NIV EXHAUSTIVE BIBLE CONCORDANCE

NIV EXHAUSTIVE BIBLE CONCORDANCE

John R. Kohlenberger III
EDITOR

ZONDERVAN ACADEMIC

The NIV Exhaustive Bible Concordance, Third Edition

Requests for information should be addressed to:
Zondervan, *3900 Sparks Dr. SE, Grand Rapids, Michigan 49546*

ISBN 978-0-310-26293-0

Cover design: Tammy Johnson
Interior design: John R. Kohlenberger III/Blue Heron Bookcraft, Inc.

Printed in the United States of America

---

23 24 25 26 27 28 29 30 31 32 33 /TRM/ 21 20 19 18 17 16 15 14 13 12 11 10 9

TABLE OF CONTENTS

ACKNOWLEDGMENTS

So many people have encouraged me by word and with prayer over the past decade that I cannot possibly begin to thank you all. But I do want to acknowledge those who have had direct involvement in the planning, shaping, and production of this concordance.

I must start by acknowledging the late Edward W. Goodrick, my co-editor for the original edition of the *NIV Exhaustive Concordance*. Dr. Goodrick was my Greek teacher for three years at Multnomah Bible College (now University), then Ed became my mentor, my co-writer, and my dear friend. His insistence on careful scholarship, hard work, and attention to detail made our six concordances to the NIV works of high quality and set the standards for my career as a researcher and writer. My education and my output would have been much poorer without his input and guidance.

The original edition of the *NIV Exhaustive Concordance* was acquired by Bob De Vries, former publisher of Zondervan. The leadership of Zondervan in the 1980s, especially Stan Gundry, Bruce Ryskamp, Peter Kladder, and Jim Buick and were strongly committed to the project throughout the decade. Editor Ed van der Maas was close to the project for its last three years and personally worked through its final marathon typesetting sessions. Dennis Thomas, Barbara Perz, and Bob Lind, formerly of Control Data, provided the technical expertise to computerize our manual labor. Jim Swanson and Don Potts spent many long hours helping us develop and correct the data from which the concordance was generated.

My wife, Carolyn, and my children, Joshua and Sarah, were all under the same roof during the decade in which the original edition was created. Although Josh and Sarah now maintain their own homes, my family continues their unrelenting love and encouragement.

My family of faith at Cascade View Covenant Church and at Christians for Biblical Equality have supported me regularly with prayer and encouragement. The scientists and physicians, nurses, and staff at the Cancer Center at Providence Hospital—especially Dr. Brendan D. Curti and Dr. Bernard A. Fox and their teams—have done everything in their significant power to keep me going these last ten years.

For this third edition, Roy and Helen Brown of Oak Tree Software generously provided software so that I could update my work on the 1984 NIV Old Testament, rather than building that whole database from scratch. Programmers Rick Bennett and Joel Brown integrated the revised New Testament database with the Old Testament and updated Oak Tree's excellent Accordance software to display all the details of the 2011 NIV database, so that I could generate specialized concordances on the way to creating the exhaustive contexts for typesetting. They also generated the dictionary-indexes from the revised database.

Bob Pritchett, Dale Pritchett, and Bill Nienhuis of Logos Research Systems provided text-alignment software so I could re-create the New Testament database from scratch. I did this in light of having an official Greek text for the NIV New Testament, thanks to Dr. Gordon Fee working through our list of variant readings from the original project and from the TNIV and 2011 NIV revisions. Rick Brannan of Logos extracted the finalized New Testament database, which the programmers at Oak Tree then converted into a database format consistent with the Old Testament.

Dr. Gordon Fee and Dr. Douglas J. Moo from the Committee on Bible Translation put in many hours to help me establish, as closely as possible, the Greek and Hebrew texts from which the NIV was translated. For the original edition, Dr. Kenneth Barker, Dr. Ronald Youngblood, and Dr. Walter Wessel had provided valuable guidance on textual variants.

As always, the leadership and editors at Zondervan have provided for my needs and have regularly encouraged my progress. Acquistions Editor Madison Trammel kept open the lines of communication between me, the publisher, and the programmers. Verlyn Verbrugge, Senior Production Editor at Large, was involved in all details of design and content and proofreading. Stan Gundry, Senior Vice President and Publisher, CARR, and Editor-in-Chief, Zondervan, was unfailing in his support of this project, as he was of the original. For his thirty years of friendship and advocacy, the revised edition of the NIV Exhaustive Bible Concordance is gratefully dedicated.

DEDICATION

To Dr. Stanley N. Gundry
Publisher, Mentor, Friend

INTRODUCTION

What Is a Concordance?

A concordance is an index to a book. It is usually arranged in alphabetical order and shows the location of each word in the book. In addition, it usually supplies several words of the context in which each word is found.

There are two kinds of Bible concordances for the nonspecialist: those that deal only with the English text of the Bible version on which they are based, and those that also deal with the Hebrew, Aramaic, and Greek texts from which the Bible version was translated.

Examples of English-only concordances are *Cruden's Complete Concordance* for the King James Version and the *NIV Bible Concordance* (Zondervan, 2012). The best-known examples of multilingual concordances are Young's *Analytical Concordance*, Strong's *Exhaustive Concordance* and its revision the *Strongest Strong's Exhaustive Concordance* (Zondervan, 2001), all based on the King James Version, and the original edition of *The NIV Exhaustive Concordance* (Zondervan, 1990, 1999).

An *analytical* concordance is organized in English alphabetical order and shows a complete index of all the different words of a given translation (with the exception of the most common articles, conjunctions, prepositions, and pronouns, such as *a, and, to,* and *he*). Each entry is subdivided according to the Hebrew, Aramaic, or Greek words that underlie the English. Each reference in these subdivisions is listed with a brief context. The analytical concordance also contains index-lexicons of biblical language vocabulary, showing the various English words that translate them.

An *exhaustive* concordance by definition should contain every reference to every word of the Bible version on which it is based. This is true of Strong's *Exhaustive Concordance to the Bible*, but not of Thomas's *New American Standard Exhaustive Concordance of the Bible*, which did not index the most common articles, conjunctions, prepositions, and pronouns. An exhaustive concordance is organized in English alphabetical order, indexes every word of the Bible, and lists every single biblical reference in which that word appears. For all but the most common words, a context is also given with each reference. (In Strong's work, the more common words are exhaustively indexed but without contexts.) Unlike the analytical concordance, an exhaustive concordance lists the references for each English word in biblical order, from Genesis to Revelation.

In Strong's *Concordance* and the NAS *Concordance*, the relationship of the English to the originals is indicated by a numbering system that was originally devised for Strong's concordance. Strong made a list of the Hebrew and "Chaldee" (Aramaic) words used in the Old Testament and of the Greek words used in the New. To each word he assigned a number. This number appears at the end of each context line to indicate the word the English translates. By consulting the dictionaries in the back of these exhaustive concordances, the user can match numbers in order to identify the biblical word, to see its "root" definition, and to find its range of translation in the English Bible.

The *NIVEBC* adopts the simple format of the exhaustive concordance for the main concordance. Like Strong's, it is truly exhaustive, indexing even the most frequent articles, conjunctions, prepositions, and pronouns in their own special section. Like Strong's, the *NIVEBC* uses a numbering system but, for reasons explained below (page xvii), it is an entirely new system. Two indexes cross-reference Strong's numbers to the new numbers and vice versa. For its biblical language Dictionary-Indexes, the *NIVEBC* adopts the format of the analytical concordance. It has three separate indexes—Hebrew, Aramaic, and Greek—that list every word in the original-language texts and every word and phrase used to translate them in the NIV. Thus the *NIVEBC* combines the best features of Young's and Strong's concordances.

Features of *The NIV Exhaustive Bible Concordance*

The *NIVEBC* is divided into four major sections: (1) the Main Concordance, (2) the Index of Articles, Conjunctions, Particles, Prepositions, and Pronouns, (3) the Biblical Language Dictionary-Indexes, and (4) the Numbering System Indexes.

The Main Concordance

Below is a typical entry from the Main Concordance:

AARON (318) [AARON'S, AARONIC]

Ex	4:14	"What about your brother, **A** the Levite?	H195
Ac	7:40	They told **A**, 'Make us gods who will go	*G2*

The heading consists of:
(1) the indexed word (AARON);
(2) the frequency count in parentheses (318);
(3) the list of related words (AARON'S, AARONIC).

The context lines consist of:
(1) the book-chapter-verse reference;
(2) the context for the indexed word;
(3) the number key to the Dictionary-Index.

Headings

There are four kinds of headings: (1) NIV word headings, (2) NIV "See" references, (3) NIV84 "See" references, and (4) KJV "See" references.

NIV Word Headings

The North American Edition of the NIV contains 727,145 total words, with a unique vocabulary of 14,408. The *NIVEBC* is an exhaustive alphabetic index to every word and numeral of the NIV.

The simplest heading is composed of the NIV word and its frequency count, for example:

ABBA (3)

The frequency count lists the total number of times the word appears in the NIV, which is also the number of contexts listed in the concordance. The original edition of the *NIVEBC* was the first exhaustive concordance to provide this information.

The headings show the indexed words exactly as they are spelled in the NIV. If the word occurs in other forms or spellings, these words appear in square brackets following the frequency count:

ABANDON (13) [ABANDONED, ABANDONS]

ABANDONED (35) [ABANDON]

ABANDONS (1) [ABANDON]

Rather than listing all related words after each indexed word, the editor chose one indexed word to act as the "group heading." All related words are listed after the group heading, and each of the related word headings points back to the group heading. In the example above, ABANDON serves as the group heading for ABANDONED and ABANDONS.

The headings also group together words that share common elements. For example:

ABLE (145) [ABILITY, ABLE-BODIED, DISABLED, ENABLE, ENABLED, ENABLES, ENABLING]

Place names composed of more than one word have a single, multiple-word heading:

BAAL GAD (3) [BAAL, GAD]

If the second or third term of a multiple-word place name is not indexed as an NIV word in its own right, it still appears in the Main Concordance as a heading that refers to the multiple-word heading:

AMMONI See KEPHAR AMMONI

(Multiple-word headings appear only for place names generated by transliteration. They are not used for place names that combine a geographic term and a proper noun, such as the Jordan River, the Sea of Galilee or Mount Sinai.)

NIV "See" References

78 words occur a total of 363,233 times—almost half the bulk of the NIV! These words are exhaustively indexed in their own section: the Index of Articles, Conjunctions, Particles, Prepositions, and Pronouns (see page xv). These words are also represented by headings in the Main Concordance, with a message referring to this special index:

A (9013) [AN] See Index of Articles Etc.

Eight of these 78 words have a selected listing of contexts in the Main Concordance.

HAD, HAS, and HAVE are usually used as auxiliary verbs to indicate the English perfect tense, as in the clause "everything I **have** commanded you." As auxiliary verbs, these words are not indexed in the Main Concordance. But these words also occur as verbs in their own right, expressing the idea of ownership, "He **had** so many flocks," or causing action, "God **had** me wander." In these latter cases, the words are indexed in the Main Concordance: HAD 597 of 2808 occurrences, HAS 303 of 2328, HAVE 1002 of 4448.

Neither I nor AM is indexed in the Main Concordance, but many important passages containing the self-revelation of God contain the phrase I AM, such as Exodus 3:14, "**I AM** WHO **I AM**," and John 8:58, "before Abraham was born, **I am**!" 70 highly significant verses have been selected from the 1038 occurrences of the phrase I AM for the Main Concordance.

When ON is used as a proper name (4 of 4894 occurrences), it is indexed in the Main Concordance, as is SO (1 of 3102). When WILL is used other than as an auxiliary verb, as in "the **will** of God" (177 of 10,122 occurrences), it is indexed in the Main Concordance.

NIV84 "See" References

Because there were many changes in the 2011 edition of the NIV to the spelling of proper names and to key terms, more than 200 words are referenced from their spellings in the 1984 NIV (NIV84). Among the more common proper names, "Abimelech" was changed to "Abimelek." The well-known translation of the Greek word σάρξ (*sarx*, G/K *G4922*), often "sinful nature" in the first editions of the NIV, is now usually translated by the more traditional term "flesh." These changes are noted in the following "See" references:

ABIMELECH (NIV84) ABIMELEK

(SINFUL) NATURE (NIV84) FLESH

SINFUL NATURE (NIV84) FLESH

KJV "See" References

The King James or Authorized Version has been the dominant English Bible translation from the early seventeenth century to the latter half of the twentieth century. Because of this, the KJV has had profound impact on the language of both the Church and English-speaking society. To help users familiar with KJV vocabulary find the proper NIV terms, more than 2100 KJV words appear in 836 KJV "See" references. These include such headings as:

COMFORTER (KJV) ADVOCATE, COMFORT

(GAVE/GIVE UP THE] GHOST (KJV) BREATHED HIS LAST, DIE, DIED, DYING, GAVE UP HIS SPIRIT, PERISH, PERISHED

(HOLY) GHOST (KJV) (HOLY) SPIRIT

Context Lines

Concordances are word indexes. At the very least, they index the book, chapter, and verse in which these words are located. Most concordances also show each word within a brief phrase or clause: a context. This gives the user a better idea of the use of the word and helps to locate a specific verse that contains that word.

Most concordances limit their contexts to a single line. This is generally true of the *NIVEBC*; however, it has many two-line and several three-line contexts. These longer contexts help give a better glimpse into a word's function within the English text and give a better idea of the relationship of the English to the original languages.

The purpose of context lines in a concordance is merely to help the reader recognize or find a specific verse in the Bible. For word study—or any kind of Bible study—the context offered by a concordance is rarely enough to go on. Nevertheless, sometimes a short sentence or a whole verse fits on one line, as in the case of John 11:35: "Jesus wept." Under the heading PRAISE, the *NIVEBC* was able to present the entirety of Psalm 150 on thirteen consecutive lines!

Taken by themselves, context lines can and do misrepresent the teaching of Scripture by omitting key words. "There is no God" is a context taken straight from Psalm 14:1. Of course the Bible does not teach this; it is what "the fool says in his heart"! Similarly, a context for Leviticus 24:16 might read "the LORD is to be put to death" while the text actually says "anyone who blasphemes the name of the LORD is to be put to death."

Great care has been taken by the editor, programmers, and proofreader of the *NIVEBC* to create contexts that are informative and accurate. But the reader should always check word contexts by looking them up in the NIV itself. "The Wicked Bible," a KJV edition of 1631, accidentally omitted the word "not" from the seventh commandment, for which the printers were fined 300 pounds sterling! Though there are no such fines for misleading contexts, the editor is still deeply concerned that the *NIVEBC* be used discerningly.

Bible Translating and Concordance Making

Traduttore traditore, "the translator is a traitor," is an ancient proverb oft quoted in books about Bible translations. To a degree this proverb is true, for no translation can perfectly bring over all the meaning and nuances of one language into another. Because no two languages share identical grammar and an identical range of word meanings, not even the best-intentioned word-for-word translation can claim to perfectly represent the original.

If the translator is a traitor, the concordance maker must be a partner in crime. For no multilingual concordance can perfectly represent both the English translation and the biblical language texts it indexes. It can perfectly represent the vocabulary of the English text, for it needs only to list the location of each of its words. In this respect a concordance is either absolutely right or absolutely wrong. But when a concordance attempts to display the relationship between the English text and the biblical languages, it falls heir to the same difficulties that face the Bible translator.

Much of Bible translation involves one-to-one relationships. More often than not, אֱלֹהִים is translated "God," Ἰησοῦς "Jesus," and ἀγαπάω "love." This part of translating and concordance making is easy.

Often, however, more than one word is needed in English to render a word in the originals. For example, the Greek word τεκνίον is regularly translated "little children" in the KJV and NAS and "dear children" in the NIV. Conversely, one English word can translate several words from the originals. Thus the infamous number "666" of Revelation 13:18 translates three Greek words.

Sometimes, because of differences in idiom, it takes several English words to translate two or more words from the original languages. This is called "dynamic equivalence" or "functional equivalence." For example, the famous KJV expletive "God forbid!" translates one word in Hebrew and two words in Greek—neither of which has either "God" or "forbid" as part of its "literal" meaning! Nevertheless, "God forbid!" is the *functional* equivalent of the Greek and Hebrew phrases.

Multilingual concordances of the past have tended to display the relationship between English and the original languages as if it were almost always one-to-one. Scan a few columns of Strong's *Concordance*, and you see context after context presenting one indexed word followed by one number. Over the years, this has lent support to the misconception that the KJV is an absolutely "literal," word-for-word translation. However, the original preface to the KJV stated, "We have not tied our selves to an uniformity of phrasing, or to an identity of words, as some peradventure would wish that we had done. . . ." Young's *Analytical Concordance*, and more so *Eerdmans' Analytical Concordance to the RSV* that followed it, attempt to show multiple-word translation by means of multiple-word headings. However, nothing within the context itself shows how the indexed word relates to the original Greek or Hebrew.

The *NIVEBC*, by means of three different typefaces in the context line and a more nuanced use of its entirely new numbering system, shows more fully than any previous concordance the interrelation of the English text and the biblical languages.

Context Lines: Word-for-Word Translation

The simplest context line presents four items of information. First, the location of the indexed word by book, chapter, and verse. (A complete list of NIV book abbreviations appears at the beginning of the Main Concordance.) Second, the context line. Third, within the context line, the indexed word is abbreviated by its first letter and is *usually* in bold type. Fourth, a letter and number at the right margin indicates the Hebrew, Aramaic, or Greek word the indexed word translates. For example, under the heading DANIEL on page 248:

Da	1: 8	But **D** resolved not to defile himself with	H1975
Da	6:23	And when **D** was lifted from the den, no	A10181
Mt	24:15	spoken of through the prophet **D**—let the	*G1248*

The numbering system indicates which biblical language is translated. Hebrew words are represented by numbers in normal "roman" type, preceded by the letter "H," from H1 through H9597. Aramaic word numbers are also in roman type, preceded by the letter "A," from 10001 through 10779. Greek word numbers are in italics, preceded by the letter "*G*," from *1* through *6068*. This "Goodrick/Kohlenberger numbering system," named after its developers, is hereafter referred to as "G/K numbers."

Context Lines: Multiple-Word Translation

One English Word—Multiple Original Words. When the indexed word translates more than one word from the original, this is indicated by an appropriate number of G/K numbers at the end of the line. This is especially true of numerals, for example:

Rev	7: 5	tribe of Judah **12,000** were sealed,	*G1557+5942*
Nu	1:46	number was **603,550**.	H9252+4395+547+2256
			+8993+547+2256+2822+4395+2256+2822

The second example is a rare occurrence of a string of G/K numbers too long to fit on one line. In this case, the string of numbers is broken to fit on two lines; the second line begins with a plus (+) to show that it is a continuation of the previous line.

In some cases, multiple English words are needed to define a Hebrew, Aramaic, or Greek word or phrase. We will refer to this as "multiple-word translation." In other cases, multiple English words are needed to translate the inflection of the original, to express, for example, the tense of a verb or the number and gender of a noun. We will refer to this as "assisting in translation." These two concepts are explained below.

Multiple-word Translation. As mentioned above, the Greek word τεκνίον is regularly translated "little children" in the KJV and NAS and "dear children" in the NIV. If you were to look up the word "little" in either Strong's or the NAS *Concordance* and look at the context for 1 John 2:1, you would find the word abbreviated by its first letter with the number *5040* at the end of the line. However, if you looked up the word "children" you would find the same thing:

1Jo 2: 1	My *l.* children, these things write	*5040*
1Jo 2: 1	My little *c.*, these things write I	*5040*

In these examples (reproduced from Strong's *Concordance*), it would appear that the Greek word number *5040* meant only "little" or "children," depending on which entry you looked up first. Nothing in the context line would inform you that Greek word *5040* actually means "little children." Young's *Concordance*, on the other hand, does not list 1 John 2:1 under the word "little," but has a heading "CHILD or children, little—" under which the verse is indexed.

The *NIVEBC* has solved the problem of indicating such multiple-word translations by putting *all* the words in bold type. Using the same example of 1 John 2:1, under the headings "dear" and "children":

1Jn 2: 1	My **d children**, I write this to you so that	*G5448*
1Jn 2: 1	My **dear c**, I write this to you so that you	*G5448*

If more than one English word is used to render several words from the original, the typefaces and the G/K numbers show all the words involved in this multiple-word translation. Such is the case with "give...children" in Genesis 19:31, as indexed under both words:

Ge 19:31	no man around here to **give** us **c**—	H995+6584
Ge 19:31	man around here to **g** us **children**—	H995+6584

This unique convention shows at a glance all the words involved in a multiple-word translation, the English words as well as the original-language words.

Assist in Translation. The biblical languages use spelling (or "inflection") to indicate such things as the subject and tense of a verb, or the number and gender of a noun. Such inflections are not part of the definition of a word, but are necessary to reflect in translation.

English does not inflect to the same degree as the biblical languages. Thus translators have to use auxiliary or "assisting" words to render these inflections. Common assisting words are pronouns such as "he" and "she," auxiliary verbs such as "shall" and "will" and quantifying words such as "many," "some," and even "two."

If you were to look up the word "will" in either Strong's or the NAS *Concordance*, you would notice that for most of the several thousand references to the word, there is no number at the end of the context line. Some might take this to mean that the word does not represent any word in the original but was simply supplied by the translators. But for the most part this is not true. The word "will" was used to translate the inflection of a Hebrew, Aramaic, or Greek verb, not the verb itself. But the editors did not put the number of that verb at the end of the context line lest the user misinterpret "will" as the *definition* of that number.

The *NIVEBC* has solved this problem by means of different typefaces and a code. If an indexed word is a word that "assists in translation," the context line displays it in three ways, as shown in the following example, found under the heading LET:

Ge 1:26	God said, "*L us* **make** mankind in our image	AIT

First, the abbreviation of the indexed word is in italics, because it is not the main word but a word that assists in the translation of "make." Second, the word it assists ("make") is in bold. Third, the code AIT ("Assisting In Translation") appears at the end of the line in the place of a G/K number.

On the other hand, if the indexed word is assisted by other NIV words, the indexed word is abbreviated and in bold type, but the assisting words are in italics. Using the same example, but looking now under the heading MAKE:

Ge 1:26	"*Let us* **m** mankind in our image	H6913

In both examples, the auxiliary verb "Let" and the pronoun "us" are marked as assisting words by the italic typeface. In both contexts, the verb "make" is shown to be the main, "defining" word by the bold typeface. Under their own headings, the code AIT also marks the assisting word, while the G/K number identifies the defining word.

By using these conventions to identify multiple-word translations and to distinguish between defining words and assisting words, the *NIVEBC* more thoroughly displays the relationship between the English and the biblical languages than any previous concordance.

Context Lines: "Substitution" Translation

Bible translators often substitute nouns for pronouns and pronouns for nouns for clarity. For example, John 8:1 in the KJV reads "Jesus went unto the mount of Olives." Strong tells us that here "Jesus" translates Greek word *846*, which is not the proper name Ἰησοῦς (Strong's word *2424*), but the pronoun αὐτός, often translated "he." Such "substitutionary" translations are common and acceptable in Bible translations, but other concordances treat them as if they were one-to-one translations.

The *NIVEBC* indicates substitutionary translation by attaching a raised "S" to the G/K number or numbers at the end of the context line. For example, under AARON:

Ex	9:12	he would not listen to **Moses and A**,	H2157[S]
Lev	8: 7	He put the tunic on **A**, tied the sash	H2257[S]

In the first example, the phrase "Moses and Aaron" substitutes for the masculine plural pronominal suffix הֶם-, often translated "they," "their," or "them." In the second example, "Aaron" substitutes for the masculine singular pronominal suffix וֹ-, often translated "he," "him," or "his."

Similarly, the NIV often uses forms of the verb "do" to substitute for a more specific verb repeated in the context. For example, Deuteronomy 6:16 reads "Do not put the LORD your God to the test as you **did** at Massah" rather than "Do not put the LORD your God to the test as you **tested** him at Massah." This substitutionary translation is indicated under DID:

Dt	6:16	your God to the test as *you* **d** at Massah.	H5814[S]

The NIV is not unique in using substitutionary translation. The *NIVEBC* is unique in displaying it.

Context Lines: "Not Directly Translated"

Because modern English and ancient Hebrew, Aramaic, and Greek do not have identical rules of grammar and style, translators must often add words for the sake of clarity. For example, Mark 16:9 in the KJV begins "Now when Jesus was risen early. . . ." Strong has no number at the end of this context line because there is no Greek word for "Jesus" in this verse; it was supplied by the translators to give a subject to the verb.

The *NIVEBC* follows this practice of indicating NIV words that are not in the originals by using the code NDT, "Not Directly Translated," for both the Hebrew and Aramaic of the Old Testament and for the Greek of the New Testament. Under the heading ABRAHAM, for example, we find:

Ge	21:33	**A** planted a tamarisk tree in Beersheba, and	NDT
Heb	6:15	patiently, **A** received what was promised.	NDT

As in the case of "Jesus" in the KJV in Mark 16:9, these proper names were supplied from the context for clarity, for the benefit of the reader. This practice has always been considered acceptable in Bible translation.

Context Lines: "Double Use" of NIV Words

Sometimes a single NIV word is used in combination with two NIV words to form a pair of multiple-word translations. This is especially seen in the case of "male and female" in such phrases as "male and female servants" = "male servants and female servants." To show this "double use" of the NIV word "servants" requires duplicating relevant contexts. And to show that a context is duplicated, it is surrounded by square brackets:

Dt	16:11	your **male** and female **s**, the Levites	H6269
[Dt	16:11	your male and **female s**, the Levites	H563]

The bolded words "**male...s**" in the first context show that Hebrew word H6269 is translated as "male servants," not just "male" or "servants." The bracketed second context shows it is a duplicate of the first, and its bolded words "**female s**" show that Hebrew word H563 is translated as "female servants," not just "female" or "servants." This convention occurs 50 times in the *NIVEBC*.

A Note on NIV Typefaces

In the NIV text itself, italics are used when a Hebrew, Aramaic, or Greek word is not translated, but merely spelled out in English letters. These "transliterated" words include *"Eli, eli, lema sabachthani?"* in Matthew 27:46 and "*Talitha koum!*" in Mark 5:41. However, the NIV italic typeface could be confused with the italics used in the concordance for words that assist in translation (AIT). Therefore, all italics used in the NIV text are printed as normal "roman" type in context lines.

The NIV uses a typographical convention to distinguish between two different Hebrew words, both of which are usually translated "Lord" in English versions. For the proper name of God, יהוה ("Yahweh"), the NIV uses "LORD." For the title אֲדֹנָי, it uses "Lord." The *NIVEBC* also distinguishes these two words under two separate headings. "Lord" and its possessive form "Lord's" are indexed under the headings LORD and

LORD'S (pages 685–688, 709). "LORD" and "LORD'S" are indexed under the headings LORD* and LORD'S* (pages 688–710). In context lines, these words appear as in the NIV text.

The 1984 NIV used half brackets (⌞ ⌟) to indicate certain words supplied for clarity, but these are no longer used in the 2011 NIV, and thus do not appear in contexts.

The Index of Articles, Conjunctions, Particles, Prepositions and Pronouns

The Main Concordance indexes 366,066 references to 14,339 NIV words, numerals, and compound proper names. The Index of Articles, Conjunctions, Particles, Prepositions, and Pronouns indexes 363,233 references to 78 NIV words. These include 55 words that appear more than 1000 times each, such as "I," "me," and "my," and 23 less frequent words that are related to them, such as "myself," "I'll," and "I'm." This index makes the *NIVEBC* the first truly exhaustive concordance since Strong's.

The format of the Index of Articles Etc. is very simple. Each of the 78 words has its own heading, followed by a frequency count. For example:

A (9013)

The eight words that are partially indexed in the Main Concordance (AM, HAD, HAS, HAVE, I, ON, SO and WILL, see above pages x-xi) also have the message "See also selected list in the Main Concordance."

The 78 words of this section are indexed without contexts, since providing contexts would be of little benefit to the reader and would double the size of the *NIVEBC*! Book, chapter and verse references appear in biblical order. Books and chapters are set in bold print for easy location:

Lev 1:3,3,9,9,10,10,13,13,14,14,14,17,17; **2:**1,2,2,2,3,4,5,6,7, 9,10,11,12,14,15,16;

Verses within the same chapter are set off by commas. The final verse of the chapter is followed by a semicolon. The final verse of the entry is followed by a period.

The Biblical Language Dictionary-Indexes

At the end of each context line in the Main Concordance is a code or a G/K number, describing the relationship of the NIV to the original languages. The three Biblical Language Dictionary-Indexes list all of the words that are found in the Hebrew, Aramaic, and Greek texts from which the NIV was translated. These lists are in the alphabetical order of each of the three languages, which is also the order of the G/K numbering system.

In the first edition of the *NIVEBC* these lists were called "Index-Lexicons" and followed the pattern of Young's *Analytical Concordance* rather than that of Strong's dictionaries. The editors felt that Young's system more accurately interrelated the original languages to the NIV and was easier to read. So great was the demand from the public, however, that editors John R. Kohlenberger III and James A. Swanson completely reworked this section for the second edition of 1999, which was also published as *The Strongest NIV Exhaustive Concordance*. The Greek Dictionary-Index from the second edition is used in this third edition, but the updated *Kohlenberger/Mounce Concise Hebrew-Aramaic Dictionary of the Old Testament*, developed for Accordance software, replaces the Hebrew and Aramaic Dictionary-Indexes from the second edition. All three Dictionary-Indexes that have more information than Strong's dictionaries and are still exhaustive indexes to the NIV translations.

The Dictionary-Indexes to the *NIVEBC* have three features not found in the indexes or dictionaries of any other concordance. First, the *NIVEBC* provides frequency statistics of both the biblical languages and the English, including words that are not directly translated. Second, each entry lists exhaustively all the NIV words and phrases that translate each word of the original, showing multiple-word translation and substitution translation. Third, the NIV words and phrases indexed are in their exact textual spelling, so the user can locate its heading in the Main Concordance without any further cross-referencing.

The entries for Greek words *G26* and *G27* can serve as an example for most features of all three Dictionary-Indexes:

> ***G26*** **ἀγαπάω *agapaō***, v. [143] [→*27, 28*]. to love; in the NT usually the active love of God for his Son and his people, and the active love his people are to have for God, each other, and even enemies:– love (76), loved (39), loves (22), dearly loved (1), have^{S} (1), longed for (1), love shown (1), loving (1), NDT (1)

> ***G27*** **ἀγάπη *agapē***, n. [115] [√*26*]. love, in the NT usually the active love of God for his Son and his people, and the active love his people are to have for God, each other, and even enemies; love feast, the common meal shared by Christians in

connection with church meetings:– love (111), love (2 [+*2400*]), love feasts (1), loves (1)

The entry for *G27* begins with the G/K number, in bold type for easy location. Next is the lexical form or dictionary form of the word, followed its transliteration (in bold italics), the part of speech (abbreviated), the total number of occurrences in the biblical text (in square brackets), and related words (listed by G/K number in square brackets, see below for more on related words). Note that the transliteration follows the system used in Zondervan's *New International Dictionary of New Testament Theology and Exegesis* and *New International Dictionary of Old Testament Theology and Exegesis*. A complete transliteration and pronunication guide, as well as a list of abbreviations, appears before each index.

The six heading elements are concluded by a period. Following the period is an essential definition for the word as it is used in the NT. These definitions can be as brief as one or two words. In the case of hundreds of theologically and culturally significant words, like ἀγάπη, the definition functions as a concise expository dictionary. In the case of a proper name, like "Bethlehem," the definition will include the possible meaning of the name in the original languages: "*house of bread* possibly *temple of Lakhmu*" in the case of Bethlehem.

The definition ends with a colon and a dash (:–). Following this symbol is a list of all the ways in which the word is translated in the NIV, in descending order of frequency. If two words (or phrases) have the same frequency, they are listed in alphabetical order. Following the NIV word is its frequency count, in parentheses.

One-to-one translations are indicated by one NIV word, as in the case of the first and last NIV words in the example above. Multiple-word translations are indicated in two ways: by multiple NIV words and/or multiple G/K numbers. The next-to-the-last word, "love feasts (1)," indicates a multiple-word NIV translation. If you look up "love" and "feasts" in the Main Concordance, you will find the following contexts under Jude 12:

Jude	12	These people are blemishes at your **l feasts**	*G27*
Jude	12	These people are blemishes at your **love f**	*G27*

Under both headings, the phrase "love feasts" is shown to be the definition of Greek word *G27*. (Multiple-word translation is described above on page xiii.)

When an NIV word or phrase translates more than one word of the original, the G/K number of the additional word (or words) follows the frequency count in square brackets. That is why there are two separate statistics for "love" in the example above. The first is a one-to-one translation. The second shows that "love" translates Greek words *G27* and *G2400*. In all three Index-Dictionaries, the entry has the letter "H" (Hebrew), "A" (Aramaic), or "G" (Greek) at the beginning of the entry. But all internal references to G/K numbers have no letters, because the numbers are usually in the same language as the entry. In the cases where Hebrew words reference Aramaic words by G/K, and Aramaic words reference Hebrew, all 5-digit numbers starting with "10" are Aramaic and 1- to 4-digit numbers are Hebrew.

Words that "assist in translation" (see above, page xiii) do not appear in the Dictionary-Indexes. This is because they do not *define* words. Rather, they assist words in translating tense, number, gender, and mood.

"Substitution" translation (see above, page xiv) is noted with a raised "S," as in the Main Concordance. In the entry for *G26*, the fifth indexed word (have[S]) indicates that "have" is a substitution translation for Greek word *G27*.

Words Not Directly Translated

There is one other category of words in the Dictionary-Indexes that cannot be looked up in the Main Concordance. If a word in the original is not translated in the NIV, either directly or in multiple-word translation, this is noted by the abbreviation "NDT." This word is always last in the index list and includes a frequency count, as seen above in the entry for *G26*.

The Hebrew word שָׁנָה (G/K H9102, Strong 8141) is usually translated "year(s)" in English versions. But its use with numbers is so repetitious in the Hebrew text that no English version translates it every time it appears. A word-for-word translation of Genesis 23:1 would be: "And the life of Sarah was one hundred **year** and twenty **year** and seven **years**—the **years** of the life of Sarah." Though שָׁנָה appears four times in this verse, "year(s)" appears only twice in the KJV and NAS, and once in the NIV.

According to the Hebrew Index-Lexicon to Young's *Analytical Concordance*, שָׁנָה is translated 805 times in the KJV. The Hebrew-Aramaic Dictionary of the NAS *Concordance* has a total of 789 occurrences. Actually, the word appears 868 times in the Hebrew text. The Hebrew Dictionary-Index of the *NIVEBC* lists this word (H9102) as translated 868 times and Not Directly Translated 92 times. Although all Bible translations leave words untranslated, the *NIVEBC* is the first multilingual concordance to indicate this.

Related Words

The Dictionary-Indexes of the *NIVEBC* list all biblical words that are related by common elements. Rather than list all related words in every heading, the editors chose a major word (usually a verb or a noun) to act as an organizing head, just as in the case of NIV words (see page x). Each related word points back to the organizing word with a root symbol (√), as in the case of ἀγάπη on page xv, while each organizing word points to all related words with an arrow symbol (→), as in the case of ἀγαπάω also on page xv.

Please note that although the root symbol is used to organize related words, this does *not* mean that this word is the root from which all related words are derived and to which all must relate in meaning. This is one of the methodological errors found in Strong's dictionaries, which as also been popularized in Vine's *Expository Dictionary of New Testament Words.* Defining a word by the sum of its parts ("etymology") does not always work in English—try it with "butterfly"—and does not always work in the biblical languages. The related words lists are provided to allow the user to do more thorough word studies. These studies, however, should be done carefully with more attention paid to contextual definitions than fanciful etymologies.

"Not used in NIVEBC"

The Dictionary-Indexes of the *NIVEBC* list several thousand words that are alternate spellings of Hebrew, Aramaic, and Greek words, or words not found in the original-language texts translated by the NIV. The three word lists were compiled from several standard lexicons and grammars in the hope that the G/K numbering system could be used in a multitude of reference works, describing the textual base of most Bible translations.

Because these words are not translated by the NIV, they have no NIV words to index. So instead of a frequency statistic is the phrase "Not used in NIVEBC":

> **G15 ἀγαθοεργός** ***agathoergos***, a. Not used in NIVEBC. [√*19* + *2240*]. one who does good

Note that even these words are included in the related words lists and are given definitions.

Dictionary Definition versus NIV Translation

The dictionaries in Strong's *Concordance* and the NAS *Concordance* usually give a single "root" definition for each word. This is often misunderstood as the *only* definition or the "literal" meaning of the word and can be misused to criticize other valid translations of the word—even in the KJV and NAS themselves! For example, Young's Dictionary-Index to the New Testament lists 57 different KJV translations of the Greek word ποιέω (*poieō*). Strong's dictionary defines this word as "to *make* or *do*." Either the KJV translators were wrong in 96% of their definitions or there is more to the meaning of ποιέω than "to *make* or *do*"!

The NIV translations that follow the definition are listed in order from most used to least used. They represent careful choices the NIV translators made to render each word accurately and understandably in its context. The NIV translations list is as good an indicator of the range of a word's meaning as is the dictionary definition that precedes the list. Use these resources together, not in opposition.

For further and more detailed word studies, please consult Zondervan's *Mounce's Complete Expository Dictionary of Old and New Testament Words, New International Encyclopedia of Bible Words*, *New International Dictionary of New Testament Theology and Exegesis, The NIV Theological Dictionary of New Testament Words,* and *New International Dictionary of Old Testament Theology and Exegesis.* These books are keyed to the G/K numbering system, either by entry or by index.

The Numbering System Indexes

You may have noticed in the examples above that the "Goodrick/Kohlenberger" numbering system differs from that of Strong. Advances in biblical scholarship have made it difficult, if not impossible, to use Strong's century-old system. In the first place, Strong's system indexes only the vocabulary of the original-language texts that underlie the KJV. Second, modern analysis of the biblical languages divides many words of identical spelling into two or three or more unique "homographs"—words with the same spelling but different meanings (such as the English word "bow"). This is especially true of biblical Hebrew. Third, Strong mixed the Hebrew and Aramaic ("Chaldee") vocabularies together into one numbering scheme, whereas all modern lexicons and grammars treat them as different languages. Fourth, even after a century and dozens of corrected editions, Strong's system still suffers from numerous typographical and factual errors. These factors demand both expansion and revision of Strong's system.

The general editor of the NAS *Concordance* opted

to retain Strong's numbers. Typographical and factual errors were corrected while indexing the dictionaries to the NAS. To overcome the need for additional words and numbers, letters of the alphabet were added to Strong's existing numbers. For example, to number a word not included in Strong's original list that should be alphabetized between words 112 and 113, the NAS altered Strong's numbers to 112a, 112b, and 113.

Rather than attempt to similarly patch up Strong's well-worn system, the editors of the original *NIVEBC* decided to make a clean break and develop a new standard for use in up-to-date biblical language reference works. But for the benefit of those who want to cross-reference to Strong's system, the editors also created two sets of indexes to show the relationship of these two numbering schemes.

Index of Strong to Goodrick/Kohlenberger Numbers

The first index is organized according to Strong's numbering system. It first indexes Strong's Hebrew and Aramaic ("Chaldee") numbers, then his Greek numbers.

Most of the index involves a one-to-one correspondence:

Strong .... G/K
1 .... H3
2 .... A10003
3 .... H4
4 .... A10004

The first four words of Strong's Hebrew/Aramaic numbering system consist of two Hebrew and two Aramaic words.

Sometimes a single Strong's number corresponds to more than one G/K number, due to spelling variations. In this case, each corresponding G/K number is listed on its own line, but Strong's is replaced by a ditto mark (").

11 .... H10
" H11

Sometimes Strong assigned a number to a compound name that the NIV treats as two separate words. The plus sign (+) marks this relationship:

25 .... H3+1500

Index of Goodrick/Kohlenberger to Strong Numbers

This set of indexes has one for each of the biblical languages: Hebrew, Aramaic, and Greek. Each index is organized according to the G/K numbering system.

As in the case of the previous set, most relationships are one-to-one:

G1 1
G2 2
G3 3
G4 4

Sometimes a G/K number corresponds to more than one Strong number. In this case, each corresponding Strong number is listed on its own line, but the G/K number is replaced by a ditto mark (").

G41 39
" 40

Sometimes a G/K number is assigned to a compound word that Strong treated only as two separate words. The plus sign (+) marks this relationship:

G15 .... 18+2041

In many cases, a G/K number has no corresponding Strong number. In this case, the G/K number is simply followed by blank space, as is the case with Greek numbers *G112* and *G207*.

In Conclusion

To Ralph Waldo Emerson, "A foolish consistency is the hobgoblin of little minds." To the editors of the *NIVEBC*, there is no such thing as a foolish consistency in a biblical reference book. Every effort has been made by the editors, programmers, and proofreaders to make the *NIVEBC* consistent and error-free. Strong's and Young's *Concordances* have each been through more than two dozen revisions, and we realize that our work has not been perfect either.

If you find anything that appears to be an error, write to The NIV Concordance Project, c/o Zondervan, 3900 Sparks Drive S.E., Grand Rapids, Michigan 49546.

INDEX OF SPELLING DIFFERENCES BETWEEN THE NORTH AMERICAN AND ANGLICISED EDITIONS OF THE NIV

The two editions of the New International Version—North American and Anglicised—are more identical than they are different. Most differences are in the spelling of certain words, such as "honor/honour" and "center/centre." There are also differences in wording, such as "heads of grain/ears of corn." And there are differences in punctuation and the use of quotation marks.

The following indexes deal with all spelling and wording differences, other than for conjunctions and prepositions that are not indexed in the Main Concordance. Hopefully this will allow readers of the Anglicised NIV to use the *NIVEBC* as fully as readers of the North American edition.

To use the index of 286 spelling and hyphenation differences, look up the word in the left column (Anglicised spelling), go to the entry in the right column (North American spelling).

NIVA 2011	NIV NA 2011
advisor	adviser
advisors	advisers
afterwards	afterward
algum-wood	algumwood
almug-wood	almugwood
any more	anymore
any one	anyone
armour	armor
armour-bearer	armor-bearer
armour-bearers	armor-bearers
armoury	armory
authorisation	authorization
authorised	authorized
axe	ax
axe-head	axhead
backwards	backward
baptise	baptize
baptised	baptized
baptising	baptizing
battering-rams	battering rams
battle-bow	battle bow
behaviour	behavior
Benjaminite	Benjamite
Benjaminites	Benjamites
birth-pains	birth pains
blood-relative	blood relative
bow-shot	bowshot
bow-strings	bowstrings
broken-hearted	brokenhearted
burnt-out	burned-out
cancelled	canceled
cancelling	canceling
cauldron	caldron
cauldrons	caldrons

NIVA 2011	NIV NA 2011
centre	center
centres	centers
channelled	channeled
chiselled	chiseled
chiselling	chiseling
clamour	clamor
coloured	colored
colourful	colorful
colours	colors
commander-in-chief	commander in chief
counsellor	counselor
counsellors	counselors
criticised	criticized
dark-coloured	dark-colored
defence	defense
defences	defenses
dishonour	dishonor
dishonoured	dishonored
dishonours	dishonors
distil	distill
door-frame	doorframe
door-frames	doorframes
door-post	doorpost
drag-net	dragnet
dwelling-place	dwelling place
dwelling-places	dwelling places
ear lobe	earlobe
elder	older
eldest	oldest
enquire	inquire
enquired	inquired
enquirer	inquirer
enquirers	inquirers
enquiring	inquiring

NIVA 2011	NIV NA 2011
enrol	enroll
enrolment	enrollment
equalled	equaled
ever-flowing	ever flowing
eye-witnesses	eyewitnesses
face down	facedown
faint-hearted	fainthearted
fault-finders	faultfinders
favour	favor
favourable	favorable
favourably	favorably
favoured	favored
favourite	favorite
favouritism	favoritism
favours	favors
fertilise	fertilize
fervour	fervor
fig-tree	fig tree
fig-trees	fig trees
flavour	flavor
for ever	forever
for evermore	forevermore
fulfil	fulfill
fulfilment	fulfillment
fulfils	fulfills
grape-pickers	grape pickers
grey	gray
grey-haired	gray-haired
half-dead	half dead
harbour	harbor
harboured	harbored
hare	rabbit
hard-hearted	hardhearted
head-dresses	headdresses
heavenwards	heavenward
herdsmen	herders
hiding-place	hiding place
hiding-places	hiding places
home town	hometown
honour	honor
honourable	honorable
honourably	honorably
honoured	honored
honouring	honoring
honours	honors
jewellery	jewelry
kind-hearted	kindhearted
labour	labor
laboured	labored
labourer	laborer
labourers	laborers
labouring	laboring
labours	labors
laughing-stock	laughingstock
law-breaker	lawbreaker
law-breakers	lawbreakers
legalising	legalizing
levelled	leveled

NIVA 2011	NIV NA 2011
licence	license
lustre	luster
market-place	marketplace
market-places	marketplaces
marshalled	marshaled
marvelled	marveled
marvelling	marveling
marvellous	marvelous
Michmash	Mikmash
mid-air	midair
misdemeanour	misdemeanor
mobilised	mobilized
mould	mold
moulded	molded
moulding	molding
moulds	molds
mouldy	moldy
money-changers	money changers
money-lender	moneylender
multicoloured	multicolored
moustache	mustache
naïve	naive
near by	nearby
neighbour	neighbor
neighbourís	neighborís
neighbouring	neighboring
neighbours	neighbors
neighboursí	neighborsí
Nephussim	Nephusim
newly-built	newly built
nine-and-a-half	nine and a half
North-easter	Northeaster
north-west	northwest
odour	odor
offence	offense
offences	offenses
open-handed	openhanded
over-righteous	overrighteous
ox-goad	oxgoad
panelled	paneled
panelling	paneling
paralysed	paralyzed
parcelled	parceled
pasture-land	pastureland
pasture-lands	pasturelands
per cent	percent
plough	plow
ploughed	plowed
ploughing	plowing
ploughman	plowman
ploughmen	plowmen
ploughs	plows
plumb-line	plumb line
practise	practice
practised	practiced
practises	practices
practising	practicing
pre-eminent	preeminent

NIVA 2011	NIV NA 2011
pretence	pretense
quarrelled	quarreled
quarrelling	quarreling
re-entered	reentered
re-established	reestablished
realise	realize
realised	realized
realises	realizes
realising	realizing
recognise	recognize
recognised	recognized
recognises	recognizes
recognising	recognizing
resting-place	resting place
revelled	reveled
revellers	revelers
revelling	reveling
river bed	riverbed
round	around
rumour	rumor
rumours	rumors
sandalled	sandaled
sand-bar	sandbar
sand-bars	sandbars
saviour	savior
sceptre	scepter
sceptres	scepters
servant-girl	servant girl
sheep-shearers	sheepshearers
shield-bearer	shield bearer
shrine-prostitute	shrine prostitute
shrine-prostitutes	shrine prostitutes
shrivelled	shriveled
sick-bed	sickbed
side walls	sidewalls
signalled	signaled
signalling	signaling
skilful	skillful
skilfully	skillfully
smoulder	smolder
smouldering	smoldering
smoulders	smolders
sombre	somber
south-east	southeast
south-west	southwest
splendour	splendor
storey	story
stumbling-block	stumbling block
sub-division	subdivision
sub-divisions	subdivisions
sulphur	sulfur

NIVA 2011	NIV NA 2011
symbolises	symbolizes
sympathise	sympathize
tambourine	timbrel
tambourines	timbrels
terrorised	terrorized
thank-offering	thank offering
thank-offerings	thank offerings
theatre	theater
thorn-bush	thornbush
thorn-bushes	thornbushes
threshing-cart	threshing cart
threshing-floor	threshing floor
threshing-floors	threshing floors
threshing-sledge	threshing sledge
threshing-sledges	threshing sledges
tight-fisted	tightfisted
totalled	totaled
towards	toward
travelled	traveled
traveller	traveler
travellers	travelers
travelling	traveling
treasure-house	treasure house
tumble-weed	tumbleweed
tumours	tumors
two-and-a-half	two and a half
unauthorised	unauthorized
under age	underage
unequalled	unequaled
unfavourable	unfavorable
unploughed	unplowed
unsandalled	unsandaled
untravelled	untraveled
upside-down	upside down
upwards	upward
vapour	vapor
vigour	vigor
war-horses	warhorses
warder	warden
water-carriers	water carriers
wilful	willful
wilfully	willfully
wind-blown	windblown
wing-span	wingspan
woollen	woolen
worshipped	worshiped
worshipper	worshiper
worshippers	worshipers
worshipping	worshiping
worth while	worthwhile

INDEX OF WORDING DIFFERENCES BETWEEN THE NORTH AMERICAN AND ANGLICISED EDITIONS OF THE NIV

The index of 509 wording differences already indexes these words by book, chapter and verse. To find the Hebrew and Greek words underlying these NIV words, look up the word in the left column (Anglicised spelling), go to the entry in the right column (North American spelling).

NIVA 2011	NIV NA 2011	Reference
360	three hundred and sixty	2Sa 2:31
[in] advance	ahead of time	Mt 24:25
[in] advance	ahead of time	Mk 13:23
[land] allotted	allotment	Dt 12:12
[land] allotted	allotment	Dt 14:27, 29
[land] allotted	allotment	Dt 18:1
[land] allotted to	allotment for	Jos 15:1
[land] allotted to	allotment for	Jos 16:1
[land] allotted to	allotment for	Jos 17:1, 2
allotted	given	Jos 17:14
[portion of land] allotted	allotment	Jos 17:17
[be] allotted a portion of land	have an allotment	Eze 48:13
allowance	allotment	Ge 47:22
allowed	had	Eze 32:32
among you	in your midst	1Co 3:16
assistant	aide	Ex 24:13
assistant	aide	Ex 33:11
assistant	aide	Nu 11:28
assistant	aide	Jos 1:1
assistant	aide	Ne 6:5
at this very moment	right now	1Ki 1:25
avoid	keep from	Ge 38:9
bade	bid	2Sa 19:39
[put … on] bail	made … post bond	Ac 17:9
banqueting	banquet	Est 7:8
beards	beard	Isa 7:20
bind	obligate	Nu 30:2
binds	obligates	Nu 30:3, 6, 8, 8, 10
bitumen	tar	Ge 11:3
[uttered] blasphemies against	blasphemed	1Sa 3:13
[use] … blasphemously	blaspheme	Lev 24:17
[used] … blasphemously	blasphemed	Lev 24:11
[uses] … blasphemously	blasphemes	Lev 24:16
[utters] blasphemy against	blasphemes	Nu 15:30
block	stop	2Ki 3:19
bound	obligated	Nu 30:4, 5, 7, 11
brazier	firepot	Ge 15:17
brazier	fire pot	Jer 36:22, 23
brazier	fire pot	Zec 12:6
break forth	shout for joy	Gal 4:27
bring up	rear	Hos 9:12
bringing them up	rearing them	2Ki 10:6
brought	hadÖcome	1Ki 20:33
brought up	reared	Isa 51:18
bruises	welts	Isa 1:6
call	get	Nu 20:25
came on	started	1Ki 18:45
camp	encamp	Ex 14:2, 2
camp round	encamp around	Nu 1:50
camp	encamp	Nu 2:3
[set up] camp	encamp	Nu 2:17

NIVA 2011	NIV NA 2011	Reference
[set up] camp	encamp	Nu 9:20
[set up] camp	encamped	Nu 9:17, 18, 23
[set up] camp	are encamped	Dt 23:9
camped	encamped	Ge 26:17
camped	encamped	Nu 2:34
camped	encamped	Nu 12:16
camped	encamped	1Sa 26:5
camped	encamped	2Ki 25:1
cartwheel	wheel of a cart	Isa 28:27
caused me to wander	had me wander	Ge 20:13
caused	raised	Ac 9:21
chief ministers	administrators	Da 2:49
chief ministers	administrators	Da 6:2, 3, 4, 6
children	offspring	Job 14:21
cities	towns	Jos 18:21
cities	towns	Jos 19:35
cock	rooster	Mt 25:34
cock	rooster	Mt 26:74, 75
cock	rooster	Mk 13:35
cock	rooster	Mk 14:30, 72, 72
cock	rooster	Lk 22:34, 60, 61
cock	rooster	Jn 13:38
cock	rooster	Jn 18:27
cockerel	rooster	Job 38:36
corn	grain	Ge 37:7
corn	grain	Ge 41:5, 6, 7, 22, 24, 26, 27
corn	grain	Ex 22:6
corn	grain	Nu 20:5
corn	grain	Dt 7:13
corn	grain	Dt 11:14
corn	grain	Dt 12:17
corn	grain	Dt 14:23
corn	grain	Dt 16:9
corn	grain	Dt 18:4
corn	grain	Dt 23:25
corn	grain	Dt 28:51
corn	grain	Jdg 15:5, 5
corn	grain	Jdg 16:21
corn	grain	2Sa 17:19
corn	grain	2Ki 4:42, 42
corn	grain	Job 24:24
corn	grain	Ps 65:9, 13
corn	grain	Ps 72:16
corn	grain	Isa 17:5, 5, 5
corn	grain	Isa 36:17
corn	grain	Jer 9:22
corn	grain	Jer 50:11
corn	grain	Eze 36:29
corn	grain	Hos 2:9
corn	grain	Hos 14:7
corn	grain	Mt 12:1

NIVA 2011	NIV NA 2011	Reference
corn	grain	Mk 2:23
corn	grain	Mk 4:28, 29
corn	grain	Lk 6:1
corn	grain	Lk 17:35
cornfield	grainfield	Dt 23:25
cornfields	grainfields	Mt 12:1
cornfields	grainfields	Mk 2:23
cornfields	grainfields	Lk 6:1
covering	long lobe	Ex 29:13
craftsmen	artisans	Jer 24:1
craftsmen	artisans	Jer 29:2
cricket, cicada or	katydid, cricket, or	Lev 11:22
debtor	obligated	Ro 1:14
desert	wilderness	Mt 24:26
desert	wilderness	Rev 17:3
disease	sickness	Ex 23:25
dish	small serving	Pr 15:17
dish	platter	Mt 14:8, 11
dish	platter	Mk 6:25, 28
dishes	basins	1Ki 7:50
doctors	physicians	2Ch 16:12
done	did	Jn 4:29, 39
dumb	mute	1Co 12:2
duties	service	Nu 8:25
ear	headed	Ex 9:31
ear	head	Mk 4:28
ears	heads	Ge 41:7, 23, 24
ears	kernels	Dt 23:25
ears	heads	2Ki 4:42
ears	heads	Mt 13:26
ears of corn	heads of grain	Ge 41:5, 6, 7, 22, 24, 26, 27
ears of corn	heads of grain	Job 24:24
ears of corn	heads of grain	Isa 17:5
ears of corn	heads of grain	Mt 12:1
ears of corn	heads of grain	Mk 2:23
ears of corn	heads of grain	Lk 6:1
eighty to a hundred and twenty litres	twenty to thirty gallons	Jn 2:6
entrance	entryway	2Ki 16:18
entrance	entryway	Mk 14:68
even more to	would rather have	1Co 14:5
excluded	banned	2Ch 26:21
expend	spend	Dt 32:23
Feast	festival	Ps 81:3
feed	nurse	Isa 66:11, 12
feel sympathy for	empathize with	Heb 4:15
feigned insanity	pretended to be insane	1Sa 21:13
fellow-worker	co-worker	Ro 16:9
fellow-worker	co-worker	2Co 8:23
fellow-workers	co-workers	Ro 16:3
fellow-workers	co-workers	1Co 3:9
fellow-workers	co-workers	2Co 6:1
fellow-workers	co-workers	Col 4:11
[stones from the] field	fieldstones	Dt 27:6
fifteen hundred	four hundred and fifty	Lk 15:6
finished	done	1Pe 4:1
[on] fire	afire	Dt 32:22
fishing nets	fishnets	Eze 26:5, 14
fixed allowance	regular allotment	Ge 47:22
in flood	at flood stage	Jos 3:15
in flood	at flood stage	Jos 4:18
[break] forth	shout for joy	Gal 4:27
forty kilograms	hundred pounds	Rev 16:21
forty metres	hundred and twenty feet	Ac 27:28
forwards	forward	Nu 8:3
[to and] fro	back and forth	Est 2:11
[to and] fro	back and forth	Job 1:7
[to and] fro	back and forth	Job 2:2
[to and] fro	back and forth	Eze 37:2
further	farther	Lk 24:28
gave	delivered	1Sa 24:10, 18
gave	delivered	1Sa 26:23
generations	generation	Job 8:8
get	have	1Ki 21:10
get	have	Mk 15:11
give	seat	1Ki 21:9
given	delivered	1Sa 26:8
gourd plant	vine	2Ki 4:39
grain in the ear	kernel in the head	Mk 4:28
grain	kernels	Lk 6:1
grain	kernel	Jn 12:24
grains	kernels	Dt 32:14
half a litre	a pint	Jn 12:3
hand	turn	Ps 27:12
handcrafted	crafted	Nu 31:51
handed	turned	Jer 39:14
handed	delivered	Lk 18:32
heap	pile	Lk 14:35
here and now	right now	Nu 22:29
human race	mankind	Ps 115:16
human race	mankind	Pr 8:31
human race	mankind	Pr 30:14
humanity	mankind	Pr 8:4
[eighty to a] hundred and twenty litres	twenty to thirty gallons	Jn 2:6
[one who is] ill	sick person	Isa 10:18
ill	sick	Eze 34:4
ill	sick	Mt 8:16
ill	sick	Mt 9:12
ill	sick	Mt 10:8
ill	sick	Mt 14:14, 35, 36
ill	sick	Mt 25:36, 39, 43, 44
ill	sick	Mk 1:32
ill	sick	Mk 2:17
ill	sick	Mk 6:5, 13, 55, 56
ill	sick	Lk 5:17, 31
ill	sick	Lk 7:2
ill	sick	Lk 9:2
ill	sick	Lk 10:9
ill	sick	Jn 4:46
ill	sick	Jn 6:2
ill	sick	Jn 11:1, 2, 3, 6
ill	sick	Ac 5:15, 16
ill	sick	Ac 9:37
ill	sick	Ac 19:12
ill	sick	Ac 28:8, 9
ill	sick	1Co 11:30
ill	sick	2Ti 4:20
ill	sick	Jas 5:14
ill-treat	mistreat	Ge 31:50
ill-treat	mistreat	Ex 22:21
ill-treat	mistreat	Lev 19:33
ill-treat	mistreat	1Sa 25:7, 15
ill-treat	mistreat	Jer 38:19
ill-treat	mistreat	Eze 22:29
ill-treat	mistreat	Lk 6:28
ill-treat	mistreat	Ac 14:5
ill-treated	mistreated	Ge 15:13
ill-treated	mistreated	Ge 16:6
ill-treated	mistreated	Nu 20:15
ill-treated	mistreated	Dt 26:6
ill-treated	mistreated	Jer 13:22
ill-treated	mistreated	Eze 22:7
ill-treated	mistreated	Mt 22:6
ill-treated	mistreated	Ac 7:6, 24
ill-treated	mistreated	Heb 11:25, 37
ill-treated	mistreated	Heb 13:3
ill-treating	mistreating	Eze 18:17
ill-treating	mistreating	Ac 7:27

NIVA 2011	NIV NA 2011	Reference
[times of] illness	sickness	Pr 18:14
illness	sickness	Mt 4:23
illness	sickness	Mt 9:35
illness	sickness	Mt 10:1
illness	sickness	Lk 4:40
illness	sickness	Jn 11:4
illnesses	sicknesses	Lk 5:15
illnesses	sicknesses	Lk 7:21
behind	in back	Rev 4:6
in flood	at flood stage	Jos 3:15
in flood	at flood stage	Jos 4:18
[feigned] insanity	pretended to be insane	1Sa 21:13
instructed	directed	Ge 45:19
instructed	directed	1Ki 17:4, 9
instructions	directions	1Co 11:35
Joash	Jehoash	Hos 1:1
just as	even as	3Jn 2
[has been] laid to	is already at	Mt 3:10
[has been] laid to	is already at	Lk 3:9
kerb	rim	Eze 43:13, 17
[a] kilogram	two pounds	Rev 6:6
[forty] kilograms	a hundred pounds	Rev 16:21
[thirty] kilograms	sixty pounds	Mt 13:33
[thirty] kilograms	sixty pounds	Lk 13:21
[thirty-five] kilograms	seventy-five pounds	Jn 19:39
[three] kilograms	six pounds	Rev 6:6
land allotted	allotment	Dt 12:12
land allotted	allotment	Dt 14:27, 29
land allotted	allotment	Dt 18:1
land allotted to	allotment for	Jos 15:1
land allotted to	allotment for	Jos 16:1
land allotted to	allotment for	Jos 17:1, 2
[portion of] land	allotment	Jos 17:14
[portion of] land allotted	allotment	Jos 17:17
[be allotted a portion of] land	have an allotment	Eze 48:13
leafy	shade	Ne 8:15
legally made over	deeded	Ge 23:17
legally made over	deeded	Ge 23:20
let her be burned	have her burned	Ge 38:24
let	have	Ex 9:8
let	have	Ex 10:11
let	have	Ex 18:22, 22
let	have	Ex 20:19
let	have	Ex 25:8, 10
let	have	Ex 28:1
let	have	1Sa 5:8
let	have	1Sa 17:8
let	have	2Ki 20:10
let	have	Ne 4:22
let	have	Est 6:8
let	have	Isa 21:6
let	have	2Co 1:16
[way of] life	walk	Ps 15:2
[way of] life	walk	Ps 84:11
[way of] life	walk	Ps 101:6
[way of] life	walk	Pr 2:7
[way of] life	walk	Pr 19:1
[way of] life	walk	Pr 28:6, 18
[half a] litre	a pint	Jn 12:3
[eighty to a hundred and twenty] litres	twenty to thirty gallons	Jn 2:6
[three thousand] litres	nine hundred gallons	Lk 16:6
live	walk	Gal 5:16
live a life	walk in the way	Eph 5:2
lives among you	dwells in your midst	1Co 3:16
loosed	loosened	Mk 7:35
made	had	Ge 24:11
made	had	Ge 41:43
made	had	Lev 23:43
made	had	Nu 5:18
made	had	Nu 11:24
made	had	Nu 27:22
made	had	Jos 7:16, 17, 18
made	had	1Sa 16:8, 9, 10
made	had	1Sa 20:17
made	had	2Ki 10:16
made	had	2Ch 34:32, 33
made	had	Lk 9:47
make	have	Ge 45:1
make	have	Ex 19:10
make	have	Ex 28:5
make	have	Nu 5:16, 26, 30
make	have	Nu 8:7, 8, 13
make	have	Nu 9:2
make	have	Nu 11:16
make	have	Nu 16:5
make	have	Nu 27:19
make	have	Dt 21:12
make	have	Dt 31:19
make	have	Jos 6:4, 5, 6
make	have	2Ki 5:8
make	have	2Ki 7:13
make	have	2Ki 17:27
make	have	2Ki 22:4, 5, 5, 6
make	have	Ne 7:3
make	have	Eze 34:15
make	have	Mk 6:39
make	have	Lk 9:14
make	have	Lk 12:39
make	have	Jn 6:10
makes	has	1Sa 2:8
men	people	Job 34:23
metres	yards	Jn 21:8
[forty] metres	hundred and twenty feet	Ac 27:28
[thirty] metres	ninety feet	Ac 27:28
ministers	administrators	Da 6:7
[at this very] moment	right now	1Ki 1:25
[even] more to	would rather have	1Co 14:5
nowhere	no place	Mt 8:20
nowhere	no place	Lk 9:58
oaths	vows	Mt 5:23
obnoxious	stench	Pr 13:5
on fire	afire	Dt 32:22
once	one time	Job 9:3
one	person	Lev 27:29
one who is ill	sick person	Isa 10:18
one-fifth	two-tenths	Lev 23:13, 17
one-fifth	two-tenths	Lev 24:5
one-fifth	two-tenths	Nu 15:6
one-fifth	two-tenths	Nu 28:9, 12, 20, 28
one-fifth	two-tenths	Nu 29:3, 9, 14
opposite	across from	Nu 22:1
opposite	across from	Nu 26:3, 63
opposite	across from	Nu 31:12
opposite	across from	Nu 33:48, 50
opposite	across from	Nu 34:15
opposite	across from	Nu 35:1
opposite	across from	Nu 36:13
opposite	across from	Dt 32:49
opposite	across from	Dt 34:1
ordinary	regular	Lev 16:24
ordinary	regular	Lev 23:7, 8, 21, 25, 35, 36
ordinary	regular	Nu 28:18, 25, 26
ordinary	regular	Nu 29:1, 12, 35
ox	cow	Nu 18:17
oxen	cows	Dt 15:19
passed	came	2Ki 4:8
passing	going	Mt 20:30
pence	cents	Mk 12:42
people	persons	Lk 15:7

NIVA 2011	NIV NA 2011	Reference
person	persons	Ac 4:34
pile	stack	Lev 24:6, 7
piles	stacks	Lev 24:6
pinions	aloft	Dt 32:11
[gourd] plant	vine	2Ki 4:39
plant	plants	Job 40:21
[young] plant	sprout	Isa 61:11
ploughshares	plow points	1Sa 13:20, 21
ploughshares	plowshares	Isa 2:4
ploughshares	plowshares	Joel 3:10
ploughshares	plowshares	Mic 4:3
poll-tax	imperial tax	Mt 22:17
poll-tax	imperial tax	Mk 12:14
portion of land	allotment	Jos 17:14
portion of land allotted	allotment	Jos 17:17
[be allotted a] portion of land	have an allotment	Eze 48:13
[you are] progressing spiritually	your soul is getting along well	3Jn 2
pushes	shoves	Nu 35:20
put	seat	1Ki 21:10
put … on	have … mount	1Ki 1:33
put … on	had … mount	1Ki 1:38
put … on bail	made … post bond	Ac 17:9
quarter	fourth	1Ki 6:33
quarter	fourth	Rev 6:8
quietened	quieted	Ps 131:2
quietened	quieted	Ac 19:35
[human] race	mankind	Ps 115:16
[human] race	mankind	Pr 8:31
[human] race	mankind	Pr 30:14
rainstorm came on	rain started falling	1Ki 18:45
rattles	sistrums	2Sa 6:5
rebels	insurrectionists	Mk 15:7
regular	perpetual	Ex 29:28
remain	remaining	Jer 27:18
required	obligated	Gal 5:3
restriction	restrictions	Est 1:8
sank	melted in fear	Jos 2:11
sawn	sawed	Heb 11:37
scrawny	rawboned	Ge 49:14
seat	place	1Ki 21:9
seen	saw	2Sa 18:10
set him	had him stand	Mt 4:5
set him	had him stand	Ac 22:30
set up camp	encamp	Nu 2:17
set up camp	encamp	Nu 9:20
set up camp	encamped	Nu 9:17, 18, 23
set up camp	are encamped	Dt 23:9
share	portion	Jos 17:14
sheaves of corn	shocks of grain	Ex 22:6
sheepfold	pen	Mic 2:12
sheepfold	pen	Hab 3:17
sheepfold	sheep pen	Jn 10:1, 16
sheepfolds	sheep pens	Ge 49:14
sheepfolds	sheep pens	Jdg 5:16
sheepfolds	sheep pens	1Sa 24:3
sheepfolds	sheep pens	Ps 68:13
sheepfolds	sheep pens	Ps 78:70
sheepfolds	pens	Zep 2:6
short-sighted	nearsighted	2Pe 1:9
should	would	1Sa 20:2
should	have	Est 9:21
should	might	Ac 15:7
sink	melt in fear	Jos 14:8
slaughtered	butchered	1Sa 28:24
slaughtered	butchered	Mt 22:4

NIVA 2011	NIV NA 2011	Reference
snake	serpent	Ge 3:1, 2, 4, 13, 14
snake	serpent	Rev 12:9, 15
snake	serpent	Rev 20:2
snakeís	serpentís	2Co 11:3
snakeís	serpentís	Rev 12:14
someone	one	Da 11:7
sound	have … sounded	Lev 25:9
spat	spit	Nu 12:14
spat	spit	Mt 26:67
spat	spit	Mt 27:30
spat	spit	Mk 7:33
spat	spit	Mk 8:23
spat	spit	Mk 15:19
spat	spit	Jn 9:6
[you are progressing] spiritually	your soul is getting along well	3Jn 2
stings	stingers	Rev 9:10
stingy	begrudging	Pr 23:6
stones from the field	fieldstones	Dt 27:6
[violent] storm	windstorm	Eze 1:4
sunset	sundown	Da 6:14
supple	limber	Ge 49:24
[feel] sympathy for	empathize with	Heb 4:15
thirty tons	a thousand bushels	Lk 16:7
thirty kilograms	sixty pounds	Mt 13:33
thirty kilograms	sixty pounds	Lk 13:21
thirty metres	ninety feet	Ac 27:28
thirty-five kilograms	seventy-five pounds	Jn 19:39
three kilograms	six pounds	Rev 6:6
three thousand litres	nine hundred gallons	Lk 16:6
timber	lumber	2Ch 2:9
timber	timbers	Ezr 6:4
times of illness	sickness	Pr 18:14
to and fro	back and forth	Est 2:11
to and fro	back and forth	Job 1:7
to and fro	back and forth	Job 2:2
to and fro	back and forth	Eze 37:2
told	directed	Mt 14:19
told	directed	Mk 6:39
[thirty] tons	a thousand bushels	Lk 16:7
[eighty to a hundred and] twenty litres	twenty to thirty gallons	Jn 2:6
twenty-four	eight hundred	Lk 16:7
two thousand seven hundred	twenty-seven hundred	1Ch 26:32
two thousand six hundred	twenty-six hundred	2Ch 35:8
use … blasphemously	blaspheme	Lev 24:17
used … blasphemously	blasphemed	Lev 24:11
uses … blasphemously	blasphemes	Lev 24:16
usual	regular	Lev 14:32
usual	regular	Nu 8:25
usual	regular	2Ch 30:16
until	through	Ex 12:15
uttered blasphemies against	blasphemed	1Sa 3:13
utters blasphemy against	blasphemes	Nu 15:30
violent storm	windstorm	Eze 1:4
[caused me to] wander	had me wander	Ge 20:13
washing	bathing	2Sa 11:2
way of life	walk	Ps 15:2
way of life	walk	Ps 84:11
way of life	walk	Ps 101:6
way of life	walk	Pr 2:7
way of life	walk	Pr 19:1
way of life	walk	Pr 28:6, 18
whirlwind	windstorm	Isa 29:6
without restriction	with no restrictions	Est 1:8
young plant	sprout	Isa 61:11

FEATURES OF THE MAIN CONCORDANCE

NIV WORD HEADING
The indexed word as spelled in the NIV (see the introduction, pages, x, xi).

FREQUENCY COUNT
Total number of occurrences in the NIV (see the introduction, page x).

RELATED WORD LIST
Other spellings and related words in the NIV (see the introduction, page x).

ABLE (145) [ABILITY, ABLE-BODIED, DISABLED, ENABLE, ENABLED, ENABLES, ENABLING]

Ge 13: 6 so great that *they were* not **a** to stay H3523

G/K NUMBER
Refers to the biblical-language Index-Lexicons: "H" followed by one- to four-digit non-italic number is Hebrew; "A" followed by a five-digit number is Aramaic; "*G*" with *italic* number is Greek (see the introduction, pages xii, xv-xviii). For G/K number with raised "S" (3523S), see the introduction, page xiv.

INDEXED WORD
Abbreviated by its first letter, usually in **bold** type (see the introduction, page xii).

ITALIC TYPEFACE
Indicates words that "assist in translation" (see the introduction, page xiii).

BIBLICAL REFERENCE
See the abbreviations below.

1Ch 9:13 They were **a men**, responsible for H1475+2657

ADDITIONAL G/K NUMBERS
Indicates more than one Hebrew, Aramaic, or Greek word is represented by the NIV translation (see pp. xii-xiii).

BOLD TYPEFACE
In addition to the indexed word, indicates multiple-word translation (see p. xiii).

Dt 7:24 No one *will be a to* **stand up** against you AIT

AIT
Indicates the indexed word "assists in translation"; the indexed word abbreviation is in *italics*, the word it assists is in **bold** (see p. xiii).

Hos 5:13 able to cure you, not **a** to heal your sores. NDT

NDT
"Not Directly Translated" indicates the indexed word was supplied for clarity in translation (see p. xiv).

A (9013) [AN] SEE INDEX OF ARTICLES ETC.

NIV "See" REFERENCES
Refers to the Index of Articles following the Main Concordance (see pp. x-xi).

ABIB (NIV84) AVIV

NIV84 "See" REFERENCES
Cross-references key words and spellings from the 1984 NIV (see p. xi).

ABATED (KJV) GONE, RECEDED

KJV "See" REFERENCES
Cross-references key KJV words to NIV vocabulary (see p. xi).

ABBREVIATIONS FOR THE BOOKS OF THE BIBLE

Genesis ... Ge	2 Kings ... 2Ki	Isaiah ... Isa	Nahum ... Na	Romans ... Ro	Titus ... Titus
Exodus ... Ex	1 Chronicles ... 1Ch	Jeremiah ... Jer	Habakkuk ... Hab	1 Corinthians ... 1Co	Philemon ... Phm
Leviticus ... Lev	2 Chronicles ... 2Ch	Lamentations ... La	Zephaniah ... Zep	2 Corinthians ... 2Co	Hebrews ... Heb
Numbers ... Nu	Ezra ... Ezr	Ezekiel ... Eze	Haggai ... Hag	Galatians ... Gal	James ... Jas
Deuteronomy ... Dt	Nehemiah ... Ne	Daniel ... Da	Zechariah ... Zec	Ephesians ... Eph	1 Peter ... 1Pe
Joshua ... Jos	Esther ... Est	Hosea ... Hos	Malachi ... Mal	Philippians ... Php	2 Peter ... 2Pe
Judges ... Jdg	Job ... Job	Joel ... Joel	Matthew ... Mt	Colossians ... Col	1 John ... 1Jn
Ruth ... Ru	Psalms ... Ps	Amos ... Am	Mark ... Mk	1 Thessalonians ... 1Th	2 John ... 2Jn
1 Samuel ... 1Sa	Proverbs ... Pr	Obadiah ... Ob	Luke ... Lk	2 Thessalonians ... 2Th	3 John ... 3Jn
2 Samuel ... 2Sa	Ecclesiastes ... Ecc	Jonah ... Jnh	John ... Jn	1 Timothy ... 1Ti	Jude ... Jude
1 Kings ... 1Ki	Song of Songs ... SS	Micah ... Mic	Acts ... Ac	2 Timothy ... 2Ti	Revelation ... Rev

The NIV EXHAUSTIVE BIBLE CONCORDANCE

A

A (9013) [AN] See Index of Articles Etc.

AARON (318) [AARON'S, AARONIC]

Ex 4:14 “What about your brother, A the Levite? H195
Ex 4:27 The LORD said to A, “Go into the wilderness H195
Ex 4:28 Then Moses told A everything the LORD had H195
Ex 4:29 Moses and A brought together all the H195
Ex 4:30 A told them everything the LORD had H195
Ex 5: 1 Moses and A went to Pharaoh and H195
Ex 5: 4 “Moses and A, why are you taking H195
Ex 5:20 found Moses and A waiting to meet them H195
Ex 6:13 spoke to Moses and A about the Israelites H195
Ex 6:20 Jochebed, who bore him A and Moses. H195
Ex 6:23 A married Elisheba, daughter of H195
Ex 6:25 Eleazar son of A married one of the H195
Ex 6:26 It was this A and Moses to whom the LORD H195
Ex 6:27 out of Egypt—this same Moses and A. H195
Ex 7: 1 your brother A will be your prophet. H195
Ex 7: 2 your brother A is to tell Pharaoh to let H195
Ex 7: 6 Moses and A did just as the LORD H195
Ex 7: 7 eighty years old and A eighty-three when H195
Ex 7: 8 The LORD said to Moses and A, H195
Ex 7: 9 miracle,' then say to A, 'Take your staff H195
Ex 7:10 So Moses and A went to Pharaoh and did H195
Ex 7:10 A threw his staff down in front of Pharaoh H195
Ex 7:19 said to Moses, “Tell A, 'Take your staff H195
Ex 7:20 Moses and A did just as the LORD had H195
Ex 7:22 he would not listen to **Moses and A**, just H2157S
Ex 8: 5 said to Moses, “Tell A, 'Stretch out your H195
Ex 8: 6 So A stretched out his hand over the waters H195
Ex 8: 8 summoned Moses and A and said, H195
Ex 8:12 After Moses and A left Pharaoh, Moses H195
Ex 8:15 would not listen to **Moses and A**, H2157S
Ex 8:16 said to Moses, “Tell A, 'Stretch out your H195
Ex 8:17 when A stretched out his hand with H195
Ex 8:25 summoned Moses and A and said, H195
Ex 9: 8 Then the LORD said to Moses and A, “Take H195
Ex 9:12 he would not listen to **Moses and A**, H2157S
Ex 9:27 Then Pharaoh summoned Moses and A H195
Ex 10: 3 So Moses and A went to Pharaoh and said H195
Ex 10: 8 Then Moses and A were brought back to H195
Ex 10:11 Then **Moses and A** were driven out of H4392S
Ex 10:16 quickly summoned Moses and A and said, H195
Ex 11:10 Moses and A performed all these wonders H195
Ex 12: 1 The LORD said to Moses and A in Egypt, H195
Ex 12:28 what the LORD commanded Moses and A. H195
Ex 12:31 summoned Moses and A and said, H195
Ex 12:43 The LORD said to Moses and A, “These are H195
Ex 12:50 the LORD had commanded Moses and A. H195
Ex 16: 2 grumbled against Moses and A. H195
Ex 16: 6 So Moses and A said to all the Israelites H195
Ex 16: 9 Then Moses told A, “Say to the entire H195
Ex 16:10 While A was speaking to the whole H195
Ex 16:33 So Moses said to A, “Take a jar and put an H195
Ex 16:34 A put the manna with the tablets of the H195
Ex 17:10 A and Hur went to the top of the hill. H195
Ex 17:12 A and Hur held his hands up—one on one H195
Ex 18:12 A came with all the elders of Israel to H195
Ex 19:24 “Go down and bring A up with you. H195
Ex 24: 1 to the LORD, you and A, Nadab and Abihu, H195
Ex 24: 9 Moses and A, Nadab and Abihu, and the H195
Ex 24:14 A and Hur are with you, and anyone H195
Ex 27:21 A and his sons are to keep the lamps H195
Ex 28: 1 “Have A your brother brought to you from H195
Ex 28: 2 your brother A to give him dignity and H195
Ex 28: 3 that they are to make garments for A, H195
Ex 28: 4 garments for your brother A and his sons, H195
Ex 28:12 A is to bear the names on his shoulders as H195
Ex 28:29 “Whenever A enters the Holy Place, he will H195
Ex 28:30 Thus A will always bear the means of H195
Ex 28:35 A must wear it when he ministers. The H195
Ex 28:41 clothes on your brother A and his sons, H195
Ex 28:43 A and his sons must wear them whenever H195
Ex 28:43 ordinance for A and his descendants. H2257S
Ex 29: 4 Then bring A and his sons to the entrance H195
Ex 29: 5 the garments and dress A with the tunic, H195
Ex 29: 9 Then tie sashes on A and his sons. The H195
Ex 29: 9 “Then you shall ordain A and his sons. H195
Ex 29:10 A and his sons shall lay their hands on H195
Ex 29:15 A and his sons shall lay their hands on H195
Ex 29:19 A and his sons shall lay their hands on H195
Ex 29:20 lobes of the right ears of A and his sons, H195
Ex 29:21 sprinkle it on A and his garments and H195
Ex 29:24 in the hands of A and his sons and have H195
Ex 29:27 ram that belong to A and his sons: H195
Ex 29:28 share from the Israelites for A and his sons. H195
Ex 29:32 A and his sons are to eat the meat of the H195
Ex 29:35 “Do for A and his sons everything I have H195
Ex 29:44 will consecrate A and his sons to serve H195
Ex 30: 7 “A must burn fragrant incense on the altar H195
Ex 30:10 Once a year A shall make atonement on its H195
Ex 30:19 A and his sons are to wash their hands H195
Ex 30:21 ordinance for A and his descendants H2257S
Ex 30:30 “Anoint A and his sons and consecrate H195
Ex 31:10 sacred garments for A the priest and the H195
Ex 32: 1 they gathered around A and said, “Come, H195
Ex 32: 2 A answered them, “Take off the gold H195
Ex 32: 3 off their earrings and brought them to A. H195
Ex 32: 5 When A saw this, he built an altar in front H195
Ex 32:21 He said to A, “What did these people do H195
Ex 32:22 be angry, my lord,” A answered. “You know H195
Ex 32:25 wild and that A had let them get out H195
Ex 32:35 of what they did with the calf A had made. H195
Ex 34:30 When A and all the Israelites saw Moses H195
Ex 34:31 so A and all the leaders of the community H195
Ex 35:19 sacred garments for A the priest and the H195
Ex 38:21 under the direction of Ithamar son of A, H195
Ex 39: 1 They also made sacred garments for A, as H195
Ex 39:27 For A and his sons, they made tunics of H195
Ex 39:41 sacred garments for A the priest and the H195
Ex 40:12 “Bring A and his sons to the entrance to H195
Ex 40:13 Then dress A in the sacred garments H195
Ex 40:31 Moses and A and his sons used it to H195
Lev 1: 7 The sons of A the priest are to put fire on H195
Lev 2: 3 grain offering belongs to A and his sons; H195
Lev 2:10 grain offering belongs to A and his sons; H195
Lev 6: 9 “Give A and his sons this command: 'These H195
Lev 6:16 A and his sons shall eat the rest of it, but it H195
Lev 6:18 Any male descendant of A may eat it. For H195
Lev 6:20 “This is the offering A and his sons are to H195
Lev 6:25 “Say to A and his sons: 'These are the H195
Lev 7:10 belongs equally to all the sons of A. H195
Lev 7:31 the breast belongs to A and his sons. H195
Lev 7:33 The son of A who offers the blood and the H195
Lev 7:34 have given them to A the priest and his H195
Lev 7:35 that were allotted to A and his sons on the H195
Lev 8: 2 “Bring A and his sons, their garments, the H195
Lev 8: 6 Moses brought A and his sons forward H195
Lev 8: 7 He put the tunic on A, tied the sash H2257S
Lev 8:14 A and his sons laid their hands on its H195
Lev 8:18 A and his sons laid their hands on its H195
Lev 8:22 A and his sons laid their hands on its H195
Lev 8:27 all these in the hands of A and his sons, H195
Lev 8:30 sprinkled them on A and his garments H195
Lev 8:30 So he consecrated A and his garments H195
Lev 8:31 Moses then said to A and his sons, “Cook H195
Lev 8:31 'A and his sons are to eat it H195
Lev 8:36 So A and his sons did everything the LORD H195
Lev 9: 1 day Moses summoned A and his sons and H195
Lev 9: 2 He said to A, “Take a bull calf for your sin H195
Lev 9: 7 Moses said to A, “Come to the altar and H195
Lev 9: 8 So A came to the altar and slaughtered the H195
Lev 9:15 A then brought the offering that was for the NDT
Lev 9:20 then A burned the fat on the altar. NDT
Lev 9:21 A waved the breasts and the right thigh H195
Lev 9:22 Then A lifted his hands toward the people H195
Lev 9:23 Moses and A then went into the tent of H195
Lev 10: 3 Moses then said to A, “This is what the LORD H195
Lev 10: 3 I will be honored.' ” A remained silent. H195
Lev 10: 6 Then Moses said to A and his sons Eleazar H195
Lev 10: 8 Then the LORD said to A, H195
Lev 10:12 Moses said to A and his remaining sons H195
Lev 10:19 A replied to Moses, “Today they sacrificed H195
Lev 11: 1 The LORD said to Moses and A, H195
Lev 13: 1 The LORD said to Moses and A, H195
Lev 13: 2 must be brought to A the priest or to one of H195
Lev 14:33 The LORD said to Moses and A, H195
Lev 15: 1 The LORD said to Moses and A, H195
Lev 16: 1 of the two sons of A who died when they H195
Lev 16: 2 “Tell your brother A that he is not to come H195
Lev 16: 3 “This is how A is to enter the Most Holy H195
Lev 16: 6 “A is to offer the bull for his own sin H195
Lev 16: 9 A shall bring the goat whose lot falls to the H195
Lev 16:11 “A shall bring the bull for his own sin H195
Lev 16:17 from the time A goes in to make H2257S
Lev 16:20 “When A has finished making atonement NDT
Lev 16:23 “Then A is to go into the tent of meeting H195
Lev 17: 2 “Speak to A and his sons and to all the H195
Lev 21: 1 the priests, the sons of A, and say to them: H195
Lev 21:17 “Say to A: 'For the generations to come H195
Lev 21:21 No descendant of A the priest who has any H195
Lev 21:24 So Moses told this to A and his sons and to H195
Lev 22: 2 “Tell A and his sons to treat with respect H195
Lev 22: 4 “ 'If a descendant of A has a defiling skin H195
Lev 22:18 “Speak to A and his sons and to all the H195
Lev 24: 3 A is to tend the lamps before the LORD from H195
Lev 24: 9 It belongs to A and his sons, who are to eat H195
Nu 1: 3 You and A are to count according to their H195
Nu 1:17 Moses and A took these men whose H195
Nu 1:44 counted by Moses and A and the twelve H195
Nu 2: 1 The LORD said to Moses and A: H195
Nu 3: 1 of the family of A and Moses at the time H195
Nu 3: 2 names of the sons of A were Nadab the H195
Nu 3: 4 priests during the lifetime of their father A. H195
Nu 3: 6 present them to A the priest to assist H195
Nu 3: 9 Give the Levites to A and his sons; they are H195
Nu 3:10 Appoint A and his sons to serve as priests H195
Nu 3:32 leader of the Levites was Eleazar son of A, H195
Nu 3:38 Moses and A and his sons were to camp to H195
Nu 3:39 by Moses and A according to their H195
Nu 3:48 the additional Israelites to A and his sons.” H195
Nu 3:51 the redemption money to A and his sons, H195
Nu 4: 1 The LORD said to Moses and A: H195
Nu 4: 5 A and his sons are to go in and take down H195
Nu 4:15 “After A and his sons have finished H195
Nu 4:16 “Eleazar son of A, the priest, is to have H195
Nu 4:17 The LORD said to Moses and A, H195
Nu 4:19 A and his sons are to go into the sanctuary H195
Nu 4:27 done under the direction of A and his sons. H195
Nu 4:28 be under the direction of Ithamar son of A, H195
Nu 4:33 under the direction of Ithamar son of A, H195
Nu 4:34 A and the leaders of the community H195
Nu 4:37 Moses and A counted them according to H195
Nu 4:41 Moses and A counted them according to H195
Nu 4:45 Moses and A counted them according to H195

Nu 4:46 A and the leaders of Israel counted all the H195
Nu 6:23 "Tell A and his sons, 'This is how you are to H195
Nu 7: 8 all under the direction of Ithamar son of A, H195
Nu 8: 2 "Speak to A and say to him, 'When you set H195
Nu 8: 3 A did so; he set up the lamps so that they H195
Nu 8:11 A is to present the Levites before the LORD H195
Nu 8:13 stand in front of A and his sons and then H195
Nu 8:19 Levites as gifts to A and his sons to do the H195
Nu 8:20 A and the whole Israelite community did H195
Nu 8:21 Then A presented them as a wave offering H195
Nu 8:22 under the supervision of A and his sons. H195
Nu 9: 6 they came to Moses and A that same day H195
Nu 10: 8 "The sons of A, the priests, are to blow the H195
Nu 12: 1 Miriam and A began to talk against Moses H195
Nu 12: 4 LORD said to Moses, A and Miriam, "Come H195
Nu 12: 5 to the tent and summoned A and Miriam. H195
Nu 12:10 A turned toward her and saw that she had H195
Nu 13:26 came back to Moses and A and the whole H195
Nu 14: 2 Israelites grumbled against Moses and A, H195
Nu 14: 5 Then Moses and A fell facedown in front of H195
Nu 14:26 The LORD said to Moses and A: H195
Nu 15:33 him to Moses and A and the whole H195
Nu 16: 3 to oppose Moses and A and said to them, H195
Nu 16:11 Who is A that you should grumble against H195
Nu 16:16 the LORD tomorrow—you and they and A. H195
Nu 16:17 You and A are to present your censers also." H195
Nu 16:18 stood with Moses and A at the entrance to H195
Nu 16:20 The LORD said to Moses and A, H195
Nu 16:22 But Moses and A fell facedown and cried NDT
Nu 16:37 "Tell Eleazar son of A, the priest, to remove H195
Nu 16:40 a descendant of A should come to burn H195
Nu 16:41 grumbled against Moses and A. H195
Nu 16:42 to Moses and A and turned toward the H195
Nu 16:43 Then Moses and A went to the front of the H195
Nu 16:46 Then Moses said to A, "Take your censer H195
Nu 16:47 So A did as Moses said, and ran into the H195
Nu 16:47 A offered the incense and made NDT
Nu 16:50 Then A returned to Moses at the entrance H195
Nu 18: 1 The LORD said to A, "You, your sons and H195
Nu 18: 8 Then the LORD said to A, "I myself have put H195
Nu 18:20 The LORD said to A, "You will have no H195
Nu 18:28 must give the LORD's portion to A the priest. H195
Nu 19: 1 The LORD said to Moses and A: H195
Nu 20: 2 gathered in opposition to Moses and A. H195
Nu 20: 6 Moses and A went from the assembly to H195
Nu 20: 8 your brother A gather the assembly H195
Nu 20:10 He and A gathered the assembly together H195
Nu 20:12 But the LORD said to Moses and A H195
Nu 20:23 of Edom, the LORD said to Moses and A, H195
Nu 20:24 "A will be gathered to his people. He will H195
Nu 20:25 Get A and his son Eleazar and take them H195
Nu 20:26 A will be gathered to his people H195
Nu 20:28 And A died there on top of the mountain H195
Nu 20:29 whole community learned that A had died, H195
Nu 25: 7 son of Eleazar, the son of A, the priest, H195
Nu 25:11 son of Eleazar, the son of A, the priest, H195
Nu 26: 1 LORD said to Moses and Eleazar son of A, H195
Nu 26: 9 against Moses and A and were among H195
Nu 26:59 To Amram she bore A, Moses and their H195
Nu 26:60 A was the father of Nadab and Abihu H195
Nu 26:64 by Moses and A the priest when they H195
Nu 27:13 to your people, as your brother A was, H195
Nu 33: 1 under the leadership of Moses and A. H195
Nu 33:38 the LORD's command A the priest went up H195
Nu 33:39 A was a hundred and twenty-three years H195
Dt 9:20 was angry enough with A to destroy him, H195
Dt 9:20 but at that time I prayed for A too. H195
Dt 10: 6 There A died and was buried, and Eleazar H195
Dt 32:50 just as your brother A died on Mount Hor H195
Jos 21: 4 who were descendants of A the priest were H195
Jos 21:10 to the descendants of A who were from the H195
Jos 21:13 the descendants of A the priest they gave H195
Jos 21:19 the descendants of A, came to thirteen, H195
Jos 24: 5 " 'Then I sent Moses and A, and I afflicted H195
Jos 24:33 And Eleazar son of A died and was buried H195
Jdg 20:28 Eleazar, the son of A, ministering before it H195
1Sa 12: 6 appointed Moses and A and brought your H195
1Sa 12: 8 the LORD sent Moses and A, who H195
1Ch 6: 3 children of Amram: A, Moses and Miriam H195
1Ch 6: 3 The sons of A: Nadab, Abihu, H195
1Ch 6:49 But A and his descendants were the ones H195
1Ch 6:50 These were the descendants of A: Eleazar H195
1Ch 6:54 to the descendants of A who were from the H195
1Ch 6:57 the descendants of A were given Hebron H195
1Ch 12:27 leader of the family of A, with 3,700 men, H195
1Ch 15: 4 the descendants of A and the Levites: H195
1Ch 23:13 The sons of Amram: A and Moses. Aaron H195
1Ch 23:13 A was set apart, he and his descendants H195
1Ch 23:32 under their relatives the descendants of A H195
1Ch 24: 1 were the divisions of the descendants of A: H195
1Ch 24: 1 The sons of A were Nadab, Abihu, Eleazar H195
1Ch 24:19 prescribed for them by their ancestor A, H195
1Ch 24:31 as their relatives the descendants of A did, H195
1Ch 27:17 Hashabiah son of Kemuel; over A: Zadok; H195
2Ch 13: 9 of the LORD, the sons of A, and the Levites, H195
2Ch 13:10 priests who serve the LORD are sons of A, H195
2Ch 26:18 the descendants of A, who have been H195
2Ch 29:21 the descendants of A, to offer these on the H195
2Ch 31:19 the descendants of A, who lived on the H195
2Ch 35:14 the descendants of A, were sacrificing the H195
Ezr 7: 5 of Eleazar, the son of A the chief priest— H195
Ne 10:38 descended from A is to accompany the H195
Ne 12:47 aside the portion for the descendants of A. H195
Ps 77:20 like a flock by the hand of Moses and A. H195
Ps 99: 6 Moses and A were among his priests H195
Ps 105:26 his servant, and A, whom he had chosen. H195
Ps 106:16 they grew envious of Moses and of A, H195
Ps 115:10 House of A, trust in the LORD—he is their H195
Ps 115:12 he will bless the house of A, H195
Ps 118: 3 Let the house of A say: "His love endures H195
Ps 135:19 the LORD; house of A, praise the LORD; H195
Mic 6: 4 Moses to lead you, also A and Miriam. H195
Lk 1: 5 wife Elizabeth was also a descendant of A. G2
Ac 7:40 They told A, 'Make us gods who will go before G2
Heb 5: 4 receives it when called by God, just as A was. G2
Heb 7:11 order of Melchizedek, not in the order of A? G2

AARON'S (35) [AARON]
Ex 7:12 But A staff swallowed up their staffs H195
Ex 15:20 Miriam the prophet, A sister, took a timbrel H195
Ex 28:30 so they may be over A heart whenever he H195
Ex 28:38 It will be on A forehead, and he will bear H195
Ex 28:38 It will be on A forehead continually so H2257S
Ex 28:40 sashes and caps for A sons to give them H195
Ex 29:26 take the breast of the ram for A ordination, H195
Ex 29:29 "A sacred garments will belong to H4200+195
Lev 1: 5 then A sons the priests shall bring the H195
Lev 1: 8 Then A sons the priests shall arrange the H195
Lev 1:11 A sons the priests shall splash its H195
Lev 2: 2 take it to A sons the priests. The priest H195
Lev 3: 2 Then A sons the priests shall splash the H195
Lev 3: 5 Then A sons are to burn it on the altar on H195
Lev 3: 8 Then A sons shall splash its blood against H195
Lev 3:13 Then A sons shall splash its blood against H195
Lev 6:14 A sons are to bring it before the LORD, in H195
Lev 8: 9 placed the turban on A head and set the H2257S
Lev 8:12 the anointing oil on A head and anointed H195
Lev 8:13 Then he brought A sons forward, put tunics H195
Lev 8:23 blood and put it on the lobe of A right ear, H195
Lev 8:24 Moses also brought A sons forward and put H195
Lev 10: 1 A sons Nadab and Abihu took their censers H195
Lev 10: 4 Elzaphan, sons of A uncle Uzziel, and H195
Lev 10:16 Ithamar, A remaining sons, and H195
Nu 3: 3 Those were the names of A sons, the H195
Nu 17: 3 On the staff of Levi write A name, for there H195
Nu 17: 6 and A staff was among them. H195
Nu 17: 8 entered the tent and saw that A staff, H195
Nu 17:10 "Put back A staff in front of the ark of the H195
Nu 20:26 Remove A garments and put them on his H195
Nu 20:28 Moses removed A garments and put them H195
1Ch 23:28 Levites was to help A descendants in the H195
Ps 133: 2 running down on A beard, down on the H195
Heb 9: 4 gold jar of manna, A staff that had budded G2

AARONIC (1) [AARON]
2Ch 35:14 themselves and for the A priests. H1201+195

AARONITES (KJV) AARON

ABADDON (1)
Rev 9:11 whose name in Hebrew is A and in Greek is G3

ABAGTHA (1)
Est 1:10 Harbona, Bigtha, A, Zethar and Karkas— H5

ABANA (1)
2Ki 5:12 Are not A and Pharpar, the rivers of H76

ABANDON (13) [ABANDONED, ABANDONS]
Dt 4:31 he will not a or destroy you or forget the H8332
Jos 10: 6 "Do not a your servants H8332+3338+4946
1Ki 6:13 Israelites and will not a my people Israel." H6440
2Ch 12: 5 therefore, I now a you to Shishak. H6440
Ne 9:19 compassion you did not a them in the H6440
Ne 9:31 you did not put an end to them or a them, H6440
Ps 16:10 because you will not a me to the realm of H6440
Ps 138: 8 do not a the works of your hands. H8332
Jer 12: 7 forsake my house, a my inheritance; I will H5759
Jer 48:28 A your towns and dwell among the rocks H6440
Eze 27:29 handle the oars will a their ships; H3718+4946
Ac 2:27 because you will not a me to the realm of G1593
1Ti 4: 1 in later times some will a the faith and G923

ABANDONED (35) [ABANDON]
Ge 24:27 who has not a his kindness and H6440
Dt 29:25 because this people a the covenant of the H6440
Dt 32:15 They a the God who made them and H5759
Jdg 5: 6 the highways were a; travelers took H2532
Jdg 6:13 ' But now the LORD has a us and given us H5759
1Sa 30:13 My master a me when I became ill three H6440
1Sa 31: 7 had died, they a their towns and fled. H6440
2Sa 5:21 The Philistines a their idols there, and H6440
1Ki 18:18 You have a the LORD's commands and H6440
2Ki 7: 7 fled in the dusk and a their tents and their H6440
1Ch 10: 7 had died, they a their towns and fled. H6440
1Ch 14:12 The Philistines had a their gods there, and H6440
2Ch 11:14 The Levites even a their pasturelands and H6440
2Ch 12: 1 he and all Israel with him a the law of the H6440
2Ch 12: 5 the LORD says, 'You have a me; therefore, H6440
2Ch 16: 5 stopped building Ramah and a his work. H8697
2Ch 24:18 They a the temple of the LORD, the God of H6440
Ne 9:28 Then you a them to the hand of their H6440
Job 18: 4 is the earth to be a for your sake? H6440
Ps 78:60 He a the tabernacle of Shiloh, the tent he H5759
Isa 2: 6 You, LORD, have a your people, the H5759
Isa 10:14 as people gather a eggs, so I gathered all H6440
Isa 17: 9 will be like places a to thickets and H6440
Isa 27:10 stands desolate, an a settlement H8938
Isa 32:14 The fortress will be a, the noisy city H5759
Isa 54: 7 "For a brief moment I a you, but with H6440
Jer 7:29 has rejected and a this generation that H5759
Jer 49:25 Why has the city of renown not been a H6440
La 2: 7 has rejected his altar and a his sanctuary. H5545
Mic 5: 3 Therefore Israel will be a until the time H5989
Zep 2: 4 Gaza will be a and Ashkelon left in ruins H6440
Ac 2:31 that he was not a to the realm of the G1593
Ro 1:27 same way the men also a natural relations G918
2Co 4: 9 persecuted, but not a; struck down, but not G1593
Jude 6 of authority but a their proper dwelling— G657

ABANDONS (1) [ABANDON]
Jn 10:12 coming, he a the sheep and runs away. G918

ABARIM (5) [IYE ABARIM]
Nu 27:12 this mountain in the A Range and see the H6305
Nu 33:47 camped in the mountains of A, H6305
Nu 33:48 the mountains of A and camped on the H6305
Dt 32:49 "Go up into the A Range to Mount Nebo H6305
Jer 22:20 Bashan, cry out from A, for all your allies H6305

ABASE, ABASED, ABASING (KJV) DISTURBED, HUMBLE, HUMBLED, IN NEED, LOW

ABATED (KJV) GONE, RECEDED

ABBA (3)
Mk 14:36 "A, Father," he said, "everything is possible G5
Ro 8:15 And by him we cry, "A, Father." G5
Gal 4: 6 the Spirit who calls out, "A, Father. G5

ABDA (2)
1Ki 4: 6 Adoniram son of A—in charge of forced H6272
Ne 11:17 associates; and A son of Shammua, the H6272

ABDEEL (1)
Jer 36:26 Shelemiah son of A to arrest Baruch the H6274

ABDI (3)
1Ch 6:44 of Kishi, the son of A, the son of Malluk, H6279
2Ch 29:12 Kish son of A and Azariah son of H6279
Ezr 10:26 Zechariah, Jehiel, A, Jeremoth and Elijah. H6279

ABDIEL (1)
1Ch 5:15 Ahi son of A, the son of Guni, was head H6280

ABDOMEN (3)
Nu 5:21 your womb miscarry and your a swell. H1061
Nu 5:22 body so that your a swells or your womb H1061
Nu 5:27 her a will swell and her womb will H1061

ABDON (9)
Jos 19:28 It went to A, Rehob, Hammon and Kanah H6278
Jos 21:30 from the tribe of Asher, Mishal, A, H6278
Jdg 12:13 After him, A son of Hillel, from Pirathon H6277
Jdg 12:15 Then A son of Hillel died and was buried H6277
1Ch 6:74 tribe of Asher they received Mashal, A, H6278
1Ch 8:23 A, Zikri, Hanan, H6277
1Ch 8:30 his firstborn son was A, followed by H6277
1Ch 9:36 his firstborn son was A, followed by H6277
2Ch 34:20 son of Shaphan, A son of Micah H6277

ABEDNEGO (14)
Da 1: 7 to Mishael, Meshach; and to Azariah, A. H6284
Da 2:49 Meshach and A administrators over the A10524
Da 3:12 Shadrach, Meshach and A—who pay no A10524
Da 3:13 summoned Shadrach, Meshach and A. A10524
Da 3:14 Meshach and A, that you do not A10524
Da 3:16 Meshach and A replied to him A10524
Da 3:19 Meshach and A, and his attitude A10524
Da 3:20 Meshach and A and throw them into the A10524
Da 3:22 who took up Shadrach, Meshach and A, A10524
Da 3:26 Meshach and A, servants of the Most A10524
Da 3:26 Meshach and A came out of the fire A10524
Da 3:28 Meshach and A, who has sent his A10524
Da 3:29 Meshach and A be cut into pieces and A10524
Da 3:30 Meshach and A in the province of A10524

ABEL (14)
Ge 4: 2 Later she gave birth to his brother A. Now H2040
Ge 4: 2 Now A kept flocks, and Cain worked the H2040
Ge 4: 4 And A also brought an offering—fat H2040
Ge 4: 4 looked with favor on A and his offering, H2040
Ge 4: 8 Now Cain said to his brother A, "Let's go H2040
Ge 4: 8 attacked his brother A and killed him. H2040
Ge 4: 9 said to Cain, "Where is your brother A?" H2040
Ge 4:25 granted me another child in place of A, H2040
2Sa 20:18 'Get your answer at A,' and that settled it. H64
Mt 23:35 from the blood of righteous A to the blood of G6
Lk 11:51 from the blood of A to the blood of Zechariah G6
Heb 11: 4 By faith A brought God a better offering than G6
Heb 11: 4 And by faith A still speaks, even though he NDT
Heb 12:24 that speaks a better word than the blood of A. G6

ABEL BETH MAAKAH (4)
2Sa 20:14 of Israel to A and through the H68
2Sa 20:15 besieged Sheba in A. H68
1Ki 15:20 A and all Kinnereth in H68
2Ki 15:29 took Ijon, A, Janoah, H68

ABEL KERAMIM (1)
Jdg 11:33 the vicinity of Minnith, as far as **A**. H70

ABEL MAIM (1)
2Ch 16: 4 **A** and all the store cities of Naphtali. H72

ABEL MEHOLAH (3) [MEHOLAH]
Jdg 7:22 as the border of **A** near Tabbath. H71
1Ki 4:12 from Beth Shan to **A** across to H71
1Ki 19:16 of Shaphat from **A** to succeed you H71

ABEL MIZRAIM (1) [MIZRAIM]
Ge 50:11 place near the Jordan is called **A**. H73

ABEL SHITTIM (1) [SHITTIM]
Nu 33:49 Jordan from Beth Jeshimoth to **A**. H69

ABHOR (8) [ABHORRED, ABHORRENT]
Lev 26:11 place among you, and I *will* not **a** you. H1718
Lev 26:15 my decrees and **a** my laws and fail to H1718
Lev 26:30 forms of your idols, and I *will* **a** you. H1718
Lev 26:44 not reject them or **a** them so as to destroy H1718
Ps 26: 5 *I* **a** the assembly of evildoers and refuse H8533
Ps 139:21 **a** those who are in rebellion against H7752
Am 6: 8 "I **a** the pride of Jacob and detest his H9290
Ro 2:22 You *who* **a** idols, do you rob *G1009*

ABHORRED (4) [ABHOR]
Lev 20:23 they did all these things, *I* **a** them. H7762
Lev 26:43 they rejected my laws and **a** my decrees. H1718
Ps 106:40 with his people and **a** his inheritance. H9493
Isa 49: 7 who was despised and **a** *by* the nation, H9493

ABHORRENT (4) [ABHOR]
Jer 15: 4 I will make them **a** to all the kingdoms of H2317
Jer 24: 9 I will make them **a** and an offense to all H2317
Jer 29:18 will make them **a** to all the kingdoms H2317
Jer 34:17 I will make you **a** to all the kingdoms of H2317

ABI-ALBON (1)
2Sa 23:31 **A** the Arbathite, Azmaveth the Barhumite, H50

ABIA, ABIAH (KJV) ABIJAH

ABIASAPH (1)
Ex 6:24 sons of Korah were Assir, Elkanah and **A**. H25

ABIATHAR (29) [ABIATHAR'S]
1Sa 22:20 of Ahitub, named **A**, escaped and fled to H59
1Sa 22:22 Then David said to **A**, "That day, when Doeg H59
1Sa 23: 6 Now **A** son of Ahimelek had brought the H59
1Sa 23: 9 he said to **A** the priest, "Bring the H59
1Sa 30: 7 Then David said to **A** the priest, the son of H59
1Sa 30: 7 "Bring me the ephod." **A** brought it to him, H59
2Sa 8:17 Ahitub and Ahimelek son of **A** were priests; H59
2Sa 15:24 **A** offered sacrifices until all the people H59
2Sa 15:27 You and **A** return with your two sons NDT
2Sa 15:29 So Zadok and **A** took the ark of God back to H59
2Sa 15:35 the priests Zadok and **A** be there with you? H59
2Sa 15:36 son of Zadok and Jonathan son of **A**, H59
2Sa 17:15 Hushai told Zadok and **A**, the priests H59
2Sa 19:11 David sent this message to Zadok and **A**, H59
2Sa 20:25 was secretary; Zadok and **A** were priests; H59
1Ki 1: 7 Joab son of Zeruiah and with **A** the priest, H59
1Ki 1:19 **A** the priest and Joab the commander of the H59
1Ki 1:25 commanders of the army and **A** the priest. H59
1Ki 1:42 Jonathan son of **A** the priest arrived. H59
1Ki 2:22 him and for **A** the priest and Joab son of H59
1Ki 2:26 To **A** the priest the king said, "Go back to H59
1Ki 2:27 So Solomon removed **A** from the priesthood H59
1Ki 2:35 replaced **A** with Zadok the priest H59
1Ki 4: 4 commander in chief; Zadok and **A**—priests; H59
1Ch 15:11 David summoned Zadok and **A** the priests, H59
1Ch 18:16 Ahitub and Ahimelek son of **A** were priests; H59
1Ch 24: 6 Ahimelek son of **A** and the heads of H59
1Ch 27:34 by Jehoiada son of Benaiah and by **A**. H59
Mk 2:26 In the days of **A** the high priest, he entered *G8*

ABIATHAR'S (1) [ABIATHAR]
2Sa 15:27 with you, and also **A** son Jonathan. H59

ABIB (NIV84) AVIV

ABIDA (2)
Ge 25: 4 were Ephah, Epher, Hanok, **A** and Eldaah. H30
1Ch 1:33 Epher, Hanok, **A** and Eldaah. All H30

ABIDAN (5)
Nu 1:11 from Benjamin, **A** son of Gideoni; H29
Nu 2:22 the people of Benjamin is **A** son of Gideoni. H29
Nu 7:60 On the ninth day **A** son of Gideoni, the H29
Nu 7:65 This was the offering of **A** son of Gideoni. H29
Nu 10:24 **A** son of Gideoni was over the division H29

ABIDE, ABIDES, ABIDETH, ABIDING (KJV) CONTINUE, CONTINUES, DWELL, ENDURE, ENDURES, LIVE, LIVES, REMAIN, REMAINS, STAY, STAYS

ABIEL (3)
1Sa 9: 1 whose name was Kish son of **A**, the son of H24
1Sa 14:51 Kish and Abner's father Ner were sons of **A**. H24
1Ch 11:32 from the ravines of Gaash, **A** the Arbathite, H24

ABIEZER (6) [ABIEZRITE, ABIEZRITES]
Jos 17: 2 people of Manasseh—the clans of **A**, Helek, H48
Jdg 8: 2 better than the full grape harvest of **A**? H48
2Sa 23:27 **A** from Anathoth, Sibbekai the Hushathite, H48
1Ch 7:18 gave birth to Ishhod, **A** and Mahlah. H48
1Ch 11:28 son of Ikkesh from Tekoa, **A** from Anathoth, H48
1Ch 27:12 the ninth month, was **A** the Anathothite, a H48

ABIEZRITE (1) [ABIEZER]
Jdg 6:11 oak in Ophrah that belonged to Joash the **A**, H49

ABIEZRITES (3) [ABIEZER]
Jdg 6:24 To this day it stands in Ophrah of the **A**. H49
Jdg 6:34 a trumpet, summoning the **A** to follow him. H48
Jdg 8:32 tomb of his father Joash in Ophrah of the **A**. H49

ABIGAIL (17)
1Sa 25: 3 was Nabal and his wife's name was **A**. H28
1Sa 25:14 One of the servants told **A**, Nabal's wife H28
1Sa 25:18 **A** acted quickly. She took two hundred H28
1Sa 25:23 When **A** saw David, she quickly got off her H28
1Sa 25:32 David said to **A**, "Praise be to the LORD, the H28
1Sa 25:36 When **A** went to Nabal, he was in the house H28
1Sa 25:39 Then David sent word to **A**, asking her to H28
1Sa 25:40 His servants went to Carmel and said to **A** H28
1Sa 25:42 **A** quickly got on a donkey and, attended by H28
1Sa 27: 3 Ahinoam of Jezreel and **A** of Carmel, the H28
1Sa 30: 5 Ahinoam of Jezreel and **A**, the widow of H28
2Sa 2: 2 Ahinoam of Jezreel and **A**, the widow of H28
2Sa 3: 3 Kileab the son of **A** the widow of Nabal of H28
2Sa 17:25 an Ishmaelite who had married **A**, the NDT
1Ch 2:16 Their sisters were Zeruiah and **A**. Zeruiah's H28
1Ch 2:17 **A** was the mother of Amasa, whose father H28
1Ch 3: 1 the second, Daniel the son of **A** of Carmel; H28

ABIHAIL (6)
Nu 3:35 of the Merarite clans was Zuriel son of **A**; H38
1Ch 2:29 Abishur's wife was named **A**, who bore him H35
1Ch 5:14 These were the sons of **A** son of Huri, the H38
2Ch 11:18 daughter of David's son Jerimoth and of **A**, H35
Est 2:15 the daughter of his uncle **A**) to go to the H38
Est 9:29 daughter of **A**, along with Mordecai H38

ABIHU (12)
Ex 6:23 she bore him Nadab and **A**, Eleazar H33
Ex 24: 1 Nadab and **A**, and seventy of the H33
Ex 24: 9 Aaron, Nadab and **A**, and the seventy H33
Ex 28: 1 along with his sons Nadab and **A**, Eleazar H33
Lev 10: 1 sons Nadab and **A** took their censers, H33
Nu 3: 2 of Aaron were Nadab the firstborn and **A**, H33
Nu 3: 4 Nadab and **A**, however, died before the LORD H33
Nu 26:60 Aaron was the father of Nadab and **A** H33
Nu 26:61 But Nadab and **A** died when they made an H33
1Ch 6: 3 Nadab, **A**, Eleazar and Ithamar. H33
1Ch 24: 1 Aaron were Nadab, **A**, Eleazar and Ithamar H33
1Ch 24: 2 But Nadab and **A** died before their father did, H33

ABIHUD (3)
1Ch 8: 3 The sons of Bela were: Addar, Gera, **A**, H34
Mt 1:13 Zerubbabel the father of **A**, Abihud the *G10*
Mt 1:13 the father of Abihud, **A** the father of Eliakim *G10*

ABIJAH (32) [ABIJAH'S]
1Sa 8: 2 was Joel and the name of his second was **A**, H31
1Ki 14: 1 At that time **A** son of Jeroboam became ill, H31
1Ki 14:31 And **A** his son succeeded him as king H31
1Ki 15: 1 son of Nebat, **A** became king of Judah, H31
1Ki 15: 6 There was war between **A** and Jeroboam H31
1Ki 15: 7 There was war between **A** and Jeroboam. H31
1Ki 15: 8 And **A** rested with his ancestors and was H31
2Ki 18: 2 mother's name was **A** daughter of Zechariah H23
1Ch 2:24 **A** the wife of Hezron bore him Ashhur the H31
1Ch 3:10 son was Rehoboam, **A** his son, Asa his son, H31
1Ch 6:28 Joel the firstborn and **A** the second son. H31
1Ch 7: 8 Jeremoth, **A**, Anathoth and Alemeth. H31
1Ch 24:10 the seventh to Hakkoz, the eighth to **A**, H31
2Ch 11:20 of Absalom, who bore him **A**, Attai, H31
2Ch 11:22 Rehoboam appointed **A** son of Maakah as H31
2Ch 12:16 And **A** his son succeeded him as king H31
2Ch 13: 1 reign of Jeroboam, **A** became king of Judah H31
2Ch 13: 2 There was war between **A** and Jeroboam. H31
2Ch 13: 3 **A** went into battle with an army of four H31
2Ch 13: 4 **A** stood on Mount Zemaraim, in the hill H31
2Ch 13:15 all Israel before **A** and Judah. H31
2Ch 13:17 **A** and his troops inflicted heavy losses on H31
2Ch 13:19 **A** pursued Jeroboam and took from him the H31
2Ch 13:20 did not regain power during the time of **A**. H32
2Ch 13:21 But **A** grew in strength. He married fourteen H32
2Ch 14: 1 And **A** rested with his ancestors and was H31
2Ch 29: 1 mother's name was **A** daughter of Zechariah H31
Ne 10: 7 Meshullam, **A**, Mijamin, H31
Ne 12: 4 Ginnethon, **A**, H31
Mt 1: 7 Rehoboam the father of **A**, Abijah the father *G7*
Mt 1: 7 the father of Abijah, **A** the father of Asa, *G7*
Lk 1: 5 who belonged to the priestly division *of* **A**; his *G7*

ABIJAH'S (4) [ABIJAH]
1Ki 15: 6 Jeroboam throughout **A** lifetime. H2257S
1Ki 15: 7 As for the other events of **A** reign, and all he H31
2Ch 13:22 The other events of **A** reign, what he did H31
Ne 12:17 of **A**, Zikri; of Miniamin's and of Moadiah's H31

ABILENE (1)
Lk 3: 1 Traconitis, and Lysanias tetrarch *of* **A**— *G9*

ABILITY (14) [ABLE]
Ge 47: 6 know of any among them with **special a**, H2657
Ex 31: 6 Also I have given **a** to all the skilled H2683
Ex 35:34 of the tribe of Dan, the **a** to teach others. H4213
Ex 36: 1 has given skill and **a** to know how to carry H9312
Ex 36: 2 had given **a** and who was H2683+928+4213
Dt 8:18 who gives you the **a** to produce wealth, H3946
Ezr 2:69 According to their **a** they gave to the H3946
Ecc 5:19 possessions, and the **a** to enjoy them, to H8948
Ecc 6: 2 God *does* not **grant** them **the a** to H8948
Da 5:12 also the *a to* **interpret** dreams, explain AIT
Mt 25:15 another one bag, each according to his **a**. *G1539*
Ac 8:19 "Give me also this **a** so that everyone on *G2026*
2Co 1: 8 far beyond our **a** *to endure*, so that we *G1539*
2Co 8: 3 they were able, and even beyond their **a**. *G1539*

ABIMAEL (2)
Ge 10:28 Obal, **A**, Sheba, H42
1Ch 1:22 Obal, **A**, Sheba, H42

ABIMELECH (NIV84) ABIMELEK

ABIMELEK (61) [ABIMELEK'S]
Ge 20: 2 Then **A** king of Gerar sent for Sarah and took H43
Ge 20: 3 But God came to **A** in a dream one night H43
Ge 20: 4 Now **A** had not gone near her, so he said H43
Ge 20: 8 Early the next morning **A** summoned all his H43
Ge 20: 9 Then **A** called Abraham in and said, "What H43
Ge 20:10 And **A** asked Abraham, "What was your H43
Ge 20:14 Then **A** brought sheep and cattle and male H43
Ge 20:15 And **A** said, "My land is before you; live H43
Ge 20:17 and God healed **A**, his wife and his H43
Ge 21:22 At that time **A** and Phicol the commander of H43
Ge 21:25 complained to **A** about a well of water H43
Ge 21:26 But **A** said, "I don't know who has done this H43
Ge 21:27 sheep and cattle and gave them to **A**, H43
Ge 21:29 **A** asked Abraham, "What is the H43
Ge 21:32 **A** and Phicol the commander of his forces H43
Ge 26: 1 Isaac went to **A** king of the Philistines in H43
Ge 26: 8 **A** king of the Philistines looked down from a H43
Ge 26: 9 So **A** summoned Isaac and said, "She is H43
Ge 26:10 Then **A** said, "What is this you have done to H43
Ge 26:11 So **A** gave orders to all the people: "Anyone H43
Ge 26:16 Then **A** said to Isaac, "Move away from us H43
Ge 26:26 Meanwhile, **A** had come to him from Gerar H43
Jdg 8:31 also bore him a son, whom he named **A**. H43
Jdg 9: 1 **A** son of Jerub-Baal went to his mother's H43
Jdg 9: 3 they were inclined to follow **A**, for they said, H43
Jdg 9: 4 **A** used it to hire reckless scoundrels H43
Jdg 9: 6 at the pillar in Shechem to crown **A** king. H43
Jdg 9:16 in good faith by making **A** king? H43
Jdg 9:18 sons on a single stone and have made **A**, H43
Jdg 9:19 If you have, may **A** be your joy, and may you H43
Jdg 9:20 let fire come out from **A** and consume you H43
Jdg 9:20 Shechem and Beth Millo, and consume **A**!" H43
Jdg 9:21 because he was afraid of his brother **A**. H43
Jdg 9:22 After **A** had governed Israel three years, H43
Jdg 9:23 up animosity between **A** and the citizens of H43
Jdg 9:23 so that they acted treacherously against **A**. H43
Jdg 9:24 on their brother **A** and on the citizens of H43
Jdg 9:25 who passed by, and this was reported to **A**. H43
Jdg 9:27 were eating and drinking, they cursed **A**. H43
Jdg 9:28 of Ebed said, "Who is **A**, and why should we H43
Jdg 9:28 Why should we serve **A**? H5647S
Jdg 9:29 I would say to **A**, 'Call out your whole H43
Jdg 9:31 Under cover he sent messengers to **A**, saying, H43
Jdg 9:34 So **A** and all his troops set out by night and H43
Jdg 9:35 the city gate just as **A** and his troops came H43
Jdg 9:38 'Who is **A** that we should be subject to him? H43
Jdg 9:39 out the citizens of Shechem and fought **A**. H43
Jdg 9:40 **A** chased him all the way to the entrance of H43
Jdg 9:41 Then **A** stayed in Arumah, and Zebul drove H43
Jdg 9:42 out to the fields, and this was reported to **A**. H43
Jdg 9:44 **A** and the companies with him rushed H43
Jdg 9:45 All that day **A** pressed his attack against the H43
Jdg 9:47 When **A** heard that they had assembled H43
Jdg 9:49 So all the men cut branches and followed **A** H43
Jdg 9:50 Next **A** went to Thebez and besieged it and H43
Jdg 9:52 **A** went to the tower and attacked it. But as H43
Jdg 9:55 When the Israelites saw that **A** was dead H43
Jdg 9:56 the wickedness that **A** had done to his father H43
Jdg 10: 1 After the time of **A**, a man of Issachar H43
2Sa 11:21 Who killed **A** son of Jerub-Besheth? Didn't a H43
Ps 34: T When he pretended to be insane before **A** H43

ABIMELEK'S (2) [ABIMELEK]
Ge 20:18 kept all the women in **A** household from H43
Ge 21:25 a well of water that **A** servants had seized. H43

ABINADAB (9) [ABINADAB'S]
1Sa 16: 8 Then Jesse called **A** and had him pass in H44
1Sa 17:13 was Eliab; the second, **A**; and the third H44
1Sa 31: 2 killed his sons Jonathan, **A** and Malki-Shua. H44
2Sa 6: 3 new cart and brought it from the house of **A**, H44
2Sa 6: 3 Ahio, sons of **A**, were guiding the new H44
1Ch 2:13 the second son was **A**, the third Shimea, H44
1Ch 8:33 of Jonathan, Malki-Shua, **A** and Esh-Baal. H44
1Ch 9:39 of Jonathan, Malki-Shua, **A** and Esh-Baal. H44
1Ch 10: 2 killed his sons Jonathan, **A** and Malki-Shua. H44

ABINADAB'S (2) [ABINADAB]
1Sa 7: 1 They brought it to A house on the hill and H44
1Ch 13: 7 the ark of God from A house on a new cart, H44

ABINOAM (4)
Jdg 4: 6 sent for Barak son of A from Kedesh in H45
Jdg 4:12 that Barak son of A had gone up to Mount H45
Jdg 5: 1 Deborah and Barak son of A sang this song: H45
Jdg 5:12 Take captive your captives, son of A.' H45

ABIRAM (11)
Nu 16: 1 Reubenites—Dathan and A, sons of Eliab, H53
Nu 16:12 Then Moses summoned Dathan and A, the H53
Nu 16:24 away from the tents of Korah, Dathan and A. H53
Nu 16:25 Moses got up and went to Dathan and A H53
Nu 16:27 away from the tents of Korah, Dathan and A. H53
Nu 16:27 Dathan and A had come out and were H53
Nu 26: 9 sons of Eliab were Nemuel, Dathan and A. H53
Nu 26: 9 same Dathan and A were the community H53
Dt 11: 6 what he did to Dathan and A, sons of H53
1Ki 16:34 foundations at the cost of his firstborn son A, H53
Ps 106:17 it buried the company of A. H53

ABISHAG (5)
1Ki 1: 3 a beautiful young woman and found A, H54
1Ki 1:15 where A the Shunammite was attending H54
1Ki 2:17 to give me A the Shunammite as my wife." H54
1Ki 2:21 "Let A the Shunammite be given in H54
1Ki 2:22 "Why do you request A the Shunammite H54

ABISHAI (26)
1Sa 26: 6 Ahimelek the Hittite and A son of Zeruiah, H57
1Sa 26: 6 with me to Saul?" "I'll go with you," said A. H57
1Sa 26: 7 So David and A went to the army by night H57
1Sa 26: 8 A said to David, "Today God has delivered H57
1Sa 26: 9 But David said to A, "Don't destroy him H57
2Sa 2:18 Joab, A and Asahel. Now H57
2Sa 2:24 But Joab and A pursued Abner, and as the H57
2Sa 3:30 Joab and his brother A murdered Abner H57
2Sa 10:10 under the command of A his brother and H93
2Sa 10:14 they fled before A and went inside the city. H57
2Sa 16: 9 Then A son of Zeruiah said to the king H57
2Sa 16:11 David then said to A and all his officials H57
2Sa 18: 2 third under Joab's brother A son of Zeruiah, H57
2Sa 18: 5 king commanded Joab, A and Ittai, "Be H57
2Sa 18:12 the king commanded you and A and Ittai, H57
2Sa 19:21 Then A son of Zeruiah said, "Shouldn't H57
2Sa 20: 6 David said to A, "Now Sheba son of Bikri H57
2Sa 20: 7 went out under the command of A. H2257S
2Sa 20:10 his brother A pursued Sheba son of H57
2Sa 21:17 But A son of Zeruiah came to David's rescue H57
2Sa 23:18 A the brother of Joab son of Zeruiah was H57
1Ch 2:16 Zeruiah's three sons were A, Joab and H93
1Ch 11:20 A the brother of Joab was chief of the Three H93
1Ch 18:12 A son of Zeruiah struck down eighteen H93
1Ch 19:11 men under the command of A his brother, H93
1Ch 19:15 before his brother A and went inside the H93

ABISHALOM (2)
1Ki 15: 2 mother's name was Maakah daughter of A. H58
1Ki 15:10 name was Maakah daughter of A. H58

ABISHUA (5)
1Ch 6: 4 of Phinehas, Phinehas the father of A, H55
1Ch 6: 5 A the father of Bukki, Bukki the father of H55
1Ch 6:50 Phinehas his son, A his son, H55
1Ch 8: 4 A, Naaman, Ahoah, H55
Ezr 7: 5 the son of A, the son of Phinehas, the son of H55

ABISHUR (1) [ABISHUR'S]
1Ch 2:28 The sons of Shammai: Nadab and A. H56

ABISHUR'S (1) [ABISHUR]
1Ch 2:29 A wife was named Abihail, who bore him H56

ABITAL (2)
2Sa 3: 4 Haggith; the fifth, Shephatiah the son of A; H40
1Ch 3: 3 Shephatiah the son of A; and the sixth, H40

ABITUB (1)
1Ch 8:11 By Hushim he had A and Elpaal. H39

ABIUD (KJV, NIV84) ABIHUD

ABLAZE (12)
Dt 5:23 while the mountain was a with fire, all H1277
Dt 9:15 the mountain while it was a with fire. H1277
Job 41:21 Its breath sets coals a, and flames dart H4265
Ps 83:14 forest or a flame sets the mountains a, H4265
Isa 9:18 it sets the forest thickets a, so that H3675
Isa 30:33 like a stream of burning sulfur, sets it a. H1277
Isa 33:12 they will be set a. H3675+928+2021+836
Isa 43: 2 be burned; the flames will not set you a. H1277
Isa 50:11 fires and of the torches you have set a. H1277
Isa 64: 2 As when fire sets twigs a and causes H7706
Da 7: 9 and its wheels were all a. A10178+10471
Rev 8: 8 huge mountain, all a, was thrown G4786+2794

ABLE (145) [ABILITY, ABLE-BODIED, DISABLED, ENABLE, ENABLED, ENABLES, ENABLING]
Ge 11:30 because she was not a to conceive. H2263
Ge 13: 6 so great that they were not a to stay H3523
Ge 14:23 so that you will never be a to say, 'I made AIT
Ge 45: 3 But his brothers were not a to answer him H3523
Ex 7:18 the Egyptians will not be a to drink its H4206
Ex 18:23 you will be a to stand the strain H3523
Lev 26:26 ten women will be a to bake your bread in AIT
Lev 26:37 So you will not be a to stand before your H9538
Nu 1: 3 years old or more and a to serve in the army. AIT
Nu 1:20 old or more who were a to serve in the army AIT
Nu 1:22 old or more who were a to serve in the army AIT
Nu 1:24 old or more who were a to serve in the army AIT
Nu 1:26 old or more who were a to serve in the army AIT
Nu 1:28 old or more who were a to serve in the army AIT
Nu 1:30 old or more who were a to serve in the army AIT
Nu 1:32 old or more who were a to serve in the army AIT
Nu 1:34 old or more who were a to serve in the army AIT
Nu 1:36 old or more who were a to serve in the army AIT
Nu 1:38 old or more who were a to serve in the army AIT
Nu 1:40 old or more who were a to serve in the army AIT
Nu 1:42 old or more who were a to serve in the army AIT
Nu 1:45 old or more who were a to serve in Israel's AIT
Nu 5:28 and will be a to have children. H2445+2446
Nu 14:16 'The LORD was not a to bring these people H3523
Nu 22: 6 Perhaps then I will be a to defeat them H3523
Nu 22:11 Perhaps then I will be a to fight them H3523
Nu 22:37 Am I really not a to reward you? H3523
Nu 26: 2 old or more who are a to serve in the army of AIT
Dt 7:24 No one will be a to stand up against you AIT
Dt 9:28 'Because the LORD was not a to take them H3523
Dt 11:25 No one will be a to stand against you. The AIT
Dt 31: 2 old and I am no longer a to lead you. H3523
Jos 1: 5 No one will be a to stand against you all the AIT
Jos 10: 8 Not one of them will be a to withstand you." AIT
Jos 17:12 the Manassites were not a to occupy H3523
Jos 22:27 your descendants will not be a to say to ours, AIT
Jos 23: 9 this day no one has been a to withstand you. AIT
Jos 24:19 people, "You are not a to serve the LORD. H3523
Jdg 2:14 whom they were no longer a to resist. H3523
Jdg 8: 3 What was I a to do compared to you?" H3523
Jdg 20:15 seven hundred a young men from those H1047
Jdg 20:34 of Israel's a young men made a frontal H1047
1Sa 17: 9 If he is a to fight and kill me, we will H3523
1Sa 17:33 "You are not a to go out against this H3523
1Sa 24: 2 took three thousand a young men from all H1047
2Sa 6: 1 together all the a young men of Israel— H1047
1Ki 3: 9 For who is a to govern this great people of H3523
1Ki 12:21 eighty thousand a young men— H1033
2Ki 2:16 "we your servants have fifty a men. H1201+2657
2Ki 9:37 so that no one will be a to say, 'This is AIT
2Ki 18:35 countries has been a to save his land from AIT
1Ch 9:13 They were a men, responsible for H1475+2657
1Ch 12: 2 with bows and were a to shoot arrows or to NDT
1Ch 12: 8 battle and a to handle the shield and AIT
1Ch 26: 7 and Semakiah were also a men. H1201+2657
1Ch 26: 9 who were a men—18 in all. H1201+2657
1Ch 26:30 seventeen hundred a men—were H1201+2657
1Ch 26:32 who were a men and heads of H1201+2657
1Ch 29:14 that we should be a to give as H6806+3946
2Ch 1:10 who is a to govern this great people of AIT
2Ch 2: 6 But who is a to build a temple for H6806+3946
2Ch 11: 1 eighty thousand a young men— H1033
2Ch 13: 3 of four hundred thousand a fighting men, H1033
2Ch 13: 3 with eight hundred thousand a troops. H1033
2Ch 13:17 casualties among Israel's a men. H1033
2Ch 20:37 were wrecked and were not a to set sail to H6806
2Ch 25: 5 service, a to handle the spear and shield. AIT
2Ch 30: 3 They had not been a to celebrate it at the H3523
2Ch 32:13 Were the gods of those nations ever a H3523+3523
2Ch 32:14 destroyed has been a to save his people H3523
2Ch 32:15 kingdom has been a to deliver his H3523
Ne 8: 2 women and all who were a to understand H1067
Ne 10:28 daughters who are a to understand— H3359
Job 41:10 Who then is a to stand against me? AIT
Ps 36:12 lie fallen—thrown down, not a to rise! H3523
Pr 17:16 when they are not a to understand it? H4213
Isa 36:20 countries have been a to save their lands AIT
Eze 7:19 gold will not be a to deliver them H3523
Da 2:26 "Are you a to tell me what I saw in my A10346
Da 2:47 for you were a to reveal this mystery." A10321
Da 3:15 what god will be a to rescue you from my AIT
Da 3:17 the God we serve is a to deliver us from A10321
Da 4:37 who walk in pride he is a to humble. A10321
Da 5:16 Now I have heard that you are a to give A10321
Da 6:20 has your God, whom you serve continually, been a A10321
Da 11:16 no one will be a to stand against him. AIT
Da 11:25 but he will not be a to stand because of the AIT
Hos 5:13 But he is not a to cure you, not able to H3523
Hos 5:13 able to cure you, not a to heal your sores. NDT
Zep 1:18 their gold will be a to save them on H3523
Mt 9:28 "Do you believe that I am a to do this?" G1538
Mt 18:25 Since he was not a to pay, the master G2400
Mt 26:61 'I am a to destroy the temple of God and G1538
Mk 3:20 his disciples were not even a to eat. G1538
Mk 6:19 wanted to kill him. But she was not a to, G1538
Lk 1: 7 because Elizabeth was not a to conceive, G5096
Lk 1:20 be silent and not a to speak until the day G1538
Lk 8:19 but they were not a to get near him G1538
Lk 13:24 will try to enter and will not be a to. G2710
Lk 14:29 the foundation and are not a to finish it, G2710
Lk 14:30 began to build and wasn't a to finish. G2710
Lk 14:31 whether he is a with ten thousand men G1543
Lk 14:32 If he is not a, he will send a delegation NDT
Lk 21:15 of your adversaries will be a to resist or G1538
Lk 21:36 pray that you may be a to escape all G2996
Lk 21:36 that you may be a to stand before the NDT
Jn 18:28 because they wanted to be a to eat the AIT
Ac 5:39 you will not be a to stop these men G1538
Ac 11:29 as each one was a, decided to provide G2344
Ac 13:11 not even a to see the light of the sun." AIT
Ac 13:39 a justification you were not a to obtain G1538
Ac 15:10 our ancestors have been a to bear? G2710
Ac 19:40 In that case we would not be a to account G1538
Ac 22:13 at that very moment I was a to see him. G329
Ac 24: 8 him yourself you will be a to learn the G1538
Ac 27:16 we were hardly a to make the lifeboat G2710
Ro 8:39 will be a to separate us from the love of G1538
Ro 9:19 For who is a to resist his will?" AIT
Ro 11:23 for God is a to graft them in again. G1543
Ro 12: 2 Then you will be a to test and G1650+3836
Ro 14: 4 the Lord is a to make them stand. G1542
Ro 16:25 Now to him who is a to establish you in G1538
1Co 9:10 threshes should be a to do so in the hope of AIT
2Co 8: 3 that they gave as much as they were a, G1539
2Co 9: 8 And God is a to bless you abundantly, so G1542
Eph 3: 4 you will be a to understand my insight G1538
Eph 3:20 Now to him who is a to do immeasurably G1538
Eph 6:13 you may be a to stand your ground G1538
Php 1:10 so that you may be a to discern what is best AIT
Php 2:16 And then I will be a to boast on the day G1650
1Ti 3: 2 respectable, hospitable, a to teach, G1434
2Ti 1:12 that he is a to guard what I have G1543
2Ti 2:24 kind to everyone, a to teach, not resentful. G1434
2Ti 3: 7 learning but never a to come to a G1538
2Ti 3:15 which are a to make you wise for G1538
Heb 2:18 he is a to help those who are being G1538
Heb 3:19 So we see that they were not a to enter G1538
Heb 5: 2 He is a to deal gently with those who are G1538
Heb 7:25 Therefore he is a to save completely those G1538
Heb 9: 9 being offered were not a to clear the G1538
Jas 3: 2 a to keep their whole body in check. G1543
Jas 4:12 the one who is a to save and destroy. G1538
2Pe 1:15 you will always be a to remember G2400
Jude 24 To him who is a to keep you from G1538
Rev 5: 5 He is a to open the scroll and its seven seals." AIT

ABLE-BODIED (3) [ABLE]
Dt 3:18 But all your a men, armed for battle, must H2657
2Sa 24: 9 hundred thousand a men who could H2657
1Ch 5:18 a men who could handle shield H1201+2657

ABNER (56) [ABNER'S]
1Sa 14:50 of Saul's army was A son of Ner, H46
1Sa 17:55 he said to A, commander of the army H79
1Sa 17:55 of the army, "A, whose son is that H79
1Sa 17:55 A replied, "As surely as you live, Your H79
1Sa 17:57 A took him and brought him before Saul H79
1Sa 20:25 Jonathan, and A sat next to Saul, but H79
1Sa 26: 5 He saw where Saul and A son of Ner, the H79
1Sa 26: 7 A and the soldiers were lying around him H79
1Sa 26:14 called out to the army and to A son of Ner, H79
1Sa 26:14 "Aren't you going to answer me, A? H79
1Sa 26:14 A replied, "Who are you who calls to the H79
2Sa 2: 8 Meanwhile, A son of Ner, the commander of H79
2Sa 2:12 A son of Ner, together with the men of H79
2Sa 2:14 Then A said to Joab, "Let's have some of H79
2Sa 2:17 A and the Israelites were defeated by H79
2Sa 2:19 He chased A, turning neither to the right H79
2Sa 2:20 A looked behind him and asked, "Is that you H79
2Sa 2:21 Then A said to him, "Turn aside to the right H79
2Sa 2:22 Again A warned Asahel, "Stop chasing me H79
2Sa 2:23 so A thrust the butt of his spear into H79
2Sa 2:24 But Joab and Abishai pursued A, and as the H79
2Sa 2:25 Then the men of Benjamin rallied behind A H79
2Sa 2:26 A called out to Joab, "Must the sword H79
2Sa 2:29 All that night A and his men marched H79
2Sa 2:30 stopped pursuing A and assembled the H79
2Sa 2:31 sixty Benjamites who were with A. H79
2Sa 3: 6 A had been strengthening his own position H79
2Sa 3: 7 And Ish-Bosheth said to A, "Why did you H79
2Sa 3: 8 A was very angry because of what H79
2Sa 3: 9 May God deal with A, be it ever so severely H79
2Sa 3:11 did not dare to say another word to A, H79
2Sa 3:12 Then A sent messengers on his behalf to H79
2Sa 3:16 way to Bahurim. Then A said to him, "Go H79
2Sa 3:17 A conferred with the elders of Israel and H79
2Sa 3:19 A also spoke to the Benjamites in person H79
2Sa 3:20 When A, who had twenty men with him H79
2Sa 3:21 Then A said to David, "Let me go at once H79
2Sa 3:21 So David sent A away, and he went in H79
2Sa 3:22 But A was no longer with David in Hebron H79
2Sa 3:23 he was told that A son of Ner had come to H79
2Sa 3:24 Look, A came to you. Why did H79
2Sa 3:25 You know A son of Ner; he came to deceive H79
2Sa 3:26 then left David and sent messengers after A, H79
2Sa 3:27 Now when A returned to Hebron, Joab took H79
2Sa 3:28 LORD concerning the blood of A son of Ner. H79
2Sa 3:30 Abishai murdered A because he had killed H79
2Sa 3:31 sackcloth and walk in mourning in front of A." H79
2Sa 3:32 They buried A in Hebron, and the king wept H79
2Sa 3:33 The king sang this lament for A: "Should H79
2Sa 3:33 "Should A have died as the lawless die H79
2Sa 3:37 had no part in the murder of A son of Ner. H79
2Sa 4: 1 of Saul heard that A had died in Hebron, H79
1Ki 2: 5 A son of Ner and Amasa son of Jether. H79
1Ki 2:32 Both of them—A son of Ner, commander of H79

1Ch 26:28 **A** son of Ner and Joab son of Zeruiah H79
1Ch 27:21 Zechariah; over Benjamin: Jaasiel son of **A**; H79

ABNER'S (3) [ABNER]
1Sa 14:51 Saul's father Kish and **A** father Ner were sons H79
2Sa 3:32 and the king wept aloud at **A** tomb. H79
2Sa 4:12 buried it in **A** tomb at Hebron. H79

ABNORMAL (1) [ABNORMALLY, NORMALLY]
Lk 14: 2 man **suffering from a swelling of** *his* **body**. G5622

ABNORMALLY (1) [ABNORMAL]
1Co 15: 8 appeared to me also, as *to* one **a born**. G1765

ABOARD (6) [BOARD]
Eze 27: 8 skilled men, Tyre, were **a** as your sailors. H928
Jnh 1: 3 *he* **went a** and sailed for Tarshish to H3718+928
Ac 20:13 where we were going to **take** Paul **a**. G377
Ac 20:14 *we* **took** him **a** and went on to Mitylene. G377
Ac 21: 6 to each other, *we* **went a** the ship, and they G326
Ac 27:17 so the men **hoisted** it **a**. Then they passed G149

ABODE (2)
Job 38:19 "What is the way to the **a** *of* light? H8905
Isa 33:20 a peaceful **a**, a tent that will not H5659

ABODEST (KJV) STAY

ABOLISH (4) [ABOLISHED]
Da 11:31 temple fortress and *will* **a** the daily H6073
Hos 2:18 sword and battle *I will* **a** from the land, H8689
Mt 5:17 think that I have come *to* **a** the Law or the G2907
Mt 5:17 I have not come *to* **a** them but to fulfill G2907

ABOLISHED (2) [ABOLISH]
Da 12:11 the daily sacrifice **is a** and the H6073
Gal 5:11 case the offense of the cross *has been* **a**. G2934

ABOMINABLE (1) [ABOMINATION]
Rev 17: 4 filled with **a** *things* and the filth of her G1007

ABOMINATION (5) [ABOMINABLE, ABOMINATIONS]
Da 9:27 he will set up an **a** that causes desolation H9199
Da 11:31 they will set up the **a** that causes H9199
Da 12:11 is abolished and the **a** that causes H9199
Mt 24:15 the holy place 'the **a** that causes G1007
Mk 13:14 "When you see 'the **a** that causes G1007

ABOMINATIONS (3) [ABOMINATION]
Pr 26:25 believe them, for seven **a** fill their hearts. H9359
Isa 66: 3 own ways, and they delight in their **a**; H9199
Rev 17: 5 PROSTITUTES AND OF THE **A** OF THE EARTH. G1007

ABOUND (7) [ABOUNDING, ABOUNDS]
2Ki 9:22 **all** the idolatry and witchcraft of your mother Jezebel **a** H8041
Ps 4: 7 with joy when their grain and new wine **a**. H8045
Ps 72: 7 prosperity **a** till the moon is no H8044
Ps 72:16 *May* grain **a** throughout the land H2118+7172
2Co 9: 8 you need, *you will* **a** in every good work. G4355
Php 1: 9 that your love *may* **a** more and more in G4355
Php 1:26 in Christ Jesus *will* **a** on account of me. G4355

ABOUNDED, ABOUNDETH, ABOUNDING (KJV) ABOUNDS, EXCEL, INCREASE, INCREASED, INCREASING, OVERFLOW, OVERFLOWING, RICHLY

ABOUNDING (9) [ABOUND]
Ex 34: 6 slow to anger, **a** *in* love and faithfulness, H8041
Nu 14:18 **a** *in* love and forgiving sin and rebellion. H8041
Dt 33:23 "Naphtali is **a** *with* the favor of the LORD H8428
Ne 9:17 slow to anger and **a** *in* love. H8041
Ps 86: 5 good, **a** *in* love to all who call to you. H8041
Ps 86:15 slow to anger, **a** *in* love and faithfulness. H8041
Ps 103: 8 gracious, slow to anger, **a** *in* love. H8041
Joel 2:13 slow to anger and **a** *in* love, and he H8041
Jnh 4: 2 slow to anger and **a** *in* love, a God who H8041

ABOUNDS (2) [ABOUND]
Hab 1: 3 before me; there is strife, and conflict **a**. H5951
2Co 1: 5 so also our comfort **a** through Christ. G4355

ABOUT (901)
Ge 1:21 the water teems and that **moves a** in it, H8253
Ge 3:17 fruit from the tree *a* which *I* **commanded** you, AIT
Ge 9: 3 that lives and **moves a** will be food for H8254
Ge 12:11 As *he was* **a** to enter Egypt, he said to his H7928
Ge 12:20 Pharaoh gave orders **a** Abram to his men, H6584
Ge 13: 5 Now Lot, who *was* **moving a** with Abram H2143
Ge 18:10 surely return to you **a** this time next year, H3869
Ge 18:17 I hide from Abraham what I *am a to* **do**? AIT
Ge 18:19 so that the LORD *will* **bring a** for Abraham H995
Ge 19:14 because the LORD *is a to* **destroy** the city!" AIT
Ge 21: 6 everyone who **hears** *a* this will laugh AIT
Ge 21:12 not be so distressed **a** the boy and your H6584
Ge 21:16 went off and sat down **a** a bowshot away, H3869
Ge 21:25 to Abimelek **a** a well of water that H6584+128
Ge 21:26 did not tell me, and I **heard** *a* it only today." AIT
Ge 22: 3 he set out for the place God *had* **told** him *a*. AIT
Ge 22: 9 they reached the place God *had* **told** him *a*, AIT
Ge 24:28 her mother's household **a** these things. H3869
Ge 24:57 "Let's call the young woman and **ask** her *a* it." AIT
Ge 25:32 I *am* **a** to die," Esau said. "What H2143
Ge 26: 7 men of that place asked him **a** his wife, H4200
Ge 26:32 and told him **a** the well they had H6584+128
Ge 29:13 As soon as Laban heard the **news** *a* Jacob AIT
Ge 31:43 what can I do today **a** these daughters of H4200
Ge 31:43 or **a** the children they have borne? H4200
Ge 34: 5 so he **did nothing** *a* it until they came home. AIT
Ge 37: 2 he brought their father a bad **report** *a* them. AIT
Ge 38:24 **A** three months later Judah was told H3869
Ge 41:25 has revealed to Pharaoh what *he is a to* **do**. AIT
Ge 41:28 God has shown Pharaoh what *he is a to* **do**. AIT
Ge 42: 9 his dreams **a** them and said to them H4200
Ge 43: 7 questioned us closely **a** ourselves and our H4200
Ge 43:27 "How is your aged father *you* **told** me *a*? AIT
Ge 43:29 As he **looked a** and saw his brother H6524+5951
Ge 43:29 youngest brother, the one *you* **told** me *a*?" AIT
Ge 45: 2 and Pharaoh's household **heard** *a* it. AIT
Ge 45:13 **Tell** my father *a* all the honor accorded me in AIT
Ge 45:13 me in Egypt and **a** everything you have seen NDT
Ge 45:20 Never mind **a** your belongings, because H6584
Ge 48:21 to Joseph, "I *am a to* **die**, but God will be AIT
Ge 49:29 "I *am a to* **be gathered** to my people AIT
Ge 50: 5 oath and said, "I *am a to* **die**; bury me in the AIT
Ge 50:24 Joseph said to his brothers, "I *am a to* **die**. AIT
Ex 2:25 the Israelites and *was* **concerned a** them. H3359
Ex 3: 7 and *I am* **concerned a** their suffering. H3359
Ex 4:14 and he said, "**What a** your brother H2022+4202
Ex 4:24 the LORD met Moses and *was* **a to** kill him. H1335
Ex 4:28 **told** Aaron everything the LORD had sent him to say, and also *a* AIT
Ex 4:31 the LORD *was* **concerned a** them and had H7212
Ex 6:13 to Moses and Aaron **a** the Israelites and H448
Ex 6:27 *were the ones who* **spoke** to Pharaoh king of Egypt *a* AIT
Ex 8:12 out to the LORD **a** the frogs he had H6584+1821
Ex 10:23 else or **move a** for three H7756+4946+9393
Ex 11: 4 '**A** midnight I will go throughout Egypt. H3869
Ex 12:37 There were **a** six hundred thousand men H3869
Ex 14: 5 changed their minds **a** them and said, H448
Ex 18: 8 Moses **told** his father-in-law *a* everything the AIT
Ex 18: 8 Israel's sake and **a** all the hardships they NDT
Ex 18: 9 delighted to hear **a** all the good things H6584
Ex 22: 9 other lost property *a* **which** somebody says, AIT
Ex 32:28 that day **a** three thousand of the H3869
Lev 5: 1 something they have seen or **learned a**, H3359
Lev 5: 4 in any matter one might carelessly swear **a** NDT
Lev 6: 2 a neighbor **a** something entrusted H928
Lev 6: 2 left in their care or **a** something stolen, H928
Lev 6: 3 if they find lost property and lie **a** it, or if H928
Lev 6: 3 if they swear falsely **a** any such sin that H6584
Lev 6: 5 whatever it was they swore falsely **a** H6584
Lev 10:16 When Moses **inquired a** the goat H2011+2011
Lev 11:46 living thing that **moves a** in the water H8253
Lev 15: 3 discharge *will* **bring a** uncleanness: H2118+928
Lev 19:16 " '*Do* not **go a** spreading slander among H2143
Nu 10:29 out for the place *a* **which** the LORD said, AIT
Nu 11: 1 Now the people **complained** *a* their AIT
Nu 13:32 the Israelites **a bad report** *a* the land they AIT
Nu 14:10 the whole assembly **talked** *a* stoning them. AIT
Nu 14:13 the LORD, "Then the Egyptians *will* **hear** *a* it! AIT
Nu 14:14 *they will* **tell** the inhabitants of this land *a* AIT
Nu 14:15 who have heard this **report** *a* you will say, AIT
Nu 14:36 him by spreading a bad report **a** it— H6584
Nu 14:37 spreading the bad **report** *a* the land were AIT
Nu 16:30 But if the LORD **brings a** something totally H1343
Nu 20:14 You **know a** all the hardships that have H3359
Nu 21:17 "Spring up, O well! Sing **a** it, H4200
Nu 21:18 **a** the well that the princes dug, that the NDT
Nu 30: 4 her father **hears** *a* her vow or pledge but AIT
Nu 30: 5 if her father forbids her when he **hears** *a* it, AIT
Nu 30: 7 her husband **hears** *a* it but says nothing AIT
Nu 30: 8 her husband forbids her when he **hears** *a* it, AIT
Nu 30:11 her husband **hears** *a* it but says nothing AIT
Nu 30:12 nullifies them when he **hears** *a* them, AIT
Nu 30:14 her husband **says nothing** to her *a* it from day AIT
Nu 30:14 saying nothing to her when he **hears** *a* them. AIT
Nu 30:15 them some time after he **hears** *a* them, AIT
Nu 32:28 Moses gave orders **a** them to Eleazar the H4200
Dt 1:22 us and bring back a **report** *a* the route we are AIT
Dt 2: 4 'You *are a to* **pass** through the territory of AIT
Dt 3:26 "Do not speak to me anymore **a** this matter. H928
Dt 4: 1 the decrees and laws I *am a to* **teach** you. AIT
Dt 4: 6 who *will* **hear** *a* all these decrees and say AIT
Dt 4:22 you *are a to* **cross over** and take AIT
Dt 4:32 Ask now **a** the former days, long before H4200
Dt 6: 7 Talk **a** them when you sit at home and H928
Dt 9: 1 You *are* now *a to* **cross** the Jordan to go in AIT
Dt 9: 2 You **know a** them and have heard it said H3359
Dt 11:19 talking **a** them when you sit at home and H928
Dt 11:31 You *are a to* **cross** the Jordan to enter and AIT
Dt 12:29 nations you *are a to* **invade** and dispossess AIT
Dt 12:30 to be ensnared by inquiring **a** their gods, H4200
Dt 13:12 If you hear it said **a** one of the towns the H928
Dt 20: 2 When you *are a to* **go** into battle, the priest AIT
Dt 23:14 LORD your God **moves a** in your camp to H2143
Dt 24: 1 he finds something indecent **a** her, H928
Dt 28:29 At midday *you will* **grope a** like a blind H5491
Dt 33: 7 And this he said **a** Judah: "Hear, LORD, the H4200
Dt 33: 8 **A** Levi he said: "Your Thummim and Urim H4200
Dt 33:12 **A** Benjamin he said: "Let the beloved of H4200
Dt 33:13 **A** Joseph he said: "May the LORD bless his H4200
Dt 33:18 **A** Zebulun he said: "Rejoice, Zebulun, in H4200
Dt 33:20 **A** Gad he said: "Blessed is he who H4200
Dt 33:22 **A** Dan he said: "Dan is a lion's cub H4200
Dt 33:23 **A** Naphtali is H4200
Dt 33:24 **A** Asher he said: "Most blessed of sons is H4200
Jos 1: 2 River into the land I *am a to* **give** to them— AIT
Jos 3: 4 keep a distance of **a** two thousand cubits H3869
Jos 4:13 **A** forty thousand armed for battle crossed H3869
Jos 5: 6 The Israelites *had* **moved a** in the H2143
Jos 6:18 *you will* not **bring a** *your own* **destruction** H3049
Jos 7: 4 So **a** three thousand went up; but they H3869
Jos 7: 5 who killed **a** thirty-six of them. They H3869
Jos 7: 9 of the country *will* **hear** *a* this and they will AIT
Jos 8:12 Joshua had taken **a** five thousand men H3869
Jos 9: 1 west of the Jordan **heard** *a* these things— AIT
Jos 10:13 sky and delayed going down **a** a full day. H3869
Jos 14: 6 at Kadesh Barnea **a** you and me. H6584+128
Jos 14:10 while Israel **moved a** in the wilderness. H2143
Jos 22:33 And *they* **talked** no more **a** going to war AIT
Jos 23:14 "Now I *am a to* **go** the way of all the earth AIT
Jdg 3:16 a double-edged sword **a a cubit** long, H1688
Jdg 3:29 they struck down **a** ten thousand Moabites H3869
Jdg 6:13 that our ancestors **told** us *a* when they said, AIT
Jdg 8:10 with a force of **a** fifteen thousand men, H3869
Jdg 8:15 *a* **whom** you taunted me by saying AIT
Jdg 9: 7 When Jotham *was* **told** *a* this, he climbed up AIT
Jdg 9:49 Shechem, **a** a thousand men and women H3869
Jdg 16:27 on the roof were **a** three thousand men H3869
Jdg 17: 2 taken from you and **a** which I heard you NDT
Jdg 20:12 "**What** *a* this awful crime that was committed AIT
Jdg 20:31 so that **a** thirty men fell in the open field H3869
Jdg 20:39 on the Israelites (**a** thirty), and they said, H3869
Ru 1: 4 After they had lived there **a** ten years, H3869
Ru 2:11 "I've **been told** all **a** what you have H5583+5583
Ru 2:17 it amounted to **a** an ephah. H3869
Ru 2:19 Then Ruth **told** her mother-in-law *a* the one AIT
1Sa 2:22 **heard** *a* everything his sons were doing to all AIT
1Sa 2:23 I **hear** from all the people *a* these wicked AIT
1Sa 3:11 I *am a to* **do** something in Israel that will AIT
1Sa 3:11 the ears of everyone *who* **hears** *a* it tingle. AIT
1Sa 3:13 forever because of the sin *he* **knew a**; H3359
1Sa 4: 2 who killed **a** four thousand of them on the H3869
1Sa 9: 5 will stop thinking **a** the donkeys and start H4946
1Sa 9: 5 about the donkeys and start worrying **a** us." H4200
1Sa 9:13 up now; you should find him **a** this time." H3869
1Sa 9:16 "**A** this time tomorrow I will send you a H3869
1Sa 9:17 "This is the man *I* **spoke** to you *a*; he will AIT
1Sa 9:20 do not worry **a** them; they have been H4200
1Sa 9:22 who were invited—**a** thirty in number. H3869
1Sa 9:26 They rose **a** daybreak, and Samuel called H3869
1Sa 10: 2 your father *has* **stopped thinking** *a* them AIT
1Sa 10: 2 thinking about them and is worried **a** you. H4200
1Sa 10: 2 is asking, "What shall I do **a** my son?" H4200
1Sa 10:16 uncle what Samuel *had* **said** *a* the kingship. AIT
1Sa 12:16 thing the LORD *is a to* **do** before your eyes! AIT
1Sa 13: 3 at Geba, and the Philistines **heard** *a* it. AIT
1Sa 13:15 They numbered **a** six hundred. H3869
1Sa 14: 2 With him were **a** six hundred men, H3869
1Sa 14:14 twenty men in an area of **a** half an acre. H3869
1Sa 14:45 *he* who *has* **brought a** this great H6913
1Sa 16: 2 If Saul **hears** *a* it, he will kill me. AIT
1Sa 18:20 and when *they* **told** Saul *a* it, he was AIT
1Sa 19: 3 I'll speak to him **a** you and will tell you H928
1Sa 19:21 Saul *was* **told** *a* it, and he sent more men AIT
1Sa 20:23 And **a** the matter you and I discussed NDT
1Sa 20:39 The boy **knew** nothing **a** all this; only H3359
1Sa 21: 2 'No one *is to* **know** anything **a** the mission H3359
1Sa 21:11 he the one they sing **a** in their dances: H4200
1Sa 22: 1 his father's household **heard** *a* it, AIT
1Sa 22: 2 **A** four hundred men were with him H3869
1Sa 22: 8 of you is concerned **a** me or tells me that H6584
1Sa 22:15 knows nothing at all **a** this whole affair." H928
1Sa 23:13 his men, **a** six hundred in number H3869
1Sa 23:23 Find out **a** all the hiding places he uses H4946
1Sa 23:25 when David *was* **told** *a* it, he went down AIT
1Sa 24:18 You *have* just now **told** me *a* the good you AIT
1Sa 25:13 **A** four hundred men went up with David H3869
1Sa 25:38 **A** ten days later, the LORD struck Nabal H3869
1Sa 26:12 No one saw or **knew a** it, nor did anyone H3359
1Sa 28: 9 set a trap for my life to **bring a** my **death**?" H4637
1Sa 29: 3 "**What a** these Hebrews? H4537
1Sa 29: 5 this the David they sang **a** in their dances: H4200
2Sa 3:28 when David **heard** *a* this, he said, "I AIT
2Sa 4: 4 old when the **news** *a* Saul and Jonathan AIT
2Sa 5:17 David **heard** *a* it and went down to the AIT
2Sa 7:19 you have also spoken **a** the future of the H4200
2Sa 10: 5 When David *was* **told** *a* this, he sent AIT
2Sa 11: 3 David sent someone to find out **a** her H4200
2Sa 13:13 **What a** me? Where could I get rid of my H2256
2Sa 13:13 **And what a** you? You would H2256
2Sa 13:33 *should* not *be* **concerned a** H8492+448+4213
2Sa 15:11 innocently, **knowing** nothing **a** the matter. H3359
2Sa 15:20 today *shall I* **make** you **wander a** with us, H5675
2Sa 17: 9 whoever **hears** *a* it will say, 'There AIT
2Sa 17:19 No *one* **knew** anything **a** it. H3359
2Sa 18: 3 to flee, *they* won't **care a** us. H8492+4213+448
2Sa 18:29 just as Joab was **a** to send the king's servant NDT
2Sa 19:10 So why *do* you **say nothing** *a* bringing the AIT
2Sa 19:42 Why are you angry **a** it? Have we eaten H6584
2Sa 22: 5 The waves of death **swirled a** me; the H705
2Sa 23:10 LORD **brought a** a great victory that day H6913
2Sa 23:12 the LORD **brought a** a great victory. H6913
1Ki 1:11 and our lord David **knows** nothing *a* it? AIT
1Ki 1:18 *you*, my lord the king, *do* not **know a** it. H3359

1Ki 2: 2 "*I am a to* **go** the way of all the earth," AIT
1Ki 2:27 had spoken at Shiloh **a** the house of Eli. H6584
1Ki 4:33 He spoke **a** plant life, from the cedar of H6584
1Ki 4:33 He also spoke **a** animals and birds H6584
1Ki 8: 5 that had gathered **a** him were before the H6584
1Ki 10: 1 the queen of Sheba **heard** *a* the fame of AIT
1Ki 10: 2 Solomon and **talked** with him *a* all that she AIT
1Ki 10: 6 in my own country **a** your achievements H6584
1Ki 11: 2 were from nations *a* **which** the LORD had told AIT
1Ki 11:29 **A** that time Jeroboam was going out of H928
1Ki 14: 5 wife is coming to ask you **a** her son, H448
1Ki 16: 3 So I *am a to* **wipe out** Baasha and his house AIT
1Ki 19:11 of the LORD, for the LORD *is a to* **pass by**." AIT
1Ki 20: 6 But **a** this time tomorrow I am going to H3869
1Ki 22: 6 the prophets—**a** four hundred men—and H3869
1Ki 22: 8 he never prophesies anything good **a** me, H6584
1Ki 22:18 he never prophesies anything good **a** me, H6584
2Ki 2: 1 the LORD *was a to* **take** Elijah **up** to heaven in AIT
2Ki 3:20 **a** the time for offering the sacrifice H3869
2Ki 4:16 "**A** this time next year," Elisha said, "you H4200
2Ki 4:17 the next year **a** that same time she H4200
2Ki 7: 1 **A** this time tomorrow, a seah of the finest H3869
2Ki 7:18 "**A** this time tomorrow, a seah of the H3869
2Ki 8: 4 "**Tell** me *a* all the great things Elisha has AIT
2Ki 8: 6 The king **asked** the woman *a* it, and she told AIT
2Ki 9:23 Joram **turned a** and fled, calling H2200+3338
2Ki 9:30 When Jezebel **heard** *a* it, she put on eye AIT
2Ki 11: 2 royal princes, who *were a to* **be murdered**. AIT
2Ki 12:17 **A this time** Hazael king of Aram went up H255
2Ki 14:13 a section **a** four hundred cubits long. NDT
2Ki 22:13 for all Judah **a** what is written in this H6584
2Ki 23:27 this temple, *a* **which** I said, 'My Name AIT
1Ch 11:14 the LORD **brought a** a great **victory**. H3828+9591
1Ch 14: 8 David **heard** *a* it and went out to meet AIT
1Ch 15:13 *We did* not **inquire of** him *a* how to do it in AIT
1Ch 17:17 you have spoken **a** the future of the house H4200
1Ch 19: 5 came and told David **a** the men, H6584
2Ch 2: 4 Now I *am a to* **build** a temple for the Name AIT
2Ch 5: 6 that had gathered **a** him were before the H6584
2Ch 9: 1 Solomon and **talked** with him *a* all she had AIT
2Ch 9: 5 in my own country **a** your achievements H6584
2Ch 15: 5 it was not safe to **travel a**, H3655+2256+995
2Ch 15:15 All Judah rejoiced **a** the oath because H6584
2Ch 18: 7 he never prophesies anything good **a** me, H6584
2Ch 18:17 he never prophesies anything good **a** me, H6584
2Ch 21:14 So now the LORD *is a to* **strike** your people AIT
2Ch 22: 7 God **brought a** Ahaziah's downfall. H2118+4946
2Ch 22:11 princes who *were a to* **be murdered** and put AIT
2Ch 24:27 the many prophecies **a** him, and the H6584
2Ch 25: 9 "But what **a** the hundred talents I paid H4200
2Ch 25:23 a section **a** four hundred cubits long. NDT
2Ch 29:36 at what God *had* **brought a** for his people, H3922
2Ch 31: 9 asked the priests and Levites **a** the heaps; H6584
2Ch 32: 3 military staff **a** blocking off the water H4200
2Ch 32:19 They spoke **a** the God of Jerusalem as they H448
2Ch 32:19 as they did **a** the gods of the other H6584
2Ch 32:20 Amoz cried out in prayer to heaven **a** this. H6584
2Ch 32:31 of Babylon to **ask** him *a* the miraculous sign AIT
2Ch 34:21 in Israel and Judah **a** what is written in H6584
2Ch 35: 3 It is not to be **carried a** on your shoulders H5362
Ezr 7:14 to inquire **a** Judah and Jerusalem A10542
Ezr 8:23 we fasted and petitioned our God **a** this, H6584
Ne 1: 2 I questioned them **a** the Jewish remnant H6584
Ne 1: 2 survived the exile, and also **a** Jerusalem. H6584
Ne 2:10 Tobiah the Ammonite official **heard** *a* this, AIT
Ne 2:18 *I* also **told** them *a* the gracious hand of my AIT
Ne 2:19 official and Geshem the Arab **heard** *a* it, AIT
Ne 6: 6 these reports you *are a to* **become** their king AIT
Ne 6: 7 this proclamation **a** you in Jerusalem: H6584
Ne 6:16 When all our enemies **heard** *a* this, all the AIT
Ne 13: 7 Here I learned **a** the evil thing Eliashib had H928
Est 1:18 of the nobility who *have* **heard** *a* the queen's AIT
Est 2: 1 done and what he had decreed **a** her. H6584
Est 2:22 But Mordecai **found out** *a* the plot and told AIT
Est 3: 4 Therefore *they* **told** Haman *a* it to see AIT
Est 4: 4 attendants came and **told** her *a* Mordecai, AIT
Est 5:11 Haman **boasted** to them *a* his vast wealth, his AIT
Est 6: 4 of the palace to **speak** to the king *a* impaling AIT
Est 9:32 decree confirmed these **regulations** *a* Purim, AIT
Job 2:11 **heard** *a* all the troubles that had come upon AIT
Job 3: 4 *may* God above not **care a** it; may H2011
Job 11:18 *you will* **look a** you and take your rest in H2916
Job 15:23 He **wanders a** for food like a vulture; he H5610
Job 21: 6 When *I* **think a** this, I am terrified H2349
Job 21:11 as a flock; their little ones **dance a**. H8376
Job 21:21 For what do they care **a** the families they H928
Job 22:14 not see us as *he* **goes a** *in* the vaulted H2143
Job 24: 5 the poor **go a** their labor of foraging food H3655
Job 24:10 Lacking clothes, *they* **go a** naked; they H2143
Job 27:11 "I will teach you **a** the power of God; the H928
Job 30:22 the wind; *you* **toss** me **a** in the storm. H4570
Job 30:28 *I* **go a** blackened, but not by the sun; I H2143
Job 33: 2 *I am a to* **open** my mouth; my words are on AIT
Job 36:30 See how he scatters his lightning **a** him H6584
Job 38:41 out to God and **wander a** for lack of food? H9494
Job 41:14 its mouth, **ringed a** *with* fearsome teeth? H6017
Job 42: 7 you have not spoken the truth **a** me, H448
Job 42: 8 You have not spoken the truth **a** me, as my H448
Ps 10: 3 He boasts **a** the cravings of his heart; he H6584
Ps 12: 8 who freely strut **a** when what is vile is H6017
Ps 22:30 future generations will be told **a** the Lord. H4200
Ps 26: 6 in innocence, and **go a** your altar, LORD, H6015
Ps 35:11 question me on things *I* **know** nothing **a**. H3359
Ps 35:14 *I* **went a** mourning as though for my friend H2143
Ps 38: 6 very low; all day long *I* **go a** mourning. H2143
Ps 38:17 For I *am* **a to** fall, and my pain is ever with H3922
Ps 39: 6 phantom; in vain *they* **rush a**, heaping up H2159
Ps 40: 7 come—it is written **a** me in the scroll. H6584
Ps 42: 9 Why *must I* **go a** mourning, oppressed by H2143
Ps 43: 2 Why *must I* **go a** mourning, oppressed by H2143
Ps 48:12 **Walk a** Zion, go around her, count her H6015
Ps 55:10 Day and night *they* **prowl a** on its walls H6015
Ps 55:14 *as we* **walked a** among the worshipers. H2143
Ps 59: 6 snarling like dogs, and **prowl a** the city. H6015
Ps 59:14 snarling like dogs, and **prowl a** the city. H6015
Ps 59:15 They **wander a** for food and howl if not H5675
Ps 64: 5 in evil plans, *they* **talk** *a* hiding their snares AIT
Ps 69:26 you wound and talk **a** the pain of those you H448
Ps 77: 5 *I* **thought** *a* the former days, the years of long AIT
Ps 82: 5 *They* **walk a** in darkness; all the H2143
Ps 109:19 May it be like a cloak wrapped **a** him, like H4200
Ps 118:13 I was pushed back and *a to* **fall**, but the LORD AIT
Ps 119:45 *I will* **walk a** in freedom, for I have sought H2143
Ps 142: 7 the righteous *will* **gather a** me because of H4193
Pr 6:12 a villain, *who* **goes a** with a corrupt mouth H2143
Pr 20:14 then goes off and **boasts** *a* the purchase. AIT
Pr 23: 7 of person who is always thinking **a** the cost. H928
Pr 24: 2 violence, and their lips **talk** *a* making trouble. AIT
Pr 24:12 "But *we* **knew** nothing **a** this," does H3359
Pr 27: 1 Do not boast **a** tomorrow, for you do not H928
Pr 29: 7 The righteous **care a** justice for the poor H3359
Pr 31:17 *She* **sets a** her **work** vigorously; her H5516+2520
Ecc 7:14 no one *can* **discover** anything *a* their future. AIT
Ecc 12: 5 home and mourners **go a** the streets. H6015
SS 3: 2 I will get up now and **go a** the city H6015
Isa 3: 1 *is a to* **take** from Jerusalem and Judah both AIT
Isa 5: 1 the one I love a song **a** his vineyard: H4200
Isa 8: 7 the Lord *is a to* **bring** against them the AIT
Isa 13:21 there the wild goats *will* **leap a**. H8376
Isa 22:17 the LORD *is a to* **take firm hold** *of* you AIT
Isa 26:17 As a pregnant woman **a** to give birth H7928
Isa 27: 2 In that day—"Sing **a** a fruitful vineyard: H4200
Isa 35: 8 wicked fools *will* not **go a** on it. H9494
Isa 38:19 tell their children **a** your faithfulness. H448
Isa 45:11 do you question me **a** my children, or give H6584
Isa 45:11 give me orders **a** the work of my hands? H6584
Isa 45:20 are those *who* **carry a** idols of wood, H5951
Isa 46: 1 The **images that are carried a** are H5953
Isa 46:11 I have said, that *I will* **bring a**; what I have H995
Isa 48: 5 'My images **brought** them **a**; my wooden H6913
Isa 57:10 You wearied yourself by such **going a**, but H2006
Isa 60: 4 "Lift up your eyes and look **a** you: All H6017
Isa 66:18 *am a to* **come** and gather the people of all AIT
Jer 1:15 I *am a to* **summon** all the peoples of the AIT
Jer 2:36 Why *do you* **go a** so much, changing your H261
Jer 5:12 They have lied **a** the LORD; they said, "He H928
Jer 6:20 **What do I care a** H4200+4537+2296+4200+3276
Jer 6:24 We have heard **reports** *a* them, and our AIT
Jer 6:28 all hardened rebels, **going a** to slander. H2143
Jer 7:22 them commands **a** burnt offerings H6584+1821
Jer 9:24 let the one who boasts boast **a** this H928
Jer 11:21 is what the LORD says **a** the people of H6584
Jer 12: 1 Yet I would speak with you **a** your justice NDT
Jer 12: 3 you see me and test my thoughts **a** you. H907
Jer 14:10 This is what the LORD says **a** this people H4200
Jer 14:15 what the LORD says **a** the prophets who are H6584
Jer 16: 3 is what the LORD says **a** the sons and H6584
Jer 16: 3 in this land and **a** the women who are H6584
Jer 21: 4 I *am a to* **turn against** you the weapons of AIT
Jer 22: 6 is what the LORD says **a** the palace of the H6584
Jer 22:11 what the LORD says **a** Shallum son of Josiah H448
Jer 22:18 is what the LORD says **a** Jehoiakim son of H448
Jer 26:10 the officials of Judah **heard** *a* these things, AIT
Jer 26:19 We *are a to* **bring** a terrible disaster on AIT
Jer 27:19 is what the LORD Almighty says **a** the pillars, H448
Jer 27:21 says **a** the things that are left in the house H6584
Jer 28:16 'I *am a to* **remove** you from the face of the AIT
Jer 29:16 is what the LORD says **a** the king who sits on H448
Jer 29:21 says **a** Ahab son of Kolaiah and Zedekiah H448
Jer 29:31 is what the LORD says **a** Shemaiah the H448
Jer 31:24 farmers and *those who* **move a** with their H5825
Jer 32: 3 I *am a to* **give** this city into the hands of the AIT
Jer 32:28 I *am a to* **give** this city into the hands of the AIT
Jer 32:36 "You are saying **a** this city, 'By the sword H448
Jer 33: 4 says **a** the houses in this city and the royal H6584
Jer 33:10 'You say **a** this place, "It is a desolate H928
Jer 34: 2 I *am a to* **give** this city into the hands of the AIT
Jer 36: 3 *when* the people of Judah **hear** *a* every AIT
Jer 36:30 is what the LORD says **a** Jehoiakim king of H6584
Jer 37: 5 Jerusalem heard the **report** *a* them, AIT
Jer 38:24 not let anyone know **a** this conversation, H928
Jer 39:11 given these orders **a** Jeremiah through H6584
Jer 39:16 I *am a to* **fulfill** my words against this city AIT
Jer 40: 3 And now the LORD *has* **brought** it **a**; he has H995
Jer 40:16 What you are saying **a** Ishmael is not true." H448
Jer 41: 4 assassination, before anyone **knew a** it, H3359
Jer 41:11 who were with him **heard** *a* all the crimes AIT
Jer 46:13 the LORD **spoke** to Jeremiah the prophet *a* the AIT
Jer 46:25 "I *am a to* **bring punishment** on Amon god of AIT
Jer 47: 4 The LORD *is a to* **destroy** the Philistines, the AIT
Jer 50:43 king of Babylon has heard **reports** *a* them, AIT
Jer 51:60 Jeremiah *had* **written** on a scroll *a* all the AIT
La 3:54 my head, and I thought *I was a to* **perish**. AIT
La 4:15 When they flee and **wander a**, people H5675
Eze 4:16 I *am a to* **cut off** the food supply in Jerusalem AIT
Eze 6: 3 I *am a to* **bring** a sword against you, and I AIT
Eze 7: 8 I am **a to** pour out my wrath H6964+4946+7940
Eze 8:16 the altar, were **a** twenty-five men. H3869
Eze 10:11 the wheels *did* not **turn a** as the cherubim H6015
Eze 12:19 the Sovereign LORD says **a** those living in H4200
Eze 12:27 he prophesies **a** the distant future. H4200
Eze 16: 6 by and saw you **kicking a** in your blood, H1008
Eze 16:22 naked and bare, **kicking a** in your blood. H1008
Eze 16:44 proverbs will quote this proverb **a** you: H6584
Eze 18: 2 quoting this proverb **a** the land of Israel: H6584
Eze 19: 4 The nations heard **a** him, and he was H448
Eze 19: 8 against him, those from regions **round a**. H6017
Eze 20:47 I *am a to* **set fire** to you, and it will consume AIT
Eze 21:28 Sovereign LORD says **a** the Ammonites and H448
Eze 21:29 you and lying divinations **a** you, H4200
Eze 23:28 I *am a to* **deliver** you into the hands of those AIT
Eze 23:43 Then I said **a** the one worn out by adultery, H4200
Eze 24:16 one blow I *am a to* **take away** from you the AIT
Eze 24:21 I *am a to* **desecrate** my sanctuary—the AIT
Eze 25:16 I *am a to* **stretch out** my hand against the AIT
Eze 32: 2 in the seas **thrashing a** in your streams, H1631
Eze 32: 9 peoples when I **bring a** your destruction H995
Eze 33:30 are talking together **a** you by the walls H928
Eze 38: 7 you and all the hordes gathered **a** you H6584
Da 1:20 understanding *a* **which** the king AIT
Da 2:27 to the king the mystery he *has* **asked** *a*, AIT
Da 4: 2 It is my pleasure to **tell** you *a* the miraculous AIT
Da 4:33 had been said **a** Nebuchadnezzar was A10542
Da 6:12 spoke to him **a** his royal decree: A10542
Da 7: 8 "While I was thinking **a** the horns, there A10089
Da 7:20 also wanted to know **a** the ten horns on A10542
Da 7:20 horns on its head and **a** the other horn that NDT
Da 8: 5 As I was thinking **a** this, suddenly a goat NDT
Da 8:27 Then I got up and **went a** the king's H6913
Da 9:21 to me in swift flight **a** the time of the H3869
Da 10:11 carefully the words I *am a to* **speak** to you, AIT
Hos 3: 2 shekels of silver and **a** a homer and a lethek NDT
Hos 5: 3 I **know all a** Ephraim; Israel is not hidden H3359
Hos 7:13 redeem them but they speak **a** me falsely. H6584
Joel 1:18 The herds **mill a** because they have no H1003
Am 4: 5 as a thank offering and **brag** *a* your freewill AIT
Am 4: 5 freewill offerings—**boast** *a* them, you AIT
Ob 1 is what the Sovereign LORD says **a** Edom— H4200
Jnh 2: 3 the currents **swirled a** me; all your H6015
Jnh 4: 6 Jonah was very happy **a** the plant. H6584
Jnh 4: 9 "Is it right for you to be angry **a** the plant?" H6584
Jnh 4:10 "You have been concerned **a** this plant H6584
Mic 1: 8 wail; *I will* **go a** barefoot and naked. H2143
Mic 2: 6 "Do not prophesy **a** these things; disgrace H4200
Na 2: 4 flaming torches; *they* **dart a** like lightning. H8132
Na 3:19 All who hear the **news** *a* you clap their hands AIT
Hab 3:14 gloating as though **a** to devour the wretched NDT
Zep 1:17 people that *they will* **grope a** like those H2143
Zec 8:10 one *could* **go a** *their* **business** H3655+2256+995
Mal 3:14 requirements and **going a** like mourners H2143
Mt 1:18 the birth of Jesus the Messiah **came a**: *G1639*
Mt 4:24 News **a him** spread all over Syria, and people AIT
Mt 6:25 I tell you, *do* not **worry a** your life, what *G3534*
Mt 6:25 will eat or drink; or **a** your body, what you NDT
Mt 6:28 "And why do you worry **a** clothes? See *G4309*
Mt 6:34 Therefore do not worry **a** tomorrow, for *G1650*
Mt 6:34 tomorrow, for tomorrow *will* **worry a** itself. *G3534*
Mt 9:30 "See that no one **knows a** this. *G1182*
Mt 9:31 spread the news *a* **him** all over that AIT
Mt 10:19 *do* not **worry a** what to say or how to say it. *G3534*
Mt 11: 2 *When* John, who was in prison, **heard** *a* the AIT
Mt 11: 7 Jesus began to speak to the crowd **a** John: *G4309*
Mt 11:10 This is the one **a** whom it is written: " 'I *G4309*
Mt 12:16 them not *to* **tell** others **a** him. *G5745+4472*
Mt 13:19 the message *a* the **kingdom** and does not AIT
Mt 13:33 mixed into **a sixty pounds** of flour *G4929+5552*
Mt 14: 1 Herod the tetrarch heard the reports *a* **Jesus**, AIT
Mt 14:21 those who ate was **a** five thousand men, *G6059*
Mt 15: 7 was right when he prophesied **a** you: *G4309*
Mt 16: 8 among yourselves **a** having no bread? *G4022*
Mt 16:11 that I was not talking to you **a** bread? *G4309*
Mt 16:15 "But what **a** you?" he asked. "Who do you NDT
Mt 17:13 he was talking to them **a** John the Baptist. *G4309*
Mt 18:13 he is happier **a** that one sheep than *G2093*
Mt 18:13 that one sheep than **a** the ninety-nine *G2093*
Mt 18:19 you on earth agree **a** anything they ask for *G4309*
Mt 19:17 "Why do you ask me **a** what is good?" *G4309*
Mt 20: 3 "**A** nine in the morning he went out and *G4309*
Mt 20: 5 "He went out again **a** noon and about *G4309*
Mt 20: 5 again about noon and **a** three in the NDT
Mt 20: 6 **A** five in the afternoon he went out and *G4309*
Mt 20: 9 who were hired **a** five in the afternoon *G4309*
Mt 20:24 *When* the ten **heard a** this, they were *G201*
Mt 21:45 they knew he was talking **a** them. *G4309*
Mt 22:31 But **a** the resurrection of the dead—have *G4309*
Mt 22:42 "What do you think **a** the Messiah? Whose *G4309*
Mt 24:36 "But **a** that day or hour no one knows, not *G4309*
Mt 24:39 they knew nothing **a** what would happen NDT
Mt 26:24 of Man will go just as it is written **a** him. *G4309*
Mt 26:70 "I don't know what *you're* **talking a**," *G3306*
Mt 27:46 **A** three in the afternoon Jesus cried out in *G4309*
Mk 1: 1 of the good news *a* **Jesus** the Messiah, AIT
Mk 1:28 News *a* **him** spread quickly over the whole AIT
Mk 1:30 they immediately told Jesus **a** her. *G4309*
Mk 3: 8 When they heard *a* **all** he was doing, many AIT
Mk 3:12 strict orders not to **tell** others **a** him. *G5745+4472*

Mk 3:21 When his family heard a this, they went to G201
Mk 4:10 others around him asked him a the parables. AIT
Mk 5:13 The herd, a two thousand in number G6055
Mk 5:16 and told a the pigs as well. G4309
Mk 5:27 When she heard a Jesus, she came up G4309
Mk 5:43 strict orders not to let anyone know a this, AIT
Mk 6:14 King Herod heard a this, for Jesus' name G201
Mk 6:48 He was a to pass by them, G2527
Mk 6:52 they had not understood a the loaves G2093
Mk 7: 6 when he prophesied a you hypocrites; G4309
Mk 7:17 his disciples asked him a this parable. G2089
Mk 7:25 as soon as she heard a him, a woman G4309
Mk 7:36 he did so, the more they kept talking a it. G3062
Mk 8: 9 A four thousand were present. After he G6055
Mk 8:17 "Why are you talking a having no bread G1368
Mk 8:29 "But what a you?" he asked. "Who do you NDT
Mk 8:30 warned them not to tell anyone a him. G4309
Mk 8:32 He spoke plainly a this, and Peter took G3281
Mk 9:13 they wished, just as it is written a him." G2093
Mk 9:16 "What are you arguing with them a?" G5184
Mk 9:32 he meant and were afraid to ask him a it. G2089
Mk 9:33 "What were you arguing a on the road?" G1368
Mk 9:34 on the way they had argued a who was G1363
Mk 9:39 the next moment say anything bad a me, G2800
Mk 10:10 the disciples asked Jesus a this. G4309
Mk 10:41 When the ten heard a this, they became G201
Mk 12:26 Now a the dead rising—have you not read G4309
Mk 13: 4 the sign that they are all a to be fulfilled?" G3516
Mk 13:11 do not worry beforehand a what to say. G4628
Mk 13:32 "But a that day or hour no one knows, not G4309
Mk 14:21 of Man will go just as it is written a him. G4309
Mk 14:68 know or understand what you're talking a," G3306
Mk 14:71 "I don't know this man you're talking a." G3306
Lk 1:56 with Elizabeth for a three months and G6055
Lk 1:65 of Judea people were talking a all these G1362
Lk 1:66 this wondered a it, G5502+1877+3836+2840
Lk 2:15 happened, which the Lord has told us a." G1192
Lk 2:17 what had been told them a this child, G4309
Lk 2:33 mother marveled at what was said a him. G4309
Lk 2:38 to God and spoke a the child to all who G4309
Lk 3:23 Jesus himself was a thirty years old when G6059
Lk 4:14 news a him spread through the G4309
Lk 4:37 And the news a him spread throughout G4309
Lk 5:15 Yet the news a him spread all the more G4309
Lk 7: 2 valued highly, was sick and a to die. G3516
Lk 7:17 This news a Jesus spread throughout G4309
Lk 7:18 disciples told him a all these things. G4309
Lk 7:24 Jesus began to speak to the crowd a John: G4309
Lk 7:27 This is the one a whom it is written: " 'I G4309
Lk 8: 1 Jesus traveled a from one town and G1476
Lk 8:42 daughter, a girl of a twelve, was dying. G6055
Lk 9: 7 Herod the tetrarch heard a all that was G201
Lk 9: 9 is this I hear such things a?" And he tried G4309
Lk 9:11 the crowds learned a it and followed G1182
Lk 9:11 spoke to them a the kingdom of God, G4309
Lk 9:14 (A five thousand men were there.) But he G6059
Lk 9:14 them sit down in groups of a fifty each." G6059
Lk 9:20 "But what a you?" he asked. "Who do you NDT
Lk 9:28 A eight days after Jesus said this, he took G6059
Lk 9:31 They spoke a his departure, which he was AIT
Lk 9:31 which he was a to bring to fulfillment at G3516
Lk 9:44 "Listen carefully to what I am a to tell you NDT
Lk 9:45 and they were afraid to ask him a it. G4309
Lk 10: 1 town and place where he was a to go. G3516
Lk 10:41 "you are worried and upset a many things, G4309
Lk 12:11 do not worry a how you will defend G3534
Lk 12:22 I tell you, do not worry a your life, what G3534
Lk 12:22 you will eat; or a your body, what you will AIT
Lk 12:26 little thing, why do you worry a the rest? G4309
Lk 12:29 you will eat or drink; do not worry a it. G3577
Lk 13: 1 who told Jesus a the Galileans whose G4309
Lk 13:21 mixed into a sixty pounds of flour G4929+5552
Lk 14:31 "Or suppose a king is a to go to war G4513
Lk 16: 2 asked him, 'What is this I hear a you? G4309
Lk 18: 7 And will not God bring a justice for his G4472
Lk 18:31 by the prophets a the Son of Man will be AIT
Lk 18:34 they did not know what he was talking a. G3306
Lk 21: 5 were remarking a how the temple was G4309
Lk 21: 7 be the sign that they are a to take place?" G3516
Lk 21:36 be able to escape all that is a to happen, G3516
Lk 22:37 what is written a me is reaching its G4309
Lk 22:41 He withdrew a a stone's throw beyond G6059
Lk 22:59 A an hour later another asserted G6059
Lk 22:60 I don't know what you're talking a! G3306
Lk 23: 8 From what he had heard a him, he hoped G4309
Lk 23:44 It was now a noon, and darkness came G6059
Lk 23:54 and the Sabbath was a to begin. G2216
Lk 24: 4 While they were wondering a this G4309
Lk 24:13 a seven miles from Jerusalem G600+5084+2008
Lk 24:14 with each other a everything that had G4309
Lk 24:19 "A Jesus of Nazareth," they G4309
Lk 24:36 While they were still talking a this, Jesus AIT
Lk 24:44 that is written a me in the Law of Moses, G4309
Jn 1:15 "This is the one I spoke a when I said, 'He AIT
Jn 1:22 What do you say a yourself?" G4309
Jn 1:39 It was a four in the afternoon G6055
Jn 1:45 found the one Moses wrote a in the Law, G1211
Jn 1:45 and a whom the prophets also wrote NDT
Jn 2:25 He did not need any testimony a mankind G4309
Jn 3:26 of the Jordan—the one you testified a—look, AIT
Jn 4: 6 sat down by the well. It was a noon. G6055
Jn 4:32 have food to eat that you know nothing a." G3857
Jn 5:31 "If I testify a myself, my testimony is not G4309
Jn 5:32 I know that his testimony a me is true. G4309
Jn 5:39 are the very Scriptures that testify a me, G4309
Jn 5:46 you would believe me, for he wrote a me. G4309
Jn 6:10 down (a five thousand men were there). G6055
Jn 6:19 When they had rowed a three or four G6055
Jn 6:41 began to grumble a him because he said, G4309
Jn 6:61 that his disciples were grumbling a this, G4309
Jn 7: 1 He did not want to go a in Judea because G4344
Jn 7:12 there was widespread whispering a him. G4309
Jn 7:13 say anything publicly a him for fear of the G4309
Jn 7:18 man of truth; there is nothing false a him. G1877
Jn 7:32 the crowd whispering such things a him. G4309
Jn 8:27 that he was telling them a his Father. AIT
Jn 9:17 blind man, "What have you to say a him? G4309
Jn 10:25 I do in my Father's name testify a me, G4309
Jn 10:36 what a the one whom the Father set apart as NDT
Jn 10:41 all that John said a this man was true." G4309
Jn 11:54 Jesus no longer moved a publicly among G4344
Jn 12: 3 Then Mary took a a pint of pure nard, an G3354
Jn 12: 6 because he cared a the poor but because G4309
Jn 12:16 had been written a him and that these G2093
Jn 12:41 he saw Jesus' glory and spoke a him. G4309
Jn 13:27 told him, "What you are a to do, do quickly." AIT
Jn 15:26 out from the Father—he will testify a me. G4309
Jn 16: 4 you will remember that I warned you a them. AIT
Jn 16: 8 to be in the wrong a sin and G4309
Jn 16: 9 a sin, because people do not believe in G4309
Jn 16:10 a righteousness, because I am going to G4309
Jn 16:11 a judgment, because the prince of G4309
Jn 16:19 saw that they wanted to ask him a this, NDT
Jn 16:25 will tell you plainly a my Father. G4309
Jn 18:19 questioned Jesus a his disciples and his G4309
Jn 18:32 what Jesus had said a the kind of death G4955s
Jn 18:34 "or did others talk to you a me? G4309
Jn 19:14 of the Passover; it was a noon. G6055
Jn 19:39 myrrh and aloes, a seventy-five pounds. G6055
Jn 21: 8 not far from shore, a a hundred yards. G6055
Jn 21:21 Peter saw him, he asked, "Lord, what a him?" AIT
Ac 1: 1 I wrote a all that Jesus began to do and G4309
Ac 1: 3 days and spoke a the kingdom of God. G4309
Ac 1: 4 promised, which you have heard me speak a. AIT
Ac 1:15 a group numbering a a hundred and G6059
Ac 1:19 Everyone in Jerusalem heard a this G1196+1181
Ac 2:25 David said a him: " 'I saw the Lord always G1650
Ac 2:41 a three thousand were added to their G6059
Ac 3: 3 When he saw Peter and John a to enter G3516
Ac 4: 4 who believed grew to a five thousand. G6055
Ac 4:20 help speaking a what we have seen and AIT
Ac 5: 7 A three hours later his wife came in, not G6055
Ac 5:11 church and all who heard a these events. AIT
Ac 5:20 the people all a this new G4246+3836+4839
Ac 5:36 a four hundred men rallied to him. G6055
Ac 7:13 and Pharaoh learned a Joseph's G5745+1181
Ac 8:25 the word of the Lord and testified a Jesus, NDT
Ac 8:34 who is the prophet talking a, himself or G4309
Ac 8:35 told him the good news a Jesus. AIT
Ac 8:40 appeared at Azotus and traveled a G1451
Ac 9:13 heard many reports a this man and all the G4309
Ac 9:28 them and moved a freely in G1660+2779+1744
Ac 9:32 As Peter traveled a the country, he went G1451
Ac 9:37 A that time she became sick and died G1877
Ac 10: 3 One day at a three in the afternoon he G6059
Ac 10: 9 A noon the following day as they were on G4309
Ac 10:17 was wondering a the meaning of the vision, AIT
Ac 10:19 While Peter was still thinking a the vision G4309
Ac 10:43 the prophets testify a him that everyone who AIT
Ac 11:12 me to have no hesitation a going with them. AIT
Ac 11:20 telling them the good news a the Lord Jesus. AIT
Ac 12: 1 It was a this time that King Herod arrested G2848
Ac 12:17 the other brothers and sisters a this, AIT
Ac 13:11 over him, and he groped a, seeking G4310
Ac 13:12 he was amazed at the teaching a the Lord. AIT
Ac 13:18 a forty years he endured their conduct G6055
Ac 13:20 All this took a 450 years. "After this, God G6055
Ac 13:29 had carried out all that was written a him, G4309
Ac 13:42 to speak further a these things on the next AIT
Ac 14: 6 But they found out a it and fled to the AIT
Ac 15: 2 the apostles and elders a this question. G4309
Ac 15:12 Barnabas and Paul telling a the signs G2007
Ac 16:25 A midnight Paul and Silas were praying G2848
Ac 16:27 drew his sword and was a to kill himself G3516
Ac 17:18 the good news a Jesus and the resurrection. AIT
Ac 17:21 doing nothing but talking a and listening to AIT
Ac 17:32 they heard a the resurrection of the dead, AIT
Ac 18:14 Just as Paul was a to speak, Gallio said to G3516
Ac 18:14 you Jews were making a complaint a some AIT
Ac 18:15 involves questions a words and names G4309
Ac 18:25 great fervor and taught a Jesus accurately, G4309
Ac 19: 7 There were a twelve men in all. G6059
Ac 19: 8 persuasively a the kingdom of God. G4309
Ac 19:15 and Paul I know a, but who are G2179
Ac 19:23 A that time there arose a great G2848
Ac 19:23 arose a great disturbance a the Way. G4309
Ac 19:34 they all shouted in unison for a two hours: G6055
Ac 20: 3 against him just as he was a to sail for G3516
Ac 20:25 among whom I have gone a preaching G1451
Ac 21:24 there is no truth in these reports a you, G4309
Ac 21:37 As the soldiers were a to take Paul into G3516
Ac 22: 6 "A noon as I came near Damascus G4309
Ac 22:18 here will not accept your testimony a me. G4309
Ac 22:29 Those who were a to interrogate him G3516
Ac 23: 5 'Do not speak evil a the ruler of your people.' AIT
Ac 23:11 As you have testified a me in Jerusalem G4309
Ac 23:15 more accurate information a his case. AIT
Ac 23:20 wanting more accurate information a him. G4309
Ac 23:27 by the Jews and they were a to kill him, G3516
Ac 23:29 had to do with questions a their law, AIT
Ac 24: 2 your foresight has brought a reforms in G1181
Ac 24: 8 to learn the truth a all these charges we G4309
Ac 24:24 to him as he spoke a faith in Christ Jesus. G4309
Ac 24:25 As Paul talked a righteousness G4309
Ac 25:19 of dispute with him a their own religion G4309
Ac 25:19 own religion and a a dead man named G4309
Ac 25:24 has petitioned me a him in Jerusalem G4309
Ac 25:26 definite to write to His Majesty a him. G4309
Ac 26:13 A noon, King Agrippa, as I was on G2465+3545
Ac 27: 2 from Adramyttium a to sail for ports along G3516
Ac 27:27 when a midnight the sailors sensed they G2848
Ac 28:21 has reported or said anything bad a you. G4309
Ac 28:23 explaining a the kingdom of God G1758
Ac 28:23 he tried to persuade them a Jesus. G4309
Ac 28:31 of God and taught a the Lord Jesus Christ G4309
Ro 1:19 what may be known a God is plain to them, AIT
Ro 1:25 They exchanged the truth a God for a lie, and AIT
Ro 4: 2 he had something to boast a—but not G3017
Ro 4:19 since he was a a hundred years old G4543
Ro 7:13 it used what is good to bring a my death G2981
Ro 8:15 you received brought a your adoption to NDT
Ro 10: 2 For I can testify a them that they are zealous AIT
Ro 10: 5 writes this a the righteousness that is by the AIT
Ro 10:17 message is heard through the word a Christ. AIT
Ro 11: 2 what Scripture says in the passage a Elijah— AIT
Ro 13:14 and do not think a how to gratify G4630+4472
Ro 14:22 whatever you believe a these things keep NDT
Ro 15:21 "Those who were not told a him will see G4309
Ro 16:19 Everyone has heard a your G1650+919
Ro 16:19 I want you to be wise a what is good G1650
Ro 16:19 what is good, and innocent a what is evil. G1650
Ro 16:25 the message I proclaim a Jesus Christ, in AIT
1Co 1: 6 confirming our testimony a Christ among AIT
1Co 2: 1 as I proclaimed to you the testimony a God. AIT
1Co 2:15 the Spirit makes judgments a all things, G373
1Co 3:21 no more boasting a human leaders! G1877
1Co 6: 4 if you have disputes a such matters, do you AIT
1Co 7: 1 Now for the matters you wrote a: "It is G4309
1Co 7:25 Now a virgins: I have no command from G4309
1Co 7:32 unmarried man is concerned a the Lord's G3534
1Co 7:33 a married man is concerned a the affairs G3534
1Co 7:34 woman or virgin is concerned a the Lord's G3534
1Co 7:34 married woman is concerned a the affairs G3534
1Co 8: 1 Now a food sacrificed to idols: We know G4309
1Co 8: 4 So then, a eating food sacrificed to idols G4309
1Co 9: 9 Is it a oxen that God is concerned? G3508
1Co 11:16 If anyone wants to be contentious a this, we NDT
1Co 12: 1 Now a the gifts of the Spirit, brothers and G4309
1Co 14:35 If they want to inquire a something, they G3443
1Co 15:15 are then found to be false witnesses a God, AIT
1Co 15:15 we have testified a God that he raised G2848
1Co 15:31 as surely as I boast a you in Christ Jesus our AIT
1Co 16: 1 Now a the collection for the Lord's people: G4309
1Co 16:12 Now a our brother Apollos: I strongly G4309
2Co 1: 8 a the troubles we experienced in the G5642
2Co 7: 7 He told us a your longing for me, your G334
2Co 7:14 I had boasted to him a you, and you have G5642
2Co 7:14 so our boasting a you to Titus has proved to NDT
2Co 8: 1 want you to know a the grace that God has AIT
2Co 8:10 here is my judgment a what is best for you AIT
2Co 9: 1 me to write to you a this service to the G4309
2Co 9: 2 I have been boasting a it to the G5642
2Co 9: 3 that our boasting a you in this matter G5642
2Co 9: 4 not to say anything a you—would be AIT
2Co 10: 8 boast somewhat freely a the authority the G4309
2Co 10:16 not want to boast a work already done in G1650
2Co 11:12 equal with us in the things they boast a. AIT
2Co 11:21 Whatever anyone else dares to boast a—I AIT
2Co 11:21 speaking as a fool—I also dare to boast a. AIT
2Co 12: 5 I will boast a a man like that, but I will not G5642
2Co 12: 5 I will not boast a myself, except about G5642
2Co 12: 5 about myself, except a my weaknesses. G1877
2Co 12: 9 all the more gladly a my weaknesses, G1877
Gal 4:20 my tone, because I am perplexed a you! G1877
Gal 6:13 that they may boast a your circumcision in G1877
Eph 1:15 since I heard a your faith in the Lord Jesus AIT
Eph 3: 2 you have heard a the administration of God's AIT
Eph 4:21 when you heard a Christ and were taught in G201
Eph 5:32 I am talking a Christ and the church. G1650
Php 1: 7 is right for me to feel this way a all of you, G5642
Php 1:27 see you or only hear a you in my absence, G4309
Php 2:19 be cheered when I receive news a you. G4309
Php 4: 6 Do not be anxious a anything, but in every AIT
Php 4: 8 praiseworthy—think a such things. G3357
Col 1: 5 you in heaven and a which you have already AIT
Col 1: 9 since the day we heard a you, we have not NDT
Col 2:18 goes into great detail a what they have seen; AIT
Col 4: 7 Tychicus will tell you all the news a me G2848
Col 4: 8 that you may know a our circumstances G4309
Col 4:10 You have received instructions a him; if he G4309
1Th 1: 8 we do not need to say anything a it, NDT
1Th 3: 5 it no longer, I sent to find out a your faith. AIT
1Th 3: 6 has brought good news a your faith and love. AIT
1Th 3: 7 we were encouraged a you because of G2093
1Th 4: 9 Now a your love for one another we do G4309
1Th 4:13 to be uninformed a those who sleep in G4309

1Th 5: 1 **a** times and dates we do not need to G4309
2Th 1: 4 churches we boast **a** your perseverance G5642
1Ti 1: 7 not know what *they are* **talking** *a* or what they AIT
1Ti 1:18 with the prophecies once made **a** you, G2093
1Ti 5:13 of being idle and **going a** from house to G4320
1Ti 6: 4 and **quarrels a words** that result in G3363
1Ti 6:15 which God *will* **bring a** in his own time G1259
2Ti 1: 8 of the testimony *a* our **Lord** or of me his AIT
2Ti 2:14 before God against **quarreling a words**; G3362
2Ti 3:10 however, **know all a** my teaching, my way G4158
Titus 2: 8 they have nothing bad to say **a** us. G4309
Titus 2:10 make the teaching *a* **God** our Savior AIT
Titus 3: 9 arguments and quarrels **a** *the* **law**, G3788
Phm 5 because I hear *a* your **love** for all his holy AIT
Heb 1: 8 But **a** the Son he says, "Your throne, O G4639
Heb 2: 5 world to come, **a** which we are speaking. G4309
Heb 4: 4 he has spoken **a** the seventh day in G4309
Heb 4: 8 not have spoken later **a** another day. G4309
Heb 5:11 We have much to say **a** this, but it is hard G4309
Heb 5:13 with the teaching *a* **righteousness**. AIT
Heb 6: 1 teachings *a* **Christ** and be taken forward AIT
Heb 6: 2 instruction *a* **cleansing rites**, the laying on of AIT
Heb 7:14 to that tribe Moses said nothing **a** priests. G4309
Heb 8: 5 was warned *when he was* **a to** build the G3516
Heb 10: 7 it is written **a** me in the scroll—I G4309
Heb 10:15 The Holy Spirit also testifies to us **a** this NDT
Heb 11: 1 and assurance *a* **what** we do not see. AIT
Heb 11: 7 when warned **a** things not yet seen G4309
Heb 11:17 the promises *was a to* **sacrifice** his one and AIT
Heb 11:22 spoke **a** the exodus of the Israelites from G4309
Heb 11:32 I do not have time to tell **a** Gideon, Barak G4309
Heb 11:32 **a** David and Samuel and the prophets NDT
Heb 11:37 *They* **went a** in sheepskins and goatskins G4320
Jas 1:11 away even while they **go a** their **business**. G4512
Jas 2:16 does nothing *a* their physical **needs** AIT
Jas 3:14 do not boast **a** it or deny the truth. NDT
Jas 5:11 have seen what the Lord **finally brought a**. G5465
2Pe 1:16 stories *when we* **told** you *a* the coming of AIT
2Pe 1:20 of Scripture **came a** by the prophet's own G1181
2Pe 3:12 That day will **bring a** the destruction of G1328
1Jn 2:26 these things to you **a** those who are trying G4309
1Jn 2:27 anointing teaches you **a** all things and as G4309
1Jn 5: 9 which he has given **a** his Son. G4309
1Jn 5:10 the testimony God has given **a** his Son. G4309
1Jn 5:16 am not saying that you should pray **a** that. G4309
3Jn 3 came and **testified a** your faithfulness G3455
3Jn 6 They *have* **told** the church **a** your love G3455
3Jn 10 is doing, spreading malicious nonsense *a* **us**. AIT
Jude 3 eager to write to you **a** the salvation we G4309
Jude 4 condemnation *was* **written a** long ago G4592
Jude 9 with the devil **a** the body of Moses, G4309
Jude 14 the seventh from Adam, prophesied *a* **them**: AIT
Jude 16 they boast **a** themselves and flatter others NDT
Rev 2: 9 I know **a** the slander of those who say they NDT
Rev 2:10 not be afraid of what *you are* **a to** suffer. G3516
Rev 3: 2 Strengthen what remains and *is* **a to** die G3516
Rev 3:16 cold—*I am* **a to** spit you out of my mouth. G3516
Rev 8: 1 was silence in heaven for **a** half an hour. G6055
Rev 8:13 the trumpet blasts **a to be** sounded by the G3516
Rev 10: 4 thunders spoke, *I was* **a to** write; but I G3516
Rev 10: 7 the seventh angel *is* **a to** sound his G3516
Rev 10:11 must prophesy again **a** many peoples, G2093
Rev 12: 2 cried out in pain *as she was a to* **give birth**. AIT
Rev 12: 4 of the woman who *was* **a to** give birth, G3516
Rev 12:17 hold fast their testimony *a* **Jesus**. AIT
Rev 16:21 each weighing **a** a hundred pounds, fell G6055
Rev 20: 4 of their testimony *a* **Jesus** and because of the AIT

ABOVE (147)

Ge 1: 7 under the vault from the water **a** it. H4946+6584
Ge 1:20 let birds fly **a** the earth across the H6584
Ge 3:14 "Cursed are you **a** all livestock and all H4946
Ge 7:17 they lifted the ark high **a** the earth. H4946+6584
Ge 27:39 away from the dew of heaven **a**. H4946+6584
Ge 28:13 There **a** it stood the LORD, and he said: "I H6584
Ge 32:31 The sun rose **a** him as he passed Peniel H4200
Ge 49:25 you with blessings of the skies **a**, H4946+6584
Ex 20: 4 in heaven **a** or on the earth H4946+5087
Ex 25:22 **a** the cover between the two H4946+6584
Ex 28:27 to the seam **just a** the waistband of H4946+5087
Ex 39:20 to the seam **just a** the waistband of H4946+5087
Ex 40:36 the cloud lifted from **a** the tabernacle, H6584
Lev 16:13 the atonement cover **a** the tablets of the H6584
Lev 26:19 pride and make the **sky** *a* you like iron and AIT
Nu 7:89 the two cherubim **a** the atonement H4946+6584
Nu 9:15 morning the cloud **a** the tabernacle H6584
Nu 9:17 Whenever the cloud lifted from **a** the tent H6584
Nu 10:11 cloud lifted from **a** the tabernacle of the H6584
Nu 12:10 When the cloud lifted from **a** the tent H6584
Nu 16: 3 you set yourselves **a** the LORD's assembly?" H6584
Dt 4:39 God in heaven **a** and on the earth H4946+5087
Dt 5: 8 in heaven **a** or on the earth H4946+5087
Dt 10:15 their descendants, **a** all the nations—as it H4946
Dt 11:21 the days that the heavens are **a** the earth. H6584
Dt 26:19 fame and honor high **a** all the nations he H6584
Dt 28: 1 God will set you high **a** all the nations on H6584
Dt 28:43 among you will rise **a** you higher and H6584
Dt 33:13 the precious dew **from** heaven *a* and with the AIT
Jos 2:11 God in heaven **a** and on the earth H4946+5087
2Sa 22:49 You exalted me **a** my foes; from a violent H4946
1Ki 7: 3 with cedar **a** the beams that H4946+5087+6584
1Ki 7:11 **A** were high-grade H4946+4200+5087+2025
1Ki 7:20 **a** the bowl-shaped part H4946+5087+4946+4200+6645
1Ki 7:29 **A** and below the lions and bulls H4946+5087
1Ki 8:23 you in heaven **a** or on earth below H4946+5087
2Ki 19:30 root below and bear fruit **a**. H4200+5087+2025
1Ch 4:38 The men listed **a** by name were leaders of NDT
1Ch 11:21 was doubly honored **a** the Three and H4946
1Ch 16:25 of praise; he is to be feared **a** all gods. H6584
1Ch 29: 3 **over and a** everything I have H4200+5087+2025
2Ch 7: 3 the glory of the LORD **a** the temple, H6584
2Ch 34: 4 altars that were **a** them, H4200+5087+2025
Ne 3:28 **A** the Horse Gate, the priests made H4946+6584
Ne 3:31 as far as the **room a** the corner; H6608
Ne 3:32 between the **room a** the corner and H6608
Ne 8: 5 because he was standing **a** them; H4946+6584
Ne 9: 5 may it be exalted **a** all blessing and H6584
Ne 12:37 wall and passed **a** the site of H4946+6584
Est 5:11 he had elevated him **a** the other nobles H6584
Job 3: 4 may God **a** not care about it H4946+5087
Job 11: 8 They are higher than the **heavens a** H9028
Job 18:16 below and his branches wither **a**. H4946+5087
Job 19: 5 would exalt yourselves **a** me and use my H6584
Job 31: 2 For what is our lot from God **a**, our H4946+5087
Job 35: 5 gaze at the clouds so high **a** you. H4946
Ps 18:48 You exalted me **a** my foes; from a violent H4946
Ps 27: 6 head will be exalted **a** the enemies who H6584
Ps 45: 7 has set you **a** your companions by H4946
Ps 50: 4 He summons the heavens **a**, and H4946+6584
Ps 57: 5 **a** the heavens; let your glory be H6584
Ps 57:11 **a** the heavens; let your glory be H6584
Ps 78:23 to the skies **a** and opened the H4946+5087
Ps 89: 6 For who in the **skies a** can compare with H8836
Ps 95: 3 the great God, the great King **a** all gods. H6584
Ps 96: 4 of praise; he is to be feared **a** all gods. H6584
Ps 97: 9 the earth; you are exalted far **a** all gods. H6584
Ps 103:11 as high as the heavens are **a** the earth, H6584
Ps 104: 6 the waters stood **a** the mountains. H6584
Ps 108: 5 **a** the heavens; let your glory be H6584
Ps 113: 4 all the nations, his glory **a** the heavens. H6584
Ps 148: 1 the heavens; praise him in the **heights a**. H5294
Ps 148: 4 and you waters **a** the skies. H4946+6584
Ps 148:13 his splendor is **a** the earth and the H6584
Pr 4:23 **A** all else, guard your heart, for everything H4946
Pr 8:28 the clouds **a** and fixed securely the H4946+5087
Isa 2: 2 it will be exalted **a** the hills, and all H4946
Isa 6: 2 **A** him were seraphim, each with six H4946+5087
Isa 10:15 the ax raise itself **a** the person who H6584
Isa 14:13 raise my throne **a** the stars of God; H4946+5087
Isa 14:14 I will ascend **a** the tops of the clouds; I H6584
Isa 24:21 the heavens **a** and the kings H928+2021+5294
Isa 37:31 root below and bear fruit **a**. H4200+5087+2025
Isa 40:22 He sits enthroned **a** the circle of the earth H6584
Isa 45: 8 "You heavens **a**, rain down my H4946+5087
Jer 4:28 and the heavens **a** grow dark, H4946+5087
Jer 17: 9 heart is deceitful **a** all things and beyond H4946
Jer 21:13 you *who* **live** *a* this valley *on* the rocky AIT
Jer 31:37 if the heavens **a** can be H4946+4200+5087+2025
Jer 43:10 he will spread his royal canopy **a** them. H6584
Jer 52:23 of pomegranates **a** the surrounding H6584
Eze 1:22 Spread out **a** the heads of the living H6584
Eze 1:25 came a voice from **a** the vault over their H6584
Eze 1:26 **A** the vault over their heads was H4946+5087
Eze 1:26 and **high a** on the H4946+4200+5087+2025
Eze 9: 3 of Israel went up from **a** the cherubim, H6584
Eze 10: 1 throne of lapis lazuli **a** the vault that was H448
Eze 10: 4 of the LORD rose from **a** the cherubim and H6584
Eze 10:18 the temple and stopped **a** the cherubim. H6584
Eze 10:19 of Israel was **a** them. H4946+4200+5087+2025
Eze 11:22 of Israel was **a** them. H4946+4200+5087+2025
Eze 11:23 city and stopped **a** the mountain east of H6584
Eze 19:11 It towered high **a** the thick foliage H6584+1068
Eze 29:15 again exalt itself **a** the other nations. H6584
Eze 31: 3 on high, its top **a** the thick foliage. H1068
Eze 31:14 lifting their tops **a** the thick foliage. H448+1068
Eze 41: 6 on three levels, one **a** another, thirty on H448
Eze 41:17 In the space **a** the outside of the H4946+6584
Eze 41:20 floor to the area **a** the entrance, H4946+6584
Eze 43:15 **A** that, the altar hearth is four cubits high NDT
Da 11:36 magnify himself **a** every god and will H6584
Da 11:37 any god, but will exalt himself **a** them all. H6584
Da 12: 6 who was **a** the waters of the river H4946+5087
Da 12: 7 who was **a** the waters of the river H4946+5087
Am 2: 9 their fruit **a** and their roots below H4946+5087
Am 9: 2 Though they climb up to the **heavens** *a*, from AIT
Mic 4: 1 it will be exalted **a** the hills, and peoples H4946
Mt 10:24 "The student is not **a** the teacher, nor a G5642
Mt 10:24 the teacher, nor a servant **a** his master. G5642
Mt 27:37 **A** his head they placed the written charge G2062
Mk 2: 4 in the roof **a Jesus** by digging G3963+1639S
Lk 6:40 The student is not **a** the teacher, but G5642
Lk 23:38 There was a written notice **a** him, which G2093
Jn 3:31 The one who comes **from a** is above all G540
Jn 3:31 The one who comes from above is **a** all G2062
Jn 3:31 The one who comes from heaven is **a** all. G2062
Jn 8:23 "You are from below; I am from **a**. G539
Jn 19:11 over me if it were not given to you **from a**. G540
Ac 2:19 in the heavens **a** and signs on the earth G539
Ro 12:10 Honor one another **a** *yourselves*. G4605
Gal 4:26 But the Jerusalem that is **a** is free, and she G539
Eph 1:21 **far a** all rule and authority, power and G5645
Php 2: 3 in humility value others **a** yourselves, G5660
Php 2: 9 gave him the name that is **a** every name, G5642
Col 3: 1 set your hearts on things **a**, where Christ is, G539
Col 3: 2 Set your minds on things **a**, not on earthly G539
1Ti 3: 2 Now the overseer is to be **a reproach** G455
Heb 1: 9 has *set* you **a** your companions by G4123
Heb 4: 5 And again in the *passage a* he says, "They AIT
Heb 7:26 apart from sinners, **exalted a** the heavens. G5734
Heb 9: 5 **A** the ark were the cherubim of the Glory G5645
Jas 1:17 Every good and perfect gift is **from a** G540
Jas 5:12 **A** all, my brothers and sisters, do not G4574
1Pe 4: 8 **A** all, love each other deeply, because G4574
2Pe 1:20 **A all**, you must understand that no G4047+4754
2Pe 3: 3 **A all**, you must understand that in G4047+4754
Rev 10: 1 with a rainbow **a** his head; his face G2093

ABRAHAM (229) [ABRAHAM'S, ABRAM, ABRAM'S]

Ge 17: 5 your name will be **A**, for I have made you a H90
Ge 17: 9 Then God said to **A**, "As for you, you must H90
Ge 17:15 God also said to **A**, "As for Sarai your wife H90
Ge 17:17 **A** fell facedown; he laughed and said to H90
Ge 17:18 And **A** said to God, "If only Ishmael might H90
Ge 17:22 When he had finished speaking with **A**, God H90
Ge 17:23 On that very day **A** took his son Ishmael H90
Ge 17:24 **A** was ninety-nine years old when he was H90
Ge 17:26 **A** and his son Ishmael were both circumcised H90
Ge 18: 1 LORD appeared to **A** near the great trees H2257S
Ge 18: 2 **A** looked up and saw three men standing H2257S
Ge 18: 6 So **A** hurried into the tent to Sarah. "Quick," H90
Ge 18:11 **A** and Sarah were already very old, and H90
Ge 18:13 Then the LORD said to **A**, "Why did Sarah H90
Ge 18:16 **A** walked along with them to see them H90
Ge 18:17 "Shall I hide from **A** what I am about to do? H90
Ge 18:18 **A** will surely become a great and powerful H90
Ge 18:19 will bring about for **A** what he has promised H90
Ge 18:22 **A** remained standing before the LORD. H90
Ge 18:23 Then **A** approached him and said: "Will you H90
Ge 18:27 Then **A** spoke up again: "Now that I have H90
Ge 18:31 **A** said, "Now that I have been so bold as to NDT
Ge 18:33 the LORD had finished speaking with **A**, H90
Ge 18:33 Abraham, he left, and **A** returned home. H90
Ge 19:27 the next morning **A** got up and returned to H90
Ge 19:29 he remembered **A**, and he brought Lot H90
Ge 20: 1 Now **A** moved on from there into the region H90
Ge 20: 2 there **A** said of his wife Sarah, "She is H90
Ge 20: 9 Then Abimelek called **A** in and said, "What H90
Ge 20:10 And Abimelek asked **A**, "What was your H90
Ge 20:11 **A** replied, "I said to myself, 'There is surely H90
Ge 20:14 female slaves and gave them to **A**, H90
Ge 20:17 Then **A** prayed to God, and God healed H90
Ge 21: 2 pregnant and bore a son to **A** in his old age, H90
Ge 21: 3 **A** gave the name Isaac to the son Sarah bore H90
Ge 21: 4 was eight days old, **A** circumcised him, as H90
Ge 21: 5 **A** was a hundred years old when his son H90
Ge 21: 7 would have said to **A** that Sarah would H90
Ge 21: 8 day Isaac was weaned **A** held a great feast. H90
Ge 21: 9 the Egyptian had borne to **A** was mocking, H90
Ge 21:10 she said to **A**, "Get rid of that slave H90
Ge 21:11 The matter distressed **A** greatly because it H90
Ge 21:14 the next morning **A** took some food and a H90
Ge 21:22 the commander of his forces said to **A**, H90
Ge 21:24 **A** said, "I swear it." H90
Ge 21:25 Then **A** complained to Abimelek about a H90
Ge 21:27 So **A** brought sheep and cattle and gave H90
Ge 21:28 **A** set apart seven ewe lambs from the flock, H90
Ge 21:29 Abimelek asked **A**, "What is the H90
Ge 21:33 **A** planted a tamarisk tree in Beersheba, and NDT
Ge 21:34 And **A** stayed in the land of the Philistines H90
Ge 22: 1 Some time later God tested **A**. He said to H90
Ge 22: 1 He said to him, "**A**!" "Here I am, H90
Ge 22: 3 the next morning **A** got up and loaded his H90
Ge 22: 4 On the third day **A** looked up and saw the H90
Ge 22: 6 **A** took the wood for the burnt offering and H90
Ge 22: 7 Isaac spoke up and said to his father **A** H90
Ge 22: 7 **A** replied. "The fire and wood are NDT
Ge 22: 8 **A** answered, "God himself will provide the H90
Ge 22: 9 **A** built an altar there and arranged the H90
Ge 22:11 the LORD called out to him from heaven, "**A**! H90
Ge 22:11 "Abraham! **A**!" "Here I am," he H90
Ge 22:13 **A** looked up and there in a thicket he saw a H90
Ge 22:14 So **A** called that place The LORD Will Provide H90
Ge 22:15 the LORD called to **A** from heaven a second H90
Ge 22:19 Then **A** returned to his servants, and they set H90
Ge 22:19 Beersheba. And **A** stayed in Beersheba. H90
Ge 22:20 Some time later **A** was told, "Milkah is also H90
Ge 23: 2 **A** went to mourn for Sarah and to weep H90
Ge 23: 3 Then **A** rose from beside his dead wife and H90
Ge 23: 5 The Hittites replied to **A**, H90
Ge 23: 7 Then **A** rose and bowed down before the H90
Ge 23:10 he replied to **A** in the hearing of all H90
Ge 23:12 Again **A** bowed down before the people of H90
Ge 23:14 Ephron answered **A**, H90
Ge 23:16 **A** agreed to Ephron's terms and weighed H90
Ge 23:18 to **A** as his property in the presence of all the H90
Ge 23:19 Afterward **A** buried his wife Sarah in the cave H90
Ge 23:20 in it were deeded to **A** by the Hittites as a H90
Ge 24: 1 **A** was now very old, and the LORD had H90
Ge 24: 6 you do not take my son back there," **A** said. H90
Ge 24: 9 thigh of his master **A** and swore an oath to H90
Ge 24:12 God of my master **A**, make me successful H90
Ge 24:12 and show kindness to my master **A**. H90
Ge 24:27 the God of my master **A**, who has not H90
Ge 24:42 God of my master **A**, if you will, please H90
Ge 24:48 the God of my master **A**, who had led me on H90

Ge 25: 1 A had taken another wife, whose name was H90
Ge 25: 5 A left everything he owned to Isaac. H90
Ge 25: 7 A lived a hundred and seventy-five years. H90
Ge 25: 8 Then A breathed his last and died at a good H90
Ge 25:10 the field A had bought from the Hittites H90
Ge 25:10 There A was buried with his wife Sarah H90
Ge 25:12 Hagar the Egyptian, bore to A. H90
Ge 25:19 A became the father of Isaac H90
Ge 26: 3 confirm the oath I swore to your father A. H90
Ge 26: 5 because A obeyed me and did everything I H90
Ge 26:15 servants had dug in the time of his father A, H90
Ge 26:18 had been dug in the time of his father A, H90
Ge 26:18 the Philistines had stopped up after A died, H90
Ge 26:24 "I am the God of your father A. H90
Ge 26:24 descendants for the sake of my servant A." H90
Ge 28: 4 your descendants the blessing given to A, H90
Ge 28: 4 as a foreigner, the land God gave to A." H90
Ge 28: 9 Nebaioth and daughter of Ishmael son of A, H90
Ge 28:13 God of your father A and the God of Isaac. H90
Ge 31:42 the God of A and the Fear of Isaac H90
Ge 31:53 May the God of A and the God of Nahor, the H90
Ge 32: 9 "O God of my father A, God of my father H90
Ge 35:12 The land I gave to A and Isaac I also give to H90
Ge 35:27 Hebron), where A and Isaac had stayed. H90
Ge 48:15 before whom my fathers A and Isaac walked H90
Ge 48:16 the names of my fathers A and Isaac, H90
Ge 49:30 which A bought along with the field as a H90
Ge 49:31 There A and his wife Sarah were buried H90
Ge 50:13 which A had bought along with the field as H90
Ge 50:24 land to the land he promised on oath to A, H90
Ex 2:24 he remembered his covenant with A, H90
Ex 3: 6 the God of A, the God of Isaac and H90
Ex 3:15 fathers—the God of A, the God of Isaac H90
Ex 3:16 fathers—the God of A, Isaac and Jacob— H90
Ex 4: 5 fathers—the God of A, the God of Isaac H90
Ex 6: 3 I appeared to A, to Isaac and to Jacob as H90
Ex 6: 8 land I swore with uplifted hand to give to A, H90
Ex 32:13 Remember your servants A, Isaac and Israel H90
Ex 33: 1 go up to the land I promised on oath to A, H90
Lev 26:42 with Isaac and my covenant with A, H90
Nu 32:11 will see the land I promised on oath to A, H90
Dt 1: 8 to your fathers—to A, Isaac and Jacob— H90
Dt 6:10 swore to your fathers, to A, Isaac and Jacob, H90
Dt 9: 5 swore to your fathers, to A, Isaac and Jacob. H90
Dt 9:27 Remember your servants A, Isaac and Jacob H90
Dt 29:13 he swore to your fathers, A, Isaac and Jacob. H90
Dt 30:20 to give to your fathers, A, Isaac and Jacob. H90
Dt 34: 4 "This is the land I promised on oath to A H90
Jos 24: 2 including Terah the father of A and Nahor H90
Jos 24: 3 But I took your father A from the land beyond H90
1Ki 18:36 the God of A, Isaac and Israel, let it H90
2Ki 13:23 them because of his covenant with A, H90
1Ch 1:27 Abram (that is, A). H90
1Ch 1:28 The sons of A: Isaac and Ishmael. H90
1Ch 1:34 A was the father of Isaac. The sons of Isaac H90
1Ch 16:16 the covenant he made with A, the oath he H90
1Ch 29:18 the God of our fathers A, Isaac and Israel, H90
2Ch 20: 7 forever to the descendants of A your friend? H90
2Ch 30: 6 to the LORD, the God of A, Isaac and Israel, H90
Ne 9: 7 of Ur of the Chaldeans and named him A. H90
Ps 47: 9 assemble as the people of the God of A, H90
Ps 105: 6 the descendants of A, his chosen ones, H90
Ps 105: 9 the covenant he made with A, the oath he H90
Ps 105:42 his holy promise given to his servant A. H90
Isa 29:22 the LORD, who redeemed A, says to the H90
Isa 41: 8 you descendants of A my friend, H90
Isa 51: 2 look to A, your father, and to Sarah, who H90
Isa 63:16 though A does not know us or Israel H90
Jer 33:26 his sons to rule over the descendants of A, H90
Eze 33:24 Israel are saying, 'A was only one man, yet H90
Mic 7:20 show love to A, as you pledged on oath H90
Mt 1: 1 the Messiah the son of David, the son *of* A: G11
Mt 1: 2 A was the father of Isaac, Isaac the father of G11
Mt 1:17 fourteen generations in all from A to David, G11
Mt 3: 9 say to yourselves, 'We have A as our father. G11
Mt 3: 9 stones God can raise up children *for* A. G11
Mt 8:11 will take their places at the feast with A G11
Mt 22:32 'I am the God *of* A, the God of Isaac, and the G11
Mk 12:26 'I am the God *of* A, the God of Isaac, G11
Lk 1:55 *to* A and his descendants forever, just as he G11
Lk 1:73 the oath he swore to our father A: G11
Lk 3: 8 say to yourselves, 'We have A as our father. G11
Lk 3: 8 stones God can raise up children *for* A. G11
Lk 3:34 son of Isaac, the son *of* A, the son of Terah, G11
Lk 13:16 a daughter *of* A, whom Satan has G11
Lk 13:28 when you see A, Isaac and Jacob and G11
Lk 16:23 he looked up and saw A far away, with G11
Lk 16:24 'Father A, have pity on me and G11
Lk 16:25 "But A replied, 'Son, remember that in your G11
Lk 16:29 "A replied, 'They have Moses and the G11
Lk 16:30 father A,' he said, 'but if someone G11
Lk 19: 9 because this man, too, is a son *of* A. G11
Lk 20:37 he calls the Lord 'the God *of* A, and the G11
Jn 8:39 "A is our father," they answered. "If you G11
Jn 8:39 said Jesus, "then you would do what A did. G11
Jn 8:40 I heard from God. A did not do such things. G11
Jn 8:52 A died and so did the prophets, yet you say G11
Jn 8:53 Are you greater than our father A? He died G11
Jn 8:56 Your father A rejoiced at the thought of G11
Jn 8:57 they said to him, "and you have seen A!" G11
Jn 8:58 Jesus answered, "before A was born, I am!" G11
Ac 3:13 The God *of* A, Isaac and Jacob, the God of G11
Ac 3:25 He said to A, 'Through your offspring all G11
Ac 7: 2 to our father A while he was still in G11
Ac 7: 5 even though at that time A had no child. G899S
Ac 7: 8 Then he gave A the covenant of G899S
Ac 7: 8 And A became the father of Isaac and NDT
Ac 7:16 in the tomb that A had bought from the G11
Ac 7:17 drew near for God to fulfill his promise *to* A, G11
Ac 7:32 your fathers, the God *of* A, Isaac and Jacob. G11
Ac 13:26 "Fellow children *of* A and you God-fearing G11
Ro 4: 1 What then shall we say that A, our G11
Ro 4: 2 A was justified by works, he had G11
Ro 4: 3 "A believed God, and it was credited to him G11
Ro 4:12 the faith that our father A had before he was G11
Ro 4:13 not through the law that A and his offspring G11
Ro 4:16 also to those who have the faith *of* A. G11
Ro 4:18 A in hope believed and so became the G4005S
Ro 11: 1 a descendant of A, from the tribe of G11
Gal 3: 6 So also A "believed God, and it was credited G11
Gal 3: 7 that those who have faith are children *of* A. G11
Gal 3: 8 announced the gospel in advance *to* A: G11
Gal 3: 9 who rely on faith are blessed along with A, G11
Gal 3:14 the blessing *given to* A might come to the G11
Gal 3:16 promises were spoken *to* A and to his seed. G11
Gal 3:18 in his grace gave it *to* A through a promise. G11
Gal 4:22 For it is written that A had two sons, one by G11
Heb 6:13 When God made his promise *to* A, since G11
Heb 6:15 patiently, A received what was promised. NDT
Heb 7: 1 He met A returning from the defeat of the G11
Heb 7: 2 A gave him a tenth of everything. First G11
Heb 7: 4 Even the patriarch A gave him a tenth of the G11
Heb 7: 5 even though they also are descended from A. G11
Heb 7: 6 collected a tenth *from* A and blessed him G11
Heb 7: 9 collects the tenth, paid the tenth through A, G11
Heb 7:10 because when Melchizedek met A, Levi G899S
Heb 11: 8 By faith A, when called to go to a place he G11
Heb 11:17 By faith A, when God tested him, offered G11
Heb 11:19 A reasoned that God could even raise the NDT
Jas 2:21 Was not our father A considered righteous G11
Jas 2:23 fulfilled that says, "A believed God, and it G11
1Pe 3: 6 who obeyed A and called him her lord. G11

ABRAHAM'S (23) [ABRAHAM]

Ge 17:27 And every male in A household H2257S
Ge 20:18 from conceiving because of A wife Sarah. H90
Ge 22:23 bore these eight sons to A brother Nahor. H90
Ge 24:15 who was the wife of A brother Nahor. H90
Ge 24:34 So he said, "I am A servant. H90
Ge 24:52 When A servant heard what they said, he H90
Ge 24:59 with her nurse and A servant and his men. H90
Ge 25:11 After A death, God blessed his son Isaac H90
Ge 25:12 account of the family line of A son Ishmael, H90
Ge 25:19 the account of the family line of A son Isaac. H90
Ge 26: 1 besides the previous famine in A time—and H90
1Ch 1:32 sons born to Keturah, A concubine: Zimran, H90
Lk 16:22 died and the angels carried him to A side. G11
Jn 8:33 "We are A descendants and have never G11
Jn 8:37 I know that you are A descendants. Yet you G11
Jn 8:39 "If you were A children," said Jesus, "then G11
Ro 4: 9 been saying that A faith was credited to G11
Ro 4:16 may be guaranteed to all A offspring— G3836S
Ro 9: 7 are his descendants are they all A children. G11
Ro 9: 8 promise who are regarded as A offspring. NDT
2Co 11:22 Are they A descendants? So am I. G11
Gal 3:29 to Christ, then you are A seed, and heirs G11
Heb 2:16 it is not angels he helps, but A descendants. G11

ABRAM (60) [ABRAHAM]

Ge 11:26 he became the father of A, Nahor and H92
Ge 11:27 Terah became the father of A, Nahor and H92
Ge 11:29 A and Nahor both married. The name of H92
Ge 11:31 Terah took his son A, his grandson Lot son H92
Ge 11:31 the wife of his son A, and together they set H92
Ge 12: 1 The LORD had said to A, "Go from your H92
Ge 12: 4 So A went, as the LORD had told him; and Lot H92
Ge 12: 4 A was seventy-five years old when he set H92
Ge 12: 6 A traveled through the land as far as the site H92
Ge 12: 7 The LORD appeared to A and said, "To your H92
Ge 12: 9 Then A set out and continued toward the H92
Ge 12:10 A went down to Egypt to live there for a H92
Ge 12:14 When A came to Egypt, the Egyptians saw H92
Ge 12:16 He treated A well for her sake, and Abram H92
Ge 12:16 and A acquired sheep and cattle H2257S
Ge 12:18 So Pharaoh summoned A. "What have you H92
Ge 12:20 gave orders about A to his men, H2257S
Ge 13: 1 So A went up from Egypt to the Negev, with H92
Ge 13: 2 A had become very wealthy in livestock and H92
Ge 13: 4 There A called on the name of the LORD. H92
Ge 13: 5 who was moving about with A, also had H92
Ge 13: 8 So A said to Lot, "Let's not have any H92
Ge 13:12 A lived in the land of Canaan, while Lot lived H92
Ge 13:14 The LORD said to A after Lot had parted from H92
Ge 13:18 So A went to live near the great trees of H92
Ge 14:13 came and reported this to A the Hebrew. H92
Ge 14:13 Now A was living near the great trees of H2085S
Ge 14:13 Aner, all of whom were allied with A. H92
Ge 14:14 When A heard that his relative had been H92
Ge 14:15 During the night A divided his men to H2085S
Ge 14:17 After A returned from defeating H2257S
Ge 14:19 he blessed A, saying, "Blessed be H2084S
Ge 14:19 "Blessed be A by God Most High H92
Ge 14:20 Then A gave him a tenth of everything. NDT
Ge 14:21 The king of Sodom said to A, "Give me the H92
Ge 14:22 But A said to the king of Sodom, "With H92
Ge 14:23 you will never be able to say, 'I made A rich. H92
Ge 15: 1 the word of the LORD came to A in a vision: H92
Ge 15: 1 "Do not be afraid, A. I am your shield, H92
Ge 15: 2 But A said, "Sovereign LORD, what can you H92
Ge 15: 3 And A said, "You have given me no children H92
Ge 15: 6 A believed the LORD, and he credited it to NDT
Ge 15: 8 A said, "Sovereign LORD, how can I know NDT
Ge 15:10 A brought all these to him, cut them in two NDT
Ge 15:11 on the carcasses, but A drove them away. H92
Ge 15:12 the sun was setting, A fell into a deep sleep H92
Ge 15:18 the LORD made a covenant with A and said, H92
Ge 16: 2 so she said to A, "The LORD has kept me H92
Ge 16: 2 A agreed to what Sarai said H92
Ge 16: 3 So after A had been living in Canaan ten H92
Ge 16: 5 Then Sarai said to A, "You are responsible H92
Ge 16: 6 slave is in your hands," A said. "Do with her H92
Ge 16:15 So Hagar bore A a son, and Abram gave the H92
Ge 16:15 A gave the name Ishmael to the son H92
Ge 16:16 A was eighty-six years old when Hagar bore H92
Ge 17: 1 When A was ninety-nine years old, the LORD H92
Ge 17: 3 A fell facedown, and God said to him, H92
Ge 17: 5 No longer will you be called A; your name H92
1Ch 1:27 A (that is, Abraham). H92
Ne 9: 7 who chose A and brought him out of Ur of H92

ABRAM'S (5) [ABRAHAM]

Ge 11:29 The name of A wife was Sarai, and the H92
Ge 12:17 his household because of A wife Sarai. H92
Ge 13: 7 arose between A herders and Lot's. H92
Ge 14:12 They also carried off A nephew Lot and his H92
Ge 16: 1 Now Sarai, A wife, had borne him no H92

ABRONAH (2)

Nu 33:34 They left Jotbathah and camped at A. H6307
Nu 33:35 They left A and camped at Ezion Geber. H6307

ABSALOM (92) [ABSALOM'S]

2Sa 3: 3 A the son of Maakah daughter of Talmai H94
2Sa 13: 1 the beautiful sister of A son of David. H94
2Sa 13:20 Her brother A said to her, "Has that Amnon H94
2Sa 13:22 And A never said a word to Amnon, either H94
2Sa 13:24 A went to the king and said, "Your servant H94
2Sa 13:25 Although A urged him, he still refused to NDT
2Sa 13:26 Then A said, "If not, please let my brother H94
2Sa 13:27 But A urged him, so he sent with him Amnon H94
2Sa 13:28 A ordered his men, "Listen! When Amnon is H94
2Sa 13:29 men did to Amnon what A had ordered. H94
2Sa 13:30 "A has struck down all the king's sons; not H94
2Sa 13:34 Meanwhile, A had fled. Now the man H94
2Sa 13:37 A fled and went to Talmai son of Ammihud H94
2Sa 13:38 After A fled and went to Geshur, he stayed H94
2Sa 13:39 And King David longed to go to A, for he H94
2Sa 14: 1 knew that the king's heart longed for A. H94
2Sa 14:21 Go, bring back the young man A." H94
2Sa 14:23 to Geshur and brought A back to Jerusalem. H94
2Sa 14:24 So A went to his own house and did not see H94
2Sa 14:25 praised for his handsome appearance as A. H94
2Sa 14:27 Three sons and a daughter were born to A H94
2Sa 14:28 A lived two years in Jerusalem without H94
2Sa 14:29 Then A sent for Joab in order to send him to H94
2Sa 14:32 A said to Joab, "Look, I sent word to you H94
2Sa 14:33 Then the king summoned A, and he came H94
2Sa 14:33 before the king. And the king kissed A. H94
2Sa 15: 1 A provided himself with a chariot and horses H94
2Sa 15: 2 king for a decision, A would call out to him H94
2Sa 15: 3 Then A would say to him, "Look, your claims H94
2Sa 15: 4 And A would add, "If only I were appointed H94
2Sa 15: 5 before him, A would reach out his hand NDT
2Sa 15: 6 A behaved in this way toward all the H94
2Sa 15: 7 the end of four years, A said to the king, "Let H94
2Sa 15:10 Then A sent secret messengers throughout H94
2Sa 15:10 the trumpets, then say, 'A is king in Hebron. H94
2Sa 15:11 men from Jerusalem had accompanied A. H94
2Sa 15:12 While A was offering sacrifices, he also sent H94
2Sa 15:13 hearts of the people of Israel are with A." H94
2Sa 15:14 must flee, or none of us will escape from A. H94
2Sa 15:19 Go back and stay with King A. You are a NDT
2Sa 15:31 is among the conspirators with A. H94
2Sa 15:34 But if you return to the city and say to A H94
2Sa 15:37 at Jerusalem as A was entering the city. H94
2Sa 16: 8 the kingdom into the hands of your son A. H94
2Sa 16:15 A and all the men of Israel came to H94
2Sa 16:16 confidant, went to A and said to him, "Long H94
2Sa 16:17 A said to Hushai, "So this is the love you H94
2Sa 16:18 Hushai said to A, "No, the one chosen by H94
2Sa 16:20 A said to Ahithophel, "Give us your advice H94
2Sa 16:22 So they pitched a tent for A on the roof, and H94
2Sa 16:23 was how both David and A regarded all of H94
2Sa 17: 1 Ahithophel said to A, "I would choose H94
2Sa 17: 4 plan seemed good to A and to all the elders H94
2Sa 17: 5 But A said, "Summon also Hushai the Arkite, H94
2Sa 17: 6 Hushai came to him, A said, "Ahithophel H94
2Sa 17: 7 Hushai replied to A, "The advice Ahithophel H94
2Sa 17: 9 a slaughter among the troops who follow A. H94
2Sa 17:14 A and all the men of Israel said, "The H94
2Sa 17:14 Ahithophel in order to bring disaster on A. H94
2Sa 17:15 "Ahithophel has advised A and the elders of H94
2Sa 17:18 But a young man saw them and told A. H94
2Sa 17:24 A crossed the Jordan with all the men H94
2Sa 17:25 A had appointed Amasa over the army in H94
2Sa 17:26 The Israelites and A camped in the land of H94

2Sa 18: 5 gentle with the young man **A** for my sake." H94
2Sa 18: 5 giving orders concerning **A** to each of the H94
2Sa 18: 9 Now **A** happened to meet David's men. He H94
2Sa 18:10 "I just saw **A** hanging in an oak tree." H94
2Sa 18:12 'Protect the young man **A** for my sake. H94
2Sa 18:14 heart while **A** was still alive in H5647S
2Sa 18:15 ten of Joab's armor-bearers surrounded **A**, H94
2Sa 18:17 They took **A**, threw him into a big pit in the H94
2Sa 18:18 During his lifetime **A** had taken a pillar and H94
2Sa 18:29 "Is the young man **A** safe?" Ahimaaz H94
2Sa 18:32 the Cushite, "Is the young man **A** safe?" H94
2Sa 18:33 "O my son **A**! My son, my son H94
2Sa 18:33 my son **A**! If only I had died H94
2Sa 18:33 I had died instead of you—O **A**, my son, H94
2Sa 19: 1 "The king is weeping and mourning for **A**." H94
2Sa 19: 4 his face and cried aloud, "O my son **A**! H94
2Sa 19: 4 "O my son Absalom! O **A**, my son, my son!" H94
2Sa 19: 6 would be pleased if **A** were alive today and H94
2Sa 19: 9 he has fled the country to escape from **A**; H94
2Sa 19:10 **A**, whom we anointed to rule over us H94
2Sa 20: 6 son of Bikri will do us more harm than **A** did. H94
1Ki 1: 6 very handsome and was born next after **A**.) H94
1Ki 2: 7 stood by me when I fled from your brother **A**. H94
1Ki 2:28 conspired with Adonijah though not with **A**, H94
1Ch 3: 2 **A** the son of Maakah daughter of Talmai H94
2Ch 11:20 Then he married Maakah daughter of **A**, who H94
2Ch 11:21 Maakah daughter of **A** more than any of his H94
Ps 3: T When he fled from his son **A**. H94

ABSALOM'S (12) [ABSALOM]

2Sa 13: 4 "I'm in love with Tamar, my brother **A** sister." H94
2Sa 13:20 And Tamar lived in her brother **A** house, a H94
2Sa 13:23 when **A** sheepshearers were at Baal H4200+94
2Sa 13:29 So **A** men did to Amnon what Absalom had H94
2Sa 13:32 This has been **A** express intention ever since H94
2Sa 14:30 So **A** servants set the field on fire. H94
2Sa 14:31 Then Joab did go to **A** house, and he said H94
2Sa 15:12 **A** following kept on increasing. H94
2Sa 17:20 When **A** men came to the woman at the H94
2Sa 18: 9 large oak, **A** hair got caught in the tree. H2257S
2Sa 18:14 plunged them into **A** heart while Absalom H94
2Sa 18:18 it is called **A** Monument to this day. H94

ABSENCE (3) [ABSENT]

Ac 24:17 "After an **a** of several years, I came to NDT
Php 1:27 see you or only hear about you **in** my **a**, *G582*
Php 2:12 now much more in my **a**—continue to *G707*

ABSENT (4) [ABSENCE]

2Co 10:11 what we are in our letters *when we are* **a**, *G582*
2Co 13: 2 I now repeat it *while* **a**: On my return I will *G582*
2Co 13:10 This is why I write these things *when I am* **a**, *G582*
Col 2: 5 For though *I am* **a** from you in body, I am *G582*

ABSOLUTE (1) [ABSOLUTELY]

1Ti 5: 2 younger women as sisters, with **a** purity. *G4246*

ABSOLUTELY (3) [ABSOLUTE]

Ex 22:17 If her father **a refuses** to give her to H4412+4412
Gal 2:17 that Christ promotes sin? **A not**! *G3590+1181*
Gal 3:21 **A not**! For if a law *G3590+1181*

ABSTAIN (7) [ABSTAINS]

Ex 19:15 **A from sexual relations**." H440+5602+448+851
Nu 6: 3 *they must* **a** from wine and other H5693
Ac 15:20 telling them *to* **a** from food polluted by *G600*
Ac 15:29 *You are to* **a** from food sacrificed to idols *G600*
Ac 21:25 our decision *that* they *should* **a** from food *G5875*
1Ti 4: 3 to marry and **order** them **to a** from certain *G600*
1Pe 2:11 exiles, *to* **a from** sinful desires, which *G600*

ABSTAINS (1) [ABSTAIN]

Ro 14: 6 and whoever **a** does so to the Lord *G3590+2266*

ABSTINENCE (KJV) GONE WITHOUT FOOD

ABUNDANCE (33) [ABUNDANT]

Ge 27:28 richness—an **a** *of* grain and new wine. H8044
Ge 41:29 Seven years of great **a** are coming H8426
Ge 41:30 Then all the **a** in Egypt will be forgotten H8426
Ge 41:31 The **a** in the land will not be remembered H8426
Ge 41:34 of Egypt during the seven years of **a**. H8426
Ge 41:47 the seven years of **a** the land produced H8426
Ge 41:48 those seven years of **a** in Egypt and stored it NDT
Ge 41:53 The seven years of **a** in Egypt came to an H8426
Dt 33:19 they will feast on the **a** *of* the seas, on the H9179
1Ch 29:16 all this **a** that we have provided for H2162
1Ch 29:21 other sacrifices **in a** for all Israel. H4200+8044
2Ch 29:35 There were burnt offerings **in a** H4200+8044
Ne 9:25 olive groves and fruit trees **in a**. H4200+8044
Job 36:31 the nations and provides food in **a**. H3892
Ps 36: 8 They feast on the **a** *of* your house; you H2016
Ps 65:11 and your carts overflow with **a**. H2016
Ps 66:12 but you brought us to a **place of a**. H8122
Ps 73:10 turn to them and drink up waters in **a**. H4849
Pr 20:15 there is, and rubies **in a**, but lips that H8044
Ecc 5:12 the rich, their **a** permits them no sleep. H8426
Isa 7:22 And because of the **a** of the milk they give, H8044
Isa 30:33 wide, with an **a** of fire and wood; the H2221
Isa 33:23 Then an **a** *of* spoils will be divided and H5269
Isa 66:11 deeply and delight in her overflowing **a**." H3883
Jer 2:22 with soap and **use an a** *of* cleansing H8049
Jer 31:14 I will satisfy the priests with **a**, and my H2016
Jer 40:12 they harvested an **a** of wine and H2221+4394
Mt 13:12 be given more, and *they will* **have an a**. *G4355*
Mt 25:29 be given more, and *they will* **have an a**. *G4355*
Lk 12:15 does not consist in an **a** of possessions." *G4355*
1Pe 1: 2 Grace and peace *be* yours **in a**. *G4437*
2Pe 1: 2 peace *be* yours **in a** through the *G4437*
Jude 2 peace and love *be* yours **in a**. *G4437*

ABUNDANT (32) [ABUNDANCE, ABUNDANTLY]

Nu 24: 7 their buckets; their seed will have **a** water. H8041
Dt 28:11 The LORD *will* **grant** you **a** prosperity—in H3855
Dt 32: 2 on new grass, like **a rain** on tender plants. H8053
2Ch 11:23 He gave them **a** provisions and H4200+8044
Ne 5:18 every ten days an **a supply** of wine of all H2221
Ne 9:37 its **a** harvest goes to the kings you have H8049
Est 1: 7 the royal wine was **a**, in keeping with H8041
Job 36:28 their moisture and **a** showers fall on H8041
Ps 31:19 How **a** are the good things that you have H8041
Ps 68: 9 You gave **a** showers, O God; you H5607
Ps 78:15 gave them water as **a** as the seas; H8041
Ps 132:15 *I will* **bless** her *with* **a** provisions H1385+1385
Ps 145: 7 They celebrate your **a** goodness and H8041
Pr 12:11 who work their land *will* **have a** food, H8425
Pr 14: 4 the strength of an ox come **a** harvests. H8044
Pr 28:19 who work their land *will* **have a** food, H8425
Isa 23:18 the LORD, for **a** food and fine clothes. H8429
Jer 33: 6 will let them enjoy **a** peace and security. H6988
Jer 33: 9 will tremble at the **a** prosperity and peace H3972
Eze 17: 5 He planted it like a willow by **a** water, H8041
Eze 17: 8 in good soil by **a** water so that it would H8041
Eze 19:10 full of branches because of **a** water. H8041
Eze 31: 5 spreading because of **a** waters. H8041
Eze 31: 7 its roots went down to **a** waters. H8041
Eze 31: 9 I made it beautiful with **a** branches, the H8044
Eze 31:15 streams, and its **a** waters were restrained. H8041
Eze 32:13 cattle from beside **a** waters no longer to H8041
Da 4:12 beautiful, its fruit **a**, and on it was food A10678
Da 4:21 with beautiful leaves and **a** fruit A10678
Joel 2:23 He sends you **a showers**, both autumn H1773
Lk 12:16 of a certain rich man **yielded an a harvest**. *G2369*
Ro 5:17 receive God's **a provision** of grace and of *G4353*

ABUNDANTLY (7) [ABUNDANT]

Ge 24:35 The LORD has blessed my master **a**, and he H4394
Jos 17:14 LORD has blessed us **a**." H6330+889+6330+3907
Ps 65: 9 the land and water it; you enrich it **a**. H8041
Ps 78:20 streams **flowed a**, but can he also H8851
2Co 1: 5 For just as we share **a** in the sufferings of *G4355*
2Co 9: 8 God is able *to* **bless** you **a**, *G4246+5921+4355*
1Ti 1:14 of our Lord *was* **poured out** on me **a**, *G5670*

ABUSE (9) [ABUSED, ABUSIVE]

1Sa 31: 4 will come and run me through and **a** me." H6618
1Ch 10: 4 fellows will come and **a** me. H6618
Ps 55:10 on its walls; malice and **a** are within it. H6662
Pr 9: 7 whoever rebukes the wicked incurs **a**. H4583
Ac 13:45 Paul was saying and **heaped a** on him. *G1059*
1Pe 4: 4 wild living, and *they* **heap a** on you. *G1059*
2Pe 2:10 they are not afraid *to* **heap a** on celestial *G1059*
2Pe 2:11 do not heap **a** on such beings when *G1061*
Jude 8 authority and **heap a on** celestial beings. *G1059*

ABUSED (1) [ABUSE]

Jdg 19:25 they raped her and **a** her throughout the H6618

ABUSIVE (2) [ABUSE]

Ac 18: 6 when they opposed Paul and *became* **a**, *G1059*
2Ti 3: 2 boastful, proud, **a**, disobedient to their *G1061*

ABUTTED (1)

Eze 40:18 It **a** the sides of the gateways and was as H448

ABYSS (9)

Lk 8:31 not to order them to go into the **A**. *G12*
Rev 9: 1 star was given the key to the shaft *of* the **A**. *G12*
Rev 9: 2 When he opened the **A**, smoke rose from it *G12*
Rev 9: 2 were darkened by the smoke *from* the **A**. *G5853*
Rev 9:11 had as king over them the angel *of* the **A**, *G12*
Rev 11: 7 that comes up from the **A** will attack them, *G12*
Rev 17: 8 will come up out of the **A** and go to its *G12*
Rev 20: 1 having the key *to* the **A** and holding in his *G12*
Rev 20: 3 He threw him into the **A**, and locked and *G12*

ACACIA (28) [ACACIAS]

Ex 25: 5 another type of durable leather; **a** wood; H8847
Ex 25:10 "Have them make an ark of **a** wood—two H8847
Ex 25:13 Then make poles of **a** wood and overlay H8847
Ex 25:23 "Make a table of **a** wood—two cubits long H8847
Ex 25:28 Make the poles of **a** wood, overlay them H8847
Ex 26:15 upright frames of **a** wood for the H8847
Ex 26:26 "Also make crossbars of **a** wood: five for H8847
Ex 26:32 on four posts of **a wood** overlaid with gold H8847
Ex 26:37 five posts of **a wood** overlaid with H8847
Ex 27: 1 "Build an altar of **a** wood, three cubits H8847
Ex 27: 6 Make poles of **a** wood for the altar and H8847
Ex 30: 1 "Make an altar of **a** wood for burning H8847
Ex 30: 5 Make the poles of **a** wood and overlay H8847
Ex 35: 7 another type of durable leather; **a** wood; H8847
Ex 35:24 everyone who had **a** wood for any part of H8847
Ex 36:20 made upright frames of **a** wood for the H8847
Ex 36:31 They also made crossbars of **a** wood: five H8847
Ex 36:36 made four posts of **a wood** for it and H8847
Ex 37: 1 Bezalel made the ark of **a** wood—two H8847
Ex 37: 4 he made poles of **a** wood and overlaid H8847
Ex 37:10 They made the table of **a** wood—two H8847
Ex 37:15 table were made of **a** wood and were H8847
Ex 37:25 made the altar of incense out of **a** wood. H8847
Ex 37:28 made the poles of **a** wood and overlaid H8847
Ex 38: 1 built the altar of burnt offering of **a** wood, H8847
Ex 38: 6 made the poles of **a** wood and overlaid H8847
Dt 10: 3 made the ark out of **a** wood and chiseled H8847
Isa 41:19 will put in the desert the cedar and the **a**, H8847

ACACIAS (1) [ACACIA]

Joel 3:18 house and will water the valley of **a**. H8847

ACBOR (NIV84) AKBOR

ACCAD (KJV) AKKAD

ACCENT (1)

Mt 26:73 are one of them; your **a** gives you away." *G3282*

ACCEPT (77) [ACCEPTABLE, ACCEPTABLY, ACCEPTANCE, ACCEPTED, ACCEPTING, ACCEPTS]

Ge 14:23 that *I will* **a** nothing belonging to you, not H4374
Ge 14:24 I will **a** nothing but what my men have eaten NDT
Ge 21:30 "**A** these seven lambs from my hand as a H4374
Ge 23:13 **A** it from me so I can bury my dead there." H4374
Ge 33:10 favor in your eyes, **a** this gift from me. H4374
Ge 33:11 Please **a** the present that was brought to H4374
Ex 22:11 The owner is *to* **a** this, and no restitution H4374
Ex 23: 8 "*Do* not **a** a bribe, for a bribe blinds those H4374
Lev 22:25 you must not **a** such animals from the NDT
Lev 26:23 things *you do* not **a** my **correction** but H3579
Nu 7: 5 "**A** these from them, that they may be H4374
Nu 16:15 said to the LORD, "*Do* not **a** their offering. H7155
Nu 32:30 *they must* **a** *their* **possession** with you in H296
Nu 35:31 " '*Do* not **a** a ransom for the life of a H4374
Nu 35:32 " '*Do* not **a** a ransom for anyone who has H4374
Dt 16:19 *Do* not **a** a bribe, for a bribe blinds the H4374
Dt 20:11 If *they* **a** and open their gates, all the H6699
Dt 21: 8 **A** *this* **atonement** for your people Israel H4105
1Sa 2:15 to roast; *he* won't **a** boiled meat from you H4374
1Sa 10: 4 of bread, which *you will* **a** from them. H4374
1Sa 26:19 against me, then *may he* **a** an offering. H8193
2Sa 24:23 "*May* the LORD your God **a** you. H8354
2Ki 5:15 So please **a** a gift from your servant." H4374
2Ki 5:16 whom I serve, *I will* not **a** a thing. H4374
2Ki 5:23 He urged Gehazi to **a** them, and then tied NDT
2Ki 5:26 the time to take money or to **a** clothes— H4374
Est 4: 4 of his sackcloth, but *he would* not **a** them. H7691
Job 2:10 *Shall we* **a** good from God, and not H7691
Job 22:22 **A** instruction from his mouth and lay up H4374
Job 42: 8 and *I will* **a** his prayer and not deal H5951+7156
Ps 15: 5 *who does* not **a** a bribe against the H4374
Ps 20: 3 your sacrifices and **a** your burnt offerings. H2014
Ps 119:108 **A**, LORD, the willing praise of my mouth H8354
Pr 1:25 all my advice and *do* not **a** my rebuke, H14
Pr 1:30 Since *they would* not **a** my advice and H14
Pr 2: 1 if *you* **a** my words and store up my H4374
Pr 4:10 my son, **a** what I say, and the years of H4374
Pr 6:35 *He will* not **a** any compensation H5951+7156
Pr 10: 8 The wise in heart **a** commands, but a H4374
Pr 17:23 The wicked **a** bribes in secret to pervert H4374
Pr 19:20 Listen to advice and **a** discipline, and at H7691
Ecc 5:19 to **a** their lot and be happy in their toil H5951
Isa 29:24 those who complain *will* **a** instruction." H4340
Jer 14:10 So the LORD *does* not **a** them; he will now H8354
Jer 14:12 grain offerings, *I will* not **a** them. H8354
Eze 20:40 will serve me, and there *I will* **a** them. H8354
Eze 20:41 *I will* **a** you as fragrant incense when I H8354
Eze 22:12 In you *are people who* **a** bribes to shed H4374
Eze 43:27 Then *I will* **a** you, declares the Sovereign H8354
Da 4:27 Your Majesty, be pleased to **a** my advice: NDT
Am 5:22 grain offerings, *I will* not **a** them. H8354
Zep 3: 7 'Surely you will fear me and **a** correction! H4374
Mal 1: 8 *Would he* **a** you?" says H5951+7156
Mal 1: 9 from your hands, *will he* **a** you?" H5951+7156
Mal 1:10 "and *I will* **a** no offering from your hands. H8354
Mal 1:13 *should I* **a** them from your hands? H8354
Mt 11:14 And if you are willing *to* **a** it, he is the *G1312*
Mt 19:11 "Not everyone *can* **a** this word, but only *G6003*
Mt 19:12 The one who can **a** this should accept it." *G6003*
Mt 19:12 The one who can accept this *should* **a** it." *G6003*
Mk 4:20 hear the word, **a** it, and produce a *G4138*
Jn 3:11 but *still you people do* not **a** our *G3284*
Jn 5:34 Not *that* I **a** human testimony; but I *G3284*
Jn 5:41 "*I do* not **a** glory from human beings, *G3284*
Jn 5:43 and *you do* not **a** me; but if *G3284*
Jn 5:43 comes in his own name, *you will* **a** him. *G3284*
Jn 5:44 you believe *since you* **a** glory from one *G3284*
Jn 6:60 "This is a hard teaching. Who can **a** it?" *G201*
Jn 12:48 who rejects me and *does* not **a** my words; *G3284*
Jn 14:17 The world cannot **a** him, because it *G3284*
Ac 16:21 unlawful for us Romans *to* **a** or practice." *G4138*
Ac 22:18 because *the people* here *will* not **a** your *G4138*
Ro 14: 1 **A** the one whose faith is weak, without *G4689*
Ro 15: 7 **A** one another, then, just as Christ *G4689*
1Co 2:14 the Spirit *does* not **a** the things that *G1312*
Jas 1:21 humbly **a** the word planted in *G1312*
1Jn 5: 9 *We* **a** human testimony, but God's *G3284*

ACCEPTABLE (16) [ACCEPT]

Ex 28:38 so that they will be **a** to the LORD. H8356
Lev 1: 3 of meeting so that it will be **a** to the LORD. H8356

Lev 22:21 be without defect or blemish to be **a**. H8356
Lev 22:27 *it will* **be a** as a food offering presented to H8354
Lev 27: 9 is an animal that *is* **a** as an offering to the H7928
Lev 27:11 one that *is* not **a** as an offering to the LORD H7928
Jdg 14: 3 "Isn't there an **a** woman among your NDT
Pr 21: 3 is right and just *is* more **a** to the LORD than H1047
Isa 58: 5 what you call a fast, a day **a** to the LORD? H8356
Jer 6:20 Your burnt offerings are not **a**; your H8356
Mal 1:14 the cheat who has an **a** male in his flock NDT
Mal 3: 4 Jerusalem *will be* **a** to the LORD, H6844
Ro 15:16 might become an offering **a** to God, *G2347*
2Co 8:12 the gift is **a** according to what one has *G2347*
Php 4:18 fragrant offering, an **a** sacrifice, pleasing *G1283*
1Pe 2: 5 spiritual sacrifices **a** to God through Jesus *G2347*

ACCEPTABLY (1) [ACCEPT]

Heb 12:28 so worship God **a** with reverence and *G2299*

ACCEPTANCE (3) [ACCEPT]

Ro 11:15 what will their **a** be but life from the dead *G4691*
1Ti 1:15 is a trustworthy saying that deserves full **a**: *G628*
1Ti 4: 9 is a trustworthy saying that deserves full **a**. *G628*

ACCEPTED (34) [ACCEPT]

Ge 4: 7 will you not be **a**? But if you do not do H8420
Ge 33:11 And because Jacob insisted, Esau **a** it. H4374
Lev 1: 4 and *it will* **be a** on your behalf to make H8354
Lev 7:18 the one who offered it *will* not **be a**. H8354
Lev 19: 5 a way that it will be **a** *on your behalf.* H8356
Lev 19: 7 third day, it is impure and *will* not **be a**. H8354
Lev 22:19 in order that it may be **a** *on your behalf.* H8356
Lev 22:20 because it will not be **a** on your behalf. H8356
Lev 22:23 but *it will* not **be a** in fulfillment of a vow. H8354
Lev 22:25 *They will* not **be a** on your behalf H8354
Lev 22:29 a way that it will be **a** *on your behalf.* H8356
Lev 23:11 the LORD so it will be **a** *on your behalf;* H8356
Nu 31:51 Eleazar the priest **a** from them the gold— H4374
Nu 31:54 Eleazar the priest **a** the gold from the H4374
Jdg 13:23 *he would* not *have* **a** a burnt offering and H4374
1Sa 8: 3 dishonest gain and **a** bribes and H4374
1Sa 12: 3 From whose hand *have I* **a** a bribe to H4374
1Sa 25:35 Then David **a** from her hand what she H4374
Job 42: 9 and the LORD **a** Job's prayer. H5951+906+7156
Isa 56: 7 sacrifices *will be* **a** on my altar; H8356
Isa 60: 7 they will be **a** as offerings on my altar H8356
Lk 4:24 "no prophet is **a** in his hometown. *G1283*
Jn 3:33 Whoever *has* **a** it has certified that God is *G3284*
Jn 17: 8 the words you gave me and they **a** them. *G3284*
Ac 2:41 Those *who* **a** his message were baptized *G622*
Ac 8:14 that Samaria *had* **a** the word of God, *G1312*
Ac 15: 8 **showed that** *he* **a** them by giving the Holy *G3455*
Ro 10:16 But not all the Israelites **a** the good news *G5634*
Ro 14: 3 the one who does, for God *has* **a** them. *G4689*
Ro 15: 7 just as Christ **a** you, in order to bring *G4689*
2Co 11: 4 a different gospel from the one *you* **a** *G1312*
Gal 1: 9 to you a gospel other than what *you* **a**, *G4161*
1Th 2:13 from us, *you* **a** it not as a human word *G1312*
Heb 10:34 in prison and joyfully **a** the confiscation of *G4657*

ACCEPTING (2) [ACCEPT]

2Ki 5:20 by not **a** from him what he brought. H4374
Isa 33:15 keep their hands from **a** bribes, H9461

ACCEPTS (15) [ACCEPT]

Dt 10:17 who shows no partiality and **a** no bribes. H4374
Dt 27:25 "Cursed is *anyone who* **a** a bribe to kill an H4374
Ps 6: 9 my cry for mercy; the LORD **a** my prayer. H4374
Mic 7: 3 the judge **a** bribes, the powerful NDT
Zep 3: 2 She obeys no one, *she* **a** no correction H4374
Mal 2:13 on your offerings or **a** them with pleasure H4374
Jn 3:32 heard, but no one **a** his testimony. *G3284*
Jn 13:20 whoever **a** anyone I send accepts me *G3284*
Jn 13:20 whoever accepts anyone I send **a** me; and *G3284*
Jn 13:20 whoever **a** me accepts the one who *G3284*
Jn 13:20 whoever accepts me **a** the one who sent *G3284*
Ac 10:35 **a** from every nation the one *G1283+1639*
Heb 12: 6 he chastens everyone *he* **a** as his son." *G4138*
Jas 1:27 God our Father **a** *as* pure and faultless *G4123*
1Jn 5:10 Son of God **a** this testimony *G2400+1877+1571*

ACCESS (3)

Est 1:14 Media *who* **had special a** to the H8011+7156
Ro 5: 2 whom we have gained **a** by faith into this *G4643*
Eph 2:18 him we both have **a** to the Father by one *G4643*

ACCESSORIES (7)

Ex 25:39 used for the lampstand and all these **a**. H3998
Ex 30:27 the lampstand and its **a**, the altar of H3998
Ex 31: 8 the pure gold lampstand and all its **a**, the H3998
Ex 35:14 the lampstand that is for light with its **a** H3998
Ex 37:24 lampstand and all its **a** from one talent of H3998
Ex 39:37 with its row of lamps and all its **a**, H3998
Nu 4:10 to wrap it and all its **a** in a covering of the H3998

ACCHO (KJV) AKKO

ACCIDENTALLY (4)

Nu 35:11 who has killed someone **a** may flee. H928+8705
Nu 35:15 has killed another **a** can flee there. H928+8705
Jos 20: 3 who kills a person **a** and H928+8705
Jos 20: 9 who killed someone **a** could flee to H928+8705

ACCLAIM (2) [ACCLAMATION]

Ps 89:15 are those who have learned to **a** you, H9558
Isa 24:14 from the west *they* **a** the LORD's majesty. H7412

ACCLAMATION (1) [ACCLAIM]

2Ch 15:14 They took an oath to the LORD with loud **a** H7754

ACCO (NIV84) AKKO

ACCOMPANIED (23) [ACCOMPANY]

Ge 50: 7 All Pharaoh's officials **a** him—the H6590+907
Ru 1:22 from Moab **a by** Ruth the Moabite, H6640
1Sa 10:26 **a by** valiant men whose hearts God H2143+6640
2Sa 15:11 from Jerusalem *had* **a** Absalom. H2143+907
2Sa 15:18 Gittites who *had* **a** him from Gath H995+8079
1Ki 20: 1 **A by** thirty-two kings with their horses and H907
1Ch 25: 1 of prophesying, **a by** harps, lyres and H928
2Ch 5:12 They were **a by** 120 priests sounding H6640
2Ch 5:13 **A by** trumpets, cymbals and other H928
2Ch 29:27 **a** by trumpets and the instruments H6584+3338
2Ch 29:35 drink offerings that **a** the burnt offerings. H4200
Jer 17:25 **a** by the men of Judah and those living in NDT
Jer 22: 4 **a by** their officials and their people. H2256
Mk 6: 1 went to his hometown, **a**, *by* his disciples. *G199*
Mk 16:20 confirmed his word by the signs *that* **a** it. *G2051*
Jn 19:39 *He was* **a** *by* Nicodemus, the man who *G2262*
Ac 18:18 sailed for Syria, **a by** Priscilla and Aquila. *G5250*
Ac 20: 4 He *was* **a** *by* Sopater son of Pyrrhus from *G5299*
Ac 20:38 Then *they* **a** him to the ship. *G4636*
Ac 21: 5 wives and children, **a** us out of the city *G4636*
Ac 21:16 from Caesarea **a** us and brought us to *G5302*
1Co 10: 4 drank from the spiritual rock *that* **a** them, *G199*
Jas 2:17 by itself, if *it is* not **a by** action, is dead. *G2400*

ACCOMPANIES (3) [ACCOMPANY]

Isa 40:10 and his recompense **a** him. H4200+7156
Isa 62:11 and his recompense **a** him. H4200+7156
2Co 9:13 that *a* your **confession** of the gospel AIT

ACCOMPANY (9) [ACCOMPANIED, ACCOMPANIES, ACCOMPANYING]

Ge 33:12 us be on our way; *I'll* **a** you." H2143+4200+5584
Dt 28: 2 come on you and **a** you if you obey the H5952
1Sa 28: 1 and your men *will* **a** me in the army." H3655+907
Ne 10:38 from Aaron is to **a** the Levites when they H6640
Est 5:12 Esther invited to **a** the king to the banquet H6640
Ecc 8:15 Then joy *will* **a** them in their toil all the H4277
Mk 16:17 And these signs *will* **a** those who believe *G4158*
1Co 16: 4 me to go also, *they will* **a** me. *G5250+4513*
2Co 8:19 by the churches to **a** us as we carry the *G5292*

ACCOMPANYING (1) [ACCOMPANY]

Nu 28: 7 The **a** drink offering is to be a quarter of a NDT

ACCOMPLICES (1)

Pr 29:24 The **a** *of* thieves are their own H2745+6640

ACCOMPLISH (11) [ACCOMPLISHED, ACCOMPLISHES, ACCOMPLISHING]

Ge 50:20 it for good to **a** what is now being done, H6913
Dt 9: 5 to **a** what he swore to your fathers H7756
2Ki 8:13 "How *could* your servant, a mere dog, **a** H6913
2Ki 19:31 "The zeal of the LORD Almighty *will* **a** this. H6913
Ecc 2: 2 And what *does* pleasure **a**?" H6913
Isa 9: 7 The zeal of the LORD Almighty *will* **a** this. H6913
Isa 37:32 The zeal of the LORD Almighty *will* **a** this. H6913
Isa 44:28 is my shepherd and *will* **a** all that I please H8966
Isa 55:11 but *will* **a** what I desire and achieve the H6913
Jer 48:30 the LORD, "and her boasts **a** nothing. H6913
Rev 17:17 it into their hearts *to* **a** his purpose by *G4472*

ACCOMPLISHED (6) [ACCOMPLISH]

Jdg 8: 2 "What *have I* **a** compared to you? H6913
Isa 26:12 all *that* we have **a** you have done for us. H5126
Mt 5:18 from the Law until everything *is* **a**. *G1181*
Ro 15:18 except what Christ *has* **a** through me in *G2981*
Eph 3:11 purpose that *he* **a** in Christ Jesus our *G4472*
Rev 10: 7 the mystery of God *will be* **a**, just as he *G5464*

ACCOMPLISHES (2) [ACCOMPLISH]

Jer 23:20 until he **fully a** the purposes H6913+2256+7756
Jer 30:24 until he **fully a** the purposes H6913+2256+7756

ACCOMPLISHING (2) [ACCOMPLISH]

2Ki 10:30 have done well in **a** what is right in my H6913
Jn 11:47 "What *are we* **a**?" they asked. *G4472*

ACCORD (4) [ACCORDED, ACCORDANCE, ACCORDING, ACCORDINGLY]

Nu 24:13 I could not do anything of my own **a** H4213
2Ki 10:15 "Are you **in a with** me, as I am H4222+3838
Jer 5: 5 But **with one a** they too had broken off the H3481
Jn 10:18 it from me, but I lay it down **of** my own **a**. *G608*

ACCORDANCE (65) [ACCORD]

Ex 12: 4 lamb needed **in a with** *what* each H4200+7023
Ex 24: 8 made with you **in a with** all these words." H6584
Ex 34:27 for **in a with** these words I have H6584+7023
Nu 6:21 to the LORD **in a with** their dedication, H6584
Nu 9: 3 **in a with** all its rules and regulations." H3869
Nu 9:14 the LORD's Passover **in a with** its rules and H3869
Nu 9:23 **in a with** his command through Moses. H6584
Nu 14:19 **In a with** your great love, forgive the sin of H3869
Dt 2:37 But **in a with** the command of the H3972+889
Jos 6:22 **in a with** your oath to her. H3869+889
Jos 15:13 **In a with** the LORD's command to him H448
Jos 22: 9 had acquired **in a with** the command of H6584
1Ki 8:32 by treating them **in a with** their innocence H3869
1Ki 16:12 **in a with** the word of the LORD spoken H3869
1Ki 16:34 **in a with** the word of the LORD spoken by H3869
2Ki 9:26 that plot, **in a with** the word of the LORD." H3869
2Ki 14: 6 **in a with** what is written in the Book of the H3869
2Ki 14:25 Dead Sea, **in a with** the word of the LORD H3869
2Ki 16:11 built an altar **in a with** all the plans that H3869
2Ki 17:13 **in a with** the entire Law that I H3869
2Ki 17:33 their own gods **in a with** the customs of H3869
2Ki 22:13 they have not acted **in a with** all that is H3869
2Ki 23:16 **in a with** the word of the LORD proclaimed H3869
2Ki 23:25 strength, **in a with** all the Law of Moses. H3869
2Ki 24: 2 **in a with** the word of the LORD proclaimed H3869
1Ch 5: 1 record **in a with** his birthright, H4200
1Ch 6:49 **in a with** all that Moses the servant of H3869
1Ch 15:15 had commanded **in a with** the word of the H3869
1Ch 16:40 **in a with** everything written in the Law of H4200
2Ch 6:23 by treating them **in a with** their innocence H3869
2Ch 25: 4 acted **in a with** what is written in the H3869
2Ch 34:21 they have not acted **in a with** all that is H3869
2Ch 34:32 did this **in a with** the covenant of H3869
2Ch 35:26 acts of devotion **in a with** what is written H3869
Ezr 3: 2 **in a with** what is written in the Law of H3869
Ezr 3: 4 Then **in a with** what is written, they H3869
Ezr 7:18 gold, **in a with** the will of your God. A10341
Ezr 7:25 **in a with** the wisdom of your God A10341
Ezr 10: 3 **in a with** the counsel of my lord and of H928
Ezr 10: 8 **in a with** the decision of the officials and H3869
Ne 8:18 the eighth day, **in a with** the regulation H3869
Ps 119:149 Hear my voice **in a with** your love H3869
Ps 119:159 my life, LORD, **in a with** your love. H3869
Jer 42: 5 we do not act **in a with** everything H3869+4027
Eze 25:14 deal with Edom **in a with** my anger and H3869
Eze 35:11 I will treat you **in a with** the anger and H3869
Da 1:13 treat your servants **in a with** what you see." H3869
Da 6: 8 **in a with** the law of the Medes and A10341
Da 6:12 **in a with** the law of the Medes and A10341
Mt 2:16 **in a with** the time he had learned from *G2848*
Mt 22:16 teach the way of God **in a with** the truth. *G1877*
Mk 12:14 teach the way of God **in a with** the truth. *G2093*
Lk 20:21 teach the way of God **in a with** the truth. *G2093*
Jn 19:40 This was **in a with** Jewish burial customs. *G2777*
Ac 24:14 that is **in a with** the Law and that *G2848*
Ro 8: 5 those who live **in a with** the Spirit have *G2848*
Ro 8:27 God's people **in a with the will of** God. *G2848*
Ro 12: 3 **in a with** the faith God has *G6055+3586*
Ro 12: 6 prophesy **in a with** your faith; *G2848+3836+381*
Ro 16:25 able to establish you **in a with** my gospel, *G2848*
Eph 1: 5 **in a with** his pleasure and will *G2848*
Eph 1: 7 **in a with** the riches of God's grace *G2848*
Eph 4:21 taught in him **in a with** the truth that is *G2777*
2Th 2: 9 one will be **in a with** how Satan works. *G2848*
Heb 10: 8 though they were offered **in a with** the law. *G2848*

ACCORDED (1) [ACCORD]

Ge 45:13 father about all the **honor** *a* me in Egypt AIT

ACCORDING (317) [ACCORD]

Ge 1:11 with seed in it, **a to** their various kinds." H4200
Ge 1:12 plants bearing seed **a to** their kinds and H4200
Ge 1:12 fruit with seed in it **a to** their kinds. H4200
Ge 1:21 moves about in it, **a to** their kinds, and H4200
Ge 1:21 and every winged bird **a to** its kind. H4200
Ge 1:24 produce living creatures **a to** their kinds: H4200
Ge 1:24 the wild animals, each **a to** its kind." H4200
Ge 1:25 made the wild animals **a to** their kinds, H4200
Ge 1:25 the livestock **a to** their kinds, and H4200
Ge 1:25 move along the ground **a to** their kinds. H4200
Ge 7:14 with them every wild animal **a to** its kind, H4200
Ge 7:14 its kind, all livestock **a to** their kinds, every H4200
Ge 7:14 along the ground **a to** its kind and every H4200
Ge 7:14 to its kind and every bird **a to** its kind, H4200
Ge 10:32 of Noah's sons, **a to** their lines of descent H4200
Ge 23:16 **a to the weight current** among the H6296
Ge 25:16 twelve tribal rulers **a to** their settlements H928
Ge 36:30 the Horite chiefs, **a to** their divisions, in H4200
Ge 36:40 by name, **a to** their clans and regions: H4200
Ge 36:43 **a to** their settlements in the land they H4200
Ge 47:12 **a to** the number of their children. H4200
Ex 6:16 of the sons of Levi **a to** their records: H4200
Ex 6:19 were the clans of Levi **a to** their records. H4200
Ex 25:40 that you make them **a to** the pattern shown H928
Ex 26:30 up the tabernacle **a to** the plan shown H3869
Ex 30:13 a half shekel, **a to** the sanctuary shekel H928
Ex 30:24 of cassia—all **a to** the sanctuary shekel H928
Ex 38:24 730 shekels, **a to** the sanctuary shekel. H928
Ex 38:25 1,775 shekels, **a to** the sanctuary shekel H928
Ex 38:26 half a shekel, **a to** the sanctuary shekel H928
Lev 5:15 value in silver, **a to** the sanctuary shekel. H928
Lev 20:23 You must not live **a to** the customs of the H928
Lev 27: 3 shekels of silver, **a to** the sanctuary shekel; H928
Lev 27: 8 will set the value **a to** what the one H6584+7023
Lev 27:16 value is to be set **a to** the amount of seed H4200
Lev 27:18 the value **a to** the number of years H6584
Lev 27:25 value is to be set **a to** the sanctuary shekel, H928
Nu 1: 3 Aaron are to count **a to** their divisions all H4200
Nu 1:20 **a to** the records of their clans and families H4200
Nu 1:22 **a to** the records of their clans and families H4200
Nu 1:24 **a to** the records of their clans and families H4200
Nu 1:26 **a to** the records of their clans and families H4200
Nu 1:28 **a to** the records of their clans and families H4200

Nu 1:30 **a to** the records of their clans and families H4200
Nu 1:32 **a to** the records of their clans and families H4200
Nu 1:34 **a to** the records of their clans and families H4200
Nu 1:36 **a to** the records of their clans and families H4200
Nu 1:38 **a to** the records of their clans and families H4200
Nu 1:40 **a to** the records of their clans and families H4200
Nu 1:42 **a to** the records of their clans and families H4200
Nu 1:45 army were counted **a to** their families. H4200
Nu 2: 9 to the camp of Judah, **a to** their divisions H4200
Nu 2:16 the camp of Reuben, **a to** their divisions H4200
Nu 2:24 the camp of Ephraim, **a to** their divisions H4200
Nu 2:32 the Israelites, counted **a to** their families. H4200
Nu 3:20 were the Levite clans, **a to** their families. H4200
Nu 3:39 by Moses and Aaron **a to** their clans, H4200
Nu 3:47 each one, **a to** the sanctuary shekel H928
Nu 3:50 1,365 shekels, **a to** the sanctuary shekel. H928
Nu 4:37 Aaron counted them **a to** the LORD's H6584
Nu 4:41 Aaron counted them **a to** the LORD's H6584
Nu 4:45 Aaron counted them **a to** the LORD's H6584
Nu 6:21 have made, **a to** the law of the Nazirite. H6584
Nu 7:13 shekels, both **a to** the sanctuary shekel H928
Nu 7:19 shekels, both **a to** the sanctuary shekel H928
Nu 7:25 shekels, both **a to** the sanctuary shekel H928
Nu 7:31 shekels, both **a to** the sanctuary shekel H928
Nu 7:37 shekels, both **a to** the sanctuary shekel H928
Nu 7:43 shekels, both **a to** the sanctuary shekel H928
Nu 7:49 shekels, both **a to** the sanctuary shekel H928
Nu 7:55 shekels, both **a to** the sanctuary shekel H928
Nu 7:61 shekels, both **a to** the sanctuary shekel H928
Nu 7:67 shekels, both **a to** the sanctuary shekel H928
Nu 7:73 shekels, both **a to** the sanctuary shekel H928
Nu 7:79 shekels, both **a to** the sanctuary shekel H928
Nu 7:85 hundred shekels, **a to** the sanctuary shekel. H928
Nu 7:86 ten shekels each, **a to** the sanctuary shekel. H928
Nu 18:16 shekels of silver, **a to** the sanctuary shekel H928
Nu 26:54 its inheritance **a to** the number of those H4200
Nu 26:55 inherits will be **a to** the names for its H4200
Nu 29:18 drink offerings **a to** the number H928
Nu 29:21 drink offerings **a to** the number H928
Nu 29:24 drink offerings **a to** the number H928
Nu 29:27 drink offerings **a to** the number H928
Nu 29:30 drink offerings **a to** the number H928
Nu 29:33 drink offerings **a to** the number H928
Nu 29:37 drink offerings **a to** the number H928
Nu 33:54 the land by lot, **a to** your clans. To a H4200
Nu 33:54 Distribute it **a to** your ancestral tribes. H4200
Nu 35:24 avenger of blood **a to** these regulations. H6584
Dt 12:15 **a to** the blessing the LORD your God gives H3869
Dt 17:10 You must act **a to** the decisions they H6584+7023
Dt 17:11 Act **a to** whatever they teach you H6584+7023
Dt 26:13 the widow, **a to** all you commanded. H3869
Dt 29:21 **a to** all the curses of the covenant written H3869
Dt 30: 2 with all your soul **a to** everything I H3869
Dt 32: 8 the peoples **a to** the number of the H4200
Jos 4: 5 **a to** the number of the tribes of the H4200
Jos 4: 8 **a to** the number of the tribes of the H4200
Jos 8:31 He built it **a to** what is written in the Book H3869
Jos 11:23 inheritance to Israel **a to** their tribal H3869
Jos 12: 7 the tribes of Israel **a to** their tribal H3869
Jos 13:15 to the tribe of Reuben, **a to** its clans: H4200
Jos 13:23 of the Reubenites, **a to** their clans. H4200
Jos 13:24 given to the tribe of Gad, **a to** its clans: H4200
Jos 13:28 of the Gadites, **a to** their clans. H4200
Jos 13:29 descendants of Manasseh, **a to** its clans: H4200
Jos 13:31 half of the sons of Makir, **a to** their clans. H4200
Jos 14: 7 back a report **a to** my convictions, H3869+889
Jos 15: 1 the tribe of Judah, **a to** its clans, extended H4200
Jos 15:20 of the tribe of Judah, **a to** its clans: H4200
Jos 16: 5 was the territory of Ephraim, **a to** its clans: H4200
Jos 16: 8 the tribe of the Ephraimites, **a to** its clans. H4200
Jos 17: 4 of their father, **a to** the LORD's command. H448
Jos 18: 4 of it, **a to** the inheritance of each. H4200+7023
Jos 18:10 land to the Israelites **a to** their tribal H3869
Jos 18:11 up for the tribe of Benjamin **a to** its clans. H4200
Jos 18:21 tribe of Benjamin, **a to** its clans, had the H4200
Jos 19: 1 out for the tribe of Simeon **a to** its clans. H4200
Jos 19: 8 the tribe of the Simeonites, **a to** its clans. H4200
Jos 19:10 lot came up for Zebulun **a to** its clans: H4200
Jos 19:16 the inheritance of Zebulun, **a to** its clans. H4200
Jos 19:17 lot came out for Issachar **a to** its clans. H4200
Jos 19:23 of the tribe of Issachar, **a to** its clans. H4200
Jos 19:24 out for the tribe of Asher **a to** its clans. H4200
Jos 19:31 of the tribe of Asher, **a to** its clans. H4200
Jos 19:32 lot came out for Naphtali **a to** its clans: H4200
Jos 19:39 of the tribe of Naphtali, **a to** its clans. H4200
Jos 19:40 out for the tribe of Dan **a to** its clans. H4200
Jos 19:48 of the tribe of Dan, **a to** its clans. H4200
Jos 21: 4 out for the Kohathites, **a to** their clans. H4200
Jos 21: 7 of Merari, **a to** their clans, received H4200
1Sa 2:35 who will do **a to** what is in my heart and H3869
1Sa 6: 4 a to the number of the Philistine rulers NDT
1Sa 6:18 of the gold rats was a to the number of NDT
2Sa 3:39 repay the evildoer **a to** his evil deeds!" H3869
2Sa 7:21 the sake of your word and **a to** your will, H3869
2Sa 22:21 has dealt with me **a to** my righteousness; H3869
2Sa 22:21 **a to** the cleanness of my hands he has H3869
2Sa 22:25 has rewarded me **a to** my righteousness, H3869
2Sa 22:25 **a to** my cleanness in his sight. H3869
1Ki 2: 6 Deal with him **a to** your wisdom, but do H3869
1Ki 3: 3 the LORD by walking **a to** the instructions H928
1Ki 6:38 in all its details **a to** its specifications. H4200
1Ki 8:39 deal with everyone **a to** all they do, since H3869
1Ki 8:59 of his people Israel **a to** each day's need, H928
1Ki 13: 5 ashes poured out **a to** the sign given by H3869
1Ki 15:29 **a to** the word of the LORD given through H3869
2Ki 1:17 **a to** the word of the LORD that Elijah had H3869
2Ki 2:22 this day, **a to** the word Elisha had spoken. H3869
2Ki 4:44 some left over, **a to** the word of the LORD. H3869
2Ki 10:17 **a to** the word of the LORD spoken to Elijah. H3869
2Ki 22:16 **a to** everything written in the book the king H907
2Ki 23:35 people of the land **a to** their assessments. H3869
2Ki 24: 3 happened to Judah **a to** the LORD's H6584
1Ch 5: 7 listed **a to** their genealogical records: H4200
1Ch 6:19 of the Levites listed **a to** their fathers: H4200
1Ch 6:32 their duties **a to** the regulations laid H3869
1Ch 7: 4 **A to** their family genealogy, they had H4200
1Ch 15:20 were to play the lyres **a to** alamoth, H6584
1Ch 15:21 play the harps, directing **a to** sheminith. H6584
1Ch 16:37 regularly, **a to** each day's requirements. H4200
1Ch 17:19 the sake of your servant and **a to** your will, H3869
1Ch 23:27 **A to** the last instructions of David, the H928
1Ch 24:19 **a to** the regulations prescribed for them H3869
1Ch 24:30 These were the Levites, **a to** their families. H4200
1Ch 26:13 cast for each gate, **a to** their families H4200
1Ch 26:31 was their chief **a to** the genealogical H4200
1Ch 28:15 its lamps, **a to** the use of each lampstand H3869
2Ch 4: 7 gold lampstands **a to** the specifications H3869
2Ch 6:16 all they do to walk before me **a to** my law, H928
2Ch 6:30 deal with everyone **a to** all they do H3869
2Ch 8:13 **a to** the daily requirement for offerings H928
2Ch 8:14 to assist the priests **a to** each day's H4200
2Ch 24:13 the temple of God **a to** its original design H6584
2Ch 25: 5 assigned them **a to** their families to H4200
2Ch 26:11 to go out by divisions **a to** their numbers as H928
2Ch 30: 5 in large numbers **a to** what was written. H3869
2Ch 30:19 are not clean **a to the rules** *of* the H3869
2Ch 31: 2 each of them **a to** their duties as H3869+7023
2Ch 31:15 to their fellow priests **a to** their divisions, H928
2Ch 31:16 **a to** their responsibilities and their H928
2Ch 31:17 **a to** their responsibilities and their H928
2Ch 35: 4 **a to** the instructions written by David king H928
Ezr 2:69 **A to** their ability they gave to the treasury H3869
Ezr 6:14 the temple **a to** the command of the A10427
Ezr 6:18 **a to** what is written in the Book of Moses. A10341
Ezr 10: 3 Let it be done **a to** the Law. H3869
Ne 6: 6 **a to** these reports you are about to H3869
Ne 12:45 **a to** the commands of David and his son H3869
Ne 13:22 show mercy to me **a to** your great love. H3869
Est 1:15 "**A to** law, what must be done to Queen H3869
Job 42: 8 prayer and not deal with you a to your folly. NDT
Ps 6: T **A to** sheminith. A psalm of H6584
Ps 7: 8 **a to** my righteousness, according to H3869
Ps 7: 8 my righteousness, **a to** my integrity, O H3869
Ps 8: T director of music. **A to** gittith. A psalm of H6584
Ps 12: T director of music. **A to** sheminith. A psalm H6584
Ps 18:20 has dealt with me **a to** my righteousness; H3869
Ps 18:20 **a to** the cleanness of my hands he has H3869
Ps 18:24 has rewarded me **a to** my righteousness, H3869
Ps 18:24 **a to** the cleanness of my hands in his H3869
Ps 25: 7 **a to** your love remember me H3869
Ps 46: T the Sons of Korah. **A to** alamoth. A song. H6584
Ps 51: 1 **a to** your unfailing love; according H3869
Ps 51: 1 **a to** your great compassion blot out my H3869
Ps 53: T director of music. **A to** mahalath. A maskil H6584
Ps 62:12 reward everyone **a to** what they have H3869
Ps 81: T director of music. **A to** gittith. Of Asaph. H6584
Ps 84: T director of music. **A to** gittith. Of the Sons H6584
Ps 88: T director of music. **A to** mahalath leannoth H6584
Ps 103:10 deserve or repay us **a to** our iniquities. H3869
Ps 109:26 my God; save me **a to** your unfailing love. H3869
Ps 119: 1 who walk **a to** the law of the LORD. H928
Ps 119: 9 path of purity? By living **a to** your word. H3869
Ps 119:25 the dust; preserve my life **a to** your word. H3869
Ps 119:28 strengthen me **a to** your word. H3869
Ps 119:37 preserve my life **a to** your word. H928
Ps 119:41 your salvation, **a to** your promise; H3869
Ps 119:58 be gracious to me **a to** your promise. H3869
Ps 119:65 Do good to your servant **a to** your word H3869
Ps 119:76 comfort, **a to** your promise to your servant. H3869
Ps 119:107 preserve my life, LORD, **a to** your word. H3869
Ps 119:116 my God, **a to** your promise, and I H3869
Ps 119:124 with your servant **a to** your love and teach H3869
Ps 119:133 Direct my footsteps **a to** your word; let no H928
Ps 119:149 preserve my life, LORD, **a to** your laws. H3869
Ps 119:154 preserve my life **a to** your promise. H4200
Ps 119:156 is great; preserve my life **a to** your laws. H3869
Ps 119:169 give me understanding **a to** your word. H3869
Ps 119:170 before you; deliver me **a to** your promise. H3869
Ps 122: 4 the name of the LORD a to the statute given NDT
Ps 137: 8 who repays you **a to what** you have done H1691S
Pr 12: 8 is praised **a to** their prudence, H4200+7023
Pr 24:12 not repay everyone **a to** what they have H3869
Pr 26: 4 Do not answer a fool **a to** his folly, or you H3869
Pr 26: 5 Answer a fool **a to** his folly, or he will be H3869
Isa 8:20 If anyone does not speak **a to** this word H3869
Isa 59:18 **A to** what they have done, so will H3869+6584
Isa 63: 7 **a to** all the LORD has done for us H3869+6584
Isa 63: 7 **a to** his compassion and many kindnesses H3869
Jer 17:10 to reward each person **a to** their conduct H3869
Jer 17:10 conduct, **a to** what their deeds deserve." H3869
Jer 25:14 I will repay them **a to** their deeds and the H3869
Jer 32:19 reward each person **a to** their conduct H3869
Eze 7: 3 I will judge you **a to** your conduct and H3869
Eze 7: 8 I will judge you **a to** your conduct and H3869
Eze 7:27 I will deal with them **a to** their conduct H4946
Eze 18:30 judge each of you **a to** your own ways, H3869
Eze 20:44 sake and not **a to** your evil ways and H3869
Eze 23:24 they will punish you **a to** their standards. H928
Eze 24:14 You will be judged **a to** your conduct and H3869
Eze 31:11 him to deal with **a to** its wickedness. H3869
Eze 33:20 judge each of you **a to** your own ways." H3869
Eze 36:19 I judged them **a to** their conduct and their H3869
Eze 39:24 I dealt with them **a to** their uncleanness H3869
Eze 44:24 judges and decide it **a to** my ordinances. H928
Eze 45: 8 Israel to possess the land **a to** their tribes. H4200
Eze 47:21 among yourselves **a to** the tribes of Israel H4200
Da 6:15 that a to the law of the Medes and Persians NDT
Da 9: 2 **a to** the word of the LORD given to Jeremiah H889
Hos 12: 2 will punish Jacob **a to** his ways and repay H3869
Hos 12: 2 to his ways and repay him **a to** his deeds. H3869
Zec 5: 3 for **a to** what it says on one side H4017
Zec 5: 3 and **a to** what it says on the other H4017
Mt 9:29 "**A to** your faith let it be done to you"; *G2848*
Mt 16:27 reward each person **a to** what they have *G2848*
Mt 25:15 to another one bag, each **a to** his ability. *G2848*
Mk 7: 5 your disciples live **a to** the tradition of the *G2848*
Lk 1: 9 by lot, **a to** the custom of the priesthood *G2848*
Lk 2:42 went up to the festival, **a to** the custom. *G2848*
Jn 19: 7 have a law, and **a to** that law he must die *G2848*
Ac 7:44 **a to** the pattern he had seen. *G2848*
Ac 15: 1 circumcised, *a to* the **custom** taught by Moses AIT
Ac 21:21 their children or live *a to* our **customs**. AIT
Ac 23: 3 You sit there to judge me **a to** the law, yet *G2848*
Ro 2: 6 repay each person **a to** what they have *G2848*
Ro 4: 1 our forefather **a to** the flesh, discovered *G2848*
Ro 8: 4 who do not live **a to** the flesh but *G2848*
Ro 8: 4 according to the flesh but **a to** the Spirit. *G2848*
Ro 8: 5 Those who live **a to** the flesh have their *G2848*
Ro 8:12 it is not to the flesh, to live **a to** it. *G2848*
Ro 8:13 For if you live **a to** the flesh, you will die *G2848*
Ro 8:28 who have been called **a to** his purpose. *G2848*
Ro 12: 6 gifts, **a to** the grace given to each of us. *G2848*
1Co 3: 8 each be rewarded **a to** their own labor. *G2848*
1Co 15: 3 Christ died for our sins **a to** the Scriptures, *G2848*
1Co 15: 4 raised on the third day **a to** the Scriptures, *G2848*
2Co 8:11 by your completion of it, **a to** your means. *G1666*
2Co 8:12 is acceptable **a to what** one has, *G2771+1569*
2Co 8:12 not **a to what** one does not have. *G2771*
Gal 1: 4 age, **a to** the will of our God and Father, *G2848*
Gal 3:29 and heirs **a to** the promise. *G2848*
Gal 4:23 the slave woman was born **a to** the flesh, *G2848*
Gal 4:29 time the son born **a to** the flesh *G2848*
Eph 1: 9 mystery of his will **a to** his good pleasure, *G2848*
Eph 1:11 been predestined **a to** the plan of him *G2848*
Eph 3:11 **a to** his eternal purpose that he *G2848*
Eph 3:20 **a to** his power that is at work within us *G2848*
Eph 4:29 building others up *a to* their **needs**, AIT
Php 4:19 meet all your needs **a to** the riches of his *G2848*
Col 1:11 with all power **a to** his glorious might so *G2848*
1Th 4:15 **A to** the Lord's word, we tell you that we *G1877*
2Th 1:12 **a to** the grace of our God and the Lord *G2848*
2Th 3: 6 does not live **a to** the teaching you *G2848*
2Ti 2: 5 crown except by competing **a to the rules**. *G3789*
Heb 2: 4 of the Holy Spirit distributed **a to** his will. *G2848*
Heb 8: 5 make everything **a to** the pattern shown *G2848*
1Pe 1: 2 have been chosen **a to** the foreknowledge *G2848*
1Pe 4: 6 might be judged **a to** human standards in *G2848*
1Pe 4: 6 live **a to** God in regard to the spirit. *G2848*
1Pe 4:19 those who suffer **a to** God's will should *G2848*
1Jn 5:14 that if we ask anything **a to** his will, he *G2848*
Rev 2:23 I will repay each of you **a to** your deeds. *G2848*
Rev 20:12 dead were judged **a to** what they had *G2848*
Rev 20:13 person was judged **a to** what they had *G2848*
Rev 22:12 give to each person **a to** what they have *G6055*

ACCORDINGLY (4) [ACCORD]

Lev 25:52 and pay for their redemption **a.** H3869+7023
1Ki 20:25 He agreed with them and acted **a.** H4027
1Ch 24: 4 among Ithamar's, and they *were* **divided** *a*: AIT
Mt 5:19 teaches others **a** will be called least *G4048*

ACCOUNT (73) [ACCOUNTABLE, ACCOUNTED, ACCOUNTING, ACCOUNTS]

Ge 2: 4 This is the **a** *of* the heavens and the earth H9352
Ge 5: 1 This is the written **a of** Adam's **family line**. H9352
Ge 6: 9 This is the **a of** Noah and his **family** H9352
Ge 10: 1 This is the **a** *of* Shem, Ham and Japheth H9352
Ge 11:10 This is the **a of** Shem's **family line**. Two H9352
Ge 11:27 This is the **a of** Terah's **family line**. Terah H9352
Ge 25:12 is the **a of the family line** *of* Abraham's H9352
Ge 25:19 is the **a of the family line** *of* Abraham's H9352
Ge 26: 7 this place might kill me **on a of** Rebekah, H6584
Ge 26: 9 I thought I might lose my life **on a of** her." H6584
Ge 36: 1 This is the **a of the family line** *of* Esau H9352
Ge 36: 9 This is the **a of the family line** *of* Esau the H9352
Ge 37: 2 This is the **a of** Jacob's **family line** H9352
Ex 12: 4 having **taken into** a the number of people H928
Nu 3: 1 This is the **a of the family** *of* Aaron and H9352
Nu 6: 7 ceremonially unclean **on a of** them, H4200
Nu 9: 6 unclean **on a of** a dead body. H4200
Nu 13:27 *They* **gave** Moses *this* **a**: "We went into H6218
Dt 9: 4 it is **on a of** the wickedness of these H928
Dt 9: 5 but **on a of** the wickedness of these nations H928
Dt 18:19 *I* myself *will* **call to a** anyone H2011+4946+6640
Jos 22:23 *may* the LORD himself **call** us **to a.** H1335
1Sa 17:32 no one lose heart **on a of** this Philistine; H6584

1Sa 20:16 *May* the LORD **call** David's enemies **to a** H1335+4946+3338
1Sa 23:10 and destroy the town **on a of** me. H928+6288
2Sa 11:18 Joab sent David a full **a** *of* the battle. H1821
2Sa 11:19 giving the king this **a** *of* the battle, H1821
2Sa 21: 1 "It is **on a of** Saul and his blood-stained H448
1Ki 9:15 Here is the **a** *of* the forced labor King H1821
1Ki 11:27 Here is the **a** of how he rebelled against H1821
2Ki 22: 7 But they *need* not **a for** the money H3108+907
1Ch 27:24 came on Israel **on a of** this numbering, H928
2Ch 24:22 "May the LORD see this and **call** you **to a**." H2011
2Ch 24:27 The **a** of his sons, the many prophecies NDT
Est 10: 2 together with a **full a** *of* the greatness of H7308
Job 13:10 *He would* **surely call** you **to a** if you H3519+3519
Job 31:14 What will I answer when **called to a**? H7212
Job 31:37 I would give him an **a** *of* my every step; I H5031
Ps 10:13 say to himself, "*He* won't **call** me **to a**"? H2011
Ps 10:15 **call** the evildoer **to a** *for* his wickedness H2011
Ps 119:26 *I* **gave an a** *of* my ways and you answered H6218
Ecc 3:15 and God *will* **call** the past **to a**. H1335
Isa 23:13 this people that is now **of no a**! H4202
Eze 16:14 among the nations **on a of** your beauty, H928
Eze 28:17 heart became proud **on a of** your beauty, H928
Mt 10:18 **On** my **a** you will be brought before *G1915*
Mt 11: 6 who does not stumble **on a of** me. *G1877*
Mt 12:36 will have to give **a** on the day of *G3364*
Mt 26:31 night you will all fall away **on a of** me, *G1877*
Mt 26:33 "Even if all fall away **on a of** you, I never *G1877*
Mk 12:26 of Moses, **in the a of** the burning bush *G2093*
Mk 13: 9 **On a of** me you will stand before *G1915*
Lk 1: 1 to draw up an **a** of the things that have *G1456*
Lk 1: 3 I too decided *to* **write an** orderly **a** for you *G1211*
Lk 7:23 who does not stumble **on a of** me. *G1877*
Lk 16: 2 Give an **a** of your management, because *G3364*
Lk 20:37 But **in the a of** the burning bush, even *G2093*
Lk 21:12 governors, and **all on a of** my name. *G1915*
Jn 12:11 for **on a of** him many of the Jews were *G1328*
Ac 4: 9 If we *are being* **called to a** today for an act *G373*
Ac 19:40 would not be able *to* **a** for this *G625+3364*
Ro 5:13 sin *is* not **charged against** anyone's **a** *G1824*
Ro 11:28 they are loved **on a of** the patriarchs, *G1328*
Ro 14:12 of us will give an **a** of ourselves to God. *G3364*
2Co 7:12 it was neither **on a of** the one who did the *G1915*
2Co 7:12 did the wrong nor **on a of** the injured *G1915*
Php 1:26 in Christ Jesus will abound **on a of** me. *G1877*
Php 4:17 I desire is that more be credited to your **a**. *G3364*
Heb 4:13 the eyes of him to whom we must give **a**. *G3364*
Heb 13:17 over you as those who must give an **a**. *G3364*
1Pe 4: 5 will have to give **a** to him who is ready to *G3364*
1Jn 2:12 sins have been forgiven **on a of** his name. *G1328*
Rev 16:21 they cursed God **on a of** the plague of *G1666*

ACCOUNTABLE (8) [ACCOUNT]
Eze 3:18 and *I will* **hold** you **a** *for* H1335+4946+3338
Eze 3:20 and *I will* **hold** you **a** *for* H1335+4946+3338
Eze 33: 6 *I will* **hold** the watchman **a** *for* H2011+4946+3338
Eze 33: 8 and *I will* **hold** you **a** *for* H1335+4946+3338
Eze 34:10 and *will* **hold** them **a** *for* my H2011+4946+3338
Da 6: 2 satraps were made **a** to them so that the A10302
Jnh 1:14 *Do* not **hold** us **a** *for* killing an H5989+6584
Ro 3:19 the whole world held **a** to God. *G5688*

ACCOUNTED (1) [ACCOUNT]
Ezr 8:34 Everything was **a** for by number and weight NDT

ACCOUNTING (5) [ACCOUNT]
Ge 9: 5 your lifeblood *I will* surely **demand an a**. H2011
Ge 9: 5 *I will* **demand an a** from every animal H2011
Ge 9: 5 *I will* **demand an a** for the life of another H2011
Ge 42:22 Now *we must* **give an a** *for* his blood." H2011
2Ki 12:15 *They did* not **require an a** *from* those to H3108

ACCOUNTS (3) [ACCOUNT]
Job 21:29 Have you paid no regard to their **a**— H253
Mt 18:23 who wanted to settle **a** with his servants. *G3364*
Mt 25:19 servants returned and settled **a** with them. *G3364*

ACCREDITED (1) [CREDIT]
Ac 2:22 of Nazareth *was* a man **a** by God to you by *G617*

ACCUMULATE (1) [ACCUMULATED]
Dt 17:17 *He must* not **a large amounts** *of* H8049+4394

ACCUMULATED (4) [ACCUMULATE]
Ge 12: 5 possessions *they had* **a** and the people H8223
Ge 31:18 all the goods *he had* **a** in Paddan Aram, H8223
1Ki 10:26 Solomon **a** chariots and horses; he had H665
2Ch 1:14 Solomon **a** chariots and horses; he had H665

ACCURATE (7) [ACCURATELY]
Dt 25:15 You must have **a** and honest weights and H8969
Pr 11: 1 but **a** weights find favor with him. H8969
Eze 45:10 You are to use **a** scales, an accurate H7406
Eze 45:10 an **a** ephah and an accurate bath. H7406
Eze 45:10 an accurate ephah and an **a** bath. H7406
Ac 23:15 of wanting **more a** information about *G209*
Ac 23:20 of wanting **more a** information about *G209*

ACCURATELY (1) [ACCURATE]
Ac 18:25 with great fervor and taught about Jesus **a**, *G209*

ACCURSED (4) [CURSE]
Ps 119:21 the arrogant, *who are* **a**, those who stray H826
Isa 65:20 to reach a hundred *will* **be considered a**. H7837
Mic 6:10 and the short ephah, which *is* **a**? H2404
2Pe 2:14 they are experts in greed—an **a** brood! *G2932*

ACCUSATION (6) [ACCUSE]
Ezr 4: 6 they lodged an **a** against the people of H8478
Mic 6: 2 mountains, the LORD's **a**; listen, you H8190
Ac 23:29 I found that the **a** had to do with *G1592*
Ac 24: 9 The other Jews joined in the **a**, asserting NDT
Col 1:22 without blemish and **free from a**— *G441*
1Ti 5:19 Do not entertain an **a** against an elder *G2990*

ACCUSATIONS (5) [ACCUSE]
Ps 27:12 rise up against me, **spouting** malicious **a**. H3641
Ps 35:20 devise false **a** against those who live H1821
Ps 38:20 my good with evil **lodge a against** me, H8476
Ps 50:21 now arraign you and **set** *my* **a** before you. H6885
Ac 26: 2 my defense against all the **a** of the Jews, *G1592*

ACCUSE (16) [ACCUSATION, ACCUSATIONS, ACCUSED, ACCUSER, ACCUSERS, ACCUSES, ACCUSING]
Dt 19:16 takes the stand to **a** someone of a crime, H6699
1Sa 22:15 *Let* not the king **a** your servant H8492+1821+928
2Sa 3: 8 Yet now *you* **a** me *of* an offense H7212+6584
Ps 103: 9 *He will* not always **a**, nor will he harbor H8189
Ps 109: 4 In return for my friendship *they* **a** me, but I H8476
Pr 3:30 *Do* not **a** anyone for no reason—when H8189
Isa 57:16 *I will* not **a** them forever, nor will I always H8189
Hos 4: 4 bring a charge, *let* no one **a** another, for H3519
Zec 3: 1 Satan standing at his right side to **a** him. H8476
Mk 3: 2 *Some* of them *were looking* for a reason *to* **a** *G2989*
Lk 3:14 extort money and don't **a** *people* **falsely**— *G5193*
Lk 6: 7 law were looking for a reason *to* **a** Jesus, *G2989*
Lk 23: 2 And they began *to* **a** him, saying, "We *G2989*
Jn 5:45 "But do not think I *will* **a** you before the *G2989*
Jn 10:36 Why then *do* you **a** me *of* blasphemy *G3306*
1Pe 2:12 though *they* **a** you of doing wrong *G2895*

ACCUSED (20) [ACCUSE]
Nu 35:12 so that anyone **a of murder** may not die H8357
Nu 35:24 judge between the **a** and the avenger of H5782S
Nu 35:25 must protect the *one* **a of murder** from the H8357
Nu 35:25 of blood and send the **a** back to the city H2257S
Nu 35:25 The **a** must stay there until the death of the NDT
Nu 35:26 " 'But if the **a** ever goes outside the limits H8357
Nu 35:27 blood may kill the **a** without being guilty H8357
Nu 35:28 The **a** must stay in the city of refuge until the NDT
Dt 19:15 to convict anyone **a of** any crime or H4200
Jos 21:13 a city of refuge for *one* **a of murder**), H8357
Jos 21:21 a city of refuge for *one* **a of murder**) and H8357
Jos 21:27 a city of refuge for *one* **a of murder**) and H8357
Jos 21:32 a city of refuge for *one* **a of murder**), H8357
Jos 21:38 a city of refuge for *one* **a of murder**), H8357
Ne 5: 7 in my mind and then **a** the nobles and H8189
Da 6:24 men who *had* **falsely a** Daniel A10030+10642
Mt 27:12 When he *was* **a** by the chief priests and *G2989*
Mk 15: 3 The chief priests **a** him of many things. *G2989*
Lk 16: 1 man whose manager *was* **a** of wasting his *G1330*
Ac 22:30 exactly why Paul *was being* **a** by the Jews. *G2989*

ACCUSER (5) [ACCUSE]
Job 31:35 let my **a** put his indictment in writing H408+8190
Ps 109: 6 let an **a** stand at his right hand. H8477
Isa 50: 8 Who is my **a**? Let him H1251+5477
Jn 5:45 Your **a** is Moses, on whom your hopes are *G2989*
Rev 12:10 For the **a** of our brothers and sisters, who *G2992*

ACCUSERS (10) [ACCUSE]
Ps 71:13 May my **a** perish in shame; may those H8476
Ps 109:20 May this be the LORD's payment to my **a** H8476
Ps 109:25 I am an object of scorn to **my a**; when H2157S
Ps 109:29 May my **a** be clothed with disgrace and H8476
Jer 18:19 LORD; hear what my **a** are saying! H3742
Ac 23:30 I also ordered his **a** to present to you their *G2991*
Ac 23:35 will hear your case when your **a** get here." *G2991*
Ac 24:12 My **a** did not find me arguing with anyone at NDT
Ac 25:16 they have faced their **a** and have had an *G2991*
Ac 25:18 When his **a** got up to speak, they did not *G2991*

ACCUSES (3) [ACCUSE]
Job 40: 2 Let him *who* **a** God answer him!" H3519
Isa 54:17 every tongue *that* **a** you. H7756+4200+2021+5477
Rev 12:10 who **a** them before our God day and night *G2989*

ACCUSING (7) [ACCUSE]
Ps 31:20 safe in your dwelling from **a** tongues. H8190
Mk 15: 4 See how many things *they are* **a** you of." *G2989*
Lk 23:10 were standing there, vehemently **a** him. *G2989*
Jn 8: 6 in order to have a **basis for a** him. *G2989*
Ac 23:28 I wanted to know why *they were* **a** him, so *G1592*
Ac 26: 7 of this hope *that* these Jews *are* **a** *me*. *G1592*
Ro 2:15 thoughts sometimes **a** them and at other *G2989*

ACCUSTOMED (3) [CUSTOM]
Jer 2:24 a wild donkey **a to** the desert, sniffing the H4341
Jer 13:23 can you do good *who* are **a to** doing evil. H4341
1Co 8: 7 people are still *so* **a** *to* idols that when *G5311*

ACELDAMA (KJV) AKELDAMA

ACHAIA (10)
Ac 18:12 While Gallio was proconsul *of* **A**, the Jews *G938*
Ac 18:27 When Apollos wanted to go to **A**, the *G938*
Ac 19:21 passing through Macedonia and **A**. *G938*
Ro 15:26 For Macedonia and **A** were pleased to *G938*
1Co 16:15 of Stephanas were the first converts *in* **A**, *G938*
2Co 1: 1 with all his holy people throughout **A**: *G938*
2Co 9: 2 since last year you *in* **A** were ready to give; *G938*
2Co 11:10 nobody in the regions *of* **A** will stop this *G938*
1Th 1: 7 to all the believers in Macedonia and **A**. *G938*
1Th 1: 8 from you not only in Macedonia and **A**— *G938*

ACHAICUS (1)
1Co 16:17 Fortunatus and **A** arrived, because they *G939*

ACHAN (7)
Jos 7: 1 the devoted things; **A** son of Karmi, the H6575
Jos 7:18 man by man, and **A** son of Karmi, the son H6575
Jos 7:19 Then Joshua said to **A**, "My son, give H6575
Jos 7:20 **A** replied, "It is true! I have sinned H6575
Jos 7:24 with all Israel, took **A** son of Zerah, the H6575
Jos 7:26 Over **A** they heaped up a large pile of H2257S
Jos 22:20 When **A** son of Zerah was unfaithful in H6575

ACHAR (1)
1Ch 2: 7 **A**, who brought trouble on Israel by H6580

ACHAZ (KJV) AHAZ

ACHBOR (KJV) AKBOR

ACHE (1)
Pr 14:13 Even in laughter the heart *may* **a**, and H3872

ACHIEVE (5) [ACHIEVED, ACHIEVEMENT, ACHIEVEMENTS, ACHIEVING]
Job 5:12 so that their hands **a** no success. H6913
Ps 45: 4 *let* your right hand **a** awesome deeds. H3723
Ecc 2:11 had done and what I had toiled to **a**, H6913
Isa 55:11 I desire and **a** *the* **purpose** for which I sent H7503
Da 11:24 invade them and *will* **a** what neither his H6913

ACHIEVED (5) [ACHIEVE]
1Ki 9: 1 and had **a** all he had desired to do NDT
1Ki 16:27 what he did and the things *he* **a**, are they H6913
1Ki 22:45 the things he **a** and his military exploits H6913
Isa 59:16 so his own arm **a salvation** for him, and H3828
Isa 63: 5 so my own arm **a salvation** for me, and H3828

ACHIEVEMENT (1) [ACHIEVE]
Ecc 4: 4 all toil and all **a** spring from one H4179+5126

ACHIEVEMENTS (10) [ACHIEVE]
1Ki 10: 6 country about your **a** and your wisdom is H1821
1Ki 15:23 Asa's reign, all his **a**, all he did and the H1476
1Ki 16: 5 what he did and his **a**, are they not H1476
2Ki 10:34 and all his **a**, are they not written H1476
2Ki 13: 8 all he did and his **a**, are they not written H1476
2Ki 13:12 all he did and his **a**, including his war H1476
2Ki 14:15 what he did and his **a**, including his war H1476
2Ki 14:28 and his military **a**, including how he H1476
2Ki 20:20 all his **a** and how he made the pool and H1476
2Ch 9: 5 country about your **a** and your wisdom is H1821

ACHIEVING (1) [ACHIEVE]
2Co 4:17 troubles *are* **a** for us an eternal *G2981*

ACHIM (KJV) AKIM

ACHISH (20)
1Sa 21:10 fled from Saul and went to **A** king of Gath. H429
1Sa 21:11 But the servants of **A** said to him, "Isn't this H429
1Sa 21:12 was very much afraid of **A** king of Gath. H429
1Sa 21:14 **A** said to his servants, "Look at the man H429
1Sa 27: 2 left and went over to **A** son of Maok king of H429
1Sa 27: 3 David and his men settled in Gath with **A** H429
1Sa 27: 5 Then David said to **A**, "If I have found favor H429
1Sa 27: 6 So on that day **A** gave him Ziklag, and it H429
1Sa 27: 9 Then he returned to **A**. H429
1Sa 27:10 When **A** asked, "Where did you go raiding H429
1Sa 27:12 **A** trusted David and said to himself, "He H429
1Sa 28: 1 **A** said to David, "You must understand that H429
1Sa 28: 2 **A** replied, "Very well, I will make you my H429
1Sa 29: 2 his men were marching at the rear with **A**. H429
1Sa 29: 3 **A** replied, "Is this not David, who was an H429
1Sa 29: 4 were angry with **A** and said, H2257S
1Sa 29: 6 So **A** called David and said to him, "As H429
1Sa 29: 9 **A** answered, "I know that you have been as H429
1Ki 2:39 Shimei's slaves ran off to **A** son of Maakah, H429
1Ki 2:40 donkey and went to **A** at Gath in search of H429

ACHMETHA (KJV) ECBATANA

ACHOR (5)
Jos 7:24 all that he had, to the Valley of **A**. H6574
Jos 7:26 been called the Valley of **A** ever since. H6574
Jos 15: 7 from the Valley of **A** and turned north to H6574
Isa 65:10 the Valley of **A** a resting place for H6574
Hos 2:15 will make the Valley of **A** a door of hope. H6574

ACHSAH (KJV) AKSAH

ACHSHAPH (KJV) AKSHAPH

ACHZIB (KJV) AKZIB

ACKNOWLEDGE (42) [ACKNOWLEDGED, ACKNOWLEDGES, ACKNOWLEDGMENT]
Dt 4:39 **A** and take to heart this day that the LORD H3359
Dt 21:17 *He must* **a** the son of his unloved wife as H5795
Dt 33: 9 his brothers or **a** his own children, H3359
1Ch 28: 9 my son Solomon, **a** the God of your father H3359
Ps 79: 6 wrath on the nations that *do* not **a** you, H3359
Ps 87: 4 Babylon among *those who* **a** me— H3359
Isa 19:21 in that day they *will* **a** the LORD. H3359
Isa 29:23 *they will* **a** *the* **holiness** *of* the Holy One of H7727
Isa 33:13 you who are near, **a** my power! H3359
Isa 45: 4 a title of honor, though *you do* not **a** me. H3359
Isa 59:12 are ever with us, and *we* **a** our iniquities: H3359
Isa 61: 9 All who see them *will* **a** that they are a H5795
Isa 63:16 Abraham does not know us or Israel **a** us; H5795
Jer 3:13 Only **a** your guilt—you have rebelled H3359
Jer 9: 3 to another; *they do* not **a** me," declares H3359
Jer 9: 6 in their deceit they refuse *to* **a** me, H3359
Jer 10:25 wrath on the nations that *do* not **a** you, H3359
Jer 14:20 *We* **a** our wickedness, LORD, and the guilt H3359
Eze 12:16 where they go *they may* **a** all their H6218
Da 4:25 by for you until *you* **a** that the Most High A10313
Da 4:26 to you when *you* **a** that Heaven rules. A10313
Da 4:32 by for you until *you* **a** that the Most High A10313
Da 11:39 will greatly honor *those who* **a** him. H5795
Hos 2:20 in faithfulness, and *you will* **a** the LORD. H3359
Hos 5: 4 is in their heart; *they do* not **a** the LORD. H3359
Hos 6: 3 *Let us* **a** the LORD; let us press on to H3359
Hos 6: 3 the LORD; let us press on to **a** him. H3359
Hos 8: 2 cries out to me, 'Our God, *we* **a** you!' H3359
Hos 13: 4 *You shall* **a** no God but me, no Savior H3359
Mt 10:32 I *will* also **a** before my Father in heaven. G3933
Lk 12: 8 the Son of Man *will* also **a** before the G3933
Jn 12:42 *they would* not **openly a** *their* **faith** for fear G3933
Ac 24: 3 *we* **a** this with profound gratitude. G622
Ro 14:11 bow before me; every tongue *will* **a** God. G2018
1Co 14:37 *let them* **a** that what I am writing to you is G2105
Php 2:11 every tongue **a** that Jesus Christ is G2018
1Th 5:12 *to* **a** those who work hard among you G3857
Heb 3: 1 whom we **a** as our apostle and high priest G3934
1Jn 4: 3 every spirit that *does* not **a** Jesus is not G3933
2Jn 7 who *do* not **a** Jesus Christ as coming in G3933
Rev 3: 5 but *will* **a** that name before my Father G3933
Rev 3: 9 at your feet and **a** that I have loved you G1182

ACKNOWLEDGED (8) [ACKNOWLEDGE]
Lev 22:32 for *I must* **be a as holy** by the Israelites. H7727
1Ch 29:22 *they* **a** Solomon son of David **as king** a H4887
Ps 32: 5 Then *I* **a** my sin *to* you and did not cover H3359
Isa 45: 5 though *you have* not **a** me, H3359
Da 5:21 until *he* **a** that the Most High God is A10313
Hos 2: 8 She *has* not **a** that I was the one who H3359
Lk 7:29 **a** *that* God's **way** was **right** G1467
Jn 9:22 that anyone *who* **a** that Jesus was the G3933

ACKNOWLEDGES (6) [ACKNOWLEDGE]
Ps 91:14 I will protect him, for *he* **a** my name. H3359
Mt 10:32 "Whoever **a** me before others, I will also G3933
Lk 12: 8 whoever **publicly a** me before others G3933
1Jn 2:23 whoever **a** the Son has the Father also. G3933
1Jn 4: 2 Every spirit that **a** that Jesus Christ has G3933
1Jn 4:15 If anyone **a** that Jesus is the Son of God G3933

ACKNOWLEDGMENT (2) [ACKNOWLEDGE]
Hos 4: 1 no love, no **a** *of* God in the land. H1981
Hos 6: 6 and **a** *of* God rather than burnt offerings. H1981

ACQUAINTANCE (1) [ACQUAINTANCES, ACQUAINTED]
Php 4:15 in the early days *of* your *a* **with** the **gospel** AIT

ACQUAINTANCES (1) [ACQUAINTANCE]
Job 19:13 my **a** are completely estranged from me. H3359

ACQUAINTED (4) [ACQUAINTANCE]
Ac 24:22 Then Felix, *who was* well **a with** the Way G3857
Ac 26: 3 so because you are **well a** with all the G1195
Gal 1:18 up to Jerusalem *to* **get a with** Cephas G2707
Heb 5:13 is **not a with** the teaching about G586

ACQUIRE (6) [ACQUIRED, ACQUIRES]
Ge 34:10 Live in it, trade in it, and **a property** in it." H296
Lev 25:26 on they prosper and **a** sufficient means to H5162
Lev 25:28 But if they *do* not **a** the means to repay H5162
Dt 17:16 *must* not **a great numbers** *of* horses for H8049
Ru 4: 5 Naomi, *you* also **a** Ruth the Moabite H7864+907
Ne 5:16 there for the work; *we did* not **a** any land. H7864

ACQUIRED (13) [ACQUIRE]
Ge 12: 5 the people *they had* **a** in Harran, H6913
Ge 12:16 and Abram **a** sheep and cattle H2118+4200
Ge 36: 6 all the goods *he had* **a** in Canaan, H8223
Ge 46: 6 the possessions *they had* **a** in Canaan. H8223
Ge 47:27 *They* **a property** there and were fruitful H296
Nu 31:50 the LORD the gold articles each of us **a**— H5162
Jos 22: 9 which *they had* **a** in accordance with the H296
Ru 4:10 *I have* also **a** Ruth the Moabite, Mahlon's H7864
2Ch 32:29 He built villages and **a** great numbers of H5238
Ecc 2: 8 *I* **a** male and female singers, and a H6913
Isa 15: 7 So the wealth *they have* **a** and stored up H6913
Jer 48:36 The wealth *they* **a** is gone. H6913
Rev 3:17 *I have* **a wealth** and do not need a thing. G4456

ACQUIRES (1) [ACQUIRE]
Pr 18:15 The heart of the discerning **a** knowledge H7864

ACQUIT (3) [ACQUITTED, ACQUITTING]
Ex 23: 7 person to death, for *I will* not **a** the guilty. H7405
Isa 5:23 *who* **a** the guilty for a bribe, but deny H7405
Mic 6:11 *Shall I* **a** someone with dishonest scales H2342

ACQUITTED (1) [ACQUIT]
Mt 12:37 For by your words *you will be* **a**, and by G1467

ACQUITTING (2) [ACQUIT]
Dt 25: 1 **a** the innocent and condemning the guilty H7405
Pr 17:15 **A** the guilty and condemning the H7405

ACRE (1) [TEN-ACRE]
1Sa 14:14 men in an area of about half an **a**. H5103+7538

ACROSS (58) [CROSS]
Ge 1:20 above the earth **a** the vault of the H6584+7156
Ge 9:23 a garment and laid it **a** their shoulders; H6584
Ge 32:23 After *he had* **sent** them **a** the stream, he H6296
Ex 10:13 an east wind blow **a** the land all that day H928
Ex 23: 4 "If *you* **come a** your enemy's ox or donkey H7003
Nu 22: 1 along the Jordan **a from** Jericho. H4946+6298
Nu 26: 3 plains of Moab by the **Jordan** *a from* Jericho, AIT
Nu 26:63 plains of Moab by the **Jordan** *a from* Jericho. AIT
Nu 31:12 plains of Moab, by the **Jordan** *a from* Jericho. AIT
Nu 33:48 plains of Moab by the **Jordan** *a from* Jericho. AIT
Nu 33:50 of Moab by the **Jordan** *a from* Jericho the AIT
Nu 34:15 east of the Jordan **a** from Jericho, H6298
Nu 35: 1 plains of Moab by the **Jordan** *a from* Jericho, AIT
Nu 36:13 plains of Moab by the **Jordan** *a from* Jericho. AIT
Dt 3:20 God is giving them **a** the Jordan. H928+6298
Dt 3:28 he *will* **lead** this people **a** H6296+4200+7156
Dt 9: 3 God is the *one who* **goes a** ahead of you H6296
Dt 11:30 these mountains are **a** the Jordan H928+6298
Dt 22: 6 If you **come a** a bird's nest H7925+4200+7156
Dt 32:49 Nebo in Moab, **a from** Jericho, and H6584+7156
Dt 33:26 *who* **rides a** the heavens to help you and H8206
Dt 34: 1 the top of Pisgah, **a from** Jericho. H6584+7156
Jos 7: 7 *did you ever* **bring** this people **a** H6296+6296
Jos 13:32 plains of Moab **a** the Jordan east H4946+6298
Jdg 20:48 All the towns they **came a** they set on fire. H5162
1Sa 31: 7 valley and those **a** the Jordan saw H928+6298
2Sa 19:15 the king and **bring** him **a** the Jordan. H6296
2Sa 19:41 and **bring** him and his household **a** the H6296
1Ki 4:12 to Abel Meholah **a** to Jokmeam; H4946+6298
1Ki 6:21 extended gold chains **a** the front of the H4200
1Ki 7:38 forty baths and measuring four cubits **a**, NDT
2Ki 3:22 To the Moabites **a the way**, the H4946+5584
1Ch 6:78 tribe of Reuben **a** the Jordan east H4946+6298
2Ch 3: 4 cubits long **a** the width of the H6584+7156
Job 38: 5 Who stretched a measuring line **a** it? H6584
Ps 68:33 to him who rides **a** the highest heavens H928
Ecc 11: 1 Ship your grain **a** the sea; after H6584+7156
SS 2: 8 Here he comes, leaping **a** the mountains H6584
Isa 9: 4 burdens them, the **bar** *a* their shoulders, the AIT
Isa 16: 1 from Sela, **a** the desert, to the mount of H2025
Jer 25:22 kings of the coastlands **a** the sea; H928+6298
Eze 39:14 They will spread out **a** the land and, along H928
Eze 41: 4 was twenty cubits **a** the end of the main H448
Joel 2: 2 Like dawn spreading **a** the mountains a H6584
Mic 5: 6 invade our land and march **a** our borders. H928
Hab 1: 6 who sweep **a** the whole earth to seize H4200
Mt 4:25 Judea and the **region a** the Jordan G4305
Mt 16: 5 When they went **a the lake** G1650+3836+4305
Mk 3: 8 the **regions a** the Jordan and around G4305
Mk 5: 1 They went **a** the lake to the G1650+3836+4305
Mk 10: 1 the region of Judea and **a** the Jordan. G4305
Lk 8:26 which is **a** *the lake* **from** Galilee. G527
Jn 6:17 a boat and set off **a** the lake for G4305
Jn 10:40 Then Jesus went back **a** the Jordan to the G4305
Jn 11:38 a cave with a stone **laid a** the entrance. G2130
Ac 27: 5 *When we had* **sailed a** the open sea off G1386
Ac 27:27 we were *still being* **driven a** the Adriatic G1422
Rev 20: 9 They marched **a** the breadth of the earth G2093

ACSAH (NIV84) AKSAH

ACSHAPH (NIV84) AKSHAPH

ACT (46) [ACTED, ACTING, ACTION, ACTIONS, ACTIVE, ACTIVITY, ACTS]
Ex 8:29 *let* Pharaoh *be sure that he does* not
a deceitfully H9438
Lev 20:21 it is an **a of impurity**; he has H5614
Nu 5:13 her and she *has* not **been caught in the a**), H9530
Nu 23:19 Does he speak and then not **a**? Does he H6913
Dt 17:10 *You must* **a** according to the decisions they H6913
Dt 17:11 **A** according to whatever they teach you H6913
Dt 24:13 regarded as a **righteous a** in the sight of H7407
Jdg 20: 6 this **lewd** and outrageous **a** in Israel. H2365
Jdg 20:10 this **outrageous a** done in Israel. H5576
1Sa 14: 6 Perhaps the LORD *will* **a** in our behalf H6913
2Sa 6: 7 against Uzzah because of his **irreverent a**; H8915
2Sa 14: 2 **A** like a woman who has spent many days H2118
1Ki 2: 2 "So be strong, **a** *like* a man, H2118+4200
1Ki 8:32 then hear from heaven and **a**. Judge H6913
1Ki 8:39 Forgive and **a**; deal with everyone H6913
1Ki 21: 7 "Is this how you **a** as king over Israel? H6913
2Ch 6:23 then hear from heaven and **a**. Judge H6913
2Ch 19:11 **A** with courage, and may the LORD be with H6913
2Ch 22: 3 his mother encouraged him to **a wickedly**. H8399
2Ch 24: 5 But the Levites *did* not **a at once**. H4554
Ezr 10:14 *Let* our officials **a** for the whole assembly H6641
Ne 5:15 of reverence for God I *did* not **a** like that. H6913
Ps 36: 3 deceitful; they fail to **a wisely** or do good. H8505
Ps 106: 3 Blessed are *those who* **a** justly, who H9068
Ps 119:126 It is time for you to **a**, LORD; your law is H6913
Pr 3:27 it is due, when it is in your power to **a**. H6913
Pr 13:16 All who are prudent **a** with knowledge H6913
Isa 43:13 out of my hand. *When I* **a**, who can H7188
Isa 52:13 my servant *will* **a wisely**; he will be H8505
Jer 6:28 are bronze and iron; they all **a corruptly**. H8845
Jer 42: 5 against us if we *do* not **a** in accordance H6913
Eze 24:14 The time has come *for me to* **a**. I will not H6913
Da 9:19 hear and **a**! For your sake, my God, H6913
Da 11:23 with him, *he will* **a** deceitfully, and H6913
Mic 6: 8 *To* **a** justly and to love mercy and to walk H6913
Zep 3: 7 still eager *to* **a corruptly** in all they did. H8845
Mal 3:17 "On the day when I **a**," says the LORD H6913
Mal 4: 3 the soles of your feet on the day when I **a**," H6913
Jn 8: 4 this woman was caught in the **a** of adultery. G900
Ac 4: 9 today for an **a of kindness** shown to a G2307
Ro 5:18 so also one **righteous a** resulted in G1468
2Co 8: 6 to completion this **a of grace** on your part. G5921
2Co 10: 6 ready to punish every **a of disobedience**, G4157
Php 2:13 in you to will and *to* **a** in order to fulfill his G1919
Col 4: 5 Be wise *in* **the way** *you* **a** toward outsiders G4344
Jas 2:12 Speak and **a** as those who are going to G4472

ACTED (25) [ACT]
Jdg 9:16 "*Have you* **a** honorably and in good faith H6913
Jdg 9:19 So *have you* **a** honorably and in good faith H6913
Jdg 9:23 so that they **a treacherously** against H953
Jdg 15: 7 to them, "Since *you've* **a** like this, I swear H6913
1Sa 21:13 was in their hands *he* **a like a madman**, H2147
1Sa 25:18 Abigail **a quickly**. She took two hundred H4554
1Sa 26:21 Surely *I have* **a like a fool** and have been H6118
1Ki 8:47 have done wrong, *we have* **a wickedly**'; H8399
1Ki 20:25 He agreed with them and **a** accordingly. H6913
2Ki 12:15 because they **a** with complete honesty. H6913
2Ki 22:13 they *have* not **a** in accordance with all H6913
2Ch 6:37 we have done wrong and **a wickedly**'; H8399
2Ch 11:23 He **a wisely**, dispersing some of his sons H1067
2Ch 25: 4 **a** in accordance with what is written in NDT
2Ch 34:21 they *have* not **a** in accordance with all H6913
Ne 1: 7 *We have* **a very wickedly** toward H2472+2472
Ne 9:33 righteous; *you have* **a** faithfully, while H6913
Ne 9:33 have acted faithfully, while we **a wickedly**. H8399
Ps 106: 6 we have done wrong and **a wickedly**. H8399
Isa 48: 3 then suddenly *I* **a**, and they came to H6913
Jer 38: 9 these men *have* **a wickedly** in all they H8317
Eze 25:15 the Philistines **a** in vengeance and took H6913
Lk 16: 8 manager because *he had* **a** shrewdly. G4472
Ac 3:17 I know that *you* **a** in ignorance, as did G4556
1Ti 1:13 mercy because *I* **a** in ignorance and G4472

ACTING (8) [ACT]
2Sa 12:21 asked him, "Why *are you* **a** this way? H6913
2Ki 10:19 But Jehu *was* **a** deceptively in order to H6913
Eze 16:30 all these things, **a** *like* a brazen prostitute! H5126
Eze 24:19 to do with us? Why *are you* **a** like this?" H6913
Ro 14:15 what you eat, *you are* no longer **a** in love. G4344
1Co 3: 3 *Are you* not **a** like mere humans G4344
1Co 7:36 *that he might* **not be a honorably** toward G858
Gal 2:14 I saw that *they were* not **a in line** with the G3980

ACTION (6) [ACT]
Jer 32:39 I will give them singleness of heart and **a** H2006
Da 11:28 *He will* **take a** against it and then return H6913
Lk 23:51 not consented to their decision and **a**. G4552
Ac 7:22 was powerful in speech and **a**. G2240
2Co 9: 2 enthusiasm *has* **stirred** most of them **to a**. G2241
Jas 2:17 if it is not accompanied by **a**, is dead. G2240

ACTIONS (21) [ACT]
Pr 20:11 Even small children are known by their **a** H5095
Jer 4:18 own conduct and **a** have brought this on H5095
Jer 7: 3 Reform your ways and your **a**, and I will H5095
Jer 7: 5 your ways and your **a** and deal with each H5095
Jer 18:11 and reform your ways and your **a**. H5095
Jer 26:13 your ways and your **a** and obey the LORD H5095
Jer 35:15 from your wicked ways and reform your **a**; H5095
Jer 44:22 endure your wicked **a** and the detestable H5095
Eze 14:22 when you see their conduct and their **a**, H6613
Eze 14:23 when you see their conduct and their **a**, H6613
Eze 20:43 conduct and all the **a** by which you have H6613
Eze 24:14 according to your conduct and your **a**, H6613
Eze 36:17 they defiled it by their conduct and their **a**. H6613
Eze 36:19 according to their conduct and their **a**. H6613
2Co 10:11 we will be *in* our **a** when we are present. G2240
2Co 11:15 Their end will be what their **a** deserve. G2240
Gal 6: 4 Each one should test their own **a**. Then G2240
Titus 1:16 know God, but *by* their **a** they deny him. G2240
Jas 2:22 his faith and his **a** were working together, G2240
1Jn 3:12 Because his own **a** were evil and his G2240
1Jn 3:18 words or speech but with **a** and in truth. G2240

ACTIVE (1) [ACT]
Heb 4:12 For the word of God is alive and **a** G1921

ACTIVITY (5) [ACT]
Ne 11:23 which regulated their daily **a**. H1821
Ecc 3: 1 a season for every **a** under the heavens: H2914

Ecc 3:17 there will be a time for every **a**, a time H2914
Ac 5:38 if their purpose or **a** is of human origin, *G2240*
2Co 10:15 our **sphere of a** among you will greatly *G2834*

ACTS (38) [ACT]
Ex 6: 6 arm and with mighty **a of judgment**. H9150
Ex 7: 4 with mighty **a of judgment** I will bring H9150
1Sa 12: 7 as to all the **righteous a** performed by the H7407
1Ch 16: 9 sing praise to him; tell of all his **wonderful** *a.* AIT
2Ch 32:32 reign and his **a of devotion** are written in H2876
2Ch 35:26 reign and his **a of devotion** in accordance H2876
Est 10: 2 And all his **a** *of* power and might, together H5126
Ps 9:16 The LORD is known by his **a of justice**; the H5477
Ps 40: 9 I proclaim your **saving a** in the great H7406
Ps 71:15 of your **saving a** all day long H9591
Ps 71:16 I will come and proclaim your **mighty a** H1476
Ps 71:18 your **mighty a** to all who are to come. H1476
Ps 71:24 will tell of your **righteous a** all day long, H7407
Ps 105: 2 sing praise to him; tell of all his **wonderful** *a.* AIT
Ps 106: 2 can proclaim the **mighty a** *of* the LORD H1476
Ps 145: 4 to another; they tell of your **mighty a**. H1476
Ps 145:12 may know of your **mighty a** and the H1476
Ps 150: 2 Praise him for his **a of power**; praise him H1476
Pr 12:10 the **kindest a** *of* the wicked are cruel. H8171
Isa 5:16 will be proved holy by his **righteous a**. H7407
Isa 59: 6 and **a** *of* violence are in their hands. H7189
Isa 59: 7 **a of violence** mark their H8719+2256+8691
Isa 64: 4 *who* **a** on behalf of those who wait for H6913
Isa 64: 6 all our **righteous a** are like filthy rags H7407
Jer 13:27 I have seen your **detestable a** on the hills H9199
Jer 29:26 any maniac *who* **a like a prophet** into the H5547
Eze 22: 9 the mountain shrines and commit **lewd a**. H2365
Da 9:16 in keeping with all your **righteous a**, turn H7407
Mic 6: 5 may know the **righteous a** *of* the LORD." H7407
Jn 7: 4 to become a public figure **a** in secret. *G4472*
Ro 1:27 Men committed **shameful a** with other men *G859*
Gal 5:19 The **a** of the flesh are obvious: sexual *G2240*
Heb 6: 1 of repentance from **a** that lead to death, *G2240*
Heb 9:14 our consciences from **a** that lead to death, *G2240*
Heb 10:17 "Their sins and **lawless a** I will remember *G490*
Jude 15 of all the ungodly **a** they have committed *G2240*
Rev 15: 4 your **righteous a** have been revealed." *G1468*
Rev 19: 8 stands for the **righteous a** of God's holy *G1468*

ACTUAL (1) [ACTUALLY]
Dt 21:16 wife he loves in preference to his **a** firstborn, NDT

ACTUALLY (9) [ACTUAL]
Ge 37: 8 *Will you* **a rule** us?" And H5440+5440
Ge 37:10 *Will* your mother and I and your brothers **a come** H995+995
Jos 9:22 way from you,' while **a** you live near us? NDT
Jer 8: 8 when **a** the lying pen of the scribes has H434
Jn 7:22 (**though a** it did not come from Moses *G4022*
Ro 7:10 was intended to bring life **a** brought death. NDT
1Co 5: 1 It is **a** reported that there is sexual *G3914*
Php 1:12 happened to me has **a** served to advance *G3437*
1Th 2:13 but as it **a** is, the word of God, *G242*

ACZIB (NIV84) AKZIB

ADADAH (1)
Jos 15:22 Dimonah, **A**, H6368

ADAH (8)
Ge 4:19 one named **A** and the other Zillah. H6336
Ge 4:20 **A** gave birth to Jabal; he was the father of H6336
Ge 4:23 said to his wives, "**A** and Zillah, listen to H6336
Ge 36: 2 **A** daughter of Elon the Hittite, and H6336
Ge 36: 4 **A** bore Eliphaz to Esau, Basemath bore H6336
Ge 36:10 the son of Esau's wife **A**, and Reuel, H6336
Ge 36:12 These were grandsons of Esau's wife **A**. H6336
Ge 36:16 in Edom; they were grandsons of **A**. H6336

ADAIAH (9)
2Ki 22: 1 name was Jedidah daughter of **A**; H6347
1Ch 6:41 of Ethni, the son of Zerah, the son of **A**, H6347
1Ch 8:21 **A**, Beraiah and Shimrath were the sons of H6347
1Ch 9:12 **A** son of Jeroham, the son of Pashhur, the H6347
2Ch 23: 1 Maaseiah son of **A**, and Elishaphat son H6348
Ezr 10:29 Meshullam, Malluch, **A**, Jashub, Sheal H6347
Ezr 10:39 Shelemiah, Nathan, **A**, H6347
Ne 11: 5 Hazaiah, the son of **A**, the son of Joiarib, H6347
Ne 11:12 822 men; **A** son of Jeroham, the son of H6347

ADALIA (1)
Est 9: 8 Poratha, **A**, Aridatha, H130

ADAM (22) [ADAM'S]
Ge 2:20 But for **A** no suitable helper was found H134
Ge 2:25 **A** and his wife were both naked, and they H132
Ge 3:17 To **A** he said, "Because you listened to H134
Ge 3:20 **A** named his wife Eve, because she would H134
Ge 3:21 garments of skin for **A** and his wife and H134
Ge 4: 1 **A** made love to his wife Eve, and she H134
Ge 4:25 **A** made love to his wife again, and she H134
Ge 5: 3 When **A** had lived 130 years, he had a son H134
Ge 5: 4 **A** lived 800 years and had other sons and H134
Ge 5: 5 Altogether, **A** lived a total of 930 years, and H134
Jos 3:16 at a town called **A** in the vicinity of H136
1Ch 1: 1 **A**, Seth, Enosh, H134
Hos 6: 7 As *at* **A**, they have broken the covenant H136
Lk 3:38 son of Seth, the son *of* **A**, the son of God. *G77*
Ro 5:14 from the time of **A** to the time of Moses, *G77*
Ro 5:14 a command, as did **A**, who is a pattern of *G77*
1Co 15:22 For as in **A** all die, so in Christ all will be *G77*
1Co 15:45 "The first man **A** became a living being"; *G77*
1Co 15:45 living being"; the last **A**, a life-giving spirit. *G77*
1Ti 2:13 For **A** was formed first, then Eve. *G77*
1Ti 2:14 And **A** was not the one deceived; it was the *G77*
Jude 14 the seventh from **A**, prophesied about them: *G77*

ADAM'S (1) [ADAM]
Ge 5: 1 This is the written account of **A** family line H134

ADAMAH (1)
Jos 19:36 **A**, Ramah, Hazor, H142

ADAMANT (KJV) FLINT

ADAMI NEKEB (1)
Jos 19:33 passing **A** and Jabneel to Lakkum H146

ADAR (9)
Ezr 6:15 on the third day of the month **A**, A10009
Est 3: 7 fell on the twelfth month, the month of **A**. H160
Est 3:13 the month of **A**, and to plunder H160
Est 8:12 day of the twelfth month, the month of **A**. H160
Est 9: 1 the month of **A**, the edict H160
Est 9:15 on the fourteenth day of the month of **A**, H160
Est 9:17 on the thirteenth day of the month of **A**, H160
Est 9:19 of the month of **A** as a day of joy and H160
Est 9:21 fifteenth days of the month of **A** H160

ADBEEL (2)
Ge 25:13 firstborn of Ishmael, Kedar, **A**, Mibsam, H118
1Ch 1:29 firstborn of Ishmael, Kedar, **A**, Mibsam, H118

ADD (31) [ADDED, ADDING, ADDITION, ADDITIONAL, ADDS]
Ge 30:24 "*May* the LORD **a** to me another son." H3578
Lev 2:13 grain offerings; **a** salt to all your offerings. H7928
Lev 6: 5 **a** a fifth of the value to it and give it all to H3578
Lev 6:12 morning the priest *is to* **a** firewood and H6584
Lev 22:14 the offering and **a** a fifth of the value H3578
Lev 27:15 redeem it, *they must* **a** a fifth to its value H3578
Lev 27:19 redeem it, *they must* **a** a fifth to its value H3578
Lev 27:31 any of their tithe *must* **a** a fifth of the H3578
Nu 5: 7 **a** a fifth of the value to it and give it all to H3578
Dt 4: 2 *Do* not **a** to what I command you and do H3578
Dt 12:32 *do* not **a** to it or take away from it. H3578
Dt 20: 8 Then the officers *shall* **a**, "Is anyone afraid H3578
2Sa 15: 4 And Absalom *would* **a**, "If only I were H606
1Ki 1:14 come in and **a** *my* **word** to what you have H4848
2Ki 20: 6 *I will* **a** fifteen years to your life. And I will H3578
1Ch 22:14 wood and stone. And *you may* **a** to them. H3578
2Ch 28:13 Do you intend to **a** to our sin and guilt H3578
Pr 1: 5 let the wise listen and **a** *to* their learning H3578
Pr 9: 9 righteous and *they will* **a** *to* their learning. H3578
Pr 30: 6 *Do* not **a** to his words, or he will rebuke H3578
Isa 5: 8 Woe to you *who* **a** house to house and H5595
Isa 29: 1 **A** year to year and let your cycle of H3578
Isa 38: 5 I *will* **a** fifteen years to your life. H3578
Jer 7:21 *Go ahead*, **a** your burnt offerings to your H3578
Jer 30:19 *I will* **a to** their **numbers**, and they will not H8049
Eze 16:43 *Did you* not **a** lewdness to all your other H6913
Mt 6:27 of you by worrying **a** a single hour to your *G4707*
Lk 12:25 you by worrying can **a** a single hour to *G4707*
Gal 3:15 can set aside or **a** to a human covenant *G2112*
2Pe 1: 5 make every effort *to* **a** to your faith *G2220*
Rev 22:18 God *will* **a** to that person the plagues *G2202*

ADDAR (2) [ATAROTH ADDAR, HAZAR ADDAR]
Jos 15: 3 past Hezron up to **A** and curved around to H162
1Ch 8: 3 The sons of Bela were: **A**, Gera, Abihud, H161

ADDED (38) [ADD]
Ge 16:10 The angel **a**, "I will increase your H606
Ge 21: 7 And *she* **a**, "Who would have said to H606
Ge 24:25 And *she* **a**, "We have plenty of straw and H606
Ge 30:28 *He* **a**, "Name your wages, and I will pay H606
Ge 38:25 And *she* **a**, "See if you recognize whose H606
Ex 12:34 took their dough before the **yeast** *was* **a**, H2806
Lev 10: 1 put fire in them and **a** incense; and they H8492
Lev 27:13 the animal, a fifth *must be* **a** to its value. H3578
Nu 36: 3 inheritance and **a** to that of the tribe they H3578
Nu 36: 4 their inheritance *will* **be a** to that of the H3578
Dt 5:22 deep darkness; and *he* **a** nothing more. H3578
Jdg 19:13 *He* **a**, "Come, let's try to reach Gibeah or H606
Ru 2:20 She **a**, "That man is our close relative; he H606
Ru 3:17 **a**, "He gave me these six measures of H606
1Sa 12:19 for *we have* **a** to all our other sins the evil H3578
1Sa 26:18 And *he* **a**, "Why is my lord pursuing his H606
2Sa 19:35 your servant be an **a** burden to my lord H6388
1Ki 2:14 Then *he* **a**, "I have something to say to you." H606
1Ki 22:28 Then *he* **a**, "Mark my words, all you H606
2Ch 2:12 And Hiram **a**: "Praise be to the LORD, the H606
2Ch 18:27 Then *he* **a**, "Mark my words, all you H606
Est 5:12 Haman **a**. "I'm the only person H606
Pr 9:11 be many, and years *will be* **a** to your life. H3578
Ecc 3:14 nothing *can be* **a** to it and nothing taken H3578
Jer 36:32 similar words **were a** to them. H3578+6388
Jer 40: 5 Nebuzaradan **a**, "Go back to NDT
Jer 44:19 The women **a**, "When we burned incense to NDT
Jer 45: 3 The LORD *has* **a** sorrow to my pain; I am H3578
Zec 5: 6 And *he* **a**, "This is the iniquity of the H606
Lk 3:20 Herod **a** this to them all: He locked John *G4707*
Jn 1:51 *He* then **a**, "Very truly I tell you, you will *G3306*
Ac 1:26 so *he was* **a** to the eleven apostles. *G5164*
Ac 2:41 thousand *were* **a** to *their* **number** that day. *G4707*
Ac 2:47 And the Lord **a** to their number daily *G4707*
Ac 5:14 in the Lord and *were* **a** to their number. *G4707*
Gal 2: 6 they **a** nothing to my message. *G4651*
Gal 3:19 *It was* **a** because of transgressions until *G4707*
Rev 19: 9 And *he* **a**, "These are the true words of *G3306*

ADDER (2) [ADDERS]
Job 20:16 of serpents; the fangs of an **a** will kill him. H704
Isa 59: 5 when one is broken, an **a** is hatched. H704

ADDERS (1) [ADDER]
Isa 30: 6 lionesses, of **a** and darting snakes, the H704

ADDI (1)
Lk 3:28 of Melki, the son *of* **A**, the son of Cosam, *G79*

ADDICTED (1)
Titus 2: 3 not to be slanderers or **a to** much wine *G1530*

ADDING (5) [ADD]
Lev 27:27 at its set value, **a** a fifth of the value to it. H3578
2Sa 14:11 of blood from **a** to the destruction, H8049
1Ki 11:25 **a** to the trouble caused by Hadad. H2256+907
Ezr 10:10 married foreign women, **a** to Israel's guilt. H3578
Ecc 7:27 "**A** one thing to another to discover the NDT

ADDITION (37) [ADD]
Ge 28: 9 **in a to** the wives he already had. H6584
Lev 9:17 on the altar **in a to** the H4946+4200+963
Lev 23:38 offerings are **in a to** those for H4946+4200+963
Lev 23:38 and **in a to** your gifts H4946+4200+963
Nu 6:21 **in a to** whatever else they can H4946+963+4200
Nu 16:49 **in a to** those who had died H4946+4200+963
Nu 28:10 **in a to** the regular burnt offering and its H6584
Nu 28:23 Offer these **in a to** the regular H4946+4200+963
Nu 28:24 it is to be offered **in a to** the regular burnt H6584
Nu 28:31 **in a to** the regular burnt H4946+4200+963
Nu 29: 6 These are **in a to** the monthly H4946+4200+963
Nu 29:11 **in a to** the sin offering for H4946+4200+963
Nu 29:16 **in a to** the regular burnt H4946+4200+963
Nu 29:19 **in a to** the regular burnt H4946+4200+963
Nu 29:22 **in a to** the regular burnt H4946+4200+963
Nu 29:25 **in a to** the regular burnt H4946+4200+963
Nu 29:28 **in a to** the regular burnt H4946+4200+963
Nu 29:31 **in a to** the regular burnt H4946+4200+963
Nu 29:34 **in a to** the regular burnt H4946+4200+963
Nu 29:38 **in a to** the regular burnt H4946+4200+963
Nu 29:39 " '**In a to** what you vow and your H4200+963
Nu 35: 6 someone may flee. **In a**, give them H2256
Dt 29: 1 **in a to** the covenant he had H4946+4200+963
Jos 13:22 **In a to** those slain in battle, the Israelites H448
Jdg 20:15 **in a to** seven hundred able young H4200+963
1Ki 5:11 **in a to** twenty thousand baths of pressed H2256
1Ki 15:20 all Kinnereth **in a to** Naphtali. H6584
2Ch 31:16 **In a**, they distributed to the H4946+4200+963
Ezr 1: 6 **in a to** all the freewill offerings. H4200+963
Ne 5:15 of silver from them **in a to** food and wine. H339
Ecc 12:12 warned, my son, of **anything in a** to them. H3463
Eze 16:23 **In a to** all your other wickedness H339
Eze 44: 7 **In a to** all your other detestable practices H448
Lk 24:22 **In a**, some of our women amazed us *G247+2779*
2Co 7:13 **In a to** our own encouragement, we were *G2093*
2Co 8:22 **In a**, we are sending with them our *G1254*
Eph 6:16 **In a to** all this, take up the shield of faith *G1877*

ADDITIONAL (4) [ADD]
Ge 43:22 We have also brought **a** silver with us to H337
Ex 26:12 As for the **a** length of the tent curtains, the H6369
Lev 5:16 **pay an a** *penalty of* a fifth of its value H3578
Nu 3:48 redemption of the **a** Israelites to Aaron H6369

ADDON (2)
Ezr 2:59 **A** and Immer, but they could not H150
Ne 7:61 **A** and Immer, but they could not H124

ADDRESS (3) [ADDRESSED, ADDRESSES]
Dt 20: 2 priest shall come forward and **a** the army. H1819
Ac 12:21 throne and **delivered a public a** to the *G1319*
1Co 3: 1 I could not **a** you as people who live by *G3281*

ADDRESSED (3) [ADDRESS]
Ac 2:14 raised his voice and **a** the crowd: *G710*
Ac 5:35 Then *he* **a** the Sanhedrin: "Men of Israel *G3306*
Ac 15: 7 discussion, Peter got up and **a** them: *G3306*

ADDRESSES (2) [ADDRESS]
Heb 12: 5 of encouragement that **a** you as a father *G1363*
Heb 12: 5 that addresses you as a father **a** his son? NDT

ADDS (4) [ADD]
Job 34:37 To his sin *he* **a** rebellion; scornfully he H3578
Pr 10:27 The fear of the LORD **a length** *to* life, but H3578
Heb 10:17 Then he **a**: "Their sins and lawless acts I NDT
Rev 22:18 If anyone **a** anything to them, God will *G2202*

ADEQUATELY (1)
Ac 18:26 explained to him the way of God **more a**. *G209*

ADER (KJV) EDER

A

ADHERE (1)
2Ki 17:34 the LORD nor a to the decrees and H6913+3869

ADIEL (3)
1Ch 4:36 Asaiah, A, Jesimiel, Benaiah, H6346
1Ch 9:12 Maasai son of A, the son of Jahzerah H6346
1Ch 27:25 Azmaveth son of A was in charge of the H6346

ADIN (4)
Ezr 2:15 of A 454 H6350
Ezr 8: 6 of the descendants of A, Ebed son of H6350
Ne 7:20 of A 655 H6350
Ne 10:16 Adonijah, Bigvai, A, H6350

ADINA (1)
1Ch 11:42 A son of Shiza the Reubenite, who was H6351

ADITHAIM (1)
Jos 15:36 Shaaraim, A and Gederah (or H6353

ADJOINING (5) [JOIN]
Ne 3: 2 men of Jericho built the a section, H6584+3338
Ne 3:10 A this, Jedaiah son of Harumaph H6584+3338
Eze 41:11 the base a the open area was five cubits AIT
Eze 42:10 a the temple courtyard and opposite H448+7156
Eze 45: 6 cubits long, a the sacred portion H4200+6645

ADJOURNED (1)
Ac 24:22 with the Way, a the proceedings. G327

ADJURE, ADJURED (KJV) CHARGE, COMMAND, OATH, SWEAR

ADLAI (1)
1Ch 27:29 Shaphat son of A was in charge of the H6354

ADMAH (5)
Ge 10:19 Gomorrah, A and Zeboyim, as far H144
Ge 14: 2 Shinab king of A, Shemeber king of H144
Ge 14: 8 the king of A, the king of Zeboyim H144
Dt 29:23 Gomorrah, A and Zeboyim, which H144
Hos 11: 8 How can I treat you like A? How can I make H144

ADMATHA (1)
Est 1:14 Karshena, Shethar, A, Tarshish, Meres H148

ADMINISTER (7) [ADMINISTERED, ADMINISTERING, ADMINISTRATION, ADMINISTRATOR, ADMINISTRATORS]
1Ki 3:28 that he had wisdom from God to a justice. H6913
2Ch 19: 8 Israelite families to a the law of the LORD NDT
Ezr 7:25 judges to a justice to all the people A10169
Jer 21:12 " 'A justice every morning; rescue from H1906
Zec 7: 9 'A true justice; show mercy and H9149
2Co 8:19 which we a in order to honor the Lord G1354
2Co 8:20 criticism of the way we a this liberal gift. G1354

ADMINISTERED (1) [ADMINISTER]
Heb 11:33 kingdoms, a justice, and gained G2237

ADMINISTERING (1) [ADMINISTER]
1Ki 3:11 enemies but for discernment in a justice, H9048

ADMINISTRATION (2) [ADMINISTER]
Eph 3: 2 you have heard about the a of God's G3873
Eph 3: 9 plain to everyone the a of this mystery, G3873

ADMINISTRATOR (11) [ADMINISTER]
1Ki 4: 6 Ahishar—palace a; Adoniram son of H6584
1Ki 16: 9 of Arza, the palace a at Tirzah. H889+6584
1Ki 18: 3 summoned Obadiah, his palace a. H889+6584
2Ki 10: 5 So the palace a, the city governor H889+6584
2Ki 18:18 Eliakim son of Hilkiah the palace a, H889+6584
2Ki 18:37 Eliakim son of Hilkiah the palace a, H889+6584
2Ki 19: 2 He sent Eliakim the palace a H889+6584
Isa 22:15 steward, to Shebna the palace a: H889+6584
Isa 36: 3 Eliakim son of Hilkiah the palace a H889+6584
Isa 36:22 Eliakim son of Hilkiah the palace a, H889+6584
Isa 37: 2 He sent Eliakim the palace a H889+6584

ADMINISTRATORS (9) [ADMINISTER]
Ezr 4: 9 officials and a over the people from A10305
Est 3: 9 silver to the king's a for the royal H6913+4856
Est 9: 3 and the king's a helped the Jews, H6913+4856
Da 2:49 Abednego a over the province of A10525
Da 6: 2 with three a over them, one of whom was A10518
Da 6: 3 himself among the a and the satraps by A10518
Da 6: 4 the a and the satraps tried to find A10518
Da 6: 6 So these a and satraps went as a group A10518
Da 6: 7 The royal a, prefects, satraps, advisers A10518

ADMIRABLE (1) [ADMIRED]
Php 4: 8 is lovely, whatever is a—if anything is G2368

ADMIRED (1) [ADMIRABLE]
2Sa 1:23 in life they were loved and a, and in H5833

ADMIT (6) [ADMITTED, ADMITTING]
Jos 20: 4 Then the elders are to a the fugitive into H665
Job 27: 5 I will never a you are in the right; till I die H7405
Job 40:14 Then I myself will a to you that your own H3344
Isa 48: 6 Will you not a them? "From H5583
Ac 24:14 I a that I worship the God of our ancestors G3933
2Co 11:21 To my shame I a that we were too weak G3306

ADMITTED (1) [ADMIT]
Ne 13: 1 Moabite should ever be a into the H995

ADMITTING (1) [ADMIT]
Heb 11:13 a that they were foreigners and strangers G3933

ADMONISH (2) [ADMONISHING]
Col 3:16 as you teach and a one another with all G3805
1Th 5:12 care for you in the Lord and who a you. G3805

ADMONISHING (1) [ADMONISH]
Col 1:28 a and teaching everyone with all wisdom G3805

ADNA (2)
Ezr 10:30 A, Kelal, Benaiah, Maaseiah, Mattaniah H6363
Ne 12:15 of Harim's, A; of Meremoth's, Helkai; H6363

ADNAH (2)
1Ch 12:20 A, Jozabad, Jediael, Michael, Jozabad H6367
2Ch 17:14 A the commander, with 300,000 fighting H6365

ADO (KJV) COMMOTION

ADONI-BEZEK (3) [BEZEK]
Jdg 1: 5 there that they found A and fought against H152
Jdg 1: 6 A fled, but they chased him and caught him H152
Jdg 1: 7 Then A said, "Seventy kings with their H152

ADONI-ZEDEK (2)
Jos 10: 1 Now A king of Jerusalem heard that H155
Jos 10: 3 So A king of Jerusalem appealed to Hoham H155

ADONIJAH (26) [ADONIJAH'S]
2Sa 3: 4 the fourth, A the son of Haggith; the fifth H153
1Ki 1: 5 Now A, whose mother was Haggith, put H153
1Ki 1: 7 A conferred with Joab son of Zeruiah and H153
1Ki 1: 8 David's special guard did not join A. H154
1Ki 1: 9 A then sacrificed sheep, cattle and H154
1Ki 1:11 "Have you not heard that A, the son of H154
1Ki 1:13 Why then has A become king?' H154
1Ki 1:18 But now A has become king, and you, my H153
1Ki 1:24 declared that A shall be king after you H154
1Ki 1:25 with him and saying, 'Long live King A! H154
1Ki 1:41 A and all the guests who were with him H154
1Ki 1:42 the priest arrived. A said, "Come in. A H154
1Ki 1:50 But A, in fear of Solomon, went and took H154
1Ki 1:51 "A is afraid of King Solomon and is H154
1Ki 1:53 And A came and bowed down to King NDT
1Ki 2:13 Now A, the son of Haggith, went to H154
1Ki 2:19 to King Solomon to speak to him for A, H154
1Ki 2:21 be given in marriage to your brother A." H154
1Ki 2:22 request Abishag the Shunammite for A? H154
1Ki 2:23 if A does not pay with his life for this H154
1Ki 2:24 promised—A shall be put to death today!" H154
1Ki 2:25 he struck down A and he died. H2257S
1Ki 2:28 who had conspired with A though not with H153
1Ch 3: 2 the fourth, A the son of Haggith; H153
2Ch 17: 8 Jehonathan, A, Tobijah and Tob-Adonijah H154
Ne 10:16 A, Bigvai, Adin, H153

ADONIJAH'S (1) [ADONIJAH]
1Ki 1:49 all A guests rose in alarm and H4200+154

ADONIKAM (3)
Ezr 2:13 of A 666 H156
Ezr 8:13 of the descendants of A, the last ones H156
Ne 7:18 of A 667 H156

ADONIRAM (5)
2Sa 20:24 A was in charge of forced labor H157
1Ki 4: 6 palace administrator; A son of Abda—in H157
1Ki 5:14 A was in charge of the forced labor H157
1Ki 12:18 King Rehoboam sent out A, who was in H157
2Ch 10:18 King Rehoboam sent out A, who was in H2067

ADOPT (1) [ADOPTED, ADOPTION]
Job 15: 5 you a the tongue of the crafty. H1047

ADOPTED (2) [ADOPT]
Est 2:15 woman Mordecai had a, H4374+4200+1426
Ps 106:35 with the nations and a their customs. H4340

ADOPTION (5) [ADOPT]
Ro 8:15 received brought about your a to sonship. G5625
Ro 8:23 as we wait eagerly for our a to sonship, G5625
Ro 9: 4 Theirs is the a to sonship; theirs the G5625
Gal 4: 5 that we might receive a to sonship. G5625
Eph 1: 5 us for a to sonship through Jesus G5625

ADORAIM (1)
2Ch 11: 9 A, Lachish, Azekah, H126

ADORE (1)
SS 1: 4 How right they are to a you! H170

ADORN (8) [ADORNED, ADORNING, ADORNMENT, ADORNS]
Job 40:10 Then a yourself with glory and splendor H6335
Ps 144:12 will be like pillars carved to a a palace. H9322
Pr 1: 9 grace your head and a chain to a your neck. NDT
Isa 60: 7 my altar, and I will a my glorious temple. H6995
Isa 60:13 cypress together, to a my sanctuary; and I H6995
Jer 4:30 with makeup? You a yourself in vain. Your H3636
Jer 10: 4 They a it with silver and gold; they fasten H3636
1Pe 3: 5 their hope in God used to a themselves. G3175

ADORNED (14) [ADORN]
2Sa 1:24 who a your garments with H6590+6584
1Ki 7:17 of interwoven chains a the capitals on top H1544
1Ki 22:39 the palace he built and a with ivory, and the AIT
2Ch 3: 6 He a the temple with H7596+4200+9514
Ps 45: 8 from palaces a with ivory the music of the AIT
Ps 132:18 his head will be a with a radiant crown." H6584
Eze 16:11 I a you with jewelry: I put bracelets on your H6335
Eze 16:13 So you were a with gold and silver; your H6335
Eze 27: 6 of Cyprus they made your deck, a with ivory. AIT
Eze 28:13 every precious stone a you: H5010
Hos 10: 1 land prospered, he a his sacred stones. H3512
Am 3:15 the houses a with ivory will be destroyed AIT
Am 6: 4 You lie on beds a with ivory and lounge on AIT
Lk 21: 5 how the temple was a with beautiful G3175

ADORNING (1) [ADORN]
1Ti 2: 9 propriety, a themselves, not with G3175

ADORNMENT (1) [ADORN]
1Pe 3: 3 beauty should not come from outward a, G3180

ADORNS (4) [ADORN]
Ps 93: 5 holiness a your house for endless days. H5533
Pr 15: 2 The tongue of the wise a knowledge, but H3512
Isa 61:10 as a bridegroom a his head like a priest H6996
Isa 61:10 as a bride a herself with her jewels. H6335

ADRAMMELECH (NIV84) ADRAMMELEK

ADRAMMELEK (3)
2Ki 17:31 the fire as sacrifices to A and Anammelek, H165
2Ki 19:37 his sons A and Sharezer killed him with the H166
Isa 37:38 his sons A and Sharezer killed him with the H166

ADRAMYTTIUM (1)
Ac 27: 2 We boarded a ship from A about to sail G101

ADRIATIC (1)
Ac 27:27 were still being driven across the A Sea, G102

ADRIEL (2)
1Sa 18:19 was given in marriage to A of Meholah. H6377
2Sa 21: 8 she had borne to A son of Barzillai the H6377

ADULLAM (9) [ADULLAMITE]
Ge 38: 1 to stay with a man of A named Hirah. H6356
Jos 12:15 the king of Libnah one the king of A one H6355
Jos 15:35 Jarmuth, A, Sokoh, Azekah, H6355
1Sa 22: 1 left Gath and escaped to the cave of A. H6355
2Sa 23:13 came down to David at the cave of A, H6355
1Ch 11:15 to David to the rock at the cave of A, H6355
2Ch 11: 7 Beth Zur, Soko, A, H6355
Ne 11:30 Zanoah, A and their villages, in Lachish H6355
Mic 1:15 The nobles of Israel will flee to A. H6355

ADULLAMITE (2) [ADULLAM]
Ge 38:12 his friend Hirah the A went with him. H6356
Ge 38:20 goat by his friend the A in order to get his H6356

ADULTERER (3) [ADULTERY]
Lev 20:10 both the a and the adulteress are to be H5537
Job 24:15 The eye of the a watches for dusk; he H5537
Heb 13: 4 God will judge the a and all the sexually G3659

ADULTERERS (8) [ADULTERY]
Ps 50:18 join with him; you throw in your lot with a. H5537
Isa 57: 3 you offspring of a and prostitutes! H5537
Jer 9: 2 from them; for they are all a, a crowd of H5537
Jer 23:10 The land is full of a; because of the curse H5537
Hos 7: 4 They are all a, burning like an oven H5537
Mal 3: 5 against sorcerers, a and perjurers, against H5537
Lk 18:11 evildoers, a—or even like this tax collector G3659
1Co 6: 9 idolaters nor a nor men who have sex G3659

ADULTERESS (4) [ADULTERY]
Lev 20:10 the adulterer and the a are to be put to H5537
Hos 3: 1 she is loved by another man and is an a. H5537
Ro 7: 3 husband is still alive, she is called an a. G3655
Ro 7: 3 law and is not an a if she marries another G3655

ADULTERIES (7) [ADULTERY]
Jer 3: 8 sent her away because of all her a. H5537
Jer 13:27 your a and lustful neighings, your H5539
Rev 14: 8 drink the maddening wine of her a." G4518
Rev 17: 2 were intoxicated with the wine of her a." G4518
Rev 17: 4 abominable things and the filth of her a. G4518
Rev 18: 3 have drunk the maddening wine of her a. G4518
Rev 19: 2 who corrupted the earth by her a. G4518

ADULTEROUS (15) [ADULTERY]
Pr 2:16 save you also from the a woman, H851+2424
Pr 5: 3 For the lips of the a woman drip honey H2424
Pr 7: 5 will keep you from the a woman, H851+2424
Pr 22:14 The mouth of an a woman is a deep pit H2424
Pr 23:27 an a woman is a deep pit, and a H2390
Pr 30:20 "This is the way of an a woman: She eats H5537
Eze 6: 9 how I have been grieved by their a hearts H2388
Eze 16:32 " 'You a wife! You prefer strangers to your H5537
Eze 23:45 because they are a and blood is on their H5537
Hos 1: 2 for like an a wife this land is guilty of H2388
Hos 2: 2 her remove the a look from her face and H2393

Mt 12:39 "A wicked and **a** generation asks for a G3655
Mt 16: 4 A wicked and **a** generation looks for a sign G3655
Mk 8:38 my words in this **a** and sinful G3655
Jas 4: 4 *You* **a** *people*, don't you know that G3655

ADULTERY (48) [ADULTERER, ADULTERERS, ADULTERESS, ADULTERIES, ADULTEROUS]

Ex 20:14 "*You shall* not **commit a**. H5537
Lev 20:10 " 'If a man **commits a** with another man's H5537
Dt 5:18 "*You shall* not **commit a**. H5537
Ps 51: T David *had* **committed a with** H995+448
Pr 6:32 But *a man who* **commits a** has no H5537+851
Jer 3: 6 tree and *has* **committed a** there. H2388
Jer 3: 8 she also went out and **committed a**. H2388
Jer 3: 9 the land and **committed a** with stone and H5537
Jer 5: 7 yet *they* **committed a** and thronged to the H5537
Jer 7: 9 murder, **commit a** and perjury, burn H5537
Jer 23:14 They **commit a** and live a lie H5537
Jer 29:23 *they have* **committed a** with their H5537
Eze 16:38 of *women who* **commit a** and who shed H5537
Eze 23:37 for *they have* **committed a** and blood is on H5537
Eze 23:37 *They* **committed a** with their idols; they H5537
Eze 23:43 Then I said about the one worn out by **a** H5539
Eze 23:45 of *women who* **commit a** and shed H5537
Hos 2: 4 because they are the children of **a**. H2393
Hos 4: 2 murder, stealing and **a**; they break all H5537
Hos 4:13 your daughters-in-law *to* **a**. H5537
Hos 4:14 daughters-in-law when *they* **commit a**, H5537
Hos 4:15 **commit a**, do not let Judah H2388
Mt 5:27 that it was said, '*You shall* not **commit a**. G3658
Mt 5:28 lustfully *has* already **committed a** with her G3658
Mt 5:32 makes her the **victim of a**, and anyone G3658
Mt 5:32 marries a divorced woman **commits a**. G3656
Mt 15:19 thoughts—murder, **a**, sexual immorality G3657
Mt 19: 9 marries another woman **commits a**." G3656
Mt 19:18 murder, *you shall* not **commit a**, you shall G3658
Mk 7:22 **a**, greed, malice, deceit, lewdness, envy G3657
Mk 10:11 another woman **commits a** against her. G3656
Mk 10:12 marries another man, *she* **commits a**." G3656
Mk 10:19 murder, *you shall* not **commit a**, you shall G3658
Lk 16:18 marries another woman **commits a**, G3658
Lk 16:18 marries a divorced woman **commits a**. G3658
Lk 18:20 '*You shall* not **commit a**, you shall not G3658
Jn 8: 3 brought in a woman caught in **a**. G3657
Jn 8: 4 this woman was caught in the act *of* **a**. G3658
Ro 2:22 who say *that people should* not **commit a**, G3658
Ro 2:22 not commit adultery, *do you* **commit a**? G3658
Ro 13: 9 "*You shall* not *commit* **a**," "You shall G3658
Jas 2:11 who said, "*You shall* not **commit a**," G3658
Jas 2:11 If *you do* not **commit a** but do commit G3658
2Pe 2:14 With eyes full of **a**, they never stop sinning G3655
Rev 2:22 will make those *who* **commit a** with her G3658
Rev 17: 2 her the kings of the earth **committed a**, G4519
Rev 18: 3 kings of the earth **committed a** with her, G4519
Rev 18: 9 the earth who **committed a** with her and G4519

ADULTS (1)

1Co 14:20 evil be infants, but in your thinking be **a**. G5455

ADUMMIM (2)

Jos 15: 7 faces the Pass of **A** south of the gorge. H147
Jos 18:17 which faces the Pass of **A**, and ran down to H147

ADVANCE (20) [ADVANCED, ADVANCES, ADVANCING]

Dt 1: 7 Break camp and **a** *into* the hill country of H5825
Jos 6: 7 ordered the army, "**A**! March around the H6296
Jos 8: 5 I and all those with me *will* **a** on the city H7928
Jdg 4:15 **At** Barak's **a**, the LORD routed Sisera H4200+7156
Jdg 9:33 the morning at sunrise, **a** against the city. H7320
2Sa 22:30 With your help *I can* **a** *against* a troop H8132
Job 19:12 His troops **a** in force; they build a siege H995
Job 30:14 *They* **a** as *through* a gaping breach; amid H910
Ps 18:29 With your help *I can* **a** *against* a troop H8132
Ps 27: 2 When the wicked **a** against me to devour H7928
Pr 30:27 no king, yet they **a** together in ranks; H3655
Eze 38:16 *You will* **a** against my people Israel like a H6590
Da 11:13 *he will* **a** with a huge army fully equipped. H995
Joel 3:12 *let them* **a** into the Valley of Jehoshaphat H6590
Hab 1: 9 Their hordes **a** like a desert wind H7156+2025
Ro 9:23 whom *he* **prepared in a** for glory— G4602
2Co 9: 5 you **in a** and **finish the arrangements** for G4616
Gal 3: 8 and **announced the gospel in a** to G4603
Eph 2:10 which God **prepared in a** for us to do. G4602
Php 1:12 to me has actually served to **a** the gospel. G4620

ADVANCED (11) [ADVANCE]

Jdg 1:10 They **a** against the Canaanites living in H2143
Jdg 1:11 From there *they* **a** against the people H2143
Jdg 11:29 from there *he* **a** *against* the Ammonites H6296
2Sa 10:13 the troops with him **a** to fight the H5602
1Ki 20:21 The king of Israel **a** and overpowered the H3655
2Ki 24:10 king of Babylon **a** *on* Jerusalem and laid H6590
1Ch 19:14 the troops with him **a** to fight the H5602
1Ch 19:17 *he* **a** against them and formed his battle H995
Job 32: 7 **a** years should teach wisdom. H8044
Ps 18:12 of the brightness of his presence clouds **a**, H6296
Ps 48: 4 kings joined forces, when *they* **a** together, H6296

ADVANCES (3) [ADVANCE]

Jer 4:13 *He* **a** like the clouds, his chariots come H6590
Jer 46:22 a fleeing serpent as the enemy **a** in force; H2143
Na 2: 1 An attacker **a** against you, Nineveh H6590

ADVANCING (4) [ADVANCE]

1Ki 20:17 who reported, "Men *are* **a** from Samaria." H3655
Eze 38: 9 with you will go up, **a** like a storm; you will H995
Gal 1:14 *I was* **a** in Judaism beyond many of my G4621
1Ti 1: 4 speculations rather than **a** God's work— NDT

ADVANTAGE (15)

Ge 27:36 is the second time *he has* **taken a of** me: H6810
Ex 22:22 "*Do* not **take a of** the widow or the H6700
Lev 25:14 from them, *do* not **take a of** each other. H3561
Lev 25:17 *Do* not **take a of** each other, but fear your H3561
Dt 24:14 *Do* not **take a** *of* a hired worker who is H6943
Ecc 3:19 humans have no **a** over animals. H4639
Ecc 6: 8 What **a** have the wise over fools? What H3463
Ecc 7:12 a shelter, but the **a** *of* knowledge is this: H3862
Isa 30: 5 who bring neither help nor **a**, but only H3603
Ro 3: 1 What **a**, then, is there in being a Jew, or G4356
Ro 3: 9 *Do we have any* **a**? Not at all! G4604
2Co 11:20 exploits you or **takes a** *of* you or puts on G3284
Php 2: 6 God **something** to be **used to** his **own a**; G772
1Th 4: 6 one should wrong or **take a of** a brother G4430
Jude 16 flatter others for their own **a**. G6066

ADVERSARIES (13) [ADVERSARY]

Dt 32:41 vengeance on my **a** and repay those who H7640
2Sa 22:40 battle; you humbled my **a** before me. H7756
Ps 18:39 battle; you humbled my **a** before me. H7756
Ps 44: 7 our enemies, you put our **a** to shame. H8533
Ps 44:10 the enemy, and our **a** have plundered us. H8533
Ps 56: 2 My **a** pursue me all day long; in their H8806
Ps 74:23 Do not ignore the clamor of your **a**, the H7675
Ps 89:23 his foes before him and strike down his **a**. H8533
Ps 92:11 My eyes have seen the defeat of my **a**; my H8806
Ps 106:11 The waters covered their **a**; not one of H7640
Ps 139:20 with evil intent; your **a** misuse your name. H6839
Da 4:19 your enemies and its meaning to your **a**! A10568
Lk 21:15 wisdom that none *of* your **a** will be able to G512

ADVERSARY (12) [ADVERSARIES, ADVERSITY]

Dt 32:27 lest the **a** misunderstand and say H7640
1Ki 5: 4 every side, and there is no **a** or disaster. H8477
1Ki 11:14 the LORD raised up against Solomon an **a**, H8477
1Ki 11:23 raised up against Solomon another **a**, H8477
1Ki 11:25 Rezon was Israel's **a** as long as Solomon H8477
Est 7: 6 Esther said, "An **a** and enemy! This vile H7640
Job 27: 7 be like the wicked, my **a** like the unjust! H7756
Mt 5:25 *with* your **a who is taking** you **to court**. G508
Mt 5:25 your **a** may hand you over to the judge G508
Lk 12:58 are going with your **a** to the magistrate, G508
Lk 12:58 or your **a** may drag you off to the judge NDT
Lk 18: 3 the plea, 'Grant me justice against my **a**. G508

ADVERSITIES (KJV) ANXIETY, CALAMITY, TROUBLE

ADVERSITY (2) [ADVERSARY]

Pr 17:17 a brother is born for a time of **a**. H7650
Isa 30:20 gives you the bread of **a** and the water of H7639

ADVICE (37) [ADVISE]

Ex 18:19 now to me and *I will* **give** you *some* **a**, H3619
Nu 31:16 who followed Balaam's **a** and enticed the H1821
2Sa 15:34 can help me by frustrating Ahithophel's **a**. H6783
2Sa 16:20 said to Ahithophel, "Give us your **a**. H6783
2Sa 16:23 days the **a** Ahithophel **gave** was H3619+6783
2Sa 16:23 Absalom regarded all of Ahithophel's **a**. H6783
2Sa 17: 6 "Ahithophel has given this **a**. H1821
2Sa 17: 7 "The **a** Ahithophel *has* **given** is not H3619+6783
2Sa 17:14 "The **a** *of* Hushai the Arkite is better than H6783
2Sa 17:14 frustrate the good **a** *of* Ahithophel in H6783
2Sa 17:23 saw that his **a** had not been followed, H6783
2Sa 20:22 went to all the people with her **wise a**, H2683
1Ki 12: 8 the **a** the elders **gave** him and H6783+3619
1Ki 12: 9 "What *is* your **a**? How should we H3619
1Ki 12:13 Rejecting the **a given** him by the H3619+6783
1Ki 12:14 he followed the **a** *of* the young men and H6783
1Ki 12:28 After **seeking a**, the king made two H3619
2Ch 10: 8 the **a** the elders **gave** him and H3619+6783
2Ch 10: 9 "What *is* your **a**? How should we H3619
2Ch 10:13 Rejecting the **a** *of* the elders, H6783
2Ch 10:14 he followed the **a** *of* the young men and H6783
Est 1:21 his nobles were pleased with this **a**, H1821
Est 2: 4 This **a** appealed to the king, and he H1821
Job 26: 3 What **a** *you have* **offered** to one without H3619
Pr 1:25 disregard all my **a** and do not accept my H6783
Pr 1:30 would not accept my **a** and spurned my H6783
Pr 12: 5 but the **a** *of* the wicked is deceitful. H9374
Pr 12:15 right to them, but the wise listen to **a**. H6783
Pr 13:10 wisdom is found in *those who* **take a**. H3619
Pr 19:20 Listen to **a** and accept discipline, and at H6783
Pr 20:18 Plans are established by seeking **a**; so if H6783
Pr 27: 9 of a friend springs from their heartfelt **a**. H6783
Isa 19:11 counselors of Pharaoh give senseless **a**. H6783
Eze 11: 2 evil and **giving** wicked **a** in this city. H3619+6783
Da 4:27 Your Majesty, be pleased to accept my **a**: A10422
Ac 27:11 **followed the a** of the pilot and of the G4275
Ac 27:21 you should have **taken** my **a** not to sail G4272

ADVISABLE (1) [ADVISE]

1Co 16: 4 If it seems **a** for me to go also, they will G545

ADVISE (5) [ADVICE, ADVISABLE, ADVISED, ADVISER, ADVISERS]

2Sa 17:11 "So *I* **a** you: Let all Israel, from Dan to H3619
1Ki 1:12 *let me* **a** you how you can save H3619+6783
1Ki 12: 6 "How *would* you **a** me to answer these H3619
2Ch 10: 6 "How *would* you **a** me to answer these H3619
Ac 5:38 in the present case *I* **a** you: Leave these G3306

ADVISED (5) [ADVISE]

2Sa 17:15 "Ahithophel *has* **a** Absalom and the H3619
2Sa 17:15 but I *have* **a** them to do so and so. H3619
2Sa 17:21 Ahithophel *has* **a** such and such against H3619
1Ki 20:23 the officials of the king of Aram **a** him H606
Jn 18:14 was the *one who had* **a** the Jewish G5205

ADVISER (4) [ADVISE]

Ge 26:26 Ahuzzath his **personal a** and Phicol the H5335
2Sa 13: 3 Now Amnon had an **a** named Jonadab H8276
1Ki 4: 5 of Nathan—a priest and **a** *to* the king; H8291
2Ch 25:16 "Have we appointed you an **a** to the king? H3446

ADVISERS (19) [ADVISE]

2Ki 25:19 the fighting men, and five royal **a**. H8011+7156
2Ch 22: 4 after his father's death they became his **a**, H3446
2Ch 25:17 Amaziah king of Judah **consulted** *his* **a**, H3619
Ezr 7:14 king and his seven **a** to inquire about A10325
Ezr 7:15 the king and his **a** have freely given to A10325
Ezr 7:28 the king and his **a** and all the king's H3446
Ezr 8:25 that the king, his **a**, his officials and all H3446
Est 6:13 His **a** and his wife Zeresh said to him H2682
Job 12:20 the lips of **trusted a** and takes away the H586
Pr 11:14 but victory is won through many **a**. H3446
Pr 15:22 of counsel, but with many **a** they succeed. H3446
Pr 24: 6 and victory is won through many **a**. H3446
Jer 52:25 fighting men, and seven royal **a**. H8011+7156
Da 3: 2 prefects, governors, **a**, treasurers, judges A10011
Da 3: 3 prefects, governors, **a**, treasurers, judges A10011
Da 3:24 his feet in amazement and asked his **a**, A10196
Da 3:27 royal **a** crowded around them A10196
Da 4:36 My **a** and nobles sought me out, and I A10196
Da 6: 7 **a** and governors have all agreed that the A10196

ADVOCATE (6) [ADVOCATING]

Job 16:19 my witness is in heaven; my **a** is on high. H8446
Jn 14:16 you another **a to help** you and be with G4156
Jn 14:26 But the **A**, the Holy Spirit, whom the Father G4156
Jn 15:26 "When the **A** comes, whom I will send to G4156
Jn 16: 7 I go away, the **A** will not come to you G4156
1Jn 2: 1 does sin, we have an **a** with the Father G4156

ADVOCATING (2) [ADVOCATE]

Ac 16:21 *by* **a** customs unlawful for us Romans to G2859
Ac 17:18 "He seems to be **a** foreign gods. G2858

AENEAS (3)

Ac 9:33 There he found a man named **A**, who was G138
Ac 9:34 "**A**," Peter said to him, "Jesus Christ heals G138
Ac 9:34 roll up your mat." Immediately **A** got up. NDT

AENON (1)

Jn 3:23 John also was baptizing at **A** near Salim, G143

AFAR (16) [FAR]

Job 36: 3 I get my knowledge from **a**; I will ascribe H8158
Job 36:25 has seen it; mortals gaze on it from **a**. H8158
Job 39:25 ' It catches the scent of battle from **a**, the H8158
Job 39:29 it looks for food; its eyes detect it from **a**. H8158
Ps 138: 6 though lofty, he sees them from **a**. H5305
Ps 139: 2 you perceive my thoughts from **a**. H8158
Pr 31:14 merchant ships, bringing her food from **a**. H5305
Isa 10: 3 reckoning, when disaster comes from **a**? H5305
Isa 30:27 the Name of the LORD comes from **a**, with H5305
Isa 33:17 beauty and view a land that **stretches a**. H5305
Isa 43: 6 ' Bring my sons from **a** and my daughters H8158
Isa 49:12 they will come from **a**—some from the H8158
Isa 60: 4 your sons come from **a**, and your H8158
Isa 60: 9 bringing your children from **a**, with their H8158
Jer 50:26 Come against her from **a**. Break open her H7891
Hab 1: 8 headlong; their horsemen come from **a**. H8158

AFFAIR (1) [AFFAIRS]

1Sa 22:15 knows nothing at all about this whole **a**." H1821

AFFAIRS (13) [AFFAIR]

1Ch 26:32 to God and for the **a** *of* the king. H1821
Ne 11:24 king's agent in all **a** relating to the H1821
Ps 101: 2 *I will* **conduct the a** *of* my H2143+928+7931
Ps 112: 5 who conduct their **a** with justice. H1821
Pr 31:27 watches over the **a** *of* her household and H2142
Da 3:12 have set over the **a** *of* the province of A10525
Da 6: 4 Daniel in his conduct of **government a**, A10424
1Co 7:32 man is concerned about the Lord's **a**— G3836
1Co 7:33 is concerned about **the a** of this world— G3836
1Co 7:34 virgin is concerned about the Lord's **a**: G3836
1Co 7:34 is concerned about **the a** of this world— G3836
1Ti 5:17 The elders *who* **direct** *the* **a** of the church G4613
2Ti 2: 4 soldier gets entangled in **civilian a**, G1050+4548

AFFECT (1) [AFFECTED, AFFECTS]

Job 35: 6 If you sin, how *does that* **a** him? If your H7188

AFFECTED (8) [AFFECT]

Lev 13: 4 is to isolate the **a person** for seven days. H5596
Lev 13:12 the skin of the **a person** from head to foot, H5596
Lev 13:17 priest shall pronounce the **a person** clean; H5596
Lev 13:31 to isolate the **a person** for seven H5596+5999
Lev 13:33 except for the **a area**, and the priest is to H5999

A

Lev 13:37 has grown in it, the **a person** is healed. H5999
Lev 13:49 if the **a area** in the fabric, the leather, the H5596
Lev 13:50 is to examine the **a area** and isolate the H5596

AFFECTION (8)

Dt 7: 7 The LORD *did* not **set** *his* **a** on you and H3137
Dt 10:15 Yet the LORD **set** *his* **a** on your ancestors H3137
Eze 24:21 delight of your eyes, the object of your **a**. H5883
2Co 6:12 We are not withholding our **a** from you *G5073*
2Co 7:15 And his **a** for you is all the greater when *G5073*
Php 1: 8 all of you with the **a** of Christ Jesus. *G5073*
2Pe 1: 7 to godliness, **mutual a**; and to mutual *G5789*
2Pe 1: 7 mutual affection; and to **mutual a**, love. *G5789*

AFFECTS (1) [AFFECT]

Job 35: 8 wickedness only **a** humans like yourself H4200

AFFIRM (1) [REAFFIRM, REAFFIRM]

1Ti 1: 7 about or what *they so* **confidently a**. *G1331*

AFFIXING (1) [FIX]

Ne 9:38 our priests *are* **a** their **seals** to it. H3159

AFFLICT (5) [AFFLICTED, AFFLICTING, AFFLICTION, AFFLICTIONS]

Lev 26:24 toward you and *will* **a** you for your sins H5782
Dt 28:27 The LORD *will* **a** you with the boils of Egypt H5782
Dt 28:28 The LORD *will* **a** you with madness H5782
Dt 28:35 The LORD *will* **a** your knees and legs with H5782
Na 1:12 afflicted you, Judah, *I will* **a** you no more. H6700

AFFLICTED (47) [AFFLICT]

Dt 29:22 the diseases with which the LORD *has* **a** it. H2703
Jos 24: 5 and *I* **a** the Egyptians by what I did there H5597
Jdg 2:18 under those who oppressed and **a** them. H1895
Ru 1:21 The LORD *has* **a** me; the Almighty has H6700
1Sa 5: 6 on them and **a** them with tumors. H5782
1Sa 5: 9 *He* **a** the people of the city, both young H5782
1Sa 5:12 Those who did not die **were a** with tumors H5782
1Ki 8:35 from their sin because *you have* **a** them, H6700
2Ki 15: 5 The LORD **a** the king *with* leprosy until the H5595
2Ki 17:20 *he* **a** them and gave them into the hands H6700
2Ch 6:26 from their sin because *you have* **a** them, H6700
2Ch 16:12 reign Asa *was* **a with a disease** in his feet H2688
2Ch 21:18 the LORD **a** Jehoram with an incurable H5597
2Ch 26:20 to leave, because the LORD *had* **a** him. H5595
Job 2: 7 of the LORD and **a** Job with painful sores H5782
Job 30:11 that God has unstrung my bow and **a** me, H6700
Job 36: 6 wicked alive but gives the **a** their rights. H6714
Ps 9:12 he does not ignore the cries of the **a**. H6705
Ps 9:18 the hope of the **a** will never perish. H6714+6705
Ps 10:14 see the trouble of the **a**; you consider their NDT
Ps 10:17 hear the desire of the **a**; you encourage H6705
Ps 22:24 scorned the suffering of the **a** *one*; H6714
Ps 25:16 be gracious to me, for I am lonely and **a**. H6714
Ps 34: 2 in the LORD; let the **a** hear and rejoice. H6705
Ps 41: 8 "A vile disease *has* **a** him; he will never H3668
Ps 69:29 But as for me, **a** and in pain—may your H6714
Ps 72: 2 in righteousness, your **a** *ones* with justice. H6714
Ps 72: 4 he defend the **a** *among* the people and H6714
Ps 72:12 the **a** who have no one to help. H6714
Ps 73:14 All day long I have been **a**, and every H5595
Ps 74:19 forget the lives of your **a** *people* forever. H6714
Ps 76: 9 up to judge, to save all the **a** *of* the land. H6705
Ps 90:15 glad for as many days as *you have* **a** us, H6700
Ps 102: T A prayer of an **a** *person* who has grown H6714
Ps 116:10 in the LORD when I said, "I *am* greatly **a**"; H6700
Ps 119:67 Before *I was* **a** I went astray, but now I H6700
Ps 119:71 It was good for me *to* **be a** so that I might H6700
Ps 119:75 that in faithfulness *you have* **a** me. H6700
Isa 1: 5 head is injured, your whole heart **a**. H1868
Isa 14:32 in her his **a** people will find refuge." H6714
Isa 49:13 will have compassion on his **a** *ones*. H6714
Isa 51:21 hear this, you **a** *one*, made drunk, H6714
Isa 53: 4 punished by God, stricken by him, and **a**. H6700
Isa 53: 7 He was oppressed and **a**, yet he did not H6700
Isa 54:11 "**A** city, lashed by storms and not H6714
Jer 14:19 Why *have you* **a** us so that we cannot be H5782
Na 1:12 Although *I have* **a** you, Judah, I will afflict H6700

AFFLICTING (1) [AFFLICT]

2Sa 24:16 said to the angel who *was* **a** the people, H8845

AFFLICTION (21) [AFFLICT]

Dt 16: 3 the bread of **a**, because you left H6715
Job 10:15 I am full of shame and drowned in my **a**. H6715
Job 36: 8 bound in chains, held fast by cords of **a**, H6715
Job 36:15 suffering; he speaks to them in their **a**. H4316
Job 36:21 which you seem to prefer to **a**. H6715
Ps 25:18 Look on my **a** and my distress and take H6715
Ps 31: 7 you saw my **a** and knew the anguish of H6715
Ps 31:10 my strength fails because of my **a**, and my H6411
Ps 107:17 ways and **suffered a** because of their H6700
Ps 107:41 needy out of their **a** and increased their H6715
Ps 119:92 delight, I would have perished in my **a**. H6715
Ecc 5:17 with great frustration, **a** and anger. H2716
Isa 30:20 the bread of adversity and the water of **a**, H4316
Isa 48:10 I have tested you in the furnace of **a**. H6715
La 1: 3 After **a** and harsh labor, Judah has gone H6715
La 1: 7 In the days of her **a** and wandering H6715
La 1: 9 on my **a**, for the enemy has H6715
La 3: 1 the man who has seen **a** by the rod of the H6715
La 3:19 I remember my **a** and my wandering, the H6715
La 3:33 For *he does* not willingly **bring a** or grief H6700
Ro 12:12 in hope, patient *in* **a**, faithful in prayer. *G2568*

AFFLICTIONS (5) [AFFLICT]

Lev 26:21 I will multiply your **a** seven times over, as H4804
1Ki 8:38 being aware of the **a** *of* their own hearts H5596
2Ch 6:29 being aware of their **a** and pains, and H5596
Col 1:24 what is still lacking *in regard to* Christ's **a**, *G2568*
Rev 2: 9 I know your **a** and your poverty—yet you *G2568*

AFFORD (9) [AFFORDED]

Lev 5: 7 *who* cannot **a** a lamb H5595+3338+1896
Lev 5:11 they cannot **a** two doves or two H5952+3338
Lev 12: 8 But if she cannot **a** a lamb H5162+3338+1896
Lev 14:21 they are poor and cannot **a** these H5952+3338
Lev 14:22 such as they *can* **a**, one for a sin H5952+3338
Lev 14:30 pigeons, such as the person *can* **a**, H5952+3338
Lev 14:32 and who cannot **a** the regular H5952+3338
Lev 27: 8 the one making the vow *can* **a**. H5952+3338
Nu 6:21 to whatever else they *can* **a**. H5952+3338

AFFORDED (2) [AFFORD]

Ro 7: 8 the opportunity **a by** the commandment, *G1328*
Ro 7:11 the opportunity **a by** the commandment, *G1328*

AFFRIGHT, AFFRIGHTED (KJV) AFRAID, ALARMED, HORROR, TERRIFIED, TERRIFY

AFIRE (1) [FIRE]

Dt 32:22 its harvests and **set a** the foundations of H4265

AFLAME (1) [FLAME]

Isa 13: 8 look aghast at each other, their faces **a**. H4258

AFOOT (1) [FOOT]

Ac 14: 5 *There was* a plot **a** among both Gentiles *G1181*

AFOREHAND (KJV) BEFOREHAND

AFORETHOUGHT (5) [THINK]

Nu 35:20 If anyone with **malice a** shoves another H8534
Dt 4:42 without **malice a**. H8533+4946+9453+8997
Dt 19: 4 without **malice a**. H8533+4946+9453+8997
Dt 19: 6 without **malice a**. H8533+4946+9453+8997
Jos 20: 5 and without **malice a**. H8533+4946+9453+8997

AFRAID (212) [FEAR]

Ge 3:10 garden, and *I was* **a** because I was naked H3707
Ge 15: 1 "*Do* not *be* **a**, Abram. I am H3707
Ge 18:15 Sarah *was* **a**, so she lied and said, "I did H3707
Ge 19:30 mountains, for *he was* **a** to stay in Zoar. H3707
Ge 20: 8 had happened, they *were* very much **a**. H3707
Ge 21:17 *Do* not *be* **a**; God has heard the boy H3707
Ge 26: 7 because *he was* **a** to say, "She is my wife H3707
Ge 26:24 *Do* not *be* **a**, for I am with you; I will bless H3707
Ge 28:17 *He was* **a** and said, "How awesome is this H3707
Ge 31:31 answered Laban, "*I was* **a**, because I H3707
Ge 32:11 I *am* **a** he will come and attack me H3707
Ge 42: 4 because *he was* **a** that harm might come H6065
Ge 43:23 "Don't *be* **a**. Your God, the God H3707
Ge 46: 3 "*Do* not *be* **a** to go down to Egypt, for I H3707
Ge 50:19 to them, "Don't *be* **a**. Am I in the place H3707
Ge 50:21 So then, don't *be* **a**. I will provide for you H3707
Ex 2:14 Then Moses *was* **a** and thought, "What I H3707
Ex 3: 6 because *he was* **a** to look at God. H3707
Ex 14:13 answered the people, "*Do* not *be* **a**. H3707
Ex 20:20 the people, "*Do* not *be* **a**. God has come H3707
Ex 34:30 and *they were* **a** to come near him. H3707
Lev 26: 6 will lie down and no *one will* **make** you **a**. H3006
Nu 12: 8 Why then *were you* not **a** to speak against H3707
Nu 14: 9 And *do* not *be* **a** *of* the people of the land H3707
Nu 14: 9 the LORD is with us. *Do* not *be* **a** *of* them." H3707
Nu 21:34 to Moses, "*Do* not *be* **a** *of* him, for I have H3707
Dt 1:17 *Do* not *be* **a** of anyone, for judgment H1593
Dt 1:21 *Do* not *be* **a**; do not be H3707
Dt 1:29 "Do not be terrified; *do* not *be* **a** of them. H3707
Dt 2: 4 *They will be* **a** of you, but be H3707
Dt 3: 2 said to me, "*Do* not *be* **a** *of* him, for I H3707
Dt 3:22 *Do* not *be* **a** *of* them; the LORD your God H3707
Dt 5: 5 because *you were* **a** of the fire and did H3707
Dt 7:18 But *do* not *be* **a** of them; remember well H3707
Dt 13:11 Then all Israel will hear and *be* **a**, and no H3707
Dt 17:13 All the people will hear and *be* **a**, and will H3707
Dt 19:20 of the people will hear of this and *be* **a**, H3707
Dt 20: 1 than yours, *do* not *be* **a** of them, because H3707
Dt 20: 3 Do not be fainthearted or **a**; do not panic H3707
Dt 20: 8 shall add, "Is anyone **a** or fainthearted? H3710
Dt 21:21 All Israel will hear of it and *be* **a**. H3707
Dt 31: 6 Do not *be* **a** or terrified because of them H3707
Dt 31: 8 forsake you. Do not *be* **a**; do not be H3707
Jos 1: 9 *Do* not *be* **a**; do not be discouraged, for H6907
Jos 8: 1 said to Joshua, "*Do* not *be* **a**; do not be H3707
Jos 10: 8 to Joshua, "*Do* not *be* **a** of them; I have H3707
Jos 10:25 said to them, "*Do* not *be* **a**; do not be H3707
Jos 11: 6 to Joshua, "*Do* not *be* **a** of them, because H3707
Jdg 4:18 Don't *be* **a**." So he entered her H3707
Jdg 6:23 *Do* not *be* **a**. You are not going to H3707
Jdg 6:27 But because *he was* **a** *of* his family and H3707
Jdg 7:10 If you are **a** to attack, go down to the camp H3710
Jdg 8:20 because he was only a boy and *was* **a**. H3707
Jdg 9:21 there because he was **a** of his brother NDT
Ru 3:11 my daughter, don't *be* **a**. I will do for you H3707
1Sa 3:15 He *was* **a** to tell Eli the vision H3707
1Sa 4: 7 the Philistines *were* **a**. "A god has come H3707
1Sa 7: 7 *they were* **a** because of the Philistines. H3707
1Sa 12:20 "*Do* not *be* **a**," Samuel replied. "You have H3707
1Sa 15:24 *I was* **a** *of* the men and so I gave in to H3707
1Sa 18:12 Saul *was* **a** of David, because the LORD H3707
1Sa 18:15 how successful he was, *he was* **a** of him. H1593
1Sa 18:29 Saul became still more **a** of him, and he H3707
1Sa 21:12 to heart and *was* very much **a** of Achish H3707
1Sa 22:23 Stay with me; don't *be* **a**. The man who H3707
1Sa 23: 3 said to him, "Here in Judah we are **a**. H3710
1Sa 23:17 "Don't *be* **a**," he said. "My father Saul will H3707
1Sa 28: 5 Philistine army, *he was* **a**; terror filled his H3707
1Sa 28:13 "Don't *be* **a**. What do you see? H3707
2Sa 1:14 "Why weren't *you* **a** to lift your hand to H3707
2Sa 3:11 word to Abner, because he *was* **a** *of* him. H3707
2Sa 6: 9 David *was* **a** *of* the LORD that day and said H3707
2Sa 9: 7 "Don't *be* **a**," David said to him, "for I will H3707
2Sa 10:19 So the Arameans *were* **a** to help the H3707
2Sa 12:18 David's attendants *were* **a** to tell him that H3707
2Sa 13:28 Don't *be* **a**. Haven't I given H3707
2Sa 14:15 because the people *have* **made** me **a**. H3707
1Ki 1:51 "Adonijah *is* **a** *of* King Solomon and is H3707
1Ki 17:13 "Don't *be* **a**. Go home and do as H3707
1Ki 19: 3 Elijah *was* **a** and ran for his life. When he H3707
2Ki 1:15 "Go down with him; *do* not *be* **a** of him." H3707
2Ki 6:16 "Don't *be* **a**," the prophet answered H3707
2Ki 19: 6 *Do* not *be* **a** of what you have heard H3707
2Ki 25:24 "*Do* not *be* **a** of the Babylonian officials," H3707
1Ch 13:12 David *was* **a** *of* God that day and asked H3707
1Ch 21:30 because *he was* **a** of the sword of the H1286
1Ch 22:13 courageous. *Do* not *be* **a** or discouraged H3707
1Ch 28:20 *Do* not *be* **a** or discouraged, for the LORD H3707
2Ch 20:15 '*Do* not *be* **a** or discouraged because of H3707
2Ch 20:17 Jerusalem. *Do* not *be* **a**; do not be H3707
2Ch 32: 7 *Do* not *be* **a** or discouraged because of H3707
2Ch 32:18 terrify them and **make** them **a** in order to H987
Ezr 4: 4 of Judah and **make** them **a** to go on H987
Ne 2: 2 sadness of heart." *I was* very much **a**, H3707
Ne 4:14 rest of the people, "Don't *be* **a** of them. H3707
Ne 6:16 surrounding nations *were* **a** and lost their H3707
Est 9: 2 nationalities *were* **a** *of* them. H5877+7065+6584
Job 6:21 you see something dreadful and *are* **a**. H3707
Job 11:19 with no *one to* **make** you **a**, and many H3006
Job 39:22 It laughs at fear, **a** *of* nothing; it does not H3169
Ps 27: 1 of my life—of whom *shall I be* **a**? H7064
Ps 56: 3 When I *am* **a**, I put my trust in you. H3707
Ps 56: 4 I praise—in God I trust and *am* not **a**. H3707
Ps 56:11 in God I trust and *am* not **a**. What can H3707
Ps 118: 6 is with me; *I will* not *be* **a**. What can mere H3707
Pr 3:24 you lie down, *you will* not *be* **a**; when you H7064
Ecc 9: 2 so with *those who are* **a** to take them. H3707
Ecc 12: 5 when *people are* **a** of heights and of H3707
Isa 7: 4 'Be careful, keep calm and don't *be* **a**. H3707
Isa 10:24 live in Zion, *do* not *be* **a** of the Assyrians H3707
Isa 12: 2 is my salvation; I will trust and not *be* **a**. H7064
Isa 17: 2 lie down, with no *one to* **make** them **a**. H3006
Isa 37: 6 Do not *be* **a** of what you have heard H3707
Isa 40: 9 lift it up, *do* not *be* **a**; say to the towns of H3707
Isa 41:14 *Do* not *be* **a**, *you* worm Jacob, little Israel H3707
Isa 43: 5 *Do* not *be* **a**, for I am with you; I will bring H3707
Isa 44: 2 *Do* not *be* **a**, Jacob, my servant, Jeshurun H3707
Isa 44: 8 Do not tremble, *do* not *be* **a**. Did I not H3724
Isa 54: 4 "*Do* not *be* **a**; you will not be put to H3707
Jer 1: 8 *Do* not *be* **a** of them, for I am with you H3707
Jer 23: 4 and *they will* no longer *be* **a** or terrified H3707
Jer 30:10 " 'So *do* not *be* **a**, Jacob my servant; do H3707
Jer 30:10 security, and no *one will* **make** him **a**. H3006
Jer 38:19 "I *am* **a** *of* the Jews who have gone over H1793
Jer 40: 9 "*Do* not *be* **a** to serve the Babylonians," H3707
Jer 41:18 *They were* **a** of them because Ishmael H3707
Jer 42:11 *Do* not *be* **a** of the king of Babylon, whom H3707
Jer 42:11 *Do* not *be* **a** of him, declares the LORD, for H3707
Jer 46:27 "*Do* not *be* **a**, Jacob my servant; do not be H3707
Jer 46:27 security, and no *one will* **make** him **a**. H3006
Jer 46:28 *Do* not *be* **a**, Jacob my servant, for I am H3707
Jer 51:46 not lose heart or *be* **a** when rumors are H3707
Eze 2: 6 *do* not *be* **a** of them or their words. H3707
Eze 2: 6 *Do* not *be* **a**, though briers and thorns are H3707
Eze 2: 6 *Do* not *be* **a** of what they say or be H3707
Eze 3: 9 *Do* not *be* **a** *of* them or terrified by them H3707
Eze 34:28 in safety, and no *one will* **make** them **a**. H3006
Eze 39:26 in their land with no *one to* **make** them **a**. H3006
Da 1:10 told Daniel, "I am **a** *of* my lord the king H3710
Da 4: 5 I had a dream *that* **made** me **a**. As I was A10167
Da 10:12 he continued, "*Do* not *be* **a**, Daniel. Since H3707
Da 10:19 "*Do* not *be* **a**, *you* who are highly H3707
Joel 2:21 *Do* not *be* **a**, land of Judah; be glad and H3707
Joel 2:22 *Do* not *be* **a**, *you* wild animals, for the H3707
Jnh 1: 5 All the sailors *were* **a** and each cried out H3707
Mic 4: 4 no *one will* **make** them **a**, for the H3006
Mic 7:17 to the LORD our God and *will be* **a** of you. H3707
Zep 3:13 lie down and no *one will* **make** them **a**." H3006
Zec 8:13 be a blessing. *Do* not *be* **a**, but let your H3707
Zec 8:15 to Jerusalem and Judah. *Do* not *be* **a**. H3707
Mt 1:20 *do* not *be* **a** to take Mary home as your *G5828*
Mt 2:22 of his father Herod, *he was* **a** to go there. *G5828*
Mt 8:26 "You of little faith, why are you *so* **a**?" *G1264*
Mt 10:26 "So *do* not *be* **a** of them, for there is *G5828*
Mt 10:28 *Do* not *be* **a** of those who kill the body *G5828*
Mt 10:28 *be* **a** of the One who can destroy both *G5828*
Mt 10:31 So don't *be* **a**; you are worth more than *G5828*
Mt 14: 5 to kill John, but *he was* **a** of the people *G5828*
Mt 14:27 "Take courage! It is I. Don't *be* **a**." *G5828*

Mt 14:30 saw the wind, *he was* a and, beginning G5828
Mt 17: 7 "Get up," he said. "Don't *be* a." G5828
Mt 21:26 human origin'—*we are* a of the people G5828
Mt 21:46 but *they were* a of the crowd because the G5828
Mt 25:25 So *I was* a and went out and hid your gold G5828
Mt 28: 4 The guards were so a of him that they G5832
Mt 28: 5 to the women, "*Do* not *be* a, for I know G5828
Mt 28: 8 away from the tomb, a yet filled with joy G5832
Mt 28:10 said to them, "*Do* not *be* a. Go and tell G5828
Mk 4:40 said to his disciples, "Why are you so a? G1264
Mk 5:15 in his right mind; and *they were* a. G5828
Mk 5:36 Jesus told him, "Don't *be* a; just believe." G5828
Mk 6:50 "Take courage! It is I. Don't *be* a." G5828
Mk 9:32 he meant and *were* a to ask him about G5828
Mk 10:32 while those who followed *were* a. G5828
Mk 12:12 But *they were* a of the crowd; so they left G5828
Mk 16: 8 nothing to anyone, because *they were* a. G5828
Lk 1:13 "*Do* not *be* a, Zechariah; your prayer has G5828
Lk 1:30 the angel said to her, "*Do* not *be* a, Mary; G5828
Lk 2:10 said to them, "*Do* not *be* a. I bring you G5828
Lk 5:10 to Simon, "Don't *be* a; from now on you G5828
Lk 8:35 in his right mind; and *they were* a. G5828
Lk 8:50 said to Jairus, "Don't *be* a; just believe, G5828
Lk 9:34 and *they were* a as they entered the cloud G5828
Lk 9:45 and *they were* a to ask him about it. G5828
Lk 12: 4 *do* not *be* a of those who kill the body G5828
Lk 12: 7 Don't *be* a; you are worth more than G5828
Lk 12:32 "*Do* not *be* a, little flock, for your Father G5828
Lk 19:21 *I was* a of you, because you are a hard G5828
Lk 20:19 But *they were* a of the people. G5828
Lk 22: 2 rid of Jesus, for *they were* a of the people. G5828
Jn 6:20 But he said to them, "It is I; don't *be* a." G5828
Jn 9:22 this because *they were* a of the Jewish G5828
Jn 12:15 "*Do* not *be* a, Daughter Zion; see, your G5828
Jn 14:27 your hearts be troubled and *do* not *be* a. G1262
Jn 19: 8 Pilate heard this, *he was* even more a, G5828
Ac 9:26 disciples, but *they were* all a of him, not G5828
Ac 18: 9 "*Do* not *be* a; keep on speaking, do not G5828
Ac 23:10 so violent *that* the commander *was* a Paul G5828
Ac 24:25 to come, Felix was a and said, "That's G1873
Ac 27:17 Because *they were* a they would run G5828
Ac 27:24 said, '*Do* not *be* a, Paul. You must G5828
Ro 13: 4 But if you do wrong, *be* a, for rulers do not G5828
2Co 11: 3 But *I am* a *that* just as Eve was deceived G5828
2Co 12:20 For *I am* a that when I come I may not find G5828
2Co 12:21 I am a that when I come again my God will NDT
Gal 2:12 Gentiles *because he was* a *of* those who G5828
1Th 3: 5 I was a that in some way the tempter had G3590
Heb 11:23 and *they were* not a of the king's edict. G5828
Heb 13: 6 "The Lord is my helper; *I will* not *be* a. G5828
2Pe 2:10 *they are* not a to heap abuse on celestial G5554
Rev 1:17 me and said: "*Do* not *be* a. I am the First G5828
Rev 2:10 *Do* not *be* a of what you are about to G5828

AFTER (729) [AFTERWARD]

Ge 3:24 A he drove the man out, he placed on the H2256
Ge 4:17 and he named it a his son Enoch. H3869
Ge 5: 4 A Seth was born, Adam lived 800 years H339
Ge 5: 7 A he became the father of Enosh, Seth H339
Ge 5:10 A he became the father of Kenan, Enosh H339
Ge 5:13 A he became the father of Mahalalel H339
Ge 5:16 A he became the father of Jared, Mahalalel H339
Ge 5:19 A he became the father of Enoch, Jared H339
Ge 5:22 A he became the father of Methuselah H339
Ge 5:26 A he became the father of Lamech H339
Ge 5:30 A Noah was born, Lamech lived 595 years H339
Ge 5:32 A Noah was 500 years old, he became H2256
Ge 7:10 And a the seven days the floodwaters H4200
Ge 8: 6 A forty days Noah opened a H4946+7891
Ge 8:19 the ark, one kind a another. H4200+5476+2157
Ge 9: 9 with you and with your descendants a you H339
Ge 9:28 A the flood Noah lived 350 years. H339
Ge 10: 1 who themselves had sons a the flood. H339
Ge 10:32 spread out over the earth a the flood. H339
Ge 11:10 Two years a the flood, when Shem was H339
Ge 11:11 And a he became the father of Arphaxad H339
Ge 11:13 And a he became the father of Shelah H339
Ge 11:15 And a he became the father of Eber H339
Ge 11:17 And a he became the father of Peleg, Eber H339
Ge 11:19 And a he became the father of Reu, Peleg H339
Ge 11:21 And a he became the father of Serug, Reu H339
Ge 11:23 And a he became the father of Nahor H339
Ge 11:25 And a he became the father of Terah H339
Ge 11:26 A Terah had lived 70 years, he became H2256
Ge 13:14 LORD said to Abram a Lot had parted from H339
Ge 14:17 A Abram returned from defeating H339
Ge 15: 1 A this, the word of the LORD came to Abram H339
Ge 16: 3 So a Abram had been living in H4946+7891
Ge 17: 7 your descendants a you for the H339
Ge 17: 7 the God of your descendants a you. H339
Ge 17: 8 to you and your descendants a you; H339
Ge 17: 9 your descendants a you for the H339
Ge 17:10 with you and your descendants a you, H339
Ge 17:19 covenant for his descendants a him. H339
Ge 18:12 "A I am worn out and my lord is old H339
Ge 18:19 his household a him to keep the way H339
Ge 21:32 A the treaty had been made at Beersheba H2256
Ge 24:19 A she had given him a drink, she said H3983
Ge 24:67 Isaac was comforted a his mother's *death*. H339
Ge 25:11 A Abraham's death, God blessed his son H339
Ge 25:26 A this, his brother came out, with his hand H339
Ge 26:18 had stopped up a Abraham died, H339
Ge 27:30 A Isaac finished blessing him, and H3869+889
Ge 29:14 A Jacob had stayed with him for a whole H2256
Ge 30:25 A Rachel gave birth to Joseph H3869+889
Ge 31:33 A he came out of Leah's tent, he entered H2256
Ge 31:54 A they had eaten, they spent the night H2256
Ge 32:23 A he had sent them across the stream, he H2256
Ge 33:18 A Jacob came from Paddan Aram, he H928
Ge 35: 9 A Jacob returned from Paddan Aram, God H928
Ge 35:12 give this land to your descendants a you." H339
Ge 37:17 So Joseph went a his brothers and found H339
Ge 37:27 our hands on him; a all, he is our brother, H3954
Ge 38:12 A a long time Judah's wife, the daughter H2256
Ge 38:19 A she left, she took off her veil and put on H2256
Ge 38:23 A all, I did send her this young goat, but H2180
Ge 39: 7 and a a while his H339+2021+1821+2021+465
Ge 39:10 And though she spoke to Joseph day *a* day AIT
Ge 40: 4 A they had been in custody for some time, H2256
Ge 41: 3 A them, seven other cows, ugly and gaunt H339
Ge 41: 6 A them, seven other heads of grain H339
Ge 41:19 A them, seven other cows came up H339
Ge 41:21 But even a they ate them, no one could H2256
Ge 41:23 A them, seven other heads sprouted H339
Ge 42:25 their journey. A this was done for them H2256
Ge 43:31 A he had washed his face, he came out H2256
Ge 44: 4 to his steward, "Go a those men at once H339
Ge 47: 7 A Jacob blessed Pharaoh, H2256
Ge 48: 4 possession to your descendants a you. H339
Ge 48: 6 children born to you a them will be yours; H339
Ge 50:14 A burying his father, Joseph returned to H339
Ge 50:26 And a they embalmed him, he was H2256
Ex 2:11 One day, a Moses had grown up, he went H2256
Ex 3:20 perform among them. A that, he will let H339
Ex 7:25 Seven days passed a the LORD struck the H339
Ex 8:12 A Moses and Aaron left Pharaoh, Moses H2256
Ex 10: 5 devour what little you have left a the hail, H4946
Ex 10:15 They devoured all that was left a the hail NDT
Ex 11: 1 A that, he will let you go from here, and H339
Ex 11: 8 people who follow you!' A that I will leave." H339
Ex 12:44 bought may eat it a you have circumcised H255
Ex 13:10 at the appointed time year a year. H2025
Ex 13:11 "A the LORD brings you into the land of the H3954
Ex 13:20 A leaving Sukkoth they camped at Etham H2256
Ex 14:10 were the Egyptians, marching a them. H339
Ex 14:17 Egyptians so that they will go in a them. H339
Ex 16: 1 of the second month a they had come out of NDT
Ex 18: 2 A Moses had sent away his wife Zipporah H339
Ex 19: 1 day of the third month a the Israelites left NDT
Ex 19: 2 A they set out from Rephidim, they H2256
Ex 19:14 A Moses had gone down the mountain to H2256
Ex 21:21 if the slave recovers a a day or two, NDT
Ex 22: 3 if it happens *a* sunrise, the defender is AIT
Ex 28:41 A you put these clothes on your brother H2256
Ex 29:26 A you take the breast of the ram for H2256
Ex 36: 3 bring freewill offerings morning a morning. H928
Lev 8:25 A that, he took the fat, the fat tail, all the H2256
Lev 13: 7 spread in their skin a they have shown H339
Lev 13:35 spread in the skin a they are pronounced H339
Lev 13:55 A the article has been washed, the priest is H339
Lev 13:56 the mold has faded a the article has been H339
Lev 14: 7 A that, he is to release the live bird in the H2256
Lev 14: 8 A this they may come into the camp, but H339
Lev 14:19 A that, the priest shall slaughter the burnt H339
Lev 14:36 A this the priest is to go in and inspect the H339
Lev 14:43 in the house a the stones have been H339
Lev 14:48 mold has not spread a the house has been H339
Lev 15:28 and a that she will be ceremonially clean. H339
Lev 16: 1 LORD spoke to Moses a the death of the two H339
Lev 22: 7 and a that he may eat the sacred offerings H339
Lev 23:11 is to wave it on the day a the Sabbath. H4740
Lev 23:15 " 'From the day a the Sabbath, the day H4740
Lev 23:16 days up to the day a the seventh Sabbath H4740
Lev 23:39 a you have gathered the crops of the land H928
Lev 24: 8 the LORD regularly, Sabbath a Sabbath, H928+3427+2021+8701+928+3427+2021+8701
Lev 25:29 right of redemption a full year a its sale. H6330
Lev 25:48 the right of redemption a they have sold H339
Lev 26:18 " 'If a all this you will not listen to me, I H6330
Lev 27:18 But if they dedicate a field a the Jubilee H339
Nu 1: 1 of the second year a the Israelites came H4200
Nu 4:15 "A Aaron and his sons have finished H2256
Nu 5:18 A the priest has had the woman stand H2256
Nu 5:26 it on the altar; a that, he is to have the H339
Nu 6:19 " 'A the Nazirite has shaved off the hair H339
Nu 6:20 was presented. A that, the Nazirite may H339
Nu 7:88 dedication of the altar a it was anointed. H339
Nu 8:15 "A you have purified the Levites and H339+4027
Nu 8:22 A that, the Levites came to do their work at H339
Nu 9: 1 of the second year a they came out of H4200
Nu 12:14 a that she can be brought back. H339
Nu 12:16 A that, the people left Hazeroth and H339
Nu 15: 2 'A you enter the land I am giving you as a H3954
Nu 15:39 by chasing a the lusts of your own H339
Nu 19: 7 A that, the priest must wash his clothes H2256
Nu 19:13 themselves *a* touching a human corpse, AIT
Nu 21:32 A Moses had sent spies to Jazer, the H2256
Nu 26: 1 A the plague the LORD said to Moses and H339
Nu 27:13 A you have seen it, you too will be H2256
Nu 30: 6 "If she marries a she makes a vow or after H2256
Nu 30: 6 she makes a vow or a her lips utter a rash NDT
Nu 30:15 nullifies them some time a he hears about H339
Nu 31: 2 A that, you will be gathered to your people." H339
Nu 32: 9 A they went up to the Valley of Eshkol H2256
Nu 32:42 settlements and called it Nobah a himself. H928
Nu 33: 3 of the first month, the day a the Passover. H4740
Nu 33:38 of the fortieth year a the Israelites came H4200
Nu 35:28 only a the death of the high priest may H339
Dt 1: 4 This was a he had defeated Sihon king of H339
Dt 1: 8 Jacob—and to their descendants a them." H339
Dt 3:14 it was named a him, so that to this day H6584
Dt 3:20 A that, each of you may go back to the H2256
Dt 4: 9 your children and to their children a them. NDT
Dt 4:25 A you have had children and H3954
Dt 4:37 chose their descendants a them, H339
Dt 4:40 your children a you and that you may H339
Dt 6: 2 their children a them may fear the LORD NDT
Dt 9: 4 A the LORD your God has driven them out H928
Dt 12:25 go well with you and your children a you, H339
Dt 12:28 go well with you and your children a you, H339
Dt 12:30 a they have been destroyed before you H339
Dt 16:13 seven days a you have gathered the H928
Dt 21:13 A she has lived in your house and H339+4027
Dt 22:13 man takes a wife and, a sleeping with her H2256
Dt 24: 2 and if a she leaves his house she H2256
Dt 24: 4 to marry her again a she has been defiled. H339
Dt 24: 9 Miriam along the way a you came out of H928
Dt 28:29 day a day you will be H3972+2021+3427
Dt 28:32 watching for them day a day, H3972+2021+3427
Dt 31:24 A Moses finished writing in a book the H3869
Dt 31:27 how much more will you rebel a I die! H339
Dt 31:29 For I know that a my death you are sure to H339
Jos 1: 1 A the death of Moses the servant of the H339
Jos 1:13 the servant of the LORD gave you *a he* said, AIT
Jos 1:15 A that, you may go back and occupy your H2256
Jos 2: 5 way they went. Go a them quickly. You may H339
Jos 3: 2 A three days the officers went H4946+7895
Jos 5: 4 the wilderness on the way a leaving Egypt. H928
Jos 5: 8 And a the whole nation had been H3869+889
Jos 5:11 The day a the Passover, that very day, they H4740
Jos 5:12 manna stopped the day a they ate this H4740
Jos 7:25 and a they had stoned the rest H2256
Jos 8:17 in Ai or Bethel who did not go a Israel. H339
Jos 9:16 Three days a they made the treaty with the H339
Jos 10: 9 A an all-night march from Gilgal, Joshua H2256
Jos 14:15 used to be called Kiriath Arba a Arba, NDT
Jos 18: 6 A you have written descriptions of the H2256
Jos 19:47 and named it Dan a their ancestor.) H3869+9005
Jos 23: 1 A a long time had passed and the LORD H339
Jos 24:20 an end of you, a he has been good to you." H339
Jos 24:29 A these things, Joshua son of Nun, the H339
Jdg 1: 1 A the death of Joshua, the Israelites asked H339
Jdg 1: 9 A that, Judah went down to fight against H339
Jdg 2: 6 A Joshua had dismissed the Israelites H2256
Jdg 2:10 A that whole generation had been H2256+1685
Jdg 3:18 A Ehud had presented the tribute, he H3869+889
Jdg 3:22 Even the handle sank in a the blade, and H339
Jdg 3:24 A he had gone, the servants came and H2256
Jdg 3:31 A Ehud came Shamgar son of Anath, who H339
Jdg 7:19 just a they had changed the guard. H421
Jdg 9:22 A Abimelek had governed Israel three H2256
Jdg 9:27 A they had gone out into the fields and H2256
Jdg 10: 1 A the time of Abimelek, a man of Issachar H339
Jdg 11:39 A the two months, she returned to H4946+7891
Jdg 12: 8 A him, Ibzan of Bethlehem led Israel. H339
Jdg 12:11 A him, Elon the Zebulunite led Israel ten H339
Jdg 12:13 A him, Abdon son of Hillel, from Pirathon H339
Jdg 16:16 him day a day until he H3972+2021+3427
Jdg 16:19 *A* putting him to sleep on her lap, she called AIT
Jdg 16:22 to grow again a it had been shaved. H3869+889
Jdg 17: 4 So *a he* returned the silver to his mother, she AIT
Jdg 18:23 As they shouted a them, the Danites turned H448
Jdg 18:29 They named it Dan a their ancestor H928+9005
Jdg 19: 2 A she had been there four months, H2256
Jdg 19:21 A they had washed their feet, they had H2256
Jdg 20: 5 of Gibeah came a me and surrounded H6584
Jdg 20:45 They kept pressing a the Benjamites as far H339
Ru 1: 4 A they had lived there about ten years H2256
Ru 2: 9 harvesting, and follow along a the women. H339
Ru 2:18 she had left over a she had eaten enough H4946
Ru 3:10 You have not run a the younger men H339
1Sa 1: 3 Year a year this man went up from his H2025
1Sa 1: 7 This went on year a year. Whenever H928
1Sa 1:22 to her husband, "A the boy is weaned, I H6330
1Sa 1:24 A he was weaned, she took the boy H3869+889
1Sa 5: 1 A the Philistines had captured the ark of H2256
1Sa 5: 9 But a they had moved it, the LORD's hand H339
1Sa 8: 3 They turned aside a dishonest gain and H339
1Sa 9:25 A they came down from the high place to H2256
1Sa 10: 5 "A that you will go to Gibeah of God H339
1Sa 10:13 A Saul stopped prophesying, he went to H2256
1Sa 12: 8 "A Jacob entered Egypt, they cried H3869+889
1Sa 12:21 Do not turn away a useless idols. They can H339
1Sa 13:14 sought out a man a his own heart and H3869
1Sa 14:12 "Climb up a me; the LORD has given H339
1Sa 14:31 a the Israelites had struck down the H2256
1Sa 14:47 A Saul had assumed rule over Israel, he H2256
1Sa 17:35 I went a it, struck it and rescued the sheep H339
1Sa 17:51 A he killed him, he cut off his head with H2256
1Sa 18: 1 A David had finished talking with Saul H3869
1Sa 18: 6 were returning home a David had killed H928
1Sa 20: 5 until the evening of the day a tomorrow. H8958
1Sa 20:12 my father by this time the day a tomorrow! H8958
1Sa 20:19 The day a tomorrow, toward evening, go H8992
1Sa 20:37 Jonathan called out a him, "Isn't the arrow H339
1Sa 20:41 A the boy had gone, David got up from the NDT

1Sa 23:14 Day a day Saul searched for H3972+2021+3427
1Sa 24: 1 A Saul returned from pursuing the H3869+889
2Sa 1: 1 A the death of Saul, David returned from H339
2Sa 1:10 because I knew that a he had fallen he H339
2Sa 3:26 left David and sent messengers a Abner, H339
2Sa 4: 7 A they stabbed and killed him, they cut H2256
2Sa 5:13 A he left Hebron, David took more H339
2Sa 6:18 A he had finished sacrificing the burnt H2256
2Sa 7: 1 A the king was settled in his palace and H3954
2Sa 8:13 David became famous a he returned from H928
2Sa 10:15 A the Arameans saw that they had been H2256
2Sa 11: 8 a gift from the king was sent a him. H339
2Sa 11:27 A the time of mourning was over, David H2256
2Sa 12:15 A Nathan had gone home, the LORD struck H2256
2Sa 12:20 A he had washed, put on lotions and H2256
2Sa 12:28 take the city, and it will be named a me." H6584
2Sa 13: 4 look so haggard morning a morning? H928
2Sa 13:17 out of my sight and bolt the door a her." H339
2Sa 13:18 put her out and bolted the door a her. H339
2Sa 13:38 A Absalom fled and went to Geshur, he H2256
2Sa 17:21 A they had gone, the two climbed out of H339
2Sa 18:18 He named the pillar a himself, and it is H6584
2Sa 20:13 A Amasa had been removed from H3869+889
2Sa 21:12 had hung them a they struck Saul H928+3427
2Sa 21:14 A that, God answered prayer in behalf of H339
2Sa 23: 4 like the brightness a rain that brings grass H4946
2Sa 24: 5 A crossing the Jordan, they camped near H2256
2Sa 24: 8 A they had gone through the entire land H2256
2Sa 24:10 a he had counted the H339+4027
1Ki 1: 6 handsome and was born next a Absalom.) H339
1Ki 1:13 Solomon your son shall be king a me, H339
1Ki 1:17 'Solomon your son shall be king a me, and H339
1Ki 1:20 sit on the throne of my lord the king a him. H339
1Ki 1:24 declared that Adonijah shall be king a you H339
1Ki 1:27 sit on the throne of my lord the king a him?" H339
1Ki 1:30 Solomon your son shall be king a me, and H339
1Ki 1:40 And all the people went up a him, playing H339
1Ki 2:22 kingdom for him—a all, he is my older H3954
1Ki 3:18 The third day a my child was born, this H4200
1Ki 5:11 continued to do this for Hiram year a year. H928
1Ki 6: 1 eightieth year a the Israelites came H4200
1Ki 8: 9 with the Israelites a they came out of Egypt H928
1Ki 9:24 A Pharaoh's daughter had come up from H421
1Ki 10:25 Year a year, everyone who came H1821+928
1Ki 11: 2 will surely turn your hearts a their gods." H339
1Ki 11: 4 his wives turned his heart a other gods H339
1Ki 12:16 Look a your own house, David!" So H8011
1Ki 12:28 A seeking advice, the king made two H2256
1Ki 13:14 rode a the man of God. He found him H339
1Ki 13:31 A burying him, he said to his sons, "When H339
1Ki 13:33 Even a this, Jeroboam did not change his H339
1Ki 16:24 calling it Samaria, a Shemer, the name of H6584
1Ki 18: 1 A a long time, in the third year, the word H2256
1Ki 19:11 A the wind there was an earthquake, but H339
1Ki 19:12 A the earthquake came a fire, but the LORD H339
1Ki 19:12 And a the fire came a gentle whisper. H339
1Ki 19:20 Elisha then left his oxen and ran a Elijah H339
1Ki 20:36 And a the man went away, a lion found H2256
1Ki 21:26 in the vilest manner by going a idols, H339
1Ki 22:46 who remained there even a the reign of his H928
2Ki 1: 1 A Ahab's death, Moab rebelled against H339
2Ki 3: 5 But a Ahab died, the king of Moab H3869
2Ki 3: 9 A a roundabout march of seven days, the H2256
2Ki 4:20 A the servant had lifted him up and H2256
2Ki 5:19 A Naaman had traveled some distance H2256
2Ki 5:20 I will run a him and get something from H339
2Ki 5:21 So Gehazi hurried a Naaman. When H339
2Ki 6: 8 A conferring with his officers, he said, "I H2256
2Ki 6:20 A they entered the city, Elisha said, "LORD H3869
2Ki 6:23 and a they had finished eating and H2256
2Ki 7:14 the king sent them a the Aramean army. H339
2Ki 10:15 A he left there, he came upon Jehonadab H2256
2Ki 14: 5 A the kingdom was firmly in his H3869+889
2Ki 14:17 fifteen years a the death of Jehoash H339
2Ki 14:19 they sent men a him to Lachish and H339
2Ki 14:22 restored it to Judah a Amaziah rested with H339
2Ki 18: 5 kings of Judah, either before him or a him. H339
2Ki 23:25 Neither before nor a Josiah was there a H339
1Ch 2:24 A Hezron died in Caleb Ephrathah, Abijah H339
1Ch 6:31 house of the LORD a the ark came to rest H4946
1Ch 8: 8 Shaharaim in Moab a he had divorced his H4946
1Ch 12:19 Philistines because, a consultation, their H928
1Ch 12:22 Day a day men came to help David, until H928
1Ch 14:14 "Do not go directly a them, but circle H339
1Ch 15: 1 A David had constructed buildings for H2256
1Ch 16: 2 A David had finished sacrificing the burnt H2256
1Ch 16:23 the earth; proclaim his salvation day a day. H448
1Ch 17: 1 A David was settled in his palace H3869+889
1Ch 19:16 A the Arameans saw that they had been H2256
2Ch 1:12 you ever had and none a you will have." H339
2Ch 2:17 a the census his father David had taken H339
2Ch 5:10 with the Israelites a they came out of Egypt H928
2Ch 9:24 Year a year, everyone who came brought a H928
2Ch 10:16 Look a your own house, David!" So H8011
2Ch 12: 1 A Rehoboam's position as king was H3869
2Ch 20: 1 A this, the Moabites and Ammonites with H339
2Ch 20:21 A consulting the people, Jehoshaphat H2256
2Ch 20:23 A they finished slaughtering the men H3869
2Ch 20:36 A these were built at Ezion Geber H2256
2Ch 21:18 A all this, the LORD afflicted Jehoram with H339
2Ch 22: 4 a his father's death they became his H339
2Ch 24:17 A the death of Jehoiada, the officials of H339
2Ch 25: 3 A the kingdom was firmly in his H3869+889
2Ch 25:17 A Amaziah king of Judah consulted his H2256
2Ch 25:25 fifteen years a the death of Jehoash H339
2Ch 25:27 they sent men a him to Lachish and H339
2Ch 26: 2 restored it to Judah a Amaziah rested with H339
2Ch 26:16 But a Uzziah became powerful, his pride H3869
2Ch 31: 1 A they had destroyed all of them, the H6330
2Ch 32: 1 A all that Hezekiah had so faithfully done H339
2Ch 35:14 A this, they made preparations for H339
2Ch 35:20 A all this, when Josiah had set the temple H339
Ezr 3: 5 A that, they presented the regular burnt H339
Ezr 3: 8 of the second year a their arrival at the H4200
Ezr 7: 1 A these things, during the reign of H339
Ezr 9: 1 A these things had been done, the H3869
Ezr 9:10 what can we say a this? For we have H339
Ne 2:11 to Jerusalem, and a staying there three days NDT
Ne 4:14 A I looked things over, I stood up and said H2256
Ne 7: 1 A the wall had been rebuilt and I H3869+889
Ne 8:18 Day a day, from the first day to the last H928
Ne 9:28 you delivered them time a time. H8041+6961
Est 3: 1 A these events, King Xerxes honored H339
Est 3: 4 Day a day they spoke to him but he H2256
Job 3: 1 A this, Job opened his mouth and cursed H339
Job 5: 5 and the thirsty pant a his wealth. AIT
Job 10: 6 search out my faults and probe a my sin— H4200
Job 13:25 windblown leaf? Will you chase a dry chaff? AIT
Job 19:26 And a my skin has been destroyed, yet in H339
Job 21: 3 while I speak, and a I have spoken, mock H339
Job 21:33 everyone follows a them, and a countless H339
Job 29:22 A I had spoken, they spoke no more; my H339
Job 31: 5 my foot has hurried a deceit— H6584
Job 37: 4 A that comes the sound of his roar; he H339
Job 37:21 as it is in the skies a the wind has swept H2256
Job 42: 7 A the LORD had said these things to Job, he H339
Job 42:10 A Job had prayed for his friends, the LORD H928
Job 42:16 A this, Job lived a hundred and forty years H339
Ps 13: 2 my thoughts and day a day have sorrow in H3429
Ps 16: 4 Those who run a other gods will suffer more AIT
Ps 19: 2 Day a day they pour forth speech; night H4200
Ps 19: 2 night a night they reveal knowledge. H4200
Ps 49:11 they had named lands a themselves. H928
Ps 51: T Nathan came to him a David had H3869+889
Ps 59: 2 save me from those who are a my blood. AIT
Ps 61: 8 of your name and fulfill my vows day a day. AIT
Ps 68:25 front are the singers, a them the musicians H339
Ps 78:38 Time a time he restrained his anger and H8049
Ps 96: 2 proclaim his salvation day a day. H4200
Pr 1:19 of all who go a ill-gotten gain; H1298+1299
Pr 6:25 Do not lust in your heart a her beauty H2773
Pr 8:30 I was filled with delight day a day, rejoicing AIT
Pr 20: 7 blessed are their children a them. H339
Pr 24:27 your fields ready; a that, build your house. H339
Pr 29: 1 remains stiff-necked a many rebukes will NDT
Ecc 1:14 are meaningless, a chasing a the wind. H8296
Ecc 1:17 that this, too, is a chasing a the wind. H8301
Ecc 2:11 meaningless, a chasing a the wind H8296
Ecc 2:17 it is meaningless, a chasing a the wind. H8296
Ecc 2:18 leave them to the one who comes a me. H339
Ecc 2:26 too is meaningless, a chasing a the wind. H8296
Ecc 3:22 them to see what will happen a them? H339
Ecc 4: 4 too is meaningless, a chasing a the wind. H8296
Ecc 4: 6 handfuls with toil and chasing a the wind. H8296
Ecc 4:16 too is meaningless, a chasing a the wind. H8301
Ecc 6: 9 too is meaningless, a chasing a the wind. H8296
Ecc 6:12 happen under the sun a they are gone? H339
Ecc 10:14 else what will happen a them? H4946+339
Ecc 11: 1 a many days you may receive a return. H928
Ecc 12: 2 and the clouds return a the rain; H339
Isa 1:23 they all love bribes and chase a gifts. H8103
Isa 5:11 early in the morning to run a their drinks, H8103
Isa 21: 8 shouted, "Day a day, my lord, H9458+3429
Isa 24:13 are left a the grape harvest. H3983+561
Isa 24:22 in prison and be punished a many days. H4946
Isa 28:19 you away; morning a morning, by day and H928
Isa 38: 9 Hezekiah king of Judah a his illness and H928
Isa 43:10 was formed, nor will there be one a me. H339
Isa 53:11 A he has suffered, he will see the light of H4946
Isa 58: 2 For day a day they seek me out; they seem AIT
Isa 62:12 you will be called Sought A, the City H2011
Isa 64:12 A all this, LORD, will you hold yourself H6584
Jer 2:23 am not defiled; I have not run a the Baals'? H339
Jer 2:25 I love foreign gods, and I must go a them.' H339
Jer 3: 7 I thought that a she had done all this she H339
Jer 3:15 I will give you shepherds a my own heart, H3869
Jer 7:25 until now, day a day, again and again H3427
Jer 12:15 But a I uproot them, I will again have H339
Jer 13:10 of their hearts and go a other gods to serve H339
Jer 16:16 A that I will send for many hunters, and H339
Jer 21: 7 A that, declares the LORD, I will give H339
Jer 24: 1 A Jehoiachin son of Jehoiakim king of H339
Jer 25:26 near and far, one a the other—all the H448
Jer 25:26 And a all of them, the king of Sheshak will H339
Jer 28:12 A the prophet Hananiah had broken the H339
Jer 29: 2 This was a King Jehoiachin and the queen H339
Jer 31:19 A I strayed, I repented; after I came to H339
Jer 31:19 I repented; a I came to understand, I beat H339
Jer 31:33 make with the people of Israel a that time," H339
Jer 32:16 "A I had given the deed of purchase to H339
Jer 32:18 sins into the laps of their children a them. H339
Jer 32:39 well for them and for their children a them. H339
Jer 34: 8 from the LORD a King Zedekiah had made H339
Jer 34:14 A they have served you six years, you H2256
Jer 36:13 A Micaiah told them everything he had H2256
Jer 36:20 A they put the scroll in the room of H2256
Jer 36:27 A the king burned the scroll containing the H339
Jer 37:11 A the Babylonian army had withdrawn from H928
Jer 39:12 "Take him and look a him H8492+6524+6584
Jer 40: 1 from the LORD a Nebuzaradan commander H339
Jer 40: 4 and I will look a you; but H8492+6524+6584
Jer 41: 4 The day a Gedaliah's assassination H9108
Jer 41:16 son of Nethaniah a Ishmael had H339
La 1: 3 A affliction and harsh labor, Judah has H4946
Eze 4: 6 "A you have finished this, lie down again H2256
Eze 6: 9 their eyes, which have lusted a their idols. H339
Eze 15: 4 And a it is thrown on the fire as fuel and the NDT
Eze 16:28 were insatiable; and even a that, you still H2256
Eze 16:34 no one runs a you for your favors. H2388+339
Eze 20:24 their eyes lusted a their parents' idols. H339
Eze 20:30 did and lust a their vile images H2388+339
Eze 23: 5 and she lusted a her lovers H6311+6584
Eze 23: 7 all the idols of everyone she lusted a. H6311
Eze 23:12 She too lusted a the Assyrians H6311+448
Eze 23:16 she lusted a them and sent H6311+6584
Eze 23:17 A she had been defiled by them, she H2256
Eze 23:20 There she lusted a her lovers H6311+6584
Eze 23:30 because you lusted a the nations H2388+339
Eze 34:11 will search for my sheep and look a them. H1329
Eze 34:12 As a shepherd looks a his scattered flock H1333
Eze 34:12 he is with them, so will I look a my sheep. H1329
Eze 38: 8 A many days you will be called to arms. In H4946
Eze 39:14 " 'A the seven months they will H4946+7895
Eze 40: 1 in the fourteenth year a the fall of the city— H339
Eze 44:10 who wandered from me a their idols must H339
Eze 44:26 A he is cleansed, he must wait seven days. H339
Eze 46:12 shall go out, and a he has gone out, the H339
Eze 48:31 city will be named a the tribes of Israel. H6584
Da 1: 5 and a that they were to enter the H4946+7921
Da 2:39 "A you, another kingdom will arise A10092
Da 4: 8 Belteshazzar, a the name of my god A10341
Da 7: 6 "A that, I looked, and there before me A10092
Da 7: 7 "A that, in my vision at night I looked A10092
Da 7:24 A them another king will arise, different A10021
Da 8: 1 a the one that had already appeared to me H339
Da 9:26 A the sixty-two 'sevens,' the Anointed One H339
Da 11: 4 A he has arisen, his empire will be broken H3869
Da 11: 6 A some years, they will become H4200+7891
Da 11:13 the first; and a several years, he H4200+7891
Da 11:19 A this, he will turn back toward the H2256
Da 11:23 A coming to an agreement with him, he H4946
Hos 1: 8 A she had weaned Lo-Ruhamah, Gomer H2256
Hos 2: 5 She said, 'I will go a my lovers, who give H339
Hos 2: 7 She will chase a her lovers but not catch H8103
Hos 2:13 jewelry, and went a her lovers, but me H339
Hos 6: 2 A two days he will revive us; on the third H4946
Am 7: 1 swarms of locusts a the king's share had H339
Jnh 1: 3 A paying the fare, he went aboard and H2256
Zec 2: 8 "A the Glorious One has sent me against H339
Zec 14:16 go up year a year to worship H4946+1896+928
Mt 1:12 A the exile to Babylon: Jeconiah was the G3552
Mt 1:20 But a he had considered this, an angel of the AIT
Mt 2: 1 A Jesus was born in Bethlehem in Judea AIT
Mt 2: 9 A they had heard the king, they went on their AIT
Mt 2:19 A Herod died, an angel of the Lord appeared AIT
Mt 3:11 But a me comes one who is more G3958
Mt 4: 2 A fasting forty days and forty nights, he G5731
Mt 6:32 For the pagans run a all these things, and G2118
Mt 9:25 A the crowd had been put outside, he G4021
Mt 11: 1 A Jesus had finished instructing his G4021
Mt 14:23 A he had dismissed them, he went up on a AIT
Mt 15:23 her away, for she keeps crying out a us." G3957
Mt 15:39 A Jesus had sent the crowd away, he got into AIT
Mt 17: 1 A six days Jesus took with him Peter G3552
Mt 17:24 A Jesus and his disciples arrived in AIT
Mt 21:32 And even a you saw this, you did not G5731
Mt 24:29 "Immediately a the distress of those days G3552
Mt 25:19 "A a long time the master of those G3552
Mt 25:36 I was sick and you looked a me, I was in G2170
Mt 25:43 in prison and you did not look a me. G2170
Mt 26:22 sad and began to say to him one a the other, AIT
Mt 26:32 But a I have risen, I will go ahead G3552+3836
Mt 26:73 A a little while, those standing there went G3552
Mt 27:31 A they had mocked him, they took off the G4021
Mt 27:34 with gall; but a tasting it, he refused to AIT
Mt 27:53 out of the tombs a Jesus' resurrection G3552
Mt 27:62 next day, the one a Preparation Day, the G3552
Mt 27:63 'A three days I will rise again.' G3552
Mt 28: 1 A the Sabbath, at dawn on the first day of G4067
Mk 1: 7 "A me comes the one more powerful than G3958
Mk 1:14 A John was put in prison, Jesus went into G3552
Mk 1:32 That evening a sunset the people brought G4021
Mk 5:40 A he put them all out, he took the child's AIT
Mk 6:46 A leaving them, he went up on a AIT
Mk 7:17 A he had left the crowd and entered the G4021
Mk 7:33 A he took him aside, away from the crowd AIT
Mk 8: 9 A he had sent them away, AIT
Mk 8:31 must be killed and a three days rise again G3552
Mk 9: 2 A six days Jesus took Peter, James and G3552
Mk 9:28 A Jesus had gone indoors, his disciples AIT
Mk 9:31 will kill him, and a three days he will rise." G3552
Mk 14:28 But a I have risen, I will go ahead G3552+3836
Mk 14:70 A a little while, those standing near said G3552
Mk 16: 2 the week, just a sunrise, they G422+3836+2463
Mk 16:14 those who had seen him a he had risen. AIT
Mk 16:19 A the Lord Jesus had spoken to G3552+3836

Lk 1:24 **A** this his wife Elizabeth became pregnant *G3552*
Lk 1:59 going to name him **a** his father Zechariah *G2093*
Lk 2:36 her husband seven years **a** her marriage, *G608*
Lk 2:43 *A* the festival *was* **over**, while his parents AIT
Lk 2:46 **A** three days they found him in the temple *G3552*
Lk 5:27 **A** this, Jesus went out and saw a tax *G3552*
Lk 5:39 And no one *a* **drinking** old wine wants the AIT
Lk 7:24 *A* John's messengers **left**, Jesus began to AIT
Lk 8: 1 **A this**, Jesus traveled about *G1877+3836+2759*
Lk 8: 4 coming to Jesus **from town a town**, *G2848+4484*
Lk 9:28 About eight days **a** Jesus said this, he *G3552*
Lk 10: 1 **A** this the Lord appointed seventy-two *G3552*
Lk 10:35 '**Look a** him,' he said, 'and when I return *G2150*
Lk 12: 4 kill the body and **a** that can do no more. *G3552*
Lk 12: 5 him who, **a** your body has been killed *G3552*
Lk 12:30 For the pagan world **runs a** all such things *G2118*
Lk 15: 4 open country and go **a** the lost sheep *G2093*
Lk 15:13 "Not long **a** that, the younger son got *G3552*
Lk 15:14 *A* he *had* **spent** everything, there was a AIT
Lk 17: 7 a servant plowing or **looking a the sheep**. *G4477*
Lk 17: 8 drink; **a** that you may eat and drink'? *G3552*
Lk 17:23 ' Do not go **running off a** them. *G1503*
Lk 19:14 him and sent a delegation **a** him to say, *G3958*
Lk 19:28 *A* Jesus *had* **said** this, he went on ahead AIT
Lk 22:17 *A* **taking** the cup, he gave thanks and said AIT
Lk 22:20 same way, **a** the supper he took the cup *G3552*
Jn 1:15 'He who comes **a** me has surpassed me *G3958*
Jn 1:27 He is the one who comes **a** me, the straps *G3958*
Jn 1:30 'A man who comes **a** me has surpassed *G3958*
Jn 2:10 the cheaper wine **a** the guests have had *G4020*
Jn 2:12 **A** this he went down to Capernaum with *G3552*
Jn 2:22 **A** he was raised from the dead, his *G4021*
Jn 3:22 **A** this, Jesus and his disciples went out *G3552*
Jn 4:43 **A** the two days he left for Galilee. *G3552*
Jn 4:54 Jesus performed *a* **coming** from Judea to AIT
Jn 6: 1 **Some time a this**, Jesus crossed to *G3552+4047*
Jn 6:14 *A* the people **saw** the sign Jesus performed AIT
Jn 6:23 eaten the bread *a* the Lord *had* **given thanks**. AIT
Jn 7: 1 **A** this, Jesus went around in Galilee. He *G3552*
Jn 7: 9 *A he had* **said** this, he stayed in Galilee. AIT
Jn 7:10 **a** his brothers had left for the festival *G6055*
Jn 9: 6 *A* **saying** this, he spit on the ground, made AIT
Jn 11:11 **A** he had said this, he went on to tell *G3552*
Jn 11:28 *A she had* **said** this, she went back and AIT
Jn 12:16 Only **a** Jesus was glorified did they realize *G4021*
Jn 12:19 how the whole world has gone **a** him!" *G3958*
Jn 12:37 Even *a* Jesus *had* **performed** so many signs AIT
Jn 13: 5 **A that**, he poured water into a basin and *G1663*
Jn 13:21 *A he had* **said** this, Jesus was troubled in AIT
Jn 14: 9 even *a I have* **been** among you such a long AIT
Jn 16:16 then *a a* **little while** you will see me. AIT
Jn 16:17 then *a a* **little while** you will see me AIT
Jn 16:19 then *a a* **little while** you will see me'? AIT
Jn 17: 1 *A* Jesus **said** this, he looked toward heaven AIT
Jn 20:20 *A he* **said** this, he showed them his hands AIT
Jn 21:14 his disciples *a he was* **raised** from the dead. AIT
Ac 1: 2 *a* **giving instructions** through the Holy Spirit AIT
Ac 1: 3 **A** his suffering, he presented himself to *G3552*
Ac 1: 9 *A he* **said** this, he was taken up before their AIT
Ac 4:21 *A* **further threats** they let them go. AIT
Ac 4:31 *A* they **prayed**, the place where they were AIT
Ac 5: 4 And *a it was* **sold**, wasn't the money at your AIT
Ac 5:37 **A** him, Judas the Galilean appeared in *G3552*
Ac 5:42 **Day a day**, in the temple courts and *G4246+2465*
Ac 7: 4 **A** the death of his father, God sent him to *G3552*
Ac 7: 5 his descendants **a** him would possess *G3552*
Ac 7: 8 circumcised him eight **days** *a* his birth. AIT
Ac 7:14 **A this**, Joseph sent for his father Jacob *G1254*
Ac 7:30 "*A* forty years *had* **passed**, an angel AIT
Ac 7:45 *A* **receiving** the tabernacle, our ancestors AIT
Ac 8:25 *A* they *had further* **proclaimed** the word of AIT
Ac 9:19 and *a* **taking** some food, he regained his AIT
Ac 9:23 **A** many days had gone by, there was a *G6055*
Ac 10:37 beginning in Galilee **a** the baptism that *G3552*
Ac 10:41 drank with him **a** he rose from the *G3552+3836*
Ac 12: 4 *A* **arresting** him, he put him in prison AIT
Ac 12: 4 him out for public trial **a** the Passover. *G3552*
Ac 12:19 *A* Herod *had* **a thorough search made** for him AIT
Ac 12:20 *A* **securing** *the* **support** *of* Blastus, a trusted AIT
Ac 13: 3 So *a they had* **fasted** and prayed, they placed AIT
Ac 13:15 **A** the reading from the Law and the *G3552*
Ac 13:20 "**A** this, God gave them judges until the *G3552*
Ac 13:22 *A* **removing** Saul, he made David their king AIT
Ac 13:22 son of Jesse, a man **a** my own heart; he *G2848*
Ac 13:25 is one coming **a** me whose sandals I *G3552*
Ac 14:20 But *a* the disciples *had* **gathered around** him AIT
Ac 14:24 *A* **going through** Pisidia, they came into AIT
Ac 15: 7 **A** much discussion, Peter got up and *G1181*
Ac 15:16 " '**A** this I will return and rebuild David's *G3552*
Ac 15:33 *A* **spending** some time there, they were sent AIT
Ac 16:10 **A** Paul had seen the vision, we got ready *G6055*
Ac 16:23 *A* they *had been* severely **flogged**, they were AIT
Ac 16:40 *A* Paul and Silas **came out** of the prison, they AIT
Ac 18: 1 **A** this, Paul left Athens and went to *G3552*
Ac 18:23 *A* **spending** some time in Antioch, Paul set AIT
Ac 19: 4 to believe in the one coming **a** him, *G3552*
Ac 19:21 **A** all this had happened, Paul decided to *G6055*
Ac 19:21 "**A** I have been there," he said, "I *G3552+3836*
Ac 19:41 *A he had* **said** this, he dismissed the AIT
Ac 20: 1 disciples and, *a* **encouraging** them, said AIT
Ac 20: 6 we sailed from Philippi **a** the Festival of *G3552*
Ac 20:11 bread and ate. *A* **talking** until daylight, he AIT
Ac 20:15 The **day a that** we crossed over to Samos *G2283s*
Ac 20:29 I know that **a** I leave, savage wolves will *G3552*
Ac 20:30 in order to draw away disciples **a** them. *G3958*
Ac 21: 1 **A** we had torn ourselves away from them *G6055*
Ac 21: 3 *A* **sighting** Cyprus and passing to the south of AIT
Ac 21: 6 *A* **saying goodbye** to each other, we went AIT
Ac 21:10 *A we had* **been there** a number of days, a AIT
Ac 21:15 **A** this, we started on our way up to *G3552*
Ac 21:40 *A* **receiving** the commander's **permission** AIT
Ac 24:17 "**A** an absence of several years, I came to *G1328*
Ac 25: 1 Three days **a** arriving in the province *G3552*
Ac 25: 6 *A* **spending** eight or ten days with them AIT
Ac 25:12 **A** Festus had conferred with his council *G5538*
Ac 26:31 *A they* **left** the room, they began saying to AIT
Ac 27: 9 because by now *it was* **a** the Day of *G4216*
Ac 27:21 *A they had* **gone** a long time without food AIT
Ac 27:35 *A he* **said** this, he took some bread and gave AIT
Ac 28: 6 but *a* **waiting** a long time and seeing AIT
Ac 28: 8 in to see him and, *a* **prayer**, placed his hands AIT
Ac 28:11 **A** three months we put out to sea in a *G3552*
Ac 28:25 leave *a* Paul *had* **made** this final **statement**: AIT
Ro 4:10 Was it *a he* **was** circumcised, or AIT
Ro 4:10 It was not **a**, but before! *G1877+4364s*
Ro 11:24 **A all**, if you were cut out of an olive tree *G1142*
Ro 15:24 **a** I have enjoyed your company for a *G4754*
Ro 15:28 So *a I have* **completed** this task and have AIT
1Co 3: 5 **a all**, is Apollos? And what is Paul *G4036*
1Co 9:27 my slave so that *a I have* **preached** to others, AIT
1Co 11:25 **a** supper he took the cup *G3552+3836*
1Co 15: 6 **A that**, he appeared to more than five *G2083*
1Co 15:24 to God the Father **a** he has destroyed all *G4020*
1Co 15:46 the natural, **and a that** the spiritual. *G2083*
1Co 16: 5 **A** I go through Macedonia, I will come to *G4020*
2Co 12:14 **A all**, children should not have to save up *G1142*
Gal 1:18 Then **a** three years, I went up to *G3552*
Gal 2: 1 Then **a** fourteen years, I went up again to *G1328*
Gal 3: 3 *A* **beginning** by means of the Spirit, are you AIT
Eph 5:29 **A all**, no one ever hated their own body *G1142*
Eph 6:13 and *a you have* **done** everything, to AIT
Col 4:16 **A** this letter has been read to you, see *G4020*
1Th 4:17 **A that**, we who are still alive and are left *G2083*
Titus 3:10 them a second time. **A** that, have nothing *G3552*
Heb 1: 3 *A he had* **provided** purification for sins, he AIT
Heb 6:15 And so *a* **waiting patiently**, Abraham received AIT
Heb 7:27 need to offer sacrifices **day a day**, *G2848+2465*
Heb 7:28 the oath, which *came* **a** the law *G3552*
Heb 8:10 with the people of Israel **a** that time, *G3552*
Heb 9:27 to die once, and **a** that to face judgment, *G3552*
Heb 10: 1 repeated endlessly **year a year**, *G2848+1929*
Heb 10:11 **Day a day** every priest stands and *G2848+2465*
Heb 10:16 I will make with them **a** that time, *G3552*
Heb 10:26 keep on sinning **a** we have *G3552+3836*
Heb 10:32 earlier days *a you had* **received** *the* **light**, AIT
Heb 11:23 hid him for three months *a he was* **born**, AIT
Heb 11:30 *a the army had* **marched around** them for AIT
Jas 1:15 *a* desire *has* **conceived**, it gives birth to AIT
Jas 1:24 *a* **looking at** himself, goes away and AIT
Jas 1:27 *to* **look a** orphans and widows in their *G2170*
1Pe 3:19 *A being* **made alive**, he went and made AIT
1Pe 5:10 in Christ, *a you have* **suffered** a little while AIT
2Pe 1:15 effort to see that **a** my departure you will *G3552*
2Pe 2: 8 living among them **day a day**, was *G1666*
Rev 4: 1 **A** this I looked, and there before me was *G3552*
Rev 4: 1 will show you what must take place **a** this." *G3552*
Rev 7: 1 **A** this I saw four angels standing at the *G3552*
Rev 7: 9 **A** this I looked, and there before me was *G3552*
Rev 11:11 But **a** the three and a half days the breath *G3552*
Rev 15: 5 **A** this I looked, and I saw in heaven the *G3552*
Rev 18: 1 **A** this I saw another angel coming down *G3552*
Rev 19: 1 **A** this I heard what sounded like the roar *G3552*
Rev 20: 3 **A** that, he must be set free for a short *G3552*

AFTERBIRTH (1)

Dt 28:57 the **a** from her womb and the children she H8953

AFTERNOON (15)

Jdg 19: 8 Wait till **a**!" So the two of H5742+2021+3427
Mt 20: 5 about **three in the a** and did the *G1888*
Mt 20: 6 About **five in the a** he went out and found *G1895*
Mt 20: 9 hired about **five in the a** came and *G1895+6052*
Mt 27:45 noon until **three in the a** darkness *G6052+1888*
Mt 27:46 About **three in the a** Jesus cried out *G1888+6052*
Mk 15:33 the whole land until **three in the a.** *G6052+1888*
Mk 15:34 And *at* **three in the a** Jesus *G3836+1888+6052*
Lk 9:12 **Late in the a** the Twelve *G3836+2465+806+3111*
Lk 23:44 the whole land until **three in the a,** *G6052+1888*
Jn 1:39 It was about **four in the a.** *G6052+1281*
Jn 4:52 *at* **one in the a,** the fever *G6052+1575*
Ac 3: 1 time of prayer—*at* **three in the a.** *G3836+1888*
Ac 10: 3 about **three in the a** he *G6052+1888+3836+2465*
Ac 10:30 at this hour, *at* **three in the a.** *G3836+1888*

AFTERWARD (35) [AFTER]

Ge 4: 4 days—and also **a**—when the sons of H339+4027
Ge 15:14 and **a** they will come out with great H339+4027
Ge 23:19 **A** Abraham buried his wife Sarah in H339+4027
Ge 41:27 ugly cows that came up **a** are seven years H339
Ge 45:15 **A** his brothers talked with him. H339+4027
Ex 5: 1 **A** Moses and Aaron went to Pharaoh and H339
Ex 32: 6 **A** they sat down to eat and drink and got H2256
Ex 34:32 **A** all the Israelites came near him H339+4027
Lev 16:26 **a** he may come into the camp. H339+4027
Lev 16:28 **a** he may come into the camp. H339+4027
Jos 8:34 **A**, Joshua read all the words of the H339+4027
Jdg 7:11 **A**, you will be encouraged to attack the H339
Jdg 19: 6 **A** the woman's father said, "Please stay H2256
1Sa 9:13 bless the sacrifice; **a**, those who are H339+4027
1Sa 24: 5 **A**, David was conscience-stricken H339+4027
1Ki 14:28 **and a** they returned them to the H2256
1Ki 20:22 **A**, the prophet came to the king of Israel H2256
2Ch 12:11 **and a** they returned them to the H2256
2Ch 33:14 **A** he rebuilt the outer wall of the H339+4027
Est 6:12 **A** Mordecai returned to the king's gate H2256
Ps 73:24 counsel, and **a** you will take me into glory. H339
Ecc 9: 3 while they live, and **a** they join the dead. H339
Isa 1:26 **A** you will be called the City of H339+4027
Jer 34:11 But **a** they changed their minds and H339+4027
Jer 49: 6 "Yet **a**, I will restore the fortunes of H339+4027
Eze 20:39 But **a** you will surely listen to me and no H339
Hos 3: 5 **A** the Israelites will return and seek the LORD H339
Joel 2:28 "And **a**, I will pour out my Spirit on H339+4027
Mt 15:37 **A** the disciples picked up seven basketfuls *G2779*
Mk 8: 8 **A** the disciples picked up seven basketfuls *G2779*
Mk 16:12 **A** Jesus appeared in a different *G3552+4047*
Lk 7:11 **Soon a**, Jesus went to a *G1877+3836+2009*
Jn 21: 1 **A** Jesus appeared again to his *G3552+4047*
Ac 7: 7 'and **a** they will come out of that *G3552+4047*
Heb 12:17 **A**, as you know, when he wanted to inherit *G3575*

AGABUS (2)

Ac 11:28 One of them, named **A**, stood up and *G13*
Ac 21:10 a prophet named **A** came down from Judea. *G13*

AGAG (7) [AGAGITE]

Nu 24: 7 "Their king will be greater than **A**; their H97
1Sa 15: 8 He took **A** king of the Amalekites alive, and H97
1Sa 15: 9 the army spared **A** and the best of the H97
1Sa 15:20 Amalekites and brought back **A** their king. H97
1Sa 15:32 "Bring me **A** king of the Amalekites." H97
1Sa 15:32 of the Amalekites." **A** came to him in chains H97
1Sa 15:33 And Samuel put **A** to death before the LORD H97

AGAGITE (5) [AGAG]

Est 3: 1 of Hammedatha, the **A**, elevating him and H98
Est 3:10 of Hammedatha, the **A**, the enemy of the H98
Est 8: 3 put an end to the evil plan of Haman the **A**, H98
Est 8: 5 of Hammedatha, the **A**, devised and wrote H98
Est 9:24 of Hammedatha, the **A**, the enemy of all the H98

AGAIN (457)

Ge 4:25 Adam made love to his wife **a**, and she H6388
Ge 8:10 seven more days and **a** sent out the dove H3578
Ge 8:12 seven more days and sent the dove out **a**, H6388
Ge 8:21 "Never **a** will I curse the ground H3578+6388
Ge 8:21 And never **a** will I destroy all living H3578+6388
Ge 9:11 Never **a** will all life be destroyed by the H6388
Ge 9:11 never **a** will there be a flood to destroy H6388
Ge 9:15 Never **a** will the waters become a flood to H6388
Ge 18:27 Then Abraham spoke up **a**: "Now that I NDT
Ge 18:29 **Once a** he spoke to him, "What if H3578+6388
Ge 19:34 Let's get him to drink wine **a** tonight, and H1685
Ge 19:35 **A** he was not aware of it when she lay H2256
Ge 20:17 female slaves so they could have children **a**, NDT
Ge 23:12 **A** Abraham bowed down before the H2256
Ge 24:16 to the spring, filled her jar **and** came up *a.* AIT
Ge 29:33 She conceived **a**, and when she gave H6388
Ge 29:34 **A** she conceived, and when she gave H6388
Ge 29:35 She conceived **a**, and when she gave H6388
Ge 30: 7 Bilhah conceived **a** and bore Jacob a H6388
Ge 30:19 Leah conceived **a** and bore Jacob a sixth H6388
Ge 35: 9 God appeared to him **a** and blessed him. H6388
Ge 35:21 Israel moved on **a** and pitched his tent H2256
Ge 38: 4 She conceived **a** and gave birth to a son H6388
Ge 38:19 her veil **and** put on her widow's clothes **a**. H2256
Ge 38:26 And he did not sleep with her **a**. H3578+6388
Ge 40:21 so that *he once a* **put** the cup into Pharaoh's AIT
Ge 41: 5 He fell asleep **a** and had a second dream: H2256
Ge 42:24 then came back and spoke to them **a**. NDT
Ge 43: 3 will not see my face **a** unless your brother is NDT
Ge 43: 5 will not see my face **a** unless your brother is NDT
Ge 44:23 with you, you will not see my face **a**. H3578
Ge 46: 4 and I will surely bring you back **a**. H1685
Ge 48:11 "I never expected to see your face **a**, and NDT
Ex 8:29 not act deceitfully **a** by not letting the H3578
Ex 9:34 thunder had stopped, he sinned **a**: H3578
Ex 10:14 plague of locusts, nor will there ever be **a**. H339
Ex 10:28 sure you do not appear before me **a**! H3578
Ex 10:29 "I will never appear before you **a**." H3578+6388
Ex 11: 6 there has ever been or *ever will be* **a**. H3578
Ex 14:13 you see today you will never see **a**. H3578+6388
Ex 30: 8 must burn incense **a** when he lights the H2256
Lev 13: 6 day the priest is to examine them **a**, H9108
Lev 13: 7 they must appear before the priest **a**. H9108
Lev 13:55 the priest *is to* **examine** it *a*, and if the mold AIT
Lev 13:58 is rid of the mold, must be washed **a**. H9108
Lev 27:15 and the house *will a* **become** theirs. AIT
Lev 27:19 its value, and the field *will a* **become** theirs. AIT
Nu 6:11 day *they are to* **consecrate** their head *a.* AIT
Nu 11: 4 **a** the Israelites started wailing and H8740
Nu 11:25 they prophesied—but *did* not **do** *so* **a**. H3578
Nu 18: 5 my wrath will not fall on the Israelites **a**. H6388
Nu 20:20 **A** they answered: "You may not pass H2256
Nu 22:25 foot against it. So he beat the donkey **a**. H3578
Nu 32:15 he *will* **a** leave all this people in H3578+6388
Dt 9:18 Then **once a** I fell prostrate H3869+2021+8037

Dt 9:19 But **a** the LORD listened H1685+928+2021+7193+2021+2085
Dt 13:11 among you will do such an evil thing **a**. H3578
Dt 17:13 and will not be contemptuous **a**. H3578
Dt 17:16 "You are not to go back that way **a**." H3578+6388
Dt 19:20 and never **a** will such an evil thing H3578+6388
Dt 24: 4 allowed to marry her **a** after she has been H8740
Dt 24:21 your vineyard, *do* not **go over the vines a**. H6618
Dt 28:68 I said you *should* never **make a**. H3578+6388
Dt 30: 3 you and gather you **a** from all the nations H8740
Dt 30: 8 You will **a** obey the LORD and follow all his H8740
Dt 30: 9 The LORD will **a** delight in you and make H8740
Jos 5: 2 and circumcise the Israelites **a**." H8740+9108
Jos 24:10 so *he* **blessed** you **a and again** H1385+1385
Jos 24:10 so *he* **blessed** you **again and a** H1385+1385
Jdg 3:12 **A** the Israelites did evil in the eyes of the H3578
Jdg 3:15 **A** the Israelites cried out to the LORD, and H2256
Jdg 4: 1 **A** the Israelites did evil in the eyes of the H3578
Jdg 8:28 the Israelites and did not raise its head **a**. H3578
Jdg 8:33 than the Israelites **a** prostituted H8740
Jdg 9:37 But Gaal spoke up **a**: "Look, people H3578+6388
Jdg 10: 6 **A** the Israelites did evil in the eyes of the H3578
Jdg 13: 1 **A** the Israelites did evil in the eyes of the H3578
Jdg 13: 8 you sent to us come **a** to teach us how to H6388
Jdg 13: 9 angel of God came **a** to the woman while H6388
Jdg 13:21 the LORD *did* not show himself **a** to H3578+6388
Jdg 16:14 **A** she called to him, "Samson, the H2256
Jdg 16:22 hair on his head **began** to grow *a* after it had AIT
Jdg 20:22 one another and **a** took up their positions H3578
Jdg 20:23 "*Shall we* go up **a** to fight against the H3578
Jdg 20:28 "*Shall we* go up **a** to fight against H3578+6388
Ru 1:14 At this they wept aloud **a**. Then Orpah H6388
1Sa 3: 6 **A** the LORD called, "Samuel!" And H3578+6388
1Sa 9: 8 The servant answered him **a**. "Look," H3578
1Sa 15:35 he did not go to see Saul **a**, though H3578
1Sa 20:27 of the month, David's place was empty **a**. H2256
1Sa 23: 4 **Once a** David inquired of the LORD H3578+6388
1Sa 23:12 **A** David asked, "Will the citizens of H2256
1Sa 26:21 I will not try to harm you **a**. H6388
2Sa 2:22 **A** Abner warned Asahel, "Stop H3578+6388
2Sa 3:34 And all the people wept over him **a**. H3578
2Sa 6: 1 David **a** brought together all the able H6388
2Sa 12:23 Can I bring him back **a**? I will go to him, H6388
2Sa 14:10 and they will not bother you **a**." H3578+6388
2Sa 15:25 let me see it and his dwelling place **a**. NDT
2Sa 18:22 son of Zadok **a** said to Joab, H3578+6388
2Sa 20:10 Without being stabbed **a**, Amasa died H9101
2Sa 21:15 **Once a** there was a battle between the H6388
2Sa 21:17 "Never **a** will you go out with us to battle H6388
2Sa 24: 1 **A** the anger of the LORD burned against H3578
1Ki 10:10 Never **a** were so many spices brought in H6388
1Ki 12:24 the word of the LORD and went home **a**, H8740
1Ki 12:27 they *will* **a give** their **allegiance** to H8740+4213
1Ki 18:34 "**Do** *it* **a**," he said, and they did it again H9101
1Ki 18:34 he said, and *they* **did** *it* **a**. "Do it a third H9101
1Ki 18:37 that you are turning their hearts back **a**." NDT
1Ki 19: 6 He ate and drank and then lay down **a**. H8740
1Ki 20: 5 The messengers **came a** and said, "This H8740
1Ki 20:22 spring the king of Aram will attack you **a**." NDT
2Ki 2:21 Never **a** will it cause death or make the H6388
2Ki 5:17 servant will never **a** make burnt offerings H6388
2Ki 6:10 **Time and a** Elisha H4202+285+2256+4202+9109
2Ki 19: 9 So *he* **a** sent messengers to Hezekiah H8740
2Ki 21: 8 *I will* not **a** make the feet of the Israelites H3578
2Ki 24: 7 march out from his own country **a**, H3578+6388
1Ch 7:23 Then he made love to his wife **a**, and she NDT
1Ch 14:14 so David inquired of God **a**, and God H6388
2Ch 19: 4 he went out **a** among the people H8740
2Ch 28:17 The Edomites had **a** come and attacked H6388
2Ch 33: 8 *I will* not **a** make the feet of the Israelites H3578
2Ch 36:15 messengers **a and again**, H8899+2256+8938
2Ch 36:15 messengers **again and a**, H8899+2256+8938
Ezr 9:14 your commands **a** and intermarry with H8740
Ne 9:28 *they* **a** did what was evil in your sight. H8740
Ne 9:28 And when they cried out to you **a**, you H8740
Ne 13:21 If *you* **do** *this* **a**, I will arrest H9101
Est 1:19 that Vashti is **never** *a* to enter the presence of AIT
Est 5: 6 the king **a** asked Esther, "Now what H2256
Est 7: 2 the king **a** asked, "Queen Esther H1685
Est 8: 3 Esther **a** pleaded with the king, falling at H3578
Job 7: 7 my eyes will never see happiness **a**. H8740
Job 7:10 He will never come to his house **a**; his H6388
Job 10: 9 *Will you* now **turn** me to dust **a**? H8740
Job 10:16 me like a lion and **a** display your H8740
Job 14: 7 it will sprout **a**, and its new shoots H6388
Job 14:14 *will they* **live a**? All the days H2649
Job 16:14 **A and again** *he* **bursts** upon H7287+7288+7288
Job 16:14 **Again and a** *he* **bursts** upon H7287+7288+7288
Job 17:10 come on, all of you, **try a**! I will not find a H8740
Job 20: 9 The eye that saw him *will* not see him **a** H3578
Job 34:32 if I have done wrong, *I will* not **do** so **a**. H3578
Job 41: 8 remember the struggle and never **do** *it* **a**! H3578
Ps 3: 5 down and sleep; I wake **a**, because the LORD NDT
Ps 10:18 earthly mortals will never **a** strike terror. H3578
Ps 28: 5 tear them down and never **build** them **up** *a*. AIT
Ps 39:13 that *I may* **enjoy life** *a* before I depart and AIT
Ps 49:19 who will **never a** see the H6330+5905+4202
Ps 71:20 you will restore my life **a**; from the depths H8740
Ps 71:20 of the earth *you will* **a** bring me up. H8740
Ps 77: 7 Will he never show his favor **a**? H3578+6388
Ps 78:34 seek him; *they* eagerly **turned** *to* him **a**. H8740
Ps 78:41 **A and again** they put God to the test; they H8740
Ps 78:41 **Again and a** they put God to the test; they H8740
Ps 85: 4 **Restore** us **a**, God our Savior, and put H8740
Ps 85: 6 Will you not revive us **a**, that your people H8740
Ps 94:15 Judgment *will* **a** be founded on H8740
Ps 104: 9 never **a** will they cover the earth. H8740
Pr 19:19 and *you will have to* **do** it **a**. H3578+6388
Pr 24:16 seven times, they rise **a**, but the wicked H2256
Ecc 1: 7 streams come from, there they return **a**. H8740
Ecc 1: 9 What has been *will* **be** *a*, what has been AIT
Ecc 1: 9 what has been done *will* **be done** *a*; there is AIT
Ecc 4: 1 **A** I looked and saw all the oppression H8740
Ecc 4: 7 **A** I saw something meaningless under H8740
Ecc 9: 6 never **a** will they have a part in anything H6388
SS 5: 3 have taken off my robe—must I put it on **a**? NDT
SS 5: 3 have washed my feet—must I soil them **a**? NDT
Isa 6:13 in the land, *it will* **a** be laid waste. H8740
Isa 7:10 **A** the LORD spoke to Ahaz, H3578
Isa 8: 5 The LORD spoke to me **a**: H3578+6388
Isa 14: 1 **once a** he will choose Israel and will H6388
Isa 14:20 the wicked never be mentioned **a**. H4200+6409
Isa 21:12 would ask, then ask; and come **back** yet **a**." H8740
Isa 24:20 its rebellion that it falls—never to rise **a**. H3578
Isa 34:10 will **ever** pass through it **a**. H4200+5905+5905
Isa 38:11 "I will not **a** see the LORD himself in the land NDT
Isa 43:17 they lay there, never *to* **rise** *a*, extinguished, AIT
Isa 51:22 goblet of my wrath, you will never drink **a**. H6388
Isa 52: 1 and defiled will not enter you **a**. H3578+6388
Isa 54: 9 of Noah would never **a** cover the earth. H6388
Isa 54: 9 to be angry with you, never to rebuke you **a**. NDT
Isa 60:20 Your sun will never set **a**, and your moon H6388
Isa 62: 8 "Never **a** will I give your grain as food H6388
Isa 62: 8 never **a** will foreigners drink the new NDT
Isa 65:20 "Never **a** will there be in it an infant who H6388
Jer 1:13 The word of the LORD came to me **a** H9108
Jer 2: 9 "Therefore I bring charges against you **a**," H6388
Jer 3: 1 another man, should he return to her **a**? H6388
Jer 6: 9 **pass** your hand over the branches **a**, like H8740
Jer 7:13 I spoke to you **a and again**, but you did H8899
Jer 7:13 I spoke to you **again and a**, but you did H8899
Jer 7:25 **a and again** I sent you my servants the H8899
Jer 7:25 **again and a** I sent you my servants the H8899
Jer 11: 7 I warned them **a and again**, saying, H8899
Jer 11: 7 I warned them **again and a**, saying, H8899
Jer 12:15 *I will* **a** have compassion and will bring H8740
Jer 22:10 will never return nor see his native land **a**. NDT
Jer 22:12 him captive; he will not see this land **a**." H6388
Jer 23:36 not mention 'a message from the LORD' **a**, H6388
Jer 25: 3 I have spoken to you **a and again**, H8899
Jer 25: 3 I have spoken to you **again and a**, H8899
Jer 25: 4 servants the prophets to you **a and again**, H8899
Jer 25: 4 servants the prophets to you **again and a**, H8899
Jer 26: 5 whom I have sent to you **a and again** H8899
Jer 26: 5 whom I have sent to you **again and a** H8899
Jer 29:19 I sent to them **a and again** by my servants H8899
Jer 29:19 I sent to them **again and a** by my servants H8899
Jer 30:10 Jacob *will* **a** have peace and security, and H8740
Jer 31: 4 I will build you up **a**, and you, Virgin H6388
Jer 31: 4 **A** you will take up your timbrels and go H6388
Jer 31: 5 **A** you will plant vineyards on the hills of H6388
Jer 31:23 in its towns will **once a** use these words: H6388
Jer 31:40 The city will never **a** be uprooted or H6388
Jer 32:15 vineyards will **a** be bought in this H6388
Jer 32:33 though I taught them **a and again**, they H8899
Jer 32:33 though I taught them **again and a**, they H8899
Jer 33:12 all its towns there will **a** be pastures for H6388
Jer 33:13 flocks will **a** pass under the hand of the H6388
Jer 34:11 slaves they had freed and enslaved them **a**. NDT
Jer 34:16 have forced them to become your slaves **a**. NDT
Jer 35:14 But I have spoken to you **a and again**, yet H8899
Jer 35:14 But I have spoken to you **again and a**, yet H8899
Jer 35:15 **A and again** I sent all my servants the H8899
Jer 35:15 **Again and a** I sent all my servants the H8899
Jer 42:18 reproach; you will never see this place **a**. H6388
Jer 44: 4 **A and again** I sent my servants the H8899
Jer 44: 4 **Again and a** I sent my servants the H8899
Jer 44:26 in Egypt will **ever a** invoke my name or H6388
Jer 46:27 Jacob *will* **a** have peace and security, and H8740
Jer 50:39 It will never **a** be inhabited or lived in H6388
La 3: 3 turned his hand against me **a and again**, H8740
La 3: 3 turned his hand against me **again and a**, H8740
Eze 3:20 "**A**, when a righteous person turns from H2256
Eze 4: 6 finished this, lie down **a**, this time on your H2256
Eze 5: 4 **A**, take a few of these and throw them into H6388
Eze 5: 9 never done before and will never do **a**. H6388
Eze 8:13 **A**, he said, "You will see them doing H2256
Eze 11:17 I will give you back the land of Israel **a**. NDT
Eze 16:63 ashamed and never **a** open your mouth H6388
Eze 17:14 unable *to* **rise a**, surviving only by H5951
Eze 21: 5 sword from its sheath; it will not return **a**. H6388
Eze 22:23 **A** the word of the LORD came to me: H2256
Eze 24:13 you will not be clean **a** until my wrath H6388
Eze 26:21 you will never **a** be found, declares H6388
Eze 29:15 will never **a** exalt itself above the H6388
Eze 29:15 so weak that it will **never** *a* rule over the AIT
Eze 36:12 *you will* never **a** deprive them of H3578+6388
Eze 36:16 **A** the word of the LORD came to me: H2256
Eze 36:37 Once **a** I will yield to Israel's plea and do H6388
Eze 37:22 they will never **a** be two nations or be H6388
Eze 43: 7 Israel will never **a** defile my holy name— H6388
Da 10:18 **A** the one who looked like a man touched H3578
Da 11:29 time he will invade the South **a**, H8740
Hos 1: 6 Gomer conceived **a** and gave birth to a H6388
Hos 3: 1 show your love to your wife **a**, though she H6388
Hos 10: 9 *Will* not war **a overtake** the evildoers in AIT
Hos 11: 9 nor *will I* devastate Ephraim **a**. H8740
Hos 12: 9 I will make you live in tents **a**, as in the H6388
Hos 14: 3 We will never **a** say 'Our gods' to what H6388
Hos 14: 7 People will dwell **a** in his shade; they will H8740
Joel 2:19 never **a** will I make you an object of scorn H6388
Joel 2:26 **never a** will my people be H4202+4200+6409
Joel 2:27 **never a** will my people be H4202+4200+6409
Joel 3:17 never **a** will foreigners invade her. H6388
Am 5: 2 never to rise **a**, deserted in her own H3578
Am 8:14 they will fall, never to rise **a**. H6388
Am 9:15 never **a** to be uprooted from the land I H6388
Jnh 2: 4 yet *I will* look **a** toward your holy temple. H3578
Mic 1: 7 wages of prostitutes *they will* **a be used**." H8740
Mic 7:19 *You will* **a** have compassion on us; you H8740
Zep 3:11 Never **a** will you be haughty on my H6388+3578
Zep 3:15 with you; never **a** will you fear any harm. H6388
Zec 1:17 'My towns will **a** overflow with prosperity H6388
Zec 1:17 the LORD will **a** comfort Zion and H6388
Zec 2:12 holy land and will **a** choose Jerusalem. H6388
Zec 4:12 **A** I asked him, "What are these two olive H9108
Zec 5: 1 I looked **a**, and there before me was a H8740
Zec 6: 1 I looked up **a**, and there before me were H8740
Zec 7: 8 the word of the LORD came **a** to Zechariah: NDT
Zec 8: 4 "**Once a** men and women of ripe old age H6388
Zec 8:15 to do good **a** *to* Jerusalem and Judah. H8740
Zec 9: 8 Never **a** will an oppressor overrun my H6388
Zec 11:15 "Take **a** the equipment of a foolish H6388
Zec 14:11 be inhabited; never **a** will it be destroyed. H6388
Mal 3:18 And you will **a** see the distinction between H8740
Mt 4: 8 **A**, the devil took him to a very high *G4099*
Mt 5:13 its saltiness, how can it be made salty **a**? NDT
Mt 5:22 **A**, anyone who says to a brother or sister *G1254*
Mt 5:33 "**A**, you have heard that it was said to the *G4099*
Mt 12:29 "**Or a**, how can anyone enter a strong *G2445*
Mt 13:44 man found it, he hid it **a**, and then in his joy NDT
Mt 13:45 "**A**, the kingdom of heaven is like a *G4099*
Mt 13:47 "**Once a**, the kingdom of heaven is like a *G4099*
Mt 18:19 "**A**, truly I tell you that if two of you on *G4099*
Mt 19:24 **A** I tell you, it is easier for a camel to go *G4099*
Mt 20: 5 "He went out **a** about noon and about *G4099*
Mt 21:19 "May you never bear fruit **a**!" *G1650+3836+172*
Mt 22: 1 Jesus spoke to them **a** in parables, saying: *G4099*
Mt 23:39 you will not see me **a** until you say *G608+785*
Mt 24:21 now—and **never** to be equaled **a**. *G4024+3590*
Mt 25:14 "**A**, it will be like a man going on a *G1142*
Mt 26:43 he came back, he **a** found them sleeping *G4099*
Mt 26:72 He denied it **a**, with an oath: "I don't *G4099*
Mt 27:30 and **struck** him on the head *a and again*. AIT
Mt 27:30 and **struck** him on the head *again and a*. AIT
Mt 27:50 Jesus had cried out **a** in a loud voice, *G4099*
Mt 27:63 'After three days *I will* **rise a**. *G1586*
Mk 2: 1 when Jesus **a** entered Capernaum *G4099*
Mk 2:13 Once **a** Jesus went out beside the lake. A *G4099*
Mk 3:20 a house, and **a** a crowd gathered, so *G4099*
Mk 4: 1 **A** Jesus began to teach by the lake. The *G4099*
Mk 4:30 **A** he said, "What shall we say the *G2779*
Mk 5:10 he begged Jesus **a and again** not to send *G4498*
Mk 5:10 he begged Jesus **again and a** not to send *G4498*
Mk 5:21 When Jesus had **a** crossed over by boat to *G4099*
Mk 7:14 **A** Jesus called the crowd to him and said *G4099*
Mk 8:31 must be killed and after three days **rise a**. *G482*
Mk 9:25 come out of him and **never** enter him **a**." *G3600*
Mk 9:50 its saltiness, how can you make it salty **a**? NDT
Mk 10: 1 **A** crowds of people came to him, and as *G4099*
Mk 10:10 When they were in the house **a**, the *G4099*
Mk 10:24 But Jesus said **a**, "Children, how hard it is *G4099*
Mk 10:32 **A** he took the Twelve aside and told them *G4099*
Mk 11:14 "May no one ever eat fruit from you **a**." *G3600*
Mk 11:27 They arrived **a** in Jerusalem, and while *G4099*
Mk 13:19 now—and **never** to be equaled **a**. *G4024+3590*
Mk 14:25 I will not drink **a** from the fruit of the vine *G4033*
Mk 14:40 he came back, he **a** found them sleeping *G4099*
Mk 14:61 **A** the high priest asked him, "Are you the *G4099*
Mk 14:69 she said **a** to those standing around *G4099*
Mk 14:70 **A** he denied it. After a little while, those *G4099*
Mk 15: 4 So **a** Pilate asked him, "Aren't you going *G4099*
Mk 15:19 *A and again they* **struck** him on the head with AIT
Mk 15:19 *Again and a they* **struck** him on the head with AIT
Lk 13:20 **A** he asked, "What shall I compare the *G4099*
Lk 13:35 you will **not** see me **a** until you say *G4024+3590*
Lk 14:34 its saltiness, how *can it be* **made salty** *a*? AIT
Lk 15:24 this son of mine was dead and *is* **alive a**; *G348*
Lk 15:32 brother of yours was dead and *is* **alive a**; *G2409*
Lk 18:33 On the third day *he will* **rise a**." *G482*
Lk 22:16 I will **not** eat it **a** until it finds *G4024+3590*
Lk 22:18 I will not drink **a** from the fruit *G608+3836+3814*
Lk 23:20 release Jesus, Pilate appealed to them **a**. *G4099*
Lk 24: 7 crucified and on the third day *be* **raised a**. *G482*
Jn 1:35 next day John was there **a** with two of his *G4099*
Jn 2:19 temple, and *I will* **raise** it **a** in three days." *G1586*
Jn 3: 3 the kingdom of God unless they are born **a**." *G540*
Jn 3: 7 at my saying, 'You must be born **a**. *G540*
Jn 4:13 who drinks this water will be thirsty **a**, *G4099*
Jn 5:14 said to him, "See, *you* **are** well *a*. AIT
Jn 6:15 withdrew **a** to a mountain by himself. *G4099*
Jn 8: 2 At dawn he appeared **a** in the temple *G4099*
Jn 8: 8 **A** he stooped down and wrote on the *G4099*
Jn 8:12 When Jesus spoke **a** to the people, he *G4099*
Jn 9:17 Then they turned **a** to the blind man *G4099*
Jn 9:27 Why do you want to hear it **a**? Do you *G4099*

Jn 10: 7 Therefore Jesus said **a**, "Very truly I tell *G4099*
Jn 10:17 I lay down my life—only to take it up **a**. *G4099*
Jn 10:18 lay it down and authority to take it up **a**. *G4099*
Jn 10:19 who heard these words were **a** divided. *G4099*
Jn 10:31 **A** his Jewish opponents picked up stones *G4099*
Jn 10:39 **A** they tried to seize him, but he escaped *G4099*
Jn 11:23 Jesus said to her, "Your brother *will* **rise a**." *G482*
Jn 11:24 "I know he *will* **rise a** in the resurrection at *G482*
Jn 12:28 "I have glorified it, and will glorify it **a**." *G4099*
Jn 16:22 I will see you **a** and you will rejoice *G4099*
Jn 18: 7 **A** he asked them, "Who is it you want?" *G4099*
Jn 18:27 **A** Peter denied it, and at that moment a *G4099*
Jn 18:38 this he went out **a** to the Jews gathered *G4099*
Jn 19: 3 and **went** up to him *a and again*, saying AIT
Jn 19: 3 and **went** up to him *again and a*, saying AIT
Jn 20:21 **A** Jesus said, "Peace be with you! As the *G4099*
Jn 20:26 later his disciples were in the house **a**, *G4099*
Jn 21: 1 Jesus appeared **a** to his disciples, *G4099*
Jn 21:16 **A** Jesus said, "Simon son of John *G4099+1309*
Ac 4:18 Then *they* **called** them **in** *a* and commanded AIT
Ac 8:39 the eunuch did not see him **a**, but *G4033*
Ac 9:17 me so that *you may* **see a** and be filled *G329*
Ac 9:18 fell from Saul's eyes, and *he could* **see a**. *G329*
Ac 11:10 then it was all pulled up to heaven **a**. *G4099*
Ac 17:32 "We want to hear you **a** on this subject." *G4099*
Ac 20:11 Then *he* **went upstairs** *a* and broke bread AIT
Ac 20:25 **none** of you … will **ever** see me **a** *G4033+4246*
Ac 20:38 that they would **never** see his face **a**. *G4033*
Ac 27: 4 From there *we* **put out to sea** *a* and passed to AIT
Ac 27:28 they took soundings **a** and found it was *G4099*
Ro 6: 9 the dead, he **cannot** die **a**; death no *G4033*
Ro 8:15 so that you live in fear **a**; rather, *G4099*
Ro 10:19 **A** I ask: Did Israel not understand? First *G247*
Ro 11:11 **A** I ask: Did they stumble so as to fall *G4036*
Ro 11:23 for God is able to graft them in **a**. *G4099*
Ro 15:10 **A**, it says, "Rejoice, you Gentiles, with his *G4099*
Ro 15:11 And **a**, "Praise the Lord, all you Gentiles *G4099*
Ro 15:12 And **a**, Isaiah says, "The Root of Jesse *G4099*
Ro 15:15 on some points to **remind** you of them **a**, *G2057*
1Co 3:20 **a**, "The Lord knows that the thoughts *G4099*
1Co 7: 5 Then come together **a** so that Satan will *G4099*
1Co 8:13 I will **never** eat meat **a** *G4024+3590+1650+3836+172*
1Co 14: 8 **A**, if the trumpet does not sound a clear *G2779*
2Co 1:10 such a deadly peril, and *he will* **deliver** us *a*. AIT
2Co 3: 1 we beginning to commend ourselves **a**? *G4099*
2Co 5:12 not trying to commend ourselves to you **a**, *G4099*
2Co 5:15 him who died for them and *was* **raised a**. *G1586*
2Co 10: 7 they should consider **a** that we belong to *G4099*
2Co 11:23 been exposed to death **a and again**. *G4490*
2Co 11:23 been exposed to death **again and a**. *G4490*
2Co 12:21 that when I come **a** my God will humble *G4099*
Gal 1: 9 so now I say **a**: If anybody is *G4099*
Gal 2: 1 I went up **a** to Jerusalem, this time *G4099*
Gal 3: 5 So **a** I ask, does God give you his Spirit and NDT
Gal 4: 9 to be enslaved by them **all over a**? *G4099+540*
Gal 4:19 whom I am **a** in the pains of childbirth *G4099*
Gal 5: 1 be burdened **a** by a yoke of slavery. *G4099*
Gal 5: 3 **A** I declare to every man who lets himself *G4099*
Php 1:26 my being with you **a** your boasting in *G4099*
Php 2:28 when you see him **a** you may be glad *G4099*
Php 3: 1 me to write the **same** *things* to you *a*, AIT
Php 3:18 you before and **now** tell you *a* even with AIT
Php 4: 4 in the Lord always. I will say it **a**: Rejoice! *G4099*
1Th 2:18 **a** and again—but Satan blocked our *G562*
1Th 2:18 again and **a**—but Satan blocked our *G1489*
1Th 3:10 earnestly that *we may* **see** you *a* and supply AIT
1Th 4:14 For we believe that Jesus died and **rose a** *G482*
Heb 1: 5 Or **a**, "I will be his Father, and he will be *G4099*
Heb 1: 6 And **a**, when God brings his firstborn into *G4099*
Heb 2:13 And **a**, "I will put my trust in him." And *G4099*
Heb 2:13 And **a** he says, "Here am I, and the *G4099*
Heb 4: 5 And **a** in the passage above he says *G4099*
Heb 4: 7 God **a** set a certain day, calling it "Today." *G4099*
Heb 5:12 truths of God's word **all over a**. *G4099*
Heb 6: 1 not laying **a** the foundation of repentance *G4099*
Heb 6: 6 *they are* **crucifying** the Son of God **all over a** *G416*
Heb 9:25 heaven to offer himself **a and again**, *G4490*
Heb 9:25 heaven to offer himself **again and a**, *G4490*
Heb 10:11 **a and again** he offers the same sacrifices *G4490*
Heb 10:11 **again and a** he offers the same sacrifices *G4490*
Heb 10:30 I will repay," and **a**, "The Lord will judge *G4099*
Heb 11:35 received back their dead, **raised to life a**. *G414*
Jas 5:18 **A** he prayed, and the heavens gave rain *G4099*
1Pe 1:23 *For you have been* **born a**, not of perishable *G335*
2Pe 2:20 Jesus Christ and are **a** entangled in it *G4099*
Rev 2: 8 the Last, who died and **came to life a**. *G2409*
Rev 3:12 Never **a** will they leave it. I *G2285*
Rev 7:16 'Never **a** will they hunger; never again *G2285*
Rev 7:16 will they hunger; never **a** will they thirst. *G2285*
Rev 10:11 must prophesy **a** about many peoples *G4099*
Rev 18:21 will be thrown down, never to be found **a**. *G2285*
Rev 18:22 trumpeters, will never be heard in you **a**. *G2285*
Rev 18:22 of any trade will ever be found in you **a**. *G2285*
Rev 18:22 a millstone will never be heard in you **a**. *G2285*
Rev 18:23 light of a lamp will never shine in you **a**. *G2285*
Rev 18:23 bride will never be heard in you **a**. *G2285*
Rev 19: 3 And **a** they shouted: "Hallelujah! The *G1309*

AGAINST (1324)

Ge 13:13 were sinning greatly **a** the LORD. H4200
Ge 14: 2 kings **went to war** *a* Bera king of Sodom, AIT
Ge 14: 9 **a** Kedorlaomer king of Elam, Tidal king of H907
Ge 14: 9 Arioch king of Ellasar—four kings **a** five. H907
Ge 16:12 his hand will be **a** everyone and everyone's H928
Ge 16:12 everyone and everyone's hand **a** him, H928
Ge 18:20 "The **outcry** *a* Sodom and Gomorrah is so AIT
Ge 19:13 The **outcry** to the LORD *a* its people is so great AIT
Ge 20: 6 so I have kept you from sinning **a** me. H4200
Ge 20:16 to cover the offense **a** you before all who H4200
Ge 27:41 Esau **held a grudge a** Jacob because of H8475
Ge 34:30 if they join forces **a** me and attack me, H6584
Ge 39: 9 I do such a wicked thing and sin **a** God?" H4200
Ge 42:22 "Didn't I tell you not to sin **a** the boy? H928
Ge 42:36 to take Benjamin. Everything is **a** me!" H6584
Ge 50:15 if Joseph **holds a grudge a** us and pays us H8475
Ex 1:10 enemies, fight **a** us and leave the country." H928
Ex 4:14 LORD's anger burned **a** Moses and he said, H928
Ex 7: 5 stretch out my hand **a** Egypt and bring the H6584
Ex 9:14 force of my plagues **a** you and against your H448
Ex 9:14 against you and **a** your officials and your H928
Ex 9:17 You still set yourself **a** my people and will H928
Ex 10:16 "I have sinned **a** the LORD your God and H4200
Ex 10:16 against the LORD your God and **a** you. H4200
Ex 14:25 The LORD is fighting for them **a** Egypt." H928
Ex 14:31 hand of the LORD displayed **a** the Egyptians, H928
Ex 15:24 So the people grumbled **a** Moses, saying H6584
Ex 16: 2 community grumbled **a** Moses and Aaron. H6584
Ex 16: 7 he has heard your grumbling **a** him. H6584
Ex 16: 7 that you should grumble **a** us? H6584
Ex 16: 8 he has heard your grumbling **a** him. H6584
Ex 16: 8 You are not grumbling against us, but against H6584
Ex 16: 8 not grumbling against us, but **a** the LORD." H6584
Ex 17: 3 water there, and they grumbled **a** Moses. H6584
Ex 17:16 hands were lifted up **a** the throne of the H6584
Ex 17:16 LORD will be at war **a** the Amalekites from H928
Ex 19:22 the LORD will break out **a** them. H928
Ex 19:24 up to the LORD, or he will break out **a** them." H928
Ex 20:16 not give false testimony **a** your neighbor. H928
Ex 23:21 Do not rebel **a** him; he will not forgive your H928
Ex 23:33 land or they will cause you to sin **a** me, H4200
Ex 24: 6 the other half he splashed **a** the altar. H6584
Ex 24:11 not raise his hand **a** these leaders of the H448
Ex 29:16 blood and splash it **a** the sides of the H6584
Ex 29:20 Then splash blood **a** the sides of the altar. H6584
Ex 32:10 my anger may burn **a** them and that I may H928
Ex 32:11 "why should your anger burn **a** your people, H928
Ex 32:29 you were **a** your own sons and brothers H928
Ex 32:33 "Whoever has sinned **a** me I will blot out H4200
Lev 1: 5 blood and splash it **a** the sides of the H6584
Lev 1:11 splash its blood **a** the sides of the altar H6584
Lev 3: 2 splash the blood **a** the sides of the altar H6584
Lev 3: 8 splash its blood **a** the sides of the altar H6584
Lev 3:13 splash its blood **a** the sides of the altar H6584
Lev 5: 9 of the sin offering **a** the side of the altar; H6584
Lev 5:19 been guilty of wrongdoing **a** the LORD." H4200
Lev 7: 2 is to be splashed **a** the sides of the altar. H6584
Lev 7:14 blood of the fellowship offering **a** the altar. NDT
Lev 8:19 splashed the blood **a** the sides of the H6584
Lev 8:24 he splashed blood **a** the sides of the altar H6584
Lev 9:12 he splashed it **a** the sides of the altar. H6584
Lev 9:18 he splashed it **a** the sides of the altar. H6584
Lev 17: 6 to splash the blood **a** the altar of the LORD H6584
Lev 17:10 " 'I will set my face **a** any Israelite or any H928
Lev 19:18 revenge or **bear a grudge a** anyone H5757
Lev 20: 3 will set my face **a** him and will cut him H928
Lev 20: 5 will set my face **a** him and his family and H928
Lev 20: 6 " 'I will set my face **a** anyone who turns to H928
Lev 26:17 I will set my face **a** you so that you will be H928
Lev 26:22 I will send wild animals **a** you, and they will H928
Nu 5:13 there is no witness **a** her and she has not H928
Nu 10: 9 in your own land **a** an enemy who is H6584
Nu 11:33 the anger of the LORD burned **a** the people H928
Nu 12: 1 Aaron began to talk **a** Moses because of H928
Nu 12: 8 not afraid to speak **a** my servant Moses?" H928
Nu 12: 9 The anger of the LORD burned **a** them, and H928
Nu 12:11 ask you not to hold **a** us the sin we have H6584
Nu 14: 2 Israelites grumbled **a** Moses and Aaron, H6584
Nu 14: 9 Only do not rebel **a** the LORD. And do not be H928
Nu 14:27 this wicked community grumble **a** me? H6584
Nu 14:29 the census and who has grumbled **a** me. H6584
Nu 14:34 know what it is like to have me **a** you. H9481
Nu 14:35 which has banded together **a** me. H6584
Nu 14:36 community grumble **a** him by spreading a H6584
Nu 16: 2 rose up **a** Moses. With them H4200+7156
Nu 16:11 It is **a** the LORD that you and all your H6584
Nu 16:11 is Aaron that you should grumble **a** him?" H6584
Nu 16:41 community grumbled **a** Moses and Aaron. H6584
Nu 17: 5 constant grumbling **a** you by the Israelites H6584
Nu 17:10 an end to their grumbling **a** me, H4946+6584
Nu 18:17 Splash their blood **a** the altar and burn H6584
Nu 18:23 any offenses they commit **a** it. NDT
Nu 20:20 Then Edom came out **a** them with a large H7925
Nu 20:24 both of you rebelled **a** my command at the H907
Nu 21: 5 they spoke **a** God and against Moses, and H928
Nu 21: 5 they spoke against God and **a** Moses, and H928
Nu 21: 7 when we spoke **a** the LORD and against H928
Nu 21: 7 when we spoke against the LORD and **a** you. H928
Nu 21:23 marched out into the wilderness **a** Israel. H7925
Nu 21:26 who had fought **a** the former king of Moab H928
Nu 22:25 to the wall, crushing Balaam's foot **a** it. H448
Nu 23:23 There is no divination **a** Jacob, no evil H928
Nu 23:23 against Jacob, no evil omens **a** Israel. H928
Nu 24:10 Then Balak's anger burned **a** Balaam. He H448
Nu 25: 3 And the LORD's anger burned **a** them. H928
Nu 25: 8 Then the plague **a** the Israelites H4946+6584
Nu 26: 9 who rebelled **a** Moses and Aaron and H6584
Nu 26: 9 followers when they rebelled **a** the LORD. H6584
Nu 27: 3 who banded together **a** the LORD, but he H6584
Nu 31: 3 your men to go to war **a** the Midianites so H6584
Nu 31: 7 They fought **a** Midian, as the LORD H6584
Nu 32:13 LORD's anger burned **a** Israel and he made H928
Nu 32:23 you will be sinning **a** the LORD; and you H4200
Dt 1:26 you rebelled **a** the command of the LORD H907
Dt 1:41 you replied, "We have sinned **a** the LORD. H4200
Dt 1:43 You rebelled **a** the LORD's command and in H907
Dt 1:44 who lived in those hills came out **a** you; H7925
Dt 2:15 The LORD's hand was **a** them until he had H928
Dt 4:26 earth as witnesses **a** you this day that you H928
Dt 5:20 not give false testimony **a** your neighbor. H928
Dt 6:15 jealous God and his anger will burn **a** you, H928
Dt 7: 4 anger will burn **a** you and will quickly H928
Dt 7:24 one will be able to stand up **a** you; H928+7156
Dt 8:19 I testify **a** you today that you will surely be H928
Dt 9: 2 "Who can stand up **a** the Anakites?" H4200+7156
Dt 9: 7 you have been rebellious **a** the LORD. H6640
Dt 9:16 that you had sinned **a** the LORD your God; H4200
Dt 9:23 But you rebelled **a** the command of the H907
Dt 9:24 been rebellious **a** the LORD ever since H6640
Dt 11:17 Then the LORD's anger will burn **a** you, and H928
Dt 11:25 No one will be able to stand **a** you H7156+928
Dt 13: 5 inciting rebellion **a** the LORD your God, H6584
Dt 15: 9 They may then appeal to the LORD **a** you H6584
Dt 19:18 giving false testimony **a** a fellow Israelite, H928
Dt 20: 1 When you go to war **a** your enemies and H6584
Dt 20: 3 you are going into battle **a** your enemies. H6584
Dt 20: 4 you to fight for you **a** your enemies to give H6640
Dt 20:18 you will sin **a** the LORD your God. H4200
Dt 20:19 a long time, fighting **a** it to capture it, do H6584
Dt 21:10 When you go to war **a** your enemies and H6584
Dt 23: 9 When you are encamped **a** your enemies H6584
Dt 24:15 Otherwise they may cry to the LORD **a** you H6584
Dt 28: 7 enemies who rise up **a** you will be H6584
Dt 28:48 serve the enemies the LORD sends **a** you. H928
Dt 28:49 will bring a nation **a** you from far away, H6584
Dt 29: 7 Og king of Bashan came out to fight **a** us, H7925
Dt 29:20 his wrath and zeal will burn **a** them. H928
Dt 29:27 the LORD's anger burned **a** this land, H928
Dt 30:19 the earth as witnesses **a** you that I have set H928
Dt 31:19 so that it may be a witness for me **a** them. H928
Dt 31:21 this song will testify **a** them H4200+7156
Dt 31:26 There it will remain as a witness **a** you. H928
Dt 31:27 been rebellious **a** the LORD while I am H6640
Dt 31:28 heavens and the earth to testify **a** them. H928
Dt 32:23 on them and spend my arrows **a** them. H928
Dt 32:24 I will send wasting famine **a** them H928
Dt 32:24 I will send **a** them the fangs of wild beasts NDT
Dt 33: 7 Oh, be his help **a** his foes!" H4946
Dt 33:11 Strike down *those who* **rise** *a* him, his foes till AIT
Jos 1: 5 be able to stand **a** you all the days H4200+7156
Jos 1:18 Whoever rebels **a** your word and does not H907
Jos 7: 1 So the LORD's anger burned **a** Israel. H928
Jos 7: 3 "Not all the army *will have to* **go up** *a* Ai. AIT
Jos 7:12 cannot stand **a** their enemies; H4200+7156
Jos 7:13 You cannot stand **a** your enemies H4200+7156
Jos 7:20 I have sinned **a** the LORD, the God of Israel H4200
Jos 8: 5 when the men come out **a** us, as they H7925
Jos 8:14 had been set **a** him behind the city H4200
Jos 8:20 had turned back **a** their pursuers. H448
Jos 8:22 ambush also came out of the city **a** them, H7925
Jos 9: 2 together to wage war **a** Joshua and Israel. H6640
Jos 9:18 whole assembly grumbled **a** the leaders, H6584
Jos 10: 5 took up positions **a** Gibeon and attacked H6584
Jos 10: 6 the hill country have joined forces **a** us." H448
Jos 10:21 no one uttered a word **a** the Israelites. H4200
Jos 10:31 he took up positions **a** it and attacked it. H6584
Jos 10:34 they took up positions **a** it and attacked it. H6584
Jos 11: 5 at the Waters of Merom to fight **a** Israel. H6640
Jos 11: 7 his whole army came **a** them suddenly at H6584
Jos 11:18 Joshua waged war **a** all these kings for a H907
Jos 11:20 hardened their hearts to **wage war** *a* Israel, AIT
Jos 15:15 there he marched **a** the people living in H448
Jos 22:12 gathered at Shiloh to go to war **a** them. H6584
Jos 22:16 yourselves an altar in rebellion **a** him now? H928
Jos 22:18 " 'If you rebel **a** the LORD today, tomorrow H928
Jos 22:19 But do not rebel **a** the LORD or against us by H928
Jos 22:19 against the LORD or **a** us by building an H907
Jos 22:29 it from us to rebel **a** the LORD and turn away H928
Jos 22:33 about going to war **a** them to devastate H6584
Jos 23:16 the LORD's anger will burn **a** you, and you H928
Jos 24: 8 They fought **a** you, but I gave them into H907
Jos 24: 9 prepared to fight **a** Israel, he sent for H928
Jos 24:11 The citizens *of* Jericho fought **a** you, as did H928
Jos 24:22 "You are witnesses **a** yourselves that you H928
Jos 24:27 "This stone will be a witness **a** us. It has H928
Jos 24:27 It will be a witness **a** you if you are untrue H928
Jdg 1: 1 is to go up first to fight **a** the Canaanites?" H448
Jdg 1: 3 allotted to us, to fight **a** the Canaanites. H928
Jdg 1: 5 they found Adoni-Bezek and fought **a** him, H928
Jdg 1: 9 went down to fight **a** the Canaanites living H928
Jdg 1:10 They advanced **a** the Canaanites living in H448
Jdg 1:11 there they advanced **a** the people living in H448
Jdg 2:14 In his anger **a** Israel the LORD gave them H928
Jdg 2:15 of the LORD was **a** them to defeat them, H928
Jdg 3: 8 of the LORD burned **a** Israel so that he sold H928
Jdg 4:24 harder and harder **a** Jabin king of Canaan H6584

A

Jdg 5:13 of the LORD came down to me **a** the mighty. H928
Jdg 5:20 from their courses they fought **a** Sisera. H6640
Jdg 5:23 the LORD, to help the LORD **a** the mighty. H928
Jdg 7: 2 Israel *would* boast **a** me, 'My own H6584
Jdg 7: 9 "Get up, go down **a** the camp, because I H928
Jdg 7:24 "Come down **a** the Midianites and seize H7925
Jdg 8: 3 their resentment **a** him subsided. H4946+6584
Jdg 9:18 you have revolted **a** my father's family. H6584
Jdg 9:23 that they acted treacherously **a** Abimelek. H928
Jdg 9:24 in order that the **crime** *a* Jerub-Baal's seventy AIT
Jdg 9:31 are stirring up the city **a** you. H6584
Jdg 9:33 morning at sunrise, advance **a** the city. H6584
Jdg 9:33 When Gaal and his men come out **a** you H448
Jdg 9:45 pressed his attack **a** the city until he had H928
Jdg 9:49 They piled them **a** the stronghold and set H6584
Jdg 10: 9 also crossed the Jordan to fight **a** Judah, H928
Jdg 10:10 "We have sinned **a** you, forsaking our H4200
Jdg 11: 4 the Ammonites were fighting **a** Israel, H6640
Jdg 11:12 "What do you have **a** me that you have H4200
Jdg 11:27 are doing me wrong by waging war **a** me. H928
Jdg 11:29 from there *he* **advanced** *a* the Ammonites AIT
Jdg 12: 4 the men of Gilead and fought **a** Ephraim. H907
Jdg 16:26 the temple, so that I may lean **a** them." H6584
Jdg 16:29 Bracing himself **a** them, his right hand on H6584
Jdg 18:27 to Laish, **a** a people at peace and secure. H6584
Jdg 20: 9 We'll go up **a** it in the order decided by H6584
Jdg 20:11 got together and united as one **a** the city. H448
Jdg 20:14 at Gibeah to fight **a** the Israelites. H6640
Jdg 20:18 is to go up first to fight **a** the Benjamites?" H6640
Jdg 20:20 took up battle positions **a** them at Gibeah. H907
Jdg 20:23 we go up again to fight **a** the Benjamites, H6640
Jdg 20:23 The LORD answered, "Go up **a** them." H448
Jdg 20:28 we go up again to fight **a** the Benjamites, H6640
Jdg 20:30 They went up **a** the Benjamites on the third H448
Jdg 20:30 took up positions **a** Gibeah as they had H448
Ru 1:13 because the LORD's hand has turned **a** me!" H928
1Sa 2:25 If one person sins **a** another, God may H4200
1Sa 2:25 if anyone sins **a** the LORD, who will H4200
1Sa 3:12 time I will carry out **a** Eli everything I spoke H448
1Sa 3:12 Eli everything I spoke **a** his family— H448
1Sa 4: 1 went out to fight **a** the Philistines. H7925
1Sa 5: 9 the LORD's hand was **a** that city, throwing it H928
1Sa 7: 6 confessed, "We have sinned **a** the LORD." H4200
1Sa 7:10 with loud thunder **a** the Philistines and H6584
1Sa 7:13 the hand of the LORD was **a** the Philistines. H928
1Sa 12: 3 Testify **a** me in the presence of the LORD H928
1Sa 12: 5 "The LORD is witness **a** you, and also his H928
1Sa 12: 9 the king of Moab, who fought **a** them. H928
1Sa 12:12 king of the Ammonites was moving **a** you, H6584
1Sa 12:14 him and do not rebel **a** his commands, H907
1Sa 12:15 if you rebel **a** his commands, his hand H907
1Sa 12:15 his hand will be **a** you, as it was against H928
1Sa 12:15 be against you, as it was **a** your ancestors. H928
1Sa 12:23 me that I should sin **a** the LORD by failing H4200
1Sa 13:12 Philistines will come down **a** me at Gilgal, H448
1Sa 14:33 the men are sinning **a** the LORD by eating H4200
1Sa 14:34 Do not sin **a** the LORD by eating meat with H4200
1Sa 14:47 he fought **a** their enemies on every side: H928
1Sa 15:18 wage war **a** them until you have wiped H928
1Sa 17:19 Valley of Elah, fighting **a** the Philistines." H6640
1Sa 17:33 are not able to go out **a** this Philistine and H448
1Sa 17:45 "You come **a** me with sword and spear H448
1Sa 17:45 I come **a** you in the name of the LORD H448
1Sa 18:17 to himself, "I will not raise a hand **a** him. H928
1Sa 18:21 the hand of the Philistines may be **a** him." H928
1Sa 22: 8 Is that why you have all conspired **a** me H6584
1Sa 22:13 "Why have you conspired **a** me, you and H6584
1Sa 22:13 that he has rebelled **a** me and lies in wait H448
1Sa 23: 1 are fighting **a** Keilah and are looting H928
1Sa 23: 3 if we go to Keilah **a** the Philistine forces!" H448
1Sa 23: 9 learned that Saul was plotting **a** him, H6584
1Sa 24:14 "**A** whom has the king of Israel come out H339
1Sa 25:39 upheld my cause **a** Nabal for H4946+3338
1Sa 26:19 If the LORD has incited you **a** me, then may H928
1Sa 27:10 David would say, "**A** the Negev of Judah H6584
1Sa 27:10 of Judah" or "**A** the Negev of Jerahmeel H6584
1Sa 27:10 Jerahmeel" or "**A** the Negev of the Kenites." H448
1Sa 28: 1 gathered their forces to fight **a** Israel. H928
1Sa 28:15 "The Philistines are fighting **a** me, and H928
1Sa 28:18 carry out his fierce wrath **a** the Amalekites, H928
1Sa 29: 4 or *he will* **turn** *a* us during H2118+4200+8477
1Sa 29: 8 "What have you found **a** your servant from H928
1Sa 29: 8 can't I go and fight **a** the enemies of my H928
1Sa 30:23 hands the raiding party that came **a** us. H6584
1Sa 31: 1 Now the Philistines fought **a** Israel; the H928
2Sa 1:16 own mouth testified **a** you when you said, H928
2Sa 4: 8 my lord the king **a** Saul and his offspring." H4946
2Sa 5:20 the LORD *has* **broken out** *a* my enemies AIT
2Sa 6: 7 LORD's anger burned **a** Uzzah because of H928
2Sa 6: 8 the LORD's wrath had broken out **a** Uzzah, H928
2Sa 10: 9 deployed them **a** the Arameans. H7925
2Sa 10:10 deployed them **a** the Ammonites. H7925
2Sa 10:17 lines to meet David and fought **a** him. H6640
2Sa 11:17 of the city came out and fought **a** Joab, H907
2Sa 11:23 us and came out **a** us in the open, H448
2Sa 11:25 Press the attack **a** the city and destroy it.' H448
2Sa 12: 5 burned with anger **a** the man and said to H928
2Sa 12:13 said to Nathan, "I have sinned **a** the LORD." H4200
2Sa 12:26 Meanwhile Joab fought **a** Rabbah of the H928
2Sa 12:27 "I have fought **a** Rabbah and taken its H928
2Sa 14: 7 whole clan has risen up **a** your servant; H6584
2Sa 14:13 a thing like this **a** the people of God? H6584
2Sa 17:21 has advised such and such **a** you. H6584
2Sa 18:28 who lifted their hands **a** my lord the king." H928
2Sa 18:31 from the hand of all who rose up **a** you." H6584
2Sa 20:10 not on his guard **a** the dagger in Joab's H928
2Sa 20:15 and it stood **a** the outer fortifications. H928
2Sa 20:21 has lifted up his hand **a** the king, against H928
2Sa 20:21 up his hand against the king, **a** David. H928
2Sa 21: 5 us and plotted **a** us so that we have been H4200
2Sa 21:15 down with his men *to* **fight** *a* the Philistines, AIT
2Sa 22:30 With your help *I can* **advance** *a* a troop; with AIT
2Sa 23: 8 he raised his spear **a** eight hundred men H6584
2Sa 23:18 He raised his spear **a** three hundred men H6584
2Sa 23:21 his hand, Benaiah went **a** him with a club. H448
2Sa 24: 1 the anger of the LORD burned **a** Israel, H928
2Sa 24: 1 he incited David **a** them, saying, H928
2Sa 24:12 one of them for me to carry out **a** you. H4200
1Ki 5: 3 **waged a** my father David **from all sides**, H6015
1Ki 6: 5 **A** the walls of the main hall and inner H6584
1Ki 8:33 enemy because they have sinned **a** you, H4200
1Ki 8:35 because your people have sinned **a** you, H4200
1Ki 8:44 your people go to war **a** their enemies, H6584
1Ki 8:46 "When they sin **a** you—for there is no one H4200
1Ki 8:50 who have sinned **a** you; forgive all the H4200
1Ki 8:50 the offenses they have committed **a** you, H928
1Ki 11:14 the LORD raised up **a** Solomon an H4200
1Ki 11:23 And God raised up **a** Solomon another H4200
1Ki 11:26 Jeroboam son of Nebat rebelled **a** the king. H928
1Ki 11:27 the account of how he rebelled **a** the king: H928
1Ki 12:19 been in rebellion **a** the house of David to H928
1Ki 12:21 to go to war **a** Israel and to regain the H6640
1Ki 12:24 Do not go up to fight **a** your brothers, the H6640
1Ki 13: 2 word of the LORD he cried out **a** the altar: H6584
1Ki 13: 4 of God cried out **a** the altar at Bethel, H6584
1Ki 13:32 the word of the LORD **a** the altar in Bethel H6584
1Ki 13:32 altar in Bethel and **a** all the shrines on H6584
1Ki 15:17 of Israel went up **a** Judah and fortified H6584
1Ki 15:20 of his forces **a** the towns of Israel. H6584
1Ki 15:27 from the tribe of Issachar plotted **a** him, H6584
1Ki 16: 9 of half his chariots, plotted **a** him. H6584
1Ki 16:12 of the LORD spoken **a** Baasha through the H448
1Ki 16:16 heard that Zimri *had* **plotted** *a* the king and AIT
1Ki 17:18 "What do you have **a** me, man of God? H4200
1Ki 20:26 went up to Aphek to fight **a** Israel. H6640
1Ki 21:13 him and **brought charges a** Naboth before H6386
1Ki 22: 4 you go with me to fight **a** Ramoth Gilead?" NDT
1Ki 22: 6 "Shall I go to war **a** Ramoth Gilead, or H6584
1Ki 22:15 shall we go to war **a** Ramoth Gilead, or not H448
2Ki 1: 1 After Ahab's death, Moab rebelled **a** Israel. H928
2Ki 3: 5 king of Moab rebelled **a** the king of Israel. H928
2Ki 3: 7 "The king of Moab has rebelled **a** me. Will H928
2Ki 3: 7 Will you go with me to fight **a** Moab?" H448
2Ki 3:21 that the kings had come to fight **a** them; H928
2Ki 3:26 saw that the battle had gone **a** him, H4946
2Ki 3:27 The fury **a** Israel was great; they withdrew H6584
2Ki 6:32 shut the door and **hold** it **shut** *a* him. AIT
2Ki 8:20 rebelled **a** Judah and set H4946+9393+3338
2Ki 8:22 been in rebellion **a** Judah. H4946+9393+3338
2Ki 8:28 son of Ahab to war **a** Hazael king of Aram H6640
2Ki 9:14 the son of Nimshi, conspired **a** Joram. H448
2Ki 9:14 Ramoth Gilead **a** Hazael king of H4946+7156
2Ki 9:25 when the LORD spoke this prophecy **a** him: H6584
2Ki 10: 9 was I who conspired **a** my master and H6584
2Ki 10:10 the LORD has spoken **a** the house of Ahab H6584
2Ki 12:20 His officials **conspired** *a* him and AIT
2Ki 13: 3 So the LORD's anger burned **a** Israel, and H928
2Ki 13:12 including his war **a** Amaziah king of H6640
2Ki 14:15 including his war **a** Amaziah king of H6640
2Ki 14:19 They conspired **a** him in Jerusalem, and H6584
2Ki 15:10 son of Jabesh conspired **a** Zechariah. H6584
2Ki 15:25 Pekah son of Remaliah, conspired **a** him. H6584
2Ki 15:30 of Elah conspired **a** Pekah son of H6584
2Ki 15:37 Aram and Pekah son of Remaliah **a** Judah.) H928
2Ki 16: 5 of Israel **marched up** to fight *a* Jerusalem AIT
2Ki 16:13 of his fellowship offerings **a** the altar. H6584
2Ki 16:15 Splash **a** this altar the blood of all the H6584
2Ki 17: 5 **marched** *a* Samaria and laid siege to it for AIT
2Ki 17: 7 Israelites had sinned **a** the LORD their God, H4200
2Ki 17: 9 secretly did things **a** the LORD their God H6584
2Ki 18: 7 He rebelled **a** the king of Assyria and did H928
2Ki 18: 9 of Assyria marched **a** Samaria and laid H6584
2Ki 18:20 are you depending, that you rebel **a** me? H928
2Ki 18:25 told me to march **a** this country and H6584
2Ki 19: 8 found the king fighting **a** Libnah. H6584
2Ki 19: 9 of Cush, was marching out to fight **a** him. H907
2Ki 19:21 the word that the LORD has spoken **a** him: H6584
2Ki 19:22 **A** whom have you raised your voice and H6584
2Ki 19:22 eyes in pride? **A** the Holy One of Israel H6584
2Ki 19:27 you come and go and how you rage **a** me. H448
2Ki 19:28 Because you rage **a** me and because your H448
2Ki 19:32 it with shield or build a siege ramp **a** it. H6584
2Ki 21:13 the **measuring line** *used a* Samaria and AIT
2Ki 21:13 the **plumb line** *used a* the house of AIT
2Ki 21:23 officials conspired **a** him and H6584
2Ki 21:24 killed all who had plotted **a** King Amon, H6584
2Ki 22:13 anger that burns **a** us because those who H928
2Ki 22:17 my anger will burn **a** this place and will not H928
2Ki 22:19 what I have spoken **a** this place and its H6584
2Ki 23:17 pronounced **a** the altar of Bethel H6584
2Ki 23:26 which burned **a** Judah because of all that H928
2Ki 24: 1 But then he turned **a** Nebuchadnezzar and H928
2Ki 24: 2 Ammonite raiders **a** him to destroy Judah H928
2Ki 24:20 Zedekiah rebelled **a** the king of Babylon. H928
2Ki 25: 1 of Babylon marched **a** Jerusalem with his H6584
1Ch 5:10 reign they waged war **a** the Hagrites, H6640
1Ch 5:19 They waged war **a** the Hagrites, Jetur H6640
1Ch 10: 1 Now the Philistines fought **a** Israel; the H928
1Ch 11:11 he raised his spear **a** three hundred men H6584
1Ch 11:20 He raised his spear **a** three hundred men H6584
1Ch 11:23 his hand, Benaiah went **a** him with a club. H448
1Ch 12:19 went with the Philistines to fight **a** Saul. H6584
1Ch 12:21 They helped David **a** raiding bands, for all H6584
1Ch 13:10 The LORD's anger burned **a** Uzzah, and he H928
1Ch 13:11 the LORD's wrath had broken out **a** Uzzah, H928
1Ch 14:11 God *has* **broken out** *a* my enemies by my AIT
1Ch 15:13 the LORD our God broke out in anger **a** us. H928
1Ch 19:10 deployed them **a** the Arameans. H7925
1Ch 19:11 they were deployed **a** the Ammonites. H7925
1Ch 19:17 he advanced **a** them and formed his battle H448
1Ch 19:17 in battle, and they fought **a** him. H6640
1Ch 21: 1 Satan rose up **a** Israel and incited David H6584
1Ch 21:10 one of them for me to carry out **a** you. H4200
2Ch 6:24 they have sinned **a** you and when they H4200
2Ch 6:26 because your people have sinned **a** you, H4200
2Ch 6:34 your people go to war **a** their enemies, H6584
2Ch 6:36 "When they sin **a** you—for there is no one H4200
2Ch 6:39 your people, who have sinned **a** you. H4200
2Ch 10:19 been in rebellion **a** the house of David to H928
2Ch 11: 1 to go to war **a** Israel and to regain the H6640
2Ch 11: 4 Do not go up to fight **a** your fellow H6640
2Ch 11: 4 turned back from marching **a** Jeroboam. H448
2Ch 13: 3 drew up a battle line **a** him with eight H6640
2Ch 13: 6 son of David, rebelled **a** his master. H6584
2Ch 13:12 trumpets will sound the battle cry **a** you. H6584
2Ch 13:12 do not fight **a** the LORD, the God of H6640
2Ch 14: 9 Cushite marched out **a** them with an army H448
2Ch 14:11 you to help the powerless **a** the mighty. H1068
2Ch 14:11 name we have come **a** this vast army. H6584
2Ch 14:11 do not let mere mortals prevail **a** you." H6640
2Ch 16: 1 of Israel went up **a** Judah and fortified H6584
2Ch 16: 4 of his forces **a** the towns of Israel. H448
2Ch 17: 1 as king and strengthened himself **a** Israel. H6584
2Ch 17:10 they did not go to war **a** Jehoshaphat. H6640
2Ch 18: 3 "*Will you* **go** with me *a* Ramoth Gilead?" AIT
2Ch 18: 5 "Shall we go to war **a** Ramoth Gilead, or H448
2Ch 18:14 shall we go to war **a** Ramoth Gilead, or H448
2Ch 19:10 you are to warn them not to sin **a** the LORD H4200
2Ch 20: 1 came to wage war **a** Jehoshaphat. H6584
2Ch 20: 2 "A vast army is coming **a** you from Edom H6584
2Ch 20:16 Tomorrow march down **a** them. They will H6584
2Ch 20:22 LORD set ambushes **a** the men of Ammon H6584
2Ch 20:23 Moabites rose up **a** the men from Mount H6584
2Ch 20:29 the LORD had fought **a** the enemies of H6640
2Ch 20:37 of Mareshah prophesied **a** Jehoshaphat, H6584
2Ch 21: 8 rebelled **a** Judah and set H4946+9393+3338
2Ch 21:10 been in rebellion **a** Judah. H4946+9393+3338
2Ch 21:16 The LORD aroused **a** Jehoram the hostility H6584
2Ch 22: 5 Israel to wage war **a** Hazael king of Aram H6584
2Ch 24:19 though they testified **a** them, they H928
2Ch 24:21 But they plotted **a** him, and by order of H6584
2Ch 24:23 the army of Aram marched **a** Joash; it H6584
2Ch 24:25 officials conspired **a** him for murdering H6584
2Ch 24:26 Those who conspired **a** him were Zabad H6584
2Ch 25:15 The anger of the LORD burned **a** Amaziah H928
2Ch 25:27 they conspired **a** him in Jerusalem and he H6584
2Ch 26: 6 He went to war **a** the Philistines and broke H928
2Ch 26: 7 God helped him **a** the Philistines and H6584
2Ch 26: 7 the Philistines and **a** the Arabs who lived H6584
2Ch 26: 7 who lived in Gur Baal and **a** the Meunites. NDT
2Ch 26:13 force to support the king **a** his enemies. H6584
2Ch 27: 5 Jotham waged war **a** the king of the H6640
2Ch 28:10 also guilty of sins **a** the LORD your God? H4200
2Ch 29:22 took the blood and splashed it **a** the altar; H2025
2Ch 29:22 rams and splashed their blood **a** the altar; H2025
2Ch 29:22 splashed their blood **a** the altar. H2025
2Ch 30:16 The priests splashed **a** the altar the blood NDT
2Ch 32: 2 he intended to wage war **a** Jerusalem, H6584
2Ch 32:16 officers spoke further **a** the LORD God and H6584
2Ch 32:16 the LORD God and **a** his servant Hezekiah. H6584
2Ch 32:17 the God of Israel, and saying this **a** him: H6584
2Ch 33:11 So the LORD brought **a** them the army H6584
2Ch 33:24 officials conspired **a** him and H6584
2Ch 33:25 killed all who had plotted **a** King Amon, H6584
2Ch 34:27 heard what he spoke **a** this place and its H6584
2Ch 35:11 the priests splashed **a** the altar the blood NDT
2Ch 36: 8 he did and all that was found **a** him, H6584
2Ch 36:13 He also rebelled **a** King Nebuchadnezzar H928
2Ch 36:16 LORD was aroused **a** his people and there H928
2Ch 36:17 He brought up **a** them the king of the H6584
Ezr 4: 5 officials to work **a** them and frustrate their H6584
Ezr 4: 6 an accusation **a** the people of Judah H6584
Ezr 4: 8 wrote a letter **a** Jerusalem to Artaxerxes A10542
Ezr 4:19 history of revolt **a** kings and has been a A10542
Ezr 8:22 his great anger is **a** all who forsake him." H6584
Ne 1: 6 my father's family, have committed **a** you. H4200
Ne 2:19 "Are you rebelling **a** the king?" H6584
Ne 4: 8 to come and fight **a** Jerusalem and stir up H928
Ne 4: 8 against Jerusalem and stir up trouble **a** it. H4200
Ne 5: 1 raised a great outcry **a** their fellow Jews. H448
Ne 6:12 he had prophesied **a** me because Tobiah H6584
Ne 9:10 You sent signs and wonders **a** Pharaoh H928
Ne 9:10 **a** all his officials and all the people of his H928
Ne 9:26 they were disobedient and rebelled **a** you; H928
Ne 9:29 They sinned **a** your ordinances, of which H928
Ne 13:15 Therefore *I* **warned** them *a* selling food on AIT

Ne 13:18 up more wrath **a** Israel by desecrating H6584
Est 1:16 not only **a** the king but also against all H6584
Est 1:16 the king but also **a** all the nobles and the H6584
Est 4:16 even though it is **a** the law. H4202+3869
Est 5: 9 he was filled with rage **a** Mordecai. H6584
Est 6:13 you cannot stand **a** him—you will surely H4200
Est 8: 3 which he had devised **a** the Jews. H6584
Est 9: 2 No one could stand **a** them H4200+7156
Est 9:24 had plotted **a** the Jews to destroy them H6584
Est 9:25 Haman had devised **a** the Jews should H6584
Job 2: 3 though you incited me **a** him to ruin him H928
Job 6: 4 God's terrors *are* **marshaled** *a* me. AIT
Job 8: 4 When your children sinned **a** him, he H4200
Job 10: 2 tell me what **charges** *you have a* me. AIT
Job 10:16 again display your awesome power **a** me. H928
Job 10:17 bring new witnesses **a** me and increase H5584
Job 10:17 your forces come **a** me wave upon wave. H6640
Job 11: 5 that he would open his lips **a** you H6640
Job 13:19 Can anyone bring charges **a** me? If so, I H6643
Job 13:26 down bitter things **a** me and make me H6584
Job 15: 6 not mine; your own lips testify **a** you. H928
Job 15:13 you vent your rage **a** God and pour out H448
Job 15:25 at God and vaunts himself **a** the Almighty, H448
Job 15:26 defiantly charging **a** him with a thick H448
Job 16: 4 make fine speeches **a** you and shake my H6584
Job 16: 8 rises up and testifies **a** me. H928+7156
Job 16:10 cheek in scorn and unite together **a** me. H6584
Job 17: 8 the innocent are aroused **a** the ungodly. H6584
Job 19: 5 above me and use my humiliation **a** me, H6584
Job 19:11 His anger burns **a** me; he counts me H6584
Job 19:12 build a siege ramp **a** me and encamp H6584
Job 19:19 detest me; those I love have turned **a** me. H928
Job 20:23 his burning anger **a** him and rain down his H928
Job 20:27 his guilt; the earth will rise up **a** him. H4200
Job 22: 4 he rebukes you and brings charges **a** you? H6640
Job 23: 6 he would not press charges **a** me. H928
Job 23:14 He carries out his **decree** *a* me, and many AIT
Job 24:13 "There are those *who* **rebel** *a* the light, who AIT
Job 27:22 It hurls itself **a** him without mercy as he H6584
Job 30:12 they build their siege ramps **a** me. H6584
Job 31:13 female, when they had a grievance **a** me, H6643
Job 31:21 if I have raised my hand **a** the fatherless H6584
Job 31:30 mouth to sin by **invoking** a curse *a* their life— AIT
Job 31:38 "if my land cries out **a** me and all its H6584
Job 32:14 But Job has not marshaled his words **a** me H448
Job 34:37 us and multiplies his words **a** God." H4200
Job 39:23 The quiver rattles **a** its **side**, along with H6584
Job 40:23 the Jordan should surge **a** its mouth. H448
Job 41:10 Who then is able to stand **a** me? H4200+7156
Job 41:11 Who **has a claim a** me that I must pay H7709
Ps 2: 2 band together **a** the LORD and against H6584
Ps 2: 2 against the LORD and **a** his anointed, H6584
Ps 3: 1 How many rise up **a** me! H6584
Ps 5:10 many sins, for they have rebelled **a** you. H928
Ps 7: 6 rise up **a** the rage of my enemies. H928
Ps 8: 2 a stronghold **a** your enemies, H4200+5100
Ps 11: 2 they set their arrows **a** the strings to shoot H6584
Ps 15: 5 does not accept a bribe **a** the innocent. H6584
Ps 18:29 With your help *I can* **advance** *a* a troop; with AIT
Ps 21:11 they plot evil **a** you and devise wicked H6584
Ps 22:13 their prey open their mouths wide **a** me. H6584
Ps 27: 2 the wicked advance **a** me to devour me, H6584
Ps 27: 3 though war break out **a** me, even then I H6584
Ps 27:12 false witnesses rise up **a** me, spouting H928
Ps 31:13 They conspire **a** me and plot to take my H6584
Ps 31:18 they speak arrogantly **a** the righteous. H6584
Ps 32: 2 LORD does not count **a** them and in whose H4200
Ps 34:16 the face of the LORD is **a** those who do evil, H928
Ps 35: 1 fight **a** those who fight against me. H907
Ps 35: 1 with me; fight against *those who* **fight** *a* me. AIT
Ps 35: 3 spear and javelin **a** those who pursue me. H7925
Ps 35:15 assailants gathered **a** me without my H6584
Ps 35:20 false accusations **a** those who live quietly H6584
Ps 36:11 *May* the foot of the proud not **come** *a* me AIT
Ps 37:12 The wicked plot **a** the righteous and H4200
Ps 38:20 good with evil **lodge accusations a** me, H8476
Ps 41: 4 heal me, for I have sinned **a** you. H4200
Ps 41: 7 All my enemies whisper together **a** me H6584
Ps 41: 9 who shared my bread, has turned **a** me. H6584
Ps 43: 1 plead my cause **a** an unfaithful H4946
Ps 50: 7 I will speak; I will testify **a** you, Israel: H928
Ps 50: 8 *I* **bring** no **charges** *a* you concerning your AIT
Ps 50:20 You sit and testify **a** your brother and H928
Ps 51: 4 **A** you, you only, have I sinned and done H4200
Ps 55:12 if a foe were rising **a** me, I could hide. H6584
Ps 55:18 unharmed from the battle waged **a** me, H4200
Ps 59: 1 be my fortress **a** those who are attacking H4946
Ps 59: 3 Fierce men conspire **a** me for no offense H6584
Ps 60: 4 a banner to be unfurled **a** the bow. H4946+7156
Ps 60:11 Give us aid **a** the enemy, for human help H4946
Ps 61: 3 refuge, a strong tower **a** the foe. H4946+7156
Ps 64: 8 their own tongues **a** them and bring them H6584
Ps 66: 7 let not the rebellious rise up **a** him. H4200
Ps 71:10 For my enemies speak **a** me; those who H4200
Ps 74: 1 your anger smolder **a** the sheep of your H928
Ps 75: 5 Do not lift your horns **a** heaven; do not H4200
Ps 76:10 Surely your **wrath** *a* mankind brings you AIT
Ps 78:17 But they continued to sin **a** him, rebelling H4200
Ps 78:17 **rebelling** in the wilderness *a* the Most High. AIT
Ps 78:19 They spoke **a** God; they said, "Can God H928
Ps 78:21 his fire broke out **a** Jacob, and his wrath H928
Ps 78:21 against Jacob, and his wrath rose **a** Israel, H928
Ps 78:31 God's anger rose **a** them; he put to death H928
Ps 78:40 How often *they* **rebelled** *a* him in the AIT
Ps 78:49 He unleashed **a** them his hot anger, his H928
Ps 78:56 to the test and rebelled **a** the Most High; H907
Ps 79: 8 Do not hold **a** us the sins of past H4200
Ps 80: 4 your anger smolder **a** the prayers of your H928
Ps 81: 5 When God went out **a** Egypt, he H6584
Ps 81:14 enemies and turn my hand **a** their foes! H6584
Ps 83: 3 With cunning they conspire **a** your people; H6584
Ps 83: 3 people; they plot **a** those you cherish. H6584
Ps 83: 5 together; they form an alliance **a** you— H6584
Ps 91:12 that you will not strike your foot **a** a stone. H928
Ps 94:16 Who will rise up for me **a** the wicked H6640
Ps 94:16 Who will take a stand for me **a** evildoers? H6640
Ps 94:21 wicked band together **a** the righteous H6584
Ps 102: 8 *those who* **rail** *a* me use my name as a curse. AIT
Ps 105:25 hate his people, to conspire **a** his servants. H928
Ps 105:28 had they not rebelled **a** his words? H907
Ps 106:33 they rebelled **a** the Spirit of God, and H907
Ps 107:11 *because they* **rebelled** *a* God's commands AIT
Ps 108:12 Give us aid **a** the enemy, for human help H4946
Ps 109: 2 deceitful have opened their mouths **a** me; H6584
Ps 109: 2 they have spoken **a** me with lying tongues. H907
Ps 119:11 in my heart that I might not sin **a** you. H4200
Ps 124: 3 us alive when their anger flared **a** us; H928
Ps 135: 9 **a** Pharaoh and all his servants. H928
Ps 137: 9 your infants and dashes them **a** the rocks. H448
Ps 138: 7 out your hand **a** the anger of my foes; H6584
Ps 139:21 abhor *those who are* **in rebellion** *a* you? AIT
Ps 141: 5 prayer will still be **a** the deeds of evildoers. H928
Ps 149: 9 to carry out the sentence written **a** them H928
Pr 3:29 Do not plot harm **a** your neighbor, who H6584
Pr 17:11 Evildoers foster **rebellion** *a God*; the AIT
Pr 17:11 messenger of death will be sent **a** them. H928
Pr 18: 1 selfish ends and **a** all sound judgment H928
Pr 19: 3 their ruin, yet their heart rages **a** the LORD. H6584
Pr 21:22 One who is wise *can* **go up** *a* the city of the AIT
Pr 21:30 plan that can **succeed a** the LORD. H4200+5584
Pr 23:11 is strong; he will take up their case **a** you. H907
Pr 24:28 Do not testify **a** your neighbor without H928
Pr 25:10 shame you and the **charge** *a* you will stand. AIT
Pr 25:18 who gives false testimony **a** a neighbor. H928
Pr 30:31 he-goat, and a king **secure** a revolt. H440+6640
Ecc 9:14 And a powerful king came **a** it, surrounded H448
Ecc 9:14 it and built huge siege works **a** it. H6584
Ecc 10: 4 If a ruler's anger rises **a** you, do not leave H6584
Isa 1: 2 them up, but they have rebelled **a** me. H928
Isa 1:25 I will turn my hand **a** you; I will thoroughly H6584
Isa 2: 4 Nation will not take up sword **a** nation, nor H448
Isa 3: 5 each other—man **a** man, neighbor against H928
Isa 3: 5 man against man, neighbor **a** neighbor. H928
Isa 3: 5 The young will rise up **a** the old, the H928
Isa 3: 5 against the old, the nobody **a** the honored. H928
Isa 3: 8 their words and deeds are **a** the LORD H448
Isa 3: 9 The look on their faces testifies **a** them H928
Isa 3:14 enters into judgment **a** the elders and H6640
Isa 5:25 the LORD's anger burns **a** his people; H928
Isa 7: 1 of Israel marched up to fight **a** Jerusalem, H6584
Isa 8: 7 Lord is about to bring **a** them the mighty H6584
Isa 9: 8 The Lord has sent a message **a** Jacob; it H928
Isa 9:11 Rezin's foes **a** them and has spurred H6584
Isa 9:21 together they will turn **a** Judah. H6584
Isa 10: 6 I send him **a** a godless nation, I dispatch H928
Isa 10: 6 I dispatch him **a** a people who anger me H6584
Isa 10:12 finished all his work **a** Mount Zion and H928
Isa 10:15 or the saw boast **a** the one who uses it? H6584
Isa 10:24 you with a rod and lift up a club **a** you, H6584
Isa 10:25 Very soon my anger **a** you will end and my NDT
Isa 13: 1 A **prophecy** *a* Babylon that Isaiah son of AIT
Isa 13:17 I will stir up **a** them the Medes, who H6584
Isa 14: 4 take up this taunt **a** the king of Babylon: H6584
Isa 14:22 "I will rise up **a** them," declares the LORD H6584
Isa 15: 1 A **prophecy** *a* Moab: Ar in Moab is ruined AIT
Isa 17: 1 A **prophecy** *a* Damascus: "See, Damascus AIT
Isa 19: 1 A **prophecy** *a* Egypt: See, the LORD rides on a AIT
Isa 19: 2 "I will stir up Egyptian **a** Egyptian—brother H928
Isa 19: 2 brother will fight **a** brother, neighbor H928
Isa 19: 2 neighbor **a** neighbor, city against H928
Isa 19: 2 neighbor, city **a** city, kingdom against H928
Isa 19: 2 city against city, kingdom **a** kingdom. H928
Isa 19:12 the LORD Almighty has planned **a** Egypt. H6584
Isa 19:16 that the LORD Almighty raises **a** them. H6584
Isa 19:17 the LORD Almighty is planning **a** them. H6584
Isa 20: 3 as a sign and portent **a** Egypt and Cush, H6584
Isa 21: 1 A **prophecy** *a* the Desert by the Sea: Like AIT
Isa 21:11 A **prophecy** *a* Dumah: Someone calls to me AIT
Isa 21:13 A prophecy **a** Arabia: You caravans of H928
Isa 22: 1 A **prophecy** *a* the Valley of Vision: What AIT
Isa 23: 1 A **prophecy** *a* Tyre: Wail, you ships of AIT
Isa 23: 8 Who planned this **a** Tyre, the bestower of H6584
Isa 25: 4 of the ruthless is like a **storm** *driving* a a wall AIT
Isa 27: 4 I would march **a** them in battle; I would set H928
Isa 28:22 the destruction decreed **a** the whole land. H6584
Isa 29: 3 I will encamp **a** you on all sides; I will H6584
Isa 29: 3 towers and set up my siege works **a** you. H6584
Isa 29: 7 hordes of all the nations that fight **a** Ariel, H6584
Isa 29: 8 of all the nations that fight **a** Mount Zion. H6584
Isa 31: 2 He will rise up **a** that wicked nation H6584
Isa 31: 2 **a** those who help evildoers. H6584
Isa 31: 4 band of shepherds is called together **a** it, H6584
Isa 31: 6 to the One you have so greatly **revolted a**. H6240
Isa 33:15 who stop their ears **a** plots of murder and H4946
Isa 33:15 shut their eyes **a** contemplating evil— H4946
Isa 36: 5 are you depending, that you rebel **a** me? H928
Isa 36:10 told me to march **a** this country and destroy H448
Isa 37: 8 found the king fighting **a** Libnah. H6584
Isa 37: 9 of Cush, was marching out to fight **a** him. H907
Isa 37:22 this is the word the LORD has spoken **a** him H6584
Isa 37:23 **A** whom have you raised your voice and H6584
Isa 37:23 your eyes in pride? **A** the Holy One of Israel H448
Isa 37:28 you come and go and how you rage **a** me. H448
Isa 37:29 Because you rage **a** me and because your H448
Isa 37:33 it with shield or build a siege ramp **a** it. H6584
Isa 41:11 "All who rage **a** you will surely be H928
Isa 41:12 Those who wage **war** *a* you will be as AIT
Isa 42:24 it not the LORD, **a** whom we have sinned? H4200
Isa 43:27 those I sent to teach you rebelled **a** me. H928
Isa 45:24 All who have raged **a** him will come to him H928
Isa 48:14 ally will carry out his purpose **a** Babylon; H928
Isa 48:14 Babylon; his arm will be **a** the Babylonians. NDT
Isa 50: 8 Who then will bring charges **a** me? Let us H907
Isa 54:17 no weapon forged **a** you will prevail, and H6584
Isa 59:12 in your sight, and our sins testify **a** us. H928
Isa 59:13 rebellion and treachery **a** the LORD, turning H928
Isa 63:10 their enemy and he himself fought **a** them. H928
Isa 64: 5 But when we continued to sin **a** them, you H928
Isa 66:24 dead bodies of those who rebelled **a** me; H928
Jer 1:15 they will come **a** all her surrounding walls H6584
Jer 1:15 surrounding walls and **a** all the towns of H6584
Jer 1:18 a bronze wall to stand **a** the whole land— H6584
Jer 1:18 the whole land—**a** the kings of Judah H4200
Jer 1:19 They will fight **a** you but will not overcome H448
Jer 2: 8 not know me; the leaders rebelled **a** me. H928
Jer 2: 9 "Therefore I bring charges **a** you again," H907
Jer 2: 9 I will bring charges **a** your children's H907
Jer 2:21 How then did you turn **a** me into a corrupt, H4200
Jer 2:29 "Why do you bring charges **a** me? You H448
Jer 2:29 You have all rebelled **a** me," declares the H928
Jer 3:13 you have rebelled **a** the LORD your God, you H928
Jer 3:25 We have sinned **a** the LORD our God, both H4200
Jer 4:12 Now I pronounce my judgments **a** them." H907
Jer 4:16 raising a war cry **a** the cities of Judah. H6584
Jer 4:17 because she has rebelled **a** me,' " H907
Jer 5:15 "I am bringing **a** distant nation **a** you H6584
Jer 6: 3 Shepherds with their flocks will come **a** her H448
Jer 6: 4 "Prepare for battle **a** her! Arise, let us H6584
Jer 6: 6 trees and build siege ramps **a** Jerusalem. H6584
Jer 6:12 stretch out my hand **a** those who live in H6584
Jer 8:14 to drink, because we have sinned **a** him. H4200
Jer 11:19 not realize that they had plotted **a** me, H6584
Jer 12: 6 they have raised a loud cry **a** you. H339
Jer 13:14 I will smash them one **a** the other, parents H448
Jer 14: 7 Although our sins testify **a** us, do H928
Jer 14: 7 often rebelled; we have sinned **a** you. H4200
Jer 14:20 ancestors; we have indeed sinned **a** you. H4200
Jer 15: 3 will send four kinds of destroyers **a** them," H6584
Jer 15: 8 bring a destroyer **a** the mothers of their H6584
Jer 15:14 will kindle a fire that will burn **a** you." H6584
Jer 15:20 they will fight **a** you but will not overcome H448
Jer 16:10 LORD decreed such a great disaster **a** us? H6584
Jer 16:10 have we committed **a** the LORD our God? H4200
Jer 18:11 you and devising a plan **a** you. H6584
Jer 18:18 let's make plans **a** Jeremiah; for the H6584
Jer 18:22 you suddenly bring invaders **a** them, H6584
Jer 19: 9 the siege so hard **a** them to destroy them. H4200
Jer 19:15 it every disaster I pronounced **a** them, H6584
Jer 21: 4 I *am about to* **turn a** you the weapons of H6015
Jer 21: 5 myself will fight **a** you with an outstretched H907
Jer 21:13 I am **a** you, Jerusalem, you who live above H448
Jer 21:13 you who say, "Who can come **a** us? H6584
Jer 22: 7 I will send destroyers **a** you, each man H6584
Jer 23:30 "I am **a** the prophets who steal from one H6584
Jer 23:31 "I am **a** the prophets who wag their own H6584
Jer 23:32 I am **a** those who prophesy false dreams," H6584
Jer 24:10 famine and plague **a** them until they are H928
Jer 25: 9 "and I will bring them **a** this land and its H6584
Jer 25: 9 its inhabitants and **a** all the surrounding H6584
Jer 25:13 that land all the things I have spoken **a** it, H6584
Jer 25:13 prophesied by Jeremiah **a** all the nations. H6584
Jer 25:30 all these words **a** them and say to them: H448
Jer 25:30 dwelling and roar mightily **a** his land. H6584
Jer 25:30 shout **a** all who live on the earth. H448
Jer 25:31 the LORD will bring charges **a** the nations; H928
Jer 26:11 because he has prophesied **a** this city. H448
Jer 26:12 sent me to prophesy **a** this house and this H448
Jer 26:13 the disaster he has pronounced **a** you. H6584
Jer 26:19 bring the disaster he pronounced **a** them? H6584
Jer 26:20 the same things **a** this city and this land H6584
Jer 28: 8 disaster and plague **a** many countries and H448
Jer 28:16 you have preached rebellion **a** the LORD. H448
Jer 29:17 famine and plague **a** them and I will make H928
Jer 29:32 because he has preached rebellion **a** me. H6584
Jer 31:20 Though I often speak **a** him, I still H928
Jer 32: 5 If you fight **a** the Babylonians, you will not H907
Jer 33: 4 down to be used **a** the siege ramps and H448
Jer 33: 8 have committed **a** me and will forgive H4200
Jer 33: 8 will forgive all their sins of rebellion **a** me. H928
Jer 34: 1 ruled were fighting **a** Jerusalem and all H6584
Jer 34: 7 Babylon was fighting **a** Jerusalem and the H6584
Jer 34:22 They will fight **a** it, take it and burn it H6584
Jer 35:17 every disaster I pronounced **a** them. H6584
Jer 36: 7 wrath pronounced **a** this people by the H448
Jer 36:31 Judah every disaster I pronounced **a** them, H448
Jer 37:18 have I committed **a** you or your attendants H4200

A

Jer 39: 1 of Babylon marched **a** Jerusalem with his H448
Jer 39:16 I am about to fulfill my words **a** this city H448
Jer 40: 3 you people sinned **a** the LORD and did not H4200
Jer 41: 9 part of his **defense** **a** Baasha king H7156+4946
Jer 42: 5 faithful witness **a** us if we do not act in H928
Jer 43: 3 is inciting you **a** us to hand us over to H928
Jer 44: 6 it raged **a** the towns of Judah and the H928
Jer 44:23 have sinned **a** the LORD and have not H4200
Jer 44:29 my threats of harm **a** you will surely stand. H6584
Jer 46: 2 is the message **a** the army of Pharaoh H6584
Jer 46:20 a gadfly is coming **a** her from the north. H928
Jer 46:22 they will come **a** her with axes, like H4200
Jer 48: 8 The destroyer will come **a** every town, and H448
Jer 48:18 Moab will come up **a** you and ruin your H928
Jer 49: 2 sound the battle cry **a** Rabbah of the H448
Jer 49:19 what shepherd can stand **a** me?" H4200+7156
Jer 49:20 hear what the LORD has planned **a** Edom H448
Jer 49:20 what he has purposed **a** those who live in H448
Jer 49:30 king of Babylon has plotted **a** you; H6584
Jer 49:30 against you; he has devised a plan **a** you. H6584
Jer 49:36 I will bring **a** Elam the four winds from the H448
Jer 50: 7 they sinned **a** the LORD, their verdant H4200
Jer 50: 9 stir up and bring **a** Babylon an alliance of H6584
Jer 50: 9 They will take up their positions **a** her H4200
Jer 50:14 no arrows, for she has sinned **a** the LORD. H4200
Jer 50:15 Shout **a** her on every side! She surrenders H6584
Jer 50:26 Come **a** her from afar. Break open her H4200
Jer 50:29 "Summon archers **a** Babylon, all those who H448
Jer 50:31 I am **a** you, you arrogant one, H448
Jer 50:35 "A sword **a** the Babylonians!" declares the H6584
Jer 50:35 "**a** those who live in Babylon and against H448
Jer 50:35 live in Babylon and **a** her officials and wise H448
Jer 50:36 A sword **a** her false prophets! They will H448
Jer 50:36 become fools. A sword **a** her warriors! They H448
Jer 50:37 A sword **a** her horses and chariots and all H448
Jer 50:37 A sword **a** her treasures! They H448
Jer 50:44 what shepherd can stand **a** me?" H4200+7156
Jer 50:45 hear what the LORD has planned **a** Babylon H448
Jer 50:45 what he has purposed **a** the land of the H448
Jer 51: 1 spirit of a destroyer **a** Babylon and the H6584
Jer 51:12 Lift up a banner **a** the walls of Babylon H448
Jer 51:12 his decree **a** the people of Babylon. H448
Jer 51:25 "I am **a** you, you destroying mountain, you H448
Jer 51:25 "I will stretch out my hand **a** you, roll you H6584
Jer 51:27 Prepare the nations for battle **a** her H6584
Jer 51:27 summon **a** her these kingdoms: H6584
Jer 51:27 Appoint a commander **a** her; send up H6584
Jer 51:28 Prepare the nations for battle **a** her—the H6584
Jer 51:29 the LORD's purposes **a** Babylon stand H6584
Jer 51:46 violence in the land and of ruler **a** ruler. H6584
Jer 51:53 I will send destroyers **a** her," declares the H4200
Jer 51:56 A destroyer will come **a** Babylon; her H6584
Jer 52: 3 Zedekiah rebelled **a** the king of Babylon. H928
Jer 52: 4 of Babylon marched **a** Jerusalem with his H6584
La 1:15 summoned an army **a** me to crush my H6584
La 1:18 is righteous, yet *I* **rebelled** *a* his command. AIT
La 2:16 enemies open their mouths wide **a** you; H6584
La 2:22 so you summoned *a* me **terrors** on every side. AIT
La 3: 3 turned his hand **a** me again and again, H928
La 3:46 have opened their mouths wide **a** us. H6584
La 3:60 of their vengeance, all their plots **a** me. H4200
La 3:61 heard their insults, all their plots **a** me— H6584
La 3:62 whisper and mutter **a** me all day long. H6584
Eze 2: 3 a rebellious nation that has rebelled **a** me; H928
Eze 2: 3 have been in revolt **a** me to this very day. H928
Eze 3:13 creatures brushing **a** each other and the H448
Eze 4: 2 Erect siege works **a** it, build a ramp up to H6584
Eze 4: 2 set up camps **a** it and put battering rams H6584
Eze 4: 7 with bared arm prophesy **a** her. H6584
Eze 5: 6 she has rebelled **a** my laws and decrees H907
Eze 5: 8 I myself am **a** you, Jerusalem, and I will H6584
Eze 5:13 cease and my wrath **a** them will subside, H928
Eze 5:17 I will send famine and wild beasts **a** you H6584
Eze 5:17 and I will bring the sword **a** you. H6584
Eze 6: 2 set your face **a** the mountains of Israel H448
Eze 6: 2 the mountains of Israel; prophesy **a** them H448
Eze 6: 3 I am about to bring a sword **a** you, and I H6584
Eze 6:14 stretch out my hand **a** them and make the H6584
Eze 7: 3 and I will unleash my anger **a** you. H928
Eze 7: 6 It has roused itself **a** you. See, H448
Eze 7: 8 wrath on you and spend my anger **a** you. H928
Eze 11: 4 Therefore prophesy **a** them; prophesy, son H6584
Eze 11: 8 the sword is what I will bring **a** you H6584
Eze 13: 2 prophesy **a** the prophets of Israel who are H448
Eze 13: 8 lying visions, I am **a** you, declares the H448
Eze 13: 9 My hand will be **a** the prophets who see H448
Eze 13:15 pour out my wrath **a** the wall and against H928
Eze 13:15 the wall and **a** those who covered it H928
Eze 13:17 set your face **a** the daughters of your H448
Eze 13:17 their own imagination. Prophesy **a** them H6584
Eze 13:20 I am **a** your magic charms with which you H448
Eze 14: 8 I will set my face **a** them and make them an H928
Eze 14: 9 out my hand **a** him and destroy him H6584
Eze 14:13 if a country sins **a** me by being unfaithful H4200
Eze 14:13 I stretch out my hand **a** it to cut off its food H6584
Eze 14:17 if I bring a sword **a** that country and say, H6584
Eze 14:21 will it be when I send **a** Jerusalem my four H448
Eze 15: 7 I will set my face **a** them. Although they H928
Eze 15: 7 And when I set my face **a** them, you will H928
Eze 16:27 out my hand **a** you and reduced your H6584
Eze 16:30 " '*I am* **filled with fury** **a** you H582+4226
Eze 16:37 I will gather them **a** you from all around H6584
Eze 16:40 They will bring a mob **a** you, who will H6584
Eze 16:42 Then my wrath **a** you will subside and my H928
Eze 17:15 But the king rebelled **a** him by sending his H928
Eze 18:20 of the wicked will be **charged** **a** them. H6584
Eze 18:22 committed will be remembered **a** them. H4200
Eze 19: 8 Then the nations came **a** him, those from H6584
Eze 20: 8 " 'But they rebelled **a** me and would not H928
Eze 20: 8 them and spend my anger **a** them in Egypt. H928
Eze 20:13 of Israel rebelled **a** me in the wilderness. H928
Eze 20:21 " 'But the children rebelled **a** me: They did H928
Eze 20:21 spend my anger **a** them in the H928
Eze 20:38 you of those who revolt and rebel **a** me. H928
Eze 20:46 preach **a** the south and prophesy against H448
Eze 20:46 the south and prophesy **a** the forest of the H448
Eze 21: 2 set your face **a** Jerusalem and preach H448
Eze 21: 2 Jerusalem and preach **a** the sanctuary. H448
Eze 21: 2 Prophesy **a** the land of Israel H448
Eze 21: 3 I am **a** you. I will draw my H448
Eze 21: 4 will be unsheathed **a** everyone from south H448
Eze 21:12 son of man, for it is **a** my people; it is H928
Eze 21:12 my people; it is **a** all the princes of Israel. H928
Eze 21:20 the sword to come **a** Rabbah of the H907
Eze 21:20 another **a** Judah and fortified H907
Eze 21:22 to set battering rams **a** the gates, to build H6584
Eze 21:31 you and breathe out my fiery anger **a** you; H6584
Eze 23:22 I will stir up your lovers **a** you, those you H6584
Eze 23:22 I will bring them **a** you from every side— H6584
Eze 23:24 They will come **a** you with weapons H6584
Eze 23:24 take up positions **a** you on every side with H6584
Eze 23:25 I will direct my jealous anger **a** you, and H928
Eze 23:46 Bring a mob **a** them and give them over H6584
Eze 24:13 again until my wrath **a** you has subsided. H928
Eze 25: 2 set your face **a** the Ammonites and H448
Eze 25: 2 the Ammonites and prophesy **a** them. H6584
Eze 25: 6 malice of your heart **a** the land of Israel, H448
Eze 25: 7 stretch out my hand **a** you and give you as H6584
Eze 25:13 stretch out my hand **a** Edom and kill both H6584
Eze 25:16 to stretch out my hand **a** the Philistines, H6584
Eze 26: 3 I am **a** you, Tyre, and I will bring many H6584
Eze 26: 3 I will bring many nations **a** you, like H6584
Eze 26: 7 I am going to bring **a** Tyre Nebuchadnezzar H448
Eze 26: 8 he will set up siege works **a** you, build a H6584
Eze 26: 8 to your walls and raise his shields **a** you. H6584
Eze 26: 9 of his battering rams **a** your walls and H928
Eze 28: 7 I am going to bring foreigners **a** you, the H6584
Eze 28: 7 draw their swords **a** your beauty and H6584
Eze 28:21 set your face **a** Sidon; prophesy H448
Eze 28:21 your face against Sidon; prophesy **a** her H6584
Eze 28:22 " 'I am **a** you, Sidon, and among you I H6584
Eze 28:23 with the sword **a** you on every side. H6584
Eze 29: 2 set your face **a** Pharaoh king of Egypt and H6584
Eze 29: 2 Egypt and prophesy **a** him and against all H6584
Eze 29: 2 prophesy against him and **a** all Egypt. H6584
Eze 29: 3 " 'I am **a** you, Pharaoh king of Egypt, you H6584
Eze 29: 8 I will bring a sword **a** you and kill both H6584
Eze 29:10 therefore I am **a** you and against your H448
Eze 29:10 I am against you and **a** your streams, H448
Eze 29:18 drove his army in a hard campaign **a** Tyre; H448
Eze 29:18 reward from the campaign he led **a** Tyre. H6584
Eze 30: 4 A sword will come **a** Egypt, and anguish H928
Eze 30:11 will draw their swords **a** Egypt and fill the H6584
Eze 30:22 I am **a** Pharaoh king of Egypt. I H448
Eze 30:25 of Babylon and he brandishes it **a** Egypt. H448
Eze 32:11 sword of the king of Babylon *will* **come** *a* you. AIT
Eze 33: 2 'When I bring the sword **a** a land, and the H6584
Eze 33: 3 the sword coming **a** the land and blows H6584
Eze 33:16 committed will be remembered **a** them. H4200
Eze 34: 2 prophesy **a** the shepherds of Israel H6584
Eze 34:10 I am **a** the shepherds and will hold them H448
Eze 35: 2 set your face **a** Mount Seir; prophesy H6584
Eze 35: 2 face against Mount Seir; prophesy **a** it H6584
Eze 35: 3 I am **a** you, Mount Seir, and I will stretch H448
Eze 35: 3 out my hand **a** you and make you a H6584
Eze 35:12 things you have said **a** the mountains of H6584
Eze 35:13 You boasted **a** me and spoke against me H6584
Eze 35:13 me and spoke **a** me without restraint H6584
Eze 36: 5 zeal I have spoken **a** the rest of the H6584
Eze 36: 5 of the nations, and **a** all Edom, for with H6584
Eze 38: 2 set your face **a** Gog, of the land of H448
Eze 38: 2 of Meshek and Tubal; prophesy **a** him H6584
Eze 38: 3 I am **a** you, Gog, chief prince of Meshek H448
Eze 38:12 turn my hand **a** the resettled ruins H6584
Eze 38:16 You will advance **a** my people Israel like a H6584
Eze 38:16 I will bring you **a** my land, so that the H6584
Eze 38:17 years that I would bring you **a** them. H6584
Eze 38:21 I will summon a sword **a** Gog on all my H6584
Eze 38:21 Every man's sword will be **a** his brother. H928
Eze 39: 1 of man, prophesy **a** Gog and say: 'This is H6584
Eze 39: 1 I am **a** you, Gog, chief prince of Meshek H448
Eze 39: 2 far north and send you **a** the mountains of H6584
Eze 43:18 splashing blood **a** the altar when it is H6584
Da 3:29 who say anything **a** the God of Shadrach A10542
Da 4:24 Most High has issued **a** my lord the king: A10542
Da 5:23 set yourself up **a** the Lord of heaven. A10542
Da 6: 4 grounds for charges **a** Daniel in his A10378
Da 6: 5 any basis for charges **a** this man Daniel A10378
Da 7:21 was waging war **a** the holy people and A10554
Da 7:25 He will speak **a** the Most High A10378+10608
Da 8: 4 No animal could stand **a** it, and H4200+7156
Da 8: 7 ram was powerless to stand **a** it; H4200+7156
Da 8:25 take his stand **a** the Prince of princes. H6584
Da 9: 8 because we have sinned **a** you. H4200
Da 9: 9 even though we have rebelled **a** him; H928
Da 9:11 out on us, because we have sinned **a** you. H4200
Da 9:12 the words spoken **a** us and against our H6584
Da 9:12 spoken against us and **a** our rulers by H6584
Da 10:20 I will return to fight **a** the prince of Persia, H6640
Da 10:21 No one supports me **a** them except H6584
Da 11: 2 stir up everyone **a** the kingdom of Greece H907
Da 11: 7 he will fight **a** them and be victorious. H928
Da 11:11 in a rage and fight **a** the king of the North H6640
Da 11:14 times many will rise **a** the king of the H6584
Da 11:16 no one will be able to stand **a** him. H4200+7156
Da 11:25 strength and courage **a** the king of the H6584
Da 11:25 stand because of the plots devised **a** him. H6584
Da 11:28 his heart will be **set** **a** the holy covenant. H6584
Da 11:28 He will take action **a** it and then return to NDT
Da 11:30 vent his fury **a** the holy covenant. H6584
Da 11:36 say unheard-of things **a** the God of gods. H6584
Da 11:40 North will storm out **a** him with chariots H6584
Hos 4: 1 a charge to bring **a** you who live in the H6640
Hos 4: 4 are like *those who* **bring charges** *a* a priest. AIT
Hos 4: 7 the more they sinned **a** me; they H4200
Hos 5: 1 This judgment is **a** you: You have been a H4200
Hos 5: 5 Israel's arrogance testifies **a** them H928+7156
Hos 7:10 Israel's arrogance testifies **a** him H928+7156
Hos 7:13 to them, because they have rebelled **a** me! H928
Hos 7:15 their arms, but they plot evil **a** me. H448
Hos 8: 1 my covenant and rebelled **a** my law. H6584
Hos 8: 5 My anger burns **a** them. How long H928+6330
Hos 10:10 will be gathered **a** them to put them in H6584
Hos 10:14 the roar of battle will rise **a** your people, so H928
Hos 11: 9 I will not come **a** their cities. H928
Hos 11:12 And Judah is unruly **a** God, even against H6640
Hos 11:12 even **a** the faithful Holy One. H6640
Hos 12: 2 The LORD has a charge to bring **a** Judah H6640
Hos 13: 9 because you are **a** me, against your helper H928
Hos 13: 9 because you are against me, **a** your helper. H928
Hos 13:16 because they have rebelled **a** their God. H928
Joel 3: 4 "Now what have you **a** me, Tyre and H4200
Am 1: 8 I will turn my hand **a** Ekron, till the last of H6584
Am 3: 1 the word the LORD has spoken **a** you H6584
Am 3: 1 **a** the whole family I brought up out of H6584
Am 3:13 "Hear this and testify **a** the descendants of H928
Am 6:14 "I will stir up a nation **a** you, Israel, H6584
Am 7: 9 my sword I will rise **a** the house of H6584
Am 7:10 raising a conspiracy **a** you in the very H6584
Am 7:16 " 'Do not prophesy **a** Israel, and stop H6584
Am 7:16 stop preaching **a** the descendants of H6584
Ob 1 "Rise, let us go **a** her for battle"— H6584
Ob 10 Because of the **violence** *a* your brother Jacob AIT
Jnh 1: 2 the great city of Nineveh and preach **a** it, H6584
Mic 1: 2 the Sovereign LORD may bear witness **a** you, H928
Mic 1:15 will bring a conqueror **a** you who live in H4200
Mic 2: 3 "I am planning disaster **a** this people H6584
Mic 3: 5 to wage war **a** anyone who refuses H6584
Mic 4: 3 Nation will not take up sword **a** nation, nor H448
Mic 4:11 But now many nations are gathered **a** you. H6584
Mic 5: 1 city of troops, for a siege is laid **a** us. H6584
Mic 5: 5 We will raise **a** them seven shepherds H6584
Mic 6: 2 For the LORD has a case **a** his people; he is H6640
Mic 6: 2 people; he is lodging a charge **a** Israel. H6640
Mic 7: 6 a daughter rises up **a** her mother, a H928
Mic 7: 6 a daughter-in-law **a** her mother-in-law—a H928
Mic 7: 9 Because I have sinned **a** him, I will bear H4200
Na 1: 2 foes and vents his wrath **a** his enemies. H4200
Na 1: 9 Whatever they plot **a** the LORD he will bring H448
Na 1:11 forth who plots evil **a** the LORD and devises H6584
Na 2: 1 An attacker advances **a** you H6584+7156
Na 2:13 "I am **a** you," declares the LORD Almighty. "IH448
Na 3: 5 "I am **a** you," declares the LORD Almighty. "IH448
Hab 3: 8 Was your wrath **a** the streams? Did you H928
Hab 3: 8 Did you rage **a** the sea when you rode your H928
Zep 1: 4 stretch out my hand **a** Judah and against H6584
Zep 1: 4 hand against Judah and **a** all who live in H6584
Zep 1:16 trumpet and battle cry **a** the fortified cities H6584
Zep 1:16 the fortified cities and **a** the corner towers. H6584
Zep 1:17 because they have sinned **a** the LORD. H4200
Zep 2: 5 the word of the LORD is **a** you, Canaan, H6584
Zep 2: 8 my people and made threats **a** their land. H6584
Zep 2:13 stretch out his hand **a** the north and H6584
Zec 1:21 lifted up their horns **a** the land of Judah to H448
Zec 2: 8 One has sent me **a** the nations that have H448
Zec 2: 9 surely raise my hand **a** them so that their H6584
Zec 7:10 the poor. *Do not* **plot** evil *a* each other.' AIT
Zec 8:10 I had turned everyone **a** their neighbor. H928
Zec 8:17 *do* not **plot** evil **a** each other H3108+928+4222
Zec 9: 1 word of the LORD is **a** the land of Hadrak H928
Zec 9: 8 my temple to guard it **a** marauding forces. H4946
Zec 9:13 your sons, Zion, **a** your sons, Greece, and H6584
Zec 10: 3 "My anger burns **a** the shepherds, and I H6584
Zec 12: 3 nations of the earth are gathered **a** her, H6584
Zec 13: 7 **a** my shepherd, against the man H6584
Zec 13: 7 shepherd, **a** the man who is close to me!" H6584
Zec 13: 7 I will turn my hand **a** the little ones. H6584
Zec 14: 2 all the nations to Jerusalem to fight **a** it; NDT
Zec 14: 3 LORD will go out and fight **a** those nations, H928
Zec 14:12 all the nations that fought **a** Jerusalem: H6584
Mal 3: 5 I will be quick to testify **a** sorcerers H928
Mal 3: 5 **a** those who defraud laborers of their H928
Mal 3:13 "You have spoken arrogantly **a** me," H6584
Mal 3:13 "Yet you ask, 'What have we said **a** you?' H6584
Mt 4: 6 that you will not strike your foot **a** a stone. *G4639*
Mt 5:11 say all kinds of evil **a** you because of me. *G2848*

Mt 5:23 brother or sister has something **a** you, G2848
Mt 6:14 forgive other people when they sin **a** you, NDT
Mt 7:25 the winds blew and **beat a** that house; G4700
Mt 7:27 the winds blew and **beat a** that house, G4684
Mt 10:21 children will rebel **a** their parents and G2093
Mt 10:35 I have come to turn " 'a man **a** his father, G2848
Mt 10:35 his father, a daughter **a** her mother, a G2848
Mt 10:35 a daughter-in-law **a** her mother-in-law— G2848
Mt 12:10 *Looking* for a reason *to* **bring charges a** G2989
Mt 12:25 kingdom divided **a** itself will be ruined, G2848
Mt 12:25 household divided **a** itself will not G2848
Mt 12:26 drives out Satan, he is divided **a** himself. G2093
Mt 12:30 "Whoever is not with me is **a** me, and G2848
Mt 12:31 blasphemy *a* the **Spirit** will not be AIT
Mt 12:32 who speaks a word **a** the Son of Man will G2848
Mt 12:32 anyone who speaks **a** the Holy Spirit will G2848
Mt 14:24 by the waves because the wind was **a** it. G1885
Mt 16: 6 "Be on your guard **a** the yeast of the G608
Mt 16:11 But be on your guard **a** the yeast of the G608
Mt 16:12 telling them to guard **a** the yeast used in G608
Mt 16:12 **a** the teaching of the Pharisees and G608
Mt 18:21 my brother or sister who sins **a** me? G1650
Mt 20:11 they began to grumble **a** the landowner. G2848
Mt 23:31 So you testify *a* **yourselves** that you are the AIT
Mt 24: 7 Nation will rise **a** nation, and kingdom G2093
Mt 24: 7 against nation, and kingdom **a** kingdom. G2093
Mt 26:59 false evidence **a** Jesus so that they G2848
Mt 26:62 *is* **this testimony** that these men
are **bringing a** G2909
Mt 27: 6 "It is **a** the law to put this into the treasury, G4024
Mt 27:13 *the* **testimony** *they are* **bringing a** you?" G2909
Mt 27:37 head they placed the written charge *a* **him**: AIT
Mk 3:24 If a kingdom is divided **a** itself, that G2093
Mk 3:25 If a house is divided **a** itself, that house G2093
Mk 3:29 whoever blasphemes **a** the Holy Spirit will G1650
Mk 5:31 "You see the people **crowding a** you," G5315
Mk 6:11 the dust off your feet as a testimony *a* **them**." AIT
Mk 6:19 So Herodias **nursed a grudge a** John and G1923
Mk 6:48 the oars, because the wind was **a** them. G1885
Mk 9:40 whoever is not **a** us is for us. G2848
Mk 10:11 another woman commits adultery **a** her. G2093
Mk 11:25 if you hold anything **a** anyone, forgive G2848
Mk 12:12 knew he had spoken the parable **a** them. G4639
Mk 13: 8 Nation will rise **a** nation, and kingdom G2093
Mk 13: 8 against nation, and kingdom **a** kingdom. G2093
Mk 13:12 Children will rebel **a** their parents and G2093
Mk 14:55 looking for evidence **a** Jesus so that they G2848
Mk 14:56 Many testified falsely **a** him, but their G2848
Mk 14:57 up and gave this false testimony **a** him: G2848
Mk 14:60 What is *this* **testimony** that these men
are **bringing a** G2909
Mk 15:26 The written notice of the charge *a* **him** read AIT
Mk 15:46 he rolled a stone **a** the entrance of the G2093
Lk 2:34 to be a sign *that will be* **spoken a**, G515
Lk 4:11 so that *you will* not **strike** your foot **a a** G4684
Lk 8:45 people are crowding and **pressing a** you." G632
Lk 9: 5 dust off your feet as a testimony **a** them." G2093
Lk 9:50 "for whoever is not **a** you is for you." G2848
Lk 11: 4 we also forgive everyone *who* **sins a** us. G4053
Lk 11:17 "Any kingdom divided **a** itself will be G2093
Lk 11:17 a house divided **a** itself will fall. G2093
Lk 11:18 If Satan is divided **a** himself, how can his G2093
Lk 11:23 "Whoever is not with me is **a** me, and G2848
Lk 12: 1 "Be on your guard **a** the yeast of the G608
Lk 12:10 who speaks a word **a** the Son of Man will G1650
Lk 12:10 who blasphemes **a** the Holy Spirit will G1650
Lk 12:15 Be on your guard **a** all kinds of greed; life G608
Lk 12:52 be five in one family **divided** *a each other*, AIT
Lk 12:52 three **a** two and two against three. G2093
Lk 12:52 three against two and two **a** three. G2093
Lk 12:53 father **a** son and son against father G2093
Lk 12:53 father against son and son **a** father G1923
Lk 12:53 mother **a** daughter and daughter against G2093
Lk 12:53 against daughter and daughter **a** mother, G2093
Lk 12:53 mother-in-law **a** daughter-in-law and G2093
Lk 12:53 daughter-in-law **a** mother-in-law. G2093
Lk 14:31 a king is about to go to war *a* another **king**. AIT
Lk 14:31 oppose the one coming **a** him with twenty G2093
Lk 15:18 I have sinned **a** heaven and against you. G1650
Lk 15:18 I have sinned against heaven and **a** you. G1967
Lk 15:21 I have sinned **a** heaven and against you. G1650
Lk 15:21 I have sinned against heaven and **a** you. G1967
Lk 17: 3 "If your brother or sister sins *a* **you**, rebuke AIT
Lk 17: 4 Even if they sin **a** you seven times in a day G1650
Lk 18: 3 the plea, 'Grant me justice **a** my adversary.' G608
Lk 19:43 build an embankment *a* **you** and encircle you AIT
Lk 20:19 knew he had spoken this parable **a** them. G4639
Lk 21:10 "Nation will rise **a** nation, and kingdom G2093
Lk 21:10 against nation, and kingdom **a** kingdom. G2093
Lk 21:23 distress in the land and wrath *a* this **people**. AIT
Lk 23: 4 "I find no basis for a charge **a** this man." G1877
Lk 23:14 found no basis for your charges **a** him. G2848
Jn 13:18 bread *has* **turned a** me. G2048+3836+4761+899
Jn 13:25 Leaning back **a** Jesus, he G2093+3836+5111
Jn 18:29 charges are you bringing **a** this man?" G2848
Jn 18:38 "I find no basis for a charge **a** him. G1877
Jn 19: 4 that I find no basis for a charge **a** him." G1877
Jn 19: 6 I find no basis for a charge **a** him. G1877
Jn 21:20 leaned back **a** Jesus at the G2093+3836+5111
Ac 4:26 band together **a** the Lord and against G2848
Ac 4:26 against the Lord and **a** his anointed one. G2848
Ac 4:27 in this city *to conspire* **a** your holy servant G2093
Ac 5:39 will only find yourselves **fighting a God**." G2534
Ac 6: 1 them complained **a** the Hebraic Jews G4639
Ac 6:10 they could not **stand up a** the wisdom the G468
Ac 6:11 blasphemous words **a** Moses and against G1650
Ac 6:11 words against Moses and **a** God. NDT
Ac 6:13 stops speaking **a** this holy place and G2848
Ac 6:13 against this holy place and **a** the law. NDT
Ac 7:60 cried out, "Lord, do not hold this sin *a* **them**." AIT
Ac 8: 1 persecution broke out **a** the church in G2093
Ac 9: 1 murderous threats **a** the Lord's disciples. G1650
Ac 10:28 well aware that it is **a** our **law** for a Jew to G116
Ac 13:11 Now the hand of the Lord is **a** you. You are G2093
Ac 13:50 up persecution **a** Paul and Barnabas, G2093
Ac 14: 2 poisoned their minds **a** the brothers. G2848
Ac 16:22 joined in the attack **a** Paul and Silas, G2848
Ac 19:38 craftsmen have a grievance **a** anybody, G4639
Ac 20: 3 Jews had plotted *a* **him** just as he was about AIT
Ac 21:28 everywhere **a** our people and our G2848
Ac 23:29 there was no charge **a** him that deserved NDT
Ac 23:30 of a plot to be carried out **a** the man, G1650
Ac 23:30 to present to you their case **a** him. G4639
Ac 24: 1 brought their charges **a** Paul before the G2848
Ac 24: 8 all these charges we are bringing *a* **him**." AIT
Ac 24:13 you the charges they are now making *a* **me**. AIT
Ac 24:19 bring charges if they have anything **a** me. G4639
Ac 25: 2 him and presented the charges **a** Paul. G2848
Ac 25: 5 they can press charges *a* **him** there. AIT
Ac 25: 7 They brought many serious charges **a** him NDT
Ac 25: 8 done nothing wrong **a** the Jewish law G1650
Ac 25: 8 the Jewish law or **a** the temple or against G1650
Ac 25: 8 law or against the temple or **a** Caesar." G1650
Ac 25:11 the charges brought *a* **me** by these Jews are AIT
Ac 25:15 brought charges **a** him and asked that G2848
Ac 25:16 to defend themselves **a** the charges. G4309
Ac 25:27 without specifying the charges **a** him." G2848
Ac 26: 2 I make my defense **a** all the accusations G4309
Ac 26:10 were put to death, *I* **cast** my vote **a** them. G2965
Ac 26:14 It is hard for you to kick **a** the goads.' G4639
Ac 27: 4 of Cyprus because the winds were **a** us. G1885
Ac 27:29 that we would be dashed **a** the rocks, G2848
Ac 28:17 I have done nothing **a** our people or G1885
Ac 28:17 against our people or **a** the customs of our NDT
Ac 28:19 not intend *to* **bring** any **charge a** my own G2989
Ac 28:22 that *people* everywhere *are* **talking a** this G515
Ro 1:18 from heaven **a** all the godlessness G2093
Ro 2: 2 that God's judgment **a** those who do such G2093
Ro 2: 5 are storing up wrath *a* **yourself** for the day of AIT
Ro 2:21 You who preach **a** stealing, do you steal? G3590
Ro 4: 8 sin the Lord *will* never **count a** them." G3357
Ro 4:18 **A** all hope, Abraham in hope believed G4123
Ro 5:13 sin *is* not **charged a** anyone's **account** G1824
Ro 7:23 **waging war a** the law of my mind and G529
Ro 8:31 If God is for us, who can be **a** us? G2848
Ro 8:33 bring any charge **a** those whom God has G2848
Ro 11: 2 Elijah—how he appealed to God **a** Israel: G2848
Ro 13: 2 whoever **rebels a** the authority is rebelling G530
Ro 13: 2 the authority *is* **rebelling a** what God has G468
1Co 4: 6 a follower of one of us **over a** the other. G2848
1Co 6:18 sins sexually, sins **a** their own body. G1650
1Co 8:12 When you sin **a** them in this way and G1650
1Co 8:12 their weak conscience, you sin **a** Christ. G1650
1Co 11:27 guilty of sinning *a* the **body** and blood of the AIT
2Co 5:19 in Christ, not counting people's sins *a* **them**. AIT
2Co 10: 5 that sets itself up **a** the knowledge of God G2848
2Co 13: 8 For we cannot do anything **a** the truth, but G2848
Gal 5:23 **A** such things there is no law. G2848
Eph 6:11 can take your stand **a** the devil's schemes. G4639
Eph 6:12 For our struggle is not **a** flesh and blood G4639
Eph 6:12 flesh and blood, but **a** the rulers, against G4639
Eph 6:12 against the rulers, **a** the authorities G4639
Eph 6:12 **a** the powers of this dark world and G4639
Eph 6:12 this dark world and **a** the spiritual forces G4639
Col 2:14 which stood **a** us **and condemned** us; he G5641
Col 3:13 if any of you has a grievance **a** someone. G4639
1Ti 3:10 then if there is **nothing a** them, let G441
1Ti 5:19 an accusation **a** an elder unless it is G2848
2Ti 2:14 them before God **a** quarreling about G3590
2Ti 4:15 You too should be on your guard *a* **him** AIT
2Ti 4:16 May it not be held *a* **them**. AIT
Heb 12: 4 *In your* **struggle a** sin, you have not yet G497
Jas 4: 4 with the world means enmity *a* **God**? AIT
Jas 4:11 Anyone *who* **speaks a** a brother or sister G2895
Jas 4:11 judges them **speaks a** the law and G2895
Jas 5: 3 corrosion will testify *a* **you** and eat your flesh AIT
Jas 5: 4 mowed your fields are crying out **a** you. G608
Jas 5: 9 Don't grumble **a** one another, brothers G2848
1Pe 2:11 desires, which wage war **a** your soul. G2848
1Pe 3:12 face of the Lord is **a** those who do evil." G2093
1Pe 3:16 those *who* **speak maliciously a** your good G2092
Jude 15 ungodly sinners have spoken **a** him." G2848
Rev 2: 4 Yet I hold this **a** you: You have forsaken G2848
Rev 2:14 I have a few things **a** you: There are some G2848
Rev 2:16 you and will fight **a** them with the sword G3552
Rev 2:20 Nevertheless, I *have* this **a** you: You G2848
Rev 12: 7 his angels fought **a** the dragon, G3552
Rev 12:17 went off to wage war **a** the rest of her G3552
Rev 13: 4 like the beast? Who can wage war **a** it?" G3552
Rev 13: 7 power to wage war **a** God's holy people G3552
Rev 17:14 They will wage war **a** the Lamb, but the G3552
Rev 19:19 together to wage war **a** the rider on the G3552

AGAR (KJV) HAGAR

AGATE (3)

Ex 28:19 row shall be jacinth, **a** and amethyst; H8648
Ex 39:12 the third row was jacinth, **a** and amethyst; H8648
Rev 21:19 sapphire, the third **a**, the fourth emerald, G5907

AGE (68) [AGE-OLD, AGED, AGES, UNDERAGE]

Ge 15:15 in peace and be buried at a good **old a**. H8484
Ge 17:17 bear a child *at* the **a** *of* ninety?" H1426+9102
Ge 18:11 the **a of childbearing**. H784+3869+2021+851
Ge 21: 2 bore a son to Abraham in his **old a**, H2421
Ge 21: 7 Yet I have borne him a son in his **old a**." H2421
Ge 24:36 Sarah has borne him a son in her **old a**, H2420
Ge 25: 8 his last and died at a good **old a**, H8484
Ge 37: 3 he had been born to him in his **old a**; H2421
Ge 44:20 is a young son born to him in his **old a**. H2421
Ge 48:10 eyes were failing because of **old a**, H2419
Ge 50:26 died at the **a** *of* a hundred and ten H1201+9102
Nu 4: 3 to fifty years *of* **a** who come to serve in H1201
Nu 4:23 to fifty years *of* **a** who come to serve in H1201
Nu 4:30 to fifty years *of* **a** who come to serve in H1201
Nu 4:35 to fifty years *of* **a** who came to serve in H1201
Nu 4:39 to fifty years *of* **a** who came to serve in H1201
Nu 4:43 to fifty years *of* **a** who came to serve in H1201
Nu 4:47 to fifty years *of* **a** who came to do the H1201
Nu 8:25 at the **a** *of* fifty, they must retire from H1201
Jos 5: 4 all the men of **military a**—died in the H4878
Jos 5: 6 men who were of **military a** when they left H4878
Jos 24:29 died at the **a** *of* a hundred and ten. H1201+9102
Jdg 2: 8 died at the **a** *of* a hundred and ten. H1201+9102
Jdg 8:32 died at a good **old a** and was buried in H8484
Ru 4:15 your life and sustain you in your **old a**. H8484
1Sa 2:31 so that no one in it will reach **old a**, H2418
1Sa 2:32 in your family line will ever reach **old a**. H2418
2Sa 19:32 Barzillai was very old, eighty years *of* **a**. H1201
1Ki 14: 4 his sight was gone because of his **a**. H8483
1Ki 15:23 In his **old a**, however, his feet became H2420
1Ch 29:28 He died at a good **old a**, having enjoyed H8484
2Ch 24:15 he died at the **a** *of* a hundred and H1201+9102
Job 32: 7 I thought, '**A** should speak; advanced H3427
Ps 92:14 They will still bear fruit in **old a**, they will H8484
Isa 46: 4 Even to your **old a** and gray hairs I am he H2420
Da 1:10 worse than the other young men your **a**? H1636
Da 5:31 kingdom, at the **a** of sixty-two. A10120+10732
Zec 8: 4 again *men* and women **of ripe old a** will H2418
[Zec 8: 4 again men and *women* **of ripe old a** will H2418]
Zec 8: 4 cane in hand because of their **a**. H8044+3427
Mt 12:32 either in this **a** or in the age to come. G172
Mt 12:32 either in this age or in the **a** to come. NDT
Mt 13:39 The harvest is the end *of* the **a**, and the G172
Mt 13:40 in the fire, so it will be at the end *of* the **a**. G172
Mt 13:49 This is how it will be at the end *of* the **a** G172
Mt 24: 3 of your coming and of the end *of* the **a**?" G172
Mt 28:20 with you always, to the very end *of* the **a**." G172
Mk 10:30 hundred times as much in this present **a**: G2789
Mk 10:30 in the **a** to come eternal life. G172
Lk 1:36 is going to have a child in her **old a**, G1179
Lk 18:30 to receive many times as much in this **a**, G2789
Lk 18:30 this age, and in the **a** to come eternal life." G172
Lk 20:34 "The people *of* this **a** marry and are given G172
Lk 20:35 of taking part *in* the **a** to come and in the G172
Jn 9:21 He *is* **of a**; he will speak for himself G2461+2400
Jn 9:23 parents said, "He *is* **of a**; ask him." G2461+2400
1Co 1:20 Where is the philosopher *of* this **a**? Has not G172
1Co 2: 6 not the wisdom *of* this **a** or of the rulers G172
1Co 2: 6 wisdom of this age or of the rulers *of* this **a**, G172
1Co 2: 8 None of the rulers *of* this **a** understood it G172
1Co 3:18 you are wise by the standards *of* this **a**, G172
2Co 4: 4 The god *of* this **a** has blinded the minds of G172
Gal 1: 4 sins to rescue us from the present evil **a**, G172
Gal 1:14 beyond many of *my* **own a** among my G5312
Eph 1:21 only in the present **a** but also in the one to G172
1Ti 6:19 as a firm foundation for the **coming** *a*, AIT
Titus 2:12 upright and godly lives in this present **a**, G172
Heb 6: 5 of God and the powers *of* the coming **a** G172
Heb 11:11 who was past **childbearing a**, was G2789+2461

AGE-OLD (4) [AGE]

Ge 49:26 mountains, than the bounty of the **a** hills. H6409
Jdg 5:21 swept them away, the **a** river, the river H7704
Isa 58:12 raise up the **a** foundations; H1887+2256+1887
Hab 3: 6 crumbled and the **a** hills collapsed— H6409

AGED (11) [AGE]

Ge 43:27 "How is your **a** father you told me about? H2418
Ge 44:20 'We have an **a** father, and there is H2418
Lev 19:32 " 'Stand up in the presence of the **a**, show H8484
1Ki 1:15 went to see the **a** king in his room, H2416+4394
Job 12:12 Is not wisdom found among the **a**? Does H3813
Job 15:10 gray-haired and the **a** are on our side, H3813
Job 32: 9 not only the **a** who understand what is H2418
Pr 17: 6 Children's children are a crown to the **a** H2418
Pr 30:17 that scorns an **a** mother, will be pecked H4272
Isa 25: 6 a banquet of **a wine**—the best of meats H9069
Isa 47: 6 Even on the **a** you laid a very heavy yoke. H2418

AGEE (1)

2Sa 23:11 to him was Shammah son of **A** the Hararite. H96

AGENT (1) [AGENTS]

Ne 11:24 was the king's **a** in all affairs H4200+3338

AGENTS (1) [AGENT]
Ro 13: 4 a of wrath to bring punishment on the G1690

AGES (13) [AGE]
Ge 43:33 before him in the order of their a, H1148+7584
Lev 27: 3 male between the a of twenty and H1201+9102
Lev 27: 5 between the a of five and twenty, H1201+9102
Pr 8:23 I was formed long a ago, at the H4946+6409
Isa 45:17 to shame or disgraced, to a everlasting. H6409
Joel 2: 2 times nor ever will be in a to come. H9102
Ro 16:25 of the mystery hidden for long a past, G173
1Co 10:11 whom the culmination of the a has come. G172
Eph 2: 7 that in the coming a he might show the G172
Eph 3: 9 which for a past was kept hidden in God G172
Col 1:26 been kept hidden for a and generations, G172
Heb 9:26 at the culmination of the a to do away with G172
Jude 25 our Lord, before all a, now and forevermore G172

AGGRESSION (1) [AGGRESSIVE, AGGRESSOR]
Isa 14: 6 in fury subdued nations with relentless a. H5284

AGGRESSIVE (2) [AGGRESSION]
Isa 18: 2 wide, an a nation of strange speech H4431
Isa 18: 7 wide, an a nation of strange speech H4431

AGGRESSOR (1) [AGGRESSION]
Isa 16: 4 the a will vanish from the land. H8252

AGHAST (2)
Job 26:11 of the heavens quake, a at his rebuke. H9449
Isa 13: 8 They will look a at each other, their faces H9449

AGITATING (1) [AGITATORS]
Ac 17:13 a the crowds and stirring them up. G4888

AGITATORS (1) [AGITATING]
Gal 5:12 As for those a, I wish they would go the G415

AGO (52)
Jos 24: 2 'Long a your ancestors, including H4946+6409
1Sa 9:20 the donkeys you lost three days a, H2021+3427
1Sa 30:13 me when I became ill three days a. AIT
2Sa 20:18 "Long a they used to say H928+2021+8037
2Ki 19:25 Long a I ordained it H4200+4946+8158
Ezr 5:11 was built many years a, A10427+10622+10180
Ne 12:46 For long a, in the days of David and H4946+7710
Ps 44: 1 what you did in their days, in days long a. H7710
Ps 74: 2 the nation you purchased long a, H7710
Ps 74:12 But God is my King from long a; he brings H7710
Ps 77: 5 the former days, the years of long a; H6409
Ps 77:11 I will remember your miracles of long a. H7710
Ps 93: 2 Your throne was established long a H4946+255
Ps 119:152 Long a I learned from your statutes that H7710
Ps 143: 5 I remember the days of long a; I meditate H7710
Pr 8:23 I was formed long ages a, at the H4946+6409
Ecc 1:10 here already, long a; it was here H4200+6409
Isa 22:11 the One who planned it long a. H4946+8158
Isa 25: 1 things, things planned long a. H4946+8158
Isa 37:26 Long a I ordained it H4200+4946+8158
Isa 44: 8 proclaim this and foretell it long a? H4946+255
Isa 45:21 Who foretold this long a, who H4946+7710
Isa 46: 9 former things, those of long a; I am God, H6409
Isa 48: 3 I foretold the former things long a H4946+255
Isa 48: 5 I told you these things long a; H4946+255
Isa 48: 7 and not long a; you have not H4946+255
Jer 2:20 "Long a you broke off your yoke H4946+6409
La 2:17 which he decreed long a. H4946+3427+7710
Eze 26:20 down to the pit, to the people of long a. H6409
Mic 7:14 in Bashan and Gilead as in days long a. H6409
Mic 7:20 on oath to our ancestors in days long a. H7710
Mt 5:21 heard that it was said to the people long a, G792
Mt 5:33 heard that it was said to the people long a, G792
Mt 11:21 have repented long a in sackcloth and G4093
Mk 6:15 a prophet, like one of the prophets of long a." AIT
Lk 1:70 said through his holy prophets of long a), G172
Lk 9: 8 of the prophets of long a had come back to G792
Lk 9:19 of the prophets of long a has come back to G792
Lk 10:13 they would have repented long a, sitting G4093
Jn 11: 8 "a short while a the Jews there tried to G3814
Ac 1:16 Holy Spirit spoke long a through David G4625
Ac 3:21 as he promised long a through his G608+172
Ac 5:36 Some time a Theudas G4574+4047+3836+2465
Ac 10:30 "Three days a I was in my house G608+5480
Ac 15: 7 that some time a God made G608+2465+792
Ac 15:18 things known from long a. G172
Ac 21:38 wilderness some time a?" G4574+4047+3836+2465
Ac 24:11 than twelve days a I went up to G608+4005
2Co 12: 2 who fourteen years a was caught up to G4574
1Pe 3:20 disobedient long a when God waited G4537
2Pe 3: 5 forget that long a by God's word the G1732
Jude 4 was written about long a have secretly G4093

AGONE (KJV) AGO

AGONY (11)
Ps 6: 2 heal me, LORD, for my bones are in a. H987
Ps 42:10 My bones suffer mortal a as my foes taunt H8358
Jer 4:19 Oh, the a of my heart! My heart H7815
Eze 30:16 to Egypt; Pelusium will writhe in a. H2655+2655
Mic 4:10 Writhe in a, Daughter Zion, like a woman H1631
Zec 9: 5 Gaza will writhe in a, and Ekron H2655+4394
Lk 16:24 my tongue, because I am in a in this fire. G3849
Lk 16:25 he is comforted here and you are in a. G3849
Ac 2:24 freeing him from the a of death G6047
Rev 9: 5 And the a they suffered was like that of the G990
Rev 16:10 People gnawed their tongues in a G4506

AGREE (14) [AGREED, AGREEING, AGREEMENT, AGREEMENTS, AGREES, DISAGREE, DISAGREEMENT]
Ge 34:17 But if you will not a to be circumcised H9048
Ge 34:22 But the men will a to live with us as one H252
Ge 34:23 So let us a to their terms, and they will H252
2Sa 14:16 Perhaps the king will a to deliver his H9048
1Ki 20: 8 "Don't listen to him or a to his demands." H14
1Ki 22:13 Let your word a with theirs H2118+3869+285
2Ch 18:12 Let your word a with theirs H2118+3869+285
Mt 18:19 two of you on earth a about anything they G5244
Mt 20:13 Didn't you a to work for a denarius? G5244
Mk 14:56 but their statements did not a. G2698
Mk 14:59 Yet even then their testimony did not a. G2698
Ro 7:16 not want to do, I a that the law is good. G5238
1Co 1:10 of you a with one another in what you say G3836+899+3306
1Ti 6: 3 otherwise and does not a to the sound G4665

AGREED (27) [AGREE]
Ge 16: 2 Abram a to what Sarai said H9048
Ge 23:16 Abraham a to Ephron's terms and H9048
Ge 30:34 "A," said Laban. "Let it be as you have H2176
Ge 34:24 out of the city gate a with Hamor and his H9048
Ge 37:27 our own flesh and blood." His brothers a. H9048
Ex 2:21 Moses a to stay with the man, who gave H3283
Jos 2:21 "A," she replied. "Let it be as you say." H4026
Jdg 15:13 "A," they answered. "We will only tie you H4202
Jdg 17:11 So the Levite a to live with him, and the H3283
1Ki 15:20 Ben-Hadad a with King Asa and sent the H9048
1Ki 20:25 He a with them and acted H9048+4200+7754
2Ki 12: 8 The priests a that they would not collect any H252
1Ch 13: 4 The whole assembly a to do this, because it H606
2Ch 16: 4 Ben-Hadad a with King Asa and sent the H9048
2Ch 20:36 He a with him to construct a fleet of H2489
2Ch 30:23 whole assembly then a to celebrate the H3619
Est 9:23 So the Jews a to continue the celebration H7691
Jer 34:10 into this covenant a that they would free H9048
Jer 34:10 them in bondage. They a, and set them H9048
Da 1:14 So he a to this and tested them for ten H9048
Da 6: 7 governors have all a that the king A10324
Am 3: 3 together unless they have a to do so? H3359
Mt 20: 2 He a to pay them a denarius for the day G5244
Lk 22: 5 were delighted and a to give him money. G5338
Ac 15:25 So we all a to choose some G1506+1181+3924
Ac 23:20 "Some Jews have a to ask you to bring G5338
Gal 2: 9 They a that we should go to the Gentiles NDT

AGREEING (1) [AGREE]
Rev 17:17 his purpose by a to hand G4472+1651+1191

AGREEMENT (13) [AGREE]
Ge 26:28 ought to be a sworn a between us'— H460
Ge 34:15 We will enter into an a with you on one H252
2Sa 3:12 Make an a with me, and I will help you H1382
2Sa 3:13 "I will make an a with you. But I demand H1382
Ne 9:38 we are making a binding a, putting it in H591
Job 2:11 homes and met together by a to go and H3585
Job 41: 4 Will it make an a with you for you to take H1382
Isa 28:15 realm of the dead we have made an a. H2603
Isa 28:18 your a with the realm of the dead will not H2607
Da 11:23 After coming to an a with him, he will act H2489
Ac 15:15 words of the prophets are in a with this, G5244
2Co 6:16 What a is there between the temple of G5161
1Jn 5: 8 and the three are in a. G1650+3836+1651

AGREEMENTS (1) [AGREE]
Hos 10: 4 take false oaths and make a; therefore H1382

AGREES (2) [AGREE]
Ac 7:42 This a with what is written in the book of G2777
1Co 4:17 which a with what I teach everywhere in G2777

AGRIPPA (13)
Ac 25:13 A few days later King A and Bernice arrived G68
Ac 25:22 Then A said to Festus, "I would like to hear G68
Ac 25:23 The next day A and Bernice came with great G68
Ac 25:24 "King A, and all who are present with us G68
Ac 25:26 before you, King A, so that as a result of G68
Ac 26: 1 Then A said to Paul, "You have permission G68
Ac 26: 2 "King A, I consider myself fortunate to stand G68
Ac 26: 7 King A, it is because of this hope that these NDT
Ac 26:13 About noon, King A, as I was on the road, I NDT
Ac 26:19 "So then, King A, I was not disobedient to G68
Ac 26:27 King A, do you believe the prophets? I know G68
Ac 26:28 Then A said to Paul, "Do you think that in G68
Ac 26:32 A said to Festus, "This man could have been G68

AGROUND (4) [GROUND]
Ac 27:17 were afraid they would run a on the G1738
Ac 27:26 we must run a on some island. G1738
Ac 27:39 they decided to run the ship a if they G2034
Ac 27:41 But the ship struck a sandbar and ran a G2131

AGUE (KJV) FEVER

AGUR (1)
Pr 30: 1 The sayings of A son of Jakeh—an inspired H101

AH (4) [AHA]
Ge 27:27 him and said, "A, the smell of my son H8011
Isa 1:24 "A! I will vent my wrath on my H2098
Isa 44:16 warms himself and says, "A! I am warm; H2027
Jer 32:17 "A, Sovereign LORD, you have made the H177

AHA (11) [AH]
Job 39:25 trumpet it snorts, 'A!' It catches the scent H2027
Ps 35:21 at me and say, "A! Aha! With our own H2027
Ps 35:21 A! With our own eyes we have H2027
Ps 35:25 let them think, "A, just what we wanted H2027
Ps 40:15 who say to me, "A! Aha!" be appalled at H2027
Ps 40:15 A!" be appalled at their own H2027
Ps 70: 3 those who say to me, "A! Aha!" turn back H2027
Ps 70: 3 A!" turn back because of their H2027
Eze 25: 3 Because you said "A!" over my sanctuary H2027
Eze 26: 2 because Tyre has said of Jerusalem, 'A! H2027
Eze 36: 2 enemy said of you, "A! The ancient H2027

AHAB (85) [AHAB'S]
1Ki 16:28 And A his son succeeded him as king H281
1Ki 16:29 A son of Omri became king of Israel H281
1Ki 16:30 A son of Omri did more evil in the eyes of H281
1Ki 16:33 A also made an Asherah pole and did H281
1Ki 17: 1 Tishbe in Gilead, said to A, "As the LORD, H281
1Ki 18: 1 "Go and present yourself to A, and I will H281
1Ki 18: 2 So Elijah went to present himself to A. Now H281
1Ki 18: 3 A had summoned Obadiah, his palace H281
1Ki 18: 5 A had said to Obadiah, "Go through the H281
1Ki 18: 6 A going in one direction and Obadiah in H281
1Ki 18: 9 your servant over to A to be put to death? H281
1Ki 18:12 If I go and tell A and he doesn't find you H281
1Ki 18:15 I will surely present myself to A today." H2257S
1Ki 18:16 So Obadiah went to meet A and told him H281
1Ki 18:16 told him, and A went to meet Elijah. H281
1Ki 18:20 So A sent word throughout all Israel and H281
1Ki 18:41 And Elijah said to A, "Go, eat and drink H281
1Ki 18:42 So A went off to eat and drink, but Elijah H281
1Ki 18:44 "Go and tell A, 'Hitch up your chariot H281
1Ki 18:45 started falling and A rode off to Jezreel. H281
1Ki 18:46 he ran ahead of A all the way to Jezreel. H281
1Ki 19: 1 Now A told Jezebel everything Elijah had H281
1Ki 20: 2 messengers into the city to A king of Israel, H281
1Ki 20:10 Ben-Hadad sent another message to A: H2257S
1Ki 20:13 a prophet came to A king of Israel and H281
1Ki 20:14 asked A. The prophet replied, H281
1Ki 20:15 So A summoned the 232 junior officers NDT
1Ki 20:33 A had him come up into his chariot. NDT
1Ki 20:34 A said, "On the basis of a treaty I will set NDT
1Ki 21: 1 close to the palace of A king of Samaria. H281
1Ki 21: 2 A said to Naboth, "Let me have your H281
1Ki 21: 4 So A went home, sullen and angry H281
1Ki 21:15 to death, she said to A, "Get up and take H281
1Ki 21:16 When A heard that Naboth was dead, he H281
1Ki 21:18 "Go down to meet A king of Israel, who H281
1Ki 21:20 A said to Elijah, "So you have found me H281
1Ki 21:21 cut off from A every last male in Israel H281
1Ki 21:24 those belonging to A who die in the city, H281
1Ki 21:25 There was never anyone like A, who sold H281
1Ki 21:27 When A heard these words, he tore his H281
1Ki 21:29 you noticed how A has humbled himself H281
1Ki 22:20 'Who will entice A into attacking Ramoth H281
1Ki 22:40 A rested with his ancestors. And Ahaziah H281
1Ki 22:41 Judah in the fourth year of A king of Israel. H281
1Ki 22:49 time Ahaziah son of A said to Jehoshaphat H281
1Ki 22:51 Ahaziah son of A became king of Israel in H281
2Ki 3: 1 Joram son of A became king of Israel in H281
2Ki 3: 5 But after A died, the king of Moab rebelled H281
2Ki 8:16 fifth year of Joram son of A king of Israel, H281
2Ki 8:18 as the house of A had done, for he H281
2Ki 8:18 had done, for he married a daughter of A. H281
2Ki 8:25 year of Joram son of A king of Israel, H281
2Ki 8:27 ways of the house of A and did evil in the H281
2Ki 8:27 as the house of A had done, for he was H281
2Ki 8:28 with Joram son of A to war against Hazael H281
2Ki 8:29 down to Jezreel to see Joram son of A, H281
2Ki 9: 7 are to destroy the house of A your master, H281
2Ki 9: 8 The whole house of A will perish. I will cut H281
2Ki 9: 8 I will cut off from A every last male in Israel H281
2Ki 9: 9 I will make the house of A like the house of H281
2Ki 9:25 in chariots behind A his father when the H281
2Ki 9:29 In the eleventh year of Joram son of A H281
2Ki 10: 1 in Samaria seventy sons of the house of A. H281
2Ki 10:10 has spoken against the house of A will fail. H281
2Ki 10:11 in Jezreel who remained of the house of A, H281
2Ki 10:18 said to them, "A served Baal a little H281
2Ki 10:30 done to the house of A all I had in mind to H281
2Ki 21: 3 as A king of Israel had done. H281
2Ki 21:13 plumb line used against the house of A. H281
2Ch 18: 1 he allied himself with A by marriage. H281
2Ch 18: 2 later he went down to see A in Samaria. H281
2Ch 18: 2 A slaughtered many sheep and cattle for H281
2Ch 18: 3 A king of Israel asked Jehoshaphat king of H281
2Ch 18:19 'Who will entice A king of Israel into H281
2Ch 21: 6 as the house of A had done, for he H281
2Ch 21: 6 had done, for he married a daughter of A. H281
2Ch 21:13 themselves, just as the house of A did. H281
2Ch 22: 3 too followed the ways of the house of A, H281
2Ch 22: 4 as the house of A had done, for after H281
2Ch 22: 5 with Joram son of A king of Israel to wage H281
2Ch 22: 6 see Joram son of A because he had been H281
2Ch 22: 7 had anointed to destroy the house of A. H281

2Ch 22: 8 executing judgment on the house of A, H281
Jer 29:21 says about A son of Kolaiah and Zedekiah H281
Jer 29:22 the LORD treat you like Zedekiah and A, H282

AHAB'S (8) [AHAB]

1Ki 16:34 In A time, Hiel of Bethel rebuilt Jericho H2257S
1Ki 21: 8 So she wrote letters in A name, placed his H281
1Ki 22:39 As for the other events of A reign H281
2Ki 1: 1 After A death, Moab rebelled against H281
2Ki 8:27 he was related by marriage to A family. H281
2Ki 10: 1 elders and to the guardians of A children. H281
2Ki 10:17 killed all who were left there of A family; H281
Mic 6:16 of Omri and all the practices of A house; H281

AHARAH (1)

1Ch 8: 1 Ashbel the second son, A the third, H341

AHARHEL (1)

1Ch 4: 8 of the clans of A son of Harum. H342

AHASAI (KJV) AHZAI

AHASBAI (1)

2Sa 23:34 Eliphelet son of A the Maakathite, Eliam H335

AHASUERUS (KJV) XERXES

AHAVA (3)

Ezr 8:15 them at the canal that flows toward A, H178
Ezr 8:21 by the A Canal, I proclaimed a fast H178
Ezr 8:31 we set out from the A Canal to go to H178

AHAZ (44)

2Ki 15:38 And A his son succeeded him as king H298
2Ki 16: 1 A son of Jotham king of Judah began to H298
2Ki 16: 2 A was twenty years old when he became H298
2Ki 16: 5 to fight against Jerusalem and besieged A, H298
2Ki 16: 7 A sent messengers to say to Tiglath-Pileser H298
2Ki 16: 8 And A took the silver and gold found in the H298
2Ki 16:10 Then King A went to Damascus to meet H298
2Ki 16:11 the plans that King A had sent from H298
2Ki 16:11 finished it before King A returned. H298
2Ki 16:15 King A then gave these orders to Uriah the H298
2Ki 16:16 the priest did just as King A had ordered. H298
2Ki 16:17 King A cut off the side panels and removed H298
2Ki 16:19 As for the other events of the reign of A H298
2Ki 16:20 A rested with his ancestors and was buried H298
2Ki 17: 1 In the twelfth year of A king of Judah H298
2Ki 18: 1 Hezekiah son of A king of Judah began to H298
2Ki 20:11 it had gone down on the stairway of A. H298
2Ki 23:12 on the roof near the upper room of A, H298
1Ch 3:13 A his son, Hezekiah his son, Manasseh his H298
1Ch 8:35 Pithon, Melek, Tarea and A. H298
1Ch 8:36 A was the father of Jehoaddah, Jehoaddah H298
1Ch 9:41 Pithon, Melek, Tahrea and A. H298
1Ch 9:42 A was the father of Jadah, Jadah was the H298
2Ch 27: 9 And A his son succeeded him as king H298
2Ch 28: 1 A was twenty years old when he became H298
2Ch 28:16 At that time King A sent to the kings of H298
2Ch 28:19 Judah because of A king of Israel, H298
2Ch 28:21 A took some of the things from the temple H298
2Ch 28:22 time of trouble King A became even more H298
2Ch 28:24 A gathered together the furnishings from H298
2Ch 28:27 A rested with his ancestors and was buried H298
2Ch 29:19 all the articles that King A removed in his H298
Isa 1: 1 of Uzziah, Jotham, A and Hezekiah, kings H298
Isa 7: 1 When A son of Jotham, the son of Uzziah H298
Isa 7: 2 so the hearts of A and his people were H2257S
Isa 7: 3 to meet A at the end of the aqueduct of H298
Isa 7:10 Again the LORD spoke to A, H298
Isa 7:12 But A said, "I will not ask; I will not put the H298
Isa 14:28 prophecy came in the year King A died: H298
Isa 38: 8 it has gone down on the stairway of A. H298
Hos 1: 1 of Uzziah, Jotham, A and Hezekiah, kings H298
Mic 1: 1 reigns of Jotham, A and Hezekiah, kings H298
Mt 1: 9 Jotham the father of A, Ahaz the father of G937
Mt 1: 9 father of Ahaz, A the father of Hezekiah G937

AHAZIAH (39) [AHAZIAH'S]

1Ki 22:40 And A his son succeeded him as king H302
1Ki 22:49 At that time A son of Ahab said to H302
1Ki 22:51 A son of Ahab became king of Israel in H302
2Ki 1: 2 Now A had fallen through the lattice of his H301
2Ki 1:17 Because A had no son, Joram H2257S
2Ki 8:24 And A his son succeeded him as king H302
2Ki 8:25 A son of Jehoram king of Judah began to H302
2Ki 8:26 A was twenty-two years old when he H302
2Ki 8:28 A went with Joram son of Ahab to war NDT
2Ki 8:29 Then A son of Jehoram king of Judah went H302
2Ki 9:16 was resting there and A king of Judah had H301
2Ki 9:21 king of Israel and A king of Judah rode out, H302
2Ki 9:23 fled, calling out to A, "Treachery, H302
2Ki 9:23 calling out to Ahaziah, "Treachery, A!" H301
2Ki 9:27 When A king of Judah saw what had H301
2Ki 9:29 son of Ahab, A had become king of Judah.) H301
2Ki 10:13 met some relatives of A king of Judah and H302
2Ki 10:13 "We are relatives of A, and we have come H302
2Ki 11: 1 the mother of A saw that her son was H302
2Ki 11: 2 daughter of King Jehoram and sister of A, H302
2Ki 11: 2 took Joash son of A and stole him away H301
2Ki 12:18 Jehoram and A, the kings of Judah— H302
2Ki 13: 1 year of Joash son of A king of Judah, H302
2Ki 14:13 of Joash, the son of A, at Beth Shemesh. H302
1Ch 3:11 Jehoram his son, A his son, Joash his son, H302
2Ch 20:35 made an alliance with A king of Israel, H301
2Ch 20:37 you have made an alliance with A, H302
2Ch 21:17 Not a son was left to him except A, the H3370
2Ch 22: 1 The people of Jerusalem made A H302
2Ch 22: 1 So A son of Jehoram king of Judah began H302
2Ch 22: 2 A was twenty-two years old when he H302
2Ch 22: 6 Then A son of Jehoram king of Judah went H302
2Ch 22: 7 When A arrived, he went out with Joram H2257S
2Ch 22: 8 who had been attending A, and he killed H302
2Ch 22: 9 He then went in search of A, and his men H302
2Ch 22: 9 one in the house of A powerful enough to H302
2Ch 22:10 the mother of A saw that her son was H302
2Ch 22:11 took Joash son of A and stole him away H302
2Ch 25:23 of Joash, the son of A, at Beth Shemesh. H3370

AHAZIAH'S (5) [AHAZIAH]

2Ki 1:18 As for all the other events of A reign, and H302
2Ch 22: 7 Through A visit to Joram, God brought NDT
2Ch 22: 7 to Joram, God brought about A downfall. H302
2Ch 22: 8 of Judah and the sons of A relatives, H302
2Ch 22:11 priest Jehoiada, was A sister, she hid the H302

AHBAN (1)

1Ch 2:29 Abihail, who bore him A and Molid. H283

AHEAD (97) [HEAD]

Ge 31:18 and he drove all his livestock a of him H5627
Ge 32: 3 sent messengers a of him to his H4200+7156
Ge 32:16 servants, "Go a of me, and keep H7156+4200
Ge 32:20 with these gifts I am sending on a; H4200+7156
Ge 32:21 So Jacob's gifts went on a of him H6584+7156
Ge 33: 3 went on a and bowed down H7156+4200
Ge 33:14 let my lord go on a of his servant, H7156+4200
Ge 45: 5 lives that God sent me a of you. H7156+4200
Ge 45: 7 But God sent me a of you to H7156+4200
Ge 46:28 sent Judah a of him to Joseph H7156+4200
Ge 48:20 So he put Ephraim a of Manasseh. H7156+4200
Ex 13:21 the LORD went a of them in a pillar H7156+4200
Ex 23:20 sending an angel a of you to guard H7156+4200
Ex 23:23 My angel will go a of you and bring H7156+4200
Ex 23:27 send my terror a of you and throw H7156+4200
Ex 23:28 send the hornet a of you to drive H7156+4200
Nu 11:15 treat me, please go a and kill me—if I have AIT
Nu 22:26 of the LORD moved on a and stood in a H6296
Nu 32:17 battle and go a of the Israelites H4200+7156
Dt 1:22 "Let us send men a to spy out the H4200+7156
Dt 1:33 who went a of you on your journey H4200+7156
Dt 3:18 must cross over a of the other H4200+7156
Dt 9: 3 who goes across a of you like a H4200+7156
Dt 31: 3 himself will cross over a of you. H4200+7156
Dt 31: 3 Joshua also will cross over a of you, H4200+7156
Jos 1:14 must cross over a of your fellow H4200+7156
Jos 3: 6 and pass on a of the people. H4200+7156
Jos 3: 6 they took it up and went a of them. H4200+7156
Jos 3:11 will go into the Jordan a of you. H4200+7156
Jos 3:14 ark of the covenant went a of them. H4200+7156
Jos 6: 7 guard going a of the ark of the H4200+7156
Jos 6: 9 guard marched a of the priests who H4200+7156
Jos 6:13 men went a of them and the H4200+7156
Jos 24:12 I sent the hornet a of you, which H4200+7156
Jdg 4:14 Has not the LORD gone a of you?" H4200+7156
Jdg 7:24 of the Jordan a of them as far as Beth H4200
Ru 2: 2 Naomi said to her, "Go a, my daughter." H2143
1Sa 9:12 "He's a of you. Hurry now H4200+7156
1Sa 9:19 "Go up a of me to the high place H4200+7156
1Sa 9:27 "Tell the servant to go on a of us"— H4200+7156
1Sa 10: 8 "Go down a of me to Gilgal. I will H4200+7156
1Sa 14: 7 armor-bearer said. "Go a; I am with you H5742
1Sa 17: 7 His shield bearer went a of him. H4200+7156
1Sa 23:24 set out and went to Ziph a of Saul. H4200+7156
1Sa 25:19 servants, "Go on a; I'll follow you." H4200+7156
1Sa 30:20 his men drove them a of the other H4200+7156
2Sa 7: 3 you have in mind, go a and do it, for the H2143
2Sa 15: 1 and with fifty men to run a of him. H4200+7156
2Sa 15:22 said to Ittai, "Go a, march on." So Ittai H2143
1Ki 1: 5 with fifty men to run a of him. H4200+7156
1Ki 18:46 he ran a of Ahab all the way to H4200+7156
2Ki 4:31 Gehazi went on a and laid the staff H4200+7156
2Ki 5:23 and they carried them a of Gehazi. H4200+7156
2Ki 6:32 king sent a messenger a, H4946+4200+7156
Ne 4: 7 walls had gone a and that the H6590
Pr 4:25 Let your eyes look straight a; fix H4200+5790
Jer 7:21 Go a, add your burnt offerings to your other AIT
Jer 44:25 "'Go a then, do what you promised AIT
Eze 1: 9 Each one went straight a H448+6298+7156
Eze 1:12 Each one went straight a H448+6298+7156
Eze 10:22 Each one went straight a. H448+6298+7156
Joel 2: 8 each other; each marches straight a. H5019
Mt 2: 9 seen when it rose went a of them until it G4575
Mt 11:10 'I will send my messenger a of you, G4574+4725
Mt 14:22 into the boat and go on a of him to the G4575
Mt 21: 2 "Go to the village a of you, and at once G2978
Mt 21: 9 The crowds that went a of him and those G4575
Mt 21:31 are entering the kingdom of God a of you. G4575
Mt 23:32 Go a, then, and complete what your ancestors AIT
Mt 24:25 I have told you a of time. G4625
Mt 26:32 have risen, I will go a of you into Galilee." G4575
Mt 28: 7 from the dead and is going a of you into G4575
Mk 1: 2 "I will send my messenger a of you, G4574+4725
Mk 6:33 all the towns and got there a of them. G4601
Mk 6:45 into the boat and go on a of him to G4575
Mk 11: 2 "Go to the village a of you, and just as G2978
Mk 11: 9 Those who went a and those who G4575
Mk 13:23 I have told you everything a of time. G4625
Mk 14:28 have risen, I will go a of you into Galilee." G4575
Mk 16: 7 'He is going a of you into Galilee. G4575
Lk 7:27 'I will send my messenger a of you, G4574+4725
Lk 9:52 And he sent messengers on a, who G4574+4725
Lk 10: 1 them two by two a of him to every G4574+4725
Lk 19: 4 So he ran a and climbed G4731+1650+3836+1869
Lk 19:28 said this, he went on a, going up to G1869
Lk 19:30 "Go to the village a of you, and as you G2978
Lk 19:32 Those who were sent a went and found it NDT
Jn 3:28 am not the Messiah but am sent a of him. G1869
Jn 5: 7 someone else goes down a of me." G4574
Jn 10: 4 his own, he goes on a of them, and his G1869
Ac 20: 5 These men went on a and waited for us at G4601
Ac 20:13 We went on a to the ship and sailed for G4601
1Co 11:21 some of you go a with your own private G4624
Php 3:13 is behind and straining toward what is a, G1869
1Ti 5:24 reaching the place of judgment a of them; G4575
Heb 11:26 because he was looking a to his reward. G611
2Jn 9 Anyone who runs a and does not continue G4575

AHER (1)

1Ch 7:12 and the Hushites the descendants of A. H338

AHI (2)

1Ch 5:15 A son of Abdiel, the son of Guni, was head H306
1Ch 7:34 sons of Shomer: A, Rohgah, Hubbah and H306

AHIAH (1)

Ne 10:26 A, Hanan, Anan, H308

AHIAM (2)

2Sa 23:33 the Hararite, A son of Sharar the Hararite H307
1Ch 11:35 A son of Sakar the Hararite, Eliphal son of H307

AHIAN (1)

1Ch 7:19 of Shemida were: A, Shechem, Likhi and H319

AHIEZER (6)

Nu 1:12 from Dan, A son of Ammishaddai; H323
Nu 2:25 people of Dan is A son of Ammishaddai. H323
Nu 7:66 On the tenth day A son of Ammishaddai H323
Nu 7:71 was the offering of A son of Ammishaddai. H323
Nu 10:25 A son of Ammishaddai was in command. H323
1Ch 12: 3 A their chief and Joash the sons of H323

AHIHUD (2)

Nu 34:27 A son of Shelomi, the leader from the tribe H310
1Ch 8: 7 who was the father of Uzza and A. H312

AHIJAH (21) [AHIJAH'S]

1Sa 14: 3 among whom was A, who was wearing an H308
1Sa 14:18 Saul said to A, "Bring the ark of God." H308
1Ki 4: 3 Elihoreph and A, sons of Shisha H308
1Ki 11:29 A the prophet of Shiloh met him on H308
1Ki 11:30 A took hold of the new cloak he was H308
1Ki 12:15 son of Nebat through A the Shilonite. H308
1Ki 14: 2 A the prophet is there—the one who told H308
1Ki 14: 4 Now A could not see; his sight was gone H309
1Ki 14: 5 But the LORD had told A, "Jeroboam's wife H309
1Ki 14: 6 So when A heard the sound of her H309
1Ki 14:18 had said through his servant the prophet A. H309
1Ki 15:27 Baasha son of A from the tribe of Issachar H308
1Ki 15:29 given through his servant A the Shilonite. H308
1Ki 15:33 Baasha son of A became king of all Israel H308
1Ki 21:22 son of Nebat and that of Baasha son of A, H308
2Ki 9: 9 like the house of Baasha son of A. H308
1Ch 2:25 his firstborn, Bunah, Oren, Ozem and A. H308
1Ch 8: 7 Naaman, A, and Gera, who deported them H308
1Ch 11:36 Hepher the Mekerathite, A the Pelonite, H308
2Ch 9:29 in the prophecy of A the Shilonite and in H308
2Ch 10:15 son of Nebat through A the Shilonite. H309

AHIJAH'S (1) [AHIJAH]

1Ki 14: 4 he said and went to A house in Shiloh. H308

AHIKAM (20)

2Ki 22:12 Hilkiah the priest, A son of Shaphan, Akbor H324
2Ki 22:14 Hilkiah the priest, A, Akbor, Shaphan and H324
2Ki 25:22 of Babylon appointed Gedaliah son of A, H324
2Ch 34:20 orders to Hilkiah, A son of Shaphan H324
Jer 26:24 A son of Shaphan supported Jeremiah H324
Jer 39:14 They turned him over to Gedaliah son of A H324
Jer 40: 5 "Go back to Gedaliah son of A, the son of H324
Jer 40: 6 to Gedaliah son of A at Mizpah and stayed H324
Jer 40: 7 Gedaliah son of A as governor over the H324
Jer 40: 9 Gedaliah son of A, the son of Shaphan H324
Jer 40:11 had appointed Gedaliah son of A, H324
Jer 40:14 But Gedaliah son of A did not believe H324
Jer 40:16 But Gedaliah son of A said to Johanan son H324
Jer 41: 1 ten men to Gedaliah son of A at Mizpah. H324
Jer 41: 2 got up and struck down Gedaliah son of A, H324
Jer 41: 6 he said, "Come to Gedaliah son of A." H324
Jer 41:10 guard had appointed Gedaliah son of A. H324
Jer 41:16 had assassinated Gedaliah son of A— H324
Jer 41:18 of Nethaniah had killed Gedaliah son of A, H324
Jer 43: 6 guard had left with Gedaliah son of A, H324

AHILUD (5)

2Sa 8:16 Jehoshaphat son of A was recorder; H314
2Sa 20:24 Jehoshaphat son of A was recorder; H314
1Ki 4: 3 Jehoshaphat son of A—recorder; H314

1Ki 4:12 Baana son of A—in Taanach and Megiddo, H314
1Ch 18:15 Jehoshaphat son of A was recorder; H314

AHIMAAZ (15)
1Sa 14:50 wife's name was Ahinoam daughter of A. H318
2Sa 15:27 Take your son A with you, and also H318
2Sa 15:36 A son of Zadok and Jonathan son of H318
2Sa 17:17 Jonathan and A were staying at En Rogel H318
2Sa 17:20 they asked, "Where are A and Jonathan?" H318
2Sa 18:19 Now A son of Zadok said, "Let me run and H318
2Sa 18:22 A son of Zadok again said to Joab, "Come H318
2Sa 18:23 Then A ran by way of the plain and outran H318
2Sa 18:27 that the first one runs like A son of Zadok." H318
2Sa 18:28 Then A called out to the king, "All is well!" H318
2Sa 18:29 A answered, "I saw great confusion just as H318
1Ki 4:15 A—in Naphtali (he had married Basemath H318
1Ch 6: 8 the father of Zadok, Zadok the father of A, H318
1Ch 6: 9 A the father of Azariah, Azariah the father H318
1Ch 6:53 Zadok his son and A his son. H318

AHIMAN (4)
Nu 13:22 to Hebron, where A, Sheshai and Talmai, H317
Jos 15:14 Anakites—Sheshai, A and Talmai, the H317
Jdg 1:10 defeated Sheshai, A and Talmai. H317
1Ch 9:17 Talmon, A and their fellow Levites H317

AHIMELECH (NIV84) AHIMELEK

AHIMELEK (19)
1Sa 21: 1 went to Nob, to A the priest. Ahimelek H316
1Sa 21: 1 A trembled when he met him, and asked H316
1Sa 21: 2 David answered A the priest, "The king H316
1Sa 21: 8 David asked A, "Don't you have a spear H316
1Sa 22: 9 of Jesse come to A son of Ahitub at Nob H316
1Sa 22:10 A inquired of the LORD for him; he also gave NDT
1Sa 22:11 sent for the priest A son of Ahitub and all H316
1Sa 22:14 A answered the king, "Who of all your H316
1Sa 22:16 "You will surely die, A, you and your whole H316
1Sa 22:20 But one son of A son of Ahitub, named H316
1Sa 23: 6 Now Abiathar son of A had brought the H316
1Sa 26: 6 David then asked A the Hittite and Abishai H316
1Sa 30: 7 the son of A, "Bring me the ephod. H316
2Sa 8:17 son of Ahitub and A son of Abiathar were H316
1Ch 18:16 son of Ahitub and A son of Abiathar were H316
1Ch 24: 3 of Eleazar and A a descendant of Ithamar, H316
1Ch 24: 6 A son of Abiathar and the heads of H316
1Ch 24:31 David and of Zadok, A, and the heads of H316
Ps 52: T "David has gone to the house of A." H316

AHIMOTH (1)
1Ch 6:25 The descendants of Elkanah: Amasai, A, H315

AHINADAB (1)
1Ki 4:14 A son of Iddo—in Mahanaim; H320

AHINOAM (7)
1Sa 14:50 His wife's name was A daughter of H321
1Sa 25:43 David had also married A of Jezreel, and H321
1Sa 27: 3 A of Jezreel and Abigail of Carmel, the H321
1Sa 30: 5 been captured—A of Jezreel and Abigail H321
2Sa 2: 2 his two wives, A of Jezreel and Abigail H321
2Sa 3: 2 was Amnon the son of A of Jezreel; H321
1Ch 3: 1 was Amnon the son of A of Jezreel; H321

AHIO (6)
2Sa 6: 3 Uzzah and A, sons of Abinadab, were H311
2Sa 6: 4 God on it, and A was walking in front of it. H311
1Ch 8:14 A, Shashak, Jeremoth, H311
1Ch 8:31 A, Zeker H311
1Ch 9:37 A, Zechariah and Mikloth. H311
1Ch 13: 7 on a new cart, with Uzzah and A guiding it. H311

AHIRA (5)
Nu 1:15 from Naphtali, A son of Enan." H327
Nu 2:29 of the people of Naphtali is A son of Enan. H327
Nu 7:78 On the twelfth day A son of Enan, the H327
Nu 7:83 This was the offering of A son of Enan. H327
Nu 10:27 A son of Enan was over the division of H327

AHIRAM (1) [AHIRAMITE]
Nu 26:38 through A, the Ahiramite clan; H325

AHIRAMITE (1) [AHIRAM]
Nu 26:38 through Ahiram, the A clan; H326

AHISAMACH (NIV84) AHISAMAK

AHISAMAK (3)
Ex 31: 6 I have appointed Oholiab son of A, of the H322
Ex 35:34 has given both him and Oholiab son of A, H322
Ex 38:23 with him was Oholiab son of A, of the tribe H322

AHISHAHAR (1)
1Ch 7:10 Kenaanah, Zethan, Tarshish and A. H328

AHISHAR (1)
1Ki 4: 6 A—palace administrator; Adoniram son of H329

AHITHOPHEL (17) [AHITHOPHEL'S]
2Sa 15:12 he also sent for A the Gilonite, David's H330
2Sa 15:31 "A is among the conspirators with Absalom H330
2Sa 16:15 came to Jerusalem, and A was with him. H330
2Sa 16:20 Absalom said to A, "Give us your advice H330
2Sa 16:21 A answered, "Sleep with your father's H330
2Sa 16:23 days the advice A gave was like that of H330
2Sa 17: 1 A said to Absalom, "I would choose twelve H330
2Sa 17: 6 Absalom said, "A has given this advice. H330
2Sa 17: 7 "The advice A has given is not good this H330
2Sa 17:14 Hushai the Arkite is better than that of A." H330
2Sa 17:14 the good advice of A in order to bring H330
2Sa 17:15 "A has advised Absalom and the elders of H330
2Sa 17:21 A has advised such and such against you." H330
2Sa 17:23 When A saw that his advice had not been H330
2Sa 23:34 Maakathite, Eliam son of A the Gilonite, H330
1Ch 27:33 A was the king's counselor. Hushai the H330
1Ch 27:34 A was succeeded by Jehoiada son of H330

AHITHOPHEL'S (3) [AHITHOPHEL]
2Sa 15:31 turn A counsel into foolishness. H330
2Sa 15:34 you can help me by frustrating A advice. H330
2Sa 16:23 Absalom regarded all of A advice. H330

AHITUB (15)
1Sa 14: 3 of Ichabod's brother A son of Phinehas, H313
1Sa 22: 9 Jesse come to Ahimelek son of A at Nob. H313
1Sa 22:11 Ahimelek son of A and all the men of his H313
1Sa 22:12 "Listen now, son of A." "Yes, my lord," H313
1Sa 22:20 But one son of Ahimelek son of A, named H313
2Sa 8:17 Zadok son of A and Ahimelek son of H313
1Ch 6: 7 of Amariah, Amariah the father of A, H313
1Ch 6: 8 A the father of Zadok, Zadok the father of H313
1Ch 6:11 of Amariah, Amariah the father of A, H313
1Ch 6:12 A the father of Zadok, Zadok the father of H313
1Ch 6:52 Amariah his son, A his son, H313
1Ch 9:11 Meraioth, the son of A, the official in H313
1Ch 18:16 Zadok son of A and Ahimelek son of H313
Ezr 7: 2 Shallum, the son of Zadok, the son of A, H313
Ne 11:11 Meraioth, the son of A, the official in H313

AHLAB (1)
Jdg 1:31 in Akko or Sidon or A or Akzib or Helbah H331

AHLAI (2)
1Ch 2:31 Sheshan was the father of A. H333
1Ch 11:41 Uriah the Hittite, Zabad son of A, H333

AHOAH (1)
1Ch 8: 4 Abishua, Naaman, A, H291

AHOHITE (5)
2Sa 23: 9 him was Eleazar son of Dodai the A. H1201+292
2Sa 23:28 Zalmon the A, Maharai the Netophathite, H292
1Ch 11:12 to him was Eleazar son of Dodai the A, H292
1Ch 11:29 Sibbekai the Hushathite, Ilai the A, H292
1Ch 27: 4 the second month was Dodai the A; H292

AHOLAH (KJV) OHOLAH

AHOLIAB (KJV) OHOLIAB

AHOLIBAH (KJV) OHOLAH

AHOLIBAMAH (KJV) OHOLIBAMAH

AHUMAI (1)
1Ch 4: 2 Jahath the father of A and Lahad. H293

AHUZZAM (1)
1Ch 4: 6 Naarah bore him A, Hepher, Temeni and H303

AHUZZATH (1)
Ge 26:26 with A his personal adviser and Phicol the H304

AHZAI (1)
Ne 11:13 of Azarel, the son of A, the son of H300

AI (36)
Ge 12: 8 Bethel on the west and A on the east. H6504
Ge 13: 3 between Bethel and A where his tent had H6504
Jos 7: 2 Now Joshua sent men from Jericho to A H6504
Jos 7: 2 So the men went up and spied out A. H6504
Jos 7: 3 all the army will have to go up against A. H6504
Jos 7: 4 but they were routed by the men of A, H6504
Jos 8: 1 army with you, and go up and attack A. H6504
Jos 8: 1 delivered into your hands the king of A, H6504
Jos 8: 2 You shall do to A and its king as you did H6504
Jos 8: 3 the whole army moved out to attack A. H6504
Jos 8: 9 lay in wait between Bethel and A, H6504
Jos 8: 9 to the west of A—but Joshua spent H6504
Jos 8:10 of Israel marched before them to A. H6504
Jos 8:11 They set up camp north of A, with the H6504
Jos 8:12 them in ambush between Bethel and A, H6504
Jos 8:14 When the king of A saw this, he and all H6504
Jos 8:16 All the men of A were called to pursue H6504
Jos 8:17 a man remained in A or Bethel who did H6504
Jos 8:18 "Hold out toward A the javelin that is in H6504
Jos 8:20 The men of A looked back and saw the H6504
Jos 8:21 turned around and attacked the men of A. H6504
Jos 8:23 took the king of A alive and brought him H6504
Jos 8:24 all the men of A in the fields and in H6504
Jos 8:24 returned to A and killed those who H6504
Jos 8:25 women fell that day—all the people of A. H6504
Jos 8:26 until he had destroyed all who lived in A. H6504
Jos 8:28 So Joshua burned A and made it a H6504
Jos 8:29 body of the king of A on a pole and left it H6504
Jos 9: 3 what Joshua had done to Jericho and A, H6504
Jos 10: 1 Joshua had taken A and totally destroyed H6504
Jos 10: 1 doing to A and its king as he had done to H6504
Jos 10: 2 it was larger than A, and all its men were H6504
Jos 12: 9 the king of Jericho one the king of A (near H6504
Ezr 2:28 of Bethel and A 223 H6504
Ne 7:32 of Bethel and A 123 H6504
Jer 49: 3 Heshbon, for A is destroyed! Cry H6504

AIAH (4) [AIAH'S]
Ge 36:24 The sons of Zibeon: A and Anah. This is H371
2Sa 3: 7 a concubine named Rizpah daughter of A. H371
2Sa 21:10 Rizpah daughter of A took sackcloth and H371
1Ch 1:40 The sons of Zibeon: A and Anah. H371

AIAH'S (2) [AIAH]
2Sa 21: 8 the two sons of A daughter Rizpah, whom H371
2Sa 21:11 David was told what A daughter Rizpah, H371

AIATH (1)
Isa 10:28 They enter A; they pass through Migron H6569

AID (10) [AIDE]
Ge 50:24 God *will* **surely come to** your a and H7212+7212
Ge 50:25 "God *will* **surely come to** your a H7212+7212
Ex 13:19 "God *will* **surely come to** your a H7212+7212
Ru 1: 6 the LORD *had* **come to the a of** his people H7212
Ps 35: 2 armor; arise and come to my a. H6476
Ps 60:11 Give us a against the enemy, for human H6476
Ps 106: 4 **come to** my a when you save them H7212
Ps 108:12 Give us a against the enemy, for human H6476
Isa 38:14 am being threatened; Lord, **come to** my a! H6842
Php 4:16 you sent me a more than once when I was NDT

AIDE (5) [AID]
Ex 24:13 Then Moses set out with Joshua his a H9250
Ex 33:11 his young a Joshua son of Nun did H9250
Nu 11:28 Nun, *who had been* Moses' a since youth H9250
Jos 1: 1 LORD said to Joshua son of Nun, Moses' a: H9250
Ne 6: 5 Sanballat sent his a to me with the same H5853

AIJA (1)
Ne 11:31 Geba lived in Mikmash, A, Bethel and its H6509

AIJALON (10)
Jos 10:12 you, moon, over the Valley of A. H389
Jos 19:42 Shaalabbin, A, Ithlah, H389
Jos 21:24 A and Gath Rimmon, together with their H389
Jdg 1:35 out in Mount Heres, A and Shaalbim, but H389
Jdg 12:12 was buried in A in the land of Zebulun H389
1Sa 14:31 down the Philistines from Mikmash to A, H389
1Ch 6:69 A and Gath Rimmon, together with their H389
1Ch 8:13 of those living in A and who drove out the H389
2Ch 11:10 A and Hebron. These were fortified H389
2Ch 28:18 Beth Shemesh, A and Gederoth, as well H389

AILS (1)
Job 16: 3 What a you that you keep on arguing? H5344

AIM (4) [AIMLESSLY]
Ps 21:12 their backs when *you* a at them with H3922
Ps 64: 3 like swords and a cruel words like deadly H2005
Ac 20:24 my only a is to finish the race and complete NDT
1Co 7:34 Her **a is** to be devoted to the Lord in both *G2671*

AIMLESSLY (2) [AIM]
Pr 5: 6 her paths **wander a**, but she does not H5675
1Co 9:26 I do not run like someone running **a**; *G85*

AIN (5)
Nu 34:11 on the east side of A and continue along H6526
Jos 15:32 Shilhim, A and Rimmon—a total of H6526
Jos 19: 7 A, Rimmon, Ether and Ashan—four towns H6526
Jos 21:16 A, Juttah and Beth Shemesh, together H6526
1Ch 4:32 villages were Etam, A, Rimmon, H6526

AIR (11) [AIRING, AIRS, MIDAIR]
Ex 9: 8 Moses toss it into the a in the presence of H9028
Ex 9:10 Moses tossed it into the a, and festering H9028
Dt 4:17 on earth or any bird that flies in the a, H9028
Job 41:16 to the next that no a can pass between. H8120
Mt 6:26 Look at the birds *of* the a; they do not sow *G4041*
Ac 22:23 off their cloaks and flinging dust into the a, *G113*
1Co 9:26 I do not fight like a boxer beating the a. *G113*
1Co 14: 9 You will just be speaking into the a. *G113*
Eph 2: 2 of the ruler of the kingdom *of* the a, *G113*
1Th 4:17 in the clouds to meet the Lord in the a. *G113*
Rev 16:17 angel poured out his bowl into the a, *G113*

AIRING (1) [AIR]
Pr 18: 2 delight in **a** their own opinions. H1655

AIRS (1) [AIR]
2Co 11:20 of you or **puts on a** or slaps you in the *G2048*

AJALON (KJV) AIJALON

AKAN (2)
Ge 36:27 The sons of Ezer: Bilhan, Zaavan and A. H6826
1Ch 1:42 Zaavan and A. The sons of H6826

AKBOR (7)
Ge 36:38 Baal-Hanan son of A succeeded him as H6570
Ge 36:39 When Baal-Hanan son of A died, Hadad H6570
2Ki 22:12 son of Shaphan, A son of Micaiah H6570
2Ki 22:14 Ahikam, A, Shaphan and Asaiah went to H6570
1Ch 1:49 Baal-Hanan son of A succeeded him as H6570
Jer 26:22 sent Elnathan son of A to Egypt, along H6570
Jer 36:12 Elnathan son of A, Gemariah son of H6570

AKELDAMA (1) [FIELD, BLOOD]
Ac 1:19 they called that field in their language A, G192

AKIM (2)
Mt 1:14 Zadok the father of A, Akim the father of G943
Mt 1:14 the father of Akim, A the father of Elihud, G943

AKKAD (1)
Ge 10:10 were Babylon, Uruk, A and Kalneh, in H422

AKKO (1)
Jdg 1:31 out those living in A or Sidon or Ahlab H6573

AKKUB (8)
1Ch 3:24 Eliashib, Pelaiah, A, Johanan, Delaiah H6822
1Ch 9:17 Shallum, A, Talmon, Ahiman and their H6822
Ezr 2:42 Talmon, A, Hatita and Shobai H6822
Ezr 2:45 Lebanah, Hagabah, A, H6822
Ne 7:45 Talmon, A, Hatita and Shobai H6822
Ne 8: 7 Sherebiah, Jamin, A, Shabbethai, Hodiah H6822
Ne 11:19 A, Talmon and their associates, who kept H6822
Ne 12:25 Talmon and A were gatekeepers who H6822

AKSAH (5)
Jos 15:16 give my daughter A in marriage to the H6578
Jos 15:17 gave his daughter A to him in marriage. H6578
Jdg 1:12 give my daughter A in marriage to the H6578
Jdg 1:13 gave his daughter A to him in marriage. H6578
1Ch 2:49 Caleb's daughter was A. H6578

AKSHAPH (3)
Jos 11: 1 of Madon, to the kings of Shimron and A, H439
Jos 12:20 of Shimron Meron one the king of A one H439
Jos 19:25 territory included: Helkath, Hali, Beten, A, H439

AKZIB (4)
Jos 15:44 A and Mareshah—nine towns and H424
Jos 19:29 the Mediterranean Sea in the region of A, H424
Jdg 1:31 Sidon or Ahlab or A or Helbah or Aphek H424
Mic 1:14 The town of A will prove deceptive to the H424

ALABASTER (3)
Mt 26: 7 came to him with an **a jar** of very expensive G223
Mk 14: 3 came with an **a jar** of very expensive G223
Lk 7:37 so she came there with an **a jar** of perfume. G223

ALAMMELECH (KJV) ALLAMMELEK

ALAMOTH (2)
1Ch 15:20 were to play the lyres according to a, H6628
Ps 46: T Sons of Korah. According to a. A song. H6628

ALARM (10) [ALARMED]
1Ki 1:49 guests rose *in* a and dispersed. H3006
Job 33: 7 No fear of me *should* a you, nor should H1286
Job 40:23 A raging river *does* not a it; it is secure H2905
Ps 31:22 In my a I said, "I am cut off from your H2905
Ps 116:11 in my a I said, "Everyone is a liar. H2905
Da 4:19 *do* not *let* the dream or its meaning a A10097
Da 11:44 from the east and the north *will* a him, H987
Joel 2: 1 in Zion; **sound** *the* a on my holy hill. H8131
Mic 7: 4 the day your watchmen sound the a. NDT
2Co 7:11 indignation, what a, what longing, what G5832

ALARMED (13) [ALARM]
Dt 18:22 spoken presumptuously, so *do* not *be* a. H1593
Jos 10: 2 *He and his people were* very much a at H3707
2Sa 4: 1 he lost courage, and all Israel *became* a. H987
2Ch 20: 3 A, Jehoshaphat resolved to inquire of the H3707
Da 5:10 "Don't *be* a! Don't look so pale A10097
Mt 24: 6 of wars, but see to it *that you are* not a. G2583
Mk 13: 7 of wars and rumors of wars, *do* not *be* a. G2583
Mk 16: 5 sitting on the right side, and *they were* a. G1701
Mk 16: 6 "Don't *be* a," he said. "You are looking G1701
Ac 16:38 Silas were Roman citizens, *they were* a. G5828
Ac 20:10 "Don't *be* a," he said. "He's G2572
Ac 22:29 The commander *himself was* a when he G5828
2Th 2: 2 easily unsettled or a by the teaching G2583

ALAS (21)
Nu 24:23 spoke his message: "A! Who can live when H208
Jos 7: 7 And Joshua said, "A, Sovereign LORD, why H177
Jdg 6:22 he exclaimed, "A, Sovereign LORD! H177
1Ki 13:30 over him and said, "A, my brother! H2098
Jer 1: 6 "A, Sovereign LORD," I said, "I do not know H177
Jer 4:10 Then I said, "A, Sovereign LORD! How H177
Jer 4:31 stretching out her hands and saying, "A! H208
Jer 6: 4 a, the daylight is fading, and the H208
Jer 14:13 But I said, "A, Sovereign LORD! The H177
Jer 15:10 A, my mother, that you gave me birth, a H208
Jer 22:18 not mourn for him: 'A, my brother! Alas, H2098
Jer 22:18 A, my sister!' They will not H2098
Jer 22:18 not mourn for him: 'A, my master! Alas, H2098
Jer 22:18 'Alas, my master! A, his splendor!' H2098
Jer 34: 5 fire in your honor and lament, "A, master!" H2098
Jer 47: 6 " 'A, sword of the LORD, how long till you H2098
Eze 6:11 stamp your feet and cry out "A! H277
Eze 9: 8 facedown, crying out, "A, Sovereign LORD! H177
Eze 11:13 out in a loud voice, "A, Sovereign LORD! H177
Eze 30: 2 " 'Wail and say, "A for that day!" H2081
Joel 1:15 A for that day! For the day of the LORD is H177

ALCOVE (2) [ALCOVES]
Eze 40:12 In front of each a was a wall one cubit H9288
Eze 40:13 of the rear wall of one a to the top of the H9288

ALCOVES (9) [ALCOVE]
Eze 40: 7 The **a for the guards** were one rod long H9288
Eze 40: 7 walls between the a were five cubits thick. H9288
Eze 40:10 the east gate were three a on each side; H9288
Eze 40:12 and the a were six cubits square. H9288
Eze 40:16 The a and the projecting walls inside the H9288
Eze 40:21 Its a—three on each side—its projecting H9288
Eze 40:29 Its a, its projecting walls and its portico H9288
Eze 40:33 Its a, its projecting walls and its portico H9288
Eze 40:36 as did its a, its projecting walls and its H9288

ALEMETH (4)
1Ch 6:60 A and Anathoth, together with H6630
1Ch 7: 8 Jeremoth, Abijah, Anathoth and A. H6631
1Ch 8:36 Jehoaddah was the father of A, Azmaveth H6631
1Ch 9:42 Jadah was the father of A, Azmaveth and H6631

ALERT (9)
Jos 8: 4 go very far from it. All of you be **on the a.** H3922
Ps 17:11 with eyes a, to throw me to the H8883
Isa 21: 7 on camels, *let him be* a, fully alert." H7992+7993
Isa 21: 7 riders on camels, let him be alert, fully a." H7993
Mk 13:33 *Be* a! You do not know when G70
Eph 6:18 *be* a and always keep on praying for all the G70
1Pe 1:13 *with* minds that *are* a and G350+3836+4019
1Pe 4: 7 Therefore *be* a and of sober mind so that G5404
1Pe 5: 8 *Be* a and of sober mind. Your enemy the G3768

ALEXANDER (5)
Mk 15:21 the father *of* A and Rufus, was G235
Ac 4: 6 A and others of the high priest's family. G235
Ac 19:33 Jews in the crowd pushed A to the front, G235
1Ti 1:20 Among them are Hymenaeus and A, whom G235
2Ti 4:14 A the metalworker did me a great deal of G235

ALEXANDRIA (2) [ALEXANDRIAN]
Ac 6: 9 Jews of Cyrene and A as well as the G233
Ac 18:24 Apollos, a native **of** A, came to Ephesus. G233

ALEXANDRIAN (2) [ALEXANDRIA]
Ac 27: 6 centurion found an A ship sailing for Italy G234
Ac 28:11 it was an A ship with the figurehead of the G234

ALGUM (1) [ALGUMWOOD, ALMUGWOOD]
2Ch 2: 8 juniper and a logs from Lebanon, for H454

ALGUMWOOD (2) [ALGUM]
2Ch 9:10 they also brought a and precious H6770+454
2Ch 9:11 The king used the a to make steps H6770+454

ALIAH (KJV) ALVAH

ALIEN (1) [ALIENATE, ALIENATED]
Isa 28:21 and perform his task, his a task. H5799

ALIENATE (1) [ALIEN]
Gal 4:17 What they want is *to* a you from us, so G1710

ALIENATED (3) [ALIEN]
Job 19:13 "*He has* a my family from me; my H8178
Gal 5: 4 by the law *have been* a from Christ; G1467
Col 1:21 Once you were a **from** God and were G558

ALIGHTING (1)
Mt 3:16 descending like a dove and a on him. G2262

ALIKE (24) [LIKE]
Ge 18:25 treating the righteous and the wicked a. H3869
Ex 11: 2 people that men **and** women a are to ask H2256
Ex 35:22 men **and** women a, came and H6584
Ex 36:29 into a single ring; both were made a. H4027
Nu 5: 3 Send away male **and** female a; send them H6330
Dt 1:17 in judging; hear **both** small *and* great a. H3869
1Sa 30:24 down to the battle. All will share a." H3481
1Ch 25: 8 Young and old a, teacher as well as H4200+6645
1Ch 26:13 to their families, young and old a. H3869
2Ch 31:15 to their divisions, old and young a. H3869
Job 34:29 Yet he is over individual and nation a, H3480
Ps 49: 2 both low and high, rich and poor a: H3480
Ps 115:13 who fear the LORD—small **and** great a. H6640
Jer 6:13 prophets **and** priests a, all practice H6330
Jer 6:21 Parents and children a will stumble over H3481
Jer 8:10 prophets **and** priests a, all practice H6330
Jer 13:14 parents and children a, declares the LORD. H3481
Eze 1:16 sparkled like topaz, and all four looked a. H285
Eze 10:10 the four of them looked a; each was like a H285
Eze 18: 4 as well as the child—**both** *a* belong to me. AIT
Lk 14:18 "But they all a began to make G608+1651
Ac 26:22 here and testify to small and great a. G5445
Ro 3: 9 that Jews and Gentiles a are all under the G5445
Ro 14: 5 than another; another considers **every** day *a.* AIT

ALIVE (91) [LIVE]
Ge 6:19 female, to **keep them** a with you. H2649
Ge 6:20 the ground will come to you to *be* **kept** a. H2649
Ge 7: 3 to **keep** their various kinds a throughout H2649
Ge 11:28 **While** his father Terah was **still** a H6584+7156
Ge 43:28 "Your servant our father is still a and well." H2645
Ge 45:26 "Joseph is still a! In fact, he is ruler H2645
Ge 45:28 My son Joseph is still a. I will go and see H2645
Ge 46:30 I have seen for myself that you are still a." H2645
Ex 4:18 in Egypt to see if any of them are still a." H2645
Ex 22: 4 animal is found a in their possession— H2645
Lev 16:10 shall be presented a before the LORD to be H2645
Nu 14:15 to death, **leaving none** a, the H3869+408+285
Nu 16:30 they go down a into the realm of the H2645
Nu 16:33 They went down a into the realm of the H2645
Dt 4: 4 fast to the LORD your God are still a today. H2645
Dt 5: 3 with all of us who are a here today. H2645
Dt 6:24 we might always prosper and *be* **kept** a, H2649
Dt 20:16 *do* not **leave** a anything that breathes. H2649
Dt 31:27 the LORD while I am still a and with you, H2645
Jos 8:23 took the king of Ai a and brought him to H2645
Jos 14:10 *he has* **kept** me a for forty-five years since H2649
Jdg 6:16 Midianites, **leaving none** a." H3869+408+285
1Sa 2: 6 "The LORD brings death and **makes** a; he H2649
1Sa 14:36 and *let us* not **leave** one of them a." H8636
1Sa 15: 8 He took Agag king of the Amalekites a H2645
1Sa 25:22 if by morning *I* **leave** a one male of all H8636
1Sa 25:34 to Nabal *would have* **been left** a by H3855
1Sa 27: 9 *he did* not **leave** a man or woman a, but H2649
1Sa 27:11 He *did* not **leave** a man or woman a to be H2649
2Sa 1: 9 in the throes of death, but I'm still a. H5883+928
2Sa 9: 3 there no one still a from the house of Saul NDT
2Sa 12:21 While the child was a, you fasted and H2645
2Sa 12:22 "While the child was still a, I fasted and H2645
2Sa 17:12 he nor any of his men *will* **be left** a. H3855
2Sa 18:14 while Absalom was still a in the oak tree. H2645
2Sa 19: 6 if Absalom were a today and all of us H2645
1Ki 3:23 'My son is a and your son is dead H2645
1Ki 3:23 Your son is dead and mine is a.' " H2645
1Ki 3:26 whose son was a was deeply moved H2645
1Ki 17:23 his mother and said, "Look, your son is a!" H2645
1Ki 18: 5 *to* **keep** the horses and mules a so we H2649
1Ki 20:18 peace, take them a; if they have come H2645
1Ki 20:18 they have come out for war, take them a." H2645
1Ki 20:32 answered, "Is he still a? He is my brother." H2645
1Ki 21:15 He is no longer a, but dead." H2645
2Ki 7:12 we will take them a and get into the city. H2645
2Ki 10:14 "Take them a!" he ordered. So they took H2645
2Ki 10:14 So they took them a and slaughtered H2645
2Ch 25:12 Judah also captured ten thousand *men* a, H2645
Ne 5: 2 in order for us to eat and **stay** a, we must H2649
Job 36: 6 *He does* not **keep** the wicked a but gives H2649
Ps 22:29 *those who* cannot **keep** themselves a. H2649
Ps 33:19 from death and **keep** them a in famine. H2649
Ps 55:15 let them go down a to the realm of the H2645
Ps 124: 3 have swallowed us a when their anger H2645
Pr 1:12 let's swallow them a, like the grave, and H2645
Ecc 4: 2 happier than the living, who are still a. H2645
Isa 7:21 a person *will* **keep** a a young cow and two H2649
Jer 49:11 fatherless children; I *will* **keep** them a. H2649
La 1:11 food to **keep themselves** a. H8740+5883
La 1:19 *to* **keep themselves** a. H8740+906+5883+4392
Da 2:30 greater wisdom than anyone else a, A10261
Mt 27:63 remember that *while he was* still a that G2409
Mk 16:11 heard that Jesus *was* a and that she had G2409
Lk 15:24 this son of mine was dead and *is* **a again;** G348
Lk 15:32 brother of yours was dead and *is* **a again;** G2409
Lk 20:38 of the living, for to him all *are* a. G2409
Lk 24:23 a vision of angels, who said he *was* a. G2409
Jn 21:22 "If I want him *to* **remain** *a* until I return, what AIT
Jn 21:23 "If I want him *to* **remain** *a* until I return AIT
Ac 1: 3 many convincing proofs *that he was* a. G2409
Ac 9:41 the widows, and presented her to them a. G2409
Ac 20:10 he said. "He's a!" G3836+6034+1877+899+1639
Ac 20:12 the young man home a and were greatly G2409
Ac 25:19 named Jesus who Paul claimed *was* a. G2409
Ro 6:11 dead to sin but a to God in Christ Jesus. G2409
Ro 7: 2 bound to her husband *as long as he is* a, G2409
Ro 7: 3 another man *while* her husband *is still* a, G2409
Ro 7: 9 Once I *was* a apart from the law; but when G2409
1Co 15:22 so in Christ all *will be* **made** a. G2443
2Co 4:11 For we who *are* a are always being given G2409
Eph 2: 5 **made us** a **with** Christ even when we were G5188
Col 2:13 of your flesh, God **made** you a **with** Christ. G5188
1Th 4:15 we tell you that we who *are still* a, who G2409
1Th 4:17 we who *are still* a and are left will be G2409
Heb 4:12 For the word of God *is* a and active G2409
1Pe 3:18 in the body but **made** a in the Spirit. G2443
1Pe 3:19 *After being* **made** a, he went and G1877+4005S
Rev 1:18 now look, I am a for ever and ever! G2409
Rev 3: 1 you have a reputation *of being* a, but you G2409
Rev 19:20 of them were thrown a into the fiery lake G2409

ALL (4702)
Ge 1:25 a the creatures that move along the H3972
Ge 1:26 over the livestock and a the wild animals H3972
Ge 1:26 over a the creatures that move along H3972
Ge 1:30 And to a the beasts of the earth and all H3972
Ge 1:30 of the earth and a the birds in the sky H3972
Ge 1:30 birds in the sky and a the creatures that H3972
Ge 1:31 God saw a that he had made, and it was H3972
Ge 2: 1 earth were completed in a their vast array. H3972
Ge 2: 2 the seventh day he rested from a his work. H3972
Ge 2: 3 on it he rested from a the work of creating H3972
Ge 2: 9 LORD God made a *kinds of* trees grow out H3972
Ge 2:19 out of the ground a the wild animals and H3972
Ge 2:19 wild animals and a the birds in the sky H3972
Ge 2:20 So the man gave names to a the livestock H3972
Ge 2:20 birds in the sky and a the wild animals. H3972
Ge 3:14 "Cursed are you above a livestock and all H3972
Ge 3:14 above all livestock and a wild animals! H3972
Ge 3:14 you will eat dust a the days of your life H3972

A

Book	Ref	Context	Number
Ge	3:17	will eat food from it **a** the days of your life	H3972
Ge	3:20	would become the mother of **a** the living.	H3972
Ge	4:21	he was the father of **a** who play stringed	H3972
Ge	4:22	who forged **a** *kinds of* tools out of bronze	H3972
Ge	6: 5	the human heart was only evil **a** the time.	H3972
Ge	6:12	**a** the people on earth had corrupted	H3972
Ge	6:13	"I am going to put an end to **a** people, for	H3972
Ge	6:16	one cubit high **a around.**	H4946+4200+5087
Ge	6:17	the earth to destroy **a** life under the	H3972
Ge	6:19	bring into the ark two of **a** living creatures,	H3972
Ge	7: 5	And Noah did **a** that the LORD	H3972
Ge	7: 8	of birds and of **a** creatures that move	H3972
Ge	7:11	on that day **a** the springs of the great deep	H3972
Ge	7:14	**a** livestock according to their kinds	H3972
Ge	7:15	Pairs of **a** creatures that have the breath of	H3972
Ge	7:19	**a** the high mountains under the	H3972
Ge	7:21	**a** the creatures that swarm over the earth	H3972
Ge	7:21	swarm over the earth, and **a** mankind.	H3972
Ge	8: 1	Noah and **a** the wild animals	H3972
Ge	8: 9	there was water over **a** the surface of the	H3972
Ge	8:17	**a** the creatures that move along the	H3972
Ge	8:19	**A** the animals and all the creatures that	H3972
Ge	8:19	All the animals and **a** the creatures that	H3972
Ge	8:19	move along the ground and **a** the birds—	H3972
Ge	8:20	taking some of **a** the clean animals and	H3972
Ge	8:21	again will I destroy **a** living creatures,	H3972
Ge	9: 2	of you will fall on **a** the beasts of the	H3972
Ge	9: 2	of the earth, and on **a** the birds in the sky	H3972
Ge	9: 2	the ground, and on **a** the fish in the sea	H3972
Ge	9:10	the livestock and **a** the wild animals, all	H3972
Ge	9:10	**a** those that came out of the ark with you	H3972
Ge	9:11	Never again will **a** life be destroyed by	H3972
Ge	9:12	a covenant for **a** generations to come:	NDT
Ge	9:15	me and you and **a** living creatures of	H3972
Ge	9:15	waters become a flood to destroy **a** life.	H3972
Ge	9:16	between God and **a** living creatures of	H3972
Ge	9:17	between me and **a** life on the earth."	H3972
Ge	10:21	was the ancestor of **a** the sons of Eber.	H3972
Ge	10:29	**A** these were sons of Joktan	H3972
Ge	11: 8	them from there over **a** the earth,	H3972
Ge	12: 3	**a** peoples on earth will be blessed	H3972
Ge	12: 5	**a** the possessions they had accumulated	H3972
Ge	13:15	**A** the land that you see I will give to you	H3972
Ge	14: 3	**A** these latter kings joined forces in the	H3972
Ge	14:11	four kings seized **a** the goods of Sodom	H3972
Ge	14:11	of Sodom and Gomorrah and **a** their food;	H3972
Ge	14:13	**a** *of whom* were allied with Abram.	H2156S
Ge	14:16	He recovered **a** the goods and brought	H3972
Ge	15:10	Abram brought **a** these to him, cut them	H3972
Ge	16:12	will live in hostility toward **a** his brothers."	H3972
Ge	17:23	his son Ishmael and **a** those born in his	H3972
Ge	18: 4	then *you may a* **wash** your feet and rest	AIT
Ge	18:18	**a** nations on earth will be blessed	H3972
Ge	18:25	Will not the Judge of **a** the earth do right?"	H3972
Ge	19: 4	**a** the men from every part of the city of	H3972
Ge	19:25	destroying **a** those living in the cities	H3972
Ge	19:28	Gomorrah, toward **a** the land of the plain	H3972
Ge	19:31	as is the custom **a** *over* the earth.	H3972
Ge	20: 7	be sure that you and **a** who belong to you	H3972
Ge	20: 8	Abimelek summoned **a** his officials,	H3972
Ge	20: 8	when he told them **a** that had happened,	H3972
Ge	20:16	against you before **a** who are with you;	H3972
Ge	20:18	the LORD had kept **a** the women in	H3972
Ge	22:18	your offspring **a** nations on earth will	H3972
Ge	23:10	in the hearing of **a** the Hittites who had	H3972
Ge	23:17	**a** the trees within the borders of the	H3972
Ge	23:18	in the presence of **a** the Hittites who had	H3972
Ge	24: 2	the one in charge of **a** that he had, "Put	H3972
Ge	24:10	loaded with **a** *kinds of* good things from	H3972
Ge	24:20	and drew enough for **a** his camels.	H3972
Ge	24:66	the servant told Isaac **a** he had done.	H3972
Ge	25: 4	**A** these were descendants of Keturah	H3972
Ge	25:18	in hostility toward **a** the tribes related to	H3972
Ge	26: 3	I will give **a** these lands and will	H3972
Ge	26: 4	the sky and will give them **a** these lands,	H3972
Ge	26: 4	your offspring **a** nations on earth will	H3972
Ge	26:11	So Abimelek gave orders to **a** the people	H3972
Ge	26:15	So **a** the wells that his father's servants	H3972
Ge	27:37	you and have made **a** his relatives his	H3972
Ge	28:14	**A** peoples on earth will be blessed	H3972
Ge	28:22	of **a** that you give me I will give you a	H3972
Ge	29: 3	When **a** the flocks were gathered there	H3972
Ge	29: 8	"until **a** the flocks are gathered and the	H3972
Ge	29:13	there Jacob told him **a** these things.	H3972
Ge	29:22	brought together **a** the people of the	H3972
Ge	30:32	Let me go through **a** your flocks today and	H3972
Ge	30:35	same day he removed **a** the male goats that	NDT
Ge	30:35	**a** the speckled or spotted female	H3972
Ge	30:35	female goats (**a** that had white on them	H3972
Ge	30:35	on them) and **a** the dark-colored lambs	H3972
Ge	30:38	peeled branches in **a** the watering troughs,	NDT
Ge	31: 1	owned and has gained **a** this wealth from	H3972
Ge	31: 6	worked for your father with **a** my strength,	H3972
Ge	31: 8	' then **a** the flocks gave birth to speckled	H3972
Ge	31: 8	' then **a** the flocks bore streaked young.	H3972
Ge	31:12	up and see that **a** the male goats mating	H3972
Ge	31:12	I have seen **a** that Laban has been	H3972
Ge	31:16	Surely **a** the wealth that God took away	H3972
Ge	31:18	he drove **a** his livestock ahead of him	H3972
Ge	31:18	along with **a** the goods he had	H3972
Ge	31:21	So he fled with **a** he had, crossed the	H3972
Ge	31:37	you have searched through **a** my goods,	H3972
Ge	31:43	are my flocks. **A** you see is mine. Yet	H3972
Ge	32:10	I am unworthy of **a** the kindness and	H3972
Ge	32:17	who owns **a** these animals in front of	NDT
Ge	32:19	the third and **a** the others who followed	H3972
Ge	32:23	the stream, he sent over **a** his possessions.	NDT
Ge	33: 7	**Last of a** came Joseph and Rachel, and	H339
Ge	33: 8	the meaning of **a** these flocks and herds	H3972
Ge	33:11	been gracious to me and I have **a** I *need.*"	H3972
Ge	33:13	hard just one day, **a** the animals will die.	H3972
Ge	34:15	like us by circumcising **a** your males.	H3972
Ge	34:19	the most honored of **a** his father's family,	H3972
Ge	34:23	their property and **a** their other animals	H3972
Ge	34:24	**A** the men who went out of the city gate	H3972
Ge	34:25	days later, while **a** of them were still in pain	NDT
Ge	34:29	They carried off **a** their wealth and all their	H3972
Ge	34:29	all their wealth and **a** their women and	H3972
Ge	35: 2	household and to **a** who were with him,	H3972
Ge	35: 4	So they gave Jacob **a** the foreign gods	H3972
Ge	35: 5	on the towns **a around** them so that no	H6017
Ge	35: 6	Jacob and **a** the people with him came to	H3972
Ge	36: 6	daughters and **a** the members of his	H3972
Ge	36: 6	as his livestock and **a** his other animals	H3972
Ge	36: 6	his other animals and **a** the goods he had	H3972
Ge	37: 5	they hated him **a the more.**	H3578+6388
Ge	37: 8	hated him **a the more** because of	H3578+6388
Ge	37:14	"Go and see if **a** is well with your brothers	NDT
Ge	37:27	our hands on him; **after a**, he is our	H3954
Ge	37:35	**A** his sons and daughters came to comfort	H3972
Ge	38:23	**After a**, I did send her this young goat	H2180
Ge	39: 5	of his household and of **a** that he owned,	H3972
Ge	39:22	Joseph in charge of **a** those held in the	H3972
Ge	39:22	responsible for **a** that was done there.	H3972
Ge	40:14	But when *a* **goes well** with you, remember me	AIT
Ge	40:17	basket were **a kinds** *of* baked	H4946+3972
Ge	40:20	he gave a feast for **a** his officials.	H3972
Ge	41: 8	so he sent for **a** the magicians and wise	H3972
Ge	41:19	such ugly cows in **a** the land of Egypt.	H3972
Ge	41:30	Then **a** the abundance in Egypt will be	H3972
Ge	41:35	They should collect **a** the food of these	H3972
Ge	41:37	good to Pharaoh and to **a** his officials.	H3972
Ge	41:39	"Since God has made **a** this known to you,	H3972
Ge	41:40	**a** my people are to submit to your	H3972
Ge	41:44	no one will lift hand or foot in **a** Egypt."	H3972
Ge	41:48	Joseph collected **a** the food produced in	H3972
Ge	41:51	has made me forget **a** my trouble and all	H3972
Ge	41:51	all my trouble and **a** my father's	H3972
Ge	41:54	There was famine in **a** the other lands	H3972
Ge	41:55	When **a** Egypt began to feel the famine	H3972
Ge	41:55	Then Pharaoh told **a** the Egyptians, "Go	H3972
Ge	41:56	Joseph opened **a** the storehouses and	H3972
Ge	41:57	And **a** the world came to Egypt to buy	H3972
Ge	42: 6	the person who sold grain to **a** its people.	H3972
Ge	42:11	We are **a** the sons of one man. Your	H3972
Ge	42:17	And he put **them** *a* in custody for three days.	AIT
Ge	42:29	they told him **a** that had happened to	H3972
Ge	43: 2	when they had eaten **a** the grain they had	H3983
Ge	43: 9	I will bear the blame before you **a** my life.	H3972
Ge	43:23	"It's **a right**," he said. "Don't be afraid	H8934
Ge	44:13	Then they **a** loaded their donkeys and	H408
Ge	44:32	blame before you, my father, **a** my life!	H3972
Ge	45: 1	control himself before **a** his attendants,	H3972
Ge	45: 8	his entire household and ruler of **a** Egypt.	H3972
Ge	45: 9	God has made me lord of **a** Egypt. Come	H3972
Ge	45:10	your flocks and herds, and **a** you have.	H3972
Ge	45:11	your household and **a** who belong to you	H3972
Ge	45:13	Tell my father about **a** the honor accorded	H3972
Ge	45:15	And he kissed **a** his brothers and wept	H3972
Ge	45:16	Pharaoh and **a** his officials were pleased.	NDT
Ge	45:20	because the best of **a** Egypt will be yours.	H3972
Ge	45:26	he is ruler of **a** Egypt." Jacob was	H3972
Ge	46: 1	So Israel set out with **a** that was his, and	H3972
Ge	46: 6	So Jacob and **a** his offspring went to Egypt,	H3972
Ge	46: 7	granddaughters—**a** his offspring.	H3972
Ge	46:15	daughters of his were thirty-three *in* **a**.	H3972
Ge	46:18	given to his daughter Leah—sixteen *in* **a**.	H5883
Ge	46:22	who were born to Jacob—fourteen *in* **a**.	H3972
Ge	46:25	given to his daughter Rachel—seven *in* **a**.	H3972
Ge	46:26	**A** those who went to Egypt with Jacob	H3972
Ge	46:27	which went to Egypt, were seventy *in* **a**.	H3972
Ge	46:34	**a** shepherds are detestable to the	H3972
Ge	47:12	his brothers and **a** his father's	H3972
Ge	47:14	Joseph collected **a** the money that was to	H3972
Ge	47:15	**a** Egypt came to Joseph and said	H3972
Ge	47:15	before your eyes? Our money *is* **a gone**."	H699
Ge	47:17	with food in exchange for **a** their livestock.	H3972
Ge	47:20	So Joseph bought **a** the land in Egypt	H3972
Ge	47:20	The Egyptians, **one and a**, sold their fields	H408
Ge	48:15	my shepherd **a** my **life** to this day,	H4946+6388
Ge	48:16	who has delivered me from **a** harm—	H3972
Ge	49:26	*Let a these* **rest** on the head of Joseph, on	AIT
Ge	49:28	**A** these are the twelve tribes of Israel	H3972
Ge	50: 7	**A** Pharaoh's officials accompanied him	H3972
Ge	50: 7	of his court and **a** the dignitaries of Egypt	H3972
Ge	50: 8	besides **a** *the members of* Joseph's	H3972
Ge	50:14	his brothers and **a** the others who had	H3972
Ge	50:15	pays us back for **a** the wrongs we did to	H3972
Ge	50:22	in Egypt, along with **a** his father's family.	NDT
Ex	1: 5	of Jacob numbered seventy *in* **a**;	H3972
Ex	1: 6	Now Joseph and **a** his brothers and all	H3972
Ex	1: 6	his brothers and **a** that generation died	H3972
Ex	1:14	mortar and with **a** *kinds of* work in the	H3972
Ex	1:14	in **a** their harsh labor the Egyptians	H3972
Ex	1:22	Pharaoh gave this order to **a** his people:	H3972
Ex	3:20	the Egyptians with **a** the wonders that I	H3972
Ex	4:19	**a** those who wanted to kill you are	H3972
Ex	4:21	before Pharaoh **a** the wonders I have	H3972
Ex	4:28	also about **a** the signs he had	H3972
Ex	4:29	brought together **a** the elders of the	H3972
Ex	5:11	but your work will not be reduced **at a.**	H1821
Ex	5:12	people scattered **a** over Egypt to gather	H3972
Ex	5:23	*you have* not **rescued** your people **at a**	H5911+5911
Ex	7:19	over the ponds and **a** the reservoirs—and	H3972
Ex	7:20	**a** the water was changed into blood.	H3972
Ex	7:24	And **a** the Egyptians dug along the Nile to	H3972
Ex	8: 4	you and your people and **a** your officials.	H3972
Ex	8:17	**A** the dust throughout the land of Egypt	H3972
Ex	9: 6	**A** the livestock of the Egyptians died, but	H3972
Ex	9:11	were on them and on **a** the Egyptians.	H3972
Ex	9:14	there is no one like me in **a** the earth.	H3972
Ex	9:16	name might be proclaimed in **a** the earth.	H3972
Ex	9:22	the sky so that hail will fall **a** over Egypt—	H3972
Ex	9:24	was the worst storm in **a** the land of Egypt	H3972
Ex	10: 6	houses and those of **a** your officials and	H3972
Ex	10: 6	of all your officials and **a** the Egyptians—	H3972
Ex	10:13	blow across the land **a** that day and all	H3972
Ex	10:13	the land all that day and **a** that night.	H3972
Ex	10:14	they invaded **a** Egypt and settled down in	H3972
Ex	10:15	They covered **a** the ground until it was	H3972
Ex	10:15	They devoured **a** that was left after the	H3972
Ex	10:15	on tree or plant in **a** the land of Egypt.	H3972
Ex	10:22	darkness covered **a** Egypt for three days.	H3972
Ex	10:23	Yet **a** the Israelites had light in the places	H3972
Ex	11: 5	**a** the firstborn of the cattle as well.	H3972
Ex	11: 8	**A** these officials of yours will come to me	H3972
Ex	11: 8	you and **a** the people who follow you!	H3972
Ex	11:10	Aaron performed **a** these wonders	H3972
Ex	12: 6	when **a** the members of the community of	H3972
Ex	12:12	bring judgment on **a** the gods of Egypt.	H3972
Ex	12:16	Do no work **at a** on these days, except to	H3972
Ex	12:16	that is **a** you may do.	H4200+963
Ex	12:21	Then Moses summoned **a** the elders of	H3972
Ex	12:29	the LORD struck down **a** the firstborn in	H3972
Ex	12:29	the firstborn of **a** the livestock as well.	H3972
Ex	12:30	Pharaoh and **a** his officials and all the	H3972
Ex	12:30	all his officials and **a** the Egyptians got up	H3972
Ex	12:33	otherwise," they said, "we will **a** die!"	H3972
Ex	12:41	very day, **a** the LORD's divisions left Egypt.	H3972
Ex	12:42	on this night **a** the Israelites are to keep	H3972
Ex	12:48	Passover must have **a** the males in his	H3972
Ex	12:50	**A** the Israelites did just what the LORD had	H3972
Ex	13:12	**A** the firstborn males of your livestock	H3972
Ex	14: 4	myself through Pharaoh and **a** his army,	H3972
Ex	14: 7	along with **a** the other chariots of Egypt	H3972
Ex	14: 7	of Egypt, with officers over **a** *of* them.	H3972
Ex	14: 9	**a** Pharaoh's horses and chariots	H3972
Ex	14:17	glory through Pharaoh and **a** his army,	H3972
Ex	14:20	neither went near the other **a** night *long*.	H3972
Ex	14:21	**a** that night the LORD drove the sea	H3972
Ex	14:23	**a** Pharaoh's horses and chariots and	H3972
Ex	15:20	her hand, and **a** the women followed her	H3972
Ex	15:26	to his commands and keep **a** his decrees,	H3972
Ex	16: 3	of meat and ate **a** the food we **wanted,**	H8427
Ex	16: 6	Moses and Aaron said to **a** the Israelites,	H3972
Ex	16: 8	evening and **a** the bread you **want** in the	H8425
Ex	18: 8	sake and about **a** the hardships they had	H3972
Ex	18: 9	to hear about **a** the good things the	H3972
Ex	18:11	that the LORD is greater than **a** other gods,	H3972
Ex	18:12	Aaron came with **a** the elders of	H3972
Ex	18:14	father-in-law saw **a** that Moses was doing	H3972
Ex	18:14	while **a** these people stand around you	H3972
Ex	18:21	select capable men from **a** the people—	H3972
Ex	18:22	serve as judges for the people at **a** times,	H3972
Ex	18:23	**a** these people will go home	H3972
Ex	18:25	capable men from **a** Israel and made	H3972
Ex	18:26	as judges for the people at **a** times.	H3972
Ex	19: 5	then out of **a** nations you will be my	H3972
Ex	19: 7	set before them **a** the words the LORD	H3972
Ex	19: 8	The people **a** responded together, "We	H3972
Ex	19:11	Mount Sinai in the sight of **a** the people.	H3972
Ex	20: 1	And God spoke **a** these words:	H3972
Ex	20: 9	days you shall labor and do **a** your work,	H3972
Ex	20:11	the sea, and **a** that is in them, but he	H3972
Ex	22: 9	In **a** cases of illegal possession of an ox, a	H3972
Ex	23:17	"Three times a year **a** the men are to	H3972
Ex	23:22	to what he says and do **a** that I say,	H3972
Ex	23:27	I will make **a** your enemies turn their	H3972
Ex	24: 3	told the people **a** the LORD's words	H3972
Ex	24: 8	you in accordance with **a** these words."	H3972
Ex	25: 9	this tabernacle and **a** its furnishings	H3972
Ex	25:22	you and give you **a** my commands for the	H3972
Ex	25:30	on this table to be before me **at a times.**	H9458
Ex	25:33	the same for **a** six branches extending	NDT
Ex	25:35	bud under the third pair—six branches in **a.**	NDT
Ex	25:36	branches shall **a** be of one piece with	H3972
Ex	25:39	the lampstand and **a** these accessories.	H3972
Ex	26: 2	**A** the curtains are to be the same size	H3972
Ex	26: 8	**A** eleven curtains are to be the same size	NDT
Ex	26:17	Make **a** the frames of the tabernacle in	H3972
Ex	26:24	from the bottom **a the way to** the top and	H6584
Ex	27: 3	Make **a** its utensils of bronze—its pots to	H3972
Ex	27:17	**A** the posts around the courtyard are to	H3972
Ex	27:19	**A** the other articles used in the service of	H3972
Ex	27:19	including **a** the tent pegs for it and those	H3972

Ex 28: 3 Tell **a** the skilled workers to whom I have H3972
Ex 29:13 Then take **a** the fat on the internal organs H3972
Ex 29:24 Put **a** these in the hands of Aaron and his H3972
Ex 30: 3 Overlay the top and **a** the sides and the H6017
Ex 30:14 **A** who cross over, those twenty years old H3972
Ex 30:24 cassia—**a** according to the sanctuary shekel NDT
Ex 30:27 the table and **a** its articles, the lampstand H3972
Ex 30:28 altar of burnt offering and **a** its utensils, H3972
Ex 30:34 pure frankincense, **a** in equal amounts, NDT
Ex 31: 3 knowledge and with **a** *kinds of* skills— H3972
Ex 31: 5 and to engage in **a** *kinds of* crafts. H3972
Ex 31: 6 have given ability to **a** the skilled workers H3972
Ex 31: 7 and **a** the other furnishings of the tent H3972
Ex 31: 8 gold lampstand and **a** its accessories, H3972
Ex 31: 9 altar of burnt offering and **a** its utensils, H3972
Ex 32: 3 So **a** the people took off their earrings H3972
Ex 32:13 your descendants **a** this land I promised H3972
Ex 32:26 And **a** the Levites rallied to him H3972
Ex 33: 8 **a** the people rose and stood at the H3972
Ex 33:10 to the tent, they **a** stood and worshiped H3972
Ex 33:16 your people from **a** the other people on H3972
Ex 33:19 "I will cause **a** my goodness to pass in H3972
Ex 34:10 Before **a** your people I will do wonders H3972
Ex 34:10 before done in any nation in **a** the world. H3972
Ex 34:19 including **a** the firstborn males of your H3972
Ex 34:20 Redeem **a** your firstborn sons H3972
Ex 34:23 Three times a year **a** your men are to H3972
Ex 34:30 When Aaron and **a** the Israelites saw H3972
Ex 34:31 so Aaron and **a** the leaders of the H3972
Ex 34:32 Afterward **a** the Israelites came near him H3972
Ex 34:32 he gave them **a** the commands the H3972
Ex 35:10 "**A** who are skilled among you are to H3972
Ex 35:13 with its poles and **a** its articles and the H3972
Ex 35:16 grating, its poles and **a** its utensils; the H3972
Ex 35:21 tent of meeting, for **a** its service, and for H3972
Ex 35:22 **A** *who* were willing, men and women H3972
Ex 35:22 came and brought gold jewelry of **a** *kinds*: H3972
Ex 35:22 They **a** presented their gold as a wave H3972
Ex 35:26 And **a** the women who were willing and H3972
Ex 35:29 **A** the Israelite men and women who were H3972
Ex 35:29 freewill offerings for **a** the work the LORD H3972
Ex 35:31 knowledge and with **a** *kinds of* skills— H3972
Ex 35:33 wood and to engage in **a** kinds of artistic H3972
Ex 35:35 with skill to do **a** *kinds of* work as H3972
Ex 35:35 **a** *of* them skilled workers and designers. H3972
Ex 36: 1 know how to carry out **a** the work of H3972
Ex 36: 3 received from Moses **a** the offerings the H3972
Ex 36: 4 So **a** the skilled workers who were doing H3972
Ex 36: 4 workers who were doing **a** the work on the H3972
Ex 36: 7 was more than enough to do **a** the work. H3972
Ex 36: 8 **A** *those who* were skilled among the H3972
Ex 36: 9 **A** the curtains were the same size H285
Ex 36:15 **A** eleven curtains were the same size H285
Ex 36:22 They made **a** the frames of the tabernacle H3972
Ex 36:29 from the bottom **a the way to** the top and H448
Ex 37:19 the same for **a** six branches extending NDT
Ex 37:21 bud under the third pair—six branches in **a**. NDT
Ex 37:22 the branches were **a** of one piece with the H3972
Ex 37:24 the lampstand and **a** its accessories from H3972
Ex 37:26 overlaid the top and **a** the sides and the H6017
Ex 38: 3 They made **a** its utensils of bronze—its H3972
Ex 38:16 **A** the curtains around the courtyard were H3972
Ex 38:17 so **a** the posts of the courtyard had silver H3972
Ex 38:20 **A** the tent pegs of the tabernacle and of H3972
Ex 38:24 wave offering used for **a** the work on the H3972
Ex 38:30 with its bronze grating and **a** its utensils, H3972
Ex 38:31 its entrance and **a** the tent pegs for the H3972
Ex 39:32 So **a** the work on the tabernacle, the tent H3972
Ex 39:33 the tent and **a** its furnishings, its clasps H3972
Ex 39:36 the table with **a** its articles and the bread H3972
Ex 39:37 its row of lamps and **a** its accessories, H3972
Ex 39:39 grating, its poles and **a** its utensils; the H3972
Ex 39:40 **a** the furnishings for the tabernacle H3972
Ex 39:42 Israelites had done **a** the work just as the H3972
Ex 40: 9 consecrate it and **a** its furnishings, and H3972
Ex 40:10 altar of burnt offering and **a** its utensils; H3972
Ex 40:36 In **a** the travels of the Israelites, whenever H3972
Ex 40:38 in the sight of **a** the Israelites during all H3972
Ex 40:38 of all the Israelites during **a** their travels. H3972
Lev 1: 9 the priest is to burn **a** *of* it on the altar. H3972
Lev 1:13 priest is to bring **a** *of* them and burn them H3972
Lev 2: 2 together with **a** the incense, and burn H3972
Lev 2:13 Season **a** your grain offerings with salt. Do H3972
Lev 2:13 offerings; add salt to **a** your offerings. H3972
Lev 2:16 together with **a** the incense, as a food H3972
Lev 3: 3 the internal organs and **a** the fat that is H3972
Lev 3: 9 the internal organs and **a** the fat that is H3972
Lev 3:14 the internal organs and **a** the fat that is H3972
Lev 3:16 a pleasing aroma. **A** the fat is the LORD's. H3972
Lev 4: 8 He shall remove **a** the fat from the bull of H3972
Lev 4: 8 **a** the fat that is connected to the internal H3972
Lev 4:11 But the hide of the bull and **a** its flesh, as H3972
Lev 4:12 **a** *the rest of* the bull—he must take H3972
Lev 4:19 He shall remove **a** the fat from it and burn H3972
Lev 4:26 He shall burn **a** the fat on the altar as he H3972
Lev 4:31 They shall remove **a** the fat, just as the fat H3972
Lev 4:35 They shall remove **a** the fat, just as the fat H3972
Lev 5:16 a fifth of its value and give it **a** to the priest. NDT
Lev 6: 5 to it and give it **a** to the owner on the day NDT
Lev 6:15 together with **a** the incense on the grain H3972
Lev 6:18 For *a* **generations to come** it is his perpetual AIT
Lev 7: 3 **A** its fat shall be offered: the fat tail and H3972
Lev 7:10 belongs equally to **a** the sons of Aaron. H3972
Lev 8:11 the altar and **a** its utensils and the H3972
Lev 8:15 finger he put it on **a** the horns of the altar H6017
Lev 8:16 Moses also took **a** the fat around the H3972
Lev 8:25 **a** the fat around the internal organs H3972
Lev 8:27 He put **a** these in the hands of Aaron and H3972
Lev 9:23 of the LORD appeared to **a** the people. H3972
Lev 9:24 And when **a** the people saw it, they H3972
Lev 10: 3 in the sight of **a** the people I will be H3972
Lev 10: 6 But your relatives, **a** the Israelites, may H3972
Lev 10:11 teach the Israelites **a** the decrees the LORD H3972
Lev 11: 2 'Of **a** the animals that live on land, these H3972
Lev 11: 9 " 'Of **a** the creatures living in the water of H3972
Lev 11:10 But **a** creatures in the seas or streams that H3972
Lev 11:10 whether among **a** the swarming things H3972
Lev 11:10 things or among **a** the other living H3972
Lev 11:20 " '**A** flying insects that walk on all fours H3972
Lev 11:20 that walk on **a fours** are to be regarded H752
Lev 11:21 that walk on **a fours** that you may eat: H752
Lev 11:23 But **a** other flying insects that have four H3972
Lev 11:27 Of **a** the animals that walk on all fours H3972
Lev 11:27 Of all the animals that walk on **a fours** H752
Lev 11:31 Of **a** those that move along the ground H3972
Lev 11:42 belly or walks on **a fours** or on many feet; H752
Lev 13:12 disease **breaks out a over** their skin H7255+7255
Lev 13:12 it covers **a** the skin of the affected person H3972
Lev 13:13 Since it has **a** turned white, they are clean H3972
Lev 14: 8 shave off **a** their hair and bathe with H3972
Lev 14: 9 day they must shave off **a** their hair; H3972
Lev 14:41 He must have **a** the inside walls of the H6017
Lev 14:45 timbers and **a** the plaster—and H3972
Lev 16:18 blood and put it on **a** the horns of the H6017
Lev 16:21 confess over it **a** the wickedness and H3972
Lev 16:21 of the Israelites—**a** their sins—and put H3972
Lev 16:22 will carry on itself **a** their sins to a remote H3972
Lev 16:30 you will be clean from **a** your sins. H3972
Lev 16:33 the priests and **a** the members of the H3972
Lev 16:34 be made once a year for **a** the sins of the H3972
Lev 17: 2 his sons and to **a** the Israelites and H3972
Lev 18:27 **a** these things were done by the H3972
Lev 19:24 In the fourth year **a** its fruit will be holy, an H3972
Lev 19:37 " 'Keep **a** my decrees and all my laws H3972
Lev 19:37 all my decrees and **a** my laws and follow H3972
Lev 20: 5 people together with **a** who follow him in H3972
Lev 20:22 " 'Keep **a** my decrees and laws and follow H3972
Lev 20:23 Because they did **a** these things, I H3972
Lev 21:24 his sons and to **a** the Israelites. H3972
Lev 22:18 his sons and to **a** the Israelites and H3972
Lev 23:31 You shall do no work **at a**. This is to be a H3972
Lev 23:38 you have vowed and **a** the freewill H3972
Lev 23:42 **A** native-born Israelites are to live in such H3972
Lev 24:14 **A** those who heard him are to lay their H3972
Lev 25:10 throughout the land to **a** its inhabitants. H3972
Lev 26: 5 will eat **a** the food you **want** and live in H8427
Lev 26:14 to me and carry out **a** these commands, H3972
Lev 26:15 fail to carry out **a** my commands and so H3972
Lev 26:18 " 'If after **a this** you will not listen to me, I H465
Lev 26:34 its sabbath years **a** the time that it lies H3972
Lev 26:35 **A** the time that it lies desolate, the land H3972
Nu 1: 3 to their divisions **a** the men in Israel who H3972
Nu 1:20 **A** the men twenty years old or more who H3972
Nu 1:22 **A** the men twenty years old or more who H3972
Nu 1:24 **A** the men twenty years old or more who H3972
Nu 1:26 **A** the men twenty years old or more who NDT
Nu 1:28 **A** the men twenty years old or more who H3972
Nu 1:30 **A** the men twenty years old or more who H3972
Nu 1:32 **A** the men twenty years old or more who H3972
Nu 1:34 **A** the men twenty years old or more who H3972
Nu 1:36 **A** the men twenty years old or more who H3972
Nu 1:38 **A** the men twenty years old or more who H3972
Nu 1:40 **A** the men twenty years old or more who H3972
Nu 1:42 **A** the men twenty years old or more who H3972
Nu 1:45 **A** the Israelites twenty years old or more H3972
Nu 1:50 over **a** its furnishings and everything H3972
Nu 1:50 carry the tabernacle and **a** its furnishings; H3972
Nu 1:54 The Israelites did **a** this just as the LORD H3972
Nu 2: 9 **A** the men assigned to the camp of Judah H3972
Nu 2:16 **A** the men assigned to the camp of H3972
Nu 2:24 **A** the men assigned to the camp of H3972
Nu 2:31 **A** the men assigned to the camp of Dan H3972
Nu 2:32 **A** *the men in* the camps, by their divisions H3972
Nu 3: 8 are to take care of **a** the furnishings of the H3972
Nu 3:13 **a** the firstborn are mine. When I struck H3972
Nu 3:13 When I struck down **a** the firstborn in H3972
Nu 3:22 The number of **a** the males a month old H3972
Nu 3:28 The number of **a** the males a month old H3972
Nu 3:34 The number of **a** the males a month old H3972
Nu 3:36 **a** its equipment, and everything H3972
Nu 3:40 "Count **a** the firstborn Israelite males who H3972
Nu 3:41 me in place of **a** the firstborn of the H3972
Nu 3:41 Levites in place of **a** the firstborn of the H3972
Nu 3:42 So Moses counted **a** the firstborn of the H3972
Nu 3:45 Levites in place of **a** the firstborn of Israel H3972
Nu 4: 3 Count **a** the men from thirty to fifty years of H3972
Nu 4: 9 **a** its jars for the olive oil used to H3972
Nu 4:10 are to wrap it and **a** its accessories in a H3972
Nu 4:12 "They are to take **a** the articles used for H3972
Nu 4:14 are to place on it **a** the utensils used for H3972
Nu 4:15 holy furnishings and **a** the holy articles, H3972
Nu 4:23 Count **a** the men from thirty to fifty years of H3972
Nu 4:26 the ropes and **a** the equipment used in H3972
Nu 4:26 are to do **a** that needs to be done H3972
Nu 4:27 **A** their service, whether carrying or doing H3972
Nu 4:27 as their responsibility **a** they are to carry. H3972
Nu 4:30 Count **a** the men from thirty to fifty years of H3972
Nu 4:31 As part of **a** their service at the tent, they H3972
Nu 4:32 **a** their equipment and everything related H3972
Nu 4:35 **A** the men from thirty to fifty years of age H3972
Nu 4:37 was the total of **a** *those in* the Kohathite H3972
Nu 4:39 **A** the men from thirty to fifty years of age H3972
Nu 4:43 **A** the men from thirty to fifty years of age H3972
Nu 4:46 of Israel counted **a** the Levites by their H3972
Nu 4:47 **A** the men from thirty to fifty years of age H3972
Nu 5: 7 to it and give it **a** to the person they have NDT
Nu 5: 9 **A** the sacred contributions the Israelites H3972
Nu 6:16 priest is to present **a** these before the LORD NDT
Nu 7: 1 consecrated it and **a** its furnishings. H3972
Nu 7: 1 consecrated the altar and **a** its utensils. H3972
Nu 7: 8 They were **a** under the direction of Ithamar NDT
Nu 8: 2 see that *a* **seven** light up the area in front of AIT
Nu 8: 6 from among *a* the **Israelites** and make them AIT
Nu 8:17 When I struck down **a** the firstborn in H3972
Nu 8:18 Levites in place of **a** the firstborn sons in H3972
Nu 8:19 From among *a* the **Israelites**, I have given AIT
Nu 9: 3 in accordance with **a** its rules and H3972
Nu 9:12 they must follow **a** the regulations. H3972
Nu 10:25 as the rear guard for **a** the units, the H3972
Nu 11:11 put the burden of **a** these people on me? H3972
Nu 11:12 Did I conceive **a** these people? Did I give H3972
Nu 11:13 Where can I get meat for **a** these people H3972
Nu 11:14 I cannot carry **a** these people by myself H3972
Nu 11:22 they have enough if **a** the fish in the sea H3972
Nu 11:29 I wish that **a** the LORD's people were H3972
Nu 11:31 up to two cubits deep **a around** the camp, H6017
Nu 11:32 **A** that day and night and all the next day H3972
Nu 11:32 that day and night and **a** the next day the H3972
Nu 11:32 they spread them out **a around** the camp. H6017
Nu 12: 4 out to the tent of meeting, *a* **three** *of* you." AIT
Nu 12: 7 he is faithful in **a** my house. H3972
Nu 13: 3 **A** *of* them were leaders of the Israelites. H3972
Nu 13:32 **A** the people we saw there are of great H3972
Nu 14: 1 That night **a** the members *of* the H3972
Nu 14: 2 **A** the Israelites grumbled against Moses H3972
Nu 14:10 at the tent of meeting to **a** the Israelites. H3972
Nu 14:11 in spite of **a** the signs I have performed H3972
Nu 14:15 If you put *a* **these** people to death, leaving AIT
Nu 14:39 Moses reported this to **a** the Israelites, H3972
Nu 14:45 beat them down **a the way to** Hormah. H6330
Nu 15:26 because **a** the people were involved in H3972
Nu 15:39 you will remember **a** the commands of H3972
Nu 15:40 remember to obey **a** my commands and H3972
Nu 16: 5 Then he said to Korah and **a** his followers H3972
Nu 16: 6 and **a** your followers are to do this: H3972
Nu 16:10 has brought you and **a** your fellow Levites H3972
Nu 16:11 LORD that you and **a** your followers have H3972
Nu 16:16 "You and **a** your followers are to appear H3972
Nu 16:17 250 censers in **a**—and present it NDT
Nu 16:19 Korah had gathered **a** his followers in H3972
Nu 16:22 God who gives breath to **a** living things, H3972
Nu 16:26 be swept away because of **a** their sins." H3972
Nu 16:28 has sent me to do **a** these things and that H3972
Nu 16:29 death and suffer the fate of **a** mankind, H3972
Nu 16:31 As soon as he finished saying **a** this, the H3972
Nu 16:32 **a** those associated with Korah H3972
Nu 16:34 **a** the Israelites around them fled H3972
Nu 17: 9 Moses brought out **a** the staffs from the H3972
Nu 17: 9 the LORD's presence to **a** the Israelites. H3972
Nu 17:12 We are lost, we are **a** lost! H3972
Nu 17:13 the LORD will die. *Are we* **a** going to die?" H9462
Nu 18: 3 are to perform **a** the duties of the tent H3972
Nu 18: 4 tent of meeting—**a** the work at the tent H3972
Nu 18: 8 **a** the holy offerings the Israelites give me H3972
Nu 18: 9 From **a** the gifts they bring me as most H3972
Nu 18:11 from the gifts of **a** the wave offerings of H3972
Nu 18:12 "I give you **a** the finest olive oil and all H3972
Nu 18:12 finest olive oil and **a** the finest new wine H3972
Nu 18:13 **A** the land's firstfruits that they bring to the H3972
Nu 18:21 "I give to the Levites **a** the tithes in Israel H3972
Nu 18:28 to the LORD from **a** the tithes you receive H3972
Nu 19:18 the tent and **a** the furnishings and H3972
Nu 20:14 You know about **a** the hardships that have H3972
Nu 20:29 **a** the Israelites mourned for him thirty H3972
Nu 21:25 Israel captured **a** the cities of the Amorites H3972
Nu 21:25 including Heshbon and **a** its surrounding H3972
Nu 21:26 had taken from him **a** his land as far as H3972
Nu 21:30 has been destroyed **a the way to** Dibon. H6330
Nu 22: 2 son of Zippor saw **a** that Israel had done H3972
Nu 22:18 gave me **a** the silver and gold *in* his H4850
Nu 23: 6 his offering, with **a** the Moabite officials. H3972
Nu 23:13 you will not see them **a** but only the H3972
Nu 23:25 "Neither **curse** them **at a** nor bless H7686+7686
Nu 23:25 them at all nor **bless** them **at a**!" H1385+1385
Nu 24:13 gave me **a** the silver and gold *in* his H4850
Nu 24:17 the skulls of **a** the people of Sheth. H3972
Nu 25: 4 "Take **a** the leaders of these people H3972
Nu 26: 2 **a** *those* twenty years old or more who are H3972
Nu 26:43 **A** *of* them were Shuhamite clans; and H3972
Nu 26:62 **A** the male Levites a month old or more H3972
Nu 27:16 God who gives breath to **a** living things, H3972
Nu 28:11 male lambs a year old, *a* **without defect**. AIT
Nu 28:19 male lambs a year old, *a* **without defect**. AIT
Nu 29: 2 male lambs a year old, *a* **without defect**. AIT
Nu 29: 8 male lambs a year old, *a* **without defect**. AIT
Nu 29:13 male lambs a year old, *a* **without defect**. AIT

A

Nu 29:17 male lambs a year old, *a* **without defect.** AIT
Nu 29:20 male lambs a year old, *a* **without defect.** AIT
Nu 29:23 male lambs a year old, *a* **without defect.** AIT
Nu 29:26 male lambs a year old, *a* **without defect.** AIT
Nu 29:29 male lambs a year old, *a* **without defect.** AIT
Nu 29:32 male lambs a year old, *a* **without defect.** AIT
Nu 29:36 male lambs a year old, *a* **without defect.** AIT
Nu 29:40 told the Israelites a that the LORD H3972
Nu 30: 4 then a her vows and every pledge by H3972
Nu 30:11 then a her vows or the pledges by which H3972
Nu 30:14 then he confirms a her vows or the H3972
Nu 31: 9 children and took a the Midianite herds, H3972
Nu 31:10 They burned a the towns where the H3972
Nu 31:10 had settled, as well as a their camps. H3972
Nu 31:11 They took a the plunder and spoils H3972
Nu 31:13 Eleazar the priest and a the leaders of the H3972
Nu 31:15 "Have you allowed a the women to live?" H3972
Nu 31:17 Now kill a the boys. And kill every woman H3972
Nu 31:26 are to count a the people and animals H4917S
Nu 31:51 them the gold—a the crafted articles. H3972
Nu 31:52 A the gold from the commanders of H3972
Nu 32:15 he will again leave a this people in the H3972
Nu 32:21 if a of you who are armed cross over H3972
Nu 33: 3 defiantly in full view of a the Egyptians, H3972
Nu 33: 4 who were burying a their firstborn, whom H3972
Nu 33:52 drive out a the inhabitants of the land H3972
Nu 33:52 Destroy a their carved images and their H3972
Nu 33:52 and demolish a their high places. H3972
Nu 35: 3 cattle they own and a their other animals. H3972
Nu 35: 7 *In* a you must give the Levites forty-eight H3972
Dt 1: 1 words Moses spoke to a Israel in the H3972
Dt 1: 3 to the Israelites a that the LORD had H3972
Dt 1: 7 go to a the neighboring peoples in the H3972
Dt 1:12 your disputes **a by myself**? H4200+963+3276
Dt 1:19 the Amorites through a that vast and H3972
Dt 1:22 Then a *of* you came to me and said, "Let H3972
Dt 1:31 a the way you went until you reached this H3972
Dt 1:44 you down from Seir a **the way to** Hormah. H6330
Dt 1:46 many days—a the time you spent there. H3869
Dt 2: 7 has blessed you in a the work of your H3972
Dt 2:25 fear of you on a the nations under H3972
Dt 2:32 When Sihon and a his army came out to H3972
Dt 2:34 At that time we took a his towns and H3972
Dt 2:36 The LORD our God gave us a of them. H3972
Dt 3: 3 hands Og king of Bashan and a his army. H3972
Dt 3: 4 At that time we took a his cities. There H3972
Dt 3: 5 A these cities were fortified with high H3972
Dt 3: 7 But a the livestock and the plunder from H3972
Dt 3:10 We took a the towns on the plateau, and H3972
Dt 3:10 on the plateau, and a Gilead, and all H3972
Dt 3:10 a Bashan as far as Salekah and Edrei, H3972
Dt 3:13 The rest of Gilead and also a *of* Bashan H3972
Dt 3:18 But a your able-bodied men, armed for H3972
Dt 3:21 with your own eyes a that the LORD your H3972
Dt 3:21 will do the same to a the kingdoms over H3972
Dt 4: 4 but a *of* you who held fast to the LORD your H3972
Dt 4: 6 who will hear about a these decrees and H3972
Dt 4:19 moon and the stars—a the heavenly array H3972
Dt 4:19 has apportioned to a the nations under H3972
Dt 4:29 if you seek him with a your heart and with H3972
Dt 4:29 with all your heart and with a your soul. H3972
Dt 4:30 are in distress and a these things have H3972
Dt 4:34 like a the things the LORD your God did H3972
Dt 4:40 the LORD your God gives you for a time. H3972
Dt 4:49 included a the Arabah east of the H3972
Dt 5: 1 Moses summoned a Israel and said: Hear, H3972
Dt 5: 3 with a *of* us who are alive here today. H3972
Dt 5:13 days you shall labor and do a your work, H3972
Dt 5:23 a the leaders of your tribes and your H3972
Dt 5:27 Go near and listen to a that the LORD our H3972
Dt 5:29 fear me and keep a my commands always H3972
Dt 5:31 so that I may give you a the commands, H3972
Dt 5:33 Walk in obedience to a that the LORD your H3972
Dt 6: 2 as you live by keeping a his decrees and H3972
Dt 6: 5 LORD your God with a your heart and with H3972
Dt 6: 5 your heart and with a your soul and with H3972
Dt 6: 5 all your soul and with a your strength. H3972
Dt 6:11 filled with a *kinds of* good things you H3972
Dt 6:19 thrusting out a your enemies before you H3972
Dt 6:24 us to obey a these decrees and to H3972
Dt 6:25 are careful to obey a this law before the H3972
Dt 7: 6 chosen you out of a the peoples on the H3972
Dt 7: 7 you were the fewest of a peoples. H3972
Dt 7:15 he will inflict them on a who hate you. H3972
Dt 7:16 You must destroy a the peoples the LORD H3972
Dt 7:18 your God did to Pharaoh and to a Egypt. H3972
Dt 7:19 do the same to a the peoples you now H3972
Dt 7:22 be allowed to eliminate them **a at once,** H4554
Dt 8: 2 LORD your God led you a the way in the H3972
Dt 8:13 gold increase and a you have is H3972
Dt 9:10 On them were a the commandments the H3972
Dt 9:18 because of a the sin you had committed H3972
Dt 10:12 LORD your God with a your heart and with H3972
Dt 10:12 with all your heart and with a your soul, H3972
Dt 10:15 descendants, above a the nations—as it H3972
Dt 10:22 went down into Egypt were seventy **in a,** H5883S
Dt 11: 6 in the middle of a Israel and swallowed H3972
Dt 11: 7 own eyes that saw a these great things H3972
Dt 11: 8 Observe therefore a the commands I am H3972
Dt 11:13 to serve him with a your heart and with H3972
Dt 11:13 with all your heart and with a your soul— H3972
Dt 11:22 carefully observe a these commands I am H3972
Dt 11:23 LORD will drive out a these nations before H3972
Dt 11:32 sure that you obey a the decrees and laws H3972
Dt 12: 2 Destroy completely a the places on the H3972
Dt 12: 5 choose from among a your tribes to put H3972
Dt 12:10 give you rest from a your enemies around H3972
Dt 12:11 a the choice possessions you have H3972
Dt 12:28 Be careful to obey a these regulations I H3972
Dt 12:31 they do a *kinds of* detestable things the H3972
Dt 12:32 See that you do a I command you; do not H3972
Dt 13: 3 you love him with a your heart and with H3972
Dt 13: 3 with all your heart and with a your soul. H3972
Dt 13: 9 then the hands of a the people. H3972
Dt 13:11 Then a Israel will hear and be afraid, and H3972
Dt 13:15 put to the sword a who live in that town. NDT
Dt 13:16 You are to gather a the plunder of the H3972
Dt 13:16 burn the town and a its plunder as a H3972
Dt 13:18 God by keeping a his commands that I H3972
Dt 14: 2 Out of a the peoples on the face of the H3972
Dt 14: 9 Of a the creatures living in the water, you H3972
Dt 14:19 A flying insects are unclean to you; do not H3972
Dt 14:22 to set aside a tenth of a that your fields H3972
Dt 14:28 bring a the tithes of that year's produce H3972
Dt 14:29 God may bless you in a the work of your H3972
Dt 15: 5 careful to follow a these commands I am H3972
Dt 15:10 God will bless you in a your work and in H3972
Dt 16: 3 so that a the days of your life you may H3972
Dt 16: 4 your possession in a your land for seven H3972
Dt 16:15 will bless you in a your harvest and in H3972
Dt 16:15 your harvest and in a the work of your H3972
Dt 16:16 Three times a year a your men must H3972
Dt 17: 7 then the hands of a the people. H3972
Dt 17:13 A the people will hear and be afraid, and H3972
Dt 17:14 a king over us like a the nations around H3972
Dt 17:19 he is to read it a the days of his life H3972
Dt 17:19 follow carefully a the words of this H3972
Dt 18: 5 descendants out of a your tribes to stand H3972
Dt 18: 6 comes in a earnestness to the place H3972
Dt 18: 7 the LORD his God like a his fellow Levites H3972
Dt 19: 9 carefully follow a these laws I command H3972
Dt 20:11 a the people in it shall be subject to H3972
Dt 20:13 put to the sword a the men in it. H3972
Dt 20:15 how you are to treat a the cities that are H3972
Dt 20:18 teach you to follow a the detestable H3972
Dt 21: 5 LORD and to decide a cases of dispute H3972
Dt 21: 6 Then a the elders of the town nearest the H3972
Dt 21:17 by giving him a double share of a he has. H3972
Dt 21:21 Then a the men of his town are to stone H3972
Dt 21:21 A Israel will hear of it and be afraid. H3972
Dt 23:24 you may eat a the grapes you **want,** but H8427
Dt 24:19 God may bless you in a the work of your H3972
Dt 25:18 journey and attacked a who were lagging H3972
Dt 25:19 gives you rest from a the enemies around H3972
Dt 26: 2 of the firstfruits of a that you produce from H3972
Dt 26:11 you shall rejoice in a the good things the H3972
Dt 26:12 aside a tenth of a your produce in the H3972
Dt 26:13 according to a you commanded. H3972
Dt 26:16 observe them with a your heart and with H3972
Dt 26:16 with all your heart and with a your soul. H3972
Dt 26:18 that you are to keep a his commands. H3972
Dt 26:19 honor high above a the nations he has H3972
Dt 27: 1 "Keep a these commands that I give you H3972
Dt 27: 3 Write on them a the words of this law H3972
Dt 27: 8 write very clearly a the words of this law H3972
Dt 27: 9 the Levitical priests said to a Israel, H3972
Dt 27:14 shall recite to a the people of Israel in H3972
Dt 27:15 Then a the people shall say H3972
Dt 27:16 Then a the people shall say H3972
Dt 27:17 Then a the people shall say H3972
Dt 27:18 Then a the people shall say H3972
Dt 27:19 Then a the people shall say H3972
Dt 27:20 Then a the people shall say H3972
Dt 27:21 Then a the people shall say H3972
Dt 27:22 Then a the people shall say H3972
Dt 27:23 Then a the people shall say H3972
Dt 27:24 Then a the people shall say H3972
Dt 27:25 Then a the people shall say H3972
Dt 27:26 Then a the people shall say H3972
Dt 28: 1 carefully follow a his commands I give H3972
Dt 28: 1 set you high above a the nations on earth H3972
Dt 28: 2 A these blessings will come on you and H3972
Dt 28:10 Then a the peoples on earth will see that H3972
Dt 28:12 season and to bless a the work of your H3972
Dt 28:15 not carefully follow a his commands and H3972
Dt 28:15 a these curses will come on you and H3972
Dt 28:25 a thing of horror to a the kingdoms on H3972
Dt 28:26 will be food for a the birds and the wild H3972
Dt 28:33 nothing but cruel oppression a your days. H3972
Dt 28:37 of ridicule among a the peoples where H3972
Dt 28:42 locusts will take over a your trees and the H3972
Dt 28:45 A these curses will come on you. They H3972
Dt 28:52 will lay siege to a the cities throughout H3972
Dt 28:52 They will besiege a the cities throughout H3972
Dt 28:55 It will be a he has left because of the H3972
Dt 28:55 on you during the siege of a your cities. H3972
Dt 28:58 not carefully follow a the words of this law H3972
Dt 28:60 He will bring on you a the diseases of H3972
Dt 28:64 the LORD will scatter you among a nations, H3972
Dt 29: 2 Moses summoned a the Israelites and H3972
Dt 29: 2 Your eyes have seen a that the LORD did in H3972
Dt 29: 2 to a his officials and to all his land. H3972
Dt 29: 2 to all his officials and to a his land. H3972
Dt 29:10 A *of* you are standing today in the H3972
Dt 29:10 officials, and a the other men of Israel H3972
Dt 29:20 A the curses written in this book will fall H3972
Dt 29:21 single them out from a the tribes of Israel H3972
Dt 29:21 according to a the curses of the covenant H3972
Dt 29:24 A the nations will ask: "Why has the LORD H3972
Dt 29:27 he brought on it a the curses written in H3972
Dt 29:29 that we may follow a the words of this law H3972
Dt 30: 1 When a these blessings and curses I have H3972
Dt 30: 2 obey him with a your heart and with H3972
Dt 30: 2 your heart and with a your soul according H3972
Dt 30: 3 you again from a the nations where he H3972
Dt 30: 6 may love him with a your heart and with H3972
Dt 30: 6 with all your heart and with a your soul, H3972
Dt 30: 7 your God will put a these curses on your H3972
Dt 30: 8 the LORD and follow a his commands I am H3972
Dt 30: 9 most prosperous in a the work of your H3972
Dt 30:10 LORD your God with a your heart and with H3972
Dt 30:10 with all your heart and with a your soul. H3972
Dt 31: 1 out and spoke these words to a Israel: H3972
Dt 31: 5 you must do to them a that I have H3972
Dt 31: 7 said to him in the presence of a Israel, H3972
Dt 31: 9 of the LORD, and to a the elders of Israel. H3972
Dt 31:11 when a Israel comes to appear before the H3972
Dt 31:12 follow carefully a the words of this H3972
Dt 31:18 that day because of a their wickedness in H3972
Dt 31:28 Assemble before me a the elders of your H3972
Dt 31:28 the elders of your tribes and a your officials, NDT
Dt 32: 4 works are perfect, and a his ways are just. H3972
Dt 32: 8 when he divided a mankind, he set up NDT
Dt 32:27 triumphed; the LORD has not done a this. H3972
Dt 32:44 son of Nun and spoke a the words of this H3972
Dt 32:45 finished reciting a these words to all H3972
Dt 32:45 reciting all these words to a Israel, H3972
Dt 32:46 "Take to heart a the words I have H3972
Dt 32:46 to obey carefully a the words of this law. H3972
Dt 33: 3 people; a the holy ones are in your hand. H3972
Dt 33: 3 At your feet they a bow down, and from you NDT
Dt 33:11 Bless a his skills, LORD, and be pleased with NDT
Dt 33:12 he shields him a day long, and the H3972
Dt 33:16 *Let a these* **rest** on the head of Joseph, on AIT
Dt 34: 2 a *of* Naphtali, the territory of Ephraim and H3972
Dt 34: 2 a the land of Judah as far as the H3972
Dt 34:11 who did a those signs and wonders the H3972
Dt 34:11 to Pharaoh and to a his officials and to his H3972
Dt 34:12 that Moses did in the sight of a Israel. H3972
Jos 1: 2 Now then, you and a these people, get H3972
Jos 1: 4 the Euphrates—a the Hittite country—to H3972
Jos 1: 5 to stand against you a the days of your H3972
Jos 1: 7 Be careful to obey a the law my servant H3972
Jos 1:14 of the Jordan, but a your fighting men H3972
Jos 2: 9 so that a who live in this country are H3972
Jos 2:13 sisters, and a who belong to them H3972
Jos 2:18 your brothers and a your family into your H3972
Jos 2:22 had searched a along the road and H3972
Jos 2:24 a the people are melting in fear because H3972
Jos 3: 1 morning Joshua and a the Israelites set H3972
Jos 3: 7 begin to exalt you in the eyes of a Israel, H3972
Jos 3:11 of the Lord of a the earth will go into H3972
Jos 3:13 the LORD—the Lord of a the earth—set foot H3972
Jos 3:15 Jordan is at flood stage a during harvest. H3972
Jos 3:17 while a Israel passed by until the whole H3972
Jos 4:11 as soon as a *of* them had crossed, the H3972
Jos 4:14 exalted Joshua in the sight of a Israel; H3972
Jos 4:14 stood in awe of him a the days of his life, H3972
Jos 4:24 He did this so that a the peoples of the H3972
Jos 5: 1 Now when a the Amorite kings west of H3972
Jos 5: 1 of the Jordan and a the Canaanite kings H3972
Jos 5: 4 A those who came out of Egypt—all the H3972
Jos 5: 4 out of Egypt—a the men of military age H3972
Jos 5: 5 A the people that came out had been H3972
Jos 5: 5 a the people born in the wilderness H3972
Jos 5: 6 forty years until a the men who were of H3972
Jos 6: 3 the city once with a the armed men. H3972
Jos 6: 9 **A this time** the trumpets were sounding. H2143
Jos 6:17 The city and a that is in it are to be H3972
Jos 6:17 the prostitute and a who are with her in H3972
Jos 6:19 A the silver and gold and the articles of H3972
Jos 6:22 bring her out and a who belong to her, H3972
Jos 6:23 sisters and a who belonged to her. H3972
Jos 6:25 her family and a who belonged to her H3972
Jos 7: 3 "Not a the army will have to go up H3972
Jos 7:15 along with a that belongs to him. H3972
Jos 7:23 them to Joshua and a the Israelites and H3972
Jos 7:24 Joshua, together with a Israel, took Achan H3972
Jos 7:24 his tent and a that he had, to the H3972
Jos 7:25 Then a Israel stoned him, and after they H3972
Jos 8: 4 very far from it. A *of* you be on the alert H3972
Jos 8: 5 I and a those with me will advance on the H3972
Jos 8:14 he and a the men of the city hurried out H3972
Jos 8:15 Joshua and a Israel let themselves be H3972
Jos 8:16 A the men of Ai were called to pursue H3972
Jos 8:21 For when Joshua and a Israel saw that the H3972
Jos 8:24 had finished killing a the men of Ai in the H3972
Jos 8:24 a the Israelites returned to Ai and killed H3972
Jos 8:25 women fell that day—a the people of Ai. H3972
Jos 8:26 until he had destroyed a who lived in Ai. H3972
Jos 8:33 A the Israelites, with their elders, officials H3972
Jos 8:34 Joshua read a the words of the law H3972
Jos 8:35 There was not a word of a that Moses had H3972
Jos 9: 1 Now when a the kings west of the Jordan H3972
Jos 9: 5 A the bread of their food supply was dry H3972
Jos 9: 9 reports of him: a that he did in Egypt, H3972

Jos 9:10 a that he did to the two kings of the H3972
Jos 9:11 And our elders and a those living in our H3972
Jos 9:19 a the leaders answered, "We have H3972
Jos 9:24 to wipe out a its inhabitants from H3972
Jos 10: 2 and a its men were good fighters. H3972
Jos 10: 5 They moved up with a their troops and H3972
Jos 10: 6 because a the Amorite kings from the hill H3972
Jos 10: 7 including a the best fighting men. H3972
Jos 10:10 cut them down a the way to Azekah and H6330
Jos 10:15 Joshua returned with a Israel to the camp H3972
Jos 10:24 he summoned a the men of Israel and H3972
Jos 10:25 the LORD will do to a the enemies you are H3972
Jos 10:29 Then Joshua and a Israel with him moved H3972
Jos 10:31 Then Joshua and a Israel with him moved H3972
Jos 10:34 Then Joshua and a Israel with him moved H3972
Jos 10:36 Then Joshua and a Israel with him went H3972
Jos 10:38 Then Joshua and a Israel with him turned H3972
Jos 10:40 together with a their kings. H3972
Jos 10:40 He totally destroyed a who breathed, just H3972
Jos 10:42 A these kings and their lands Joshua H3972
Jos 10:43 Joshua returned with a Israel to the camp H3972
Jos 11: 4 They came out with a their troops and a H3972
Jos 11: 5 A these kings joined forces and made H3972
Jos 11: 6 this time tomorrow I will hand a *of* them, H3972
Jos 11: 8 pursued them a the way to Greater Sidon, H6330
Jos 11:10 had been the head of a these kingdoms.) H3972
Jos 11:12 Joshua took a these royal cities and their H3972
Jos 11:14 off for themselves a the plunder and H3972
Jos 11:14 a the people they put to the sword H3972
Jos 11:15 left nothing undone of a that the LORD H3972
Jos 11:16 the hill country, a the Negev, the whole H3972
Jos 11:17 He captured a their kings and put them to H3972
Jos 11:18 waged war against a these kings for a H3972
Jos 11:19 the Israelites, who took them a in battle. H3972
Jos 11:21 from a the hill country of Judah H3972
Jos 11:21 from a the hill country of Israel. H3972
Jos 12: 1 including a the eastern side of the H3972
Jos 12: 5 a *of* Bashan to the border of the people of H3972
Jos 12:24 king of Tirzah one thirty-one kings in a. H3972
Jos 13: 2 a the regions of the Philistines and H3972
Jos 13: 3 *a of it* counted as Canaanite though held by AIT
Jos 13: 4 the south; a the land of the Canaanites H3972
Jos 13: 5 area of Byblos; and a Lebanon to the east H3972
Jos 13: 6 "As for a the inhabitants of the mountain H3972
Jos 13: 6 a the Sidonians, I myself will drive H3972
Jos 13:10 a the towns of Sihon king of the H3972
Jos 13:11 a *of* Mount Hermon and all Bashan as far H3972
Jos 13:11 of Mount Hermon and a Bashan as far as H3972
Jos 13:17 to Heshbon and a its towns on the H3972
Jos 13:21 a the towns on the plateau and the entire H3972
Jos 13:25 a the towns of Gilead and half the H3972
Jos 13:30 Mahanaim and including a *of* Bashan, H3972
Jos 13:30 a the settlements of Jair in Bashan H3972
Jos 15:46 a that were in the vicinity of Ashdod H3972
Jos 16: 9 It also included a the towns and their H3972
Jos 17:16 a the Canaanites who live in the H3972
Jos 18:20 of the clans of Benjamin on a sides. H6017
Jos 19: 8 a the villages around these towns as H3972
Jos 21:26 A these ten towns and their pasturelands H3972
Jos 21:39 with their pasturelands—four towns *in* a. H3972
Jos 21:41 by the Israelites were forty-eight *in* a, H3972
Jos 21:42 this was true for a these towns. H3972
Jos 21:43 the LORD gave Israel a the land he had H3972
Jos 21:44 the LORD gave a their enemies into their H3972
Jos 21:45 Not one of a the LORD's good promises to H3972
Jos 22: 2 "You have done a that Moses the servant H3972
Jos 22: 5 to serve him with a your heart and with H3972
Jos 22: 5 with all your heart and with a your soul." H3972
Jos 23: 1 Israel rest from a their enemies around H3972
Jos 23: 2 summoned a Israel—their elders, leaders H3972
Jos 23: 3 your God has done to a these nations H3972
Jos 23: 4 your tribes a the land of the nations H3972
Jos 23: 6 be careful to obey a that is written in the H3972
Jos 23:14 I am about to go the way of a the earth. H3972
Jos 23:14 You know with a your heart and soul that H3972
Jos 23:14 soul that not one of a the good promises H3972
Jos 23:15 But just as a the good things the LORD your H3972
Jos 23:15 he will bring on you a the evil things he H3972
Jos 24: 1 Joshua assembled a the tribes of Israel H3972
Jos 24: 2 Joshua said to a the people, "This is what H3972
Jos 24:14 LORD and serve him with a faithfulness. H9459
Jos 24:17 journey and among a the nations through H3972
Jos 24:18 LORD drove out before us a the nations, H3972
Jos 24:27 he said to a the people. "This H3972
Jos 24:27 It has heard a the words the LORD has said H3972
Jdg 2: 4 spoken these things to a the Israelites, H3972
Jdg 2: 7 who had seen a the great things the H3972
Jdg 2:14 hands of their enemies a around, H4946+6017
Jdg 3: 1 LORD left to test a *those* Israelites who had H3972
Jdg 3: 3 of the Philistines, a the Canaanites, the H3972
Jdg 3:19 attendants, "Leave us!" And they a left. H3972
Jdg 3:29 thousand Moabites, a vigorous and strong H3972
Jdg 4:13 to the Kishon River a his men and his H3972
Jdg 4:15 routed Sisera and a his chariots and army H3972
Jdg 4:16 a Sisera's troops fell by the sword H3972
Jdg 5:30 garments for my neck—a this as plunder? NDT
Jdg 5:31 "So may a your enemies perish, LORD! But H3972
Jdg 5:31 But *may a who* love you be like the sun when AIT
Jdg 6: 4 the crops a the way to Gaza and did H6330
Jdg 6: 9 you from the hand of a your oppressors; H3972
Jdg 6:13 is with us, why has a this happened to us? H3972
Jdg 6:13 Where are a his wonders that our H3972
Jdg 6:16 you will strike down *a* the Midianites AIT
Jdg 6:33 Now a the Midianites, Amalekites and H3972
Jdg 6:37 on the fleece and a the ground is dry, H3972
Jdg 6:40 a the ground was covered with dew. H3972
Jdg 7: 1 a his men camped at the spring of H3972
Jdg 7: 6 A the rest got down on their knees to H3972
Jdg 7: 7 Let a the others go home." H3972
Jdg 7:12 the Amalekites and a the other eastern H3972
Jdg 7:16 empty jars in the hands of a *of* them, H3972
Jdg 7:18 When I and a who are with me blow our H3972
Jdg 7:18 then from a around the camp blow yours H3972
Jdg 7:21 around the camp, a the Midianites ran H3972
Jdg 7:23 Asher and a Manasseh were called out H3972
Jdg 7:24 So a the men of Ephraim were called out H3972
Jdg 8:10 a that were left of the armies of the H3972
Jdg 8:27 A Israel prostituted themselves by H3972
Jdg 8:34 from the hands of a their enemies on H3972
Jdg 8:35 in spite of a the good things he had done H3972
Jdg 9: 1 said to them and to a his mother's clan, H3972
Jdg 9: 2 "Ask a the citizens of Shechem, 'Which is H3972
Jdg 9: 2 to have a seventy of Jerub-Baal's sons H3972
Jdg 9: 3 the brothers repeated a this to the citizens H3972
Jdg 9: 6 Then a the citizens of Shechem and Beth H3972
Jdg 9:14 "Finally a the trees said to the thornbush H3972
Jdg 9:34 So Abimelek and a his troops set out by H3972
Jdg 9:40 chased him a the way to the entrance of H6330
Jdg 9:45 A that day Abimelek pressed his attack H3972
Jdg 9:48 he and a his men went up Mount Zalmon H3972
Jdg 9:49 So a the men cut branches and followed H3972
Jdg 9:49 So a the people in the tower of Shechem H3972
Jdg 9:51 to which a the men and women H3972
Jdg 9:51 women—a the people of the city H3972
Jdg 9:57 of Shechem pay for a their wickedness. H3972
Jdg 10: 8 years they oppressed a the Israelites on H3972
Jdg 10:18 will be head over a who live in Gilead." H3972
Jdg 11: 8 you will be head over a of us who live in H3972
Jdg 11:11 And he repeated a his words before the H3972
Jdg 11:13 to the Jabbok, a the way to the Jordan. H6330
Jdg 11:20 He mustered a his troops and encamped H3972
Jdg 11:21 Israel took over a the land of the Amorites H3972
Jdg 11:22 capturing a *of* it from the Arnon to the H3972
Jdg 11:26 settlements and a the towns along the H3972
Jdg 12: 6 they said, "A right, say 'Shibboleth.'" If he H5528
Jdg 13:13 "Your wife must do a that I have told her. H3972
Jdg 13:23 shown us a these things or now told H3972
Jdg 14: 3 your relatives or among a our people? H3972
Jdg 16: 2 lay in wait for him a night at the city gate. H3972
Jdg 16: 3 and tore them loose, bar and a. H6640
Jdg 16:13 "A this time you have been making H6330+2178
Jdg 16:27 a the rulers of the Philistines were there H3972
Jdg 16:30 Then he pushed with a his might, and down NDT
Jdg 16:30 on the rulers and a the people in it. H3972
Jdg 18: 2 These men represented a the Danites H7896
Jdg 18:31 a the time the house of God was in H3972
Jdg 19:29 sent them into a the areas of Israel. H3972
Jdg 20: 1 Then a Israel from Dan to Beersheba and H3972
Jdg 20: 2 The leaders of a the people of the tribes H3972
Jdg 20: 7 a you Israelites, speak up and tell H3972
Jdg 20: 8 A the men rose up together as one H3972
Jdg 20:10 every hundred from a the tribes of Israel, H3972
Jdg 20:11 So a the Israelites got together and united H3972
Jdg 20:16 Among a these soldiers there were seven H3972
Jdg 20:17 swordsmen, a *of* them fit for battle. H3972
Jdg 20:25 Israelites, a *of* them armed with swords. H3972
Jdg 20:26 Then a the Israelites, the whole army H3972
Jdg 20:33 A the men of Israel moved from their H3972
Jdg 20:35 25,100 Benjamites, a armed with swords. H3972
Jdg 20:44 Benjamites fell, a *of* them valiant fighters. H3972
Jdg 20:46 swordsmen fell, a *of* them valiant fighters. H3972
Jdg 20:48 to Benjamin and put a the towns to the H5507
Jdg 20:48 A the towns they came across they set on H3972
Jdg 21: 5 "Who from a the tribes of Israel has failed H3972
Jdg 21:14 But there were not enough for a of them. NDT
Ru 2:11 "I've been told a about what you have H3972
Ru 2:14 She ate a *she* wanted and had some left H8425
Ru 2:21 until they finish harvesting a my grain. H3972
Ru 3:11 I will do for you a you ask. All the people H3972
Ru 3:11 A the people of my town know that you H3972
Ru 4: 9 to the elders and a the people, H3972
Ru 4: 9 have bought from Naomi a the property of H3972
Ru 4:11 Then the elders and a the people at the H3972
1Sa 1: 4 wife Peninnah and to a her sons and H3972
1Sa 1:11 him to the LORD for a the days of his life, H3972
1Sa 1:21 Elkanah went up with a his family to offer H3972
1Sa 2:14 is how they treated a the Israelites who H3972
1Sa 2:22 sons were doing to a Israel and how they H3972
1Sa 2:23 I hear from a the people about these H3972
1Sa 2:28 your ancestor out of a the tribes of Israel H3972
1Sa 2:28 your ancestor's family a the food offerings H3972
1Sa 2:33 a your descendants will die in the H3972
1Sa 3:20 And a Israel from Dan to Beersheba H3972
1Sa 4: 1 And Samuel's word came to a Israel. Now H3972
1Sa 4: 5 a Israel raised such a great shout that the H3972
1Sa 4: 6 "What's a this shouting in the Hebrew H1524
1Sa 4: 8 Egyptians with a *kinds of* plagues in the H3972
1Sa 5: 8 So they called together a the rulers of the H3972
1Sa 5:11 So they called together a the rulers of the H3972
1Sa 6: 3 by a means send a guilt offering to H8740+8740
1Sa 6:12 keeping on the road and lowing a the way H2143+2143
1Sa 6:16 the Philistines saw a this and then returned NDT
1Sa 7: 2 Jearim a long time—twenty years in a. H2118
1Sa 7: 2 Then a the people of Israel turned back to H3972
1Sa 7: 3 So Samuel said to a the Israelites, "If you H3972
1Sa 7: 3 returning to the LORD with a your hearts, H3972
1Sa 7: 5 "Assemble a Israel at Mizpah, and H3972
1Sa 7:15 as Israel's leader a the days of his life. H3972
1Sa 7:16 Mizpah, judging Israel in a those places. H3972
1Sa 8: 4 So a the elders of Israel gathered H3972
1Sa 8: 5 lead us, such as a the other nations have." H3972
1Sa 8: 7 "Listen to a that the people are saying to H3972
1Sa 8:10 Samuel told a the words of the LORD to the H3972
1Sa 8:20 Then we will be like a the other nations H3972
1Sa 8:21 When Samuel heard a that the people H3972
1Sa 9:19 will tell you a that is in your heart H3972
1Sa 9:20 And to whom is a the desire of Israel H3972
1Sa 9:21 my clan the least of a the clans of the H3972
1Sa 10: 9 a these signs were fulfilled that day. H3972
1Sa 10:11 When a those who had formerly known H3972
1Sa 10:18 power of Egypt and a the kingdoms that H3972
1Sa 10:19 who saves you out of a your disasters and H3972
1Sa 10:20 When Samuel had a Israel come forward H3972
1Sa 10:24 Samuel said to a the people, "Do you see H3972
1Sa 10:24 is no one like him among a the people." H3972
1Sa 11: 1 And a the men of Jabesh said to him H3972
1Sa 11: 2 of you and so bring disgrace on a Israel." H3972
1Sa 11: 4 terms to the people, they a wept aloud. H3972
1Sa 11:15 So a the people went to Gilgal and made H3972
1Sa 11:15 Saul and a the Israelites held a great H3972
1Sa 12: 1 Samuel said to a Israel, "I have listened H3972
1Sa 12: 7 before the LORD as to a the righteous acts H3972
1Sa 12:11 of your enemies a around you, H4946+6017
1Sa 12:18 So a the people stood in awe of the LORD H3972
1Sa 12:19 The people a said to Samuel, "Pray to the H3972
1Sa 12:19 we have added to a our other sins the H3972
1Sa 12:20 "You have done a this evil; yet do not turn H3972
1Sa 12:20 but serve the LORD with a your heart. H3972
1Sa 12:24 serve him faithfully with a your heart; H3972
1Sa 13: 4 So a Israel heard the news: "Saul has H3972
1Sa 13: 7 a the troops with him were quaking H3972
1Sa 13:13 your kingdom over Israel for a time. H6409
1Sa 13:20 So a Israel went down to the Philistines to H3972
1Sa 14: 7 "Do a that you have in mind," his H3972
1Sa 14:16 the army melting away in a directions. H2151
1Sa 14:20 Then Saul and a his men assembled and H3972
1Sa 14:22 When a the Israelites who had hidden in H3972
1Sa 14:38 a you who are leaders of the army H3972
1Sa 14:40 Saul then said to a the Israelites, "You H3972
1Sa 14:52 A the days of Saul there was bitter war H3972
1Sa 15: 3 totally destroy a that belongs to them H3972
1Sa 15: 6 showed kindness to a the Israelites when H3972
1Sa 15: 7 Amalekites a the way from Havilah to Shur, H995
1Sa 15: 8 a his people he totally destroyed with H3972
1Sa 15:11 he cried out to the LORD a that night. H3972
1Sa 16:11 "*Are these* a the sons you have? H9462
1Sa 17:11 Saul and a the Israelites were dismayed H3972
1Sa 17:19 are with Saul and a the men of Israel in H3972
1Sa 17:24 they a fled from him in great fear. H3972
1Sa 17:47 A those gathered here will know that it is H3972
1Sa 17:47 he will give a of you into our hands. NDT
1Sa 18: 5 This pleased a the troops, and Saul's H3972
1Sa 18: 6 came out from a the towns of Israel H3972
1Sa 18:16 But a Israel and Judah loved David H3972
1Sa 18:22 his attendants a love you; now H3972
1Sa 19: 1 his son Jonathan and a the attendants to H3972
1Sa 19: 5 The LORD won a great victory for a Israel H3972
1Sa 19:18 told him a that Saul had done H3972
1Sa 19:24 He lay naked a that day and all that night. H3972
1Sa 19:24 He lay naked all that day and a that night. H3972
1Sa 20: 6 If your father misses me at a, tell H7212+7212
1Sa 20:39 The boy knew nothing about a this; only H4399
1Sa 22: 2 A those who were in distress or in debt H3972
1Sa 22: 6 with a his officials standing at his side. H3972
1Sa 22: 7 the son of Jesse give a *of* you fields and H3972
1Sa 22: 7 Will he make a *of* you commanders of H3972
1Sa 22: 8 Is that why you have a conspired against H3972
1Sa 22:11 of Ahitub and a *the men of* his family, H3972
1Sa 22:11 and they a came to the king. H3972
1Sa 22:14 "Who of a your servants is as loyal as H3972
1Sa 22:15 knows nothing at a about this H7785+196+1524
1Sa 23: 8 And Saul called up a his forces for battle H3972
1Sa 23:23 Find out about a the hiding places he uses H3972
1Sa 23:23 him down among a the clans of Judah." H3972
1Sa 24: 2 able young men from a Israel and set out H3972
1Sa 25: 1 a Israel assembled and mourned for H3972
1Sa 25: 6 And good health to a that is yours! H3972
1Sa 25:21 a my watching over this fellow's property H3972
1Sa 25:22 alive one male of a who belong to him!" H3972
1Sa 25:26 and *a* who *are* intent on harming my AIT
1Sa 25:36 him nothing at a until H7785+2256+1524
1Sa 25:37 his wife told him a these things, and his NDT
1Sa 26:12 They were a sleeping, because the LORD H3972
1Sa 26:24 my life and deliver me from a trouble." H3972
1Sa 28: 3 a Israel had mourned for him and H3972
1Sa 28: 4 while Saul gathered a Israel and set up H3972
1Sa 28:20 he had eaten nothing a that day and all H3972
1Sa 28:20 nothing all that day and a that night. H3972
1Sa 29: 1 Philistines gathered a their forces at H3972
1Sa 30:20 He took a the flocks and herds, and his H3972
1Sa 30:22 But a the evil men and troublemakers H3972
1Sa 30:24 went down to the battle. *A will* share alike." AIT
1Sa 30:31 to those in a the other places where H3972
1Sa 31: 6 his armor-bearer and a his men died H3972
1Sa 31:12 a their valiant men marched through the H3972

A

2Sa	1:11	Then David and **a** the men with him took	H3972
2Sa	2: 9	also over Ephraim, Benjamin and **a** Israel.	H3972
2Sa	2:14	"**A right**, *let them* **do it**," Joab	H7756S
2Sa	2:28	trumpet, and **a** the troops came to a halt	H3972
2Sa	2:29	**A** that night Abner and his men marched	H3972
2Sa	2:32	his men marched **a** night and arrived	H3972
2Sa	3:12	I will help you bring **a** Israel over to you."	H3972
2Sa	3:16	behind her **a the way** to Bahurim.	H2143
2Sa	3:18	from the hand of **a** their enemies.	H3972
2Sa	3:21	at once and assemble **a** Israel for my lord	H3972
2Sa	3:21	that you may rule over **a** that your heart	H3972
2Sa	3:23	When Joab and **a** the soldiers with him	H3972
2Sa	3:31	said to Joab and **a** the people with him,	H3972
2Sa	3:32	at Abner's tomb. **A** the people wept also.	H3972
2Sa	3:34	And **a** the people wept over him again	H3972
2Sa	3:35	Then they **a** came and urged David to eat	H3972
2Sa	3:36	**A** the people took note and were pleased;	H3972
2Sa	3:37	So on that day **a** the people there and all	H3972
2Sa	3:37	people there and **a** Israel knew that the	H3972
2Sa	4: 1	courage, and **a** Israel became alarmed.	H3972
2Sa	4: 7	they traveled **a** night by way of the	H3972
2Sa	5: 1	**A** the tribes of Israel came to David at	H3972
2Sa	5: 3	When **a** the elders of Israel had come to	H3972
2Sa	5: 5	he reigned over **a** Israel and Judah	H3972
2Sa	5:25	**a the way** from Gibeon **to** Gezer.	H6330+995
2Sa	6: 1	brought together **a** the able young men of	H3972
2Sa	6: 2	He and **a** his men went to Baalah in	H3972
2Sa	6: 5	David and **a** Israel were celebrating with	H3972
2Sa	6: 5	with **a** their *might* before the LORD	H3972
2Sa	6:14	dancing before the LORD with **a** his might,	H3972
2Sa	6:15	while he and **a** Israel were bringing up the	H3972
2Sa	6:19	And **a** the people went to their homes	H3972
2Sa	7: 1	given him rest from **a** his enemies around	H3972
2Sa	7: 7	I have moved with **a** the Israelites,	H3972
2Sa	7: 9	I have cut off **a** your enemies from	H3972
2Sa	7:11	also give you rest from **a** your enemies.	H3972
2Sa	7:17	reported to David **a** the words of this	H3972
2Sa	8: 4	He hamstrung **a** but a hundred of the	H3972
2Sa	8:11	silver and gold from **a** the nations he had	H3972
2Sa	8:14	**a** the Edomites became subject to	H3972
2Sa	8:15	David reigned over **a** Israel, doing what	H3972
2Sa	8:15	what was just and right for **a** his people.	H3972
2Sa	9: 7	I will restore to you **a** the land that	H3972
2Sa	9:12	**a** the members of Ziba's household	H3972
2Sa	10:17	he gathered **a** Israel, crossed the	H3972
2Sa	10:19	When **a** the kings who were vassals of	H3972
2Sa	11: 9	to the palace with **a** his master's servants	H3972
2Sa	12: 8	I gave you **a** Israel and Judah	H1074S
2Sa	12: 8	And if **a** this had been too little, I would	NDT
2Sa	12:12	thing in broad daylight before **a** Israel.	H3972
2Sa	12:31	David did this to **a** the Ammonite towns	H3972
2Sa	13:21	When King David heard **a** this, he was	H3972
2Sa	13:23	he invited **a** the king's sons to come there.	H3972
2Sa	13:25	"**A** *of* us should not go; we would only be	H3972
2Sa	13:29	Then **a** the king's sons got up, mounted	H3972
2Sa	13:30	has struck down **a** the king's sons;	H3972
2Sa	13:31	**a** his attendants stood by with their	H3972
2Sa	13:32	not think that they killed **a** the princes;	H3972
2Sa	13:33	about the report that **a** the king's sons are	H3972
2Sa	13:36	**a** his attendants wept very bitterly.	H3972
2Sa	14:19	"Isn't the hand of Joab with you in **a** this?"	H3972
2Sa	14:19	do this and who put **a** these words into	H3972
2Sa	14:25	In **a** Israel there was not a man so highly	H3972
2Sa	15: 6	in this way toward **a** the Israelites who	H3972
2Sa	15:14	Then David said to **a** his officials who	H3972
2Sa	15:17	with **a** the people following him	H3972
2Sa	15:18	**A** his men marched past him, along with	H3972
2Sa	15:18	along with **a** the Kerethites and Pelethites	H3972
2Sa	15:18	**a** the six hundred Gittites who had	H3972
2Sa	15:22	marched on with **a** his men and the	H3972
2Sa	15:23	wept aloud as **a** the people passed by.	H3972
2Sa	15:23	**a** the people moved on toward the	H3972
2Sa	15:24	**a** the Levites who were with him were	H3972
2Sa	15:24	sacrifices until **a** the people had finished	H3972
2Sa	15:30	**A** the people with him covered their	H3972
2Sa	16: 4	"**A** that belonged to Mephibosheth is now	H3972
2Sa	16: 6	He pelted David and **a** the king's officials	H3972
2Sa	16: 6	though **a** the troops and the special guard	H3972
2Sa	16: 8	has repaid you for **a** the blood you shed	H3972
2Sa	16:11	then said to Abishai and **a** his officials,	H3972
2Sa	16:14	The king and **a** the people with him	H3972
2Sa	16:15	Absalom and **a** the men of Israel came to	H3972
2Sa	16:18	these people, and by **a** the men of Israel	H3972
2Sa	16:21	Then **a** Israel will hear that you have	H3972
2Sa	16:22	concubines in the sight of **a** Israel.	H3972
2Sa	16:23	Absalom regarded **a** *of* Ahithophel's	H3972
2Sa	17: 2	then **a** the people with him will flee.	H3972
2Sa	17: 3	bring **a** the people back to you. The	H3972
2Sa	17: 3	man you seek will mean the return of **a**;	H3972
2Sa	17: 3	**a** the people will be unharmed.	H3972
2Sa	17: 4	to Absalom and to **a** the elders of Israel.	H3972
2Sa	17:10	**a** Israel knows that your father is a	H3972
2Sa	17:11	Let **a** Israel, from Dan to Beersheba—as	H3972
2Sa	17:13	then **a** Israel will bring ropes to that city	H3972
2Sa	17:14	Absalom and **a** the men of Israel said	H3972
2Sa	17:16	the king and **a** the people with him will	H3972
2Sa	17:22	So David and **a** the people with him set	H3972
2Sa	17:24	the Jordan with **a** the men of Israel.	H3972
2Sa	18: 4	the gate while **a** his men marched out	H3972
2Sa	18: 5	And **a** the troops heard the king giving	H3972
2Sa	18:17	**a** the Israelites fled to their homes.	H3972
2Sa	18:28	called out to the king, "**A is well**!	H8934
2Sa	18:31	from the hand of **a** who rose up against	H3972
2Sa	18:32	lord the king and **a** who rise up to harm	H3972
2Sa	19: 5	"Today you have humiliated **a** your men	H3972
2Sa	19: 6	were alive today and **a** *of* us were dead.	H3972
2Sa	19: 7	worse for you than **a** the calamities that	H3972
2Sa	19: 8	in the gateway," they **a** came before him.	H3972
2Sa	19: 9	**a** the people were arguing among	H3972
2Sa	19:14	of Judah so that they were **a** of one mind.	H3972
2Sa	19:14	to the king, "Return, you and **a** your men."	H3972
2Sa	19:28	**A** my grandfather's descendants deserved	H3972
2Sa	19:39	So **a** the people crossed the Jordan, and	H3972
2Sa	19:40	**A** the troops of Judah and half the troops	H3972
2Sa	19:41	Soon **a** the men of Israel were coming to	H3972
2Sa	19:41	the Jordan, together with **a** his men?"	H3972
2Sa	19:42	**A** the men of Judah answered the men of	H3972
2Sa	20: 2	So **a** the men of Israel deserted David to	H3972
2Sa	20: 2	by their king **a the way from** the Jordan to	H4946
2Sa	20: 7	Pelethites and **a** the mighty warriors	H3972
2Sa	20:12	the man saw that **a** the troops came to a	H3972
2Sa	20:14	passed through **a** the tribes of Israel	H3972
2Sa	20:15	**A** the troops with Joab came and	H3972
2Sa	20:22	the woman went to **a** the people with her	H3972
2Sa	21: 9	*A* **seven** *of* them fell together; they were put	AIT
2Sa	21:20	six toes on each foot—twenty-four **in a**.	H5031
2Sa	22: 1	from the hand of **a** his enemies and from	H3972
2Sa	22:23	**A** his laws are before me; I have not	H3972
2Sa	22:31	he shields **a** who take refuge in him.	H3972
2Sa	22:46	**They** *a* lose heart; they come trembling from	AIT
2Sa	23: 6	But evil men are **a** to be cast aside like	H3972
2Sa	23:39	There were thirty-seven **in a**.	H3972
2Sa	24: 7	fortress of Tyre and **a** the towns of the	H3972
2Sa	24:23	Majesty, Araunah gives **a** this to the king."	H3972
1Ki	1: 9	He invited **a** his brothers, the king's sons	H3972
1Ki	1: 9	and **a** the royal officials of Judah	H3972
1Ki	1:19	and has invited **a** the king's sons	H3972
1Ki	1:20	the eyes of **a** Israel are on you, to	H3972
1Ki	1:25	He has invited **a** the king's sons, the	H3972
1Ki	1:39	the trumpet and **a** the people shouted,	H3972
1Ki	1:40	And **a** the people went up after him	H3972
1Ki	1:41	Adonijah and **a** the guests who were with	H3972
1Ki	1:41	the meaning of **a** the noise in the city?"	NDT
1Ki	1:43	"**Not at a**!" Jonathan answered. "Our lord	H66
1Ki	1:49	**a** Adonijah's guests rose in alarm and	H3972
1Ki	2: 2	"I am about to go the way of **a** the earth,"	H3972
1Ki	2: 3	you may prosper in **a** you do and	H3972
1Ki	2: 4	before me with **a** their heart and soul,	H3972
1Ki	2:15	**A** Israel looked to me as their king	H3972
1Ki	2:22	kingdom for him—**after a**, he is my older	H3954
1Ki	2:26	David and shared **a** my father's hardships."	H3972
1Ki	2:44	know in your heart **a** the wrong you did to	H3972
1Ki	3:15	Then he gave a feast for **a** his court.	H3972
1Ki	3:28	When **a** Israel heard the verdict the king	H3972
1Ki	4: 1	So King Solomon ruled over **a** Israel.	H3972
1Ki	4: 7	had twelve district governors over **a** Israel,	H3972
1Ki	4:10	Sokoh and **a** the land of Hepher were his);	H3972
1Ki	4:12	in **a** *of* Beth Shan next to Zarethan	H3972
1Ki	4:21	Solomon ruled over **a** the kingdoms from	H3972
1Ki	4:21	were Solomon's subjects **a** his life.	H3972
1Ki	4:24	For he ruled over **a** the kingdoms west of	H3972
1Ki	4:24	to Gaza, and had peace on **a** sides.	H3972
1Ki	4:27	King Solomon and **a** who came to the	H3972
1Ki	4:30	than the wisdom of **a** the people of the	H3972
1Ki	4:30	greater than **a** the wisdom of Egypt.	H3972
1Ki	4:31	And his fame spread to **a** the surrounding	H3972
1Ki	4:34	From **a** nations people came to listen to	H3972
1Ki	4:34	wisdom, sent by **a** the kings of the world	H3972
1Ki	5: 3	**waged against** my father David **from a sides**	H6015
1Ki	5: 8	sent me and will do **a** you want in	H3972
1Ki	5:10	supplied with **a** the cedar and juniper	H3972
1Ki	5:13	conscripted laborers from **a** Israel—	H3972
1Ki	6:10	built the side rooms **a** along the temple.	H3972
1Ki	6:12	my laws and keep **a** my commands and	H3972
1Ki	6:29	On the walls **a** around the temple, in both	H3972
1Ki	6:38	was finished in **a** its details according	H3972
1Ki	7: 5	**A** the doorways had rectangular frames	H3972
1Ki	7: 9	**A** these structures, from the outside to the	H3972
1Ki	7:14	knowledge to do **a** *kinds of* bronze work.	H3972
1Ki	7:14	Solomon and did **a** the work assigned to	H3972
1Ki	7:20	hundred pomegranates in rows **a around**.	H6017
1Ki	7:33	spokes and hubs were **a** *of* cast metal.	H3972
1Ki	7:36	available space, with wreaths **a around**.	H6017
1Ki	7:37	They were **a** cast in the same molds and	H3972
1Ki	7:40	So Huram finished **a** the work he had	H3972
1Ki	7:45	**A** these objects that Huram made for King	H3972
1Ki	7:47	Solomon left **a** these things unweighed	H3972
1Ki	7:48	Solomon also made **a** the furnishings that	H3972
1Ki	7:51	When **a** the work King Solomon had done	H3972
1Ki	8: 1	**a** the heads of the tribes and the chiefs of	H3972
1Ki	8: 2	**A** the Israelites came together to King	H3972
1Ki	8: 3	When **a** the elders of Israel had arrived	H3972
1Ki	8: 4	tent of meeting and **a** the sacred	H3972
1Ki	8:25	are careful in **a** they **do** to walk before me	H2006
1Ki	8:39	deal with everyone according to **a** they do,	H3972
1Ki	8:40	they will fear you **a** the time they live in	H3972
1Ki	8:43	so that **a** the peoples of the earth may	H3972
1Ki	8:48	back to you with **a** their heart and soul	H3972
1Ki	8:50	forgive **a** the offenses they have	H3972
1Ki	8:53	them out from **a** the nations of the	H3972
1Ki	8:54	had finished **a** these prayers and	H3972
1Ki	8:56	word has failed of **a** the good promises	H3972
1Ki	8:60	so that **a** the peoples of the earth may	H3972
1Ki	8:62	Then the king and **a** Israel with him	H3972
1Ki	8:63	So the king and **a** the Israelites dedicated	H3972
1Ki	8:65	at that time, and **a** Israel with him—a vast	H3972
1Ki	8:65	seven days more, fourteen days in **a**.	NDT
1Ki	8:66	glad in heart for **a** the good things the	H3972
1Ki	9: 1	had achieved **a** he had desired to do	H3972
1Ki	9: 4	do **a** I command and observe my	H3972
1Ki	9: 7	an object of ridicule among **a** peoples.	H3972
1Ki	9: 8	**A** who pass by will be appalled and will	H3972
1Ki	9: 9	why the LORD brought **a** this disaster on	H3972
1Ki	9:11	supplied him with **a** the cedar and juniper	H3972
1Ki	9:19	as well as **a** his store cities and the towns	H3972
1Ki	9:19	throughout **a** the territory he ruled	H3972
1Ki	9:21	descendants of *a these* **peoples** remaining in	AIT
1Ki	10: 2	with him about **a** that she had on her	H3972
1Ki	10: 3	Solomon answered **a** her questions	H3972
1Ki	10: 4	queen of Sheba saw **a** the wisdom of	H3972
1Ki	10:13	the queen of Sheba **a** she desired and	H3972
1Ki	10:15	traders and from **a** the Arabian kings	H3972
1Ki	10:21	**A** King Solomon's goblets were gold, and	H3972
1Ki	10:21	**a** the household articles in the	H3972
1Ki	10:23	wisdom than **a** the other kings of the	H3972
1Ki	10:29	also exported them to **a** the kings of the	H3972
1Ki	11: 8	He did the same for **a** his foreign wives	H3972
1Ki	11:15	had struck down **a** the men in Edom.	H3972
1Ki	11:16	Joab and **a** the Israelites stayed there for	H3972
1Ki	11:16	they had destroyed **a** the men in Edom.	H3972
1Ki	11:32	I have chosen out of **a** the tribes of Israel,	H3972
1Ki	11:34	have made him ruler **a** the days of his life	H3972
1Ki	11:37	you will rule over **a** that your heart	H3972
1Ki	11:41	**a** he did and the wisdom he displayed	H3972
1Ki	11:42	in Jerusalem over **a** Israel forty years.	H3972
1Ki	12: 1	**a** Israel had gone there to make him	H3972
1Ki	12:12	later Jeroboam and **a** the people returned	H3972
1Ki	12:16	When **a** Israel saw that the king refused	H3972
1Ki	12:18	but **a** Israel stoned him to death.	H3972
1Ki	12:20	When **a** the Israelites heard that	H3972
1Ki	12:20	made him king over **a** Israel.	H3972
1Ki	12:21	he mustered **a** Judah and the tribe of	H3972
1Ki	12:23	king of Judah, to **a** Judah and Benjamin	H3972
1Ki	12:31	appointed priests from **a sorts** *of* people,	H7896
1Ki	13:11	came and told him **a** that the man of God	H3972
1Ki	13:32	in Bethel and against **a** the shrines on the	H3972
1Ki	13:33	the high places from **a sorts** *of* people.	H7896
1Ki	14: 8	followed me with **a** his heart,	H3972
1Ki	14: 9	done more evil than **a** who lived before	H3972
1Ki	14:10	as one burns dung, until it *is* **a gone**.	H9462
1Ki	14:13	**A** Israel will mourn for him and bury him	H3972
1Ki	14:18	buried him, and **a** Israel mourned for him	H3972
1Ki	14:21	had chosen out of **a** the tribes of Israel	H3972
1Ki	14:24	the people engaged in **a** the detestable	H3972
1Ki	14:26	including **a** the gold shields Solomon had	H3972
1Ki	14:29	and **a** he did, are they not	H3972
1Ki	15: 3	He committed **a** the sins his father had	H3972
1Ki	15: 5	the LORD's commands **a** the days of his life	H3972
1Ki	15: 7	Abijah's reign, and **a** he did, are they not	H3972
1Ki	15:12	land and got rid of **a** the idols his	H3972
1Ki	15:14	was fully committed to the LORD **a** his life.	H3972
1Ki	15:18	Asa then took **a** the silver and gold that	H3972
1Ki	15:20	Abel Beth Maakah and **a** Kinnereth in	H3972
1Ki	15:22	King Asa issued an order to **a** Judah—	H3972
1Ki	15:23	As for **a** the other events of Asa's reign	H3972
1Ki	15:23	of Asa's reign, **a** his achievements, all	H3972
1Ki	15:23	**a** he did and the cities he built	H3972
1Ki	15:27	while Nadab and **a** Israel were besieging	H3972
1Ki	15:29	destroyed them **a**, according to the word	NDT
1Ki	15:31	Nadab's reign, and **a** he did, are they not	H3972
1Ki	15:33	Ahijah became king of **a** Israel in Tirzah,	H3972
1Ki	16: 7	because of **a** the evil he had done in the	H3972
1Ki	16:13	because of **a** the sins Baasha and his son	H3972
1Ki	16:14	of Elah's reign, and **a** he did, are they not	H3972
1Ki	16:17	Then Omri and **a** the Israelites with him	H3972
1Ki	16:25	sinned more than **a** those before him.	H3972
1Ki	16:33	than did **a** the kings of Israel before him.	H3972
1Ki	18: 5	through the land to **a** the springs and	H3972
1Ki	18:19	the people from **a over** Israel to meet me	H3972
1Ki	18:20	word throughout **a** Israel and assembled	H3972
1Ki	18:24	Then **a** the people said, "What you say	H3972
1Ki	18:30	Then Elijah said to **a** the people, "Come	H3972
1Ki	18:36	have done **a** these things at your	H3972
1Ki	18:39	When **a** the people saw this, they fell	H3972
1Ki	18:46	of Ahab **a the way to** Jezreel.	H6330+995+3870
1Ki	19: 1	how he had killed **a** the prophets with the	H3972
1Ki	19: 5	**A at once** an angel touched him	H2180+2296
1Ki	19:18	**a** whose knees have not bowed down to	H3972
1Ki	20: 4	I and **a** I have are yours."	H3972
1Ki	20: 7	of Israel summoned **a** the elders of the	H3972
1Ki	20: 8	The elders and the people **a** answered	H3972
1Ki	20: 9	'Your servant will do **a** you demanded the	H3972
1Ki	20:15	the rest of the Israelites, 7,000 **in a**.	H3972
1Ki	20:24	Remove **a** the kings from their commands	H408
1Ki	22:10	with **a** the prophets prophesying before	H3972
1Ki	22:12	**A** the other prophets were prophesying	H3972
1Ki	22:17	"I saw **a** Israel scattered on the hills like	H3972
1Ki	22:19	on his throne with **a** the multitudes of	H3972
1Ki	22:22	spirit in the mouths of **a** his prophets,	H3972
1Ki	22:23	in the mouths of **a** these prophets of yours	H3972
1Ki	22:28	he added, "Mark my words, **a** you people!"	H3972
1Ki	22:35	**A day long** the battle raged,	H928+2021+3427+2021+2085
1Ki	22:39	including **a** he did, the palace he	H3972
2Ki	1:14	the first two captains and *a* their **men**.	AIT

2Ki 1:18 As for *a* the **other** events of Ahaziah's reign AIT
2Ki 3: 6 out from Samaria and mobilized a Israel. H3972
2Ki 3:19 good tree, stop up a the springs, and ruin H3972
2Ki 3:21 Now a the Moabites had heard that the H3972
2Ki 3:25 They stopped up a the springs and cut H3972
2Ki 4: 2 "Your servant has nothing there **at a**," H3972
2Ki 4: 3 "Go around and ask a your neighbors H3972
2Ki 4: 4 Pour oil into a the jars, and as each is H3972
2Ki 4: 6 When a the jars were full, she said to her NDT
2Ki 4:13 'You have gone to a this trouble for us. H3972
2Ki 4:23 "That's **a right**," she said. H8934
2Ki 4:26 to meet her and ask her, 'Are you **a right**? H8934
2Ki 4:26 Is your husband **a right**? Is your child all H8934
2Ki 4:26 husband all right? Is your child **a right**?' " H8934
2Ki 4:26 ' " "Everything is **a right**," she said. H8934
2Ki 5: 5 "**By a means, go**," the king of Aram H2143+995
2Ki 5:12 better than a the waters of Israel? H3972
2Ki 5:15 Then Naaman and a his attendants went H3972
2Ki 5:15 there is no God in a the world except in H3972
2Ki 5:21 "Is everything **a right**?" he asked. H8934
2Ki 5:22 "Everything is **a right**," Gehazi answered H8934
2Ki 5:23 "**By a means**, take two talents," said H3283
2Ki 6:17 chariots of fire **a around** Elisha. H6017
2Ki 7:13 be like that of a the Israelites left H3972+2162
2Ki 7:13 will only be like a these Israelites H3972+2162
2Ki 8: 4 "Tell me about a the great things Elisha H3972
2Ki 8: 6 including a the income from her land H3972
2Ki 8: 7 man of God has come **a the way up** here," H6330
2Ki 8: 9 forty camel-loads of a the finest wares of H3972
2Ki 8:21 Jehoram went to Zair with a his chariots. H3972
2Ki 8:23 and a he did, are they not H3972
2Ki 9: 7 the blood of a the LORD's servants H3972
2Ki 9:11 of them asked him, "Is everything **a right**? H8934
2Ki 9:14 Now Joram and a Israel had been H3972
2Ki 9:22 a the idolatry and witchcraft of your mother Jezebel **abound** H8041
2Ki 10: 7 princes and slaughtered a seventy of them. NDT
2Ki 10: 9 He stood before a the people and said H3972
2Ki 10: 9 killed him, but who killed a these? H3972
2Ki 10:11 of Ahab, as well as a his chief men, his H3972
2Ki 10:17 he killed a who were left there of Ahab's H3972
2Ki 10:18 Then Jehu brought a the people together H3972
2Ki 10:19 Now summon a the prophets of Baal, all H3972
2Ki 10:19 of Baal, a his servants and all his priests. H3972
2Ki 10:19 of Baal, all his servants and a his priests. H3972
2Ki 10:21 and a the servants of Baal came H3972
2Ki 10:22 "Bring robes for a the servants of Baal." H3972
2Ki 10:30 the house of Ahab a I had in mind to do, H3972
2Ki 10:31 the God of Israel, with a his heart. H3972
2Ki 10:33 east of the Jordan in a the land of Gilead H3972
2Ki 10:34 of Jehu's reign, a he did, and all his H3972
2Ki 10:34 all he did, and a his achievements, are H3972
2Ki 11: 7 Sabbath duty are a to guard the temple H3972
2Ki 11:14 a the people of the land were H3972
2Ki 11:18 A the people of the land went to the H3972
2Ki 11:19 the guards and a the people of the land H3972
2Ki 11:20 A the people of the LORD rejoiced, and the H3972
2Ki 12: 2 the eyes of the LORD a the years Jehoiada H3972
2Ki 12: 4 "Collect a the money that is brought as H3972
2Ki 12: 9 put into the chest a the money that was H3972
2Ki 12:12 met a the other expenses of restoring H3972
2Ki 12:18 king of Judah took a the sacred objects H3972
2Ki 12:18 had dedicated and a the gold found in H3972
2Ki 12:19 reign of Joash, and a he did, are they not H3972
2Ki 13: 8 Jehoahaz, a he did and his achievements H3972
2Ki 13:12 Jehoash, a he did and his achievements H3972
2Ki 14:14 He took a the gold and silver and all the H3972
2Ki 14:14 gold and silver and a the articles found in H3972
2Ki 14:21 Then a the people of Judah took Azariah H3972
2Ki 14:28 of Jeroboam's reign, a he did, and his H3972
2Ki 15: 6 and a he did, are they not H3972
2Ki 15:16 ripped open a the pregnant women. H3972
2Ki 15:21 and a he did, are they not H3972
2Ki 15:26 and a he did, are written H3972
2Ki 15:29 Galilee, including a the land of Naphtali H3972
2Ki 15:31 Pekah's reign, and a he did, are they not H3972
2Ki 16:11 in accordance with a the plans that King H3972
2Ki 16:15 the burnt offering of a the people of the H3972
2Ki 16:15 altar the blood of a the burnt offerings H3972
2Ki 17: 7 *A this* **took place** because the Israelites had AIT
2Ki 17: 9 themselves high places in a their towns. H3972
2Ki 17:13 Judah through a his prophets and H3972
2Ki 17:16 They forsook a the commands of the LORD H3972
2Ki 17:16 They bowed down to a the starry hosts H3972
2Ki 17:20 the LORD rejected a the people of Israel; H3972
2Ki 17:22 persisted in a the sins of Jeroboam H3972
2Ki 17:23 he had warned through a his servants the H3972
2Ki 17:32 **a sorts** *of* their own *people* to H4946+7896
2Ki 17:39 you from the hand of a your enemies." H3972
2Ki 18: 5 one like him among a the kings of Judah, H3972
2Ki 18:12 a that Moses the servant of the LORD H3972
2Ki 18:13 of Assyria attacked a the fortified cities of H3972
2Ki 18:15 Hezekiah gave him a the silver that was H3972
2Ki 18:21 king of Egypt to a who depend on him. H3972
2Ki 18:35 Who of a the gods of these countries has H3972
2Ki 19: 2 leading priests, **a wearing** sackcloth, to the AIT
2Ki 19: 4 your God will hear a the words of the field H3972
2Ki 19:11 of Assyria have done to a the countries, H3972
2Ki 19:15 alone are God over a the kingdoms of the H3972
2Ki 19:19 so that a the kingdoms of the earth may H3972
2Ki 19:24 I have dried up a the streams of Egypt H3972
2Ki 19:35 morning—there were a the dead bodies! H3972
2Ki 20:13 showed them a that was *in* his H3972
2Ki 20:13 in his palace or in a his kingdom that H3972
2Ki 20:17 a that your predecessors have stored up NDT
2Ki 20:20 a his achievements and how he made the H3972
2Ki 21: 3 He bowed down to a the starry hosts and H3972
2Ki 21: 5 he built altars to a the starry hosts. H3972
2Ki 21: 7 I have chosen out of a the tribes of Israel, H3972
2Ki 21:14 looted and plundered by a their enemies; H3972
2Ki 21:17 and a he did, including the H3972
2Ki 21:24 of the land killed a who had plotted H3972
2Ki 22:13 the people and for a Judah about what is H3972
2Ki 22:13 in accordance with a that is written there H3972
2Ki 22:17 aroused my anger by a the idols their H3972
2Ki 22:20 Your eyes will not see a the disaster I am H3972
2Ki 23: 1 king called together a the elders of Judah H3972
2Ki 23: 2 a the people from the least to the greatest. H3972
2Ki 23: 2 in their hearing a the words of the Book H3972
2Ki 23: 3 decrees with a his heart and all his H3972
2Ki 23: 3 decrees with all his heart and a his soul, H3972
2Ki 23: 3 Then a the people pledged themselves to H3972
2Ki 23: 4 temple of the LORD a the articles made H3972
2Ki 23: 4 Baal and Asherah and a the starry hosts. H3972
2Ki 23: 5 constellations and to a the starry hosts. H3972
2Ki 23: 8 Josiah brought a the priests from the H3972
2Ki 23:19 Josiah removed a the shrines at the high H3972
2Ki 23:20 Josiah slaughtered a the priests of those H3972
2Ki 23:21 The king gave this order to a the people H3972
2Ki 23:24 the idols and a the other detestable H3972
2Ki 23:25 with a his heart and with all his soul and H3972
2Ki 23:25 his heart and with a his soul and with all H3972
2Ki 23:25 with all his soul and with a his strength, H3972
2Ki 23:25 in accordance with a the Law of Moses. H3972
2Ki 23:26 Judah because of a that Manasseh had H3972
2Ki 23:28 Josiah's reign, and a he did, are they not H3972
2Ki 24: 3 the sins of Manasseh and a he had done, H3972
2Ki 24: 5 and a he did, are they not H3972
2Ki 24: 7 king of Babylon had taken a his territory, H3972
2Ki 24:12 nobles and his officials *a* **surrendered** to him. AIT
2Ki 24:14 He carried a Jerusalem into exile: all the H3972
2Ki 24:14 a the officers and fighting men, and all H3972
2Ki 24:14 a the skilled workers and artisans H3972
2Ki 24:20 anger that *a this* **happened** to Jerusalem AIT
2Ki 25: 1 the city and built siege works **a around** it. H6017
2Ki 25: 5 A his soldiers were separated from him H3972
2Ki 25: 9 the royal palace and a the houses of H3972
2Ki 25:14 dishes and a the bronze articles used in H3972
2Ki 25:15 a that were made of pure gold or silver. NDT
2Ki 25:17 pomegranates of bronze a around. H3972
2Ki 25:20 commander took **them** *a* and brought them AIT
2Ki 25:23 When a the army officers and their men H3972
2Ki 25:26 a the people from the least to the H3972
1Ch 1:23 A these were sons of Joktan H3972
1Ch 1:33 A these were descendants of Keturah H3972
1Ch 2: 4 Zerah to Judah. He had five sons *in* a. H3972
1Ch 2: 6 Heman, Kalkol and Darda—five *in* a. H3972
1Ch 2:23 A these were descendants of Makir the H3972
1Ch 3: 8 Elishama, Eliada and Eliphelet—nine in a. NDT
1Ch 3: 9 A *these* were the sons of David, besides H3972
1Ch 3:22 Bariah, Neariah and Shaphat—six in a. NDT
1Ch 3:23 Elioenai, Hizkiah and Azrikam—three in a. NDT
1Ch 3:24 Johanan, Delaiah and Anani—seven in a. NDT
1Ch 4:33 a the villages around these towns as H3972
1Ch 5:13 Jakan, Zia and Eber—seven in a. NDT
1Ch 5:16 on a the pasturelands of Sharon as H3972
1Ch 5:17 A these were entered in the genealogical H3972
1Ch 5:20 the Hagrites and a their allies into their H3972
1Ch 6:48 were assigned to a the other duties of the H3972
1Ch 6:49 in connection with a that was done in the H3972
1Ch 6:49 in accordance with a that Moses the H3972
1Ch 7: 1 Jashub and Shimron—four in a. NDT
1Ch 7: 3 A five *of* them were chiefs H3972
1Ch 7: 5 men belonging to a the clans of Issachar, H3972
1Ch 7: 5 in their genealogy, were 87,000 in a. H3972
1Ch 7: 7 heads of families—five in a. NDT
1Ch 7: 8 A these were the sons of Beker H3972
1Ch 7:11 A these sons of Jediael were heads of H3972
1Ch 7:28 its villages **a the way to** Ayyah and its H6330
1Ch 7:40 A these were descendants of Asher H3972
1Ch 8:28 *A* **these** were heads of families, chiefs as AIT
1Ch 8:38 A these were the sons of Azel H3972
1Ch 8:40 had many sons and grandsons—150 in a. NDT
1Ch 8:40 A these were the descendants of H3972
1Ch 9: 1 A Israel was listed in the genealogies H3972
1Ch 9: 9 A these men were heads of their families H3972
1Ch 9:29 the furnishings and a the other articles of H3972
1Ch 9:34 *A* **these** were heads of Levite families, chiefs AIT
1Ch 10: 6 sons died, and a his house died together. H3972
1Ch 10: 7 When a the Israelites in the valley saw H3972
1Ch 10:11 When a the inhabitants of Jabesh Gilead H3972
1Ch 10:12 a their valiant men went and took the H3972
1Ch 11: 1 A Israel came together to David at H3972
1Ch 11: 3 When a the elders of Israel had come to H3972
1Ch 11: 4 David and a the Israelites marched to H3972
1Ch 11:10 together with a Israel, gave his H3972
1Ch 12:15 when it was overflowing a its banks, H3972
1Ch 12:21 for a *of* them were brave warriors H3972
1Ch 12:32 with a their relatives under their H3972
1Ch 12:38 A these were fighting men who H3972
1Ch 12:38 to make David king over a Israel. H3972
1Ch 12:38 A the rest of the Israelites were also of H3972
1Ch 13: 4 because it seemed right to a the people. H3972
1Ch 13: 5 So David assembled a Israel, from the H3972
1Ch 13: 6 David and a Israel went to Baalah of H3972
1Ch 13: 8 David and a the Israelites were H3972
1Ch 13: 8 were celebrating with a their might before H3972
1Ch 14: 8 had been anointed king over a Israel, H3972
1Ch 14:16 **a the way** from Gibeon **to** Gezer. H6330
1Ch 14:17 the LORD made a the nations fear him. H3972
1Ch 15: 3 David assembled a Israel in Jerusalem to H3972
1Ch 15:27 as were a the Levites who were carrying H3972
1Ch 15:28 So a Israel brought up the ark of the H3972
1Ch 16: 9 praise to him; tell of a his wonderful acts. H3972
1Ch 16:14 our God; his judgments are in a the earth. H3972
1Ch 16:23 Sing to the LORD, a the earth; proclaim his H3972
1Ch 16:24 his marvelous deeds among a peoples. H3972
1Ch 16:25 he is to be feared above a gods. H3972
1Ch 16:26 For a the gods of the nations are idols H3972
1Ch 16:28 to the LORD, *a you* **families** *of* nations, ascribe AIT
1Ch 16:30 Tremble before him, a the earth! The H3972
1Ch 16:32 sea resound, and **a that is in** it; let the H4850
1Ch 16:36 Then a the people said "Amen" and H3972
1Ch 16:43 Then a the people left, each for their own H3972
1Ch 17: 6 I have moved with a the Israelites, H3972
1Ch 17: 8 I have cut off a your enemies from H3972
1Ch 17:10 I will also subdue a your enemies. " 'I H3972
1Ch 17:15 reported to David a the words of this H3972
1Ch 17:19 made known a these great promises H3972
1Ch 18: 4 He hamstrung a but a hundred of the H3972
1Ch 18:10 Hadoram brought a *kinds of* articles of H3972
1Ch 18:11 gold he had taken from a these nations: H3972
1Ch 18:13 a the Edomites became subject to H3972
1Ch 18:14 David reigned over a Israel, doing what H3972
1Ch 18:14 what was just and right for a his people. H3972
1Ch 19:17 he gathered a Israel and crossed the H3972
1Ch 20: 3 David did this to a the Ammonite towns H3972
1Ch 20: 6 six toes on each foot—twenty-four in a. NDT
1Ch 21: 3 are they not a my lord's subjects? H3972
1Ch 21: 5 In a Israel there were one million one H3972
1Ch 21:23 the grain offering. I will give a this." H3972
1Ch 22: 5 splendor in the sight of a the nations. H3972
1Ch 22: 9 give him rest from a his enemies on every H3972
1Ch 22:17 Then David ordered a the leaders of H3972
1Ch 23: 2 gathered together a the leaders of Israel, H3972
1Ch 23: 8 Zetham and Joel—three in a. NDT
1Ch 23: 9 Haran—three in a. These were the NDT
1Ch 23:10 These were the sons of Shimei—four in a. NDT
1Ch 23:12 Izhar, Hebron and Uzziel—four in a. NDT
1Ch 23:23 Eder and Jerimoth—three in a. NDT
1Ch 23:28 the purification of a sacred things and the H3972
1Ch 23:29 a measurements of quantity and size. H3972
1Ch 25: 3 Mattithiah, six in a, under the supervision NDT
1Ch 25: 5 A these were sons of Heman the king's H3972
1Ch 25: 6 A these men were under the supervision H3972
1Ch 25: 7 a *of* them trained and skilled in music H3972
1Ch 26: 8 A these were descendants of Obed-Edom; H3972
1Ch 26: 8 descendants of Obed-Edom, 62 in a. NDT
1Ch 26: 9 relatives, who were able men—18 in a. NDT
1Ch 26:11 sons and relatives of Hosah were 13 *in* a. H3972
1Ch 26:26 were in charge of a the treasuries for the H3972
1Ch 26:28 a the other dedicated things were in H3972
1Ch 26:30 of the Jordan for a the work of the LORD H3972
1Ch 27: 1 served the king in a that concerned the H3972
1Ch 27: 3 Perez and chief of a the army officers for H3972
1Ch 27:31 A these were the officials in charge of H3972
1Ch 28: 1 David summoned a the officials of Israel H3972
1Ch 28: 1 officials in charge of a the property and H3972
1Ch 28: 1 the warriors and a the brave fighting men. H3972
1Ch 28: 4 pleased to make me king over a Israel. H3972
1Ch 28: 5 Of a my sons—and the LORD has given me H3972
1Ch 28: 8 you in the sight of a Israel and of the H3972
1Ch 28: 8 careful to follow a the commands of the H3972
1Ch 28:12 him the plans of a that the Spirit had H3972
1Ch 28:12 of the LORD and a the surrounding rooms, H3972
1Ch 28:13 for a the work of serving in the H3972
1Ch 28:13 as well as for a the articles to be used in H3972
1Ch 28:14 weight of gold for a the gold articles to H3972
1Ch 28:14 weight of silver for a the silver articles to H3972
1Ch 28:19 "A this," David said, "I have in writing as H3972
1Ch 28:19 me to understand a the details of the H3972
1Ch 28:20 forsake you until a the work for the H3972
1Ch 28:21 Levites are ready for a the work on the H3972
1Ch 28:21 in any craft will help you in a the work. H3972
1Ch 28:21 The officials and a the people will obey H3972
1Ch 29: 2 With a my resources I have provided for H3972
1Ch 29: 2 and a *kinds of* fine stone and marble H3972
1Ch 29: 2 marble—a of these in large quantities. NDT
1Ch 29: 5 for a the work to be done by the H3972
1Ch 29:11 kingdom; you are exalted as head over a. H3972
1Ch 29:12 from you; you are the ruler of a *things*. H3972
1Ch 29:12 power to exalt and give strength to a. H3972
1Ch 29:15 in your sight, as were a our ancestors. H3972
1Ch 29:16 a this abundance that we have provided H3972
1Ch 29:16 your hand, and a of it belongs to you. H3972
1Ch 29:17 A these things I have given willingly and H3972
1Ch 29:20 So they a praised the LORD, the God of H3972
1Ch 29:21 other sacrifices in abundance for a Israel. H3972
1Ch 29:23 He prospered and a Israel obeyed him. H3972
1Ch 29:24 A the officers and warriors, as well as all H3972
1Ch 29:24 warriors, as well as a *of* King David's sons H3972
1Ch 29:25 in the sight of a Israel and bestowed on H3972
1Ch 29:26 David son of Jesse was king over a Israel. H3972
1Ch 29:30 the kingdoms of a the other lands. H3972
2Ch 1: 2 Then Solomon spoke to a Israel—to the H3972
2Ch 1: 2 to the judges and to a the leaders in H3972

2Ch 1:17 also exported them to **a** the kings of the H3972
2Ch 2: 5 our God is greater than **a** other gods. H3972
2Ch 2:14 experienced in **a** *kinds of* engraving and H3972
2Ch 2:16 we will cut **a** the logs from Lebanon H3972
2Ch 2:17 took a census of **a** the foreigners residing H3972
2Ch 4:16 shovels, meat forks and **a** related articles. H3972
2Ch 4:16 **A** the objects that Huram-Abi made for King NDT
2Ch 4:18 **A** these things that Solomon made H3972
2Ch 4:19 Solomon also made **a** the furnishings that H3972
2Ch 5: 1 When **a** the work Solomon had done for H3972
2Ch 5: 1 the silver and gold and **a** the furnishings H3972
2Ch 5: 2 **a** the heads of the tribes and the chiefs of H3972
2Ch 5: 3 And **a** the Israelites came together to the H3972
2Ch 5: 4 When **a** the elders of Israel had arrived H3972
2Ch 5: 5 tent of meeting and **a** the sacred H3972
2Ch 5:11 **A** the priests who were there had H3972
2Ch 5:12 **A** the Levites who were musicians—Asaph, H3972
2Ch 6:16 are careful in **a** they **do** to walk before me H2006
2Ch 6:30 with everyone according to **a** they do, H3972
2Ch 6:31 in obedience to you **a** the time they live H3972
2Ch 6:33 so that **a** the peoples of the earth may H3972
2Ch 6:38 back to you with **a** their heart and soul H3972
2Ch 7: 3 When **a** the Israelites saw the fire coming H3972
2Ch 7: 4 Then the king and **a** the people offered H3972
2Ch 7: 5 So the king and **a** the people dedicated H3972
2Ch 7: 6 **a** the Israelites were standing. H3972
2Ch 7: 8 seven days, and **a** Israel with him—a H3972
2Ch 7:11 in carrying out **a** he had in mind to do in H3972
2Ch 7:17 father did, and do **a** I command, and H3972
2Ch 7:20 an object of ridicule among **a** peoples. H3972
2Ch 7:21 **A** who pass by will be appalled and say H3972
2Ch 7:22 is why he brought **a** this disaster on them H3972
2Ch 8: 4 in the desert and **a** the store cities he had H3972
2Ch 8: 6 as well as Baalath and **a** his store cities H3972
2Ch 8: 6 **a** the cities for his chariots and for his H3972
2Ch 8: 6 throughout **a** the territory he ruled H3972
2Ch 8: 8 descendants of *a* **these** *people* remaining in AIT
2Ch 8:16 **A** Solomon's work was carried out, from H3972
2Ch 9: 1 with him about **a** she had on her mind. H3972
2Ch 9: 2 Solomon answered **a** her questions H3972
2Ch 9:12 the queen of Sheba **a** she desired and H3972
2Ch 9:14 Also **a** the kings of Arabia and the H3972
2Ch 9:20 **A** King Solomon's goblets were gold, and H3972
2Ch 9:20 **a** the household articles in the H3972
2Ch 9:22 wisdom than **a** the other kings of the H3972
2Ch 9:23 **A** the kings of the earth sought audience H3972
2Ch 9:26 He ruled over **a** the kings from the H3972
2Ch 9:28 from Egypt and from **a** other countries. H3972
2Ch 9:30 in Jerusalem over **a** Israel forty years. H3972
2Ch 10: 1 **a** Israel had gone there to make him H3972
2Ch 10: 3 he and **a** Israel went to Rehoboam H3972
2Ch 10:12 later Jeroboam and **a** the people returned H3972
2Ch 10:16 When **a** Israel saw that the king refused H3972
2Ch 10:16 So **a** the Israelites went home. H3972
2Ch 11: 3 of Judah and to **a** Israel in Judah and H3972
2Ch 11:12 He put shields and spears in **a** the cities H3972
2Ch 11:13 priests and Levites from **a** their districts H3972
2Ch 11:21 *In* **a**, he had eighteen wives and sixty H3954
2Ch 11:23 Benjamin, and to **a** the fortified cities. H3972
2Ch 12: 1 he and **a** Israel with him abandoned the H3972
2Ch 12:13 had chosen out of **a** the tribes of Israel H3972
2Ch 13: 4 "Jeroboam and **a** Israel, listen to me H3972
2Ch 13:15 routed Jeroboam and **a** Israel before H3972
2Ch 14: 8 **A** these were brave fighting men H3972
2Ch 14:14 They destroyed **a** the villages around H3972
2Ch 14:14 They looted **a** these villages, since there H3972
2Ch 15: 2 Asa and **a** Judah and Benjamin. H3972
2Ch 15: 5 **a** the inhabitants of the lands were in H3972
2Ch 15: 9 Then he assembled **a** Judah and H3972
2Ch 15:12 ancestors, with **a** their heart and soul. H3972
2Ch 15:13 **A** who would not seek the LORD, the God ofH3972
2Ch 15:15 **A** Judah rejoiced about the oath because H3972
2Ch 15:17 was fully committed to the LORD **a** his life. H3972
2Ch 16: 4 Abel Maim and **a** the store cities of H3972
2Ch 16: 6 King Asa brought **a** the men of Judah, H3972
2Ch 17: 2 He stationed troops in **a** the fortified cities H3972
2Ch 17: 5 **a** Judah brought gifts to Jehoshaphat, H3972
2Ch 17: 9 they went around to **a** the towns of Judah H3972
2Ch 17:10 of the LORD fell on **a** the kingdoms of the H3972
2Ch 18: 9 with **a** the prophets prophesying before H3972
2Ch 18:11 **A** the other prophets were prophesying H3972
2Ch 18:16 "I saw **a** Israel scattered on the hills like H3972
2Ch 18:18 on his throne with **a** the multitudes of H3972
2Ch 18:21 spirit in the mouths of **a** his prophets, H3972
2Ch 18:27 he added, "Mark my words, **a** you people!" H3972
2Ch 18:34 **A day long** the battle raged, H928+2021+3427+2021+2085
2Ch 20: 3 he proclaimed a fast for **a** Judah. H3972
2Ch 20: 6 You rule over **a** the kingdoms of the H3972
2Ch 20:13 **A** the men of Judah, with their wives and H3972
2Ch 20:15 Jehoshaphat and **a** who live in Judah H3972
2Ch 20:18 **a** the people of Judah and Jerusalem H3972
2Ch 20:27 **a** the men of Judah and Jerusalem H3972
2Ch 20:29 fear of God came on **a** the surrounding H3972
2Ch 21: 2 **A** these were sons of Jehoshaphat king of H3972
2Ch 21: 4 he put **a** his brothers to the sword along H3972
2Ch 21: 9 there with his officers and **a** his chariots. H3972
2Ch 21:17 it and carried off **a** the goods found in the H3972
2Ch 21:18 After **a** this, the LORD afflicted Jehoram H3972
2Ch 22: 1 the camp, had killed **a** the older sons. H3972
2Ch 22: 9 who sought the LORD with **a** his heart." H3972
2Ch 23: 2 of Israelite families from **a** the towns. H3972
2Ch 23: 5 **a** the others are to be in the H3972
2Ch 23: 6 **a** the others are to observe the LORD's H3972
2Ch 23: 8 The Levites and **a** the men of Judah did H3972
2Ch 23:10 He stationed **a** the men, each with his H3972
2Ch 23:13 **a** the people of the land were H3972
2Ch 23:17 **A** the people went to the temple of Baal H3972
2Ch 23:20 of the people and **a** the people of the H3972
2Ch 23:21 **A** the people of the land rejoiced, and the H3972
2Ch 24: 2 the eyes of the LORD **a** the years of H3972
2Ch 24: 5 the money due annually from **a** Israel, H3972
2Ch 24:10 **A** the officials and all the people brought H3972
2Ch 24:10 All the officials and **a** the people brought H3972
2Ch 24:23 Jerusalem and killed **a** the leaders of the H3972
2Ch 24:23 They sent **a** the plunder to their king in H3972
2Ch 25: 5 of hundreds for **a** Judah and Benjamin. H3972
2Ch 25:12 them down so that **a** were dashed to H3972
2Ch 25:24 He took **a** the gold and silver and all the H3972
2Ch 25:24 gold and silver and **a** the articles found in H3972
2Ch 26: 1 Then **a** the people of Judah took Uzziah H3972
2Ch 26:20 the chief priest and **a** the other priests H3972
2Ch 27: 7 including **a** his wars and the other things H3972
2Ch 28:14 of the officials and **a** the assembly. H3972
2Ch 28:15 plunder they clothed **a** who were naked. H3972
2Ch 28:15 **A** those who were weak they put on H3972
2Ch 28:23 his downfall and the downfall of **a** Israel. H3972
2Ch 28:26 other events of his reign and **a** his ways, H3972
2Ch 29: 5 Remove *a* **defilement** from the sanctuary AIT
2Ch 29:18 altar of burnt offering with **a** its utensils, H3972
2Ch 29:18 the consecrated bread, with **a** its articles. H3972
2Ch 29:19 consecrated **a** the articles that King H3972
2Ch 29:24 a sin offering to atone for **a** Israel, H3972
2Ch 29:24 offering and the sin offering for **a** Israel. H3972
2Ch 29:28 **A** this continued until the sacrifice of the H3972
2Ch 29:31 and **a** *whose* hearts were willing brought H3972
2Ch 29:32 **a** *of* them for burnt offerings to the LORD. H3972
2Ch 29:34 were too few to skin **a** the burnt offerings H3972
2Ch 29:36 Hezekiah and **a** the people rejoiced at H3972
2Ch 30: 1 sent word to **a** Israel and Judah and H3972
2Ch 30:17 Passover lambs for **a** those who were not H3972
2Ch 30:22 spoke encouragingly to **a** the Levites, H3972
2Ch 30:25 Levites and **a** who had assembled H3972
2Ch 31: 1 When **a** this had ended, the Israelites H3972
2Ch 31: 1 After they had destroyed **a** of them, the NDT
2Ch 31: 5 olive oil and honey and **a** that the fields H3972
2Ch 31:13 **A** these served by appointment of King NDT
2Ch 31:16 **a** who would enter the temple of the LORD H3972
2Ch 31:18 They included **a** the little ones, the wives H3972
2Ch 31:19 among them and to **a** who were recorded H3972
2Ch 32: 1 After *a* that Hezekiah had so faithfully **done** AIT
2Ch 32: 4 people who blocked **a** the springs and the H3972
2Ch 32: 5 hard repairing **a** the broken sections H3972
2Ch 32: 9 king of Assyria and **a** his forces were H3972
2Ch 32: 9 of Judah and for **a** the people of Judah H3972
2Ch 32:13 have done to **a** the peoples of the other H3972
2Ch 32:14 Who of **a** the gods of these nations that H3972
2Ch 32:21 who annihilated **a** the fighting men and H3972
2Ch 32:22 of Assyria and from the hand of **a** others. H3972
2Ch 32:23 he was highly regarded by **a** the nations. H3972
2Ch 32:27 shields and **a** kinds of valuables. H3972
2Ch 32:33 **A** Judah and the people of Jerusalem H3972
2Ch 33: 3 He bowed down to **a** the starry hosts and H3972
2Ch 33: 5 he built altars to **a** the starry hosts. H3972
2Ch 33: 7 I have chosen out of **a** the tribes of Israel, H3972
2Ch 33: 8 commanded them concerning **a** the laws, H3972
2Ch 33:14 commanders in **a** the fortified cities H3972
2Ch 33:15 as well as **a** the altars he had built on the H3972
2Ch 33:19 as well as **a** his sins and unfaithfulness H3972
2Ch 33:19 **a** *these* are written in the records of the H4392S
2Ch 33:22 offered sacrifices to **a** the idols Manasseh H3972
2Ch 33:25 of the land killed **a** who had plotted H3972
2Ch 34: 7 cut to pieces **a** the incense altars H3972
2Ch 34: 9 of Israel and from **a** the people of Judah H3972
2Ch 34:12 **a** who were skilled in playing musical H3972
2Ch 34:13 supervised **a** the workers from job to H3972
2Ch 34:21 in accordance with **a** that is written in this H3972
2Ch 34:24 **a** the curses written in the book that has H3972
2Ch 34:25 aroused my anger by **a** that their hands H3972
2Ch 34:28 Your eyes will not see **a** the disaster I am H3972
2Ch 34:29 king called together **a** the elders of Judah H3972
2Ch 34:30 **a** the people from the least to the greatest. H3972
2Ch 34:30 in their hearing **a** the words of the Book H3972
2Ch 34:31 decrees with **a** his heart and all his H3972
2Ch 34:31 decrees with all his heart and **a** his soul, H3972
2Ch 34:33 Josiah removed **a** the detestable idols H3972
2Ch 34:33 detestable idols from **a** the territory H3972
2Ch 34:33 he had **a** who were present in Israel H3972
2Ch 35: 3 who instructed **a** Israel and who had been H3972
2Ch 35: 7 Josiah provided for **a** the lay people who H3972
2Ch 35: 7 **a** from the king's own possessions. H465S
2Ch 35:13 served them quickly to **a** the people. H3972
2Ch 35:18 the Levites and **a** Judah and Israel who H3972
2Ch 35:20 After **a** this, when Josiah had set the H3972
2Ch 35:24 **a** Judah and Jerusalem mourned for H3972
2Ch 35:25 to this day **a** the male and female H3972
2Ch 35:27 **a** the events, from beginning to end, are NDT
2Ch 36: 8 things he did and **a** that was found against NDT
2Ch 36:14 **a** the leaders of the priests and the H3972
2Ch 36:14 following **a** the detestable practices of the H3972
2Ch 36:17 God gave them **a** into the hands of H3972
2Ch 36:18 He carried to Babylon **a** the articles from H3972
2Ch 36:19 they burned **a** the palaces and destroyed H3972
2Ch 36:21 **a** the time of its desolation it rested H3972
2Ch 36:23 has given me **a** the kingdoms of the earth H3972
Ezr 1: 2 has given me **a** the kingdoms of the earth H3972
Ezr 1: 6 **A** their neighbors assisted them with H3972
Ezr 1: 6 in addition to **a** the freewill offerings. H3972
Ezr 1:11 *In* **a**, there were 5,400 articles of gold H3972
Ezr 1:11 Sheshbazzar brought **a** these along with H3972
Ezr 3: 5 the sacrifices for **a** the appointed sacred H3972
Ezr 3: 8 the Levites and **a** who had returned H3972
Ezr 3: 9 sons and brothers—**a** Levites—joined NDT
Ezr 3:11 And **a** the people gave a great shout of H3972
Ezr 6:17 as a sin offering for **a** Israel, twelve male A10353
Ezr 6:20 were **a** ceremonially clean. H3972
Ezr 6:20 the Passover lamb for **a** the exiles, H3972
Ezr 6:21 together with **a** who had separated H3972
Ezr 7:16 together with **a** the silver and gold you A10353
Ezr 7:19 of Jerusalem *a* the **articles** entrusted to you AIT
Ezr 7:21 decree that **a** the treasurers of A10353
Ezr 7:25 to administer justice to **a** the people of A10353
Ezr 7:25 **a** who know the laws of your God. A10353
Ezr 7:28 his advisers and **a** the king's powerful H3972
Ezr 8:18 Sherebiah's sons and brothers, 18 in **a**; NDT
Ezr 8:19 his brothers and nephews, **20** *in a*. AIT
Ezr 8:20 **A** were registered by name H3972
Ezr 8:21 our children, with **a** our possessions. H3972
Ezr 8:22 great anger is against **a** who forsake him." H3972
Ezr 8:25 his officials and **a** Israel present there had H3972
Ezr 8:35 twelve bulls for **a** Israel, ninety-six rams H3972
Ezr 8:35 **A** this was a burnt offering to the LORD H3972
Ezr 10: 3 God to send away **a** these women and H3972
Ezr 10: 5 Levites and **a** Israel under oath to do H3972
Ezr 10: 7 Jerusalem for **a** the exiles to H3972
Ezr 10: 8 three days would forfeit **a** his property, H3972
Ezr 10: 9 **a** the men of Judah and Benjamin had H3972
Ezr 10: 9 **a** the people were sitting in the square H3972
Ezr 10:16 and **a** *of* them designated by name. H3972
Ezr 10:17 finished dealing with **a** the men who had H3972
Ezr 10:19 *They a* **gave** their hands **in pledge** to put AIT
Ezr 10:44 **A** these had married foreign women, and H3972
Ne 4: 6 rebuilt the wall till **a** *of* it reached half its H3972
Ne 4: 6 the people worked *with a* their **heart**. AIT
Ne 4: 8 They **a** plotted together to come and fight H3972
Ne 4:15 had frustrated it, we **a** returned to the wall H3972
Ne 4:16 themselves behind **a** the people of Judah H3972
Ne 5:16 **A** my men were assembled there for the H3972
Ne 5:18 an abundant supply of wine of **a** *kinds*. H3972
Ne 5:18 In spite of **a** this, I never demanded the NDT
Ne 5:19 for **a** I have done for these people. H3972
Ne 6: 9 They were **a** trying to frighten us, thinking H3972
Ne 6:16 When **a** our enemies heard about this, all H3972
Ne 6:16 **a** the surrounding nations were afraid H3972
Ne 8: 1 **a** the people came together as one in the H3972
Ne 8: 2 men and women and **a** who were able to H3972
Ne 8: 3 And **a** the people listened attentively to H3972
Ne 8: 5 **A** the people could see him because he H3972
Ne 8: 5 as he opened it, the people **a** stood up. H3972
Ne 8: 6 **a** the people lifted their hands and H3972
Ne 8: 9 instructing the people said to them **a**, H3972
Ne 8: 9 For **a** the people had been weeping as H3972
Ne 8:11 The Levites calmed **a** the people, saying H3972
Ne 8:12 Then **a** the people went away to eat and H3972
Ne 8:13 the heads of **a** the families, along H3972
Ne 9: 2 separated themselves from **a** foreigners. H3972
Ne 9: 5 it be exalted above **a** blessing and praise. H3972
Ne 9: 6 highest heavens, and **a** their starry host H3972
Ne 9: 6 the earth and **a** that is on it, the H3972
Ne 9: 6 the seas and **a** that is in them. H3972
Ne 9:10 against **a** his officials and all the people H3972
Ne 9:10 all his officials and **a** the people of his H3972
Ne 9:25 houses filled with **a** *kinds of* good things, H3972
Ne 9:32 do not let **a** this hardship seem trifling in H3972
Ne 9:32 on our ancestors and **a** your people, from H3972
Ne 9:33 In **a** that has happened to us, you have H3972
Ne 9:38 "In view of **a** this, we are making a H3972
Ne 10:28 temple servants and **a** who separated H3972
Ne 10:28 with their wives and **a** their sons and H3972
Ne 10:29 **a** these now join their fellow Israelites the NDT
Ne 10:29 to obey carefully **a** the commands, H3972
Ne 10:31 working the land and will cancel **a** debts. H3972
Ne 10:33 for **a** the duties of the house of our H3972
Ne 10:37 of the fruit of **a** our trees and of our new H3972
Ne 10:37 collect the tithes in **a** the towns where we H3972
Ne 11: 2 commended **a** who volunteered H3972+2021+408
Ne 11:20 Levites, were in **a** the towns of Judah H3972
Ne 11:24 the king's agent in **a** affairs relating to the H3972
Ne 11:30 living **a the way** from Beersheba **to** the H6330
Ne 12:47 **a** Israel contributed the daily portions H3972
Ne 13: 3 from Israel **a** who were of foreign H3972
Ne 13: 6 But while **a** this was going on, I was not H3972
Ne 13: 8 threw **a** Tobiah's household H3972
Ne 13:10 that **a** the Levites and musicians H408
Ne 13:12 **A** Judah brought the tithes of grain, new H3972
Ne 13:15 figs and **a** *other kinds of* loads. H3972
Ne 13:15 they were bringing **a** this into Jerusalem on NDT
Ne 13:16 in fish and **a** *kinds of* merchandise and H3972
Ne 13:18 that our God brought **a** this calamity on us H3972
Ne 13:20 sellers of **a** *kinds of* goods spent the H3972
Ne 13:26 God made him king over **a** Israel, but H3972
Ne 13:27 that you too are doing **a** this terrible H3972
Est 1: 3 he gave a banquet for **a** his nobles and H3972
Est 1: 5 **a** the people from the least to the H3972
Est 1: 8 the king instructed **a** the wine stewards to H3972
Est 1:16 also against **a** the nobles and the H3972

Est 1:16 the peoples of **a** the provinces of H3972
Est 1:17 will become known to **a** the women, H3972
Est 1:18 will respond to **a** the king's nobles in H3972
Est 1:20 is proclaimed throughout **a** his vast realm, H3972
Est 1:20 **a** the women will respect their husbands H3972
Est 1:22 sent dispatches to **a** parts of the kingdom H3972
Est 2: 3 his realm to bring **a** these beautiful young H3972
Est 2:18 banquet, for **a** his nobles and officials. H3972
Est 2:23 *A this* **was recorded** in the book of the annals AIT
Est 3: 1 higher than that of **a** the other nobles. H3972
Est 3: 2 **A** the royal officials at the king's gate knelt H3972
Est 3: 6 a way to destroy **a** Mordecai's people, H3972
Est 3: 8 among the peoples in **a** the provinces of H3972
Est 3: 8 are different from those of **a** other people, H3972
Est 3:12 of each people **a** Haman's orders to the H3972
Est 3:13 sent by couriers to **a** the king's provinces H3972
Est 3:13 kill and annihilate **a** the Jews—young H3972
Est 4: 1 learned of **a** that had been done, H3972
Est 4:11 "**A** the king's officials and the people of H3972
Est 4:13 house you alone of **a** the Jews will H3972
Est 4:16 gather together **a** the Jews who are in H3972
Est 4:17 away and carried out **a** *of* Esther's H3972
Est 5:11 **a** the ways the king had honored him H3972
Est 5:12 "And that's not **a**," Haman added. "I'm the H677
Est 5:13 But **a** this gives me no satisfaction as long H3972
Est 5:14 His wife Zeresh and **a** his friends said to H3972
Est 6:13 Zeresh his wife and **a** his friends H3972
Est 8: 5 destroy the Jews in **a** the king's provinces. H3972
Est 8: 9 They wrote out **a** Mordecai's orders to the H3972
Est 8:12 Jews to do this in **a** the provinces of King H3972
Est 9: 2 in their cities in **a** the provinces of King H3972
Est 9: 2 because the people of **a** the other H3972
Est 9: 3 And **a** the nobles of the provinces, the H3972
Est 9: 5 Jews struck down **a** their enemies with H3972
Est 9:20 he sent letters to **a** the Jews throughout H3972
Est 9:24 the enemy of **a** the Jews, had plotted H3972
Est 9:27 descendants and **a** who join them should H3972
Est 9:30 sent letters to **a** the Jews in the 127 H3972
Est 10: 2 And **a** his acts of power and might H3972
Est 10: 3 spoke up for the welfare of **a** the Jews. H3972
Job 1: 3 greatest man among **a** the people of the H3972
Job 1:22 In **a** this, Job did not sin by charging God H3972
Job 2: 4 "A man will give **a** he has for his own life H3972
Job 2:10 not trouble?" In **a** this, Job did not sin H3972
Job 2:11 heard about **a** the troubles that had come H3972
Job 4:14 seized me and made **a** my bones shake. H8044
Job 6: 2 be weighed and **a** my misery be placed H3480
Job 8:13 Such is the destiny of **a** who forget God H3972
Job 9:22 It is **a the same**; that is why I say, 'He H285
Job 9:28 I still dread **a** my sufferings, for I know you H3972
Job 11: 2 "Are **a** these words to go unanswered? Is H8044
Job 12: 3 Who does not know **a** these things? H4017
Job 12: 9 Which of **a** these does not know that the H3972
Job 12:10 creature and the breath of **a** mankind. H3972
Job 13: 1 "My eyes have seen **a** *this*, my ears have H3972
Job 13: 4 you are worthless physicians, **a** *of* you! H3972
Job 13:27 close watch on **a** my paths by putting H3972
Job 14:14 **A** the days of my hard service I will wait H3972
Job 14:20 You overpower them **once for a** H4200+5905
Job 15:20 **A** his days the wicked man suffers torment H3972
Job 15:20 man through **a** the years stored up H5031
Job 15:21 fill his ears; when **a** seems well, marauders NDT
Job 16: 2 you are miserable comforters, **a** *of* you! H3972
Job 16:12 *A* was **well** with me, but he shattered me; he AIT
Job 17:10 "But come on, **a** *of* you, try again! I will H3972
Job 19:19 **A** my intimate friends detest me; those I H3972
Job 22:10 That is why snares are **a around** you, why H6017
Job 23:15 when I think of **a** this, I fear him. NDT
Job 24: 4 the path and force **a** the poor of the land H3480
Job 24:17 For **a** of them, midnight is their morning H3481
Job 24:24 low and gathered up like **a** *others*; H3972
Job 26: 5 beneath the waters and *a that* **live in** them. AIT
Job 27:10 Will they call on God at **a** times? H3972
Job 27:12 You have **a** seen this yourselves. Why H3972
Job 27:19 when he opens his eyes, **a** is gone. H5647S
Job 28:10 the rock; their eyes see **a** its treasures. H3972
Job 29:19 the dew *will* **lie a night** on my H4328
Job 30:23 to the place appointed for **a** the living. H3972
Job 31:38 out against me and **a** its furrows are wet H3480
Job 33:11 he keeps close watch on **a** my paths. H3972
Job 33:29 "God does **a** these things to a person H3972
Job 34:15 **a** humanity would perish together and H3972
Job 34:19 for they are **a** the work of his hands? H3972
Job 36:19 your wealth or even **a** your mighty efforts H3972
Job 36:25 **A** humanity has seen it; mortals gaze on H3972
Job 37: 7 he stops **a** people from their labor. H3972
Job 37:24 not have regard for **a** the wise in heart?" H3972
Job 38: 7 sang together and **a** the angels shouted H3972
Job 38:18 Tell me, if you know **a** this. H3972
Job 40:11 look at **a** who are proud and bring them H3972
Job 40:12 look at **a** who are proud and humble H3972
Job 40:13 Bury **them** *a* in the dust together; shroud their AIT
Job 40:20 **a** the wild animals play nearby. H3972
Job 41:34 It looks down on **a** that are haughty; it is H3972
Job 41:34 haughty; it is king over **a** that are proud." H3972
Job 42: 2 "I know that you can do **a** *things*; no H3972
Job 42:11 **A** his brothers and sisters and everyone H3972
Job 42:11 consoled him over **a** the trouble the LORD H3972
Job 42:15 Nowhere in **a** the land were there found H3972
Ps 2:12 Blessed are **a** who take refuge in him H3972
Ps 3: 7 Strike **a** my enemies on the jaw; break the H3972
Ps 5: 5 your presence. You hate **a** who do wrong; H3972
Ps 5:11 But let **a** who take refuge in you be glad H3972
Ps 6: 6 **A** night *long* I flood my bed with weeping H3972
Ps 6: 7 they fail because of **a** my foes. H3972
Ps 6: 8 Away from me, **a** you who do evil, for the H3972
Ps 6:10 **A** my enemies will be overwhelmed with H3972
Ps 7: 1 deliver me from **a** who pursue me, H3972
Ps 8: 1 how majestic is your name in **a** the earth! H3972
Ps 8: 7 **a** flocks and herds, and the animals of the H3972
Ps 8: 8 **a** that swim the paths of the seas. NDT
Ps 8: 9 how majestic is your name in **a** the earth! H3972
Ps 9: 1 with **a** my heart; I will tell of all your H3972
Ps 9: 1 I will tell of **a** your wonderful deeds. H3972
Ps 9:17 the dead, **a** the nations that forget God. H3972
Ps 10: 4 in **a** his thoughts there is no room for God. H3972
Ps 10: 5 he sneers at **a** his enemies. H3972
Ps 12: 3 May the LORD silence **a** flattering lips and H3972
Ps 14: 2 from heaven on *a* **mankind** to see if there AIT
Ps 14: 3 **A** have turned away, all have become H3972
Ps 14: 3 have turned away, **a** have become corrupt H3481
Ps 14: 4 Do **a** these evildoers know nothing? They H3972
Ps 16: 3 the noble ones in whom is **a** my delight." H3972
Ps 18: T from the hand of **a** his enemies and from H3972
Ps 18:22 **A** his laws are before me; I have not H3972
Ps 18:30 he shields **a** who take refuge in him. H3972
Ps 18:45 **They** *a* lose heart; they come trembling from AIT
Ps 19: 4 Yet their voice goes out into **a** the earth H3972
Ps 19: 9 are firm, and **a of them** are righteous. H3481
Ps 20: 3 May he remember **a** your sacrifices and H3972
Ps 20: 4 heart and make **a** your plans succeed. H3972
Ps 20: 5 May the LORD grant **a** your requests. H3972
Ps 21: 8 hand will lay hold on **a** your enemies; H3972
Ps 22: 7 **A** who see me mock me; they hurl insults H3972
Ps 22:14 and **a** my bones are out of joint. H3972
Ps 22:17 **A** my bones are on display; people stare H3972
Ps 22:23 **A** you descendants of Jacob H3972
Ps 22:23 Revere him, **a** you descendants of Israel H3972
Ps 22:27 **A** the ends of the earth will remember H3972
Ps 22:27 **a** the families of the nations will bow H3972
Ps 22:29 **A** the rich of the earth will feast and H3972
Ps 22:29 **a** who go down to the dust will kneel H3972
Ps 23: 6 love will follow me **a** the days of my life, H3972
Ps 24: 1 the world, and *a who* **live** in it; AIT
Ps 25: 5 and my hope is in you **a** day long. H3972
Ps 25:10 **A** the ways of the LORD are loving and H3972
Ps 25:18 my distress and take away **a** my sins. H3972
Ps 25:22 O God, from **a** their troubles! H3972
Ps 26: 7 telling of **a** your wonderful deeds. H3972
Ps 27: 4 house of the LORD **a** the days of my life, H3972
Ps 29: 9 And in his temple **a** cry, "Glory!" H3972
Ps 31:11 Because of **a** my enemies, I am the utter H3972
Ps 31:19 that you bestow in the sight of **a**, on H1201+132
Ps 31:20 you hide them from *a* human **intrigues**; AIT
Ps 31:23 Love the LORD, **a** his faithful people! The H3972
Ps 31:24 take heart, **a** you who hope in the LORD. H3972
Ps 32: 3 away through my groaning **a** day long. H3972
Ps 32: 6 Therefore let **a** the faithful pray to you H3972
Ps 32:11 **a** you who are upright in heart! H3972
Ps 33: 4 right and true; he is faithful in **a** he does. H3972
Ps 33: 8 Let **a** the earth fear the LORD; let all the H3972
Ps 33: 8 let **a** the people of the world revere him. H3972
Ps 33:11 heart through **a generations**. H1887+2256+1887
Ps 33:13 the LORD looks down and sees **a** mankind; H3972
Ps 33:14 place he watches **a** who live on earth— H3972
Ps 33:15 he who forms the hearts of **a**, who H3480
Ps 33:17 despite *a* its **great** strength it cannot save. AIT
Ps 34: 1 I will extol the LORD at **a** times; his praise H3972
Ps 34: 4 he delivered me from **a** my fears. H3972
Ps 34: 6 he saved him out of **a** his troubles. H3972
Ps 34:17 he delivers them from **a** their troubles. H3972
Ps 34:19 the LORD delivers him from them **a**; H3972
Ps 34:20 he protects **a** his bones, not one of them H3972
Ps 35:26 May **a** who gloat over my distress be put H3481
Ps 35:26 may *a who* **exalt** *themselves* over me be AIT
Ps 35:28 righteousness, your praises **a** day long. H3972
Ps 37:38 But **a** sinners will be destroyed; there will H3481
Ps 38: 6 very low; **a** day long I go about mourning. H3972
Ps 38: 9 **A** my longings lie open before you, Lord H3972
Ps 38:12 my ruin; **a** day long they scheme and lie. H3972
Ps 39: 8 Save me from **a** my transgressions; do not H3972
Ps 39:12 a stranger, as **a** my ancestors were. H3972
Ps 40:14 May **a** who want to take my life be put to H3480
Ps 40:14 may *a who* **desire** my ruin be turned back in AIT
Ps 40:16 But may **a** who seek you rejoice and be H3972
Ps 41: 7 **A** my enemies whisper together against H3972
Ps 42: 3 while people say to me **a** day long H3972
Ps 42: 7 **a** your waves and breakers have swept H3972
Ps 42:10 saying to me **a** day long, "Where is H3972
Ps 44: 8 In God we make our boast **a** day long H3972
Ps 44:15 I live in disgrace **a** day long, and my face H3972
Ps 44:17 **A** this came upon us, though we had not H3972
Ps 44:22 your sake we face death **a** day long; H3972
Ps 45: 8 **A** your robes are fragrant with myrrh and H3972
Ps 45:13 **A** glorious is the princess within her H3972
Ps 45:17 your memory through **a** generations; H3972
Ps 47: 1 Clap your hands, **a** you nations; shout to H3972
Ps 47: 2 awesome, the great King over **a** the earth. H3972
Ps 47: 7 For God is the King of **a** the earth; sing to H3972
Ps 49: 1 Hear this, **a** you peoples; listen, all who H3972
Ps 49: 1 peoples; listen, **a** who live in this world, H3972
Ps 49:10 For *a can* **see** that the wise die, that the AIT
Ps 50:12 the world is mine, and **a that** is **in** it. H4850
Ps 51: 2 Wash away **a** my iniquity and cleanse me H2221
Ps 51: 9 from my sins and blot out **a** my iniquity. H3972
Ps 52: 1 Why do you boast **a** day long, you who H3972
Ps 53: 2 from heaven on *a* **mankind** to see if there AIT
Ps 53: 3 has turned away, **a** have become corrupt H3481
Ps 53: 4 *Do a these* evildoers **know** nothing? They AIT
Ps 54: 7 have delivered me from **a** my troubles, H3972
Ps 56: 1 **a** day long they press their attack. H3972
Ps 56: 2 My adversaries pursue me **a** day long; in H3972
Ps 56: 5 **A** day long they twist my words; all their H3972
Ps 56: 5 my words; **a** their schemes are for my ruin. H3972
Ps 57: 5 let your glory be over **a** the earth. H3972
Ps 57:11 let your glory be over **a** the earth. H3972
Ps 59: 5 rouse yourself to punish **a** the nations H3972
Ps 59: 8 LORD; you scoff at **a** those nations. H3972
Ps 62: 3 Would **a** *of* you throw me down—this H3972
Ps 62: 8 Trust in him at **a** times, you people; pour H3972
Ps 63:11 **a** who swear by God will glory in him H3972
Ps 64: 8 **a** who see them will shake their heads in H3972
Ps 64: 9 **A** people will fear; they will proclaim the H3972
Ps 64:10 **a** the upright in heart will glory in him! H3972
Ps 65: 2 answer prayer, to you **a** people will come. H3972
Ps 65: 5 the hope of **a** the ends of the earth and of H3972
Ps 66: 1 Shout for joy to God, **a** the earth! H3972
Ps 66: 4 **A** the earth bows down to you; they sing H3972
Ps 66: 8 Praise our God, *a* **peoples**, let the sound of AIT
Ps 66:16 Come and hear, **a** you who fear God; let H3972
Ps 67: 2 on earth, your salvation among **a** nations. H3972
Ps 67: 3 God; may **a** the peoples praise you. H3972
Ps 67: 5 God; may **a** the peoples praise you. H3972
Ps 67: 7 so that **a** the ends of the earth will fear H3972
Ps 69:19 shamed; **a** my enemies are before you. H3972
Ps 69:34 the seas and **a** that move in them, H3972
Ps 70: 2 may *a who* **desire** my ruin be turned back in AIT
Ps 70: 4 But may **a** who seek you rejoice and be H3972
Ps 71: 8 declaring your splendor **a** day long. H3972
Ps 71:15 of your saving acts **a** day long—though I H3972
Ps 71:15 though I know not how to relate them **a**. NDT
Ps 71:18 your mighty acts to **a** who are to come. H3972
Ps 71:24 will tell of your righteous acts **a** day long, H3972
Ps 72: 5 the moon, **through a generations**. H1887+1887
Ps 72:11 May **a** kings bow down to him and all H3972
Ps 72:11 down to him and **a** nations serve him. H3972
Ps 72:15 pray for him and bless him **a** day long. H3972
Ps 72:17 Then **a** nations will be blessed through H3972
Ps 73:14 **A** day long I have been afflicted, and H3972
Ps 73:16 When I tried to understand *a* **this**, it troubled AIT
Ps 73:27 you destroy **a** who are unfaithful to you. H3972
Ps 73:28 LORD my refuge; I will tell of **a** your deeds. H3972
Ps 74: 3 **a** this destruction the enemy has brought H3972
Ps 74: 6 They smashed **a** the carved paneling with H3480
Ps 74:17 It was you who set **a** the boundaries of H3972
Ps 74:22 remember how fools mock you **a** day long. H3972
Ps 75: 3 When the earth and **a** its people quake, it H3972
Ps 75: 8 **a** the wicked of the earth drink it H3972
Ps 75:10 "I will cut off the horns of **a** the wicked H3972
Ps 76: 9 to save **a** the afflicted of the land. H3972
Ps 76:11 let **a** the neighboring lands bring gifts to H3972
Ps 77: 8 promise failed for **a time**? H1887+2256+1887
Ps 77:12 I will consider **a** your works and meditate H3972
Ps 77:12 works and meditate on **a** your mighty deeds." NDT
Ps 78:14 by day and with light from the fire **a** night. H3972
Ps 78:25 he sent them **a** the food they **could eat**. H8427
Ps 78:28 inside their camp, **a around** their tents. H6017
Ps 78:32 In spite of **a** this, they kept on sinning; in H3972
Ps 78:51 He struck down **a** the firstborn of Egypt H3972
Ps 79: 3 out blood like water **a around** Jerusalem, H6017
Ps 80:12 its walls so that **a** who pass by pick its H3972
Ps 82: 5 **a** the foundations of the earth are shaken. H3972
Ps 82: 6 you are **a** sons of the Most High. H3972
Ps 82: 8 **a** the nations are your inheritance. H3972
Ps 83:11 **a** their princes like Zebah and Zalmunna, H3972
Ps 83:18 alone are the Most High over **a** the earth. H3972
Ps 85: 2 of your people and covered **a** their sins. H3972
Ps 85: 3 You set aside **a** your wrath and turned H3972
Ps 85: 5 through **a generations**? H1887+2256+1887
Ps 86: 3 Lord, for I call to you **a** day long. H3972
Ps 86: 5 abounding in love to **a** who call to you. H3972
Ps 86: 9 **A** the nations you have made will come H3972
Ps 86:12 my God, with **a** my heart; I will glorify H3972
Ps 87: 2 Zion more than **a** the *other* dwellings of H3972
Ps 87: 7 they will sing, "**A** my fountains are in you." H3972
Ps 88: 7 have overwhelmed me with **a** your waves. H3972
Ps 88:17 **A** day long they surround me like a flood H3972
Ps 89: 1 through **a generations**. H1887+2256+1887
Ps 89: 4 firm through **a generations**. H1887+2256+1887
Ps 89: 7 more awesome than **a** who surround him. H3972
Ps 89:11 you founded the world and **a that is in** it. H4850
Ps 89:16 They rejoice in your name **a** day long H3972
Ps 89:35 **Once for a**, I have sworn by my holiness H285
Ps 89:40 have broken through **a** his walls and H3972
Ps 89:41 **A** who pass by have plundered him; he H3972
Ps 89:42 you have made **a** his enemies rejoice. H3972
Ps 89:47 what futility you have created **a** humanity! H3972
Ps 89:50 in my heart the taunts of **a** the nations, H3972
Ps 90: 1 throughout **a generations**. H1887+2256+1887
Ps 90: 9 **A** our days pass away under your wrath H3972
Ps 90:14 may sing for joy and be glad **a** our days. H3972
Ps 91:11 you to guard you in **a** your ways; H3972
Ps 92: 7 up like grass and **a** evildoers flourish, H3972
Ps 92: 9 will perish; **a** evildoers will be scattered. H3972
Ps 93: 2 long; you are from **a eternity**. H6409
Ps 94: 4 **a** the evildoers are full of boasting. H3972

Ps 94:11 The LORD knows a human plans; he knows AIT
Ps 94:15 a the upright in heart will follow it. H3972
Ps 95: 3 great God, the great King above a gods. H3972
Ps 96: 1 a new song; sing to the LORD, a the earth. H3972
Ps 96: 3 his marvelous deeds among a peoples. H3972
Ps 96: 4 he is to be feared above a gods. H3972
Ps 96: 5 For a the gods of the nations are idols H3972
Ps 96: 7 Ascribe to the LORD, a you families of nations AIT
Ps 96: 9 holiness; tremble before him, a the earth. H3972
Ps 96:11 let the sea resound, and a that is in it. H4850
Ps 96:12 let a the trees of the forest sing for joy. H3972
Ps 96:13 Let a creation rejoice before the LORD, for he NDT
Ps 97: 5 the LORD, before the Lord of a the earth. H3972
Ps 97: 6 a peoples see his glory. H3972
Ps 97: 7 A who worship images are put to shame H3972
Ps 97: 7 boast in idols—worship him, a you gods! H3972
Ps 97: 9 are the Most High over a the earth; you H3972
Ps 97: 9 you are exalted far above a gods. H3972
Ps 98: 3 a the ends of the earth have seen the H3972
Ps 98: 4 joy to the LORD, a the earth, burst into H3972
Ps 98: 7 the world, and a who live in it. AIT
Ps 99: 2 in Zion; he is exalted over a the nations. H3972
Ps 100: 1 Shout for joy to the LORD, a the earth. H3972
Ps 100: 5 through a generations. H1887+2256+1887
Ps 101: 8 I will put to silence a the wicked in the H3972
Ps 102: 8 A day long my enemies taunt me; those H3972
Ps 102:12 through a generations. H1887+2256+1887
Ps 102:15 a the kings of the earth will revere your H3972
Ps 102:24 years go on through a generations. H1887+1887
Ps 102:26 they will a wear out like a garment. H3972
Ps 103: 1 my soul; a my inmost being, praise his H3972
Ps 103: 2 my soul, and forget not a his benefits— H3972
Ps 103: 3 who forgives a your sins and heals all H3972
Ps 103: 3 all your sins and heals a your diseases, H3972
Ps 103: 6 justice for a the oppressed. H3972
Ps 103:19 in heaven, and his kingdom rules over a. H3972
Ps 103:21 Praise the LORD, a his heavenly hosts, you H3972
Ps 103:22 a his works everywhere in his dominion. H3972
Ps 104:11 They give water to a the beasts of the H3972
Ps 104:20 a the beasts of the forest prowl. H3972
Ps 104:24 In wisdom you made them a; the earth is H3972
Ps 104:27 A creatures look to you to give them their H3972
Ps 104:33 I will sing to the LORD a my life; I will sing H928
Ps 105: 2 praise to him; tell of a his wonderful acts. H3972
Ps 105: 7 our God; his judgments are in a the earth. H3972
Ps 105:16 land and destroyed a their supplies of H3972
Ps 105:21 his household, ruler over a he possessed, H3972
Ps 105:36 Then he struck down a the firstborn in H3972
Ps 105:36 the firstfruits of a their manhood. H3972
Ps 106:46 He caused a who held them captive to H3972
Ps 106:48 to everlasting. Let a the people say H3972
Ps 107:18 They loathed a food and drew near the H3972
Ps 107:42 a the wicked shut their mouths. H3972
Ps 108: 1 I will sing and make music with a my soul. H677
Ps 108: 5 let your glory be over a the earth. H3972
Ps 109:11 May a creditor seize a he has; may H3972
Ps 111: 1 extol the LORD with a my heart in the H3972
Ps 111: 2 are pondered by a who delight in them. H3972
Ps 111: 7 just; a his precepts are trustworthy. H3972
Ps 111:10 a who follow his precepts have good H3972
Ps 113: 4 The LORD is exalted over a the nations, his H3972
Ps 115: 8 like them, and so will a who trust in them. H3972
Ps 115: 9 A you Israelites, trust in the LORD— AIT
Ps 116:12 to the LORD for a his goodness to me? H3972
Ps 116:14 the LORD in the presence of a his people. H3972
Ps 116:18 the LORD in the presence of a his people, H3972
Ps 117: 1 Praise the LORD, a you nations; extol him H3972
Ps 117: 1 all you nations; extol him, a you peoples. H3972
Ps 118:10 A the nations surrounded me, but in the H3972
Ps 119: 2 statutes and seek him with a their heart— H3972
Ps 119: 6 shame when I consider a your commands. H3972
Ps 119:10 I seek you with a my heart; do not let me H3972
Ps 119:13 my lips I recount a the laws that come H3972
Ps 119:20 with longing for your laws at a times. H3972
Ps 119:34 your law and obey it with a my heart. H3972
Ps 119:58 I have sought your face with a my heart H3972
Ps 119:63 I am a friend to a who fear you, to all who H3972
Ps 119:63 who fear you, to a who follow your precepts. AIT
Ps 119:69 I keep your precepts with a my heart. H3972
Ps 119:86 A your commands are trustworthy; help H3972
Ps 119:90 through a generations; H1887+2256+1887
Ps 119:91 endure to this day, for a things serve you. H3972
Ps 119:96 To a perfection I see a limit, but your H3972
Ps 119:97 I meditate on it a day long. H3972
Ps 119:99 I have more insight than a my teachers H3972
Ps 119:118 You reject a who stray from your decrees H3972
Ps 119:119 A the wicked of the earth you discard like H3972
Ps 119:128 because I consider a your precepts right, H3972
Ps 119:145 I call with a my heart; answer me, LORD H3972
Ps 119:151 and a your commands are true. H3972
Ps 119:160 A your words are true; all your righteous H8031
Ps 119:160 a your righteous laws are eternal. H3972
Ps 119:168 statutes, for a my ways are known to you. H3972
Ps 119:172 for a your commands are righteous. H3972
Ps 121: 7 The LORD will keep you from a harm—he H3972
Ps 128: 1 Blessed are a who fear the LORD, who walk H3972
Ps 128: 5 of Jerusalem a the days of your life. H3972
Ps 129: 5 May a who hate Zion be turned back in H3972
Ps 130: 8 will redeem Israel from a their sins. H3972
Ps 132: 1 remember David and a his self-denial. H3972
Ps 134: 1 a you servants of the LORD who minister by H3972
Ps 135: 5 that our Lord is greater than a gods. H3972
Ps 135: 6 the earth, in the seas and a their depths. H3972
Ps 135: 9 against Pharaoh and a his servants. H3972
Ps 135:11 of Bashan, and a the kings of Canaan H3972
Ps 135:13 through a generations. H1887+2256+1887
Ps 135:18 like them, and so will a who trust in them. H3972
Ps 135:19 A you Israelites, praise the LORD; house of AIT
Ps 138: 1 LORD, with a my heart; before the H3972
Ps 138: 4 May a the kings of the earth praise you H3972
Ps 139: 3 you are familiar with a my ways. H3972
Ps 139:16 a the days ordained for me were written H3972
Ps 143: 5 I meditate on a your works and consider H3972
Ps 143:12 my enemies; destroy a my foes, for I am H3972
Ps 145: 9 The LORD is good to a; he has compassion H3972
Ps 145: 9 he has compassion on a he has made. H3972
Ps 145:10 A your works praise you, LORD; H3972
Ps 145:12 so that a people may know of H1201+2021+132
Ps 145:13 dominion endures through a generations. H3972
Ps 145:13 LORD is trustworthy in a he promises and H3972
Ps 145:13 all he promises and faithful in a he does. H3972
Ps 145:14 The LORD upholds a who fall and lifts up H3972
Ps 145:14 fall and lifts up a who are bowed down. H3972
Ps 145:15 The eyes of a look to you, and you give H3972
Ps 145:17 LORD is righteous in a his ways and faithful H3972
Ps 145:17 in all his ways and faithful in a he does. H3972
Ps 145:18 The LORD is near to a who call on him, to H3972
Ps 145:18 call on him, to a who call on him in truth. H3972
Ps 145:20 The LORD watches over a who love him H3972
Ps 145:20 love him, but a the wicked he will destroy. H3972
Ps 146: 2 I will praise the LORD a my life; I will sing H928
Ps 146:10 O Zion, for a generations. H1887+2256+1887
Ps 148: 2 Praise him, a his angels; praise him, all H3972
Ps 148: 2 praise him, a his heavenly hosts. H3972
Ps 148: 3 praise him, a you shining stars. H3972
Ps 148: 7 great sea creatures and a ocean depths, H3972
Ps 148: 9 you mountains and a hills, fruit trees and H3972
Ps 148: 9 all hills, fruit trees and a cedars, H3972
Ps 148:10 wild animals and a cattle, small creatures H3972
Ps 148:11 kings of the earth and a nations, you H3972
Ps 148:11 you princes and a rulers on earth, H3972
Ps 148:14 the praise of a his faithful servants H3972
Ps 149: 9 this is the glory of a his faithful people. H3972
Pr 1:13 we will get a sorts of valuable things and H3972
Pr 1:14 lots with us; we will a share the loot"— H3972
Pr 1:19 Such are the paths of a who go after H3972
Pr 1:25 since you disregard a my advice and do H3972
Pr 3: 5 in the LORD with a your heart and lean H3972
Pr 3: 6 in a your ways submit to him, and he will H3972
Pr 3: 9 with the firstfruits of a your crops; H3972
Pr 3:17 and a her paths are peace. H3972
Pr 4: 4 "Take hold of my words with a your heart NDT
Pr 4: 7 Though it cost a you have, get H3972
Pr 4:23 Above a else, guard your heart, for H3972
Pr 4:26 your feet and be steadfast in a your ways. H3972
Pr 5:21 the LORD, and he examines a your paths. H3972
Pr 6:31 though it costs him a the wealth of his H3972
Pr 7:22 A at once he followed her like an ox H7328
Pr 8: 4 I raise my voice to a mankind. H1201+132
Pr 8: 8 A the words of my mouth are just; none of H3972
Pr 8: 9 To the discerning a of them are right; they H3972
Pr 8:16 and nobles—a who rule on earth. H3972
Pr 8:36 themselves; a who hate me love death." H3972
Pr 9: 4 "Let a who are simple come to my house!" AIT
Pr 9:16 "Let a who are simple come to my house!" AIT
Pr 10:12 up conflict, but love covers over a wrongs. H3972
Pr 11: 7 a the promise of their power comes to AIT
Pr 13:16 A who are prudent act with knowledge H3972
Pr 14:23 A hard work brings a profit, but mere talk H3972
Pr 15:15 A the days of the oppressed are wretched H3972
Pr 16: 2 A a person's ways seem pure to them, but H3972
Pr 16: 5 The LORD detests a the proud of heart. Be H3972
Pr 16:11 a the weights in the bag are of his H3972
Pr 17:17 A friend loves at a times, and a brother is H3972
Pr 18: 1 ends and against a sound judgment starts H3972
Pr 19: 7 poor are shunned by a their relatives— H3972
Pr 20: 8 he winnows out a evil with his eyes. H3972
Pr 21: 1 he channels toward a who please him. H3972
Pr 21:26 A day long he craves for more, but the H3972
Pr 22: 2 The LORD is the Maker of them a. H3972
Pr 22:18 heart and have a of them ready on your H3481
Pr 27:24 not secure for a generations. H1887+2256+1887
Pr 29:12 a his officials become wicked. H3972
Pr 30: 4 Who has established a the ends of the H3972
Pr 31: 5 deprive a the oppressed of their H3972
Pr 31: 8 the rights of a who are destitute. H3972
Pr 31:12 not harm, a the days of her life. H3972
Pr 31:21 for a of them are clothed in scarlet. H3972
Pr 31:29 do noble things, but you surpass them a." H3972
Pr 31:31 Honor her for a that her hands have done H7262
Ecc 1: 3 do people gain from a their labors at H3972
Ecc 1: 7 A streams flow into the sea, yet the sea is H3972
Ecc 1: 8 A things are wearisome, more than one H3972
Ecc 1:13 to explore by wisdom a that is done under H3972
Ecc 1:14 I have seen a the things that are done H3972
Ecc 1:14 under the sun; a of them are meaningless H3972
Ecc 2: 5 parks and planted a kinds of fruit trees in H3972
Ecc 2: 9 me. In a this my wisdom stayed with me H677
Ecc 2:10 My heart took delight in a my labor, and H3972
Ecc 2:10 this was the reward for a my toil. H3972
Ecc 2:11 Yet when I surveyed a that my hands had H3972
Ecc 2:17 A of it is meaningless, a chasing after the H3972
Ecc 2:18 I hated a the things I had toiled for under H3972
Ecc 2:19 will have control over a the fruit of my toil H3972
Ecc 2:20 to despair over a my toilsome labor H3972
Ecc 2:21 they must leave a they own to another who AIT
Ecc 2:22 do people get for a the toil and anxious H3972
Ecc 2:23 A their days their work is grief and pain H3972
Ecc 3:13 find satisfaction in a their toil—this is H3972
Ecc 3:19 A have the same breath; humans have no H3972
Ecc 3:20 A go to the same place; all come from H3972
Ecc 3:20 to the same place; a come from dust, and H3972
Ecc 3:20 all come from dust, and to dust a return. H3972
Ecc 4: 1 I looked and saw a the oppression that H3972
Ecc 4: 4 And I saw that a toil and all achievement H3972
Ecc 4: 4 saw that all toil and a achievement spring H3972
Ecc 4: 8 There was a man a alone; he had H401+9108
Ecc 4:15 I saw that a who lived and walked under H3972
Ecc 4:16 There was no end to a the people who H3972
Ecc 5: 9 The increase from the land is taken by a H3972
Ecc 5:17 A their days they eat in darkness, with H3972
Ecc 6: 6 Do not a go to the same place? H3972
Ecc 7:18 Whoever fears God will avoid a extremes. H3972
Ecc 7:23 A this I tested by wisdom and I said, "I H3972
Ecc 7:28 not one upright woman among them a. H3972
Ecc 8: 9 A this I saw, as I applied my mind to H3972
Ecc 8:15 them in their toil a the days of the life God NDT
Ecc 8:17 then I saw a that God has done. No one H3972
Ecc 8:17 Despite a their efforts to search it out, no one AIT
Ecc 9: 1 So I reflected on a this and concluded H3972
Ecc 9: 2 A share a common destiny—the righteous H3972
Ecc 9: 3 The same destiny overtakes a. The hearts H3972
Ecc 9: 9 a the days of this meaningless life that H3972
Ecc 9: 9 under the sun—a your meaningless days. H3972
Ecc 9:10 do it with a your might, for in the NDT
Ecc 9:11 time and chance happen to them a. H3972
Ecc 11: 5 the work of God, the Maker of a things. H3972
Ecc 11: 8 anyone may live, let them enjoy them a. H3972
Ecc 11: 9 know that for a these things God will H3972
Ecc 12: 4 of birds, but a their songs grow faint; H3972
Ecc 12:13 Now a has been heard; here is the H3972
Ecc 12:13 this is the duty of a mankind. H3972
SS 3: 1 A night long on my bed I H928+2021+4326
SS 3: 6 incense made from a the spices of the H3972
SS 3: 8 a of them wearing the sword, all H3972
SS 3: 8 wearing the sword, a experienced in battle NDT
SS 4: 4 shields, a of them shields of warriors. H3972
SS 4:14 myrrh and aloes and a the finest spices. H3972
SS 8: 7 If one were to give a the wealth of one's H3972
Isa 1:14 festivals I hate with a my being. H5883
Isa 1:23 they a love bribes and chase after gifts. H3972
Isa 1:25 your dross and remove a your impurities. H3972
Isa 2: 2 the hills, and a nations will stream to it. H3972
Isa 2:12 a day in store for a the proud and lofty, H3972
Isa 2:12 proud and lofty, for a that is exalted (and H3972
Isa 2:13 a the cedars of Lebanon, tall and lofty H3972
Isa 2:13 tall and lofty, and a the oaks of Bashan, H3972
Isa 2:14 a the towering mountains and all the H3972
Isa 2:14 towering mountains and a the high hills, H3972
Isa 3: 1 a supplies of food and all supplies of H3972
Isa 3: 1 supplies of food and a supplies of water, H3972
Isa 4: 3 a who are recorded among the living in H3972
Isa 4: 5 will create over a of Mount Zion and over H3972
Isa 5:14 masses with a their brawlers and NDT
Isa 5:25 Yet for a this, his anger is not turned away H3972
Isa 5:28 arrows are sharp, a their bows are strung H3972
Isa 7: 9 firm in your faith, you will not stand at a. H3954
Isa 7:19 They will a come and settle in the steep H3972
Isa 7:19 on a the thornbushes and at all the water H3972
Isa 7:19 the thornbushes and at a the water holes. H3972
Isa 7:22 A who remain in the land will eat curds H3972
Isa 7:25 As for a the hills once cultivated by the H3972
Isa 8: 7 the king of Assyria with a his pomp. H3972
Isa 8: 7 It will overflow a its channels, run over all H3972
Isa 8: 7 all its channels, run over a its banks H3972
Isa 8: 9 Listen, a you distant lands H3972
Isa 9: 9 A the people will know it—Ephraim and H3972
Isa 9:12 Yet for a this, his anger is not turned away H3972
Isa 9:17 Yet for a this, his anger is not turned away H3972
Isa 9:21 Yet for a this, his anger is not turned away H3972
Isa 10: 4 Yet for a this, his anger is not turned away H3972
Isa 10: 8 'Are not my commanders a kings?' he H3481
Isa 10:12 the Lord has finished a his work against H3972
Isa 10:14 so I gathered a the countries; not H3972
Isa 11: 9 harm nor destroy on a my holy mountain, H3972
Isa 12: 5 let this be known to a the world. H3972
Isa 13: 7 Because of this, a hands will go limp H3972
Isa 13:14 they will a return to their own people AIT
Isa 13:15 a who are caught will fall by the sword. H3972
Isa 13:20 in through a generations; H1887+2256+1887
Isa 14: 7 A the lands are at rest and at peace; they H3972
Isa 14: 9 the dead below is a astir to meet you at H8074
Isa 14: 9 a those who were leaders in the world H3972
Isa 14: 9 a those who were kings over the nations. H3972
Isa 14:10 They will a respond, they will say to you H3972
Isa 14:11 A your pomp has been brought down to the NDT
Isa 14:18 A the kings of the nations lie in state H3972
Isa 14:26 is the hand stretched out over a nations. H3972
Isa 14:29 Do not rejoice, a you Philistines, that the H3972
Isa 14:31 Melt away, a you Philistines! A H3972
Isa 15: 3 in the public squares they a wail, H3972
Isa 15: 4 their voices are heard a the way to Jahaz. H6330
Isa 16:14 Moab's splendor and a her many people H3972
Isa 17: 9 undergrowth. And a will be desolation. AIT
Isa 18: 3 A you people of the world, you who live H3972
Isa 18: 6 They will a be left to the mountain birds H3481

Isa 18: 6 the birds *will* feed on them **a summer**, the H7810
Isa 18: 6 all summer, the wild animals **a winter**. H3069
Isa 19: 8 lament, **a** who cast hooks into the Nile H3972
Isa 19:10 **a** the wage earners will be sick at H3972
Isa 19:14 make Egypt stagger in **a** that she does, H3972
Isa 21: 2 I will bring to an end **a** the groaning she H3972
Isa 21: 9 **A** the images of its gods lie shattered on H3972
Isa 21:16 **a** the splendor of Kedar will come to an H3972
Isa 22: 1 that you have **a** gone up on the roofs, H3972
Isa 22: 3 **A** your leaders have fled together; they H3972
Isa 22: 3 **A** you who were caught were taken H3972
Isa 22:24 **A** the glory of his family will hang on him H3972
Isa 22:24 offshoots—**a** its lesser vessels H3972
Isa 22:24 vessels, from the bowls to **a** the jars. H3972
Isa 23: 9 down her pride in **a** her splendor and to H3972
Isa 23: 9 to humble **a** who are renowned on H3972
Isa 23:17 ply her trade with **a** the kingdoms on the H3972
Isa 24: 7 vine withers; **a** the merrymakers groan. H3972
Isa 24:11 they cry out for wine; **a** joy turns to gloom H3972
Isa 24:11 **a** joyful sounds are banished from the earth. NDT
Isa 25: 6 prepare a feast of rich food for **a** peoples, H3972
Isa 25: 7 destroy the shroud that enfolds **a** peoples, H3972
Isa 25: 7 peoples, the sheet that covers **a** nations; H3972
Isa 25: 8 will wipe away the tears from **a** faces; H3972
Isa 25: 8 his people's disgrace from **a** the earth. H3972
Isa 26:12 **a** that we have accomplished you have H3972
Isa 26:14 you wiped out **a** memory of them. H3972
Isa 26:15 you have extended **a** the borders of the H3972
Isa 27: 4 them in battle; I would set them **a** on fire. H3480
Isa 27: 6 blossom and fill **a** the world with fruit H7156
Isa 27: 9 When he makes **a** the altar stones to be H3972
Isa 28: 8 **A** the tables are covered with vomit and H3972
Isa 28:29 *A* **this** also comes from the LORD Almighty AIT
Isa 29: 3 against you **on a sides**; H3869+2021+1885
Isa 29: 7 Then the hordes of **a** the nations that H3972
Isa 29: 8 be with the hordes of **a** the nations that H3972
Isa 29:20 **a** who have an eye for evil will be cut H3972
Isa 30:17 at the threat of five *you will a* **flee away**, till AIT
Isa 30:18 Blessed are **a** who wait for him! H3972
Isa 31: 3 are helped will fall; **a** will perish together. H3972
Isa 32:13 mourn for **a** houses of merriment and H3972
Isa 34: 1 earth hear, and **a that is in** it, the world, H4850
Isa 34: 1 the world, and **a** that comes out of it! H3972
Isa 34: 2 The LORD is angry with **a** nations; his wrath H3972
Isa 34: 2 all nations; his wrath is on **a** their armies. H3972
Isa 34: 4 **A** the stars in the sky will be dissolved H3972
Isa 34: 4 **a** the starry host will fall like withered H3972
Isa 34:12 kingdom, **a** her princes will vanish away. H3972
Isa 36: 1 of Assyria attacked **a** the fortified cities of H3972
Isa 36: 6 king of Egypt to **a** who depend on him. H3972
Isa 36:20 Who of **a** the gods of these countries have H3972
Isa 37: 2 leading priests, *a* **wearing** sackcloth, to the AIT
Isa 37:11 of Assyria have done to **a** the countries, H3972
Isa 37:16 alone are God over **a** the kingdoms of the H3972
Isa 37:17 listen to **a** the words Sennacherib has H3972
Isa 37:18 have laid waste **a** these peoples and H3972
Isa 37:20 so that **a** the kingdoms of the earth may H3972
Isa 37:25 I have dried up **a** the streams of Egypt H3972
Isa 37:36 morning—there were **a** the dead bodies! H3972
Isa 38:13 like a lion he broke **a** my bones; day H3972
Isa 38:15 I will walk humbly **a** my years because of H3972
Isa 38:17 you have put **a** my sins behind your back. H3972
Isa 38:20 stringed instruments **a** the days of our H3972
Isa 39: 2 in his palace or in **a** his kingdom that H3972
Isa 39: 6 **a** that your predecessors have stored up NDT
Isa 40: 2 the LORD's hand double for **a** her sins. H3972
Isa 40: 5 **a** people will see it together. H3972
Isa 40: 6 "**A** people are like grass, and all their H3972
Isa 40: 6 **a** their faithfulness is like the flowers H3972
Isa 40:17 Before him **a** the nations are as nothing H3972
Isa 40:26 Who created *a* **these**? He who brings out AIT
Isa 41:11 "**A** who rage against you will surely be H3972
Isa 41:12 you will be as **nothing at a**. H401+2256+700
Isa 41:29 they are **a** false! Their deeds amount H3972
Isa 42: 5 out the earth with **a that springs from** it, H7368
Isa 42:10 to the sea, and **a that is in** it, you islands, H4850
Isa 42:10 you islands, and *a who* **live in** them. AIT
Isa 42:15 hills and dry up **a** their vegetation; H3972
Isa 42:22 **a** *of* them trapped in pits or hidden away H3972
Isa 43: 9 **A** the nations gather together and the H3972
Isa 43:14 down as fugitives **a** the Babylonians, H3972
Isa 44: 9 **A** who make idols are nothing, and the H3972
Isa 44:11 Let them **a** come together and take their H3972
Isa 44:13 human form in *a* its **glory**, that it may dwell AIT
Isa 44:23 you forests and **a** your trees, for the LORD H3972
Isa 44:24 the Maker of **a** *things*, who stretches H3972
Isa 44:28 will accomplish **a** that I please; H3972
Isa 45: 7 disaster; I, the LORD, do **a** these things. H3972
Isa 45:13 I will make **a** his ways straight. He will H3972
Isa 45:16 **A** the makers of idols will be put to H3972
Isa 45:22 me and be saved, **a** you ends of the earth H3972
Isa 45:23 has uttered *in a* **integrity** a word that will AIT
Isa 45:24 **A** who have raged against him will come H3972
Isa 45:25 But **a** the descendants of Israel will find H3972
Isa 46: 3 **a** the remnant of the people of Israel H3972
Isa 46:10 will stand, and I will do **a** that I please. H3972
Isa 47: 9 many sorceries and **a** your potent spells. H4394
Isa 47:13 **A** the counsel you have received has only H8044
Isa 47:15 **That is a** they are to you—these you have AIT
Isa 47:15 **A** of them go on in their error; there is not H408
Isa 48: 6 have heard these things; look at them **a**. H3972
Isa 48:13 I summon them, *they a* **stand up** together. AIT
Isa 48:14 "Come together, **a** *of* you, and listen H3972
Isa 49: 4 my strength for **nothing at a**. H9332+2256+2039
Isa 49:11 I will turn **a** my mountains into roads, and H3972
Isa 49:18 **a** your children gather and come to you. H3972
Isa 49:18 "you will wear them **a** as ornaments; you H3972
Isa 49:21 I was left **a alone**, but these—where H4200+963
Isa 49:26 Then **a** mankind will know that I, the LORD H3972
Isa 50: 9 They will **a** wear out like a garment; the H3972
Isa 50:11 **a** you who light fires and provide H3972
Isa 51: 3 will look with compassion on **a** her ruins; H3972
Isa 51: 8 salvation through **a generations**." H1887+1887
Isa 51:18 Among **a** the children she bore there was H3972
Isa 51:18 among **a** the children she reared there H3972
Isa 52: 5 "And **a** day long my name is constantly H3972
Isa 52:10 his holy arm in the sight of **a** the nations, H3972
Isa 52:10 **a** the ends of the earth will see the H3972
Isa 53: 6 We **a**, like sheep, have gone astray, each H3972
Isa 53: 6 LORD has laid on him the iniquity of us **a**. H3972
Isa 54: 5 he is called the God of **a** the earth. H3972
Isa 54:12 **a** your walls of precious stones. H3972
Isa 54:13 **A** your children will be taught by the LORD H3972
Isa 55: 1 **a** you who are thirsty, come to the H3972
Isa 55:12 **a** the trees of the field will clap their H3972
Isa 56: 6 **a** who keep the Sabbath without H3972
Isa 56: 7 be called a house of prayer for **a** nations." H3972
Isa 56: 9 **a** you beasts of the field, come H3972
Isa 56: 9 devour, **a** you beasts of the forest! H3972
Isa 56:10 are blind, they **a** lack knowledge; they are H3972
Isa 56:10 knowledge; they are **a** mute dogs, they H3972
Isa 56:11 they **a** turn to their own way H3972
Isa 57: 6 In view of **a this**, should I relent? AIT
Isa 57:13 The wind will carry **a** *of* them off, a mere H3972
Isa 58: 3 as you please and exploit **a** your workers. H3972
Isa 59: 9 We look for light, but **a** is darkness; for NDT
Isa 59:11 We **a** growl like bears; we moan H3972
Isa 60: 4 **A** assemble and come to you; your sons H3972
Isa 60: 6 And **a** from Sheba will come, bearing H3972
Isa 60: 7 **A** Kedar's flocks will be gathered to you H3972
Isa 60:14 **a** who despise you will bow down at your H3972
Isa 60:15 the joy of **a generations**. H1887+2256+1887
Isa 60:21 Then **a** your people will be righteous and H3972
Isa 61: 2 of our God, to comfort **a** who mourn, H3972
Isa 61: 9 **A** who see them will acknowledge that H3972
Isa 61:11 praise spring up before **a** nations. H3972
Isa 62: 2 vindication, and **a** kings your glory; you H3972
Isa 63: 3 my garments, and I stained **a** my clothing. H3972
Isa 63: 7 according to **a** the LORD has done for us H3972
Isa 63: 9 In **a** their distress he too was distressed H3972
Isa 63: 9 up and carried them **a** the days of old. H3972
Isa 64: 6 **A** *of* us have become like one who is H3972
Isa 64: 6 **a** our righteous acts are like filthy H3972
Isa 64: 6 like filthy rags; we **a** shrivel up like a leaf H3972
Isa 64: 8 we are **a** the work of your hand. H3972
Isa 64: 9 we pray, for we are **a** your people. H3972
Isa 64:11 and **a** that we treasured lies in ruins. H3972
Isa 64:12 After *a* **this**, LORD, will you hold yourself AIT
Isa 65: 2 **A** day long I have held out my hands to H3972
Isa 65: 5 nostrils, a fire that keeps burning **a** day. H3972
Isa 65: 8 of my servants; I will not destroy them **a**. H3972
Isa 65:12 and **a** *of* you will fall in the slaughter H3972
Isa 65:25 harm nor destroy on **a** my holy mountain," H3972
Isa 66: 2 Has not my hand made **a** these things H3972
Isa 66: 6 LORD repaying his enemies *a* they **deserve**. AIT
Isa 66:10 be glad for her, **a** you who love her H3972
Isa 66:10 with her, **a** you who mourn over her. H3972
Isa 66:16 LORD will execute judgment on **a** people, H3972
Isa 66:18 gather the people of **a** nations and H3972
Isa 66:20 And they will bring **a** your people, from all H3972
Isa 66:20 all your people, from **a** the nations, to my H3972
Isa 66:23 **a** mankind will come and bow down H3972
Isa 66:24 they will be loathsome to **a** mankind." H3972
Jer 1:14 be poured out on **a** who live in the land. H3972
Jer 1:15 about to summon **a** the peoples of the H3972
Jer 1:15 will come against **a** her surrounding walls H3972
Jer 1:15 walls and against **a** the towns of Judah. H3972
Jer 2: 3 **a** who devoured her were held guilty H3972
Jer 2: 4 of Jacob, **a** you clans of Israel. H3972
Jer 2:11 Yet they are **not** gods *at a*.) But my people AIT
Jer 2:29 You have **a** rebelled against me, H3972
Jer 2:34 them breaking in. Yet in spite of **a** this H3972
Jer 3: 5 how you talk, but you do *a* the **evil** you can." AIT
Jer 3: 7 after she had done **a** this she would H3972
Jer 3: 8 her away because of **a** her adulteries. H3972
Jer 3:10 In spite of **a** this, her unfaithful sister H3972
Jer 3:10 did not return to me with **a** her heart, H3972
Jer 3:17 **a** nations will gather in Jerusalem to H3972
Jer 4:24 were quaking; **a** the hills were swaying. H3972
Jer 4:26 **a** its towns lay in ruins before the LORD H3972
Jer 4:29 **A** the towns are deserted; no one lives in H3972
Jer 5: 7 *I* **supplied a** their **needs**, yet they H8425
Jer 5:16 **a** *of* them are mighty warriors. H3972
Jer 5:19 has the LORD our God done **a** this to us? H3972
Jer 6:13 least to the greatest, **a** are greedy for gain H3972
Jer 6:13 priests alike, **a** practice deceit. H3972
Jer 6:15 *they* **have** no **shame at a**; they H1017+1017
Jer 6:28 They are **a** hardened rebels, going about H3972
Jer 6:28 are bronze and iron; they **a** act corruptly. H3972
Jer 7: 2 **a** you people of Judah who come through H3972
Jer 7:10 safe to do **a** these detestable things? H3972
Jer 7:13 While you were doing **a** these things H3972
Jer 7:15 just as I did **a** your fellow Israelites H3972
Jer 7:23 Walk in obedience to **a** I command you H3972
Jer 7:27 "When you tell them **a** this, they will not H3972
Jer 8: 2 sun and the moon and **a** the stars of the H3972
Jer 8: 3 **a** the survivors of this evil nation will H3972
Jer 8:10 least to the greatest, **a** are greedy for gain H3972
Jer 8:10 priests alike, **a** practice deceit. H3972
Jer 8:12 *they* **have** no **shame at a**; they H1017+1017
Jer 8:16 everything in it, the city and *a who* **live** there. AIT
Jer 9: 2 for they are **a** adulterers, a crowd of H3972
Jer 9: 8 With their mouths *they a* **speak** cordially to AIT
Jer 9:10 The birds *have a* **fled** and the animals are AIT
Jer 9:25 "when I will punish **a** who are circumcised H3972
Jer 9:26 Moab and **a** who live in the wilderness in H3972
Jer 9:26 For **a** these nations are really H3972
Jer 10: 7 Among **a** the wise leaders of the nations H3972
Jer 10: 7 of the nations and in **a** their kingdoms, H3972
Jer 10: 8 They are **a** senseless and foolish H928+285
Jer 10: 9 purple—**a** made by skilled workers. H3972
Jer 10:16 he is the Maker of **a** *things*, including H3972
Jer 10:20 tent is destroyed; **a** its ropes are snapped. H3972
Jer 10:21 they do not prosper and **a** their flock is H3972
Jer 11: 6 "Proclaim **a** these words in the towns of H3972
Jer 11: 8 So I brought on them **a** the curses of the H3972
Jer 11:12 but *they will* not **help** them **at a** H3828+3828
Jer 12: 1 Why do **a** the faithless live at ease H3972
Jer 12: 9 Go and gather **a** the wild beasts; bring H3972
Jer 12:12 Over **a** the barren heights in the desert H3972
Jer 12:14 "As for **a** my wicked neighbors who seize H3972
Jer 13:11 so I bound **a** the people of Israel and all H3972
Jer 13:11 of Israel and **a** the people of Judah H3972
Jer 13:13 with drunkenness **a** who live in this land H3972
Jer 13:13 the prophets and **a** those living in H3972
Jer 13:19 **A** Judah will be carried into exile, carried H3972
Jer 14:22 for you are the one who does **a** this. H3972
Jer 15: 4 them abhorrent to **a** the kingdoms of the H3972
Jer 15:13 because of **a** your sins throughout your H3972
Jer 16:10 tell these people **a** this and they ask you H3972
Jer 16:12 See how **a** of you are following the H408
Jer 16:15 the north and out of **a** the countries where H3972
Jer 16:17 My eyes are on **a** their ways; they are not H3972
Jer 17: 3 your wealth and **a** your treasures I H3972
Jer 17: 9 deceitful above **a** *things* and beyond cure. H3972
Jer 17:13 **a** who forsake you will be put to shame. H3972
Jer 17:19 stand also at **a** the other gates of H3972
Jer 17:20 kings of Judah and **a** people of Judah H3972
Jer 18:12 we will **a** follow the stubbornness of our H408s
Jer 18:16 **a** who pass by will be appalled and will H3972
Jer 18:23 you, LORD, know **a** their plots to kill me. H3972
Jer 19: 8 **a** who pass by will be appalled and will H3972
Jer 19: 8 will scoff because of **a** its wounds. H3972
Jer 19:13 **a** the houses where they burned incense H3972
Jer 19:13 on the roofs to **a** the starry hosts and H3972
Jer 19:14 LORD's temple and said to **a** the people, H3972
Jer 19:15 on this city and **a** the villages around it H3972
Jer 20: 4 a terror to yourself and to **a** your friends; H3972
Jer 20: 4 I will give **a** Judah into the hands of the H3972
Jer 20: 5 I will deliver **a** the wealth of this city into H3972
Jer 20: 5 of their enemies—**a** its products, all its H3972
Jer 20: 5 **a** its valuables and all the treasures of the H3972
Jer 20: 5 all its valuables and **a** the treasures of the H3972
Jer 20: 6 **a** who live in your house will go into H3972
Jer 20: 6 you and **a** your friends to whom you have H3972
Jer 20: 7 I am ridiculed **a** day long; everyone mocks H3972
Jer 20: 8 me insult and reproach **a** day long. H3972
Jer 20:10 **A** my friends are waiting for me to slip H3972
Jer 22:15 was right and just, so **a** went well with him. NDT
Jer 22:16 of the poor and needy, and so **a** went well. NDT
Jer 22:20 from Abarim, for **a** your allies are crushed. H3972
Jer 22:22 wind will drive **a** your shepherds away H3972
Jer 22:22 disgraced because of **a** your wickedness. H3972
Jer 23: 3 of my flock out of **a** the countries where I H3972
Jer 23: 8 the north and out of **a** the countries where H3972
Jer 23: 9 is broken within me; **a** my bones tremble. H3972
Jer 23:14 They are **a** like Sodom to me; the people H3972
Jer 23:17 ' And to **a** who follow the stubbornness of H3972
Jer 24: 7 they will return to me with **a** their heart. H3972
Jer 24: 9 an offense to **a** the kingdoms of the H3972
Jer 25: 1 concerning **a** the people of Judah H3972
Jer 25: 2 the prophet said to **a** the people of Judah H3972
Jer 25: 2 people of Judah and to **a** those living in H3972
Jer 25: 4 the LORD has sent **a** his servants the H3972
Jer 25: 9 I will summon **a** the peoples of the north H3972
Jer 25: 9 against **a** the surrounding nations H3972
Jer 25:13 will bring on that land **a** the things I have H3972
Jer 25:13 **a** that are written in this book and H3972
Jer 25:13 by Jeremiah against **a** the nations. H3972
Jer 25:15 my wrath and make **a** the nations to H3972
Jer 25:17 hand and made **a** the nations to whom H3972
Jer 25:19 attendants, his officials and **a** his people, H3972
Jer 25:20 **a** the foreign people there; all the H3972
Jer 25:20 people there; **a** the kings of Uz; all H3972
Jer 25:20 kings of Uz; **a** the kings of the Philistines H3972
Jer 25:22 **a** the kings of Tyre and Sidon; the kings of H3972
Jer 25:23 Buz and **a** who are in distant places; H3972
Jer 25:24 **a** the kings of Arabia and all the kings of H3972
Jer 25:24 the kings of Arabia and **a** the kings of the H3972
Jer 25:25 **a** the kings of Zimri, Elam and Media; H3972
Jer 25:26 **a** the kings of the north, near and far H3972
Jer 25:26 **a** the kingdoms on the face of the earth. H3972
Jer 25:26 And after **a** of them, the king of Sheshak NDT
Jer 25:29 down a sword on **a** who live on the earth, H3972
Jer 25:30 "Now prophesy **a** these words against H3972
Jer 25:30 shout against **a** who live on the earth. H3972

A

Jer 25:31 bring judgment on **a** mankind and put the H3972
Jer 26: 2 house and speak to **a** the people of the H3972
Jer 26: 6 city a curse among **a** the nations of the H3972
Jer 26: 7 the prophets and **a** the people heard H3972
Jer 26: 8 finished telling **a** the people everything H3972
Jer 26: 8 the prophets and **a** the people seized him H3972
Jer 26: 9 And **a** the people crowded around H3972
Jer 26:11 said to the officials and **a** the people, H3972
Jer 26:12 Jeremiah said to **a** the officials and all H3972
Jer 26:12 said to all the officials and **a** the people: H3972
Jer 26:12 house and this city **a** the things you have H3972
Jer 26:15 me to you to speak **a** these words in your H3972
Jer 26:16 the officials and **a** the people said to the H3972
Jer 26:18 He told **a** the people of Judah, 'This is H3972
Jer 26:21 King Jehoiakim and **a** his officers and H3972
Jer 27: 6 Now I will give **a** your countries into the H3972
Jer 27: 7 **A** nations will serve him and his son and H3972
Jer 27:16 I said to the priests and **a** these people, H3972
Jer 27:20 along with **a** the nobles of Judah and H3972
Jer 28: 1 presence of the priests and **a** the people: H3972
Jer 28: 3 back to this place **a** the articles of the H3972
Jer 28: 4 king of Judah and **a** the other exiles from H3972
Jer 28: 5 the priests and **a** the people who were H3972
Jer 28: 6 the LORD's house and **a** the exiles back to H3972
Jer 28: 7 in the hearing of **a** the people: H3972
Jer 28:11 he said before **a** the people, "This is H3972
Jer 28:11 off the neck of **a** the nations within two H3972
Jer 28:14 yoke on the necks of **a** these nations to H3972
Jer 29: 1 the prophets and **a** the other people H3972
Jer 29: 4 says to **a** those I carried into exile from H3972
Jer 29:13 me when you seek me with **a** your heart. H3972
Jer 29:14 will gather you from **a** the nations and H3972
Jer 29:16 David's throne and **a** the people who H3972
Jer 29:18 them abhorrent to **a** the kingdoms of the H3972
Jer 29:18 among **a** the nations where I drive them. H3972
Jer 29:20 **a** you exiles whom I have sent away from H3972
Jer 29:22 **a** the exiles from Judah who are in H3972
Jer 29:25 in your own name to **a** the people in H3972
Jer 29:25 of Maaseiah, and to **a** the other priests. H3972
Jer 29:31 "Send this message to **a** the exiles: 'This H3972
Jer 30: 2 'Write in a book **a** the words I have H3972
Jer 30:11 I completely destroy **a** the nations among H3972
Jer 30:14 **A** your allies have forgotten you; they care H3972
Jer 30:16 " 'But **a** who devour you will be devoured H3972
Jer 30:16 **a** your enemies will go into exile. H3972
Jer 30:16 **a** who make spoil of you I will despoil. H3972
Jer 30:20 I will punish **a** who oppress them. H3972
Jer 31: 1 "I will be the God of **a** the families of H3972
Jer 31:24 live together in Judah and **a** its towns— H3972
Jer 31:34 ' because they will **a** know me, from the H3972
Jer 31:37 out will I reject **a** the descendants of H3972
Jer 31:37 of Israel because of **a** they have done," H3972
Jer 31:40 **a** the terraces out to the Kidron Valley H3972
Jer 32:12 the deed and of **a** the Jews sitting in H3972
Jer 32:19 eyes are open to the ways of **a** mankind; H3972
Jer 32:20 in Israel and among **a** mankind, and have NDT
Jer 32:23 So you brought **a** this disaster on them H3972
Jer 32:27 the God of **a** mankind. Is anything H3972
Jer 32:32 have provoked me by **a** the evil they have H3972
Jer 32:37 gather them from **a** the lands where I H3972
Jer 32:39 me and that *a* will then go **well** for them AIT
Jer 32:41 in this land with **a** my heart and soul. H3972
Jer 32:42 As I have brought **a** this great calamity on H3972
Jer 32:42 so I will give them **a** the prosperity I have H3972
Jer 33: 5 from this city because of **a** its wickedness. H3972
Jer 33: 8 cleanse them from **a** the sin they have H3972
Jer 33: 8 me and will forgive **a** their sins of H3972
Jer 33: 9 honor before **a** nations on earth that H3972
Jer 33: 9 earth that hear of **a** the good things I do H3972
Jer 33:12 in **a** its towns there will again be pastures H3972
Jer 34: 1 king of Babylon and **a** his army and all H3972
Jer 34: 1 all his army and **a** the kingdoms and H3972
Jer 34: 1 Jerusalem and **a** its surrounding towns H3972
Jer 34: 6 the prophet told **a** this to Zedekiah king of H3972
Jer 34: 8 made a covenant with **a** the people in H3972
Jer 34:10 So **a** the officials and people who entered H3972
Jer 34:17 you abhorrent to **a** the kingdoms of the H3972
Jer 34:19 the priests and **a** the people of the land H3972
Jer 35: 3 his brothers and **a** his sons—the H3972
Jer 35:15 Again and again I sent **a** my servants the H3972
Jer 35:18 have followed **a** his instructions and H3972
Jer 36: 2 scroll and write on it **a** the words I have H3972
Jer 36: 2 Judah and **a** the other nations from the H3972
Jer 36: 4 Jeremiah dictated **a** the words the LORD H3972
Jer 36: 6 Read them to **a** *the people of* Judah who H3972
Jer 36: 9 was proclaimed for **a** the people in H3972
Jer 36:10 Baruch read to **a** the people at the LORD's H3972
Jer 36:11 heard **a** the words of the LORD from the H3972
Jer 36:12 where **a** the officials were sitting: H3972
Jer 36:12 of Hananiah, and **a** the other officials. H3972
Jer 36:14 **a** the officials sent Jehudi son of H3972
Jer 36:16 When they heard **a** these words, they H3972
Jer 36:16 "We must report **a** these words to the king H3972
Jer 36:17 "Tell us, how did you come to write **a** this? H3972
Jer 36:18 replied, "he dictated **a** these words to me H3972
Jer 36:21 it to the king and **a** the officials standing H3972
Jer 36:24 The king and **a** his attendants who heard H3972
Jer 36:24 who heard **a** these words showed H3972
Jer 36:28 write on it **a** the words that were on H3972
Jer 36:32 Baruch wrote on it **a** the words of the H3972
Jer 37:21 each day until **a** the bread in the city H3972
Jer 38: 1 was telling **a** the people when he H3972

Jer 38: 4 in this city, as well as **a** the people, by the H3972
Jer 38: 9 acted wickedly *in* **a** they have done to H3972
Jer 38:22 **A** the women left in the palace of the king H3972
Jer 38:23 "**A** your wives and children will be H3972
Jer 38:27 **A** the officials did come to Jeremiah and H3972
Jer 39: 3 Then **a** the officials of the king of Babylon H3972
Jer 39: 3 a high official and **a** the other officials of H3972
Jer 39: 4 king of Judah and **a** the soldiers saw H3972
Jer 39: 6 also killed **a** the nobles of Judah. H3972
Jer 39:13 a high official and **a** the other officers of H3972
Jer 40: 1 in chains among **a** the captives from H3972
Jer 40: 3 *A* **this** happened because you people sinned AIT
Jer 40: 7 When **a** the army officers and their men H3972
Jer 40:11 When **a** the Jews in Moab, Ammon H3972
Jer 40:11 Edom and **a** the other countries heard H3972
Jer 40:12 they **a** came back to the land of Judah, to H3972
Jer 40:12 from **a** the countries where they had been H3972
Jer 40:13 son of Kareah and **a** the army officers still H3972
Jer 40:15 your life and cause **a** the Jews who are H3972
Jer 41: 3 Ishmael also killed **a** the men of Judah H3972
Jer 41: 9 where he threw **a** the bodies of the men H3972
Jer 41:10 made captives of **a** the rest of the people H3972
Jer 41:10 along with **a** the others who were H3972
Jer 41:11 son of Kareah and **a** the army officers who H3972
Jer 41:11 him heard about **a** the crimes Ishmael H3972
Jer 41:12 they took **a** their men and went to fight H3972
Jer 41:13 When **a** the people Ishmael had with him H3972
Jer 41:14 **A** the people Ishmael had taken captive at H3972
Jer 41:16 son of Kareah and **a** the army officers who H3972
Jer 41:16 with him led away **a** the people of H3972
Jer 42: 1 Then **a** the army officers, including H3972
Jer 42: 1 **a** the people from the least to the H3972
Jer 42: 8 son of Kareah and **a** the army officers who H3972
Jer 42: 8 were with him and **a** the people from the H3972
Jer 42:17 **a** who are determined to go to Egypt to H3972
Jer 42:21 the LORD your God in **a** he sent me to tell H3972
Jer 43: 1 telling the people **a** the words of the LORD H3972
Jer 43: 2 son of Kareah and **a** the arrogant men H3972
Jer 43: 4 son of Kareah and **a** the army officers H3972
Jer 43: 4 army officers and **a** the people disobeyed H3972
Jer 43: 5 son of Kareah and **a** the army officers led H3972
Jer 43: 5 officers led away **a** the remnant of Judah H3972
Jer 43: 5 land of Judah from **a** the nations where H3972
Jer 43: 6 They also led away **a** those whom H3972
Jer 44: 1 Jeremiah concerning **a** the Jews living in H3972
Jer 44: 2 Jerusalem and on **a** the towns of Judah. H3972
Jer 44: 8 of reproach among **a** the nations on earth H3972
Jer 44:11 disaster on you and to destroy **a** Judah. H3972
Jer 44:12 They will **a** perish in Egypt; they will fall H3972
Jer 44:15 Then **a** the men who knew that their H3972
Jer 44:15 along with **a** the women who were H3972
Jer 44:15 **a** the people living in Lower and H3972
Jer 44:20 Then Jeremiah said to **a** the people, both H3972
Jer 44:24 Then Jeremiah said to **a** the people H3972
Jer 44:24 the LORD, **a** you people of Judah in Egypt. H3972
Jer 44:26 of the LORD, **a** you Jews living in Egypt: H3972
Jer 44:27 famine until they are **a** destroyed. H3972
Jer 45: 5 For I will bring disaster on **a** people H3972
Jer 46:28 I completely destroy **a** the nations among H3972
Jer 47: 2 **a** who dwell in the land will wail H3972
Jer 47: 4 has come to destroy **a** the Philistines and H3972
Jer 47: 4 to remove **a** survivors who could help H3972
Jer 48:17 Mourn for her, **a** who live around her, all H3972
Jer 48:17 live around her, **a** who know her fame H3972
Jer 48:24 Bozrah—to **a** the towns of Moab, far H3972
Jer 48:31 I wail over Moab, for **a** Moab I cry out, I H3972
Jer 48:38 On **a** the roofs in Moab and in the public H3972
Jer 48:39 an object of horror to **a** those around her." H3972
Jer 49: 5 terror on you from **a** those around you," H3972
Jer 49:13 **a** its towns will be in ruins forever. H3972
Jer 49:17 **a** who pass by will be appalled and will H3972
Jer 49:17 will scoff because of **a** its wounds. H3972
Jer 49:26 **a** her soldiers will be silenced in that day," H3972
Jer 49:29 be carried off with **a** their goods and H3972
Jer 50:10 **a** who plunder her will have their fill," H3972
Jer 50:13 **A** who pass Babylon will be appalled H3972
Jer 50:13 they will scoff because of **a** her wounds. H3972
Jer 50:14 around Babylon, **a** you who draw the bow. H3972
Jer 50:27 Kill **a** her young bulls; let them go down H3972
Jer 50:29 Babylon, **a** those who draw the bow. H3972
Jer 50:29 Encamp **a around** her; let no H6017
Jer 50:30 **a** her soldiers will be silenced in that day," H3972
Jer 50:32 that will consume **a** who are around her." H3972
Jer 50:33 **A** their captors hold them fast, refusing to H3972
Jer 50:37 chariots and **a** the foreigners in her H3972
Jer 51:19 he is the Maker of **a** *things*, including H3972
Jer 51:24 repay Babylon and **a** who live in H3972
Jer 51:24 in Babylonia for **a** the wrong they have H3972
Jer 51:28 their governors and **a** their officials, and H3972
Jer 51:28 officials, and **a** the countries they rule. H3972
Jer 51:38 Her people **a** roar like young lions, they H3481
Jer 51:47 her slain will **a** lie fallen within her. H3972
Jer 51:48 earth and **a** that is in them will H3972
Jer 51:49 just as the slain in **a** the earth have fallen H3972
Jer 51:60 on a scroll about **a** the disasters that H3972
Jer 51:60 **a** that had been recorded concerning H3972
Jer 51:61 see that you read **a** these words aloud. H3972
Jer 52: 3 anger that *a this* **happened** to Jerusalem AIT
Jer 52: 4 the city and built siege works **a around** it. H6017
Jer 52: 8 **A** his soldiers were separated from him H3972
Jer 52:10 he also killed **a** the officials of Judah. H3972
Jer 52:13 the royal palace and **a** the houses of H3972

Jer 52:14 broke down **a** the walls around Jerusalem. H3972
Jer 52:17 they carried **a** the bronze to Babylon H3972
Jer 52:18 dishes and **a** the bronze articles used in H3972
Jer 52:19 *a* **that** were made of pure gold or silver. AIT
Jer 52:22 pomegranates of bronze **a** around. H3972
Jer 52:26 commander took **them** *a* and brought them AIT
Jer 52:30 There were 4,600 people *in* **a**. H3972
La 1: 2 Among **a** her lovers there is no one to H3972
La 1: 2 **A** her friends have betrayed her; they H3972
La 1: 3 **A** who pursue her have overtaken her in H3972
La 1: 4 **A** her gateways are desolate, her priests H3972
La 1: 6 **A** the splendor has departed from H3972
La 1: 7 Jerusalem remembers **a** the treasures that H3972
La 1: 8 **A** who honored her despise her, for they H3972
La 1: 8 for *they have a* **seen** her naked; she AIT
La 1:10 The enemy laid hands on **a** her treasures H3972
La 1:11 **A** her people groan as they search for H3972
La 1:12 it nothing to you, **a** you who pass by? Look H3972
La 1:13 made me desolate, faint **a** the day long. H3972
La 1:15 Lord has rejected **a** the warriors in my H3972
La 1:18 **a** you peoples; look on my H3972
La 1:21 **A** my enemies have heard of my distress H3972
La 1:22 "Let **a** their wickedness come before you H3972
La 1:22 have dealt with me because of **a** my sins. H3972
La 2: 2 Lord has swallowed up **a** the dwellings of H3972
La 2: 4 a foe he has slain **a** who were pleasing to H3972
La 2: 5 He has swallowed up **a** her palaces and H3972
La 2:15 **A** who pass your way clap their hands at H3972
La 2:16 **A** your enemies open their mouths wide H3972
La 3: 3 against me again and again, **a** day long. H3972
La 3:14 the laughingstock of **a** my people; H3972
La 3:14 people; they mock me in song **a** day long. H3972
La 3:18 is gone and *a that* I had **hoped** from the LORD AIT
La 3:34 To crush underfoot **a** prisoners in the land, H3972
La 3:46 "**A** our enemies have opened their H3972
La 3:51 my soul because of **a** the women of my H3972
La 3:60 their vengeance, **a** their plots against me. H3972
La 3:61 their insults, **a** their plots against me H3972
La 3:62 mutter against me **a** day long. H3972
Eze 1: 8 *A* **four** *of* them had faces and wings, AIT
Eze 1:16 sparkled like topaz, and *a* **four** looked alike. AIT
Eze 1:18 and *a* **four** rims were full of eyes all around. AIT
Eze 1:18 all four rims were full of eyes **a around**. H6017
Eze 2: 6 thorns are **a around** you and you live H907
Eze 3: 7 **a** the Israelites are hardened and H3972
Eze 3:10 take to heart **a** the words I speak to H3972
Eze 5: 2 strike it with the sword **a around** the city. H6017
Eze 5: 4 A fire will spread from there to **a** Israel. H3972
Eze 5: 5 the nations, with countries **a around** her. H6017
Eze 5: 9 Because of **a** your detestable idols, I will H3972
Eze 5:10 you and will scatter **a** your survivors to the H3972
Eze 5:11 my sanctuary with **a** your vile images and H3972
Eze 5:14 around you, in the sight of **a** who pass by. H3972
Eze 6: 9 they have done and for **a** their detestable H3972
Eze 6:11 because of **a** the wicked and detestable H3972
Eze 6:13 high hill and on **a** the mountaintops, H3972
Eze 6:13 offered fragrant incense to **a** their idols. H3972
Eze 7: 3 repay you for **a** your detestable H3972
Eze 7: 8 repay you for **a** your detestable H3972
Eze 7:14 they have made **a** *things* ready, but no H3972
Eze 7:16 they will **a** moan, each for their H3972
Eze 8:10 portrayed **a over** the walls H6017+6017+6584
Eze 8:10 all over the walls **a** kinds of crawling H3972
Eze 8:10 unclean animals and **a** the idols of Israel. H3972
Eze 9: 4 lament over **a** the detestable things H3972
Eze 11:15 fellow exiles and **a** the *other* Israelites, H3972
Eze 11:18 to it and remove **a** its vile images and H3972
Eze 12:10 in Jerusalem and **a** the Israelites who are H3972
Eze 12:14 scatter to the winds **a** those around him— H3972
Eze 12:14 his staff and **a** his troops—and I will H3972
Eze 12:16 they may acknowledge **a** their detestable H3972
Eze 12:19 of the violence of **a** who live there. H3972
Eze 13:18 sew magic charms on **a** their wrists and H3972
Eze 14: 3 *Should I* **let** them **inquire** of *me* **at a** H2011+4200+2011
Eze 14: 5 who have **a** deserted me for their idols. H3972
Eze 14: 6 your idols and renounce **a** your detestable H3972
Eze 14:11 themselves anymore with **a** their sins. H3972
Eze 16:22 In **a** your detestable practices and your H3972
Eze 16:23 In addition to **a** your other wickedness H3972
Eze 16:30 when you do **a** these things, acting H3972
Eze 16:33 **A** prostitutes receive gifts, but you give H3972
Eze 16:33 you give gifts to **a** your lovers, bribing H3972
Eze 16:36 because of **a** your detestable idols H3972
Eze 16:37 I am going to gather **a** your lovers, H3972
Eze 16:37 against you from **a around** and will strip H6017
Eze 16:43 enraged me with **a** these things, H3972
Eze 16:43 not add lewdness to **a** your other H3972
Eze 16:47 in **a** your ways you soon became more H3972
Eze 16:51 seem righteous by **a** these things you H3972
Eze 16:54 be ashamed of **a** you have done in H3972
Eze 16:57 of Edom and **a** her neighbors and the H3972
Eze 16:57 **a** those around you who despise you. NDT
Eze 16:63 atonement for you for **a** you have done, H3972
Eze 17: 9 **A** its new growth will wither H3972
Eze 17:18 in pledge and yet did **a** these things, H3972
Eze 17:21 **A** his choice troops will fall by the sword H3972
Eze 17:24 **A** the trees of the forest will know that I H3972
Eze 18:13 Because he has done **a** these detestable H3972
Eze 18:14 has a son who sees **a** the sins his father H3972
Eze 18:19 has been careful to keep **a** my decrees, H3972
Eze 18:21 turns away from **a** the sins they have H3972

Eze 18:21 keeps a my decrees and does H3972
Eze 18:28 Because they consider a the offenses they H3972
Eze 18:30 Turn away from a your offenses; then sin H3972
Eze 18:31 Rid yourselves of a the offenses you have H3972
Eze 19: 7 The land and a who were in it were H4850
Eze 20: 6 honey, the most beautiful of a lands. H3972
Eze 20:15 the most beautiful of a lands— H3972
Eze 20:31 yourselves with a your idols to this day H3972
Eze 20:40 there in the land a the people of Israel H3972
Eze 20:40 along with a your holy sacrifices. H3972
Eze 20:43 your conduct and a the actions by which H3972
Eze 20:43 loathe yourselves for a the evil you have H3972
Eze 20:47 it will consume a your trees, both H3972
Eze 21: 5 Then a people will know that I the LORD H3972
Eze 21:12 it is against a the princes of Israel. H3972
Eze 21:15 the sword for slaughter at a their gates. H3972
Eze 21:24 revealing your sins in a that you do H3972
Eze 22: 2 Then confront her with a her detestable H3972
Eze 22: 4 a laughingstock to a the countries. H3972
Eze 22:18 dross to me; a of them are the copper H3972
Eze 22:19 'Because you have a become dross, I will H3972
Eze 22:31 down on their own heads a they have done, AIT
Eze 23: 6 a of them handsome young men H3972
Eze 23: 7 as a prostitute to a the elite of the H3972
Eze 23: 7 defiled herself with a the idols of H3972
Eze 23:12 horsemen, a handsome young men. H3972
Eze 23:15 a of them looked like Babylonian chariot H3972
Eze 23:23 the Babylonians and a the Chaldeans, the H3972
Eze 23:23 Koa, and a the Assyrians with them H3972
Eze 23:23 a of them governors and commanders H3972
Eze 23:23 men of high rank, a mounted on horses. H3972
Eze 23:43 use her as a prostitute, for that is a she is. NDT
Eze 23:48 that a women may take warning and not H3972
Eze 24: 4 the pieces of meat, a the choice pieces H3972
Eze 24:12 It has frustrated a efforts; its heavy deposit AIT
Eze 25: 6 rejoicing with a the malice of your heart H3972
Eze 25: 8 has become like a the other nations," H3972
Eze 26:11 of his horses will trample a your streets; H3972
Eze 26:16 Then a the princes of the coast will step H3972
Eze 26:17 you put your terror on a who lived there. H3972
Eze 27: 5 They made a your timbers of juniper from H3972
Eze 27: 9 A the ships of the sea and their sailors H3972
Eze 27:21 " 'Arabia and a the princes of Kedar were H3972
Eze 27:22 the finest of a kinds of spices and H3972
Eze 27:27 your merchants and a your soldiers, and H3972
Eze 27:29 A who handle the oars will abandon their H3972
Eze 27:29 the mariners and a the sailors will stand H3972
Eze 27:34 your wares and a your company have H3972
Eze 27:35 A who live in the coastlands are appalled H3972
Eze 28:18 in the sight of a who were watching. H3972
Eze 28:19 A the nations who knew you are appalled H3972
Eze 28:26 punishment on a their neighbors who H3972
Eze 29: 2 against him and against a Egypt. H3972
Eze 29: 4 with a the fish sticking to your scales. H3972
Eze 29: 5 you and a the fish of your streams. H3972
Eze 29: 6 Then a who live in Egypt will know that I H3972
Eze 30: 5 Lydia and a Arabia, Kub and the H3972
Eze 30: 8 set fire to Egypt and a her helpers are H3972
Eze 31: 4 streams flowed a around its base and H6017
Eze 31: 4 their channels to a the trees of the field H3972
Eze 31: 5 towered higher than a the trees of the H3972
Eze 31: 6 A the birds of the sky nested in its boughs, H3972
Eze 31: 6 a the animals of the wild gave birth under H3972
Eze 31: 6 a the great nations lived in its shade. H3972
Eze 31: 9 the envy of a the trees of Eden in the H3972
Eze 31:12 on the mountains and in a the valleys; H3972
Eze 31:12 lay broken in a the ravines of the H3972
Eze 31:12 A the nations of the earth came out from H3972
Eze 31:13 A the birds settled on the fallen tree, and H3972
Eze 31:13 a the wild animals lived among its H3972
Eze 31:14 a height; they are a destined for death H3972
Eze 31:15 a the trees of the field withered away. H3972
Eze 31:16 Then a the trees of Eden, the choicest H3972
Eze 31:18 " 'This is Pharaoh and a his hordes H3972
Eze 32: 4 I will let a the birds of the sky settle on H3972
Eze 32: 4 sky settle on you and a the animals of the H3972
Eze 32: 6 flowing blood a the way to the mountains, H448
Eze 32: 8 A the shining lights in the heavens I will H3972
Eze 32:12 the most ruthless of a nations. H3972
Eze 32:12 a her hordes will be overthrown. H3972
Eze 32:13 I will destroy a her cattle from beside H3972
Eze 32:15 when I strike down a who live there, then H3972
Eze 32:16 Egypt and a her hordes they will chant H3972
Eze 32:20 let her be dragged off with a her hordes. H3972
Eze 32:22 is surrounded by the graves of a her slain, H3972
Eze 32:22 her slain, a who have fallen by the sword. NDT
Eze 32:23 A who had spread terror in the land of the H3972
Eze 32:24 with a her hordes around her grave. H3972
Eze 32:24 around her grave. A of them are slain H3972
Eze 32:24 A who had spread terror in the land of the NDT
Eze 32:25 with a her hordes around her grave. H3972
Eze 32:25 A of them are uncircumcised, killed by the H3972
Eze 32:26 with a their hordes around their graves. H3972
Eze 32:26 A of them are uncircumcised, killed by the H3972
Eze 32:29 her kings and a her princes; despite H3972
Eze 32:30 "A the princes of the north and all the H3972
Eze 32:30 of the north and a the Sidonians are there H3972
Eze 32:31 "Pharaoh—he and a his army—will see H3972
Eze 32:31 be consoled for a his hordes that were H3972
Eze 32:32 Pharaoh and a his hordes will be laid H3972
Eze 33:29 waste because of a the detestable things H3972
Eze 33:33 "When a this comes true—and it surely H2023S
Eze 34: 5 they became food for a the wild animals. H3972
Eze 34: 6 wandered over a the mountains and H3972
Eze 34: 8 has become food for a the wild animals, H3972
Eze 34:12 rescue them from a the places where they H3972
Eze 34:13 in the ravines and in a the settlements in H3972
Eze 34:21 butting a the weak sheep with your horns H3972
Eze 35: 7 waste and cut off from it a who come and go. AIT
Eze 35: 8 in your valleys and in a your ravines. H3972
Eze 35:12 I the LORD have heard a the contemptible H3972
Eze 35:15 desolate, Mount Seir, you and a of Edom. H3972
Eze 36: 5 against a Edom, for with glee H3972
Eze 36:10 people to live on you—yes, a of Israel. H3972
Eze 36:24 I will gather you from a the countries and H3972
Eze 36:25 cleanse you from a your impurities and H3972
Eze 36:25 all your impurities and from a your idols. H3972
Eze 36:29 I will save you from a your uncleanness. I H3972
Eze 36:33 On the day I cleanse you from a your sins H3972
Eze 36:34 in the sight of a who pass through it. H3972
Eze 37:16 a the Israelites associated with him. H3972
Eze 37:21 them from a around and bring them H6017
Eze 37:22 be one king over a of them and they will H3972
Eze 37:23 I will save them from a their sinful H3972
Eze 37:24 and they will a have one shepherd. H3972
Eze 38: 4 a of them brandishing their swords. H3972
Eze 38: 5 be with them, a with shields and helmets H3972
Eze 38: 6 also Gomer with a its troops, and Beth H3972
Eze 38: 6 from the far north with a its troops— H3972
Eze 38: 7 you and a the hordes gathered about you H3972
Eze 38: 8 nations, and now a of them live in safety. H3972
Eze 38: 9 You and a your troops and the many H3972
Eze 38:11 a of them living without walls and without H3972
Eze 38:13 of Tarshish and a her villages will say to H3972
Eze 38:15 with you, a of them riding on horses H3972
Eze 38:20 a the people on the face of the earth H3972
Eze 38:21 a sword against Gog on a my mountains, H3972
Eze 39: 4 you and a your troops and the nations H3972
Eze 39: 4 give you as food to a kinds of carrion birds H3972
Eze 39:11 because Gog and a his hordes will be H3972
Eze 39:13 A the people of the land will bury them H3972
Eze 39:17 every kind of bird and a the wild animals: H3972
Eze 39:17 together from a around to the sacrifice H6017
Eze 39:18 a of them fattened animals from Bashan. H3972
Eze 39:21 a the nations will see the H3972
Eze 39:23 enemies, and they a fell by the sword. H3972
Eze 39:25 have compassion on a the people of H3972
Eze 39:26 their shame and a the unfaithfulness H3972
Eze 40:14 walls a around the inside of H6017+6017
Eze 40:16 narrow parapet openings a around, H6017+6017
Eze 40:16 the openings a around faced H6017+6017
Eze 40:17 constructed a around the court; H6017+6017
Eze 40:25 had narrow openings a around, H6017+6017
Eze 40:29 its portico had openings a around. H6017+6017
Eze 40:33 its portico had openings a around. H6017+6017
Eze 40:36 and it had openings a around. H6017+6017
Eze 40:41 eight tables in a—on which the NDT
Eze 40:43 were attached to the wall a around. H6017+6017
Eze 41: 6 were ledges a around the wall of H6017+6017
Eze 41: 7 The side rooms a around the temple were H6015
Eze 41: 8 had a raised base a around it, H6017+6017
Eze 41:10 cubits wide a around the temple. H6017+6017
Eze 41:11 area was five cubits wide a around. H6017+6050
Eze 41:12 was five cubits thick a around, H6017+6017
Eze 41:17 intervals a around the inner and H6017+6017
Eze 41:19 were carved a around the whole H6017+6017
Eze 42:15 and measured the area a around: H6017+6017
Eze 42:20 So he measured the area on a four sides. It AIT
Eze 43:11 if they are ashamed of a they have done, H3972
Eze 43:11 its whole design and a its regulations and H3972
Eze 43:11 to its design and follow a its regulations. H3972
Eze 43:12 A the surrounding area on top of the H3972
Eze 43:17 A around the altar is a gutter of one cubit H6017
Eze 43:20 of the upper ledge and a around the rim, H6017
Eze 44: 5 tell you concerning a the regulations and H3972
Eze 44: 5 to the temple and a the exits of the H3972
Eze 44: 7 In addition to a your other detestable H3972
Eze 44:14 guard the temple for a the work that is to H3972
Eze 44:24 my decrees for a my appointed H3972
Eze 44:30 The best of a the firstfruits and of all your H3972
Eze 44:30 the firstfruits and of a your special gifts H3972
Eze 45: 6 sacred portion; it will belong to a Israel. H3972
Eze 45:16 A the people of the land will be required H3972
Eze 45:17 at a the appointed festivals of Israel. H3972
Eze 45:22 himself and for a the people of the H3972
Eze 46: 4 six male lambs and a ram, a without defect. AIT
Eze 46: 6 six lambs and a ram, a without defect. AIT
Eze 46:23 fire built a around under the ledge. H6017
Eze 47:12 Fruit trees of a kinds will grow on both H3972
Eze 48:19 it will come from a the tribes of Israel. H3972
Eze 48:35 "The distance a around will be 18,000 H6017
Da 1:17 understanding of a kinds of literature and H3972
Da 1:17 understand visions and dreams of a kinds. H3972
Da 1:20 ten times better than a the magicians H3972
Da 2:12 the execution of a the wise men of A10353
Da 2:35 the gold were a broken to pieces A10341+10248
Da 2:38 has placed a mankind and the A10120+10050
Da 2:38 he has made you ruler over them a. A10353
Da 2:40 so it will crush and break a the others. A10353
Da 2:44 It will crush a those kingdoms and bring A10353
Da 2:48 placed him in charge of a its wise men. A10353
Da 3: 2 magistrates and a the other provincial A10353
Da 3: 3 magistrates and a the other provincial A10353
Da 3: 5 pipe and a kinds of music, you A10353
Da 3: 7 harp and a kinds of music, all the A10353
Da 3: 7 a the nations and peoples of every A10353
Da 3:10 pipe and a kinds of music must fall A10353
Da 3:15 pipe and a kinds of music, if you A10353
Da 4: 1 every language, who live in a the earth: A10353
Da 4: 6 So I commanded that a the wise men of A10353
Da 4:12 fruit abundant, and on it was food for a. A10353
Da 4:17 is sovereign over a kingdoms on earth and AIT
Da 4:21 providing food for a, giving shelter to the A10353
Da 4:25 is sovereign over a kingdoms on earth and AIT
Da 4:28 A this happened to King A10353
Da 4:32 is sovereign over a kingdoms on earth and AIT
Da 4:35 A the peoples of the earth are regarded A10353
Da 4:37 he does is right and a his ways are just. NDT
Da 5: 8 Then a the king's wise men came in, but A10353
Da 5:19 a the nations and peoples of every A10353
Da 5:21 sovereign over a kingdoms on earth and sets AIT
Da 5:22 yourself, though you knew a this. A10353
Da 5:23 in his hand your life and a your ways. A10353
Da 6: 7 governors have a agreed that the A10353
Da 6:24 them and crushed a their bones. A10353
Da 6:25 King Darius wrote to a the nations and A10353
Da 6:25 of every language in a the earth: A10353
Da 7: 7 It was different from a the former beasts A10353
Da 7: 9 and its wheels were a ablaze. A10178+10471
Da 7:14 a nations and peoples of every A10353
Da 7:16 asked him the meaning of a this. A10353
Da 7:19 was different from a the others and most A10353
Da 7:23 be different from a the other kingdoms A10353
Da 7:27 greatness of a the kingdoms under A10353
Da 7:27 a rulers will worship and obey him. A10353
Da 9: 6 to a the people of the land. H3972
Da 9: 7 the inhabitants of Jerusalem and a Israel, H3972
Da 9: 7 in a the countries where you have H3972
Da 9:11 A Israel has transgressed your law and H3972
Da 9:13 of Moses, a this disaster has come on us H3972
Da 9:16 in keeping with a your righteous acts H3972
Da 9:16 an object of scorn to a those around us. H3972
Da 10: 3 and I used no lotions at a until the H6057+6057
Da 11: 2 who will be far richer than a the others. H3972
Da 11:37 but will exalt himself above them a. H3972
Da 11:43 gold and silver and a the riches of Egypt, H3972
Da 12: 7 a these things will be completed. H3972
Da 12: 8 lord, what will the outcome of a this be?" AIT
Hos 1: 6 that I should at a forgive them. H5951+5951
Hos 2:11 I will stop a her celebrations: her yearly H3972
Hos 2:11 Sabbath days—a her appointed festivals. H3972
Hos 2:18 so that a may lie down in safety. H4392S
Hos 4: 2 adultery; they break a bounds, and H7287
Hos 4: 3 dries up, and a who live in it waste away H3972
Hos 5: 2 I will discipline a of them. H3972
Hos 5: 3 I know a about Ephraim; Israel is not H3359
Hos 7: 2 realize that I remember a their evil deeds. H3972
Hos 7: 4 They are a adulterers, burning like an H3972
Hos 7: 6 Their passion smolders a night; in the H3972
Hos 7: 7 A of them are hot as an oven; they devour H3972
Hos 7: 7 A their kings fall, and none of them calls H3972
Hos 7:10 despite a this he does not return to H3972
Hos 9: 4 a who eat them will be unclean. H3972
Hos 9: 8 snares await him on a his paths, and H3972
Hos 9:15 "Because of a their wickedness in Gilgal, I H3972
Hos 9:15 love them; a their leaders are rebellious. H3972
Hos 10:14 so that a your fortresses will be H3972
Hos 11: 8 within me; a my compassion is aroused. H3480
Hos 12: 1 the east wind a day and multiplies H3972
Hos 12: 8 With a my wealth they will not find in me H3972
Hos 13: 2 images, a of them the work of craftsmen. H3972
Hos 13:10 Where are your rulers in a your towns, of H3972
Hos 13:15 will be plundered of a its treasures. H3972
Hos 14: 2 "Forgive a our sins and receive us H3972
Joel 1: 2 you elders; listen, a who live in the land. H3972
Joel 1: 5 a you drinkers of wine; wail H3972
Joel 1:12 the apple tree—a the trees of the field H3972
Joel 1:14 the elders and a who live in the land H3972
Joel 1:19 flames have burned up a the trees of the H3972
Joel 2: 1 Let a who live in the land tremble, for the H3972
Joel 2: 7 They a march in line, not swerving from their AIT
Joel 2:12 "return to me with a your heart, with H3972
Joel 2:28 I will pour out my Spirit on a people. H3972
Joel 3: 2 I will gather a nations and bring them H3972
Joel 3: 4 Tyre and Sidon and a you regions of H3972
Joel 3: 9 Let a the fighting men draw near and H3972
Joel 3:11 a you nations from every side H3972
Joel 3:12 I will sit to judge a the nations on every H3972
Joel 3:18 a the ravines of Judah will run with water. H3972
Joel 3:20 through a generations. H1887+2256+1887
Am 2: 3 her ruler and kill a her officials with him," H3972
Am 3: 2 only have I chosen of a the families of the H3972
Am 3: 2 therefore I will punish you for a your sins." H3972
Am 5:16 will be wailing in a the streets and cries H3972
Am 5:17 There will be wailing in a the vineyards H3972
Am 6:14 that will oppress you a the way from Lebo NDT
Am 7:10 The land cannot bear a his words. H3972
Am 8: 8 this, and a who live in it mourn? H3972
Am 8:10 into mourning and a your singing into H3972
Am 8:10 I will make a of you wear sackcloth and H3972
Am 9: 1 them down on the heads of a the people; H3972
Am 9: 5 it melts, and a who live in it mourn H3972
Am 9: 9 of Israel among a the nations as grain H3972
Am 9:10 A the sinners among my people will die H3972
Am 9:10 will die by the sword, a those who say NDT
Am 9:12 remnant of Edom and a the nations that H3972

Am 9:13 the mountains and flow from **a** the hills, H3972
Ob 7 **A** your allies will force you to the border H3972
Ob 15 "The day of the LORD is near for **a** nations H3972
Ob 16 so **a** the nations will drink continually H3972
Jnh 1: 5 **A** the sailors were afraid and each cried out NDT
Jnh 1: 8 responsible for making **a** this trouble for us? NDT
Jnh 2: 3 **a** your waves and breakers swept over me. H3972
Jnh 3: 5 was proclaimed, and **a** of them, from the NDT
Mic 1: 2 you peoples, **a** *of* you, listen, earth H3972
Mic 1: 2 earth and **a who live in** it, that the H4850
Mic 1: 5 **A** this is because of Jacob's transgression H3972
Mic 1: 7 **A** her idols will be broken to pieces; all H3972
Mic 1: 7 **a** her temple gifts will be burned with fire H3972
Mic 1: 7 with fire; I will destroy **a** her images. H3972
Mic 1:10 not in Gath; **weep** not **at a**. In Beth H1134+1134
Mic 2:10 is defiled, it is ruined, **beyond a remedy**. H5344
Mic 2:12 "I will surely gather **a** *of* you, Jacob; I will H3972
Mic 3: 7 They will **a** cover their faces because H3972
Mic 3: 9 despise justice and distort **a** that is right; H3972
Mic 4: 5 **A** the nations may walk in the name of H3972
Mic 4:13 their wealth to the Lord of **a** the earth. H3972
Mic 5: 9 **a** your foes will be destroyed. H3972
Mic 5:11 land and tear down **a** your strongholds. H3972
Mic 6:16 statutes of Omri and **a** the practices of H3972
Mic 7: 3 what they desire—*they* **a conspire** *together*. AIT
Mic 7:16 be ashamed, deprived of **a** their power. H3972
Mic 7:19 underfoot and hurl **a** our iniquities into H3972
Na 1: 4 dries it up; he makes **a** the rivers run dry. H3972
Na 1: 5 presence, the world and **a** who live in it. H3972
Na 2: 1 brace yourselves, marshal **a** your strength! H4394
Na 2: 9 is endless, the wealth from **a** its treasures! H3972
Na 3: 4 **a** because of the wanton lust of a H8044
Na 3: 7 **A** who see you will flee from you and say H3972
Na 3:10 **a** her great men were put in chains. H3972
Na 3:12 **A** your fortresses are like fig trees with H3972
Na 3:13 troops—they are **a** weaklings. The gates NDT
Na 3:19 **A** who hear the news about you clap their H3972
Hab 1: 9 they **a** come intent on violence. Their H3972
Hab 1:10 They laugh at **a** fortified cities; by H3972
Hab 1:15 wicked foe pulls **a** *of* them up with hooks, H3972
Hab 2: 5 gathers to himself **a** the nations and takes H3972
Hab 2: 5 nations and takes captive **a** the peoples. H3972
Hab 2: 6 "Will not **a** *of* them taunt him with H3972
Hab 2:20 let **a** the earth be silent before him. H3972
Zep 1: 3 "When I destroy **a** mankind on the face H2021S
Zep 1: 4 Judah and against **a** who live in H3972
Zep 1: 8 the king's sons and **a** those clad in H3972
Zep 1: 9 day I will punish **a** who avoid stepping on H3972
Zep 1:11 **a** your merchants will be wiped out H3972
Zep 1:11 **a** who trade with silver will be destroyed. H3972
Zep 1:17 such distress on **a** people that they will H2021S
Zep 1:18 make a sudden end of **a** who live on the H3972
Zep 2: 3 Seek the LORD, **a** you humble of the land H3972
Zep 2:11 when he destroys **a** the gods of the earth H3972
Zep 2:11 down to him, **a** *of them* in their own lands. H408
Zep 2:15 **A** who pass by her scoff and shake their H3972
Zep 3: 7 **a** my punishments come upon her. H3972
Zep 3: 7 still eager to act corruptly in **a** they did. H3972
Zep 3: 8 my wrath on them—**a** my fierce anger. H3972
Zep 3: 9 that **a** *of* them may call on the name of H3972
Zep 3:11 put to shame for **a** the wrongs you have H3972
Zep 3:14 Be glad and rejoice with **a** your heart H3972
Zep 3:18 from you *a who* **mourn** *over* the loss of AIT
Zep 3:19 I will deal with **a** who oppressed you. H3972
Zep 3:20 praise among **a** the peoples of the H3972
Hag 1:11 on **a** the labor of your hands. H3972
Hag 2: 4 Be strong, **a** you people of the land,' H3972
Hag 2: 7 I will shake **a** nations, and what is desired H3972
Hag 2: 7 what is desired by **a** nations will come, H3972
Hag 2:17 I struck **a** the work of your hands with H3972
Zec 2:13 before the LORD, **a** mankind, because he H3972
Zec 4:14 anointed to serve the Lord of **a** the earth." H3972
Zec 6: 3 the fourth dappled—*a of them* **powerful**. AIT
Zec 7: 5 "Ask **a** the people of the land and the H3972
Zec 7:14 with a whirlwind among **a** the nations, H3972
Zec 8:12 I will give **a** these things as an H3972
Zec 8:17 swear falsely. I hate **a** this," declares the H3972
Zec 8:23 days ten people from **a** languages and H3972
Zec 9: 1 the eyes of *a* **people** and all the tribes of AIT
Zec 9: 1 of all people and **a** the tribes of Israel H3972
Zec 10: 1 He gives showers of rain to *a* **people**, and AIT
Zec 10:11 will be subdued and **a** the depths of the H3972
Zec 11:10 covenant I had made with **a** the nations. H3972
Zec 12: 2 a cup that sends **a** the surrounding H3972
Zec 12: 3 when **a** the nations of the earth are H3972
Zec 12: 3 an immovable rock for **a** the nations. H3972
Zec 12: 3 **A** who try to move it will injure H3972
Zec 12: 4 I will blind **a** the horses of the nations. H3972
Zec 12: 6 They will consume **a** the surrounding H3972
Zec 12: 9 set out to destroy **a** the nations that attack H3972
Zec 12:14 **a** the rest of the clans and their wives. H3972
Zec 14: 2 I will gather **a** the nations to Jerusalem to H3972
Zec 14: 5 will come, and **a** the holy ones with him. H3972
Zec 14:12 the LORD will strike **a** the nations that H3972
Zec 14:14 The wealth of **a** the surrounding nations H3972
Zec 14:15 **a** the animals in those camps. H3972
Zec 14:16 the survivors from **a** the nations that have H3972
Zec 14:19 the punishment of **a** the nations that do H3972
Zec 14:21 **a** who come to sacrifice will take H3972
Mal 2: 9 humiliated before **a** the people, H3972
Mal 2:10 Do we not **a** have one Father? Did not H3972
Mal 2:17 "**A** who do evil are good in the eyes of H3972
Mal 3:12 "Then **a** the nations will call you blessed H3972
Mal 4: 1 **A** the arrogant and every evildoer will be H3972
Mal 4: 4 laws I gave him at Horeb for **a** Israel. H3972
Mt 1:17 generations *in* **a** from Abraham to G4246
Mt 1:22 **A** this took place to fulfill what the Lord G3910
Mt 2: 3 was disturbed, and **a** Jerusalem with him. G4246
Mt 2: 4 had called together **a** the people's chief G4246
Mt 2:16 gave orders to kill **a** the boys in G4246
Mt 3: 5 from Jerusalem and **a** Judea and the G4246
Mt 3:15 us to do this to fulfill **a** righteousness." G4246
Mt 4: 8 showed him **a** the kingdoms of the G4246
Mt 4: 9 "**A** this I will give you," he said, "if you G4246
Mt 4:24 about him spread **a over** Syria, G1650+3910
Mt 4:24 people brought to him **a** who were ill with G4246
Mt 5:11 you and falsely say **a** *kinds* of evil against G4246
Mt 5:34 do not swear an oath **at a**: either by G3914
Mt 5:37 **A** you need to say is simply 'Yes' or 'No' G1254
Mt 6:29 not even Solomon in **a** his splendor was G4246
Mt 6:32 For the pagans run after **a** these things G4246
Mt 6:33 **a** these things will be given to you as G4246
Mt 7: 4 '**when** *a the time* there is a plank in your own AIT
Mt 8:16 spirits with a word and healed **a** the sick. G4246
Mt 8:33 went into the town and reported **a** *this* G4246
Mt 9:26 News of this spread through **a** that region. G3910
Mt 9:31 news about him **a over** that region. G1877+3910
Mt 9:35 Jesus went through **a** the towns and G4246
Mt 10:30 very hairs of your head are **a** numbered. G4246
Mt 11:13 For **a** the Prophets and the Law prophesied G4246
Mt 11:27 "**A** *things* have been committed to me by G4246
Mt 11:28 **a** you who are weary and burdened G4246
Mt 12:15 and he healed **a** who were ill. G4246
Mt 12:23 **A** the people were astonished and said G4246
Mt 13: 2 while **a** the people stood on the shore. G4246
Mt 13:32 Though it is the smallest *of* **a** seeds, yet G4246
Mt 13:33 flour until it worked **a** through the dough." G3910
Mt 13:34 Jesus spoke **a** these things to the crowd in G4246
Mt 13:41 that causes sin and **a** who do evil. NDT
Mt 13:44 joy went and sold **a** he had and bought G4246
Mt 13:47 into the lake and caught **a** kinds of fish. G4246
Mt 13:51 "Have you understood **a** these things?" G4246
Mt 13:56 Aren't **a** his sisters with us? Where then G4246
Mt 13:56 then did this man get **a** these things?" G4246
Mt 14:20 They **a** ate and were satisfied, and the G4246
Mt 14:35 they sent word to **a** the surrounding G3910
Mt 14:35 People brought **a** their sick to him G4246
Mt 14:36 and **a** who touched it were healed. G4012
Mt 15:37 They **a** ate and were satisfied. Afterward G4246
Mt 17:11 Elijah comes and will restore **a** *things*. G4246
Mt 18:25 his children and **a** that he had be sold G4246
Mt 18:32 'I canceled **a** that debt of yours because G4246
Mt 18:34 until he should pay back **a** he owed. G4246
Mt 19:20 "**A** these I have kept," the young man G4246
Mt 19:26 with God **a** *things* are possible. G4246
Mt 19:28 at the **renewal of a things**, when the G4098
Mt 20: 6 standing here **a** day *long* doing nothing? G3910
Mt 20:31 they shouted **a the louder**, "Lord, G3505
Mt 21:12 drove out **a** who were buying and G4246
Mt 21:26 they **a** hold that John was a prophet." G4246
Mt 21:37 **Last of a**, he sent his son to them. 'They G5731
Mt 22:10 streets and gathered **a** the people they G4246
Mt 22:28 since **a** *of them* were married to her?" G4246
Mt 22:37 Lord your God with **a** your heart and with G3910
Mt 22:37 your heart and with **a** your soul and with G3910
Mt 22:37 with all your soul and with **a** your mind. G3910
Mt 22:40 **A** the Law and the Prophets hang on these G3910
Mt 23: 8 one Teacher, and you are **a** brothers. G4246
Mt 23:35 upon you will come **a** the righteous blood G4246
Mt 23:36 **a** this will come on this generation. G4246
Mt 24: 2 "Do you see **a** these things?" he asked G4246
Mt 24: 8 **A** these are the beginning of birth pains. G4246
Mt 24: 9 you will be hated by **a** nations because of G4246
Mt 24:14 whole world as a testimony *to* **a** nations, G4246
Mt 24:30 And then **a** the peoples of the earth will G4246
Mt 24:33 Even so, when you see **a** these things, you G4246
Mt 24:34 not pass away until **a** these things have G4246
Mt 24:39 the flood came and took *them* **a** away. G570
Mt 24:47 put him in charge of **a** his possessions. G4246
Mt 25: 5 they **a** became drowsy and fell G4246
Mt 25: 7 "Then **a** the virgins woke up and trimmed G4246
Mt 25:31 in his glory, and **a** the angels with him G4246
Mt 25:32 **A** the nations will be gathered before him G4246
Mt 26: 1 Jesus had finished saying **a** these things, G4246
Mt 26:27 it to them, saying, "Drink from it, **a** of you. G4246
Mt 26:31 very night you will **a** fall away on account G4246
Mt 26:33 "Even if **a** fall away on account of you G4246
Mt 26:35 And **a** the other disciples said the same G4246
Mt 26:52 "for **a** who draw the sword will die by the G4246
Mt 26:56 But this has **a** taken place that the writings G3910
Mt 26:56 Then **a** the disciples deserted him and G4246
Mt 26:64 "But I say *to a of* **you**: From now on you AIT
Mt 26:70 But he denied it before *them* **a**. "I don't G4246
Mt 27: 1 **a** the chief priests and the elders of the G4246
Mt 27:22 They **a** answered, "Crucify G4246
Mt 27:23 But they shouted **a the louder**, "Crucify G4360
Mt 27:25 **A** the people answered, "His blood is on G4246
Mt 27:45 afternoon darkness came over **a** the land. G4246
Mt 27:54 the earthquake and **a** that had happened, G3836
Mt 28:18 "**A** authority in heaven and on earth has G4246
Mt 28:19 go and make disciples *of* **a** nations, G4246
Mk 1: 5 Judean countryside and **a** the people of G4246
Mk 1:27 The people were **a** so amazed that they G570
Mk 1:32 people brought to Jesus **a** the sick and G4246
Mk 2:12 walked out in full view of *them* **a**. G4246
Mk 3: 8 When they heard *about* **a** he was doing G4012
Mk 3:28 can be forgiven **a** their sins and every G4246
Mk 4: 1 while **a** the people were along the shore G4246
Mk 4:28 **A by itself** the soil produces grain—first the G897
Mk 4:31 which is the smallest *of* **a** seeds on earth. G4246
Mk 4:32 becomes the largest *of* **a** garden plants, G4246
Mk 5:20 And **a** *the people* were amazed. G4246
Mk 5:26 of many doctors and had spent **a** she had, G4246
Mk 5:39 "Why *a this* **commotion** and wailing? AIT
Mk 5:40 After he put *them* **a** out, he took the G4246
Mk 6:30 reported to him **a** they had done and G4246
Mk 6:33 ran on foot from **a** the towns and got G4246
Mk 6:39 them to have **a** *the people* sit down in G4246
Mk 6:41 also divided the two fish *among them* **a**. G4246
Mk 6:42 They **a** ate and were satisfied, G4246
Mk 6:50 because they **a** saw him and were terrified. G4246
Mk 6:56 and **a** who touched it were healed. G4012+323
Mk 7: 3 The Pharisees and **a** the Jews do not eat G4246
Mk 7:19 saying this, Jesus declared **a** foods clean.) G4246
Mk 7:23 **A** these evils come from inside and defile G4246
Mk 7:27 "First let the children **eat a** *they* **want**," G5963
Mk 9: 2 where they were **a alone**. G2848+2625+3668
Mk 9:12 does come first, and restores **a** *things*. G4246
Mk 9:15 As soon as **a** the people saw Jesus, they G4246
Mk 9:35 be the very last, and the servant *of* **a**." G4246
Mk 10:20 "**a** these I have kept since I was a boy." G4246
Mk 10:27 with God; **a** *things* are possible with God." G4246
Mk 10:44 wants to be first must be slave *of* **a**. G4246
Mk 10:48 he shouted **a the more**, "Son of G4498+3437
Mk 11:17 be called a house of prayer for **a** nations'? G4246
Mk 12: 6 He sent him **last of a**, saying, 'They will G2274
Mk 12:22 Last *of* **a**, the woman died G4246
Mk 12:28 he asked him, "*Of* **a** the commandments G4246
Mk 12:30 Lord your God with **a** your heart and with G3910
Mk 12:30 your heart and with **a** your soul and with G3910
Mk 12:30 your soul and with **a** your mind and with G3910
Mk 12:30 all your mind and with **a** your strength. G3910
Mk 12:33 To love him with **a** your heart, with all your G3910
Mk 12:33 with **a** your understanding and with all G3910
Mk 12:33 understanding and with **a** your strength, G3910
Mk 12:33 is more important *than* **a** burnt offerings G4246
Mk 12:43 more into the treasury *than* **a** the others. G4246
Mk 12:44 *They* **a** gave out of their wealth; but she G4246
Mk 12:44 put in everything—**a** she had to live on." G3910
Mk 13: 2 "Do you see *a* **these** great buildings? AIT
Mk 13: 4 sign that they are **a** about to be fulfilled?" G4246
Mk 13:10 must first be preached to **a** nations. G4246
Mk 13:30 not pass away until **a** these things have G4246
Mk 14:23 gave it to them, and they **a** drank from it. G4246
Mk 14:27 "You will **a** fall away," Jesus told them G4246
Mk 14:29 declared, "Even if **a** fall away, I will not." G4246
Mk 14:31 And **a** *the others* said the same. G4246
Mk 14:53 the high priest, and **a** the chief priests G4246
Mk 14:64 They **a** condemned him as worthy of G4246
Mk 15:14 But they shouted **a the louder**, "Crucify G4360
Mk 16:15 "Go into **a** the world and preach the gospel G570
Mk 16:15 preach the gospel *to* **a** creation. G4246
Mk 16:18 it will **not** hurt them **at a**; they will G4024+3590
Lk 1: 6 observing **a** the Lord's commands and G4246
Lk 1:10 **a** the assembled worshipers were praying G4246
Lk 1:48 From now on **a** generations will call me G4246
Lk 1:65 **A** the neighbors were filled with awe, and G4246
Lk 1:65 people were talking about **a** these things. G4246
Lk 1:71 from the hand *of* **a** who hate us— G4246
Lk 1:75 righteousness before him **a** our days. G4246
Lk 2:10 that will cause great joy *for* **a** the people. G4246
Lk 2:18 **a** who heard it were amazed at what G4246
Lk 2:19 But Mary treasured up **a** these things and G4246
Lk 2:20 praising God for **a** the things they had G4246
Lk 2:31 have prepared in the sight *of* **a** nations: G4246
Lk 2:38 about the child *to* **a** who were looking G4246
Lk 2:51 his mother treasured **a** these things in her G4246
Lk 3: 3 He went into **a** the country around the G4246
Lk 3: 6 And **a** people will see God's salvation.'" G4246
Lk 3:15 expectantly and were **a** wondering in their G4246
Lk 3:16 John answered *them* **a**, "I baptize you with G4246
Lk 3:19 and *a* the **other** evil things he had done AIT
Lk 3:20 Herod added this to *them* **a**: He locked G4246
Lk 3:21 When **a** the people were being baptized G570
Lk 4: 5 him in an instant **a** the kingdoms of the G4246
Lk 4: 6 "I will give you **a** their authority and G570
Lk 4: 7 If you worship me, it will **a** be yours." G4246
Lk 4:13 the devil had finished **a** *this* tempting, G4246
Lk 4:22 **A** spoke well of him and were amazed at G4246
Lk 4:28 **A** the people in the synagogue were G4246
Lk 4:35 down before them **a** and came out without NDT
Lk 4:36 **A** *the people* were amazed and said to G4246
Lk 4:40 brought to Jesus **a** who had various kinds G570
Lk 5: 5 we've worked hard **a** night and haven't G3910
Lk 5: 9 For he and **a** his companions were G4246
Lk 5:15 the news about him spread **a the more**, G3437
Lk 6:10 He looked around *at* them **a**, and then G4246
Lk 6:17 number of people from **a over** Judea, G4246
Lk 6:19 the people **a** tried to touch him G4246
Lk 6:19 coming from him and healing *them* **a**. G4246
Lk 7: 1 had finished saying **a** this to the people G4246
Lk 7:16 *They* were **a** filled with awe and praised G4246
Lk 7:18 disciples told him about **a** these things. G4246
Lk 7:29 (**A** the people, even the tax collectors G4246
Lk 7:35 wisdom is proved right by **a** her children." G4246
Lk 8:24 the storm subsided, and *a* **was** calm. AIT

Lk 8:37 Then **a** the people of the region of the G570
Lk 8:39 away and told **a over** town how G2848+3910
Lk 8:40 for they were **a** expecting him. G4246
Lk 8:45 When they **a** denied it, Peter said G4246
Lk 8:47 In the presence of **a** the people, she told G4246
Lk 8:52 **a** *the people* were wailing and mourning G4246
Lk 9: 1 to drive out **a** demons and to cure G4246
Lk 9: 7 tetrarch heard about **a** that was going on. G4246
Lk 9:13 we go and buy food for **a** this crowd." G4246
Lk 9:17 They **a** ate and were satisfied, and the G4246
Lk 9:23 Then he said to *them* **a**: "Whoever wants G4246
Lk 9:43 And they were **a** amazed at the greatness G4246
Lk 9:43 was marveling at **a** that Jesus did, G4246
Lk 9:48 is least among you **a** who is the greatest." G4246
Lk 10:19 to overcome **a** the power of the G4246
Lk 10:22 "**A** *things* have been committed to me by G4246
Lk 10:27 Lord your God with **a** your heart and with G3910
Lk 10:27 your heart and with **a** your soul and with G3910
Lk 10:27 your soul and with **a** your strength and G3910
Lk 10:27 all your strength and with **a** your mind'; G3910
Lk 10:40 was distracted by **a** the preparations that G4498
Lk 11:42 rue and **a** *other kinds of* garden herbs G4246
Lk 11:50 the blood *of* **a** the prophets that has G4246
Lk 11:51 generation will be held responsible for it **a**. NDT
Lk 12: 7 very hairs of your head are **a** numbered. G4246
Lk 12:15 Be on your guard against **a** *kinds of* greed; G4246
Lk 12:27 not even Solomon in **a** his splendor was G4246
Lk 12:30 the pagan world runs after **a** such things, G4246
Lk 12:44 put him in charge of **a** his possessions. G4246
Lk 13: 2 worse sinners than **a** the other Galileans G4246
Lk 13: 3 unless you repent, you too will **a** perish. G4246
Lk 13: 4 more guilty than **a** the others living in G4246
Lk 13: 5 unless you repent, you too will **a** perish." G4246
Lk 13:11 could not straighten up **at a**. G1650+3836+4117
Lk 13:17 **a** his opponents were humiliated G4246
Lk 13:17 were delighted with **a** the wonderful G4246
Lk 13:21 flour until it worked **a** through the dough." G3910
Lk 13:27 Away from me, **a** you evildoers!' G4246
Lk 13:28 Isaac and Jacob and **a** the prophets in the G4246
Lk 14:10 in the presence of **a** the other guests. G4246
Lk 14:11 For **a** those who exalt themselves will be G4246
Lk 14:18 "But they **a** alike began to make excuses G4246
Lk 15: 1 sinners were **a** gathering around to G4246
Lk 15:13 the younger son got together **a** he had G4246
Lk 15:29 **A these** years I've been slaving for you G5537
Lk 16:14 heard **a** this and were sneering at Jesus. G4246
Lk 16:26 And besides **a** this, between us and you **a** G4246
Lk 17:17 "Were not **a** ten cleansed? Where G3836
Lk 17:27 the flood came and destroyed *them* **a**. G4246
Lk 17:29 down from heaven and destroyed *them* **a**. G4246
Lk 18:12 twice a week and give a tenth *of* **a** I get. G4246
Lk 18:14 For **a** those who exalt themselves will be G4246
Lk 18:21 "**A** these I have kept since I was a boy," G4246
Lk 18:28 "We have left **a** *we* **had** to follow G3836+2625
Lk 18:39 he shouted **a the more**, "Son of G4498+3437
Lk 18:43 When **a** the people saw it, they also G4246
Lk 19: 7 **A** *the people* saw this and began to G4246
Lk 19:37 in loud voices for **a** the miracles they had G4246
Lk 19:48 because **a** the people hung on his words. G570
Lk 20: 6 human origin,' **a** the people will stone us G570
Lk 20:38 of the living, for to him **a** are alive." G4246
Lk 20:45 While **a** the people were listening, Jesus G4246
Lk 21: 3 widow has put in more *than* **a** *the others.* G4246
Lk 21: 4 **A** these people gave their gifts out of their G4246
Lk 21: 4 of her poverty put in **a** she had to live on." G4246
Lk 21:12 "But before **a** this, they will seize you and G4246
Lk 21:12 governors, and **a on account of** my name. G1915
Lk 21:22 in fulfillment of **a** that has been written. G4246
Lk 21:24 be taken as prisoners to **a** the nations. G4246
Lk 21:29 "Look at the fig tree and **a** the trees. G4246
Lk 21:32 away until **a** *these things* have happened. G4246
Lk 21:35 For it will come on **a** those who live on the G4246
Lk 21:36 may be able to escape **a** that is about to G4246
Lk 21:38 **a** the people came early in the G4246
Lk 22:12 you a large room upstairs, **a furnished**. G5143
Lk 22:31 Satan has asked to sift *a of* **you** as wheat. AIT
Lk 22:70 They **a** asked, "Are you then the Son of G4246
Lk 23: 5 up the people **a over** Judea by his G2848+3910
Lk 23: 5 in Galilee and has come **a the way** here." G2401
Lk 23:48 When **a** the people who had gathered to G4246
Lk 23:49 But **a** those who knew him, including the G4246
Lk 24: 9 they told **a** these things to the Eleven G4246
Lk 24: 9 things to the Eleven and *to* **a** the others. G4246
Lk 24:19 deed before God and **a** the people. G4246
Lk 24:21 it is the third day since *a* **this** took place. AIT
Lk 24:25 how slow to believe **a** that the prophets G4246
Lk 24:27 with Moses and **a** the Prophets, G4246
Lk 24:27 to them what was said in **a** the Scriptures G4246
Lk 24:47 be preached in his name to **a** nations, G4246
Jn 1: 3 Through him **a** *things* were made; without G4246
Jn 1: 4 and that life was the light *of a* **mankind**. AIT
Jn 1: 7 so that through him **a** might believe. G4246
Jn 1:12 Yet *to* **a** who did receive him, to those who G4012
Jn 1:16 his fullness we have **a** received grace in G4246
Jn 1:28 **This** *a* happened at Bethany on the other AIT
Jn 2:15 and drove **a** from the temple courts G4246
Jn 2:18 show us to prove your authority to do *a* **this**?" AIT
Jn 2:24 himself to them, for he knew **a** *people*. G4246
Jn 3:31 one who comes from above is above **a**; G4246
Jn 3:31 one who comes from heaven is above **a**. G4246
Jn 4:45 They had seen **a** that he had done in G4246
Jn 5:18 reason they tried **a the more** to kill him; G3437
Jn 5:20 loves the Son and shows him **a** he does. G4246
Jn 5:22 has entrusted **a** judgment to the Son, G4246
Jn 5:23 that **a** may honor the Son just as they G4246
Jn 5:28 a time is coming when **a** who are in their G4246
Jn 6:12 When *they had a* **had enough to eat**, he said AIT
Jn 6:37 **A** those the Father gives me will come to G4246
Jn 6:39 I shall lose none of **a** those he has given G4246
Jn 6:45 'They will **a** be taught by God.' G4246
Jn 7:21 "I did one miracle, and you are **a** amazed. G4246
Jn 7:53 Then they **a** went home, G1667
Jn 8: 2 where **a** the people gathered around him G4246
Jn 10: 4 When he has brought out **a** his own, he G4246
Jn 10: 8 **A** who have come before me are thieves G4246
Jn 10:29 is greater *than* **a**; no one can G4246
Jn 10:41 **a** that John said about this man was true." G4246
Jn 11:49 spoke up, "You know **nothing at a**! G4024+4029
Jn 11:56 **Isn't** he coming to the festival **at a**?" G4024+3590
Jn 12:16 At first his disciples did not understand *a* **this**. AIT
Jn 12:32 the earth, will draw **a** *people* to myself." G4246
Jn 12:49 commanded me to say *a* **that** I have spoken. AIT
Jn 13: 3 Father had put **a** *things* under his power, G4246
Jn 13:18 "I am not referring to **a** of you; I know G4246
Jn 14:25 "*A* **this** I have spoken while still with you. AIT
Jn 14:26 will teach you **a** *things* and will remind G4246
Jn 16: 1 "*A* **this** I have told you so that you will not AIT
Jn 16:13 he will guide you into **a** the truth. G4246
Jn 16:15 **A** that belongs to the Father is mine. That G4246
Jn 16:30 that you know **a** *things* and that you do G4246
Jn 16:32 You will leave me **a alone**. Yet I am not G3668
Jn 17: 2 him authority *over* **a** people that he might G4246
Jn 17: 2 give eternal life *to* **a** those you have given G4246
Jn 17:10 **A** I have is yours, and all you have is G4246
Jn 17:10 I have is yours, and you have is mine. And NDT
Jn 17:21 that **a** *of them* may be one, Father, just as G4246
Jn 18: 4 knowing **a** that was going to happen to G4246
Jn 18:20 temple, where **a** the Jews come together. G4246
Jn 21:17 you know **a** *things*; you know that I G4246
Ac 1: 1 I wrote about **a** that Jesus began to do G4246
Ac 1: 8 Jerusalem, and in **a** Judea and Samaria G4246
Ac 1:14 They **a** joined together constantly in prayer G4246
Ac 1:18 body burst open and **a** his intestines G4246
Ac 2: 1 they were **a** together in one place. G4246
Ac 2: 4 **A** of them were filled with the Holy Spirit G4246
Ac 2: 7 "Aren't **a** these who are speaking G570
Ac 2:14 "Fellow Jews and **a** of you who live in G4246
Ac 2:17 I will pour out my Spirit on **a** people. G4246
Ac 2:32 Jesus to life, and we are **a** witnesses of it. G4246
Ac 2:36 "Therefore let **a** Israel be assured of this G4246
Ac 2:39 your children and *for* **a** who are far off— G4246
Ac 2:39 *for* **a whom** the Lord our God will call." G4012+323
Ac 2:44 **A** the believers were together and had G4246
Ac 2:47 enjoying the favor of **a** the people. G3910
Ac 3: 9 When **a** the people saw him walking and G4246
Ac 3:11 **a** the people were astonished and came G4246
Ac 3:16 completely healed him, as you can **a** see. G4246
Ac 3:18 he had foretold through **a** the prophets, G4246
Ac 3:24 **a** the prophets who have spoken have G4246
Ac 3:25 your offspring **a** peoples on earth will G4246
Ac 4:10 know this, you and **a** the people of Israel: G4246
Ac 4:18 to speak or teach **at a** in the name of G2773
Ac 4:21 because **a** the people were praising God G4246
Ac 4:23 reported **a that** the chief priests G4012
Ac 4:31 And they were **a** filled with the Holy Spirit G570
Ac 4:32 **A** the believers were one in heart and G4436
Ac 4:33 grace was so powerfully at work in them **a** G4246
Ac 5: 5 great fear seized **a** who heard what had G4246
Ac 5:11 the whole church and **a** who heard about G4246
Ac 5:12 And **a** the believers used to meet together G570
Ac 5:16 impure spirits, and **a** of them were healed. G570
Ac 5:17 Then the high priest and **a** his associates G4246
Ac 5:20 the people **a about** this new G4246+3836+4839
Ac 5:34 who was honored *by* **a** the people, stood G4246
Ac 5:36 **a** his followers were dispersed G4246+4012
Ac 5:36 were dispersed, and *it a* **came** to nothing. AIT
Ac 5:37 and **a** his followers were scattered. G4246+4012
Ac 6: 2 So the Twelve gathered **a** the disciples G4436
Ac 6:15 **A** who were sitting in the Sanhedrin G4246
Ac 7:10 rescued him from **a** his troubles. He G4246
Ac 7:10 him ruler over Egypt and **a** his palace. G3910
Ac 7:11 a famine struck **a** Egypt and Canaan, G3910
Ac 7:14 his whole family, seventy-five in **a**. G6034S
Ac 7:22 was educated in **a** the wisdom of the G4246
Ac 7:50 Has not my hand made **a** these things? G4246
Ac 7:57 top of their voices, they **a** rushed at him, G3924
Ac 8: 1 **a** except the apostles were scattered G4246
Ac 8: 6 they **a** paid close attention to what he G3924
Ac 8: 9 city and amazed *a* the **people** of Samaria. AIT
Ac 8:10 **a** the people, both high and low G4246
Ac 8:27 official in charge of **a** the treasury of the G4246
Ac 8:40 the gospel in **a** the towns until he G4246
Ac 9:13 about this man and **a** the harm he has G4012
Ac 9:14 priests to arrest **a** who call on your name." G4246
Ac 9:21 **A** those who heard him were astonished G4246
Ac 9:26 they were **a** afraid of him, not G4246
Ac 9:35 **A** those who lived in Lydda and Sharon G4246
Ac 9:39 **A** the widows stood around him, crying G4246
Ac 9:40 Peter sent *them* **a** out of the room; then G4246
Ac 9:42 This became known **a over** Joppa G2848+3910
Ac 10: 2 He and **a** his family were devout and G4246
Ac 10:12 It contained **a** *kinds of* four-footed animals G4246
Ac 10:22 who is respected by **a** the Jewish people. G3910
Ac 10:33 Now we are **a** here in the presence of G4246
Ac 10:36 through Jesus Christ, who is Lord *of* **a**. G4246
Ac 10:38 good and healing **a** who were under the G4246
Ac 10:41 He was not seen *by* **a** the people, but by G4246
Ac 10:43 **A** the prophets testify about him that G4246
Ac 10:44 Holy Spirit came on **a** who heard the G4246
Ac 11:10 then it was **a** pulled up to heaven G570
Ac 11:14 which you and **a** your household will G4246
Ac 11:23 encouraged *them* **a** to remain true to G4246
Ac 11:23 to remain true to the Lord *with a* their **hearts**. AIT
Ac 13:10 You are full of **a** *kinds of* deceit and G4246
Ac 13:20 **A** this took about 450 years. "After this, God NDT
Ac 13:24 baptism *to* **a** the people of Israel. G4246
Ac 13:29 they had carried out **a** that was written G4246
Ac 13:48 **a** who were appointed for eternal life G4012
Ac 14:16 he let **a** nations go their own way. G4246
Ac 14:27 reported *a* **that** God had done through AIT
Ac 15: 3 This news made **a** the believers very glad G4246
Ac 15:17 even **a** the Gentiles who bear my name G4246
Ac 15:25 So **we** *a* agreed to choose some men and AIT
Ac 15:36 the believers in **a** the towns where we G4246
Ac 16: 3 they **a** knew that his father was a Greek. G570
Ac 16:26 At once **a** the prison doors flew open, and G4246
Ac 16:28 "Don't harm yourself! We are **a** here!" G570
Ac 16:32 the Lord to him and *to* **a** the others in his G4246
Ac 16:33 he and **a** his household were G4246
Ac 17: 6 trouble **a over** the **world** have now come G3876
Ac 17: 7 They are **a** defying Caesar's decrees G4246
Ac 17:21 **A** the Athenians and the foreigners who G4246
Ac 17:26 From one man he made **a** the nations G4246
Ac 17:30 now he commands **a** people everywhere G4246
Ac 18: 2 had ordered **a** Jews to leave Rome. G4246
Ac 18:23 Phrygia, strengthening **a** the disciples. G4246
Ac 19: 7 There were about twelve men *in* **a**. G4246
Ac 19:10 so that **a** the Jews and Greeks who lived G4246
Ac 19:16 jumped on them and overpowered *them* **a**. G317
Ac 19:17 Ephesus, they were **a** seized with fear G4246
Ac 19:21 After *a* **this** had happened, Paul decided to AIT
Ac 19:26 made by human hands are **no** gods **at a**. G4024
Ac 19:29 **a** of them rushed into the theater **together** G3924
Ac 19:34 they **a** shouted in unison for about two G4246
Ac 19:35 doesn't **a** the world know that the city of G5515
Ac 20:28 over yourselves and **a** the flock of which G4246
Ac 20:32 an inheritance among **a** those who are G4246
Ac 20:36 he knelt down with **a** of them and prayed. G4246
Ac 20:37 They **a** wept as they embraced him and G4246
Ac 21: 5 **A** *of them*, including wives and children G4246
Ac 21:18 and **a** the elders were present. G4246
Ac 21:20 and **a** *of them* are zealous for the law. G4246
Ac 21:21 that you teach **a** the Jews who live among G4246
Ac 21:30 people came **running from a directions**. G5282
Ac 21:40 When they were **a** silent, he said to them G4498
Ac 22: 5 as the high priest and **a** the Council can G4246
Ac 22:10 you will be told **a** that you have been G4246
Ac 22:12 highly respected by **a** the Jews living G4246
Ac 22:15 be his witness to **a** people of what you G4246
Ac 22:30 chief priests and **a** the members of the G4246
Ac 23: 1 my duty to God in **a** good conscience to G4246
Ac 23: 8 the Pharisees believe **a** these **things**.) G317
Ac 24: 5 up riots among the Jews **a** over the world. G4246
Ac 24: 8 the truth about **a** these charges we are G4246
Ac 25:24 Agrippa, and **a** who are present with us G4246
Ac 25:26 Therefore I have brought him before *a of* **you**, AIT
Ac 26: 2 my defense against **a** the accusations of G4246
Ac 26: 3 well acquainted *with* **a** the Jewish G4246
Ac 26: 4 "The Jewish people **a** know the way I G4246
Ac 26: 9 ought to do **a** *that was possible* to oppose G4498
Ac 26:14 We **a** fell to the ground, and I heard a G4246
Ac 26:20 to those in Jerusalem and *in* **a** Judea, G4246
Ac 26:29 not only you but **a** who are listening to G4246
Ac 27:20 we finally gave up **a** hope of being saved. G4246
Ac 27:24 given you the lives of **a** who sail with you. G4246
Ac 27:33 Just before dawn Paul urged *them* **a** to eat G570
Ac 27:35 gave thanks to God in front of *them* **a**. G4246
Ac 27:36 They were **a** encouraged and ate some G4246
Ac 28: 2 fire and welcomed us **a** because it was G4246
Ac 28:30 house and welcomed **a** who came to see G4246
Ac 28:31 with **a** boldness and without hindrance! G4246
Ro 1: 5 apostleship to call **a** the Gentiles to the G4246
Ro 1: 7 *To* **a** in Rome who are loved by God and G4246
Ro 1: 8 my God through Jesus Christ for **a** of you, G4246
Ro 1: 8 faith is being reported **a** over the world. G3910
Ro 1:10 in my prayers **at a times**; and I pray that G4121
Ro 1:18 heaven against **a** the godlessness and G4246
Ro 2:12 **A** who sin apart from the law will also G4012
Ro 2:12 **a** who sin under the law will be G4012
Ro 3: 2 **First of a**, the Jews have been entrusted G4754
Ro 3: 4 **Not at a**! Let God be true, and every G3590+1181
Ro 3: 9 any advantage? Not **at a**! For we have G4122
Ro 3: 9 Gentiles alike are **a** under the power of G4246
Ro 3:12 **A** have turned away, they have together G4246
Ro 3:22 faith in Jesus Christ to **a** who believe. G4246
Ro 3:23 **a** have sinned and fall short of the G4246
Ro 3:24 and *a* **are justified** freely by his grace through AIT
Ro 3:31 law by this faith? **Not at a**! Rather, G3590+1181
Ro 4:11 he is the father *of* **a** who believe but have G4246
Ro 4:16 may be guaranteed *to* **a** Abraham's G4246
Ro 4:16 faith of Abraham. He is the father *of* us **a**. G4246
Ro 4:18 Against **a** hope, Abraham in hope believed NDT
Ro 5:12 in this way death came to **a** people G4246
Ro 5:12 came to all people, because **a** sinned— G4246
Ro 5:18 resulted in condemnation for **a** people, G4246

Ro 5:18 in justification and life for **a** people. G4246
Ro 5:20 increased, grace **increased a the more,** G5668
Ro 6: 3 Or don't you know that **a** of us who were G4012
Ro 6:10 he died to sin **once for a**; but the life he G2384
Ro 8:24 But hope that is seen is **no** hope *at a*. Who AIT
Ro 8:28 we know that *in* **a** *things* God works for G4246
Ro 8:32 gave him up for us **a**—how will he not G4246
Ro 8:32 graciously give us **a things**? G3836+4246
Ro 8:36 "For your sake we face death **a** day *long* G3910
Ro 8:37 in **a** these things we are more than G4246
Ro 8:39 anything else *in a* **creation**, will be able AIT
Ro 9: 5 who is God over **a**, forever praised! G4246
Ro 9: 6 For not **a** who are descended from Israel G4246
Ro 9: 7 descendants are *they* **a** Abraham's G4246
Ro 9:14 Is God unjust? **Not at a**! G3590+1181
Ro 9:17 name might be proclaimed in **a** the earth." G4246
Ro 10:12 same Lord is Lord *of* **a** and richly blesses G4246
Ro 10:12 all and richly blesses **a** who call on him, G4246
Ro 10:16 But not **a** the Israelites accepted the good G4246
Ro 10:18 "Their voice has gone out into **a** the earth, G4246
Ro 10:21 "**A** day *long* I have held out my hands to G3910
Ro 11:11 beyond recovery? **Not at a**! Rather, G3590+1181
Ro 11:24 **After a**, if you were cut out of an olive tree G1142
Ro 11:26 in this way **a** Israel will be saved. As it G4246
Ro 11:32 so that he may have mercy *on* them **a**. G4246
Ro 11:36 him and for him are **a things**. G3836+4246
Ro 12: 4 these members do not **a** have the same G4246
Ro 12: 5 each member *belongs to a the* **others**. AIT
Ro 14:10 For we will **a** stand before God's G4246
Ro 14:20 **A** food is clean, but it is wrong for **a** G4246
Ro 15:11 "Praise the Lord, **a** you Gentiles; let all G4246
Ro 15:11 you Gentiles; let **a** the peoples extol him." G4246
Ro 15:13 hope fill you with **a** joy and peace as you G4246
Ro 15:19 Jerusalem **a the way** around to Illyricum, G3588
Ro 15:33 The God of peace be with you **a**. Amen. G4246
Ro 16: 4 Not only I but **a** the churches of the G4246
Ro 16:15 Olympas and **a** the Lord's people G4246
Ro 16:16 **A** the churches of Christ send greetings G4246
Ro 16:26 so that **a** the Gentiles might come to the G4246
1Co 1: 2 together with **a** those everywhere who call G4246
1Co 1: 5 with **a** *kinds of* speech and with all G4246
1Co 1: 5 kinds of speech and with **a** knowledge— G4246
1Co 1:10 that **a** of you agree with one another in G4246
1Co 2:10 The Spirit searches **a** *things*, even the G4246
1Co 2:15 Spirit makes judgments about **a** *things*, G4246
1Co 3: 5 **after a**, is Apollos? And what is G4036
1Co 3:21 about human leaders! **A** *things* are yours, G4246
1Co 3:22 the present or the future—**a** are yours, G4246
1Co 4: 8 Already *you* **have a** *you* **want** G3170+1639
1Co 5:10 not **at a** meaning the people of this world G4122
1Co 6:18 **A** *other* sins a person commits are outside G4246
1Co 7: 7 I wish that **a** of you were as I am. But each G4246
1Co 7:17 is the rule I lay down in **a** the churches. G4246
1Co 8: 1 We know that "We **a** possess knowledge." G4246
1Co 8: 4 that "An idol is **nothing at a** in the world" G4029
1Co 8: 6 from whom **a things** came and for G3836+4246
1Co 8: 6 through whom **a things** came and G3836+4246
1Co 8:10 with *a* your **knowledge**, eating in an AIT
1Co 9:12 shouldn't we have it **a the more?** G3437
1Co 9:22 I have become **a** *things* to all people so G4246
1Co 9:22 all things *to* **a** *people* so that by all G4246
1Co 9:22 so that **by a possible means** I might save G4122
1Co 9:23 I do **a** *this* for the sake of the gospel, that I G4246
1Co 9:24 not know that in a race **a** the runners run, G4246
1Co 10: 1 our ancestors were **a** under the cloud and G4246
1Co 10: 1 cloud and that they **a** passed through the G4246
1Co 10: 2 They were **a** baptized into Moses in the G4246
1Co 10: 3 They **a** ate the same spiritual food G4246
1Co 10:17 are one body, for we **a** share the one loaf. G4246
1Co 10:31 do *it* **a** for the glory of God. G4246
1Co 11:33 gather to eat, you should **a** eat together. G253
1Co 12: 6 *in* **a** of them and in everyone it is the G4246
1Co 12:11 **A** these are the work of one and the same G4246
1Co 12:12 but **a** its many parts form one body G4246
1Co 12:13 For we were **a** baptized by one Spirit so as G4246
1Co 12:13 we were **a** given the one Spirit to G4246
1Co 12:19 If they were **a** one part, where would the G4246
1Co 12:28 placed in the church **first of a** apostles, G4754
1Co 12:29 Are **a** apostles? Are all prophets? Are all G4246
1Co 12:29 Are all apostles? Are **a** prophets? Are all G4246
1Co 12:29 Are **a** teachers? Do all work G4246
1Co 12:29 Are all teachers? Do **a** work miracles? G4246
1Co 12:30 Do **a** have gifts of healing? Do all speak in G4246
1Co 12:30 Do **a** speak in tongues? Do G4246
1Co 12:30 Do all speak in tongues? Do **a** interpret? G4246
1Co 13: 2 can fathom **a** mysteries and all G4246
1Co 13: 2 fathom all mysteries and **a** knowledge, G4246
1Co 13: 3 If I give **a** I possess to the poor and give G4246
1Co 14:10 there are **a** sorts of languages G5537
1Co 14:18 I speak in tongues more *than* **a** of you. G4246
1Co 14:24 sin and are brought under judgment by **a**, G4246
1Co 14:31 For you can **a** prophesy in turn so that G4246
1Co 14:33 as in **a** the congregations of the Lord's G4246
1Co 15: 7 to James, then *to* **a** the apostles, G4246
1Co 15: 8 last *of* **a** he appeared to me also, as G4246
1Co 15:10 I worked harder than **a** of them—yet not I, G4246
1Co 15:19 we are *of* **a** people most to be pitied. G4246
1Co 15:22 For as in Adam **a** die, so in Christ all will G4246
1Co 15:22 so in Christ **a** will be made alive. G4246
1Co 15:24 Father after he has destroyed **a** dominion, G4246
1Co 15:25 until he has put **a** his enemies under his G4246
1Co 15:28 under him, so that God may be **a** in all. G4246
1Co 15:28 under him, so that God may be all in **a**. G4246
1Co 15:29 If the dead are not raised **at a**, why are G3914
1Co 15:39 Not **a** flesh is the same: People have one G4246
1Co 15:51 We will not **a** sleep, but we will all be G4246
1Co 15:51 not all sleep, but we will **a** be changed— G4246
1Co 16:20 **A** the brothers and sisters here send you G4246
1Co 16:24 My love to **a** of you in Christ Jesus. Amen. G4246
2Co 1: 1 together with **a** his holy people G4246
2Co 1: 3 of compassion and the God of **a** comfort, G4246
2Co 1: 4 who comforts us in **a** our troubles, so that G4246
2Co 2: 3 I had confidence in **a** of you, that you G4246
2Co 2: 3 all of you, that you would **a** share my joy. G4246
2Co 2: 5 me as he has grieved **a** of you to some G4246
2Co 3:18 And we **a**, who with unveiled faces G4246
2Co 4:15 **A** this is for your benefit, so that the grace G4246
2Co 4:17 glory *that* **far outweighs them a** G2848+5651+1650+5651+983
2Co 5:10 For we must **a** appear before the judgment G4246
2Co 5:14 we are convinced that one died for **a**, G4246
2Co 5:14 one died for all, and therefore **a** died. G4246
2Co 5:15 And he died for **a**, that those who live G4246
2Co 5:18 **A** this is from God, who reconciled us to G4246
2Co 7: 4 in **a** our troubles my joy knows no bounds. G4246
2Co 7:13 By *a* **this** we are encouraged. In addition to AIT
2Co 7:13 his spirit has been refreshed by **a** of you. G4246
2Co 7:15 you is **a the greater** when he G4359
2Co 7:15 he remembers that you were **a** obedient, G4246
2Co 8: 5 gave themselves **first of a** to the Lord, G4754
2Co 8:18 who is praised by **a** the churches for his G4246
2Co 9: 8 so that in **a** *things* at all times, having G4246
2Co 9: 8 so that in all things **at a times**, having all G4121
2Co 9: 8 at all times, having **a** that you need, you G4246
2Co 11:28 pressure of my concern *for* **a** the churches. G4246
2Co 12: 9 I will boast **a the more** gladly about my G3437
2Co 12:14 **After a**, children should not have to save G1142
2Co 12:19 you been thinking **a along** that we have G4093
2Co 13:13 **A** God's people here send their greetings. G4246
2Co 13:14 of the Holy Spirit be with you **a**. G4246
Gal 1: 2 **a** the brothers and sisters with me, To G4246
Gal 1: 7 which is really **no** gospel **at a**. Evidently G4024
Gal 2:10 **A** they asked was that we should continue G3667
Gal 2:10 very thing *I had been* **eager** to do *a along*. AIT
Gal 2:14 I said to Cephas in front of *them* **a**, "You G4246
Gal 3: 8 "**A** nations will be blessed through you." G4246
Gal 3:10 For **a** *who* rely on the works of the law are G4012
Gal 3:19 was the law given at **a**? It was added NDT
Gal 3:26 Christ Jesus you are **a** children of God G4246
Gal 3:27 for **a** *of* you who were baptized into Christ G4012
Gal 3:28 female, for you are **a** one in Christ Jesus. G4246
Gal 4: 9 be enslaved by them **a over again**? G4099+540
Gal 5: 2 Christ will be of **no** value to you **at a**. G4029
Gal 6: 6 the word should share **a** good things with G4246
Gal 6:10 let us do good to **a** *people*, especially to G4246
Gal 6:16 Peace and mercy *to* **a** who follow this rule G4012
Eph 1: 8 With **a** wisdom and understanding G4246
Eph 1:10 to bring unity *to* **a things** in heaven G3836+4246
Eph 1:15 Jesus and your love for **a** God's people, G4246
Eph 1:21 far above **a** rule and authority, power and G4246
Eph 1:22 And God placed **a** *things* under his feet G4246
Eph 2: 3 **A** of us also lived among them at one G4246
Eph 3: 8 less than the least *of* **a** the Lord's people, G4246
Eph 3: 9 in God, who created **a things**. G3836+4246
Eph 3:18 together with **a** the Lord's holy people G4246
Eph 3:19 to the measure of **a** the fullness of God. G4246
Eph 3:20 more than **a** we ask or imagine, G4246
Eph 3:21 in Christ Jesus throughout **a** generations, G4246
Eph 4: 6 one God and Father *of* **a**, who is over all G4246
Eph 4: 6 who is over **a** and through all and in all. G4246
Eph 4: 6 who is over all and through **a** and in all. G4246
Eph 4: 6 who is over all and through all and in **a**. G4246
Eph 4:10 who ascended higher *than* **a** the heavens, G4246
Eph 4:13 we **a** reach unity in the faith and in G4246
Eph 4:19 *Having* **lost a sensitivity**, they have given G556
Eph 4:25 neighbor, for *we* **are** *a* members of one body. AIT
Eph 4:31 Get rid of **a** bitterness, rage and anger G4246
Eph 5: 9 fruit of the light consists in **a** goodness, G4246
Eph 5:29 **After a**, no one ever hated their own body G1142
Eph 6:16 In addition to **a** *this*, take up the shield of G4246
Eph 6:16 you can extinguish **a** the flaming arrows G4246
Eph 6:18 pray in the Spirit on **a** occasions with all G4246
Eph 6:18 all occasions with **a** *kinds of* prayers and G4246
Eph 6:18 keep on praying for **a** the Lord's people. G4246
Eph 6:24 Grace to **a** who love our Lord Jesus Christ G4246
Php 1: 1 *To* **a** God's holy people in Christ Jesus at G4246
Php 1: 4 In **a** my prayers for all of you, I always pray G4246
Php 1: 4 In all my prayers for **a** of you, I always pray G4246
Php 1: 7 me to feel this way about **a** of you, G4246
Php 1: 7 **a** of you share in God's grace with me. G4246
Php 1: 8 testify how I long for **a** of you with the G4246
Php 1:14 Lord and dare **a the more** to proclaim the G4359
Php 1:25 I will continue *with* **a** of you for your G4246
Php 2:17 I am glad and rejoice with **a** of you. G4246
Php 2:26 For he longs for **a** of you and is distressed G4246
Php 2:28 Therefore *I am* **a the more eager** to send G5081
Php 3: 8 whose sake I have lost **a things**. G3836+4246
Php 3:12 Not that I have already obtained **a** this, or NDT
Php 3:15 **A** *of us*, then, who are mature should take G4012
Php 4: 5 Let your gentleness be evident *to* **a** G4246+476
Php 4: 7 which transcends **a** understanding, will G4246
Php 4:13 I can do **a** *this* through him who gives me G4246
Php 4:19 And my God will meet **a** your needs G4246
Php 4:21 Greet **a** God's people in Christ Jesus. The G4246
Php 4:22 **A** God's people here send you greetings G4246
Col 1: 4 of the love you have for **a** God's people— G4246
Col 1: 9 of his will through **a** the wisdom and G4246
Col 1:11 strengthened with **a** power according to G4246
Col 1:15 the firstborn over **a** creation. G4246
Col 1:16 For in him **a things** were created G3836+4246
Col 1:16 **a things** have been created G3836+4246
Col 1:17 He is before **a** *things*, and in him all G4246
Col 1:17 and in him **a things** hold together. G3836+4246
Col 1:19 was pleased to have **a** his fullness dwell G4246
Col 1:20 to reconcile to himself **a things,** G3836+4246
Col 1:28 teaching everyone with **a** wisdom, G4246
Col 1:29 contend with *a the* **energy** Christ so AIT
Col 2: 1 and *for* **a** who have not met me G4012
Col 2: 3 in whom are hidden **a** the treasures of G4246
Col 2: 9 For in Christ **a** the fullness of the Deity G4246
Col 2:13 alive with Christ. He forgave us **a** our sins, G4246
Col 2:22 with things that are **a** destined to perish G4246
Col 3: 8 of **a** *such* **things** *as these*: G3836+4246
Col 3:11 free, but Christ is **a**, and is in all. G3836+4246
Col 3:11 slave or free, but Christ is all, and is in **a**. G4246
Col 3:14 And over **a** these virtues put on love G4246
Col 3:14 which binds them **a** together in perfect unity. NDT
Col 3:16 one another with **a** wisdom through G4246
Col 3:17 do it **a** in the name of the Lord Jesus G4246
Col 3:23 work at it with *a* your **heart**, as working for AIT
Col 4: 7 will tell you **a** the news about me. G4246
Col 4:12 you may stand firm in **a** the will of God, G4246
1Th 1: 2 always thank God for **a** of you and G4246
1Th 1: 7 you became a model *to* **a** the believers in G4246
1Th 3: 7 in **a** our distress and persecution we were G4246
1Th 3: 9 you in return for **a** the joy we have in G4246
1Th 3:13 Lord Jesus comes with **a** his holy ones. G4246
1Th 4: 6 Lord will punish **a** *those* who commit such G4246
1Th 4:10 you do love **a** of God's family throughout G4246
1Th 5: 5 You are **a** children of the light and G4246
1Th 5:18 give thanks in **a** *circumstances*; for this is G4246
1Th 5:21 test *them* **a**; hold on to what is good, G4246
1Th 5:26 Greet **a** God's people with a holy kiss. G4246
1Th 5:27 have this letter read *to* **a** the brothers and G4246
2Th 1: 3 the love **a** of you have for one G4246
2Th 1: 4 faith in **a** the persecutions and G4246
2Th 1: 5 **A** this is evidence that God's judgment is NDT
2Th 1:10 be marveled at among **a** those who have G4246
2Th 2: 9 He will use **a** *sorts of* displays of power G4246
2Th 2:10 **a** *the ways* that wickedness deceives G4246
2Th 2:12 so that **a** will be condemned who G4246
2Th 3:16 you peace **at a times** and in every G1328+4246
2Th 3:16 The Lord be with **a** of you. G4246
2Th 3:17 is the distinguishing mark in **a** my letters. G4246
2Th 3:18 of our Lord Jesus Christ be with you **a**. G4246
1Ti 2: 1 then, first *of* **a**, that petitions G4246
1Ti 2: 1 thanksgiving be made for **a** people— G4246
1Ti 2: 2 kings and **a** those in authority, that we G4246
1Ti 2: 2 quiet lives in **a** godliness and G4246
1Ti 2: 4 who wants **a** people to be saved and to G4246
1Ti 2: 6 gave himself as a ransom for **a** *people*. G4246
1Ti 3:16 **Beyond a question**, the mystery from G3935
1Ti 4: 8 godliness has value for **a** *things* G4246
1Ti 4:10 who is the Savior of **a** people, and G4246
1Ti 5: 4 these should learn **first of a** to put their G4754
1Ti 5: 5 in need and **left a alone** puts her hope in G3670
1Ti 5:10 devoting herself to **a** *kinds of* good deeds. G4246
1Ti 6: 1 **A** who are under the yoke of slavery G4012
1Ti 6:10 love of money is a root *of* **a** *kinds* of evil. G4246
1Ti 6:11 man of God, flee *from a* **this**, and pursue AIT
1Ti 6:21 departed from the faith. Grace be with **you** *a*. AIT
2Ti 2: 7 the Lord will give you insight into **a** *this*. G4246
2Ti 3: 6 are swayed by **a kinds** *of* evil desires, G4476
2Ti 3:10 however, **know a about** my teaching, my G4158
2Ti 3:11 Yet the Lord rescued me from **a** *of them*. G4246
2Ti 3:16 **A** Scripture is God-breathed and is useful G4246
2Ti 4: 5 keep your head in **a** *situations*, endure G4246
2Ti 4: 5 **discharge a the duties** of your ministry. G4442
2Ti 4: 8 also *to* **a** who have longed for his G4246
2Ti 4:17 fully proclaimed and **a** the Gentiles might G4246
2Ti 4:21 Claudia and **a** the brothers and sisters. G4246
2Ti 4:22 Lord be with your spirit. Grace be with **you** *a*. AIT
Titus 1:15 To the pure, **a** *things* are pure, but to G4246
Titus 2:11 that offers salvation to **a** people. G4246
Titus 2:14 us to redeem us from **a** wickedness and to G4246
Titus 2:15 Encourage and rebuke with **a** authority G4246
Titus 3: 3 enslaved by **a kinds** *of* passions and G4476
Titus 3:15 love us in the faith. Grace be with you **a**. G4246
Phm 5 about your love for **a** his holy people and G4246
Heb 1: 2 whom he appointed heir *of* **a** *things*, and G4246
Heb 1: 3 sustaining **a things** by his powerful G3836+4246
Heb 1: 6 he says, "Let **a** God's angels worship him." G4246
Heb 1:11 they will **a** wear out like a garment. G4246
Heb 1:14 Are not **a** angels ministering spirits sent G4246
Heb 2:15 free those who **a** their lives were held G4246
Heb 3: 2 as Moses was faithful in **a** God's house. G3910
Heb 3: 5 faithful as a servant in **a** God's house," G3910
Heb 3:16 Were they not **a** those Moses led out of G4246
Heb 4: 4 seventh day God rested from **a** his works." G4246
Heb 4:13 Nothing *in a* **creation** is hidden from God's AIT
Heb 5: 9 of eternal salvation *for* **a** who obey him G4246
Heb 5:12 truths of God's word **a over again**. G4099
Heb 6: 6 *they are* **crucifying** the Son of God **a over again** G416
Heb 6:16 is said and puts an end to **a** argument. G4246
Heb 7:27 their sins **once for a** when he offered G2384

Heb 7:28 as high priests men **in a** their weakness; G2400
Heb 8:11 ' because they will **a** know me, from the G4246
Heb 9:12 Most Holy Place **once for a** by his own G2384
Heb 9:19 command of the law to **a** the people, G4246
Heb 9:19 sprinkled the scroll and **a** the people. G4246
Heb 9:26 he has appeared **once for a** at the G562
Heb 10: 2 would have been cleansed **once for a**, G562
Heb 10:10 of the body of Jesus Christ **once for a**. G2384
Heb 10:12 had offered **for a time** one G1650+3836+1457
Heb 10:25 and **a the more** as you see the Day G5537+3437
Heb 11:13 **A** these people were still living by faith G4246
Heb 11:39 These were **a** commended for their faith G4246
Heb 12: 8 not true sons and daughters **at a**. G2779
Heb 12: 9 we *have a* **had** human fathers who AIT
Heb 12:23 the Judge *of* **a**, to the spirits of G4246
Heb 13: 4 Marriage should be honored by **a**, and G4246
Heb 13: 4 the adulterer and *a* the **sexually immoral**. AIT
Heb 13: 9 carried away by **a kinds of** strange G4476
Heb 13:24 Greet **a** your leaders and all the Lord's G4246
Heb 13:24 all your leaders and **a** the Lord's people. G4246
Heb 13:25 Grace be with you **a**. G4246
Jas 1: 5 who gives generously *to* **a** without finding G4246
Jas 1: 8 unstable in **a** they do. G4246
Jas 1:18 might be a kind of firstfruits *of a* he **created**. AIT
Jas 1:21 get rid of **a** moral filth and the evil that is G4246
Jas 2:10 just one point is guilty *of* breaking **a** of it. G4246
Jas 3: 2 We **a** stumble in many ways. Anyone who G570
Jas 3: 7 **A** kinds of animals, birds, reptiles and sea G4246
Jas 3:17 that comes from heaven is **first** *of a* pure; AIT
Jas 4:16 arrogant schemes. **A** such boasting is evil. G4246
Jas 5:12 Above **a**, my brothers and sisters, do not G4246
Jas 5:12 *A* you *need to* **say** is a simple "Yes AIT
1Pe 1: 6 In *a* **this** you greatly rejoice, though now for a AIT
1Pe 1: 6 have had to suffer grief in **a kinds** of trials. G4476
1Pe 1:15 called you is holy, so be holy in **a** you do; G4246
1Pe 1:24 "**A** people are like grass, and all their G4246
1Pe 1:24 **a** their glory is like the flowers of the G4246
1Pe 2: 1 rid yourselves of **a** malice and all deceit G4246
1Pe 2: 1 rid yourselves of all malice and **a** deceit G4246
1Pe 3: 8 **a** *of you*, be like-minded, be G4246
1Pe 3:20 few people, eight **in a**, were saved G4047+1639
1Pe 4: 7 The end *of* **a** *things* is near. Therefore be G4246
1Pe 4: 8 Above **a**, love each other deeply, because G4246
1Pe 4:11 so that in **a** *things* God may be praised G4246
1Pe 5: 5 **A** of you, clothe yourselves with humility G4246
1Pe 5: 7 Cast **a** your anxiety on him because he G4246
1Pe 5:10 And the God of **a** grace, who called you G4246
1Pe 5:14 Peace *to* **a** of you who are in Christ G4246
2Pe 1:20 **Above a**, you must understand that G4047+4754
2Pe 3: 3 **Above a**, you must understand that G4047+4754
2Pe 3:16 He writes the same way in **a** his letters G4246
1Jn 1: 5 in him there is **no** darkness **at a**. G4024+4029
1Jn 1: 7 of Jesus, his Son, purifies us from **a** sin. G4246
1Jn 1: 9 sins and purify us from **a** unrighteousness. G4246
1Jn 2:20 Holy One, and **a** *of* you know the truth. G4246
1Jn 2:27 teaches you about **a** *things* and as that G4246
1Jn 3: 3 **A** who have this hope in him purify G4246
1Jn 5:17 **A** wrongdoing is sin, and there is sin that G4246
2Jn 1 but also **a** who know the truth— G4246
3Jn 2 health and that **a** may go well with you G4246
Jude 3 the faith that was **once for a** entrusted to G562
Jude 5 Though you already know **a** *this*, I want to G4246
Jude 15 to convict **a** of them of all the G4246
Jude 15 of all of them of **a** the ungodly acts they G4246
Jude 15 of **a** the defiant words ungodly G4246
Jude 25 Christ our Lord, before **a** ages, now and G4246
Rev 1: 7 **a** peoples on earth "will mourn G4246
Rev 1:16 was like the sun shining in *a* its **brilliance**. AIT
Rev 2:11 will **not** be hurt **at a** by the second G4024+3590
Rev 2:23 Then **a** the churches will know that I am G4246
Rev 4: 8 was covered with eyes **a around**, G3239
Rev 4:11 you created **a things**, and by G3836+4246
Rev 5: 6 spirits of God sent out into **a** the earth. G4246
Rev 5:13 on the sea, and **a** that is in them G4246
Rev 7: 4 144,000 from **a** the tribes of Israel G4246
Rev 7:11 **A** the angels were standing around the G4246
Rev 8: 3 with the prayers of **a** God's people, on the G4246
Rev 8: 7 and **a** the green grass was burned up. G4246
Rev 8: 8 mountain, **a ablaze**, was thrown G4786+2794
Rev 10: 6 created the heavens and *a* **that** is in them, AIT
Rev 10: 6 the earth and *a* **that** is in it, and the AIT
Rev 10: 6 and the sea and *a* **that** is in it, and said, AIT
Rev 12: 5 who "will rule **a** the nations with an iron G4246
Rev 13: 8 **A** inhabitants of the earth will worship the G4246
Rev 13: 8 *a* **whose** names have not been written in the AIT
Rev 13:12 It exercised **a** the authority of the first G4246
Rev 13:15 speak and cause **a** *who* refused to G4012
Rev 13:16 It also forced **a** *people*, great and small G4246
Rev 14: 8 ' which made **a** the nations drink the G4246
Rev 15: 4 **A** nations will come and worship before G4246
Rev 18: 3 For **a** the nations have drunk the G4246
Rev 18:14 **A** your luxury and splendor have vanished, G4246
Rev 18:17 sea captain, and **a** who travel by ship, the G4246
Rev 18:17 **a** who earn their living from the sea G4012
Rev 18:19 where **a** who had ships on the sea G4246
Rev 18:23 By your magic spell **a** the nations were G4246
Rev 18:24 of **a** who have been slaughtered on the G4246
Rev 19: 5 "Praise our God, **a** you his servants, you G4246
Rev 19:17 in a loud voice *to* **a** the birds flying in G4246
Rev 19:18 the flesh *of* **a** *people*, free and slave, G4246
Rev 19:21 **a** the birds gorged themselves on G4246
Rev 21: 7 Those who are victorious will inherit *a* **this** AIT
Rev 21: 8 the idolaters and **a** liars—they will be G4246
Rev 22: 9 prophets and *with a* who **keep** the words of AIT

ALL-NIGHT (1) [NIGHT]

Jos 10: 9 After an **a** march from Gilgal H3972+2021+4326

ALL-SURPASSING (1) [SURPASS]

2Co 4: 7 to show that this **a** power is from God G5651

ALLAMMELECH (NIV84) ALLAMMELEK

ALLAMMELEK (1)

Jos 19:26 **A**, Amad and Mishal. On the west the H526

ALLEGEDLY (1)

2Th 2: 2 alarmed by the teaching **a** from us— G6055

ALLEGIANCE (4) [ALLY]

1Ki 12:27 they *will* **again give** their **a** to their H8740+4213
Isa 19:18 of Canaan and **swear a** to the LORD H8678
Eze 21:23 to those *who have* **sworn a** to him, H8678+8652
Ro 6:17 of teaching that *has now* **claimed** *your* **a**. G4140

ALLEGORY (1)

Eze 17: 2 set forth an **a** and tell it to the Israelites H2648

ALLELUIA (KJV) HALLELUJAH

ALLEYS (1)

Lk 14:21 into the streets and **a** of the town and G4860

ALLIANCE (9) [ALLY]

Jdg 4:17 there was an **a** between Jabin king H8934
1Ki 3: 1 Solomon **made an a** with Pharaoh king of H3161
2Ch 20:35 king of Judah **made an a** with Ahaziah H2489
2Ch 20:37 "Because you *have* **made an a** with H2489
Ps 83: 5 together; they form an **a** against you— H1382
Isa 30: 1 not mine, **forming an a**, but not by H5818+5011
Jer 50: 9 against Babylon an **a** *of* great nations H7736
Da 11: 6 go to the king of the North to make an **a**, H4797
Da 11:17 will make an **a** with the king of the H3838

ALLIANCES (1) [ALLY]

Hos 10: 6 Israel will be ashamed of its *foreign* **a**. H6783

ALLIED (8) [ALLY]

Ge 14: 5 the kings **a with** him went out and H907
Ge 14:13 all of whom were **a** *with* Abram. H1251+1382
Ge 14:17 Kedorlaomer and the kings **a with** him, H907
Jos 13:21 Hur and Reba—**princes** *a with* Sihon—who AIT
1Ki 20:16 the 32 kings **a with** him were in their H6468
2Ch 18: 1 and *he* **a himself** with Ahab **by marriage**. H3161
Ps 94:20 *Can* a corrupt throne *be* **a with** you—a H2489
Isa 7: 2 "Aram *has* **a** *itself* with Ephraim" H5663

ALLIES (14) [ALLY]

Jos 10: 1 and *had* **become** their **a**. H2118+928+7931
1Ch 5:20 and all their **a** into their hands, H8611+6640S
Jer 13:21 you those you cultivated as your special **a**? H476
Jer 22:20 out from Abarim, for all your **a** are crushed. H170
Jer 22:22 and your **a** will go into exile. H170
Jer 30:14 All your **a** have forgotten you; they care H170
Jer 49:10 destroyed, also his **a** and neighbors, so H278
La 1:19 "I called to my **a** but they betrayed me. My H170
Eze 30: 6 " 'The **a** *of* Egypt will fall and her proud H6164
Eze 32:21 leaders will say of Egypt and her **a**, H6468
Da 11: 6 some years, *they will become* **a**. The H2489
Ob 7 All your **a** will force you to the H408+1382
Na 1:12 "Although *they have* **a** and are numerous H8969
Na 3: 9 Put and Libya were among her **a**. H6476

ALLOCATE (1)

Jos 13: 6 Be sure *to* **a** this land to Israel for an H5877

ALLON (1)

1Ch 4:37 of Shiphi, the son of **A**, the son of Jedaiah, H474

ALLON BACUTH (1)

Ge 35: 8 outside Bethel. So it was named **A**. H475

ALLOT (3) [ALLOTMENT, ALLOTS, ALLOTTED, ALLOTTING]

Eze 45: 1 " 'When you **a** the land as an inheritance H5877
Eze 47:22 *You are to* **a** it as an inheritance for H5877
Eze 48:29 is the land *you are to* **a** as an inheritance H5877

ALLOTMENT (13) [ALLOT]

Ge 47:22 they received a **regular a** from Pharaoh H2976
Ge 47:22 enough from the **a** Pharaoh gave them. H2976
Dt 12:12 towns who have no **a** or inheritance of H2750
Dt 14:27 they have no **a** or inheritance of their H2750
Dt 14:29 who have no **a** or inheritance of their own H2750
Dt 18: 1 are to have no **a** or inheritance with Israel. H2750
Jos 15: 1 The **a** for the tribe of Judah, according to H1598
Jos 16: 1 The **a** for Joseph began at the Jordan H1598
Jos 17: 1 This was the **a** for the tribe of Manasseh H1598
Jos 17: 2 So this **a** was for the rest of the people of NDT
Jos 17:14 given us only one **a** and one portion for H1598
Jos 17:17 You will have not only one **a** H1598
Eze 48:13 Levites will have an **a** 25,000 cubits long NDT

ALLOTS (4) [ALLOT]

Job 20:29 Such is the fate God **a** the wicked, the H4946
Job 21:17 upon them, the fate God **a** in his anger? H2745
Job 27:13 "Here is the fate God **a to** the wicked, the H6640
Isa 34:17 He **a** their portions; his hand distributes H5877

ALLOTTED (32) [ALLOT]

Lev 7:35 **portion** of the food offerings presented to the LORD that were *a to* AIT
Nu 26:53 "The land *is to* **be a** to them as an H2745
Nu 34: 2 the land that *will be* **a** to you as an H5877
Nu 36: 3 of the inheritance **a** to us will be taken H1598
Dt 32: 9 is his people, Jacob his **a** inheritance. H2475
Jos 14: 1 of the tribal clans of Israel **a** *to* them. H5706
Jos 18:11 Their **a** territory lay between the tribes of H1598
Jos 19:49 dividing the land into its **a portions**, H1474
Jos 21: 4 priest *were* **a** thirteen H2118+1598+928+2021
Jos 21: 5 were **a** ten towns from H928+2021+1598
Jos 21: 6 Gershon were **a** thirteen H928+2021+1598
Jos 21: 8 Israelites **a** to the Levites H5989+928+2021+1598
Jos 21: 9 of Judah and Simeon *they* **a** the following H5989
Jos 21:20 the Levites *were* **a** towns from the H2118+1598
Jos 21:40 number of towns **a** to the Merarite H2118+1598
Jos 23: 4 Remember how *I have* **a** as an inheritance H5877
Jos 24:33 which *had* **been a** to his son Phinehas in H5989
Jdg 1: 3 "Come up with us into the **territory a** *to* us H1598
1Sa 18:26 So before the **a time** elapsed, H3427
1Ch 6:54 of their settlements **a** as their **territory** H1473
1Ch 6:61 were **a** ten towns from H928+2021+1598
1Ch 6:62 were **a** thirteen towns from the tribes of H4200
1Ch 6:63 were **a** twelve towns from the H928+2021+1598
1Ch 6:65 and Benjamin *they* **a** the H5989+928+2021+1598
Ne 5:14 my brothers ate the **food** *a to* the governor. AIT
Ne 5:18 I never demanded the **food** *a to* the governor, AIT
Job 7: 3 so I *have* **been a** months of futility, and H5706
Job 21:21 behind when their **a** months come to an H5031
Ps 78:55 them and **a** their lands *to* them as an H5877
Ps 125: 3 remain over the *land* **a** *to* the righteous, H1598
Eze 47:22 along with you *they are to be* **a** an H5877
Da 12:13 you will rise to receive your **a inheritance**."H1598

ALLOTTING (1) [ALLOT]

Ne 9:22 **a** *to* them even the remotest frontiers. H2745

ALLOW (19) [ALLOWANCE, ALLOWED, ALLOWING, ALLOWS]

Ex 10:25 "You *must* **a** us to have sacrifices and H5989
Ex 22:18 "*Do* not **a** a sorceress **to live**. H2649
Nu 33:55 those *you* **a to remain** will become barbs H3855
Nu 35:32 refuge and so **a** them *to* **go back** and live on AIT
Jdg 6:39 *A me* one more **test** with the fleece, but this AIT
1Sa 16:22 "*A* David *to* **remain** in my service, for AIT
1Sa 24: 7 his men and *did* not **a** them to attack H5989
2Ch 20:10 whose territory *you would* not **a** Israel to H5989
Job 11:14 hand and **a** no evil **to dwell** in your tent H8905
Ps 132: 4 *I will* **a** no sleep to my eyes or slumber to H5989
Pr 6: 4 **A** no sleep to your eyes, no slumber to H5989
Jer 13:14 *I will* **a** no **pity** or mercy or compassion to H2798
Eze 45: 8 but *will* **a** the people of Israel **to possess** H5989
Mk 5:12 us among the pigs; **a** us to go into them." G2671
Mk 11:16 and *would* not **a** anyone to carry G918
Lk 4:41 them and *would* not **a** them to speak, G1572
Ac 16: 7 the Spirit of Jesus *would* not **a** them to. G1572
Ac 27: 7 *When* the wind *did* not **a** us **to hold our course** G4661
1Co 9:15 rather die than **a** anyone to deprive me NDT

ALLOWANCE (3) [ALLOW]

2Ki 25:30 Jehoiachin a regular **a** as long as he lived. H786
Jer 52:34 Jehoiachin a regular **a** as long as he lived, H786
Lk 12:42 to give them their **food a** at the proper G4991

ALLOWED (29) [ALLOW]

Ge 3:22 He must **not be a** to reach out his hand H7153
Ge 31: 7 However, God *has* not **a** him to harm me. H5989
Ge 46:34 ' Then *you will be* **a** *to* **settle** in the region of AIT
Ge 48:11 now God *has* **a** me **to see** your H8011
Lev 11:34 Any food you *are a* **to eat** that has come into AIT
Lev 11:39 " 'If an animal that you are **a** to eat dies H4200
Nu 31:15 "*Have you* **a** all the women **to live**?" H2649
Dt 7:22 *You will* not *be* **a to** eliminate them all at H3523
Dt 24: 4 *is* not **a** to marry her again after she has H3523
Jdg 2:23 The LORD *had* **a** those nations **to remain** H5663
Jdg 3:28 led to Moab; *they* **a** no one to cross over. H5989
2Sa 8: 2 and the third length *was* **a to live**. H2649
1Ki 1:48 who *has* **a** my eyes to see a successor on H5989
1Ch 16:21 *He* **a** no one to oppress them; for their H5663
2Ch 25:13 back and *had* not *a to* **take part** in the war AIT
2Ch 34:11 the kings of Judah *had* **a to fall into ruin**. H8845
Est 1: 8 each guest *was* **a** to drink with no H401+646
Est 4: 2 one clothed in sackcloth was **a** to enter it. NDT
Job 31:30 *I have* not **a** my mouth to sin by invoking H5989
Ps 105:14 *He* **a** no one to oppress them; for their H5663
Jer 36: 5 *I am* not **a** to go to the LORD's temple. H3523
Eze 33:12 person who sins *will* not *be* **a** to live even H3523
Da 7:12 but **were a** to live for a period of time.) A10314
Ac 27: 3 **a** him to go to his friends so they might G2205
Ac 28: 4 the goddess Justice *has* not **a** him to live." G1572
Ac 28:16 got to Rome, Paul *was* **a** to live by himself G2205
1Co 14:34 They *are* not **a** to speak, but must be in G2205
Rev 9: 5 They *were* not **a** to kill them but only to G1443
Rev 16: 8 the sun *was* **a** to scorch people with G1443

ALLOWING (2) [ALLOW]

Lev 22:16 by **a** them *to* **eat** the sacred offerings and so AIT
Jdg 1:34 not **a** them to come down into the plain. H5989

A

ALLOWS (2) [ALLOW]
Ex 21:22 husband demands and the court a. H5989
Ro 14: 2 One person's faith *a them* to eat anything AIT

ALLURE (1) [ALLURING]
Hos 2:14 "Therefore I *am* now *going to* a her; I will H7331

ALLURING (1) [ALLURE]
Na 3: 4 of a prostitute, a, the mistress of H3202+2834

ALLY (3) [ALLEGIANCE, ALLIANCE, ALLIANCES, ALLIED, ALLIES]
Jos 23:12 you turn away and a *yourselves* with the H1815
Ps 7: 4 if I have repaid my a with evil or without H8966
Isa 48:14 The LORD's chosen a will carry out his H170

ALMIGHTY (345) [MIGHT]
Ge 17: 1 said, "I am God A; walk before me H8724
Ge 28: 3 May God A bless you and make you H8724
Ge 35:11 said to him, "I am God A; be fruitful and H8724
Ge 43:14 And may God A grant you mercy before H8724
Ge 48: 3 "God A appeared to me at Luz in the land H8724
Ge 49:25 because of the A, who blesses you H8724
Ex 6: 3 to Isaac and to Jacob as God A, but by my H8724
Nu 24: 4 who sees a vision from the A, who falls H8724
Nu 24:16 who sees a vision from the A, who falls H8724
Ru 1:20 because the A has made my life very H8724
Ru 1:21 the A has brought misfortune upon me." H8724
1Sa 1: 3 sacrifice to the LORD A at Shiloh, H7372
1Sa 1:11 "LORD A, if you will only look on H7372
1Sa 4: 4 the ark of the covenant of the LORD A, H7372
1Sa 15: 2 is what the LORD A says: 'I will punish H7372
1Sa 17:45 against you in the name of the LORD A, H7372
2Sa 5:10 because the LORD God A was with him. H7372
2Sa 6: 2 the name of the LORD A, who is enthroned H7372
2Sa 6:18 the people in the name of the LORD A. H7372
2Sa 7: 8 'This is what the LORD A says: H7372
2Sa 7:26 will say, 'The LORD A is God over Israel! H7372
2Sa 7:27 "LORD A, God of Israel, you have revealed H7372
1Ki 18:15 "As the LORD A lives, whom I serve, H7372
1Ki 19:10 been very zealous for the LORD God A. H7372
1Ki 19:14 been very zealous for the LORD God A. H7372
2Ki 3:14 "As surely as the LORD A lives, whom I H7372
2Ki 19:31 zeal of the LORD A will accomplish this. H7372
1Ch 11: 9 because the LORD A was with him. H7372
1Ch 17: 7 'This is what the LORD A says: H7372
1Ch 17:24 will say, 'The LORD A, the God over Israel, H7372
Job 5:17 so do not despise the discipline of the A. H8724
Job 6: 4 The arrows of the A are in me, my spirit H8724
Job 6:14 from a friend forsakes the fear of the A. H8724
Job 8: 3 Does the A pervert what is right? H8724
Job 8: 5 seek God earnestly and plead with the A, H8724
Job 11: 7 Can you probe the limits of the A? H8724
Job 13: 3 to speak to the A and to argue my case H8724
Job 15:25 at God and vaunts himself against the A, H8724
Job 21:15 Who is the A, that we should serve him H8724
Job 21:20 them drink the cup of the wrath of the A. H8724
Job 22: 3 would it give the A if you were righteous? H8724
Job 22:17 What can the A do to us?' H8724
Job 22:23 If you return to the A, you will be restored H8724
Job 22:25 then the A will be your gold, the choicest H8724
Job 22:26 find delight in the A and will lift up your H8724
Job 23:16 my heart faint; the A has terrified me. H8724
Job 24: 1 "Why does the A not set times for H8724
Job 27: 2 me justice, the A, who has made my life H8724
Job 27:10 Will they find delight in the A? Will they H8724
Job 27:11 the ways of the A I will not conceal. H8724
Job 27:13 a ruthless man receives from the A: H8724
Job 29: 5 when the A was still with me and my H8724
Job 31: 2 our heritage from the A on high? H8724
Job 31:35 my defense—let the A answer me; let my H8724
Job 32: 8 the breath of the A, that gives them H8724
Job 33: 4 the breath of the A gives me life. H8724
Job 34:10 God to do evil, from the A to do wrong. H8724
Job 34:12 that the A would pervert justice. H8724
Job 35:13 empty plea; the A pays no attention to it. H8724
Job 37:23 The A is beyond our reach and exalted in H8724
Job 40: 2 one who contends with the A correct him? H8724
Ps 24:10 The LORD A—he is the King of H7372
Ps 46: 7 The LORD A is with us; the God of Jacob is H7372
Ps 46:11 The LORD A is with us; the God of Jacob is H7372
Ps 48: 8 so we have seen in the city of the LORD A H7372
Ps 59: 5 LORD God A, you who are the God of H7372
Ps 68:14 When the A scattered the kings in the H8724
Ps 69: 6 the LORD A, may those who hope in H7372
Ps 80: 4 How long, LORD God A, will your anger H7372
Ps 80: 7 Restore us, God A; make your face shine H7372
Ps 80:14 Return to us, God A! Look down from H7372
Ps 80:19 Restore us, LORD God A; make your face H7372
Ps 84: 1 lovely is your dwelling place, LORD A! H7372
Ps 84: 3 your altar, LORD A, my King and my God. H7372
Ps 84: 8 my prayer, LORD God A; listen to me, God H7372
Ps 84:12 LORD A, blessed is the one who trusts in H7372
Ps 89: 8 is like you, LORD God A? You, LORD, are H7372
Ps 91: 1 High will rest in the shadow of the A. H8724
Isa 1: 9 Unless the LORD A had left us some H7372
Isa 1:24 the Lord, the LORD A, the Mighty One of H7372
Isa 2:12 The LORD A has a day in store for all the H7372
Isa 3: 1 the Lord, the LORD A, is about to take H7372
Isa 3:15 declares the Lord, the LORD A. H7372
Isa 5: 7 vineyard of the LORD A is the nation of H7372
Isa 5: 9 The LORD A has declared in my hearing H7372
Isa 5:16 But the LORD A will be exalted by his H7372
Isa 5:24 the law of the LORD A and spurned the H7372
Isa 6: 3 holy is the LORD A; the whole earth is H7372
Isa 6: 5 my eyes have seen the King, the LORD A." H7372
Isa 8:13 The LORD A is the one you are to regard as H7372
Isa 8:18 symbols in Israel from the LORD A, H7372
Isa 9: 7 zeal of the LORD A will accomplish this H7372
Isa 9:13 nor have they sought the LORD A. H7372
Isa 9:19 By the wrath of the LORD A the land will H7372
Isa 10:16 the Lord, the LORD A, will send a wasting H7372
Isa 10:23 The Lord, the LORD A, will carry out the H7372
Isa 10:24 this is what the Lord, the LORD A, says: H7372
Isa 10:26 The LORD A will lash them with a whip, as H7372
Isa 10:33 the Lord, the LORD A, will lop off the H7372
Isa 13: 4 The LORD A is mustering an army for war H7372
Isa 13: 6 it will come like destruction from the A. H8724
Isa 13:13 from its place at the wrath of the LORD A, H7372
Isa 14:22 up against them," declares the LORD A. H7372
Isa 14:23 of destruction," declares the LORD A. H7372
Isa 14:24 The LORD A has sworn, "Surely, as I have H7372
Isa 14:27 For the LORD A has purposed, and who can H7372
Isa 17: 3 of the Israelites," declares the LORD A. H7372
Isa 18: 7 brought to the LORD A from a people tall H7372
Isa 18: 7 the place of the Name of the LORD A. H7372
Isa 19: 4 over them," declares the Lord, the LORD A. H7372
Isa 19:12 what the LORD A has planned against H7372
Isa 19:16 hand that the LORD A raises against them. H7372
Isa 19:17 of what the LORD A is planning against H7372
Isa 19:18 swear allegiance to the LORD A. H7372
Isa 19:20 witness to the LORD A in the land of Egypt. H7372
Isa 19:25 The LORD A will bless them, saying H7372
Isa 21:10 you what I have heard from the LORD A, H7372
Isa 22: 5 The Lord, the LORD A, has a day of tumult H7372
Isa 22:12 The Lord, the LORD A, called you on that H7372
Isa 22:14 The LORD A has revealed this in my H7372
Isa 22:14 be atoned for," says the Lord, the LORD A. H7372
Isa 22:15 is what the Lord, the LORD A, says: "Go, H7372
Isa 22:25 declares the LORD A, "the peg driven into H7372
Isa 23: 9 The LORD A planned it, to bring down her H7372
Isa 24:23 the LORD A will reign on Mount Zion H7372
Isa 25: 6 mountain the LORD A will prepare a feast H7372
Isa 28: 5 In that day the LORD A will be a glorious H7372
Isa 28:22 the Lord, the LORD A, has told me of the H7372
Isa 28:29 All this also comes from the LORD A, H7372
Isa 29: 6 the LORD A will come with thunder and H7372
Isa 31: 4 so the LORD A will come down to do battle H7372
Isa 31: 5 the LORD A will shield Jerusalem H7372
Isa 37:16 "LORD A, the God of Israel, enthroned H7372
Isa 37:32 zeal of the LORD A will accomplish this H7372
Isa 39: 5 Hezekiah, "Hear the word of the LORD A: H7372
Isa 44: 6 Israel's King and Redeemer, the LORD A: H7372
Isa 45:13 not for a price or reward, says the LORD A." H7372
Isa 47: 4 Redeemer—the LORD A is his name—is H7372
Isa 48: 2 God of Israel—the LORD A is his name: H7372
Isa 51:15 its waves roar—the LORD A is his name. H7372
Isa 54: 5 husband—the LORD A is his name—the H7372
Jer 2:19 awe of me," declares the Lord, the LORD A. H7372
Jer 5:14 this is what the LORD God A says: H7372
Jer 6: 6 This is what the LORD A says: "Cut down H7372
Jer 6: 9 This is what the LORD A says: "Let them H7372
Jer 7: 3 This is what the LORD A, the God of Israel H7372
Jer 7:21 " 'This is what the LORD A, the God of H7372
Jer 8: 3 prefer death to life, declares the LORD A. H7372
Jer 9: 7 Therefore this is what the LORD A says H7372
Jer 9:15 Therefore this is what the LORD A, H7372
Jer 9:17 This is what the LORD A says: "Consider H7372
Jer 10:16 his inheritance—the LORD A is his name. H7372
Jer 11:17 The LORD A, who planted you, has H7372
Jer 11:20 But you, LORD A, who judge righteously H7372
Jer 11:22 therefore this is what the LORD A says: "I H7372
Jer 15:16 for I bear your name, LORD God A. H7372
Jer 16: 9 For this is what the LORD A, the God of H7372
Jer 19: 3 This is what the LORD A, the God of Israel H7372
Jer 19:11 say to them, 'This is what the LORD A says: H7372
Jer 19:15 is what the LORD A, the God of Israel H7372
Jer 20:12 LORD A, you who examine the righteous H7372
Jer 23:15 is what the LORD A says concerning the H7372
Jer 23:16 This is what the LORD A says: "Do not H7372
Jer 23:36 of the living God, the LORD A, our God. H7372
Jer 25: 8 Therefore the LORD A says this: "Because H7372
Jer 25:27 'This is what the LORD A, the God of Israel, H7372
Jer 25:28 tell them, 'This is what the LORD A says: H7372
Jer 25:29 live on the earth, declares the LORD A. H7372
Jer 25:32 This is what the LORD A says: "Look H7372
Jer 26:18 of Judah, 'This is what the LORD A says: H7372
Jer 27: 4 is what the LORD A, the God of Israel, H7372
Jer 27:18 plead with the LORD A that the articles H7372
Jer 27:19 this is what the LORD A says about the H7372
Jer 27:21 this is what the LORD A, the God of Israel, H7372
Jer 28: 2 "This is what the LORD A, the God of Israel H7372
Jer 28:14 This is what the LORD A, the God of Israel H7372
Jer 29: 4 This is what the LORD A, the God of Israel H7372
Jer 29: 8 this is what the LORD A, the God of Israel, H7372
Jer 29:17 this is what the LORD A says: "I will send H7372
Jer 29:21 This is what the LORD A, the God of Israel H7372
Jer 29:25 "This is what the LORD A, the God of Israel H7372
Jer 30: 8 declares the LORD A, 'I will break the yoke H7372
Jer 31:23 This is what the LORD A, the God of Israel H7372
Jer 31:35 its waves roar—the LORD A is his name: H7372
Jer 32:14 'This is what the LORD A, the God of Israel H7372
Jer 32:15 For this is what the LORD A, the God of H7372
Jer 32:18 mighty God, whose name is the LORD A, H7372
Jer 33:11 "Give thanks to the LORD A, for the LORD H7372
Jer 33:12 "This is what the LORD A says: 'In this H7372
Jer 35:13 is what the LORD A, the God of Israel H7372
Jer 35:17 "Therefore this is what the LORD God A H7372
Jer 35:18 is what the LORD A, the God of Israel H7372
Jer 35:19 this is what the LORD A, the God H7372
Jer 38:17 "This is what the LORD God A, the God of H7372
Jer 39:16 is what the LORD A, the God of Israel, H7372
Jer 42:15 This is what the LORD A, the God of Israel H7372
Jer 42:18 This is what the LORD A, the God of Israel H7372
Jer 43:10 is what the LORD A, the God of Israel, H7372
Jer 44: 2 is what the LORD A, the God of Israel H7372
Jer 44: 7 "Now this is what the LORD God A, the H7372
Jer 44:11 "Therefore this is what the LORD A, the H7372
Jer 44:25 This is what the LORD A, the God of Israel H7372
Jer 46:10 the Lord, the LORD A—a day of vengeance H7372
Jer 46:10 the Lord, the LORD A, will offer sacrifice H7372
Jer 46:18 whose name is the LORD A, "one will H7372
Jer 46:25 The LORD A, the God of Israel, says: "I am H7372
Jer 48: 1 This is what the LORD A, the God of Israel H7372
Jer 48:15 the King, whose name is the LORD A. H7372
Jer 49: 5 declares the Lord, the LORD A. H7372
Jer 49: 7 This is what the LORD A says: "Is there no H7372
Jer 49:26 silenced in that day," declares the LORD A. H7372
Jer 49:35 This is what the LORD A says: "See, I will H7372
Jer 50:18 Therefore this is what the LORD A, the God H7372
Jer 50:25 the Sovereign LORD A has work to do in H7372
Jer 50:31 the Lord, the LORD A, "for your day has H7372
Jer 50:33 This is what the LORD A says: "The people H7372
Jer 50:34 is strong; the LORD A is his name. H7372
Jer 51: 5 their God, the LORD A, though their land is H7372
Jer 51:14 The LORD A has sworn by himself: I will H7372
Jer 51:19 his inheritance—the LORD A is his name. H7372
Jer 51:33 This is what the LORD A, the God of Israel H7372
Jer 51:57 the King, whose name is the LORD A. H7372
Jer 51:58 This is what the LORD A says: "Babylon's H7372
Eze 1:24 like the voice of the A, like the tumult of H8724
Eze 10: 5 like the voice of God A when he speaks. H8724
Hos 12: 5 the LORD God A, the LORD is his name! H7372
Joel 1:15 it will come like destruction from the A. H8724
Am 3:13 declares the Lord, the LORD God A. H7372
Am 4:13 the earth—the LORD God A is his name. H7372
Am 5:14 Then the LORD God A will be with you, H7372
Am 5:15 the LORD God A will have mercy on H7372
Am 5:16 is what the Lord, the LORD God A, says: H7372
Am 5:27 says the LORD, whose name is God A. H7372
Am 6: 8 by himself—the LORD God A declares: H7372
Am 6:14 the LORD God A declares, "I will stir up H7372
Am 9: 5 The Lord, the LORD A—he touches the H7372
Mic 4: 4 them afraid, for the LORD A has spoken. H7372
Na 2:13 declares the LORD A. "I will burn up your H7372
Na 3: 5 declares the LORD A. "I will lift your H7372
Hab 2:13 Has not the LORD A determined that the H7372
Zep 2: 9 declares the LORD A, the God of Israel H7372
Zep 2:10 mocking the people of the LORD A. H7372
Hag 1: 2 This is what the LORD A says: "These H7372
Hag 1: 5 Now this is what the LORD A says: "Give H7372
Hag 1: 7 is what the LORD A says: "Give careful H7372
Hag 1: 9 declares the LORD A. "Because of my H7372
Hag 1:14 began to work on the house of the LORD A, H7372
Hag 2: 4 For I am with you,' declares the LORD A. H7372
Hag 2: 6 "This is what the LORD A says: 'In a little H7372
Hag 2: 7 fill this house with glory,' says the LORD A. H7372
Hag 2: 8 the gold is mine,' declares the LORD A. H7372
Hag 2: 9 of the former house,' says the LORD A. H7372
Hag 2: 9 I will grant peace,' declares the LORD A." H7372
Hag 2:11 "This is what the LORD A says: 'Ask the H7372
Hag 2:23 ' declares the LORD A, 'I will take you, H7372
Hag 2:23 I have chosen you,' declares the LORD A." H7372
Zec 1: 3 This is what the LORD A says: 'Return to H7372
Zec 1: 3 ' declares the LORD A, 'and I will return to H7372
Zec 1: 3 'and I will return to you,' says the LORD A. H7372
Zec 1: 4 This is what the LORD A says: 'Turn from H7372
Zec 1: 6 'The LORD A has done to us what our ways H7372
Zec 1:12 the LORD said, "LORD A, how long will H7372
Zec 1:14 This is what the LORD A says: 'I am very H7372
Zec 1:16 out over Jerusalem,' declares the LORD A. H7372
Zec 1:17 This is what the LORD A says: 'My towns H7372
Zec 2: 8 For this is what the LORD A says: "After H7372
Zec 2: 9 will know that the LORD A has sent me. H7372
Zec 2:11 know that the LORD A has sent me to you. H7372
Zec 3: 7 "This is what the LORD A says: 'If you will H7372
Zec 3: 9 ' says the LORD A, 'and I will remove H7372
Zec 3:10 vine and fig tree,' declares the LORD A." H7372
Zec 4: 6 but by my Spirit,' says the LORD A. H7372
Zec 4: 9 know that the LORD A has sent me to you. H7372
Zec 5: 4 The LORD A declares, 'I will send it out H7372
Zec 6:12 Tell him this is what the LORD A says: H7372
Zec 6:15 know that the LORD A has sent me to you. H7372
Zec 7: 3 the house of the LORD A and the prophets, H7372
Zec 7: 4 Then the word of the LORD A came to me: H7372
Zec 7: 9 "This is what the LORD A said: 'Administer H7372
Zec 7:12 words that the LORD A had sent by his H7372
Zec 7:12 So the LORD A was very angry. H7372
Zec 7:13 I would not listen,' says the LORD A. H7372
Zec 8: 1 The word of the LORD A came to me. H7372
Zec 8: 2 This is what the LORD A says: "I am very H7372
Zec 8: 3 mountain of the LORD A will be called the H7372
Zec 8: 4 This is what the LORD A says: "Once again H7372
Zec 8: 6 This is what the LORD A says: "It may H7372
Zec 8: 6 marvelous to me?" declares the LORD A. H7372
Zec 8: 7 This is what the LORD A says: "I will save H7372

Zec 8: 9 This is what the LORD **A** says: "Now hear H7372
Zec 8: 9 was laid for the house of the LORD **A**. H7372
Zec 8:11 as I did in the past," declares the LORD **A**. H7372
Zec 8:14 This is what the LORD **A** says: "Just as I H7372
Zec 8:14 ancestors angered me," says the LORD **A**, H7372
Zec 8:18 The word of the LORD **A** came to me. H7372
Zec 8:19 This is what the LORD **A** says: "The fasts H7372
Zec 8:20 This is what the LORD **A** says: "Many H7372
Zec 8:21 to entreat the LORD and seek the LORD **A**. H7372
Zec 8:22 to seek the LORD **A** and to entreat him." H7372
Zec 8:23 This is what the LORD **A** says: "In those H7372
Zec 9:15 the LORD **A** will shield them. They will H7372
Zec 10: 3 the LORD **A** will care for his flock H7372
Zec 12: 5 because the LORD **A** is their God. H7372
Zec 13: 2 no more," declares the LORD **A**. H7372
Zec 13: 7 declares the LORD **A**. "Strike the shepherd H7372
Zec 14:16 the King, the LORD **A**, and to celebrate the H7372
Zec 14:17 the King, the LORD **A**, they will have no H7372
Zec 14:21 Judah will be holy to the LORD **A**, H7372
Zec 14:21 a Canaanite in the house of the LORD **A**. H7372
Mal 1: 4 But this is what the LORD **A** says: "They H7372
Mal 1: 6 says the LORD **A**. "It is you priests H7372
Mal 1: 8 Would he accept you?" says the LORD **A**. H7372
Mal 1: 9 will he accept you?"—says the LORD **A**. H7372
Mal 1:10 says the LORD **A**, "and I will accept no H7372
Mal 1:11 among the nations," says the LORD **A**. H7372
Mal 1:13 at it contemptuously," says the LORD **A**. H7372
Mal 1:14 says the LORD **A**, "and my name is to be H7372
Mal 2: 2 says the LORD **A**, "I will send a curse on H7372
Mal 2: 4 with Levi may continue," says the LORD **A**. H7372
Mal 2: 7 messenger of the LORD **A** and people seek H7372
Mal 2: 8 the covenant with Levi," says the LORD **A**. H7372
Mal 2:12 he brings an offering to the LORD **A**. H7372
Mal 2:16 one he should protect," says the LORD **A**. H7372
Mal 3: 1 you desire, will come," says the LORD **A**. H7372
Mal 3: 5 do not fear me," says the LORD **A**. H7372
Mal 3: 7 I will return to you," says the LORD **A**. H7372
Mal 3:10 says the LORD **A**, "and see if I will not H7372
Mal 3:11 fruit before it is ripe," says the LORD **A**. H7372
Mal 3:12 will be a delightful land," says the LORD **A**. H7372
Mal 3:14 about like mourners before the LORD **A**? H7372
Mal 3:17 says the LORD **A**, "they will be my H7372
Mal 4: 1 will set them on fire," says the LORD **A**. H7372
Mal 4: 3 on the day when I act," says the LORD **A**. H7372
Ro 9:29 "Unless the Lord **A** had left us *G4877*
2Co 6:18 my sons and daughters, says the Lord **A**." *G4120*
Jas 5: 4 have reached the ears of the Lord **A**. *G4877*
Rev 1: 8 who was, and who is to come, the **A**." *G4120*
Rev 4: 8 holy is the Lord God **A**,' who was, and is, *G4120*
Rev 11:17 Lord God **A**, the One who is and *G4120*
Rev 15: 3 marvelous are your deeds, Lord God **A**. *G4120*
Rev 16: 7 Lord God **A**, true and just are your *G4120*
Rev 16:14 the battle on the great day of God **A**. *G4120*
Rev 19: 6 For our Lord God **A** reigns. *G4120*
Rev 19:15 of the fury of the wrath of God **A**. *G4120*
Rev 21:22 the Lord God **A** and the Lamb are its *G4120*

ALMODAD (2)

Ge 10:26 Joktan was the father of **A**, Sheleph H525
1Ch 1:20 Joktan was the father of **A**, Sheleph H525

ALMON (1)

Jos 21:18 Anathoth and **A**, together with their H6626

ALMON DIBLATHAIM (2) [BETH DIBLATHAIM]

Nu 33:46 Dibon Gad and camped at **A**. H6627
Nu 33:47 They left **A** and camped in H6627

ALMOND (7) [ALMONDS]

Ge 30:37 **a** and plane trees and made white stripes H4280
Ex 25:33 Three cups **shaped like a flowers** with H5481
Ex 25:34 four cups **shaped like a flowers** with buds H5481
Ex 37:19 Three cups **shaped like a flowers** with H5481
Ex 37:20 four cups **shaped like a flowers** with buds H5481
Ecc 12: 5 when the **a tree** blossoms and the H9196
Jer 1:11 "I see the branch of an **a tree**," I replied. H9196

ALMONDS (2) [ALMOND]

Ge 43:11 myrrh, some pistachio nuts and **a**. H9196
Nu 17: 8 had budded, blossomed and produced **a**. H9196

ALMOST (14)

Ex 17: 4 They are **a** ready to stone me." H5071+6388
Jdg 19: 9 said, "Now look, it's **a** evening. H8332
Jdg 19:11 were near Jebus and the day was **a** gone, H4394
Job 10:20 *Are* not my few days *a* **over**? Turn away from AIT
Ps 73: 2 my feet had **a** slipped; I had H3869+5071
Ps 119:87 They **a** wiped me from the earth H3869+5071
Lk 8:42 was on his way, the crowds *a* **crushed** him. AIT
Lk 24:29 it is nearly evening; the day is **a** over." *G2453*
Jn 2:13 When it was **a time** for the Jewish *G1584*
Jn 11:55 When it was **a time for** the Jewish *G1584*
Ac 13:44 On the next Sabbath **a** the whole city *G5385*
Ro 13:12 the day is **a here**. So let us put *G1581*
Php 2:27 he was ill, and **a** died. But God had *G4180*
Php 2:30 because *he* **a** died for the work of *G3588+1581*

ALMS (KJV) BEG, GENEROUS, PRACTICE RIGHTEOUSNESS

ALMSDEEDS (KJV) HELPING THE POOR

ALMUGWOOD (3) [ALGUM]

1Ki 10:11 great cargoes of **a** and precious H6770+523
1Ki 10:12 king used the **a** to make supports H6770+523
1Ki 10:12 So much **a** has never been imported H6770+523

ALOES (5)

Nu 24: 6 beside a river, like **a** planted by the LORD H193
Ps 45: 8 are fragrant with myrrh and **a** and cassia; H189
Pr 7:17 my bed with myrrh, **a** and cinnamon. H193
SS 4:14 with myrrh and **a** and all the finest spices. H189
Jn 19:39 brought a mixture of myrrh and **a**, *G264*

ALOFT (1)

Dt 32:11 to catch them and carries them **a**. H6584+89

ALONE (113) [LONELY]

Ge 2:18 "It is not good for the man to be **a**. H4200+963
Ge 32:24 So Jacob was left **a**, and a man H4200+963
Ex 4:26 So the LORD **let** him **a**. (At that time she H8332
Ex 14:12 in Egypt, '**Leave** us **a**; let us serve H2532+4946
Ex 18:14 Why do you **a** sit as judge, while all H4200+963
Ex 18:18 you; you cannot handle it **a**. H4200+963
Ex 21: 3 If he comes **a**, he is to go free H928+1727+2257
Ex 21: 3 he is to go free **a**; but if he H928+1727+2257
Ex 24: 2 Moses **a** is to approach the LORD H4200+963
Ex 32:10 Now **leave** me **a** so that my anger may H5663
Lev 13:46 They must live **a**; they must live outside the H970
Nu 11:17 so that you will not have to carry it **a**. H4200+963
Nu 18: 1 you and your sons **a** are to bear the NDT
Dt 1: 9 too heavy a burden *for* me to carry **a**. H963+4200
Dt 8: 3 live on bread **a** but on every word H4200+963
Dt 9:14 **Let** me **a**, so that I may destroy them and H8332
Dt 16:20 Follow justice and **justice** *a*, so that you may AIT
Dt 32:12 The LORD **a** led him; no foreign god was H970
Jdg 3:20 he was sitting **a** in the upper room H4200+963
1Sa 21: 1 and asked, "Why are you **a**? H4200+963
2Sa 16:11 **Leave** him **a**; let him curse, for the LORD H5663
2Sa 18:24 he saw a man running **a**. H4200+963
2Sa 18:25 "If he is **a**, he must have good H4200+963
2Sa 18:26 another man running **a**! H4200+963
1Ki 3:18 We were **a**; there was no one in the H3481
1Ki 8:39 you **a** know every human heart), H4200+963
1Ki 11:29 two of them were **a** out in the H4200+963
2Ki 4:27 the man of God said, "**Leave** her **a**! H8332
2Ki 19:15 you **a** are God over all the kingdoms H4200+963
2Ki 19:19 of the earth may know that you **a**, H4200+963
2Ki 23:18 "**Leave** it **a**," he said. "Don't let anyone H5663
2Ch 6:30 you **a** know the human heart) H4200+963
Ezr 4: 3 We **a** will build it for the LORD, the God of H3480
Ne 9: 6 You **a** are the LORD. You made the H4200+963
Est 4:13 in the king's house you **a** of all the Jews will NDT
Job 7:16 **Let** me **a**; my days have no H2532
Job 7:19 from me, or **let** me **a** even for an instant? H8332
Job 9: 8 He **a** stretches out the heavens and H4200+963
Job 14: 6 So look away from him and **let** him **a**, till H2532
Job 15:19 to whom **a** the land was given when H4200+963
Job 19: 4 gone astray, my error remains **my** concern *a*. AIT
Job 21:14 to God, '**Leave** us **a**! We have no H6073+4946
Job 22:17 to God, '**Leave** us **a**! What can the H6073+4946
Job 23:13 "But he stands **a**, and who can H928+285
Job 28:23 the way to it and **he a** knows where it H2085
Ps 4: 8 lie down and sleep, for you **a**, LORD, H4200+970
Ps 16: 5 you **a** are my portion and my cup; you NDT
Ps 71:16 your righteous deeds, yours **a**. H4200+963
Ps 72:18 who **a** does marvelous deeds. H4200+963
Ps 76: 7 It is **you a** who are to be feared. Who H911+911
Ps 83:18 that you **a** are the Most High over all H4200+963
Ps 86:10 do marvelous deeds; you **a** are God. H4200+963
Ps 102: 7 I have become like a bird **a** on a roof. H969
Ps 136: 4 to him who **a** does great wonders H4200+963
Ps 148:13 for his name **a** is exalted; his H4200+963
Pr 5:17 Let them be yours **a**, never to be H4200+963
Pr 9:12 if you are a mocker, you **a** will suffer. H4200+963
Ecc 4: 8 There was a man **all a**; he had H401+9108
Ecc 4:11 But how can **one** keep warm *a*? AIT
SS 4: 2 Each has its twin; not one of them is **a**. H8891
Isa 2:11 the LORD **a** will be exalted in that day H4200+963
Isa 2:17 the LORD **a** will be exalted in that day H4200+963
Isa 5: 8 is left and you live **a** in the land. H4200+963
Isa 26:13 but your name **a** do we honor. H4200+963
Isa 37:16 you **a** are God over all the kingdoms H4200+963
Isa 45:24 'In the LORD **a** are deliverance and strength. NDT
Isa 49:21 I was left **all a**, but these—where H4200+963
Isa 63: 3 "I have trodden the winepress **a** H4200+963
Jer 15:17 I sat **a** because your hand was on me and H970
Jer 41: 8 So *he* **let** them **a** and did not kill them H2532
La 3:28 Let him sit **a** in silence, for the LORD has H970
Eze 9: 8 While they were killing and I *was* **left a**, I H8636
Eze 14:16 They **a** would be saved, but the land H4200+963
Eze 14:18 They **a** would be saved. H4200+963
Eze 37: 3 I said, "Sovereign LORD, **you** *a* know." AIT
Eze 44:16 **They** *a* are to enter my sanctuary; they alone AIT
Eze 44:16 **they** *a* are to come near my table to minister AIT
Da 10: 8 So I was left **a**, gazing at this great H4200+963
Da 11: 8 *will* **leave** the king of the North **a**. H6641+4946
Hos 4:17 Ephraim is joined to idols; **leave** him **a**! H5663
Hos 8: 9 to Assyria like a wild donkey **wandering a**. H969
Mt 4: 4 'Man shall not live on bread **a**, but on *G3668*
Mt 14:23 Later that night, he was there **a**, *G3668*
Mt 27:49 The rest said, "*Now* **leave** him **a**. Let's see if *G918*
Mk 2: 7 Who can forgive sins but God **a**?" *G1651*
Mk 4:10 When he was **a**, the Twelve and *G2848+3668*
Mk 4:34 But when he was **a** with his own *G2848+2625*
Mk 6:47 middle of the lake, and he was **a** on land. *G3668*
Mk 9: 2 where they were **all a**. *G2848+2625+3668*
Mk 10:18 "No one is good—except God **a**. *G1651*
Mk 14: 6 "**Leave** her **a**," said Jesus. "Why are you *G918*
Mk 15:36 "Now **leave** *him* **a**. Let's see if *G918*
Lk 4: 4 'Man shall not live on bread **a**.'" *G3668*
Lk 5:21 Who can forgive sins but God **a**?" *G3668*
Lk 9:36 had spoken, they found that Jesus was **a**. *G3668*
Lk 13: 8 man replied, '**leave** it **a** for one more year *G918*
Lk 18:19 "No one is good—except God **a**. *G1651*
Jn 6:22 disciples, but that they had gone away **a**. *G3668*
Jn 8:16 my decisions are true, because I am not **a**. *G3668*
Jn 8:29 he has not left me **a**, for I always do what *G3668*
Jn 12: 7 "**Leave** her **a**," Jesus replied. "It was *G918*
Jn 16:32 You will leave me **all a**. Yet I am not *G3668*
Jn 16:32 Yet I am not **a**, for my Father is *G3668*
Jn 17:20 "My prayer is not for them **a**. I pray also *G3667*
Ac 5:38 **Leave** these men **a**! Let them *G923*
Ro 4:23 were written not for him **a**, *G3667*
Ro 14: 7 For none of us lives *for* **ourselves** *a*, AIT
Ro 14: 7 and none of us dies *for* **ourselves** *a*. AIT
Gal 6: 4 Then they can take pride in themselves **a** *G3668*
1Ti 5: 5 in need and **left all a** puts her hope in *G3670*
1Ti 6:16 who **a** is immortal and who lives in *G3668*
Jas 2:24 by what they do and not by faith **a**. *G3667*
Rev 15: 4 For you **a** are holy. All nations *G3668*

ALONG (321) [ALONGSIDE]

Ge 1:24 the creatures that move **a** the ground, and NDT
Ge 1:25 all the **creatures that move** *a* the ground AIT
Ge 1:26 all the creatures that move **a** the ground." H6584
Ge 1:30 the creatures that move **a** the ground— H6584
Ge 2:14 the Tigris; it **runs a** the east side of Ashur. H2143
Ge 6: 7 the **creatures that move a the ground**— H8254
Ge 6:20 kind of **creature that moves** *a* the ground AIT
Ge 7: 8 of all creatures that move **a** the ground, H6584
Ge 7:14 creature that moves **a** the ground H6584
Ge 7:23 creatures that move **a** the ground and the NDT
Ge 8:17 the creatures that move **a** the ground— H6584
Ge 8:19 creatures that move **a** the ground and all NDT
Ge 9: 2 every creature *that* **moves a** the ground, H8253
Ge 15: 9 old, **a with** a dove and a young pigeon." H2256
Ge 18:16 Abraham **walked a** with them to see H2143
Ge 24:59 **a with** her nurse and Abraham's servant H2256
Ge 31:18 **a with** all the goods he had accumulated H2256
Ge 33:14 while I **move a** slowly at the pace of the H5633
Ge 43: 4 If you will send our brother **a with** us, we H907
Ge 43: 8 "Send the boy **a with** me and we will go at H907
Ge 44: 2 one's sack, **a with** the silver for his grain." H2256
Ge 46:32 and *they have* **brought** *a* their flocks and AIT
Ge 48: 1 sons Manasseh and Ephraim **a with** him. H6640
Ge 49:17 the roadside, a viper **a** the path, that bites H6584
Ge 49:30 Abraham bought **a with** the field as a H907
Ge 50:13 Abraham had bought **a with** the field as a H907
Ge 50:22 in Egypt, **a with** all his father's family. H2256
Ex 2: 3 it among the reeds **a** the bank of the Nile. H6584
Ex 2: 5 attendants were walking **a** the riverbank. H6584
Ex 2:17 Some shepherds **came a** and drove them H995
Ex 7:24 all the Egyptians dug **a** the Nile to get H6017
Ex 10:10 **a with** your women and children! H2256
Ex 12: 8 over the fire, **a with** bitter herbs, and H6584
Ex 14: 7 **a with** all the other chariots of Egypt H2256
Ex 18: 8 they had met **a** the way and how the H928
Ex 23:18 a sacrifice to me **a with** anything H6584
Ex 23:20 of you to guard you **a** the way and to bring H928
Ex 26: 4 of blue material **a** the edge of the end H6584
Ex 26:10 Make fifty loops **a** the edge of the end H6584
Ex 26:10 in one set and also **a** the edge of the end H6584
Ex 28: 1 **a with** his sons Nadab and Abihu H907
Ex 29: 3 present them **a with** the bull and the H2256
Ex 29:25 them on the altar **a with** the burnt offering H6584
Ex 34:25 a sacrifice to me **a with** anything H6584
Ex 36:11 of blue material **a** the edge of the end H6584
Ex 36:17 made fifty loops **a** the edge of the end H6584
Ex 36:17 in one set and also **a** the edge of the end H6584
Lev 5: 2 **creature that moves a the ground**) H9238
Lev 7:12 then **a with** this thank offering they are to H6584
Lev 7:13 **A with** their fellowship offering of H6584
Lev 7:21 **creature that moves a the ground**— H9238
Lev 11:29 " 'Of the animals that move **a** the ground H6584
Lev 11:31 Of all those *that* **move a** the ground, these H9238
Lev 11:41 creature that moves **a** the ground is to be H6584
Lev 11:42 eat any creature that moves **a** the ground, H6584
Lev 11:44 by any creature that moves **a** the ground. H6584
Lev 11:46 every creature that moves **a** the ground. H6584
Lev 14:10 **a with** three-tenths of an ephah of the H2256
Lev 14:12 a guilt offering, **a with** the log of oil; he H2256
Lev 20:25 anything that **moves a** the ground— H8253
Nu 1:47 was not counted **a with** the others. H928+9348
Nu 2:33 were not counted **a with** the other H928+9348
Nu 5: 8 **a with** the ram with which H4946+4200+963
Nu 13:23 **a with** some pomegranates and figs. H2256
Nu 13:29 live near the sea and **a** the Jordan." H6584+3338
Nu 14:25 toward the desert *a* the **route** *to* the Red Sea." AIT
Nu 15:24 **a with** its prescribed grain offering and H2256
Nu 16:46 **a with** burning coals from the altar H2256
Nu 20:17 *We will* **travel** a the King's Highway and H2143
Nu 20:19 "We will go **a** the main road, and if we H928
Nu 21: 1 heard that Israel *was* **coming** *a* the road to AIT
Nu 21: 4 *They* **traveled** from Mount Hor *a* the route to AIT
Nu 21:15 of Ar and lie **a** the border of Moab." H4200

A

Nu 21:22 We will travel **a** the King's Highway until H928
Nu 21:33 they turned and **went up** *a* the road toward AIT
Nu 21:34 **a with** his whole army and his land. H2256
Nu 22: 1 of Moab and camped **a** the Jordan across H4200
Nu 26:10 mouth and swallowed them **a with** Korah, H2256
Nu 26:62 were not counted **a with** the other H928+9348
Nu 28: 8 **a** with the same kind of grain offering and NDT
Nu 31: 6 each tribe, **a with** Phinehas son of Eleazar H2256
Nu 33:49 of Moab they camped **a** the Jordan from H6584
Nu 34: 3 of the Desert of Zin **a** the border of Edom. H6584
Nu 34:11 of Ain and continue **a** the slopes east of H6584
Nu 34:12 will go down **a** the Jordan and end at H2025
Dt 1: 7 in the Negev and **a** the coast, to the land H928
Dt 1:40 and **set out** toward the desert *a* the route AIT
Dt 2: 1 back and **set out** toward the wilderness *a* the AIT
Dt 2: 8 and **traveled a** the desert road of Moab. H6296
Dt 2:37 neither the land **a** the course of the H3338
Dt 3: 1 we turned and **went up** *a* the road toward AIT
Dt 3: 2 **a with** his whole army and his land. H2256
Dt 4:18 creature that moves **a** the ground or any H928
Dt 6: 7 sit at home and when you walk **a** the road, H928
Dt 11:19 sit at home and when you walk **a** the road, H928
Dt 24: 9 God did to Miriam **a** the way after you H928
Dt 25:17 did to you **a** the way when you came H928
Dt 31: 4 whom he destroyed **a with** their land. H2256
Dt 33: 5 assembled, **a with** the tribes of Israel. H3480
Jos 2:22 had searched all **a** the road and returned H928
Jos 5: 1 Canaanite kings **a** the coast heard how H6584
Jos 6: 2 **a with** its king and its fighting men. H2256
Jos 7:15 **a with** all that belongs to him. H2256
Jos 9: 1 **a** the entire coast of the H928
Jos 10:10 Israel **pursued** them *a* the road going up to AIT
Jos 15: 4 *It* then **passed a** to Azmon and joined the H6296
Jos 15: 7 It **continued a** to the waters of En H6296
Jos 15: 8 Valley of Ben Hinnom **a** the southern slope H448
Jos 15:10 ran **a** the northern slope of Mount Jearim H448
Jos 15:11 **passed a** *to* Mount Baalah and reached H6296
Jos 17: 4 an inheritance **a with** the brothers of H928+9348
Jos 18:14 turned south **a** the western side and H4200
Jos 18:16 the Hinnom Valley **a** the southern slope of H448
Jos 22: 7 west side of the Jordan **a with** their fellow H6640
Jdg 5:10 you who walk **a** the road, consider H6584
Jdg 11:18 passed **a** the eastern side of the country H4946
Jdg 11:26 and all the towns **a** the Arnon. H6584+3338
Jdg 14: 9 his hands and ate as *he* **went a**. H2143+2143
Jdg 18:20 the idol and went **a with** the people. H928+7931
Jdg 20:45 cut down five thousand men **a** the roads. H928
Ru 2: 9 harvesting, and **follow a** after the women. H2143
Ru 4: 1 he had mentioned **came a**. H6296
1Sa 1:24 as he was, **a with** a three-year-old bull H928
1Sa 6:11 the LORD on the cart and **a** with it the chest NDT
1Sa 7:11 slaughtering them **a** the way to a point NDT
1Sa 15: 6 so that I do not destroy you **a with** them; H6640
1Sa 17:18 **Take a** these ten cheeses to the H995
1Sa 17:52 dead were strewn **a** the Shaaraim road to H928
1Sa 18: 4 gave it to David, **a with** his tunic, and H2256
1Sa 19:23 and *he* **walked a** prophesying until H2143+2143
1Sa 23:26 Saul was going **a** one side of the H4946
1Sa 24: 3 He came to the sheep pens **a** the way; a H6584
1Sa 29:10 **a with** your master's servants who have H2256
1Sa 31: 7 When the Israelites **a** the valley and H928+6298
2Sa 5:11 **a with** cedar logs and carpenters and H2256
2Sa 15:18 **a with** all the Kerethites and Pelethites H2256
2Sa 15:19 "Why should you come **a with** us? H907
2Sa 16:13 his men continued **a** the road while Shimei H928
2Sa 16:13 Shimei was going **a** the hillside opposite H928
2Sa 19:17 Benjamites, **a with** Ziba, the steward of H2256
1Ki 6:10 he built the side rooms all **a** the temple. H6584
1Ki 9:25 incense before the LORD **a with** them, H907
1Ki 10:22 ships at sea **a with** the ships of Hiram. H6640
1Ki 18: 7 As Obadiah was **walking a** H928+2021+2006
2Ki 2:11 **walking a** and talking *together*, H2143+2143
2Ki 2:23 As he was walking **a** the road, some boys H928
2Ki 4:42 **a with** some heads of new grain. H2256
2Ki 6:30 As he went **a** the wall, the people looked H6584
2Ki 10:16 Then *he* **had** him **ride a** in his chariot H8206
2Ki 14: 9 beast in Lebanon **came a** and trampled H6296
2Ki 15:25 Pekahiah, **a with** Argob and Arieh, in H907
2Ki 25:11 **a with** the rest of the populace and those H2256
1Ch 7:29 **A** the borders of Manasseh were Beth H6584
1Ch 14: 1 messengers to David, **a with** cedar logs H2256
1Ch 25: 7 **A with** their relatives—all of them trained H6640
2Ch 21: 4 to the sword **a with** some of the H2256+1685
2Ch 25:18 beast in Lebanon **came a** and trampled H6296
2Ch 30:25 **a with** the priests and Levites and all who H2256
2Ch 35: 9 Also Konaniah **a with** Shemaiah and H2256
Ezr 1:11 Sheshbazzar **brought** all these **a** with the H6590
Ezr 2:70 **a with** some of the other people H2256
Ezr 8:31 us from enemies and bandits **a** the way. H6584
Ezr 10:14 **a with** the elders and judges of each town H6640
Ne 4:19 separated from each other **a** the wall. H6584
Ne 7: 2 **a with** Hananiah the commander of the H2256
Ne 7:73 **a with** certain of the people and the rest H2256
Ne 8:13 families, **a** with the priests and the Levites NDT
Ne 9:24 **a with** their kings and the peoples of the H2256
Ne 12:33 **a with** Azariah, Ezra, Meshullam, H2256
Est 5:12 has invited me **a with** the king tomorrow H6640
Est 9:29 of Abihail, **a with** Mordecai the Jew H2256
Job 11:10 "If *he* **comes a** and confines you in prison H2736
Job 39:23 **a** with the flashing spear and lance. NDT
Job 40:15 which I made **a with** you and which feeds H6640
Job 42:15 an inheritance **a with** their brothers. H928+9348
Ps 23: 3 He guides me **a** the right paths for his H928
Ps 26: 9 Do not take away my soul **a with** sinners H6640
Ps 58: 8 like a slug that melts away *as it* **moves a**, H2143
Ps 87: 4 and Tyre, **a with** Cush—and will say H6640
Ps 110: 7 He will drink from a brook **a** the way, and H928
Ps 140: 5 have set traps for me **a** my path. H4200+3338
Ps 141: 4 part in wicked deeds **a with** those who are H907
Pr 1:11 If they say, "Come **a with** us; let's lie in H907
Pr 1:15 do not go **a with** them, do not set H907
Pr 4:11 of wisdom and lead you **a** straight paths. H928
Pr 7: 8 **walking a** *in* the direction of her house H7575
Pr 8: 2 At the highest point **a** the way, where the H6584
Pr 8:20 righteousness, **a** the paths of justice H928+9348
Pr 12:28 there is life; **a** that path is immortality. H2006
Pr 16:19 be lowly in spirit **a with** the oppressed than H907
Pr 28:10 leads the upright **a** an evil path will fall H928
Ecc 10: 3 Even as fools walk **a** the road, they lack H928
Ecc 12: 5 grasshopper **drags itself a** and desire no H6022
Isa 3:16 **walking a** with outstretched necks H2143
Isa 3:16 **strutting a with swaying hips**, H2143+2256+3262
Isa 5:18 Woe to *those who* **draw** sin **a** with cords H5432
Isa 14:11 to the grave, **a** with the noise of your harps NDT
Isa 15: 8 Their outcry **echoes a** the border of Moab H5938
Isa 18: 1 of whirring wings **a** the rivers of H4946+6298
Isa 19: 7 also the plants **a** the Nile, at the mouth of H6584
Isa 19: 7 Every **sown field** *a* the Nile will become AIT
Isa 19:24 will be the third, **a** with Egypt and Assyria H4200
Isa 23:10 Till your land as they do **a** the Nile NDT
Isa 42:16 **a** unfamiliar paths I will guide them H928
Isa 59: 8 no one who walks **a** them will know peace. H928
Isa 59:10 Like the blind *we* **grope a** the wall H1779
Isa 59:19 flood that the breath of the LORD **drives a**. H5674
Isa 60: 8 "Who are these *that* **fly a** like clouds, like H6414
Jer 19: 1 Take **a** some of the elders of the people NDT
Jer 23:39 out of my presence **a with** the city I gave H2256
Jer 26:22 of Akbor to Egypt, **a with** some other men. H907
Jer 27:20 **a with** all the nobles of Judah and H2256
Jer 32:29 **a with** the houses where the people H2256
Jer 39: 9 **a with** those who had gone over to him H2256
Jer 41: 9 he had killed **a with** Gedaliah was H928+3338
Jer 41:10 king's daughters **a with** all the others who H2256
Jer 43: 6 Baruch son of Neriah **a** with them. NDT
Jer 44:15 **a with** all the women who were present H2256
Jer 49:18 **a with** their neighboring towns, H2256
Jer 50:40 Gomorrah **a with** their neighboring H2256
Jer 52:15 **a with** the rest of the craftsmen and those H2256
Eze 1:20 the wheels would rise **a with** them, H4200+6645
Eze 1:21 the wheels rose **a with** them H4200+6645
Eze 16:53 and your fortunes **a with** them, H928+9348
Eze 20:40 choice gifts, **a with** all your holy sacrifices. H928
Eze 21:12 are thrown to the sword **a with** my people. H907
Eze 23:42 from the desert **a with** men from the rabble H448
Eze 25:10 I will give Moab **a with** the Ammonites to H6584
Eze 25:16 destroy those **remaining** *a* the coast. AIT
Eze 30: 5 land will fall by the sword **a with** Egypt. H907
Eze 31:17 **a with** the armed men who lived in its H2256
Eze 32:18 **a with** those who go down to the pit. H907
Eze 38:20 every creature that moves **a** the ground H6584
Eze 39: 2 I will turn you around and **drag** you **a**. I H9255
Eze 39:14 across the land and, **a with** others, they will H907
Eze 40:14 *He* **measured** *a* the faces of the projecting AIT
Eze 40:17 there were thirty rooms **a** the pavement. H448
Eze 42:10 On the south side **a** the length of the wall H928
Eze 45:24 **a with** a hin of olive oil for each ephah. H2256
Eze 46: 5 **a with** a hin of olive oil for each ephah. H2256
Eze 46: 7 **a with** a hin of oil for each ephah. H2256
Eze 46:11 **a with** a hin of oil for each ephah. H2256
Eze 47:10 Fishermen will stand **a** the shore; from En H6584
Eze 47:17 **a** the northern border of Damascus NDT
Eze 47:18 **a** the Jordan between Gilead and the land NDT
Eze 47:19 then **a** the Wadi of Egypt to the NDT
Eze 47:22 **a with** you they are to be allotted an H907
Eze 48:20 **a with** the property of the city. H448
Eze 48:28 then **a** the Wadi of Egypt to the NDT
Da 1: 2 **a with** some of the articles from the H2256
Da 6:24 lions' den, **a** with their wives and children. NDT
Hos 2:18 and the **creatures that move** *a* the ground AIT
Hos 9: 8 The prophet, **a with** my God, is the H6640
Joel 2: 4 of horses; *they* **gallop a** like cavalry. H8132
Joel 2: 9 They rush upon the city; they run **a** the wall. H928
Am 3:15 winter house **a with** the summer house H6584
Am 4:10 the sword, **a with** your captured horses. H6640
Mt 13: 4 the seed, some fell **a** the path, and the G4123
Mt 13:19 This is the seed sown **a** the path. G4123
Mt 15:29 left there and went **a** the Sea of Galilee. G4123
Mt 18:16 **take** one or two others **a**, so that G4161
Mt 22:16 disciples to him **a with** the Herodians. G3552
Mt 25: 4 took oil in jars **a with** their lamps. G3552
Mt 26:37 *He* **took** Peter and the two sons of Zebedee **a with** G4161
Mk 2:14 *As he* **walked a**, he saw Levi son of G4135
Mk 2:23 and *as* his disciples **walked a**, they G3847+4472
Mk 4: 1 all the people were **a** the shore at the G2093
Mk 4: 4 the seed, some fell **a** the path, and the G4123
Mk 4:15 Some people are like seed **a** the path G4123
Mk 4:36 crowd behind, *they* **took** him **a**, just as he G4161
Mk 8:34 the crowd to him **a with** his disciples and G5250
Mk 10:30 fields—**a with** persecutions—and in G3552
Mk 10:52 his sight and followed Jesus **a** the road. G1877
Mk 11:20 the morning, *as they* **went a**, they saw the G4182
Mk 14:33 James and John **a with** him, and he G3552
Lk 1:18 old man and my wife *is* **well a** in years." G4581
Lk 5:12 a man **came a** who was covered G2779+2627
Lk 7:11 a large crowd **went a with** him. G5233
Lk 8: 5 the seed, some fell **a** the path; it was G4123
Lk 8:12 Those **a** the path are the ones who hear G4123
Lk 9:57 As they were walking **a** the road, a man G1877
Lk 17: 7 '**Come a** now and sit down to eat'? G4216
Lk 17:11 Jesus **traveled a** the border between G1451
Lk 19:36 *As* he **went a**, people spread their cloaks G4513
Lk 23:33 him there, **a with** the criminals—one on G2779
Lk 24:15 himself came up and **walked a with** them; G5233
Lk 24:17 you discussing together *as you* **walk a**?" G4344
Jn 9: 1 *As he* **went a**, he saw a man blind from G4135
Jn 11:33 the Jews *who had* **come a with** her also G5302
Jn 20: 6 Then Simon Peter **came a** behind him G2262
Ac 1:14 **a with** the women and Mary the mother of G5250
Ac 8:36 As they traveled **a** the road, they came to G2848
Ac 10:23 some of the believers from Joppa **went a**. G5302
Ac 15: 2 appointed, **a with** some other believers G2779
Ac 16: 3 Paul wanted to take him **a** on the journey G5250
Ac 19:25 **a with** the workers in related trades G2779
Ac 21:26 men and purified himself **a with** them. G5250
Ac 25: 3 an ambush to kill him **a** the way. G2848
Ac 27: 2 sail for ports **a the coast of** the province of G2848
Ac 27: 8 *We* **moved a** the coast with difficulty and G4162
Ac 27:13 anchor and sailed **a the shore** of Crete. G839
Ac 27:15 so we gave way to it and *were* **driven a**. G5770
Ac 27:17 sea anchor and *let* the ship *be* **driven a**. G5770
Ro 8:32 will he not also, **a with** him, graciously G5250
1Co 9: 5 right *to* **take** a believing wife **a with** us, G4310
1Co 16:11 I am expecting him **a with** the brothers. G3552
2Co 8:18 And *we are* **sending a** with him the G5225
2Co 12:19 you been thinking **all a** that we have G4093
Gal 2: 1 time with Barnabas. *I* **took** Titus **a** also. G5221
Gal 2:10 the very thing *I had been* **eager** to do *all a*. AIT
Gal 3: 9 rely on faith are blessed **a with** Abraham, G5250
Eph 4:31 slander, **a with** every form of malice. G5250
Php 4: 3 **a with** Clement and the rest of my G3552
1Ti 1:14 **a with** the faith and love that are in Christ G3552
2Ti 2:22 **a with** those who call on the Lord out of a G3552
Heb 10:34 *You* **suffered a with** those in prison and G5217
Heb 11:25 He chose *to be* **mistreated a with** the G5156
2Pe 1:21 from God *as they were* **carried a** by the G5770
3Jn 2 even as your soul *is* **getting a well**. G2338
Jude 12 without rain, **blown a** by the wind G4195
Rev 17:12 authority as kings **a with** the beast. G3552

ALONGSIDE (5) [ALONG]

Ex 20:23 Do not make any gods to be **a** me; do not H907
Nu 21:13 there and camped **a** the Arnon, H4946+6298
1Ch 26:16 and Hosah. Guard was **a of** guard: H4200+6645
Eze 27: 9 their sailors came **a** to trade for your H928
Eze 48:13 "**A** the territory of the priests, the H4200+6645

ALOOF (4)

Job 21:16 so I **stand a** from the plans of the wicked. H8178
Job 22:18 so I **stand a** from the plans of the wicked. H8178
Ps 83: 1 turn a deaf ear, *do* not **stand a**, O God. H9200
Ob 11 the day you stood **a** while strangers H4946+5584

ALOTH (1)

1Ki 4:16 Baana son of Hushai—in Asher and in **A**; H6599

ALOUD (35) [LOUD]

Ge 27:38 my father!" Then Esau wept **a**. H5951+7754
Ge 29:11 Rachel and began to weep **a**. H5951+906+7754
Nu 14: 1 community raised their voices and **wept a**. H1134
Jdg 2: 4 Israelites, the people wept **a**, H5951+906+7754
Ru 1: 9 them goodbye and they wept **a** H5951+7754
Ru 1:14 At this *they* **wept a** again. Then Orpah H1134
1Sa 11: 4 the people, they all wept **a**. H5951+906+7754
1Sa 24:16 David my son?" And he wept **a**. H5951+7754
1Sa 30: 4 his men wept **a** until they had H5951+906+7754
2Sa 3:32 the king wept **a** at Abner's H5951+906+7754
2Sa 13:19 went away, **weeping a** as she went. H2410
2Sa 15:23 countryside wept **a** as all the H7754+1524
2Sa 19: 4 king covered his face and cried **a**, H7754+1524
Ezr 3:12 wept **a** when they saw the H928+7754+1524
Ne 8: 3 *He* **read** it **a** from daybreak till noon as he H7924
Ne 13: 1 Book of Moses **was read a** in the hearing H7924
Job 2:12 they began to weep **a**, and they H5951+7754
Ps 26: 7 proclaiming **a** your praise and H928+7754
Ps 81: 1 our strength; **shout a** to the God of Jacob! H8131
Ps 95: 1 *let us* **shout a** to the Rock of our salvation. H8131
Ps 102: 5 my distress I groan **a** and am reduced to H7754
Ps 142: 1 I cry **a** to the LORD; I lift up my voice to the H7754
Pr 1:20 Out in the open wisdom **calls a**, she H8264
Pr 2: 3 insight and **cry a** for H5989+7754
Pr 8: 3 into the city, at the entrance, *she* **cries a**: H8264
Isa 12: 6 **Shout a** and sing for joy, people of Zion H7412
Isa 33: 7 their brave men **cry a** in the streets; the H7590
Isa 44:23 done this; **shout a**, *you* earth beneath. H8131
Isa 58: 1 "**Shout** it **a**, do not hold back H7924+928+1744
Jer 4: 5 ' Cry **a** and say: 'Gather together H4848
Jer 51:61 see that *you* **read** all these words **a**. H7924
Mic 4: 9 Why *do you* now **cry a**—have you H8131+8275
Zep 3:14 Daughter Zion; **shout a**, Israel! Be glad H8131
Gal 4:27 shout for joy and **cry a**, you who were G1066
Rev 1: 3 Blessed is the *one who* **reads a** the words of G336

ALPHA (3)

Rev 1: 8 "I am the **A** and the Omega," says the Lord G270
Rev 21: 6 I am the **A** and the Omega, the Beginning G270
Rev 22:13 I am the **A** and the Omega, the First and G270

ALPHAEUS (5)

Mt 10: 3 collector; James son of A, and Thaddaeus; G271
Mk 2:14 he saw Levi son of A sitting at the tax G271
Mk 3:18 Thomas, James son of A, Thaddaeus G271
Lk 6:15 Thomas, James son of A, Simon who was G271
Ac 1:13 James son of A and Simon the Zealot G271

ALREADY (92) [READY]

Ge 18:11 Abraham and Sarah were a very old, and NDT
Ge 28: 9 Abraham, in addition to the wives he a had. AIT
Ge 33: 9 But Esau said, "I a have plenty, my brother AIT
Ex 1: 5 seventy in all; Joseph was a in Egypt. AIT
Ex 4:14 He is a on his way to meet you, and he H2180
Ex 30:13 over to those a counted is to give a half AIT
Ex 36: 7 because what they a had was more than AIT
Lev 13:11 isolate them, because they are a unclean. NDT
Lev 27:26 since the firstborn a belongs to the LORD NDT
Nu 14:14 They have a heard that you, LORD, are with AIT
Nu 16:47 The plague had a started among the people AIT
Dt 14:21 Do not eat anything you find a dead. H5577
Jos 18: 7 of Manasseh have a received their AIT
Jdg 8: 6 "Do you a have the hands of Zebah and H6964
Jdg 8:15 'Do you a have the hands of Zebah and H6964
1Sa 29: 3 He has a been with me for over a year, and AIT
2Sa 13:16 wrong than what you have a done to me." AIT
2Ch 20: 2 It is a in Hazezon Tamar" (that is, En Gedi H2180
2Ch 28:13 For our guilt is a great, and his fierce anger NDT
Ne 5: 5 of our daughters have a been enslaved, AIT
Ne 9:25 kinds of good things, wells a dug, vineyards, AIT
Est 7: 7 realizing that the king had a decided his fate, AIT
Job 9:29 Since I am a found guilty, why should I AIT
Job 38:21 for you were a born! You have lived H255
Pr 3:28 give it to you"—when you a have it with you. AIT
Ecc 1:10 It was here a, long ago; it was here H3893
Ecc 2:12 successor do than what has a been done? H3893
Ecc 2:16 the days have a come when H928+8611+3893
Ecc 3:15 Whatever is has a been, and what will be H3893
Ecc 4: 2 the dead, who had a died, are happier H3893
Ecc 6:10 Whatever exists has a been named, and H3893
Ecc 9: 7 God has a approved what you do. H3893
Isa 16:13 the LORD has a spoken concerning H4946+255
Isa 56: 8 still others to them besides those a gathered." AIT
Da 8: 1 one that had a appeared to H9378+928+2021
Jnh 1:10 the LORD, because he had a told them so.) AIT
Mal 2: 2 I have a cursed them, because you have AIT
Mt 3:10 The ax is a at the root of the trees, and G2453
Mt 5:28 woman lustfully has a committed adultery G2453
Mt 14:15 is a remote place, and it's a getting late. G2453
Mt 14:24 the boat was a a considerable G2453
Mt 15:32 they have a been with me three days and G2453
Mt 17:12 tell you, Elijah has a come, and they did G2453
Mk 6:35 they said, "and it's a very late. G2453
Mk 8: 2 they have a been with me three days and G2453
Mk 11:11 since it was a late, he went out to G2453
Mk 15:44 was surprised to hear that he was a dead. G2453
Mk 15:44 he asked him if Jesus had a died. G4093
Lk 3: 9 The ax is a at the root of the trees, and G2453
Lk 6:24 for you have a received your comfort. AIT
Lk 11: 7 The door is a locked, and my children G2453
Lk 12:49 and how I wish it were a kindled! G2453
Lk 19:25 ' they said, 'he a has ten! AIT
Jn 1:16 received grace in place of grace a given. G505
Jn 3:18 stands condemned a because they have G2453
Jn 6: 6 he a had in mind what he was going to AIT
Jn 9:22 who a had decided that anyone who G2453
Jn 9:27 "I have told you a and you did not listen. G2453
Jn 11:17 that Lazarus had a been in the tomb for G2453
Jn 13: 2 the devil had a prompted Judas, the G2453
Jn 15: 3 You are a clean because of the word I G2453
Jn 19:33 to Jesus and found that he was a dead, G2453
Ac 10:41 by witnesses whom God had a chosen— G4742
Ac 27: 9 sailing had a become dangerous G2453
Ro 3: 9 For we have a made the charge that Jews G4577
Ro 8:24 Who hopes for what they a have? G1063
Ro 13:11 The hour has a come for you to wake up G2453
1Co 3:11 lay any foundation other than the one a laid, AIT
1Co 4: 8 A you have all you want! Already you G2453
1Co 4: 8 A you have become rich G2453
1Co 5: 3 I have a passed judgment in the name of G2453
1Co 6: 7 you have been completely defeated a. G2453
1Co 7:18 Was a man a circumcised when he was AIT
2Co 10:16 to boast about work a done in someone G2289
2Co 13: 2 I a gave you a warning when I was with G4625
Gal 1: 9 As we have a said, so now I say again: If G4625
Eph 3: 3 by revelation, as I have a written briefly. G4592
Php 3:12 Not that I have a obtained all this, or G2453
Php 3:12 or have a arrived at my goal, but I G2453
Php 3:16 let us live up to what we have a attained. AIT
Col 1: 5 about which you have a heard in the true G4578
2Th 2: 2 asserting that the day of the Lord has a come. AIT
2Th 2: 7 secret power of lawlessness is a at work; G2453
1Ti 5:15 Some have in fact a turned away to follow G2453
2Ti 2:18 that the resurrection has a taken place, G2453
2Ti 4: 6 For I am a being poured out like a drink G2453
Heb 4: 7 as in the passage a quoted: G4625
Heb 8: 4 for there are a priests who offer the gifts AIT
Heb 9:11 priest of the good things that are now a here, AIT
1Jn 2: 8 is passing and the true light is a shining. G2453
1Jn 4: 3 is coming and even now is a in the world. G2453
Jude 5 Though you a know all this, I want to remind AIT

ALSO (832)

Ge 1:16 to govern the night. He a made the stars. H2256
Ge 2:12 aromatic resin and onyx are a there. NDT
Ge 3: 6 and a desirable for gaining wisdom H2256
Ge 3: 6 She a gave some to her husband, who H1685
Ge 3:22 his hand and take a from the tree of life H1685
Ge 4: 4 And Abel a brought an offering—fat H1685
Ge 4:22 Zillah a had a son, Tubal-Cain, who H1685
Ge 4:26 Seth a had a son, and he named him H1685
Ge 6: 4 in those days—and a afterward—when H1685
Ge 7: 3 and a seven pairs of every kind of bird H1685
Ge 9:26 He a said, "Praise be to the LORD, the God H2256
Ge 10:21 Sons were a born to Shem, whose older H1685
Ge 13: 5 a had flocks and herds and tents. H1685
Ge 13: 7 Perizzites were a living in the land at H2256
Ge 14:12 They a carried off Abram's nephew Lot H2256
Ge 15: 7 He a said to him, "I am the LORD, who H2256
Ge 16:11 The angel of the LORD a said to her: "You H2256
Ge 17:15 God a said to Abraham, "As for Sarai your H2256
Ge 19:25 cities—and a the vegetation in the land. H2256
Ge 19:35 got their father to drink wine that night a, H1685
Ge 19:38 The younger daughter a had a son, and H1685
Ge 20: 5 and didn't she a say, 'He is my brother' H1685
Ge 21:13 son of the slave into a nation a, H2256+1685
Ge 22:20 was told, "Milkah is a a mother; she has H1685
Ge 22:24 whose name was Reumah, a had sons: H1685
Ge 24:46 So I drank, and she watered the camels a. H1685
Ge 24:53 he a gave costly gifts to her brother and to H2256
Ge 24:64 Rebekah a looked up and saw Isaac. She H2256
Ge 25:30 That is why he was a called Edom.) NDT
Ge 26:21 they quarreled over that one a; so he H1685
Ge 26:34 and a Basemath daughter of Elon the H2256
Ge 27:16 She a covered his hands and the smooth H2256
Ge 29:27 then we will give you the younger one a H1685
Ge 29:30 Jacob made love to Rachel a, and his love H1685
Ge 31:49 It was a called Mizpah, because he said H2256
Ge 31:51 Laban a said to Jacob, "Here is this heap H2256
Ge 32: 1 Jacob a went on his way, and the angels H2256
Ge 32:11 and a the mothers with their children. NDT
Ge 32:19 He a instructed the second, the third and H1685
Ge 35:12 I gave to Abraham and Isaac I a give to you, NDT
Ge 35:14 drink offering on it; he a poured oil on it. H2256
Ge 36: 3 a Basemath daughter of Ishmael and H2256
Ge 36:12 Esau's son Eliphaz a had a concubine H2256
Ge 38:10 so the LORD put him to death a. H1685
Ge 42: 5 there was famine in the land of Canaan a. NDT
Ge 43:13 Take your brother a and go back to the H2256
Ge 43:15 the amount of silver, and Benjamin a. H2256
Ge 43:22 We have a brought additional silver with H2256
Ge 44: 5 master drinks from and a uses for H2256
Ge 45:19 "You are a directed to tell them, 'Do this H2256
Ge 45:21 and he a gave them provisions for their H2256
Ge 47: 4 They a said to him, "We have come to live H2256
Ge 47:12 Joseph a provided his father and his H2256
Ge 50: 9 horsemen a went up with him. H1685
Ge 50:23 A the children of Makir son of Manasseh H1685
Ex 3:15 God a said to Moses, "Say to the H6388
Ex 4:28 and a about all the signs he had H2256
Ex 4:30 He a performed the signs before the H2256
Ex 6: 2 God a said to Moses, "I am the LORD. H2256
Ex 6: 4 I a established my covenant with H2256+1685
Ex 7:11 Egyptian magicians a did the same things H1685
Ex 8: 7 they a made frogs come up on the land of H2256
Ex 8:32 But this time a Pharaoh hardened his H1685
Ex 12:32 you have said, and go. And a bless me." H1685
Ex 12:38 with them, and a large droves of livestock H2256
Ex 14:19 The pillar of cloud a moved from in front H2256
Ex 16: 8 Moses a said, "You will know that it was H2256
Ex 21:29 stoned and its owner a is to be put to H1685
Ex 21:31 This law a applies if the bull gores a son NDT
Ex 25:25 A make around it a rim a handbreadth H2256
Ex 26:10 in one set and a along the edge of H2256
Ex 26:26 "A make crossbars of acacia wood: five H2256
Ex 26:29 A overlay the crossbars with gold H2256
Ex 27:11 The north side shall a be a hundred cubits H4027
Ex 27:13 the courtyard shall a be fifty cubits wide. H2256
Ex 28:30 A put the Urim and the Thummim in the H2256
Ex 29:43 there a I will meet with the Israelites, and H2256
Ex 30:20 A, when they approach the altar to minister H196
Ex 31: 6 A I have given ability to all the skilled H2256
Ex 31:10 and a the woven garments, both the H2256
Ex 35:28 They a brought spices and olive oil for the H2256
Ex 36:12 They a made fifty loops on one curtain and NDT
Ex 36:17 in one set and a along the edge of H2256
Ex 36:31 They a made crossbars of acacia wood H2256
Ex 36:34 They a overlaid the crossbars with gold H2256
Ex 37:12 They a made around it a rim a H2256
Ex 37:29 They a made the sacred anointing oil H2256
Ex 38:11 The north side was a a hundred cubits H2256
Ex 38:13 toward the sunrise, was a fifty cubits wide. H2256
Ex 39: 1 They a made sacred garments for Aaron H2256
Lev 6:19 The LORD a said to Moses, H2256
Lev 8: 7 He a fastened the ephod with a H2256
Lev 8:16 Moses a took all the fat around the H2256
Lev 8:24 Moses a brought Aaron's sons forward H2256
Lev 8:29 Moses a took the breast, which was his H2256
Lev 9:17 He a brought the grain offering, took a H2256
Lev 16:25 He shall a burn the fat of the sin offering H2256
Lev 20:18 of her flow, and she has a uncovered it. H2256
Lev 22: 4 He will a be unclean if he touches H2256
Lev 23:39 and the eighth day a is a day of sabbath H2256
Lev 25:45 You may a buy some of the H2256+1685
Lev 26:39 a because of their ancestors' sins H2256+677
Nu 3:11 The LORD a said to Moses, H2256
Nu 3:44 The LORD a said to Moses, H2256
Nu 4:22 "Take a census a of the Gershonites by H1685
Nu 5:15 He must a take an offering of a tenth of H2256
Nu 7: 1 He a anointed and consecrated the altar H2256
Nu 9:14 residing among you is a to celebrate the H2256
Nu 10:10 A at your times of rejoicing—your H2256
Nu 11: 5 in Egypt at no cost—a the cucumbers NDT
Nu 11: 9 camp at night, the manna a came down. NDT
Nu 11:26 Yet the Spirit a rested on them, and they H2256
Nu 12: 2 "Hasn't he a spoken through us?" H1685
Nu 15:10 and a bring half a hin of wine as a drink H2256
Nu 16: 8 Moses a said to Korah, "Now listen, you H2256
Nu 16:13 And now you a want to lord it over us! H1685
Nu 16:17 Aaron are to present your censers a." H2256
Nu 18:11 "This a is yours: whatever is set aside H2256
Nu 18:28 In this way you a will present an offering H1685
Nu 19: 8 who burns it must a wash his clothes and H2256
Nu 19:10 of the heifer must a wash his clothes, H2256
Nu 19:18 He must a sprinkle anyone who has H2256
Nu 19:21 of cleansing must a wash his clothes, H2256
Nu 26:58 These a were Levite clans: the Libnite clan NDT
Nu 31: 8 They a killed Balaam son of Beor with the H2256
Nu 31:23 But it must a be purified with the water of H421
Dt 1:37 LORD became angry with me a and said, H1685
Dt 3: 3 the LORD our God a gave into our hands H1685
Dt 3: 5 and there were a a great many H963+4200
Dt 3:13 The rest of Gilead and a all of Bashan, the H2256
Dt 9:21 A I took that sinful thing of yours, the calf H2256
Dt 9:22 You a made the LORD angry at Taberah, at H2256
Dt 10: 1 on the mountain. A make a wooden ark. H2256
Dt 10:10 the LORD listened to me at this time a. H1685
Dt 14: 8 The pig is a unclean; although it has a H2256
Dt 22: 9 the crops you plant but a the fruit of the H2256
Dt 28:61 The LORD will a bring on you every kind of H1685
Dt 29:15 the LORD our God but a with those who are H2256
Dt 31: 3 Joshua a will cross over ahead of you, as NDT
Jos 8:22 Those in the ambush a came out of the H2256
Jos 10:30 The LORD a gave that city and its king into H1685
Jos 12: 3 He a ruled over the eastern Arabah from H2256
Jos 13:11 It a included Gilead, the territory of the H2256
Jos 15:19 in the Negev, give me a springs of water." H2256
Jos 16: 9 It a included all the towns and their H2256
Jos 17:11 Asher, Manasseh a had Beth Shan H2256
Jos 21:23 A from the tribe of Dan they received H2256
Jos 24:11 against you, as did a the Amorites H2256
Jos 24:12 out before you—a the two Amorite kings. NDT
Jdg 1: 8 Judah attacked Jerusalem a and took it. H2256
Jdg 1:15 in the Negev, give me a springs of water." H2256
Jdg 1:18 Judah a took Gaza, Ashkelon and Ekron H2256
Jdg 1:35 And the Amorites were determined a to H2256
Jdg 2: 3 And I have a said, 'I will not drive them H1685
Jdg 4:10 Deborah a went up with him. H2256
Jdg 6:35 them to arms, and a into Asher, Zebulun H1685
Jdg 7:25 They a captured two of the Midianite H2256
Jdg 8:17 He a pulled down the tower of Peniel and H2256
Jdg 8:31 lived in Shechem, a bore him a son H1685
Jdg 8:35 They a failed to show any loyalty to the H2256
Jdg 9:49 a thousand men and women, a, died. H1685
Jdg 9:57 God a made the people of Shechem pay H2256
Jdg 10: 9 The Ammonites a crossed the Jordan to H1685
Jdg 11: 2 Gilead's wife a bore him sons, and when H2256
Jdg 11:17 They sent a to the king of Moab, and he H1685
Jdg 18: 7 A, they lived a long way from the H2256
Ru 1: 5 both Mahlon and Kilion a died, and H1685
Ru 2:18 Ruth a brought out and gave her what she H2256
Ru 3:15 He a said, "Bring me the shawl you are H2256
Ru 4: 5 you a acquire Ruth the Moabite H1685
Ru 4:10 I have a acquired Ruth the Moabite H1685
1Sa 2:28 I a gave your ancestor's family all the H2256
1Sa 4:17 A your two sons, Hophni and H2256+1685
1Sa 7:17 and there he a held court for Israel. H2256
1Sa 10:11 Is Saul a among the prophets?" H1685
1Sa 10:12 "Is Saul a among the prophets?" H1685
1Sa 10:26 Saul a went to his home in Gibeah H1685
1Sa 12: 5 and a his anointed is witness this day H2256
1Sa 17:25 He will a give him his daughter in H2256
1Sa 19:20 on Saul's men, and they a prophesied. H1685
1Sa 19:21 men a third time, and they a prophesied. H1685
1Sa 19:24 "Is Saul a among the prophets? H1685
1Sa 22:10 he a gave him provisions and the sword H2256
1Sa 22:19 He a put to the sword Nob, the town of the H2256
1Sa 25:43 David had a married Ahinoam of Jezreel H2256
1Sa 28:19 The LORD will a give the army of Israel into H1685
2Sa 2: 3 David a took the men who were with him H2256
2Sa 2: 9 Ashuri and Jezreel, and a over Ephraim H2256
2Sa 3:19 Abner a spoke to the Benjamites in H1685
2Sa 3:32 at Abner's tomb. All the people wept a. H2256
2Sa 7:11 I will a give you rest from all your H2256
2Sa 7:19 you have a spoken about the future of the H1685
2Sa 8: 2 David a defeated the Moabites. He made H2256
2Sa 8:12 He a dedicated the plunder taken from H2256
2Sa 10: 6 and a twelve thousand men from Tob. H2256
2Sa 10:18 He a struck down Shobak the commander H2256
2Sa 15: 5 A, whenever anyone approached him to H2256
2Sa 15:12 he a sent for Ahithophel the Gilonite H2256
2Sa 15:23 The king a crossed the Kidron Valley, and H2256
2Sa 15:27 The king a said to Zadok the priest, "Do H2256
2Sa 15:27 with you, and a Abiathar's son Jonathan. H2256
2Sa 17: 5 "Summon a Hushai the Arkite, so H1685
2Sa 17:28 They a brought wheat and barley, flour H2256

2Sa 19:24 grandson, **a** went down to meet the king. H2256
2Sa 19:31 the Gileadite **a** came down from Rogelim H2256
2Sa 21:20 He **a** was descended from Rapha. H1685
2Sa 23:20 He **a** went down into a pit on a snowy day H2256
2Sa 24:23 Araunah **a** said to him, "May the LORD H2256
1Ki 1: 6 He was **a** very handsome and was born H1685
1Ki 1:47 **A**, the royal officials have come to H2256+1685
1Ki 2:44 The king **a** said to Shimei, "You know in H2256
1Ki 3:18 child was born, this woman **a** had a baby. H1685
1Ki 4:28 They **a** brought to the proper place their H2256
1Ki 4:33 He **a** spoke about animals and birds H2256
1Ki 6:20 **and** he **a** overlaid the altar of cedar. H2256
1Ki 6:22 He **a** overlaid with gold the altar that H2256
1Ki 6:25 The second cherub **a** measured ten cubits H2256
1Ki 6:30 He **a** covered the floors of both the inner H2256
1Ki 6:34 He **a** made two doors out of juniper wood H2256
1Ki 7: 8 Solomon **a** made a palace like this hall H2256
1Ki 7:16 He **a** made two capitals of cast bronze to H2256
1Ki 7:27 He **a** made ten movable stands of bronze H2256
1Ki 7:40 He **a** made the pots and shovels and H2256
1Ki 7:48 Solomon **a** made all the furnishings that H2256
1Ki 7:50 **a** for the doors of the main hall of the NDT
1Ki 9:23 They were **a** the chief officials in charge of NDT
1Ki 9:26 King Solomon **a** built ships at Ezion H2256
1Ki 10:17 He **a** made three hundred small shields of H2256
1Ki 10:26 in the chariot cities **and a** with him in H2256
1Ki 10:29 They **a** exported them to all the kings of H2256
1Ki 11:21 **and** that Joab the commander of the army was **a** H2256
1Ki 11:26 **A**, Jeroboam son of Nebat rebelled H2256
1Ki 12:32 **And** at Bethel he **a** installed priests at the H2256
1Ki 13: 5 **A**, the altar was split apart and its ashes H2256
1Ki 13:11 They **a** told their father what he had said H2256
1Ki 14:23 They **a** set up for themselves high places H1685
1Ki 15:22 up Geba in Benjamin, **and a** Mizpah. H2256
1Ki 16: 7 **and a** because he destroyed it. H2256
1Ki 16:31 **but** he **a** married Jezebel daughter of H2256
1Ki 16:33 Ahab **a** made an Asherah pole and did H2256
1Ki 18:38 **and a** licked up the water in the trench. H2256
1Ki 19:16 **A**, anoint Jehu son of Nimshi king over H2256
1Ki 20:25 You must **a** raise an army like the one you H2256
1Ki 20:27 **When** the Israelites were **a** mustered and H2256
1Ki 21:23 "And **a** concerning Jezebel the LORD says H1685
1Ki 22: 5 **But** Jehoshaphat **a** said to the king of H2256
1Ki 22:44 Jehoshaphat was **a** at peace with the king H2256
2Ki 3: 7 He **a** sent this message to Jehoshaphat H2256
2Ki 3:18 he will **a** deliver Moab into your hands. H2256
2Ki 5:18 on my arm **and** I have to bow there **a**— H2256
2Ki 7: 8 took some things from it and hid them **a**. H2256
2Ki 11:17 He **a** made a covenant between the king H2256
2Ki 13: 6 **A**, the Asherah pole remained H2256+1685
2Ki 14:10 your own downfall and that of Judah **a**?" H6640
2Ki 14:14 He **a** took hostages and returned to H2256
2Ki 17:32 **but** they **a** appointed all sorts of their own H2256
2Ki 17:33 **but** they **a** served their own gods in H2256
2Ki 21: 3 he **a** erected altars to Baal and made an H2256
2Ki 21:16 Manasseh **a** shed so much innocent H2256
2Ki 22: 6 **A** have them purchase timber and H2256
2Ki 22:19 in my presence, I **a** have heard you H2256+1685
2Ki 23: 7 He **a** tore down the quarters of the male H2256
2Ki 23:13 The king **a** desecrated the high places that H2256
2Ki 23:15 powder, **and** burned the Asherah pole **a**. H2256
2Ki 23:27 will remove Judah **a** from my presence as H1685
2Ki 24:15 He **a** took from Jerusalem to Babylon the H2256
2Ki 24:16 The king of Babylon **a** deported to Babylon H2256
2Ki 25:14 They **a** took away the pots, shovels, wick H2256
2Ki 25:19 He **a** took the secretary who was chief H2256
2Ki 25:25 Gedaliah **and a** the men of Judah and H2256
1Ch 1:51 Hadad **a** died. The chiefs of Edom were H2256
1Ch 2:49 She **a** gave birth to Shaaph the father of H2256
1Ch 3: 6 There were **a** Ibhar, Elishua, Eliphelet, H2256
1Ch 3:20 There were **a** five others: Hashubah, Ohel, H2256
1Ch 4:36 **a** Elioenai, Jaakobah, Jeshohaiah H2256
1Ch 4:41 their dwellings **and a** the Meunites who H2256
1Ch 5:21 They **a** took one hundred thousand H2256
1Ch 6:71 Golan in Bashan **and a** Ashtaroth, H2256
1Ch 11:22 He **a** went down into a pit on a snowy day H2256
1Ch 12:16 some men from Judah **a** came to David in H2256
1Ch 12:38 the Israelites were **a** of one mind to make H1685
1Ch 12:40 **A**, their neighbors from as far away H2256+1685
1Ch 13: 2 **and a** to the priests and Levites who are H2256
1Ch 15:24 Jehiah were **a** to be doorkeepers for H2256
1Ch 15:27 David **a** wore a linen ephod. H2256
1Ch 16:38 He **a** left Obed-Edom and his sixty-eight H2256
1Ch 16:38 son of Jeduthun, **and a** Hosah, were H2256
1Ch 17:10 I will **a** subdue all your enemies H2256
1Ch 18: 2 David **a** defeated the Moabites, and they H2256
1Ch 19:18 He **a** killed Shophak the commander of H2256
1Ch 20: 6 He **a** was descended from Rapha H1685
1Ch 21: 7 This command was **a** evil in the sight of H2256
1Ch 22: 1 **and a** the altar of burnt offering for Israel." H2256
1Ch 22: 4 He **a** provided more cedar logs than could H2256
1Ch 23: 2 He **a** gathered together all the leaders of H2256
1Ch 23:30 They were **a** to stand every morning to H2256
1Ch 24:31 They **a** cast lots, just as their relatives the H1685
1Ch 26: 4 Obed-Edom **a** had sons: Shemaiah the H2256
1Ch 26: 6 Obed-Edom's son Shemaiah **a** had sons H2256
1Ch 26: 7 Elihu and Semakiah were **a** able men. NDT
1Ch 28:18 He **a** gave him the plan for the chariot H2256
1Ch 28:20 David **a** said to Solomon his son, "Be H2256
1Ch 29: 9 David the king **a** rejoiced greatly. H2256+1685
2Ch 1:12 **And** I will **a** give you wealth, possessions H2256
2Ch 1:14 in the chariot cities **and a** with him in H2256
2Ch 1:17 They **a** exported them to all the kings of H2256
2Ch 2: 8 "Send me **a** cedar, juniper and algum H2256
2Ch 3: 9 He **a** overlaid the upper parts with gold H2256
2Ch 3:11 while its other wing, **a** five cubits long NDT
2Ch 3:12 its other wing, **a** five cubits long NDT
2Ch 3:16 He **a** made a hundred pomegranates H2256
2Ch 4: 8 He **a** made a hundred gold sprinkling H2256
2Ch 4:11 **And** Huram **a** made the pots and shovels H2256
2Ch 4:19 Solomon **a** made all the furnishings that H2256
2Ch 8: 4 He **a** built up Tadmor in the desert and all H2256
2Ch 8:10 They were **a** King Solomon's chief officials H2256
2Ch 8:14 He **a** appointed the gatekeepers by H2256
2Ch 9:10 they **a** brought algumwood and H2256+1685
2Ch 9:14 **A** all the kings of Arabia and the H2256
2Ch 9:16 He **a** made three hundred small shields of H2256
2Ch 9:25 in the chariot cities **and a** with him in H2256
2Ch 14:15 They **a** attacked the camps of the H2256+1685
2Ch 15:16 King Asa **a** deposed his H2256+1685
2Ch 17:13 He **a** kept experienced fighting men in H2256
2Ch 18: 4 **But** Jehoshaphat **a** said to the king of H2256
2Ch 19: 8 In Jerusalem **a**, Jehoshaphat H2256+1685
2Ch 20:25 clothing **and a** articles of value— H2256
2Ch 21:11 He had **a** built high places on the hills of H1685
2Ch 21:13 You have **a** murdered your own H2256+1685
2Ch 22: 5 He **a** followed their counsel when he went H1685
2Ch 23:19 He **a** stationed gatekeepers at the gates of H2256
2Ch 24:12 **a** workers in iron and bronze to repair H1685
2Ch 24:14 **and a** dishes and other objects of gold H2256
2Ch 25: 6 He **a** hired a hundred thousand fighting H2256
2Ch 25:12 The army of Judah **a** captured ten H2256
2Ch 25:19 your own downfall and that of Judah **a**?" H6640
2Ch 26:10 He **a** built towers in the wilderness and H2256
2Ch 27: 5 the same amount **a** in the second and H2256
2Ch 28: 2 the kings of Israel and **a** made idols for H1685
2Ch 28: 5 He was **a** given into the hands of H2256+1685
2Ch 28: 8 They **a** took a great deal of plunder H2256+1685
2Ch 28:10 **But** aren't you **a** guilty of sins against the H8370
2Ch 29: 7 They **a** shut the doors of the portico and H1685
2Ch 29:27 singing to the LORD began **a** H2256
2Ch 30: 1 Israel and Judah and **a** wrote letters to H1685
2Ch 30:12 **A** in Judah the hand of God was on the H1685
2Ch 30:25 come from Israel **and a** those who resided H2256
2Ch 31: 6 in the towns of Judah **a** brought a tithe of H1685
2Ch 31:14 made to the LORD **and a** the consecrated H2256
2Ch 32: 5 He **a** made large numbers of weapons H2256
2Ch 32:17 The king **a** wrote letters ridiculing the LORD H2256
2Ch 32:28 He **a** made buildings to store the harvest H2256
2Ch 33: 3 he **a** erected altars to the Baals and made H2256
2Ch 33:14 hill of Ophel; he **a** made it much higher. H2256
2Ch 34:11 They **a** gave money to the carpenters and H2256
2Ch 35: 7 offerings, **and a** three thousand cattle H2256
2Ch 35: 8 His officials **a** contributed voluntarily to H2256
2Ch 35: 9 **A** Konaniah along with Shemaiah and H2256
2Ch 36: 7 Nebuchadnezzar **a** took to Babylon articles H2256
2Ch 36:13 He **a** rebelled against King H2256+1685
2Ch 36:22 his realm and **a** to put it in writing: H1685
Ezr 1: 1 his realm and **a** to put it in writing: H1685
Ezr 2:65 **and** they **a** had 200 male and female H2256
Ezr 5: 4 They **a** asked, "What are the A10008+10358
Ezr 5:10 We **a** asked them their names A10221+10059
Ezr 6: 5 **A**, the gold and silver articles of A10221+10059
Ezr 7: 7 **a** came up to Jerusalem in the seventh H2256
Ezr 7:24 You are **a** to know that you have no A10221
Ezr 8:20 They **a** brought 220 of the temple servants H2256
Ezr 8:36 They **a** delivered the king's orders to the H2256
Ne 1: 2 the exile, **and a** about Jerusalem. H2256
Ne 2: 7 I **a** said to him, "If it pleases the king H2256
Ne 2: 9 The king had **a** sent army officers and H2256
Ne 2:18 I **a** told them about the gracious hand of H2256
Ne 3: 4 **and** next to him Zadok son of Baana **a** H2256
Ne 3:13 They **a** repaired a thousand cubits of the H2256
Ne 3:15 He **a** repaired the wall of the Pool of H2256
Ne 4:11 **A** our enemies said, "Before they know it H2256
Ne 4:22 At that time I **a** said to the people, "Have H1685
Ne 5:10 and my men are **a** lending the H2256+1685
Ne 5:11 **and a** the interest you are charging them H2256
Ne 5:13 I **a** shook out the folds of my robe and said H1685
Ne 5:15 Their assistants **a** lorded it over the H1685
Ne 6:14 remember **a** the prophet Noadiah H2256+1685
Ne 6:17 **A**, in those days the nobles of Judah were H1685
Ne 7: 3 **A** appoint residents of Jerusalem as H2256
Ne 7:67 **and** they **a** had 245 male and female H2256
Ne 10:35 "We **a** assume responsibility for bringing H2256
Ne 10:36 "As it is **a** written in the Law, we will bring H2256
Ne 10:39 gatekeepers and the musicians are **a** kept. NDT
Ne 12: 8 Sherebiah, Judah, and **a** Mattaniah, who NDT
Ne 12:28 The musicians **a** were brought together H2256
Ne 12:31 I **a** assigned two large choirs to give H2256
Ne 12:35 trumpets, and **a** Zechariah son of Jonathan NDT
Ne 12:42 **and a** Maaseiah, Shemaiah, Eleazar, Uzzi H2256
Ne 12:43 women and children **a** rejoiced. H2256+1685
Ne 12:45 as did **a** the musicians and gatekeepers H2256
Ne 12:47 They **a** set aside the portion for the other H2256
Ne 13: 5 temple articles, **and a** the tithes of grain H2256
Ne 13:10 I **a** learned that the portions assigned to H2256
Ne 13:22 Remember me for this **a**, my God, and H1685
Ne 13:31 I **a** made provision for contributions of H2256
Est 1: 9 Queen Vashti **a** gave a banquet for the H1685
Est 1:16 against the king but **a** against all the nobles NDT
Est 1:19 **A** let the king give her royal position to H2256
Est 2: 7 who was **a** known as Esther, had NDT
Est 2: 8 Esther **a** was taken to the king's palace H2256
Est 4: 8 He **a** gave him a copy of the text of the H2256
Est 8: 9 of each people **and a** to the Jews in their H2256
Est 9: 7 They **a** killed Parshandatha, Dalphon H2256
Est 9:12 is your request? It will **a** be granted." H6388
Est 9:13 to carry out this day's edict tomorrow **a**, H1685
Est 9:16 king's provinces **a** assembled to protect H2256
Job 1: 6 the LORD, and Satan **a** came with them. H1685
Job 2: 1 Satan **a** came with them to present H1685
Job 3:18 Captives **a** enjoy their ease; they no H3480
Job 5:18 For he wounds, **but** he **a** binds up; he H2256
Job 5:18 he injures, **but** his hands **a** heal. H2256
Job 13: 2 What you know, I **a** know; I am not H1685
Job 16: 4 I **a** could speak like you, if you were in my H1685
Job 31:28 then these **a** would be sins to be judged H1685
Job 32: 3 He was **a** angry with the three friends H2256
Job 42:13 **And** he **a** had seven sons and three H2256
Ps 16: 9 tongue rejoices; my body **a** will rest secure, H677
Ps 19:13 Keep your servant **a** from willful sins; may H1685
Ps 49:10 the foolish and the senseless **a** perish, H3480
Ps 74:16 The day is yours, **and** yours **a** the night; you H677
Ps 78:20 abundantly, **but** can he **a** give us bread? H1685
Ps 84: 6 the autumn rains **a** cover it with pools. H1685
Ps 89:11 are yours, **and** yours **a** the earth; you H677
Pr 2:16 Wisdom will save you **a** from the adulterous NDT
Pr 9: 2 mixed her wine; she has **a** set her table. H677
Pr 21:13 cry of the poor will **a** cry out and not be H1685
Pr 24:14 Know **a** that wisdom is like honey for you: If NDT
Pr 24:23 These **a** are sayings of the wise: To show H1685
Pr 31:28 blessed; her husband **a**, and he praises her: NDT
Ecc 1:17 of wisdom, **and a** of madness and folly H2256
Ecc 2: 1 But that **a** proved to be meaningless H1685
Ecc 2: 7 I **a** owned more herds and flocks than H1685
Ecc 2:12 wisdom, **and a** madness and folly. H2256
Ecc 2:15 "The fate of the fool will overtake me **a**. H1685
Ecc 3:11 He has **a** set eternity in the human heart H1685
Ecc 3:18 I **a** said to myself, "As for humans, God tests NDT
Ecc 4:11 **A**, if two lie down together, they will keep H1685
Ecc 9:13 I **a** saw under the sun this example of H1685
Ecc 12: 9 **but** he **a** imparted knowledge to the H6388
Isa 7:13 Will you try the patience of my God **a**? H1685
Isa 7:20 private parts, and to cut off your beard **a**. H1685
Isa 14:10 say to you, "You **a** have become weak, as H1685
Isa 16: 8 of Heshbon wither, the vines of Sibmah **a**. NDT
Isa 19: 7 **a** the plants along the Nile, at the mouth of NDT
Isa 21:12 "Morning is coming, but **a** the night. H1685
Isa 28: 7 And these **a** stagger from wine and reel H1685
Isa 28:29 All this **a** comes from the LORD Almighty H1685
Isa 30:23 He will **a** send you rain for the seed you H2256
Isa 34:14 night creatures will **a** lie down and find H421
Isa 34:15 of her wings; there **a** the falcons will gather H421
Isa 44:15 **But** he **a** fashions a god and worships it; he H677
Isa 44:16 He **a** warms himself and says H677
Isa 49: 6 I will **a** make you a light for the Gentiles H2256
Isa 57:15 **but a** with the one who is contrite and H2256
Isa 66: 4 so I **a** will choose harsh treatment for H1685
Isa 66:21 select some of them **a** to be priests and H1685
Jer 2:16 **A**, the men of Memphis and Tahpanhes H1685
Jer 2:37 You will **a** leave that place with your H1685
Jer 3: 8 she **a** went out and committed adultery. H1685
Jer 17:19 stand **a** at all the other gates of H2256
Jer 28: 4 I will **a** bring back to this place Jehoiachin H2256
Jer 29: 7 **A**, seek the peace and prosperity of the H2256
Jer 35: 7 **A** you must never build houses, sow seed H2256
Jer 36:29 **A** tell Jehoiakim king of Judah, 'This is H2256
Jer 39: 6 before his eyes **and a** killed all the nobles H2256
Jer 41: 3 Ishmael **a** killed all the men of Judah who H2256
Jer 43: 6 They **a** led away all those whom H2256
Jer 46:14 proclaim it **a** in Memphis and Tahpanhes: H2256
Jer 48: 2 of Madmen, will **a** be silenced; the sword H1685
Jer 49:10 are destroyed, **a** his allies and neighbors H2256
Jer 52:10 he **a** killed all the officials of Judah H2256+1685
Jer 52:18 They **a** took away the pots, shovels, wick H2256
Jer 52:25 He **a** took the secretary who was chief H2256
La 4:21 **But** to you **a** the cup will be passed; you H1685
Eze 1:10 of an ox; each **a** had the face of an eagle. H2256
Eze 1:19 rose from the ground, the wheels **a** rose. NDT
Eze 1:21 creatures moved, they **a** moved; when the NDT
Eze 1:21 stood still, they **a** stood still; and when the NDT
Eze 4:11 **A** measure out a sixth of a hin of water H2256
Eze 8:17 Must they **a** fill the land with violence and NDT
Eze 10:17 stood still, they **a** stood still; and when the NDT
Eze 16:17 You **a** took the fine jewelry I gave you, the H2256
Eze 16:19 **A** the food I provided for you—the flour H2256
Eze 17:13 He **a** carried away the leading men of the H2256
Eze 20:12 **A** I gave them my Sabbaths as a H2256+1685
Eze 20:15 **A** with uplifted hand I swore to H2256+1685
Eze 20:23 **A** with uplifted hand I swore to them in H1685
Eze 20:27 In this **a** your ancestors blasphemed me H6388
Eze 23:26 They will **a** strip you of your clothes and H2256
Eze 23:38 They have **a** done this to me: At that same H6388
Eze 32:27 though these warriors **a** had terrorized the NDT
Eze 34:18 Must you **a** trample the rest of your H2256
Eze 34:18 Must you **a** muddy the rest with your feet H2256
Eze 36: 7 the nations around you will **a** suffer scorn. NDT
Eze 38: 6 **a** Gomer with all its troops, and Beth NDT
Eze 40:27 The inner court **a** had a gate facing south H2256
Eze 40:42 There were **a** four tables of dressed stone H2256
Eze 41: 2 He **a** measured the main hall; it was forty H2256
Eze 41:13 with its walls were **a** a hundred cubits long. NDT
Eze 41:26 rooms of the temple **a** had overhangs. H2256
Eze 43:14 **and** that ledge is **a** a cubit wide. H2256

Eze 43:17 The upper ledge **a** is square, fourteen H2256
Eze 43:25 you are **a** to provide a young bull and a H2256
Eze 45:15 **A** one sheep is to be taken from every H2256
Eze 46:14 You are **a** to provide with it morning by H2256
Eze 46:16 his sons, it will **a** belong to his descendants NDT
Da 2:26 king asked Daniel (**a** called Belteshazzar), NDT
Da 4:19 Then Daniel (**a** called Belteshazzar) was NDT
Da 5:12 **a** the ability to interpret dreams NDT
Da 7:20 I **a** wanted to know about the ten horns A10221
Da 11:8 He will **a** seize their gods, their H2256+1685
Da 11:41 He will **a** invade the Beautiful Land. Many H2256
Hos 4:6 knowledge, I **a** reject you as my priests H2256
Hos 4:6 of your God, I **a** will ignore your children. H1685
Hos 5:5 in their sin; Judah **a** stumbles with them. H1685
Hos 6:11 "**A** for you, Judah, a harvest is appointed H1685
Am 2:11 "I **a** raised up prophets from among your H2256
Am 4:7 "I **a** withheld rain from you when H2256+1685
Am 7:14 **and** I **a** took care of sycamore-fig trees. H2256
Jnh 4:11 from their left—**and a** many animals?" H2256
Mic 6:4 Moses to lead you, **a** Aaron and Miriam. NDT
Zep 1:5 by the LORD **and** who **a** swear by Molek, H2256
Zec 4:3 **A** there are two olive trees by it, one on H2256
Zec 4:9 this temple; his hands will **a** complete it. H2256
Zec 8:9 ' This is **a** what the prophets said who were NDT
Mt 4:7 answered him, "It is **a** written: 'Do not put *G4099*
Mt 5:39 turn to them the other cheek **a**. *G2779*
Mt 6:12 as we **a** have forgiven our debtors. *G2779*
Mt 6:14 your heavenly Father will **a** forgive you. *G2779*
Mt 6:21 your treasure is, there your heart will be **a**. *G2779*
Mt 10:32 **I** will **a** acknowledge before my Father in *G2743*
Mt 13:26 then the weeds **a** appeared. *G2779*
Mt 19:28 followed me will **a** sit on twelve thrones *G2779*
Mt 20:4 'You **a** go and work in my vineyard *G2779*
Mt 20:7 'You **a** go and work in my vineyard.' *G2779*
Mt 20:10 each one of them **a** received a denarius. *G2779*
Mt 21:21 but **a** you can say to this mountain *G2829*
Mt 21:24 replied, "**I** will **a** ask you one question. *G2743*
Mt 23:18 You **a** say, 'If anyone swears by the altar, it *G2779*
Mt 23:26 **and** then the outside **a** will be clean. *G2779*
Mt 24:44 So you **a** must be ready, because the Son *G2779*
Mt 25:11 "Later the others **a** came. 'Lord, Lord,' they *G2779*
Mt 25:17 **So a**, the one with two bags of gold *G6058*
Mt 25:22 "The man with two bags of gold **a** came *G2779*
Mt 25:44 "They **a** will answer, 'Lord, when did we *G2779*
Mt 26:13 what she has done will **a** be told, in *G2779*
Mt 26:69 "You **a** were with Jesus of Galilee," she *G2779*
Mt 27:44 crucified with him **a** heaped insults on *G2779*
Mk 1:34 He **a** drove out many demons, but he *G2779*
Mk 1:38 nearby villages—so I can preach there **a**. *G2779*
Mk 2:26 And he **a** gave some to his companions." *G2779*
Mk 4:26 He **a** said, "This is what the kingdom of *G2779*
Mk 4:36 There were **a** other boats with him *G2779*
Mk 6:41 He **a** divided the two fish among them all. *G2779*
Mk 8:7 gave thanks for them **a** and told the *G2779*
Mk 12:21 the widow, **but** he **a** died, leaving no *G2779*
Mk 14:9 what she has done will **a** be told, in *G2779*
Mk 14:67 "You **a** were with that Nazarene, Jesus," *G2779*
Mk 15:32 crucified with him **a** heaped insults on *G2779*
Mk 15:41 up with him to Jerusalem were **a** there. *G2779*
Lk 1:5 wife Elizabeth was **a** a descendant of *G2779*
Lk 2:4 So Joseph **a** went up from the town of *G2779*
Lk 2:36 There was **a** a prophet, Anna, the *G2779*
Lk 4:43 the kingdom of God to the other towns **a**, *G2779*
Lk 6:4 **And** he **a** gave some to his companions." *G2779*
Lk 6:13 of them, whom he **a** designated apostles: *G2779*
Lk 6:29 on one cheek, turn to them the other **a**. *G2779*
Lk 6:39 He **a** told them this parable: "Can the *G2779*
Lk 8:2 **and a** some women who had been cured *G2779*
Lk 11:4 we **a** forgive everyone who sins *G2779*
Lk 11:30 so **a** will the Son of Man be to this *G2779*
Lk 11:34 healthy, your whole body **a** is full of light. *G2779*
Lk 11:34 unhealthy, your body **a** is full of darkness. *G2779*
Lk 11:40 who made the outside make the inside **a**? *G2779*
Lk 11:45 you say these things, you insult us **a**." *G2779*
Lk 12:8 Son of Man will **a** acknowledge before *G2779*
Lk 12:34 your treasure is, there your heart will be **a**. *G2779*
Lk 12:40 You **a** must be ready, because the Son of *G2779*
Lk 16:10 with very little can **a** be trusted with much, *G2779*
Lk 16:10 with very little will **a** be dishonest with *G2779*
Lk 16:22 The rich man **a** died and was buried. *G2779*
Lk 16:28 that they will not **a** come to this place of *G2779*
Lk 17:10 So you **a**, when you have done everything *G2779*
Lk 17:26 so **a** will it be in the days of the Son of *G2779*
Lk 18:15 People were **a** bringing babies to Jesus *G1254*
Lk 18:43 all the people saw it, they **a** praised God. *G2779*
Lk 20:3 He replied, "**I** will **a** ask you a question *G2743*
Lk 20:11 **but** that one **a** they beat and treated *G1254*
Lk 21:2 He **a** saw a poor widow put in two very *G1254*
Lk 22:24 A dispute **a** arose among them as to *G2779*
Lk 22:36 and **a** a bag; and if you don't have *G3931*
Lk 22:58 him and said, "You **a** are one of them." *G2779*
Lk 23:7 who was **a** in Jerusalem at that time. *G2779*
Lk 23:32 were **a** led out with him to be executed. *G2779*
Lk 23:36 The soldiers **a** came up and mocked him *G2779*
Jn 1:45 **and** about whom the prophets **a** wrote *G2779*
Jn 2:2 his disciples had **a** been invited to the *G1254*
Jn 3:23 Now John **a** was baptizing at Aenon near *G2779*
Jn 4:12 as did **a** his sons and his livestock? *G2779*
Jn 4:45 Festival, for they **a** had been there. *G2779*
Jn 5:19 whatever the Father does the Son **a** does. *G3931*
Jn 5:26 he has granted the Son **a** to have life in *G2779*
Jn 7:10 the festival, he went **a**, not publicly, *G2779*
Jn 7:47 "You mean he has deceived you **a**?" *G2779*
Jn 8:19 knew me, you would know my Father **a**." *G2779*
Jn 9:15 the Pharisees **a** asked him how he had *G2779*
Jn 10:16 I must bring **them a**. They too will *G2797*
Jn 11:16 Then Thomas (**a** known as Didymus) said to NDT
Jn 11:16 disciples, "Let us **a** go, that we may die *G2779*
Jn 11:33 **and** the Jews who had come along with her **a** *G2779*
Jn 11:52 only for that nation but **a** for the scattered *G2779*
Jn 12:9 only because of him but **a** to see Lazarus, *G2779*
Jn 12:26 and where I am, my servant **a** will be. *G2779*
Jn 13:14 you **a** should wash one another's feet. *G2779*
Jn 14:1 You believe in God; believe **a** in me. *G2779*
Jn 14:3 with me that you **a** may be where I am. *G2779*
Jn 14:19 Because I live, you **a** will live. *G2779*
Jn 15:4 Remain in me, as **I a** remain in you. No *G2743*
Jn 15:20 persecuted me, they will persecute you **a**. *G2779*
Jn 15:20 my teaching, they will obey yours **a**. *G2779*
Jn 15:27 And you **a** must testify, for you have been *G1254*
Jn 17:20 I pray **a** for those who will believe in me *G2779*
Jn 17:21 May they **a** be in us so that the world may *G2779*
Jn 18:18 Peter **a** was standing with them, warming *G2779*
Jn 19:35 he testifies so that you **a** may believe. *G2779*
Jn 20:8 had reached the tomb first, **a** went inside. *G2779*
Jn 20:24 Now Thomas (**a** known as Didymus), NDT
Jn 21:2 Thomas (**a** known as Didymus), Nathanael NDT
Ac 1:23 called Barsabbas (**a** known as Justus) and NDT
Ac 2:26 rejoices; my body **a** will rest in hope, *G2779*
Ac 5:1 wife Sapphira, **a** sold a piece of property. NDT
Ac 5:9 at the door, **and** they will carry you out **a**." *G2779*
Ac 5:16 Crowds gathered **a** from the towns around *G2779*
Ac 6:5 of the Holy Spirit; **a** Philip, Procorus, *G2779*
Ac 8:19 "Give **me a** this ability so that everyone *G2743*
Ac 11:1 that the Gentiles **a** had received the word *G2779*
Ac 11:12 These six brothers **a** went with me, and *G2779*
Ac 11:20 Antioch and began to speak to Greeks **a**, *G2779*
Ac 12:3 the Jews, he proceeded to seize Peter **a**. *G2779*
Ac 12:12 the mother of John, **a** called Mark, where NDT
Ac 12:25 taking with them John, *a* **called** Mark. AIT
Ac 13:9 Then Saul, who was **a** called Paul, filled *G2779*
Ac 13:35 So it is **a** stated elsewhere: " 'You will not *G2779*
Ac 15:37 wanted to take John, **a** called Mark, with *G2779*
Ac 17:12 **as** did **a** a number of prominent Greek *G2779*
Ac 17:34 Areopagus, **a** a woman named Damaris *G2779*
Ac 19:21 he said, "I must visit Rome **a**." *G2779*
Ac 19:27 **a** that the temple of the great *G2779*
Ac 20:4 from Derbe, Timothy **a**, and Tychicus and *G2779*
Ac 21:13 **a** to die in Jerusalem for the name of *G2779*
Ac 23:11 Jerusalem, so you must **a** testify in Rome." *G2779*
Ac 23:30 I **a** ordered his accusers to present to you *G2779*
Ac 26:4 in my own country, **and a** in Jerusalem. *G5445*
Ac 27:10 to ship and cargo, and to our own lives **a**." *G2779*
Ro 1:6 **And** you **a** are among those Gentiles who *G2779*
Ro 1:15 to preach the gospel **a** to you who are in *G2779*
Ro 1:27 same way the men **a** abandoned natural *G2779*
Ro 1:32 very things but **a** approve of those who *G2779*
Ro 2:12 from the law will **a** perish apart from the *G2779*
Ro 2:15 their consciences **a bearing witness**, and *G5210*
Ro 4:9 circumcised, or **a** for the uncircumcised? *G2779*
Ro 4:12 **And** he is **then a** the father of the *G2779*
Ro 4:12 circumcised but who **a** follow in the *G2779*
Ro 4:16 are of the law but **a** to those who have *G2779*
Ro 4:19 old—**and** that Sarah's womb was **a** dead. *G2779*
Ro 4:24 **a** for us, to whom God will credit *G2779*
Ro 5:3 only so, but we **a** glory in our sufferings *G2779*
Ro 5:11 we **a** boast in God through our Lord *G2779*
Ro 5:18 so **a** one righteous act resulted in *G2779*
Ro 5:19 so **a** through the obedience of the one *G2779*
Ro 5:21 so **a** grace might reign through *G2779*
Ro 6:5 we will certainly **a** be united with him in a *G2779*
Ro 6:8 we believe that we will **a** live with him. *G2779*
Ro 7:4 you **a** died to the law through the body of *G2779*
Ro 8:11 from the dead will **a** give life to your *G2779*
Ro 8:17 in order that we may **a** share in his glory. *G2779*
Ro 8:29 God foreknew he **a** predestined to be *G2779*
Ro 8:30 he predestined, he **a** called; those he *G2779*
Ro 8:30 those he called, he **a** justified; those he *G2779*
Ro 8:30 justified; those he justified, he **a** glorified. *G2779*
Ro 8:32 us all—how will he not **a**, along with him, *G2779*
Ro 8:34 right hand of God **and** is **a** interceding *G2779*
Ro 9:24 even us, whom he **a** called, not only from *G2779*
Ro 9:24 from the Jews but **a** from the Gentiles? *G2779*
Ro 11:22 Otherwise, you **a** will be cut off. *G2779*
Ro 13:5 possible punishment but **a** as a matter of *G2779*
Ro 13:6 This is **a** why you pay taxes, for the *G2779*
Ro 16:5 Greet **a** the church that meets at their *G2779*
1Co 1:8 He will **a** keep you firm to the end, so that *G2779*
1Co 1:16 I **a** baptized the household of Stephanas *G2779*
1Co 4:8 to reign so that we **a** might reign with you *G2779*
1Co 6:14 from the dead, **and** he will raise us **a**. *G2779*
1Co 7:37 the virgin—this man **a** does the right thing. NDT
1Co 10:13 he will **a** provide a way out so that you *G2779*
1Co 11:12 from man, so **a** man is born of woman. *G2779*
1Co 11:23 from the Lord what I **a** passed on to you: *G2779*
1Co 14:15 I will **a** pray with my understanding *G2779*
1Co 14:15 I will **a** sing with my understanding. *G2779*
1Co 15:8 last of all he appeared *to* **me a**, as to *G2743*
1Co 15:18 Then those **a** who have fallen asleep in *G2779*
1Co 15:21 of the dead comes **a** through a man. *G2779*
1Co 15:40 There are **a** heavenly bodies and there are *G2779*
1Co 15:44 a natural body, there is **a** a spiritual body. *G2779*
1Co 15:48 so **a** are those who are of heaven. *G2779*
1Co 16:4 If it seems advisable *for* **me** to go **a**, they *G2743*
1Co 16:18 For they refreshed my spirit **and** yours **a** *G2779*
2Co 1:5 so **a** our comfort abounds through Christ. *G2779*
2Co 1:7 sufferings, so **a** you share in our comfort. *G2779*
2Co 2:10 Anyone you forgive, **I a** forgive. And what I *G2743*
2Co 4:10 the life of Jesus may **a** be revealed in our *G2779*
2Co 4:11 so that his life may **a** be revealed in our *G2779*
2Co 4:13 of faith, we **a** believe and therefore speak *G2779*
2Co 4:14 from the dead will **a** raise us with Jesus *G2779*
2Co 5:11 I hope it is **a** plain to your conscience. *G2779*
2Co 6:13 to my children—open wide your hearts **a**. *G2779*
2Co 7:7 by his coming but **a** by the comfort you *G2779*
2Co 8:5 **and then** by the will of God **a** to us. *G2779*
2Co 8:6 to bring **a** to completion this act of grace *G2779*
2Co 8:7 see that you **a** excel in this grace of giving. *G2779*
2Co 8:10 not only to give but **a** to have the desire *G2779*
2Co 8:21 eyes of the Lord but **a** in the eyes of man. *G2779*
2Co 9:6 sows sparingly will **a** reap sparingly, *G2779*
2Co 9:6 sows generously will **a** reap generously. *G2779*
2Co 9:10 bread for food will **a** supply and increase NDT
2Co 9:12 people but is **a** overflowing in many *G2779*
2Co 10:13 a sphere that **a** includes you. *G2779*
2Co 11:15 if his servants **a** masquerade as servants *G2779*
2Co 11:21 as a fool—**I a** dare to boast about. *G2743*
Gal 2:1 time with Barnabas. I took Titus along **a**. *G2779*
Gal 2:8 was **a** at work in me as an apostle to the *G2779*
Gal 2:17 Jews find ourselves **a** among the sinners, *G2779*
Gal 3:6 **So a** Abraham "believed God, and it was *G2777*
Gal 4:3 So **a**, when we were underage, we were in *G2779*
Gal 4:7 his child, God has made you **a** an heir. *G2779*
Gal 6:1 yourselves, or you **a** may be tempted. *G2779*
Eph 1:11 In him we were **a** chosen, having been *G2779*
Eph 1:13 **And** you **a** were included in Christ when *G2779*
Eph 1:21 the present age but **a** in the one to come. *G2779*
Eph 2:3 All of us **a** lived among them at one time *G2779*
Eph 2:19 with God's people **and a** members of his *G2779*
Eph 4:9 mean except that he **a** descended to the *G2779*
Eph 5:24 so **a** wives should submit to their *G2779*
Eph 5:33 each one of you **a** must love his wife as *G2779*
Eph 6:19 Pray **a** for me, that whenever I speak *G2779*
Eph 6:21 so that you **a** may know how I am and *G2779*
Php 1:29 to believe in him, but **a** to suffer for him, *G2779*
Php 2:19 that **I a** may be cheered when I receive *G2743*
Php 2:25 who is **a** your messenger, whom *G1254*
Php 2:27 not on him only but **a** on me, to *G2779*
Col 1:8 **and** who **a** told us of your love in the Spirit. *G2779*
Col 2:11 In him you were **a** circumcised with a *G2779*
Col 2:12 in which you were **a** raised with him *G2779*
Col 2:18 Such a person **a** goes into great detail NDT
Col 3:4 then you **a** will appear with him in glory. *G2779*
Col 3:8 But now you must **a** rid yourselves of all *G2779*
Col 4:1 you know that you **a** have a Master in *G2779*
Col 4:11 who is called Justus, **a** sends greetings. *G2779*
Col 4:16 see that it is **a** read in the church of the *G2779*
1Th 1:5 not simply with words but **a** with power, *G2779*
1Th 2:13 And we **a** thank God continually because *G2779*
1Th 2:15 the prophets **and a** drove us out. *G2779*
1Th 3:6 to see us, just as we **a** long to see you. *G2779*
1Ti 1:9 We **a** know that the law is made not for the NDT
1Ti 2:9 I **a** want the women to dress modestly *G6058*
1Ti 3:7 He must **a** have a good reputation with *G2779*
1Ti 5:13 **a** busybodies who talk nonsense *G2779*
2Ti 1:5 I am persuaded, now lives in you **a**. *G2779*
2Ti 2:2 people who will **a** be qualified to teach *G2779*
2Ti 2:11 we died with him, we will **a** live with him; *G2779*
2Ti 2:12 we endure, we will **a** reign with him. If we *G2779*
2Ti 2:12 If we disown him, **he** will **a** disown us; *G2797*
2Ti 2:20 gold and silver, but **a** of wood and clay *G2779*
2Ti 3:8 so **a** these teachers oppose the truth. *G2779*
2Ti 4:8 **a** to all who have longed for his *G2779*
Phm 2 **a** to Apphia our sister and Archippus our *G2779*
Phm 9 an old man and now **a** a prisoner of Christ *G2779*
Heb 1:2 through whom **a** he made the *G2779*
Heb 1:10 He **a** says, "In the beginning, Lord, you *G2779*
Heb 2:4 God **a** testified to it by signs, wonders and *G5445*
Heb 4:2 For we **a** have had the good news *G2779*
Heb 4:10 who enters God's rest **a** rests from their *G2779*
Heb 7:2 righteousness"; then **a**, "king of Salem *G2779*
Heb 7:5 though *they a are* **descended from** Abraham. AIT
Heb 7:12 is changed, the law must be changed **a**. *G2779*
Heb 8:3 this one **a** to have something to *G2779*
Heb 9:1 worship **and a** an earthly sanctuary. *G5445*
Heb 10:15 The Holy Spirit **a** testifies to us about this *G2779*
Heb 12:26 not only the earth but **a** the heavens." *G2779*
Heb 13:12 **And** so Jesus **a** suffered outside the city *G2779*
Jas 2:2 poor man in filthy old clothes **a** comes in. *G2779*
Jas 2:11 commit adultery," **a** said, "You shall not *G2779*
Jas 3:6 The tongue **a** is a fire, a world of evil *G2779*
1Pe 2:5 you **a**, like living stones, are being built *G2779*
1Pe 2:8 which is **a** what they were destined for. *G2779*
1Pe 2:18 considerate, but **a** to those who are harsh. *G2779*
1Pe 3:18 For Christ **a** suffered once for sins, the *G2779*
1Pe 3:21 baptism that now saves you **a**— *G2779*
1Pe 4:1 arm yourselves **a** with the same attitude *G2779*
1Pe 5:1 sufferings who **a** will share in the glory *G2779*
2Pe 1:19 We **a** have the prophetic message as *G2779*
2Pe 2:1 But there were **a** false prophets among *G2779*
2Pe 3:6 By these waters **a** the world of that time was NDT
2Pe 3:15 our dear brother Paul **a** wrote you with the *G2779*
1Jn 1:3 so that you **a** may have fellowship with us. *G2779*
1Jn 2:2 not only for ours but **a** for the sins of the *G2779*
1Jn 2:23 acknowledges the Son has the Father **a**. *G2779*

A

1Jn 2:24 you **a** will remain in the Son and in the *G2779*
1Jn 4:11 loved us, we **a** ought to love one another. *G2779*
1Jn 4:21 who loves God must **a** love their brother *G2779*
1Jn 5:20 We know **a** that the Son of God has come *G1254*
2Jn 1 not I only, but **a** all who know the truth *G2779*
3Jn 10 He **a** stops those who want to do so and *G2779*
3Jn 12 We **a** speak well of him, and you know *G2779*
Rev 2: 6 of the Nicolaitans, which **I a** hate. *G2743*
Rev 2:15 you **a** have those who hold to the *G2779*
Rev 2:17 I will **a** give that person a white stone *G2779*
Rev 2:28 I will **a** give that one the morning star. *G2779*
Rev 3:10 I will **a** keep you from the hour of trial that *G2743*
Rev 3:12 **and** I will **a** write on them my new name. *G2779*
Rev 4: 6 **A** in front of the throne there was what *G2779*
Rev 8:12 without light, and **a** a third of the night. *G3931*
Rev 11: 8 Egypt—where **a** their Lord was crucified. *G2779*
Rev 13: 4 **and** they **a** worshiped the beast and *G2779*
Rev 13:16 It **a** forced all people, great and small, rich *G2779*
Rev 17:10 They are **a** seven kings. Five have fallen *G2779*

ALTAR (388) [ALTARS]

Ge 8:20 Then Noah built an **a** to the LORD and H4640
Ge 12: 7 So he built an **a** there to the LORD, who H4640
Ge 12: 8 There he built an **a** to the LORD and called H4640
Ge 13: 4 where he had first built an **a**. There H4640
Ge 13:18 There he built an **a** to the LORD. H4640
Ge 22: 9 Abraham built an **a** there and arranged H4640
Ge 22: 9 his son Isaac and laid him on the **a**, H4640
Ge 26:25 Isaac built an **a** there and called on the H4640
Ge 33:20 There he set up an **a** and called it El H4640
Ge 35: 1 and build an **a** there to God, who H4640
Ge 35: 3 where I will build an **a** to God, who H4640
Ge 35: 7 There he built an **a**, and he called the H4640
Ex 17:15 Moses built an **a** and called it The LORD is H4640
Ex 20:24 " 'Make an **a** *of* earth for me and sacrifice H4640
Ex 20:25 If you make an **a** *of* stones for me, do not H4640
Ex 20:26 And do not go up to my **a** on steps, or your H4640
Ex 21:14 is to be taken from my **a** and put to death. H4640
Ex 24: 4 morning and built an **a** at the foot of the H4640
Ex 24: 6 the other half he splashed against the **a**. H4640
Ex 27: 1 "Build an **a** *of* acacia wood, three cubits H4640
Ex 27: 2 the horns and **the a** are of one piece, H5647S
Ex 27: 2 and overlay **the a** with bronze. H2257S
Ex 27: 5 the ledge of the **a** so that it is halfway H4640
Ex 27: 5 of the altar so that it is halfway up the **a**. H4640
Ex 27: 6 acacia wood for the **a** and overlay them H4640
Ex 27: 7 on two sides of the **a** when it is carried. H4640
Ex 27: 8 Make **the a** hollow, out of boards. It is to H2257S
Ex 28:43 approach the **a** to minister in the Holy H4640
Ex 29:12 it on the horns of the **a** with your finger, H4640
Ex 29:12 pour out the rest of it at the base of the **a**. H4640
Ex 29:13 the fat on them, and burn them on the **a**. H4640
Ex 29:16 splash it against the sides of the **a**. H4640
Ex 29:18 Then burn the entire ram on the **a**. It is a H4640
Ex 29:20 splash blood against the sides of the **a**. H4640
Ex 29:21 some blood from the **a** and some of the H4640
Ex 29:25 burn them on the **a** along with the burnt H4640
Ex 29:36 Purify the **a** by making atonement for it H4640
Ex 29:37 atonement for the **a** and consecrate it. H4640
Ex 29:37 Then the **a** will be most holy, and H4640
Ex 29:38 are to offer on the **a** regularly each day: H4640
Ex 29:44 of meeting and the **a** and will consecrate H4640
Ex 30: 1 "Make an **a** *of* acacia wood *for* burning H4640
Ex 30: 4 gold rings for **the a** below the molding H2257S
Ex 30: 6 Put **the a** in front of the curtain that H2257S
Ex 30: 7 incense on **the a** every morning when H2257S
Ex 30: 9 Do not offer on **this a** any other incense H2257S
Ex 30:18 it between the tent of meeting and the **a**, H4640
Ex 30:20 when they approach the **a** to minister by H4640
Ex 30:27 its accessories, the **a** *of* incense, H4640
Ex 30:28 the **a** *of* burnt offering and all its utensils H4640
Ex 31: 8 all its accessories, the **a** *of* incense, H4640
Ex 31: 9 the **a** *of* burnt offering and all its utensils H4640
Ex 32: 5 he built an **a** in front of the calf and H4640
Ex 35:15 the **a** *of* incense with its poles, the H4640
Ex 35:16 the **a** *of* burnt offering with its bronze H4640
Ex 37:25 They made the **a** *of* incense out of acacia H4640
Ex 38: 1 They built the **a** *of* burnt offering of acacia H4640
Ex 38: 2 the horns and **the a** were of one piece H5647S
Ex 38: 2 they overlaid **the a** with bronze. H2257S
Ex 38: 4 They made a grating for the **a**, a bronze H4640
Ex 38: 4 to be under its ledge, halfway up **the a**. H2257S
Ex 38: 7 be on the sides of the **a** for carrying it. H4640
Ex 38:30 the bronze **a** with its bronze grating and H4640
Ex 39:38 the gold **a**, the anointing oil, the fragrant H4640
Ex 39:39 the bronze **a** with its bronze grating, its H4640
Ex 40: 5 Place the gold **a** of incense in front of the H4640
Ex 40: 6 "Place the **a** *of* burnt offering in front of H4640
Ex 40: 7 of meeting and the **a** and put water in it. H4640
Ex 40:10 Then anoint the **a** *of* burnt offering and all H4640
Ex 40:10 consecrate the **a**, and it will be most H4640
Ex 40:26 Moses placed the gold **a** in the tent of H4640
Ex 40:29 He set the **a** *of* burnt offering near the H4640
Ex 40:30 of meeting and the **a** and put water in it H4640
Ex 40:32 the tent of meeting or approached the **a**, H4640
Ex 40:33 the tabernacle and **a** and put up the H4640
Lev 1: 5 the sides of the **a** at the entrance to the H4640
Lev 1: 7 to put fire on the **a** and arrange wood on H4640
Lev 1: 8 on the wood that is burning on the **a**. H4640
Lev 1: 9 the priest is to burn all of it on the **a**. H4640
Lev 1:11 at the north side of the **a** before the LORD, H4640
Lev 1:11 its blood against the sides of the **a**. H4640
Lev 1:12 on the wood that is burning on the **a**. H4640
Lev 1:13 bring all of them and burn them on the **a**. H4640
Lev 1:15 The priest shall bring it to the **a**, wring off H4640
Lev 1:15 wring off the head and burn it on the **a**. H4640
Lev 1:15 shall be drained out on the side of the **a**. H4640
Lev 1:16 down east of the **a** where the ashes are. H4640
Lev 1:17 it on the wood that is burning on the **a**. H4640
Lev 2: 2 burn this as a memorial portion on the **a**, H4640
Lev 2: 8 it to the priest, who shall take it to the **a**. H4640
Lev 2: 9 burn it on the **a** as a food offering, H4640
Lev 2:12 be offered on the **a** as a pleasing aroma. H4640
Lev 3: 2 the blood against the sides of the **a**. H4640
Lev 3: 5 are to burn it on the **a** on top of the burnt H4640
Lev 3: 8 its blood against the sides of the **a**. H4640
Lev 3:11 burn them on the **a** as a food offering H4640
Lev 3:13 its blood against the sides of the **a**. H4640
Lev 3:16 burn them on the **a** as a food offering, H4640
Lev 4: 7 on the horns of the **a** *of* fragrant incense H4640
Lev 4: 7 at the base of the **a** *of* burnt offering at H4640
Lev 4:10 shall burn them on the **a** *of* burnt offering. H4640
Lev 4:18 on the horns of the **a** that is before the H4640
Lev 4:18 at the base of the **a** *of* burnt offering at H4640
Lev 4:19 all the fat from it and burn it on the **a**, H4640
Lev 4:25 on the horns of the **a** *of* burnt offering H4640
Lev 4:25 the rest of the blood at the base of the **a**. H4640
Lev 4:26 all the fat on the **a** as he burned the fat of H4640
Lev 4:30 on the horns of the **a** *of* burnt offering H4640
Lev 4:30 the rest of the blood at the base of the **a**. H4640
Lev 4:31 burn it on the **a** as an aroma pleasing H4640
Lev 4:34 on the horns of the **a** *of* burnt offering H4640
Lev 4:34 the rest of the blood at the base of the **a**. H4640
Lev 4:35 shall burn it on the **a** on top of the food H4640
Lev 5: 9 the sin offering against the side of the **a**; H4640
Lev 5: 9 must be drained out at the base of the **a**. H4640
Lev 5:12 burn it on the **a** on top of the food H4640
Lev 6: 9 is to remain on the **a** hearth throughout H4640
Lev 6: 9 the fire must be kept burning on the **a**. H4640
Lev 6:10 has consumed on the **a** and place them H4640
Lev 6:10 on the altar and place them beside the **a**. H4640
Lev 6:12 The fire on the **a** must be kept burning; it H4640
Lev 6:13 be kept burning on the **a** continuously; H4640
Lev 6:14 bring it before the LORD, in front of the **a**. H4640
Lev 6:15 portion on the **a** as an aroma pleasing to H4640
Lev 7: 2 to be splashed against the sides of the **a**. H4640
Lev 7: 5 burn them on the **a** as a food offering H4640
Lev 7:14 of the fellowship offering against the **a**. NDT
Lev 7:31 The priest shall burn the fat on the **a**, but H4640
Lev 8:11 some of the oil on the **a** seven times, H4640
Lev 8:11 anointing the **a** and all its utensils and H4640
Lev 8:15 all the horns of the **a** to purify the altar. H4640
Lev 8:15 all the horns of the altar to purify the **a**. H4640
Lev 8:15 the rest of the blood at the base of the **a**. H4640
Lev 8:16 their fat, and burned it on the **a**. H4640
Lev 8:19 the blood against the sides of the **a**. H4640
Lev 8:21 burned the whole ram on the **a**. H4640
Lev 8:24 splashed blood against the sides of the **a**. H4640
Lev 8:28 burned them on the **a** on top of the burnt H4640
Lev 8:30 the blood from the **a** and sprinkled them H4640
Lev 9: 7 "Come to the **a** and sacrifice your sin H4640
Lev 9: 8 Aaron came to the **a** and slaughtered the H4640
Lev 9: 9 the blood and put it on the horns of the **a**; H4640
Lev 9: 9 blood he poured out at the base of the **a**. H4640
Lev 9:10 On the **a** he burned the fat, the kidneys H4640
Lev 9:12 he splashed it against the sides of the **a**. H4640
Lev 9:13 the head, and he burned them on the **a**. H4640
Lev 9:14 on top of the burnt offering on the **a**. H4640
Lev 9:17 burned it on the **a** in addition to the H4640
Lev 9:18 he splashed it against the sides of the **a**. H4640
Lev 9:20 then Aaron burned the fat on the **a**. H4640
Lev 9:24 offering and the fat portions on the **a**. H4640
Lev 10:12 to the LORD and eat it beside the **a**, H4640
Lev 14:20 offer it on the **a**, together with the H4640
Lev 16:12 coals from the **a** before the LORD and H4640
Lev 16:18 shall come out to the **a** that is before the H4640
Lev 16:18 blood and put it on all the horns of the **a**. H4640
Lev 16:20 the tent of meeting and the **a**, he shall H4640
Lev 16:25 burn the fat of the sin offering on the **a**. H4640
Lev 16:33 the tent of meeting and the **a**, and for H4640
Lev 17: 6 the blood against the **a** *of* the LORD at the H4640
Lev 17:11 make atonement for yourselves on the **a**; H4640
Lev 21:23 not go near the curtain or approach the **a**, H4640
Lev 22:22 any of these on the **a** as a food offering H4640
Nu 3:26 surrounding the tabernacle and **a**, H4640
Nu 4:11 "Over the gold **a** they are to spread a blue H4640
Nu 4:13 from the bronze **a** and spread a purple H4640
Nu 4:14 utensils used for ministering at **the a**, H2257S
Nu 4:26 surrounding the tabernacle and **a**, H4640
Nu 5:25 it before the LORD and bring it to the **a**. H4640
Nu 5:26 a memorial offering and burn it on the **a**; H4640
Nu 7: 1 consecrated the **a** and all its utensils. H4640
Nu 7:10 When the **a** was anointed, the leaders H4640
Nu 7:10 presented them before the **a**. H4640
Nu 7:11 his offering for the dedication of the **a**." H4640
Nu 7:84 dedication of the **a** when it was anointed: H4640
Nu 7:88 dedication of the **a** after it was anointed H4640
Nu 16:38 the censers into sheets to overlay the **a**, H4640
Nu 16:39 had them hammered out to overlay the **a**, H4640
Nu 16:46 along with burning coals from the **a**, and H4640
Nu 18: 3 the furnishings of the sanctuary or the **a**, H4640
Nu 18: 5 the care of the sanctuary and the **a**, H4640
Nu 18: 7 everything at the **a** and inside the curtain H4640
Nu 18:17 blood against the **a** and burn their fat as H4640
Nu 23: 2 them offered a bull and a ram on each **a**. H4640
Nu 23: 4 on each **a** I have offered a bull and a H4640
Nu 23:14 offered a bull and a ram on each **a**. H4640
Nu 23:30 offered a bull and a ram on each **a**. H4640
Dt 12:27 offerings on the **a** *of* the LORD your God, H4640
Dt 12:27 poured beside the **a** *of* the LORD your God, H4640
Dt 16:21 pole beside the **a** you build to the LORD H4640
Dt 26: 4 in front of the **a** *of* the LORD your God. H4640
Dt 27: 5 Build there an **a** to the LORD your God, an H4640
Dt 27: 5 altar to the LORD your God, an **a** *of* stones. H4640
Dt 27: 6 Build the **a** *of* the LORD your God with H4640
Dt 33:10 you and whole burnt offerings on your **a**. H4640
Jos 8:30 built on Mount Ebal an **a** to the LORD, H4640
Jos 8:31 Law of Moses—an **a** *of* uncut stones, on H4640
Jos 9:27 the needs of the **a** *of* the LORD at the H4640
Jos 22:10 built an imposing **a** there by the Jordan. H4640
Jos 22:11 they had built the **a** on the border of H4640
Jos 22:16 build yourselves an **a** in rebellion against H4640
Jos 22:19 against us by building an **a** for yourselves, H4640
Jos 22:19 other than the **a** *of* the LORD our God. H4640
Jos 22:23 have built our own **a** to turn away from H4640
Jos 22:26 'Let us get ready and build an **a**—but not H4640
Jos 22:28 Look at the replica of the LORD's **a**, which H4640
Jos 22:29 today by building an **a** for burnt offerings, H4640
Jos 22:29 other than the **a** *of* the LORD our God that H4640
Jos 22:34 the Gadites gave the **a** this name: H4640
Jdg 6:24 So Gideon built an **a** to the LORD there H4640
Jdg 6:25 down your father's **a** *to* Baal and cut down H4640
Jdg 6:26 a proper kind of **a** to the LORD your God H4640
Jdg 6:28 there was Baal's **a**, demolished, H4640
Jdg 6:28 bull sacrificed on the newly built **a**! H4640
Jdg 6:30 broken down Baal's **a** and cut down the H4640
Jdg 6:31 when someone breaks down his **a**." H4640
Jdg 6:32 So because Gideon broke down Baal's **a** H4640
Jdg 13:20 blazed up from the **a** toward heaven, H4640
Jdg 21: 4 the people built an **a** and presented burnt H4640
1Sa 2:28 to go up to my **a**, to burn incense, H4640
1Sa 2:33 from serving at my **a** I will spare only to H4640
1Sa 7:17 And he built an **a** there to the LORD. H4640
1Sa 14:35 Then Saul built an **a** to the LORD; it was the H4640
2Sa 24:18 "Go up and build an **a** to the LORD on the H4640
2Sa 24:21 "so I can build an **a** to the LORD, that the H4640
2Sa 24:25 David built an **a** to the LORD there and H4640
1Ki 1:50 went and took hold of the horns of the **a**. H4640
1Ki 1:51 is clinging to the horns of the **a**. H4640
1Ki 1:53 they brought him down from the **a**. H4640
1Ki 2:28 LORD and took hold of the horns of the **a**. H4640
1Ki 2:29 the tent of the LORD and was beside the **a**. H4640
1Ki 3: 4 a thousand burnt offerings on that **a**. H4640
1Ki 6:20 and he also overlaid the **a** *of* cedar. H4640
1Ki 6:22 with gold the **a** that belonged to the H4640
1Ki 7:48 the golden **a**; the golden table on which H4640
1Ki 8:22 stood before the **a** *of* the LORD in front of H4640
1Ki 8:31 the oath before your **a** in this temple, H4640
1Ki 8:54 he rose from before the **a** *of* the LORD H4640
1Ki 8:64 because the bronze **a** that stood before H4640
1Ki 9:25 offerings on the **a** he had built for the H4640
1Ki 12:32 in Judah, and offered sacrifices on the **a**. H4640
1Ki 12:33 sacrifices on the **a** he had built at Bethel. H4640
1Ki 12:33 went up to the **a** to make offerings. H4640
1Ki 13: 1 was standing by the **a** to make an offering H4640
1Ki 13: 2 of the LORD he cried out against the **a**: H4640
1Ki 13: 2 against the altar: "**A**, altar! This is what H4640
1Ki 13: 2 "Altar, **a**! This is what the LORD H4640
1Ki 13: 3 The **a** will be split apart and the ashes on H4640
1Ki 13: 4 of God cried out against the **a** at Bethel, H4640
1Ki 13: 4 out his hand from the **a** and said, H4640
1Ki 13: 5 the **a** was split apart and its ashes poured H4640
1Ki 13:32 the LORD against the **a** in Bethel and H4640
1Ki 16:32 He set up an **a** for Baal in the temple of H4640
1Ki 18:26 they danced around the **a** they had made. H4640
1Ki 18:30 he repaired the **a** *of* the LORD, which H4640
1Ki 18:32 stones he built an **a** in the name of the H4640
1Ki 18:35 down around the **a** and even filled the H4640
2Ki 11:11 the king—near the **a** and the temple H4640
2Ki 12: 9 He placed it beside the **a**, on the right H4640
2Ki 16:10 He saw an **a** in Damascus and sent to H4640
2Ki 16:10 sent to Uriah the priest a sketch of the **a**, H4640
2Ki 16:11 the priest built an **a** in accordance with all H4640
2Ki 16:12 came back from Damascus and saw the **a**, H4640
2Ki 16:13 of his fellowship offerings against the **a**. H4640
2Ki 16:14 As for the bronze **a** that stood before the H4640
2Ki 16:14 between the new **a** and the temple of H4640
2Ki 16:14 put it on the north side of the new **a**. H4640
2Ki 16:15 "On the large new **a**, offer the morning H4640
2Ki 16:15 Splash against **this a** the blood of all the H2257S
2Ki 16:15 will use the bronze **a** for seeking H4640
2Ki 18:22 must worship before this **a** in Jerusalem"? H4640
2Ki 23: 9 did not serve at the **a** *of* the LORD in H4640
2Ki 23:15 Even the **a** at Bethel, the high place H4640
2Ki 23:15 even that **a** and high place he demolished H4640
2Ki 23:16 them and burned on the **a** to defile it, H4640
2Ki 23:17 against the **a** *of* Bethel the very H4640
1Ch 6:49 offerings on the **a** *of* burnt offering and on H4640
1Ch 6:49 offering and on the **a** *of* incense in H4640
1Ch 16:40 to the LORD on the **a** *of* burnt offering H4640
1Ch 21:18 to go up and build an **a** to the LORD on the H4640
1Ch 21:22 floor so I can build an **a** to the LORD, H4640
1Ch 21:26 David built an **a** to the LORD there and H4640
1Ch 21:26 from heaven on the **a** *of* burnt offering. H4640
1Ch 21:29 the **a** *of* burnt offering were at that H4640
1Ch 22: 1 also the **a** of burnt offering for Israel." H4640

1Ch 28:18 of the refined gold for the a *of* incense. H4640
2Ch 1: 5 But the bronze a that Bezalel son of Uri H4640
2Ch 1: 6 went up to the bronze a before the LORD in H4640
2Ch 4: 1 He made a bronze a twenty cubits long H4640
2Ch 4:19 the golden a; the tables on which was the H4640
2Ch 5:12 stood on the east side of the a, dressed in H4640
2Ch 6:12 stood before the a *of* the LORD in front of H4640
2Ch 6:22 the oath before your a in this temple, H4640
2Ch 7: 7 because the bronze a he had made could H4640
2Ch 7: 9 the dedication of the a for seven days H4640
2Ch 8:12 On the a *of* the LORD that he had built in H4640
2Ch 15: 8 He repaired the a *of* the LORD that was in H4640
2Ch 23:10 the king—near the a and the temple H4640
2Ch 26:16 LORD to burn incense on the a *of* incense. H4640
2Ch 26:19 before the incense a in the LORD's temple, H4640
2Ch 29:18 the a *of* burnt offering with all its utensils H4640
2Ch 29:19 They are now in front of the LORD's a." H4640
2Ch 29:21 to offer these on the a *of* the LORD. H4640
2Ch 29:22 the blood and splashed it against the a; H4640
2Ch 29:22 splashed their blood against the a; H4640
2Ch 29:22 splashed their blood against the a. H4640
2Ch 29:24 their blood on the a for a sin offering to H4640
2Ch 29:27 to sacrifice the burnt offering on the a. H4640
2Ch 30:16 splashed against the a the blood handed to NDT
2Ch 32:12 worship before one a and burn sacrifices H4640
2Ch 33:16 Then he restored the a *of* the LORD and H4640
2Ch 35:11 splashed against the a the blood handed to NDT
2Ch 35:16 of burnt offerings on the a *of* the LORD, H4640
Ezr 3: 2 began to build the a *of* the God of Israel H4640
Ezr 3: 3 they built the a on its foundation and H4640
Ezr 7:17 them on the a of the temple of your A10401
Ne 10:34 to burn on the a *of* the LORD our God, H4640
Ps 26: 6 in innocence, and go about your a, LORD, H4640
Ps 43: 4 Then I will go to the a *of* God, to God, my H4640
Ps 51:19 then bulls will be offered on your a. H4640
Ps 84: 3 a place near your a, LORD Almighty, H4640
Ps 118:27 festal procession up to the horns of the a. H4640
Isa 6: 6 which he had taken with tongs from the a. H4640
Isa 19:19 day there will be an a to the LORD in the H4640
Isa 27: 9 he makes all the a stones to be like H4640
Isa 29: 2 she will be to me like an a **hearth**. H789
Isa 36: 7 "You must worship before this a"? H4640
Isa 40:16 Lebanon is not sufficient for *a* **fires**, nor its AIT
Isa 56: 7 sacrifices will be accepted on my a; H4640
Isa 60: 7 will be accepted as offerings on my a, H4640
La 2: 7 has rejected his a and abandoned his H4640
Eze 8: 5 north of the gate of the a I saw this idol of H4640
Eze 8:16 between the portico and the a, were H4640
Eze 9: 2 came in and stood beside the bronze a. H4640
Eze 40:46 north is for the priests who guard the a. H4640
Eze 40:47 And the a was in front of the temple. H4640
Eze 41:22 There was a wooden a three cubits high H4640
Eze 43:13 the measurements of the a in long cubits, H4640
Eze 43:13 And this is the height of the a: H4640
Eze 43:14 that goes around the a it is two cubits high, NDT
Eze 43:14 that goes around the a it is four cubits high, NDT
Eze 43:15 Above that, the a **hearth** is four cubits high H2219
Eze 43:16 The a **hearth** is square, twelve cubits long H789
Eze 43:17 All around **the a** is a gutter of one cubit H2023S
Eze 43:17 The steps of **the a** face east." H2084S
Eze 43:18 blood against the a when it is built: H4640
Eze 43:20 the four horns of **the a** and on the four H2257S
Eze 43:20 so purify **the a** and make atonement H2257S
Eze 43:22 the a is to be purified as it was H4640
Eze 43:26 make atonement for the a and cleanse it; H4640
Eze 43:27 fellowship offerings on the a. H4640
Eze 45:19 upper ledge of the a and on the H4640
Eze 47: 1 south side of the temple, south of the a. H4640
Joel 1:13 you who minister before the a. H4640
Joel 2:17 weep between the portico and the a. H4640
Am 2: 8 down beside every a on garments taken H4640
Am 3:14 the horns of the a will be cut off and fall H4640
Am 9: 1 I saw the Lord standing by the a, and he H4640
Zec 9:15 used for sprinkling the corners of the a. H4640
Zec 14:20 be like the sacred bowls in front of the a. H4640
Mal 1: 7 "By offering defiled food on my a. "But H4640
Mal 1:10 you would not light useless fires on my a! H4640
Mal 2:13 You flood the LORD's a with tears. You H4640
Mt 5:23 your gift at the a and there remember that *G2603*
Mt 5:24 leave your gift there in front of the a. First *G2603*
Mt 23:18 'If anyone swears by the a, it means *G2603*
Mt 23:18 by the gift on **the a** is bound by that *G899S*
Mt 23:19 or the a that makes the gift sacred? *G2603*
Mt 23:20 who swears by the a swears by it and by *G2603*
Mt 23:35 murdered between the temple and the a. *G2603*
Lk 1:11 at the right side *of* the a of incense. *G2603*
Lk 11:51 killed between the a and the sanctuary. *G2603*
Ac 17:23 I even found an a with this inscription: *G1117*
1Co 9:13 those who serve *at* the a share in what is *G2603*
1Co 9:13 altar share in what is offered *on* the a? *G2603*
1Co 10:18 who eat the sacrifices participate in the a? *G2603*
Heb 7:13 from that tribe has ever served at the a. *G2603*
Heb 9: 4 had the golden a **of incense** and the *G2593*
Heb 13:10 We have an a from which those who *G2603*
Jas 2:21 when he offered his son Isaac on the a? *G2603*
Rev 6: 9 I saw under the a the souls of those who *G2603*
Rev 8: 3 golden censer, came and stood at the a. *G2603*
Rev 8: 3 on the golden a in front of the throne. *G2603*
Rev 8: 5 filled it with fire *from* the a, and hurled it *G2603*
Rev 9:13 the four horns *of* the golden a that is *G2603*
Rev 11: 1 measure the temple of God and the a, *G2603*
Rev 14:18 came from the a and called in a loud *G2603*
Rev 16: 7 And I heard the a respond: "Yes, Lord *G2603*

ALTARS (61) [ALTAR]

Ex 34:13 Break down their a, smash their sacred H4640
Lev 26:30 cut down your **incense** a and pile your H2802
Nu 3:31 the lampstand, the a, the articles of the H4640
Nu 23: 1 "Build me seven a here, and prepare H4640
Nu 23: 4 "I have prepared seven a, and on each H4640
Nu 23:14 there he built seven a and offered a bull H4640
Nu 23:29 "Build me seven a here, and prepare H4640
Dt 7: 5 Break down their a, smash their sacred H4640
Dt 12: 3 Break down their a, smash their sacred H4640
Jdg 2: 2 but you shall break down their a. H4640
1Ki 19:10 torn down your a, and put your prophets H4640
1Ki 19:14 torn down your a, and put your prophets H4640
2Ki 11:18 They smashed the a and idols to pieces H4640
2Ki 11:18 Mattan the priest of Baal in front of the a. H4640
2Ki 18:22 high places and a Hezekiah removed, H4640
2Ki 21: 3 he also erected a to Baal and made an H4640
2Ki 21: 4 He built a in the temple of the LORD, of H4640
2Ki 21: 5 the LORD, he built a to all the starry hosts. H4640
2Ki 23:12 He pulled down the a the kings of Judah H4640
2Ki 23:12 the a Manasseh had built in the two H4640
2Ki 23:20 high places on the a and burned human H4640
2Ch 14: 3 the foreign a and the high places H4640
2Ch 14: 5 high places and **incense** a in every town H2802
2Ch 23:17 They smashed the a and idols and killed H4640
2Ch 23:17 Mattan the priest of Baal in front of the a. H4640
2Ch 28:24 temple and set up a at every street corner H4640
2Ch 30:14 They removed the a in Jerusalem and H4640
2Ch 30:14 away the **incense** a and threw them H5232
2Ch 31: 1 high places and the a throughout Judah H4640
2Ch 32:12 remove this god's high places and a, H4640
2Ch 33: 3 he also erected a to the Baals and made H4640
2Ch 33: 4 He built a in the temple of the LORD, of H4640
2Ch 33: 5 the LORD, he built a to all the starry hosts. H4640
2Ch 33:15 as well as all the a he had built on the H4640
2Ch 34: 4 his direction the a *of* the Baals were torn H4640
2Ch 34: 4 to pieces the **incense** a that were above H2802
2Ch 34: 5 burned the bones of the priests on their a, H4640
2Ch 34: 7 he tore down the a and the Asherah poles H4640
2Ch 34: 7 to pieces all the **incense** a throughout H2802
Isa 17: 8 They will not look to the a, the work of H4640
Isa 17: 8 poles and the **incense** a their fingers have H2802
Isa 27: 9 no Asherah poles or **incense** a will be left H2802
Isa 36: 7 high places and a Hezekiah removed, H4640
Isa 65: 3 burning incense on a **of brick**; H4246
Jer 11:13 the a you have set up to burn incense H4640
Jer 17: 1 of their hearts and on the horns of their a. H4640
Jer 17: 2 remember their a and Asherah poles H4640
Eze 6: 4 Your a will be demolished and your H4640
Eze 6: 4 your **incense** a will be smashed; H2802
Eze 6: 5 I will scatter your bones around your a. H4640
Eze 6: 6 so that your a will be laid waste and H4640
Eze 6: 6 ruined, your **incense** a broken down H2802
Eze 6:13 lie slain among their idols around their a, H4640
Hos 8:11 Ephraim built many a for sin offerings, H4640
Hos 8:11 these have become a for sinning. H4640
Hos 10: 1 he built more a; as his land prospered, H4640
Hos 10: 2 will demolish their a and destroy their H4640
Hos 10: 8 thistles will grow up and cover their a. H4640
Hos 12:11 Their a will be like piles of stones on a H4640
Am 3:14 I will destroy the a *of* Bethel; the horns of H4640
Ro 11: 3 killed your prophets and torn down your a; *G2603*

ALTER (1) [ALTERED]

Ps 89:34 my covenant or a what my lips have H9101

ALTERED (1) [ALTER]

Da 6: 8 put it in writing so that *it* cannot *be* a— A10731

ALTERNATE (1) [ALTERNATED]

Ex 28:34 *are to* a around the H7194+2298+2256+8232S

ALTERNATED (2) [ALTERNATE]

Ex 39:26 a around the hem H7194+2256+8232S
Eze 41:18 Palm trees a **with** cherubim. Each H1068

ALTHOUGH (62) [THOUGH]

Ge 42: 8 A Joseph recognized his brothers, they H2256
Ex 19: 5 A the whole earth is mine H3954
Ex 34: 9 A this is a stiff-necked people, forgive our H3954
Dt 14: 7 A they chew the cud, they do not have a H3954
Dt 14: 8 is also unclean; a it has a divided hoof H3954
Jdg 12: 2 Ammonites, and *a I* **called**, you didn't save AIT
Ru 3:12 A it is true that I am a guardian-redeemer H3954
1Sa 2:32 A good will be done to Israel H928+3972+889
1Sa 15:17 "A you were once small in your own eyes H561
2Sa 13:25 A Absalom urged him, he still refused to H2256
2Sa 23:21 A the Egyptian had a spear in his hand H2256
1Ki 11:10 A he had forbidden Solomon to follow H2256
1Ki 15:14 A he did not remove the high places H2256
2Ki 17:15 nations around them a the LORD had H889
2Ki 23: 9 A the priests of the high places did not H421
1Ch 11:23 A the Egyptian had a spear like a H2256
1Ch 26:10 Shimri the first (a he was not the firstborn H3954
2Ch 15:17 A he did not remove the high places from H8370
2Ch 24:19 A the LORD sent prophets to the people to H2256
2Ch 24:24 A the Aramean army had come with only H3954
2Ch 30:18 A most of the many people who came H3954
Ne 5: 5 A we are of the same flesh and blood as H6964
Job 9:21 "A I am blameless, I have no concern for NDT
Job 34: 6 A I am right, I am considered a liar H6584
Job 34: 6 I am considered a liar; a I am guiltless, his NDT
Ecc 8:12 A a wicked person who commits a hundred H889
Isa 12: 1 A you were angry with me, your anger has H3954
Isa 17:13 A the peoples roar like the roar of surging NDT
Isa 30:20 A the Lord gives you the bread of adversity H2256
Isa 60:15 "A you have been forsaken and hated H9393
Jer 2:22 A you wash yourself with soap and H3954+561
Jer 5: 2 A they say, 'As surely as the LORD lives,' H561
Jer 11:11 A they cry out to me, I will not listen to H2256
Jer 14: 7 A our sins testify against us, do something H561
Jer 14:12 A they fast, I will not listen to their cry H3954
Jer 23:38 A you claim, 'This is a message from the H561
Jer 48:33 A there are shouts, they are not shouts of NDT
Eze 8:18 A they shout in my ears, I will not listen to H2256
Eze 11:16 A I sent them far away among the nations H3954
Eze 15: 7 A they have come out of the fire, the fire NDT
Eze 20:38 A I will bring them out of the land where NDT
Eze 32:32 A I had him spread terror in the land of H3954
Hos 8:10 A they have sold themselves H1685+3954
Na 1:12 "A they have allies and are numerous, they H561
Na 1:12 A I have afflicted you, Judah, I will afflict H2256
Lk 14:14 A they cannot repay you, you will be *G4022*
Jn 4: 2 a **in fact** it was not Jesus who baptized *G2793*
Ac 28:17 *a I have* **done** nothing against our people AIT
Ro 1:21 For *a they* **knew** God, they neither glorified AIT
Ro 1:22 *A they* **claimed** to be wise, they became fools AIT
Ro 1:32 *A they* **know** God's righteous decree that AIT
Ro 7:21 *A I* **want** to do good, evil is right there with AIT
Ro 9:22 *a* **choosing** to show his wrath and make his AIT
1Co 7:21 you—a if you can gain your freedom *G247*
2Co 12: 1 *A there is* nothing *to be* **gained**, I will go on AIT
Gal 4: 1 from a slave, *a he* **owns** the whole estate. AIT
Eph 3: 8 A I am less than the least of all the Lord's NDT
1Ti 3:14 *A I* **hope** to come to you soon, I am writing AIT
Phm 8 a in Christ *I could be* **bold** and order you to AIT
Jas 3: 4 *A they* **are** so large and are driven by strong AIT
2Pe 2:11 *a they* **are** stronger and more powerful AIT
Jude 3 *a I* **was** very eager to write to you about the AIT

ALTOGETHER (18) [TOGETHER]

Ge 5: 5 A, Adam lived a **total** *of* 930 years H3972+3427
Ge 5: 8 A, Seth lived a **total** *of* 912 years, and H3972
Ge 5:11 A, Enosh lived a **total** *of* 905 years, and H3972
Ge 5:14 A, Kenan lived a **total** *of* 910 years, and H3972
Ge 5:17 A, Mahalalel lived a **total** *of* 895 years H3972
Ge 5:20 A, Jared lived a **total** *of* 962 years, and H3972
Ge 5:23 A, Enoch lived a **total** *of* 365 years. H3972
Ge 5:27 A, Methuselah lived a **total** *of* 969 years H3972
Ge 5:31 A, Lamech lived a **total** *of* 777 years, and H3972
Ex 26: 7 the tent over the tabernacle—eleven a. NDT
Ex 36:14 the tent over the tabernacle—eleven a. NDT
Nu 7:85 A, the silver dishes weighed two H3972
Nu 7:86 A, the gold dishes weighed a hundred H3972
1Ch 9:22 A, those chosen to be gatekeepers at the H3972
Job 13: 5 If only *you would be* a **silent**! For H3087+3087
SS 4: 7 You are a beautiful, my darling; there is H3972
SS 5:16 mouth is sweetness itself; he is a lovely. H3972
Ac 27:37 A there were 276 of us on board. *G3836+4246*

ALUSH (2)

Nu 33:13 They left Dophkah and camped at A. H478
Nu 33:14 They left A and camped at Rephidim H478

ALVAH (2)

Ge 36:40 clans and regions: Timna, A, Jetheth, H6595
1Ch 1:51 chiefs of Edom were: Timna, A, Jetheth, H6595

ALVAN (2)

Ge 36:23 The sons of Shobal: A, Manahath, Ebal H6597
1Ch 1:40 The sons of Shobal: A, Manahath, Ebal H6597

ALWAYS (141)

Ge 26:29 not harm you but a treated you well and H8370
Ex 19: 9 with you and will a put their trust in H4200+6409
Ex 28:30 Thus Aaron will a bear the means of H9458
Ex 29:28 This is a to be the perpetual share from H6409
Lev 25:32 " 'The Levites a have the right to redeem H6409
Nu 22:30 which you have a ridden, to this H4946+6388
Dt 5:29 keep all my commands a, H3972+2021+3427
Dt 6:24 that we might a prosper and H3972+2021+3427
Dt 11: 1 laws and his commands a. H3972+2021+3427
Dt 12:28 so that it may a go well with you H6330+6409
Dt 14:23 revere the LORD your God a. H3972+2021+3427
Dt 15:11 *There will* a **be** poor people in the H2532+4202
Dt 18: 5 in the LORD's name a. H3972+2021+3427
Dt 19: 9 and to walk a in obedience H3972+2021+3427
Dt 28:13 you will a be at the top, never H8370
Jos 1: 8 **Keep** this Book of the Law *a* on your lips AIT
Jos 4:24 you might a fear the LORD H3972+2021+3427
1Sa 1:22 the LORD, and he will live there a." H6330+6409
1Sa 2:35 before my anointed one a. H3972+2021+3427
1Sa 7:17 But he a went back to Ramah, where his NDT
2Sa 9: 7 and you will a eat at my table. H9458
2Sa 9:10 of your master, will a eat at my table." H9458
2Sa 9:13 because he a ate at the king's table H9458
1Ki 5: 1 because he had a been on H3972+2021+3427
1Ki 9: 3 my heart will a be there. H3972+2021+3427
1Ki 11:36 servant may a have a lamp H3972+2021+3427
1Ki 12: 7 they will a be your servants." H3972+2021+3427
1Ki 22: 8 anything good about me, but a bad. NDT
2Ki 17:37 You must a be careful to H3972+2021+3427
1Ch 16:11 the LORD and his strength; seek his face a. H9458
2Ch 7:16 my heart will a be there. H3972+2021+3427

2Ch 10: 7 they will **a** be your servants." H3972+2021+3427
2Ch 18: 7 good about me, but **a** bad. H3972+3427
Job 31:32 my door *was a* open to the traveler— AIT
Ps 10: 5 His ways are **a** prosperous H928+3972+6961
Ps 16: 8 I keep my eyes **a** on the LORD. With him at H9458
Ps 26: 3 I have **a** been mindful of your unfailing NDT
Ps 34: 1 all times; his praise will **a** be on my lips. H9458
Ps 35:27 gladness; may they **a** say, "The LORD be H9458
Ps 37:26 They are **a** generous and H3972+2021+3427
Ps 40:11 your love and faithfulness **a** protect me. H9458
Ps 40:16 those who long for your saving help **a** say, H9458
Ps 51: 3 transgressions, and my sin is **a** before me. H9458
Ps 52: 9 have done I will **a** praise you in the H4200+6409
Ps 70: 4 those who long for your saving help **a** say, H9458
Ps 71: 3 to which I can **a** go; give the command H9458
Ps 71:14 As for me, I will **a** have hope; I will praise H9458
Ps 73:12 the wicked are like—**a** free of care, they H6409
Ps 73:23 Yet I am **a** with you; you hold me by my H9458
Ps 103: 9 He will not **a** accuse, nor will he H4200+5905
Ps 105: 4 the LORD and his strength; seek his face **a**. H9458
Ps 106: 3 justly, who **a** do what is right. H928+3972+6961
Ps 109:15 May their sins **a** remain before the LORD H9458
Ps 119:44 I will **a** obey your law, for ever and ever. H9458
Ps 119:98 commands are **a** with me and H4200+6409
Ps 119:117 I will **a** have regard for your decrees. H9458
Ps 119:132 as you **a do** to those who love your name. H5477
Ps 119:144 Your statutes are **a** righteous; give H4200+6409
Pr 5:19 may her breasts satisfy you **a** H928+3972+6961
Pr 6:14 heart—he **a** stirs up conflict. H928+3972+6961
Pr 6:21 Bind them **a** on your heart; fasten them H9458
Pr 8:30 rejoicing **a** in his presence H928+3972+6961
Pr 23: 7 kind of *person who is a* **thinking** about the AIT
Pr 23:17 but **a** be zealous for the fear H3972+2021+3427
Pr 28:14 is the one who **a** trembles before God, H9458
Ecc 9: 8 **A** be clothed in white, and H928+3972+6961
Ecc 9: 8 and **a** anoint your head with oil. H440+2893
Isa 57:16 will I **a** be angry, for then H4200+5905
Isa 58:11 The LORD will guide you **a**; he will satisfy H9458
Isa 59:21 in your mouth *will* **a be** on your lips H4202+4631
Isa 60:11 Your gates will **a** stand open, they will H9458
Jer 3: 5 will you **a** be angry? Will your H4200+6409
Jer 8: 5 Why **does** Jerusalem **a** turn away H5904
Jer 12: 1 You are **a** righteous, LORD, when I bring **a** NDT
Jer 12: 2 You are **a** on their lips but far from their H7940
Jer 17: 8 when heat comes; its leaves **are** *a* green. AIT
Jer 32:39 that they will **a** fear me and H3972+2021+3427
Jer 35: 7 things, but must **a** live in tents. H3972+3427
La 5:20 Why do you **a** forget us? Why do H4200+5905
Hos 7: 2 sins engulf them; they are **a** before me. H6964
Hos 12: 6 love and justice, and wait for your God **a**. H9458
Mal 1: 4 **a** people under the wrath of the H6330+6409
Mt 18:10 angels in heaven **a** see the face of G1328+4246
Mt 26:11 The poor you will **a** have with you, but you G4121
Mt 26:11 with you, but you will not **a** have me. G4121
Mt 28:20 And surely I am with you **a** G4246+3836+2465
Mk 14: 7 The poor you will **a** have with you, and G4121
Mk 14: 7 But you will not **a** have me. G4121
Lk 15:31 father said, 'you are **a** with me, and G4121
Lk 18: 1 that they should **a** pray and not give up. G4121
Lk 21:36 Be **a** on the watch, and pray G1877+4246+2789
Jn 5:17 "My Father *is a* **at** *his* **work** to this very day AIT
Jn 6:34 they said, "**a** give us this bread. G4121
Jn 8:29 me alone, for I **a** do what pleases him." G4121
Jn 11:42 I knew that you **a** hear me, but I said this G4121
Jn 12: 8 You will **a** have the poor among you, but G4121
Jn 12: 8 among you, but you will not **a** have me." G4121
Jn 18:20 "I **a** taught in synagogues or at the G4121
Ac 2:25 " 'I saw the Lord **a** before me G1328+4246
Ac 7:51 your ancestors: You **a** resist the Holy Spirit! G107
Ac 9:36 she was **a** doing good and helping the G4441
Ac 24:16 So I strive **a** to keep my conscience G1328+4246
Ro 15:20 It *has a been my* **ambition** to preach the AIT
1Co 1: 4 I **a** thank my God for you because of his G4121
1Co 13: 7 It **a** protects, always trusts, always hopes G4246
1Co 13: 7 It always protects, **a** trusts, always hopes G4246
1Co 13: 7 always trusts, **a** hopes, always perseveres G4246
1Co 13: 7 always trusts, always hopes, **a** perseveres. G4246
1Co 15:58 **A** give yourselves fully to the work of the G4121
2Co 1:19 "No," but in him *it has a* **been** "Yes. AIT
2Co 2:14 who **a** leads us as captives in Christ's G4121
2Co 4:10 We **a** carry around in our body the death G4121
2Co 4:11 we who are alive are **a** being given over to G107
2Co 5: 6 Therefore we are **a** confident and know G4121
2Co 6:10 sorrowful, yet **a** rejoicing; poor, yet making G107
Gal 4:18 and to be so **a**, not just when I am G4121
Eph 5:20 **a** giving thanks to God the Father for G4121
Eph 6:18 be alert and **a** keep on praying for all the G4246
Php 1: 4 my prayers for all of you, I **a** pray with joy G4121
Php 1:20 so that now as **a** Christ will be exalted G4121
Php 2:12 as you have **a** obeyed—not only in G4121
Php 4: 4 Rejoice in the Lord **a**. I will say it again G4121
Col 1: 3 We **a** thank God, the Father of our Lord G4121
Col 4: 6 Let your conversation be **a** full of grace G4121
Col 4:12 He is **a** wrestling in prayer for you, that G4121
1Th 1: 2 We **a** thank God for all of you and G4121
1Th 2:16 In this way they **a** heap up their sins to G4121
1Th 3: 6 has told us that you **a** have pleasant G4121
1Th 5:15 **a** strive to do what is good for each G4121
1Th 5:16 Rejoice **a**, G4121
2Th 1: 3 We ought **a** to thank God for you, brothers G4121
2Th 2:13 But we ought **a** to thank God for you G4121
2Ti 3: 7 **a** learning but never able to come to **a** G4121
Titus 1:12 "Cretans are **a** liars, evil brutes, lazy G107
Titus 3: 2 **a** to be gentle toward everyone. G4246
Phm 4 I **a** thank my God as I remember you in G4121
Heb 3:10 'Their hearts are **a** going astray, and they G107
Heb 7:25 because he **a** lives to intercede for them. G4121
1Pe 3:15 **A** be prepared to give an answer to G107
2Pe 1:12 So I will **a** remind you of these things, even G107
2Pe 1:15 departure you will **a** be able to remember G1668

AM (1130) [BE] See Index of Articles Etc.

AMAD (1)

Jos 19:26 Allammelek, **A** and Mishal. On the west H6675

AMAL (1)

1Ch 7:35 Zophah, Imna, Shelesh and **A**. H6663

AMALEK (12) [AMALEKITE, AMALEKITES]

Ge 36:12 named Timna, who bore him **A**. H6667
Ge 36:16 Gatam and **A**. These were the H6667
Ex 17:14 out the name of **A** from under heaven." H6667
Nu 24:20 Then Balaam saw **A** and spoke his H6667
Nu 24:20 "**A** was first among the nations, but their H6667
Dt 25:19 out the name of **A** from under heaven. H6667
Jdg 5:14 whose roots were in **A**; Benjamin was H6667
1Sa 15: 5 went to the city of **A** and set an ambush H6667
2Sa 8:12 Ammonites and the Philistines, and **A**. H6667
1Ch 1:36 Gatam and Kenaz; by Timna: **A**. H6667
1Ch 18:11 Ammonites and the Philistines, and **A**. H6667
Ps 83: 7 Ammon and **A**, Philistia, with the H6667

AMALEKITE (4) [AMALEK]

Ex 17:13 overcame the **A** army with the sword H6667
1Sa 30:13 "I am an Egyptian, the slave of an **A**. H6668
2Sa 1: 8 'Who are you?' " 'An **A**,' I answered. H6668
2Sa 1:13 son of a foreigner, an **A**," he answered. H6668

AMALEKITES (34) [AMALEK]

Ge 14: 7 conquered the whole territory of the **A**, H6668
Ex 17: 8 The **A** came and attacked the Israelites at H6667
Ex 17: 9 of our men and go out to fight the **A**. H6667
Ex 17:10 Joshua fought the **A** as Moses had H6667
Ex 17:11 lowered his hands, the **A** were winning. H6667
Ex 17:16 at war against the **A** from generation to H6667
Nu 13:29 The **A** live in the Negev; the Hittites H6667
Nu 14:25 Since the **A** and the Canaanites are living H6668
Nu 14:43 the **A** and the Canaanites will face you H6668
Nu 14:45 Then the **A** and the Canaanites who lived H6668
Dt 25:17 Remember what the **A** did to you along H6667
Jdg 3:13 Getting the Ammonites and **A** to join him H6667
Jdg 6: 3 **A** and other eastern peoples invaded the H6667
Jdg 6:33 **A** and other eastern peoples joined forces H6667
Jdg 7:12 the **A** and all the other eastern peoples H6667
Jdg 10:12 the **A** and the Maonites oppressed you H6667
Jdg 12:15 in Ephraim, in the hill country of the **A**. H6668
1Sa 14:48 He fought valiantly and defeated the **A** H6667
1Sa 15: 2 'I will punish the **A** for what they did to H6667
1Sa 15: 3 attack the **A** and totally destroy all that H6667
1Sa 15: 6 leave the **A** so that I do not destroy you H6668
1Sa 15: 6 So the Kenites moved away from the **A**. H6667
1Sa 15: 7 Then Saul attacked the **A** all the way from H6667
1Sa 15: 8 He took Agag king of the **A** alive, and all H6667
1Sa 15:15 "The soldiers brought them from the **A** H6668
1Sa 15:18 wicked people, the **A**; wage war against H6667
1Sa 15:20 destroyed the **A** and brought back Agag H6667
1Sa 15:32 "Bring me Agag king of the **A**. H6667
1Sa 27: 8 the Geshurites, the Girzites and the **A**. H6668
1Sa 28:18 carry out his fierce wrath against the **A**, H6667
1Sa 30: 1 Now the **A** had raided the Negev and H6668
1Sa 30:18 recovered everything the **A** had taken, H6667
2Sa 1: 1 striking down the **A** and stayed in Ziklag H6667
1Ch 4:43 killed the remaining **A** who had escaped, H6667

AMAM (1)

Jos 15:26 **A**, Shema, Moladah, H585

AMANA (1)

SS 4: 8 Descend from the crest of **A**, from the top H592

AMARIAH (15) [AMARIAH'S]

1Ch 6: 7 Meraioth the father of **A**, Amariah the H618
1Ch 6: 7 father of Amariah, **A** the father of Ahitub, H618
1Ch 6:11 Azariah the father of **A**, Amariah the father H618
1Ch 6:11 father of Amariah, **A** the father of Ahitub, H618
1Ch 6:52 Meraioth his son, **A** his son, Ahitub his son, H618
1Ch 23:19 Jeriah the first, **A** the second, Jahaziel the H618
1Ch 24:23 Jeriah the first, **A** the second, Jahaziel the H619
2Ch 19:11 "**A** the chief priest will be over you in any H619
2Ch 31:15 **A** and Shekaniah assisted him faithfully in H619
Ezr 7: 3 the son of **A**, the son of Azariah, the son of H618
Ezr 10:42 Shallum, **A** and Joseph. H618
Ne 10: 3 Pashhur, **A**, Malkijah, H618
Ne 11: 4 Zechariah, the son of **A**, the son of H618
Ne 12: 2 **A**, Malluk, Hattush, H618
Zep 1: 1 the son of **A**, the son of Hezekiah H618

AMARIAH'S (1) [AMARIAH]

Ne 12:13 of Ezra's, Meshullam; of **A**, Jehohanan; H618

AMASA (18)

2Sa 17:25 had appointed **A** over the army in H6690
2Sa 17:25 **A** was the son of Jether, an Ishmaelite H6690
2Sa 19:13 And say to **A**, 'Are you not my own flesh H6690
2Sa 20: 4 Then the king said to **A**, "Summon the H6690
2Sa 20: 5 But when **A** went to summon Judah, he H6690
2Sa 20: 8 rock in Gibeon, **A** came to meet them. H6690
2Sa 20: 9 Joab said to **A**, "How are you, my brother?" H6690
2Sa 20: 9 Then Joab took **A** by the beard with his H6690
2Sa 20:10 **A** was not on his guard against the dagger H6690
2Sa 20:10 stabbed again, **A** died. Then Joab and NDT
2Sa 20:11 of Joab's men stood beside **A** and said, H2257S
2Sa 20:12 **A** lay wallowing in his blood in the middle H6690
2Sa 20:12 that everyone who came up to **A** stopped, H6690
2Sa 20:13 After **A** had been removed from the road NDT
1Ki 2: 5 Abner son of Ner and **A** son of Jether. H6690
1Ki 2:32 of Israel's army, and **A** son of Jether H6690
1Ch 2:17 Abigail was the mother of **A**, whose H6690
2Ch 28:12 son of Shallum, and **A** son of Hadlai H6690

AMASAI (5)

1Ch 6:25 The descendants of Elkanah: **A**, Ahimoth, H6691
1Ch 6:35 the son of Mahath, the son of **A**, H6691
1Ch 12:18 Then the Spirit came on **A**, chief of the H6691
1Ch 15:24 Nethanel, **A**, Zechariah, Benaiah H6691
2Ch 29:12 Mahath son of **A** and Joel son of Azariah H6691

AMASHSAI (1)

Ne 11:13 242 men; **A** son of Azarel, the son of H6692

AMASIAH (1)

2Ch 17:16 **A** son of Zikri, who volunteered H6674

AMASSED (2) [AMASSES]

Ecc 2: 8 *I* **a** silver and gold for myself, and the H4043
Eze 28: 4 yourself and **a** gold and silver in your H6913

AMASSES (1) [AMASSED, AMASSING]

Pr 28: 8 profit from the poor **a** it for another, H7695

AMASSING (1) [AMASSES]

Ps 73:12 always free of care, *they* **go on a** wealth. H8436

AMAZED (42) [AMAZEMENT]

Isa 29: 9 Be stunned and **a**, blind yourselves and H9449
Hab 1: 5 and watch—and *be* **utterly a**. H9449+9449
Mt 7:28 the crowds *were* **a** at his teaching, G1742
Mt 8:10 *he was* **a** and said to those following him G2513
Mt 8:27 The men *were* **a** and asked, "What kind G2513
Mt 9:33 The crowd *was* **a** and said, "Nothing like G2513
Mt 13:54 in their synagogue, and they *were* **a**. G1742
Mt 15:31 The people *were* **a** when they saw the G2513
Mt 21:20 saw this, *they were* **a**. "How did the fig G2513
Mt 22:22 they heard this, *they were* **a**. So they left G2513
Mk 1:22 *The people were* **a** at his teaching G1742
Mk 1:27 *The people were* all so **a** that they asked G2501
Mk 2:12 *This* **a** everyone and they praised God G2014
Mk 5:20 done for him. And all the people *were* **a**. G2513
Mk 6: 2 many who heard him *were* **a**. G1742
Mk 6: 6 *He was* **a** at their lack of faith. Then Jesus G2513
Mk 6:51 They *were* completely **a**, G2014
Mk 10:24 The disciples *were* **a** at his words. But G2501
Mk 10:26 The disciples *were* even more **a**, and said G1742
Mk 11:18 the whole crowd *was* **a** at his teaching. G1742
Mk 12:17 what is God's." And *they were* **a** at him. G1703
Mk 15: 5 still made no reply, and Pilate *was* **a**. G2513
Lk 2:18 all who heard it *were* **a** at what the G2513
Lk 2:47 who heard him *was* **a** at his G2014
Lk 4:22 well of him and *were* **a** at the gracious G2513
Lk 4:32 *They were* **a** at his teaching, because his G1742
Lk 4:36 All the people were **a** and said to each G2502
Lk 5:26 Everyone *was* **a** and gave praise to G1749+3284
Lk 7: 9 Jesus heard this, *he was* **a** at him, and G2513
Lk 9:43 And *they were* all **a** at the greatness of G1742
Lk 11:14 been mute spoke, and the crowd *was* **a**. G2513
Lk 24:22 some of our women **a** us. They went to G2014
Jn 5:20 works than these, so that you *will be* **a**. G2513
Jn 5:28 "*Do not be* **a** at this, for a time is coming G2513
Jn 7:15 The Jews there *were* **a** and asked, "How G2513
Jn 7:21 "I did one miracle, and *you are* all **a**. G2513
Ac 2: 7 **Utterly a**, they asked: "Aren't G2014+2779+2513
Ac 2:12 **A** and perplexed, they asked one another G2014
Ac 7:31 he saw this, *he was* **a** at the sight. As G2513
Ac 8: 9 sorcery in the city and **a** all the people of G2014
Ac 8:11 him because *he had* **a** them for a long G2014
Ac 13:12 *for he was* **a** at the teaching about the G1742

AMAZEMENT (6) [AMAZED, AMAZING]

Da 3:24 to his feet in **a** and asked his A10755+10097
Mt 27:14 charge—to the great **a** of the governor. G2513
Mk 7:37 *People were* overwhelmed *with* **a**. "He has G1742
Lk 8:25 In fear and **a** they asked one another G2513
Lk 24:41 did not believe it because of joy and **a**, G2513
Ac 3:10 with wonder and **a** at what had happened G1749

AMAZIAH (40) [AMAZIAH'S]

2Ki 12:21 And **A** his son succeeded him as king H604
2Ki 13:12 including his war against **A** king of Judah H604
2Ki 14: 1 **A** son of Joash king of Judah began to H605
2Ki 14: 8 Then **A** sent messengers to Jehoash son of H604
2Ki 14: 9 king of Israel replied to **A** king of Judah: H605
2Ki 14:11 **A**, however, would not listen, so Jehoash H605
2Ki 14:11 He and **A** king of Judah faced each other H605
2Ki 14:13 king of Israel captured **A** king of Judah, H605
2Ki 14:15 including his war against **A** king of Judah H605
2Ki 14:17 **A** son of Joash king of Judah lived for H605
2Ki 14:21 made him king in place of his father **A**. H605
2Ki 14:22 it to Judah after **A** rested with his H2021+4889S

2Ki 14:23 the fifteenth year of A son of Joash king of H605
2Ki 15: 1 Azariah son of A king of Judah began to H604
2Ki 15: 3 of the LORD, just as his father A had done. H605
1Ch 3:12 A his son, Azariah his son, Jotham his son, H605
1Ch 4:34 Meshobab, Jamlech, Joshah son of A, H604
1Ch 6:45 the son of A, the son of Hilkiah, H604
2Ch 24:27 And A his son succeeded him as king H605
2Ch 25: 1 A was twenty-five years old when he H605
2Ch 25: 5 A called the people of Judah together H605
2Ch 25: 9 A asked the man of God, "But what about H605
2Ch 25:10 So A dismissed the troops who had come H605
2Ch 25:11 A then marshaled his strength and led his H605
2Ch 25:13 the troops that A had sent back and had H605
2Ch 25:14 When A returned from slaughtering the H605
2Ch 25:15 The anger of the LORD burned against A H605
2Ch 25:17 After A king of Judah consulted his H605
2Ch 25:18 king of Israel replied to A king of Judah: H605
2Ch 25:20 A, however, would not listen, for God so H605
2Ch 25:21 He and A king of Judah faced each other H605
2Ch 25:23 king of Israel captured A king of Judah, H605
2Ch 25:25 A son of Joash king of Judah lived for H605
2Ch 25:27 From the time that A turned away from H605
2Ch 26: 1 made him king in place of his father A. H605
2Ch 26: 2 it to Judah after A rested with his H2021+4889S
2Ch 26: 4 of the LORD, just as his father A had done. H605
Am 7:10 Then A the priest of Bethel sent a message H604
Am 7:12 Then A said to Amos, "Get out, you seer H604
Am 7:14 Amos answered A, "I was neither a H604

AMAZIAH'S (2) [AMAZIAH]

2Ki 14:18 As for the other events of A reign, are they H605
2Ch 25:26 As for the other events of A reign, from H605

AMAZING (3) [AMAZEMENT]

Jos 3: 5 the LORD will do a *things* among you." H7098
Jdg 13:19 the LORD did an a *thing* while Manoah H7098
Pr 30:18 are three things *that are* too a for me, H7098

AMBASSADOR (1) [AMBASSADORS]

Eph 6:20 which *I am an* a in chains. Pray that I *G4563*

AMBASSADORS (2) [AMBASSADOR]

Isa 57: 9 You sent your a far away; you descended H7495
2Co 5:20 *We are* therefore Christ's a, as though God *G4563*

AMBASSAGE (KJV) DELEGATION

AMBER (KJV) GLOWING METAL

AMBITION (8)

Ro 15:20 It *has always been my* a to preach the *G5818*
2Co 12:20 fits of rage, **selfish a**, slander, gossip, *G2249*
Gal 5:20 fits of rage, **selfish a**, dissensions, factions *G2249*
Php 1:17 The former preach Christ out of **selfish a** *G2249*
Php 2: 3 Do nothing out of **selfish a** or vain conceit *G2249*
1Th 4:11 and *to* **make it** *your* a to lead a quiet life *G5818*
Jas 3:14 bitter envy and **selfish a** in your hearts, *G2249*
Jas 3:16 For where you have envy and **selfish a** *G2249*

AMBUSH (27) [AMBUSHES]

Jos 8: 2 yourselves. Set an a behind the city." H741
Jos 8: 4 You *are to* **set an a** behind the city H741
Jos 8: 7 you are to rise up from a and take the city H741
Jos 8: 9 they went to the **place of a** and lay in wait H4422
Jos 8:12 men and set them **in a** between Bethel H741
Jos 8:13 of the city and the a to the west of it. H6811
Jos 8:14 know that an a *had been* **set** against him H741
Jos 8:19 the *men* **in** *the* a rose quickly from their H741
Jos 8:21 Israel saw that the a had taken the city H741
Jos 8:22 Those in the a also came out of the city NDT
Jdg 9:25 men on the hilltops *to* a and rob everyone H741
Jdg 9:43 three companies and **set an a** in the fields. H741
Jdg 20:29 Then Israel set an a around Gibeah. H741
Jdg 20:33 the Israelite a charged out of its place H741
Jdg 20:36 they relied on the a they had set near H741
Jdg 20:37 Those *who had been* **in** a made a sudden H741
Jdg 20:38 arranged with the a that they should send H741
1Sa 15: 5 city of Amalek and **set an a** in the ravine. H741
2Ch 13:13 in front of Judah the a was behind them. H4422
Ps 10: 8 villages; from a he murders the innocent. H5041
Ps 64: 4 They shoot from a at the innocent; they H5041
Pr 1:11 *let's* a some harmless soul H7621
Pr 1:18 their own blood; *they* a only themselves! H7621
Jer 51:12 station the watchmen, prepare an a! H741
Hos 6: 9 As marauders **lie in** a *for* a victim, so do H2675
Ac 23:21 forty of them *are* **waiting in** a for him. *G1910*
Ac 25: 3 were preparing an a to kill him along the *G1909*

AMBUSHES (1) [AMBUSH]

2Ch 20:22 the LORD set a against the men of Ammon H741

AMEN (57)

Nu 5:22 the woman is to say, "**A. So be it.**" H589+589
Dt 27:15 Then all the people shall say, "A!" H589
Dt 27:16 Then all the people shall say, "A!" H589
Dt 27:17 Then all the people shall say, "A!" H589
Dt 27:18 Then all the people shall say, "A!" H589
Dt 27:19 Then all the people shall say, "A!" H589
Dt 27:20 Then all the people shall say, "A!" H589
Dt 27:21 Then all the people shall say, "A!" H589
Dt 27:22 Then all the people shall say, "A!" H589
Dt 27:23 Then all the people shall say, "A!" H589
Dt 27:24 Then all the people shall say, "A!" H589
Dt 27:25 Then all the people shall say, "A!" H589
Dt 27:26 Then all the people shall say, "A!" H589
1Ki 1:36 son of Jehoiada answered the king, "A! H589
1Ch 16:36 Then all the people said "A" and "Praise H589
Ne 5:13 whole assembly said, "A," and praised the H589
Ne 8: 6 lifted their hands and responded, "A! H589
Ne 8: 6 A!" Then they bowed down and H589
Ps 41:13 everlasting to everlasting. A and Amen. H589
Ps 41:13 everlasting to everlasting. Amen and A. H589
Ps 72:19 earth be filled with his glory. A and Amen. H589
Ps 72:19 earth be filled with his glory. Amen and A. H589
Ps 89:52 Praise be to the LORD forever! A and Amen. H589
Ps 89:52 Praise be to the LORD forever! Amen and A. H589
Ps 106:48 Let all the people say, "A!" Praise the LORD. H589
Jer 11: 5 you possess today." I answered, "A, LORD." H589
Jer 28: 6 "A! May the LORD do so! May the H589
Ro 1:25 the Creator—who is forever praised. A. *G297*
Ro 9: 5 who is God over all, forever praised! A. *G297*
Ro 11:36 To him be the glory forever! A. *G297*
Ro 15:33 The God of peace be with you all. A. *G297*
Ro 16:27 be glory forever through Jesus Christ! A. *G297*
1Co 14:16 of an inquirer, say "A" to your thanksgiving, *G297*
1Co 16:24 My love to all of you in Christ Jesus. A. *G297*
2Co 1:20 And so through him the "A" is spoken by *G297*
Gal 1: 5 to whom be glory for ever and ever. A. *G297*
Gal 6:18 be with your spirit, brothers and sisters. A. *G297*
Eph 3:21 all generations, for ever and ever! A. *G297*
Php 4:20 Father be glory for ever and ever. A. *G297*
Php 4:23 the Lord Jesus Christ be with your spirit. A. *G297*
1Ti 1:17 be honor and glory for ever and ever. A. *G297*
1Ti 6:16 To him be honor and might forever. A. *G297*
2Ti 4:18 To him be glory for ever and ever. A. *G297*
Heb 13:21 to whom be glory for ever and ever. A. *G297*
1Pe 4:11 glory and the power for ever and ever. A. *G297*
1Pe 5:11 To him be the power for ever and ever. A. *G297*
2Pe 3:18 To him be glory both now and forever! A. *G297*
Jude 25 before all ages, now and forevermore! A. *G297*
Rev 1: 6 be glory and power for ever and ever! A. *G297*
Rev 1: 7 mourn because of him." So shall it be! A. *G297*
Rev 3:14 These are the words of the A, the faithful *G297*
Rev 5:14 creatures said, "A," and the elders fell *G297*
Rev 7:12 "A! Praise and glory and wisdom *G297*
Rev 7:12 be to our God for ever and ever. A!" *G297*
Rev 19: 4 And they cried: "A, Hallelujah!" *G297*
Rev 22:20 I am coming soon." A. Come, Lord Jesus. *G297*
Rev 22:21 of the Lord Jesus be with God's people. A. *G297*

AMENDS (2)

Job 20:10 His children *must* **make a** *to* the poor; his H8355
Pr 14: 9 Fools mock at **making a for sin**, but H871

AMETHYST (3)

Ex 28:19 the third row shall be jacinth, agate and a; H334
Ex 39:12 the third row was jacinth, agate and a; H334
Rev 21:20 the eleventh jacinth, and the twelfth a. *G287*

AMI (1)

Ezr 2:57 Pokereth-Hazzebaim and A H577

AMIABLE (KJV) LOVELY

AMID (7) [MIDDLE]

Job 4:13 A disquieting dreams in the night, when H928
Job 30:14 a the ruins they come rolling in. H9393
Ps 47: 5 God has ascended a shouts of joy, the LORD H928
Ps 47: 5 the LORD a the sounding of trumpets. H928
Am 1:14 her fortresses a war cries on the day H928
Am 1:14 of battle, a violent winds on a stormy day. H928
Am 2: 2 down in great tumult a war cries and the H928

AMINADAB (KJV) AMMINADAB

AMISS (KJV) WRONG

AMITTAI (2)

2Ki 14:25 spoken through his servant Jonah son of A H624
Jnh 1: 1 word of the LORD came to Jonah son of A: H624

AMMAH (1) [METHEG AMMAH]

2Sa 2:24 they came to the hill of A, near Giah on H565

AMMI (KJV) MY PEOPLE

AMMIEL (6)

Nu 13:12 from the tribe of Dan, A son of Gemalli; H6653
2Sa 9: 4 the house of Makir son of A in Lo Debar." H6653
2Sa 9: 5 from the house of Makir son of A. H6653
2Sa 17:27 Makir son of A from Lo Debar, and H6653
1Ch 3: 5 four were by Bathsheba daughter of A. H6653
1Ch 26: 5 A the sixth, Issachar the seventh and H6653

AMMIHUD (10)

Nu 1:10 Elishama son of A; from Manasseh, H6654
Nu 2:18 people of Ephraim is Elishama son of A. H6654
Nu 7:48 On the seventh day Elishama son of A, H6654
Nu 7:53 was the offering of Elishama son of A. H6654
Nu 10:22 Elishama son of A was in command. H6654
Nu 34:20 Shemuel son of A, from the tribe of H6654
Nu 34:28 Pedahel son of A, the leader from the H6654
2Sa 13:37 fled and went to Talmai son of A, H6654
1Ch 7:26 Ladan his son, A his son, Elishama his son H6654
1Ch 9: 4 Uthai son of A, the son of Omri, the son H6654

AMMINADAB (16)

Ex 6:23 daughter of A and sister of Nahshon H6657
Nu 1: 7 from Judah, Nahshon son of A; H6657
Nu 2: 3 the people of Judah is Nahshon son of A. H6657
Nu 7:12 was Nahshon son of A of the tribe of H6657
Nu 7:17 was the offering of Nahshon son of A. H6657
Nu 10:14 Nahshon son of A was in command. H6657
Ru 4:19 the father of Ram, Ram the father of A, H6657
Ru 4:20 A the father of Nahshon, Nahshon the H6657
1Ch 2:10 Ram was the father of A, and H6657
1Ch 2:10 A the father of Nahshon H6657
1Ch 6:22 A his son, Korah his son H6657
1Ch 15:10 of Uzziel, A the leader and 112 relatives. H6657
1Ch 15:11 Shemaiah, Eliel and A the Levites. H6657
Mt 1: 4 Ram the father of A, Amminadab the *G300*
Mt 1: 4 of Amminadab, A the father of Nahshon *G300*
Lk 3:33 the son *of* A, the son of Ram, the son of *G300*

AMMISHADDAI (5)

Nu 1:12 from Dan, Ahiezer son of A; H6659
Nu 2:25 of the people of Dan is Ahiezer son of A. H6659
Nu 7:66 On the tenth day Ahiezer son of A, the H6659
Nu 7:71 This was the offering of Ahiezer son of A. H6659
Nu 10:25 Ahiezer son of A was in command. H6659

AMMIZABAD (1)

1Ch 27: 6 His son A was in charge of his division H6655

AMMON (15) [AMMONITE, AMMONITES]

Jdg 11:28 The king of A, however, paid no H1201+6648
Jdg 11:33 Thus Israel subdued A. H1201+6648
2Ki 23:13 the detestable god of the people of A. H6648
2Ch 20:10 "But now here are men from A, Moab H6648
2Ch 20:22 the men of A and Moab and Mount H6648
Ne 13:23 women from Ashdod, A and Moab. H6649
Ps 83: 7 A and Amalek, Philistia, with the H6648
Jer 9:26 Edom, A, Moab and all who live in H1201+6648
Jer 25:21 Moab and A; H1201+6648
Jer 27: 3 Moab, A, Tyre and Sidon through H1201+6648
Jer 40:11 Jews in Moab, A, Edom and all the H1201+6648
Jer 49: 4 Unfaithful Daughter A, you trust in your NDT
Eze 25: 5 camels and A into a resting H1201+6648
Da 11:41 the leaders of A will be delivered H1201+6648
Am 1:13 "For three sins of A, even for four, I H1201+6648

AMMONI See KEPHAR AMMONI

AMMONITE (21) [AMMON]

Dt 23: 3 No A or Moabite or any of their H6649
Jos 13:25 and half the A country as far as H1201+6648
Jdg 11:12 messengers to the A king with the H1201+6648
Jdg 11:14 back messengers to the A king, H1201+6648
1Sa 11: 1 Nahash the A went up and besieged H6649
1Sa 11: 2 But Nahash the A replied, "I will make a H6649
2Sa 10: 3 the A commanders said to Hanun H1201+6648
2Sa 12:31 David did this to all the A towns H1201+6648
2Sa 23:37 Zelek the A, Naharai the Beerothite, the H6649
1Ki 14:21 name was Naamah; she was an A. H6649
1Ki 14:31 name was Naamah; she was an A. H6649
2Ki 24: 2 Moabite and A raiders against him H1201+6648
1Ch 11:39 Zelek the A, Naharai the Berothite, the H6649
1Ch 19: 3 the A commanders said to Hanun H1201+6648
1Ch 20: 3 David did this to all the A towns H1201+6648
2Ch 12:13 name was Naamah; she was an A. H6649
2Ch 24:26 son of Shimeath an A *woman*, and H6649
Ne 2:10 Tobiah the A official heard about H6649
Ne 2:19 Tobiah the A official and Geshem the H6649
Ne 4: 3 Tobiah the A, who was at his side, said H6649
Ne 13: 1 found written that no A or Moabite should H6649

AMMONITES (89) [AMMON]

Ge 19:38 he is the father of the A of today. H1201+6648
Nu 21:24 only as far as the A, because H1201+6648
Dt 2:19 When you come to the A, do not H1201+6648
Dt 2:19 of any land belonging to the A. H1201+6648
Dt 2:20 the A called them Zamzummites. H6649
Dt 2:21 LORD destroyed them from before **the A**, H2157S
Dt 2:37 on any of the land of the A, H1201+6648
Dt 3:11 It is still in Rabbah of the A.) H1201+6648
Dt 3:16 which is the border of the A. H1201+6648
Jos 12: 2 which is the border of the A. H1201+6648
Jos 13:10 out to the border of the A. H1201+6648
Jdg 3:13 Getting the A and Amalekites to H1201+6648
Jdg 10: 6 the gods of the A and the gods of H1201+6648
Jdg 10: 7 hands of the Philistines and the A, H1201+6648
Jdg 10: 9 The A also crossed the Jordan to H1201+6648
Jdg 10:11 the Amorites, the A, the Philistines, H1201+6648
Jdg 10:17 When the A were called to arms H1201+6648
Jdg 10:18 in attacking the A will be head H1201+6648
Jdg 11: 4 when the A were fighting against H1201+6648
Jdg 11: 6 commander, so we can fight the A." H1201+6648
Jdg 11: 8 come with us to fight the A, and H1201+6648
Jdg 11: 9 back to fight the A and the LORD H1201+6648
Jdg 11:13 The king of the A answered H1201+6648
Jdg 11:15 land of Moab or the land of the A. H1201+6648
Jdg 11:27 between the Israelites and the A." H1201+6648
Jdg 11:29 there he advanced against the A. H1201+6648
Jdg 11:30 "If you give the A into my hands, H1201+6648
Jdg 11:31 triumph from the A will be the H1201+6648
Jdg 11:32 Jephthah went over to fight the A, H1201+6648
Jdg 11:36 you of your enemies, the A. H1201+6648
Jdg 12: 1 go to fight the A without calling us H1201+6648
Jdg 12: 2 in a great struggle with the A, H1201+6648
Jdg 12: 3 and crossed over to fight the A, H1201+6648
1Sa 11:10 They said to the A, "Tomorrow we will NDT

1Sa 11:11 the camp of the A and slaughtered them H6648
1Sa 12:12 king of the A was moving against H1201+6648
1Sa 14:47 Moab, the A, Edom, the kings of H1201+6648
2Sa 8:12 Moab, the A and the Philistines H1201+6648
2Sa 10: 1 the king of the A died, and his son H1201+6648
2Sa 10: 2 men came to the land of the A, H1201+6648
2Sa 10: 6 When the A realized that they had H1201+6648
2Sa 10: 8 The A came out and drew up in H1201+6648
2Sa 10:10 and deployed them against the A. H1201+6648
2Sa 10:11 if the A are too strong for you H1201+6648
2Sa 10:14 When the A realized that the H1201+6648
2Sa 10:14 from fighting the A and came to H1201+6648
2Sa 10:19 were afraid to help the A anymore. H1201+6648
2Sa 11: 1 destroyed the A and besieged H1201+6648
2Sa 12: 9 killed him with the sword of the A. H1201+6648
2Sa 12:26 Rabbah of the A and captured the H1201+6648
2Sa 17:27 of Nahash from Rabbah of the A, H1201+6648
1Ki 11: 1 daughter—Moabites, A, Edomites H6649
1Ki 11: 5 Molek the detestable god of the A. H6649
1Ki 11: 7 Molek the detestable god of the A. H1201+6648
1Ki 11:33 and Molek the god of the A, and H1201+6648
1Ch 18:11 Moab, the A and the Philistines H1201+6648
1Ch 19: 1 Nahash king of the A died, and his H1201+6648
1Ch 19: 2 in the land of the A to express H1201+6648
1Ch 19: 6 When the A realized that they had H1201+6648
1Ch 19: 6 Hanun and the A sent a thousand H1201+6648
1Ch 19: 7 while the A were mustered from H1201+6648
1Ch 19: 9 The A came out and drew up in H1201+6648
1Ch 19:11 they were deployed against the A. H1201+6648
1Ch 19:12 if the A are too strong for you H1201+6648
1Ch 19:15 When the A realized that the H1201+6648
1Ch 19:19 not willing to help the A anymore. H1201+6648
1Ch 20: 1 the land of the A and went to H1201+6648
2Ch 20: 1 Moabites and A with some of the H1201+6648
2Ch 20:23 The A and Moabites rose up H1201+6648
2Ch 26: 8 The A brought tribute to Uzziah, and his H6649
2Ch 27: 5 the king of the A and conquered H1201+6648
2Ch 27: 5 That year the A paid him a H1201+6648
2Ch 27: 5 The A brought him the same H1201+6648
Ezr 9: 1 Jebusites, A, Moabites, Egyptians H6649
Ne 4: 7 the A and the people of Ashdod heard H6649
Isa 11:14 and the A will be subject to them. H1201+6648
Jer 40:14 king of the A has sent Ishmael H1201+6648
Jer 41:10 and set out to cross over to the A. H1201+6648
Jer 41:15 from Johanan and fled to the A. H1201+6648
Jer 49: 1 Concerning the A: This is what the H1201+6648
Jer 49: 2 battle cry against Rabbah of the A; H1201+6648
Jer 49: 6 I will restore the fortunes of the A," H1201+6648
Eze 21:20 Rabbah of the A and another H1201+6648
Eze 21:28 says about the A and their insults: H1201+6648
Eze 25: 2 face against the A and prophesy H1201+6648
Eze 25:10 along with the A to the people of H1201+6648
Eze 25:10 so that the A will not be H1201+6648
Zep 2: 8 of Moab and the taunts of the A, H1201+6648
Zep 2: 9 like Sodom, the A like Gomorrah H1201+6648

AMNON (28) [AMNON'S]

2Sa 3: 2 His firstborn was A the son of Ahinoam of H596
2Sa 13: 1 A son of David fell in love with Tamar H596
2Sa 13: 2 A became so obsessed with his sister H596
2Sa 13: 3 Now A had an adviser named Jonadab son H596
2Sa 13: 4 He asked A, "Why do you, the king's son H2257S
2Sa 13: 4 A said to him, "I'm in love with Tamar, my H596
2Sa 13: 6 So A lay down and pretended to be ill H596
2Sa 13: 6 came to see him, A said to him, "I would H596
2Sa 13: 7 of your brother A and prepare some food H596
2Sa 13: 8 Tamar went to the house of her brother A, H596
2Sa 13: 9 out of here," A said. So everyone left H596
2Sa 13:10 Then A said to Tamar, "Bring the food here H596
2Sa 13:10 brought it to her brother A in his bedroom. H596
2Sa 13:15 Then A hated her with intense hatred. In H596
2Sa 13:15 he had loved her. A said to her, "Get up H596
2Sa 13:20 said to her, "Has that A, your brother, H578
2Sa 13:22 And Absalom never said a word to A, either H596
2Sa 13:22 he hated A because he had disgraced his H596
2Sa 13:26 please let my brother A come with us." H596
2Sa 13:27 so he sent with him A and the rest of the H596
2Sa 13:28 When A is in high spirits from drinking H596
2Sa 13:28 I say to you, 'Strike A down,' then kill him. H596
2Sa 13:29 men did to A what Absalom had H596
2Sa 13:32 they killed all the princes; only A is dead. H596
2Sa 13:32 ever since the day A raped his sister H2257S
2Sa 13:33 the king's sons are dead. Only A is dead." H596
1Ch 3: 1 The firstborn was A the son of Ahinoam of H596
1Ch 4:20 sons of Shimon: A, Rinnah, Ben-Hanan H596

AMNON'S (1) [AMNON]

2Sa 13:39 he was consoled concerning A death. H596

AMOK (1) [AMOK'S]

Ne 12: 7 A, Hilkiah and Jedaiah. These H6651

AMOK'S (1) [AMOK]

Ne 12:20 of Sallu's, Kallai; of A, Eber; H6651

AMON (18) [AMON'S]

1Ki 22:26 send him back to A the ruler of the city H571
2Ki 21:18 And A his son succeeded him as king H571
2Ki 21:19 A was twenty-two years old when he H571
2Ki 21:24 killed all who had plotted against King A, H571
1Ch 3:14 A his son, Josiah his son. H571
2Ch 18:25 send him back to A the ruler of the city H571
2Ch 33:20 And A his son succeeded him as king H571
2Ch 33:21 A was twenty-two years old when he H571
2Ch 33:22 A worshiped and offered sacrifices to all H571
2Ch 33:23 before the LORD; A increased his guilt. H571
2Ch 33:25 killed all who had plotted against King A, H571
Ne 7:59 Pokereth-Hazzebaim and A H571
Jer 1: 2 the reign of Josiah son of A king of Judah, H571
Jer 25: 3 year of Josiah son of A king of Judah until H571
Jer 46:25 to bring punishment on A god of Thebes, H572
Zep 1: 1 the reign of Josiah son of A king of Judah: H571
Mt 1:10 Manasseh the father of A, Amon the father G322
Mt 1:10 the father of Amon, A the father of Josiah, G322

AMON'S (3) [AMON]

2Ki 21:23 A officials conspired against him and H571
2Ki 21:25 As for the other events of A reign, and H571
2Ch 33:24 A officials conspired against him and H2257S

AMONG (836)

Ge 3: 8 from the LORD God a the trees of the H928+9348
Ge 6: 9 blameless a the people of his time H928
Ge 13:12 while Lot lived a the cities of the plain H928
Ge 17:10 Every male a you shall be circumcised. H4200
Ge 17:12 to come every male a you who is eight H4200
Ge 23: 4 "I am a foreigner and stranger a you. Sell H6640
Ge 23: 6 You are a mighty prince a us. Bury H928+9348
Ge 23: 9 the full price as a burial site a you." H928+9348
Ge 23:10 was sitting a his people and he H928+9348
Ge 23:16 to the weight current a the merchants. H4200
Ge 24: 3 the Canaanites, a whom I am living, H928+7931
Ge 25:27 was content *to* **stay at home** *a* the tents. AIT
Ge 27:46 takes a wife **from a** the women of this H4946
Ge 28: 2 **from a** the daughters of Laban H4946
Ge 33: 1 so he divided the children a Leah, Rachel H6584
Ge 34:10 You can settle a us; the land is open to you H907
Ge 34:16 We'll settle a you and become one people H907
Ge 34:23 to their terms, and they will settle a us." H907
Ge 35:11 kings *will be* a your descendants. H3655S
Ge 36:15 These were the **chiefs** *a* Esau's descendants AIT
Ge 41: 2 sleek and fat, and they grazed a the reeds. H928
Ge 41:18 fat and sleek, and they grazed a the reeds. H928
Ge 42: 5 sons were a those who went to H928+9348
Ge 47: 6 And if you know of any a them with special H928
Ge 49:14 donkey lying down a the sheep pens. H1068
Ge 49:26 on the brow of the **prince** *a* his brothers. AIT
Ex 2: 3 child in it and put it a the reeds along the H928
Ex 2: 5 saw the basket a the reeds and sent H928+9348
Ex 3:20 wonders that I will perform a them. H928+7931
Ex 10: 1 perform these signs of mine a them H928+7931
Ex 10: 2 how I performed my signs a them, H928
Ex 11: 7 But a the Israelites not a dog will H4200+3972
Ex 12:48 "A foreigner residing a you who wants to H907
Ex 12:49 and to the foreigner residing a you." H928+9348
Ex 13: 2 of every womb a the Israelites belongs H928
Ex 13: 7 with yeast in it is to be seen a you, H4200
Ex 13:13 Redeem every firstborn a your sons. H928
Ex 15:11 Who a the gods is like you, LORD? Who is H928
Ex 17: 7 saying, "Is the LORD a us or not?" H928+7931
Ex 22:25 to one of my people a you who is needy, H6640
Ex 23:11 Then the **poor** *a* your people may get food AIT
Ex 23:12 the **foreigner living** a you may be H1731
Ex 23:25 I will take away sickness from a you, H7931
Ex 25: 8 me, and I will dwell a them. H928+9348
Ex 27:21 lasting ordinance a the Israelites H4946+907
Ex 28: 1 brought to you from a the Israelites, H9348
Ex 29:45 Then I will dwell a the Israelites and H928+9348
Ex 29:46 Egypt so that I might dwell a them. H928+9348
Ex 34:10 The people you live a will see how H928+7931
Ex 34:12 or they will be a snare a you. H928+7931
Ex 35:10 "All who are skilled a you are to come H928
Ex 36: 8 who were skilled a the workers made the H928
Lev 1: 2 'When anyone a you brings an offering to H4946
Lev 10: 3 " 'A those who approach me I will be H928
Lev 11:10 whether a all the swarming things or H4946
Lev 11:10 swarming things or a all the other living H4946
Lev 15:31 my dwelling place, which is a them. H928+9348
Lev 16:16 which *is* a them in the midst of their H8905+907
Lev 16:29 a foreigner residing a you— H928+9348
Lev 17: 8 residing a them who offers a H928+9348
Lev 17:10 foreigner residing a them who eats H928+9348
Lev 17:12 foreigner residing a you eat blood." H928+9348
Lev 17:13 residing a you who hunts any H928+9348
Lev 18:26 residing a you must not do any H928+9348
Lev 19:16 go about spreading slander a your people. H928
Lev 19:18 bear a grudge against **anyone** *a* your people, AIT
Lev 19:33 a foreigner resides a you in your land, H907
Lev 19:34 foreigner residing a you must be treated H907
Lev 20:14 so that no wickedness will be a you. H928+9348
Lev 20:27 a medium or spiritist a you must be put to H928
Lev 21:10 the one a his brothers who has had the H4946
Lev 21:15 will not defile his offspring a his people. H928
Lev 23:22 the poor and for the **foreigner residing** *a* you. AIT
Lev 23:30 I will destroy from a their people anyone H7931
Lev 24:10 father went out a the Israelites, H928+9348
Lev 25: 6 temporary resident who live a you, H6640
Lev 25:33 are their property a the Israelites. H928+9348
Lev 25:35 are unable to support themselves a you, H6640
Lev 25:35 so they can continue to live a you. H6640
Lev 25:36 so that they may continue to live a you. H6640
Lev 25:40 workers or temporary residents a you; H6640
Lev 25:45 residents living a you and members of H6640
Lev 25:47 foreigner residing a you becomes rich H6640
Lev 26:11 I will put my dwelling place a you H928+9348
Lev 26:12 I will walk a you and be your God H928+9348
Lev 26:25 I will send a plague a you, and you H928+9348
Lev 26:33 I will scatter you a the nations and will draw H928
Lev 26:38 You will perish a the nations; the land of H928
Nu 3:12 taken the Levites from a the Israelites in H9348
Nu 4:18 not destroyed **from a** the Levites. H4946+9348
Nu 5: 3 their camp, where I dwell a them." H928+9348
Nu 5:21 become a curse a your people when H928+9348
Nu 8: 6 "Take the Levites from a all the Israelites H9348
Nu 8:19 From a all the Israelites, I have given the H9348
Nu 9:14 " 'A foreigner residing a you is also to H907
Nu 11: 1 the LORD burned a them and consumed H928
Nu 11: 3 fire from the LORD had burned a them. H928
Nu 11:16 to you as leaders and **officials** *a* the people. AIT
Nu 11:20 the LORD, who is a you, and have H928+7931
Nu 11:21 "Here I am a six hundred thousand H928+7931
Nu 11:26 They were listed a the elders, but did not H928
Nu 12: 6 "**When** there is a prophet *a* you, I, the LORD AIT
Nu 13:32 And they spread a the Israelites a bad H448
Nu 14: 6 who were a those who had explored the H4946
Nu 14:11 the signs I have performed a them? H928+7931
Nu 14:13 brought these people up from a them. H7931
Nu 15:14 anyone else living a you presents a food H907
Nu 15:15 you and for the foreigner residing a you; NDT
Nu 15:16 to you and to the foreigner residing a you. H907
Nu 15:26 foreigners residing a them will be H928+9348
Nu 15:29 a foreigner residing a you. H928+9348
Nu 16:47 plague had already started a the people, H928
Nu 17: 6 and Aaron's staff was a them. H928+9348
Nu 18: 6 fellow Levites from a the Israelites as a H9348
Nu 18:20 will you have any share a them H928+9348
Nu 18:20 and your inheritance a the Israelites. H928+9348
Nu 18:23 no inheritance a the Israelites. H928+9348
Nu 18:24 have no inheritance a the Israelites. H928+9348
Nu 19:10 the foreigners residing a them. H928+9348
Nu 20:13 where he was proved holy a them. H928
Nu 21: 6 the LORD sent venomous snakes a them; H928
Nu 23:21 with them; the shout of the King is a them. H928
Nu 24:20 "Amalek was **first** *a* the nations, but their end AIT
Nu 25:11 my honor a them as I am, H928+9348
Nu 26: 9 Aaron and were a Korah's followers H928
Nu 26:56 be distributed by lot a the larger and H1068
Nu 26:62 they received no inheritance a them. H928+9348
Nu 26:64 Not one of them was a those counted by H4946
Nu 27: 3 He was not a Korah's followers, who H928+9348
Nu 27: 4 Give us property a our father's H928+9348
Nu 27: 7 as an inheritance a their father's H928+9348
Nu 31: 8 A their victims were Evi, Rekem, Zur, Hur H6584
Nu 33: 4 whom the LORD had struck down a them; for H928
Nu 35:15 and for foreigners residing a them, H928+9348
Nu 35:34 the LORD, dwell a the Israelites. H928+9348
Dt 1:16 an Israelite and a **foreigner residing** *a* you. AIT
Dt 2:16 fighting men a the people had H4946+7931
Dt 4: 3 God destroyed from a you everyone who H7931
Dt 4:27 The LORD will scatter you a the peoples, and H928
Dt 4:27 of you will survive a the nations to which H928
Dt 6:15 your God, who is a you, is a jealous H928+7931
Dt 7:20 will send the hornet a them until even the H928
Dt 7:21 your God, who is a you, is a great H928+7931
Dt 10: 9 share or inheritance a their fellow H6640
Dt 10:18 loves the **foreigner residing** *a* you, giving AIT
Dt 12: 5 God will choose **from a** all your tribes to H4946
Dt 13: 1 appears a you and announces to H928+7931
Dt 13: 5 You must purge the evil from a you. H7931
Dt 13:11 and no one a you will do such an H928+7931
Dt 13:13 have arisen a you and have led the H4946+7931
Dt 13:14 thing has been done a you, H928+7931
Dt 15: 2 **anyone** a their own **people**, H8276+2256+278
Dt 15: 4 there need be no poor people a you, for in H928
Dt 15: 7 If anyone is poor a your fellow Israelites in H928
Dt 15: 9 ill will toward the **needy** *a* your fellow AIT
Dt 16:11 and the widows living a you. H928+7931
Dt 17: 2 woman living a you in one of the H928+7931
Dt 17: 7 You must purge the evil from a you. H7931
Dt 17:15 He must be from a your fellow Israelites H7931
Dt 18: 2 have no inheritance a their fellow H928+7931
Dt 18:10 Let no one be found a you who sacrifices H928
Dt 18:15 up for you a prophet like me from a you, H7931
Dt 18:18 prophet like you from a their fellow H7931
Dt 19:19 You must purge the evil from a you. H7931
Dt 19:20 such an evil thing be done a you. H928+7931
Dt 21:11 if you notice a the captives a beautiful H928
Dt 21:21 You must purge the evil from a you. All H7931
Dt 22:21 You must purge the evil from a you. H7931
Dt 22:24 You must purge the evil from a you. H7931
Dt 23:14 that he will not see a you anything H928
Dt 23:16 Let them live a you wherever they H928+7931
Dt 24: 7 You must purge the evil from a you. H7931
Dt 26:11 residing a you shall rejoice H928+7931
Dt 28:37 object of ridicule a all the peoples where H928
Dt 28:43 who reside a you will rise above H928+7931
Dt 28:54 sensitive man a you will have no H928
Dt 28:56 most gentle and sensitive woman a you— H928
Dt 28:64 Then the LORD will scatter you a all nations H928
Dt 28:65 A those nations you will find no repose, no H928
Dt 29:17 You saw a them their detestable images H6640
Dt 29:18 clan or tribe a you today whose heart turns H928
Dt 29:18 sure there is no root a you that produces H928
Dt 30: 1 LORD your God disperses you a the nations, H928
Dt 31: 7 *must* **divide** it *a* them **as their inheritance**. AIT
Dt 32:51 uphold my holiness a the Israelites. H928+9348
Dt 33:16 on the brow of the **prince** *a* his brothers. AIT

Jos 3: 5 LORD will do amazing things **a** you." H928+7931
Jos 3:10 the living God is **a** you and that he H928+7931
Jos 4: 2 "Choose twelve men **from a** the people H4946
Jos 4: 6 to serve as a sign **a** you. In the future, H928+7931
Jos 6:25 she lives **a** the Israelites to this H928+7931
Jos 7:12 destroy whatever **a** you is devoted H4946+7931
Jos 7:13 There are devoted things **a** you H928+7931
Jos 8:33 Both the **foreigners living a** them and the H1731
Jos 8:35 and the foreigners who lived **a** them. H928+7931
Jos 13: 7 it as an inheritance **a** the nine tribes and H4200
Jos 13:13 continue to live **a** the Israelites to H928+7931
Jos 14: 3 the Levites an inheritance **a** the rest, H928+9348
Jos 14:15 who was the greatest man **a** the Anakites.) H928
Jos 16:10 the Canaanites live **a** the people of H928+7931
Jos 17: 4 us an inheritance **a** our relatives." H928+9348
Jos 17: 6 received an inheritance **a** the sons. H928+9348
Jos 17: 9 to Ephraim lying **a** the towns of H928+9348
Jos 18: 7 do not get a portion **a** you, because H928+7931
Jos 19:49 son of Nun an inheritance **a** them, H928+9348
Jos 20: 4 city and provide a place to live **a** them. H6640
Jos 20: 9 foreigner residing **a** them who killed H928+9348
Jos 22:14 of a family division **a** the Israelite clans. H4200
Jos 23: 7 with these nations that remain **a** you; H907
Jos 23:12 nations that remain **a** you and if you H907
Jos 24:17 our entire journey and **a** all the nations H928
Jos 24:23 gods that are **a** you and yield your H928+7931
Jdg 1:16 of Judah to live **a** the inhabitants of the H907
Jdg 1:29 continued to live there **a** them. H928+7931
Jdg 1:30 so these Canaanites lived **a** them H928+7931
Jdg 1:32 The Asherites lived **a** the Canaanite H928+7931
Jdg 1:33 too lived **a** the Canaanite H928+7931
Jdg 3: 5 Israelites lived **a** the Canaanites, H928+7931
Jdg 5: 8 spear was seen **a** forty thousand in Israel H928
Jdg 5: 9 with the willing volunteers **a** the people. H928
Jdg 5:16 Why did you stay **a** the sheep pens to H1068
Jdg 10:16 foreign gods **a** them and served H4946+7931
Jdg 14: 3 an acceptable woman **a** your relatives or H928
Jdg 14: 3 among your relatives or **a** all our people? H928
Jdg 16:25 When they stood him **a** the pillars, H1068
Jdg 18: 1 into an inheritance **a** the tribes of H928+9348
Jdg 20:12 this awful crime that was committed **a** you? H928
Jdg 20:16 **A** all these soldiers there were seven H4946
Jdg 21:12 They found **a** the people living in Jabesh H4946
Ru 2: 7 me glean and gather **a** the sheaves behind H928
Ru 2:15 "Let her gather **a** the sheaves and don't H1068
Ru 4:10 not disappear from **a** his family or from H6640
1Sa 2:24 the report I hear **spreading a** the LORD's H6296
1Sa 10:11 Is Saul also **a** the prophets?" H928
1Sa 10:12 "Is Saul also **a** the prophets?" H928
1Sa 10:22 he has hidden himself **a** the supplies." H448
1Sa 10:23 and as he stood **a** the people he H928+9348
1Sa 10:24 There is no one like him **a** all the people." H928
1Sa 13: 6 caves and thickets, **a** the rocks, and in pits H928
1Sa 14: 3 **a** whom was Ahijah, who was wearing an NDT
1Sa 14:34 he said, "Go out **a** the men and tell them H928
1Sa 15:33 so will your mother be childless **a** women." H4946
1Sa 19:24 people say, "Is Saul also **a** the prophets?" H928
1Sa 23:19 "Is not David hiding **a** us in the H6640
1Sa 23:23 I will track him down **a** all the clans of H928
1Sa 30:22 troublemakers **a** David's followers H4946
1Sa 31: 9 temple of their idols and **a** their people. H907
2Sa 11:13 to sleep on his mat **a** his master's H6640
2Sa 12:19 attendants *were* **whispering a themselves,** H4317
2Sa 15:31 "Ahithophel is **a** the conspirators with H928
2Sa 17: 9 has been a slaughter **a** the troops who H928
2Sa 19: 9 all the people *were* **arguing a themselves,** H1906
2Sa 19:28 your servant a place **a** those who eat at H928
2Sa 22:50 **a** the nations; I will sing the praises H928
2Sa 23:19 even though he was not included **a** them. H6330
2Sa 23:23 he was not included **a** the Three. H448
2Sa 23:24 **A** the Thirty were: Asahel the brother of H928
1Ki 2: 7 let them be **a** those who eat at your H928
1Ki 3: 8 servant is here **a** the people you H928+9348
1Ki 3:13 lifetime you will have no equal **a** kings. H928
1Ki 6:13 And I will live **a** the Israelites and H928+9348
1Ki 8:38 is made by anyone **a** your people Israel— H4200
1Ki 9: 7 an object of ridicule **a** all peoples. H928
1Ki 14: 7 'I raised you up from **a** the people and H9348
1Ki 21: 9 Naboth in a **prominent place** *a* the people. AIT
1Ki 21:12 Naboth in a **prominent place** *a* the people. AIT
2Ki 4:13 "I have a home **a** my own people." H928+9348
2Ki 11: 2 stole him away from **a** the royal princes, H9348
2Ki 17:25 so he sent lions **a** them and they killed H928
2Ki 17:26 He has sent lions **a** them, which are killing H928
2Ki 18: 5 was no one like him **a** all the kings of H928
2Ki 20:13 everything found **a** his treasures. H928
2Ki 20:15 "There is nothing **a** my treasures that I did H928
1Ch 6:60 of towns **distributed a** the Kohathite H928
1Ch 7:15 Makir took a wife **from a** the Huppites H4200
1Ch 10: 9 Philistines to **proclaim the news** *a* their idols AIT
1Ch 11:21 even though he was not included **a** them. H6330
1Ch 11:25 he was not included **a** the Three. H448
1Ch 12: 1 they were **a** the warriors who helped him in H928
1Ch 12: 4 a mighty warrior **a** the Thirty, who was a H928
1Ch 16: 8 make known **a** the nations what he has H928
1Ch 16:24 Declare his glory **a** the nations, his H928
1Ch 16:24 his marvelous deeds **a** all peoples. H928
1Ch 16:31 be glad; let them say **a** the nations, "The H928
1Ch 22: 2 from **a** them he appointed stonecutters NDT
1Ch 24: 4 number of leaders **were found** *a* Eleazar's AIT
1Ch 24: 4 Eleazar's descendants than **a** Ithamar's, NDT
1Ch 24: 5 officials of God **a** the descendants of H4946
1Ch 26:31 capable men **a** the Hebronites were H928
1Ch 27: 6 who was a **mighty warrior** *a* the Thirty and AIT
2Ch 6:29 plea is made by **anyone** *a* your people AIT
2Ch 7:13 the land or send a plague **a** my people, H928
2Ch 7:20 an object of ridicule **a** all peoples. H928
2Ch 11:22 of Maakah as crown prince **a** his brothers, H928
2Ch 13:17 thousand casualties **a** Israel's able men. H4946
2Ch 15: 9 Simeon who had settled **a** them, H6640
2Ch 19: 4 he went out again **a** the people from H928
2Ch 20:25 they found **a** them a great amount of H928
2Ch 22:11 stole him away from **a** the royal princes H9348
2Ch 26: 6 Ashdod and elsewhere **a** the Philistines. H928
2Ch 31:19 to every male **a** them and to all who H928
2Ch 36:23 Any of his people **a** you may go up, and H928
Ezr 1: 3 Any of his people **a** you may go up to H928
Ezr 2:61 And **from a** the priests: The descendants H4946
Ezr 8:15 When I checked **a** the people and the H928
Ezr 10:18 **A** the descendants of the priests, the H4946
Ezr 10:23 **A** the Levites: Jozabad, Shimei, Kelaiah H4946
Ezr 10:25 And **a** the other Israelites: From the H4946
Ne 1: 8 unfaithful, I will scatter you **a** the nations, H928
Ne 4:11 be right there **a** them and will kill H448+9348
Ne 6: 6 "It is reported **a** the nations—and Geshem H928
Ne 7:63 And **from a** the priests: the descendants H4946
Ne 9:17 the miracles you performed **a** them. H6640
Ne 11:17 Bakbukiah, second **a** his associates; and H4946
Ne 12:23 The family heads **a** the descendants of Levi NDT
Ne 13:26 **A** the many nations there was no king like H928
Est 2: 6 **a** those taken captive with Jehoiachin H6640
Est 3: 8 people dispersed **a** the peoples in all the H1068
Est 4: 3 there was great mourning **a** the Jews H4200
Est 8:17 there was joy and gladness **a** the Jews H4200
Est 9:28 of these days die out **a** their descendants. H4946
Est 10: 3 preeminent **a** the Jews, and held H4200
Job 1: 3 was the greatest man **a** all the people of H4946
Job 2: 8 himself with it as he sat **a** the ashes. H928+9348
Job 3: 6 it not be included **a** the days of the year H928
Job 5: 5 taking it even from **a** thorns, and the thirsty H448
Job 8:17 rocks and looks for a *place* **a** the stones. H1075
Job 12:12 Is not wisdom found **a** the aged? Does not H928
Job 15:19 when no foreigners moved **a** them): H928+9348
Job 17:10 I will not find a wise man **a** you. H928
Job 18:19 no offspring or descendants **a** his people, H928
Job 19:11 against me; he counts me **a** his enemies. H3869
Job 24:11 They crush olives **a** the terraces; they H1068
Job 29:25 I dwelt as a king **a** his troops; I was like H928
Job 30: 6 **a** the rocks and in holes in the ground. NDT
Job 30: 7 They brayed **a** the bushes and huddled in H1068
Job 30: 9 in song; I have become a byword **a** them. H4200
Job 34:37 he claps his hands **a** us and multiplies his H1068
Job 36:14 **a** male prostitutes of the shrines. H928
Job 40:19 It ranks **first** *a* the works of God, yet its Maker AIT
Job 40:21 **hidden** *a* the reeds in the marsh. AIT
Job 41: 6 Will they divide it up **a** the merchants? H1068
Ps 6: 5 **A** the dead no one proclaims your name H928
Ps 9:11 proclaim **a** the nations what he has done. H928
Ps 18:49 **a** the nations; I will sing the praises H928
Ps 22:18 divide my clothes **a** them and cast lots H4200
Ps 35:18 assembly; **a** the throngs I will praise you. H928
Ps 41: 2 *they are* **counted a the blessed** in the land H887
Ps 42: 4 shouts of joy and praise **a** the festive throng. NDT
Ps 44:11 sheep and have scattered us **a** the nations. H928
Ps 44:14 You have made us a byword **a** the nations H928
Ps 45: 9 of kings are **a** your honored women; H928
Ps 46:10 I will be exalted **a** the nations, I will be H928
Ps 54: T Saul and said, "Is not David hiding **a** us?" H6640
Ps 55:14 as we walked about **a** the worshipers. H928
Ps 55:15 for evil finds lodging **a** them. H928+7931
Ps 57: 4 I am forced to dwell **a** ravenous beasts NDT
Ps 57: 9 **a** the nations; I will sing of you H928
Ps 57: 9 nations; I will sing of you **a** the peoples. H928
Ps 67: 2 on earth, your salvation **a** all nations. H928
Ps 68:13 Even while you sleep **a** the sheep pens H1068
Ps 68:30 Rebuke the **beast** *a* the reeds, the herd of AIT
Ps 68:30 the herd of bulls **a** the calves of the nations H928
Ps 72: 4 he defend the **afflicted** *a* the people and AIT
Ps 77:14 you display your power **a** the peoples. H928
Ps 78:31 he put to death the sturdiest **a** them H928
Ps 78:60 the tent he had set up **a** humans. H928
Ps 79:10 make known **a** the nations that you avenge H928
Ps 81: 9 You shall have no foreign god **a** you; you H928
Ps 82: 1 he renders judgment **a** the "gods": H928+7931
Ps 86: 8 **A** the gods there is none like you, Lord; no H928
Ps 87: 4 Rahab and Babylon **a** those who H4200
Ps 88: 4 I am counted **a** those who go down to the H6640
Ps 89: 6 Who is like the LORD **a** the heavenly beings? H928
Ps 89:19 up a young man **from a** the people. H4946
Ps 94: 8 you senseless ones **a** the people; you fools H928
Ps 96: 3 Declare his glory **a** the nations, his H928
Ps 96: 3 his marvelous deeds **a** all peoples. H928
Ps 96:10 Say **a** the nations, "The LORD reigns." H928
Ps 99: 6 Moses and Aaron were **a** his priests H928
Ps 99: 6 Samuel was **a** those who called on his H928
Ps 102: 6 I am like a desert owl, like an **owl** *a* the ruins. AIT
Ps 104:12 waters; they sing **a** the branches. H4946+1068
Ps 105: 1 make known **a** the nations what he has H928
Ps 105:27 They performed his signs **a** them, his H928
Ps 105:37 from **a** their tribes no one faltered. H928
Ps 106:15 but sent a wasting disease **a** them. H928
Ps 106:18 Fire blazed **a** their followers; a flame H928
Ps 106:27 their descendants fall **a** the nations and H928
Ps 106:29 and a plague broke out **a** them. H928
Ps 108: 3 **a** the nations; I will sing of you H928
Ps 108: 3 nations; I will sing of you **a** the peoples. H928
Ps 120: 5 in Meshek, that I live **a** the tents of Kedar! H6640
Ps 120: 6 long have I lived **a** those who hate peace. H6640
Ps 126: 2 Then it was said **a** the nations, "The LORD H928
Ps 136:11 Israel out from **a** them His love endures H9348
Pr 7: 7 I saw **a** the simple, I noticed among the H928
Pr 7: 7 the simple, I noticed **a** the young men, a H928
Pr 14: 9 but goodwill is found **a** the upright. H1068
Pr 14:33 discerning and even **a** fools she lets H928+7931
Pr 15:31 will be at home **a** the wise. H928+7931
Pr 19:20 at the end *you will be* **counted a the wise**. H2681
Pr 23:28 wait and multiplies the unfaithful **a** men. H928
Pr 25: 6 do not claim a place **a** his great men; H928
Pr 30:14 the earth and the needy **from a** mankind. H4946
Pr 30:30 mighty **a** beasts, who retreats before H928
Pr 31:23 he takes his seat **a** the elders of the land. H6640
Ecc 7:28 I found one upright man **a** a thousand H4946
Ecc 7:28 not one upright woman **a** them all. H928
Ecc 9: 4 Anyone who *is* **a** the living has hope H2489
SS 1: 9 to a mare **a** Pharaoh's chariot horses. H928
SS 2: 2 Like a lily **a** thorns is my darling among H1068
SS 2: 2 thorns is my darling **a** the young women. H1068
SS 2: 3 Like an apple tree **a** the trees of the forest H928
SS 2: 3 the forest is my beloved **a** the young men. H1068
SS 2:16 mine and I am his; he browses **a** the lilies. H928
SS 4: 5 fawns of a gazelle that browse **a** the lilies. H928
SS 5:10 ruddy, outstanding **a** ten thousand. H4946
SS 6: 3 beloved is mine; he browses **a** the lilies. H928
SS 6:12 my desire **set** me *a* the royal chariots of my AIT
Isa 4: 3 all who are recorded **a** the living in H4200
Isa 5:17 lambs *will* **feed** *a* the ruins of the rich. AIT
Isa 6: 5 and I live **a** a people of unclean lips, H928+9348
Isa 7: 6 let us tear it apart and divide it **a** ourselves H448
Isa 8:16 seal up God's instruction **a** my disciples. H928
Isa 10: 4 remain but to cringe **a** the captives or fall H9393
Isa 10: 4 among the captives or fall **a** the slain. H9393
Isa 12: 4 make known **a** the nations what he has H928
Isa 12: 6 great is the Holy One of Israel **a** you." H928+7931
Isa 13: 4 an **uproar** *a* the kingdoms, like AIT
Isa 24:13 it be on the earth and **a** the nations, H928+9348
Isa 29:23 When they see **a** them their children H928+7931
Isa 30:14 so mercilessly that **a** its pieces not a H928
Isa 39: 2 everything found **a** his treasures. H928
Isa 39: 4 "There is nothing **a** my treasures that I did H928
Isa 41:28 no one **a** the gods to give counsel H4946
Isa 43:12 and not some foreign god **a** you. H928
Isa 44:14 He let it grow **a** the trees of the forest, or H928
Isa 45: 9 potsherds **a** the potsherds on the H907
Isa 50:10 Who **a** you fears the LORD and obeys the H928
Isa 51:18 **A** all the children she bore there was H4946
Isa 51:18 **a** all the children she reared there was H4946
Isa 53:12 I will give him a portion **a** the great, H928
Isa 57: 5 You burn with lust **a** the oaks and under H928
Isa 57: 6 The idols **a** the smooth stones of the H928
Isa 59:10 if it were twilight; **a** the strong, we are like H928
Isa 61: 9 will be known **a** the nations and their H928
Isa 61: 9 and their offspring **a** the peoples. H928+9348
Isa 63:11 is he who set his Holy Spirit **a** them, H928+7931
Isa 65: 4 who sit **a** the graves and spend their nights H928
Isa 66:17 one who is **a** those who eat H928+2021+9348
Isa 66:19 "I will set a sign **a** them, and I will send H928
Isa 66:19 They will proclaim my glory **a** the nations. H928
Jer 4: 3 unplowed ground and do not sow **a** thorns. H448
Jer 4:29 the thickets; some climb up **a** the rocks. H928
Jer 5:26 "**A** my people are the wicked who lie in H928
Jer 6:15 So they will fall **a** the fallen; they will be H928
Jer 8:12 So they will fall **a** the fallen; they will be H928
Jer 8:17 I will send venomous snakes **a** you, vipers H928
Jer 9:16 I will scatter them **a** nations that neither H928
Jer 10: 7 **A** all the wise leaders of the nations and in H928
Jer 11: 9 is a conspiracy **a** the people of Judah H928
Jer 12:14 uproot the people of Judah from **a** them. H9348
Jer 12:16 will be established **a** my people. H928+9348
Jer 14: 9 You are **a** us, LORD, and we bear your H928+7931
Jer 18:13 "Inquire **a** the nations: Who has H928
Jer 23:13 "**A** the prophets of Samaria I saw this H928
Jer 23:14 And **a** the prophets of Jerusalem I have H928
Jer 25:16 because of the sword I will send **a** them." H1068
Jer 25:27 because of the sword I will send **a** you. H1068
Jer 26: 6 this city a curse **a** all the nations of H4200
Jer 29: 1 to the surviving **elders** *a* the exiles and to the AIT
Jer 29: 8 and diviners **a** you deceive you. H928+7931
Jer 29:18 **a** all the nations where I drive them. H928
Jer 29:27 Anathoth, who poses as a prophet **a** you? H4200
Jer 29:32 will have no one left **a** this people, H928+9348
Jer 30:11 all the nations **a which** I scatter you, H9004S
Jer 30:21 their ruler will arise from **a** them. H7931
Jer 31: 8 **A** them will be the blind and the lame H928
Jer 32:20 in Israel and **a** all mankind, and have H928
Jer 37: 4 free to come and go **a** the people, H928+9348
Jer 37:12 of the property **a** the people there. H928+9348
Jer 39:14 So he remained **a** his own people. H928+9348
Jer 40: 1 bound in chains **a** all the captives H928+9348
Jer 40: 5 and live with him **a** the people, or H928+9348
Jer 40: 6 stayed with him **a** the people who H928+9348
Jer 44: 8 an object of reproach **a** all the nations on H928
Jer 46:18 come who is like Tabor **a** the mountains, H928
Jer 46:28 all the nations **a** which I scatter you, H2025
Jer 48:27 Was she caught **a** thieves, that you shake H928
Jer 48:28 Abandon your towns and dwell **a** the rocks H928
Jer 49:15 "Now I will make you small **a** the nations H928

Jer 50: 2 "Announce and proclaim **a** the nations, lift H928
Jer 50:23 How desolate is Babylon **a** the nations! H928
Jer 50:46 tremble; its cry will resound **a** the nations. H928
Jer 51:27 Blow the trumpet **a** the nations! Prepare H928
Jer 51:41 desolate Babylon will be **a** the nations! H928
La 1: 1 who once was great **a** the nations! H928
La 1: 1 She who was queen **a** the provinces has H928
La 1: 2 **A** all her lovers there is no one to comfort H4946
La 1: 3 She dwells **a** the nations; she finds no H928
La 1:17 has become an unclean thing **a** them. H1068
La 2: 9 her princes are exiled **a** the nations, H928
La 3:45 us scum and refuse **a** the nations. H928+7931
La 4:15 wander about, people **a** the nations say H928
La 4:20 his shadow we would live **a** the nations. H928
Eze 1: 1 while I was **a** the exiles by the Kebar H928+9348
Eze 1:13 Fire moved back and forth **a** the creatures H1068
Eze 2: 5 that a prophet has been **a** them. H928+9348
Eze 2: 6 all around you and you live **a** scorpions. H448
Eze 3:15 I sat **a** them for seven days H928+9348
Eze 3:25 that you cannot go out **a** the people. H928+9348
Eze 4:13 will eat defiled food **a** the nations where I H928
Eze 5:14 a ruin and a reproach **a** the nations around H928
Eze 6: 7 Your people will fall slain **a** you, and H928+9348
Eze 6: 8 you are scattered **a** the lands and nations. H928
Eze 6:13 people lie slain **a** their idols around H928+9348
Eze 7: 4 the detestable practices **a** you. H928+9348
Eze 7: 9 the detestable practices **a** you. H928+9348
Eze 8:11 of Shaphan was standing **a** them. H928+9348
Eze 10: 2 "Go in **a** the wheels beneath the H1068
Eze 10: 2 burning coals from **a** the cherubim and H1068
Eze 10: 6 "Take fire from **a** the wheels, from among H1068
Eze 10: 6 the wheels, from **a** the cherubim," the H1068
Eze 10: 7 out his hand to the fire that was **a** them. H1068
Eze 11: 1 and I saw **a** them Jaazaniah son of H928+9348
Eze 11:16 I sent them far away **a** the nations and H928
Eze 11:16 nations and scattered them **a** the countries, H928
Eze 12: 2 you are living **a** a rebellious people. H928+9348
Eze 12:12 "The prince **a** them will put his H928+9348
Eze 12:15 when I disperse them **a** the nations and H928
Eze 12:24 divinations **a** the people of Israel. H928+9348
Eze 13: 4 prophets, Israel, are like jackals **a** ruins. H928
Eze 13:19 have profaned me **a** my people for a few H448
Eze 14: 9 destroy him from **a** my people Israel. H9348
Eze 15: 6 the wood of the vine **a** the trees of the H928
Eze 16:14 And your fame spread **a** the nations on H928
Eze 18:18 did what was wrong **a** his people. H928+9348
Eze 19: 2 a lioness was your mother **a** the lions! H1068
Eze 19: 2 She lay down **a** them and reared her H928+9348
Eze 19: 6 He prowled **a** the lions, for he was H928+9348
Eze 20: 9 of the nations **a** whom they lived H928+9348
Eze 20:23 I would disperse them **a** the nations and H928
Eze 22:15 I will disperse you **a** the nations and scatter H928
Eze 22:26 so that I am profaned **a** them. H928+9348
Eze 22:30 looked for someone **a** them who would H4946
Eze 23:10 She became a byword **a** women, and H4200
Eze 24:23 sins and groan **a yourselves.** H408+448+278
Eze 25: 4 up their camps and pitch their tents **a** you; H928
Eze 25: 7 I will wipe you out **from a** the nations H4946
Eze 25:10 will not be remembered **a** the nations; H928
Eze 27:36 The merchants **a** the nations scoff at you H928
Eze 28:14 you walked **a** the fiery stones. H928+9348
Eze 28:16 guardian cherub, from **a** the fiery stones. H9348
Eze 28:22 and **a** you I will display my glory. H928+9348
Eze 29: 3 great monster lying **a** your streams. H928+9348
Eze 29: 4 I will pull you out from **a** your streams H9348
Eze 29:12 Egypt desolate **a** devastated lands, H928+9348
Eze 29:12 desolate forty years **a** ruined cities. H928+9348
Eze 29:12 disperse the Egyptians **a** the nations and H928
Eze 29:21 and I will open your mouth **a** them. H928+9348
Eze 30: 7 will be desolate **a** desolate lands, H928+9348
Eze 30: 7 their cities will lie **a** ruined cities. H928+9348
Eze 30:23 disperse the Egyptians **a** the nations and H928
Eze 30:26 disperse the Egyptians **a** the nations and H928
Eze 31:13 all the wild animals lived **a** its branches. H448
Eze 31:14 **a** mortals who go down to the realm H928+9348
Eze 31:17 who lived in its shade **a** the nations. H928+9348
Eze 31:18 you will lie **a** the uncircumcised H928+9348
Eze 32: 2 " 'You are like a **lion** *a* the nations; you are AIT
Eze 32: 9 bring about your destruction **a** the nations, H928
Eze 32: 9 the nations, **a** lands you have not known. H6584
Eze 32:19 Go down and be laid **a** the uncircumcised.' H907
Eze 32:20 They will fall **a** those killed by the H928+9348
Eze 32:25 A bed is made for her **a** the slain H928+9348
Eze 32:25 to the pit; they are laid **a** the slain. H928+9348
Eze 32:28 and will lie **a** the uncircumcised, H928+9348
Eze 32:32 will be laid **a** the uncircumcised, H928+9348
Eze 33:33 that a prophet has been **a** them." H928+9348
Eze 34:24 servant David will be prince **a** them. H928+9348
Eze 35:11 make myself known **a** them when I judge H928
Eze 36:19 I dispersed them **a** the nations, and they H928
Eze 36:20 And wherever they went **a** the nations they H448
Eze 36:21 of Israel profaned **a** the nations where they H928
Eze 36:22 you have profaned **a** the nations where you H928
Eze 36:23 which has been profaned **a** the nations H928
Eze 36:23 name you have profaned **a** them. H928+9348
Eze 36:30 suffer disgrace **a** the nations because of H928
Eze 37: 2 He led me back and forth **a** them, and I H6584
Eze 37:26 will put my sanctuary **a** them forever. H928+9348
Eze 37:28 when my sanctuary is **a** them forever. H928+9348
Eze 39: 7 my holy name **a** my people Israel. H928+9348
Eze 39:21 "I will display my glory **a** the nations, and H928
Eze 39:28 though I sent them into exile **a** the nations, H448

Eze 43: 7 is where I will live **a** the Israelites H928+9348
Eze 43: 9 and I will live **a** them forever. H928+9348
Eze 44: 9 foreigners who live **a** the Israelites. H928+9348
Eze 46:10 The prince is to be **a** them, going in H928+9348
Eze 47:13 that you will divide **a** the twelve tribes of H4200
Eze 47:14 divide it **equally a them.** H408+3869+278+2257
Eze 47:21 distribute this land **a** yourselves according H4200
Eze 47:22 residing **a** you and who have H928+9348
Eze 47:22 an inheritance **a** the tribes of Israel. H928+9348
Da 1: 6 **A** those who were chosen were some from H928
Da 2:11 and they do not live **a** humans. A10554
Da 2:25 "I have found a man **a** the exiles from A10427
Da 4:15 live with the animals **a** the plants of the A10089
Da 6: 3 himself **a** the administrators A10542
Da 7: 8 which came up **a** them; and three of A10099
Da 11:14 Those who are **violent** *a* your own people AIT
Da 11:24 plunder, loot and wealth **a** his followers. H4200
Hos 5: 9 **A** the tribes of Israel I proclaim what is H928
Hos 8: 8 now she is **a** the nations like something no H928
Hos 8:10 they have sold themselves **a** the nations, H928
Hos 9:17 they will be wanderers **a** the nations. H928
Hos 11: 9 not a man—the Holy One **a** you. H928+7931
Hos 13:15 even though he thrives **a** his brothers. An H1068
Joel 2:17 an object of scorn, a byword **a** the nations. H928
Joel 2:17 Why should they say **a** the peoples H928
Joel 2:25 swarm—my great army that I sent **a** you. H928
Joel 2:32 even **a** the survivors whom the LORD calls. H928
Joel 3: 2 scattered my people **a** the nations and H928
Joel 3: 9 Proclaim this **a** the nations: Prepare for war! H928
Am 2:11 up prophets **from a** your children and H4946
Am 2:11 children and Nazirites **from a** your youths. H4946
Am 3: 9 and the oppression **a** her people." H7931+928
Am 4:10 "I sent plagues **a** you as I did to Egypt. I H928
Am 6: 7 Therefore you will be **a** the first to go into H928
Am 7: 8 a plumb line **a** my people Israel; H7931+928
Am 9: 9 the people of Israel **a** all the nations as H928
Am 9:10 All the **sinners** *a* my people will die by the AIT
Ob 2 I will make you small **a** the nations; you H928
Ob 4 the eagle and make your nest **a** the stars, H1068
Mic 3:11 and say, "Is not the LORD **a** us? H7931+928
Mic 5: 2 though you are small **a** the clans of Judah H928
Mic 5: 8 The remnant of Jacob will be **a** the nations, H928
Mic 5: 8 like a lion **a** the beasts of the forest H928
Mic 5: 8 like a young lion **a** flocks of sheep, which H928
Mic 5:10 your horses from **a** you and demolish your H7931
Mic 5:13 idols and your sacred stones from **a** you; H7931
Mic 5:14 I will uproot from **a** you your Asherah H7931
Na 1:10 will be entangled **a** thorns and drunk from H6330
Na 3: 9 strength; Put and Libya were **a** her allies. H928
Zep 3:20 you honor and praise **a** all the peoples of H928
Hag 2: 5 And my Spirit remains **a** you. Do not H928+9348
Zec 1: 8 He was standing **a** the myrtle trees in a H1068
Zec 1:10 Then the man standing **a** the myrtle trees H1068
Zec 1:11 LORD who was standing **a** the myrtle trees, H1068
Zec 2:10 and I will live **a** you," declares the H928+9348
Zec 2:11 I will live **a** you and you will know H928+9348
Zec 3: 7 give you a place **a** these standing here. H1068
Zec 7:14 them with a whirlwind **a** all the nations, H6584
Zec 8:13 have been a curse **a** the nations, so I will H928
Zec 10: 9 Though I scatter them **a** the peoples, yet in H928
Zec 12: 6 a woodpile, like a flaming torch **a** sheaves. H928
Zec 12: 8 so that the feeblest **a** them will be like H928
Mal 1:11 My name will be great **a** the nations, from H928
Mal 1:11 my name will be great **a** the nations," H928
Mal 1:14 my name is to be feared **a** the nations. H928
Mal 3: 5 deprive the foreigners **a** you of justice NDT
Mt 2: 6 by no means least **a** the rulers of Judah; *G1877*
Mt 4:23 every disease and sickness **a** the people. *G1877*
Mt 10: 5 "Do not go **a** the Gentiles or enter *G1650+3847*
Mt 10:16 you out like sheep **a** wolves. *G1877+3545*
Mt 11:11 **a** those born of women there has not *G1877*
Mt 13: 7 Other seed fell **a** thorns, which grew up *G2093*
Mt 13:22 The seed falling **a** the thorns refers to *G1650*
Mt 13:25 and sowed weeds **a** the wheat, *G324+3545*
Mt 16: 7 discussed this **a** themselves and said *G1877*
Mt 16: 8 why are you talking **a** yourselves about *G1877*
Mt 18: 2 and placed the child **a** them. *G1877+3545*
Mt 20:26 to become great **a** you must be your *G1877*
Mt 21:25 They discussed it **a** themselves and said *G1877*
Mt 22:25 Now there were seven brothers **a** us. The *G4123*
Mt 23:11 The greatest *a* **you** will be your servant. AIT
Mt 26: 5 "or there may be a riot **a** the people." *G1877*
Mt 27:56 **A** them were Mary Magdalene, Mary the *G1877*
Mt 28:15 widely circulated **a** the Jews to this very *G4123*
Mk 4: 7 Other seed fell **a** thorns, which grew up *G1650*
Mk 4:18 like seed sown **a** thorns, hear the word; *G1650*
Mk 5: 5 Night and day **a** the tombs and in the hills *G1877*
Mk 5:12 "Send us **a** the pigs; allow us to *G1650*
Mk 6: 4 **a** his relatives and in his own home." *G1877*
Mk 6:41 He also divided the two fish *a them* **all**. AIT
Mk 9:36 child whom he placed **a** them. *G1877+3545*
Mk 9:50 Have salt **a** yourselves, and be at peace *G1877*
Mk 10:43 to become great **a** you must be your *G1877*
Mk 11:31 They discussed it **a** themselves and said *G4639*
Mk 15:31 of the law mocked him **a** themselves. *G4639*
Mk 15:40 **A** them were Mary Magdalene, Mary the *G1877*
Lk 1: 1 of the things that have been fulfilled **a** us, *G1877*
Lk 1:25 taken away my disgrace **a** the people." *G1877*
Lk 1:42 "Blessed are you **a** women, and blessed *G1877*
Lk 1:61 "There is no one **a** your relatives who has *G1666*
Lk 2:44 looking for him **a** their relatives and *G1877*
Lk 2:46 courts, sitting **a** the teachers *G1877+3545*

Lk 7:16 "A great prophet has appeared **a** us," *G1877*
Lk 7:28 **a** those born of women there is no one *G1877*
Lk 7:49 other guests began to say **a** themselves, *G1877*
Lk 8: 7 Other seed fell **a** thorns, which grew *G1877+3545*
Lk 8:14 The seed that fell **a** thorns stands for those *G1650*
Lk 9:46 An argument started **a** the disciples as to *G1877*
Lk 9:48 the one who is least **a** you all who is the *G1877*
Lk 10: 3 you out like lambs **a** wolves. *G1877+3545*
Lk 19:47 the leaders *a* the **people** were trying to AIT
Lk 20: 5 They discussed it **a** themselves and said *G4639*
Lk 22:17 said, "Take this and divide it **a** you. *G1650*
Lk 22:23 began to question **a** themselves which of *G4639*
Lk 22:24 dispute also arose **a** them as to which of *G1877*
Lk 22:26 the greatest **a** you should be like the *G1877*
Lk 22:27 But I am **a** you as one who serves. *G1877+3545*
Lk 24: 5 do you look for the living **a** the dead? *G3552*
Lk 24:36 himself stood **a** them and said to *G1877+3545*
Jn 1:14 flesh and made his dwelling **a** us. *G1877*
Jn 1:26 "but **a** you stands one you do not know. *G3545*
Jn 6: 9 but how far will they go **a** so many?" *G1650*
Jn 6:43 "Stop grumbling **a** yourselves," Jesus *G3552*
Jn 6:52 began to argue sharply **a** themselves, *G4639*
Jn 7:12 **A** the crowds there was widespread *G1877*
Jn 7:35 where our people live scattered *a* the **Greeks**, AIT
Jn 11:54 about publicly **a** the people of Judea. *G1877*
Jn 12: 2 while Lazarus was **a** those reclining at the *G1666*
Jn 12: 8 You will always have the poor **a** you, but *G3552*
Jn 12:20 were some Greeks **a** those who went up *G1666*
Jn 12:42 same time many even **a** the leaders *G1666*
Jn 14: 9 after I have been **a** you such a long time? *G3552*
Jn 15:24 If I had not done **a** them the works no one *G1877*
Jn 19:24 divided my clothes *a* **them** and cast lots for AIT
Jn 20:19 and stood **a** them and said, *G1650+3836+3545*
Jn 20:26 and stood **a** them and said, *G1650+3836+3545*
Jn 21:23 the rumor spread **a** the believers that this *G1650*
Ac 1:15 Peter stood up **a** the believers *G1877+3545*
Ac 1:21 whole time the Lord Jesus was living **a** us, *G2093*
Ac 2:22 which God did **a** you through him *G1877+3545*
Ac 3:22 prophet like me **from a** your own people; *G1666*
Ac 4:17 from spreading any further **a** the people, *G1650*
Ac 4:34 that there were no needy persons **a** them *G1877*
Ac 5:12 many signs and wonders **a** the people. *G1877*
Ac 6: 1 the Hellenistic Jews **a** them complained NDT
Ac 6: 3 choose seven men **from a** you who are *G1666*
Ac 6: 8 great wonders and signs **a** the people. *G1877*
Ac 9:21 in Jerusalem *a* those *who* **call on** this name? AIT
Ac 9:23 *there was a* **conspiracy** *a* the Jews to kill him, AIT
Ac 11:19 Antioch, spreading the word only *a* **Jews**. AIT
Ac 12: 3 saw that this met with approval *a* the **Jews**, AIT
Ac 12:18 no small commotion **a** the soldiers as to *G1877*
Ac 14: 5 was a plot afoot *a* both **Gentiles** and Jews, AIT
Ac 15: 7 God made a choice **a** you that the *G1877*
Ac 15:12 God had done **a** the Gentiles through *G1877*
Ac 15:22 men who were leaders **a** the believers. *G1877*
Ac 17:34 **A** them was Dionysius, a member of the *G1877*
Ac 20:25 that none of you **a** whom I have gone *G1877*
Ac 20:29 wolves will come in **a** you and will not *G1650*
Ac 20:32 you an inheritance **a** all those who are *G1877*
Ac 21:19 what God had done **a** the Gentiles *G1877*
Ac 21:21 all the Jews who *live* **a** the Gentiles to *G2848*
Ac 24: 5 stirring up riots *a* the **Jews** all over the world. AIT
Ac 26:18 of sins and a place **a** those who are *G1877*
Ac 28:25 They disagreed **a** themselves and began *G4639*
Ro 1: 6 And you also are **a** those Gentiles who are *G1877*
Ro 1:13 in order that I might have a harvest **a** you *G1877*
Ro 1:13 just as I have had **a** the other Gentiles. *G1877*
Ro 2:24 name is blasphemed **a** the Gentiles *G1877*
Ro 8:29 be the firstborn **a** many brothers and *G1877*
Ro 11: 7 The elect **a** them did, but the others were NDT
Ro 11:17 been grafted in **a** the others and now *G1877*
Ro 15: 9 "Therefore I will praise you **a** the Gentiles; *G1877*
Ro 15:26 the poor *a* **the Lord's people** in Jerusalem AIT
Ro 16: 7 They are outstanding **a** the apostles, and *G1877*
1Co 1: 6 our testimony about Christ **a** you. *G1877*
1Co 1:10 say and that there be no divisions **a** you, *G1877*
1Co 1:11 me that there are quarrels **a** you. *G1877*
1Co 2: 6 speak a message of wisdom **a** the mature, *G1877*
1Co 3: 3 there is jealousy and quarreling **a** you, *G1877*
1Co 5: 1 that there is sexual immorality **a** you, *G1877*
1Co 5:13 "Expel the wicked person **from a** you." *G1666*
1Co 6: 5 that there is nobody **a** you wise enough to *G1877*
1Co 6: 7 you have lawsuits **a** you means you have *G3552*
1Co 9:11 If we have sown spiritual seed *a* **you**, is it too AIT
1Co 11:18 there are divisions **a** you, and to some *G1877*
1Co 11:19 to be differences **a** you to show which of *G1877*
1Co 11:30 That is why many **a** you are weak and sick *G1877*
1Co 14:25 exclaiming, "God is really **a** you! *G1877*
2Co 1:19 who was preached **a** you by us—by me *G1877*
2Co 2:15 aroma of Christ **a** those who are being *G1877*
2Co 6:16 "I will live with them and **walk a** them *G1853*
2Co 8:23 he is my partner and co-worker **a** you; as *G1650*
2Co 10:15 our sphere of activity **a** you will greatly *G1877*
2Co 12:12 in demonstrating **a** you the marks of a *G1877*
2Co 13: 3 in dealing with you, but is powerful **a** you. *G1877*
Gal 1:14 of my own age **a** my people and was *G1877*
Gal 1:16 so that I might preach him **a** the Gentiles, *G1877*
Gal 2: 2 the gospel that I preach **a** the Gentiles. *G1877*
Gal 2:17 we Jews find ourselves also *a* the **sinners** AIT
Gal 3: 5 work miracles **a** you by the works of *G1877*
Eph 2: 3 All of us also lived **a** them at one time *G1877*
Eph 5: 3 But **a** you there must not be even a hint of *G1877*
Php 2:15 Then you will shine **a** them like stars in *G1877*

Col 1: 6 as it has been doing a you since the day G1877
Col 1:18 beginning and the firstborn from a the dead, AIT
Col 1:27 chosen to make known a the Gentiles the G1877
Col 3:16 of Christ dwell a you richly as you teach G1877
Col 4:11 are the only Jews a my co-workers for the NDT
1Th 1: 5 know how we lived a you for your sake. G1877
1Th 2: 7 we were like young children a you. G1877+3545
1Th 2:10 blameless we were a you who believed. AIT
1Th 5:12 acknowledge those who work hard a you, G1877
2Th 1: 4 a God's churches we boast about your G1877
2Th 1:10 to be marveled at a all those who have G1877
2Th 3:11 We hear that some a you are idle and G1877
1Ti 1:20 A them are Hymenaeus and Alexander AIT
1Ti 3:16 was preached a the nations, was G1877
2Ti 2:17 A them are Hymenaeus and Philetus AIT
Heb 5: 1 priest is selected from a the people and is G1666
Jas 1: 1 the twelve tribes scattered a the nations: G1402
Jas 2: 4 not discriminated a yourselves and G1877
Jas 3: 6 a world of evil a the parts of the body. G1877
Jas 3:13 Who is wise and understanding a you G1877
Jas 4: 1 What causes fights and quarrels a you G1877
Jas 5:13 Is anyone a you in trouble? Let them pray G1877
Jas 5:14 Is anyone a you sick? Let them call the G1877
1Pe 2:12 Live such good lives a the pagans that G1877
1Pe 5: 1 To the elders a you, I appeal as a fellow G1877
2Pe 2: 1 were also false prophets a the people, G1877
2Pe 2: 1 just as there will be false teachers a you. G1877
2Pe 2: 8 man, living a them day after day G1594
1Jn 4: 9 This is how God showed his love a us: He G1877
1Jn 4:17 is made complete a us so that we will G3552
Jude 4 long ago have secretly slipped in a you. NDT
Rev 1:13 a the lampstands was G1877+3545
Rev 2: 1 hand and walks a the seven G1877+3545
Rev 2:14 There are some a you who hold to the G1695
Rev 6: 6 like a voice a the four living G1877+3545
Rev 6:15 hid in caves and a the rocks of the G1650
Rev 14: 4 They were purchased from a mankind and G608
Rev 21: 3 God's dwelling place is now a the people, G3552

AMORITE (9) [AMORITES]

Ge 14:13 living near the great trees of Mamre the A, H616
Nu 21:13 in the wilderness extending into A territory. H616
Dt 2:24 I have given into your hand Sihon the A H616
Dt 4:47 Bashan, the two A kings east of the Jordan. H616
Jos 5: 1 Now when all the A kings west of the H616
Jos 10: 6 because all the A kings from the hill H616
Jos 24:12 them out before you—also the two A kings. H616
Eze 16: 3 your father was an A and your mother a H616
Eze 16:45 mother was a Hittite and your father an A. H616

AMORITES (77) [AMORITE]

Ge 10:16 Jebusites, A, Girgashites, H616
Ge 14: 7 as well as the A who were living in H616
Ge 15:16 the sin of the A has not yet reached its H616
Ge 15:21 A, Canaanites, Girgashites and Jebusites." H616
Ge 48:22 I took from the A with my sword and my H616
Ex 3: 8 Canaanites, Hittites, A, Perizzites, Hivites H616
Ex 3:17 Canaanites, Hittites, A, Perizzites, Hivites H616
Ex 13: 5 Canaanites, Hittites, A, Hivites and H616
Ex 23:23 of you and bring you into the land of the A, H616
Ex 33: 2 drive out the Canaanites, A, Hittites, H616
Ex 34:11 I will drive out before you the A H616
Nu 13:29 Jebusites and A live in the hill country H616
Nu 21:13 border of Moab, between Moab and the A. H616
Nu 21:21 messengers to say to Sihon king of the A: H616
Nu 21:25 all the cities of the A and occupied them, H616
Nu 21:26 Heshbon was the city of Sihon king of the A, H616
Nu 21:29 as captives to Sihon king of the A. H616
Nu 21:31 So Israel settled in the land of the A. H616
Nu 21:32 drove out the A who were there. H616
Nu 21:34 to him what you did to Sihon king of the A, H616
Nu 22: 2 saw all that Israel had done to the A, H616
Nu 32:33 of Sihon king of the A and the kingdom of H616
Nu 32:39 it and drove out the A who were there. H616
Dt 1: 4 after he had defeated Sihon king of the A, H616
Dt 1: 7 advance into the hill country of the A; H616
Dt 1:19 hill country of the A through all that vast H616
Dt 1:20 "You have reached the hill country of the A, H616
Dt 1:27 us into the hands of the A to destroy us. H616
Dt 1:44 The A who lived in those hills came out H616
Dt 3: 2 to him what you did to Sihon king of the A, H616
Dt 3: 8 these two kings of the A the territory east of H616
Dt 3: 9 Sirion by the Sidonians; the A call it Senir.) H616
Dt 4:46 in the land of Sihon king of the A, who H616
Dt 7: 1 Girgashites, A, Canaanites H616
Dt 20:17 the Hittites, A, Canaanites H616
Dt 31: 4 the kings of the A, whom he destroyed H616
Jos 2:10 the two kings of the A east of the Jordan H616
Jos 3:10 Perizzites, Girgashites, A and Jebusites. H616
Jos 7: 7 us into the hands of the A to destroy us? H616
Jos 9: 1 kings of the Hittites, A, Canaanites H616
Jos 9:10 the two kings of the A east of the Jordan— H616
Jos 10: 5 Then the five kings of the A—the kings of H616
Jos 10:12 the day the LORD gave the A over to Israel, H616
Jos 11: 3 in the east and west; to the A, Hittites, H616
Jos 12: 2 Sihon king of the A, who reigned in H616
Jos 12: 8 the lands of the Hittites, A, Canaanites, H616
Jos 13: 4 as far as Aphek and the border of the A; H616
Jos 13:10 all the towns of Sihon king of the A H616
Jos 13:21 the entire realm of Sihon king of the A, H616
Jos 24: 8 to the land of the A who lived east of the H616
Jos 24:11 against you, as did also the A, Perizzites, H616
Jos 24:15 the gods of the A, in whose land you are H616
Jos 24:18 including the A, who lived in the land H616
Jdg 1:34 The A confined the Danites to the hill H616
Jdg 1:35 And the A were determined also to hold H616
Jdg 1:36 The boundary of the A was from Scorpion H616
Jdg 3: 5 Canaanites, Hittites, A, Perizzites, Hivites H616
Jdg 6:10 do not worship the gods of the A, in whose H616
Jdg 10: 8 of the Jordan in Gilead, the land of the A. H616
Jdg 10:11 the Egyptians, the A, the Ammonites, H616
Jdg 11:19 sent messengers to Sihon king of the A, H616
Jdg 11:21 over all the land of the A who lived in that H616
Jdg 11:23 has driven the A out before his people H616
1Sa 7:14 there was peace between Israel and the A. H616
2Sa 21: 2 a part of Israel but were survivors of the A; H616
1Ki 4:19 of Sihon king of the A and the country of H616
1Ki 9:20 There were still people left from the A H616
1Ki 21:26 like the A the LORD drove out before Israel.) H616
2Ki 21:11 more evil than the A who preceded him H616
1Ch 1:14 Jebusites, A, Girgashites, H616
2Ch 8: 7 people left from the Hittites, A, Perizzites, H616
Ezr 9: 1 Ammonites, Moabites, Egyptians and A. H616
Ne 9: 8 Canaanites, Hittites, A, Perizzites H616
Ps 135:11 Sihon king of the A, Og king of Bashan H616
Ps 136:19 Sihon king of the A His love endures H616
Am 2: 9 "Yet I destroyed the A before them, though H616
Am 2:10 wilderness to give you the land of the A. H616

AMOS (8)

Am 1: 1 The words of A, one of the shepherds of H6650
Am 7: 8 the LORD asked me, "What do you see, A?" H6650
Am 7:10 "A is raising a conspiracy against you in H6650
Am 7:11 For this is what A is saying: " 'Jeroboam H6650
Am 7:12 Then Amaziah said to A, "Get out, you H6650
Am 7:14 A answered Amaziah, "I was neither a H6650
Am 8: 2 "What do you see, A?" he asked. "A H6650
Lk 3:25 the son of A, the son of Nahum, G322

AMOUNT (22) [AMOUNTED, AMOUNTS]

Ge 43:12 Take double *the a of* silver with you, for you AIT
Ge 43:15 men took the gifts and double *the a of* silver, AIT
Ex 12: 4 *You are to* determine the a *of* lamb needed H4082
Ex 38:24 The total *a of* the gold from the wave offering AIT
Lev 25: 8 seven sabbath years a to a period of H2118
Lev 27: 8 the vow is too poor to pay the specified a, H6886
Lev 27:16 set according to the a *of* seed required H7023
1Sa 30:16 because of the great a of plunder they H1524
2Ki 12:10 that there was a large a *of* money in the H8041
2Ki 12:11 When the a *had* been determined, they H9419
1Ch 22: 3 He provided a large a of iron to H4200+8044
2Ch 14:13 carried off a large a of plunder. H2221+4394
2Ch 20:25 among them a great a of H4200+8044
2Ch 24:11 saw that there was a large a *of* money, H8041
2Ch 24:11 and collected a great a of money. H4200+8044
2Ch 27: 5 brought him the same a also in the H2296[S]
2Ch 31: 5 They brought a great a, a tithe of H4200+8044
2Ch 31:10 his people, and this great a is left over." H2162
Est 4: 7 including the exact a *of* money Haman H7308
Isa 41:29 Their deeds a to nothing; their images are H700
Da 1: 5 them a daily a of food and wine from H1821
Lk 19: 8 of anything, I will pay back four times *the a*." AIT

AMOUNTED (3) [AMOUNT]

Ru 2:17 gathered, and *it* a to about an ephah. H2118
2Ch 4:18 that Solomon made a to so much that the NDT
2Ch 29:33 as sacrifices a to six hundred bulls and NDT

AMOUNTS (5) [AMOUNT]

Ex 30:34 frankincense, all in equal a, H963+928+963
Ex 38:21 These are the a *of* the materials used H7217
Dt 17:17 *He must* not accumulate large a *of* H8049+4394
Mk 12:41 Many rich people threw in large *a*. AIT
2Co 10:10 his speaking a to nothing. G2024

AMOZ (13)

2Ki 19: 2 sackcloth, to the prophet Isaiah son of A. H576
2Ki 19:20 Then Isaiah son of A sent a message to H576
2Ki 20: 1 Isaiah son of A went to him and said, H576
2Ch 26:22 recorded by the prophet Isaiah son of A. H576
2Ch 32:20 prophet Isaiah son of A cried out in prayer H576
2Ch 32:32 prophet Isaiah son of A in the book of the H576
Isa 1: 1 that Isaiah son of A saw during the reigns H576
Isa 2: 1 what Isaiah son of A saw concerning Judah H576
Isa 13: 1 against Babylon that Isaiah son of A saw: H576
Isa 20: 2 the LORD spoke through Isaiah son of A. H576
Isa 37: 2 sackcloth, to the prophet Isaiah son of A. H576
Isa 37:21 Then Isaiah son of A sent a message to H576
Isa 38: 1 Isaiah son of A went to him and said, H576

AMPHIPOLIS (1)

Ac 17: 1 had passed through A and Apollonia, G315

AMPLIATUS (1)

Ro 16: 8 Greet A, my dear friend in the Lord. G309

AMPLY (1)

Php 4:18 *I am* a supplied, now that I have received G4444

AMRAM (13) [AMRAM'S, AMRAMITES]

Ex 6:18 The sons of Kohath were A, Izhar, Hebron H6688
Ex 6:20 A married his father's sister Jochebed H6688
Ex 6:20 him Aaron and Moses. A lived 137 years. H6688
Nu 3:19 The Kohathite clans: A, Izhar, Hebron H6688
Nu 26:58 (Kohath was the forefather of A; H6688
Nu 26:59 To A she bore Aaron, Moses and their H6688
1Ch 6: 2 The sons of Kohath: A, Izhar, Hebron and H6688
1Ch 6: 3 The children of A: Aaron, Moses and H6688
1Ch 6:18 The sons of Kohath: A, Izhar, Hebron and H6688
1Ch 23:12 The sons of Kohath: A, Izhar, Hebron and H6688
1Ch 23:13 The sons of A: Aaron and Moses. Aaron H6688
1Ch 24:20 from the sons of A: Shubael; H6688
Ezr 10:34 the descendants of Bani: Maadai, A, Uel, H6688

AMRAM'S (1) [AMRAM]

Nu 26:59 the name of A wife was Jochebed, a H6688

AMRAMITES (2) [AMRAM]

Nu 3:27 To Kohath belonged the clans of the A H6689
1Ch 26:23 From the A, the Izharites, the Hebronites H6689

AMRAPHEL (2)

Ge 14: 1 At the time when A was king of Shinar H620
Ge 14: 9 A king of Shinar and Arioch king of Ellasar H620

AMZI (2)

1Ch 6:46 the son of A, the son of Bani, the son of H603
Ne 11:12 Pelaliah, the son of A, the son of H603

AN (1100) [A] See Index of Articles Etc.

ANAB (2)

Jos 11:21 Hebron, Debir and A, from all the hill H6693
Jos 15:50 A, Eshtemoh, Anim, H6693

ANAH (12)

Ge 36: 2 daughter of A and granddaughter of H6704
Ge 36:14 daughter of A and granddaughter of H6704
Ge 36:18 Esau's wife Oholibamah daughter of A. H6704
Ge 36:20 in the region: Lotan, Shobal, Zibeon, A, H6704
Ge 36:24 Aiah and A. This is the Anah H6704
Ge 36:24 This is the A who discovered the hot H6704
Ge 36:25 The children of A: Dishon and H6704
Ge 36:25 Dishon and Oholibamah daughter of A. H6704
Ge 36:29 Lotan, Shobal, Zibeon, A, H6704
1Ch 1:38 Shobal, Zibeon, A, Dishon, Ezer and H6704
1Ch 1:40 The sons of Zibeon: Aiah and A. H6704
1Ch 1:41 The son of A: Dishon. The sons of Dishon: H6704

ANAHARATH (1)

Jos 19:19 Hapharaim, Shion, A, H637

ANAIAH (2)

Ne 8: 4 Mattithiah, Shema, A, Uriah, Hilkiah and H6717
Ne 10:22 Pelatiah, Hanan, A, H6717

ANAK (7) [ANAKITES]

Nu 13:22 Talmai, the descendants of A, lived. H6737
Nu 13:28 We even saw descendants of A there. H6737
Nu 13:33 the descendants of A come from the H6737
Jos 15:13 (Arba was the forefather of A.) H6737
Jos 15:14 Ahiman and Talmai, the sons of A. H6737
Jos 21:11 (Arba was the forefather of A.) H6710
Jdg 1:20 who drove from it the three sons of A. H6737

ANAKIMS (KJV) ANAKITE

ANAKITES (11) [ANAK]

Dt 1:28 We even saw the A there.' " H1201+6737
Dt 2:10 numerous, and as tall as the A. H6737
Dt 2:11 Like the A, they too were considered H6737
Dt 2:21 numerous, and as tall as the A. H6737
Dt 9: 2 and tall—A! You know about H1201+6737
Dt 9: 2 "Who can stand up against the A?" H1201+6737
Jos 11:21 destroyed the A from the hill country: H6737
Jos 11:22 No A were left in Israelite territory; only in H6737
Jos 14:12 heard then that the A were there and H6737
Jos 14:15 who was the greatest man among the A.) H6737
Jos 15:14 Caleb drove out the three A— H1201+6737

ANAMIM (KJV) ANAMITES

ANAMITES (2)

Ge 10:13 the father of the Ludites, A, Lehabites, H6723
1Ch 1:11 the father of the Ludites, A, Lehabites, H6723

ANAMMELECH (NIV84) ANAMMELEK

ANAMMELEK (1)

2Ki 17:31 fire as sacrifices to Adrammelek and A, H6724

ANAN (1)

Ne 10:26 Hanan, A, H6728

ANANI (1)

1Ch 3:24 Johanan, Delaiah and A—seven in all. H6730

ANANIAH (2)

Ne 3:23 the son of A, made repairs beside H6731
Ne 11:32 in Anathoth, Nob and A, H6732

ANANIAS (13)

Ac 5: 1 Now a man named A, together with his G393
Ac 5: 3 Then Peter said, "A, how is it that Satan G393
Ac 5: 5 When A heard this, he fell down and died G393
Ac 5: 8 is this the price you and A got for the land?" NDT
Ac 9:10 Damascus there was a disciple named A. G393
Ac 9:10 Lord called to him in a vision, "A!" "Yes, G393
Ac 9:12 seen a man named A come and place his G393
Ac 9:13 A answered, "I have heard many reports G393

A

Ac 9:15 But the Lord said to **A**, "Go! This man is G899S
Ac 9:17 Then **A** went to the house and entered it G393
Ac 22:12 "A man named **A** came to see me. He was G393
Ac 23: 2 this the high priest **A** ordered those G393
Ac 24: 1 the high priest **A** went down to Caesarea G393

ANATH (2)

Jdg 3:31 After Ehud came Shamgar son of **A**, who H6742
Jdg 5: 6 "In the days of Shamgar son of **A**, in the H6742

ANATHEMA (KJV) CURSED

ANATHOTH (18) [ANATHOTHITE]

Jos 21:18 **A** and Almon, together with their H6743
2Sa 23:27 Abiezer **from A**, Sibbekai the Hushathite, H6745
1Ki 2:26 the king said, "Go back to your fields in **A**. H6743
1Ch 6:60 Alemeth and **A**, together with their H6743
1Ch 7: 8 Jeremoth, Abijah, **A** and Alemeth. H6744
1Ch 11:28 son of Ikkesh from Tekoa, Abiezer **from A**, H6745
Ezr 2:23 of **A** 128 H6743
Ne 7:27 of **A** 128 H6743
Ne 10:19 **A**, Nebai, H6744
Ne 11:32 in **A**, Nob and Ananiah, H6743
Isa 10:30 Daughter Gallim! Listen, Laishah! Poor **A**! H6743
Jer 1: 1 one of the priests at **A** in the territory of H6743
Jer 11:21 the people of **A** who are threatening H6743
Jer 11:23 on the people of **A** in the year of their H6743
Jer 29:27 you not reprimanded Jeremiah **from A**, H6745
Jer 32: 7 'Buy my field at **A**, because as nearest H6743
Jer 32: 8 'Buy my field at **A** in the territory of H6743
Jer 32: 9 I bought the field at **A** from my cousin H6743

ANATHOTHITE (2) [ANATHOTH]

1Ch 12: 3 sons of Azmaveth; Berakah, Jehu the **A**, H6745
1Ch 27:12 was Abiezer the **A**, a Benjamite. H6745

ANCESTOR (7) [ANCESTOR'S, ANCESTORS, ANCESTORS', ANCESTRAL, ANCESTRY]

Ge 10:21 Shem was the **a** *of* all the sons of Eber. H3
Jos 17: 1 Makir was the **a** *of* the Gileadites, who had H3
Jos 19:47 in Leshem and named it Dan after their **a**.) H3
Jdg 18:29 They named it Dan after their **a** Dan, who was H3
1Sa 2:28 I chose **your a** out of all the tribes of H2257S
1Ch 24:19 prescribed for them by their **a** Aaron, H3
Heb 7:10 Levi was still in the body *of* his **a**. G4252

ANCESTOR'S (2) [ANCESTOR]

1Sa 2:27 reveal myself to your **a** family when they were H3
1Sa 2:28 I also gave your **a** family all the food offerings H3

ANCESTORS (314) [ANCESTOR]

Ge 15:15 will go to your **a** in peace and be buried at a H3
Ex 10: 6 parents nor your **a** have ever seen from H3+3
Ex 13: 5 the land he swore to your **a** to give you, a land H3
Ex 13:11 as he promised on oath to you and your **a**, H3
Lev 25:41 their own clans and to the property of their **a**. H3
Lev 26:40 will confess their sins and the sins of their **a**— H3
Lev 26:45 covenant with their **a** whom I brought out H8037
Nu 11:12 to the land you promised on oath to their **a**? H3
Nu 14:23 see the land I promised on oath to their **a**. H3
Nu 20:15 Our **a** went down into Egypt, and we lived H3
Nu 20:15 The Egyptians mistreated us and our **a**, H3
Nu 36: 4 be taken from the tribal inheritance of our **a**." H3
Nu 36: 7 shall keep the tribal inheritance of their **a**. H3
Nu 36: 8 will possess the inheritance of their **a**. H3
Dt 1:11 the God of your **a**, increase you a H3
Dt 1:21 of it as the LORD, the God of your **a**, told you. H3
Dt 1:35 see the good land I swore to give your **a**, H3
Dt 4: 1 the LORD, the God of your **a**, is giving you. H3
Dt 4:31 destroy you or forget the covenant with your **a**, H3
Dt 4:37 Because he loved your **a** and chose their H3
Dt 5: 3 It was not with our **a** that the LORD made this H3
Dt 6: 3 as the LORD, the God of your **a**, promised you. H3
Dt 6:18 land the LORD promised on oath to your **a**, H3
Dt 6:23 us the land he promised on oath to our **a**. H3
Dt 7: 8 oath he swore to your **a** that he brought you H3
Dt 7:12 of love with you, as he swore to your **a**. H3
Dt 7:13 in the land he swore to your **a** to give you. H3
Dt 8: 1 the land the LORD promised on oath to your **a**. H3
Dt 8: 3 which neither you nor your **a** had known, to H3
Dt 8:16 something your **a** had never known, to H3
Dt 8:18 which he swore to your **a**, as it is today. H3
Dt 10:11 the land I swore to their **a** to give them." H3
Dt 10:15 set his affection on your **a** and loved them, H3
Dt 10:22 Your **a** who went down into Egypt were H3
Dt 11: 9 the LORD swore to your **a** to give to them and H3
Dt 11:21 in the land the LORD swore to give your **a**, H3
Dt 12: 1 the God of your **a**, has given you to H3
Dt 13: 6 gods that neither you nor your **a** have known, H3
Dt 13:17 numbers, as he promised on oath to your **a**— H3
Dt 19: 8 as he promised on oath to your **a**, and gives H3
Dt 26: 3 to the land the LORD swore to our **a** to give us." H3
Dt 26: 7 the God of our **a**, and the LORD heard our H3
Dt 26:15 given us as you promised on oath to our **a**, H3
Dt 27: 3 as the LORD, the God of your **a**, promised you. H3
Dt 28:11 in the land he swore to your **a** to give you. H3
Dt 28:36 you to a nation unknown to you or your **a**. H3
Dt 28:64 which neither you nor your **a** have known. H3
Dt 29:25 the God of their **a**, the covenant he made H3
Dt 30: 5 bring you to the land that belonged to your **a**, H3
Dt 30: 5 more prosperous and numerous than your **a**. H3
Dt 30: 9 prosperous, just as he delighted in your **a**, H3
Dt 31: 7 that the LORD swore to their **a** to give them, H3
Dt 31:16 "You are going to rest with your **a**, and these H3
Dt 31:20 the land I promised on oath to their **a**, and H3
Dt 32:17 recently appeared, gods your **a** did not fear. H3
Jos 1: 6 the land I swore to their **a** to give them. H3
Jos 5: 6 he had solemnly promised their **a** to give us, H3
Jos 18: 3 the LORD, the God of your **a**, has given you? H3
Jos 21:43 all the land he had sworn to give their **a**, H3
Jos 21:44 on every side, just as he had sworn to their **a**. H3
Jos 22:28 LORD's altar, which our **a** built, not for burnt H3
Jos 24: 2 'Long ago your **a**, including Terah the father H3
Jos 24:14 away the gods your **a** worshiped beyond the H3
Jos 24:15 whether the gods your **a** served beyond the H3
Jdg 2: 1 led you into the land I swore to give to your **a**. H3
Jdg 2:10 generation had been gathered to their **a**, H3
Jdg 2:12 the God of their **a**, who had brought them H3
Jdg 2:17 They quickly turned from the ways of their **a** H3
Jdg 2:19 ways even more corrupt than those of their **a**, H3
Jdg 2:20 I ordained for their **a** and has not listened to H3
Jdg 2:22 way of the LORD and walk in it as their **a** did." H3
Jdg 3: 4 which he had given their **a** through Moses. H3
Jdg 6:13 his wonders that our **a** told us about when H3
1Sa 12: 6 Aaron and brought your **a** up out of Egypt. H3
1Sa 12: 7 acts performed by the LORD for you and your **a**. H3
1Sa 12: 8 who brought your **a** out of Egypt and settled H3
1Sa 12:15 will be against you, as it was against your **a**. H3
2Sa 7:12 your days are over and you rest with your **a**, H3
1Ki 1:21 as my lord the king is laid to rest with his **a**, H3
1Ki 2:10 David rested with his **a** and was buried in the H3
1Ki 8:21 he made with our **a** when he brought them H3
1Ki 8:34 them back to the land you gave to their **a**. H3
1Ki 8:40 the time they live in the land you gave our **a**. H3
1Ki 8:48 pray to you toward the land you gave their **a**, H3
1Ki 8:53 Sovereign LORD, brought our **a** out of Egypt." H3
1Ki 8:57 LORD our God be with us as he was with our **a**; H3
1Ki 8:58 commands, decrees and laws he gave our **a**. H3
1Ki 9: 9 who brought their **a** out of Egypt, and have H3
1Ki 11:21 that David rested with his **a** and that Joab the H3
1Ki 11:43 he rested with his **a** and was buried in the H3
1Ki 13:22 body will not be buried in the tomb of your **a**. H3
1Ki 14:15 that he gave to their **a** and scatter them H3
1Ki 14:20 twenty-two years and then rested with his **a**. H3
1Ki 14:31 rested with his **a** and was buried with them H3
1Ki 15: 8 rested with his **a** and was buried in the H3
1Ki 15:12 got rid of all the idols his **a** had made. H3
1Ki 15:24 Asa rested with his **a** and was buried with H3
1Ki 16: 6 Baasha rested with his **a** and was buried in H3
1Ki 16:28 Omri rested with his **a** and was buried in H3
1Ki 19: 4 "Take my life; I am no better than my **a**." H3
1Ki 21: 3 that I should give you the inheritance of my **a**." H3
1Ki 21: 4 "I will not give you the inheritance of my **a**." H3
1Ki 22:40 Ahab rested with his **a**. And Ahaziah his son H3
1Ki 22:50 rested with his **a** and was buried with them in H3
2Ki 8:24 Jehoram rested with his **a** and was buried with H3
2Ki 9:28 buried him with his **a** in his tomb in the City H3
2Ki 10:35 Jehu rested with his **a** and was buried in H3
2Ki 12:21 was buried with his **a** in the City of David. H3
2Ki 13: 9 Jehoahaz rested with his **a** and was buried in H3
2Ki 13:13 Jehoash rested with his **a**, and Jeroboam H3
2Ki 14:16 Jehoash rested with his **a** and was buried in H3
2Ki 14:20 horse and was buried in Jerusalem with his **a**, H3
2Ki 14:22 it to Judah after Amaziah rested with his **a**. H3
2Ki 14:29 Jeroboam rested with his **a**, the kings of Israel H3
2Ki 15: 7 Azariah rested with his **a** and was buried near H3
2Ki 15:22 Menahem rested with his **a**. And Pekahiah his H3
2Ki 15:38 Jotham rested with his **a** and was buried with H3
2Ki 16:20 Ahaz rested with his **a** and was buried with H3
2Ki 17:13 that I commanded your **a** to obey and that I H3
2Ki 17:14 not listen and were as stiff-necked as their **a**, H3
2Ki 17:15 he had made with their **a** and the statutes he H3
2Ki 17:41 grandchildren continue to do as their **a** did. H3
2Ki 20:21 Hezekiah rested with his **a**. And Manasseh his H3
2Ki 21: 8 Israelites wander from the land I gave their **a**, H3
2Ki 21:15 from the day their **a** came out of Egypt until H3
2Ki 21:18 rested with his **a** and was buried in his H3
2Ki 21:22 the LORD, the God of his **a**, and did not walk in H3
2Ki 22:20 Therefore I will gather you to your **a**, and you H3
2Ki 24: 6 Jehoiakim rested with his **a**. And Jehoiachin H3
1Ch 5:25 to the God of their **a** and prostituted H3
1Ch 9:19 the tent just as their **a** had been responsible H3
1Ch 12:17 may the God of our **a** see it and judge you." H3
1Ch 17:11 days are over and you go to be with your **a**, H3
1Ch 29:15 strangers in your sight, as were all our **a**. H3
2Ch 6:25 to the land you gave to them and their **a**. H3
2Ch 6:31 the time they live in the land you gave our **a**. H3
2Ch 6:38 pray toward the land you gave their **a** H3
2Ch 7:22 the God of their **a**, who brought them out H3
2Ch 9:31 he rested with his **a** and was buried in the H3
2Ch 11:16 offer sacrifices to the LORD, the God of their **a**. H3
2Ch 12:16 rested with his **a** and was buried in the H3
2Ch 13:12 the God of your **a**, for you will not H3
2Ch 13:18 they relied on the LORD, the God of their **a**. H3
2Ch 14: 1 rested with his **a** and was buried in the H3
2Ch 14: 4 the God of their **a**, and to obey his laws H3
2Ch 15:12 the God of their **a**, with all their heart H3
2Ch 16:13 of his reign Asa died and rested with his **a**. H3
2Ch 19: 4 them back to the LORD, the God of their **a**. H3
2Ch 20: 6 the God of our **a**, are you not the God H3
2Ch 20:33 had not set their hearts on the God of their **a**. H3
2Ch 21: 1 rested with his **a** and was buried with them in H3
2Ch 21:10 had forsaken the LORD, the God of his **a**. H3
2Ch 24:18 the God of their **a**, and worshiped Asherah H3
2Ch 24:24 the God of their **a**, judgment was executed H3
2Ch 25:28 was buried with his **a** in the City of Judah. H3
2Ch 26: 2 it to Judah after Amaziah rested with his **a**. H3
2Ch 26:23 Uzziah rested with his **a** and was buried near H3
2Ch 27: 9 rested with his **a** and was buried in the H3
2Ch 28: 6 had forsaken the LORD, the God of their **a**. H3
2Ch 28: 9 the God of your **a**, was angry with Judah H3
2Ch 28:25 the anger of the LORD, the God of his **a**. H3
2Ch 28:27 Ahaz rested with his **a** and was buried in the H3
2Ch 29: 5 the temple of the LORD, the God of your **a**. H3
2Ch 30: 7 the God of their **a**, so that he made them H3
2Ch 30: 8 stiff-necked, as your **a** were; submit to the H3
2Ch 30:19 the God of their **a**—even if they are not H3
2Ch 30:22 praised the LORD, the God of their **a**. H3
2Ch 32:33 rested with his **a** and was buried on the H3
2Ch 33: 8 Israelites leave the land I assigned to your **a**, H3
2Ch 33:12 himself greatly before the God of his **a**. H3
2Ch 33:20 rested with his **a** and was buried in his H3
2Ch 34:28 Now I will gather you to your **a**, and you will H3
2Ch 34:32 with the covenant of God, the God of their **a**. H3
2Ch 34:33 not fail to follow the LORD, the God of their **a**. H3
2Ch 35:24 He was buried in the tombs of his **a**, and all H3
2Ch 36:15 the God of their **a**, sent word to them H3
Ezr 5:12 But because our **a** angered the God of A10003
Ezr 7:27 the God of our **a**, who has put it into the H3
Ezr 8:28 offering to the LORD, the God of your **a**. H3
Ezr 9: 7 From the days of our **a** until now, our guilt has H3
Ezr 10:11 the LORD, the God of your **a**, and do his will. H3
Ne 2: 3 when the city where my **a** are buried lies in H3
Ne 2: 5 city in Judah where my **a** are buried so that I H3
Ne 9: 2 confessed their sins and the sins of their **a**. H3
Ne 9: 9 "You saw the suffering of our **a** in Egypt; you H3
Ne 9:16 "But they, our **a**, became arrogant and H3
Ne 9:32 prophets, on our **a** and all your people H3
Ne 9:34 our priests and our **a** did not follow your law H3
Ne 9:36 the land you gave our **a** so they could eat its H3
Ne 13:18 Didn't your **a** do the same things, so that our H3
Job 8: 8 generation and find out what their **a** learned, H3
Job 15:18 declared, hiding nothing received from their **a** H3
Ps 22: 4 In you our **a** put their trust; they trusted and H3
Ps 39:12 as a foreigner, a stranger, as all my **a** were. H3
Ps 44: 1 our **a** have told us what you did in their days H3
Ps 44: 2 drove out the nations and planted **our a**; H4392S
Ps 44: 2 the peoples and made **our a** flourish. H4392S
Ps 78: 3 heard and known, things our **a** have told us. H3
Ps 78: 5 which he commanded our **a** to teach their H3
Ps 78: 8 They would not be like their **a**—a stubborn H3
Ps 78:12 in the sight of their **a** in the land of Egypt, H3
Ps 78:57 Like their **a** they were disloyal and faithless H3
Ps 95: 9 where your **a** tested me; they tried me H3
Ps 106: 6 even as our **a** did; we have done H3
Ps 106: 7 When our **a** were in Egypt, they gave no H3
Pr 22:28 an ancient boundary stone set up by your **a**. H3
Isa 14:21 to slaughter his children for the sins of their **a**; H3
Isa 64:11 where our **a** praised you, has been H3
Isa 65: 7 both your sins and the sins of your **a**," says H3
Jer 2: 5 "What fault did your **a** find in me, that they H3
Jer 3:18 to the land I gave your **a** as an inheritance. H3
Jer 3:25 both we and our **a**; from our youth till H3
Jer 7: 7 in the land I gave your **a** for ever and ever. H3
Jer 7:14 the place I gave to you and your **a**. H3
Jer 7:22 when I brought your **a** out of Egypt and spoke H3
Jer 7:25 From the time your **a** left Egypt until now, day H3
Jer 7:26 stiff-necked and did more evil than their **a**. H3
Jer 9:14 followed the Baals, as their **a** taught them." H3
Jer 9:16 that neither they nor their **a** have known, H3
Jer 11: 4 I commanded your **a** when I brought them H3
Jer 11: 5 Then I will fulfill the oath I swore to your **a**, to H3
Jer 11: 7 the time I brought your **a** up from Egypt until H3
Jer 11:10 have returned to the sins of their **a**, H3+8037
Jer 11:10 have broken the covenant I made with their **a**. H3
Jer 14:20 the guilt of our **a**; we have indeed sinned H3
Jer 16:11 'It is because your **a** forsook me,' declares the H3
Jer 16:12 you have behaved more wickedly than your **a**. H3
Jer 16:13 a land neither you nor your **a** have known, H3
Jer 16:15 I will restore them to the land I gave their **a**. H3
Jer 16:19 "Our **a** possessed nothing but false gods H3
Jer 17:22 Sabbath day holy, as I commanded your **a**. H3
Jer 19: 4 neither they nor their **a** nor the kings of Judah H3
Jer 23:27 just as their **a** forgot my name through Baal H3
Jer 23:39 along with the city I gave to you and your **a**. H3
Jer 24:10 from the land I gave to them and their **a**. H3
Jer 25: 5 LORD gave to you and your **a** for ever and ever. H3
Jer 30: 3 them to the land I gave their **a** to possess, H3
Jer 31:32 I made with their **a** when I took them by the H3
Jer 32:22 them this land you had sworn to give their **a**, H3
Jer 34:13 a covenant with your **a** when I brought them H3
Jer 34:14 'Your **a**, however, did not listen to me or pay H3
Jer 35:15 in the land I have given to you and your **a**." H3
Jer 44: 3 neither they nor you nor your **a** ever knew. H3
Jer 44: 9 committed by your **a** and by the kings and H3
Jer 44:10 the decrees I set before you and your **a**. H3
Jer 44:17 out drink offerings to her just as we and our **a**, H3
Jer 44:21 the streets of Jerusalem by you and your **a**, H3
Jer 50: 7 verdant pasture, the LORD, the hope of their **a**. H3
La 5: 7 Our **a** sinned and are no more, and we bear H3
Eze 2: 3 they and their **a** have been in revolt against H3
Eze 20: 4 them with the detestable practices of their **a** H3
Eze 20:27 In this also your **a** blasphemed me by being H3
Eze 20:30 yourselves the way your **a** did and lust after H3
Eze 20:36 As I judged your **a** in the wilderness of the H3
Eze 20:42 sworn with uplifted hand to give to your **a**. H3
Eze 36:28 Then you will live in the land I gave your **a** H3

Eze 37:25 servant Jacob, the land where your **a** lived. H3
Eze 47:14 I swore with uplifted hand to give it to your **a**, H3
Da 2:23 God of my **a**: You have given me A10003
Da 9: 6 our princes and our **a**, and to all the people H3
Da 9: 8 our princes and our **a** are covered with shame, H3
Da 9:16 the iniquities of our **a** have made Jerusalem H3
Da 11:37 the gods of his **a** or for the one desired by H3
Da 11:38 a god unknown to his **a** he will honor with H3
Hos 9:10 when I saw your **a**, it was like seeing the H3
Joel 1: 2 in your days or in the days of your **a**? H3
Am 2: 4 by false gods, the gods their **a** followed, H3
Mic 7:20 pledged on oath to our **a** in days long ago. H3
Zec 1: 2 "The LORD was very angry with your **a**. H3
Zec 1: 4 Do not be like your **a**, to whom the earlier H3
Zec 1: 5 Where are your **a** now? And the prophets, do H3
Zec 1: 6 my servants the prophets, overtake your **a**? H3
Zec 8:14 showed no pity when your **a** angered me," H3
Mal 2:10 the covenant of our **a** by being unfaithful to H3
Mal 3: 7 since the time of your **a** you have turned away H3
Mt 23:30 'If we had lived in the days *of* our **a**, we G4252
Mt 23:32 and complete what your **a** started! G4252
Lk 1:55 just as he promised our **a**. G4252
Lk 1:72 show mercy to our **a** and to remember his G4252
Lk 6:23 that is how their **a** treated the prophets. G4252
Lk 6:26 that is how their **a** treated the false G4252
Lk 11:47 it was your **a** who killed them. G4252
Lk 11:48 that you approve of what your **a** did; G4252
Jn 4:20 Our **a** worshiped on this mountain, but you G4252
Jn 6:31 Our **a** ate the manna in the wilderness; as G4252
Jn 6:49 Your **a** ate the manna in the wilderness G4252
Jn 6:58 Your **a** ate manna and died, but whoever G4252
Ac 5:30 The God *of* our **a** raised Jesus from the G4252
Ac 7:11 suffering, and our **a** could not find food. G4252
Ac 7:15 down to Egypt, where he and our **a** died. G4252
Ac 7:19 oppressed our **a** by forcing them to G4252
Ac 7:38 and *with* our **a**; and he received G4252
Ac 7:39 "But our **a** refused to obey him. Instead G4252
Ac 7:44 **a** had the tabernacle of the covenant law *with* G4252
Ac 7:45 our **a** under Joshua brought it with them G4252
Ac 7:51 You are just like your **a**: You always resist G4252
Ac 7:52 ever a prophet your **a** did not persecute? G4252
Ac 13:17 God of the people of Israel chose our **a**; G4252
Ac 13:32 the good news: What God promised our **a** G4252
Ac 13:36 was buried with his **a** and his body G4252
Ac 15:10 neither we nor our **a** have been able to G4252
Ac 22: 3 thoroughly trained in the law *of* our **a**. G4262
Ac 22:14 'The God *of* our **a** has chosen you to know G4252
Ac 24:14 I worship the God **of** *our* **a** as a follower of G4262
Ac 26: 6 God has promised our **a** that I am on trial G4252
Ac 28:17 people or against the customs *of* our **a**, G4262
Ac 28:25 the truth to your **a** when he said through G4252
1Co 10: 1 that our **a** were all under the cloud and G4252
2Ti 1: 3 whom I serve, as my **a** did, with a clear G4591
Heb 1: 1 the past God spoke *to* our **a** through the G4252
Heb 3: 9 where your **a** tested and tried me, though G4252
Heb 8: 9 covenant I made *with* their **a** when I took G4252
1Pe 1:18 of life **handed down** to you **from** your **a**, G4261
2Pe 3: 4 Ever since our **a** died, everything goes on G4252

ANCESTORS' (2) [ANCESTOR]
Lev 26:39 also because of their **a** sins they will waste H3
Jer 3:24 have consumed the fruits of our **a** labor— H3

ANCESTRAL (11) [ANCESTOR]
Nu 1:16 the community, the leaders of their **a** tribes. H3
Nu 1:47 The **a** tribe of the Levites, however, was not H3
Nu 13: 2 From each **a** tribe send one of its leaders." H3
Nu 17: 2 one from the leader of each of their **a** tribes. H3
Nu 17: 3 must be one staff for the head of each **a** tribe. H3
Nu 17: 6 one for the leader of each of their **a** tribes H3
Nu 18: 2 Levites from your **a** tribe to join you and H3
Nu 26:55 will be according to the names for its **a** tribe. H3
Nu 33:54 Distribute it according to your **a** tribes. H3
Nu 36: 3 be taken from our **a** inheritance and added H3
Ne 11:20 towns of Judah, each on their **a property**. H5709

ANCESTRY (6) [ANCESTOR]
Nu 1:18 The people **registered** *their* **a** by their H3528
Eze 16: 3 Your **a** and birth were in the land of the H4808
Eze 21:30 in the land of your **a**, I will judge you. H4808
Eze 29:14 them to Upper Egypt, the land of their **a**. H4808
Ro 9: 5 is traced the **human a** of the G2848+4922
Heb 7:16 of a regulation **as to** his **a** but on the G4921

ANCHOR (3) [ANCHORED, ANCHORS]
Ac 27:13 so *they* **weighed a** and sailed along the G149
Ac 27:17 they lowered the **sea a** and let the ship G5007
Heb 6:19 We have this hope as an **a** for the soul, firm G46

ANCHORED (1) [ANCHOR]
Mk 6:53 they landed at Gennesaret and **a** there. G4694

ANCHORS (3) [ANCHOR]
Ac 27:29 they dropped four **a** from the stern and G46
Ac 27:30 were going to lower some **a** from the bow. G46
Ac 27:40 Cutting loose the **a**, they left them in the sea G46

ANCIENT (33) [ANCIENTS]
Ge 49:26 than the blessings of the **a** mountains, H6329
Dt 33:15 choicest gifts of the **a** mountains and the H7710
1Sa 27: 8 From **a times** these peoples had lived in H6409
1Ch 4:22 (These records are **from a times**.) H6972
Ps 24: 7 be lifted up, you **a** doors, that the King of H6409
Ps 24: 9 lift them up, you **a** doors, that the King of H6409
Ps 68:33 highest heavens, the **a** heavens, who H7710
Ps 119:52 your **a** laws, and I find H4946+6409
Pr 22:28 Do not move an **a** boundary stone set up H6409
Pr 23:10 Do not move an **a** boundary stone or H6409
Isa 19:11 the wise men, a disciple of the **a** kings"? H7710
Isa 43:13 and from **a** days I am he. No one can NDT
Isa 44: 7 since I established my **a** people, H6409
Isa 46:10 beginning, from **a times**, what is still to H7710
Isa 58:12 will rebuild the **a** ruins and will raise up H6409
Isa 61: 4 will rebuild the **a** ruins and restore the H6409
Isa 64: 4 Since **a times** no one has heard, no ear H6409
Jer 5:15 an **a** and enduring nation H4946+6409
Jer 6:16 ask for the **a** paths, ask where the H6409
Jer 18:15 stumble in their ways, in the **a** paths. H6409
Eze 25:15 with **a** hostility sought to destroy H6409
Eze 26:20 below, as in **a** ruins, with those H4946+6409
Eze 35: 5 you harbored an **a** hostility and delivered H6409
Eze 36: 2 The **a** heights have become our H6409
Da 7: 9 and the **A** *of* Days took his seat. A10578
Da 7:13 approached the **A** *of* Days and was led A10578
Da 7:22 the **A** *of* Days came and A10578
Joel 2: 2 as never was in **a times** nor ever will be in H6409
Mic 5: 2 origins are from of old, from **a** times." H6409
Hab 3: 6 The **a** mountains crumbled and the H6329
2Pe 2: 5 he did not spare the **a** world when he G792
Rev 12: 9 that **a** serpent called the devil G792
Rev 20: 2 the dragon, that **a** serpent, who is the G792

ANCIENTS (1) [ANCIENT]
Heb 11: 2 This is what the **a** were commended for. G4565

ANCLE, ANCLES (KJV) ANKLE, ANKLES

AND (29510) See Index of Articles Etc.

ANDREW (14)
Mt 4:18 Simon called Peter and his brother **A**. G436
Mt 10: 2 his brother **A**; James son of Zebedee, G436
Mk 1:16 Simon and his brother **A** casting a net into G436
Mk 1:29 John to the home of Simon and **A**. G436
Mk 3:18 **A**, Philip, Bartholomew, Matthew, Thomas G436
Mk 13: 3 John and **A** asked him privately, G436
Lk 6:14 named Peter), his brother **A**, James, John, G436
Jn 1:40 **A**, Simon Peter's brother, was one of the G436
Jn 1:41 The first thing **A** did was to find his G4047S
Jn 1:44 *like* **A** and Peter, was from the town G436
Jn 6: 8 of his disciples, **A**, Simon Peter's brother, G436
Jn 12:22 Philip went to tell **A**; Andrew and Philip in G436
Jn 12:22 Andrew; **A** and Philip in turn told Jesus. G436
Ac 1:13 James and **A**; Philip and Thomas G436

ANDRONICUS (1)
Ro 16: 7 Greet **A** and Junia, my fellow Jews who G438

ANEM (1)
1Ch 6:73 Ramoth and **A**, together with their H6722

ANER (3)
Ge 14:13 a brother of Eshkol and **A**, all of whom H6738
Ge 14:24 went with me—to **A**, Eshkol and Mamre. H6738
1Ch 6:70 the Israelites gave **A** and Bileam, H6739

ANGEL (207) [ANGEL'S, ANGELS, ARCHANGEL]
Ge 16: 7 The **a** *of* the LORD found Hagar near a H4855
Ge 16: 9 Then the **a** *of* the LORD told her, "Go back H4855
Ge 16:10 **The a** added, "I will increase your H4855+3378
Ge 16:11 The **a** *of* the LORD also said to her: "You H4855
Ge 21:17 the **a** *of* God called to Hagar from H4855
Ge 22:11 But the **a** *of* the LORD called out to him H4855
Ge 22:15 The **a** *of* the LORD called to Abraham from H4855
Ge 24: 7 he will send his **a** before you so that you H4855
Ge 24:40 will send his **a** with you and make your H4855
Ge 31:11 The **a** *of* God said to me in the dream H4855
Ge 48:16 the **A** who has delivered me from all H4855
Ex 3: 2 There the **a** *of* the LORD appeared to him in H4855
Ex 14:19 Then the **a** *of* God, who had been H4855
Ex 23:20 I am sending an **a** ahead of you to guard H4855
Ex 23:23 My **a** will go ahead of you and bring you H4855
Ex 32:34 I spoke of, and my **a** will go before you. H4855
Ex 33: 2 I will send an **a** before you and drive out H4855
Nu 20:16 our cry and sent an **a** and brought us out H4855
Nu 22:22 the **a** *of* the LORD stood in the road to H4855
Nu 22:23 the donkey saw the **a** *of* the LORD standing H4855
Nu 22:24 Then the **a** *of* the LORD stood in a narrow H4855
Nu 22:25 When the donkey saw the **a** *of* the LORD, it H4855
Nu 22:26 Then the **a** *of* the LORD moved on ahead H4855
Nu 22:27 When the donkey saw the **a** *of* the LORD, it H4855
Nu 22:31 he saw the **a** *of* the LORD standing in H4855
Nu 22:32 The **a** *of* the LORD asked him, "Why have H4855
Nu 22:34 Balaam said to the **a** *of* the LORD, "I have H4855
Nu 22:35 The **a** *of* the LORD said to Balaam, "Go H4855
Jdg 2: 1 The **a** *of* the LORD went up from Gilgal to H4855
Jdg 2: 4 When the **a** *of* the LORD had spoken these H4855
Jdg 5:23 ' said the **a** *of* the LORD. 'Curse its H4855
Jdg 6:11 The **a** *of* the LORD came and sat down H4855
Jdg 6:12 When the **a** *of* the LORD appeared to H4855
Jdg 6:20 The **a** *of* God said to him, "Take the meat H4855
Jdg 6:21 Then the **a** *of* the LORD touched the meat H4855
Jdg 6:21 And the **a** *of* the LORD disappeared. H4855
Jdg 6:22 realized that it was the **a** *of* the LORD, H4855
Jdg 6:22 I have seen the **a** *of* the LORD face to face!" H4855
Jdg 13: 3 The **a** *of* the LORD appeared to her and H4855
Jdg 13: 6 He looked like an **a** *of* God, very H4855
Jdg 13: 9 the **a** *of* God came again to the H4855
Jdg 13:13 The **a** *of* the LORD answered, "Your wife H4855
Jdg 13:15 Manoah said to the **a** *of* the LORD, "We H4855
Jdg 13:16 The **a** *of* the LORD replied, "Even though H4855
Jdg 13:16 not realize that it was the **a** *of* the LORD.) H4855
Jdg 13:17 Manoah inquired of the **a** *of* the LORD, H4855
Jdg 13:20 the **a** *of* the LORD ascended in the flame. H4855
Jdg 13:21 When the **a** *of* the LORD did not show H4855
Jdg 13:21 realized that it was the **a** *of* the LORD. H4855
1Sa 29: 9 as pleasing in my eyes as an **a** *of* God; H4855
2Sa 14:17 the king is like an **a** *of* God in discerning H4855
2Sa 14:20 has wisdom like that of an **a** *of* God— H4855
2Sa 19:27 My lord the king is like an **a** *of* God; so do H4855
2Sa 24:16 When the **a** stretched out his hand to H4855
2Sa 24:16 said to the **a** who was afflicting the H4855
2Sa 24:16 The **a** *of* the LORD was then at the H4855
2Sa 24:17 When David saw the **a** who was striking H4855
1Ki 13:18 And an **a** said to me by the word of the H4855
1Ki 19: 5 All at once an **a** touched him and said H4855
1Ki 19: 7 The **a** *of* the LORD came back a second H4855
2Ki 1: 3 But the **a** *of* the LORD said to Elijah the H4855
2Ki 1:15 The **a** *of* the LORD said to Elijah, "Go down H4855
2Ki 19:35 That night the **a** *of* the LORD went out and H4855
1Ch 21:12 with the **a** *of* the LORD ravaging every part H4855
1Ch 21:15 And God sent an **a** to destroy Jerusalem H4855
1Ch 21:15 But as the **a** was doing so, the LORD saw it NDT
1Ch 21:15 said to the **a** who was destroying the H4855
1Ch 21:15 The **a** *of* the LORD was then standing at H4855
1Ch 21:16 up and saw the **a** *of* the LORD standing H4855
1Ch 21:18 Then the **a** *of* the LORD ordered Gad to tell H4855
1Ch 21:20 he turned and saw the **a**; his four sons H4855
1Ch 21:27 Then the LORD spoke to the **a**, and he put H4855
1Ch 21:30 afraid of the sword of the **a** *of* the LORD. H4855
2Ch 32:21 And the LORD sent an **a**, who annihilated H4855
Job 33:23 Yet if there is an **a** at their side, a H4855
Ps 34: 7 The **a** *of* the LORD encamps around those H4855
Ps 35: 5 with the **a** *of* the LORD driving them away H4855
Ps 35: 6 with the **a** *of* the LORD pursuing them. H4855
Isa 37:36 Then the **a** *of* the LORD went out and put H4855
Isa 63: 9 the **a** *of* his presence saved them. H4855
Da 3:28 who has sent his **a** and rescued his A10417
Da 6:22 My God sent his **a**, and he shut the A10417
Hos 12: 4 struggled with the **a** and overcame him; H4855
Zec 1: 9 The **a** who was talking with me answered H4855
Zec 1:11 they reported to the **a** *of* the LORD who was H4855
Zec 1:12 Then the **a** *of* the LORD said, "LORD H4855
Zec 1:13 words to the **a** who talked with me. H4855
Zec 1:14 Then the **a** who was speaking to me said H4855
Zec 1:19 I asked the **a** who was speaking to me H4855
Zec 2: 3 While the **a** who was speaking to me was H4855
Zec 2: 3 was leaving, another **a** came to meet him H4855
Zec 3: 1 priest standing before the **a** *of* the LORD, H4855
Zec 3: 3 in filthy clothes as he stood before the **a**. H4855
Zec 3: 4 The **a** said to those who were standing NDT
Zec 3: 5 while the **a** *of* the LORD stood by. H4855
Zec 3: 6 The **a** *of* the LORD gave this charge to H4855
Zec 4: 1 Then the **a** who talked with me returned H4855
Zec 4: 4 I asked the **a** who talked with me, "What H4855
Zec 4:11 Then I asked **the a**, "What are these two H2257S
Zec 5: 5 Then the **a** who was speaking to me H4855
Zec 5:10 I asked the **a** who was speaking to me H4855
Zec 6: 4 I asked the **a** who was speaking to me H4855
Zec 6: 5 The **a** answered me, "These are the four H4855
Zec 12: 8 like the **a** *of* the LORD going before them. H4855
Mt 1:20 an **a** of the Lord appeared to him in a dream G34
Mt 1:24 he did what the **a** of the Lord had G34
Mt 2:13 an **a** of the Lord appeared to Joseph in a G34
Mt 2:19 an **a** of the Lord appeared in a dream to G34
Mt 28: 2 an **a** of the Lord came down from heaven G34
Mt 28: 5 The **a** said to the women, "Do not be afraid G34
Lk 1:11 Then an **a** of the Lord appeared to him G34
Lk 1:13 But the **a** said to him: "Do not be afraid G34
Lk 1:18 Zechariah asked the **a**, "How can I be sure G34
Lk 1:19 The **a** said to him, "I am Gabriel. I stand in G34
Lk 1:26 God sent the **a** Gabriel to Nazareth, a G34
Lk 1:28 The **a** went to her and said, "Greetings, you NDT
Lk 1:30 But the **a** said to her, "Do not be afraid, Mary; G34
Lk 1:34 Mary asked the **a**, "since I am a virgin?" G34
Lk 1:35 The **a** answered, "The Holy Spirit will come G34
Lk 1:38 to me be fulfilled." Then the **a** left her. G34
Lk 2: 9 An **a** of the Lord appeared to them, and the G34
Lk 2:10 But the **a** said to them, "Do not be afraid. I G34
Lk 2:13 of the heavenly host appeared with the **a**, G34
Lk 2:21 the name the **a** had given him before he G34
Lk 22:43 An **a** from heaven appeared to him and G34
Jn 12:29 others said an **a** had spoken to him. G34
Ac 5:19 during the night an **a** of the Lord opened the G34
Ac 6:15 saw that his face was like the face *of* an **a**. G34
Ac 7:30 an **a** appeared to Moses in the flames of a G34
Ac 7:35 through the **a** who appeared to him in the G34
Ac 7:38 with the **a** who spoke to him on Mount Sinai, G34
Ac 8:26 Now an **a** of the Lord said to Philip, "Go G34
Ac 10: 3 He distinctly saw an **a** of God, who came to G34
Ac 10: 4 The **a** answered, "Your prayers and gifts to NDT
Ac 10: 7 When the **a** who spoke to him had gone G34
Ac 10:22 A holy **a** told him to ask you to come to his G34
Ac 11:13 how he had seen an **a** appear in his house G34
Ac 12: 7 Suddenly an **a** of the Lord appeared and a G34
Ac 12: 8 Then the **a** said to him, "Put on your clothes G34
Ac 12: 8 around you and follow me," the **a** told him. NDT

Ac 12: 9 idea that what the a was doing was really G34
Ac 12:10 length of one street, suddenly the a left him. G34
Ac 12:11 the Lord has sent his a and rescued me from G34
Ac 12:15 that it was so, they said, "It must be his a." G34
Ac 12:23 an a of the Lord struck him down G34
Ac 23: 9 "What if a spirit or an a has spoken to him?" G34
Ac 27:23 Last night an a of the God to whom I belong G34
1Co 10:10 and were killed by the destroying a. AIT
2Co 11:14 Satan himself masquerades as an a of light. G34
Gal 1: 8 But even if we or an a from heaven should G34
Gal 4:14 you welcomed me as if I were an a of God G34
Rev 1: 1 known by sending his a to his servant John, G34
Rev 2: 1 "To the a of the church in Ephesus write G34
Rev 2: 8 "To the a of the church in Smyrna write G34
Rev 2:12 "To the a of the church in Pergamum write G34
Rev 2:18 "To the a of the church in Thyatira write G34
Rev 3: 1 "To the a of the church in Sardis write G34
Rev 3: 7 "To the a of the church in Philadelphia write: G34
Rev 3:14 "To the a of the church in Laodicea write G34
Rev 5: 2 And I saw a mighty a proclaiming in a loud G34
Rev 7: 2 Then I saw another a coming up from the G34
Rev 8: 3 Another a, who had a golden censer, came G34
Rev 8: 5 Then the a took the censer, filled it with fire G34
Rev 8: 7 The first a sounded his trumpet, and there NDT
Rev 8: 8 The second a sounded his trumpet, and G34
Rev 8:10 The third a sounded his trumpet, and a G34
Rev 8:12 The fourth a sounded his trumpet, and a G34
Rev 9: 1 The fifth a sounded his trumpet, and I saw a G34
Rev 9:11 had as king over them the a of the Abyss, G34
Rev 9:13 The sixth a sounded his trumpet, and I G34
Rev 9:14 It said to the sixth a who had the trumpet G34
Rev 10: 1 I saw another mighty a coming down from G34
Rev 10: 5 Then the a I had seen standing on the sea G34
Rev 10: 7 when the seventh a is about to sound his G34
Rev 10: 8 open in the hand of the a who is standing G34
Rev 10: 9 So I went to the a and asked him to give me G34
Rev 11:15 The seventh a sounded his trumpet, and G34
Rev 14: 6 Then I saw another a flying in midair, and G34
Rev 14: 8 A second a followed and said, " 'Fallen G34
Rev 14: 9 A third a followed them and said in a loud G34
Rev 14:15 Then another a came out of the temple and G34
Rev 14:17 Another a came out of the temple in heaven G34
Rev 14:18 Still another a, who had charge of the fire G34
Rev 14:19 The a swung his sickle on the earth G34
Rev 16: 2 The first a went and poured out his bowl on NDT
Rev 16: 3 The second a poured out his bowl on the NDT
Rev 16: 4 The third a poured out his bowl on the rivers NDT
Rev 16: 5 Then I heard the a in charge of the waters G34
Rev 16: 8 The fourth a poured out his bowl on the sun, NDT
Rev 16:10 The fifth a poured out his bowl on the NDT
Rev 16:12 The sixth a poured out his bowl on the great NDT
Rev 16:17 The seventh a poured out his bowl into the NDT
Rev 17: 3 Then the a carried me away in the Spirit NDT
Rev 17: 7 Then the a said to me: "Why are you G34
Rev 17:15 Then the a said to me, "The waters you saw, NDT
Rev 18: 1 this I saw another a coming down from G34
Rev 18:21 Then a mighty a picked up a boulder the G34
Rev 19: 9 Then the a said to me, "Write this: Blessed NDT
Rev 19:17 And I saw an a standing in the sun, who G34
Rev 20: 1 And I saw an a coming down out of heaven G34
Rev 21:15 The a who talked with me had a measuring NDT
Rev 21:17 The a measured the wall using human G34
Rev 22: 1 Then the a showed me the river of the water NDT
Rev 22: 6 The a said to me, "These words are NDT
Rev 22: 6 sent his a to show his servants the things G34
Rev 22: 8 worship at the feet of the a who had been G34
Rev 22:16 have sent my a to give you this testimony G34

ANGEL'S (2) [ANGEL]

Rev 8: 4 went up before God from the a hand. G34
Rev 10:10 the little scroll from the a hand and ate it. G34

ANGELS (97) [ANGEL]

Ge 19: 1 The two a arrived at Sodom in the H4855
Ge 19:15 coming of dawn, the a urged Lot, saying, H4855
Ge 28:12 the a of God were ascending and H4855
Ge 32: 1 on his way, and the a of God met him. H4855
Job 1: 6 One day the a came to H1201+2021+466
Job 2: 1 day the a came to present H1201+2021+466
Job 4:18 his servants, if he charges his a with error, H4855
Job 38: 7 and all the a shouted for joy? H1201+466
Ps 8: 5 lower than the a and crowned them with H466
Ps 78:25 Human beings ate the bread of a; he sent H52
Ps 78:49 hostility—a band of destroying a. H4855
Ps 91:11 he will command his a concerning you to H4855
Ps 103:20 the LORD, you his a, you mighty ones who H4855
Ps 148: 2 Praise him, all his a; praise him, all his H4855
Mt 4: 6 " 'He will command his a concerning you G34
Mt 4:11 left him, and a came and attended him. G34
Mt 13:39 the end of the age, and the harvesters are a. G34
Mt 13:41 The Son of Man will send out his a, and they G34
Mt 13:49 The a will come and separate the wicked G34
Mt 16:27 to come in his Father's glory with his a, G34
Mt 18:10 I tell you that their a in heaven always see G34
Mt 22:30 marriage; they will be like the a in heaven. G34
Mt 24:31 And he will send his a with a loud trumpet G34
Mt 24:36 not even the a in heaven, nor the G34
Mt 25:31 his glory, and all the a with him, he will sit G34
Mt 25:41 eternal fire prepared for the devil and his a. G34
Mt 26:53 my disposal more than twelve legions of a? G34
Mk 1:13 with the wild animals, and a attended him. G34
Mk 8:38 comes in his Father's glory with the holy a." G34
Mk 12:25 marriage; they will be like the a in heaven. G34
Mk 13:27 And he will send his a and gather his elect G34
Mk 13:32 not even the a in heaven, nor the G34
Lk 2:15 When the a had left them and gone into G34
Lk 4:10 " 'He will command his a concerning you to G34
Lk 9:26 in the glory of the Father and of the holy a. G34
Lk 12: 8 will also acknowledge before the a of God. G34
Lk 12: 9 others will be disowned before the a of God. G34
Lk 15:10 the presence of the a of God over one sinner G34
Lk 16:22 the beggar died and the a carried him to G34
Lk 20:36 can no longer die; for they are like the a. G2694
Lk 24:23 told us that they had seen a vision of a, G34
Jn 1:51 the a of God ascending and descending G34
Jn 20:12 saw two a in white, seated where Jesus' G34
Ac 7:53 was given through a but have not obeyed it G34
Ac 23: 8 that there are neither a nor spirits, but G34
Ro 8:38 neither a nor demons, neither the G34
1Co 4: 9 universe, to a as well as to human beings. G34
1Co 6: 3 Do you not know that we will judge a? How G34
1Co 11:10 over her own head, because of the a. G34
1Co 13: 1 If I speak in the tongues of men or of a, but G34
Gal 3:19 law was given through a and entrusted to a G34
Col 2:18 humility and the worship of a disqualify you. G34
2Th 1: 7 heaven in blazing fire with his powerful a. G34
1Ti 3:16 was seen by a, was preached among G34
1Ti 5:21 of God and Christ Jesus and the elect a, G34
Heb 1: 4 as much superior to the a as the name he G34
Heb 1: 5 For to which of the a did God ever say, "You G34
Heb 1: 6 he says, "Let all God's a worship him." G34
Heb 1: 7 In speaking of the a he says, "He makes his G34
Heb 1: 7 "He makes his a spirits, and his G34
Heb 1:13 To which of the a did God ever say, "Sit at G34
Heb 1:14 Are not all a ministering spirits sent to serve NDT
Heb 2: 2 the message spoken through a was binding, G34
Heb 2: 5 It is not to a that he has subjected the world G34
Heb 2: 7 You made them a little lower than the a G34
Heb 2: 9 was made lower than the a for a little while, G34
Heb 2:16 For surely it is not a he helps, but Abraham's G34
Heb 12:22 upon thousands of a in joyful assembly, G34
Heb 13: 2 shown hospitality to a without knowing it. G34
1Pe 1:12 Even a long to look into these things G34
1Pe 3:22 at God's right hand—with a, authorities G34
2Pe 2: 4 For if God did not spare a when they sinned G34
2Pe 2:11 even a, although they are stronger and G34
Jude 6 And the a who did not keep their positions of G34
Rev 1:20 seven stars are the a of the seven churches, G34
Rev 3: 5 that name before my Father and his a. G34
Rev 5:11 I looked and heard the voice of many a, G34
Rev 7: 1 After this I saw four a standing at the four G34
Rev 7: 2 in a loud voice to the four a who had been G34
Rev 7:11 All the a were standing around the throne G34
Rev 8: 2 And I saw the seven a who stand before G34
Rev 8: 6 Then the seven a who had the seven G34
Rev 8:13 about to be sounded by the other three a!" G34
Rev 9:14 "Release the four a who are bound at the G34
Rev 9:15 And the four a who had been kept ready G34
Rev 12: 7 Michael and his a fought against the dragon G34
Rev 12: 7 the dragon and his a fought back. G34
Rev 12: 9 was hurled to the earth, and his a with him. G34
Rev 14:10 the presence of the holy a and of the Lamb. G34
Rev 15: 1 seven a with the seven last plagues—last G34
Rev 15: 6 temple came the seven a with the seven G34
Rev 15: 7 creatures gave to the seven a seven golden G34
Rev 15: 8 seven plagues of the seven a were G34
Rev 16: 1 voice from the temple saying to the seven a, G34
Rev 17: 1 One of the seven a who had the seven G34
Rev 21: 9 One of the seven a who had the seven G34
Rev 21:12 twelve gates, and with twelve a at the gates. G34

ANGER (261) [ANGERED, ANGRY]

Ge 39:19 your slave treated me," he burned with a. H678
Ge 49: 6 killed men in their a and hamstrung oxen H678
Ge 49: 7 Cursed be their a, so fierce, and their fury H678
Ex 4:14 Then the LORD's a burned against Moses H678
Ex 11: 8 Then Moses, hot with a, left Pharaoh. H678
Ex 15: 7 You unleashed your burning a; it H3019
Ex 22:24 My a will be aroused, and I will kill you with H678
Ex 32:10 me alone so that my a may burn against H678
Ex 32:11 "why should your a burn against your H678
Ex 32:12 Turn from your fierce a; relent and do not H678
Ex 32:19 his a burned and he threw the tablets out H678
Ex 34: 6 gracious God, slow to a, abounding in love H678
Lev 26:28 then in my a I will be hostile toward you H2779
Nu 11: 1 when he heard them his a was aroused. H678
Nu 11:33 the a of the LORD burned against the H678
Nu 12: 9 The a of the LORD burned against them H678
Nu 14:18 'The LORD is slow to a, abounding in love H678
Nu 24:10 Then Balak's a burned against Balaam. He H678
Nu 25: 3 And the LORD's a burned against them H678
Nu 25: 4 that the LORD's fierce a may turn away from H678
Nu 25:11 has turned my a away from the Israelites. H2779
Nu 32:10 The LORD's a was aroused that day and he H678
Nu 32:13 The LORD's a burned against Israel and he H678
Dt 4:25 of the LORD your God and arousing his a, H4087
Dt 6:15 jealous God and his a will burn against H678
Dt 7: 4 the LORD's a will burn against you and H678
Dt 9: 7 how you aroused the a of the LORD your H7911
Dt 9:18 in the LORD's sight and so arousing his a. H4087
Dt 9:19 I feared the a and wrath of the LORD, for he H678
Dt 11:17 Then the LORD's a will burn against you, and H678
Dt 13:17 Then the LORD will turn from his fierce a H678
Dt 29:23 which the LORD overthrew in fierce a. H678
Dt 29:24 Why this fierce, burning a?" H678
Dt 29:27 Therefore the LORD's a burned against this H678
Dt 29:28 In furious a and in great wrath the LORD H678
Dt 31:29 of the LORD and arouse his a by what your H4087
Jos 7: 1 So the LORD's a burned against Israel. H678
Jos 7:26 Then the LORD turned from his fierce a H678
Jos 23:16 to them, the LORD's a will burn against you H678
Jdg 2:12 around them. They aroused the LORD's a H4087
Jdg 2:14 In his a against Israel the LORD gave H678+3013
Jdg 3: 8 The a of the LORD burned against Israel so H678
Jdg 14:19 Burning with a, he returned to his father's H678
1Sa 11: 6 upon him, and he burned with a. H678
1Sa 17:28 he burned with a at him and asked H678
1Sa 20:30 Saul's a flared up at Jonathan and he said H678
1Sa 20:34 Jonathan got up from the table in fierce a H678
2Sa 6: 7 The LORD's a burned against Uzzah because H678
2Sa 11:20 the king's a may flare up, and he may ask H2779
2Sa 12: 5 David burned with a against the man and H678
2Sa 24: 1 Again the a of the LORD burned against H678
1Ki 14: 9 you have aroused my a and turned your H4087
1Ki 14:15 because they aroused the LORD's a by H4087
1Ki 14:22 they stirred up his jealous a more H7861
1Ki 15:30 he aroused the a of the LORD, H4087+4088
1Ki 16: 2 to sin and to arouse my a by their sins. H4087
1Ki 16: 7 arousing his a by the things he did H4087
1Ki 16:13 so that they aroused the a of the LORD, the H4087
1Ki 16:26 so that they aroused the a of the LORD, the H4087
1Ki 16:33 did more to arouse the a of the LORD, H4087
1Ki 21:22 you have aroused my a and H4087+4088
1Ki 22:53 Baal and aroused the a of the LORD, H4087
2Ki 13: 3 So the LORD's a burned against Israel, and H678
2Ki 17:11 wicked things that aroused the LORD's a. H4087
2Ki 17:17 in the eyes of the LORD, arousing his a. H4087
2Ki 21: 6 in the eyes of the LORD, arousing his a. H4087
2Ki 21:15 eyes and have aroused my a from the day H4087
2Ki 22:13 Great is the LORD's a that burns against us H2779
2Ki 22:17 other gods and aroused my a by all the H4087
2Ki 22:17 my a will burn against this place and will H2779
2Ki 23:19 that had aroused the LORD's a. H4087
2Ki 23:26 not turn away from the heat of his fierce a, H678
2Ki 23:26 had done to arouse his a. H4087+4088
2Ki 24:20 because of the LORD's a that all this H678
1Ch 13:10 The LORD's a burned against Uzzah, and he H678
1Ch 15:13 LORD our God broke out in a against us. H7287
2Ch 12:12 himself, the LORD's a turned from him, and H678
2Ch 24:18 God's a came on Judah and Jerusalem. H7912
2Ch 25:15 The a of the LORD burned against Amaziah H678
2Ch 28:11 the LORD's fierce a rests on you. H678
2Ch 28:13 and his fierce a rests on Israel. H678
2Ch 28:25 other gods and aroused the a of the LORD, H4087
2Ch 29: 8 the a of the LORD has fallen on Judah and H7912
2Ch 29:10 so that his fierce a will turn away from us. H678
2Ch 30: 8 so that his fierce a will turn away from you. H678
2Ch 33: 6 in the eyes of the LORD, arousing his a. H4087
2Ch 34:21 Great is the LORD's a that is poured out on H2779
2Ch 34:25 other gods and aroused my a by all that H4087
2Ch 34:25 my a will be poured out on this place H2779
Ezr 8:22 his great a is against all who forsake H678
Ezr 10:14 the fierce a of our God in this matter H678
Ne 9:17 slow to a and abounding in love. H678
Est 1:12 king became furious and burned with a. H2779
Job 4: 9 at the blast of his a they are no more. H678
Job 9: 5 knowing it and overturns them in his a. H678
Job 9:13 God does not restrain his a; even the H678
Job 10:17 me and increase your a toward me; H4089
Job 14:13 conceal me till your a has passed! H678
Job 16: 9 tears me in his a and gnashes his H678
Job 18: 4 You who tear yourself to pieces in your a, H678
Job 19:11 His a burns against me; he counts me H678
Job 20:23 vent his burning a against him and rain H678
Job 21:17 upon them, the fate God allots in his a? H678
Job 32: 5 nothing more to say, his a was aroused. H678
Job 35:15 that his a never punishes and he does not H678
Ps 2: 5 rebukes them in his a and terrifies them in H678
Ps 6: 1 not rebuke me in your a or discipline me in H678
Ps 7: 6 in your a; rise up against the rage of H678
Ps 27: 9 do not turn your servant away in a; you H678
Ps 30: 5 For his a lasts only a moment, but his favor H678
Ps 37: 8 Refrain from a and turn from wrath; do not H678
Ps 38: 1 rebuke me in your a or discipline me in H7912
Ps 55: 3 suffering on me and assail me in their a. H678
Ps 56: 7 do not let them escape; in your a, God, H678
Ps 69:24 on them; let your fierce a overtake them. H678
Ps 74: 1 Why does your a smolder against the H678
Ps 77: 9 Has he in a withheld his compassion?" H678
Ps 78:31 God's a rose against them; he put to death H678
Ps 78:38 time he restrained his a and did not stir up H678
Ps 78:49 He unleashed against them his hot a, his H678
Ps 78:50 He prepared a path for his a; he did not H678
Ps 80: 4 will your a smolder against the prayers of H6939
Ps 85: 3 your wrath and turned from your fierce a. H678
Ps 85: 5 Will you prolong your a through all H678
Ps 86:15 gracious God, slow to a, abounding in love H678
Ps 90: 7 are consumed by your a and terrified by H678
Ps 90:11 If only we knew the power of your a! Your H678
Ps 95:11 So I declared on oath in my a, 'They shall H678
Ps 103: 8 gracious, slow to a, abounding in love. H678
Ps 103: 9 nor will he harbor his a forever; H5757
Ps 106:29 they aroused the LORD's a by their wicked H4087
Ps 124: 3 us alive when their a flared against us; H678
Ps 138: 7 out your hand against the a of my foes; H678
Ps 145: 8 compassionate, slow to a and rich in love. H678

Pr 15: 1 away wrath, but a harsh word stirs up a. H678
Pr 20: 2 those who a him forfeit their lives. H6297
Pr 21:14 A gift given in secret soothes a, and a H678
Pr 27: 4 A is cruel and fury overwhelming, but who H2779
Pr 29: 8 stir up a city, but the wise turn away a. H678
Pr 30:33 so stirring up a produces strife. H678
Ecc 5:17 with great frustration, affliction and a. H7912
Ecc 7: 9 your spirit, for a resides in the lap of fools. H4088
Ecc 10: 4 If a ruler's a rises against you, do not H8120
Isa 5:25 Therefore the LORD's a burns against his H678
Isa 5:25 Yet for all this, his a is not turned away, his H678
Isa 7: 4 of the fierce a of Rezin and Aram and H678
Isa 9:12 Yet for all this, his a is not turned away, his H678
Isa 9:17 Yet for all this, his a is not turned away, his H678
Isa 9:21 Yet for all this, his a is not turned away, his H678
Isa 10: 4 Yet for all this, his a is not turned away, his H678
Isa 10: 5 the rod of my a, in whose hand is the H678
Isa 10: 6 dispatch him against a people who a me, H6301
Isa 10:25 Very soon my a against you will end and H2405
Isa 12: 1 your a has turned away and you have H678
Isa 13: 9 with wrath and fierce a—to make the land H678
Isa 13:13 LORD Almighty, in the day of his burning a. H678
Isa 14: 6 which in a struck down peoples with H6301
Isa 30:27 with burning a and dense clouds of smoke H678
Isa 30:30 down with raging a and consuming fire, H678
Isa 42:25 So he poured out on them his burning a H678
Isa 54: 8 In a surge of a I hid my face from you H7912
Isa 57:17 hid my face in a, yet they kept on in H7911
Isa 60:10 Though in a I struck you, in favor I will H7912
Isa 63: 3 them in my a and trod them down H678
Isa 63: 6 I trampled the nations in my a; in my wrath H678
Isa 66:15 he will bring down his a with fury, and his H678
Jer 4: 8 the fierce a of the LORD has not turned H678
Jer 4:26 in ruins before the LORD, before his fierce a. H678
Jer 7:18 offerings to other gods to arouse my a. H4087
Jer 7:20 My a and my wrath will be poured out on H678
Jer 8:19 "Why have they aroused my a with their H4087
Jer 10:24 measure—not in your a, or you will reduce H678
Jer 11:17 done evil and aroused my a by burning H4087
Jer 12:13 their harvest because of the LORD's fierce a." H678
Jer 15:14 my a will kindle a fire that will burn H678
Jer 17: 4 you have kindled my a, and it will burn H678
Jer 18:23 deal with them in the time of your a. H678
Jer 21: 5 mighty arm in furious a and in great wrath. H678
Jer 23:20 The a of the LORD will not turn back until he H678
Jer 25: 6 do not arouse my a with what your hands H4087
Jer 25: 7 "and you have aroused my a with what H4087
Jer 25:37 waste because of the fierce a of the LORD. H678
Jer 25:38 because of the LORD's fierce a. H678
Jer 30:24 The fierce a of the LORD will not turn back H678
Jer 32:29 where the people aroused my a by H4087
Jer 32:30 nothing but arouse my a with what their H4087
Jer 32:31 has so aroused my a and wrath that I must H678
Jer 32:37 them in my furious a and great wrath; H678
Jer 33: 5 of the people I will slay in my a and wrath. H678
Jer 36: 7 the a and wrath pronounced against H678
Jer 42:18 'As my a and wrath have been poured out H678
Jer 44: 3 They aroused my a by burning incense to H4087
Jer 44: 6 Therefore, my fierce a was poured out; it H678
Jer 44: 8 Why arouse my a with what your hands H4087
Jer 49:37 even my fierce a," declares the LORD. H678
Jer 50:13 Because of the LORD's a she will not be H7912
Jer 51:45 Run from the fierce a of the LORD. H678
Jer 52: 3 because of the LORD's a that all this H678
La 1:12 brought on me in the day of his fierce a? H678
La 2: 1 Daughter Zion with the cloud of his a! H678
La 2: 1 his footstool in the day of his a. H678
La 2: 3 In fierce a he has cut off every horn of H678
La 2: 6 in his fierce a he has spurned both king H678
La 2:21 You have slain them in the day of your a H678
La 2:22 the day of the LORD's a no one escaped H678
La 3:43 covered yourself with a and pursued us; H678
La 3:66 Pursue them in a and destroy them from H678
La 4:11 to his wrath; he has poured out his fierce a. H678
Eze 3:14 in bitterness and in the a of my spirit, H2779
Eze 5:13 "Then my a will cease and my wrath H678
Eze 5:15 punishment on you in a and in wrath and H678
Eze 7: 3 and I will unleash my a against you. H678
Eze 7: 8 wrath on you and spend my a against you. H678
Eze 8:17 violence and continually arouse my a? H4087
Eze 8:18 Therefore I will deal with them in a; I will H2779
Eze 13:13 in my a hailstones and torrents of rain H678
Eze 16:26 aroused my a with your increasing H4087
Eze 16:38 vengeance of my wrath and jealous a. H7863
Eze 16:42 subside and my jealous a will turn away H7863
Eze 20: 8 on them and spend my a against them in H678
Eze 20:21 them and spend my a against them in the H678
Eze 20:28 made offerings that aroused my a H4088
Eze 21:31 breathe out my fiery a against you; H6301
Eze 22:20 I gather you in my a and my wrath and put H678
Eze 22:31 them and consume them with my fiery a, H6301
Eze 23:25 I will direct my jealous a against you, and H7863
Eze 25:14 in accordance with my a and my wrath; H678
Eze 35:11 in accordance with the a and jealousy you H678
Eze 38:18 land of Israel, my hot a will be aroused H678
Eze 43: 8 So I destroyed them in my a. H678
Da 9:16 turn away your a and your wrath from H678
Da 11:20 will be destroyed, yet not in a or in battle. H678
Hos 8: 5 out your calf-idol! My a burns against them H678
Hos 11: 9 I will not carry out my fierce a, nor will I H678
Hos 12:14 But Ephraim has aroused his bitter a; his H4087
Hos 13:11 So in my a I gave you a king, and in my H678
Hos 14: 4 for my a has turned away from them. H678
Joel 2:13 slow to a and abounding in love H678
Am 1:11 because his a raged continually and his H678
Jnh 3: 9 turn from his fierce a so that we will not H678
Jnh 4: 2 slow to a and abounding in love, a H678
Mic 5:15 will take vengeance in a and wrath on the H678
Na 1: 3 The LORD is slow to a but great in power H678
Na 1: 6 Who can endure his fierce a? His wrath is H678
Hab 3:12 the earth and in a you threshed the nations H678
Zep 2: 2 before the LORD's fierce a comes upon you H678
Zep 2: 3 will be sheltered on the day of the LORD's a. H678
Zep 3: 8 out my wrath on them—all my fierce a. H678
Zep 3: 8 be consumed by the fire of my jealous a. H7863
Zec 10: 3 "My a burns against the shepherds, and I H678
Mt 18:34 In a his master handed him over to the G3974
Mk 3: 5 He looked around at them in a and G3973
Ro 2: 8 follow evil, there will be wrath and a. G2596
Eph 4:26 "In your a do not sin": Do not let the sun G3974
Eph 4:31 bitterness, rage and a, brawling and G3973
Col 3: 8 a, rage, malice, slander, and filthy G3973
1Ti 2: 8 up holy hands without a or disputing. G3973
Heb 3:11 So I declared on oath in my a, 'They shall G3973
Heb 4: 3 "So I declared on oath in my a, 'They G3973
Heb 11:27 not fearing the king's a; he persevered G2596
Jas 1:20 because human a does not produce the G3973

ANGERED (9) [ANGER]

Dt 32:16 their foreign gods and a him with their H4087
Dt 32:19 them because he was a by his sons and H4088
Dt 32:21 by what is no god and a me with their H4087
Ezr 5:12 our ancestors a the God of heaven, A10653
Ps 78:58 They a him with their high places; they H4087
Ps 106:32 By the waters of Meribah they a the LORD H7911
Pr 22:24 do not associate with one easily a, H2779
Zec 8:14 no pity when your ancestors a me, H7911
1Co 13: 5 self-seeking, it is not easily a, it keeps no G4236

ANGLE (5)

2Ch 26: 9 the Valley Gate and at the a of the wall, H5243
Ne 3:19 to the armory as far as the a of the wall. H5243
Ne 3:20 from the a to the entrance of the house of H5243
Ne 3:24 Azariah's house to the a and the corner, H5243
Ne 3:25 worked opposite the a and the tower H5243

ANGRY (115) [ANGER]

Ge 4: 5 So Cain was very a, and his face was H3013
Ge 4: 6 the LORD said to Cain, "Why are you a? H3013
Ge 18:30 he said, "May the Lord not be a, but let H3013
Ge 18:32 he said, "May the Lord not be a, but let H3013
Ge 27:45 brother is no longer a with you and forgets H678
Ge 30: 2 Jacob became a with her and said H3013+678
Ge 31:35 father, "Don't be a, my lord, H3013+928+6524
Ge 31:36 Jacob was a and took Laban to task H3013
Ge 40: 2 Pharaoh was a with his two officials, the H7911
Ge 41:10 Pharaoh was once a with his servants, and H7911
Ge 44:18 Do not be a with your servant H3013+678
Ge 45: 5 distressed and do not be a with H3013
Ex 16:20 So Moses was a with them. H7911
Ex 32:22 "Do not be a, my lord," Aaron H3013+678
Lev 10: 6 die and the LORD will be a with the whole H7911
Lev 10:16 he was a with Eleazar and Ithamar H7911
Nu 11:10 The LORD became exceedingly a H3013+678
Nu 16:15 Then Moses became very a and said to H3013
Nu 16:22 will you be a with the entire assembly H7911
Nu 22:22 But God was very a when he went H3013+678
Nu 22:27 and he was a and beat it with his H3013+678
Nu 31:14 Moses was a with the officers of the army H7911
Nu 32:14 the LORD even more a with Israel. H3019+678
Dt 1:34 you said, he was a and solemnly swore: H7911
Dt 1:37 of you the LORD became a with me also H647
Dt 3:26 of you the LORD was a with me and would H6297
Dt 4:21 The LORD was a with me because of you H647
Dt 9: 8 so that he was a enough to destroy you. H647
Dt 9:19 for he was a enough with you to destroy H7911
Dt 9:20 And the LORD was a enough with Aaron to H647
Dt 9:22 You also made the LORD a at H2118+7911
Dt 31:17 that day I will become a with them H3013+678
Dt 32:21 I will make them a by a nation that has H4087
Jos 22:18 tomorrow he will be a with the whole H7911
Jdg 2:20 the LORD was very a with Israel and H3013+678
Jdg 6:39 said to God, "Do not be a with me. H3013+678
Jdg 9:30 son of Ebed said, he was very a. H3013+678
Jdg 10: 7 he became a with them. He sold H3013+678
Jdg 18:25 the men may get a and attack you, H5253+5883
1Sa 15:11 Samuel was a, and he cried out to the H3013
1Sa 18: 8 Saul was very a; this refrain displeased H3013
1Sa 29: 4 commanders were a with Achish and said H7911
2Sa 3: 8 Abner was very a because of what H3013
2Sa 6: 8 Then David was a because the LORD's H3013
2Sa 19:42 Why are you a about it? Have we H3013
2Sa 22: 8 they trembled because he was a. H3013
1Ki 8:46 and you become a with them and give H647
1Ki 11: 9 The LORD became a with Solomon because H647
1Ki 20:43 Sullen and a, the king of Israel went to his H2409
1Ki 21: 4 sullen and a because Naboth the H2409
2Ki 5:11 But Naaman went away a and said, "I H7911
2Ki 13:19 The man of God was a with him and said H7911
2Ki 17:18 So the LORD was very a with Israel and H647
1Ch 13:11 Then David was a because the LORD's H3013
2Ch 6:36 and you become a with them and give H647
2Ch 16:10 Asa was a with the seer because of this H4087
2Ch 26:19 hand ready to burn incense, became a. H2406
2Ch 28: 9 your ancestors, was a with Judah, he gave H2779
Ezr 9:14 Would you not be a enough with us to H647
Ne 4: 1 he became a and was greatly incensed. H3013
Ne 4: 7 gaps were being closed, they were very a. H3013
Ne 5: 6 outcry and these charges, I was very a. H3013
Est 2:21 became a and conspired to assassinate H7911
Job 32: 2 became very a with Job for justifying H3013+678
Job 32: 3 He was also a with the three friends H3013+678
Job 42: 7 "I am a with you and your two H3013+678
Ps 2:12 or he will be a and your way will lead to H647
Ps 18: 7 they trembled because he was a. H3013
Ps 60: 1 upon us; you have been a—now restore us H647
Ps 76: 7 Who can stand before you when you are a? H678
Ps 79: 5 Will you be a forever? How long will H647
Ps 85: 5 Will you be a with us forever? Will you H647
Ps 89:38 you have been very a with your anointed H6297
Ps 95:10 For forty years I was a with that generation H7752
Ps 106:40 the LORD was a with his people H3013+678
Pr 29:22 An a person stirs up conflict, and a H678
Ecc 5: 6 Why should God be a at what you say H7911
SS 1: 6 My mother's sons were a with me and H5723
Isa 12: 1 Although you were a with me, your anger H647
Isa 27: 4 I am not a. If only there were briers and H2779
Isa 34: 2 The LORD is a with all nations; his wrath is H7912
Isa 47: 6 I was a with my people and desecrated H7911
Isa 54: 9 So now I have sworn not to be a with you H7911
Isa 57:16 nor will I always be a, for then H7911
Isa 64: 5 to sin against them, you were a. H7911
Isa 64: 9 Do not be a beyond measure, LORD; do H7911
Jer 2:35 'I am innocent; he is not a with me. H8740+678
Jer 3: 5 will you always be a? Will your wrath H5757
Jer 3:12 ' declares the LORD, 'I will not be a forever. H5757
Jer 10:10 When he is a, the earth trembles; the H7912
Jer 37:15 They were a with Jeremiah and had him H7911
La 5:22 rejected us and are a with us beyond H7911
Eze 16:42 from you; I will be calm and no longer a. H4087
Da 2:12 made the king so a and furious that he A10113
Jnh 4: 1 seemed very wrong, and he became a. H3013
Jnh 4: 4 LORD replied, "Is it right for you to be a?" H3013
Jnh 4: 9 "Is it right for you to be a about the plant?" H3013
Jnh 4: 9 "And I'm so a I wish I were dead. H3013
Mic 7:18 You do not stay a forever but delight to H678
Hab 3: 8 Were you a with the rivers, LORD? Was H3013
Zec 1: 2 "The LORD was very a with your H7911+7912
Zec 1:12 which you have been a with these seventy H2404
Zec 1:15 I am very a with the nations H7911+7912
Zec 1:15 I was only a little a, but they went too far H7911
Zec 7:12 So the LORD Almighty was very a. H7912
Mt 5:22 you that anyone who is a with a brother G3974
Lk 14:21 of the house became a and ordered his G3974
Lk 15:28 older brother became a and refused to go G3974
Jn 7:23 why are you a with me for healing a G5957
Ro 10:19 I will make you a by a nation that has no G4239
Eph 4:26 let the sun go down while you are still a, G4240
Heb 3:10 That is why I was a with that generation; I G4696
Heb 3:17 And with whom was he a for forty years G4696
Jas 1:19 slow to speak and slow to become a, G3973
Rev 11:18 The nations were a, and your wrath has G3974

ANGUISH (45) [ANGUISHED]

Ex 15:14 a will grip the people of Philistia. H2659
Dt 2:25 will tremble and be in a because of you." H2655
1Sa 1:10 In her deep a Hannah prayed to the H5253+5883
1Sa 1:16 praying here out of my great a and grief." H8490
Job 6: 2 "If only my a could be weighed and all H4089
Job 7:11 I will speak out in the a of my spirit, I will H7639
Job 15:24 Distress and a fill him with terror; troubles H5188
Job 26: 5 "The dead are in deep a, those beneath H2655
Ps 6: 3 My soul is in deep a. How long, LORD, how H987
Ps 6:10 be overwhelmed with shame and a; H987+4394
Ps 22: 1 from saving me, so far from my cries of a? H8614
Ps 25:17 of my heart and free me from my a. H5188
Ps 31: 7 my affliction and knew the a of my soul. H7650
Ps 31:10 My life is consumed by a and my years by H3326
Ps 38: 8 utterly crushed; I groan in a of heart. H5639
Ps 39: 2 anything good. But my a increased; H3873
Ps 55: 4 My heart is in a within me; the terrors of H2655
Ps 116: 3 the a of the grave came over me H5210
Pr 31: 6 wine for those who are in a! H5253+5883
Isa 13: 8 pain and a will grip them; they H2477
Isa 23: 5 they will be in a at the report from Tyre. H2655
Isa 38:15 all my years because of this a of my soul. H5253
Isa 38:17 was for my benefit that I suffered such a. H5253
Isa 65:14 you will cry out from a of heart and wail in H3873
Jer 4:19 my a, my anguish! I writhe in pain H5055
Jer 4:19 my anguish, my a! I writhe in pain H5055
Jer 6:24 A has gripped us, pain like that of a H7650
Jer 15: 8 I will bring down on them a and terror. H6552
Jer 48: 3 Cries of a arise from Horonaim H7754+7591
Jer 49:24 gripped her; a and pain have seized her H7650
Jer 50:43 A has gripped him, pain like that of a H7650
La 1: 4 women grieve, and she is in bitter a. H5352
Eze 27:31 weep over you with a of soul and with H5253
Eze 30: 4 and a will come upon Cush. H2714
Eze 30: 9 A will take hold of them on the day of H2714
Da 10:16 "I am overcome with a because of the H7496
Joel 2: 6 of them, nations are in a; every face turns H2655
Am 5:16 and cries of a in every public H2082+2082
Hab 3: 7 in distress, the dwellings of Midian in a. H8074
Zep 1:15 a day of distress and a, a day of trouble H5188
Lk 21:25 nations will be in a and perplexity at the G5330
Lk 22:44 And being in a, he prayed more earnestly G75

A

Jn 16:21 born she forgets the **a** because of her joy *G2568*
Ro 9: 2 great sorrow and unceasing **a** in my heart. *G3850*
2Co 2: 4 of great distress and **a** of heart and with *G5330*

ANGUISHED (2) [ANGUISH]

Jer 48: 5 road down to Horonaim **a** cries over the H7639
Da 6:20 he called to Daniel in an **a** voice A10565

ANIAM (1)

1Ch 7:19 Ahian, Shechem, Likhi and **A**. H642

ANIM (1)

Jos 15:50 Eshtemoh, **A**, H6719

ANIMAL (83) [ANIMALS]

Ge 6:20 of every kind of **a** and of every kind of H989
Ge 7: 2 you seven pairs of every kind of clean **a**, H989
Ge 7: 2 one pair of every kind of unclean **a**, a H989
Ge 7:14 with them every **wild a** according to its H2651
Ge 9: 5 I will demand an accounting from every **a** H2651
Ge 37:20 say that a ferocious **a** devoured him. H2651
Ge 37:33 Some ferocious **a** has devoured him H2651
Ge 43:16 slaughter an **a** and prepare a meal H3181
Ex 9: 4 so that no **a** belonging to the Israelites H1821S
Ex 9: 6 not one **a** belonging to the Israelites H5238
Ex 9:19 on every person and **a** that has not been H989
Ex 11: 7 not a dog will bark at any person or **a**. H989
Ex 13: 2 belongs to me, whether human or **a**." H989
Ex 19:13 No person or **a** shall be permitted to live H989
Ex 21:34 the loss and take the **dead** *a* in exchange. AIT
Ex 21:35 both the money and the **dead** *a* equally. AIT
Ex 21:36 the owner must pay, **a** for animal, and H8802
Ex 21:36 must pay, animal for **a**, and take the dead H8802
Ex 21:36 animal, and take the **dead** *a* in exchange. AIT
Ex 22: 4 If the **stolen** *a* is found alive in their AIT
Ex 22:10 a sheep or any other **a** to their neighbor H989
Ex 22:12 But if the **a** was stolen from the neighbor NDT
Ex 22:13 If *it* **was torn to pieces by a wild a** H3271+3271
Ex 22:13 shall not be required to pay for the torn **a**. NDT
Ex 22:14 "If anyone borrows an **a** from their neighbor NDT
Ex 22:15 But if the owner is with **the a**, the H2257S
Ex 22:15 If **the a** was hired, the money paid for H2085S
Ex 22:19 relations with an **a** is to be put to death. H989
Ex 22:31 eat the meat of an **a torn by** wild **beasts**; H3274
Lev 1: 2 as your offering an **a** from either the herd H989
Lev 3: 1 you offer an **a** from the herd, whether NDT
Lev 3: 1 before the LORD an **a** without defect. H5647S
Lev 3: 6 " 'If you offer an **a** from the flock as a NDT
Lev 5: 2 carcass of an unclean **a**, **wild** or domestic, H2651
Lev 7:21 an unclean **a** or any unclean creature H989
Lev 7:24 The fat of an **a found dead** or torn by wild H5577
Lev 7:25 who eats the fat of an **a** from which a food H989
Lev 7:26 you must not eat the blood of any bird or **a**. H989
Lev 11: 3 You may eat any **a** that has a divided hoof H989
Lev 11:26 " 'Every **a** that does not have a divided H989
Lev 11:39 " 'If an **a** that you are allowed to eat dies H989
Lev 17:13 who hunts any **a** or bird that may H7473+2651
Lev 18:23 relations with an **a** and defile yourself with H989
Lev 18:23 present herself to an **a** to have sexual H989
Lev 20:15 " 'If a man has sexual relations with an **a** H989
Lev 20:15 to be put to death, and you must kill the **a**. H989
Lev 20:16 a woman approaches an **a** to have sexual H989
Lev 20:16 kill both the woman and the **a**. H989
Lev 20:25 yourselves by any **a** or bird or anything that H989
Lev 22:24 not offer to the LORD an **a** whose testicles are NDT
Lev 24:18 life of someone's **a** must make restitution H989
Lev 24:21 Whoever kills an **a** must make restitution H989
Lev 27: 9 they vowed is an **a** that is acceptable as H989
Lev 27: 9 such an **a** given to the LORD becomes H5647S
Lev 27:10 if they should substitute *one* **a** for another H989
Lev 27:11 they vowed is a ceremonially unclean **a**— H989
Lev 27:11 the **a** must be presented to the priest H989
Lev 27:13 If the owner wishes to redeem **the a**, a H5626S
Lev 27:26 may dedicate the firstborn of an **a**, since H989
Lev 27:28 a human being or an **a** or family land— H989
Lev 27:32 every tenth **a** that passes under the NDT
Lev 27:33 both **the a** and its substitute become H2085S
Nu 3:13 firstborn in Israel, whether human or **a**. H989
Nu 8:17 in Israel, whether human or **a**, is mine. H989
Nu 18:15 both human and **a**, that is offered to H989
Dt 4:17 like any **a** on earth or any bird that flies H989
Dt 14: 6 You may eat any **a** that has a divided hoof H989
Dt 15:21 If an **a** has a defect, is lame or blind, or H2257S
Dt 16: 2 your God an **a from** your **flock** or herd at H7366
Dt 27:21 who has sexual relations with any **a**." H989
Job 39:15 that some wild **a** may trample them. H2651
Ps 50:10 every **a** *of* the forest is mine, and the H2651
Ecc 3:21 if the spirit of the **a** goes down into the H989
Eze 44:31 whether bird or **a**, found dead or torn by H989
Da 4:16 let him be given the mind of an **a**, A10263
Da 5:21 from people and given the mind of an **a**; A10263
Da 8: 4 No **a** could stand against it, and none H2651
Hos 13: 8 a wild **a** will tear them apart. H2651
Mal 1:14 then sacrifices a **blemished** *a* to the Lord. AIT
Heb 12:20 "If even an **a** touches the mountain, it *G2563*
Jas 3: 3 them obey us, we can turn the whole **a**. *G5393*
2Pe 2:16 by a donkey—an **a** without speech—who NDT
Rev 18: 2 haunt *for* every unclean and detestable **a**. *G2563*

ANIMALS (172) [ANIMAL]

Ge 1:24 ground, and the wild **a**, each according to H2651
Ge 1:25 God made the wild **a** according to their H2651
Ge 1:26 over the livestock and all the wild **a**, and H2651
Ge 2:19 ground all the wild **a** and all the birds in H2651
Ge 2:20 the birds in the sky and all the wild **a**. H2651
Ge 3: 1 than any of the wild **a** the LORD God had H2651
Ge 3:14 are you above all livestock and all wild **a**! H2651
Ge 6: 7 with them the **a**, the birds and the H989
Ge 7: 8 Pairs of clean and unclean **a**, of birds and H989
Ge 7:16 The *a* **going in** were male and female of AIT
Ge 7:21 livestock, **wild a**, all the creatures that H2651
Ge 7:23 people and **a** and the creatures that move H989
Ge 8: 1 Noah and all the **wild a** and the livestock H2651
Ge 8:17 the birds, the **a**, and all the creatures that H989
Ge 8:19 All the **a** and all the creatures that move H2651
Ge 8:20 some of all the clean **a** and clean birds, H989
Ge 9:10 the livestock and all the wild **a**, all those H2651
Ge 30:40 dark-colored **a** *that belonged to* Laban. H7366
Ge 30:40 did not put them with Laban's **a**. H7366
Ge 30:41 in front of the **a** so they would mate near H7366
Ge 30:42 if the **a** were weak, he would not place H7366
Ge 30:42 So the weak **a** went to Laban and the strong NDT
Ge 31:39 I did not bring you **a torn by wild beasts**; H3274
Ge 32:17 who owns all these **a** in front of you? NDT
Ge 33:13 hard just one day, all the **a** will die. H7366
Ge 34:23 property and all their *other* **a** become ours? H989
Ge 36: 6 all his *other* **a** and all the goods he H989
Ge 45:17 Load your **a** and return to the land of H1248
Ex 8:17 the ground, gnats came on people and **a**. H989
Ex 8:18 gnats were on people and **a** everywhere, H989
Ex 9: 7 not even one of the **a** *of* the Israelites had H5238
Ex 9: 9 out on people and **a** throughout the land." H989
Ex 9:10 festering boils broke out on people and **a**. H989
Ex 9:22 on people and **a** and on everything growing H989
Ex 9:25 both people and **a**; it beat down H989
Ex 12: 5 The **a** you choose must be year-old males H8445
Ex 12:12 down every firstborn of both people and **a**, H989
Ex 12:21 once and select the **a** for your families H7366
Ex 13:15 the firstborn of both people and **a** in Egypt. H989
Ex 20:10 nor your **a**, nor any foreigner H989
Ex 23:11 and the wild **a** may eat what is left. H2651
Ex 23:29 the wild **a** too numerous for you. H2651
Lev 7:24 found dead or **torn by wild** **a** may be used H3274
Lev 11: 2 'Of all the **a** that live on land, these are the H989
Lev 11:27 Of all the **a** that walk on all fours, those H2651
Lev 11:28 till evening. **These** *a* are unclean for you AIT
Lev 11:29 " 'Of the **a** that move along the ground H9238
Lev 11:46 " 'These are the regulations concerning **a** H989
Lev 17:15 found dead or **torn by wild a** must wash H3274
Lev 19:19 " 'Do not mate different kinds of **a**. " 'Do H989
Lev 20:25 clean and unclean **a** and between unclean H989
Lev 22: 8 eat anything found dead or **torn by wild a**, H3274
Lev 22:25 must not accept such **a** from the hand of a H465S
Lev 25: 7 your livestock and the **wild a** in your land. H2651
Lev 26:22 I will send wild **a** against you, and they H2651
Lev 27:27 If it is one of the unclean **a**, it may be H989
Nu 7:87 The total number of **a** for the burnt H1330
Nu 7:88 The total number of **a** *for* the sacrifice of H1330
Nu 18:15 son and every firstborn male of unclean **a**. H989
Nu 28:31 Be sure the **a** are without defect. NDT
Nu 31:11 spoils, including the people and **a**, H989
Nu 31:26 all the people and **a** that were captured. H989
Nu 31:30 cattle, donkeys, sheep or other **a**. H989
Nu 31:47 one out of every fifty people and **a**, H989
Nu 35: 3 the cattle they own and all their *other* **a**. H2651
Dt 5:14 your donkey or any of your **a**, nor any H989
Dt 7:22 the wild **a** will multiply around you. H2651
Dt 12:15 may slaughter your **a** in any of your towns NDT
Dt 12:21 you may slaughter **a** from the herds and NDT
Dt 14: 4 These are the **a** you may eat: the ox, the H989
Dt 28:26 food for all the birds and the **wild a**, H989+824
Jdg 20:48 including the **a** and everything else they H989
1Sa 17:44 give your flesh to the birds and the wild **a**!" H989
1Sa 17:46 army to the birds and the wild **a**, H2651
2Sa 21:10 touch them by day or the wild **a** by night. H2651
1Ki 4:33 He also spoke about **a** and birds, reptiles H989
1Ki 18: 5 so we will not have to kill any of our **a**." H989
2Ki 3: 9 water for themselves or for the **a** with them. H989
2Ki 3:17 your cattle and your other **a** will drink. H989
2Ch 29:33 The *a* **consecrated** as sacrifices amounted to AIT
2Ch 35:11 to them, while the Levites skinned the **a**. NDT
2Ch 35:13 They roasted the **Passover a** over the fire H7175
Job 5:22 famine, and need not fear the wild **a**. H2651
Job 5:23 the wild **a** will be at peace with you. H2651
Job 12: 7 "But ask the **a**, and they will teach you, or H989
Job 37: 8 The **a** take cover; they remain in their H2651
Job 40:20 produce, and all the wild **a** play nearby. H2651
Ps 8: 7 all flocks and herds, and the **a** *of* the wild, H989
Ps 36: 6 LORD, preserve both people and **a**. H989
Ps 66:15 I will sacrifice **fat a** to you and an offering H4671
Ps 79: 2 of your own people for the **a** *of* the wild. H2651
Ps 135: 8 of Egypt, the firstborn of people and **a**. H989
Ps 148:10 **wild a** and all cattle, small creatures and H2651
Pr 12:10 The righteous care for the needs of their **a** H989
Ecc 3:18 that they may see that they are like the **a**. H989
Ecc 3:19 fate of human beings is like that of the **a**; H989
Ecc 3:19 humans have no advantage over **a**. H989
Isa 1:11 of rams and the fat of **fattened a**; I have H5309
Isa 18: 6 mountain birds of prey and to the wild **a**; H989
Isa 18: 6 on them all summer, the wild **a** all winter. H989
Isa 30: 6 A prophecy concerning the **a** *of* the Negev H989
Isa 40:16 nor its **a** enough for burnt offerings. H2651
Isa 43:20 The wild **a** honor me, the jackals and the H2651
Jer 7:33 become food for the birds and the wild **a**, H989
Jer 9:10 The birds have all fled and the **a** are gone H989
Jer 12: 4 are wicked, the **a** and birds have perished. H989
Jer 15: 3 birds and the wild **a** to devour and destroy. H989
Jer 16: 4 become food for the birds and the wild **a**." H989
Jer 19: 7 as food to the birds and the wild **a**. H989
Jer 27: 5 its people and the **a** that are on it, H989
Jer 27: 6 I will make even the wild **a** subject to him. H2651
Jer 28:14 will even give him control over the wild **a**. H2651
Jer 31:27 with the offspring of people and of **a**. H989
Jer 32:43 without people or **a**, for it has been given H989
Jer 33:10 "It is a desolate waste, without people or **a**." H989
Jer 33:10 inhabited by neither people nor **a**, there H989
Jer 33:12 desolate and without people or **a**—in all H989
Jer 34:20 become food for the birds and the wild **a**. H989
Jer 50: 3 live in it; both people and **a** will flee away. H989
Jer 51:62 so that neither people nor **a** will live in it; it H989
Eze 4:14 anything found dead or **torn by wild a**. H3274
Eze 8:10 things and unclean **a** and all the idols of H989
Eze 14:13 upon it and kill its people and their **a**, H989
Eze 14:17 the land,' and I kill its people and their **a**, H989
Eze 14:19 bloodshed, killing its people and their **a**, H989
Eze 14:21 plague—to kill its men and their **a**! H989
Eze 31: 6 all the **a** *of* the wild gave birth under its H2651
Eze 31:13 all the wild **a** lived among its H2651
Eze 32: 4 on you and all the **a** *of* the wild gorge H2651
Eze 33:27 I will give to the **wild a** to be devoured, H2651
Eze 34: 3 with the wool and slaughter the **choice** *a*, AIT
Eze 34: 5 they became food for all the wild **a**. H2651
Eze 34: 8 has become food for all the wild **a**, H2651
Eze 34:28 the nations, nor will wild **a** devour them. H2651
Eze 36:11 the number of people and **a** living on you, H989
Eze 39: 4 all kinds of carrion birds and to the wild **a**. H2651
Eze 39:17 to every kind of bird and all the wild **a**: H2651
Eze 39:18 all of them **fattened** *a from* Bashan. H5309
Eze 44:31 animal, found dead or **torn by wild a**. H3274
Da 4:12 Under it the wild **a** found shelter, and A10263
Da 4:14 Let the **a** flee from under it and the birds A10263
Da 4:15 him live with the **a** among the plants of A10263
Da 4:21 giving shelter to the wild **a**, and having A10263
Da 4:23 let him live with the wild **a**, until seven A10263
Da 4:25 people and will live with the wild **a**; A10263
Da 4:32 people and will live with the wild **a**; A10263
Hos 2:12 a thicket, and wild **a** will devour them. H2651
Joel 1:20 Even the wild **a** pant for you; the streams of H989
Joel 2:22 be afraid, you wild **a**, for the pastures in H989
Jnh 3: 7 Do not let people or **a**, herds or flocks H989
Jnh 3: 8 But let people and **a** be covered with H989
Jnh 4:11 hand from their left—and also many **a**?" H989
Hab 2:17 your destruction of **a** will terrify you. H989
Zec 2: 4 of the great number of people and **a** in it. H989
Zec 8:10 were no wages for people or hire for **a**. H989
Zec 14:15 donkeys, and all the **a** in those camps. H989
Mal 1: 8 When you offer **blind** *a* for sacrifice, is that AIT
Mal 1: 8 When you sacrifice lame or **diseased** *a*, is AIT
Mal 1:13 lame or **diseased** *a* and offer them as AIT
Mk 1:13 He was with the **wild a**, and angels *G2563*
Ac 10:12 It contained all kinds of **four-footed a**, as *G5488*
Ac 11: 6 into it and saw **four-footed a** of the earth, *G5488*
Ac 15:20 *from* the *meat of* **strangled** *a* and from blood. AIT
Ac 15:29 *from the meat of* **strangled** *a* and from sexual AIT
Ac 21:25 *from the meat of* **strangled** *a* and from sexual AIT
Ro 1:23 being and birds and **a** and reptiles. *G5488*
1Co 15:39 one kind of flesh, **a** have another, birds *G3229*
Heb 13:11 carries the blood *of* **a** into the Most Holy *G2442*
Jas 3: 7 All kinds *of* **a**, birds, reptiles and sea *G2563*
2Pe 2:12 They are like unreasoning **a**, creatures of *G2442*
2Pe 2:12 destroyed, and like **a** they too will perish. *G899S*
Jude 10 as irrational **a** do—will destroy them. *G2442*

ANIMOSITY (1)

Jdg 9:23 God stirred up **a** between Abimelek H8273+8120

ANISE (KJV) DILL

ANKLE-DEEP (1) [ANKLES, DEEP]

Eze 47: 3 then led me through water that was **a**. H701

ANKLES (4) [ANKLE-DEEP, ANKLETS]

2Sa 22:37 my feet, so that my **a** do not give way. H7972
Ps 18:36 my feet, so that my **a** do not give way. H7972
Isa 3:16 with ornaments jingling on their **a**. H8079
Ac 3: 7 the man's feet and **a** became strong. *G5383*

ANKLETS (1) [ANKLES]

Isa 3:20 the headdresses and **a** and sashes, the H7578

ANNA (1)

Lk 2:36 was also a prophet, **A**, the daughter of *G483*

ANNALS (40)

1Ki 11:41 written in the book of the **a** *of* Solomon? H1821
1Ki 14:19 in the book of the **a** of the kings of H1821+3427
1Ki 14:29 in the book of the **a** of the kings of H1821+3427
1Ki 15: 7 in the book of the **a** of the kings of H1821+3427
1Ki 15:23 in the book of the **a** of the kings of H1821+3427
1Ki 15:31 in the book of the **a** of the kings of H1821+3427
1Ki 16: 5 in the book of the **a** of the kings of H1821+3427
1Ki 16:14 in the book of the **a** of the kings of H1821+3427
1Ki 16:20 in the book of the **a** of the kings of H1821+3427
1Ki 16:27 in the book of the **a** of the kings of H1821+3427
1Ki 22:39 in the book of the **a** of the kings of H1821+3427
1Ki 22:45 in the book of the **a** of the kings of H1821+3427
2Ki 1:18 in the book of the **a** of the kings of H1821+3427
2Ki 8:23 in the book of the **a** of the kings of H1821+3427

2Ki 10:34 in the book of the a of the kings of H1821+3427
2Ki 12:19 in the book of the a of the kings of H1821+3427
2Ki 13: 8 in the book of the a of the kings of H1821+3427
2Ki 13:12 in the book of the a of the kings of H1821+3427
2Ki 14:15 in the book of the a of the kings of H1821+3427
2Ki 14:18 in the book of the a of the kings of H1821+3427
2Ki 14:28 in the book of the a of the kings of H1821+3427
2Ki 15: 6 in the book of the a of the kings of H1821+3427
2Ki 15:11 in the book of the a of the kings of H1821+3427
2Ki 15:15 in the book of the a of the kings of H1821+3427
2Ki 15:21 in the book of the a of the kings of H1821+3427
2Ki 15:26 in the book of the a of the kings of H1821+3427
2Ki 15:31 in the book of the a of the kings of H1821+3427
2Ki 15:36 in the book of the a of the kings of H1821+3427
2Ki 16:19 in the book of the a of the kings of H1821+3427
2Ki 20:20 in the book of the a of the kings of H1821+3427
2Ki 21:17 in the book of the a of the kings of H1821+3427
2Ki 21:25 in the book of the a of the kings of H1821+3427
2Ki 23:28 in the book of the a of the kings of H1821+3427
2Ki 24: 5 in the book of the a of the kings of H1821+3427
1Ch 27:24 in the book of the a of King David. H1821+3427
2Ch 20:34 are written in the a *of* Jehu son of Hanani, H1821
2Ch 33:18 are written in the a *of* the kings of Israel. H1821
Ne 12:23 were recorded in the book of the a. H1821+3427
Est 2:23 the book of the a in the presence H1821+3427
Est 10: 2 in the book of the a of the kings of H1821+3427

ANNAS (4)
Lk 3: 2 the high-priesthood *of* **A** and Caiaphas, *G484*
Jn 18:13 brought him first to **A**, who was the *G484*
Jn 18:24 Then **A** sent him bound to Caiaphas the *G484*
Ac 4: 6 **A** the high priest was there, and so were *G484*

ANNIHILATE (6) [ANNIHILATED, ANNIHILATION]
Dt 9: 3 you will drive them out and a them quickly, H6
2Sa 21: 2 Israel and Judah had tried to a them.) H5782
2Ch 20:23 from Mount Seir to destroy and a them. H9012
Est 3:13 to destroy, kill and a all the Jews—young H6
Est 8:11 kill and a the armed men of any nationality H6
Da 11:44 out in a great rage to destroy and a many. H3049

ANNIHILATED (2) [ANNIHILATE]
2Ch 32:21 *who* a all the fighting men and the H3948
Est 7: 4 have been sold to be destroyed, killed and a. H6

ANNIHILATION (1) [ANNIHILATE]
Est 4: 8 a copy of the text of the edict for their a, H9012

ANNIVERSARY (1)
Dt 16: 6 on the a *of* your departure from Egypt. H4595

ANNOTATIONS (2) [NOTE]
2Ch 13:22 are written in the a *of* the prophet Iddo. H4535
2Ch 24:27 are written in the a *on* the book of the H4535

ANNOUNCE (13) [ANNOUNCED, ANNOUNCEMENT, ANNOUNCES, ANNOUNCING]
Jdg 7: 3 Now a to the army, 'Anyone who trembles H7924
Isa 42: 9 they spring into being *I* a them *to* you." H9048
Isa 48:20 **A** this with shouts of joy and proclaim it H5583
Jer 4: 5 "**A** in Judah and proclaim in Jerusalem H5583
Jer 5:20 "**A** this to the descendants of Jacob and H5583
Jer 18: 7 If at any time *I* a that a nation or kingdom H1819
Jer 18: 9 And if at another time *I* a that a nation H1819
Jer 46:14 "**A** this in Egypt, and proclaim it in Migdol H5583
Jer 48:20 **A** by the Arnon that Moab is destroyed H5583
Jer 50: 2 "**A** and proclaim among the nations, lift H5583
Jer 51:31 follows messenger to a to the king of H5583
Zec 9:12 even now I a that I will restore twice as H5583
Mt 6: 2 *do* not a it **with trumpets**, as the *G4895*

ANNOUNCED (13) [ANNOUNCE]
Ex 32: 5 he built an altar in front of the calf and a H7924
Lev 23:44 So Moses a to the Israelites the H1819
Ru 4: 9 Then Boaz a to the elders and all the H606
1Ki 20:13 prophet came to Ahab king of Israel and a, H606
2Ki 10:10 LORD has done what *he* a through his H1819
Isa 48: 3 my mouth a them and I made them H3655
Isa 48: 5 they happened *I* a them *to* you so that H9048
La 1:21 you bring the day *you have* a so they may H7924
Da 4:17 " 'The decision is a *by* messengers, the A10141
Lk 23: 4 Then Pilate a to the chief priests and the *G3306*
Gal 3: 8 and **a the gospel in advance** to Abraham: *G4603*
Heb 2: 3 which *was* first a by the Lord *G3284+3281*
Rev 10: 7 just as *he* a to his servants the prophets." *G2294*

ANNOUNCEMENT (1) [ANNOUNCE]
Isa 48:16 "From the first a I have not spoken in secret NDT

ANNOUNCES (3) [ANNOUNCE]
Dt 13: 1 among you and a to you a sign or H5989
Job 36:33 His thunder a the coming storm; even the H5583
Ps 68:11 The Lord a the word, and the women who H5989

ANNOUNCING (2) [ANNOUNCE]
Jer 4:15 A voice *is* a from Dan, proclaiming H5583
Ac 10:36 **a the good news** of peace through Jesus *G2294*

ANNOYANCE (1) [ANNOYED]
Pr 12:16 Fools show their a at once, but the H4088

ANNOYED (1) [ANNOYANCE]
Ac 16:18 Finally Paul *became so* a that he turned *G1387*

ANNUAL (7) [ANNUALLY]
Ex 30:10 This a atonement must H285+928+2021+9102
Jdg 21:19 there is the a festival of H4946+3427+3427+2025
1Sa 1:21 family to offer the a sacrifice to the LORD H3427
1Sa 2:19 with her husband to offer the a sacrifice. H3427
1Sa 20: 6 because an a sacrifice is being made H3427
2Ch 8:13 the three a festivals— H7193+928+2021+9102
Heb 10: 3 sacrifices are an a reminder of sins. *G2848+1929*

ANNUALLY (2) [ANNUAL]
2Ch 24: 5 money **due** a from all H4946+1896+9102+928+9102
Est 9:21 celebrate a the H928+3972+9102+2256+9102

ANNULLED (1) [NULLIFY]
Isa 28:18 Your covenant with death *will* **be** a; your H4105

ANOINT (28) [ANOINTED, ANOINTING]
Ex 28:41 Aaron and his sons, a and ordain them. H5417
Ex 29: 7 anointing oil and a him by pouring it on H5417
Ex 29:36 atonement for it, and a it to consecrate it. H5417
Ex 30:26 Then use it *to* a the tent of meeting, the H5417
Ex 30:30 "**A** Aaron and his sons and consecrate H5417
Ex 40: 9 anointing oil and a the tabernacle and H5417
Ex 40:10 Then a the altar of burnt offering and all H5417
Ex 40:11 **A** the basin and its stand and consecrate H5417
Ex 40:13 a him and consecrate him so he may H5417
Ex 40:15 A them just as you anointed their father H5417
Jdg 9: 8 trees went out to a a king for themselves H5417
Jdg 9:15 'If you really *want to* a me king over you H5417
1Sa 9:16 **A** him ruler over my people Israel; he will H5417
1Sa 15: 1 one the LORD sent to a you king over his H5417
1Sa 16: 3 *You are to* a for me the one I indicate." H5417
1Sa 16:12 LORD said, "Rise and a him; this is the one H5417
1Ki 1:34 *have* Zadok the priest and Nathan the prophet a H5417
1Ki 19:15 you get there, a Hazael king over Aram. H5417
1Ki 19:16 a Jehu son of Nimshi king over Israel H5417
1Ki 19:16 a Elisha son of Shaphat from Abel H5417
2Ki 9: 3 the LORD says: *I* a you king over Israel H5417
2Ki 9: 6 '*I* a you king over the LORD's people Israel H5417
2Ki 9:12 the LORD says: *I* a you king over Israel H5417
Ps 23: 5 of my enemies. *You* a my head with oil H2014
Ecc 9: 8 in white, and always a your head *with* oil. H6584
Da 9:24 prophecy and to a the Most Holy Place H5417
Mk 16: 1 so that they might go *to* a Jesus' body. *G230*
Jas 5:14 pray over them and a them with oil in the *G230*

ANOINTED (83) [ANOINT]
Ge 31:13 where *you* a a pillar and where you made H5417
Ex 29:29 so that they *can be* a and ordained in H5417
Ex 40:15 Anoint them just as *you* a their father, so H5417
Lev 4: 3 " 'If the a priest sins, bringing guilt on the H5431
Lev 4: 5 Then the a priest shall take some of the H5431
Lev 4:16 Then the a priest is to take some of the H5431
Lev 6:20 are to bring to the LORD on the day he *is* a: H5417
Lev 6:22 is to succeed him as a priest shall prepare H5431
Lev 7:36 On the day they *were* a, the LORD H5417
Lev 8:10 anointing oil and a the tabernacle and H5417
Lev 8:12 on Aaron's head and a him to consecrate H5417
Lev 16:32 The priest who *is* a and ordained to H5417
Nu 3: 3 of Aaron's sons, the a priests, who were H5417
Nu 7: 1 *he* a and consecrated it and all its H5417
Nu 7: 1 *He* also a and consecrated the altar and H5417
Nu 7:10 When the altar *was* a, the leaders H5417
Nu 7:84 the dedication of the altar when it **was** a: H5417
Nu 7:88 the dedication of the altar after it **was** a. H5417
Nu 35:25 high priest, who *was* a with the holy oil. H5417
1Sa 2:10 to his king and exalt the horn of his a." H5431
1Sa 2:35 they will minister before my a *one* always. H5431
1Sa 10: 1 "*Has* not the LORD a you ruler over his H5417
1Sa 12: 3 me in the presence of the LORD and his a. H5431
1Sa 12: 5 and also his a is witness this day H5431
1Sa 15:17 The LORD a you king over Israel. H5417
1Sa 16: 6 "Surely the LORD's a stands here before H5431
1Sa 16:13 the horn of oil and a him in the presence H5417
1Sa 24: 6 the LORD's a, or lay my hand on H5431
1Sa 24: 6 hand on him; for he is the a *of* the LORD." H5431
1Sa 24:10 on my lord, because he is the LORD's a. H5431
1Sa 26: 9 a hand on the LORD's a and be guiltless? H5431
1Sa 26:11 that I should lay a hand on the LORD's a. H5431
1Sa 26:16 did not guard your master, the LORD's a. H5431
1Sa 26:23 I would not lay a hand on the LORD's a. H5431
2Sa 1:14 to lift your hand to destroy the LORD's a?" H5431
2Sa 1:16 you when you said, 'I killed the LORD's a.' H5431
2Sa 2: 4 there *they* a David king over the tribe H5417
2Sa 2: 7 people of Judah *have* a me king over H5417
2Sa 3:39 though I *am* the a king, I am weak, H5417
2Sa 5: 3 and *they* a David king over Israel. H5417
2Sa 5:17 heard that David *had been* a king over H5417
2Sa 12: 7 'I a you king over Israel, and I delivered H5417
2Sa 19:10 Absalom, whom *we* a to rule over us H5417
2Sa 19:21 to death for this? He cursed the LORD's a." H5431
2Sa 22:51 he shows unfailing kindness to his a, to H5431
2Sa 23: 1 the man a *by* the God of Jacob H5431
1Ki 1:39 oil from the sacred tent and a Solomon. H5417
1Ki 1:45 the prophet *have* a him king at Gihon H5417
1Ki 5: 1 that Solomon *had been* a king to succeed H5417
2Ki 11:12 *They* a him, and the people clapped their H5417
2Ki 23:30 son of Josiah and a him and made him H5417
1Ch 11: 3 the LORD, and *they* a David king over Israel H5417
1Ch 14: 8 heard that David *had* **been** a king over all H5417
1Ch 16:22 "Do not touch my a *ones*; do my prophets H5431
2Ch 6:42 do not reject your a *one*. Remember the H5431
2Ch 22: 7 whom the LORD *had* a to destroy the house H5417
2Ch 23:11 *They* a him and shouted, "Long live the H5417
Ps 2: 2 against the LORD and against his a, H5431
Ps 18:50 he shows unfailing love to his a, to David H5431
Ps 20: 6 The LORD gives victory to his a. H5431
Ps 28: 8 a fortress of salvation for his a *one*. H5431
Ps 45: 2 your lips *have* **been** a *with* grace, H3668
Ps 84: 9 look with favor on your a *one*. H5431
Ps 89:20 servant; with my sacred oil *I have* a him. H5417
Ps 89:38 you have been very angry with your a *one*. H5431
Ps 89:51 have mocked every step of your a *one*. H5431
Ps 105:15 "Do not touch my a *ones*; do my prophets H5431
Ps 132:10 servant David, do not reject your a *one*. H5431
Ps 132:17 David and set up a lamp for my a *one*. H5431
Isa 45: 1 "This is what the LORD says to his a, to H5431
Isa 61: 1 because the LORD *has* a me to proclaim H5417
La 4:20 The LORD's a, our very life breath, was H5431
Eze 28:14 You were a as a guardian cherub, for so I H4937
Da 9:25 rebuild Jerusalem until the **A** *One*, H5431
Da 9:26 ' the **A** *One* will be put to death and will H5431
Hab 3:13 to deliver your people, to save your a *one*. H5431
Zec 4:14 the two *who are* a to serve H3658+1201+2021
Mk 6:13 out many demons and a many sick people *G230*
Lk 4:18 because *he has* a me to proclaim good *G5987*
Ac 4:26 against the Lord and against his a *one*. *G5986*
Ac 4:27 your holy servant Jesus, whom *you* a. *G5987*
Ac 10:38 how God a Jesus of Nazareth with the *G5987*
2Co 1:21 us and you stand firm in Christ. *He* a us, *G5987*

ANOINTING (30) [ANOINT]
Ex 25: 6 spices for the a oil and for the fragrant H5418
Ex 29: 7 Take the a oil and anoint him by pouring H5418
Ex 29:21 altar and some of the a oil and sprinkle it H5418
Ex 30:25 Make these into a sacred a oil, a fragrant H5418
Ex 30:25 of a perfumer. It will be the sacred a oil. H5418
Ex 30:31 is to be my sacred a oil for the H5418
Ex 31:11 the a oil and fragrant incense for the H5418
Ex 35: 8 spices for the a oil and for the fragrant H5418
Ex 35:15 the a oil and the fragrant incense H5418
Ex 35:28 the light and for the a oil and for the H5418
Ex 37:29 also made the sacred a oil and the pure, H5418
Ex 39:38 the gold altar, the a oil, the fragrant H5418
Ex 40: 9 "Take the a oil and anoint the tabernacle H5418
Ex 40:15 Their a will be to a priesthood that will H5420
Lev 8: 2 their garments, the a oil, the bull for the H5418
Lev 8:10 Then Moses took the a oil and anointed H5418
Lev 8:11 a the altar and all its utensils and the H5417
Lev 8:12 poured some of the a oil on Aaron's head H5418
Lev 8:30 took some of the a oil and some of the H5418
Lev 10: 7 because the LORD's a oil is on you. H5418
Lev 21:10 who has had the a oil poured on his head H5418
Lev 21:12 been dedicated by the a oil of his God. H5418
Nu 4:16 the regular grain offering and the a oil. H5418
1Ch 29:22 a him before the LORD to be ruler and H5417
Ps 45: 7 your companions by a you with the oil of H5417
Heb 1: 9 your companions *by* a you with the oil of *G5987*
1Jn 2:20 But you have an a from the Holy One, and *G5984*
1Jn 2:27 the a you received from him remains in *G5984*
1Jn 2:27 But as his a teaches you about all things *G5984*
1Jn 2:27 you about all things and as that a is real, NDT

ANON (KJV) AT ONCE, IMMEDIATELY

ANOTH See BETH ANOTH

ANOTHER (368) [ANOTHER'S]
Ge 4:25 "God has granted me a child in place of H337
Ge 8:19 of the ark, **one kind after a**. H4200+5476+2157
Ge 9: 5 the life of a human being. H2021[S]
Ge 25: 1 Abraham had taken a wife, whose name H3578
Ge 26:21 Then they dug a well, but they quarreled H337
Ge 26:22 He moved on from there and dug a well H337
Ge 29:27 in return for a seven years of work." H6388+337
Ge 29:30 he worked for Laban a seven years. H6388+337
Ge 30:24 said, "May the LORD add to me a son." H337
Ge 35:17 "Don't despair, for you have a son." H1685
Ge 37: 9 Then he had a dream, and he told it H337+6388
Ge 37: 9 he said, "I had a dream, and this time the H6388
Ge 38: 5 gave birth to **still** a son and named H3578+6388
Ge 42:21 They said to one a, "Surely we are being H278[S]
Ge 43: 6 me by telling the man you had a brother?" H6388
Ge 43: 7 'Do you have a brother?' We simply NDT
Ex 12:16 and a *one* on the seventh day. H5246+7731[S]
Ex 21:10 If he marries a *woman*, he must not deprive H337
Ex 21:18 one person hits a with a stone or H8276[S]
Ex 25: 5 dyed red and a **type** *of* durable leather; H9391[S]
Ex 26: 9 one set and the other six **into a set**. H4200+963
Ex 35: 7 dyed red and a **type** *of* durable leather; H9391[S]
Ex 36:16 into one set and the other six into *a* **set**. AIT
Ex 39:34 the covering of a durable leather and H9391[S]
Lev 13: 5 he is to isolate them for a seven days. H9108
Lev 13:33 is to keep them isolated a seven days. H9108
Lev 13:54 Then he is to isolate it for a seven days. H9108
Lev 19:11 " 'Do not deceive one a. H6660[S]
Lev 19:20 who is promised to a man but who has not NDT
Lev 20:10 man commits adultery with a man's wife— NDT
Lev 26:37 will stumble over one a as though fleeing H278[S]
Lev 27:10 if they should substitute one animal for a H989[S]
Nu 5: 6 who wrongs a in any way and H2021+132[S]
Nu 5:13 so that a man has sexual relations with her NDT
Nu 23:13 "Come with me to a place where you can H337

Nu 23:27 let me take you to a place. H337
Nu 35:15 who has killed a accidentally can flee H5883S
Nu 35:20 shoves a or throws something H5647S
Nu 35:21 enmity one person hits a with their fist so H2084
Nu 35:22 suddenly pushes a or throws something H2257S
Nu 36: 7 in Israel is to pass from one tribe to a, H4751S
Nu 36: 9 may pass from one tribe to a, H4751S
Dt 4:34 take for himself one nation out of a nation, NDT
Dt 22:22 a man is found sleeping with a man's wife, NDT
Dt 22:24 man because he violated a *man's* wife. H8276S
Dt 24: 2 his house she becomes the wife of a man, H337
Dt 28:30 a woman, but a will take her and rape her. H337
Dt 28:32 daughters will be given to a nation, H337
Dt 29:28 from their land and thrust them into a land, H337
Jdg 2:10 a generation grew up who knew neither H337
Jdg 11: 2 "because you are the son of a woman." H337
Jdg 19:10 unwilling to stay a night, the man left NDT
Jdg 19:30 Everyone who saw it was saying to one a NDT
Jdg 20:22 encouraged **one a** and again took H2021+6639
Jdg 20:25 they cut down a eighteen thousand H6388
Ru 1: 9 will find rest in the home of a husband." H2023S
Ru 1:12 daughters; I am too old to have a husband. NDT
Ru 2: 8 Don't go and glean in a field and don't go H337
Ru 3:12 there is a *who is* more closely related H1457S
1Sa 2:25 If one person sins against a, God may H408
1Sa 10: 3 young goats, a three loaves of bread H285S
1Sa 10: 3 loaves of bread, and a a skin of wine. H285S
1Sa 13:18 a toward Beth Horon, and the third toward H285S
1Sa 17: 3 hill and the Israelites a, H2021+2215+4946+2296S
2Sa 3:11 did not dare to say a word to Abner, H6388
2Sa 11:25 the sword devours one as well as a. H2296S
2Sa 18:20 "You may take the news a time, but you H337
2Sa 18:26 Then the watchman saw a runner, and he H337
2Sa 18:26 gatekeeper, "Look, a man running alone!" NDT
2Sa 21:18 there was a battle with the Philistines H6388
2Sa 21:19 In a battle with the Philistines at Gob H6388
2Sa 21:20 In **still** a battle, which took place at Gath H6388
1Ki 11:23 God raised up against Solomon a adversary, NDT
1Ki 13:10 So he took a road and did not return by the H337
1Ki 18: 6 going in one direction and Obadiah in a. H285S
1Ki 20:10 Then Ben-Hadad sent a message to Ahab NDT
1Ki 20:37 The prophet found a man and said, "Strike H337
1Ki 21: 6 I will give you a vineyard in its place. NDT
1Ki 22:20 ' "One suggested this, and a that. H2296S
2Ki 1:11 king sent to Elijah a captain with his fifty H337
2Ki 4: 6 she said to her son, "Bring me a one." H6388
2Ki 7: 6 so that they said to one a, "Look, H278S
2Ki 7: 8 returned and entered a tent and took some H337
1Ch 2:26 Jerahmeel had a wife, whose name was H337
1Ch 7:15 **A** descendant was named Zelophehad H9108
1Ch 16:20 nation to nation, from one kingdom to a. H337
1Ch 17: 5 I have moved from one tent site to a, from H185S
1Ch 17: 5 to another, from one dwelling place to a. NDT
1Ch 20: 5 In a battle with the Philistines, Elhanan H6388
1Ch 20: 6 In **still** a battle, which took place at Gath H6388
2Ch 15: 6 was being crushed by a and one city by H1580S
2Ch 15: 6 crushed by another and one city by a, H6551S
2Ch 18:19 ' "One suggested this, and a that. H2296S
2Ch 20:23 from Seir, they helped to destroy one a. H8276S
2Ch 30:23 so for a seven days they celebrated joyfully. NDT
2Ch 32: 5 He built a wall outside that one and H337
Ne 3:11 Pahath-Moab repaired a section and the H9108
Ne 3:19 of Mizpah, repaired a section, from a H9108
Ne 3:20 of Zabbai zealously repaired a section, H9108
Ne 3:21 of Hakkoz, repaired a section, from the H9108
Ne 3:24 Binnui son of Henadad repaired a section, H9108
Ne 3:27 the men of Tekoa repaired a section, from H9108
Ne 3:30 sixth son of Zalaph, repaired a section. H9108
Ne 9: 3 spent a quarter in confession and in NDT
Est 2:14 return to a **part** *of* the harem to the H9108
Est 4:14 the Jews will arise from a place, H337
Est 8: 8 Now write a decree in the king's name in NDT
Est 9:22 of food to one a and gifts to the poor. H8276S
Job 1:16 speaking, **a messenger** came and said H2296S
Job 1:17 speaking, **a messenger** came and said H2296
Job 1:18 yet **a messenger** came and said H2296S
Job 2: 1 On a day the angels came to present H2021S
Job 19:27 see him with my own eyes—I, and not a. H2424
Job 21:25 **A** dies in bitterness of soul, never having H2296S
Job 31:10 then may my wife grind a *man's* grain, and H337
Job 33:14 now one way, now a—though no one H9109
Job 41:17 They are joined fast to one a; they cling H278S
Ps 49: 7 can redeem the life of a or give to God a H278S
Ps 75: 7 He brings one down, he exalts a. H2296S
Ps 105:13 nation to nation, from one kingdom to a. H337
Ps 109: 8 may a take his place of leadership. H337
Ps 145: 4 generation commends your works to a; H1887S
Pr 5:10 your toil enrich the house of a. H5799
Pr 5:20 my son, be intoxicated with a *man's wife*? H2424
Pr 6:26 but a **man's** wife preys on your very life. AIT
Pr 6:29 So is he who sleeps with a *man's* wife H8276S
Pr 11:24 gains even more; *a* **withholds** unduly, but AIT
Pr 13: 7 has nothing; **a pretends to be poor**, yet has AIT
Pr 23:35 will I wake up so I can find a drink?" H3578+6388
Pr 27:17 so one person sharpens a. H8276S
Pr 28: 8 it for *a, who will be* **kind** *to* the poor. AIT
Ecc 2:21 leave all they own to a who has not toiled H132
Ecc 4: 4 spring from one person's envy of a. H8276S
Ecc 6: 1 I have seen a evil under the sun, and it NDT
Ecc 7:27 "Adding one thing to a to discover the H285S
Isa 6: 3 And they were calling to one a: "Holy H2296S
Isa 9:19 fuel for the fire; they will not spare one a. H278S
Isa 42: 8 not yield my glory to a or my praise to idols H337
Isa 48:11 I will not yield my glory to a. H337
Isa 65:15 to his servants he will give a name. H337
Isa 66:23 From one New Moon to a and from one H2544S
Isa 66:23 to another and from one Sabbath to a, H8701S
Jer 3: 1 she leaves him and marries a man, H337
Jer 3:16 not be missed, nor will a one be made. H6388
Jer 5: 8 stallions, each neighing for a *man's* wife. H8276
Jer 9: 3 They go from one sin to a; they do not H8288S
Jer 9:20 how to wail; teach one a a lament. H8295S
Jer 18: 4 so the potter formed it into a pot, shaping H337
Jer 18: 9 And if **at a time** I announce that a nation H8092
Jer 22: 8 will pass by this city and will ask one a, H8276S
Jer 22:26 mother who gave you birth into a country, H337
Jer 23:27 they tell one a will make my people H8276S
Jer 23:30 who steal from one a words supposedly H8276S
Jer 26:20 Kiriath Jearim was a man who prophesied H1685
Jer 31:34 neighbor, or say to one a, 'Know the LORD,' H278S
Jer 36:28 "Take a scroll and write on it all the words H337
Jer 36:32 So Jeremiah took a scroll and gave it to the H337
Jer 46:12 One warrior will stumble over a; both H1475S
Jer 48:11 not poured from one jar to a—she has H3998S
Jer 51:31 One courier follows a and messenger H8132S
Jer 51:46 this year, a the next, rumors H2021+9019S
Eze 1: 9 the wings of one touched the wings of a. H295S
Eze 12: 3 out and go from where you are to a place. H337
Eze 17: 7 " 'But there was a great eagle with H285
Eze 19: 5 she took a of her cubs and made him a H285S
Eze 21:20 of the Ammonites and a against Judah NDT
Eze 22:11 a shamefully defiles his daughter-in-law H408
Eze 22:11 daughter-in-law, and a violates his sister H408
Eze 34:17 I will judge between one sheep and a H8445S
Eze 34:22 I will judge between one sheep and a. H8445S
Eze 37:16 ' Then take a stick of wood, and write on it, H285S
Eze 40:44 a at the side of the south gate and H285
Eze 41: 6 one above a, thirty on each level. H7521S
Eze 41:11 one on the north and a on the south; and H285S
Eze 46:21 and I saw in each corner a court. NDT
Eze 47: 4 He measured off a thousand cubits and led NDT
Eze 47: 4 He measured off a thousand and led me NDT
Eze 47: 5 He measured off a thousand, but now it was NDT
Da 2:39 "After you, a kingdom will arise, inferior A10023
Da 2:44 destroyed, nor will it be left to a people. A10025
Da 7: 6 there before me was a beast, one A10023
Da 7: 8 there before me was a horn, a little one, A10023
Da 7:24 After them a king will arise, different A10025
Da 8: 9 Out of one of them came a horn, which H285S
Da 8:13 one speaking, and a holy one said to him H285S
Da 11:13 the king of the North will muster a army, H8740
Hos 1: 8 weaned Lo-Ruhamah, Gomer had a son. NDT
Hos 3: 1 she is loved by a *man* and is an H8276
Hos 4: 4 let no one accuse a, for your people are like NDT
Am 4: 7 rain on one town, but withheld it from a. H285S
Am 4: 7 field had rain; a had none and dried up. H2754S
Hag 2:15 stone was laid on a in the LORD's temple. H74S
Zec 2: 3 was leaving, a angel came to meet him H337
Zec 7: 9 show mercy and compassion to one a. H278S
Zec 8:21 of one city will go to a and say, H285S
Zec 14:13 other by the hand and attack one a. H8276S
Mal 2:10 ancestors by being unfaithful to one a? H278S
Mal 2:13 **A** thing you do: You flood the LORD's altar H9108
Mt 2:12 they returned to their country by a route. *G257*
Mt 8:21 **A** disciple said to him, "Lord, first let me *G2283*
Mt 10:23 are persecuted in one place, flee to a. *G2283*
Mt 13:24 Jesus told them a parable: "The kingdom *G257*
Mt 13:31 He told them a parable: "The kingdom of *G257*
Mt 13:33 He told them *still* a parable: "The kingdom *G257*
Mt 19: 9 marries a *woman* commits adultery." *G257*
Mt 21:33 "Listen to a parable: There was a *G257*
Mt 21:33 to some farmers and **moved to a place**. *G623*
Mt 21:35 beat one, killed a, and stoned a *G4005+1254*
Mt 22: 5 one to his field, a to his business. *G4005+1254*
Mt 24: 2 not one stone here will be left on a *G3345S*
Mt 25:15 bags of gold, *to* a two bags, and to *G4005+1254*
Mt 25:15 another two bags, and *to* a one bag, each *G4005*
Mt 25:32 the people **one** from a as a shepherd *G253*
Mt 26:71 where a servant *girl* saw him and said to *G257*
Mk 3: 1 **A time** Jesus went into the synagogue *G4099*
Mk 8: 1 During those days a large crowd gathered. *G4099*
Mk 8:16 They discussed this with **one a** and said, "It *G253*
Mk 10:11 wife and marries a *woman* commits *G257*
Mk 10:12 divorces her husband and marries a *man*, *G257*
Mk 12: 1 to some farmers and **moved to a place**. *G623*
Mk 12: 4 Then he sent a servant to them; they struck *G257*
Mk 12: 5 He sent still a, and that one they killed. He *G257*
Mk 12: 7 "But the tenants said to **one a**, 'This is the *G1571*
Mk 13: 2 "Not one stone here will be left on a *G3345S*
Mk 14: 4 present were saying indignantly to **one a**, *G1571*
Mk 14:58 hands and in three days will build a, *G257*
Lk 2:15 the shepherds said to **one a**, "Let's go to *G253*
Lk 6: 6 On a Sabbath he went into the *G2283*
Lk 6:11 to discuss with **one a** what they might do *G253*
Lk 8: 1 about **from one** town and village **to a**, *G2848*
Lk 8:25 In fear and amazement they asked **one a** *G253*
Lk 9:56 he and his disciples went to a village. *G2283*
Lk 9:59 He said to a *man*, "Follow me." But he *G2283*
Lk 9:61 Still a said, "I will follow you, Lord; but *G2283*
Lk 12: 1 so that they were trampling on **one a** *G253*
Lk 14:19 "**A** said, 'I have just bought five yoke of *G2283*
Lk 14:20 "Still a said, 'I just got married, so I can't *G2283*
Lk 14:31 king is about to go to war against a king. *G2283*
Lk 16:18 wife and marries a *woman* commits *G2283*
Lk 19:20 "Then a servant came and said, 'Sir, here *G2283*
Lk 19:44 They will not leave one stone on a *G3345S*
Lk 20:11 He sent a servant, but that one also they *G2283*
Lk 21: 6 when not one stone will be left on a; *G3345S*
Lk 22:59 About an hour later a asserted *G257+5516*
Jn 4:37 the saying 'One sows and a reaps' is true. *G257*
Jn 5:32 There is a who testifies in my favor, and I *G257*
Jn 5:44 accept glory from **one a** but do not seek the *G253*
Jn 6: 8 **A** of his disciples, Andrew, Simon Peter's *G1651*
Jn 7:35 The Jews said to **one a**, "Where does this *G1571*
Jn 11:56 in the temple courts they asked **one a**, *G253*
Jn 12:19 So the Pharisees said to **one a**, "See, this *G1571*
Jn 13:22 His disciples stared at **one a**, at a loss to *G253*
Jn 13:34 Love **one a**. As I have loved you, *G253*
Jn 13:34 I have loved you, so you must love **one a**. *G253*
Jn 13:35 that you are my disciples, if you love **one a**." *G253*
Jn 14:16 he will give you a advocate to help you *G257*
Jn 16:17 some of his disciples said to **one a**, "What *G253*
Jn 16:19 "Are you asking **one a** what I meant when I *G253*
Jn 18:15 Simon Peter and a disciple were following *G257*
Jn 18:36 now my kingdom is **from a place**." *G4024+1949*
Jn 19:24 they said to **one a**. "Let's decide by lot *G253*
Jn 19:37 as a scripture says, "They will look on *G2283*
Ac 1:20 " 'May a take his place of leadership.' *G2283*
Ac 2:12 they asked **one a**, "What does *G257+4639+257*
Ac 12:17 he said, and then he left for a place. *G2283*
Ac 17: 7 saying that there is a king, one called *G2283*
Ac 19:32 one thing, some a. Most of the people did *G257*
Ac 21:34 the crowd shouted one thing and some a, *G257*
Ac 22:19 that I went **from one** synagogue **to a** to *G2848*
Ac 26:11 I went **from one** synagogue **to a** to *G2848+4246*
Ac 26:31 they began saying to **one a**, "This man is *G253*
Ro 1:24 the degrading of their bodies with **one a**. *G899*
Ro 1:27 were inflamed with lust for **one a**. *G253*
Ro 2: 1 at whatever point you judge a, you are *G2283*
Ro 7: 3 relations with a man while her husband *G2283*
Ro 7: 3 is not an adulteress if she marries a man. *G2283*
Ro 7: 4 that you might belong *to* a, to him who *G2283*
Ro 7:23 I see a law at work in me, waging war *G2283*
Ro 12:10 Be devoted to **one a** in love. Honor one *G253*
Ro 12:10 Honor **one a** above yourselves. *G253*
Ro 12:16 Live in harmony with **one a**. Do not be *G253*
Ro 13: 8 except the continuing debt to love **one a** *G253*
Ro 14: 2 eat anything, but a, whose faith is weak *G3836*
Ro 14: 5 considers one day more sacred than a; *G2465S*
Ro 14: 5 a considers every day alike. *G4005+1254*
Ro 14:13 let us stop passing judgment *on* **one a**. *G253*
Ro 15: 7 Accept **one a**, then, just as Christ accepted *G253*
Ro 15:14 competent to instruct **one a**. *G253*
Ro 16:12 *a woman* **who** has worked very hard in the AIT
Ro 16:16 Greet **one a** with a holy kiss. All the *G253*
1Co 1:10 all *of you* **agree** *with one a* **in what** *you* **say** AIT
1Co 1:12 "I follow Paul"; a, "I follow Apollos"; *G1254*
1Co 1:12 "I follow Apollos"; a, "I follow Cephas"; *G1254*
1Co 1:12 "I follow Cephas"; **still**, a, "I follow Christ." *G1254*
1Co 3: 4 "I follow Paul," and a, "I follow Apollos," *G2283*
1Co 6: 1 If any of you has a dispute with a, do you *G2283*
1Co 6: 6 one brother takes a to court—and this in *G81S*
1Co 7: 7 one has this gift, a has that. *G3836+1254*
1Co 11:21 person remains hungry and a gets drunk. *G4005*
1Co 12: 8 *to* a a message of knowledge by means of *G257*
1Co 12: 9 *to* a faith by the same Spirit, to another *G2283*
1Co 12: 9 *to* a gifts of healing by that one Spirit *G257*
1Co 12:10 *to* a miraculous powers, to another *G257*
1Co 12:10 miraculous powers, *to* a prophecy, to *G257*
1Co 12:10 *to* a distinguishing between spirits *G257*
1Co 12:10 *to* a speaking in different kinds of tongues *G2283*
1Co 12:10 and *to* still a the interpretation of tongues. *G257*
1Co 15:39 of flesh, animals have a, birds another *G257*
1Co 15:39 have another, birds a and fish another. *G257*
1Co 15:39 have another, birds another and fish a. *G257*
1Co 15:40 the splendor of the earthly bodies is a. *G2283*
1Co 15:41 splendor, the moon a and the stars another *G257*
1Co 15:41 the moon another and the stars a; and star *G257*
1Co 16:20 you greetings. Greet **one a** with a holy kiss. *G253*
2Co 2: 1 I would not make a painful visit to you. *G4099*
2Co 2: 9 **A** reason I wrote you was to see if you *G2779*
2Co 13:11 restoration, **encourage** *one a*, be of one AIT
2Co 13:12 Greet **one a** with a holy kiss. *G253*
Gal 5:13 rather, serve **one a** humbly in love. *G253*
Eph 4: 2 be patient, bearing with **one a** in love. *G253*
Eph 4:32 Be kind and compassionate to **one a** *G253*
Eph 5:19 speaking *to* **one a** with psalms, hymns *G1571*
Eph 5:21 Submit *to* **one a** out of reverence for Christ. *G253*
Php 2: 5 **In your relationships with one a** *G1877+5148*
Col 3:13 other and forgive **one a** if any of you has *G1571*
Col 3:16 admonish **one a** with all wisdom *G1571*
1Th 4: 9 Now about your **love for one a** we do not *G5789*
1Th 4:18 encourage **one a** with these words. *G253*
1Th 5:11 Therefore encourage **one a** and build each *G253*
2Th 1: 3 love all of you have for **one a** is increasing. *G253*
Titus 3: 3 envy, being hated and hating **one a**. *G253*
Heb 3:13 But encourage **one a** daily, as long as it is *G1571*
Heb 4: 8 would not have spoken later about a day. *G257*
Heb 5: 6 And he says in a *place*, "You are a priest *G2283*
Heb 7:11 was there still need for a priest to come, *G2283*
Heb 7:15 is even more clear if a priest like *G2283*
Heb 8: 7 no place would have been sought *for* a. *G1311*
Heb 8:11 neighbor, or say *to* **one a**, 'Know the Lord,' *G81*
Heb 10:24 how we may spur **one a** on toward love *G253*
Heb 10:25 encouraging one a—and all the more NDT
Heb 13: 1 **on loving one a as brothers and sisters**. *G5789*

Jas 4:11 do not slander **one a**. Anyone who speaks *G253*
Jas 5: 9 Don't grumble against **one a**, brothers and *G253*
1Pe 1:22 each other, love **one a** deeply, from the *G253*
1Pe 3: 8 be sympathetic, **love one a**, be *G5790*
1Pe 4: 9 Offer hospitality to **one a** without grumbling. *G253*
1Pe 5: 5 yourselves with humility *toward* **one a**, *G253*
1Pe 5:14 Greet **one a** with a kiss of love. Peace to all *G253*
1Jn 1: 7 we have fellowship with **one a**, and the *G253*
1Jn 3:11 from the beginning: We should love **one a**. *G253*
1Jn 3:23 to love **one a** as he commanded us. *G253*
1Jn 4: 7 let us love **one a**, for love comes *G253*
1Jn 4:11 so loved us, we also ought to love **one a**. *G253*
1Jn 4:12 but if we love **one a**, God lives in us *G253*
2Jn 5 the beginning. I ask that we love **one a**. *G253*
Rev 6: 4 Then **a** horse came out, a fiery red one. Its *G257*
Rev 7: 2 Then I saw **a** angel coming up from the *G257*
Rev 8: 3 **A** angel, who had a golden censer, came *G257*
Rev 10: 1 Then I saw **a** mighty angel coming down *G257*
Rev 12: 3 Then **a** sign appeared in heaven: an *G257*
Rev 14: 6 Then I saw **a** angel flying in midair, and he *G257*
Rev 14:15 Then **a** angel came out of the temple and *G257*
Rev 14:17 **A** angel came out of the temple in heaven *G257*
Rev 14:18 Still **a** angel, who had charge of the fire *G257*
Rev 15: 1 I saw in heaven **a** great and marvelous *G257*
Rev 18: 1 After this I saw **a** angel coming down from *G257*
Rev 18: 4 Then I heard **a** voice from heaven say: *G257*
Rev 20:12 **A** book was opened, which is the book of *G257*

ANOTHER'S (5) [ANOTHER]

Pr 25: 9 to court, do not betray **a** confidence, H337
Jer 19: 9 they will eat one **a** flesh because their H8276S
Zec 11: 9 Let those who are left eat one **a** flesh." H8295S
Jn 13:14 your feet, you also should wash **one a** feet. *G253*
1Co 10:29 my freedom being judged by **a** conscience? *G257*

ANSWER (161) [ANSWERABLE, ANSWERED, ANSWERING, ANSWERS]

Ge 41:16 "but God *will* **give** Pharaoh *the* **a** he H6699
Ge 45: 3 But his brothers were not able to **a** him H6699
Ge 46:34 *you should* **a**, 'Your servants have tended H606
Ex 19: 8 So Moses brought their **a** back to the LORD. H1821
Nu 22: 8 back to you with the **a** the LORD gives me." H1821
Dt 29:25 And *the* **a** *will be*: "It is because this H606
Jos 22:28 this to us, or to our descendants, *we will* **a**: H606
Jdg 5:29 The wisest of her ladies **a** her; indeed H6699
Jdg 14:12 "If *you can* **give** me *the* **a** within H5583+5583
Jdg 14:13 If you can't **tell** me *the* **a**, you must give H5583
Jdg 14:14 For three days they could not give the **a**. H2648
Jdg 14:16 a riddle, but *you* haven't **told** me *the* **a**." H5583
Jdg 19:28 But there was no **a**. Then the man put H6699
1Sa 2:16 the servant *would* **a**, "No, hand it H606
1Sa 8:18 the LORD *will* not **a** you in that day. H6699
1Sa 14:37 But God *did* not **a** him that day. H6699
1Sa 26:14 "Aren't *you going to* **a** me, Abner? H6699
1Sa 28: 6 the LORD *did* not **a** him by dreams or H6699
2Sa 14:18 keep from me the **a** to what I am going to H1821
2Sa 15: 2 *He would* **a**, "Your servant is from one of H606
2Sa 20:18 to say, '**Get** *your* **a** at Abel,' and H8626+8626
2Sa 22:42 save them—to the LORD, but *he did* not **a**. H6699
2Sa 24:13 decide how *I should* **a** the one who H8740+1821
1Ki 9: 9 *People will* **a**, 'Because they have forsaken H606
1Ki 12: 6 you advise me to **a** these people?" H8740+1821
1Ki 12: 7 them and **give** them **a** favorable **a**, H1819+1821
1Ki 12: 9 How *should we* **a** these people H8740+1821
1Ki 14: 5 *you are to* **give** her such and such **an a**. H1819
1Ki 18:26 "Baal, **a** us!" they shouted. H6699
1Ki 18:37 **A** me, LORD, answer me, so these people H6699
1Ki 18:37 **a** me, so these people will know H6699
1Ki 20: 9 left and took the **a** back to Ben-Hadad. H1821
2Ki 4:29 and if anyone greets you, *do* not **a**. H6699
2Ki 18:36 the king had commanded, "*Do* not **a** him." H6699
2Ki 22:20 So they took her **a** back to the king. H1821
1Ch 21:12 decide how *I should* **a** the one who H8740+1821
2Ch 7:22 *People will* **a**, 'Because they have forsaken H606
2Ch 10: 6 you advise me to **a** these people?" H8740+1821
2Ch 10: 7 them and **give** them **a** favorable **a**, H1819+1821
2Ch 10: 9 How *should we* **a** these people H8740+1821
2Ch 34:28 So they took her **a** back to the king. H1821
Ezr 5:11 This is the **a** they gave us: "We are the A10601
Ne 6: 4 each time I gave them the same **a**. H1821
Est 4:13 he sent back *this* **a**: "Do not think that H606
Est 5: 8 Then *I will* **a** the king's question. H6913
Job 5: 1 you will, but *who will* **a** you? To which of H6699
Job 9: 3 *they could* not **a** him one time out of a H6699
Job 9:15 I were innocent, *I could* not **a** him; I could H6699
Job 9:32 a mere mortal like me that *I might* **a** him, H6699
Job 13:22 Then summon me and I *will* **a**, or let me H6699
Job 14:15 You will call and I *will* **a** you; you will H6699
Job 15: 2 "*Would* a wise person **a** *with* empty H6699
Job 19:16 servant, but *he does* not **a**, though I beg H6699
Job 20: 2 thoughts **prompt** me **to a** because I am H8740
Job 23: 5 I would find out what *he would* **a** me, and H6699
Job 30:20 God, but *you do* not **a**; I stand up H6699
Job 31:14 What *will I* **a** when called to account? H8740
Job 31:35 defense—*let* the Almighty **a** me; let my H6699
Job 32:14 and *I will* not **a** him with your arguments. H8740
Job 33: 5 **A** me then, if you can; stand up and H8740
Job 33:32 you have anything to say, **a** me; speak up, H8740
Job 35:12 *He does* not **a** when people cry out H6699
Job 38: 3 I will question you, and *you shall* **a** me. H3359
Job 40: 2 *Let him* who accuses God **a** him!" H6699
Job 40: 5 spoke once, but *I* **have** no **a**—twice, but I H6699
Job 40: 7 I will question you, and *you shall* **a** me. H3359
Job 42: 4 I will question you, and *you shall* **a** me. H3359
Ps 4: 1 **A** me when I call to you, my righteous H6699
Ps 13: 3 Look on me and **a**, LORD my God. Give H6699
Ps 17: 6 my God, for *you will* **a** me; turn your ear to H6699
Ps 18:41 save them—to the LORD, but *he did* not **a**. H6699
Ps 20: 1 *May* the LORD **a** you when you are in H6699
Ps 20: 9 victory to the king! **A** us when we call! H6699
Ps 22: 2 I cry out by day, but *you do* not **a**, by night, H6699
Ps 27: 7 LORD; be merciful to me and **a** me. H6699
Ps 38:15 I wait for you; you *will* **a**, Lord my God. H6699
Ps 55: 2 hear me and **a** me. My thoughts trouble H6699
Ps 65: 2 You *who* **a** prayer, to you all people will H9048
Ps 65: 5 *You* **a** us with awesome and righteous H6699
Ps 69:13 **a** me with your sure salvation. H6699
Ps 69:16 **A** me, LORD, out of the goodness of your H6699
Ps 69:17 from your servant; **a** me quickly, for I am H6699
Ps 86: 1 Hear me, LORD, and **a** me, for I am poor H6699
Ps 86: 7 distress, I call to you, because *you* **a** me. H6699
Ps 91:15 call on me, and *I will* **a** him; I will be with H6699
Ps 102: 2 your ear to me; when I call, **a** me quickly. H6699
Ps 119:42 then *I can* **a** anyone who taunts me H6699+1821
Ps 119:145 with all my heart; **a** me, LORD, and I will H6699
Ps 143: 7 **A** me quickly, LORD; my spirit fails. Do not H6699
Pr 1:28 "Then they will call to me but *I will* not **a** H6699
Pr 15: 1 A gentle **a** turns away wrath, but a harsh H5101
Pr 16: 1 LORD comes the *proper* **a** *of* the tongue. H5101
Pr 18:13 *To* **a** before listening—that is folly H8740+1821
Pr 18:23 plead for mercy, but the rich **a** harshly. H6699
Pr 24:26 An honest **a** is like a kiss on the H8740+1821
Pr 26: 4 *Do* not **a** a fool according to his folly, or H6699
Pr 26: 5 **A** a fool according to his folly, or he will H6699
Pr 26:16 eyes than seven *people who* **a** discreetly. H8740
Pr 27:11 then *I can* **a** anyone who treats me H8740+1821
Pr 31: 2 my son, the **a to** my **prayers**! H5624
Ecc 10:19 and money *is the* **a** *for* everything. H6699
SS 5: 6 I called him but *he did* not **a**. H6699
Isa 14:32 What **a** *shall be* **given** *to* the envoys of H6699
Isa 21: 9 And *he* **gives back** *the* **a**: 'Babylon H6699
Isa 29:11 please," *they will* **a**, "I can't; it is H606
Isa 29:12 *they will* **a**, "I don't know how to H606
Isa 30:19 As soon as he hears, *he will* **a** you. H6699
Isa 36:21 the king had commanded, "*Do* not **a** him." H6699
Isa 41:17 But I the LORD *will* **a** them; I, the God of H6699
Isa 41:28 no one to give **a** when I ask them. H1821
Isa 46: 7 cries out to it, *it* cannot **a**; it cannot save H6699
Isa 49: 8 "In the time of my favor *I will* **a** you, and H6699
Isa 50: 2 I called, why was there no *one to* **a**? H6699
Isa 58: 9 and the LORD *will* **a**; you will cry for H6699
Isa 65:12 I called but *you did* not **a**, I spoke but H6699
Isa 65:24 Before they call I *will* **a**; while they are H6699
Jer 7:13 not listen; I called you, but *you did* not **a**. H6699
Jer 7:27 when you call to them, *they will* not **a**. H6699
Jer 22: 9 And *the* **a** *will be*: 'Because they have H606
Jer 23:35 'What *is* the LORD's **a**?' or 'What has H6699
Jer 23:37 'What *is* the LORD's **a** *to* you?' or H6699
Jer 33: 3 'Call to me and *I will* **a** you and tell you H6699
Jer 35:17 I called to them, but *they did* not **a**. H6699
Jer 38:15 Zedekiah, "If *I* **give** you **an a**, will you not H5583
Eze 14: 4 I the LORD *will* **a** them myself in keeping H6699
Eze 14: 7 I the LORD *will* **a** them myself. H6699
Hos 14: 8 I *will* **a** him and care for him H6699
Mic 3: 4 cry out to the LORD, but *he will* not **a** them. H6699
Mic 3: 7 faces because there is no **a** *from* God." H5101
Mic 6: 3 How have I burdened you? **A** me. H6699
Hab 2: 1 what **a** *I am to* **give** to this complaint. H8740
Zec 10: 6 I am the LORD their God and *I will* **a** them. H6699
Zec 13: 6 ' *they will* **a**, 'The wounds I was given at the H606
Zec 13: 9 will call on my name and I *will* **a** them; H6699
Mt 15:23 Jesus *did* not **a** a word. So his disciples *G646*
Mt 21:24 If *you* **a** me, I will tell you by what *G3306*
Mt 25:37 "Then the righteous *will* **a** him, 'Lord, when *G646*
Mt 25:44 "*They* also *will* **a**, 'Lord, when did we see *G646*
Mt 26:62 said to Jesus, "*Are you* not *going to* **a**? *G646*
Mt 27:12 chief priests and the elders, *he* **gave** no **a**. *G646*
Mk 11:29 **A** me, and I will tell you by what authority I *G646*
Mk 12:28 that Jesus *had* **given** them **a** good **a**, *G646*
Mk 14:60 asked Jesus, "*Are you* not *going to* **a**? *G646*
Mk 14:61 But Jesus remained silent and **gave** no **a** *G646*
Mk 15: 4 Pilate asked him, "Aren't *you going to* **a**? *G646*
Lk 13:25 ' "But *he will* **a**, 'I don't know you or where *G646*
Lk 20:26 And astonished by his **a**, they became *G647*
Lk 22:68 if I asked you, *you would* not **a**. *G646*
Lk 23: 9 many questions, but Jesus **gave** him no **a**. *G646*
Jn 1:22 Give us an **a** to take back to those who sent *G647*
Jn 5:19 Jesus **gave** them *this* **a**: "Very truly I tell you *G646*
Jn 18:22 "Is this the way *you* **a** the high priest?" *G646*
Jn 19: 9 he asked Jesus, but Jesus gave him no **a**. *G647*
Ac 12:13 servant named Rhoda came *to* **a** the door. *G5634*
Ro 11: 4 And what was **God's a** to him? "I have *G5977*
1Co 4:13 are slandered, *we* **a kindly**. We have *G4151*
2Co 1:11 favor granted us **in a to** the prayers of *G1328*
2Co 5:12 so that *you can* **a** those who take *G2400+4639*
Col 4: 6 so that you may know how *to* **a** everyone. *G646*
Phm 22 to be restored to you **in a to** your prayers. *G1328*
1Pe 3:15 prepared to give an **a** to everyone who asks *G665*

ANSWERABLE (1) [ANSWER]

Mt 5:22 a brother or sister, 'Raca,' is **a** to the court. *G1944*

ANSWERED (393) [ANSWER]

Ge 3:10 *He* **a**, "I heard you in the garden, and I was H606
Ge 16: 8 away from my mistress Sarai," *she* **a**. H606
Ge 18: 5 "Very well," *they* **a**, "do as you say." H606
Ge 18:30 can be found there?" *He* **a**, "I will not do it H606
Ge 18:32 *He* **a**, "For the sake of ten, I will not H606
Ge 19: 2 *they* **a**, "we will spend the night in the H606
Ge 22: 8 Abraham **a**, "God himself will provide the H606
Ge 23:14 Ephron **a** Abraham, H6699
Ge 24:24 *She* **a** him, "I am the daughter of Bethuel H606
Ge 24:50 Laban and Bethuel **a**, "This is from the H6699
Ge 24:65 the servant **a**. So she took her veil H606
Ge 25:21 The LORD **a** his **prayer**, and his wife H6983
Ge 26: 9 Isaac **a** him, "Because I thought I might H606
Ge 26:28 *They* **a**, "We saw clearly that the LORD was H606
Ge 27: 1 said to him, "My son." "Here I am," *he* **a**. H606
Ge 27:18 "Yes, my son," *he* **a**. "Who is it? H606
Ge 27:32 "I am your son," *he* **a**, "your firstborn, Esau H606
Ge 27:37 Isaac **a** Esau, "I have made him lord over H6699
Ge 27:39 His father Isaac **a** him, "Your dwelling will H6699
Ge 29: 5 "Yes, we know him," *they* **a**. H606
Ge 31:11 me in the dream, 'Jacob.' *I* **a**, 'Here I am.' H606
Ge 31:31 Jacob **a** Laban, "I was afraid, because I H6699
Ge 31:43 Laban **a** Jacob, "The women are my H6699
Ge 32:27 "What is your name?" "Jacob," *he* **a**. H606
Ge 33: 5 Jacob **a**, "They are the children God has H606
Ge 35: 3 who **a** me in the day of my distress and H6699
Ge 37:17 have moved on from here," the man **a**. H606
Ge 38:18 and the staff in your hand," *she* **a**. H606
Ge 40: 8 *they* **a**, "but there is no one to interpret H606
Ge 42:10 my lord," *they* **a**. "Your servants have H606
Ge 43: 7 ' *We* simply **a** his questions H5583
Ge 44:20 And *we* **a**, 'We have an aged father, and H606
Ex 1:19 The midwives **a** Pharaoh, "Hebrew women H606
Ex 2: 8 go," she **a**. So the girl went and got H606
Ex 2:19 *They* **a**, "An Egyptian rescued us from the H606
Ex 4: 1 Moses **a**, "What if they do not believe me H6699
Ex 8:29 Moses **a**, "As soon as I leave you, I will H606
Ex 10: 9 Moses **a**, "We will go with our young and H606
Ex 14:13 Moses **a** the people, "Do not be afraid H606
Ex 17: 5 The LORD **a** Moses, "Go out in front of the H606
Ex 18:15 Moses **a** him, "Because the people come H606
Ex 19:19 Moses spoke and the voice of God **a** him. H6699
Ex 32: 2 Aaron **a** them, "Take off the gold earrings H606
Ex 32:22 my lord," Aaron **a**. "You know how prone H606
Nu 9: 8 Moses **a** them, "Wait until I find out what H606
Nu 10:30 *He* **a**, "No, I will not go; I am going back to H606
Nu 11:23 The LORD **a** Moses, "Is the LORD's arm too H606
Nu 20:18 But Edom **a**: "You may not pass through H606
Nu 20:20 Again *they* **a**: "You may not pass through." H606
Nu 22:18 But Balaam **a** them, "Even if Balak gave H6699
Nu 22:29 Balaam **a** the donkey, "You have made a H606
Nu 23:12 *He* **a**, "Must I not speak what the LORD H6699
Nu 23:26 Balaam **a**, "Did I not tell you I must do H6699
Nu 24:12 Balaam **a** Balak, "Did I not tell the H606
Nu 32:31 The Gadites and Reubenites **a**, "Your H6699
Dt 1:14 *You* **a** me, "What you propose to do is H6699
Jos 1:16 Then *they* **a** Joshua, "Whatever you have H6699
Jos 9: 9 *They* **a**: "Your servants have come from a H606
Jos 9:19 all the leaders **a**, "We have given them H606
Jos 9:24 *They* **a** Joshua, "Your servants were H6699
Jos 17:15 Joshua **a**, "and if the hill country of H606
Jos 24:16 Then the people **a**, "Far be it from us to H6699
Jdg 1: 2 The LORD **a**, "Judah shall go up; I have H606
Jdg 6:16 The LORD **a**, "I will be with you, and you H606
Jdg 8: 2 But *he* **a** them, "What have I accomplished H606
Jdg 8: 8 they **a** as the men of Sukkoth had. H6699
Jdg 8:18 *they* **a**, "each one with the bearing of a H606
Jdg 8:25 *They* **a**, "We'll be glad to give them." H606
Jdg 9: 9 "But the olive tree **a**, 'Should I give up my H606
Jdg 9:13 "But the vine **a**, 'Should I give up my wine H606
Jdg 11: 9 Jephthah **a**, "Suppose you take me back to H606
Jdg 11:13 of the Ammonites **a** Jephthah's H606
Jdg 12: 2 Jephthah **a**, "I and my people were H606
Jdg 13:13 The angel of the LORD **a**, "Your wife must H606
Jdg 13:23 his wife **a**, "If the LORD had meant to kill H606
Jdg 15:10 Samson prisoner," *they* **a**, "to do to him as H606
Jdg 15:11 *He* **a**, "I merely did to them what they did H606
Jdg 15:13 "Agreed," *they* **a**. "We will only tie you up H606
Jdg 16: 7 Samson **a** her, "If anyone ties me with H606
Jdg 18: 6 The priest **a** them, "Go in peace. Your H606
Jdg 18: 9 *They* **a**, "Come on, let's attack them! We H606
Jdg 18:19 *They* **a** him, "Be quiet! Don't say a word H606
Jdg 18:25 The Danites **a**, "Don't argue with us, or H606
Jdg 19:18 *He* **a**, "We are on our way from Bethlehem H606
Jdg 20:23 The LORD **a**, "Go up against them. H606
Ru 2: 4 "The LORD bless you!" *they* **a**. H606
Ru 3: 5 "I will do whatever you say," Ruth **a**. H606
1Sa 1:17 Eli **a**, "Go in peace, and may the God of H6699
1Sa 3: 4 called Samuel. Samuel **a**, "Here I am." H606
1Sa 3:16 "Samuel, my son." Samuel **a**, "Here I am." H606
1Sa 5: 8 *They* **a**, "Have the ark of the god of Israel H606
1Sa 6: 3 *They* **a**, "If you return the ark of the god of H606
1Sa 7: 9 on Israel's behalf, and the LORD **a** him. H6699
1Sa 8:22 The LORD **a**, "Listen to them and give them H606
1Sa 9: 8 The servant **a** him again. "Look," he said H6699
1Sa 9:12 *they* **a**. "He's ahead of you. Hurry H6699
1Sa 9:21 Saul **a**, "But am I not a Benjamite, from H6699
1Sa 10:12 A man who lived there **a**, "And who is H6699
1Sa 14:41 "Why *have you* not **a** your servant today? H6699
1Sa 15:15 Saul **a**, "The soldiers brought them from H606
1Sa 16:11 the youngest," Jesse **a**. "He is tending the H606
1Sa 16:18 One of the servants **a**, "I have seen a son H6699
1Sa 17:30 and the men **a** him as before. H8740+1821

1Sa 20:28 Jonathan a, "David earnestly asked me H6699
1Sa 21: 2 David a Ahimelek the priest, "The king H606
1Sa 21: 4 But the priest a David, "I don't have any H6699
1Sa 22:12 son of Ahitub." "Yes, my lord," he a. H606
1Sa 22:14 Ahimelek a the king, "Who of all your H6699
1Sa 23: 2 The LORD a him, "Go, attack the Philistines H606
1Sa 23: 4 and the LORD a him, "Go down to H6699
1Sa 25:10 Nabal a David's servants, "Who is this H6699
1Sa 26:22 king's spear," David a. "Let one of your H6699
1Sa 29: 9 Achish a, "I know that you have been as H6699
1Sa 30: 8 "Pursue them," he a. "You will certainly H606
1Sa 30:15 He a, "Swear to me before God that you H606
2Sa 1: 3 He a, "I have escaped from the Israelite H606
2Sa 1: 8 'Who are you?' " 'An Amalekite,' I a. H606
2Sa 1:13 son of a foreigner, an Amalekite," he a. H606
2Sa 2: 1 "To Hebron," the LORD a. H606
2Sa 2:20 "Is that you, Asahel?" "It is," he a. H606
2Sa 2:27 Joab a, "As surely as God lives, if you had H606
2Sa 3: 8 So he a, "Am I a dog's head—on Judah's H606
2Sa 4: 9 David a Rekab and his brother Baanah H6699
2Sa 5:19 The LORD a him, "Go, for I will surely H606
2Sa 5:23 of the LORD, and he a, "Do not go straight H606
2Sa 9: 3 Ziba a the king, "There is still a son of H606
2Sa 9: 4 Ziba a, "He is at the house of Makir son of H606
2Sa 12:22 He a, "While the child was still alive, I H606
2Sa 14:19 The woman a, "As surely as you live, my H6699
2Sa 15:15 The king's officials a him, "Your servants H606
2Sa 16: 2 Ziba a, "The donkeys are for the king's H606
2Sa 16:21 Ahithophel a, "Sleep with your father's H606
2Sa 17:20 The woman a them, "They crossed over H606
2Sa 18: 4 The king a, "I will do whatever seems best H606
2Sa 18:29 Ahimaaz a, "I saw great confusion just as H606
2Sa 19:34 But Barzillai a the king, "How many more H606
2Sa 19:42 All the men of Judah a the men of Israel H6699
2Sa 19:43 the men of Israel a the men of Judah, H6699
2Sa 20:17 "I am," he a. She said, "Listen H606
2Sa 21: 4 The Gibeonites a him, "We have no right H606
2Sa 21: 5 They a the king, "As for the man who H606
2Sa 21:14 God a prayer in behalf of the land. H6983
2Sa 24:21 David a, "so I can build an altar to the H606
2Sa 24:25 Then the LORD a his prayer in behalf of the H6983
1Ki 1:36 Benaiah son of Jehoiada a the king H6699
1Ki 1:43 Jonathan a. "Our lord King David H6699
1Ki 2:13 come peacefully?" He a, "Yes, peacefully." H606
1Ki 2:22 King Solomon a his mother, "Why do you H6699
1Ki 2:30 ' " But he a, "No, I will die here. H606
1Ki 2:30 to the king, "This is how Joab a me." H6699
1Ki 2:38 Shimei a the king, "What you say is good H606
1Ki 3: 6 Solomon a, "You have shown great H606
1Ki 10: 3 Solomon a all her questions; nothing was H5583
1Ki 12: 5 Rehoboam a, "Go away for three days and H606
1Ki 12:13 The king a the people harshly. Rejecting H6699
1Ki 12:16 to listen to them, they a the king: H8740+1821
1Ki 13: 8 But the man of God a the king, "Even if you H606
1Ki 13:18 The old prophet a, "I too am a prophet, as H606
1Ki 18:26 no response; no one a. And they danced H6699
1Ki 18:29 was no response, no one a, no one paid H6699
1Ki 20: 4 The king of Israel a, "Just as you say, my H6699
1Ki 20: 8 The elders and the people all a, "Don't H606
1Ki 20:11 The king of Israel a, "Tell him: 'One who H6699
1Ki 20:14 The prophet a, "You will." H606
1Ki 20:32 ' " The king a, "Is he still alive? He H606
1Ki 21: 6 He a her, "Because I said to Naboth the H1819
1Ki 21:20 he a, "because you have sold yourself to H606
1Ki 22: 6 they a, "for the Lord will give it into the H606
1Ki 22: 8 The king of Israel a Jehoshaphat, "There is H606
1Ki 22:15 he a, "for the LORD will give it into the H606
1Ki 22:17 Then Micaiah a, "I saw all Israel scattered H606
2Ki 1:10 Elijah a the captain, "If I am a man of H6699
2Ki 3: 8 "Through the Desert of Edom," he a. H606
2Ki 3:11 An officer of the king of Israel a, "Elisha H6699
2Ki 3:13 the king of Israel a, "because it was the H606
2Ki 4:43 But Elisha a, "Give it to the people H606
2Ki 5:16 The prophet a, "As surely as the LORD lives H606
2Ki 5:22 is all right," Gehazi a. "My master sent me H606
2Ki 5:25 servant didn't go anywhere," Gehazi a. H606
2Ki 6:16 the prophet a. "Those who are with H606
2Ki 6:22 "Do not kill them," he a. "Would you kill H606
2Ki 6:28 She a, "This woman said to me, 'Give up H606
2Ki 7: 2 with your own eyes," a Elisha, "but you will H606
2Ki 7:13 One of his officers a, "Have some men H6699
2Ki 8:10 Elisha a, "Go and say to him, 'You will H606
2Ki 8:12 harm you will do to the Israelites," he a. H606
2Ki 8:13 you will become king of Aram," a Elisha. H606
2Ki 10:15 "I am," Jehonadab a. "If so, H606
2Ki 20: 9 Isaiah a, "This is the LORD's sign to you that H606
1Ch 5:20 He a their prayers, because they trusted in H6983
1Ch 14:10 The LORD a him, "Go, I will deliver them H606
1Ch 14:14 of God again, and God a him, "Do not go H606
1Ch 21:26 the LORD a him with fire from heaven H6699
1Ch 21:28 saw that the LORD had a him on the H6699
2Ch 1: 8 Solomon a God, "You have shown great H606
2Ch 9: 2 Solomon a all her questions; nothing was H5583
2Ch 10: 5 Rehoboam a, "Come back to me in three H606
2Ch 10:13 The king a them harshly. Rejecting the H6699
2Ch 10:16 refused to listen to them, they a the king: H8740
2Ch 18: 5 they a, "for God will give it into the king's H606
2Ch 18: 7 The king of Israel a Jehoshaphat, "There is H606
2Ch 18:14 he a, "for they will be given into your H606
2Ch 18:16 Then Micaiah a, "I saw all Israel scattered H606
2Ch 31:10 the family of Zadok, a, "Since the people H606
2Ch 32:24 who a him and gave him a miraculous sign H606
Ezr 4: 3 rest of the heads of the families of Israel a, H606
Ezr 8:23 our God about this, and he a our prayer. H6983
Ne 2: 5 and I a the king, "If it pleases the king and H606
Ne 2:20 I a them by saying, "The God of H8740+1821
Est 6: 3 has been done for him," his attendants a. H606
Est 6: 5 His attendants a, "Haman is standing in H606
Est 6: 7 So he a the king, "For the man the king H606
Est 7: 3 Then Queen Esther a, "If I have found H6699
Est 9:13 Esther a, "give the Jews in Susa H606
Job 1: 7 Satan a the LORD, "From roaming H6699
Job 2: 2 Satan a the LORD, "From roaming H6699
Job 12: 4 though I called on God and he a—a H6699
Job 32:12 none of you has a his arguments. H6699
Job 40: 3 Then Job a the LORD: H6699
Ps 34: 4 the LORD, and he a me; he delivered me H6699
Ps 81: 7 rescued you, I a you out of a thundercloud H6699
Ps 99: 6 they called on the LORD and he a them. H6699
Ps 99: 8 LORD our God, you a them; you were to H6699
Ps 118:21 you thanks, for you a me; you have H6699
Ps 119:26 an account of my ways and you a me; H6699
Ps 138: 3 When I called, you a me; you greatly H6699
Pr 21:13 of the poor will also cry out and not be a. H6699
Isa 6:11 And he a: "Until the cities lie ruined H606
Isa 66: 4 For when I called, no one a, when I spoke, H6699
Jer 1:13 pot that is boiling," I a. "It is tilting toward H606
Jer 11: 5 you possess today." I a, "Amen, LORD." H6699
Jer 21: 3 But Jeremiah a them, "Tell Zedekiah, H606
Jer 24: 3 "Figs," I a. "The good ones are H606
Jer 38: 5 King Zedekiah a. "The king can do H606
Eze 9: 9 He a me, "The sin of the people of Israel H606
Da 2: 4 Then the astrologers a the king, "May the H1819
Da 2: 8 Then the king a, "I am certain that you A10558
Da 2:10 The astrologers a the king, "There is no A10558
Da 4:19 Belteshazzar a, "My lord, if only the A10558
Da 5:17 Then Daniel a the king, "You may keep A10558
Da 6:12 The king a, "The decree stands—in A10558
Da 6:21 Daniel a, "May the king live forever! A10425
Am 7:14 Amos a Amaziah, "I was neither a H6699
Am 8: 2 of ripe fruit," I a. Then the LORD said to H606
Jnh 1: 9 He a, "I am a Hebrew and I worship the H606
Jnh 2: 2 distress I called to the LORD, and he a me. H6699
Mic 6: 5 plotted and what Balaam son of Beor a. H6699
Hag 2:12 ' " The priests a, "No." H6699
Zec 1: 9 The angel who was talking with me a, "I H606
Zec 1:19 He a me, "These are the horns that H606
Zec 1:21 He a, "These are the horns that scattered H606
Zec 2: 2 He a me, "To measure Jerusalem, to find H606
Zec 4: 2 I a, "I see a solid gold lampstand with a H606
Zec 4: 5 He a, "Do you not know what these are?" H6699
Zec 5: 2 I a, "I see a flying scroll, twenty cubits H606
Zec 6: 5 The angel a me, "These are the four H6699
Mt 4: 4 Jesus a, "It is written: 'Man shall not live G646
Mt 4: 7 Jesus a him, "It is also written: 'Do not G5774
Mt 9:15 Jesus a, "How can the guests of the G3306
Mt 12: 3 He a, "Haven't you read what David did G3306
Mt 12:39 He a, "A wicked and adulterous generation G646
Mt 13:29 ' he a, 'because while you are G5774
Mt 13:37 He a, "The one who sowed the good seed G646
Mt 14:17 five loaves of bread and two fish," they a. G3306
Mt 15:24 He a, "I was sent only to the lost sheep of G646
Mt 15:33 His disciples a, "Where could we get G3306
Mt 16:16 Simon Peter a, "You are the Messiah, the G646
Mt 17:26 "From others," Peter a. "Then the children G3306
Mt 18:22 Jesus a, "I tell you, not seven times, but G3306
Mt 19:21 Jesus a, "If you want to be perfect, go G5774
Mt 19:27 Peter a him, "We have left everything to G646
Mt 20: 7 has hired us,' they a. "He said to them, G3306
Mt 20:13 "But he a one of them, 'I am not being G646
Mt 20:22 I am going to drink?" "We can," they a. G3306
Mt 20:33 they a, "we want our sight." G3306
Mt 21:11 The crowds a, "This is Jesus, the prophet G3306
Mt 21:27 So they a Jesus, "We don't know." Then he G646
Mt 21:29 " 'I will not,' he a, but later he changed his G646
Mt 21:30 the same thing. He a, 'I will, sir,' but he G646
Mt 21:31 "The first," they a. Jesus said to them, G3306
Mt 24: 4 Jesus a: "Watch out that no one deceives G646
Mt 26:25 Jesus a, "You have said so." G3306
Mt 26:34 I tell you," Jesus a, "this very night, before G5774
Mt 26:66 "He is worthy of death," they a. G646
Mt 27:21 asked the governor. "Barabbas," they a. G3306
Mt 27:22 Pilate asked. They all a, "Crucify him!" G3306
Mt 27:25 All the people a, "His blood is on us and G646
Mt 27:65 a guard," Pilate a. "Go, make the tomb as G5774
Mk 2:19 Jesus a, "How can the guests of the G3306
Mk 2:25 He a, "Have you never read what David G3306
Mk 5:31 his disciples a, "and yet you can ask G3306
Mk 6:24 "The head of John the Baptist," she a. G3306
Mk 6:37 But he a, "You give them something to eat." G646
Mk 8: 4 His disciples a, "But where in this remote G646
Mk 8:20 did you pick up?" They a, "Seven." G3306
Mk 8:29 Peter a, "You are the G646
Mk 9:17 A man in the crowd a, "Teacher, I brought G646
Mk 9:21 been like this?" "From childhood," he a. G3306
Mk 10:11 He a, "Anyone who divorces his wife and G3306
Mk 10:18 Jesus a. "No one is good— G3306
Mk 10:39 "We can," they a. Jesus said to them G3306
Mk 11: 6 They a as Jesus had told them to, and the G3306
Mk 11:22 "Have faith in God," Jesus a. G646
Mk 11:33 So they a Jesus, "We don't know." Jesus G646
Mk 12:29 most important one," a Jesus, "is this G646
Mk 12:34 When Jesus saw that he had a wisely, he G646
Mk 14:30 I tell you," Jesus a, "today—yes, tonight— G3306
Lk 1:35 The angel a, "The Holy Spirit will come on G646
Lk 1:38 servant," Mary a. "May your word to me G3306
Lk 3:11 John a, "Anyone who has two shirts should G646
Lk 3:16 John a them all, "I baptize you with water G646
Lk 4: 4 Jesus a, "It is written: 'Man shall not live G646
Lk 4: 8 Jesus a, "It is written: 'Worship the Lord G646
Lk 4:12 Jesus a, "It is said: 'Do not put the Lord G646
Lk 5: 5 Simon a, "Master, we've worked hard all G646
Lk 5:31 Jesus a them, "It is not the healthy who G646
Lk 5:34 Jesus a, "Can you make the friends of the G3306
Lk 6: 3 Jesus a them, "Have you never read what G646
Lk 7:40 Jesus a him, "Simon, I have something to G646
Lk 9:13 They a, "We have only five loaves of G3306
Lk 9:20 Peter a, "God's Messiah." G646
Lk 10:27 He a, " 'Love the Lord your God with all G646
Lk 10:28 "You have a correctly," Jesus replied. "Do G646
Lk 10:41 the Lord a, "you are worried and upset G646
Lk 11:45 One of the experts in the law a him G646
Lk 12:42 The Lord a, "Who then is the faithful and G3306
Lk 13: 2 Jesus a, "Do you think that these Galileans G646
Lk 13:15 The Lord a him, "You hypocrites! Doesn't G646
Lk 15:29 But he a his father, 'Look! All these years G646
Lk 16:27 "He a, 'Then I beg you, father, send G3306
Lk 18:19 Jesus a. "No one is good— G3306
Lk 19:19 His master a, 'You take charge of five G3306
Lk 20: 7 So they a, "We don't know where it was G646
Lk 22:34 Jesus a, "I tell you, Peter, before the G3306
Lk 22:35 did you lack anything?" "Nothing," they a. G3306
Lk 22:51 But Jesus a, "No more of this!" And he G646
Lk 22:67 Jesus a, "If I tell you, you will not believe G3306
Lk 23:43 Jesus a him, "Truly I tell you, today you G3306
Jn 1:21 "Are you the Prophet?" He a, "No." G646
Jn 1:48 Jesus a, "I saw you while you were still G646
Jn 2:19 Jesus a them, "Destroy this temple, and I G646
Jn 3: 5 Jesus a, "Very truly I tell you, no one can G646
Jn 4:10 Jesus a her, "If you knew the gift of God G646
Jn 4:13 Jesus a, "Everyone who drinks this water G646
Jn 6: 7 Philip a him, "It would take more than half G646
Jn 6:26 Jesus a, "Very truly I tell you, you are G646
Jn 6:29 Jesus a, "The work of God is this: to G646
Jn 6:43 grumbling among yourselves," Jesus a. G646
Jn 6:68 Simon Peter a him, "Lord, to whom shall G646
Jn 7:16 Jesus a, "My teaching is not my own. It G646
Jn 7:20 the crowd a. "Who is trying to kill you G646
Jn 8:14 Jesus a, "Even if I testify on my own behalf G646
Jn 8:33 They a him, "We are Abraham's G646
Jn 8:39 is our father," they a. "If you were G646
Jn 8:48 The Jews a him, "Aren't we right in saying G646
Jn 8:58 I tell you," Jesus a, "before Abraham was G3306
Jn 9:20 the parents a, "and we know he was born G646
Jn 9:27 He a, "I have told you already and you did G646
Jn 9:30 The man a, "Now that is remarkable! You G646
Jn 10:25 Jesus a, "I did tell you, but you do not G646
Jn 10:34 Jesus a them, "Is it not written in your Law G646
Jn 11: 9 Jesus a, "Are there not twelve hours of G646
Jn 11:24 Martha a, "I know he will rise again in the G3306
Jn 13: 8 Jesus a, "Unless I wash you, you have no G646
Jn 13:10 Jesus a, "Those who have had a bath G3306
Jn 13:26 Jesus a, "It is the one to whom I will give G646
Jn 13:38 Then Jesus a, "Will you really lay down G646
Jn 14: 6 Jesus a, "I am the way and the truth and G3306
Jn 14: 9 Jesus a: "Don't you know me, Philip, even G3306
Jn 18: 8 Jesus a, "I told you that I am he. If you are G646
Jn 18:37 Jesus a, "You say that I am a G646
Jn 19: 6 But Pilate a, "You take him and crucify G3306
Jn 19:11 Jesus a, "You would have no power over G646
Jn 19:15 no king but Caesar," the chief priests a. G646
Jn 19:22 Pilate a, "What I have written, I have G646
Jn 21: 5 haven't you any fish?" "No," they a. G646
Jn 21:16 He a, "Yes, Lord, you know that I love G3306
Jn 21:22 Jesus a, "If I want him to remain alive G3306
Ac 8:20 Peter a: "May your money perish with you G3306
Ac 8:24 Then Simon a, "Pray to the Lord for me so G646
Ac 9:10 in a vision, "Ananias!" "Yes, Lord," he a. G3306
Ac 9:13 Ananias a, "I have heard many reports G646
Ac 10: 4 The angel a, "Your prayers and gifts to G3306
Ac 10:30 Cornelius a: "Three days ago I was in my G5774
Ac 13:46 Then Paul and Barnabas a them boldly G4245
Ac 19: 2 They a, "No, we have not even heard that NDT
Ac 19:15 One day the evil spirit a them, "Jesus I G646
Ac 21:13 Then Paul a, "Why are you weeping and G646
Ac 21:39 Paul a, "I am a Jew, from Tarsus in Cilicia, G3306
Ac 22:27 you a Roman citizen?" "Yes, I am," he a. G5774
Ac 25: 4 Festus a, "Paul is being held at Caesarea G646
Ac 25:10 Paul a: "I am now standing before G3306
Rev 7:14 I a, "Sir, you know." And he said, "These G3306

ANSWERING (3) [ANSWER]

Job 32: 1 So these three men stopped a Job H6699
Job 34:36 to the utmost for a like a wicked man! H9588
Jer 44:20 both men and women, who were a him, H6699

ANSWERS (10) [ANSWER]

1Sa 20:10 will tell me if your father a you harshly?" H6699
1Sa 28:15 He no longer a me, either by prophets H6699
1Ki 18:24 The god who a by fire—he is God. H6699
Job 21:34 Nothing is left of your a but falsehood!" H9588
Ps 3: 4 and he a me from his holy mountain. H6699
Ps 20: 6 He a him from his heavenly sanctuary H6699
Ps 120: 1 on the LORD in my distress, and he a me. H6699
Pr 15:28 The heart of the righteous weighs its a H6699
Lk 2:47 amazed at his understanding and his a. G647

Lk 11: 7 And suppose the one inside a, 'Don't G646

ANT (1) [ANTS]
Pr 6: 6 Go to the a, you sluggard; consider its H5805

ANTELOPE (2)
Dt 14: 5 the ibex, the a and the mountain sheep. H9293
Isa 51:20 every street corner, like a caught in a net. H9293

ANTHOTHIJAH (1)
1Ch 8:24 Hananiah, Elam, A, H6746

ANTICHRIST (4) [ANTICHRISTS]
1Jn 2:18 as you have heard that the a is coming, G532
1Jn 2:22 Such a person is the a—denying the Father G532
1Jn 4: 3 This is the spirit of the a, which you have G532
2Jn 7 Any such person is the deceiver and the a. G532

ANTICHRISTS (1) [ANTICHRIST]
1Jn 2:18 is coming, even now many a have come. G532

ANTIOCH (21)
Ac 6: 5 Parmenas, and Nicolas from A, a convert to G523
Ac 11:19 Cyprus and A, spreading the word G522
Ac 11:20 went to A and began to speak to Greeks G522
Ac 11:22 in Jerusalem, and they sent Barnabas to A. G522
Ac 11:26 when he found him, he brought him to A. G522
Ac 11:26 disciples were called Christians first at A. G522
Ac 11:27 prophets came down from Jerusalem to A. G522
Ac 13: 1 Now in the church at A there were prophets G522
Ac 13:14 From Perga they went on to Pisidian A. On G522
Ac 14:19 Jews came from A and Iconium and won G522
Ac 14:21 they returned to Lystra, Iconium and A, G522
Ac 14:26 From Attalia they sailed back to A, where G522
Ac 15: 1 down from Judea to A and were teaching NDT
Ac 15:22 men and send them to A with Paul and G522
Ac 15:23 To the Gentile believers in A, Syria and G522
Ac 15:30 the men were sent off and went down to A, G522
Ac 15:35 But Paul and Barnabas remained in A G522
Ac 18:22 the church and then went down to A. G522
Ac 18:23 After spending some time in A, Paul set out NDT
Gal 2:11 When Cephas came to A, I opposed him to G522
2Ti 3:11 what kinds of things happened to me in A G522

ANTIPAS (1)
Rev 2:13 not even in the days of A, my faithful G525

ANTIPATRIS (1)
Ac 23:31 the night and brought him as far as A. G526

ANTS (1) [ANT]
Pr 30:25 A are creatures of little strength, yet they H5805

ANUB (1)
1Ch 4: 8 was the father of A and Hazzobebah and H6707

ANVIL (1)
Isa 41: 7 spurs on the one who strikes the a. H7193

ANXIETIES (1) [ANXIOUS]
Lk 21:34 drunkenness and the a of life, and that G3533

ANXIETY (7) [ANXIOUS]
Ps 94:19 When a was great within me, your H8595
Pr 12:25 A weighs down the heart, but a kind word H1796
Ecc 11:10 banish a from your heart and cast off the H4088
Eze 4:16 eat rationed food in a and drink rationed H1796
Eze 12:19 eat their food in a and drink their water H1796
Php 2:28 you may be glad and I may have less a. G267
1Pe 5: 7 Cast all your a on him because he cares G3533

ANXIOUS (4) [ANXIETIES, ANXIETY, ANXIOUSLY]
Dt 28:65 There the LORD will give you an a mind H8076
Ps 139:23 test me and know my a thoughts. H8595
Ecc 2:22 the toil and a striving with which H8301+4213
Php 4: 6 Do not be a about anything, but in every G3534

ANXIOUSLY (1) [ANXIOUS]
Lk 2:48 I have been a searching for you. G3849

ANY (584) [ANYBODY, ANYMORE, ANYONE, ANYONE'S, ANYTHING, ANYWHERE]
Ge 2:16 are free to eat from a tree in the garden; H3972
Ge 3: 1 more crafty than a of the wild animals H3972
Ge 3: 1 must not eat from a tree in the garden'?" H3972
Ge 6: 2 they married a of them they chose. H3972
Ge 13: 8 "Let's not have a quarreling between you NDT
Ge 17:14 A uncircumcised male, who has not been NDT
Ge 27:36 "Haven't you reserved a blessing for me?" NDT
Ge 30: 1 that she was not bearing Jacob a children, NDT
Ge 30:33 A goat in my possession that is not H3972
Ge 30:33 spotted, or a lamb that is not dark-colored H928
Ge 31:14 "Do we still have a share in the inheritance NDT
Ge 31:50 daughters or if you take a wives besides my NDT
Ge 36:31 in Edom before a Israelite king reigned NDT
Ge 37: 3 Joseph more than a of his other sons, H3972
Ge 37: 4 father loved him more than a of them, H3972
Ge 37:22 "Don't shed a blood. Throw him into this NDT
Ge 38:21 "There hasn't been a shrine prostitute here," NDT
Ge 38:22 'There hasn't been a shrine prostitute here.' NDT
Ge 44: 9 If a of your servants is found to have it, he H889
Ge 47: 6 if you know of a among them with special H408
Ge 48: 6 A children born to you after them will be NDT
Ex 3: 5 "Do not come a closer," God said. "Take off AIT
Ex 3:22 neighbor and a woman living in her house AIT
Ex 4:18 in Egypt to see if a of them are still alive." AIT
Ex 5:10 'I will not give you a more straw. NDT
Ex 5:18 You will not be given a straw, yet you must NDT
Ex 9:28 you don't have to stay a longer. H3578
Ex 11: 7 not a dog will bark at a person or animal. H4946
Ex 12: 4 If a household is too small for a whole H2021
Ex 12:10 Do not leave a of it till morning; if some is H4946
Ex 12:44 A slave you have bought may eat it after H3972
Ex 12:46 Do not break a of the bones. NDT
Ex 13: 7 shall a yeast be seen anywhere within AIT
Ex 15:26 will not bring on you a of the diseases I H3972
Ex 16:19 "No one is to keep a of it until morning." H4946
Ex 16:25 You will not find a of it on the ground today. AIT
Ex 16:26 the Sabbath, there will not be a. H928
Ex 20:10 On it you shall not do a work, neither you H3972
Ex 20:10 a foreigner residing in your towns. H3870S
Ex 20:23 Do not make a gods to be alongside me; do NDT
Ex 21:11 without a payment of money. H2855+401
Ex 21:19 the injured person for a loss of time and see NDT
Ex 22: 9 a other lost property about which H3972
Ex 22:10 a sheep or a other animal to their H3972
Ex 22:20 sacrifices to a god other than the H2021
Ex 29:34 And if a of the meat of the ordination ram H4946
Ex 29:34 the ordination ram or a bread is left over H4946
Ex 30: 9 not offer on this altar a other incense or any NDT
Ex 30: 9 any other incense or a burnt offering or NDT
Ex 30:32 body and do not make a other oil using the NDT
Ex 30:37 Do not make a incense with this formula H2021
Ex 31:14 those who do a work on that day must be NDT
Ex 31:15 Whoever does a work on the Sabbath day is NDT
Ex 32:24 'Whoever has a gold jewelry, take it NDT
Ex 33: 4 mourn and no one put on a ornaments. H2257S
Ex 34:10 never before done in a nation in all the H3972
Ex 34:14 Do not worship a other god, for the LORD AIT
Ex 34:17 "Do not make a idols. NDT
Ex 34:25 do not let a of the sacrifice from the NDT
Ex 35: 2 Whoever does a work on it is to be put to NDT
Ex 35: 3 not light a fire in a of your dwellings on H3972
Ex 35:24 had acacia wood for a part of the work H3972
Lev 2:11 you are not to burn a yeast or honey in a H3972
Lev 3:17 You must not eat a fat or any blood.' H3972
Lev 3:17 You must not eat any fat or a blood.'" H3972
Lev 4: 2 is forbidden in a of the LORD's commands H3972
Lev 4:13 is forbidden in a of the LORD's H285+3972
Lev 4:22 is forbidden in a of the commands H285+3972
Lev 4:27 "'If a member of the community sins H285
Lev 4:27 what is forbidden in a of the LORD's H285
Lev 5: 2 of a unclean creature that moves along NDT
Lev 5: 4 in a matter one might carelessly swear H3972
Lev 5: 5 that they are guilty in a of these matters, H285
Lev 5:13 atonement for them for a of these sins they H285
Lev 5:15 in regard to a of the LORD's holy things, NDT
Lev 5:17 is forbidden in a of the LORD's H285+3972
Lev 6: 3 swear falsely about a such sin that people H285
Lev 6: 4 when they sin in a of these ways and realize NDT
Lev 6: 7 will be forgiven for a of the things they did H285
Lev 6:18 A male descendant of Aaron may eat it H3972
Lev 6:27 Whatever touches a of the flesh will become NDT
Lev 6:27 if a of the blood is spattered on a H4946
Lev 6:29 A male in a priest's family may eat it; it is H3972
Lev 6:30 But a sin offering whose blood is brought H3972
Lev 7: 6 A male in a priest's family may eat it, but H3972
Lev 7:17 A meat of the sacrifice left over till the H4946
Lev 7:18 If a meat of the fellowship offering is H4946
Lev 7:18 the person who eats a of it will be held H4946
Lev 7:20 who is unclean eats a meat of the NDT
Lev 7:21 an unclean animal or a unclean creature H3972
Lev 7:21 then eats a of the meat of the H4946
Lev 7:23 'Do not eat a of the fat of cattle, sheep H3972
Lev 7:24 animals may be used for a other purpose, H3972
Lev 7:26 not eat the blood of a bird or animal. H3972
Lev 11: 3 You may eat a animal that has a divided H3972
Lev 11: 9 streams you may eat a that have fins and H3972
Lev 11:14 the red kite, a kind of black kite, NDT
Lev 11:15 a kind of raven, H3972
Lev 11:16 the screech owl, the gull, a kind of hawk, NDT
Lev 11:19 the stork, a kind of heron, the hoopoe and NDT
Lev 11:22 Of these you may eat a kind of locust NDT
Lev 11:26 touches the carcass of a of them will be NDT
Lev 11:29 the weasel, the rat, a kind of great lizard, NDT
Lev 11:34 A food you are allowed to eat that has H3972
Lev 11:34 with water from a such pot is unclean, H3972
Lev 11:34 a liquid that is drunk from such a pot H3972
Lev 11:37 If a carcass falls on a seeds that are to be H3972
Lev 11:42 You are not to eat a creature that moves H3972
Lev 11:43 defile yourselves by a of these creatures. H3972
Lev 11:44 unclean by a creature that moves H3972
Lev 13:47 "As for a fabric that is spoiled with a H2021
Lev 13:47 a defiling mold—a woolen or linen clothing NDT
Lev 13:48 a woven or knitted material of linen or wool NDT
Lev 13:48 a leather or anything made of leather NDT
Lev 13:49 knitted material, or a leather article, is H3972
Lev 13:52 a leather article that has been spoiled H3972
Lev 13:58 A fabric, woven or knitted material, or any H2021
Lev 13:58 a leather article that has been washed H3972
Lev 13:59 knitted material, or a leather article, for H3972
Lev 14: 2 the regulations for a diseased person at H2021
Lev 14:54 the regulations for a defiling skin disease, H3972
Lev 15: 2 'When a man has an unusual bodily H408+408
Lev 15: 4 "'A bed the man with a discharge lies on H3972
Lev 15:10 touches a of the things that were under H3972
Lev 15:12 a wooden article is to be rinsed with H3972
Lev 15:17 A clothing or leather that has semen on it H3972
Lev 15:24 a bed he lies on will be unclean. H3972
Lev 15:26 A bed she lies on while her discharge H3972
Lev 16:29 must deny yourselves and not do a work— H3972
Lev 17: 3 A Israelite who sacrifices an ox, a lamb H408
Lev 17: 7 must no longer offer a of their sacrifices to NDT
Lev 17: 8 'A Israelite or any foreigner residing H408
Lev 17: 8 'Any Israelite or a foreigner residing H4946
Lev 17:10 will set my face against a Israelite or any H408
Lev 17:10 any Israelite or a foreigner residing H4946
Lev 17:12 may a foreigner residing among you H2021
Lev 17:13 "'A Israelite or any foreigner residing H408
Lev 17:13 "'Any Israelite or a foreigner residing H4946
Lev 17:13 among you who hunts a animal or bird that NDT
Lev 17:14 "You must not eat the blood of a creature H3972
Lev 18: 6 one is to approach a close relative to H3972
Lev 18:21 "'Do not give a of your children to be H4946
Lev 18:24 not defile yourselves in a of these ways, H3972
Lev 18:26 you must not do a of these detestable H3972
Lev 18:29 'Everyone who does a of these detestable H3972
Lev 18:30 do not follow a of the detestable H4946
Lev 19: 7 If a of it is eaten on the third day, it is impure AIT
Lev 19:23 the land and plant a kind of fruit tree, H3972
Lev 19:26 "'Do not eat a meat with the blood still in it NDT
Lev 20: 2 'A Israelite or any foreigner residing in H408
Lev 20: 2 'Any Israelite or a foreigner residing in H4946
Lev 20: 2 Israel who sacrifices a of his children to H4946
Lev 20:25 defile yourselves by a animal or bird or H2021
Lev 21: 1 unclean for a of his people who die, NDT
Lev 21:18 No man who has a defect may come near NDT
Lev 21:20 or who has a eye defect, or who NDT
Lev 21:21 the priest who has a defect is to come near NDT
Lev 22: 3 if a of your descendants is H3972+408
Lev 22: 5 if he touches a crawling thing that H3972
Lev 22: 5 a person who makes him unclean AIT
Lev 22: 6 who touches a such thing will be H2257S
Lev 22: 6 He must not eat a of the sacred offerings H4946
Lev 22:12 she may not eat a of the sacred H928
Lev 22:18 'If a of you—whether an Israelite or a H408
Lev 22:22 Do not place a of these on the altar as a H4946
Lev 23: 3 You are not to do a work; wherever you H3972
Lev 23:14 You must not eat a bread, or roasted or new NDT
Lev 23:28 Do not do a work on that day, because it is H3972
Lev 23:30 anyone who does a work on that day. H3972
Lev 25:14 "'If you sell land to a of your own people NDT
Lev 25:33 a house sold in a town they hold—and is NDT
Lev 25:35 "'If a of your fellow Israelites become poor NDT
Lev 25:36 Do not take interest or a profit from them NDT
Lev 25:39 "'If a of your fellow Israelites become poor NDT
Lev 25:47 you becomes rich and a of your fellow NDT
Lev 25:49 An uncle or a cousin or a blood relative in H4946
Lev 25:54 is not redeemed in a of these ways, NDT
Lev 27:31 would redeem a of their tithe must H4946
Lev 27:33 from the bad or make a substitution. H5647S
Nu 5: 2 skin disease or a discharge of a kind, H3972
Nu 5: 6 'A man or woman who wrongs another in AIT
Nu 5: 6 wrongs another in a way and so is H3972
Nu 5:31 husband will be innocent of a wrongdoing, NDT
Nu 7: 9 But Moses did not give a to the Kohathites NDT
Nu 9:10 'When a of you or your descendants H408+408
Nu 9:12 They must not leave a of it till morning H4946
Nu 9:12 any of it till morning or break a of its bones. NDT
Nu 11:31 a day's walk in a direction. H3907+2256+3907
Nu 15:22 fail to keep a of these commands the LORD H3972
Nu 15:23 a of the LORD's commands to you through H3972
Nu 16:15 from them, nor have I wronged a of them." H285
Nu 18:20 will you have a share among them; I am NDT
Nu 18:23 the responsibility for a offenses they commit AIT
Nu 20:17 We will not go through a field or vineyard NDT
Nu 20:17 field or vineyard, or drink water from a well. NDT
Nu 20:19 if we or our livestock drink a of your water, NDT
Nu 21:22 will not turn aside into a field or vineyard, NDT
Nu 21:22 field or vineyard, or drink water from a well. NDT
Nu 30: 9 "A vow or obligation taken by a widow H3972
Nu 30:13 confirm or nullify a vow she makes or any H3972
Nu 30:13 vow she makes or a sworn pledge to deny H3972
Nu 32:19 We will not receive a inheritance with them AIT
Nu 36: 8 who inherits land in a Israelite tribe must NDT
Dt 1:17 Bring me a case too hard for you, and I H2021
Dt 2: 5 I will not give you a of their land, H4946
Dt 2: 9 I will not give you a part of their land. H4946
Dt 2:19 you possession of a land belonging to the H4946
Dt 2:37 did not encroach on a of the land of the H3972
Dt 4:15 You saw no form of a kind the day the H3972
Dt 4:16 an idol, an image of a shape, whether H3972
Dt 4:17 like a animal on earth or any bird that H3972
Dt 4:17 animal on earth or a bird that flies in the H3972
Dt 4:18 like a creature that moves along the H3972
Dt 4:18 along the ground or a fish in the waters H3972
Dt 4:25 become corrupt and make a kind of idol, H3972
Dt 4:33 Has a other people heard the voice of God NDT
Dt 4:34 Has a god ever tried to take for himself one NDT
Dt 5:14 On it you shall not do a work, neither you H3972
Dt 5:14 your donkey or a of your animals, nor H3972
Dt 5:14 a foreigner residing in your towns H3870S
Dt 5:25 voice of the LORD our God a longer. H3578+6388
Dt 7:14 will be blessed more than a other people; H3972
Dt 7:14 will a of your livestock be without young. NDT
Dt 10:16 do not be stiff-necked a longer. H6388
Dt 12:15 your animals in a of your towns and eat H3972
Dt 14: 3 Do not eat a detestable thing. H3972

Dt 14: 6 You may eat **a** animal that has a divided H3972
Dt 14: 9 you may eat **a** that has fins and scales. H3972
Dt 14:11 You may eat **a** clean bird. H3972
Dt 14:13 the red kite, the black kite, **a** kind of falcon, NDT
Dt 14:14 **a** kind of raven, H3972
Dt 14:15 the screech owl, the gull, **a** kind of hawk, NDT
Dt 14:18 the stork, **a** kind of heron, the hoopoe and NDT
Dt 14:20 But **a** winged creature that is clean you H3972
Dt 14:21 to the foreigner residing in **a** of your towns, NDT
Dt 14:21 or you may sell it to **a** other foreigner. NDT
Dt 15: 2 cancel *a* **loan** *they have* **made** to a fellow AIT
Dt 15: 3 you *must* **cancel** *a* **debt** your fellow AIT
Dt 15: 7 fellow Israelites in **a** *of* the towns of the H285
Dt 15:12 If **a** of your people—Hebrew men or women NDT
Dt 15:21 lame or blind, or has **a** serious flaw, you H3972
Dt 16: 4 Do not let **a** *of* the meat you sacrifice on H4946
Dt 16: 5 the Passover in **a** town the LORD your God H285
Dt 16:21 Do not set up **a** wooden Asherah pole H3972
Dt 17: 1 a sheep that has **a** defect or flaw in it, H3972
Dt 19:15 anyone accused of **a** crime or offense they H3972
Dt 23: 2 marriage nor **a** *of* their descendants may H4200
Dt 23: 3 Moabite or **a** *of* their descendants may H4200
Dt 23:18 house of the LORD your God to pay **a** vow, H3972
Dt 23:24 you want, but do not put **a** in your basket. NDT
Dt 24: 5 sent to war or have **a** other duty laid on H3972
Dt 24:10 make a loan of **a kind** to your neighbor, H4399
Dt 26:13 commands nor have I forgotten **a** of them. NDT
Dt 26:14 I have not eaten **a** *of* the sacred portion H4946
Dt 26:14 have I removed **a** *of* it while I was H4946
Dt 26:14 have I offered **a** *of* it to the dead. H4946
Dt 27: 5 Do not use **a** iron tool on them. NDT
Dt 27:21 who has sexual relations with **a** animal." H3972
Dt 28:14 not turn aside from **a** *of* the commands I H3972
Dt 28:51 **a** calves of your herds or lambs of your NDT
Dt 28:55 give to one of them **a** *of* the flesh of his H4946
Jos 2:19 If **a** *of* them go outside your house into the H3972
Jos 5:12 there was no longer **a** manna for the NDT
Jos 6:18 your own destruction by taking **a** *of* them. H4946
Jos 8:20 to escape **in a direction**; H2178+2256+2178
Jos 11:13 Israel did not burn **a** *of* the cities built on H3972
Jos 11:22 only in Gaza, Gath and Ashdod *did a* **survive**. AIT
Jos 20: 9 **A** *of* the Israelites or any foreigner residing H3972
Jos 20: 9 Any of the Israelites or **a** foreigner residing H3972
Jdg 2:21 out before them **a** of the nations Joshua H408
Jdg 3: 1 not experienced **a** *of* the wars in Canaan H3972
Jdg 8:35 also failed to show *a* **loyalty** to the family of AIT
Jdg 11: 2 "*You are* not *going to* **get** *a* **inheritance** in AIT
Jdg 11:25 Are you **a better** than Balak son of H3201+3201
Jdg 13:14 drink **a** wine or other fermented drink NDT
Jdg 13:16 you detain me, I will not eat **a** *of* your food. H928
Jdg 16: 7 I'll become as weak as **a** other man." H285
Jdg 16:11 I'll become as weak as **a** other man." H285
Jdg 16:13 I'll become as weak as **a** other man." H285
Jdg 16:17 I would become as weak as **a** other man." H3972
Jdg 19:12 We won't go into **a** city whose people H5799S
Jdg 21: 7 not to give them **a** *of* our daughters in H4946
Ru 1:11 Am I going to have **a more** sons, who H6388
1Sa 2:13 whenever **a** of the people offered **a** H3972+408
1Sa 4:20 But she did not respond or pay *a* **attention**. AIT
1Sa 5: 5 priests of Dagon nor **a** others who enter H3972
1Sa 10:23 he was a head taller than **a** *of* the others. H3972
1Sa 12: 3 If I have done **a** of these things, I will make NDT
1Sa 21: 4 "I don't have **a** ordinary bread on hand NDT
1Sa 21: 8 brought my sword or **a** other weapon, NDT
1Sa 22:15 your servant or **a** *of* his father's family, H3972
1Sa 30:12 he had not eaten *a* **food** or drunk any water AIT
1Sa 30:12 any food or drunk *a* **water** for three days and AIT
2Sa 6:20 of his servants as **a** vulgar fellow would!" H285
2Sa 7: 7 did I ever say to **a** *of* their rulers whom I H285
2Sa 12:17 he would not eat **a** food with them. NDT
2Sa 14: 2 and don't use **a** cosmetic lotions. NDT
2Sa 17:12 Neither he nor **a** *of* his men will be left H3972
2Sa 18:22 You don't have **a** news that will bring you **a** NDT
2Sa 19:28 do I have to make **a more** appeals to the H6388
2Sa 19:42 Have we eaten **a** *of* the king's provisions H4946
2Sa 23:23 held in greater honor than **a** of the Thirty, NDT
1Ki 6: 7 chisel or **a** other iron tool was heard at H3972
1Ki 8:16 not chosen a city in **a** tribe of Israel to H3972
1Ki 8:37 an enemy besieges them in **a** of their cities, NDT
1Ki 9:22 did not make slaves of **a** of the Israelites; NDT
1Ki 10:20 had ever been made for **a** other kingdom. H3972
1Ki 15: 5 not failed to keep **a** *of* the LORD's H3972
1Ki 16:30 of the LORD than **a** *of* those before him. H3972
1Ki 17:12 "I don't have **a** bread—only a handful NDT
1Ki 18: 5 we will not have to kill **a** *of* our animals." H4946
1Ki 19:17 will put to death **a** who escape the sword H2021
1Ki 19:17 will put to death **a** who escape the sword H2021
2Ki 3:14 *I would* not **pay a attention** H5564+2256+8011
2Ki 5:17 sacrifices to *a* **other** god but the LORD. AIT
2Ki 6:33 Why should I wait for the LORD **a longer**?" H6388
2Ki 7: 2 "but you will not eat **a** *of* it! H4946
2Ki 7:19 your own eyes, but you will not eat **a** *of* it!" H4946
2Ki 10:24 "If one of you lets **a** of the men I am H408
2Ki 12: 8 would not collect **a** more money from the NDT
2Ki 12:13 trumpets or **a** other articles of gold or H3972
2Ki 13:11 not turn away from **a** *of* the sins of H3972
2Ki 14:24 not turn away from **a** *of* the sins of H3972
2Ki 17:35 "Do not worship *a* **other** gods or bow down to AIT
2Ki 18:33 Has the god of **a** nation ever delivered his H2021
2Ki 23:22 kings of Judah had **a** such Passover been H2021
1Ch 1:43 in Edom before **a** Israelite king reigned NDT
1Ch 11:25 held in greater honor than **a** of the Thirty, NDT
1Ch 17: 6 did I ever say to **a** *of* their leaders whom I H285
1Ch 23:26 the tabernacle or **a** *of* the articles used in H3972
1Ch 28:21 person skilled in **a** craft will help you in H3972
2Ch 2:14 can execute **a** design given to him. H3972
2Ch 6: 5 not chosen a city in **a** tribe of Israel to H3972
2Ch 6:28 enemies besiege them in **a** of their cities, NDT
2Ch 8:15 to the priests or to the Levites in **a** matter, H3972
2Ch 9:19 had ever been made for **a** other kingdom. H3972
2Ch 11:21 Absalom more than **a** *of* his other wives H3972
2Ch 19:11 will be over you in **a** matter concerning H3972
2Ch 19:11 will be over you in **a** matter concerning H3972
2Ch 23: 8 priest had not released **a** of the divisions. NDT
2Ch 23:19 no one who was in **a** way unclean might H3972
2Ch 25: 7 not with **a** *of* the people of Ephraim. H3972
2Ch 29: 7 incense or present **a** burnt offerings at the NDT
2Ch 31:19 around their towns or in **a** *other* towns, H3972
2Ch 32:15 no god of **a** nation or kingdom has H3972
2Ch 36:23 **A** of his people among you may go H4769+3972
Ezr 1: 3 **A** of his people among you may go H4769+3972
Ezr 1: 4 And in **a** locality where survivors may now H3972
Ezr 2:63 them not to eat **a** *of* the most sacred food H4946
Ezr 6:12 overthrow **a** king or people who lifts a A10353
Ezr 7:13 Now I decree that **a** of the Israelites in A10353
Ezr 7:24 tribute or duty on **a** *of* the priests, Levites A10353
Ezr 7:25 you are to teach *a* **who** do not know them. AIT
Ezr 9:12 a treaty of friendship with them at **a time**, H6409
Ne 2:16 officials or *a* **others** who would be doing AIT
Ne 2:20 share in Jerusalem or **a** claim or historic NDT
Ne 5:16 there for the work; we did not acquire *a* **land**. AIT
Ne 7:65 them not to eat **a** *of* the most sacred food H4946
Ne 10:31 from them on the Sabbath or on **a** holy day. NDT
Est 2:17 more than to **a** *of* the other women, H3972
Est 2:17 approval more than **a** *of* the other virgins. H3972
Est 4:11 know that for **a** man or woman who H3972
Est 8:11 the armed men of **a** nationality or H3972
Job 2: 3 against him to ruin him **without a reason**." H2855
Job 3: 6 year nor be entered in **a** *of* the months. H5031
Job 6:13 Do I have **a** power to help myself, now H401S
Job 6:30 Is there **a** wickedness on my lips? Can my NDT
Job 10:18 I wish I had died before **a** eye saw me. NDT
Job 17:15 is my hope—who can see **a** hope for me? NDT
Job 31:13 "If I have denied justice to *a of* **my** servants AIT
Job 33:12 not right, for God is greater than *a* **mortal**. AIT
Job 34:27 him and had no regard for **a** *of* his ways. H3972
Job 39: 8 its pasture and searches for **a** green thing. H3972
Job 41: 9 **A** hope of subduing it is false; the mere NDT
Ps 14: 2 to see if there are *a who* **understand**, AIT
Ps 14: 2 are any who understand, *a who* **seek** God. AIT
Ps 53: 2 to see if there are *a who* **understand**, AIT
Ps 53: 2 are any who understand, *a who* **seek** God. AIT
Ps 81: 9 you shall not worship **a** god other than me. NDT
Ps 139:24 See if there is **a** offensive way in me, and NDT
Pr 3:31 envy the violent or choose **a** *of* their ways. H3972
Pr 6:35 He will not accept **a** compensation; he H3972
Pr 8:26 its fields or **a** *of* the dust of the earth H8031
Pr 12:27 The lazy do not roast **a** game, but the H2257S
Pr 14:34 exalts a nation, but sin condemns **a** people. NDT
Pr 26:10 is one who hires a fool or **a** passer-by. NDT
SS 4:10 of your perfume more than **a** spice! H3972
Isa 7:17 father a time unlike **a** since Ephraim broke NDT
Isa 33:20 be pulled up, nor **a** *of* its ropes broken. H3972
Isa 35: 9 be there, nor *a* ravenous **beast**; they will not AIT
Isa 36:18 ' Have the gods of **a** nations ever H2021
Isa 41:26 foretold it, no one heard *a* **words** *from* you. AIT
Isa 43:24 have not bought *a* **fragrant calamus** for me, AIT
Isa 44: 8 Is there **a** God besides me? No, NDT
Isa 52:14 beyond that of *a* **human being** and his form AIT
Isa 53: 9 no violence, nor was **a** deceit in his mouth. NDT
Isa 56: 2 keeps their hands from doing **a** evil." H3972
Isa 64: 4 no eye has seen **a** God besides you, who NDT
Jer 2:24 **A** males that pursue her need not tire H3972
Jer 3: 2 Is there *a place* **where** you have not been AIT
Jer 3:19 the most beautiful inheritance of *a* **nation**. AIT
Jer 5: 6 towns to tear to pieces **a** who venture out, H3972
Jer 7:16 this people nor offer **a** plea or petition for NDT
Jer 10: 5 they can do no harm nor *can* they **do** *a* **good**." AIT
Jer 11:14 this people or offer **a** plea or petition for NDT
Jer 12:17 But if **a** nation does not listen, I will H2085S
Jer 14:22 Do **a** *of* the worthless idols of the nations H928
Jer 17:22 your houses or do **a** work on the Sabbath, H3972
Jer 17:24 day holy by not doing **a** work on it, H3972
Jer 17:27 holy by not carrying **a** load as you come NDT
Jer 18: 7 If **at a time** I announce that a nation or H8092
Jer 23: 4 terrified, nor *will a* **be missing**," declares the AIT
Jer 25: 4 or **paid a attention**. H5742+265+4200+9048
Jer 27: 8 **a** nation or kingdom will not serve H2021
Jer 27:11 But if **a** nation will bow its neck under the H2021
Jer 27:13 LORD has threatened **a** nation that will not H2021
Jer 29:26 you should put **a** maniac who acts like a H3972
Jer 34:14 of you must free **a** fellow Hebrews who H2257S
Jer 35: 7 you must never have **a** of these things, but NDT
Jer 37: 2 of the land **paid** *a* **attention** to the words the AIT
Jer 37:17 privately, "Is there **a** word from the LORD?" NDT
Jer 38: 9 there is no longer **a** bread in the city." H2021
Jer 51:26 a cornerstone, nor **a** stone for a foundation NDT
La 1:12 Is **a** suffering like my suffering that was NDT
La 4:12 did **a** *of* the peoples of the world H3972
Eze 1:17 they would go in **a** one of the four directions NDT
Eze 10:11 they would go in **a** one of the four directions NDT
Eze 12:28 of my words will be delayed **a longer**; H6388
Eze 14: 4 When **a** of the Israelites set up idols H408+408
Eze 14: 7 " 'When **a** of the Israelites or any H408+408
Eze 14: 7 of the Israelites or **a** foreigner residing in H2021
Eze 15: 2 that of a branch from **a** of the trees in the H3972
Eze 16: 5 enough to do **a** of these things for you H285
Eze 18:10 sheds blood or does **a** of these other things H285
Eze 18:23 *Do I* **take a pleasure** in the death of H2911+2911
Eze 20:28 them and they saw **a** high hill or any leafy H3972
Eze 20:28 they saw any high hill or **a** leafy tree, H3972
Eze 24:16 do not lament or weep or shed **a** tears. H3870S
Eze 37:23 vile images or with **a** *of* their offenses, H3972
Eze 39:14 they will bury **a** bodies that are lying on the NDT
Eze 39:28 own land, not leaving **a** behind. H6388+4946
Eze 44:13 come near **a** *of* my holy things or my H3972
Eze 44:17 they must not wear **a** woolen garment while NDT
Eze 44:24 " 'In **a** dispute, the priests are to serve as NDT
Eze 46:18 must not take **a** *of* the inheritance of H4946
Eze 48:14 They must not sell or exchange **a** *of* it H4946
Da 1: 4 young men without **a** physical defect H3972
Da 1:15 nourished than **a** *of* the young men who H3972
Da 2:10 such a thing of **a** magician or enchanter A10353
Da 2:43 **a more than** iron mixes A10195+10341+10168
Da 3:28 serve or worship **a** god except their own A10353
Da 3:29 that the people of **a** nation or language A10353
Da 6: 5 "We will never find **a** basis for charges A10353
Da 6: 7 who prays to **a** god or human being A10353
Da 6:12 who prays to **a** god or human being A10353
Da 6:18 eating and without **a** entertainment being NDT
Da 6:22 Nor have I ever done **a** wrong before you NDT
Da 11:37 will he regard **a** god, but will exalt H3972
Hos 3: 3 be a prostitute or be intimate with **a** man, NDT
Hos 12: 8 they will not find in me **a** iniquity or sin." NDT
Zep 3:15 with you; never again will you fear **a** harm. NDT
Hag 2:19 Is there yet **a** seed left in the barn? Until now NDT
Zec 14:17 If **a of** the peoples of the earth do H4946+907
Mt 5:18 **not** the least stroke of a pen, will **by a means** *G4024+3590*
Mt 6:27 Can **a** one of you by worrying add a single *G5515*
Mt 10: 5 the Gentiles or enter **a** town of the NDT
Mt 10: 9 "Do not get **a** gold or silver or copper to take NDT
Mt 12:11 "If **a** of you has a sheep and *G5515+5516+476*
Mt 16: 7 "It is because we didn't bring *a* **bread**." AIT
Mt 18:14 is not willing that **a** of these little ones *G1651*
Mt 19: 3 divorce his wife for **a and every** reason?" *G4246*
Mt 22:46 one dared to ask him **a more** questions. *G4033*
Mt 25: 3 their lamps but did not take *a* **oil** with them. AIT
Mt 26:60 But they did not find **a**, though many false NDT
Mt 26:65 Why do we need **a more** witnesses? Look, *G2285*
Mk 4:13 How then will you understand **a** parable? *G4246*
Mk 6: 5 He could not do **a** miracles there, except *G4029*
Mk 6:11 And **if a** place will not welcome you *G4005+323*
Mk 11:13 he went to find out if it had *a* **fruit**. *G5516*
Mk 12:20 married and died without leaving *a* **children**. AIT
Mk 12:22 none of the seven left *a* **children**. Last of all, AIT
Mk 12:34 on no one dared **ask** him *a more* **questions**. AIT
Mk 14: 7 you can help them **a time** you want. *G4020*
Mk 14:55 put him to death, but they did not find **a**. NDT
Mk 14:63 "Why do we need **a more** witnesses?" *G2285*
Lk 3:13 "**Don't** collect **a** more than you are *G3594*
Lk 4:26 Yet Elijah was **not** sent to **a** of them, but to *G4029*
Lk 7:44 You did not give me *a* **water** for my feet, but AIT
Lk 10:35 reimburse you *for* **a** extra *G4005+5516+323*
Lk 11:17 "**A** kingdom divided against itself will be *G4246*
Lk 13: 6 went to look for fruit on it but did not find **a**. NDT
Lk 13: 7 fruit on this fig tree and haven't found **a**. NDT
Lk 13:33 **In a case**, I must press on today and *G4440*
Lk 16: 2 because you cannot be manager **a longer**. *G2285*
Lk 18:34 The disciples did **not** understand **a** of this *G4029*
Lk 19:48 they could not find **a way** to do it, *G3836+5515*
Lk 20:40 one dared to ask him **a more** questions. *G4033*
Lk 22:71 "Why do we need **a more** testimony? *G2285*
Jn 2:25 He did not need **a** testimony about *G5516*
Jn 7: 6 is not yet here; for you **a** time will do. *G4121*
Jn 7:48 "Have **a** of the rulers or of the Pharisees *G5516*
Jn 8: 7 "Let *a one* of you **who** is without sin be the AIT
Jn 8:46 Can **a** of you prove me guilty of sin? If I am *G5515*
Jn 10:33 "We are not stoning you for **a** good work," NDT
Jn 17:14 the world **a more than** I am of the *G2777+4024*
Jn 21: 5 out to them, "Friends, haven't you **a** fish?" *G5516*
Ac 4:17 spreading **a further** among the *G2093+4498*
Ac 4:32 No one claimed that **a** of their *G5516*
Ac 8:16 Spirit had not yet come on **a** of them; *G4029*
Ac 9: 2 so that if he found **a** there who belonged *G5516*
Ac 10:29 sent for, I came **without raising a objection**. *G395*
Ac 17:27 though he is not far from **a** one of us. *G1667*
Ac 20:26 I am innocent of the blood *of* **a** *of you*. *G4246*
Ac 22: 3 as zealous for God as **a** of you are today. *G4246*
Ac 24:18 nor was I involved in **a** disturbance. NDT
Ac 25:10 I have **not** done **a** wrong to the Jews, as *G4029*
Ac 25:18 they did **not** charge him with **a** of the *G4029*
Ac 25:24 that he ought not to live **a longer**. *G3600*
Ac 26: 8 Why should **a of** you consider it incredible *G4123*
Ac 27:42 prisoners to prevent **a** of them from *G5516*
Ac 28:18 because I was **not** guilty of **a** crime *G3594*
Ac 28:19 not intend to bring **a** charge against my *G5516*
Ac 28:21 "We have not received **a** letters from Judea NDT
Ro 3: 9 *Do we have a* **advantage**? Not at all! AIT
Ro 6: 2 how can we live in it **a longer**? *G2285*
Ro 6:13 Do not offer **a** part of yourself to sin as an *G3836*
Ro 8:33 Who *will* **bring a charge** against those *G1592*
Ro 8:38 the present nor the future, nor **a** powers, NDT
Ro 14:13 your mind not to put **a** stumbling block *G3836*
Ro 16: 2 and to give her **a** help she may *G4005+323*
1Co 1: 7 you do not lack **a** spiritual gift as you *G3594*

1Co 1:14 God that I did **not** baptize **a** of you except G4029
1Co 3:11 one can lay **a** foundation **other** than the G257
1Co 3:18 If **a** of you think you are wise by the G5516
1Co 4: 3 if I am judged by you or by **a** human court; NDT
1Co 6: 1 If **a** of you has a dispute with another, do G5516
1Co 7:12 If **a** brother has a wife who is not a G5516
1Co 9:15 But I have not used **a** of these rights. And G4029
2Co 1: 4 we can comfort those in **a** trouble with the G4246
2Co 7: 9 so were **not** harmed in **a way** by us. G3594
2Co 8:20 We want to avoid **a** criticism of the way we G5516
2Co 9: 4 For if **a** Macedonians come with me and find NDT
2Co 11: 9 from being a burden to you in **a** *way,* G4246
2Co 12:17 exploit you through **a** of the men I sent to G5516
2Co 13: 2 who sinned earlier or **a** of the others, G4246
Gal 1:12 I did not receive it from **a** man, nor was I NDT
Gal 1:16 response was not to consult **a** human being. NDT
Gal 5: 6 uncircumcision has **a** value. G5516
Eph 4:29 Do not let **a** unwholesome talk come out G4246
Eph 5: 3 immorality, or of **a** *kind of* impurity, or of G4246
Eph 5: 5 has **a** inheritance in the kingdom of Christ NDT
Eph 5:27 stain or wrinkle or **a** *other* blemish, G5516
Php 1:28 being frightened in **a way** by those who G3594
Php 2: 1 if you have **a** encouragement from G5516
Php 2: 1 with Christ, if **a** comfort from his love G5516
Php 2: 1 his love, if **a** common sharing in the Spirit G5516
Php 2: 1 if **a** tenderness and compassion, G5516
Php 4:12 of being content in **a** and every situation, G4246
Col 2:23 they lack **a** value in restraining G5516
Col 3:13 one another if **a** *of you* has a grievance G5516
2Th 2: 3 Don't let anyone deceive you in **a** way, for G3594
2Th 3: 8 we would not be a burden *to* **a** of you. G5516
1Ti 1: 3 people not *to* **teach false doctrines** *a* longer AIT
1Ti 5:16 If **a** woman who is a believer has widows G5516
2Ti 2:21 Master and prepared to do **a** good work. G4246
Phm 14 so that **a** favor you do would not seem G3836
Phm 18 If he has done you **a** wrong or owes you G5516
Heb 4:12 Sharper than **a** double-edged sword, it G4246
Heb 7:20 Others became priests without **a** oath, NDT
Jas 1: 5 If **a** of you lacks wisdom, you should ask G5516
1Pe 3: 1 if **a** of them do not believe the word G5516
1Pe 4:15 murderer or thief or *a other kind of* **criminal**, AIT
1Jn 5:16 If you see **a** brother or sister commit a sin G3836
2Jn 7 *A* **such** *person* is the deceiver and the AIT
Rev 2:24 'I will not impose **a other** burden on you, AIT
Rev 7: 1 the earth to prevent **a** wind from blowing on NDT
Rev 7: 1 on the land or on the sea or on **a** tree. G4246
Rev 7:16 down on them,' nor **a** scorching heat. G4246
Rev 9: 4 the grass of the earth or **a** plant or tree, G4246
Rev 18: 4 that you will not receive **a** of her plagues; G3836
Rev 18:22 No worker of **a** trade will ever be found in G4246
Rev 21: 1 and there was no longer **a** sea. G3836
Rev 22: 3 No longer will there be **a** curse. The G4246
Rev 22:19 from that person **a** share in the tree of G3836

ANYBODY (5) [ANY]

Lk 19: 8 if I have cheated **a** out of anything, I G5516
Ac 19:38 craftsmen have a grievance against **a**, G5516
Gal 1: 9 If **a** is preaching to you a gospel other G5516
1Th 4:12 so that you will **not** be dependent on **a**. G3594
1Jn 2: 1 But if **a** does sin, we have an advocate G5516

ANYMORE (23) [ANY]

Dt 3:26 not speak to me **a** about this H3578+6388
Dt 18:16 our God nor see this great fire **a**, H3578+6388
Jos 7:12 I will not be with you **a** unless you destroy H3578
2Sa 2:28 pursued Israel, nor *did they* fight **a**. H3578+6388
2Sa 7:10 Wicked people will not oppress them **a** H3578
2Sa 10:19 were afraid to help the Ammonites **a**. H6388
1Ch 17: 9 Wicked people will not oppress them **a** H3578
1Ch 19:19 not willing to help the Ammonites **a**. H6388
Ps 12: 1 for **no** one is faithful **a**; those who H1698
Isa 1: 5 Why should you be beaten **a**? Why do H6388
Isa 2: 4 nor will they train for war **a**. H6388
Jer 20: 9 mention his word or speak **a** in his name," H6388
Jer 22:30 on the throne of David or rule **a** in Judah." H6388
Eze 14:11 defile themselves **a** with all their sins. H6388
Eze 23:27 things with longing or remember Egypt **a**. H6388
Am 7:13 Don't prophesy **a** at Bethel H6388+3578
Mic 4: 3 nor will they train for war **a**. H6388
Mk 5: 3 no one could bind him **a**, not even G4033
Mk 5:35 "Why bother the teacher **a**?" G2285
Lk 8:49 **"Don't** bother the teacher **a**." G3600
Jn 14:19 the world will not see me **a**, but you will G4033
Rev 18:11 because no one buys their cargoes **a**— G4033
Rev 20: 3 the nations **a** until the thousand G2285

ANYONE (501) [ANY]

Ge 4:15 **a** who kills Cain will suffer vengeance H3972
Ge 13:16 the earth, so that if **a** could count the dust H408
Ge 19:12 "Do you have **a** else here H4769
Ge 19:12 **a** else in the city who belongs to you? H3972
Ge 26:11 "**A** who harms this man or his wife shall H2021
Ge 31:32 But if you find *a* **who** has your gods, that AIT
Ge 41:38 "Can we find **a** like this man, one in NDT
Ge 43:34 was five times as much as **a** else's. H3972
Ex 10:23 No one could see **a** else or move about H278s
Ex 12:19 And **a**, whether foreigner or native-born H3972
Ex 20: 7 will not hold *a* guiltless **who** misuses his AIT
Ex 21:12 "*A who* **strikes** a person with a fatal blow is AIT
Ex 21:14 But if **a** schemes and kills someone H408
Ex 21:15 "*A who* **attacks** their father or mother is to be AIT
Ex 21:16 "*A who* **kidnaps** someone is to be put to AIT
Ex 21:17 "*A who* **curses** their father or mother is to be AIT
Ex 21:20 "**A** who beats their male or female slave H408
Ex 21:33 "If **a** uncovers a pit or digs one and fails to H408
Ex 22: 3 "**A** who steals must certainly make NDT
Ex 22: 5 "If **a** grazes their livestock in a field or H408
Ex 22: 7 "If **a** gives a neighbor silver or goods for H408
Ex 22:10 "If **a** gives a donkey, an ox, a sheep or any H408
Ex 22:14 "If **a** borrows an animal from their neighbor H408
Ex 22:19 "**A** who has sexual relations with an H3972
Ex 24:14 **a** involved in a dispute can go to H4769
Ex 30:32 Do not pour it on **a else's** body and do not H132
Ex 30:33 puts it on **a other than a priest** must be H2424
Ex 31:14 *A who* **desecrates** it is to be put to death AIT
Ex 33: 7 **A** inquiring of the LORD would go to the H3972
Ex 33:16 How *will a* **know** that you are pleased with AIT
Lev 1: 2 'When **a** among you brings an offering to H132
Lev 2: 1 " 'When **a** brings a grain offering to the H5883
Lev 4: 2 'When **a** sins unintentionally and does H5883
Lev 5: 1 " 'If **a** sins because they do not speak up H5883
Lev 5: 2 " 'If **a** becomes aware that they are guilty H5883
Lev 5: 4 if **a** thoughtlessly takes an oath to do H5883
Lev 5: 5 when *a becomes* **aware that** *they are* **guilty** in AIT
Lev 5: 7 " '**A** who cannot afford a lamb is to bring H2257
Lev 5:15 "When **a** is unfaithful to the LORD by H5883
Lev 5:17 "If **a** sins and does what is forbidden in H5883
Lev 6: 2 'If **a** sins and is unfaithful to the LORD by H5883
Lev 7: 8 a burnt offering for **a** may keep its hide H408
Lev 7:11 offering *a may* **present** to the LORD: AIT
Lev 7:19 **a** ceremonially clean may eat it. H3972
Lev 7:20 But if **a** who is unclean eats any H2021+5883
Lev 7:21 **A** who touches something unclean H5883
Lev 7:25 **A** who eats the fat of an animal from H3972
Lev 7:27 **A** who eats blood must be cut off H3972+5883
Lev 7:29 '**A** who brings a fellowship offering to the H2021
Lev 11:28 **A** who picks up their carcasses must wash H2021
Lev 11:36 but *a who* **touches** one of these carcasses is AIT
Lev 11:39 **a** who touches its carcass will be unclean H2021
Lev 11:40 **A** who eats some of its carcass must wash H2021
Lev 11:40 **A** who picks up the carcass must wash H2021
Lev 13: 2 "When **a** has a swelling or a rash or a shiny H132
Lev 13: 9 "When **a** has a defiling skin disease, they H132
Lev 13:45 "**A** with such a defiling disease must wear H2021
Lev 14:32 the regulations for **a** who has a defiling H2257
Lev 14:46 "**A** who goes into the house while it is H2021
Lev 14:47 **A** who sleeps or eats in the house must H2021
Lev 15: 5 **A** who touches his bed must wash their H408
Lev 15: 8 the discharge spits on **a** *who* is clean, H2021
Lev 15:11 " '**A** the man with a discharge touches H3972
Lev 15:19 **a** who touches her will be unclean till H3972
Lev 15:21 **A** who touches her bed will be unclean H3972
Lev 15:22 **A** who touches anything she sits on will be H3972
Lev 15:23 was sitting on, when **a** touches it, they H2257
Lev 15:27 **A** who touches them will be unclean; they H3972
Lev 15:32 for *a made* **unclean** by an emission of semen AIT
Lev 17:14 is its blood; **a** who eats it must be cut off." H3972
Lev 17:15 " '**A**, whether native-born or H3972+5883
Lev 19:18 a grudge against **a** *among* your people, H1201
Lev 20: 6 set my face against **a** who turns to H5883
Lev 20: 9 " '**A** who curses their father or mother H408+408
Lev 22: 4 by a corpse or by **a** who has an emission of H408
Lev 22:12 daughter marries **a other than a priest**, H2424
Lev 22:14 " '**A** who eats a sacred offering by mistake H408
Lev 22:21 When **a** brings from the herd or flock a H408
Lev 23:30 their people **a** who does any H3972+2021+5883
Lev 24:15 '**A** who curses their God will be held H408+408
Lev 24:16 *a who* **blasphemes** the name of the LORD is to AIT
Lev 24:17 " '**A** who takes the life of a human being is H408
Lev 24:18 *A who* **takes the life** *of* someone's animal AIT
Lev 24:19 **A** who injures their neighbor is to be H408
Lev 25:29 " '**A** who sells a house in a walled city H408
Lev 27: 2 'If **a** makes a special vow to dedicate a H408
Lev 27: 8 If **a** making the vow is too poor to pay the H2085
Lev 27:14 " 'If **a** dedicates their house as something H408
Lev 27:16 " 'If **a** dedicates to the LORD part of their H408
Lev 27:22 " 'If *a* **dedicates** to the LORD a field they have AIT
Lev 27:33 If *a does* **make a substitution**, both the AIT
Nu 1:51 **A else** who approaches it is to be put to H2424
Nu 3:10 **a else** who approaches the sanctuary is to H2424
Nu 3:38 **A else** who approached the sanctuary was H2424
Nu 5: 2 away from the camp **a** who has a defiling H3972
Nu 9:13 But if **a** who is ceremonially clean H2021+408
Nu 12: 3 more humble than **a** else on the face of H3972
Nu 15:14 a foreigner or **a** *else* living among you H889
Nu 15:30 " 'But **a** who sins defiantly, whether H2021+5883
Nu 17:13 **A** who even comes near the tabernacle of H3972
Nu 18: 7 **A else** who comes near the sanctuary is to H2424
Nu 19:14 **A** who enters the tent and anyone who is H3972
Nu 19:14 enters the tent and **a** who is in it will be H3972
Nu 19:16 "**A** out in the open who touches someone H3972
Nu 19:16 **a** who touches a human bone or a grave NDT
Nu 19:18 must also sprinkle **a** who has touched a H2021
Nu 19:18 bone or a grave or **a** who has been killed H2021
Nu 19:18 has been killed or **a** who has died a H2021
Nu 19:21 **a** who touches the water of cleansing H2021
Nu 19:22 and **a** who touches it becomes H2021+5883
Nu 21: 8 **a** who is bitten can look at it and live." H3972
Nu 21: 9 Then when **a** was bitten by a snake and H408
Nu 31:19 "**A** who has killed someone or touched H3972
Nu 35:12 so that **a** accused of murder may not die H2021
Nu 35:15 so that **a** who has killed another H3972
Nu 35:16 " 'If *a* **strikes** someone **a** fatal **blow** with an AIT
Nu 35:17 Or if **a** is holding a stone and strikes NDT
Nu 35:18 Or if **a** is holding a wooden object and NDT
Nu 35:20 If **a** with malice aforethought **shoves** another AIT
Nu 35:30 " '**A** who kills a person is to be put to H3972
Nu 35:32 a ransom for *a who has* **fled** to a city of AIT
Nu 36: 6 They may marry **a** they please as long as H2021
Dt 1:17 Do not be afraid of **a**, for judgment H408
Dt 4:42 to which *a* who *had* **killed a person** could flee AIT
Dt 5:11 LORD will not hold **a** guiltless who misuses H889
Dt 15: 2 **a among** their own **people**, H8276+2256+278
Dt 15: 7 If **a** is poor among your fellow Israelites in H285
Dt 17:12 **A** who shows contempt for the judge H2021+408
Dt 18:12 **A** who does these things is detestable to H3972
Dt 18:19 call to account **a** who does not listen H2021+408
Dt 19: 4 the rule concerning **a** who kills a person H2021
Dt 19: 4 *a* who **kills** a neighbor unintentionally AIT
Dt 19:15 enough to convict **a** accused of any crime H408
Dt 20: 5 "Has **a** built a new house and H4769+2021+408
Dt 20: 6 Has **a** planted a vineyard and H4769+2021+408
Dt 20: 7 Has **a** become pledged to a H4769+2021+408
Dt 20: 8 "Is **a** afraid or fainthearted? H4769+2021+408
Dt 21:23 because *a who* **is hung** on a pole is under AIT
Dt 22: 5 LORD your God detests **a** who does this. H3972
Dt 25:16 your God detests **a** who does these things H3972
Dt 25:16 these things, **a** who deals dishonestly. H3972
Dt 27:15 "Cursed is **a** who makes an idol—a thing H408
Dt 27:16 "Cursed is *a who* **dishonors** their father or AIT
Dt 27:17 "Cursed is *a who* **moves** their neighbor's AIT
Dt 27:18 is *a who* **leads** the blind **astray** on the AIT
Dt 27:19 "Cursed is *a who* **withholds** justice from the AIT
Dt 27:20 "Cursed is *a who* **sleeps with** his father's wife, AIT
Dt 27:21 is *a who* **has sexual relations with** any AIT
Dt 27:22 "Cursed is *a who* **sleeps with** his sister, the AIT
Dt 27:23 "Cursed is *a who* **sleeps with** his AIT
Dt 27:24 "Cursed is *a who* **kills** their neighbor secretly." AIT
Dt 27:25 "Cursed is *a who* **accepts** a bribe to kill an AIT
Dt 27:26 "Cursed is *a* **who** does not uphold the words AIT
Jos 11:11 not sparing **a** that breathed, and he H3972
Jos 11:14 not sparing **a** that breathed. H3972
Jos 20: 3 so that **a** who kills a person accidentally H8357s
Jdg 4:20 comes by and asks you, 'Is **a** in there?' H408
Jdg 7: 3 '**A** who trembles with fear may turn back H4769
Jdg 16: 7 "If *a* **ties** me with seven fresh bowstrings that AIT
Jdg 16:11 "If *a* **ties** me **securely** with new ropes that AIT
Jdg 18: 7 had no relationship with **a** else. H132
Jdg 18:28 Sidon and had no relationship with **a** else. H132
Jdg 21: 5 a solemn oath that *a* **who** failed to assemble AIT
Jdg 21:18 'Cursed be *a who* **gives** a wife to a Benjamite AIT
Ru 2: 2 leftover grain behind **a** in whose eyes I find H889
Ru 3:14 got up before **a** could be recognized H408
1Sa 2:25 the offender; but if **a** sins against the LORD H408
1Sa 9: 2 he was a head taller than **a** else. H3972
1Sa 11: 7 to the oxen of **a** who does not follow H2257
1Sa 14:24 "Cursed be **a** who eats food before evening H408
1Sa 14:28 'Cursed be **a** who eats food today! H408
1Sa 26:12 one saw or knew about it, nor *did a* **wake up**. AIT
2Sa 5: 8 "**A** who conquers the Jebusites will have H3972
2Sa 6:21 your father or **a** *from* his house when he H3972
2Sa 9: 1 "Is there **a** still left of the house of Saul to H889
2Sa 14:10 king replied, "If **a** says anything to you H2021
2Sa 15: 2 Whenever **a** came with a H3972+2021+408
2Sa 15: 5 whenever **a** approached him to bow down H408
2Sa 19:22 Should **a** be put to death in Israel today H408
2Sa 21: 4 have the right to put **a** in Israel to death." H408
1Ki 3:12 that there will never have been **a** like you, NDT
1Ki 4:31 He was wiser than **a** else, including Ethan H3972
1Ki 8:31 "When **a** wrongs their neighbor and is H408
1Ki 8:38 is made by **a** among your H3972+2021+132
1Ki 13:33 **A** who wanted to become a priest he H2021
1Ki 15:17 to prevent *a* from **leaving** or entering the AIT
1Ki 15:29 did not leave Jeroboam **a** that breathed, H3972
1Ki 18:40 Don't let **a** get away!" They seized H408
1Ki 21:25 (*There* **was** never *a* like Ahab, who sold AIT
1Ki 22:31 "Do not fight with **a**, small or great, H4200+963
2Ki 4:29 Don't greet **a** you meet, and if anyone H408
2Ki 4:29 you meet, and if **a** greets you, do not H408
2Ki 7:10 not a sound of **a**—only tethered horses H132
2Ki 9:15 don't let **a** slip out of the city to go and H7127s
2Ki 10: 5 We will not appoint **a** as king; you do H408
2Ki 10:19 **A** who fails to come will no longer live." H3972
2Ki 11: 8 **A** who approaches your ranks is to be put H2021
2Ki 11:15 put to the sword **a** who follows her." H2021
2Ki 18:21 pierces the hand of **a** who leans on it! H408
2Ki 23:18 "Don't let **a** disturb his bones." So H408
1Ch 29: 8 **A** who had precious stones gave them to H2257s
2Ch 6: 5 have I chosen **a** to be ruler over my H408
2Ch 6:22 "When **a** wrongs their neighbor and is H408
2Ch 6:29 is made by **a** among your H3972+2021+132
2Ch 16: 1 to prevent *a* from **leaving** or entering the AIT
2Ch 18:30 "Do not fight with **a**, small or great, NDT
2Ch 23: 7 **A** who enters the temple is to be put to H2021
2Ch 23:14 put to the sword **a** who follows her." H2021
Ezr 6:11 I decree that if **a** defies this edict A10353+10050
Ezr 10: 8 **A** who failed to appear within three days H3972
Ne 2:12 I had not told **a** what my God had put in H132
Ne 5:13 possessions **a** who does not H3972+2021+408
Job 6:14 "**A** who withholds kindness from a friend H2021
Job 13:19 Can **a** bring charges against me? If so, I H4769
Job 17: 5 If *a* **denounces** their friends for reward, the AIT
Job 21:22 "*Can a* **teach** knowledge to God, since he AIT
Job 31:19 if I have seen *a* **perishing** for lack of clothing AIT
Job 32:21 I will show no partiality, nor will I flatter **a**; H132
Job 34: 7 Is there **a** like Job, who drinks scorn like H1505

Job 37:20 Would a ask to be swallowed up H408
Job 40:24 Can a capture it by the eyes, or trap it and AIT
Ps 39:11 you rebuke and discipline a for their sin, H408
Ps 119:42 then I can answer a who taunts me, for I trust AIT
Pr 3:30 Do not accuse a for no reason—when they H132
Pr 15:10 discipline awaits a who leaves the path; AIT
Pr 20:19 a confidence; so avoid a who talks too much. AIT
Pr 20:24 How then can a understand their own way? H132
Pr 27: 8 flees its nest is a who flees from home. H408
Pr 27:11 I can answer a who treats me with contempt. AIT
Pr 27:14 If a loudly blesses their neighbor early in the AIT
Pr 28: 9 If a turns a deaf ear to my instruction, even AIT
Pr 28:17 A tormented by the guilt of murder will H132
Ecc 1:16 wisdom more than a who has ruled over H3972
Ecc 2: 7 flocks than a in Jerusalem before H3972
Ecc 2: 9 greater by far than a in Jerusalem before H3972
Ecc 4:10 But pity a who falls and has no one to help H285
Ecc 6:11 the meaning, and how does that profit a? H132
Ecc 9: 4 A who is among the living has hope H4769
Ecc 11: 8 However many years a may live, let them H132
Isa 8:20 If a does not speak according to this word AIT
Isa 11:15 streams so that a can cross over in sandals. AIT
Isa 36: 6 pierces the hand of a who leans on it! H408
Isa 54:15 If a does attack you, it will not be my doing AIT
Jer 9: 4 of your friends; do not trust a in your clan. H3972
Jer 16: 7 nor will a give them a drink to console them. AIT
Jer 23:34 If a prophet or a priest or a else claims H6639S
Jer 26:19 king of Judah or a else in Judah put him H3972
Jer 27: 5 that are on it, and I give it to a I please. H889
Jer 36:19 Don't let a know where you are. H408
Jer 38:24 "Do not let a know about this conversation H408
Jer 41: 4 assassination, before a knew about it, H408
Jer 48:10 "A curse on a who is lax in doing the LORD's AIT
Jer 48:10 A curse on a who keeps their sword from AIT
La 3:33 willingly bring affliction or grief to a. H1201+408
Eze 6:12 a who survives and is spared will H2021S
Eze 9: 6 do not touch a who has the mark H3972+408
Eze 16:15 your favors on a who passed by and your H3972
Eze 16:25 promiscuity to a who passed by. H3972
Eze 18: 7 He does not oppress a, but returns what he H408
Eze 18:16 He does not oppress a or require a pledge H408
Eze 18:32 no pleasure in the death of a, H2021+4637S
Eze 33: 4 then if a hears the trumpet but does not heed AIT
Eze 39:15 a who sees a human bone will leave a AIT
Eze 45:20 day of the month for a who sins H408
Da 2:30 have greater wisdom than a else alive, H10353S
Da 4:17 gives them to a he wishes and A10426+10168
Da 4:25 and gives them to a he wishes. A10426+10168
Da 4:32 and gives them to a he wishes." A10426+10168
Da 5:21 and sets over them a he wishes. A10426+10168
Da 6: 7 the decree that a who prays to any god A10353
Da 6:12 thirty days a who prays to any A10353+10050
Am 6:10 to burn them asks a who might be hiding H889
Am 6:10 might be hiding there, "Is a else with you?" AIT
Mic 3: 5 wage war against a who refuses to feed H2257
Mic 5: 7 which do not wait for a or depend on man. H408
Na 3: 7 ' Where can I find a to comfort you?" AIT
Hag 2:16 When a came to a heap of twenty H4392
Hag 2:16 When a went to a wine vat to draw fifty AIT
Zec 5: 4 the house of a who swears falsely H2021S
Zec 11: 6 I will not rescue a from their hands. NDT
Zec 13: 3 And if a still prophesies, their father and H408
Mt 5:19 Therefore a who sets aside one of G4005+1569
Mt 5:21 and a who murders will be subject G4005+323
Mt 5:22 But I tell you that a who is angry with a G4246
Mt 5:22 a who says to a brother or sister G4005+323
Mt 5:22 to the court. And a who says, 'You G4005+323
Mt 5:28 But I tell you that a who looks at a woman G4246
Mt 5:31 'A who divorces his wife must give G4005+323
Mt 5:32 But I tell you that a who divorces his wife G4246
Mt 5:32 and a who marries a divorced G4005+1569
Mt 5:39 If a slaps you on the right cheek, turn to G4015
Mt 5:40 And if a wants to sue you and take your G3836
Mt 5:41 If a forces you to go one mile, go with G4015
Mt 8: 4 said to him, "See that you don't tell a. G3594
Mt 8:10 I have not found a in Israel with such G4029
Mt 10:14 If a will not welcome you or listen to your G4005
Mt 10:37 "A who loves their father or mother more G3836
Mt 10:37 a who loves their son or daughter more G3836
Mt 10:40 "A who welcomes you welcomes me, and G3836
Mt 10:40 a who welcomes me welcomes the G3836
Mt 10:42 And if a gives even a cup of cold water to G4005
Mt 11: 6 Blessed is a who does not stumble G4005+1569
Mt 11:11 there has not risen a greater than John the NDT
Mt 12:29 how can a enter a strong man's house G5516
Mt 12:32 A who speaks a word against the G4005+1569
Mt 12:32 a who speaks against the Holy G4005+323
Mt 13:19 When a hears the message about the G4246
Mt 15: 4 mother' and 'A who curses their G3836
Mt 15: 5 But you say that if a declares that what G4005
Mt 16:20 his disciples not to tell a that he was the G3594
Mt 16:26 Or what can a give in exchange for their G476
Mt 17: 9 "Don't tell a what you have seen G3594
Mt 18: 6 "If a causes one of these little ones G4005+323
Mt 19: 9 I tell you that a who divorces his wife, G4005+323
Mt 21: 3 If a says anything to you, say that the Lord G5516
Mt 21:44 A who falls on this stone will be broken to G3836
Mt 21:44 a on whom it falls will be crushed. G323
Mt 22: 9 invite to the banquet a you find. G4012+1569
Mt 23: 9 And do not call a on earth 'father,' for you NDT
Mt 23:16 You say, 'If a swears by the temple, it G4005
Mt 23:16 a who swears by the gold of the temple G323
Mt 23:18 You also say, 'If a swears by the altar, it G4005
Mt 23:18 a who swears by the gift on the altar is G323
Mt 23:20 a who swears by the altar swears by it G3836
Mt 23:21 And a who swears by the temple swears G3836
Mt 23:22 And a who swears by heaven swears by G3836
Mt 24:23 At that time if a says to you, 'Look, here is G5516
Mt 24:26 "So if a tells you, 'There he is, out in the AIT
Mk 1:44 "See that you don't tell this to a. But go G3594
Mk 4:23 If a has ears to hear, let them hear." G5516
Mk 5:37 He did not let a follow him except Peter G4029
Mk 5:43 strict orders not to let a know about this, G3594
Mk 7:10 'A who curses their father or mother is to G3836
Mk 7:11 But you say that if a declares that what G4005
Mk 7:24 a house and did not want a to know it; G4029
Mk 7:36 Jesus commanded them not to tell a. But G3594
Mk 8: 4 remote place can a get enough bread to G5516
Mk 8:30 warned them not to tell a about him. G3594
Mk 8:37 Or what can a give in exchange for their G476
Mk 8:38 If a is ashamed of me and my words in G4005
Mk 9: 3 whiter than a in the world could bleach G1187S
Mk 9: 8 they no longer saw a with them except G4029
Mk 9: 9 them orders not to tell a what they had G3594
Mk 9:30 Jesus did not want a to know where they G5516
Mk 9:35 "A who wants to be first must be the very G5516
Mk 9:41 a who gives you a cup of water in G4005+323
Mk 9:42 "If a causes one of these little ones G4005
Mk 10:11 "A who divorces his wife and G4005+323
Mk 10:15 a who will not receive the kingdom G4005+323
Mk 11: 3 If a asks you, 'Why are you doing this?' say G5516
Mk 11:16 would not allow a to carry G5516
Mk 11:23 "Truly I tell you, if a says to this mountain G4005
Mk 11:25 if you hold anything against a, forgive G5516
Mk 13:21 At that time if a says to you, 'Look, here is G5516
Mk 16: 8 They said nothing to a, because they G4029
Lk 3:11 "A who has two shirts should share with G3836
Lk 3:11 a who has food should do the same." G3836
Lk 4: 6 and I can give it to a I want to. G4005+1569
Lk 5:14 Jesus ordered him, "Don't tell a, but go, G3594
Lk 6:30 and if a takes what belongs to you G3836
Lk 7:23 Blessed is a who does not stumble G4005+1569
Lk 8:51 he did not let a go in with him except G5516
Lk 8:56 he ordered them not to tell a what had G3594
Lk 9:21 strictly warned them not to tell this to a. G3594
Lk 9:36 did not tell a at that time what G4029
Lk 10: 4 sandals; and do not greet a on the road. G3594
Lk 12:10 a who blasphemes against the Holy G3836
Lk 14:26 "If a comes to me and does not hate G5516
Lk 16:18 "A who divorces his wife and marries G4246
Lk 16:26 nor can a cross over from there to us. AIT
Lk 17: 1 woe to a through whom they come. AIT
Lk 18:17 a who will not receive the kingdom G4005+323
Lk 19:31 If a asks you, 'Why are you untying it?' say G5516
Lk 20:18 a on whom it falls will be crushed." G4005+323
Jn 6:50 heaven, which a may eat and not die. G5516
Jn 7:17 A who chooses to do the will of God will G5516
Jn 7:37 "Let a who is thirsty come to me and drink. G5516
Jn 8:33 have never been slaves of a. G4029
Jn 9:22 decided that a who acknowledged G1569+5516
Jn 10: 1 a who does not enter the sheep pen by G3836
Jn 11: 9 A who walks in the daytime will G1569+5516
Jn 11:57 given orders that a who found out G1569+5516
Jn 12:25 A who loves their life will lose it, while G3836
Jn 12:25 while a who hates their life in this world G3836
Jn 12:47 "If a hears my words but does not keep G5516
Jn 13:20 whoever accepts a I send accepts G323+5516
Jn 14: 9 A who has seen me has seen the Father G3836
Jn 14:23 "A who loves me will obey my G1569+5516
Jn 14:24 A who does not love me will not obey my G3836
Jn 16: 2 time is coming when a who kills you will G4246
Jn 16:30 even need to have a ask you questions. G5516
Jn 18:31 "But we have no right to execute a," G4029
Jn 19:12 A who claims to be a king opposes G4246
Ac 2:45 possessions to give to a who had need. G4246
Ac 3:23 A who does not listen to him will G4246+6034
Ac 4:17 speak no longer to a in this name." G3594+476
Ac 4:35 it was distributed to a who had need. G1667
Ac 9: 7 they heard the sound but did not see a. G3594
Ac 10:28 that I should not call a impure or unclean. G476
Ac 23:22 "Don't tell a that you have reported this to G3594
Ac 24:12 not find me arguing with a at the temple, G5516
Ac 25:16 to hand over a before they have G5516+476
Ro 5: 7 Very rarely will a die for a righteous person G5516
Ro 6: 7 because a who has died has been set free G3836
Ro 8: 9 And if a does not have the Spirit of Christ G5516
Ro 10:11 "A who believes in him will never be put G4246
Ro 10:15 And how can a preach unless they are sent AIT
Ro 12:17 Do not repay a evil for evil. Be careful to G3594
Ro 14:14 But if a regards something as unclean G3836
Ro 14:18 because a who serves Christ in this way is G3836
1Co 1:16 I don't remember if I baptized a else.) G5516
1Co 3:12 If a builds on this foundation using gold G5516
1Co 3:17 If a destroys God's temple, God will G5516
1Co 4: 7 For who makes you different from a else NDT
1Co 5:11 associate with a who claims to be G1569+5516
1Co 7:36 If a is worried that he might not be acting G5516
1Co 7:39 she is free to marry a she wishes, but he G4005
1Co 9:15 die than allow a to deprive me of this G4029
1Co 10:32 Do not cause a to stumble, whether Jews NDT
1Co 11:16 If a wants to be contentious about this, we G5516
1Co 11:34 A who is hungry should eat something at G5516
1Co 14: 2 For a who speaks in a tongue does not G3836
1Co 14: 4 A who speaks in a tongue edifies G3836
1Co 14: 7 how will a know what tune is being played AIT
1Co 14: 9 how will a know what you are saying? AIT
1Co 14:27 If a speaks in a tongue, two—or at the G5516
1Co 14:37 If a thinks they are a prophet or otherwise G5516
1Co 14:38 But if a ignores this, they will themselves G5516
1Co 16:22 If a does not love the Lord, let that person G5516
2Co 2: 5 If a has caused grief, he has not so much G5516
2Co 2:10 A you forgive, I also forgive. And G4005+5516
2Co 3:16 But whenever a turns to the Lord, the veil is AIT
2Co 5:17 Therefore, if a is in Christ, the new G5516
2Co 10: 7 If a is confident that they belong to Christ G5516
2Co 11: 9 I was not a burden to a, for the brothers G4029
2Co 11:20 even put up with a who enslaves you or G5516
2Co 11:21 Whatever a else dares to boast about—I G5516
Gal 6: 3 If a thinks they are something when they G5516
Eph 4:28 A who has been stealing must steal no G3836
Col 2:16 Therefore do not let a judge you by what G5516
Col 2:18 Do not let a who delights in false humility G3594
Col 3:25 A who does wrong will be repaid for their G3836
1Th 2: 6 not from you or a else, even though as G257
1Th 2: 9 to be a burden to a while we preached G5516
1Th 4: 8 a who rejects this instruction does not G3836
2Th 2: 3 Don't let a deceive you in any way, for that G5516
2Th 3:14 Take special note of a who does not obey G5516
1Ti 3: 5 If a does not know how to manage his G5516
1Ti 4:12 Don't let a look down on you because you G3594
1Ti 5: 8 A who does not provide for their relatives G5516
1Ti 6: 3 If a teaches otherwise and does not agree G5516
2Ti 2: 5 a who competes as an athlete does not G5516
Titus 2:15 Do not let a despise you. G3594
Heb 4:10 a who enters God's rest also rests from G3836
Heb 5:13 A who lives on milk, being still an infant G4246
Heb 10:28 A who rejected the law of Moses died G5516
Heb 11: 6 because a who comes to him must G3836
Jas 1:13 be tempted by evil, nor does he tempt a; G4029
Jas 1:23 A who listens to the word but does not do G5516
Jas 2:13 will be shown to a who has not been G3836
Jas 3: 2 A who is never at fault in what they say is G5516
Jas 4: 4 a who chooses to be a friend of the G4005+1569
Jas 4:11 A who speaks against a brother or sister G3836
Jas 4:17 If a, then, knows the good they ought to do AIT
Jas 5:13 Is a among you in trouble? Let them pray G5516
Jas 5:13 Let them pray. Is a happy? Let them sing G5516
Jas 5:14 Is a among you sick? Let them call the G5516
1Pe 4:11 If a speaks, they should do so as one who G5516
1Pe 4:11 If a serves, they should do so with the G5516
2Pe 3: 9 with you, not wanting a to perish, but G5516
1Jn 2: 5 But if a obeys his word, love for God is G4005
1Jn 2: 9 A who claims to be in the light but hates G3836
1Jn 2:10 A who loves their brother and sister lives G3836
1Jn 2:11 But a who hates a brother or sister is in the G3836
1Jn 2:15 If a loves the world, love for the Father is G5516
1Jn 2:27 and you do not need a to teach you. G5516
1Jn 3: 7 children, do not let a lead you astray. G3594
1Jn 3:10 A who does not do what is right is not G4246
1Jn 3:10 is a who does not love their brother G3836
1Jn 3:14 A who does not love remains in death. G3836
1Jn 3:15 A who hates a brother or sister is a G4246
1Jn 3:17 If a has material possessions and sees a G4005
1Jn 4:15 If a acknowledges that Jesus is the Son of G4005
1Jn 4:21 A who loves God must also love their G3836
1Jn 5:18 We know that a born of God does not G4246
2Jn 9 A who runs ahead and does not continue G4246
2Jn 10 If a comes to you and does not bring this G5516
2Jn 11 A who welcomes them shares in their G3836
3Jn 11 A who does what is good is from God G3836
3Jn 11 A who does what is evil has not seen God G3836
Rev 3:20 If a hears my voice and opens the door, I G5516
Rev 11: 5 If a tries to harm them, fire comes from G5516
Rev 11: 5 This is how a who wants to harm them G5516
Rev 13:10 "If a is to go into captivity, into captivity G5516
Rev 13:10 If a is to be killed with the sword, with the G5516
Rev 14: 9 "If a worships the beast and its image G5516
Rev 14:11 for a who receives the mark of its name." G5516
Rev 20:15 A whose name was not found written in G5516
Rev 21:27 will a who does what is shameful or G3836
Rev 22:18 If a adds anything to them, God will add G5516
Rev 22:19 And if a takes words away from this scroll G5516

ANYONE'S (8) [ANY]

Ex 21:35 "If a bull injures someone else's bull and it H408
1Sa 12: 4 "You have not taken anything from a hand." H408
Pr 16: 7 When the LORD takes pleasure in a way, he H408
Jn 20:23 If you forgive a sins, their sins are forgiven G5516
Ac 20:33 I have not coveted a silver or gold or G4029
Ro 5:13 not charged against a account where there NDT
2Co 6: 3 We put no stumbling block in a path, so G3594
2Th 3: 8 did we eat a food without G4123+5516

ANYTHING (209) [ANY]

Ge 18:14 Is a too hard for the LORD? I will return to H1821
Ge 19: 8 But don't do a to these men, for they have H1821
Ge 19:22 because I cannot do a until you reach it." H1821
Ge 22:12 "Do not do a to him. Now I know H4399
Ge 30:31 "Don't give me a," Jacob replied. "But H4399
Ge 31:24 "Be careful not to say a to Jacob, either AIT
Ge 31:29 'Be careful not to say a to Jacob, either NDT
Ge 31:32 whether there is a of yours here with me; NDT
Ge 39: 6 concern himself with a except the food he H4399
Ge 39: 8 not concern himself with a in the house; H4537
Ge 39:23 no attention to a under Joseph's H3972+4399
Ge 44: 7 be it from your servants to do a like that! H1821

Ex 12:15 whoever eats **a with yeast in it** from the H2809
Ex 12:19 who eats **a with yeast in it** must be cut off H4721
Ex 20: 4 image in the form *of* a in heaven above H3972
Ex 20:17 **a** that belongs to your neighbor. H3972
Ex 21: 2 he shall go free, **without paying a**. H2855
Ex 23:18 to me along with **a containing yeast**. H2809
Ex 34:25 to me along with **a containing yeast**, H2809
Ex 36: 6 woman is to make **a** else as an offering H4856
Lev 5: 2 unwittingly touch **a** ceremonially H3972+1821
Lev 5: 3 (**a** that would make them unclean H3972
Lev 5: 4 anyone thoughtlessly takes an oath to do **a**, NDT
Lev 7:16 **a** left over may be eaten on the next H2021
Lev 7:19 'Meat that touches **a** ceremonially H3972
Lev 11:12 **A** living in the water that does not have H3972
Lev 11:35 **A** that one of their carcasses falls on H3972
Lev 12: 4 She must not touch **a** sacred or go to the H3972
Lev 13:48 any leather or **a** made of leather— H3972
Lev 15: 4 and **a** he sits on will be H3972+2021+3998
Lev 15: 6 Whoever sits on **a** that the man with a H3998
Lev 15:20 " '**A** she lies on during her period will be H3972
Lev 15:20 **a** she sits on will be unclean. H3972
Lev 15:22 who touches **a** she sits on will H3972+3998
Lev 15:23 it is the bed or **a** she was sitting on, H3998
Lev 15:26 and **a** she sits on will be H3972+2021+3998
Lev 17:15 who eats **a found dead** or torn by wild H5577
Lev 19: 6 **a** left over until the third day must be H2021
Lev 19:16 *Do* not **do a that endangers** your neighbor's **life** H6641+6584+1947
Lev 20:25 animal or bird or **a** that moves along the H3972
Lev 22: 8 He must not eat **a found dead** or torn by H5577
Lev 22:20 Do not bring **a** with a defect, because it H3972
Lev 22:22 or **a with warts** or festering or running H3301
Nu 6: 4 they must not eat **a** that comes from the H3972
Nu 11: 6 appetite; we never see **a** but this manna!" H3972
Nu 16:26 Do not touch **a** belonging to them, or you H3972
Nu 19:22 **A** that an unclean person touches H3972
Nu 22:16 *Do* not *let a* **keep** *you* from coming to me AIT
Nu 22:18 I could not do *a* **great** or small to go beyond AIT
Nu 24:13 not do *a* of my own accord, **good** or bad, AIT
Nu 31:23 **a** else that can withstand fire H3972+1821
Dt 2: 7 with you, and you have not lacked **a**. H1821
Dt 4:23 idol in the form of **a** the LORD your God H3972
Dt 4:32 Has **a** so great as this ever happened, or H1821
Dt 4:32 has **a** like it ever been heard of? NDT
Dt 5: 8 in the form of **a** in heaven above or H3972
Dt 5:21 **a** that belongs to your neighbor. H3972
Dt 14:10 But **a** that does not have fins and scales H3972
Dt 14:21 Do not eat **a** you find already dead. You H3972
Dt 14:26 other fermented drink, or **a** you wish. H3972
Dt 18:20 to speak in my name **a** I have not H1821
Dt 20:16 do not leave alive **a** that breathes. H3972
Dt 22: 3 donkey or cloak or **a** *else* they have lost. H3972
Dt 23:14 not see among you **a** indecent and turn H1821
Dt 23:19 money or food or **a** else that may H3972+1821
Jdg 13: 4 drink and that you do not eat **a** unclean. H3972
Jdg 13: 7 drink and do not eat **a** unclean, H3972
Jdg 13:14 She must not eat **a** that comes from the H3972
Jdg 13:14 other fermented drink nor eat **a** unclean. H3972
Jdg 19:19 man with us. We don't need **a**." H3972+1821
1Sa 3:17 from me **a** he told you." H1821+4946+3972+2021+1821
1Sa 12: 4 have not taken **a** from anyone's hand." H4399
1Sa 12: 5 that you have not found **a** in my hand." H4399
1Sa 20: 2 my father doesn't do **a**, great or small, H1821
1Sa 21: 2 'No one is to know **a** about the mission I H4399
1Sa 30:19 plunder or **a** *else* they had taken. H3972
2Sa 3:35 taste bread or **a** *else* before the H3972+4399
2Sa 13: 2 seemed impossible for him to do **a** to her. H4399
2Sa 14:10 "If anyone says **a** to you, bring them to me NDT
2Sa 14:19 to the left from **a** my lord the king says. H3972
2Sa 14:32 if I am guilty of **a**, let him put me to NDT
2Sa 15:35 Tell them **a** you hear in the H3972+2021+1821
2Sa 15:36 Send them to me with **a** you hear." H3972+1821
2Sa 17:19 No one knew **a** about it. H1821
2Sa 19:38 And **a** you desire from me I will do for you H3972
2Sa 19:42 *Have we* **taken a** for ourselves?" H5951+5951
1Ki 14:13 the God of Israel, has found **a** good. H1821
1Ki 22: 8 he never prophesies *a* **good** about me, AIT
1Ki 22:18 that he never prophesies *a* **good** about me, AIT
2Ki 10: 5 your servants and we will do **a** you say. H3972
2Ch 18: 7 he never prophesies *a* **good** about me, AIT
2Ch 18:17 that he never prophesies *a* **good** about me, AIT
Ezr 7:20 And **a** else needed for the temple of A10692
Ne 5:12 we will not demand **a** more from them. NDT
Est 2:13 **A** she wanted was given her to take H3972+889
Est 6:10 Do not neglect **a** you have H1821+4946+3972
Job 21:25 never having enjoyed **a** good. H2021S
Job 27: 4 my lips will not say **a wicked**, and my H6406
Job 33:32 If you have **a to say**, answer me; speak up, H4863
Ps 39: 2 utterly silent, not even saying *a* **good**. AIT
Ps 73:11 Does the Most High know **a**?" NDT
Ps 101: 3 not look with approval on **a** *that* is vile. H1821
Pr 14:15 The simple believe **a**, but the H3972+1821
Ecc 1:10 Is there **a** of which one can say, "Look H1821
Ecc 5: 2 hasty in your heart to utter **a** before God. H1821
Ecc 6: 5 Though it never saw the sun or knew **a**, it H4202S
Ecc 7:14 no one can discover **a** about their future. H4399
Ecc 9: 6 they have **a** part in **a** that happens under H3972
Ecc 12:12 warned, my son, of **a in addition** to them. H3463
Jer 2:10 see if there has ever been **a** like this: NDT
Jer 18:13 Who has ever heard **a** like this? A most NDT
Jer 18:18 pay no attention to **a** he says. H3972
Jer 32:27 all mankind. Is **a** too hard for me? H3972+1821
Jer 38:14 "Do not hide **a** from me." H1821
Eze 4:14 never eaten **a found dead** or torn by wild H5577
Eze 15: 3 wood ever taken from it to make **a useful**? H4856
Eze 15: 4 chars the middle, is it then useful for **a**? H4856
Eze 15: 5 it was not useful for **a** when it was whole, H4856
Eze 44:18 They must not wear **a** that makes them NDT
Eze 44:31 The priests must not eat **a**, whether bird H3972
Da 3:29 language who say **a** against the God of A10712
Joel 1: 2 Has **a** like this ever happened in your days NDT
Am 3: 5 up from the ground if it has **not** caught *a*? AIT
Am 8: 7 "I will never forget **a** they have done. H3972
Jnh 3: 7 flocks, taste **a**; do not let them eat H4399
Mt 5:13 It is **no** longer good for **a**, except to be G4029
Mt 5:37 **a** beyond this comes from the evil one. G3836
Mt 12:34 how can you who are evil say *a* **good**? AIT
Mt 13:34 he did **not** say **a** to them without using a G4029
Mt 18:19 earth agree about **a** they ask for, G4246+4547
Mt 21: 3 If anyone says **a** to you, say that the Lord G5516
Mt 24:17 go down to take **a** out of the house. G3836
Mt 27:19 "**Don't** have **a** to do with that innocent G3594
Mk 2:12 "We have **never** seen **a** like this! G4030
Mk 4:34 He did not say **a** to them without using a NDT
Mk 6:22 "Ask me for **a** you want, and G4005+1569
Mk 7:12 no longer let them do **a** for their father G4029
Mk 8:23 on him, Jesus asked, "Do you see **a**?" G5516
Mk 9:22 But if you can do **a**, take pity on us and G5516
Mk 9:39 can in the next moment **say** *a* **bad about** me, AIT
Mk 11:25 praying, if you hold **a** against anyone G5516
Mk 13:15 go down or enter the house to take **a** out. G5516
Lk 5: 5 hard all night and **haven't** caught **a**. G4029
Lk 6:35 to them **without** expecting to get **a** back. G3594
Lk 11: 7 I can't get up and give you **a**.' NDT
Lk 15:16 pigs were eating, but no one gave him **a**. NDT
Lk 17:31 no one in the field *should* **go back** *for a*. AIT
Lk 19: 8 if I have cheated anybody out of **a**, I G5516
Lk 22:35 bag or sandals, did you lack **a**?" G3590+5516
Lk 24:41 asked them, "Do you have **a** here to eat?" G5516
Jn 1:46 Can **a** good come from there? G5516
Jn 7:13 But no one would say **a** publicly about him NDT
Jn 14:14 You may ask me for **a** in my name, and I G5516
Jn 16:23 In that day you will no longer ask me **a** G4029
Jn 16:24 you have not asked *for* **a** in my name. G4029
Ac 9: 9 he was blind, and did not eat or drink **a**. NDT
Ac 10:14 "I have never eaten **a** impure or unclean." G4246
Ac 10:15 "Do not call **a** impure that God has made G4005
Ac 11: 9 'Do not call **a** impure *that* God has made G4005
Ac 15:28 to us **not** to burden you *with* **a** beyond G3594
Ac 17:25 by human hands, as if he needed **a**. G5516
Ac 19:36 ought to calm down and **not** do **a** rash. G3594
Ac 19:39 If there is **a** further you want to bring up, it G5516
Ac 20:20 I have **not** hesitated to preach **a** that G4029
Ac 23:14 oath not to eat **a** until we have killed NDT
Ac 24:19 bring charges if they have **a** against me. G5516
Ac 25: 5 if the man has done **a** wrong, they G5516
Ac 25:11 I am guilty of doing **a** deserving death, I G5516
Ac 26:31 man is not doing **a** that deserves death G5516
Ac 27:33 gone without food—you **haven't** eaten **a**. G3594
Ac 28:21 has reported or said **a** bad about you. G5516
Ro 8:39 depth, nor **a** else in all creation G5516
Ro 9:11 were born or had done **a** good or bad— G5516
Ro 14: 2 One person's faith allows them to eat **a** G4246
Ro 14:20 a person to eat **a** that causes someone NDT
Ro 14:21 drink wine or to do **a** else that will cause NDT
Ro 15:18 venture to speak *of* **a** except what Christ G5516
1Co 3: 7 who plants nor the one who waters is **a**, G5516
1Co 6:12 "I have the right to do **a**," you say—but G4246
1Co 6:12 "I have the right to do **a**"—but I will not G4246
1Co 6:12 I will not be mastered by **a**. G5516
1Co 9:12 we put up with **a** rather than hinder the G4246
1Co 10:19 then that food sacrificed to an idol is **a**, G5515
1Co 10:19 to an idol is anything, or that an idol is **a**? G5515
1Co 10:23 "I have the right to do **a**," you say—but G4246
1Co 10:23 "I have the right to do **a**"—but not G4246
1Co 10:25 Eat **a** sold in the meat market without G4246
2Co 1:13 we do not write you **a** you cannot read G4005
2Co 2:10 forgiven—if there was **a** to forgive—I have G5516
2Co 3: 5 in ourselves to claim **a** for ourselves, G5516
2Co 9: 4 not to **say** *a about* you—would be AIT
2Co 13: 7 to God that you will not do **a** wrong— G3594
2Co 13: 8 For we cannot do **a** against the truth, but G5516
Gal 6:15 circumcision nor uncircumcision means **a**; G5516
Php 4: 6 Do **not** be anxious *about* **a**, but in every G3594
Php 4: 8 if **a** is excellent or praiseworthy G5516
1Th 1: 8 we do not need to say **a** about it, G5516
2Ti 1: 9 not because of **a** we have done but G3836
2Ti 2:23 **Don't have a to do with** foolish and stupid G4148
Titus 1:16 disobedient and unfit for doing **a** good. G4246
Phm 14 But I did **not** want to do **a** without your G4029
Phm 18 If he has done you any wrong or owes you **a** NDT
Jas 1: 4 be mature and complete, **not** lacking **a**. G3594
Jas 1: 7 not expect to receive **a** from the Lord. G5516
Jas 5:12 not by heaven or by earth or *by* **a** else. G5516
1Jn 2:15 Do not love the world or **a** in the world. If G3836
1Jn 3:22 receive from him **a** we ask G4005+1569
1Jn 5:14 that if we ask **a** according to his will, he G5516
Rev 22:18 If anyone adds **a** to them, God will add to NDT

ANYWHERE (16) [ANY]

Ge 19:17 look back, and don't stop **a** in the plain! H3972
Ex 10:19 Not a locust was left **a** in Egypt. H3972
Ex 13: 7 any yeast be seen **a** within your borders. H3972
Ex 34: 3 with you or be seen **a** on the mountain; H3972
Nu 18:31 may eat the rest of it **a**, H928+3972+5226
Dt 12:13 burnt offerings **a** you please. H928+3972+5226
Dt 18: 6 one of your towns **a** in Israel where he is H3972
1Sa 9: 2 man as could be found **a in** Israel, H4946+1201
1Sa 27: 1 up searching for me **a in** Israel, H3972+1473
2Sa 21: 5 and have no place **a in** Israel, H928+3972+1473
1Ki 2:36 but do not go **a else**. H625+2025+2256+625+2025
1Ki 2:42 you leave to go **a else**, H625+2025+2256+625+2025
2Ki 5:25 servant didn't go **a**, H625+2025+2256+625+2025
Jer 40: 5 the people, or go **a** *else* you please." H3972
Jer 44:26 one from Judah living **a** in Egypt will ever H3972
Ac 24:12 in the synagogues or **a else in** the city. G2848

APART (58) [PART]

Ge 21:28 Abraham set **a** seven ewe lambs H963+4200
Ge 21:29 you have set **a** by themselves? H4200+963
Ge 30:40 **set a** the young of the flock **by themselves** H7233
Ex 19:23 around the mountain and **set it a as holy**. H7727
Ex 32:29 "You *have been* **set a** to the LORD H4848+3338
Lev 20:24 who *has* set you **a** from the nations. H976
Lev 20:25 those that *I have* **set a** as unclean for you. H976
Lev 20:26 and *I have* **set** you **a** from the nations to be H976
Nu 3:13 *I* **set a** for myself every firstborn in Israel H7727
Nu 8:14 this way *you are to* **set** the Levites **a** from H976
Nu 8:17 firstborn in Egypt, *I* **set** them **a** for myself. H7727
Nu 16:31 the ground under them **split a** H1324
Nu 23: 9 a people who live **a** and do not H4200+970
Nu 31:28 **set a** as tribute for the LORD one out of H8123
Nu 31:42 which Moses **set a** from that of the H2936
Dt 7:26 like it, will be **set a for destruction**. H3051
Dt 7:26 detest it, for it is **set a for destruction**. H3051
Dt 10: 8 At that time the LORD **set a** the tribe of Levi H976
Dt 15:19 **Set a** for the LORD your God every firstborn H7727
Jos 20: 7 So *they* **set a** Kedesh in Galilee in the hill H7727
Jdg 14: 6 him so that *he* **tore** the lion **a** with his H9117
Jdg 20:17 **a** from Benjamin, mustered H4200+963
1Ki 13: 3 The altar *will* **be split a** and the ashes on H7973
1Ki 13: 5 the altar **was split a** and its ashes poured H7973
1Ki 19:11 powerful wind **tore** the mountains **a** and H7293
1Ch 23:13 Aaron **was set a**, he and his descendants H976
1Ch 25: 1 the army, **set a** some of the sons of Asaph H976
Ezr 8:24 Then *I* **set a** twelve of the leading priests H976
Ps 4: 3 Know that the LORD *has* **set a** his faithful H7111
Ps 7: 2 or *they will* **tear** me **a** like a lion and rip H3271
Ps 16: 2 Lord; **a from** you I have no good thing." H6584
Ps 88: 5 I am **set a** with the dead, like the slain H2930
Pr 18:18 disputes and **keeps** strong opponents **a**. H7233
Isa 7: 6 *let us* **tear** it **a** and divide it among H7763
Isa 23:18 her earnings will be **set a** for the LORD; H7731
Isa 43:11 and **a from** me there is no savior. H4946+1187
Isa 44: 6 **a from** me there is no God. H4946+1187
Isa 45: 5 is no other; **a from** me there is no God. H2314
Isa 45:21 And there is no God **a from** me, a H4946+1187
Jer 1: 5 before you were born *I* **set** you **a**; I H7727
Jer 12: 3 **Set** them **a** for the day of slaughter! H7727
Hos 13: 8 a wild animal *will* **tear** them **a**. H1324
Mic 1: 4 melt beneath him and the valleys **split a**, H1324
Mk 5: 4 he **tore** the chains **a** and broke the G1400
Jn 10:36 the Father **set a as** *his* **very own** and sent G39
Jn 15: 5 much fruit; **a from** me you can do nothing. G6006
Ac 13: 2 "**Set a** for me Barnabas and Saul for the G928
Ro 1: 1 to be an apostle and **set a** for the gospel of G928
Ro 2:12 All who sin **a from the law** will also perish G492
Ro 2:12 the law will also perish **a from the law**, G492
Ro 3:21 But now **a from** the law the righteousness G6006
Ro 3:28 justified by faith **a from** the works of the G6006
Ro 4: 6 God credits righteousness **a from** works: G6006
Ro 7: 8 For **a from** the law, sin was G6006
Ro 7: 9 Once I was alive **a from** the law; but when G6006
2Co 12: 3 in the body or **a from** the body I do not G6006
Gal 1:15 who set me **a** from my mother's womb G928
Heb 7:26 **set a** from sinners, exalted above G6004

APARTMENT (1)

Jer 36:22 the king was sitting in the winter **a**, H1074

APELLES (1)

Ro 16:10 Greet **A**, whose fidelity to Christ has stood G593

APES (2)

1Ki 10:22 silver and ivory, and **a** and baboons. H7761
2Ch 9:21 silver and ivory, and **a** and baboons. H7761

APHARSACHITES, APHARSATHCHITES (KJV) OFFICIALS

APHARSITES (KJV) PERSIA

APHEK (9)

Jos 12:18 the king of **A** one the king of Lasharon one H707
Jos 13: 4 Sidonians as far as **A** and the border of the H707
Jos 19:30 Ummah, **A** and Rehob. There were H707
Jdg 1:31 Ahlab or Akzib or Helbah or **A** or Rehob. H707
1Sa 4: 1 at Ebenezer, and the Philistines at **A**. H707
1Sa 29: 1 Philistines gathered all their forces at **A**, H707
1Ki 20:26 went up to **A** to fight against Israel H707
1Ki 20:30 The rest of them escaped to the city of **A** H707
2Ki 13:17 will completely destroy the Arameans at **A**." H707

APHEKAH (1)

Jos 15:53 Beth Tappuah, **A**, H708

APHIAH (1)
1Sa 9: 1 son of Bekorath, the son of **A** *of* Benjamin. H688

APHRAH (KJV) BETH OPHRAH

APHSES (KJV) HAPPIZZEZ

APOLLONIA (1)
Ac 17: 1 had passed through Amphipolis and **A**, *G662*

APOLLOS (11)
Ac 18:24 Meanwhile a Jew named **A**, a native of *G663*
Ac 18:27 When **A** wanted to go to Achaia, the *G899S*
Ac 19: 1 While **A** was at Corinth, Paul took the road *G663*
1Co 1:12 another, "I follow **A**"; another, "I follow *G663*
1Co 3: 4 another, "I follow **A**," are you not mere *G663*
1Co 3: 5 after all, is **A**? And what is Paul *G663*
1Co 3: 6 I planted the seed, **A** watered it, but God *G663*
1Co 3:22 whether Paul or **A** or Cephas or the world *G663*
1Co 4: 6 things to myself and **A** for your benefit, *G663*
1Co 16:12 Now about our brother **A**: I strongly urged *G663*
Titus 3:13 the lawyer and **A** on their way and see *G663*

APOLLYON (1)
Rev 9:11 in Hebrew is Abaddon and in Greek is **A** *G661*

APOSTLE (21) [APOSTLES, APOSTLES', APOSTLESHIP, APOSTOLIC, SUPER-APOSTLES]
Ro 1: 1 called to be an **a** and set apart for the *G693*
Ro 11:13 Inasmuch as I am the **a** to the Gentiles, I *G693*
1Co 1: 1 called to be an **a** of Christ Jesus by the will *G693*
1Co 9: 1 Am I not an **a**? Have I not seen *G693*
1Co 9: 2 Even though I may not be an **a** to others *G693*
1Co 15: 9 do not even deserve to be called an **a**, *G693*
2Co 1: 1 an **a** of Christ Jesus by the will of God *G693*
2Co 12:12 among you the marks *of a true* **a**, *G693*
Gal 1: 1 an **a**—sent not from men nor by a *G693*
Gal 2: 8 at work in Peter as an **a** to the circumcised, *G692*
Gal 2: 8 also at work in me as an **a** to the Gentiles. NDT
Eph 1: 1 an **a** of Christ Jesus by the will of God *G693*
Col 1: 1 an **a** of Christ Jesus by the will of God *G693*
1Ti 1: 1 an **a** of Christ Jesus by the command of *G693*
1Ti 2: 7 I was appointed a herald and an **a**— *G693*
2Ti 1: 1 an **a** of Christ Jesus by the will of God *G693*
2Ti 1:11 a herald and an **a** and a teacher. *G693*
Titus 1: 1 a servant of God and an **a** of Jesus Christ to *G693*
Heb 3: 1 we acknowledge *as* our **a** and high priest. *G693*
1Pe 1: 1 an **a** of Jesus Christ, To God's elect *G693*
2Pe 1: 1 a servant and **a** of Jesus Christ, To *G693*

APOSTLES (57) [APOSTLE]
Mt 10: 2 These are the names *of* the twelve **a**: first *G693*
Mk 6:30 The **a** gathered around Jesus and reported *G693*
Lk 6:13 of them, whom he also designated **a**: *G693*
Lk 9:10 When the **a** returned, they reported to *G693*
Lk 11:49 'I will send them prophets and **a**, some of *G693*
Lk 17: 5 The **a** said to the Lord, "Increase our faith!" *G693*
Lk 22:14 Jesus and his **a** reclined at the table. *G693*
Lk 24:10 the others with them who told this to the **a**. *G693*
Ac 1: 2 the Holy Spirit *to* the **a** he had chosen. *G693*
Ac 1:12 Then the **a** returned to Jerusalem from the NDT
Ac 1:26 Matthias; so he was added to the eleven **a**. *G693*
Ac 2:37 the heart and said to Peter and the other **a**, *G693*
Ac 2:43 wonders and signs performed by the **a**. *G693*
Ac 4: 2 disturbed because **the a** were teaching *G899S*
Ac 4:33 With great power the **a** continued to testify *G693*
Ac 4:36 from Cyprus, whom the **a** called Barnabas *G693*
Ac 5:12 The **a** performed many signs and wonders *G693*
Ac 5:18 They arrested the **a** and put them in the *G693*
Ac 5:21 of Israel—and sent to the jail for **the a**. *G899S*
Ac 5:26 went with his officers and brought **the a**. *G899S*
Ac 5:27 **The a** were brought in and made to *G899S*
Ac 5:29 Peter and the other **a** replied: "We must *G693*
Ac 5:40 They called the **a** in and had them flogged. *G693*
Ac 5:41 **The a** left the Sanhedrin, rejoicing *G3836S*
Ac 6: 6 They presented these men to the **a**, who *G693*
Ac 8: 1 all except the **a** were scattered *G693*
Ac 8:14 When the **a** in Jerusalem heard that *G693*
Ac 9:27 took him and brought him to the **a**. *G693*
Ac 11: 1 The **a** and the believers throughout Judea *G693*
Ac 14: 4 sided with the Jews, others with the **a**. *G693*
Ac 14:14 But when the **a** Barnabas and Paul heard *G693*
Ac 15: 2 Jerusalem to see the **a** and elders about *G693*
Ac 15: 4 by the church and the **a** and elders, *G693*
Ac 15: 6 The **a** and elders met to consider this *G693*
Ac 15:22 Then the **a** and elders, with the whole *G693*
Ac 15:23 The **a** and elders, your brothers, To the *G693*
Ac 16: 4 reached by the **a** and elders in Jerusalem *G693*
Ro 16: 7 They are outstanding among the **a**, and *G693*
1Co 4: 9 that God has put us **a** on display at the end *G693*
1Co 9: 5 as do the other **a** and the Lord's brothers *G693*
1Co 12:28 God has placed in the church first of all **a**, *G693*
1Co 12:29 Are all **a**? Are all prophets? Are all teachers *G693*
1Co 15: 7 he appeared to James, then to all the **a**, *G693*
1Co 15: 9 For I am the least *of* the **a** and do not even *G693*
2Co 11:13 For such people are **false a**, deceitful *G6013*
2Co 11:13 workers, masquerading as **a** of Christ. *G693*
Gal 1:17 to see those who were **a** before I was, *G693*
Gal 1:19 I saw none *of* the other **a**—only James, the *G693*
Eph 2:20 on the foundation *of* the **a** and prophets, *G693*
Eph 3: 5 by the Spirit *to* God's holy **a** and prophets. *G693*
Eph 4:11 So Christ himself gave the **a**, the prophets *G693*
1Th 2: 6 even though as **a** of Christ we could have *G693*
2Pe 3: 2 by our Lord and Savior *through* your **a**. *G693*
Jude 17 remember what the **a** of our Lord Jesus *G693*
Rev 2: 2 tested those who claim to be **a** but are not, *G693*
Rev 18:20 Rejoice, **a** and prophets! For God *G693*
Rev 21:14 the names *of* the twelve **a** of the Lamb. *G693*

APOSTLES' (5) [APOSTLE]
Ac 2:42 themselves to the **a** teaching and to *G693*
Ac 4:35 put it at the **a** feet, and it was *G693*
Ac 4:37 brought the money and put it at the **a** feet. *G693*
Ac 5: 2 brought the rest and put it at the **a** feet. *G693*
Ac 8:18 was given at the laying on of the **a** hands, *G693*

APOSTLESHIP (2) [APOSTLE]
Ro 1: 5 we received grace and **a** to call all the *G692*
1Co 9: 2 For you are the seal *of* my **a** in the Lord. *G692*

APOSTOLIC (1) [APOSTLE]
Ac 1:25 to take over this **a** ministry, which Judas left *G692*

APOTHECARIES, APOTHECARIES', APOTHECARY (KJV) PERFUME, PERFUME-MAKERS, PERFUMER, PERFUMES

APPAIM (2)
1Ch 2:30 Seled and **A**. Seled died without H691
1Ch 2:31 The son of **A**: Ishi, who was the father of H691

APPALLED (26)
Lev 26:32 your enemies who live there *will be* **a**. H9037
1Ki 9: 8 All who pass by *will be* **a** and will scoff H9037
2Ch 7:21 All who pass by *will be* **a** and say, 'Why H9037
Ezr 9: 3 from my head and beard and sat down **a**. H9037
Ezr 9: 4 And I sat there **a** until the evening H9037
Job 17: 8 The upright *are* **a** at this; the innocent are H9037
Job 18:20 People of the west **are a** at his fate; those H9037
Job 21: 5 Look at me and *be* **a**; clap your hand over H9037
Ps 40:15 *May* those who say to me, "Aha! Aha!" *be* **a** H9037
Isa 52:14 as there were many *who were* **a** at him— H9037
Isa 59:16 *he was* **a** that there was no one to H9037
Isa 63: 5 to help, *I was* **a** that no one gave support H9037
Jer 2:12 *Be* **a** at this, *you* heavens, and shudder H9037
Jer 4: 9 be horrified, and the prophets *will be* **a**." H9449
Jer 18:16 all who pass by *will be* **a** and will shake H9037
Jer 19: 8 all who pass by *will be* **a** and will scoff H9037
Jer 49:17 all who pass by *will be* **a** and will scoff H9037
Jer 49:20 their pasture *will be* **a** at their fate. H9037
Jer 50:13 All who pass Babylon *will be* **a**; they will H9037
Jer 50:45 their pasture *will be* **a** at their fate. H9037
Eze 4:17 *They will be* **a** at the sight of each other H9037
Eze 26:16 trembling every moment, **a** at you. H9037
Eze 27:35 who live in the coastlands *are* **a** at you; H9037
Eze 28:19 the nations who knew you *are* **a** at you; H9037
Eze 32:10 *I will* **cause** many peoples **to be a** at you H9037
Da 8:27 *I was* **a** by the vision; it was beyond H9037

APPEAL (17) [APPEALED, APPEALING, APPEALS]
Dt 15: 9 *They may* then **a** to the LORD against you H7924
2Ki 8: 3 went to **a** to the king for her H7590
2Ki 8: 5 back to life came *to* **a** to the king for her H7590
Job 5: 8 if I were you, *I would* **a** to God; I would H2011
Ps 77:10 I thought, "*To* this I *will* **a**: the years when H2704
Ac 25:11 to hand me over to them. *I* **a** to Caesar!" *G2126*
Ac 25:21 But *when* Paul **made** *his* **a** to be held over *G2126*
Ac 25:25 but *because* he **made** his **a** to the *G2126*
Ac 28:19 I was compelled *to* **make an a** to Caesar. *G2126*
1Co 1:10 *I* **a** to you, brothers and sisters, in the *G4151*
2Co 5:20 though God *were* **making** *his* **a** through us *G4151*
2Co 8:17 For Titus not only welcomed our **a**, but he *G4155*
2Co 10: 1 gentleness of Christ, I **a** to you—I, *G4151*
1Th 2: 3 For the **a** we make does not spring from *G4155*
Phm 9 *yet I* prefer *to* **a** to you on the basis of love *G4151*
Phm 10 *that I* **a** to you for my son Onesimus, who *G4151*
1Pe 5: 1 *I* **a** as a fellow elder and a witness of *G4151*

APPEALED (7) [APPEAL]
Ex 5:15 Israelite overseers went and **a** to Pharaoh: H7590
Jos 10: 3 king of Jerusalem **a** to Hoham king of H8938
Est 2: 4 This advice **a to** the king H3512+928+6524
Lk 23:20 to release Jesus, Pilate **a to** them again. *G4715*
Ac 25:12 "*You have* **a** to Caesar. To *G2126*
Ac 26:32 been set free if *he had* not **a** to Caesar." *G2126*
Ro 11: 2 Elijah—how *he* **a** to God against Israel: *G1961*

APPEALING (2) [APPEAL]
Hos 7:14 *They* **slash themselves, a to their gods** H1517
2Pe 2:18 **by a to** the lustful desires of the flesh *G1877*

APPEALS (1) [APPEAL]
2Sa 19:28 do I have to **make** any more **a** to the king?" H2410

APPEAR (49) [APPEARANCE, APPEARANCES, APPEARED, APPEARING, APPEARS, REAPPEARS]
Ge 1: 9 to one place, and *let* dry ground **a**." H8011
Ge 27:12 *I would* **a** to be tricking H2118+928+6524+3869
Ex 4: 1 me and say, 'The LORD *did* not **a** to you'?" H8011
Ex 10:28 Make sure *you do* not **a** before me again H8011
Ex 10:29 "*I will* never **a** before you again. H8011
Ex 22: 8 of the house *must* **a** before the judges H7928
Ex 23:15 "No *one is to* **a** before me empty-handed. H8011
Ex 23:17 a year all the men *are to* **a** before the H8011
Ex 34:20 "No *one is to* **a** before me empty-handed. H8011
Ex 34:23 a year all your men *are to* **a** before the H8011
Ex 34:24 times each year to **a** before the LORD your H8011
Lev 9: 4 For today the LORD *will* **a** to you.'" H8011
Lev 9: 6 so that the glory of the LORD *may* **a** to you." H8011
Lev 13: 4 white but does not **a** to be more than skin H5260
Lev 13: 7 *they must* **a** before the priest again. H8011
Lev 13:32 it and it does not **a** to be more than skin H5260
Lev 14:37 depressions that **a** to be deeper than the H5260
Lev 16: 2 For *I will* **a** in the cloud over the H8011
Nu 16:16 all your followers *are to* **a** before the LORD H2118
Dt 16:16 year all your men *must* **a** before the LORD H8011
Dt 16:16 No *one should* **a** before the LORD H8011
Dt 31:11 all Israel comes to **a** before the LORD your H8011
1Sa 3:21 The LORD continued to **a** at Shiloh, and H8011
2Sa 9: 2 They summoned him to **a** before David, and NDT
Ezr 10: 8 Anyone who failed *to* **a** within three days H995
Job 19:18 boys scorn me; *when I* **a**, they ridicule me. H7756
Ps 21: 9 When you **a** for battle, you will burn them H7156
Ps 102:16 LORD will rebuild Zion and **a** in his glory. H8011
SS 2:12 Flowers **a** on the earth; the season of H8011
Isa 1:12 When you come to **a before** me H8011+7156
Isa 58: 8 your healing *will* quickly **a**; then your H7541
Eze 16:52 *they* **a** more **righteous** than you. H7405
Eze 16:52 you *have* **made** your sisters **a righteous**. H7405
Da 7:23 is a fourth kingdom *that will* **a** on earth. A10201
Hos 6: 3 sun rises, he *will* **a**; he will come to H4604+3922
Zec 9:14 Then the LORD *will* **a** over them; his arrow H8011
Mt 23:28 on the outside you **a** to people as *G5743*
Mt 24:11 false prophets *will* **a** and deceive many *G1586*
Mt 24:24 false prophets *will* **a** and perform great *G1586*
Mt 24:30 "Then *will* **a** the sign of the Son of Man in *G5743*
Mk 13:22 false prophets *will* **a** and perform signs *G1586*
Lk 19:11 kingdom of God was going to **a** at once. *G428*
Ac 5:27 were brought in and *made to* **a** before the *G2705*
Ac 11:13 had seen an angel **a** in his house and say *G2705*
Ac 19:30 Paul wanted *to* **a** before the crowd, but the *G1656*
2Co 5:10 For we must all **a** before the judgment *G5746*
Col 3: 4 then you also *will* **a** with him in glory. *G5746*
Heb 9:24 now *to* **a** for us in God's presence. *G1872*
Heb 9:28 sins of many; and *he will* **a** a second time *G3972*

APPEARANCE (29) [APPEAR]
Lev 13:55 if the mold has not changed its **a** H6524
1Sa 16: 7 "Do not consider his **a** or his height, for I H5260
1Sa 16: 7 People look at the **outward a**, but the LORD H6524
1Sa 16:12 had a fine **a** and handsome features H6524
2Sa 14:25 praised for his **handsome a** as Absalom. H3637
Ecc 8: 1 their face and changes its hard **a**. H7156
SS 5:15 His **a** is like Lebanon, choice H5260
Isa 52:14 his **a** was so disfigured beyond that of any H5260
Isa 53: 2 nothing in his **a** that we should desire H5260
La 4: 7 ruddy than rubies, their **a** like lapis lazuli. H1619
Eze 1: 5 *In* **a** their form was human, H5260
Eze 1:13 The **a** *of* the living creatures was like H5260
Eze 1:16 This was the **a** and structure of the wheels H5260
Eze 1:28 Like the **a** *of* a rainbow in the clouds on a H5260
Eze 1:28 This was the **a** *of* the likeness of the glory H5260
Eze 8: 2 from there up his **a** was as bright as H5260
Eze 10:10 As for their **a**, the four of them looked H5260
Eze 10:22 faces had the same **a** as those I had seen H1952
Eze 40: 3 I saw a man whose **a** was like bronze; H5260
Da 1:13 Then compare our **a** with that of the young H5260
Da 2:31 dazzling statue, awesome in **a**. A10657
Joel 2: 4 They have the **a** *of* horses; they gallop H5260
Mt 16: 3 know how to interpret the **a** of the sky, *G4725*
Mt 28: 3 His **a** was like lightning, and his clothes *G1624*
Lk 9:29 he was praying, the **a** of his face changed *G1626*
Lk 12:56 how to interpret the **a** of the earth and the *G4725*
Php 2: 8 And being found *in* **a** as a man, he *G5386*
Col 2:23 regulations indeed have an **a** of wisdom, *G3364*
Rev 4: 3 sat there had the **a of** jasper and ruby. *G3970*

APPEARANCES (2) [APPEAR]
Jn 7:24 Stop judging by *mere* **a**, but instead judge *G4071*
2Co 10: 7 You are judging by **a**. If anyone is *G4725*

APPEARED (95) [APPEAR]
Ge 2: 5 Now no shrub *had* yet **a** on the earth and H2118
Ge 12: 7 The LORD **a** to Abram and said, "To your H8011
Ge 12: 7 altar there to the LORD, who *had* **a** to him. H8011
Ge 15:17 a blazing torch **a** and passed between H2180
Ge 17: 1 years old, the LORD **a** to him and said, "I H8011
Ge 18: 1 The LORD **a** to Abraham near the great H8011
Ge 26: 2 The LORD **a** to Isaac and said, "Do not go H8011
Ge 26:24 That night the LORD **a** to him and said, "I H8011
Ge 35: 1 who **a** to you when you were fleeing from H8011
Ge 35: 9 God **a** to him again and blessed him. H8011
Ge 46:29 As soon as Joseph **a** before him, he threw H8011
Ge 48: 3 "God Almighty **a** to me at Luz in the land H8011
Ex 3: 2 angel of the LORD **a** to him in flames of H8011
Ex 3:16 Isaac and Jacob—**a** to me and said: H8011
Ex 4: 5 the God of Jacob—*has* **a** to you. H8011
Ex 6: 3 *I* **a** to Abraham, to Isaac and to Jacob as H8011
Ex 16:14 frost on the ground **a** on the desert floor. H2180
Lev 9:23 the glory of the LORD **a** to all the people. H8011
Nu 14:10 the glory of the LORD **a** at the tent of H8011
Nu 16:19 the glory of the LORD **a** to the entire H8011
Nu 16:42 covered it and the glory of the LORD **a**. H8011
Nu 20: 6 the glory of the LORD **a** to them. H8011
Dt 31:15 Then the LORD **a** at the tent in a pillar of H8011
Dt 32:17 gods that recently **a**, gods your ancestors H995
Jdg 6:12 When the angel of the LORD **a** to Gideon H8011
Jdg 13: 3 The angel of the LORD **a** to her and said H8011

Jdg 13:10 The man who a to me the other day!" H8011
1Ki 3: 5 At Gibeon the LORD a to Solomon during H8011
1Ki 9: 2 the LORD a to him a second time, as he H8011
1Ki 9: 2 as he had a to him at Gibeon. H8011
1Ki 11: 9 the God of Israel, who had a to him twice. H8011
2Ki 2:11 **suddenly** a chariot of fire and horses of fire a H2180
2Ch 1: 7 That night God a to Solomon and said to H8011
2Ch 3: 1 where the LORD had a to his father David. H8011
2Ch 7:12 the LORD a to him at night and said: "I H8011
Jer 31: 3 The LORD a to us in the past, saying: "I H8011
Eze 1:16 Each a to be made like a wheel H5260
Eze 1:27 I saw that from what a to be his waist up H5260
Eze 8: 2 From what a to be his waist down he was H5260
Eze 37: 8 tendons and flesh a on them and skin H6590
Da 5: 5 of a human hand a and wrote on the A10485
Da 8: 1 after the one that had already a to me. H8011
Mt 1:20 an angel of the Lord a to him in a dream G5743
Mt 2: 7 from them the exact time the star had a. G5743
Mt 2:13 angel of the Lord a to Joseph in a dream G5743
Mt 2:19 angel of the Lord a in a dream to Joseph G5743
Mt 13:26 formed heads, then the weeds also a. G5743
Mt 17: 3 Just then there a before them Moses and G3972
Mt 27:53 into the holy city and a to many people. G1872
Mk 1: 4 so John the Baptist a in the wilderness, G1181
Mk 9: 4 And there a before them Elijah and Moses G3972
Mk 9: 7 Then a cloud a and covered them, and a G1181
Mk 14:43 speaking, Judas, one of the Twelve, a. G4134
Mk 16: 9 of the week, he a first to Mary Magdalene G5743
Mk 16:12 Afterward Jesus a in a different form to G5746
Mk 16:14 Later Jesus a to the Eleven as they were G5746
Lk 1:11 Then an angel of the Lord a to him G3972
Lk 1:80 the wilderness until he a **publicly** to Israel. G345
Lk 2: 9 An angel of the Lord a to them, and the G2392
Lk 2:13 of the heavenly host a with the angel, G1181
Lk 7:16 "A great prophet has a among us," they G1586
Lk 9: 8 others that Elijah had a, and still others G5743
Lk 9:30 Moses and Elijah, a in glorious splendor G3972
Lk 9:34 speaking, a cloud a and covered them G1181
Lk 22:43 An angel from heaven a to him and G3972
Lk 24:34 The Lord has risen and has a to Simon." G3972
Jn 8: 2 At dawn he a again in the temple courts G4134
Jn 21: 1 Afterward Jesus a again to his disciples G5746
Jn 21:14 the third time Jesus a to his disciples after G5746
Ac 1: 3 He a to them over a period of forty days G3964
Ac 5:36 Some time ago Theudas a, claiming to be G482
Ac 5:37 Judas the Galilean a in the days of the G482
Ac 7: 2 The God of glory a to our father Abraham G3972
Ac 7:30 an angel a to Moses in the flames of a G3972
Ac 7:35 the angel who a to him in the bush. G3972
Ac 8:40 however, a at Azotus and traveled about G2351
Ac 9:17 who a to you on the road as you were G3972
Ac 12: 7 angel of the Lord a and a light shone in G2392
Ac 25: 2 a before him **and presented *the* charges** G1872
Ac 26:16 I have a to you to appoint you as a G3972
Ac 27:20 When neither sun nor stars a for many G2210
1Co 15: 5 that he a to Cephas, and then to the G3972
1Co 15: 6 he a to more than five hundred of the G3972
1Co 15: 7 Then he a to James, then to all the G3972
1Co 15: 8 last of all he a to me also, as to one G3972
1Ti 3:16 He a in the flesh, was vindicated by the G5746
Titus 2:11 For the grace of God has a that offers G2210
Titus 3: 4 kindness and love of God our Savior a, G2210
Heb 9:26 But he has a once for all at the G5746
1Jn 1: 2 The life a; we have seen it and testify to it G5746
1Jn 1: 2 which was with the Father and has a to us. G5746
1Jn 3: 5 But you know that he a so that he might G5746
1Jn 3: 8 the Son of God a was to destroy the G5746
Rev 12: 1 A great sign a in heaven: a woman G3972
Rev 12: 3 Then another sign a in heaven: an G3972

APPEARING (8) [APPEAR]

Ex 16:10 was the glory of the LORD a in the cloud. H8011
Zec 5: 5 said to me, "Look up and see what is a." H3655
Jn 8:13 "Here you are, a as your own **witness**; your AIT
1Ti 6:14 spot or blame until the a of our Lord Jesus G2211
2Ti 1:10 revealed through the a of our Savior, G2211
2Ti 4: 1 in view of his a and his kingdom, I G2211
2Ti 4: 8 also to all who have longed for his a. G2211
Titus 2:13 the a of the glory of our great God and G2211

APPEARS (26) [APPEAR]

Ge 9:14 the earth and the rainbow a in the clouds, H8011
Ge 9:16 Whenever the rainbow a in the clouds, I H2118
Lev 13: 3 white and the sore a to be more than skin H5260
Lev 13:14 But whenever raw flesh a on them, they H8011
Lev 13:19 a white swelling or reddish-white spot a H2118
Lev 13:20 if it a to be more than skin deep and H5260
Lev 13:24 white spot a in the raw flesh of the H2118
Lev 13:25 and it a to be more than skin deep H5260
Lev 13:30 if it a to be more than skin deep and H5260
Lev 13:34 in the skin and a to be no more than H5260
Dt 13: 1 a among you and announces to you a H7756
Ps 84: 7 to strength, till each a before God in Zion. H8011
Pr 14:12 There is a way that a to be right H4200+7156
Pr 16:25 There is a way that a to be right H4200+7156
Pr 27:25 new growth a and the grass from the H8011
SS 6:10 Who is this that a like the dawn, fair as H9207
Isa 16:12 When Moab a at her high place, she only H8011
Isa 60: 2 rises upon you and his glory a over you. H8011
Na 3:17 when the sun a they fly away, and no H2436
Mal 3: 2 Who can stand when he a? For he will be H8011

Col 3: 4 who is your life, a, then you also will G5746
Heb 7:15 clear if another priest like Melchizedek a, G482
Jas 4:14 You are a mist that a for a little while G5743
1Pe 5: 4 And when the Chief Shepherd a, you will G5746
1Jn 2:28 so that when he a we may be confident G5746
1Jn 3: 2 But we know that when Christ a, we shall G5746

APPEASE (2)

Pr 16:14 messenger of death, but the wise will a it. H4105
Ac 16:39 They came to a them and escorted them G4151

APPETITE (7) [APPETITES]

Nu 11: 6 But now we have lost our a; we never see H5883
Pr 13: 2 the unfaithful have an a for violence. H5883
Pr 13: 4 A sluggard's a is never filled, but H203+5883
Pr 16:26 The a of laborers works for them; their H5883
Ecc 6: 7 their mouth, yet their a is never satisfied. H5883
Ecc 6: 9 the eye sees than the roving of the a. H5883
Jer 50:19 their a will be satisfied on the hills of H5883

APPETITES (2) [APPETITE]

Isa 56:11 They are dogs with mighty a; they never H5883
Ro 16:18 serving our Lord Christ, but their own a. G3120

APPHIA (1)

Phm 2 also to A our sister and Archippus our G722

APPIUS (1)

Ac 28:15 as far as the Forum of A and the Three G716

APPLE (7) [APPLES]

Dt 32:10 he guarded him as the a of his eye, H413
Ps 17: 8 Keep me as the a of your eye; hide H413+1426
Pr 7: 2 guard my teachings as the a of your eye. H413
SS 2: 3 Like an a **tree** among the trees of the H9515
SS 8: 5 Under the a **tree** I roused you; there your H9515
Joel 1:12 the palm and the a **tree**—all the trees of H9515
Zec 2: 8 touches you touches the a of his eye— H949

APPLES (3) [APPLE]

Pr 25:11 Like a of gold in settings of silver is a H9515
SS 2: 5 refresh me with a, for I am faint with H9515
SS 7: 8 the fragrance of your breath like a, H9515

APPLICATION (1) [APPLY]

Heb 11:28 he kept the Passover and the a of blood, G4717

APPLIED (9) [APPLY]

2Ki 20: 7 They did so and a it to the boil, and he H8492
Pr 24:32 I a my heart to what I observed and H8883
Ecc 1:13 I a my mind to study and to explore by H5989
Ecc 1:17 Then I a myself to the understanding of H5989
Ecc 8: 9 as I a my mind to everything done under H5989
Ecc 8:16 When I a my mind to know wisdom and H5989
Eze 23:40 a eye **makeup** and put on your jewelry. H3949
Da 4:19 if only the dream a **to** your enemies and A10378
1Co 4: 6 I have a these things to myself and G3571

APPLIES (6) [APPLY]

Ex 12:49 The same law a both to the native-born H2118
Ex 21:31 This law also a if the bull gores a son or H6913
Lev 7: 7 " 'The same law a **to** both the sin offering H4200
Nu 8:24 "This a **to** the Levites: Men twenty-five H4200
Nu 15:29 One and the same law a to everyone who H2118
Nu 19:14 is the law that a when a person dies in NDT

APPLY (6) [APPLICATION, APPLIED, APPLIES, APPLYING]

Nu 5:30 the LORD and is to a this entire law to H6913
Nu 15:16 regulations will a both to you and to H2118
Job 5:27 So hear it and a it to yourself." H3359
Pr 22:17 of the wise; a your heart to what I teach, H8883
Pr 23:12 A your heart to instruction and your ears to H995
Isa 38:21 a poultice of figs and a it to the boil, H5302

APPLYING (2) [APPLY]

Pr 2: 2 your ear to wisdom and a your heart to H5742
Heb 9:10 external regulations a until the time of the G2130

APPOINT (33) [APPOINTED, APPOINTING, APPOINTMENT, APPOINTS]

Ge 41:34 Let Pharaoh a commissioners over the H7212
Ex 18:21 a them as officials over thousands H8492
Nu 1:50 a the Levites to be in charge of the H7212
Nu 3:10 A Aaron and his sons to serve as priests H7212
Nu 27:16 a someone over this community H7212
Nu 34:18 And a one leader from each tribe to help H4374
Dt 16:18 A judges and officials for each of your H5989
Dt 17:15 **be sure to** a over you a king the H8492+8492
Dt 20: 9 they shall a commanders over it. H7212
Jos 18: 4 A three men from each tribe. I will send H2035
1Sa 2:36 "A me to some priestly office so I can H6202
1Sa 8: 5 follow your ways; now a a king to lead us H8492
1Sa 10:19 you have said, 'No, a a king over us.' So H8492
2Ki 10: 5 We will not a anyone **as king**; you do H4887
1Ch 15:16 to a their fellow Levites as musicians H6641
Ezr 7:25 a magistrates and judges to administer A10431
Ne 7: 3 Also a residents of Jerusalem as guards H6641
Est 2: 3 Let the king a commissioners in every H7212
Ps 61: 7 a your love and faithfulness to protect him H4948
Ps 89:27 And I will a him to be my firstborn, the H5989
Ps 109: 6 A someone evil to oppose my enemy; let H7212
Jer 1:10 today I a you over nations and kingdoms H7212
Jer 23:32 reckless lies, yet I did not send or a them. H7422

Jer 49:19 Who is the chosen one I will a for this H7212
Jer 50:44 Who is the chosen one I will a for this H7212
Jer 51:27 A a commander against her; send up H7212
Eze 44:14 And I will a them to guard the temple H5989
Da 6: 1 It pleased Darius to a 120 satraps to rule A10624
Hos 1:11 they will a one leader and will come up H8492
Ac 26:16 appeared to you to a you as a servant G4741
1Th 5: 9 For God did not a us to suffer wrath but to G5502
Titus 1: 5 left unfinished and a elders in every town, G2770
Rev 11: 3 And I will a my two witnesses, and they G1443

APPOINTED (157) [APPOINT]

Ge 18:14 I will return to you at the a time next year H4595
Ex 5:14 beat the Israelite overseers they had a, H8492
Ex 13:10 ordinance at the a **time** year after year. H4595
Ex 23:15 Do this at the a **time** in the month of Aviv H4595
Ex 31: 6 I have a Oholiab son of Ahisamak H5989
Ex 34:18 Do this at the a **time** in the month of Aviv H4595
Lev 16:21 in the care of someone a **for the task**. H6967
Lev 23: 2 'These are my a **festivals**, the appointed H4595
Lev 23: 2 festivals, the a **festivals** of the LORD, which H4595
Lev 23: 4 " 'These are the LORD's a **festivals**, the H4595
Lev 23: 4 you are to proclaim at their a **times**: H4595
Lev 23:37 " 'These are the LORD's a **festivals**, which H4595
Lev 23:44 to the Israelites the a **festivals** of the LORD. H4595
Nu 1:16 These **were** the men a from the H7924
Nu 3:32 He was a over those who were H7213
Nu 3:36 The Merarites were a to take care of the H7213
Nu 9: 2 celebrate the Passover at the a **time**. H4595
Nu 9: 3 Celebrate it at the a **time**, at twilight on H4595
Nu 9: 7 with the other Israelites at the a **time**?" H4595
Nu 9:13 the LORD's offering at the a **time**. H4595
Nu 10:10 your a **festivals** and New Moon feasts H4595
Nu 16: 2 leaders who had been a members of the H7951
Nu 28: 2 to me at the a **time** my food offerings, H4595
Nu 29:39 offer these to the LORD at your a **festivals**: H4595
Dt 1:15 a them to have authority over you H5989
Jos 4: 4 the twelve men he had a from the H3922
1Sa 8: 1 he a his sons as Israel's leaders. H8492
1Sa 12: 6 is the LORD who a Moses and Aaron and H6913
1Sa 13:14 his own heart and a him ruler of his H7422
1Sa 25:30 concerning him and has a him ruler over H7422
2Sa 6:21 his house when he a me ruler over the H7422
2Sa 7: 8 a you ruler over my people Israel. H2118S
2Sa 7:11 ever since the time I a leaders over my H7422
2Sa 15: 4 "If only I were a judge in the land! H8492
2Sa 17:25 Absalom had a Amasa over the army in H8492
2Sa 18: 1 were with him and a over them H8492
1Ki 1:35 I have a him ruler over Israel and Judah." H7422
1Ki 12:31 on high places and a priests from all sorts H6913
1Ki 13:33 once more a priests for the high H6913
1Ki 14: 7 the people and a you ruler over my H5989
1Ki 16: 2 up from the dust and a you ruler over my H5989
2Ki 12:11 the money to the men a to supervise the H7212
2Ki 17:32 but they also a all sorts of their own H6913
2Ki 22: 5 entrust it to the men a to supervise the H7212
2Ki 23: 5 idolatrous priests a by the kings of Judah H5989
2Ki 25:22 king of Babylon a Gedaliah son of H7212
2Ki 25:23 of Babylon had a Gedaliah **as governor**, H7212
1Ch 15:17 So the Levites a Heman son of Joel; from H6641
1Ch 16: 4 He a some of the Levites to minister H5989
1Ch 16: 7 David first a Asaph and his H5989+928+3338
1Ch 17: 7 a you ruler over my people Israel. H2118
1Ch 17:10 ever since the time I a leaders over my H7422
1Ch 22: 2 from among them he a stonecutters to H6641
1Ch 23:31 New Moon feasts and at the a **festivals**. H4595
1Ch 24: 3 divisions for their a **order** of ministering. H7213
1Ch 24:19 This was their a **order** of ministering when H7213
1Ch 26:10 firstborn, his father had a him the first), H8492
2Ch 2: 4 at the a **festivals** of the LORD our H4595
2Ch 8:14 he a the divisions of the priests for their H6641
2Ch 8:14 He also a the gatekeepers by divisions for NDT
2Ch 11:15 when he a his own priests for the high H6641
2Ch 11:22 Rehoboam a Abijah son of Maakah as H6641
2Ch 19: 5 He a judges in the land, in each of the H6641
2Ch 19: 8 Jehoshaphat a some of the Levites H6641
2Ch 20:21 Jehoshaphat a men to sing to the LORD H6641
2Ch 25:16 "Have we a you an adviser to the king? H5989
2Ch 31: 3 Moons and at the a **festivals** as written in H4595
2Ch 32: 6 He a military officers over the people and H5989
2Ch 34:10 entrusted it to the men a to supervise the H7212
2Ch 35: 2 He a the priests to their duties and H6641
2Ch 36:23 of the earth and he has a me to build a H7212
Ezr 1: 2 of the earth and he has a me to build a H7212
Ezr 3: 5 all the a sacred **festivals** of the LORD, H4595
Ezr 3: 8 They a Levites twenty years old and older H6641
Ezr 5:14 Sheshbazzar, whom he had a governor, A10682
Ne 5:14 when I was a to be their governor in the H7422
Ne 6: 7 and have even a prophets to make this H6641
Ne 7: 1 the musicians and the Levites **were** a. H7212
Ne 9:17 in their rebellion a a leader in order to H5989
Ne 10:33 New Moon feasts and at the a **festivals**; H4595
Ne 12:44 At that time men **were** a to be in charge H7212
Est 8: 2 And Esther a him over Haman's estate. H8492
Est 8:12 The day a for the Jews to do this in all the H285
Est 9:27 in the way prescribed and at the **time** a. H2375
Job 20:29 the wicked, the heritage a for them by God." H609
Job 30:23 to death, to the place a for all the living. H4595
Job 34:13 Who a him over the earth? Who put him H7212
Ps 75: 2 "I choose the a **time**; it is I who judge H4595
Ps 102:13 to show favor to her; the a **time** has come. H4595
Isa 1:14 feasts and your a **festivals** I hate with all H4595

Jer 1: 5 *I* **a** you as a prophet to the nations." H5989
Jer 6:17 *I* **a** watchmen over you and said, 'Listen to H7756
Jer 8: 7 the stork in the sky knows her **a seasons,** H4595
Jer 14:14 not sent them or **a** them or spoken to H7422
Jer 29:26 'The LORD *has* **a** you priest in place of H5989
Jer 33:20 night no longer come at their **a time,** H6961
Jer 40: 5 king of Babylon *has* **a** over the towns of H7212
Jer 40: 7 *had* **a** Gedaliah son of Ahikam **as governor** H7212
Jer 40:11 *had* **a** Gedaliah son of Ahikam, the son of Shaphan, **as governor** H7212
Jer 41: 2 of Babylon *had* **a as governor** over the H7212
Jer 41:10 *over* whom Nebuzaradan commander of the imperial guard *had* **a** H7212
Jer 41:18 of Babylon *had* **a as governor** over the H7212
La 1: 4 no one comes to her **a festivals.** H4595
La 2: 6 Zion forget her **a festivals** and her H4595
La 2: 7 of the LORD as on the day of an **a festival.** H4595
Eze 9: 1 *those who* are **a to execute judgment** *on* H7213
Eze 21:11 " 'The sword *is* **a** to be polished, to be H5989
Eze 36:38 at Jerusalem during her **a festivals.** H4595
Eze 44:24 laws and my decrees for all my **a festivals,** H4595
Eze 45:17 Sabbaths—at all the **a festivals** *of* Israel. H4595
Eze 46: 9 come before the LORD at the **a festivals,** H4595
Eze 46:11 At the feasts and the **a festivals,** the grain H4595
Da 1:11 whom the chief official *had* **a** over Daniel, H4948
Da 2:24 whom the king *had* **a** to execute the A10431
Da 2:49 at Daniel's request the king **a** Shadrach A10431
Da 5:11 **a** him chief of the magicians A10624
Da 8:19 the vision concerns the **a time** *of* the end. H4595
Da 11:27 an end will still come at the **a time.** H4595
Da 11:29 "At the **a time** he will invade the South H4595
Da 11:35 the end, for it will still come at the **a time.** H4595
Hos 2:11 her Sabbath days—all her **a festivals.** H4595
Hos 6:11 a harvest *is* **a**. "Whenever I would H8883
Hos 9: 5 will you do on the day of your **a festivals,** H4595
Hos 12: 9 as in the days of your **a festivals.** H4595
Mic 6: 9 "Heed the rod and the One who **a** it. H3585
Hab 1:12 *You,* LORD, *have* **a** them to execute H8492
Hab 2: 3 For the revelation awaits an **a time;** it H4595
Zep 3:18 mourn over the loss of your **a festivals,** H4595
Mt 8:29 come here to torture us before the **a time?"** *G2789*
Mt 26:18 Teacher says: My **a time** is near. I am *G2789*
Mk 3:14 *He* **a** twelve that they might be with him *G4472*
Mk 3:16 These are the twelve *he* **a**: Simon (to *G4472*
Lk 1:20 which will come true at their **a time."** *G2789*
Lk 10: 1 After this the Lord **a** seventy-two others *G344*
Lk 12:14 who **a** me a judge or an arbiter between *G2770*
Lk 19:12 country *to have* himself **a king** and *G3284+993*
Jn 15:16 I chose you and **a** you so that you *G5502*
Ac 3:20 the Messiah, *who has been* **a** for you *G4741*
Ac 10:42 he is the *one whom* God **a** as judge of *G3988*
Ac 12:21 On the **a** day Herod, wearing his royal *G5414*
Ac 13:48 all who were **a** for eternal life *G5435*
Ac 14:23 Paul and Barnabas **a** elders for them in *G5936*
Ac 15: 2 So Paul and Barnabas *were* **a**, along with *G5435*
Ac 17:26 he marked out their **a** times in history *G4705*
Ac 17:31 world with justice by the man *he has* **a**. *G3988*
Ro 1: 4 Spirit of holiness *was* **a** the Son of God in *G3988*
Ro 9: 9 "At the **a** time I will return, and Sarah *G4047S*
1Co 4: 5 Therefore judge nothing before the **a time;** *G2789*
Eph 1:22 under his feet and **a** him to be head over *G1443*
1Ti 2: 7 this purpose I *was* **a** a herald and an *G5502*
2Ti 1:11 And of this gospel I *was* **a** a herald and an *G5502*
Titus 1: 3 which now *at* his **a season** he has *G2789*
Heb 1: 2 by his Son, whom *he* **a** heir of all things *G5502*
Heb 3: 2 He was faithful *to the one who* **a** him, just *G4472*
Heb 5: 1 the people and *is* **a** to represent the *G2770*
Heb 7:28 came after the law, **a** the Son, who has NDT
Heb 8: 3 Every high priest *is* **a** to offer both gifts *G2770*

APPOINTING (1) [APPOINT]
1Ti 1:12 me trustworthy, **a** me to his service. *G5502*

APPOINTMENT (1) [APPOINT]
2Ch 31:13 these served by **a** *of* King Hezekiah and H5152

APPOINTS (2) [APPOINT]
Jer 31:35 *he who* **a** the sun to shine by day H5989
Heb 7:28 For the law **a** as high priests men in all *G2770*

APPORTIONED (2) [PORTION]
Dt 4:19 the LORD your God *has* **a** to all the nations H2745
Eph 4: 7 of us grace has been given as Christ **a** it. *G3586*

APPRAISED (1)
Job 28:27 then he looked at wisdom and **a** it; he H6218

APPREHEND, APPREHENDED (KJV) ARREST, ARRESTING, HOLD

APPREHENSIVE (1)
Lk 21:26 **a** of what is coming on the world *G4660*

APPROACH (21) [APPROACHED, APPROACHES, APPROACHING]
Ex 19:12 careful that you *do* not **a** the mountain H6590
Ex 19:13 a long blast *may* they **a** the mountain." H6590
Ex 19:22 Even the priests, who **a** the LORD, must H5602
Ex 24: 2 Moses alone *is to* **a** the LORD; the H5602
Ex 28:43 tent of meeting or **a** the altar to minister H5602
Ex 30:20 when they **a** the altar to minister by H5602
Lev 10: 3 " 'Among *those who* **a** me I will be H7940
Lev 18: 6 " 'No one *is to* **a** any close relative to H7928
Lev 18:19 " '*Do* not **a** a woman to have sexual H7928
Lev 21:23 not go near the curtain or **a** the altar, H5602
1Sa 10: 5 As you **a** the town, you will meet a H995
Job 36:33 even the cattle make known *its* **a**. H6590
Job 40:19 yet its Maker *can* **a** it with his sword. H5602
Ecc 12: 1 come and the years **a** when you will say, H5595
Isa 5:19 One of Israel—*let it* **a**, let it come into H7928
Isa 41: 5 earth tremble. *They* **a** and come forward; H7928
La 2: 3 his right hand at the **a** *of* the enemy. H7156
Eze 42:13 the priests who **a** the LORD will eat the H7940
Hos 7: 6 are like an oven; *they* **a** him with intrigue. H7928
Eph 3:12 faith in him *we may* **a** God with *G2400+4643*
Heb 4:16 *Let us* then **a** God's throne of grace with *G4665*

APPROACHED (44) [APPROACH]
Ge 18:23 Then Abraham **a** him and said: "Will you H5602
Ge 33: 3 ground seven times as he **a** his brother. H5602
Ge 33: 6 their children **a** and bowed down. H5602
Ex 14:10 As Pharaoh **a**, the Israelites looked up H7928
Ex 20:21 while Moses **a** the thick darkness where H5602
Ex 32:19 When Moses **a** the camp and saw the calf H7928
Ex 40:32 entered the tent of meeting or **a** the altar, H7928
Lev 16: 1 of Aaron who died when they **a** the LORD. H7928
Nu 3:38 Anyone else who **a** the sanctuary was to H7929
Dt 22:14 woman, but when *I* **a** her, I did not find H7928
Jos 8:11 him marched up and **a** the city and H5602
Jos 14: 6 the people of Judah **a** Joshua at Gilgal, H5602
Jos 21: 1 heads of the Levites **a** Eleazar the priest, H5602
Jdg 3:20 Ehud then **a** him while he was sitting H995+448
Jdg 9:52 But *as he* **a** the entrance to the tower to H5602
Jdg 14: 5 As *they* **a** the vineyards of Timnah H995+6330
Jdg 15:14 *As he* **a** Lehi, the Philistines came H995+6330
Ru 3: 7 Ruth **a** quietly, uncovered his feet and lay H995
1Sa 9:18 Saul **a** Samuel in the gateway and asked H5602
1Sa 17:40 with his sling in his hand, **a** the Philistine. H5602
1Sa 30:21 As David and his men **a**, he asked them H5602
2Sa 15: 5 whenever anyone **a** him to bow down H7928
2Sa 16: 5 As King David **a** Bahurim, a man H995+6330
2Ki 16:12 he **a** it and presented offerings on it. H7928
1Ch 21:21 Then David **a**, and when Araunah H995+6330
Est 5: 2 So Esther **a** and touched the tip of the H7928
Jer 42: 1 people from the least to the greatest **a** H5602
Da 3:26 then **a** the opening of the A10638
Da 7:13 *He* **a** the Ancient of Days and was led A10413
Da 7:16 *I* **a** one of those standing there and A10638
Mt 14:15 *As* evening **a**, the disciples came to him *G1181*
Mt 17:14 **a** man **a** Jesus and knelt before him. *G4665*
Mt 21: 1 As *they* **a** Jerusalem and came to *G1581*
Mt 21:34 When the harvest time **a**, he sent his *G1581*
Mt 27:57 *As* evening **a**, there came a rich man from *G1181*
Mk 11: 1 As *they* **a** Jerusalem and came to *G1581*
Mk 15:42 the Sabbath). So as evening **a**, *G2453+1181*
Lk 7:12 As *he* **a** the town gate, a dead person was *G1581*
Lk 9:51 As the time **a** for him to be taken up to *G5230*
Lk 18:35 As Jesus **a** Jericho, a blind man was *G1581*
Lk 19:29 As *he* **a** Bethphage and Bethany at the hill *G1581*
Lk 19:41 As *he* **a** Jerusalem and saw the city, he *G1581*
Lk 22:47 was leading them. *He* **a** Jesus to kiss him *G1581*
Lk 24:28 *As they* **a** the village to which they were *G1581*

APPROACHES (6) [APPROACH]
Lev 20:16 " 'If a woman **a** an animal to have sexual H7928
Nu 1:51 Anyone else who **a** it is to be put to death H7929
Nu 3:10 anyone else who **a** the sanctuary is to be H7929
Dt 23:11 But as evening **a** he is to wash himself H7155
2Ki 11: 8 Anyone *who* **a** your ranks is to be put H995+448
Est 4:11 man or woman who **a** the king in the H995+448

APPROACHING (10) [APPROACH]
Ge 24:63 as he looked up, he saw camels **a**. H995
Lev 18:14 father's brother by **a** his wife to have H7928
2Ki 9:17 the tower in Jezreel saw Jehu's troops **a**, H995
Lk 22: 1 called the Passover, *was* **a**, *G1581*
Jn 1:47 When Jesus saw Nathanael **a**, he said of *G2262*
Jn 6:19 they saw Jesus **a** the boat, walking *G1584+1181*
Ac 10: 9 they were on their journey and **a** the city, *G1581*
Ac 27:27 the sailors sensed they *were* **a** land. *G4642*
Heb 10:25 all the more as you see the Day **a**. *G1581*
1Jn 5:14 This is the confidence we have *in* **a** God *G4639*

APPROPRIATE (4)
Ge 49:28 giving each the blessing **a** *to* him. H3869
Ecc 5:18 that it is **a** for a person to eat, to drink H3637
1Ti 2:10 **a for** women who profess to worship God. *G4560*
Titus 2: 1 must teach what *is* **a** to sound doctrine. *G4560*

APPROVAL (10) [APPROVE]
Jdg 18: 6 Your journey has the LORD's **a**." H5790
Est 2:17 won his favor and **a** more than any of the H2876
Ps 101: 3 will not **look with a** *on* H8883+4200+5584+6524
Hos 8: 4 they choose princes without *my* **a**. H3359
Jn 6:27 God the Father *has* **placed** *his* **seal of a**." *G5381*
Ac 12: 3 saw that this met with **a** among the Jews, *G744*
Ac 22:20 I stood there **giving** *my* **a** and guarding *G5306*
Ro 14:18 is pleasing to God and receives human **a**. *G1511*
1Co 11:19 you to show which of you have God's **a**. *G1511*
Gal 1:10 *Am I* now *trying to* **win** the **a** of human *G4275*

APPROVE (7) [APPROVAL, APPROVED, APPROVES]
1Sa 29: 6 but the rulers don't **a** of you. H3202+928+6524
Ps 49:13 of their followers, *who* **a** their sayings. H8354
Lk 11:48 So you testify that *you* **a of** what your *G5306*
Ro 1:32 things but also **a of** those who practice *G5306*
Ro 2:18 know his will and **a of** what is superior *G1507*
Ro 12: 2 will be able to **test and a** what God's will *G1507*
1Co 16: 3 to the men *you* **a** and send them with *G1507*

APPROVED (5) [APPROVE]
Ecc 9: 7 for God *has* already **a** what you do. H8354
Ac 8: 1 And Saul **a** of their killing him. On *G1639+5306*
2Co 10:18 the one who commends himself who is **a**, *G1511*
1Th 2: 4 we speak as *those* **a** by God to be *G1507*
2Ti 2:15 best to present yourself to God *as one* **a**, *G1511*

APPROVES (1) [APPROVE]
Ro 14:22 does not condemn himself by what *he* **a**. *G1507*

APRONS (1)
Ac 19:12 handkerchiefs and **a** that had touched *G4980*

APT (1) [APTITUDE]
Pr 15:23 finds joy in **giving an a reply**— H5101+7023

APTITUDE (1) [APT]
Da 1: 4 **showing a** for every kind of learning H8505

AQUEDUCT (3)
2Ki 18:17 stopped at the **a** *of* the Upper Pool, H9498
Isa 7: 3 at the end of the **a** *of* the Upper Pool, H9498
Isa 36: 2 stopped at the **a** *of* the Upper Pool, H9498

AQUILA (7)
Ac 18: 2 There he met a Jew named **A**, a native of *G217*
Ac 18:18 Syria, accompanied by Priscilla and **A**. *G217*
Ac 18:19 Ephesus, where Paul left **Priscilla and A**. *G2797*
Ac 18:26 When Priscilla and **A** heard him, they *G217*
Ro 16: 3 Greet Priscilla and **A**, my co-workers in *G217*
1Co 16:19 **A** and Priscilla greet you warmly in the Lord *G217*
2Ti 4:19 Greet Priscilla and **A** and the household of *G217*

AR (6)
Nu 21:15 to the settlement of **A** and lie along the H6840
Nu 21:28 It consumed **A** *of* Moab, the citizens of H6840
Dt 2: 9 I have given **A** to the descendants of Lot H6840
Dt 2:18 are to pass by the region of Moab at **A**. H6840
Dt 2:29 the Moabites, who live in **A**, did for us— H6840
Isa 15: 1 against Moab: **A** *in* Moab is ruined H6840

ARA (1)
1Ch 7:38 sons of Jether: Jephunneh, Pispah and **A**. H736

ARAB (3) [ARABIA, ARABIAN, ARABS]
Jos 15:52 **A**, Dumah, Eshan, H742
Ne 2:19 official and Geshem the **A** heard about it, H6861
Ne 6: 1 Geshem the **A** and the rest of our H6861

ARABAH (30) [BETH ARABAH]
Dt 1: 1 in the **A**—opposite Suph, between H6858
Dt 1: 7 to all the neighboring peoples in the **A**, H6858
Dt 2: 8 We turned from the **A** road, which comes H6858
Dt 3:17 Its western border was the Jordan in the **A** H6858
Dt 3:17 from Kinnereth to the Sea of the **A** (that is H6858
Dt 4:49 included all the **A** east of the Jordan H6858
Dt 11:30 living in the **A** in the vicinity of H6858
Jos 3:16 water flowing down to the Sea of the **A** H6858
Jos 8:14 at a certain place overlooking the **A**. H6858
Jos 11: 2 mountains, in the **A** south of Kinnereth H6858
Jos 11:16 the **A** and the mountains of Israel with H6858
Jos 12: 1 including all the eastern side of the **A**: H6858
Jos 12: 3 ruled over the eastern **A** from the Sea of H6858
Jos 12: 3 the Sea of Galilee to the Sea of the **A** H6858
Jos 12: 8 foothills, the **A**, the mountain slopes, H6858
Jos 18:18 of Beth Arabah and on down into the **A**. H6858
1Sa 23:24 of Maon, in the **A** south of Jeshimon. H6858
2Sa 2:29 his men marched through the **A**. H6858
2Sa 4: 7 they traveled all night by way of the **A**. H6858
2Ki 25: 4 They fled toward the **A**, H6858
Isa 33: 9 Sharon is like the **A**, and Bashan and H6858
Jer 39: 4 the two walls, and headed toward the **A**. H6858
Jer 52: 7 They fled toward the **A**, H6858
Eze 47: 8 eastern region and goes down into the **A**, H6858
Am 6:14 from Lebo Hamath to the valley of the **A**." H6858
Zec 14:10 of Jerusalem, will become like the **A**. H6858

ARABIA (8) [ARAB]
2Ch 9:14 all the kings of **A** and the governors of H6851
Isa 21:13 A prophecy against **A**: You caravans of H6851
Isa 21:13 who camp in the thickets of **A**, H6851
Jer 25:24 all the kings of **A** and all the kings of the H6851
Eze 27:21 " '**A** and all the princes of Kedar were H6851
Eze 30: 5 Lydia and all **A**, Kub and the people H6851
Gal 1:17 apostles before I was, but I went into **A**. *G728*
Gal 4:25 Mount Sinai in **A** and corresponds to *G728*

ARABIAN (1) [ARAB]
1Ki 10:15 from all the **A** kings and the H6851

ARABS (6) [ARAB]
2Ch 17:11 as tribute, and the **A** brought him flocks: H6861
2Ch 21:16 of the **A** who lived near the H6861
2Ch 22: 1 who came with the **A** into the camp, had H6861
2Ch 26: 7 against the **A** who lived in Gur Baal H6861
Ne 4: 7 Tobiah, the **A**, the Ammonites and the H6861
Ac 2:11 Cretans and **A**—we hear them declaring *G732*

ARAD (5)
Nu 21: 1 When the Canaanite king of **A**, who lived H6866

Nu 33:40 The Canaanite king of **A**, who lived in the H6866
Jos 12:14 the king of Hormah one the king of **A** one H6866
Jdg 1:16 the Desert of Judah in the Negev near **A**. H6866
1Ch 8:15 Zebadiah, **A**, Eder, H6865

ARAH (5)

Jos 13: 4 from **A** of the Sidonians as far as Aphek H6869
1Ch 7:39 The sons of Ulla: **A**, Hanniel and Rizia. H783
Ezr 2: 5 of **A** 775 H783
Ne 6:18 he was son-in-law to Shekaniah son of **A**, H783
Ne 7:10 of **A** 652 H783

ARAM (69) [ARAM MAAKAH, ARAM NAHARAIM, ARAM ZOBAH, ARAMAIC, ARAMEAN, ARAMEANS, PADDAN ARAM]

Ge 10:22 Elam, Ashur, Arphaxad, Lud and **A**. H806
Ge 10:23 The sons of **A**: Uz, Hul, Gether and Meshek H806
Ge 22:21 Buz his brother, Kemuel (the father of **A**), H806
Nu 23: 7 "Balak brought me from **A**, the king of H806
Jdg 3:10 king of **A** into the hands of Othniel H806
Jdg 10: 6 the gods of **A**, the gods of Sidon, H806
2Sa 15: 8 your servant was living at Geshur in **A**, H806
1Ki 11:25 So Rezon ruled in **A** and was hostile H806
1Ki 15:18 of Hezion, the king of **A**, who was ruling in H806
1Ki 19:15 you get there, anoint Hazael king over **A**. H806
1Ki 20: 1 Ben-Hadad king of **A** mustered his entire H806
1Ki 20:20 Ben-Hadad king of **A** escaped on H806
1Ki 20:22 spring the king of **A** will attack you again." H806
1Ki 20:23 the officials of the king of **A** advised him H806
1Ki 22: 1 there was no war between **A** and Israel. H806
1Ki 22: 3 nothing to retake it from the king of **A**?" H806
1Ki 22:31 Now the king of **A** had ordered his H806
2Ki 5: 1 commander of the army of the king of **A**. H806
2Ki 5: 1 him the LORD had given victory to **A**. H806
2Ki 5: 2 of raiders from **A** had gone out and had H806
2Ki 5: 5 the king of **A** replied. "I will send a H806
2Ki 6: 8 Now the king of **A** was at war with Israel H806
2Ki 6:11 This enraged the king of **A**. He summoned H806
2Ki 6:23 So the bands from **A** stopped raiding H806
2Ki 6:24 Ben-Hadad king of **A** mobilized his entire H806
2Ki 8: 7 Ben-Hadad king of **A** was ill. H806
2Ki 8: 9 Ben-Hadad king of **A** has sent me to ask, H806
2Ki 8:13 shown me that you will become king of **A**," H806
2Ki 8:28 Hazael king of **A** at Ramoth Gilead. H806
2Ki 8:29 Ramoth in his battle with Hazael king of **A**. H806
2Ki 9:14 Ramoth Gilead against Hazael king of **A**, H806
2Ki 9:15 on him in the battle with Hazael king of **A**.) H806
2Ki 12:17 time Hazael king of **A** went up and H806
2Ki 12:18 he sent them to Hazael king of **A**, who H806
2Ki 13: 3 of Hazael king of **A** and Ben-Hadad his H806
2Ki 13: 4 severely the king of **A** was oppressing H806
2Ki 13: 5 they escaped from the power of **A**. H806
2Ki 13: 7 the king of **A** had destroyed the rest and H806
2Ki 13:17 of victory, the arrow of victory over **A**!" H806
2Ki 13:19 would have defeated **A** and completely H806
2Ki 13:22 Hazael king of **A** oppressed Israel H806
2Ki 13:24 Hazael king of **A** died, and Ben-Hadad his H806
2Ki 15:37 to send Rezin king of **A** and Pekah son of H806
2Ki 16: 5 Then Rezin king of **A** and Pekah son of H806
2Ki 16: 6 Rezin king of **A** recovered Elath for Aram H806
2Ki 16: 6 recovered Elath for **A** by driving out the H806
2Ki 16: 7 the hand of the king of **A** and of the king of H806
1Ch 1:17 Arphaxad, Lud and **A**. The sons of Aram: H806
1Ch 1:17 Lud and Aram. The sons of **A**: Uz, Hul, H806
1Ch 2:23 But Geshur and **A** captured Havvoth Jair H806
1Ch 7:34 Ahi, Rohgah, Hubbah and **A**. H806
2Ch 16: 2 palace and sent it to Ben-Hadad king of **A**, H806
2Ch 16: 7 relied on the king of **A** and not on the LORD H806
2Ch 16: 7 army of the king of **A** has escaped from H806
2Ch 18:30 Now the king of **A** had ordered his chariot H806
2Ch 22: 5 Hazael king of **A** at Ramoth Gilead. H806
2Ch 22: 6 Ramoth in his battle with Hazael king of **A**. H806
2Ch 24:23 the army of **A** marched against Joash H806
2Ch 28: 5 him into the hands of the king of **A**. H806
2Ch 28:23 gods of the kings of **A** have helped them, H806
Isa 7: 1 King Rezin of **A** and Pekah son of H806
Isa 7: 2 was told, "**A** has allied itself with Ephraim"; H806
Isa 7: 4 anger of Rezin and **A** and of the son of H806
Isa 7: 5 **A**, Ephraim and Remaliah's son have H806
Isa 7: 8 the head of **A** is Damascus, and the H806
Isa 17: 3 the remnant of **A** will be like the glory of H806
Eze 27:16 " '**A** did business with you because of your H806
Hos 12:12 Jacob fled to the country of **A**; Israel served H806
Am 1: 5 The people of **A** will go into exile to Kir," H806

ARAM MAAKAH (1) [ABEL BETH MAAKAH, ARAM, MAAKAH]

1Ch 19: 6 Aram Naharaim, **A** and Zobah. H807

ARAM NAHARAIM (5) [ARAM]

Ge 24:10 He set out for **A** and made his H808
Dt 23: 4 from Pethor in **A** to pronounce a H808
Jdg 3: 8 of Cushan-Rishathaim king of **A**, H808
1Ch 19: 6 chariots and charioteers from **A**, H808
Ps 60: T he fought **A** and Aram Zobah H808

ARAM ZOBAH (1) [ARAM, ZOBAH]

Ps 60: T he fought Aram Naharaim and **A**, H809

ARAMAIC (12) [ARAM]

2Ki 18:26 "Please speak to your servants **in A**, since H811
Ezr 4: 7 The letter was written **in A** script and in the H811
Ezr 4: 7 in Aramaic script and **in** the **A** language. H811
Isa 36:11 "Please speak to your servants **in A**, since H811
Jn 5: 2 which *in* **A** is called Bethesda and which *G1580*
Jn 19:13 Pavement (which *in* **A** is Gabbatha). *G1580*
Jn 19:17 the Skull (which *in* **A** is called Golgotha). *G1580*
Jn 19:20 the sign was written *in* **A**, Latin and *G1580*
Jn 20:16 She turned toward him and cried out *in* **A** *G1580*
Ac 21:40 all silent, he said to them *in* **A**: *G1579+1365*
Ac 22: 2 they heard him speak to them *in* **A**, *G1579+1365*
Ac 26:14 I heard a voice saying to me *in* **A**, *G1579+1365*

ARAMEAN (17) [ARAM]

Ge 25:20 of Bethuel the **A** from Paddan Aram and H812
Ge 25:20 Paddan Aram and sister of Laban the **A**. H812
Ge 28: 5 to Laban son of Bethuel the **A**, the brother H812
Ge 31:20 deceived Laban the **A** by not telling him he H812
Ge 31:24 came to Laban the **A** in a dream at night H812
Dt 26: 5 "My father was a wandering **A**, and he H812
2Sa 8: 6 garrisons in the **A kingdom** *of* Damascus, H806
2Sa 10: 6 thousand **A** foot soldiers *from* Beth Rehob H806
1Ki 20:29 casualties on the **A** foot soldiers in one day H806
2Ki 5:20 easy on Naaman, this **A**, by not accepting H812
2Ki 7:10 "We went into the **A** camp and no one was H806
2Ki 7:14 the king sent them after the **A** army. H806
2Ki 24: 2 sent Babylonian, **A**, Moabite and H806
1Ch 7:14 his descendant through his **A** concubine. H812
1Ch 18: 6 garrisons in the **A kingdom** *of* Damascus, H806
2Ch 24:24 Although the **A** army had come with only a H806
Jer 35:11 to escape the Babylonian and **A** armies. H806

ARAMEANS (48) [ARAM]

2Sa 8: 5 When the **A** *of* Damascus came to help H806
2Sa 8: 6 the **A** became subject to him and H806
2Sa 10: 8 while the **A** *of* Zobah and Rehob and the H806
2Sa 10: 9 in Israel and deployed them against the **A**. H806
2Sa 10:11 Joab said, "If the **A** are too strong for me H806
2Sa 10:13 troops with him advanced to fight the **A**, H806
2Sa 10:14 realized that the **A** were fleeing, H806
2Sa 10:15 After the **A** saw that they had been routed H806
2Sa 10:16 Hadadezer had **A** brought from beyond the H806
2Sa 10:17 The **A** formed their battle lines to meet H806
2Sa 10:19 So the **A** were afraid to help the H806
1Ki 10:29 to all the kings of the Hittites and of the **A**. H806
1Ki 20:20 the **A** fled, with the Israelites in H806
1Ki 20:21 inflicted heavy losses on the **A**. H806
1Ki 20:26 mustered the **A** and went up to Aphek H806
1Ki 20:27 while the **A** covered the countryside. H806
1Ki 20:28 'Because the **A** think the LORD is a god of H806
1Ki 22:11 these you will gore the **A** until they are H806
1Ki 22:35 was propped up in his chariot facing the **A**. H806
2Ki 6: 9 because the **A** are going down there." H806
2Ki 7: 4 over to the camp of the **A** and surrender. H806
2Ki 7: 5 they got up and went to the camp of the **A**. H806
2Ki 7: 6 Lord had caused the **A** to hear the sound of H806
2Ki 7:12 "I will tell you what the **A** have done to us. H806
2Ki 7:15 equipment the **A** had thrown away in H806
2Ki 7:16 went out and plundered the camp of the **A**. H806
2Ki 8:28 at Ramoth Gilead. The **A** wounded Joram; H812
2Ki 8:29 from the wounds the **A** had inflicted on H812
2Ki 9:15 from the wounds the **A** had inflicted on H812
2Ki 13:17 will completely destroy the **A** at Aphek." H806
1Ch 18: 5 When the **A** *of* Damascus came to help H806
1Ch 18: 6 the **A** became subject to him and H806
1Ch 19:10 in Israel and deployed them against the **A**. H806
1Ch 19:12 Joab said, "If the **A** are too strong for me H806
1Ch 19:14 troops with him advanced to fight the **A**, H806
1Ch 19:15 realized that the **A** were fleeing, H806
1Ch 19:16 After the **A** saw that they had been routed H806
1Ch 19:16 messengers and had **A** brought from H806
1Ch 19:17 formed his lines to meet the **A** in battle, H806
1Ch 19:19 So the **A** were not willing to help the H806
2Ch 1:17 to all the kings of the Hittites and of the **A**. H806
2Ch 18:10 these you will gore the **A** until they are H806
2Ch 18:34 up in his chariot facing the **A** until evening. H806
2Ch 22: 5 at Ramoth Gilead. The **A** wounded Joram; H812
2Ch 24:25 When **the A** withdrew, they left Joash H4392S
2Ch 28: 5 The **A** defeated him and took many of his NDT
Isa 9:12 **A** from the east and Philistines from the H806
Am 9: 7 from Caphtor and the **A** from Kir? H806

ARAMITESS (KJV) ARAMEAN

ARAN (2)

Ge 36:28 The sons of Dishan: Uz and **A**. H814
1Ch 1:42 The sons of Dishan: Uz and **A**. H814

ARARAT (4)

Ge 8: 4 the ark came to rest on the mountains of **A**. H827
2Ki 19:37 and they escaped to the land of **A**. H827
Isa 37:38 and they escaped to the land of **A**. H827
Jer 51:27 these kingdoms: **A**, Minni and Ashkenaz H827

ARAUNAH (17)

2Sa 24:16 at the threshing floor of **A** the Jebusite. H779
2Sa 24:18 on the threshing floor of **A** the Jebusite." H779
2Sa 24:20 When **A** looked and saw the king and his H779
2Sa 24:21 **A** said, "Why has my lord the king come to H779
2Sa 24:22 **A** said to David, "Let my lord the king take H779
2Sa 24:23 Your Majesty, **A** gives all this to the king." H779
2Sa 24:23 **A** also said to him, "May the LORD your H779
2Sa 24:24 But the king replied to **A**, "No, I insist on H779
1Ch 21:15 at the threshing floor of **A** the Jebusite. H821
1Ch 21:18 on the threshing floor of **A** the Jebusite. H821
1Ch 21:20 While **A** was threshing wheat, he turned H821
1Ch 21:21 when **A** looked and saw him H821
1Ch 21:23 **A** said to David, "Take it! Let my lord the H821
1Ch 21:24 But King David replied to **A**, "No, I insist on H821
1Ch 21:25 So David paid **A** six hundred shekels of H821
1Ch 21:28 on the threshing floor of **A** the Jebusite, H821
2Ch 3: 1 on the threshing floor of **A** the Jebusite, H821

ARBA (3) [KIRIATH ARBA]

Jos 14:15 used to be called Kiriath Arba after **A**, NDT
Jos 15:13 (**A** was the forefather of Anak. NDT
Jos 21:11 (**A** was the forefather of Anak. NDT

ARBATHITE (2)

2Sa 23:31 Abi-Albon the **A**, Azmaveth the H6863
1Ch 11:32 from the ravines of Gaash, Abiel the **A**, H6863

ARBEL See BETH ARBEL

ARBITE (1)

2Sa 23:35 Hezro the Carmelite, Paarai the **A**, H750

ARBITER (1)

Lk 12:14 me a judge or an **a** between you? *G3537*

ARCHANGEL (2) [ANGEL]

1Th 4:16 with the voice *of* the **a** and with the *G791*
Jude 9 But even the **a** Michael, when he was *G791*

ARCHELAUS (1)

Mt 2:22 when he heard that **A** was reigning in *G793*

ARCHER (4) [ARCHERS]

Ge 21:20 in the desert and became an **a**. H8050+8009
Pr 26:10 Like an **a** who wounds at random is one H8043
Jer 51: 3 Let not the **a** string his bow, nor let him H2005
Am 2:15 The **a** will not stand his ground H9530+8008

ARCHERS (10) [ARCHER]

Ge 49:23 With bitterness **a** attacked him H1251+2932
1Sa 31: 3 when the **a** overtook him H4619+408+928+2021+8008
2Sa 11:24 Then the **a** shot arrows at your servants H4619
1Ch 10: 3 when the **a** overtook him H4619+928+2021+8008
2Ch 35:23 **A** shot King Josiah, and he told his H3452
Job 16:13 his **a** surround me. Without pity, he H8043
Isa 21:17 The survivors of the **a**, the warriors H5031+8008
Isa 66:19 famous as **a**), to Tubal and H5432+8008
Jer 4:29 of horsemen and **a** every town H8227+8008
Jer 50:29 "Summon **a** against Babylon, all those H8043

ARCHES (KJV) PORTICO

ARCHEVITES (KJV) URUK

ARCHI, ARCHITE (KJV) ARKITE, ARKITES

ARCHIPPUS (2)

Col 4:17 Tell **A**: "See to it that you complete the *G800*
Phm 2 our sister and **A** our fellow soldier— *G800*

ARCHITECT (1)

Heb 11:10 foundations, whose **a** and builder is God. *G5493*

ARCHIVES (3)

Ezr 4:15 may be made in the **a** of your A10515+10177
Ezr 5:17 in the royal **a** of Babylon to see A10103+10148
Ezr 6: 1 searched in the **a** stored in the A10103+10515

ARCTURUS (KJV) BEAR

ARD (3) [ARDITE]

Ge 46:21 Rosh, Muppim, Huppim and **A**. H764
Nu 26:40 of Bela through **A** and Naaman were: H764
Nu 26:40 through **A**, the Ardite clan; through H764

ARDENT (1)

2Co 7: 7 your **a concern** for me, so that *G2419*

ARDITE (1) [ARD]

Nu 26:40 through Ard, the **A** clan; through Naaman H766

ARDON (1)

1Ch 2:18 were her sons: Jesher, Shobab and **A**. H765

ARE (4117) [BE] See Index of Articles Etc.

AREA (53) [AREAS]

Ge 25:18 settled in the **a** from Havilah to Shur, NDT
Ge 34: 2 the Hivite, the ruler of that **a**, saw her, H824
Ex 10:14 down in every **a** *of* the country in great H1473
Lev 6:16 be eaten without yeast in the sanctuary **a**; H5226
Lev 6:26 it is to be eaten in the sanctuary **a**, in the H5226
Lev 6:27 you must wash it in the sanctuary **a**. H5226
Lev 7: 6 it must be eaten in the sanctuary **a**; it H5226
Lev 10:13 Eat it in the sanctuary **a**, because it is your H5226
Lev 10:17 eat the sin offering in the sanctuary **a**? H5226
Lev 10:18 have eaten the goat in the sanctuary **a**, NDT
Lev 13:33 except for the **affected a**, and the priest is H5999
Lev 13:49 if the **affected a** in the fabric, the leather H5596
Lev 13:50 to examine the **affected a** and isolate the H5596
Lev 14:13 lamb in the sanctuary **a** where the sin H5226
Lev 16:24 in the sanctuary **a** and put on his regular H5226
Lev 24: 9 who are to eat it in the sanctuary **a** H5226
Nu 8: 2 all seven light up the **a** in front of the NDT
Nu 35: 5 They will have **this** *a* as pastureland for the AIT

Jos 13: 5 the a *of* Byblos; and all Lebanon to the H824
Jos 19:46 Rakkon, with the a facing Joppa. H1473
Jdg 19: 1 who lived in a **remote a** *in* the hill country H3752
Jdg 19:18 in Judah to a **remote a** *in* the hill country H3752
1Sa 9: 4 through the a *around* Shalisha, H824
1Sa 14:14 twenty men in an a of about half an acre H8441
1Sa 23:23 if he is in the **a**, I will track him down H824
1Sa 27: 9 Whenever David attacked an a, he did not H824
2Sa 5: 9 He built up the **a around** it, from the H6017
1Ch 5: 8 They settled in the a from Aroer to Nebo NDT
Ne 12:29 from the a *of* Geba and Azmaveth H8441
Eze 40: 5 surrounding the temple **a**. H4946+2575
Eze 41: 9 The **open a** between the side rooms of H4965
Eze 41:11 to the side rooms from the **open a**, H4965
Eze 41:11 base adjoining the **open a** was five cubits H4965
Eze 41:20 From the floor to the a above the entrance NDT
Eze 42:15 measuring what was inside the **temple a**, H1074
Eze 42:15 gate and measured **the a** all around: H2257[S]
Eze 42:20 So he measured **the a** on all four sides. It H2257[S]
Eze 43:12 All the surrounding a on top of the H1473
Eze 43:21 part of the **temple a** outside the sanctuary H1074
Eze 45: 1 cubits wide; the entire a will be holy. H1473
Eze 45: 5 An a 25,000 cubits long and 10,000 cubits NDT
Eze 45: 6 as its property an a 5,000 cubits wide and NDT
Eze 45: 7 each side of the a formed by the sacred NDT
Eze 48:15 "The **remaining** *a*, 5,000 cubits wide and AIT
Eze 48:18 What remains of the **a**, bordering on the NDT
Eze 48:21 on both sides of the a formed by the sacred NDT
Eze 48:22 lie in the center of the a that belongs to the NDT
Eze 48:22 The a belonging to the prince will lie NDT
Mt 4:13 was by the lake in the a of Zebulun and *G3990*
Mk 5:10 again not to send them out of the **a**. *G6001*
Lk 4:37 him spread throughout the surrounding **a**. *G5536*
Ac 16: 3 because of the Jews who lived in that **a**, *G5536*
Ac 20: 2 He traveled through that **a**, speaking many *G3538*

AREAS (6) [AREA]

Jos 13: 1 still very large **a of land** to be taken over. H824
Jos 14: 1 Now these are **the a** the Israelites H889[S]
Jdg 19:29 sent them into all the a *of* Israel. H1473
1Ki 20:34 set up your own **market a** in Damascus, H2575
2Ch 27: 4 forts and towers in the **wooded a**. H3091
Eze 48:21 Both these a running the length of the tribal NDT

ARELI (2) [ARELITE]

Ge 46:16 Shuni, Ezbon, Eri, Arodi and **A**. H739
Nu 26:17 Arodite clan; through **A**, the Arelite clan. H739

ARELITE (1) [ARELI]

Nu 26:17 the Arodite clan; through Areli, the **A** clan. H740

AREN'T (19) [BE, NOT]

Jdg 8: 2 **A** the gleanings of Ephraim's grapes H4202
Jdg 9:38 ' **A** these the men you ridiculed H4202
Jdg 18: 9 **A** you *going to* **do something** H3120
1Sa 26:14 son of Ner, "**A** you going to answer me H4202
1Sa 26:15 "You're a man, a you? And who is like H4202
2Ki 12: 7 "Why **a** you repairing the damage done to H401
2Ch 28:10 But a you also guilty of sins against the H4202
Mt 13:55 name Mary, and a his brothers James NDT
Mt 13:56 **A** all his sisters with us? Where *G4049+1639*
Mt 22:16 You a swayed by others, because you pay *G4024*
Mk 6: 3 **A** his sisters here with us? *G4024+1639*
Mk 12:14 You a swayed by others, because you pay *G4024*
Mk 15: 4 asked him, "**A** you going to answer? *G4024*
Lk 23:39 insults at him: "**A** you the Messiah *G4049+1639*
Jn 8:48 "**A** we right in saying that you are a *G4024*
Jn 18:17 **a** one of this man's disciples too, *are you* *G3590+1639*
Jn 18:25 **a** one of his disciples too, *are you*?" *G3590+1639*
Ac 2: 7 "**A** all these who are speaking Galileans? *G4024*
Ac 21:38 "**A** you the Egyptian who started a *G4024+1639*

ARENA (1)

1Co 4: 9 like those condemned to die in the **a**. NDT

AREOPAGITE (KJV) AREOPAGUS

AREOPAGUS (3)

Ac 17:19 brought him to a **meeting of the A**, *G740*
Ac 17:22 stood up in the **meeting of the A** and said: *G740*
Ac 17:34 Dionysius, a **member of the A**, also a *G741*

ARETAS (1)

2Co 11:32 governor under King **A** had the city of the *G745*

ARGOB (5)

Dt 3: 4 the whole region of **A**, Og's kingdom in H758
Dt 3:13 The whole region of **A** in Bashan used to H758
Dt 3:14 the whole region of **A** as far as the border H758
1Ki 4:13 well as the region of **A** in Bashan and its H758
2Ki 15:25 Pekahiah, along with **A** and Arieh, in the H759

ARGUE (10) [ARGUED, ARGUING, ARGUMENT, ARGUMENTS]

Jdg 18:25 "Don't **a** with us, or some H9048+7754
Job 9:14 How can I find words to **a** with him? NDT
Job 13: 3 the Almighty and *to* **a** my **case** with God. H3519
Job 13: 8 *Will you* **a the case** for God? H8189
Job 15: 3 *Would* they **a** with useless words, with H3519
Job 33: 5 stand up and **a** *your* **case** before me. H3656
Isa 43:26 past for me, *let us* **a** *the matter* together H9149
Jn 6:52 Then the Jews *began to* **a sharply** among *G3481*

Ac 6: 9 Asia—*who began to* **a with** Stephen. *G5184*
Ro 3: 7 Someone might **a**, "If my falsehood NDT

ARGUED (3) [ARGUE]

1Ki 3:22 And so *they* **a** before the king. H1819
Mk 9:34 on the way *they had* **a about** who was the *G1363*
Ac 23: 9 were Pharisees stood up and **a vigorously**. *G1372*

ARGUING (8) [ARGUE]

2Sa 19: 9 all the people *were* **a among themselves** H1906
Job 16: 3 What ails you that *you keep on* **a**? H6699
Mk 9:14 the teachers of the law **a** with them. *G5184*
Mk 9:16 "What *are you* **a** with them **about**?" he *G5184*
Mk 9:33 "What *were you* **a about** on the road?" *G1368*
Ac 19: 8 **a** persuasively about the kingdom of God. *G1363*
Ac 24:12 did not find me **a** with anyone at the *G1363*
Php 2:14 Do everything without grumbling or **a**, *G1369*

ARGUMENT (5) [ARGUE]

Job 13: 6 Hear now my **a**; listen to the pleas of my H9350
Lk 9:46 An **a** started among the disciples as to *G1369*
Jn 3:25 An **a** developed between some of John's *G2428*
Ro 3: 5 (I am using a **human a**.) *G2848+476*
Heb 6:16 what is said and puts an end *to* all **a**. *G517*

ARGUMENTS (10) [ARGUE]

Job 6:25 honest words! But what do your **a** prove? H3519
Job 23: 4 case before him and fill my mouth with **a**. H9350
Job 32:12 none of you has answered his **a**. H609
Job 32:14 and I will not answer him with your **a**. H609
Isa 41:21 "Set forth your **a**," says Jacob's King. H6802
Isa 59: 4 They rely on empty **a**, they utter lies; they NDT
2Co 10: 5 We demolish **a** and every pretension that *G3361*
Col 2: 4 one may deceive you by **fine-sounding a**. *G4391*
2Ti 2:23 anything to do with foolish and stupid **a**, *G2428*
Titus 3: 9 genealogies and **a** and quarrels about *G2251*

ARID (2)

Mt 12:43 it goes through **a** places seeking rest and *G536*
Lk 11:24 it goes through **a** places seeking rest and *G536*

ARIDAI (1)

Est 9: 9 Parmashta, Arisai, **A** and Vaizatha, H767

ARIDATHA (1)

Est 9: 8 Adalia, **A**, H792

ARIEH (1)

2Ki 15:25 along with Argob and **A**, in the citadel of H794

ARIEL (5)

Ezr 8:16 summoned Eliezer, **A**, Shemaiah, Elnathan H791
Isa 29: 1 Woe to you, **A**, Ariel, the city where David H790
Isa 29: 1 Woe to you, Ariel, **A**, the city where David H790
Isa 29: 2 Yet I will besiege **A**; she will mourn and H790
Isa 29: 7 of all the nations that fight against **A**, H790

ARIMATHEA (4)

Mt 27:57 there came a rich man from **A**, named *G751*
Mk 15:43 Joseph of **A**, a prominent member of the *G751*
Lk 23:51 He came from the Judean town *of* **A**, and *G751*
Jn 19:38 Joseph of **A** asked Pilate for the body of *G751*

ARIOCH (6)

Ge 14: 1 was king of Shinar, **A** king of Ellasar H796
Ge 14: 9 king of Shinar and **A** king of Ellasar— H796
Da 2:14 When **A**, the commander of the king's A10070
Da 2:15 **A** then explained the matter to Daniel A10070
Da 2:24 Then Daniel went to **A**, whom the king A10070
Da 2:25 **A** took Daniel to the king at once and A10070

ARISAI (1)

Est 9: 9 Parmashta, **A**, Aridai and Vaizatha, H798

ARISE (37) [RISE]

Nu 23:18 "**A**, Balak, and listen; hear me, son of H7756
Jdg 5:12 break out in song! **A**, Barak! Take captive H7756
2Ch 6:41 "Now **a**, LORD God, and come to your H7756
Est 4:14 the Jews *will* **a** from another place, H6641
Ps 3: 7 **A**, LORD! Deliver me, my God! Strike all H7756
Ps 7: 6 **A**, LORD, in your anger; rise up against the H7756
Ps 9:19 **A**, LORD, do not let mortals triumph; let the H7756
Ps 10:12 **A**, LORD! Lift up your hand, O God. Do not H7756
Ps 12: 5 needy groan, *I will* now **a**," says the LORD. H7756
Ps 35: 2 shield and armor; **a and come** to my aid. H7756
Ps 59: 4 ready to attack me. **A** to help me; look on H6424
Ps 68: 1 *May* God **a**, may his enemies be scattered H7756
Ps 73:20 when one awakes; when you **a**, Lord, H6424
Ps 102:13 You *will* **a** and have compassion on Zion H7756
Ps 132: 8 '**A**, LORD, and come to your resting place H7756
Pr 31:28 Her children **a** and call her blessed; her H7756
SS 2:10 spoke and said to me, "**A**, my darling, H7756
SS 2:13 **A**, come, my darling; my beautiful one H7756
Isa 33:10 "Now *will I* **a**," says the LORD. "Now will I H7756
Isa 60: 1 "**A**, shine, for your light has come, and H7756
Jer 6: 4 battle against her! **A**, let us attack at noon H7756
Jer 6: 5 So **a**, let us attack at night and destroy her H7756
Jer 30:21 their ruler *will* **a** from among them. H3655
Jer 48: 3 Cries of anguish *a* **from** Horonaim, cries of AIT
Jer 49:28 "**A**, and attack Kedar and destroy the H7756
Jer 49:31 "**A** and attack a nation at ease, which H7756
La 2:19 **A**, cry out in the night, as the watches of H7756
Da 2:39 another kingdom *will* **a**, inferior to yours. A10624
Da 7:24 After them another king *will* **a**, different A10624

Da 8:23 a master of intrigue, *will* **a**. H6641
Da 11: 2 Three more kings *will* **a** in Persia, and H6641
Da 11: 3 Then a mighty king *will* **a**, who will rule H6641
Da 11: 7 "*One* from her family line *will* **a** to take H6641
Da 12: 1 prince who protects your people, *will* **a**. H6641
Hab 2: 7 *Will* not your creditors suddenly **a**? Will H7756
Ac 20:30 own number men *will* **a** and distort the *G482*
Ro 15:12 one *who will* **a** to rule over the nations *G482*

ARISEN (3) [RISE]

Dt 13:13 that troublemakers *have* **a** among you H3655
Eze 7:11 Violence *has* **a**, a rod to punish the H7756
Da 11: 4 After he *has* **a**, his empire will be broken H6641

ARISES (1) [RISE]

Ecc 10: 5 the sort of error that **a** from a ruler: H3655

ARISTARCHUS (5)

Ac 19:29 The people seized Gaius and **A**, Paul's *G752*
Ac 20: 4 **A** and Secundus from Thessalonica *G752*
Ac 27: 2 **A**, a Macedonian from Thessalonica, was *G752*
Col 4:10 My fellow prisoner **A** sends you his *G752*
Phm 24 And so do Mark, **A**, Demas and Luke, my *G752*

ARISTOBULUS (1)

Ro 16:10 those who belong to the household *of* **A**. *G755*

ARK (227)

Ge 6:14 So make yourself an **a** *of* cypress wood H9310
Ge 6:15 The **a** is to be three hundred cubits long H9310
Ge 6:16 door in the side of the **a** and make lower, H9310
Ge 6:18 you will enter the **a**—you and your H9310
Ge 6:19 You are to bring into the **a** two of all living H9310
Ge 7: 1 "Go into the **a**, you and your whole H9310
Ge 7: 7 wives entered the **a** to escape the waters H9310
Ge 7: 9 came to Noah and entered the **a**, as God H9310
Ge 7:13 the wives of his three sons, entered the **a**. H9310
Ge 7:15 in them came to Noah and entered the **a**. H9310
Ge 7:17 they lifted the **a** high above the earth. H9310
Ge 7:18 the **a** floated on the surface of the H9310
Ge 7:23 was left, and those with him in the **a**. H9310
Ge 8: 1 the livestock that were with him in the **a**, H9310
Ge 8: 4 seventh month the **a** came to rest on the H9310
Ge 8: 6 opened a window he had made in the **a** H9310
Ge 8: 9 the earth; so it returned to Noah in the **a**. H9310
Ge 8: 9 brought it back to himself in the **a**. H9310
Ge 8:10 again sent out the dove from the **a**. H9310
Ge 8:13 the covering from the **a** and saw that the H9310
Ge 8:16 "Come out of the **a**, you and your wife H9310
Ge 8:19 came out of the **a**, one kind after H9310
Ge 9:10 those that came out of the **a** with you— H9310
Ge 9:18 Noah who came out of the **a** were Shem, H9310
Ex 25:10 "Have them make an **a** *of* acacia wood H778
Ex 25:14 the rings on the sides of the **a** to carry it. H778
Ex 25:15 poles are to remain in the rings of this **a**; H778
Ex 25:16 Then put in the **a** the tablets of the H778
Ex 25:21 cover on top of the **a** and put in the ark the H778
Ex 25:21 the ark and put in the **a** the tablets of the H778
Ex 25:22 that are over the **a** *of* the covenant law, H778
Ex 26:33 clasps and place the **a** *of* the covenant law H778
Ex 26:34 cover on the **a** *of* the covenant law in H778
Ex 27:21 that shields the **a** of the covenant law, NDT
Ex 30: 6 that shields the **a** *of* the covenant law— H778
Ex 30:26 tent of meeting, the **a** *of* the covenant law, H778
Ex 30:36 it in front of the **a** of the covenant law in NDT
Ex 31: 7 the **a** *of* the covenant law with the H778
Ex 35:12 the **a** with its poles and the atonement H778
Ex 37: 1 Bezalel made the **a** of acacia wood—two H778
Ex 37: 5 the rings on the sides of the **a** to carry it. H778
Ex 39:35 the **a** *of* the covenant law with its poles H778
Ex 40: 3 Place the **a** *of* the covenant law in it and H778
Ex 40: 3 law in it and shield the **a** with the curtain. H778
Ex 40: 5 in front of the **a** *of* the covenant law and H778
Ex 40:20 covenant law and placed them in the **a**, H778
Ex 40:20 the poles to the **a** and put the atonement H778
Ex 40:21 Then he brought the **a** into the tabernacle H778
Ex 40:21 shielded the **a** *of* the covenant law, H778
Lev 16: 2 in front of the atonement cover on the **a**, H778
Lev 24: 3 that shields the **a** of the covenant law in NDT
Nu 3:31 They were responsible for the care of the **a** H778
Nu 4: 5 put it over the **a** *of* the covenant law. H778
Nu 7:89 cover on the **a** *of* the covenant law. H778
Nu 10:33 The **a** *of* the covenant of the LORD went H778
Nu 10:35 Whenever the **a** set out, Moses said, "Rise H778
Nu 14:44 Moses nor the **a** *of* the LORD's covenant H778
Nu 17: 4 in front of the **a** of the covenant law, NDT
Nu 17:10 staff in front of the **a** of the covenant law, NDT
Dt 10: 1 on the mountain. Also make a wooden **a**. H778
Dt 10: 2 Then you are to put them in the **a**." H778
Dt 10: 3 So I made the **a** out of acacia wood and H778
Dt 10: 5 put the tablets in the **a** I had made, H778
Dt 10: 8 of Levi to carry the **a** *of* the covenant of the H778
Dt 31: 9 who carried the **a** *of* the covenant of the H778
Dt 31:25 who carried the **a** *of* the covenant of the H778
Dt 31:26 place it beside the **a** *of* the covenant of the H778
Jos 3: 3 "When you see the **a** *of* the covenant of H778
Jos 3: 4 thousand cubits between you and **the a**; H2257[S]
Jos 3: 6 "Take up the **a** *of* the covenant and pass H778
Jos 3: 8 the priests who carry the **a** *of* the covenant: H778
Jos 3:11 the **a** *of* the covenant of the Lord of all the H778
Jos 3:13 as the priests who carry the **a** *of* the LORD— H778
Jos 3:14 priests carrying the **a** *of* the covenant went H778
Jos 3:15 who carried the **a** reached the Jordan and H778

Jos 3:17 who carried the a of the covenant of the H778
Jos 4: 5 "Go over before the a of the LORD your God H778
Jos 4: 7 cut off before the a of the covenant of the H778
Jos 4: 9 who carried the a of the covenant had H778
Jos 4:10 who carried the a remained standing in H778
Jos 4:11 the a of the LORD and the priests came to H778
Jos 4:16 priests carrying the a of the covenant law to H778
Jos 4:18 river carrying the a of the covenant of the H778
Jos 6: 4 trumpets of rams' horns in front of the a. H778
Jos 6: 6 "Take up the a of the covenant of the LORD H778
Jos 6: 7 guard going ahead of the a of the LORD." H778
Jos 6: 8 the a of the LORD's covenant followed H778
Jos 6: 9 the rear guard followed the a. H778
Jos 6:11 So he had the a of the LORD carried around H778
Jos 6:12 the priests took up the a of the LORD. H778
Jos 6:13 marching before the a of the LORD and H778
Jos 6:13 the rear guard followed the a of the LORD, H778
Jos 7: 6 to the ground before the a of the LORD, H778
Jos 8:33 both sides of the a of the covenant of the H778
Jdg 20:27 In those days the a of the covenant of God H778
1Sa 3: 3 house of the LORD, where the a of God was. H778
1Sa 4: 3 Let us bring the a of the LORD's covenant H778
1Sa 4: 4 brought back the a of the covenant of the H778
1Sa 4: 4 were there with the a of the covenant of H778
1Sa 4: 5 When the a of the LORD's covenant came H778
1Sa 4: 6 learned that the a of the LORD had come H778
1Sa 4:11 The a of God was captured, and Eli's two H778
1Sa 4:13 because his heart feared for the a of God. H778
1Sa 4:17 and the a of God has been captured." H778
1Sa 4:18 When he mentioned the a of God, Eli fell H778
1Sa 4:19 the news that the a of God had been H778
1Sa 4:21 the capture of the a of God and the deaths H778
1Sa 4:22 for the a of God has been captured." H778
1Sa 5: 1 the Philistines had captured the a of God, H778
1Sa 5: 2 they carried the a into Dagon's temple H778
1Sa 5: 3 on the ground before the a of the LORD! H778
1Sa 5: 4 on the ground before the a of the LORD! H778
1Sa 5: 7 "The a of the god of Israel must not stay H778
1Sa 5: 8 shall we do with the a of the god of Israel?" H778
1Sa 5: 8 "Have the a of the god of Israel moved to H778
1Sa 5: 8 So they moved the a of the God of Israel. H778
1Sa 5:10 So they sent the a of God to Ekron. As the H778
1Sa 5:10 As the a of God was entering Ekron, the H778
1Sa 5:10 have brought the a of the god of Israel H778
1Sa 5:11 "Send the a of the god of Israel away H778
1Sa 6: 1 When the a of the LORD had been in H778
1Sa 6: 2 "What shall we do with the a of the LORD? H778
1Sa 6: 3 "If you return the a of the god of Israel, do H778
1Sa 6: 8 Take the a of the LORD and put it on the cart H778
1Sa 6:11 They placed the a of the LORD on the cart H778
1Sa 6:13 when they looked up and saw the a H778
1Sa 6:15 The Levites took down the a of the LORD H778
1Sa 6:18 the Levites set the a of the LORD is a witness H778
1Sa 6:19 because they looked into the a of the LORD. H778
1Sa 6:20 To whom will the a go up from here?" NDT
1Sa 6:21 Philistines have returned the a of the LORD. H778
1Sa 7: 1 Jearim came and took up the a of the LORD. H778
1Sa 7: 1 Eleazar his son to guard the a of the LORD. H778
1Sa 7: 2 The a remained at Kiriath Jearim a long H778
1Sa 14:18 "Bring the a of God." (At that time H778
2Sa 6: 2 Judah to bring up from there the a of God, H778
2Sa 6: 2 between the cherubim on the a. H2257S
2Sa 6: 3 They set the a of God on a new cart and H778
2Sa 6: 4 with the a of God on it, and Ahio was H778
2Sa 6: 6 reached out and took hold of the a of God, H778
2Sa 6: 7 he died there beside the a of God. H778
2Sa 6: 9 "How can the a of the LORD ever come to H778
2Sa 6:10 willing to take the a of the LORD to be with H778
2Sa 6:11 The a of the LORD remained in the house of H778
2Sa 6:12 because of the a of God. H778
2Sa 6:12 to bring up the a of God from the house H778
2Sa 6:13 were carrying the a of the LORD had taken H778
2Sa 6:15 were bringing up the a of the LORD with H778
2Sa 6:16 As the a of the LORD was entering the City H778
2Sa 6:17 They brought the a of the LORD and set it in H778
2Sa 7: 2 while the a of God remains in a tent." H778
2Sa 11:11 "The a and Israel and Judah are staying in H778
2Sa 15:24 were carrying the a of the covenant of God. H778
2Sa 15:24 They set down the a of God, and Abiathar H778
2Sa 15:25 "Take the a of God back into the city. H778
2Sa 15:29 Abiathar took the a of God back to H778
1Ki 2:26 you carried the a of the Sovereign LORD H778
1Ki 3:15 stood before the a of the Lord's covenant H778
1Ki 6:19 temple to set the a of the covenant of the H778
1Ki 8: 1 to bring up the a of the LORD's covenant H778
1Ki 8: 3 had arrived, the priests took up the a, H778
1Ki 8: 4 they brought up the a of the LORD and the H778
1Ki 8: 5 had gathered about him were before the a, H778
1Ki 8: 6 then brought the a of the LORD's covenant H778
1Ki 8: 7 the place of the a and overshadowed the H778
1Ki 8: 7 overshadowed the a and its carrying H778
1Ki 8: 9 was nothing in the a except the two stone H778
1Ki 8:21 I have provided a place there for the a, in H778
1Ch 6:31 of the LORD after the a came to rest there. H778
1Ch 13: 3 Let us bring the a of our God back to us, for H778
1Ch 13: 5 to bring the a of God from Kiriath Jearim. H778
1Ch 13: 6 bring up from there the a of God the LORD, H778
1Ch 13: 6 cherubim—the a that is called by the Name. NDT
1Ch 13: 7 They moved the a of God from Abinadab's H778
1Ch 13: 9 reached out his hand to steady the a, H778
1Ch 13:10 because he had put his hand on the a. H778
1Ch 13:12 "How can I ever bring the a of God to me?" H778
1Ch 13:13 He did not take the a to be with him in the H778
1Ch 13:14 The a of God remained with the family of H778
1Ch 15: 1 a place for the a of God and pitched a tent H778
1Ch 15: 2 one but the Levites may carry the a of God, H778
1Ch 15: 2 chose them to carry the a of the LORD and to H778
1Ch 15: 3 to bring up the a of the LORD to the place H778
1Ch 15:12 yourselves and bring up the a of the LORD, H778
1Ch 15:14 in order to bring up the a of the LORD, H778
1Ch 15:15 Levites carried the a of God with the poles H778
1Ch 15:23 Elkanah were to be doorkeepers for the a. H778
1Ch 15:24 were to blow trumpets before the a of God. H778
1Ch 15:24 were also to be doorkeepers for the a. H778
1Ch 15:25 to bring up the a of the covenant of the H778
1Ch 15:26 were carrying the a of the covenant of the H778
1Ch 15:27 all the Levites who were carrying the a, H778
1Ch 15:28 brought up the a of the covenant of the H778
1Ch 15:29 As the a of the covenant of the LORD was H778
1Ch 16: 1 They brought the a of God and set it inside H778
1Ch 16: 4 Levites to minister before the a of the LORD, H778
1Ch 16: 6 before the a of the covenant of God H778
1Ch 16:37 before the a of the covenant of the H778
1Ch 17: 1 while the a of the covenant of the LORD is H778
1Ch 22:19 you may bring the a of the covenant of the H778
1Ch 28: 2 of rest for the a of the covenant of the H778
1Ch 28:18 overshadow the a of the covenant of H778
2Ch 1: 4 had brought up the a of God from Kiriath H778
2Ch 5: 2 to bring up the a of the LORD's covenant H778
2Ch 5: 4 had arrived, the Levites took up the a, H778
2Ch 5: 5 they brought up the a and the tent of H778
2Ch 5: 6 had gathered about him were before the a, H778
2Ch 5: 7 then brought the a of the LORD's covenant H778
2Ch 5: 8 over the place of the a and covered the ark H778
2Ch 5: 8 ark and covered the a and its carrying poles H778
2Ch 5: 9 extending from the a, could be seen from H778
2Ch 5:10 was nothing in the a except the two tablets H778
2Ch 6:11 There I have placed the a, in which is the H778
2Ch 6:41 resting place, you and the a of your might. H778
2Ch 8:11 the places the a of the LORD has entered H778
2Ch 35: 3 "Put the sacred a in the temple that H778
Ps 78:61 He sent the a of his **might** into captivity, his AIT
Ps 132: 8 resting place, you and the a of your might. H778
Jer 3:16 'The a of the covenant of the LORD. H778
Mt 24:38 up to the day Noah entered the a; G3066
Lk 17:27 up to the day Noah entered the a. G3066
Heb 9: 4 the gold-covered a of the covenant. G3066
Heb 9: 4 **This** a contained the gold jar of manna G4005S
Heb 9: 5 Above **the** a were the cherubim of the G899S
Heb 11: 7 in holy fear built an a to save his family. G3066
1Pe 3:20 days of Noah while the a was being built. G3066
Rev 11:19 temple was seen the a of his covenant. G3066

ARKITE (5) [ARKITES]

2Sa 15:32 Hushai the A was there to meet him H805
2Sa 16:16 Then Hushai the A, David's confidant, went H805
2Sa 17: 5 "Summon also Hushai the A, so we can H805
2Sa 17:14 advice of Hushai the A is better than that H805
1Ch 27:33 Hushai the A was the king's confidant H805

ARKITES (3) [ARKITE]

Ge 10:17 A, Sinites, H6909
Jos 16: 2 over to the territory of the A in Ataroth, H805
1Ch 1:15 A, Sinites, H6909

ARM (75) [ARMED, ARMIES, ARMLETS, ARMOR, ARMOR-BEARER, ARMOR-BEARERS, ARMORY, ARMRESTS, ARMS, ARMY]

Ex 6: 6 an outstretched a and with mighty acts H2432
Ex 15:16 By the power of your a they will be as still H2432
Nu 11:23 "Is the LORD's a too short? H3338
Nu 20:11 Moses raised his a and struck the rock H3338
Nu 31: 3 "A some of your men to go to war against H2741
Nu 32:17 But we *will* a **ourselves** for battle and go H2741
Nu 32:20 if *you will* a **yourselves** before the LORD H2741
Dt 4:34 by a mighty hand and an outstretched a H2432
Dt 5:15 a mighty hand and an outstretched a. H2432
Dt 7:19 the mighty hand and outstretched a, with H2432
Dt 9:29 your great power and your outstretched a." H2432
Dt 11: 2 his mighty hand, his outstretched a; H2432
Dt 26: 8 a mighty hand and an outstretched a, H2432
Dt 33:20 there like a lion, tearing at a or head. H2432
2Sa 1:10 the band on his a and have brought H2432
1Ki 8:42 mighty hand and your outstretched a— H2432
2Ki 5:18 he is leaning on my a and I have to bow H3338
2Ki 7: 2 officer on whose a the king was leaning H3338
2Ki 7:17 officer on whose a he leaned in charge H3338
2Ki 17:36 with mighty power and outstretched a, H2432
2Ch 6:32 mighty hand and your outstretched a— H2432
2Ch 32: 8 With him is only the a of flesh, but with us H2432
Job 26: 2 How you have saved the a that is feeble! H2432
Job 31:22 then let my a fall from the shoulder, let it H4190
Job 35: 9 plead for relief from the a of the powerful. H2432
Job 38:15 their light, and their upraised a is broken. H2432
Job 40: 9 Do you have an a like God's, and can H2432
Ps 10:15 Break the a of the wicked man; call the H2432
Ps 44: 3 nor did their a bring them victory; it H2432
Ps 44: 3 your right hand, your a, and the light of H2432
Ps 77:15 With your mighty a you redeemed your H2432
Ps 79:11 with your strong a preserve those H2432
Ps 89:10 with your strong a you scattered your H2432
Ps 89:13 Your a is endowed with power; your hand H2432
Ps 89:21 surely my a will strengthen him. H2432
Ps 98: 1 hand and his holy a have worked H2432
Ps 136:12 with a mighty hand and outstretched a H2432
SS 2: 6 His left a is under my head, and his right NDT
SS 2: 6 my head, and his **right** *a* embraces me. AIT
SS 8: 3 His left a is under my head and his right NDT
SS 8: 3 under my head and his **right** *a* embraces me. AIT
SS 8: 6 like a seal on your a; for love is as strong H2432
Isa 30:30 make them see his a coming down with H2432
Isa 30:32 fights them in battle with the blows of his a. NDT
Isa 40:10 with power, and he rules with a *mighty* a. H2432
Isa 44:12 he forges it with the might of his a. H2432
Isa 48:14 his a will be against the Babylonians. H2432
Isa 50: 2 Was my a too short to deliver you H3338
Isa 51: 5 my a will bring justice to the nations. H2432
Isa 51: 5 will look to me and wait in hope for my a. H2432
Isa 51: 9 awake, a of the LORD, clothe yourself with H2432
Isa 52:10 will lay bare his holy a in the sight of all H2432
Isa 53: 1 to whom has the a of the LORD been H2432
Isa 59: 1 Surely the a of the LORD is not too short to H3338
Isa 59:16 so his own a achieved salvation for him H2432
Isa 62: 8 by his right hand and by his mighty a: H2432
Isa 63: 5 so my own a achieved salvation for me H2432
Isa 63:12 his glorious a **of power** to be at Moses' H2432
Isa 66:12 be carried on her a and dandled on her H7396
Jer 21: 5 hand and a mighty a in furious anger H2432
Jer 27: 5 outstretched a I made the earth and H2432
Jer 32:17 by your great power and outstretched a. H2432
Jer 32:21 an outstretched a and with great terror. H274
Jer 48:25 horn is cut off; her a is broken," declares H2432
Eze 4: 7 of Jerusalem and *with* bared a prophesy H2432
Eze 17: 9 not take a strong a or many people to pull H2432
Eze 20:33 an outstretched a and with outpoured H2432
Eze 20:34 an outstretched a and with outpoured H2432
Eze 30:21 I have broken the a of Pharaoh king of H2432
Eze 30:22 the good a as well as the broken one NDT
Zec 11:17 the sword strike his a and his right eye! H2432
Zec 11:17 May his a be completely withered, his H2432
Lk 1:51 has performed mighty deeds with his a; G1098
Jn 12:38 to whom has the a of the Lord been G1098
1Pe 4: 1 a yourselves also with the same attitude G3959

ARMAGEDDON (1)

Rev 16:16 to the place that in Hebrew is called A. G762

ARMED (47) [ARM]

Nu 31: 5 So twelve thousand *men* a *for* battle, a H2741
Nu 32:21 if all of you *who are* a cross over the H2741
Nu 32:27 every *man who is* a *for* battle, will H2741
Nu 32:29 Reubenites, every *man* a for battle, cross H2741
Nu 32:30 But if they do not cross over with you a H2741
Nu 32:32 cross over before the LORD into Canaan a, H2741
Dt 3:18 a **for battle**, must cross over H2741
Jos 4:13 About forty thousand a *for* battle crossed H2741
Jos 6: 3 around the city once with all the a men. H4878
Jos 6: 7 with an a **guard** going ahead of the ark of H2741
Jos 6: 9 The a **guard** marched ahead of the priests H2741
Jos 6:13 The a *men* went ahead of them and the H2741
Jdg 18:11 of the Danites, a *for* battle, set out H2520+3998
Jdg 18:16 Danites, a *for* battle, stood H2520+3998
Jdg 18:17 the six hundred a men stood at the H2520+3998
Jdg 20: 2 hundred thousand men a *with* swords. H8990
Jdg 20:25 Israelites, all of them a *with* swords. H8990
Jdg 20:35 25,100 Benjamites, all a *with* swords. H8990
1Sa 2: 4 those who stumbled *are* a *with* strength. H273
2Sa 21:16 shekels and who **was** a *with* a new sword, H2520
2Sa 22:40 *You* a me *with* strength for battle; you H273
2Ki 3:25 **men** a **with slings** surrounded it and H7847
1Ch 12: 2 *they were* a *with* bows and were able to H5976
1Ch 12:23 numbers of the men a for battle who H2741
1Ch 12:24 shield and spear—6,800 a *for* battle; H2741
1Ch 12:37 of Manasseh, *a* **with** every type of weapon AIT
1Ch 20: 1 to war, Joab led out the a **forces**. H2657+7372
2Ch 14: 8 a *with* small shields and with bows. H5951
2Ch 17:17 with 200,000 *men* a *with* bows and H5976
2Ch 17:18 with 180,000 *men* a *for* battle. H2741
Est 8:11 annihilate the a *men of* any nationality H2657
Ps 18:39 *You* a me *with* strength for battle; you H273
Ps 65: 6 your power, *having* a **yourself** with strength, H273
Ps 78: 9 though a *with* bows, turned H5976+8227
Ps 93: 1 is robed in majesty and a *with* strength; H273
Pr 6:11 you like a thief and scarcity like an a man. H4482
Pr 24:34 you like a thief and scarcity like an a man. H4482
Isa 15: 4 Therefore the a *men of* Moab cry out, and H2741
Jer 6:23 *They are* a *with* bow and spear; they are H2616
Jer 49:10 His a **men** are destroyed, also his allies H2446
Jer 50:42 *They are* a *with* bows and spears; they are H2616
Eze 31:17 along with the a *men* who lived in its H2432
Eze 38: 4 your horsemen fully a, and a great horde H4229
Da 11:31 "His a **forces** will rise up to desecrate the H2432
Mt 26:47 was a large crowd *a* **with** swords and clubs, AIT
Mk 14:43 him was a crowd *a* **with** swords and clubs, AIT
Lk 11:21 a strong man, **fully** a, guards his own G2774

ARMENIA (KJV) ARARAT

ARMIES (17) [ARM]

Ex 14:20 coming between the a of Egypt and Israel H4722
Jdg 8:10 were left of the a of the eastern peoples; H4722
1Sa 17:10 "This day I defy the a of Israel! H5120
1Sa 17:26 he should defy the a of the living God?" H5120
1Sa 17:36 he has defied the a of the living God. H5120
1Sa 17:45 the God of the a of Israel, whom you have H5120
1Ki 2: 5 did to the two commanders of Israel's a, H7372
Ps 44: 9 you no longer go out with our a. H7372

Ps 60:10 us and no longer go out with our a? H7372
Ps 68:12 "Kings and a flee in haste; the women at H7372
Ps 108:11 us and no longer go out with our a? H7372
Isa 34: 2 with all nations; his wrath is on all their a. H7372
Jer 35:11 escape the Babylonian and Aramean a. H2657
Lk 21:20 see Jerusalem being surrounded by a, *G5136*
Heb 11:34 powerful in battle and routed foreign a. *G4213*
Rev 19:14 The a of heaven were following him *G5128*
Rev 19:19 the earth and their a gathered together to *G5128*

ARMLETS (1) [ARM]
Nu 31:50 articles each of us acquired—a, bracelets, H731

ARMONI (1)
2Sa 21: 8 But the king took A and Mephibosheth, the H813

ARMOR (20) [ARM]
1Sa 17: 5 wore a **coat of scale a** *of* bronze H9234+7989
1Sa 17:38 He put a **coat of a** on him and a bronze H9234
1Sa 31: 9 cut off his head and stripped off his a, H3998
1Sa 31:10 They put his a in the temple of the H3998
1Ki 20:11 '*One who* **puts on** *his* a should not boast H2520
1Ki 22:34 of Israel between the sections of his a. H9234
1Ch 10: 9 stripped him and took his head and his a, H3998
1Ch 10:10 They put his a *in* the temple of their gods H3998
2Ch 18:33 between the breastplate and the **scale** a. H9234
2Ch 26:14 helmets, **coats of** a, bows and slingstones H9234
Ne 4:16 with spears, shields, bows and a. H9234
Job 41:13 Who can penetrate its double **coat of** a? H6246
Ps 35: 2 Take up shield and a; arise and come to H7558
Isa 45: 1 before him and to strip kings of their a, H5516
Jer 46: 4 Polish your spears, put on your a! H6246
Jer 51: 3 string his bow, nor let him put on his a. H6246
Lk 11:22 he takes away the a in which the man *G4110*
Ro 13:12 of darkness and put on the a of light. *G3960*
Eph 6:11 Put on the **full** a of God, so that you can *G4110*
Eph 6:13 Therefore put on the **full** a of God, so that *G4110*

ARMOR-BEARER (19) [ARM]
Jdg 9:54 Hurriedly he called to his a, "Draw H5951+3998
1Sa 14: 1 son of Saul said to his young a, H3998+5951
1Sa 14: 6 Jonathan said to his young a H5951+3998
1Sa 14: 7 that you have in mind," his a said. H5951+3998
1Sa 14:12 shouted to Jonathan and his a, H5951+3998
1Sa 14:12 So Jonathan said to his a, "Climb H5951+3998
1Sa 14:13 with his a right behind him. H5951+3998
1Sa 14:13 and his a followed and killed H5951+3998
1Sa 14:14 Jonathan and his a killed some H5951+3998
1Sa 14:17 Jonathan and his a who were not H5951+3998
1Sa 31: 4 Saul said to his a, "Draw your H5951+3998
1Sa 31: 4 But his a was terrified and would H5951+3998
1Sa 31: 5 When the a saw that Saul was H5951+3998
1Sa 31: 6 sons and his a and all his men H5951+3998
2Sa 23:37 the a *of* Joab son of Zeruiah H5951+3998
1Ch 10: 4 Saul said to his a, "Draw your H5951+3998
1Ch 10: 4 But his a was terrified and would H5951+3998
1Ch 10: 5 When the a saw that Saul was H5951+3998
1Ch 11:39 the a *of* Joab son of Zeruiah H5951+3998

ARMOR-BEARERS (2) [ARM]
1Sa 16:21 and David became one of his a. H5951+3998
2Sa 18:15 And ten of Joab's a surrounded H5951+3998

ARMORY (3) [ARM]
2Ki 20:13 his a and everything found among H1074+3998
Ne 3:19 the ascent to the a as far as the angle of H5977
Isa 39: 2 his entire a and everything found H1074+3998

ARMRESTS (2) [ARM]
1Ki 10:19 On both sides of the seat were a, with a H3338
2Ch 9:18 On both sides of the seat were a, with a H3338

ARMS (51) [ARM]
Ge 16: 5 I put my slave in your a, and now that she H2668
Ge 24:30 the bracelets on his sister's a, and H3338
Ge 24:47 in her nose and the bracelets on her a, H3338
Ge 33: 4 *he* **threw** *his* **a around** his neck and H5877+6584
Ge 45:14 *he* **threw** *his* **a around** his H5877+6584+7418
Ge 46:29 *he* **threw** *his* **a around** his H5877+6584+7418
Ge 48:14 crossing his a, he put his left hand on H3338
Ge 49:24 steady, his **strong** a stayed limber H2432+3338
Nu 11:12 Why do you tell me to carry them in my a H2668
Dt 33:27 underneath are the everlasting a. H2432
Jdg 6:35 **calling** them **to** a, and also H2410+339
Jdg 10:17 Ammonites **were called to** a and camped H7590
Jdg 15:14 The ropes on his a became like charred H2432
Jdg 16:12 the ropes off his a as if they were threads. H2432
Ru 4:16 took the child in her a and cared for him. H2668
2Sa 12: 3 drank from his cup and even slept in his a. H2668
2Sa 12: 8 and your master's wives into your a. H2668
2Sa 22:33 It is God *who* a me *with* strength and keeps H273
2Sa 22:35 my a can bend a bow of bronze. H2432
1Ki 17:19 He took him from her a, carried him to the H2668
2Ki 3:21 *who could* **bear** a was called up H2520+2514
2Ki 4:16 Elisha said, "you *will* **hold** a son **in** your a." H2485
Ps 18:32 It is God who a me *with* strength and keeps H273
Ps 18:34 my a can bend a bow of bronze. H2432
Ps 129: 7 nor one who gathers fill his a. H2950
Pr 31:17 vigorously; her a are strong for her tasks. H2432
Pr 31:20 She opens her a to the poor and extends H4090
SS 5:14 His a are rods of gold set with topaz. His H3338
Isa 17: 5 gathering the grain in their a—as when H2432
Isa 40:11 the lambs in his a and carries them close H2432
Isa 49:22 your sons in their a and carry your H2950
Jer 38:12 under your a to pad the ropes." H723+3338
La 2:12 as their lives ebb away in their mothers' a. H2668
Eze 13:20 like birds and I will tear them from your a; H2432
Eze 16:11 bracelets on your a and a necklace H3338
Eze 30:22 I will break *both* his a, the good arm as H2432
Eze 30:24 will strengthen the a *of* the king of H2432
Eze 30:24 I will break the a *of* Pharaoh, and he H2432
Eze 30:25 will strengthen the a *of* the king of H2432
Eze 30:25 the a *of* Pharaoh will fall limp. H2432
Eze 38: 8 After many days *you will* **be called to** a. In H7212
Da 2:32 its chest and a of silver, its belly A10185
Da 10: 6 his a and legs like the gleam of H2432
Hos 7:15 I trained them and strengthened their a H2432
Hos 11: 3 taking them by the a; but they did not H2432
Mk 9:36 **Taking** the child **in** *his* a, he said to them, *G1878*
Mk 10:16 And *he* **took** the children **in** *his* a, placed *G1878*
Lk 2:28 Simeon took him in his a and praised God *G44*
Lk 15:20 to his son, **threw** *his* **a around** him *G2158+2093+3836+5549*
Ac 20:10 the young man and **put** *his* **a around** him. *G5227*
Heb 12:12 strengthen your feeble a and weak knees. *G5931*

ARMY (269) [ARM]
Ex 14: 4 myself through Pharaoh and all his a, H2657
Ex 14: 6 made ready and took his a with him. H6639
Ex 14:17 gain glory through Pharaoh and all his a, H2657
Ex 14:19 had been traveling in front of Israel's a, H4722
Ex 14:24 cloud at the Egyptian a and threw it into H4722
Ex 14:28 the entire a *of* Pharaoh that had followed H2657
Ex 15: 4 chariots and his a he has hurled into the H2657
Ex 17:13 overcame the Amalekite a with the sword. H6639
Nu 1: 3 old or more and able to serve in the a. H7372
Nu 1:20 to serve in the a were listed by name, H7372
Nu 1:22 able to serve in the a were counted and H7372
Nu 1:24 to serve in the a were listed by name, H7372
Nu 1:26 to serve in the a were listed by name, H7372
Nu 1:28 to serve in the a were listed by name, H7372
Nu 1:30 to serve in the a were listed by name, H7372
Nu 1:32 to serve in the a were listed by name, H7372
Nu 1:34 to serve in the a were listed by name, H7372
Nu 1:36 to serve in the a were listed by name, H7372
Nu 1:38 to serve in the a were listed by name, H7372
Nu 1:40 to serve in the a were listed by name, H7372
Nu 1:42 to serve in the a were listed by name, H7372
Nu 1:45 to serve in Israel's a were counted H7372
Nu 20:20 against them with a large and powerful a. H6639
Nu 21:23 mustered his entire a and marched out H6639
Nu 21:33 his whole a marched out to meet H6639
Nu 21:34 along with his whole a and his land. H6639
Nu 21:35 together with his sons and his whole a H6639
Nu 26: 2 who are able to serve in the a of Israel." H7372
Nu 31:14 was angry with the officers of the a— H2657
Nu 31:48 officers who were over the units of the a— H7372
Dt 2:32 Sihon and all his a came out to meet us H6639
Dt 2:33 together with his sons and his whole a. H6639
Dt 3: 1 with his whole a marched out to meet H6639
Dt 3: 2 along with his whole a and his land. H6639
Dt 3: 3 hands Og king of Bashan and all his a. H6639
Dt 11: 4 what he did to the Egyptian a, to its horses H2657
Dt 20: 1 chariots and an a greater than yours, H6639
Dt 20: 2 shall come forward and address the a. H6639
Dt 20: 5 The officers shall say to the a: "Has H6639
Dt 20: 9 officers have finished speaking to the a, H6639
Jos 5:14 as commander of the a *of* the LORD I have H7372
Jos 5:15 The commander of the LORD's a replied H7372
Jos 6: 5 have the whole a give a loud shout; then H6639
Jos 6: 5 the city will collapse and the a will go up, H6639
Jos 6: 7 And he ordered the a, "Advance! March H6639
Jos 6:10 But Joshua had commanded the a, "Do H6639
Jos 6:11 Then the a returned to camp and spent the NDT
Jos 6:16 Joshua commanded the a, "Shout! H6639
Jos 6:20 sounded, the a shouted, and at the H6639
Jos 7: 3 "Not all the a will have to go up against H6639
Jos 7: 3 to take it and do not weary the whole a, H6639
Jos 8: 1 Take the whole a with you, and go H6639+4878
Jos 8: 3 and the whole a moved out to H6639+4878
Jos 8:10 the next morning Joshua mustered his a, H6639
Jos 10: 7 up from Gilgal with his entire a, H6639+4878
Jos 10:21 The whole a then returned safely to H6639
Jos 10:24 and said to the a commanders who H408+4878
Jos 10:33 Joshua defeated him and his a—until H6639
Jos 11: 4 chariots—a huge a, as numerous as the H6639
Jos 11: 7 and his whole a came against H6639+4878
Jdg 4: 2 the commander of his a, was based in H7372
Jdg 4: 7 the commander of Jabin's a, with his H7372
Jdg 4:15 all his chariots and a by the sword, H4722
Jdg 4:16 the chariots and a as far as Harosheth H4722
Jdg 7: 3 Now announce to the a, 'Anyone who H6639
Jdg 7:22 The a fled to Beth Shittah toward Zererah H4722
Jdg 8:11 attacked the unsuspecting a. H4722
Jdg 8:12 captured them, routing their entire a. H4722
Jdg 9:29 say to Abimelek, 'Call out your whole a! H7372
Jdg 11:21 Sihon and his whole a into Israel's hands, H6639
Jdg 20:10 ten thousand, to get provisions for the a. H6639
Jdg 20:10 when **the** a arrives at Gibeah in H4392S
Jdg 20:26 Israelites, the whole a, went up to Bethel, H6639
1Sa 4:17 the a has suffered heavy losses. H6639
1Sa 12: 9 the commander of the a *of* Hazor, and H7372
1Sa 13: 6 critical and that their a was hard pressed, H6639
1Sa 14:15 Then panic struck the whole a—those in H6639
1Sa 14:16 Benjamin saw the a melting away in all H2162
1Sa 14:25 The entire a entered the woods, and there H824
1Sa 14:28 father bound the a under a strict oath, H6639
1Sa 14:38 all you who are leaders of the a, and let H6639
1Sa 14:50 commander of Saul's a was Abner son of H7372
1Sa 15: 9 But Saul and the a spared Agag and the H6639
1Sa 17:20 the camp as the a was going out to its H2657
1Sa 17:46 of the Philistine a to the birds and the H4722
1Sa 17:55 to Abner, commander of the a, "Abner, H7372
1Sa 18: 5 Saul gave him a high rank in the a. H408+4878
1Sa 26: 5 the commander of the a, had lain down. H7372
1Sa 26: 5 with the a encamped around him. H6639
1Sa 26: 7 David and Abishai went to the a by night, H6639
1Sa 26:14 He called out to the a and to Abner son of H6639
1Sa 28: 1 your men will accompany me in the a." H4722
1Sa 28: 5 When Saul saw the Philistine a, he was H4722
1Sa 28:19 will also give the a *of* Israel into the H4722
1Sa 29: 6 to have you serve with me in the a. H4722
1Sa 31: 7 that the Israelite a had fled and that Saul H408
2Sa 1:12 for the a *of* the LORD and for the H6639
2Sa 2: 8 the commander of Saul's a, had taken H7372
2Sa 2:30 Abner and assembled the whole a. H6639
2Sa 5:24 in front of you to strike the Philistine a." H4722
2Sa 8: 9 had defeated the entire a *of* Hadadezer, H2657
2Sa 8:16 Joab son of Zeruiah was over the a H7372
2Sa 10: 7 out with the entire a of fighting men. H7372
2Sa 10:16 of Hadadezer's a leading them. H7372
2Sa 10:18 down Shobak the commander of their a, H7372
2Sa 11: 1 the king's men and the whole Israelite a. NDT
2Sa 11:17 some of the men in David's a fell H6639
2Sa 12:29 the entire a and went to Rabbah, H6639
2Sa 12:31 he and his entire a returned to Jerusalem. H6639
2Sa 17:25 Amasa over the a in place of Joab. H7372
2Sa 18: 6 David's a marched out of the city to fight H6639
2Sa 19: 2 And for the whole a the victory that day H6639
2Sa 19:13 the commander of my a for life in place of H7372
2Sa 20:23 Joab was over Israel's entire a; Benaiah H7372
2Sa 24: 2 to Joab and the a commanders with him, H2657
2Sa 24: 4 overruled Joab and the a commanders; so H2657
1Ki 1:19 priest and Joab the commander of the a, H7372
1Ki 1:25 commanders of the a and Abiathar the H7372
1Ki 2:32 commander of Israel's a, and Amasa son H7372
1Ki 2:32 commander of Judah's a—were better H7372
1Ki 2:35 of Jehoiada over the a in Joab's position H7372
1Ki 11:15 Joab the commander of the a, who had H7372
1Ki 11:21 the commander of the a was also dead. H7372
1Ki 11:24 When David destroyed Zobah's a, Rezon H4392S
1Ki 16:15 The a was encamped near Gibbethon, a H6639
1Ki 16:16 the commander of the a, king over Israel H7372
1Ki 20: 1 king of Aram mustered his entire a. H2657
1Ki 20:13 'Do you see this vast a? I will give it into H2162
1Ki 20:19 out of the city with the a behind them H2657
1Ki 20:25 must also raise an a like the one you lost H2657
1Ki 20:28 I will deliver this vast a into your hands H2162
1Ki 22:36 was setting, a cry spread through the a: H4722
2Ki 3: 9 the a had no more water for themselves H4722
2Ki 4:13 to the king or the commander of the a? H7372
2Ki 5: 1 commander of the a *of* the king of Aram. H7372
2Ki 6:15 an a with horses and chariots had H2657
2Ki 6:18 to the LORD, "Strike this a with blindness." H1580
2Ki 6:24 his entire a and marched up and H4722
2Ki 7: 6 of chariots and horses and a great a, H2657
2Ki 7:14 the king sent them after the Aramean a. H4722
2Ki 8:21 broke through by night; his a, however, H6639
2Ki 9: 5 he found the a officers sitting together. H2657
2Ki 13: 7 had been left of the a of Jehoahaz except H6639
2Ki 18:17 his field commander with a large a, H2657
2Ki 25: 1 against Jerusalem with his whole a. H2657
2Ki 25: 4 and the whole a fled at night H408+4878
2Ki 25: 5 the Babylonian a pursued the king and H2657
2Ki 25:10 whole Babylonian a under the H2657
2Ki 25:23 When all the a officers and their men H2657
2Ki 25:26 together with the a officers, fled to Egypt H2657
1Ch 10: 7 valley saw that the a had fled and that Saul NDT
1Ch 12:14 These Gadites were a commanders; the H7372
1Ch 12:21 they were commanders in his a. H7372
1Ch 12:22 until he had a great a, like the army of H4722
1Ch 12:22 he had a great army, like the a *of* God. H4722
1Ch 14:15 in front of you to strike the Philistine a." H4722
1Ch 14:16 they struck down the Philistine a, all H4722
1Ch 18: 9 the entire a *of* Hadadezer king of H2657
1Ch 18:15 Joab son of Zeruiah was over the a H7372
1Ch 19: 8 out with the entire a *of* fighting men. H7372
1Ch 19:16 of Hadadezer's a leading them. H7372
1Ch 19:18 killed Shophak the commander of their a. H7372
1Ch 20: 3 David and his entire a returned to H6639
1Ch 25: 1 together with the commanders of the a H7372
1Ch 26:26 by the other a commanders. H7372
1Ch 27: 1 concerned the a **divisions** that were on H4713
1Ch 27: 3 chief of all the a officers for the first H7372
1Ch 27: 5 The third a commander, for the third H7372
1Ch 27:34 Joab was the commander of the royal a. H7372
2Ch 13: 3 into battle with an a of four hundred H2657
2Ch 13: 8 are indeed a vast a and have with you the H2162
2Ch 14: 8 Asa had an a of three hundred thousand H2657
2Ch 14: 9 them with an a *of* thousands upon H2657
2Ch 14:11 name we have come against this **vast** a. H2162
2Ch 14:13 Asa and his a pursued them as far as H6639
2Ch 16: 7 the a *of* the king of Aram has escaped H2657
2Ch 16: 8 Libyans a mighty a with great numbers H2657
2Ch 20: 2 "A vast a is coming against you from H2162
2Ch 20:12 to face this vast a that is attacking us. H2162
2Ch 20:15 discouraged because of this vast a. H2162

2Ch 20:21 as they went out at the head of the **a**, H2741
2Ch 20:24 the desert and looked toward the **vast a**, H2162
2Ch 24:23 the **a** *of* Aram marched against Joash H2657
2Ch 24:24 the Aramean **a** had come with only H2657
2Ch 24:24 into their hands a much larger **a**. H2657
2Ch 25:11 strength and led his **a** to the Valley of Salt H6639
2Ch 25:12 The **a** *of* Judah also captured ten H1201
2Ch 26:11 Uzziah had a well-trained **a**, ready to go H2657
2Ch 26:13 was an **a** of 307,500 men H2657+7372
2Ch 26:14 bows and slingstones for the entire **a**. H7372
2Ch 28: 9 out to meet the **a** when it returned to H7372
2Ch 32: 7 king of Assyria and the vast **a** with him, H2162
2Ch 33:11 against them the **a** commanders of the H7372
Ne 2: 9 king had also sent **a** officers and cavalry H2657
Ne 4: 2 of his associates and the **a** *of* Samaria, H2657
Ps 27: 3 Though an **a** besiege me, my heart will H4722
Ps 33:16 No king is saved by the size of his **a**; no H2657
Ps 136:15 Pharaoh and his **a** into the Red Sea; H2657
Isa 13: 4 LORD Almighty is mustering an **a** *for* war. H7372
Isa 33: 3 At the uproar of your **a**, the peoples flee H2162
Isa 36: 2 with a large **a** from Lachish to King H2657
Isa 43:17 the **a** and reinforcements together H2657
Jer 4:16 'A **besieging** *a* is coming from a distant land AIT
Jer 6:22 an **a** is coming from the land of the north H6639
Jer 32: 2 The **a** *of* the king of Babylon was then H2657
Jer 34: 1 Babylon and all his **a** and all the H2657
Jer 34: 7 while the **a** *of* the king of Babylon was H2657
Jer 34:21 kill them, to the **a** *of* the king of Babylon H2657
Jer 37: 5 Pharaoh's **a** had marched out of Egypt H2657
Jer 37: 7 'Pharaoh's **a**, which has marched H2657
Jer 37:10 entire Babylonian **a** that is attacking you H2657
Jer 37:11 the Babylonian **a** had withdrawn from H2657
Jer 37:11 from Jerusalem because of Pharaoh's **a**, H2657
Jer 38: 3 the hands of the **a** *of* the king of Babylon, H2657
Jer 39: 1 with his whole **a** and laid siege to it. H2657
Jer 39: 5 But the Babylonian **a** pursued them and H2657
Jer 40: 7 When all the **a** officers and their men H2657
Jer 40:13 of Kareah and all the **a** officers still in the H2657
Jer 41:11 of Kareah and all the **a** officers who were H2657
Jer 41:13 son of Kareah and the **a** officers who were H2657
Jer 41:16 of Kareah and all the **a** officers who were H2657
Jer 42: 1 Then all the **a** officers, including Johanan H2657
Jer 42: 8 of Kareah and all the **a** officers who were H2657
Jer 43: 4 Kareah and all the **a** officers and all the H2657
Jer 43: 5 Kareah and all the **a** officers led away all H2657
Jer 46: 2 against the **a** *of* Pharaoh Necho king H2657
Jer 50:41 An **a** is coming from the north; a great H6639
Jer 51: 3 her young men; completely destroy her **a**. H7372
Jer 52: 4 against Jerusalem with his whole **a**. H2657
Jer 52: 7 through, and the whole **a** fled. H408+4878
Jer 52: 8 the Babylonian **a** pursued King H2657
Jer 52:14 The whole Babylonian **a**, under the H2657
La 1:15 he has summoned an **a** against me to H4595
Eze 1:24 of the Almighty, like the tumult of an **a**. H4722
Eze 17:15 to Egypt to get horses and a large **a**. H6639
Eze 17:17 with his mighty **a** and great horde will H2657
Eze 26: 7 horsemen and a great **a**. H7736+2256+6639
Eze 27:10 Lydia and Put served as soldiers in your **a**. H2657
Eze 29:18 Babylon drove his **a** in a hard campaign H2657
Eze 29:18 Yet he and his **a** got no reward from the H2657
Eze 29:19 loot and plunder the land as pay for his **a**. H2657
Eze 29:20 his efforts because *he and his a* **did** it for me, AIT
Eze 30:11 He and his **a**—the most ruthless of H6639
Eze 32:22 "Assyria is there with her whole **a**; she is H7736
Eze 32:23 of the pit and her **a** lies around her grave. H7736
Eze 32:31 he and all his **a**—will see them and he H2657
Eze 37:10 life and stood up on their feet—a vast **a**. H2657
Eze 38: 4 bring you out with your whole **a**— H2657
Eze 38:15 on horses, a great horde, a mighty **a**. H2657
Da 3:20 soldiers in his **a** to tie up Shadrach, A10264
Da 8:11 as the commander of the **a** of the LORD; H7372
Da 11:10 war and assemble a great **a**, H2162+2657
Da 11:11 who will raise a large **a**, but it will be H2162
Da 11:12 When the **a** is carried off, the king of the H2162
Da 11:13 king of the North will muster another **a**, H2162
Da 11:13 advance with a huge **a** fully equipped. H2657
Da 11:22 an overwhelming **a** will be swept away H2432
Da 11:25 "With a large **a** he will stir up his strength H2657
Da 11:25 war with a large and very powerful **a**, H2657
Da 11:26 to destroy him; his **a** will be swept away H2657
Joel 1: 6 invaded my land, a **mighty** *a* without number AIT
Joel 2: 2 mountains a large and mighty **a** comes, H6639
Joel 2: 5 like a mighty **a** drawn up for battle. H6639
Joel 2:11 The LORD thunders at the head of his **a** H2657
Joel 2:11 mighty is the **a** that obeys his command NDT
Joel 2:25 my great **a** that I sent among you. H2657
Mt 22: 7 He sent his **a** and destroyed those *G5128*
Heb 11:30 *after the a had* **marched around** them for AIT
Rev 19:19 against the rider on the horse and his **a**. *G5128*

ARNAN (1)

1Ch 3:21 sons of Rephaiah, of **A**, of Obadiah and of H820

ARNON (24) [ARNON'S]

Nu 21:13 from there and camped alongside the **A**, H818
Nu 21:13 The **A** is the border of Moab, between H818
Nu 21:14 Zahab in Suphah and the ravines, the **A** H818
Nu 21:24 over his land from the **A** to the Jabbok, H818
Nu 21:26 taken from him all his land as far as the **A**. H818
Nu 22:36 him at the Moabite town on the **A** border, H818
Dt 2:24 "Set out now and cross the **A** Gorge. See, I H818
Dt 2:36 From Aroer on the rim of the **A** Gorge, and H818
Dt 3: 8 from the **A** Gorge as far as Mount Hermon. H818
Dt 3:12 the territory north of Aroer by the **A** Gorge, H818
Dt 3:16 from Gilead down to the **A** Gorge H818
Dt 4:48 on the rim of the **A** Gorge to Mount Sirion H818
Jos 12: 1 from the **A** Gorge to Mount Hermon H818
Jos 12: 2 from Aroer on the rim of the **A** Gorge— H818
Jos 13: 9 from Aroer on the rim of the **A** Gorge, H818
Jos 13:16 from Aroer on the rim of the **A** Gorge, H818
Jdg 11:13 away my land from the **A** to the Jabbok, H818
Jdg 11:18 camped on the other side of the **A**. H818
Jdg 11:18 territory of Moab, for the **A** was its border. H818
Jdg 11:22 all of it from the **A** to the Jabbok and from H818
Jdg 11:26 settlements and all the towns along the **A**. H818
2Ki 10:33 from Aroer by the **A** Gorge through Gilead H818
Isa 16: 2 the women of Moab at the fords of the **A**. H818
Jer 48:20 Announce by the **A** that Moab is destroyed H818

ARNON'S (1) [ARNON]

Nu 21:28 Ar of Moab, the citizens of **A** heights. H818

ARODI (2) [ARODITE]

Ge 46:16 Shuni, Ezbon, Eri, **A** and Areli. H771
Nu 26:17 through **A**, the Arodite clan; through Areli H771

ARODITE (1) [ARODI]

Nu 26:17 through Arodi, the **A** clan; through Areli H772

AROER (16) [AROERITE]

Nu 32:34 The Gadites built up Dibon, Ataroth, **A**, H6876
Dt 2:36 From **A** on the rim of the Arnon Gorge H6876
Dt 3:12 territory north of **A** by the Arnon Gorge, H6876
Dt 4:48 land extended from **A** on the rim of the H6876
Jos 12: 2 He ruled from **A** on the rim of the Arnon H6876
Jos 13: 9 It extended from **A** on the rim of the H6876
Jos 13:16 The territory from **A** on the rim of the H6876
Jos 13:25 half the Ammonite country as far as **A**, H6876
Jdg 11:26 occupied Heshbon, **A**, the surrounding H6876
Jdg 11:33 twenty towns from **A** to the vicinity of H6876
1Sa 30:28 to those in **A**, Siphmoth, Eshtemoa H6876
2Sa 24: 5 they camped near **A**, south of the town in H6876
2Ki 10:33 from **A** by the Arnon Gorge through H6876
1Ch 5: 8 in the area from **A** to Nebo and Baal H6876
Isa 17: 2 The cities of **A** will be deserted and left to H6876
Jer 48:19 by the road and watch, you who live in **A**. H6876

AROERITE (1) [AROER]

1Ch 11:44 Jeiel the sons of Hotham the **A**, H6901

AROMA (44) [AROMATIC]

Ge 8:21 smelled the pleasing **a** and said in his H8194
Ex 29:18 to the LORD, a pleasing **a**, a food offering H8194
Ex 29:25 burnt offering for a pleasing **a** to the LORD, H8194
Ex 29:41 morning—a pleasing **a**, a food offering H8194
Lev 1: 9 a food offering, an **a** pleasing to the LORD. H8194
Lev 1:13 a food offering, an **a** pleasing to the LORD. H8194
Lev 1:17 a food offering, an **a** pleasing to the LORD. H8194
Lev 2: 2 a food offering, an **a** pleasing to the LORD. H8194
Lev 2: 9 a food offering, an **a** pleasing to the LORD. H8194
Lev 2:12 to be offered on the altar as a pleasing **a**. H8194
Lev 3: 5 a food offering, an **a** pleasing to the LORD. H8194
Lev 3:16 the altar as a food offering, a pleasing **a**. H8194
Lev 4:31 on the altar as an **a** pleasing to the LORD. H8194
Lev 6:15 on the altar as an **a** pleasing to the LORD. H8194
Lev 6:21 in pieces as an **a** pleasing to the LORD. H8194
Lev 8:21 offering, a pleasing **a**, a food offering H8194
Lev 8:28 offering, a pleasing **a**, a food offering H8194
Lev 17: 6 burn the fat as an **a** pleasing to the LORD. H8194
Lev 23:13 the LORD, a pleasing **a**—and its drink H8194
Lev 23:18 a food offering, an **a** pleasing to the LORD. H8194
Lev 26:31 delight in the pleasing **a** *of* your offerings. H8194
Nu 15: 3 the flock, as an **a** pleasing to the LORD H8194
Nu 15: 7 Offer it as an **a** pleasing to the LORD. H8194
Nu 15:10 a food offering, an **a** pleasing to the LORD. H8194
Nu 15:13 food offering as an **a** pleasing to the LORD. H8194
Nu 15:14 food offering as an **a** pleasing to the LORD, H8194
Nu 15:24 burnt offering as an **a** pleasing to the LORD H8194
Nu 18:17 a food offering, an **a** pleasing to the LORD. H8194
Nu 28: 2 food offerings, as an **a** pleasing to me. H8194
Nu 28: 6 instituted at Mount Sinai as a pleasing **a**, H8194
Nu 28: 8 a food offering, an **a** pleasing to the LORD. H8194
Nu 28:13 offering, a pleasing **a**, a food offering H8194
Nu 28:24 seven days as an **a** pleasing to the LORD H8194
Nu 28:27 a year old as an **a** pleasing to the LORD. H8194
Nu 29: 2 As an **a** pleasing to the LORD, offer a burnt H8194
Nu 29: 6 presented to the LORD, a pleasing **a**. H8194
Nu 29: 8 Present as an **a** pleasing to the LORD a H8194
Nu 29:13 Present as an **a** pleasing to the LORD a H8194
Nu 29:36 Present as an **a** pleasing to the LORD a H8194
Jer 48:11 as she did, and her **a** is unchanged. H8194
2Co 2:14 us to spread the **a** of the knowledge of *G4011*
2Co 2:15 are to God the **pleasing a** of Christ among *G2380*
2Co 2:16 To the one we are an **a** that brings death *G4011*
2Co 2:16 to the other, an **a** that brings life. *G4011*

AROMATIC (1) [AROMA]

Ge 2:12 is good; **a resin** and onyx are also there.) H978

AROSE (11) [RISE]

Ge 13: 7 And quarreling **a** between Abram's H2118
Jdg 5: 7 they held back until *I*, Deborah, **a**, until I H7756
Jdg 5: 7 until *I* **a**, a mother in Israel. H7756
1Sa 1:19 **Early** the next morning *they* **a** and H8899
Est 8: 4 to Esther and she **a** and stood before him. H7756
SS 5: 5 I **a** to open for my beloved, and my hands H7756
Jnh 1: 4 such a violent storm **a** that the ship H2118
Lk 22:24 A dispute also **a** among them as to which *G1181*
Ac 6: 9 **Opposition a**, however, from members of *G482*
Ac 19:23 About that time *there* **a** a great *G1181*
Gal 2: 4 This matter **a** because some false believers NDT

AROUND (407) [ROUNDABOUT]

Ge 6:16 one cubit high **all a**. H4946+4200+5087
Ge 13:10 Lot looked **a** and saw that the whole plain H5951
Ge 13:14 "**Look a** from where you H5951+6524+2256+8011
Ge 19:31 there is no man **a** here to give us H928
Ge 33: 4 *he* **threw** *his* **arms a** his neck and H5877+6584
Ge 35: 5 fell on the towns **all a** them so that no H6017
Ge 37: 7 your sheaves **gathered a** mine and bowed H6015
Ge 37:15 man found him **wandering a** in the fields H9494
Ge 41:42 linen and put a gold chain **a** his neck. H6584
Ge 45:14 *he* **threw** *his* **arms a** his H5877+6584+7418
Ge 46:29 *he* **threw** *his* **arms a** his H5877+6584+7418
Ge 49: 1 "**Gather a** so I can tell you what will H665
Ex 13:18 **led** the people **a** *by* the desert road *toward* H6015
Ex 14: 3 *are* **wandering a** the land **in confusion**, H1003
Ex 16: 3 There we sat **a** pots of meat and ate all H6584
Ex 16:13 there was a layer of dew **a** the camp. H6017
Ex 18:13 they stood **a** him from morning till H6584
Ex 18:14 these people stand **a** you from morning H6584
Ex 19:12 the people **a** the mountain and tell H6017
Ex 19:23 '**Put limits a** the mountain and set it apart H1487
Ex 21:19 can get up and **walk a** outside with a H2143
Ex 25:11 out, and make a gold molding **a** it. H6017
Ex 25:24 pure gold and make a gold molding **a** it. H6017
Ex 25:25 Also make **a** it a rim a handbreadth wide H6017
Ex 27:17 All the posts **a** the courtyard are to have H6017
Ex 28:32 a woven edge like a collar **a** this opening, H6017
Ex 28:33 scarlet yarn **a** the hem of the robe, H6017
Ex 28:34 are to alternate **a** the hem of the robe. H6017
Ex 30: 3 pure gold, and make a gold molding **a** it. H6017
Ex 32: 1 they gathered **a** Aaron and said, "Come, H6584
Ex 37: 2 out, and made a gold molding **a** it. H6017
Ex 37:11 pure gold and made a gold molding **a** it. H6017
Ex 37:12 They also made **a** it a rim a handbreadth H6017
Ex 37:26 pure gold, and made a gold molding **a** it. H6017
Ex 38:16 All the curtains **a** the courtyard were of H6017
Ex 39:23 a collar, and a band **a** this opening, so H6017
Ex 39:24 finely twisted linen **a** the hem of the robe. H6584
Ex 39:25 attached them **a** the hem between H6017
Ex 39:26 alternated **a** the hem of the robe to H6017
Ex 40: 8 Set up the courtyard **a** it and put the H6017
Ex 40:33 set up the courtyard **a** the tabernacle and H6017
Lev 8: 7 on Aaron, **tied** the sash **a** him, clothed H2520
Lev 8: 7 waistband, which he tied **a** him. H4200
Lev 8:13 **tied** sashes **a** them and fastened caps on H2520
Lev 8:16 also took all the fat **a** the internal organs, H6584
Lev 8:25 all the fat **a** the internal organs H6584
Lev 16: 4 *he is to* **tie** the linen sash **a** him and put H2520
Lev 25:31 villages without walls **a** them are to be H6017
Lev 25:44 are to come from the nations **a** you; H6017
Nu 1:50 they are to take care of it and encamp **a** it. H6017
Nu 1:53 set up their tents **a** the tabernacle of the H6017
Nu 2: 2 are to camp **a** the tent of meeting H6017
Nu 11: 8 The people **went a** gathering it, and then H8763
Nu 11:24 elders and had them stand **a** the tent. H6017
Nu 11:31 up to two cubits deep **all a** the camp, H6017
Nu 11:32 they spread them out **all a** the camp. H6017
Nu 16:34 all the Israelites **a** them fled, shouting, H6017
Nu 21: 4 the route to the Red Sea, to **go a** Edom. H6015
Nu 22: 4 horde is going to lick up everything **a** us, H6017
Nu 32:33 with its cities and the territory **a** them. H6017
Nu 35: 2 And give them pasturelands **a** the towns. H6017
Nu 35: 4 "The pasturelands **a** the towns that you H6017
Dt 1:40 **turn a** and set out toward the desert along H7155
Dt 2: 1 a long time *we* **made** *our* **way a** the hill H6015
Dt 2: 3 "You *have* **made** *your* **way a** this hill H6015
Dt 2:37 the Jabbok nor that **a** the towns in the hills NDT
Dt 6:14 the gods of the peoples **a** you; H6017
Dt 7:22 the wild animals will multiply **a** you. H6584
Dt 12:10 all your enemies **a** you so that you H4946+6017
Dt 13: 7 gods of the peoples **a** you, whether near H6017
Dt 17:14 set a king over us like all the nations **a** us," H6017
Dt 22: 8 make a parapet **a** your roof so that you H4200
Dt 25:19 all the enemies **a** you in the land H4946+6017
Jos 6: 3 **March a** the city once with all the H5938+6015
Jos 6: 4 seventh day, **march a** the city seven times H6015
Jos 6: 7 **March a** the city, with an armed guard H6015
Jos 6:11 So *he had* the ark of the LORD **carried a** the H6015
Jos 6:14 second day *they* **marched a** the city once H6015
Jos 6:15 at daybreak and **marched a** the city seven H6015
Jos 6:16 The seventh time **a**, when the priests NDT
Jos 8:21 *they* **turned a** and attacked the men of Ai. H8740
Jos 10:38 Israel with him **turned a** and attacked H8740
Jos 15: 3 up to Addar and **curved a** to Karka. H6015
Jos 15:12 are the boundaries **a** the people of Judah H6017
Jos 19: 8 all the villages **a** these towns as far H6017
Jos 19:14 the boundary **went a** on the north to H6015
Jos 21:12 But the fields and **villages** *a* the city they had AIT
Jos 23: 1 rest from all their enemies **a** them, H4946+6017
Jdg 2:12 various gods of the peoples **a** them. H6017
Jdg 2:14 the hands of their enemies **all a**, H4946+6017
Jdg 6:31 Joash replied to the hostile crowd **a** him, H6584
Jdg 7:18 then from all **a** the camp blow yours and H6017
Jdg 7:21 each man held his position **a** the camp, H6017
Jdg 11: 3 scoundrels gathered **a** him and followed H448

Jdg 18:26 him, **turned a** and went back home. H7155
Jdg 20:29 Then Israel set an ambush **a** Gibeah. H6017
1Sa 5:10 *They have* **brought** the ark of the god of Israel **a** H6015
1Sa 9: 4 of Ephraim and through the **area** *a* Shalisha, AIT
1Sa 12:11 hands of your enemies **all a** you, H4946+6017
1Sa 17:39 sword over the tunic and tried **walking a**, H2143
1Sa 22: 2 in debt or discontented gathered **a** him, H448
1Sa 25:12 David's men **turned a** and went back H2200
1Sa 25:16 they were a wall **a** us the whole time we H6584
1Sa 26: 5 with the army encamped **a** him. H6017
1Sa 26: 7 Abner and the soldiers were lying **a** him. H6017
1Sa 26:16 LORD's anointed. **Look a** you. Where are H8011
1Sa 31: 3 The fighting grew fierce **a** Saul, and when H448
2Sa 1: 7 When he turned **a** and saw me, he called H339
2Sa 5: 9 He built up the **area a** it, from the terraces H6017
2Sa 5:23 but **circle a** behind them and attack them H6015
2Sa 6:20 **going a half-naked** in full view of the H1655
2Sa 7: 1 rest from all his enemies **a** him, H4946+6017
2Sa 11: 2 from his bed and **walked a** on the roof of H2143
2Sa 22: 6 The cords of the grave **coiled a** me; the H6015
2Sa 22:12 He made darkness his canopy **a** him H6017
2Sa 24: 6 on to Dan Jaan and **a** toward Sidon. H6017
1Ki 2: 5 he stained the belt **a** his waist and the H928
1Ki 3: 1 of the LORD, and the wall **a** Jerusalem. H6017
1Ki 6: 5 he built a structure **a** the building, H6017
1Ki 6: 6 made offset ledges **a** the outside of the H6017
1Ki 6:29 On the walls all **a** the temple, in both the H4990
1Ki 7:20 two hundred pomegranates in rows **all a**. H6017
1Ki 7:23 line of thirty cubits *to* **measure a** it. H6015+6017
1Ki 7:31 **A** its opening there was engraving H6584
1Ki 7:36 every available space, with wreaths **all a**. H6017
1Ki 8:14 the king **turned a** and blessed them. H6015
1Ki 11:24 a band of men **a** him and became their H6584
1Ki 16:18 palace and set the palace on fire **a** him. H6584
1Ki 18:26 And they danced **a** the altar they had H6584
1Ki 18:32 he dug a trench **a** it large enough to H6017
1Ki 18:35 The water ran down **a** the altar and even H6017
1Ki 19: 6 *He* **looked a**, and there by his head was H5564
1Ki 19:19 went up to him and threw his cloak **a** him. H448
1Ki 20:31 Israel with sackcloth **a** our waists and ropes H928
1Ki 20:31 around our waists and ropes **a** our heads. H928
1Ki 20:32 Wearing sackcloth **a** their waists and ropes H928
1Ki 20:32 their waists and ropes **a** their heads, H928
1Ki 21:27 He lay in sackcloth and **went a** meekly. H2143
1Ki 22:19 of heaven standing **a** him on his right H6584
1Ki 22:34 **"Wheel a** and get me out of the H2200+3338
2Ki 1: 8 of hair and had a leather belt **a** his waist." H928
2Ki 2:24 He turned **a**, looked at them and called H339
2Ki 4: 3 "Go **a** and ask all your H4946+2021+2575
2Ki 6:17 of horses and chariots of fire **all a** Elisha. H6017
2Ki 10:23 **"Look a** and see that no one who serves H2924
2Ki 11: 8 Station yourselves **a** the king, each of you H6017
2Ki 11:11 stationed themselves **a** the king—near H6017
2Ki 17:15 imitated the nations **a** them although the H6017
2Ki 23: 5 of Judah and on *those* **a** Jerusalem— H4990
2Ki 23:16 Then Josiah **looked a**, and when he saw H7155
2Ki 25: 1 the city and built siege works **all a** it. H6017
2Ki 25:10 guard broke down the walls **a** Jerusalem. H6017
2Ki 25:17 pomegranates of bronze all **a**. H6017
1Ch 4:33 all the villages **a** these towns as far as H6017
1Ch 6:56 But the fields and **villages** *a* the city were AIT
1Ch 9:27 spend the night **stationed a** the house of H6017
1Ch 10: 3 The fighting grew fierce **a** Saul, and when H6584
1Ch 11: 8 He built up the city **a** it, from the terraces H6017
1Ch 14:14 but **circle a** them and attack them in front H6015
2Ch 4: 2 line of thirty cubits *to* **measure a** it. H6015+6017
2Ch 6: 3 the king **turned a** and blessed them. H6015
2Ch 13: 7 scoundrels gathered **a** him and opposed H6584
2Ch 13:13 Jeroboam *had* **sent** troops **a** to the rear H6015
2Ch 14: 7 to Judah, "and **put** walls **a** them, with H6015
2Ch 14:14 They destroyed all the villages **a** Gerar, for H6017
2Ch 17: 9 *they* **went a** to all the towns of Judah and H6015
2Ch 18:33 **"Wheel a** and get me out of the H2200+3338
2Ch 23: 7 are to station themselves **a** the king, H6017
2Ch 23:10 weapon in his hand, **a** the king—near the H6017
2Ch 31:19 who lived on the **farmlands** *a* their towns AIT
2Ch 34: 6 far as Naphtali, and in the ruins **a** them, H6017
Ezr 3: 3 Despite their fear of the peoples **a** them H824S
Ezr 4: 4 Then the peoples **a** them set out to H824S
Ezr 9: 2 the holy race with the peoples **a** them. H824S
Ezr 9: 4 of Israel gathered **a** me because of this H448
Ezr 10: 1 women and children—gathered **a** him. H448
Ezr 10: 2 foreign women from the peoples **a** us. H824S
Ezr 10:11 from the peoples **a** you and from your H824S
Ne 8:13 gathered **a** Ezra the teacher to give H448
Ne 10:30 marriage to the peoples **a** us or take their H824S
Ne 12:28 together from the region **a** Jerusalem— H6017
Ne 12:29 built villages for themselves **a** Jerusalem. H6017
Ne 12:44 From the **fields** *a* the towns they were to AIT
Job 1:10 put a hedge **a** him and his H6017+4946+1237
Job 8:17 it entwines its roots **a** a pile of rocks and H6584
Job 12:18 by kings and ties a loincloth **a** their waist. H928
Job 19: 6 has wronged me and drawn his net **a** me. H6584
Job 19:12 ramp against me and encamp **a** my tent. H6017
Job 21: 8 see their children established **a** them, H6640
Job 22:10 That is why snares are **all a** you, why H6017
Job 29: 5 still with me and my children were **a** me, H6017
Job 37:12 direction they swirl **a** over the face of the H4991
Ps 3: 3 are a shield **a** me, my glory, the One H1237
Ps 7: 7 *Let* the assembled peoples **gather a** you H6015
Ps 18: 5 The cords of the grave **coiled a** me; the H6015
Ps 18:11 covering, his canopy **a** him—the dark rain H6017
Ps 34: 7 the LORD encamps **a** those who fear him, H6017
Ps 39: 6 "Surely everyone **goes a** like a mere H2143
Ps 41: 6 goes out and spreads it **a**. H4200+2021+2575
Ps 44:13 the scorn and derision of *those* **a** us. H6017
Ps 48:12 Walk about Zion, **go a** her, count her H5938
Ps 50: 3 before him, and **a** him a tempest rages. H6017
Ps 78:28 down inside their camp, **all a** their tents. H6017
Ps 79: 3 out blood like water **all a** Jerusalem, H6017
Ps 79: 4 of scorn and derision to *those* **a** us. H6017
Ps 109:19 about him, like a belt **tied** forever **a** him. H2520
Ps 118:12 *They* **swarmed a** me like bees, but they H6015
Ps 128: 3 will be like olive shoots **a** your table. H6017
Ps 139:11 me and the light become night **a** me," H1237
Pr 3: 3 leave you; bind them **a** your neck, write H6584
Pr 6:21 on your heart; fasten them **a** your neck. H6584
Isa 11: 5 his belt and faithfulness the **sash** *a* his waist. AIT
Isa 19:14 as a drunkard **staggers a** in his vomit. H9494
Isa 20: 2 he did so, **going a** stripped and barefoot. H2143
Isa 22:21 robe and **fasten** your sash *a* him and hand AIT
Isa 28:20 the blanket too narrow *to* **wrap a** *you*. H4043
Isa 49:18 Lift up your eyes and look **a**; all your H6017
Isa 56:10 cannot bark; *they* **lie a** and dream, they H8886
Jer 5: 1 of Jerusalem, **look a** and consider, search H8011
Jer 6: 3 they will pitch their tents **a** her, each H6017
Jer 13: 1 buy a linen belt and put it **a** your waist, H6584
Jer 13: 2 as the LORD directed, and put it **a** my waist. H6584
Jer 13: 4 you bought and are **wearing a** your waist, H6584
Jer 13:11 For as a belt is bound **a** the waist, so I H448
Jer 17:26 and the villages **a** Jerusalem, H4946+6017
Jer 19:15 city and all the **villages** *a* it every disaster I AIT
Jer 21:14 that will consume everything **a** you. H6017
Jer 26: 9 the people crowded **a** Jeremiah in the H448
Jer 31:26 At this I awoke and **looked** *a*. My sleep had AIT
Jer 32:44 in the villages **a** Jerusalem, in the towns H6017
Jer 33:13 in the villages **a** Jerusalem and in the H6017
Jer 34:16 But now *you have* **turned a** and profaned H8740
Jer 40:15 who are gathered **a** you to be scattered H448
Jer 46:14 for the sword devours *those* **a** you. H6017
Jer 48:17 all who live **a** her, all who know her H6017
Jer 48:39 an object of horror to all *those* **a** her." H6017
Jer 49: 5 bring terror on you from all *those* **a** you," H6017
Jer 50:14 "Take up your positions **a** Babylon, all you H6017
Jer 50:29 Encamp **all a** her; let no one H6017
Jer 50:32 that will consume all who are **a** her." H6017
Jer 52: 4 the city and built siege works **all a** it. H6017
Jer 52:14 broke down all the walls **a** Jerusalem. H6017
Jer 52:22 pomegranates of bronze all **a**. H6017
La 1:12 you who pass by? **Look a** and see. Is any H5564
La 2: 3 flaming fire that consumes **everything a** it. H6017
La 2: 8 to tear down the **wall** *a* Daughter Zion. AIT
Eze 1:18 all four rims were full of eyes **all a**. H6017
Eze 1:28 a rainy day, so was the radiance **a** him. H6017
Eze 2: 6 briers and thorns are **all a** you and you live H907
Eze 4: 2 against it and put battering rams **a** it. H6017
Eze 5: 2 strike it with the sword **all a** the city. H6017
Eze 5: 5 of the nations, with countries **all a** her. H6017
Eze 5: 6 than the nations and countries **a** her. H6017
Eze 5: 7 than the nations **a** you and have not H6017
Eze 5: 7 to the standards of the nations **a** you. H6017
Eze 5:14 a reproach among the nations **a** you, H6017
Eze 5:15 horror to the nations **a** you when I inflict H6017
Eze 6: 5 I will scatter your bones **a** your altars. H6017
Eze 6:13 lie slain among their idols **a** their altars, H6017
Eze 11:12 to the standards of the nations **a** you." H6017
Eze 12:14 I will scatter to the winds all those **a** him H6017
Eze 16:11 on your arms and a necklace **a** your neck, H6584
Eze 16:37 against you from **all a** and will strip you H6017
Eze 16:57 all *those* **a** you who despise you. H6017
Eze 23:15 with belts **a** their waists and flowing turbans H928
Eze 23:42 "The noise of a carefree crowd was **a** her H928
Eze 27:11 They hung their shields **a** your walls; they H6017
Eze 31: 4 streams flowed **all a** its base and sent H6017
Eze 32:23 of the pit and her army lies **a** her grave. H6017
Eze 32:24 is there, with all her hordes **a** her grave. H6017
Eze 32:25 the slain, with all her hordes **a** her grave. H6017
Eze 32:26 with all their hordes **a** their graves. H6017
Eze 36: 4 by the rest of the nations **a** you— H4946+6017
Eze 36: 7 that the nations **a** you will also H4946+6017
Eze 36:36 Then the nations **a** you that remain will H6017
Eze 37:21 gather them from **all a** and bring them H6017
Eze 38: 4 *I will* **turn** you **a**, put hooks in your jaws H8740
Eze 39: 2 *I will* **turn** you **a** and drag you along. I will H8740
Eze 39:17 come together from **all a** to the sacrifice I H6017
Eze 40:14 projecting walls **all a** the inside of H6017+6017
Eze 40:16 by narrow parapet openings **all a**, H6017+6017
Eze 40:16 the openings **all a** faced inward. H6017+6017
Eze 40:17 been constructed **all a** the court; H6017+6017
Eze 40:25 portico had narrow openings **all a**, H6017+6017
Eze 40:29 and its portico had openings **all a**. H6017+6017
Eze 40:30 of the gateways **a** the inner court H6017+6017
Eze 40:33 and its portico had openings **all a**. H6017+6017
Eze 40:36 portico, and it had openings **all a**. H6017+6017
Eze 40:43 were attached to the wall **all a**. H6017+6017
Eze 41: 5 each side room **a** the temple was H6017+6017
Eze 41: 6 were ledges **all a** the wall of the H6017+6017
Eze 41: 7 The side rooms **all a** the temple were H6015
Eze 41: 8 temple had a raised base **all a** it, H6017+6017
Eze 41:10 cubits wide **all a** the temple. H6017+6017
Eze 41:11 area was five cubits wide **all a**. H6017+6017
Eze 41:12 building was five cubits thick **all a**, H6017+6017
Eze 41:16 galleries **a** the three of them— H6017
Eze 41:17 regular intervals **all a** the inner and H6017+6017
Eze 41:19 They were carved **all a** the whole H6017+6017
Eze 42:15 gate and measured the area **all a**: H6017+6017
Eze 42:20 It had a wall **a** it, five hundred H6017+6017
Eze 43:13 with a rim of one span **a** the edge. H6017
Eze 43:14 to the lower **ledge that goes a** the altar it H6478
Eze 43:14 to the upper **ledge that goes a** the altar it H6478
Eze 43:17 **All a** the altar is a gutter of one cubit with H6017
Eze 43:20 of the upper ledge and **all a** the rim, H6017
Eze 44:18 linen undergarments **a** their waists. H6584
Eze 45: 2 with 50 cubits **a** it for open land. H6017
Eze 46:21 the outer court and **led** me **a** to its four H6296
Eze 46:23 **A** the inside of each of the four courts was H6017
Eze 46:23 places for fire built **all a** under the ledge. H6017
Eze 47: 2 north gate and **led** me **a** the outside to H6015
Eze 48:35 "The distance **all a** will be 18,000 cubits H6017
Da 3:25 I see four men **walking a** in the fire A10207
Da 3:27 royal advisers **crowded a** them. A10359
Da 5: 7 have a gold chain placed **a** his neck, A10542
Da 5:16 have a gold chain placed **a** your neck, A10542
Da 5:29 a gold chain was placed **a** his neck, and A10542
Da 9:16 an object of scorn to all *those* **a** us. H6017
Da 10: 5 a belt of fine gold from Uphaz **a** his waist. NDT
Jnh 2: 5 seaweed *was* **wrapped a** my head. H2502
Na 3: 8 situated on the Nile, with water **a** her? H6017
Hab 2:16 the LORD's right hand *is* **coming a** to you, H6015
Zec 2: 5 And I myself will be a wall of fire **a** it,' H6017
Mt 3: 4 he had a leather belt **a** his waist. *G4309*
Mt 8:18 When Jesus saw the crowd **a** him, he *G4309*
Mt 13: 2 large crowds **gathered a** him that he got *G5251*
Mt 18: 6 millstone hung **a** their neck and to be *G4309*
Mt 20: 6 out and found still others **standing a**. *G2705*
Mt 21:33 *He* **put** a wall **a** it, dug a winepress in it *G4363*
Mt 27:27 the whole company of soldiers **a** him. *G2093*
Mk 1: 6 with a leather belt **a** his waist, and he ate *G4309*
Mk 3: 5 *He* **looked a** at them in anger and, deeply *G4315*
Mk 3: 8 across the Jordan and **a** Tyre and Sidon. *G4309*
Mk 3:32 A crowd was sitting **a** him, and they told *G4309*
Mk 3:34 at those seated in a circle **a** him and said, *G4309*
Mk 4: 1 crowd that gathered **a** him was so large *G4639*
Mk 4:10 the others **a** him asked him about *G4309*
Mk 5:21 crowd gathered **a** him while he was by *G2093*
Mk 5:24 large crowd followed and **pressed a** him. *G5315*
Mk 5:30 *He* **turned a** in the crowd and asked *G2188*
Mk 5:32 But Jesus *kept* **looking a** to see who had *G4315*
Mk 5:42 the girl stood up and *began to* **walk a** *G4344*
Mk 6: 6 Then Jesus *went* **a** teaching from village *G4310*
Mk 6:30 apostles gathered **a** Jesus and reported to *G4639*
Mk 7: 1 come from Jerusalem gathered **a** Jesus *G4639*
Mk 8:24 see people; they look like trees **walking a**." *G4344*
Mk 8:27 went on to the villages *a* **Caesarea** Philippi. AIT
Mk 9: 8 Suddenly, *when they* **looked a**, they no *G4315*
Mk 9:14 saw a large crowd **a** them and the *G4309*
Mk 9:20 He fell to the ground and **rolled a** *G3244*
Mk 9:42 millstone were hung **a** their neck and they *G4309*
Mk 10:23 Jesus **looked a** and said to his disciples *G4315*
Mk 11:11 *He* **looked a** at everything, but since it *G4315*
Mk 12: 1 *He* **put** a wall **a** it, dug a pit for the *G4363*
Mk 12:38 They like *to* **walk a** in flowing robes and *G4344*
Mk 14:69 she said again *to* those **standing a**, "This *G4225*
Lk 2: 9 the glory of the Lord **shone a** them *G4334*
Lk 3: 3 He went into all the **country a** the Jordan *G4369*
Lk 5: 1 the people *were* **crowding a** him and *G2130*
Lk 6:10 *He* **looked a** at them all, and then said to *G4315*
Lk 6:17 from the coastal region *a* Tyre and **Sidon**, AIT
Lk 10: 7 *Do* not **move a** from house to house *G3553*
Lk 13: 8 more year, and I'll dig **a** it and fertilize it. *G4309*
Lk 15: 1 were all **gathering a** to hear Jesus. *G1581*
Lk 15:20 **threw** *his* **arms a** him *G2158+2093+3836+5549*
Lk 17: 2 with a millstone **tied a** their neck than to *G4329*
Lk 20:46 They like *to* **walk a** in flowing robes and *G4344*
Jn 1:38 **Turning a**, Jesus saw them following and *G5138*
Jn 7: 1 After this, Jesus *went* **a** in Galilee. He did *G4344*
Jn 8: 2 where all the people gathered **a** him, and *G4639*
Jn 10:24 The Jews who were there **gathered a** him *G3240*
Jn 11:44 with strips of linen, and a cloth **a** his face. *G4317*
Jn 13: 4 **wrapped** a towel **a** his **waist**. *G1346*
Jn 13: 5 with the towel that was **wrapped a** him. *G1346*
Jn 18:18 officials stood *a* a **fire** they had made to AIT
Jn 20: 7 that had been **wrapped a** Jesus' head. *G1962*
Jn 20:14 she turned **a** and saw Jesus *G1650+3836+3958*
Jn 21: 7 *he* **wrapped** his outer garment **a** him (for *G1346*
Ac 1: 6 Then they **gathered a** him and asked him *G5302*
Ac 5:16 also from the towns **a** Jerusalem, *G4339*
Ac 9: 3 a light from heaven **flashed a** him. *G4313*
Ac 9:39 All the widows **stood a** him, crying and *G4225*
Ac 10:38 how he **went a** doing good and *G1451*
Ac 12: 8 **"Wrap** your cloak **a** you and follow me," *G4314*
Ac 14:20 But *after* the disciples *had* **gathered a** him *G3240*
Ac 16:18 so annoyed that *he* **turned a** and said to *G2188*
Ac 17:23 For *as I* **walked a** and looked carefully at *G1451*
Ac 19:13 Some Jews who **went a** driving out evil *G4320*
Ac 20:10 the young man and **put** *his* **arms a** him. *G5227*
Ac 22: 6 a bright light from heaven **flashed a** me. *G4313*
Ac 25: 7 come down from Jerusalem **stood a** him. *G4325*
Ac 26:13 **blazing a** me and my companions. *G4334*
Ro 15:19 from Jerusalem all the way **a** to Illyricum, *G3241*
2Co 4:10 *We* always **carry a** in our body the death of *G4367*
Eph 6:14 *with* the **belt** of truth **buckled a** your waist *G4322*
2Ti 4: 3 *they will* **gather a** them **a great number** of *G2197*
Heb 11:30 *after the army had* **marched a** them for *G3240*
1Pe 5: 8 enemy the devil **prowls a** like a roaring *G4344*

1Jn 2:11 the darkness and walks a in the darkness. G4344
Rev 1:12 I turned a to see the voice that was G2188
Rev 1:13 feet and with a golden sash a his chest. G4322
Rev 4: 6 In the center, a the throne, were four G3241
Rev 4: 8 six wings and was covered with eyes all a, G3239
Rev 7:11 angels were standing a the throne and G3241
Rev 7:11 around the throne and a the elders and the NDT
Rev 15: 6 wore golden sashes a their chests. G4309

AROUSE (14) [ROUSE]
Dt 31:29 of the LORD and a his anger by what your H4087
1Ki 16: 2 to sin and to a my anger by their sins. H4087
1Ki 16:33 did more to a the anger of the LORD, H4087
2Ki 23:26 had done to a his anger. H4087+4088
SS 2: 7 Do not a or awaken love until it so desires H6424
SS 3: 5 Do not a or awaken love until it so desires H6424
SS 8: 4 Do not a or awaken love until it so desires H6424
Jer 7:18 offerings to other gods to a my anger. H4087
Jer 25: 6 do not a my anger with what your hands H4087
Jer 32:30 nothing but a my anger with what their H4087
Jer 44: 8 Why a my anger with what your hands H4087
Eze 8:17 with violence and continually a my anger? H4087
Ro 11:14 I may somehow a my own people to envy G4143
1Co 10:22 Are we trying to a the Lord's jealousy? Are G4143

AROUSED (39) [ROUSE]
Ex 22:24 My anger will be a, and I will kill you with H3013
Nu 11: 1 when he heard them his anger was a. H3013
Nu 32:10 The LORD's anger was a that day and he H3013
Dt 9: 7 how you a the anger of the LORD your H7911
Dt 9: 8 At Horeb you a the LORD's wrath so that he H7911
Jdg 2:12 around them. They a the LORD's anger H4087
1Ki 14: 9 you have a my anger and turned your H4087
1Ki 14:15 because they a the LORD's anger by H4087
1Ki 15:30 he a the anger of the LORD, H4087+4088
1Ki 16:13 so that they a the anger of the LORD, the H4087
1Ki 16:26 so that they a the anger of the LORD, the H4087
1Ki 21:22 because you have a my anger and H4087+4088
1Ki 22:53 Baal and a the anger of the LORD, H4087
2Ki 17:11 did wicked things that a the LORD's anger. H4087
2Ki 21:15 eyes and have a my anger from the day H4087
2Ki 22:17 other gods and a my anger by all the H4087
2Ki 23:19 Samaria and that had a the LORD's anger. H4087
2Ch 21:16 The LORD a against Jehoram the hostility H6424
2Ch 28:25 to other gods and a the anger of the LORD, H4087
2Ch 34:25 other gods and a my anger by all that H4087
2Ch 36:16 wrath of the LORD was a against his H6590
Job 17: 8 the innocent are a against the ungodly. H6424
Job 32: 5 had nothing more to say, his anger was a. H3013
Ps 78:58 they a his jealousy with their idols. H7861
Ps 106:29 they a the LORD's anger by their wicked H4087
Jer 8:19 "Why have they a my anger with their H4087
Jer 11:17 done evil and a my anger by burning H4087
Jer 25: 7 "and you have a my anger with what your H4087
Jer 32:29 where the people a my anger by burning H4087
Jer 32:31 this city has so a my anger and H2118+6584
Jer 44: 3 They a my anger by burning incense to H4087
Jer 51:39 But while they are a, I will set out a feast H2801
Eze 16:26 a my anger with your increasing H4087
Eze 20:28 made offerings that a my anger H4088
Eze 38:18 my hot anger will be a, declares the H6590
Hos 11: 8 within me; all my compassion is a. H4023
Hos 12:14 But Ephraim has a his bitter anger; his H4087
Ac 21:30 The whole city was a, and the people G3075
Ro 7: 5 the sinful passions a by the law were at G1328

AROUSES (2) [ROUSE]
Pr 6:34 For jealousy a a husband's fury, and he will NDT
Pr 14:35 servant, but a shameful servant a his fury. H2118

AROUSING (6) [ROUSE]
Dt 4:25 of the LORD your God and a his anger, H4087
Dt 9:18 evil in the LORD's sight and so a his anger. H4087
1Ki 16: 7 the LORD, a his anger by the things he did H4087
2Ki 17:17 evil in the eyes of the LORD, a his anger. H4087
2Ki 21: 6 evil in the eyes of the LORD, a his anger. H4087
2Ch 33: 6 evil in the eyes of the LORD, a his anger. H4087

ARPAD (6)
2Ki 18:34 Where are the gods of Hamath and A H822
2Ki 19:13 is the king of Hamath or the king of A? H822
Isa 10: 9 Is not Hamath like A, and Samaria like H822
Isa 36:19 Where are the gods of Hamath and A H822
Isa 37:13 is the king of Hamath or the king of A? H822
Jer 49:23 "Hamath and A are dismayed, for they H822

ARPHAXAD (10)
Ge 10:22 Elam, Ashur, A, Lud and Aram. H823
Ge 10:24 A was the father of Shelah, and Shelah the H823
Ge 11:10 100 years old, he became the father of A. H823
Ge 11:11 And after he became the father of A, Shem H823
Ge 11:12 When A had lived 35 years, he became H823
Ge 11:13 A lived 403 years and had other sons and H823
1Ch 1:17 Elam, Ashur, A, Lud and Aram. The H823
1Ch 1:18 A was the father of Shelah, and Shelah the H823
1Ch 1:24 A, Shelah, H823
Lk 3:36 of Cainan, the son of A, the son of Shem, G790

ARRAIGN (1)
Ps 50:21 But I now a you and set my accusations H3519

ARRANGE (5) [ARRANGED, ARRANGEMENT, ARRANGEMENTS]
Lev 1: 7 fire on the altar and a wood on the fire. H6885
Lev 1: 8 sons the priests shall a the pieces, H6885
Lev 1:12 the priest shall a them, including the H6885
Lev 6:12 to add firewood and a the burnt offering H6885
Lev 24: 6 A them in two stacks, six in each stack, on H8492

ARRANGED (11) [ARRANGE]
Ge 15:10 cut them in two and a the halves opposite H5989
Ge 22: 9 built an altar there and a the wood on it. H6885
Jdg 20:38 The Israelites had a with the H2118+4595
2Sa 23: 5 covenant, a and secured in every part H6885
1Ki 18:33 He a the wood, cut the bull into pieces H6885
2Ki 9:30 a her hair and looked out of a window. H3512
2Ch 35:10 The service was a and the priests stood in H3922
Mt 26:48 Now the betrayer had a a signal with them G1443
Mk 14:44 Now the betrayer had a a signal with G1443
Ac 28:23 They a to meet Paul on a certain day, and G5435
Heb 9: 6 When everything had been a like this, the G2941

ARRANGEMENT (2) [ARRANGE]
Eze 43:11 of the temple—its a, its exits and H9414
Ac 20:13 He had made this a because he was G1411

ARRANGEMENTS (2) [ARRANGE]
Job 1: 5 Job would make a for them to be purified. H8938
2Co 9: 5 you in advance and finish the a for the G4616

ARRAY (2) [ARRAYED]
Ge 2: 1 earth were completed in all their vast a. H7372
Dt 4:19 all the heavenly a—do not be enticed into H7372

ARRAYED (2) [ARRAY]
Ps 110: 3 A in holy splendor, your young men will H928
Isa 61:10 of salvation and a me in a robe of his H3598

ARREST (17) [ARRESTED, ARRESTING]
Ne 13:21 do this again, I will a you." H8938+3338+928
Jer 36:26 son of Abdeel to a Baruch the scribe and H4374
Mt 10:19 But when they a you, do not worry about G4140
Mt 21:46 They looked for a way to a him, but they G3195
Mt 26: 4 they schemed to a Jesus secretly and G3195
Mt 26:48 "The one I kiss is the man; a him." G3195
Mt 26:55 courts teaching, and you did not a me. G3195
Mk 12:12 looked for a way to a him because they G3195
Mk 14: 1 law were scheming to a Jesus secretly G3195
Mk 14:44 a him and lead him away under guard." G3195
Mk 14:49 the temple courts, and you did not a me. G3195
Lk 20:19 for a way to a him G2095+2093+3836+5931
Jn 7:32 Pharisees sent temple guards to a him. G4389
Jn 11:57 should report it so that they might a him. G4389
Jn 18:36 fight to prevent my a by the Jewish G4140
Ac 9:14 the chief priests to a all who call on your G1313
2Co 11:32 Damascenes guarded in order to a me. G4389

ARRESTED (14) [ARREST]
Jer 37:13 son of Hananiah, a him and said, "You H9530
Jer 37:14 he a Jeremiah and brought him to the H9530
Mt 14: 3 Now Herod had a John and bound him G3195
Mt 26:50 stepped forward, seized Jesus and a him. G3195
Mt 26:57 Those who had a Jesus took him to G3195
Mk 6:17 himself had given orders to have John a, G3195
Mk 13:11 Whenever you are a and brought to trial G4140
Mk 14:46 The men seized Jesus and a him. G3195
Jn 18:12 the Jewish officials a Jesus. G5197
Ac 1:16 served as guide for those who a Jesus. G5197
Ac 5:18 They a the apostles and G2095+3836+5931+2093
Ac 12: 1 that King Herod a some who G2095+3836+5931
Ac 21:33 came up and a him and ordered him G2138
Ac 28:17 I was a in Jerusalem and handed over to G1300

ARRESTING (2) [ARREST]
Ac 12: 4 After a him, he put him in prison, handing G4389
Ac 22: 4 a both men and women and throwing G1297

ARRIVAL (3) [ARRIVE]
Ge 43:25 prepared their gifts for Joseph's a at noon, H995
Ezr 3: 8 year after their a at the house of God in H995
Jn 11:17 On his a, Jesus found that Lazarus had G2262

ARRIVE (4) [ARRIVAL, ARRIVED, ARRIVES, ARRIVING]
Ex 1:19 give birth before the midwives a." H995+448
Ne 2: 7 provide me safe-conduct until I a in Judah? H995
Job 6:20 been confident; they a there, only to H995+6330
1Co 16: 3 when I a, I will give letters of G4134

ARRIVED (87) [ARRIVE]
Ge 12: 5 the land of Canaan, and they a there. H995
Ge 19: 1 The two angels a at Sodom in the evening H995
Ge 33:18 he a safely at the city of Shechem in H995
Ge 37:14 When Joseph a at Shechem, H995
Ge 42: 6 So when Joseph's brothers a, they bowed H995
Ge 46:28 When they a in the region of Goshen H995
Nu 10:21 tabernacle was to be set up before they a. H995
Nu 20: 1 Israelite community a at the Desert of Zin, H995
Dt 9: 7 day you left Egypt until you a here, H995+6330
Dt 11: 5 in the wilderness until you a at this place, H995
Jos 8:11 approached the city and a in front of it. H995
Jdg 3:27 When he a there, he blew a trumpet in the H995
Jdg 7:13 Gideon a just as a man was telling a friend H995
Ru 1:19 When they a in Bethlehem, the whole H995
Ru 2: 4 Just then Boaz a from Bethlehem and H995
1Sa 4:13 When he a, there was Eli sitting on his H995
1Sa 10:10 When he and his servant a at Gibeah, a H995
1Sa 13:10 the offering, Samuel a, and Saul went out H995
1Sa 16: 4 When he a at Bethlehem, the elders of the H995
1Sa 16: 6 When they a, Samuel saw Eliab and H995
1Sa 25: 9 When David's men a, they gave Nabal this H995
1Sa 25:12 went back. When they a, they reported H995
1Sa 26: 4 learned that Saul had definitely a. H995
2Sa 1: 2 the third day a man a from Saul's camp H995
2Sa 2:32 all night and a at Hebron by daybreak NDT
2Sa 3:23 When Joab and all the soldiers with him a H995
2Sa 4: 5 and they a there in the heat of the day H995
2Sa 11:22 when he a he told David everything H995
2Sa 15:32 When David a at the summit, where H995
2Sa 15:37 a at Jerusalem as Absalom was entering H995
2Sa 16:14 the people with him a at their destination H995
2Sa 18:31 Then the Cushite a and said, "My lord the H995
1Ki 1:22 with the king, Nathan the prophet a. H995
1Ki 1:42 Jonathan son of Abiathar the priest a. H995
1Ki 8: 3 When all the elders of Israel had a, the H995
1Ki 12:21 When Rehoboam a in Jerusalem, he H995
1Ki 22:15 When he a, the king asked him H995+448
2Ki 6:32 before he a, Elisha said to the H995+448
2Ki 9: 5 When he a, he found the army officers H995
2Ki 10: 7 When the letter a, these men took the H995+448
2Ki 10: 8 When the messenger a, he told Jehu H995
2Ch 5: 4 When all the elders of Israel had a, the H995
2Ch 11: 1 When Rehoboam a in Jerusalem, he H995
2Ch 18:14 When he a, the king asked him H995+448
2Ch 22: 7 When Ahaziah a, he went out with Joram H995
Ezr 2:68 When they a at the house of the LORD in H995
Ezr 7: 8 Ezra a in Jerusalem in the fifth month of H995
Ezr 7: 9 and he a in Jerusalem on the first day of H995
Ezr 8:32 So we a in Jerusalem, where we rested H995
Est 6:14 the king's eunuchs a and hurried Haman H5595
Isa 30: 4 Zoan and their envoys have a in Hanes, H5595
Eze 7:12 The day has a! Let not the H5595
Eze 23:40 when they a you bathed yourself for H995
Eze 33:22 Now the evening before the man a, the H995
Eze 47: 7 When I a there, I saw a great number of H8740
Zec 6:10 Jedaiah, who have a from Babylon. H995
Mt 8:28 When he a at the other side in the region G2262
Mt 17:24 After Jesus and his disciples a in G2262
Mt 25:10 their way to buy the oil, the bridegroom a. G2262
Mt 26:47 speaking, Judas, one of the Twelve, a. G2262
Mk 3:31 Then Jesus' mother and brothers a G2262
Mk 11:27 They a again in Jerusalem, and while G2262
Mk 14:17 evening came, Jesus a with the Twelve. G2262
Lk 8:51 When he a at the house of Jairus, he did G2262
Jn 4:45 When he a in Galilee, the Galileans G2262
Jn 4:47 heard that Jesus had a in Galilee from G2457
Ac 1:13 When they a, they went upstairs to the G1656
Ac 5:21 When the high priest and his associates a G4134
Ac 8:15 When they a, they prayed for the new G2849
Ac 9:39 and when he a he was taken upstairs to G4134
Ac 10:24 The following day he a in Caesarea G1656
Ac 11:23 When he a and saw what the grace of G4134
Ac 13: 5 When they a at Salamis, they proclaimed G1181
Ac 18:19 They a at Ephesus, where Paul left G2918
Ac 18:27 When he a, he was a great help to those G4134
Ac 19: 1 through the interior and a at Ephesus. G2262
Ac 20: 2 to the people, and finally a in Greece, G2262
Ac 20:15 day we set sail from there and a off Chios. G2918
Ac 20:15 on the following day a at Miletus. G2262
Ac 20:18 When they a, he said to them: "You know G4134
Ac 21:17 When we a at Jerusalem, the brothers G1181
Ac 23:33 When the cavalry a in Caesarea, they G1656
Ac 25:13 Agrippa and Bernice a at Caesarea to pay G2918
Ac 28:13 From there we set sail and a at Rhegium G2918
1Co 16:17 Fortunatus and Achaicus a, because they G4242
Gal 2:12 But when they a, he began to draw back G2262
Php 3:12 or have already a at my goal, but I G5457

ARRIVES (7) [ARRIVE]
Jdg 20:10 when the army a at Gibeah in Benjamin H995
1Sa 16:11 we will not sit down until he a." H995+7024
1Ki 14: 5 When she a, she will pretend to be H995
Hos 13:13 when the time a, he doesn't have the NDT
Mt 12:44 'When it a, it finds the house unoccupied G2262
Lk 11:25 When it a, it finds the house swept clean G2262
Heb 13:23 If he a soon, I will come with him to see G2262

ARRIVING (9) [ARRIVE]
Ru 1:22 a in Bethlehem as the barley harvest was H995
1Ki 10: 2 A at Jerusalem with a very great caravan H995
2Ch 9: 1 A with a very great caravan—with camels NDT
2Ch 28:12 confronted those who were a from the war. H995
Ac 5:22 But on a at the jail, the officers did not G4134
Ac 14:27 On a there, they gathered the church G4134
Ac 17:10 On a there, they went to the Jewish G4134
Ac 25: 1 Three days after a in the province, Festus G2094
Ac 27: 7 many days and had difficulty a off Cnidus. G1181

ARROGANCE (18) [ARROGANT]
Dt 1:43 command and in your a you marched up H2326
1Sa 2: 3 so proudly or let your mouth speak such a, H6981
1Sa 15:23 divination, and a like the evil of idolatry. H7210
Job 35:12 cry out because of the a of the wicked. H1454
Ps 10: 2 In his a the wicked man hunts down the H1452
Ps 17:10 and their mouths speak with a. H1455
Ps 73: 8 with a they threaten oppression. H5294
Pr 8:13 I hate pride and a, evil behavior and H1454

Isa 2:17 The a *of* man will be brought low and H1471
Isa 9: 9 who say with pride and a *of* heart, H1542
Isa 13:11 put an end to the a *of* the haughty and H1454
Isa 16: 6 of Moab's pride—how great is her a!— H1447
Jer 48:29 of Moab's pride—how great is her a!— H1450
Eze 7:10 the rod has budded, a has blossomed! H2295
Hos 5: 5 Israel's a testifies against them; the H1454
Hos 7:10 Israel's a testifies against him, but H1454
Mk 7:22 lewdness, envy, slander, a and folly. *G5661*
2Co 12:20 ambition, slander, gossip, a and disorder. *G5883*

ARROGANT (39) [ARROGANCE, ARROGANTLY]

2Ki 14:10 defeated Edom and now you *are* a. H5951+4213
2Ch 25:19 and now you *are* a and proud. H5951+4213
Ne 9:16 our ancestors, *became* a and stiff-necked H2326
Ne 9:29 they *became* a and disobeyed your H2326
Ps 5: 5 The a cannot stand in your presence. You H2147
Ps 54: 3 **A foes** are attacking me; ruthless people H2424
Ps 73: 3 For I envied the a when I saw the H2147
Ps 75: 4 To the a I say, 'Boast no more,' and to the H2147
Ps 86:14 **A foes** are attacking me, O God; ruthless H2294
Ps 94: 4 They pour out a words; all the evildoers H6981
Ps 119:21 You rebuke the a, who are accursed H2294
Ps 119:51 The a mock me unmercifully, but I do not H2294
Ps 119:69 Though the a have smeared me with lies H2294
Ps 119:78 May the a be put to shame for wronging H2294
Ps 119:85 The a dig pits to trap me, contrary to your H2294
Ps 119:122 well-being; do not let the a oppress me. H2294
Ps 123: 4 endured no end of ridicule from the a, H8633
Ps 140: 5 The a have hidden a snare for me; they H1450
Pr 21:24 The proud and a *person*—"Mocker" is his H3400
Isa 2:11 The eyes of the a will be humbled H1471+132
Isa 5:15 humbled, the eyes of the a humbled. H1469
Isa 33:19 You will see those a people no more H3594
Jer 13:15 pay attention, *do* not be a, for the LORD H1467
Jer 43: 2 Kareah and all the a men said to H2294
Jer 50:31 am against you, you a *one*," declares the H2295
Jer 50:32 The a *one* will stumble and fall and no H2295
Eze 16:49 She and her daughters were a, overfed H1454
Da 5:20 when his heart *became* a and hardened A10659
Hab 2: 5 betrays him; he is a and never at rest. H3400
Zep 3:11 I will remove from you your a boasters. H1452
Mal 3:15 But now we call the a blessed. Certainly H2294
Mal 4: 1 All the a and every evildoer will be H2294
Ro 1:30 insolent, a and boastful; they invent ways *G5662*
Ro 11:20 by faith. *Do* not *be* a, but tremble. *G5734+5858*
1Co 4:18 Some *of you have become* a, as if I were *G5881*
1Co 4:19 not only how these a *people* are talking, *G5881*
1Ti 6:17 present world not *to be* a nor to put their *G5735*
Jas 4:16 you boast in your a **schemes**. All such *G224*
2Pe 2:10 Bold and a, they are not afraid to heap *G881*

ARROGANTLY (5) [ARROGANT]

Ex 18:11 did this to *those* who *had* **treated** Israel a." H2326
Ne 9:10 knew how a the Egyptians **treated** them. H2326
Job 36: 9 have done—that they have sinned a. H1504
Ps 31:18 contempt they speak a against the H6981
Mal 3:13 "You *have* spoken a against me," says the H2616

ARROW (18) [ARROWS]

1Sa 20:36 As the boy ran, he shot an a beyond him. H2943
1Sa 20:37 the place where Jonathan's a had fallen, H2943
1Sa 20:37 out after him, "Isn't the a beyond you?" H2943
1Sa 20:38 boy picked up the a and returned to his H2943
2Ki 9:24 The a pierced his heart and he slumped H2943
2Ki 13:17 "The LORD's a *of* victory, the arrow of H2932
2Ki 13:17 of victory, the a *of* victory over Aram!" H2932
2Ki 19:32 will not enter this city or shoot an a here. H2932
Job 20:24 weapon, a bronze-tipped a pierces him. H8008
Job 34: 6 his a inflicts an incurable wound. H2932
Ps 91: 5 terror of night, nor the a that flies by day, H2932
Pr 7:23 till an a pierces his liver, like a bird H2932
Pr 25:18 a sword or a sharp a is one who gives H2932
Isa 7:24 Hunters will go there with bow and a, for H2932
Isa 37:33 will not enter this city or shoot an a here. H2932
Isa 49: 2 me into a polished a and concealed me H2932
Jer 9: 8 Their tongue is a deadly a; it speaks H2932
Zec 9:14 over them; his a will flash like lightning. H2932

ARROWS (46) [ARROW]

Ex 19:13 are to be stoned or **shot with** a; H3721+3721
Nu 24: 8 in pieces; with their a they pierce them. H2932
Dt 32:23 on them and spend my a against them. H2932
Dt 32:42 I will make my a drunk with blood, while H2932
1Sa 20:20 I will shoot three a to the side of it, as H2932
1Sa 20:21 I will send a boy and say, 'Go, find the a. H2932
1Sa 20:21 the a are on this side of you; bring H2932
1Sa 20:22 the a are beyond you,' then you H2932
1Sa 20:36 to the boy, "Run and find the a I shoot." H2932
2Sa 11:20 you know *they would* **shoot** a from the H3721
2Sa 11:24 Then the archers **shot** a at your servants H3721
2Sa 22:15 He shot his a and scattered the enemy H2932
2Ki 13:15 "Get a bow and *some* a," and he did so. H2932
2Ki 13:18 he said, "Take the a," and the king took H2932
1Ch 12: 2 were able to shoot a or to sling stones H2932
2Ch 26:15 soldiers could shoot a and hurl large H2932
Job 6: 4 The a *of* the Almighty are in me, my spirit H2932
Job 41:28 A do not make it flee; slingstones H1201+8008
Ps 7:13 weapons; he makes ready his flaming a. H2932
Ps 11: 2 they set their a against the strings to H2932
Ps 18:14 He shot his a and scattered the enemy H2932
Ps 38: 2 Your a have pierced me, and your hand H2932
Ps 45: 5 Let your sharp a pierce the hearts of the H2932
Ps 57: 4 men whose teeth are spears and a H2932
Ps 58: 7 they draw the bow, let their a fall short. H2932
Ps 64: 3 swords and aim cruel words like *deadly* a. H2932
Ps 64: 7 But God will shoot them with his a; they H2932
Ps 76: 3 There he broke the flashing a, the shields H8008
Ps 77:17 thunder; your a flashed back and forth. H2932
Ps 120: 4 will punish you with a warrior's sharp a, H2932
Ps 127: 4 Like a in the hands of a warrior are H2932
Ps 144: 6 the enemy; shoot your a and rout them. H2932
Pr 26:18 Like a maniac shooting flaming a of death H2932
Isa 5:28 Their a are sharp, all their bows are H2932
Jer 50: 9 Their a will be like skilled warriors who do H2932
Jer 50:14 Spare no a, for she has sinned against H2932
Jer 51:11 "Sharpen the a, take up the shields! The H2932
La 3:12 his bow and made me the target for his a. H2932
La 3:13 pierced my heart with a *from* his quiver. H1201S
Eze 5:16 my deadly and destructive a *of* famine, H2932
Eze 21:21 He will cast lots with a, he will consult his H2932
Eze 39: 3 hand and make your a drop from your H2932
Eze 39: 9 the bows and a, the war clubs and H2932
Hab 3: 9 your bow, you called for many a. H4751
Hab 3:11 the heavens at the glint of your flying a, H2932
Eph 6:16 all the flaming a of the evil one. *G1018*

ARSENAL (1)

Jer 50:25 LORD has opened his a and brought out the H238

ART (1) [ARTISANS, ARTIST'S, ARTISTIC, ARTS]

2Ch 2: 7 experienced in the a **of engraving**, H7338+7334

ARTAXERXES (15)

Ezr 4: 7 And in the days of A king of Persia H831
Ezr 4: 7 rest of his associates wrote a letter to A. H831
Ezr 4: 8 Jerusalem to A the king as follows: A10078
Ezr 4:11 To King A, From your servants in A10078
Ezr 4:23 the letter of King A was read to Rehum A10078
Ezr 6:14 of Cyrus, Darius and A, kings of Persia. A10078
Ezr 7: 1 during the reign of A king of Persia, Ezra H831
Ezr 7: 7 to Jerusalem in the seventh year of King A. H831
Ezr 7:11 of the letter King A had given to Ezra the H831
Ezr 7:12 A, king of kings, To Ezra the priest A10078
Ezr 7:21 King A, decree that all the A10078
Ezr 8: 1 from Babylon during the reign of King A: H831
Ne 2: 1 of Nisan in the twentieth year of King A, H831
Ne 5:14 from the twentieth year of King A, when I H831
Ne 13: 6 year of A king of Babylon I had H831

ARTEMAS (1)

Titus 3:12 As soon as I send A or Tychicus to you, do *G782*

ARTEMIS (5)

Ac 19:24 who made silver shrines *of* A, brought in a *G783*
Ac 19:27 of the great goddess A will be discredited; *G783*
Ac 19:28 "Great is A of the Ephesians!" *G783*
Ac 19:34 "Great is A of the Ephesians!" *G783*
Ac 19:35 temple of the great A and of her image, *G783*

ARTICLE (14) [ARTICLES]

Lev 11:32 on something, that a, whatever its use, H3998
Lev 13:49 any leather a, is greenish or reddish, H3998
Lev 13:50 area and isolate the a for seven days. H5596S
Lev 13:51 defiling mold; the a is unclean. H5596S
Lev 13:52 any leather a that has been spoiled H3998
Lev 13:52 mold is persistent, the a must be burned. NDT
Lev 13:53 knitted material, or the leather a, H3998
Lev 13:54 shall order that the **spoiled** a be washed. H5596
Lev 13:55 After the a has been washed, the priest H5596S
Lev 13:56 has faded after the a has been washed, H2257S
Lev 13:57 in the leather a, it is a spreading mold; H3998
Lev 13:58 any leather a that has been washed H3998
Lev 13:59 any leather a, for pronouncing them H3998
Lev 15:12 any wooden a is to be rinsed with H3998

ARTICLES (82) [ARTICLE]

Ge 24:53 jewelry and a **of clothing** and gave them to H955
Ex 3:22 in her house for a *of* silver and gold and H3998
Ex 11: 2 their neighbors for a *of* silver and gold." H3998
Ex 12:35 the Egyptians for a *of* silver and gold and H3998
Ex 27:19 All the other a *used* in the service of the H3998
Ex 30:27 the table and all its a, the lampstand and H3998
Ex 31: 8 the table and its a, the pure gold H3998
Ex 35:13 its poles and all its a and the bread of the H3998
Ex 37:16 made from pure gold the a for the table— H3998
Ex 39:36 table with all its a and the bread of the H3998
Nu 3:31 the a *of* the sanctuary used in ministering H3998
Nu 4:12 are to take all the a used for ministering H3998
Nu 4:15 the holy furnishings and all the holy a, H3998
Nu 4:16 including its holy furnishings and a." H3998
Nu 31: 6 took with him a *from* the sanctuary and H3998
Nu 31:50 the LORD the gold a each of us acquired— H3998
Nu 31:51 from them the gold—all the crafted a. H3998
Jos 6:19 gold and the a *of* bronze and iron are H3998
Jos 6:24 gold and the a *of* bronze and iron H3998
2Sa 8:10 Joram brought with him a *of* silver, of H3998
2Sa 8:11 David dedicated **these** a to the LORD, H4392S
2Sa 17:28 bedding and bowls and a *of* pottery. H3998
1Ki 10:21 all the **household** a *in* the Palace of H3998
1Ki 10:25 came brought a gift—a *of* silver and gold H3998
1Ki 15:15 gold and the a that he and his father H3998
2Ki 12:13 any other a *of* gold or silver for H3998
2Ki 14:14 silver and all the a found in the temple of H3998
2Ki 23: 4 of the LORD all the a made for Baal and H3998
2Ki 24:13 cut up the gold a that Solomon king H3998
2Ki 25:14 all the bronze a used in the temple H3998
1Ch 9:28 in charge of the a *used in* the temple H3998
1Ch 9:29 all the other a *of* the sanctuary, H3998
1Ch 18: 8 the pillars and various bronze a. H3998
1Ch 18:10 Hadoram brought all kinds of a *of* gold, of H3998
1Ch 18:11 David dedicated **these** a to the LORD, H4392S
1Ch 22:19 the sacred a *belonging to* God into the H3998
1Ch 23:26 any of the a used in its service. H3998
1Ch 28:13 as for all the a *to be used in* its service. H3998
1Ch 28:14 all the gold a *to be used in* various kinds H3998
1Ch 28:14 all the silver a *to be used in* various kinds H3998
2Ch 4:16 shovels, meat forks and all related a. H3998
2Ch 9:20 all the **household** a *in* the Palace of H3998
2Ch 9:24 came brought a gift—a *of* silver and gold H3998
2Ch 15:18 gold and the a that he and his father H3998
2Ch 20:25 clothing and also a *of* value— H3998
2Ch 21: 3 gifts of silver and gold and a **of value**, H4458
2Ch 24:14 with it were made a for the LORD's temple H3998
2Ch 24:14 a *for* the service and for the burnt H3998
2Ch 25:24 silver and all the a found in the temple of H3998
2Ch 29:18 out the consecrated bread, with all its a. H3998
2Ch 29:19 consecrated all the a that King Ahaz H3998
2Ch 36: 7 took to Babylon a *from* the temple of the H3998
2Ch 36:10 together with a *of* value from the temple H3998
2Ch 36:18 Babylon all the a *from* the temple of God H3998
Ezr 1: 6 assisted them with a *of* silver and gold, H3998
Ezr 1: 7 out the a *belonging to* the temple of H3998
Ezr 1:10 matching silver bowls 410 other a 1,000 H3998
Ezr 1:11 there were 5,400 a of gold and of silver. H3998
Ezr 5:14 gold and silver a of the house of God A10398
Ezr 5:15 'Take these a and go and deposit them A10398
Ezr 6: 5 gold and silver a *of* the house of God, A10398
Ezr 7:19 of Jerusalem *all* the a entrusted to you A10398
Ezr 8:25 of silver and gold and the a that the king, H3998
Ezr 8:26 of silver, silver a weighing 100 talents H3998
Ezr 8:27 two fine a *of* polished bronze, as H3998
Ezr 8:28 as well as these a are consecrated to H3998
Ezr 8:30 gold and sacred a that had been H3998
Ezr 8:33 gold and the sacred a into the hands of H3998
Ne 10:39 where the a *for* the sanctuary and for the H3998
Ne 13: 5 grain offerings and incense and temple a, H3998
Isa 52:11 you who carry the a *of* the LORD's *house*. H3998
Jer 27:16 soon now the a *from* the LORD's house H3998
Jer 27:18 Almighty that the a remaining in the H3998
Jer 27:19 stands and the other a that are left in this H3998
Jer 28: 3 to this place all the a *of* the LORD's house H3998
Jer 28: 6 by bringing the a *of* the LORD's house and H3998
Jer 52:18 all the bronze a used in the temple H3998
Eze 27:13 human beings and a *of* bronze for your H3998
Da 1: 2 with some of the a *from* the temple of H3998
Da 11: 8 their valuable a *of* silver and gold H3998
2Ti 2:20 house there are a not only of gold and *G5007*
Rev 18:12 and a of every kind made of ivory *G5007*

ARTIFICER, ARTIFICERS (KJV) CARPENTER, CRAFTSMAN, CRAFTSMEN

ARTIFICIAL (1)

Ne 3:16 as far as the a pool and the House of the H6913

ARTILLERY (KJV) WEAPONS

ARTISANS (4) [ART]

2Ki 24:14 all the skilled workers and a—a total H4994
2Ki 24:16 a thousand skilled workers and a. H4994
Jer 24: 1 workers and the a *of* Judah were carried H4994
Jer 29: 2 workers and the a had gone into exile H4994

ARTIST'S (1) [ART]

SS 7: 1 are like jewels, the work of an a hands. H588

ARTISTIC (3) [ART]

Ex 31: 4 to make a **designs** for work in gold, silver H4742
Ex 35:32 to make a **designs** for work in gold, silver H4742
Ex 35:33 to engage in all kinds of a **crafts**. H4742

ARTS (7) [ART]

Ex 7:11 also did the same things by their **secret** a: H4268
Ex 7:22 did the same things by their **secret** a, H4319
Ex 8: 7 did the same things by their **secret** a; H4319
Ex 8:18 tried to produce gnats by their **secret** a, H4319
Rev 9:21 their murders, their **magic** a, their sexual *G5760*
Rev 21: 8 immoral, **those who practice magic** a, the *G5761*
Rev 22:15 those **who practice magic** a, the *G5761*

ARUBBOTH (1)

1Ki 4:10 Ben-Hesed—in A (Sokoh and all the land H749

ARUMAH (1)

Jdg 9:41 Then Abimelek stayed in A, and Zebul H777

ARVAD (2) [ARVADITES]

Eze 27: 8 Men of Sidon and A were your oarsmen H770
Eze 27:11 Men of A and Helek guarded your walls on H770

ARVADITES (2) [ARVAD]

Ge 10:18 A, Zemarites and Hamathites. Later the H773
1Ch 1:16 A, Zemarites and Hamathites. H773

ARZA (1)

1Ki 16: 9 getting drunk in the home of A, the palace H825

AS (4068) See Index of Articles Etc.

ASA (52) [ASA'S]
1Ki 15: 8 And **A** his son succeeded him as king H654
1Ki 15: 9 king of Israel, **A** became king of Judah, H654
1Ki 15:11 **A** did what was right in the eyes of the LORD H654
1Ki 15:13 **A** cut it down and burned it in the Kidron H654
1Ki 15:16 was war between **A** and Baasha king of H654
1Ki 15:17 entering the territory of **A** king of Judah. H654
1Ki 15:18 **A** then took all the silver and gold that was H654
1Ki 15:20 agreed with King **A** and sent the H654
1Ki 15:22 Then King **A** issued an order to all Judah H654
1Ki 15:22 With them King **A** built up Geba in H654
1Ki 15:24 Then **A** rested with his ancestors and was H654
1Ki 15:25 in the second year of **A** king of Judah, H654
1Ki 15:28 in the third year of **A** king of Judah and H654
1Ki 15:32 was war between **A** and Baasha king of H654
1Ki 15:33 In the third year of **A** king of Judah, Baasha H654
1Ki 16: 8 In the twenty-sixth year of **A** king of Judah H654
1Ki 16:10 the twenty-seventh year of **A** king of Judah. H654
1Ki 16:15 the twenty-seventh year of **A** king of Judah, H654
1Ki 16:23 In the thirty-first year of **A** king of Judah H654
1Ki 16:29 In the thirty-eighth year of **A** king of Judah H654
1Ki 22:41 Jehoshaphat son of **A** became king of H654
1Ki 22:43 ways of his father **A** and did not stray from H654
1Ki 22:46 there even after the reign of his father **A**. H654
1Ch 3:10 Abijah his son, **A** his son, Jehoshaphat his H654
1Ch 9:16 Berekiah son of **A**, the son of Elkanah, H654
2Ch 14: 1 **A** his son succeeded him as king, and in H654
2Ch 14: 2 **A** did what was good and right in the eyes H654
2Ch 14: 8 **A** had an army of three hundred thousand H654
2Ch 14:10 **A** went out to meet him, and they took up H654
2Ch 14:11 Then **A** called to the LORD his God and said, H654
2Ch 14:12 down the Cushites before **A** and Judah. H654
2Ch 14:13 **A** and his army pursued them as far as H654
2Ch 15: 2 He went out to meet **A** and said to him H654
2Ch 15: 2 **A** and all Judah and Benjamin. H654
2Ch 15: 8 When **A** heard these words and the H654
2Ch 15:16 King **A** also deposed his grandmother H654
2Ch 15:16 **A** cut it down, broke it up and burned it in H654
2Ch 16: 1 entering the territory of **A** king of Judah. H654
2Ch 16: 2 **A** then took the silver and gold out of the H654
2Ch 16: 4 agreed with King **A** and sent the H654
2Ch 16: 6 Then King **A** brought all the men of Judah H654
2Ch 16: 7 the seer came to **A** king of Judah and said H654
2Ch 16:10 **A** was angry with the seer because of this H654
2Ch 16:10 At the same time **A** brutally oppressed H654
2Ch 16:12 year of his reign **A** was afflicted with a H654
2Ch 16:13 year of his reign **A** died and rested with his H654
2Ch 17: 2 of Ephraim that his father **A** had captured. H654
2Ch 20:32 ways of his father **A** and did not stray from H654
2Ch 21:12 father Jehoshaphat or of **A** king of Judah. H654
Jer 41: 9 was the one King **A** had made as part of H654
Mt 1: 7 father of Abijah, Abijah the father of **A**, *G811*
Mt 1: 8 **A** the father of Jehoshaphat, Jehoshaphat *G811*

ASA'S (7) [ASA]
1Ki 15:14 **A** heart was fully committed to the LORD all H654
1Ki 15:23 As for all the other events of **A** reign, all H654
2Ch 15:10 third month of the fifteenth year of **A** reign. H654
2Ch 15:17 **A** heart was fully committed to the LORD all H654
2Ch 15:19 war until the thirty-fifth year of **A** reign. H654
2Ch 16: 1 thirty-sixth year of **A** reign Baasha king of H654
2Ch 16:11 The events of **A** reign, from beginning to H654

ASAHEL (18) [ASAHEL'S]
2Sa 2:18 Abishai and **A**. Now Asahel was as H6915
2Sa 2:18 Now **A** was as fleet-footed as a wild H6915
2Sa 2:20 behind him and asked, "Is that you, **A**?" H6915
2Sa 2:21 But **A** would not stop chasing him H6915
2Sa 2:22 Again Abner warned **A**, "Stop chasing me H6915
2Sa 2:23 But **A** refused to give up the pursuit; so NDT
2Sa 2:23 to the place where **A** had fallen and died. H6915
2Sa 2:30 Besides **A**, nineteen of David's men were H6915
2Sa 2:32 They took **A** and buried him in his father's H6915
2Sa 3:27 to avenge the blood of his brother **A** H6915
2Sa 3:30 killed their brother **A** in the battle at H6915
2Sa 23:24 **A** the brother of Joab, Elhanan son of H6915
1Ch 2:16 three sons were Abishai, Joab and **A**. H6915
1Ch 11:26 **A** the brother of Joab, Elhanan son of H6915
1Ch 27: 7 fourth month, was **A** the brother of Joab H6915
2Ch 17: 8 Nethaniah, Zebadiah, **A**, Shemiramoth H6915
2Ch 31:13 Azaziah, Nahath, **A**, Jerimoth, Jozabad H6915
Ezr 10:15 Jonathan son of **A** and Jahzeiah son of H6915

ASAHEL'S (1) [ASAHEL]
2Sa 2:23 the butt of his spear into **A** stomach, H2084S

ASAIAH (8)
2Ki 22:12 the secretary and **A** the king's attendant: H6919
2Ki 22:14 Shaphan and **A** went to speak to the H6919
1Ch 4:36 Jaakobah, Jeshohaiah, **A**, Adiel, Jesimiel, H6919
1Ch 6:30 his son, Haggiah his son and **A** his son. H6919
1Ch 9: 5 **A** the firstborn and his sons H8989
1Ch 15: 6 of Merari, **A** the leader and 220 relatives; H6919
1Ch 15:11 the priests, and Uriel, **A**, Joel, Shemaiah, H6919
2Ch 34:20 the secretary and **A** the king's attendant: H6919

ASAPH (45) [ASAPH'S]
2Ki 18:18 Joah son of **A** the recorder went out to H666
2Ki 18:37 Joah son of **A** the recorder went to H666
1Ch 6:39 Heman's associate **A**, who served at H666
1Ch 6:39 at his right hand: **A** son of Berekiah, the H666
1Ch 9:15 son of Mika, the son of Zikri, the son of **A**; H666
1Ch 15:17 from his relatives, **A** son of Berekiah; and H666
1Ch 15:19 **A** and Ethan were to sound the bronze H666
1Ch 16: 5 **A** was the chief, and next to him in rank H666
1Ch 16: 5 harps, **A** was to sound the cymbals H666
1Ch 16: 7 first appointed **A** and his associates to H666
1Ch 16:37 David left **A** and his associates before the H666
1Ch 25: 1 set apart some of the sons of **A**, Heman H666
1Ch 25: 2 From the sons of **A**: Zakkur, Joseph H666
1Ch 25: 2 The sons of **A** were under the supervision H666
1Ch 25: 2 of Asaph were under the supervision of **A**, H666
1Ch 25: 6 **A**, Jeduthun and Heman were under the H666
1Ch 25: 9 The first lot, which was for **A**, fell to Joseph, H666
1Ch 26: 1 son of Kore, one of the sons of **A**. H666
2Ch 5:12 Levites who were musicians—**A**, Heman, H666
2Ch 20:14 a Levite and descendant of **A**, as he stood H666
2Ch 29:13 from the descendants of **A**, Zechariah and H666
2Ch 29:30 with the words of David and of **A** the seer. H666
2Ch 35:15 the descendants of **A**, were in the places H666
2Ch 35:15 by David, **A**, Heman and Jeduthun H666
Ezr 2:41 The musicians: the descendants of **A** 128 H666
Ezr 3:10 the Levites (the sons of **A**) with cymbals, H666
Ne 2: 8 And may I have a letter to **A**, keeper of the H666
Ne 7:44 The musicians: the descendants of **A** 148 H666
Ne 11:17 of Zabdi, the son of **A**, the director who led H666
Ne 12:35 Micaiah, the son of Zakkur, the son of **A**, H666
Ne 12:46 in the days of David and **A**, there had been H666
Ps 50: T A psalm of **A**. H666
Ps 73: T A psalm of **A**. H666
Ps 74: T A maskil of **A**. H666
Ps 75: T of "Do Not Destroy." A psalm of **A**. A song. H666
Ps 76: T A psalm of **A**. A song. H666
Ps 77: T For Jeduthun. Of **A**. A psalm. H666
Ps 78: T A maskil of **A**. H666
Ps 79: T A psalm of **A**. H666
Ps 80: T Lilies of the Covenant." Of **A**. A psalm. H666
Ps 81: T According to gittith. Of **A**. H666
Ps 82: T A psalm of **A**. H666
Ps 83: T A psalm of **A**. H666
Isa 36: 3 Joah son of **A** the recorder went out to H666
Isa 36:22 Joah son of **A** the recorder went to H666

ASAPH'S (1) [ASAPH]
Ne 11:22 Uzzi was one of **A** descendants, who were H666

ASAREL (1)
1Ch 4:16 Ziph, Ziphah, Tiria and **A**. H832

ASARELAH (1)
1Ch 25: 2 Nethaniah and **A**. The sons of Asaph H833

ASCEND (7) [ASCENDED, ASCENDING, ASCENDS, ASCENT, ASCENTS]
Dt 30:12 "Who *will* **a** into heaven to get it and H6590
Ps 24: 3 Who *may* **a** the mountain of the LORD H6590
Isa 14:13 in your heart, "*I will* **a** *to* the heavens; I H6590
Isa 14:14 *I will* **a** above the tops of the clouds; I will H6590
Jn 6:62 see the Son of Man **a** to where he was *G326*
Ac 2:34 For David *did* not **a** to heaven, and yet he *G326*
Ro 10: 6 say in your heart, 'Who *will* **a** into heaven? *G326*

ASCENDED (10) [ASCEND]
Jdg 13:20 the angel of the LORD **a** in the flame. H6590
2Ki 19:23 my many chariots I *have* **a** the heights of H6590
Ps 47: 5 God *has* **a** amid shouts of joy, the LORD H6590
Ps 68:18 *When you* **a** on high, you took many H6590
Isa 37:24 my many chariots I *have* **a** the heights of H6590
Jn 20:17 on to me, for *I have* not yet **a** to the Father. *G326*
Eph 4: 8 "*When he* **a** on high, he took many *G326*
Eph 4: 9 What does "*he* **a**" mean except that he *G326*
Eph 4:10 is the very one who **a** higher than all the *G326*
Heb 4:14 great high priest *who has* **a into** heaven, *G1451*

ASCENDING (4) [ASCEND]
Ge 28:12 the angels of God *were* **a** and descending H6590
Eze 41: 7 the temple was built **in a stages**, H4200+5087+2025+4200+5087+2025
Jn 1:51 the angels of God **a** and descending on' *G326*
Jn 20:17 '*I am* **a** to my Father and your Father *G326*

ASCENDS (1) [ASCEND]
Jer 51:53 Even if Babylon **a** *to* the heavens and H6590

ASCENT (2) [ASCEND]
Ne 3:19 a point facing the **a** *to* the armory as far H6590
Ne 12:37 City of David on the **a** to the wall and H5090

ASCENTS (15) [ASCEND]
Ps 120: T A song of **a**. H5092
Ps 121: T A song of **a**. H5092
Ps 122: T A song of **a**. Of David. H5092
Ps 123: T A song of **a**. H5092
Ps 124: T A song of **a**. Of David. H5092
Ps 125: T A song of **a**. H5092
Ps 126: T A song of **a**. H5092
Ps 127: T A song of **a**. Of Solomon. H5092
Ps 128: T A song of **a**. H5092
Ps 129: T A song of **a**. H5092
Ps 130: T A song of **a**. H5092
Ps 131: T A song of **a**. Of David. H5092
Ps 132: T A song of **a**. H5092
Ps 133: T A song of **a**. Of David. H5092
Ps 134: T A song of **a**. H5092

ASCRIBE (10)
1Ch 16:28 **A** to the LORD, all you families of nations H2035
1Ch 16:28 nations, **a** to the LORD glory and strength. H2035
1Ch 16:29 **A** to the LORD the glory due his name H2035
Job 36: 3 from afar; *I will* **a** justice to my Maker. H5989
Ps 29: 1 **A** to the LORD, *you* heavenly beings H2035
Ps 29: 1 **a** to the LORD glory and strength. H2035
Ps 29: 2 **A** to the LORD the glory due his name H2035
Ps 96: 7 **A** to the LORD, *all you* families of nations H2035
Ps 96: 7 nations, **a** to the LORD glory and strength. H2035
Ps 96: 8 **A** to the LORD the glory due his name H2035

ASENATH (3)
Ge 41:45 gave him **A** daughter of Potiphera, H664
Ge 41:50 born to Joseph by **A** daughter of Potiphera, H664
Ge 46:20 born to Joseph by **A** daughter of Potiphera, H664

ASER (KJV) ASHER

ASH (4) [ASHES]
Lev 4:12 burn it there in a wood fire on the **a** heap. H2016
1Sa 2: 8 dust and lifts the needy from the **a heap**; H883
Ps 113: 7 dust and lifts the needy from the **a heap**; H883
La 4: 5 up in royal purple now lie on **a heaps**. H883

ASHAMED (48) [SHAME]
2Sa 19: 3 as men steal in who *are* **a** when they flee H4007
2Ch 30:15 the Levites *were* **a** and consecrated H4007
Ezr 8:22 *I was* **a** to ask the king for soldiers and H1017
Ezr 9: 6 "*I am too* **a** and disgraced, my God, to lift H1017
Ps 83:17 *May they* ever *be* **a** and dismayed; may H1017
Isa 1:29 "*You will be* **a** because of the sacred oaks H1017
Isa 23: 4 *Be* **a**, Sidon, and you fortress of the sea H1017
Isa 24:23 be dismayed, the sun **a**; for the LORD H1017
Isa 29:22 "No longer *will* Jacob *be* **a**; no longer will H1017
Isa 33: 9 Lebanon *is* **a** and withers; Sharon H2917
Isa 41:11 against you *will* surely *be* **a** and disgraced H1017
Jer 6:15 *Are they* **a** *of* their detestable conduct? No H1017
Jer 8:12 *Are they* **a** *of* their detestable conduct? No H1017
Jer 22:22 Then *you will be* **a** and disgraced H1017
Jer 31:19 *I was* **a** and humiliated because I bore H1017
Jer 48:13 Then Moab *will be* **a** of Chemosh, as H1017
Jer 48:13 as Israel *was* **a** when they trusted in H1017
Jer 50:12 your mother *will be* greatly **a**; she who H1017
Eze 16:52 So then, *be* **a** and bear your disgrace, for H1017
Eze 16:54 your disgrace and *be* **a** of all you have H4007
Eze 16:61 your ways and *be* **a** when you receive your H4007
Eze 16:63 will remember and *be* **a** and never again H1017
Eze 36:32 *Be* **a** and disgraced for your conduct H1017
Eze 43:10 of Israel, that *they may be* **a** of their sins. H4007
Eze 43:11 if *they are* **a** of all they have done H4007
Hos 10: 6 Israel *will be* **a** of its foreign alliances. H1017
Mic 3: 7 The seers *will be* **a** and the diviners H1017
Mic 7:16 Nations will see and *be* **a**, deprived of all H1017
Zec 13: 4 day every prophet *will be* **a** of their H1017
Mk 8:38 If anyone *is* **a** of me and my words in this *G2049*
Mk 8:38 the Son of Man *will be* **a** of them when *G2049*
Lk 9:26 Whoever *is* **a** of me and my words, the *G2049*
Lk 9:26 the Son of Man *will be* **a** of them when *G2049*
Lk 16: 3 strong enough to dig, and *I'm* **a** to beg— *G159*
Ro 1:16 For *I am* not **a** of the gospel, because it is *G2049*
Ro 6:21 time from the things *you are* now **a of**? *G2049*
2Co 9: 4 *would be* **a** *of* having been so confident. *G2875*
2Co 10: 8 than tearing you down, *I will* not *be* **a** of it. *G159*
Php 1:20 expect and hope that *I will* in no way *be* **a**, *G159*
2Th 3:14 with them, in order that *they may* **feel a**. *G1956*
2Ti 1: 8 So *do* not *be* **a** of the testimony about our *G2049*
2Ti 1:16 refreshed me and *was* not **a** of my chains. *G2049*
2Ti 2:15 worker *who does* **not** *need to be* **a** and who *G454*
Titus 2: 8 who oppose you *may be* **a** because they *G1956*
Heb 2:11 So Jesus *is* not **a** to call them brothers *G2049*
Heb 11:16 Therefore God *is* not **a** to be called their *G2049*
1Pe 3:16 in Christ *may be* **a** of their slander. *G2875*
1Pe 4:16 as a Christian, *do* not *be* **a**, but praise God *G159*

ASHAN (4) [BOR ASHAN]
Jos 15:42 Ether, **A**, H6941
Jos 19: 7 Rimmon, Ether and **A**—four towns and H6941
1Ch 4:32 Rimmon, Token and **A**—five towns— H6941
1Ch 6:59 **A**, Juttah and Beth Shemesh, together H6941

ASHBEA See BETH ASHBEA

ASHBEL (3) [ASHBELITE]
Ge 46:21 Beker, **A**, Gera, Naaman, Ehi, Rosh H839
Nu 26:38 Belaite clan; through **A**, the Ashbelite clan; H839
1Ch 8: 1 Bela his firstborn, **A** the second son H839

ASHBELITE (1) [ASHBEL]
Nu 26:38 through Ashbel, the **A** clan; through H840

ASHDOD (21)
Jos 11:22 only in Gaza, Gath and **A** did any survive. H846
Jos 13: 3 five Philistine rulers in Gaza, **A**, Ashkelon, H847
Jos 15:46 all that were in the vicinity of **A**, together H846
Jos 15:47 **A**, its surrounding settlements and villages H846
1Sa 5: 1 ark of God, they took it from Ebenezer to **A**. H846
1Sa 5: 3 When the **people of A** rose early the next H847
1Sa 5: 5 Dagon's temple at **A** step on the threshold. H846
1Sa 5: 6 was heavy on the **people of A** and its H847
1Sa 5: 7 When the people of **A** saw what was H846
1Sa 6:17 offering to the LORD—one each for **A**, Gaza, H846
2Ch 26: 6 down the walls of Gath, Jabneh and **A**. H846

2Ch 26: 6 rebuilt towns near **A** and elsewhere among H846
Ne 4: 7 the **people of A** heard that the H847
Ne 13:23 of Judah who had married women **from A**, H847
Ne 13:24 spoke the **language of A** or the language H848
Isa 20: 1 came to **A** and attacked and captured it H846
Jer 25:20 Ekron, and the people left at **A**); H846
Am 1: 8 destroy the king of **A** and the one who H846
Am 3: 9 to the fortresses of **A** and to the fortresses H846
Zep 2: 4 At midday **A** will be emptied and Ekron H846
Zec 9: 6 A mongrel people will occupy **A**, and I will H846

ASHER (44) [ASHER'S, ASHERITES]

Ge 30:13 will call me happy." So she named him **A**. H888
Ge 35:26 Gad and **A**. These were the sons of H888
Ge 46:17 The sons of **A**: Imnah, Ishvah, Ishvi and H888
Ex 1: 4 Dan and Naphtali; Gad and **A**. H888
Nu 1:13 from **A**, Pagiel son of Okran; H888
Nu 1:40 From the descendants of **A**: All the men H888
Nu 1:41 number from the tribe of **A** was 41,500. H888
Nu 2:27 The tribe of **A** will camp next to them. The H888
Nu 2:27 of the people of **A** is Pagiel son of Okran. H888
Nu 7:72 the leader of the people of **A**, brought his H888
Nu 10:26 over the division of the tribe of **A**, H1201+888
Nu 13:13 from the tribe of **A**, Sethur son of Michael; H888
Nu 26:44 The descendants of **A** by their clans were H888
Nu 26:46 (**A** had a daughter named Serah.) H888
Nu 26:47 These were the clans of **A**; those H1201+888
Nu 34:27 the leader from the tribe of **A**; H1201+888
Dt 27:13 Reuben, Gad, **A**, Zebulun, Dan and H888
Dt 33:24 About **A** he said: "Most blessed of sons is H888
Dt 33:24 "Most blessed of sons is **A**; let him be H888
Jos 17: 7 extended from **A** to Mikmethath east of H888
Jos 17:10 Sea and bordered **A** on the north and H888
Jos 17:11 Within Issachar and **A**, Manasseh also had H888
Jos 19:24 out for the tribe of **A** according to its H1201+888
Jos 19:31 the inheritance of the tribe of **A**, H1201+888
Jos 19:34 **A** on the west and the Jordan on the east. H888
Jos 21: 6 the tribes of Issachar, **A**, Naphtali and the H888
Jos 21:30 from the tribe of **A**, Mishal, Abdon, H888
Jdg 1:31 Nor did **A** drive out those living in Akko H888
Jdg 5:17 **A** remained on the coast and stayed in his H888
Jdg 6:35 and also into **A**, Zebulun and H888
Jdg 7:23 **A** and all Manasseh were called out H888
1Ki 4:16 Baana son of Hushai—in **A** and in Aloth; H888
1Ch 2: 2 Benjamin, Naphtali, Gad and **A**. H888
1Ch 6:62 tribes of Issachar, **A** and Naphtali, and H888
1Ch 6:74 from the tribe of **A** they received Mashal H888
1Ch 7:30 The sons of **A**: Imnah, Ishvah, Ishvi and H888
1Ch 7:40 All these were descendants of **A**—heads of H888
1Ch 12:36 from **A**, experienced soldiers prepared H888
2Ch 30:11 some from **A**, Manasseh and Zebulun H888
Eze 48: 2 "**A** will have one portion; it will border the H888
Eze 48: 3 border the territory of **A** from east to west. H888
Eze 48:34 the gate of **A** and the gate of Naphtali. H888
Lk 2:36 the daughter of Penuel, of the tribe *of* **A**. *G818*
Rev 7: 6 from the tribe *of* **A** 12,000, from the tribe of *G818*

ASHER'S (1) [ASHER]

Ge 49:20 "**A** food will be rich; he will provide H888+4946

ASHERAH (39) [ASHERAHS]

Ex 34:13 sacred stones and cut down their **A poles**. H895
Dt 7: 5 cut down their **A poles** and burn their idols H895
Dt 12: 3 stones and burn their **A poles** in the fire; H895
Dt 16:21 set up any wooden **A pole** beside the altar H895
Jdg 6:25 to Baal and cut down the **A pole** beside it. H895
Jdg 6:26 the wood of the **A pole** that you cut down, H895
Jdg 6:28 with the **A pole** beside it cut down and the H895
Jdg 6:30 altar and cut down the **A pole** beside it." H895
1Ki 14:15 the LORD's anger by making **A poles**. H895
1Ki 14:23 sacred stones and **A poles** on every high H895
1Ki 15:13 a repulsive image for the worship of **A**. H895
1Ki 16:33 Ahab also made an **A pole** and did more to H895
1Ki 18:19 Baal and the four hundred prophets of **A**, H895
2Ki 13: 6 the **A pole** remained standing in Samaria. H895
2Ki 17:10 sacred stones and **A poles** on every high H895
2Ki 17:16 cast in the shape of calves, and an **A pole**. H895
2Ki 18: 4 sacred stones and cut down the **A poles**. H895
2Ki 21: 3 erected altars to Baal and made an **A pole**, H895
2Ki 21: 7 took the carved **A pole** he had made and H895
2Ki 23: 4 made for Baal and **A** and all the starry H895
2Ki 23: 6 He took the **A pole** from the temple of the H895
2Ki 23: 7 quarters where women did weaving for **A**. H895
2Ki 23:14 cut down the **A poles** and covered the H895
2Ki 23:15 it to powder, and burned the **A pole** also. H895
2Ch 14: 3 sacred stones and cut down the **A poles**. H895
2Ch 15:16 a repulsive image for the worship of **A**. H895
2Ch 17: 6 high places and the **A poles** from Judah. H895
2Ch 19: 3 the land of the **A poles** and have set your H895
2Ch 24:18 worshiped **A poles** and idols. H895
2Ch 31: 1 sacred stones and cut down the **A poles**. H895
2Ch 33: 3 altars to the Baals and made **A poles**. H895
2Ch 33:19 places and set up **A poles** and idols before H895
2Ch 34: 3 of high places, **A poles** and idols. H895
2Ch 34: 4 smashed the **A poles** and the idols. H895
2Ch 34: 7 the altars and the **A poles** and crushed the H895
Isa 17: 8 no regard for the **A poles** and the incense H895
Isa 27: 9 no **A poles** or incense altars will be left H895
Jer 17: 2 their altars and **A poles** beside the H895
Mic 5:14 among you your **A poles** when I demolish H895

ASHERAHS (1) [ASHERAH]

Jdg 3: 7 their God and served the Baals and the **A**. H895

ASHERITES (1) [ASHER]

Jdg 1:32 The **A** lived among the Canaanite H896

ASHES (37) [ASH]

Ge 18:27 though I am nothing but dust and **a**, H709
Ex 27: 3 its pots to **remove** the **a**, and its shovels, H2014
Lev 1:16 down east of the altar where the **a** are. H2016
Lev 4:12 where the **a** are thrown, and burn it H2016
Lev 6:10 shall remove the **a** of the burnt H2016
Lev 6:11 carry the **a** outside the camp to a H2016
Nu 4:13 "*They are to* **remove** the **a** *from* the H2014
Nu 19: 9 shall gather up the **a** *of* the heifer and put H709
Nu 19:10 who gathers up the **a** *of* the heifer must H709
Nu 19:17 put some **a** *from* the burned purification H6760
2Sa 13:19 Tamar put **a** on her head and tore the H709
1Ki 13: 3 split apart and the **a** on it will be poured H2016
1Ki 13: 5 split apart and its **a** poured out according H2016
2Ki 23: 4 Kidron Valley and took the **a** to Bethel. H6760
Est 4: 1 put on sackcloth and **a**, and went out into H709
Est 4: 3 Many lay in sackcloth and **a**. H709
Job 2: 8 himself with it as he sat among the **a**. H709
Job 13:12 Your maxims are proverbs of **a**; your H709
Job 30:19 the mud, and I am reduced to dust and **a**. H709
Job 42: 6 I despise myself and repent in dust and **a**." H709
Ps 102: 9 For I eat **a** as my food and mingle my drink H709
Ps 147:16 snow like wool and scatters the frost like **a**. H709
Isa 33:12 The peoples will be burned to **a**; like cut H8487
Isa 44:20 Such a person feeds on **a**; a deluded heart H709
Isa 58: 5 like a reed and for lying in sackcloth and **a**? H709
Isa 61: 3 on them a crown of beauty instead of **a**, H709
Jer 6:26 my people, and roll in **a**; mourn with bitter H709
Jer 31:40 where dead bodies and **a** are thrown, H2016
Eze 27:30 sprinkle dust on their heads and roll in **a**. H709
Eze 28:18 I reduced you to **a** on the ground in the H709
Da 9: 3 petition, in fasting, and in sackcloth and **a**. H709
Am 2: 1 he burned to **a** the bones of Edom's H8487
Mal 4: 3 they will be **a** under the soles of your feet H709
Mt 11:21 repented long ago in sackcloth and **a**. *G5075*
Lk 10:13 long ago, sitting in sackcloth and **a**. *G5075*
Heb 9:13 bulls and the **a** of a heifer sprinkled *G5075*
2Pe 2: 6 Gomorrah *by* **burning them to a**, *G5491*

ASHHUR (2)

1Ch 2:24 of Hezron bore him **A** the father of Tekoa. H858
1Ch 4: 5 **A** the father of Tekoa had two wives, Helah H858

ASHIMA (1)

2Ki 17:30 and those from Hamath made **A**; H860

ASHKELON (13)

Jos 13: 3 in Gaza, Ashdod, **A**, Gath and Ekron; the H885
Jdg 1:18 also took Gaza, **A** and Ekron—each city H884
Jdg 14:19 He went down to **A**, struck down thirty of H884
1Sa 6:17 each for Ashdod, Gaza, **A**, Gath and Ekron. H884
2Sa 1:20 proclaim it not in the streets of **A**, lest the H884
Jer 25:20 kings of the Philistines (those of **A**, Gaza, H884
Jer 47: 5 her head in mourning; **A** will be silenced. H884
Jer 47: 7 he has ordered it to attack **A** and the coast?" H884
Am 1: 8 the one who holds the scepter in **A**. H884
Zep 2: 4 will be abandoned and **A** left in ruins. H884
Zep 2: 7 they will lie down in the houses of **A**. H884
Zec 9: 5 **A** will see it and fear; Gaza will writhe in H884
Zec 9: 5 will lose her king and **A** will be deserted. H884

ASHKENAZ (3)

Ge 10: 3 The sons of Gomer: **A**, Riphath and H867
1Ch 1: 6 The sons of Gomer: **A**, Riphath and H867
Jer 51:27 Minni and **A**. Appoint a H867

ASHNAH (2)

Jos 15:33 In the western foothills: Eshtaol, Zorah, **A**, H877
Jos 15:43 **A**, Nezib, H877

ASHORE (2) [SHORE]

Lk 8:27 When Jesus stepped **a**, he *G2093+3836+1178*
Jn 21:11 boat and dragged the net **a**. *G1650+3836+1178*

ASHPENAZ (1)

Da 1: 3 Then the king ordered **A**, chief of his court H881

ASHTAROTH (6)

Dt 1: 4 Og king of Bashan, who reigned in **A**. H6958
Jos 9:10 Og king of Bashan, who reigned in **A**. H6958
Jos 12: 4 Rephaites, who reigned in **A** and Edrei. H6958
Jos 13:12 Bashan, who had reigned in **A** and Edrei. H6958
Jos 13:31 half of Gilead, and **A** and Edrei (the royal H6958
1Ch 6:71 received Golan in Bashan and also **A**, H6958

ASHTERATHITE (1)

1Ch 11:44 Uzzia the **A**, Shama and Jeiel the sons of H6960

ASHTEROTH KARNAIM (1)

Ge 14: 5 defeated the Rephaites in **A**, H6959

ASHTORETH (3) [ASHTORETHS]

1Ki 11: 5 He followed **A** the goddess of the H6956
1Ki 11:33 me and worshiped **A** the goddess of the H6956
2Ki 23:13 Israel had built for **A** the vile goddess of H6956

ASHTORETHS (6) [ASHTORETH]

Jdg 2:13 forsook him and served Baal and the **A**. H6956
Jdg 10: 6 They served the Baals and the **A**, and the H6956
1Sa 7: 3 foreign gods and the **A** and commit H6956
1Sa 7: 4 the Israelites put away their Baals and **A**, H6956
1Sa 12:10 the LORD and served the Baals and the **A**. H6956
1Sa 31:10 in the temple of the **A** and fastened his H6956

ASHUR (7)

Ge 2:14 the Tigris; it runs along the east side of **A**. H855
Ge 10:22 sons of Shem: Elam, **A**, Arphaxad, Lud H855
Ge 25:18 border of Egypt, as you go toward **A**. H855
Nu 24:22 be destroyed when **A** takes you captive." H855
Nu 24:24 they will subdue **A** and Eber, but they too H855
1Ch 1:17 sons of Shem: Elam, **A**, Arphaxad, Lud H855
Eze 27:23 of Sheba, **A** and Kilmad traded with you. H855

ASHURBANIPAL (1)

Ezr 4:10 great and honorable **A** deported and A10055

ASHURI (1)

2Sa 2: 9 king over Gilead, **A** and Jezreel, and also H856

ASHURITES (1)

Ge 25: 3 the descendants of Dedan were the **A**, the H857

ASHVATH (1)

1Ch 7:33 Bimhal and **A**. These were H6937

ASIA (19)

Ac 2: 9 Judea and Cappadocia, Pontus and **A**, *G823*
Ac 6: 9 as well as the provinces of Cilicia and **A**— *G823*
Ac 16: 6 preaching the word in the **province of A**. *G823*
Ac 19:10 lived in the **province of A** heard the word *G823*
Ac 19:22 stayed in the **province of A** a little longer *G823*
Ac 19:26 and *in* practically the whole **province of A**. *G823*
Ac 19:27 throughout the **province of A** and the world *G823*
Ac 20: 4 Trophimus **from the province of A**. *G824*
Ac 20:16 avoid spending time in the **province of A**, *G823*
Ac 20:18 the first day I came into the **province of A**. *G823*
Ac 21:27 Jews from the **province of A** saw Paul at *G823*
Ac 24:19 are some Jews from the **province of A**, *G823*
Ac 27: 2 ports along the coast of the **province of A**, *G823*
Ro 16: 5 first convert to Christ *in* the **province of A**. *G823*
1Co 16:19 The churches *in* the **province of A** send you *G823*
2Co 1: 8 we experienced in the **province of A**. *G823*
2Ti 1:15 everyone in the **province of A** has deserted *G823*
1Pe 1: 1 **provinces of** Pontus, Galatia, Cappadocia, **A** *G823*
Rev 1: 4 To the seven churches in the **province of A**: *G823*

ASIDE (72) [SIDE]

Ge 19: 2 "please **turn a** to your servant's house. H6073
Nu 18:11 *whatever* is **set a** *from* the gifts of all the H9556
Nu 18:19 Whatever is **set a** *from* the holy offerings H9556
Nu 21:22 *We will* not **turn a** into any field or H5742
Nu 23: 3 here beside your offering while *I* **go a**. H2143
Dt 2:27 *we will* not **turn a** *to* the right or *to* the left. H6073
Dt 4:41 Then Moses **set a** three cities east of the H976
Dt 5:32 *do* not **turn a** *to* the right or to the left. H6073
Dt 9:16 *You had* **turned a** quickly from the way H6073
Dt 14:22 **Be sure to set a a tenth** *of* all that H6923+6923
Dt 17:11 *Do* not **turn a** from what they tell you, to H6073
Dt 19: 2 then **set a** for yourselves three cities in the H976
Dt 19: 7 why I command you *to* **set a** for yourselves H976
Dt 19: 9 then you are to set **a** three more cities. NDT
Dt 21:13 and **put a** the clothes she was wearing H6073
Dt 26:12 **setting a a tenth** *of* all your H6923+5130
Dt 26:13 *I have* not **turned a** from your commands H6296
Dt 28:14 *Do* not **turn a** from any of the commands I H6073
Jos 16: 9 villages that were **set a** for the H4426
Jos 23: 6 without **turning a** to the right or to the left. H6073
Jdg 14: 8 *he* **turned a** to look at the lion's carcass H6073
1Sa 8: 3 *They* **turned a** after dishonest gain and H5742
1Sa 9:23 I gave you, the one I told you to **lay a**." H6640
1Sa 9:24 because *it* **was set a** for you for this H9068
2Sa 2:21 "**Turn a** to the right or to the left H5742
2Sa 3:27 Joab **took** him **a** into an inner chamber H5742
2Sa 18:30 The king said, "**Stand a** and wait here." H6015
2Sa 18:30 So *he* **stepped a** and stood there H6015
2Sa 23: 6 evil men are all *to* **be cast a** like thorns, H5610
2Ki 22: 2 not **turning a** *to* the right or *to* the left. H6073
2Ki 25:29 So Jehoiachin **put a** his prison clothes H9101
2Ch 34: 2 not **turning a** *to* the right or *to* the left. H6073
2Ch 35:12 *They* **set a** the burnt offerings to give them H6073
Ne 12:47 *They* also **set a** the portion for the other H7727
Ne 12:47 the Levites **set a** the portion for the H7727
Job 6:18 Caravans **turn a** *from* their routes; they go H4369
Job 23:11 I have kept to his way without **turning a**. H5742
Job 29: 8 men saw me and **stepped a** and the old H2461
Job 36:18 *do* not *let* a large bribe **turn** you **a**. H5742
Ps 40: 4 to *those who* **turn a** *to* false gods. H8454
Ps 85: 3 *You* **set a** all your wrath and turned from H665
Ps 102:10 you have taken me up and **thrown** me **a**. H8959
Pr 5: 7 listen to me; *do* not **turn a** from what I say. H6073
Jer 5:23 *they have* **turned a** and gone away. H6073
Jer 52:33 So Jehoiachin **put a** his prison clothes H9101
Eze 26:16 their thrones and **lay a** their robes and H6073
Eze 31:11 according to its wickedness. *I* **cast** it **a**, H1763
Eze 48:20 **As a special gift** *you will* **set a** the sacred H8123
Mt 5:19 Therefore anyone *who* **sets a** one of the *G3395*
Mt 16:22 Peter **took** him **a** and began to rebuke *G4689*
Mt 20:17 took the Twelve **a** and said to them *G2848+2625*
Mk 7: 9 "*You have* a fine way of **setting a** the *G119*
Mk 7:33 After he **took** him **a**, away from the *G2848+2625*
Mk 8:32 Peter **took** him **a** and began to *G4689*
Mk 10:32 Again *he* **took** the Twelve **a** and told *G4161*
Mk 10:50 **Throwing** his cloak **a**, he jumped to his feet *G610*

Lk 18:31 Jesus **took** the Twelve **a** and told them *G4161*
Jn 2: 9 Then he **called** the bridegroom **a** *G5888*
Jn 10:35 came—and Scripture cannot *be* **set a**— *G3395*
Jn 11:28 went back and called her sister Mary **a**. *G3277*
Ac 7:27 the other **pushed** Moses **a** and said, *G723*
Ac 23:19 drew him **a** and asked *G2848+2625*
Ro 13:12 So *let us* **put a** the deeds of darkness and *G700*
1Co 16: 2 one of you *should* **set a** a sum of money *G5502*
Gal 2:21 *I do* not **set a** the grace of God, for if *G119*
Gal 3:15 Just as no one *can* **set a** or add to a human *G119*
Gal 3:17 *does* not **set a** the covenant previously *G218*
Eph 2:15 *by* **setting a** in his flesh the law with its *G2934*
2Ti 4: 4 away from the truth and **turn a** to myths. *G1762*
Heb 7:18 regulation is **set a** because it was weak *G120*
Heb 10: 9 *He* **sets a** the first to establish the second *G359*
2Pe 1:14 I know that *I will* soon **put** it **a**, *G1639+629*

ASIEL (1)

1Ch 4:35 the son of Seraiah, the son of **A**, H6918

ASK (190) [ASKED, ASKING, ASKS]

Ge 23: 9 **A** him to sell it to me for the full price as a NDT
Ge 24:57 call the young woman and **a** her *about* it." H8626
Ge 32:29 replied, "Why *do you* **a** my name?" Then H8626
Ge 34:11 and I will give you whatever *you* **a**. H606
Ge 34:12 as you like, and I'll pay whatever *you* **a** me. H606
Ge 50:17 **I a** you to forgive your brothers the sins H626
Ex 3:13 me to you,' and *they* **a** me, 'What is his H606
Ex 3:22 *is to* **a** her neighbor and any woman living in her house *for* H8626
Ex 11: 2 alike *are to* **a** their neighbors *for* articles H8626
Ex 12:26 And when your children **a** you, 'What does H606
Lev 25:20 *You may* **a**, "What will we eat in the H606
Nu 12:11 **I a** you not to hold against us the sin we H5528
Dt 4:32 **A** now about the former days, long before H8626
Dt 4:32 **a** from one end of the heavens to the other. NDT
Dt 10:12 what *does* the LORD your God **a** of you H8626
Dt 29:24 All the nations *will* **a**: "Why has the LORD H606
Dt 30:12 so that you *have to* **a**, "Who will ascend H606
Dt 30:13 so that you *have to* **a**, "Who will cross H606
Dt 31:17 in that day *they will* **a**, 'Have not these H606
Dt 32: 7 **A** your father and he will tell you, your H8626
Jos 4: 6 when your children **a** you, 'What do these H8626
Jos 4:21 when your descendants **a** their parents, H8626
Jos 15:18 she urged him to **a** her father for a H8626+907
Jdg 1:14 she urged him to **a** her father *for* a field. H8626
Jdg 9: 2 "**A** all the citizens of Shechem, 'Which is H1819
Jdg 13: 6 *I* didn't **a** him where he came from, and H8626
Jdg 13:18 He replied, "Why *do you* **a** my name? It is H8626
Jdg 18:24 How *can you* **a**, 'What's the matter with H606
Ru 3:11 I will do for you all *you* **a**. All the people of H606
1Sa 25: 8 **A** your own servants and they will tell you H8626
2Sa 11:20 may flare up, and *he may* **a** you, 'Why did H606
2Sa 14:18 the answer to what I *am going to* **a** you." H8626
2Sa 14:32 here so I can send you to the king to **a**, H606
2Sa 16:10 'Curse David,' who *can* **a**, 'Why do you do H606
2Sa 19:11 "**A** the elders of Judah, 'Why should you H1819
1Ki 2:17 continued, "Please **a** King Solomon—he H606
1Ki 3: 5 "**A** *for* whatever you want me to give you." H8626
1Ki 14: 5 is coming to **a** you about her son H2011+1821
2Ki 1: 3 of the king of Samaria and **a** them, H1819
2Ki 4: 3 "Go around and **a** all your neighbors for H8626
2Ki 4: 3 empty jars. Don't **a** for just a few. NDT
2Ki 4:26 Run to meet her and **a** her, 'Are you all H606
2Ki 4:28 "*Did I* **a** you for a son, my lord?" she said H8626
2Ki 8: 8 the LORD through him; **a** him, 'Will I recover H606
2Ki 8: 9 Ben-Hadad king of Aram has sent me to **a**, H606
2Ki 9:17 "Send him to meet them and **a**, 'Do you H606
2Ki 14:10 Why **a** for trouble and cause your own H1741
2Ch 1: 7 "**A** *for* whatever you want me to give you." H8626
2Ch 25:19 Why **a** for trouble and cause your own H1741
2Ch 32:31 of Babylon to **a** him *about* the miraculous H2011
Ezr 7:21 of the God of heaven, *may* **a** *of* you— A10689
Ezr 8:21 our God and **a** him **for** a safe journey for H1335
Ezr 8:22 ashamed to **a** the king *for* soldiers and H8626
Est 5:14 **a** the king in the morning to have H606
Job 8: 8 "**A** the former generation and find out H8626
Job 12: 7 "But **a** the animals, and they will teach H8626
Job 35: 3 Yet *you* **a** him, 'What profit is it to me, and H606
Job 37:20 *Would* anyone **a** to be swallowed up H606
Ps 2: 8 **A** me, and I will make the nations your H8626
Ps 27: 4 One thing *I* **a** from the LORD, this only do I H8626
Pr 30: 7 "Two things *I* **a** of you, LORD; do not refuse H8626
Ecc 7:10 For it is not wise *to* **a** such questions. H8626
Isa 7:11 "**A** the LORD your God for a sign, whether H8626
Isa 7:12 But Ahaz said, "*I will* not **a**; I will not put H8626
Isa 21:12 If *you would* **a**, then ask; and come back H1239
Isa 21:12 you would ask, then **a**; and come back H1239
Isa 41:28 no one to give answer when *I* **a** them. H8626
Isa 58: 2 *They* **a** me *for* just decisions and seem H8626
Isa 65: 1 myself to *those who did* not **a** for me; H8626
Jer 2: 6 *They did* not **a**, 'Where is the LORD, who H606
Jer 2: 8 The priests *did* not **a**, 'Where is the LORD?' H606
Jer 5:19 And when *the people* **a**, 'Why has the LORD H606
Jer 6:16 look; **a** for the ancient paths H8626
Jer 6:16 the ancient paths, **a** where the good way is NDT
Jer 13:22 And if *you* **a** yourself, "Why has this H606
Jer 15: 2 And if *they* **a** you, 'Where shall we go?' tell H606
Jer 15: 5 Who will stop to **a** how you are? H8626
Jer 16:10 tell these people all this and *they* **a** you, H606
Jer 22: 8 pass by this city and *will* **a** one another, H606
Jer 23:33 a prophet or a priest, **a** you, 'What is the H8626
Jer 30: 6 **A** and see: Can a man bear children H8626
Jer 38:14 "*I am going to* **a** you something," the king H8626
Jer 48:19 **A** the man fleeing and the woman H8626
Jer 48:19 the woman escaping, **a** them, 'What has H606
Jer 50: 5 *They will* **a** the way to Zion and turn their H8626
Eze 12: 9 rebellious people, **a** you, 'What are you H606
Eze 13:12 collapses, *will* people not **a** you, "Where is H606
Eze 18:19 "Yet *you* **a**, 'Why does the son not share H606
Eze 21: 7 And when *they* **a** you, 'Why are you H606
Eze 37:18 "When your people **a** you, 'Won't you tell H606
Hag 2: 2 to the remnant of the people. **A** them, H606
Hag 2:11 '**A** the priests what the law says H8626
Zec 7: 5 "**A** all the people of the land and the H606
Zec 10: 1 **A** the LORD *for* rain in the springtime; it is H8626
Mal 1: 2 "But *you* **a**, 'How have you H606
Mal 1: 6 "But *you* **a**, 'How have we shown contempt H606
Mal 1: 7 "But *you* **a**, 'How have we H606
Mal 2:14 *You* **a**, "Why?" It is because the LORD is the H606
Mal 2:17 have we wearied him?" *you* **a**. By saying, H606
Mal 3: 7 LORD Almighty. "But *you* **a**, 'How are we to H606
Mal 3: 8 Yet you rob me. "But *you* **a**, 'How are we H606
Mal 3:13 "Yet *you* **a**, 'What have we said against H606
Mt 6: 8 knows what you need before you **a** him. *G160*
Mt 7: 7 "**A** and it will be given to you; seek and *G160*
Mt 7:11 heaven give good gifts *to* those *who* **a** him! *G160*
Mt 9:38 **A** the Lord of the harvest, therefore, to *G1289*
Mt 11: 3 *to* **a** him, "Are you the one who is to come, *G3306*
Mt 18:19 on earth agree about anything *they* **a for**, *G160*
Mt 19:17 "Why *do you* **a** me about what is good?" *G2263*
Mt 21:22 will receive whatever *you* **a for** in prayer." *G160*
Mt 21:24 replied, "I *will* also **a** you one question. *G2263*
Mt 21:25 'From heaven,' *he will* **a**, 'Then why didn't *G3306*
Mt 22:46 one dared *to* **a** him any more **questions**. *G2089*
Mt 27:20 the crowd to **a for** Barabbas and to have *G160*
Mk 5:31 "and yet *you can* **a**, 'Who touched me? *G3306*
Mk 6:22 to the girl, "**A** me **for** anything you want *G160*
Mk 6:23 an oath, "Whatever *you* **a** I will give you *G160*
Mk 6:24 said to her mother, "What *shall I* **a for**?" *G160*
Mk 8:12 "Why *does* this generation **a for** a sign? *G2426*
Mk 9:32 meant and were afraid *to* **a** him **about** it. *G2089*
Mk 10:35 "we want you to do for us whatever *we* **a**." *G160*
Mk 11:24 whatever *you* **a for** in prayer, believe *G160*
Mk 11:29 Jesus replied, "*I will* **a** you one question *G2089*
Mk 11:31 'From heaven,' *he will* **a**, 'Then why didn't *G3306*
Mk 12:34 no one dared **a** him *any more* **questions**. *G2089*
Lk 6: 9 said to them, "*I* **a** you, which is lawful *G2089*
Lk 7:19 he sent them to the Lord *to* **a**, "Are you the *G3306*
Lk 7:20 "John the Baptist sent us to you *to* **a**, 'Are *G3306*
Lk 9:45 and they were afraid *to* **a** him about it. *G1263*
Lk 10: 2 **A** the Lord of the harvest, therefore, to *G1289*
Lk 11: 9 **A** and it will be given to you; seek and you *G160*
Lk 11:13 give the Holy Spirit to those *who* **a** him!" *G160*
Lk 14:32 a long way off and *will* **a** for terms of *G2263*
Lk 20: 3 He replied, "I *will* also **a** you a question *G2263*
Lk 20: 5 'From heaven,' *he will* **a**, 'Why didn't you *G3306*
Lk 20:40 one dared *to* **a** him any more **questions**. *G2089*
Jn 1:19 priests and Levites to **a** him who he was. *G2263*
Jn 4: 9 How *can you* **a** me *for* a drink?" *G160*
Jn 7:25 of the people of Jerusalem *began to* **a**, *G3306*
Jn 8:22 This made the Jews **a**, "Will he kill *G3306*
Jn 9:21 we don't know. **A** him. He is of age *G2263*
Jn 9:23 his parents said, "He is of age; **a** him." *G2089*
Jn 11:22 now God will give you whatever *you* **a**." *G160*
Jn 13:24 said, "**A** him which one he means." *G4785*
Jn 14:13 And I will do whatever *you* **a** in my name *G160*
Jn 14:14 *You* may **a** me *for* anything in my name *G160*
Jn 14:16 And I *will* **a** the Father, and he will give *G2263*
Jn 15: 7 words remain in you, **a** whatever you wish *G160*
Jn 15:16 so that whatever *you* **a** in my name the *G160*
Jn 16:19 saw that they wanted *to* **a** him about this, *G2263*
Jn 16:23 In that day *you will* no longer **a** me *G2263*
Jn 16:23 will give you whatever *you* **a** in my name. *G160*
Jn 16:24 **A** and you will receive, and your joy will be *G160*
Jn 16:26 In that day *you will* **a** in my name. I am not *G160*
Jn 16:26 not saying that I *will* **a** the Father on your *G2263*
Jn 16:30 need to *have* anyone **a** you **questions**. *G2263*
Jn 18:21 Why question me? **A** those who heard me *G2263*
Jn 21:12 None of the disciples dared **a** him, "Who *G2004*
Ac 9:11 Street and **a for** a man from Tarsus *G2426*
Ac 10:22 A holy angel **told** him **to a** you to come to *G5976*
Ac 10:29 *May I* **a** why you sent for me? *G4785*
Ac 23:20 Jews have agreed *to* **a** you to bring Paul *G2263*
Ro 10:18 But *I* **a**: Did they not hear? Of course they *G3306*
Ro 10:19 Again *I* **a**: Did Israel not understand? First *G3306*
Ro 10:20 myself to those *who did* not **a for** me." *G2089*
Ro 11: 1 *I* **a** then: Did God reject his people? By no *G3306*
Ro 11:11 Again *I* **a**: Did they stumble so as to fall *G3306*
Ro 16: 2 **I a** you to receive her in the Lord in a way NDT
1Co 6: 4 *do you* **a for a ruling** from those whose *G2767*
1Co 14:35 *they should* **a** their own husbands at *G2089*
1Co 15:35 But someone *will* **a**, "How are the dead *G3306*
Gal 3: 5 So again I **a**, does God give you his Spirit NDT
Eph 3:13 *I* **a** you, therefore, not to be discouraged *G160*
Eph 3:20 more than all *we* **a** or imagine, *G160*
Php 4: 3 and *I* **a** you, my true companion, help *G2263*
Col 1: 9 *We continually* **a** God to fill you with the *G160*
1Th 4: 1 *Now we* **a** you and urge you in the Lord *G2263*
1Th 5:12 Now *we* **a** you, brothers and sisters, to *G2263*
2Th 2: 1 gathered to him, *we* **a** you, brothers and *G2263*
1Ti 5: 5 day to pray and to **a** God **for help**. *G1255*
Phm 21 that you will do even more than *I* **a**. *G3306*
Jas 1: 5 lacks wisdom, *you should* **a** God, who gives *G160*
Jas 1: 6 But *when you* **a**, you must believe and not *G160*
Jas 4: 2 do not have because you *do* not **a** God. *G160*
Jas 4: 3 *When you* **a**, you do not receive, because *G160*
Jas 4: 3 because *you* **a** with wrong motives *G160*
1Jn 3:22 receive from him anything *we* **a** *G160*
1Jn 5:14 that if *we* **a** anything according to his will *G160*
1Jn 5:15 whatever *we* **a**—we know that we *G160*
2Jn 5 beginning. *I* **a** that we love one another *G2263*

ASKED (554) [ASK]

Ge 18: 9 is your wife Sarah?" *they* **a** him. "There, H606
Ge 20:10 And Abimelek **a** Abraham, "What was your H606
Ge 21:29 Abimelek **a** Abraham, "What is the H606
Ge 24: 5 The servant **a** him, "What if the woman is H606
Ge 24:23 Then *he* **a**, "Whose daughter are you H606
Ge 24:39 "Then *I* **a** my master, 'What if the woman H606
Ge 24:47 "*I* **a** her, 'Whose daughter are you?' "She H8626
Ge 24:58 So they called Rebekah and **a** her, "Will H606
Ge 24:65 **a** the servant, "Who is that man in the H606
Ge 26: 7 men of that place **a** him about his wife, H8626
Ge 26:27 Isaac **a** them, "Why have you come to me H606
Ge 27:20 Isaac **a** his son, "How did you find it so H606
Ge 27:24 *he* **a**. "I am," he replied. H606
Ge 27:32 His father Isaac **a** him, "Who are you?" H606
Ge 27:36 Then *he* **a**, "Haven't you reserved any H606
Ge 29: 4 Jacob **a** the shepherds, "My brothers H606
Ge 29: 6 Then Jacob **a** them, "Is he well?" "Yes, he H606
Ge 30:31 shall I give you?" *he* **a**. "Don't give me H606
Ge 31:36 he **a** Laban. "How have I H6699
Ge 32:27 The man **a** him, "What is your name?" H606
Ge 33: 5 are these with you?" *he* **a**. Jacob answered, H606
Ge 33: 8 Esau **a**, "What's the meaning of all these H606
Ge 33:15 Jacob **a**. "Just let me find H606
Ge 37:15 around in the fields and **a** him, H8626
Ge 38:16 will you give me to sleep with you?" *she* **a**. H606
Ge 38:17 as a pledge until you send it?" *she* **a**. H606
Ge 38:21 *He* **a** the men who lived there, "Where is H8626
Ge 40: 7 So *he* **a** Pharaoh's officials who were in H8626
Ge 41:38 So Pharaoh **a** them, "Can we find anyone H606
Ge 42: 7 do you come from?" *he* **a**. "From the land H606
Ge 43: 6 Israel **a**, "Why did you bring this trouble on H606
Ge 43: 7 father still living?' *he* **a** us. 'Do you have H606
Ge 43:27 *He* **a** them **how they were** H4200+8934+8626
Ge 43:29 his own mother's son, *he* **a**, "Is this your H606
Ge 44:19 My lord **a** his servants, 'Do you have a H8626
Ge 47: 3 Pharaoh **a** the brothers, "What is your H606
Ge 47: 8 Pharaoh **a** him, "How old are you?" H606
Ge 48: 8 the sons of Joseph, *he* **a**, "Who are these?" H606
Ex 1:18 summoned the midwives and **a** them, H606
Ex 2: 7 Then his sister **a** Pharaoh's daughter H606
Ex 2:13 *He* **a** the one in the wrong, "Why are you H606
Ex 2:18 their father, *he* **a** them, "Why have you H606
Ex 2:20 Reuel **a** his daughters. "Why H606
Ex 8:13 And the LORD did what Moses **a**. The frogs H1821
Ex 8:31 the LORD did what Moses **a**. The flies H1821
Ex 12:35 and **a** the Egyptians *for* articles of H8626
Ex 12:36 and *they* **gave** them **what** they **a for**; so H8626
Ex 33:17 "I will do the very thing *you have* **a** H1819
Lev 10:16 Ithamar, Aaron's remaining sons, and **a**, H606
Nu 11:11 He **a** the LORD, "Why have you brought this H606
Nu 12: 2 through Moses?" *they* **a**. "Hasn't he also H606
Nu 14:20 replied, "I have forgiven them, as you **a**. H1821
Nu 22: 9 God came to Balaam and **a**, "Who are H606
Nu 22:32 The angel of the LORD **a** him, "Why have H606
Nu 23:17 Balak **a** him, "What did the LORD H606
Nu 31:15 all the women to live?" he **a** them. H606
Dt 18:16 For this is what *you* **a** of the LORD your God H8626
Jos 5:13 Joshua went up to him and **a**, "Are you H606
Jos 5:14 in reverence, and **a** him, "What message H606
Jos 9: 8 But Joshua **a**, "Who are you and where do H606
Jos 15:18 off her donkey, Caleb **a** her, "What can I do H606
Jos 19:50 They gave him the town *he* **a** *for* H8626
Jdg 1: 1 the Israelites **a** the LORD, "Who of us H8626
Jdg 1:14 off her donkey, Caleb **a** her, "What can I do H606
Jdg 5:25 *He* **a** *for* water, and she gave him milk; in H8626
Jdg 6:29 *They* **a** each other, "Who did this?" When H606
Jdg 8: 1 Now the Ephraimites **a** Gideon, "Why have H606
Jdg 8:18 Then *he* **a** Zebah and Zalmunna, "What H606
Jdg 8:26 the gold rings *he* **a** *for* came to seventeen H8626
Jdg 12: 5 the men of Gilead **a** him, "Are you an H606
Jdg 13:12 So Manoah **a** him, "When your words are H606
Jdg 15: 6 When the Philistines **a**, "Who did this?" H606
Jdg 15:10 The people of Judah **a**, "Why have you H606
Jdg 17: 9 Micah **a** him, "Where are you from?" "I'm a H606
Jdg 18: 3 so they turned in there and **a** him, "Who H606
Jdg 18: 8 their fellow Danites **a** them, "How did you H606
Jdg 19:17 the old man **a**, "Where are you H606
Jdg 20:28 They **a**, "Shall we go up again to fight H606
Jdg 21: 5 Then the Israelites **a**, "Who from all the H606
Jdg 21: 8 Then *they* **a**, "Which one of the tribes of H606
Ru 2: 5 Boaz **a** the overseer of his harvesters, "Who H606
Ru 2:10 *She* **a** him, "Why have I found such favor in H606
Ru 2:19 Her mother-in-law **a** her, "Where did you H606
Ru 3: 9 "Who are you?" *he* **a**. "I am your servant H606
Ru 3:16 mother-in-law, Naomi **a**, "How did it go, H606
1Sa 1:17 Israel grant you what *you have* **a** of him." H8626
1Sa 1:20 "Because *I* **a** the LORD *for* him. H8626
1Sa 1:27 the LORD has granted me what *I* **a** of him. H8626
1Sa 3:17 he said to you?" Eli **a**. "Do not hide it from H606
1Sa 4: 3 the elders of Israel **a**, "Why did the LORD H606
1Sa 4: 6 the Philistines **a**, "What's all this H606
1Sa 4:14 Eli heard the outcry and **a**, "What is the H606

1Sa 4:16 Eli **a**, "What happened, my H606
1Sa 5: 8 all the rulers of the Philistines and **a** them, H606
1Sa 6: 4 The Philistines **a**, "What guilt offering H606
1Sa 6:20 And the people of Beth Shemesh **a**, "Who H606
1Sa 9:11 to draw water, and *they* **a** them, "Is the H606
1Sa 9:18 approached Samuel in the gateway and **a**, H606
1Sa 10:11 the prophets, they **a** each other, "What is H606
1Sa 10:14 Now Saul's uncle **a** him and his servant H606
1Sa 11: 5 his oxen, and he **a**, "What is wrong with H606
1Sa 11:12 "Who was it that **a**, 'Shall Saul reign over H606
1Sa 12:13 you have chosen, the one *you* **a** *for*; see, H8626
1Sa 12:17 eyes of the LORD when you **a** for a king." H8626
1Sa 13:11 have you done?" **a** Samuel. Saul replied, H606
1Sa 14:37 So Saul **a** God, "Shall I go down and H8626
1Sa 16: 4 *They* **a**, "Do you come in H606
1Sa 16:11 So he **a** Jesse, "Are these all the sons you H606
1Sa 17:22 **a** his brothers **how** they **were** H8626+4200+8934
1Sa 17:26 David **a** the men standing near him, "What H606
1Sa 17:28 he burned with anger at him and **a**, "Why H606
1Sa 17:58 Saul **a** him. David said, "I H606
1Sa 19:22 And *he* **a**, "Where are Samuel and David?" H8626
1Sa 20: 1 at Ramah and went to Jonathan and **a**, H606
1Sa 20: 6 **earnestly a** my **permission** to H8626+8626
1Sa 20:10 David **a**, "Who will tell me if your father H606
1Sa 20:28 **earnestly a** me **for permission** to go H8626+8626
1Sa 20:32 has he done?" Jonathan **a** his father. H6699
1Sa 21: 1 he met him, and **a**, "Why are you alone? H606
1Sa 21: 8 David **a** Ahimelek, "Don't you have a spear H606
1Sa 23:12 Again David **a**, "Will the citizens of Keilah H606
1Sa 24:16 saying this, Saul **a**, "Is that your voice, H606
1Sa 26: 6 David then **a** Ahimelek the Hittite and H6699
1Sa 27:10 When Achish **a**, "Where did you go raiding H606
1Sa 28:11 Then the woman **a**, "Whom shall I bring H606
1Sa 28:14 does he look like?" *he* **a**. "An old man H606
1Sa 29: 3 The commanders of the Philistines **a** H606
1Sa 29: 8 what have I done?" **a** David. "What have H606
1Sa 30:13 David **a** him, "Who do you belong to H606
1Sa 30:15 David **a** him, "Can you lead me down to H606
1Sa 30:21 approached, *he* **a** them how they were. H8626
2Sa 1: 3 David **a** him. He answered, H606
2Sa 1: 4 David **a**. "Tell me." "The men H606
2Sa 1: 8 "*He* **a** me, 'Who are you?' " 'An Amalekite H606
2Sa 1:14 David **a** him, "Why weren't you afraid to lift H606
2Sa 2: 1 the towns of Judah?" he **a**. The LORD said, H606
2Sa 2: 1 David **a**, "Where shall I go?" "To H606
2Sa 2:20 Abner looked behind him and **a**, "Is that H606
2Sa 9: 1 David **a**, "Is there anyone still left of the H606
2Sa 9: 3 The king **a**, "Is there no one still alive from H606
2Sa 9: 4 the king **a**. Ziba answered, "He is H606
2Sa 11: 7 came to him, David **a** him how Joab was H8626
2Sa 11:10 So he **a** Uriah, "Haven't you just come H606
2Sa 12:19 the child dead?" he **a**. "Yes," they replied, H606
2Sa 12:21 His attendants **a** him, "Why are you acting H606
2Sa 13: 4 *He* **a** Amnon, "Why do you, the king's son H606
2Sa 13:26 The king **a** him, "Why should he go with H606
2Sa 14: 5 The king **a** her, "What is troubling you?" H606
2Sa 14:19 The king **a**, "Isn't the hand of Joab with H606
2Sa 16: 2 The king **a** Ziba, "Why have you brought H606
2Sa 16: 3 The king then **a**, "Where is your master's H606
2Sa 17:20 at the house, *they* **a**, "Where are Ahimaaz H606
2Sa 18:29 The king **a**, "Is the young man Absalom H606
2Sa 18:32 The king **a** the Cushite, "Is the young man H606
2Sa 19:25 the king, the king **a** him, "Why didn't you H606
2Sa 20:17 toward her, and she **a**, "Are you Joab?" H606
2Sa 21: 3 David **a** the Gibeonites, "What shall I do H606
2Sa 21: 4 do you want me to do for you?" David **a**. H606
1Ki 1:11 Then Nathan **a** Bathsheba, Solomon's H606
1Ki 1:16 "What is it you want?" the king **a**. H606
1Ki 1:41 the trumpet, Joab **a**, "What's the meaning H606
1Ki 2:13 Bathsheba **a** him, "Do you come peacefully H606
1Ki 3:10 was pleased that Solomon *had* **a** *for* this. H8626
1Ki 3:11 "Since *you have* **a** *for* this and not for long H8626
1Ki 3:11 nor *have* **a** *for* the death of your enemies H8626
1Ki 3:12 I will do what you have **a**. I will give you a H1821
1Ki 3:13 I will give you what *you have* not **a** *for* H8626
1Ki 9:13 *he* **a**. And he called them the H606
1Ki 10:13 queen of Sheba all she desired and **a** *for*, H8626
1Ki 11:22 to your own country?" Pharaoh **a**. "Nothing," H606
1Ki 12: 6 advise me to answer these people?" he **a**. H606
1Ki 12: 9 *He* **a** them, "What is your advice? How H606
1Ki 13:12 Their father **a** them, "Which way did he go H1819
1Ki 13:14 found him sitting under an oak tree and **a**, H606
1Ki 17:10 He called to her and **a**, "Would you bring H606
1Ki 18: 9 **a** Obadiah, "that you are handing your H606
1Ki 20:14 who will do this?" **a** Ahab. The prophet H606
1Ki 20:14 start the battle?" *he* **a**. The prophet H606
1Ki 21: 5 His wife Jezebel came in and **a** him H1819
1Ki 22: 4 So *he* **a** Jehoshaphat, "Will you go with H606
1Ki 22: 6 hundred men—and **a** them, "Shall I go to H606
1Ki 22: 7 But Jehoshaphat **a**, "Is there no longer a H606
1Ki 22:15 he arrived, the king **a** him, "Micaiah, shall H606
1Ki 22:22 ' the LORD **a**. " 'I will go out and H606
1Ki 22:24 he went from me to speak to you?" *he* **a**. H606
2Ki 1: 5 to the king, *he* **a** them, "Why have you H606
2Ki 1: 7 The king **a** them, "What kind of man was H1819
2Ki 2: 3 at Bethel came out to Elisha and **a**, H606
2Ki 2: 5 at Jericho went up to Elisha and **a** him, H606
2Ki 2:10 "*You have* **a** a difficult thing," Elijah said H8626
2Ki 2:14 God of Elijah?" *he* **a**. When he struck the H606
2Ki 3: 8 shall we attack?" *he* **a**. "Through the Desert H606
2Ki 3:11 But Jehoshaphat **a**, "Is there no prophet of H606
2Ki 4:14 be done for her?" Elisha **a**. Gehazi said, H606
2Ki 4:23 go to him today?" *he* **a**. "It's not the New H606
2Ki 4:43 his servant **a**. But Elisha answered, H606
2Ki 5:21 "Is everything all right?" *he* **a**. H606
2Ki 5:25 his master, Elisha **a** him, "Where have you H606
2Ki 6: 6 The man of God **a**, "Where did it fall?" H606
2Ki 6:15 What shall we do?" the servant **a**. H606
2Ki 6:18 them with blindness, as Elisha had **a**. H1821
2Ki 6:21 of Israel saw them, *he* **a** Elisha, "Shall I kill H606
2Ki 6:28 Then he **a** her, "What's the matter?" She H606
2Ki 8: 6 The king **a** the woman *about* it, and she H8626
2Ki 8:12 is my lord weeping?" **a** Hazael. "Because I H606
2Ki 8:14 When Ben-Hadad **a**, "What did Elisha say H606
2Ki 9: 5 "For which of us?" **a** Jehu. "For you H606
2Ki 9:11 fellow officers, *one* of them **a** him, "Is H606
2Ki 9:22 When Joram saw Jehu *he* **a**, "Have you H606
2Ki 9:31 entered the gate, *she* **a**, "Have you come H606
2Ki 10:13 relatives of Ahaziah king of Judah and **a**, H606
2Ki 12: 7 the priest and the other priests and **a** them, H606
2Ki 20: 8 Hezekiah *had* **a** Isaiah, "What will be the H606
2Ki 20:14 the prophet went to King Hezekiah and **a**, H606
2Ki 20:15 The prophet **a**, "What did they see in your H606
2Ki 23:17 The king **a**, "What is that tombstone I see?" H606
1Ch 13:12 David was afraid of God that day and **a** H606
2Ch 1:11 desire and *you have* not **a** *for* wealth, H8626
2Ch 1:11 since *you have* not **a** *for* a long life H8626
2Ch 9:12 queen of Sheba all she desired and **a** *for*; H8626
2Ch 10: 6 advise me to answer these people?" he **a**. H606
2Ch 10: 9 *He* **a** them, "What is your advice? How H606
2Ch 18: 3 Ahab king of Israel **a** Jehoshaphat king of H606
2Ch 18: 5 hundred men—and **a** them, "Shall we go H606
2Ch 18: 6 But Jehoshaphat **a**, "Is there no longer a H606
2Ch 18:14 he arrived, the king **a** him, "Micaiah, shall H606
2Ch 18:20 ' " 'By what means?' the LORD **a**. H606
2Ch 18:23 he went from me to speak to you?" *he* **a**. H606
2Ch 25: 9 Amaziah **a** the man of God, "But what H606
2Ch 31: 9 Hezekiah **a** the priests and Levites about H2011
Ezr 5: 3 their associates went to them and **a**, A10042
Ezr 5: 4 *They* also **a**, "What are the names of A10042
Ezr 5: 9 We questioned the elders and **a** them A10042
Ezr 5:10 *We* also **a** them their names, so that we A10689
Ezr 7: 6 king had granted him everything he **a**, H1336
Ne 2: 2 so the king **a** me, "Why does your face look H606
Ne 2: 6 sitting beside him, **a** me, "How long will H606
Ne 2:19 you are doing?" *they* **a**. "Are you rebelling H606
Ne 13: 6 Some time later *I* **a** his permission H8626
Ne 13:11 So I rebuked the officials and **a** them, "Why H606
Est 1:15 Queen Vashti?" he **a**. "She has not obeyed NDT
Est 2:15 *she* **a for** nothing other than what Hegai H1335
Est 3: 3 officials at the king's gate **a** Mordecai, H606
Est 5: 3 Then the king **a**, "What is it, Queen Esther H606
Est 5: 6 the king again **a** Esther, "Now what is H606
Est 6: 3 the king **a**. "Nothing has been H606
Est 6: 6 entered, the king **a** him, "What should be H606
Est 7: 2 the king again **a**, "Queen Esther, H606
Est 7: 5 King Xerxes **a** Queen Esther, "Who is he H606
Job 42: 3 You **a**, 'Who is this that obscures my plans NDT
Ps 21: 4 *He* **a** you *for* life, and you gave it to him H8626
Ps 77: 6 My heart meditated and my spirit **a**: H2924
Ps 105:40 *They* **a**, and he brought them quail; he H8626
Ps 106:15 So he gave them **what** they **a for**, but sent H8629
Ps 137: 3 there our captors **a** us *for* songs, our H8626
Ecc 4: 8 he **a**, "and why am I depriving myself of NDT
Isa 1:12 before me, who *has* **a** this of you, this H1335
Isa 38:22 Hezekiah *had* **a**, "What will be the sign H606
Isa 39: 3 the prophet went to King Hezekiah and **a**, H606
Isa 39: 4 The prophet **a**, "What did they see in your H606
Jer 24: 3 Then the LORD **a** me, "What do you see H606
Jer 36:17 Then *they* **a** Baruch, "Tell us, how did you H8626
Jer 37:17 the palace, where he **a** him privately, "Is H8626
Eze 24:19 Then the people **a** me, "Won't you tell us H606
Eze 37: 3 *He* **a** me, "Son of man, can these bones H606
Eze 47: 6 *He* **a** me, "Son of man, do you see this?" H606
Da 1: 8 and *he* **a** the chief official **for permission** H1335
Da 2:10 *has ever* **a** such a thing of any magician A10689
Da 2:15 *He* **a** the king's officer, "Why did the king A10558
Da 2:16 went in to the king and **a for** time, A10114
Da 2:23 made known to me what *we* **a** of you, A10114
Da 2:26 The king **a** Daniel (also called A10558
Da 2:27 to the king the mystery he *has* **a** *about*, A10689
Da 3:24 feet in amazement and **a** his advisers, A10558
Da 7:16 there and **a** him the meaning of A10114
Da 12: 8 So *I* **a**, "My lord, what will the outcome of H606
Am 7: 8 And the LORD **a** me, "What do you see H606
Am 8: 2 do you see, Amos?" *he* **a**. "A basket of ripe H606
Jnh 1: 8 So *they* **a** him, "Tell us, who is responsible H606
Jnh 1:10 This terrified them and *they* **a**, "What have H606
Jnh 1:11 So *they* **a** him, "What should we do to you H606
Zec 1: 9 *I* **a**, "What are these, my lord?" The angel H606
Zec 1:19 *I* **a** the angel who was speaking to me H606
Zec 1:21 *I* **a**, "What are these coming to do?" He H606
Zec 2: 2 *I* **a**, "Where are you going?" He answered H606
Zec 4: 2 *He* **a** me, "What do you see?" I answered H606
Zec 4: 4 *I* **a** the angel who talked with me, "What H6699
Zec 4:11 Then *I* **a** the angel, "What are these two H6699
Zec 4:12 Again *I* **a** him, "What are these two olive H6699
Zec 5: 2 *He* **a** me, "What do you see?" I answered H606
Zec 5: 6 *I* **a**, "What is it?" He replied, "It is a basket." H606
Zec 5:10 *I* **a** the angel who was speaking to me H606
Zec 6: 4 *I* **a** the angel who was speaking to me H6699
Mt 2: 2 **a**, "Where is the one who has been G3306
Mt 2: 4 *he* **a** them where the Messiah was to be G4785
Mt 8:27 The men were amazed and **a**, "What kind G3306
Mt 9:11 saw this, *they* **a** his disciples, "Why G3306
Mt 9:14 Then John's disciples came and **a** him G3306
Mt 9:28 came to him, and he **a** them, "Do you G3306
Mt 12:10 against Jesus, *they* **a** him, "Is it lawful to G2089
Mt 13:10 The disciples came to him and **a**, "Why G3306
Mt 13:28 "The servants **a** him, 'Do you want us to G3306
Mt 13:51 understood all these things?" Jesus **a**. "Yes," NDT
Mt 13:54 these miraculous powers?" *they* **a**. G3306
Mt 14: 7 with an oath to give her whatever *she* **a**. G160
Mt 15: 1 law came to Jesus from Jerusalem and **a**, G3306
Mt 15:12 Then the disciples came to him and **a** G3306
Mt 15:16 "Are you still so dull?" Jesus **a** them. G3306
Mt 15:34 loaves do you have?" Jesus **a**. "Seven," G3306
Mt 16: 8 discussion, Jesus **a**, "You of little faith, G3306
Mt 16:13 Caesarea Philippi, *he* **a** his disciples G2263
Mt 16:15 what about you?" *he* **a**. "Who do you say I G3306
Mt 17:10 The disciples **a** him, "Why then do the G2089
Mt 17:19 disciples came to Jesus in private and **a**, G3306
Mt 17:24 temple tax came to Peter and **a**, G3306
Mt 17:25 he **a**. "From whom do the kings of NDT
Mt 18: 1 time the disciples came to Jesus and **a**, G3306
Mt 18:21 Then Peter came to Jesus and **a**, "Lord G3306
Mt 19: 3 *They* **a**, "Is it lawful for a man to divorce G3306
Mt 19: 7 *they* **a**, "did Moses command that a man G3306
Mt 19:16 Just then a man came up to Jesus and **a** G3306
Mt 19:25 they were greatly astonished and **a**, "Who G3306
Mt 20: 6 *He* **a** them, 'Why have you been standing G3306
Mt 20:20 sons and, kneeling down, **a** a favor of him. G160
Mt 20:21 is it you want?" he **a**. She said, "Grant G3306
Mt 20:32 do you want me to do for you?" *he* **a**. G3306
Mt 21:10 the whole city was stirred and **a**, "Who is G3306
Mt 21:16 children are saying?" *they* **a** him. "Yes," G3306
Mt 21:20 did the fig tree wither so quickly?" *they* **a**. G3306
Mt 21:23 *they* **a**. "And who gave you G3306
Mt 22:12 *He* **a**, 'How did you get in here without G3306
Mt 22:20 and *he* **a** them, "Whose image is this G3306
Mt 22:41 were gathered together, Jesus **a** them, G2089
Mt 24: 2 all these things?" he **a**. "Truly I tell you, G646
Mt 26: 8 "Why this waste?" *they* **a**. G3306
Mt 26:15 **a**, "What are you willing to give me if G3306
Mt 26:17 the disciples came to Jesus and **a** G3306
Mt 26:40 watch with me for one hour?" *he* **a** Peter. G3306
Mt 27:11 the governor **a** him, "Are you the king G2089
Mt 27:13 Then Pilate **a** him, "Don't you hear the G3306
Mt 27:17 gathered, Pilate **a** them, "Which one do G3306
Mt 27:21 me to release to you?" **a** the governor G646
Mt 27:22 Pilate **a**. They all answered, G3306
Mt 27:23 has he committed?" **a** Pilate. But they G5774
Mt 27:58 Going to Pilate, he **a** for Jesus' body, and G160
Mk 1:27 all so amazed that *they* **a** each other, G5184
Mk 2:16 tax collectors, *they* **a** his disciples: G3306
Mk 2:18 Some people came and **a** Jesus, "How is G3306
Mk 3: 4 Then Jesus **a** them, "Which is lawful on G3306
Mk 3:33 are my mother and my brothers?" *he* **a**. G646
Mk 4:10 the others around him **a** him about the G2263
Mk 4:41 They were terrified and **a** each other G3306
Mk 5: 9 Then Jesus **a** him, "What is your name?" G2089
Mk 5:30 He turned around in the crowd and **a** G3306
Mk 6: 2 get these things?" *they* **a**. "What's this G3306
Mk 6:38 loaves do you have?" he **a**. "Go and see." G3306
Mk 7: 5 teachers of the law **a** Jesus, G2089
Mk 7:17 his disciples **a** him **about** this parable. G2089
Mk 7:18 "Are you so dull?" *he* **a**. "Don't you see G3306
Mk 8: 5 loaves do you have?" Jesus **a**. "Seven," G2263
Mk 8:11 *they* **a** him **for** a sign from heaven. G2426
Mk 8:17 discussion, Jesus **a** them: "Why are you G3306
Mk 8:23 hands on him, Jesus **a**, "Do you see G2089
Mk 8:27 On the way *he* **a** them, "Who do people G2089
Mk 8:29 what about you?" *he* **a**. "Who do you say I G2089
Mk 9:11 And *they* **a** him, "Why do the teachers of G2089
Mk 9:16 are you arguing with them about?" *he* **a**. G2089
Mk 9:18 *I* **a** your disciples to drive out the spirit G3306
Mk 9:21 Jesus **a** the boy's father, "How long has G2089
Mk 9:28 his disciples **a** him privately, "Why G2089
Mk 9:33 was in the house, *he* **a** them, "What were G2089
Mk 10:10 the disciples **a** Jesus about this. G2089
Mk 10:17 *he* **a**, "what must I do to inherit eternal G2089
Mk 10:36 do you want me to do for you?" he **a**. G3306
Mk 10:51 to do for you?" Jesus **a** him. The blind man G646
Mk 11: 5 some people standing there **a**, "What are G3306
Mk 11:28 *they* **a**. "And who gave you G3306
Mk 12:15 trying to trap me?" *he* **a**. "Bring me a G3306
Mk 12:16 the coin, and *he* **a** them, "Whose image G3306
Mk 12:28 a good answer, *he* **a** him, "Of all the G2089
Mk 12:35 in the temple courts, *he* **a**, "Why do the G646
Mk 13: 3 John and Andrew **a** him privately, G2089
Mk 14:12 Jesus' disciples **a** him, "Where do you G3306
Mk 14:60 priest stood up before them and **a** Jesus, G2089
Mk 14:61 Again the high priest **a** him, "Are you the G2089
Mk 14:63 do we need any more witnesses?" *he* **a**. G3306
Mk 15: 2 king of the Jews?" **a** Pilate. "You have G2089
Mk 15: 4 So again Pilate **a** him, "Aren't you going G2089
Mk 15: 8 The crowd came up and **a** Pilate to do for G160
Mk 15: 9 to you the king of the Jews?" **a** Pilate, G646
Mk 15:12 call the king of the Jews?" Pilate **a** them. G646
Mk 15:14 has he committed?" **a** Pilate. But they G3306
Mk 15:43 went boldly to Pilate and **a for** Jesus' body. G160
Mk 15:44 *he* **a** him if Jesus had already died. G2089
Mk 16: 3 and *they* **a** each other, "Who will roll the G3306
Lk 1:18 Zechariah **a** the angel, "How can I be G3306
Lk 1:34 will this be," Mary **a** the angel, "since I G3306
Lk 1:63 *He* **a for** a writing tablet, and to everyone's G160

Lk 2:49 searching for me?" he a. "Didn't you know G3306
Lk 3:10 "What should we do then?" the crowd a. G2089
Lk 3:12 "Teacher," they a, "what should we do?" G3306
Lk 3:14 Then some soldiers a him, "And what G2089
Lk 4:22 "Isn't this Joseph's son?" they a. G3306
Lk 4:38 a high fever, and they a Jesus to help her. G2263
Lk 5: 3 a him to put out a little from shore. G2263
Lk 5:22 Jesus knew what they were thinking and a G646
Lk 6: 2 Some of the Pharisees a, "Why are you G3306
Lk 8: 9 His disciples a him what this parable G2089
Lk 8:25 he a his disciples. In G3306
Lk 8:25 fear and amazement they a one another, G3306
Lk 8:30 Jesus a him, "What is your name? G2089
Lk 8:37 of the Gerasenes a Jesus to leave them, G2263
Lk 8:45 Jesus a. When they all G3306
Lk 9:18 were with him, he a them, "Who do the G2089
Lk 9:20 what about you?" he a. "Who do you say I G3306
Lk 9:54 James and John saw this, they a, "Lord, G3306
Lk 10:25 he a, "what must I do to inherit eternal G3306
Lk 10:29 justify himself, so he a Jesus, "And who is G3306
Lk 10:40 She came to him and a, "Lord, don't you G3306
Lk 12:41 Peter a, "Lord, are you telling this parable G3306
Lk 12:48 entrusted with much, much more will be a. G160
Lk 13:18 Then Jesus a, "What is the kingdom of G3306
Lk 13:20 Again he a, "What shall I compare the G3306
Lk 13:23 Someone a him, "Lord, are only a few G3306
Lk 14: 3 Jesus a the Pharisees and experts in the G646
Lk 14: 5 Then he a them, "If one of you has a G3306
Lk 15:26 of the servants and a him what was going G4785
Lk 16: 2 So he called him in and a him, 'What is G3306
Lk 16: 5 He a the first, 'How much do you owe my G3306
Lk 16: 7 "Then he a the second, 'And how much G3306
Lk 17:17 Jesus a, "Were not all ten cleansed G646
Lk 17:20 on being a by the Pharisees when the G2089
Lk 17:37 "Where, Lord?" they a. He replied, "Where G646
Lk 18:18 A certain ruler a him, "Good teacher G2089
Lk 18:26 Those who heard this a, "Who then can G3306
Lk 18:36 going by, he a what was happening. G4785
Lk 18:40 When he came near, Jesus a him, G2089
Lk 19:33 the colt, its owners a them, "Why are you G3306
Lk 20:17 Jesus looked directly at them and a G3306
Lk 21: 7 "Teacher," they a, "when will these things G2089
Lk 22: 9 do you want us to prepare for it?" they a. G3306
Lk 22:31 Satan has a to sift all of you as wheat. G1977
Lk 22:35 Then Jesus a them, "When I sent you G3306
Lk 22:46 you sleeping?" he a them. "Get up and G3306
Lk 22:48 Jesus a him, "Judas, are you betraying G3306
Lk 22:68 if I a you, you would not answer. G2263
Lk 22:70 They all a, "Are you then the Son of God?" G3306
Lk 23: 3 So Pilate a Jesus, "Are you the king of the G2263
Lk 23: 6 Pilate a if the man was a Galilean. G2089
Lk 23:25 the one they a for, and G160
Lk 23:52 Going to Pilate, he a for Jesus' body. G160
Lk 24:17 He a them, "What are you discussing G3306
Lk 24:18 named Cleopas, a him, "Are you the only G646
Lk 24:19 "What things?" he a. "About Jesus of G3306
Lk 24:32 They a each other, "Were not our hearts G3306
Lk 24:41 amazement, he a them, "Do you G3306
Jn 1:21 They a him, "Then who are you? Are you G2263
Jn 1:38 Jesus saw them following and a, "What G3306
Jn 1:46 Nathanael a. "Come and see, G3306
Jn 1:48 Nathanael a. Jesus answered, G3306
Jn 3: 4 Nicodemus a. "Surely they G3306
Jn 3: 9 "How can this be?" Nicodemus a. G646
Jn 4:10 you would have a him and he would have G160
Jn 4:27 But no one a, "What do you want G3306
Jn 5: 6 a long time, he a him, "Do you want G3306
Jn 5:12 So they a him, "Who is this fellow who G2263
Jn 6: 6 He a this only to test him, for he already G3306
Jn 6:25 other side of the lake, they a him, "Rabbi, G3306
Jn 6:28 Then they a him, "What must we do to do G3306
Jn 6:30 So they a him, "What sign then will you G3306
Jn 6:67 leave too, do you?" Jesus a the Twelve. G3306
Jn 7:15 The Jews there were amazed and a, "How G3306
Jn 7:41 Still others a, "How can the Messiah G3306
Jn 7:45 the Pharisees, who a them, "Why didn't G3306
Jn 7:50 who was one of their own number, a, G3306
Jn 8:10 Jesus straightened up and a her, "Woman, G3306
Jn 8:19 Then they a him, "Where is your father?" G3306
Jn 8:25 "Who are you?" they a. "Just what I have G3306
Jn 9: 2 His disciples a him, "Rabbi, who sinned G2263
Jn 9: 8 who had formerly seen him begging a, G3306
Jn 9:10 then were your eyes opened?" they a. G3306
Jn 9:12 they a him. "I don't know, G3306
Jn 9:15 the Pharisees also a him how he had G2263
Jn 9:16 But others a, "How can a sinner perform G3306
Jn 9:19 "Is this your son?" they a. "Is this the one G2263
Jn 9:26 Then they a him, "What did he do to you G3306
Jn 9:36 the man a. "Tell me so that I may G646
Jn 9:40 were with him heard him say this and a, G3306
Jn 11:34 you laid him?" he a. "Come and see, G3306
Jn 11:47 accomplishing?" they a. "Here is this man G3306
Jn 11:56 in the temple courts they a one another, G3306
Jn 13:12 what I have done for you?" he a them. G3306
Jn 13:25 back against Jesus, he a him, "Lord, G3306
Jn 13:36 Simon Peter a him, "Lord, where are you G3306
Jn 13:37 Peter a, "Lord, why can't I follow you now G3306
Jn 16:24 Until now you have not a for anything in my G160
Jn 18: 4 went out and a them, "Who is it you G3306
Jn 18: 7 Again he a them, "Who is it you want?" G2089
Jn 18:17 are you?" she a Peter. He replied, "I G3306
Jn 18:25 So they a him, "You aren't one of his G3306
Jn 18:29 So Pilate came out to them and a, "What G5774
Jn 18:33 summoned Jesus and a him, "Are you the G3306
Jn 18:34 Jesus a, "or did others talk to you about G646
Jn 19: 9 he a Jesus, but Jesus gave him no G3306
Jn 19:15 Pilate a. "We have no king G3306
Jn 19:31 they a Pilate to have the legs broken and G2263
Jn 19:38 Joseph of Arimathea a Pilate for the body G2263
Jn 20:13 They a her, "Woman, why are you crying?" G3306
Jn 20:15 He a her, "Woman, why are you crying G3306
Jn 21:17 hurt because Jesus a him the third time, G3306
Jn 21:21 Peter saw him, he a, "Lord, what about G3306
Ac 1: 6 they gathered around him and a him, G2263
Ac 2: 7 Utterly amazed, they a: "Aren't all these G3306
Ac 2:12 perplexed, they a one another, "What G3306
Ac 3: 3 about to enter, he a them for money. G2263
Ac 3:14 Righteous One and a that a murderer be G160
Ac 4: 9 lame and are being a how he was healed, NDT
Ac 4:16 with these men?" they a. "Everyone living G3306
Ac 5: 8 Peter a her, "Tell me, is this the price you G646
Ac 7: 1 Then the high priest a Stephen, "Are G3306
Ac 7:46 God's favor and a that he might provide a G160
Ac 8:30 what you are reading?" Philip a. G3306
Ac 8:34 The eunuch a Philip, "Tell me, please G646
Ac 9: 2 a him for letters to the synagogues in G160
Ac 9: 5 are you, Lord?" Saul a. "I am Jesus, whom G3306
Ac 9:21 who heard him were astonished and a, G3306
Ac 10: 4 he a. The angel answered G3306
Ac 10:48 Then they a Peter to stay with them for a G2263
Ac 12:20 of the king, they a for peace, because G160
Ac 13:21 Then the people a for a king, and he gave G160
Ac 13:28 they a Pilate to have him executed. G160
Ac 16:30 He then brought them out and a, "Sirs G5774
Ac 17:18 Some of them a, "What is this babbler G3306
Ac 18:20 When they a him to spend more time with G2263
Ac 19: 2 a them, "Did you receive the Holy G3306
Ac 19: 3 So Paul a, "Then what baptism did you G3306
Ac 21:33 Then he a who he was and what he had G4785
Ac 21:37 into the barracks, he a the commander G3306
Ac 22: 8 " 'Who are you, Lord?' I a. " 'I am Jesus of G646
Ac 22:10 shall I do, Lord?' I a. " 'Get up,' the Lord G3306
Ac 22:26 you going to do?" he a. "This man is a G3306
Ac 22:27 The commander went to Paul and a, "Tell G3306
Ac 23:18 sent for me and a me to bring this young G2263
Ac 23:19 drew him aside and a, "What is it you G4785
Ac 23:34 read the letter and a what province he G2089
Ac 25:15 against him and a that he be condemned. G160
Ac 25:20 so I a if he would be willing to go to G3306
Ac 26:15 "Then I a, 'Who are you, Lord?' " 'I am G3306
Ac 28:20 For this reason I have a to see you and talk G4151
Gal 2:10 All they a was that we should continue to NDT
1Jn 5:15 we know that we have what we a of him. G160
Rev 7:13 Then one of the elders a me, "These in G646
Rev 10: 9 to the angel and a him to give me the G3306
Rev 13: 4 they also worshiped the beast and a G3306

ASKING (25) [ASK]

Ex 10:11 since that's what you have been a for." H1335
1Sa 8:10 to the people who were a him for a king. H8626
1Sa 10: 2 He is a, "What shall I do H606
1Sa 12:19 all our other sins the evil of a for a king." H8626
1Sa 25:39 word to Abigail, a her to become his wife. H1819
2Sa 15: 6 Israelites who came to the king a for justice, NDT
1Ki 1: 6 His father had never rebuked him by a H606
Ps 4: 6 LORD, are a, "Who will bring us H606
Da 6:11 Daniel praying and a God for help. A10274
Zec 7: 3 by a the priests of the house of the LORD H606
Mt 8: 5 a centurion came to him, a for help. G4151
Mt 16: 1 tested him by a him to show them a G2089
Mt 20:22 "You don't know what you are a," Jesus G160
Mk 10: 2 Pharisees came and tested him by a, G2089
Mk 10:38 "You don't know what you are a," Jesus G160
Lk 1:66 wondered about it, a, "What then is this G3306
Lk 2:46 listening to them and a them questions. G2089
Lk 7: 3 a him to come and heal his servant. G2263
Lk 11:16 Others tested him by a for a sign from G2426
Jn 7:11 leaders were watching for Jesus and a, G3306
Jn 11:28 she said, "and is a for you. G5888
Jn 16:18 They kept a, "What does he mean by 'a G3306
Jn 16:19 "Are you a one another what I meant G2426
Ac 10:18 a if Simon who was known as Peter was G4785
Eph 1:17 I keep a that the God of our Lord Jesus NDT

ASKS (31) [ASK]

Ge 32:17 "When my brother Esau meets you and a H8626
Ge 46:33 When Pharaoh calls you in and a, 'What is H606
Ex 13:14 when your son a you, 'What does H8626
Dt 6:20 when your son a you, "What is the H8626
Jdg 4:20 "If someone comes by and a you, 'Is H8626
2Sa 11:21 ' If he a you this, then say to him, 'Moreover NDT
1Ki 8:43 Do whatever the foreigner a of you, so H7924
2Ch 6:33 Do whatever the foreigner a of you, so H7924
Est 5: 5 "so that we may do what Esther a." H1821
Jer 39:12 harm him but do for him whatever he a." H1819
Da 2:10 on earth who can do what the king a! A10418
Da 2:11 What the king a is too difficult. No one A10689
Am 6:10 house to burn them a anyone who might H606
Zec 13: 6 If someone a, 'What are these wounds on H606
Mt 5:42 Give to the one who a you, and do not turn G160
Mt 7: 8 For everyone who a receives; the one who G160
Mt 7: 9 if your son a for bread, will give him G160
Mt 7:10 Or if he a for a fish, will give him a snake? G160
Mt 12:39 adulterous generation a for a sign! G2118
Mk 11: 3 If anyone a you, 'Why are you doing this?' G3306
Mk 14:14 of the house he enters, 'The Teacher a: G3306
Lk 6:30 Give to everyone who a you, and if anyone G160
Lk 11:10 For everyone who a receives; the one who G160
Lk 11:11 of you fathers, if your son a for a fish, will G160
Lk 11:12 Or if he a for an egg, will give him a G160
Lk 11:29 It a for a sign, but none will be given it G2426
Lk 19:31 If anyone a you, 'Why are you untying it?' G2263
Lk 22:11 the owner of the house, 'The Teacher a: G3306
Jn 4:10 of God and who it is that a you for a drink, G3306
Jn 16: 5 None of you a me, 'Where are you G2263
1Pe 3:15 everyone who a you to give the reason G160

ASLEEP (26) [SLEEP]

Ge 41: 5 He fell a again and had a second dream H3822
Jdg 4:21 went quietly to him while he lay fast a, H8101
1Sa 26: 7 lying a inside the camp with his spear H3825
1Ki 3:20 from my side while I your servant was a. H3825
1Ki 19: 5 he lay down under the bush and fell a. H3822
Job 3:13 down in peace; I would be a and at rest H3822
Mt 9:24 The girl is not dead but a." But they G2761
Mt 25: 5 they all became drowsy and fell a. G2761
Mt 28:13 stole him away while we were a. G3121
Mk 5:39 The child is not dead but a." G2761
Mk 14:37 said to Peter, "are you a? Couldn't you G2761
Lk 8:23 As they sailed, he fell a. A squall came G934
Lk 8:52 "She is not dead but a." G2761
Lk 22:45 he found them a, exhausted from sorrow. G3121
Jn 11:11 "Our friend Lazarus has fallen a; but I am G3121
Ac 7:60 When he had said this, he fell a. G3121
Ac 13:36 own generation, he fell a; he was buried G3121
Ac 20: 9 When he was sound a G2965+608+3836+5678
1Co 11:30 and a number of you have fallen a. G3121
1Co 15: 6 still living, though some have fallen a. G3121
1Co 15:18 those also who have fallen a in Christ are G3121
1Co 15:20 the firstfruits of those who have fallen a. G3121
1Th 4:14 Jesus those who have fallen a in him. G3121
1Th 4:15 not precede those who have fallen a. G3121
1Th 5: 6 let us not be like others, who are a, but G2761
1Th 5:10 whether we are awake or a, we may live G2761

ASNAH (1)

Ezr 2:50 A, Meunim, Nephusim, H663

ASNAPPAR (KJV) ASHURBANIPAL

ASP, ASPS (KJV) COBRA'S, COBRAS, SERPENTS

ASPATHA (1)

Est 9: 7 They also killed Parshandatha, Dalphon, A, H672

ASPIRES (1)

1Ti 3: 1 Whoever a to be an overseer desires a G3977

ASRIEL (3) [ASRIELITE]

Nu 26:31 through A, the Asrielite clan; through H835
Jos 17: 2 of Abiezer, Helek, A, Shechem, Hepher H835
1Ch 7:14 A was his descendant through his H835

ASRIELITE (1) [ASRIEL]

Nu 26:31 through Asriel, the A clan; through H834

ASS, ASSES (KJV) DONKEY, DONKEYS

ASSAIL (2) [ASSAILANT, ASSAILANTS, ASSAILS]

Ps 3: 6 of thousands a me on every side. H8883+6584
Ps 55: 3 suffering on me and a me in their anger. H8475

ASSAILANT (1) [ASSAIL]

Dt 25:11 comes to rescue her husband from his a, H5782

ASSAILANTS (1) [ASSAIL]

Ps 35:15 a gathered against me without my H5782

ASSAILS (1) [ASSAIL]

Job 16: 9 God a me and tears me in his anger and H8475

ASSAR See TEL ASSAR

ASSASSINATE (2) [ASSASSINATED, ASSASSINATION, ASSASSINS]

Est 2:21 conspired to a King Xerxes. H8938+3338+928
Est 6: 2 conspired to a King Xerxes. H8938+3338+928

ASSASSINATED (9) [ASSASSINATE]

2Ki 12:20 against him and a him at Beth Millo, H5782
2Ki 15:10 a him and succeeded him as king. H4637
2Ki 15:14 a him and succeeded him as king. H4637
2Ki 15:25 of Gilead with him, he a Pekahiah, along H5782
2Ki 15:30 He attacked and a him, and then H4637
2Ki 21:23 against him and a the king in his palace. H4637
2Ki 25:25 ten men and a Gedaliah H5782+2256+4637
2Ch 33:24 against him and a him in his palace. H4637
Jer 41:16 after Ishmael had a Gedaliah son of H5782

ASSASSINATION (1) [ASSASSINATE]

Jer 41: 4 The day after Gedaliah's a, before H4637

ASSASSINS (1) [ASSASSINATE]

2Ki 14: 6 did not put the children of the a to death, H5782

ASSAULT (3) [ASSAULTS]

Dt 21: 5 to decide all cases of dispute and a. H5596
Job 28: 9 People a the flinty rock with their H8938+928
Ps 62: 3 How long will you a me? Would all of you H2109

ASSAULTS (2) [ASSAULT]

Dt 17: 8 lawsuits or **a**—take them to H5596+4200+5596
Dt 19:11 lies in wait, **a** and kills a neighbor H7756+6584

ASSAY, ASSAYED (KJV) TRIED, VENTURES

ASSEMBLE (33) [ASSEMBLED, ASSEMBLIES, ASSEMBLING, ASSEMBLY]

Ge 49: 2 "**A** and listen, sons of Jacob; listen to your H7695
Ex 3:16 **a** the elders of Israel and say to them H665
Nu 8: 9 tent of meeting and **a** the whole Israelite H7735
Nu 10: 3 whole community *is to* **a** before you at the H3585
Nu 10: 4 of the clans of Israel—*are to* **a** before you. H3585
Dt 4:10 "**A** the people before me to hear my H7735
Dt 31:12 **A** the people—men, women and children H7735
Dt 31:28 **A** before me all the elders of your tribes H7735
Jdg 21: 5 *has* failed *to* **a** before H6590+928+2021+7736
Jdg 21: 5 anyone who failed *to* **a** before the LORD at H6590
Jdg 21: 8 of Israel failed *to* **a** before the LORD at H6590
1Sa 7: 5 Then Samuel said, "**A** all Israel at Mizpah H7695
2Sa 3:21 me go at once and **a** all Israel for my lord H7695
1Ch 22: 2 David gave orders to **a** the foreigners H4043
1Ch 28: 1 **summoned** all the officials of Israel **to a** H7735
Ezr 10: 7 all the exiles to **a** *in* Jerusalem. H7695
Ne 7: 5 God put it into my heart *to* **a** the nobles, H7695
Est 8:11 city the right to **a** and protect themselves; H7735
Ps 47: 9 of the nations **a** as the people of the H665
Ps 102:22 and the kingdoms **a** to worship the H7695+3481
Isa 4: 5 Zion and over *those who* **a** there a cloud H5246
Isa 11:12 *he will* **a** the scattered people of Judah H7695
Isa 43: 9 nations gather together and the peoples **a**. H665
Isa 45:20 **a**, *you* fugitives from the nations. H5602+3481
Isa 60: 4 All **a** and come to you; your sons come H7695
Jer 49:14 nations to say, "**A yourselves** to attack it! H7695
Eze 39:17 '**A** and come together from all around to H7695
Da 11:10 will prepare for war and **a** a great army, H665
Joel 3:11 you nations from every side, and **a** there. H7695
Am 3: 9 "**A** *yourselves* on the mountains of Samaria H665
Mic 4: 6 *I will* **a** the exiles and those I have H7695
Zep 3: 8 I have decided to **a** the nations, to gather H665
Ac 22:30 all the members of the Sanhedrin *to* **a**. *G5302*

ASSEMBLED (46) [ASSEMBLE]

Ex 35: 1 Moses **a** the whole Israelite community H7735
Dt 33: 5 when the leaders of the people **a**, H665
Dt 33:21 When the heads of the people **a**, he H910
Jos 24: 1 Then Joshua **a** all the tribes of Israel at H665
Jdg 9:47 Abimelek heard that they *had* **a** there, H7695
Jdg 10:17 the Israelites **a** and camped at Mizpah. H665
Jdg 16:23 rulers of the Philistines **a** to offer a great H665
Jdg 20: 1 together as one and **a** before the LORD in H7735
1Sa 7: 6 When *they had* **a** at Mizpah, they drew H7695
1Sa 7: 7 heard that Israel *had* **a** at Mizpah, H7695
1Sa 13: 5 The Philistines **a** to fight Israel, with three H665
1Sa 14:20 Saul and all his men **a** and went to the H2410
1Sa 17: 1 forces for war and **a** *at* Sokoh in Judah. H665
1Sa 17: 2 Saul and the Israelites **a** and camped in the H665
1Sa 25: 1 all Israel **a** and mourned for him H7695
1Sa 28: 4 The Philistines **a** and came and set up H7695
2Sa 2:30 pursuing Abner and **a** the whole army. H7695
1Ki 18:20 all Israel and **a** the prophets on Mount H7695
1Ki 20:15 Then *he* **a** the rest of the Israelites, 7,000 H7212
1Ch 13: 5 So David **a** all Israel, from the Shihor H7735
1Ch 15: 3 David **a** all Israel in Jerusalem to bring up H7735
2Ch 12: 5 of Judah who *had* **a** in Jerusalem for H665
2Ch 15: 9 Then *he* **a** all Judah and Benjamin and H7695
2Ch 15:10 *They* **a** *at* Jerusalem in the third month of H7695
2Ch 20:26 On the fourth day *they* **a** in the Valley of H7735
2Ch 29: 4 **a** them in the square on the east side H665
2Ch 29:15 When *they had* **a** their fellow Levites and H665
2Ch 30: 3 the people *had* not **a** in Jerusalem. H665
2Ch 30:13 large crowd of people **a** *in* Jerusalem to H665
2Ch 30:25 and all who *had* **a** from Israel, H7736+995
2Ch 32: 6 over the people and **a** them before him in H7695
Ezr 3: 1 the people **a together** as one in Jerusalem. H665
Ezr 8:15 *I* **a** them at the canal that flows toward H7695
Ne 5:16 All my men **were a** there for the work; we H7695
Est 2:19 When the virgins **were a** a second time H7695
Est 9: 2 The Jews **a** in their cities in all the H7735
Est 9:16 provinces also **a** to protect themselves H7735
Est 9:18 *had* **a** on the thirteenth and fourteenth H7735
Ps 7: 7 Let the **a** peoples gather around you H6337
Da 3: 3 provincial officials **a** for the dedication of A10359
Mt 26: 3 of the people **a** in the palace of the *G5251*
Mt 26:57 teachers of the law and the elders *had* **a**. *G5251*
Lk 1:10 all the **a worshipers** were *G4436+3836+3295*
Lk 24:33 the Eleven and those with them, **a together** *G125*
Ac 28:17 leaders. *When* they *had* **a**, Paul said to *G5302*
1Co 5: 4 *So when* you *are* **a** and I am with you in *G5251*

ASSEMBLIES (5) [ASSEMBLE]

Lev 23: 2 which you are to proclaim as sacred **a**. H5246
Lev 23: 4 the sacred **a** you are to proclaim at their H5246
Lev 23:37 to proclaim as sacred **a** for bringing food H5246
Isa 1:13 I cannot bear your worthless **a**. H6809
Am 5:21 festivals; your **a** are a stench to me. H6809

ASSEMBLING (1) [ASSEMBLE]

1Sa 13:11 that the Philistines *were* **a** at Mikmash, H665

ASSEMBLY (163) [ASSEMBLE]

Ge 49: 6 let me not join their **a**, for they have killed H7736
Ex 12:16 On the first day hold a sacred **a**, and H5246
Ex 16: 3 this desert to starve this entire **a** to death." H7736
Lev 4:14 the **a** must bring a young bull as a sin H7736
Lev 8: 3 gather the entire **a** at the entrance to H6337
Lev 8: 4 the **a** gathered at the entrance to the H6337
Lev 8: 5 Moses said to the **a**, "This is what the H6337
Lev 9: 5 the entire **a** came near and stood H6337
Lev 19: 2 "Speak to the entire **a** *of* Israel and say to H6337
Lev 23: 3 is a day of sabbath rest, a day of sacred **a**. H5246
Lev 23: 7 day hold a sacred **a** and do no regular H5246
Lev 23: 8 day hold a sacred **a** and do no regular H5246
Lev 23:21 to proclaim a sacred **a** and do no regular H5246
Lev 23:24 a sacred **a** commemorated with trumpet H5246
Lev 23:27 Hold a sacred **a** and deny yourselves, and H5246
Lev 23:35 The first day is a sacred **a**; do no regular H5246
Lev 23:36 day hold a sacred **a** and present a food H5246
Lev 23:36 It is the **closing special a**; do no regular H6809
Lev 24:14 his head, and the entire **a** is to stone him. H6337
Lev 24:16 The entire **a** must stone them H6337
Nu 10: 7 To gather the **a**, blow the trumpets, but H7736
Nu 13:26 to the whole **a** and showed them the H6337
Nu 14: 2 and the whole **a** said to them, "If H6337
Nu 14: 5 of the whole Israelite **a** gathered there. H6337
Nu 14: 7 said to the entire Israelite **a**, "The H6337
Nu 14:10 But the whole **a** talked about stoning H6337
Nu 15:33 to Moses and Aaron and the whole **a**, H6337
Nu 15:35 The whole **a** must stone him outside the H6337
Nu 15:36 So the **a** took him outside the camp and H6337
Nu 16: 3 do you set yourselves above the LORD's **a**?" H7736
Nu 16:19 glory of the LORD appeared to the entire **a**. H6337
Nu 16:21 yourselves from this **a** so I can put an end H6337
Nu 16:22 with the entire **a** when only one man H6337
Nu 16:24 "Say to the **a**, 'Move away from the tents H6337
Nu 16:26 He warned the **a**, "Move back from the H6337
Nu 16:42 But when the **a** gathered in opposition to H6337
Nu 16:45 "Get away from this **a** so I can put an end H6337
Nu 16:46 hurry to the **a** to make atonement for H6337
Nu 16:47 and ran into the midst of the **a**. H7736
Nu 20: 6 Aaron went from the **a** to the entrance to H7736
Nu 20: 8 your brother Aaron gather the **a** together. H6337
Nu 20:10 Aaron gathered the **a** together in front of H7736
Nu 25: 6 the whole **a** *of* Israel while they H6337
Nu 25: 7 saw this, he left the **a**, took a spear in his H6337
Nu 27: 2 the whole **a** at the entrance to H6337
Nu 27:19 the entire **a** and commission him in H6337
Nu 27:22 before Eleazar the priest and the whole **a**. H6337
Nu 28:18 day hold a sacred **a** and do no regular H5246
Nu 28:25 day hold a sacred **a** and do no regular H5246
Nu 28:26 hold a sacred **a** and do no regular work. H5246
Nu 29: 1 month hold a sacred **a** and do no regular H5246
Nu 29: 7 of this seventh month hold a sacred **a**. H5246
Nu 29:12 hold a sacred **a** and do no regular work. H5246
Nu 29:35 day hold a **closing special a** and do no H6809
Nu 31:12 the Israelite **a** at their camp on the H6337
Nu 35:12 die before they stand trial before the **a**. H6337
Nu 35:24 the **a** must judge between the accused H6337
Nu 35:25 The **a** must protect the one accused of H6337
Dt 5:22 voice to your whole **a** there on the H7736
Dt 9:10 out of the fire, on the day of the **a**. H7736
Dt 10: 4 out of the fire, on the day of the **a**. H7736
Dt 16: 8 seventh day hold an **a** to the LORD your H6809
Dt 18:16 Horeb on the day of the **a** when you said, H7736
Dt 23: 1 cutting may enter the **a** *of* the LORD. H7736
Dt 23: 2 descendants may enter the **a** *of* the LORD, H7736
Dt 23: 3 descendants may enter the **a** *of* the LORD, H7736
Dt 23: 8 born to them may enter the **a** *of* the LORD. H7736
Dt 31:30 in the hearing of the whole **a** *of* Israel: H7736
Dt 33: 4 gave us, the possession of the **a** *of* Jacob. H7737
Jos 8:35 did not read to the whole **a** *of* Israel, H7736
Jos 9:15 the leaders of the **a** ratified it by oath. H6337
Jos 9:18 the leaders of the **a** had sworn an oath to H6337
Jos 9:18 The whole **a** grumbled against the H6337
Jos 9:21 carriers in the service of the whole **a**." H6337
Jos 9:27 woodcutters and water carriers for the **a**, H6337
Jos 18: 1 The whole **a** *of* the Israelites gathered at H6337
Jos 20: 6 trial before the **a** and until the death of H6337
Jos 20: 9 blood prior to standing trial before the **a**. H6337
Jos 22:12 the whole **a** *of* Israel gathered at Shiloh to H6337
Jos 22:16 "The whole **a** *of* the LORD says: 'How could H6337
Jdg 20: 2 took their places in the **a** *of* God's people, H7736
Jdg 21: 8 Gilead had come to the camp for the **a**. H7736
Jdg 21:10 So the **a** sent twelve thousand fighting H6337
Jdg 21:13 Then the whole **a** sent an offer of peace H6337
Jdg 21:16 And the elders of the **a** said, "With the H6337
1Ki 8: 5 the entire **a** *of* Israel that had H6337
1Ki 8:14 While the whole **a** *of* Israel was standing H7736
1Ki 8:22 the LORD in front of the whole **a** *of* Israel, H7736
1Ki 8:55 blessed the whole **a** *of* Israel in a loud H7736
1Ki 8:65 with him—a vast **a**, people from Lebo H7736
1Ki 12: 3 he and the whole **a** *of* Israel went to H7736
1Ki 12:20 called him to the **a** and made him king H6337
2Ki 10:20 Jehu said, "Call an **a** in honor of Baal." H6809
1Ch 13: 2 He then said to the whole **a** *of* Israel, "If it H7736
1Ch 13: 4 The whole **a** agreed to do this, because it H7736
1Ch 28: 8 sight of all Israel and of the **a** *of* the LORD, H7736
1Ch 29: 1 Then King David said to the whole **a**: "My H7736
1Ch 29:10 the LORD in the presence of the whole **a**, H7736
1Ch 29:20 Then David said to the whole **a**, "Praise H7736
2Ch 1: 3 the whole **a** went to the high H7736
2Ch 1: 5 so Solomon and the **a** inquired of him H7736
2Ch 5: 6 the entire **a** *of* Israel that had H6337
2Ch 6: 3 While the whole **a** *of* Israel was standing H7736
2Ch 6:12 front of the whole **a** *of* Israel and spread H7736
2Ch 6:13 before the whole **a** *of* Israel and spread H7736
2Ch 7: 8 with him—a vast **a**, people from Lebo H7736
2Ch 7: 9 On the eighth day they held an **a**, for they H6809
2Ch 20: 5 stood up in the **a** *of* Judah and Jerusalem H7736
2Ch 20:14 of Asaph, as he stood in the **a**. H7736
2Ch 23: 3 the whole **a** made a covenant with the H7736
2Ch 24: 6 the LORD and by the **a** of Israel for the tent H7736
2Ch 28:14 the presence of the officials and all the **a**. H7736
2Ch 29:23 were brought before the king and the **a**, H7736
2Ch 29:28 The whole **a** bowed in worship, while the H7736
2Ch 29:31 So the **a** brought sacrifices and thank H7736
2Ch 29:32 burnt offerings the **a** brought was seventy H7736
2Ch 30: 2 the whole **a** in Jerusalem decided to H7736
2Ch 30: 4 right both to the king and to the whole **a**. H7736
2Ch 30:23 The whole **a** then agreed to celebrate the H7736
2Ch 30:24 thousand sheep and goats for the **a**, H7736
2Ch 30:25 The entire **a** *of* Judah rejoiced, along with H7736
Ezr 10: 8 be expelled from the **a** *of* the exiles. H7736
Ezr 10:12 The whole **a** responded with a loud voice H7736
Ezr 10:14 Let our officials act for the whole **a**. Then H7736
Ne 5:13 At this the whole **a** said, "Amen," and H7736
Ne 8: 2 the priest brought the Law before the **a**, H7736
Ne 8:18 with the regulation, there was an **a**. H6809
Ne 13: 1 ever be admitted into the **a** *of* God, H7736
Job 30:28 I stand up in the **a** and cry for help. H7736
Ps 1: 5 sinners in the **a** *of* the righteous. H6337
Ps 22:22 to my people; in the **a** I will praise you. H7736
Ps 22:25 the theme of my praise in the great **a**; H7736
Ps 26: 5 I abhor the **a** *of* evildoers and refuse to sit H7736
Ps 35:18 I will give you thanks in the great **a** H7736
Ps 40: 9 I proclaim your saving acts in the great **a** H7736
Ps 40:10 your faithfulness from the great **a**. H7736
Ps 68:26 praise the LORD in the **a** *of* Israel. H5227
Ps 82: 1 God presides in the great **a**; he renders H6337
Ps 89: 5 faithfulness too, in the **a** *of* the holy ones. H7736
Ps 107:32 them exalt him in the **a** *of* the people H7736
Ps 111: 1 in the council of the upright and in the **a**. H6337
Ps 149: 1 his praise in the **a** *of* his faithful people. H7736
Pr 5:14 serious trouble in the **a** *of* God's people." H7736
Pr 24: 7 in the **a at the gate** they must not open H9133
Pr 26:26 their wickedness will be exposed in the **a**. H7736
Isa 14:13 I will sit enthroned on the mount of **a**, on H4595
Jer 26:17 said to the entire **a** *of* people, H7736
Jer 44:15 present—a large **a**—and all the people H7736
La 1:10 those you had forbidden to enter your **a**. H7736
Joel 1:14 holy fast; call a **sacred a**. Summon the H6809
Joel 2:15 declare a holy fast, call a **sacred a**. H6809
Joel 2:16 consecrate the **a**; bring together the H7736
Mic 2: 5 have no one in the **a** *of* the LORD to divide H7736
Lk 23: 1 Then the whole **a** rose and led him off to *G4436*
Ac 5:21 the full **a of the elders** of Israel—and *G1172*
Ac 7:38 He was in the **a** in the wilderness, with the *G1711*
Ac 15:12 The whole **a** became silent as they *G4436*
Ac 19:32 The **a** was in confusion: Some were *G1711*
Ac 19:39 bring up, it must be settled in a legal **a**. *G1711*
Ac 19:41 After he had said this, he dismissed the **a**. *G1711*
Ac 23: 7 the Sadducees, and the **a** was divided. *G4436*
Heb 2:12 in the **a** I will sing your praises. *G1711*
Heb 12:22 upon thousands of angels *in* **joyful a**, *G4108*

ASSERTED (2) [ASSERTING]

Lk 22:59 About an hour later another **a**, "Certainly *G1462*
1Th 2: 6 could have **a** our **authority**. *G1877+983+1639*

ASSERTING (2) [ASSERTED]

Ac 24: 9 accusation, **a** that these things were true. *G5763*
2Th 2: 2 **a** that the day of the Lord has already *G6055*

ASSESSMENTS (1)

2Ki 23:35 people of the land according to their **a**. H6886

ASSHUR (NIV84) ASHUR

ASSHURITES (NIV84) ASHURITES

ASSIGN (12) [ASSIGNED, ASSIGNMENT, ASSIGNMENTS, ASSIGNS, REASSIGN]

Nu 4:19 the sanctuary and **a** to each man his work H8492
Nu 4:27 *You shall* **a** to them as their responsibility H7212
Nu 4:32 **A** to each man the specific things he is to H7212
Nu 8:26 is how *you are to* **a** the responsibilities of H6913
Nu 34:13 "**A** this land by lot **as an inheritance**. The H5706
Nu 34:17 *are to* **a** the land for you **as an inheritance** H5706
Nu 34:18 leader from each tribe to **help a** the land. H5706
Nu 34:29 commanded to **a** *the* **inheritance** *to* the H5706
1Sa 8:12 Some he *will* **a** to be commanders of H8492
Job 22:24 **a** your nuggets to the dust, your gold H8883
Mt 24:51 him to pieces and **a** him a place with the *G5502*
Lk 12:46 him to pieces and **a** him a place with the *G5502*

ASSIGNED (45) [ASSIGN]

Ge 40: 4 captain of the guard **a** them *to* Joseph, H7212
Nu 2: 9 All the *men* **a** to the camp of Judah H7212
Nu 2:16 All the *men* **a** to the camp of Reuben H7212
Nu 2:24 All the *men* **a** to the camp of Ephraim H7212
Nu 2:31 All the *men* **a** to the camp of Dan number H7212
Nu 4:49 each *was* **a** his work and told what to carry H7212
Jos 13: 8 the servant of the LORD, *had* **a** it to them. H5989
Jos 14: 2 inheritances were **a** by lot to the nine and NDT
Jos 19:51 tribal clans of Israel **a** by lot at Shiloh in H5706
Jos 21:10 these towns were **a to** the descendants of H4200
Jos 24: 4 *I* **a** the hill country of Seir to Esau, but H5989

1Sa 15:20 "I went on the mission the LORD **a** me. I H8938
1Sa 27: 5 *let* a place *be* **a** to me in one of the H5989
1Sa 29: 4 that he may return to the place *you* **a** him. H7212
1Ki 7:14 King Solomon and did all the **work** *a to* him. AIT
1Ki 14:27 to replace them and **a** these to the H7212
2Ki 8: 6 Then he **a** an official to her case and said H5989
1Ch 6:48 Their fellow Levites **were a** to all the other H5989
1Ch 6:54 they were **a to** the descendants of Aaron H4200
1Ch 9:22 *had been* **a to** their **positions** of trust *by* H3569
1Ch 9:29 Others **were a** to take care of the H4948
1Ch 26:29 his sons were **a** duties away from the H4200
2Ch 2:18 *He* **a** 70,000 of them to be carriers and H6913
2Ch 12:10 to replace them and **a** these to the H7212
2Ch 25: 5 Judah together and **a** them according to H6641
2Ch 30:22 days they ate their **a portion** and offered H4595
2Ch 31: 2 Hezekiah **a** the priests and Levites to H6641
2Ch 33: 8 leave the land *I* **a** to your ancestors, H6641
Ne 12:31 *I* also **a** two large choirs to give thanks H6641
Ne 13:10 learned that the **portions** *a to* the Levites had AIT
Ne 13:30 foreign, and **a** them duties, each to H6641
Est 2: 9 He **a** to her seven female attendants H5989
Est 4: 5 one of the king's eunuchs **a** to attend her H6641
Job 7: 3 nights of misery *have been* **a** to me. H4948
Ps 104: 8 the valleys, to the place *you* **a** for them. H3569
Isa 53: 9 He *was* **a** a grave with the wicked, and H5989
Eze 4: 5 I *have* **a** you the same number of days as H5989
Eze 4: 6 people of Judah. *I have* **a** you 40 days, a H5989
Da 1: 5 The king **a** them a daily amount of food H4948
Da 1:10 the king, who *has* **a** your food and drink. H4948
Mk 13:34 each *with* their **a task**, and tells *G2240*
Ac 22:10 be told all that you *have been* **a** to do. *G5435*
1Co 3: 5 as the Lord *has* **a** to each his **task**. *G1443*
1Co 7:17 whatever situation the Lord *has* **a** to them, *G3532*
2Co 10:13 sphere of service God himself *has* **a** to us, *G3532*

ASSIGNMENT (1) [ASSIGN]

1Ch 23:11 were counted as one family with one **a**. H7213

ASSIGNMENTS (1) [ASSIGN]

2Ch 23:18 *to* whom David *had* **made a** in the temple H2745

ASSIGNS (1) [ASSIGN]

Mic 2: 4 takes it from me! *He* **a** our fields to traitors H2745

ASSIR (4)

Ex 6:24 The sons of Korah were **A**, Elkanah and H661
1Ch 6:22 Korah his son, **A** his son, H661
1Ch 6:23 Ebiasaph his son, **A** his son, H661
1Ch 6:37 the son of **A**, the son of Ebiasaph, H661

ASSIST (9) [ASSISTANCE, ASSISTANT, ASSISTANTS, ASSISTED]

Nu 1: 5 names of the men who *are to* **a** you: H6641+907
Nu 3: 6 present them to Aaron the priest *to* **a** him. H9250
Nu 8:26 *They may* **a** their brothers in performing H9250
Nu 18: 2 to join you and **a** you when you and your H9250
2Ch 8:14 the praise and to **a** the priests according H9250
2Ch 13:10 sons of Aaron, and the Levites **a** them. H4856
Ezr 8:20 officials had established to **a** the Levites. H6275
Job 29:12 the fatherless who had none *to* **a** them. H6468
Ro 15:24 and *to have* you **a** me **on** my **journey** *G4636*

ASSISTANCE (1) [ASSIST]

Ezr 8:36 *who* then **gave a** *to* the people and *to* the H5951

ASSISTANT (2) [ASSIST]

Dt 1:38 But your **a**, Joshua son of H6641+4200+7156
Ne 13:13 Mattaniah, their **a**, because they H6584+3338

ASSISTANTS (2) [ASSIST]

2Ch 31:13 Benaiah were **a** of Konaniah and H7224
Ne 5:15 Their **a** also lorded it over the people H5853

ASSISTED (3) [ASSIST]

2Ch 31:15 and Shekaniah **a** him faithfully in H6584+3338
Ezr 1: 6 their neighbors **a** them with H2616+928+3338
Ezr 6:22 so that he **a** them in the work H2616+928+3338

ASSOCIATE (11) [ASSOCIATED, ASSOCIATES]

Jos 23: 7 *Do* not **a with** these nations that H995+928
Jos 23:12 with them and **a with** them, H995+928
1Ch 6:39 Heman's **a** Asaph, who served at his H278
Ps 26: 4 the deceitful, nor *do I* **a** with hypocrites. H995
Pr 22:24 *do* not **a** with one easily angered H995
Jn 4: 9 For Jews *do* not **a with** Samaritans.) *G5178*
Ac 10:28 our law for a Jew *to* **a with** or visit a *G3140*
Ro 12:16 but *be willing to* **a with** people of low *G5270*
1Co 5: 9 in my letter not *to* **a with** sexually immoral *G5264*
1Co 5:11 to you *that you must* not **a with** anyone *G5264*
2Th 3:14 *Do* not **a** with them, in order that they *G5264*

ASSOCIATED (5) [ASSOCIATE]

Nu 16:32 all those **a with** Korah, together with H4200
Ne 13: 4 He was **closely a** with Tobiah, H7940
Eze 37:16 to Judah and the Israelites **a with** him. H2492
Eze 37:16 Ephraim) and all the Israelites **a with** him. H2492
Eze 37:19 of the Israelite tribes **a with** him, and H2492

ASSOCIATES (29) [ASSOCIATE]

1Ch 6:44 from their **a**, the Merarites, at his left H278
1Ch 16: 7 Asaph and his **a** to give praise to the H278
1Ch 16:37 left Asaph and his **a** before the ark of the H278
1Ch 16:38 his sixty-eight **a** to minister with them. H278
Ezr 3: 2 of Shealtiel and his **a** began to build the H278
Ezr 4: 7 the rest of his **a** wrote a letter to H4056
Ezr 4: 9 together with the rest of their **a**—the A10360
Ezr 4:17 the rest of their **a** living in Samaria and A10360
Ezr 4:23 Shimshai the secretary and their **a**, A10360
Ezr 5: 3 their **a** went to them and asked, A10360
Ezr 5: 6 Shethar-Bozenai and their **a**, the A10360
Ezr 6:13 their **a** carried it out with A10360
Ne 4: 2 in the presence of his **a** and the army of H278
Ne 10:10 their **a**: Shebaniah, Hodiah, Kelita H278
Ne 11:12 their **a**, who carried on work for the H278
Ne 11:13 his **a**, who were heads of families H278
Ne 11:14 his **a**, who were men of standing—128 H278
Ne 11:17 second among his **a**; and Abda son of H278
Ne 11:19 Talmon and their **a**, who kept watch at the H278
Ne 12: 7 priests and their **a** in the days of Joshua H278
Ne 12: 8 together with his **a**, was in charge of the H278
Ne 12: 9 Unni, their **a**, stood opposite them in H278
Ne 12:24 Kadmiel, and their **a**, who stood opposite H278
Ne 12:36 his **a**—Shemaiah, Azarel, Milalai H278
Job 34: 8 with evildoers; he **a** with the wicked. H2143
Zec 3: 8 Joshua, you and your **a** seated before you H8276
Ac 5:17 Then the high priest and all his **a** *G3836+5250*
Ac 5:21 the high priest and his **a** arrived, *G3836+5250*
Ac 22: 5 letters from them to their **a** in Damascus, *G81*

ASSOS (2)

Ac 20:13 on ahead to the ship and sailed for **A**, *G840*
Ac 20:14 When he met us at **A**, we took him aboard *G840*

ASSUME (3) [ASSUMED]

Ne 10:32 *We* **a the responsibility for carrying out** H6641+6584
Ne 10:35 "We also **a** responsibility for bringing to the NDT
1Ti 2:12 to teach or *to* **a authority over** a man; *G883*

ASSUMED (2) [ASSUME]

1Sa 14:47 After Saul *had* **a** rule over Israel, he H4334
Ac 21:29 city with Paul and **a** that Paul had brought *G3787*

ASSUR (KJV) ASSYRIA

ASSURANCE (6) [ASSURE]

1Sa 17:18 are and bring back *some* **a** *from* them. H6859
Est 9:30 kingdom—words of goodwill and **a**— H622
Job 24:22 become established, *they* **have** no **a** of life. H586
1Ti 3:13 standing and great **a** in their faith in *G4244*
Heb 10:22 heart and with the **full a** that faith brings, *G4443*
Heb 11: 1 we hope for and **a** about what we do not *G1793*

ASSURE (2) [ASSURANCE, ASSURED, ASSUREDLY, ASSURES, REASSURE, REASSURED]

Lk 4:25 *I* **a** you that there were many *G2093+237+3306*
Gal 1:20 **I a you** before God that what I am writing *G2627*

ASSURED (7) [ASSURE]

Dt 9: 3 But *be* **a** today that the LORD your God is H3359
Jos 2:14 the men **a** her. "If you don't tell H606
1Sa 10:16 "*He* **a** us that the donkeys had H5583+5583
Job 36: 4 **Be a** that my words are not false; one who H597
Jer 26:15 *Be* **a**, however, that if you put me to H3359+3359
Ac 2:36 "Therefore let all Israel be **a** of this: God *G857*
Col 4:12 in all the will of God, mature and **fully a**. *G4442*

ASSUREDLY (1) [ASSURE]

Jer 32:41 good and will **a** plant them in this H928+622

ASSURES (1) [ASSURE]

Jer 5:24 *who* **a** us *of* the regular weeks of harvest. H9068

ASSWAGE, ASSWAGED (KJV) RECEDED, RELIEF, RELIEVED

ASSYRIA (122) [ASSYRIA'S, ASSYRIAN, ASSYRIANS]

Ge 10:11 From that land he went to **A**, where he built H855
2Ki 15:19 Then Pul king of **A** invaded the land, and H855
2Ki 15:20 of silver to be given to the king of **A**. H855
2Ki 15:20 So the king of **A** withdrew and stayed in H855
2Ki 15:29 king of **A** came and took Ijon, H855
2Ki 15:29 of Naphtali, and deported the people to **A**. H855
2Ki 16: 7 to say to Tiglath-Pileser king of **A**, H855
2Ki 16: 8 palace and sent it as a gift to the king of **A**. H855
2Ki 16: 9 The king of **A** complied by attacking H855
2Ki 16:10 to meet Tiglath-Pileser king of **A**. H855
2Ki 16:18 of the LORD, in deference to the king of **A**. H855
2Ki 17: 3 Shalmaneser king of **A** came up to attack H855
2Ki 17: 4 But the king of **A** discovered that Hoshea H855
2Ki 17: 4 he no longer paid tribute to the king of **A**, H855
2Ki 17: 5 The king of **A** invaded the entire land H855
2Ki 17: 6 the king of **A** captured Samaria and H855
2Ki 17: 6 Samaria and deported the Israelites to **A**. H855
2Ki 17:23 taken from their homeland into exile in **A**, H855
2Ki 17:24 The king of **A** brought people from Babylon H855
2Ki 17:26 It was reported to the king of **A**: "The H855
2Ki 17:27 Then the king of **A** gave this order: "Have H855
2Ki 18: 7 against the king of **A** and did not serve him H855
2Ki 18: 9 Shalmaneser king of **A** marched against H855
2Ki 18:11 The king of **A** deported Israel to Assyria H855
2Ki 18:11 deported Israel to **A** and settled them in H855
2Ki 18:13 Sennacherib king of **A** attacked all the H855
2Ki 18:14 this message to the king of **A** at Lachish: H855
2Ki 18:14 The king of **A** exacted from Hezekiah king H855
2Ki 18:16 of the LORD, and gave it to the king of **A**. H855
2Ki 18:17 The king of **A** sent his supreme H855
2Ki 18:19 is what the great king, the king of **A**, says: H855
2Ki 18:23 a bargain with my master, the king of **A**: H855
2Ki 18:28 the word of the great king, the king of **A**! H855
2Ki 18:30 not be given into the hand of the king of **A**. H855
2Ki 18:31 This is what the king of **A** says: Make H855
2Ki 18:33 his land from the hand of the king of **A**? H855
2Ki 19: 4 the king of **A**, has sent to ridicule H855
2Ki 19: 6 of the king of **A** have blasphemed me. H855
2Ki 19: 8 heard that the king of **A** had left Lachish, H855
2Ki 19:10 be given into the hands of the king of **A**. H855
2Ki 19:11 what the kings of **A** have done to all the H855
2Ki 19:20 prayer concerning Sennacherib king of **A**. H855
2Ki 19:32 the LORD says concerning the king of **A**: H855
2Ki 19:36 So Sennacherib king of **A** broke camp and H855
2Ki 20: 6 this city from the hand of the king of **A**. H855
2Ki 23:29 the Euphrates River to help the king of **A**. H855
1Ch 5: 6 Tiglath-Pileser king of **A** took into exile. H855
1Ch 5:26 Israel stirred up the spirit of Pul king of **A** H855
1Ch 5:26 Tiglath-Pileser king of **A**), who took the H855
2Ch 28:16 King Ahaz sent to the kings of **A** for help. H855
2Ch 28:20 Tiglath-Pileser king of **A** came to him, but H855
2Ch 28:21 presented them to the king of **A**, H855
2Ch 30: 6 escaped from the hand of the kings of **A**. H855
2Ch 32: 1 Sennacherib king of **A** came and invaded H855
2Ch 32: 4 should the kings of **A** come and find plenty H855
2Ch 32: 7 of the king of **A** and the vast army with H855
2Ch 32: 9 Sennacherib king of **A** and all his forces H855
2Ch 32:10 "This is what Sennacherib king of **A** says H855
2Ch 32:11 will save us from the hand of the king of **A**, H855
2Ch 32:22 Sennacherib king of **A** and from the hand H855
2Ch 33:11 the army commanders of the king of **A**, H855
Ezr 4: 2 since the time of Esarhaddon king of **A**, H855
Ezr 6:22 attitude of the king of **A** so that he assisted H855
Ne 9:32 from the days of the kings of **A** until today. H855
Ps 83: 8 Even **A** has joined them to reinforce Lot's H855
Isa 7:17 from Judah—he will bring the king of **A**." H855
Isa 7:18 in Egypt and for bees from the land of **A**. H855
Isa 7:20 the king of **A**—to shave your head H855
Isa 8: 4 Samaria will be carried off by the king of **A**." H855
Isa 8: 7 the king of **A** with all his pomp. H855
Isa 10:12 punish the king of **A** for the willful pride H855
Isa 11:11 the surviving remnant of his people from **A**, H855
Isa 11:16 remnant of his people that is left from **A**, H855
Isa 19:23 there will be a highway from Egypt to **A**. H855
Isa 19:23 will go to Egypt and the Egyptians to **A**. H855
Isa 19:24 along with Egypt and **A**, a blessing on the H855
Isa 19:25 be Egypt my people, **A** my handiwork, and H855
Isa 20: 1 sent by Sargon king of **A**, came to Ashdod H855
Isa 20: 4 so the king of **A** will lead away stripped H855
Isa 20: 6 help and deliverance from the king of **A**! H855
Isa 27:13 were perishing in **A** and those who H824+855
Isa 30:31 The voice of the LORD will shatter **A**; with H855
Isa 31: 8 "**A** will fall by no human sword; a sword H855
Isa 36: 1 Sennacherib king of **A** attacked all the H855
Isa 36: 2 Then the king of **A** sent his field H855
Isa 36: 4 is what the great king, the king of **A**, says: H855
Isa 36: 8 a bargain with my master, the king of **A**: H855
Isa 36:13 the words of the great king, the king of **A**! H855
Isa 36:15 not be given into the hand of the king of **A**. H855
Isa 36:16 This is what the king of **A** says: Make H855
Isa 36:18 their lands from the hand of the king of **A**? H855
Isa 37: 4 the king of **A**, has sent to ridicule H855
Isa 37: 6 of the king of **A** have blasphemed me. H855
Isa 37: 8 heard that the king of **A** had left Lachish, H855
Isa 37:10 be given into the hands of the king of **A**. H855
Isa 37:11 what the kings of **A** have done to all the H855
Isa 37:21 to me concerning Sennacherib king of **A**, H855
Isa 37:33 the LORD says concerning the king of **A**: H855
Isa 37:37 So Sennacherib king of **A** broke camp and H855
Isa 38: 6 this city from the hand of the king of **A**. H855
Isa 52: 4 Egypt to live; lately, **A** has oppressed them. H855
Jer 2:18 And why go to **A** to drink water from the H855
Jer 2:36 disappointed by Egypt as you were by **A**. H855
Jer 50:17 The first to devour them was the king of **A** H855
Jer 50:18 his land as I punished the king of **A**. H855
La 5: 6 to Egypt and **A** to get enough bread. H855
Eze 31: 3 Consider **A**, once a cedar in Lebanon, with H855
Eze 32:22 "**A** is there with her whole army; she is H855
Hos 5:13 then Ephraim turned to **A**, and sent to the H855
Hos 7:11 now calling to Egypt, now turning to **A**. H855
Hos 8: 9 they have gone up to **A** like a wild donkey H855
Hos 9: 3 return to Egypt and eat unclean food in **A**. H855
Hos 10: 6 It will be carried to **A** as tribute for the H855
Hos 11: 5 to Egypt and will not **A** rule over them H855
Hos 11:11 like sparrows, from **A**, fluttering like H824+855
Hos 12: 1 makes a treaty with **A** and sends olive oil H855
Hos 14: 3 **A** cannot save us; we will not mount H855
Mic 5: 6 who will rule the land of **A** with the sword H855
Mic 7:12 will come to you from **A** and the cities of H855
Na 3:18 King of **A**, your shepherds slumber; your H855
Zep 2:13 his hand against the north and destroy **A**, H855
Zec 10:10 back from Egypt and gather them from **A**. H855

ASSYRIA'S (1) [ASSYRIA]

Zec 10:11 **A** pride will be brought down and Egypt's H855

ASSYRIAN (7) [ASSYRIA]

2Ki 19:17 that the **A** kings have laid waste these H855
2Ki 19:35 eighty-five thousand in the **A** camp. H855
2Ch 32:21 officers in the camp of the **A** king. H855
Isa 10: 5 "Woe to the **A**, the rod of my anger, in H855
Isa 14:25 I will crush the **A** in my land; on my H855
Isa 37:18 that the **A** kings have laid waste all these H855

A

Isa 37:36 eighty-five thousand in the **A** camp. H855

ASSYRIANS (13) [ASSYRIA]

2Ki 18:10 At the end of three years the **A** took it. So NDT
Isa 10:24 do not be afraid of the **A**, who beat you H855
Isa 19:23 The **A** will go to Egypt and the Egyptians to H855
Isa 19:23 The Egyptians and **A** will worship together H855
Isa 23:13 The **A** have made it a place for desert H855
Eze 16:28 in prostitution with the **A** too, H1201+855
Eze 23: 5 she lusted after her lovers, the **A**—warriors H855
Eze 23: 7 the elite of the **A** and defiled herself H1201+855
Eze 23: 9 of her lovers, the **A**, for whom she H1201+855
Eze 23:12 She too lusted after the **A** H1201+855
Eze 23:23 and all the **A** with them H1201+855
Mic 5: 5 our peace when the **A** invade our land H855
Mic 5: 6 deliver us from the **A** when they invade our H855

ASTIR (1) [STIR]

Isa 14: 9 of the dead below *is* **all a** to meet you at H8074

ASTONISHED (19) [ASTONISHMENT]

Mt 12:23 All the people *were* **a** and said, "Could *G2014*
Mt 19:25 heard this, *they were* greatly **a** and asked *G1742*
Mt 22:33 heard this, *they were* **a** at his teaching. *G1742*
Mk 5:42 At this *they were* completely **a**. *G2014+1749*
Mk 10:32 the disciples *were* **a**, while those who *G2501*
Lk 2:48 saw him, *they were* **a**. His mother said *G1742*
Lk 5: 9 his companions *were* **a** at the catch *G2502+4321*
Lk 8:56 Her parents *were* **a**, but he ordered them *G2014*
Lk 20:26 there in public. And **a** by his answer, they *G2513*
Ac 3:11 the people were **a** and came running to *G1702*
Ac 4:13 *they were* **a** and they took note that these *G2513*
Ac 8:13 **a** *by* the great signs and miracles he saw. *G2014*
Ac 9:21 those who heard him *were* **a** and asked, *G2014*
Ac 10:45 come with Peter *were* **a** that the gift of *G2014*
Ac 12:16 the door and saw him, *they were* **a**. *G2014*
Gal 1: 6 *I am* **a** that you are so quickly deserting *G2513*
Rev 17: 6 I saw her, *I was* **greatly a**. *G2513+2512+3489*
Rev 17: 7 "Why *are you* **a**? I will explain *G2513*
Rev 17: 8 of the world *will be* **a** when they see the *G2513*

ASTONISHING (1) [ASTONISHMENT]

Da 12: 6 it be before these **a things** are fulfilled?" H7099

ASTONISHMENT (2) [ASTONISHED, ASTONISHING]

Ge 43:33 they **looked** at each other **in a**. H9449
Lk 1:63 and *to* everyone's **a** he wrote, "His *G2513*

ASTOUND (1) [ASTOUNDED, ASTOUNDING]

Isa 29:14 once more I *will* **a** these people with H7098

ASTOUNDED (1) [ASTOUND]

Ps 48: 5 they saw her and *were* **a**; they fled in H9449

ASTOUNDING (2) [ASTOUND]

La 1: 9 Her fall was **a**; there was none to comfort H7099
Da 8:24 He will cause **a** devastation and will H7098

ASTRAY (49) [STRAY]

Nu 5:12 'If a man's wife **goes a** and is unfaithful H8474
Nu 5:19 you and *you have* not **gone a** and H8474
Nu 5:20 But if you *have* **gone a** while married to H8474
Nu 5:29 when a woman **goes a** and makes herself H8474
Dt 13:13 and *have* **led** the people of their town **a**, H5615
Dt 17:17 many wives, or his heart *will be* **led a**. H6073
Dt 27:18 is *anyone who* **leads** the blind **a** on the H8706
1Ki 11: 3 and his wives **led** him **a**. H5742+4213
2Ki 21: 9 Manasseh **led** them **a**, so that they did H9494
2Ch 21:11 themselves and *had* **led** Judah **a**. H5615
2Ch 33: 9 **led** Judah and the people of Jerusalem **a**, H9494
Job 19: 4 If it is true that *I have* **gone a**, my error H8706
Ps 58: 3 Even from birth the wicked **go a**; from the H2319
Ps 95:10 'They are a people whose hearts **go a** H9494
Ps 119:67 Before I was afflicted I **went a**, but now I H8704
Pr 5:23 will die, **led a** by their own great folly. H8706
Pr 7:21 With persuasive words *she* **led** him **a**; she H5742
Pr 10:17 whoever ignores correction **leads** others **a**. H9494
Pr 12:26 the way of the wicked **leads** them **a**. H9494
Pr 14:22 *Do* not those who plot evil **go a**? But H9494
Pr 20: 1 whoever *is* **led a** by them is not wise. H8706
Isa 3:12 your guides **lead** you **a**; they turn you H9494
Isa 9:16 those who are guided **are led a**. H1182
Isa 19:13 of her peoples *have* **led** Egypt **a**. H9494
Isa 30:28 of the peoples a bit *that* **leads** them **a**. H9494
Isa 53: 6 like sheep, *have* **gone a**, each of us has H9494
Jer 4: 1 idols out of my sight and no longer **go a**, H5653
Jer 23:13 by Baal and **led** my people Israel **a**. H9494
Jer 23:32 tell them and **lead** my people **a** with their H9494
Jer 50: 6 shepherds *have* **led** them **a** and caused H9494
Eze 13:10 " 'Because *they* **lead** my people **a**, saying H3246
Eze 44:10 me when Israel **went a** and who H9494
Eze 44:15 when the Israelites **went a** from me, H9494
Eze 48:11 me and *did* not **go a** as the Levites H9494
Eze 48:11 the Levites did when the Israelites **went a**. H9494
Hos 4:12 A spirit of prostitution **leads** them **a**; they H9494
Am 2: 4 they *have been* **led a** *by* false gods, H9494
Mic 3: 5 the prophets *who* **lead** my people **a**, H9494
Ac 19:26 has convinced and **led a** large numbers of *G3496*
1Co 12: 2 were influenced and **led a** to mute idols. *G552*
2Co 11: 3 minds *may* somehow *be* **led a** from your *G5780*
Gal 2:13 their hypocrisy even Barnabas *was* **led a**. *G5270*
Heb 3:10 'Their hearts *are* always **going a**, and they *G4414*
Heb 5: 2 those who are ignorant and *are* **going a**, *G4414*
1Pe 2:25 For "you were like sheep **going a**," but *G4414*
1Jn 2:26 about those *who are trying to* **lead** you **a**. *G4414*
1Jn 3: 7 children, *do* not *let* anyone **lead** you **a**. *G4414*
Rev 12: 9 Satan, who **leads** the whole world **a**. *G4414*
Rev 18:23 magic spell all the nations *were* **led a**. *G4414*

ASTROLOGER (1) [ASTROLOGERS]

Da 2:10 thing of any magician or enchanter or **a**. A10373

ASTROLOGERS (9) [ASTROLOGER]

Isa 47:13 Let your **a** come forward, those H2042+9028
Da 2: 2 sorcerers and **a** to tell him what he had H4169
Da 2: 4 Then the **a** answered the king, "May the H4169
Da 2: 5 The king replied to the **a**, "This is what I A10373
Da 2:10 The **a** answered the king, "There is no A10373
Da 3: 8 At this time some **a** came forward and A10373
Da 4: 7 enchanters, **a** and diviners came, I told A10373
Da 5: 7 the enchanters, **a** and diviners. A10373
Da 5:11 magicians, enchanters, **a** and diviners. A10373

ASUNDER (2)

Ps 136:13 divided the Red Sea **a** His love endures H1617
Isa 24:19 the earth **is split a**, the earth is H7297+7297

ASUPPIM (KJV) SHUPPIM, STOREHOUSE

ASWAN (3)

Isa 49:12 from the west, some from the region of **A**." H6059
Eze 29:10 a desolate waste from Migdol to **A**, H6059
Eze 30: 6 From Migdol to **A** they will fall by the H6059

ASYNCRITUS (1)

Ro 16:14 Greet **A**, Phlegon, Hermes, Patrobas *G850*

AT (2255) See Index of Articles Etc.

ATAD (2)

Ge 50:10 they reached the threshing floor of **A**, H354
Ge 50:11 the mourning at the threshing floor of **A**, H354

ATARAH (1)

1Ch 2:26 whose name was **A**; she was the mother H6499

ATAROTH (4) [ATAROTH ADDAR]

Nu 32: 3 "**A**, Dibon, Jazer, Nimrah, Heshbon H6500
Nu 32:34 The Gadites built up Dibon, **A**, Aroer, H6500
Jos 16: 2 over to the territory of the Arkites in **A**, H6500
Jos 16: 7 went down from Janoah to **A** and Naarah, H6500

ATAROTH ADDAR (2) [ADDAR, ATAROTH]

Jos 16: 5 went from **A** in the east to Upper H6501
Jos 18:13 went down to **A** on the hill H6501

ATE (108) [EAT]

Ge 3: 6 gaining wisdom, she took some and **a** it. H430
Ge 3: 6 husband, who was with her, and *he* **a** it. H430
Ge 3:12 me some fruit from the tree, and *I* **a** it." H430
Ge 3:13 "The serpent deceived me, and *I* **a**. H430
Ge 3:17 to your wife and **a** fruit from the tree about H430
Ge 18: 8 While *they* **a**, he stood near them under a H430
Ge 19: 3 baking bread without yeast, and *they* **a**. H430
Ge 24:54 who were with him **a** and drank and spent H430
Ge 25:34 some lentil stew. *He* **a** and drank, and then H430
Ge 26:30 a feast for them, and *they* **a** and drank. H430
Ge 27:25 Jacob brought it to him and *he* **a**; and he H430
Ge 27:33 *I* **a** it just before you came and I blessed H430
Ge 31:46 in a heap, and *they* **a** there by the heap. H430
Ge 39: 6 himself with anything except the food he **a**. H430
Ge 41: 4 were ugly and gaunt **a up** the seven sleek, H430
Ge 41:20 ugly cows **a up** the seven fat cows that H430
Ge 41:21 But even after they **a** *them*, no H995+448+7931
Ge 43:32 the Egyptians who **a** with him by H430
Ex 16: 3 pots of meat and **a** all the food we wanted, H430
Ex 16:35 The Israelites **a** manna forty years, until H430
Ex 16:35 *they* **a** manna until they reached the border H430
Ex 24:11 they saw God, and *they* **a** and drank. H430
Nu 11: 5 remember the fish *we* **a** in Egypt at no cost H430
Nu 25: 2 The people **a** the sacrificial meal and H430
Dt 9: 9 *I* **a** no bread and drank no water. H430
Dt 9:18 *I* **a** no bread and drank no water H430
Dt 29: 6 *You* **a** no bread and drank no wine or other H430
Dt 32:38 the gods who **a** the fat of their sacrifices H430
Jos 5:11 *they* **a** some of the produce of the land: H430
Jos 5:12 the day after they **a** this food from the land; H430
Jos 5:12 that year *they* **a** the produce of Canaan. H430
Jdg 14: 9 with his hands and **a** as he went along. H430
Jdg 14: 9 he gave them some, and *they* too **a** it. H430
Jdg 19: 8 So the two of them **a** together. H430
Ru 2:14 *She* **a** all she wanted and had some left H430
1Sa 1:18 Then she went her way and **a** something H430
1Sa 14:32 butchered them on the ground and **a** them, H430
1Sa 28:25 set it before Saul and his men, and *they* **a**. H430
1Sa 30:12 *He* **a** and was revived, for he had not eaten H430
2Sa 9:11 So Mephibosheth **a** at David's table like H430
2Sa 9:13 because he always **a** at the king's table; he H430
2Sa 11:13 David's invitation, *he* **a** and drank with him H430
2Sa 12:20 his request they served him food, and *he* **a**. H430
1Ki 4:20 on the seashore; *they* **a**, they drank and H430
1Ki 13:19 returned with him and **a** and drank in his H430
1Ki 13:22 You came back and **a** bread and drank H430
1Ki 19: 6 *He* **a** and drank and then lay down again H430
1Ki 19: 8 So he got up and **a** and drank H430
1Ki 19:21 gave it to the people, and *they* **a**. H430
2Ki 4:44 and *they* **a** and had some left over H430
2Ki 6:29 So we cooked my son and **a** him. The next H430
2Ki 7: 8 entered one of the tents and **a** and drank. H430
2Ki 9:34 Jehu went in and **a** and drank. "Take care H430
2Ki 23: 9 *they* **a** unleavened bread with their fellow H430
2Ki 25:29 the rest of his life **a** regularly at the king's H430
1Ch 29:22 *They* **a** and drank with great joy in the H430
2Ch 30:18 themselves, yet *they* **a** the Passover H430
2Ch 30:22 For the seven days *they* **a** their assigned H430
Ezr 6:21 who had returned from the exile **a** it, H430
Ezr 10: 6 *he* **a** no food and drank no water H430
Ne 5:14 my brothers **a** the food allotted to the H430
Ne 5:17 fifty Jews and officials **a** at my table, NDT
Ne 9:25 *They* **a** to the full and were well-nourished H430
Job 42:11 him before came and **a** with him in his H430
Ps 78:25 Human beings **a** the bread of angels; he H430
Ps 78:29 *They* **a** till they were gorged—he had H430
Ps 105:35 *they* **a up** every green thing in their land H430
Ps 105:35 in their land, **a up** the produce of their soil. H430
Ps 106:28 the Baal of Peor and **a** sacrifices offered to H430
Isa 44:19 bread over its coals, I roasted meat and *I* **a**. H430
Jer 15:16 your words came, *I* **a** them; they were my H430
Jer 52:33 the rest of his life **a** regularly at the king's H430
La 4: 5 Those *who once* **a** delicacies are destitute H430
Eze 3: 3 So *I* **a** it, and it tasted as sweet as honey H430
Da 1:15 of the young men who **a** the royal food. H430
Da 4:33 from people and **a** grass like the ox. A10030
Da 5:21 the wild donkeys and **a** grass like the ox; A10301
Da 10: 3 *I* **a** no choice food; no meat or wine H430
Mt 9:10 sinners came and **a with** him and his *G5263*
Mt 12: 4 and *he* and his companions **a** the *G2266*
Mt 13: 4 the path, and the birds came and **a** it **up**. *G2983*
Mt 14:20 *They* all **a** and were satisfied, and the *G2266*
Mt 14:21 The number of those *who* **a** was about five *G2266*
Mt 15:37 *They* all **a** and were satisfied. Afterward *G2266*
Mt 15:38 number of those *who* **a** was four thousand *G2266*
Mk 1: 6 and *he* **a** locusts and wild honey. *G2266*
Mk 2:26 the house of God and **a** the consecrated *G2266*
Mk 4: 4 the path, and the birds came and **a** it **up**. *G2983*
Mk 6:42 *They* all **a** and were satisfied, *G2266*
Mk 8: 8 *The people* **a** and were satisfied *G2266*
Lk 4: 2 *He* **a** nothing during those days, and at *G2266*
Lk 6: 4 *he* **a** what is lawful only for priests to eat. *G2266*
Lk 8: 5 it was trampled on, and the birds **a** it **up**. *G2983*
Lk 9:17 *They* all **a** and were satisfied, and the *G2266*
Lk 13:26 you will say, '*We* **a** and drank with you *G2266*
Lk 24:43 he took it and **a** it in their presence. *G2266*
Jn 6:26 because *you* **a** the loaves and had *G2266*
Jn 6:31 Our ancestors **a** the manna in the *G2266*
Jn 6:49 Your ancestors **a** the manna in the *G2266*
Jn 6:58 Your ancestors **a** manna and died, but *G2266*
Ac 2:46 homes and **a together** with glad *G3561+5575*
Ac 10:41 by us who **a** and drank **with** him after he *G5303*
Ac 11: 3 of uncircumcised men and **a with** them." *G5303*
Ac 20:11 upstairs again and broke bread and **a**. *G1174*
Ac 27:36 all encouraged and **a** some food *G4689*
1Co 10: 3 *They* all **a** the same spiritual food *G2266*
Rev 2:14 to sin *so that they* **a** food sacrificed *G2266*
Rev 10:10 little scroll from the angel's hand and **a** it. *G2983*

ATER (5)

Ezr 2:16 of **A** (through Hezekiah) 98 H359
Ezr 2:42 of Shallum, **A**, Talmon, Akkub, H359
Ne 7:21 of **A** (through Hezekiah) 98 H359
Ne 7:45 of Shallum, **A**, Talmon, Akkub, H359
Ne 10:17 **A**, Hezekiah, Azzur, H359

ATHACH (NIV84) ATHAK

ATHAIAH (1)

Ne 11: 4 **A** son of Uzziah, the son of Zechariah, the H6970

ATHAK (1)

1Sa 30:30 to those in Hormah, Bor Ashan, **A** H6973

ATHALIAH (17)

2Ki 8:26 His mother's name was **A**, a H6976
2Ki 11: 1 When **A** the mother of Ahaziah saw that H6975
2Ki 11: 2 nurse in a bedroom to hide him from **A**; H6976
2Ki 11: 3 LORD for six years while **A** ruled the land. H6975
2Ki 11:13 When **A** heard the noise made by the H6975
2Ki 11:14 Then **A** tore her robes and called out H6975
2Ki 11:20 because **A** had been slain with the sword H6976
1Ch 8:26 Shamsherai, Shehariah, **A**, H6975
2Ch 22: 2 His mother's name was **A**, a H6976
2Ch 22:10 When **A** the mother of Ahaziah saw that H6976
2Ch 22:11 hid the child from **A** so she could not kill H6976
2Ch 22:12 God for six years while **A** ruled the land. H6975
2Ch 23:12 When **A** heard the noise of the people H6976
2Ch 23:13 Then **A** tore her robes and shouted H6976
2Ch 23:21 because **A** had been slain with the sword. H6976
2Ch 24: 7 that wicked woman **A** had broken into the H6976
Ezr 8: 7 Jeshaiah son of **A**, and with him 70 men; H6975

ATHARIM (1)

Nu 21: 1 that Israel was coming along the road to **A**, H926

ATHENIANS (1) [ATHENS]

Ac 17:21 All the **A** and the foreigners who lived there *G122*

ATHENS (5) [ATHENIANS]

Ac 17:15 Paul brought him to **A** and then left with *G121*
Ac 17:16 While Paul was waiting for them in **A**, he *G121*
Ac 17:22 "People **of A**! I see that in every *G122*

Ac 18: 1 After this, Paul left A and went to Corinth. G121
1Th 3: 1 thought it best to be left by ourselves in A. G121

ATHLAI (1)

Ezr 10:28 Jehohanan, Hananiah, Zabbai and A. H6974

ATHLETE (1)

2Ti 2: 5 anyone who competes as an a does not G123

ATONE (3) [ATONEMENT]

Ex 30:15 the offering to the LORD to a for your lives. H4105
2Ch 29:24 altar for a sin offering to a for all Israel, H4105
Da 9:24 an end to sin, to a for wickedness, to H4105

ATONED (6) [ATONEMENT]

Dt 21: 8 Then the bloodshed will be a for, H4105
1Sa 3:14 Eli's house will never be a for by sacrifice H4105
Pr 16: 6 Through love and faithfulness sin is a for H4105
Isa 6: 7 your guilt is taken away and your sin a for." H4105
Isa 22:14 your dying day this sin will not be a for," H4105
Isa 27: 9 will Jacob's guilt be a for, and this H4105

ATONEMENT (107) [ATONE, ATONED, ATONING]

Ex 25:17 "Make an a cover of pure gold—two and H4114
Ex 26:34 Put the a cover on the ark of the covenant H4114
Ex 29:33 offerings by which a was made for their H4105
Ex 29:36 bull each day as a sin offering to make a. H4113
Ex 29:36 Purify the altar by making a for it, and H4105
Ex 29:37 For seven days make a for the altar and H4105
Ex 30: 6 before the a cover that is over the tablets H4114
Ex 30:10 a year Aaron shall make a on its horns. H4105
Ex 30:10 This annual a must be made with the H4105
Ex 30:16 Receive the a money from the Israelites H4113
Ex 30:16 before the LORD, making a for your lives." H4105
Ex 31: 7 of the covenant law with the a cover on it, H4114
Ex 32:30 perhaps I can make a for your sin. H4105
Ex 35:12 its poles and the a cover and the curtain H4114
Ex 37: 6 He made the a cover of pure gold—two H4114
Ex 39:35 law with its poles and the a cover; H4114
Ex 40:20 to the ark and put the a cover over it. H4114
Lev 1: 4 on your behalf to make a for you. H4105
Lev 4:20 way the priest will make a for the H4105
Lev 4:26 way the priest will make a for the leader's H4105
Lev 4:31 In this way the priest will make a for them, H4105
Lev 4:35 way the priest will make a for them for the H4105
Lev 5: 6 the priest shall make a for them for H4105
Lev 5:10 way and make a for them for the H4105
Lev 5:13 way the priest will make a for them for H4105
Lev 5:16 The priest will make a for them with the H4105
Lev 5:18 way the priest will make a for them for the H4105
Lev 6: 7 way the priest will make a for them before H4105
Lev 6:30 of meeting to make a in the Holy Place H4105
Lev 7: 7 to the priest who makes a with them. H4105
Lev 8:15 So he consecrated it to make a for it. H4105
Lev 8:34 by the LORD to make a for you. H4105
Lev 9: 7 burnt offering and make a for yourself H4105
Lev 9: 7 is for the people and make a for them, H4105
Lev 10:17 community by making a for them before H4105
Lev 12: 7 them before the LORD to make a for her, H4105
Lev 12: 8 In this way the priest will make a for her H4105
Lev 14:18 be cleansed and make a for them before H4105
Lev 14:19 sin offering and make a for the one to be H4105
Lev 14:20 offering, and make a for them, and they H4105
Lev 14:21 offering to be waved to make a for them, H4105
Lev 14:29 to make a for them before the LORD. H4105
Lev 14:31 way the priest will make a before the LORD H4105
Lev 14:53 In this way he will make a for the house H4105
Lev 15:15 In this way he will make a before the LORD H4105
Lev 15:30 In this way he will make a for her before H4105
Lev 16: 2 curtain in front of the a cover on the ark, H4114
Lev 16: 2 I will appear in the cloud over the a cover. H4114
Lev 16: 6 sin offering to make a for himself and H4105
Lev 16:10 to be used for making a by sending it into H4105
Lev 16:11 sin offering to make a for himself and H4105
Lev 16:13 will conceal the a cover above the tablets H4114
Lev 16:14 sprinkle it on the front of the a cover; H4114
Lev 16:14 his finger seven times before the a cover. H4114
Lev 16:15 sprinkle it on the a cover and in front of it. H4114
Lev 16:16 In this way he will make a for the Most H4105
Lev 16:17 Aaron goes in to make a in the Most Holy H4105
Lev 16:17 he comes out, having made a for himself H4105
Lev 16:18 that is before the LORD and make a for it. H4105
Lev 16:20 has finished making a for the Most Holy H4105
Lev 16:24 to make a for himself and for the people. H4105
Lev 16:27 into the Most Holy Place to make a, H4105
Lev 16:30 on this day a will be made for you, H4105
Lev 16:32 his father as high priest is to make a. H4105
Lev 16:33 and make a for the Most Holy Place, for H4105
Lev 16:34 A is to be made once a year for all the H4105
Lev 17:11 given it to you to make a for yourselves on H4105
Lev 17:11 it is the blood that makes a for one's life. H4105
Lev 19:22 the priest is to make a for him before the H4105
Lev 23:27 day of this seventh month is the Day of A. H4113
Lev 23:28 because it is the Day of A, when H4113
Lev 23:28 when a is made for you before the LORD H4105
Lev 25: 9 on the Day of A sound the trumpet H4113
Nu 5: 8 ram with which a is made for the H4113+4105
Nu 6:11 a burnt offering to make a for the Nazirite H4105
Nu 7:89 above the a cover on the ark of the H4114
Nu 8:12 a burnt offering, to make a for the Levites. H4105
Nu 8:19 Israelites and to make a for them so that H4105
Nu 8:21 the LORD and made a for them to purify H4105
Nu 15:25 The priest is to make a for the whole H4105
Nu 15:28 The priest is to make a before the LORD H4105
Nu 15:28 when a has been made, that person H4105
Nu 16:46 hurry to the assembly to make a for them. H4105
Nu 16:47 offered the incense and made a for them. H4105
Nu 25:13 of his God and made a for the Israelites." H4105
Nu 28:22 goat as a sin offering to make a for you. H4105
Nu 28:30 Include one male goat to make a for you. H4105
Nu 29: 5 goat as a sin offering to make a for you. H4105
Nu 29:11 the sin offering for a and the regular burnt H4113
Nu 31:50 to make a for ourselves before the LORD." H4105
Nu 35:33 and a cannot be made for the land on H4105
Dt 21: 8 Accept this a for your people Israel, whom H4105
Dt 32:43 his enemies and make a for his land and H4105
2Sa 21: 3 How shall I make a so that you will bless H4105
1Ch 6:49 Most Holy Place, making a for Israel, in H4105
1Ch 28:11 its inner rooms and the place of a. H4114
Ne 10:33 sin offerings to make a for Israel; and H4105
Eze 16:63 when I make a for you for all you have H4105
Eze 43:20 so purify the altar and make a for it. H4105
Eze 43:26 days they are to make a for the altar H4105
Eze 45:15 offerings to make a for the people, H4105
Eze 45:17 offerings to make a for the Israelites. H4105
Eze 45:20 so you are to make a for the temple. H4105
Ac 27: 9 because by now it was after the Day of A. G3763
Ro 3:25 God presented Christ as a sacrifice of a G2663
Heb 2:17 that he might make a for the sins of G2661
Heb 9: 5 of the Glory, overshadowing the a cover. G2663

ATONING (3) [ATONEMENT]

Ex 30:10 with the blood of the a sin offering for the H4113
1Jn 2: 2 He is the a sacrifice for our sins, and not G2662
1Jn 4:10 sent his Son as an a sacrifice for our sins. G2662

ATROTH BETH JOAB (1)

1Ch 2:54 the Netophathites, A, half the H6502

ATROTH SHOPHAN (1)

Nu 32:35 A, Jazer, Jogbehah, H6503

ATTACH (7) [ATTACHED, ATTACHING]

Ex 28:14 and a the chains to the settings. H5989
Ex 28:26 two gold rings and a them to the other H8492
Ex 28:27 more gold rings and a them to the bottom H5989
Ex 28:37 a blue cord to it to a it to the turban; H2118
Ex 29: 6 on his head and a the sacred emblem to H5989
Ex 39:31 a blue cord to it to a it to the turban, H5989
Eze 37: 6 I will a tendons to you and make flesh H5989

ATTACHED (15) [ATTACH]

Ge 29:34 at last my husband will become a to me, H4277
Ge 32:32 not eat the tendon a to the socket of the H6584
Ex 28: 7 two shoulder pieces a to two of its corners H2489
Ex 39: 4 which were a to two of its corners H2489
Ex 39:19 two gold rings and a them to the other H8492
Ex 39:20 more gold rings and a them to the bottom H5989
Ex 39:25 of pure gold and a them around the hem H5989
Ex 40:20 a the poles to the ark and put the H8492
1Ki 6:10 and they were a to the temple by beams of H297
1Ki 7:28 They had side panels a to uprights. H1068
1Ki 7:32 axles of the wheels were a to the stand. H928
1Ki 7:35 panels were a to the top of the stand. H6584
2Ch 3:16 pomegranates and a them to the chains. H5989
2Ch 9:18 and a footstool of gold was a to it. H297
Eze 40:43 were a to the wall all around. H3922

ATTACHING (2) [ATTACH]

Ex 28:25 a them to the shoulder pieces of the H5989
Ex 39:18 a them to the shoulder pieces of the H5989

ATTACK (101) [ATTACKED, ATTACKER, ATTACKING, ATTACKS, COUNTERATTACK, COUNTERATTACKED]

Ge 14:15 divided his men to a them and he routed H6584
Ge 32:11 I am afraid he will come and a me H5782
Ge 34:30 if they join forces against me and a me, H5782
Ge 43:18 He wants to a us and overpower us and H1670
Ge 49:19 but he will a them at their heels. H1574
Nu 13:31 "We can't a those people; they H6590+448
Nu 20:18 will march out and a you with the sword." H7925
Dt 20:10 When you march up to a a city, make its H4309
Jos 8: 1 whole army with you, and go up and a Ai. H6590
Jos 8: 3 the whole army moved out to a Ai. H6590
Jos 9:18 But the Israelites did not a them, because H5782
Jos 10: 4 "Come up and help me a Gibeon," he H5782
Jos 10:19 A them from the rear and don't let them H2386
Jdg 7:10 If you are afraid to a, go down to the camp H3718
Jdg 7:11 will be encouraged to a the camp." H3718+928
Jdg 9:33 seize the opportunity to a them." H6913+4200
Jdg 9:43 coming out of the city, he rose to a them. H5782
Jdg 9:45 day Abimelek pressed his a against the H4309
Jdg 18: 9 answered, "Come on, let's a them! H6590+6584
Jdg 18:25 of the men may get angry and a you, H7003
Jdg 20:34 young men made a frontal a on Gibeah. H995
1Sa 7: 7 rulers of the Philistines came up to a them. H448
1Sa 14:14 In that first a Jonathan and his H4804
1Sa 15: 3 a the Amalekites and totally destroy all H5782
1Sa 17:48 As the Philistine moved closer to a him H7925
1Sa 23: 2 "Shall I go and a these Philistines?" H5782
1Sa 23: 2 a the Philistines and save Keilah. H5782
1Sa 24: 7 and did not allow them to a Saul. H7756+448
2Sa 5: 6 marched to Jerusalem to a the Jebusites, H448
2Sa 5:19 the LORD, "Shall I go and a the Philistines? H448
2Sa 5:23 behind them and a them in front of H995+4200
2Sa 11:25 Press the a against the city and destroy it H4878
2Sa 17: 2 I would a him while he is weary and H995+6584
2Sa 17: 9 If he should a your troops first H5877+928
2Sa 17:12 Then we will a him wherever he may H995+448
1Ki 20:12 "Prepare to a." So they prepared to NDT
1Ki 20:12 So they prepared to a the city. H6584
1Ki 20:22 the king of Aram will a you again." H6590+6584
1Ki 22:12 "A Ramoth Gilead and be victorious," H6590
1Ki 22:15 "A and be victorious," he answered, "for H6590
1Ki 22:32 So they turned to a him, but when H4309
2Ki 3: 8 "By what route shall we a?" he asked H6590
2Ki 7: 6 Hittite and Egyptian kings to a us!" H995+6584
2Ki 12:17 Then he turned to a Jerusalem. H6590+6584
2Ki 17: 3 king of Assyria came up to a Hoshea, H6584
2Ki 18:25 have I come to a and destroy this place H6584
1Ch 11: 6 "Whoever leads the a on the Jebusites H5782
1Ch 14:10 "Shall I go and a the Philistines H6584
1Ch 14:14 around them and a them in front of H995+4200
2Ch 18: 2 and urged him to a Ramoth Gilead. H6590+448
2Ch 18:11 "A Ramoth Gilead and be victorious," H6590
2Ch 18:14 "A and be victorious," he answered, "for H6590
2Ch 18:31 So they turned to a him, but H4309
Ne 4:12 "Wherever you turn, they will a us. H6584
Est 8:11 province who might a them and their H7444
Est 9: 2 King Xerxes to a those H8938+3338+928
Job 15:21 when all seems well, marauders a him. H995
Job 15:24 overwhelm him, like a king poised to a, H3960
Job 19: 3 reproached me; shamelessly you a me. H2686
Job 30:21 with the might of your hand you a me. H8475
Ps 56: 1 hot pursuit; all day long they press their a. H4309
Ps 59: 4 no wrong, yet they are ready to a me. H8132
Ps 109: 3 surround me; they a me without cause. H4309
Ps 109:28 may those who a me be put to shame H7756
Isa 21: 2 Elam, a! Media, lay siege! H6590
Isa 29: 7 that a her and her fortress and besiege H7371
Isa 36:10 have I come to a and destroy this land H6584
Isa 54:15 If anyone does a you, it will not be H1592+1592
Jer 5: 6 a lion from the forest will a them, H5782
Jer 6: 4 Arise, let us a at noon! But, H6590
Jer 6: 5 let us a at night and destroy her fortresses!" H6590
Jer 6:23 like men in battle formation to a you, H6584
Jer 12: 9 that other birds of prey surround and a? H6584
Jer 18:18 let's a him with our tongues and pay no H5782
Jer 37: 8 the Babylonians will return and a this city; H4309
Jer 37:19 king of Babylon will not a you or this H995+6584
Jer 43:11 He will come and a Egypt, bringing death H5782
Jer 46:13 king of Babylon to a Egypt: H5782
Jer 47: 7 he has ordered it to a Ashkelon and the H448
Jer 49: 4 your riches and say, 'Who will a me? H995+448
Jer 49:14 "Assemble yourselves to a it! H995+6584
Jer 49:28 and a Kedar and destroy the people H6590+448
Jer 49:31 "Arise and a a nation at ease, which H6590+448
Jer 50: 3 from the north will a her and lay H6590+6584
Jer 50:21 "A the land of Merathaim and H6590+6584
Jer 50:42 like men in battle formation to a you, H6584
Jer 51:48 out of the north destroyers will a her," H995+4200
Eze 38:11 I will a a peaceful and unsuspecting H995
Da 8: 7 I saw it a the ram furiously, striking the H5595
Da 11: 7 He will a the forces of the king of the H995+448
Da 11:39 He will a the mightiest fortresses H6913+4200
Hos 13: 8 her cubs, I will a them and rip them open H7008
Joel 3: 9 Let all the fighting men draw near and a. H6590
Zec 12: 9 all the nations that a Jerusalem. H995+6584
Zec 14:13 hand and a one another. H6590+6584+3338
Lk 18: 5 that she won't eventually come and a me! G5724
Ac 16:22 The crowd joined in the a against Paul G5308
Ac 18:10 no one is going to a and harm you G2202
Ac 18:12 of Corinth made a united a on Paul and G2987
2Ti 4:18 me from every evil a and will bring me G2240
Rev 11: 7 up from the Abyss will a them, G4472+4483

ATTACKED (66) [ATTACK]

Ge 4: 8 Cain a his brother Abel and killed H7756+448
Ge 34:25 their swords and a the unsuspecting H995+6584
Ge 49:19 "Gad will be a by a band of raiders, but H1574
Ge 49:23 With bitterness archers a him; they shot at H5352
Ex 17: 8 Amalekites came and a the Israelites at H4309
Nu 14:45 came down and a them and beat them H5782
Nu 21: 1 he a the Israelites and captured some of H4309
Dt 25:18 on your journey and a all who were H2386
Jos 8:21 they turned around and a the men of Ai. H5782
Jos 10: 5 took up positions against Gibeon and a it. H4309
Jos 10:29 on from Makkedah to Libnah and a it. H4309
Jos 10:31 he took up positions against it and a it. H4309
Jos 10:34 they took up positions against it and a it. H4309
Jos 10:36 went up from Eglon to Hebron and a it. H4309
Jos 10:38 with him turned around and a Debir. H4309
Jos 11: 7 at the Waters of Merom and a them, H5877+928
Jos 19:47 they went up and a Leshem, took it, H4309
Jdg 1: 4 When Judah a, the LORD gave the H6590
Jdg 1: 8 The men of Judah a Jerusalem also and H4309
Jdg 1:17 Israelites and a the Canaanites living H5782
Jdg 1:22 Now the tribes of Joseph a Bethel, and H6590
Jdg 3:13 Eglon came and a Israel, and they H5782
Jdg 8:11 Jogbehah and a the unsuspecting H5782
Jdg 9:44 Then two companies a those in the H7320+6584
Jdg 9:52 Abimelek went to the tower and a it. But H4309
Jdg 11:12 against me that you have a my country?" H4309
Jdg 15: 8 He a them viciously H5782+8797+6584+3751
Jdg 18:27 They a them with the sword and burned H5782
1Sa 13: 3 Jonathan a the Philistine outpost at Geba, H5782
1Sa 13: 4 "Saul has a the Philistine outpost, and H5782
1Sa 15: 7 Then Saul a the Amalekites all the way H5782

1Sa 27: 9 Whenever David a an area, he did not H5782
1Sa 30: 1 *They had* a Ziklag and burned it H5782
2Sa 12:29 went to Rabbah, and a and captured it. H4309
1Ki 2:32 David knowing it *he* a two men and killed H7003
1Ki 9:16 king of Egypt *had* a and captured Gezer. H6590
1Ki 14:25 Shishak king of Egypt a Jerusalem. H6590+6584
1Ki 20: 1 went up and besieged Samaria and a it. H4309
2Ki 3:25 armed with slings surrounded it and a it. H5782
2Ki 12:17 Aram went up and a Gath and captured H4309
2Ki 14:11 not listen, so Jehoash king of Israel a. H6590
2Ki 15:10 *He* a him in front of the people H5782
2Ki 15:14 *He* a Shallum son of Jabesh in Samaria H5782
2Ki 15:16 a Tiphsah and everyone in the city and its H5782
2Ki 15:30 *He* a and assassinated him, and then H5782
2Ki 18:13 king of Assyria a all the fortified H6590+6584
1Ch 4:41 *They* a the Hamites in their dwellings H5782
1Ch 20: 1 Joab a Rabbah and left it in ruins. H5782
2Ch 12: 2 king of Egypt a Jerusalem in the H6590+6584
2Ch 12: 9 Shishak king of Egypt a Jerusalem, H6590+6584
2Ch 13:14 that they were being a at both front and H4878
2Ch 14:15 *They* also a the camps of the herders and H5782
2Ch 21:17 *They* a Judah, invaded it and carried H6590+928
2Ch 25:21 So Jehoash king of Israel a. He and H6590
2Ch 28:17 had again come and a Judah and carried H5782
2Ch 36: 6 king of Babylon a him and bound H6590+6584
Est 8: 7 "Because Haman a the Jews H8938+3338+928
Job 1:15 the Sabeans a and made off with H5877
Ps 53: 5 scattered the bones of *those who* a you; H2837
Ps 124: 2 on our side when people a us, H7756+6584
Isa 20: 1 came to Ashdod and a and captured it— H4309
Isa 36: 1 king of Assyria a all the fortified H6590+6584
Jer 47: 1 the Philistines before Pharaoh a Gaza: H5782
Jer 49:28 which Nebuchadnezzar king of Babylon a: H5782
Zec 14:16 nations that *have* a Jerusalem will H995+6584
Lk 10:30 to Jericho, when *he was* a by robbers. *G4346*

ATTACKER (1) [ATTACK]

Na 2: 1 An a advances against you, Nineveh H7046

ATTACKING (15) [ATTACK]

Jdg 10:18 take the lead in a the Ammonites will be H4309
1Ki 22:20 entice Ahab into a Ramoth Gilead and H6590
2Ki 16: 7 of the king of Israel, who *are* a me." H7756+6584
2Ki 16: 9 complied by a Damascus and H6590+448
2Ch 18:19 king of Israel into a Ramoth Gilead and H6590
2Ch 20:12 to face this vast army that *is* a us. H995+6584
2Ch 35:21 It is not you I am a at this time, but the H6584
Ps 54: 3 Arrogant foes *are* a me; ruthless H7756+6584
Ps 56: 2 day long; in their pride many *are* a me. H4309
Ps 59: 1 my fortress against *those who are* a me. H7756
Ps 86:14 Arrogant foes *are* a me, O God H7756+6584
Jer 21: 2 Nebuchadnezzar king of Babylon *is* a us. H4309
Jer 32:24 hands of the Babylonians who *are* a it. H4309
Jer 32:29 The Babylonians who *are* a this city will H4309
Jer 37:10 Babylonian army that *is* a you and only H4309

ATTACKS (13) [ATTACK]

Ge 32: 8 "If Esau comes and a one group, the H5782
Ex 21:15 "*Anyone who* a their father or mother is to H5782
Dt 22:26 of someone *who* a and murders a H7756+6584
Jos 15:16 to the man who a and captures Kiriath H5782
Jdg 1:12 to the man who a and captures Kiriath H5782
2Sa 22:44 delivered me from the a *of* the peoples; H8190
Job 30:12 On my right the tribe a; they lay snares H7756
Ps 18:43 delivered me from the a *of* the people; H8190
Ps 55:20 My companion a his friends H8938+3338+928
Isa 54:15 whoever a you will surrender to you. H1592
Eze 38:18 When Gog a the land of Israel, my H995+6584
Lk 11:22 someone stronger a and overpowers him, *G2088*
Jn 10:12 Then the wolf a the flock and scatters it. *G773*

ATTAI (4)

1Ch 2:35 to his servant Jarha, and she bore him A. H6968
1Ch 2:36 A was the father of Nathan, Nathan the H6968
1Ch 12:11 A the sixth, Eliel the seventh, H6968
2Ch 11:20 bore him Abijah, A, Ziza and Shelomith. H6968

ATTAIN (3) [ATTAINED, ATTAINING]

Ps 139: 6 wonderful for me, too lofty for *me to* a. H3523
Pr 2:19 who go to her return or a the paths of life. H5952
Pr 11:19 Truly the righteous a life, but whoever H4200

ATTAINED (5) [ATTAIN]

Pr 16:31 *it is* a in the way of righteousness. H5162
Pr 30: 3 nor *have I* a to the **knowledge** *of* H3359+1981
Ro 9:31 *have* not a their goal. *G1650+5777*
Php 3:16 let us live up to what *we have already* a. *G5777*
Heb 7:11 perfection *could have been* a through the *G1639*

ATTAINING (2) [ATTAIN]

Eph 4:13 a to the whole measure of the fullness of *G1650*
Php 3:11 a to the resurrection from the dead. *G2918*

ATTALIA (2)

Ac 14:25 the word in Perga, they went down to A. *G877*
Ac 14:26 **From A** they sailed back to Antioch *G2796S*

ATTEMPT (1)

Ac 27:30 *In an* a to escape from the ship, the sailors *G2426*

ATTEND (2) [ATTENDANCE, ATTENDANT, ATTENDANTS, ATTENDED, ATTENDING, ATTENDS]

Ge 39:11 he went into the house to a to his duties, H6913
Est 4: 5 king's eunuchs assigned to a her, H4200+7156

ATTENDANCE (1) [ATTEND]

SS 8:13 dwell in the gardens with friends *in* a, H7992

ATTENDANT (7) [ATTEND]

Ge 29:24 servant Zilpah to his daughter as her a. H9148
Ge 29:29 Bilhah to his daughter Rachel as her a. H9148
Ge 39: 4 found favor in his eyes and *became* his a. H9250
2Ki 22:12 the secretary and Asaiah the king's a: H6269
2Ch 34:20 the secretary and Asaiah the king's a: H6269
Lk 4:20 gave it back *to* the a and sat down. *G5677*
Ac 13: 7 who was an a of the proconsul, Sergius *G5250*

ATTENDANTS (39) [ATTEND]

Ge 24:61 Then Rebekah and her a got ready and H5855
Ge 45: 1 no longer control himself before all his a, H5893
Ex 2: 5 her a were walking along the H5855
Jdg 3:19 The king said *to* his a, "Leave us!" H6641+6584
1Sa 8:14 olive groves and give them to his a. H6269
1Sa 8:15 vintage and give it to his officials and a. H6269
1Sa 16:15 Saul's a said to him, "See, an evil spirit H6269
1Sa 16:17 So Saul said to his a, "Find someone who H6269
1Sa 18:22 Then Saul ordered his a: "Speak to David H6269
1Sa 18:22 king likes you, and his a all love you; now H6269
1Sa 18:26 When the a told David these things, he H6269
1Sa 19: 1 son Jonathan and all the a to kill David. H6269
1Sa 28: 7 Saul then said to his a, "Find me a woman H6269
2Sa 12:18 David's a were afraid to tell him that the H6269
2Sa 12:19 noticed that his a were whispering among H6269
2Sa 12:21 His a asked him, "Why are you acting this H6269
2Sa 13:24 Will the king and his a please join me?" H6269
2Sa 13:31 all his a stood by with their clothes H6269
2Sa 13:36 too, and all his a wept very bitterly. H6269
1Ki 1: 2 So his a said to him, "Let us look for a H6269
2Ki 5:15 Naaman and all his a went back to the H4722
2Ki 24:12 his mother, his a, his nobles and his H6269
Ezr 8:17 that they might bring a to us for the house H9250
Est 1:12 But when the a delivered the king's H6247
Est 2: 2 the king's **personal** a proposed, H5853+9250
Est 2: 9 to her seven **female** a selected from the H5855
Est 2: 9 moved her and her a into the best place H5855
Est 4: 4 eunuchs and **female** a came and told her H5855
Est 4:16 I and my a will fast as you do H5855
Est 6: 3 done for him," his a answered. H5853+9250
Est 6: 5 His a answered, "Haman is standing in H5853
Jer 25:19 king of Egypt, his a, his officials and all H6269
Jer 36:24 The king and all his a who heard all these H6269
Jer 36:31 his children and his a for their wickedness H6269
Jer 37: 2 Neither he nor his a nor the people of the H6269
Jer 37:18 against you or your a or this people, H6269
Mt 14: 2 he said *to* his a, "This is John the *G4090*
Mt 22:13 "Then the king told the a, 'Tie him hand *G1356*
Ac 10: 7 a devout soldier who *was one of* his a. *G4674*

ATTENDED (6) [ATTEND]

Ge 40: 4 assigned them to Joseph, and *he* a them. H9250
Jdg 14:20 companions who *had* a him **at the feast**. H8287
1Sa 25:42 a **by** her five female servants H2143+4200+8079
Da 7:10 Thousands upon thousands a him; ten A10727
Mt 4:11 left him, and angels came and a him. *G1354*
Mk 1:13 with the wild animals, and angels a him. *G1354*

ATTENDING (6) [ATTEND]

1Sa 4:20 was dying, the *women* a her said, "Don't H5893
1Ki 1:15 Abishag the Shunammite *was* a him. H9250
1Ki 10: 5 his officials, the a servants in their robes H5096
2Ch 9: 4 his officials, the a servants in their robes H5096
2Ch 22: 8 relatives, *who had been* a Ahaziah, and H9250
Est 7: 9 one of the eunuchs a the king, said H4200+7156

ATTENDS (1) [ATTEND]

Jn 3:29 The friend who *a* the **bridegroom** waits and AIT

ATTENTION (81) [ATTENTIVE, ATTENTIVELY]

Ge 39:23 The warden **paid** no a *to* anything under H8011
Ex 4: 8 not believe you or **pay** a to the first sign, H9048
Ex 5: 9 they keep working and **pay** no a to lies." H9120
Ex 15:26 if *you* **pay** a to his commands and keep all H263
Ex 16:20 some of them **paid** no a to Moses; they H9048
Ex 23:21 **Pay** a to him and listen to what he says H9068
Nu 5:15 *to* **draw** a **to** wrongdoing. H2349
Dt 1:45 he **paid** no a to your weeping and H9048
Dt 7:12 If *you* **pay** a *to* these laws and are careful H9048
Dt 17: 4 *this has* **been brought to** your a
H5583+2256+9048
Dt 28:13 If *you* **pay** a to the commands of the LORD H9048
Jdg 11:28 **paid** no a to the message Jephthah sent H9048
Ru 4: 4 *I should* **bring** the matter **to** your a H1655+265
1Sa 4:20 But she did not respond or pay *any* a. H4213
1Sa 25:25 Please pay no a, my lord, to that wicked H4213
1Ki 8:28 Yet **give** a to your servant's prayer and his H7155
1Ki 18:29 no one answered, no one **paid** a. H7993
2Ki 3:14 *I would* not **pay any** a to you. H5564+2256+8011
2Ch 6:19 **give** a to your servant's prayer and his H7155
2Ch 33:10 his people, but *they* **paid** no a. H7992
Ne 8:13 Ezra the teacher to **give** a to the words of H8505
Ne 9:30 Yet *they* **paid** no a, so you gave them into H263
Ne 9:34 *they did* not **pay** a to your commands or H7992
Est 9:25 when the plot came to the king's a, H4200+7156
Job 7:17 of them, that you give them so much a, H4213
Job 32:12 *I* **gave** you *my* **full** a. But not one of you H1067
Job 33: 1 to my words; **pay** a *to* everything I say. H263
Job 33:31 "**Pay** a, Job, and listen to me; be silent H7992
Job 35:13 empty plea; the Almighty **pays** no a *to* it. H8800
Ps 45:10 and **pay careful** a: H8011+2256+5742+265
Pr 1:24 I call and no *one* **pays** a when I stretch H7992
Pr 4: 1 **pay** a and gain understanding. H7992
Pr 4:20 My son, **pay** a to what I say; turn your ear H7992
Pr 5: 1 My son, **pay** a to my wisdom, turn your ear H7992
Pr 7:24 my sons, listen to me; **pay** a to what I say. H7992
Pr 17: 4 a liar **pays** a to a destructive tongue. H263
Pr 21:11 by **paying** a to the wise they get H8505
Pr 22:17 **Pay** a and turn your ear to the sayings of H9048
Pr 27:23 your flocks, give **careful** a to your herds; H4213
Ecc 7:21 *Do* not pay a to every word people say, or H4213
Isa 28:23 hear my voice; **pay** a and hear what I say. H7992
Isa 34: 1 nations, and listen; **pay** a, *you* peoples! H7992
Isa 42:20 but *you* **pay** no a; your ears are H9068
Isa 42:23 to this or **pay close** a in time H7992+2256+9048
Isa 48:18 If only *you had* **paid** a to my commands H7992
Jer 7:24 But they did not listen or **pay** a H5742+265
Jer 7:26 But they did not listen to me or **pay** a. H5742+265
Jer 11: 8 But they did not listen or **pay** a H5742+265
Jer 13:15 Hear and **pay** a, do not be arrogant, for the H263
Jer 17:23 Yet they did not listen or **pay** a; they H5742+265
Jer 18:18 our tongues and **pay** no a to anything he H7992
Jer 25: 4 listened or **paid any** a. H5742+265+4200+9048
Jer 34:14 did not listen to me or **pay** a to me. H5742+265
Jer 35:15 But *you have* not **paid** a or listened H5742+265
Jer 37: 2 of the land **paid** *any* a to the words the H9048
Jer 44: 5 But they did not listen or **pay** a; they H5742+265
Eze 40: 4 listen closely and pay a to everything I am H4213
Eze 44: 5 closely and give a to everything I tell H4213
Eze 44: 5 Give a to the entrance to the temple and H4213
Da 3:12 Abednego—who pay no a to you, Your A10302
Da 6:13 from Judah, pays no a to you, Your A10302
Da 9:13 from our sins and **giving** a to your truth. H8505
Da 11:18 Then he will turn his a to the coastlands H7156
Hos 5: 1 **Pay** a, *you* Israelites! Listen H7992
Zec 1: 4 ' But they would not listen or **pay** a to me H7992
Zec 7:11 "But they refused to **pay** a; stubbornly they H7992
Mt 7: 3 brother's eye and **pay** no a **to** the plank in *G2917*
Mt 22: 5 "But they **paid** no a and went off—one to *G288*
Mt 22:16 *you* **pay** no a **to who they are**
G1063+1650+4725+476
Mt 24: 1 up to him *to* **call** his a **to** its buildings *G2109*
Mk 12:14 because *you* **pay** no a to who they are *G1063*
Lk 6:41 brother's eye and **pay** no a **to** the plank in *G2917*
Ac 3: 5 So the man **gave** them *his* a, expecting to *G2091*
Ac 6: 4 *will* **give** *our* a to prayer and the *G4674*
Ac 8: 6 they all **paid close** a to what he said. *G4668*
Ac 8:10 low, **gave** him *their* a and exclaimed *G4668*
Titus 1:14 and *will* **pay** no a **to** Jewish myths or to the *G4668*
Heb 2: 1 We must **pay** the most careful a, therefore *G4668*
Jas 2: 3 *If you* **show special** a to the man wearing *G2098*
2Pe 1:19 you will do well *to* **pay** a to it, as to a *G4668*
3Jn 10 I come, *I will* **call** a **to** what he is doing *G5703*

ATTENTIVE (7) [ATTENTION]

2Ch 6:40 be open and your ears a to the prayers H7995
2Ch 7:15 be open and my ears a to the prayers H7995
Ne 1: 6 let your ear be a and your eyes open to H7994
Ne 1:11 let your ear be a to the prayer of this your H7994
Ps 34:15 righteous, and his ears are a **to** their cry; H448
Ps 130: 2 Let your ears be a to my cry for mercy. H7995
1Pe 3:12 righteous and his ears are *a* to their prayer, AIT

ATTENTIVELY (2) [ATTENTION]

Ne 8: 3 the people **listened** a **to** the Book of H265+448
Jer 8: 6 I have listened a, but they do not say H7992

ATTESTED (1)

1Sa 3:20 that Samuel **was** a as a prophet of the H586

ATTITUDE (8) [ATTITUDES]

Ge 31: 2 that Laban's a toward him was not H7156
Ge 31: 5 that your father's a toward me is not what H7156
1Ki 11:11 "Since this is your a and you have not H6640
Ezr 6:22 joy by changing the a *of* the king of H7156
Da 3:19 and his a toward them changed. A10614+10049
Ro 15: 5 give you the same a **of mind** toward each *G5858*
Eph 4:23 to be made new *in* the a of your minds; *G4460*
1Pe 4: 1 arm yourselves also *with* the same a *G1936*

ATTITUDES (1) [ATTITUDE]

Heb 4:12 it judges the thoughts and a of the heart. *G1936*

ATTRACT (1) [ATTRACTED, ATTRACTIVE, ATTRACTS]

Isa 53: 2 had no beauty or majesty *to* a *us to* him, H8011

ATTRACTED (2) [ATTRACT]

Dt 21:11 a beautiful woman and *are* a to her, H3137
Est 2:17 Now the king *was* a to Esther more than to H170

ATTRACTIVE (3) [ATTRACT]

Jdg 15: 2 Isn't her younger sister more a? Take her H3202
Zec 9:17 How a and beautiful they will be! Grain H3206
Titus 2:10 *they will* **make** the teaching about
God our Savior a *G3175*

ATTRACTS (1) [ATTRACT]

Pr 19: 4 Wealth a many friends, but even the H3578

AUDACITY (1)

Lk 11: 8 because of your **shameless** a he will surely *G357*

AUDIENCE (5)
1Ki 10:24 world sought **a** *with* Solomon to hear H7156
2Ch 9:23 the earth sought **a** *with* Solomon to hear H7156
Pr 29:26 Many **seek an a with** a ruler, but it H1335+7156
Ac 12:20 *they* now joined together and **sought an a** G4205
Ac 25:23 pomp and entered the **a room** with the G211

AUGUSTUS (1)
Lk 2: 1 those days Caesar **A** issued a decree that G880

AUL (KJV) AWL

AUNT (2)
Lev 18:14 to have sexual relations; she is your **a**. H1860
Lev 20:20 " 'If a man has sexual relations with his **a** H1860

AUSTERE (KJV) HARD

AUTHOR (1)
Ac 3:15 You killed the **a** of life, but God raised him G795

AUTHORITIES (13) [AUTHORITY]
Lk 12:11 rulers and **a**, do not worry about G2026
Jn 7:26 Have the **a** really concluded that he is the G807
Ac 16:19 them into the marketplace to face the **a**. G807
Ro 13: 1 everyone be subject *to* the governing **a**, G2026
Ro 13: 1 The **a** that exist have been established by NDT
Ro 13: 5 it is necessary to submit to the **a**, not only NDT
Ro 13: 6 you pay taxes, for the **a** are God's servants NDT
Eph 3:10 to the rulers and **a** in the heavenly realms G2026
Eph 6:12 against the **a**, against the powers G2026
Col 1:16 whether thrones or powers or rulers or **a** G2026
Col 2:15 And having disarmed the powers and **a** G2026
Titus 3: 1 the people to be subject to rulers and **a**, G2026
1Pe 3:22 **a** and powers in submission to him. G2026

AUTHORITY (97) [AUTHORITIES, AUTHORIZATION, AUTHORIZE, AUTHORIZED]
Ge 41:35 store up the grain under the **a** *of* Pharaoh, H3338
Nu 27:20 Give him some of your **a** so the whole H2086
Dt 1:15 appointed them to have **a** over you H8031
Ezr 7:24 that you have no **a** to impose taxes, A10718
Ne 3: 7 places under the **a** *of* the governor of H4058
Est 9:29 wrote with full **a** to confirm this second H9549
Isa 22:21 around him and hand your **a** over to him. H4939
Jer 5:31 the priests rule by their own **a**, and my H3338
Da 4:31 Your **royal a** has been taken from you. A10424
Da 7: 6 four heads, and it was given **a to rule**. A10717
Da 7:12 beasts had been stripped of their **a**, A10717
Da 7:14 He was given **a**, glory and sovereign A10717
Mt 7:29 because he taught as one who had **a**, and G2026
Mt 8: 9 For I myself am a man under **a**, with G2026
Mt 9: 6 the Son of Man has **a** on earth to forgive G2026
Mt 9: 8 who had given such **a** to man. G2026
Mt 10: 1 him and gave them **a** to drive out impure G2026
Mt 20:25 their high officials **exercise a over** them. G2980
Mt 21:23 "By what **a** are you doing these things?" G2026
Mt 21:23 "And who gave you this **a**?" G2026
Mt 21:24 will tell you by what **a** I am doing these G2026
Mt 21:27 I tell you by what **a** I am doing these G2026
Mt 28:18 "All **a** in heaven and on earth has been G2026
Mk 1:22 he taught them as one who had **a**, G2026
Mk 1:27 teaching—and with **a**! He even gives G2026
Mk 2:10 the Son of Man has **a** on earth to forgive G2026
Mk 3:15 to have **a** to drive out demons. G2026
Mk 6: 7 two and gave them **a** over impure spirits. G2026
Mk 10:42 their high officials **exercise a over** them. G2980
Mk 11:28 "By what **a** are you doing these things?" G2026
Mk 11:28 "And who gave you **a** to do this?" G2026
Mk 11:29 will tell you by what **a** I am doing these G2026
Mk 11:33 I tell you by what **a** I am doing these G2026
Lk 4: 6 "I will give you all their **a** and splendor; it G2026
Lk 4:32 at his teaching, because his words had **a**. G2026
Lk 4:36 With **a** and power he gives orders to G2026
Lk 5:24 the Son of Man has **a** on earth to forgive G2026
Lk 7: 8 For I myself am a man under **a**, with G2026
Lk 9: 1 he gave them power and **a** to drive out all G2026
Lk 10:19 I have given you **a** to trample on snakes G2026
Lk 12: 5 been killed, has **a** to throw you into hell. G2026
Lk 20: 2 "Tell us by what **a** you are doing these G2026
Lk 20: 2 "Who gave you this **a**?" G2026
Lk 20: 8 I tell you by what **a** I am doing these G2026
Lk 20:20 hand him over *to* the power and **a** of the G2026
Lk 22:25 those *who* **exercise a over** them call G2027
Jn 2:18 sign *can you* **show** us **to prove** *your* **a** to G1259
Jn 5:27 he has given him **a** to judge because he G2026
Jn 7:28 I am not here **on** my own **a**, but he who G608
Jn 10:18 I have **a** to lay it down and authority to G2026
Jn 10:18 to lay it down and **a** to take it up again. G2026
Jn 14:10 to you I do not speak **on my own a**. G608+1831
Jn 17: 2 For you granted him **a** over all people that G2026
Ac 1: 7 dates the Father has set by his own **a**. G2026
Ac 9:14 he has come here with **a** from the chief G2026
Ac 26:10 **On** the **a** of the chief priests I put G2026+3284
Ac 26:12 Damascus with the **a** and commission of G2026
Ro 7: 1 that the law **has a over** someone only as G3259
Ro 13: 1 there is no **a** except that which God G2026
Ro 13: 2 rebels against the **a** is rebelling against G2026
Ro 13: 3 want to be free from fear of the one *in* **a**? G2026
Ro 13: 4 For the one in **a** is God's servant for your NDT
1Co 7: 4 The wife *does* not **have a** over her own G2027
1Co 7: 4 the husband *does* not **have a** over his G2027
1Co 9: 8 Do I say this merely **on** human **a**? Doesn't G2848
1Co 11:10 ought to have **a** over her own head, G2026
1Co 15:24 has destroyed all dominion, **a** and power. G2026
2Co 10: 8 freely about the **a** the Lord gave us for G2026
2Co 13:10 not have to be harsh in my use of **a**— G2026
2Co 13:10 **the a** the Lord gave me for building you G4005S
Eph 1:21 far above all rule and **a**, power and G2026
Col 2:10 He is the head over every power and **a**. G2026
1Th 2: 6 we could have **asserted** our **a**. G1877+983+1639
1Th 4: 2 we gave you **by the a of** the Lord Jesus. G1328
1Ti 2: 2 kings and all those in **a**, that we may G5667
1Ti 2:12 to teach or *to* **assume a over** a man; G883
Titus 2:15 Encourage and rebuke with all **a**. Do not G2198
Heb 13:17 in your leaders and **submit to** their **a**, G5640
1Pe 2:13 the Lord's sake to every human **a**: G3232
1Pe 2:13 to the emperor, as the **supreme a**, G5660
2Pe 2:10 corrupt desire of the flesh and despise **a**. G3262
Jude 6 keep their **positions of a** but abandoned G794
Jude 8 reject **a** and heap abuse on celestial G3262
Jude 25 majesty, power and **a**, through Jesus G2026
Rev 2:26 to the end, I will give **a** over the nations— G2026
Rev 2:27 just as I have received **a** from my Father. NDT
Rev 12:10 of our God, and the **a** of his Messiah. G2026
Rev 13: 2 his power and his throne and great **a**. G2026
Rev 13: 4 because he had given **a** to the beast, G2026
Rev 13: 5 to exercise its **a** for forty-two months. G2026
Rev 13: 7 And it was given **a** over every tribe G2026
Rev 13:12 It exercised all the **a** of the first beast on G2026
Rev 17:12 hour will receive **a** as kings along with G2026
Rev 17:13 will give their power and **a** to the beast. G2026
Rev 17:17 to hand over to the beast their **royal a**, G993
Rev 18: 1 He had great **a**, and the earth was G2026
Rev 20: 4 those who had been given **a** to judge. NDT

AUTHORIZATION (1) [AUTHORITY]
Ac 15:24 from us without *our* **a** and disturbed you, G1403

AUTHORIZE (1) [AUTHORITY]
Jer 29:23 they have uttered lies—which *I did* not **a**. H7422

AUTHORIZED (3) [AUTHORITY]
Ezr 3: 7 to Joppa, as **a** *by* Cyrus king of Persia. H8397
Ezr 5: 3 "Who **a** you to rebuild this A10682+10302
Ezr 5: 9 "Who **a** you to rebuild this A10682+10302

AUTUMN (7)
Dt 11:14 in its season, both **a** and spring **rains**, so H3453
Ps 84: 6 the **a rains** also cover it with pools. H4620
Jer 5:24 who gives **a** and spring **rains** in season H3453
Joel 2:23 has given you the **a rains** because he is H4620
Joel 2:23 showers, both **a** and spring **rains**, as H4620
Jas 5: 7 waiting for the **a** and spring **rains**. G4611
Jude 12 along by the wind; **a** trees, without fruit G5781

AVAIL (2) [AVAILABLE]
Isa 16:12 goes to her shrine to pray, *it is to* no **a**. H3523
Da 11:27 each other, but *to* no **a**, because an end H7503

AVAILABLE (2) [AVAIL]
1Ki 7:36 in every **a space**, with wreaths all H5113
Lk 2: 7 because there was no guest room *a for* **them**. AIT

AVEN (1) [BETH AVEN]
Am 1: 5 is in the Valley of **A** and the one who holds H225

AVENGE (19) [VENGEANCE]
Ge 27:42 Esau *is* **planning to a himself** by killing H5714
Lev 26:25 sword on you *to* **a** the breaking of H5933+5934
Dt 32:35 It is mine to **a**; I will repay. In due time H5934
Dt 32:43 for *he will* **a** the blood of his servants H5933
1Sa 24:12 *may* the LORD **a** the **wrongs** you have *done to* H5933
2Sa 3:27 **to a** the blood of his brother Asahel H928
2Ki 9: 7 and *I will* **a** the blood of my servants the H5933
Est 8:13 on that day to **a themselves** on their H5933
Ps 79:10 the nations that *you* **a** the outpoured H5935
Pr 20:22 Wait for the LORD, and *he will* **a** you. H3828
Isa 1:24 on my foes and **a myself** on my enemies. H5933
Jer 5: 9 "*Should I* not **a** myself on such a nation H5933
Jer 5:29 "*Should I* not **a** myself on such a nation H5933
Jer 9: 9 "*Should I* not **a** myself on such a nation H5933
Jer 15:15 care for me. **A** me on my persecutors H5933
Jer 51:36 I will defend your cause and **a** you H5933+5935
Ro 12:19 "It is mine to **a**; I will repay," says the Lord G1689
Heb 10:30 who said, "It is mine to **a**; I will repay," G1689
Rev 6:10 inhabitants of the earth and **a** our blood?" G1688

AVENGED (11) [VENGEANCE]
Ge 4:24 If Cain **is a** seven times, then Lamech H5933
Jos 10:13 till the nation **a** *itself on* its enemies, as it H5933
Jdg 9:24 *might be* **a** on their brother Abimelek H8492
Jdg 11:36 now that the LORD *has* **a** you of your H5935+6913
1Sa 14:24 before *I have* **a myself** on my enemies!" H5933
1Sa 25:31 bloodshed or of *having* **a** himself. H3828
2Sa 4: 8 day the LORD *has* **a** my lord the king H5989+5935
Ps 58:10 righteous will be glad when they are **a**, H5934
Eze 5:13 against them will subside, and *I will* **be a**. H5714
Ac 7:24 his defense and **a** him by killing G4472+1689
Rev 19: 2 *He has* **a** on her the blood of his servants." G1688

AVENGER (16) [VENGEANCE]
Nu 35:12 They will be places of refuge from the **a** H1457
Nu 35:19 The **a** *of* blood shall put the murderer to H1457
Nu 35:19 when **the a** comes upon the murderer H2257S
Nu 35:19 **the a** shall put the murderer to death. H2085S
Nu 35:21 The **a** *of* blood shall put the murderer to H1457
Nu 35:24 accused and the **a** *of* blood according to H1457
Nu 35:25 of murder from the **a** *of* blood and send H1457
Nu 35:27 the **a** *of* blood finds them outside the H1457
Nu 35:27 the **a** *of* blood may kill the accused H1457
Dt 19: 6 the **a** *of* blood might pursue him in a rage H1457
Dt 19:12 be handed over to the **a** *of* blood to die. H1457
Jos 20: 3 find protection from the **a** *of* blood. H1457
Jos 20: 5 If the **a** *of* blood comes in pursuit, the H1457
Jos 20: 9 not be killed by the **a** *of* blood prior to H1457
2Sa 14:11 to prevent the **a** *of* blood from adding H1457
Ps 8: 2 enemies, to silence the foe and the **a**. H5933

AVENGES (5) [VENGEANCE]
2Sa 22:48 He is the God who **a** me, who puts H5989+5935
Ps 9:12 For *he who* **a** blood remembers; he does H2011
Ps 18:47 He is the God who **a** me, who H5989+5935
Ps 94: 1 The LORD is a God who **a**. O God who H5935
Ps 94: 1 who avenges. O God who **a**, shine forth. H5935

AVENGING (3) [VENGEANCE]
1Sa 25:26 bloodshed and from **a** yourself with your H3828
1Sa 25:33 this day and from **a** myself with my own H3828
Na 1: 2 The LORD is a jealous and **a** God; the LORD H5933

AVERT (1)
Jer 11:15 *Can* consecrated meat **a** your *punishment* H6296+4946+6584

AVITH (2)
Ge 36:35 His city was named **A**. H6400
1Ch 1:46 His city was named **A**. H6400

AVIV (5) [TEL AVIV]
Ex 13: 4 in the month of **A**, you are leaving. H26
Ex 23:15 at the appointed time in the month of **A**, H26
Ex 34:18 at the appointed time in the month of **A**, H26
Dt 16: 1 Observe the month of **A** and celebrate the H26
Dt 16: 1 in the month of **A** he brought you out of H26

AVOID (18) [AVOIDED, AVOIDS]
Ne 5: 9 fear of our God to **a** the reproach of our H4946
Ps 38:11 companions **a** me because of my H6641
Pr 4:15 **A** it, do not travel on it; turn from it and H7277
Pr 15:12 correction, so *they* **a** the wise. H4202+2143+448
Pr 19: 7 how much more *do* their friends **a** them! H8178
Pr 20: 3 It is to one's honor *to* **a** strife, but H3782+4946
Pr 20:19 so **a** anyone who talks too H4202+6843+4200
Ecc 7:18 Whoever fears God *will* **a** all extremes. H3655
Eze 46:20 to **a** bringing them into the outer court H1194
Zep 1: 9 punish all who **a stepping** on the H1925
Jn 18:28 to **a** ceremonial uncleanness they did G3590
Ac 15:29 You will do well *to* **a** these things G1413
Ac 20:16 past Ephesus to **a** spending time in the G3590
2Co 8:20 *We want to* **a** any criticism of the way we G5097
Gal 6:12 they do this is to **a** being persecuted for G3590
1Th 4: 3 *that* you *should* **a** sexual immorality; G600
2Ti 2:16 **A** godless chatter, because those who G4325
Titus 3: 9 But **a** foolish controversies and G4325

AVOIDED (1) [AVOIDS]
Pr 16: 6 through the fear of the LORD evil *is* **a**. H6073

AVOIDS (1) [AVOID]
Pr 16:17 The highway of the upright **a** evil; those H6073

AVVA (1)
2Ki 17:24 Kuthah, **A**, Hamath and Sepharvaim and H6379

AVVIM (1)
Jos 18:23 **A**, Parah, Ophrah, H6399

AVVITES (3)
Dt 2:23 And as for the **A** who lived in villages as H6398
Jos 13: 3 Gath and Ekron; the territory of the **A** H6398
2Ki 17:31 the **A** made Nibhaz and Tartak, and the H6398

AWAIT (5) [WAIT]
Isa 24:17 Terror and pit and snare **a** you, people of H6584
Jer 48:43 Terror and pit and snare **a** you, you H6584
Hos 9: 8 Ephraim, yet snares **a** him on all his paths NDT
Gal 5: 5 through the Spirit we **eagerly a** by faith the G587
Php 3:20 And *we* **eagerly a** a Savior from there, the G587

AWAITS (9) [WAIT]
Job 17: 1 my days are cut short, the grave **a** me. H4200
Ps 37:37 upright; a future **a** those who seek peace. H4200
Ps 65: 1 Praise **a** you, our God, in Zion; to you our H1875
Pr 15:10 Stern discipline **a** anyone who leaves the H4200
Pr 28:22 rich and are unaware that poverty **a** them. H995
Ecc 3:19 the animals; the same fate **a** them both: H4200
Ecc 9: 1 whether love or hate **a** them. H4200+7156
Ob 5 in the night—oh, what a **disaster a** *you*!— H1950
Hab 2: 3 For the revelation **a** an appointed time; it H6388

AWAKE (29) [WAKE]
Job 14:12 people *will* not **a** or be roused from their H7810
Ps 7: 6 rage of my enemies. **A**, my God; decree H6424
Ps 17:15 see your face; when *I* **a**, I will be satisfied H7810
Ps 35:23 **A**, and rise to my defense! Contend for H6424
Ps 44:23 **A**, Lord! Why do you sleep? Rouse H6424
Ps 57: 8 **A**, my soul! Awake, harp and lyre! I will H6424
Ps 57: 8 **A**, harp and lyre! I will awaken H6424

Ps 102: 7 *I* **lie a**; I have become like a bird alone on H9193
Ps 108: 2 **A**, harp and lyre! I will awaken the dawn. H6424
Ps 139:18 grains of sand—*when I* **a**, I am still with H7810
Pr 6:22 over you; when *you* **a**, they will speak to H7810
Pr 20:13 **stay a** and you will have food to H7219+6524
SS 4:16 **A**, north wind, and come, south wind H6424
SS 5: 2 I slept but my heart *was* **a**. Listen! My H6424
Isa 51: 9 **A**, awake, arm of the LORD, clothe yourself H6424
Isa 51: 9 **a**, arm of the LORD, clothe yourself H6424
Isa 51: 9 **A**, as in days gone by, as in generations H6424
Isa 51:17 **A**, awake! Rise up, Jerusalem, you who H6424
Isa 51:17 **a**! Rise up, Jerusalem, you who H6424
Isa 52: 1 **A**, awake, Zion, clothe yourself with H6424
Isa 52: 1 **a**, Zion, clothe yourself with H6424
Jer 51:39 then sleep forever and not **a**," declares H7810
Jer 51:57 they will sleep forever and not **a**, H7810
Da 12: 2 who sleep in the dust of the earth *will* **a**: H7810
Zec 13: 7 "**A**, sword, against my shepherd, against H6424
Lk 9:32 but *when they became* **fully a**, they saw *G1340*
1Th 5: 6 who are asleep, but *let us be* **a** and sober. *G1213*
1Th 5:10 whether *we are* **a** or asleep, we *G1213*
Rev 16:15 is the *one who* **stays a** and remains *G1213*

AWAKEN (6) [WAKE]

Ps 57: 8 harp and lyre! *I will* **a** the dawn. H6424
Ps 80: 2 Manasseh. **A** your might; come and H6424
Ps 108: 2 harp and lyre! *I will* **a** the dawn. H6424
SS 2: 7 Do not arouse or **a** love until it so desires. H6424
SS 3: 5 Do not arouse or **a** love until it so desires. H6424
SS 8: 4 Do not arouse or **a** love until it so desires. H6424

AWAKENED (3) [WAKE]

1Ki 18:27 Maybe he is sleeping and *must be* **a**." H3699
2Ki 4:31 Elisha and told him, "The boy *has* not **a**." H7810
Zec 4: 1 woke me up, like someone **a** from sleep. H6424

AWAKENS (2) [WAKE]

Isa 29: 8 of eating, but **a** hungry still; as when H7810
Isa 29: 8 of drinking, but **a** faint and thirsty still. H7810

AWAKES (1) [WAKE]

Ps 73:20 They are like a dream when *one* **a**; when H7810

AWARD (1)

2Ti 4: 8 righteous Judge, *will* **a** to me on that day *G625*

AWARE (20)

Ge 19:33 *He was* not **a** *of it* when she lay down H3359
Ge 19:35 Again *he was* not **a** *of it* when she lay H3359
Ge 28:16 LORD is in this place, and I *was* not **a** *of* it." H3359
Ex 34:29 he *was* not **a** that his face was radiant H3359
Lev 5: 2 " 'If anyone becomes **a** that they are guilty— NDT
Lev 5: 5 *anyone becomes* **a that** *they are* **guilty** in H870
Nu 15:24 **without** the community **being a** *of* H4946+6524
1Sa 14: 3 No one *was* **a** that Jonathan had left H3359
1Ki 8:38 *being* **a** *of* the afflictions of their own H3359
2Ch 6:29 *being* **a** *of* their afflictions and pains H3359
Ne 4:15 heard that we *were* **a** *of* their plot and H3359
Mt 12:15 **A** of this, Jesus withdrew from that place *G1182*
Mt 16: 8 **A** *of* their discussion, Jesus asked, "You of *G1182*
Mt 24:50 expect him and at an hour *he is* not **a of**. *G1182*
Mt 26:10 **A** *of this*, Jesus said to them, "Why are *G1182*
Mk 8:17 **A of** their discussion, Jesus asked them *G1182*
Lk 12:46 expect him and at an hour *he is* not **a of**. *G1182*
Jn 6:61 **A** that his disciples were *G3857+1877+1571*
Ac 10:28 "You *are* **well a** that it is against our law *G2179*
Gal 4:21 law, *are you* not **a of what** the law **says**? *G201*

AWAY (777)

Ge 5:24 was no more, because God **took him a**. H4374
Ge 6:21 is to be eaten and **store** it **a** as food for you H665
Ge 14:11 all their food; then *they* **went a**. H2143
Ge 15:11 the carcasses, but Abram **drove** them **a**. H5959
Ge 16: 8 "I'm **running a** from my mistress Sarai," H1368
Ge 18:22 The men turned **a** and went toward H4946+9004
Ge 18:23 "*Will you* **sweep a** the righteous with the H6200
Ge 18:24 *Will you* really **sweep** it **a** and not spare H6200
Ge 19:15 or *you will* **be swept a** when the city is H6200
Ge 19:17 to the mountains or *you will* **be swept a**!" H6200
Ge 21:16 went off and sat down about a bowshot **a**, H8178
Ge 25: 6 concubines and **sent** them **a** from his son H8938
Ge 26:16 "Move **a from** us; you have H4946+6640
Ge 26:17 So Isaac moved **a from** there and H4946
Ge 26:27 were hostile to me and sent me **a**?" H4946+907
Ge 26:29 you well and **sent** you **a** peacefully. H8938
Ge 26:31 and they went **a** peacefully. H4946+907
Ge 27:39 dwelling will be **a from** the earth's H4946
Ge 27:39 **a from** the dew of heaven above. H4946
Ge 29: 3 roll the stone **a from** the well's H4946+6584
Ge 29: 8 been rolled **a from** the mouth of H4946+6584
Ge 29:10 the stone **a from** the mouth of H4946+6584
Ge 30:15 it enough that you **took a** my husband? H4374
Ge 30:23 said, "God *has* **taken a** my disgrace." H665
Ge 31: 9 So God *has* **taken a** your father's livestock H5911
Ge 31:16 the wealth that God **took a** from our father H5911
Ge 31:20 by not telling him he *was* **running a**. H1368
Ge 31:27 so *I could* **send** you **a** with joy and singing H8938
Ge 31:31 your daughters **a from** me by force. H4946+6640
Ge 31:42 *you would* surely *have* **sent** me **a** H8938
Ge 31:49 you and me when *we are* **a** from each H6259
Ge 40:19 And the birds *will* **eat a** your flesh." H430
Ge 42:24 *He* **turned a** from them and began to H6015
Ge 44:28 One of them **went a** from me, and I said H3655
Ge 45:24 Then *he* **sent** his brothers **a**, and as they H8938
Ge 47:13 Canaan **wasted a** because of the H3532
Ex 2:17 shepherds came along and **drove** them **a**, H1763
Ex 5: 4 why *are you* **taking** the people **a** from H7277
Ex 8: 8 the LORD *to* **take** the frogs **a** from me and H6073
Ex 10:17 God *to* **take** this deadly plague **a** from me H6073
Ex 14:25 "*Let's* **get a** from the Israelites! H5674
Ex 15:15 the people of Canaan *will* **melt a**; H4570
Ex 16:21 when the sun grew hot, *it* **melted a**. H5022
Ex 18: 2 After Moses had **sent a** his wife Zipporah H8933
Ex 22:10 is injured or **is taken a** while no one is H8647
Ex 23:25 *I will* **take a** sickness from among you H6073
Ex 32: 8 They have been quick *to* **turn a** from what I H6073
Ex 33: 7 outside the camp **some distance a**, H8178+4946
Lev 10: 4 **a from** the front of the sanctuary." H4946+907
Lev 10:17 was given to you to **take a** the guilt of the H5951
Lev 16:21 *He shall* **send** the goat **a** into the H8938
Lev 26:39 who are left *will* **waste a** in the lands of H5245
Lev 26:39 of their ancestors' sins *they will* **waste a**. H5245
Nu 5: 2 the Israelites *to* **send a** from the camp H8938
Nu 5: 3 **Send a** male and female alike; send them H8938
Nu 9:10 of a dead body or are **a** on a journey, H8158
Nu 12:12 mother's womb with its flesh half **eaten a**." H430
Nu 14:43 Because *you have* **turned a** from the LORD H8740
Nu 16:24 assembly, '**Move a** from the tents of Korah H6590
Nu 16:26 or *you will* **be swept a** because of all their H6200
Nu 16:27 So *they* **moved a** from the tents of Korah H6590
Nu 16:37 scatter the coals **some distance a**, H2134
Nu 16:45 "**Get a** from this assembly so I can put an H8250
Nu 20:21 territory, Israel turned **a from** them. H4946+6584
Nu 21: 7 the LORD *will* **take** the snakes **a** from us." H6073
Nu 22:11 be able to fight them and **drive** them **a**. H1763
Nu 22:33 saw me and **turned a** from me these H5742
Nu 22:33 If *it had* not **turned a**, I would certainly H5742
Nu 25: 4 fierce anger *may* **turn a** from Israel." H8740
Nu 25:11 *has* **turned** my anger **a** from the Israelites. H8740
Nu 32:15 If *you* **turn a** from following him, he will H8740
Nu 36: 3 inheritance allotted to us *will* **be taken a**. H1757
Dt 7: 4 for *they will* **turn** your children **a** from H6073
Dt 9:12 *They have* **turned a** quickly from what I H6073
Dt 11:16 will be enticed *to* **turn a** and worship H6073
Dt 12:21 to put his Name *is too* **far a** from you, H8178
Dt 12:32 do not add to it or **take a** from it. H1757
Dt 13:10 they tried to **turn** you **a** from the LORD your H5615
Dt 14:24 will choose to put his Name *is so* **far a**), H8178
Dt 15:13 do not send them **a** empty-handed. H4946+6640
Dt 23: 9 enemies, keep **a from** everything impure. H4946
Dt 23:14 indecent and turn **a from** you. H4946+339
Dt 28:26 there will be no *one to* **frighten** them **a**. H3006
Dt 28:49 will bring a nation against you from **far a**, H8158
Dt 29:18 whose heart **turns a** from the LORD our H7155
Dt 30:17 But if your heart **turns a** and you are not H7155
Dt 30:17 if *you* **are drawn a** to bow down to H5615
Jos 2:21 So *she* **sent** them **a**, and they H8938
Jos 3:16 It piled up in a heap a great **distance a** H8178
Jos 5: 9 "Today *I have* **rolled a** the reproach of H1670
Jos 6:18 But **keep a** from the devoted things, so H9068
Jos 8: 6 us until *we have* **lured** them **a** from the H5998
Jos 8: 6 '*They are* **running a** from us as they did H5674
Jos 8:16 Joshua and **were lured a** from the city. H5998
Jos 22: 6 Joshua blessed them and **sent** them **a**, H8938
Jos 22:16 How could you **turn a** from the LORD and H8740
Jos 22:18 And *are* you now **turning a** from the LORD H8740
Jos 22:23 our own altar to **turn a** from the LORD and H8740
Jos 22:29 the LORD and **turn a** from him today by H8740
Jos 23:12 "But if *you* **turn a** and ally H8740+8740
Jos 24:14 **Throw a** the gods your ancestors H6073
Jos 24:23 "**throw a** the foreign gods that are among H6073
Jdg 3:26 they waited, Ehud **got a**. He passed by H4880
Jdg 5:21 The river Kishon **swept** them **a**, the H1759
Jdg 6:18 Please *do* not **go a** until I come back and H4631
Jdg 11: 2 were grown up, *they* **drove** Jephthah **a**. H1763
Jdg 11:13 they **took a** my land from the Arnon to the H4374
Jdg 12: 9 *He* **gave** his daughters **a in marriage** to H8938
Jdg 15:17 speaking, *he* **threw a** the jawbone; and H8959
Jdg 18:21 in front of them, *they* **turned a** and left. H7155
Jdg 18:24 gods I made, and my priest, and **went a**. H2143
Jdg 20:31 meet them and **were drawn a** from the H5998
Jdg 20:32 retreat and **draw** them **a** from the city to H5998
Ru 1:21 I **went a** full, but the LORD has brought me H2143
Ru 2: 8 in another field and don't **go a** from here. H6296
1Sa 1:14 going to stay drunk? **Put a** your wine." H6073
1Sa 2: 5 she who has had many sons **pines a**. H581
1Sa 5:11 "**Send** the ark of the god of Israel **a**; let H8938
1Sa 6: 7 but **take** their calves **a** and pen them up. H8740
1Sa 7: 4 So the Israelites **put a** their Baals and H6073
1Sa 12:20 this evil; yet *do* not **turn a** from the LORD H6073
1Sa 12:21 *Do* not **turn a** after useless idols. They can H6073
1Sa 14:16 the army **melting a** in all H4570+2256+2143
1Sa 15: 6 to the Kenites, "Go **a**, leave the H6073
1Sa 15: 6 So the Kenites **moved a** from the H6073
1Sa 15:11 he has turned **a from** me and has H4946+339
1Sa 17:30 He then turned **a** to someone else H4946+725
1Sa 18:13 So he **sent** David **a** from him and gave H6073
1Sa 19:17 like this and **send** my enemy **a** so that he H8938
1Sa 19:17 told him, "He said to me, '**Let** me **get a**. H8938
1Sa 20:13 let you know and send you **a** in peace. H2143
1Sa 20:22 must go, because the LORD *has* **sent** you **a**. H8938
1Sa 20:29 **let** *me* **get a** to see my brothers. H4880
1Sa 21: 6 by hot bread on the day it **was taken a**. H4374
1Sa 23:26 other side, hurrying to **get a** from Saul. H2143
1Sa 24:19 *does he* **let** him **get a** H8938+928+2006
1Sa 25:10 Many servants *are* **breaking a** from their H7287
1Sa 25:29 of your enemies *he will* **hurl a** as from the H7843
1Sa 26:13 on top of the hill **some distance a**; H4946+8158
1Sa 30:17 none of them **got a**, except four H4880
2Sa 3:15 gave orders and *had* her **taken a** from her H4374
2Sa 3:21 So David **sent** Abner **a**, and he went in H8938
2Sa 3:22 because David *had* **sent** him **a**, and he H8938
2Sa 3:23 that the king *had* **sent** him **a** and that he H8938
2Sa 4: 6 Rekab and his brother Baanah **slipped a**. H4880
2Sa 7:15 my love *will* never **be taken a** from him, H6073
2Sa 7:15 from him, as *I* **took** it **a** from Saul, whom H6073
2Sa 10: 4 at the buttocks, and **sent** them **a**. H8938
2Sa 12:13 replied, "The LORD *has* **taken a** your sin. H6296
2Sa 13:16 "**Sending** me **a** would be a greater wrong H8938
2Sa 13:19 put her hands on her head and **went a**, H2143
2Sa 19:41 *did* our brothers, the men of Judah,
steal the king **a** H1704
2Sa 22:23 *I have* not **turned a** from his decrees. H6073
2Sa 24:10 I beg you, **take a** the guilt of your servant. H6296
1Ki 2:40 So Shimei **went a** and brought the slaves H2143
1Ki 5: 9 separate them and you *can* **take** them **a**. H5951
1Ki 8:46 captive to their own lands, **far a** or near; H8158
1Ki 8:66 On the following day *he* **sent** the people **a**. H8938
1Ki 9: 6 descendants **turn a** from me and H8740+8740
1Ki 11: 9 his heart *had* **turned a** from the LORD, H5742
1Ki 11:11 *I will* **most certainly tear** the kingdom **a** H7973+7973
1Ki 12: 5 "**Go a** for three days and then come back H2143
1Ki 12: 5 come back to me." So the people **went a**. H2143
1Ki 14: 8 *I* **tore** the kingdom **a** from the house of H7973
1Ki 15:22 and *they* **carried a** from Ramah the stones H5951
1Ki 17:15 *She* **went a** and did as Elijah had told her. H2143
1Ki 18:40 Don't **let** anyone **get a**!" They H4880
1Ki 20: 6 seize everything you value and **carry** it **a**. H4374
1Ki 20:36 And after the man went **a**, a lion H4946+725
2Ki 3: 3 to commit; *he did* not **turn a** from them. H6073
2Ki 4:27 Gehazi came over to **push** her **a**, but the H2074
2Ki 4:35 Elisha **turned a** and walked back and forth H8740
2Ki 5:11 But Naaman **went a** angry and said, "I H2143
2Ki 5:24 the servants and **put** them **a** in the house. H7212
2Ki 5:24 *He* **sent** the men **a** and they left H8938
2Ki 6:23 drinking, *he* **sent** them **a**, and they H8938
2Ki 7:15 the Arameans *had* **thrown a** in their H8959
2Ki 8: 1 "**Go a** with your family and stay for a H2143
2Ki 8: 2 her family **went a** and stayed in the H2143
2Ki 9: 2 **get** him **a** from his companions and take H7756
2Ki 10:21 of Baal came; not one **stayed a**. H4202+995
2Ki 10:29 he *did* not **turn a** from the sins of H6073
2Ki 10:31 *He did* not **turn a** from the sins of H6073
2Ki 11: 2 of Ahaziah and **stole** him **a** from among H1704
2Ki 13: 2 commit, and *he did* not **turn a** from them. H6073
2Ki 13: 6 But *they did* not **turn a** from the sins of the H6073
2Ki 13:11 of the LORD and *did* not **turn a** from any of H6073
2Ki 14:24 of the LORD and *did* not **turn a** from any of H6073
2Ki 15: 9 *He did* not **turn a** from the sins of H6073
2Ki 15:18 entire reign *he did* not **turn a** from the H6073
2Ki 15:24 *He did* not **turn a** from the sins of H6073
2Ki 15:28 *He did* not **turn a** from the sins of H6073
2Ki 16:18 *He* **took a** the Sabbath canopy that had H6015
2Ki 17:21 When *he* **tore** Israel **a** from the house of H7973
2Ki 17:21 enticed Israel **a from** following the LORD H4946
2Ki 17:22 of Jeroboam and *did* not **turn a** from them H6073
2Ki 20:18 born to you, *will be* **taken a**, and they will H4374
2Ki 23: 5 *He* **did a with** the idolatrous priests H8697
2Ki 23:26 the LORD *did* not **turn a** from the heat of H8740
2Ki 25:14 *They* also **took a** the pots, shovels, wick H4374
2Ki 25:15 the imperial guard **took a** the censers H4374
2Ki 25:21 went into captivity, **a from** her land. H4946+6584
1Ch 12:19 after consultation, their rulers **sent** him **a**. H8938
1Ch 12:40 their neighbors from **as far a** as Issachar H6330
1Ch 17:13 *I will* never **take** my love **a** from him, as I H6073
1Ch 17:13 as *I* **took** it **a** from your predecessor. H6073
1Ch 19: 4 at the buttocks, and **sent** them **a**. H8938
1Ch 21: 8 I beg you, **take a** the guilt of your servant. H6296
1Ch 21:12 months of **being swept a** before your H6200
1Ch 26:29 were assigned duties **a from** the temple, H2667
2Ch 6:36 takes them captive to a land **far a** or near; H8158
2Ch 7:19 "But if you **turn a** and forsake the decrees H8740
2Ch 10: 5 me in three days." So the people **went a**. H2143
2Ch 16: 6 and *they* **carried a** from Ramah the stones H5951
2Ch 18:31 God **drew** them **a** from him, H6077
2Ch 20:10 so *they* **turned a** from them and did not H6073
2Ch 20:25 more than *they could* **take a**. H5911+5362
2Ch 21:20 *He* **passed a**, to no one's regret, and was H2143
2Ch 22:11 of Ahaziah and **stole** him **a** from among H1704
2Ch 25:27 that Amaziah **turned a** from following H6073
2Ch 28:17 attacked Judah and **carried a** prisoners, H8647
2Ch 29: 6 *They* **turned** their faces **a** from the LORD's H6015
2Ch 29:10 so that his fierce anger *will* **turn a** from us. H8740
2Ch 30: 8 that his fierce anger *will* **turn a** from you. H8740
2Ch 30:14 in Jerusalem and **cleared a** the incense H6073
2Ch 35:22 *would* not **turn a** from him H6015+7156
2Ch 35:23 his officers, "**Take** me **a**; I am badly H6296
Ezr 1: 7 Nebuchadnezzar *had* **carried a** from H3655
Ezr 3:13 sound was heard **far a**. H6330+4200+4946+8158
Ezr 6: 6 of that province, stay **a** from there. A10663
Ezr 10: 3 our God to **send a** all these women H3655
Ezr 10:14 our God in this matter *is* **turned a** from us." H8740
Ezr 10:19 their hands in pledge to **put a** their wives, H3655
Ne 6:11 "*Should* a man like me **run a**? Or H1368
Ne 8:12 all the people **went a** to eat and drink, H2143
Ne 12:43 in Jerusalem could be heard **far a**. H4946+8158

Ne 13:28 And *I* **drove** him **a** from me. H1368
Est 4:17 So Mordecai **went a** and carried out all of H6296
Est 6:14 hurried Haman **a** to the banquet H995
Job 1:21 The LORD gave and the LORD *has* **taken a** H4374
Job 3:16 Or why was I not **hidden a** in the ground H3243
Job 5:13 the schemes of the wily **are swept a**. H4554
Job 6:27 the fatherless and **barter a** your friend. H4126
Job 7:19 Will you never look **a from** me, or let me H4946
Job 8:19 Surely its life **withers a**, and from the soil H5376
Job 9:12 If *he* **snatches a**, who can stop him? Who H3166
Job 9:25 *they* **fly a** without a glimpse of joy. H1368
Job 10:20 Turn **a from** me so I can have a moment's H4946
Job 11:14 if *you* **put a** the sin that is in your hand H8178
Job 12:17 *He* **leads** rulers **a** stripped and makes H2143
Job 12:19 *He* **leads** priests **a** stripped and H2143
Job 12:20 advisers and **takes a** the discernment of H4374
Job 13:28 "So man **wastes a** like something rotten H1162
Job 14: 2 They spring up like flowers and **wither a** H4908
Job 14: 6 So look **a from** him and let him H4946+6584
Job 14:19 as water **wears a** stones and torrents wash H8835
Job 14:19 away stones and torrents **wash a** the soil, H8851
Job 14:20 their countenance and **send** them **a**. H8938
Job 15:12 Why *has* your heart **carried** you **a**, and H4374
Job 15:30 breath of God's mouth *will* **carry** *him* **a**. H6073
Job 16: 6 relieved; and if I refrain, it does not go **a**. H4946
Job 18:13 *It* **eats a** parts of his skin; death's firstborn H430
Job 19:14 My relatives *have* **gone a**; my closest H2532
Job 20: 8 Like a dream *he* **flies a**, no more to be H6414
Job 21:18 the wind, like chaff **swept a** *by* a gale? H1704
Job 22: 9 And *you* **sent** widows **a** empty-handed H8938
Job 22:16 their foundations **washed a** *by* a flood. H3668
Job 24: 3 *They* **drive a** the orphan's donkey and H5627
Job 24:19 drought **snatch a** the melted snow H1608
Job 24:19 the grave snatches **a** those who have sinned NDT
Job 24:22 But God **drags a** the mighty by his power H5432
Job 27: 8 are cut off, when God **takes a** their life? H8923
Job 27:20 a tempest **snatches** him **a** in the night. H1704
Job 30:15 my dignity *is* **driven a** as *by* the wind, my H8103
Job 30:16 "And now my life **ebbs a**; days of H9161
Job 32:22 my Maker *would* soon **take** me **a**. H5951
Job 33:21 Their flesh **wastes a** to nothing, and their H3983
Job 34:20 the people are shaken and *they* **pass a** H6296
Job 36:20 to **drag** people **a** *from* their homes. H6590
Job 39:22 nothing; *it does* not **shy a** from the sword. H8740
Ps 1: 4 They are like chaff that the wind **blows a**. H5622
Ps 6: 8 **A** from me, all you who do evil, for the H6073
Ps 14: 3 All *have* **turned a**, all have become H6073
Ps 18:22 *I have* not **turned a** from his decrees. H6073
Ps 25:18 my distress and **take a** all my sins. H5951
Ps 26: 9 *Do* not **take a** my soul along with sinners H665
Ps 27: 9 *do* not **turn** your servant **a** in anger H5742
Ps 28: 3 *Do* not **drag** me **a** with the wicked, with H5432
Ps 32: 3 my bones **wasted a** through my groaning H1162
Ps 34: T Abimelek, *who* **drove** him **a**, and he left. H1763
Ps 35: 5 with the angel of the LORD **driving** them **a**; H1890
Ps 36:11 the hand of the wicked **drive** me **a**. H5653
Ps 37: 2 like green plants *they will* soon **die a**. H5570
Ps 37:36 but *he* soon **passed a** and was no more H6296
Ps 38:11 wounds; my neighbors stay **far a**. H4946+8158
Ps 39:13 Look **a from** me, that I may enjoy life H4946
Ps 51: 2 **Wash a** all my iniquity and cleanse me H3891
Ps 53: 3 Everyone *has* **turned a**, all have become H6047
Ps 55: 6 *I would* **fly a** and be at rest. H6414
Ps 55: 7 *I would* flee **far a** and stay in the desert; H8178
Ps 58: 7 Let them vanish like water *that* **flows a** H2143
Ps 58: 8 be like a slug *that* **melts a** as it moves H9468
Ps 58: 9 green or dry—the wicked *will be* **swept a**. H8548
Ps 68: 2 *May you* **blow** them **a** like smoke—as H5622
Ps 71: 9 *Do* not **cast** me **a** when I am old; do not H8959
Ps 73:19 destroyed, completely **swept a** by terrors! H6200
Ps 80:18 Then *we will* not **turn a** from you; revive H6047
Ps 85: 4 and **put a** your displeasure toward us. H7296
Ps 90: 5 Yet *you* **sweep** people **a** in the sleep of H2441
Ps 90: 9 All our days **pass a** under your wrath; we H7155
Ps 90:10 for they quickly pass, and *we* **fly a**. H6414
Ps 102:11 the evening shadow; I **wither a** like grass. H3312
Ps 102:24 "*Do* not **take** me **a**, my God, in the midst H6590
Ps 104:22 sun rises, and *they* **steal a**; they return and H665
Ps 104:29 are terrified; *when you* **take a** their breath H665
Ps 106:43 rebellion and *they* **wasted a** in their sin. H4812
Ps 107: 5 thirsty, and their lives **ebbed a**. H6494
Ps 107:14 utter darkness, and **broke a** their chains. H5998
Ps 107:26 in their peril their courage **melted a**. H4570
Ps 109:23 *I* **fade a** like an evening shadow; I am H2143
Ps 112:10 they will gnash their teeth and **waste a** H5022
Ps 119:37 **Turn** my eyes **a** from worthless things H6296
Ps 119:39 **Take a** the disgrace I dread, for your laws H6296
Ps 119:115 **A** from me, *you* evildoers, that I may keep H6073
Ps 124: 5 the raging waters *would have* **swept** us **a**. H6296
Ps 139:19 **A** from me, *you* who are bloodthirsty! H6073
Ps 148: 6 he issued a decree *that will* never **pass a**. H6296
Pr 1:19 *it* **takes a** the life of those who get it. H4374
Pr 4: 5 not forget my words or turn **a from** them. H4946
Pr 6:33 and his shame *will* never **be wiped a**. H4681
Pr 13:11 Dishonest money **dwindles a**, but H5070
Pr 13:23 the poor, but injustice **sweeps** it **a**. H6200
Pr 14: 7 Stay **a from** a fool, for you will not H4946+5584
Pr 15: 1 A gentle answer **turns a** wrath, but a H8740
Pr 20:30 Blows and wounds **scrub a** evil, and H9475
Pr 21: 7 violence of the wicked *will* **drag** them **a**, H1760
Pr 22:15 the rod of discipline will drive it far **a**. H4946
Pr 24:11 Rescue *those* **being led a** to death; hold H4374
Pr 24:18 and **turn** his wrath **a** from them. H8740
Pr 25:20 Like *one who* **takes a** a garment on a cold H6334
Pr 27:10 a neighbor nearby than a relative **far a**. H8158
Pr 29: 8 stir up a city, but the wise **turn a** anger. H8740
Ecc 3: 6 a time to keep and a time to **throw a**, H8959
SS 1: 4 **Take** me **a** with you—let us hurry! Let the H5432
SS 5: 7 they took **a** my cloak, those H4946+6584
SS 8: 7 quench love; rivers cannot **sweep** it **a**. H8851
SS 8:14 **Come a**, my beloved, and be like a H1368
Isa 1:25 *I will* **thoroughly purge a** your dross H7671+3869+2021+1342
Isa 2:20 that day people *will* **throw a** to the moles H8959
Isa 3:18 that day the Lord *will* **snatch a** their finery: H6073
Isa 4: 1 by your name. **Take a** our disgrace!" H665
Isa 4: 4 The Lord *will* **wash a** the filth of the H8175
Isa 5: 5 I *will* **take a** its hedge, and it will be H6073
Isa 5:24 decay and their flowers **blow a** like dust; H6590
Isa 5:25 his anger *is* not **turned a**, his hand is H8740
Isa 6: 7 your guilt *is* **taken a** and your sin atoned H6073
Isa 6:12 the LORD *has* **sent** everyone **far a** and the H8178
Isa 7:17 any since Ephraim **broke a** from Judah— H6073
Isa 9:12 his anger *is* not **turned a**, his hand is H8740
Isa 9:17 his anger *is* not **turned a**, his hand is H8740
Isa 9:21 his anger *is* not **turned a**, his hand is H8740
Isa 10: 4 his anger *is* not **turned a**, his hand is H8740
Isa 10:18 destroy, as *when* a sick person **wastes a**. H5022
Isa 12: 1 your anger *has* **turned a** and you have H8740
Isa 14:31 **Melt a**, all you Philistines! A H4570
Isa 15: 7 stored up *they* **carry a** over the Ravine H5951
Isa 16:10 Joy and gladness **are taken a** from the H665
Isa 17: 4 will fade; the fat of his body *will* **waste a**. H8135
Isa 17:13 he rebukes them they flee **far a**, H4946+5305
Isa 18: 5 cut down and **take a** the spreading H6073
Isa 19: 7 parched, *will* **blow a** and be no more. H5622
Isa 19: 8 who throw nets on the water *will* **pine a**. H581
Isa 20: 4 king of Assyria *will* **lead a** stripped and H5627
Isa 22: 3 while the enemy was still **far a**. H4946+8158
Isa 22: 4 Therefore I said, "**Turn a** from me; let me H9120
Isa 22: 8 The Lord **stripped a** the defenses of Judah H1655
Isa 22:17 firm hold of you and **hurl** you **a**, H3214+3232
Isa 24:16 But I said, "I **waste a**, I waste away! Woe H8140
Isa 24:16 "I waste away, I **waste a**! Woe to me! H8140
Isa 25: 8 Sovereign LORD *will* **wipe a** the tears from H4681
Isa 28:17 plumb line; hail *will* **sweep a** your refuge H3589
Isa 28:19 As often as it comes *it will* **carry** you **a** H4374
Isa 30:17 at the threat of five *you will all* **flee a**, till H5674
Isa 30:22 *you will* **throw** them **a** like a menstrual H2430
Isa 30:22 cloth and say to them, "**A** *with you*!" H3655
Isa 33: 9 The land dries up and **wastes a**, Lebanon H581
Isa 33:13 You *who* are **far a**, hear what I have done H8158
Isa 34:12 a kingdom, all her princes will **vanish a**. H700
Isa 35:10 and sorrow and sighing *will* **flee a**. H5674
Isa 39: 7 born to you, *will be* **taken a**, and they will H4374
Isa 40:24 a whirlwind **sweeps** them **a** like chaff. H5951
Isa 41:16 them up, and a gale *will* **blow** them **a**. H7046
Isa 42:22 trapped in pits or **hidden a** in prisons. H2461
Isa 44:22 *I have* **swept a** your offenses like a cloud H4681
Isa 46:13 *it is* not **far a**; and my salvation H8178
Isa 47:11 you will not know how *to* **conjure** it **a**. H8838
Isa 49:19 those who devoured you *will be* **far a**. H8178
Isa 50: 1 of divorce with which *I* **sent** her **a**? H8938
Isa 50: 1 transgressions your mother **was sent a**. H8938
Isa 50: 5 not been rebellious, I have not turned **a**. H294
Isa 51:11 and sorrow and sighing *will* **flee a**. H5674
Isa 52: 5 my people *have* **been taken a** for nothing, H4374
Isa 53: 8 oppression and judgment *he* **was taken a**. H4374
Isa 57: 1 the devout **are taken a**, and no one H665
Isa 57: 1 the righteous **are taken a** to be spared from H665
Isa 57: 9 You sent your ambassadors **far a** H4946+8158
Isa 57:13 them off, a mere breath *will* **blow** them **a**. H4374
Isa 57:16 then they *would* **faint a** because of me H6494
Isa 58: 7 not *to* **turn a** from your own flesh and H6623
Isa 58: 9 "If *you* **do a with** the yoke of H6073+4946+9348
Isa 59:11 find none; for deliverance, but *it is* **far a**. H8178
Isa 64: 6 like the wind our sins **sweep** us **a**. H5951
Isa 65: 5 who say, '**Keep a**; don't come H7928+448+3870
Jer 3: 8 of divorce and **sent** her **a** because of all H8938
Jer 3:19 'Father' and not **turn a** from following me. H8740
Jer 4: 8 of the LORD *has* not **turned a** from us. H8740
Jer 4:25 people; every bird in the sky *had* **flown a**. H5610
Jer 5:23 they have turned aside and **gone a**. H2143
Jer 5:25 Your wrongdoings *have* **kept** these **a**; your H5742
Jer 6: 8 I *will* **turn a** from you and make your H3697
Jer 6:29 blow fiercely *to* **burn a** the lead with fire, H9462
Jer 7:29 " 'Cut off your hair and **throw** it **a**; take up H8959
Jer 7:33 there will be no *one to* **frighten** them **a**. H3006
Jer 8: 4 When *someone* **turns a**, do they not H8740
Jer 8: 5 Why then *have* these people **turned a** H8740
Jer 8: 5 Why does Jerusalem always **turn a**? They H5412
Jer 8:13 " '*I will* **take a** their harvest, declares the H665
Jer 8:19 to the cry of my people from a land **far a**: H5305
Jer 9: 2 my people and go **a from** them; H4946+907
Jer 13:19 be carried into exile, **carried** completely **a**. H1655
Jer 15: 1 people. **Send** them **a** from my presence H8938
Jer 15: 3 the dogs to **drag a** and the birds and H6079
Jer 15:15 *do* not **take** me **a**; think of how H4374
Jer 17: 3 all your treasures *I will* **give a** as plunder, H5989
Jer 17: 5 whose heart **turns a** from the LORD. H6073
Jer 17:13 *Those who* **turn a** *from* you will be written H6073
Jer 17:16 I have not run **a from** being your shepherd H4946
Jer 18:20 behalf to **turn** your wrath **a** from them. H8740
Jer 20: 4 *who will* **carry** them **a** to Babylon or put H1655
Jer 20: 5 *They will* **take** it **a** as plunder and carry it H4374
Jer 22:19 **dragged a** and thrown outside the gates H6079
Jer 22:22 The wind *will* **drive** all your shepherds **a** H8286
Jer 23: 2 my flock and **driven** them **a** and have not H5615
Jer 23:23 the LORD, "and not a God **far a**? H4946+8158
Jer 24: 5 whom *I* **sent a** from this place *to* the land H8938
Jer 27:20 king of Babylon *did* not **take a** when he H4374
Jer 29:20 exiles whom *I have* **sent a** from Jerusalem H8938
Jer 32:40 so that they *will* never **turn a** from me. H6073
Jer 41:16 who were with him **led a** all the people of H4374
Jer 43: 5 the army officers **led a** all the remnant of H4374
Jer 43: 6 They also led **a** all those whom NDT
Jer 44:12 *I will* **take a** the remnant of Judah who H4374
Jer 46:16 **a from** the sword of the oppressor. H4946+7156
Jer 49: 5 "Every one of *you will* **be driven a**, and no H5615
Jer 49:20 The young of the flock *will be* **dragged a** H6079
Jer 49:30 "Flee quickly **a**! Stay in deep caves, you H5653
Jer 50: 3 both people and animals will flee **a**. H2143
Jer 50:17 a scattered flock that lions *have* **chased a**. H5615
Jer 50:45 The young of the flock *will be* **dragged a** H6079
Jer 52:18 *They* also **took a** the pots, shovels, wick H4374
Jer 52:19 of the imperial guard **took a** the basins, H4374
Jer 52:27 went into captivity, **a from** her land. H4946+6584
La 1: 8 her naked; she herself groans and turns **a**. H294
La 2: 8 walls lament; together *they* **wasted a**. H581
La 2:12 as their lives **ebb a** in their mothers' arms. H9161
La 3: 2 *He has* **driven** me **a** and made me walk in H5627
La 4: 9 *they* **waste a** for lack of food from the field H2307
La 4:15 "**Go a**! You are unclean!" people cry to H6073
La 4:15 people cry to them. "**A**! Away! Don't touch H6073
La 4:15 "Away! **A**! Don't touch us!" H6073
Eze 3:14 Spirit then lifted me up and **took** me **a**, H4374
Eze 4:17 each other and *will* **waste a** because of H5245
Eze 5: 3 a few hairs and **tuck** them **a** in the folds of H7443
Eze 6: 9 which have turned **a from** me, and H4946+6584
Eze 6:12 One *who* is **far a** will die of the plague H8158
Eze 7:22 I will turn my face **a from** the people, and H4946
Eze 10: 5 could be heard **as far a as** the outer court, H6330
Eze 11:15 Israelites, '*They are* **far a** from the LORD H8178
Eze 11:16 Although *I* **sent** them **far a** among the H8178
Eze 16:42 my jealous anger *will* **turn a** from you; H6073
Eze 16:50 Therefore *I* **did a with** them as you have H6073
Eze 17: 4 topmost shoot and **carried** it **a** to a land of H995
Eze 17:10 it—**wither a** in the plot where it grew? H3312
Eze 17:13 *He* also **carried a** the leading men of the H4374
Eze 18:21 if a wicked person **turns a** from all the sins H8740
Eze 18:27 if a wicked person **turns a** from the H8740
Eze 18:28 have committed and **turn a** from them, H8740
Eze 18:30 **Turn a** from all your offenses; then sin will H8740
Eze 22: 5 those *who* are **far a** will mock you H8158
Eze 23:10 **took a** her sons and daughters and killed H4374
Eze 23:17 she **turned a** from them **in disgust**. H3697
Eze 23:18 I **turned a** from her **in disgust**, just H3697
Eze 23:18 just as I *had* **turned a** from her sister. H5936
Eze 23:22 those you **turned a** from **in disgust**, and I H5936
Eze 23:25 They *will* **take a** your sons and daughters H4374
Eze 23:28 to those you **turned a** from **in disgust**. H5936
Eze 23:29 you in hatred and **take a** everything you H4374
Eze 23:40 messengers for men who came from **far a**, H5305
Eze 24: 6 encrusted, whose deposit will not go **a**! H4946
Eze 24:11 may be melted and its deposit **burned a**. H9462
Eze 24:16 one blow I *am about to* **take a** from you H4374
Eze 24:23 weep but *will* **waste a** because of your H5245
Eze 24:25 on the day I **take a** their stronghold H4374
Eze 26: 4 *I will* **scrape a** her rubble and make her a H6081
Eze 30: 4 her wealth *will be* **carried a** and her H4374
Eze 31:15 all the trees of the field **withered a**. H6634
Eze 33:10 we *are* **wasting a** because of them. H5245
Eze 33:14 ' but *they* then **turn a** from their sin and do H8740
Eze 33:19 And if a wicked person **turns a** from their H8740
Eze 34:21 you have driven them **a**, H448+2021+2575+2025
Eze 38:13 to **take a** livestock and goods and to seize H4374
Eze 43: 9 Now *let them* **put a** from me their H8178
Da 1:16 So the guard **took a** their choice food and H5951
Da 2:35 The wind **swept** them **a** without leaving A10492
Da 4:25 You *will be* **driven a** from people and A10304
Da 4:32 You *will be* **driven a** from people and A10304
Da 4:33 *He* **was driven a** from people and ate A10304
Da 5:21 *He* **was driven a** from people and given A10304
Da 7:14 dominion that *will* not **pass a**, A10528
Da 7:26 his power *will be* **taken a** and A10528
Da 8:11 *it* **took a** the daily sacrifice from the LORD H8123
Da 9: 5 we *have* **turned a** from your commands H6073
Da 9:11 has transgressed your law and **turned a**, H6073
Da 9:16 **turn a** your anger and your wrath from H8740
Da 11:22 army *will* **be swept a** before him; H8851
Da 11:26 his army *will be* **swept a**, and many H8851
Hos 2: 9 "Therefore *I will* **take a** my grain when it H4374
Hos 4: 3 all who live in it **waste a**; the beasts of H581
Hos 4: 3 the sky and the fish in the sea *are* **swept a**. H665
Hos 4:11 wine and new wine **take a** their H4374
Hos 4:19 whirlwind *will* **sweep** them **a**, H7674+928+4053
Hos 5:14 I will tear them to pieces and **go a**; I will H2143
Hos 7:14 new wine, but *they* **turn a** from me. H6073
Hos 8:10 They will begin to **waste a** under the H5071
Hos 9:11 Ephraim's glory *will* **fly a** like a bird—no H6414
Hos 9:12 Woe to them when I **turn a** from them! H6073
Hos 10: 7 swept **a** like a twig on the surface of the NDT
Hos 11: 2 the more they went **a from** me. H4946+7156
Hos 13:11 you a king, and in my wrath *I* **took** him **a**. H4374
Hos 14: 4 my anger *has* **turned a** from them. H8740
Joel 1: 7 has stripped off their bark and **thrown** it **a**, H8959

A

Joel 1:12 Surely the people's joy *is* **withered a**. H3312
Joel 3: 8 sell them to the Sabeans, a nation **far a**." H8158
Am 2:15 the fleet-footed soldier *will* not **get a**, and H4880
Am 4: 2 when you *will* **be taken a** with hooks, H5951
Am 4: 7 when the harvest was still three months **a**. NDT
Am 5:23 **A** *with* the noise of your songs! I will not H6073
Am 6: 5 *You* **strum a** on your harps like David and H7260
Am 7:11 into exile, **a from** their native land. H4946+6584
Am 7:17 into exile, **a from** their native land. H4946+6584
Am 8: 4 the needy and **do a with** the poor of the H8697
Am 9: 1 Not one *will* **get a**, none will H5674+5674
Jnh 1: 3 But Jonah **ran a** from the LORD and H1368
Jnh 1:10 knew he *was* **running a** from the LORD, H1368
Jnh 2: 7 "When my life *was* **ebbing a**, I H6494
Jnh 2: 8 worthless idols **turn a from** God's love H6440
Jnh 4: 3 take **a** my life, for it is better for me H4946
Mic 2: 9 *You* **take a** my blessing from their children H4374
Mic 2:10 **go a**! For this is not your resting H2143
Mic 4: 7 remnant, those **driven a** a strong nation. H2133
Na 1: 5 quake before him and the hills **melt a**. H4570
Na 1:12 they will be destroyed and **pass a**. H6296
Na 1:13 from your neck and **tear** your shackles **a**." H5998
Na 2: 7 that Nineveh be exiled and **carried a**. H6590
Na 2: 8 is like a pool whose water *is* **draining a**. H5674
Na 3:16 locusts they strip the land and then **fly a**. H6414
Na 3:17 when the sun appears *they* **fly a**, and H5610
Zep 1: 2 "*I will* **sweep a** everything from the H6066+665
Zep 1: 3 "*I will* **sweep a** both man and beast; I will H6066
Zep 1: 3 *I will* **sweep a** the birds in the sky and the H6066
Zep 3:15 The LORD *has* **taken a** your punishment, he H6073
Hag 1: 9 What you brought home, *I* **blew a**. Why?" H5870
Zec 3: 4 *I have* **taken a** your sin, and I will H6296
Zec 6:15 *Those who are* **far a** will come and help to H8158
Zec 9: 4 the Lord *will* **take a** her **possessions** and H3769
Zec 9:10 *I will* **take a** the chariots from Ephraim H4162
Zec 10:11 down and Egypt's scepter *will* **pass a**. H6073
Mal 3: 7 your ancestors *you have* **turned a** from my H6073
Mal 3:15 they put God to the test, *they* **get a with** it. H4880
Mt 4:10 said to him, "**A from** me, Satan! For it G5632
Mt 5:29 you to stumble, gouge it out and throw it **a**. G608
Mt 5:30 you to stumble, cut it off and throw it **a**. G608
Mt 5:42 and *do* not **turn a** from the one who wants G695
Mt 6:26 do not sow or reap or **store a** in barns, G5251
Mt 7:23 'I never knew you. **A** from me, you G713
Mt 9:16 the patch *will* **pull a** from the garment G149
Mt 9:24 "**Go a**. The girl is not dead but G432
Mt 13:19 one comes and **snatches a** what was sown G773
Mt 13:21 because of the word, *they* quickly **fall a**. G4997
Mt 13:25 weeds among the wheat, and **went a**. G599
Mt 13:46 *he* **went a** and sold everything he had and G599
Mt 13:48 good fish in baskets, but threw the bad **a**. G2032
Mt 14:15 **Send** the crowds **a**, so they can go to the G668
Mt 14:16 "They do not need *to* **go a**. You give them G599
Mt 15:23 urged him, "**Send** her **a**, for she keeps G668
Mt 15:32 I do not want *to* **send** them **a** hungry, or G668
Mt 15:39 *After* Jesus *had* **sent** the crowd **a**, he got G668
Mt 16: 4 Jesus then left them and **went a**. G599
Mt 18: 8 you to stumble, cut it off and throw it **a**. G608
Mt 18: 9 you to stumble, gouge it out and throw it **a**. G608
Mt 18:12 one of them **wanders a**, will he not G4414
Mt 19: 7 wife a certificate of divorce and **send** her **a**?" G668
Mt 19:22 man heard this, *he* **went a** sad, because he G599
Mt 21: 3 and he will send them **right a**. G2317
Mt 21:43 of God *will be* **taken a** from you and G149
Mt 22:22 were amazed. So they left him and **went a**. G599
Mt 24: 1 the temple and *was* **walking a** when his G4513
Mt 24:10 many *will* **turn a from the faith** and will G4997
Mt 24:34 *will* certainly not **pass a** until all G4216
Mt 24:35 Heaven and earth *will* **pass a**, but my G4216
Mt 24:35 but my words *will* never **pass a**. G4216
Mt 24:39 the flood came and **took** them all **a**. G149
Mt 24:48 'My master *is* **staying a a long time**,' G5988
Mt 25:46 "Then they *will* **go a** to eternal punishment, G599
Mt 26: 2 the Passover is two days **a**—and the Son G3552
Mt 26:31 very night you *will* all **fall a** on account of G4997
Mt 26:33 "Even if all **fall a** on account of you, I G4997
Mt 26:42 *He* **went a** a second time and prayed, "My G599
Mt 26:42 this cup *to be* **taken a** unless I drink it, G4216
Mt 26:44 So he left them and **went a** once more and G599
Mt 26:73 of them; your accent **gives** you **a**." G1316+4472
Mt 27: 2 **led** him **a** and handed him over to Pilate G552
Mt 27: 5 Then *he* **went a** and hanged himself. G599
Mt 27:31 Then **they led** him **a** to crucify him. G552
Mt 27:60 of the entrance to the tomb and **went a**. G599
Mt 28: 8 So the women hurried **a** from the tomb G599
Mt 28:13 the night and **stole** him **a** while we were G3096
Mk 1:43 Jesus **sent** him **a** at once with a strong G1675
Mk 2:21 the new piece *will* **pull a** from the old G149
Mk 4:15 Satan comes and **takes a** the word that was G149
Mk 4:17 because of the word, *they* quickly **fall a**. G4997
Mk 5:20 So *the man* **went a** and began to tell in the G599
Mk 6:32 So *they* **went a** by themselves in a boat to G599
Mk 6:36 **Send** the people **a** so that they can go to G668
Mk 7:33 *After he* **took** him aside, **a** from the crowd G655
Mk 8: 9 *After he had* **sent** them **a**, G668
Mk 10: 4 a certificate of divorce and **send** her **a**." G668
Mk 10:22 *He* **went a** sad, because he had great G599
Mk 12: 3 beat him and **sent** him **a** empty-handed. G690
Mk 12:12 of the crowd; so they left him and **went a**. G599
Mk 13:30 *will* certainly not **pass a** until all G4216
Mk 13:31 Heaven and earth *will* **pass a**, but my G4216
Mk 13:31 but my words *will* never **pass a**. G4216
Mk 13:34 It's like a man **going a**: He leaves his house G624
Mk 14: 1 Unleavened Bread were only two days **a**, G3552
Mk 14:27 "*You will* all **fall a**," Jesus told them, "for G4997
Mk 14:29 declared, "Even if all **fall a**, I will not." G4997
Mk 14:39 Once more *he* **went a** and prayed the same G599
Mk 14:44 arrest him and **lead** him **a** under guard." G552
Mk 15: 1 **led** him **a** and handed him over to Pilate. G708
Mk 15:16 The soldiers **led** Jesus **a** into the palace G552
Mk 16: 3 "Who **will roll** the stone **a** from the G653
Mk 16: 4 which was very large, *had been* **rolled a**. G653
Lk 1:25 his favor and **taken a** my disgrace among G904
Lk 1:53 good things but *has* **sent** the rich **a** empty. G1990
Lk 4:34 "**Go a**! What do you want with us, Jesus of G1568
Lk 5: 8 knees and said, "**Go a** from me, Lord; G2002
Lk 8:12 the devil comes and **takes a** the word from G149
Lk 8:13 but in the time of testing *they* **fall a**. G923
Lk 8:38 go with him, but Jesus **sent** him **a**, saying, G668
Lk 8:39 So *the man* **went a** and told all over town G599
Lk 9:12 "**Send** the crowd **a** so they can go to the G668
Lk 10:30 beat him and **went a**, leaving him half G599
Lk 10:42 and it *will* not *be* **taken a** from her. G904
Lk 11:22 *he* **takes a** the armor in which the man G149
Lk 11:52 because *you have* **taken a** the key to G149
Lk 13:27 where you come from. **A** from me, all you G923
Lk 16: 3 My master *is* **taking a** my job. I'm not G904
Lk 16:23 looked up and saw Abraham **far a**, G608+3427
Lk 19:20 I have kept it **laid a** in a piece of cloth. G641
Lk 19:24 '**Take** his mina **a** from him and give it to G149
Lk 19:26 even what they have *will be* **taken a**. G149
Lk 20: 9 some farmers and **went a** for a long time. G623
Lk 20:10 beat him and **sent** him **a** empty-handed. G1990
Lk 20:11 shamefully and **sent a** empty-handed. G1990
Lk 21: 9 but the end will not come **right a**. G2311
Lk 21:32 *will* certainly not **pass a** until all G4216
Lk 21:33 Heaven and earth *will* **pass a**, but my G4216
Lk 21:33 but my words *will* never **pass a**. G4216
Lk 22:54 *they* **led** him **a** and took him into the house G72
Lk 23:18 whole crowd shouted, "**A with** this man! G149
Lk 23:26 As the soldiers **led** him **a**, they seized G552
Lk 23:48 they beat their breasts and **went a**. G5715
Lk 24: 2 found the stone **rolled a** from the tomb, G653
Lk 24:12 themselves, and *he* **went a**, wondering to G599
Jn 1:29 who **takes a** the sin of the world! G149
Jn 5:13 Jesus *had* **slipped a** into the crowd G1728
Jn 5:15 The man **went a** and told the Jewish G599
Jn 6:22 disciples, but that they *had* **gone a** alone. G599
Jn 6:37 whoever comes to me I will never **drive a**. G2032
Jn 8: 9 who heard *began to* **go a** one at a time, G2002
Jn 8:21 said to them, "I *am* **going a**, and you will G5632
Jn 8:59 **slipping a** from the temple grounds. G2002
Jn 10: 5 *they will* **run a** from him because they do G5771
Jn 10:12 he abandons the sheep and **runs a**. G5771
Jn 10:13 The man runs **a** because he is a hired hand NDT
Jn 11:39 "**Take a** the stone," he said. "But, Lord," G149
Jn 11:41 So *they* **took a** the stone. Then Jesus G149
Jn 11:48 will come and **take a** both our temple and G149
Jn 14:28 '*I am* **going a** and I am coming back to G5632
Jn 15: 6 like a branch that is thrown **a** and withers; G2032
Jn 16: 1 I have told you so that *you will* not **fall a**. G4997
Jn 16: 7 it is for your good that I *am* **going a**. G599
Jn 16: 7 Unless *I* **go a**, the Advocate will not come G599
Jn 16:22 and no one *will* **take a** your joy. G149
Jn 18:11 Peter, "Put your sword **a**! G1650+3836+2557S
Jn 19:15 they shouted, "**Take** him **a**! Take him away! G149
Jn 19:15 "Take him away! **Take** him **a**! Crucify him!" G149
Jn 19:38 permission, he came and **took** the body **a**. G149
Jn 20:13 "*They have* **taken** my Lord **a**," she said G149
Jn 20:15 if you *have* **carried** him **a**, tell me G1002
Ac 7:42 But God **turned a from** them and gave G5138
Ac 8:39 Spirit of the Lord **suddenly took** Philip **a**, G773
Ac 17:10 believers **sent** Paul and Silas **a** to Berea. G1734
Ac 20:30 the truth *in order to* **draw a** disciples after G685
Ac 21: 1 After *we had* **torn** *ourselves* **a** from them G685
Ac 21:21 among the Gentiles to **turn a** from Moses, G686
Ac 22:16 be baptized and **wash** your sins **a**, calling G666
Ac 22:21 I *will* **send** you far **a** to the Gentiles. G1990
Ac 23:10 and take him **a from** them by force G1666+3545
Ac 27:32 that held the lifeboat and let it **drift a**. G1738
Ac 27:42 any *of them* from **swimming a** and G1713
Ro 3:12 All *have* **turned a**, they have together G1712
Ro 6: 6 body ruled by sin *might be* **done a with**, G2934
Ro 11:26 *he will* **turn** godlessness **a** from Jacob. G695
Ro 11:27 with them when *I* **take a** their sins. G904
Ro 16:17 you have learned. **Keep a** from them. G1712
1Co 7:31 this world in its present form *is* **passing a**. G4135
1Co 13: 8 where there is knowledge, *it will* **pass a**. G2934
2Co 3:13 seeing the end *of* what *was* **passing a**. G2934
2Co 3:14 because only in Christ *is it* **taken a**. G2934
2Co 3:16 turns to the Lord, the veil *is* **taken a**. G4311
2Co 4:16 Though outwardly we *are* **wasting a**, yet G1425
2Co 5: 6 home in the body *we are* **a** from the Lord. G1685
2Co 5: 8 would prefer *to be* **a** from the body G1685
2Co 5: 9 we are at home in the body or **a from** it. G1685
2Co 10: 1 with you, but "bold" toward you *when* **a**! G582
2Co 12: 8 pleaded with the Lord to **take** it **a** from me. G923
Gal 3:17 by God and thus **do a with** the promise. G2934
Gal 5: 4 from Christ; *you have* **fallen a from** grace. G1738
Eph 2:13 you who once were **far a** have been G3426
Eph 2:17 to you who were **far a** and peace to those G3426
Col 2:14 he has taken it **a**, nailing it G1666+3836+3545
2Th 3: 6 *to* **keep a** from every believer who is idle G5097
1Ti 5:15 Some *have* in fact already **turned a** to G1762
1Ti 6:20 **Turn a from** godless chatter and the G1762
2Ti 2:19 of the Lord *must* **turn a** from wickedness G923
2Ti 4: 4 *They will* **turn** their ears **a** from the truth G695
Heb 2: 1 we have heard, so that *we do* not **drift a**. G4184
Heb 3:12 heart that **turns a** from the living God. G923
Heb 6: 6 and *who have* **fallen a**, to be brought back G4178
Heb 8: 9 I **turned a from** them, declares G288
Heb 9:26 of the ages to **do a with** sin by the sacrifice G120
Heb 9:28 sacrificed once to **take a** the sins of many; G429
Heb 10: 4 the blood of bulls and goats *to* **take a** sins. G904
Heb 10:11 sacrifices, which can never **take a** sins. G4311
Heb 10:35 So *do* not **throw a** your confidence; it will be G610
Heb 11: 5 be found, because God *had* **taken** him **a**." G3572
Heb 12:25 if we **turn a from** him who warns us from G695
Heb 13: 9 *Do* not *be* **carried a** by all kinds of strange G4195
Jas 1:10 since *they will* **pass a** like a wild flower. G4216
Jas 1:11 the rich *will* **fade a** even while they go G3447
Jas 1:14 tempted *when they are* **dragged a** by their G1999
Jas 1:24 **goes a** and immediately forgets what he G599
1Pe 5: 4 the crown of glory that will **never fade a**. G277
2Pe 3:17 so that *you may* not *be* **carried a** by the G5270
1Jn 2:17 The world and its desires **pass a**, but G4135
1Jn 3: 5 appeared so that *he might* **take a** our sins. G149
Rev 7:17 ' 'And God *will* **wipe a** every tear from G1981
Rev 12:15 and **sweep** her **a with the torrent**. G4533+4472
Rev 16:20 Every island **fled a** and the mountains G5771
Rev 17: 3 Then the angel **carried** me **a** in the Spirit G708
Rev 21: 1 heaven and the first earth *had* **passed a**, G599
Rev 21: 4 the old order of things *has* **passed a**." G599
Rev 21:10 And *he* **carried** me **a** in the Spirit to a G708
Rev 22:19 And if anyone **takes** words **a** from this scroll G904
Rev 22:19 God *will* **take a** from that person any share G904

AWE (18) [AWESOME, OVERAWED]

Jos 4:14 and *they* **stood in a** *of* him all the days of H3707
Jos 4:14 just as *they had* **stood in a** *of* Moses. H3707
1Sa 12:18 the people **stood in a** *of* the LORD H3707+4394
1Ki 3:28 *they* **held** the king **in a**, because H3707
Job 25: 2 "Dominion and **a** belong to God; he H7065
Ps 65: 8 The whole earth *is* **filled with a** at your H3707
Ps 119:120 in fear of you; *I* **stand in a** of your laws. H3707
Isa 29:23 and *will* **stand in a** *of* the God of Israel. H6907
Jer 2:19 the LORD your God and have no **a** *of* me," H7067
Jer 33: 9 and *they will be* **in a** and will tremble at H7064
Hab 3: 2 of your fame; *I* **stand in a** *of* your deeds H3707
Mal 2: 5 revered me and **stood in a** of my name. H3169
Mt 9: 8 saw this, *they were* **filled with a**; and they G5828
Lk 1:65 All the neighbors were filled with **a**, and G5832
Lk 5:26 They were filled with **a** and said, "We G5832
Lk 7:16 were all filled with **a** and praised God. G5832
Ac 2:43 was filled with **a** at the many wonders G5832
Heb 12:28 God acceptably with reverence and **a**, G1290

AWEL-MARDUK (2) [MARDUK]

2Ki 25:27 in the year **A** became king of Babylon H213
Jer 52:31 in the year **A** became king of Babylon H213

AWESOME (34) [AWE]

Ge 28:17 was afraid and said, "How **a** is this place! H3707
Ex 15:11 majestic in holiness, **a** *in* glory, working H3707
Ex 34:10 among will see how **a** *is* the work that I, H3707
Dt 4:34 or by great and **a deeds**, like all the H4616
Dt 7:21 who is among you, is a great and **a** God. H3707
Dt 10:17 great God, mighty and **a**, who shows no H3707
Dt 10:21 those great and **a wonders** you saw with H3707
Dt 28:58 do not revere this glorious and **a** name— H3707
Dt 34:12 performed the **a** deeds that Moses did H4616
Jdg 13: 6 an angel of God, very **a**. I didn't ask him H3707
2Sa 7:23 great and **a wonders** by driving out H3707
1Ch 17:21 great and **a wonders** by driving out H3707
Ne 1: 5 the great and **a** God, who keeps his H3707
Ne 4:14 who is great and **a**, and fight for your H3707
Ne 9:32 great God, mighty and **a**, who keeps his H3707
Job 10:16 again **display** *your* **a power** against H7098
Job 37:22 splendor; God comes in **a** majesty. H3707
Ps 45: 4 let your right hand achieve **a** *deeds*. H3707
Ps 47: 2 the LORD Most High *is* **a**, the great King H3707
Ps 65: 5 You answer us with **a** and righteous H3707
Ps 66: 3 Say to God, "How **a** are your deeds! So H3707
Ps 66: 5 God has done, his **a** deeds for mankind! H3707
Ps 68:35 *You*, God, *are* **a** in your sanctuary; the H3707
Ps 89: 7 *he is* **more a** than all who surround him. H3707
Ps 99: 3 Let them praise your great and **a** name H3707
Ps 106:22 land of Ham and **a** *deeds* by the Red Sea. H3707
Ps 111: 9 forever—holy and **a** *is* his name. H3707
Ps 145: 6 They tell of the power of your **a works** H3707
Isa 64: 3 For when you did **a** *things* that we did not H3707
Eze 1:18 Their rims were high and **a**, and all four H3711
Eze 1:22 like a vault, sparkling like crystal, and **a**. H3707
Da 2:31 dazzling statue, **a** in appearance. A10167
Da 9: 4 the great and **a** God, who keeps his H3707
Zep 2:11 The LORD *will be* **a** to them when he H3707

AWFUL (5)

Jdg 20: 3 "Tell us how this **a thing** happened." H8288
Jdg 20:12 "What about this **a crime** that was H8288
Ne 9:18 when they committed **a** blasphemies. H1524
Ne 9:26 they committed **a** blasphemies. H1524
Jer 30: 7 How **a** that day will be! No other H2098+1524

AWL (2)

Ex 21: 6 the doorpost and pierce his ear with an **a**. H5345
Dt 15:17 then take an **a** and push it through his H5345

AWNINGS (1)
Eze 27: 7 your **a** were of blue and purple from the H4833

AWOKE (7) [WAKE]
Ge 9:24 When Noah **a** from his wine and found H3699
Ge 28:16 When Jacob **a** from his sleep, he thought H3699
Jdg 16:14 *He* **a** from his sleep and pulled up the pin H3699
Jdg 16:20 *He* **a** from his sleep and thought, "I'll go H3699
1Ki 3:15 Then Solomon **a**—and he realized it had H3699
Ps 78:65 Then the Lord **a** as from sleep, as a H3699
Jer 31:26 At this *I* **a** and looked around. My sleep H7810

AX (8) [AXES, AXHEAD]
Dt 19: 5 as he swings his **a** to fell a tree, the H1749
Dt 20:19 destroy its trees by putting an **a** to them, H1749
Jdg 9:48 He took an **a** and cut off some branches H7935
Ecc 10:10 If the **a** is dull and its edge unsharpened H1366
Isa 10:15 Does the **a** raise itself above the person H1749
Isa 10:34 will cut down the forest thickets with an **a**; H1366
Mt 3:10 The **a** is already at the root of the trees, and *G544*
Lk 3: 9 The **a** is already at the root of the trees, and *G544*

AXES (7) [AX]
1Sa 13:20 mattocks, **a** and sickles sharpened. H7935
1Sa 13:21 sharpening forks and **a** and for repointing H7935
2Sa 12:31 labor with saws and with iron picks and **a**, H4477
1Ch 20: 3 labor with saws and with iron picks and **a**. H4490
Ps 74: 5 like men wielding **a** to cut through a H7935
Ps 74: 6 carved paneling with their **a** and hatchets. H4172
Jer 46:22 they will come against her with **a**, like H7935

AXHEAD (1) [AX]
2Ki 6: 5 down a tree, the **iron a** fell into the water. H1366

AXLES (3)
1Ki 7:30 had four bronze wheels with bronze **a**, H6248
1Ki 7:32 the **a** *of* the wheels were attached to H3338
1Ki 7:33 made like chariot wheels; the **a**, rims, H3338

AXLETREES (KJV) AXELS

AYYAH (1)
1Ch 7:28 villages all the way to **A** and its villages. H6509

AZALIAH (2)
2Ki 22: 3 Shaphan son of **A**, the son of Meshullam, H729
2Ch 34: 8 sent Shaphan son of **A** and Maaseiah the H729

AZANIAH (1)
Ne 10: 9 Jeshua son of **A**, Binnui of the sons of H271

AZAREL (6)
1Ch 12: 6 **A**, Joezer and Jashobeam the H6475
1Ch 25:18 the eleventh to **A**, his sons and relatives H6475
1Ch 27:22 **A** son of Jeroham. These were H6475
Ezr 10:41 **A**, Shelemiah, Shemariah, H6475
Ne 11:13 Amashsai son of **A**, the son of Ahzai, H6475
Ne 12:36 Shemaiah, **A**, Milalai, Gilalai, H6475

AZARIAH (46) [AZARIAH'S]
1Ki 4: 2 his chief officials: **A** son of Zadok—the H6482
1Ki 4: 5 **A** son of Nathan—in charge of the district H6482
2Ki 14:21 Then all the people of Judah took **A**, who H6481
2Ki 15: 1 **A** son of Amaziah king of Judah began to H6481
2Ki 15: 7 **A** rested with his ancestors and was buried H6481
2Ki 15: 8 the thirty-eighth year of **A** king of Judah, H6482
2Ki 15:17 In the thirty-ninth year of **A** king of Judah H6481
2Ki 15:23 In the fiftieth year of **A** king of Judah H6481
2Ki 15:27 In the fifty-second year of **A** king of Judah, H6481
1Ch 2: 8 The son of Ethan: **A**. H6481
1Ch 2:38 the father of Jehu, Jehu the father of **A**, H6481
1Ch 2:39 **A** the father of Helez, Helez the father of H6481
1Ch 3:12 Amaziah his son, **A** his son, Jotham his H6481
1Ch 6: 9 Ahimaaz the father of **A**, Azariah the H6481
1Ch 6: 9 father of Azariah, **A** the father of Johanan H6481
1Ch 6:10 Johanan the father of **A** (it was he who H6481
1Ch 6:11 **A** the father of Amariah, Amariah the H6481
1Ch 6:13 father of Hilkiah, Hilkiah the father of **A**, H6481
1Ch 6:14 **A** the father of Seraiah, and Seraiah the H6481
1Ch 6:36 the son of **A**, the son of H6481
1Ch 9:11 **A** son of Hilkiah, the son of Meshullam H6481
2Ch 15: 1 The Spirit of God came on **A** son of Oded. H6482
2Ch 15: 8 the prophecy of **A** son of Oded the H6482
2Ch 21: 2 Jehoshaphat, were **A**, Jehiel, Zechariah, H6481
2Ch 23: 1 **A** son of Jeroham, Ishmael son of H6482
2Ch 23: 1 son of Jehohanan, **A** son of Obed H6482
2Ch 26:17 **A** the priest with eighty other courageous H6482
2Ch 26:20 When **A** the chief priest and all the other H6482
2Ch 28:12 leaders in Ephraim—**A** son of Jehohanan H6482
2Ch 29:12 Mahath son of Amasai and Joel son of **A** H6482
2Ch 29:12 Kish son of Abdi and **A** son of Jehallelel H6482
2Ch 31:10 **A** the chief priest, from the family of H6482
2Ch 31:13 of King Hezekiah and **A** the official in H6482
Ezr 7: 1 Seraiah, the son of **A**, the son of Hilkiah, H6481
Ezr 7: 3 Amariah, the son of **A**, the son of H6481
Ne 3:23 next to them, **A** son of Maaseiah, the H6481
Ne 7: 7 Joshua, Nehemiah, **A**, Raamiah H6481
Ne 8: 7 Maaseiah, Kelita, **A**, Jozabad, Hanan H6481
Ne 10: 2 Seraiah, **A**, Jeremiah, H6481
Ne 12:33 along with **A**, Ezra, Meshullam, H6481
Jer 43: 2 **A** son of Hoshaiah and Johanan son of H6481
Da 1: 6 Daniel, Hananiah, Mishael and **A**. H6481
Da 1: 7 Mishael, Meshach; and to **A**, Abednego. H6481
Da 1:11 over Daniel, Hananiah, Mishael and **A**, H6481
Da 1:19 Mishael and **A**; so they entered the H6481
Da 2:17 to his friends Hananiah, Mishael and **A**. A10538

AZARIAH'S (2) [AZARIAH]
2Ki 15: 6 As for the other events of **A** reign, and all H6482
Ne 3:24 from **A** house to the angle and the corner H6481

AZARIAHU (1)
2Ch 21: 2 Zechariah, **A**, Michael and H6482

AZAZ (1)
1Ch 5: 8 Bela son of **A**, the son of Shema, the H6452

AZAZIAH (3)
1Ch 15:21 Jeiel and **A** were to play the harps H6453
1Ch 27:20 Hoshea son of **A**; over half the tribe of H6453
2Ch 31:13 **A**, Nahath, Asahel, Jerimoth H6453

AZBUK (1)
Ne 3:16 Nehemiah son of **A**, ruler of a H6443

AZEKAH (7)
Jos 10:10 down all the way to **A** and Makkedah. H6467
Jos 10:11 on the road down from Beth Horon to **A**, H6467
Jos 15:35 Jarmuth, Adullam, Sokoh, **A**, H6467
1Sa 17: 1 Ephes Dammim, between Sokoh and **A**. H6467
2Ch 11: 9 Adoraim, Lachish, **A**, H6467
Ne 11:30 its fields, and in **A** and its settlements. H6467
Jer 34: 7 were still holding out—Lachish and **A**. H6467

AZEL (7)
1Ch 8:37 Eleasah his son and **A** his son. H727
1Ch 8:38 **A** had six sons, and these were their H727
1Ch 8:38 All these were the sons of **A**. H727
1Ch 9:43 Eleasah his son and **A** his son. H727
1Ch 9:44 **A** had six sons, and these were their H727
1Ch 9:44 These were the sons of **A**. H727
Zec 14: 5 my mountain valley, for it will extend to **A**. H728

AZEM (KJV) EZEM

AZGAD (4)
Ezr 2:12 of **A** 1,222 H6444
Ezr 8:12 of the descendants of **A**, Johanan son of H6444
Ne 7:17 of **A** 2,322 H6444
Ne 10:15 **A**, Bebai, H6444

AZIEL (NIV84) JAAZIEL

AZIZA (1)
Ezr 10:27 Mattaniah, Jeremoth, Zabad and **A**. H6461

AZMAVETH (8) [BETH AZMAVETH]
2Sa 23:31 the Arbathite, **A** the Barhumite, H6462
1Ch 8:36 father of Alemeth, **A** and Zimri, and Zimri H6462
1Ch 9:42 father of Alemeth, **A** and Zimri, and Zimri H6462
1Ch 11:33 **A** the Baharumite, Eliahba the H6462
1Ch 12: 3 Jeziel and Pelet the sons of **A**; Berakah, H6462
1Ch 27:25 **A** son of Adiel was in charge of the royal H6462
Ezr 2:24 of **A** 42 H6463
Ne 12:29 from the area of Geba and **A**, for the H6463

AZMON (2)
Nu 34: 4 it will go to Hazar Addar and over to **A**, H6801
Jos 15: 4 passed along to **A** and joined the Wadi H6801

AZNOTH TABOR (1) [TABOR]
Jos 19:34 ran west through **A** and came out at H268

AZOR (2)
Mt 1:13 father of Eliakim, Eliakim the father of **A**, *G110*
Mt 1:14 **A** the father of Zadok, Zadok the father of *G110*

AZOTUS (1)
Ac 8:40 appeared at **A** and traveled about *G111*

AZRIEL (3)
1Ch 5:24 Eliel, **A**, Jeremiah, Hodaviah and H6480
1Ch 27:19 over Naphtali: Jerimoth son of **A**; H6480
Jer 36:26 Seraiah son of **A** and Shelemiah son of H6480

AZRIKAM (6)
1Ch 3:23 Elioenai, Hizkiah and **A**—three in all. H6483
1Ch 8:38 **A**, Bokeru, Ishmael, Sheariah, Obadiah H6483
1Ch 9:14 Hasshub, the son of **A**, the son of H6483
1Ch 9:44 **A**, Bokeru, Ishmael, Sheariah, Obadiah H6483
2Ch 28: 7 **A** the officer in charge of the palace H6483
Ne 11:15 Hasshub, the son of **A**, the son of H6483

AZUBAH (4)
1Ki 22:42 mother's name was **A** daughter of Shilhi. H6448
1Ch 2:18 son of Hezron had children by his wife **A** H6448
1Ch 2:19 When **A** died, Caleb married Ephrath H6448
2Ch 20:31 mother's name was **A** daughter of Shilhi. H6448

AZZAH (KJV) GAZA

AZZAN (1)
Nu 34:26 Paltiel son of **A**, the leader from the tribe H6464

AZZUR (3)
Ne 10:17 Hezekiah, **A**, H6473
Jer 28: 1 the prophet Hananiah son of **A**, who was H6473
Eze 11: 1 Jaazaniah son of **A** and Pelatiah son of H6473

B

BAAL (63) [BAAL GAD, BAAL HAMON, BAAL HAZOR, BAAL HERMON, BAAL MEON, BAAL PEOR, BAAL PERAZIM, BAAL SHALISHAH, BAAL TAMAR, BAAL ZEPHON, BAAL'S, BAAL-BERITH, BAAL-HANAN, BAAL-ZEBUB, BAALS, BAMOTH BAAL, GUR BAAL, KIRIATH BAAL]
Nu 25: 3 Israel yoked themselves to the **B** *of* Peor. H1251
Nu 25: 5 have yoked themselves to the **B** *of* Peor." H1251
Dt 4: 3 you everyone who followed the **B** *of* Peor, H1251
Jdg 2:13 him and served **B** and the Ashtoreths. H1251
Jdg 6:25 your father's altar to **B** and cut down the H1251
Jdg 6:31 If **B** really is a god, he can defend H2085S
Jdg 6:32 that day, saying, "Let **B** contend with him." H1251
1Ki 16:31 began to serve **B** and worship him. H1251
1Ki 16:32 set up an altar for **B** *in* the temple of Baal H1251
1Ki 16:32 Baal in the temple of **B** that he built in H1251
1Ki 18:19 fifty prophets of **B** and the four hundred H1251
1Ki 18:21 follow him; but if **B** is God, follow him." H1251
1Ki 18:22 **B** has four hundred and fifty prophets. H1251
1Ki 18:25 Elijah said to the prophets of **B**, "Choose H1251
1Ki 18:26 called on the name of **B** from morning till H1251
1Ki 18:26 morning till noon. "**B**, answer us!" they H1251
1Ki 18:40 "Seize the prophets of **B**. H1251
1Ki 19:18 not bowed down to **B** and whose mouths H1251
1Ki 22:53 served and worshiped **B** and aroused the H1251
2Ki 3: 2 the sacred stone of **B** that his father had H1251
2Ki 10:18 to them, "Ahab served **B** a little; Jehu will H1251
2Ki 10:19 Now summon all the prophets of **B**, all his H1251
2Ki 10:19 I am going to hold a great sacrifice for **B**. H1251
2Ki 10:19 in order to destroy the servants of **B**. H1251
2Ki 10:20 "Call an assembly in honor of **B**. H1251
2Ki 10:21 all the servants of **B** came; not one H1251
2Ki 10:21 into the temple of **B** until it was full from H1251
2Ki 10:22 "Bring robes for all the servants of **B**." H1251
2Ki 10:23 son of Rekab went into the temple of **B**. H1251
2Ki 10:23 Jehu said to the servants of **B**, "Look H1251
2Ki 10:23 is here with you—only servants of **B**." H1251
2Ki 10:25 the inner shrine of the temple of **B**. H1251
2Ki 10:26 out of the temple of **B** and burned it. H1251
2Ki 10:27 the sacred stone of **B** and tore down the H1251
2Ki 10:27 of Baal and tore down the temple of **B**, H1251
2Ki 10:28 So Jehu destroyed **B worship** in Israel. H1251
2Ki 11:18 went to the temple of **B** and tore it down. H1251
2Ki 11:18 Mattan the priest of **B** in front of the altars H1251
2Ki 17:16 all the starry hosts, and they worshiped **B**. H1251
2Ki 21: 3 erected altars to **B** and made an Asherah H1251
2Ki 23: 4 articles made for **B** and Asherah and all H1251
2Ki 23: 5 those who burned incense to **B**, to the sun H1251
1Ch 5: 5 Micah his son, Reaiah his son, **B** his son, H1252
1Ch 8:30 followed by Zur, Kish, **B**, Ner, Nadab, H1252
1Ch 9:36 followed by Zur, Kish, **B**, Ner, Nadab, H1252
2Ch 23:17 went to the temple of **B** and tore it down. H1251
2Ch 23:17 Mattan the priest of **B** in front of the altars H1251
Ps 106:28 yoked themselves to the **B** *of* Peor and ate H1251
Jer 2: 8 The prophets prophesied by **B**, following H1251
Jer 7: 9 burn incense to **B** and follow other gods H1251
Jer 11:13 that shameful god **B** are as many as the H1251
Jer 11:17 my anger by burning incense to **B**. H1251
Jer 12:16 once taught my people to swear by **B**— H1251
Jer 19: 5 the high places of **B** to burn their children H1251
Jer 19: 5 children in the fire as offerings to **B**— H1251
Jer 23:13 They prophesied by **B** and led my people H1251
Jer 23:27 forgot my name through **B worship**. H1251
Jer 32:29 on the roofs to **B** and by pouring out H1251
Jer 32:35 built high places for **B** in the Valley of Ben H1251
Hos 2: 8 silver and gold—which they used for **B**. H1251
Hos 13: 1 he became guilty of **B worship** and died. H1251
Zep 1: 4 every remnant of **B worship** in this place, H1251
Ro 11: 4 who have not bowed the knee *to* **B**. *G955*

BAAL GAD (3) [BAAL, GAD]
Jos 11:17 to **B** in the Valley of Lebanon below H1254
Jos 12: 7 from **B** in the Valley of Lebanon to H1254
Jos 13: 5 from **B** below Mount Hermon to Lebo H1254

BAAL HAMON (1) [BAAL]
SS 8:11 Solomon had a vineyard in **B**; H1255

BAAL HAZOR (1) [BAAL, HAZOR]
2Sa 13:23 were at **B** near the border of H1258

BAAL HERMON (2) [BAAL, HERMON, SENIR]
Jdg 3: 3 from Mount **B** to Lebo Hamath. H1259
1Ch 5:23 in the land from Bashan to **B**, H1259

BAAL MEON (3) [BETH BAAL MEON, BETH MEON]
Nu 32:38 as well as Nebo and **B** (these H1260
1Ch 5: 8 the area from Aroer to Nebo and **B**. H1260
Eze 25: 9 Beth Jeshimoth, **B** and Kiriathaim H1260

BAAL PEOR (2) [BAAL, PEOR]
Dt 4: 3 own eyes what the LORD did at **B**. H1261
Hos 9:10 But when they came to **B**, they H1261

BAAL PERAZIM (4) [BAAL, PERAZIM]
2Sa 5:20 So David went to **B**, and there he H1262
2Sa 5:20 So that place was called **B**. H1262

1Ch 14:11 David and his men went up to **B**, H1262
1Ch 14:11 So that place was called **B**. H1262

BAAL SHALISHAH (1) [BAAL]

2Ki 4:42 A man came from **B**, bringing H1264

BAAL TAMAR (1) [BAAL, TAMAR]

Jdg 20:33 places and took up positions at **B Tamar**, H1265

BAAL ZEPHON (3) [BAAL, ZEPHON]

Ex 14: 2 by the sea, directly opposite **B**. H1263
Ex 14: 9 sea near Pi Hahiroth, opposite **B**. H1263
Nu 33: 7 to the east of **B**, and camped H1263

BAAL'S (5) [BAAL]

Jdg 6:28 there was **B** altar, demolished, H1251
Jdg 6:30 he has broken down **B** altar and cut down H1251
Jdg 6:31 "Are you going to plead **B** cause? H1251
Jdg 6:32 So because Gideon broke down **B** altar H2257S
1Ki 18:23 Let **B** prophets choose one for themselves NDT

BAAL-BERITH (2) [BAAL]

Jdg 8:33 They set up **B** as their god H1253
Jdg 9: 4 shekels of silver from the temple of **B**, H1253

BAAL-HANAN (5) [BAAL]

Ge 36:38 **B** son of Akbor succeeded him as king. H1257
Ge 36:39 When **B** son of Akbor died, Hadad H1257
1Ch 1:49 **B** son of Akbor succeeded him as king. H1257
1Ch 1:50 When **B** died, Hadad succeeded him as H1257
1Ch 27:28 **B** the Gederite was in charge of the olive H1257

BAAL-ZEBUB (4) [BAAL, BEELZEBUL]

2Ki 1: 2 "Go and consult **B**, the god of Ekron, H1256
2Ki 1: 3 Israel that you are going off to consult **B**, H1256
2Ki 1: 6 you are sending messengers to consult **B**, H1256
2Ki 1:16 you have sent messengers to consult **B**, H1256

BAALAH (6) [KIRIATH JEARIM]

Jos 15: 9 Mount Ephron and went down toward **B** H1267
Jos 15:10 it curved westward from **B** to Mount Seir, H1267
Jos 15:11 along to Mount **B** and reached Jabneel. H1267
Jos 15:29 **B**, Iyim, Ezem, H1267
2Sa 6: 2 all his men went to **B** *in* Judah to bring up H1267
1Ch 13: 6 David and all Israel went to **B** of Judah H1267

BAALATH (4) [BAALATH BEER]

Jos 19:44 Eltekeh, Gibbethon, **B**, H1272
1Ki 9:18 **B**, and Tadmor in the desert, within his H1272
1Ch 4:33 villages around these towns as far as **B**. H1272
2Ch 8: 6 as well as **B** and all his store cities, and all H1272

BAALATH BEER (1) [BAALATH]

Jos 19: 8 around these towns as far as **B Beer** H1273

BAALI (KJV) MY MASTER

BAALIM (KJV) BAALS

BAALIS (1)

Jer 40:14 "Don't you know that **B** king of the H1271

BAALS (18) [BAAL]

Jdg 2:11 in the eyes of the LORD and served the **B**. H1251
Jdg 3: 7 God and served the **B** and the Asherahs. H1251
Jdg 8:33 again prostituted themselves to the **B**. H1251
Jdg 10: 6 They served the **B** and the Ashtoreths H1251
Jdg 10:10 forsaking our God and serving the **B**." H1251
1Sa 7: 4 Israelites put away their **B** and Ashtoreths, H1251
1Sa 12:10 LORD and served the **B** and the Ashtoreths. H1251
1Ki 18:18 commands and have followed the **B**. H1251
2Ch 17: 3 He did not consult the **B** H1251
2Ch 24: 7 had used even its sacred objects for the **B**. H1251
2Ch 28: 2 also made idols for worshiping the **B**. H1251
2Ch 33: 3 erected altars to the **B** and made Asherah H1251
2Ch 34: 4 the altars of the **B** were torn down; H1251
Jer 2:23 not defiled; I have not run after the **B**'? H1251
Jer 9:14 they have followed the **B**, as their H1251
Hos 2:13 the days she burned incense to the **B**; H1251
Hos 2:17 remove the names of the **B** from her lips; H1251
Hos 11: 2 They sacrificed to the **B** and they burned H1251

BAANA (3)

1Ki 4:12 **B** son of Ahilud—in Taanach and H1275
1Ki 4:16 **B** son of Hushai—in Asher and in Aloth; H1275
Ne 3: 4 to him Zadok son of **B** also made repairs. H1275

BAANAH (9)

2Sa 4: 2 One was named **B** and the other Rekab H1276
2Sa 4: 5 Now Rekab and **B**, the sons of Rimmon H1276
2Sa 4: 6 Rekab and his brother **B** slipped away. H1276
2Sa 4: 9 David answered Rekab and his brother **B** H1276
2Sa 23:29 Heled son of **B** the Netophathite, Ithai H1276
1Ch 11:30 Heled son of **B** the Netophathite, H1276
Ezr 2: 2 Rehum and **B**): The list of the men H1276
Ne 7: 7 Nehum and **B**): The list of the men H1276
Ne 10:27 Harim and **B**. H1276

BAARA (1)

1Ch 8: 8 he had divorced his wives Hushim and **B**. H1281

BAASEIAH (1)

1Ch 6:40 Michael, the son of **B**, the son of Malkijah H1283

BAASHA (25) [BAASHA'S]

1Ki 15:16 was war between Asa and **B** king of Israel H1284
1Ki 15:17 **B** king of Israel went up against Judah H1284
1Ki 15:19 your treaty with **B** king of Israel so he H1284
1Ki 15:21 When **B** heard this, he stopped building H1284
1Ki 15:22 stones and timber **B** had been using there H1284
1Ki 15:27 **B** son of Ahijah from the tribe of Issachar H1284
1Ki 15:28 **B** killed Nadab in the third year of Asa H1284
1Ki 15:32 was war between Asa and **B** king of Israel H1284
1Ki 15:33 **B** son of Ahijah became king of all Israel H1284
1Ki 16: 1 to Jehu son of Hanani concerning **B**: H1284
1Ki 16: 3 I am about to wipe out **B** and his house, H1284
1Ki 16: 4 those belonging to **B** who die in the city, H1284
1Ki 16: 6 **B** rested with his ancestors and was buried H1284
1Ki 16: 7 Jehu son of Hanani to **B** and his house, H1284
1Ki 16: 8 Elah son of **B** became king of Israel H1284
1Ki 16:12 So Zimri destroyed the whole family of **B** H1284
1Ki 16:12 spoken against **B** through the prophet H1284
1Ki 16:13 of all the sins **B** and his son Elah had H1284
1Ki 21:22 son of Nebat and that of **B** son of Ahijah, H1284
2Ki 9: 9 like the house of **B** son of Ahijah. H1284
2Ch 16: 1 year of Asa's reign **B** king of Israel went H1284
2Ch 16: 3 your treaty with **B** king of Israel so he H1284
2Ch 16: 5 When **B** heard this, he stopped building H1284
2Ch 16: 6 the stones and timber **B** had been using. H1284
Jer 41: 9 of his defense against **B** king of Israel. H1284

BAASHA'S (2) [BAASHA]

1Ki 16: 5 As for the other events of **B** reign, what he H1284
1Ki 16:11 the throne, he killed off **B** whole family. H1284

BABBLER (1) [BABBLING]

Ac 17:18 them asked, "What is this **b** trying to say?" *G5066*

BABBLING (1) [BABBLER]

Mt 6: 7 you pray, *do not keep on* **b** like pagans *G1006*

BABBLINGS (KJV) CHATTER

BABE, BABES (KJV) BABY, CHILDREN

BABEL (1) [BABYLON]

Ge 11: 9 That is why it was called **B**—because there H951

BABIES (5) [BABY]

Ge 25:22 The **b** jostled each other within her, and H1201
Ex 2: 6 "This is one of the Hebrew **b**," she said. H3529
Lk 18:15 were also bringing **b** to Jesus for him to *G1100*
Ac 7:19 throw out their **newborn b** so that they *G1100*
1Pe 2: 2 Like newborn **b**, crave pure spiritual milk *G1100*

BABOONS (2)

1Ki 10:22 silver and ivory, and apes and **b**. H9415
2Ch 9:21 silver and ivory, and apes and **b**. H9415

BABY (17) [BABIES, BABY'S]

Ex 1:16 if you see that **the b** is a boy, kill him; H2085S
Ex 2: 6 She opened it and saw the **b**. H3529
Ex 2: 7 Hebrew women to nurse the **b** for you?" H3529
Ex 2: 9 "Take this **b** and nurse him for me H3529
Ex 2: 9 So the woman took the **b** and nursed him. H3529
1Ki 3:17 and ***I* had a b** while she was there with H3528
1Ki 3:18 child was born, this woman also **had a b**. H3528
1Ki 3:26 "Please, my lord, give her the living **b**! H3528
1Ki 3:27 "Give the living **b** to the first woman. H3528
Isa 49:15 forget the **b at** her **breast** and have no H6403
Lk 1:41 greeting, the **b** leaped in her womb *G1100*
Lk 1:44 my ears, the **b** in my womb leaped for joy. *G1100*
Lk 1:57 it was time for Elizabeth ***to* have** her **b**, *G5503*
Lk 2: 6 the time came *for the* **b to be born**, *G5503*
Lk 2:12 You will find a **b** wrapped in cloths and *G1100*
Lk 2:16 Joseph, and the **b**, who was lying in *G1100*
Jn 16:21 when her **b** is born she forgets the *G4086*

BABY'S (1) [BABY]

Ex 2: 8 So the girl went and got the **b** mother. H3529

BABYLON (280) [BABEL, BABYLON'S, BABYLONIA, BABYLONIAN, BABYLONIANS]

Ge 10:10 The first centers of his kingdom were **B** H951
2Ki 17:24 The king of Assyria brought people from **B** H951
2Ki 17:30 The people from **B** made Sukkoth Benoth H951
2Ki 20:12 of Baladan king of **B** sent Hezekiah letters H951
2Ki 20:14 Hezekiah replied. "They came from **B**." H951
2Ki 20:17 up until this day, will be carried off to **B**. H951
2Ki 20:18 eunuchs in the palace of the king of **B**." H951
2Ki 24: 1 king of **B** invaded the land, H951
2Ki 24: 7 because the king of **B** had taken all his H951
2Ki 24:10 king of **B** advanced on Jerusalem H951
2Ki 24:12 eighth year of the reign of the king of **B**, H951
2Ki 24:15 took Jehoiachin captive to **B**. H951
2Ki 24:15 took from Jerusalem to **B** the king's mother, H951
2Ki 24:16 The king of **B** also deported to Babylon the H951
2Ki 24:16 also deported to **B** the entire force of H951
2Ki 24:20 Zedekiah rebelled against the king of **B**. H951
2Ki 25: 1 Nebuchadnezzar king of **B** marched against H951
2Ki 25: 6 He was taken to the king of **B** at Riblah H951
2Ki 25: 7 with bronze shackles and took him to **B**. H951
2Ki 25: 8 year of Nebuchadnezzar king of **B**, H951
2Ki 25: 8 an official of the king of **B**, came to H951
2Ki 25:11 those who had deserted to the king of **B**. H951
2Ki 25:13 the LORD and they carried the bronze to **B**. H951
2Ki 25:20 brought them to the king of **B** at Riblah. H951
2Ki 25:22 king of **B** appointed Gedaliah son H951
2Ki 25:23 that the king of **B** had appointed Gedaliah H951
2Ki 25:24 down in the land and serve the king of **B**, H951
2Ki 25:27 in the year Awel-Marduk became king of **B** H951
2Ki 25:28 of the other kings who were with him in **B**. H951
1Ch 9: 1 were taken captive to **B** because of their H951
2Ch 32:31 sent by the rulers of **B** to ask him about the H951
2Ch 33:11 with bronze shackles and took him to **B**. H951
2Ch 36: 6 Nebuchadnezzar king of **B** attacked him H951
2Ch 36: 6 him with bronze shackles to take him to **B**. H951
2Ch 36: 7 also took to **B** articles from the temple H951
2Ch 36:10 sent for him and brought him to **B**, H951
2Ch 36:18 He carried to **B** all the articles from the H951
2Ch 36:20 He carried into exile to **B** the remnant, who H951
Ezr 1:11 when they came up from **B** to Jerusalem. H951
Ezr 2: 1 king of **B** had taken captive to H951
Ezr 2: 1 king of Babylon had taken captive to **B** H951
Ezr 4: 9 Uruk and **B**, the Elamites of Susa A10094
Ezr 5:12 Chaldean, king of **B**, who destroyed this A10093
Ezr 5:12 temple and deported the people to **B**. A10093
Ezr 5:13 in the first year of Cyrus king of **B**, King A10093
Ezr 5:14 from the temple of **B** the gold and silver A10093
Ezr 5:14 brought to the temple in **B**. A10093
Ezr 5:17 royal archives of **B** to see if King Cyrus A10093
Ezr 6: 1 the archives stored in the treasury at **B**. A10093
Ezr 6: 5 temple in Jerusalem and brought to **B**, A10093
Ezr 7: 6 this Ezra came up from **B**. He was a teacher H951
Ezr 7: 9 begun his journey from **B** on the first day of H951
Ezr 7:16 you may obtain from the province of **B**, A10093
Ezr 8: 1 up with me from **B** during the reign of H951
Ne 7: 6 king of **B** had taken captive H951
Ne 13: 6 of Artaxerxes king of **B** I had returned to the H951
Est 2: 6 Jerusalem by Nebuchadnezzar king of **B**, H951
Ps 87: 4 will record Rahab and **B** among those who H951
Ps 137: 1 By the rivers of **B** we sat and wept when we H951
Ps 137: 8 Daughter **B**, doomed to destruction, happy H951
Isa 13: 1 A prophecy against **B** that Isaiah son of H951
Isa 13:19 **B**, the jewel of kingdoms, the pride and H951
Isa 14: 4 will take up this taunt against the king of **B**: H951
Isa 21: 9 back the answer: '**B** has fallen, has fallen H951
Isa 39: 1 of Baladan king of **B** sent Hezekiah letters H951
Isa 39: 3 "They came to me from **B**." H951
Isa 39: 6 up until this day, will be carried off to **B**. H951
Isa 39: 7 eunuchs in the palace of the king of **B**." H951
Isa 43:14 sake I will send to **B** and bring down as H951
Isa 47: 1 Virgin Daughter **B**; sit on the ground H951
Isa 48:14 ally will carry out his purpose against **B**; H951
Isa 48:20 Leave **B**, flee from the Babylonians H951
Jer 20: 4 all Judah into the hands of the king of **B**, H951
Jer 20: 4 will carry them away to **B** or put them to the H951
Jer 20: 5 take it away as plunder and carry it off to **B**. H951
Jer 20: 6 live in your house will go into exile to **B**. H951
Jer 21: 2 Nebuchadnezzar king of **B** is attacking us. H951
Jer 21: 4 to fight the king of **B** and the Babylonians H951
Jer 21: 7 king of **B** and to their enemies H951
Jer 21:10 be given into the hands of the king of **B**, H951
Jer 22:25 king of **B** and the Babylonians. H951
Jer 24: 1 from Jerusalem to **B** by Nebuchadnezzar H951
Jer 24: 1 to Babylon by Nebuchadnezzar king of **B**, H951
Jer 25: 1 the first year of Nebuchadnezzar king of **B**. H951
Jer 25: 9 my servant Nebuchadnezzar king of **B**," H951
Jer 25:11 will serve the king of **B** seventy years. H951
Jer 25:12 I will punish the king of **B** and his nation H951
Jer 27: 6 of my servant Nebuchadnezzar king of **B**; H951
Jer 27: 8 king of **B** or bow its neck under H951
Jer 27: 9 tell you, 'You will not serve the king of **B**.' H951
Jer 27:11 the yoke of the king of **B** and serve him, H951
Jer 27:12 your neck under the yoke of the king of **B**; H951
Jer 27:13 any nation that will not serve the king of **B**? H951
Jer 27:14 'You will not serve the king of **B**,' for they H951
Jer 27:16 LORD's house will be brought back from **B**. H951
Jer 27:17 Serve the king of **B**, and you will live. H951
Jer 27:18 Judah and in Jerusalem not be taken to **B**. H951
Jer 27:20 king of **B** did not take away when H951
Jer 27:20 of Judah into exile from Jerusalem to **B**, H951
Jer 27:22 'They will be taken to **B** and there they will H951
Jer 28: 2 'I will break the yoke of the king of **B**. H951
Jer 28: 3 king of **B** removed from here and H951
Jer 28: 3 Babylon removed from here and took to **B**. H951
Jer 28: 4 the other exiles from Judah who went to **B**, H951
Jer 28: 4 'for I will break the yoke of the king of **B**.' H951
Jer 28: 6 all the exiles back to this place from **B**. H951
Jer 28:11 king of **B** off the neck of all H951
Jer 28:14 them serve Nebuchadnezzar king of **B**, H951
Jer 29: 1 had carried into exile from Jerusalem to **B**. H951
Jer 29: 3 Judah sent to King Nebuchadnezzar in **B**. H951
Jer 29: 4 I carried into exile from Jerusalem to **B**: H951
Jer 29:10 "When seventy years are completed for **B**, H951
Jer 29:15 LORD has raised up prophets for us in **B**," H951
Jer 29:20 I have sent away from Jerusalem to **B**. H951
Jer 29:21 the hands of Nebuchadnezzar king of **B**, H951
Jer 29:22 from Judah who are in **B** will use this curse: H951
Jer 29:22 whom the king of **B** burned in the fire. H951
Jer 29:28 He has sent this message to us in **B**: It will H951
Jer 32: 2 army of the king of **B** was then besieging H951
Jer 32: 3 this city into the hands of the king of **B**, H951
Jer 32: 4 be given into the hands of the king of **B**, H951
Jer 32: 5 He will take Zedekiah to **B**, where he will H951
Jer 32:28 to Nebuchadnezzar king of **B**, H951
Jer 32:36 be given into the hands of the king of **B**'; H951
Jer 34: 1 king of **B** and all his army and H951
Jer 34: 2 this city into the hands of the king of **B**, H951

Jer 34: 3 will see the king of **B** with your own eyes, H951
Jer 34: 3 with you face to face. And you will go to **B**. H951
Jer 34: 7 army of the king of **B** was fighting against H951
Jer 34:21 to the army of the king of **B**, which has H951
Jer 35:11 king of **B** invaded this land, H951
Jer 36:29 it that the king of **B** would certainly come H951
Jer 37: 1 of Judah by Nebuchadnezzar king of **B**; H951
Jer 37:17 delivered into the hands of the king of **B**." H951
Jer 37:19 'The king of **B** will not attack you or this H951
Jer 38: 3 into the hands of the army of the king of **B**, H951
Jer 38:17 surrender to the officers of the king of **B**, H951
Jer 38:18 surrender to the officers of the king of **B**, H951
Jer 38:22 brought out to the officials of the king of **B**. H951
Jer 38:23 hands but will be captured by the king of **B**; H951
Jer 39: 1 Nebuchadnezzar king of **B** marched against H951
Jer 39: 3 of the king of **B** came and took seats in H951
Jer 39: 3 all the other officials of the king of **B**. H951
Jer 39: 5 king of **B** at Riblah in the land H951
Jer 39: 6 Riblah the king of **B** slaughtered the sons H951
Jer 39: 7 him with bronze shackles to take him to **B**. H951
Jer 39: 9 carried into exile to **B** the people who H951
Jer 39:11 king of **B** had given these orders H951
Jer 39:13 all the other officers of the king of **B** H951
Jer 40: 1 who were being carried into exile to **B**. H951
Jer 40: 4 Come with me to **B**, if you like, and I will H951
Jer 40: 5 whom the king of **B** has appointed over the H951
Jer 40: 7 that the king of **B** had appointed Gedaliah H951
Jer 40: 7 who had not been carried into exile to **B**, H951
Jer 40: 9 down in the land and serve the king of **B**, H951
Jer 40:11 that the king of **B** had left a remnant in H951
Jer 41: 2 one whom the king of **B** had appointed as H951
Jer 41:18 whom the king of **B** had appointed as H951
Jer 42:11 Do not be afraid of the king of **B**, whom you H951
Jer 43: 3 they may kill us or carry us into exile to **B**." H951
Jer 43:10 my servant Nebuchadnezzar king of **B**, H951
Jer 44:30 the hands of Nebuchadnezzar king of **B**, H951
Jer 46: 2 king of **B** in the fourth year of H951
Jer 46:13 Nebuchadnezzar king of **B** to attack Egypt: H951
Jer 46:26 Nebuchadnezzar king of **B** and his officers. H951
Jer 49:28 which Nebuchadnezzar king of **B** attacked: H951
Jer 49:30 king of **B** has plotted against you H951
Jer 50: 1 prophet concerning **B** and the land of the H951
Jer 50: 2 '**B** will be captured; Bel will be put H951
Jer 50: 8 "Flee out of **B**; leave the land of the H951
Jer 50: 9 up and bring against **B** an alliance of great H951
Jer 50:13 All who pass **B** will be appalled; they will H951
Jer 50:14 "Take up your positions around **B**, all you H951
Jer 50:16 Cut off from **B** the sower, and the reaper H951
Jer 50:17 their bones was Nebuchadnezzar king of **B**." H951
Jer 50:18 will punish the king of **B** and his land as I H951
Jer 50:23 How desolate is **B** among the nations! H951
Jer 50:24 I set a trap for you, **B**, and you were caught H951
Jer 50:28 refugees from **B** declaring in Zion H824+951
Jer 50:29 "Summon archers against **B**, all those who H951
Jer 50:34 but unrest to those who live in **B**. H951
Jer 50:35 those who live in **B** and against her H951
Jer 50:42 battle formation to attack you, Daughter **B**. H951
Jer 50:43 The king of **B** has heard reports about them H951
Jer 50:44 I will chase **B** from its land in an instant. H4392S
Jer 50:45 hear what the LORD has planned against **B** H951
Jer 51: 1 a destroyer against **B** and the people of H951
Jer 51: 2 send foreigners to **B** to winnow her and to H951
Jer 51: 4 They will fall down slain in **B**, fatally H824+4169
Jer 51: 6 "Flee from **B**! Run for your lives! Do not be H951
Jer 51: 7 **B** was a gold cup in the LORD's hand; she H951
Jer 51: 8 **B** will suddenly fall and be broken. H951
Jer 51: 9 " 'We would have healed **B**, but she H951
Jer 51:11 because his purpose is to destroy **B**. H951
Jer 51:12 Lift up a banner against the walls of **B** H951
Jer 51:12 his decree against the people of **B**. H951
Jer 51:24 your eyes I will repay **B** and all who live in H951
Jer 51:29 the LORD's purposes against **B** stand—to H951
Jer 51:29 lay waste the land of **B** so that no one will H951
Jer 51:31 to the king of **B** that his entire city is H951
Jer 51:33 "Daughter **B** is like a threshing floor at the H951
Jer 51:34 king of **B** has devoured us, H951
Jer 51:35 May the violence done to our flesh be on **B**," H951
Jer 51:37 **B** will be a heap of ruins, a haunt of jackals H951
Jer 51:41 How desolate **B** will be among the nations H951
Jer 51:42 The sea will rise over **B**; its roaring waves H951
Jer 51:44 I will punish Bel in **B** and make him spew H951
Jer 51:44 stream to him. And the wall of **B** will fall. H951
Jer 51:47 come when I will punish the idols of **B**; H951
Jer 51:48 all that is in them will shout for joy over **B**, H951
Jer 51:49 "**B** must fall because of Israel's slain, just H951
Jer 51:49 in all the earth have fallen because of **B**. H951
Jer 51:53 Even if **B** ascends to the heavens and H951
Jer 51:54 "The sound of a cry comes from **B**, the H951
Jer 51:55 The LORD will destroy **B**; he will silence her H951
Jer 51:56 A destroyer will come against **B**; her H951
Jer 51:59 when he went to **B** with Zedekiah king of H951
Jer 51:60 all the disasters that would come upon **B**— H951
Jer 51:60 all that had been recorded concerning **B**. H951
Jer 51:61 "When you get to **B**, see that you read all H951
Jer 51:64 'So will **B** sink to rise no more because of H951
Jer 52: 3 Zedekiah rebelled against the king of **B**. H951
Jer 52: 4 Nebuchadnezzar king of **B** marched against H951
Jer 52: 9 taken to the king of **B** at Riblah in the land H951
Jer 52:10 at Riblah the king of **B** killed the sons of H951
Jer 52:11 with bronze shackles and took him to **B**, H951
Jer 52:12 year of Nebuchadnezzar king of **B**, H951
Jer 52:12 who served the king of **B**, came to H951
Jer 52:15 those who had deserted to the king of **B**. H951
Jer 52:17 LORD and they carried all the bronze to **B**. H951
Jer 52:26 brought them to the king of **B** at Riblah. H951
Jer 52:31 in the year Awel-Marduk became king of **B** H951
Jer 52:32 of the other kings who were with him in **B**. H951
Jer 52:34 Day by day the king of **B** gave Jehoiachin a H951
Eze 17:12 'The king of **B** went to Jerusalem and H951
Eze 17:12 bringing them back with him to **B**. H951
Eze 17:16 he shall die in **B**, in the land of the H951
Eze 17:20 I will bring him to **B** and execute judgment H951
Eze 19: 9 a cage and brought him to the king of **B**. H951
Eze 21:19 roads for the sword of the king of **B** to take, H951
Eze 21:21 For the king of **B** will stop at the fork in the H951
Eze 24: 2 because the king of **B** has laid siege to H951
Eze 26: 7 against Tyre Nebuchadnezzar king of **B**, H951
Eze 29:18 king of **B** drove his army in a H951
Eze 29:19 to give Egypt to Nebuchadnezzar king of **B**, H951
Eze 30:10 by the hand of Nebuchadnezzar king of **B**. H951
Eze 30:24 arms of the king of **B** and put my sword in H951
Eze 30:25 I will strengthen the arms of the king of **B** H951
Eze 30:25 hand of the king of **B** and he brandishes it H951
Eze 32:11 sword of the king of **B** will come against H951
Da 1: 1 king of **B** came to Jerusalem and H951
Da 2:12 the execution of all the wise men of **B**. A10093
Da 2:14 out to put to death the wise men of **B**, A10093
Da 2:18 with the rest of the wise men of **B**. A10093
Da 2:24 appointed to execute the wise men of **B**, A10093
Da 2:24 "Do not execute the wise men of **B**. A10093
Da 2:48 entire province of **B** and placed him in A10093
Da 2:49 administrators over the province of **B**, A10093
Da 3: 1 on the plain of Dura in the province of **B**. A10093
Da 3:12 set over the affairs of the province of **B**— A10093
Da 3:30 Abednego in the province of **B**. A10093
Da 4: 6 all the wise men of **B** be brought before A10093
Da 4:29 on the roof of the royal palace of **B**, A10093
Da 4:30 "Is not this the great **B** I have built as the A10093
Da 5: 7 Then he said to these wise men of **B** A10093
Da 7: 1 In the first year of Belshazzar king of **B** A10093
Mic 4:10 You will go to **B**; there you will be H951
Zec 2: 7 Escape, you who live in Daughter **B**!" H951
Zec 6:10 Jedaiah, who have arrived from **B**. H951
Mt 1:11 his brothers at the time of the exile *to* **B**. G956
Mt 1:12 After the exile *to* **B**: Jeconiah was the G956
Mt 1:17 fourteen from David to the exile *to* **B**, and G956
Ac 7:43 I will send you into exile' beyond **B**. G956
1Pe 5:13 She who is in **B**, chosen together with you G956
Rev 14: 8 Fallen is **B** the Great,' which made all the G956
Rev 16:19 God remembered **B** the Great and gave her G956
Rev 17: 5 **B** THE GREAT THE MOTHER OF PROSTITUTES G956
Rev 18: 2 Fallen is **B** the Great!' She has G956
Rev 18:10 you mighty city *of* **B**! In one hour your G956
Rev 18:21 the great city *of* **B** will be thrown down, G956

BABYLON'S (4) [BABYLON]

Isa 14:22 "I will wipe out **B** name and survivors, her H951
Jer 50:46 At the sound of **B** capture the earth will H951
Jer 51:30 **B** warriors have stopped fighting; they H951
Jer 51:58 "**B** thick wall will be leveled and her high H951

BABYLONIA (10) [BABYLON]

Jos 7:21 in the plunder a beautiful robe from **B**, H9114
Isa 11:11 from Elam, from **B**, from Hamath and from H9114
Jer 50:10 So **B** will be plundered; all who plunder H4169
Jer 51:24 all who live in **B** for all the wrong H4169
Jer 51:35 "May our blood be on those who live in **B**," H4169
Eze 11:24 me to the exiles in **B** in the vision given H4169
Eze 12:13 I will bring him to **B**, the land of the H951
Eze 16:29 increased your promiscuity to include **B**, H4169
Da 1: 2 of his god in **B** and put in the H824+9114
Zec 5:11 "To the country of **B** to build a house for it. H9114

BABYLONIAN (13) [BABYLON]

2Ki 24: 2 The LORD sent **B**, Aramean, Moabite and H4169
2Ki 25: 5 the **B** army pursued the king and H4169
2Ki 25:10 The whole **B** army under the commander H4169
2Ki 25:24 "Do not be afraid of the **B** officials," H4169
Jer 35:11 to escape the **B** and Aramean armies. H4169
Jer 37:10 to defeat the entire **B** army that is H4169
Jer 37:11 After the **B** army had withdrawn from H4169
Jer 39: 5 But the **B** army pursued them and H4169
Jer 41: 3 as well as the **B** soldiers who were there. H4169
Jer 52: 8 the **B** army pursued King Zedekiah and H4169
Jer 52:14 The whole **B** army, under the commander H4169
Eze 23:15 them looked like **B** chariot officers, H1201+951
Da 9: 1 who was made ruler over the **B** kingdom— H4169

BABYLONIANS (54) [BABYLON]

2Ki 25: 4 though the **B** were surrounding the city. H4169
2Ki 25:13 The **B** broke up the bronze pillars, the H4169
2Ki 25:25 of Judah and the **B** who were with him at H4169
2Ki 25:26 officers, fled to Egypt for fear of the **B**. H4169
2Ch 36:17 up against them the king of the **B**, H4169
Isa 13:19 the pride and glory of the **B**, will be H4169
Isa 23:13 Look at the land of the **B**, this people that H4169
Isa 43:14 bring down as fugitives all the **B**, H4169
Isa 47: 1 without a throne, queen city of the **B**. H4169
Isa 47: 5 queen city of the **B**; no more will you be H4169
Isa 48:14 Babylon; his arm will be against the **B**. H4169
Isa 48:20 flee from the **B**! Announce this with H4169
Jer 21: 4 of Babylon and the **B** who are outside the H4169
Jer 21: 9 surrenders to the **B** who are besieging you H4169
Jer 22:25 king of Babylon and the **B**. H4169
Jer 24: 5 away from this place to the land of the **B**. H4169
Jer 25:12 the land of the **B**, for their guilt, H4169
Jer 32: 4 will not escape the **B** but will certainly be H4169
Jer 32: 5 If you fight against the **B**, you will not H4169
Jer 32:24 the hands of the **B** who are attacking it. H4169
Jer 32:25 city will be given into the hands of the **B**, H4169
Jer 32:28 the hands of the **B** and to H4169
Jer 32:29 The **B** who are attacking this city will come H4169
Jer 32:43 it has been given into the hands of the **B**. H4169
Jer 33: 5 in the fight with the **B**: 'They will be filled H4169
Jer 37: 5 when the **B** who were besieging H4169
Jer 37: 8 Then the **B** will return and attack this city H4169
Jer 37: 9 thinking, 'The **B** will surely leave us. H4169
Jer 37:13 him and said, "You are deserting to the **B**!" H4169
Jer 37:14 "I am not deserting to the **B**." But Irijah H4169
Jer 38: 2 whoever goes over to the **B** will live. H4169
Jer 38:18 the hands of the **B** and they will burn it H4169
Jer 38:19 of the Jews who have gone over to the **B**, H4169
Jer 38:19 the **B** may hand me over to them and NDT
Jer 38:23 children will be brought out to the **B**. H4169
Jer 39: 8 The **B** set fire to the royal palace and the H4169
Jer 40: 9 "Do not be afraid to serve the **B**," he said H4169
Jer 40:10 you before the **B** who come to us, H4169
Jer 41:18 to escape the **B**. They were afraid of them H4169
Jer 43: 3 you against us to hand us over to the **B**, H4169
Jer 50: 1 concerning Babylon and the land of the **B**: H4169
Jer 50: 8 leave the land of the **B**, and be like the H4169
Jer 50:25 has work to do in the land of the **B**. H4169
Jer 50:35 "A sword against the **B**!" declares the LORD H4169
Jer 50:45 has purposed against the land of the **B**: H4169
Jer 51:54 great destruction from the land of the **B**. H4169
Jer 52: 7 though the **B** were surrounding the city. H4169
Jer 52:17 The **B** broke up the bronze pillars, the H4169
Eze 1: 3 by the Kebar River in the land of the **B**. H4169
Eze 23:17 Then the **B** came to her, to the bed H1201+951
Eze 23:23 the **B** and all the Chaldeans, the H1201+951
Da 1: 4 the language and literature of the **B**. H4169
Da 5:30 Belshazzar, king of the **B**, was slain, A10373
Hab 1: 6 I am raising up the **B**, that ruthless and H4169

BACA (NIV84) BAKA

BACHRITES (KJV) BEKERITE

BACK (612) [BACKBONE, BACKGROUND, BACKS, BACKSLIDING, BACKSLIDINGS, BACKWARD]

Ge 3:24 sword **flashing b and forth** to guard the H2200
Ge 8: 7 it kept flying **b** and forth until the H8740
Ge 8: 9 took the dove and **brought** it **b** to himself in H995
Ge 14: 7 Then *they* **turned b** and went to En H8740
Ge 14:16 the goods and **brought b** his relative Lot H8740
Ge 15:16 your descendants *will* **come b** here, H8740
Ge 16: 9 "**Go b** to your mistress and submit to her." H8740
Ge 19:10 out and **pulled** Lot **b** into the house H995
Ge 19:17 Don't look **b**, and don't stop anywhere in H339
Ge 19:26 But Lot's wife looked **b**, and she H4946+339
Ge 22: 5 worship and then *we will* **come b** to you." H8740
Ge 24: 5 unwilling to come **b** *with* me to this land? H339
Ge 24: 5 *Shall I then* **take** your son **b** to the H8740+8740
Ge 24: 6 sure that *you do* not **take** my son **b** there," H8740
Ge 24: 8 woman is unwilling to come **b** *with* you, H339
Ge 24: 8 Only *do* not **take** my son **b** there." H8740
Ge 24:20 ran **b** to the well to draw more water H6388
Ge 24:39 if the woman will not come **b** *with* me? H339
Ge 24:61 the camels and went **b** *with* the man. H339
Ge 27: 5 open country to hunt game and **bring** it **b**, H995
Ge 27:45 send word for you *to* **come b** from there. H4374
Ge 28:15 and *I will* **bring** you **b** to this land. H8740
Ge 29: 7 the sheep and **take** them **b** *to* pasture." H2143
Ge 30:25 me on my way so *I can* **go b** to my own H2143
Ge 31: 3 "**Go b** to the land of your fathers and to H8740
Ge 31:13 land at once and **go b** to your native land. H8740
Ge 32: 9 '**Go b** to your country and your relatives H8740
Ge 33:16 that day Esau **started** on his way **b** to Seir. H8740
Ge 37:14 with the flocks, and **bring** word **b** to me." H8740
Ge 37:22 from them and **take** him **b** to his father. H8740
Ge 37:30 *He* **went b** to his brothers and said, "The H8740
Ge 37:32 *They* **took** the ornate robe **b** to H8938+2256+995
Ge 38:20 in order to **get** his pledge **b** from the H4374
Ge 38:22 So *he* **went b** to Judah and said, "I didn't H8740
Ge 38:29 But when *he* **drew b** his hand, his brother H8740
Ge 42:19 of you go and **take** grain **b** *for* your starving H995
Ge 42:24 then **came b** and spoke to them again H8740
Ge 42:25 to **put** each man's silver **b** in his sack H8740
Ge 42:34 Then *I will* **give** your brother **b** to you, and H5989
Ge 42:37 sons to death if *I do* not **bring** him **b** to you. H995
Ge 42:37 him to my care, and I *will* **bring** him **b**." H8740
Ge 43: 2 "**Go b** and buy us a little more food." H8740
Ge 43: 9 If *I do* not **bring** him **b** to you and set him H995
Ge 43:12 the silver that *was* **put b** into the mouths H8740
Ge 43:13 brother also and **go b** to the man at once. H8740
Ge 43:14 *he will let* your other brother and Benjamin **come b** H8938
Ge 43:18 of the silver that *was* **put b** into our sacks H8740
Ge 43:21 So *we have* **brought** it **b** with us. H8740
Ge 44: 8 *We* even **brought b** to you from the land of H8740
Ge 44:17 rest of you, **go b** to your father in peace." H6590
Ge 44:24 When *we* **went b** to your servant my father H6590
Ge 44:25 '**Go b** and buy a little more food. H8740
Ge 44:30 not with us when I **go b** to your servant my H995
Ge 44:32 'If *I do* not **bring** him **b** to you, I will H995
Ge 44:34 How *can I* **go b** to my father if the boy is H6590
Ge 45: 9 Now hurry **b** to my father and say to him H6590
Ge 45:18 bring your father and your families **b** to me. H995

Ge 45:27 the carts Joseph had sent to **carry** him **b**, H5951
Ge 46: 4 and I *will* **surely bring** you **b** again. H6590+6590
Ge 48:21 be with you and **take** you **b** to the land of H8740
Ge 50:15 against us and **pays** us **b** *for* all the H8740+8740
Ex 4: 4 of the snake and *it* **turned** *b* **into** a staff in his AIT
Ex 4: 7 "Now **put** it **b** into your cloak," he said. H8740
Ex 4: 7 So Moses **put** his hand **b** into his cloak H8740
Ex 4:18 Then Moses went **b** to Jethro his H8740
Ex 4:19 Moses in Midian, "Go **b** *to* Egypt, for all H8740
Ex 4:20 them on a donkey and **started b** to Egypt. H8740
Ex 5: 4 from their labor? **Get b** to your work!" H2143
Ex 9: 2 let them go and continue *to* **hold** them **b**, H2616
Ex 9:24 lightning **flashed b and forth.** H4374+928+9348
Ex 10: 8 Aaron **were brought b** to Pharaoh. H8740
Ex 14: 2 the Israelites *to* **turn b** and encamp near H8740
Ex 14:21 the LORD **drove** the sea **b** with a strong H2143
Ex 14:26 so that the waters *may* **flow b** over the H8740
Ex 14:27 at daybreak the sea **went b** to its place. H8740
Ex 14:28 The water **flowed b** and covered the H8740
Ex 15:19 LORD **brought** the waters of the sea **b** over H8740
Ex 19: 7 So Moses **went b** and summoned the H995
Ex 19: 8 So Moses **brought** their answer **b** to the H8740
Ex 22: 1 sells it *must* **pay b** five head of cattle H8966
Ex 22: 4 sheep—*they must* **pay b** double. H8966
Ex 22: 7 the thief, if caught, *must* **pay b** double. H8966
Ex 22: 9 declare guilty *must* **pay b** double to the H8966
Ex 22:29 "*Do* not **hold b** offerings from your H336
Ex 24:14 "Wait here for us until *we* **come b** to you. H8740
Ex 32:15 inscribed on both sides, front and **b**. H2296S
Ex 32:27 **Go b** and forth through the camp from H8740
Ex 32:31 So Moses **went b** to the LORD and said H8740
Ex 33:23 remove my hand and you will see my **b**; H294
Ex 34:31 leaders of the community **came b** to him, H8740
Ex 34:35 Then Moses *would* **put** the veil **b** over his H8740
Lev 19:13 *Do* not **hold b** the wages of a hired worker **overnight** H4328+6330+1332
Lev 25:27 *they can* then **go b** to their own property. H8740
Lev 25:28 and *they can* then **go b** to their property. H8740
Lev 25:41 and *they will* **go b** to their own clans and H8740
Lev 27:27 it *may be* **bought b** at its set value H7009
Nu 10:30 *I am* **going b** to my own land and my own H2143
Nu 12:14 after that *she can* **be brought b**. H665
Nu 12:15 did not move on till she *was* **brought b**. H665
Nu 13:20 Do your best *to* **bring b** some of the fruit H4374
Nu 13:26 *They* **came b** to Moses and H2143+2256+995
Nu 14: 3 it be better for us *to* **go b** to Egypt? H8740
Nu 14: 4 choose a leader and **go b** to Egypt." H8740
Nu 14:25 **turn b** tomorrow and set out toward the H7155
Nu 16:26 "**Move b** from the tents of these wicked H6073
Nu 17:10 "**Put b** Aaron's staff in front of the ark of H8740
Nu 22: 8 "and *I will* **report b** *to* you *with* the answer H8740
Nu 22:13 officials, "**Go b** to your own country H2143
Nu 22:23 Balaam beat it to **get** it **b on** the road. H5742
Nu 22:34 Now if you are displeased, *I will* **go b**." H8740
Nu 23: 5 "**Go b** to Balak and give him this word." H8740
Nu 23: 6 So *he* **went b** to him and found him H8740
Nu 23:16 "**Go b** to Balak and give him this word." H8740
Nu 24:14 Now I *am* **going b** to my people, but come, H2143
Nu 33: 7 They left Etham, **turned b** to Pi Hahiroth H8740
Nu 35:25 blood and **send** the accused **b** to the city H8740
Nu 35:32 so *allow* them *to* **go b** and live on H8740
Dt 1:22 land for us and **bring b** a report about the H8740
Dt 1:45 *You* **came b** and wept before the LORD, but H8740
Dt 2: 1 Then *we* **turned b** and set out toward the H7155
Dt 3:20 each of you *may* **go b** to the possession I H8740
Dt 10: 5 Then *I came* **b** down the mountain and H7155
Dt 17:16 "*You* are not to **go b** that way again." H8740
Dt 19:12 town elders, *be* **brought b** from the city H4374
Dt 22: 1 it but **be sure to take** it **b** to its H8740+8740
Dt 22: 2 they come looking for it. Then **give** it **b**. H8740
Dt 24:19 overlook a sheaf, *do* not **go b** to get it. H8740
Dt 28:68 The LORD *will* **send** you **b** in ships *to* Egypt H8740
Dt 30: 4 your God will gather you and **bring** you **b**. H4374
Jos 1:15 *you may* **go b** and occupy your own land H8740
Jos 2:23 Then the two men **started b**. H8740
Jos 8:15 Israel **let themselves be driven b** before H5595
Jos 8:20 men of Ai looked **b** and saw the H7155+339
Jos 8:20 the wilderness *had* **turned b** against their H2200
Jos 8:26 For Joshua *did* not **draw b** the hand that H8740
Jos 11:10 that time Joshua **turned b** and captured H8740
Jos 14: 7 And *I* **brought** him **b** a report according to H8740
Jos 19:29 then **turned b** *toward* Ramah and H8740
Jos 20: 6 Then they *may* **go b** to their own home in H8740
Jdg 1: 7 Now God *has* **paid** me **b** *for* what I did to H8966
Jdg 3:19 near Gilgal *he* himself **went b** to Eglon H8740
Jdg 5: 7 not fight; *they* **held s** until I, Deborah H2532
Jdg 6:18 not go away until I **come b** and bring my H995
Jdg 7: 3 with fear *may* **turn b** and leave Mount H8740
Jdg 8:29 son of Joash **went b** home to live. H2143
Jdg 11: 9 "Suppose you **take** me **b** to fight the H8740
Jdg 11:13 to the Jordan. Now **give** it **b** peaceably." H8740
Jdg 11:14 Jephthah sent **b** messengers to the H3578+6388
Jdg 14: 8 time later, when *he* **went b** to marry her H8740
Jdg 16:18 Philistines, "**Come b** once more; he has H6590
Jdg 16:31 *They* **brought** him **b** and buried him H6590
Jdg 17: 3 *I will* **give** it **b** to you." H8740
Jdg 18:26 him, turned around and **went b** home. H8740
Jdg 19: 2 left him and went **b** to her parents' home NDT
Jdg 19:26 the woman **went b** *to* the house where H995
Jdg 20:48 The men of Israel **went b** to Benjamin H8740
Ru 1: 7 road that *would* **take** them **b** to the land H8740
Ru 1: 8 two daughters-in-law, "Go **b**, each of you, H8740
Ru 1:10 "*We will* **go b** with you to your people." H8740
Ru 1:15 sister-in-law *is* **going b** to her people H8740
Ru 1:15 her people and her gods. **Go b** with her." H8740
Ru 1:16 me to leave you or to **turn b** from you. H8740
Ru 1:21 but the LORD *has* **brought** me **b** empty. H8740
Ru 2: 6 the Moabite who **came b** from Moab with H8740
Ru 2:18 She carried it **b** *to* town, and her H995
Ru 3:15 bundle on her. Then *he* **went b** *to* town. H995
Ru 3:17 'Don't **go b** to your mother-in-law H995
Ru 4: 3 "Naomi, who *has* **come b** from Moab, is H8740
1Sa 1:19 LORD and then went **b** to their home at H8740
1Sa 3: 5 "I did not call; **go b** and lie down. H8740
1Sa 3: 6 Eli said, "I did not call; **go b** and lie down." H8740
1Sa 4: 4 and they brought **b** the ark of the H4946+9004
1Sa 5: 3 took Dagon and **put** him **b** in his place. H8740
1Sa 5:11 of Israel away; *let* it **go b** to its own place H8740
1Sa 6: 2 Tell us how *we should* **send** it **b** to its H8938
1Sa 6: 3 *do* not **send** it **b** to him without a gift H8938
1Sa 6: 8 objects *you are* **sending b** to him as a H8740
1Sa 7: 2 the people of Israel turned **b to** the LORD. H339
1Sa 7:17 But he always **went b** to Ramah, where his H9588
1Sa 8:22 "Everyone **go b** to your own town. H2143
1Sa 9: 5 *let's* **go b**, or my father will stop H8740
1Sa 13: 2 rest of the men *he* **sent b** to their homes. H8938
1Sa 15:20 Amalekites and **brought b** Agag their king. H995
1Sa 15:25 forgive my sin and **come b** with me, so H8740
1Sa 15:26 said to him, "*I will* not **go b** with you. H8740
1Sa 15:30 before Israel; **come b** with me, so that I H8740
1Sa 15:31 So Samuel **went b** with Saul, and Saul H8740
1Sa 17: 6 bronze javelin was **slung on** his **b**. H1068+4190
1Sa 17:15 David went **b** and forth from Saul to H8740
1Sa 17:18 brothers are and **bring b** some assurance H4374
1Sa 18:27 Philistines and **brought b** their foreskins. H995
1Sa 19:15 Then Saul **sent** the men **b** to see David H8938
1Sa 20:40 boy and said, "Go, **carry** them **b** *to* town." H995
1Sa 20:42 and Jonathan **went b** *to* the town. H995
1Sa 23:23 places he uses and **come b** to me with H8740
1Sa 24: 3 and his men were **far b in** the cave. H928+3752
1Sa 25:12 David's men turned around and **went b** H8740
1Sa 25:21 *He has* **paid** me **b** evil for good H8740
1Sa 26:21 "I have sinned. **Come b**, David my son H8740
1Sa 29: 4 said, "**Send** the man **b**, that he may H8740
1Sa 29: 7 Now **turn b** and go in peace; do nothing to H8740
1Sa 29:11 in the morning to **go b** to the land of the H8740
1Sa 30:19 David **brought** everything **b**. H8740
2Sa 1:22 the bow of Jonathan did not turn **b**, the H294
2Sa 2:23 the spear came out through his **b**. H339
2Sa 3:16 said to him, "Go **b** home!" So he went H8740
2Sa 3:16 "Go back home!" So *he* **went b**. H8740
2Sa 3:26 and *they* **brought** him **b** from the cistern at H8740
2Sa 10: 5 beards have grown, and then **come b**." H8740
2Sa 11: 4 Then *she* **went b** home. H8740
2Sa 11:12 more day, and tomorrow *I will* **send** you **b**." H8938
2Sa 11:23 but *we* **drove** them **b** to the H2118+6584
2Sa 12:23 Can I **bring** him **b** again? I will go H8740
2Sa 14:13 the king *has* not **brought b** his H8740
2Sa 14:21 **bring b** the young man Absalom. H8740
2Sa 14:23 and **brought** Absalom **b** *to* Jerusalem H995
2Sa 15: 8 the LORD **takes** me **b** *to* Jerusalem, H8740+8740
2Sa 15:19 **Go b** and stay with King Absalom H8740
2Sa 15:20 where I am going? **Go b**, and take your H8740
2Sa 15:25 "**Take** the ark of God **b** *into* the city. H8740
2Sa 15:25 *he will* **bring** me **b** and let me see it and H8740
2Sa 15:27 **Go b** *to* the city with my blessing H8740
2Sa 15:29 Abiathar **took** the ark of God **b** *to* H8740
2Sa 17: 3 and **bring** all the people **b** to you. H8740
2Sa 19:10 say nothing about **bringing** the king **b**?" H8740
2Sa 19:11 the last to **bring** the king **b** to his palace H8740
2Sa 19:12 should you be the last to **bring b** the king? H8740
2Sa 19:43 the first to speak of **bringing b** our king?" H8740
2Sa 20:22 And Joab **went b** to the king in Jerusalem. H8740
2Sa 22:38 *I did* not **turn b** till they were destroyed. H8740
2Sa 23:16 of Bethlehem and carried it **b** to David. H995
2Sa 24: 8 *they* **came b** *to* Jerusalem at the end of H995
1Ki 2:26 "**Go b** to your fields in Anathoth. H2143
1Ki 2:40 away and **brought** the slaves **b** from Gath. H995
1Ki 5: 2 Solomon **sent b** this message to Hiram: H8938
1Ki 7: 8 to live, **set farther b**, was H2958+2021+337
1Ki 8:33 when *they* **turn b** to you and give H8740
1Ki 8:34 Israel and **bring** them **b** to the land you H8740
1Ki 8:48 if *they* **turn b** to you with all their H8740
1Ki 9:28 Ophir and **brought b** 420 talents of H4946+9004
1Ki 10:19 and its **b** had a rounded top. H4946+339
1Ki 11:22 that you want to **go b** to your own country?" H2143
1Ki 12: 5 three days and then **come b** to me." H8740
1Ki 12:12 had said, "**Come b** to me in three days." H8740
1Ki 13: 4 so that he could not **pull** it **b**. H8740
1Ki 13:16 "I cannot **turn b** and go with you H8740
1Ki 13:18 '**Bring** him **b** with you to your house so H8740
1Ki 13:20 the old prophet who *had* **brought** him **b**. H8740
1Ki 13:22 *You* **came b** and ate bread and drank H8740
1Ki 13:23 prophet who *had* **brought** him **b** saddled H8740
1Ki 13:26 prophet who *had* **brought** him **b** from his H8740
1Ki 13:29 and **brought** it **b** to his own city to mourn H8740
1Ki 14: 9 my anger and turned your **b** on me. H1567
1Ki 14:12 "As for you, **go b** home. When you set H2143
1Ki 18:37 that you are turning their hearts **b** again." H345
1Ki 18:43 Seven times Elijah said, "**Go b**." H8740
1Ki 19: 7 angel of the LORD **came b** a second time H8740
1Ki 19:15 said to him, "Go **b** the way you came, and H8740
1Ki 19:20 come with you." "Go **b**," Elijah replied H8740
1Ki 19:21 So Elisha left him and **went b**. He took his H8740
1Ki 20: 9 left and **took** the answer **b** *to* Ben-Hadad. H8740
1Ki 22:26 Micaiah and **send** him **b** to Amon the H8740
2Ki 1: 5 he asked them, "Why *have you* **come b**?" H8740
2Ki 1: 6 'Go **b** to the king who sent you and tell H8740
2Ki 2:13 from him and **went b** and stood on the H8740
2Ki 4:31 So Gehazi **went b** to meet Elisha and told H8740
2Ki 4:35 walked **b and forth** in the room H285+2178+2256+285+2178
2Ki 5: 7 Can I kill and **bring b to life**? Why does H2649
2Ki 5:15 his attendants **went b** to the man of God H8740
2Ki 6:13 *The* **report came b**: "He is in H5583
2Ki 6:22 drink and then **go b** to their master." H2143
2Ki 8: 3 seven years she **came b** from the land of H8740
2Ki 8: 5 son Elisha *had* **brought b to life** came to H2649
2Ki 8: 6 "**Give b** everything that belonged to her H8740
2Ki 8:21 by night; his army, however, **fled b** home. H5674
2Ki 9:18 has reached them, but *he* isn't **coming b**." H8740
2Ki 9:20 but *he* isn't **coming b** either. H8740
2Ki 9:36 *They* **went b** and told Jehu, who said H8740
2Ki 14:20 *He was* **brought b** by horse and was buried H5951
2Ki 16:12 When the king **came b** from Damascus H995
2Ki 17:27 from Samaria go **b** to live there H9004+2025S
2Ki 20: 5 "**Go b** and tell Hezekiah, the ruler of my H8740
2Ki 20: 9 ten steps, or *shall it* **go b** ten steps?" H8740
2Ki 20:10 "Rather, *have* it **go b** ten steps." H8740+345
2Ki 20:11 the LORD **made** the shadow **go b** the ten H8740
2Ki 22:20 So *they* **took** her answer **b** *to* the king. H8740
2Ki 23:20 Then *he* **went b** *to* Jerusalem. H8740
1Ch 11:18 of Bethlehem and carried it **b** to David. H995
1Ch 11:19 Because they risked their lives *to* **bring** it **b** H995
1Ch 13: 3 *Let us* **bring** the ark of our God **b** to us, for H6015
1Ch 19: 5 beards have grown, and then **come b**." H8740
1Ch 19:15 So Joab **went b** *to* Jerusalem. H995
1Ch 21: 2 Then **report b** to me so that I may know H995
1Ch 21: 4 Israel and then **came b** *to* Jerusalem. H995
1Ch 21:27 and *he* **put** his sword **b** into its sheath. H8740
2Ch 6:24 you and when *they* **turn b** and give praise H8740
2Ch 6:25 Israel and **bring** them **b** to the land you H8740
2Ch 6:38 if *they* **turn b** to you with all their H8740
2Ch 8:18 and brought **b** four hundred and H4946+9004
2Ch 10: 5 answered, "**Come b** to me in three days." H8740
2Ch 10:12 had said, "**Come b** to me in three days." H8740
2Ch 11: 4 of the LORD and **turned b** from marching H8740
2Ch 15:11 goats from the plunder *they had* **brought b**. H995
2Ch 18:25 Micaiah and **send** him **b** to Amon the H8740
2Ch 19: 4 of Ephraim and **turned** them **b** to the LORD, H8740
2Ch 24:11 empty the chest and carry it **b** to its place. H8740
2Ch 24:19 to the people to **bring** them **b** to him, H8740
2Ch 25:13 that Amaziah *had* **sent b** and had not H8740
2Ch 25:14 *he* **brought b** the gods of the people of Seir H995
2Ch 25:28 He *was* **brought b** by horse and was buried H5951
2Ch 28: 8 plunder, which *they* **carried b** to Samaria. H995
2Ch 28:11 **Send b** your fellow Israelites you have H8740
2Ch 28:15 So *they* **took** them **b** to their fellow H995
2Ch 33:13 so *he* **brought** him **b** *to* Jerusalem and to H8740
2Ch 34: 7 Then *he* **went b** to Jerusalem. H8740
2Ch 34:28 So *they* **took** her answer **b** *to* the king. H8740
Ne 1: 3 the exile and are **b** in the province are in H9004
Ne 2: 6 journey take, and when *will you* **get b**?" H8740
Ne 2:15 *I* **turned b** and reentered through the H8740
Ne 4: 2 *Can they* **bring** the stones **b to life** from H2649
Ne 4: 4 **Turn** their insults **b** on their own heads H8740
Ne 5: 8 we *have* **bought b** our fellow Jews who H7864
Ne 5: 8 people, only for *them to* **be sold b** to us!" H4835
Ne 5:11 **Give b** to them immediately their fields H8740
Ne 5:12 "*We will* **give** it **b**," they said. "And we H8740
Ne 6: 7 Now this report *will* **get b** to the king; so H9048
Ne 8:15 hill country and **bring b** branches from olive H995
Ne 8:16 went out and **brought b** branches and built H995
Ne 9:26 them in order to **turn** them **b** to you; H8740
Ne 9:29 them in order to **turn** them **b** to your law, H8740
Ne 13: 7 and **came b** to Jerusalem. Here I learned H995
Ne 13: 9 then *I* **put b** *into* them the equipment H8740
Ne 13:10 the service *had* **gone b** to their own H1368
Est 2:11 Every day he **walked b and forth** near the H2143
Est 4: 9 Hathak **went b** and reported to Esther what H995
Est 4:13 he **sent b** this answer: "Do not think that H8740
Est 9:25 the Jews *should* **come b** onto his own H8740
Job 1: 7 the earth, **going b and forth** on it. H2143
Job 2: 2 the earth, **going b and forth** on it. H2143
Job 12:15 If *he* **holds b** the waters, there is drought H6806
Job 20:10 his own hands *must* **give b** his wealth. H8740
Job 20:18 he toiled for *he must* **give b** uneaten; H8740
Job 20:25 He pulls it out of his **b**, the gleaming H1576
Job 33:30 to **turn** them **b** from the pit, that the light H8740
Job 37: 4 his voice resounds, *he* **holds** nothing **b**. H6810
Job 41:15 Its **b** has rows of shields tightly sealed H1568
Ps 6:10 *they will* **turn b** and suddenly be put to H8740
Ps 9: 3 My enemies turn **b**; they stumble and H294
Ps 18:37 *I did* not **turn b** till they were destroyed. H8740
Ps 28: 4 have done and **bring b** on them what they H8740
Ps 31:23 but the proud *he* **pays b** in full. H8966
Ps 35: 4 who plot my ruin be turned **b** in dismay. H294
Ps 38: 7 My **b** is filled with searing pain; there is H4072
Ps 40:14 who desire my ruin be turned **b** in disgrace. H294
Ps 44: 5 Through you *we* **push b** our enemies H5590
Ps 44:18 Our hearts had not turned **b**; our feet had H294
Ps 51:13 so that sinners *will* **turn b** to you. H8740
Ps 56: 9 my enemies will turn **b** when I call for help. H294
Ps 70: 2 who desire my ruin be turned **b** in disgrace. H294
Ps 70: 3 *May* those who say to me, "Aha! Aha!" **turn b** H8740

Ps 74:11 Why do you hold b your hand, your right H8740
Ps 77:17 thunder; your arrows flashed b and forth. H2143
Ps 78: 9 with bows, turned b on the day of battle; H2200
Ps 78:66 He beat b his enemies; he put them to H294
Ps 79:12 Pay b into the laps of our neighbors seven H8740
Ps 89:43 you have turned b the edge of his sword H8740
Ps 90: 3 You turn people b to dust, saying, "Return H8740
Ps 94: 2 pay b to the proud what they deserve. H8740
Ps 109:17 a curse—may it come b on him. H995
Ps 114: 3 sea looked and fled, the Jordan turned b; H294
Ps 114: 5 Why, Jordan, did you turn b? H294
Ps 118:13 I was pushed b and about to fall H1890+1890
Ps 129: 3 have plowed my b and made their furrows H1461
Ps 129: 5 all who hate Zion be turned b in shame. H294
Pr 3:28 "Come b tomorrow and I'll give it to you" H8740
Pr 10:13 a rod is for the b of one who has no H1568
Pr 17:13 the house of one who pays b evil for good H8740
Pr 19:24 he will not even bring it b to his mouth! H8740
Pr 20:22 Do not say, "I'll pay you b for this wrong!" H8966
Pr 22:21 so that you bring b truthful reports to H8740
Pr 24:11 hold b those staggering toward slaughter. H3104
Pr 24:29 I'll pay them b for what they did. H8740
Pr 26:15 he is too lazy to bring it b to his mouth. H8740
Pr 26:27 rolls a stone, it will roll b on them. H8740
Pr 28:17 in the grave; let no one hold them b. H9461
Ecc 1: 5 sun sets, and hurries b to where it rises. H8634
SS 6:13 Come b, come back, O Shulammite; come H8740
SS 6:13 Come back, come b, O Shulammite; come H8740
SS 6:13 O Shulammite; come b, come back, that H8740
SS 6:13 come back, come b, that we may gaze on H8740
Isa 3:11 They will be paid b for what their hands H6913
Isa 14:27 is stretched out, and who can turn it b? H8740
Isa 21: 9 And he gives b the answer: 'Babylon H6699
Isa 21:12 then ask; and come b yet again. H8740
Isa 28: 6 strength to those who turn b the battle at H8740
Isa 31: 2 disaster; he does not take b his words. H6073
Isa 38: 8 cast by the sun go b the ten steps it has H345
Isa 38: 8 So the sunlight went b the ten steps it H8740
Isa 38:17 you have put all my sins behind your b. H1568
Isa 42:14 I have been quiet and held myself b. H706
Isa 42:17 our gods,' will be turned b in utter shame. H294
Isa 42:22 with no one to say, "Send them b. H8740
Isa 43: 6 the south, 'Do not hold them b.' Bring my H3973
Isa 48: 9 the sake of my praise I hold it b from you, H2641
Isa 49: 5 be his servant to bring Jacob b to him H8740
Isa 49: 6 of Jacob and bring b those of Israel I H8740
Isa 49:17 Your children hasten b, and those who laid NDT
Isa 50: 6 I offered my b to those who beat me, my H1568
Isa 51:23 And you made your b like the ground H1568
Isa 54: 2 do not hold b; lengthen your H3104
Isa 54: 6 The LORD will call you b as if you were a H7924
Isa 54: 7 with deep compassion I will bring you b. H7695
Isa 58: 1 "Shout it aloud, do not hold b. Raise your H3104
Isa 59:14 So justice is driven b, and H6047+294
Isa 64:12 LORD, will you hold yourself b? Will you H706
Isa 65: 6 I will not keep silent but will pay b in full H8966
Isa 65: 6 back in full; I will pay it b into their laps H8966
Jer 4:28 I have decided and will not turn b. H8740
Jer 12:15 and will bring each of them b to their own H8740
Jer 15: 6 destroy you; I am tired of holding b. H5714
Jer 18:17 I will show them my b and not my face in H6902
Jer 22:27 You will never come b to the land you H8740
Jer 23: 3 driven them and will bring them b to their H8740
Jer 23:20 of the LORD will not turn b until he fully H8740
Jer 24: 6 and I will bring them b to this land. H8740
Jer 27:16 LORD's house will be brought b from H8740
Jer 27:22 'Then I will bring them b and restore H6590
Jer 28: 3 Within two years I will bring b to this place H8740
Jer 28: 4 I will also bring b to this place Jehoiachin H8740
Jer 28: 6 bringing the articles of the LORD's house
and all the exiles b H8740
Jer 29:10 good promise to bring you b to this place. H8740
Jer 29:14 "and will bring you b from captivity. H8740
Jer 29:14 "and will bring you b to the place from H8740
Jer 30: 3 I will bring my people Israel and Judah b from
H8740
Jer 30:24 of the LORD will not turn b until he fully H8740
Jer 31: 9 weeping; they will pray as I bring them b. H3297
Jer 31:23 "When I bring them b from captivity, the H8740
Jer 32:37 I will bring them b to this place and let H8740
Jer 33: 7 I will bring Judah and Israel b from H8740
Jer 34:11 their minds and took b the slaves they H8740
Jer 34:16 each of you has taken b the male and H8740
Jer 34:22 and I will bring them b to this city. H8740
Jer 37: 7 to support you, will go b to its own land H8740
Jer 37:20 Do not send me b to the house of H8740
Jer 38:26 the king not to send me b to Jonathan's H8740
Jer 39:14 of Shaphan, to take him b to his home. H3655
Jer 40: 5 "Go b to Gedaliah son of Ahikam H8740
Jer 40:12 they all came b to the land of Judah, to H8740
Jer 42: 4 says and will keep nothing b from you." H4979
Jer 43: 5 of Judah who had come b to live in the H8740
Jer 46: 5 They flee in haste without looking b, and H7155
Jer 46:16 let us go b to our own people and our H8740
Jer 48:39 How Moab turns her b in shame! Moab H6902
Jer 50: 2 proclaim it; keep nothing b, but say, H3948
Jer 50:19 But I will bring Israel b to their own H8740
La 1:13 spread a net for my feet and turned me b. H294
La 3:64 Pay them b what they deserve, LORD, for H8740
Eze 1:13 Fire moved b and forth among the H2143
Eze 1:14 The creatures sped b and forth like flashes H8740
Eze 9:11 the writing kit at his side brought b word, H8740
Eze 11:17 the nations and bring you b from the H665
Eze 11:17 and I will give you b the land of Israel H5989
Eze 17:12 bringing them b with him to Babylon. AIT
Eze 23:35 forgotten me and turned your b on me, H1567
Eze 24:14 I will not hold b; I will not have pity, nor H7277
Eze 29:14 I will bring them b from captivity and H8740
Eze 31:15 mourning for it; I held b its streams, and H4979
Eze 33:15 if they give b what they took in pledge H8740
Eze 34: 4 You have not brought b the strays or H8740
Eze 34:16 search for the lost and bring b the strays. H8740
Eze 36:24 the countries and bring you b into your own H995
Eze 37: 2 He led me b and forth among them, H6017+6017
Eze 37:12 I will bring you b to the land of Israel. H995
Eze 37:21 all around and bring them b into their own H995
Eze 39:27 When I have brought them b from the H8740
Eze 40:49 and twelve cubits from front to b. H8145
Eze 44: 1 Then the man brought me b to the outer H8740
Eze 47: 1 The man brought me b to the entrance to H8740
Eze 47: 6 Then he led me b to the bank of the river. H8740
Da 4:35 No one can hold b his hand or say to A10411
Da 7: 6 And on its b it had four wings like those A10128
Da 11:18 will turn his insolence b on him. H8740
Da 11:19 he will turn b toward the fortresses of his H8740
Da 11:30 Then he will turn b and vent his fury H8740
Hos 2: 7 'I will go b to my husband as at first H8740
Hos 2: 9 I will take b my wool and my linen H5911
Hos 2:15 There I will give her b her vineyards, and H5989
Joel 3: 4 If you are paying me b, I will swiftly and H1694
Am 7:12 you seer! Go b to the land of Judah. H1368
Am 9:14 and I will bring my people Israel b from H8740
Jnh 1:13 the men did their best to row b to land. H8740
Na 2: 4 rushing b and forth through the squares. H9212
Na 2: 8 they cry, but no one turns b. H7155
Zep 1: 6 those who turn b from following the LORD H6047
Zep 3:15 punishment, he has turned b your enemy. H7155
Zec 5: 8 and he pushed her b into the basket and H8959
Zec 8: 8 I will bring them b to live in Jerusalem; they H995
Zec 10:10 I will bring them b from Egypt and gather H8740
Mt 2:12 warned in a dream not to go b to Herod, G366
Mt 11: 4 "Go b and report to John what you hear G4513
Mt 18:26 he begged, 'and I will pay b everything. G625
Mt 18:28 'Pay b what you owe me!' he G625
Mt 18:29 'Be patient with me, and I will pay it b. G625
Mt 18:34 tortured, until he should pay b all he owed. G625
Mt 21:18 as Jesus was on his way b to the city G2056
Mt 22:21 "So give b to Caesar what is Caesar's G625
Mt 24:18 no one in the field go b to get their cloak. G3958
Mt 25:27 I returned I would have received it b with G3152
Mt 26:43 When he came b, he again found them G2262
Mt 26:52 "Put your sword b in its place," Jesus said G695
Mt 28: 2 the tomb, rolled b the stone and sat on it. G653
Mk 6:28 and brought b his head on a platter. G5770
Mk 8:13 got b into the boat and crossed to the G4099
Mk 11: 3 needs it and will send it b here shortly. G4099
Mk 12:17 "Give b to Caesar what is Caesar's and to G625
Mk 13:16 in the field go b to get their G1650+3836+3958
Mk 13:35 the owner of the house will come b— G2262
Mk 14:40 When he came b, he again found them G2262
Lk 1:16 He will bring b many of the people of G2188
Lk 2:45 they went b to Jerusalem to look for him. G5715
Lk 4:20 gave it b to the attendant and sat down. G625
Lk 6:30 what belongs to you, do not demand it b. G555
Lk 6:35 them without expecting to get anything b. G594
Lk 7:15 and Jesus gave him b to his mother. G1443
Lk 7:22 "Go b and report to John what you have G4513
Lk 7:42 of them had the money to pay him b, G625
Lk 9: 8 prophets of long ago had come b to life. G482
Lk 9:19 prophets of long ago has come b to life." G482
Lk 9:42 the boy and gave him b to his father. G625
Lk 9:61 first let me go b and say goodbye to my NDT
Lk 9:62 plow and looks b is fit for G1650+3836+3958
Lk 14:12 they may invite you b and so you will be G511
Lk 14:21 "The servant came b and reported this to G4134
Lk 15:18 I will set out and go b to my father and say to AIT
Lk 15:27 calf because he has him b safe and sound. G655
Lk 17: 4 seven times come b to you saying 'I G2188
Lk 17:15 he was healed, came b, praising God in a G5715
Lk 17:31 in the field should go b for anything.
G2188+1650+3836+3958
Lk 19: 8 I will pay b four times the amount. G625
Lk 19:13 money to work,' he said, 'until I come b. G2262
Lk 19:23 so that when I came b, I could have G2262
Lk 20:25 "Then give b to Caesar what is Caesar's G625
Lk 22:32 And when you have turned b, strengthen G2188
Lk 22:45 from prayer and went b to the disciples, G4639
Lk 23:11 an elegant robe, they sent him b to Pilate. G402
Lk 23:15 has Herod, for he sent him b to us; as you G402
Lk 24: 9 When they came b from the tomb, they G5715
Jn 1:22 Give us an answer to take b to those who G1443
Jn 4: 3 So he left Judea and went b once more to G599
Jn 4:16 "Go, call your husband and come b." G1924
Jn 4:28 the woman went b to the town and said to G599
Jn 6:66 turned b and no longer G1650+3836+3958
Jn 7:45 temple guards went b to the chief priests G4639
Jn 10:40 Then Jesus went b across the Jordan to the G599
Jn 11: 7 to his disciples, "Let us go b to Judea." G4099
Jn 11: 8 to stone you, and yet you are going b?" G4099
Jn 11:28 she went b and called her sister Mary aside G599
Jn 13:25 Leaning b against Jesus, he asked him G404
Jn 14: 3 I will come b and take you to be with me G4099
Jn 14:28 going away and I am coming b to you. G4639
Jn 16:28 the world and going b to the Father." G4639
Jn 18: 6 they drew b and fell to G599+1650+3836+3958
Jn 18:16 to the high priest, came b, spoke to the G2002
Jn 18:33 Pilate then went b inside the palace G4099
Jn 18:40 They shouted b, "No, not him! Give us G4099
Jn 19: 9 he went b inside the palace. G4099
Jn 20:10 Then the disciples went b to where they G599
Jn 21:11 So Simon Peter climbed b into the boat G326
Jn 21:20 the one who had leaned b against Jesus G404
Ac 1:11 will come b in the same way you have G2262
Ac 4:23 Peter and John went b to their own people AIT
Ac 5: 2 he kept b part of the money for himself, G3802
Ac 5:22 So they went b and reported, G418
Ac 7:16 Their bodies were brought b to Shechem G3572
Ac 7:34 Now come, I will send you b to Egypt.' G1650
Ac 7:39 him and in their hearts turned b to Egypt. G5138
Ac 10: 5 men to Joppa to bring b a man named G3569
Ac 10:16 the sheet was taken b to heaven. G377
Ac 12:14 so overjoyed she ran b without opening G1661
Ac 14:20 he got up and went b into the city. G1656
Ac 14:26 From Attalia they sailed b to Antioch G676
Ac 15:36 "Let us go b and visit the believers in all G2188
Ac 18:21 promised, "I will come b if it is God's will." G366
Ac 20: 3 he decided to go b through Macedonia. G5715
Ro 9:20 are you, a human being, to talk b to God? G503
1Co 15:34 Come b to your senses as you ought, and G1729
2Co 1:16 to come b to you from Macedonia G4099
Gal 2:12 he began to draw b and separate himself G5713
Gal 4: 9 that you are turning b to those weak and G4099
Eph 4:14 tossed b and forth by the waves, and G3115
Php 2:25 it is necessary to send b to you Epaphroditus, AIT
1Th 5:15 Make sure that nobody pays b wrong for G625
2Th 1: 6 He will pay b trouble to those who trouble G500
2Th 2: 6 And now you know what is holding him b G2988
2Th 2: 7 the one who now holds it b will G2988
Titus 2: 9 to try to please them, not to talk b to them, G515
Phm 12 I am sending him—who is my very heart—b G402
Phm 15 was that you might have him b forever— G600
Phm 19 I will pay it b—not to mention that you owe G702
Heb 6: 6 to be brought b to repentance. G4099+362
Heb 10:38 no pleasure in the one who shrinks b." G5713
Heb 10:39 not belong to those who shrink b and are G5714
Heb 11:19 speaking he did receive Isaac b from G3152
Heb 11:35 Women received b their dead, raised to G1666
Heb 13:20 eternal covenant brought b from the dead G343
Jas 5:19 someone should bring that person b, G2188
2Pe 2:13 They will be paid b with harm for the G3635
Rev 4: 6 were covered with eyes, in front and in b. G3957
Rev 7: 1 holding b the four winds of the earth to G3195
Rev 12: 7 the dragon and his angels fought b. G4482
Rev 18: 6 Give b to her as she has given; pay her G625
Rev 18: 6 pay her b double for what she has done. G1488

BACKBITERS, BACKBITING, BACKBITINGS
(KJV) SLY, SLANDER, SLANDERS

BACKBONE (1) [BACK, BONE]
Lev 3: 9 the entire fat tail cut off close to the b, the H6782

BACKGROUND (2) [BACK]
Est 2:10 not revealed her nationality and family b, H4580
Est 2:20 kept secret her family b and nationality H4580

BACKS (24) [BACK]
Ex 23:27 all your enemies turn their b and run. H6902
Jos 7:12 they turn their b and run because they H6902
Jos 23:13 whips on your b and thorns in your eyes H7396
2Sa 22:41 made my enemies turn their b in flight, H6902
2Ch 29: 6 dwelling place and turned their b on him. H6902
Ne 9:26 they turned their b on your law. H1567
Ne 9:29 Stubbornly they turned their b on you H4190
Ps 18:40 made my enemies turn their b in flight, H6902
Ps 21:12 them turn their b when you aim at them H8900
Ps 66:11 us into prison and laid burdens on our b. H5516
Ps 69:23 cannot see, and their b be bent forever. H5516
Pr 19:29 mockers, and beatings for the b of fools. H1568
Pr 26: 3 the donkey, and a rod for the b of fools! H1568
Isa 1: 4 One of Israel and turned their b on him. H294
Isa 30: 6 the envoys carry their riches on donkeys' b, H4190
Isa 59:13 the LORD, turning our b on our God, H339
Jer 2:27 have turned their b to me and not their H6902
Jer 32:33 They turned their b to me and not their H6902
Eze 8:16 With their b toward the temple of the LORD H294
Eze 10:12 including their b, their hands and their H1461
Eze 29: 7 you broke and their b were wrenched. H5516
Zec 7:11 they turned their b and covered their ears. H4190
Ro 11:10 cannot see, and their b be bent forever." G3822
2Pe 2:21 it and then to turn their b on the sacred G5715

BACKSLIDER, BACKSLIDING (KJV) FAITHLESS, STUBBORN, UNFAITHFUL

BACKSLIDING (4) [BACK]
Jer 2:19 will punish you; your b will rebuke you. H5412
Jer 3:22 faithless people; I will cure you of b." H5412
Jer 15: 6 "You keep on b. So I will reach out H294
Eze 37:23 I will save them from all their sinful b H5412

BACKSLIDINGS (1) [BACK]
Jer 5: 6 their rebellion is great and their b many. H5412

BACKWARD (5) [BACK]
Ge 9:23 then they walked in b and covered their H345
Ge 49:17 horse's heels so that its rider tumbles b. H294

1Sa 4:18 Eli fell **b** off his chair by the side of the H345
Isa 28:13 so that as they go they will fall **b**; they will H294
Jer 7:24 They went **b** and not forward. H4200+294

BACUTH (NIV84) See ALLON BAKUTH

B

BAD (64) [BADLY]
Ge 18:21 they have done is as **b** as the outcry that H3986
Ge 31:24 to say anything to Jacob, either good or **b**." H8273
Ge 31:29 to say anything to Jacob, either good or **b**. H8273
Ge 37: 2 their father a **b** report about them. H8273
Ex 7:21 the river **smelled** so **b** that the H944
Lev 27:10 substitute a good one for a **b** *one*, H8273
Lev 27:10 a bad one, or a **b** *one* for a good one; if H8273
Lev 27:12 who will judge its quality as good or **b** H8273
Lev 27:14 priest will judge its quality as good or **b**. H8273
Lev 27:33 out the good from the **b** or make any H8273
Nu 13:19 Is it good or **b**? What kind of towns do H8273
Nu 13:32 Israelites a **b report** *about* the land they H1804
Nu 14:36 him by spreading a **b report** about it— H1804
Nu 14:37 spreading the **b** report about the land H8273
Nu 24:13 own accord, good or **b**, to go beyond the H8288
Dt 1:39 who do not yet know good from **b**— H8273
Dt 22:14 slanders her and gives her a **b** name H8273
Dt 22:19 has given an Israelite virgin a **b** name. H8273
2Sa 13:22 either good or **b**; he hated Amnon H8273
1Ki 14: 6 I have been sent to you with **b news**. H7997
1Ki 22: 8 anything good about me, but always **b**. H8273
1Ki 22:18 anything good about me, but only **b**?" H8273
2Ki 2:19 the water is **b** and the land is H8273
2Ch 18: 7 anything good about me, but always **b**. H8288
2Ch 18:17 anything good about me, but only **b**?" H8273
Ne 6:13 would give me a **b** name to discredit me H8273
Ps 112: 7 They will have no fear of **b** news; their H8273
Ecc 7:14 when times are **b**, consider this: H8288
Ecc 8: 3 Do not stand up for a **b** cause, for he will H8273
Ecc 9: 2 the good and the **b**, the clean and the H8273
Ecc 10: 1 dead flies **give** perfume **a b smell**, H944+5580
Isa 5: 2 of good grapes, but it yielded only **b fruit**. H946
Isa 5: 4 good grapes, why did it yield only **b**? H946
Isa 41:23 whether good or **b**, so that we will be H8317
Jer 24: 2 the other basket had very **b** figs, so bad H8273
Jer 24: 2 bad figs, so **b** they could not be eaten. H8278
Jer 24: 3 the **b** *ones* are so bad they cannot be H8273
Jer 24: 3 the bad ones are so **b** they cannot be H8278
Jer 24: 8 " 'But like the **b** figs, which are so bad H8273
Jer 24: 8 which are so **b** they cannot be eaten H8278
Jer 29:17 figs that are so **b** they cannot be eaten. H8278
Jer 49:23 dismayed, for they have heard **b** news. H8273
Zep 1:12 LORD will do nothing, either good or **b**. H8317
Mt 7:17 good fruit, but a **b** tree bears bad fruit. *G4911*
Mt 7:17 good fruit, but a bad tree bears **b** fruit. *G4505*
Mt 7:18 A good tree cannot bear **b** fruit, and a bad *G4505*
Mt 7:18 and a **b** tree cannot bear good fruit. *G4911*
Mt 12:33 make a tree **b** and its fruit will be bad *G4911*
Mt 12:33 make a tree bad and its fruit will be **b** *G4911*
Mt 13:48 fish in baskets, but threw the **b** away. *G4911*
Mt 22:10 they could find, the **b** as well as the good *G4505*
Mk 9:39 next moment **say** *anything* **b about** me, *G2800*
Lk 6:43 "No good tree bears **b** fruit, nor does a *G4911*
Lk 6:43 nor does a **b** tree bear good fruit. *G4911*
Lk 16:25 while Lazarus received **b** *things*, but now *G2805*
Jn 11:39 "by this time *there is a* **b odor**, for he has *G3853*
Ac 17: 5 rounded up some **b** characters from the *G4505*
Ac 28:21 reported or said anything **b** about you. *G4505*
Ro 9:11 born or had done anything good or **b**— *G5765*
1Co 15:33 "**B** company corrupts good character." *G2805*
2Co 5:10 while in the body, whether good or **b**. *G5765*
2Co 6: 8 dishonor, **b report** and good report *G1556*
2Ti 3:13 impostors will go *from* **b** to **worse**, AIT
Titus 2: 8 they have nothing **b** to say about us. *G5765*

BADGERS' SKINS (KJV) DURABLE LEATHER

BADLY (4) [BAD]
Ge 50:17 they committed in treating you *so* **b**. H8288
1Sa 24:17 treated me well, but I have treated you **b**. H8288
2Ch 35:23 officers, "Take me away; I am **b** wounded." H4394
Mk 12:27 of the living. You are **b** mistaken!" *G4498*

BAFFLED (2)
Da 5: 9 grew more pale. His nobles *were* **b**. A10698
Ac 9:22 more powerful and **b** the Jews living in *G5177*

BAG (17) [BAGS]
Dt 25:13 not have two differing weights in your **b**— H3967
1Sa 17:40 in the pouch of his shepherd's **b** and, H3998
1Sa 17:49 Reaching into his **b** and taking out a stone, H3998
Job 14:17 My offenses will be sealed up in a **b**; you H7655
Pr 16:11 all the weights in the **b** are of his making. H3967
Mic 6:11 with a **b** *of* false weights? H3967
Mt 10:10 no **b** for the journey or extra shirt or *G4385*
Mt 25:15 to another one **b**, each according to his NDT
Mt 25:18 the man who had received one **b** went off, NDT
Mt 25:24 who had received one **b of gold** came. *G5419*
Mt 25:28 " 'So take the **b of gold** from him and give *G5419*
Mk 6: 8 a staff—no bread, no **b**, no money in your *G4385*
Lk 9: 3 no **b**, no bread, no money, *G4385*
Lk 10: 4 Do not take a purse or **b** or sandals; and *G4385*
Lk 22:35 you without purse, **b** or sandals, did you *G4385*
Lk 22:36 and also a **b**; and if you don't *G4385*
Jn 12: 6 as keeper *of* the **money b**, he used to *G1186*

BAGS (16) [BAG]
Ge 42:25 gave orders to fill their **b** with grain, H3998
Ge 43:11 of the land in your **b** and take them down H3998
2Ki 5:23 tied up the two talents of silver in two **b**, H3038
2Ki 12:10 the temple of the LORD and **put** it **into b**. H7443
Isa 46: 6 out gold from their **b** and weigh out silver H3967
Mt 18:24 ten thousand **b of gold** was brought to *G5419*
Mt 25:15 To one he gave five **b of gold**, to another *G5419*
Mt 25:15 to another two **b**, and to another one NDT
Mt 25:16 received five **b of gold** went at once and *G5419*
Mt 25:16 his money to work and gained five **b** more. NDT
Mt 25:17 the one with two **b** of gold gained two more. NDT
Mt 25:20 had received five **b of gold** brought the *G5419*
Mt 25:20 'you entrusted me with five **b of gold**. *G5419*
Mt 25:22 "The man with two **b of gold** also came *G5419*
Mt 25:22 'you entrusted me with two **b of gold**; see, *G5419*
Mt 25:28 him and give it to the one who has ten **b**. *G5419*

BAHARUMITE (1)
1Ch 11:33 Azmaveth the **B**, Eliahba the Shaalbonite, H1049

BAHURIM (5)
2Sa 3:16 weeping behind her all the way to **B**. H1038
2Sa 16: 5 As King David approached **B**, a man from H1038
2Sa 17:18 went to the house of a man in **B**. H1038
2Sa 19:16 the Benjamite from **B**, hurried down with H1038
1Ki 2: 8 the Benjamite from **B**, who called down H1038

BAIT (1)
Am 3: 5 a trap on the ground when no **b** is there? H4613

BAJITH (KJV) TEMPLE

BAKA (1)
Ps 84: 6 As they pass through the Valley of **B**, they H1133

BAKBAKKAR (1)
1Ch 9:15 **B**, Heresh, Galal and Mattaniah son of H1320

BAKBUK (2)
Ezr 2:51 **B**, Hakupha, Harhur, H1317
Ne 7:53 **B**, Hakupha, Harhur, H1317

BAKBUKIAH (3)
Ne 11:17 prayer; **B**, second among his H1319
Ne 12: 9 **B** and Unni, their associates, stood H1319
Ne 12:25 Mattaniah, **B**, Obadiah, Meshullam H1319

BAKE (9) [BAKED, BAKER, BAKERS, BAKES, BAKING]
Ge 11: 3 and **b** them **thoroughly**. H8596+4200+8599
Ge 18: 6 flour and knead it and **b** some bread." H6913
Ex 16:23 So **b** what you want to bake and boil what H684
Ex 16:23 So bake what *you want to* **b** and boil what H684
Lev 24: 5 the finest flour and **b** twelve loaves of H684
Lev 26:26 ten women *will be able to* **b** your bread in H684
Eze 4:12 **b** it in the sight of the people H6383
Eze 4:15 "I will let you **b** your bread over cow dung H6913
Eze 46:20 the sin offering and **b** the grain offering, H684

BAKED (14) [BAKE]
Ge 40:17 kinds of **b goods** *for* Pharaoh, H4407+5126+685
Ex 12:39 *they* **b** loaves of unleavened bread. H684
Lev 2: 4 'If you bring a grain offering **b** *in* an oven, H4418
Lev 6:17 *It must* not **be b** *with* yeast; I have given it H684
Lev 7: 9 Every grain offering **b** in an oven or cooked H684
Lev 23:17 of the finest flour, **b** *with* yeast, as a wave H684
1Sa 28:24 kneaded it and **b** bread without yeast. H684
2Sa 13: 8 made the bread in his sight and **b** it. H1418
1Ki 19: 6 head was some bread **b over hot coals**, H8363
2Ki 4:42 of barley bread **b** *from* the first ripe grain, H4312
Isa 44:19 I used for fuel; *I* even **b** bread over its coals H684
Da 2:33 its feet partly of iron and partly of **b clay**. A10279
Da 2:41 were partly of **b clay** and partly of iron, A10279
Da 2:43 saw the iron mixed with **b clay**, A10279+10298

BAKER (8) [BAKE]
Ge 40: 1 cupbearer and the **b** of the king of Egypt H685
Ge 40: 2 the chief cupbearer and the chief **b**, H685
Ge 40: 5 the cupbearer and the **b** of the king of Egypt H685
Ge 40:16 When the chief **b** saw that Joseph had H685
Ge 40:20 the chief **b** in the presence of his H685
Ge 40:22 he impaled the chief **b**, just as Joseph H685
Ge 41:10 me and the chief **b** in the house of the H685
Hos 7: 4 oven whose fire the **b** need not stir from H685

BAKERS (2) [BAKE]
1Sa 8:13 to be perfumers and cooks and **b**. H685
Jer 37:21 the street of the **b** each day until all the H685

BAKES (1) [BAKE]
Isa 44:15 himself, he kindles a fire and **b** bread. H684

BAKING (3) [BAKE]
Ge 19: 3 a meal for them, **b** bread without yeast H684
1Ch 9:31 the responsibility for **b** the offering bread. H5126
1Ch 23:29 without yeast, the **b** and the mixing, and H4679

BAKUTH See ALLON BAKUTH

BALAAM (59) [BALAAM'S]
Nu 22: 5 sent messengers to summon **B** son of Beor, H1189
Nu 22: 7 When they came to **B**, they told him what H1189
Nu 22: 8 **B** said to them, "and I will report back to H1189
Nu 22: 9 God came to **B** and asked, "Who are H1189
Nu 22:10 **B** said to God, "Balak son of Zippor, king H1189
Nu 22:12 But God said to **B**, "Do not go with them H1189
Nu 22:13 The next morning **B** got up and said to H1189
Nu 22:14 said, "**B** refused to come with us." H1189
Nu 22:16 They came to **B** and said: "This is what H1189
Nu 22:18 But **B** answered them, "Even if Balak gave H1189
Nu 22:20 That night God came to **B** and said H1189
Nu 22:21 **B** got up in the morning, saddled his H1189
Nu 22:22 **B** was riding on his donkey, and his two H2085S
Nu 22:23 **B** beat it to get it back on the road H1189
Nu 22:27 it lay down under **B**, and he was angry H1189
Nu 22:28 it said to **B**, "What have I done to H1189
Nu 22:29 **B** answered the donkey, "You have made H1189
Nu 22:30 The donkey said to **B**, "Am I not your own H1189
Nu 22:34 **B** said to the angel of the LORD, "I have H1189
Nu 22:35 The angel of the LORD said to **B**, "Go with H1189
Nu 22:35 So **B** went with Balak's officials H1189
Nu 22:36 When Balak heard that **B** was coming, he H1189
Nu 22:37 Balak said to **B**, "Did I not send you an H1189
Nu 22:38 I have come to you now," **B** replied. H1189
Nu 22:39 Then **B** went with Balak to Kiriath Huzoth. H1189
Nu 22:40 gave some to **B** and the officials who H1189
Nu 22:41 morning Balak took **B** up to Bamoth Baal, H1189
Nu 23: 1 **B** said, "Build me seven altars here, and H1189
Nu 23: 2 Balak did as **B** said, and the two of them H1189
Nu 23: 3 Then **B** said to Balak, "Stay here beside H1189
Nu 23: 4 God met with him, and **B** said, "I have H1189
Nu 23: 7 Then **B** spoke his message: "Balak brought NDT
Nu 23:11 Balak said to **B**, "What have you done to H1189
Nu 23:15 **B** said to Balak, "Stay here beside your NDT
Nu 23:16 The LORD met with **B** and put a word in his H1189
Nu 23:25 Then Balak said to **B**, "Neither curse them H1189
Nu 23:26 **B** answered, "Did I not tell you I must do H1189
Nu 23:27 Then Balak said to **B**, "Come, let me take H1189
Nu 23:28 And Balak took **B** to the top of Peor H1189
Nu 23:29 **B** said, "Build me seven altars here, and H1189
Nu 23:30 Balak did as **B** had said, and offered a bull H1189
Nu 24: 1 Now when **B** saw that it pleased the LORD H1189
Nu 24: 2 When **B** looked out and saw Israel H1189
Nu 24: 3 "The prophecy of **B** son of Beor, the H1189
Nu 24:10 Then Balak's anger burned against **B**. H1189
Nu 24:12 **B** answered Balak, "Did I not tell the H1189
Nu 24:15 "The prophecy of **B** son of Beor, the H1189
Nu 24:20 Then **B** saw Amalek and spoke his message: NDT
Nu 24:25 Then **B** got up and returned home, and H1189
Nu 31: 8 They also killed **B** son of Beor with the H1189
Dt 23: 4 they hired **B** son of Beor from Pethor H1189
Dt 23: 5 would not listen to **B** but turned the curse H1189
Jos 13:22 had put to the sword **B** son of Beor, H1189
Jos 24: 9 he sent for **B** son of Beor to put a curse on H1189
Jos 24:10 But I would not listen to **B**, so he blessed H1189
Ne 13: 2 water but had hired **B** to call a curse down H1189
Mic 6: 5 plotted and what **B** son of Beor answered. H1189
2Pe 2:15 off to follow the way *of* **B** son of Bezer, *G962*
Rev 2:14 among you who hold to the teaching *of* **B**, *G962*

BALAAM'S (5) [BALAAM]
Nu 22:25 to the wall, crushing **B** foot against it. H1189
Nu 22:31 Then the LORD opened **B** eyes, and he saw H1189
Nu 23: 5 The LORD put a word in **B** mouth and said H1189
Nu 31:16 ones who followed **B** advice and enticed H1189
Jude 11 they have rushed for profit into **B** error; they *G962*

BALADAN (2) [MARDUK-BALADAN]
2Ki 20:12 son of **B** king of Babylon sent H1156
Isa 39: 1 son of **B** king of Babylon sent H1156

BALAH (1)
Jos 19: 3 Hazar Shual, **B**, Ezem, H1163

BALAK (35) [BALAK'S]
Nu 22: 2 Now **B** son of Zippor saw all that Israel H1192
Nu 22: 4 So **B** son of Zippor, who was king of H1192
Nu 22: 5 in his native land. **B** said: "A people has NDT
Nu 22: 7 to Balaam, they told him what **B** had said. H1192
Nu 22:10 said to God, "**B** son of Zippor, king H1192
Nu 22:14 Moabite officials returned to **B** and said, H1192
Nu 22:15 Then **B** sent other officials, more H1192
Nu 22:16 "This is what **B** son of Zippor says H1192
Nu 22:18 "Even if **B** gave me all the silver and gold H1192
Nu 22:36 When **B** heard that Balaam was coming H1192
Nu 22:37 **B** said to Balaam, "Did I not send you an H1192
Nu 22:39 Balaam went with **B** to Kiriath Huzoth. H1192
Nu 22:40 **B** sacrificed cattle and sheep, and gave H1192
Nu 22:41 The next morning **B** took Balaam up to H1192
Nu 23: 2 **B** did as Balaam said, and the two of them H1192
Nu 23: 3 Then Balaam said to **B**, "Stay here beside H1192
Nu 23: 5 "Go back to **B** and give him this word." H1192
Nu 23: 7 "**B** brought me from Aram, the king of H1192
Nu 23:11 **B** said to Balaam, "What have you done H1192
Nu 23:13 Then **B** said to him, "Come with me to H1192
Nu 23:15 Balaam said to **B**, "Stay here beside your H1192
Nu 23:16 "Go back to **B** and give him this word." H1192
Nu 23:17 Moabite officials. **B** asked him, "What did H1192
Nu 23:18 **B**, and listen; hear me, son of H1192
Nu 23:25 Then **B** said to Balaam, "Neither curse H1192
Nu 23:27 Then **B** said to Balaam, "Come, let me H1192
Nu 23:28 And **B** took Balaam to the top of Peor H1192
Nu 23:30 **B** did as Balaam had said, and offered a H1192
Nu 24:12 Balaam answered **B**, "Did I not tell the H1192
Nu 24:13 'Even if **B** gave me all the silver and gold H1192
Nu 24:25 returned home, and **B** went his own way. H1192
Jos 24: 9 When **B** son of Zippor, the king of Moab H1192

Jdg 11:25 Are you any better than **B** son of Zippor H1192
Mic 6: 5 remember what **B** king of Moab plotted H1192
Rev 2:14 who taught **B** to entice the Israelites to sin *G963*

BALAK'S (3) [BALAK]
Nu 22:13 Balaam got up and said to **B** officials, H1192
Nu 22:35 So Balaam went with **B** officials. H1192
Nu 24:10 Then **B** anger burned against Balaam. H1192

BALANCE (3) [BALANCES]
Lev 25:27 it and refund the **b** to the one to whom H6369
Ps 62: 9 If weighed on a **b**, they are nothing H4404
Isa 40:12 on the scales and the hills in a **b**? H4404

BALANCES (1) [BALANCE]
Pr 16:11 Honest scales and **b** belong to the LORD H7144

BALD (5) [BALDNESS, BALDY]
Lev 13:40 who has lost his hair and is **b** is clean. H7944
Lev 13:41 front of his scalp and has a **b forehead**, H1477
Lev 13:42 sore on his **b head** or forehead, H7949
Isa 3:17 of Zion; the LORD *will* **make** their scalps **b**." H6867
Mic 1:16 **make** yourself as **b** as the vulture H8143+7947

BALDNESS (1) [BALD]
Isa 3:24 of well-dressed hair, **b**; instead of fine H7947

BALDY (2) [BALD]
2Ki 2:23 "Get out of here, **b**!" they said. H7944
2Ki 2:23 they said. "Get out of here, **b**!" H7944

BALL (1)
Isa 22:18 up tightly like a **b** and throw you into a H1885

BALM (7)
Ge 37:25 loaded with spices, **b** and myrrh, and they H7661
Ge 43:11 man as a gift—a little **b** and a little honey H7661
2Ch 28:15 sandals, food and drink, and **healing b**. H6057
Jer 8:22 Is there no **b** in Gilead? Is there no H7661
Jer 46:11 "Go up to Gilead and get **b**, Virgin H7661
Jer 51: 8 Get **b** for her pain; perhaps she can be H7661
Eze 27:17 olive oil and **b** for your wares. H7661

BALSAM (NIV84) POPLAR

BAMAH (1)
Eze 20:29 (It is called **B** to this day.) H1196

BAMOTH (2) [BAMOTH BAAL]
Nu 21:19 to Nahaliel, from Nahaliel to **B**, H1199
Nu 21:20 from **B** to the valley in Moab where H1199

BAMOTH BAAL (2) [BAAL, BAMOTH]
Nu 22:41 morning Balak took Balaam up to **B Baal**, H1200
Jos 13:17 including Dibon, **B Baal**, Beth Baal Meon, H1200

BAN (1) [BANNED]
1Ch 2: 7 on Israel *by* **violating the b** on taking H5085

BAND (16) [BANDED, BANDS]
Ge 49:19 "Gad will be attacked by a **b of raiders** H1522
Ex 39:23 of a collar, and a **b** around this opening H8557
2Sa 1:10 on his head and the **b** on his arm and have H731
2Sa 23:13 while a **b** *of* Philistines was encamped in H2653
1Ki 7:35 there was a **circular b** half a cubit H6318+6017
1Ki 11:24 Rezon gathered a **b** *of* men around him H1522
2Ki 13:21 suddenly they saw a **b of raiders**; so they H1522
2Ki 19:31 out of Mount Zion a **b of survivors**. H7129
1Ch 11:15 while a **b** *of* Philistines was encamped in H4722
Ps 2: 2 up and the rulers **b** together against the H3570
Ps 78:49 hostility—a **b** *of* destroying angels. H5449
Ps 94:21 The wicked **b together** against the H1518
Isa 31: 4 though a **whole b** *of* shepherds is H4850
Isa 37:32 out of Mount Zion a **b of survivors**. H7129
Ac 4:26 up and the rulers **b** together against the *G5251*
Ac 5:37 census and led a **b of people** in revolt. *G3295*

BANDAGED (2)
Isa 1: 6 not cleansed or **b** or soothed with olive oil H2502
Lk 10:34 He went to him and **b** his wounds, pouring *G2866*

BANDED (4) [BAND]
Nu 14:35 which *has* **b together** against me. H3585
Nu 16:11 all your followers *have* **b together**. H3585
Nu 27: 3 followers, who **b together** against the LORD H3585
2Sa 23:11 **b together** at a place H665+4200+2021+2653

BANDIT (1) [BANDITS]
Pr 23:28 Like a **b** she lies in wait and multiplies H3167

BANDITS (3) [BANDIT]
Ezr 8:31 us from enemies and **b** along the way. H741
Hos 7: 1 break into houses, **b** rob in the streets; H1522
2Co 11:26 in danger *from* **b**, in danger from *G3334*

BANDS (17) [BAND]
Ex 27:10 with silver hooks and **b** on the posts. H3122
Ex 27:11 with silver hooks and **b** on the posts. H3122
Ex 27:17 courtyard are to have silver **b** and hooks, H3138
Ex 36:38 the posts and their **b** with gold and made H3122
Ex 38:10 with silver hooks and **b** on the posts. H3122
Ex 38:11 with silver hooks and **b** on the posts. H3122
Ex 38:12 with silver hooks and **b** on the posts. H3122
Ex 38:17 The hooks and **b** on the posts were silver H3122
Ex 38:17 all the posts of the courtyard had silver **b**. H3138
Ex 38:19 Their hooks and **b** were silver, and their H3122
Ex 38:28 the tops of the posts, and *to* **make** their **b**. H3138
2Sa 4: 2 two men who were leaders of **raiding b**. H1522
2Ki 5: 2 Now **b of raiders** from Aram had gone out H1522
2Ki 6:23 So the **b** *from* Aram stopped raiding H1522
1Ch 12:18 made them leaders of his **raiding b**. H1522
1Ch 12:21 They helped David against **raiding b**, for H1522
Hos 6: 9 a victim, so do **b** *of* priests; they H2490

BANGLES (1)
Isa 3:18 the **b** and headbands and crescent H6577

BANI (14)
1Ch 6:46 of Amzi, the son of **B**, the son of Shemer, H1220
1Ch 9: 4 the son of **B**, a descendant of H1220
Ezr 2:10 of **B** 642 H1220
Ezr 8:10 of the descendants of **B**, Shelomith son of H1220
Ezr 10:29 From the descendants of **B**: Meshullam H1220
Ezr 10:34 From the descendants of **B**: Maadai H1220
Ne 3:17 by the Levites under Rehum son of **B**. H1220
Ne 8: 7 Levites—Jeshua, **B**, Sherebiah, Jamin, H1220
Ne 9: 4 of the Levites were Jeshua, **B**, Kadmiel, H1220
Ne 9: 4 Sherebiah, **B** and Kenani. H1220
Ne 9: 5 Kadmiel, **B**, Hashabneiah H1220
Ne 10:13 Hodiah, **B** and Beninu. H1220
Ne 10:14 Pahath-Moab, Elam, Zattu, **B**, H1220
Ne 11:22 Levites in Jerusalem was Uzzi son of **B**, H1220

BANISH (11) [BANISHED, BANISHMENT]
2Ki 13:23 to destroy them or **b** them from his H8959
Ps 5:10 **B** them for their many sins, for they have H5615
Ps 125: 5 ways the LORD *will* **b** with the evildoers. H2143
Ecc 11:10 **b** anxiety from your heart and cast off the H6073
Jer 8: 3 Wherever *I* **b** them, all the survivors of this H5615
Jer 24: 9 an object of ridicule, wherever *I* **b** them. H5615
Jer 25:10 *I will* **b** from them the sounds of joy and H6
Jer 27:10 *I will* **b** you and you will perish. H5615
Jer 27:15 Therefore, I *will* **b** you and you will perish H5615
Jer 32:37 all the lands where *I* **b** them in my furious H5615
Zec 13: 2 *I will* **b** the names of the idols from the H4162

BANISHED (17) [BANISH]
Ge 3:23 So the LORD God **b** him from the Garden of H8938
Dt 30: 4 Even if you *have* **been b** to the most H5615
2Sa 14:13 the king has not brought back his **b** son? H5615
2Sa 14:14 ways so that a **b** *person* does not remain H5615
2Sa 14:14 person *does* not *remain* **b** from him. H5615
1Ch 12: 1 while *he* **was b** from the presence of Saul H6806
Job 18:18 realm of darkness and *is* **b** from the world. H5610
Job 20: 8 to be found, **b** like a vision of the night. H5610
Job 30: 5 *They* **were b** from human society, shouted H1763
Isa 24:11 all joyful sounds *are* **b** *from* the earth. H1655
Jer 16:15 of all the countries where *he had* **b** them. H5615
Jer 23: 8 of all the countries where *he had* **b** them. H5615
Jer 23:12 *they will be* **b** to darkness and there they H1890
Jer 29:14 nations and places where *I have* **b** you," H5615
Jnh 2: 4 '*I have* **been b** from your sight; yet I H1763
Zec 5: 3 every thief *will* **be b**, and according H5927
Zec 5: 3 everyone who swears falsely *will* **be b**. H5927

BANISHMENT (1) [BANISH]
Ezr 7:26 be punished by death, **b**, confiscation of A10744

BANK (12) [BANKERS, BANKS, EMBANKMENT]
Ge 41:17 I was standing on the **b** *of* the Nile, H8557
Ex 2: 3 among the reeds along the **b** *of* the Nile. H8557
Ex 7:15 Confront him on the **b** *of* the Nile, and H8557
Jos 13:23 the Reubenites was the **b** *of* the Jordan. H1473
2Ki 2:13 back and stood on the **b** *of* the Jordan. H8557
Eze 47: 6 Then he led me back to the **b** *of* the river. H8557
Da 10: 4 I was standing on the **b** *of* the great river, H3338
Da 12: 5 one on this **b** *of* the river and one on the H8557
Da 12: 5 of the river and one on the opposite **b**. H8557
Mt 8:32 rushed down the **steep b** into the lake *G3204*
Mk 5:13 rushed down the **steep b** into the lake *G3204*
Lk 8:33 rushed down the **steep b** into the lake *G3204*

BANKERS (1) [BANK]
Mt 25:27 have put my money on deposit *with* the **b**, *G5545*

BANKS (3) [BANK]
1Ch 12:15 month when it was overflowing all its **b**, H1536
Isa 8: 7 overflow all its channels, run over all its **b** H1536
Eze 47:12 all kinds will grow on both **b** *of* the river. H8557

BANNED (1) [BAN]
2Ch 26:21 and **b** from the temple of the LORD. H1615

BANNER (15) [BANNERS]
Ex 17:15 an altar and called it The LORD is my **B**. H5812
Ps 60: 4 you have raised a **b** to be unfurled H5812
SS 2: 4 and let his **b** over me be love. H1840
Isa 5:26 He lifts up a **b** for the distant nations, he H5812
Isa 11:10 of Jesse will stand as a **b** *for* the peoples; H5812
Isa 11:12 He will raise a **b** for the nations and H5812
Isa 13: 2 Raise a **b** on a bare hilltop, shout to them; H5812
Isa 18: 3 when a **b** is raised on the mountains H5812
Isa 30:17 on a mountaintop, like a **b** on a hill." H5812
Isa 49:22 I will lift up my **b** to the peoples; they will H5812
Isa 62:10 Raise a **b** for the nations. H5812
Jer 50: 2 nations, lift up a **b** and proclaim it; keep H5812
Jer 51:12 Lift up a **b** against the walls of Babylon H5812
Jer 51:27 "Lift up a **b** in the land! Blow the trumpet H5812
Eze 27: 7 Egypt was your sail and served as your **b**; H5812

BANNERS (3) [BANNER]
Nu 2: 2 standard and holding the **b** of their family." H253
Ps 20: 5 victory and **lift up** *our* **b** in the name of H1839
SS 6: 4 Jerusalem, as majestic as **troops with b**. H1839

BANQUET (33) [BANQUETS]
1Sa 25:36 the house holding a **b** like that of a king. H5492
Est 1: 3 his reign he gave a **b** for all his nobles H5492
Est 1: 5 the king gave a **b**, lasting seven days, H5492
Est 1: 9 Vashti also gave a **b** *for* the women in the H5492
Est 2:18 And the king gave a great **b**, Esther's H5492
Est 2:18 banquet, Esther's **b**, for all his nobles H5492
Est 5: 4 come today to a **b** I have prepared for him H5492
Est 5: 5 Haman went to the **b** Esther had prepared H5492
Est 5: 8 come tomorrow to the **b** I will prepare H5492
Est 5:12 to accompany the king to the **b** she gave. H5492
Est 5:14 with the king to the **b** and enjoy yourself." H5492
Est 6:14 Haman away to the **b** Esther had H5492
Est 7: 1 Haman went to Queen Esther's **b**, H9272
Est 7: 8 the palace garden to the **b hall**, and H5492+3516
SS 2: 4 Let him lead me to the **b hall**, and H1074+3516
Isa 25: 6 all peoples, a **b** *of* aged wine—the H5492
Da 5: 1 gave a great **b** for a thousand of his A10389
Da 5:10 his nobles, came into the **b** hall. A10447
Mt 22: 2 who prepared a **wedding b** for his son. *G1141*
Mt 22: 3 been invited to the **b** to tell them to come *G1141*
Mt 22: 4 Come to the **wedding b**.' *G1141*
Mt 22: 8 his servants, 'The **wedding b** is ready, but *G1141*
Mt 22: 9 invite to the **b** anyone you find. *G1141*
Mt 25:10 ready went in with him to the **wedding b**. *G1141*
Mk 6:21 birthday Herod gave a **b** for his high *G1270*
Lk 5:29 Levi held a great **b** for Jesus at his house *G1531*
Lk 12:36 their master to return from a **wedding b**, *G1141*
Lk 14:13 But when you give a **b**, invite the poor, the *G1531*
Lk 14:16 was preparing a great **b** and invited many *G1270*
Lk 14:17 At the time *of* the **b** he sent his servant to *G1270*
Lk 14:24 who were invited will get a taste *of* my **b**. *G1270*
Jn 2: 8 some out and take it *to* the **master of the b**." *G804*
Jn 2: 9 the **master of the b** tasted the water *G804*

BANQUETS (4) [BANQUET]
Isa 5:12 They have harps and lyres at their **b** H5492
Mt 23: 6 the place of honor at **b** and the most *G1270*
Mk 12:39 synagogues and the places of honor at **b**. *G1270*
Lk 20:46 synagogues and the places of honor at **b**. *G1270*

BAPTISM (20) [BAPTIZE]
Mt 21:25 John's **b**—where did it come from? Was it *G967*
Mk 1: 4 preaching a **b** of repentance for the *G967*
Mk 10:38 be baptized *with* the **b** I am baptized *G967*
Mk 10:39 be baptized *with* the **b** I am baptized *G967*
Mk 11:30 John's **b**—was it from heaven, or of human *G967*
Lk 3: 3 preaching a **b** of repentance for the *G967*
Lk 12:50 But I have a **b** to undergo, and what *G967*
Lk 20: 4 John's **b**—was it from heaven, or of human *G967*
Ac 1:22 beginning from John's **b** to the time when *G967*
Ac 10:37 in Galilee after the **b** that John preached— *G967*
Ac 13:24 repentance and **b** to all the people of *G967*
Ac 18:25 though he knew only the **b** of John. *G967*
Ac 19: 3 Paul asked, "Then what **b** *did you* receive?" *G966*
Ac 19: 3 did you receive?" "John's **b**," they replied. *G967*
Ac 19: 4 "John's **b** *was* a baptism of repentance. *G966*
Ac 19: 4 "John's baptism was a **b** of repentance. *G967*
Ro 6: 4 with him through **b** into death in order *G967*
Eph 4: 5 one Lord, one faith, one **b**; *G967*
Col 2:12 having been buried with him in **b**, in which *G968*
1Pe 3:21 this water symbolizes **b** that now saves you *G967*

BAPTIST (15) [BAPTIZE]
Mt 3: 1 In those days John the **B** came, preaching *G969*
Mt 11:11 not risen anyone greater than John the **B**; *G969*
Mt 11:12 From the days of John the **B** until now, the *G969*
Mt 14: 2 "This is John the **B**; he has risen from the *G969*
Mt 14: 8 here on a platter the head of John the **B**." *G969*
Mt 16:14 "Some say John the **B**; others say Elijah; *G969*
Mt 17:13 he was talking to them about John the **B**. *G969*
Mk 1: 4 And so John the **B** appeared in the *G966*
Mk 6:14 "John the **B** has been raised from the dead, *G966*
Mk 6:24 "The head of John the **B**," she answered. *G966*
Mk 6:25 now the head of John the **B** on a platter." *G969*
Mk 8:28 "Some say John the **B**; others say Elijah; *G969*
Lk 7:20 they said, "John the **B** sent us to you to ask *G969*
Lk 7:33 For John the **B** came neither eating bread *G969*
Lk 9:19 "Some say John the **B**; others say Elijah; *G969*

BAPTIZE (12) [BAPTISM, BAPTIST, BAPTIZED, BAPTIZING]
Mt 3:11 "I **b** you with water for repentance. But after *G966*
Mt 3:11 He *will* **b** you with the Holy Spirit and fire. *G966*
Mk 1: 8 I **b** you with water, but he will baptize you *G966*
Mk 1: 8 he *will* **b** you with the Holy Spirit. *G966*
Lk 3:16 answered them all, "I **b** you with water. *G966*
Lk 3:16 He *will* **b** you with the Holy Spirit and fire. *G966*
Jn 1:25 "Why then *do you* **b** if you are not the *G966*
Jn 1:26 "I **b** with water," John replied, "but among *G966*
Jn 1:33 one who sent me *to* **b** with water told me *G966*
Jn 1:33 remain is the *one who will* **b** with the Holy *G966*
1Co 1:14 I thank God that *I did* not **b** any of you *G966*
1Co 1:17 For Christ did not send me *to* **b**, but to *G966*

BAPTIZED (50) [BAPTIZE]

Mt 3: 6 they were b by him in the Jordan River. G966
Mt 3:13 from Galilee to the Jordan to be b by John. G966
Mt 3:14 "I need to be b by you, and do you G966
Mt 3:16 As soon as Jesus was b, he went up out of G966
Mk 1: 5 they were b by him in the Jordan River. G966
Mk 1: 9 in Galilee and was b by John in the Jordan G966
Mk 10:38 the cup I drink or be b with the baptism I G966
Mk 10:38 be baptized with the baptism I am b with?" G966
Mk 10:39 the cup I drink and be b with the baptism I G966
Mk 10:39 be baptized with the baptism I am b with, G966
Mk 16:16 Whoever believes and is b will be saved G966
Lk 3: 7 to the crowds coming out to be b by him, G966
Lk 3:12 Even tax collectors came to be b. "Teacher," G966
Lk 3:21 When all the people were being b, Jesus G966
Lk 3:21 were being baptized, Jesus was b too. G966
Lk 7:29 because they had been b by G966+3836+967
Lk 7:30 because they had not been b by John.) G966
Jn 3:22 he spent some time with them, and b. G966
Jn 3:23 people were coming and being b. G966
Jn 4: 2 although in fact it was not Jesus who b, but G966
Ac 1: 5 For John b with water, but in a few days you G966
Ac 1: 5 in a few days you will be b with the Holy G966
Ac 2:38 "Repent and be b, every one of you, G966
Ac 2:41 Those who accepted his message were b G966
Ac 8:12 of Jesus Christ, they were b, both men and G966
Ac 8:13 Simon himself believed and was b. G966
Ac 8:16 they had simply been b in the name of the G966
Ac 8:36 What can stand in the way of my being b?" G966
Ac 8:38 went down into the water and Philip b him. G966
Ac 9:18 he could see again. He got up and was b, G966
Ac 10:47 in the way of their being b with water. G966
Ac 10:48 he ordered that they be b in the name of G966
Ac 11:16 'John b with water, but you will be G966
Ac 11:16 you will be b with the Holy Spirit. G966
Ac 16:15 she and the members of her household were b G966
Ac 16:33 he and all his household were b. G966
Ac 18: 8 who heard Paul believed and were b. G966
Ac 19: 5 they were b in the name of the Lord Jesus. G966
Ac 22:16 be b and wash your sins away G966
Ro 6: 3 know that all of us who were b into Christ G966
Ro 6: 3 into Christ Jesus were b into his death? G966
1Co 1:13 Were you b in the name of Paul? G966
1Co 1:15 one can say that you were b in my name. G966
1Co 1:16 I also b the household of Stephanas G966
1Co 1:16 I don't remember if I b anyone else.) G966
1Co 10: 2 They were all b into Moses in the cloud G966
1Co 12:13 For we were all b by one Spirit so as to form G966
1Co 15:29 what will those do who are b for the dead? G966
1Co 15:29 raised at all, why are people b for them? G966
Gal 3:27 all of you who were b into Christ have G966

BAPTIZING (8) [BAPTIZE]

Mt 3: 7 Sadducees coming to where he was b, G967
Mt 28:19 b them in the name of the Father and of G966
Jn 1:28 side of the Jordan, where John was b. G966
Jn 1:31 the reason I came b with water was that G966
Jn 3:23 Now John also was b at Aenon near Salim G966
Jn 3:26 about—look, he is b, and everyone is G966
Jn 4: 1 he was gaining and b more disciples than G966
Jn 10:40 where John had been b in the early days. G966

BAR (5) [BARRED, BARS]

Jos 7:21 of silver and a b of gold weighing fifty H4383
Jos 7:24 the robe, the gold b, his sons and H4383
Jdg 16: 3 two posts, and tore them loose, b and all. H1378
Ne 7: 3 have them shut the doors and b them. H296
Isa 9: 4 the b across their shoulders H4751

BAR-JESUS (1)

Ac 13: 6 sorcerer and false prophet named B, G979

BARABBAS (12)

Mt 27:16 prisoner whose name was Jesus B. G972
Mt 27:17 Jesus B, or Jesus who is called the Messiah G972
Mt 27:20 the crowd to ask for B and to have Jesus G972
Mt 27:21 asked the governor. "B," they answered. G972
Mt 27:26 Then he released B to them. But he had G972
Mk 15: 7 A man called B was in prison with the G972
Mk 15:11 the crowd to have Pilate release B instead. G972
Mk 15:15 the crowd, Pilate released B to them. G972
Lk 23:18 "Away with this man! Release B to us!" G972
Lk 23:19 B had been thrown into prison for an G4015S
Jn 18:40 Give us B!" Now Barabbas had G972
Jn 18:40 Now B had taken part in an uprising. G972

BARACHIAS (KJV) BEREKIAH

BARAH See BETH BARAH

BARAK (14) [BARAK'S]

Jdg 4: 6 She sent for B son of Abinoam from H1399
Jdg 4: 8 B said to her, "If you go with me, I will go H1399
Jdg 4: 9 So Deborah went with B to Kedesh. H1399
Jdg 4:10 There B summoned Zebulun and Naphtali, H1399
Jdg 4:12 told Sisera that B son of Abinoam had H1399
Jdg 4:14 Then Deborah said to B, "Go! This is the H1399
Jdg 4:14 So B went down Mount Tabor, with ten H1399
Jdg 4:16 B pursued the chariots and army as far as H1399
Jdg 4:22 Just then B came by in pursuit of Sisera H1399
Jdg 5: 1 day Deborah and B son of Abinoam sang H1399
Jdg 5:12 Arise, B! Take captive your H1399
Jdg 5:15 Issachar was with B, sent under his H1399
1Sa 12:11 sent Jerub-Baal, B, Jephthah and Samuel H1399
Heb 11:32 tell about Gideon, B, Samson and G973

BARAK'S (1) [BARAK]

Jdg 4:15 At B advance, the LORD routed Sisera and H1399

BARAKEL (2)

Job 32: 2 But Elihu son of B the Buzite, of the family H1387
Job 32: 6 So Elihu son of B the Buzite said: "I am H1387

BARBARIAN (1)

BARBARIAN, BARBARIANS (KJV) FOREIGNER, ISLANDERS, NON-GREEKS

Col 3:11 uncircumcised, b, Scythian, slave or free, G975

BARBER'S (1)

Eze 5: 1 use it as a b razor to shave your H1647

BARBS (1)

Nu 33:55 to remain will become b in your eyes and H8493

BARE (25) [BARED, BAREFOOT, BARELY, BARREN]

Jdg 14: 6 apart with his b hands as he H4399+401+928
2Sa 22:16 of the earth laid b at the rebuke of the H1655
2Ki 9:13 spread them under him on the b steps. H1752
Job 28: 9 with their hands and lay b the roots of the H2200
Ps 18:15 of the earth laid b at your rebuke, H1655
Ps 29: 9 twists the oaks and strips the forests b. H3106
Isa 13: 2 Raise a banner on a b hilltop, shout to H9142
Isa 23:13 they stripped its fortresses b and turned it H6910
Isa 27:10 they lie down; they strip its branches b. H3983
Isa 47: 2 Lift up your skirts, b your legs, and wade H1655
Isa 52:10 The LORD will lay b his holy arm in the H3106
Jer 2:25 until your feet are b and your throat is dry. H3504
Jer 49:10 But I will strip Esau b; I will uncover his H3106
Eze 13:14 so that its foundation will be laid b. H1655
Eze 16:22 when you were naked and b, kicking H6880
Eze 24: 7 She poured it on the b rock; she did not H7460
Eze 24: 8 revenge I put her blood on the b rock, H7460
Eze 26: 4 away her rubble and make her a b rock. H7460
Eze 26:14 I will make you a b rock, and you will H7460
Eze 29:18 every head was rubbed b and every H7942
Hos 2: 3 her naked and make her as b as on the H3657
Mic 1: 6 into the valley and lay b her foundations. H1655
1Co 14:25 as the secrets of their hearts are laid b. G5745
Heb 4:13 is uncovered and laid b before the eyes of G5548
2Pe 3:10 everything done in it will be laid b. G2351

BARED (2) [BARE]

Isa 20: 4 with buttocks b—to Egypt's shame. H3106
Eze 4: 7 Jerusalem and with b arm prophesy H3106

BAREFOOT (5) [BARE, FOOT]

2Sa 15:30 his head was covered and he was b. H3504
Isa 20: 2 he did so, going around stripped and b. H3504
Isa 20: 3 has gone stripped and b for three years, H3504
Isa 20: 4 away stripped and b the Egyptian captives H3504
Mic 1: 8 wail; I will go about b and naked. H8768

BARELY (2) [BARE]

1Sa 3: 2 becoming so weak that he could b see, H4202
Isa 26:16 they could b whisper a prayer. H4318+7440

BARGAIN (2)

2Ki 18:23 " 'Come now, make a b with my master H6842
Isa 36: 8 " 'Come now, make a b with my master H6842

BARHUMITE (1)

2Sa 23:31 Abi-Albon the Arbathite, Azmaveth the B, H1372

BARIAH (1)

1Ch 3:22 Hattush, Igal, B, Neariah and Shaphat H1377

BARK (4)

Ge 30:37 made white stripes on them by peeling the b AIT
Ex 11: 7 not a dog will b at any person or H3076+4383
Isa 56:10 they cannot b; they lie around and H5560
Joel 1: 7 It has stripped off their b and H3106+3106

BARKOS (2)

Ezr 2:53 B, Sisera, Temah, H1401
Ne 7:55 B, Sisera, Temah, H1401

BARLEY (36)

Ex 9:31 The flax and b were destroyed, since the H8555
Ex 9:31 since the b had headed and the flax was H8555
Lev 27:16 fifty shekels of silver to a homer of b seed. H8555
Nu 5:15 of an ephah of b flour on her behalf. H8555
Dt 8: 8 a land with wheat and b, vines and fig H8555
Jdg 7:13 "A round loaf of b bread came tumbling H8555
Ru 1:22 in Bethlehem as the b harvest was H8555
Ru 2:17 she threshed the b she had gathered, H8555
Ru 2:23 to glean until the b and wheat harvests H8555
Ru 3: 2 he will be winnowing b on the threshing H8555
Ru 3:15 it six measures of b and placed the H8555
Ru 3:17 "He gave me these six measures of b H8555
2Sa 14:30 field is next to mine, and he has b there. H8555
2Sa 17:28 They also brought wheat and b, flour and H8555
2Sa 21: 9 just as the b harvest was beginning. H8555
1Ki 4:28 place their quotas of b and straw for the H8555
2Ki 4:42 twenty loaves of b bread baked from the H8555
2Ki 7: 1 two seahs of b for a shekel at the H8555
2Ki 7:16 two seahs of b sold for a shekel, as H8555
2Ki 7:18 two seahs of b for a shekel at the H8555
1Ch 11:13 a place where there was a field full of b, H8555
2Ch 2:10 twenty thousand cors of b, twenty H8555
2Ch 2:15 the wheat and b and the olive oil and H8555
2Ch 27: 5 cors of wheat and ten thousand cors of b. H8555
Job 31:40 of wheat and stinkweed instead of b." H8555
Isa 28:25 wheat in its place, b in its plot, and spelt H8555
Jer 41: 8 We have wheat and b, olive oil and H8555
Eze 4: 9 "Take wheat and b, beans and lentils H8555
Eze 4:12 the food as you would a loaf of b bread; H8555
Eze 13:19 a few handfuls of b and scraps of bread. H8555
Eze 45:13 a sixth of an ephah from each homer of b. H8555
Hos 3: 2 about a homer and a lethek of b. H8555
Joel 1:11 grieve for the wheat and the b, because H8555
Jn 6: 9 boy with five small b loaves and two G3209
Jn 6:13 the pieces of the five b loaves left over by G3209
Rev 6: 6 six pounds of b for a day's wages G3208

BARN (5) [BARNS]

Hag 2:19 Is there yet any seed left in the b? Until H4476
Mt 3:12 his wheat into the b and burning up the G630
Mt 13:30 gather the wheat and bring it into my b. G630
Lk 3:17 floor and to gather the wheat into his b, G630
Lk 12:24 they have no storeroom or b; yet God feeds G630

BARNABAS (34)

Ac 4:36 whom the apostles called B (which means G982
Ac 9:27 But B took him and brought him to the G982
Ac 11:22 in Jerusalem, and they sent B to Antioch. G982
Ac 11:25 Then B went to Tarsus to look for Saul, NDT
Ac 11:26 a whole year B and Saul met with the G899S
Ac 11:30 their gift to the elders by B and Saul. G982
Ac 12:25 When B and Saul had finished their G982
Ac 13: 1 B, Simeon called Niger, Lucius of Cyrene G982
Ac 13: 2 "Set apart for me B and Saul for the work to G982
Ac 13: 7 sent for B and Saul because he wanted to G982
Ac 13:42 As Paul and B were leaving the G899S
Ac 13:43 converts to Judaism followed Paul and B, G982
Ac 13:46 Then Paul and B answered them boldly G982
Ac 13:50 stirred up persecution against Paul and B, G982
Ac 14: 1 At Iconium Paul and B went as usual into G899S
Ac 14: 3 So Paul and B spent considerable time there, NDT
Ac 14:12 B they called Zeus, and Paul they called G982
Ac 14:14 But when the apostles B and Paul heard of G982
Ac 14:20 The next day he and B left for Derbe. G982
Ac 14:23 Paul and B appointed elders for them in NDT
Ac 15: 2 This brought Paul and B into sharp dispute G982
Ac 15: 2 So Paul and B were appointed, along with G982
Ac 15:12 as they listened to B and Paul telling about G982
Ac 15:22 send them to Antioch with Paul and B. G982
Ac 15:25 to you with our dear friends B and Paul— G982
Ac 15:35 But Paul and B remained in Antioch, where G982
Ac 15:36 Some time later Paul said to B, "Let us go G982
Ac 15:37 B wanted to take John, also called Mark G982
Ac 15:39 B took Mark and sailed for Cyprus G982
1Co 9: 6 Or is it only I and B who lack the right to not G982
Gal 2: 1 up again to Jerusalem, this time with B. G982
Gal 2: 9 gave me and B the right hand of fellowship G982
Gal 2:13 by their hypocrisy even B was led astray. G982
Col 4:10 greetings, as does Mark, the cousin of B. G982

BARNEA See KADESH BARNEA

BARNS (5) [BARN]

Dt 28: 8 a blessing on your b and on everything you H662
Ps 144:13 Our b will be filled with every kind of H4646
Pr 3:10 then your b will be filled to overflowing H662
Mt 6:26 they do not sow or reap or store away in b G630
Lk 12:18 I will tear down my b and build bigger G630

BARRACKS (6)

Ac 21:34 he ordered that Paul be taken into the b. G4213
Ac 21:37 were about to take Paul into the b, G4213
Ac 22:24 ordered that Paul be taken into the b. G4213
Ac 23:10 them by force and bring him into the b. G4213
Ac 23:16 he went into the b and told Paul. G4213
Ac 23:32 on with him, while they returned to the b. G4213

BARRED (5) [BAR]

Jos 6: 1 Jericho were securely b H6037+2256+6037
Pr 18:19 disputes are like the b gates of a citadel. H1378
Isa 24:10 the entrance to every house is b. H6037
La 3: 9 He has b my way with blocks of stone; he H1553
Jnh 2: 6 the earth beneath b me in forever. H1378+1237

BARREL, BARRELS (KJV) JAR, JARS, JUG

BARREN (22) [BARE]

Ex 23:26 none will miscarry or be b in your land. H6829
Nu 23: 3 Then he went off to a b height. H9155
Dt 32:10 he found him, in a b and howling waste. H9332
Jdg 13: 3 said, "You are b and childless, but H6829
1Sa 2: 5 She who was b has borne seven children H6829
Job 3: 7 May that night be b; may no shout of joy H1678
Job 15:34 For the company of the godless will be b, H1678
Job 24:21 They prey on the b and childless woman H6829
Pr 30:16 the grave, the b womb, land, which is H6808
Isa 41:18 I will make rivers flow on b heights, and H9155
Isa 49: 9 the roads and find pasture on every b hill. H9155
Isa 49:21 I was bereaved and b; I was exiled and H1678
Isa 54: 1 b woman, you who never bore a H6829
Jer 2: 6 led us through the b wilderness, H4497

Jer 3: 2 "Look up to the **b heights** and see. H9155
Jer 3:21 A cry is heard on the **b heights**, the H9155
Jer 4:11 wind from the **b heights** in the desert H9155
Jer 7:29 take up a lament on the **b heights**, for the H9155
Jer 12:12 Over all the **b heights** in the desert H9155
Jer 14: 6 stand on the **b heights** and pant like H9155
Joel 2:20 pushing it into a parched and **b** land; its H9039
Gal 4:27 "Be glad, **b** *woman*, you who never bore a *G5096*

BARRIER (2)

Jer 5:22 the sea, an everlasting **b** it cannot cross. H2976
Eph 2:14 two groups one and has destroyed the **b**, *G5850*

BARS (22) [BAR]

Lev 26:13 I broke the **b** *of* your yoke and enabled H4574
Dt 3: 5 with high walls and with gates and **b**, H1378
1Sa 23: 7 by entering a town with gates and **b**." H1378
1Ki 4:13 large walled cities with bronze **gate b**); H1378
2Ch 8: 5 with walls and with gates and **b**, H1378
2Ch 14: 7 around them, with towers, gates and **b**. H1378
Ne 3: 3 put its doors and bolts and **b** in place. H1378
Ne 3: 6 its doors with their bolts and **b** in place. H1378
Ne 3:13 its doors with their bolts and **b** in place. H1378
Ne 3:14 its doors with their bolts and **b** in place. H1378
Ne 3:15 putting its doors and bolts and **b** in place. H1378
Job 38:10 it and set its doors and **b** in place, H1378
Ps 68:30 may the beast bring **b** *of* silver. H8349
Ps 107:16 of bronze and cuts through **b** *of* iron. H1378
Ps 147:13 He strengthens the **b** *of* your gates and H1378
Isa 45: 2 gates of bronze and cut through **b** *of* iron. H1378
Jer 49:31 "a nation that has neither gates nor **b**; its H1378
Jer 51:30 set on fire; the **b** *of* her **gates** are broken. H1378
La 2: 9 their **b** he has broken and destroyed. H1378
Eze 34:27 when I break the **b** *of* their yoke and H4574
Eze 38:11 without walls and without gates and **b**. H1378
Na 3:13 fire has consumed the **b** *of* your gates. H1378

BARSABBAS (2)

Ac 1:23 Joseph called **B** (also known as Justus) and *G984*
Ac 15:22 chose Judas (called **B**) and Silas, men who *G984*

BARTER (3)

Job 6:27 the fatherless and **b away** your friend. H4126
Job 41: 6 *Will* traders **b** for it? Will they divide it up H4126
La 1:11 *they* **b** their treasures for food to keep H5989

BARTHOLOMEW (4)

Mt 10: 3 Philip and **B**; Thomas and Matthew the tax *G978*
Mk 3:18 Philip, **B**, Matthew, Thomas *G978*
Lk 6:14 his brother Andrew, James, John, Philip, **B**, *G978*
Ac 1:13 Philip and Thomas, **B** and Matthew; James *G978*

BARTIMAEUS (1) [TIMAEUS]

Mk 10:46 a blind man, **B** (which means "son of *G985*

BARUCH (28)

Ne 3:20 **B** son of Zabbai zealously repaired H1358
Ne 10: 6 Ginnethon, **B**, H1358
Ne 11: 5 Maaseiah son of **B**, the son of H1358
Jer 32:12 I gave this deed to **B** son of Neriah H1358
Jer 32:13 their presence I gave **B** these instructions: H1358
Jer 32:16 the deed of purchase to **B** son of Neriah, H1358
Jer 36: 4 So Jeremiah called **B** son of Neriah, and H1358
Jer 36: 4 spoken to him, **B** wrote them on the scroll. H1358
Jer 36: 5 Then Jeremiah told **B**, "I am restricted; H1358
Jer 36: 8 **B** son of Neriah did everything Jeremiah H1358
Jer 36:10 **B** read to all the people at the LORD's H1358
Jer 36:13 he had heard **B** read to the people from H1358
Jer 36:14 of Cushi, to say to **B**, "Bring the scroll from H1358
Jer 36:14 So **B** son of Neriah went to them with the H1358
Jer 36:15 read it to us." So **B** read it to them. H1358
Jer 36:16 looked at each other in fear and said to **B**, H1358
Jer 36:17 Then they asked **B**, "Tell us, how did you H1358
Jer 36:18 **B** replied, "he dictated all these words to H1358
Jer 36:19 Then the officials said to **B**, "You and H1358
Jer 36:26 of Abdeel to arrest **B** the scribe and H1358
Jer 36:27 the words that **B** had written at Jeremiah's H1358
Jer 36:32 gave it to the scribe **B** son of Neriah, H1358
Jer 36:32 **B** wrote on it all the words of the scroll that NDT
Jer 43: 3 But **B** son of Neriah is inciting you against H1358
Jer 43: 6 the prophet and **B** son of Neriah along H1358
Jer 45: 1 When **B** son of Neriah wrote on a scroll H1358
Jer 45: 1 king of Judah, Jeremiah said this to **B**: H2257S
Jer 45: 2 the LORD, the God of Israel, says to you, **B**: H1358

BARZILLAI (13)

2Sa 17:27 and **B** the Gileadite from Rogelim H1367
2Sa 19:31 **B** the Gileadite also came down from H1367
2Sa 19:32 Now **B** was very old, eighty years of age H1367
2Sa 19:33 The king said to **B**, "Cross over with me H1367
2Sa 19:34 But **B** answered the king, "How many H1367
2Sa 19:39 The king kissed **B** and bid him farewell H1367
2Sa 19:39 him farewell, and **B** returned to his home. NDT
2Sa 21: 8 borne to Adriel son of **B** the Meholathite. H1367
1Ki 2: 7 to the sons of **B** of Gilead and let them H1367
Ezr 2:61 Hobaiah, Hakkoz and **B** (a man who had H1367
Ezr 2:61 a daughter of **B** the Gileadite and was H1367
Ne 7:63 Hobaiah, Hakkoz and **B** (a man who had H1367
Ne 7:63 a daughter of **B** the Gileadite and was H1367

BASE (20) [BASED, BASES, BASING, BASIS]

Ex 25:31 Hammer out its **b** and shaft, and make its H3751
Ex 29:12 pour out the rest of it at the **b** *of* the altar. H3572
Ex 37:17 They hammered out its **b** and shaft, and H3751
Ex 38:27 from the 100 talents, one talent for each **b**. H149
Lev 4: 7 shall pour out at the **b** *of* the altar of burnt H3572
Lev 4:18 shall pour out at the **b** *of* the altar of burnt H3572
Lev 4:25 the rest of the blood at the **b** *of* the altar. H3572
Lev 4:30 the rest of the blood at the **b** *of* the altar. H3572
Lev 4:34 the rest of the blood at the **b** *of* the altar. H3572
Lev 5: 9 must be drained out at the **b** *of* the altar. H3572
Lev 8:15 the rest of the blood at the **b** *of* the altar. H3572
Lev 9: 9 blood he poured out at the **b** *of* the altar. H3572
Nu 8: 4 from its **b** to its blossoms. H3751
2Ki 16:17 that supported it and set it on a stone **b**. H5346
Job 30: 8 A **b** and nameless brood, they were H5572
SS 3:10 made of silver, its **b** *of* gold. Its seat was H8339
Eze 31: 4 flowed all around its **b** and sent their H4760
Eze 41: 8 that the temple had a **raised** *b* all around it, AIT
Eze 41:11 the **b** *adjoining* the open area was H5226
Eze 41:22 its corners, its **b** and its sides were of wood. H149

BASED (10) [BASE]

Lev 25:50 to be **b on the rate paid** *to* a hired H3869+3427
Nu 26:53 as an inheritance **b on** the number of H928
Jdg 4: 2 his army, *was* **b** in Harosheth Haggoyim. H3782
Isa 29:13 worship of me **is** *b on* merely human rules AIT
Ro 2: 2 those who do such things is **b on** truth. *G2848*
Ro 10: 2 but their zeal is not **b on** knowledge. *G2848*
Ro 11: 6 then it cannot be **b on** works; if it were, *G1666*
Gal 3:12 The law is not **b on** faith; on the contrary *G1666*
Php 3: 6 as for righteousness **b on the** law *G1877*
Col 2:22 are **b on** merely human commands and *G2848*

BASEMATH (7)

Ge 26:34 also **B** daughter of Elon the Hittite. H1412
Ge 36: 3 also **B** daughter of Ishmael and sister of H1412
Ge 36: 4 Adah bore Eliphaz to Esau, **B** bore Reuel, H1412
Ge 36:10 Reuel, the son of Esau's wife **B**. H1412
Ge 36:13 These were grandsons of Esau's wife **B**. H1412
Ge 36:17 they were grandsons of Esau's wife **B**. H1412
1Ki 4:15 he had married **B** daughter of Solomon); H1412

BASES (41) [BASE]

Ex 26:19 make forty silver **b** to go under them H149
Ex 26:19 go under them—two **b** for each frame, one H149
Ex 26:21 forty silver **b**—two under each frame. H149
Ex 26:25 will be eight frames and sixteen silver **b**— H149
Ex 26:32 with gold and standing on four silver **b**. H149
Ex 26:37 And cast five bronze **b** for them. H149
Ex 27:10 twenty bronze **b** and with silver hooks H149
Ex 27:11 twenty bronze **b** and with silver hooks H149
Ex 27:12 have curtains, with ten posts and ten **b**. H149
Ex 27:14 the entrance, with three posts and three **b**, H149
Ex 27:15 other side, with three posts and three **b**. H149
Ex 27:16 embroiderer—with four posts and four **b**. H149
Ex 27:17 have silver bands and hooks, and bronze **b**. H149
Ex 27:18 linen five cubits high, and with bronze **b**. H149
Ex 35:11 frames, crossbars, posts and **b**; H149
Ex 35:17 of the courtyard with its posts and **b**, H149
Ex 36:24 made forty silver **b** to go under them H149
Ex 36:24 go under them—two **b** for each frame, one H149
Ex 36:26 forty silver **b**—two under each frame. H149
Ex 36:30 were eight frames and sixteen silver **b**— H149
Ex 36:36 hooks for them and cast their four silver **b**. H149
Ex 36:38 with gold and made their five **b** *of* bronze. H149
Ex 38:10 with twenty posts and twenty bronze **b**, and H149
Ex 38:11 had twenty posts and twenty bronze **b**, H149
Ex 38:12 with ten posts and ten **b**, with silver hooks H149
Ex 38:14 the entrance, with three posts and three **b**, H149
Ex 38:15 the courtyard, with three posts and three **b**. H149
Ex 38:17 The **b** for the posts were bronze. The hooks H149
Ex 38:19 with four posts and four bronze **b**. H149
Ex 38:27 used to cast the **b** *for* the sanctuary and H149
Ex 38:27 the curtain—100 **b** from the 100 talents H149
Ex 38:30 used it to make the **b** *for* the entrance to H149
Ex 38:31 the **b** *for* the surrounding courtyard and H149
Ex 39:33 its clasps, frames, crossbars, posts and **b**; H149
Ex 39:40 of the courtyard with its posts and **b**, H149
Ex 40:18 he put the **b** in place, erected the H149
Nu 3:36 its crossbars, posts, **b**, all its equipment H149
Nu 3:37 of the surrounding courtyard with their **b**, H149
Nu 4:31 the tabernacle, its crossbars, posts and **b**, H149
Nu 4:32 of the surrounding courtyard with their **b**, H149
SS 5:15 are pillars of marble set on **b** *of* pure gold. H149

BASEST (KJV) LOWLIEST

BASEWORK (1)

1Ki 7:31 and with its **b** it measured a cubit H5126+4029

BASHAN (60)

Nu 21:33 went up along the road toward **B**, H1421
Nu 21:33 Og king of **B** and his whole army H1421
Nu 32:33 the kingdom of Og king of **B**— H1421
Dt 1: 4 at Edrei had defeated Og king of **B** H1421
Dt 3: 1 went up along the road toward **B**, H1421
Dt 3: 1 Og king of **B** with his whole army H1421
Dt 3: 3 our hands Og king of **B** and all his army. H1421
Dt 3: 4 region of Argob, Og's kingdom in **B**. H1421
Dt 3:10 all **B** as far as Salekah and Edrei H1421
Dt 3:10 Edrei, towns of Og's kingdom in **B**. H1421
Dt 3:11 Og king of **B** was the last of the Rephaites H1421
Dt 3:13 The rest of Gilead and also all of **B**, the H1421
Dt 3:13 region of Argob in **B** used to be known as H1421
Dt 3:14 so that to this day **B** is called Havvoth Jair. H1421
Dt 4:43 Golan in **B**, for the Manassites. H1421
Dt 4:47 of his land and the land of Og king of **B**, H1421
Dt 29: 7 Og king of **B** came out to fight H1421
Dt 32:14 with choice rams of **B** and the finest H1421
Dt 33:22 "Dan is a lion's cub, springing out of **B**." H1421
Jos 9:10 Og king of **B**, who reigned in H1421
Jos 12: 4 And the territory of Og king of **B**, one of H1421
Jos 12: 5 all of **B** to the border of the people of H1421
Jos 13:11 Hermon and all **B** as far as Salekah— H1421
Jos 13:12 the whole kingdom of Og in **B**, who had H1421
Jos 13:30 from Mahanaim and including all of **B**, H1421
Jos 13:30 the entire realm of Og king of **B**—all the H1421
Jos 13:30 all the settlements of Jair in **B**, sixty towns, H1421
Jos 13:31 the royal cities of Og in **B**). This was for the H1421
Jos 17: 1 received Gilead and **B** because the H1421
Jos 17: 5 besides Gilead and **B** east of the Jordan, H1421
Jos 20: 8 Golan in **B** in the tribe of Manasseh. H1421
Jos 21: 6 the half-tribe of Manasseh in **B**. H1421
Jos 21:27 Manasseh, Golan in **B** (a city of refuge H1421
Jos 22: 7 of Manasseh Moses had given land in **B**, H1421
1Ki 4:13 the region of Argob in **B** and its sixty large H1421
1Ki 4:19 Amorites and the country of Og king of **B**). H1421
2Ki 10:33 by the Arnon Gorge through Gilead to **B**. H1421
1Ch 5:11 The Gadites lived next to them in **B** H824+1421
1Ch 5:12 the second, then Janai and Shaphat, in **B**. H1421
1Ch 5:16 in Gilead, in **B** and its outlying villages H1421
1Ch 5:23 in the land from **B** to Baal Hermon, H1421
1Ch 6:62 part of the tribe of Manasseh that is in **B**. H1421
1Ch 6:71 received Golan in **B** and also Ashtaroth, H1421
Ne 9:22 Heshbon and the country of Og king of **B**. H1421
Ps 22:12 strong bulls of **B** encircle me. H1421
Ps 68:15 Mount **B**, majestic mountain, Mount H1421
Ps 68:15 mountain, Mount **B**, rugged mountain, H1421
Ps 68:22 "I will bring them from **B**; I will bring them H1421
Ps 135:11 Amorites, Og king of **B**, and all the kings H1421
Ps 136:20 Og king of **B**—His love endures H1421
Isa 2:13 tall and lofty, and all the oaks of **B**, H1421
Isa 33: 9 **B** and Carmel drop their leaves. H1421
Jer 22:20 let your voice be heard in **B**, cry out from H1421
Jer 50:19 they will graze on Carmel and **B**; their H1421
Eze 27: 6 Of oaks from **B** they made your oars; of H1421
Eze 39:18 all of them fattened animals from **B**. H1421
Am 4: 1 you cows of **B** on Mount Samaria H1421
Mic 7:14 Let them feed in **B** and Gilead as in days H1421
Na 1: 4 **B** and Carmel wither and the blossoms of H1421
Zec 11: 2 oaks of **B**; the dense forest has H1421

BASIN (14) [BASINS, WASHBASIN]

Ex 12:22 the blood in the **b** and put some of the H6195
Ex 30:18 "Make a bronze **b**, with its bronze stand H3963
Ex 30:28 all its utensils, and the **b** with its stand. H3963
Ex 31: 9 all its utensils, the **b** with its stand— H3963
Ex 35:16 its utensils; the bronze **b** with its stand; H3963
Ex 38: 8 made the bronze **b** and its bronze stand H3963
Ex 39:39 all its utensils; the **b** with its stand; H3963
Ex 40: 7 place the **b** between the tent of meeting H3963
Ex 40:11 Anoint the **b** and its stand and consecrate H3963
Ex 40:30 He placed the **b** between the tent of H3963
Lev 8:11 all its utensils and the **b** with its stand, H3963
1Ki 7:30 each had a **b** resting on four supports, H3963
1Ki 7:38 one **b** to go on each of the ten stands. H3963
Jn 13: 5 poured water into a **b** and began to wash *G3781*

BASING (3) [BASE]

2Ki 18:19 **On** what *are you* **b** this confidence of H1053
2Ch 32:10 On what *are* you **b** your **confidence**, that H1053
Isa 36: 4 **On** what *are you* **b** this confidence of H1053

BASINS (8) [BASIN]

1Ki 7:38 He then made ten bronze **b**, each holding H3963
1Ki 7:43 the ten stands with their ten **b**; H3963
1Ki 7:50 the pure gold **b**, wick trimmers, sprinkling H6195
2Ki 12:13 temple was not spent for making silver **b**, H6195
2Ki 16:17 removed the **b** from the movable H3963
2Ch 4: 6 He then made ten **b** for washing and H3963
2Ch 4:14 the stands with their **b**; H3963
Jer 52:19 of the imperial guard took away the **b**, H6195

BASIS (15) [BASE]

Lev 25:15 your own people **on the b of** the number of H928
Lev 25:15 are to sell to you **on the b of** the number of H928
1Ki 20:34 **"On the b of** a treaty I will set you free." H928
Eze 16:61 not **on the b of** my covenant with you. H4946
Da 6: 5 never find any **b for charges** against this A10544
Lk 23: 4 "I find no **b for a charge** against this man." *G165*
Lk 23:14 have found no **b** for your charges *G165*
Jn 8: 6 in order to have a **b for accusing** him. *G2989*
Jn 18:38 "I find no **b for a charge** against him. *G162*
Jn 19: 4 that I find no **b for a charge** against him." *G162*
Jn 19: 6 I find no **b for a charge** against him." *G162*
Php 3: 9 that comes from God **on the b of** faith. *G2093*
Phm 9 I prefer to appeal to you **on the b of** love. *G1328*
Heb 7:16 a priest not **on the b of** a regulation as to *G2848*
Heb 7:16 ancestry but **on the b of** the power of an *G2848*

BASKET (34) [BASKETFULS, BASKETS]

Ge 40:17 In the top **b** were all kinds of baked goods H6130
Ge 40:17 eating them out of the **b** on my head." H6130
Ex 2: 3 she got a papyrus **b** for him and coated it H9310
Ex 2: 5 She saw the **b** among the reeds and sent H9310
Ex 29: 3 Put them in a **b** and present them along H6130
Ex 29:23 From the **b** *of* bread made without yeast H6130
Ex 29:32 of the ram and the bread that is in the **b**. H6130

Lev 8: 2 rams and the **b** *containing* bread made H6130
Lev 8:26 And from the **b** *of* bread made without H6130
Lev 8:31 the bread from the **b** *of* ordination H6130
Nu 6:15 a **b** *of* bread made with the finest H6130
Nu 6:17 is to present the **b** *of* unleavened bread H6130
Nu 6:19 thick loaf and one thin loaf from the **b**, H6130
Dt 23:24 you want, but do not put any in your **b**. H3998
Dt 26: 2 God is giving you and put them in a **b**. H3244
Dt 26: 4 shall take the **b** from your hands and H3244
Dt 26:10 Place **the b** before the LORD your God H2257S
Dt 28: 5 Your **b** and your kneading trough will be H3244
Dt 28:17 Your **b** and your kneading trough will be H3244
Jdg 6:19 Putting the meat in a **b** and its broth in a H6130
Ps 81: 6 their hands were set free from the **b**. H1857
Isa 40:12 Who has held the dust of the earth in a **b** H8955
Jer 24: 2 One **b** had very good figs, like those that H1857
Jer 24: 2 the other **b** had very bad figs, so H1857
Am 8: 1 LORD showed me: a **b** *of* ripe fruit. H3990
Am 8: 2 "A **b** *of* ripe fruit," I answered H3990
Zec 5: 6 He replied, "It is a **b**." And he added, H406
Zec 5: 7 and there in the **b** sat a woman! H406
Zec 5: 8 her back into the **b** and pushed its lead H406
Zec 5: 9 they lifted up the **b** between heaven and H406
Zec 5:10 "Where are they taking the **b**?" I asked the H406
Zec 5:11 is ready, the **b** will be set there in its place." NDT
Ac 9:25 lowered him in a **b** through an opening *G5083*
2Co 11:33 I was lowered in a **b** from a window in the *G4914*

BASKETFULS (9) [BASKET]

Mt 14:20 up twelve **b** of broken pieces *G3186+4441*
Mt 15:37 picked up seven **b** of broken pieces *G5083+4441*
Mt 16: 9 thousand, and how many **b** you gathered? *G3186*
Mt 16:10 thousand, and how many **b** you gathered? *G5083*
Mk 6:43 up twelve **b** of broken pieces *G3186+4445*
Mk 8: 8 picked up seven **b** of broken pieces that *G5083*
Mk 8:19 how many **b** of pieces did you pick *G3186+4441*
Mk 8:20 how many **b** of pieces did you pick *G5083+4445*
Lk 9:17 picked up twelve **b** of broken pieces that *G3186*

BASKETS (6) [BASKET]

Ge 40:16 On my head were three **b** *of* bread. H6130
Ge 40:18 "The three **b** are three days. H6130
2Ki 10: 7 put their heads in **b** and sent them to H1857
Jer 24: 1 LORD showed me two **b** *of* figs placed in H1857
Mt 13:48 sat down and collected the good fish in **b**, *G35*
Jn 6:13 filled twelve **b** with the pieces of the *G3186*

BASON, BASONS (KJV) BASIN, BOWLS, DISH

BASTARD, BASTARDS (KJV) BORN OF A FORBIDDEN MARRIAGE, MONGREL, NOT LEGITIMATE

BAT (2) [BATS]

Lev 11:19 any kind of heron, the hoopoe and the **b**. H6491
Dt 14:18 any kind of heron, the hoopoe and the **b**. H6491

BATCH (4)

Ro 11:16 then the *whole* **b** is holy; if the *G5878*
1Co 5: 6 little yeast leavens the whole **b of dough**? *G5878*
1Co 5: 7 so that you may be a new unleavened **b**— *G5878*
Gal 5: 9 works through the whole **b of dough**." *G5878*

BATH (7) [BATHE]

Isa 5:10 vineyard will produce only a **b** of wine; H1427
Eze 45:10 an accurate ephah and an accurate **b**. H1427
Eze 45:11 The ephah and the **b** are to be the same H1427
Eze 45:11 the **b** containing a tenth of a homer and H1427
Eze 45:14 measured by the **b**, is a tenth of a H1427
Eze 45:14 is a tenth of a **b** from each cor (which H1427
Jn 13:10 "Those *who have* **had a b** need only to *G3374*

BATH RABBIM (1)

SS 7: 4 of Heshbon by the gate of **B Rabbim**. H1442

BATHE (25) [BATH, BATHED, BATHING, BATHS]

Ex 2: 5 daughter went down to the Nile to **b**, H8175
Lev 14: 8 shave off all their hair and **b** with water H8175
Lev 14: 9 their clothes and **b** themselves with water, H8175
Lev 15: 5 must wash their clothes and **b** with water, H8175
Lev 15: 6 must wash their clothes and **b** with water, H8175
Lev 15: 7 must wash their clothes and **b** with water, H8175
Lev 15: 8 must wash their clothes and **b** with water, H8175
Lev 15:10 must wash their clothes and **b** with water, H8175
Lev 15:11 must wash their clothes and **b** with water, H8175
Lev 15:13 wash his clothes and **b** himself with fresh H8175
Lev 15:16 *he must* **b** his whole body with water H8175
Lev 15:18 of semen, *both of them must* **b** with water H8175
Lev 15:21 must wash their clothes and **b** with water, H8175
Lev 15:22 must wash their clothes and **b** with water, H8175
Lev 15:27 must wash their clothes and **b** with water, H8175
Lev 16: 4 so *he must* **b** himself with water before he H8175
Lev 16:24 *He shall* **b** himself with water in the H8175
Lev 16:26 his clothes and **b** himself with water; H8175
Lev 16:28 his clothes and **b** himself with water; H8175
Lev 17:15 must wash their clothes and **b** with water, H8175
Lev 17:16 not wash their clothes and **b** themselves, H8175
Nu 19: 7 his clothes and **b** himself with water. H8175
Nu 19: 8 also wash his clothes and **b** with water, H8175
Nu 19:19 must wash their clothes and **b** with water, H8175
Dt 33:24 his brothers, and *let him* **b** his feet in oil. H3188

BATHED (5) [BATHE]

Lev 22: 6 offerings unless *he has* **b** himself with H8175
1Ki 22:38 where the prostitutes **b**), and the dogs H8175
Isa 34: 6 The sword of the LORD *is* **b in** blood, it is H4848
Eze 16: 9 " '*I* **b** you with water and washed the H8175
Eze 23:40 when they arrived *you* **b** *yourself* for them, H8175

BATHING (2) [BATHE]

2Sa 11: 2 From the roof he saw a woman **b**. H8175
Job 36:30 about him, **b** the depths of the sea. H4059

BATHS (10) [BATHE]

1Ki 5:11 to twenty thousand **b** *of* pressed olive oil. H1427
1Ki 7:26 like a lily blossom. It held two thousand **b**. H1427
1Ki 7:38 each holding forty **b** and measuring four H1427
2Ch 2:10 twenty thousand **b** of wine and twenty H1427
2Ch 2:10 wine and twenty thousand **b** of olive oil." H1427
2Ch 4: 5 a lily blossom. It held three thousand **b**. H1427
Ezr 7:22 a hundred **b** of wine, a hundred A10126
Ezr 7:22 of wine, a hundred **b** of olive oil, and A10126
Eze 45:14 which consists of ten **b** or one homer, for H1427
Eze 45:14 ten **b** are equivalent to a homer). H1427

BATHSHEBA (13)

2Sa 11: 3 The man said, "She is **B**, the daughter of H1444
2Sa 12:24 Then David comforted his wife **B**, and he H1444
1Ki 1:11 Then Nathan asked **B**, Solomon's mother H1444
1Ki 1:15 So **B** went to see the aged king in his H1444
1Ki 1:16 **B** bowed down, prostrating herself before H1444
1Ki 1:28 David said, "Call in **B**." So she came into H1444
1Ki 1:31 Then **B** bowed down with her face to the H1444
1Ki 2:13 of Haggith, went to **B**, Solomon's mother. H1444
1Ki 2:13 Solomon's mother. **B** asked him, "Do you NDT
1Ki 2:18 **B** replied, "I will speak to the king for you H1444
1Ki 2:19 When **B** went to King Solomon to speak H1444
1Ch 3: 5 These four were by **B** daughter of Ammiel. H1444
Ps 51: T David had committed adultery with **B**. H1444

BATS (1) [BAT]

Isa 2:20 to the moles and **b** their idols of silver H6491

BATTERED (1) [BATTERING]

Isa 24:12 left in ruins, its gate *is* **b to pieces**. H4198+8625

BATTERING (7) [BATTERED]

2Sa 20:15 While *they were* **b** the wall to bring it H8845
Isa 22: 5 a day of **b down** walls and of crying out to H7982
Eze 4: 2 against it and put **b rams** around it. H4119
Eze 21:22 where he is to set up **b rams**, to give the H4119
Eze 21:22 battle cry, to set **b rams** against the gates H4119
Eze 26: 9 the blows of his **b rams** against your walls H7692
Ac 27:18 **We took such a** violent **b from the storm** *G5928*

BATTLE (217) [BATTLEMENTS, BATTLES]

Ge 14: 8 out and drew up their **b** lines in the Valley H4878
Ex 13:18 Israelites went up out of Egypt **ready for b**. H2821
Nu 10: 9 When you go into **b** in your own land H4878
Nu 21:33 marched out to meet them in **b** at Edrei. H4878
Nu 31: 4 Send into **b** a thousand men from each of H7372
Nu 31: 5 So twelve thousand men armed for **b**, H7372
Nu 31: 6 Moses sent them into **b**, a thousand from H7372
Nu 31:14 who returned from the **b**. H7372+4878
Nu 31:21 said to the soldiers who had gone into **b**, H4878
Nu 31:27 who took part in the **b** and the rest of the H7372
Nu 31:28 From the soldiers who fought in the **b**, set H7372
Nu 31:36 share of those who fought in the **b** was: H7372
Nu 32:17 will arm ourselves *for* **b** and go ahead of H2821
Nu 32:20 will arm yourselves before the LORD for **b** H4878
Nu 32:27 every man who is armed for **b**, will cross H7372
Nu 32:29 every man armed for **b**, cross over the H4878
Dt 2:24 possession of it and engage him in **b**. H4878
Dt 2:32 army came out to meet us in **b** at Jahaz, H4878
Dt 3: 1 marched out to meet us in **b** at Edrei. H4878
Dt 3:18 **armed for b**, must cross over H2741
Dt 20: 2 When you are about to go into **b**, the H4878
Dt 20: 3 you are going into **b** against your H4878
Dt 20: 5 he may die in **b** and someone else H4878
Dt 20: 6 he may die in **b** and someone else H4878
Dt 20: 7 he may die in **b** and someone else H4878
Dt 20:12 to make peace and they engage you in **b**, H4878
Jos 1:14 fighting men, **ready for b**, must cross over H2821
Jos 4:12 crossed over, **ready for b**, in front of the H2821
Jos 4:13 thousand armed for **b** crossed over before H7372
Jos 8:14 to meet Israel in **b** at a certain place H4878
Jos 11:19 with the Israelites, who took them all in **b**. H4878
Jos 13:22 In addition to *those* **slain in b**, the H2728
Jos 14:11 vigorous to go out to **b** now as I was then. H4878
Jdg 3: 2 who had not had previous **b** experience): H4392S
Jdg 8:13 returned from the **b** by the Pass of Heres. H4878
Jdg 18:11 Danites, armed for **b**, set out from Zorah H4878
Jdg 18:16 Danites, armed for **b**, stood at the H4878
Jdg 20:17 swordsmen, all of them **fit for b**. H4878+408
Jdg 20:20 took up **b** positions against them H4878
Jdg 20:39 "We are defeating them as in the first **b**." H4878
Jdg 20:42 they could not escape the **b**. H4878
1Sa 4: 2 and as the **b** spread, Israel was H4878
1Sa 4:12 ran from the **b line** and went to Shiloh H5120
1Sa 4:16 "I have just come from the **b line**; I fled H5120
1Sa 7:10 drew near to engage Israel in **b**. H4878
1Sa 13:22 So on the day of the **b** not a soldier with H4878
1Sa 14:20 all his men assembled and went to the **b**. H4878
1Sa 14:22 the run, they joined the **b** in hot pursuit. H4878
1Sa 14:23 the **b** moved on beyond Beth Aven. H4878
1Sa 17: 2 Elah and drew up their **b** line to meet the H4878
1Sa 17: 8 "Why do you come out and line up for **b**? H4878
1Sa 17:20 the army was going out to its **b positions**, H5120
1Sa 17:22 ran to the **b lines** and asked his brothers H5120
1Sa 17:28 you came down only to watch the **b**." H4878
1Sa 17:47 LORD saves; for the **b** is the LORD's, and he H4878
1Sa 17:48 ran quickly toward the **b line** to meet him. H5120
1Sa 18:30 commanders continued to go out to **b**, NDT
1Sa 23: 8 And Saul called up all his forces for **b**, to H4878
1Sa 26:10 will die, or he will go into **b** and perish. H4878
1Sa 29: 4 He must not go with us into **b**, or he will H4878
1Sa 29: 9 'He must not go up with us into **b**.' H4878
1Sa 30:24 as that of him who went down to the **b**. H4878
2Sa 1: 4 "The men fled from the **b**," he replied H4878
2Sa 1:25 "How the mighty have fallen in **b** H4878
2Sa 2:17 The **b** that day was very fierce, and Abner H4878
2Sa 3:30 their brother Asahel in the **b** at Gibeon.) H4878
2Sa 8:10 him on his victory *in* **b** over Hadadezer, H4309
2Sa 10: 8 drew up in **b formation** at the H4878
2Sa 10: 9 that there were **b lines** in front of him H4878
2Sa 10:17 Arameans **formed** *their* **b lines** to meet H6885
2Sa 11:18 Joab sent David a full account of the **b**. H4878
2Sa 11:19 giving the king this account of the **b**, H4878
2Sa 17:11 with you yourself leading them into **b**. H7930
2Sa 18: 6 the **b** took place in the forest of H4878
2Sa 18: 8 The **b** spread out over the whole H4878
2Sa 19: 3 who are ashamed when they flee from **b**. H4878
2Sa 19:10 anointed to rule over us, has died in **b**. H4878
2Sa 21:15 Once again there was a **b** between the H4878
2Sa 21:17 "Never again will you go out with us to **b** H4878
2Sa 21:18 there was another **b** with the Philistines H4878
2Sa 21:19 In another **b** with the Philistines at Gob H4878
2Sa 21:20 In still another **b**, which took place at H4878
2Sa 22:35 He trains my hands for **b**; my arms can H4878
2Sa 22:40 You armed me with strength for **b**; you H4878
2Sa 23: 9 gathered at Pas Dammim for **b**. H4878
1Ki 2: 5 their blood in peacetime as if in **b**, H4878
1Ki 20:14 "And who will start the **b**?" he asked. H4878
1Ki 20:29 on the seventh day the **b** was joined. H4878
1Ki 20:39 "Your servant went into the thick of the **b** H4878
1Ki 22:30 "I will enter the **b** in disguise, but you H4878
1Ki 22:30 Israel disguised himself and went into **b**. H4878
1Ki 22:35 All day long the **b** raged, and the king was H4878
2Ki 3:26 Moab saw that the **b** had gone against H4878
2Ki 8:29 at Ramoth in his **b** with Hazael king of H4309
2Ki 9:15 on him in the **b** with Hazael king of H4309
2Ki 13:25 towns he had taken in **b** from his father H4878
2Ki 14: 7 the Valley of Salt and captured Sela in **b**, H4878
2Ki 14: 8 *let us* **face each other in b**." H8011+7156
2Ki 23:29 Josiah marched out to **meet** him **in b**, H7925
1Ch 5:18 use a bow, and who were trained for **b**. H4878
1Ch 5:20 they cried out to him during the **b**. H4878
1Ch 5:22 fell slain, because the **b** was God's. H4878
1Ch 7: 4 had 36,000 **men ready for b**, H1522+7372+4878
1Ch 7:40 of men **ready for b**, H7372+928+2021+4878
1Ch 11:13 when the Philistines gathered there for **b**. H4878
1Ch 12: 1 among the warriors who helped him in **b**; H4878
1Ch 12: 8 **ready for b** and able to handle H408+7372+4200+2021+4878
1Ch 12:23 the men armed for **b** who came to David H7372
1Ch 12:24 shield and spear—6,800 armed for **b**; H7372
1Ch 12:25 from Simeon, warriors ready for **b**—7,100; H7372
1Ch 12:33 soldiers prepared for **b** with every type of H4878
1Ch 12:35 from Dan, ready for **b**—28,600; H4878
1Ch 12:36 experienced soldiers prepared for **b** H4878
1Ch 14:15 move out to **b**, because that will H4878
1Ch 18:10 him on his victory *in* **b** over Hadadezer, H4309
1Ch 19: 7 from their towns and moved out for **b**. H4878
1Ch 19: 9 drew up in **b formation** at the H4878
1Ch 19:10 that there were **b lines** in front of him H4878
1Ch 19:17 them and **formed** *his* **b lines** opposite H6885
1Ch 19:17 his lines to meet the Arameans *in* **b**, H4878
1Ch 20: 5 In another **b** with the Philistines, Elhanan H4878
1Ch 20: 6 In still another **b**, which took place at H4878
1Ch 26:27 the plunder taken in **b** they dedicated H4878
2Ch 13: 3 Abijah went into **b** with an army of four H4878
2Ch 13: 3 Jeroboam drew up a **b** line against him H4878
2Ch 13:12 trumpets will sound the **b cry** against you. H9558
2Ch 13:15 the men of Judah **raised the b cry**. H8131
2Ch 13:15 At the **sound of** their **b cry**, God routed H8131
2Ch 14:10 they took up **b** positions in the Valley H4878
2Ch 17:18 with 180,000 men armed for **b**. H7372
2Ch 18:29 "I will enter the **b** in disguise, but you H4878
2Ch 18:29 Israel disguised himself and went into **b**. H4878
2Ch 18:34 All day long the **b** raged, and the king of H4878
2Ch 20:15 For the **b** is not yours, but God's H4878
2Ch 20:17 You *will* not *have* to **fight** this **b**. Take up H4309
2Ch 22: 6 at Ramoth in his **b** with Hazael king of H4309
2Ch 25: 8 Even if you go and fight courageously in **b** H4878
2Ch 25:17 *let us* **face each other in b**." H8011+7156
2Ch 35:20 Josiah marched out to **meet** him **in b**. H7925
2Ch 35:22 disguised himself to **engage** him **in b**. H4309
Job 5:20 in **b** from the stroke of the sword. H4878
Job 38:23 times of trouble, for days of war and **b**? H4878
Job 39:25 It catches the scent of **b** from afar, the H4878
Job 39:25 the shout of commanders and the **b cry**. H9558
Ps 18:34 He trains my hands for **b**; my arms can H4878
Ps 18:39 You armed me with strength for **b**; you H4878
Ps 21: 9 When you appear for **b**, you will burn them NDT
Ps 24: 8 strong and mighty, the LORD mighty in **b**. H4878
Ps 55:18 unharmed from the **b** waged against me, H7930
Ps 78: 9 with bows, turned back on the day of **b**; H7930

Ps 89:43 sword and have not supported him in b. H4878
Ps 110: 3 troops will be willing on your day of b. H2657
Ps 140: 7 you shield my head in the day of b. H5977
Ps 144: 1 trains my hands for war, my fingers for b. H4878
Pr 21:31 The horse is made ready for the day of b H4878
Ecc 9:11 is not to the swift or the b to the strong, H4878
SS 3: 8 all experienced in b, each with his sword H4878
Isa 3:25 will fall by the sword, your warriors in b. H4878
Isa 8: 9 Prepare for b, and be H273
Isa 8: 9 Prepare for b, and be H273
Isa 9: 5 boot used in b and every garment H8323
Isa 13: 3 I have commanded *those* I prepared *for b*; AIT
Isa 21:15 from the bent bow and from the heat of b. H4878
Isa 22: 2 killed by the sword, nor did they die in b. H4878
Isa 27: 4 I would march against them in b; I would H4878
Isa 28: 6 to those who turn back the b at the gate. H4878
Isa 30:32 as he fights them in b with the blows of H4878
Isa 31: 4 will come down to do b on Mount Zion H7371
Isa 31: 9 the sight of the b standard their H5812
Isa 42:13 a shout *he will* raise the b cry and will H7658
Jer 4:19 of the trumpet; I have heard the b cry. H4878
Jer 4:21 must I see the b standard and hear the H5812
Jer 6: 4 "Prepare for b against her! Arise, let us H4878
Jer 6:23 come like men in b formation to attack H4878
Jer 8: 6 own course like a horse charging into b. H4878
Jer 18:21 their young men slain by the sword in b. H4878
Jer 20:16 wailing in the morning, a b cry at noon. H9558
Jer 46: 3 both large and small, and march out for b! H4878
Jer 48:14 'We are warriors, men valiant in b'? H4878
Jer 49: 2 I will sound the b cry against Rabbah of H4878
Jer 49:14 yourselves to attack it! Rise up for b!" H4878
Jer 50:22 The noise of b is in the land, the noise of H4878
Jer 50:42 come like men in b formation to attack H4878
Jer 51:20 my weapon for b—with you I shatter H4878
Jer 51:27 Prepare the nations for b against her NDT
Jer 51:28 Prepare the nations for b against her—the NDT
Eze 7:14 no one will go into b, for my wrath is H4878
Eze 13: 5 stand firm in the b on the day of the LORD H4878
Eze 21:22 to sound the b cry, to set battering rams H9558
Da 11:10 flood and carry the b as far H8740+2256+1741
Da 11:20 will be destroyed, yet not in anger or in b. H4878
Da 11:26 and many *will* fall in b. H5877+2728
Da 11:40 king of the South *will* engage him in b, H5590
Hos 1: 7 not by bow, sword or b, or by horses and H4878
Hos 2:18 Bow and sword and b I will abolish from H4878
Hos 5: 8 Raise the b cry in Beth Aven; lead on H8131
Hos 10:14 the roar of b will rise against your people H8623
Hos 10:14 devastated Beth Arbel on the day of b, H4878
Joel 2: 5 like a mighty army drawn up for b. H4878
Am 1:14 fortresses amid war cries on the day of b, H4878
Ob 1 "Rise, let us go against her for b"— H4878
Mic 2: 8 without a care, like men returning from b. H4878
Zep 1:14 the Mighty Warrior shouts *his* b cry. H7658
Zep 1:16 a day of trumpet and b cry against the H9558
Zec 9:10 Jerusalem, and the b bow will be broken. H4878
Zec 10: 3 make them like a proud horse in b. H4878
Zec 10: 4 from him the b bow, from him every H4878
Zec 10: 5 be like warriors in b trampling their H4878
Zec 14: 3 those nations, as he fights on a day of b. H7930
1Co 14: 8 a clear call, who will get ready for b? G4483
1Ti 1:18 recalling them you may fight the b well, G5127
Heb 11:34 became powerful in b and routed foreign G4483
Jas 4: 1 come from your desires that b within you? G5129
Rev 9: 7 locusts looked like horses prepared for b. G4483
Rev 9: 9 many horses and chariots rushing into b. G4483
Rev 16:14 gather them for the b on the great day of G4483
Rev 20: 8 Magog—and to gather them for b. G4483

BATTLEFIELD (2) [FIELD]
Jdg 20:21 thousand Israelites on the b that day. H824
1Sa 4: 2 four thousand of them on the b. H5120+8441

BATTLEMENT, BATTLEMENTS (KJV) BRANCHES, PARAPET

BATTLEMENTS (1) [BATTLE]
Isa 54:12 I will make your b of rubies, your gates of H9087

BATTLES (4) [BATTLE]
1Sa 8:20 to go out before us and fight our b." H4878
1Sa 18:17 me bravely and fight the b *of* the LORD." H4878
1Sa 25:28 because you fight the LORD's b, and no H4878
2Ch 32: 8 our God to help us and to fight our b." H4878

BAVAI (KJV) BINNUI

BAY (4)
Jos 15: 2 started from the b at the southern end of H4383
Jos 15: 5 started from the b *of* the sea at the mouth H4383
Jos 18:19 out at the northern b *of* the Dead Sea, H4383
Ac 27:39 but they saw a b with a sandy beach G3146

BAZLUTH (2)
Ezr 2:52 B, Mehida, Harsha, H1296
Ne 7:54 B, Mehida, Harsha, H1296

BDELLIUM (KJV) RESIN

BE (5152) [AM, ARE, AREN'T, BEEN, BEING, WAS, WERE] See Index of Articles Etc.

BE ESHTERAH (1)
Jos 21:27 and B, together with their pasturelands— H1285

BEACH (3)
Ac 21: 5 and there on the b we knelt to pray. G129
Ac 27:39 they saw a bay with a sandy b, where G129
Ac 27:40 foresail to the wind and made for the b. G129

BEACON (KJV) FLAGSTAFF

BEAK (1)
Ge 8:11 there in its b was a freshly plucked olive H7023

BEALIAH (1)
1Ch 12: 5 Jerimoth, B, Shemariah and Shephatiah H1270

BEALOTH (1)
Jos 15:24 Telem, B, H1268

BEAM (1) [BEAMS]
Ezr 6:11 a b is to be pulled from their house and A10058

BEAMS (18) [BEAM]
1Ki 6: 9 roofing it with b and cedar planks. H1464
1Ki 6:10 attached to the temple by b *of* cedar. H6770
1Ki 6:36 stone and one course of trimmed cedar b. H4164
1Ki 7: 2 columns supporting trimmed cedar b. H4164
1Ki 7: 3 with cedar above the b that rested on the H7521
1Ki 7: 3 the columns—forty-five b, fifteen to a row. NDT
1Ki 7:11 high-grade stones, cut to size, and cedar *b*. AIT
1Ki 7:12 stone and one course of trimmed cedar b, H4164
2Ch 3: 7 He overlaid the ceiling b, doorframes H7771
2Ch 34:11 joists and b *for* the buildings that H7936
Ne 2: 8 me timber to make b *for* the gates of the H7936
Ne 3: 3 They laid its b and put its doors and bolts H7936
Ne 3: 6 They laid its b and put its doors with their H7936
Ps 104: 3 lays *the* b *of* his upper chambers on H7936
SS 1:17 The b *of* our house are cedars; our rafters H7771
Jer 22: 7 cut up your fine cedar *b* and throw them into AIT
Hab 2:11 the b of the woodwork will echo it. H4096
Zep 2:14 doorways, the b of cedar will be exposed. H781

BEANS (2)
2Sa 17:28 flour and roasted grain, b and lentils, H7038
Eze 4: 9 wheat and barley, b and lentils, millet H7038

BEAR (129) [AFTERBIRTH, BEARABLE, BEARER, BEARERS, BEARING, BEARS, BIRTH, BIRTHDAY, BIRTHDAYS, BIRTHRIGHT, BORE, BORN, BORNE, CHILDBEARING, CHILDBIRTH, CUPBEARER, CUPBEARERS, FIRSTBORN, HIGHBORN, LOWBORN, NATIVE-BORN, NEWBORN, REBIRTH, STILLBORN, UNBORN]
Ge 1:11 trees on the land *that* b fruit with seed in H6913
Ge 4:13 "My punishment is more than I *can* b. H5951
Ge 17:17 *Will* Sarah b a child at the age of ninety?" H3528
Ge 17:19 your wife Sarah *will* b you a son, and H3528
Ge 17:21 whom Sarah *will* b to you by this time H3528
Ge 30: 3 her so that *she can* b children for me and H3528
Ge 43: 9 *I will* b the blame before you all my life. H2627
Ge 44:32 back to you, *I will* b the blame before you H2627
Ex 16:29 B in mind that the LORD has given you the H8011
Ex 28:12 Aaron *is to* b the names on his shoulders H5951
Ex 28:29 he *will* b the names of the sons of Israel H5951
Ex 28:30 Thus Aaron *will* always b the means of H5951
Ex 28:38 he *will* b the guilt involved in the H5951
Lev 19:18 revenge or b a grudge against anyone H5757
Nu 5:31 the woman *will* b the consequences H5951
Nu 9:13 They *will* b the consequences of their sin H5951
Nu 18: 1 your family *are to* b the responsibility H5951
Nu 18: 1 your sons alone *are to* b the responsibility H5951
Nu 18:22 they *will* b the consequences of their H5951
Nu 18:23 tent of meeting and b the responsibility H5951
Nu 30:15 then *he must* b the consequences *of* her H5951
Dt 1:12 But how *can I* b your problems and your H5951
Dt 21:15 both b him sons but the firstborn is H3528
Jdg 5:14 from Zebulun *those who* b a H5432
Jdg 10:16 And he *could* b Israel's misery no longer. H7918
1Sa 17:34 When a lion or a b came and carried off a H1800
1Sa 17:36 servant has killed both the lion and the b; H1800
1Sa 17:37 the paw of the b will rescue me from H1800
2Sa 17: 8 as fierce as a wild b robbed of her cubs. H1800
2Ki 3:21 *who could* b arms was called up H2520+2514
2Ki 19:30 will take root below and b fruit above. H6913
Est 8: 6 For how *can I* b to see disaster fall on my H3523
Est 8: 6 How *can I* b to see the destruction of my H3523
Job 9: 9 He is the Maker of the B and Orion, the H6933
Job 20:13 though *he* cannot b to let it go and lets it H2798
Job 21: 3 B with me while I speak, and after I have H5951
Job 36: 2 "B with me a little longer and I will show H4192
Job 38:32 seasons or lead out the B with its cubs? H6568
Job 39: 2 Do you count the months till *they* b? Do H4848
Ps 38: 4 me like a burden too heavy to b. NDT
Ps 89:50 how I b in my heart the taunts of all the H5951
Ps 92:14 *They will* still b fruit in old age, they will H5649
Pr 17:12 Better to meet a b robbed of her cubs H1800
Pr 18:14 sickness, but a crushed spirit who *can* b? H5951
Pr 28:15 lion or a charging b is a wicked ruler over H1800
Pr 30:21 earth trembles, under four it cannot b up: H5951
Isa 1:13 *I* cannot b your worthless H4202+3523
Isa 11: 1 from his roots a Branch *will* b fruit. H7238
Isa 11: 7 The cow will feed with the b, their young H1800
Isa 24: 6 the earth; its people *must* b *their* guilt. H870
Isa 37:31 will take root below and b fruit above. H6913
Isa 53:11 justify many, and he *will* b their iniquities. H6022
Isa 65:23 nor *will they* b children doomed to H3528
Jer 12: 2 have taken root; they grow and b fruit. H6913
Jer 12:13 *They will* b *the* shame of their harvest H1017
Jer 14: 9 and we b your name; do not H7924+6584
Jer 15:16 delight, for I b your name, LORD H7924+6584
Jer 17: 8 a year of drought and never fails *to* b fruit." H6913
Jer 30: 6 *Can* a man b children? Then why H3528
La 3:10 Like a b lying in wait, like a lion in hiding, H1800
La 3:27 is good for a man *to* b the yoke while he H5951
La 5: 7 are no more, and we b their punishment. H6022
Eze 4: 4 *You are to* b their sin for the number of H5951
Eze 4: 5 So for 390 days *you will* b the sin of the H5951
Eze 4: 6 b the sin of the people of Judah. H5951
Eze 14:10 *They will* b their guilt—the prophet will be H5951
Eze 16:52 B your disgrace, for you have furnished H5951
Eze 16:52 be ashamed and b your disgrace, for H5951
Eze 16:54 so that *you may* b your disgrace and be H5951
Eze 16:58 You *will* b the consequences of your H5951
Eze 17: 8 b fruit and become a splendid vine. H5951
Eze 17:23 branches and b fruit and become a H6913
Eze 23:35 you *must* b the consequences of your H5951
Eze 23:49 your lewdness and b the consequences of H5951
Eze 32:24 *They* b their shame with those who go H5951
Eze 32:25 *they* b their shame with those who go H5951
Eze 32:30 by the sword and b their shame with H5951
Eze 34:29 famine in the land or b the scorn of the H5951
Eze 44:10 after their idols *must* b the consequences H5951
Eze 44:12 hand that *they must* b the consequences H5951
Eze 44:13 *they must* b the shame of their detestable H5951
Eze 47:12 Every month *they will* b fruit, because the H1144
Da 7: 5 a second beast, which looked like a b. A10155
Da 9:19 city and your people b your Name." H7924+6584
Hos 9:16 Even if *they* b children, I will slay their H3528
Hos 10: 2 deceitful, and now *they must* b *their* guilt. H870
Hos 13: 8 Like a b robbed of her cubs, I will attack H1800
Hos 13:16 The people of Samaria *must* b *their* guilt H870
Am 5:19 a man fled from a lion only to meet a b, H1800
Am 7:10 The land cannot b all his words. H3920
Am 9:12 all the nations that b my name," H7924+6584
Mic 1: 2 Sovereign LORD *may* b witness H2118+4200
Mic 6:16 *you will* b the scorn of the nations. H5951
Mic 7: 9 against him, *I will* b the LORD's wrath H5951
Na 1:14 will have no descendants to b your name. NDT
Mt 7:18 A good tree cannot b bad fruit, and a bad G4472
Mt 7:18 and a bad tree cannot b good fruit. G4472
Mt 7:19 Every tree *that does* not b good fruit is cut G4472
Mt 21:19 "*May* you never b fruit again! G1666+1181
Mk 4: 7 the plants, so that *they did* not b grain. G1443
Lk 1:13 Your wife Elizabeth *will* b you a son, and G1164
Lk 1:42 is the child you will b! G2843+3836+3120
Lk 6:43 bad fruit, nor *does* a bad tree b good fruit. G4472
Lk 21:13 so you *will* b testimony to me. G609+1650+3457
Jn 15: 2 every branch that *does* b fruit he prunes G5770
Jn 15: 4 No branch can b fruit by itself; it must G5770
Jn 15: 4 Neither *can* you b fruit unless you G4048S
Jn 15: 5 I in you, you *will* b much fruit; apart G5770
Jn 15: 8 that *you* b much fruit, showing G5770
Jn 15:16 you so that you might go and b fruit— G5770
Jn 16:12 to say to you, more than you can now b. G1002
Ac 15:10 our ancestors have been able *to* b? G1002
Ac 15:17 even all the Gentiles who b my name G2126
Ro 7: 4 in order that *we might* b fruit for God. G2844
Ro 13: 4 rulers do not b the sword for no reason. G5841
Ro 15: 1 are strong ought *to* b with the failings of G1002
1Co 10:13 you be tempted beyond what *you* can b. G1538
1Co 15:49 so *shall we* b the image of the heavenly G5841
Gal 6:17 I b on my body the marks of Jesus. G1002
Col 3:13 B with each other and forgive one another if G462
Heb 9:28 a second time, not to b sin, but to bring NDT
Heb 11:11 enabled *to* b children G1650+2856+5065+3284
Heb 12:20 because *they could* not b what was G5770
Heb 13:22 I urge you *to* b with my word of exhortation G462
Jas 3:12 can a fig tree b olives, or a grapevine G4472
Jas 3:12 a fig tree bear olives, or a grapevine b figs? NDT
1Pe 4:16 praise God that you b that name. G1877
2Pe 3:15 B in mind *that* our Lord's patience means G2451
Rev 13: 2 had feet like those *of* a b and a mouth like G759

BEARABLE (5) [BEAR]
Mt 10:15 it will be more b for Sodom and Gomorrah G445
Mt 11:22 it will be more b for Tyre and Sidon on the G445
Mt 11:24 you that it will be more b for Sodom on the G445
Lk 10:12 it will be more b on that day for Sodom G445
Lk 10:14 But it will be more b for Tyre and Sidon at G445

BEARD (15) [BEARDS]
Lev 14: 9 their head, their b, their eyebrows and the H2417
Lev 19:27 your head or clip off the edges of your b. H2417
1Sa 21:13 gate and letting saliva run down his b. H2417
2Sa 10: 4 shaved off half of each man's b, cut off H2417
2Sa 20: 9 took Amasa by the b with his right hand H2417
Ezr 9: 3 from my head and b and sat down H2417
Ps 133: 2 running down on the b, running down on H2417
Ps 133: 2 running down on Aaron's b, down on the H2417
Isa 7:20 private parts, and to cut off your b also. H2417
Isa 15: 2 Every head is shaved and every b cut off. H2417
Isa 50: 6 my cheeks to *those who* pulled out my b; H5307
Jer 48:37 Every head is shaved and every b cut off H2417
Eze 5: 1 razor to shave your head and your b. H2417
Eze 24:17 not cover your mustache and b or eat the H8559
Eze 24:22 not cover your mustache and b or eat the H8559

BEARDS (4) [BEARD]
Lev 21: 5 off the edges of their **b** or cut their bodies. H2417
2Sa 10: 5 "Stay at Jericho till your **b** have grown H2417
1Ch 19: 5 "Stay at Jericho till your **b** have grown H2417
Jer 41: 5 eighty men who had shaved off their **b** H2417

BEARER (2) [BEAR]
1Sa 17: 7 His shield **b** went ahead of him. H5951
1Sa 17:41 with his shield **b** in front of him, kept H5951

BEARERS (1) [BEAR]
Lk 7:14 carrying him on, and the **b** stood still. *G1002*

BEARING (18) [BEAR]
Ge 1:12 plants **b** seed according to their kinds H2445
Ge 1:12 their kinds and trees **b** fruit with seed in it H6913
Ge 30: 1 that *she was* not **b** Jacob any **children**, H3528
Nu 13:23 they cut off a branch **b** a single cluster of H2256
Jdg 8:18 "each one with the **b** *of* a prince. H9307
2Ch 12:11 guards went with him, **b** the shields, and H5951
Pr 30:29 their stride, four that move *with* **stately b**: H3512
Isa 1:14 a burden to me; I am weary of **b** them. H5951
Isa 60: 6 **b** gold and incense and proclaiming the H5951
Jer 4:31 a groan as of *one* **b** *her* **first child**—the H1144
Joel 2:22 The trees *are* **b** their fruit; the fig tree and H5951
Ro 2:15 their consciences **also b witness**, and their *G5210*
Eph 4: 2 be patient, **b with** one another in love. *G462*
Col 1: 6 the gospel is **b fruit** and growing *G2844*
Col 1:10 **b fruit** in every good work, growing in the *G2844*
Heb 3: 5 **b** witness to what would be spoken by *G1650*
Heb 13:13 outside the camp, **b** the disgrace he bore. *G5770*
Rev 22: 2 the tree of life, **b** twelve crops of fruit *G4472*

BEARS (28) [BEAR]
Ge 49:21 is a doe set free that **b** beautiful fawns. H5989
Ex 21: 4 gives him a wife and *she* **b** him sons or H3528
Dt 25: 6 The first son *she* **b** shall carry on the name H3528
Dt 28:57 from her womb and the children *she* **b**. H3528
1Ki 8:43 house I have built **b** your Name. H7924+6584
2Ki 2:24 Then two **b** came out of the woods and H1800
2Ch 6:33 house I have built **b** your Name. H7924+6584
2Ch 20: 9 this temple that **b** your Name and will cry H928
Job 39: 1 Do you watch when the doe **b** her fawn? H2655
Ps 68:19 God our Savior, *who* daily **b** our **burdens**. H6673
Isa 59:11 We all growl like **b**; we moan mournfully H1800
Jer 7:10 house, which **b** my Name, and say, H7924+6584
Jer 7:11 house, which **b** my Name, become H7924+6584
Jer 7:14 do to the house that **b** my Name, H7924+6584
Jer 7:30 the house that **b** my Name and H7924+6584
Jer 25:29 on the city that **b** my Name, H7924+6584
Jer 32:34 in the house that **b** my Name and H7924+6584
Jer 34:15 me in the house that **b** my Name. H7924+6584
Da 9:18 of the city that **b** your Name. H7924+6584
Mic 5: 3 time when she who is in labor **b a son**, H3528
Mt 7:17 every good tree **b** good fruit, but a bad *G4472*
Mt 7:17 good fruit, but a bad tree **b** bad fruit. *G4472*
Lk 6:43 "No good tree **b** bad fruit, nor does *G1639+4472*
Lk 13: 9 If *it* **b** fruit next year, fine! If not, then cut it *G4472*
Jn 15: 2 cuts off every branch in me *that* **b** no fruit, *G5770*
Gal 4:24 Mount Sinai and **b children** who are to be *G1164*
1Pe 2:19 commendable if *someone* **b up** under the *G5722*
Rev 19:10 of prophecy who **b testimony** to Jesus." *G3456*

BEAST (61) [BEASTS]
2Ki 14: 9 Then a wild **b** in Lebanon came along H2651
2Ch 25:18 Then a wild **b** in Lebanon came along H2651
Ps 68:30 Rebuke the **b** *among* the reeds, the herd H2651
Ps 68:30 Humbled, may the **b** bring bars of silver NDT
Ps 73:22 ignorant; I was a **brute b** before you. H989
Isa 35: 9 be there, nor *any* ravenous **b**; they will not H2651
Jer 7:20 on man and **b**, on the trees of the H989
Jer 21: 6 both man and **b**—and they will die of H989
Jer 36:29 this land and wipe from it both man and **b**?" H989
Eze 25:13 against Edom and kill both man and **b**. H989
Eze 29: 8 sword against you and kill both man and **b**. H989
Eze 29:11 of neither man nor **b** will pass through it; H989
Da 7: 5 "And there before me was a second **b** A10263
Da 7: 6 there before me was another **b**, one NDT
Da 7: 6 This **b** had four heads, and it was given A10263
Da 7: 7 there before me was a fourth **b** A10263
Da 7:11 looking until the **b** was slain and its A10263
Da 7:19 to know the meaning of the fourth **b**, A10263
Da 7:19 the **b** that crushed and devoured its victims NDT
Da 7:23 'The fourth **b** is a fourth kingdom that A10263
Zep 1: 3 "I will sweep away both man and **b**; I will H989
Rev 11: 7 the **b** that comes up from the Abyss will *G2563*
Rev 13: 1 And I saw a **b** coming out of the sea *G2563*
Rev 13: 2 The **b** I saw resembled a leopard, but had *G2563*
Rev 13: 2 The dragon gave the **b** his power and his *G899S*
Rev 13: 3 One of the heads *of* the **b** seemed to have *G899S*
Rev 13: 3 filled with wonder and followed the **b**. *G2563*
Rev 13: 4 because he had given authority *to* the **b**, *G2563*
Rev 13: 4 they also worshiped the **b** and asked *G2563*
Rev 13: 4 the beast and asked, "Who is like the **b**? *G2563*
Rev 13: 5 The **b** was given a mouth to utter proud *G899S*
Rev 13: 8 of the earth will worship the **b**— *G899S*
Rev 13:11 Then I saw a second **b**, coming out of the *G2563*
Rev 13:12 all the authority of the first **b** on its behalf, *G2563*
Rev 13:12 its inhabitants worship the first **b**, *G2563*
Rev 13:14 power to perform on behalf of the first **b**, *G2563*
Rev 13:14 up an image *in honor of* the **b** who was *G2563*
Rev 13:15 The **second b** was given power to give *G899S*
Rev 13:15 to give breath to the image *of* the first **b**, *G2563*
Rev 13:17 is the name *of* the **b** or the number of *G2563*
Rev 13:18 has insight calculate the number *of* the **b**, *G2563*
Rev 14: 9 anyone worships the **b** and its image and *G2563*
Rev 14:11 those who worship the **b** and its image, *G2563*
Rev 15: 2 victorious over the **b** and its image and *G2563*
Rev 16: 2 who had the mark *of* the **b** and worshiped *G2563*
Rev 16:10 out his bowl on the throne *of* the **b**, *G2563*
Rev 16:13 out of the mouth *of* the **b** and out of the *G2563*
Rev 17: 3 sitting on a scarlet **b** that was covered *G2563*
Rev 17: 7 of the woman and *of* the **b** she rides, *G2563*
Rev 17: 8 The **b**, which you saw, once was, now is *G2563*
Rev 17: 8 will be astonished when they see the **b**, *G2563*
Rev 17:11 The **b** who once was, and now is not, is an *G2563*
Rev 17:12 authority as kings along with the **b**. *G2563*
Rev 17:13 give their power and authority *to* the **b**. *G2563*
Rev 17:16 The **b** and the ten horns you saw will hate *G2563*
Rev 17:17 agreeing to hand over *to* the **b** their royal *G2563*
Rev 19:19 Then I saw the **b** and the kings of the *G2563*
Rev 19:20 But the **b** was captured, and with it the *G2563*
Rev 19:20 received the mark *of* the **b** and worshiped *G2563*
Rev 20: 4 not worshiped the **b** or its image and had *G2563*
Rev 20:10 where the **b** and the false prophet had *G2563*

BEASTS (38) [BEAST]
Ge 1:30 And to all the **b** *of* the earth and all the H2651
Ge 9: 2 of you will fall on all the **b** *of* the earth, H2651
Ge 31:39 I did not bring you **animals torn by wild b** H3274
Ex 22:31 eat the meat of an **animal torn by** wild **b**; H3274
Lev 26: 6 I will remove wild **b** from the land, and H2651
Dt 32:24 will send against them the fangs of **wild b**, H989
Job 28: 8 **Proud b** do not set foot on it, and H1201+8832
Job 35:11 than he teaches the **b** *of* the earth and H989
Ps 49:12 not endure; they are like the **b** that perish. H989
Ps 49:20 understanding are like the **b** that perish. H989
Ps 57: 4 I am forced to dwell among **ravenous b** H4266
Ps 74:19 hand over the life of your dove to **wild b**; H2651
Ps 104:11 They give water to all the **b** *of* the field H2651
Ps 104:20 and all the **b** *of* the forest prowl. H2651
Pr 30:30 mighty among **b**, who retreats before H989
Isa 46: 1 are borne by **b of burden**. H2651+2256+989
Isa 56: 9 all you **b** *of* the field, come and H2651
Isa 56: 9 come and devour, all you **b** of the forest! H2651
Jer 12: 9 Go and gather all the wild **b**; bring them H2651
Eze 5:17 I will send famine and wild **b** against you H2651
Eze 14:15 "Or if I send wild **b** through that country H2651
Eze 14:15 one can pass through it because of the **b**, H2651
Eze 14:21 famine and wild **b** and plague— H2651
Eze 29: 5 you as food to the **b** *of* the earth and the H2651
Eze 34:25 the land of savage **b** so that they may live H2651
Eze 38:20 birds in the sky, the **b** *of* the field, every H2651
Da 2:38 mankind and the **b** *of* the field and the A10263
Da 7: 3 Four great **b**, each different from the A10263
Da 7: 7 It was different from all the former **b** A10263
Da 7:12 The other **b** had been stripped of their A10263
Da 7:17 'The four great **b** are four kings that will A10263
Hos 2:18 covenant for them with the **b** *of* the field, H2651
Hos 4: 3 it waste away; the **b** *of* the field, the birds H2651
Mic 5: 8 like a lion among the **b** *of* the forest, like a H989
Zep 2:15 a ruin she has become, a lair for **wild b**! H2651
Ac 11: 6 of the earth, **wild b**, reptiles and birds. *G2563*
1Co 15:32 If *I* **fought wild b** in Ephesus with no more *G2562*
Rev 6: 8 plague, and by the **wild b** of the earth. *G2563*

BEAT (42) [BEATEN, BEATING, BEATINGS, BEATS]
Ex 5:14 slave drivers **b** the Israelite overseers H5782
Ex 9:25 it **b down** everything growing in the fields H5782
Nu 14:45 them and **b** them **down** all the way to H4198
Nu 22:23 Balaam **b** it to get it back on the road H5782
Nu 22:25 foot against it. So *he* **b** the donkey again. H5782
Nu 22:27 he was angry and **b** it with his staff. H5782
Nu 22:28 I done to you *to make you* **b** me these H5782
Dt 1:44 of bees and **b** *you* **down** from Seir all H4198
Dt 24:20 When *you* **b** the olives from your trees, do H2468
2Sa 22:43 *I* **b** them as **fine** as the dust of the earth; H8835
Ne 13:25 *I* **b** some of the men and pulled out their H5782
Ps 18:42 *I* **b** them as **fine** as windblown dust; H8835
Ps 78:66 *He* **b** back his enemies; he put them to H5782
Pr 23:35 "but I'm not hurt! *They* **b** me, but I don't H2150
SS 5: 7 *They* **b** me, they bruised me; they took H5782
Isa 2: 4 *They will* **b** their swords into plowshares H4198
Isa 10:24 *who* **b** you with a rod and lift up a club H5782
Isa 32:12 **B** your breasts for the pleasant fields, for H6199
Isa 49:10 *will* the desert heat or the sun **b down** *on* H5782
Isa 50: 6 I offered my back to *those who* **b** me, my H5782
Jer 31:19 after I came to understand, *I* **b** my breast. H6215
Eze 21:12 with my people. Therefore **b** your breast. H6215
Joel 3:10 **B** your plowshares into swords and your H4198
Mic 4: 3 *They will* **b** their swords into plowshares H4198
Na 2: 7 moan like doves and **b** on their breasts. H9528
Mt 7:25 the winds blew and **b against** that house; *G4700*
Mt 7:27 the winds blew and **b against** that house, *G4684*
Mt 21:35 his servants; *they* **b** one, killed another, *G1296*
Mt 24:49 he then begins *to* **b** his fellow *G5597*
Mk 12: 3 **b** him and sent him away empty-handed. *G1296*
Mk 12: 5 some of them *they* **b**, others they killed *G1296*
Mk 14:65 And the guards took him and **b** him. *G4825*
Lk 10:30 his clothes, **b** him and went away *G4435+2202*
Lk 12:45 he then begins *to* **b** the other *G5597*
Lk 18:13 up to heaven, but **b** his breast and said *G5597*
Lk 20:10 But the tenants **b** him and sent him away *G1296*
Lk 20:11 that one also *they* **b** and treated *G1296*
Lk 23:48 *they* **b** their breasts and went away. *G5597*
Ac 16:37 "*They* **b** us publicly without a trial, even *G1296*
Ac 18:17 leader and **b** him in front of the *G5597*
Ac 22:19 to imprison and **b** those who believe in *G1296*
Rev 7:16 The sun *will* not **b down** on them,' nor *G4406*

BEATEN (16) [BEAT]
Ex 5:16 Your servants *are* **being b**, but the fault is H5782
Nu 22:32 "Why *have you* **b** your donkey these three H5782
Dt 25: 2 If the guilty person deserves *to be* **b**, the H5782
Jdg 20:36 Then the Benjamites saw that *they* **were b** H5597
Isa 1: 5 Why *should you* **be b** anymore? Why do H5782
Isa 17: 6 as when an olive tree is **b**, leaving two H5939
Isa 24:13 as when an olive tree is **b**, or as when H5939
Isa 28:18 sweeps by, you will be **b down** by it. H5330
Isa 28:27 caraway **is b out** with a rod, and H2468
Jer 20: 2 he **had** Jeremiah the prophet **b** and put in H5782
Jer 37:15 Jeremiah and **had** him **b** and imprisoned H5782
Lk 12:47 master wants *will be* **b with** many **blows**. *G1296*
Lk 12:48 punishment *will be* **b with** few **blows**. *G1296*
Ac 16:22 them to be stripped and **b with rods**. *G4810*
2Co 6: 9 yet we live on; **b**, and yet not killed; *G4084*
2Co 11:25 Three times *I was* **b with rods**, once I was *G4810*

BEATING (7) [BEAT]
Ex 2:11 He saw an Egyptian **b** a Hebrew, one of H5782
Pr 18: 6 them strife, and their mouths invite a **b**. H4547
Lk 22:63 Jesus began mocking and **b** him. *G1296*
Ac 19:16 *He* **gave** them such **a b** that they ran out *G2710*
Ac 21:32 his soldiers, they stopped **b** Paul. *G5597*
1Co 9:26 I do not fight like a *boxer* **b** the air. *G1296*
1Pe 2:20 your credit if *you* **receive a b** for doing *G3139*

BEATINGS (3) [BEAT]
Pr 19:29 mockers, and **b** for the backs of fools. H4547
Pr 20:30 away evil, and **b** purge the inmost being. H4804
2Co 6: 5 in **b**, imprisonments and riots; in hard work *G4435*

BEATS (1) [BEAT]
Ex 21:20 "Anyone *who* **b** their male or female H5782

BEAUTIFUL (69) [BEAUTY]
Ge 6: 2 saw that the daughters of humans were **b**, H3202
Ge 12:11 "I know what a **b** woman you are. H3637+5260
Ge 12:14 saw that Sarai was a very **b** woman. H3637
Ge 24:16 The woman was very **b**, a virgin; no H3202+5260
Ge 26: 7 of Rebekah, because she is **b**." H3202+5260
Ge 29:17 had a lovely figure and was **b**. H3637+5260
Ge 49:21 is a doe set free that bears **b** fawns. H9183
Nu 24: 5 "How **b** *are* your tents, Jacob, your H3201
Dt 21:11 the captives a **b** woman and are H3637+9307
Jos 7:21 in the plunder a **b** robe from Babylonia, H3202
1Sa 25: 3 was an intelligent and **b** woman, H3637+9307
2Sa 11: 2 The woman was very **b**, H3202+5260
2Sa 13: 1 the **b** sister of Absalom son of David. H3637
2Sa 14:27 and she became a **b** woman. H3637+5260
1Ki 1: 3 Israel for a **b** young woman and found H3637
1Ki 1: 4 The woman was very **b**; she took care of H3637
Est 2: 2 be made for **b** young virgins for H3202+5260
Est 2: 3 bring all these **b** young women H3202+5260
Est 2: 7 had a lovely figure and was **b**. H3202+5260
Job 42:15 found women as **b** as Job's daughters, H3637
Ps 48: 2 **B** *in* its loftiness, the joy of the whole H3637
Pr 11:22 a pig's snout is a **b** woman who shows no H3637
Pr 24: 4 rooms are filled with rare and **b** treasures. H5833
Ecc 3:11 He has made everything **b** in its time. H3637
SS 1: 8 do not know, *most* **b** of women, follow H3637
SS 1:10 Your cheeks *are* **b** with earrings, your neck H5533
SS 1:15 How **b** you are, my darling! Oh, how H3637
SS 1:15 Oh, how **b**! Your eyes are H3637
SS 2:10 my darling, my **b** *one*, come with me. H3637
SS 2:13 my darling; my **b** *one*, come with me." H3637
SS 4: 1 How **b** you are, my darling! Oh, how H3637
SS 4: 1 Oh, how **b**! Your eyes behind H3637
SS 4: 7 You are altogether **b**, my darling; there is H3637
SS 5: 9 better than others, *most* **b** of women? H3637
SS 6: 1 your beloved gone, *most* **b** of women? H3637
SS 6: 4 You are as **b** as Tirzah, my darling, as H3637
SS 7: 1 How **b** your sandaled feet, O prince's H3636
SS 7: 6 How **b** *you are* and how pleasing, my love H3636
Isa 4: 2 Branch of the LORD will be **b** and glorious, H7382
Isa 28: 5 a **b** wreath for the remnant of his people. H7382
Isa 52: 7 How **b** on the mountains *are* the feet of H5533
Jer 3:19 the **most b** inheritance of any H7382+7382
Jer 6: 2 destroy Daughter Zion, so **b** and delicate. H5534
Jer 11:16 a thriving olive tree with fruit **b** *in* form. H3637
Jer 46:20 "Egypt is a **b** heifer, but a gadfly is H3645
Eze 7:20 pride in their **b jewelry** and used it H7382+6344
Eze 16:12 on your ears and a **b** crown on your head. H9514
Eze 16:13 *You became* very **b** and rose to be a H3636
Eze 20: 6 milk and honey, the **most b** of all lands. H7382
Eze 20:15 milk and honey, the **most b** of all lands— H7382
Eze 23:42 her sister and **b** crowns on their H9514
Eze 27:24 they traded with you **b garments**, H4815
Eze 31: 3 *with* **b** branches overshadowing the forest H3637
Eze 31: 9 I made it **b** with abundant branches, the H3637
Eze 33:32 love songs with a **b** voice and plays an H3637
Da 4:12 Its leaves were **b**, its fruit abundant, and A10736
Da 4:21 with **b** leaves and abundant fruit A10736
Da 8: 9 to the east and toward the **B** Land. H7382
Da 11:16 himself in the **B** Land and will have the H7382
Da 11:41 He will also invade the **B** Land. H7382
Da 11:45 between the seas at the **b** holy mountain. H7382

Zec 9:17 How attractive and b they will be! Grain H3642
Mt 23:27 which look b on the outside but on the G6053
Mt 26:10 She has done a b thing to me. G2819
Mk 14: 6 She has done a b thing to me. G2819
Lk 21: 5 was adorned with b stones and with gifts G2819
Ac 3: 2 being carried to the temple gate called B, G6053
Ac 3:10 sit begging at the temple gate called B, G6053
Ro 10:15 "How b are the feet of those who bring G6053

BEAUTIFULLY (1) [BEAUTY]

Rev 21: 2 as a bride b dressed for her husband. G3175

BEAUTY (33) [BEAUTIFUL, BEAUTIFULLY]

Est 1:11 order to display her b to the people and H3642
Est 2: 3 let b treatments be given to them. H9475
Est 2: 9 her with her b treatments and special H9475
Est 2:12 months of b treatments prescribed for H5299
Ps 27: 4 to gaze on the b of the LORD and to seek H5840
Ps 45:11 Let the king be enthralled by your b H3642
Ps 50: 2 From Zion, perfect in b, God shines forth. H3642
Pr 6:25 your heart after her b or let her captivate H3642
Pr 31:30 is deceptive, and b is fleeting; but a H3642
Isa 3:24 sackcloth; instead of b, branding. H3642
Isa 28: 1 his glorious b, set on the head of H7382
Isa 28: 4 his glorious b, set on the head of H7382
Isa 33:17 see the king in his b and view a land that H3642
Isa 53: 2 He had no b or majesty to attract us to H9307
Isa 61: 3 bestow on them a crown of b instead of H6996
La 2:15 city that was called the perfection of b, H3642
Eze 16:14 among the nations on account of your b, H3642
Eze 16:14 I had given you made your b perfect, NDT
Eze 16:15 you trusted in your b and used your fame H3642
Eze 16:15 who passed by and your b became his. NDT
Eze 16:16 You went to him, and he possessed your b. NDT
Eze 16:25 your lofty shrines and degraded your b, H3642
Eze 27: 3 " 'You say, Tyre, "I am perfect in b." H3642
Eze 27: 4 your builders brought your b to perfection. H3642
Eze 27:11 they brought your b to perfection. H3642
Eze 28: 7 swords against your b and wisdom and H3642
Eze 28:12 full of wisdom and perfect in b. H3642
Eze 28:17 heart became proud on account of your b, H3642
Eze 31: 7 It was majestic in b, with its spreading H1542
Eze 31: 8 in the garden of God could match its b. H3642
Jas 1:11 falls and its b is destroyed. G2346+3836+4725
1Pe 3: 3 Your b should not come from outward NDT
1Pe 3: 4 the unfading b of a gentle and quiet spirit NDT

BEBAI (6)

Ezr 2:11 of B 623 H950
Ezr 8:11 of the descendants of B, Zechariah son of H950
Ezr 8:11 Zechariah son of B, and with him 28 men; H950
Ezr 10:28 From the descendants of B: Jehohanan H950
Ne 7:16 of B 628 H950
Ne 10:15 Azgad, B, H950

BECAME (334) [BECOME]

Ge 2: 7 and the man b a living being. H2118
Ge 4: 1 and she b pregnant and gave birth to Cain. AIT
Ge 4:17 and she b pregnant and gave birth to Enoch. AIT
Ge 5: 6 lived 105 years, he b the father of Enosh. AIT
Ge 5: 7 After he b the father of Enosh, Seth lived 807 AIT
Ge 5: 9 had lived 90 years, he b the father of Kenan. AIT
Ge 5:10 After he b the father of Kenan, Enosh lived AIT
Ge 5:12 lived 70 years, he b the father of Mahalalel. AIT
Ge 5:13 After he b the father of Mahalalel, Kenan AIT
Ge 5:15 had lived 65 years, he b the father of Jared. AIT
Ge 5:16 After he b the father of Jared, Mahalalel lived AIT
Ge 5:18 lived 162 years, he b the father of Enoch. AIT
Ge 5:19 After he b the father of Enoch, Jared lived AIT
Ge 5:21 65 years, he b the father of Methuselah. AIT
Ge 5:22 After he b the father of Methuselah, Enoch AIT
Ge 5:25 lived 187 years, he b the father of Lamech. AIT
Ge 5:26 After he b the father of Lamech, Methuselah AIT
Ge 5:32 years old, he b the father of Shem, Ham AIT
Ge 8: 5 month the tops of the mountains b visible. AIT
Ge 9:21 he b drunk and lay uncovered inside his tent. AIT
Ge 10: 8 who b a mighty warrior on H2725+4200+2118
Ge 11:10 100 years old, he b the father of Arphaxad. AIT
Ge 11:11 And after he b the father of Arphaxad, Shem AIT
Ge 11:12 had lived 35 years, he b the father of Shelah. AIT
Ge 11:13 And after he b the father of Shelah, Arphaxad AIT
Ge 11:14 had lived 30 years, he b the father of Eber. AIT
Ge 11:15 And after he b the father of Eber, Shelah AIT
Ge 11:16 had lived 34 years, he b the father of Peleg. AIT
Ge 11:17 And after he b the father of Peleg, Eber lived AIT
Ge 11:18 had lived 30 years, he b the father of Reu. AIT
Ge 11:19 And after he b the father of Reu, Peleg lived AIT
Ge 11:20 had lived 32 years, he b the father of Serug. AIT
Ge 11:21 And after he b the father of Serug, Reu lived AIT
Ge 11:22 had lived 30 years, he b the father of Nahor. AIT
Ge 11:23 And after he b the father of Nahor, Serug AIT
Ge 11:24 had lived 29 years, he b the father of Terah. AIT
Ge 11:25 And after he b the father of Terah, Nahor AIT
Ge 11:26 70 years, he b the father of Abram, Nahor AIT
Ge 11:27 Terah b the father of Abram, Nahor and AIT
Ge 11:27 And Haran b the father of Lot. AIT
Ge 19:26 looked back, and she b a pillar of salt. H2118
Ge 19:36 of Lot's daughters b pregnant by their father. AIT
Ge 20:12 not of my mother; and she b my wife. H2118
Ge 21: 2 Sarah b pregnant and bore a son to Abraham AIT
Ge 21:20 He lived in the desert and b an archer. H2118
Ge 22:23 Bethuel b the father of Rebekah. Milkah bore AIT
Ge 24:67 So she b his wife, and he loved her; and H2118
Ge 25:19 Abraham b the father of Isaac, AIT
Ge 25:21 his prayer, and his wife Rebekah b pregnant. AIT
Ge 25:27 grew up, and Esau b a skillful hunter, H2118
Ge 26:13 The man b rich, and his wealth continued to AIT
Ge 26:13 continued to grow until he b very wealthy. AIT
Ge 29:32 Leah b pregnant and gave birth to a son. AIT
Ge 30: 1 any children, she b jealous of her sister. AIT
Ge 30: 2 Jacob b angry with her and said, "Am I in the AIT
Ge 30: 5 she b pregnant and bore him a son. AIT
Ge 30:17 and she b pregnant and bore Jacob a fifth AIT
Ge 30:23 She b pregnant and gave birth to a son and AIT
Ge 36:32 Bela son of Beor b king of Edom. His city was AIT
Ge 38: 3 she b pregnant and gave birth to a son, who AIT
Ge 38:18 slept with her, and she b pregnant by him. AIT
Ge 39: 4 found favor in his eyes and b his attendant. AIT
Ge 47:20 severe for them. The land b Pharaoh's, H2118
Ex 1: 7 in numbers and b so numerous that the land AIT
Ex 1:20 increased and b even more numerous. AIT
Ex 2: 2 she b pregnant and gave birth to a son AIT
Ex 2:10 to Pharaoh's daughter and he b her son. H2118
Ex 4: 3 threw it on the ground and it b a snake, H2118
Ex 7:10 his officials, and it b a snake. H2118
Ex 7:12 one threw down his staff and it b a snake. H2118
Ex 7:13 Yet Pharaoh's heart b hard and he would not AIT
Ex 7:22 Pharaoh's heart b hard; he would not AIT
Ex 8:17 dust throughout the land of Egypt b gnats. H2118
Ex 15:25 it into the water, and the water b fit to drink. AIT
Lev 18:24 going to drive out before you b defiled. H3237
Lev 18:27 the land before you, and the land b defiled. AIT
Nu 6:12 because they b defiled during their period of AIT
Nu 11:10 The LORD b exceedingly angry, and Moses AIT
Nu 12:10 skin was leprous—it b as white as snow. NDT
Nu 16: 1 of Eliab, and On son of Peleth—b insolent AIT
Nu 16:15 Moses b very angry and said to the LORD AIT
Dt 1:37 of you the LORD b angry with me also and AIT
Dt 26: 5 lived there and b a great nation, H2118
Dt 32:15 filled with food, they b heavy and sleek. AIT
Jos 7: 5 people melted in fear and b like water. H2118
Jos 24:32 This b the inheritance of Joseph's H2118
Jdg 1:28 When Israel b strong, they pressed the AIT
Jdg 1:33 Beth Anath b forced laborers for H2118
Jdg 3:10 so that he b Israel's judge and went to war. AIT
Jdg 8:27 and it b a snare to Gideon and his family. H2118
Jdg 9: 4 hire reckless scoundrels, who b his followers. AIT
Jdg 10: 7 he b angry with them. He sold them into the AIT
Jdg 15:14 The ropes on his arms b like charred flax H2118
Jdg 17:11 the young man b like one of his sons H2118
Jdg 17:12 the young man b his priest and lived H2118
Ru 4:13 So Boaz took Ruth and she b his wife H2118
1Sa 1:20 of time Hannah b pregnant and gave birth to AIT
1Sa 10:12 is their father?" So it b a saying: "Is Saul H2118
1Sa 13: 1 Saul was thirty years old when he b king, and AIT
1Sa 16:21 David b one of his armor-bearers. H2118
1Sa 18: 1 Jonathan b one in spirit with David, and H8003
1Sa 18:29 Saul b still more afraid of him, and he AIT
1Sa 18:30 Saul's officers, and his name b well known. AIT
1Sa 22: 2 around him, and he b their commander. H2118
1Sa 25:37 his heart failed him and he b like a stone. H2118
1Sa 25:42 with David's messengers and b his wife. H2118
1Sa 30:13 abandoned me when I b ill three days ago. AIT
2Sa 2:10 forty years old when he b king over Israel, AIT
2Sa 4: 1 he lost courage, and all Israel b alarmed. AIT
2Sa 4: 4 hurried to leave, he fell and b disabled. H7174
2Sa 5: 4 David was thirty years old when he b king AIT
2Sa 5:10 he b more and more powerful H2143+2143+2256+1524
2Sa 8: 2 So the Moabites b subject to David and H2118
2Sa 8: 6 the Arameans b subject to him and H2118
2Sa 8:13 And David b famous after he H6913+9005
2Sa 8:14 all the Edomites b subject to David. H2118
2Sa 10:19 with the Israelites and b subject to them. AIT
2Sa 11:27 and she b his wife and bore him a son. H2118
2Sa 12:15 Uriah's wife had borne to David, and he b ill. AIT
2Sa 13: 2 Amnon b so obsessed with his sister Tamar AIT
2Sa 14:26 a year because it b too heavy for him— NDT
2Sa 14:27 and she b a beautiful woman. H2118
2Sa 21:15 against the Philistines, and he b exhausted. AIT
2Sa 23:18 so he b as famous as the Three. H4200
2Sa 23:19 He b their commander, even though he H2118
1Ki 11: 9 The LORD b angry with Solomon because his AIT
1Ki 11:24 of men around him and b their leader; H2118
1Ki 12:30 And this thing b a sin; the people came to H2118
1Ki 13: 6 hand was restored and b as it was before. H2118
1Ki 14: 1 At that time Abijah son of Jeroboam b ill, AIT
1Ki 14:21 He was forty-one years old when he b king AIT
1Ki 15: 1 son of Nebat, Abijah b king of Judah, AIT
1Ki 15: 9 king of Israel, Asa b king of Judah, AIT
1Ki 15:23 In his old age, however, his feet b diseased. AIT
1Ki 15:25 son of Jeroboam b king of Israel in the AIT
1Ki 15:33 Baasha son of Ahijah b king of all Israel in AIT
1Ki 16: 8 Elah son of Baasha b king of Israel, and he AIT
1Ki 16:22 So Tibni died and Omri b king. AIT
1Ki 16:23 king of Judah, Omri b king of Israel, and he AIT
1Ki 16:29 Ahab son of Omri b king of Israel, and he AIT
1Ki 17:17 of the woman who owned the house b ill. AIT
1Ki 19:21 he set out to follow Elijah and b his servant. AIT
1Ki 22:41 son of Asa b king of Judah in the AIT
1Ki 22:42 was thirty-five years old when he b king, AIT
1Ki 22:51 Ahaziah son of Ahab b king of Israel in AIT
2Ki 3: 1 Joram son of Ahab b king of Israel in AIT
2Ki 4:17 But the woman b pregnant, and the next year AIT
2Ki 5:14 was restored and b clean like that of a young AIT
2Ki 8:17 He was thirty-two years old when he b king AIT
2Ki 8:26 was twenty-two years old when he b king, AIT
2Ki 12: 1 year of Jehu, Joash b king, and he reigned in AIT
2Ki 13: 1 Jehoahaz son of Jehu b king of Israel in AIT
2Ki 13:10 son of Jehoahaz b king of Israel in Samaria, AIT
2Ki 14: 2 He was twenty-five years old when he b king AIT
2Ki 14:23 of Jehoash king of Israel b king in Samaria, AIT
2Ki 15: 2 He was sixteen years old when he b king, and AIT
2Ki 15: 8 son of Jeroboam b king of Israel in Samaria, AIT
2Ki 15:13 son of Jabesh b king in the thirty-ninth AIT
2Ki 15:17 Menahem son of Gadi b king of Israel, and AIT
2Ki 15:23 son of Menahem b king of Israel in Samaria, AIT
2Ki 15:27 son of Remaliah b king of Israel in Samaria AIT
2Ki 15:33 He was twenty-five years old when he b king AIT
2Ki 16: 2 Ahaz was twenty years old when he b king AIT
2Ki 17: 1 Hoshea son of Elah b king of Israel in AIT
2Ki 17:15 worthless idols and themselves b worthless. AIT
2Ki 18: 2 He was twenty-five years old when he b king AIT
2Ki 20: 1 those days Hezekiah b ill and was at the AIT
2Ki 21: 1 was twelve years old when he b king, AIT
2Ki 21:19 was twenty-two years old when he b king, AIT
2Ki 22: 1 Josiah was eight years old when he b king AIT
2Ki 23:31 was twenty-three years old when he b king, AIT
2Ki 23:36 was twenty-five years old when he b king, AIT
2Ki 24: 1 Jehoiakim b his vassal for three years. H2118
2Ki 24: 8 was eighteen years old when he b king, AIT
2Ki 24:18 was twenty-one years old when he b king, AIT
2Ki 25:27 in the year Awel-Marduk b king of Babylon AIT
1Ch 1:10 who b a mighty warrior on H2725+4200+2118
1Ch 7:23 and she b pregnant and gave birth to a son. AIT
1Ch 11: 9 David b more and more powerful H2143+2143+2256+1524
1Ch 11:20 and so he b as famous as the Three. NDT
1Ch 11:21 above the Three and b their commander, H2118
1Ch 14: 3 wives and b the father of more sons and AIT
1Ch 18: 2 they b subject to him and brought H2118
1Ch 18: 6 the Arameans b subject to him and H2118
1Ch 18:13 all the Edomites b subject to David. H2118
1Ch 19:19 peace with David and b subject to him. AIT
2Ch 12:13 He was forty-one years old when he b king AIT
2Ch 13: 1 reign of Jeroboam, Abijah b king of Judah, AIT
2Ch 17:12 Jehoshaphat b more and more powerful H2118
2Ch 20:31 thirty-five years old when he b king of Judah, AIT
2Ch 21: 5 was thirty-two years old when he b king, AIT
2Ch 21:20 was thirty-two years old when he b king, AIT
2Ch 22: 2 was twenty-two years old when he b king, AIT
2Ch 22: 4 after his father's death they b his advisers, H2118
2Ch 24: 1 Joash was seven years old when he b king AIT
2Ch 25: 1 was twenty-five years old when he b king, AIT
2Ch 26: 3 Uzziah was sixteen years old when he b king AIT
2Ch 26:15 he was greatly helped until he b powerful. AIT
2Ch 26:16 But after Uzziah b powerful, his pride led H2621
2Ch 26:19 in his hand ready to burn incense, b angry. AIT
2Ch 27: 1 was twenty-five years old when he b king, AIT
2Ch 27: 8 He was twenty-five years old when he b king AIT
2Ch 28: 1 Ahaz was twenty years old when he b king AIT
2Ch 28:22 trouble King Ahaz b even more unfaithful to AIT
2Ch 29: 1 was twenty-five years old when he b king, AIT
2Ch 32:24 those days Hezekiah b ill and was at the AIT
2Ch 33: 1 was twelve years old when he b king, AIT
2Ch 33:21 was twenty-two years old when he b king, AIT
2Ch 34: 1 Josiah was eight years old when he b king AIT
2Ch 35:25 These b a tradition in Israel and are H5989
2Ch 36: 2 was twenty-three years old when he b king, AIT
2Ch 36: 5 was twenty-five years old when he b king, AIT
2Ch 36: 9 was eighteen years old when he b king, AIT
2Ch 36:11 was twenty-one years old when he b king, AIT
2Ch 36:13 He b stiff-necked and hardened his heart AIT
2Ch 36:14 the people b more and more unfaithful, AIT
2Ch 36:20 and they b servants to him and his H2118
Ne 4: 1 he b angry and was greatly incensed. AIT
Ne 9:16 our ancestors, b arrogant and stiff-necked AIT
Ne 9:17 They b stiff-necked and in their rebellion AIT
Ne 9:29 they b arrogant and disobeyed your AIT
Ne 9:29 b stiff-necked and refused to listen. AIT
Est 1:12 Then the king b furious and burned with AIT
Est 2:21 b angry and conspired to assassinate King AIT
Est 8:17 other nationalities b Jews because fear of H3366
Est 9: 4 b more and more powerful. H2143+2256+1524
Job 26:13 By his breath the skies b fair; his hand NDT
Job 32: 2 b very angry with Job for justifying himself AIT
Ps 83:10 perished at Endor and b like dung on the H2118
Ps 106:36 their idols, which b a snare to them. H2118
Ps 107:17 Some b fools through their rebellious ways NDT
Ps 114: 2 Judah b God's sanctuary, Israel his H2118
Ecc 2: 9 I b greater by far than anyone in Jerusalem AIT
Isa 23: 3 and she b the marketplace of the nations. H2118
Isa 38: 1 those days Hezekiah b ill and was at the AIT
Isa 63: 8 be true to me"; and so he b their Savior. H2118
Isa 63:10 So he turned and b their enemy and he H2200
Jer 2: 5 worthless idols and b worthless themselves. AIT
Jer 44:22 your land b a curse and a desolate waste H2118
Jer 52: 1 was twenty-one years old when he b king, AIT
Jer 52:31 the year Awel-Marduk b king of Babylon, H4895
La 3:14 I b the laughingstock of all my people H2118
La 4:10 who b their food when my people were H2118
Eze 16: 8 the Sovereign LORD, and you b mine. H2118
Eze 16:13 You b very beautiful and rose to be a queen. AIT
Eze 16:15 who passed by and your beauty b his. H2118
Eze 16:47 your ways you soon b more depraved than AIT
Eze 17: 6 it sprouted and b a low, spreading H2118
Eze 17: 6 So it b a vine and produced branches H2118

Eze 19: 3 one of her cubs, and he b a strong lion. H2118
Eze 19: 3 to tear the prey and he b a man-eater. AIT
Eze 19: 6 to tear the prey and he b a man-eater. AIT
Eze 23: 3 They b prostitutes in Egypt, engaging in AIT
Eze 23:10 She b a byword among women, and H2118
Eze 23:19 Yet she b more and more promiscuous as she AIT
Eze 25:12 on Judah and b very guilty by doing so, AIT
Eze 28:17 Your heart b proud on account of your beauty, AIT
Eze 34: 5 they were scattered they b food for all the H2118
Eze 35:15 when the inheritance of Israel b desolate, AIT
Eze 36: 3 side so that you b the possession of the H2118
Da 2:35 all broken to pieces and b like chaff on a A10201
Da 2:35 struck the statue b a huge mountain A10201
Da 4:36 and b even greater than A10650+10339+10323
Da 5: 6 that his legs b weak and his knees were AIT
Da 5: 9 Belshazzar b even more terrified and his face AIT
Da 5:20 But when his heart b arrogant and hardened AIT
Da 8: 4 It did as it pleased and b great. AIT
Da 8: 8 The goat b very great, but at the height of its AIT
Hos 9:10 shameful idol and b as vile as the thing H2118
Hos 13: 1 But he b guilty of Baal worship and died AIT
Hos 13: 6 were satisfied, they b proud; then they forgot AIT
Jnh 4: 1 this seemed very wrong, and he b angry. AIT
Mt 17: 2 his clothes b as white as the light. G1181
Mt 25: 5 and they all b drowsy and fell asleep. AIT
Mt 28: 4 him that they shook and b like dead men. G1181
Mk 9: 3 His clothes b dazzling white, whiter than G1181
Mk 10:41 they b indignant with James and John. G806
Lk 1:24 his wife Elizabeth b pregnant and for five AIT
Lk 1:80 And the child grew and b strong in spirit; and AIT
Lk 2:40 And the child grew and b strong; he was AIT
Lk 6:16 and Judas Iscariot, who b a traitor. G1181
Lk 9:29 his clothes b as bright as a flash of NDT
Lk 9:32 but when they b fully awake, they saw AIT
Lk 13:19 It grew and b a tree, and the birds G1181+1650
Lk 14:21 owner of the house b angry and ordered his AIT
Lk 15:28 "The older brother b angry and refused to go AIT
Lk 18:23 he heard this, he b very sad, because G1181
Lk 20:26 And astonished by his answer, they b silent. AIT
Lk 23:12 That day Herod and Pilate b friends G1181
Jn 1:14 The Word b flesh and made his dwelling G1181
Jn 4:41 because of his words many more b believers. AIT
Ac 3: 7 instantly the man's feet and ankles b strong. AIT
Ac 6: 7 number of priests b obedient to the faith. AIT
Ac 7: 8 And Abraham b the father of Isaac and AIT
Ac 7: 8 Later Isaac b the father of Jacob, and Jacob NDT
Ac 7: 8 Jacob b the father of the twelve NDT
Ac 9:37 About that time she b sick and died, and her AIT
Ac 9:42 This b known all over Joppa, and many G1181
Ac 10:10 He b hungry and wanted something to eat, G1181
Ac 15:12 The whole assembly b silent as they listened AIT
Ac 16:18 Finally Paul b so annoyed that he turned AIT
Ac 17:34 Some of the people b followers of Paul and AIT
Ac 18: 6 But when they opposed Paul and b abusive AIT
Ac 19: 9 But some of them b obstinate; they refused to AIT
Ac 19:17 When this b known to the Jews and G1181
Ac 22: 2 to them in Aramaic, they b very quiet. G4218
Ac 23:10 The dispute b so violent that the G1181
Ro 1:21 their thinking b futile and their foolish AIT
Ro 1:22 they claimed to be wise, they b fools AIT
Ro 4:18 believed and so b the father of many G1181
1Co 4:15 in Christ Jesus I b your father through the AIT
1Co 9:20 To the Jews I b like a Jew, to win the Jews. G1181
1Co 9:20 those under the law I b like one under the NDT
1Co 9:21 not having the law I b like one not having NDT
1Co 9:22 To the weak I b weak, to win the weak. G1181
1Co 13:11 When I b a man, I put the ways of G1181
1Co 15:45 first man Adam b a living being"; G1181+1650
2Co 7: 9 For you b sorrowful as God intended and so AIT
2Co 8: 9 for your sake he b poor, so that you AIT
Gal 4:12 sisters, become like me, for I b like you. NDT
Eph 3: 7 I b a servant of this gospel by the gift of G1181
1Th 1: 6 You b imitators of us and of the Lord, for G1181
1Th 1: 7 And so you b a model to all the believers G1181
1Th 2:14 b imitators of God's churches in Judea G1181
1Ti 2:14 woman who was deceived and b a sinner. G1181
Phm 10 who b my son while I was in chains. G1164S
Heb 1: 4 So he b as much superior to the angels as G1181
Heb 5: 9 he b the source of eternal salvation for all G1181
Heb 7:20 Others b priests without any oath G1639+1181
Heb 7:21 he b a priest with an oath when God NDT
Heb 11: 7 condemned the world and b heir of the G1181
Heb 11:34 and who b powerful in battle and routed G1181
Rev 16: 4 springs of water, and they b blood. G1181
Rev 18:19 ships on the sea b rich through her wealth! AIT

BECAUSE (1664)

Ge 2: 3 b on it he rested from all the work of H3954
Ge 3:10 I was afraid b I was naked; so I hid." H3954
Ge 3:14 said to the serpent, "B you have done this H3954
Ge 3:17 "B you listened to your wife and ate fruit H3954
Ge 3:17 "Cursed is the ground b of you H928+6288
Ge 3:20 b she would become the mother of all the H3954
Ge 5:24 he was no more, b God took him away. H3954
Ge 6:13 is filled with violence b of them. H4946+7156
Ge 7: 1 b I have found you righteous in this H3954
Ge 8: 9 nowhere to perch b there was water over H3954
Ge 8:21 will I curse the ground b of humans, H928+6288
Ge 10:25 b in his time the earth was divided H3954
Ge 11: 9 b there the LORD confused the language of H3954
Ge 11:30 Sarai was childless b she was not able to NDT
Ge 12:10 there for a while b the famine was severe. H3954
Ge 12:13 and my life will be spared b of you." H928+1673
Ge 12:17 his household b of Abram's wife H6584+1821
Ge 19:13 b we are going to destroy this place. H3954
Ge 19:14 b the LORD is about to destroy the city!" H3954
Ge 19:22 b I cannot do anything until you reach it." H3954
Ge 20: 3 as good as dead b of the woman you H6584
Ge 20:11 and they will kill me b of my wife. H6584+1821
Ge 20:18 conceiving b of Abraham's wife H6584+1821
Ge 21:11 Abraham greatly b it concerned his son. H6584
Ge 21:12 b it is through Isaac that your offspring H3954
Ge 21:13 into a nation also, b he is your offspring." H3954
Ge 21:31 b the two men swore an oath there. H3954
Ge 22:12 b you have not withheld from me your son H2256
Ge 22:16 that b you have done this and have H3610+889
Ge 22:18 be blessed, b you have obeyed me." H6813+889
Ge 25:21 on behalf of his wife, b she was childless. H3954
Ge 26: 5 b Abraham obeyed me and did H6813+889
Ge 26: 7 "She is my sister," b he was afraid to say H3954
Ge 26: 7 on account of Rebekah, b she is beautiful." H3954
Ge 26: 9 "B I thought I might lose my life on H3954
Ge 26:12 a hundredfold, b the LORD blessed him. H2256
Ge 26:20 the well Esek, b they disputed with him. H3954
Ge 27:41 against Jacob b of the blessing his H6584
Ge 27:46 with living b of these Hittite H4946+7156
Ge 28:11 stopped for the night b the sun had set. H3954
Ge 29: 2 of sheep lying near it b the flocks were H3954
Ge 29:15 "Just b you are a relative of mine H3954
Ge 29:20 only a few days to him b of his love for her. H928
Ge 29:32 "It is b the LORD has seen my misery. H3954
Ge 29:33 "B the LORD heard that I am not loved H3954
Ge 29:34 b I have borne him three sons. H3954
Ge 30: 6 B of this she named him Dan. H6584
Ge 30:20 with honor, b I have borne him six sons." H3954
Ge 30:27 the LORD has blessed me b of you." H928+1673
Ge 31:30 you have gone off b you longed to return H3954
Ge 31:31 b I thought you would take your daughters H3954
Ge 31:49 also called Mizpah, b he said, "May the H889
Ge 32:28 b you have struggled with God and with H3954
Ge 32:30 "It is b I saw God face to face, and H3954
Ge 32:31 and he was limping b of his hip. H6584
Ge 32:32 b the socket of Jacob's hip was touched H3954
Ge 33:11 I have all I need." And b Jacob insisted H2256
Ge 34: 7 b Shechem had done an outrageous H3954
Ge 34:13 B their sister Dinah had been defiled H889
Ge 34:19 b he was delighted with Jacob's daughter. H3954
Ge 35: 7 b it was there that God revealed himself H3954
Ge 36: 7 them both b of their livestock. H4946+7156
Ge 37: 3 b he had been born to him in his old age H3954
Ge 37: 8 him all the more b of his dream and what H6584
Ge 39: 5 of the Egyptian b of Joseph. H928+1673
Ge 39: 9 me except you, b you are his wife. H928+889
Ge 39:23 b the LORD was with Joseph and gave H928+889
Ge 41:31 b the famine that follows it will be H4946+7156
Ge 41:49 keeping records b it was beyond measure. H3954
Ge 41:51 "It is b God has made me forget all my H3954
Ge 41:52 "It is b God has made me fruitful in the H3954
Ge 41:57 b the famine was severe everywhere. H3954
Ge 42: 4 b he was afraid that harm might come to H3954
Ge 42:21 we are being punished b of our brother. H6584
Ge 43: 5 we will not go down, b the man said to us H3954
Ge 43:18 brought here b of the silver that H6584+1821
Ge 43:25 b they had heard that they were to eat H3954
Ge 43:32 b Egyptians could not eat with Hebrews H3954
Ge 45: 3 b they were terrified at his presence. H3954
Ge 45: 5 b it was to save lives that God sent me H3954
Ge 45:11 b five years of famine are still to come. H3954
Ge 45:20 b the best of all Egypt will be yours. H3954
Ge 47: 4 b the famine is severe in Canaan and H3954
Ge 47:13 in the whole region b the famine was H3954
Ge 47:13 wasted away b of the famine. H4946+7156
Ge 47:20 b the famine was too severe for them. H3954
Ge 47:22 b they received a regular allotment from H3954
Ge 48:10 Israel's eyes were failing b of old age, H4946
Ge 49:24 b of the hand of the Mighty One of Jacob H4946
Ge 49:24 One of Jacob, b of the Shepherd H4946+9004
Ge 49:25 b of your father's God, who helps you H4946
Ge 49:25 who helps you, b of the Almighty, who H907
Ex 1:21 And b the midwives feared God, he gave H3954
Ex 2:23 their cry for help b of their slavery went up H4946
Ex 3: 6 his face, b he was afraid to look at God. H3954
Ex 3: 7 them crying out b of their slave H4946+7156
Ex 6: 1 B of my mighty hand he will let them go H928
Ex 6: 1 b of my mighty hand he will drive them out H928
Ex 6: 9 not listen to him b of their H4946
Ex 7:24 b they could not drink the water of the H3954
Ex 9:11 before Moses b of the boils that H4946+7156
Ex 9:19 b the hail will fall on every person and H2256
Ex 9:32 were not destroyed, b they ripen later.) H3954
Ex 10: 9 b we are to celebrate a festival to the LORD H3954
Ex 12:17 b it was on this very day that I brought H3954
Ex 12:39 was without yeast b they had been driven H3954
Ex 12:42 B the LORD kept vigil that night to bring them NDT
Ex 13: 3 b the LORD brought you out of it with a H3954
Ex 13: 8 'I do this b of what the LORD did for H928+6288
Ex 13:19 of Joseph with him b Joseph had made H3954
Ex 14:11 "Was it b there were no graves in Egypt H4946
Ex 15:23 could not drink its water b it was bitter. H3954
Ex 16: 7 b he has heard your grumbling against him H928
Ex 16: 8 b he has heard your grumbling against him H928
Ex 16:25 "b today is a sabbath to the LORD. H3954
Ex 17: 7 Massah and Meribah b the Israelites H6584
Ex 17: 7 quarreled and b they tested the LORD H6584
Ex 17:14 b I will completely blot out the name of H3954
Ex 17:16 "B hands were lifted up against the H3954
Ex 18:15 "B the people come to me to seek God's H3954
Ex 18:22 load lighter, b they will share it with you. H2256
Ex 19:11 b on that day the LORD will come down on H3954
Ex 19:18 b the LORD descended on it in fire. H4946+7156
Ex 19:23 up Mount Sinai, b you yourself warned us H3954
Ex 21: 8 foreigners, b he has broken faith with her. H928
Ex 22:27 b that cloak is the only covering your H3954
Ex 23: 9 foreigners, b you were foreigners in Egypt. H3954
Ex 23:29 b the land would become desolate and H7153
Ex 23:33 b the worship of their gods will certainly H3954
Ex 29:33 one else may eat them, b they are sacred. H3954
Ex 29:34 It must not be eaten, b it is sacred. H3954
Ex 31:14 " 'Observe the Sabbath, b it is holy to you H3954
Ex 32: 7 "Go down, b your people, whom you H3954
Ex 32:35 with a plague b of what they did with H6584
Ex 33: 3 b you are a stiff-necked people and I H3954
Ex 33:17 b I am pleased with you and I know you H3954
Ex 34:29 his face was radiant b he had spoken with H928
Ex 36: 7 b what they already had was more than H2256
Ex 40:35 the tent of meeting b the cloud had H3954
Lev 5: 1 " 'If anyone sins b they do not speak up H561
Lev 5:11 oil or incense on it, b it is a sin offering. H3954
Lev 10: 7 b the LORD's anointing oil is on you." H3954
Lev 10:13 b it is your share and your sons' share of H3954
Lev 11:13 as unclean and not eat b they are unclean: NDT
Lev 11:44 yourselves and be holy, b I am holy. H3954
Lev 11:45 your God; therefore be holy, b I am holy. H3954
Lev 13:11 isolate them, b they are already unclean. H3954
Lev 13:44 him unclean b of the sore on his head H928
Lev 13:52 spoiled; b the defiling mold is persistent H3954
Lev 14:48 house clean, b the defiling mold is gone. H3954
Lev 15:15 the LORD for the man b of his discharge. H4946
Lev 16:16 the Most Holy Place b of the uncleanness H4946
Lev 16:30 b on this day atonement will be made H3954
Lev 17:14 b the life of every creature is its blood H3954
Lev 17:14 b the life of every creature is its blood H3954
Lev 18:13 b she is your mother's close relative. H3954
Lev 18:24 b this is how the nations that I am going H3954
Lev 19: 2 'Be holy b I, the LORD your God H3954
Lev 19: 8 be held responsible b they have H3954
Lev 19:20 put to death, b she had not been freed. H3954
Lev 20: 7 be holy, b I am the LORD your God. H3954
Lev 20: 9 B they have cursed their father or mother NDT
Lev 20:23 B they did all these things, I abhorred H3954
Lev 20:26 You are to be holy to me b I, the LORD, am H3954
Lev 21: 6 B they present the food offerings to the H3954
Lev 21: 7 husbands, b priests are holy to their God. H3954
Lev 21: 8 b they offer up the food of your God. H3954
Lev 21: 8 Consider them holy, b I the LORD am holy H3954
Lev 21:12 b he has been dedicated by the anointing H3954
Lev 21:23 yet b of his defect, he must not go near H3954
Lev 22:20 b it will not be accepted on your behalf. H3954
Lev 22:25 b they are deformed and have defects. H3954
Lev 23:28 on that day, b it is the Day of Atonement H3954
Lev 24: 9 b it is a most holy part of their perpetual H3954
Lev 25:16 b what is really being sold to you is the H3954
Lev 25:23 b the land is mine and you reside in my H3954
Lev 25:33 b the houses in the towns of the Levites H3954
Lev 25:42 B the Israelites are my servants, whom I H3954
Lev 26:16 seed in vain, b your enemies will eat it. H2256
Lev 26:20 b your soil will not yield its crops H2256
Lev 26:39 the lands of their enemies b of their sins; H928
Lev 26:39 also b of their ancestors' sins they will H928
Lev 26:43 their sins b they rejected H3610+2256+928+3610
Nu 5: 2 is ceremonially unclean b of a dead body. H4200
Nu 5:15 b it is a grain offering for jealousy H3954
Nu 5:30 come over a man b he suspects his wife. H2256
Nu 6: 7 b the symbol of their dedication to God is H3954
Nu 6:11 the Nazirite b they sinned by H4946+889
Nu 6:12 b they became defiled during their period H3954
Nu 7: 9 b they were to carry on their shoulders the H3954
Nu 9: 6 Passover on that day b they were NDT
Nu 9: 7 have become unclean b of a dead body, H4200
Nu 9:10 are unclean b of a dead body or are H4200
Nu 11: 3 b fire from the LORD had burned among H3954
Nu 11:20 it—b you have rejected the LORD H3610+3954
Nu 11:34 b there they buried the people who had H3954
Nu 12: 1 against Moses b of his Cushite wife, H6584+128
Nu 13:24 Valley of Eshkol b of the cluster of H6584+128
Nu 14: 9 of the land, b we will devour them. H3954
Nu 14:24 But b my servant Caleb has a different H6813
Nu 14:42 Do not go up, b the LORD is not with you H3954
Nu 14:43 B you have turned away H3954+6584+4027
Nu 15:26 b all the people were involved in the H3954
Nu 15:31 B they have despised the LORD's word and H3954
Nu 15:34 b it was not clear what should be done to H3954
Nu 16:26 you will be swept away b of all their sins." H928
Nu 16:49 to those who had died b of Korah. H6584+1821
Nu 19:13 B the water of cleansing has not been H3954
Nu 19:20 b they have defiled the sanctuary of the H3954
Nu 20:12 "B you did not trust in me enough to H3610
Nu 20:24 b both of you rebelled against my H6584+889
Nu 21:24 Ammonites, b their border was fortified. H3954
Nu 22: 3 was terrified b there were so many H4946+7156
Nu 22: 3 filled with dread b of the Israelites. H4946+7156
Nu 22: 6 people, b they are too powerful for me. H3954
Nu 22:12 on those people, b they are blessed." H3954
Nu 22:17 b I will reward you handsomely and do H3954
Nu 22:32 here to oppose you b your path is a H3954
Nu 25:13 b he was zealous for the honor of H9393+889

Nu 26:62 the other Israelites **b** they received no H3954
Nu 27: 4 disappear from his clan **b** he had no son? H3954
Nu 30: 5 LORD will release her **b** her father has H3954
Nu 32:11 '**B** they have not followed me H3954
Nu 32:19 **b** our inheritance has come to us on the H3954
Nu 34:14 **b** the families of the tribe of Reuben, the H3954
Dt 1:36 **b** he followed the LORD H3610+889
Dt 1:37 **B of** you the LORD became angry with H928+1673
Dt 1:38 **b** he will lead Israel to inherit it. H3954
Dt 1:42 go up and fight, **b** I will not be with you. H3954
Dt 2:25 and be in anguish **b of** you. H4946+7156
Dt 3:26 But **b of** you the LORD was angry H4200+5100
Dt 4:21 LORD was angry with me **b of** you, H6584+1821
Dt 4:37 **B** he loved your ancestors and H9393+3954
Dt 5: 5 **b** you were afraid of the fire and did not H3954
Dt 7: 7 on you and choose you **b** you were more H4946
Dt 7: 8 But it was **b** the LORD loved you and kept H4946
Dt 9: 4 of this land **b of** my righteousness. H928
Dt 9: 5 It is not **b of** your righteousness or your H928
Dt 9: 6 that it is not **b of** your righteousness that H928
Dt 9:12 **b** your people whom you brought out of H3954
Dt 9:18 water, **b of** all the sin you had committed H6584
Dt 9:25 forty nights **b** the LORD had said he H3954
Dt 9:28 '**B** the LORD was not able to take them into H4946
Dt 9:28 promised them, and **b** he hated them, he H4946
Dt 12: 7 **b** the LORD your God has blessed you. H889
Dt 12:23 not eat the blood, **b** the blood is the life H3954
Dt 12:25 **b** you will be doing what is right in the H3954
Dt 12:28 **b** you will be doing what is good and H3954
Dt 12:31 in their way, **b** in worshiping their gods H3954
Dt 13:10 **b** they tried to turn you away from the LORD H3954
Dt 13:18 **b** you obey the LORD your God by keeping H3954
Dt 14:24 **b** the place where the LORD will choose to H3954
Dt 15: 2 **b** the LORD's time for canceling debts has H3954
Dt 15:10 then **b of** this the LORD your God will H928+1673
Dt 15:16 **b** he loves you and your family and is well H3954
Dt 15:18 **b** their service to you these six years has H3954
Dt 16: 1 **b** in the month of Aviv he brought you out H3954
Dt 16: 3 of affliction, **b** you left Egypt in haste H3954
Dt 18:12 **b of** these same detestable practices H928+1673
Dt 19: 9 **b** you carefully follow all these laws I H3954
Dt 20: 1 be afraid of them, **b** the LORD your God H3954
Dt 20:19 an ax to them, **b** you can eat their fruit. H3954
Dt 21:23 **b** anyone who is hung on a pole is under H3954
Dt 22:19 **b** this man has given an Israelite virgin a H3954
Dt 22:24 the young woman **b** she was in a H6584+1821
Dt 22:24 and the man **b** he violated another H6584+1821
Dt 23: 5 **b** the LORD your God loves you. H3954
Dt 23: 7 **b** you resided as foreigners in their H3954
Dt 23:10 your men is unclean **b** of a nocturnal H4946
Dt 23:18 **b** the LORD your God detests them both. H3954
Dt 23:23 **b** you made your vow freely to the LORD NDT
Dt 24: 1 displeasing to him **b** he finds something H3954
Dt 24: 6 **b** that would be taking a person's H3954
Dt 24:15 **b** they are poor and are counting on it. H3954
Dt 28:20 to sudden ruin **b of** the evil you H4946+7156
Dt 28:38 will harvest little, **b** locusts will devour it. H3954
Dt 28:39 gather the grapes, **b** worms will eat them. H3954
Dt 28:40 not use the oil, **b** the olives will drop off. H3954
Dt 28:41 keep them, **b** they will go into captivity. H3954
Dt 28:45 **b** you did not obey the LORD your God and H3954
Dt 28:47 **B** you did not serve the LORD your H9393+889
Dt 28:53 **B of** the suffering your enemy will inflict on H928
Dt 28:55 be all he has left **b of** the suffering your H928
Dt 28:57 to eat them secretly **b of** the suffering your H928
Dt 28:62 **b** you did not obey the LORD your God. H3954
Dt 28:67 **b of** the terror that will fill your hearts and H4946
Dt 29:25 "It is **b** this people abandoned the H6584
Dt 31: 6 not be afraid or terrified **b of** them, H4946+7156
Dt 31:17 come on us **b** our God is not with H6584+3954
Dt 31:18 my face in that day **b of** all their H6584
Dt 31:21 **b** it will not be forgotten by their H3954
Dt 31:29 will fall on you **b** you will do evil in the H3954
Dt 32:19 rejected them **b** he was angered by H4946
Dt 32:51 This is **b** both of you broke faith with me in H6584
Dt 32:51 Desert of Zin and **b** you did not uphold H6584
Dt 34: 9 the spirit of wisdom **b** Moses had laid his H3954
Jos 1: 6 **b** you will lead these people to inherit the H3954
Jos 2: 3 **b** they have come to spy out the whole H3954
Jos 2: 9 are melting in fear **b of** you. H4946+7156
Jos 2:11 everyone's courage failed **b of** you, H4946+7156
Jos 2:12 **b** I have shown kindness to you. H3954
Jos 2:24 people are melting in fear **b of** us." H4946+7156
Jos 5: 7 still uncircumcised **b** they had not been H3954
Jos 6: 1 securely barred **b of** the Israelites. H4946+7156
Jos 6:17 be spared, **b** she hid the spies we sent. H3954
Jos 6:25 **b** she hid the men Joshua had sent as H3954
Jos 7:12 backs and run **b** they have been made H3954
Jos 9: 9 very distant country **b of** the fame of the H4200
Jos 9:18 **b** the leaders of the assembly had sworn H3954
Jos 9:24 So we feared for our lives **b of** you H4946+7156
Jos 10: 2 **b** Gibeon was an important city H3954
Jos 10: 4 "**b** it has made peace with Joshua and H3954
Jos 10: 6 **b** all the Amorite kings from the hill H3954
Jos 10:42 in one campaign, **b** the LORD, the God of H3954
Jos 11: 6 **b** by this time tomorrow I will hand all of H3954
Jos 14: 9 **b** you have followed the LORD my God H3954
Jos 14:14 ever since, **b** he followed the LORD H3610+889
Jos 17: 1 Gilead and Bashan **b** the Makirites were H3954
Jos 17: 6 **b** the daughters of the tribe of Manasseh H3954
Jos 18: 7 **b** the priestly service of the LORD is their H3954
Jos 19: 9 **b** Judah's portion was more than they H3954
Jos 20: 5 **b** the fugitive killed their neighbor H3954
Jos 21:10 of the Levites, **b** the first lot fell to them): H3954
Jos 22:31 **b** you have not been unfaithful to the LORD H889
Jos 23:10 **b** the LORD your God fights for you H3954
Jos 24:18 too will serve the LORD, **b** he is our God." H3954
Jdg 1:19 **b** they had chariots fitted with iron. H3954
Jdg 1:32 of the land **b** they did not drive them H3954
Jdg 2:13 **b** they forsook him and served Baal and H2256
Jdg 2:18 the LORD relented **b of** their groaning H4946
Jdg 2:20 "**B** this nation has violated the H3610+889
Jdg 3:12 and **b** they did this evil the LORD H3954+6584
Jdg 4: 3 **B** he had nine hundred chariots fitted with H3954
Jdg 4: 9 "But **b of** the course you are taking, the H6584
Jdg 4:17 **b** there was an alliance between Jabin H3954
Jdg 5:23 **b** they did not come to help the LORD H3954
Jdg 6: 2 **B** the power of Midian was so H4946+7156
Jdg 6: 7 cried out to the LORD **b of** Midian, H6584+128
Jdg 6:27 But **b** he was afraid of his family and H3869+889
Jdg 6:30 **b** he has broken down Baal's altar and cut H3954
Jdg 6:32 So **b** Gideon broke down Baal's altar, they H3954
Jdg 7: 9 **b** I am going to give it into your hands. H3954
Jdg 8:20 **b** he was only a boy and was afraid. H3954
Jdg 8:22 **b** you have saved us from the hand of H3954
Jdg 9:18 citizens of Shechem **b** he is related to you H3954
Jdg 9:21 lived there **b** he was afraid **of** his H4946+7156
Jdg 10: 6 **And b** the Israelites forsook the LORD and H2256
Jdg 11: 2 "**b** you are the son of another woman." H3954
Jdg 11:37 with my friends, **b** I will never marry." H6584
Jdg 11:38 the hills and wept **b** she would never H6584
Jdg 12: 4 struck them down **b** the Ephraimites had H3954
Jdg 12: 6 **b** he could not pronounce the word H2256
Jdg 13: 5 be touched by a razor **b** the boy is to be a H3954
Jdg 13: 7 **b** the boy will be a Nazirite of God from H3954
Jdg 14:17 told her, **b** she continued to press him. H3954
Jdg 15: 6 **b** his wife was given to his companion." H3954
Jdg 15:18 **B** he was very thirsty, he cried out to the H2256
Jdg 16:17 "**b** I have been a Nazirite dedicated to H3954
Jdg 18: 1 **b** they had not yet come into an H3954
Jdg 18:28 one to rescue them **b** they lived a long H3954
Jdg 20: 6 **b** they committed this lewd and H3954
Jdg 20:36 **b** they relied on the ambush they had set H3954
Jdg 20:41 **b** they realized that disaster had come on H3954
Jdg 21:15 **b** the LORD had made a gap in the tribes H3954
Jdg 21:22 **b** we did not get wives for them during H3954
Jdg 21:22 breaking your oath **b** you did not give your H3954
Ru 1:13 **b** the LORD's hand has turned against me!" H3954
Ru 1:19 the whole town was stirred **b of** them, and H6584
Ru 1:20 **b** the Almighty has made my life very H3954
Ru 2:22 **b** in someone else's field you H2256+4202
Ru 4: 6 I cannot redeem it **b** I might endanger my H7153
1Sa 1: 5 he gave a double portion **b** he loved her, H3954
1Sa 1: 6 **B** the LORD had closed Hannah's womb H3954
1Sa 1:20 "**B** I asked the LORD for him. H3954
1Sa 3:13 his family forever **b of** the sin he knew H928
1Sa 4:13 **b** his heart feared for the ark of God. H3954
1Sa 4:21 **b of** the capture of the ark of God and the H448
1Sa 5: 7 **b** his hand is heavy on us and on Dagon H3954
1Sa 6: 4 **b** the same plague has struck both you H3954
1Sa 6:19 of them to death **b** they looked into the H3954
1Sa 6:19 The people mourned **b of** the heavy blow H3954
1Sa 7: 7 they were afraid **b of** the Philistines H4946+7156
1Sa 9: 9 **b** the prophet of today used to be called a H3954
1Sa 9:13 he comes, **b** he must bless the sacrifice H3954
1Sa 9:24 **b** it was set aside for you for this occasion H3954
1Sa 12: 7 **b** I am going to confront you with H2256
1Sa 12:21 can they rescue you, **b** they are useless. H3954
1Sa 12:22 **b** the LORD was pleased to make you his H3954
1Sa 13:14 **b** you have not kept the LORD's command." H3954
1Sa 13:19 land of Israel, **b** the Philistines had said H3954
1Sa 14:10 **b** that will be our sign that the LORD has H2256
1Sa 14:24 **b** Saul had bound the people under an H2256
1Sa 14:26 to his mouth, **b** they feared the oath. H3954
1Sa 15:11 **b** he has turned away from me and has H3954
1Sa 15:23 **B** you have rejected the word of the LORD H3610
1Sa 17:36 **b** he has defied the armies of the living H3954
1Sa 17:39 around, **b** he was not used to them. H3954
1Sa 17:39 he said to Saul, "**b** I am not used to them." H3954
1Sa 18: 3 a covenant with David **b** he loved him as H928
1Sa 18:12 **b** the LORD was with David but had H3954
1Sa 18:14 great success, **b** the LORD was with him. H2256
1Sa 18:16 **b** he led them in their campaigns. H3954
1Sa 20: 6 **b** an annual sacrifice is being made there H3954
1Sa 20:17 **b** he loved him as he loved himself. H3954
1Sa 20:18 will be missed, **b** your seat will be empty. H3954
1Sa 20:21 then come, **b**, as surely as the LORD H3954
1Sa 20:22 must go, **b** the LORD has sent you away. H3954
1Sa 20:29 **b** our family is observing a sacrifice in the H3954
1Sa 20:34 **b** he was grieved at his father's shameful H3954
1Sa 21: 8 weapon, **b** the king's mission was urgent." H3954
1Sa 22:17 **b** they too have sided with David. H3954
1Sa 24:10 on my lord, **b** he is the LORD's anointed. H3954
1Sa 25:17 **b** disaster is hanging over our master and H3954
1Sa 25:28 my lord, **b** you fight the LORD's battles H3954
1Sa 26:12 **b** the LORD had put them into a deep H3954
1Sa 26:16 must die, **b** you did not guard your master H889
1Sa 26:21 **B** you considered my life precious H9393+889
1Sa 28:18 **B** you did not obey the LORD or carry H3869+889
1Sa 28:20 filled with fear **b of** Samuel's words. H4946
1Sa 30: 6 greatly distressed **b** the men were talking H3954
1Sa 30: 6 was bitter in spirit **b of** his sons and H6584
1Sa 30:16 reveling **b of** the great amount of H928
1Sa 30:22 "**B** they did not go out with us H3610+889
2Sa 1:10 **b** I knew that after he had fallen he could H3954
2Sa 1:12 of Israel, **b** they had fallen by the sword. H3954
2Sa 2: 6 you the same favor **b** you have done this. H889
2Sa 3: 8 was very angry **b of** what Ish-Bosheth H6584
2Sa 3:11 word to Abner, **b** he was afraid of him. H4946
2Sa 3:22 in Hebron, **b** David had sent him away H3954
2Sa 3:30 murdered Abner **b** he had killed their H6584
2Sa 4: 3 **b** the people of Beeroth fled to Gittaim H2256
2Sa 5:10 **b** the LORD God Almighty was with him. H2256
2Sa 5:24 **b** that will mean the LORD has gone out in H3954
2Sa 6: 6 of the ark of God, **b** the oxen stumbled. H3954
2Sa 6: 7 against Uzzah **b of** his irreverent act; H6584
2Sa 6: 8 David was angry **b** the LORD's wrath had H6584
2Sa 6:12 he has, **b of** the ark of God. H928+6288
2Sa 9:13 **b** he always ate at the king's table H3954
2Sa 12: 6 **b** he did such a thing and had no H6813+889
2Sa 12:10 **b** you despised me and took the H6813+3954
2Sa 12:14 But **b** by doing this you have shown utter H3954
2Sa 12:25 **b** the LORD loved him, he sent H928+6288
2Sa 13:22 **b** he hated Amnon **b** he had H6584+1821
2Sa 14:15 to my lord the king **b** the people have H3954
2Sa 14:22 **b** the king has granted his servant's request H889
2Sa 14:26 hair once a year **b** it became too heavy H3954
2Sa 16: 3 in Jerusalem, **b** he thinks, 'Today the H3954
2Sa 16: 8 have come to ruin **b** you are a murderer!" H3954
2Sa 16:10 If he is cursing **b** the LORD said to him H3954
2Sa 18:20 **b** the king's son is dead." H3954+6584+4027
2Sa 19: 2 **b** on that day the troops heard it said H3954
2Sa 19:42 "We did this **b** the king is closely related H3954
2Sa 21: 1 it is **b** he put the Gibeonites to H6584+889
2Sa 21: 7 **b of** the oath before the LORD between H6584
2Sa 22: 8 they trembled **b** he was angry. H3954
2Sa 22:20 he rescued me **b** he delighted in me. H3954
1Ki 2:26 **b** you carried the ark of the Sovereign LORD H3954
1Ki 2:32 **b** without my father David knowing it he H889
1Ki 3: 2 **b** a temple had not yet been built for the H3954
1Ki 3: 6 **b** he was faithful to you and H3869+889
1Ki 3:19 this woman's son died **b** she lay on him. H889
1Ki 3:28 **b** they saw that he had wisdom from God H3954
1Ki 5: 1 **b** he had always been on friendly terms H3954
1Ki 5: 3 "You know that **b of** the wars H4946+7156
1Ki 7:47 things unweighed, **b** there were so many H4946
1Ki 8:11 perform their service **b of** the cloud, H4946+7156
1Ki 8:33 defeated by an enemy **b** they have sinned H889
1Ki 8:35 there is no rain **b** your people have H3954
1Ki 8:35 turn from their sin **b** you have afflicted H3954
1Ki 8:41 a distant land **b of** your name— H4200+5100
1Ki 8:64 **b** the bronze altar that stood before the H3954
1Ki 9: 9 '**B** they have forsaken the LORD their H6584+889
1Ki 9:11 **b** Hiram had supplied him with all the cedar NDT
1Ki 10: 9 **B of** the LORD's eternal love for Israel, he H928
1Ki 10:21 **b** silver was considered of little value in NDT
1Ki 11: 2 **b** they will **surely** turn your hearts after their H434
1Ki 11: 9 angry with Solomon **b** his heart had H3954
1Ki 11:33 I will do this **b** they have forsaken me H3610+889
1Ki 11:39 David's descendants **b of** this, H4200+5100
1Ki 14: 4 not see; his sight was gone **b of** his age. H4946
1Ki 14:10 " '**B of this**, I am going to bring H4200+4027
1Ki 14:13 **b** he is the only one in the house of H3610
1Ki 14:15 **b** they aroused the LORD's anger by H3610+889
1Ki 14:16 give Israel up **b of** the sins H928+1673
1Ki 15:13 **b** she had made a repulsive image for the H889
1Ki 15:30 This happened **b of** the sins Jeroboam H6584
1Ki 15:30 **b** he aroused the anger of the LORD H928
1Ki 16: 7 **b of** all the evil he had done in the eyes H6584
1Ki 16: 7 also **b** he destroyed it. H6584+889
1Ki 16:13 **b of** all the sins Baasha and his son Elah H448
1Ki 16:19 **b of** the sins he had committed, doing evil H6584
1Ki 17: 7 the brook dried up **b** there had been no H3954
1Ki 20:22 **b** next spring the king of Aram will attack H3954
1Ki 20:28 '**B** the Arameans think the LORD is a H3610+889
1Ki 20:36 "**B** you have not obeyed the LORD H3610+889
1Ki 21: 4 sullen and angry **b** Naboth the Jezreelite H6584
1Ki 21: 6 "**B** I said to Naboth the Jezreelite H3954
1Ki 21:20 "**b** you have sold yourself to do evil in the H3610
1Ki 21:22 **b** you have aroused my anger and have H448
1Ki 21:29 **B** he has humbled himself, I will H3610+3954
1Ki 22: 8 I hate him **b** he never prophesies H3954
1Ki 22:52 **b** he followed the ways of his father and H2256
2Ki 1: 3 'Is it **b** there is no God in Israel that you H4946
2Ki 1: 6 Is it **b** there is no God in Israel that you H4946
2Ki 1:16 Is it **b** there is no God in Israel for you to H4946
2Ki 1:16 **B** you have done this, you will never H3610+889
2Ki 1:17 **B** Ahaziah had no son, Joram succeeded H3954
2Ki 3:13 "**b** it was the LORD who called us three H3954
2Ki 5: 1 **b** through him the LORD had given victory H3954
2Ki 6: 9 **b** the Arameans are going down there." H3954
2Ki 8: 1 **b** the LORD has decreed a famine in the H3954
2Ki 8:12 "**B** I know the harm you will do to the H3954
2Ki 8:29 son of Ahab, **b** he had been wounded. H3954
2Ki 9:16 **b** Joram was resting there and Ahaziah H3954
2Ki 10:19 **b** I am going to hold a great sacrifice for H3954
2Ki 10:30 "**B** you have done well in H3610+889
2Ki 11:20 **b** Athaliah had been slain with the sword H2256
2Ki 12:15 **b** they acted with complete honesty. H3954
2Ki 13:23 concern for them **b of** his covenant H4200+5100
2Ki 15:16 **b** they refused to open their gates. H3954
2Ki 17: 7 All this took place **b** the Israelites had H3954
2Ki 17:26 **b** the people do not know what he H3869+889
2Ki 18:12 This happened **b** they had not H6584+889
2Ki 18:36 in reply, **b** the king had commanded H3954
2Ki 19:28 **B** you rage against me and because your H3610

2Ki 19:28 rage against me and **b** your insolence has NDT
2Ki 20: 1 house in order, **b** you are going to die H3954
2Ki 20:12 **b** he had heard of Hezekiah's illness. H3954
2Ki 22: 7 **b** they are honest in their dealings." H3954
2Ki 22:13 burns against us **b** those who have H6584+889
2Ki 22:17 **B** they have forsaken me and burned H9393+889
2Ki 22:19 **B** your heart was responsive and you H3610
2Ki 22:19 **b** you tore your robes and wept in my NDT
2Ki 23:26 against Judah **b of** all that Manasseh H6584
2Ki 24: 3 from his presence **b of** the sins of H928
2Ki 24: 7 **b** the king of Babylon had taken all his H3954
2Ki 24:20 It was **b of** the LORD's anger that all this H6584
1Ch 1:19 **b** in his time the earth was divided H3954
1Ch 4:14 It was called this **b** its people were skilled H3954
1Ch 4:41 **b** there was pasture for their flocks. H3954
1Ch 5: 9 **b** their livestock had increased in Gilead. H3954
1Ch 5:20 **b** they cried out to him during the battle. H3954
1Ch 5:20 their prayers, **b** they trusted in him. H3954
1Ch 5:22 others fell slain, **b** the battle was God's. H3954
1Ch 6:54 **b** the first lot was for them) H3954
1Ch 7:23 **b** there had been misfortune in his family. H3954
1Ch 9: 1 captive to Babylon **b of** their unfaithfulness. H928
1Ch 9:27 the house of God, **b** they had to guard it H3954
1Ch 9:33 from other duties **b** they were responsible H3954
1Ch 10:13 Saul died **b** he was unfaithful to the LORD H928
1Ch 11: 9 **b** the LORD Almighty was with him. H2256
1Ch 11:19 **B** they risked their lives to bring it back H3954
1Ch 12:19 his men did not help the Philistines **b**, H3954
1Ch 13: 4 **b** it seemed right to all the people. H3954
1Ch 13: 9 to steady the ark, **b** the oxen stumbled. H3954
1Ch 13:10 he struck him down **b** he had put his H6584+889
1Ch 13:11 David was angry **b** the LORD's wrath had H3954
1Ch 14:15 **b that will mean** God has gone out in H3954
1Ch 15: 2 **b** the LORD chose them to carry the ark of H3954
1Ch 15:13 It was **b** you, the Levites, did H3954+4200+4537
1Ch 15:22 his responsibility **b** he was skillful at it. H3954
1Ch 15:26 **B** God had helped the Levites who were H928
1Ch 19: 2 **b** his father showed kindness to me." H3954
1Ch 21: 6 **b** the king's command was repulsive to H3954
1Ch 21:30 **b** he was afraid of the sword of the angel H3954
1Ch 22: 8 **b** you have shed much blood on the earth H3954
1Ch 26: 6 their father's family **b** they were very H3954
1Ch 27:23 **b** the LORD had promised to make Israel as H3954
1Ch 28: 3 **b** you are a warrior and have shed blood. H3954
1Ch 29: 1 **b** this palatial structure is not for man H3954
2Ch 1: 4 **b** he had pitched a tent for it in Jerusalem H3954
2Ch 2: 5 **b** our God is greater than all other gods. H3954
2Ch 2: 9 **b** the temple I build must be large and H3954
2Ch 2:11 "**B** the LORD loves his people, he has made H928
2Ch 5:14 perform their service **b of** the cloud, H4946+7156
2Ch 6:24 defeated by an enemy **b** they have sinned H3954
2Ch 6:26 there is no rain **b** your people have H3954
2Ch 6:26 turn from their sin **b** you have afflicted H3954
2Ch 6:32 a distant land **b of** your great name H4200+5100
2Ch 7: 2 temple of the LORD **b** the glory of the LORD H3954
2Ch 7: 7 **b** the bronze altar he had made could not H3954
2Ch 7:22 '**B** they have forsaken the LORD H6584+889
2Ch 8:11 **b** the places the ark of the LORD has H3954
2Ch 8:14 **b** this was what David the man of God H3954
2Ch 9: 8 **B of** the love of your God for Israel and his H928
2Ch 9:20 **b** silver was considered of little value in NDT
2Ch 11:14 **b** Jeroboam and his sons had rejected H3954
2Ch 12: 2 **B** they had been unfaithful to the LORD H3954
2Ch 12:12 **B** Rehoboam humbled himself, the LORD's H928
2Ch 12:14 He did evil **b** he had not set his heart on H3954
2Ch 13:18 Judah were victorious **b** they relied on the H3954
2Ch 14: 7 **b** we have sought the LORD our God H3954
2Ch 15: 6 **b** God was troubling them with every kind H3954
2Ch 15:15 about the oath **b** they had sworn it H3954
2Ch 15:16 **b** she had made a repulsive image for the H889
2Ch 16: 7 "**B** you relied on the king of Aram H6584+4027
2Ch 16:10 Asa was angry with the seer **b of** this; he H6584
2Ch 17: 3 with Jehoshaphat **b** he followed the ways H3954
2Ch 18: 7 I hate him **b** he never prophesies H3954
2Ch 19: 2 who hate the LORD? **B of** this, the wrath of H928
2Ch 19: 6 **b** you are not judging for mere mortals H3954
2Ch 20:15 discouraged **b of** this vast army. H4946+7156
2Ch 20:37 "**B** you have made an alliance with H3869
2Ch 21: 3 kingdom to Jehoram **b** he was his H3954
2Ch 21: 7 **b of** the covenant the LORD had H4200+5100
2Ch 21:10 **b** Jehoram had forsaken the LORD H3954
2Ch 21:19 his bowels came out **b of** the disease H6640
2Ch 22: 6 Joram son of Ahab **b** he had been H3954
2Ch 22:11 **B** Jehosheba, the daughter of King H2256
2Ch 23: 6 they may enter **b** they are consecrated H3954
2Ch 23:21 **b** Athaliah had been slain with the sword. H2256
2Ch 24:16 **b of** the good he had done in Israel for H3954
2Ch 24:18 **B of** their guilt, God's anger came on H928
2Ch 24:20 **B** you have forsaken the LORD, he has H3954
2Ch 24:24 **B** Judah had forsaken the LORD, the God of H3954
2Ch 25:16 **b** you have done this and have not H3954
2Ch 25:20 Jehoash, **b** they sought the gods of Edom. H3954
2Ch 26: 8 of Egypt, **b** he had become very powerful. H3954
2Ch 26:10 **b** he had much livestock in the foothills H3954
2Ch 26:20 to leave, **b** the LORD had afflicted him. H3954
2Ch 27: 6 Jotham grew powerful **b** he walked H3954
2Ch 28: 6 in Judah—**b** Judah had forsaken the LORD H928
2Ch 28: 9 He said to them, "**B** the LORD, the God of H928
2Ch 28:19 humbled Judah **b of** Ahaz king of H928+6288
2Ch 29:24 **b** the king had ordered the burnt offering H3954
2Ch 29:36 his people, **b** it was done so quickly. H3954
2Ch 30: 3 at the regular time **b** not enough priests H3954
2Ch 31:10 **b** the LORD has blessed his people H3954
2Ch 32: 7 discouraged **b of** the king of H4946+7156
2Ch 34:21 poured out on us **b** those who have H6584+889
2Ch 34:25 **B** they have forsaken me and burned H9393+889
2Ch 34:27 **B** your heart was responsive and you H3610
2Ch 34:27 **b** you humbled yourself before me and NDT
2Ch 35:14 for the priests, **b** the priests, the H3954
2Ch 35:15 **b** their fellow Levites made the H3954
2Ch 36:15 **b** he had pity on his people and on his H3954
Ezr 3:11 **b** the foundation of the house of the LORD H6584
Ezr 3:13 **b** the people made so much noise. H3954
Ezr 4: 2 "Let us help you build **b**, like you, H3954
Ezr 5:12 But **b** our ancestors angered the A10427+10168
Ezr 6:13 **b of** the decree King A10378+10619+10168
Ezr 6:22 **b** the LORD had filled them with joy by H3954
Ezr 7:28 **B** the hand of the LORD my God was on me H3869
Ezr 8:18 **B** the gracious hand of our God was on us H3869
Ezr 8:22 on the road, **b** we had told the king H3954
Ezr 9: 4 gathered around me **b of** this H6584
Ezr 9: 6 **b** our sins are higher than our heads and H3954
Ezr 9: 7 **B of** our sins, we and our kings and our H928
Ezr 9:15 though **b of** it not one of us can stand in H6584
Ezr 10: 6 **b** he continued to mourn over the H3954
Ezr 10: 9 by the occasion and **b of** the rain. H4946
Ezr 10:13 **b** we have sinned greatly in this thing. H3954
Ne 2: 8 And **b** the gracious hand of my God was H3869
Ne 2:16 **b** as yet I had said nothing to the Jews H2256
Ne 5: 5 **b** our fields and our vineyards belong to H2256
Ne 5: 8 **b** they could find nothing to say. H2256
Ne 5:18 **b** the demands were heavy on these H3954
Ne 6:10 **b** men are coming to kill you H3954
Ne 6:12 against me **b** Tobiah and Sanballat H2256
Ne 6:14 my God, **b of** what they have done H3869
Ne 6:16 **b** they realized that this work had been H2256
Ne 7: 2 **b** he was a man of integrity and feared H3954
Ne 8: 5 people could see him **b** he was standing H3954
Ne 8:12 **b** they now understood the words that had H3954
Ne 9: 8 kept your promise **b** you are righteous. H3954
Ne 9:19 "**B of** your great compassion you did not H928
Ne 9:37 **B of** our sins, its abundant harvest goes to H928
Ne 12:43 rejoicing **b** God had given them great joy. H3954
Ne 13: 2 **b** they had not met the Israelites with food H3954
Ne 13:13 **b** they were considered trustworthy. H3954
Ne 13:26 Was it not **b of** marriages like these that H6584
Ne 13:29 **b** they defiled the priestly office and the H6584
Est 2: 7 he had brought up **b** she had neither H3954
Est 2:10 **b** Mordecai had forbidden her to do so. H3954
Est 4: 2 **b** no one clothed in sackcloth was H3954
Est 4:13 "Do not think that **b** you are in the king's NDT
Est 7: 4 **b** no such distress would justify disturbing H3954
Est 8: 7 "**B** Haman attacked the Jews H6584+889
Est 8:17 became Jews **b** fear of the Jews had H3954
Est 9: 2 **b** the people of all the other nationalities H3954
Est 9: 3 **b** fear of Mordecai had seized them. H3954
Est 9:26 **B of** everything written in this letter H6584+4027
Est 9:26 this letter and **b of** what they had H6584+3970
Est 10: 3 **b** he worked for the good of his people and NDT
Job 2:13 **b** they saw how great his suffering was. H3954
Job 6:20 are distressed, **b** they had been confident H3954
Job 11:18 You will be secure, **b** there is hope; you H3954
Job 15:25 **b** he shakes his fist at God and vaunts H3954
Job 20: 2 prompt me to answer **b** I am greatly H928+6288
Job 29:12 **b** I rescued the poor who cried for help H3954
Job 31:34 **b** I so feared the crowd and so dreaded H3954
Job 32: 1 **b** he was righteous in his own eyes. H3954
Job 32: 3 **b** they had found no way to refute H6584+889
Job 32: 4 speaking to Job **b** they were older than H3954
Job 34:25 **B** he takes note of their deeds, he H4200+4027
Job 34:27 **b** they turned from following him H6584+4027
Job 35:12 people cry out **b of** the arrogance H4946+7156
Job 37:19 draw up our case **b of** our darkness. H4946+7156
Job 42: 7 **b** you have not spoken the truth about me, H3954
Ps 3: 5 I wake again, **b** the LORD sustains me. H3954
Ps 5: 8 righteousness **b of** my enemies— H4200+5100
Ps 6: 4 save me **b of** your unfailing love. H4200+5100
Ps 6: 7 weak with sorrow; they fail **b of** all my foes. H928
Ps 7:17 thanks to the LORD **b of** his righteousness; H3869
Ps 12: 5 "**B** the poor are plundered and the needy H4946
Ps 16:10 **b** you will not abandon me to the realm H3954
Ps 18: 7 they trembled **b** he was angry. H3954
Ps 18:19 he rescued me **b** he delighted in me. H3954
Ps 25:21 uprightness protect me, **b** my hope, LORD, H3954
Ps 27:11 a straight path **b of** my oppressors. H4200+5100
Ps 28: 5 **B** they have no regard for the deeds of the H3954
Ps 31:10 my strength fails **b of** my affliction, and my H928
Ps 31:11 **B of** all my enemies, I am the utter H4946
Ps 37: 1 Do not fret **b of** those who are evil or be H928
Ps 37:40 saves them, **b** they take refuge in him. H3954
Ps 38: 3 **B of** your wrath there is no health H4946+7156
Ps 38: 3 in my bones **b of** my sin. H4946+7156
Ps 38: 5 are loathsome **b of** my sinful folly. H4946+7156
Ps 38:11 avoid me **b of** my wounds; H4946+5584
Ps 41:12 **B of** my integrity you uphold me and set H928
Ps 44:16 revile me, **b of** the enemy, who H4946+7156
Ps 44:26 rescue us **b of** your unfailing love. H4200+5100
Ps 48:11 are glad **b of** your judgments H4200+5100
Ps 55: 3 **b of** what my enemy is saying, because of H4946
Ps 55: 3 **b of** the threats of the wicked H4946+7156
Ps 55:19 humble them, **b** they have no fear of God. H2256
Ps 56: 7 **B of** their wickedness do not let them H6584
Ps 63: 3 **B** your love is better than life, my lips will H3954
Ps 63: 7 **B** you are my help, I sing in the shadow of H3954
Ps 68:29 **B of** your temple at Jerusalem kings will H4946
Ps 69: 6 who hope in you not be disgraced **b of** me; H928
Ps 69: 6 who seek you not be put to shame **b of** me. H928
Ps 69:18 deliver me **b of** my foes. H4200+5100
Ps 70: 3 turn back **b of** their shame. H6584+6813
Ps 74:20 **b** haunts of violence fill the dark places of H3954
Ps 86: 7 in distress, I call to you, **b** you answer me. H3954
Ps 86:16 **b** I serve you just as my mother did. NDT
Ps 91:14 "**B** he loves me," says the LORD, "I will H3954
Ps 97: 8 are glad **b of** your judgments H4200+5100
Ps 102:10 **b of** your great wrath, for you have H4946+7156
Ps 105:38 **b** dread of Israel had fallen on them. H3954
Ps 106:32 trouble came to Moses **b of** them; H928+6288
Ps 107:11 *b they* **rebelled** *against* God's commands AIT
Ps 107:17 suffered affliction **b of** their iniquities. H4946
Ps 107:34 **b of** the wickedness of those who lived H4946
Ps 115: 1 the glory, **b of** your love and faithfulness. H6584
Ps 116: 2 **B** he turned his ear to me, I will call on H3954
Ps 119:47 I delight in your commands **b** I love them. H889
Ps 119:53 Indignation grips me **b of** the wicked, who H4946
Ps 119:127 **B** I love your commands more than H6584+4027
Ps 119:128 and **b** I consider all your precepts H6584+4027
Ps 139:14 I praise you **b** I am fearfully and H6584+3954
Ps 142: 7 gather about me **b of** your goodness to H3954
Pr 3:12 **b** the LORD disciplines those he loves, as a H3954
Pr 21:25 death of him, **b** his hands refuse to work. H3954
Pr 22:22 exploit the poor **b** they are poor and do H3954
Pr 24:19 Do not fret **b of** evildoers or be envious of H928
Ecc 2:17 **b** the work that is done under the sun was H3954
Ecc 2:18 **b** I must leave them to the one who H8611
Ecc 3:22 than to enjoy their work, **b** that is their lot. H3954
Ecc 4: 9 **b** they have a good return for their labor: H889
Ecc 5:20 **b** God keeps them occupied with H3954
Ecc 7: 3 **b** a sad face is good for the heart. H3954
Ecc 8: 2 **b** you took an oath before God. H6584+1826
Ecc 8:13 Yet **b** the wicked do not fear God, it will not H889
Ecc 8:15 **b** there is nothing better for a person under H889
Ecc 10:18 the rafters sag; **b of** idle hands, the house H928
Ecc 10:20 **b** a bird in the sky may carry your words H3954
Ecc 12: 3 when the grinders cease **b** they are few H3954
SS 1: 6 Do not stare at me **b** I am dark, because I H8611
SS 1: 6 I am dark, **b** I am darkened by the sun. H8611
Isa 1:29 will be ashamed **b of** the sacred oaks in H4946
Isa 1:29 will be disgraced **b of** the gardens that H4946
Isa 7: 4 Do not lose heart **b of** these two H4946
Isa 7: 4 **b of** the fierce anger of Rezin and Aram H928
Isa 7:22 And **b of** the abundance of the milk they H4946
Isa 8: 6 "**B** this people has rejected the H3610+3954
Isa 10:13 by my wisdom, **b** I have understanding. H3954
Isa 10:27 will be broken **b** you have grown so H4946+7156
Isa 13: 7 **B of this**, all hands will go limp H6584+4027
Isa 17: 9 which they left **b of** the Israelites H4946+7156
Isa 19:17 **b of** what the LORD Almighty is H4946+7156
Isa 19:20 out to the LORD **b of** their oppressors H4946+7156
Isa 26: 3 minds are steadfast, **b** they trust in you. H3954
Isa 30: 5 be put to shame **b of** a people useless to H6584
Isa 30:12 "**B** you have rejected this message, relied H3610
Isa 31: 9 Their stronghold will fall **b of** terror; at the H4946
Isa 36:21 in reply, **b** the king had commanded H3954
Isa 37:21 **B** you have prayed to me concerning H889
Isa 37:29 **B** you rage against me and because your H3610
Isa 37:29 rage against me and **b** your insolence has NDT
Isa 38: 1 house in order, **b** you are going to die H3954
Isa 38:15 all my years **b of** this anguish of my H6584
Isa 39: 1 **b** he had heard of his illness and recovery. H2256
Isa 40: 7 **b** the breath of the LORD blows on them. H3954
Isa 40:26 **B of** his great power and mighty strength H4946
Isa 43: 4 in my sight, and **b** I love you, I will give NDT
Isa 43:20 **b** I provide water in the wilderness and H3954
Isa 49: 7 and bow down, **b of** the LORD, who H4200+5100
Isa 50: 1 **B of** your sins you were sold; because of H928
Isa 50: 1 **b of** your transgressions your mother was H928
Isa 50: 7 **B** the Sovereign LORD helps me, H6584+4027
Isa 51:13 every day **b of** the wrath of the H4946+7156
Isa 52:15 kings will shut their mouths **b of** him. H6584
Isa 53:12 **b** he poured out his life unto death H9393+889
Isa 54: 1 **b** more are the children of the desolate H3954
Isa 55: 5 to you, **b of** the LORD your God H4200+5100
Isa 57:11 Is it not **b** I have long been silent that you NDT
Isa 57:16 would faint away **b of** me— H4946+4200+7156
Isa 61: 1 **b** the LORD has anointed me to proclaim H3610
Isa 65: 7 "**B** they burned sacrifices on the mountains H889
Isa 66: 5 and exclude you **b of** my name H4200+5100
Isa 66:18 **b of** what they have planned and done NDT
Jer 1:16 on my people **b of** their wickedness in H6584
Jer 2:35 But I will pass judgment on you **b** you say, H6584
Jer 3: 8 and sent her away **b of** all her H6584+128
Jer 3: 9 **B** Israel's immorality mattered so little to H2256
Jer 3:21 **b** they have perverted their ways and have H3954
Jer 4: 4 burn like fire **b of** the evil you have H4946+7156
Jer 4:17 **b** she has rebelled against me H3954
Jer 4:28 **b** I have spoken and will not relent H6584+3954
Jer 5:14 "**B** the people have spoken these words, H3610
Jer 6:19 **b** they have not listened to my words and H3954
Jer 6:30 **b** the LORD has rejected them. H3954
Jer 7:12 what I did to it **b of** the wickedness H4946+7156
Jer 8:14 to drink, **b** we have sinned against him. H3954
Jer 9: 7 else can I do **b of** the sin of my H4946+7156
Jer 9:13 "It is **b** they have forsaken my law H6584
Jer 9:19 must leave our land **b** our houses are in H3954
Jer 10: 5 they must be carried **b** they cannot walk. H3954
Jer 10:19 Woe to me **b of** my injury! My wound is H6584

Jer 11:14 **b** I will not listen when they call to me in H3954
Jer 11:17 **b** the people of both Israel and H928+1673
Jer 11:18 **B** the LORD revealed their plot to me, H2256
Jer 11:23 **b** I will bring disaster on the people of H3954
Jer 12: 4 **B** those who live in it are wicked, the H4946
Jer 12:11 will be laid waste **b** there is no one who H3954
Jer 12:13 of their harvest **b of** the LORD's fierce H4946
Jer 13:17 I will weep in secret **b of** your pride; H4946+7156
Jer 13:17 **b** the LORD's flock will be taken captive. H3954
Jer 13:22 it is **b of** your many sins that your skirts H928
Jer 13:25 "**b** you have forgotten me and trusted in H889
Jer 14: 4 The ground is cracked **b** there is no rain in H3954
Jer 14: 5 her newborn fawn **b** there is no grass. H3954
Jer 14:16 of Jerusalem **b of** the famine and H4946+7156
Jer 15: 4 of the earth **b of** what Manasseh son H928+1673
Jer 15:13 **b of** all your sins throughout your country. H928
Jer 15:17 I sat alone **b** your hand was on me H4946+7156
Jer 16: 5 sympathy, **b** I have withdrawn my blessing H3954
Jer 16:11 'It is **b** your ancestors forsook me H6584+889
Jer 16:18 **b** they have defiled my land with the H6584
Jer 17: 3 **b of** sin throughout your country. H928
Jer 17:13 written in the dust **b** they have forsaken H3954
Jer 19: 8 will scoff **b of** all its wounds. H6584
Jer 19: 9 one another's flesh **b** their enemies will H928
Jer 19:15 **b** they were stiff-necked and would not H3954
Jer 21: 2 of the LORD for us **b** Nebuchadnezzar king H3954
Jer 21:12 burn like fire **b of** the evil you have H4946+7156
Jer 22: 9 '**B** they have forsaken the covenant H6584+889
Jer 22:10 **b** he will never return nor see his native H3954
Jer 22:22 disgraced **b of** all your wickedness. H4946
Jer 23: 2 "**B** you have scattered my flock and driven NDT
Jer 23: 9 **b of** the LORD and his holy words. H4946+7156
Jer 23:10 **b of** the curse the land lies H3954+4946+7156
Jer 23:15 **b** from the prophets of Jerusalem H3954
Jer 23:36 **b** each one's word becomes their own H3954
Jer 25: 8 "**B** you have not listened to my H3610+889
Jer 25:16 and go mad **b of** the sword I will H4946+7156
Jer 25:27 to rise no more **b of** the sword I will H4946+7156
Jer 25:37 be laid waste **b of** the fierce anger H4946+7156
Jer 25:38 become desolate **b of** the sword of H4946+7156
Jer 25:38 the oppressor and **b of** the LORD's H4946+7156
Jer 26: 3 I was planning **b of** the evil they H4946+7156
Jer 26:11 sentenced to death **b** he has prophesied H3954
Jer 28:16 **b** you have preached rebellion against H3954
Jer 29: 7 to the LORD for it, **b** if it prospers, you too H3954
Jer 29:22 **B of** them, all the exiles from Judah who H4946
Jer 29:31 **B** Shemaiah has prophesied to you H3610+889
Jer 29:32 **b** he has preached rebellion against me. H3954
Jer 30:14 **b** your guilt is so great and your sins so H6584
Jer 30:15 **B of** your great guilt and many sins I have H6584
Jer 30:17 the LORD, '**b** you are called an outcast H3954
Jer 31: 9 will not stumble, **b** I am Israel's father H3954
Jer 31:15 to be comforted, **b** they are no more." H3954
Jer 31:18 I will return, **b** you are the LORD my God. H3954
Jer 31:19 humiliated **b** I bore the disgrace of H3954
Jer 31:32 out of Egypt, **b** they broke my covenant H889
Jer 31:34 'Know the LORD,' **b** they will all know me H3954
Jer 31:37 of Israel **b of** all they have done, H6584
Jer 32: 7 **b** as nearest relative it is your right and H3954
Jer 32:24 **B of** the sword, famine and plague H4946+7156
Jer 32:44 of the Negev, **b** I will restore their fortunes H3954
Jer 33: 5 face from this city **b of** all its wickedness. H6584
Jer 35: 6 **b** our forefather Jehonadab son of Rekab H3954
Jer 35:14 **b** they obey their forefather's command. H3954
Jer 36:31 against them, **b** they have not listened. H2256
Jer 37:11 from Jerusalem **b of** Pharaoh's H4946+7156
Jer 39:18 escape with your life, **b** you trust in me H3954
Jer 40: 3 All this happened **b** you people sinned NDT
Jer 41:18 were afraid of them **b** Ishmael son of H3954
Jer 44: 3 **b of** the evil they have done. H4946+7156
Jer 44:23 **B** you have burned incense and H4946+7156
Jer 48: 8 plateau destroyed, **b** the LORD has spoken. H889
Jer 48:42 as a nation **b** she defied the LORD. H3954
Jer 49:17 will scoff **b of** all its wounds. H6584
Jer 50:11 "**B** you rejoice and are glad, you who H3954
Jer 50:11 **b** you frolic like a heifer threshing grain H3954
Jer 50:13 **B of** the LORD's anger she will not be H4946
Jer 50:13 they will scoff **b of** all her wounds. H6584
Jer 50:16 **B of** the sword of the oppressor let H4946+7156
Jer 50:24 found and captured **b** you opposed the H3954
Jer 51: 6 Do not be destroyed **b of** her sins. It is time H928
Jer 51:11 **b** his purpose is to destroy Babylon. H3954
Jer 51:49 "Babylon must fall **b of** Israel's slain, just as NDT
Jer 51:49 in all the earth have fallen **b of** Babylon. H4200
Jer 51:51 **b** foreigners have entered the holy places H3954
Jer 51:64 to rise no more **b of** the disaster I H4946+7156
Jer 52: 3 It was **b of** the LORD's anger that all this H6584
La 1: 5 has brought her grief **b of** her many sins. H6584
La 1:16 children are destitute **b** the enemy has H3954
La 1:22 you have dealt with me **b of** all my sins. H6584
La 2:11 out on the ground **b** my people are H6584
La 2:11 **b** children and infants faint in the streets of H928
La 3:22 **B of** the LORD's great love we are not NDT
La 3:48 flow from my eyes **b** my people are H6584
La 3:51 grief to my soul **b of** all the women of my H4946
La 4: 4 **B of** thirst the infant's tongue sticks to the H928
La 4:13 But it happened **b of** the sins of her H4946
La 5: 9 of our lives **b of** the sword in the H4946+7156
La 5:17 **B of** this our hearts are faint, because of H6584
La 5:17 **b of** these things our eyes grow dim H6584
Eze 1:20 **b** the spirit of the living creatures was in H3954
Eze 1:21 **b** the spirit of the living creatures was in H3954
Eze 3: 7 to listen to you **b** they are not willing to H3954
Eze 3:21 they will surely live **b** they took warning H3954
Eze 4:17 other and will waste away **b of** their sin. H928
Eze 5: 9 **B of** all your detestable idols, I will do to H3610
Eze 5:11 **b** you have defiled my H561+4202+3610
Eze 6:11 **b of** all the wicked and detestable practices H448
Eze 7:13 **B of** their sins, not one of them will H928
Eze 10:17 **b** the spirit of the living creatures was in H3954
Eze 12:19 of everything in it **b of** the violence of all H4946
Eze 13: 8 **B of** your false words and lying visions, H3610
Eze 13:10 " '**B** they lead my people astray, saying H3610
Eze 13:10 is no peace, and **b**, when a flimsy H928+3610
Eze 13:22 **B** you disheartened the righteous with your H3610
Eze 13:22 **b** you encouraged the wicked not to NDT
Eze 14:15 can pass through it **b of** the beasts, H4946+7156
Eze 15: 8 make the land desolate **b** they have been H3610
Eze 16:14 **b** the splendor I had given you made your H3954
Eze 16:28 the Assyrians too, **b** you were insatiable H4946
Eze 16:31 a prostitute, **b** you scorned payment. H4200
Eze 16:36 **B** you poured out your lust and exposed H3610
Eze 16:36 and **b of** all your detestable idols H6584
Eze 16:36 **b** you gave them your children's H3869
Eze 16:43 " '**B** you did not remember the days H3610+889
Eze 16:52 **B** your sins were more vile than theirs, they H928
Eze 16:59 **b** you have despised my oath by breaking H889
Eze 16:63 open your mouth **b of** your H4946+7156
Eze 17:18 **B** he had given his hand in pledge and H2256
Eze 17:20 on him there **b** he was unfaithful to H889
Eze 18:13 **B** he has done all these detestable things NDT
Eze 18:18 his own sin, **b** he practiced extortion H3954
Eze 18:22 **B of** the righteous things they have done H928
Eze 18:24 **B of** the unfaithfulness they are guilty of H928
Eze 18:24 are guilty of and **b of** the sins they have H928
Eze 18:26 **b of** the sin they have committed they will H928
Eze 18:28 **B** they consider all the offenses they have H2256
Eze 19:10 full of branches **b of** abundant water. H4946
Eze 20:16 **b** they rejected my laws and did not follow H3610
Eze 20:24 **b** they had not obeyed my laws but had H3610
Eze 21: 4 **B** I am going to cut off the righteous H3610+889
Eze 21: 7 shall say, '**B of** the news that is coming. H448
Eze 21:24 '**B** you people have brought to mind your H3610
Eze 21:24 in all that you do—**b** you have done this H3610
Eze 22: 4 have become guilty **b of** the blood you H928
Eze 22:19 '**B** you have all become dross, I will H3610
Eze 23:30 **b** you lusted after the nations and defiled H928
Eze 23:45 **b** they are adulterous and blood is on H3954
Eze 24: 2 **b** the king of Babylon has laid siege to NDT
Eze 24:13 **B** I tried to cleanse you but you would not H3610
Eze 24:23 will waste away **b of** your sins and H928
Eze 25: 3 **B** you said "Aha!" over H3610
Eze 25: 6 **B** you have clapped your hands and H3610
Eze 25: 8 '**B** Moab and Seir said, "Look, Judah has H3610
Eze 25:12 '**B** Edom took revenge on Judah and H3610
Eze 25:15 '**B** the Philistines acted in vengeance and H3610
Eze 26: 2 **b** Tyre has said of Jerusalem H3610+889
Eze 27:12 business with you **b of** your great wealth H4946
Eze 27:16 business with you **b of** your many products H4946
Eze 27:18 business with you **b of** your many products H928
Eze 27:31 shave their heads **b of** you and will put on H448
Eze 28: 5 and **b of** your wealth your heart has grown H928
Eze 28: 6 " '**B** you think you are wise, as wise as a H3610
Eze 28:17 corrupted your wisdom **b of** your splendor. H6584
Eze 29: 9 " '**B** you said, "The Nile is mine; I made it,"H3610
Eze 29:20 his efforts **b** he and his army did it H889
Eze 31: 5 spreading **b of** abundant waters. H4946
Eze 31:10 **B** the great cedar towered over the H3610+889
Eze 31:10 and **b** it was proud of its height NDT
Eze 31:15 **B of** it I clothed Lebanon with gloom, and H6584
Eze 32:10 shudder with horror **b of** you when I H6584
Eze 32:25 **B** their terror had spread in the land of the H3954
Eze 32:26 killed by the sword **b** they spread their H3954
Eze 33: 6 person's life will be taken **b of** their sin, H928
Eze 33:10 and we are wasting away **b of** them. H928
Eze 33:29 a desolate waste **b of** all the detestable H6584
Eze 34: 5 they were scattered **b** there was no H4946
Eze 34: 8 **b** my flock lacks a shepherd and so has H4946
Eze 34: 8 **b** my shepherds did not search for my NDT
Eze 34:21 **B** you shove with flank and shoulder H3610
Eze 35: 5 " '**B** you harbored an ancient hostility and H3610
Eze 35:10 " '**B** you have said, "These two nations H3610
Eze 35:15 **B** you rejoiced when the inheritance of H3869
Eze 36: 3 **B** they ravaged and crushed H3610+928+3610
Eze 36: 6 in my jealous wrath **b** you have suffered H3610
Eze 36:13 **B** some say to you, "You devour people H3610
Eze 36:18 my wrath on them **b** they had shed blood H6584
Eze 36:18 blood in the land and **b** they had defiled it NDT
Eze 36:30 suffer **disgrace** among the nations *b of* AIT
Eze 39:10 **b** they will use the weapons for fuel. H3954
Eze 39:11 **b** Gog and all his hordes will be buried H2256
Eze 39:23 **b** they were unfaithful to me. H6584+889
Eze 44: 2 It is to remain shut **b** the LORD, the God of H3954
Eze 44:12 But **b** they served them in the H3610+889
Eze 47: 5 **b** the water had risen and was deep H3954
Eze 47: 9 **b** this water flows there and makes the H3954
Eze 47:12 **b** the water from the sanctuary flows to H3954
Eze 47:14 **B** I swore with uplifted hand to give it to H889
Eze 48:14 into other hands, **b** it is holy to the LORD. H3954
Da 1:10 king would then have my head **b of** *you*." H2549
Da 2: 8 **b** you realize that this is A10353+10619+10168
Da 2:30 not **b** I have greater wisdom than A10089
Da 4:18 **b** the spirit of the holy gods is in you." A10168
Da 4:37 **b** everything he does is right and all his A10168
Da 5:12 He did this **b** Daniel A10353+10619+10168
Da 5:19 **B of** the high position he gave him, all A10427
Da 6: 4 **b** he was trustworthy and A10353+10619+10168
Da 6:22 **b** I was found innocent A10353+10619+10168
Da 6:23 on him, **b** he had trusted in his God. A10168
Da 7:11 continued to watch **b of** the boastful A10427
Da 8:12 **B of** rebellion, the LORD's people and the H928
Da 8:19 **b** the vision concerns the appointed time H3954
Da 9: 7 have scattered us **b of** our unfaithfulness H928
Da 9: 8 **b** we have sinned against you. H889
Da 9:11 out on us, **b** we have sinned against you. H3954
Da 9:18 make requests of you **b** we are righteous, H6584
Da 9:18 are righteous, but **b of** your great mercy. H6584
Da 9:19 **b** your city and your people bear your H3954
Da 10:13 **b** I was detained there with the king of H2256
Da 10:16 am overcome with anguish **b of** the vision, H928
Da 11: 4 **b** his empire will be uprooted and given H3954
Da 11:25 be able to stand **b of** the plots devised H3954
Da 11:27 **b** an end will still come at the appointed H3954
Da 12: 9 **b** the words are rolled up and sealed until H3954
Hos 1: 4 **b** I will soon punish the house of Jehu H3954
Hos 2: 4 **b** they are the children of adultery. H3954
Hos 4: 1 **b** the LORD has a charge to bring against H3954
Hos 4: 3 **B of** this the land dries up, and all who H6584
Hos 4: 6 "**B** you have rejected knowledge, I also H3954
Hos 4: 6 **b** you have ignored the law of your God H2256
Hos 4:10 **b** they have deserted the LORD to give H3954
Hos 4:14 **b** the men themselves consort with harlots H3954
Hos 7:13 to them, **b** they have strayed from me! H3954
Hos 7:13 to them, **b** they have rebelled against me! H3954
Hos 7:16 fall by the sword **b of** their insolent words. H4946
Hos 8: 1 the house of the LORD **b** the people have H3610
Hos 9: 7 **B** your sins are so many and your hostility H6584
Hos 9:15 "**B of** all their wickedness in Gilgal, I hated NDT
Hos 9:15 **B of** their sinful deeds, I will drive them H6584
Hos 9:17 will reject them **b** they have not obeyed H3954
Hos 10: 3 "We have no king **b** we did not revere the H3954
Hos 10: 5 **b** it is taken from them into exile. H3954
Hos 10:13 **B** you have depended on your own H3954
Hos 10:15 Bethel, **b** your wickedness is great. H4946+7156
Hos 11: 5 rule over them **b** they refuse to repent? H3954
Hos 13: 9 **b** you are against me, against your H3954
Hos 13:16 **b** they have rebelled against their God. H3954
Joel 1: 5 of wine; wail **b of** the new wine, for it H6584
Joel 1:11 **b** the harvest of the field is destroyed. H3954
Joel 1:18 herds mill about **b** they have no pasture H3954
Joel 2:23 you the autumn rains **b** he is faithful. H4200
Joel 3: 2 **b** they scattered my people among the NDT
Joel 3:19 **b of** violence done to the people of Judah H4946
Am 1: 3 **B** she threshed Gilead with sledges H6584
Am 1: 6 **B** she took captive whole communities H6584
Am 1: 9 **B** she sold whole communities of captives H6584
Am 1:11 **B** he pursued his brother with a sword H6584
Am 1:11 **b** his anger raged continually and his fury H2256
Am 1:13 **B** he ripped open the pregnant women of H6584
Am 2: 1 **B** he burned to ashes the bones of H6584
Am 2: 4 **B** they have rejected the law of the LORD H6584
Am 2: 4 **b** they have been led astray by false gods H2256
Am 4:12 and **b** I will do this to you H6813+3954
Am 7:13 **b** this is the king's sanctuary and the H3954
Am 8:13 strong young men will faint **b of** thirst. H928
Ob 10 **B of** the violence against your brother H4946
Jnh 1: 2 **b** its wickedness has come up before me." H3954
Jnh 1:10 the LORD, **b** he had already told them so.) H3954
Mic 1: 5 All this is **b of** Jacob's transgression H928
Mic 1: 5 **b of** the sins of the people of Israel. H928
Mic 1: 8 **B of** this I will weep and wail; I will go H6584
Mic 1:12 **b** disaster has come from the LORD H3954
Mic 2: 1 they carry it out **b** it is in their power to H3954
Mic 2:10 your resting place, **b** it is defiled, it H928+6288
Mic 3: 4 face from them **b of** the evil they H3869+889
Mic 3: 7 all cover their faces **b** there is no answer H3954
Mic 3:12 Therefore **b of** you, Zion will be H928+1673
Mic 6:13 to destroy you, to ruin you **b of** your sins. H6584
Mic 6:14 **b** what you save I will give to the sword. H2256
Mic 7: 9 **B** I have sinned against him, I will bear H3954
Mic 7:13 will become desolate **b of** its inhabitants, H6584
Na 3: 4 all **b of** the wanton lust of a prostitute H4946
Hab 2: 5 **B** he is as greedy as the grave and like H889
Hab 2: 8 **B** you have plundered many nations, the H3954
Zep 1:17 **b** they have sinned against the LORD. H3954
Zep 3:11 **b** I will remove from you your arrogant H3954
Hag 1: 9 "**B of** my house, which remains a ruin H3610
Hag 1:10 **b of** you the heavens have withheld their H6584
Hag 1:12 **b** the LORD their God had sent him. H3869+889
Zec 2: 4 city without walls **b of** the great number of H4946
Zec 2:13 **b** he has roused himself from his holy H3954
Zec 8: 4 of them with cane in hand **b of** their age. H4946
Zec 8:10 their business safely **b of** their enemies, H4946
Zec 8:23 **b** we have heard that God is with you. H3954
Zec 9:11 **b of** the blood of my covenant with you H928
Zec 10: 5 They will fight **b** the LORD is with them H3954
Zec 10: 6 I will restore them **b** I have compassion H3954
Zec 12: 5 **b** the LORD Almighty is their God. H928
Zec 13: 3 **b** you have told lies in the LORD's name. H3954
Mal 1:11 **b** my name will be great among the H3954
Mal 2: 2 **b** you have not resolved to honor me. H3954
Mal 2: 3 "**B of** you I will rebuke your descendants; H4200
Mal 2: 7 **b** he is the messenger of the LORD H3954
Mal 2: 9 **b** you have not followed my H3869+7023+889
Mal 2:13 You weep and wail **b** he no longer looks H4946
Mal 2:14 It is **b** the LORD is the witness H6584+3954

Mal 3: 9 your whole nation—**b** you are robbing me. H2256
Mt 1:19 *B* Joseph her husband **was** faithful to the law AIT
Mt 1:20 **b** what is conceived in her is from the G1142
Mt 1:21 **b** he will save his people from their sins." G1142
Mt 2:18 to be comforted, **b** they are no more." G4022
Mt 5:10 who are persecuted **b of** righteousness, G1915
Mt 5:11 say all kinds of evil against you **b of** me. G1915
Mt 5:12 be glad, **b** great is your reward in heaven G4022
Mt 6: 7 they will be heard **b of** their many words. G1877
Mt 7:25 **b** it had its foundation on the rock. G1142
Mt 7:29 **b** he taught as one who had authority, and G1142
Mt 9:36 **b** they were harassed and helpless G4022
Mt 10:22 You will be hated by everyone **b of** me G1328
Mt 11:20 been performed, **b** they did not repent. G4022
Mt 11:25 **b** you have hidden these things from the G4022
Mt 13: 5 up quickly, **b** the soil was shallow. G1328+3836
Mt 13: 6 they withered **b** they had no root. G1328+3836
Mt 13:11 "**B** the knowledge of the secrets of the G4022
Mt 13:16 But blessed are your eyes **b** they see, and G4022
Mt 13:16 they see, and your ears **b** they hear. G4022
Mt 13:21 persecution comes **b of** the word, G1328
Mt 13:29 '*b while you are* **pulling** the weeds AIT
Mt 13:58 many miracles there **b of** their lack of faith G1328
Mt 14: 3 him and put him in prison **b of** Herodias, G1328
Mt 14: 5 **b** they considered John a prophet. G4022
Mt 14: 9 but **b of** his oaths and his dinner guests G1328
Mt 14:24 by the waves **b** the wind was against G1142
Mt 16: 7 "It is **b** we didn't bring any bread. G4022
Mt 17:20 He replied, "**B** you have so little faith G1328
Mt 18: 7 Woe to the world **b of** the things that cause G608
Mt 18:32 all that debt of yours **b** you begged me to. G2075
Mt 19: 8 divorce your wives **b** your hearts were hard G4639
Mt 19:22 he went away sad, **b** he had great wealth. G1142
Mt 20: 7 "'**B** no one has hired us,' they answered G4022
Mt 20:15 Or are you envious **b** I am generous?' G4022
Mt 21:46 afraid of the crowd **b** the people held that G2075
Mt 22:16 **b** you pay no attention to who they are. G1142
Mt 22:29 are in error *b you do* not **know** the Scriptures AIT
Mt 24: 9 you will be hated by all nations **b of** me. G1328
Mt 24:12 **B of** the increase of wickedness, the love G1328
Mt 24:42 **b** you do not know on what day your Lord G4022
Mt 24:44 **b** the Son of Man will come at an hour G4022
Mt 25:13 **b** you do not know the day or the hour. G4022
Mt 26:43 them sleeping, **b** their eyes were heavy. G1142
Mt 27:19 a great deal today in a dream **b of** him." G1328
Mk 1:22 **b** he taught them as one who had G1142
Mk 1:34 the demons speak **b** they knew who he G4022
Mk 2: 4 could not get him to Jesus **b of** the crowd, G1328
Mk 3: 9 **B of** the crowd he told his disciples to have G1328
Mk 3:30 He said this **b** they were saying, "He has G4022
Mk 4: 5 up quickly, **b** the soil was shallow. G1328+3836
Mk 4: 6 they withered **b** they had no root. G1328+3836
Mk 4:17 persecution comes **b of** the word, G1328
Mk 4:29 the sickle to it, **b** the harvest has come." G4022
Mk 5:28 **b** she thought, "If I just touch his clothes, G1142
Mk 6:17 He did this **b of** Herodias, his brother G1328
Mk 6:20 **b** Herod feared John and protected him G1142
Mk 6:26 but **b of** his oaths and his dinner guests G1328
Mk 6:31 **b** so many people were coming and G1142
Mk 6:34 **b** they were like sheep without a G4022
Mk 6:48 at the oars, **b** the wind was against them. G1142
Mk 6:50 **b** they all saw him and were terrified G1142
Mk 8: 3 **b** some of them have come a long G2779
Mk 8:16 said, "It is **b** we have no bread. G4022
Mk 9:31 **b** he was teaching his disciples. He said to G1142
Mk 9:34 But they kept quiet **b** on the way they had G1142
Mk 9:38 told him to stop, **b** he was not one of us." G4022
Mk 9:41 of water in my name **b** you belong to the G4022
Mk 10: 5 "It was **b** your hearts were hard that G4639
Mk 10:22 He went away sad, **b** he had great wealth. G1142
Mk 11:13 **b** it was not the season for figs. G1142
Mk 11:18 **b** the whole crowd was amazed at his G1142
Mk 12:12 a way to arrest him **b** they knew he had G1142
Mk 12:14 **b** you pay no attention to who they are G1142
Mk 12:24 you not in error **b** you do not know G1328+4047
Mk 13:13 Everyone will hate you **b of** me, but the G1328
Mk 13:19 **b** those will be days of distress unequaled G1142
Mk 13:35 keep watch **b** you do not know when G1142
Mk 14:40 them sleeping, **b** their eyes were heavy. G1142
Mk 16: 8 nothing to anyone, **b** they were afraid. G1142
Lk 1: 7 they were childless **b** Elizabeth was not G2776
Lk 1:14 and many will rejoice **b of** his birth, G2093
Lk 1:20 **b** you did not believe my words G505+4005
Lk 1:68 **b** he has come to his people and G4022
Lk 1:78 **b of** the tender mercy of our God, by G1328
Lk 2: 4 **b** he belonged to the house and G1328+3836
Lk 2: 7 **b** there was no guest room available for G1484
Lk 3:19 Herod the tetrarch **b of** his marriage to G4309
Lk 4:18 **b** he has anointed me to proclaim G4005+1641
Lk 4:32 at his teaching, **b** his words had authority. G4022
Lk 4:41 **b** they knew he was the Messiah. G4022
Lk 4:43 other towns also, **b** that is why I was sent." G4022
Lk 5: 5 caught anything. But **b** you say so, I will G2093
Lk 5:19 not find a way to do this **b of** the crowd, G1328
Lk 6:19 **b** power was coming from him and G4022
Lk 6:22 your name as evil, **b of** the Son of Man. G1915
Lk 6:23 **b** great is your reward in heaven. G1142
Lk 6:35 **b** he is kind to the ungrateful and wicked. G4022
Lk 6:48 not shake it, **b** it was well built. G1328+3836
Lk 7: 5 **b** he loves our nation and has built our G1142
Lk 7:29 was right, *b they had been* **baptized** by John. AIT
Lk 7:30 *b they had* not *been* **baptized** by John.) AIT
Lk 8: 6 the plants withered **b** they had no G1328+3836
Lk 8:19 not able to get near him **b of** the crowd. G1328
Lk 8:30 **b** many demons had gone into him. G4022
Lk 8:37 **b** they were overcome with fear. G4022
Lk 8:42 **b** his only daughter, a girl of about twelve G4022
Lk 9: 7 was perplexed **b** some were saying G1328+3836
Lk 9:12 lodging, **b** we are in a remote place here." G4022
Lk 9:49 tried to stop him, **b** he is not one of us." G4022
Lk 9:53 **b** he was heading for Jerusalem. G4022
Lk 10:21 **b** you have hidden these things from the G4022
Lk 11: 8 give you the bread **b of** friendship, G1328+3836
Lk 11: 8 yet **b of** your shameless audacity he will G1328
Lk 11:18 I say this **b** you claim that I drive out G4022
Lk 11:42 **b** you give God a tenth of your mint G4022
Lk 11:43 **b** you love the most important seats in the G4022
Lk 11:44 **b** you are like unmarked graves G4022
Lk 11:46 **b** you load people down with burdens G4022
Lk 11:47 **b** you build tombs for the prophets G4022
Lk 11:49 **B of** this, God in his wisdom said, 'I will G1328
Lk 11:52 **b** you have taken away the key to G4022
Lk 12:40 **b** the Son of Man will come at an hour G4022
Lk 13: 2 the other Galileans **b** they suffered this G4022
Lk 13:14 Indignant **b** Jesus had healed on the G4022
Lk 13:24 the narrow door, **b**, many, I tell you, G4022
Lk 15:27 the fattened calf **b** he has him back safe G4022
Lk 15:32 **b** this brother of yours was dead and is G4022
Lk 16: 2 **b** you cannot be manager any longer. G1142
Lk 16: 8 dishonest manager **b** he had acted G4022
Lk 16:24 my tongue, **b** I am in agony in this fire. G4022
Lk 17: 9 thank the servant **b** he did what he was G4022
Lk 17:21 **b** the kingdom of God is in your midst." G1142
Lk 18: 5 **b** this widow keeps bothering G1328+3836
Lk 18:23 became very sad, **b** he was very wealthy. G1142
Lk 19: 3 **b** he was short he could not see over G4022
Lk 19: 9 has come to this house, **b** this man, too, G2776
Lk 19:11 **b** he was near Jerusalem and the G1328+3836
Lk 19:17 '**B** you have been trustworthy in a very G4022
Lk 19:21 I was afraid of you, **b** you are a hard man G4022
Lk 19:44 **b** you did not recognize the time of G505+4005
Lk 19:48 **b** all the people hung on his words. G1142
Lk 20: 6 **b** they are persuaded that John was a G1142
Lk 20:19 **b** they knew he had spoken this parable G1142
Lk 21:17 Everyone will hate you **b of** me. G1328
Lk 21:28 **b** your redemption is drawing near." G1484
Lk 23: 8 **b** for a long time he had been wanting to G1142
Lk 24:11 **b** their words seemed to them like G2779
Lk 24:41 did not believe it **b of** joy and amazement, G608
Jn 1:15 has surpassed me **b** he was before me. G4022
Jn 1:30 has surpassed me **b** he was before me. G4022
Jn 1:50 "You believe **b** I told you I saw you under G4022
Jn 3:18 condemned already **b** they have not G4022
Jn 3:19 instead of light **b** their deeds were evil. G1142
Jn 3:23 near Salim, **b** there was plenty of water G4022
Jn 4:39 town believed in him **b of** the woman's G1328
Jn 4:41 And **b of** his words many more became G1328
Jn 4:42 no longer believe *just* **b of** what you said; G1328
Jn 5:16 **b** Jesus was doing these things on the G4022
Jn 5:19 **b** whatever the Father does the Son also G1142
Jn 5:27 authority to judge **b** he is the Son of Man. G4022
Jn 5:39 Scriptures diligently **b** you think that in G4022
Jn 6: 2 people followed him **b** they saw the signs G4022
Jn 6:26 not **b** you saw the signs I performed but G4022
Jn 6:26 signs I performed but **b** you ate the loaves G4022
Jn 6:41 began to grumble about him **b** he said, G4022
Jn 6:57 Father sent me and I live **b of** the Father, G1328
Jn 6:57 one who feeds on me will live **b of** me. G1328
Jn 7: 1 to go about in Judea **b** the Jewish leaders G4022
Jn 7: 7 it hates me **b** I testify that its works are G4022
Jn 7: 8 festival, **b** my time has not yet fully come." G4022
Jn 7:22 **b** Moses gave you circumcision G1328+4047
Jn 7:29 I know him **b** I am from him and he G4022
Jn 7:30 on him, **b** his hour had not yet come. G4022
Jn 7:43 Thus the people were divided **b of** Jesus. G1328
Jn 8:16 my decisions are true, **b** I am not alone. G4022
Jn 8:20 seized him, **b** his hour had not yet come. G4022
Jn 8:37 **b** you have no room for my word. G4022
Jn 8:43 **B** you are unable to hear what I say. G4022
Jn 8:45 Yet **b** I tell the truth, you do not believe G4022
Jn 9:22 His parents said this **b** they were afraid of G4022
Jn 10: 4 sheep follow him **b** they know his voice. G4022
Jn 10: 5 run away from him **b** they do not G4022
Jn 10:13 The man runs away **b** he is a hired hand G4022
Jn 10:26 you do not believe **b** you are not my G4022
Jn 10:33 "but for blasphemy, **b** you, a mere man G4022
Jn 10:36 do you accuse me of blasphemy **b** I said, G4022
Jn 12: 6 He did not say this **b** he cared about the G4022
Jn 12: 6 cared about the poor but **b** he was a thief; G4022
Jn 12: 9 not only **b of** him but also to see Lazarus G1328
Jn 12:18 **b** they had heard that he had performed G4022
Jn 12:39 they could not believe, **b**, as Isaiah says G4022
Jn 12:41 Isaiah said this **b** he saw Jesus' glory and G4022
Jn 12:42 But **b of** the Pharisees they would not G1328
Jn 14:12 than these, **b** I am going to the Father. G4022
Jn 14:17 **b** it neither sees him nor knows him. G4022
Jn 14:19 you will see me. **B** I live, you also will G4022
Jn 15: 3 You are already clean **b of** the word I have G1328
Jn 15:15 **b** a servant does not know his master's G4022
Jn 15:21 They will treat you this way **b of** my name G1328
Jn 16: 3 will do such things **b** they have not known G4022
Jn 16: 4 this from the beginning **b** I was with you, G4022
Jn 16: 6 are filled with grief **b** I have said these G4022
Jn 16: 9 about sin, **b** people do not believe in me; G4022
Jn 16:10 righteousness, **b** I am going to the Father G4022
Jn 16:11 **b** the prince of this world now stands G4022
Jn 16:14 He will glorify me **b** it is from me that he G4022
Jn 16:17 see me,' and '**B** I am going to the Father'?" G4022
Jn 16:21 to a child has pain **b** her time has come; G4022
Jn 16:21 forgets the anguish **b of** her joy that a G1328
Jn 16:27 himself loves you **b** you have loved me G4022
Jn 17:24 you have given me **b** you loved me before G4022
Jn 18: 2 **b** Jesus had often met there with his G4022
Jn 18:15 **B** this disciple was known to the high G1254
Jn 18:28 **b** they wanted to be able to eat the G247
Jn 19: 7 **b** he claimed to be the Son of God." G4022
Jn 19:31 **B** the Jewish leaders did not want the G2671
Jn 19:38 secretly **b** he feared the Jewish G1328
Jn 19:42 **B** it was the Jewish day of Preparation G1328
Jn 20:29 Jesus told him, "**B** you have seen me, you G4022
Jn 21: 6 to haul the net in **b of** the large number of G608
Jn 21:17 Peter was hurt **b** Jesus asked him the third G4022
Jn 21:23 **B of** this, the rumor spread among the G4036
Ac 2: 6 **b** each one heard their own language G4022
Ac 2:24 **b** it was impossible for death to keep its G2776
Ac 2:25 **B** he is at my right hand, I will not be G4022
Ac 2:27 **b** you will not abandon me to the realm G4022
Ac 4: 2 disturbed **b** the apostles were G1328+3836
Ac 4: 3 Peter and John and, **b** it was evening G1142
Ac 4:21 **b** all the people were praising God for G4022
Ac 5:26 **b** they feared that the people would stone G1142
Ac 5:41 rejoicing **b** they had been counted worthy G4022
Ac 6: 1 the Hebraic Jews **b** their widows were G4022
Ac 7: 9 "**B** the patriarchs were jealous of Joseph G2779
Ac 8:11 followed him **b** he had amazed G1328+3836
Ac 8:16 **b** the Holy Spirit had not yet come on any G1142
Ac 8:20 **b** you thought you could buy the gift of G4022
Ac 8:21 **b** your heart is not right before God. G1142
Ac 10:38 power of the devil, **b** God was with him. G4022
Ac 12:20 **b** they depended on the king's G1328+3836
Ac 12:23 **b** Herod did not give praise to God G505+4005
Ac 13: 7 Saul *b he* **wanted** to **hear** the word of AIT
Ac 14:12 they called Hermes **b** he was the chief G2076
Ac 14:13 city gates *b he* and the crowd **wanted** to offer AIT
Ac 15:38 *b he had* **deserted** them in Pamphylia and AIT
Ac 16: 3 he circumcised him **b of** the Jews who G1328
Ac 16:27 to kill himself *b he* **thought** the prisoners had AIT
Ac 16:34 with joy *b he had come to* **believe** in God— AIT
Ac 17:18 They said this **b** Paul was preaching the G4022
Ac 18: 2 **b** Claudius had ordered all Jews to G1328+3836
Ac 18: 3 **b** he was a tentmaker as they G1328+3836
Ac 18:10 **b** I have many people in this city. G1484
Ac 18:18 off at Cenchreae **b of** a vow he had taken. G1142
Ac 19:40 with rioting **b of** what happened today G4309
Ac 20: 3 *B* some Jews *had* **plotted** against him just as AIT
Ac 20: 7 *b he* **intended to** leave the next day AIT
Ac 20:13 this arrangement **b** he was going there on G1142
Ac 21:34 could not get at the truth **b of** the uproar, G1328
Ac 22:11 **b** the brilliance of the light had blinded G6055
Ac 22:18 **b** the people here will not accept your G1484
Ac 23: 6 I stand on trial **b of** the hope of the G4309
Ac 23:18 young man to you *b he* **has** something to tell AIT
Ac 23:21 **b** more than forty of them are waiting in G1142
Ac 24:27 but *b* Felix **wanted** to grant a favor to the AIT
Ac 25:25 but *b* he **made** his **appeal** to the Emperor I AIT
Ac 26: 3 especially so *b* you **are** well acquainted AIT
Ac 26: 6 And now it is **b of** my hope in what God G2093
Ac 26: 7 it is **b of** this hope that these Jews are G4309
Ac 26:26 his notice, **b** it was not done in a corner. G1142
Ac 27: 4 the lee of Cyprus **b** the winds were G1328+3836
Ac 27: 9 become dangerous **b** by now it was G1328+3836
Ac 27:17 **B** they were afraid they would run G5445
Ac 27:22 your courage, **b** not one of you will be lost G1142
Ac 28: 2 welcomed us all **b** it was raining G1328+3836
Ac 28:18 **b** I was not guilty of any crime G1328+3836
Ac 28:20 It is **b of** the hope of Israel that I am G1915
Ro 1: 8 **b** your faith is being reported all over the G4022
Ro 1:16 **b** it is the power of God that brings G1142
Ro 1:19 **b** God has made it plain to them. G1142
Ro 1:26 **B of** this, God gave them over to shameful G1328
Ro 2: 1 **b** you who pass judgment do the same G1142
Ro 2: 5 But **b of** your stubbornness and your G2848
Ro 2:18 is superior *b you are* **instructed** by the law; AIT
Ro 2:20 *b you* **have** in the law the embodiment of AIT
Ro 2:24 among the Gentiles **b of** you. G1328
Ro 3:25 *b* **in** his forbearance he had left the sins AIT
Ro 3:27 It is excluded. **B of** what law? The law that G1328
Ro 3:27 No, **b of** the law that requires faith G1328
Ro 4:15 **b** the law brings wrath. And where there is G1142
Ro 5: 3 *b we* **know** that suffering produces AIT
Ro 5: 5 **b** God's love has been poured out into G4022
Ro 5:12 came to all people, **b** all sinned— G2093+4005
Ro 6: 7 **b** anyone who has died has been set free G1142
Ro 6:14 your master, **b** you are not under the law G1142
Ro 6:15 Shall we sin **b** we are not under the law G4022
Ro 6:19 from everyday life **b of** your human G1328
Ro 8: 2 **b** through Christ Jesus the law of the Spirit G1142
Ro 8: 3 powerless to do **b** it was weakened G1877+4005
Ro 8:10 your body is subject to death **b of** sin, G1328
Ro 8:10 the Spirit gives life **b of** righteousness. G1328
Ro 8:11 your mortal bodies **b of** his Spirit who G1328
Ro 8:27 **b** the Spirit intercedes for God's people in G4022
Ro 9: 7 Nor **b** they are his descendants are they all G4022
Ro 9:32 **B** they pursued it not by faith but as if it G4022
Ro 11:11 *b of* their **transgression**, salvation has AIT
Ro 11:20 But they were broken off *b of* **unbelief**, and AIT

Ro 13: 5 not only **b of** possible punishment but G1328
Ro 13:11 **b** our salvation is nearer now than when G1142
Ro 14:15 sister is distressed **b of** what you eat, G1328
Ro 14:18 **b** anyone who serves Christ in this way is G1142
Ro 14:23 if they eat, **b** their eating is not from faith G4022
Ro 15:15 them again, **b of** the grace God gave me G1328
Ro 16:19 so I rejoice **b of** you; but I want you to G2093
1Co 1: 4 my God for you **b of** his grace given you G2093
1Co 1:30 It is **b of** him that you are in Christ Jesus G1666
1Co 2:14 understand them **b** they are discerned G4022
1Co 3:13 what it is, **b** the Day will bring it to light. G1142
1Co 7: 5 Satan will not tempt you **b of** your lack of G1328
1Co 7:26 **B of** the present crisis, I think that it is G1328
1Co 9:10 **b** whoever plows and threshes should be G4022
1Co 10:17 **B** there is one loaf, we, who are many, are G4022
1Co 10:30 am I denounced **b of** something I thank G5642
1Co 11:10 over her own head, **b of** the angels. G1328
1Co 12:15 foot should say, "**B** I am not a hand, I do G4022
1Co 12:16 the ear should say, "**B** I am not an eye, G4022
1Co 15: 9 apostle, **b** I persecuted the church of God. G1484
1Co 15:58 *b you* **know** that your labor in the Lord is not AIT
1Co 16: 9 **b** a great door for effective work has G1142
1Co 16:17 **b** they have supplied what was lacking G4022
2Co 1: 7 *b we* **know** that just as you share in our AIT
2Co 1:15 **B** I was confident of this, I wanted to visit G2779
2Co 1:24 your joy, **b** it is by faith you stand firm. G1142
2Co 2:13 *b I did* not **find** my brother Titus there. AIT
2Co 3: 7 steadily at the face of Moses **b of** its glory, G1328
2Co 3:14 removed, **b** only in Christ is it taken away. G4022
2Co 4:14 *b we* **know** that the one who raised the Lord AIT
2Co 5: 3 **b** when we are clothed, we G1623+1145+2779
2Co 5: 4 **b** we do not wish to be unclothed G2093+4005
2Co 5:14 *b we are* **convinced** that one died for all AIT
2Co 7: 9 I am happy, not **b** you were made sorry G4022
2Co 7: 9 **b** your sorrow led you to repentance. G4022
2Co 7:13 **b** his spirit has been refreshed by all of G4022
2Co 8:22 more so *b of* his great **confidence** in you. AIT
2Co 9:13 **B of** the service by which you have proved G1328
2Co 9:14 **b of** the surpassing grace God has given G1328
2Co 11:11 **B** I do not love you? God knows I do! G4022
2Co 12: 6 be a fool, **b** I would be speaking the truth. G1142
2Co 12: 7 *b of* these surpassingly great **revelations** AIT
2Co 12:14 **b** what I want is not your possessions but G1142
Gal 1:24 And they praised God **b of** me. G1877
Gal 2: 4 This matter arose **b** some false believers G1328
Gal 2:11 him to his face, **b** he stood condemned. G4022
Gal 2:12 the Gentiles *b he was* **afraid** *of* those who AIT
Gal 2:16 **b** by the works of the law no one will be G4022
Gal 3:11 **b** "the righteous will live by faith. G4022
Gal 3:19 It was added **b of** transgressions until the G5920
Gal 4: 6 **B** you are his sons, God sent the Spirit of G4022
Gal 4:13 it was **b of** an illness that I first preached G1328
Gal 4:20 my tone, **b** I am perplexed about you! G4022
Gal 4:25 **b** she is in slavery with her children. G1142
Gal 4:27 **b** more are the children of the desolate G4022
Eph 2: 4 But **b of** his great love for us, God, who is G1328
Eph 3:13 to be discouraged **b of** my sufferings for G1877
Eph 4:18 the life of God **b of** the ignorance that G1328
Eph 5: 3 **b** these are improper for God's holy G2777
Eph 5: 6 for **b of** such things God's wrath comes on G1328
Eph 5:16 of every opportunity, **b** the days are evil. G4022
Eph 6: 8 *b you* **know** that the Lord will reward each one AIT
Php 1: 5 **b of** your partnership in the gospel from G2093
Php 1:14 And *b of* my **chains**, most of the brothers AIT
Php 1:18 And **b of** this I rejoice. Yes, G1877
Php 2:22 **b** as a son with his father he has served G4022
Php 2:26 is distressed **b** you heard he was ill. G1484
Php 2:30 **b** he almost died for the work of Christ. G4022
Php 3: 8 a loss **b of** the surpassing G1328+3836
Php 4:11 I am not saying this **b** I am in need, for I G4022
Col 1: 4 *b we have* **heard** of your faith in Christ Jesus AIT
Col 1:21 in your minds **b of** your evil behavior. G1877
Col 3: 6 **B of** these, the wrath of God is coming. G1328
Col 4: 1 *b you* **know** that you also have a Master in AIT
1Th 1: 5 **b** our gospel came to you not simply with G4022
1Th 2: 8 **B** we loved you so much, we were G1484
1Th 2:13 And we also thank God continually **b** G4022
1Th 3: 7 encouraged about you **b of** your faith. G1328
1Th 3: 9 have in the presence of our God **b of** you? G1328
1Th 5:13 the highest regard in love **b of** their work. G1328
2Th 1: 3 **b** your faith is growing more and more G4022
2Th 1:10 **b** you believed our testimony to you. G4022
2Th 2:10 They perish **b** they refused to love G505+4005
2Th 2:13 **b** God chose you as firstfruits to be saved G4022
2Th 3: 9 not **b** we do not have the right to such G4022
1Ti 1:13 I was shown mercy **b** I acted in ignorance G4022
1Ti 4: 5 **b** it is consecrated by the word of God and G1142
1Ti 4:10 **b** we have put our hope in the living God G4022
1Ti 4:12 anyone look down on you **b** you are young, NDT
1Ti 4:16 Persevere in them, **b** if you do, you will G1142
1Ti 5:12 **b** they have broken their first pledge. G4022
1Ti 5:23 use a little wine **b of** your stomach and G1328
1Ti 6: 2 them disrespect *just* **b** they are fellow G4022
1Ti 6: 2 them even better **b** their masters are dear G4022
2Ti 1: 9 not **b of** anything we have done but G2848
2Ti 1: 9 we have done but **b of** his own purpose G2848
2Ti 1:12 **b** I know whom I have believed G1142
2Ti 1:16 **b** he often refreshed me and was not G4022
2Ti 2:16 **b** those who indulge in it will become G1142
2Ti 2:23 *b you* **know** they produce quarrels. AIT
2Ti 3: 9 But they will not get very far **b**, as in the G1142
2Ti 3:14 *b you* **know** those from whom you learned it, AIT
2Ti 4:10 Demas, *b he* **loved** this world, has AIT
2Ti 4:11 **b** he is helpful to me in my ministry. G1142
2Ti 4:15 **b** he strongly opposed our message. G1142
Titus 1:11 *b they are* **disrupting** whole households by AIT
Titus 2: 8 may be ashamed *b they* **have** nothing bad to AIT
Titus 3: 5 not **b of** righteous things we had done G1666
Titus 3: 5 things we had done, but **b of** his mercy. G2848
Titus 3: 9 **b** these are unprofitable and useless. G1142
Titus 3:12 **b** I have decided to winter there. G1142
Phm 5 *b I* **hear** about your love for all his holy AIT
Phm 7 joy and encouragement, **b** you, brother, G4022
Phm 22 **b** I hope to be restored to you in answer G1142
Heb 2: 9 with glory and honor **b** he suffered death, G1328
Heb 2:18 **B** he himself suffered when he was G1142
Heb 3:19 were not able to enter, **b of** their unbelief. G1328
Heb 4: 2 *b they did* not **share** the faith of those who AIT
Heb 4: 6 them did not go in **b of** their G1328
Heb 5: 7 he was heard **b of** his reverent G608
Heb 5:11 make it clear to you **b** you no longer try to G2075
Heb 6:17 **B** God wanted to make the G1877+4005
Heb 7:10 **b** when Melchizedek met Abraham, Levi G1142
Heb 7:18 is set aside **b** it was weak and G1328+3836
Heb 7:22 **B** of this oath, Jesus has become the G2848
Heb 7:24 **b** Jesus lives forever, he has a G1328+3836
Heb 7:25 *b he* always **lives** to intercede for them. AIT
Heb 8: 9 **b** they did not remain faithful to my G4022
Heb 8:11 'Know the Lord,' **b** they will all know me G4022
Heb 9:17 **b** a will is in force only when somebody G1142
Heb 10:34 *b you* **knew** that you yourselves had better AIT
Heb 11: 5 not be found, **b** God had taken him away." G1484
Heb 11: 6 **b** anyone who comes to him must believe G1142
Heb 11:11 to bear children **b** she considered him G2075
Heb 11:23 **b** they saw he was no ordinary child G1484
Heb 11:26 **b** he was looking ahead to his reward. G1142
Heb 11:27 he persevered **b** he saw him who is G1142
Heb 11:31 *b she* **welcomed** the spies, was AIT
Heb 12: 6 **b** the Lord disciplines the one he loves G1142
Heb 12:20 **b** they could not bear what was G1142
Heb 13: 5 with what you have, **b** God has said G1142
Heb 13:17 **b** they keep watch over you as those who G1142
Jas 1: 3 *b you* **know** that the testing of your faith AIT
Jas 1: 6 **b** the one who doubts is like a wave of G1142
Jas 1:12 is the one who perseveres under trial **b**, G4022
Jas 1:20 **b** human anger does not produce the G1142
Jas 2:13 **b** judgment without mercy will be shown G1142
Jas 3: 1 *b you* **know** that we who teach will be judged AIT
Jas 4: 2 You do not have **b** you do not ask G1328+3836
Jas 4: 3 not receive, **b** you ask with wrong motives G1484
Jas 5: 1 weep and wail **b of** the misery that is G2093
Jas 5: 8 stand firm, **b** the Lord's coming is near. G4022
1Pe 1:16 it is written: "Be holy, **b** I am holy." G4022
1Pe 2: 8 They stumble *b they* **disobey** the message AIT
1Pe 2:19 of unjust suffering **b** they are conscious of G1328
1Pe 2:21 you were called, **b** Christ suffered for you G4022
1Pe 3: 9 **b** to this you were called so that you may G4022
1Pe 4: 1 **b** whoever suffers in the body is done with G4022
1Pe 4: 8 **b** love covers over a multitude of sins. G4022
1Pe 4:14 If you are insulted **b of** the name of Christ G1877
1Pe 5: 2 over them—not **b** you must, but because NDT
1Pe 5: 2 because you must, but **b** you are willing, as NDT
1Pe 5: 5 toward one another, **b**, "God opposes the G4022
1Pe 5: 7 all your anxiety on him **b** he cares for you. G4022
1Pe 5: 9 *b you* **know** *that* the family of believers AIT
2Pe 1:14 *b I* **know** that I will soon put it aside, as our AIT
1Jn 2: 8 **b** the darkness is passing and the true G4022
1Jn 2:11 **b** the darkness has blinded them. G4022
1Jn 2:12 **b** your sins have been forgiven on account G4022
1Jn 2:13 **b** you know him who is from the G4022
1Jn 2:13 **b** you have overcome the evil one. G4022
1Jn 2:14 dear children, **b** you know the Father. G4022
1Jn 2:14 **b** you know him who is from the G4022
1Jn 2:14 young men, **b** you are strong, and the G4022
1Jn 2:21 I do not write to you **b** you do not know the G4022
1Jn 2:21 **b** you do know it and because no lie G4022
1Jn 2:21 you do know it and **b** no lie comes from G4022
1Jn 3: 8 **b** the devil has been sinning from the G4022
1Jn 3: 9 **b** God's seed remains in them G4022
1Jn 3: 9 sinning, **b** they have been born of God. G4022
1Jn 3:12 **B** his own actions were evil and his G4022
1Jn 3:14 from death to life, **b** we love each other. G4022
1Jn 3:22 **b** we keep his commands and do what G4022
1Jn 4: 1 **b** many false prophets have gone out into G4022
1Jn 4: 4 **b** the one who is in you is greater than G4022
1Jn 4: 8 love does not know God, **b** God is love. G4022
1Jn 4:18 **b** fear has to do with punishment. G4022
1Jn 4:19 We love **b** he first loved us. G4022
1Jn 5: 6 who testifies, **b** the Spirit is the truth. G4022
1Jn 5: 9 testimony is greater **b** it is the testimony G4022
1Jn 5:10 **b** they have not believed the testimony G4022
2Jn 2 **b of** the truth, which lives in us and will be G1328
2Jn 7 I say this **b** many deceivers, who do not G4022
Rev 1: 3 what is written in it, **b** the time is near. G1142
Rev 1: 7 all peoples on earth "will mourn **b of** him." G2093
Rev 1: 9 island of Patmos **b of** the word of God G1328
Rev 3:16 **b** you are lukewarm—neither hot nor G4022
Rev 5: 4 I wept and wept **b** no one was found who G4022
Rev 5: 9 to open its seals, **b** you were slain, and G4022
Rev 6: 9 who had been slain **b of** the word of God G1328
Rev 8:13 **b of** the trumpet blasts about to be G1666
Rev 11: 2 **b** it has been given to the Gentiles. G4022
Rev 11:10 **b** these two prophets had tormented G4022
Rev 11:17 **b** you have taken your great power and G4022
Rev 12:12 **b** the devil has gone down to you! G4022
Rev 12:12 with fury, *b he* **knows** that his time is short." AIT
Rev 13: 4 worshiped the dragon **b** he had given G4022
Rev 13:14 **B of** the signs it was given power to G1328
Rev 14: 7 **b** the hour of his judgment has come. G4022
Rev 14:15 reap, **b** the time to reap has come G4022
Rev 14:18 the earth's vine, **b** its grapes are ripe." G4022
Rev 15: 1 **b** with them God's wrath is completed. G4022
Rev 16:11 the God of heaven **b of** their pains and G1666
Rev 16:21 **b** the plague was so terrible. G4022
Rev 17: 8 they see the beast, **b** it once was, now is G4022
Rev 17:14 triumph over them **b** he is Lord of lords G4022
Rev 18:11 mourn over her **b** no one buys their G4022
Rev 20: 4 had been beheaded **b of** their testimony G1328
Rev 20: 4 about Jesus and **b of** the word of God. G1328
Rev 21:22 **b** the Lord God Almighty and the Lamb G1142
Rev 22:10 prophecy of this scroll, **b** the time is near. G1142

BECKON (2)

Isa 13: 2 **b** *to* them to enter the gates of the H5677+3338
Isa 49:22 I *will* **b** to the nations, I will H5951+3338

BECOME (413) [BECAME, BECOMES, BECOMING]

Ge 2:24 is united to his wife, and *they* **b** one flesh. H2118
Ge 3:20 because she *would* **b** the mother of all H2118
Ge 3:22 "The man *has* now **b** like one of us H2118
Ge 6: 5 of the human race had **b** on the earth, NDT
Ge 6:12 God saw *how* **corrupt** the earth *had b*, for all AIT
Ge 9:15 Never again *will* the waters **b** a flood to H2118
Ge 13: 2 Abram *had b* very **wealthy** in livestock and in AIT
Ge 18:18 Abraham *will* **surely** **b** a great and H2118+2118
Ge 24:35 master abundantly, and *he has b* **wealthy**. AIT
Ge 24:51 and *let her* **b** the wife of your master's son H2118
Ge 26:16 from us; *you have b* too **powerful** for us." AIT
Ge 28: 3 your numbers until *you* **b** a community of H2118
Ge 29:34 at last my husband *will b* **attached** to me, AIT
Ge 32:10 this Jordan, but now *I have* **b** two camps. H2118
Ge 34:15 that *you* **b** like us by circumcising all your H2118
Ge 34:16 among you and **b** one people with you. H2118
Ge 34:23 property and all their other animals **b** ours? NDT
Ge 38:23 she has, or *we will* **b** a laughingstock. H2118
Ge 44: 9 the rest of us *will* **b** my lord's slaves." H2118
Ge 44:10 is found to have it *will* **b** my slave; H2118
Ge 44:17 found to have the cup *will* **b** my slave. H2118
Ge 45:11 all who belong to you *will b* **destitute**. AIT
Ge 47:19 and that the land *may* not *b* **desolate**." AIT
Ge 47:26 of the priests that *did* not **b** Pharaoh's. H2118
Ge 48:19 He too *will* **b** a people, and he too will H2118
Ge 48:19 become a people, and he too *will b* **great**. AIT
Ge 48:19 his descendants *will* **b** a group of nations H2118
Ge 49:13 by the seashore and **b** a haven for ships; H4200
Ex 1: 9 "the Israelites have **b** far too numerous for NDT
Ex 1:10 or *they will b even more* **numerous** and, AIT
Ex 2:14 thought, "What I did *must have* **b known**." H3359
Ex 2:22 "*I have* **b** a foreigner in a foreign land." H2118
Ex 4: 6 was leprous—it had **b** as white as snow. NDT
Ex 4: 9 from the river *will* **b** blood on the ground H2118
Ex 7: 9 before Pharaoh,' and *it will* **b** a snake." H2118
Ex 8:16 the land of Egypt the dust *will* **b** gnats." H2118
Ex 9: 9 *It will* **b** fine dust over the whole land of H2118
Ex 9:24 the land of Egypt since *it had* **b** a nation. H2118
Ex 15: 2 my defense; *he has* **b** my salvation. H2118
Ex 18: 3 "*I have* **b** a foreigner in a foreign land"; H2118
Ex 22:24 your wives *will* **b** widows and your H2118
Ex 23:29 because the land *would* **b** desolate and H2118
Ex 32: 7 you brought up out of Egypt, *have b* **corrupt**. AIT
Ex 32:25 out of control and so **b** a laughingstock to H4200
Lev 5: 2 they are unaware that they *have b* **unclean**, AIT
Lev 6:18 Whatever touches them *will b* **holy**.'" AIT
Lev 6:27 Whatever touches any of the flesh *will b* **holy** AIT
Lev 7:18 their credit, for *it has* **b** impure; the person H2118
Lev 10: 6 "*Do* not *let* your hair *b* **unkempt** and do not AIT
Lev 21:10 *must* not *let* his hair *b* **unkempt** or tear his AIT
Lev 22: 8 by wild animals, and so *b* **unclean** through it. AIT
Lev 22: 9 they *do* not *b* **guilty** and die H2628+5951+6584
Lev 25:35 fellow Israelites *b* **poor** and are unable to AIT
Lev 25:39 fellow Israelites *b* **poor** and sell themselves AIT
Lev 25:45 your country, and *they will* **b** your property. H2118
Lev 25:47 fellow Israelites *b* **poor** and sell themselves AIT
Lev 27:10 another, both it and the substitute **b** holy. H2118
Lev 27:15 and the house *will again* **b** theirs. H2118
Lev 27:19 its value, and the field *will again* **b** theirs. H7756
Lev 27:21 in the Jubilee, it *will* **b** holy, like a field H2118
Lev 27:21 to the LORD; *it will* **b** priestly property. H2118
Lev 27:33 its substitute **b** holy and cannot be H2118
Nu 5:19 not gone astray and **b** impure while married NDT
Nu 5:21 "*may* the LORD **cause** you **to b** a curse H5989
Nu 5:27 miscarry, and she *will* **b** a curse. H2118+4200
Nu 9: 7 "We have **b** unclean because of a dead NDT
Nu 16:38 presented before the LORD and *have b* **holy**. AIT
Nu 16:40 or *he would* **b** like Korah and his followers H2118
Nu 33:55 allow to remain *will* **b** barbs in your eyes H2118
Dt 4:16 so that *you do* not *b* **corrupt** and make for AIT
Dt 4:25 if *you* then *b* **corrupt** and make any kind of AIT
Dt 8:14 then your heart *will b* **proud** and you will AIT
Dt 9:12 you brought out of Egypt *have b* **corrupt**. AIT
Dt 15:17 and *he will* **b** your servant for life. H2118
Dt 20: 7 *Has* anyone *b* **pledged** to a woman and not AIT
Dt 20: 8 fellow soldiers *will* not *b* **disheartened** too." AIT
Dt 23:17 man or woman *is to* **b** a shrine prostitute. H2118
Dt 27: 9 *You have* now **b** the people of the LORD H2118
Dt 28:25 and *you will* **b** a thing of horror to all the H2118

B

Dt 28:37 *You will* **b** a thing of horror, a byword and H2118
Dt 31:17 And in that day I *will b* **angry** with them and AIT
Dt 31:29 *you are* **sure to b utterly corrupt** H8845+8845
Jos 10: 1 Israel and *had* **b** their **allies.** H2118+928+7931
Jos 14: 4 Joseph's descendants *had* **b** two tribes— H2118
Jos 23:13 *they will* **b** snares and traps for you H2118
Jdg 2: 3 before you; *they will* **b** traps for you H2118+4200
Jdg 2: 3 and their gods *will* **b** snares to you. H2118+4200
Jdg 13: 3 but *you are going to b* **pregnant** and give AIT
Jdg 13: 5 You *will b* **pregnant** and have a son whose AIT
Jdg 13: 7 'You *will b* **pregnant** and have a son. AIT
Jdg 16: 7 *I'll* **b** as weak as any other man. H2118
Jdg 16:11 *I'll* **b** as weak as any other man. H2118
Jdg 16:13 the pin, *I'll* **b** as weak as any other man." H2118
Jdg 16:17 *I would* **b** as weak as any other man." H2118
Jdg 17:13 since this Levite *has* **b** my priest. H2118
Ru 1:11 more sons, *who could* **b** your husbands? H2118
Ru 4: 7 transfer of property *to b* **final,** AIT
Ru 4:14 *May* he *b* **famous** throughout Israel AIT
1Sa 8:17 and *you* yourselves *will* **b** his slaves. H2118
1Sa 13: 4 now Israel *has b* **obnoxious** to the AIT
1Sa 15:17 did you not **b** the head of the tribes of Israel NDT
1Sa 17: 9 kill me, *we will* **b** your subjects; but H2118
1Sa 17: 9 *you will* **b** our subjects and serve us." H2118
1Sa 18:18 that *I should* **b** the king's son-in-law?" H2118
1Sa 18:21 *you have* a second opportunity *to b* my **son-in-law** AIT
1Sa 18:22 all love you; now *b* his **son-in-law.** AIT
1Sa 18:23 is a small matter *to b* the king's **son-in-law**? AIT
1Sa 18:26 he was pleased *to b* the king's **son-in-law.** AIT
1Sa 18:27 so that David *might b* the king's **son-in-law.** AIT
1Sa 25:39 asking her *to* **b** his **wife.** H4374+4200+851
1Sa 25:40 has sent us to you to take you *to* **b** his wife." NDT
1Sa 27:12 "*He has b* **so obnoxious** to his people AIT
1Sa 28:16 has departed from you and **b** your enemy? H2118
2Sa 5: 2 people Israel, and you *will* **b** their ruler. H2118
2Sa 6:22 *I will* **b** even more **undignified** than this H7837
2Sa 7:24 and you, LORD, *have* **b** their God. H2118
2Sa 10: 6 realized that *they had b* obnoxious **to** David, AIT
2Sa 16: 2 is to refresh those who **b** exhausted in the NDT
2Sa 17:29 "The people have **b** exhausted and hungry NDT
1Ki 1:11 son of Haggith, *has b* **king**, and our lord AIT
1Ki 1:13 my throne"? Why then *has* Adonijah *b* **king**?' AIT
1Ki 1:18 But now Adonijah *has b* **king**, and you, my AIT
1Ki 8:46 and *you b* **angry** with them and give them AIT
1Ki 9: 7 Israel *will* then **b** a byword and an object H2118
1Ki 9: 8 This temple *will* **b** a heap of rubble H2118+4200
1Ki 13:33 Anyone who wanted *to* **b** a priest he H2118
2Ki 5:27 was leprous—it had **b** as white as snow. NDT
2Ki 8:13 has shown me that you will **b** king of Aram," NDT
2Ki 9:29 son of Ahab, Ahaziah *had b* **king** of Judah.) AIT
2Ki 20:18 and *they will* **b** eunuchs in the palace of H2118
2Ki 22:19 that they *would* **b** a curse and be laid H2118
2Ki 25: 3 in the city *had b so* **severe** that there was no AIT
1Ch 4:27 entire clan *did* not *b* as **numerous** as the AIT
1Ch 11: 2 people Israel, and you *will* **b** their ruler. H2118
1Ch 11: 6 on the Jebusites *will* **b** H2118
1Ch 17:22 and you, LORD, *have* **b** their God. H2118
1Ch 19: 6 realized that *they had b* **obnoxious** to David, AIT
2Ch 6:36 and *you b* **angry** with them and give them AIT
2Ch 7:21 This temple *will* **b** a heap of rubble H2118+4200
2Ch 12: 1 was established and he had **b strong,** H2621
2Ch 12: 8 *They will,* however, **b** subject to him, so H2118
2Ch 13: 9 seven rams *may* **b** a priest of what H2118
2Ch 26: 8 of Egypt, because *he had b* very **powerful.** AIT
Ne 6: 6 these reports you *are about to* **b** their king H2093
Ne 9:21 did not wear out nor *did* their feet *b* **swollen.** AIT
Est 1:17 queen's conduct *will* **b known** to all the H3655
Job 3: 9 *May* its morning stars *b* **dark**; may it wait AIT
Job 3:24 For sighing *has* **b** my daily food; my groans H995
Job 7:20 me your target? *Have I* **b** a burden to you? H2118
Job 11:12 the witless *can* no more **b wise** than a H4220
Job 11:17 darkness *will* **b** like morning. H2118
Job 11:20 elude them; their hope will **b** a dying gasp." NDT
Job 12: 4 "*I have* **b** a laughingstock to my friends H2118
Job 16: 8 me up—and *it has* **b** a witness; my H2118
Job 20:14 it will **b** the venom of serpents within him. NDT
Job 24:22 though *they b* **established,** they have AIT
Job 30: 9 in song; *I have* **b** a byword among them. H2118
Job 30:29 *I have* **b** a brother of jackals, a companion H2118
Job 37:10 produces ice, and the broad waters **b** frozen. NDT
Job 38:30 *when* the waters **b hard** as stone, when H2461
Ps 2: 7 "You are my son; today I *have b* your **father**. AIT
Ps 14: 3 turned away, all *have b* **corrupt**; there is no AIT
Ps 31:12 I were dead; *I have* **b** like broken pottery. H2118
Ps 38:14 *I have* **b** like one who does not hear H2118
Ps 38:19 **Many** *have b* my enemies without cause AIT
Ps 53: 3 turned away, all *have b* **corrupt**; there is no AIT
Ps 63:10 over to the sword and *b* food for jackals. H2118
Ps 69:22 *May* the table set before them **b** a snare H2118
Ps 69:22 may it **b** retribution and a trap. NDT
Ps 71: 7 *I have* **b** a sign to many; you are my H2118
Ps 89:41 *he has* **b** the scorn of his neighbors. H2118
Ps 94: 8 the people; you fools, when *will you b* **wise**? AIT
Ps 94:22 But the LORD *has* **b** my fortress, and my H2118
Ps 102: 7 *I have* **b** like a bird alone on a roof. H2118
Ps 118:14 my defense; *he has* **b** my salvation. H2118
Ps 118:21 answered me; *you have* **b** my salvation. H2118
Ps 118:22 builders rejected *has* **b** the cornerstone; H2118
Ps 139:11 hide me and the light **b** night around me," NDT
Pr 13:20 Walk with the wise and *b* **wise**, for a AIT
Pr 21:17 Whoever loves pleasure will **b** poor NDT
Pr 21:18 The wicked **b** a ransom for the righteous NDT
Pr 23:21 drunkards and gluttons *b* **poor**, and AIT
Pr 29:12 ruler listens to lies, all his officials **b** wicked. NDT
Pr 30: 9 Or *I may* **b poor** and steal, and so H3769
SS 8:10 Thus *I have* **b** in his eyes like one H2118
Isa 1: 9 survivors, *we would have* **b** like Sodom H2118
Isa 1:14 *They have* **b** a burden to me; I am weary H2118
Isa 1:21 how the faithful city *has* **b** a prostitute! H2118
Isa 1:22 Your silver *has* **b** dross, your choice wine H2118
Isa 1:31 The mighty man *will* **b** tinder and his work H2118
Isa 5: 9 "Surely the great houses *will* **b** desolate H2118
Isa 7:25 *they will* **b** places where cattle are turned H2118
Isa 8:21 famished, *they will b* **enraged** and, looking AIT
Isa 10:17 The Light of Israel *will* **b** a fire, their Holy H2118
Isa 12: 2 my defense; *he has* **b** my salvation." H2118
Isa 14:10 "You also *have b* **weak**, as we are; AIT
Isa 14:10 as we are; *you have* **b like** us. H5439
Isa 17: 1 longer be a city but *will* **b** a heap of ruins. H2118
Isa 19: 7 sown field along the Nile *will b* **parched,** AIT
Isa 19:13 The officials of Zoan *have* **b fools**, the H3282
Isa 19:16 In that day the Egyptians *will* **b** weaklings H2118
Isa 21: 4 twilight I longed for *has* **b** a horror to me. H8492
Isa 22:18 were so proud of will **b** a disgrace to your NDT
Isa 22:23 *he will* **b** a seat of honor for the house of H2118
Isa 28:13 the word of the LORD to them *will* **b**: H2118
Isa 28:22 your chains *will b* **heavier**; the Lord, AIT
Isa 29: 5 your many enemies *will* **b** like fine dust, H2118
Isa 30:13 this sin *will* **b** for you like a high wall H2118
Isa 32:14 watchtower *will* **b** a wasteland forever H2118
Isa 34: 9 her land *will* **b** blazing pitch! H2118
Isa 34:13 *She will* **b** a haunt for jackals, a home H2118
Isa 35: 7 The burning sand *will* **b** a pool, the thirsty H2118
Isa 39: 7 and *they will* **b** eunuchs in the palace of H2118
Isa 40: 4 the rough ground *shall* **b** level, the H2118
Isa 42:22 *They have* **b** plunder, with no one to H2118
Isa 42:24 Who handed Jacob over to **b** loot, and NDT
Isa 51: 4 my justice will **b** a light to the nations. NDT
Isa 58:10 your night will **b** like the noonday. NDT
Isa 60:22 The least of you *will* **b** a thousand, the H2118
Isa 64: 6 All of us *have* **b** like one who is unclean H2118
Isa 64:10 Your sacred cities *have* **b** a wasteland H2118
Isa 65:10 Sharon *will* **b** a pasture for flocks, and the H2118
Jer 2:14 Why then *has he* **b** plunder? H2118
Jer 5:27 full of deceit; *they have b* **rich** and powerful AIT
Jer 7:11 *Has* this house, which bears my Name, **b** a H2118
Jer 7:33 of this people *will* **b** food for the birds H2118
Jer 7:34 of Jerusalem, for the land *will* **b** desolate. H2118
Jer 12: 8 My inheritance *has* **b** to me like a lion in H2118
Jer 12: 9 not my inheritance **b** to me like a speckled NDT
Jer 16: 4 their dead bodies *will* **b** food for the birds H2118
Jer 22: 5 by myself that this palace *will* **b** a ruin. H2118
Jer 23:12 "Therefore their path *will* **b** slippery; they H2118
Jer 25:11 This whole country *will* **b** a desolate H2118
Jer 25:38 their land *will* **b** desolate because of H2118
Jer 26:18 Jerusalem *will* **b** a heap of rubble H2118
Jer 27:17 Why *should* this city **b** a ruin? H2118
Jer 34:16 have forced them to **b** your slaves again. H2118
Jer 34:20 Their dead bodies *will* **b** food for the birds H2118
Jer 44:12 *They will* **b** a curse and an object of horror H2118
Jer 47: 2 *they will* **b** an overflowing torrent. H2118
Jer 48: 6 your lives; **b** like a bush in the desert. H2118
Jer 48: 9 her towns *will* **b** desolate, with no H2118
Jer 48:39 Moab *has* **b** an object of ridicule, an H2118
Jer 49: 2 the Ammonites; *it will* **b** a mound of ruins H2118
Jer 49:13 "that Bozrah *will* **b** a ruin and a curse H2118
Jer 49:17 "Edom *will* **b** an object of horror; all who H2118
Jer 49:24 Damascus *has b* **feeble**, she has turned to AIT
Jer 49:32 Their camels *will* **b** plunder, and their H2118
Jer 49:33 "Hazor *will* **b** a haunt of jackals, H2118
Jer 50:36 false prophets! *They will* **b fools**. A sword H3282
Jer 50:37 *They will* **b** weaklings. H2118+4200
Jer 51:30 exhausted; *they have* **b** weaklings. H2118+4200
Jer 52: 6 in the city *had b so* **severe** that there was no AIT
La 1: 1 among the provinces *has now* **b** a slave. H2118
La 1: 2 betrayed her; *they have* **b** her enemies. H2118
La 1: 5 Her foes *have* **b** her masters; her enemies H2118
La 1: 8 has sinned greatly and so *has* **b** unclean. H2118
La 1:17 Jacob that his neighbors **b** his foes; NDT
La 1:17 Jerusalem *has* **b** an unclean thing among H2118
La 1:21 have announced so *they may* **b** like me. H2118
La 4: 1 gold has lost its luster, the fine gold *b* **dull!** AIT
La 4: 3 my people have **b** heartless like NDT
La 4: 8 on their bones; *it has* **b** as dry as a stick. H2118
La 5: 3 *We have* **b** fatherless, our mothers are H2118
Eze 16:15 beauty and used your fame *to b a* **prostitute.** AIT
Eze 17: 8 bear fruit and **b** a splendid vine. H2118
Eze 17:23 bear fruit and **b** a splendid cedar. H2118
Eze 21: 7 every spirit *will b* **faint** and every leg will be AIT
Eze 22: 4 *you have b* **guilty** because of the blood you AIT
Eze 22: 4 have shed and *have b* **defiled** by the idols AIT
Eze 22:18 the people of Israel *have* **b** dross to me H2118
Eze 22:19 'Because you *have* all **b** dross, I will H2118
Eze 25: 8 Judah has **b** like all the other nations," NDT
Eze 26: 5 Out in the sea *she will* **b** a place to spread H2118
Eze 26: 5 *She will* **b** plunder for the nations, H2118
Eze 26:14 and *you will* **b** a place to spread fishnets. H2118
Eze 29: 9 Egypt *will* **b** a desolate wasteland. H2118
Eze 33:21 so that it *may b* **strong** *enough* to hold a AIT
Eze 33:28 of Israel *will b* **desolate** so that no one AIT
Eze 34: 8 been plundered and *has* **b** food for all the H2118
Eze 36: 2 ancient heights *have* **b** our possession." H2118
Eze 36:11 they will be fruitful and *b* **numerous.** AIT
Eze 36:35 was laid waste *has* **b** like the garden of H2118
Eze 37:17 stick so that *they will* **b** one in your hand H2118
Eze 37:19 of wood, and *they will* **b** one in my hand. H2118
Eze 47:11 But the swamps and marshes *will* not *b* **fresh** AIT
Eze 47:14 this land *will* **b** your inheritance. H5877
Da 4:22 *You have b* **great** and strong; your greatness AIT
Da 8:23 when rebels *have b* **completely** wicked, AIT
Da 8:24 *He will b* **very strong**, but not by his own AIT
Da 11: 5 "The king of the South *will b* **strong**, but one AIT
Da 11: 5 commanders *will b even* **stronger** than he AIT
Da 11: 6 some years, *they will b* **allies**. The daughter AIT
Hos 4:15 commit adultery, *do not let* Judah *b* **guilty**. AIT
Hos 7: 5 of our king the princes *b* **inflamed** with wine, AIT
Hos 8:11 offerings, *these have* **b** altars for sinning. H2118
Hos 12: 8 "I am very rich; *I have* **b** wealthy. H5162
Am 7:17 " 'Your wife *will b a* **prostitute** in the city, AIT
Jnh 1:12 into the sea," he replied, "and it *will b* **calm**. AIT
Mic 2: 7 it be said, "*Does* the LORD *b* **impatient**? AIT
Mic 3:12 Jerusalem *will* **b** a heap of rubble H2118
Mic 7:13 The earth *will* **b** desolate because of its H2118
Mic 7:16 over their mouths and their ears *will b* **deaf**. AIT
Na 3:11 You too *will b* **drunk**; you will go into hiding AIT
Hab 2: 7 Then *you will* **b** their prey. H2118+4200
Zep 2: 6 land by the sea *will* **b** pastures having H2118
Zep 2: 9 "surely Moab *will* **b** like Sodom, the H2118
Zep 2:15 What a ruin *she has* **b**, a lair for wild H2118
Hag 2:12 olive oil or other food, *does it b* **consecrated**? AIT
Hag 2:13 one of these things, *does it b* **defiled**?" AIT
Zec 2:11 the LORD in that day and *will* **b** my people. H2118
Zec 4: 7 Zerubbabel you will **b** level ground. H4200
Zec 8:19 tenth months *will* **b** joyful and glad H2118
Zec 9: 7 belong to our God and **b** a clan in Judah, H2118
Zec 10: 7 The Ephraimites *will* **b** like warriors, and H2118
Zec 14:10 south of Jerusalem, *will* **b** like the Arabah. H6015
Mt 4: 3 Son of God, tell these stones *to* **b** bread." *G1181*
Mt 13:15 For this people's heart *has b* **calloused**; they AIT
Mt 13:52 of the law *who has* **b a disciple** in the *G3411*
Mt 18: 3 you change and **b** like little children, *G1181*
Mt 19: 5 and the two *will* **b** one flesh'? *G1639+1650*
Mt 20:26 whoever wants *to* **b** great among you *G1181*
Mt 21:42 rejected *has* **b** the cornerstone; *G1181+1650*
Mt 27:57 who *had* himself **b a disciple** of Jesus. *G3411*
Mk 6:14 for Jesus' name *had* **b** well known. *G1181*
Mk 10: 8 the two *will* **b** one flesh.' So *G1639+1650*
Mk 10:43 whoever wants *to* **b** great among you *G1181*
Mk 12:10 rejected *has* **b** the cornerstone; *G1181+1650*
Lk 3: 5 The crooked roads *shall* **b** straight *G1639+1650*
Lk 4: 3 the Son of God, tell this stone *to* **b** bread." *G1181*
Lk 20:17 rejected *has* **b** the cornerstone'? *G1181+1650*
Jn 1:12 he gave the right *to b* children of God— *G1181*
Jn 3:30 He must **b greater**; I must become less." AIT
Jn 3:30 He must become greater; I *must b* **less**." AIT
Jn 4:14 water I give them *will* **b** in them a spring *G1181*
Jn 7: 4 No one who wants to **b** a public figure acts *G1639*
Jn 9:27 Do you want *to* **b** his disciples too? *G1181*
Jn 9:39 will see and those who see *will* **b** blind." *G1181*
Jn 12:36 so that *you may* **b** children of light." *G1181*
Ac 1:22 For one of these *must* **b** a witness with us *G1181*
Ac 4:11 which *has* **b** the cornerstone. *G1181+1650*
Ac 12:18 the soldiers as to what *had* **b** *of* Peter. *G1181*
Ac 13:33 'You are my son; today *I have b* your **father**.' AIT
Ac 26:29 listening to me today *may* **b** what I am, *G1181*
Ac 27: 9 sailing *had* already **b** dangerous *G1639*
Ac 28:27 For this people's heart *has b* **calloused**; they AIT
Ro 1:29 *They have b* **filled** with every kind of AIT
Ro 2:25 you *have* **b** as though you had not been *G1181*
Ro 3:12 *they have* together *b* **worthless**; there AIT
Ro 3:20 through the law *we b* **conscious** of our sin. AIT
Ro 6:18 from sin and *have b* **slaves** to righteousness AIT
Ro 6:22 set free from sin and *have b* **slaves** of God, AIT
Ro 7:13 *Did* that which is good, then, **b** death to *G1181*
Ro 7:13 commandment sin *might* **b** utterly sinful. *G1181*
Ro 9:29 *we* would have **b** like Sodom *G1181*
Ro 11: 9 "*May* their table **b** a snare and a *G1181+1650*
Ro 11:31 so they too *have* now *b* **disobedient** in order AIT
Ro 15: 8 For I tell you that Christ *has* **b** a servant of *G1181*
Ro 15:16 so that the Gentiles *might* **b** an offering *G1181*
1Co 1:30 who *has* **b** for us wisdom from God *G1181*
1Co 3:18 of this age, *you should* **b** "fools" so that *G1181*
1Co 3:18 become "fools" so that *you may* **b** wise. *G1181*
1Co 4: 8 Already *you have b* **rich**! You have AIT
1Co 4:13 *We have* **b** the scum of the earth, the *G1181*
1Co 4:18 Some *of you have b* **arrogant**, as if I were not AIT
1Co 6:16 it is said, "The two *will* **b** one flesh." *G1639+1650*
1Co 7:18 *He should* not *b* **uncircumcised**. AIT
1Co 7:23 a price; *do* not **b** slaves of human beings. *G1181*
1Co 8: 9 of your rights *does* not **b** a stumbling *G1181*
1Co 9:22 *I have* **b** all things to all people so that by *G1181*
2Co 5:21 so that in him we *might* **b** the *G1181*
2Co 8: 9 so that you through his poverty *might b* **rich**. AIT
Gal 4:12 sisters, **b** like me, for I became *G1181*
Gal 4:16 *Have I* now **b** your enemy by telling you *G1181*
Gal 5:26 *Let us* not **b** conceited, provoking and *G1181*
Gal 6: 9 *Let us* not *b* **weary** in doing good, for at the AIT
Eph 2:21 together and rises *to b* a holy temple in the AIT
Eph 2:22 being built together *to b* a dwelling in which AIT
Eph 4:13 knowledge of the Son of God and **b** mature, NDT
Eph 4:15 *we will* **grow to b** in every respect the **mature** *G889*
Eph 5:31 and the two *will* **b** one flesh. *G1639+1650*
Php 1:13 *it has* **b** clear throughout the whole *G1181*
Php 1:14 sisters *have b* **confident** in the Lord and AIT

Php 2:15 so that *you may* b blameless and pure G1181
Col 1:23 of which I, Paul, *have* b a servant. G1181
Col 1:25 I *have* b its servant by the commission God G1181
Col 3:21 your children, or *they will* b **discouraged**. AIT
1Th 1: 8 your faith in God *has* b **known** everywhere. AIT
2Th 2: 2 not to b easily **unsettled** or alarmed by the AIT
1Ti 3: 6 or *he may* b **conceited** and fall under the AIT
1Ti 5:13 And not only do they b idlers, but also NDT
2Ti 2:16 in it *will* b **more and more** G2093+4498+4621
2Ti 3:14 you have learned and *have* b **convinced** *of*, AIT
Titus 3: 7 *we might* b heirs having the hope of G1181
Phm 11 now he has b useful both to you and to NDT
Heb 1: 5 today I *have* b your **Father**"? Or again, AIT
Heb 2:17 in order that *he might* b a merciful and G1181
Heb 5: 5 are my Son; today I *have* b your **Father**." AIT
Heb 6:12 We do not want *you to* b lazy, but to G1181
Heb 6:20 *He has* b a high priest forever, in the G1181
Heb 7: 5 of Levi who b priests to collect a G3284
Heb 7:16 one who *has* b a priest not on the basis of G1181
Heb 7:22 Jesus *has* b the guarantor of a better G1181
Jas 1:19 to listen, slow to speak and slow to b angry, NDT
Jas 2: 4 among yourselves and b judges with evil G1181
Jas 2:11 commit murder, *you have* b a lawbreaker. G1181
Jas 3: 1 Not many *of you should* b teachers, my G1181
1Pe 2: 7 rejected *has* b the cornerstone," G1181+1650
1Pe 4:18 what *will* b **of** the ungodly and the sinner?" G5743
Rev 3:18 in the fire, so *you can* b **rich**; and white AIT
Rev 8:11 died from the waters that *had* b **bitter**. AIT
Rev 11:15 of the world *has* b the kingdom of our G1181
Rev 18: 2 *She has* b a dwelling for demons and a G1181

BECOMES (35) [BECOME]

Lev 4:14 the sin they committed *b* **known**, the AIT
Lev 4:23 the sin he has committed *b* **known**, he AIT
Lev 4:28 the sin they have committed b **known** AIT
Lev 5: 2 " 'If anyone b aware that they are guilty—if NDT
Lev 5: 5 when *anyone* b **aware that** *they are* **guilty** in AIT
Lev 11:35 that one of their carcasses falls on b **unclean**; AIT
Lev 12: 2 'A woman *who* b **pregnant** and gives birth to AIT
Lev 22:13 a priest's daughter b a widow or is H2118
Lev 25:25 fellow Israelites *b* **poor** and sells some of AIT
Lev 25:47 residing among you *b* **rich** and any of your AIT
Lev 27: 9 such an animal given to the LORD b holy. H2118
Nu 19:22 that an unclean person touches b **unclean**, AIT
Nu 19:22 who touches it *b* **unclean** till evening." AIT
Dt 24: 1 marries a woman *who* b displeasing to H2118
Dt 24: 2 leaves his house *she* b the wife of H2118
Job 14:11 lake dries up or a riverbed *b* **parched** and dry, AIT
Job 18: 6 The light in his tent *b* **dark**; the lamp beside AIT
Job 30:18 his great power God b **like** clothing to me; H2924
Job 38:38 when the dust *b* **hard** and the clods of earth AIT
Ps 104:20 You bring darkness, *it* b night, and all the H2118
Pr 30:22 a servant *who* b **king**, a godless fool who AIT
Isa 18: 5 gone and the flower b a ripening grape, H2118
Isa 32:15 and the desert b a fertile field, and H2118
Isa 59:15 and whoever shuns evil b *a* **prey**. H8964
Jer 23:36 each one's word b their own message. H2118
Eze 14:15 it childless and *it* b desolate so that no H2118
Eze 24:11 on the coals till *it b* **hot** and its copper glows AIT
Eze 47: 8 into the sea, the salty water there *b* **fresh**. AIT
Hag 2:13 the priests replied, "*it b* **defiled**." AIT
Mt 13:32 the largest of garden plants and b a tree, G1181
Mk 4:32 it grows and b the largest of all garden G1181
Mk 9:18 at the mouth, gnashes his teeth and *b* **rigid**. AIT
Eph 5:13 But everything exposed by the light *b* **visible** AIT
Eph 5:13 everything that is illuminated b a light. G1639
Jas 4: 4 a friend of the world b an enemy of God. G2770

BECOMING (9) [BECOME]

Lev 21: 9 daughter defiles herself by *b a* **prostitute**, AIT
1Sa 3: 2 whose eyes *were* b so weak that he could H2725
1Ki 16: 7 b like the house of Jeroboam H2118
Joel 2:22 the pastures in the wilderness *are b* **green**. AIT
2Co 12: 7 in order to keep *me* from *b* **conceited**, I was AIT
Gal 3:13 the curse of the law *by* b a curse for us, G1181
Php 2: 8 humbled himself *by* b obedient to death G1181
Php 3:10 in his sufferings, b **like** him in his death, G5214
Heb 5: 5 on himself the glory *of* b a high priest. G1181

BECORATH (NIV84) BEKORATH

BED (76) [BEDDING, BEDRIDDEN, BEDROOM, BEDROOMS, BEDS, SICKBED]

Ge 19: 4 Before *they had* **gone to b**, all the men H8886
Ge 39: 7 and said, "**Come to b with** me!" H8886+6640
Ge 39:10 refused to **go to b with** her or even H8886+725
Ge 39:12 and said, "**Come to b with** me!" H8886+6640
Ge 48: 2 rallied his strength and sat up on the b. H4753
Ge 49: 4 you went up onto your father's b, onto H5435
Ge 49:33 he drew his feet up into the b, breathed H4753
Ex 8: 3 your bedroom and onto your b, H4753
Ex 21:18 victim does not die but is confined to b, H5435
Lev 15: 4 " 'Any b the man with a discharge lies on H5435
Lev 15: 5 Anyone who touches his b must wash their H5435
Lev 15:21 who touches her b will be unclean; H5435
Lev 15:23 Whether it is the b or anything she was H5435
Lev 15:24 any b he lies on will be unclean. H5435
Lev 15:26 Any b she lies on while her discharge H5435
Lev 15:26 as is her b during her monthly period H5435
Dt 3:11 His b was *decorated with* iron and was H6911
Dt 22:30 *he must* not **dishonor** his father's b. H1655+4053
Dt 27:20 for *he* **dishonors** his father's b." H1655+4053
1Sa 19:13 Michal took an idol and laid it on the b, H4753
1Sa 19:15 him up to me in his b so that I may kill H4753
1Sa 19:16 there was the idol in the b, and at the H4753
2Sa 4: 7 he was lying on the b in his bedroom. H4753
2Sa 4:11 in his own house and on his own b— H5435
2Sa 11: 2 got up from his b and walked around on H5435
2Sa 13: 5 "Go to b and pretend to be ill," Jonadab H5435
2Sa 13:11 "Come *to* b **with** me, my sister H8886+6640
1Ki 1:47 And the king bowed in worship on his b H5435
1Ki 17:19 he was staying, and laid him on his b. H4753
1Ki 21: 4 He lay on his b sulking and refused to eat. H4753
2Ki 1: 4 'You will not leave the b you are lying on H4753
2Ki 1: 6 you will not leave the b you are lying on. H4753
2Ki 1:16 will never leave the b you are lying on. H4753
2Ki 4:10 on the roof and put in it a b and a table, H4753
2Ki 4:21 laid him on the b *of* the man of God, H4753
2Ki 4:34 Then he got on the b and lay on the boy NDT
2Ki 4:35 then got on the b and stretched out on NDT
1Ch 5: 1 when he defiled his father's **marriage** b, H3661
2Ch 24:25 the priest, and they killed him in his b. H4753
Job 7:13 When I think my b will comfort me and H6911
Job 17:13 if I spread out my b in the realm of H3661
Job 33:19 be chastened on a b of pain with constant H5435
Ps 6: 6 night long I flood my b with weeping and H4753
Ps 41: 3 restores them from their b of illness. H5435
Ps 63: 6 On my b I remember you; I think of you H3661
Ps 132: 3 not enter my house or go to my b, H6911+3661
Ps 139: 8 are there; if *I* **make** *my* b *in* the depths H3667
Pr 7:16 I have covered my b with colored linens H6911
Pr 7:17 I have perfumed my b with myrrh, aloes H5435
Pr 22:27 your very b will be snatched from under H5435
Pr 26:14 its hinges, so a sluggard turns on his b. H4753
Pr 31:22 She makes **coverings** for her b; she is H5267
SS 1:16 how charming! And our b is verdant. H6911
SS 3: 1 night long on my b I looked for the one H5435
Isa 28:20 The b is too short to stretch out on, the H5201
Isa 57: 7 You have made your b on a high and lofty H5435
Isa 57: 8 you uncovered your b, you climbed into it H5435
Eze 22:10 *those who* **dishonor** their father's b; H1655+6872
Eze 23:17 came to her, to the b *of* love, and in their H5435
Eze 32:25 A b is made for her among the slain, with H5435
Da 2:28 mind as you were lying in b are these: A10444
Da 4: 5 As I was lying in b, the images and A10444
Da 4:10 are the visions I saw while lying in b: A10444
Da 4:13 "In the visions I saw while lying in b, A10444
Da 7: 1 through his mind as he was lying in b. A10444
Am 3:12 only the head of a b and a piece of fabric H4753
Mt 8:14 Peter's mother-in-law **lying** *in b* with a fever. AIT
Mk 1:30 mother-in-law *was* **in b** with a fever, G2879
Mk 4:21 in a lamp to put it under a bowl or a b? G3109
Mk 7:30 home and found her child lying on the b, G3109
Lk 8:16 hides it in a clay jar or puts it under a b. G3109
Lk 11: 7 and my children and I are in b. G3130
Lk 17:34 on that night two people will be in one b G3109
Ac 28: 8 His father was sick **in b**, suffering from G2879
Heb 13: 4 and the marriage b kept pure, for God G3130
Rev 2:22 So I will cast her on a b of suffering, and I G3109

BEDAD (2)

Ge 36:35 Hadad son of B, who defeated H971
1Ch 1:46 Hadad son of B, who defeated H971

BEDAN (1)

1Ch 7:17 The son of Ulam: B. These were the sons H979

BEDDING (1) [BED]

2Sa 17:28 brought b and bowls and articles of pottery H5435

BEDEIAH (1)

Ezr 10:35 Benaiah, B, Keluhi, H973

BEDRIDDEN (1) [BED]

Ac 9:33 and *had been* b for eight G2879+2093+3187

BEDROOM (8) [BED, ROOM]

Ex 8: 3 palace and your b and onto your H2540+5435
2Sa 4: 7 he was lying on the bed in his b. H2540+5435
2Sa 13:10 the food here into my b so I may eat from H2540
2Sa 13:10 brought it to her brother Amnon in his b. H2540
2Ki 6:12 the very words you speak in your b." H2540+5435
2Ki 11: 2 his nurse in a b to hide him from H2540+4753
2Ch 22:11 and put him and his nurse in a b. H2540+4753
Ecc 10:20 curse the rich in your b, because H2540+5435

BEDROOMS (1) [BED, ROOM]

Ps 105:30 which went up into the b *of* their rulers. H2540

BEDS (12) [BED]

Job 30: 6 were forced to live in the dry **stream** b, H5707
Job 33:15 falls on people as they slumber in their b, H5435
Ps 4: 4 when you are on your b, search your H5435
Ps 36: 4 Even on their b they plot evil; they commit H5435
Ps 149: 5 in this honor and sing for joy on their b. H5435
SS 5:13 His cheeks are like b *of* spice yielding H6870
SS 6: 2 his garden, to the b *of* spices, to browse H6870
Isa 57: 8 made a pact with those whose b you love, H5435
Hos 7:14 me from their hearts but wail on their b. H5435
Am 6: 4 You lie on b *adorned with* ivory and H4753
Mic 2: 1 iniquity, to those who plot evil on their b! H5435
Ac 5:15 laid them on b and mats so that at G3108

BEELIADA (1)

1Ch 14: 7 Elishama, B and Eliphelet. H1269

BEELZEBUB (NIV84) BEELZEBUL

BEELZEBUL (7) [BAAL-ZEBUB]

Mt 10:25 the head of the house has been called B, G1015
Mt 12:24 "It is only by B, the prince of demons G1015
Mt 12:27 And if I drive out demons by B, by whom G1015
Mk 3:22 Jerusalem said, "He is possessed by B! G1015
Lk 11:15 of them said, "By B, the prince of demons, G1015
Lk 11:18 you claim that I drive out demons by B. G1015
Lk 11:19 Now if I drive out demons by B, by whom G1015

BEEN (918) [BE] See Index of Articles Etc.

BEER (13) [BAALATH BEER, BEER LAHAI ROI, BEER ELIM]

Nu 21:16 From there they continued on to B, the well H932
Jdg 9:21 escaping to B, and he lived there H932
1Sa 1:15 I have not been drinking wine or b; I was H8911
Pr 20: 1 Wine is a mocker and b a brawler H8911
Pr 31: 4 to drink wine, not for rulers to crave b, H8911
Pr 31: 6 Let b be for those who are perishing, wine H8911
Isa 24: 9 with a song; the b is bitter to its drinkers. H8911
Isa 28: 7 also stagger from wine and reel from b: H8911
Isa 28: 7 stagger from b and are befuddled H8911
Isa 28: 7 they reel from b, they stagger when H8911
Isa 29: 9 not from wine, stagger, but not from b. H8911
Isa 56:12 Let us drink our fill of b! And tomorrow H8911
Mic 2:11 prophesy for you plenty of wine and b, H8911

BEER ELIM (1) [BEER, ELIM]

Isa 15: 8 their lamentation as far as B Elim. H935

BEER LAHAI ROI (3) [BEER]

Ge 16:14 That is why the well was called B Lahai Roi H936
Ge 24:62 Now Isaac had come from B Lahai Roi, for H936
Ge 25:11 son Isaac, who then lived near B Lahai Roi. H936

BEERA (1)

1Ch 7:37 Shamma, Shilshah, Ithran and B. H938

BEERAH (2)

1Ch 5: 6 B his son, whom Tiglath-Pileser king H939
1Ch 5: 6 B was a leader of the Reubenites H2085S

BEERI (2)

Ge 26:34 he married Judith daughter of B the Hittite H941
Hos 1: 1 to Hosea son of B during the reigns of H941

BEEROTH (6) [BEEROTHITE]

Jos 9:17 Gibeon, Kephirah, B and Kiriath Jearim. H940
Jos 18:25 Gibeon, Ramah, B, H940
2Sa 4: 2 B is considered part of Benjamin H940
2Sa 4: 3 because the **people of B** fled to Gittaim H943
Ezr 2:25 of Kiriath Jearim, Kephirah and B 743 H940
Ne 7:29 of Kiriath Jearim, Kephirah and B 743 H940

BEEROTHITE (4) [BEEROTH]

2Sa 4: 2 sons of Rimmon the B from the tribe of H943
2Sa 4: 5 the sons of Rimmon the B, set out for the H943
2Sa 4: 9 the sons of Rimmon the B, "As surely as H943
2Sa 23:37 Naharai the B, the armor-bearer of H943

BEERSHEBA (34)

Ge 21:14 her way and wandered in the Desert of B. H937
Ge 21:31 So that place was called B, because the H937
Ge 21:32 After the treaty had been made at B H937
Ge 21:33 Abraham planted a tamarisk tree in B, and H937
Ge 22:19 his servants, and they set off together for B. H937
Ge 22:19 Beersheba. And Abraham stayed in B. H937
Ge 26:23 From there he went up to B. H937
Ge 26:33 this day the name of the town has been B. H937
Ge 28:10 Jacob left B and set out for Harran. H937
Ge 46: 1 when he reached B, he offered H937
Ge 46: 5 Then Jacob left B, and Israel's sons took H937
Jos 15:28 Hazar Shual, B, Biziothiah, H937
Jos 19: 2 B (or Sheba), Moladah, H937
Jdg 20: 1 Israel from Dan to B and from the land of H937
1Sa 3:20 all Israel from Dan to B recognized that H937
1Sa 8: 2 second was Abijah, and they served at B. H937
2Sa 3:10 over Israel and Judah from Dan to B." H937
2Sa 17:11 from Dan to B—as numerous as the H937
2Sa 24: 2 of Israel from Dan to B and enroll the H937
2Sa 24: 7 they went on to B in the Negev of Judah. H937
2Sa 24:15 of the people from Dan to B died. H937
1Ki 4:25 Israel, from Dan to B, lived in safety, H937
1Ki 19: 3 When he came to B in Judah, he left his H937
2Ki 12: 1 name was Zibiah; she was from B. H937
2Ki 23: 8 from Geba to B, where the priests H937
1Ch 4:28 They lived in B, Moladah, Hazar Shual, H937
1Ch 21: 2 "Go and count the Israelites from B to Dan. H937
2Ch 19: 4 the people from B to the hill country H937
2Ch 24: 1 name was Zibiah; she was from B. H937
2Ch 30: 5 from B to Dan, calling the H937
Ne 11:27 in Hazar Shual, in B and its settlements, H937
Ne 11:30 living all the way from B to the Valley of H937
Am 5: 5 do not go to Gilgal, do not journey to B. H937
Am 8:14 'As surely as the god of B lives'—they will H937

BEES (4)

Dt 1:44 you like a **swarm of** b and beat you down H1805
Jdg 14: 8 it he saw a swarm of b and some honey. H1805
Ps 118:12 They swarmed around me like b, but they H1805
Isa 7:18 delta in Egypt and for b from the land of H1805

BEETLE (KJV) CRICKET

B

BEEVES (KJV) CATTLE

BEFORE (1288) [BEFOREHAND]

Ge 10: 9 He was a mighty hunter **b** the LORD H7156+4200
Ge 10: 9 a mighty hunter **b** the LORD. H7156+4200
Ge 13: 9 Is not the whole land **b** you? Let's H7156+4200
Ge 13:10 This was **b** the LORD destroyed H7156+4200
Ge 17: 1 walk **b** me faithfully and be H4200+7156
Ge 18: 8 prepared, and set these **b** them. H7156+4200
Ge 18:22 remained standing **b** the LORD. H7156+4200
Ge 19: 4 **B** they had gone to bed, all the men from H3270
Ge 19:27 where he had stood **b** the LORD. H907+7156
Ge 20:15 "My land is **b** you; live H7156+4200
Ge 20:16 offense against you **b** all who are with H4200
Ge 21:23 Now swear to me here **b** God that you will H928
Ge 23: 7 rose and bowed down **b** the people of the H4200
Ge 23:12 bowed down **b** the people of the H7156+4200
Ge 24: 7 send his angel **b** you so that you H7156+4200
Ge 24:15 **B** he had finished praying, Rebekah came H3270
Ge 24:33 Then food was set **b** him, but he H7156+4200
Ge 24:40 **b** whom I have walked faithfully H7156+4200
Ge 24:45 "**B** I finished praying in my heart, Rebekah H3270
Ge 24:52 he bowed down to the ground **b** the LORD. H4200
Ge 27: 4 I may give you my blessing **b** I die." H928+3270
Ge 27: 7 in the presence of the LORD **b** I die. H7156+4200
Ge 27:10 give you his blessing **b** he dies." H7156+4200
Ge 27:33 I ate it **just b** you came and I H928+3270
Ge 29:26 in marriage **b** the older one. H7156+4200
Ge 30:30 The little you had **b** I came has H7156+4200
Ge 31: 5 toward me is not what it was **b**, H9453+8997
Ge 33:14 and herds **b** me and the pace H4200+7156
Ge 36:31 reigned in Edom **b** any Israelite H7156+4200
Ge 37:10 come and bow down to the ground **b** you?" H4200
Ge 37:18 distance, and **b** he reached them H928+3270
Ge 41:14 changed his clothes, he came **b** Pharaoh. H448
Ge 41:21 they looked just as ugly as **b**. H928+2021+9378
Ge 41:43 and people shouted **b** him, "Make H7156+4200
Ge 41:50 **B** the years of famine came, two H928+3270
Ge 42:24 taken from them and bound **b** their eyes. H4200
Ge 43: 9 to you and set him here **b** you, H7156+4200
Ge 43: 9 I will bear the blame **b** you all my life. H4200
Ge 43:14 grant you mercy **b** the man so that H7156+4200
Ge 43:26 they bowed down **b** him to the ground. H4200
Ge 43:28 bowed down, **prostrating** *themselves b* him. AIT
Ge 43:33 had been seated **b** him in the H7156+4200
Ge 44:14 themselves to the ground **b** him. H7156+4200
Ge 44:32 I will bear the blame **b** you, my father, H4200
Ge 45: 1 control himself **b** all his attendants, H4200
Ge 45:28 I will go and see him **b** I die." H928+3270
Ge 46:29 As soon as Joseph appeared **b** him, he H448
Ge 47: 2 and presented them **b** Pharaoh. H4200+7156
Ge 47: 6 the land of Egypt is **b** you H7156+4200
Ge 47: 7 in and presented him **b** Pharaoh. H7156+4200
Ge 47:15 Why should we die **b** your eyes? Our H5584
Ge 47:19 Why should we perish **b** your eyes—we H4200
Ge 48: 5 born to you in Egypt **b** I came to you here H6330
Ge 48:15 "May the God **b** whom my fathers H7156+4200
Ge 50:16 left these instructions **b** he died: H7156+4200
Ge 50:18 and threw themselves down **b** him. H7156+4200
Ex 1:19 and give birth **b** the midwives arrive." H928+3270
Ex 4:21 that you perform **b** Pharaoh all the H7156+4200
Ex 4:30 performed the signs **b** the people, H4200+6524
Ex 5: 8 the same number of bricks as **b**; H9453+8997
Ex 5:14 of bricks yesterday or today, as **b**?" H9453+8997
Ex 7: 9 staff and throw it down **b** Pharaoh, H7156+4200
Ex 9:10 a furnace and stood **b** Pharaoh. H7156+4200
Ex 9:11 could not stand **b** Moses because H7156+4200
Ex 10: 3 refuse to humble yourself **b** me? H7156+4946
Ex 10:14 Never **b** had there been such a H7156+4200
Ex 10:28 Make sure you do not appear **b** me again H7156
Ex 10:29 "I will never appear **b** you again." H7156
Ex 11: 8 bowing down **b** me and saying, 'Go H4200
Ex 11:10 all these wonders **b** Pharaoh, H7156+4200
Ex 12:34 took their dough **b** the yeast was added, H3270
Ex 16: 9 'Come **b** the LORD, for he H7156+4200
Ex 16:33 Then place it **b** the LORD to be kept H4200+7156
Ex 17: 6 I will stand there **b** you by the rock H4200+7156
Ex 18:19 representative **b** God and bring their H4578
Ex 19: 7 people and set **b** them all the H4200+7156
Ex 20: 3 shall have no other gods **b** me. H7156+6584
Ex 21: 1 are the laws you are to set **b** them: H4200+7156
Ex 21: 6 then his master must take him **b** the judges H448
Ex 22: 8 of the house must appear **b** the judges, H448
Ex 22: 9 are to bring their cases **b** the judges. H6330
Ex 22:11 by the taking of an **oath** *b* the LORD that the AIT
Ex 23:15 one is to appear **b** me empty-handed. H7156
Ex 23:17 men are to appear **b** the Sovereign H7156+448
Ex 23:24 Do not bow down **b** their gods or worship H4200
Ex 23:30 Little by little I will drive them out **b** you H7156
Ex 23:31 and you will drive them out **b** you. H7156
Ex 25:30 this table to be **b** me at all times. H7156+4200
Ex 27:21 the lamps burning **b** the LORD from H4200+7156
Ex 28:12 as a memorial **b** the LORD. H4200+7156
Ex 28:29 a continuing memorial **b** the LORD. H4200+7156
Ex 28:30 Israelites over his heart **b** the LORD. H4200+7156
Ex 28:35 the Holy Place **b** the LORD and H4200+7156
Ex 29:23 which is **b** the LORD, take one H4200+7156
Ex 29:24 them wave them **b** the LORD as a H4200+7156
Ex 29:26 wave it **b** the LORD as a wave H4200+7156
Ex 29:42 to the tent of meeting, **b** the LORD. H4200+7156
Ex 30: 6 **b** the atonement cover that is over H4200+7156
Ex 30: 8 burn regularly **b** the LORD for the H4200+7156
Ex 30:16 the Israelites **b** the LORD, H4200+7156
Ex 32: 1 make us gods who will go **b** us. H4200+7156
Ex 32:23 'Make us gods who will go **b** us. H4200+7156
Ex 32:34 and my angel will go **b** you. H4200+7156
Ex 33: 2 send an angel **b** you and drive out H4200+7156
Ex 34:10 **B** all your people I will do wonders never H5584
Ex 34:10 do wonders never **b** done in any nation in NDT
Ex 34:11 I will drive out **b** you the Amorites H4946+7156
Ex 34:20 one is to appear **b** me empty-handed. H7156
Ex 34:23 men are to appear **b** the Sovereign H907+7156
Ex 34:24 out nations **b** you and enlarge H4946+7156
Ex 34:24 year to appear **b** the LORD your God. H907+7156
Ex 40:23 set out the bread on it **b** the LORD, H4200+7156
Ex 40:25 set up the lamps **b** the LORD, as H4200+7156
Lev 1: 5 the young bull **b** the LORD, H4200+7156
Lev 1:11 north side of the altar **b** the LORD, H4200+7156
Lev 3: 1 are to present **b** the LORD an animal H4200+7156
Lev 3: 7 you are to present it **b** the LORD, H4200+7156
Lev 3:12 you are to present it **b** the LORD, H4200+7156
Lev 4: 4 to the tent of meeting **b** the LORD. H4200+7156
Lev 4: 4 and slaughter it there **b** the LORD. H4200+7156
Lev 4: 6 some of it seven times **b** the LORD, H4200+7156
Lev 4: 7 incense that is **b** the LORD in the H4200+7156
Lev 4:14 and present it **b** the tent of H4200+7156
Lev 4:15 on the bull's head **b** the LORD, H4200+7156
Lev 4:15 shall be slaughtered **b** the LORD. H4200+7156
Lev 4:17 and sprinkle it **b** the LORD seven H4200+7156
Lev 4:18 the altar that is **b** the LORD in the H4200+7156
Lev 4:24 offering is slaughtered **b** the LORD. H4200+7156
Lev 6: 7 atonement for them **b** the LORD, H4200+7156
Lev 6:14 sons are to bring it **b** the LORD, H4200+7156
Lev 6:25 to be slaughtered **b** the LORD in the H4200+7156
Lev 7:30 wave the breast **b** the LORD as a H7156+4200
Lev 8:26 which was **b** the LORD, he H4200+7156
Lev 8:27 they waved them **b** the LORD as a H4200+7156
Lev 8:29 and waved it **b** the LORD as a wave H4200+7156
Lev 9: 2 and present them **b** the LORD. H4200+7156
Lev 9: 4 offering to sacrifice **b** the LORD, H4200+7156
Lev 9: 5 came near and stood **b** the LORD. H4200+7156
Lev 9:21 the right thigh **b** the LORD as a wave H4200+7156
Lev 10: 1 unauthorized fire **b** the LORD, H4200+7156
Lev 10: 2 and they died **b** the LORD. H4200+7156
Lev 10:15 to be waved **b** the LORD as a wave H4200+7156
Lev 10:17 atonement for them **b** the LORD. H4200+7156
Lev 10:19 and their burnt offering **b** the LORD, H4200+7156
Lev 12: 7 shall offer them **b** the LORD to make H4200+7156
Lev 13: 7 they must appear **b** the priest again. H448
Lev 14:11 and their offerings **b** the LORD at the H4200+7156
Lev 14:12 shall wave them **b** the LORD as a H4200+7156
Lev 14:16 sprinkle some of it **b** the LORD seven H4200+7156
Lev 14:18 atonement for them **b** the LORD. H4200+7156
Lev 14:23 to the tent of meeting, **b** the LORD. H4200+7156
Lev 14:24 and wave them **b** the LORD as a H4200+7156
Lev 14:27 his palm seven times **b** the LORD. H4200+7156
Lev 14:29 atonement for them **b** the LORD. H4200+7156
Lev 14:31 make atonement **b** the LORD on H4200+7156
Lev 14:36 house to be emptied **b** he goes in to H928+3270
Lev 15:14 and come **b** the LORD to the H4200+7156
Lev 15:15 make atonement **b** the LORD for the H4200+7156
Lev 15:30 her **b** the LORD for the H4200+7156
Lev 16: 4 himself with water **b** he puts them on. H2256
Lev 16: 7 and present them **b** the LORD at the H4200+7156
Lev 16:10 be presented alive **b** the LORD to be H4200+7156
Lev 16:12 from the altar **b** the LORD and H4946+4200+7156
Lev 16:13 the incense on the fire **b** the LORD, H4200+7156
Lev 16:14 seven times **b** the atonement H4200+7156
Lev 16:18 altar that is **b** the LORD and make H4200+7156
Lev 16:23 garments he put on **b** he entered the Most H928
Lev 16:30 **b** the LORD, you will be clean H4200+7156
Lev 18:24 to drive out **b** you became defiled H4946+7156
Lev 18:27 who lived in the land **b** you, H4200+7156
Lev 18:28 out the nations that were **b** you. H4200+7156
Lev 18:30 were practiced **b** you came and do H4200+7156
Lev 19:22 him **b** the LORD for the H4200+7156
Lev 20:23 I am going to drive out **b** you. H4946+7156
Lev 23:11 to wave the sheaf **b** the LORD so it H4200+7156
Lev 23:20 the two lambs **b** the LORD as a wave H4200+7156
Lev 23:28 is made for you **b** the LORD your God. H7156
Lev 23:40 rejoice **b** the LORD your God for H4200+7156
Lev 24: 3 to tend the lamps **b** the LORD from H4200+7156
Lev 24: 4 gold lampstand **b** the LORD must be H4200+7156
Lev 24: 6 the table of pure gold **b** the LORD. H4200+7156
Lev 24: 8 is to be set out **b** the LORD regularly, H4200+7156
Lev 25:30 If it is not redeemed **b** a full year has H6330
Lev 26: 1 stone in your land to bow down **b** it. H6584
Lev 26: 7 they will fall by the sword **b** you. H4200+7156
Lev 26: 8 will fall by the sword **b** you. H4200+7156
Lev 26:37 be able to stand **b** your enemies. H4200+7156
Nu 3: 4 died **b** the LORD when they made H4200+7156
Nu 3: 4 fire **b** him in the Desert H4200+7156
Nu 5:16 her and have her stand **b** the LORD. H4200+7156
Nu 5:18 had the woman stand **b** the LORD, H4200+7156
Nu 5:25 wave it **b** the LORD and bring it to H4200+7156
Nu 5:30 to have her stand **b** the LORD and is H4200+7156
Nu 6:16 all these **b** the LORD and make H4200+7156
Nu 6:20 then wave these **b** the LORD as a H4200+7156
Nu 7: 3 as their gifts **b** the LORD six covered H4200+7156
Nu 7: 3 they presented **b** the tabernacle. H4200+7156
Nu 7:10 and presented them **b** the altar. H4200+7156
Nu 8:10 are to bring the Levites **b** the LORD, H4200+7156
Nu 8:11 the Levites **b** the LORD as a wave H4200+7156
Nu 8:21 a wave offering **b** the LORD and H4200+7156
Nu 10: 3 is to assemble **b** you at the entrance to H448
Nu 10: 4 the clans of Israel—are to assemble **b** you. H448
Nu 10:10 be a memorial for you **b** your God. H4200+7156
Nu 10:21 was to be set up **b** they arrived. H6330
Nu 10:33 of the LORD went **b** them during H4200+7156
Nu 10:35 scattered; may your foes flee **b** you." H4946+7156
Nu 11:20 and have wailed **b** him, saying, H4200+7156
Nu 11:33 their teeth and **b** it could be consumed, H3270
Nu 13:22 built seven years **b** Zoan in Egypt.) H4200+7156
Nu 13:30 silenced the people **b** Moses and said, H448
Nu 14:14 and that you go **b** them in a pillar H4200+7156
Nu 14:37 and died of a plague **b** the LORD. H4200+7156
Nu 15:15 shall be the same **b** the LORD: H4200+7156
Nu 15:28 make atonement **b** the LORD for the H4200+7156
Nu 16: 7 and incense in them **b** the LORD. H4200+7156
Nu 16: 9 and to stand **b** the community and H4200+7156
Nu 16:16 are to appear **b** the LORD tomorrow H4200+7156
Nu 16:17 in all—and present it **b** the LORD. H4200+7156
Nu 16:38 were presented **b** the LORD and H4200+7156
Nu 16:40 come to burn incense **b** the LORD, H4200+7156
Nu 17: 7 placed the staffs **b** the LORD in the H4200+7156
Nu 18: 2 your sons minister **b** the tent of the H4200+7156
Nu 18:19 covenant of salt **b** the LORD for both H4200+7156
Nu 20: 3 our brothers fell dead **b** the LORD! H4200+7156
Nu 20: 8 Speak to that rock **b** their eyes and it will H4200
Nu 22:32 your path is a reckless one **b** me. H4200+5584
Nu 25: 2 meal and bowed down **b** these gods. H4200
Nu 25: 4 expose them in broad daylight **b** the LORD, H4200
Nu 25: 6 a Midianite woman **right b** the eyes of H4200
Nu 26:61 made an offering **b** the LORD with H4200+7156
Nu 27: 2 stood **b** Moses, Eleazar the H4200+7156
Nu 27: 5 brought their case **b** the LORD, H4200+7156
Nu 27:14 to honor me as holy **b** their eyes. H4200
Nu 27:17 to go out and come in **b** them, one H4200+7156
Nu 27:19 Have him stand **b** Eleazar the priest H4200+7156
Nu 27:21 He is to stand **b** Eleazar the priest H4200+7156
Nu 27:21 by inquiring of the Urim **b** the LORD. H4200+7156
Nu 27:22 and had him stand **b** Eleazar the H4200+7156
Nu 31:50 atonement for ourselves **b** the LORD." H4200+7156
Nu 31:54 the Israelites **b** the LORD. H4200+7156
Nu 32: 4 the LORD subdued **b** the people of H4200+7156
Nu 32:20 arm yourselves **b** the LORD for battle H4200+7156
Nu 32:21 over the Jordan **b** the LORD until he H4200+7156
Nu 32:21 driven his enemies out **b** him— H4946+7156
Nu 32:22 the land is subdued **b** the LORD, H4200+7156
Nu 32:22 will be your possession **b** the LORD. H4200+7156
Nu 32:27 will cross over to fight **b** the LORD H4200+7156
Nu 32:29 the Jordan with you **b** the LORD, H4200+7156
Nu 32:29 when the land is subdued **b** you, H4200+7156
Nu 32:32 We will cross over **b** the LORD into H4200+7156
Nu 33:52 the inhabitants of the land **b** you. H4946+7156
Nu 35:12 of murder may not die **b** they stand trial H6330
Nu 35:12 they stand trial **b** the assembly. H4200+7156
Nu 35:32 on their own land **b** the death of the high H6330
Nu 36: 1 came and spoke **b** Moses and the H4200+7156
Dt 1:30 who is going **b** you, will fight H4200+7156
Dt 1:30 he did for you in Egypt, **b** your very eyes, H4200
Dt 1:45 You came back and wept **b** the LORD, H4200+7156
Dt 2:12 the Horites from **b** them and settled in H7156
Dt 2:21 destroyed them from **b** the Ammonites, H7156
Dt 2:22 he destroyed the Horites from **b** them. H7156
Dt 4: 8 of laws I am setting **b** you today? H4200+7156
Dt 4:10 day you stood **b** the LORD your God H4200+7156
Dt 4:10 the people **b** me to hear my words H4200
Dt 4:32 former days, long **b** your time, from H4200+7156
Dt 4:34 God did for you in Egypt **b** your very eyes? H4200
Dt 4:38 to drive out **b** you nations greater H4946+7156
Dt 4:44 the law Moses set **b** the Israelites. H4200+7156
Dt 5: 7 shall have no other gods **b** me. H6584+7156
Dt 6:19 out all your enemies **b** you, H4946+7156
Dt 6:22 **B** our eyes the LORD sent signs and H4200
Dt 6:25 all this law **b** the LORD our God, H4200+7156
Dt 7: 1 and drives out **b** you many nations H4946+7156
Dt 7:22 will drive out those nations **b** you, H4946+7156
Dt 8:20 nations the LORD destroyed **b** you, H4946+7156
Dt 9: 3 he will subdue them **b** you. H4200+7156
Dt 9: 4 has driven them out **b** you, H4946+4200+7156
Dt 9: 4 is going to drive them out **b** you. H4946+7156
Dt 9: 5 your God will drive them out **b** you, H4946+7156
Dt 9:17 breaking them to pieces **b** your eyes. H4200
Dt 9:18 I fell prostrate **b** the LORD for forty H4200+7156
Dt 9:25 I lay prostrate **b** the LORD those forty H4200+7156
Dt 10: 4 on these tablets what he had written **b**, H8037
Dt 10: 8 to stand **b** the LORD to minister and H4200+7156
Dt 11:23 out all these nations **b** you, H4946+4200+7156
Dt 11:26 I am setting **b** you today a blessing H4200+7156
Dt 11:32 and laws I am setting **b** you today. H4200+7156
Dt 12:12 And there rejoice **b** the LORD your H4200+7156
Dt 12:18 are to rejoice **b** the LORD your God H4200+7156
Dt 12:29 God will cut off **b** you the nations H4946+7156
Dt 12:30 they have been destroyed **b** you, H4946+7156
Dt 16:11 And rejoice **b** the LORD your God at H4200+7156
Dt 16:16 men must appear **b** the LORD your H907+7156
Dt 16:16 No one should appear **b** the LORD H907+7156
Dt 17: 8 If cases come **b** your courts that are too H928
Dt 18:12 will drive out those nations **b** you. H4946+7156
Dt 18:13 must be blameless **b** the LORD your God. H6640
Dt 19:17 of the LORD **b** the priests and the H4200+7156
Dt 22:17 display the cloth **b** the elders of the H4200+7156
Dt 24:15 Pay them their wages each day **b** sunset H4202
Dt 26: 5 shall declare **b** the LORD your God H4200+7156
Dt 26:10 Place the basket **b** the LORD your H4200+7156

Dt 26:10 your God and bow down **b** him. H4200+7156
Dt 28: 7 against you will be defeated **b** you. H4200+7156
Dt 28:25 to be defeated **b** your enemies. H4200+7156
Dt 28:31 Your ox will be slaughtered **b** your eyes H4200
Dt 30: 1 I have set **b** you come on you H4200+7156
Dt 30:15 I set **b** you today life and prosperity, H4200+7156
Dt 30:19 that I have set **b** you life and death H4200+7156
Dt 31: 3 destroy these nations **b** you, H4946+4200+7156
Dt 31: 8 himself goes **b** you and will be H4200+7156
Dt 31:11 comes to appear **b** the LORD your H907+7156
Dt 31:11 shall read this law **b** them in their hearing H5584
Dt 31:21 even **b** I bring them into the land I H928+3270
Dt 31:28 Assemble **b** me all the elders of your tribes H448
Dt 33: 1 on the Israelites **b** his death. H4200+7156
Dt 33:10 He offers incense **b** you and whole H928+678
Dt 33:27 will drive out your enemies **b** you, H4946+7156
Dt 33:29 Your enemies will cower **b** you, and you H4200
Jos 2: 8 **B** the spies lay down for the night, she H3270
Jos 3: 1 where they camped **b** crossing over. H3270
Jos 3: 4 have never been this way **b**. H4946+9453+8997
Jos 3:10 drive out **b** you the Canaanites, H4946+7156
Jos 4: 5 "Go over **b** the ark of the LORD your H4200+7156
Jos 4: 7 Jordan was cut off **b** the ark of the H4946+7156
Jos 4:13 crossed over **b** the LORD to the H4200+7156
Jos 4:18 place and ran at flood stage as **b**. H9453+8997
Jos 4:23 up the Jordan **b** you until you had H4946+7156
Jos 4:23 he dried it up **b** us until we had H4946+7156
Jos 5: 1 dried up the Jordan **b** the Israelites H4946+7156
Jos 6: 8 the seven trumpets **b** the LORD went H4200+7156
Jos 6:13 marching **b** the ark of the LORD and H4200+7156
Jos 6:26 "Cursed **b** the LORD is the one who H4200+7156
Jos 7: 6 to the ground **b** the ark of the LORD, H4200+7156
Jos 7:23 and spread them out **b** the LORD. H4200+7156
Jos 8: 5 as they did **b**, we will flee H928+2021+8037
Jos 8: 6 away from us as they did **b**. H928+2021+8037
Jos 8:10 of Israel marched **b** them to Ai. H4200+7156
Jos 8:15 themselves be driven back **b** them, H4200+7156
Jos 9:24 to wipe out all its inhabitants from **b** you. H7156
Jos 10:10 threw them into confusion **b** Israel, H4200+7156
Jos 10:11 As they fled **b** Israel on the road H4946+7156
Jos 10:14 never been a day like it **b** or since, H4200+7156
Jos 13: 6 will drive them out **b** the Israelites. H4946+7156
Jos 18: 3 "How long will you wait **b** you begin to take NDT
Jos 20: 4 state their case **b** the elders of that H928+265
Jos 20: 6 stood trial **b** the assembly and H4200+7156
Jos 20: 9 to standing trial **b** the assembly. H4200+7156
Jos 22:29 God that stands **b** his tabernacle." H4200+7156
Jos 23: 5 He will drive them out **b** you, H4946+4200+7156
Jos 23: 9 LORD has driven out **b** you great and H4946+7156
Jos 23:13 out these nations **b** you. H4946+4200+7156
Jos 24: 1 they presented themselves **b** God. H4200+7156
Jos 24: 8 I destroyed them from **b** you, and you took H7156
Jos 24:12 which drove them out **b** you—also H4946+7156
Jos 24:17 performed those great signs **b** our eyes. H4200
Jos 24:18 LORD drove out **b** us all the nations H4946+7156
Jdg 2: 3 'I will not drive them out **b** you H4946+7156
Jdg 2:21 longer drive out **b** them any of the H4946+7156
Jdg 4:23 king of Canaan **b** the Israelites. H4200+7156
Jdg 5: 5 The mountains quaked **b** the LORD H4946+7156
Jdg 5: 5 One of Sinai, **b** the LORD, the God H4946+7156
Jdg 6: 9 drove them out **b** you and gave you H4946+7156
Jdg 6:18 bring my offering and set it **b** you." H4200+7156
Jdg 8:28 was subdued **b** the Israelites and H4200+7156
Jdg 11:11 all his words **b** the LORD in Mizpah. H4200+7156
Jdg 11:23 the Amorites out **b** his people H4946+7156
Jdg 14:18 **B** sunset on the seventh day the H928+3270
Jdg 16:20 go out **as b** and shake H3869+7193+928+7193
Jdg 20: 1 one and assembled **b** the LORD in Mizpah. H448
Jdg 20:23 went up and wept **b** the LORD until H4200+7156
Jdg 20:26 there they sat weeping **b** the LORD. H4200+7156
Jdg 20:28 the son of Aaron, ministering **b** it.) H4200+7156
Jdg 20:30 **as** they had **done b**. H3869+7193+928+7193
Jdg 20:31 on the Israelites **as b**, H3869+7193+928+7193
Jdg 20:32 "We are defeating them as **b**," H928+2021+8037
Jdg 20:35 LORD defeated Benjamin **b** Israel, H4200+7156
Jdg 20:36 men of Israel had given way **b** Benjamin, H4200
Jdg 20:42 So they fled **b** the Israelites in the H4200+7156
Jdg 21: 2 where they sat **b** God until evening, H4200+7156
Jdg 21: 5 of Israel has failed to assemble **b** the LORD?" H448
Jdg 21: 5 failed to assemble **b** the LORD at Mizpah H448
Jdg 21: 8 failed to assemble **b** the LORD at Mizpah?" H448
Ru 2:11 with a people you did not know **b**. H9453+8997
Ru 3:14 got up **b** anyone could be H928+3270
1Sa 1:19 and worshiped **b** the LORD and then H4200+7156
1Sa 1:22 him and present him **b** the LORD, H907+7156
1Sa 2:11 the boy ministered **b** the LORD under Eli the H907
1Sa 2:15 But even **b** the fat was burned, the H928+3270
1Sa 2:18 was ministering **b** the LORD— H907+7156
1Sa 2:30 family would minister **b** me forever. H4200+7156
1Sa 2:35 will minister **b** my anointed one H4200+7156
1Sa 2:36 come and bow down **b** him for a piece of H4200
1Sa 3: 1 Samuel ministered **b** the LORD under Eli. H907
1Sa 4: 3 on us today **b** the Philistines? H4200+7156
1Sa 4: 7 Nothing like this has happened **b**. H919+8997
1Sa 4:17 "Israel fled **b** the Philistines, and H4200+7156
1Sa 5: 3 face on the ground **b** the ark of the H4200+7156
1Sa 5: 4 face on the ground **b** the ark of the H4200+7156
1Sa 7: 6 water and poured it out **b** the LORD. H4200+7156
1Sa 7:10 they were routed **b** the Israelites. H4200+7156
1Sa 8:20 us and to go out **b** us and fight our H4200+7156
1Sa 8:21 he repeated it **b** the LORD. H928+265
1Sa 9:13 will find him **b** he goes up to the H928+3270
1Sa 9:15 Now the day **b** Saul came, the LORD H4200+7156
1Sa 10: 5 and harps being played **b** them, H4200+7156
1Sa 10:19 yourselves **b** the LORD by your H4200+7156
1Sa 10:25 a scroll and deposited it **b** the LORD. H4200+7156
1Sa 11:15 fellowship offerings **b** the LORD, H4200+7156
1Sa 12: 7 you with evidence **b** the LORD as to H4200+7156
1Sa 12:16 thing the LORD is about to do **b** your eyes! H4200
1Sa 14:13 The Philistines fell **b** Jonathan H4200+7156
1Sa 14:24 anyone who eats food **b** evening comes, H6330
1Sa 14:24 **b** I have avenged myself on my enemies!" NDT
1Sa 15:30 But please honor me **b** the elders of my H5584
1Sa 15:30 the elders of my people and **b** Israel; H5584
1Sa 15:33 put Agag to death **b** the LORD at H4200+7156
1Sa 16: 6 LORD's anointed stands here **b** the LORD." H5584
1Sa 16:10 seven of his sons pass **b** Samuel, H4200+7156
1Sa 17:30 and the men answered him as **b**. H8037
1Sa 17:57 took him and brought him **b** Saul, H4200+7156
1Sa 18:26 So **b** the allotted time **elapsed**, H4202+4848
1Sa 19: 7 and David was with Saul as **b**. H919+8997
1Sa 19: 8 such force that they fled **b** him. H4946+7156
1Sa 20: 8 him into a **covenant** with you *b* the LORD. AIT
1Sa 20:41 the stone and **bowed** down *b* Jonathan three AIT
1Sa 21: 6 been removed from **b** the LORD and H4200+7156
1Sa 21: 7 detained **b** the LORD; he was H4200+7156
1Sa 23:18 them made a covenant **b** the LORD. H4200+7156
1Sa 25:23 and bowed down **b** David with her H4200+678
1Sa 26:19 may they be cursed **b** the LORD! H4200+7156
1Sa 28:25 Then she set it **b** Saul and his men H4200+7156
1Sa 30:15 "Swear to me **b** God that you will not kill H928
1Sa 31: 1 the Israelites fled **b** them, and H4946+7156
2Sa 2:26 How long **b** you order your men to stop H4202
2Sa 3:28 forever innocent **b** the LORD H4946+6640
2Sa 3:34 You fell as one falls **b** the wicked." H4200+7156
2Sa 3:35 anything else **b** the sun sets! H4200+7156
2Sa 5: 3 with them at Hebron **b** the LORD, H4200+7156
2Sa 5:20 out against my enemies **b** me." H4200+7156
2Sa 6: 5 with all their might **b** the LORD, H4200+7156
2Sa 6:14 was dancing **b** the LORD with all H4200+7156
2Sa 6:16 leaping and dancing **b** the LORD, H4200+7156
2Sa 6:17 and fellowship offerings **b** the LORD. H4200+7156
2Sa 6:21 to Michal, "It was **b** the LORD, who H4200+7156
2Sa 6:21 Israel—I will celebrate **b** the LORD. H4200+7156
2Sa 7: 9 I have cut off all your enemies from **b** you. H7156
2Sa 7:15 whom I removed from **b** you. H4200+7156
2Sa 7:16 kingdom will endure forever **b** me; H4200+7156
2Sa 7:18 David went in and sat **b** the LORD, H4200+7156
2Sa 7:23 their gods from **b** your people, H7156
2Sa 9: 2 They summoned him to appear **b** David H448
2Sa 10:13 Arameans, and they fled **b** him. H4946+7156
2Sa 10:14 they fled **b** Abishai and went H4946+7156
2Sa 10:18 But they fled **b** Israel, and David H4946+7156
2Sa 12:11 **B** your very eyes I will take your wives and H4200
2Sa 12:12 do this thing in broad daylight **b** all Israel. H5584
2Sa 14:33 his face to the ground **b** the king. H4200+7156
2Sa 15: 2 complaint to be placed **b** the king for a H448
2Sa 15: 5 approached him to bow down **b** him, H4200
2Sa 15:18 him from Gath marched **b** the king. H6584+7156
2Sa 18:21 Cushite bowed down **b** Joab and ran off. H4200
2Sa 18:28 He bowed down **b** the king with his face H4200
2Sa 19: 8 the gateway," they all came **b** him. H4200+7156
2Sa 19:18 Jordan, he fell prostrate **b** the king H4200+7156
2Sa 21: 6 their bodies exposed **b** the LORD at Gibeah H4200
2Sa 21: 7 because of the **oath** *b* the LORD between AIT
2Sa 21: 9 their bodies on a hill **b** the LORD. H4200+7156
2Sa 22:23 All his laws are **b** me; I have not H4200+5584
2Sa 22:24 been blameless **b** him and have kept H4200
2Sa 22:40 you humbled my adversaries **b** me. H9393
2Sa 22:45 foreigners cower **b** me; as soon as they H4200
2Sa 23:16 instead, he poured it out **b** the LORD. H4200
2Sa 24:11 **B** David got up the next morning, the H2256
2Sa 24:20 out and bowed down **b** the king with his H4200
1Ki 1:16 prostrating herself **b** the king. H4200
1Ki 1:23 So he went **b** the king and bowed H4200+7156
1Ki 1:28 king's presence and stood **b** him. H4200+7156
1Ki 1:31 prostrating herself **b** the king, and said, H4200
1Ki 1:32 When they came **b** the king, H4200+7156
1Ki 2: 4 walk faithfully **b** me with all their H4200+7156
1Ki 2:26 Sovereign LORD **b** my father David H4200+7156
1Ki 2:45 remain secure **b** the LORD forever." H4200+7156
1Ki 3:15 stood **b** the ark of the Lord's H4200+7156
1Ki 3:16 came to the king and stood **b** him. H4200+7156
1Ki 3:22 And so they argued **b** the king. H4200+7156
1Ki 8: 5 gathered about him were **b** the ark, H4200+7156
1Ki 8:22 Solomon stood **b** the altar of the H4200+7156
1Ki 8:25 to sit **b** me on the throne H4946+4200+7156
1Ki 8:25 they do to walk **b** me faithfully as H4200+7156
1Ki 8:31 swear the oath **b** your altar in this H4200+7156
1Ki 8:54 he rose from **b** the altar of the LORD H4200+7156
1Ki 8:59 which I have prayed **b** the LORD, be H4200+7156
1Ki 8:62 him offered sacrifices **b** the LORD. H4200+7156
1Ki 8:64 altar that **stood b** the LORD was too H4200+7156
1Ki 8:65 celebrated it **b** the LORD our God H4200+7156
1Ki 9: 3 and plea you have made **b** me; H4200+7156
1Ki 9: 4 if you walk **b** me faithfully with H4200+7156
1Ki 9:25 burning incense **b** the LORD along H4200+7156
1Ki 10: 8 **stand b** you and hear your H4200+7156
1Ki 11:36 have a lamp **b** me in Jerusalem, H4200+7156
1Ki 13: 6 and became as it was **b**. H928+2021+8037
1Ki 14: 9 more evil than all who lived **b** you. H4200+7156
1Ki 14:22 than those who were **b** them had done. H3S
1Ki 14:24 LORD had driven out **b** the Israelites. H4946+7156
1Ki 15: 3 the sins his father had done **b** him; H4200+7156
1Ki 16:25 sinned more than all those **b** him. H4200+7156
1Ki 16:30 the LORD than any of those **b** him. H4200+7156
1Ki 16:33 did all the kings of Israel **b** him. H4200+7156
1Ki 18:21 Elijah went **b** the people and said, "How H448
1Ki 18:44 chariot and go down **b** the rain stops you. H4202
1Ki 19:11 and shattered the rocks **b** the LORD, H4200+7156
1Ki 21:13 charges against Naboth **b** the people, H5584
1Ki 21:26 the LORD drove out **b** Israel. H4946+7156
1Ki 21:29 has humbled himself **b** me? H4946+4200+7156
1Ki 22:10 the prophets prophesying **b** them. H4200+7156
1Ki 22:21 forward, stood **b** the LORD and said H4200+7156
2Ki 1:13 up and fell on his knees **b** Elijah. H4200+5584
2Ki 2: 9 can I do for you **b** I am taken from H928+3270
2Ki 2:15 him and bowed to the ground **b** him. H4200
2Ki 4:12 called her, and she stood **b** him. H4200+7156
2Ki 4:43 can I set this **b** a hundred men?" H4200+7156
2Ki 4:44 Then he set it **b** them, and they ate H4200+7156
2Ki 5:15 He stood **b** him and said, "Now I H4200+7156
2Ki 5:25 When he went in and stood **b** his master H448
2Ki 6:22 food and water **b** them so that they H4200+7156
2Ki 6:32 ahead, but **b** he arrived, Elisha H928+3270
2Ki 8: 9 He went in and stood **b** him, and H4200+7156
2Ki 10: 9 He stood **b** all the people and said, "You H448
2Ki 13: 5 in their own homes as they had **b**. H9453+8997
2Ki 16: 3 LORD had driven out **b** the Israelites. H4946+7156
2Ki 16:11 finished it **b** King Ahaz returned. H6330
2Ki 16:14 bronze altar that stood **b** the LORD, H4200+7156
2Ki 17: 8 the LORD had driven out **b** them, H4946+7156
2Ki 17:11 had driven out **b** them had done. H4946+7156
2Ki 18: 5 of Judah, either **b** him or after him. H4200+7156
2Ki 18:22 "You must worship **b** this altar in H4200+7156
2Ki 19:14 LORD and spread it out **b** the LORD. H4200+7156
2Ki 19:26 on the roof, scorched **b** it grows up. H4200+7156
2Ki 19:32 *He will* not **come b** it with shield or build H7709
2Ki 20: 3 how I have walked **b** you faithfully H4200+7156
2Ki 20: 4 **B** Isaiah had left the middle court, the H4202
2Ki 21: 2 LORD had driven out **b** the Israelites. H4946+7156
2Ki 21: 9 LORD had destroyed **b** the Israelites. H4946+7156
2Ki 22:13 us because **those who have gone b** us have H3
2Ki 22:19 humbled yourself **b** the LORD when H4946+7156
2Ki 23:25 Neither **b** nor after Josiah was there H4200+7156
2Ki 25: 7 killed the sons of Zedekiah **b** his eyes. H4200
1Ch 1:43 reigned in Edom **b** any Israelite H4200+7156
1Ch 5:25 whom God had destroyed **b** them. H4946+7156
1Ch 6:32 with music **b** the tabernacle, H4200+7156
1Ch 10: 1 the Israelites fled **b** them, and H4946+7156
1Ch 11: 3 with them at Hebron **b** the LORD, H4200+7156
1Ch 13: 8 with all their might **b** God, H4200+7156
1Ch 13:10 So he died there **b** God. H4200+7156
1Ch 15: 2 of the LORD and to **minister** *b* him forever." AIT
1Ch 15:24 to blow trumpets **b** the ark of God. H4200+7156
1Ch 16: 1 and fellowship offerings **b** God. H4200+7156
1Ch 16: 4 to minister **b** the ark of the LORD H4200+7156
1Ch 16: 6 trumpets regularly **b** the ark of the H4200+7156
1Ch 16:27 Splendor and majesty are **b** him H4200+7156
1Ch 16:29 bring an offering and come **b** him. H4200+7156
1Ch 16:30 Tremble **b** him, all the earth! H4946+4200+7156
1Ch 16:33 them sing for joy **b** the LORD, H4946+4200+7156
1Ch 16:37 and his associates **b** the ark of the H4200+7156
1Ch 16:39 fellow priests **b** the tabernacle of H4200+7156
1Ch 17: 8 I have cut off all your enemies from **b** you. H7156
1Ch 17:16 David went in and sat **b** the LORD, H4200+7156
1Ch 17:21 by driving out nations from **b** your people, H7156
1Ch 17:24 David will be established **b** you. H4200+7156
1Ch 19:14 Arameans, and they fled **b** him. H4946+7156
1Ch 19:15 they too fled **b** his brother Abishai H4946+7156
1Ch 19:18 But they fled **b** Israel, and H4946+4200+7156
1Ch 21:12 being swept away **b** your enemies, H4946+7156
1Ch 21:21 bowed down **b** David with his face H4200
1Ch 21:30 could not go **b** it to inquire of H4200+7156
1Ch 22: 5 extensive preparations **b** his death. H4200+7156
1Ch 23:13 to offer sacrifices **b** the LORD, to H4200+7156
1Ch 23:13 to **minister** *b* him and to pronounce blessings AIT
1Ch 23:31 were to serve **b** the LORD regularly H4200+7156
1Ch 24: 2 and Abihu died **b** their father did, H4200+7156
1Ch 29:20 themselves **b** the LORD and the king. H4200
1Ch 29:22 anointing him **b** the LORD to be ruler and H4200
1Ch 29:25 as no king over Israel ever had **b**. H4200+7156
2Ch 1: 6 to the bronze altar **b** the LORD in the H4200+7156
2Ch 1:12 no king who was **b** you ever had H4200+7156
2Ch 1:13 from **b** the tent of meeting. H4200+7156
2Ch 2: 4 burning fragrant incense **b** him, H4200+7156
2Ch 2: 6 as a place to burn sacrifices **b** him? H4200+7156
2Ch 5: 6 gathered about him were **b** the ark, H4200+7156
2Ch 6:12 Solomon stood **b** the altar of the H4200+7156
2Ch 6:13 then knelt down **b** the whole assembly H5584
2Ch 6:16 to sit **b** me on the throne H4946+4200+7156
2Ch 6:16 they do to walk **b** me according to H4200+7156
2Ch 6:22 swear the oath **b** your altar in this H4200+7156
2Ch 6:24 supplication **b** you in this temple, H4200+7156
2Ch 7: 4 offered sacrifices **b** the LORD. H4200+7156
2Ch 7:17 if you walk **b** me faithfully as David H4200+7156
2Ch 9: 7 stand **b** you and hear your H4200+7156
2Ch 13:15 and all Israel **b** Abijah and Judah. H4200+7156
2Ch 13:16 The Israelites fled **b** Judah, and H4946+7156
2Ch 14:12 the Cushites **b** Asa and Judah. H4200+7156
2Ch 14:13 were crushed **b** the LORD and his H4200+7156
2Ch 17: 3 the ways of his father David **b** him. H8037
2Ch 18: 9 the prophets prophesying **b** them. H4200+7156
2Ch 18:20 forward, stood **b** the LORD and said H4200+7156
2Ch 19:10 case that comes **b** you from your people H6584
2Ch 19:11 Levites will serve as officials **b** you. H4200+7156

2Ch 20: 7 of this land **b** your people H4946+4200+7156
2Ch 20: 9 in your presence **b** this temple that H4200+7156
2Ch 20:13 little ones, stood there **b** the LORD. H4200+7156
2Ch 20:18 fell down in worship **b** the LORD. H4200+7156
2Ch 24:20 He stood **b** the people and said H4946+6584
2Ch 25: 8 will overthrow you **b** the enemy, H4200+7156
2Ch 26:19 their presence **b** the incense altar H4946+6584
2Ch 27: 6 steadfastly **b** the LORD his God. H4200+7156
2Ch 28: 3 LORD had driven out **b** the Israelites. H4946+7156
2Ch 28:13 they said, "or we will be **guilty** *b* the LORD. AIT
2Ch 29:11 you to stand **b** him and serve him, H4200+7156
2Ch 29:11 to minister **b** him and to burn incense." H4200
2Ch 29:23 were brought **b** the king and the H4200+7156
2Ch 31:20 and faithful **b** the LORD his God. H4200+7156
2Ch 32: 6 assembled them **b** him in the square H448
2Ch 32:12 'You must worship **b** one altar and H4200+7156
2Ch 33: 2 LORD had driven out **b** the Israelites. H4946+7156
2Ch 33: 9 LORD had destroyed **b** the Israelites. H4946+7156
2Ch 33:12 greatly **b** the God of his H4946+4200+7156
2Ch 33:19 poles and idols **b** he humbled H4200+7156
2Ch 33:23 humble himself **b** the LORD; H4946+4200+7156
2Ch 34:21 us because **those who have gone b** us have H3
2Ch 34:27 yourself **b** God when you H4946+4200+7156
2Ch 34:27 yourself **b** me and tore your H4200+7156
2Ch 36:12 himself **b** Jeremiah the H4946+4200+7156
Ezr 7:28 favor to me **b** the king and his H4200+7156
Ezr 8:21 ourselves **b** our God and ask H4200+7156
Ezr 8:29 LORD in Jerusalem **b** the leading H4200+7156
Ezr 9:15 Here we are **b** you in our guilt H4200+7156
Ezr 10: 1 himself down **b** the house of God, H4200+7156
Ezr 10: 3 us make a covenant **b** our God to send H4200
Ezr 10: 6 withdrew from **b** the house of God H4200+7156
Ezr 10: 9 sitting in the **square** *b* the house of God, AIT
Ne 1: 4 and prayed **b** the God of heaven H4200+7156
Ne 1: 6 is praying **b** you day and night H4200+7156
Ne 2: 1 I had not been sad in his presence **b**, NDT
Ne 4:11 enemies said, "**B** they know it or see us H4202
Ne 8: 1 in the square **b** the Water Gate. H4200+7156
Ne 8: 2 brought the Law **b** the assembly, H4200+7156
Ne 8: 3 faced the square **b** the Water Gate H4200+7156
Ne 9:11 You divided the sea **b** them, so H4200+7156
Ne 9:24 You subdued **b** them the H4200+7156
Ne 13: 4 **B** this, Eliashib the priest had been H4200+7156
Ne 13:19 gates of Jerusalem **b** the Sabbath, H4200+7156
Est 1:11 to bring **b** him Queen Vashti H4200+7156
Est 1:17 Queen Vashti to be brought **b** him, H4200+7156
Est 2:12 **B** a young woman's turn came to go in to H928
Est 6: 9 proclaiming **b** him, 'This is what H4200+7156
Est 6:11 proclaiming **b** him, "This is what H4200+7156
Est 6:13 **b** whom your downfall has started H4200+7156
Est 7: 6 was terrified **b** the king and H4946+4200+7156
Est 8: 4 and she arose and stood **b** him. H4200+7156
Job 1: 6 came to present themselves **b** the LORD, H6584
Job 2: 1 came to present themselves **b** the LORD, H6584
Job 2: 1 came with them to present himself **b** him. H6584
Job 4:16 A form stood **b** my eyes, and I H4200+5584
Job 5: 8 I would lay my cause **b** him. H448
Job 7: 4 I lie down I think, '**How long** *b* I get up? AIT
Job 9: 2 mortals prove their innocence **b** God? H6640
Job 10:18 I wish I had died **b** any eye saw me. H4202
Job 10:21 **b** I go to the place of no return, to H928+3270
Job 13:16 person would dare come **b** him! H4200+7156
Job 14: 3 Will you bring them **b** you for judgment? H6640
Job 15: 7 Were you brought forth **b** the hills? H4200+7156
Job 15:32 **B** his time he will wither, and his H928+4202
Job 16:22 few years will pass **b** I take the path of no H2256
Job 21: 8 around them, their offspring **b** their eyes. H4200
Job 21:18 are they like straw **b** the wind, H4200+7156
Job 21:33 a countless throng goes **b** them. H4200+7156
Job 22:16 They were carried off **b** their time, their H4202
Job 23: 4 state my case **b** him and fill my H4200+7156
Job 23: 7 can establish their innocence **b** him, H6640
Job 23:15 That is why I am terrified **b** him H4946+7156
Job 25: 4 then can a mortal be righteous **b** God? H6640
Job 26: 6 The realm of the dead is naked **b** God H5584
Job 30:22 You snatch me up and drive me **b** the wind; H448
Job 32: 4 Now Elihu had waited **b** speaking to Job NDT
Job 33: 5 up and argue your case **b** me. H4200+7156
Job 34:23 that they should come **b** him for judgment. H448
Job 34:28 caused the cry of the poor to come **b** him, H6584
Job 35:14 your case is **b** him and you must H4200+7156
Job 41:22 in its neck; dismay goes **b** it. H4200+7156
Job 41:25 are terrified; they retreat **b** its thrashing. H4946
Job 42:10 gave him twice as much as he had **b**. NDT
Job 42:11 had known him **b** came and ate H4200+7156
Ps 5: 3 I lay my requests **b** you and wait H4200
Ps 5: 8 make your way straight **b** me. H4200+7156
Ps 9: 3 they stumble and perish **b** you. H4946+7156
Ps 18: 6 my cry came **b** him, into his ears H4200+7156
Ps 18:22 All his laws are **b** me; I have not H4200+5584
Ps 18:23 been blameless **b** him and have kept H6640
Ps 18:39 you humbled my adversaries **b** me. H9393
Ps 18:44 foreigners cower **b** me; as soon as they H4200
Ps 22:25 **b** those who fear you I will fulfill my vows. H5584
Ps 22:27 the nations will bow down **b** him, H4200+7156
Ps 22:29 to the dust will kneel **b** him— H4200+7156
Ps 23: 5 prepare a table **b** me in the H4200+7156
Ps 34: T to be insane **b** Abimelek, H4200+7156
Ps 35: 5 May they be like chaff **b** the wind H4200+7156
Ps 36: 1 is no fear of God **b** their eyes. H4200+5584
Ps 37: 7 Be still **b** the LORD and wait patiently for H4200
Ps 38: 9 All my longings lie open **b** you, Lord; my H5584
Ps 39: 5 the span of my years is as nothing **b** you. H5584
Ps 39:13 enjoy life again **b** I depart and am H928+3270
Ps 44:10 You made us retreat **b** the enemy, and H4974
Ps 49:19 will join *those* **who have gone b** them, H1887+3
Ps 50: 3 a fire devours **b** him, and around H4200+7156
Ps 50: 8 offerings, which are ever **b** me. H4200+5584
Ps 50:21 you and set my accusations **b** you. H4200+6524
Ps 51: 3 my sin is always **b** me. H5584
Ps 56:13 that I may walk **b** God in the light H4200+7156
Ps 58: 9 **B** your pots can feel the heat of the H928+3270
Ps 59:10 God *will* **go b** me and will let me gloat H7709
Ps 66: 3 power that your enemies cringe **b** you. H4200
Ps 68: 1 scattered; may his foes flee **b** him. H4946+7156
Ps 68: 2 as wax melts **b** the fire, may the H4946+7156
Ps 68: 2 may the wicked perish **b** God. H4946+7156
Ps 68: 3 be glad and rejoice **b** God; H4200+7156
Ps 68: 4 clouds; rejoice **b** him—his name is H4200+7156
Ps 68: 7 went out **b** your people, when H4200+7156
Ps 68: 8 down rain, **b** God, the One of H4946+7156
Ps 68: 8 One of Sinai, **b** God, the God of H4946+7156
Ps 68:28 your strength, our God, as you have done **b**. NDT
Ps 69:19 shamed; all my enemies are **b** you. H5584
Ps 69:22 the table set **b** them become a H7156+4200
Ps 72: 9 desert tribes bow **b** him and his H4200+7156
Ps 73:22 ignorant; I was a brute beast **b** you. H6640
Ps 76: 7 Who can stand **b** you when you are H4200+7156
Ps 78:30 But **b** they turned from what they craved H4202
Ps 78:55 out nations **b** them and allotted H4946+7156
Ps 79:10 **B** our eyes, make known among the H4200
Ps 79:11 of the prisoners come **b** you; H4200+7156
Ps 80: 2 **b** Ephraim, Benjamin and H4200+7156
Ps 81:15 who hate the LORD would cringe **b** him, H4200
Ps 83:13 my God, like chaff **b** the wind. H4200+7156
Ps 84: 7 strength, till each appears **b** God in Zion. H448
Ps 85:13 goes **b** him and prepares H4200+7156
Ps 86: 9 will come and worship **b** you, H4200+7156
Ps 88: 2 May my prayer come **b** you; turn H4200+7156
Ps 88:13 in the morning my prayer **comes b** you. H7709
Ps 89:14 love and faithfulness go **b** you. H7156
Ps 89:23 crush his foes **b** him and strike H4946+7156
Ps 89:36 his throne endure **b** me like the sun; H5584
Ps 90: 2 **B** the mountains were born or you H928+3270
Ps 90: 8 You have set our iniquities **b** you H4200+5584
Ps 95: 2 Let us come **b** him with thanksgiving and H7156
Ps 95: 6 let us kneel **b** the LORD our Maker; H4200+7156
Ps 96: 6 Splendor and majesty are **b** him H4200+7156
Ps 96: 9 holiness; tremble **b** him, all the H4946+7156
Ps 96:13 Let all creation rejoice **b** the LORD H4200+7156
Ps 97: 3 Fire goes **b** him and consumes his H4200+7156
Ps 97: 5 melt like wax **b** the LORD, H4946+4200+7156
Ps 97: 5 **b** the Lord of all the earth. H4946+4200+7156
Ps 98: 6 shout for joy **b** the LORD, the King. H4200+7156
Ps 98: 9 let them sing **b** the LORD, for he H4200+7156
Ps 100: 2 come **b** him with joyful songs. H4200+7156
Ps 102: T and pours out a lament **b** the LORD. H4200+7156
Ps 102:28 will be established **b** you. H4200+7156
Ps 105:17 and he sent a man **b** them H4200+7156
Ps 106:23 in the breach **b** him to keep his H4200+7156
Ps 109:14 of his fathers be remembered **b** the LORD; H448
Ps 109:15 May their sins always remain **b** the LORD H5584
Ps 116: 9 that I may walk **b** the LORD in the H4200+7156
Ps 119:46 of your statutes **b** kings and will not be H5584
Ps 119:67 **B** I was afflicted I went astray, but now I H3270
Ps 119:147 I rise **b** dawn and cry for help; I have put H928
Ps 119:169 May my cry come **b** you, LORD; H4200+7156
Ps 119:170 May my supplication come **b** you H4200+7156
Ps 129: 6 on the roof, which withers **b** it can grow; H7712
Ps 138: 1 with all my heart; **b** the "gods" I will sing H5584
Ps 139: 4 **B** a word is on my tongue you, LORD H3954+401
Ps 139: 5 You hem me in behind and **b**, and you H7710
Ps 139:16 in your book **b** one of them came to H4202
Ps 141: 2 my prayer be set **b** you like incense H4200+7156
Ps 142: 2 I pour out **b** him my complaint H4200+7156
Ps 142: 2 complaint; **b** him I tell my trouble. H4200+7156
Ps 143: 2 no one living is righteous **b** you. H4200+7156
Pr 2:17 ignored the **covenant** she *made b* God. AIT
Pr 4:25 fix your gaze directly **b** you. H5584
Pr 8:22 the first of his works, **b** his deeds of old; H7710
Pr 8:25 **b** the mountains were settled in H928+3270
Pr 8:25 settled in place, **b** the hills, I was H4200+7156
Pr 8:26 **b** he made the world or its fields H6330+4202
Pr 15:11 Destruction lie open **b** the LORD— H5584
Pr 15:33 and humility comes **b** honor. H4200+7156
Pr 16:18 Pride goes **b** destruction, a haughty H4200+7156
Pr 16:18 a haughty spirit **b** a fall. H4200+7156
Pr 17:14 drop the matter **b** a dispute breaks H4200+7156
Pr 18:12 **B** a downfall the heart is haughty H4200+7156
Pr 18:12 humility comes **b** honor. H4200+7156
Pr 18:13 To answer **b** listening—that is folly H928+3270
Pr 22:29 They will serve **b** kings; they will H4200+7156
Pr 22:29 they will not serve **b** officials of low H4200+7156
Pr 23: 1 a ruler, note well what is **b** you, H4200+7156
Pr 25: 7 him to humiliate you **b** his nobles. H4200+7156
Pr 27: 4 who can stand **b** jealousy? H4200+7156
Pr 28:14 is the one who always trembles **b** God, NDT
Pr 30: 7 LORD; do not refuse me **b** I die: H928+3270
Pr 30:30 beasts, who retreats **b** nothing; H4946+7156
Ecc 1:10 it was here **b** our **time**. H4946+4200+7156
Ecc 1:16 has ruled over Jerusalem **b** me; H4200+7156
Ecc 2: 7 than anyone in Jerusalem **b** me. H4200+7156
Ecc 2: 9 than anyone in Jerusalem **b** me. H4200+7156
Ecc 3:15 what will be has been **b**; and God H3893
Ecc 4:16 to all the people who were **b** them. H4200+7156
Ecc 5: 2 your heart to utter anything **b** God. H4200+7156
Ecc 6: 8 how to conduct themselves **b** others? H5584
Ecc 7:17 not be a fool—why die **b** your time? H928+4202
Ecc 8: 2 because you took an **oath** *b* God. AIT
Ecc 8:12 who are reverent **b** him. H4946+4200+7156
Ecc 10:11 If a snake bites **b** it is charmed, the H928+4202
Ecc 12: 1 **b** the days of trouble come H6330+889+4202
Ecc 12: 2 **b** the sun and the light and H6330+889+4202
Ecc 12: 6 **b** the silver cord is severed H6330+889+4202
Ecc 12: 6 **b** the pitcher is shattered at the spring NDT
SS 6:12 **B** I realized it, my desire set me among H4202
Isa 1: 7 stripped by foreigners **right b** you, H4200+5584
Isa 1:12 When you come to **appear b** me H8011+7156
Isa 1:23 the widow's case does not come **b** them. H448
Isa 7:16 **b** the boy knows enough to reject H928+3270
Isa 8: 4 For **b** the boy knows how to say 'My H928+3270
Isa 9: 3 they rejoice **b** you as people H4200+7156
Isa 10:34 Lebanon will fall **b** the Mighty One. H928
Isa 13:16 will be dashed to pieces **b** their eyes; H4200
Isa 17:13 driven **b** the wind like chaff on the H4200+7156
Isa 17:13 like tumbleweed **b** a gale. H4200+7156
Isa 17:14 sudden terror! **B** the morning, they H928+3270
Isa 18: 5 **b** the harvest, when the H4200+7156
Isa 19: 1 The idols of Egypt tremble **b** him H4946+7156
Isa 23:18 go to those who live **b** the LORD, H4200+7156
Isa 24:23 in Jerusalem, and **b** its elders—with great H5584
Isa 28: 4 will be like figs ripe **b** harvest—as H928+3270
Isa 31: 8 They will flee **b** the sword and their H4946+7156
Isa 36: 7 "You must worship **b** this altar"? H4200+7156
Isa 37:14 LORD and spread it out **b** the LORD. H4200+7156
Isa 37:27 on the roof, scorched **b** it grows up. H4200+7156
Isa 37:33 *He will* not **come b** it with shield or build H7709
Isa 38: 3 how I have walked **b** you faithfully H4200+7156
Isa 40:17 **B** him all the nations are as nothing; they H5584
Isa 41: 1 "Be silent **b** me, you islands! Let the H448
Isa 41: 2 to him and subdues kings **b** him. H4200+7156
Isa 41: 3 by a path his feet have not traveled **b**. NDT
Isa 42: 9 **b** they spring into being I announce H928+3270
Isa 42:16 into light **b** them and make the H4200+7156
Isa 43:10 **B** me no god was formed, nor will H4200+7156
Isa 44: 7 declare and lay out **b** me what has H4200
Isa 45: 1 subdue nations **b** him and to strip H4200+7156
Isa 45: 1 to open doors **b** him so that gates H4200+7156
Isa 45: 2 I will go **b** you and will level the H4200+7156
Isa 45:14 They will bow down **b** you and plead with H448
Isa 45:23 **B** me every knee will bow; by me every H4200
Isa 48: 5 **b** they happened I announced them H928+3270
Isa 48: 7 have not heard of them **b** today. H4200+7156
Isa 48:19 out nor destroyed from **b** me. H4200+7156
Isa 49: 1 **B** I was born the LORD called me; from my H4946
Isa 49:16 of my hands; your walls are ever **b** me. H5584
Isa 49:23 They will bow down **b** you with their faces H4200
Isa 52:12 the LORD will go **b** you, the God H4200+7156
Isa 53: 2 He grew up **b** him like a tender H4200+7156
Isa 53: 7 and as a sheep **b** its shearers is H4200+7156
Isa 55:12 and hills will burst into song **b** you, H4200+7156
Isa 58: 8 your righteousness will go **b** you, H4200+7156
Isa 60:14 of your oppressors will come bowing **b** you; H448
Isa 61:11 praise spring up **b** all nations. H5584
Isa 63:12 who divided the waters **b** them, to H4946+7156
Isa 64: 1 mountains would tremble **b** you! H4946+7156
Isa 64: 2 cause the nations to quake **b** you! H4946+7156
Isa 64: 3 and the mountains trembled **b** you. H4946+7156
Isa 65: 6 it stands written **b** me: I will not H4200+7156
Isa 65:24 **B** they call I will answer; while they are H3270
Isa 66: 7 "**B** she goes into labor, she gives H928+3270
Isa 66: 7 **b** the pains come upon her H928+3270
Isa 66:22 earth that I make will endure **b** me," H4200+7156
Isa 66:23 will come and bow down **b** me," H4200+7156
Jer 1: 5 "**B** I formed you in the womb I knew H928+3270
Jer 1: 5 **b** you were born I set you apart H928+3270
Jer 1:17 by them, or I will terrify you **b** them. H4200+7156
Jer 2:22 the stain of your guilt is still **b** me," H4200+7156
Jer 4:26 all its towns lay in ruins **b** the LORD H4946+7156
Jer 4:26 before the LORD, **b** his fierce anger. H4946+7156
Jer 6: 7 and wounds are ever **b** me. H6584+7156
Jer 6:21 "I will put obstacles **b** this people. H448
Jer 7:10 come and stand **b** me in this house H4200+7156
Jer 9:13 which I set **b** them; they have H4200+7156
Jer 12: 1 righteous, LORD, when I bring a case **b** you. H448
Jer 12:11 parched and desolate **b** me; the whole H6584
Jer 13:16 to the LORD your God **b** he brings the H928+3270
Jer 13:16 **b** your feet stumble on the H928+3270
Jer 15: 1 and Samuel were to stand **b** me, H4200+7156
Jer 15: 9 to the sword **b** their enemies," H4200+7156
Jer 16: 9 **B** your eyes and in your days I will bring H4200
Jer 17:16 What passes my lips is **open b** you H5790+7156
Jer 18:17 I will scatter them **b** their enemies H4200+7156
Jer 18:20 that I stood **b** you and spoke in H4200+7156
Jer 18:23 Let them be overthrown **b** you; deal H4200+7156
Jer 19: 7 fall by the sword **b** their enemies, H4200+7156
Jer 21: 8 I am setting **b** you the way of life H4200+7156
Jer 26: 4 my law, which I have set **b** you, H4200+7156
Jer 28: 5 Hananiah **b** the priests and H4200+6524
Jer 28:11 he said **b** all the people, "This H4200+6524
Jer 29:21 will put them to death **b** your very eyes. H4200
Jer 30:20 will be established **b** me; H4200+7156
Jer 31:36 ever cease being a nation **b** me." H4200+7156
Jer 33: 7 rebuild them as they were **b**. H928+2021+8037
Jer 33: 9 praise and honor **b** all nations on earth H4200
Jer 33:11 of the land as they were **b**, H928+2021+8037

Jer 33:18 man to stand **b** me H4946+4200+7156
Jer 33:21 Levites who are priests **ministering** *b* me— AIT
Jer 33:22 the Levites *who* **minister** *b* me as AIT
Jer 34: 5 the kings who ruled **b** you, so they H4200+7156
Jer 34:15 a covenant **b** me in the house H4200+7156
Jer 34:18 of the covenant they made **b** me, H4200+7156
Jer 35: 5 and some cups **b** the Rekabites H4200+7156
Jer 36: 7 their petition **b** the LORD and will H4200+7156
Jer 36: 9 a time of fasting **b** the LORD was H4200+7156
Jer 37:20 Let me bring my petition **b** you: Do H4200+7156
Jer 38:10 prophet out of the cistern **b** he dies." H928+3270
Jer 39: 6 the sons of Zedekiah **b** his eyes and also H4200
Jer 39:16 they will be fulfilled **b** your **eyes**. H4200+7156
Jer 40: 4 the whole country lies **b** you; go H4200+7156
Jer 40: 5 However, **b** Jeremiah turned to go H6388+4202
Jer 40:10 to represent you **b** the Babylonians H4200+7156
Jer 41: 4 assassination, **b** anyone knew about it, H4202
Jer 44:10 the decrees I set **b** you and your H4200+7156
Jer 47: 1 the Philistines **b** Pharaoh attacked H928+3270
Jer 49:37 I will shatter Elam **b** their foes H4200+7156
Jer 49:37 **b** those who want to kill them H4200+7156
Jer 50:24 you were caught **b** you knew it; you H4202
Jer 51: 5 land is full of guilt **b** the Holy One of H4946
Jer 51:24 "**B** your eyes I will repay Babylon and all H4200
Jer 52:10 killed the sons of Zedekiah **b** his eyes; H4200
La 1: 5 gone into exile, captive **b** the foe. H4200+7156
La 1: 6 they have fled **b** the pursuer. H4200+7156
La 1:22 all their wickedness come **b** you; H4200+7156
La 3:35 their rights **b** the Most High, H5584+7156
Eze 2:10 which he unrolled **b** me. H4200+7156
Eze 3: 1 of man, eat what *is* **b** *you*, eat this scroll; H5162
Eze 3:20 and I put a stumbling block **b** them, H4200+7156
Eze 5: 9 to you what *I have* never **done** *b* and will AIT
Eze 8: 1 elders of Judah were sitting **b** me, H4200+7156
Eze 8: 4 And there **b** me was the glory of the God of NDT
Eze 14: 3 put wicked stumbling blocks **b** their faces. H5790
Eze 14: 4 stumbling block **b** their faces and then H5790
Eze 14: 7 stumbling block **b** their faces and then H5790
Eze 16:18 offered my oil and incense **b** them. H4200+7156
Eze 16:19 offered as fragrant incense **b** them. H4200+7156
Eze 16:50 and did detestable things **b** me. H4200+7156
Eze 16:55 will return to *what* they were **b**; and you H7712
Eze 16:55 daughters will return to *what* you were **b**. H7712
Eze 16:57 **b** your wickedness was uncovered H928+3270
Eze 21: 6 Groan **b** them with broken heart H4200+6524
Eze 22:30 wall and stand **b** me in the gap on H4200+7156
Eze 23:41 a table spread **b** it on which you H4200+7156
Eze 28:17 I made a spectacle of you **b** kings. H4200+7156
Eze 30:24 and he will groan **b** him like a H4200+7156
Eze 32:10 when I brandish my sword **b** them. H6584+7156
Eze 33:22 Now the evening **b** the man arrived H4200+7156
Eze 33:22 opened my mouth **b** the man came to me H6330
Eze 33:31 and sit **b** you to hear your words H4200+7156
Eze 36:11 will make you prosper more than **b**. H8035
Eze 36:23 I am proved holy through you **b** their eyes. H4200
Eze 37:20 Hold **b** their eyes the sticks you have H4200
Eze 38:16 I am proved holy through you **b** their eyes. H4200
Eze 40:46 draw near to the LORD to **minister** *b* him." AIT
Eze 41:22 "This is the table that is **b** the LORD." H4200+7156
Eze 42:14 put on other clothes **b** they go near the H2256
Eze 43:11 Write these down **b** them so that H4200+6524
Eze 43:19 who come near to **minister** *b* me, declares AIT
Eze 43:24 You are to offer them **b** the LORD H4200+7156
Eze 44:11 and stand **b** the people and H4200+7156
Eze 44:15 are to come near to **minister** *b* me; they are AIT
Eze 44:15 they are to stand **b** me to offer H4200+7156
Eze 44:16 near my table to **minister** *b* me and serve me AIT
Eze 45: 4 who draw near to **minister** *b* the LORD. AIT
Eze 46: 9 of the land come **b** the LORD at the H4200+7156
Da 2: 2 they came in and stood **b** the king, H4200+7156
Da 2:31 and there **b** you stood a large A10378+10619
Da 2:46 fell prostrate **b** Daniel and paid him honor NDT
Da 3: 3 had set up, and they stood **b** it. A10378+10619
Da 3:13 So these men were brought **b** the king, A10621
Da 3:16 do not need to **defend** ourselves *b* you in this AIT
Da 4: 6 Babylon be brought **b** me to interpret the A10621
Da 4:10 there **b** me stood a tree in the middle NDT
Da 4:13 I looked, and there **b** me was a holy one, NDT
Da 4:36 my throne and became even greater than **b**. NDT
Da 5:13 So Daniel was brought **b** the king, and A10621
Da 5:15 were brought **b** me to read this writing A10621
Da 6:10 just as he had done **b**. A10427+10622+10180
Da 6:22 Nor have I ever done any wrong **b** you A10621
Da 6:24 And **b** they reached the floor of the den A10379
Da 7: 2 there **b** me were the four winds of NDT
Da 7: 5 "And there **b** me was a second beast, which NDT
Da 7: 6 I looked, and there **b** me was another beast NDT
Da 7: 7 I looked, and there **b** me was a fourth beast NDT
Da 7: 8 the horns, there **b** me was another horn, NDT
Da 7: 8 first horns were uprooted **b** it. A10427+10621
Da 7:10 fire was flowing, coming out from **b** him. A10621
Da 7:10 times ten thousand stood **b** him. A10621
Da 7:13 there **b** me was one like a son of man NDT
Da 7:20 **b** which three of them fell A10427+10621
Da 8: 3 there **b** me was a ram with two horns NDT
Da 8:15 there **b** me stood one who looked H4200+5584
Da 10: 5 looked up and there **b** me was a man NDT
Da 10:12 and to humble yourself **b** your God, H4200+7156
Da 10:16 I said to the one standing **b** me, "I H4200+5584
Da 11:22 will be swept away **b** him; H4946+4200+7156
Da 11:29 will be different from what it was **b**. H8037
Da 12: 5 and there **b** me stood two others NDT
Da 12: 6 "How long will it be **b** these astonishing NDT
Hos 2:10 expose her lewdness **b** the eyes of her H4200
Hos 7: 2 engulf them; they are always **b** me. H5584+7156
Joel 1: 9 in mourning, *those who* **minister** *b* the LORD. AIT
Joel 1:13 wail, *you who* **minister** *b* the altar. AIT
Joel 1:13 in sackcloth, *you who* **minister** *b* my God; for AIT
Joel 1:16 the food been cut off **b** our very eyes— H5584
Joel 2: 3 **B** them fire devours, behind them a H4200+7156
Joel 2: 3 **B** them the land is like the garden H4200+7156
Joel 2:10 **B** them the earth shakes, the H4200+7156
Joel 2:17 Let the priests, *who* **minister** *b* the LORD, AIT
Joel 2:23 both autumn and spring rains, as **b**. H8037
Joel 2:31 moon to blood **b** the coming of the H4200+7156
Am 1: 1 Israel two years **b** the earthquake, H4200+7156
Am 2: 9 I destroyed the Amorites **b** them, H4946+7156
Jnh 1: 2 its wickedness has come up **b** me." H4200+7156
Jnh 1:13 for the sea grew even wilder than **b**. NDT
Mic 1: 4 like wax **b** the fire, like water H4946+7156
Mic 2:13 open the way will go up **b** them; H4200+7156
Mic 2:13 King will pass through **b** them, H4200+7156
Mic 6: 1 "Stand up, **plead** *my* **case** *b* the mountains AIT
Mic 6: 6 With what *shall I* **come** **b** the LORD and H7709
Mic 6: 6 LORD and bow down **b** the exalted God? H4200
Mic 6: 6 *Shall I* **come** **b** him with burnt offerings H7709
Na 1: 5 The mountains quake **b** him and the hills H4946
Na 1: 6 out like fire; the rocks are shattered **b** him. H4946
Hab 1: 3 Destruction and violence are **b** me H4200+5584
Hab 2:20 let all the earth be silent **b** him. H4946+7156
Hab 3: 5 Plague went **b** him; pestilence H4200+7156
Zep 1: 7 Be silent **b** the Sovereign LORD, for H4946+7156
Zep 2: 2 **b** the decree takes effect and that H928+3270
Zep 2: 2 **b** the LORD's fierce anger H928+3270+4202
Zep 2: 2 **b** the day of the LORD's wrath H928+3270+4202
Zep 3:20 I restore your fortunes **b** your very eyes," H4200
Hag 2:15 how things were **b** one stone was H4946+3270
Zec 1: 8 there **b** me was a man mounted on a NDT
Zec 1:18 looked up, and there **b** me were four horns. NDT
Zec 2: 1 there **b** me was a man with a NDT
Zec 2:13 Be still **b** the LORD, all mankind H7156+4946
Zec 3: 1 priest standing **b** the angel of the H7156+4200
Zec 3: 3 clothes as he stood **b** the angel. H7156+4200
Zec 3: 4 to those who were standing **b** him, H7156+4200
Zec 3: 8 and your associates seated **b** you, H7156+4200
Zec 4: 7 **B** Zerubbabel you will become H7156+4200
Zec 5: 1 and there **b** me was a flying scroll. NDT
Zec 5: 9 and there **b** me were two women NDT
Zec 6: 1 there **b** me were four chariots coming NDT
Zec 8:10 **B** that time there were no wages H4200+7156
Zec 10: 8 they will be as numerous as **b**. H8049S
Zec 12: 8 angel of the LORD going **b** them. H4200+7156
Mal 2: 9 humiliated **b** all the people, H4200
Mal 3: 1 who will prepare the way **b** me. H7156+4200
Mal 3:11 fields *will* **not drop** *their* **fruit b it is ripe**," H8897
Mal 3:14 like mourners **b** the LORD Almighty? H7156+4946
Mal 4: 5 Elijah to you **b** that great and H7156+4200
Mt 1:18 Joseph, but **b** they came together *G4570+2445*
Mt 5:12 persecuted the prophets who were **b** you. *G4574*
Mt 5:16 let your light shine **b** others, that they may *G1869*
Mt 6: 8 knows what you need **b** you ask him. *G4574*
Mt 8: 2 leprosy came and **knelt b** him and said, *G4686*
Mt 8:29 here to torture us **b** the appointed time?" *G4574*
Mt 9:18 leader came and **knelt b** him and said, *G4686*
Mt 10:18 you will be brought **b** governors and kings *G2093*
Mt 10:23 the towns of Israel **b** the Son of Man *G2401+323*
Mt 10:32 "Whoever acknowledges me **b** others, *G1869*
Mt 10:32 also acknowledge **b** my Father in heaven. *G1869*
Mt 10:33 But whoever disowns me **b** others, I will *G1869*
Mt 10:33 I will disown **b** my Father in heaven. *G1869*
Mt 11:10 who will prepare your way **b** you. *G1869*
Mt 14:25 **Shortly b dawn** Jesus *G5480+5871+3836+3816*
Mt 15: 2 They don't wash their hands **b** they eat!" *G4020*
Mt 15:25 The woman came and **knelt b** him. "Lord *G4686*
Mt 16:28 not taste death **b** they see the Son *G2401+323*
Mt 17: 2 There he was transfigured **b** them. *G1869*
Mt 17: 3 there appeared *b* **them** Moses and Elijah, AIT
Mt 17:14 a man approached Jesus and knelt *b* **him**. AIT
Mt 18:26 this the servant fell **on** *his* **knees b** him. *G4686*
Mt 24:38 For in the days **b** the flood, people were *G4574*
Mt 25:32 All the nations will be gathered **b** him *G1869*
Mt 26:34 "this very night, **b** the rooster crows, you *G4570*
Mt 26:70 But he denied it **b** them all. "I don't know *G1869*
Mt 26:75 "**B** the rooster crows, you will disown me *G4570*
Mt 27:11 Meanwhile Jesus stood **b** the governor *G1869*
Mk 3:11 *they* **fell down b** him and cried out *G4700*
Mk 6:48 **Shortly b dawn** he went *G4309+5480+5871+3836+3816*
Mk 9: 1 not taste death **b** they see that the *G2401+323*
Mk 9: 2 There he was transfigured **b** them. *G1869*
Mk 9: 4 And there appeared *b* **them** Elijah and Moses AIT
Mk 10:17 ran up to him and **fell on** *his* **knees b** him. *G1206*
Mk 13: 9 me you will stand **b** governors and kings *G2093*
Mk 14:30 **b** the rooster crows twice you *G4570+2445*
Mk 14:60 priest stood up **b** them and asked *G1650+3545*
Mk 14:72 "**B** the rooster crows twice you will disown *G4570*
Mk 15:42 **the day b the Sabbath**). *G4640*
Lk 1: 8 duty and he was serving as priest **b** God, *G1882*
Lk 1:15 with the Holy Spirit **even b** he is born. *G2285*
Lk 1:17 And he will go on **b** the Lord, in the spirit *G1967*
Lk 1:75 righteousness **b** him all our days. *G1967*
Lk 1:76 you will go on **b** the Lord to prepare *G1967*
Lk 2:21 had given him **b** he was conceived. *G4574+3836*
Lk 2:26 would not die **b** he had seen *G4570+2445+323*
Lk 4:35 man down **b** them all and *G1650+3836+3545*
Lk 5:18 him into the house to lay him **b** Jesus. *G1967*
Lk 7:27 who will prepare your way **b** you. *G1869*
Lk 9:27 not taste death **b** they see the *G2401+323*
Lk 11:38 that Jesus did not first wash **b** the meal. *G4574*
Lk 12: 8 publicly acknowledges me **b** others, *G1869*
Lk 12: 8 also acknowledge **b** the angels of God. *G1869*
Lk 12: 9 But whoever disowns me **b** others will be *G1967*
Lk 12: 9 will be disowned **b** the angels of God. *G1967*
Lk 12:11 "When you are brought **b** synagogues *G2093*
Lk 18:14 the other, went home **justified b God**. *G1467*
Lk 21:12 "But **b** all this, they will seize you and *G4574*
Lk 21:12 you will be brought **b** kings and governors *G2093*
Lk 21:36 may be able to stand **b** the Son of Man." *G1869*
Lk 22:15 this Passover with you **b** I suffer. *G4574+3836*
Lk 22:34 **b** the rooster crows today *G4024+2401*
Lk 22:61 "**B** the rooster crows today, you will *G4570*
Lk 22:66 met together, and Jesus was led **b** them. *G1650*
Lk 23:12 friends—**b** *this* they had been enemies. *G4732*
Lk 24:19 in word and deed **b** God and all the *G1883*
Jn 1:15 has surpassed me because he was **b** me. *G4755*
Jn 1:30 has surpassed me because he was **b** me. *G4755*
Jn 1:48 the fig tree **b** Philip called you." *G4574+3836*
Jn 3:24 This was **b** John was put in prison.) *G4037*
Jn 4:49 "Sir, come down **b** my child dies." *G4570*
Jn 5:45 do not think I will accuse you **b** the Father. *G4639*
Jn 6:62 of Man ascend to where he was **b**! *G3836+4728*
Jn 8: 3 They made her stand **b the group** *G1877+3545*
Jn 8:58 Jesus answered, "**b** Abraham was born, *G4570*
Jn 10: 8 All who have come **b** me are thieves and *G4574*
Jn 11:55 ceremonial cleansing **b** the Passover. *G4574*
Jn 12: 1 Six days **b** the Passover, Jesus came to *G4574*
Jn 12:35 the light, **b** darkness overtakes you. *G2671+3590*
Jn 13: 1 It was **just b** the Passover Festival. *G4574*
Jn 13:19 "I am telling you now **b** it happens, so *G4574*
Jn 13:38 **b** the rooster crows *G4024+3590+2401+4005*
Jn 14:19 **B long**, the world will not see me *G2285+3625*
Jn 14:29 I have told you now **b** it happens, so that *G4570*
Jn 17: 5 I had with you **b** the world began. *G4574+3836*
Jn 17:24 you loved me **b** the creation of the *G4574*
Ac 1: 9 he was taken up **b** their very **eyes**, and a *G1063*
Ac 2:20 the moon to blood **b** the coming of the *G4570*
Ac 2:25 " 'I saw the Lord always **b** me. Because he *G1967*
Ac 3:13 and you disowned him **b** Pilate *G2848+4725*
Ac 4: 7 John brought **b** them and *G1877+3836+3545*
Ac 4:10 that this man stands **b** you healed. *G1967*
Ac 5: 4 Didn't it belong to you **b** *it was* **sold**? And *G3531S*
Ac 5:27 made to appear **b** the Sanhedrin to *G1877*
Ac 6:12 brought him **b** the Sanhedrin. *G1650*
Ac 7: 2 **b** he lived in Harran. *G4570+2445*
Ac 7:40 'Make us gods who *will* **go b** us. *G4638*
Ac 7:45 the nations God drove out **b** them. *G608+4725*
Ac 8:21 because your heart is not right **b** God. *G1882*
Ac 8:32 as a lamb **b** its shearer is silent *G1883*
Ac 10: 4 come up as a memorial offering **b** God. *G1869*
Ac 10:30 a man in shining clothes stood **b** me *G1967*
Ac 12: 6 The night **b** Herod was to bring him to *G4021*
Ac 13:24 **B** the coming of Jesus, John *G4574+4725*
Ac 16:20 *They* **brought** them **b** the magistrates and *G4642*
Ac 16:29 rushed in and **fell** trembling **b** Paul and *G4700*
Ac 16:34 his house and **set a meal b** them; *G4192+5544*
Ac 17: 6 some other believers **b** the city officials, *G2093*
Ac 18:18 **B** he sailed, he had his hair cut off at NDT
Ac 19:30 Paul wanted to appear **b** the crowd, but *G1650*
Ac 19:33 in order to make a defense *b* the **people**. AIT
Ac 22:30 brought Paul and had him stand **b** them. *G1650*
Ac 23:15 to bring him **b** you on the pretext of *G1650*
Ac 23:15 ready to kill him **b** he gets here." *G4574+3836*
Ac 23:20 ask you to bring Paul **b** the Sanhedrin *G1650*
Ac 24: 1 their charges against Paul *b* the **governor**. AIT
Ac 24: 2 Tertullus presented his case **b** Felix: NDT
Ac 24:16 my conscience clear **b** God and man. *G4639*
Ac 24:19 who ought to be here **b** you and bring *G2093*
Ac 24:20 in me when I stood **b** the Sanhedrin— *G2093*
Ac 24:21 of the dead that I am on trial **b** you today. *G2093*
Ac 25: 2 leaders appeared *b* **him** and presented the AIT
Ac 25: 6 ordered that Paul be brought **b** him. NDT
Ac 25: 9 stand trial **b** me there on these *G2093*
Ac 25:10 "I am now standing **b** Caesar's court *G2093*
Ac 25:16 over anyone **b** they have faced *G4570+2445*
Ac 25:26 Therefore I have brought him **b** all of you *G2093*
Ac 25:26 and especially **b** you, King Agrippa, *G2093*
Ac 26: 2 myself fortunate to *stand* **b** you today as I *G2093*
Ac 27:14 **B very long**, a wind of *G3552+4024+4498*
Ac 27:21 Paul stood up **b** them and said: *G1877+3545*
Ac 27:24 You must **stand trial b** Caesar; and God *G4225*
Ac 27:33 **Just b** dawn Paul urged them all to *G948+4005*
Ro 3:18 "There is no fear of God **b** their eyes." *G595*
Ro 4: 2 to boast about—but not **b** God. *G4639*
Ro 4:10 it after he was circumcised, or **b**? *G1877+213S*
Ro 4:10 It was not after, but **b**! *G1877+213S*
Ro 4:12 Abraham had **b** he was **circumcised**. *G1877+213*
Ro 5:13 sin was in the world **b** the law was given *G948*
Ro 9:11 **b** the twins were born or had done *G3609*
Ro 14:10 For *we will* all **stand b** God's judgment *G4225*
Ro 14:11 'every knee will bow *b* **me**; every tongue will AIT
Ro 16: 7 apostles, and they were in Christ **b** I was. *G4574*
1Co 1:29 so that no one may boast **b** him. *G1967*
1Co 2: 7 God destined for our glory **b** time *began*. *G4574*
1Co 4: 5 judge nothing **b** the appointed time; *G4574*
1Co 6: 1 do you dare to take it **b** the ungodly for *G2093*
1Co 6: 1 judgment instead of **b** the Lord's people? *G2093*

1Co 10:27 eat whatever *is* **put b** you without raising *G4192*
1Co 11:28 themselves **b** they eat of the *G2779+4048*
2Co 2:17 in Christ we speak **b** God with sincerity, as *G2978*
2Co 3: 4 confidence we have through Christ **b** God. *G4639*
2Co 5:10 we must all appear **b** the judgment seat *G1869*
2Co 7: 3 *I have* **said b** that you have such a place *G4625*
2Co 7:12 rather that **b** God you could see for *G1967*
2Co 12:21 again my God will humble me **b** you, *G4639*
Gal 1:17 to see those who were apostles **b** I was, *G4574*
Gal 1:20 I assure you **b** God that what I am writing *G1967*
Gal 2:12 For **b** certain men came from James, he *G4574*
Gal 3: 1 **B** your very eyes Jesus Christ was clearly *G2848*
Gal 3:11 who relies on the law is justified **b** God, *G4123*
Gal 3:23 **B** the coming of this faith, we were *G4574+3836*
Gal 5:21 I warn you, as *I* **did b**, that those who *G4625S*
Eph 1: 4 he chose us in him **b** the creation of the *G4574*
Eph 3:14 For this reason I kneel **b** the Father, *G4639*
Php 3:18 *as I have* often **told** you *b* and now tell you AIT
Col 1:17 He is **b** all things, and in him all things *G4574*
1Th 1: 3 We remember **b** our God and Father your *G1869*
1Th 4: 6 as *we* **told** you and warned you **b**. *G4625*
1Th 5:27 I charge you *b* the **Lord** to have this letter read AIT
1Ti 5:20 are sinning you are to reprove **b** everyone, *G1967*
1Ti 6:13 while testifying **b** Pontius Pilate made *G2093*
2Ti 1: 9 us in Christ Jesus **b** the beginning of time, *G4574*
2Ti 2:14 Warn them **b** God against quarreling *G1967*
2Ti 4:21 Do your best to get here **b** winter. *G4574*
Titus 1: 2 promised **b** the beginning of time, *G4574*
Heb 4:13 laid bare *b* the **eyes** of him to whom we AIT
Heb 6:18 hold of the hope **set b** us may be greatly *G4618*
Heb 11: 5 For **b** he was taken, he was commended *G4574*
Heb 12: 2 For the joy **set b** him he endured the cross, *G4618*
Jas 4:10 Humble yourselves **b** the Lord, and he will *G1967*
1Pe 1:20 *He was* **chosen b** the creation of the world *G4589*
1Pe 2:20 endure it, this is commendable **b** God. *G4123*
1Jn 2:28 unashamed **b** him at his coming. *G608*
1Jn 3:21 condemn us, we have confidence **b** God *G4639*
Jude 24 to present you **b** his glorious *G2979*
Jude 25 Jesus Christ our Lord, **b** all ages, now and *G4574*
Rev 1: 4 from the seven spirits **b** his throne, *G1967*
Rev 3: 5 that name **b** my Father and his *G1967*
Rev 3: 8 I have placed **b** you an open door that no *G1967*
Rev 4: 1 and **there** *b me* was a door standing open in AIT
Rev 4: 2 and **there** *b me* was a throne in heaven with AIT
Rev 4:10 elders fall down **b** him who sits on the *G1967*
Rev 4:10 lay their crowns **b** the throne and say: *G1967*
Rev 5: 8 twenty-four elders fell down **b** the Lamb. *G1967*
Rev 6: 2 and **there** *b me* was a white horse AIT
Rev 6: 5 I looked, and **there** *b me* was a black horse AIT
Rev 6: 8 and **there** *b me* was a pale horse! Its AIT
Rev 7: 9 and **there** *b me* was a great multitude that AIT
Rev 7: 9 standing **b** the throne and before the *G1967*
Rev 7: 9 before the throne and **b** the Lamb. *G1967*
Rev 7:11 down on their faces **b** the throne and *G2093*
Rev 7:15 "they are **b** the throne of God and serve *G1967*
Rev 8: 2 I saw the seven angels who stand **b** God, *G1967*
Rev 8: 4 went up **b** God from the angel's hand. *G1967*
Rev 9:13 horns of the golden altar that is **b** God. *G1967*
Rev 11: 4 "they stand **b** the Lord of the earth." *G1967*
Rev 11:16 who were seated on their thrones **b** God *G1967*
Rev 12:10 who accuses them **b** our God day and *G1967*
Rev 14: 1 Then I looked, and **there** *b me* was the Lamb AIT
Rev 14: 3 they sang a new song **b** the throne and *G1967*
Rev 14: 3 before the throne and **b** the four living *G1967*
Rev 14:14 I looked, and **there** *b me* was a white cloud AIT
Rev 15: 4 All nations will come and worship **b** you *G1967*
Rev 19:11 open and there b me was a white horse, NDT
Rev 20:12 small, standing **b** the throne, and *G1967*

BEFOREHAND (7) [BEFORE]

Isa 41:26 know, or **b**, so we could H4946+4200+7156
Mk 13:11 *do* **not worry b about** what to say. *G4628*
Mk 14: 8 perfume on my body **b** to prepare for my *G4624*
Lk 21:14 up your mind not *to* **worry b** how you will *G4627*
Ac 4:28 will *had* **decided b** should happen *G4633*
Ro 1: 2 the gospel *he* **promised b** through his *G4600*
Ro 3:25 left the sins **committed b** unpunished— *G4588*

BEFUDDLED (1)

Isa 28: 7 stagger from beer and *are* **b** with wine; H1182

BEG (18) [BEGGAR, BEGGARS, BEGGED, BEGGING]

Ge 43:20 "We **b** your **pardon**, our lord," they said H1065
Jdg 13: 8 **I b you** to let the man of God you sent to H5528
1Sa 15:25 Now **I b you**, forgive my sin and come back H5528
2Sa 24:10 **I b you**, take away the guilt of your H5528
1Ch 21: 8 **I b you**, take away the guilt of your H5528
Est 4: 8 presence to **b for mercy** and plead with H2858
Est 7: 7 stayed behind to **b** Queen Esther for his H1335
Job 19:16 though *I* **b** him with my own mouth. H2858
La 4: 4 the children **b** *for* bread, but no one H8626
Am 7: 5 I cried out, "Sovereign LORD, **I b you**, stop! H5528
Lk 8:28 the Most High God? *I* **b** you, don't torture *G1289*
Lk 9:38 "Teacher, *I* **b** you to look at my son, for he *G1289*
Lk 16: 3 enough to dig, and I'm ashamed *to* **b**— *G2050*
Lk 16:27 "He answered, 'Then *I* **b** you, father, send *G2263*
Jn 9: 8 this the same man who used to sit and **b**?" *G4644*
Ac 3: 2 put every day *to* **b** from those going *G160+1797*
Ac 26: 3 *I* **b** you to listen to me patiently. *G1289*
2Co 10: 2 *I* **b** you that when I come I may not have to *G1289*

BEGAN (180) [BEGIN]

Ge 4:26 At that time *people* **b** to call on the name H2725
Ge 6: 1 When human beings **b** to increase in H2725
Ge 16: 4 was pregnant, *she b to* **despise** her mistress. AIT
Ge 21:16 as she sat there, *she* **b** to sob. H5951+906+7754
Ge 29:11 Jacob kissed Rachel and *b to* **weep** aloud. AIT
Ge 35:16 Rachel *b to* **give birth** and had great difficulty. AIT
Ge 41:54 the seven years of famine **b**, just as H2725
Ge 41:55 When all Egypt *b to* **feel the famine**, the AIT
Ge 42:24 He turned away from them and *b to* **weep** AIT
Ex 16:20 it was full of maggots and *b to* **smell**. AIT
Ex 33: 4 *they b to* **mourn** and no one put on any AIT
Nu 11: 4 The rabble with them *b to* **crave other food** AIT
Nu 12: 1 Miriam and Aaron *b to* **talk** against Moses AIT
Nu 25: 1 the men **b** to indulge in sexual immorality H2725
Dt 1: 5 of Moab, Moses **b** to expound this law H3283
Jos 16: 1 The allotment for Joseph **b** at the Jordan H3655
Jos 18:12 north side their boundary **b** at the Jordan, H2118
Jos 18:15 The southern side **b** at the outskirts of H3655
Jdg 13:25 the Spirit of the LORD **b** to stir him while he H2725
Jdg 16:19 of his hair, and so **b** to subdue him. H2725
Jdg 16:22 on his head **b** to grow *again* after it had H2725
Jdg 20:31 *They* **b** to inflict casualties on the H2725
Jdg 20:40 the column of smoke **b** to rise from the H2725
Ru 2: 3 entered a field and *b to* **glean** behind the AIT
1Sa 13: 8 come to Gilgal, and Saul's men *b to* **scatter**. AIT
1Sa 20:19 where you hid **when** this trouble **b**, H928+3427
1Sa 23:25 Saul and his men **b** the search, and when H2143
1Ki 6: 1 *he b to* **build** the temple of the LORD. AIT
1Ki 15:29 As soon as he *b to* **reign**, he killed AIT
1Ki 16:11 As soon as he *b to* **reign** and was seated on AIT
1Ki 16:31 **b** to serve Baal and worship him. H2143
1Ki 18:27 At noon Elijah *b to* **taunt** them. AIT
2Ki 4:40 but as they *b to* **eat** it, they cried out, AIT
2Ki 6: 4 went to the Jordan and *b to* **cut down** trees. AIT
2Ki 8:11 Then the man of God *b to* **weep**. AIT
2Ki 8:16 of Jehoshaphat *b his* **reign** as king of Judah. AIT
2Ki 8:25 son of Jehoram king of Judah *b to* **reign**. AIT
2Ki 10:32 those days the LORD **b** to reduce the size of H2725
2Ki 11:21 was seven years old when he *b to* **reign**. AIT
2Ki 14: 1 son of Joash king of Judah *b to* **reign**. AIT
2Ki 15: 1 son of Amaziah king of Judah *b to* **reign**. AIT
2Ki 15:32 son of Uzziah king of Judah *b to* **reign**. AIT
2Ki 15:37 those days the LORD **b** to send Rezin king H2725
2Ki 16: 1 Ahaz son of Jotham king of Judah *b to* **reign**. AIT
2Ki 18: 1 son of Ahaz king of Judah *b to* **reign**. AIT
1Ch 27:24 Joab son of Zeruiah **b** to count the men H2725
2Ch 3: 1 Then Solomon **b** to build the temple of H2725
2Ch 3: 2 *He* **b** building on the second day of the H2725
2Ch 20:22 As *they* **b** to sing and praise, the LORD set H2725
2Ch 22: 1 son of Jehoram king of Judah *b to* **reign**. AIT
2Ch 29:17 *They* **b** the consecration on the first day of H2725
2Ch 29:27 As the offering **b**, singing to the LORD H2725
2Ch 29:27 singing to the LORD **b** also, accompanied H2725
2Ch 31: 7 *They* **b** doing this in the third month and H2725
2Ch 31:10 "Since the people **b** to bring their H2725
2Ch 34: 3 *he* **b** to seek the God of his father David. H2725
2Ch 34: 3 his twelfth year *he* **b** to purge Judah and H2725
Ezr 3: 8 his associates **b** to build the altar of H7756
Ezr 3: 6 of the seventh month *they* **b** to offer burnt H2725
Ezr 3: 8 the captivity to Jerusalem) **b** the work. H2725
Ne 2:18 So they **b** this good work. H2616+3338
Job 2:12 recognize him; *they b to* **weep** aloud, and AIT
Ecc 2:20 So my heart **b** to despair over all my H6015
SS 5: 4 latch-opening; my heart *b to* **pound** for him. AIT
Jer 36: 2 from the time *I b* **speaking** to you in the reign AIT
Eze 9: 6 So *they* **b** with the old men who were in H2725
Eze 9: 7 they went out and *b* **killing** throughout the AIT
Eze 23: 8 not give up the prostitution she **b** in Egypt, NDT
Eze 23:27 lewdness and prostitution you **b** in Egypt. NDT
Da 9:23 As soon as you **b** to pray, a word went out H9378
Da 10:16 and I opened my mouth and *b to* **speak**. AIT
Hos 1: 2 *When* the LORD **b** to speak through Hosea H9378
Jnh 3: 4 Jonah **b** by going a day's journey into the H2725
Mic 1:13 You are where the sin of Daughter Zion **b** H8040
Hag 1:14 They came and **b** *to* work on the house of H6913
Mt 4:17 From that time on Jesus **b** to preach *G806*
Mt 5: 2 and *he b* to teach them. *G487+3836+5125S*
Mt 8:15 and she got up and *b to* **wait on** him. AIT
Mt 11: 7 Jesus **b** to speak to the crowd about John: *G806*
Mt 11:20 Then Jesus **b** to denounce the towns in *G806*
Mt 12: 1 were hungry and **b** to pick some heads of *G806*
Mt 13:54 *he b* **teaching** the people in their synagogue AIT
Mt 16:21 From that time on Jesus **b** to explain to his *G806*
Mt 16:22 Peter took him aside and **b** to rebuke him *G806*
Mt 18:24 *As* he **b** the settlement, a man who owed *G806*
Mt 18:28 He grabbed him and *b to* **choke** him. AIT
Mt 20:11 *they b to* **grumble** against the landowner. AIT
Mt 26:22 They were very sad and **b** to say to him one *G806*
Mt 26:37 and *he* **b** to be sorrowful and troubled. *G806*
Mt 26:74 Then *he* **b** to call down curses, and he *G806*
Mk 1:21 went into the synagogue and *b to* **teach**. AIT
Mk 1:31 The fever left her and *she b to* **wait on** them. AIT
Mk 1:45 Instead he went out and **b** to talk freely *G806*
Mk 2:13 crowd came to him, and *he b to* **teach** them. AIT
Mk 2:23 *they* **b** to pick some heads of grain. *G806*
Mk 3: 6 went out and *b to* **plot** with the Herodians AIT
Mk 3:23 over to him and *b to* **speak** to them in AIT
Mk 4: 1 Again Jesus **b** to teach by the lake. *G806*
Mk 5:17 Then *the people* **b** to plead with Jesus to *G806*
Mk 5:20 So the man went away and **b** to tell in the *G806*
Mk 5:42 the girl stood up and *b to* **walk around** AIT
Mk 6: 2 came, *he* **b** to teach in the synagogue *G806*
Mk 6: 7 *he* **b** to send them out two by two and gave *G806*
Mk 6:34 So *he* **b** teaching them many things *G806*
Mk 7:35 was loosened and *he b to* **speak** plainly. AIT
Mk 8:11 Pharisees came and **b** to question Jesus. *G806*
Mk 8:31 *He* then **b** to teach them that the Son of *G806*
Mk 8:32 Peter took him aside and **b** to rebuke him. *G806*
Mk 10:47 Jesus of Nazareth, *he* **b** to shout, "Jesus, *G806*
Mk 11:15 temple courts and **b** driving out those who *G806*
Mk 11:18 heard this and *b* **looking for** a way to kill him AIT
Mk 12: 1 Jesus then **b** to speak to them in parables *G806*
Mk 14:33 and *he* **b** to be deeply distressed and *G806*
Mk 14:65 Then some **b** to spit at him; they *G806*
Mk 14:71 He **b** to call down curses, and he swore to *G806*
Mk 15:18 And *they* **b** to call out to him, "Hail, king of *G806*
Lk 1:64 and *he b to* **speak**, praising God. AIT
Lk 2:44 Then *they b* **looking for** him among their AIT
Lk 3:23 thirty years old *when he b his* **ministry**. *G806*
Lk 4:21 *He* **b** by saying to them, "Today this *G806*
Lk 4:39 She got up at once and *b to* **wait on** them. AIT
Lk 5: 6 number of fish that their nets *b to* **break**. AIT
Lk 5: 7 filled both boats so full that they *b to* **sink**. AIT
Lk 5:21 teachers of the law **b** thinking to *G806*
Lk 6: 1 his disciples *b to* **pick** some heads of AIT
Lk 6:11 were furious and *b to* **discuss** with one AIT
Lk 7:15 The dead man sat up and **b** to talk, and *G806*
Lk 7:24 Jesus **b** to speak to the crowd about John: *G806*
Lk 7:38 *she* **b** to wet his feet with her tears. *G806*
Lk 7:49 The other guests **b** to say among *G806*
Lk 11:53 teachers of the law **b** to oppose him *G806*
Lk 12: 1 Jesus **b** to speak first to his disciples *G806*
Lk 14:18 "But *they* all alike **b** to make excuses. *G806*
Lk 14:30 'This person **b** to build and wasn't able to *G806*
Lk 15:14 that whole country, and he **b** to be in need. *G806*
Lk 15:24 lost and is found.' So *they* **b** to celebrate. *G806*
Lk 19: 7 All the people saw this and *b to* **mutter**, "He AIT
Lk 19:37 crowd of disciples **b** joyfully to praise God *G806*
Lk 19:45 *he* **b** to drive out those who were selling. *G806*
Lk 22:23 They **b** to question among themselves *G806*
Lk 22:63 guarding Jesus **b mocking** and beating him. AIT
Lk 23: 2 And *they* **b** to accuse him, saying, "We *G806*
Lk 24:30 gave thanks, broke it and *b to* **give** it to them. AIT
Jn 5:16 the Jewish leaders *b to* **persecute** him. AIT
Jn 6:14 Jesus performed, *they b to* **say**, "Surely this is AIT
Jn 6:41 the Jews there *b to* **grumble** about him AIT
Jn 6:52 Then the Jews *b to* **argue sharply** among AIT
Jn 7:25 some of the people of Jerusalem *b to* **ask**, AIT
Jn 8: 9 those who heard *b to* **go away** one at a time AIT
Jn 13: 5 into a basin and **b** to wash his disciples' *G806*
Jn 17: 5 glory I had with you before the world **b**. *G1639*
Jn 18:27 and at that moment a rooster *b to* **crow**. AIT
Ac 1: 1 about all that Jesus **b** to do and to teach *G806*
Ac 2: 4 with the Holy Spirit and **b** to speak in other *G806*
Ac 3: 8 He jumped to his feet and *b to* **walk**. Then he AIT
Ac 4: 7 brought before them and *b to* **question** them: AIT
Ac 5:21 had been told, and *b to* **teach** the people. AIT
Ac 6: 9 Asia—*who b to* **argue with** Stephen. AIT
Ac 7:58 him out of the city and *b to* **stone** him. AIT
Ac 8: 3 But Saul *b to* **destroy** the church. Going from AIT
Ac 8:35 Then Philip **b** with that very passage of *G806*
Ac 9:20 At once *he b to* **preach** in the synagogues AIT
Ac 10:34 Then Peter **b** to **speak**: "*G487+3836+5125+3306*
Ac 11:15 "As **I b** to speak, the Holy Spirit came on *G806*
Ac 11:20 to Antioch and *b to* **speak** to Greeks also, AIT
Ac 13:45 *They b to* **contradict** what Paul was saying AIT
Ac 14:10 the man jumped up and *b to* **walk**. AIT
Ac 16:13 We sat down and *b to* **speak** to the women AIT
Ac 17:18 Stoic philosophers *b to* **debate with** him. AIT
Ac 18:26 He **b** to speak boldly in the synagogue *G806*
Ac 19:28 heard this, they were furious and *b* **shouting**: AIT
Ac 26: 1 motioned with his hand and *b his* **defense**: AIT
Ac 26:31 left the room, *they b* **saying** to one another AIT
Ac 27:13 *When* a **gentle** south wind *b to* **blow**, they AIT
Ac 27:18 the storm *that* the next day *they b to* throw *G4472*
Ac 27:35 Then he broke it and **b** to eat. *G806*
Ac 28:25 themselves and *b to* **leave** after Paul had AIT
1Co 2: 7 that God destined for our glory **before** time *b*. AIT
Gal 2:12 *he b to* **draw back** and separate himself from AIT
Php 1: 6 that he *who* **b** a good work in you will *G1887*

BEGAT, BEGET, BEGETTEST, BEGETTETH (KJV)

BORN, FATHER, HAD, HAVE

BEGGAR (2) [BEG]

Lk 16:20 At his gate was laid a **b** named Lazarus *G4777*
Lk 16:22 time came when the **b** died and the *G4777*

BEGGARS (1) [BEG]

Ps 109:10 May his children be wandering **b**; may H8626

BEGGED (23) [BEG]

2Ki 1:13 *he* **b**, "please have respect for my life H2858
Est 8: 3 *She* **b** him to put an end to the evil plan H2858
Hos 12: 4 he wept and **b for** his **favor**. H2858
Mt 8:31 The demons **b** Jesus, "If you drive us out *G4151*
Mt 14:36 **b** him to let the sick just touch the *G4151*
Mt 18:26 patient with me,' *he* **b**, 'and I will pay *G3306*
Mt 18:29 fellow servant fell to his knees and **b** him, *G4151*
Mt 18:32 that debt of yours because *you* **b** me to. *G4151*
Mk 1:40 came to him and **b** him on his knees, *G4151*
Mk 5:10 And *he* **b** Jesus again and again not to *G4151*
Mk 5:12 The demons **b** Jesus, "Send us among the *G4151*
Mk 5:18 been demon-possessed **b** to go with him. *G4151*
Mk 6:56 *They* **b** him to let them touch even the *G4151*
Mk 7:26 *She* **b** Jesus to drive the demon out of her *G2263*

Mk 7:32 and *they* **b** Jesus to place his hand on *G4151*
Mk 8:22 a blind man and **b** Jesus to touch him. *G4151*
Lk 5:12 fell with his face to the ground and **b** him, *G1289*
Lk 8:31 And *they* **b** Jesus *repeatedly* not to order *G4151*
Lk 8:32 The demons **b** Jesus to let them go into *G4151*
Lk 8:38 demons had gone out **b** to go with him, *G1289*
Lk 9:40 *I* **b** your disciples to drive it out, but they *G1289*
Jn 4:47 he went to him and **b** him to come and *G2263*
Heb 12:19 those who heard it **b** that no further word *G4148*

BEGGING (8) [BEG]

Job 41: 3 Will it keep **b** you **for mercy**? Will it speak H9384
Ps 37:25 forsaken or their children **b** bread. H1335
Mk 10:46 Timaeus"), was sitting by the roadside **b**. *G4644*
Lk 18:35 a blind man was sitting by the roadside **b**. *G2050*
Jn 9: 8 had formerly seen him **b** asked, *G4645+1639*
Ac 3:10 used to sit **b** at the temple *G4639+3836+1797*
Ac 16: 9 a man of Macedonia standing and **b** him, *G4151*
Ac 19:31 sent him a message **b** him not to venture *G4151*

BEGIN (20) [BEGAN, BEGINNING, BEGINNINGS, BEGINS, BEGUN]

Dt 2:24 **B** to take possession of it and engage him H2725
Dt 2:25 This very day *I will* **b** to put the terror and H2725
Dt 2:31 Now **b** to conquer and possess his land." H2725
Dt 16: 9 from the time you **b** to put the sickle to H2725
Dt 20: 5 battle and someone else *may b to* **live in** it. AIT
Dt 28:30 but *you will* not *even b to* **enjoy** its fruit. AIT
Jos 3: 7 "Today *I will* **b** to exalt you in the eyes of H2725
Jos 18: 3 you wait before you **b** to take possession of H995
1Sa 9:13 The people *will* not **b eating** until he comes AIT
1Ch 22:16 beyond number. Now **b** the work, and the H7756
1Ch 22:19 **B** to build the sanctuary of the LORD God H7756
Ps 81: 2 **B** the music, strike the timbrel, play the H5951
La 2:19 as the watches of the night **b**; pour out H8031
Eze 9: 6 who has the mark. **B** at my sanctuary." H2725
Hos 8:10 *They will* **b** *to* waste away under the H2725
Lk 3: 8 And *do* not **b** to say to yourselves, 'We *G806*
Lk 21:28 *When* these things **b** to take place, stand *G806*
Lk 23:54 and the Sabbath *was* **about to b**. *G2216*
Jn 7:14 go up to the temple courts and *b to* **teach**. AIT
1Pe 4:17 time for judgment *to* **b** with God's *G806*

BEGINNING (93) [BEGIN]

Ge 1: 1 In the **b** God created the heavens and the H8040
Ge 44:12 **b** with the oldest and ending with the H2725
Lev 23:39 " 'So **b with** the fifteenth day of the seventh H928
Dt 11:12 on it from the **b** *of* the year to its end. H8040
Dt 31:24 book the words of this law **from b to** end, H6330
Dt 31:30 words of this song **from b to** end in the H6330
Jdg 7:19 of the camp at the **b** *of* the middle watch, H8031
Ru 1:22 in Bethlehem as the barley harvest was **b**. H9378
1Sa 3:12 I spoke against his family—from **b** to end. H2725
2Sa 7:10 them anymore, as they did at the **b** H8037
2Sa 21: 9 harvest, just as the barley harvest was **b**. H9378
2Sa 21:10 From the **b** *of* the harvest till the rain H9378
1Ki 14:14 Even now this is **b** to happen. H2021+3427
1Ch 17: 9 them anymore, as they did at the **b** H8037
1Ch 29:29 David's reign, from **b** to end, they are H8037
2Ch 9:29 from **b** to end, are they not H8037
2Ch 12:15 from **b** to end, are they not H8037
2Ch 16:11 of Asa's reign, from **b** to end, are written H8037
2Ch 20:34 from **b** to end, are written in H8037
2Ch 25:26 from **b** to end, are they not H8037
2Ch 26:22 from **b** to end, are recorded H8037
2Ch 28:26 all his ways, from **b** to end, are written in H8037
2Ch 35:27 all the events, from **b** to end, are written in H8037
Ezr 4: 6 At the **b** *of* the reign of Xerxes, they H9378
Ps 102:25 In the **b** you laid the foundations of the H7156
Ps 111:10 The fear of the LORD is the **b** *of* wisdom H8040
Pr 1: 7 The fear of the LORD is the **b** *of* knowledge, H8040
Pr 4: 7 The **b** *of* wisdom is this: Get wisdom H8040
Pr 8:23 ages ago, at the **very b**, when the world H8031
Pr 9:10 The fear of the LORD is the **b** *of* wisdom H9378
Ecc 3:11 fathom what God has done from **b** to end. H8031
Ecc 7: 8 The end of a matter is better than its **b** H8040
Ecc 10:13 At the **b** their words are folly; at the end H9378
Isa 1:26 as in days of old, your rulers as at the **b**. H9378
Isa 40:21 Has it not been told you from the **b**? Have H8031
Isa 41: 4 calling forth the generations from the **b**? H8031
Isa 41:26 Who told of this from the **b**, so we could H8031
Isa 46:10 I make known the end from the **b**, from H8040
Jer 17:12 exalted from the **b**, is the place of our H8037
Jer 25:29 I am **b** to bring disaster on the city that H2725
Eze 25: 9 the flank of Moab, **b** at its frontier towns NDT
Eze 40: 1 of our exile, at the **b** *of* the year, on the H8031
Eze 42:12 a doorway at the **b** *of* the passageway H8031
Eze 48:30 **B** on the north side, which is 4,500 cubits NDT
Da 12: 1 happened from the **b** *of* nations until then H2118
Mt 14:30 he was afraid and, **b** to sink, cried out *G806*
Mt 19: 4 "that at the **b** the Creator 'made them male *G794*
Mt 19: 8 But it was not this way from the **b**. *G794*
Mt 20: 8 **b** with the last ones hired and going on to *G806*
Mt 24: 8 All these are the **b** of birth pains. *G794*
Mt 24:21 unequaled from the **b** of the world until *G794*
Mk 1: 1 The **b** of the good news about Jesus the *G794*
Mk 10: 6 "But at the **b** of creation God 'made them *G794*
Mk 13: 8 These are the **b** of birth pains. *G794*
Mk 13:19 be days of distress unequaled from the **b**, *G794*
Lk 1: 3 investigated everything **from the b**, *G540*
Lk 11:50 has been shed since the **b** of the world, *G2856*
Lk 24:27 And **b** with Moses and all the Prophets, he *G806*
Lk 24:47 in his name to all nations, **b** at Jerusalem. *G806*
Jn 1: 1 In the **b** was the Word, and the Word was *G794*
Jn 1: 2 He was with God in the **b**. *G794*
Jn 6:64 had known from the **b** which of them did *G794*
Jn 8:25 what I have been telling you *from* the **b**," *G794*
Jn 8:44 He was a murderer from the **b**, not holding *G794*
Jn 15:27 you have been with me from the **b**. *G794*
Jn 16: 4 you this from the **b** because I was with you *G794*
Ac 1:22 **b** from John's baptism to the time when *G806*
Ac 3:24 "Indeed, **b with** Samuel *G608+2779+3836+2759*
Ac 10:37 **b** in Galilee after the baptism that John *G806*
Ac 11: 4 **Starting from the b**, Peter told them the *G806*
Ac 11:15 on them as he had come on us at the **b**. *G794*
Ac 26: 4 from the **b** of my life in my own country *G794*
2Co 3: 1 *Are we* **b** to commend ourselves again? Or *G806*
2Co 8: 6 just as *he had* **earlier made a b**, to bring *G4599*
Gal 3: 3 *After* **b** by means of the Spirit, are you *G1887*
Col 1:18 he is the **b** and the firstborn from among *G794*
2Ti 1: 9 in Christ Jesus before the **b of time**, *G5989+173*
Titus 1: 2 promised before the **b of time**, *G5989+173*
Heb 1:10 He also says, "In the **b**, Lord, you laid the *G794*
Heb 7: 3 genealogy, without **b** of days or end of life *G794*
2Pe 2:20 off at the end *than* they were *at* the **b**. *G4755*
2Pe 3: 4 goes on as it has since the **b** of creation." *G794*
1Jn 1: 1 That which was from the **b**, which we have *G794*
1Jn 2: 7 old one, which you have had since the **b**. *G794*
1Jn 2:13 because you know him who is from the **b**. *G794*
1Jn 2:14 because you know him who is from the **b**. *G794*
1Jn 2:24 you have heard from the **b** remains in you. *G794*
1Jn 3: 8 the devil has been sinning from the **b**. *G794*
1Jn 3:11 this is the message you heard from the **b**: *G794*
2Jn 5 command but one we have had from the **b**. *G794*
2Jn 6 As you have heard from the **b**, his *G794*
Rev 21: 6 Alpha and the Omega, the **B** and the End. *G794*
Rev 22:13 the First and the Last, the **B** and the End. *G794*

BEGINNINGS (1) [BEGIN]

Job 8: 7 Your **b** will seem humble, so prosperous H8040

BEGINS (7) [BEGIN]

Lev 23: 5 The LORD's Passover **b** at twilight on the NDT
Lev 23: 6 the LORD's Festival of Unleavened Bread **b**; NDT
Lev 23:34 month the LORD's Festival of Tabernacles **b**, NDT
Eze 45:25 which **b** in the seventh month on the NDT
Mt 24:49 and *he* then **b** to beat his fellow servants *G806*
Lk 12:45 and *he* then **b** to beat the other servants *G806*
1Pe 4:17 household; and if it **b** with us, what will *G4754*

(ONLY) BEGOTTEN (KJV) ONE AND ONLY

BEGOTTEN (1)

Isa 45:10 who says to a father, 'What *have you* **b**? H3528

BEGRUDGE (1) [BEGRUDING]

Dt 28:56 *will* **b** the husband she loves and H8317+6524

BEGRUDGING (1) [BEGRUDGE]

Pr 23: 6 Do not eat the food of a **b host**, do H8273+6524

BEGUILE, BEGUILED, BEGUILING (KJV) DECEIVE, DECEIVED, DISQUALIFY, SEDUCE

BEGUN (12) [BEGIN]

Ge 11: 6 same language they *have* **b** to do this, H2725
Dt 2:31 *I have* **b** to deliver Sihon and his country H2725
Dt 3:24 you *have* **b** to show to your servant your H2725
Dt 20: 5 built a new house and not *yet b to* **live in** it? AIT
Dt 20: 6 planted a vineyard and not *b to* **enjoy** it? AIT
Jdg 20:39 The Benjamites *had* **b** to inflict casualties H2725
Ezr 7: 9 He *had* **b** his journey from Babylon on the H3569
Est 9:23 to continue the celebration *they had* **b**, H2725
Mic 6:13 Therefore, I *have* **b** to destroy you, to ruin H2725
1Co 4: 8 become rich! *You have b to* **reign**—and that AIT
1Co 4: 8 wish that *you* really *had b to* **reign** so that we AIT
Rev 11:17 taken your great power and *have b to* **reign**. AIT

BEHALF (45)

Ge 23: 8 with Ephron son of Zohar **on my b** H4200
Ge 25:21 prayed to the LORD **on b of** his wife, H4200+5790
Lev 1: 4 will be accepted **on** your **b** to make H4200
Lev 14:31 before the LORD **on b of** the one to be H6584
Lev 19: 5 such a way that it will be **accepted** *on* your **b**. AIT
Lev 22:19 in order that it may be **accepted** *on* your *b*. AIT
Lev 22:20 because it will not be accepted **on** your **b**. H4200
Lev 22:25 They will not be accepted **on** your **b** H4200
Lev 22:29 such a way that it will be **accepted** *on* your *b*. AIT
Lev 23:11 the LORD so it will be **accepted** *on* your *b*; AIT
Lev 24: 8 after Sabbath, **on b of** the Israelites H4946+907
Nu 3:38 the sanctuary **on b of** the Israelites. H4200+5466
Nu 5:15 tenth of an ephah of barley flour **on** her **b**. H6584
Nu 8:19 the **work** at the tent of meeting *on b of* the AIT
1Sa 7: 9 He cried out to the LORD **on** Israel's **b**, and H1237
1Sa 14: 6 Perhaps the LORD will act **in** our **b**. H4200
2Sa 3:12 sent messengers **on** his **b** to say to David, H9393
2Sa 14: 8 and I will issue an order **in** your **b**. H6584
2Sa 21:14 God answered prayer **in b of** the land. H4200
2Sa 24:25 LORD answered his prayer **in b of** the land, H4200
2Ki 4:13 Can we speak **on** your **b** to the king or the H4200
Est 8: 8 the king's name **in b of** the Jews as H6584
Job 6:22 'Give something **on** my **b**, pay a ransom H4200
Job 8: 6 rouse himself **on** your **b** and restore you H6584
Job 13: 7 Will you speak wickedly **on** God's **b**? Will H4200
Job 16:21 **on b of** a man he pleads with God as one H4200
Job 36: 2 that there is more to be said **in** God's **b**. H4200
Ps 86:16 show your strength **in b of** your servant H4200
Isa 8:19 Why consult the dead **on b of** the living? H1237
Isa 58:10 spend yourselves **in b of** the hungry and H4200
Isa 64: 4 who acts **on b of** those who wait for him. H4200
Isa 65: 8 so will I do **in b of** my servants; H4200+5100
Jer 18:20 and spoke **in** their **b** to turn your H6584+3208
Eze 22:30 me in the gap **on b of** the land so I would H1237
Jn 8:14 "Even if I testify **on** my own **b**, my *G4309*
Jn 16:26 saying that I will ask the Father **on** your **b**. *G4309*
Ro 15: 8 a servant of the Jews **on b of** God's truth, *G5642*
2Co 1:11 will give thanks **on** our **b** for the gracious *G5642*
2Co 5:20 We implore you **on** Christ's **b**: Be *G5642*
Php 1:29 granted to you **on b of** Christ not only to *G5642*
Col 1: 7 is a faithful minister of Christ **on** our **b**, *G5642*
Heb 6:20 forerunner, Jesus, has entered **on** our **b**. *G5642*
Rev 13:12 all the authority of the first beast **on** its **b**, *G1967*
Rev 13:14 power to perform **on b of** the first beast, *G1967*
Rev 19:20 who had performed the signs **on** its **b**. *G1967*

BEHAVE (4) [BEHAVED, BEHAVES, BEHAVIOR]

Ex 18:20 they are to live and how *they are to* **b**. H6913
1Ki 1: 6 him by asking, "Why *do you* **b** as you do?" H6913
Hos 3: 3 and I will *b the same way* **toward** you." AIT
Ro 13:13 *Let us* **b** decently, as in the daytime, not in *G4344*

BEHAVED (5) [BEHAVE]

2Sa 15: 6 Absalom **b** in this way toward all the H6913
1Ki 21:26 *He* **b in the vilest manner** by going H9493+4394
Ps 74: 5 *They* **b** like men wielding axes to cut H3359
Jer 2:23 See **how** you **b** in the valley; consider H2006
Jer 16:12 But you *have* **b** more wickedly than your H6913

BEHAVES (1) [BEHAVE]

Pr 21:24 is his name—**b** with insolent fury. H6913

BEHAVIOR (6) [BEHAVE]

Est 3: 4 whether Mordecai's **b** would be tolerated, H1821
Pr 1: 3 receiving instruction in **prudent b** H8505
Pr 8:13 arrogance, evil **b** and perverse speech. H2006
Col 1:21 in your minds because of your evil **b**. *G2240*
1Pe 3: 1 over without words by the **b** of their wives, *G419*
1Pe 3:16 against your good **b** in Christ may be *G419*

BEHEADED (5)

Mt 14:10 had John **b** in the prison. *G642*
Mk 6:16 whom I **b**, has been raised from the *G642*
Mk 6:27 The man went, **b** John in the prison, *G642*
Lk 9: 9 But Herod said, "I **b** John. Who, then, is this *G642*
Rev 20: 4 souls *of* those *who had been* **b** because *G4284*

BEHELD (1) [BEHOLD]

Ps 63: 2 the sanctuary and **b** your power and your H8011

BEHEMOTH (1)

Job 40:15 "Look at **B**, which I made along with you H990

BEHIND (97)

Ge 18:10 the entrance to the tent, which was **b** him. H339
Ge 19: 6 to meet them and shut the door **b** him H339
Ge 32:18 to my lord Esau, and he is coming **b** us. H339
Ge 32:20 'Your servant Jacob is coming **b** us. H339
Ex 10:24 only **leave** your flocks and herds **b**. H3657
Ex 10:26 must go with us; not a hoof *is to be* **left b**. H8636
Ex 14:19 withdrew and went **b** them. H4946+339
Ex 14:19 from in front and stood **b** them, H4946+339
Ex 26:33 of the covenant law **b** the curtain. H4946+1074
Lev 16: 2 Most Holy Place **b** the curtain in H4946+1074
Lev 16:12 and take them **b** the curtain. H4946+1074
Lev 16:15 take its blood **b** the curtain and do H4946+1074
Nu 3:23 to camp on the west, **b** the tabernacle. H339
Dt 25:18 attacked all who were lagging **b**; H339
Jos 8: 2 Set an ambush **b** the city." H4946+339
Jos 8: 4 You are to set an ambush **b** the city H4946+339
Jos 8:14 had been set against him **b** the city. H4946+339
Jdg 3:23 of the upper room **b** him and locked them H1237
Jdg 5:28 Sisera's mother; **b** the lattice she cried out H1237
Ru 2: 2 the leftover grain **b** anyone in whose eyes H339
Ru 2: 3 field and began to glean **b** the harvesters. H339
Ru 2: 7 among the sheaves **b** the harvesters. H339
1Sa 11: 5 from the fields, **b** his oxen, and he asked, H339
1Sa 14:13 feet, with his armor-bearer **right b** him. H339
1Sa 14:13 armor-bearer followed and killed **b** him. H339
1Sa 21: 9 it is wrapped in a cloth **b** the ephod. H339
1Sa 24: 8 When Saul looked **b** him, David bowed H339
1Sa 30: 9 to the Besor Valley, where some **stayed b**. H6641
1Sa 30:21 him and who *were* **left b** at the Besor H3782
2Sa 2:20 Abner looked **b** him and asked, "Is that you H339
2Sa 2:25 Then the men of Benjamin rallied **b** Abner H339
2Sa 3:16 weeping **b** her all the way to Bahurim. H339
2Sa 3:31 King David himself walked **b** the bier. H339
2Sa 5:23 circle around **b** them and attack them H339
2Sa 10: 9 lines in front of him and **b** him; H4946+294
2Sa 18:22 what may, please let me run **b** the Cushite." H339
1Ki 20:19 out of the city with the army **b** them H339
2Ki 4: 4 shut the door **b** you and your sons. H1237
2Ki 4: 5 him and shut the door **b** her and her sons. H1237
2Ki 6:32 the sound of his master's footsteps **b** him?" H339
2Ki 9:18 "Fall in **b** me." The lookout H339
2Ki 9:19 you have to do with peace? Fall in **b** me." H339
2Ki 9:25 together in chariots **b** Ahab his father when H339
2Ki 11: 6 a third at the gate **b** the guard, who H339
2Ki 25:12 But the commander **left b** some of the H8636

2Ki 25:22 over the people *he had* **left b** in Judah. H8636
1Ch 19:10 were battle lines in front of him and **b** him; H294
2Ch 13:13 of Judah the ambush was **b** them. H4946+339
Ne 4:13 of the people **b** the lowest points H4946+339
Ne 4:16 posted themselves **b** all the people of H339
Est 7: 7 **stayed b** to beg Queen Esther for his life. H6641
Job 21:21 the families they **leave b** when their H339
Job 38: 8 "Who shut up the sea **b** doors when it burst H928
Job 39:10 Will it till the valleys **b** you? H339
Job 41:32 It leaves a glistening wake **b** it; one would H339
Ps 50:17 my instruction and cast my words **b** you. H339
Ps 139: 5 You hem me in **b** and before, and you lay H294
SS 2: 9 There he stands **b** our wall, gazing through H339
SS 4: 1 Your eyes **b** your veil are doves H4946+1237
SS 4: 3 Your temples **b** your veil are like H4946+1237
SS 6: 7 Your temples **b** your veil are like H4946+1237
Isa 26:20 your rooms and shut the doors **b** you; H1237
Isa 30:21 your ears will hear a voice **b** you H4946+339
Isa 38:17 you have put all my sins **b** your back. H339
Isa 45:14 they will trudge **b** you, coming over to you H339
Isa 57: 8 **B** your doors and your doorposts you have H339
Jer 9:22 like cut grain **b** the reaper, with no H4946+339
Jer 39:10 of the guard **left b** in the land of Judah H8636
Jer 40: 6 the people who *were* **left b** in the land. H8636
Jer 52:16 But Nebuzaradan **left b** the rest of the H8636
Eze 3:12 I heard **b** me a loud rumbling sound H339
Eze 24:21 daughters *you* **left b** will fall by the H6440
Eze 39:28 them to their own land, not leaving any **b**. H9004
Eze 42:14 until they leave **b** the garments in which H9004
Joel 2: 3 them fire devours, **b** them a flame blazes. H339
Joel 2: 3 the garden of Eden, **b** them, a desert waste H339
Joel 2:14 turn and relent and leave **b** a blessing— H339
Zec 1: 8 trees in a ravine. **B** him were red, brown H339
Zec 7:14 The land they **left b** them was so desolate H339
Mt 9:20 years came up **b** him and touched the *G3957*
Mt 16:23 said to Peter, "Get **b** me, Satan! *G3958*
Mk 4:36 **Leaving** the crowd **b**, they took him along *G918*
Mk 5:27 she came up **b** him in the crowd and *G3957*
Mk 8:33 rebuked Peter. "Get **b** me, Satan!" he said *G3958*
Mk 14:52 he fled naked, **leaving** his garment **b**. *G2901*
Lk 2:43 the boy Jesus **stayed b** in Jerusalem, but *G5702*
Lk 7:38 As she stood **b** him at his feet weeping *G3958*
Lk 8:44 She came up **b** him and touched the edge *G3957*
Lk 23:26 on him and made him carry it **b** Jesus. *G3957*
Jn 20: 6 Peter came along **b** him and went straight *G199*
1Co 13:11 *I* **put** the ways of childhood **b** me. *G2934*
Php 3:13 Forgetting what is **b** and straining toward *G3958*
1Ti 5:24 of them; the sins of others **trail b** them. *G2051*
Heb 6:19 It enters the inner sanctuary *b* the **curtain**, AIT
Heb 9: 3 **B** the second curtain was a room called *G3552*
Rev 1:10 I heard **b** me a loud voice like a *G3958*
Rev 6: 8 Hades was following **close b** him. *G3552*

BEHOLD (1) [BEHELD]

Nu 24:17 but not now; *I* **b** him, but not near. H8800

BEHOVED (KJV) HAD TO

BEING (213) [BE, BEINGS]

Ge 2: 7 and the man became a living **b**. H5883
Ge 9: 5 And from each **human b**, too, I will H132
Ge 9: 5 accounting for the life of another **human b**. H132
Ge 38:25 *As* she **was b brought out**, she sent a AIT
Ge 40: 5 of Egypt, who **were b held** in prison—had a AIT
Ge 40:15 done nothing *to deserve b* **put** in a dungeon." AIT
Ge 42:21 "Surely we are **b** punished because of our NDT
Ge 50:20 good to accomplish what is now **b** done, NDT
Ex 5:16 Your servants *are* **b beaten**, but the fault H5782
Ex 6: 6 I will free you from **b** slaves to them, and I NDT
Ex 23: 1 a guilty person by **b** a malicious witness. H2118
Lev 24:17 takes the life of a **human b** is to be put to H132
Lev 24:21 whoever kills a **human b** is to be put to H132
Lev 25:16 because *what is really b* **sold** to you is the AIT
Lev 27: 8 **the person b dedicated** is to be presented H2257
Lev 27:28 whether a **human b** or an animal or family H132
Nu 6:11 they sinned by **b** in the presence of the NDT
Nu 15:24 **without** the community **b aware** *of* H4946+6524
Nu 19:19 Those who are **b** cleansed must wash their NDT
Nu 23:19 not a **human b**, that he should H1201+132
Nu 24:11 the LORD has kept you from **b** rewarded." NDT
Nu 35:27 kill the accused without **b** guilty of murder. NDT
Dt 3:16 the middle of the gorge **b** the border) and NDT
Dt 22:21 thing in Israel by *b* **promiscuous** while still in AIT
Jos 10:14 a day when the LORD listened to a **human b**. H408
1Sa 2:13 fork in his hand while the meat *was b* **boiled** AIT
1Sa 10: 5 pipes and harps **b** played before them, and NDT
1Sa 15:29 he is not a **human b**, that he should H132
1Sa 20: 6 an annual sacrifice is **b** made there for his NDT
2Sa 13:13 he will not keep me from **b** married to you." NDT
2Sa 17:17 could not risk **b seen** entering the city. H8011
2Sa 19:11 since what is **b** said throughout Israel has NDT
2Sa 20:10 Without **b** stabbed again NDT
1Ki 6: 7 heard at the temple site while it **was** *b* **built**. AIT
1Ki 8:38 *b* **aware** *of* the afflictions of their own hearts AIT
1Ch 9:18 **b** stationed at the King's Gate on the east NDT
1Ch 21:12 three months of **b swept away** before your H6200
1Ch 24: 6 one family **b taken** from Eleazar and then H296
1Ch 28: 7 laws, as is **b** done at this time. NDT
2Ch 6:29 Israel—*b* **aware** *of* their afflictions and pains AIT
2Ch 13:14 saw that they were **b** attacked at both front NDT
2Ch 15: 6 One nation **was b crushed** by another and AIT
Ezr 3:12 saw **the foundation** *of* this temple *b* **laid**, AIT
Ezr 5: 8 The work *is* **b carried on** with diligence A10522
Ne 4: 7 ahead and that the gaps *were* **b closed**, H6258
Ne 8: 8 the people understood what was **b** read. NDT
Ne 13:27 *are b* **unfaithful** to our God by AIT
Est 4:11 court without **b summoned** the king has H7924
Job 4: 7 "Consider now: Who, **b** innocent, has ever NDT
Job 10:19 If only *I had* never **come into b**, or H2118+2118
Job 21: 4 "Is my complaint directed to a **human b** H132
Job 25: 6 a maggot—a **human b**, who is only H1201+132
Ps 11: 3 When the foundations *are* **b destroyed** H2238
Ps 35:10 My whole **b** will exclaim, "Who is like you, H6795
Ps 63: 1 thirst for you, my **whole b** longs for you, in H1414
Ps 103: 1 my soul; all my **inmost b**, praise his holy H7931
Ps 119:86 for I am *b* **persecuted** without cause. AIT
Ps 119:126 for you to act, LORD; your law *is b* **broken**. AIT
Ps 130: 5 the LORD, my **whole b** waits, and in his H5883
Ps 139:13 For you created my **inmost b**; you knit me H4000
Pr 3:26 side and will keep your foot from **b** snared. NDT
Pr 6:27 into his lap without his clothes **b burned**? H8596
Pr 6:28 on hot coals without his feet **b scorched**? H3917
Pr 20:27 light on one's **inmost b**. H3972+2540+1061
Pr 20:30 and beatings purge the **inmost b**. H2540+1061
Pr 23:16 my **inmost b** will rejoice when your lips H4000
Pr 24:11 Rescue *those* **b led away** to death; hold H4374
Ecc 2:15 What then do I gain *by b* **wise**?" I said to AIT
Isa 1: 7 your fields *are b* **stripped** *by* foreigners right AIT
Isa 1:14 appointed festivals I hate *with* **all** my **b**. H5883
Isa 16:11 like a harp, my **inmost b** for Kir Hareseth. H7931
Isa 38:14 to the heavens. I am **b** threatened; Lord NDT
Isa 42: 9 before *they* **spring into b** I announce them H7541
Isa 50: 4 my ear to listen like one **b** instructed. NDT
Isa 52:14 beyond that of *any* **human b** and his form H408
Isa 66: 2 all these things, and so they **came into b**?" H2118
Jer 6:22 a great nation *is b* **stirred up** from the ends of AIT
Jer 17:16 I have not run away from *b* your **shepherd** AIT
Jer 31:36 Israel ever cease **b** a nation before me." H2118
Jer 40: 1 Judah who *were* **b carried into exile** to H1655
Jer 50:41 many kings *are* **b stirred up** from the ends H6424
Eze 1:10 Each of the four had the face of a **human b**, H132
Eze 3: 5 You *are* not **b sent** to a people of obscure H8938
Eze 10:13 I heard the wheels **b called** "the whirling H7924
Eze 10:14 the second the face of a **human b**, the third H132
Eze 14:13 against me by *b* **unfaithful** and I stretch out AIT
Eze 20: 9 my name from **b profaned** in the eyes of H2725
Eze 20:14 keep it from **b profaned** in the eyes of H2725
Eze 20:22 keep it from **b profaned** in the eyes of H2725
Eze 20:27 blasphemed me by *b* **unfaithful** to me: AIT
Eze 41:19 the face of a **human b** toward the palm tree H132
Eze 43:13 that cubit **b** a cubit and a handbreadth: NDT
Da 4:27 your wickedness by *b* **kind** *to* the oppressed. AIT
Da 6: 7 to any god or **human b** during the next A10050
Da 6:12 to any god or **human b** except to you, A10050
Da 6:18 without any entertainment *b* **brought** to him. AIT
Da 7: 4 that it stood on two feet like a **human b**, A10050
Da 7: 8 the eyes of a **human b** and a mouth that A10050
Mal 2:10 our ancestors by *b* **unfaithful** to one another? AIT
Mt 20:13 one of them, '*I am* not *b* **unfair** to you, friend. AIT
Mt 23:33 How will you escape **b** condemned to hell? NDT
Mk 1:10 he saw heaven *b* **torn open** and the Spirit AIT
Mk 1:13 wilderness forty days, *b* **tempted** by Satan. AIT
Lk 3:21 When all the people *were b* **baptized**, Jesus AIT
Lk 7:12 a dead person *was b* **carried out**—the only AIT
Lk 8:23 so that the boat *was b* **swamped**, and they AIT
Lk 14: 1 Pharisee, he was *b* **carefully watched**. AIT
Lk 16:16 **the good news** of the kingdom of God *is b* **preached** AIT
Lk 17:20 *on b* **asked** by the Pharisees when the AIT
Lk 17:27 marrying and *b* **given in marriage** up to the AIT
Lk 21:20 you see Jerusalem *b* **surrounded** by armies, AIT
Lk 22:44 And **b** in anguish, he prayed more *G1181*
Jn 3:23 people were coming and *b* **baptized**. AIT
Ac 2: 6 one heard their own language *b* **spoken**. AIT
Ac 2:47 their number daily those *who were b* **saved**. AIT
Ac 3: 2 lame from birth *was b* **carried** to the temple AIT
Ac 4: 9 If we *are b* **called to account** today for an act AIT
Ac 4: 9 who was lame and are **b** asked how he was NDT
Ac 6: 1 their widows *were b* **overlooked** in the daily AIT
Ac 7:24 saw one of them *b* **mistreated** by an Egyptian AIT
Ac 8:36 What can stand in the way of my *b* **baptized**?" AIT
Ac 10:10 and *while* the meal *was b* **prepared**, he AIT
Ac 10:11 like a large sheet *b* **let down** to earth by its AIT
Ac 10:47 in the way of their *b* **baptized** with water. AIT
Ac 11: 5 like a large sheet *b* **let down** from heaven by AIT
Ac 17:28 in him we live and move and **have** *our* **b**. *G1639*
Ac 17:29 not think that the **divine b** is like gold *G2521*
Ac 19:40 are in danger *of b* **charged with** rioting AIT
Ac 22:30 exactly why Paul *was b* **accused** by the Jews. AIT
Ac 25: 4 answered, "Paul *is b* **held** at Caesarea, and I AIT
Ac 27:20 we finally gave up all hope *of b* **saved**. AIT
Ac 27:27 we were *still b* **driven across** the Adriatic AIT
Ro 1: 8 because your faith *is b* **reported** all over the AIT
Ro 1:18 The wrath of God *is b* **revealed** from heaven AIT
Ro 1:20 *b* **understood** from what has been made AIT
Ro 1:23 look like a mortal **human b** and birds and *G476*
Ro 2: 3 So when you, a *mere* **human b**, pass *G476*
Ro 2: 9 every **human b** who does evil: *G6034+476*
Ro 3: 1 is there in **b** a Jew, or what value is NDT
Ro 3: 4 and every **human b** a liar. As it is *G476*
Ro 4:17 the dead and calls *into* **b** things that were *G1639*
Ro 4:21 *b* **fully persuaded** that God had power to do AIT
Ro 7:22 For in my inner **b** I delight in God's law; *G476*
Ro 9:20 But who are you, a **human b**, to talk back to *G476*
Ro 14:14 *b* **fully persuaded** in the Lord Jesus AIT
1Co 1:18 to us who *are b* **saved** it is the power of AIT
1Co 4: 6 not be puffed up in **b** a follower of one of us NDT
1Co 10:29 For why *is* my freedom *b* **judged** by another's AIT
1Co 11:32 *we are b* **disciplined** so that we will not be AIT
1Co 12:15 *it would* not for that reason stop **b** part of *G1639*
1Co 12:16 *it would* not for that reason stop **b** part of *G1639*
1Co 14: 7 know what **tune** *is b* **played** unless there is AIT
1Co 15:45 "The first man Adam became a living **b**"; *G6034*
2Co 2:15 among those *who are b* **saved** and those AIT
2Co 3:18 *are b* **transformed** into his image with AIT
2Co 4:11 are alive *are* always *b* **given over** to death AIT
2Co 4:16 inwardly we *are b* **renewed** day by day. AIT
2Co 11: 9 have kept myself from **b** a burden to you in NDT
Gal 1:16 not to consult any **human b**. *G4922+2779+135*
Gal 3:22 **b** given through faith in Jesus Christ NDT
Gal 4:24 These things are *b* **taken figuratively**: The AIT
Gal 5:11 circumcision, why *am I* still *b* **persecuted**? AIT
Gal 6:12 this is to avoid *b* **persecuted** for the cross of AIT
Eph 2:22 him you too *are b* **built together** to become a AIT
Eph 3:16 power through his Spirit in your inner **b**, *G476*
Eph 3:17 that you, *b* **rooted** and established in love AIT
Eph 4:22 which *is b* **corrupted** by its deceitful desires; AIT
Php 1: 6 *b* **confident** of this, that he who began a good AIT
Php 1:26 so that through my **b** with you again your *G4242*
Php 1:28 without *b* **frightened** in any way by those who AIT
Php 2: 1 encouragement from **b** united with Christ, NDT
Php 2: 2 then make my joy complete by *b* **like-minded** AIT
Php 2: 2 same love, *b* one in spirit and *of* one **mind**. AIT
Php 2: 6 **b** in very nature God, did not *G5639*
Php 2: 7 of a servant, *b* **made** in human likeness. AIT
Php 2: 8 And *b* **found** in appearance as a man, he AIT
Php 2:17 if *I am b* **poured out like a drink offering** on AIT
Php 4:12 learned the secret of **b** content in any and NDT
Col 1:11 *b* **strengthened** with all power according to AIT
Col 3:10 which *is b* **renewed** in knowledge in the AIT
Col 4: 2 yourselves to prayer, *b* **watchful** and thankful. AIT
1Th 2:17 we were orphaned by **b** separated from you NDT
1Th 4: 8 does not reject a **human b** but God, *G476*
2Th 2: 1 Lord Jesus Christ and our **b** gathered to him, NDT
1Ti 5:13 get into the habit of **b** idle and going about NDT
2Ti 2: 9 even to the point of **b** chained like a NDT
2Ti 3:13 bad to worse, deceiving and *b* **deceived**. AIT
2Ti 4: 6 *am* already *b* **poured out like a drink offering**, AIT
Titus 1: 6 to the charge of **b** wild and disobedient. NDT
Titus 3: 3 envy, **b** hated and hating one another. NDT
Heb 1: 3 the exact representation *of* his **b**, *G5712*
Heb 2:18 he is able to help those *who are b* **tempted**. AIT
Heb 5:13 who lives on milk, *b still* an infant, is not *G1639*
Heb 6: 8 is worthless and is in danger of **b** cursed. NDT
Heb 8: 2 set up by the Lord, not by a *mere* **human b**. *G476*
Heb 9: 9 gifts and sacrifices *b* **offered** were not able to AIT
Heb 10: 2 would they not have stopped *b* **offered**? AIT
Heb 10:14 perfect forever those *who are b* **made holy**. AIT
Jas 1:27 keep oneself **from b polluted** by the world. *G834*
Jas 3: 7 sea creatures *are b* **tamed** and have been AIT
Jas 3: 8 no **human b** can tame the tongue. It is *G476*
Jas 5:17 Elijah was a **human b**, even as we are. *G476*
1Pe 2: 5 *are b* **built** into a spiritual house to be a holy AIT
1Pe 3:19 *After b* **made alive**, he went and made AIT
1Pe 3:20 in the days of Noah *while* the ark *was b* **built**. AIT
1Pe 5: 3 but **b** examples to the flock. *G1181*
2Pe 1: 8 they will keep you from **b** ineffective and NDT
2Pe 3: 5 the heavens **came into b** and the earth *G1639*
2Pe 3: 7 *b* **kept** for the day of judgment and AIT
1Jn 5:20 in him who is true by **b** in his Son Jesus NDT
Rev 3: 1 you have a reputation *of b* **alive**, but you are AIT
Rev 4:11 will they were created and **have** *their* **b**." *G1639*
Rev 6:14 The heavens receded like a scroll *b* **rolled up** AIT

BEINGS (26) [BEING]

Ge 6: 1 When **human b** began to increase in H132
Ge 6: 6 that he had made **human b** on the earth, H132
Ex 4:11 "Who gave **human b** their mouths? H132
Dt 4:32 the day God created **human b** on the earth; H132
Ps 8: 4 **human b** that you care for them? H1201+132
Ps 29: 1 to the LORD, you **heavenly** *b*, ascribe to the AIT
Ps 78:25 **Human b** ate the bread of angels; he sent H408
Ps 89: 6 like the LORD among the **heavenly b**? H1201+446
Ps 144: 3 what are **human b** that you care for them H132
Ps 146: 3 in princes, in **human b**, who cannot H1201+132
Ecc 3:19 the fate of **human b** is like H1201+2021+132
Isa 44:11 such craftsmen are *only* **human b**. H132
Isa 51:12 mortals, **human b** who are but grass, H1201+132
Eze 27:13 they traded **human b** and articles of H5883+132
Jn 5:41 "I do not accept glory from **human b**, *G476*
Ac 5: 4 have not lied *just to* **human b** but to God." *G476*
Ac 5:29 "We must obey God rather than **human b**! *G476*
1Co 3: 4 Apollos," are you not *mere* **human b**? *G476*
1Co 4: 9 universe, to angels as well as *to* **human b**. *G476*
1Co 7:23 do not become slaves *of* **human b**. *G476*
Gal 1:10 now trying to win the approval *of* **human b**, *G476*
Jas 3: 9 with it we curse **human b**, who have *G476*
2Pe 2:10 not afraid to heap abuse *on* **celestial b**; *G1518*
2Pe 2:11 not heap abuse on **such b** when bringing NDT
Jude 8 authority and heap abuse on **celestial b**. *G1518*
Rev 18:13 carriages; and **human b** sold as slaves. *G476*

BEKA (2)

Ge 24:22 nose ring weighing a **b** and two gold H1325
Ex 38:26 *one* **b** per person, that is, half a shekel H1325

BEKER (5) [BEKERITE]
Ge 46:21 B, Ashbel, Gera, Naaman, Ehi, Rosh H1146
Nu 26:35 through B, the Bekerite clan; H1146
1Ch 7: 6 sons of Benjamin: Bela, B and Jediael. H1146
1Ch 7: 8 The sons of B: Zemirah, Joash, Eliezer H1146
1Ch 7: 8 All these were the sons of B. H1146

BEKERITE (1) [BEKER]
Nu 26:35 through Beker, the B clan; through Tahan H1151

BEKORATH (1)
1Sa 9: 1 of Zeror, the son of B, the son of Aphiah H1138

BEL (3)
Isa 46: 1 B bows down, Nebo stoops low; their H1155
Jer 50: 2 will be captured; B will be put to shame H1155
Jer 51:44 I will punish B in Babylon and make him H1155

BELA (14) [BELAITE, ZOAR]
Ge 14: 2 of Zeboyim, and the king of B (that is, H1186
Ge 14: 8 the king of Zeboyim and the king of B H1186
Ge 36:32 B son of Beor became king of Edom. H1185
Ge 36:33 When B died, Jobab son of Zerah from H1185
Ge 46:21 B, Beker, Ashbel, Gera, Naaman, Ehi H1185
Nu 26:38 through B, the Belaite clan; through H1185
Nu 26:40 The descendants of B through Ard and H1185
1Ch 1:43 B son of Beor, whose city was named H1185
1Ch 1:44 When B died, Jobab son of Zerah from H1185
1Ch 5: 8 B son of Azaz, the son of Shema, the H1185
1Ch 7: 6 sons of Benjamin: B, Beker and Jediael. H1185
1Ch 7: 7 The sons of B: Ezbon, Uzzi, Uzziel H1185
1Ch 8: 1 Benjamin was the father of B his firstborn H1185
1Ch 8: 3 The sons of B were: Addar, Gera, Abihud, H1185

BELAITE (1) [BELA]
Nu 26:38 through Bela, the B clan; through Ashbel H1188

BELIAL (1)
2Co 6:15 harmony is there between Christ and B? G1016

BELIEF (1) [BELIEVE]
2Th 2:13 of the Spirit and through b in the truth. G4411

BELIEFS (1) [BELIEVE]
Job 11: 4 'My b are flawless and I am pure in your H4375

BELIEVE (160) [BELIEF, BELIEFS, BELIEVED, BELIEVER, BELIEVERS, BELIEVES, BELIEVING]
Ge 45:26 Jacob was stunned; he did not b them. H586
Ex 4: 1 "What if they do not b me or listen to me H586
Ex 4: 5 "is so that they may b that the LORD H586
Ex 4: 8 "If they do not b you or pay attention to the H586
Ex 4: 8 to the first sign, they may b the second. H586
Ex 4: 9 But if they do not b these two signs or listen H586
Nu 14:11 How long will they refuse to b in me, in H586
1Ki 10: 7 But I did not b these things until I came H586
2Ch 9: 6 But I did not b what they said until I came H586
2Ch 32:15 Do not b him, for no god of any nation H586
Job 9:16 I do not b he would give me a hearing. H586
Ps 78:22 for they did not b in God or trust in his H586
Ps 78:32 in spite of his wonders, they did not b. H586
Ps 106:24 pleasant land; they did not b his promise. H586
Pr 14:15 The simple b anything, but the prudent H586
Pr 26:25 is charming, do not b them, for seven H586
Isa 43:10 you may know and b me and understand H586
Jer 40:14 Gedaliah son of Ahikam did not b them. H586
La 4:12 The kings of the earth did not b, nor did H586
Hab 1: 5 in your days that you would not b, H586
Mt 9:28 "Do you b that I am able to do this?" G4409
Mt 18: 6 those who b in me—to stumble G4409
Mt 21:22 If you b, you will receive whatever you ask G4409
Mt 21:25 he will ask, 'Then why didn't you b him? G4409
Mt 21:32 and you did not b him, but the tax G4409
Mt 21:32 saw this, you did not repent and b him. G4409
Mt 24:23 or, 'There he is!' do not b it. G4409
Mt 24:26 in the inner rooms,' do not b it. G4409
Mt 27:42 now from the cross, and we will b in him. G4409
Mk 1:15 Repent and b the good news!" G4409
Mk 5:36 Jesus told him, "Don't be afraid; just b." G4409
Mk 9:24 exclaimed, "I do b; help me overcome G4409
Mk 9:42 those who b in me—to stumble G4409
Mk 11:24 in prayer, b that you have received it G4409
Mk 11:31 he will ask, 'Then why didn't you b him? G4409
Mk 13:21 'Look, there he is!' do not b it. G4409
Mk 15:32 from the cross, that we may see and b." G4409
Mk 16:11 that she had seen him, they did not b it. G601
Mk 16:13 to the rest; but they did not b them either. G4409
Mk 16:14 stubborn refusal to b those who had seen G601
Mk 16:16 whoever does not b will be condemned G601
Mk 16:17 these signs will accompany those who b: G4409
Lk 1:20 because you did not b my words, which G4409
Lk 8:12 so that they may not b and be saved. G4409
Lk 8:13 They b for a while, but in the time of G4409
Lk 8:50 "Don't be afraid; just b, and she will be G4409
Lk 20: 5 he will ask, 'Why didn't you b him? G4409
Lk 22:67 "If I tell you, you will not b me, G4409
Lk 24:11 But they did not b the women, because G601
Lk 24:25 how slow to b all that the prophets G4409
Lk 24:41 And while they still did not b it because of G601
Jn 1: 7 that light, so that through him all might b. G4409
Jn 1:50 "You b because I told you I saw you under G4409
Jn 3:12 to you of earthly things and you do not b; G4409
Jn 3:12 how then will you b if I speak of heavenly G4409
Jn 3:18 whoever does not b stands G4409
Jn 4:21 Jesus replied, "b me, a time is coming G4409
Jn 4:42 "We no longer b just because of what you G4409
Jn 4:48 Jesus told him, "you will never b. G4409
Jn 5:38 for you do not b the one he sent. G4409
Jn 5:44 How can you b since you accept glory from G4409
Jn 5:46 believed Moses, you would b me, for he G4409
Jn 5:47 But since you do not b what he wrote, how G4409
Jn 5:47 how are you going to b what I say? G4409
Jn 6:29 of God is this: to b in the one he has sent." G4409
Jn 6:30 you give that we may see it and b you? G4409
Jn 6:36 you have seen me and still you do not b. G4409
Jn 6:64 Yet there are some of you who do not b." G4409
Jn 6:64 which of them did not b and who would G4409
Jn 6:69 We have come to b and to know that you G4409
Jn 7: 5 For even his own brothers did not b in him. G4409
Jn 8:24 in your sins; if you do not b that I am he G4409
Jn 8:45 because I tell the truth, you do not b me! G4409
Jn 8:46 am telling the truth, why don't you b me? G4409
Jn 9:18 They still did not b that he had been G4409
Jn 9:35 he said, "Do you b in the Son of Man?" G4409
Jn 9:36 "Tell me so that I may b in him." G4409
Jn 9:38 man said, "Lord, I b," and he worshiped G4409
Jn 10:25 "I did tell you, but you do not b. G4409
Jn 10:26 you do not b because you are not my G4409
Jn 10:37 Do not b me unless I do the works of my G4409
Jn 10:38 I do them, even though you do not b me G4409
Jn 10:38 do not believe me, b the works, that you G4409
Jn 11:15 glad I was not there, so that you may b. G4409
Jn 11:26 in me will never die. Do you b this?" G4409
Jn 11:27 she replied, "I b that you are the Messiah G4409
Jn 11:40 "Did I not tell you that if you b, you will G4409
Jn 11:42 that they may b that you sent me. G4409
Jn 11:48 like this, everyone will b in him, and then G4409
Jn 12:36 B in the light while you have the light, so G4409
Jn 12:37 presence, they still would not b in him. G4409
Jn 12:39 For this reason they could not b, because G4409
Jn 12:44 believes in me does not b in me only, G4409
Jn 13:19 it does happen you will b that I am who I G4409
Jn 14: 1 hearts be troubled. You b in God; believe G4409
Jn 14: 1 You believe in God; b also in me. G4409
Jn 14:10 Don't you b that I am in the Father, and G4409
Jn 14:11 B me when I say that I am in the Father G4409
Jn 14:11 at least b on the evidence of the works G4409
Jn 14:29 so that when it does happen you will b. G4409
Jn 16: 9 about sin, because people do not b in me; G4409
Jn 16:30 This makes us b that you came from God." G4409
Jn 16:31 "Do you now b?" Jesus replied. G4409
Jn 17:20 also for those who will b in me through G4409
Jn 17:21 so that the world may b that you have G4409
Jn 19:35 he testifies so that you also may b. G4409
Jn 20:25 put my hand into his side, I will not b." G4409
Jn 20:27 it into my side. Stop doubting and b." G4412
Jn 20:31 are written that you may b that Jesus is G4409
Ac 13:41 in your days that you would never b, G4409
Ac 14: 2 But the Jews who refused to b stirred up the G578
Ac 15: 7 my lips the message of the gospel and b. G4409
Ac 15:11 We b it is through the grace of our Lord G4409
Ac 16:31 They replied, "B in the Lord Jesus, and G4409
Ac 16:34 joy because he had come to b in God— G4409
Ac 19: 4 told the people to b in the one coming G4409
Ac 19: 9 they refused to b and publicly maligned G578
Ac 22:19 to imprison and beat those who b in you. G4409
Ac 23: 8 the Pharisees b all these things. G3933
Ac 24:14 I b everything that is in accordance with G4409
Ac 26:27 King Agrippa, do you b the prophets? G4409
Ac 28:24 by what he said, but others would not b. G601
Ro 3:22 through faith in Jesus Christ to all who b. G4409
Ro 4:11 the father of all who b but have not been G4409
Ro 4:24 us who b in him who raised Jesus our G4409
Ro 6: 8 we b that we will also live with him. G4409
Ro 10: 9 b in your heart that God raised him G4409
Ro 10:10 with your heart that you b and are G4409
Ro 10:14 And how can they b in the one of whom G4409
Ro 14:22 So whatever you b about these G4411+2400
1Co 1:21 what was preached to save those who b. G4409
1Co 3: 5 through whom you came to b—as the G4409
1Co 11:18 among you, and to some extent I b it. G4409
2Co 4:13 of faith, we also b and therefore speak, G4409
Gal 3:22 might be given to those who b. G4409
Eph 1:19 incomparably great power for us who b. G4409
Php 1:29 on behalf of Christ not only to b in him, G4409
1Th 2:13 which is indeed at work in you who b. G4409
1Th 4:14 For we b that Jesus died and rose again G4409
1Th 4:14 so we b that God will bring with Jesus NDT
2Th 2:11 delusion so that they will b the lie G4409
1Ti 1:16 those who would b in him and receive G4409
1Ti 4: 3 thanksgiving by those who b and who G4412
1Ti 4:10 all people, and especially of those who b. G4412
Titus 1: 6 man whose children b and are not open G4412
Titus 1:15 to those who are corrupted and do not b, G603
Heb 11: 6 comes to him must b that he exists and G4409
Jas 1: 6 you ask, you must b and not doubt G4411
Jas 2:19 You b that there is one God. Good! Even G4409
Jas 2:19 Even the demons b that—and shudder. G4409
1Pe 1: 8 you b in him and are filled with an G4409
1Pe 1:21 Through him you b in God, who raised G4412
1Pe 2: 7 Now to you who b, this stone is precious G4409
1Pe 2: 7 But to those who do not b, "The stone the G601
1Pe 3: 1 if any of them do not b the word, they G578
1Jn 3:23 to b in the name of his Son, Jesus Christ G4409
1Jn 4: 1 Dear friends, do not b every spirit, but test G4409
1Jn 5:10 Whoever does not b God has made him G4409
1Jn 5:13 things to you who b in the name of the G4409
Jude 5 later destroyed those who did not b. G4409

BELIEVED (69) [BELIEVE]
Ge 15: 6 Abram b the LORD, and he credited it to him H586
Ex 4:31 they b. And when they heard that the H586
Job 29:24 smiled at them, they scarcely b it; the light H586
Ps 106:12 Then they b his promises and sang his H586
Isa 53: 1 Who has b our message and to whom has H586
Jnh 3: 5 The Ninevites b God. A fast was proclaimed H586
Mt 8:13 Let it be done just as you b it would." G4409
Lk 1:45 Blessed is she who has b that the Lord G4409
Jn 1:12 to those who b in his name, he gave G4409
Jn 2:11 his glory; and his disciples b in him. G4409
Jn 2:22 Then they b the scripture and the words G4409
Jn 2:23 he was performing and b in his name. G4409
Jn 3:18 because they have not b in the name of G4409
Jn 4:39 from that town b in him because of the G4409
Jn 4:53 So he and his whole household b. G4409
Jn 5:46 If you b Moses, you would believe me, for G4409
Jn 7:31 many in the crowd b in him. They said, G4409
Jn 7:39 whom those who b in him were later to G4409
Jn 7:48 Have any of the rulers or of the Pharisees b G4409
Jn 8:30 Even as he spoke, many b in him. G4409
Jn 8:31 To the Jews who had b him, Jesus said G4409
Jn 10:42 And in that place many b in Jesus. G4409
Jn 11:45 had seen what Jesus did, b in him. G4409
Jn 12:38 who has b our message and to whom has G4409
Jn 12:42 many even among the leaders b in him. G4409
Jn 16:27 loved me and have b that I came from G4409
Jn 17: 8 from you, and they b that you sent me. G4409
Jn 20: 8 also went inside. He saw and b. G4409
Jn 20:29 have seen me, you have b; blessed are G4409
Jn 20:29 those who have not seen and yet have b." G4409
Ac 4: 4 But many who heard the message b; so G4409
Ac 4: 4 number of men who b grew to about five NDT
Ac 5:14 more men and women b in the Lord and G4409
Ac 8:12 But when they b Philip as he proclaimed G4409
Ac 8:13 Simon himself b and was baptized. G4409
Ac 9:42 and many people b in the Lord. G4409
Ac 11:17 gift he gave us who b in the Lord Jesus G4409
Ac 11:21 number of people b and turned to the G4409
Ac 13:12 had happened, he b, for he was amazed G4409
Ac 13:48 all who were appointed for eternal life b. G4409
Ac 14: 1 a great number of Jews and Greeks b. G4409
Ac 17:12 many of them b, as did also a G4409
Ac 17:34 people became followers of Paul and b. G4409
Ac 18: 8 his entire household b in the Lord G4409
Ac 18: 8 who heard Paul b and were baptized. G4409
Ac 18:27 a great help to those who by grace had b. G4409
Ac 19: 2 you receive the Holy Spirit when you b?" G4409
Ac 19:18 Many of those who b now came and G4409
Ac 21:20 how many thousands of Jews have b, and G4409
Ro 4: 3 "Abraham b God, and it was credited to G4409
Ro 4:17 in whom he b—the God who G4409
Ro 4:18 Abraham in hope b and so became the G4409
Ro 10:14 they call on the one they have not b in? G4409
Ro 10:16 "Lord, who has b our message? G4409
Ro 13:11 is nearer now than when we first b. G4409
1Co 15: 2 Otherwise, you have b in vain. G4409
1Co 15:11 is what we preach, and this is what you b. G4409
2Co 4:13 "I b; therefore I have spoken. G4409
Gal 3: 6 So also Abraham "b God, and it was G4409
Eph 1:13 When you b, you were marked in him G4409
1Th 2:10 blameless we were among you who b. G4409
2Th 1:10 marveled at among all those who have b. G4409
2Th 1:10 because you b our testimony to you. G4409
2Th 2:12 condemned who have not b the truth but G4409
1Ti 3:16 the nations, was b on in the world, was G4409
2Ti 1:12 because I know whom I have b, and am G4409
Heb 4: 3 Now we who have b enter that rest, just as G4409
Jas 2:23 that says, "Abraham b God, and it was G4409
1Jn 5:10 because they have not b the testimony G4409

BELIEVER (10) [BELIEVE]
1Ki 18: 3 Obadiah was a devout b in the LORD. H3707
Ac 16: 1 was Jewish and a b but whose father was G4412
Ac 16:15 "If you consider me a b in the Lord," G4412
1Co 7:12 has a wife who is not a b and she is willing G603
1Co 7:13 a husband who is not a b and he is willing G603
1Co 7:17 person should live as a b in whatever G4048S
2Co 6:15 Or what does a b have in common with G4412
2Th 3: 6 to keep away from every b who is idle and G81
2Th 3:15 warn them as you would a fellow b. G81
1Ti 5:16 If any woman who is a b has widows in G4412

BELIEVERS (45) [BELIEVE]
Jn 4:41 of his words many more became b. G4409
Jn 21:23 rumor spread among the b that this disciple G81
Ac 1:15 In those days Peter stood up among the b (a G81
Ac 2:44 All the b were together and had G4409
Ac 4:32 All the b were one in heart and mind. G4409
Ac 5:12 And all the b used to meet together in NDT
Ac 8:15 they prayed for the new b there that they G899S
Ac 9:30 When the b learned of this, they took him G81
Ac 9:41 Then he called for the b, especially the G41
Ac 10:23 some of the b from Joppa went along. G81
Ac 10:45 The circumcised b who had come with G4412
Ac 11: 1 The apostles and the b throughout Judea G81
Ac 11: 2 to Jerusalem, the circumcised b criticized him AIT
Ac 15: 1 Judea to Antioch and were teaching the b: G81

Ac 15: 2 along with some other **b**, to go up G1666+899S
Ac 15: 3 This news made all the **b** very glad. G81
Ac 15: 5 Then some *of* the **b** who belonged to the G4409
Ac 15:22 men who were leaders among the **b**. G81
Ac 15:23 your brothers, *To* the Gentile **b** in Antioch G81
Ac 15:32 much to encourage and strengthen the **b**. G81
Ac 15:33 were sent off by the **b** with the blessing of G81
Ac 15:36 go back and visit the **b** in all the towns G81
Ac 15:40 commended by the **b** to the grace of the G81
Ac 16: 2 The **b** at Lystra and Iconium spoke well of G81
Ac 17: 6 Jason and some other **b** before the city G81
Ac 17:10 the **b** sent Paul and Silas away to Berea. G81
Ac 17:14 The **b** immediately sent Paul to the coast G81
Ac 21:25 As for the Gentile **b**, we have written to G4409
1Co 6: 5 wise enough to judge a dispute between **b**? G81
1Co 14:22 are a sign, not *for* **b** but for unbelievers G4409
1Co 14:22 however, is not for unbelievers but *for* **b**. G4409
2Co 11:26 and in danger from **false b**. G6012
Gal 2: 4 because some **false b** had infiltrated G6012
Gal 6:10 to those who belong to the family *of* **b**. G4411
1Th 1: 7 a model to all the **b** in Macedonia and G4409
1Ti 4:12 set an example *for* the **b** in speech, in G4412
1Ti 6: 2 disrespect just because they are **fellow b**. G81
1Ti 6: 2 dear to them *as* **fellow b** and are devoted G4412
Jas 1: 9 **B** in humble circumstances ought to take G81
Jas 2: 1 **b** in our glorious Lord Jesus G2400+3836+4411
Jas 3: 1 teachers, my **fellow b**, because you know G81
1Pe 2:17 to everyone, love the **family of b**, fear God, G82
1Pe 5: 9 you know that the **family of b** throughout the G82
3Jn 3 me great joy when *some* **b** came and G81
3Jn 10 he even refuses to welcome other **b**. G81

BELIEVES (25) [BELIEVE]

Mk 9:23 "Everything is possible *for* one *who* **b**." G4409
Mk 11:23 in their heart but **b** that what they say will G4409
Mk 16:16 Whoever **b** and is baptized will be saved G4409
Jn 3:15 that everyone who **b** may have eternal life G4409
Jn 3:16 that whoever **b** in him shall not perish G4409
Jn 3:18 Whoever **b** in him is not condemned, but G4409
Jn 3:36 Whoever **b** in the Son has eternal life, but G4409
Jn 5:24 hears my word and **b** him who sent me G4409
Jn 6:35 whoever **b** in me will never be thirsty. G4409
Jn 6:40 looks to the Son and **b** in him shall have G4409
Jn 6:47 I tell you, the *one who* **b** has eternal life. G4409
Jn 7:38 Whoever **b** in me, as Scripture has said G4409
Jn 11:25 The *one who* **b** in me will live, even G4409
Jn 12:44 "Whoever **b** in me does not believe in me G4409
Jn 12:46 so that no one who **b** in me should stay in G4409
Jn 14:12 whoever **b** in me will do the works I have G4409
Ac 10:43 him that everyone who **b** in him receives G4409
Ac 13:39 him everyone who **b** is set free from every G4409
Ro 1:16 that brings salvation to everyone who **b**: G4409
Ro 9:33 the *one who* **b** in him will never be G4409
Ro 10: 4 may be righteousness for everyone who **b**. G4409
Ro 10:11 "Anyone who **b** in him will never be put G4409
1Jn 5: 1 Everyone who **b** that Jesus is the Christ is G4409
1Jn 5: 5 Only the *one who* **b** that Jesus is the Son G4409
1Jn 5:10 Whoever **b** in the Son of God accepts this G4409

BELIEVING (9) [BELIEVE]

Jn 11:26 whoever lives *by* **b** in me will never G4409
Jn 12:11 were going over to Jesus and **b** in him. G4409
Jn 20:31 that *by* **b** you may have life in his G4409
Ac 9:26 not **b** that he really was a disciple. G4409
1Co 7:14 has been sanctified through her **b** husband. NDT
1Co 9: 5 have the right to take a **b** wife along with us, G80
Gal 3: 2 works of the law, or by **b** what you heard? G4411
Gal 3: 5 of the law, or by your **b** what you heard? G4411
1Ti 6: 2 Those who have **b** masters should not G4412

BELLIES (1) [BELLY]

Ps 17:14 have stored up for the wicked fill their **b**; H1061

BELLOW (1) [BELLOWS]

Job 6: 5 has grass, or an ox **b** when it has fodder? H1716

BELLOWS (1) [BELLOW]

Jer 6:29 The **b** blow fiercely to burn away the lead H5135

BELLS (6)

Ex 28:33 of the robe, with gold **b** between them. H7194
Ex 28:34 The gold **b** and the pomegranates are to H7194
Ex 28:35 The sound of **the b** will be heard when H2257S
Ex 39:25 And they made **b** *of* pure gold and H7194
Ex 39:26 The **b** and pomegranates alternated H7194
Zec 14:20 will be inscribed on the **b** *of* the horses, H5197

BELLY (10) [BELLIES]

Ge 3:14 will crawl on your **b** and you will eat dust H1623
Lev 11:42 it moves on its **b** or walks on all fours H1623
Jdg 3:21 thigh and plunged it into the king's **b**. H1061
2Sa 20:10 Joab plunged it into his **b**, and his H2824
Job 15: 2 notions or fill their **b** with the hot east H1061
Job 20:23 When he has filled his **b**, God will vent H1061
Job 40:16 what power in the muscles of its **b**! H1061
Da 2:32 arms of silver, its **b** and thighs of bronze A10435
Jnh 1:17 Jonah was in the **b** *of* the fish three days H5055
Mt 12:40 three nights in the **b** of a huge fish, G3120

BELONG (87) [BELONGED, BELONGING, BELONGINGS, BELONGS]

Ge 20: 7 that you and all who **b to** you will die." H4200
Ge 32:17 'Who do you **b to**, and where are H4200
Ge 32:18 are to say, 'They **b to** your servant Jacob. H4200
Ge 40: 8 to them, "Do not interpretations **b to** God? H4200
Ge 45:11 all who **b to** you will become H4200
Ex 13:12 males of your livestock **b to** the LORD. H4200
Ex 21: 4 her children *shall* **b to** her master, H2118+4200
Ex 29:27 ram that **b to** Aaron and his sons H4200
Ex 29:29 sacred garments *will* **b to** his H2118+4200
Lev 5:13 of the offering *will* **b to** the priest, H2118+4200
Lev 7: 7 *They* **b to** the priest who makes H2118+4200
Lev 25:30 in the walled city *shall* **b** permanently to H7756
Lev 25:55 the Israelites **b to** me as servants. H4200
Nu 5: 9 bring to a priest *will* **b to** him. H2118+4200
Nu 5:10 Sacred things **b to** their owners, but H2118+4200
Nu 5:10 to the priest *will* **b to** the priest. H2118+4200
Nu 6:20 they are holy and **b to** the priest, together H4200
Dt 10:14 **To** the LORD your God **b** the heavens, even H4200
Dt 20:15 you and do not **b to** the nations nearby H4946
Dt 29:29 The secret things **b to** the LORD our God H4200
Dt 29:29 the things revealed **b to** us and to our H4200
Dt 33: 8 Thummim and Urim **b to** your faithful H4200
Jos 2:13 all who **b to** them—and that you H4200
Jos 6:22 bring her out and all who **b to** her, H4200
Ru 2: 5 "Who does that young woman **b to**?" H4200
1Sa 25:22 leave alive one male of all who **b to** him!" H4200
1Sa 30:13 "Who do you **b to**? Where do you H4200
1Ki 8:41 who does not **b to** your people Israel H4946
2Ch 6:32 who does not **b to** your people Israel H4946
Ne 5: 5 our fields and our vineyards **b to** others." H4200
Job 12:13 "**To** God **b** wisdom and power; counsel H6640
Job 12:16 **To** him **b** strength and insight; both H6640
Job 25: 2 "Dominion and awe **b to** God; he H6640
Ps 47: 9 the kings of the earth **b to** God; he is H4200
Ps 95: 4 and the mountain peaks **b to** him. H4200
Ps 104:18 The high mountains **b to** the wild goats H4200
Ps 115:16 The highest heavens **b to** the LORD, but H4200
Pr 16: 1 **To** humans **b** the plans of the heart, but H4200
Pr 16:11 Honest scales and balances **b to** the LORD H4200
SS 7:10 I **b to** my beloved, and his desire is for me H4200
Isa 44: 5 Some will say, 'I **b to** the LORD'; others H4200
Jer 5:10 these people do not **b to** the LORD. H4200
Eze 13: 9 *They will* not **b to** the council of my H2118+928
Eze 18: 4 as well as the child—both alike **b to** me. H4200
Eze 44:29 devoted to the LORD *will* **b to** them. H2118+4200
Eze 44:30 special gifts *will* **b to** the priests. H2118+4200
Eze 45: 5 10,000 cubits wide *will* **b to** the Levites, H2118
Eze 45: 6 sacred portion; *it will* **b to** all Israel. H2118+4200
Eze 46:16 it *will* also **b to** his descendants H2118+4200
Eze 48:21 the property of the city will **b to** the prince. H4200
Eze 48:21 of the tribal portions will **b to** the prince, H4200
Zep 2: 7 That land *will* **b to** the remnant of H2118+4200
Zec 9: 7 who are left will **b to** our God and H4200
Mal 2:15 You **b to** him in body and spirit H4200
Mt 20:23 These places *b to* **those** *for whom* they have AIT
Mk 9:41 my name because *you* **b to** the Messiah G1639
Mk 10:40 These places *b to* **those** for whom they have AIT
Mk 13:14 standing where *it does* not **b**— G1256
Jn 8:44 You **b to** your father, the devil, and G1666+1639
Jn 8:47 hear is that *you do* not **b to** God." G1666+1639
Jn 14:24 my own; they *b to* the **Father** who sent me. AIT
Jn 15:19 As it is, *you do* not **b to** the world G1666+1639
Ac 5: 4 Didn't *it* **b** to you before it was sold? And G3531
Ac 27:23 of the God to whom I **b** and whom I serve G1639
Ro 1: 6 Gentiles who are called to *b to* **Jesus** Christ. AIT
Ro 7: 4 that you *might* **b** to another, to him G1181
Ro 8: 9 the Spirit of Christ, they *do* not **b** to Christ. G1639
Ro 14: 8 whether we live or die, *we* **b** to the Lord. G1639
Ro 16:10 those who **b to** the **household** of G1666
1Co 7:39 she wishes, but he must **b to** the Lord. G1877
1Co 9:19 I am **free and b to no one**, G1801+1666+4246
1Co 12:15 not a hand, *I do* not **b to** the body," G1639+1666
1Co 12:16 not an eye, *I do* not **b to** the body," G1639+1666
1Co 15:23 when he comes, those who *b to* **him**. AIT
2Co 10: 7 If anyone is confident *that* they **b** to Christ G1639
2Co 10: 7 again that we *b to* **Christ** just as much as they AIT
Gal 3:29 If you *b to* **Christ**, then you are Abraham's AIT
Gal 5:24 Those who *b to* **Christ** Jesus have crucified AIT
Gal 6:10 to those *who* **b to the family** of believers. G3858
Php 4:22 those who **b to** Caesar's household. G1666
1Th 5: 5 *We do* not **b to** the night or to the G1639
1Th 5: 8 But *since* we **b to** the day, let us be sober G1639
Heb 10:39 But we *do* not **b** to those who shrink back G1639
Jas 2: 7 the noble name of him **to** whom you **b**? G2126
1Jn 2:19 from us, but they did not really **b to** us. G1666
1Jn 3:19 we know that *we* **b to** the truth and G1666+1639
Rev 19: 1 Salvation and glory and power *b to* our **God**, AIT

BELONGED (51) [BELONG]

Ge 30:40 dark-colored **animals** *that b to* Laban. AIT
Ge 31: 1 all this wealth from what **b to** our father." H4200
Nu 3:21 **To** Gershon **b** the clans of the Libnites H4200
Nu 3:27 **To** Kohath **b** the clans of the Amramites H4200
Nu 3:33 **To** Merari **b** the clans of the Mahlites and H4200
Nu 27: 1 **b** to the clans of Manasseh son of Joseph. H4200
Dt 11: 6 every living thing that **b to** them. H928+8079
Dt 30: 5 you to the land that **b** *to* your ancestors, H3769
Jos 6:23 brothers and sisters and all who **b to** her. H4200
Jos 6:25 with her family and all who **b to** her H4200
Jos 14:14 So Hebron *has* **b to** Caleb son of H2118+4200
Jos 17: 6 land of Gilead **b to** the rest of the H2118+4200
Jos 17: 8 of Manasseh, **b to** the Ephraimites.) H4200
Jos 17:10 On the south the land **b to** Ephraim, on H4200
Jdg 6:11 oak in Ophrah that **b to** Joash the H4200
Ru 4: 3 piece of land that **b to** our relative H4200
1Sa 27: 6 and it *has* **b to** the kings of Judah H2118+4200
2Sa 8: 7 gold shields that **b to** the officers of H2118+448
2Sa 8: 8 Berothai, **towns** *that b to* Hadadezer AIT
2Sa 9: 7 to you all the **land** *that b to* your grandfather AIT
2Sa 9: 9 everything that **b to** Saul and his H2118+4200
2Sa 12: 4 he took the **ewe lamb** *that b to* the poor man AIT
2Sa 16: 4 "All that **b to** Mephibosheth is now yours." H4200
1Ki 6:22 gold the altar that **b to** the inner sanctuary H4200
2Ki 8: 6 "Give back everything that **b to** her H4200
2Ki 9:21 at the **plot of ground** *that had b to* Naboth AIT
2Ki 9:25 throw him on the **field** *that b to* Naboth the AIT
2Ki 11:10 shields that had **b to** King David and that H4200
2Ki 12:16 of the LORD; *it* **b to** the priests. H2118+4200
2Ki 14:28 Hamath, which had **b to** Judah, are they H4200
1Ch 5: 2 the rights of the firstborn **b to** Joseph)— H4200
1Ch 18: 8 Tebah and Kun, **towns** *that b to* Hadadezer AIT
2Ch 23: 9 shields that had **b to** King David and that H4200
2Ch 26:23 them in a cemetery that **b to** the kings, H4200
Eze 23:41 the incense and **olive oil** *that b to* me. AIT
Eze 46:19 facing north, which **b to** the priests, and H448
Lk 1: 5 who **b to** the priestly division of Abijah G1666
Lk 2: 4 because he **b to** the house and G1639+1666
Lk 5:30 of the law *who b to* **their** *sect* complained to AIT
Jn 15:19 If *you* **b to** the world, it would love G1666+1639
Ac 9: 2 if he found any there *who* **b to** the Way, G1639
Ac 12: 1 Herod arrested some who **b to** the church, G608
Ac 15: 5 of the believers who **b to** the party of the G608
Ac 27: 1 who *b to* the Imperial **Regiment**. AIT
Ac 28: 7 There was an estate nearby that *b to* **Publius** AIT
Gal 2:12 afraid of those who **b** to the circumcision G1666
Col 2:20 as though *you still* **b** to the world, do G2409
Heb 7:13 *He* of whom these things are said **b to** a G3576
1Jn 2:19 For if they had **b to** us, they would have G1666
1Jn 2:19 showed that none of them **b to** us. G1639+1666
1Jn 3:12 who **b to** the evil one and G1666+1639

BELONGING (37) [BELONG]

Ge 14:23 that I will accept nothing **b to** you, not H4200
Ge 50: 8 and *those b to* his father's **household**. AIT
Ex 9: 4 so that no animal **b to** the Israelites will H4200
Ex 9: 6 not one animal **b to** the Israelites H4946
Lev 7:20 of the fellowship offering **b to** the LORD, H4200
Lev 7:21 fellowship offering **b to** the LORD must be H4200
Lev 25:31 to be considered as **b to** the open country. H6584
Lev 25:34 But the **pastureland** *b to* their towns must not AIT
Nu 1:50 all its furnishings and everything **b to** it. H4200
Nu 16:26 Do not touch anything **b to** them, or you H4200
Nu 17: 5 The **staff** *b to* the man I choose will sprout AIT
Nu 31:42 The **half** *b to* the Israelites, which Moses set AIT
Dt 2:19 possession of any **land** *b to* the Ammonites. AIT
Jos 17: 9 There were towns **b to** Ephraim lying H4200
Ru 2: 3 she was working in a field **b to** Boaz, who H4200
1Sa 6:18 of Philistine towns **b to** the five rulers— H4200
1Sa 9: 3 Now the donkeys **b to** Saul's father Kish H4200
1Sa 25:34 not one male **b to** Nabal would have H4200
1Sa 30:14 some territory **b to** Judah and the Negev H4200
1Ki 14:11 will eat those **b to** Jeroboam who die H4200
1Ki 14:13 is the only one **b to** Jeroboam who will H4200
1Ki 16: 4 will eat those **b to** Baasha who die in H4200
1Ki 21: 1 a vineyard **b to** Naboth the H2118+4200
1Ki 21:24 will eat those **b to** Ahab who die in the H4200
1Ch 7: 5 were fighting men **b to** all the clans of H4200
1Ch 9:18 the gatekeepers **b to** the camp of the H4200
1Ch 22:19 LORD and the sacred **articles** *b to* God into AIT
1Ch 23: 7 **B to** the Gershonites: Ladan and Shimei. H4200
1Ch 26:21 heads of families **b to** Ladan the H4200
1Ch 28: 1 livestock **b to** the king and his sons H4200
2Ch 25:13 in the war raided **towns** *b to* Judah from AIT
2Ch 34:33 from all the territory **b to** the Israelites, H4200
Ezr 1: 7 brought out the **articles** *b to* the temple of AIT
Eze 37:16 '**B to** Judah and the Israelites associated H4200
Eze 37:16 write on it, '**B to** Joseph (that is, to H4200
Eze 48:22 The area **b to** the prince will lie between H4200
Lk 5: 3 the boats, the one **b to** Simon, and asked G1639

BELONGINGS (7) [BELONG]

Ge 45:20 Never mind about your **b**, because the H3998
Jer 10:17 Gather up your **b** to leave the land, you H4045
Jer 46:19 Pack your **b** *for* exile, you who live in H3998
Eze 12: 3 pack your **b** *for* exile and in the daytime H3998
Eze 12: 4 bring out your **b** packed for exile. H3998
Eze 12: 5 the wall and take your **b** out through it. NDT
Eze 12: 7 I took my **b** out at dusk, carrying them on my NDT

BELONGS (59) [BELONG]

Ge 14:24 eaten and the **share** *that b to* the men who AIT
Ge 19:12 anyone else in the city who **b to** you? H4200
Ge 23: 9 which **b to** him and is at the end of his H4200
Ge 31:16 from our father **b to** us and our children H4200
Ge 31:37 have you found that **b to** your household? H4946
Ge 47:18 money is gone and our livestock **b to** you, H448
Ge 47:26 that a fifth of the produce **b to** Pharaoh. H4200
Ge 49:10 until he to whom it **b** shall come and the H4200
Ex 13: 2 every womb among the Israelites **b to** me, H4200
Ex 20:17 anything that **b to** your neighbor. H4200
Ex 34:19 "The first offspring of every womb **b to** me, H4200
Ex 40: 4 Bring in the table and set out **what b** *on* it H6886
Lev 2: 3 the grain offering **b to** Aaron and his sons H4200
Lev 2:10 the grain offering **b to** Aaron and his sons H4200
Lev 7: 9 on a griddle **b to** the priest who H2118+4200
Lev 7:10 **b** equally to all the sons of Aaron. H2118

Lev 7:14 *it* **b to** the priest who splashes the H2118+4200
Lev 7:31 the breast **b to** Aaron and his H2118+4200
Lev 14:13 the guilt offering **b to** the priest; it is most H4200
Lev 24: 9 *It* **b to** Aaron and his sons, who are H2118+4200
Lev 27:26 the **firstborn** already **b to** the LORD H1144+4200
Lev 27:30 fruit from the trees, **b to** the LORD; it is holy H4200
Nu 5: 8 the restitution **b to** the LORD and must be H4200
Nu 16: 5 LORD will show who **b to** him and who is H4200
Nu 16:30 with everything that **b to** them, and they H4200
Nu 18: 9 offerings, that part **b to** you and your sons. H4200
Dt 1:17 afraid of anyone, for judgment **b to** God. H4200
Dt 5:21 anything that **b to** your neighbor. H4200
Dt 21:17 The right of the firstborn **b to** him. H4200
Jos 7:15 along with all that **b to** him. H4200
1Sa 15: 3 totally destroy all that **b to** them. H4200
1Ki 22: 3 Ramoth Gilead **b to** us and yet we are H4200
1Ch 29:16 from your hand, and all of it **b to** you. H4200
Job 41:11 Everything under heaven **b to** me. H4200
Ps 22:28 dominion **b to** the LORD and he rules H4200
Ps 62:11 "Power **b to** you, God, H4200
Ps 89:18 Indeed, our shield **b to** the LORD, our king H4200
Ps 111:10 understanding. *To* him *b* eternal **praise**. AIT
Jer 46:10 But that day **b to** the Lord, the LORD H4200
Eze 18: 4 For everyone **b to** me, the parent as well H4200
Eze 21:27 until he to whom it rightfully **b** shall come H4200
Eze 29: 3 You say, "The Nile **b to** me; I made it H4200
Eze 46:17 His inheritance **b to** his sons only; it is theirs. NDT
Eze 48:22 the center of the area that **b to** the prince. H4200
Mt 19:14 kingdom of heaven **b** to such as these." G1639
Mt 25:25 in the ground. See, here is what **b to** you.' G2400
Mk 10:14 the kingdom of God **b to** such as these. G1639
Lk 6:30 if anyone takes what **b to you**, do not G5050
Lk 18:16 the kingdom of God **b to** such as these. G1639
Jn 3:29 The bride **b to** the bridegroom. The friend G2400
Jn 3:31 is from the earth **b to** the earth, G1666+1639
Jn 8:35 in the family, but a son **b** to it forever. G3531
Jn 8:47 Whoever **b to** God hears what God G1639+1666
Jn 16:15 All that **b to** the Father is mine. That is G2400
Ac 1:25 which Judas left to go where *he* **b**. G2625
Ro 12: 5 and each member *b to all the* **others**. AIT
Col 3: 5 therefore, whatever *b to* your earthly **nature**: AIT
Rev 7:10 "Salvation *b to* our **God**, who sits on the AIT
Rev 17:11 *He* **b to** the seven and is going to G1666+1639

BELOVED (32) [LOVE]

Dt 33:12 "Let the **b** *of* the LORD rest secure in him H3351
SS 1:13 My **b** is to me a sachet of myrrh resting H1856
SS 1:14 My **b** is to me a cluster of henna blossoms H1856
SS 1:16 you are, my **b**! Oh, how charming! H1856
SS 2: 3 the forest is my **b** among the young men H1856
SS 2: 8 My **b**! Look! Here he comes H1856
SS 2: 9 My **b** is like a gazelle or a young stag H1856
SS 2:10 My **b** spoke and said to me, "Arise, my H1856
SS 2:16 My **b** is mine and I am his; he browses H1856
SS 2:17 my **b**, and be like a gazelle or like a H1856
SS 4:16 Let my **b** come into his garden and taste H1856
SS 5: 2 My **b** is knocking: "Open to me, my H1856
SS 5: 4 My **b** thrust his hand through the H1856
SS 5: 5 I arose to open for my **b**, and my hands H1856
SS 5: 6 I opened for my **b**, but my beloved had H1856
SS 5: 6 my beloved, but my **b** had left; he was H1856
SS 5: 8 if you find my **b**, what will you tell H1856
SS 5: 9 How is your **b** better than others, most H1856
SS 5: 9 How is your **b** better than others, that you H1856
SS 5:10 My **b** is radiant and ruddy, outstanding H1856
SS 5:16 This is my **b**, this is my friend, daughters H1856
SS 6: 1 Where has your **b** gone, most beautiful of H1856
SS 6: 1 Which way did your **b** turn, that we may H1856
SS 6: 2 My **b** has gone down to his garden, to the H1856
SS 6: 3 I am my beloved's and my **b** is mine; he H1856
SS 7: 9 May the wine go straight to my **b**, flowing H1856
SS 7:10 I belong to my **b**, and his desire is for me. H1856
SS 7:11 my **b**, let us go to the countryside H1856
SS 7:13 that I have stored up for you, my **b**. H1856
SS 8: 5 up from the wilderness leaning on her **b**? H1856
SS 8:14 Come away, my **b**, and be like a gazelle H1856
Jer 11:15 "What is my **b** doing in my temple as she H3351

BELOVED'S (1) [LOVE]

SS 6: 3 I am my **b** and my beloved is mine H4200+1856

BELOW (44)

Ge 6:16 **leaving** *b* the roof *an opening* one cubit high AIT
Ge 49:25 blessings of the deep springs **b**, blessings H9393
Ex 20: 4 earth beneath or in the waters **b**. H4946+9393
Ex 30: 4 rings for the altar **b** the molding— H4946+9393
Ex 37:27 two gold rings **b** the molding— H4946+9393
Dt 3:17 the Dead Sea), **b** the slopes of Pisgah. H9393
Dt 4:18 ground or any fish in the waters **b**. H4946+9393
Dt 4:39 heaven above and on the earth **b**. H4946+9393
Dt 4:49 as the Dead Sea, **b** the slopes of Pisgah. H9393
Dt 5: 8 earth beneath or in the waters **b**. H4946+9393
Dt 32:22 burns down to the realm of the dead **b**. H9397
Dt 33:13 with the deep waters that lie **b**; H9393
Jos 2:11 heaven above and on the earth **b**. H4946+9393
Jos 11: 3 to the Hivites **b** Hermon in the region H9393
Jos 11:17 the Valley of Lebanon **b** Mount Hermon. H9393
Jos 12: 3 then southward **b** the slopes of H9393
Jos 13: 5 from Baal Gad **b** Mount Hermon to Lebo H9393
Jdg 7: 8 of Midian lay **b** him in the valley. H4946+9393
1Sa 7:11 the way to a point **b** Beth Kar. H4946+9393
1Ki 4:12 Shan next to Zarethan **b** Jezreel, H4946+9393
1Ki 7:24 **B** the rim, gourds encircled it—ten H4946+9393
1Ki 7:29 Above and **b** the lions and bulls H4946+9393
1Ki 8:23 in heaven above or on earth **b**— H4946+9393
2Ki 19:30 will take root **b** and bear fruit H4200+4752
2Ch 4: 3 **B** the rim, figures of bulls encircled it—ten H9393
Job 11: 8 They are deeper than the **depths b**—what H8619
Job 18:16 His roots dry up **b** and his branches H4946+9393
Job 28: 5 food comes, is transformed **b** as by fire; H9393
Isa 14: 9 realm of the dead **b** is all astir to H4946+9393
Isa 24:21 and the kings on the earth **b**. H6584+2021+141
Isa 37:31 will take root **b** and bear fruit H4200+4752
Jer 31:37 of the earth **b** be searched out will H4200+4752
Eze 26:20 I will make you dwell in the earth **b**, as in H9397
Eze 31:14 the earth **b**, among mortals who H9397
Eze 31:16 were consoled in the earth **b**. H9397
Eze 31:18 with the trees of Eden to the earth **b**; H9397
Eze 32:18 consign to the earth **b** both her and the H9397
Eze 32:24 went down uncircumcised to the earth **b**. H9397
Am 2: 9 their fruit above and their roots **b**. H4946+9393
Am 9: 2 Though they dig down to the **depths b** H8619
Jnh 1: 5 But Jonah had gone **b deck** H3752+2021+6208
Mk 14:66 While Peter was **b** in the courtyard, one of G3004
Jn 8:23 "You are from **b**; I am from above. G3004
Ac 2:19 heavens above and signs on the earth **b**, G3004

BELSHAZZAR (6) [BELSHAZZAR'S]

Da 5: 1 King **B** gave a great banquet for a A10109
Da 5: 2 While **B** was drinking his wine, he gave A10109
Da 5: 9 So King **B** became even more terrified A10109
Da 5:22 "But you, **B**, his son, have not humbled A10109
Da 5:30 That very night **B**, king of the A10105
Da 7: 1 In the first year of **B** king of Babylon A10105

BELSHAZZAR'S (2) [BELSHAZZAR]

Da 5:29 Then at **B** command, Daniel was clothed A10109
Da 8: 1 In the third year of King **B** reign, I, Daniel H1157

BELT (26) [BELTS]

Ex 12:11 with your **cloak tucked into** your **b** H2520+5516
1Sa 18: 4 even his sword, his bow and his **b**. H2512
2Sa 18:11 you ten shekels of silver and a **warrior's b**." H2514
2Sa 20: 8 it at his waist was a **b** with a dagger in its H2512
1Ki 2: 5 he stained the **b** around his waist and H2514
1Ki 18:46 **tucking** his **cloak into** *his* **b**, he H9113+5516
2Ki 1: 8 hair and had a leather **b** around his waist." H258
2Ki 4:29 "**Tuck** your **cloak into** your **b**, take H2520+5516
2Ki 9: 1 "**Tuck** *your* **cloak into** your **b**, take H2520+5516
Job 38:31 the Pleiades? Can you loosen Orion's **b**? H5436
Ps 109:19 like a **b** tied forever around him. H4652
Isa 5:27 sleeps; not a **b** is loosened at the waist H258
Isa 11: 5 will be his **b** and faithfulness the H258+5516
Jer 13: 1 "Go and buy a linen **b** and put it around H258
Jer 13: 2 So I bought a **b**, as the LORD directed, and H258
Jer 13: 4 "Take the **b** you bought and are wearing H258
Jer 13: 6 to Perath and get the **b** I told you to hide H258
Jer 13: 7 dug up the **b** and took it from the H258
Jer 13:10 will be like this **b**—completely useless! H258
Jer 13:11 For as a **b** is bound around the waist, so I H258
Da 10: 5 with a **b** of fine gold from Uphaz around H2520
Mt 3: 4 he had a leather **b** around his waist. G2438
Mk 1: 6 with a leather **b** around his waist G2438
Ac 21:11 he took Paul's **b**, tied his own hands G2438
Ac 21:11 the owner of this **b** and will hand him G2438
Eph 6:14 *with* the **b** of truth **buckled around** your G4322

BELTESHAZZAR (10)

Da 1: 7 to Daniel, the name **B**; to Hananiah H1171
Da 2:26 Daniel (also called **B**), "Are you able to A10108
Da 4: 8 He is called **B**, after the name of my A10108
Da 4: 9 "**B**, chief of the magicians, I know A10108
Da 4:18 **B**, tell me what it means, for none A10108
Da 4:19 Daniel (also called **B**) was greatly A10108
Da 4:19 So the king said, "**B**, do not let the A10108
Da 4:19 **B** answered, "My lord, if only the dream A10108
Da 5:12 whom the king called **B**, was found to A10108
Da 10: 1 who was called **B**). Its message was true H1171

BELTS (3) [BELT]

Eze 23:15 with **b** around their waists and H2513+258
Mt 10: 9 copper to take with you in your **b**— G2438
Mk 6: 8 no bread, no bag, no money in your **b**. G2438

BEMOAN, BEMOANED, BEMOANING (KJV)

COMFORTED, MOANING, MOURN, SHOW SYMPATHY

BEN HINNOM (10) [HINNOM]

Jos 15: 8 up the Valley of **B** along the H1208
Jos 18:16 of the hill facing the Valley of **B**, H1208
2Ki 23:10 which was in the Valley of **B**, so H1208
2Ch 28: 3 in the Valley of **B** and sacrificed H1208
2Ch 33: 6 in the fire in the Valley of **B**, H1208
Jer 7:31 in the Valley of **B** to burn their H1208
Jer 7:32 call it Topheth or the Valley of **B**, H1208
Jer 19: 2 go out to the Valley of **B** H1208
Jer 19: 6 place Topheth or the Valley of **B**, H1208
Jer 32:35 in the Valley of **B** to sacrifice their H1208

BEN-ABINADAB (1) [ABINADAB]

1Ki 4:11 **B**—in Naphoth Dor (he was married to H1203

BEN-AMMI (1)

Ge 19:38 she named him **B**; he is the father of H1214

BEN-DEKER (1)

1Ki 4: 9 **B**—in Makaz, Shaalbim, Beth Shemesh H1206

BEN-GEBER (1) [GEBER]

1Ki 4:13 **B**—in Ramoth Gilead (the settlements of H1205

BEN-HADAD (28) [BEN-HADAD'S, HADAD]

1Ki 15:18 sent them to **B** son of Tabrimmon, H1207
1Ki 15:20 **B** agreed with King Asa and sent the H1207
1Ki 20: 1 Now **B** king of Aram mustered his entire H1207
1Ki 20: 2 king of Israel, saying, "This is what **B** says: H1207
1Ki 20: 5 again and said, "This is what **B** says: H1207
1Ki 20: 9 They left and took the answer back to **B**. H2084S
1Ki 20:10 Then **B** sent another message to Ahab H1207
1Ki 20:12 **B** heard this message while he and the NDT
1Ki 20:16 set out at noon while **B** and the 32 kings H1207
1Ki 20:17 Now **B** had dispatched scouts, who H1207
1Ki 20:20 But **B** king of Aram escaped on horseback H1207
1Ki 20:26 The next spring **B** mustered the Arameans H1207
1Ki 20:30 And **B** fled to the city and hid in an inner H1207
1Ki 20:32 of Israel and said, "Your servant **B** says: H1207
1Ki 20:33 "Yes, your brother **B**!" they said. H1207
1Ki 20:33 When **B** came out, Ahab had him come H1207
1Ki 20:34 my father took from your father," **B** offered. NDT
2Ki 6:24 **B** king of Aram mobilized his entire army H1207
2Ki 8: 7 to Damascus, and **B** king of Aram was ill. H1207
2Ki 8: 9 "Your son **B** king of Aram has sent me to H1207
2Ki 8:14 When **B** asked, "What did NDT
2Ki 13: 3 of Hazael king of Aram and **B** his son. H1207
2Ki 13:24 and **B** his son succeeded him as king. H1207
2Ki 13:25 recaptured from **B** son of Hazael the H1207
2Ch 16: 2 own palace and sent it to **B** king of Aram, H1207
2Ch 16: 4 **B** agreed with King Asa and sent the H1207
Jer 49:27 it will consume the fortresses of **B**. H1207
Am 1: 4 that will consume the fortresses of **B**. H1207

BEN-HADAD'S (1) [BEN-HADAD]

1Ki 20: 9 So he replied to **B** messengers, "Tell my H1207

BEN-HAIL (1)

2Ch 17: 7 year of his reign he sent his officials **B**, H1211

BEN-HANAN (1) [HANAN]

1Ch 4:20 Amnon, Rinnah, **B** and Tilon. H1212

BEN-HESED (1)

1Ki 4:10 **B**—in Arubboth (Sokoh and all the land of H1213

BEN-HUR (1) [HUR]

1Ki 4: 8 are their names: **B**—in the hill country H1210

BEN-ONI (1)

Ge 35:18 she was dying—she named her son **B**. H1204

BEN-ZOHETH (1)

1Ch 4:20 The descendants of Ishi: Zoheth and **B**. H1209

BENAIAH (45)

2Sa 8:18 **B** son of Jehoiada was over the Kerethites H1226
2Sa 20:23 **B** son of Jehoiada was over the Kerethites H1225
2Sa 23:20 **B** son of Jehoiada, a valiant fighter from H1226
2Sa 23:21 in his hand, **B** went against him with a club. NDT
2Sa 23:22 were the exploits of **B** son of Jehoiada; H1226
2Sa 23:30 **B** the Pirathonite, Hiddai from the ravines H1226
1Ki 1: 8 But Zadok the priest, **B** son of Jehoiada H1226
1Ki 1:10 the prophet or **B** or the special guard H1226
1Ki 1:26 the priest, and **B** son of Jehoiada, and H1226
1Ki 1:32 the prophet and **B** son of Jehoiada." H1226
1Ki 1:36 **B** son of Jehoiada answered the king H1226
1Ki 1:38 Nathan the prophet, **B** son of Jehoiada H1226
1Ki 1:44 Nathan the prophet, **B** son of Jehoiada H1226
1Ki 2:25 gave orders to **B** son of Jehoiada, H1226
1Ki 2:29 Then Solomon ordered **B** son of Jehoiada, H1226
1Ki 2:30 So **B** entered the tent of the LORD and said H1226
1Ki 2:30 **B** reported to the king, "This is how Joab H1226
1Ki 2:31 Then the king commanded **B**, "Do as he H2257S
1Ki 2:34 So **B** son of Jehoiada went up and struck H1226
1Ki 2:35 The king put **B** son of Jehoiada over the H1226
1Ki 2:46 king gave the order to **B** son of Jehoiada, H1226
1Ki 4: 4 **B** son of Jehoiada—commander in chief H1226
1Ch 4:36 Jeshohaiah, Asaiah, Adiel, Jesimiel, **B**, H1225
1Ch 11:22 **B** son of Jehoiada, a valiant fighter from H1225
1Ch 11:23 in his hand, **B** went against him with a club. NDT
1Ch 11:24 were the exploits of **B** son of Jehoiada; H1226
1Ch 11:31 Gibeah in Benjamin, **B** the Pirathonite, H1225
1Ch 15:18 Unni, Eliab, **B**, Maaseiah H1226
1Ch 15:20 Maaseiah and **B** were to play the lyres H1226
1Ch 15:24 **B** and Eliezer the priests were to blow H1226
1Ch 16: 5 Mattithiah, Eliab, **B**, Obed-Edom and H1226
1Ch 16: 6 **B** and Jahaziel the priests were to H1226
1Ch 18:17 **B** son of Jehoiada was over the Kerethites H1226
1Ch 27: 5 was **B** son of Jehoiada the priest. H1226
1Ch 27: 6 This was the **B** who was a mighty warrior H1226
1Ch 27:14 eleventh month, was **B** the Pirathonite, an H1225
1Ch 27:34 by Jehoiada son of **B** and by Abiathar. H1226
2Ch 20:14 Zechariah, the son of **B**, the son of Jeiel, H1225
2Ch 31:13 Mahath and **B** were assistants of H1226
Ezr 10:25 Mijamin, Eleazar, Malkijah and **B**. H1225
Ezr 10:30 Kelal, **B**, Maaseiah, Mattaniah H1225
Ezr 10:35 **B**, Bedeiah, Keluhi, H1225

B

Ezr 10:43 Zebina, Jaddai, Joel and B. H1225
Eze 11: 1 son of Azzur and Pelatiah son of B, H1226
Eze 11:13 I was prophesying, Pelatiah son of B died. H1225

BENCHES (2)
Mt 21:12 changers and the b of those selling doves G2756
Mk 11:15 changers and the b of those selling doves G2756

BEND (8) [BENDING, BENT]
Ge 49:15 *he will* b his shoulder to the burden and H5742
2Sa 22:35 battle; my arms *can* b a bow of bronze. H5737
Ps 7:12 his sword; *he will* b and string his bow. H2005
Ps 11: 2 For look, the wicked b their bows; they set H2005
Ps 18:34 battle; my arms *can* b a bow of bronze. H5737
Ps 37:14 draw the sword and b the bow to bring H2005
Zec 9:13 *I will* b Judah as I bend my bow and fill it H2005
Zec 9:13 I will bend Judah as I b my bow and fill it NDT

BENDING (1) [BEND]
Lk 24:12 **B over**, he saw the strips of linen lying by G4160

BENE BERAK (1)
Jos 19:45 B, Gath Rimmon, H1222

BENE JAAKAN (3)
Nu 33:31 left Moseroth and camped at B. H1223
Nu 33:32 They left B and camped at Hor H1223
Dt 10: 6 from the wells of B to Moserah. H1223

BENEATH (20) [UNDERNEATH]
Ex 20: 4 on the earth b or in the waters H4946+9393
Lev 26:19 like iron and the **ground** *b* you like bronze. AIT
Dt 5: 8 on the earth b or in the waters H4946+9393
Dt 28:23 will be bronze, the ground b you iron. H9393
2Sa 22:39 they could not rise; they fell b my feet. H9393
1Ki 8: 6 put it b the wings of the cherubim. H9393
2Ch 5: 7 put it b the wings of the cherubim. H9393
Job 26: 5 those b the waters and all that live H4946+9393
Job 37: 3 his lightning b the whole heaven and H9393
Ps 18:38 they could not rise; they fell b my feet. H9393
Ps 45: 5 enemies; let the nations fall b your feet. H9393
Isa 14:11 are spread out b you and worms cover H9393
Isa 44:23 has done this; shout aloud, you earth b. H9397
Isa 51: 6 look at the earth b; the heavens H4946+9393
Eze 10: 2 "Go in among the wheels b the cherubim. H9393
Eze 10:20 I had seen b the God of Israel by H9393
Eze 24: 5 Pile wood b it for the bones; bring it to a H9393
Joel 1:17 The seeds are shriveled b the clods. H9393
Jnh 2: 6 sank down; the earth b barred me in forever. NDT
Mic 1: 4 The mountains melt b him and the H9393

BENEFACTOR (1) [BENEFACTORS]
Ro 16: 2 she has been the b of many people G4706

BENEFACTORS (1) [BENEFACTOR]
Lk 22:25 authority over them call themselves B. G2309

BENEFICIAL (2) [BENEFIT]
1Co 6:12 you say—but not everything *is* b. G5237
1Co 10:23 you say—but not everything *is* b. G5237

BENEFIT (18) [BENEFICIAL, BENEFITED, BENEFITS]
Job 22: 2 "*Can* a man **be of** b to God? Can even a H6122
Job 22: 2 *Can* even a wise person b him? H6122
Pr 11:17 Those who are kind b themselves, but the H1694
Ecc 5:11 And what b are they to the owners except H4179
Isa 38:17 Surely it was for my b that I suffered such H8934
Isa 57:12 your works, and *they will* not b you. H3603
Jer 23:32 *They do* not b these people **in the least** H3603+3603
Jn 11:42 I said this **for the** b **of** the people G1328
Jn 12:30 "This voice was **for** your b, not mine. G1328
Ro 6:21 What b did you reap at that time from the G2843
Ro 6:22 the b you reap leads to holiness G2843
1Co 4: 6 things to myself and Apollos **for** your b, G1328
2Co 1:15 you first so that *you might* b twice. G5921+2400
2Co 4:15 All this is **for** your b, so that the grace that G1328
Eph 4:29 that *it may* b those who listen. G1443+5921
Phm 20 *that I may* **have** *some* b from you in the G3949
Heb 13: 9 which *is of* no b to those who do so. G6067
Heb 13:17 a burden, for that would be **of no** b to you. G269

BENEFITED (1) [BENEFIT]
1Sa 19: 4 what he has done has b you greatly. H3202

BENEFITS (4) [BENEFIT]
Dt 18: 8 He is to share equally in their b, even H2750
Ps 103: 2 my soul, and forget not all his b— H1691
Ecc 7:11 is a good thing and b those who see the H3463
Jn 4:38 you *have* **reaped the** b **of** their labor." G1656

BENINU (1)
Ne 10:13 Hodiah, Bani and B. H1231

BENJAMIN (135) [BENJAMIN'S, BENJAMITE, BENJAMITES]
Ge 35:18 But his father named him B. H1228
Ge 35:24 The sons of Rachel: Joseph and B. H1228
Ge 42: 4 But Jacob did not send B, Joseph's brother, H1228
Ge 42:36 is no more, and now you want to take B. H1228
Ge 43:14 other brother and B come back with you. H1228
Ge 43:15 double the amount of silver, and B also. H1228
Ge 43:16 When Joseph saw B with them, he said to H1228
Ge 43:29 As he looked about and saw his brother B, H1228
Ge 45:12 so can my brother B, that it is really I H1228
Ge 45:14 his arms around his brother B and wept, H1228
Ge 45:14 wept, and B embraced him, weeping. H1228
Ge 45:22 to B he gave three hundred shekels of H1228
Ge 46:19 of Jacob's wife Rachel: Joseph and B. H1228
Ge 46:21 The sons of B: Bela, Beker, Ashbel, Gera H1228
Ge 49:27 "B is a ravenous wolf; in the morning he H1228
Ex 1: 3 Issachar, Zebulun and B; H1228
Nu 1:11 from B, Abidan son of Gideoni; H1228
Nu 1:36 From the descendants of B: All the men H1228
Nu 1:37 number from the tribe of B was 35,400. H1228
Nu 2:22 The tribe of B will be next. The leader of H1228
Nu 2:22 leader of the people of B is Abidan son of H1228
Nu 7:60 the leader of the people of B, brought his H1228
Nu 10:24 over the division of the tribe of B. H1201+1228
Nu 13: 9 from the tribe of B, Palti son of Raphu; H1228
Nu 26:38 The descendants of B by their clans were H1228
Nu 26:41 These were the clans of B; those H1201+1228
Nu 34:21 Elidad son of Kislon, from the tribe of B; H1228
Dt 27:12 Judah, Issachar, Joseph and B. H1228
Dt 33:12 About B he said: "Let the beloved of the H1228
Jos 18:11 up for the tribe of B according to its H1201+1228
Jos 18:20 of the clans of B on all sides. H1201+1228
Jos 18:21 The tribe of B, according to its H1201+1228
Jos 18:28 the inheritance of B for its clans. H1201+1228
Jos 21: 4 from the tribes of Judah, Simeon and B. H1228
Jos 21:17 from the tribe of B they gave them Gibeon H1228
Jdg 5:14 B was with the people who followed you. H1228
Jdg 10: 9 fight against Judah, B and Ephraim; Israel H1228
Jdg 19:14 the sun set as they neared Gibeah in B. H1228
Jdg 20: 4 came to Gibeah in B to spend the night. H1228
Jdg 20:10 when the army arrives at Gibeah in B, it H1228
Jdg 20:12 messengers throughout the tribe of B, H1228
Jdg 20:17 apart from B, mustered four H1228
Jdg 20:24 drew near to B the second day. H1201+1228
Jdg 20:35 The LORD defeated B before Israel, and on H1228
Jdg 20:36 the men of Israel had given way before B, H1228
Jdg 20:48 went back to B and put all the H1201+1228
Jdg 21: 6 the Israelites grieved for the **tribe of** B, H1228
Jdg 21:15 The people grieved for B, because the H1228
Jdg 21:16 "With the women of B destroyed, how H1228
Jdg 21:21 Then return to the land of B. H1228
1Sa 9: 1 the son of Aphiah of B. H1201+408+3549
1Sa 9: 4 Then he passed through the territory of B H3549
1Sa 9:16 I will send you a man from the land of B. H1228
1Sa 9:21 the least of all the clans of the tribe of B? H1228
1Sa 10: 2 at Zelzah on the border of B. H1228
1Sa 10:20 by tribes, the tribe of B was taken by lot. H1228
1Sa 10:21 Then he brought forward the tribe of B H1228
1Sa 13: 2 were with Jonathan at Gibeah in B. H1228
1Sa 13:15 left Gilgal and went up to Gibeah in B, H1228
1Sa 13:16 with them were staying in Gibeah in B, H1228
1Sa 14:16 at Gibeah in B saw the army melting H1228
1Sa 22: 7 to them, "Listen, **men of** B! Will the son of H1229
2Sa 2: 9 also over Ephraim, B and all Israel. H1228
2Sa 2:15 twelve men for B and Ish-Bosheth son of H1228
2Sa 2:25 Then the men of B rallied behind Abner H1228
2Sa 3:19 the whole tribe of B wanted to do. H1228
2Sa 4: 2 the Beerothite from the tribe of B— H1228
2Sa 4: 2 Beeroth is considered part of B, H1228
2Sa 21:14 at Zela in B, and did H824+1228
2Sa 23:29 Ithai son of Ribai from Gibeah in B H1201+1228
1Ki 4:18 Shimei son of Ela—in B; H1228
1Ki 12:21 mustered all Judah and the tribe of B— H1228
1Ki 12:23 to all Judah and B, and to the rest of the H1228
1Ki 15:22 With them King Asa built up Geba in B H1228
1Ch 2: 2 Joseph, B, Naphtali, Gad and Asher. H1228
1Ch 6:60 And from the tribe of B they were given H1228
1Ch 6:65 Simeon and B they allotted the H1201+1228
1Ch 7: 6 Three sons of B: Bela, Beker and Jediael. H1228
1Ch 7:10 B, Ehud, Kenaanah, Zethan H1228
1Ch 8: 1 B was the father of Bela his firstborn H1228
1Ch 8:40 All these were the descendants of B. H1228
1Ch 9: 3 from Judah, from B, and from H1201+1228
1Ch 9: 9 The **people from** B, as listed in their H278+2157
1Ch 11:31 Ithai son of Ribai from Gibeah in B H1201+1228
1Ch 12: 2 were relatives of Saul from the **tribe of** B): H1228
1Ch 12:29 from B, Saul's tribe—3,000, most H1201+1228
1Ch 21: 6 not include Levi and B in the numbering, H1228
1Ch 27:21 of Zechariah; over B: Jaasiel son of Abner H1228
2Ch 11: 1 he mustered Judah and B—a hundred H1228
2Ch 11: 3 of Judah and to all Israel in Judah and B, H1228
2Ch 11:10 These were fortified cities in Judah and B H1228
2Ch 11:12 So Judah and B were his. H1228
2Ch 11:23 throughout the districts of Judah and B, H1228
2Ch 14: 8 two hundred and eighty thousand from B, H1228
2Ch 15: 2 "Listen to me, Asa and all Judah and B. H1228
2Ch 15: 8 land of Judah and B and from the towns H1228
2Ch 15: 9 all Judah and B and the people from H1228
2Ch 17:17 From B: Eliada, a valiant soldier, with H1228
2Ch 25: 5 of hundreds for all Judah and B. H1228
2Ch 31: 1 Judah and B and in Ephraim and H1228
2Ch 34: 9 of Judah and B and the inhabitants H1228
2Ch 34:32 in Jerusalem and B pledge themselves to H1228
Ezr 1: 5 Then the family heads of Judah and B H1228
Ezr 4: 1 enemies of Judah and B heard that the H1228
Ezr 10: 9 the men of Judah and B had gathered in H1228
Ezr 10:32 B, Malluk and Shemariah. H1228
Ne 3:23 B and Hasshub made repairs in front of H1228
Ne 11: 4 both Judah and B lived in Jerusalem): H1228
Ne 11: 7 From the descendants of B: Sallu son of H1228
Ne 11:36 of the Levites of Judah settled in B. H1228
Ne 12:34 B, Shemaiah, Jeremiah, H1228
Est 2: 5 of Susa a Jew of the **tribe of** B, H408+3549
Ps 68:27 There is the little **tribe of** B, leading them H1228
Ps 80: 2 before Ephraim, B and Manasseh H1228
Jer 1: 1 priests at Anathoth in the territory of B. H1228
Jer 6: 1 people of B! Flee from Jerusalem! H1228
Jer 17:26 from the territory of B and the western H1228
Jer 20: 2 the Upper Gate of B at the LORD's temple H1228
Jer 32: 8 my field at Anathoth in the territory of B. H1228
Jer 32:44 sealed and witnessed in the territory of B H1228
Jer 33:13 in the territory of B, in the villages around H1228
Jer 37:12 go to the territory of B to get his share of H1228
Jer 37:13 But when he reached the B Gate, the H1228
Jer 38: 7 While the king was sitting in the B Gate, H1228
Eze 48:22 the border of Judah and the border of B. H1228
Eze 48:23 B will have one portion; it will extend H1228
Eze 48:24 border the territory of B from east to west. H1228
Eze 48:32 the gate of B and the gate of Dan. H1228
Hos 5: 8 the battle cry in Beth Aven; lead on, B. H1228
Ob 19 Samaria, and B will possess Gilead. H1228
Zec 14:10 up high from the B Gate to the site of the H1228
Ac 13:21 of the tribe *of* B, who ruled forty G1021
Ro 11: 1 of Abraham, from the tribe *of* B. G1021
Php 3: 5 of the tribe *of* B, a Hebrew of G1021
Rev 7: 8 12,000, from the tribe *of* B 12,000. G1021

BENJAMIN'S (2) [BENJAMIN]
Ge 43:34 B portion was five times as much as H1228
Ge 44:12 And the cup was found in B sack. H1228

BENJAMITE (14) [BENJAMIN]
Jdg 3:15 a left-handed man, the son of Gera the B. H1229
Jdg 20:46 twenty-five thousand B swordsmen fell, H1228
Jdg 21: 1 will give his daughter in marriage to a B." H1228
Jdg 21:17 The B survivors must have heirs," they said, H1228
Jdg 21:18 be anyone who gives a wife to a B. H1228
1Sa 4:12 That same day a B ran from the H408+1228
1Sa 9: 1 There was a B, a man of standing H4946+1228
1Sa 9:21 "But am I not a B, from the smallest tribe H1229
2Sa 16:11 then, this B! Leave him alone; H1229
2Sa 19:16 son of Gera, the B from Bahurim, hurried H1229
2Sa 20: 1 son of Bikri, a B, happened to be H408+3549
1Ki 2: 8 son of Gera, the B from Bahurim, who H1229
1Ch 27:12 was Abiezer the Anathothite, a B. H1229
Ps 7: T he sang to the LORD concerning Cush, a B. H1229

BENJAMITES (34) [BENJAMIN]
Jdg 1:21 The B, however, did not drive out H1201+1228
Jdg 1:21 the Jebusites live there with the B. H1201+1228
Jdg 19:16 the inhabitants of the place were B), H1229
Jdg 20: 3 The B heard that the Israelites had H1201+1228
Jdg 20:13 But the B would not listen to their H1201+1228
Jdg 20:15 At once the B mobilized twenty-six H1201+1228
Jdg 20:18 to go up first to fight against the B?" H1201+1228
Jdg 20:20 went out to fight the B and took up battle H1228
Jdg 20:21 The B came out of Gibeah and cut H1201+1228
Jdg 20:23 go up again to fight against the B, H1201+1228
Jdg 20:25 when the B came out from Gibeah to H1228
Jdg 20:28 go up again to fight against the B, H1201+1228
Jdg 20:30 up against the B on the third day H1201+1228
Jdg 20:31 The B came out to meet them and H1201+1228
Jdg 20:32 While the B were saying, "We are H1201+1228
Jdg 20:34 was so heavy that **the** B did not realize H2156S
Jdg 20:35 day the Israelites struck down 25,100 B, H1228
Jdg 20:36 Then the B saw that they were H1201+1228
Jdg 20:39 The B had begun to inflict casualties on H1228
Jdg 20:40 the B turned and saw the whole city going H1228
Jdg 20:41 and the B were terrified, because H408+1228
Jdg 20:43 They surrounded the B, chased them and H1228
Jdg 20:44 Eighteen thousand B fell, all of them H1228
Jdg 20:45 kept pressing after **the** B as far as Gidom H2257S
Jdg 21:13 of peace to the B at the rock of H1201+1228
Jdg 21:14 So the B returned at that time and were H1228
Jdg 21:20 So they instructed the B, saying H1201+1228
Jdg 21:23 So that is what the B did. H1201+1228
2Sa 2:31 and sixty B who were with H408+4946+1228
2Sa 3:19 Abner also spoke to the B in person. H1228
2Sa 19:17 With him were a thousand B, along H4946+1228
1Ch 9: 7 Of the B: Sallu son of Meshullam H1201+1228
1Ch 12:16 Other B and some men from Judah H1201+1228
Ne 11:31 descendants of the B from Geba lived in H1228

BENO (2)
1Ch 24:26 Mahli and Mushi. The son of Jaaziah: B. H1217
1Ch 24:27 from Jaaziah: B, Shoham, Zakkur and Ibri. H1217

BENOTH See SUKKOTH BENOTH

BENT (21) [BEND]
Ex 10:10 Clearly you are b **on** evil. H5584+7156
1Sa 24: 9 men say, 'David *is* b **on** harming you'? H1335
1Ki 18:42 b **down** to the ground and put his face H1566
Ps 44:16 of the enemy, *who is* b **on revenge**. H5933
Ps 69:23 cannot see, and their backs *be* b forever. H5048
Ps 106:43 they were b **on** rebellion and H928+6783
Pr 16:30 whoever purses their lips *is* b **on** evil. H3983
Pr 17:12 robbed of her cubs than a fool b **on** folly. H928
Isa 21:15 from the b bow and from the heat of H2005
Isa 32: 6 speak folly, their hearts *are* b **on** evil: H6913
Isa 51:13 of the oppressor, who *is* b **on** destruction? H3922
Eze 22: 9 who are b **on** shedding blood; H4200+5100
Da 11:27 with their hearts b **on** evil, will sit at the H4200
Hos 11: 4 to the cheek, and *I* b **down** to feed them. H5742

Lk 4:39 So *he* **b** over her and rebuked the fever *G2392*
Lk 13:11 She was **b over** and could not straighten *G5174*
Jn 8: 6 But Jesus **b** down and started to write on *G3252*
Jn 20: 5 *He* **b over** and looked in at the strips of *G4160*
Jn 20:11 she wept, *she* **b over to look** into the tomb *G4160*
Ro 11:10 cannot see, and their backs *be* **b** forever." *G5159*
Rev 6: 2 rode out as a conqueror **b on** conquest. *G2671*

BEON (1)
Nu 32: 3 Heshbon, Elealeh, Sebam, Nebo and **B**— H1274

BEOR (10) [BEZER]
Ge 36:32 Bela son of **B** became king of Edom. H1242
Nu 22: 5 messengers to summon Balaam son of **B**, H1242
Nu 24: 3 "The prophecy of Balaam son of **B**, the H1242
Nu 24:15 "The prophecy of Balaam son of **B**, the H1242
Nu 31: 8 killed Balaam son of **B** with the sword. H1242
Dt 23: 4 Balaam son of **B** from Pethor in Aram H1242
Jos 13:22 had put to the sword Balaam son of **B**, H1242
Jos 24: 9 Balaam son of **B** to put a curse on you. H1242
1Ch 1:43 Bela son of **B**, whose city was named H1242
Mic 6: 5 what Balaam son of **B** answered. H1242

BEQUEATH (1)
Lev 25:46 *You can* **b** them to your children as H5706

BERA (1)
Ge 14: 2 went to war against **B** king of Sodom, H1396

BERACAH (NIV84) BERAKAH

BERAIAH (1)
1Ch 8:21 **B** and Shimrath were the sons of Shimei. H1349

BERAK See BENE BERAK

BERAKAH (3)
1Ch 12: 3 sons of Azmaveth; **B**, Jehu the H1389
2Ch 20:26 day they assembled in the Valley of **B**, H1390
2Ch 20:26 why it is called the Valley of **B** to this day. H1390

BEREA (4) [BEREAN]
Ac 17:10 believers sent Paul and Silas away to **B**. *G1023*
Ac 17:13 Paul was preaching the word of God at **B**, *G1023*
Ac 17:14 but Silas and Timothy stayed **at B**. *G1695S*
Ac 20: 4 by Sopater son of Pyrrhus **from B**, *G1024*

BEREAN (1) [BEREA]
Ac 17:11 Now **the B Jews** were of more noble *G4047S*

BEREAVE (1) [BEREAVED, BEREAVEMENT, BEREAVES]
Hos 9:12 rear children, *I will* **b** them of every one. H8897

BEREAVED (4) [BEREAVE]
Ge 43:14 As for me, if *I am* **b**, I am bereaved." H8897
Ge 43:14 As for me, if I am bereaved, *I am* **b**." H8897
Ps 35:12 me evil for good and leave me like *one* **b**. H8890
Isa 49:21 I was **b** and barren; I was exiled and H8892

BEREAVEMENT (2) [BEREAVE]
Isa 49:20 born during your **b** will yet say in your H8898
Jer 15: 7 *I will* **bring b** and destruction on my H8897

BEREAVES (1) [BEREAVE]
La 1:20 Outside, the sword **b**; inside, there is only H8897

BERED (2)
Ge 16:14 it is still there, between Kadesh and **B**. H1354
1Ch 7:20 Shuthelah, **B** his son, Tahath his son H1355

BEREKIAH (12)
1Ch 3:20 Hashubah, Ohel, **B**, Hasadiah and H1392
1Ch 6:39 Asaph son of **B**, the son of Shimea, H1393
1Ch 9:16 of Jeduthun; and **B** son of Asa, the son H1392
1Ch 15:17 relatives, Asaph son of **B**; and from their H1393
1Ch 15:23 **B** and Elkanah were to be doorkeepers H1392
2Ch 28:12 son of Jehohanan, **B** son of Meshillemoth H1393
Ne 3: 4 Next to him Meshullam son of **B**, the son H1392
Ne 3:30 Meshullam son of **B** made repairs H1392
Ne 6:18 the daughter of Meshullam son of **B**. H1392
Zec 1: 1 came to the prophet Zechariah son of **B**, H1392
Zec 1: 7 came to the prophet Zechariah son of **B**, H1393
Mt 23:35 Abel to the blood of Zechariah son *of* **B**, *G974*

BERI (1)
1Ch 7:36 Harnepher, Shual, **B**, Imrah, H1373

BERIAH (11) [BERIITE]
Ge 46:17 Ishvi and **B**. Their sister was Serah H1380
Ge 46:17 The sons of **B**: Heber and Malkiel. H1380
Nu 26:44 Ishvite clan; through **B**, the Beriite clan; H1380
Nu 26:45 through the descendants of **B** H1380
1Ch 7:23 He named him **B**, because there had H1380
1Ch 7:30 Ishvi and **B**. Their sister was Serah H1380
1Ch 7:31 The sons of **B**: Heber and Malkiel, who H1380
1Ch 8:13 **B** and Shema, who were heads of H1380
1Ch 8:16 Ishpah and Joha were the sons of **B**. H1380
1Ch 23:10 Jeush and **B**. These were the sons of H1380
1Ch 23:11 Jeush and **B** did not have many sons H1380

BERIITE (1) [BERIAH]
Nu 26:44 Ishvite clan; through Beriah, the **B** clan; H1381

BERITES (NIV84) BIKRITES

BERNICE (3)
Ac 25:13 King Agrippa and **B** arrived at Caesarea to *G1022*
Ac 25:23 day Agrippa and **B** came with great pomp *G1022*
Ac 26:30 him the governor and **B** and those sitting *G1022*

BERODACH-BALADAN (KJV) MARDUK-BALADAN

BEROTHAH (1)
Eze 47:16 **B** and Sibraim (which lies on the border H1363

BEROTHAI (1) [BEROTHITE]
2Sa 8: 8 From Tebah and **B**, towns that belonged to H1408

BEROTHITE (1) [BEROTHAI]
1Ch 11:39 Naharai the **B**, the armor-bearer of H1409

BERRIES (KJV) OLIVES

BERYL (4)
Ex 28:17 row shall be carnelian, chrysolite and **b**; H1403
Ex 39:10 first row was carnelian, chrysolite and **b**; H1403
Eze 28:13 jasper, lapis lazuli, turquoise and **b**. H1404
Rev 21:20 chrysolite, the eighth **b**, the ninth topaz, *G1039*

BESAI (2)
Ezr 2:49 Uzza, Paseah, **B**, H1234
Ne 7:52 **B**, Meunim, Nephusim, H1234

BESEECH, BESEECHING, BESOUGHT (KJV) BEG, BEGGED, INTERCEDED, NOW, PLEADED, PLEASE, SOUGHT

BESET (1)
Ps 55: 5 Fear and trembling *have* **b** me; horror H995+928

BESIDE (88) [BESIDES, SIDE]
Ge 16: 7 it was the spring that is **b** the road to Shur. H928
Ge 23: 3 rose from **b** his dead wife and H6584+7156
Ge 24:13 I am standing **b** this spring, and the H6584
Ge 24:43 I am standing **b** this spring. If a H6584
Ge 38:21 prostitute who was **b** the road at Enaim?" H6584
Ge 39:15 he left his cloak **b** me and ran out of the H725
Ge 39:16 She kept his cloak **b** her until his master H725
Ge 39:18 he left his cloak **b** me and ran out of the H725
Ge 41: 3 of the Nile and stood **b** those on the H725
Ge 48: 7 So I buried her there **b** the road to Ephrath H928
Lev 6:10 on the altar and place them **b** the altar. H725
Lev 10:12 presented to the LORD and eat it **b** the altar, H725
Nu 23: 3 "Stay here **b** your offering while I go aside H6584
Nu 23: 6 found him standing **b** his offering, H6584
Nu 23:15 "Stay here **b** your offering while I meet H6584
Nu 23:17 found him standing **b** his offering, H6584
Nu 24: 6 like gardens **b** a river, like aloes H6584
Nu 24: 6 by the LORD, like cedars **b** the waters. H6584
Dt 12:27 must be poured **b** the altar of the LORD H6584
Dt 16:21 wooden Asherah pole **b** the altar you build H725
Dt 22: 6 If you come across a bird's nest **b** the road H928
Dt 31:26 Law and place it **b** the ark of the H4946+7396
Jdg 6:25 Baal and cut down the Asherah pole **b** it. H6584
Jdg 6:28 the Asherah pole **b** it cut down and the H6584
Jdg 6:30 altar and cut down the Asherah pole **b** it." H6584
Jdg 9: 6 Beth Millo gathered **b** the great tree at H6640
1Sa 1:26 who stood here **b** you praying to the H6640
1Sa 5: 2 into Dagon's temple and set it **b** Dagon. H725
1Sa 6: 8 and in a chest **b** it put the gold H4946+7396
1Sa 6:14 there it stopped **b** a large rock. H9004
1Sa 26: 3 Saul made his camp **b** the road on the hill H6584
2Sa 1:10 "So I stood **b** him and killed him, because H6584
2Sa 6: 7 and he died there **b** the ark of God. H6640
2Sa 12:17 his household stood **b** him to get him up H6584
2Sa 18: 4 So the king stood **b** the gate while H448+3338
2Sa 20:11 of Joab's men stood **b** Amasa and said, H6584
1Ki 1: 2 She can lie **b** him so that our lord H928+2668
1Ki 2:29 to the tent of the LORD and was **b** the altar. H725
1Ki 10:19 with a lion standing **b** each of them. H725
1Ki 13:24 both the donkey and the lion standing **b** it. H725
1Ki 13:25 with the lion standing **b** the body, and they H725
1Ki 13:28 with the donkey and the lion standing **b** it. H725
1Ki 13:31 of God is buried; lay my bones **b** his bones. H725
2Ki 11:14 officers and the trumpeters were **b** the king, H448
2Ki 12: 9 He placed it **b** the altar, on the right side H725
2Ch 9:18 with a lion standing **b** each of them. H725
2Ch 23:13 the trumpeters were **b** the king, H6584
Ne 2: 6 with the queen sitting **b** him, asked me, H725
Ne 3:17 **B** him, Hashabiah, ruler of half the H6584+3338
Ne 3:23 son of Ananiah, made repairs **b** his house. H725
Ne 8: 4 **B** him on his right stood Mattithiah, Shema, H725
Job 18: 6 becomes dark; the lamp **b** him goes out. H6584
Ps 23: 2 pastures, he leads me **b** quiet waters, H6584
Pr 8: 3 **b** the gate leading into the city, at H4200+3338
SS 1: 7 like a veiled woman **b** the flocks of your H6584
Isa 49: 9 "They will feed **b** the roads and find H6584
Isa 49:10 them and lead them **b** springs of water. H6584
Jer 17: 2 Asherah poles **b** the spreading trees H6584
Jer 31: 9 I will lead them **b** streams of water on a H448
Jer 36:21 all the officials standing **b** him. H4946+6584
Eze 1:15 wheel on the ground **b** each creature with H725
Eze 1:19 the wheels **b** them moved; and H725
Eze 3:13 the sound of the wheels **b** them, H4200+6645
Eze 9: 2 They came in and stood **b** the bronze altar H725
Eze 10: 6 the man went in and stood **b** a wheel. H725
Eze 10: 9 I saw **b** the cherubim four wheels H725
Eze 10: 9 four wheels, one **b** each of the cherubim H725
Eze 10:16 the wheels **b** them moved; and H725
Eze 11:22 with the wheels **b** them, spread H4200+6645
Eze 32:13 all her cattle from **b** abundant waters no H6584
Eze 39:15 bone will leave a marker **b** it until the H725
Eze 43: 6 While the man was standing **b** me, I heard H725
Eze 43: 8 their doorposts **b** my doorposts, H725
Da 8: 2 in the vision I was **b** the Ulai Canal. H6584
Da 8: 3 standing **b** the canal, and H4200+7156
Da 8: 6 had seen standing **b** the canal and H4200+7156
Am 2: 8 They lie down **b** every altar on garments H725
Zec 4:12 olive branches **b** the two gold pipes H928+3338
Mt 4:18 Jesus was walking **b** the Sea of Galilee, *G4123*
Mk 1:16 *As* Jesus **walked b** the Sea of Galilee, he *G4135*
Mk 2:13 Once again Jesus went out **b** the lake. *G4123*
Lk 9:47 a little child and had him stand **b** him. *G4123*
Lk 24: 4 that gleamed like lightning **stood b** them. *G2392*
Ac 1:10 two men dressed in white **stood b** them. *G4225*
Ac 5:10 her out and buried her **b** her husband. *G4639*
Ac 22:13 *He* **stood b** me and said, 'Brother Saul *G2392*
Ac 27:23 I belong and whom I serve **stood b** me *G4225*
Rev 15: 2 fire and, standing **b** the sea, those who *G2093*

BESIDES (41) [BESIDE]
Ge 20:12 **B**, she really is my sister, the H2256+1685
Ge 26: 1 **b** the previous famine in H4946+4200+963
Ge 31:50 if you take any wives **b** my daughters, H6584
Ge 38:22 **B**, the men who lived there said H2256+1685
Ge 46:15 in Paddan Aram, **b** his daughter Dinah. H2256
Ge 50: 8 **b** all the members of Joseph's household H2256
Ex 12:37 **b** women and children. H4200+963+4946
Nu 28:15 **B** the regular burnt offering with its drink H6584
Dt 4:35 **b** him there is no other. H4946+963+4200
Dt 32:39 There is no god **b** me. I put to death H6643
Jos 17: 5 tracts of land **b** Gilead and Bashan H4200+963
1Sa 2: 2 there is no one **b** you; there is no Rock H1194
2Sa 2:30 **B** Asahel, nineteen of David's men were H2256
2Sa 17: 8 **B**, your father is an experienced fighter H2256
2Sa 22:32 For who is God **b** the LORD? And H4946+1187
1Ki 10:13 **b** what he had given her out H4946+4200+963
1Ki 11: 1 foreign women **b** Pharaoh's daughter H2256
2Ki 21:16 **b** the sin that he had caused H4200+963+4946
1Ch 3: 9 **b** his sons by his concubines. H4946+4200+963
1Ch 29: 3 **B**, in my devotion to the temple of my God H6388
2Ch 17:19 **b** those he stationed in the H4946+4200+963
Ezr 2:65 **b** their 7,337 male and H4946+4200+963
Ezr 10:13 **B**, this matter cannot be taken care of in a H2256
Ne 7:67 **b** their 7,337 male and H4946+4200+963
Ps 18:31 For who is God **b** the LORD? And H4946+1187
Ps 73:25 And earth has nothing I desire **b** you. H6640
Ps 120: 3 do to you, and what **more b**, you deceitful H3578
Isa 26:13 other lords **b** you have ruled over us H2314
Isa 44: 8 Is there any God **b** me? No, H4946+1187
Isa 45: 6 people may know there is none **b** me. H1187
Isa 47: 8 to yourself, 'I am, and there is none **b** me. H6388
Isa 47:10 to yourself, 'I am, and there is none **b** me.' H6388
Isa 56: 8 still others to them **b** those already H4200
Isa 64: 4 no eye has seen any God **b** you, who acts H2314
Zep 2:15 And there is none **b** me." What a ruin she H6388
Mt 14:21 thousand men, **b** women and children. *G6006*
Mt 15:38 thousand men, **b** women and children. *G6006*
Lk 16:26 And **b** all this, between us and you a great *G1877*
Ac 21:28 And **b**, he has brought Greeks into the *G2285*
2Co 11:28 **B everything else**, I face daily *G6006+3836+4211*
1Ti 5:13 **B**, they get into the habit of being idle and *G275*

BESIEGE (10) [SIEGE]
Dt 20:19 that you *should* **b** them? H995+928+2021+5189
Dt 28:52 *They will* **b** all the cities throughout the H7674
1Sa 23: 8 down to Keilah to **b** David and his men. H7443
2Sa 12:28 of the troops and **b** the city and H2837+6584
2Ch 6:28 when enemies **b** them in any of their H7443
Ps 27: 3 Though an army **b** me, my heart H2837+6584
Isa 29: 2 Yet *I will* **b** Ariel; she will mourn and H7439
Isa 29: 7 that attack her and her fortress and **b** her H7439
Eze 4: 3 under siege, and *you shall* **b** it. This will H7443
Lk 11:53 and *to* **b** him **with questions**, *G694+4309+4498*

BESIEGED (10) [SIEGE]
Jdg 9:50 to Thebez and **b** it and captured it H2837+928
1Sa 11: 1 went up and **b** Jabesh Gilead. H2837+6584
2Sa 11: 1 destroyed the Ammonites and **b** Rabbah. H7443
2Sa 20:15 Joab came and **b** Sheba in Abel Beth H7443
1Ki 20: 1 he went up and **b** Samaria and attacked it H7443
2Ki 16: 5 up to fight against Jerusalem and **b** Ahaz, H7443
1Ch 20: 1 Ammonites and went to Rabbah and **b** it, H7443
La 3: 5 *He has* **b** me and surrounded me H1215+6584
Da 1: 1 of Babylon came to Jerusalem and **b** it. H7443
Zec 12: 2 Judah will be **b** as well as Jerusalem. H5189

BESIEGES (1) [SIEGE]
1Ki 8:37 when an enemy **b** them in any of their H7443

BESIEGING (7) [SIEGE]
1Ki 15:27 while Nadab and all Israel *were* **b** it. H7443
2Ki 24:11 up to the city while his officers *were* **b** it. H7443
Jer 4:16 'A **b** *army* is coming from a distant land H7443
Jer 21: 4 who *are* outside the wall **b** you. H7443
Jer 21: 9 the Babylonians who *are* **b** you will live; H7443
Jer 32: 2 king of Babylon *was* then **b** Jerusalem, H7443
Jer 37: 5 Babylonians who *were* **b** Jerusalem heard H7443

BESODEIAH (1)
Ne 3: 6 son of Paseah and Meshullam son of **B**. H1233

B

BESOM (KJV) BROOM

BESOR (2)
1Sa 30: 9 men with him came to the **B** Valley, H1410
1Sa 30:21 who were left behind at the **B** Valley. H1410

BEST (67) [GOOD]
Ge 16: 6 "Do with her whatever you think **b**." Then H3202
Ge 27:15 Rebekah took the **b** clothes of Esau her H2776
Ge 43:11 Put some of the **b products** *of* the land in H2380
Ge 45:18 I will give you the **b** *of* the land of Egypt H3206
Ge 45:20 because the **b** *of* all Egypt will be yours. H3206
Ge 45:23 loaded with the **b things** *of* Egypt, H3206
Ge 47: 6 your brothers in the **b** *part of* the land. H4774
Ge 47:11 them property in the **b** *part of* the land, H4774
Ex 14: 7 He took six hundred of the **b** chariots H1047
Ex 15: 4 The **b** *of* Pharaoh's officers are drowned H4436
Ex 22: 5 restitution from the **b** *of* their own field H4774
Ex 23:19 "Bring the **b** *of* the firstfruits of your soil to H8040
Ex 34:26 "Bring the **b** *of* the firstfruits of your soil to H8040
Nu 13:20 **Do** *your* **b** to bring back some of the fruit H2616
Nu 18:29 the LORD's portion the **b** and holiest part of H2693
Nu 18:30 'When you present the **b** part, it will be H2693
Nu 18:32 By presenting the **b** part of it you will not H2693
Dt 33:14 with the **b** the sun brings forth and the H4458
Dt 33:16 with the **b** gifts *of* the earth and its H4458
Dt 33:21 He chose the **b** land for himself; the H8040
Jos 8: 3 of his **b fighting men** and sent H2657+1475
Jos 10: 7 including all the **b fighting men**. H1475+2657
Jdg 10:15 Do with us whatever you think **b**, but H3202
Ru 3: 3 get dressed in your **b clothes**. H8529
1Sa 1:23 "Do what seems **b** to you," her husband H3202
1Sa 8:14 He will take the **b** of your fields and H3202
1Sa 8:16 servants and the **b** of your cattle and H3202
1Sa 14:36 "Do whatever seems **b** to you," they H3202
1Sa 14:40 "Do what seems **b** to you," they replied H3202
1Sa 15: 9 spared Agag and the **b** *of* the sheep and H4774
1Sa 15:15 they spared the **b** *of* the sheep and cattle H4774
1Sa 15:21 the **b** *of* what was devoted to God H8040
1Sa 27: 1 The **b** *thing* I can do is to escape to the H3202
2Sa 10: 9 some of the **b** *troops in* Israel and H1047
2Sa 18: 4 "I will do whatever seems **b** to you." H3512
1Ki 20: 3 the **b** of your wives and children are H3202
2Ki 10: 3 choose the **b** and most worthy of your H3202
2Ki 10: 5 as king; you do whatever you think **b**." H3202
1Ch 19:10 some of the **b** *troops* in Israel and H1047
Ezr 7:18 then do whatever **seems b** with the rest A10320
Est 2: 9 attendants into the **b** *place in* the harem. H3202
Est 3: 8 it is not **in** the king's **b interest** to tolerate H8750
Est 8: 8 in behalf of the Jews as seems **b** to you, H3202
Ps 90:10 the **b** *of* them are but trouble and H8106
SS 7: 9 your mouth like the **b** wine. May the H3202
Isa 25: 6 the **b** *of* meats and the finest of wines. H9043
Isa 48:17 who teaches you what *is* **b** for you, who H3603
Jer 18: 4 shaping it as seemed **b** to him. H3837
Jer 25:34 you will fall like the **b** *of* the rams. H2775
Eze 24: 4 Fill it with the **b** *of* these bones; H4436
Eze 31:16 the choicest and **b** *of* Lebanon, the H3202
Eze 44:30 The **b** *of* all the firstfruits and of all your H8040
Eze 48:14 This is the **b** *of* the land and must not H8040
Da 11:15 even their **b** troops will not have the H4436
Jnh 1:13 the men *did their* **b** *to* **row** back to land. AIT
Mic 7: 4 The **b** *of* them is like a brier, the most H3202
Zec 11:12 "If you think it **b**, give me my pay; H3202
Lk 15:22 Bring the **b** robe and put it on him *G4755*
Jn 2:10 but you have saved the **b** till now. *G2819*
2Co 8:10 judgment about what *is* **b** for you in this *G5237*
Php 1:10 to discern what *is* **b** and may be pure and *G1422*
1Th 3: 1 *we* **thought it b** to be left by ourselves in *G2305*
2Ti 2:15 **Do** *your* **b** to present yourself to God as *G5079*
2Ti 4: 9 **Do** *your* **b** to come to me quickly, *G5079*
2Ti 4:21 **Do** *your* **b** to get here before winter *G5079*
Titus 3:12 **do** *your* **b** to come to me at Nicopolis *G5079*
Heb 12:10 us for a little while as they **thought** *b*; AIT

BESTOW (5) [BESTOWED, BESTOWER, BESTOWING, BESTOWS]
Ps 31:19 who fear you, that *you* **b** in the sight of all H7188
Isa 45: 4 by name and **b** *on* you **a title of honor**, H4033
Isa 61: 3 to **b** on them a crown of beauty instead of H5989
Isa 62: 2 name that the mouth of the LORD *will* **b**. H5918
Jer 23: 2 I *will* **b punishment** on you *for* the evil you H7212

BESTOWED (4) [BESTOW]
1Ch 29:25 of all Israel and **b** on him royal splendor H5989
Ps 21: 5 *you have* **b** on him splendor and majesty. H8751
Ps 89:19 "*I have* **b** strength on a warrior; I have H8751
Jer 23: 2 them away and *have* not **b care on** them, H7212

BESTOWER (1) [BESTOW]
Isa 23: 8 the **b of crowns**, whose merchants H6497

BESTOWING (1) [BESTOW]
Pr 8:21 **b** a rich **inheritance** *on* those who love me H5706

BESTOWS (2) [BESTOW]
Ps 84:11 shield; the LORD **b** favor and honor; no H5989
Ps 133: 3 For there the LORD **b** his blessing, even life H7422

BETEN (1)
Jos 19:25 Helkath, Hali, **B**, Akshaph, H1062

BETH See following and ABEL BETH MAAKAH, ATROTH BETH JOAB

BETH ANATH (3) [ANATH]
Jos 19:38 Horem, **B** and Beth Shemesh. H1117
Jdg 1:33 those living in Beth Shemesh or **B**; H1117
Jdg 1:33 Shemesh and **B** became forced H1117

BETH ANOTH (1)
Jos 15:59 Maarath, **B** and Eltekon—six towns H1116

BETH ARABAH (4) [ARABAH]
Jos 15: 6 north of **B** to the Stone of H1098
Jos 15:61 the wilderness: **B**, Middin H1098
Jos 18:18 slope of **B** and on down into H1098
Jos 18:22 **B**, Zemaraim, Bethel, H1098

BETH ARBEL (1)
Hos 10:14 devastated **B** on the day of H1079

BETH ASHBEA (1)
1Ch 4:21 clans of the linen workers at **B**, H1080

BETH AVEN (7) [AVEN]
Jos 7: 2 which is near **B** to the east of Bethel, H1077
Jos 18:12 coming out at the wilderness of **B**. H1077
1Sa 13: 5 camped at Mikmash, east of **B**. H1077
1Sa 14:23 the battle moved on beyond **B**. H1077
Hos 4:15 not go to Gilgal; do not go up to **B**. H1077
Hos 5: 8 Raise the battle cry in **B**; lead on H1077
Hos 10: 5 Samaria fear for the calf-idol of **B**. H1077

BETH AZMAVETH (1) [AZMAVETH]
Ne 7:28 of **B** 42 H1115

BETH BAAL MEON (1) [BAAL MEON]
Jos 13:17 Bamoth Baal, **B**, H1081

BETH BARAH (2)
Jdg 7:24 Jordan ahead of them as far as **B**." H1083
Jdg 7:24 the waters of the Jordan as far as **B**. H1083

BETH BIRI (1)
1Ch 4:31 Hazar Susim, **B** and Shaaraim. H1082

BETH DAGON (2) [DAGON]
Jos 15:41 Gederoth, **B**, Naamah and H1087
Jos 19:27 It then turned east toward **B** H1087

BETH DIBLATHAIM (1) [ALMON DIBLATHAIM]
Jer 48:22 to Dibon, Nebo and **B**, H1086

BETH EDEN (1) [EDEN]
Am 1: 5 the one who holds the scepter in **B**. H1114

BETH EKED (2)
2Ki 10:12 At **B** *of* the Shepherds, H1118
2Ki 10:14 slaughtered them by the well of **B**— H1118

BETH EMEK (1)
Jos 19:27 went north to **B** and Neiel H1097

BETH EZEL (1) [EZEL]
Mic 1:11 **B** is in mourning; it no longer H1089

BETH GADER (1)
1Ch 2:51 Hareph the father of **B**. H1084

BETH GAMUL (1) [GAMUL]
Jer 48:23 to Kiriathaim, **B** and Beth Meon, H1085

BETH GILGAL (1) [GILGAL]
Ne 12:29 from **B**, and from the area of Geba H1090

BETH HAGGAN (1)
2Ki 9:27 he fled up the road to **B**. H1091

BETH HAKKEREM (2)
Ne 3:14 ruler of the district of **B**. H1094
Jer 6: 1 Raise the signal over **B**! For H1094

BETH HARAM (1)
Jos 13:27 in the valley, **B**, Beth Nimrah H1099

BETH HARAN (1) [HARAN]
Nu 32:36 Beth Nimrah and **B** as fortified cities H1100

BETH HOGLAH (3) [HOGLAH]
Jos 15: 6 went up to **B** and continued north H1102
Jos 18:19 slope of **B** and came out at H1102
Jos 18:21 Jericho, **B**, Emek Keziz, H1102

BETH HORON (14) [HORONITE]
Jos 10:10 road going up to **B** and cut them H1103
Jos 10:11 the road down from **B** to Azekah, H1103
Jos 16: 3 region of Lower **B** and on to Gezer, H1103
Jos 16: 5 Addar in the east to Upper **B** H1103
Jos 18:13 Addar on the hill south of Lower **B**. H1103
Jos 18:14 the hill facing **B** on the south the H1103
Jos 21:22 Kibzaim and **B**, together with their H1103
1Sa 13:18 another toward **B**, and the third H1103
1Ki 9:17 rebuilt Gezer.) He built up Lower **B**, H1103
1Ch 6:68 Jokmeam, **B**, H1103
1Ch 7:24 Lower and Upper **B** as well as H1103
2Ch 8: 5 He rebuilt Upper **B** and Lower Beth H1103
2Ch 8: 5 Horon and Lower **B** as fortified H1103
2Ch 25:13 to Judah from Samaria to **B**. H1103

BETH JESHIMOTH (4)
Nu 33:49 the Jordan from **B** to Abel H1093
Jos 12: 3 to **B**, and then southward H1093
Jos 13:20 the slopes of Pisgah, and **B**— H1093
Eze 25: 9 towns—**B**, Baal Meon and H1093

BETH KAR (1)
1Sa 7:11 along the way to a point below **B**. H1105

BETH LEBAOTH (1) [LEBAOTH]
Jos 19: 6 **B** and Sharuhen—thirteen towns H1106

BETH MARCABOTH (2)
Jos 19: 5 **B**, Hazar Susah, H1096
1Ch 4:31 **B**, Hazar Susim, Beth Biri and H1112

BETH MEON (1) [BAAL MEON]
Jer 48:23 to Kiriathaim, Beth Gamul and **B**, H1110

BETH MILLO (4)
Jdg 9: 6 of Shechem and **B** gathered beside H1109
Jdg 9:20 the citizens of Shechem and **B**, and H1109
Jdg 9:20 the citizens of Shechem and **B**, and H1109
2Ki 12:20 him and assassinated him at **B**, H1109

BETH NIMRAH (2) [NIMRAH]
Nu 32:36 **B** and Beth Haran as fortified cities H1113
Jos 13:27 Beth Haram, **B**, Sukkoth and H1113

BETH OPHRAH (1) [OPHRAH]
Mic 1:10 In **B** roll in the dust. H1108

BETH PAZZEZ (1)
Jos 19:21 En Gannim, En Haddah and **B**. H1122

BETH PELET (2) [PELET]
Jos 15:27 Hazar Gaddah, Heshmon, **B**, H1120
Ne 11:26 in Jeshua, in Moladah, in **B**, H1120

BETH PEOR (4) [PEOR]
Dt 3:29 So we stayed in the valley near **B**. H1121
Dt 4:46 in the valley near **B** east of the H1121
Dt 34: 6 in the valley opposite **B**, but to this H1121
Jos 13:20 **B**, the slopes of Pisgah, and Beth H1121

BETH RAPHA (1) [RAPHA]
1Ch 4:12 Eshton was the father of **B**, Paseah H1125

BETH REHOB (2) [REHOB]
Jdg 18:28 The city was in a valley near **B** H1124
2Sa 10: 6 foot soldiers from **B** and Zobah, H1124

BETH SHAN (10)
Jos 17:11 Manasseh also had **B**, Ibleam and H1126
Jos 17:16 both those in **B** and its settlements H1126
Jdg 1:27 out the people of **B** or Taanach or H1126
1Sa 31:10 fastened his body to the wall of **B**. H1126
1Sa 31:12 men marched through the night to **B**. NDT
1Sa 31:12 from the wall of **B** and went to H1126
2Sa 21:12 bodies from the public square at **B**, H1126
1Ki 4:12 in all of **B** next to Zarethan H1126
1Ki 4:12 from **B** to Abel Meholah across to H1126
1Ch 7:29 the borders of Manasseh were **B**, H1126

BETH SHEMESH (22)
Jos 15:10 down to **B** and crossed to H1127
Jos 19:22 Shahazumah and **B**, and ended H1127
Jos 19:38 Horem, Beth Anath and **B**. H1127
Jos 21:16 Juttah and **B**, together with H1127
Jdg 1:33 those living in **B** or Beth Anath; H1127
Jdg 1:33 living in **B** and Beth Anath H1127
1Sa 6: 9 territory, toward **B**, then the LORD H1127
1Sa 6:12 cows went straight up toward **B**, H1127
1Sa 6:12 them as far as the border of **B**. H1127
1Sa 6:13 the people of **B** were harvesting H1127
1Sa 6:14 to the field of Joshua **of B**, H1128
1Sa 6:15 the people of **B** offered burnt H1127
1Sa 6:18 day in the field of Joshua **of B**. H1128
1Sa 6:19 some of the inhabitants of **B**, H1127
1Sa 6:20 And the people of **B** asked H1127
1Ki 4: 9 **B** and Elon Bethhanan H1127
2Ki 14:11 faced each other at **B** in Judah. H1127
2Ki 14:13 the son of Ahaziah, at **B**. H1127
1Ch 6:59 Juttah and **B**, together with H1127
2Ch 25:21 faced each other at **B** in Judah. H1127
2Ch 25:23 the son of Ahaziah, at **B**. H1127
2Ch 28:18 They captured and occupied **B** H1127

BETH SHITTAH (1)
Jdg 7:22 The army fled to **B** toward Zererah H1101

BETH TAPPUAH (1) [TAPPUAH]
Jos 15:53 **B**, Aphekah, H1130

BETH TOGARMAH (2) [TOGARMAH]
Eze 27:14 " 'Men of **B** exchanged chariot H1129
Eze 38: 6 and **B** from the far north with H1129

BETH ZUR (4) [ZUR]
Jos 15:58 **B**, Gedor, H1123
1Ch 2:45 and Maon was the father of **B**. H1123
2Ch 11: 7 **B**, Soko, Adullam, H1123

Ne 3:16 ruler of a half-district of **B**, made H1123

BETHABARA (KJV) BETHANY

BETHANY (12)

Mt 21:17 he left them and went out of the city to **B**, *G1029*
Mt 26: 6 While Jesus was in **B** in the home of *G1029*
Mk 11: 1 came to Bethphage and **B** at the Mount of *G1029*
Mk 11:11 he went out to **B** with the Twelve. *G1029*
Mk 11:12 The next day as they were leaving **B** *G1029*
Mk 14: 3 While he was in **B**, reclining at the table *G1029*
Lk 19:29 Bethphage and **B** at the hill called the *G1029*
Lk 24:50 he had led them out to the vicinity of **B**, *G1029*
Jn 1:28 all happened at **B** on the other side of *G1029*
Jn 11: 1 He was from **B**, the village of Mary and *G1029*
Jn 11:18 Now **B** was less than two miles from *G1029*
Jn 12: 1 Jesus came to **B**, where Lazarus lived, *G1029*

BETHEL (72) [EL BETHEL, LUZ]

Ge 12: 8 the hills east of **B** and pitched his tent, H1078
Ge 12: 8 with **B** on the west and Ai on the east. H1078
Ge 13: 3 from place to place until he came to **B**, H1078
Ge 13: 3 to the place between **B** and Ai where his H1078
Ge 28:19 He called that place **B**, though the city H1078
Ge 31:13 I am the God of **B**, where you anointed a H1078
Ge 35: 1 to Jacob, "Go up to **B** and settle there H1078
Ge 35: 3 let us go up to **B**, where I will build H1078
Ge 35: 6 came to Luz (that is, **B**) in the land of H1078
Ge 35: 8 was buried under the oak outside **B**. H1078
Ge 35:15 place where God had talked with him **B**. H1078
Ge 35:16 Then they moved on from **B**. While they H1078
Jos 7: 2 which is near Beth Aven to the east of **B** H1078
Jos 8: 9 lay in wait between **B** and Ai, H1078
Jos 8:12 set them in ambush between **B** and Ai, H1078
Jos 8:17 remained in Ai or **B** who did not go after H1078
Jos 12: 9 of Jericho one the king of Ai (near **B**) one H1078
Jos 12:16 king of Makkedah one the king of **B** one H1078
Jos 16: 1 the desert into the hill country of **B**. H1078
Jos 16: 2 It went on from **B** (that is, Luz), crossed H1078
Jos 18:13 **B**) and went down to Ataroth Addar H1078
Jos 18:22 Beth Arabah, Zemaraim, **B**, H1078
Jdg 1:22 Now the tribes of Joseph attacked **B**, and H1078
Jdg 1:23 When they sent men to spy out **B** (formerly H1078
Jdg 4: 5 between Ramah and **B** in the hill country H1078
Jdg 20:18 went up to **B** and inquired of God. H1078
Jdg 20:26 went up to **B**, and there they sat H1078
Jdg 20:31 the one leading to **B** and the other to H1078
Jdg 21: 2 The people went to **B**, where they sat H1078
Jdg 21:19 which lies north of **B**, east of the road that H1078
Jdg 21:19 of the road that goes from **B** to Shechem, H1078
1Sa 7:16 on a circuit from **B** to Gilgal to Mizpah, H1078
1Sa 10: 3 to worship God at **B** will meet you there H1078
1Sa 13: 2 at Mikmash and in the hill country of **B**, H1078
1Sa 30:27 David sent it to those who were in **B** H1078
1Ki 12:29 One he set up in **B**, and the other in Dan. H1078
1Ki 12:30 to worship the one at **B** and went as far as H1078
1Ki 12:32 This he did in **B**, sacrificing to the calves H1078
1Ki 12:32 And at **B** he also installed priests at the H1078
1Ki 12:33 sacrifices on the altar he had built at **B**. H1078
1Ki 13: 1 LORD a man of God came from Judah to **B**, H1078
1Ki 13: 4 of God cried out against the altar at **B**, H1078
1Ki 13:10 not return by the way he had come to **B**. H1078
1Ki 13:11 was a certain old prophet living in **B**, H1078
1Ki 13:32 against the altar in **B** and against all the H1078
1Ki 16:34 Ahab's time, Hiel **of B** rebuilt Jericho. H1088
2Ki 2: 2 "Stay here; the LORD has sent me to **B**." H1078
2Ki 2: 2 not leave you." So they went down to **B**. H1078
2Ki 2: 3 of the prophets at **B** came out to Elisha H1078
2Ki 2:23 From there Elisha went up to **B**. As he was H1078
2Ki 10:29 of the golden calves at **B** and Dan. H1078
2Ki 17:28 came to live in **B** and taught them how to H1078
2Ki 23: 4 the Kidron Valley and took the ashes to **B**. H1078
2Ki 23:15 Even the altar at **B**, the high place made H1078
2Ki 23:17 against the altar of **B** the very things you H1078
2Ki 23:19 Just as he had done at **B**, Josiah removed H1078
1Ch 7:28 included **B** and its surrounding H1078
2Ch 13:19 took from him the towns of **B**, H1078
Ezr 2:28 of **B** and Ai 223 H1078
Ne 7:32 of **B** and Ai 123 H1078
Ne 11:31 in Mikmash, Aija, **B** and its settlements, H1078
Jer 48:13 was ashamed when they trusted in **B**. H1078
Hos 10:15 will it happen to you, **B**, because your H1078
Hos 12: 4 He found him at **B** and talked with him H1078
Am 3:14 I will destroy the altars of **B**; the horns of H1078
Am 4: 4 "Go to **B** and sin; go to Gilgal and sin H1078
Am 5: 5 do not seek **B**, do not go to Gilgal, do not H1078
Am 5: 5 and **B** will be reduced to nothing. H1078
Am 5: 6 and **B** will have no one to quench it. H1078
Am 7:10 the priest of **B** sent a message to H1078
Am 7:13 Don't prophesy anymore at **B**, because this H1078
Zec 7: 2 The people of **B** had sent Sharezer and H1078

BETHESDA (1)

Jn 5: 2 in Aramaic is called **B** and which is *G1031*

BETHHANAN See ELON BETHHANAN

BETHLEHEM (51) [BETHLEHEMITE, EPHRATH]

Ge 35:19 buried on the way to Ephrath (that is, **B**). H1107
Ge 48: 7 beside the road to Ephrath" (that is, **B**). H1107
Jos 19:15 Kattath, Nahalal, Shimron, Idalah and **B**. H1107
Jdg 12: 8 After him, Ibzan of **B** led Israel. H1107
Jdg 12:10 Then Ibzan died and was buried in **B**. H1107
Jdg 17: 7 A young Levite from **B** *in* Judah, who had H1107
Jdg 17: 9 "I'm a Levite from **B** *in* Judah," he said H1107
Jdg 19: 1 took a concubine from **B** *in* Judah. H1107
Jdg 19: 2 went back to her parents' home in **B**, H1107
Jdg 19:18 on our way from **B** *in* Judah to a remote H1107
Jdg 19:18 I have been to **B** *in* Judah and now I am H1107
Ru 1: 1 So a man from **B** *in* Judah, together with H1107
Ru 1: 2 They were Ephrathites from **B**, Judah. H1107
Ru 1:19 two women went on until they came to **B**. H1107
Ru 1:19 When they arrived in **B**, the whole town H1107
Ru 1:22 arriving in **B** as the barley harvest was H1107
Ru 2: 4 then Boaz arrived from **B** and greeted the H1107
Ru 4:11 in Ephrathah and be famous in **B**. H1107
1Sa 16: 1 your way; I am sending you to Jesse **of B**. H1095
1Sa 16: 4 When he arrived at **B**, the elders of the H1107
1Sa 16:18 a son of Jesse **of B** who knows how to H1095
1Sa 17:12 named Jesse, who was from **B** *in* Judah. H1107
1Sa 17:15 from Saul to tend his father's sheep at **B**. H1107
1Sa 17:58 "I am the son of your servant Jesse **of B**." H1095
1Sa 20: 6 asked my permission to hurry to **B**, H1107
1Sa 20:28 asked me for permission to go to **B**. H1107
2Sa 2:32 buried him in his father's tomb at **B**. H1107
2Sa 23:14 the Philistine garrison was at **B**. H1107
2Sa 23:15 of water from the well near the gate of **B**!" H1107
2Sa 23:16 well near the gate of **B** and carried it back H1107
2Sa 23:24 of Joab, Elhanan son of Dodo from **B**, H1107
1Ch 2:51 Salma the father of **B**, and Hareph the H1107
1Ch 2:54 **B**, the Netophathites, Atroth Beth Joab H1107
1Ch 4: 4 the firstborn of Ephrathah and father of **B**. H1107
1Ch 11:16 the Philistine garrison was at **B**. H1107
1Ch 11:17 of water from the well near the gate of **B**!" H1107
1Ch 11:18 well near the gate of **B** and carried it back H1107
1Ch 11:26 of Joab, Elhanan son of Dodo from **B**, H1107
2Ch 11: 6 **B**, Etam, Tekoa, H1107
Ezr 2:21 the men of **B** 123 H1107
Ne 7:26 the men of **B** and Netophah 188 H1107
Jer 41:17 at Geruth Kimham near **B** on their way to H1107
Mic 5: 2 "But you, **B** Ephrathah, though you are H1107
Mt 2: 1 After Jesus was born in **B** in Judea, during *G1033*
Mt 2: 5 "In **B** in Judea," they replied, "for this is *G1033*
Mt 2: 6 "'But you, **B**, in the land of Judah, are by *G1033*
Mt 2: 8 He sent them to **B** and said, "Go and *G1033*
Mt 2:16 to kill all the boys in **B** and its vicinity who *G1033*
Lk 2: 4 Galilee to Judea, to **B** the town of David *G1033*
Lk 2:15 "Let's go to **B** and see this thing that has *G1033*
Jn 7:42 from David's descendants and from **B**, *G1033*

BETHLEHEMITE (1) [BETHLEHEM]

2Sa 21:19 Elhanan son of Jair**the B** killed the brother H1095

BETHPHAGE (3)

Mt 21: 1 Jerusalem and came to **B** on the Mount of *G1036*
Mk 11: 1 came to **B** and Bethany at the *G1036*
Lk 19:29 As he approached **B** and Bethany at the *G1036*

BETHSAIDA (7)

Mt 11:21 Woe to you, **B**! For if the miracles *G1034*
Mk 6:45 the boat and go on ahead of him to **B**, *G1034*
Mk 8:22 They came to **B**, and some people *G1034*
Lk 9:10 by themselves to a town called **B**, *G1034*
Lk 10:13 Woe to you, **B**! For if the miracles *G1034*
Jn 1:44 Peter, was from the town of **B**. *G1034*
Jn 12:21 who was from **B** in Galilee, with a *G1034*

BETHUEL (10)

Ge 22:22 Hazo, Pildash, Jidlaph and **B**." H1432
Ge 22:23 **B** became the father of Rebekah. H1432
Ge 24:15 She was the daughter of **B** son of Milkah H1432
Ge 24:24 "I am the daughter of **B**, the son that H1432
Ge 24:47 'The daughter of **B** son of Nahor, whom H1432
Ge 24:50 Laban and **B** answered, "This is from the H1432
Ge 25:20 Rebekah daughter of **B** the Aramean from H1432
Ge 28: 2 to the house of your mother's father **B**. H1432
Ge 28: 5 to Laban son of **B** the Aramean, the H1432
1Ch 4:30 **B**, Hormah, Ziklag, H1433

BETHUL (1)

Jos 19: 4 Eltolad, **B**, Hormah, H1434

BETIMES (KJV) AGAIN, CAREFUL, EARLY, EARNESTLY

BETONIM (1)

Jos 13:26 from Heshbon to Ramath Mizpah and **B**, H1064

BETRAY (24) [BETRAYED, BETRAYER, BETRAYING, BETRAYS]

1Ch 12:17 if you have come to **b** me to my enemies H8228
Ps 89:33 from him, nor *will I ever* **b** my faithfulness. H9213
Pr 16:10 and his mouth *does* not **b** justice. H5085
Pr 25: 9 to court, *do* not **b** another's confidence H1655
Isa 16: 3 Hide the fugitives, *do* not **b** the refugees. H1655
Isa 24:16 The treacherous **b**! With treachery the H953
Isa 24:16 *With* treachery the treacherous **b**!" H953
Mt 10:21 "Brother *will* **b** brother to death, and a *G4140*
Mt 24:10 from the faith and *will* **b** and hate each *G4140*
Mt 26:21 "Truly I tell you, one of you *will* **b** me." *G4140*
Mt 26:23 his hand into the bowl with me *will* **b** me. *G4140*
Mt 26:25 the *one who would* **b** him, said, *G4140*
Mk 13:12 "Brother *will* **b** brother to death, and a *G4140*
Mk 14:10 to the chief priests to **b** Jesus to them. *G4140*
Mk 14:18 one of you *will* **b** me—one who is *G4140*
Lk 22: 4 with them how *he might* **b** Jesus. *G4140*
Lk 22:21 hand of him *who is going to* **b** me is with *G4140*
Jn 6:64 did not believe and who would **b** him. *G4140*
Jn 6:71 one of the Twelve, was later to **b** him.) *G4140*
Jn 12: 4 Iscariot, who was later *to* **b** him, objected, *G4140*
Jn 13: 2 the son of Simon Iscariot, to **b** Jesus. *G4140*
Jn 13:11 For he knew who *was going to* **b** him, and *G4140*
Jn 13:21 I tell you, one of you *is going to* **b** me." *G4140*
Jn 21:20 had said, "Lord, who is *going to* **b** you?" *G4140*

BETRAYED (16) [BETRAY]

2Sa 19:26 with the king.' But Ziba my servant **b** me. H8228
Ps 73:15 out like that, *I would have* **b** your children. H953
Isa 33: 1 betrayer, you who *have* not *been* **b**! H953
Isa 33: 1 when you stop betraying, you *will be* **b**. H953
Jer 12: 6 family—even they *have* **b** you; they have H953
La 1: 2 All her friends *have* **b** her; they have H953
La 1:19 "I called to my allies but they **b** me. H8228
Da 11: 6 In those days she *will* **be b**, together with H5989
Mt 10: 4 the Zealot and Judas Iscariot, who **b** him. *G4140*
Mt 27: 3 When Judas, who *had* **b** him, saw that *G4140*
Mt 27: 4 he said, "*for I have* **b** innocent blood." *G4140*
Mk 3:19 Judas Iscariot, who **b** him. *G4140*
Lk 21:16 *You will be* **b** even by parents, brothers *G4140*
Jn 18: 2 Now Judas, who **b** him, knew the place *G4140*
Ac 7:52 And now you have **b** and murdered him *G4595*
1Co 11:23 on the night *he was* **b**, took bread, *G4140*

BETRAYER (5) [BETRAY]

Isa 33: 1 Woe to you, **b**, you who have not been H953
Mt 26:46 Let us go! Here comes my **b**!" *G4140*
Mt 26:48 Now the **b** had arranged a signal with *G4140*
Mk 14:42 Let us go! Here comes my **b**!" *G4140*
Mk 14:44 Now the **b** had arranged a signal with *G4140*

BETRAYING (2) [BETRAY]

Isa 33: 1 when you stop **b**, you will be betrayed. H953
Lk 22:48 *are you* **b** the Son of Man with a kiss?" *G4140*

BETRAYS (7) [BETRAY]

Pr 11:13 A gossip **b** a confidence, but a trustworthy H1655
Pr 20:19 A gossip **b** a confidence; so avoid anyone H1655
Isa 21: 2 The traitor **b**, the looter takes loot H953
Hab 2: 5 wine **b** him; he is arrogant and H953
Mt 26:24 woe to that man who **b** the Son of Man! *G4140*
Mk 14:21 woe to that man who **b** the Son of Man! *G4140*
Lk 22:22 But woe to that man who **b** *him*!" *G4140*

BETROTH (3) [BETROTHED]

Hos 2:19 *I will* **b** you to me forever; I will betroth you H829
Hos 2:19 *I will* **b** you in righteousness and justice H829
Hos 2:20 *I will* **b** you in faithfulness, and you will H829

BETROTHED (3) [BETROTH]

Dt 22:27 though the **b** woman screamed, there H829
2Sa 3:14 whom *I* **b** to myself for the price of a H829
Joel 1: 8 sackcloth grieving for the **b** *of* her youth. H1251

BETTER (131) [GOOD]

Ge 29:19 "It's **b** that I give her to you than to some H3202
Ex 14:12 It would have been **b** for us to serve the H3202
Nu 11:18 We were **b off** in Egypt!" Now the H3202
Nu 14: 3 Wouldn't it be **b** for us to go back to Egypt H3202
Dt 17:20 not **consider** himself **b** than his H8123+4222
Jdg 8: 2 of Ephraim's grapes **b** than the full grape H3202
Jdg 9: 2 citizens of Shechem, 'Which is **b** for you: H3202
Jdg 11:25 Are you **any b** than Balak son of H3201+3201
Jdg 18:19 Isn't it **b** that you serve a tribe and clan in H3202
Ru 4:15 loves you and who is **b** to you than seven H3202
1Sa 14:30 **How much b** it would have been if H677+3954
1Sa 15:22 To obey is **b** than sacrifice, and to heed is H3202
1Sa 15:22 to heed is **b than** the fat of rams. H4946
1Sa 15:28 of your neighbors—to one **b** than you. H3202
1Sa 16:16 God comes on you, and you *will* **feel b**." H3201
1Sa 16:23 to Saul; he *would* **feel b**, and the evil H3201
1Sa 29: 4 **b** could he regain his master's favor **than** H4202
2Sa 14:32 It would be **b** for me if I were still there!" H3202
2Sa 17:14 Hushai the Arkite is **b** than that of H3202
2Sa 18: 3 It would be **b** now for you to give us H3202
1Ki 2:32 were **b** *men* and more upright than he. H3202
1Ki 19: 4 I am no **b** than my ancestors. H3202
1Ki 21: 2 I will give you a **b** vineyard or, H3202+4946
2Ki 5:12 Damascus, **b** than all the waters of Israel? H3202
2Ch 21:13 own family, men *who* were **b** than you. H3202
Est 1:19 to someone else who is **b** than she. H3202
Ps 37:16 **B** the little that the righteous have than H3202
Ps 63: 3 Because your love is **b** than life, my lips H3202
Ps 84:10 **B** is one day in your courts than a H3202
Ps 89:22 The enemy *will* not **get the b of** him H5957+928
Ps 118: 8 It is **b** to take refuge in the LORD than to H3202
Ps 118: 9 It is **b** to take refuge in the LORD than to H3202
Pr 3:14 than silver and yields **b** returns **than** gold. H4946
Pr 8:19 My fruit is **b** than fine gold; what I yield H3202
Pr 12: 9 **B** to be a nobody and yet have a servant H3202
Pr 15:16 **B** a little with the fear of the LORD than H3202
Pr 15:17 **B** a small serving of vegetables with love H3202
Pr 16: 8 **B** a little with righteousness than much H3202
Pr 16:16 How much **b** to get wisdom than gold, to H3202
Pr 16:19 **B** to be lowly in spirit along with the H3202
Pr 16:32 **B** a patient person than a warrior, one H3202
Pr 17: 1 **B** a dry crust with peace and quiet than a H3202
Pr 17:12 **B** to meet a bear robbed of her cubs **than** a H440
Pr 19: 1 **B** the poor whose walk is blameless than H3202
Pr 19:22 is unfailing love; **b** to be poor than a liar. H3202
Pr 21: 9 **B** to live on a corner of the roof than share H3202

Pr 21:19 **B** to live in a desert than with a H3202
Pr 22: 1 to be esteemed is **b** than silver or gold. H3202
Pr 25: 7 it is **b** for him to say to you, "Come up H3202
Pr 25:24 **B** to live on a corner of the roof than share H3202
Pr 27: 5 **B** is open rebuke than hidden love. H3202
Pr 27:10 **b** a neighbor nearby than a relative far H3202
Pr 28: 6 **B** the poor whose walk is blameless than H3202
Ecc 2:13 I saw that wisdom is **b** than folly, just as H3862
Ecc 2:13 than folly, just as light is **b** than darkness. H3862
Ecc 2:24 can do nothing **b** than to eat and drink H3202
Ecc 3:12 there is nothing **b** for people than to be H3202
Ecc 3:22 there is nothing **b** for a person than to H3202
Ecc 4: 3 But **b** than both is the one who has never H3202
Ecc 4: 6 **B** one handful with tranquillity than two H3202
Ecc 4: 9 Two are **b** than one, because they have a H3202
Ecc 4:13 **B** a poor but wise youth than an old but H3202
Ecc 5: 5 It is **b** not to make a vow than to make one H3202
Ecc 6: 3 I say that a stillborn child is **b off** than he. H3202
Ecc 6: 9 **B** what the eye sees than the roving of the H3202
Ecc 7: 1 A good name is **b** than fine perfume, and H3202
Ecc 7: 1 the day of death **b than** the day of birth. H4946
Ecc 7: 2 It is **b** to go to a house of mourning than H3202
Ecc 7: 3 Frustration is **b** than laughter, because a H3202
Ecc 7: 5 It is **b** to heed the rebuke of a wise person H3202
Ecc 7: 8 end of a matter is **b** than its beginning, H3202
Ecc 7: 8 beginning, and patience is **b** than pride. H3202
Ecc 7:10 "Why were the old days **b** than these?" H3202
Ecc 8:12 know that it will go **b** with those who fear H3202
Ecc 8:15 there is nothing **b** for a person under the H3202
Ecc 9: 4 even a live dog is **b off** than a dead lion! H3202
Ecc 9:16 So I said, "Wisdom is **b** than strength." H3202
Ecc 9:18 Wisdom is **b** than weapons of war, but H3202
SS 5: 9 How is your beloved **b than** others, most H4946
SS 5: 9 How is your beloved **b than** others, that H4946
Isa 56: 5 a memorial and a name **b** than sons and H3202
Isa 56:12 tomorrow will be like today, or even far **b**." H1524
La 4: 9 by the sword are **b off** than those who die H3202
Da 1:15 healthier and **b** nourished **than** any of the H4946
Da 1:20 them ten times **b than** all the magicians H6584
Hos 2: 7 as at first, for then I was **b off** than now. H3202
Am 6: 2 Are *they* **b off** than your two kingdoms H3202
Jnh 4: 3 for it is **b** for me to die than to live." H3202
Jnh 4: 8 "It would be **b** for me to die than to live." H3202
Na 3: 8 *Are you* **b** than Thebes, situated on the H3512
Mt 5:29 *It is* **b** for you to lose one part of your body *G5237*
Mt 5:30 *It is* **b** for you to lose one part of your body *G5237*
Mt 18: 6 *it would be* **b** for them to have a large *G5237*
Mt 18: 8 It is **b** for you to enter life maimed or *G2819*
Mt 18: 9 It is **b** for you to enter life with one eye *G2819*
Mt 19:10 a husband and wife, *it is* **b** not to marry." *G5237*
Mt 26:24 It would be **b** for him if he had not been *G2819*
Mk 5:26 instead of **getting b** she grew worse. *G6067*
Mk 9:42 it would be **b** for them if a large *G2819+3437*
Mk 9:43 It is **b** for you to enter life maimed than *G2819*
Mk 9:45 It is **b** for you to enter life crippled than to *G2819*
Mk 9:47 It is **b** for you to enter the kingdom of God *G2819*
Mk 14:21 It would be **b** for him if he had not been *G2819*
Lk 5:39 wants the new, for they say, 'The old is **b**. *G5982*
Lk 10:42 Mary has chosen what is **b**, and it will not be *G19*
Lk 14:10 say to you, 'Friend, move up *to a* **b** *place*. *G542*
Lk 17: 2 *It would be* **b** for them to be thrown into *G3387*
Jn 4:52 as to the time when his son got **b**, *G3153*
Jn 11:12 replied, "Lord, if he sleeps, *he will* **get b**." *G5392*
Jn 11:50 do not realize that *it is* **b** for you that one *G5237*
Ro 14:21 It is **b** not to eat meat or drink wine or to *G2819*
1Co 7: 9 it is **b** to marry than to burn with *G3202*
1Co 7:38 he who does not marry her does **b**. *G3202*
1Co 8: 8 worse if we do not eat, and no **b** if we do. *G4355*
Eph 1:17 revelation, so that you may **know** him **b**. *G2106*
Php 1:23 be with Christ, which is **b** by far; *G3437+3202*
1Ti 6: 2 should serve them **even b** because their *G3437*
Phm 16 as a slave, but **b than** a slave, as a dear *G5642*
Heb 6: 9 are convinced *of* **b** *things* in your case— *G3202*
Heb 7:19 and a **b** hope is introduced, by which we *G3202*
Heb 7:22 become the guarantor of a **b** covenant. *G3202*
Heb 8: 6 covenant is established on **b** promises. *G3202*
Heb 9:23 themselves with **b** sacrifices than these. *G3202*
Heb 10:34 you yourselves had **b** and lasting *G3202*
Heb 11: 4 Abel brought God a **b** offering than Cain *G4498*
Heb 11:16 they were longing for a **b** country—a *G3202*
Heb 11:35 they might gain an *even* **b** resurrection. *G3202*
Heb 11:40 planned something **b** for us so that only *G3202*
Heb 12:24 that speaks a **b** word than the blood *G3202*
1Pe 3:17 For it is **b**, if it is God's will, to suffer for *G3202*
2Pe 2:21 It would have been **b** for them not to have *G3202*

BETWEEN (223)

Ge 1: 6 "Let there be a vault **b** the waters to H928+9348
Ge 3:15 I will put enmity **b** you and the woman, H1068
Ge 3:15 the woman, and **b** your offspring and hers H1068
Ge 9:12 I am making **b** me and you and every H1068
Ge 9:13 sign of the covenant **b** me and the earth. H1068
Ge 9:15 my covenant **b** me and you and all H1068
Ge 9:16 everlasting covenant **b** God and all living H1068
Ge 9:17 I have established **b** me and all life on H1068
Ge 10:12 Resen, which is **b** Nineveh and Calah H1068
Ge 13: 3 to the place **b** Bethel and Ai where his H1068
Ge 13: 7 quarreling arose **b** Abram's herders and H1068
Ge 13: 8 not have any quarreling **b** you and me, H1068
Ge 13: 8 you and me, or **b** your herders and mine H1068
Ge 15:17 torch appeared and passed **b** the pieces. H1068
Ge 16: 5 May the LORD judge **b** you and me." H1068
Ge 16:14 it is still there, **b** Kadesh and Bered. H1068
Ge 17: 2 make my covenant **b** me and you and will H1068
Ge 17: 7 covenant **b** me and you and your H1068
Ge 17:11 the sign of the covenant **b** me and you. H1068
Ge 20: 1 the Negev and lived **b** Kadesh and Shur. H1068
Ge 23:15 of silver, but what is that **b** you and me? H1068
Ge 26:28 ought to be a sworn agreement **b** us'— H1068
Ge 26:28 agreement between us'—**b** us and you. H1068
Ge 30:36 a three-day journey **b** himself and Jacob, H1068
Ge 31:37 and let them judge **b** the two of us. H1068
Ge 31:44 and let it serve as a witness **b** us. H1068
Ge 31:48 heap is a witness **b** you and me today." H1068
Ge 31:49 LORD keep watch **b** you and me when we H1068
Ge 31:50 that God is a witness **b** you and me." H1068
Ge 31:51 is this pillar I have set up **b** you and me. H1068
Ge 31:53 the God of their father, judge **b** us." H1068
Ge 32:16 and keep some space **b** the herds. H1068
Ge 49:10 the ruler's staff from **b** his feet, until H1068
Ex 8:23 make a distinction **b** my people and your H1068
Ex 9: 4 make a distinction **b** the livestock of Israel H1068
Ex 11: 7 makes a distinction **b** Egypt and Israel. H1068
Ex 14: 2 near Pi Hahiroth, **b** Migdol and the sea. H1068
Ex 14:20 coming **b** the armies of Egypt and Israel H1068
Ex 16: 1 which is **b** Elim and Sinai, on the H1068
Ex 18:16 I decide **b** the parties and inform H1068
Ex 22:11 the issue **b** them will be settled by the H1068
Ex 25:22 above the cover **b** the two H4946+1068
Ex 28:33 of the robe, with gold bells **b** them. H928+9348
Ex 30:18 Place it **b** the tent of meeting and the H1068
Ex 31:13 This will be a sign **b** me and you for the H1068
Ex 31:17 It will be a sign **b** me and the Israelites H1068
Ex 39:25 around the hem **b** the H928+9348
Ex 40: 7 place the basin **b** the tent of meeting and H1068
Ex 40:30 He placed the basin **b** the tent of meeting H1068
Lev 10:10 you can distinguish **b** the holy and the H1068
Lev 10:10 common, **b** the unclean and the clean, H1068
Lev 11:47 must distinguish **b** the unclean and the H1068
Lev 11:47 **b** living creatures that may be eaten and H1068
Lev 20:25 make a distinction **b** clean and unclean H1068
Lev 20:25 animals and **b** unclean and clean H1068
Lev 24:10 out in the camp **b** him and an Israelite. NDT
Lev 26:46 at Mount Sinai **b** himself and the H1068
Lev 27: 3 of a male **b** the ages of H4946+2256+6330
Lev 27: 5 a person **b** the ages of H4946+2256+6330
Lev 27: 6 a person **b** one month H4946+2256+6330
Nu 7:89 speaking to him from **b** the two cherubim H1068
Nu 11:33 the meat was still **b** their teeth and before H1068
Nu 13:23 Two of them carried it on a pole **b** them H928
Nu 16:48 He stood **b** the living and the dead, and H1068
Nu 21:13 of Moab, **b** Moab and the Amorites. H1068
Nu 30:16 concerning **relationships b** a man and his H1068
Nu 30:16 **b** a father and his young daughter H1068
Nu 31:27 the spoils equally **b** the soldiers who took H1068
Nu 35:24 must judge **b** the accused and the H1068
Dt 1: 1 opposite Suph, **b** Paran and Tophel H1068
Dt 1:16 "Hear the disputes **b** your people and H1068
Dt 1:16 whether the case is **b** two Israelites or H1068
Dt 1:16 two Israelites or **b** an Israelite and a H1068
Dt 5: 5 At that time I stood **b** the LORD and you to H1068
Dt 33:12 one the LORD loves rests **b** his shoulders." H1068
Jos 3: 4 two thousand cubits **b** you and the ark; H1068
Jos 8: 9 ambush and lay in wait **b** Bethel and Ai, H1068
Jos 8:11 with the valley **b** them and the city. H1068
Jos 8:12 set them in ambush **b** Bethel and Ai, H1068
Jos 18:11 allotted territory lay **b** the tribes of Judah H1068
Jos 22:25 the Jordan a boundary **b** us and you— H1068
Jos 22:27 it is to be a witness **b** us and you and the H1068
Jos 22:28 sacrifices, but as a witness **b** us and you. H1068
Jos 22:34 A Witness **B** Us—that the LORD is H1068
Jos 23: 4 **b** the Jordan and the Mediterranean Sea H4946
Jos 24: 7 he put darkness **b** you and the H1068
Jdg 4: 5 Palm of Deborah **b** Ramah and Bethel in H1068
Jdg 4:17 was an alliance **b** Jabin king of Hazor H1068
Jdg 9:23 stirred up animosity **b** Abimelek and the H1068
Jdg 11:27 the dispute this day **b** the Israelites and H1068
Jdg 13:25 in Mahaneh Dan, **b** Zorah and Eshtaol. H1068
Jdg 16:31 back and buried him **b** Zorah and Eshtaol H1068
1Sa 4: 4 Almighty, *who is* **enthroned** *b* the cherubim. AIT
1Sa 7:12 a stone and set it up **b** Mizpah and Shen. H1068
1Sa 7:14 And there was peace **b** Israel and the H1068
1Sa 14:42 "Cast the lot **b** me and Jonathan my son." H1068
1Sa 17: 1 at Ephes Dammim, **b** Sokoh and Azekah. H1068
1Sa 17: 3 Israelites another, with the valley **b** them. H1068
1Sa 20: 3 there is only a step **b** me and death." H1068
1Sa 20:23 the LORD is witness **b** you and me forever." H1068
1Sa 20:42 'The LORD is witness **b** you and me, and H1068
1Sa 20:42 **b** your descendants and my H1068
1Sa 24:12 May the LORD judge **b** you and me. H1068
1Sa 24:15 the LORD be our judge and decide **b** us. H1068
1Sa 26:13 there was a wide space **b** them. H1068
2Sa 3: 1 The war **b** the house of Saul and the H1068
2Sa 3: 6 During the war **b** the house of Saul and H1068
2Sa 6: 2 *who is* **enthroned** *b* the cherubim on the ark. AIT
2Sa 18:24 David was sitting **b** the inner and outer H1068
2Sa 19:35 tell the difference **b** what is enjoyable H1068
2Sa 21: 7 before the LORD **b** David and Jonathan H1068
2Sa 21:15 there was a battle **b** the Philistines and H4200
1Ki 3: 9 to distinguish **b** right and wrong. H1068
1Ki 5:12 peaceful relations **b** Hiram and Solomon, H1068
1Ki 7:29 On the panels **b** the uprights were lions H1068
1Ki 7:46 plain of the Jordan **b** Sukkoth and H1068
1Ki 8:32 **Judge** *b* your servants, condemning the guilty AIT
1Ki 14:30 continual warfare **b** Rehoboam and H1068
1Ki 15: 6 There was war **b** Abijah and Jeroboam H1068
1Ki 15: 7 There was war **b** Abijah and Jeroboam H1068
1Ki 15:16 There was war **b** Asa and Baasha king of H1068
1Ki 15:19 "Let there be a treaty **b** me and you," H1068
1Ki 15:19 "as there was **b** my father and your father. H1068
1Ki 15:32 There was war **b** Asa and Baasha king of H1068
1Ki 18:21 "How long will you waver **b** two opinions? H6584
1Ki 18:42 the ground and put his face **b** his knees. H1068
1Ki 22: 1 years there was no war **b** Aram and Israel. H1068
1Ki 22:34 hit the king of Israel **b** the sections of his H1068
2Ki 9:24 his bow and shot Joram **b** the shoulders. H1068
2Ki 11:15 "Bring her out **b** the ranks and put to the H4200
2Ki 11:17 then made a covenant **b** the LORD and the H1068
2Ki 11:17 also made a covenant **b** the king and the H1068
2Ki 16:14 from **b** the new altar and the temple of the H1068
2Ki 19:15 God of Israel, **enthroned** *b* the cherubim, you AIT
2Ki 25: 4 through the gate **b** the two walls near the H1068
1Ch 13: 6 the LORD, *who is* **enthroned** *b* the cherubim AIT
1Ch 21:16 of the LORD standing **b** heaven and earth, H1068
2Ch 4:17 plain of the Jordan **b** Sukkoth and H1068
2Ch 6:23 **Judge** *b* your servants, condemning the guilty AIT
2Ch 12: 8 so that *they may* **learn the difference b** H3359
2Ch 12:15 was continual **warfare** *b* Rehoboam and AIT
2Ch 13: 2 There was war **b** Abijah and Jeroboam. H1068
2Ch 16: 3 "Let there be a treaty **b** me and you," H1068
2Ch 16: 3 "as there was **b** my father and your father. H1068
2Ch 18:33 hit the king of Israel **b** the breastplate H1068
2Ch 23:14 "**Bring** her **out** *b* the ranks and put to the AIT
2Ch 35:21 is there, king of Judah, **b** you and me? H4200
Ne 3:32 **b** the room above the corner and the H1068
Job 4:20 **B** dawn and dusk they are broken to H4946
Job 9:33 there were someone to mediate **b** us, H1068
Job 26:10 the waters for a **boundary** *b* light and AIT
Job 41:16 so close to the next that no air can pass **b**. H1068
Ps 80: 1 You *who* **sit enthroned** *b* the cherubim, shine AIT
Ps 99: 1 tremble; *he* **sits enthroned** *b* the cherubim AIT
Ps 104:10 into the ravines; it flows **b** the mountains. H1068
SS 1:13 me a sachet of myrrh resting **b** my breasts. H1068
Isa 2: 4 He will judge **b** the nations and will settle H1068
Isa 5: 3 of Judah, judge **b** me and my vineyard. H1068
Isa 22:11 built a reservoir **b** the two walls for the H1068
Isa 37:16 God of Israel, **enthroned** *b* the cherubim, you AIT
Jer 34:18 cut in two and then walked **b** its pieces. H1068
Jer 34:19 the land who walked **b** the pieces of the H1068
Jer 39: 4 through the gate **b** the two walls, and H1068
Jer 52: 7 through the gate **b** the two walls near the H1068
Eze 4: 3 it as an iron wall **b** you and the city and H1068
Eze 8: 3 Spirit lifted me up **b** earth and heaven H1068
Eze 8:16 to the temple, **b** the portico and the altar H1068
Eze 18: 8 wrong and judges fairly **b** two parties. H1068
Eze 20:12 I gave them my Sabbaths as a sign **b** us, H1068
Eze 20:20 that they may be a sign **b** us. H1068
Eze 22:26 do not distinguish **b** the holy and the H1068
Eze 22:26 there is no **difference b** the unclean and H1068
Eze 34:17 I will judge **b** one sheep and another H1068
Eze 34:17 another, and **b** rams and goats. H4200
Eze 34:20 I myself will judge **b** the fat sheep and H1068
Eze 34:22 I will judge **b** one sheep and another. H1068
Eze 40: 7 the projecting walls **b** the alcoves were H1068
Eze 41: 9 The open area **b** the side rooms of the H1075
Eze 43: 8 with only a wall **b** me and them, they H1068
Eze 44:23 my people **the difference b** the holy and H1068
Eze 44:23 how to distinguish **b** the unclean and the H1068
Eze 47:16 lies on the border **b** Damascus and H1068
Eze 47:18 boundary will run **b** Hauran and H4946+1068
Eze 47:18 along the Jordan **b** Gilead and the H4946+1068
Eze 48:22 to the prince will lie **b** the border of Judah H1068
Da 7: 5 it had three ribs in its mouth **b** its teeth. A10099
Da 8: 5 a prominent horn **b** its eyes came from H1068
Da 8:21 the large horn **b** its eyes is the first H1068
Da 11:45 pitch his royal tents **b** the seas at the H1068
Hos 2: 2 the unfaithfulness from **b** her breasts. H1068
Joel 2:17 the LORD, weep **b** the portico and the altar. H1068
Mic 4: 3 He will judge **b** many peoples and will H1068
Zec 5: 9 lifted up the basket **b** heaven and earth. H1068
Zec 6: 1 coming out from **b** two mountains— H1068
Zec 6:13 And there will be harmony **b** the two.' H1068
Zec 9: 7 the forbidden food from **b** their teeth. H1068
Zec 11:14 the family bond **b** Judah and Israel. H1068
Zec 14: 7 LORD—*with* **no** *distinction b* day and night. AIT
Mal 2:14 LORD is the witness **b** you and the wife of H1068
Mal 3:18 again see the **distinction b** the righteous H1068
Mal 3:18 **b** those who serve God and those who do H1068
Mt 18:15 point out their fault, just **b** the two of you. *G3568*
Mt 19:10 this is the situation **b** a husband and wife, *G3552*
Mt 23:35 whom you murdered **b** the temple and *G3568*
Lk 11:51 who was killed **b** the altar and the *G3568*
Lk 12:14 me a judge or an arbiter **b** you? *G2093*
Lk 15:12 So he divided his property **b them**. AIT
Lk 16:26 **b** us and you a great chasm has been set *G3568*
Lk 17:11 along **the border b** Samaria and *G1328+3545*
Jn 3:25 An argument developed **b** some of John's *G3552*
Ac 12: 6 Peter was sleeping **b** two soldiers, bound *G3568*
Ac 15: 9 He did not discriminate **b** us and them, for *G3568*
Ac 23: 7 dispute broke out *b* the **Pharisees** and the AIT
Ro 3:22 There is no difference **b** Jew and Gentile, NDT
Ro 10:12 For there is no difference *b* **Jew** and Gentile AIT
Ro 14:22 these things keep **b** yourself and God. *G1967*
1Co 6: 5 to judge a dispute **b** believers? *G324+3545*
1Co 12:10 to another **distinguishing b** spirits, to *G1360*
2Co 6:15 What harmony is there **b** Christ and Belial *G4639*

2Co 6:16 agreement is there b the temple of God G3552
Php 1:23 I am torn b the two: I desire to depart and G1666
1Ti 2: 5 God and one mediator b God and mankind, AIT
1Ti 6: 5 constant friction b people of corrupt mind, AIT

BEULAH (1)
Isa 62: 4 your land B; for the LORD will take H1241

BEWAIL, BEWAILED (KJV) GRIEVED, MOURN, MOURNED, WEEP, WEPT

BEWARE (7)
2Ki 6: 9 "B of passing that place, because the H9068
Job 36:21 B of turning to evil, which you seem H9068+440
Isa 22:17 "B, the LORD is about to take firm hold of H2180
Jer 7:32 So b, the days are coming, declares the H2180
Jer 9: 4 "B of your friends; do not trust anyone in H9068
Jer 19: 6 So b, the days are coming, declares the H2180
Lk 20:46 "B of the teachers of the law. They like to G4668

BEWILDERED (3) [BEWILDERMENT]
Est 3:15 down to drink, but the city of Susa was b. H1003
Isa 21: 3 by what I hear, I am b by what I see. H987
Mk 16: 8 Trembling and b, the women went out G1749

BEWILDERMENT (1) [BEWILDERED]
Ac 2: 6 a crowd came together in b, because G5177

BEWITCHED (1) [WITCHCRAFT]
Gal 3: 1 Who has b you? Before your G1001

BEWRAY, BEWRAYETH (KJV) BETRAY, GIVES AWAY

BEYOND (68)
Ge 35:21 and pitched his tent b Migdal Eder. H4946+2134
Ge 41:49 keeping records because it was b measure. H401
Lev 15:25 a discharge that continues b her period, H6584
Nu 22:18 great or small to go b the command of H6296
Nu 24:13 to go b the command of the LORD H6296
Dt 3:25 see the good land b the Jordan— H928+6298
Dt 30:11 is not too difficult for you or b your reach. H8158
Dt 30:13 Nor is it b the sea, so that you have H4946+6298
Jos 24: 2 lived b the Euphrates River and H928+6298
Jos 24: 3 Abraham from the land b the Euphrates H6298
Jos 24:14 worshiped b the Euphrates River H928+6298
Jos 24:15 ancestors served b the Euphrates, H928+6298
Jdg 1:36 from Scorpion Pass to Sela and b. H5087+2025
Jdg 5:17 Gilead stayed b the Jordan. H928+6298
Jdg 13:18 you ask my name? It is b understanding." H7100
1Sa 14:23 the battle moved on b Beth Aven. H6296
1Sa 20:22 the arrows are b you,' then H4946+2256+2134
1Sa 20:36 As the boy ran, he shot an arrow b him. H6296
1Sa 20:37 "Isn't the arrow b you? H4946+2256+2134
2Sa 10:16 brought from b the Euphrates River; H6298
2Sa 16: 1 had gone a short distance b the summit, H4946
1Ki 14:15 and scatter them b the Euphrates H4946+6298
1Ch 19:16 brought from b the Euphrates River, H6298
1Ch 22:16 bronze and iron—craftsmen b number. H401
Ne 3:16 B him, Nehemiah son of Azbuk, ruler of a H339
Ne 3:23 B them, Benjamin and Hasshub made H339
Job 28:18 mention; the price of wisdom is b rubies. H4946
Job 36:26 How great is God—b our understanding H4202
Job 37: 5 he does great things b our understanding. H4202
Job 37:23 The Almighty is b our reach and exalted H4202
Ps 104:25 teeming with creatures b number—living H401
Ecc 7:23 to be wise"—but this was b me. H8158
SS 6: 8 eighty concubines, and virgins b number; H401
Isa 7:20 a razor hired from b the Euphrates River— H6298
Isa 9: 1 by the Way of the Sea, b the Jordan— H6298
Isa 52:14 was so disfigured b that of any human H4946
Isa 52:14 his form marred b human likeness— H4946
Isa 64: 9 Do not be angry b measure, LORD H6330+4394
Isa 64:12 silent and punish us b measure? H6330+4394
Jer 17: 9 is deceitful above all things and b cure. H631
Jer 30:12 wound is incurable, your injury b healing. H2703
La 5:22 and are angry with us b measure. H6330+4394
Eze 41:16 everything b and including the threshold H5584
Da 8:27 by the vision; it was b understanding. H401
Joel 2:11 his forces are b number, and H4394+8041
Am 5:27 you into exile b Damascus," H4946+2134+4200
Mic 2:10 it is defiled, it is ruined, b all remedy. H5344
Zep 3:10 From b the rivers of Cush my worshipers H6298
Mal 1: 5 LORD—even b the borders of Israel! H4946+6584
Mt 4:15 the Way of the Sea, b the Jordan, Galilee G4305
Mt 5:37 anything b this comes from the evil one. G4356
Lk 22:41 He withdrew about a stone's throw b them G608
Ac 7:43 I will send you into exile' b Babylon. G2084
Ac 15:28 you with anything b the following G4498+4440
Ac 26:22 I am saying nothing b what the prophets G1760
Ro 11:11 Did they stumble so as to fall b recovery G4406
Ro 11:33 his judgments, and his paths b tracing out! G453
1Co 1:16 of Stephanas; b that, I don't remember if I G3370
1Co 4: 6 the saying, "Do not go b what is written." G5642
1Co 10:13 let you be tempted b what you can bear. G5642
2Co 1: 8 great pressure, far b our ability to endure G5642
2Co 8: 3 they were able, and even b their ability. G4123
2Co 10:13 will not boast b proper limits, but will G1650
2Co 10:15 Neither do we go b our limits by boasting G1650
2Co 10:16 preach the gospel in the regions b you. G5654
Gal 1:14 in Judaism b many of my own age G5642
1Ti 3:16 B all question, the mystery from which G3935
Heb 6: 1 Therefore let us move b the elementary G918

BEZAI (3)
Ezr 2:17 of B 323 H1291
Ne 7:23 of B 324 H1291
Ne 10:18 Hodiah, Hashum, B, H1291

BEZALEL (9)
Ex 31: 2 I have chosen B son of Uri, the son H1295
Ex 35:30 the LORD has chosen B son of Uri, the son H1295
Ex 36: 1 So B, Oholiab and every skilled person to H1295
Ex 36: 2 Moses summoned B and Oholiab and H1295
Ex 37: 1 B made the ark of acacia wood—two and H1295
Ex 38:22 B son of Uri, the son of Hur, of the tribe of H1295
1Ch 2:20 the father of Uri, and Uri the father of B. H1295
2Ch 1: 5 But the bronze altar that B son of Uri, the H1295
Ezr 10:30 Mattaniah, B, Binnui and Manasseh H1295

BEZEK (2) [ADONI-BEZEK]
Jdg 1: 4 they struck down ten thousand men at B. H1028
1Sa 11: 8 When Saul mustered them at B, the men H1028

BEZER (6) [BEOR]
Dt 4:43 B in the wilderness plateau, for the H1311
Jos 20: 8 they designated B in the wilderness on H1311
Jos 21:36 from the tribe of Reuben, B, Jahaz, H1311
1Ch 6:78 Jericho they received B in the wilderness, H1311
1Ch 7:37 B, Hod, Shamma, Shilshah, Ithran and H1310
2Pe 2:15 off to follow the way of Balaam son of B, G1082

BICRI (NIV84) BIKRI

BID (1) [BIDDING]
2Sa 19:39 king kissed Barzillai and b him farewell, H1385

BIDDING (2) [BID]
Ps 103:20 you mighty ones who do his b, who obey H1821
Ps 148: 8 clouds, stormy winds that do his b, H1821

BIDKAR (1)
2Ki 9:25 Jehu said to B, his chariot officer, "Pick him H982

BIER (3)
2Sa 3:31 King David himself walked behind the b. H4753
2Ch 16:14 They laid him on a b covered with spices H5435
Lk 7:14 up and touched the b they were carrying G5049

BIG (13) [BIGGER]
Ex 29:20 and on the b toes of their right feet. H991
Lev 8:23 hand and on the b toe of his right foot. H991
Lev 8:24 hands and on the b toes of their right feet. H991
Lev 14:14 hand and on the b toe of their right foot. H991
Lev 14:17 hand and on the b toe of their right foot, H991
Lev 14:25 hand and on the b toe of their right foot. H991
Lev 14:28 hand and on the b toe of their right foot. H991
Jdg 1: 6 and cut off his thumbs and b toes. H8079
Jdg 1: 7 their thumbs and b toes cut off have H8079
Jdg 9:38 "Where is your b talk now, you who said, H7023
2Sa 18:17 threw him into a b pit in the forest and H1524
Mt 27:60 He rolled a b stone in front of the G3489
Mk 4:32 with such b branches that the birds can G3489

BIGGER (2) [BIG]
Lk 7:43 the one who had the b debt forgiven." G4498
Lk 12:18 will tear down my barns and build b ones, G3505

BIGTHA (1)
Est 1:10 Harbona, B, Abagtha, Zethar and H960

BIGTHANA (2)
Est 2:21 at the king's gate, B and Teresh, two of the H961
Est 6: 2 that Mordecai had exposed B and Teresh, H962

BIGVAI (6)
Ezr 2: 2 Bilshan, Mispar, B, Rehum and Baanah): H958
Ezr 2:14 of B 2,056 H958
Ezr 8:14 of the descendants of B, Uthai and Zakkur H958
Ne 7: 7 Bilshan, Mispereth, B, Nehum and Baanah): H958
Ne 7:19 of B 2,067 H958
Ne 10:16 Adonijah, B, Adin, H958

BIKRI (8)
2Sa 20: 1 a troublemaker named Sheba son of B, H1152
2Sa 20: 2 deserted David to follow Sheba son of B. H1152
2Sa 20: 6 "Now Sheba son of B will do us more H1152
2Sa 20: 7 from Jerusalem to pursue Sheba son of B. H1152
2Sa 20:10 brother Abishai pursued Sheba son of B. H1152
2Sa 20:13 on with Joab to pursue Sheba son of B. H1152
2Sa 20:21 A man named Sheba son of B, from the H1152
2Sa 20:22 of Sheba son of B and threw it to Joab H1152

BIKRITES (1)
2Sa 20:14 through the entire region of the B, H1152

BILDAD (5)
Job 2:11 B the Shuhite and Zophar the Naamathite H1161
Job 8: 1 Then B the Shuhite replied: H1161
Job 18: 1 Then B the Shuhite replied: H1161
Job 25: 1 Then B the Shuhite replied: H1161
Job 42: 9 B the Shuhite and Zophar the Naamathite H1161

BILEAM (1)
1Ch 6:70 Manasseh the Israelites gave Aner and B, H1190

BILGAH (2) [BILGAH'S]
1Ch 24:14 the fifteenth to B, the sixteenth to Immer, H1159
Ne 12: 5 Mijamin, Moadiah, B, H1159

BILGAH'S (1) [BILGAH]
Ne 12:18 of B, Shammua; of Shemaiah's H1159

BILGAI (1)
Ne 10: 8 Maaziah, B and Shemaiah. These were H1160

BILHAH (10)
Ge 29:29 Laban gave his servant B to his daughter H1167
Ge 30: 3 she said, "Here is B, my servant. H1167
Ge 30: 4 So she gave him her servant B as a wife H1167
Ge 30: 7 Rachel's servant B conceived again and H1167
Ge 35:22 in and slept with his father's concubine B, H1167
Ge 35:25 The sons of Rachel's servant B: Dan and H1167
Ge 37: 2 the sons of B and the sons of Zilpah H1167
Ge 46:25 These were the sons born to Jacob by B H1167
1Ch 4:29 B, Ezem, Tolad, H1168
1Ch 7:13 Jezer and Shillem—the descendants of B. H1167

BILHAN (4)
Ge 36:27 The sons of Ezer: B, Zaavan and Akan. H1169
1Ch 1:42 The sons of Ezer: B, Zaavan and Akan H1169
1Ch 7:10 The son of Jediael: B. The sons of Bilhan H1169
1Ch 7:10 The sons of B: Jeush, Benjamin H1169

BILL (2)
Lk 16: 6 told him, 'Take your b, sit down quickly, G1207
Lk 16: 7 'Take your b and make it eight hundred. G1207

BILLOWED (1) [BILLOWS]
Ex 19:18 The smoke b up from it like smoke from a H6590

BILLOWS (2) [BILLOWED]
Joel 2:30 the earth, blood and fire and b of smoke. H9406
Ac 2:19 blood and fire and b of smoke. G874

BILSHAN (2)
Ezr 2: 2 Reelaiah, Mordecai, B, Mispar, Bigvai H1193
Ne 7: 7 Mordecai, B, Mispereth, Bigvai, H1193

BIMHAL (1)
1Ch 7:33 Pasak, B and Ashvath. H1197

BIND (19) [BINDING, BINDINGS, BINDS, BOUND]
Dt 6: 8 hands and b them on your H2118+4200+3213
Dt 11:18 hands and b them on your H2118+4200+3213
Ne 10:29 and b themselves with a curse and an H995+928
Job 38:31 "Can you b the chains of the Pleiades H8003
Ps 119:61 Though the wicked b me with ropes, I will H6386
Ps 149: 8 to b their kings with fetters, their nobles H673
Pr 3: 3 never leave you; b them around your neck H8003
Pr 6:21 B them always on your heart; fasten them H8003
Pr 7: 3 B them on your fingers; write them on the H8003
Isa 8:16 B up this testimony of warning and seal H7674
Isa 56: 6 foreigners who b themselves to the LORD H4277
Isa 61: 1 He has sent me to b up the H2502
Jer 50: 5 will come and b themselves to the LORD in H4277
Eze 34:16 I will b up the injured and strengthen the H2502
Hos 6: 1 injured us but he will b up our wounds. H2502
Mt 16:19 whatever you b on earth will be bound in G1313
Mt 18:18 whatever you b on earth will be bound in G1313
Mk 5: 3 no one could b him anymore, not G1313
Ac 21:11 in Jerusalem will b the owner of this G1313

BINDING (7) [BIND]
Ge 37: 7 We were b sheaves of grain out in the field H520
Nu 30: 9 divorced woman will be b on her. H7756
Nu 30:14 all her vows or the pledges b on her. H6584
Jos 2:17 you made us swear will not be b on us H5929
Jdg 16:21 B him with bronze shackles, they set him to H673
Ne 9:38 we are making a b agreement, putting it in H591
Heb 2: 2 message spoken through angels was b, G1010

BINDINGS (1) [BIND]
Jdg 15:14 and the b dropped from his hands. H657

BINDS (6) [BIND]
Job 5:18 he wounds, but he also b up; he injures, H2502
Job 30:18 he b me like the neck of my garment. H273
Ps 147: 3 the brokenhearted and b up their wounds. H2502
Isa 30:26 when the LORD b up the bruises of his H2502
Ro 7: 2 is released from the law that b her to him. NDT
Col 3:14 which b them all together in G1639+5278

BINEA (2)
1Ch 8:37 Moza was the father of B; Raphah was his H1232
1Ch 9:43 Moza was the father of B; Rephaiah was H1232

BINNUI (8)
Ezr 8:33 son of Jeshua and Noadiah son of B. H1218
Ezr 10:30 Mattaniah, Bezalel, B and Manasseh. H1218
Ezr 10:38 From the descendants of B: Shimei, H1218
Ne 3:18 fellow Levites under B son of Henadad, H1218
Ne 3:24 B son of Henadad repaired another H1218
Ne 7:15 of B 648 H1218
Ne 10: 9 son of Azaniah, B of the sons of Henadad H1218
Ne 12: 8 were Jeshua, B, Kadmiel, Sherebiah, H1218

BIRD (39) [BIRD'S, BIRDS]
Ge 1:21 every winged b according to its kind. H6416
Ge 6:20 Two of every kind of b, of every kind of H6416
Ge 7: 3 also seven pairs of every kind of b H6416
Ge 7:14 its kind and every b according to its kind H6416

B

Lev 7:26 not eat the blood of any **b** or animal. H6416
Lev 14: 6 He is then to take the live **b** and dip it H7606
Lev 14: 6 the blood of the **b** that was killed over H7606
Lev 14: 7 is to release the live **b** in the open fields. H7606
Lev 14:51 the scarlet yarn and the live **b**, dip them H7606
Lev 14:51 blood of the dead **b** and the fresh water, H7606
Lev 14:52 fresh water, the live **b**, the cedar wood, H7606
Lev 14:53 is to release the live **b** in the open fields H7606
Lev 17:13 hunts any animal or **b** that may be eaten H6416
Lev 20:25 by any animal or **b** or anything that moves H6416
Dt 4:17 on earth or any **b** that flies in the H7606+4053
Dt 14:11 You may eat any clean **b**. H7606
Job 28: 7 No **b of prey** knows that hidden path, no H6514
Job 41: 5 a pet of it like a **b** or put it on a leash H7606
Ps 11: 1 "Flee like a **b** to your mountain. H7606
Ps 50:11 I know every **b** *in* the mountains, and the H6416
Ps 102: 7 I have become like a **b** alone on a roof. H7606
Ps 124: 7 have escaped like a **b** from the fowler's H7606
Pr 1:17 a net where every **b** can see it! H1251+4053
Pr 6: 5 like a **b** from the snare of the fowler. H7606
Pr 7:23 his liver, like a **b** darting into a snare H7606
Pr 27: 8 Like a **b** that flees its nest is anyone who H7606
Ecc 10:20 because a **b** *in* the sky may carry your H6416
Ecc 10:20 and a **b on the wing** may report H1251+4053
Isa 46:11 From the east I summon a **b of prey**; from H6514
Jer 4:25 every **b** *in* the sky had flown away. H6416
Jer 12: 9 like a speckled **b of prey** that other birds H6514
La 3:52 without cause hunted me like a **b**. H7606
Eze 39:17 out to every kind of **b** and all the wild H7606
Eze 44:31 anything, whether **b** or animal, found H6416
Da 4:33 eagle and his nails like the claws of a **b**. A10616
Da 7: 6 back it had four wings like those of a **b**. A10533
Hos 9:11 Ephraim's glory will fly away like a **b**—no H6416
Am 3: 5 Does a **b** swoop down to a trap on the H7606
Rev 18: 2 a haunt *for* every unclean **b**, a haunt for G3997

BIRD'S (2) [BIRD]

Lev 14:52 He shall purify the house with the **b** blood H7606
Dt 22: 6 you come across a **b** nest beside the road H7606

BIRDS (95) [BIRD]

Ge 1:20 let **b** fly above the earth across the H6416
Ge 1:22 and let the **b** increase on the earth." H6416
Ge 1:26 the fish in the sea and the **b** *in* the sky, H6416
Ge 1:28 in the sea and the **b** *in* the sky and over H6416
Ge 1:30 earth and all the **b** *in* the sky and all the H6416
Ge 2:19 the wild animals and all the **b** *in* the sky. H6416
Ge 2:20 the **b** *in* the sky and all the wild animals. H6416
Ge 6: 7 the **b** and the creatures that H6416+2021+9028
Ge 7: 8 of **b** and of all creatures that move along H6416
Ge 7:21 moved on land perished—**b**, livestock, H6416
Ge 7:23 and the **b** were wiped H6416+2021+9028
Ge 8:17 that is with you—the **b**, the animals, H6416
Ge 8:19 move along the ground and all the **b**— H6416
Ge 8:20 of all the clean animals and clean **b**, H6416
Ge 9: 2 and on all the **b** *in* the sky, on every H6416
Ge 9:10 was with you—the **b**, the livestock and H6416
Ge 15:10 opposite each other; the **b**, however, H7606
Ge 15:11 Then **b of prey** came down on the H6514
Ge 40:17 the **b** were eating them out of the H6416
Ge 40:19 And the **b** will eat away your flesh." H6416
Lev 1:14 to the LORD is a burnt offering of **b**, H6416
Lev 11:13 " 'These are the **b** you are to regard as H6416
Lev 11:46 concerning animals, **b**, every living thing H6416
Lev 14: 4 two live clean **b** and some cedar wood H7606
Lev 14: 5 order that one of the **b** be killed over fresh H7606
Lev 14:49 he is to take two **b** and some cedar wood, H7606
Lev 14:50 shall kill one of the **b** over fresh water in a H7606
Lev 20:25 between unclean and clean **b**. H6416
Dt 28:26 all the **b** and the wild H6416+2021+9028
1Sa 17:44 flesh to the **b** and the wild H6416+2021+9028
1Sa 17:46 army to the **b** and the wild H6416+2021+9028
2Sa 21:10 not let the **b** touch them by H6416+2021+9028
1Ki 4:33 He also spoke about animals and **b** H6416
1Ki 14:11 and the **b** will feed on those H6416+2021+9028
1Ki 16: 4 and **b** will feed on those H6416+2021+9028
1Ki 21:24 and the **b** will feed on those H6416+2021+9028
Job 12: 7 teach you, or the **b** *in* the sky, and they H6416
Job 28:21 concealed even from the **b** *in* the sky. H6416
Job 35:11 makes us wiser than the **b** *in* the sky? H6416
Ps 8: 8 the **b** *in* the sky, and the fish in the sea H7606
Ps 78:27 **b** like sand on the seashore. H6416+4053
Ps 79: 2 your servants as food for the **b** *of* the sky, H6416
Ps 104:12 The **b** *of* the sky nest by the waters; they H6416
Ps 104:17 There the **b** make their nests; the stork H7606
Ps 148:10 all cattle, small creatures and flying **b**, H7606
Ecc 9:12 in a cruel net, or **b** are taken in a snare H7606
Ecc 12: 4 when people rise up at the sound of **b** H7606
Isa 16: 2 Like fluttering **b** pushed from the nest, so H6416
Isa 18: 6 to the mountain **b of prey** and to the wild H6514
Isa 18: 6 the **b** will feed on them all summer H6514
Isa 31: 5 Like **b** hovering overhead, the LORD H7606
Jer 5:26 in wait like **men who snare b** and like H3687
Jer 5:27 Like cages full of **b**, their houses are full H6416
Jer 7:33 food for the **b** and the wild H6416+2021+9028
Jer 9:10 The **b** have all fled and the H6416+2021+9028
Jer 12: 4 the animals and **b** have perished. H6416
Jer 12: 9 of prey that other **b of prey** surround and H6514
Jer 15: 3 away and the **b** and the wild H6416+2021+9028
Jer 16: 4 food for the **b** and the wild H6416+2021+9028
Jer 19: 7 food to the **b** and the wild H6416+2021+9028
Jer 34:20 food for the **b** and the wild H6416+2021+9028
Eze 13:20 ensnare people like **b** and I will tear them H7256
Eze 13:20 free the people that you ensnare like **b**. H7256
Eze 17:23 **B** of every kind will nest in it; they H7606+4053
Eze 29: 5 beasts of the earth and the **b** *of* the sky. H6416
Eze 31: 6 All the **b** *of* the sky nested in its boughs H6416
Eze 31:13 All the **b** settled on the H6416+2021+9028
Eze 32: 4 I will let all the **b** *of* the sky settle on you H6416
Eze 38:20 fish in the sea, the **b** *in* the sky, the beasts H6416
Eze 39: 4 to all kinds of **carrion b** and to the H6514+7606
Da 2:38 beasts of the field and the **b** *in* the sky. A10533
Da 4:12 and the **b** lived in its A10616+10002+10723
Da 4:14 under it and the **b** from its branches. A10616
Da 4:21 its branches for the **b**— A10616+10002+10723
Hos 2:18 the **b** *in* the sky and the creatures that H6416
Hos 4: 3 the **b** *in* the sky and the fish in the sea are H6416
Hos 7:12 I will pull them down like the **b** *in* the sky. H6416
Zep 1: 3 will sweep away the **b** *in* the sky and the H6416
Mt 6:26 Look at the **b** of the air; they do not sow G4374
Mt 8:20 have dens and **b** have nests, G4374+3836+4041
Mt 13: 4 the path, and the **b** came and ate it up. G4374
Mt 13:32 so that the **b** come and G4374+3836+4041
Mk 4: 4 the path, and the **b** came and ate it up. G4374
Mk 4:32 that the **b** can perch in its G4374+3836+4041
Lk 8: 5 and the **b** ate it up. G4374+3836+4041
Lk 9:58 have dens and **b** have nests, G4374+3836+4041
Lk 12:24 how much more valuable you are *than* **b**! G4374
Lk 13:19 and the **b** perched in its G4374+3836+4041
Ac 10:12 as well as reptiles and **b**. G4374+3836+4041
Ac 11: 6 wild beasts, reptiles and **b**. G4374+3836+4041
Ro 1:23 human being and **b** and animals and G4374
1Co 15:39 have another, **b** another and fish another. G4764
Jas 3: 7 All kinds of animals, **b**, reptiles and sea G4374
Rev 19:17 a loud voice to all the **b** flying in midair, G3997
Rev 19:21 all the **b** gorged themselves on their G3997

BIRI See BETH BIRI

BIRSHA (1)

Ge 14: 2 Bera king of Sodom, **B** king of Gomorrah H1407

BIRTH (136) [BEAR]

Ge 3:16 painful labor *you will* **give b** *to* children. H3528
Ge 4: 1 she became pregnant and **gave b** *to* Cain. H3528
Ge 4: 2 Later *she* **gave b** *to* his brother Abel. H3528
Ge 4:17 became pregnant and **gave b** *to* Enoch. H3528
Ge 4:20 Adah **gave b** *to* Jabal; he was the father of H3528
Ge 4:25 and *she* **gave b** *to* a son and named him H3528
Ge 11:28 Ur of the Chaldeans, in the land of his **b**. H4580
Ge 16:11 pregnant and *you will* **give b** *to* a son. H3528
Ge 25:13 of Ishmael, listed in the **order of** their **b**: H9352
Ge 25:24 When the time came for her to **give b** H3528
Ge 25:26 years old when Rebekah **gave b** *to* them. H3528
Ge 29:32 became pregnant and **gave b** *to* a son. H3528
Ge 29:33 when *she* **gave b** *to* a son she said H3528
Ge 29:34 when *she* **gave b** *to* a son she said H3528
Ge 29:35 when *she* **gave b** *to* a son she said H3528
Ge 30:21 time later *she* **gave b** *to* a daughter and H3528
Ge 30:23 pregnant and **gave b** *to* a son and said, H3528
Ge 30:25 After Rachel **gave b** *to* Joseph, Jacob said H3528
Ge 31: 8 all the flocks **gave b** *to* speckled young; H3528
Ge 35:16 Rachel *began to* **give b** and had great H3528
Ge 38: 3 she became pregnant and **gave b** *to* a son, H3528
Ge 38: 4 again and **gave b** *to* a son and named H3528
Ge 38: 5 *She* **gave b** *to* still another son and named H3528
Ge 38: 5 It was at Kezib that she **gave b** *to* him. H3528
Ge 38:27 When the time came for her *to* **give b** H3528
Ge 38:28 As she *was* **giving b**, one of them put out H3528
Ge 50:23 of Manasseh *were* **placed at b** on H3528
Ex 1:19 are vigorous and **give b** before the H3528
Ex 2: 2 became pregnant and **gave b** *to* a son. H3528
Ex 2:22 Zipporah **gave b** *to* a son, and Moses H3528
Ex 21:22 and she **gives b prematurely** but H3655+3529
Ex 28:10 in the order of their **b**—six names on one H9352
Lev 12: 2 pregnant and **gives b** *to* a son will be H3528
Lev 12: 5 If *she* **gives b** *to* a daughter, for two weeks H3528
Lev 12: 7 the *woman who* **gives b** to a boy or a H3528
Nu 11:12 *Did* I **give** them **b**? Why do you H3528
Dt 32:18 you forgot the God *who* **gave** you **b**. H2655
Jdg 13: 2 wife who was childless, unable *to* **give b**. H3528
Jdg 13: 3 to become pregnant and **give b** *to* a son. H3528
Jdg 13:24 The woman **gave b** *to* a boy and named H3528
Ru 1:12 tonight and then **gave b** *to* sons— H3528
Ru 4:13 her to conceive, and *she* **gave b** *to* a son. H3528
Ru 4:15 to you than seven sons, *has* **given** him **b**." H3528
1Sa 1:20 became pregnant and **gave b** *to* a son. H3528
1Sa 2:21 *she* **gave b** *to* three sons and two H3528
1Sa 4:19 she went into labor and **gave b**, but was H3528
1Sa 4:20 "Don't despair; *you have* **given b** *to* a son." H3528
2Sa 12:24 *She* **gave b** *to* a son, and they named him H3528
1Ki 11: 3 hundred wives **of royal b** and three H8576
2Ki 4:17 that same time *she* **gave b** *to* a son, H3528
2Ki 19: 3 come to the **moment of b** and there is no H5402
1Ch 2:49 *She* also **gave b** *to* Shaaph the father of Madmannah and *to* H3528
1Ch 4: 9 saying, "*I* **gave b** to him in pain. H3528
1Ch 4:17 One of Mered's wives **gave b** *to* Miriam H2225
1Ch 4:18 tribe of Judah **gave b** *to* Jered the father H3528
1Ch 7:14 *She* **gave b** *to* Makir the father of Gilead. H3528
1Ch 7:16 wife Maakah **gave b** *to* a son and named H3528
1Ch 7:18 His sister Hammoleketh **gave b** *to* Ishhod H3528
1Ch 7:23 became pregnant and **gave b** *to* a son. H3528
Job 3: 1 his mouth and cursed the day of his **b**. NDT
Job 3: 3 "May the day of *my* **b** perish, and the H3528
Job 3:11 "Why did I not perish at **b**, and die as I H8167
Job 15:35 They conceive trouble and **give b** *to* evil H3528
Job 31:18 and from my **b** I guided the widow H1061+562
Job 38:29 Who **gives b** *to* the frost from the heavens H3528
Job 39: 1 know when the mountain goats **give b**? H3528
Job 39: 2 Do you know the time they **give b**? H3528
Ps 7:14 trouble and **gives b** *to* disillusionment. H3528
Ps 22:10 From **b** I was cast on you; from my H8167
Ps 51: 5 Surely *I was* sinful **at b**, sinful from the H2655
Ps 58: 3 Even from **b** the wicked go astray; from H8167
Ps 71: 6 From **b** I have relied on you; you brought H1061
Pr 8:24 watery depths, *I* **was given b**, when there H2655
Pr 8:25 in place, before the hills, *I* **was given b**, H2655
Pr 23:25 may *she who* **gave** you **b** be joyful! H3528
Ecc 7: 1 the day of death better than the day of **b**. H3528
Ecc 10:17 king is of noble **b** and whose princes eat H1201
SS 8: 5 there she who was in labor **gave** you **b**. H3528
Isa 7:14 virgin *will* conceive and **give b** *to* a son, H3528
Isa 8: 3 she conceived and **gave b** *to* a son. H3528
Isa 23: 4 "I have neither been in labor nor **given b** H3528
Isa 26:17 woman about to **give b** writhes and cries H3528
Isa 26:18 writhed in labor, but *we* **gave b** *to* wind. H3528
Isa 26:19 the earth *will* **give b** *to* her dead. H5877
Isa 33:11 conceive chaff, *you* **give b** *to* straw; your H3528
Isa 37: 3 come to the **moment of b** and there is no H5402
Isa 45:10 a mother, 'What *have you* **brought** *to* **b**? H2655
Isa 46: 3 you whom I have upheld since your **b** H1061
Isa 48: 8 you are; you were called a rebel from **b**. H1061
Isa 51: 2 your father, and to Sarah, *who* **gave** you **b**. H2655
Isa 59: 4 they conceive trouble and **give b** *to* evil. H3528
Isa 66: 7 goes into labor, *she* **gives b**; before the H3528
Isa 66: 8 in labor than *she* **gives b** *to* her children. H3528
Isa 66: 9 *Do* I **bring to the moment of b** and not H8689
Jer 2:14 a servant, a **slave by b**? Why then H3535+1074
Jer 2:27 my father,' and to stone, 'You **gave** me **b**. H3528
Jer 15:10 mother, that *you* **gave** me **b**, a man with H3528
Jer 22:26 the mother who **gave** you **b** into another H3528
Jer 50:12 *she who* **gave** you **b** will be disgraced. H3528
Eze 16: 3 Your ancestry and **b** were in the land of H4580
Eze 23: 4 They were mine and **gave b** *to* sons and H3528
Eze 31: 6 of the wild **gave b** under its branches; H3528
Hos 1: 6 again and **gave b** *to* a daughter. H3528
Hos 5: 7 *they* **give b** *to* illegitimate children. H3528
Hos 9:11 fly away like a bird—no **b**, no pregnancy, H4256
Mt 1:18 This is how the **b** of Jesus the Messiah G1161
Mt 1:21 *She will* **give b** to a son, and you are to G5503
Mt 1:23 virgin will conceive and **give b to** a son, G5503
Mt 1:25 their marriage until *she* **gave b to** a son. G5503
Mt 24: 8 All these are the beginning *of* **b pains**. G6047
Mk 13: 8 These are the beginning *of* **b pains**. G6047
Lk 1:14 many will rejoice because of his **b**, G1161
Lk 1:31 You will conceive and **give b to** a son, and G5503
Lk 1:57 to have her baby, *she* **gave b to** a son. G1164
Lk 2: 7 and *she* **gave b to** her firstborn, a son. G5503
Lk 11:27 the mother who **gave** you **b** and nursed G1002
Lk 19:12 "A man **of noble b** went to a distant G2302
Jn 3: 6 Flesh **gives b to** flesh, but the Spirit gives G1164
Jn 3: 6 to flesh, but the Spirit **gives b to** spirit. G1164
Jn 9: 1 went along, he saw a man blind from **b**. G1162
Jn 9:34 "You *were* steeped in sin *at* **b**; how dare G1164
Jn 16:21 A woman **giving b to a child** has pain G5503
Ac 3: 2 was lame from **b** was being carried G3120+3613
Ac 7: 8 circumcised him eight days after his **b**. NDT
Ac 14: 8 that way from **b** and had never G3120+3613
1Co 1:26 influential; not many were **of noble b**. G2302
Gal 2:15 "We who are Jews *by* **b** and not sinful G5882
Eph 2:11 you who are Gentiles by **b** and called G4922
Jas 1:15 has conceived, *it* **gives b to** sin; and sin, G5503
Jas 1:15 when it is full-grown, **gives b to** death. G652
Jas 1:18 He chose *to* **give** us **b** through the word of G652
1Pe 1: 3 great mercy *he has* **given** us **new b** into a G335
Rev 12: 2 out in pain *as she was about to* **give b**. G5503
Rev 12: 4 of the woman who was about to **give b**, G5503
Rev 12: 5 *She* **gave b** to a son, a male child, who G5503
Rev 12:13 the woman who *had* **given b** to the male G5503

BIRTHDAY (3) [BEAR]

Ge 40:20 Now the third day was Pharaoh's **b** H3528+3427
Mt 14: 6 On Herod's **b** the daughter of Herodias G1160
Mk 6:21 On his **b** Herod gave a banquet for his G1160

BIRTHDAYS (1) [BEAR]

Job 1: 4 to hold feasts in their homes on their **b**, H3427

BIRTHRIGHT (6) [BEAR]

Ge 25:31 Jacob replied, "First sell me your **b**." H1148
Ge 25:32 "What good is the **b** to me?" H1148
Ge 25:33 an oath to him, selling his **b** to Jacob. H1148
Ge 25:34 got up and left. So Esau despised his **b**. H1148
Ge 27:36 He took my **b**, and now he's taken my H1148
1Ch 5: 1 record in accordance with his **b**, H1148

BIRZAITH (1)

1Ch 7:31 Malkiel, who was the father of **B**. H1365

BISHLAM (1)

Ezr 4: 7 Artaxerxes king of Persia, **B**, Mithredath, H1420

BISHOP, BISHOPS (KJV) OVERSEER, OVERSEERS

BISHOPRICK (KJV) PLACE OF LEADERSHIP

BIT (5) [BITES, BIT]
Nu 21: 6 they b the people and many Israelites H5966
2Ki 19:28 in your nose and my b in your mouth, H5496
Ps 32: 9 must be controlled by b and bridle or they H5496
Isa 30:28 jaws of the peoples a b that leads them H8270
Isa 37:29 in your nose and my b in your mouth, H5496

BITE (5) [BIT, BITES, BITTEN]
Jer 8:17 charmed, and they will b you," declares H5966
Am 5:19 on the wall only to have a snake b him. H5966
Am 9: 3 I will command the serpent to b them. H5966
Jn 6: 7 enough bread for each one to have a b!" G1099
Gal 5:15 If you b and devour each other, watch out G1231

BITES (3) [BITE]
Ge 49:17 that b the horse's heels so that its rider H5966
Pr 23:32 In the end it b like a snake and poisons H5966
Ecc 10:11 If a snake b before it is charmed, the H5966

BITHIAH (1)
1Ch 4:18 the children of Pharaoh's daughter B, H1437

BITHRON (NIV84) MORNING HOURS

BITHYNIA (2)
Ac 16: 7 they tried to enter B, but the Spirit of G1049
1Pe 1: 1 Galatia, Cappadocia, Asia and B, G1049

BITS (2) [BIT]
Am 6:11 into pieces and the small house into b. H1323
Jas 3: 3 When we put b into the mouths of horses G5903

BITTEN (3) [BITE]
Nu 21: 8 anyone who is b can look at it and live." H5966
Nu 21: 9 Then when anyone was b by a snake and H5966
Ecc 10: 8 through a wall may be b by a snake. H5966

BITTER (46) [BITTERLY, BITTERNESS, EMBITTER, EMBITTERED]
Ge 27:34 out with a loud and b cry and said to his H5253
Ex 1:14 They made their lives b with harsh labor in H5352
Ex 12: 8 along with b herbs, and bread made H5353
Ex 15:23 could not drink its water because it was b. H5253
Nu 5:18 he himself holds the b water that brings a H5253
Nu 5:19 may this b water that brings a curse not H5253
Nu 5:23 then wash them off into the b water. H5253
Nu 5:24 the woman drink the b water that brings a H5253
Nu 5:24 causes b suffering will enter her. H5253
Nu 5:27 that brings a curse and causes b suffering, H5253
Nu 9:11 with unleavened bread and b herbs. H5353
Dt 29:18 among you that produces such b poison. H4360
Ru 1:13 It is more b for me than for you, because H5352
Ru 1:20 the Almighty has made my life very b. H5352
1Sa 14:52 days of Saul there was b war with the H2617
1Sa 30: 6 each one was b in spirit because of his H5352
1Ki 2: 8 who called down b curses on me the day I H5344
2Ki 4:27 She is in b distress, but the LORD has H5352
Job 3:20 those in misery, and life to the b of soul, H5253
Job 13:26 you write down b things against me and H5353
Job 23: 2 "Even today my complaint is b; his hand H5308
Job 27: 2 the Almighty, who has made my life b, H5352
Ps 71:20 troubles, many and b, you will restore my H8273
Ps 107:12 So he subjected them to b labor; they H6662
Pr 5: 4 in the end she is b as gall, sharp as a H5253
Pr 27: 7 to the hungry even what is b tastes sweet. H5253
Ecc 7:26 I find more b than death the woman who H5253
Isa 5:20 who put b for sweet and sweet for bitter. H5253
Isa 5:20 who put bitter for sweet and sweet for b. H5253
Isa 24: 9 with a song; the beer is b to its drinkers. H5352
Jer 2:19 realize how evil and b it is for you when H5253
Jer 4:18 How b it is! How it pierces to H5352
Jer 6:26 mourn with b wailing as for an only son H9476
Jer 9:15 make this people eat b food and drink H4360
Jer 23:15 "I will make them eat b food and drink H4360
La 1: 4 women grieve, and she is in b anguish. H5352
La 3:15 filled me with b herbs and given me gall H5353
Eze 21: 6 them with broken heart and b grief. H5320
Eze 27:31 anguish of soul and with b mourning. H5253
Hos 12:14 But Ephraim has aroused his b anger; his H9476
Am 8:10 an only son and the end of it like a b day. H5253
Zep 1:14 The cry on the day of the LORD is b; the H5253
Heb 12:15 of God and that no b root grows up to G4394
Jas 3:14 But if you harbor b envy and selfish G4395
Rev 8:11 A third of the waters turned b, and many G952
Rev 8:11 died from the waters that had become b. G4393

BITTERLY (21) [BITTER]
Ge 50:10 they lamented loudly and b; and H3878+4394
Nu 14:39 this to all the Israelites, they mourned b. H4394
Jdg 5:23 'Curse its people b, because they did H826+826
Jdg 21: 2 raising their voices and weeping b. H1524
1Sa 1:10 prayed to the LORD, weeping b. H1134+1134
2Sa 13:36 and all his attendants wept very b. H1524
2Ki 14:26 LORD had seen how b everyone in Israel, H5253
2Ki 20: 3 And Hezekiah wept b. H1524
Ezr 10: 1 They too wept b. H1134+2221+1135
Est 4: 1 out into the city, wailing loudly and b. H5253
Isa 22: 4 "Turn away from me; let me weep b. H5352
Isa 33: 7 the streets; the envoys of peace weep b. H5253
Isa 38: 3 And Hezekiah wept b. H1524
Jer 13:17 my eyes will weep b, overflowing H1963+1963
Jer 22:10 weep b for him who is exiled H1134+1134
Jer 48: 5 to Luhith, weeping b as they go; on H1140+1140
La 1: 2 B she weeps at night, tears are on H1134+1134
Eze 27:30 will raise their voice and cry b over you; H5253
Zec 12:10 and grieve b for him as one grieves for a H5352
Mt 26:75 And he went outside and wept b. G4396
Lk 22:62 And he went outside and wept b. G4396

BITTERN (KJV) OWL, OWLS

BITTERNESS (17) [BITTER]
Ge 49:23 With b archers attacked him; they shot at H5352
Dt 32:32 with poison, and their clusters with b. H5353
1Sa 15:32 he thought, "Surely the b of death is past." H5253
2Sa 2:26 Don't you realize that this will end in b H5253
Job 7:11 I will complain in the b of my soul. H5253
Job 10: 1 speak out in the b of my soul. H5253
Job 21:25 Another dies in b of soul, never having H5253
Pr 14:10 Each heart knows its own b, and no one H5289
Pr 17:25 to his father and b to the mother who H4933
La 3: 5 surrounded me with b and hardship. H8032
La 3:19 my wandering, the b and the gall. H8032
Eze 3:14 I went in b and in the anger of my H5253
Am 5: 7 who turn justice into b and cast H4360
Am 6:12 the fruit of righteousness into b— H4360
Ac 8:23 that you are full of b and captive to sin." G4394
Ro 3:14 "Their mouths are full of cursing and b." G4394
Eph 4:31 Get rid of all b, rage and anger, brawling G4394

BIZIOTHIAH (1)
Jos 15:28 Hazar Shual, Beersheba, B, H1026

BIZTHA (1)
Est 1:10 Mehuman, B, Harbona, Bigtha, H1030

BLACK (16) [BLACKENED, BLACKER, BLACKEST, BLACKNESS]
Ex 10:15 They covered all the ground until it was b H3124
Lev 11:13 the eagle, the vulture, the b vulture, H6465
Lev 11:14 the red kite, any kind of b kite, H370
Lev 13:31 than skin deep and there is no b hair in it, H8839
Lev 13:37 can see, and if b hair has grown in it H8839
Dt 4:11 with b clouds and deep darkness. H3125
Dt 14:12 the eagle, the vulture, the b vulture, H6465
Dt 14:13 the red kite, the b kite, any kind of falcon, H370
1Ki 18:45 the sky grew b with clouds, the wind H7722
Job 30:30 My skin grows b and peels; my body burns H8837
SS 5:11 his hair is wavy and b as a raven. H8839
Zec 6: 2 first chariot had red horses, the second b, H8839
Zec 6: 6 The one with the b horses is going toward H8839
Mt 5:36 cannot make even one hair white or b. G3506
Rev 6: 5 there before me was a b horse! G3506
Rev 6:12 The sun turned b like sackcloth made of G3506

BLACKENED (1) [BLACK]
Job 30:28 I go about b, but not by the sun; I stand H7722

BLACKER (1) [BLACK]
La 4: 8 But now they are b than soot; they are not H3124

BLACKEST (3) [BLACK]
Job 28: 3 farthest recesses for ore in the b darkness. H7516
2Pe 2:17 B darkness is reserved for them. G2432
Jude 13 whom b darkness has been reserved G2432

BLACKNESS (3) [BLACK]
Job 3: 5 settle over it; may b overwhelm it. H4025+3427
Joel 2: 2 gloom, a day of clouds and b. H6906
Zep 1:15 gloom, a day of clouds and b— H6906

BLACKSMITH (3)
1Sa 13:19 Not a b could be found in the whole land H3093
Isa 44:12 The b takes a tool and works with it H3093+1366
Isa 54:16 is I who created the b who fans the coals H3093

BLADE (2)
Jdg 3:22 Even the handle sank in after the b, and H4258
Eze 21:16 then to the left, wherever your b is turned. H7156

BLAINS (KJV) BOILS

BLAME (6) [BLAMELESS, BLAMELESSLY]
Ge 43: 9 I will bear the b before you all my life. H2627
Ge 44:10 the rest of you will be free from b. H5929
Ge 44:32 back to you, I will bear the b before you H2627
Ro 9:19 "Then why does God still b us? For who G3522
1Ti 5: 7 so that no one may be open to b. G455
1Ti 6:14 without spot or b until the appearing of G455

BLAMELESS (56) [BLAME]
Ge 6: 9 b among the people of his time H9459
Ge 17: 1 walk before me faithfully and be b. H9459
Dt 18:13 You must be b before the LORD your God. H9459
2Sa 22:24 I have been b before him and have kept H9459
2Sa 22:26 to the b you show yourself H1475+9459
2Sa 22:26 to the blameless you show yourself b, H9462
Job 1: 1 This man was b and upright; he feared H9447
Job 1: 8 earth like him; he is b and upright, a man H9447
Job 2: 3 earth like him; he is b and upright, a man H9447
Job 4: 6 confidence and your b ways your hope? H9448
Job 8:20 does not reject one who is b or strengthen H9447
Job 9:20 if I were b, it would pronounce H9447
Job 9:21 "Although I am b, I have no concern for H9447
Job 9:22 'He destroys both the b and the wicked.' H9447
Job 12: 4 laughingstock, though righteous and b! H9459
Job 22: 3 What would he gain if your ways were b? H9462
Job 31: 6 scales and he will know that I am b— H9450
Ps 15: 2 The one whose walk is b, who does what H9459
Ps 18:23 I have been b before him and have kept H9459
Ps 18:25 to the b you show yourself H1505+9459
Ps 18:25 to the blameless you show yourself b, H9462
Ps 19:13 Then I will be b, innocent of great H9462
Ps 26: 1 for I have led a b life; I have trusted H9448
Ps 26:11 I lead a b life; deliver me and be merciful H9448
Ps 37:18 The b spend their days under the LORD's H9459
Ps 37:37 Consider the b, observe the upright; H9447
Ps 50:23 and to the b I will show my H9447+2006
Ps 84:11 he withhold from those whose walk is b. H9459
Ps 101: 2 I will be careful to lead a b life—when H9459
Ps 101: 2 the affairs of my house with a b heart. H9448
Ps 101: 6 one whose walk is b will minister to me. H9459
Ps 119: 1 Blessed are those whose ways are b, who H9459
Pr 2: 7 he is a shield to those whose walk is b, H9448
Pr 2:21 in the land, and the b will remain in it; H9459
Pr 10:29 The way of the LORD is a refuge for the b H9448
Pr 11: 5 righteousness of the b makes their paths H9459
Pr 11:20 he delights in those whose ways are b. H9459
Pr 19: 1 poor whose walk is b than a fool whose H9448
Pr 20: 7 The righteous lead b lives; blessed are H9448
Pr 28: 6 poor whose walk is b than the rich whose H9448
Pr 28:10 the b will receive a good inheritance. H9459
Pr 28:18 The one whose walk is b is kept safe, but H9459
Eze 28:15 You were b in your ways from the day you H9459
1Co 1: 8 so that you will be b on the day of our Lord G441
Eph 1: 4 of the world to be holy and b in his sight. G320
Eph 5:27 any other blemish, but holy and b. G320
Php 1:10 may be pure and b for the day of Christ G718
Php 2:15 so that you may become b and pure G289
1Th 2:10 righteous and b we were among you who G290
1Th 3:13 so that you will be b and holy in the G289
1Th 5:23 body be kept b at the coming of our G290
Titus 1: 6 An elder must be b, faithful to his wife, G441
Titus 1: 7 he must be b—not overbearing, G441
Heb 7:26 one who is holy, b, pure, set apart from G179
2Pe 3:14 found spotless, b and at peace with him. G318
Rev 14: 5 lie was found in their mouths; they are b. G320

BLAMELESSLY (1) [BLAME]
Lk 1: 6 all the Lord's commands and decrees b. G289

BLANKET (2) [BLANKETS]
Jdg 4:18 her tent, and she covered him with a b. H8526
Isa 28:20 the b too narrow to wrap around you. H5012

BLANKETS (2) [BLANKET]
Jdg 5:10 sitting on your saddle b, and you who H4496
Eze 27:20 'Dedan traded in saddle b with you. H955+2927

BLASPHEME (6) [BLASPHEMED, BLASPHEMER, BLASPHEMES, BLASPHEMIES, BLASPHEMING, BLASPHEMOUS, BLASPHEMY]
Ex 22:28 "Do not b God or curse the ruler of your H7837
Lev 24:16 when they b the Name they are to be put H5919
Ac 26:11 punished, and I tried to force them to b. G1059
1Ti 1:20 over to Satan to be taught not to b. G1059
2Pe 2:12 But these people b in matters they do not G1059
Rev 13: 6 It opened its mouth to b God, and to G1060

BLASPHEMED (10) [BLASPHEME]
Lev 24:11 the Israelite woman b the Name with a H5919
1Sa 3:13 his sons b God, and he failed H7837
2Ki 19: 6 of the king of Assyria have b me. H1552
2Ki 19:22 Who is it you have ridiculed and b H1552
Isa 37: 6 of the king of Assyria have b me. H1552
Isa 37:23 Who is it you have ridiculed and b H1552
Isa 52: 5 all day long my name is constantly b. H5540
Eze 20:27 also your ancestors b me by being H1552
Ac 19:37 though they have neither robbed temples nor b G1059
Ro 2:24 "God's name is b among the Gentiles G1059

BLASPHEMER (3) [BLASPHEME]
Lev 24:14 "Take the b outside the camp. H7837
Lev 24:23 they took the b outside the camp and H7837
1Ti 1:13 though I was once a b and a persecutor G1061

BLASPHEMES (4) [BLASPHEME]
Lev 24:16 anyone who b the name of the LORD is to H5919
Nu 15:30 b the LORD and must be cut off from the H1552
Mk 3:29 whoever b against the Holy Spirit will G1059
Lk 12:10 anyone who b against the Holy Spirit G1059

BLASPHEMIES (3) [BLASPHEME]
Ne 9:18 or when they committed awful b. H5542
Ne 9:26 back to you; they committed awful b. H5542
Rev 13: 5 proud words and b and to exercise its G1060

BLASPHEMING (3) [BLASPHEME]
Mt 9: 3 law said to themselves, "This fellow is b!" G1059
Mk 2: 7 He's b! Who can forgive G1059
Jas 2: 7 they not the ones who are b the noble G1059

BLASPHEMOUS (3) [BLASPHEME]
Ac 6:11 Stephen speak b words against Moses G1061
Rev 13: 1 on its horns, and on each head a b name. G1060
Rev 17: 3 was covered with b names and had seven G1060

BLASPHEMY (7) [BLASPHEME]
Mt 12:31 b against the Spirit will not be G1060

Mt 26:65 his clothes and said, "*He has* **spoken b**! *G1059*
Mt 26:65 now you have heard the **b**. *G1060*
Mk 14:64 "You have heard the **b**. What do you think?" *G1060*
Lk 5:21 "Who is this fellow who speaks **b**? *G1060*
Jn 10:33 replied, "but for **b**, because you, a mere *G1060*
Jn 10:36 do you accuse me of **b** because I said, *G1059*

BLAST (19) [BLASTS]
Ex 15: 8 By the **b** *of* your nostrils the waters piled H8120
Ex 19:13 the ram's horn **sounds a long b** may they H5432
Ex 19:16 the mountain, and a very loud trumpet **b**. H7754
Nu 10: 5 When a **trumpet b** is sounded, the tribes H9558
Nu 10: 6 At the sounding of a second **b**, the camps H9558
Nu 10: 6 The **b** will be the signal for setting out. H9558
Nu 10: 9 **sound a b** on the trumpets. H8131
Jos 6: 5 sound a long **b** on the trumpets, H7754+8795
Jos 6:16 when the priests **sounded** the trumpet **b** H9546
2Sa 22:16 at the **b** *of* breath from his nostrils. H5972
Job 4: 9 at the **b** *of* his anger they are no more. H8120
Job 39:25 **At the b** *of* the trumpet it snorts H928+1896
Ps 18:15 at the **b** *of* breath from your nostrils. H5972
Ps 98: 6 trumpets and the **b** *of* the ram's horn— H7754
Ps 147:17 Who can withstand his **icy b**? H7938
Isa 27: 8 with his fierce **b** he drives her out H8120
Eze 22:20 into a furnace to be melted with a fiery **b**, H5870
Am 2: 2 amid war cries and the **b** *of* the trumpet. H7754
Heb 12:19 *to* a trumpet **b** or to such a voice speaking *G2491*

BLASTS (2) [BLAST]
Lev 23:24 assembly commemorated with **trumpet b**. H9558
Rev 8:13 of the trumpet **b** about to be sounded by *G5889*

BLASTUS (1)
Ac 12:20 After securing the support of **B**, a trusted *G1058*

BLAZE (2) [BLAZED, BLAZES, BLAZING]
Nu 21:28 from Heshbon, a **b** from the city of Sihon. H4259
Jer 48:45 Heshbon, a **b** from the midst of Sihon H4259

BLAZED (7) [BLAZE]
Dt 4:11 mountain while it **b** with fire to the very H1277
Jdg 13:20 As the flame **b up** from the altar toward H6590
2Sa 22: 9 from his mouth, burning coals **b** out of it. H1277
2Sa 22:13 of his presence bolts of lightning **b forth**. H1277
Ps 18: 8 from his mouth, burning coals **b** out of it. H1277
Ps 106:18 Fire **b** among their followers; a flame H1277
Jnh 4: 8 the sun **b** on Jonah's head so that he H5782

BLAZES (2) [BLAZE]
Hos 7: 6 in the morning it **b** like a flaming fire. H1277
Joel 2: 3 fire devours, behind them a flame **b**. H4265

BLAZING (25) [BLAZE]
Ge 15:17 firepot with a **b** torch appeared and H836
Ps 21: 9 you will burn them up as in a **b** furnace. H836
SS 8: 6 It burns like **b** fire, like a mighty H8404
Isa 10:16 pomp a fire will be kindled like a **b** flame. H3679
Isa 34: 9 her land will become **b** pitch! H1277
Isa 62: 1 like the dawn, her salvation like a **b** torch. H1277
Eze 20:47 The **b** flame will not be quenched, and H4259
Da 3: 6 be thrown into a **b** furnace." A10471+10328
Da 3:11 will be thrown into a **b** furnace. A10471+10328
Da 3:15 immediately into a **b** furnace. A10471+10328
Da 3:17 are thrown into the **b** furnace, A10471+10328
Da 3:20 throw them into the **b** furnace. A10471+10328
Da 3:21 and thrown into the **b** furnace. A10471+10328
Da 3:23 fell into the **b** furnace. A10471+10328
Da 3:26 opening of the **b** furnace and A10471+10328
Da 7:11 destroyed and thrown into the **b** fire. A10329
Mt 13:42 They will throw them into the **b** furnace *G4786*
Mt 13:50 throw them into the **b** furnace, where *G4786*
Ac 26:13 **b around** me and my companions. *G4334*
2Th 1: 7 from heaven in **b** fire with his powerful *G5825*
Rev 1:14 as snow, and his eyes were like **b** fire. *G5825*
Rev 2:18 whose eyes are like **b** fire and whose feet *G5825*
Rev 4: 5 In front of the throne, seven lamps *were* **b**. *G2794*
Rev 8:10 a great star, **b** like a torch, fell from *G2794*
Rev 19:12 His eyes are like **b** fire, and on his head *G5825*

BLEACH (1)
Mk 9: 3 than anyone in the world could **b** them. *G3326*

BLEAT (1) [BLEATING]
Isa 34:14 wild goats *will* **b** to each other; there H7924

BLEATING (1) [BLEAT]
1Sa 15:14 "What then is this **b** *of* sheep in my ears? H7754

BLEEDING (8) [BLOOD]
Lev 12: 4 thirty-three days to be purified from her **b**. H1947
Lev 12: 5 sixty-six days to be purified from her **b**. H1947
Mt 9:20 a woman *who had been* **subject to b** for *G137*
Mk 5:25 been subject to **b** for twelve years. *G4868+135*
Mk 5:29 Immediately her **b** stopped and she *G4380+135*
Lk 8:43 had been **subject to b** for *G1877+4868+135*
Lk 8:44 and immediately her **b** stopped. *G4868+135*
Ac 19:16 they ran out of the house naked and **b**. *G5547*

BLEMISH (6) [BLEMISHED, BLEMISHES]
Lev 22:21 be without defect or **b** to be acceptable. H4583
Nu 19: 2 without defect or **b** and that has never H4583
2Sa 14:25 the sole of his foot there was no **b** in him. H4583
Eph 5:27 without stain or wrinkle or any other **b** *G5525*
Col 1:22 **without b** and free from accusation *G320*

1Pe 1:19 blood of Christ, a lamb **without b** or defect. *G320*

BLEMISHED (1) [BLEMISH]
Mal 1:14 then sacrifices a **b** *animal* to the Lord. H8845

BLEMISHES (2) [BLEMISH]
2Pe 2:13 They are blots and **b**, reveling in their *G3700*
Jude 12 These people are **b** at your love feasts *G5069*

BLEND (2) [BLENDED]
Ex 30:25 a fragrant **b**, the work of a perfumer. H8381
Ex 30:35 make a **fragrant b** *of* incense, the work H8381

BLENDED (2) [BLEND]
2Ch 16:14 with spices and various **b** perfumes, H8379
SS 7: 2 a rounded goblet that never lacks **b wine**. H4641

BLESS (94) [BLESSED, BLESSEDNESS, BLESSES, BLESSING, BLESSINGS]
Ge 12: 2 great nation, and *I will* **b** you; I will make H1385
Ge 12: 3 *I will* **b** those who bless you, and whoever H1385
Ge 12: 3 I will bless *those who* **b** you, and whoever H1385
Ge 17:16 *I will* **b** her and will surely give you a son H1385
Ge 17:16 *I will* **b** her so that she will be the mother H1385
Ge 17:20 *I will* surely **b** him; I will make him fruitful H1385
Ge 22:17 *I will* **surely b** you and make your H1385+1385
Ge 26: 3 I will be with you and *will* **b** you. H1385
Ge 26:24 *I will* **b** you and will increase the number H1385
Ge 27:23 brother Esau; so *he proceeded to* **b** him. H1385
Ge 27:29 be cursed and *those who* **b** you be H1385
Ge 27:34 cry and said to his father, "**B** me—me too, H1385
Ge 27:38 **B** me too, my father!" Then H1385
Ge 28: 3 *May* God Almighty **b** you and make you H1385
Ge 32:26 "I will not let you go unless *you* **b** me." H1385
Ge 48: 9 "Bring them to me so *I may* **b** them." H1385
Ge 48:16 me from all harm—*may he* **b** these boys. H1385
Ex 12:32 you have said, and go. And also **b** me." H1385
Ex 20:24 be honored, I will come to you and **b** you. H1385
Nu 6:23 'This is how *you are to* **b** the Israelites. H1385
Nu 6:24 " ' "The LORD **b** you and keep you; H1385
Nu 6:27 name on the Israelites, and I *will* **b** them." H1385
Nu 22: 6 For I know that whoever *you* **b** is blessed H1385
Nu 23:11 *you have* **done nothing but b** H1385+1385
Nu 23:20 I have received a command *to* **b**; he has H1385
Nu 23:25 curse them at all nor **b** them **at all**!" H1385+1385
Nu 24: 1 saw that it pleased the LORD *to* **b** Israel, H1385
Nu 24: 9 "*May those who* **b** you be blessed and H1385
Dt 1:11 a thousand times and **b** you as he has H1385
Dt 7:13 He will love you and **b** you and increase H1385
Dt 7:13 *He will* **b** the fruit of your womb, the crops H1385
Dt 14:29 the LORD your God *may* **b** you in all the H1385
Dt 15: 4 inheritance, he will **richly b** you, H1385+1385
Dt 15: 6 For the LORD your God *will* **b** you as he has H1385
Dt 15:10 the LORD your God *will* **b** you in all your H1385
Dt 15:18 the LORD your God *will* **b** you in everything H1385
Dt 16:15 For the LORD your God *will* **b** you in all H1385
Dt 23:20 LORD your God *may* **b** you in everything H1385
Dt 24:19 the LORD your God *may* **b** you in all the H1385
Dt 26:15 **b** your people Israel and the land you H1385
Dt 27:12 stand on Mount Gerizim *to* **b** the people: H1385
Dt 28: 8 The LORD your God *will* **b** you in the land H1385
Dt 28:12 in season and *to* **b** all the work of your H1385
Dt 30:16 the LORD your God *will* **b** you in the land H1385
Dt 33:11 **B** all his skills, LORD, and be pleased with H1385
Dt 33:13 "*May* the LORD **b** his land with the precious H1385
Jos 8:33 gave instructions *to* **b** the people of Israel. H1385
Jdg 17: 2 mother said, "The LORD **b** you, my son!" H1385
Ru 2: 4 "The LORD **b** you!" they answered. H1385
Ru 2:20 "The LORD **b** him!" Naomi said to her H1385
Ru 3:10 "The LORD **b** you, my daughter," he replied H1385
1Sa 2:20 Eli *would* **b** Elkanah and his wife, saying H1385
1Sa 9:13 because he *must* **b** the sacrifice H1385
1Sa 15:13 reached him, Saul said, "The LORD **b** you! H1385
1Sa 23:21 "The LORD **b** you for your concern for me. H1385
2Sa 2: 5 "The LORD **b** you for showing this kindness H1385
2Sa 6:20 David returned home *to* **b** his household, H1385
2Sa 7:29 Now be pleased *to* **b** the house of your H1385
2Sa 21: 3 atonement so that *you will* **b** the LORD's H1385
1Ch 4:10 that *you would* **b** me and enlarge H1385+1385
1Ch 16:43 David returned home *to* **b** his family. H1385
1Ch 17:27 have been pleased *to* **b** the house of your H1385
2Ch 30:27 the Levites stood *to* **b** the people, H1385
Job 31:20 their hearts *did* not **b** me for warming H1385
Ps 5:12 you **b** the righteous; you surround H1385
Ps 28: 9 Save your people and **b** your inheritance H1385
Ps 62: 4 With their mouths *they* **b**, but in their H1385
Ps 65:10 you soften it with showers and **b** its crops. H1385
Ps 67: 1 gracious to us and **b** us and make his face H1385
Ps 67: 7 *May* God **b** us *still*, so that all the ends of H1385
Ps 72:15 ever pray for him and **b** him all day long. H1385
Ps 109:28 they curse, *may* you **b**; may those who H1385
Ps 115:12 The LORD remembers us and *will* **b** us: He H1385
Ps 115:12 *He will* **b** his people Israel, he will bless H1385
Ps 115:12 *he will* **b** the house of Aaron H1385
Ps 115:13 *he will* **b** those who fear the LORD—small H1385
Ps 118:26 From the house of the LORD *we* **b** you. H1385
Ps 128: 5 *May* the LORD **b** you from Zion; may you H1385
Ps 129: 8 *we* **b** you in the name of the LORD. H1385
Ps 132:15 *I will* **b** her *with* **abundant** H1385+1385
Ps 134: 3 *May* the LORD **b** you from Zion, he who is H1385
Pr 30:11 their fathers and *do* not **b** their mothers; H1385
Isa 19:25 The LORD Almighty *will* **b** them, saying H1385
Jer 31:23 'The LORD **b** you, you prosperous city, you H1385

Hag 2:19 " 'From this day on *I will* **b** you.' " H1385
Zec 4: 7 out the capstone to shouts of 'God **b** it! H2834
Zec 4: 7 to shouts of 'God bless it! God **b** it!' " H2834
Lk 6:28 **b** those who curse you, pray for those who *G2328*
Ac 3:26 him first to you *to* **b** you by turning each *G2328*
Ro 12:14 **B** those who persecute you; bless and do *G2328*
Ro 12:14 who persecute you; **b** and do not curse. *G2328*
1Co 4:12 When we are cursed, *we* **b**; when we are *G2328*
2Co 9: 8 is able *to* **b** you **abundantly**, *G4246+5921+4355*
Heb 6:14 "*I will* surely **b** you and give you *G2328+2328*

BLESSED (229) [BLESS]
Ge 1:22 God **b** them and said, "Be fruitful and H1385
Ge 1:28 God **b** them and said to them, "Be fruitful H1385
Ge 2: 3 Then God **b** the seventh day and made it H1385
Ge 5: 2 them male and female and **b** them. H1385
Ge 9: 1 Then God **b** Noah and his sons, saying to H1385
Ge 12: 3 peoples on earth *will* **be b** through you." H1385
Ge 14:19 and *he* **b** Abram, saying, "Blessed be H1385
Ge 14:19 "**B** *be* Abram by God Most High H1385
Ge 18:18 nations on earth *will* **be b** through him. H1385
Ge 22:18 offspring all nations on earth *will* **be b**, H1385
Ge 24: 1 and the LORD *had* **b** him in every way. H1385
Ge 24:31 *you who are* **b** *by* the LORD," he H1385
Ge 24:35 The LORD *has* **b** my master abundantly, and H1385
Ge 24:60 And *they* **b** Rebekah and said to her, "Our H1385
Ge 25:11 God **b** his son Isaac, who H1385
Ge 26: 4 offspring all nations on earth *will* **be b**, H1385
Ge 26:12 a hundredfold, because the LORD **b** him. H1385
Ge 26:29 And now you are **b** *by* the LORD." H1385
Ge 27:27 of his clothes, he **b** him and said, "Ah, H1385
Ge 27:27 the smell of a field that the LORD *has* **b**. H1385
Ge 27:29 be cursed and those who bless you **be b**." H1385
Ge 27:33 I ate it just before you came and *I* **b** him— H1385
Ge 27:33 I blessed him—and indeed he will **be b**!" H1385
Ge 28: 1 So Isaac called for Jacob and **b** him. H1385
Ge 28: 6 learned that Isaac *had* **b** Jacob and had H1385
Ge 28: 6 that when he **b** him he commanded H1385
Ge 28:14 on earth *will* **be b** through you and H1385
Ge 30:27 that the LORD *has* **b** me because of you." H1385
Ge 30:30 the LORD *has* **b** you wherever I have H1385
Ge 31:55 his daughters and **b** them. H1385
Ge 32:29 you ask my name?" Then *he* **b** him there. H1385
Ge 35: 9 God appeared to him again and **b** him. H1385
Ge 39: 5 the LORD **b** the household of the Egyptian H1385
Ge 47: 7 before Pharaoh. After Jacob **b** Pharaoh, H1385
Ge 47:10 Then Jacob **b** Pharaoh and went out from H1385
Ge 48: 3 in the land of Canaan, and there *he* **b** me H1385
Ge 48:15 Then *he* **b** Joseph and said, "May the H1385
Ge 48:20 *He* **b** them that day and said, "In your H1385
Ge 49:28 their father said to them when *he* **b** them, H1385
Ex 20:11 Therefore the LORD **b** the Sabbath day H1385
Ex 32:29 and he *has* **b** you this day. H1388+5989
Ex 39:43 LORD had commanded. So Moses **b** them. H1385
Lev 9:22 his hands toward the people and **b** them. H1385
Lev 9:23 they came out, *they* **b** the people; and the H1385
Nu 22: 6 For I know that whoever you bless is **b** H1385
Nu 22:12 on those people, because they *are* **b**." H1385
Nu 23:20 command to bless; *he has* **b**, and I cannot H1385
Nu 24: 9 those who bless you **be b** and those who H1385
Nu 24:10 *you have* **b** them these three H1385+1385
Dt 2: 7 The LORD your God *has* **b** you in all the H1385
Dt 7:14 You will **be b** more than any other people H1385
Dt 12: 7 because the LORD your God *has* **b** you. H1385
Dt 14:24 you *have been* **b** *by* the LORD your H1385
Dt 15:14 to them as the LORD your God *has* **b** you. H1385
Dt 16:17 way the LORD your God *has* **b** you. H1388+5989
Dt 28: 3 You *will* **be b** in the city and blessed in H1385
Dt 28: 3 blessed in the city and **b** in the country. H1385
Dt 28: 4 The fruit of your womb *will* **be b**, and the H1385
Dt 28: 5 your kneading trough *will* **be b**. H1385
Dt 28: 6 You *will* **be b** when you come in and H1385
Dt 28: 6 you come in and **b** when you go out. H1385
Dt 33:20 "**B** *is* he who enlarges Gad's domain H1385
Dt 33:24 "*Most* **b** of sons *is* Asher; let him be H1385
Dt 33:29 **B** are you, Israel! Who is like you, a people H897
Jos 14:13 Then Joshua **b** Caleb son of Jephunneh H1385
Jos 17:14 the LORD *has* **b** us abundantly. H1385
Jos 22: 6 Then Joshua **b** them and sent them away H1385
Jos 22: 7 Joshua sent them home, *he* **b** them, H1385
Jos 24:10 so *he* **b** you **again and again**, and I H1385+1385
Jdg 5:24 "Most **b** of women *be* Jael, the wife of H1385
Jdg 5:24 most **b** of tent-dwelling women. H1385
Jdg 13:24 He grew and the LORD **b** him, H1385
Ru 2:19 **B** be the man who took notice of you!" H1385
1Sa 25:33 *May* you **be b** *for* your good judgment and H1385
1Sa 26:25 to David, "*May* you **be b**, David my son; H1385
2Sa 6:11 the LORD **b** him and his entire H1385
2Sa 6:12 "The LORD *has* **b** the household of H1385
2Sa 6:18 *he* **b** the people in the name of the LORD H1385
2Sa 7:29 house of your servant *will* **be b** forever." H1385
2Sa 14:22 to pay him honor, and *he* **b** the king. H1385
1Ki 2:45 But King Solomon *will* **be b**, and David's H1385
1Ki 8:14 the king turned around and **b** them H1385
1Ki 8:55 He stood and **b** the whole assembly of H1385
1Ki 8:66 *They* **b** the king and then went home H1385
1Ch 13:14 the LORD **b** his household and H1385
1Ch 16: 2 *he* **b** the people in the name of the LORD. H1385
1Ch 17:27 *have* **b** it, and it will be blessed H1385
1Ch 17:27 have blessed it, and *it will* **be b** forever." H1385
1Ch 26: 5 (For God *had* **b** Obed-Edom.) H1385
2Ch 6: 3 the king turned around and **b** them. H1385

2Ch 31: 8 *they* praised the LORD and **b** his people H1385
2Ch 31:10 because the LORD *has* **b** his people, and H1385
Ne 9: 5 "**B** *be* your glorious name, and may it be H1385
Job 1:10 *You have* **b** the work of his hands, so that H1385
Job 5:17 "**B** *is* the one whom God corrects; so do not H897
Job 29: 4 God's intimate friendship **b** my house, H6584
Job 29:13 The one who was dying **b** me; H995+1388
Job 42:12 The LORD **b** the latter part of Job's life H1385
Ps 1: 1 **B** is the one who does not walk in step with H897
Ps 2:12 **B** are all who take refuge in him H897
Ps 32: 1 **B** is the one whose transgressions are H897
Ps 32: 2 **B** is the one whose sin the LORD does not H897
Ps 33:12 **B** is the nation whose God is the LORD, the H897
Ps 34: 8 **b** is the one who takes refuge in him. H897
Ps 40: 4 **B** is the one who trusts in the LORD, who H897
Ps 41: 1 **B** are those who have regard for the weak H897
Ps 41: 2 *they are* **counted among the b** in the land H887
Ps 45: 2 with grace, since God *has* **b** you forever. H1385
Ps 49:18 while they live *they* **count** themselves **b**— H1385
Ps 65: 4 **B** are those you choose and bring near to H897
Ps 72:17 Then all nations *will* **be b** through him H1385
Ps 72:17 through him, and *they will* **call** him **b**. H887
Ps 84: 4 **B** are those who dwell in your house; they H897
Ps 84: 5 **B** are those whose strength is in you H897
Ps 84:12 Almighty, **b** is the one who trusts in you. H897
Ps 89:15 **B** are those who have learned to acclaim H897
Ps 94:12 **B** is the one you discipline, LORD, the one H897
Ps 106: 3 **B** are those who act justly, who always do H897
Ps 107:38 *he* **b** them, and their numbers greatly H1385
Ps 112: 1 **B** are those who fear the LORD, who find H897
Ps 112: 2 the generation of the upright *will* **be b**. H1385
Ps 115:15 *May* you **be b** by the LORD, the Maker of H1385
Ps 118:26 **B** *is* he who comes in the name of the H1385
Ps 119: 1 **B** are those whose ways are blameless H897
Ps 119: 2 **B** are those who keep his statutes and seek H897
Ps 127: 5 **B** is the man whose quiver is full of them H897
Ps 128: 1 **B** are all who fear the LORD, who walk in H897
Ps 144:15 **B** is the people of whom this is true H897
Ps 144:15 **b** is the people whose God is the LORD. H897
Ps 146: 5 **B** are those whose help is the God of Jacob H897
Pr 3:13 **B** are those who find wisdom, those who H897
Pr 3:18 those who hold her fast *will* **be b**. H887
Pr 5:18 May your fountain be **b**, and may you H1385
Pr 8:32 **b** are those who keep my ways. H897
Pr 8:34 **B** are those who listen to me, watching H897
Pr 14:21 **b** is the one who is kind to the needy. H897
Pr 16:20 **b** is the one who trusts in the LORD. H897
Pr 20: 7 **b** are their children after them. H897
Pr 20:21 claimed too soon *will* not **be b** at the end. H1385
Pr 22: 9 The generous *will* themselves **be b**, for H1385
Pr 28:14 **B** is the one who always trembles before H897
Pr 28:20 A faithful person will be richly **b**, but one H1388
Pr 29:18 **b** is the one who heeds wisdom's H890
Pr 31:28 Her children arise and **call** her **b**; her H887
Ecc 10:17 **B** is the land whose king is of noble birth H897
SS 6: 9 young women saw her and **called** her **b**; H887
Isa 19:25 "**B** *be* Egypt my people, Assyria H1385
Isa 30:18 a God of justice. **B** are all who wait for him! H897
Isa 32:20 *how* **b** you will be, sowing your seed by H897
Isa 51: 2 and *I* **b** him and made him many. H1385
Isa 56: 2 **B** is the one who does this—the person H897
Isa 61: 9 that they are a people the LORD *has* **b**." H1385
Isa 65:23 they will be a people **b** *by* the LORD H1385
Jer 17: 7 "But **b** *is* the one who trusts in the LORD H1385
Jer 20:14 May the day my mother bore me not be **b** H1385
Da 12:12 **B** is the one who waits for and reaches the H897
Mal 3:12 "Then all the nations *will* **call** you **b**, for H887
Mal 3:15 But now we **call** the arrogant **b**. H887
Mt 5: 3 "**B** are the poor in spirit, for theirs is the *G3421*
Mt 5: 4 **B** are those who mourn, for they will be *G3421*
Mt 5: 5 **B** are the meek, for they will inherit the *G3421*
Mt 5: 6 **B** are those who hunger and thirst for *G3421*
Mt 5: 7 **B** are the merciful, for they will be shown *G3421*
Mt 5: 8 **B** are the pure in heart, for they will see *G3421*
Mt 5: 9 **B** are the peacemakers, for they will be *G3421*
Mt 5:10 **B** are those who are persecuted because *G3421*
Mt 5:11 "**B** are you when people insult you *G3421*
Mt 11: 6 **B** is anyone who does not stumble on *G3421*
Mt 13:16 But **b** are your eyes because they see, and *G3421*
Mt 16:17 Jesus replied, "**B** are you, Simon son of *G3421*
Mt 21: 9 "**B** is he who comes in the name of the *G2328*
Mt 23:39 '**B** is he who comes in the name of the *G2328*
Mt 25:34 you *who are* **b** by my Father; take *G2328*
Mk 10:16 placed his hands on them and **b** them. *G2986*
Mk 11: 9 "**B** is he who comes in the name of the *G2328*
Mk 11:10 "**B** is the coming kingdom of our father *G2328*
Mk 14:61 you the Messiah, the Son *of* the **B** *One*?" *G2329*
Lk 1:42 "**B** *are* you among women, and blessed is *G2328*
Lk 1:42 women, and **b** *is* the child you will bear! *G2328*
Lk 1:45 **B** is she who has believed that the Lord *G3421*
Lk 1:48 now on all generations *will* **call** me **b**, *G3420*
Lk 2:34 Then Simeon **b** them and said to Mary, his *G2328*
Lk 6:20 "**B** are you who are poor, for yours is the *G3421*
Lk 6:21 **B** are you who hunger now, for you will be *G3421*
Lk 6:21 **B** are you who weep now, for you will *G3421*
Lk 6:22 **B** are you when people hate you, when *G3421*
Lk 7:23 **B** is anyone who does not stumble on *G3421*
Lk 10:23 "**B** are the eyes that see what you see. *G3421*
Lk 11:27 "**B** is the mother who gave you birth and *G3421*
Lk 11:28 "**B** rather are those who hear the word of *G3421*
Lk 13:35 '**B** *is* he who comes in the name of the *G2328*
Lk 14:14 you will be **b**. Although they cannot *G3421*
Lk 14:15 "**B** is the one who will eat at the feast in *G3421*
Lk 19:38 "**B** *is* the king who comes in the name of *G2328*
Lk 23:29 you will say, '**B** are the childless women *G3421*
Lk 24:50 he lifted up his hands and **b** them. *G2328*
Jn 12:13 "**B** *is* he who comes in the name of the *G2328*
Jn 12:13 name of the Lord!" "**B** is the king of Israel!" NDT
Jn 13:17 these things, you will be **b** if you do them. *G3421*
Jn 20:29 **b** are those who have not seen and yet *G3421*
Ac 3:25 offspring all peoples on earth *will be* **b**. *G1922*
Ac 20:35 'It is more **b** to give than to receive.' *G3421*
Ro 4: 7 "**B** are those whose transgressions are *G3421*
Ro 4: 8 **B** is the one whose sin the Lord will never *G3421*
Ro 14:22 **B** is the one who does not condemn *G3421*
Gal 3: 8 "All nations *will be* **b** through you." *G1922*
Gal 3: 9 who rely on faith *are* **b** along with *G2328*
Eph 1: 3 who *has* **b** us in the heavenly realms with *G2328*
1Ti 1:11 gospel concerning the glory of the **b** God, *G3421*
1Ti 6:15 the **b** and only Ruler, the King of *G3421*
Titus 2:13 while we wait for the **b** hope—the *G3421*
Heb 7: 1 from the defeat of the kings and **b** him, *G2328*
Heb 7: 6 from Abraham and **b** him who had the *G2328*
Heb 7: 7 doubt the lesser *is* **b** by the greater. *G2328*
Heb 11:20 By faith Isaac **b** Jacob and Esau in regard *G2328*
Heb 11:21 he was dying, **b** each of Joseph's sons *G2328*
Jas 1:12 **B** is the one who perseveres under trial *G3421*
Jas 1:25 doing it—they will be **b** in what they do. *G3421*
Jas 5:11 *we* **count as b** those who have persevered. *G3420*
1Pe 3:14 should suffer for what is right, you are **b**. *G3421*
1Pe 4:14 name of Christ, you are **b**, for the Spirit of *G3421*
Rev 1: 3 **B** is the one who reads aloud the words of *G3421*
Rev 1: 3 **b** are those who hear it and take to NDT
Rev 14:13 **B** are the dead who die in the Lord from *G3421*
Rev 16:15 **B** is the one who stays awake and *G3421*
Rev 19: 9 **B** are those who are invited to the *G3421*
Rev 20: 6 **B** and holy are those who share in the first *G3421*
Rev 22: 7 **B** is the one who keeps the words of the *G3421*
Rev 22:14 "**B** are those who wash their robes, that *G3421*

BLESSEDNESS (2) [BLESS]

Ro 4: 6 he speaks of the **b** of the one to whom *G3422*
Ro 4: 9 Is this **b** only for the circumcised, or also *G3422*

BLESSES (9) [BLESS]

Ge 49:25 *who* **b** you *with* blessings of the skies H1385
Ps 10: 3 *he* **b** the greedy and reviles the LORD. H1385
Ps 29:11 people; the LORD **b** his people with peace. H1385
Ps 37:22 *those* the LORD **b** will inherit the land, but H1385
Ps 67: 6 yields its harvest; God, our God, **b** us. H1385
Ps 147:13 of your gates and **b** your people within H1385
Pr 3:33 but *he* **b** the home of the righteous. H1385
Pr 27:14 If *anyone* loudly **b** their neighbor early in H1385
Ro 10:12 is Lord of all and **richly b** all who call on *G4456*

BLESSING (69) [BLESS]

Ge 12: 2 your name great, and you will be a **b**. H1388
Ge 17:18 Ishmael might live **under** your **b**!" H4200+7156
Ge 27: 4 so that I *may* **give** you *my* **b** before I die." H1385
Ge 27: 7 so that *I may* **give** you *my* **b** in the H1385
Ge 27:10 so that *he may* **give** you *his* **b** before he H1385
Ge 27:12 down a curse on myself rather than a **b**." H1388
Ge 27:19 so that you *may* **give** me your **b**. H1385
Ge 27:25 game to eat, so that I *may* **give** you my **b**." H1385
Ge 27:30 After Isaac finished **b** him, and Jacob had H1385
Ge 27:31 so that you *may* **give** me your **b**. H1385
Ge 27:35 brother came deceitfully and took your **b**." H1388
Ge 27:36 my birthright, and now he's taken my **b**!" H1388
Ge 27:36 "Haven't you reserved any **b** for me?" H1388
Ge 27:38 "Do you have only one **b**, my father? H1388
Ge 27:41 because of the **b** his father had given H1388
Ge 28: 4 descendants the **b** *given to* Abraham, H1388
Ge 39: 5 The **b** *of* the LORD was on everything H1388
Ge 48:20 "In your name *will* Israel **pronounce** *this* **b**: H1385
Ge 49:28 **giving** each the **b** appropriate to H1385+1388
Ex 23:25 and *his* **b** *will be on* your food and water. H1385
Lev 25:21 I will send you such a **b** in the sixth year H1388
Dt 11:26 before you today a **b** and a curse— H1388
Dt 11:27 the **b** if you obey the commands of the H1388
Dt 12:15 according to the **b** the LORD your God gives H1388
Dt 23: 5 turned the curse into a **b** for you, H1388
Dt 28: 8 LORD will send a **b** on your barns and on H1388
Dt 29:19 oath and *they* **invoke a b on themselves**, H1385
Dt 33: 1 This is the **b** that Moses the man of God H1388
Dt 33:23 the favor of the LORD and is full of his **b**; H1388
2Sa 7:29 with your **b** the house of your servant H1388
2Sa 13:25 he still refused to go but **gave** him *his* **b**. H1385
2Sa 15:27 Go back to the city with my **b**. Take your H8934
2Sa 16:12 to me his **covenant b** instead of his H3208
Ne 9: 5 may it be exalted above all **b** and praise. H1388
Ne 13: 2 however, turned the curse into a **b**.) H1388
Ps 3: 8 May your **b** be on your people. H1388
Ps 24: 5 They will receive **b** from the LORD and H1388
Ps 37:26 lend freely; their children will be a **b**. H1388
Ps 109:17 He found no pleasure in **b**—may it be far H1388
Ps 128: 4 this *will be the* **b** *for* the man who fears H1385
Ps 129: 8 say to them, "The **b** *of* the LORD be on you H1388
Ps 133: 3 For there the LORD bestows his **b**, even life H1388
Pr 10:22 The **b** *of* the LORD brings wealth, without H1388
Pr 11:11 Through the **b** *of* the upright a city is H1388
Pr 11:26 they pray *God's* **b** on the one who is H1388
Pr 24:25 the guilty, and rich **b** will come on them. H1388
Isa 19:24 with Egypt and Assyria, a **b** on the earth. H1388
Isa 44: 3 offspring, and my **b** on your descendants. H1388
Isa 65: 8 there is still a **b** in it,' so will I do in H1388
Isa 65:16 Whoever **invokes a b** in the land will do H1385
Jer 16: 5 because I have withdrawn my **b**, my love H8934
Eze 34:26 the places surrounding my hill a **b**. H1388
Eze 34:26 in season; there will be showers of **b**. H1388
Eze 44:30 ground meal so that a **b** may rest on your H1388
Joel 2:14 turn and relent and leave behind a **b**— H1388
Mic 2: 9 You take away my **b** from their children H2077
Zec 8:13 so I will save you, and you will be a **b**. H1388
Mal 3:10 pour out so much **b** that there will not H1388
Lk 24:51 While he *was* **b** them, he left them and *G2328*
Ac 15:33 believers with the **b of peace** to return to *G1645*
Ro 15:29 in the full measure *of* the **b** of Christ. *G2330*
Gal 3:14 us in order that the **b** given to Abraham *G2330*
Gal 4:15 then, is your **b** of me now? I can *G3422*
Eph 1: 3 realms with every spiritual **b** in Christ. *G2330*
Heb 6: 7 whom it is farmed receives the **b** of God. *G2330*
Heb 12:17 when he wanted to inherit this **b**, he was *G2330*
Heb 12:17 Even though he sought **the b** with tears *G899S*
1Pe 3: 9 contrary, repay evil *with* **b**, because to this *G2328*
1Pe 3: 9 were called so that you may inherit a **b**. *G2330*

BLESSINGS (26) [BLESS]

Ge 49:25 who blesses you with **b** *of* the skies above, H1388
Ge 49:25 skies above, **b** *of* the deep springs below H1388
Ge 49:25 springs below, **b** *of* the breast and womb. H1388
Ge 49:26 Your father's **b** are greater than the H1388
Ge 49:26 are greater than the **b** *of* the ancient H1388
Dt 10: 8 minister and to **pronounce b** in his name, H1385
Dt 11:29 are to proclaim on Mount Gerizim the **b**, H1388
Dt 16:10 to the **b** the LORD your God *has* **given** you. H1385
Dt 21: 5 to **pronounce b** in the name of H1385
Dt 28: 2 All these **b** will come on you and H1388
Dt 30: 1 When all these **b** and curses I have set H1388
Dt 30:19 before you life and death, **b** and curses. H1388
Jos 8:34 of the law—the **b** and the curses—just H1388
1Ch 23:13 him and to **pronounce b** in his name H1385
Ps 21: 3 greet him with rich **b** and placed a crown H1388
Ps 21: 6 him unending **b** and made him glad H1388
Ps 128: 2 your labor; **b** and prosperity will be yours. H897
Pr 10: 6 **B** crown the head of the righteous, but H1388
Pr 10: 7 The name of the righteous is used in **b** H1388
Jer 4: 2 the nations *will* **invoke b** by him and in H1385
Hos 3: 5 to the LORD and to his **b** in the last days. H3206
Mal 2: 2 a curse on you, and I will curse your **b**. H1388
Ac 13:34 you the **holy** and sure **b promised** to *G4008*
Ro 15:27 Gentiles have shared in the Jews' **spiritual** *b*, AIT
Ro 15:27 the Jews to share with them their **material** *b*. AIT
1Co 9:23 sake of the gospel, that I may share in **its** *b*. AIT

BLEW (13) [BLOW]

Ex 15:10 But *you* **b** with your breath, and the sea H5973
Jos 6: 9 ahead of the priests *who* **b** the trumpets, H9546
Jdg 3:27 *he* **b** a trumpet in the hill country of H9546
Jdg 6:34 came on Gideon, and *he* **b** a trumpet H9546
Jdg 7:19 *They* **b** their trumpets and broke the jars H9546
Jdg 7:20 The three companies **b** the trumpets and H9546
2Sa 2:28 So Joab **b** the trumpet, and all the troops H9546
2Ki 9:13 Then *they* **b** the trumpet and shouted H9546
2Ch 7: 6 the priests **b** *their* **trumpets**, and all the H2955
2Ch 13:14 The priests **b** their trumpets H2955
Hag 1: 9 What you brought home, *I* **b away**. Why?" H5870
Mt 7:25 the winds **b** and beat against that *G4463*
Mt 7:27 the winds **b** and beat against that *G4463*

BLIGHT (5) [BLIGHTED]

Dt 28:22 drought, with **b** and mildew, which H8730
1Ki 8:37 to the land, or **b** or mildew, locusts or H8730
2Ch 6:28 to the land, or **b** or mildew, locusts or H8730
Am 4: 9 destroying them with **b** and mildew. H8730
Hag 2:17 I struck all the work of your hands with **b** H8730

BLIGHTED (2) [BLIGHT]

Ps 102: 4 My heart is **b** and withered like grass; H5782
Hos 9:16 Ephraim *is* **b**, their root is withered, they H5782

BLIND (81) [BLINDED, BLINDFOLDED, BLINDFOLDS, BLINDING, BLINDNESS, BLINDS]

Ex 4:11 Who gives them sight or makes them **b** H6426
Lev 19:14 put a stumbling block in front of the **b**, H6426
Lev 21:18 no man who is **b** or lame, disfigured or H6426
Lev 22:22 Do not offer to the LORD the **b**, the injured H6428
Dt 15:21 a defect, is lame or **b**, or has any serious H6426
Dt 27:18 who leads the **b** astray on the road." H6426
Dt 28:29 grope about like a **b** *person* in the dark. H6426
2Sa 5: 6 even the **b** and the lame can ward you off." H6426
2Sa 5: 8 reach those 'lame and **b**' who are David's H6426
2Sa 5: 8 "The '**b** and lame' will not enter the H6426
Job 29:15 I was eyes to the **b** and feet to the lame. H6426
Ps 146: 8 the LORD gives sight to the **b**, the LORD lifts H6426
Isa 29: 9 amazed, **b yourselves** and be sightless H9129
Isa 29:18 darkness the eyes of the **b** will see. H6426
Isa 35: 5 will the eyes of the **b** be opened and the H6426
Isa 42: 7 to open eyes that are **b**, to free captives H6426
Isa 42:16 I will lead the **b** by ways they have not H6426
Isa 42:18 you deaf; look, you **b**, and see! H6426
Isa 42:19 Who is **b** but my servant, and deaf like H6426
Isa 42:19 Who is **b** like the one in covenant with H6426
Isa 42:19 with me, **b** like the servant of the LORD? H6426
Isa 43: 8 Lead out those who have eyes but are **b** H6426
Isa 44: 9 would speak up for them *are* **b**; H1153+8011
Isa 56:10 Israel's watchmen are **b**, they all lack H6426
Isa 59:10 Like the **b** we grope along the wall H6426

Jer 31: 8 Among them will be the b and the lame H6426
La 4:14 through the streets as if they were b. H6426
Zep 1:17 will grope about like those who are b, H6426
Zec 12: 4 but I will b all the horses H6427+5782+928+2021
Mal 1: 8 When you offer b animals for sacrifice, is H6426
Mt 9:27 on from there, two b men followed him G5603
Mt 9:28 indoors, the b men came to him, and G5603
Mt 11: 5 The b receive sight, the lame walk, those G5603
Mt 12:22 man who was b and mute, G5603
Mt 15:14 Leave them; they are b guides. If the blind G5603
Mt 15:14 If the b lead the blind, both will fall into a G5603
Mt 15:14 If the blind lead the b, both will fall into a G5603
Mt 15:30 bringing the lame, the b, the crippled, the G5603
Mt 15:31 the lame walking and the b seeing. G5603
Mt 20:30 Two b men were sitting by the roadside G5603
Mt 21:14 The b and the lame came to him at the G5603
Mt 23:16 "Woe to you, b guides! You say, 'If G5603
Mt 23:17 You b fools! Which is greater: the gold, or G5603
Mt 23:19 You b men! Which is greater: the gift, or G5603
Mt 23:24 You b guides! You strain out a gnat but G5603
Mt 23:26 B Pharisee! First clean the inside of the G5603
Mk 8:22 people brought a b man and begged G5603
Mk 8:23 He took the b man by the hand and led G5603
Mk 10:46 leaving the city, a b man, Bartimaeus G5603
Mk 10:49 So they called to the b man, "Cheer up G5603
Mk 10:51 The b man said, "Rabbi, G5603
Lk 4:18 prisoners and recovery of sight for the b, G5603
Lk 6:39 "Can the b lead the blind? Will G5603
Lk 6:39 "Can the blind lead the b? Will they not G5603
Lk 7:21 gave sight to many who were b. G5603
Lk 7:22 The b receive sight, the lame walk, those G5603
Lk 14:13 the poor, the crippled, the lame, the b, G5603
Lk 14:21 the crippled, the b and the lame. G5603
Lk 18:35 a b man was sitting by the roadside G5603
Jn 5: 3 people used to lie—the b, the lame, G5603
Jn 9: 1 went along, he saw a man b from birth. G5603
Jn 9: 2 man or his parents, that he was born b?" G5603
Jn 9:13 the Pharisees the man who had been b. G5603
Jn 9:17 Then they turned again to the b man G5603
Jn 9:18 that he had been b and had received his G5603
Jn 9:19 "Is this the one you say was born b? How G5603
Jn 9:20 answered, "and we know he was born b. G5603
Jn 9:24 summoned the man who had been b. G5603
Jn 9:25 thing I do know. I was b but now I see!" G5603
Jn 9:32 of opening the eyes of a man born b. G5603
Jn 9:39 so that the b will see and those G3590+1063
Jn 9:39 see and those who see will become b." G5603
Jn 9:40 this and asked, "What? Are we b too?" G5603
Jn 9:41 "If you were b, you would not be G5603
Jn 10:21 Can a demon open the eyes of the b?" G5603
Jn 11:37 the eyes of the b man have kept this G5603
Ac 9: 9 For three days he was b, and did G3590+1063
Ac 13:11 You are going to be b for a time, not even G5603
Ro 2:19 convinced that you are a guide for the b, G5603
2Pe 1: 9 does not have them is nearsighted and b, G5603
Rev 3:17 are wretched, pitiful, poor, b and naked. G5603

BLINDED (5) [BLIND]

Zec 11:17 withered, his right eye totally b!" H3908+3908
Jn 12:40 "He has b their eyes and hardened their G5604
Ac 22:11 brilliance of the light had b me. G4024+1838
2Co 4: 4 The god of this age has b the minds of G5604
1Jn 2:11 the darkness has b them. G5604+3836+4057

BLINDFOLDED (2) [BLIND]

Mk 14:65 at him; they b him, struck G4328+3836+4725
Lk 22:64 They b him and demanded, "Prophesy G4328

BLINDFOLDS (1) [BLIND]

Job 9:24 of the wicked, he b its judges. H4059+7156

BLINDING (1) [BLIND]

Am 5: 9 With a b flash he destroys the stronghold H1158

BLINDNESS (4) [BLIND]

Ge 19:11 with b so that they could not find the door. H6177
Dt 28:28 with madness, b and confusion of mind. H6427
2Ki 6:18 to the LORD, "Strike this army with b." H6177
2Ki 6:18 So he struck them with b, as Elisha had H6177

BLINDS (2) [BLIND]

Ex 23: 8 a bribe b those who see and twists the H6422
Dt 16:19 a bribe b the eyes of the wise and H6422

BLOCK (14) [BLOCKED, BLOCKING, BLOCKS]

Lev 19:14 deaf or put a stumbling b in front of the H4842
Isa 44:19 Shall I bow down to a b of wood?" H1005
Eze 3:20 and I put a stumbling b before them H4842
Eze 4: 1 son of man, take a b of clay, put it in front H4246
Eze 14: 4 put a wicked stumbling b before their H4842
Eze 14: 7 put a wicked stumbling b before their H4842
Eze 39:11 It will b the way of travelers, because Gog H2888
Hos 2: 6 Therefore I will b her path with H8455
Mt 16:23 You are a stumbling b to me; you do not G4998
Ro 11: 9 a stumbling b and a retribution for them. G4998
Ro 14:13 not to put any stumbling b or obstacle in G4682
1Co 1:23 a stumbling b to Jews and foolishness to G4998
1Co 8: 9 not become a stumbling b to the weak. G4682
2Co 6: 3 We put no stumbling b in anyone's path G4683

BLOCKED (6) [BLOCK]

Lev 15: 3 it continues flowing from his body or is b, H3159
2Ch 32: 4 group of people who b all the springs H6258
2Ch 32:30 It was Hezekiah who b the upper outlet of H6258
Job 19: 8 He has b my way so I cannot pass; he has H1553
Pr 15:19 The way of the sluggard is b with thorns H5379
1Th 2:18 again and again—but Satan b our way. G1601

BLOCKING (1) [BLOCK]

2Ch 32: 3 staff about b off the water from the H6258

BLOCKS (6) [BLOCK]

1Ki 5:17 from the quarry large b of high-grade stone H74
1Ki 6: 7 only b dressed at the quarry were used H74
1Ki 7: 9 made of b of high-grade stone cut to size AIT
2Ki 12:12 timber and b of dressed stone for the repair H74
La 3: 9 He has barred my way with b of stone; he H1607
Eze 14: 3 put wicked stumbling b before their H4842

BLOOD (408) [AKELDAMA, BLEEDING, BLOODSTAINED, BLOODSHED, BLOODSHOT, BLOODSTAINS, BLOODTHIRSTY, LIFEBLOOD]

Ge 4:10 Your brother's b cries out to me from the H1947
Ge 4:11 to receive your brother's b from your hand. H1947
Ge 9: 6 "Whoever sheds human b, by humans H1947
Ge 9: 6 by humans shall their b be shed; for in H1947
Ge 15: 4 who is your own flesh and b will be your H5055
Ge 29:14 said to him, "You are my own flesh and b." H6795
Ge 37:22 "Don't shed any b. Throw him into this H1947
Ge 37:26 if we kill our brother and cover up his b? H1947
Ge 37:27 he is our brother, our own flesh and b." H1414
Ge 37:31 a goat and dipped the robe in the b. H1947
Ge 42:22 Now we must give an accounting for his b." H1947
Ge 49:11 in wine, his robes in the b of grapes. H1947
Ex 4: 9 the river will become b on the ground." H1947
Ex 4:25 "Surely you are a bridegroom of b to me," H1947
Ex 4:26 At that time she said "bridegroom of b," H1947
Ex 7:17 of the Nile, and it will be changed into b. H1947
Ex 7:19 all the reservoirs—and they will turn to b. H1947
Ex 7:19 B will be everywhere in Egypt, even in H1947
Ex 7:20 all the water was changed into b. H1947
Ex 7:21 drink its water. B was everywhere in Egypt H1947
Ex 12: 7 to take some of the b and put it on the H1947
Ex 12:13 The b will be a sign for you on the houses H1947
Ex 12:13 when I see the b, I will pass over you. H1947
Ex 12:22 dip it into the b in the basin and put H1947
Ex 12:22 put some of the b on the top and on H1947
Ex 12:23 he will see the b on the top and sides of H1947
Ex 23:18 "Do not offer the b of a sacrifice to me H1947
Ex 24: 6 took half of the b and put it in bowls, H1947
Ex 24: 8 Moses then took the b, sprinkled it on the H1947
Ex 24: 8 "This is the b of the covenant that the H1947
Ex 29:12 Take some of the bull's b and put it on the H1947
Ex 29:16 it and take the b and splash it against H1947
Ex 29:20 take some of its b and put it on the lobes H1947
Ex 29:20 Then splash b against the sides of the H1947
Ex 29:21 And take some b from the altar and some H1947
Ex 30:10 be made with the b of the atoning sin H1947
Ex 34:25 "Do not offer the b of a sacrifice to me H1947
Lev 1: 5 shall bring the b and splash it against H1947
Lev 1:11 shall splash its b against the sides of the H1947
Lev 1:15 its b shall be drained out on the side of H1947
Lev 3: 2 shall splash the b against the sides of the H1947
Lev 3: 8 sons shall splash its b against the sides of H1947
Lev 3:13 sons shall splash its b against the sides of H1947
Lev 3:17 You must not eat any fat or any b.'" H1947
Lev 4: 5 some of the bull's b and carry it into the H1947
Lev 4: 6 his finger into the b and sprinkle some of H1947
Lev 4: 7 put some of the b on the horns of the H1947
Lev 4: 7 rest of the bull's b he shall pour out at H1947
Lev 4:16 take some of the bull's b into the tent of H1947
Lev 4:17 his finger into the b and sprinkle it before H1947
Lev 4:18 is to put some of the b on the horns of the H1947
Lev 4:18 The rest of the b he shall pour out at the H1947
Lev 4:25 take some of the b of the sin offering with H1947
Lev 4:25 out the rest of the b at the base of the H1947
Lev 4:30 to take some of the b with his finger and H1947
Lev 4:30 out the rest of the b at the base of the H1947
Lev 4:34 take some of the b of the sin offering with H1947
Lev 4:34 out the rest of the b at the base of the H1947
Lev 5: 9 to splash some of the b of the sin offering H1947
Lev 5: 9 the rest of the b must be drained out at H1947
Lev 6:27 if any of the b is spattered on a H1947
Lev 6:30 sin offering whose b is brought into the H1947
Lev 7: 2 its b is to be splashed against the H1947
Lev 7:14 who splashes the b of the fellowship H1947
Lev 7:26 you must not eat the b of any bird or H1947
Lev 7:27 Anyone who eats b must be cut off from H1947
Lev 7:33 Aaron who offers the b and the fat of the H1947
Lev 8:15 the bull and took some of the b, H1947
Lev 8:15 out the rest of the b at the base of the H1947
Lev 8:19 splashed the b against the sides of H1947
Lev 8:23 took some of its b and put it on the H1947
Lev 8:24 put some of the b on the lobes of H1947
Lev 8:24 Then he splashed b against the sides of H1947
Lev 8:30 oil and some of the b from the altar and H1947
Lev 9: 9 His sons brought the b to him, and he H1947
Lev 9: 9 his finger into the b and put it on the H1947
Lev 9: 9 the rest of the b he poured out at the H1947
Lev 9:12 His sons handed him the b, and he H1947
Lev 9:18 His sons handed him the b, and he H1947
Lev 10:18 Since its b was not taken into the Holy H1947
Lev 12: 7 be ceremonially clean from her flow of b. H1947
Lev 14: 6 into the b of the bird that was killed over H1947
Lev 14:14 to take some of the b of the guilt offering H1947
Lev 14:17 on top of the b of the guilt offering. H1947
Lev 14:25 take some of its b and put it on the H1947
Lev 14:28 places he put the b of the guilt offering— H1947
Lev 14:51 dip them into the b of the dead bird and H1947
Lev 14:52 He shall purify the house with the bird's b H1947
Lev 15:19 a woman has her regular flow of b, H1947
Lev 15:25 has a discharge of b for many days at a H1947
Lev 16:14 some of the bull's b and with his finger H1947
Lev 16:15 people and take its b behind the curtain H1947
Lev 16:15 do with it as he did with the bull's b: H1947
Lev 16:18 some of the bull's b and some of the H1947
Lev 16:18 some of the goat's b and put it on all the H1947
Lev 16:19 sprinkle some of the b on it with his finger H1947
Lev 16:27 whose b was brought into the Most Holy H1947
Lev 17: 4 they have shed b and must be cut off from H1947
Lev 17: 6 is to splash the b against the altar of H1947
Lev 17:10 residing among them who eats b, H1947
Lev 17:11 For the life of a creature is in the b, and I H1947
Lev 17:11 it is the b that makes atonement for one's H1947
Lev 17:12 "None of you may eat b, nor may any H1947
Lev 17:12 any foreigner residing among you eat b." H1947
Lev 17:13 must drain out the b and cover it with H1947
Lev 17:14 because the life of every creature is its b H1947
Lev 17:14 "You must not eat the b of any creature H1947
Lev 17:14 because the life of every creature is its b H1947
Lev 19:26 'Do not eat any meat with the b still in it. H1947
Lev 20: 9 mother, their b will be on their own head. H1947
Lev 20:11 their b will be on their own heads. H1947
Lev 20:12 their b will be on their own heads. H1947
Lev 20:13 their b will be on their own heads. H1947
Lev 20:16 their b will be on their own heads. H1947
Lev 20:27 their b will be on their own heads. H1947
Lev 25:49 cousin or any b relative in their H8638+1414
Nu 18:17 Splash their b against the altar and burn H1947
Nu 19: 4 is to take some of its b on his finger and H1947
Nu 19: 5 burned—its hide, flesh, b and intestines. H1947
Nu 23:24 its prey and drinks the b of its victims." H1947
Nu 35:19 The avenger of b shall put the murderer to H1947
Nu 35:21 The avenger of b shall put the murderer H1947
Nu 35:24 the avenger of b according to these H1947
Nu 35:25 from the avenger of b and send the H1947
Nu 35:27 the avenger of b finds them outside H1947
Nu 35:27 the avenger of b may kill the accused H1947
Nu 35:33 the land on which b has been shed, H1947
Nu 35:33 except by the b of the one who shed it. H1947
Dt 12:16 But you must not eat the b; pour it out on H1947
Dt 12:23 But be sure you do not eat the b, because H1947
Dt 12:23 because the b is the life, and you H1947
Dt 12:24 You must not eat the b; pour it out on the H5647S
Dt 12:27 LORD your God, both the meat and the b. H1947
Dt 12:27 The b of your sacrifices must be poured H1947
Dt 15:23 But you must not eat the b; pour it out on H1947
Dt 19: 6 the avenger of b might pursue him in a H1947
Dt 19:10 this so that innocent b will not be shed in H1947
Dt 19:12 handed over to the avenger of b to die. H1947
Dt 19:13 Israel the guilt of shedding innocent b, H1947
Dt 21: 7 "Our hands did not shed this b, nor did H1947
Dt 21: 8 your people guilty of the b of an innocent H1947
Dt 21: 9 the guilt of shedding innocent b, H1947
Dt 32:14 You drank the foaming b of the grape. H1947
Dt 32:42 I will make my arrows drunk with b, while H1947
Dt 32:42 the b of the slain and the captives, the H1947
Dt 32:43 he will avenge the b of his servants H1947
Jos 2:19 their b will be on their own heads H1947
Jos 2:19 their b will be on our head if a hand is H1947
Jos 20: 3 find protection from the avenger of b. H1947
Jos 20: 5 If the avenger of b comes in pursuit, the H1947
Jos 20: 9 by the avenger of b prior to standing trial H1947
Jdg 9: 2 Remember, I am your flesh and b." H6795
Jdg 9:24 the shedding of their b, might be H1947
1Sa 14:32 ground and ate them, together with the b. H1947
1Sa 14:33 the LORD by eating meat that has b in it." H1947
1Sa 14:34 the LORD by eating meat with b still in it. H1947
1Sa 26:20 Now do not let my b fall to the ground far H1947
2Sa 1:16 "Your b be on your own head. H1947
2Sa 1:22 "From the b of the slain, from the flesh of H1947
2Sa 3:27 to avenge the b of his brother Asahel H1947
2Sa 3:28 concerning the b of Abner son of Ner. H1947
2Sa 3:29 May his b fall on the head of Joab and on NDT
2Sa 4:11 now demand his b from your hand and H1947
2Sa 5: 1 said, "We are your own flesh and b. H6795
2Sa 7:12 your own flesh and b, and I H3655+4946+5055
2Sa 14:11 the avenger of b from adding to the H1947
2Sa 16: 8 all the b you shed in the household H1947
2Sa 16:11 my own flesh and b, is trying H3655+4946+5055
2Sa 19:12 my own flesh and b. So why should you H6795
2Sa 19:13 Amasa, 'Are you not my own flesh and b? H6795
2Sa 20:12 wallowing in his b in the middle of the H1947
2Sa 23:17 "Is it not the b of men who went at the H1947
1Ki 2: 5 their b in peacetime as if in battle, H1947
1Ki 2: 5 with that b he stained the belt H1947
1Ki 2: 9 his gray head down to the grave in b." H1947
1Ki 2:31 of the guilt of the innocent b that Joab H1947
1Ki 2:32 The LORD will repay him for the b he shed H1947
1Ki 2:33 May the guilt of their b rest on the head of H1947
1Ki 2:37 will die; your b will be on your own head." H1947
1Ki 8:19 your own flesh and b—he is H3655+4946+2743
1Ki 18:28 as was their custom, until their b flowed. H1947
1Ki 21:19 place where dogs licked up Naboth's b, H1947
1Ki 21:19 dogs will lick up your b—yes, H1947
1Ki 22:35 The b from his wound ran onto the floor H1947
1Ki 22:38 the dogs licked up his b, as the word H1947

2Ki 3:22 the way, the water looked red—like b. H1947
2Ki 3:23 "That's b!" they said. "Those kings must H1947
2Ki 9: 7 I will avenge the b of my servants the H1947
2Ki 9: 7 the prophets and the b of all the LORD's H1947
2Ki 9:26 'Yesterday I saw the b of Naboth and the H1947
2Ki 9:26 blood of Naboth and the b of his sons, H1947
2Ki 9:33 some of her b spattered the wall and H1947
2Ki 16:13 splashed the b of his fellowship H1947
2Ki 16:15 against this altar the b of all the burnt H1947
2Ki 20:18 your own flesh and b who H3655+4946+3870
2Ki 21:16 shed so much innocent b that he filled H1947
2Ki 24: 4 including the shedding of innocent b. H1947
2Ki 24: 4 he had filled Jerusalem with innocent b, H1947
2Ki 25:25 who was of royal b, came with ten men H2446
1Ch 11: 1 said, "We are your own flesh and b. H6795
1Ch 11:19 I drink the b of these men who went H1947
1Ch 22: 8 'You have shed much b and have fought H1947
1Ch 22: 8 you have shed much b on the earth in my H1947
1Ch 28: 3 you are a warrior and have shed b. H1947
2Ch 6: 9 your own flesh and b—he is H3655+4946+2743
2Ch 29:22 the priests took the b and splashed it H1947
2Ch 29:22 splashed their b against the altar; H1947
2Ch 29:22 splashed their b against the altar. H1947
2Ch 29:24 presented their b on the altar for a H1947
2Ch 30:16 the altar the b handed to them by the H1947
2Ch 32:21 his own flesh and b, cut him down H5055
2Ch 35:11 against the altar the b handed to them, NDT
Ne 5: 5 are of the same flesh and b as our fellow H1414
Job 16:18 do not cover my b; may my cry never be H1947
Job 39:30 Its young ones feast on b, and where the H1947
Ps 9:12 For he who avenges b remembers; he H1947
Ps 16: 4 out libations of b to such gods or take H1947
Ps 50:13 the flesh of bulls or drink the b of goats? H1947
Ps 58:10 they dip their feet in the b of the wicked. H1947
Ps 59: 2 save me from those who are after my b. H1947
Ps 68:23 your feet may wade in the b of your foes, H1947
Ps 72:14 precious is their b in his sight. H1947
Ps 78:44 He turned their river into b; they could not H1947
Ps 79: 3 They have poured out b like water all H1947
Ps 79:10 avenge the outpoured b of your servants. H1947
Ps 105:29 He turned their waters into b, causing H1947
Ps 106:38 They shed innocent b, the blood of their H1947
Ps 106:38 the b of their sons and daughters H1947
Ps 106:38 the land was desecrated by their b. H1947
Pr 1:11 let's lie in wait for innocent b, let's H1947
Pr 1:16 rush into evil, they are swift to shed b. H1947
Pr 1:18 These men lie in wait for their own b H1947
Pr 6:17 lying tongue, hands that shed innocent b, H1947
Pr 12: 6 The words of the wicked lie in wait for b H1947
Pr 30:33 as twisting the nose produces b, so H1947
Isa 1:11 no pleasure in the b of bulls and lambs H1947
Isa 1:15 am not listening. Your hands are full of b! H1947
Isa 9: 5 garment rolled in b will be destined for H1947
Isa 15: 9 The waters of Dimon are full of b, but I H1947
Isa 26:21 The earth will disclose the b shed on it H1947
Isa 34: 3 the mountains will be soaked with their b. H1947
Isa 34: 6 The sword of the LORD is bathed in b, it is H1947
Isa 34: 6 with fat—the b of lambs and goats, fat H1947
Isa 34: 7 Their land will be drenched with b, and H1947
Isa 39: 7 your own flesh and b who H3655+4946+3870
Isa 49:26 they will be drunk on their own b, as with H1947
Isa 58: 7 to turn away from your own flesh and b? H1414
Isa 59: 3 For your hands are stained with b, your H1947
Isa 59: 7 into sin; they are swift to shed innocent b. H1947
Isa 63: 3 my wrath; their b spattered my garments H5906
Isa 63: 6 drunk and poured their b on the ground." H5906
Isa 66: 3 offering is like one who presents pig's b, H1947
Jer 7: 6 do not shed innocent b in this place, H1947
Jer 19: 4 this place with the b of the innocent. H1947
Jer 22: 3 do not shed innocent b in this place. H1947
Jer 22:17 shedding innocent b and on oppression H1947
Jer 26:15 bring the guilt of innocent b on yourselves H1947
Jer 41: 1 who was of royal b and had been one of H2446
Jer 46:10 till it has quenched its thirst with b. H1947
Jer 51:35 "May our b be on those who live in H1947
La 4:13 shed within her the b of the righteous. H1947
La 4:14 are so defiled with b that no one dares to H1947
Eze 3:18 I will hold you accountable for their b. H1947
Eze 3:20 I will hold you accountable for their b. H1947
Eze 16: 6 by and saw you kicking about in your b, H1947
Eze 16: 6 as you lay there in your b I said to you, H1947
Eze 16: 9 water and washed the b from you and put H1947
Eze 16:22 naked and bare, kicking about in your b. H1947
Eze 16:36 because you gave them your children's b, H1947
Eze 16:38 who commit adultery and who shed b; H1947
Eze 16:38 on you the b vengeance of my wrath and H1947
Eze 18:10 who sheds b or does any of these other H1947
Eze 18:13 to death; his b will be on his own head. H1947
Eze 21:32 the fire, your b will be shed in your land H1947
Eze 22: 3 doom by shedding b in her midst and H1947
Eze 22: 4 because of the b you have shed and H1947
Eze 22: 6 who are in you uses his power to shed b. H1947
Eze 22: 9 slanderers who are bent on shedding b; H1947
Eze 22:12 are people who accept bribes to shed b; H1947
Eze 22:13 have made and at the b you have shed in H1947
Eze 22:27 they shed b and kill people to make H1947
Eze 23:37 adultery and b is on their hands. H1947
Eze 23:45 women who commit adultery and shed b, H1947
Eze 23:45 are adulterous and b is on their hands. H1947
Eze 24: 7 " 'For the b she shed is in her midst: She H1947
Eze 24: 8 take revenge I put her b on the bare rock, H1947
Eze 28:23 upon you and make b flow in your streets. H1947
Eze 32: 6 land with your flowing b all the way to the H1947
Eze 33: 4 their b will be on their own head. H1947
Eze 33: 5 their b will be on their own head. H1947
Eze 33: 6 the watchman accountable for their b. H1947
Eze 33: 8 I will hold you accountable for their b. H1947
Eze 33:25 you eat meat with the b still in it and look H1947
Eze 33:25 in it and look to your idols and shed b, H1947
Eze 36:18 because they had shed b in the land and H1947
Eze 39:17 There you will eat flesh and drink b. H1947
Eze 39:18 men and drink the b of the princes of the H1947
Eze 39:19 are glutted and drink b till you are drunk. H1947
Eze 43:18 splashing b against the altar when H1947
Eze 43:20 to take some of its b and put it on the four H1947
Eze 44: 7 me food, fat and b, and you broke my H1947
Eze 44:15 before me to offer sacrifices of fat and b, H1947
Eze 45:19 to take some of the b of the sin offering H1947
Hos 6: 8 of evildoers, stained with footprints of b. H1947
Joel 2:30 b and fire and billows of smoke. H1947
Joel 2:31 the moon to b before the coming of H1947
Joel 3:19 in whose land they shed innocent b. H1947
Joel 3:21 Shall I leave their innocent b unavenged H1947
Mic 7: 2 Everyone lies in wait to shed b; they hunt H1947
Na 3: 1 Woe to the city of b, full of lies, full of H1947
Hab 2: 8 For you have shed human b; you have H1947
Hab 2:17 For you have shed human b; you have H1947
Zep 1:17 Their b will be poured out like dust and H1947
Zec 9: 7 I will take the b from their mouths, the H1947
Zec 9:11 because of the b of my covenant with you H1947
Mt 16:17 this was not revealed to you by flesh and b, G135
Mt 23:30 with them in shedding the b of the G135
Mt 23:35 all the righteous b that has been shed on G135
Mt 23:35 from the b of righteous Abel to the blood G135
Mt 23:35 righteous Abel to the b of Zechariah son of G135
Mt 26:28 This is my b of the covenant, which is G135
Mt 27: 4 he said, "for I have betrayed innocent b." G135
Mt 27: 6 this into the treasury, since it is b money." G135
Mt 27: 8 it has been called the Field of B to this day. G135
Mt 27:24 "I am innocent of this man's b," he said. G135
Mt 27:25 "His b is on us and on our children! G135
Mk 14:24 "This is my b of the covenant, which is G135
Lk 11:50 responsible for the b of all the prophets G135
Lk 11:51 from the b of Abel to the blood of G135
Lk 11:51 the blood of Abel to the b of Zechariah, G135
Lk 13: 1 the Galileans whose b Pilate had mixed G135
Lk 22:20 "This cup is the new covenant in my b G135
Lk 22:44 sweat was like drops of b falling to the G135
Jn 6:53 the flesh of the Son of Man and drink his b, G135
Jn 6:54 my flesh and drinks my b has eternal life, G135
Jn 6:55 my flesh is real food and my b is real drink. G135
Jn 6:56 my flesh and drinks my b remains in me, G135
Jn 19:34 bringing a sudden flow of b and water. G135
Ac 1:19 language Akeldama, that is, Field of B.) G135
Ac 2:19 b and fire and billows of smoke. G135
Ac 2:20 the moon to b before the coming of G135
Ac 5:28 to make us guilty of this man's b. G135
Ac 15:20 the meat of strangled animals and from b. G135
Ac 15:29 sacrificed to idols, from b, from the meat of G135
Ac 18: 6 to them, "Your b be on your own heads! G135
Ac 20:26 that I am innocent of the b of any of you. G135
Ac 20:28 which he bought with his own b. G135
Ac 21:25 sacrificed to idols, from b, from the meat of G135
Ac 22:20 And when the b of your martyr Stephen was G135
Ro 3:15 "Their feet are swift to shed b; G135
Ro 3:25 through the shedding of his b—to be G135
Ro 5: 9 Since we have now been justified by his b G135
1Co 10:16 thanks a participation in the b of Christ? G135
1Co 11:25 "This cup is the new covenant in my b; do G135
1Co 11:27 sinning against the body and b of the Lord. G135
1Co 15:50 that flesh and b cannot inherit the kingdom G135
Eph 1: 7 In him we have redemption through his b G135
Eph 2:13 have been brought near by the b of Christ. G135
Eph 6:12 For our struggle is not against flesh and b G135
Col 1:20 by making peace through his b, shed on G135
Heb 2:14 Since the children have flesh and b, he too G135
Heb 9: 7 never without b, which he offered for G135
Heb 9:12 by means of the b of goats and calves; G135
Heb 9:12 Most Holy Place once for all by his own b, G135
Heb 9:13 The b of goats and bulls and the ashes of a G135
Heb 9:14 will the b of Christ, who through the G135
Heb 9:18 covenant was not put into effect without b. G135
Heb 9:19 he took the b of calves, together G135
Heb 9:20 "This is the b of the covenant G135
Heb 9:21 he sprinkled with the b both the tabernacle G135
Heb 9:22 that nearly everything be cleansed with b, G135
Heb 9:22 without the shedding of b there is no G136
Heb 9:25 Place every year with b that is not his own. G135
Heb 10: 4 It is impossible for the b of bulls and goats G135
Heb 10:19 the Most Holy Place by the b of Jesus, G135
Heb 10:29 an unholy thing the b of the covenant that G135
Heb 11:28 kept the Passover and the application of b, G135
Heb 12: 4 resisted to the point of shedding your b. G135
Heb 12:24 and to the sprinkled b that speaks a better G135
Heb 12:24 speaks a better word than the b of Abel. NDT
Heb 13:11 high priest carries the b of animals into the G135
Heb 13:12 make the people holy through his own b. G135
Heb 13:20 who through the b of the eternal covenant G135
1Pe 1: 2 to Jesus Christ and sprinkled with his b: G135
1Pe 1:19 but with the precious b of Christ, a lamb G135
1Jn 1: 7 one another, and the b of Jesus, his Son, G135
1Jn 5: 6 This is the one who came by water and b G135
1Jn 5: 6 come by water only, but by water and b. G135
1Jn 5: 8 the water and the b; and the three are in G135
Rev 1: 5 us and has freed us from our sins by his b, G135
Rev 5: 9 with your b you purchased for God G135
Rev 6:10 inhabitants of the earth and avenge our b?" G135
Rev 6:12 the whole moon turned b red, G6055+135
Rev 7:14 made them white in the b of the Lamb. G135
Rev 8: 7 there came hail and fire mixed with b G135
Rev 8: 8 A third of the sea turned into b, G135
Rev 11: 6 turn the waters into b and to strike the G135
Rev 12:11 over him by the b of the Lamb and by the G135
Rev 14:20 and b flowed out of the press G135
Rev 16: 3 it turned into b like that of a dead G135
Rev 16: 4 springs of water, and they became b. G135
Rev 16: 6 they have shed the b of your holy people G135
Rev 16: 6 you have given them b to drink as they G135
Rev 17: 6 was drunk with the b of God's holy people, G135
Rev 17: 6 the b of those who bore testimony to Jesus. G135
Rev 18:24 In her was found the b of prophets and of G135
Rev 19: 2 has avenged on her the b of his servants." G135
Rev 19:13 He is dressed in a robe dipped in b, and his G135

BLOOD-STAINED (1) [BLOOD]

2Sa 21: 1 "It is on account of Saul and his b house H1947

BLOODSHED (31) [BLOOD]

Ex 22: 2 fatal blow, the defender is not guilty of b; H1947
Ex 22: 3 after sunrise, the defender is guilty of b. H1947
Lev 17: 4 that person shall be considered guilty of b H1947
Nu 35:33 B pollutes the land, and atonement H1947
Dt 17: 8 whether b, lawsuits or H1947+4200+1947
Dt 19:10 so that you will not be guilty of b. H1947
Dt 21: 8 Then the b will be atoned for, H1947
Dt 22: 8 not bring the guilt of b on your house if H1947
1Sa 25:26 kept you from b and from H995+928+1947
1Sa 25:31 burden of needless b or of having H9161+1947
1Sa 25:33 me from b this day and H995+928+1947
2Ch 19:10 whether b or other concerns H1947+4200+1947
Ps 51:14 Deliver me from the guilt of b, O God, you H1947
Isa 5: 7 justice, but saw b; for righteousness, H5384
Jer 48:10 on anyone who keeps their sword from b! H1947
Eze 5:17 Plague and b will sweep through you H1947
Eze 7:23 For the land is full of b, and the city H5477+1947
Eze 9: 9 the land is full of b and the city is full of H1947
Eze 14:19 pour out my wrath on it through b, H1947
Eze 22: 2 Will you judge this city of b? Then H1947
Eze 24: 6 " 'Woe to the city of b, to the pot now H1947
Eze 24: 9 " 'Woe to the city of b! I, H1947
Eze 35: 6 will give you over to b and it will pursue H1947
Eze 35: 6 Since you did not hate b, bloodshed will H1947
Eze 35: 6 not hate bloodshed, b will pursue you. H1947
Eze 38:22 judgment on him with plague and b; H1947
Hos 4: 2 all bounds, and b follows bloodshed. H1947
Hos 4: 2 all bounds, and bloodshed follows b. H1947
Hos 12:14 on him the guilt of his b and will repay H1947
Mic 3:10 who build Zion with b, and Jerusalem H1947
Hab 2:12 builds a city with b and establishes a H1947

BLOODSHOT (1) [BLOOD]

Pr 23:29 has needless bruises? Who has b eyes? H2680

BLOODSTAINS (1) [BLOOD]

Isa 4: 4 he will cleanse the b from Jerusalem by a H1947

BLOODTHIRSTY (5) [BLOOD]

Ps 5: 6 The b and deceitful you H1947
Ps 26: 9 with sinners, my life with those who are b, H1947
Ps 55:23 the b and deceitful will not live out half H1947
Ps 139:19 Away from me, you who are b! H1947
Pr 29:10 The b hate a person of integrity and H1947+408

BLOOM (5)

Ex 9:31 barley had headed and the flax was in b. H1499
SS 2:15 the vineyards, our vineyards that are in b. H6163
SS 6:11 budded or the pomegranates were in b. H5914
SS 7:12 if the pomegranates are in b—there H5914
Isa 35: 2 it will burst into b; it will rejoice H7255+7255

BLOSSOM (8) [BLOSSOMED, BLOSSOMING, BLOSSOMS]

1Ki 7:26 rim was like the rim of a cup, like a lily b. H7258
2Ch 4: 5 rim was like the rim of a cup, like a lily b. H7258
Isa 18: 5 when the b is gone and the flower H7258
Isa 27: 6 Israel will bud and b and fill all the world H7255
Isa 35: 1 be glad; the wilderness will rejoice and b. H7255
Hos 14: 5 like the dew to Israel; he will b like a lily. H7255
Hos 14: 7 like the grain, they will b like the vine H7255
Jas 1:11 its b falls and its beauty is destroyed. G470

BLOSSOMED (3) [BLOSSOM]

Ge 40:10 as it budded, it b, and its clusters H6590+5890
Nu 17: 8 budded, b and produced almonds. H7437+7488
Eze 7:10 the rod has budded, arrogance has b! H7255

BLOSSOMING (1) [BLOSSOM]

SS 2:13 the b vines spread their fragrance. H6163

BLOSSOMS (12) [BLOSSOM]

Ex 25:31 buds and b of one piece with them. H7258
Ex 25:33 flowers with buds and b are to be on one H7258
Ex 25:34 like almond flowers with buds and b. H7258
Ex 37:17 buds and b of one piece with them. H7258
Ex 37:19 with buds and b were on one branch, H7258
Ex 37:20 like almond flowers with buds and b. H7258
Nu 8: 4 of hammered gold—from its base to its b. H7258

Job 15:33 like an olive tree shedding its **b**. H5900
Ecc 12: 5 the almond tree **b** and the grasshopper H5914
SS 1:14 me a cluster of **henna b** from the H4110
SS 7:12 budded, if their **b** have opened, and if H6163
Na 1: 4 Carmel wither and the **b** *of* Lebanon fade. H7258

BLOT (15) [BLOTS, BLOTTED]
Ex 17:14 because *I will* **completely b out** the H4681+4681
Ex 32:32 then **b** me **out** of the book you have H4681
Ex 32:33 sinned against me *I will* **b out** of my book. H4681
Dt 9:14 destroy them and **b out** their name from H4681
Dt 25:19 *you shall* **b out** the name of Amalek from H4681
Dt 29:20 the LORD *will* **b out** their names from H4681
2Ki 14:27 had not said he *would* **b out** the name of H4681
Ne 4: 5 up their guilt or **b out** their sins from your H4681
Ne 13:14 and *do* not **b out** what I have so faithfully H4681
Ps 34:16 to **b out** their name from the earth. H4162
Ps 51: 1 great compassion **b out** my transgressions H4681
Ps 51: 9 from my sins and **b out** all my iniquity. H4681
Ps 109:15 that *he may b* **out** their name from the earth. AIT
Jer 18:23 their crimes or **b out** their sins from your H4681
Rev 3: 5 *I will* never **b out** the name of that person *G1981*

BLOTS (2) [BLOT]
Isa 43:25 am he *who* **b out** your transgressions H4681
2Pe 2:13 They are **b** and blemishes, reveling in *G5070*

BLOTTED (6) [BLOT]
Dt 25: 6 his name *will* not **be b out** from Israel. H4681
Ps 9: 5 *you have* **b out** their name for ever and H4681
Ps 69:28 *May they* **be b out** of the book of life and H4681
Ps 109:13 their names **b out** from the next H4681
Ps 109:14 *may* the sin of his mother never **be b out**. H4681
Isa 48:19 their name *would* never **be b out** nor H4162

BLOW (36) [BLEW, BLOWING, BLOWN, BLOWS, WINDBLOWN]
Ex 10:13 the LORD **made** an east wind **b** across the H5627
Ex 21:12 a person **with a fatal b** is to be put to H4637
Ex 21:19 the *one who* **struck the b** will not be held H5782
Ex 22: 2 breaking in at night and is struck a **fatal b**, H4637
Nu 10: 7 the assembly, **b** *the* **trumpets**, but not with H9546
Nu 10: 8 the priests, *are to* **b** the trumpets. H9546
Nu 35:16 " 'If *anyone* **strikes** someone **a** fatal **b** with H5782
Nu 35:17 and **strikes** someone **a** fatal **b** with it, H5782
Nu 35:18 and **strikes** someone **a** fatal **b** with it, H5782
Jdg 7:18 I and all who are with me **b** our trumpets, H9546
Jdg 7:18 all around the camp **b** yours and shout, H9546
Jdg 7:20 right hands the trumpets *they were to* **b**, H9546
Jdg 16:28 let me with **one b** get revenge on the AIT
1Sa 6:19 because of the heavy **b** the LORD had dealt H4804
1Ki 1:34 **B** the trumpet and shout, 'Long live King H9546
1Ch 15:24 the priests *were to* **b** trumpets before H2955
1Ch 16: 6 the priests were to **b** the trumpets regularly NDT
2Ch 21:14 everything that is yours, with a heavy **b**. H4487
Ps 39:10 I am overcome by the **b** *of* your hand. H9327
Ps 68: 2 *May you* **b** them **away** like smoke—as H5622
Ps 78:26 by his power **made** the south wind **b**. H5627
SS 4:16 **B** *on* my garden, that its fragrance may H7031
Isa 5:24 decay and their flowers **b away** like dust; H6590
Isa 19: 7 parched, *will* **b away** and be no more. H5622
Isa 41:16 them up, and a gale *will* **b** them **away**. H7046
Isa 57:13 them off, a mere breath *will* **b** them **away**. H4374
Jer 6:29 The bellows **b fiercely** to burn away the H5723
Jer 14:17 suffered a grievous wound, a crushing **b**. H4804
Jer 51:27 **B** the trumpet among the nations H9546
Eze 22:21 gather you and *I will* **b** on you with my H5870
Eze 24:16 with *one* **b** I am about to take away from H4487
Eze 33: 6 coming and *does* not **b** the trumpet to H9546
Joel 2: 1 **B** the trumpet in Zion; sound the alarm on H9546
Joel 2:15 **B** the trumpet in Zion, declare a holy fast H9546
Ac 27:13 *When* a **gentle** south wind *began to* **b** *G5710*
1Co 9:27 *I* **strike a b** to my body and make it my *G5724*

BLOWING (9) [BLOW]
Jos 6: 4 with the priests **b** the trumpets. H9546
Jos 6: 8 LORD went forward, **b** their trumpets, and H9546
Jos 6:13 the ark of the LORD and **b** the trumpets. H9546
2Ki 11:14 of the land *were* rejoicing and **b** trumpets. H9546
2Ch 23:13 of the land *were* rejoicing and **b** trumpets, H9546
Hos 13:15 the LORD will come, **b in** from the desert H6590
Jn 6:18 A strong wind *was* **b** and the waters grew *G4463*
Ac 2: 2 a sound like the **b** of a violent wind came *G5770*
Rev 7: 1 any wind from **b** on the land or on the *G4463*

BLOWN (6) [BLOW]
1Sa 13: 3 Then Saul **had** the trumpet **b** throughout H9546
Isa 29: 5 fine dust, the ruthless hordes like **b** chaff. H6296
Eze 7:14 " '*They have* **b** the trumpet, they have H9546
Eph 4:14 and **b here and there** by every wind of *G4367*
Jas 1: 6 wave of the sea, **b** and tossed **by the wind**. *G448*
Jude 12 without rain, **b along** by the wind; autumn *G4195*

BLOWS (18) [BLOW]
Job 20:23 against him and rain down his **b** on him. H4303
Ps 1: 4 They are like chaff that the wind **b away**. H5622
Ps 103:16 the wind **b** over it and it is gone, and its H6296
Pr 6:33 **B** and disgrace are his lot, and his shame H5596
Pr 20:30 **B** and wounds scrub away evil, and H2467
Ecc 1: 6 The wind **b** to the south and turns to the H2143
Isa 14: 6 struck down peoples with unceasing **b**, H4804
Isa 27: 8 drives her out, as on a day the east wind **b**. NDT
Isa 30:32 fights them in battle with the **b** of his arm. H9485
Isa 40: 7 because the breath of the LORD **b** on them. H5959
Isa 40:24 than *he* **b** on them and they wither H5973
Jer 4:11 heights in the desert **b** toward my people, NDT
Eze 26: 9 He will direct the **b** *of* his battering rams H4693
Eze 33: 3 the land and **b** the trumpet to warn H9546
Lk 12:47 master wants *will be* **beaten with** many **b**. *G1296*
Lk 12:48 punishment *will be* **beaten with** few **b**. *G1296*
Lk 12:55 And when the south wind **b**, you say, 'It's *G4463*
Jn 3: 8 The wind **b** wherever it pleases. You hear *G4463*

BLUE (51)
Ex 24:10 of lapis lazuli, as **bright b** as the sky. H3198S
Ex 25: 4 **b**, purple and scarlet yarn and fine linen H9418
Ex 26: 1 ten curtains of finely twisted linen and **b**, H9418
Ex 26: 4 Make loops of **b material** along the edge H9418
Ex 26:31 "Make a curtain of **b**, purple and scarlet H9418
Ex 26:36 entrance to the tent make a curtain of **b**, H9418
Ex 27:16 cubits long, of **b**, purple and scarlet H9418
Ex 28: 5 them use gold, and **b**, purple and scarlet H9418
Ex 28: 6 of gold, and of **b**, purple and scarlet H9418
Ex 28: 8 with gold, and with **b**, purple and scarlet H9418
Ex 28:15 of gold, and of **b**, purple and scarlet yarn H9418
Ex 28:28 tied to the rings of the ephod with **b** cord, H9418
Ex 28:31 the robe of the ephod entirely of **b cloth**, H9418
Ex 28:33 Make pomegranates of **b**, purple and H9418
Ex 28:37 Fasten a **b** cord to it to attach it to the H9418
Ex 35: 6 **b**, purple and scarlet yarn and fine linen H9418
Ex 35:23 Everyone who had **b**, purple or scarlet yarn H9418
Ex 35:25 what she had spun—**b**, purple or scarlet H9418
Ex 35:35 embroiderers in **b**, purple and scarlet yarn H9418
Ex 36: 8 ten curtains of finely twisted linen and **b**, H9418
Ex 36:11 made loops of **b material** along the edge H9418
Ex 36:35 They made the curtain of **b**, purple and H9418
Ex 36:37 to the tent they made a curtain of **b**, H9418
Ex 38:18 entrance to the courtyard was made of **b**, H9418
Ex 38:23 an embroiderer in **b**, purple and H9418
Ex 39: 1 From the **b**, purple and scarlet yarn they H9418
Ex 39: 2 of gold, and of **b**, purple and scarlet H9418
Ex 39: 3 cut strands to be worked into the **b**, H9418
Ex 39: 5 with gold, and with **b**, purple and scarlet H9418
Ex 39: 8 of gold, and of **b**, purple and scarlet yarn H9418
Ex 39:21 to the rings of the ephod with **b** cord, H9418
Ex 39:22 the robe of the ephod entirely of **b cloth**— H9418
Ex 39:24 They made pomegranates of **b**, purple H9418
Ex 39:29 was made of finely twisted linen and **b**, H9418
Ex 39:31 Then they fastened a **b** cord to it to attach H9418
Nu 4: 6 a cloth of solid **b** over that and put the H9418
Nu 4: 7 they are to spread a **b** cloth and put on it H9418
Nu 4: 9 "They are to take a **b** cloth and cover the H9418
Nu 4:11 they are to spread a **b** cloth and cover that H9418
Nu 4:12 wrap them in a **b** cloth, cover that with H9418
Nu 15:38 garments, with a **b** cord on each tassel. H9418
2Ch 2: 7 crimson and **b yarn**, and experienced H9418
2Ch 2:14 purple and **b** and crimson **yarn** and fine H9418
2Ch 3:14 of **b**, purple and crimson **yarn** and fine H9418
Est 1: 6 had hangings of white and **b** linen, H9418
Est 8:15 wearing royal garments of **b** and white, H9418
Jer 10: 9 made is then dressed in **b** and purple— H9418
Eze 23: 6 clothed in **b**, governors and commanders H9418
Eze 27: 7 awnings were of **b** and purple from the H9418
Eze 27:24 beautiful garments, **b** fabric, embroidered H9418
Rev 9:17 were fiery red, **dark b**, and yellow as sulfur *G5610*

BLURTS (1)
Pr 12:23 themselves, but a fool's heart **b out** folly. H7924

BLUSH (3)
Jer 3: 3 a prostitute; you refuse *to* **b with shame**. H4007
Jer 6:15 they do not even know how *to* **b**. H4007
Jer 8:12 they do not even know how *to* **b**. H4007

BLUSTERING (1)
Job 8: 2 say such things? Your words are a **b** wind. H3888

BOANERGES (1)
Mk 3:17 to them he gave the name **B**, which *G1065*

BOARD (5) [ABOARD, BOARDED, BOARDS]
Eze 27: 9 of Byblos were **on b** as shipwrights to caulk H928
Eze 27:27 and everyone else **on b** will sink into H928+9348
Ac 21: 2 over to Phoenicia, **went on b** and set sail. *G2094*
Ac 27: 6 ship sailing for Italy and put us **on b**. *G1650+899*
Ac 27:37 there were 276 of us **on b**. *G1877+3836+4450*

BOARDED (1) [BOARD]
Ac 27: 2 *We* **b** a ship from Adramyttium about to *G2094*

BOARDS (4) [BOARD]
Ex 27: 8 altar hollow, out of **b**. It is to be made just H4283
Ex 38: 7 They made it hollow, out of **b**. H4283
1Ki 6:15 He lined its interior walls with cedar **b** H7521
1Ki 6:16 temple with cedar **b** from floor to ceiling H7521

BOARS (1)
Ps 80:13 **B** from the forest ravage it, and insects H2614

BOAST (62) [BOASTED, BOASTERS, BOASTFUL, BOASTFULLY, BOASTING, BOASTS]
Jdg 7: 2 Israel would **b** against me, 'My own H6995
1Ki 20:11 on his armor *should* not **b** like one who H2146
Ps 44: 8 In God *we* **make** *our* **b** all day long, and H2146
Ps 49: 6 in their wealth and **b** of their great riches? H2146
Ps 52: 1 Why *do you* **b** of evil, you mighty hero H2146
Ps 52: 1 Why do you **b** all day long, you who are a NDT
Ps 75: 4 the arrogant I say, '**B** no more,' and to the H2147
Ps 97: 7 to shame, those *who* **b** in idols—worship H2146
Pr 27: 1 *Do* not **b** about tomorrow, for you do not H2146
Isa 10:15 the saw **b** against the one who uses it? H1540
Isa 28:15 *You* **b**, "We have entered into a covenant H606
Isa 45:25 in the LORD and *will* **make** *their* **b** *in* him. H2146
Isa 61: 6 of nations, and in their riches *you will* **b**. H607
Jer 4: 2 blessings by him and in him *they will* **b**." H2146
Jer 9:23 "Let not the wise **b** of their wisdom or the H2146
Jer 9:23 wisdom or the strong **b** of their strength H2146
Jer 9:23 their strength or the rich **b** of their riches, H2146
Jer 9:24 let the one who boasts **b** about this H2146
Jer 49: 4 Why *do you* **b** of your valleys, boast of H2146
Jer 49: 4 of your valleys, **b** of your valleys so fruitful? NDT
Jer 51:41 captured, the **b** *of* the whole earth seized! H9335
Am 4: 5 freewill offerings—**b** *about* them, you H9048
Ob 12 nor **b so much** in the day of H1540+7023+3870
Ro 2:17 if you rely on the law and **b** in God; *G3016*
Ro 2:23 You who **b** in the law, do you dishonor *G3016*
Ro 4: 2 he had **something to b about**—but not *G3017*
Ro 5: 2 And *we* **b** in the hope of the glory of God *G3016*
Ro 5:11 but *we* also **b** in God through our Lord *G3016*
1Co 1:29 so that no one *may* **b** before him. *G3016*
1Co 1:31 "*Let* the one who boasts **b** in the Lord." *G3016*
1Co 4: 7 why *do you* **b** as though you did not? *G3016*
1Co 9:15 allow anyone to deprive me *of* this **b**. *G3017*
1Co 9:16 the gospel, I cannot **b**, since I am *G3017*
1Co 13: 3 over my body to hardship that *I may* **b**, *G3016*
1Co 13: 4 does not envy, *it does* not **b**, it is not *G4371*
1Co 15:31 just as surely as *I* **b** about you in *G3018+2400*
2Co 1:12 Now this is our **b**: Our conscience testifies *G3018*
2Co 1:14 fully that you can **b** of us just as we will NDT
2Co 1:14 of us just as *we will* **b** of you in the *G3017+1639*
2Co 10: 8 So even if *I* **b** somewhat freely about the *G3016*
2Co 10:13 however, *will* not **b** beyond proper limits *G3016*
2Co 10:16 *For we do* not *want to* **b** about work *G3016*
2Co 10:17 "*Let* the one who boasts **b** in the Lord." *G3016*
2Co 11:12 equal with us in the things *they* **b** *about*. *G3016*
2Co 11:18 in the way the world does, I too *will* **b**. *G3016*
2Co 11:21 Whatever anyone else **dares** *to* **b** *about*—I AIT
2Co 11:21 speaking as a fool—I also **dare** *to* **b** *about*. AIT
2Co 11:30 If I must **b**, I will boast of the things that *G3016*
2Co 11:30 *I will* **b** of the things that show my *G3016*
2Co 12: 5 *I will* **b** about a man like that, but I will not *G3016*
2Co 12: 5 like that, but *I will* not **b** about myself *G3016*
2Co 12: 6 Even if I should choose *to* **b**, I would not *G3016*
2Co 12: 9 Therefore *I will* **b** all the more gladly *G3016*
Gal 6:13 be circumcised that *they may* **b** about your *G3016*
Gal 6:14 *May* I never **b** except in the cross of our *G3016*
Eph 2: 9 not by works, so that no one *can* **b**. *G3016*
Php 2:16 I will be able to **b** on the day of Christ *G3017*
Php 3: 3 God by his Spirit, *who* **b** in Christ Jesus *G3016*
2Th 1: 4 God's churches we **b** about your *G1595*
Jas 3:14 *do* not **b** about it or deny the truth. *G2878*
Jas 4:16 *you* **b** in your arrogant schemes *G3016*
Jude 16 they **b** about themselves and flatter *G3281+5665*

BOASTED (7) [BOAST]
Ex 15: 9 The enemy **b**, 'I will pursue, I will overtake H606
Est 5:11 Haman **b** to them *about* his vast wealth H6218
Isa 20: 5 trusted in Cush and **b** *in* Egypt will be H9514
Jer 13:20 the sheep of which you **b**? H9514
Eze 35:13 You **b** against me and spoke H1540+928+7023
Ac 8: 9 *He* **b** that he was someone great, *G3306*
2Co 7:14 *I had* **b** to him about you, and you have *G3016*

BOASTERS (2) [BOAST]
Jer 48:45 of Moab, the skulls of the **noisy b**. H1201+8623
Zep 3:11 I will remove from you your arrogant **b**. H6611

BOASTFUL (5) [BOAST]
Ps 12: 3 flattering lips and every **b** tongue— H1819+1524
Da 7:11 because of the **b** words the horn was A10647
Ro 1:30 arrogant and **b**; they invent ways of *G225*
2Ti 3: 2 lovers of money, **b**, proud, abusive, *G225*
2Pe 2:18 For they mouth empty, **b** words and, by *G5665*

BOASTFULLY (2) [BOAST]
Da 7: 8 human being and a mouth that spoke **b**. A10647
Da 7:20 that had eyes and a mouth that spoke **b**. A10647

BOASTING (17) [BOAST]
Ps 94: 4 all the evildoers *are* **full of b**. H607
Ro 3:27 then, is **b**? It is excluded. *G3018*
1Co 3:21 So then, no more **b** about human leaders *G3016*
1Co 5: 6 Your **b** is not good. Don't you know that a *G3017*
2Co 7:14 so our **b** about you to Titus has proved to *G3018*
2Co 9: 2 and *I have been* **b** about it to the *G3016*
2Co 9: 3 in order that our **b** about you in this *G3017*
2Co 10:13 will confine our **b** to the sphere of NDT
2Co 10:14 We are not going too far in our **b**, as would NDT
2Co 10:15 go beyond our limits *by* **b** of work done by *G3016*
2Co 11:10 regions of Achaia will stop this **b** of mine. *G3018*
2Co 11:16 would a fool, so that I *may* **do** a little **b**. *G3016*
2Co 11:17 In this self-confident **b** I am not talking as *G3018*
2Co 11:18 Since many *are* **b** in the way the world *G3016*
2Co 12: 1 I must *go on* **b**. Although there is nothing *G3016*
Php 1:26 with you again your **b** in Christ Jesus will *G3017*
Jas 4:16 your arrogant schemes. All such **b** is evil. *G3018*

BOASTS (12) [BOAST]
1Sa 2: 1 My mouth **b** over my enemies, for I H8143

Ps 10: 3 He **b** about the cravings of his heart; he H2146
Pr 20:14 then goes off and **b** *about* the purchase. H2146
Pr 25:14 without rain is one *who* **b** of gifts never H2146
Isa 16: 6 her insolence; but her **b** are empty. H966
Jer 9:24 but *let* the *one who* **b** boast about this H2146
Jer 48:30 the LORD, "and her **b** accomplish nothing. H966
Hos 12: 8 Ephraim **b**, "I am very rich; I have become H606
1Co 1:31 "Let the *one who* **b** boast in the Lord." *G3016*
2Co 10:17 "Let the *one who* **b** boast in the Lord." *G3016*
Jas 3: 5 part of the body, but *it* **makes** great **b**. *G902*
Rev 18: 7 In her heart *she* **b**, 'I sit enthroned as *G3306*

BOAT (44) [BOATS, LIFEBOAT]

Mt 4:21 They were in a **b** with their father *G4450*
Mt 4:22 they left the **b** and their father and *G4450*
Mt 8:23 Then he got into the **b** and his disciples *G4450*
Mt 8:24 so that the waves swept over the **b**. *G4450*
Mt 9: 1 Jesus stepped into a **b**, crossed over and *G4450*
Mt 13: 2 him that he got into a **b** and sat in it, *G4450*
Mt 14:13 he withdrew by **b** privately to a solitary *G4450*
Mt 14:22 get into the **b** and go on ahead of him *G4450*
Mt 14:24 the **b** was already a considerable *G4450*
Mt 14:29 Then Peter got down out of the **b**, walked *G4450*
Mt 14:32 And when they climbed into the **b**, the *G4450*
Mt 14:33 those who were in the **b** worshiped him, *G4450*
Mt 15:39 he got into the **b** and went to the vicinity *G4450*
Mk 1:19 of Zebedee and his brother John in a **b**, *G4450*
Mk 1:20 Zebedee in the **b** with the hired men *G4450*
Mk 3: 9 disciples to have a **small b** ready for him, *G4449*
Mk 4: 1 that he got into a **b** and sat in it out on *G4450*
Mk 4:36 took him along, just as he was, in the **b**. *G4450*
Mk 4:37 the waves broke over the **b**, so that it *G4450*
Mk 5: 2 When Jesus got out of the **b**, a man with *G4450*
Mk 5:18 As Jesus was getting into the **b**, the man *G4450*
Mk 5:21 crossed over by **b** to the other side of *G4450*
Mk 6:32 by themselves in a **b** to a solitary place. *G4450*
Mk 6:45 get into the **b** and go on ahead of him *G4450*
Mk 6:47 the **b** was in the middle of the lake *G4450*
Mk 6:51 Then he climbed into the **b** with them *G4450*
Mk 6:54 As soon as they got out of the **b**, people *G4450*
Mk 8:10 he got into the **b** with his disciples and *G4450*
Mk 8:13 got back into the **b** and crossed to the other NDT
Mk 8:14 one loaf they had with them in the **b**. *G4450*
Lk 5: 3 down and taught the people from the **b**. *G4450*
Lk 5: 7 in the other **b** to come and help them *G4450*
Lk 8:22 So they got into a **b** and set out. *G4450*
Lk 8:23 the lake, so that the **b** was being swamped NDT
Lk 8:37 So he got into the **b** and left. *G4450*
Jn 6:17 where they got into a **b** and set off across *G4450*
Jn 6:19 they saw Jesus approaching the **b** *G4450*
Jn 6:21 they were willing to take him into the **b**, *G4450*
Jn 6:21 immediately the **b** reached the shore *G4450*
Jn 6:22 realized that only one **b** had been there, *G4449*
Jn 21: 3 So they went out and got into the **b**, but *G4450*
Jn 21: 6 on the right side *of* the **b** and you will find *G4450*
Jn 21: 8 The other disciples followed *in* the **b** *G4449*
Jn 21:11 back into the **b** and dragged the net NDT

BOATS (9) [BOAT]

Job 9:26 They skim past like **b** *of* papyrus, like H641
Isa 18: 2 envoys by sea in papyrus **b** over the water. H3998
Mk 4:36 There were also other **b** with him. *G4450*
Lk 5: 2 He saw at the water's edge two **b**, left *G4450*
Lk 5: 3 He got into one *of* the **b**, the one *G4450*
Lk 5: 7 came and filled both **b** so full that they *G4450*
Lk 5:11 So they pulled their **b** up on shore, left *G4450*
Jn 6:23 Then *some* **b** from Tiberias landed near *G4450*
Jn 6:24 they got into the **b** and went to *G4449*

BOAZ (29)

Ru 2: 1 the clan of Elimelek, whose name was **B**. H1244
Ru 2: 3 she was working in a field belonging to **B** H1244
Ru 2: 4 Just then **B** arrived from Bethlehem and H1244
Ru 2: 5 **B** asked the overseer of his harvesters H1244
Ru 2: 8 So **B** said to Ruth, "My daughter, listen to H1244
Ru 2:11 **B** replied, "I've been told all about what H1244
Ru 2:14 At mealtime **B** said to her, "Come over H1244
Ru 2:15 got up to glean, **B** gave orders to his men H1244
Ru 2:19 name of the man I worked with today is **B**," H1244
Ru 2:23 close to the women of **B** to glean until the H1244
Ru 3: 2 Now **B**, with whose women you have H1244
Ru 3: 7 When **B** had finished eating and drinking H1244
Ru 3:16 her everything **B** had done for her H2021+408S
Ru 4: 1 Meanwhile **B** went up to the town gate H1244
Ru 4: 1 **B** said, "Come over here, my friend, and H1244
Ru 4: 2 **B** took ten of the elders of the town and said NDT
Ru 4: 5 Then **B** said, "On the day you buy the H1244
Ru 4: 8 So the guardian-redeemer said to **B**, "Buy H1244
Ru 4: 9 Then **B** announced to the elders and all H1244
Ru 4:13 So **B** took Ruth and she became his wife H1244
Ru 4:21 Salmon the father of **B**, Boaz the father of H1244
Ru 4:21 the father of Boaz, **B** the father of Obed, H1244
1Ki 7:21 named Jakin and the one to the north **B**. H1245
1Ch 2:11 father of Salmon, Salmon the father of **B**, H1244
1Ch 2:12 **B** the father of Obed and Obed the father H1244
2Ch 3:17 named Jakin and the one to the north **B**. H1245
Mt 1: 5 Salmon the father of **B**, whose mother *G1067*
Mt 1: 5 mother was Rahab, **B** the father of Obed *G1067*
Lk 3:32 of Obed, the son *of* **B**, the son of Salmon, *G1078*

BOCHIM (KJV) BOKIM

BODIES (76) [BODY]

Ge 34:27 came upon the **dead b** and looted the H2728
Ge 47:18 left for our lord except our **b** and our land. H1581
Lev 19:28 " 'Do not cut your **b** for the dead or put H1414
Lev 21: 5 off the edges of their beards or cut their **b**. H1414
Lev 26:30 altars and pile your **dead b** on the lifeless H7007
Nu 8: 7 shave their whole **b** and wash their H1414
Nu 14:29 In this wilderness your **b** will fall—every H7007
Nu 14:32 you, your **b** will fall in this wilderness. H7007
Nu 14:33 the last of your **b** lies in the wilderness H7007
Jos 10:26 death and exposed **their b** on five poles, H4392S
1Sa 21: 5 The men's **b** are holy even on missions H3998
1Sa 31:12 took down the **b** *of* Saul and his sons H1581
2Sa 4:12 feet and hung the **b** by the pool in Hebron NDT
2Sa 21: 6 to be killed and **their b** exposed before H4392S
2Sa 21: 9 exposed their **b** on a hill before the NDT
2Sa 21:10 poured down from the heavens on **the b**, H2157S
2Sa 21:12 They had stolen **their b** from the public H4392S
2Ki 10:25 officers threw the **b** out and then entered NDT
2Ki 19:35 next morning—there were all the dead **b**! H7007
1Ch 10:12 went and took the **b** *of* Saul and his sons H1590
2Ch 20:24 they saw only **dead b** lying on the ground H7007
Ne 9:37 They rule over our **b** and our cattle as they H1581
Job 14:22 pain of their own **b** and mourn only for H1414
Ps 44:25 to the dust; our **b** cling to the ground. H1061
Ps 73: 4 struggles; their **b** are healthy and strong. H214
Ps 79: 2 have left the **dead b** *of* your servants as H5577
Isa 5:25 the **dead b** are like refuse in the H5577
Isa 26:19 their **b** will rise—let those who H5577
Isa 34: 3 be thrown out, their **dead b** will stink; the H7007
Isa 37:36 next morning—there were all the dead **b**! H7007
Isa 57: 8 you looked with lust on their **naked b**. H3338
Isa 66:24 look on the **dead b** *of* those who H7007
Jer 9:22 " '**Dead b** will lie like dung on the H5577+132
Jer 16: 4 their **dead b** will become food for the H5577
Jer 31:40 whole valley where **dead b** and ashes are H7007
Jer 33: 5 filled with the **dead b** *of* the people I will H7007
Jer 34:20 Their **dead b** will become food for the H5577
Jer 41: 9 he threw all the **b** *of* the men he had H7007
La 4: 7 than milk, their **b** more ruddy than rubies H6795
Eze 6: 5 I will lay the **dead b** *of* the Israelites in H7007
Eze 10:12 Their entire **b**, including their backs, their H1414
Eze 11: 7 The **b** you have thrown there are the meat H2728
Eze 39:14 they will bury any **b** that are lying on the NDT
Da 3:27 saw that the fire had not harmed their **b**, A10151
Am 6:10 comes to carry the **b** out of the house to H6795
Am 8: 3 Many, many **b**—flung everywhere H7007
Na 2:10 knees give way, **b** tremble, every face H5516
Na 3: 3 piles of dead, **b** without number, people H1581
Hab 2:15 so that he can gaze on their **naked b**! H5067
Mt 24:29 and the heavenly **b** will be shaken. *G1539*
Mt 27:52 The **b** of many holy people who had died *G5393*
Mk 13:25 and the heavenly **b** will be shaken. *G1539*
Lk 21:26 for the heavenly **b** will be shaken. *G1539*
Jn 19:31 did not want the **b** left on the crosses *G5393*
Jn 19:31 have the legs broken and the **b** taken down. NDT
Ac 7:16 *Their b were* **brought back** to Shechem and AIT
Ro 1:24 the degrading *of* their **b** with one another. *G5393*
Ro 8:11 also give life *to* your mortal **b** because of *G5393*
Ro 8:23 to sonship, the redemption *of* our **b**. *G5393*
Ro 12: 1 to offer your **b** as a living sacrifice *G5393*
1Co 6:15 not know that your **b** are members of *G5393*
1Co 6:19 not know that your **b** are temples of the *G5393*
1Co 6:20 Therefore honor God with your **b**. *G5393*
1Co 10: 5 *their b were* **scattered** in the wilderness. AIT
1Co 15:40 are also heavenly **b** and there are earthly *G5393*
1Co 15:40 heavenly bodies and there are earthly **b**; *G5393*
1Co 15:40 the splendor of the heavenly **b** is one kind, NDT
1Co 15:40 the splendor of the earthly **b** is another. NDT
Eph 5:28 ought to love their wives as their own **b**. *G5393*
Php 3:21 transform our lowly **b** so that they will be *G5393*
Heb 3:17 whose **b** perished in the wilderness? *G3265*
Heb 10:22 having our **b** washed with pure water. *G5393*
Heb 13:11 the **b** are burned outside the camp. *G5393*
Jude 8 these ungodly people pollute their own **b**, *G4922*
Rev 11: 8 Their **b** will lie in the public square of the *G4773*
Rev 11: 9 will gaze *on* their **b** and refuse them *G4773*

BODILY (4) [BODY]

Lev 15: 2 man has an unusual **b** discharge, H4946+1414
Lev 22: 4 a defiling skin disease or a **b discharge**, H2307
Lk 3:22 descended on him in **b** form like a dove. *G5394*
Col 2: 9 the fullness of the Deity lives **in b form**, *G5395*

BODY (248) [BODIES, BODILY, EMBODIMENT]

Ge 9:23 covered their father's **naked b**. H6872
Ge 25:25 his **whole** *b* was like a hairy garment AIT
Ge 40:19 your head and impale **your b** on a pole. H3870
Ex 28:42 as a covering for the **b**, H1414+6872
Ex 30:32 on anyone else's **b** and do not make any H1414
Lev 6:10 with linen undergarments next to his **b** H1414
Lev 13:13 if the disease has covered their whole **b**, H1414
Lev 15: 3 continues flowing from his **b** or is blocked, H1414
Lev 15:16 he must bathe his whole **b** with water H1414
Lev 16: 4 with linen undergarments next to his **b** H1414
Lev 21:11 not enter a place where there is a dead **b**. H5883
Nu 5: 2 unclean because of a **dead b**. H5883
Nu 5:22 a curse enter your **b** so that your abdomen H5055
Nu 6: 6 the Nazirite must not go near a dead **b**. H5883
Nu 6:11 by being in the presence of the **dead b**. H5883
Nu 9: 6 unclean on account of a dead **b**. H132
Nu 9: 7 become unclean because of a dead **b**, H132
Nu 9:10 because of a **dead b** or are away on a H5883
Dt 4: 8 laws as this **b** *of* laws I am setting H3972
Dt 21: 2 distance from the **b** to the neighboring H2728
Dt 21: 3 the town nearest the **b** shall take a heifer H2728
Dt 21: 6 the town nearest the **b** shall wash their H2728
Dt 21:22 put to death and **their b** is exposed on a H2257S
Dt 21:23 must not leave the **b** hanging on the pole H5577
Jos 8:29 He impaled *the b of* the **king** *of* Ai on a pole AIT
Jos 8:29 them to take the **b** from the pole and H5577
1Sa 5: 4 on the threshold; only **his b** remained. H1837S
1Sa 31:10 fastened his **b** to the wall of Beth H1581
1Ki 13:22 Therefore your **b** will not be buried in the H5577
1Ki 13:24 and his **b** was left lying on the road H5577
1Ki 13:25 who passed by saw the **b** lying there, H5577
1Ki 13:25 with the lion standing beside the **b**, and H5577
1Ki 13:28 out and found the **b** lying on the road, H5577
1Ki 13:28 neither eaten the **b** nor mauled the H5577
1Ki 13:29 picked up the **b** *of* the man of God, H5577
1Ki 13:30 Then he laid the **b** in his own tomb, and H5577
2Ki 4:34 out on him, the boy's **b** grew warm. H1414
2Ki 6:30 his robes, he had sackcloth on his **b**. H1414
2Ki 9:37 Jezebel's **b** will be like dung on the H5577
2Ki 13:21 so they threw the **man's b** into Elisha's H408
2Ki 13:21 When the **b** touched Elisha's bones, the NDT
2Ki 23:30 servants brought *his* **b** in a chariot from H4637
Ezr 8:20 a **b** *that* David and the officials had H8611S
Job 4:15 and the hair on my **b** stood on end. H1414
Job 7: 5 My **b** is clothed with worms and scabs, my H1414
Job 7:15 death, rather than this **b** *of* mine. H6795
Job 21: 6 I am terrified; trembling seizes my **b**. H1414
Job 21:24 well nourished *in* **b**, bones rich with H6489
Job 30:30 black and peels; my **b** burns with fever. H6795
Job 33:20 so that their **b** finds food repulsive and H2652
Ps 16: 9 rejoices; my **b** also will rest secure, H1414
Ps 31: 9 with sorrow, my soul and **b** with grief. H1061
Ps 38: 3 of your wrath there is no health in my **b**; H1414
Ps 38: 7 searing pain; there is no health in my **b**. H1414
Ps 109:18 it entered into his **b** like water, into his H7931
Ps 109:24 way from fasting; my **b** is thin and gaunt. H1414
Ps 139:16 Your eyes saw my **unformed b**; all the H1677
Pr 3: 8 bring health to your **b** and nourishment to H9219
Pr 4:22 find them and health to one's whole **b**. H1414
Pr 5:11 when your flesh and **b** are spent. H8638
Pr 14:30 A heart at peace gives life to the **b**, but H1414
Ecc 11: 5 how the **b** is formed in a mother's H6795
Ecc 11:10 heart and cast off the troubles of your **b**, H1414
Ecc 12:12 is no end, and much study wearies the **b**. H1414
SS 5:14 His **b** is like polished ivory decorated with H5055
Isa 17: 4 will fade; the fat of his **b** will waste away. H1414
Isa 20: 2 sackcloth from your **b** and the sandals H5516
Isa 21: 3 At this my **b** is racked with pain, pangs H5516
Jer 13:22 have been torn off and your **b** mistreated. H6811
Jer 26:23 with a sword and his **b** thrown into the H5577
Jer 36:30 his **b** will be thrown out and exposed to H5577
Eze 1:11 each had two other wings covering its **b**. H1581
Eze 1:23 each had two wings covering its **b**. H1581
Eze 16: 8 over you and covered your **naked b**. H6872
Eze 16:36 exposed your **naked b** in your H6872
Eze 23:18 openly and exposed her **naked b**, H6872
Da 4:33 His **b** was drenched with the dew of A10151
Da 5:21 his **b** was drenched with the dew of A10151
Da 7:11 was slain and its **b** destroyed and thrown A10151
Da 10: 6 His **b** was like topaz, his face like lightning H1581
Hos 2: 9 my linen, intended to cover her **naked b**. H6872
Mic 6: 7 the fruit of my **b** for the sin of my soul? H1061
Hag 2:13 by contact with a **dead b** touches one of H5883
Zec 13: 6 'What are these wounds on your **b**? H3338
Mal 2:15 You belong to him *in* **b** and spirit. H8638
Mt 5:29 to lose one **part of** your **b** than for your *G3517*
Mt 5:29 than for your whole **b** to be thrown into *G5393*
Mt 5:30 to lose one **part of** your **b** than for your *G3517*
Mt 5:30 body than for your whole **b** to go into hell. *G5393*
Mt 6:22 "The eye is the lamp *of* the **b**. If your eyes *G5393*
Mt 6:22 healthy, your whole **b** will be full of light. *G5393*
Mt 6:23 your whole **b** will be full of darkness. *G5393*
Mt 6:25 or about your **b**, what you will wear. *G5393*
Mt 6:25 than food, and the **b** more than clothes? *G5393*
Mt 10:28 of those who kill the **b** but cannot kill the *G5393*
Mt 10:28 who can destroy both soul and **b** in hell. *G5393*
Mt 14:12 came and took his **b** and buried it. *G4773*
Mt 15:17 and then **out of the b**? *G1650+909+1675*
Mt 26:12 When she poured this perfume on my **b** *G5393*
Mt 26:26 "Take and eat; this is my **b**." *G5393*
Mt 27:58 he asked *for* Jesus' **b**, and Pilate *G5393*
Mt 27:59 Joseph took the **b**, wrapped it in a clean *G5393*
Mt 27:64 may come and steal **the b** and tell the *G899S*
Mk 5:29 she felt *in* her **b** that she was freed *G5393*
Mk 6:29 came and took his **b** and laid it in a tomb. *G4773*
Mk 7:19 and then **out of the b**." *G1650+3836+909+1744S*
Mk 14: 8 poured perfume on my **b** beforehand to *G5393*
Mk 14:22 his disciples, saying, "Take it; this is my **b**." *G5393*
Mk 15:43 boldly to Pilate and asked for Jesus' **b**. *G5393*
Mk 15:45 that it was so, he gave the **b** to Joseph. *G4773*
Mk 15:46 took down **the b**, wrapped it in the *G899S*
Mk 16: 1 so that they might go to anoint Jesus' **b**. *G899S*
Lk 11:34 Your eye is the lamp *of* your **b**. When your *G5393*
Lk 11:34 healthy, your whole **b** also is full of light. *G5393*
Lk 11:34 unhealthy, your **b** also is full of darkness. *G5393*
Lk 11:36 if your whole **b** is full of light, and *G5393*
Lk 12: 4 those who kill the **b** and after that can do *G5393*
Lk 12: 5 him who, after your **b** has been killed, has NDT
Lk 12:22 will eat; or *about* your **b**, what you will *G5393*

B

Lk 12:23 than food, and the **b** more than clothes. G5393
Lk 14: 2 **suffering from abnormal swelling of** *his* **b**. G5622
Lk 17:37 "Where there is a **dead b**, there the G5393
Lk 22:19 "This is my **b** given for you; do this G5393
Lk 23:52 Going to Pilate, he asked for Jesus' **b**. G5393
Lk 23:55 the tomb and how his **b** was laid in it. G5393
Lk 24: 3 they did not find the **b** of the Lord Jesus. G5393
Lk 24:23 didn't find his **b**. They came and told G5393
Jn 2:21 the temple he had spoken of was his **b**. G5393
Jn 7:23 healing a man's **whole** *b* on the Sabbath? AIT
Jn 13:10 to wash their feet; their **whole** *b* is clean. AIT
Jn 19:38 Arimathea asked Pilate for the **b** of Jesus. G5393
Jn 19:38 he came and took the **b** away. G5393
Jn 19:40 Taking Jesus' **b**, the two of them wrapped G5393
Jn 20:12 seated where Jesus' **b** had been, one at G5393
Ac 1:18 *his b* **burst open** and all his intestines spilled AIT
Ac 2:26 rejoices; my **b** also will rest in hope G4922
Ac 2:31 of the dead, nor did his **b** see decay. G4922
Ac 5: 6 wrapped up **his** *b*, and carried him AIT
Ac 9:37 and **her** *b* was washed and placed in an AIT
Ac 13:36 buried with his ancestors and his **b** decayed. NDT
Ro 4:19 the fact that his **b** was as good as dead— G5393
Ro 6: 6 with him so that the **b** ruled by sin might G5393
Ro 6:12 reign in your mortal **b** so that you obey its G5393
Ro 7: 4 died to the law through the **b** of Christ, G5393
Ro 7:24 rescue me from this **b** that is subject to G5393
Ro 8:10 even though your **b** is subject to death G5393
Ro 8:13 you put to death the misdeeds *of* the **b**, G5393
Ro 12: 4 of us has one **b** with many members, G5393
Ro 12: 5 form one **b**, and each member G5393
1Co 6:13 The **b**, however, is not meant for sexual G5393
1Co 6:13 for the Lord, and the Lord *for* the **b**. G5393
1Co 6:16 with a prostitute is one with her *in* **b**? G5393
1Co 6:18 sins a person commits are outside the **b**, G5393
1Co 6:18 sins sexually, sins against their own **b**. G5393
1Co 7: 4 have authority *over* her own **b** but yields it G5393
1Co 7: 4 have authority *over* his own **b** but yields it G5393
1Co 7:34 devoted to the Lord *in* both **b** and spirit. G5393
1Co 9:27 I strike a blow *to* my **b** and make it my G5393
1Co 10:16 we break a participation *in* the **b** of Christ? G5393
1Co 10:17 are many, are one **b**, for we all share the G5393
1Co 11:24 it and said, "This is my **b**, which is for you; G5393
1Co 11:27 of sinning *against* the **b** and blood of the G5393
1Co 11:29 without discerning the **b** of Christ eat and G5393
1Co 12:12 Just as a **b**, though one, has many parts G5393
1Co 12:12 all its many parts form one **b**, so it is G5393
1Co 12:13 by one Spirit so as to form one **b**— G5393
1Co 12:14 Even so the **b** is not made up of one part G5393
1Co 12:15 I do not belong to the **b**," it would not G5393
1Co 12:15 that reason stop being part of the **b**. G5393
1Co 12:16 I do not belong to the **b**," it would not G5393
1Co 12:16 that reason stop being part of the **b**. G5393
1Co 12:17 If the whole **b** were an eye, where would G5393
1Co 12:17 If the whole **b** were an ear, where would the NDT
1Co 12:18 in fact God has placed the parts in the **b**, G5393
1Co 12:19 were all one part, where would the **b** be? G5393
1Co 12:20 there are many parts, but one **b**. G5393
1Co 12:22 those parts *of* the **b** that seem to be G5393
1Co 12:24 But God has put the **b** together, giving G5393
1Co 12:25 that there should be no division in the **b**, G5393
1Co 12:27 Now you are the **b** of Christ, and each one G5393
1Co 13: 3 poor and give over my **b** to hardship that I G5393
1Co 15:35 With what kind of **b** will they come?" G5393
1Co 15:37 you do not plant the **b** that will be, but G5393
1Co 15:38 But God gives it a **b** as he has determined G5393
1Co 15:38 to each kind of seed he gives its own **b**. G5393
1Co 15:42 The **b** that is sown is perishable, it is raised NDT
1Co 15:44 it is sown a natural **b**, it is raised a G5393
1Co 15:44 a natural body, it is raised a spiritual **b**. G5393
1Co 15:44 If there is a natural **b**, there is also a G5393
1Co 15:44 is a natural body, there is also a spiritual **b**. NDT
2Co 4:10 carry around in our **b** the death of Jesus, G5393
2Co 4:10 of Jesus may also be revealed in our **b**. G5393
2Co 4:11 life may also be revealed in our mortal **b**. G4922
2Co 5: 6 are at home in the **b** we are away from G5393
2Co 5: 8 to be away from the **b** and at home with G5393
2Co 5: 9 we are at home in the **b** or away from it. NDT
2Co 5:10 due us for the things done while in the **b**, G5393
2Co 7: 1 everything that contaminates **b** and spirit, G4922
2Co 12: 2 it was in the **b** or out of the body I G5393
2Co 12: 2 the body or out of the **b** I do not know— G5393
2Co 12: 3 whether in the **b** or apart from the body I G5393
2Co 12: 3 body or apart from the **b** I do not know, G5393
Gal 2:20 The life I now live in the **b**, I live by faith G4922
Gal 6:17 I bear on my **b** the marks of Jesus. G5393
Eph 1:23 which is his **b**, the fullness of him who fills G5393
Eph 2:11 which is done in the **b** by human hands)— G4922
Eph 2:16 in one **b** to reconcile both of them to G5393
Eph 3: 6 **members together of one b**, and G5362
Eph 4: 4 There is one **b** and one Spirit, just as you G5393
Eph 4:12 so that the **b** of Christ may be built up G5393
Eph 4:15 respect the mature **b** of him who is the head NDT
Eph 4:16 From him the whole **b**, joined and held G5393
Eph 4:25 neighbor, for we are all members *of* **one b**. G253
Eph 5:23 of the church, his **b**, of which he is the G5393
Eph 5:29 no one ever hated their own **b**, but they G4922
Eph 5:29 they feed and care for **their b**, just as G899S
Eph 5:30 we are members *of* his **b**. G5393
Php 1:20 as always Christ will be exalted in my **b**, G5393
Php 1:22 If I am to go on living in the **b**, this will G4922
Php 1:24 necessary for you that I remain *in* the **b**. G4922
Php 3:21 so that they will be like his glorious **b**. G5393
Col 1:18 And he is the head *of* the **b**, the church G5393
Col 1:22 by Christ's physical **b** through death to G5393
Col 1:24 the sake of his **b**, which is the church. G5393
Col 2: 5 For though I am absent from you *in* **b**, I am G4922
Col 2:19 from whom the whole **b**, supported and G5393
Col 2:23 their harsh treatment *of* the **b**, G5393
Col 3:15 as members of one **b** you were called to G5393
1Th 4: 4 to control your own **b** in a way that is holy G5007
1Th 5:23 soul and **b** be kept blameless at the G5393
1Ti 4:14 when the **b of elders** laid their hands G4564
Heb 7:10 Levi was still in the **b** of his ancestor. G4019
Heb 10: 5 not desire, but a **b** you prepared for me; G5393
Heb 10:10 the sacrifice *of* the **b** of Jesus Christ once G5393
Heb 10:20 us through the curtain, that is, his **b**, G4922
Jas 2:26 As the **b** without the spirit is dead, so faith G5393
Jas 3: 2 able to keep their whole **b** in check. G5393
Jas 3: 5 the tongue is a small **part of the b**, but it G3517
Jas 3: 6 a world of evil among the **parts of the b**. G3517
Jas 3: 6 It corrupts the whole **b**, sets the whole G5393
1Pe 2:24 our sins" in his **b** on the cross, so that G5393
1Pe 3:18 was put to death *in* the **b** but made alive G4922
1Pe 3:21 removal of dirt *from* the **b** but the pledge G4922
1Pe 4: 1 since Christ suffered *in* his **b**, arm G4922
1Pe 4: 1 whoever suffers *in* the **b** is done with sin. G4922
1Pe 4: 6 to human standards *in regard to* the **b**, G4922
2Pe 1:13 memory as long as I live in the **tent** *of* this *b*, AIT
Jude 9 with the devil about the **b** of Moses, G5393

BODYGUARD (4) [GUARD]

1Sa 22:14 captain of your **b** and highly respected in H5463
1Sa 28: 2 I will make you my **b** for life." H9068+4200+8031
2Sa 23:23 And David put him in charge of his **b**. H5463
1Ch 11:25 And David put him in charge of his **b**. H5463

BOHAN (2)

Jos 15: 6 Arabah to the Stone of **B** son of Reuben. H992
Jos 18:17 ran down to the Stone of **B** son of Reuben. H992

BOIL (10) [BOILED, BOILING, BOILS]

Ex 16:23 you want to bake and **b** what you want to H1418
Ex 16:23 want to bake and boil what *you want to* **b**. H1418
Lev 13:18 someone has a **b** on their skin and H8825
Lev 13:19 in the place where the **b** was, a white H8825
Lev 13:20 that has broken out where the **b** was. H8825
Lev 13:23 it is only a scar from the **b**, and the priest H8825
2Ki 20: 7 They did so and applied it to the **b**, and H8825
Isa 38:21 a poultice of figs and apply it to the **b**, H8825
Isa 64: 2 sets twigs ablaze and **causes** water **to b**, H1240
Eze 24: 5 **bring** it **to a b** and cook the bones H8409+8410

BOILED (5) [BOIL]

Ex 12: 9 not eat the meat raw or **b** in water, H1419+1418
Nu 6:19 in their hands a **b** shoulder of the ram, H1419
1Sa 2:13 in his hand while the meat *was being* **b** H1418
1Sa 2:15 he won't accept **b** meat from you, but H1418
2Ch 35:13 **b** the holy offerings in pots H1418

BOILING (3) [BOIL]

Job 41:20 nostrils as from a **b** pot over burning reeds H5870
Job 41:31 depths churn like a **b** caldron and stirs up NDT
Jer 1:13 "I see a pot *that is* **b**," I answered. H5870

BOILS (5) [BOIL]

Ex 9: 9 festering **b** will break out on people H8825
Ex 9:10 festering **b** broke out on people and H8825
Ex 9:11 because of the **b** that were on them H8825
Dt 28:27 afflict you with the **b** *of* Egypt and with H8825
Dt 28:35 legs with painful **b** that cannot be cured, H8825

BOKERU (2)

1Ch 8:38 Azrikam, **B**, Ishmael, Sheariah, Obadiah H1150
1Ch 9:44 Azrikam, **B**, Ishmael, Sheariah, Obadiah H1150

BOKIM (2)

Jdg 2: 1 LORD went up from Gilgal to **B** and said, H1141
Jdg 2: 5 they called that place **B**. There they H1141

BOLD (9) [BOLDLY, BOLDNESS, EMBOLDENED]

Ge 18:27 "Now *that I have been so* **b** *as* to speak to H3283
Ge 18:31 "Now *that I have been so* **b** *as* to speak to H3283
Pr 21:29 The wicked **put up a b front** H6451+928+7156
Pr 28: 1 the righteous *are* as **b** as a lion. H1053
2Co 3:12 have such a hope, *we are* very **b**. G4244+5968
2Co 10: 1 face with you, but "**b**" toward you when G2509
2Co 10: 2 *I may* not *have to be* **as b** as G2509+3836+4301
Phm 8 *although* in Christ *I could be* **b** G4498+4244+2400
2Pe 2:10 **B** and arrogant, they are not afraid to G5532

BOLDLY (10) [BOLD]

Ex 14: 8 who were marching out **b**. H928+3338+8123
Mk 15:43 went **b** to Pilate and asked for Jesus' body G5528
Ac 4:31 Spirit and spoke the word of God **b**. G3552+4244
Ac 9:28 **speaking b** in the name of the Lord. G4245
Ac 13:46 Paul and Barnabas **answered** them **b**: G4245
Ac 14: 3 time there, **speaking b** for the Lord, who G4245
Ac 18:26 He began *to* **speak b** in the synagogue G4245
Ac 19: 8 synagogue and **spoke b** there for three G4245
Ro 10:20 And Isaiah **b** says, "I was found by those G703
Ro 15:15 have written you *quite* **b** on some points G5529

BOLDNESS (2) [BOLD]

Ac 4:29 servants to speak your word with great **b**. G4244
Ac 28:31 Christ—with all **b** and without hindrance! G4244

BOLSTER (KJV) HEAD

BOLT (2) [BOLTED, BOLTS]

2Sa 13:17 out of my sight and **b** the door after her." H5835
SS 5: 5 flowing myrrh, on the handles of the **b**. H4980

BOLTED (1) [BOLT]

2Sa 13:18 put her out and **b** the door after her. H5835

BOLTS (12) [BOLT]

Dt 33:25 The **b of** your **gates** will be iron and H4981
2Sa 22:13 of his presence **b** *of* lightning blazed forth H1624
2Sa 22:15 *with* **great b of lightning** he routed them. H1398
Ne 3: 3 put its doors and **b** and bars in place. H4980
Ne 3: 6 its doors with their **b** and bars in place. H4980
Ne 3:13 its doors with their **b** and bars in place. H4980
Ne 3:14 its doors with their **b** and bars in place. H4980
Ne 3:15 putting its doors and **b** and bars in place. H4980
Job 38:35 Do you send the **lightning b** on their way H1398
Ps 18:12 with hailstones and **b** *of* lightning. H1624
Ps 18:14 *with* great **b of lightning** he routed them. H1398
Ps 78:48 the hail, their livestock to **b of lightning**. H8404

BOND (4) [BONDAGE, BONDS]

Eze 20:37 I will bring you into the **b** *of* the covenant. H5037
Zec 11:14 breaking the **family b** between Judah and H288
Ac 17: 9 *they* **made** Jason and the others **post b** G3284+3836+2653+4123
Eph 4: 3 unity of the Spirit through the **b** of peace. G5278

BONDAGE (7) [BOND]

Ge 47:19 we with our land will be **in b** to Pharaoh. H6269
Ge 47:25 of our lord; we will be **in b** to Pharaoh." H6269
Ezr 9: 8 to our eyes and a little relief in our **b**. H6285
Ezr 9: 9 our God has not forsaken us in our **b**. H6285
Jer 34: 9 no one was *to* **hold** a fellow Hebrew **in b**. H6268
Jer 34:10 slaves and no longer **hold** them **in b**. H6268
Ro 8:21 liberated from its **b** to decay and brought G1525

BONDMAID, BONDMAIDS (KJV) FEMALE SERVANT(S), FEMALE SLAVE(S)

BONDMAN, BONDMEN (KJV) MALE SERVANT(S), MALE SLAVE(S)

BONDS (4) [BOND]

Jer 2:20 broke off your yoke and tore off your **b**; H4593
Jer 5: 5 had broken off the yoke and torn off the **b**. H4593
Jer 30: 8 off their necks and will tear off their **b**; H4593
Hos 10:10 against them *to* **put** them **in b** for their H673

BONDSERVANT (KJV) SLAVES

BONDWOMAN, BONDWOMEN (KJV) FEMALE SLAVE(S), SLAVE WOMAN

BONE (7) [BACKBONE, BONES]

Ge 2:23 "This is now **b** of my bones and flesh of H6795
Nu 19:16 who touches a human **b** or a grave, H6795
Nu 19:18 has touched a human **b** or a grave or H6795
Pr 25:15 a gentle tongue can break a **b**. H1752
Eze 37: 7 the bones came together, **b** to bone. H6795
Eze 37: 7 the bones came together, bone to **b**. H6795
Eze 39:15 who sees a human **b** will leave a marker H6795

BONES (90) [BONE]

Ge 2:23 is now bone of my **b** and flesh of my flesh H6795
Ge 50:25 you must carry my **b** up from this place." H6795
Ex 12:46 Do not break any of the **b**. H6795
Ex 13:19 Moses took the **b** *of* Joseph with him H6795
Ex 13:19 you must carry my **b** up with you from this H6795
Nu 9:12 any of it till morning or break any of its **b**. H6795
Nu 24: 8 nations and break their **b** in pieces; H6795
Jos 24:32 And Joseph's **b**, which the Israelites had H6795
1Sa 31:13 Then they took their **b** and buried them H6795
2Sa 21:12 went and took the **b** *of* Saul and his son H6795
2Sa 21:13 David brought the **b** *of* Saul and his son H6795
2Sa 21:13 the **b** *of* those who had been killed H6795
2Sa 21:14 They buried the **b** *of* Saul and his son H6795
1Ki 13: 2 human **b** will be burned on you. H6795
1Ki 13:31 God is buried; lay my **b** beside his bones. H6795
1Ki 13:31 God is buried; lay my bones beside his **b**. H6795
2Ki 13:21 When the body touched Elisha's **b**, the H6795
2Ki 23:14 covered the sites with human **b**. H6795
2Ki 23:16 he had the **b** removed from them and H6795
2Ki 23:18 "Don't let anyone disturb his **b**." So they H6795
2Ki 23:18 So they spared his **b** and those of the H6795
2Ki 23:20 the altars and burned human **b** on them. H6795
1Ch 10:12 they buried their **b** under the great tree H6795
2Ch 34: 5 He burned the **b** *of* the priests on their H6795
Job 2: 5 out your hand and strike his flesh and **b**, H6795
Job 4:14 seized me and made all my **b** shake. H6795
Job 10:11 knit me together with **b** and sinews? H6795
Job 19:20 I am nothing but skin and **b**; I have H6795
Job 20:11 vigor that fills his **b** will lie with him in the H6795
Job 21:24 nourished in body, **b** rich with marrow. H6795
Job 30:17 Night pierces my **b**; my gnawing pains H6795
Job 33:19 of pain with constant distress in their **b**, H6795
Job 33:21 to nothing, and their **b**, once hidden, H6795
Job 40:18 Its **b** are tubes of bronze, its limbs like H6795
Ps 6: 2 heal me, LORD, for my **b** are in agony. H6795
Ps 22:14 like water, and all my **b** are out of joint. H6795
Ps 22:17 All my **b** are on display; people stare and H6795
Ps 31:10 of my affliction, and my **b** grow weak. H6795

Ps 32: 3 my **b** wasted away through my groaning H6795
Ps 34:20 he protects all his **b**, not one of them will H6795
Ps 38: 3 no soundness in my **b** because of my sin. H6795
Ps 42:10 My **b** suffer mortal agony as my foes taunt H6795
Ps 51: 8 let the **b** you have crushed rejoice. H6795
Ps 53: 5 God scattered the **b** *of* those who attacked H6795
Ps 102: 3 my **b** burn like glowing embers. H6795
Ps 102: 5 aloud and am reduced to skin and **b**. H6795
Ps 109:18 into his body like water, into his **b** like oil. H6795
Ps 141: 7 so our **b** have been scattered at the H6795
Pr 3: 8 to your body and nourishment to your **b**. H6795
Pr 12: 4 a disgraceful wife is like decay in his **b**. H6795
Pr 14:30 gives life to the body, but envy rots the **b**. H6795
Pr 15:30 good news gives health to the **b**. H6795
Pr 16:24 sweet to the soul and healing to the **b**. H6795
Pr 17:22 a crushed spirit dries up the **b**. H1752
Isa 38:13 like a lion he broke all my **b**; day and H6795
Jer 8: 1 the **b** *of* the kings and officials of Judah H6795
Jer 8: 1 the **b** *of* the priests and prophets H6795
Jer 8: 1 the **b** *of* the people of Jerusalem will H6795
Jer 20: 9 my heart like a fire, a fire shut up in my **b**. H6795
Jer 23: 9 is broken within me; all my **b** tremble. H6795
Jer 50:17 the last *to* **crush** their **b** was H6793
La 1:13 high he sent fire, sent it down into my **b**. H6795
La 3: 4 my flesh grow old and has broken my **b**. H6795
La 4: 8 Their skin has shriveled on their **b**; it has H6795
Eze 6: 5 I will scatter your **b** around your altars. H6795
Eze 24: 4 Fill it with the best of these **b**; H6795
Eze 24: 5 Pile wood beneath it for the **b**; bring it to H6795
Eze 24: 5 bring it to a boil and cook the **b** in it. H6795
Eze 24:10 in the spices; and let the **b** be charred. H6795
Eze 32:27 their shields resting on their **b**— H6795
Eze 37: 1 in the middle of a valley; it was full of **b**. H6795
Eze 37: 2 I saw a great many **b** on the floor of the NDT
Eze 37: 2 the floor of the valley, **b** that were very dry. NDT
Eze 37: 3 asked me, "Son of man, can these **b** live?" H6795
Eze 37: 4 "Prophesy to these **b** and say to them H6795
Eze 37: 4 say to them, 'Dry **b**, hear the word of the H6795
Eze 37: 5 what the Sovereign LORD says to these **b**: H6795
Eze 37: 7 and the **b** came together, bone to H6795
Eze 37:11 of man, these **b** are the people of Israel. H6795
Eze 37:11 'Our **b** are dried up and our hope is gone H6795
Da 6:24 them and crushed all their **b**. A10150
Am 2: 1 he burned to ashes the **b** *of* Edom's king, H6795
Am 3:12 mouth only two **leg b** or a piece of an ear H4157
Mic 3: 2 my people and the flesh from their **b**; H6795
Mic 3: 3 off their skin and break their **b** in pieces; H6795
Hab 3:16 decay crept into my **b**, and my legs H6795
Mt 23:27 inside are full *of* the **b** of the dead and *G4014*
Lk 24:39 a ghost does not have flesh and **b**, as you *G4014*
Jn 19:36 "Not one of his **b** will be broken," *G4014*
Heb 11:22 instructions concerning the burial *of* his **b**. *G4014*

BONNETS (KJV) CAPS, HEADDRESSES, TURBANS

BOOK (123) [BOOKS]

Ex 24: 7 Then he took the **B** *of* the Covenant and H6219
Ex 32:32 blot me out of the **b** you have written." H6219
Ex 32:33 sinned against me I will blot out of my **b**. H6219
Nu 21:14 That is why the **B** *of* the Wars of the LORD H6219
Dt 28:58 which are written in this **b**, and do not H6219
Dt 28:61 disaster not recorded in this **B** *of* the Law, H6219
Dt 29:20 curses written in this **b** will fall on them, H6219
Dt 29:21 the covenant written in this **B** *of* the Law. H6219
Dt 29:27 on it all the curses written in this **b**. H6219
Dt 30:10 are written in this **B** *of* the Law and turn to H6219
Dt 31:24 writing in a **b** the words of this law H6219
Dt 31:26 "Take this **B** *of* the Law and place it beside H6219
Jos 1: 8 Keep this **B** *of* the Law always on your lips H6219
Jos 8:31 is written in the **B** *of* the Law of Moses— H6219
Jos 8:34 just as it is written in the **B** *of* the Law. H6219
Jos 10:13 as it is written in the **B** *of* Jashar. H6219
Jos 23: 6 is written in the **B** *of* the Law of Moses, H6219
Jos 24:26 these things in the **B** *of* the Law of God. H6219
2Sa 1:18 the bow (it is written in the **B** *of* Jashar): H6219
1Ki 11:41 not written in the **b** *of* the annals of H6219
1Ki 14:19 are written in the **b** *of* the annals of the H6219
1Ki 14:29 not written in the **b** *of* the annals of the H6219
1Ki 15: 7 not written in the **b** *of* the annals of the H6219
1Ki 15:23 not written in the **b** *of* the annals of the H6219
1Ki 15:31 not written in the **b** *of* the annals of the H6219
1Ki 16: 5 not written in the **b** *of* the annals of the H6219
1Ki 16:14 not written in the **b** *of* the annals of the H6219
1Ki 16:20 not written in the **b** *of* the annals of the H6219
1Ki 16:27 not written in the **b** *of* the annals of the H6219
1Ki 22:39 not written in the **b** *of* the annals of the H6219
1Ki 22:45 not written in the **b** *of* the annals of the H6219
2Ki 1:18 not written in the **b** *of* the annals of the H6219
2Ki 8:23 not written in the **b** *of* the annals of the H6219
2Ki 10:34 not written in the **b** *of* the annals of the H6219
2Ki 12:19 not written in the **b** *of* the annals of the H6219
2Ki 13: 8 not written in the **b** *of* the annals of the H6219
2Ki 13:12 not written in the **b** *of* the annals of the H6219
2Ki 14: 6 is written in the **B** *of* the Law of Moses H6219
2Ki 14:15 not written in the **b** *of* the annals of the H6219
2Ki 14:18 not written in the **b** *of* the annals of the H6219
2Ki 14:28 not written in the **b** *of* the annals of the H6219
2Ki 15: 6 not written in the **b** *of* the annals of the H6219
2Ki 15:11 are written in the **b** *of* the annals of the H6219
2Ki 15:15 are written in the **b** *of* the annals of the H6219
2Ki 15:21 not written in the **b** *of* the annals of the H6219
2Ki 15:26 are written in the **b** *of* the annals of the H6219
2Ki 15:31 not written in the **b** *of* the annals of the H6219
2Ki 15:36 not written in the **b** *of* the annals of the H6219
2Ki 16:19 not written in the **b** *of* the annals of the H6219
2Ki 20:20 not written in the **b** *of* the annals of the H6219
2Ki 21:17 not written in the **b** *of* the annals of the H6219
2Ki 21:25 not written in the **b** *of* the annals of the H6219
2Ki 22: 8 "I have found the **B** *of* the Law in the H6219
2Ki 22:10 "Hilkiah the priest has given me a **b**." H6219
2Ki 22:11 king heard the words of the **B** *of* the Law, H6219
2Ki 22:13 is written in this **b** that has been found. H6219
2Ki 22:13 us have not obeyed the words of this **b**; H6219
2Ki 22:16 written in the **b** the king of Judah has H6219
2Ki 23: 2 all the words of the **B** *of* the Covenant, H6219
2Ki 23: 3 words of the covenant written in this **b**. H6219
2Ki 23:21 as it is written in this **B** *of* the Covenant." H6219
2Ki 23:24 the law written in the **b** that Hilkiah the H6219
2Ki 23:28 not written in the **b** *of* the annals of the H6219
2Ki 24: 5 not written in the **b** *of* the annals of the H6219
1Ch 9: 1 recorded in the **b** *of* the kings of Israel H6219
1Ch 27:24 not entered in the **b** *of* the annals of King H6219
2Ch 16:11 are written in the **b** *of* the kings of Judah H6219
2Ch 17: 9 with them the **B** *of* the Law of the LORD H6219
2Ch 20:34 are recorded in the **b** *of* the kings of Israel H6219
2Ch 24:27 in the annotations on the **b** *of* the kings. H6219
2Ch 25: 4 in the Law, in the **B** *of* Moses, where the H6219
2Ch 25:26 not written in the **b** *of* the kings of Judah H6219
2Ch 27: 7 are written in the **b** *of* the kings of Israel H6219
2Ch 28:26 are written in the **b** *of* the kings of Judah H6219
2Ch 32:32 son of Amoz in the **b** *of* the kings of H6219
2Ch 34:14 priest found the **B** *of* the Law of the LORD H6219
2Ch 34:15 "I have found the **B** *of* the Law in the H6219
2Ch 34:16 Then Shaphan took the **b** to the king and H6219
2Ch 34:18 "Hilkiah the priest has given me a **b**." H6219
2Ch 34:21 is written in this **b** that has been found. H6219
2Ch 34:21 with all that is written in this **b**. H6219
2Ch 34:24 written in the **b** that has been read in H6219
2Ch 34:30 all the words of the **B** *of* the Covenant, H6219
2Ch 34:31 words of the covenant written in this **b**. H6219
2Ch 35:12 the LORD, as it is written in the **B** *of* Moses. H6219
2Ch 35:27 are written in the **b** *of* the kings of Israel H6219
2Ch 36: 8 are written in the **b** *of* the kings of Israel H6219
Ezr 6:18 to what is written in the **B** *of* Moses. A10515
Ne 8: 1 to bring out the **B** *of* the Law of Moses, H6219
Ne 8: 3 listened attentively to the **B** *of* the Law. H6219
Ne 8: 5 Ezra opened the **b**. All the people could H6219
Ne 8: 8 They read from the **B** *of* the Law of God H6219
Ne 8:18 Ezra read from the **B** *of* the Law of God. H6219
Ne 9: 3 read from the **B** *of* the Law of the LORD H6219
Ne 12:23 were recorded in the **b** *of* the annals. H6219
Ne 13: 1 On that day the **B** *of* Moses was read H6219
Est 2:23 was recorded in the **b** *of* the annals in the H6219
Est 6: 1 so he ordered the **b** *of* the chronicles, the H6219
Est 10: 2 not written in the **b** *of* the annals of the H6219
Ps 69:28 be blotted out of the **b** *of* life and not be H6219
Ps 139:16 were written in your **b** before one of them H6219
Jer 25:13 are written in this **b** and prophesied by H6219
Jer 30: 2 'Write in a **b** all the words I have spoken H6219
Da 10:21 tell you what is written in the **B** *of* Truth. H4181
Da 12: 1 whose name is found written in the **b**— H6219
Na 1: 1 The **b** *of* the vision of Nahum the H6219
Mk 12:26 have you not read in the **B** of Moses, in *G1047*
Lk 3: 4 it is written in the **b** of the words of Isaiah *G1047*
Lk 20:42 David himself declares in the **B** of Psalms *G1047*
Jn 20:30 disciples, which are not recorded in this **b**. *G1046*
Ac 1: 1 *In* my former **b**, Theophilus, I wrote about *G3364*
Ac 1:20 said Peter, "it is written in the **B** of Psalms: *G1047*
Ac 7:42 what is written in the **b** of the prophets: *G1047*
Ac 8:28 reading the **B of Isaiah** the prophet. *G2480*
Gal 3:10 do everything written in the **B** of the Law." *G1046*
Php 4: 3 whose names are in the **b** of life. *G1047*
Rev 3: 5 the name of that person from the **b** of life, *G1047*
Rev 13: 8 not been written in the Lamb's **b** of life, *G1046*
Rev 17: 8 not been written in the **b** of life from the *G1046*
Rev 20:12 Another **b** was opened, which is the book *G1046*
Rev 20:12 book was opened, which is the **b** of life. NDT
Rev 20:15 found written in the **b** of life was thrown *G1047*
Rev 21:27 names are written in the Lamb's **b** of life. *G1046*

BOOKS (5) [BOOK]

Ecc 12:12 Of making many **b** there is no end, and H6219
Da 7:10 was seated, and the **b** were opened. A10515
Jn 21:25 not have room *for* the **b** that would be *G1046*
Rev 20:12 before the throne, and **b** were opened. *G1046*
Rev 20:12 what they had done as recorded in the **b**. *G1046*

BOOSTING (1)

Am 8: 5 **b** the price and cheating with dishonest H1540

BOOT (1)

Isa 9: 5 Every warrior's **b** used in battle and every H6007

BOOTH (3)

Mt 9: 9 Matthew sitting at the **tax collector's b**. *G5468*
Mk 2:14 of Alphaeus sitting at the **tax collector's b**. *G5468*
Lk 5:27 by the name of Levi sitting at his **tax b**. *G5468*

BOR ASHAN (1) [ASHAN]

1Sa 30:30 to those in Hormah, **B**, Athak H1016

BORDER (61) [BORDERED, BORDERING, BORDERS]

Ge 25:18 near the *eastern* **b** *of* Egypt, as you H7156
Ge 49:13 ships; his **b** will extend toward Sidon. H3752
Ex 16:35 until they reached the **b** *of* Canaan. H7895
Nu 20:23 Mount Hor, near the **b** *of* Edom, the LORD H1473
Nu 21:13 The Arnon is the **b** *of* Moab, between H1473
Nu 21:15 of Ar and lie along the **b** *of* Moab. H1473
Nu 21:24 Ammonites, because their **b** was fortified. H1473
Nu 22:36 him at the Moabite town on the Arnon **b**, H1473
Nu 33:37 camped at Mount Hor, on the **b** *of* Edom. H7895
Nu 33:44 camped at Iye Abarim, on the **b** *of* Moab. H1473
Nu 34: 3 of the Desert of Zin along the **b** *of* Edom. H3338
Dt 3:14 as far as the **b** *of* the Geshurites and H1473
Dt 3:16 the middle of the gorge being the **b**) and H1473
Dt 3:16 which is the **b** *of* the Ammonites. H1473
Dt 3:17 Its western **b** was the Jordan in the Arabah H1473
Jos 4:19 at Gilgal on the eastern **b** *of* Jericho. H7895
Jos 12: 2 which is the **b** *of* the Ammonites. H1473
Jos 12: 5 all of Bashan to the **b** *of* the people of H1473
Jos 12: 5 half of Gilead to the **b** *of* Sihon king of H1473
Jos 13: 4 far as Aphek and the **b** *of* the Amorites; H1473
Jos 13:10 Heshbon, out to the **b** *of* the Ammonites. H1473
Jos 16: 8 From Tappuah the **b** went west to the H1473
Jos 22:11 the altar on the **b** *of* Canaan at Geliloth H4578
Jdg 7:22 as far as the **b** *of* Abel Meholah near H8557
Jdg 11:18 territory of Moab, for the Arnon was its **b**. H1473
1Sa 6:12 them as far as the **b** *of* Beth Shemesh. H1473
1Sa 10: 2 at Zelzah on the **b** *of* Benjamin. H1473
1Sa 15: 7 to Shur, near the **eastern b** *of* Egypt. H7156
2Sa 13:23 were at Baal Hazor near the **b** of Ephraim, NDT
1Ki 4:21 of the Philistines, as far as the **b** *of* Egypt. H1473
2Ki 3:21 was called up and stationed on the **b**. H1473
2Ch 9:26 of the Philistines, as far as the **b** *of* Egypt. H1473
2Ch 26: 8 his fame spread as far as the **b** *of* Egypt, H995
Ps 78:54 he brought them to the **b** *of* his holy land, H1473
Isa 15: 8 Their outcry echoes along the **b** *of* Moab H1473
Isa 19:19 a monument to the LORD at its **b**. H1473
Eze 29:10 Migdol to Aswan, as far as the **b** *of* Cush. H1473
Eze 45: 7 to the eastern **b** parallel to one of the H1473
Eze 47:16 which lies on the **b** between Damascus H1473
Eze 47:16 Hattikon, which is on the **b** *of* Hauran. H1473
Eze 47:17 along the northern **b** *of* Damascus, with H1473
Eze 47:17 with the **b** *of* Hamath to the north. H1473
Eze 48: 1 the northern **b** *of* Damascus next to H1473
Eze 48: 1 will be part of its **b** *from* the east side to H6991
Eze 48: 2 it will **b** the territory of Dan from east to H6584
Eze 48: 3 it will **b** the territory of Asher from east to H6584
Eze 48: 4 it will **b** the territory of Naphtali from east H6584
Eze 48: 5 it will **b** the territory of Manasseh from H6584
Eze 48: 6 it will **b** the territory of Ephraim from east H6584
Eze 48: 7 it will **b** the territory of Reuben from east H6584
Eze 48:21 of the sacred portion to the eastern **b**, H1473
Eze 48:21 from the 25,000 cubits to the western **b**. H1473
Eze 48:22 will lie between the **b** *of* Judah and the H1473
Eze 48:22 border of Judah and the **b** *of* Benjamin. H1473
Eze 48:24 it will **b** the territory of Benjamin from east H6584
Eze 48:25 it will **b** the territory of Simeon from east H6584
Eze 48:26 it will **b** the territory of Issachar from east H6584
Eze 48:27 it will **b** the territory of Zebulun from east H6584
Ob 7 All your allies will force you to the **b**; your H1473
Lk 17:11 along **the b between** Samaria and *G1328+3545*
Ac 16: 7 When they came **to** *the* **b** of Mysia, they tried AIT

BORDERED (1) [BORDER]

Jos 17:10 Sea and **b** Asher on the north H7003

BORDERING (4) [BORDER]

Eze 45: 7 the land **b each side** of the area H4946+2296+2256+4946+2296S
Eze 48: 8 "**B** the territory of Judah from east to west H6584
Eze 48:12 holy portion, **b** the territory of the Levites. H448
Eze 48:18 **b** *on* the sacred portion and H4200+6645

BORDERLAND (1) [LAND]

1Sa 13:18 the third toward the **b** overlooking the H1473

BORDERS (14) [BORDER]

Ge 10:19 the **b** *of* Canaan reached from Sidon H1473
Ge 23:17 all the trees within the **b** of the field— H1473
Ex 13: 7 yeast be seen anywhere within your **b**. H1473
Ex 23:31 will establish your **b** from the Red Sea to H1473
1Ch 7:29 Along the **b** *of* Manasseh were Beth Shan H3338
Ps 147:14 grants peace to your **b** and satisfies you H1473
Isa 26:15 you have extended all the **b** *of* the land. H7898
Isa 60:18 ruin or destruction within your **b**, but H1473
Eze 11:10 judgment on you at the **b** *of* Israel. H1473
Eze 11:11 judgment on you at the **b** *of* Israel. H1473
Am 1:13 women of Gilead in order to extend his **b**, H1473
Mic 5: 6 invade our land and march across our **b**. H1473
Zec 9: 2 on Hamath too, *which* **b** on it, and on H1487
Mal 1: 5 is the LORD—even beyond **the b** *of* Israel! H1473

BORE (65) [BEAR]

Ge 16:15 So Hagar **b** Abram a son, and Abram H3528
Ge 16:16 years old when Hagar **b** him Ishmael. H3528
Ge 21: 2 pregnant and **b** a son to Abraham in H3528
Ge 21: 3 the name Isaac to the son Sarah **b** him. H3528
Ge 22:23 Milkah **b** these eight sons to Abraham's H3528
Ge 24:24 Bethuel, the son that Milkah **b** to Nahor." H3528
Ge 24:47 son of Nahor, whom Milkah **b** to him. H3528
Ge 25: 2 *She* **b** him Zimran, Jokshan, Medan H3528
Ge 25:12 Hagar the Egyptian, **b** to Abraham. H3528
Ge 30: 5 she became pregnant and **b** him a son. H3528
Ge 30: 7 again and **b** Jacob a second son. H3528
Ge 30:10 Leah's servant Zilpah **b** Jacob a son. H3528
Ge 30:12 servant Zilpah **b** Jacob a second son. H3528
Ge 30:17 became pregnant and **b** Jacob a fifth son. H3528

Ge 30:19 conceived again and b Jacob a sixth son. H3528
Ge 30:39 And they b young that were streaked or H3528
Ge 31: 8 then all the flocks b streaked young. H3528
Ge 31:39 torn by wild beasts; I b the loss myself. H2627
Ge 36: 4 Adah b Eliphaz to Esau, Basemath bore H3528
Ge 36: 4 bore Eliphaz to Esau, Basemath b Reuel, H3528
Ge 36: 5 Oholibamah b Jeush, Jalam and H3528
Ge 36:12 named Timna, who b him Amalek. H3528
Ge 36:14 of Zibeon, whom she b to Esau: H3528
Ge 44:27 'You know that my wife b me two sons. H3528
Ge 46:15 were the sons Leah b to Jacob in Paddan H3528
Ex 6:20 Jochebed, who b him Aaron and Moses. H3528
Ex 6:23 and she b him Nadab and Abihu H3528
Ex 6:25 of Putiel, and she b him Phinehas. H3528
Nu 26:59 To Amram she b Aaron, Moses and their H3528
Jdg 8:31 in Shechem, also b him a son, whom he H3528
Jdg 11: 2 Gilead's wife also b him sons, and when H3528
Ru 4:12 that of Perez, whom Tamar b to Judah." H3528
1Sa 20:30 to the shame of the mother who b you? AIT
2Sa 11:27 she became his wife and b him a son. H3528
1Ki 11:20 sister of Tahpenes b him a son named H3528
1Ki 14:28 temple, the guards b the shields, and H5951
1Ch 2: 4 Tamar b Perez and Zerah to H3528
1Ch 2:19 Caleb married Ephrath, who b him Hur. H3528
1Ch 2:21 made love to her, and she b him Segub. H3528
1Ch 2:24 the wife of Hezron b him Ashhur the H3528
1Ch 2:29 Abihail, who b him Ahban and Molid. H3528
1Ch 2:35 to his servant Jarha, and she b him Attai. H3528
1Ch 4: 6 Naarah b him Ahuzzam, Hepher, Temeni H3528
2Ch 11:19 She b him sons: Jeush, Shemariah and H3528
2Ch 11:20 of Absalom, who b him Abijah, Attai, H3528
Pr 17:25 bitterness to the mother who b him. H3528
SS 6: 9 mother, the favorite of the one who b her. H3528
Isa 49:21 will say in your heart, 'Who b me these? H3528
Isa 51:18 all the children she b there was none to H3528
Isa 53: 4 he took up our pain and b our suffering, H6022
Isa 53:12 For he b the sin of many, and made H5951
Isa 54: 1 woman, you who never b a child; burst H3528
Jer 20:14 the day my mother b me not be blessed! H3528
Jer 31:19 humiliated because I b the disgrace of my H5951
Eze 16:20 daughters whom you b to me and H3528
Eze 23:37 children, whom they b to me, as food H3528
Hos 1: 3 she conceived and b him a son. H3528
Mt 8:17 took up our infirmities and b our diseases." G1002
Lk 23:29 wombs that never b and the breasts that G1164
Ro 7: 5 at work in us, so that we b fruit for death. G2844
Ro 9:22 b with great patience the objects of his G5770
Gal 4:27 woman, you who never b a child; shout G5503
Heb 13:13 the camp, bearing the disgrace he b. NDT
1Pe 2:24 "He himself b our sins" in his body on the G429
Rev 17: 6 blood of those who b testimony to Jesus G3459

BORED (1) [BEAR]

2Ki 12: 9 priest took a chest and b a hole in its lid. H5918

BORN (145) [BEAR]

Ge 4:18 To Enoch was b Irad, and Irad was the H3528
Ge 5: 4 After Seth was b, Adam lived 800 years H3528
Ge 5:30 After Noah was b, Lamech lived 595 years H3528
Ge 6: 1 the earth and daughters were b to them, H3528
Ge 10:21 Sons were also b to Shem, whose older H3528
Ge 10:25 Two sons were b to Eber: One was named H3528
Ge 14:14 318 trained men b in his household and H3535
Ge 17:12 including those b in your household or H3535
Ge 17:13 Whether b in your household or bought H3535
Ge 17:17 "Will a son be b to a man a hundred H3528
Ge 17:23 Ishmael and all those b in his household H3535
Ge 17:27 including those b in his household or H3535
Ge 21: 5 old when his son Isaac was b to him. H3528
Ge 35:26 who were b to him in Paddan Aram. H3528
Ge 36: 5 of Esau, who were b to him in Canaan. H3528
Ge 37: 3 he had been b to him in his old age; H1201
Ge 41:50 two sons were b to Joseph by Asenath H3528
Ge 44:20 there is a young son b to him in his old age. AIT
Ge 46:18 were the children b to Jacob by Zilpah, H3528
Ge 46:20 Ephraim were b to Joseph by H3528
Ge 46:22 the sons of Rachel who were b to Jacob— H3528
Ge 46:25 These were the sons b to Jacob by Bilhah H3528
Ge 46:27 two sons who had been b to Joseph in H3528
Ge 48: 5 your two sons b to you in Egypt before I H3528
Ge 48: 6 Any children b to you after them will be H3528
Ex 1:22 Hebrew boy that is b you must throw into H3533
Ex 12:48 he may take part like one b in the land. H275
Ex 23:12 the slave b in your household and H1201+563
Lev 18: 9 she was b in the same home or H4580+1074
Lev 18:11 your father's wife, b to your father; she is H4580
Lev 22:11 if slaves are b in his household, they H3535
Lev 22:27 a lamb or a goat is b, it is to remain with H3528
Lev 25:45 members of their clans b in your country, H3528
Nu 26:59 who was b to the Levites in Egypt. H3528
Dt 23: 2 No one b of a forbidden marriage nor any H4927
Dt 23: 8 of children b to them may enter the H3528
Jos 5: 5 all the people b in the wilderness H3533
Jdg 13: 8 us how to bring up the boy who is to be b." H3528
Jdg 18:29 who was b to Israel—though H3528
2Sa 3: 2 Sons were b to David in Hebron: His H3528
2Sa 3: 5 These were b to David in Hebron H3528
2Sa 5:13 more sons and daughters were b to him. H3528
2Sa 5:14 the names of the children b to him there: H3533
2Sa 12:14 the LORD, the son b to you will die. H3533
2Sa 14:27 sons and a daughter were b to Absalom. H3528
1Ki 1: 6 very handsome and was b next after H3528
1Ki 3:18 The third day after my child was b, this H3528
1Ki 13: 2 named Josiah will be b to the house of H3528
2Ki 20:18 own flesh and blood who will be b to you, H3528
1Ch 1:19 Two sons were b to Eber: One was named H3528
1Ch 1:32 The sons b to Keturah, Abraham's H3528
1Ch 2: 3 These three were b to him by a Canaanite H3528
1Ch 2: 9 The sons b to Hezron were: Jerahmeel H3528
1Ch 3: 1 the sons of David b to him in Hebron: H3528
1Ch 3: 4 These six were b to David in Hebron H3528
1Ch 3: 5 these were the children b to him there: H3528
1Ch 8: 8 Sons were b to Shaharaim in Moab after H3528
1Ch 14: 4 the names of the children b to him there: H3528
Job 5: 7 Yet man is b to trouble as surely as sparks H3528
Job 8: 9 we were b only yesterday and know NDT
Job 11:12 a wild donkey's colt can be b human. H3528
Job 14: 1 "Mortals, b of woman, are of few days H3528
Job 15: 7 "Are you the first man ever b? Were you H3528
Job 15:14 be pure, or those b of woman, that they H3528
Job 25: 4 How can one b of woman be pure? H3528
Job 38:21 for you were already b! You have H3528
Ps 78: 6 even the children yet to be b, and they in H3528
Ps 87: 4 and will say, 'This one was b in Zion. H3528
Ps 87: 5 "This one and that one were b in her, and H3528
Ps 87: 6 of the peoples: "This one was b in Zion." H3528
Ps 90: 2 the mountains were b or you brought H3528
Ps 127: 4 of a warrior are children b in one's youth. AIT
Pr 17:17 a brother is b for a time of adversity. H3528
Ecc 2: 7 had other slaves who were b in my house. H1201
Ecc 3: 2 a time to be b and a time to die, a time H3528
Ecc 4: 3 than both is the one who has never been b, AIT
Ecc 4:14 or he may have been b in poverty within H3528
Isa 9: 6 For to us a child is b, to us a son is given H3528
Isa 39: 7 own flesh and blood who will be b to you, H3528
Isa 46: 3 and have carried since you were b. H8167
Isa 49: 1 Before I was b the LORD called me; from H1061
Isa 49:20 The children b during your bereavement will AIT
Isa 66: 8 Can a country be b in a day or a nation be H2655
Jer 1: 5 before you were b I set you H3655+4946+8167
Jer 16: 3 sons and daughters b in this land and H3533
Jer 20:14 Cursed be the day I was b! May the day H3528
Jer 20:15 saying, "A child is b to you—a son!" H3528
Jer 22:26 where neither of you was b, and there you H3528
Eze 16: 4 On the day you were b your cord was not H3528
Eze 16: 5 on the day you were b you were despised H3528
Hos 2: 3 her as bare as on the day she was b; H3528
Zec 13: 3 to whom they were b, will say to them, H3528
Mt 2: 1 After Jesus was b in Bethlehem in Judea G1164
Mt 2: 2 is the one who has been b king of the G5503
Mt 2: 4 them where the Messiah was to be b. G1164
Mt 11:11 among those b of women there has not G1168
Mt 19:12 who were b that way, G1666+3120+3613+1164
Mt 26:24 be better for him if he had not been b." G1164
Mk 7:26 was a Greek, b in Syrian Phoenicia. G1169
Mk 14:21 be better for him if he had not been b." G1164
Lk 1:15 Spirit even before he is b. G1666+3120+3613
Lk 1:35 So the holy one to be b will be called the G1164
Lk 2: 6 the time came for the baby to be b, G5503
Lk 2:11 town of David a Savior has been b to you; G5503
Lk 7:28 among those b of women there is no one G1168
Jn 1:13 children b not of natural descent, nor of G1164
Jn 1:13 decision or a husband's will, but b of God. NDT
Jn 3: 3 kingdom of God unless they are b again." G1164
Jn 3: 4 "How can someone be b when they are G1164
Jn 3: 4 time into their mother's womb to be b!" G1164
Jn 3: 5 of God unless they are b of water and the G1164
Jn 3: 7 at my saying, 'You must be b again. G1164
Jn 3: 8 So it is with everyone b of the Spirit." G1164
Jn 8:58 answered, "before Abraham was b, I am!" G1181
Jn 9: 2 man or his parents, that he was b blind?" G1164
Jn 9:19 "Is this the one you say was b blind? How G1164
Jn 9:20 answered, "and we know he was b blind. G1164
Jn 9:32 of opening the eyes of a man b blind. G1164
Jn 16:21 when her baby is b she forgets the G1164
Jn 16:21 of her joy that a child is b into the world. G1164
Jn 18:37 the reason I was b and came into the G1164
Ac 7:20 "At that time Moses was b, and he was G1164
Ac 22: 3 "I am a Jew, b in Tarsus of Cilicia, but G1164
Ac 22:28 "But I was b a citizen," Paul G1164
Ro 9:11 before the twins were b or had done G1164
1Co 11:12 from man, so also man is b of woman. G1328
1Co 15: 8 to me also, as to one abnormally b. G1765
Gal 4: 4 God sent his Son, b of a woman, born G1181
Gal 4: 4 born of a woman, b under the law, G1181
Gal 4:23 the slave woman was b according to the G1164
Gal 4:23 by the free woman was b as the result of a NDT
Gal 4:29 At that time the son b according to the G1164
Gal 4:29 persecuted the son b by the power of the NDT
Heb 11:23 hid him for three months after he was b, G1164
1Pe 1:23 For you have been b again, not of G335
2Pe 2:12 b only to be caught and destroyed G1164
1Jn 2:29 who does what is right has been b of him. G1164
1Jn 3: 9 No one who is b of God will continue to G1164
1Jn 3: 9 because they have been b of God. G1164
1Jn 4: 7 who loves has been b of God and knows G1164
1Jn 5: 1 that Jesus is the Christ is b of God, G1164
1Jn 5: 4 everyone b of God overcomes the world G1164
1Jn 5:18 We know that anyone b of God does not G1164
1Jn 5:18 the One who was b of God keeps them G1164
Rev 12: 4 devour her child the moment he was b. G5503

BORNE (22) [BEAR]

Ge 16: 1 Abram's wife, had b him no children. H3528
Ge 16:15 the name Ishmael to the son she had b. H3528
Ge 21: 7 Yet I have b him a son in his old age." H3528
Ge 21: 9 the Egyptian had b to Abraham was H3528
Ge 22:20 she has b sons to your brother Nahor: H3528
Ge 24:36 wife Sarah has b him a son in her H3528
Ge 29:34 because I have b him three sons. H3528
Ge 30:20 because I have b him six sons. H3528
Ge 31:43 or about the children they have b? H3528
Ge 34: 1 the daughter Leah had b to Jacob, went H3528
1Sa 2: 5 She who was barren has b seven children H3528
2Sa 12:15 the child that Uriah's wife had b to David, H3528
2Sa 21: 8 whom she had b to Saul, together H3528
2Sa 21: 8 whom she had b to Adriel son of Barzillai H3528
1Ki 3:21 I saw that it wasn't the son I had b." H3528
Ps 88:15 I have b your terrors and am in despair. H5951
Isa 46: 1 their idols are b by beasts of burden. H4200
Isa 49:15 no compassion on the child she has b? H1061
Hos 5:15 lair until they have b their guilt and seek H870
Hag 2:19 the olive tree have not b fruit. H5951
Mt 20:12 equal to us who have b the burden of the G1002
1Co 15:49 And just as we have b the image of the G5841

BORROW (5) [BORROWED, BORROWER, BORROWS]

Dt 15: 6 to many nations but will b from none. H6292
Dt 28:12 to many nations but will b from none. H4278
Ne 5: 4 "We have had to b money to pay the H4278
Ps 37:21 The wicked b and do not repay, but the H4278
Mt 5:42 from the one who wants to b from you. G1247

BORROWED (2) [BORROW]

2Ki 6: 5 "Oh no, my lord!" he cried out. "It was b!" H8626
Jer 15:10 I have neither lent nor b, yet H5957+928

BORROWER (3) [BORROW]

Ex 22:15 with the animal, the b will not have to pay. NDT
Pr 22: 7 the poor, and the b is slave to the lender. H4278
Isa 24: 2 seller as for buyer, for b as for lender, for H4278

BORROWS (1) [BORROW]

Ex 22:14 "If anyone b an animal from their H8626

BOSOM (3) [BOSOMS]

Pr 5:20 Why embrace the b of a wayward woman? H2668
Eze 23: 8 caressed her virgin b and poured out their H1843
Eze 23:21 when in Egypt your b was caressed and H1843

BOSOMS (1) [BOSOM]

Eze 23: 3 were fondled and their virgin b caressed. H1843

BOSOR (KJV) BEZER

BOTH (295)

Ge 2:25 Adam and his wife were b naked, and H9109
Ge 3: 7 Then the eyes of b of them were opened H9109
Ge 6:13 going to destroy b them and the earth. H907
Ge 11:29 Abram and Nahor b married. The name H2157S
Ge 11:29 the father of b Milkah and Iskah. H2256
Ge 17:26 son Ishmael were b circumcised on that very AIT
Ge 19: 4 city of Sodom—b young and old H2256
Ge 19:36 So b of Lot's daughters became pregnant H9109
Ge 23:17 Mamre—b the field and the cave in it H2256
Ge 27:45 Why should I lose b of you in one day?" H9109
Ge 36: 7 could not support them b because of their AIT
Ge 39: 5 b in the house and in the field. H2256
Ge 40: 8 "We b had dreams," they answered, "but AIT
Ge 42:37 "You may put b of my sons to death if I do H9109
Ge 47:13 b Egypt and Canaan wasted away H2256
Ge 48:13 And Joseph took b of them, Ephraim on H9109
Ex 4:15 will help b of you speak and H3870+2256+2084
Ex 9:25 in the fields—b people and animals; it H2256
Ex 12:12 every firstborn of b people and animals, H2256
Ex 12:22 the top and on b sides of the doorframe. H9109
Ex 12:38 droves of livestock, b flocks and herds. H2256
Ex 12:49 applies b to the native-born and to the H2256
Ex 13:15 the firstborn of b people and animals in H2256
Ex 15: 1 B horse and driver he has hurled into the H2256
Ex 15:21 B horse and driver he has hurled into the H2256
Ex 21:35 live one and divide b the money and the H2256
Ex 22: 9 b parties are to bring their cases before H9109
Ex 25:11 pure gold, b inside and out, and make a H2256
Ex 26:13 cubit longer on b sides; H4946+2296+2256+2296S
Ex 26:24 into a single ring; b shall be like that. H9109
Ex 29:13 and b kidneys with the fat on them H9109
Ex 29:22 of the liver, b kidneys with the fat on them H9109
Ex 31:10 b the sacred garments for Aaron the priest H2256
Ex 32:15 They were inscribed on b sides, front and H9109
Ex 35:19 b the sacred garments for Aaron the priest and H2256
Ex 35:34 he has given b him and Oholiab son of H2256
Ex 36:29 into a single ring; b were made alike. H9109
Ex 37: 2 pure gold, b inside and out, and made H2256
Ex 39:41 b the sacred garments for Aaron the priest and H2256
Lev 3: 4 b kidneys with the fat on them near the H9109
Lev 3:10 b kidneys with the fat on them near the H9109
Lev 3:15 b kidneys with the fat on them near the H9109
Lev 4: 9 b kidneys with the fat on them near the H9109
Lev 7: 4 b kidneys with the fat on them near the H9109
Lev 7: 7 applies to b the sin offering and the guilt H3869
Lev 8:16 of the liver, and b kidneys and their fat H9109
Lev 8:25 b kidneys and their fat and the right thigh. H9109
Lev 9: 2 burnt offering, b without defect, and present AIT
Lev 9: 3 a lamb—b a year old and without defect AIT

Lev 14:11 **b** the one to be cleansed **and** their H2256
Lev 15:18 of semen, *b of them must* **bathe** with water AIT
Lev 16:21 He is to lay **b** hands on the head of the H9109
Lev 18:17 with **b** a woman **and** her daughter. H2256
Lev 20:10 **b** the adulterer **and** the adulteress are to H2256
Lev 20:11 **B** the man and the woman are to be put H9109
Lev 20:12 **b** *of* them are to be put to death. H9109
Lev 20:13 **b** *of* them have done what is detestable. H9109
Lev 20:14 man marries **b** a woman **and** her mother, H2256
Lev 20:14 **B** he **and** they must be burned in the fire H2256
Lev 20:16 kill **b** the woman **and** the animal. H2256
Lev 20:18 **B** *of* them are to be cut off from their H9109
Lev 20:19 *b of* **you** would be held responsible. AIT
Lev 27:10 **b** it and the substitute become holy. H2256
Lev 27:33 **b** the animal and its substitute become H2256
Nu 6:19 loaf from the basket, **b** made without yeast. NDT
Nu 7:13 **b** according to the sanctuary shekel NDT
Nu 7:19 **b** according to the sanctuary shekel NDT
Nu 7:25 **b** according to the sanctuary shekel NDT
Nu 7:31 **b** according to the sanctuary shekel NDT
Nu 7:37 **b** according to the sanctuary shekel NDT
Nu 7:43 **b** according to the sanctuary shekel NDT
Nu 7:49 **b** according to the sanctuary shekel NDT
Nu 7:55 **b** according to the sanctuary shekel NDT
Nu 7:61 **b** according to the sanctuary shekel NDT
Nu 7:67 **b** according to the sanctuary shekel NDT
Nu 7:73 **b** according to the sanctuary shekel NDT
Nu 7:79 **b** according to the sanctuary shekel NDT
Nu 9:14 same regulations for **b** the foreigner and H2256
Nu 10: 3 When **b** are sounded, the whole H2177S
Nu 15:16 will apply **b** to you and to the foreigner H2256
Nu 18: 3 Otherwise **b** they and you will die. H1685
Nu 18:15 of every womb, **b** human **and** animal, that H2256
Nu 18:19 the LORD for **b** you **and** your offspring." H2256
Nu 19:10 ordinance **b** for the Israelites **and** for the H2256
Nu 20:24 because *b of you* **rebelled** against my AIT
Nu 22:24 with walls **on b sides.** H4946+2296+2256+4946+2296S
Nu 25: 8 He drove the spear into **b** *of* them, right H9109
Nu 27:14 *b of you* **disobeyed** my command to honor AIT
Dt 1:17 in judging; hear **b** small *and* great **alike.** H3869
Dt 11: 3 **b** to Pharaoh king of Egypt **and** to his H2256
Dt 11:14 in its season, **b** autumn **and** spring rains H2256
Dt 12:15 **B** the ceremonially unclean **and** the clean H2256
Dt 12:22 **B** the ceremonially unclean **and** the clean H3481
Dt 12:27 LORD your God, **b** the meat **and** the blood. H2256
Dt 13:15 completely, **b** its people **and** its livestock. H2256
Dt 15:22 **B** the ceremonially unclean **and** the clean H3481
Dt 21:15 and **b** bear him sons but H2021+170+2256+2021+8533S
Dt 22:22 **b** the man who slept with her and the H9109
Dt 22:24 you shall take **b** *of* them to the gate of that H9109
Dt 23:18 the LORD your God detests them **b.** H9109
Dt 28:66 filled with dread **b** night **and** day, never H2256
Dt 32:51 is because *b of you* **broke faith** with me in AIT
Jos 8:22 Israelites **on b sides.** H4946+2296+2256+4946+2296S
Jos 8:33 **on b sides** of the H4946+2296+2256+4946+2296S
Jos 8:33 **B** the foreigners living among them and H3869
Jos 17:16 **b** those in Beth Shan and its settlements NDT
Jdg 9: 9 by which **b** gods **and** humans are honored H2256
Jdg 9:13 which cheers **b** gods **and** humans, to hold H2256
Jdg 19:19 We have **b** straw and fodder for our H1685
Ru 1: 5 **b** Mahlon and Kilion also died, and H9109
1Sa 2:34 to you—they will **b** die on the same day. H9109
1Sa 5: 9 people of the city, **b** young and old, with H4946
1Sa 6: 4 plague has struck **b** you **and** your rulers. H2256
1Sa 12:14 if **b** you and the king who reigns over H1685
1Sa 12:25 **b** you and your king will perish. H1685
1Sa 14:11 So **b** *of* them showed themselves to the H9109
1Sa 17:36 servant has killed **b** the lion and the bear; H1685
1Sa 25:43 of Jezreel, and they **b** were his wives. H9109
1Sa 28:19 The LORD will deliver **b** Israel and you into H1685
1Sa 30: 2 everyone else in it, **b** young and old. H4946
2Sa 4: 4 of Saul had a son who was lame in *b* **feet.** AIT
2Sa 6:19 crowd of Israelites, **b** men and women. H4946
2Sa 9: 3 still a son of Jonathan; he is lame in *b* **feet."** AIT
2Sa 9:13 at the king's table; he was lame in **b** feet. H9109
2Sa 14:16 is trying to cut off **b** me and my son from H3480
2Sa 16:23 That was how **b** David and Absalom H1685
1Ki 2:32 **B** of them—Abner son of Ner, commander NDT
1Ki 3:13 have not asked for—**b** wealth and honor H1685
1Ki 6:29 temple, in **b** the inner **and** outer rooms H2256
1Ki 6:30 of **b** the inner and **outer** *rooms* of the H2667
1Ki 7:20 On the capitals of **b** pillars, above the H9109
1Ki 10:19 **On b sides** of the seat H4946+2296+2256+4946+2296S
1Ki 13:24 **with b** the donkey and the lion standing H2256
1Ki 21:10 that he has cursed **b** God **and** the king. H2256
1Ki 21:13 "Naboth has cursed **b** God **and** the king." H2256
2Ki 14:28 Israel **b** Damascus **and** Hamath, H2256
1Ch 24: 5 descendants of **b** Eleazar **and** Ithamar. H2256
2Ch 9:18 **On b sides** of the seat H4946+2296+2256+4946+2296S
2Ch 13:14 were being attacked at **b** front **and** rear. H2256
2Ch 30: 4 seemed right **b** to the king **and** to the H2256
2Ch 33: 5 In **b** courts of the temple of the LORD, he H9109
2Ch 36:18 **b** large **and** small, and the H2256
Ezr 3: 3 **b** the morning **and** evening sacrifices. H2256
Ne 11: 4 people from **b** Judah **and** Benjamin lived H2256
Job 9:22 destroys **b** the blameless **and** the wicked. H2256
Job 12:16 **b** deceived **and** deceiver are his. H2256
Job 21:26 they lie in the dust, and worms cover **them** *b.* AIT
Job 31:15 the same one form **us** *b* within our mothers? AIT
Ps 36: 6 LORD, preserve **b** people **and** animals. H2256
Ps 49: 2 **b** low and high, rich and poor alike: H1685
Ps 74:17 you made **b** summer **and** winter. H2256
Ps 76: 6 God of Jacob, **b** horse **and** chariot lie still. H2256
Ps 104:25 number—living things **b** large **and** small. H6640
Ps 113: 2 LORD be praised, **b** now **and** forevermore. H2256
Ps 115:14 you to flourish, **b** you **and** your children. H2256
Ps 115:18 extol the LORD, **b** now **and** forevermore. H2256
Ps 121: 8 going **b** now **and** forevermore. H2256
Ps 125: 2 his people **b** now **and** forevermore. H2256
Ps 131: 3 hope in the LORD **b** now **and** forevermore. H2256
Pr 17:15 the innocent—the LORD detests them **b.** H9109
Pr 20:10 measures—the LORD detests them **b.** H9109
Pr 20:12 that see—the LORD has made them **b.** H9109
Pr 22:16 gives gifts to the rich—**b** come to poverty. H421
Pr 27: 3 a fool's provocation is heavier than **b.** H9109
Pr 29:13 The LORD gives sight to the eyes of **b.** H9109
Ecc 2:14 that the same fate overtakes them **b.** H3972
Ecc 2:16 already come when **b** have been H3972
Ecc 3:17 judgment **b** the righteous **and** the wicked, H2256
Ecc 3:19 of the animals; the same fate awaits **them** *b:* AIT
Ecc 4: 3 But better than **b** is the one who has H9109
Ecc 5: 8 and over **them** *b* are others higher still. AIT
Ecc 7:15 life of mine I have seen **b** of these: H3972
Ecc 11: 6 or whether **b** will do equally well. H9109
SS 7:13 every delicacy, **b** new **and** old, that I have H1685
Isa 1:28 But rebels and sinners will **b** be broken H3481
Isa 1:31 his work a spark; **b** will burn together H9109
Isa 3: 1 Judah **b** supply **and** support: H2256
Isa 8:14 **b** Israel and Judah he will be a stone H9109
Isa 9:14 will cut off from Israel **b** head **and** tail, H2256
Isa 9:14 **b** palm branch **and** reed in a single day; H2256
Isa 47: 9 **B** *of* these will overtake you in a moment H9109
Isa 65: 7 **b** your sins and the sins of your ancestors," H3481
Jer 3:25 the LORD our God, **b** we **and** our ancestors H2256
Jer 6:11 **b** husband and wife will be caught in it H1685
Jer 11:10 **B** Israel and **Judah** have broken the H1074+3373
Jer 11:17 the people of **b** Israel **and** Judah have H2256
Jer 14:18 **B** prophet and priest have gone to a land H1685
Jer 16: 6 "**B** high and low will die in this land. H2256
Jer 21: 6 live in this city—**b** man and beast—and H2256
Jer 22:26 of you was born, and there *you b will* **die.** AIT
Jer 23:11 "**B** prophet and priest are godless; even in H1685
Jer 27:15 **b** you **and** the prophets who prophesy to H2256
Jer 32:14 **b** the sealed **and** unsealed copies of the H2256
Jer 34: 9 **b** male **and** female; no one H2256
Jer 36:29 land and wipe from it **b** man **and** beast?" H2256
Jer 44:20 the people, **b** men **and** women, who were H2256
Jer 46: 3 your shields, **b** large **and** small, and H2256
Jer 46:12 over another; **b** will fall down together." H9109
Jer 50: 3 **b** people and animals will flee away. H4946
La 2: 6 anger he has spurned **b** king **and** priest. H2256
La 3:38 High that **b** calamities **and** good things H2256
Eze 2:10 **On b sides** of it were written H7156+2256+294
Eze 7:13 was sold—as long as *b* **buyer and seller** live. AIT
Eze 15: 4 the fire burns **b** ends and chars the H9109
Eze 16:61 **b** those who are older than you **and** those H448
Eze 18: 4 well as the child—**b** *alike* belong to me. H2179
Eze 20:47 consume all your trees, **b** green **and** dry. H2256
Eze 21: 3 from you **b** the righteous **and** the wicked. H2256
Eze 21:19 **b** starting from the same country. H9109
Eze 23:13 **b** *of* them went the same way. H9109
Eze 25:13 against Edom and kill **b** man **and** beast. H2256
Eze 29: 8 against you and kill **b** man **and** beast. H2256
Eze 30:22 I will break *b* his **arms,** the good arm as well AIT
Eze 32:18 the earth below **b** her **and** the daughters H2256
Eze 41:23 **B** the main hall **and** the Most Holy Place H2256
Eze 42: 3 **B** in the section twenty cubits from the inner court **and** H2256
Eze 43:23 a ram from the flock, **b** without defect. NDT
Eze 43:25 a ram from the flock, **b without defect.** AIT
Eze 45:11 is to be the standard measure for **b.** H2257S
Eze 47:12 will grow **on b** banks of H4946+2296+2256+4946+2296
Eze 48:21 **on b sides** of the H4946+2296+2256+4946+2296S
Eze 48:21 **B** these areas running the length of the NDT
Da 9: 7 all Israel, **b** near **and** far, in all the H2256
Da 11:22 **b** it and a prince of the covenant will be H2256
Hos 4: 9 I will punish *b of* **them** for their ways and AIT
Joel 2:23 showers, **b** autumn **and** spring rains, as H2256
Joel 2:29 on my servants, **b** men **and** women, I will H2256
Mic 7: 3 *B* **hands** are skilled in doing evil; the ruler AIT
Zep 1: 3 "I will sweep away **b** man **and** beast; H2256
Zec 5: 4 it completely, **b** its timbers **and** its stones. H2256
Zec 13: 2 "I will remove **b** the prophets and the H1685
Mt 6:24 You cannot serve **b** God **and** money. *G2779*
Mt 9:17 into new wineskins, and **b** are preserved." *G317*
Mt 10:28 One who can destroy **b** soul and body in *G2779*
Mt 12:22 so that he could **b** talk **and** see. *G2779*
Mt 13:30 Let **b** grow together until the harvest. *G317*
Mt 15:14 blind lead the blind, **b** will fall into a pit." *G317*
Mt 25: 9 may not be enough for **b** us **and** you. *G2779*
Mk 2:22 and **b** the wine **and** the wineskins will be *G2779*
Lk 1: 6 **B** *of* them were righteous in the sight of *G317*
Lk 1: 7 able to conceive, and they were **b** very old. *G317*
Lk 5: 7 they came and filled **b** boats so full that *G317*
Lk 6:39 Will they not **b** fall into a pit? *G317*
Lk 7:42 pay him back, so he forgave the debts *of* **b.** *G317*
Lk 12:45 other servants, **b** men **and** women, and to *G2779*
Lk 14: 9 invited **b of you** will come *G5148+2779+899*
Lk 16:13 You cannot serve **b** God **and** money." *G2779*
Lk 22:66 **b** the chief priests and the teachers of the *G5445*
Lk 23:32 Two other men, *b* **criminals,** were also led AIT
Jn 2:15 the temple courts, **b** sheep and cattle; he *G5445*
Jn 11:48 take away **b** our temple and our *G2779*
Jn 15:24 they have hated **b** me and my Father. *G2779*
Jn 20: 4 **B** were running, but the other *G3836+1545+3938*
Ac 2:11 **b** Jews and converts to Judaism); Cretans *G5445*
Ac 2:18 on my servants, **b** men **and** women, I will *G2779*
Ac 2:36 whom you crucified, **b** Lord and Messiah." *G2779*
Ac 8: 3 he dragged off **b** men and women and *G5445*
Ac 8:10 the people, **b** high **and** low, gave *G608+2401*
Ac 8:12 they were baptized, **b** men and women. *G5445*
Ac 8:38 Then **b** Philip and the eunuch went down *G317*
Ac 14: 5 a plot afoot among **b** Gentiles and Jews, *G5445*
Ac 17:17 synagogue with **b** Jews **and** God-fearing *G2779*
Ac 20:21 I have declared to **b** Jews and Greeks that *G5445*
Ac 22: 4 arresting **b** men and women and throwing *G5445*
Ac 24:15 be a resurrection of **b** the righteous and *G5445*
Ac 27:12 facing **b** southwest **and** northwest. *G2779*
Ro 1:14 I am obligated **b** to Greeks and *G5445*
Ro 1:14 **b** to the wise and the foolish. *G5445*
Ro 14: 9 might be the Lord of **b** the dead and the *G2779*
1Co 1:24 whom God has called, **b** Jews and Greeks *G5445*
1Co 6:13 and God will destroy them **b.** *G2779+4047*
1Co 7:34 devoted to the Lord in **b** body and spirit. *G2779*
1Co 10:21 a part in **b** the Lord's table **and** the table *G2779*
1Co 10:28 **b** for the sake of the one who told you **and** *G2779*
2Co 1:17 same breath I say **b** "Yes, yes" **and** "No, *G2779*
2Co 1:21 God who makes **b** us **and** you stand firm *G5250*
Eph 2:16 body to reconcile **b** *of them* to God through *G317*
Eph 2:18 For through him we **b** have access to the *G317*
Eph 6: 9 know that he who is **b** their Master and *G2779*
1Ti 4: 8 promise for **b** the present life **and** the life *G2779*
1Ti 4:16 you will save **b** yourself and your hearers. *G2779*
Titus 1:15 **b** their minds and consciences are *G2779*
Phm 11 has become useful **b** to you and to me. *G2779*
Phm 16 **b** as a fellow man and as a brother in the *G2779*
Heb 2:11 **B** the one who makes people holy and *G5445*
Heb 8: 3 is appointed to offer **b** gifts and sacrifices, *G5445*
Heb 9:21 with the blood **b** the tabernacle and *G2779*
Jas 3:11 Can **b** fresh water **and** salt water flow from *G2779*
2Pe 3: 1 I have written *b of* **them** as reminders to AIT
2Pe 3:18 To him be glory **b** now **and** forever! Amen *G2779*
2Jn 9 in the teaching has **b** the Father and the *G2779*
Rev 5: 1 writing **on b** sides and *G2277+2779+3957*
Rev 6:15 everyone else, **b** slave **and** free, hid in *G2779*
Rev 11:18 your name, **b** great **and** small—and for *G2779*
Rev 19: 5 you who fear him, **b** great **and** small!" *G2779*

BOTHER (4) [BOTHERING]

2Sa 14:10 and *they will* not **b** you again. H5595
Mk 5:35 "Why **b** the teacher anymore?" *G5035*
Lk 8:49 "Don't **b** the teacher anymore." *G5035*
Lk 11: 7 one inside answers, 'Don't **b** me. *G3160+4218*

BOTHERING (3) [BOTHER]

Mt 26:10 "Why *are you* **b** this woman? *G3160+4218*
Mk 14: 6 "Why *are you* **b** her? She *G3160+4218*
Lk 18: 5 because this widow *keeps* **b** me *G4218+3160*

BOTTLED-UP (1)

Job 32:19 inside I am like **b** wine, like new H4202+7337

BOTTLES (1)

Isa 3:20 sashes, the perfume **b** and charms, H1074

BOTTOM (9)

Ex 26:24 be double from the **b** all the way to the H4752
Ex 28:27 them to the **b** *of* the H4946+4200+4752
Ex 36:29 were double from the **b** all the way to the H4752
Ex 39:20 them to the **b** *of* the H4946+4200+4752
Dt 28:13 will always be at the top, never at the **b.** H4752
Am 9: 3 hide from my eyes at the **b** *of* the sea, H7977
Mt 27:51 the temple was torn in two from top to **b.** *G3004*
Mk 15:38 the temple was torn in two from top to **b.** *G3004*
Jn 19:23 woven in one piece from top to **b.** *G3910*

BOTTOMLESS PIT (KJV) ABYSS

BOUGHS (9)

Ps 118:27 With **b** in hand, join in the festal H6291
Isa 10:33 will lop off the **b** with great power. H6998
Isa 17: 6 four or five on the fruitful **b,**" declares the H6187
Eze 17: 6 produced branches and put out **leafy b.** H6997
Eze 31: 5 its **b** increased and its branches grew long H6250
Eze 31: 6 All the birds of the sky nested in its **b,** all H6190
Eze 31: 7 with its spreading **b,** for its roots went H1936
Eze 31: 8 could the junipers equal its **b,** nor H6190
Eze 31:12 Its **b** fell on the mountains and in all the H1936

BOUGHT (47) [BUY]

Ge 17:12 in your household or **b** *with* money from a H5239
Ge 17:13 in your household or **b** *with* your money, H5239
Ge 17:23 in his household or **b** *with* his money, H5239
Ge 17:27 his household or **b** from a foreigner H5239+4084
Ge 25:10 the field Abraham *had* **b** from the Hittites H7864
Ge 33:19 of silver, *he* **b** from the sons of Hamor H7864
Ge 39: 1 **b** him from the Ishmaelites who had H7864
Ge 47:20 So Joseph **b** all the land in Egypt for H7864
Ge 47:23 "Now that *I have* **b** you and your land H7864
Ge 49:30 which Abraham **b** along with the field as H7864
Ge 49:32 the cave in it were **b** from the Hittites." H5238

B

Ge 50:13 which Abraham had b along with the H7864
Ex 12:44 slave you have b may eat it after H5239+4084
Ex 15:16 LORD, until the people you b pass by. H7864
Lev 27:22 dedicates to the LORD a field they have b, H5239
Lev 27:24 revert to the person from whom it was b, H7864
Lev 27:27 animals, it may be b back at its set value H7009
Jos 24:32 of land that Jacob b for a hundred pieces H7864
Ru 4: 9 witnesses that I have b from Naomi all H7864
2Sa 12: 3 except one little ewe lamb he had b. H7864
2Sa 24:24 So David b the threshing floor and the H7864
1Ki 16:24 He b the hill of Samaria from Shemer for H7864
Ne 5: 8 we have b back our fellow Jews who were H7864
Job 28:15 It cannot be b with the finest gold, nor H5989
Job 28:16 It cannot be b with the gold of Ophir, with H6137
Job 28:19 it cannot be b with pure gold. H6137
Ecc 2: 7 I b male and female slaves and had other H7864
Isa 43:24 You have not b any H7864+928+2021+4084
Jer 13: 2 So I b a belt, as the LORD directed, and put H7864
Jer 13: 4 "Take the belt you b and are wearing H7864
Jer 32: 9 so I b the field at Anathoth from my cousin H7864
Jer 32:15 vineyards will again be b in this land. H7864
Jer 32:43 Once more fields will be b in this land of H7864
Jer 32:44 Fields will be b for silver, and deeds will H7864
Hos 3: 2 So I b her for fifteen shekels of silver and H4126
Mt 13:44 went and sold all he had and b that field. G60
Mt 13:46 away and sold everything he had and b it. G60
Mk 15:46 So Joseph b some linen cloth, took down the G60
Mk 16: 1 Salome b spices so that they might go G60
Lk 14:18 The first said, 'I have just b a field, and I G60
Lk 14:19 'I have just b five yoke of oxen G60
Ac 1:18 his wickedness, Judas b a field; there he G3227
Ac 7:16 that Abraham had b from the sons of G6050
Ac 20:28 which he b with his own blood. G4347
1Co 6:20 you were b at a price. Therefore honor God G60
1Co 7:23 You were b at a price; do not become slaves G60
2Pe 2: 1 denying the sovereign Lord who b them— G60

BOULDER (1)

Rev 18:21 angel picked up a b the size of a large G3345

BOUND (57) [BIND]

Ge 22: 9 He b his son Isaac and laid him on the H6818
Ge 42:24 taken from them and b before their eyes. H673
Ge 44:30 whose life is closely b up with the boy's H8003
Jdg 15:13 So they b him with two new ropes and led H673
1Sa 14:24 Saul had b the people under an oath, H457
1Sa 14:27 his father had b the people with the oath, H8678
1Sa 14:28 b the army under a strict oath, H8678+8678
1Sa 25:29 my lord will be b securely in the bundle of H7674
2Sa 3:34 Your hands were not b, your feet were not H673
2Ki 25: 7 b him with bronze shackles and took him to H673
2Ch 33:11 b him with bronze shackles and took him to H673
2Ch 36: 6 attacked him and b him with bronze H673
Job 36: 8 But if people are b in chains, held fast by H673
Pr 22:15 Folly is b up in the heart of a child, but H8003
Isa 16:14 as a servant b by contract would count H8502
Isa 21:16 as a servant b by contract would count it H8502
Isa 24:22 together like prisoners b in a dungeon; AIT
Isa 56: 3 Let no foreigner who is b to the LORD say H4277
Jer 13:11 For as a belt is b around the waist, so I H1815
Jer 13:11 so I b all the people of Israel and all the H1815
Jer 39: 7 out Zedekiah's eyes and b him with bronze H673
Jer 40: 1 had found Jeremiah b in chains among all H673
Jer 52:11 b him with bronze shackles and took him to H673
La 1:14 "My sins have been b into a yoke; by his H8567
Eze 3:25 you will be b so that you cannot go out H673
Eze 30:21 It has not been b up to be healed or put H2502
Eze 34: 4 healed the sick or b up the injured. H2502
Da 3:21 were b and thrown into the blazing A10366
Da 4:15 its roots, b with iron and bronze A10054
Da 4:23 leave the stump, b with iron and bronze A10054
Jnh 1: 3 where he found a ship b for that port. H995
Mt 14: 3 arrested John and b him and put him in G1313
Mt 16:19 you bind on earth will be b in heaven, G1313
Mt 18:18 you bind on earth will be b in heaven, G1313
Mt 23:16 the gold of the temple is b by that oath. G4053
Mt 23:18 by the gift on the altar is b by that oath. G4053
Mt 27: 2 So they b him, led him away and handed G1313
Mk 6:17 and he had him b and put in prison. G1313
Mk 15: 1 So they b Jesus, led him away and G1313
Lk 13:16 whom Satan has kept b for eighteen long G1313
Lk 13:16 free on the Sabbath day from what b her?" G1301
Lk 17: 1 people to stumble are b to come, G450+3590
Jn 18:12 officials arrested Jesus. They b him G1313
Jn 18:24 Then Annas sent him b to Caiaphas the G1313
Ac 12: 6 two soldiers, b with two chains, and G1313
Ac 21:13 I am ready not only to be b, but also to G1313
Ac 21:33 ordered him to be b with two chains. G1313
Ac 23:12 and b themselves with an oath not to eat G354
Ac 28:20 hope of Israel that I am b with this chain." G4329
Ro 7: 2 a married woman is b to her husband as G1313
Ro 7: 6 by dying to what once b us, we have been G2988
Ro 11:32 For God has b everyone over to G5168
1Co 7:15 brother or the sister is not b in such G1530
1Co 7:39 A woman is b to her husband as long as G1313
Jude 6 b with everlasting chains for judgment on the AIT
Rev 9:14 four angels who are b at the great river G1313
Rev 20: 2 Satan, and b him for a thousand years. G1313

BOUNDARIES (11) [BOUNDARY]

Nu 34: 2 you as an inheritance is to have these b: H1474
Nu 34:12 will be your land, with its b on every side. H1474
Dt 32: 8 he set up b for the peoples according to H1474
Jos 15:12 These are the b around the people of H1473
Jos 18:20 These were the b that marked out the H1474
2Ki 14:25 who restored the b of Israel from Lebo H1473
Ps 74:17 It was you who set all the b of the earth H1474
Isa 10:13 I removed the b of nations, I plundered H1474
Eze 47:13 "These are the b of the land that you will H1473
Mic 7:11 will come, the day for extending your b. H2976
Ac 17:26 times in history and the b of their lands. G3999

BOUNDARY (60) [BOUNDARIES, BOUNDLESS, BOUNDS]

Nu 34: 3 Your southern b will start in the east from H1473
Nu 34: 6 " 'Your western b will be the coast of the H1473
Nu 34: 6 This will be your b on the west. H1473
Nu 34: 7 " 'For your northern b, run a line from the H1473
Nu 34: 8 Then the b will go to Zedad, H1473
Nu 34: 9 This will be your b on the north. H1473
Nu 34:10 " 'For your eastern b, run a line from H1473
Nu 34:11 The b will go down from Shepham to H1473
Nu 34:12 Then the b will go down along the Jordan H1473
Dt 19:14 your neighbor's b stone set up by your H1473
Dt 27:17 who moves their neighbor's b stone." H1473
Jos 13:23 The b of the Reubenites was the bank of H1473
Jos 15: 2 Their southern b started from the bay at H1473
Jos 15: 4 This is their southern b. H1473
Jos 15: 5 The eastern b is the Dead Sea as far as H1473
Jos 15: 5 The northern b started from the bay of the H1473
Jos 15: 7 The b then went up to Debir from the H1473
Jos 15: 9 From the hilltop the b headed toward the H1473
Jos 15:11 The b ended at the sea. H1473
Jos 15:12 The western b is the coastline of the H1473
Jos 15:21 in the Negev toward the b of Edom were: H1473
Jos 16: 5 The b of their inheritance went from H1473
Jos 17: 7 The b ran southward from there to include H1473
Jos 17: 8 on the b of Manasseh, belonged to H1473
Jos 17: 9 Then the b continued south to the Kanah H1473
Jos 17: 9 the b of Manasseh was the northern H1473
Jos 18:12 north side their b began at the Jordan, H1473
Jos 18:14 on the south the b turned south along the H1473
Jos 18:15 the b came out at the spring of the H1473
Jos 18:16 The b went down to the foot of the hill H1473
Jos 18:19 This was the southern b. H1473
Jos 18:20 The Jordan formed the b on the eastern H1487
Jos 19:10 The b of their inheritance went as far as H1473
Jos 19:14 There the b went around on the north to H1473
Jos 19:22 The b touched Tabor, Shahazumah and H1473
Jos 19:26 On the west the b touched Carmel and NDT
Jos 19:29 The b then turned back toward Ramah H1473
Jos 19:33 Their b went from Heleph and the large H1473
Jos 19:34 The b ran west through Aznoth Tabor H1473
Jos 22:25 made the Jordan a b between us and you H1473
Jdg 1:36 The b of the Amorites was from Scorpion H1473
Job 24: 2 There are those who move b stones; they H1474
Job 26:10 the waters for a b between light and H9417
Ps 16: 6 The b lines have fallen for me in pleasant H2475
Ps 104: 9 You set a b they cannot cross; never again H1473
Pr 8:29 he gave the sea its b so the waters would H2976
Pr 15:25 he sets the widow's b stones in place. H1473
Pr 22:28 move an ancient b stone set up by your H1473
Pr 23:10 move an ancient b stone or encroach on H1473
Jer 5:22 I made the sand a b for the sea, an H1473
Eze 47:15 "This is to be the b of the land: "On the H1473
Eze 47:17 The b will extend from the sea to Hazar H1473
Eze 47:17 This will be the northern b. H6991
Eze 47:18 "On the east side the b will run between H1473
Eze 47:18 This will be the eastern b. H6991
Eze 47:19 This will be the southern b. H6991
Eze 47:20 Sea will be the b to a point opposite Lebo H1473
Eze 47:20 Lebo Hamath. This will be the western b. H6991
Eze 48:28 "The southern b of Gad will run south H1473
Hos 5:10 leaders are like those who move b stones. H1473

BOUNDING (1)

SS 2: 8 across the mountains, b over the hills. H7890

BOUNDLESS (3) [BOUNDARY]

Ps 119:96 a limit, but your commands are b. H8146+4394
Na 3: 9 Cush and Egypt were her b strength H401+7897
Eph 3: 8 to the Gentiles the b riches of Christ, G453

BOUNDS (2) [BOUNDARY]

Hos 4: 2 adultery; they break all b, and H7287
2Co 7: 4 in all our troubles my joy knows no b. G5668

BOUNTY (7)

Ge 49:26 than the b of the age-old hills. H9294
Dt 28:12 the storehouse of his b, to send rain on H3202
1Ki 10:13 what he had given her out of his royal b. H3338
Ps 65:11 You crown the year with your b, and your H3208
Ps 68:10 people settled in it, and from your b, God, H3208
Jer 31:12 they will rejoice in the b of the LORD—the H3206
Jer 31:14 my people will be filled with my b," H3206

BOW (104) [BOWED, BOWING, BOWS, BOWSHOT, BOWSTRINGS]

Ge 27: 3 your quiver and b—and go out to the open H8008
Ge 27:29 serve you and peoples b down to you. H2556
Ge 27:29 may the sons of your mother b down to H2556
Ge 37:10 actually come and b down to the ground H2556
Ge 48:22 the Amorites with my sword and my b." H8008
Ge 49: 8 your father's sons will b down to you. H2556
Ge 49:24 But his b remained steady, his strong H8008
Ex 20: 5 You shall not b down to them or worship H2556
Ex 23:24 Do not b down before their gods or H2556
Lev 26: 1 stone in your land to b down before it. H2556
Dt 5: 9 You shall not b down to them or worship H2556
Dt 8:19 gods and worship and b down to them, H2556
Dt 11:16 worship other gods and b down to them. H2556
Dt 26:10 LORD your God and b down before him. H2556
Dt 30:17 are drawn away to b down to other gods H2556
Dt 33: 3 At your feet they all b down, and from you H9413
Jos 23: 7 must not serve them or b down to them. H2556
Jos 23:16 serve other gods and b down to them, H2556
Jos 24:12 did not do it with your own sword and b. H8008
1Sa 2:36 will come and b down before him for a H2556
1Sa 18: 4 even his sword, his b and his belt. H8008
2Sa 1:18 of Judah be taught this lament of the b H8008
2Sa 1:22 the b of Jonathan did not turn back H8008
2Sa 15: 5 approached him to b down before him, H2556
2Sa 16: 4 "I humbly b," Ziba said H2556
2Sa 22:35 my arms can bend a b of bronze. H8008
1Ki 22:34 someone drew his b at random and hit H8008
2Ki 5:18 of Rimmon to b down and he is leaning H2556
2Ki 5:18 on my arm and I have to b there also— H2556
2Ki 5:18 when I b down in the temple of Rimmon H2556
2Ki 6:22 have captured with your own sword or b? H8008
2Ki 9:24 Then Jehu drew his b and shot Joram H8008
2Ki 13:15 Elisha said, "Get a b and some arrows," H8008
2Ki 13:16 "Take the b in your hands," he said to the H8008
2Ki 17:35 any other gods or b down to them, H2556
2Ki 17:36 To him you shall b down and to him offer H2556
1Ch 5:18 who could use a b, and who were trained H8008
1Ch 8:40 brave warriors who could handle the b. H8008
2Ch 18:33 someone drew his b at random and hit H8008
Job 29:20 the b will be ever new in my hand. H8008
Job 30:11 God has unstrung my b and afflicted me, H3857
Ps 5: 7 in reverence I b down toward your holy H2556
Ps 7:12 his sword; he will bend and string his b. H8008
Ps 18:34 my arms can bend a b of bronze. H8008
Ps 21:12 when you aim at them with drawn b. H4798
Ps 22:27 of the nations will b down before him, H2556
Ps 37:14 sword and bend the b to bring down the H8008
Ps 44: 6 I put no trust in my b, my sword does not H8008
Ps 46: 9 He breaks the b and shatters the spear H8008
Ps 58: 7 when they draw the b, let their H2005
Ps 60: 4 a banner to be unfurled against the b. H8000
Ps 72: 9 May the desert tribes b before him and H4156
Ps 72:11 May all kings b down to him and all H2556
Ps 78:57 faithless, as unreliable as a faulty b. H8008
Ps 95: 6 let us b down in worship, let us H4156
Ps 138: 2 I will b down toward your holy temple H2556
Pr 14:19 Evildoers will b down in the presence of H8820
Isa 2: 8 they b down to the work of their hands H2556
Isa 7:24 Hunters will go there with b and arrow, for H8008
Isa 21:15 from the bent b and from the heat of H8008
Isa 22: 3 have been captured without using the b. H8008
Isa 41: 2 his sword, to windblown chaff with his b. H8008
Isa 44:19 Shall I b down to a block of wood? H6032
Isa 45:14 They will b down before you and plead H2556
Isa 45:23 Before me every knee will b; by me every H4156
Isa 46: 2 They stoop and b down together; unable H4156
Isa 46: 6 and they b down and worship it. H6032
Isa 49: 7 princes will see and b down, because of H2556
Isa 49:23 They will b down before you with their faces to H2556
Isa 60:14 who despise you will b down at your feet H2556
Isa 66:23 will come and b down before me, H2556
Jer 6:23 They are armed with b and spear; they H8008
Jer 9: 3 "They make ready their tongue like a b, to H8008
Jer 27: 8 king of Babylon or b its neck under his H5989
Jer 27:11 But if any nation will b its neck under the H995
Jer 27:12 "B your neck under the yoke of the king of H995
Jer 46: 9 shields, men of Lydia who draw the b. H8008
Jer 49:35 I will break the b of Elam, the mainstay of H8008
Jer 50:14 around Babylon, all you who draw the b. H8008
Jer 50:29 Babylon, all those who draw the b. H8008
Jer 51: 3 Let not the archer string his b, nor let him H8008
La 2: 4 Like an enemy he has strung his b; his H8008
La 3:12 He drew his b and made me the target H8008
Eze 39: 3 I will strike your b from your left hand H8008
Eze 46: 2 He is to b down in worship at the H2556
Hos 1: 5 I will break Israel's b in the Valley of H8008
Hos 1: 7 will save them—not by b, sword or battle, H8008
Hos 2:18 B and sword and battle I will abolish from H8008
Hos 7:16 to the Most High; they are like a faulty b. H8008
Mic 5:13 you will no longer b down to the work of H2556
Mic 6: 6 the LORD and b down before the exalted H4104
Hab 3: 9 You uncovered your b, you called for H8008
Zep 1: 5 who b down on the roofs to worship the H2556
Zep 1: 5 those who b down and swear by the LORD H2556
Zep 2:11 Distant nations will b down to him, all of H2556
Zec 9:10 the battle b will be broken. H8008
Zec 9:13 bend Judah as I bend my b and fill it with H8008
Zec 10: 4 from him the battle b, from him every H8008
Mt 4: 9 "if you will b down and worship me." G4406
Ac 27:30 going to lower some anchors from the b. G4749
Ac 27:41 The b stuck fast and would not move, and G4749
Ro 14:11 'every knee will b before me; every G2828
Php 2:10 at the name of Jesus every knee should b, G2828
Rev 6: 2 Its rider held a b, and he was given a G5534

BOWED (68) [BOW]

Ge 18: 2 to meet them and b low to the ground. H2556
Ge 19: 1 meet them and b down with his face to H2556

Ge 23: 7 Abraham rose and **b down** before the H2556
Ge 23:12 Again Abraham **b down** before the H2556
Ge 24:26 Then the man **b down** and worshiped the H7702
Ge 24:48 and *I* **b down** and worshiped the LORD. H7702
Ge 24:52 *he* **b down** to the ground before the LORD. H2556
Ge 33: 3 went on ahead and **b down** to the ground H2556
Ge 33: 6 their children approached and **b down**. H2556
Ge 33: 7 Leah and her children came and **b down**. H2556
Ge 33: 7 Joseph and Rachel, and *they* too **b down**. H2556
Ge 37: 7 gathered around mine and **b down** to it." H2556
Ge 42: 6 *they* **b down** to him *with* their faces to the H2556
Ge 43:26 and *they* **b down** before him to the H2556
Ge 43:28 And *they* **b down**, prostrating themselves H7702
Ge 48:12 knees and **b down** *with* his face to the H2556
Ex 4:31 their misery, *they* **b down** and worshiped. H7702
Ex 12:27 Then the people **b down** and worshiped. H7702
Ex 18: 7 father-in-law and **b down** and kissed him. H2556
Ex 32: 8 *They have* **b down** to it and sacrificed to it H2556
Ex 34: 8 Moses **b** to the ground at once and H7702
Nu 22:31 So *he* **b low** and fell facedown. H7702
Nu 25: 2 meal and **b down** before these gods. H2556
Dt 29:26 other gods and **b down** to them, H2556
Jdg 7:15 interpretation, *he* **b down and worshiped**. H2556
Ru 2:10 *she* **b** down with her face to the ground. H2556
1Sa 20:41 the stone and **b** down *before* Jonathan H2556
1Sa 24: 8 David **b down** and prostrated himself with H7702
1Sa 25:23 off her donkey and **b** down before David H2556
1Sa 25:41 *She* **b down** with her face to the ground H2556
1Sa 28:14 and *he* **b down** and prostrated himself H7702
2Sa 9: 6 *he* **b down** to pay him honor. H5877+6584+7156
2Sa 9: 8 Mephibosheth **b down** and said, "What is H2556
2Sa 14:33 he came in and **b down** with his face to H2556
2Sa 18:21 The Cushite **b down** before Joab and ran H2556
2Sa 18:28 *He* **b down** before the king with his face H2556
2Sa 24:20 he went out and **b down** before the king H2556
1Ki 1:16 Bathsheba **b down**, prostrating herself H7702
1Ki 1:23 before the king and **b** with his face to the H2556
1Ki 1:31 Then Bathsheba **b down** with her face to H7702
1Ki 1:47 And the king **b in worship** on his bed H2556
1Ki 1:53 came and **b down** to King Solomon, H2556
1Ki 2:19 **b down** to her and sat down on his throne. H2556
1Ki 18: 7 **b down to the ground**, and H5877+6584+7156
1Ki 19:18 whose knees *have* not **b down** to Baal H4156
2Ki 2:15 to meet him and **b** to the ground before H2556
2Ki 4:37 fell at his feet and **b** to the ground. H2556
2Ki 17:16 *They* **b down** to all the starry hosts, and H2556
2Ki 21: 3 *He* **b down** to all the starry hosts and H2556
1Ch 21:21 floor and **b down** before David with H2556
1Ch 29:20 of their fathers; *they* **b down**, prostrating H7702
2Ch 20:18 Jehoshaphat **b down** with his face to the H7702
2Ch 25:14 **b down** to them and burned sacrifices to H2556
2Ch 29:28 The whole assembly **b in worship**, while H2556
2Ch 29:30 gladness and **b down** and worshiped. H7702
2Ch 33: 3 *He* **b down** to all the starry hosts and H2556
Ne 8: 6 Then *they* **b down** and worshiped the LORD H7702
Ps 35:14 *I* **b** *my* **head** in grief as though weeping H8820
Ps 38: 6 *I am* **b down** and brought very low; all day H6390
Ps 57: 6 net for my feet—I *was* **b down in distress**. H4104
Ps 145:14 who fall and lifts up all who **are b down**. H4104
Ps 146: 8 the LORD lifts up *those who* **are b down** H4104
La 2:10 of Jerusalem *have* **b** their heads to the H3718
Da 10:15 *I* **b** with my face toward the ground and H5989
Mt 2:11 and *they* **b down** and worshiped him. G4406
Lk 24: 5 fright the women **b down** with their faces G3111
Jn 19:30 *he* **b** his head and gave up his spirit. G3111
Ro 11: 4 thousand who *have* not **b** the knee to G2828

BOWELS (5)

Jdg 3:22 in after the blade, and his **b** discharged. H7307
2Ch 21:15 very ill with a lingering disease of the **b**, H5055
2Ch 21:15 the disease causes your **b** to come out. H5055
2Ch 21:18 with an incurable disease of the **b**. H5055
2Ch 21:19 his **b** came out because of the disease H5055

BOWING (8) [BOW]

Ge 37: 9 eleven stars *were* **b down** to me. H2556
Ex 11: 8 **b down** before me and saying H2556
Dt 4:19 not be enticed into **b down** to them and H2556
Dt 17: 3 **b down** to them or to the sun or the moon H2556
2Ki 21:21 had worshiped, and **b down** to them. H2556
Isa 58: 5 Is it only for **b** one's head like a reed and H4104
Isa 60:14 of your oppressors will come **b** before you; H8820
Eze 8:16 they *were* **b down** to the sun in the east. H2556

BOWL (31) [BOWL-SHAPED, BOWLFUL, BOWLS]

Nu 7:13 one silver **sprinkling b** weighing H4670
Nu 7:19 one silver **sprinkling b** weighing H4670
Nu 7:25 one silver **sprinkling b** weighing H4670
Nu 7:31 one silver **sprinkling b** weighing H4670
Nu 7:37 one silver **sprinkling b** weighing H4670
Nu 7:43 one silver **sprinkling b** weighing H4670
Nu 7:49 one silver **sprinkling b** weighing H4670
Nu 7:55 one silver **sprinkling b** weighing H4670
Nu 7:61 one silver **sprinkling b** weighing H4670
Nu 7:67 one silver **sprinkling b** weighing H4670
Nu 7:73 one silver **sprinkling b** weighing H4670
Nu 7:79 one silver **sprinkling b** weighing H4670
Nu 7:85 each **sprinkling b** seventy shekels. H4670
Jdg 5:25 in a **b** *fit for* nobles she brought him H6210
2Ki 2:20 "Bring me a new **b**," he said, "and put H7504
Ecc 12: 6 the golden **b** is broken; before the H1657
Zec 4: 2 lampstand with a **b** at the top and seven H1657
Zec 4: 3 on the right of the **b** and the other on its H1657
Zec 9:15 full like a **b used for sprinkling** the corners H4670
Mt 5:15 people light a lamp and put it under a **b**. G3654
Mt 26:23 his hand into the **b** with me will betray G5581
Mk 4:21 in a lamp to put it under a **b** or a bed? G3654
Mk 14:20 "one who dips bread into the **b** with me. G5581
Lk 11:33 where it will be hidden, or under a **b**. G3654
Rev 16: 2 went and poured out his **b** on the land, G5786
Rev 16: 3 angel poured out his **b** on the sea, G5786
Rev 16: 4 angel poured out his **b** on the rivers and G5786
Rev 16: 8 fourth angel poured out his **b** on the sun, G5786
Rev 16:10 poured out his **b** on the throne of the G5786
Rev 16:12 angel poured out his **b** on the great river G5786
Rev 16:17 angel poured out his **b** into the air, G5786

BOWL-SHAPED (7) [BOWL]

1Ki 7:20 above the **b part** next to the network H1061
1Ki 7:41 the two **b** capitals on top of the pillars H1657
1Ki 7:41 decorating the two **b** capitals on top of H1657
1Ki 7:42 decorating the **b** capitals on top of the H1657
2Ch 4:12 the two **b** capitals on top of the pillars H1657
2Ch 4:12 decorating the two **b** capitals on top of H1657
2Ch 4:13 decorating the **b** capitals on top of the H1657

BOWLFUL (3) [BOWL]

Jdg 6:38 wrung out the dew—a **b** of water. H4850+6210
Ps 80: 5 you have made them drink tears *by* the **b**. H8955
Am 6: 6 You drink wine by the **b** and use the finest H4670

BOWLS (35) [BOWL]

Ex 24: 6 Moses took half of the blood and put it in **b** H110
Ex 25:29 as its pitchers and **b** for the pouring out of H4984
Ex 27: 3 its shovels, **sprinkling b**, meat forks and H4670
Ex 37:16 dishes and **b** and its pitchers for H4984
Ex 38: 3 shovels, **sprinkling b**, meat forks and H4670
Nu 4: 7 the plates, dishes and **b**, and the jars H4984
Nu 4:14 meat forks, shovels and **sprinkling b**. H4670
Nu 7:84 twelve silver **sprinkling b** and twelve gold H4670
2Sa 17:28 brought bedding and **b** and articles of H6195
1Ki 7:40 the pots and shovels and **sprinkling b**. H4670
1Ki 7:45 shovels and **sprinkling b**. All these H4670
1Ki 7:50 wick trimmers, **sprinkling b**, dishes and H4670
2Ki 12:13 wick trimmers, **sprinkling b**, trumpets or H4670
2Ki 25:15 took away the censers and **sprinkling b**— H4670
1Ch 28:17 the forks, **sprinkling b** and pitchers; the H4670
2Ch 4: 8 also made a hundred gold **sprinkling b**. H4670
2Ch 4:11 the pots and shovels and **sprinkling b**. H4670
2Ch 4:22 wick trimmers, **sprinkling b**, dishes and H4670
Ezr 1:10 gold **b** 30 matching silver bowls 410 other H4094
Ezr 1:10 30 matching silver **b** 410 other articles H4094
Ezr 8:27 20 **b** *of* gold valued at 1,000 darics, and H4094
Ne 7:70 50 **b** and 530 garments for priests. H4670
Pr 23:30 who go to sample **b of mixed wine**. H4932
Isa 22:24 its lesser vessels, from the **b** to all the jars. H110
Isa 65:11 fill **b of mixed wine** for Destiny, H4932
Jer 35: 5 Then I set **b** full of wine and some cups H1483
Jer 52:18 wick trimmers, **sprinkling b**, dishes and all H4670
Jer 52:19 censers, **sprinkling b**, pots H4670
Jer 52:19 dishes and **b used for drink offerings**—all H4984
Zec 14:20 will be like the **sacred b** in front of the H4670
Rev 5: 8 were holding golden **b** full of incense, G5786
Rev 15: 7 angels seven golden **b** filled with the G5786
Rev 16: 1 pour out the seven **b** of God's wrath on G5786
Rev 17: 1 who had the seven **b** came and said to G5786
Rev 21: 9 who had the seven **b** full of the seven last G5786

BOWS (19) [BOW]

1Sa 2: 4 "The **b** *of* the warriors are broken, but H8008
1Ch 12: 2 they were armed with **b** and were able to H8008
2Ch 14: 8 with small shields and **with b**. H2005+8008
2Ch 17:17 200,000 men armed with **b** and shields; H8008
2Ch 26:14 **b** and slingstones for the entire army. H8008
Ne 4:13 families, with their swords, spears and **b**. H8008
Ne 4:16 with spears, shields, **b** and armor. H8008
Ps 11: 2 the wicked bend their **b**; they set their H8008
Ps 37:15 own hearts, and their **b** will be broken. H8008
Ps 66: 4 All the earth **b down** to you; they sing H2556
Ps 78: 9 though armed with **b**, turned back on the H8008
Isa 5:28 are sharp, all their **b** are strung; their H8008
Isa 13:18 Their **b** will strike down the young men H8008
Isa 44:15 he makes an idol and **b down** to it. H6032
Isa 44:17 his idol; *he* **b down** to it and worships. H6032
Isa 46: 1 Bel **b down**, Nebo stoops low; their idols H4156
Jer 50:42 They are armed with **b** and spears; they H8008
Jer 51:56 be captured, and their **b** will be broken. H8008
Eze 39: 9 large shields, the **b** and arrows, the war H8008

BOWSHOT (1) [BOW]

Ge 21:16 off and sat down about a **b** away, H3217+8008

BOWSTRINGS (3) [BOW]

Jdg 16: 7 me with seven fresh **b** that have not been H3857
Jdg 16: 8 her seven fresh **b** that had not been dried H3857
Jdg 16: 9 But he snapped the **b** as easily as a piece H3857

BOX (KJV) CYPRESS, FLASK, JAR

BOXER (1)

1Co 9:26 I do not fight like a *b* **beating** the air. AIT

BOY (79) [BOY'S, BOYHOOD, BOYS]

Ge 21:12 about the **b** and your slave woman H5853
Ge 21:14 then sent her off with the **b**. H3529
Ge 21:15 she put the **b** under one of the bushes. H3529
Ge 21:16 she thought, "I cannot watch the **b** die." H3529
Ge 21:17 God heard the **b** crying, and the angel of H5853
Ge 21:17 God has heard the **b** crying as he lies H5853
Ge 21:18 Lift the **b** up and take him by the hand, for H5853
Ge 21:19 skin with water and gave the **b** a drink. H5853
Ge 21:20 God was with the **b** as he grew up. H5853
Ge 22: 5 donkey while I and the **b** go over there. H5853
Ge 22:12 "Do not lay a hand on the **b**," he said H5853
Ge 37:30 his brothers and said, "The **b** isn't there! H3529
Ge 42:22 "Didn't I tell you not to sin against the **b**? H3529
Ge 43: 8 "Send the **b** along with me and we will H5853
Ge 44:22 to my lord, 'The **b** cannot leave his father H5853
Ge 44:30 if the **b** is not with us when I go back to H5853
Ge 44:31 sees that the **b** isn't there, he will die H5853
Ge 44:33 here as my lord's slave in place of the **b**, H5853
Ge 44:33 and let the **b** return with his brothers. H5853
Ge 44:34 back to my father if the **b** is not with me? H5853
Ex 1:16 if you see that the baby is a **b**, kill him; H1201
Ex 1:22 "Every Hebrew **b** that is born you must H1201
Lev 12: 3 On the eighth day **the b** is to be H2257s
Lev 12: 7 woman who gives birth to a **b** or a girl. H2351
Jdg 8:20 because he was only a **b** and was afraid. H5853
Jdg 13: 5 a razor because the **b** is to be a Nazirite, H5853
Jdg 13: 7 because the **b** will be a Nazirite of God H5853
Jdg 13: 8 how to bring up the **b** who is to be born." H5853
Jdg 13:24 gave birth to a **b** and named him Samson H1201
1Sa 1:22 husband, "After the **b** is weaned, I will H5853
1Sa 1:24 she took the **b** with her, young as H5853
1Sa 1:25 been sacrificed, they brought the **b** to Eli, H5853
1Sa 2:11 the **b** ministered before the LORD H5853
1Sa 2:18 the LORD—a **b** wearing a linen ephod. H5853
1Sa 2:21 the **b** Samuel grew up in the presence of H5853
1Sa 2:26 And the **b** Samuel continued to grow in H5853
1Sa 3: 1 The **b** Samuel ministered before the LORD H5853
1Sa 3: 8 realized that the LORD was calling the **b**. H5853
1Sa 4:21 She named the **b** Ichabod, saying, "The H5853
1Sa 17:42 saw that he was little more than a **b**, H5853
1Sa 20:21 Then I will send a **b** and say, 'Go, find the H5853
1Sa 20:22 But if I say to the **b**, 'Look, the arrows are H6624
1Sa 20:35 He had a small **b** with him, H5853
1Sa 20:36 he said to the **b**, "Run and find the H5853
1Sa 20:36 As the **b** ran, he shot an arrow beyond H5853
1Sa 20:37 When the **b** came to the place where H5853
1Sa 20:38 The **b** picked up the arrow and returned to H5853
1Sa 20:39 The **b** knew nothing about all this; only H5853
1Sa 20:40 gave his weapons to the **b** and said, H5853
1Sa 20:41 After the **b** had gone, David got up from H5853
1Sa 30:19 young or old, **b** or girl, plunder or H1201
1Ki 11:17 still only a **b**, fled to Egypt with H5853+7783
1Ki 14: 3 He will tell you what will happen to the **b**." H5853
1Ki 14:12 you set foot in your city, the **b** will die. H3529
1Ki 14:17 the threshold of the house, the **b** died. H5853
1Ki 17:21 himself out on the **b** three times and cried H3529
2Ki 4:20 his mother, the **b** sat on her lap until noon NDT
2Ki 4:31 told him, "The **b** has not awakened." H5853
2Ki 4:32 there was the **b** lying dead on his couch. H5853
2Ki 4:34 Then he got on the bed and lay on the **b** H3529
2Ki 4:35 The **b** sneezed seven times and opened H5853
2Ki 5:14 became clean like that of a young **b**. H5853
Job 3: 3 the night that said, 'A **b** is conceived! H1505
Isa 7:16 before the **b** knows enough to reject H5853
Isa 8: 4 For before the **b** knows how to say 'My H5853
Mt 17:17 put up with you? Bring **the b** here to me." G899s
Mt 17:18 it came out of the **b**, and he was G4090
Mk 9:19 I put up with you? Bring **the b** to me." G899s
Mk 9:20 immediately threw **the b** into a convulsion G899s
Mk 9:26 The **b** looked so much like a corpse that NDT
Mk 10:20 "all these I have kept since I was a **b**." G3744
Lk 2:43 the **b** Jesus stayed behind in Jerusalem G4090
Lk 9:42 Even while **the b** was coming, the demon G899s
Lk 9:42 healed the **b** and gave him back to his G4090
Lk 18:21 "All these I have kept since I was a **b**," G3744
Jn 4:51 him with the news that his **b** was living. G4090
Jn 6: 9 "Here is a **b** with five small barley loaves G4081
Jn 7:22 you circumcise a **b** on the Sabbath. G476
Jn 7:23 Now if a **b** can be circumcised on the G476

BOY'S (10) [BOY]

Ge 44:30 life is closely bound up with **the b** life, H2257s
Ge 44:32 guaranteed the **b** safety to my father. H5853
Jdg 13:12 the rule that governs the **b** life and work?" H5853
1Ki 17:21 my God, let this **b** life return to him!" H3529
1Ki 17:22 Elijah's cry, and the **b** life returned to him H3529
2Ki 4:29 Lay my staff on the **b** face." H5853
2Ki 4:31 on ahead and laid the staff on the **b** face, H5853
2Ki 4:34 out on him, the **b** body grew warm. H3529
Mk 9:21 Jesus asked **the b** father, "How long has G899s
Mk 9:24 Immediately the **b** father exclaimed, "I do G4086

BOYHOOD (1) [BOY]

Ge 46:34 have tended livestock from our **b** on, H5830

BOYS (15) [BOY]

Ge 25:24 to give birth, there were **twin** *b* in her womb. AIT
Ge 25:27 The **b** grew up, and Esau became a H5853
Ge 38:27 to give birth, there were **twin** *b* in her womb. AIT
Ge 48:16 me from all harm—may he bless these **b**. H5853
Ex 1:17 had told them to do; they let the **b** live. H3529
Ex 1:18 Why have you let the **b** live?" H3529
Nu 31:17 Now kill all the **b**. And kill every H2351+3251
2Ki 2:23 *some* **b** came out of the town and H5853+7783

2Ki 2:24 the woods and mauled forty-two of the **b**. H3529
2Ki 4: 1 is coming to take my two **b** as his slaves." H3529
Job 19:18 Even the **little b** scorn me; when I appear H6396
La 5:13 **b** stagger under loads of wood. H5853
Joel 3: 3 my people and traded **b** for prostitutes; H3529
Zec 8: 5 will be filled with **b** and girls playing H3529
Mt 2:16 to kill all the **b** in Bethlehem and its *G4090*

BOZEZ (1)
1Sa 14: 4 one was called **B** and the other Seneh. H1010

BOZKATH (2)
Jos 15:39 Lachish, **B**, Eglon, H1304
2Ki 22: 1 daughter of Adaiah; she was from **B**. H1304

BOZRAH (8)
Ge 36:33 son of Zerah from **B** succeeded him as H1313
1Ch 1:44 son of Zerah from **B** succeeded him as H1313
Isa 34: 6 has a sacrifice in **B** and a great slaughter H1313
Isa 63: 1 from Edom, from **B**, with his garments H1313
Jer 48:24 to Kerioth and **B**—to all the towns of H1313
Jer 49:13 "that **B** will become a ruin and a curse H1313
Jer 49:22 swoop down, spreading its wings over **B**. H1313
Am 1:12 that will consume the fortresses of **B**." H1313

BRACE (3) [BRACING]
Job 38: 3 **B** yourself like a man; I will question H273+2743
Job 40: 7 "**B** yourself like a man; I will H273+2743
Na 2: 1 the road, **b yourselves**, marshal all H2616+5516

BRACELETS (7)
Ge 24:22 two gold **b** weighing ten H7543+6584+3338
Ge 24:30 nose ring, and the **b** on his sister's arms H7543
Ge 24:47 ring in her nose and the **b** on her arms, H7543
Nu 31:50 us acquired—armlets, **b**, signet rings H7543
Isa 3:19 the earrings and **b** and veils, H9217
Eze 16:11 I put **b** on your arms and a necklace H7543
Eze 23:42 they put **b** on the wrists of the woman H7543

BRACING (1) [BRACE]
Jdg 16:29 **B** *himself* against them, his right hand on H6164

BRAG (1)
Am 4: 5 a thank offering and **b** *about* your freewill H7924

BRAIDED (3) [BRAIDS]
Ex 28:14 two **b** chains of pure gold, like a rope H4456
Ex 28:22 breastpiece make **b** chains of pure gold, H1491
Ex 39:15 they made **b** chains of pure gold, H1491

BRAIDS (3) [BRAIDED]
Jdg 16:13 weave the seven **b** *of* my head into the H4710
Jdg 16:13 Delilah took the seven **b** *of* his head H4710
Jdg 16:19 to shave off the seven **b** *of* his hair, H4710

BRAMBLE (KJV) THORNBUSH

BRAMBLES (1)
Isa 34:13 citadels, nettles and **b** her strongholds. H2560

BRANCH (26) [BRANCHES]
Ge 49:11 his colt to the **choicest b**; he will wash his H8605
Ex 25:33 buds and blossoms are to be on one **b**, H7866
Ex 25:33 three on the next **b**, and the same for all H7866
Ex 37:19 with buds and blossoms were on one **b**, H7866
Ex 37:19 three on the next **b** and the same for all H7866
Nu 4: 2 of the Kohathite **b of** the Levites by H4946+9348
Nu 13:23 they cut off a **b** bearing a single cluster of H2367
Isa 4: 2 In that day the **B** *of* the LORD will be H7542
Isa 9:14 both **palm b** and reed in a single day; H4093
Isa 11: 1 of Jesse; from his roots a **B** will bear fruit. H5916
Isa 14:19 are cast out of your tomb like a rejected **b**; H5916
Isa 19:15 can do—head or tail, **palm b** or reed. H4093
Jer 1:11 "I see the **b** *of* an almond tree," I replied. H5234
Jer 23: 5 I will raise up for David a righteous **B**, H7542
Jer 33:15 make a righteous **B** sprout from David's H7542
Eze 8:17 Look at them putting the **b** to their nose! H2367
Eze 15: 2 from that of a **b** from any of the trees in H2367
Eze 19:14 No strong **b** is left on it fit for a ruler's H4751
Zec 3: 8 I am going to bring my servant, the **B**. H7542
Zec 6:12 'Here is the man whose name is the **B** H7542
Zec 6:12 and *he will* **b out** from his place and build H7541
Mal 4: 1 "Not a root or a **b** will be left to them. H6733
Jn 15: 2 He cuts off every **b** in me that bears no *G3097*
Jn 15: 2 while every **b** that does bear fruit he prunes NDT
Jn 15: 4 No **b** can bear fruit by itself; it must *G3097*
Jn 15: 6 you are like a **b** that is thrown away and *G3097*

BRANCHES (81) [BRANCH]
Ge 30:37 took fresh-cut **b** *from* poplar, almond and H5234
Ge 30:37 exposing the white inner wood of the **b**. H5234
Ge 30:38 placed the peeled **b** in all the watering H5234
Ge 30:39 they mated in front of the **b**. And they bore H5234
Ge 30:41 Jacob would place the **b** in the troughs in H5234
Ge 30:41 animals so they would mate near the **b**, H5234
Ge 40:10 on the vine were three **b**. As soon as H8585
Ge 40:12 "The three **b** are three days. H8585
Ge 49:22 near a spring, whose **b** climb over a wall. H1426
Ex 25:32 Six **b** are to extend from the sides of the H7866
Ex 25:33 the same for all six **b** extending from the H7866
Ex 25:35 the first pair of **b** extending from the H7866
Ex 25:35 third bud under the third pair—six **b** in all. H7866
Ex 25:36 The buds and **b** shall all be of one piece H7866
Ex 37:18 Six **b** extended from the sides of the H7866
Ex 37:19 the same for all six **b** extending from the H7866
Ex 37:21 the first pair of **b** extending from the H7866
Ex 37:21 third bud under the third pair—six **b** in all. H7866
Ex 37:22 The buds and the **b** were all of one piece H7866
Lev 23:40 you are to take **b** *from* luxuriant trees— H7262
Dt 24:20 *do* not **go over the b a second time**. H6994+339
Jdg 9:48 He took an ax and cut off *some* **b** H8457+6770
Jdg 9:49 So all the men cut **b** and followed H8456
2Sa 18: 9 went under the **thick b** *of* a large oak, H8449
Ne 8:15 bring back **b** *from* olive and wild olive H6591
Ne 8:16 brought back **b** and built themselves NDT
Job 15:32 he will wither, and his **b** will not flourish. H4093
Job 18:16 dry up below and his **b** wither above. H7908
Job 29:19 the dew will lie all night on my **b**. H7908
Ps 80:10 its shade, the mighty cedars with its **b**. H6733
Ps 80:11 Its **b** reached as far as the Sea, its shoots H7908
Ps 104:12 by the waters; they sing among the **b**. H6751
Isa 17: 6 two or three olives on the topmost **b**, H580
Isa 18: 5 cut down and take away the **spreading b**. H5746
Isa 27:10 there they lie down; they strip its **b** bare. H6187
Jer 5:10 Strip off her **b**, for these people do not H5746
Jer 6: 9 pass your hand over the **b** again, like one H6151
Jer 11:16 will set it on fire, and its **b** will be broken. H1936
Jer 48:32 Your **b** spread as far as the sea; they H5746
Eze 17: 6 Its **b** turned toward him, but its roots H1936
Eze 17: 6 a vine and produced **b** and put out leafy H964
Eze 17: 7 stretched out its **b** to him for water. H1936
Eze 17: 8 water so that it would produce **b**, H6733
Eze 17:23 it will produce **b** and bear fruit and H6733
Eze 17:23 they will find shelter in the shade of its **b**. H1936
Eze 19:10 it was fruitful and **full of b** because of H6734
Eze 19:11 Its **b** were strong, fit for a ruler's scepter. H4751
Eze 19:11 its height and for its many **b**. H1936
Eze 19:12 its strong **b** withered and fire consumed H4751
Eze 19:14 one of its **main b** and consumed H4751+964
Eze 21:19 a signpost where the road **b off** *to* the city. H8031
Eze 31: 3 with beautiful **b** overshadowing the forest H6733
Eze 31: 5 its boughs increased and its **b** grew long H6997
Eze 31: 6 animals of the wild gave birth under its **b**; H6997
Eze 31: 8 the plane trees compare with its **b**— H6997
Eze 31: 9 I made it beautiful with abundant **b**, the H1936
Eze 31:12 its **b** lay broken in all the ravines of the H6997
Eze 31:13 all the wild animals lived among its **b**. H6997
Eze 36: 8 will produce **b** and fruit for my people H6733
Da 4:12 the birds lived in its **b**; from it every A10561
Da 4:14 'Cut down the tree and trim off its **b**; strip A10561
Da 4:14 from under it and the birds from its **b**. A10561
Da 4:21 nesting places in its **b** for the birds— A10561
Joel 1: 7 thrown it away, leaving their **b** white. H8585
Zec 4:12 are these two olive **b** beside the two gold H8672
Mt 13:32 so that the birds come and perch in its **b**." *G3080*
Mt 21: 8 while others cut **b** from the trees and *G3080*
Mk 4:32 with such big **b** that the birds can perch in *G3080*
Mk 11: 8 while others spread **b** they had cut in the *G5115*
Lk 13:19 and the birds perched in its **b**. *G3080*
Jn 12:13 They took palm **b** and went out to meet him *G961*
Jn 15: 5 you are the **b**. If you remain in me *G3097*
Jn 15: 6 away and withers; **such b** are picked up *G899S*
Ro 11:16 if the root is holy, so are the **b**. *G3080*
Ro 11:17 If some *of* the **b** have been broken off *G3080*
Ro 11:18 yourself to be superior *to* those other **b**. *G3080*
Ro 11:19 "**B** were broken off so that I could be *G3080*
Ro 11:21 For if God did not spare the natural **b**, he *G3080*
Ro 11:24 the natural **b**, be grafted into their NDT
Heb 9:19 scarlet wool and **b of hyssop**, and *G5727*
Rev 7: 9 were holding **palm b** in their hands. *G5836*

BRAND (KJV) BURNING STICK

BRANDING (1)
Isa 3:24 clothing, sackcloth; instead of beauty, **b**. H3953

BRANDISH (3) [BRANDISHED, BRANDISHES, BRANDISHING]
Ps 35: 3 **B** spear and javelin against those who H8197
Isa 10:15 or a club **b** the one who is not wood! H8123
Eze 32:10 of you when I **b** my sword before them. H6758

BRANDISHED (1) [BRANDISH]
Na 2: 3 made ready; the spears of juniper *are* **b**. H8302

BRANDISHES (1) [BRANDISH]
Eze 30:25 king of Babylon and *he* **b** it against Egypt. H5742

BRANDISHING (1) [BRANDISH]
Eze 38: 4 small shields, all of them **b** their swords. H9530

BRASEN, BRASS (KJV) BRONZE

BRAVE (15) [BRAVELY, BRAVEST]
1Sa 14:52 Saul saw a mighty or **b** man, H1201+2657
1Sa 16:18 He is a **b man** and a warrior H1475+2657
2Sa 2: 7 be strong and **b**, for Saul your H1201+2657
2Sa 13:28 you this order? Be strong and **b**." H1201+2657
2Sa 17:10 and that those with him are **b**. H1201+2657
1Ch 5:24 They were **b** warriors, famous men, and H2657
1Ch 7:40 **b warriors** and outstanding leaders. H1475+2657
1Ch 8:40 of Ulam were **b warriors** who could H1475+2657
1Ch 12: 8 They were **b warriors**, ready for H1475+2657
1Ch 12:21 all of them were **b warriors**, and H1475+2657
1Ch 12:28 Zadok, a **b** young **warrior**, with 22 H1475+2657
1Ch 12:30 Ephraim, **b warriors**, famous in H1475+2657
1Ch 28: 1 the warriors and all the **b** fighting men. H2657
2Ch 14: 8 All these were **b fighting men**. H1475+2657
Isa 33: 7 their **b men** cry aloud in the streets H737

BRAVELY (3) [BRAVE]
1Sa 18:17 serve me **b** and fight the H4200+1201+2657
2Sa 10:12 and *let us* **fight b** for our people and the H2616
1Ch 19:13 and *let us* **fight b** for our people and the H2616

BRAVEST (2) [BRAVE]
2Sa 17:10 Then even the **b soldier**, whose H1201+2657
Am 2:16 Even the **b** warriors will flee naked H579+4213

BRAWLER (1) [BRAWLERS, BRAWLING]
Pr 20: 1 Wine is a mocker and beer a **b**; whoever H2159

BRAWLERS (1) [BRAWLER]
Isa 5:14 masses with all their **b** and revelers. H8623

BRAWLING (1) [BRAWLER]
Eph 4:31 rage and anger, **b** and slander, along *G3199*

BRAY (1) [BRAYED]
Job 6: 5 *Does* a wild donkey **b** when it has grass H5640

BRAYED (1) [BRAY]
Job 30: 7 *They* **b** among the bushes and huddled in H5640

BRAZEN (3)
Pr 7:13 kissed him and *with* a **b** face she said: H6451
Jer 3: 3 Yet you have the **b look** *of* a prostitute H5195
Eze 16:30 all these things, acting like a **b** prostitute! H8951

BREACH (2) [BREAK]
Job 30:14 They advance as through a gaping **b** H7288
Ps 106:23 stood in the **b** before him to keep his H7288

BREACHES (2) [BREAK]
Eze 13: 5 not gone up to the **b** in the wall to repair H7288
Am 4: 3 each go straight out through **b in the wall**, H7288

BREACHING (2) [BREAK]
Ps 144:14 There will be no **b of walls**, no going into H7288
Pr 17:14 Starting a quarrel is like **b** a dam; so drop H7080

BREAD (267)
Ge 14:18 king of Salem brought out **b** and wine. H4312
Ge 18: 6 flour and knead it and bake *some* **b**." H6314
Ge 19: 3 baking **b without yeast**, and they H5174
Ge 25:34 Jacob gave Esau *some* **b** and some lentil H4312
Ge 27:17 the tasty food and the **b** she had made. H4312
Ge 40:16 On my head were three baskets of **b**. H3035
Ge 45:23 with grain and **b** and other provisions H4312
Ex 12: 8 bitter herbs, and **b made without yeast**. H5174
Ex 12:15 days you are to eat **b made without yeast**. H5174
Ex 12:17 "Celebrate the **Festival of Unleavened B** H5174
Ex 12:18 you are to eat **b made without yeast**, H5174
Ex 12:20 you live, you must eat **unleavened b**." H5174
Ex 12:39 they baked loaves of **unleavened b**. H5174
Ex 13: 6 days eat **b made without yeast** and on the H5174
Ex 13: 7 Eat **unleavened b** during those seven days; H5174
Ex 16: 4 "I will rain down **b** from heaven for you. H4312
Ex 16: 8 evening and all the **b** you want in the H4312
Ex 16:12 in the morning you will be filled with **b**. H4312
Ex 16:15 "It is the **b** the LORD has given you to eat. H4312
Ex 16:29 the sixth day he gives you **b** for two days. H4312
Ex 16:31 The people of Israel called **the b** manna. H2257S
Ex 16:32 so they can see the **b** I gave you to eat in H4312
Ex 23:15 "Celebrate the **Festival of Unleavened B** H5174
Ex 23:15 seven days eat **b made without yeast** H5174
Ex 25:30 Put the **b** *of* the Presence on this table to H4312
Ex 29:23 From the basket of **b made without yeast** H5174
Ex 29:32 of the ram and the **b** that is in the basket. H4312
Ex 29:34 ordination ram or any **b** is left over till H4312
Ex 34:18 "Celebrate the **Festival of Unleavened B** H5174
Ex 34:18 For seven days eat **b made without yeast** H5174
Ex 34:28 nights without eating **b** or drinking water. H4312
Ex 35:13 all its articles and the **b** *of* the Presence; H4312
Ex 39:36 all its articles and the **b** *of* the Presence; H4312
Ex 40:23 set out the **b** on it before the LORD, as H4312
Lev 7:13 with thick loaves of **b** made with yeast. H4312
Lev 8: 2 basket containing **b made without yeast**, H5174
Lev 8:26 from the basket of **b made without yeast**, H5174
Lev 8:31 eat it there with the **b** from the basket of H4312
Lev 8:32 burn up the rest of the meat and the **b**. H4312
Lev 23: 6 LORD's Festival of **Unleavened B** begins; H5174
Lev 23: 6 days you must eat **b made without yeast**. H5174
Lev 23:14 You must not eat any **b**, or roasted or new H4312
Lev 23:18 Present with this **b** seven male lambs H4312
Lev 23:20 together with the **b** *of* the firstfruits. H4312
Lev 24: 5 finest flour and bake twelve **loaves of b**, H2705
Lev 24: 7 to represent the **b** and to be a food H4312
Lev 24: 8 **This b** is to be set out before the LORD H5647S
Lev 26:26 When I cut off your supply of **b**, ten H4312
Lev 26:26 will be able to bake your **b** in one oven, H4312
Lev 26:26 they will dole out the **b** by weight. H4312
Nu 4: 7 the **b** that is continually there is to remain H4312
Nu 6:15 **b** *made with* the finest flour and **without yeast** H5174
Nu 6:17 the basket of **unleavened b** and is to H5174
Nu 9:11 together with **unleavened b** and bitter H5174
Nu 21: 5 There is no **b**! There is no water! H4312
Nu 28:17 seven days eat **b made without yeast**. H5174
Dt 8: 3 does not live on **b** alone but on every H4312
Dt 8: 9 a land where **b** will not be scarce and you H4312

Dt 9: 9 I ate no **b** and drank no water. H4312
Dt 9:18 forty nights; I ate no **b** and drank no water H4312
Dt 16: 3 Do not eat it with **b made with yeast**, but H2809
Dt 16: 3 for seven days eat **unleavened b**, the H5174
Dt 16: 3 the **b** *of* affliction, because H4312
Dt 16: 8 For six days eat **unleavened b** and on the H5174
Dt 16:16 at the Festival of **Unleavened B**, the H5174
Dt 23: 4 to meet you with **b** and water on your way H4312
Dt 29: 6 You ate no **b** and drank no wine or other H4312
Jos 5:11 land: **unleavened b** and roasted grain. H5174
Jos 9: 5 All the **b** *of* their food supply was dry and H4312
Jos 9:12 This **b** *of* ours was warm when we packed H4312
Jdg 6:19 ephah of flour he made **b without yeast**. H5174
Jdg 6:20 "Take the meat and the **unleavened b** H5174
Jdg 6:21 meat and the **unleavened b** with the tip H5174
Jdg 6:21 the rock, consuming the meat and the **b**. H5174
Jdg 7:13 round loaf of barley **b** came tumbling into H4312
Jdg 8: 5 "Give my troops *some* **b**; they are H3971+4312
Jdg 8: 6 Why should we give **b** to your troops?" H4312
Jdg 8:15 Why should we give **b** to your exhausted H4312
Jdg 19:19 our donkeys and **b** and wine for H4312
Ru 2:14 Have some **b** and dip it in the wine H4312
1Sa 2:36 piece of silver and a loaf of **b** and plead, H4312
1Sa 10: 3 another three loaves of **b**, and another a H4312
1Sa 10: 4 greet you and offer you two loaves of **b**, H4312
1Sa 16:20 So Jesse took a donkey loaded with **b**, H4312
1Sa 17:17 these ten **loaves of b** for your brothers H4312
1Sa 21: 3 Give me five **loaves of b**, or whatever you H4312
1Sa 21: 4 "I don't have any ordinary **b** on hand H4312
1Sa 21: 4 there is *some* consecrated **b** here H4312
1Sa 21: 6 So the priest gave him the consecrated **b** NDT
1Sa 21: 6 since there was no **b** there except the H4312
1Sa 21: 6 there except the **b** *of* the Presence that H4312
1Sa 21: 6 replaced by hot **b** on the day it was H4312
1Sa 22:13 giving him **b** and a sword and inquiring of H4312
1Sa 25:11 Why should I take my **b** and water, and H4312
1Sa 25:18 She took two hundred **loaves of b**, two H4312
1Sa 28:24 kneaded it and baked **b without yeast**. H5174
2Sa 3:35 if I taste **b** or anything else before the sun H4312
2Sa 6:19 Then he gave a loaf of **b**, a cake of dates H4312
2Sa 13: 6 and **make** some **special b** in my H4221+4223
2Sa 13: 8 **made** *the* **b** in his sight and baked it. H4221
2Sa 13: 9 Then she took the pan and served him the **b** NDT
2Sa 13:10 And Tamar took the **b** she had prepared H4223
2Sa 16: 1 loaded with two hundred **loaves of b**, H4312
2Sa 16: 2 the **b** and fruit are for the men to eat H4312
1Ki 7:48 table on which was the **b** *of* the Presence; H4312
1Ki 13: 8 nor would I eat **b** or drink water here. H4312
1Ki 13: 9 'You must not eat **b** or drink water or H4312
1Ki 13:16 can I eat **b** or drink water with you in H4312
1Ki 13:17 'You must not eat **b** or drink water there H4312
1Ki 13:18 so that he may eat **b** and drink water. H4312
1Ki 13:22 came back and ate **b** and drank water in H4312
1Ki 14: 3 Take ten **loaves of b** with you, some cakes H4312
1Ki 17: 6 The ravens brought him **b** and meat in the H4312
1Ki 17: 6 in the morning and **b** and meat in the H4312
1Ki 17:11 "And bring me, please, a piece of **b**." H4312
1Ki 17:12 "I don't have any **b**—only a handful of H5056
1Ki 17:13 make a small **loaf of b** for me from what H6314
1Ki 19: 6 by his head was *some* **b** baked over hot H6314
1Ki 22:27 give him nothing but **b** and water until I H4312
2Ki 4:42 God twenty **loaves of** barley **b** baked from H4312
2Ki 18:32 new wine, a land of **b** and vineyards, H4312
2Ki 23: 9 they ate **unleavened b** with their fellow H5174
1Ch 9:31 responsibility for baking the **offering b**. H2503
1Ch 9:32 every Sabbath the **b** set out on the table. H4312
1Ch 16: 3 Then he gave a loaf of **b**, a cake of dates H4312
1Ch 23:29 in charge of the **b** set out on the table, H4312
1Ch 28:16 of gold for each table for **consecrated b**; H5121
2Ch 2: 4 setting out the **consecrated b** regularly H5121
2Ch 4:19 on which was the **b** *of* the Presence; H4312
2Ch 8:13 the Festival of **Unleavened B**, the Festival H5174
2Ch 13:11 They set out the **b** on the ceremonially H4312
2Ch 18:26 give him nothing but **b** and water until I H4312
2Ch 29:18 table for **setting out the consecrated b**, H5121
2Ch 30:13 Festival of **Unleavened B** in the second H5174
2Ch 30:21 Festival of **Unleavened B** for seven days H5174
2Ch 35:17 Festival of **Unleavened B** for seven days H5174
Ezr 6:22 with joy the Festival of **Unleavened B**, H5174
Ne 9:15 you gave them **b** from heaven and in H4312
Ne 10:33 the **b** set out on the table; for the H4312
Job 23:12 words of his mouth more than my **daily b**. H2976
Job 31:17 if I have kept my **b** to myself, not sharing H7326
Ps 14: 4 devour my people as though eating **b**; H4312
Ps 37:25 forsaken or their children begging **b**. H4312
Ps 41: 9 one who shared my **b**, has turned against H4312
Ps 53: 4 devour my people as though eating **b**; H4312
Ps 78:20 abundantly, but can he also give us **b**? H4312
Ps 78:25 Human beings ate the **b** *of* angels; he H4312
Ps 80: 5 You have fed them with the **b** *of* tears H4312
Ps 104:15 and **b** that sustains their hearts. H4312
Ps 105:40 he fed them well with the **b** *of* heaven. H4312
Pr 4:17 They eat the **b** *of* wickedness and drink H4312
Pr 6:26 For a prostitute can be had for a loaf of **b** H4312
Pr 28:21 a person will do wrong for a piece of **b**. H4312
Pr 30: 8 riches, but give me only my **daily b**. H4312+2976
Pr 31:27 does not eat the **b** *of* idleness. H4312
Isa 28:28 Grain must be ground to make **b**; so one H4312
Isa 30:20 Lord gives you the **b** *of* adversity and the H4312
Isa 33:16 Their **b** will be supplied, and water will H4312
Isa 36:17 new wine, a land of **b** and vineyards. H4312
Isa 44:15 himself, he kindles a fire and bakes **b**. H4312
Isa 44:19 fuel; I even baked **b** over its coals, H4312
Isa 51:14 die in their dungeon, nor will they lack **b**. H4312
Isa 55: 2 Why spend money on *what* is not **b**, and H4312
Isa 55:10 given for the sower and **b** for the eater, H4312
Jer 37:21 given a loaf of **b** from the street of H4312
Jer 37:21 day until all the **b** in the city was gone. H4312
Jer 38: 9 when there is no longer any **b** in the city." H4312
Jer 42:14 hear the trumpet or be hungry for **b**, H4312
La 1:11 All her people groan as they search for **b** H4312
La 2:12 to their mothers, "Where is **b** and wine?" H1841
La 4: 4 the children beg for **b**, but no one gives it H4312
La 5: 6 to Egypt and Assyria to get enough **b**. H4312
La 5: 9 We get our **b** at the risk of our lives H4312
Eze 4: 9 jar and use them to make **b** for yourself. H4312
Eze 4:12 the food as you would a **loaf of** barley **b**; H6314
Eze 4:15 let you bake your **b** over cow dung instead H4312
Eze 13:19 a few handfuls of barley and scraps of **b**. H4312
Eze 45:21 which you shall eat **b made without yeast**. H5174
Hos 9: 4 will be to them like the **b** *of* mourners; H4312
Am 4: 5 Burn **leavened b** as a thank offering and H2809
Am 4: 6 in every city and lack of **b** in every town, H4312
Am 7:12 Earn your **b** there and do your H4312
Ob 7 those who eat your **b** will set a trap for H4312
Hag 2:12 that fold touches some **b** or stew H4312
Mt 4: 3 Son of God, tell these stones to become **b**." *G788*
Mt 4: 4 'Man shall not live on **b** alone, but on *G788*
Mt 6:11 Give us today our daily **b**. *G788*
Mt 7: 9 if your son asks *for* **b**, will give him a *G788*
Mt 12: 4 his companions ate the consecrated **b**— *G788*
Mt 14:17 here only five **loaves of b** and two fish," *G788*
Mt 15:26 to take the children's **b** and toss it to the *G788*
Mt 15:33 could we get enough **b** in this remote *G788*
Mt 16: 5 the lake, the disciples forgot to take **b**. *G788*
Mt 16: 7 "It is because we didn't bring *any* **b**." *G788*
Mt 16: 8 among yourselves about having no **b**? *G788*
Mt 16:11 that I was not talking to you about **b**? *G788*
Mt 16:12 them to guard against the yeast *used in* **b**, *G788*
Mt 26:17 first day *of* the **Festival of Unleavened B**, *G109*
Mt 26:26 Jesus took **b**, and when he had *G788*
Mk 2:26 house of God and ate the consecrated **b**, *G788*
Mk 6: 8 the journey except a staff—no **b**, no bag, *G788*
Mk 6:37 spend that much *on* **b** and give it to *G788*
Mk 6:43 basketfuls of broken pieces of **b** and fish. NDT
Mk 7:27 to take the children's **b** and toss it to the *G788*
Mk 8: 4 can anyone get enough **b** to feed them?" *G788*
Mk 8:14 The disciples had forgotten to bring **b** *G788*
Mk 8:16 "It is because we have no **b**. *G788*
Mk 8:17 "Why are you talking about having no **b** *G788*
Mk 14: 1 the **Festival of Unleavened B** were only *G109*
Mk 14:12 first day *of* the **Festival of Unleavened B**, *G109*
Mk 14:20 "one who dips **b** into the bowl with me. NDT
Mk 14:22 Jesus took **b**, and when he had *G788*
Lk 4: 3 Son of God, tell this stone to become **b**." *G788*
Lk 4: 4 'Man shall not live on **b** alone.'" *G788*
Lk 6: 4 taking the consecrated **b**, he ate what *G788*
Lk 7:33 came neither eating **b** nor drinking wine, *G788*
Lk 9: 3 no bag, no **b**, no money, no extra *G788*
Lk 9:13 have only five **loaves of b** and two fish— *G788*
Lk 11: 3 Give us each day our daily **b**. *G788*
Lk 11: 5 'Friend, lend me three **loaves of b**; *G788*
Lk 11: 8 up and give you the **b** because of friendship NDT
Lk 22: 1 Now the Festival *of* **Unleavened B**, called *G109*
Lk 22: 7 the day *of* **Unleavened B** on which the *G109*
Lk 22:19 And he took **b**, gave thanks and broke it *G788*
Lk 24:30 table with them, he took **b**, gave thanks, *G788*
Lk 24:35 recognized by them when he broke the **b**. *G788*
Jn 6: 5 "Where shall we buy **b** for these people to *G788*
Jn 6: 7 wages to buy enough **b** for each one to *G788*
Jn 6:23 people had eaten the **b** after the Lord had *G788*
Jn 6:31 'He gave them **b** from heaven to eat.'" *G788*
Jn 6:32 who has given you the **b** from heaven, *G788*
Jn 6:32 who gives you the true **b** from heaven. *G788*
Jn 6:33 For the **b** of God is the bread that comes *G788*
Jn 6:33 bread of God is the **b** that comes down from NDT
Jn 6:34 they said, "always give us this **b**. *G788*
Jn 6:35 declared, "I am the **b** of life. *G788*
Jn 6:41 "I am the **b** that came down from heaven." *G788*
Jn 6:48 I am the **b** of life. *G788*
Jn 6:50 But here is the **b** that comes down from *G788*
Jn 6:51 I am the living **b** that came down from *G788*
Jn 6:51 Whoever eats this **b** will live forever. *G788*
Jn 6:51 This **b** is my flesh, which I will give for the *G788*
Jn 6:58 This is the **b** that came down from heaven *G788*
Jn 6:58 whoever feeds on this **b** will live forever." *G788*
Jn 13:18 'He who shared my **b** has turned against *G788*
Jn 13:26 I will give this **piece of b** when I have *G6040*
Jn 13:26 dipping the **piece of b**, he gave it to *G6040*
Jn 13:27 As soon as Judas took the **b**, Satan *G6040*
Jn 13:30 As soon as Judas had taken the **b**, he *G6040*
Jn 21: 9 coals there with fish on it, and *some* **b**. *G788*
Jn 21:13 Jesus came, took the **b** and gave it to them *G788*
Ac 2:42 to the breaking *of* **b** and to prayer. *G788*
Ac 2:46 They broke **b** in their homes and ate *G788*
Ac 12: 3 during the **Festival of Unleavened B**. *G109*
Ac 20: 6 the **Festival of Unleavened B**, *G2465+3836+109*
Ac 20: 7 of the week we came together to break **b**. *G788*
Ac 20:11 went upstairs again and broke **b** and ate. *G788*
Ac 27:35 he took *some* **b** and gave thanks to God in *G788*
1Co 5: 8 not with the old **b** leavened with malice *G2434*
1Co 5: 8 with the **unleavened b** of sincerity and *G109*
1Co 10:16 And is not the **b** that we break a *G788*
1Co 11:23 on the night he was betrayed, took **b**, *G788*
1Co 11:26 whenever you eat this **b** and drink this cup, *G788*
1Co 11:27 whoever eats the **b** or drinks the cup of the *G788*
1Co 11:28 they eat of the **b** and drink from the cup *G788*
2Co 9:10 seed to the sower and **b** for food will also *G788*
Heb 9: 2 the table with its consecrated **b**; *G788*

BREADTH (5)

Ge 13:17 walk through the length and **b** of the land, H8145
1Ki 4:29 a **b** *of* understanding as measureless H8145
Isa 8: 8 wings will cover the **b** *of* your land, H8145
Isa 40:12 with the **b of** his **hand** marked off the H2455
Rev 20: 9 marched across the **b** of the earth and *G4424*

BREAK (94) [BREACH, BREACHES, BREACHING, BREAKERS, BREAKING, BREAKS, BROKE, BROKEN, BROKENNESS, LAWBREAKER, LAWBREAKERS]

Ge 19: 9 moved forward to **b down** the door. H8689
Ex 9: 9 festering boils will **b out** on people and H7255
Ex 12:46 *Do* not **b** any of the bones. H8689
Ex 13:13 if you do not redeem it, **b** its **neck**. H6904
Ex 19:22 the LORD *will* **b out** against them. H7287
Ex 19:24 to the LORD, or *he will* **b out** against them." H7287
Ex 23:24 and **b** their sacred stones **to pieces**. H8689+8689
Ex 34:13 **B down** their altars, smash their sacred H5997
Ex 34:20 if you do not redeem it, **b** its **neck**. H6904
Lev 11:33 will be unclean, and *you must* **b** the pot. H8689
Lev 26:19 *I will* **b down** your stubborn pride and H8689
Nu 9:12 any of it till morning or **b** any of its bones. H8689
Nu 24: 8 nations and **b** their bones **in pieces**; H1751
Nu 30: 2 *he must* not **b** his word but must do H2725
Dt 1: 7 **B camp** and advance into the hill country H7155
Dt 7: 5 **B down** their altars, smash their sacred H5997
Dt 12: 3 **B down** their altars, smash their sacred H5997
Dt 21: 4 the valley *they are to* **b** the heifer's **neck**. H6904
Dt 31:16 forsake me and **b** the covenant I made H7296
Jos 22:16 'How *could you* **b faith** with the H5085+5086
Jdg 2: 1 '*I will* never **b** my covenant with you, H7296
Jdg 2: 2 but *you shall* **b down** their altars. H5997
Jdg 5:12 Wake up, wake up, **b out** in song! Arise, H1819
Jdg 11:35 made a vow to the LORD that I cannot **b**." H8740
2Sa 5:20 He said, "As waters **b out**, the LORD has H7288
1Ki 15:19 Now **b** your treaty with Baasha king of H7296
2Ki 3:26 swordsmen to **b through** to the king of H1324
1Ch 14:11 "As waters **b out**, God has broken H7288
2Ch 16: 3 Now **b** your treaty with Baasha king of H7296
Ezr 9:14 *Shall we then* **b** your commands again H7296
Ne 4: 3 up on it *would* **b down** their wall of H7287
Job 24:16 In the dark, *thieves* **b into** houses, but by H3168
Job 30:13 *They* **b up** my road; they succeed in H5995
Ps 2: 3 "*Let us* **b** their chains and throw off their H5998
Ps 2: 9 *You will* **b** them with a rod of iron; you H8318
Ps 3: 7 on the jaw; **b** the teeth of the wicked. H8689
Ps 10:15 **B** the arm of the wicked man; call the H8689
Ps 27: 3 though war **b out** against me, even H7756
Ps 46: 5 God will help her at **b of day**. H7155+1332
Ps 58: 6 **B** the teeth in their mouths, O God; LORD H2238
Pr 25:15 a gentle tongue *can* **b** a bone. H8689
Isa 5: 5 be destroyed; *I will* **b down** its wall, and it H7287
Isa 11:15 *He will* **b** it **up** into seven streams so that H5782
Isa 14: 7 at rest and at peace; *they* **b** *into* singing. H7200
Isa 30:14 It will **b in pieces** like pottery, shattered so H8691
Isa 42: 3 A bruised reed *he will* not **b**, and a H8689
Isa 45: 2 *I will* **b down** gates of bronze and cut H8689
Isa 58: 6 set the oppressed free and **b** every yoke? H5998
Isa 58: 8 Then your light *will* **b forth** like the dawn H1324
Jer 4: 3 "**B up** your unplowed ground and do not H5774
Jer 14:21 your covenant with us and *do* not **b** it. H7296
Jer 15:12 "*Can a man* **b** iron—iron from the north H8318
Jer 19:10 "Then **b** the jar while those who go with H8689
Jer 21:12 my wrath *will* **b out** and burn like fire H3655
Jer 28: 2 '*I will* **b** the yoke of the king of Babylon H8689
Jer 28: 4 'for *I will* **b** the yoke of the king of Babylon H8689
Jer 28:11 'In the same way *I will* **b** the yoke of H8689
Jer 30: 8 '*I will* **b** the yoke off their necks and will H8689
Jer 33:20 'If *you can* **b** my covenant with the day H7296
Jer 49:35 I *will* **b** the bow of Elam, the H8689
Jer 50:26 **B open** her granaries; pile her up like H7337
Eze 17:15 *Will he* **b** the treaty and yet escape? H7296
Eze 17:22 *I will* **b off** a tender sprig from its topmost H7786
Eze 26:12 *they will* **b down** your walls and demolish H2238
Eze 27:26 east wind *will* **b** you **to pieces** far out at H8689
Eze 30:18 at Tahpanhes when I **b** the yoke of Egypt; H8689
Eze 30:22 *I will* **b** both his arms, the good arm as H8689
Eze 30:24 his hand, but *I will* **b** the arms of Pharaoh H8689
Eze 34:27 when I **b** the bars of their yoke and rescue H8689
Da 2:40 so it will crush and **b** all the others. A10671
Hos 1: 5 In that day *I will* **b** Israel's bow in the H8689
Hos 4: 2 adultery; *they* **b all bounds**, and H7287
Hos 7: 1 thieves **b into** houses, bandits rob H995
Hos 10:11 and Jacob *must* **b up the ground**. H8440
Hos 10:12 and **b up** your unplowed ground H5774
Am 1: 5 *I will* **b down** the gate of Damascus; I will H8689
Jnh 1: 4 arose that the ship threatened to **b up**. H8689
Mic 2:13 *they will* **b** through the gate and go out. H7287
Mic 3: 3 off their skin and **b** their bones **in pieces**; H7200
Mic 4:13 and *you will* **b to pieces** many nations." H1990
Na 1:13 Now *I will* **b** their yoke from your neck H8689
Mt 5:33 long ago, '*Do* not **b** *your* **oath**, but fulfill *G2155*
Mt 6:19 destroy, and where thieves **b in** and steal. *G1482*
Mt 6:20 where thieves *do* not **b in** and steal. *G1482*
Mt 12:20 A bruised reed *he will* not **b**, and a *G2862*
Mt 15: 2 "Why *do* your disciples **b** the tradition of *G4124*

Mt 15: 3 "And why *do* you **b** the command of God *G4124*
Lk 5: 6 number of fish that their nets *began to* **b**. *G1396*
Jn 19:33 was already dead, *they did* not **b** his legs. *G2862*
Ac 20: 7 of the week we came together *to* **b** bread. *G3089*
Ro 2:25 the law, but if *you* **b** the law, you *G4127+1639*
1Co 10:16 not the bread that *we* **b** a participation in *G3089*
Heb 2:14 his death *he might* **b the power** of him *G2934*
Rev 5: 2 "Who is worthy *to* **b** the seals and open *G3395*

BREAKERS (3) [BREAK]

Ps 42: 7 all your waves and **b** have swept over me. H1644
Ps 93: 4 mightier than the **b** *of* the sea—the LORD H5403
Jnh 2: 3 all your waves and **b** swept over me. H5403

BREAKFAST (1)

Jn 21:12 to them, "Come and **have b**." None of the *G753*

BREAKING (24) [BREAK]

Ex 22: 2 "If a thief is caught **b in** at night and is H4747
Ex 32:19 **b** them **to pieces** at the foot of the H8689
Lev 13:42 is a defiling disease **b out** on his head H7255
Lev 26:25 on you to avenge the **b** of the covenant. NDT
Lev 26:44 completely, **b** my covenant with them. H7296
Dt 9:17 **b** them **to pieces** before your eyes. H8689
Dt 31:20 rejecting me and **b** my covenant. H7296
Jos 9:20 will not fall on us for **b** the oath we swore to NDT
Jdg 21:22 will not be guilty of **b** your oath because you NDT
1Sa 25:10 Many servants *are* **b away** from their H7287
Isa 28:24 *Does he keep on* **b up** and working the H7337
Isa 58:13 keep your feet from **b** the Sabbath and from NDT
Jer 2:34 though you did not catch them **b in**. H4747
Eze 16:59 have despised my oath by **b** the covenant. H7296
Eze 17:18 He despised the oath by **b** the covenant H7296
Eze 17:19 despising my oath and **b** my covenant. H7296
Joel 2: 8 plunge through defenses without **b ranks**. H1298
Zec 11:14 **b** the family bond between Judah and H7296
Jn 5:18 not only *was he* **b** the Sabbath, but *G3395*
Ac 2:42 *to* the **b** of bread and to prayer. *G3082*
Ac 21:13 "Why are you weeping and **b** my heart? *G5316*
Ro 2:23 do you dishonor God by **b** the law? *G4126*
Ro 5:14 those who did not sin *by* **b a command**, *G4126*
Jas 2:10 at just one point is guilty of **b** all of it. NDT

BREAKS (20) [BREAK]

Ex 1:10 numerous and, if war **b out**, will join our H7925
Ex 22: 6 "If a fire **b out** and spreads into H3655
Lev 13:12 the disease **b out all over** their skin H7255+7255
Jdg 6:31 himself when *someone* **b down** his altar." H5997
Ps 29: 5 The voice of the LORD **b** the cedars; the H8689
Ps 29: 5 the LORD **b in pieces** the cedars of H8689
Ps 46: 9 *He* **b** the bow and shatters the spear; he H8689
Ps 76:12 *He* **b** the spirit of rulers; he is feared by H1306
Ps 107:16 for *he* **b down** gates of bronze and cuts H8689
Ps 141: 7 "As one plows and **b up** the earth, so our H1324
Pr 17:14 so drop the matter before a dispute **b out**. H1679
Ecc 10: 8 *whoever* **b through** a wall may be bitten H7287
SS 2:17 Until the day **b** and the shadows flee, turn H7031
SS 4: 6 Until the day **b** and the shadows flee, H7031
Isa 66: 3 a lamb is like *one who* **b** a dog's **neck**; H6904
Jer 23:29 like a hammer *that* **b** a rock **in pieces**? H7207
Da 2:40 for iron **b** and smashes everything A10182
Da 2:40 as iron **b** things **to pieces**, so it will A10671
Mic 2:13 The *One who* **b open** the way will go up H7287
1Jn 3: 4 Everyone who sins **b the law**; in fact *G490+4472*

BREAST (22) [BREASTPIECE, BREASTPLATE, BREASTPLATES, BREASTS]

Ge 49:25 blessings of the **b** and womb. H8716
Ex 29:26 After you take the **b** of the ram for Aaron's H2601
Ex 29:27 the **b** that was waved and the thigh that H2601
Lev 7:30 together with the **b**, and wave the breast H2601
Lev 7:30 wave the **b** before the LORD as a wave H2601
Lev 7:31 the **b** belongs to Aaron and his sons. H2601
Lev 7:34 I have taken the **b** that is waved and the H2601
Lev 8:29 Moses also took the **b**, which was his H2601
Lev 10:14 may eat the **b** that was waved and H2601
Lev 10:15 presented and the **b** that was waved must H2601
Nu 6:20 together with the **b** that was waved and H2601
Nu 18:18 just as the **b** *of* the wave offering and the H2601
1Ki 3:20 She put him by her **b** and put her dead H2668
1Ki 3:20 her breast and put her dead son by my **b**. H2668
Job 24: 9 fatherless child is snatched from the **b**; H8718
Ps 22: 9 me trust in you, even at my mother's **b**. H8716
Isa 28: 9 their milk, to those just taken from the **b**? H8716
Isa 49:15 forget the **baby at** her **b** and have no H6403
Jer 31:19 after I came to understand, I beat my **b**. H3751
Eze 21:12 with my people. Therefore beat your **b**. H3751
Joel 2:16 the children, those nursing at the **b**. H8716
Lk 18:13 to heaven, but beat his **b** and said, 'God, *G5111*

BREASTPIECE (23) [BREAST]

Ex 25: 7 gems to be mounted on the ephod and **b**. H3136
Ex 28: 4 a **b**, an ephod, a robe, a woven tunic, H3136
Ex 28:15 "Fashion a **b** *for* making decisions—the H3136
Ex 28:22 "For the **b** make braided chains of pure H3136
Ex 28:23 it and fasten them to two corners of the **b**. H3136
Ex 28:24 chains to the rings at the corners of the **b**, H3136
Ex 28:26 two corners of the **b** on the inside edge H3136
Ex 28:28 The rings of the **b** are to be tied to the H3136
Ex 28:28 so that the **b** will not swing out from the H3136
Ex 28:29 over his heart on the **b** *of* decision as a H3136
Ex 28:30 put the Urim and the Thummim in the **b**, H3136
Ex 29: 5 of the ephod, the ephod itself and the **b**. H3136
Ex 35: 9 gems to be mounted on the ephod and **b**. H3136
Ex 35:27 gems to be mounted on the ephod and **b**. H3136
Ex 39: 8 They fashioned the **b**—the work of a H3136
Ex 39:15 For the **b** they made braided chains of H3136
Ex 39:16 the rings to two of the corners of the **b**. H3136
Ex 39:17 chains to the rings at the corners of the **b**, H3136
Ex 39:19 two corners of the **b** on the inside edge H3136
Ex 39:21 tied the rings of the **b** to the rings of the H3136
Ex 39:21 so that the **b** would not swing out H3136
Lev 8: 8 He placed the **b** on him and put the Urim H3136
Lev 8: 8 put the Urim and Thummim in the **b**. H3136

BREASTPLATE (4) [BREAST]

2Ch 18:33 Israel between the **b** and the scale armor. H1817
Isa 59:17 He put on righteousness as his **b**, and the H9234
Eph 6:14 with the **b** of righteousness in place, *G2606*
1Th 5: 8 putting on faith and love *as* a **b**, and the *G2606*

BREASTPLATES (3) [BREAST]

Rev 9: 9 They had **b** like breastplates of iron, and *G2606*
Rev 9: 9 They had breastplates like **b** of iron, and *G2606*
Rev 9:17 Their **b** were fiery red, dark blue, and *G2606*

BREASTS (25) [BREAST]

Lev 9:20 these they laid on the **b**, and then Aaron H2601
Lev 9:21 Aaron waved the **b** and the right thigh H2601
Job 3:12 to receive me and **b** that I might be H8716
Pr 5:19 may her **b** satisfy you always H1843
SS 1:13 a sachet of myrrh resting between my **b**. H8716
SS 4: 5 Your **b** are like two fawns, like twin fawns H8716
SS 7: 3 Your **b** are like two fawns, like twin fawns H8716
SS 7: 7 the palm, and your **b** like clusters of fruit. H8716
SS 7: 8 May your **b** be like clusters of grapes on H8716
SS 8: 1 who was nursed at my mother's **b**! H8716
SS 8: 8 a little sister, and her **b** are not yet grown. H8716
SS 8:10 I am a wall, and my **b** are like towers H8716
Isa 32:12 Beat your **b** for the pleasant fields, for the H8716
Isa 60:16 milk of nations and be nursed at royal **b**. H8718
Isa 66:11 be satisfied at her comforting **b**; H8718
La 4: 3 jackals offer their **b** to nurse their young, H8716
Eze 16: 7 Your **b** had formed and your hair had H8716
Eze 23: 3 In that land their **b** were fondled and their H8716
Eze 23:21 was caressed and your young **b** fondled. H8716
Eze 23:34 on its pieces—and you will tear your **b**. H8716
Hos 2: 2 the unfaithfulness from between her **b**. H8716
Hos 9:14 wombs that miscarry and **b** that are dry. H8716
Na 2: 7 moan like doves and beat on their **b**. H4222
Lk 23:29 never bore and the **b** that never nursed! *G3466*
Lk 23:48 they beat their **b** and went away. *G5111*

BREATH (61) [BREATHE, BREATHED, BREATHES, BREATHING, GOD-BREATHED]

Ge 1:30 everything that has the **b** *of* life in it—I H5883
Ge 2: 7 breathed into his nostrils the **b** *of* life, H5972
Ge 6:17 every creature that has the **b** *of* life in it. H8120
Ge 7:15 that have the **b** *of* life in them came to H8120
Ge 7:22 land that had the **b** *of* life in its H5972+8120
Ex 15:10 But you blew with your **b**, and the sea H8120
Nu 16:22 the God who gives **b** to all living things H8120
Nu 27:16 the God who gives **b** to all living things H8120
2Sa 22:16 the LORD, at the blast of **b** *from* his nostrils. H8120
Job 4: 9 At the **b** *of* God they perish; at the blast of H5972
Job 7: 7 that my life is but a **b**; my eyes will never H8120
Job 9:18 let me catch my **b** but would overwhelm H8120
Job 12:10 every creature and the **b** *of* all mankind. H8120
Job 15:30 the **b** *of* God's mouth will carry him H8120
Job 19:17 My **b** is offensive to my wife; I am H8120
Job 26:13 By his **b** the skies became fair; his hand H8120
Job 27: 3 life within me, the **b** *of* God in my nostrils H8120
Job 32: 8 in a person, the **b** *of* the Almighty, that H5972
Job 33: 4 the **b** *of* the Almighty gives me life. H5972
Job 34:14 he withdrew his spirit and **b**, H5972
Job 37:10 The **b** *of* God produces ice, and the broad H5972
Job 41:21 Its **b** sets coals ablaze, and flames dart H5883
Ps 18:15 at the blast of **b** *from* your nostrils. H8120
Ps 33: 6 their starry host by the **b** *of* his mouth. H8120
Ps 39: 5 Everyone is but a **b**, even those who seem H2039
Ps 39:11 like a moth—surely everyone is but a **b**. H2039
Ps 62: 9 Surely the lowborn are *but a* **b**, the H2039
Ps 62: 9 are nothing; together they are only a **b**. H2039
Ps 104:29 when you take away their **b**, they die and H8120
Ps 135:17 nor is there **b** in their mouths. H8120
Ps 144: 4 They are like a **b**; their days are like a H2039
Ps 150: 6 Let everything that has **b** praise the LORD H5972
Ecc 3:19 All have the same **b**; humans have no H8120
SS 7: 8 the fragrance of your **b** like apples, H678
Isa 2:22 who have but a **b** in their nostrils. H5972
Isa 11: 4 with the **b** *of* his lips he will slay the H8120
Isa 25: 4 For the **b** *of* the ruthless is like a storm H8120
Isa 30:28 His **b** is like a rushing torrent, rising up to H8120
Isa 30:33 of fire and wood; the **b** *of* the LORD, like a H5972
Isa 33:11 your **b** is a fire that consumes you. H8120
Isa 40: 7 because the **b** *of* the LORD blows on them. H8120
Isa 42: 5 who gives **b** to its people, and life H5972
Isa 57:13 them off, a **mere b** will blow them away. H2039
Isa 59:19 flood that the **b** *of* the LORD drives along H8120
Jer 4:31 the cry of Daughter Zion **gasping for b** H3640
Jer 10:14 are a fraud; they have no **b** in them. H8120
Jer 38:16 who has given us **b**, I will neither kill H5883
Jer 51:17 are a fraud; they have no **b** in them. H8120
La 4:20 our very **life b**, was caught in H8120+678
Eze 37: 5 I will make **b** enter you, and you will H8120
Eze 37: 6 with skin; I will put **b** in you, and you will H8120
Eze 37: 8 but there was no **b** in them. H8120
Eze 37: 9 said to me, "Prophesy to the **b**; prophesy, H8120
Eze 37: 9 **b**, from the four winds and breathe H8120
Eze 37:10 commanded me, and **b** entered them H8120
Hab 2:19 with gold and silver; there is no **b** in it." H8120
Ac 17:25 everyone life and **b** and everything else. *G4466*
2Co 1:17 so that *in the same b* I **say** both "Yes, AIT
2Th 2: 8 will overthrow *with* the **b** of his mouth *G4460*
Rev 11:11 a half days the **b** of life from God *G4460*
Rev 13:15 given power to give **b** to the image of the *G4460*

BREATHE (4) [BREATH]

Jer 15: 9 will grow faint and **b** her **last**. H5870+5883
Eze 21:31 my wrath on you and **b out** my fiery anger H7032
Eze 37: 9 from the four winds and **b** into these slain, H5870
Da 10:17 is gone and I **can hardly b**." H5972+4202+8636

BREATHED (13) [BREATH]

Ge 2: 7 of the ground and **b** into his nostrils the H5870
Ge 25: 8 Then Abraham **b his last** and died at a H1588
Ge 25:17 *He* **b his last** and died, and he was H1588
Ge 35:18 As she **b her last**—for she was H5883+3655
Ge 35:29 Then he **b his last** and died and was H1588
Ge 49:33 **b** *his* **last** and was gathered to his people. H1588
Jos 10:40 He totally destroyed all who **b**, just as the H5972
Jos 11:11 not sparing anyone that **b**, and he burned H5972
Jos 11:14 not sparing anyone that **b**. H5972
1Ki 15:29 He did not leave Jeroboam anyone that **b**, H5972
Mk 15:37 With a loud cry, Jesus **b** *his* **last**. *G1743*
Lk 23:46 When he had said this, *he* **b** *his* **last**. *G1743*
Jn 20:22 And with that *he* **b on** them and said *G1874*

BREATHES (2) [BREATH]

Dt 20:16 do not leave alive anything that **b**. H5972
Job 14:10 is laid low; he **b his last** and is no more. H1588

BREATHING (2) [BREATH]

1Ki 17:17 worse and worse, and finally stopped **b**. H5972
Ac 9: 1 Saul *was* still **b out** murderous threats *G1863*

BRED (1) [BREED]

Est 8:10 horses **especially b** for the H1201+2021+8247

BREECHES (KJV) UNDERGARMENTS

BREED (1) [BRED, BREEDING]

Job 21:10 Their bulls never fail *to* **b**; their cows calve H6296

BREEDING (1) [BREED]

Ge 31:10 "In **b** season I once had a H3501+2021+7366

BREEZE (1) [BREEZES]

Ps 78:39 a passing **b** that does not return. H8120

BREEZES (1) [BREEZE]

Ps 147:18 he stirs up his **b**, and the waters flow. H8120

BRETHREN (KJV) BROTHERS (AND SISTERS)

BRIBE (16) [BRIBED, BRIBERY, BRIBES, BRIBING]

Ex 23: 8 "Do not accept a **b**, for a bribe blinds H8816
Ex 23: 8 a **b** blinds those who see and twists H8816
Dt 16:19 Do not accept a **b**, for a bribe blinds the H8816
Dt 16:19 a **b** blinds the eyes of the wise and H8816
Dt 27:25 who accepts a **b** to kill an innocent H8816
1Sa 12: 3 have I accepted a **b** to make me shut my H4111
Job 36:18 do not let a large **b** turn you aside. H4111
Ps 15: 5 does not accept a **b** against the innocent. H8816
Ps 17: 4 Though people tried to **b** me, I have kept H7190
Pr 6:35 he will refuse a **b**, however great it is. H8816
Pr 17: 8 A **b** is seen as a charm by the one who H8816
Pr 21:14 a **b** concealed in the cloak pacifies H8816
Ecc 7: 7 into a fool, and a **b** corrupts the heart. H5510
Isa 5:23 who acquit the guilty for a **b**, but deny H8816
Mic 3:11 Her leaders judge for a **b**, her priests H8816
Ac 24:26 was hoping that Paul would offer him a **b**, *G5975*

BRIBED (1) [BRIBE]

Ezr 4: 5 *They* **b** officials to work against them and H6128

BRIBERY (1) [BRIBE]

2Ch 19: 7 is no injustice or partiality or **b**." H5228+8816

BRIBES (12) [BRIBE]

Dt 10:17 who shows no partiality and accepts no **b**. H8816
1Sa 8: 3 gain and accepted **b** and perverted justice H8816
Job 15:34 consume the tents of **those who love b**. H8816
Ps 26:10 schemes, whose right hands are full of **b**. H8816
Pr 15:27 the one who hates **b** will live. H5510
Pr 17:23 The wicked accept **b** in secret to pervert H8816
Pr 29: 4 those who are greedy for **b** tear it down. H9556
Isa 1:23 they all love **b** and chase after gifts. H8816
Isa 33:15 keep their hands from accepting **b**, H8816
Eze 22:12 are people who accept **b** to shed blood; H8816
Am 5:12 innocent and take **b** and deprive the poor H4111
Mic 7: 3 the judge accepts **b**, the powerful dictate H8936

BRIBING (1) [BRIBE]

Eze 16:33 **b** them to come to you from everywhere H8815

BRICK (4) [BRICKMAKING, BRICKS, BRICKWORK]

Ge 11: 3 They used **b** instead of stone, and tar H4246
Ex 1:14 with harsh labor in **b** and mortar and with H4246
Isa 65: 3 burning incense on **altars of b**; H4246

Jer 43: 9 in clay in the **b pavement** at the entrance H4861

BRICKMAKING (1) [BRICK]

2Sa 12:31 axes, and he made them work at **b**. H4861

BRICKS (8) [BRICK]

Ge 11: 3 *let's* **make b** and bake them H4236+4246
Ex 5: 7 the people with straw for **making b**; H4236+4246
Ex 5: 8 to make the same number of **b** as before; H4246
Ex 5:14 met your quota of **b** yesterday or today, H4236
Ex 5:16 given no straw, yet we are told, 'Make **b**! H4246
Ex 5:18 you must produce your full quota of **b**." H4246
Ex 5:19 the number of **b** *required of* you for each H4246
Isa 9:10 "The **b** have fallen down, but we will H4246

BRICKWORK (1) [BRICK]

Na 3:14 the clay, tread the mortar, repair the **b**! H4861

BRIDAL (1) [BRIDE]

Ge 29:27 Finish this daughter's **b week**; then we will H8651

BRIDE (25) [BRIDAL, BRIDE-PRICE]

Ge 34:12 Make the **price for the b** and the gift I am H4558
1Sa 18:25 wants no other **price for** *the* **b** than a H4558
Ps 45: 9 right hand is the **royal b** in gold of Ophir. H8712
SS 4: 8 from Lebanon, my **b**, come with me from H3987
SS 4: 9 my sister, my **b**; you have stolen my heart H3987
SS 4:10 delightful is your love, my sister, my **b**! H3987
SS 4:11 the honeycomb, my **b**; milk and honey are H3987
SS 4:12 my sister, my **b**; you are a spring enclosed, H3987
SS 5: 1 my sister, my **b**; I have gathered my myrrh H3987
Isa 49:18 ornaments; you will put them on, like a **b**. H3987
Isa 61:10 as a **b** adorns herself with her jewels. H3987
Isa 62: 5 as a bridegroom rejoices over his **b**, so H3987
Jer 2: 2 how as a **b** you loved me and followed H3994
Jer 2:32 her jewelry, a **b** her wedding ornaments? H3987
Jer 7:34 to the voices of **b** and bridegroom in H3987
Jer 16: 9 to the voices of **b** and bridegroom in H3987
Jer 25:10 the voices of **b** and bridegroom, the H3987
Jer 33:11 the voices of **b** and bridegroom, and the H3987
Joel 2:16 leave his room and the **b** her chamber. H3987
Jn 3:29 The **b** belongs to the bridegroom. *G3811*
Rev 18:23 of bridegroom and **b** will never be heard *G3811*
Rev 19: 7 and his **b** has made herself ready. *G1222*
Rev 21: 2 prepared as a **b** beautifully dressed for *G3811*
Rev 21: 9 I will show you the **b**, the wife of the *G3811*
Rev 22:17 The Spirit and the **b** say, "Come!" And let *G3811*

BRIDE-PRICE (2) [BRIDE]

Ex 22:16 *he* **must pay** the **b**, and she H4555+4555
Ex 22:17 he must still pay the **b** *for* virgins. H4558

BRIDECHAMBER (KJV) BRIDEGROOM

BRIDEGROOM (24) [BRIDEGROOM'S]

Ex 4:25 "Surely you are a **b** *of* blood to me," H3163
Ex 4:26 At that time she said "**b** *of* blood, H3163
Ps 19: 5 It is like a **b** coming out of his chamber H3163
Isa 61:10 as a **b** adorns his head like a priest H3163
Isa 62: 5 marry you; as a **b** rejoices over his bride H3163
Jer 7:34 voices of bride and **b** in the towns of H3163
Jer 16: 9 to the voices of bride and **b** in this place. H3163
Jer 25:10 the voices of bride and **b**, the sound of H3163
Jer 33:11 the voices of bride and **b**, and the voices H3163
Joel 2:16 Let the **b** leave his room and the bride her H3163
Mt 9:15 can the guests *of* the **b** mourn while he is *G3813*
Mt 9:15 will come when the **b** will be taken from *G3812*
Mt 25: 1 their lamps and went out to meet the **b**. *G3812*
Mt 25: 5 The **b** was a long time in coming, and *G3812*
Mt 25: 6 'Here's the **b**! Come out to meet him *G3812*
Mt 25:10 on their way to buy the oil, the **b** arrived. *G3812*
Mk 2:19 can the guests *of* the **b** fast while he is *G3813*
Mk 2:20 will come when the **b** will be taken from *G3812*
Lk 5:34 make the friends *of* the **b** fast while he is *G3813*
Lk 5:35 will come when the **b** will be taken from *G3812*
Jn 2: 9 Then he called the **b** aside *G3812*
Jn 3:29 The bride belongs to the **b**. The friend *G3812*
Jn 3:29 The friend who *attends* the **b** waits and *G3812*
Rev 18:23 The voice *of* **b** and bride will never be *G3812*

BRIDEGROOM'S (1) [BRIDEGROOM]

Jn 3:29 is full of joy when he hears the **b** voice. *G3812*

BRIDLE (2) [BRIDLES]

Ps 32: 9 by bit and **b** or they will not come H8270+6344
Pr 26: 3 the horse, a **b** for the donkey, and a H5496

BRIDLES (1) [BRIDLE]

Rev 14:20 as high as the horses' **b** for a distance of *G5903*

BRIEF (3) [BRIEFLY]

Ezr 9: 8 "But now, for a **b** moment, the LORD our H5071
Job 20: 5 that the mirth of the wicked is **b** H4946+7940
Isa 54: 7 "For a **b** moment I abandoned you, but H7785

BRIEFLY (4) [BRIEF]

Ac 24: 4 that you be kind enough to hear us **b**. *G5339*
Eph 3: 3 as I have already written **b**. *G1877+3900*
Heb 13:22 in fact I have written to you **quite b**. *G1328+1099*
1Pe 5:12 I have written to you **b** *G1328+3900*

BRIER (1) [BRIERS]

Mic 7: 4 The best of them is like a **b**, the most H2537

BRIERS (16) [BRIER]

Jdg 8: 7 tear your flesh with desert thorns and **b**." H1402
Jdg 8:16 punishing them with desert thorns and **b**. H1402
Job 31:40 then let **b** come up instead of wheat and H2560
Isa 5: 6 **b** and thorns will grow there. H9031
Isa 7:23 shekels, there will be only **b** and thorns. H9031
Isa 7:24 land will be covered with **b** and thorns. H9031
Isa 7:25 go there for fear of the **b** and thorns; H9031
Isa 9:18 it consumes **b** and thorns, it sets H9031
Isa 10:17 burn and consume his thorns and his **b**. H9031
Isa 27: 4 If only there were **b** and thorns H9031
Isa 32:13 a land overgrown with thorns and **b**—yes, H9031
Isa 55:13 instead of **b** the myrtle will grow. H6252
Eze 2: 6 though **b** and thorns are all around you H6235
Eze 28:24 who are painful **b** and sharp thorns. H6141
Hos 9: 6 treasures of silver will be taken over by **b**, H7853
Lk 6:44 figs from thornbushes, or grapes from **b**. *G1003*

BRIGANDINE, BRIGANDINES (KJV) ARMOR

BRIGHT (11) [BRIGHTENED, BRIGHTENS, BRIGHTER, BRIGHTLY, BRIGHTNESS]

Ex 24:10 of lapis lazuli, as **b blue** as the sky. H3198[S]
Job 25: 5 If even the moon *is* not **b** and the stars are H183
Job 37:21 **b** as it is in the skies after the wind has H986
SS 6:10 fair as the moon, **b** as the sun, majestic H1338
Eze 1:13 the creatures; it was **b**, and lightning H5586
Eze 8: 2 appearance was as **b** as glowing metal. H2303
Mt 17: 5 still speaking, a **b** cloud covered them *G5893*
Lk 9:29 his clothes became as **b** as a flash of *G3328*
Ac 22: 6 suddenly a **b** light from heaven flashed *G2653*
Rev 19: 8 Fine linen, **b** and clean, was given her to *G3287*
Rev 22:16 of David, and the **b** Morning Star. *G3287*

BRIGHTENED (2) [BRIGHT]

1Sa 14:27 his hand to his mouth, and his eyes **b**. H239
1Sa 14:29 See how my eyes **b** when I tasted a little of H239

BRIGHTENS (2) [BRIGHT]

Pr 16:15 When a king's face **b**, it means life; his H240
Ecc 8: 1 A person's wisdom **b** their face and H239

BRIGHTER (5) [BRIGHT]

Job 11:17 Life *will be* **b** than noonday, and darkness H7756
Pr 4:18 **shining ever b** till the full H2143+2256+239
Isa 30:26 the sunlight will be **seven** *times* **b**, like AIT
La 4: 7 Their princes *were* **b** than snow and H2348
Ac 26:13 a light from heaven, **b** than the sun *G3288*

BRIGHTLY (1) [BRIGHT]

Pr 13: 9 The light of the righteous **shines b**, but H8523

BRIGHTNESS (8) [BRIGHT]

2Sa 22:13 Out of the **b** *of* his presence bolts of H5586
2Sa 23: 4 like the **b** after rain that brings grass from H5586
Ps 18:12 Out of the **b** *of* his presence clouds H5586
Isa 59: 9 all is darkness; for **b**, but we walk in deep H5588
Isa 60: 3 and kings to the **b** *of* your dawn. H5586
Isa 60:19 will the **b** *of* the moon shine on you H5586
Da 12: 3 wise will shine like the **b** *of* the heavens, H2303
Am 5:20 not light—pitch-dark, without a **ray of b**? H5586

BRILLIANCE (3) [BRILLIANT]

Ac 22:11 because the **b** of the light had blinded *G1518*
Rev 1:16 face was like the sun shining in *all* its **b**. *G1539*
Rev 21:11 its **b** was like that of a very precious *G5891*

BRILLIANT (3) [BRILLIANCE]

Ecc 9:11 wise or wealth to the **b** or favor to the H1067
Eze 1: 4 lightning and surrounded by **b light**. H5586
Eze 1:27 like fire; and **b light** surrounded him. H5586

BRIM (2)

Pr 3:10 your vats *will* **b over** *with* new wine. H7287
Jn 2: 7 with water"; so they filled them to the **b**. *G539*

BRIMSTONE (KJV) (BURNING) SULFUR

BRING (723) [BRINGING, BRINGS, BROUGHT]

Ge 6:17 I *am going to* **b** floodwaters on the earth to H995
Ge 6:19 *You are to* **b** into the ark two of all living H995
Ge 8:17 **B out** every kind of living creature that is H3655
Ge 9:14 Whenever I **b clouds** over the earth H6725+6727
Ge 15: 9 LORD said to him, "**B** me a heifer, a goat H4374
Ge 18:19 so that the LORD *will* **b about** for Abraham H995
Ge 19: 5 **B** them **out** to us so that we can have sex H3655
Ge 19: 8 *Let me* **b** them **out** to you, and you can do H3655
Ge 27: 4 of tasty food I like and **b** it to me to eat, H995
Ge 27: 5 open country to hunt game and **b** it **back**, H995
Ge 27: 7 '**B** me some game and prepare me some H995
Ge 27: 9 to the flock and **b** me two choice young H4374
Ge 27:12 tricking him and *would* **b down** a curse on H995
Ge 27:25 "My son, **b** me some of your game to eat H5602
Ge 28:15 and *I will* **b** you **back** to this land. H8740
Ge 31:39 *I did* not **b** you animals torn by wild beasts H995
Ge 34:12 bride and the gift **I** *am to* **b** as great as you AIT
Ge 37:14 with the flocks, and **b** word **back** *to* me." H8740
Ge 38:24 "**B** her **out** and have her burned to death!" H3655
Ge 42:20 But *you must* **b** your youngest brother to me H995
Ge 42:34 But **b** your youngest brother to me so I will H995
Ge 42:37 sons to death if *I do* not **b** him **back** to you. H995
Ge 42:37 him to my care, and I *will* **b** him **back**." H8740
Ge 42:38 *you will* **b** my gray head **down** to the H3718
Ge 43: 6 "Why *did you* **b** *this* **trouble** on me by H8317
Ge 43: 7 he would say, '**B** your brother **down** here'?" H3718
Ge 43: 9 If *I do* not **b** him **back** to you and set him H995
Ge 44:21 '**B** him **down** to me so I can see him for H3718
Ge 44:29 *you will* **b** my gray head **down** to the H3718
Ge 44:31 *will* **b** the gray head of our father **down** to H3718
Ge 44:32 'If *I do* not **b** him **back** to you, I will H995
Ge 45:13 And **b** my father **down** here quickly." H3718
Ge 45:18 **b** your father and your families back to H4374
Ge 46: 4 and I *will* **surely b** you **back** again. H6590+6590
Ge 47:16 "Then **b** your livestock," said Joseph. H2035
Ge 48: 9 "**B** them to me so I may bless them." H4374
Ex 3: 8 Egyptians and to **b** them **up** out of that H6590
Ex 3:10 *to* **b** my people the Israelites **out** of H3655
Ex 3:11 Pharaoh and **b** the Israelites **out** of Egypt?" H3655
Ex 3:17 I have promised *to* **b** you **up** out of your H6590
Ex 6: 6 and *I will* **b** you **out** from under the yoke H3655
Ex 6: 8 And *I will* **b** you to the land I swore with H995
Ex 6:13 them to **b** the Israelites **out** of Egypt. H3655
Ex 6:26 "**B** the Israelites **out** of Egypt by their H3655
Ex 7: 4 acts of judgment *I will* **b out** my divisions, H3655
Ex 7: 5 Egypt and **b** the Israelites **out** of it. H3655
Ex 9: 3 hand of the LORD *will* **b** a terrible plague H2118
Ex 9:19 *to* **b** your livestock and everything you have in the field **to a place of shelter** H6395
Ex 9:20 word of the LORD **hurried to b** their slaves H5674
Ex 10: 4 I *will* **b** locusts into your country tomorrow. H995
Ex 11: 1 "*I will* **b** one more plague on Pharaoh and H995
Ex 12:12 and *I will* **b** judgment on all the gods of H6913
Ex 12:42 vigil that night to **b** them **out** of Egypt, H3655
Ex 14:13 the deliverance the LORD *will* **b** you today. H6913
Ex 15:17 *You will* **b** them *in* and plant them on the H995
Ex 15:26 *I will* not **b** on you any of the diseases I H8492
Ex 16: 5 day they are to prepare what *they* **b in**, H995
Ex 17: 3 "Why *did you* **b** us **up** out of Egypt to H6590
Ex 18:19 before God and **b** their disputes to him. H995
Ex 18:22 *have them* **b** every difficult case to you H995
Ex 19:24 "Go down and *b* Aaron **up** with you. AIT
Ex 22: 9 both parties *are to* **b** their cases before the H995
Ex 22:13 the neighbor *shall* **b in** the remains as H995
Ex 23:19 "**B** the best of the firstfruits of your soil *to* H995
Ex 23:20 along the way and to **b** you to the place I H995
Ex 23:23 go ahead of you and **b** you into the land of H995
Ex 25: 2 "Tell the Israelites *to* **b** me an offering H4374
Ex 27:20 the Israelites *to* **b** you clear oil of H4374
Ex 29: 4 Then **b** Aaron and his sons to the entrance H7928
Ex 29: 8 **B** his sons and dress them in tunics H7928
Ex 29:10 "**B** the bull to the front of the tent of H7928
Ex 32: 2 daughters are wearing, and **b** them to me." H995
Ex 32:12 **relent and do not b** disaster on your H5714
Ex 32:14 relented and did not **b** on his people the H6913
Ex 34:26 "**B** the best of the firstfruits of your soil to H995
Ex 35: 5 who is willing *is to* **b** to the LORD an offering H995
Ex 36: 3 the people continued *to* **b** freewill offerings H995
Ex 40: 4 **B in** the table and set out what belongs on H995
Ex 40: 4 Then **b in** the lampstand and set up its H995
Ex 40:12 "**B** Aaron and his sons to the entrance to H7928
Ex 40:14 **B** his sons and dress them in tunics. H7928
Lev 1: 2 **b** as your offering an animal from either H7928
Lev 1: 5 sons the priests *shall* **b** the blood and H7928
Lev 1:13 the priest *is to* **b** all of them and burn H7928
Lev 1:15 The priest *shall* **b** it to the altar, wring off H7928
Lev 2: 4 " 'If *you* **b** a grain offering baked in an H7928
Lev 2: 8 **B** the grain offering made of these things to H995
Lev 2:11 grain offering *you* **b** to the LORD must be H7928
Lev 2:12 *You may* **b** them to the LORD as an offering H7928
Lev 2:14 " 'If *you* **b** a grain offering of firstfruits to H7928
Lev 3: 3 offering *you are to* **b** a food offering to H7928
Lev 3: 9 offering *you are to* **b** a food offering to H7928
Lev 4: 3 *he must* **b** to the LORD a young bull H7928
Lev 4:14 the assembly *must* **b** a young bull as a sin H7928
Lev 4:23 *he must* **b** as his offering a male goat H995
Lev 4:28 *they must* **b** as their offering for the sin they H995
Lev 4:32 *they are to* **b** a female without defect. H995
Lev 5: 6 *they must* **b** to the LORD a female lamb H995
Lev 5: 7 afford a lamb *is to* **b** two doves or two H995
Lev 5: 8 *They are to* **b** them to the priest, who shall H995
Lev 5:11 *they are to* **b** as an offering for their sin a H995
Lev 5:12 *They are to* **b** it to the priest, who shall take H995
Lev 5:15 *they are to* **b** to the LORD as a penalty a ram H995
Lev 5:18 *They are to* **b** to the priest as a guilt offering H995
Lev 6: 6 And as a penalty *they must* **b** to the priest H995
Lev 6:14 Aaron's sons *are to* **b** it before the LORD, in H7928
Lev 6:20 his sons *are to* **b** to the LORD on the H7928
Lev 6:21 **b** it well-mixed and present the grain H995
Lev 7:14 *They are to* **b** one of each kind as an H7928
Lev 7:29 offering to the LORD *is to* **b** part of it as their H995
Lev 7:30 to the LORD; *they are to* **b** the fat, together H995
Lev 7:38 the Israelites to **b** their offerings to the H7928
Lev 8: 2 "**B** Aaron and his sons, their garments, the H4374
Lev 12: 6 *she is to* **b** to the priest at the entrance to H995
Lev 12: 8 *she is to* **b** two doves or two young H4374
Lev 14:10 the eighth day *they must* **b** two male H4374
Lev 14:23 the eighth day *they must* **b** them for their H995
Lev 15: 3 discharge *will* **b about** uncleanness: H2118+928
Lev 15:29 young pigeons and **b** them to the priest at H995
Lev 16: 3 He must first **b** a young bull for a sin H928
Lev 16: 9 Aaron *shall* **b** the goat whose lot falls to H7928
Lev 16:11 "Aaron *shall* **b** the bull for his own sin H7928
Lev 16:20 the altar, *he shall* **b forward** the live goat. H7928
Lev 17: 5 This is so the Israelites *will* **b** to the LORD the H995
Lev 17: 5 *They must* **b** them to the priest, that is, to H995

Lev 17: 9 and *does* not **b** it to the entrance to the tent H995
Lev 19:21 *must* **b** a ram to the entrance to the tent of H995
Lev 22:16 offerings and so **b upon** them guilt H5951
Lev 22:20 *Do* not **b** anything with a defect, because H7928
Lev 23:10 **b** to the priest a sheaf of the first grain you H995
Lev 23:14 the very day you **b** this offering to your H995
Lev 23:17 **b** two loaves made of two-tenths of an H995
Lev 24: 2 the Israelites *to* **b** you clear oil of H4374
Lev 26:16 *I will* **b** on you sudden terror, wasting H7212
Lev 26:25 And *I will* **b** the sword on you to avenge the H995
Nu 3: 6 "**B** the tribe of Levi and present them to H7928
Nu 5: 9 the Israelites **b** to a priest will belong to H7928
Nu 5:16 " 'The priest *shall* **b** her and have her H7928
Nu 5:25 it before the LORD and **b** it to the altar. H7928
Nu 6:10 the eighth day *they must* **b** two doves or H995
Nu 6:12 of dedication and *must* **b** a year-old male H995
Nu 7:11 day one leader *is to* **b** his offering for the H7928
Nu 8: 9 **B** the Levites to the front of the tent of H7928
Nu 8:10 *You are to* **b** the Levites before the LORD H7928
Nu 11:16 "**B** me seventy of Israel's elders who are H665
Nu 13:20 Do your best *to* **b back** some of the fruit of H4374
Nu 14:16 LORD was not able to **b** these people into H995
Nu 14:24 *I will* **b** him into the land he went to H995
Nu 14:31 *I will* **b** them **in** to enjoy the land you have H995
Nu 15: 9 **b** with the bull a grain offering of H7928
Nu 15:10 also **b** half a hin of wine as a drink H7928
Nu 15:27 *that person must* **b** a year-old female H7928
Nu 18: 2 **B** your fellow Levites from your ancestral H7928
Nu 18: 9 From all the gifts *they* **b** me as most holy H8740
Nu 18:13 firstfruits that *they* **b** to the LORD will be H995
Nu 19: 2 Tell the Israelites *to* **b** you a red heifer H4374
Nu 20: 4 Why *did you* **b** the LORD's community into H995
Nu 20: 5 Why *did you* **b** us **up** out of Egypt to this H6590
Nu 20: 8 *You will* **b** water **out** of the rock for the H3655
Nu 20:10 *must we* **b** you water **out** of this rock?" H3655
Nu 20:12 *you will* not **b** this community into the land H995
Nu 27:17 one who will lead them out and **b** them **in** H995
Dt 1:17 **B** me any case too hard for you, and I will H7928
Dt 1:22 land for us and **b back** a report about the H8740
Dt 4:38 than you and to **b** you **into** their land to H995
Dt 6:23 us out from there to **b** us **in** and give us the H995
Dt 7:26 *Do* not **b** a detestable thing into your house H995
Dt 12: 6 there **b** your burnt offerings and sacrifices H995
Dt 12:11 there *you are to* **b** everything I command H995
Dt 14:28 **b** all the tithes of that year's produce and H3655
Dt 16:17 Each of you must **b** a gift in proportion to the NDT
Dt 21:12 **B** her into your home and have her shave H995
Dt 21:19 hold of him and **b** him to the elders at H3655
Dt 22: 8 roof so that *you may* not **b** the guilt of H8492
Dt 22:15 and mother *shall* **b** to the H4374+2256+3655
Dt 23:18 *You must* not **b** the earnings of a female H995
Dt 24: 4 *Do* not **b sin** *upon* the land the LORD your H2627
Dt 24: 5 at home and **b happiness** *to* the wife he H8523
Dt 24:11 *let* the neighbor to whom you are making the loan **b** the pledge **out** H3655
Dt 26:10 now *I* **b** the firstfruits of the soil that you H995
Dt 28:49 The LORD *will* **b** a nation against you from H5951
Dt 28:60 *He will* **b** on you all the diseases of Egypt H8740
Dt 28:61 The LORD *will* also **b** on you every kind of H6623
Dt 29:19 *they will* **b disaster** *on* the watered land H6200
Dt 30: 4 your God will gather you and **b** you **back**. H4374
Dt 30: 5 He *will* **b** you to the land that belonged to H995
Dt 31:21 even before *I* **b** them into the land I H995
Dt 31:23 you *will* **b** the Israelites into the land I H995
Dt 32:39 I put to death and *I* **b to life**, I have H2649
Dt 33: 7 the cry of Judah; **b** him to his people. H995
Jos 2: 3 "**B out** the men who came to you and H3655
Jos 6:18 *you will* not **b about** *your own* **destruction** H3049
Jos 6:18 liable to destruction and **b trouble** *on* it. H6579
Jos 6:22 house and **b** her **out** and all who belong H3655
Jos 7: 7 *did you ever* **b** this people **across** H6296+6296
Jos 7:25 The LORD *will* **b trouble** *on* you today." H6579
Jos 10:22 the cave and **b** those five kings **out** to me." H3655
Jos 18: 6 **b** them here to me and I will cast lots for H995
Jos 23:15 so he *will* **b** on you all the evil things he H995
Jos 24:20 will turn and **b disaster** on you and make H8317
Jdg 6:13 '*Did* not the LORD **b** us **up** out of Egypt? H6590
Jdg 6:18 I come back and **b** my offering and set H3655
Jdg 6:30 demanded of Joash, "**B out** your son. H3655
Jdg 13: 8 to teach us how *to* **b up** the boy who is to H6913
Jdg 16:25 shouted, "**B out** Samson to entertain us." H7924
Jdg 19:22 "**B out** the man who came to your house H3655
Jdg 19:24 *I will* **b** them **out** to you now, and you can H3655
Ru 3:15 "**B** me the shawl you are wearing and H2035
Ru 4: 4 *I should* **b** the matter to your **attention** H1655+265
1Sa 4: 3 "Why *did* the LORD **b defeat on** us today H5597
1Sa 4: 3 *Let us* **b** the ark of the LORD's covenant H4374
1Sa 9:23 the cook, "**B** the piece of meat I gave you H5989
1Sa 11: 2 one of you and so **b** disgrace on all Israel." H8492
1Sa 13: 9 "**B** me the burnt offering and the H5602
1Sa 14:18 said to Ahijah, "**B** the ark of God." (At H5602
1Sa 14:34 'Each of you **b** me your cattle and sheep H5602
1Sa 15:32 "**B** me Agag king of the Amalekites." H5602
1Sa 16:17 someone who plays well and **b** him to me." H995
1Sa 17:18 brothers are and **b back** some assurance H4374
1Sa 19:15 "**B** him **up** to me in his bed so that I may H6590
1Sa 20:21 on this side of you; **b** them here,' then H4374
1Sa 20:31 Now send someone *to* **b** him to me, for H4374
1Sa 21:14 He is insane! Why **b** him to me? H995
1Sa 21:15 of madmen that *you have to* **b** this fellow H995
1Sa 23: 9 said to Abiathar the priest, "**B** the ephod." H5602
1Sa 28: 8 he said, "and **b up** for me the one I name." H6590
1Sa 28: 9 set a trap for my life to **b about** my **death**?" H4637
1Sa 28:11 "Whom *shall I* **b up** for you? H6590
1Sa 28:11 up for you?" "**B up** Samuel," he said. H6590
1Sa 30: 7 the son of Ahimelek, "**B** me the ephod." H5602
2Sa 3:12 I will help you **b** all Israel **over** to you." H6015
2Sa 3:13 presence unless you **b** Michal daughter of H995
2Sa 6: 2 Baalah in Judah to **b up** from there the H6590
2Sa 6:12 So David went *to* **b up** the ark of God from H6590
2Sa 9:10 to farm the land for him and **b in** the crops, H995
2Sa 12:11 household I *am going to* **b** calamity on H7756
2Sa 12:23 Can I **b** him **back** again? I will go H8740
2Sa 13:10 "**B** the food here **into** my bedroom so I may H995
2Sa 14:10 anything to you, **b** them to me, and they H995
2Sa 14:21 **b back** the young man Absalom. H8740
2Sa 15:14 to overtake us and **b** ruin on us and put H5616
2Sa 15:25 *he will* **b** me **back** and let me see it and H8740
2Sa 17: 3 and **b** all the people **back** to you. H8740
2Sa 17:13 then all Israel *will* **b** ropes to that city H5951
2Sa 17:14 in order to **b** disaster on Absalom. H995
2Sa 18:22 have any news *that will* **b** you **a reward**." H5162
2Sa 19:11 the last to **b** the king **back** to his palace H8740
2Sa 19:12 should you be the last to **b back** the king? H8740
2Sa 19:15 the king and **b** him **across** the Jordan. H6296
2Sa 19:41 and **b** him and his household **across** the H6296
2Sa 20:15 they were battering the wall to **b** it **down**, H5877
2Sa 22:28 eyes are on the haughty *to* **b** them **low**. H9164
2Sa 23: 5 surely *he would* not **b to fruition** my H7541
1Ki 2: 9 **B** his gray head **down** *to* the grave in H3718
1Ki 3:24 the king said, "**B** me a sword." So they H4374
1Ki 8: 1 to **b up** the ark of the LORD's covenant from H6590
1Ki 8:34 Israel and **b** them **back** to the land you H8740
1Ki 13:18 '**B** him **back** with you to your house so that H8740
1Ki 14:10 I *am going to* **b** disaster on the house of H995
1Ki 17:10 "*Would you* **b** me a little water in a jar so H4374
1Ki 17:11 he called, "And **b** me, please, a piece H4374
1Ki 17:13 me from what you have and **b** it to me, H3655
1Ki 18:19 And **b** the four hundred and fifty prophets H7695
1Ki 21:10 him and **have** *them* **b charges** that he has H6386
1Ki 21:21 'I *am going to* **b** disaster on you. H995
1Ki 21:29 himself, *I will* not **b** this disaster in his day H995
1Ki 21:29 but *I will* **b** it on his house in the days of H995
1Ki 22: 9 "**B** Micaiah son of Imlah **at once**. H4554
2Ki 2:20 "**B** me a new bowl," he said, "and put salt H4374
2Ki 3:15 But now **b** me a harpist." While the harpist H4374
2Ki 4: 6 she said to her son, "**B** me another one." H5602
2Ki 5: 7 Can I kill and **b back to life**? Why does H2649
2Ki 10:22 "**B** robes for all the servants of Baal." H3655
2Ki 11:15 "**B** her **out** between the ranks and put to H3655
2Ki 21:12 I *am going to* **b** such disaster on Jerusalem H995
2Ki 22:16 I *am going to* **b** disaster on this place and H995
2Ki 22:20 the disaster I *am going to* **b** on this place. H995
1Ch 11:19 Because they risked their lives *to* **b** it **back** H995
1Ch 13: 3 *Let us* **b** the ark of our God **back** to us, for H6015
1Ch 13: 5 to **b** the ark of God from Kiriath Jearim. H995
1Ch 13: 6 to **b up** from there the ark of God the LORD H6590
1Ch 13:12 "How *can I ever* **b** the ark of God to me?" H995
1Ch 15: 3 in Jerusalem to **b up** the ark of the LORD H6590
1Ch 15:12 yourselves and **b up** the ark of the LORD, H6590
1Ch 15:13 did not **b** it up the first time that the LORD our NDT
1Ch 15:14 in order to **b up** the ark of the LORD, H6590
1Ch 15:25 of a thousand went to **b up** the ark of the H6590
1Ch 16:29 **b** an offering and come before him. H5951
1Ch 21: 3 Why *should he* **b** guilt on Israel?" H2118+4200
1Ch 22:19 so that you *may* **b** the ark of the covenant H995
2Ch 5: 2 to **b up** the ark of the LORD's covenant from H6590
2Ch 6:25 Israel and **b** them **back** to the land you H8740
2Ch 18: 8 "**B** Micaiah son of Imlah **at once**. H4554
2Ch 23:14 "**B** her **out** *between* the ranks and put to H3655
2Ch 24: 6 required the Levites to **b in** from Judah H995
2Ch 24: 9 that they *should* **b** to the LORD the H995
2Ch 24:19 to the people to **b** them **back** to him, H8740
2Ch 28:13 "*You must* not **b** those prisoners here," H995
2Ch 29:31 Come and **b** sacrifices and thank offerings H995
2Ch 31:10 began to **b** their contributions *to* the H995
2Ch 34:24 I *am going to* **b** disaster on this place and H995
2Ch 34:28 the disaster I *am going to* **b** on this place H995
Ezr 3: 7 so that they *would* **b** cedar logs by sea from H995
Ezr 7:27 king's heart to **b honor** to the house of the H6995
Ezr 8:17 so that they *might* **b** attendants to us for H995
Ne 1: 9 them from there and **b** them to the place I H995
Ne 4: 2 *Can they* **b** the stones **back to life** from H2649
Ne 8: 1 of the Law to **b out** the Book of the Law H995
Ne 8:15 hill country and **b back** branches from olive H995
Ne 10:31 neighboring peoples **b** merchandise or H995
Ne 10:34 of our families is to **b** to the house of our H995
Ne 10:36 we *will* **b** the firstborn of our sons and of H995
Ne 10:37 *we will* **b** to the storerooms of the house of H995
Ne 10:37 And we will **b** a tithe of our crops to the NDT
Ne 10:38 *are to* **b** a tenth of the tithes **up** to the H6590
Ne 10:39 *are to* **b** their contributions of grain H995
Ne 11: 1 people cast lots to **b** one out of every ten of H995
Ne 12:44 towns they were to **b** into the storerooms H4043
Est 1:11 to **b** before him Queen Vashti, wearing her H995
Est 2: 3 of his realm *to* **b** all these beautiful H7695
Est 5: 5 "**B** Haman **at once**," the king said, "so H4554
Est 6: 5 "**B** *him* **in**," the king ordered. H995
Est 6: 8 *have them* **b** a royal robe the king has worn H995
Job 8:10 *Will they* not **b forth** words from their H3655
Job 9:33 *someone to* **b** us together, H8883+3338+6584
Job 10:17 *You* **b new** witnesses against me and H2542
Job 10:18 "Why then *did you* **b** me **out** of the womb? H3655
Job 12:12 Does not long life **b** understanding? NDT
Job 13:19 *Can* anyone **b charges** against me? If so, H8189
Job 14: 3 *Will you* **b** him before you for judgment? H995
Job 14: 4 Who *can* **b** what is pure from the impure H5989
Job 16: 5 comfort from my lips *would* **b** you **relief**. H3104
Job 19:29 wrath will **b** punishment by the sword NDT
Job 28:11 of the rivers and **b** hidden things *to* light. H3655
Job 30:23 I know *you will* **b** me **down** *to* death, to H8740
Job 38:32 *Can you* **b forth** the constellations in their H3655
Job 39: 3 They crouch down and **b forth** their young H7114
Job 39:12 in your grain and **b** it *to* your threshing floor H665
Job 40:11 look at all who are proud and **b** them **low**, H9164
Job 40:20 The hills **b** it their produce, and all the H5951
Ps 4: 6 are asking, "Who *will* **b** us prosperity?" H8011
Ps 7: 9 **B to an end** the violence of the wicked H1698
Ps 17:13 confront them, **b** them **down**; with your H4156
Ps 18:27 the humble but **b low** those whose eyes H9164
Ps 28: 4 have done and **b back** on them what they H8740
Ps 37:14 bend the bow to **b down** the poor and H5877
Ps 43: 3 *let them* **b** me to your holy mountain H995
Ps 44: 3 nor *did* their arm **b** them **victory**; it was H3828
Ps 44: 6 my bow, my sword *does* not **b** me **victory**; H3828
Ps 50: 8 *I* **b** no **charges** *against* you concerning H3519
Ps 51:16 in sacrifice, or *I would* **b** it; you do not H5989
Ps 52: 5 God *will* **b** you **down** to everlasting **ruin**: H5997
Ps 55: 3 for *they* **b down** suffering on me and H4572
Ps 55:23 *will* **b down** the wicked into the pit of H3718
Ps 56: 7 in your anger, God, **b** the nations **down**. H3718
Ps 59:11 might uproot them and **b** them **down**. H3718
Ps 60: 9 Who *will* **b** me to the fortified city? Who H3297
Ps 64: 8 tongues against them and **b** them **to ruin**; H4173
Ps 65: 4 you choose and **b near** to live in your H7928
Ps 68:22 The Lord says, "*I will* **b** them from Bashan H8740
Ps 68:22 *I will* **b** them from the depths of the sea, H8740
Ps 68:29 temple at Jerusalem kings *will* **b** you gifts. H3297
Ps 68:30 Humbled, may the beast **b** bars of silver H928
Ps 71:20 of the earth you will again **b** me **up**. H6590
Ps 72: 3 *May* the mountains **b** prosperity to the H5951
Ps 72:10 *May* the kings of Tarshish and of distant shores **b** H8740
Ps 76:11 *let* all the neighboring lands **b** gifts to the H3297
Ps 86: 4 **B joy** *to* your servant, Lord, for I put my H8523
Ps 86: 9 Lord; *they will* **b glory** to your name. H3877
Ps 96: 8 **b** an offering and come into his courts. H5951
Ps 104:20 *You* **b** darkness, it becomes night, and all H8883
Ps 108:10 Who *will* **b** me *to* the fortified city? Who H3297
Ps 143: 2 *Do* not **b** your servant into judgment H995+907
Ps 143: 8 *Let* the morning **b** me **word** *of* your H9048
Ps 143:11 in your righteousness, **b** me **out** of trouble. H3655
Pr 3: 2 life many years and **b** you peace and H3578
Pr 3: 8 *This will* **b** health to your body and H2118
Pr 10: 4 poverty, but diligent hands **b wealth**. H6947
Pr 11:17 the cruel **b ruin** *on* themselves. H6579
Pr 13: 5 a stench and **b shame** *on themselves*. H2917
Pr 15:27 The greedy **b ruin** *to* their households, but H6579
Pr 18: 6 The lips of fools **b** them strife, and their H995
Pr 19:24 *he will* not even **b** it **back** to his mouth! H8740
Pr 22:21 so that *you* **b back** truthful reports to those H8740
Pr 24:22 who knows what calamities they can **b**? NDT
Pr 25: 8 *do* not **b** hastily to court, for what will you H3655
Pr 26:15 he is too lazy to **b** it **back** to his mouth. H8740
Pr 27: 1 you do not know what a day *may* **b**. H3528
Pr 27: 9 Perfume and incense **b joy** *to* the heart H8523
Pr 27:11 my son, and **b joy** *to* my heart; then I can H8523
Pr 29:11 their rage, but the wise **b calm** in the end. H8656
Pr 29:17 *they will* **b** you the delights you desire. H5989
Pr 31:31 and *let* her works **b** her **praise** at the city H2146
Ecc 3:17 "God *will* **b into judgment** both the H9149
Ecc 3:22 For who *can* **b** them to see what will H995
Ecc 10:10 is needed, but skill *will* **b** success. H4178
Ecc 11: 9 these things God *will* **b** you into judgment. H995
Ecc 12:14 For God *will* **b** every deed into judgment H995
SS 1: 4 *Let* the king **b** me **into** his chambers H995
SS 8: 2 I would lead you and **b** you to my mother's H995
SS 8:11 Each *was to* **b** for its fruit a thousand H995
Isa 3:17 the Lord *will* **b sores on** the heads of the H8558
Isa 7:17 The LORD *will* **b** on you and on your people H995
Isa 7:17 from Judah—he will **b** the king of Assyria." NDT
Isa 8: 7 the Lord *is about to* **b** against them the H6590
Isa 14: 2 will take them and **b** them to their own H995
Isa 15: 9 but *I will* **b** still more upon Dimon H8883
Isa 17:11 plant them, *you* **b** them **to bud**, yet the H7255
Isa 19: 3 and *I will* **b** their plans **to nothing**; they H1182
Isa 19:17 land of Judah *will* **b** terror *to* the H2118+4200
Isa 21: 2 *I will* **b to an end** all the groaning she H8697
Isa 21:14 **b** water for the thirsty; you who live in H910
Isa 21:14 who live in Tema, **b** food for the fugitives. H7709
Isa 23: 9 to **b down** her pride in all her splendor H2725
Isa 25:11 God *will* **b down** their pride despite the H9164
Isa 25:12 *He will* **b down** your high fortified walls H8820
Isa 25:12 *he will* **b** them **down** to the ground H5595
Isa 28:19 of this message *will* **b** sheer terror. H2118
Isa 30: 3 Egypt's shade will **b** you disgrace. NDT
Isa 30: 5 to them, who **b** neither help nor advantage NDT
Isa 31: 2 Yet he too is wise and *can* **b** disaster; he H995
Isa 40: 9 You *who* **b good news** *to* Zion, go up on a H1413
Isa 40: 9 You *who* **b good news** *to* Jerusalem, lift H1413
Isa 42: 1 and *he will* **b** justice to the nations. H3655
Isa 42: 3 In faithfulness *he will* **b forth** justice; H3655
Isa 43: 5 *I will* **b** your children from the east and H995
Isa 43: 6 **B** my sons from afar and my daughters H995
Isa 43: 9 *Let them* **b** *in* their witnesses to prove they H5989
Isa 43:14 to Babylon and **b down** as fugitives all H3718

Isa 45: 7 I **b** prosperity and create disaster H6913
Isa 46:11 I have said, that *I will* **b about**; what I have H995
Isa 48:15 *I will* **b** him, and he will succeed in his H995
Isa 49: 5 be his servant to **b** Jacob **back** to him and H8740
Isa 49: 6 tribes of Jacob and **b back** those of Israel I H8740
Isa 49:22 *they will* **b** your sons in their arms and carry H995
Isa 50: 8 Who then *will* **b charges** against me H8189
Isa 51: 5 my arm *will* **b justice** *to* the nations. H9149
Isa 52: 7 are the feet of *those who* **b good news**, H1413
Isa 52: 7 *who* **b** good **tidings**, who proclaim H1413
Isa 54: 7 with deep compassion *I will* **b** you **back**. H7695
Isa 56: 7 these *I will* **b** to my holy mountain and give H995
Isa 60:11 so that people *may* **b** you the wealth of the H995
Isa 60:17 Instead of bronze *I will* **b** you gold, and H995
Isa 60:17 Instead of wood *I will* **b** you bronze, and H995
Isa 65: 9 *I will* **b forth** descendants from Jacob, and H3655
Isa 66: 4 them and *will* **b** on them what they H995
Isa 66: 9 *Do* I **b to the moment of birth** and not H8689
Isa 66: 9 I close up the womb when I **b to delivery**?" H3528
Isa 66:15 *he will* **b down** his anger with fury H8740
Isa 66:20 And *they will* **b** all your people, from all the H995
Isa 66:20 "They will **b** them, as the Israelites bring NDT
Isa 66:20 as the Israelites **b** their grain offerings H995
Jer 2: 9 "Therefore *I* **b charges** against you again," H8189
Jer 2: 9 "And *I will* **b charges** against your H8189
Jer 2:29 "Why *do you* **b charges** against me? You H8189
Jer 3:14 two from a clan—and **b** you *to* Zion. H995
Jer 7:34 *I will* **b an end** *to* the sounds of joy and H8697
Jer 10:18 *I will* **b distress** on them so that they may H7674
Jer 11:11 'I *will* **b** on them a disaster they cannot H995
Jer 11:23 because *I will* **b** disaster on the people of H995
Jer 12: 1 when *I* **b a case** before you. H8189
Jer 12: 9 all the wild beasts; **b** them to devour. H910
Jer 12:15 and *will* **b** each of them **back** to their own H8740
Jer 14:22 *Do* any of the worthless idols of the nations **b rain** H1772
Jer 15: 7 *I will* **b bereavement** and destruction on H8897
Jer 15: 8 At midday *I will* **b** a destroyer against the H995
Jer 15: 8 suddenly *I will* **b down** on them anguish H5877
Jer 16: 9 your days I *will* **b an end** *to* the sounds of H8697
Jer 17:18 **B** on them the day of disaster; destroy them H995
Jer 17:21 the Sabbath day or **b** it through the gates H995
Jer 17:22 *Do* not **b** a load **out** of your houses or do H3655
Jer 17:24 **b** no load through the gates of this city H995
Jer 18:22 houses when *you* suddenly **b** invaders H995
Jer 19: 3 I *am going to* **b** a disaster on this place H995
Jer 19:15 I *am going to* **b** on this city and all the H995
Jer 23: 3 driven them and *will* **b** them **back** to their H8740
Jer 23:12 *I will* **b** disaster on them in the year they H995
Jer 23:40 *I will* **b** on you everlasting disgrace H5989
Jer 24: 6 and *I will* **b** them **back** to this land. H8740
Jer 25: 9 "and *I will* **b** them against this land and its H995
Jer 25:13 *I will* **b** on that land all the things I have H995
Jer 25:29 am beginning to **b disaster** on the city H8317
Jer 25:31 the LORD will **b** charges against the NDT
Jer 25:31 he *will* **b judgment** on all mankind and H9149
Jer 26:13 the LORD *will* **relent and not b** the disaster H5714
Jer 26:15 you *will* **b** the guilt of innocent blood on H5989
Jer 26:19 *did* not the LORD **relent, so that** he *did* **not b** H5714
Jer 26:19 We *are about to* **b** a terrible disaster on H6913
Jer 27:22 'Then *I will* **b** them **back** and restore them H6590
Jer 28: 3 Within two years I *will* **b back** to this place H8740
Jer 28: 4 I *will* also **b back** to this place Jehoiachin H8740
Jer 29:10 good promise to **b** you **back** to this place. H8740
Jer 29:14 "and *will* **b** you **back** *from* captivity. H8740
Jer 29:14 "and *will* **b** you **back** to the place from H8740
Jer 30: 3 *I will* **b** my people Israel and Judah **back** *from* H8740
Jer 30:19 decreased; *I will* **b** them **honor**, and they H3877
Jer 30:21 *I will* **b** him **near** and he will come close H7928
Jer 31: 8 I *will* **b** them from the land of the north H995
Jer 31: 9 weeping; they will pray *as I* **b** them **back**. H3297
Jer 31:23 "When I **b** them **back** *from* captivity, the H8740
Jer 31:28 destroy and **b disaster**, so I will watch over H8317
Jer 32:18 but **b** *the* **punishment** *for* the parents' H8966
Jer 32:37 *I will* **b** them **back** to this place and let H8740
Jer 33: 6 I *will* **b** health and healing to it H6590
Jer 33: 7 *I will* **b** Judah and Israel **back** *from* H8740
Jer 33: 9 Then this city *will* **b** me renown, joy H2118+4200
Jer 33:11 voices of *those who* **b** thank offerings *to* the H995
Jer 34:22 and *I will* **b** them **back** to this city. H8740
Jer 35:17 I *am going to* **b** on Judah and on everyone H995
Jer 36: 7 Perhaps *they will* **b** their petition before H5877
Jer 36:14 "**B** the scroll from which you have read to H4374
Jer 36:31 *I will* **b** on them and those living in H995
Jer 37:20 *Let* me **b** my petition before you H5877
Jer 42:17 escape the disaster *I will* **b** on them. H995
Jer 44: 7 Why **b** such great disaster on yourselves H6913
Jer 44:11 I am determined to **b** disaster on you and to NDT
Jer 45: 5 For *I will* **b** disaster on all people, declares H995
Jer 46:25 "I *am about to* **b punishment** on Amon H7212
Jer 48:44 for *I will* **b** on Moab the year of her H995
Jer 49: 5 I *will* **b** terror on you from all those around H995
Jer 49: 8 for *I will* **b** disaster on Esau at the time H995
Jer 49:16 from there *I will* **b** you **down**," declares H3718
Jer 49:32 places and *will* **b** disaster *on* them from H995
Jer 49:36 *I will* **b** against Elam the four winds from H995
Jer 49:37 want to kill them; *I will* **b** disaster on them H995
Jer 50: 9 For I will stir up and **b** against Babylon an H6590
Jer 50:19 But *I will* **b** Israel **back** to their own H8740
Jer 50:34 cause so that *he may* **b rest** *to* their land, H8089
Jer 51:40 "*I will* **b** them **down** like lambs to the H3718
Jer 51:64 because of the disaster I *will* **b** on her. H995
La 1:21 *May you* **b** the day you have announced so H995
La 3:33 For *he does* not willingly **b affliction** or H6700
Eze 5:16 *I will* **b more and more** famine upon you H3578
Eze 5:17 and *I will* **b** the sword against you. H995
Eze 6: 3 I *am about to* **b** a sword against you, and I H995
Eze 6:10 threaten in vain to **b** this calamity on H6913
Eze 7:24 *I will* **b** the most wicked of nations to take H995
Eze 9: 1 "**B near** those who are appointed to H7928
Eze 9:10 but *I will* **b down** on their own heads what H5989
Eze 11: 8 the sword is what *I will* **b** against you H995
Eze 11:17 the nations and **b** you **back** from the H665
Eze 11:21 *I will* **b down** on their own heads what H5989
Eze 12: 4 **b out** your belongings packed for exile. H3655
Eze 12:13 in my snare; *I will* **b** him to Babylonia H995
Eze 14:17 "Or if *I* **b** a sword against that country and H995
Eze 16:38 *I will* **b** *on* you the blood vengeance of my H5989
Eze 16:40 *They will* **b** a mob against you, who will H6590
Eze 16:43 I *will* surely **b down** on your head what H5989
Eze 17:20 *I will* **b** him to Babylon and execute H995
Eze 17:24 that I the LORD **b down** the tall tree and H9164
Eze 20: 6 to them that *I would* **b** them **out** of Egypt H3655
Eze 20:15 wilderness that I *would* not **b** them into the H995
Eze 20:34 *I will* **b** you from the nations and gather H3655
Eze 20:35 *I will* **b** you into the wilderness of the H995
Eze 20:37 and *I will* **b** you into the bond of the H995
Eze 20:38 Although *I will* **b** them **out** of the land H3655
Eze 20:41 incense when I **b** you **out** from the nations H3655
Eze 20:42 when I **b** you into the land of Israel H995
Eze 23:22 and *I will* **b** them against you from every H995
Eze 23:32 *it will* **b** scorn and derision H2118+4200
Eze 23:46 **B** a mob against them and give them over H6590
Eze 24: 5 **b** it **to a boil** and cook the bones in H8409+8410
Eze 26: 3 and *I will* **b** many nations against you H6590
Eze 26: 7 From the north I *am going to* **b** against Tyre H995
Eze 26:19 when I **b** the ocean depths over you H6590
Eze 26:20 then *I will* **b** you **down** with those who go H3718
Eze 26:21 *I will* **b** you *to* a horrible end and you will H5989
Eze 28: 7 I *am going to* **b** foreigners against you, the H995
Eze 28: 8 *They will* **b** you **down** to the pit, and you H3718
Eze 29: 8 I *will* **b** a sword against you and kill both H995
Eze 29:14 *I will* **b** them **back** *from* captivity and return H8740
Eze 32: 8 over you; *I will* **b** darkness over your land H5989
Eze 32: 9 peoples when I **b about** your destruction H995
Eze 33: 2 'When *I* **b** the sword against a land, and H995
Eze 33:12 wickedness *will* not **b condemnation**. H4173
Eze 34:13 *I will* **b** them **out** from the nations and H3655
Eze 34:13 and *I will* **b** them into their own land. H995
Eze 34:16 search for the lost and **b back** the strays. H8740
Eze 36:24 the countries and **b** you **back** into your own H995
Eze 36:29 plentiful and *will* not **b** famine upon you H5989
Eze 37:12 your graves and **b** you **up** from them; H6590
Eze 37:12 *I will* **b** you **back** to the land of Israel. H995
Eze 37:13 your graves and **b** you **up** from them. H6590
Eze 37:21 all around and **b** them **back** into their own H995
Eze 38: 4 your jaws and **b** you **out** with your whole H3655
Eze 38:16 *I will* **b** you against my land, so that H995
Eze 38:17 years that *I would* **b** you against them. H995
Eze 39: 2 *I will* **b** you from the far north and send H6590
Da 1: 3 to **b into** the king's service some of the H995
Da 1:18 set by the king to **b** them **into** his service, H995
Da 2:44 those kingdoms and **b** them **to an end**, A10508
Da 5: 2 he gave orders to **b in** the gold and A10085
Da 9:14 did not hesitate *to* **b** the disaster on us, H995
Da 9:24 to **b in** everlasting righteousness H995
Hos 4: 1 LORD has a charge to **b** against you who live NDT
Hos 4: 4 "But *let* no one **b a charge**, let no one H8189
Hos 4: 4 are like *those who* **b charges** *against* a H8189
Hos 4:19 their sacrifices *will* **b** *them* **shame**. H1017
Hos 9:13 But Ephraim *will* **b out** their children to H3655
Hos 12: 2 The LORD has a charge to **b** against Judah NDT
Hos 12:13 used a prophet *to* **b** Israel **up** from Egypt, H6590
Joel 2:16 the assembly; **b together** the elders H7695
Joel 3: 2 all nations and **b** them **down** to the Valley H3718
Joel 3:11 assemble there. **B down** your warriors H5737
Am 4: 1 say to your husbands, "**B** us some drinks!" H995
Am 4: 4 **B** your sacrifices every morning, your tithes H995
Am 5:22 Even though *you* **b** me burnt offerings H6590
Am 5:22 Though you **b** choice fellowship offerings, NDT
Am 5:25 "*Did you* **b** me sacrifices and offerings H5602
Am 6: 3 of disaster and **b near** a reign of terror. H5602
Am 9: 1 **B** them **down** on the heads of all the H1298
Am 9: 2 from there *I will* **b** them **down**. H3718
Am 9: 7 "*Did I* not **b** Israel **up** from Egypt, the H6590
Am 9:14 and *I will* **b** my people Israel **back** *from* H8740
Ob 3 'Who *can* **b** me **down** to the ground? H3718
Ob 4 from there *I will* **b** you **down**," declares H3718
Jnh 3:10 he relented and *did* not **b** on them the H6913
Mic 1:15 *I will* **b** a conqueror against you who live in H995
Mic 2:12 *I will* **surely b together** the remnant H7695+7695
Mic 2:12 *I will* **b** them together like sheep in a pen H8492
Mic 7: 9 *He will* **b** me **out** into the light; I will see H3655
Na 1: 9 plot against the LORD he *will* **b** to an end; H6913
Zep 1:17 "*I will* **b** *such* **distress** on all people that H7674
Zep 3:10 my scattered people, *will* **b** me offerings. H3297
Zep 3:20 gather you; at that time *I will* **b** you **home**. H995
Hag 1: 8 mountains and **b down** timber and build H995
Zec 3: 8 I *am going to* **b** my servant, the H995
Zec 4: 7 Then *he will* **b out** the capstone to shouts H3655
Zec 8: 8 *I will* **b** them **back** to live in Jerusalem; they H995
Zec 8:14 had determined to **b disaster** on you and H8317
Zec 10:10 *I will* **b** them **back** from Egypt and gather H8740
Zec 10:10 *I will* **b** them to Gilead and Lebanon, and H995
Zec 14:18 The LORD *will* **b** on them the plague he H2118
Mal 1:13 "When *you* **b** injured, lame or diseased H995
Mal 3: 3 LORD will have *men who will* **b** offerings in H5602
Mal 3:10 **B** the whole tithe into the storehouse, that H995
Mt 10:34 that I have come *to* **b** peace to the earth. *G965*
Mt 10:34 I did not come *to* **b** peace, but a sword. *G965*
Mt 12:10 *Looking* for a reason *to* **b charges against** *G2989*
Mt 13:30 gather the wheat and **b** it **into** my barn. *G1650*
Mt 14:18 "**B** them here to me," he said. *G5770*
Mt 16: 7 "It is because *we* didn't **b** any bread." *G3284*
Mt 17:17 I put up with you? **B** the boy here to me." *G5770*
Mt 21: 2 Untie them and **b** them to me. *G72*
Mt 21:41 *He will* **b** those wretches **to a wretched end**," *G660*
Mk 4:21 "*Do you* **b** *in* a lamp to put it under a *G2262*
Mk 6:27 executioner with orders *to* **b** John's head. *G5770*
Mk 8:14 The disciples had forgotten *to* **b** bread *G3284*
Mk 9:19 shall I put up with you? **B** the boy to me." *G5770*
Mk 11: 2 has ever ridden. Untie it and **b** it here. *G5770*
Mk 12:15 "**B** me a denarius and let me look at it." *G5770*
Lk 1:16 *He will* **b back** many of the people of *G2188*
Lk 2:10 *I* **b** you **good news** that will cause great *G2294*
Lk 9:31 was about to **b to fulfillment** at Jerusalem *G4444*
Lk 9:41 put up with you? **B** your son here." *G4642*
Lk 12:49 "I have come *to* **b** fire on the earth, and *G965*
Lk 12:51 Do you think I came *to* **b** peace on earth *G1443*
Lk 14:21 alleys of the town and **b in** the poor, *G1652*
Lk 15:22 **B** the best robe and put it on him *G1766*
Lk 15:23 **B** the fattened calf and kill it. Let's have a *G5770*
Lk 18: 7 And *will* not God **b about** justice for his *G4472*
Lk 19:27 **b** them here and kill them in front of me. *G72*
Lk 19:30 one has ever ridden. Untie it and **b** it here. *G72*
Lk 19:42 on this day what would **b** you peace— *G4639*
Jn 7:45 who asked them, "Why didn't *you* **b** him **in**?" *G72*
Jn 10:16 this sheep pen. I must **b** them also. They too *G72*
Jn 11:52 *to* **b** them **together** and make them one. *G5251*
Jn 21:10 "**B** some of the fish you have just caught." *G5770*
Ac 5:31 Savior that *he might* **b** Israel to *G1443*
Ac 7:42 " '*Did you* **b** me sacrifices and offerings *G4712*
Ac 10: 5 men to Joppa *to* **b back** a man named *G3569*
Ac 11:14 He *will* **b** you a message through which *G3281S*
Ac 12: 4 Herod intended *to* **b** him **out** for public trial *G343*
Ac 12: 6 night before Herod was to **b him to trial**, *G4575*
Ac 13:47 that you *may* **b** salvation to the *G1639+1650*
Ac 17: 5 Silas *in order to* **b** them **out** to the *G4575*
Ac 19:39 there is anything further *you want to* **b up**, *G2118*
Ac 22: 5 went there *to* **b** these people as *G72*
Ac 23:10 them by force and **b** him into the barracks. *G72*
Ac 23:15 the commander to **b** him before you on *G2864*
Ac 23:18 me and asked me *to* **b** this young man to *G72*
Ac 23:20 agreed to ask you to **b** Paul before the *G2864*
Ac 24:17 I came to Jerusalem *to* **b** my people gifts *G4472*
Ac 24:19 before you and **b charges** if they have *G2989*
Ac 26:23 would **b** *the* **message** of light to his own *G2859*
Ac 27:10 to be disastrous and **b** great loss to ship *G3552*
Ac 28:19 intend *to* **b** any **charge against** my own *G2989*
Ro 5:21 righteousness **to b** eternal life through *G1650*
Ro 7:10 that was intended **to b** life actually *G1650*
Ro 7:13 it used what is good *to* **b about** my death *G2981*
Ro 8:33 Who *will* **b any charge** against those *G1592*
Ro 10: 6 (that is, *to* **b** Christ **down**) *G2864*
Ro 10: 7 that is, *to* **b** Christ **up** from the dead). *G343*
Ro 10:15 are the feet *of* those *who* **b** good **news**!" *G2294*
Ro 11:12 greater riches will their full inclusion **b**! NDT
Ro 13: 2 those who do so *will* **b** judgment on *G3284*
Ro 13: 4 **agents** of wrath to **b** to **punishment** on the *G1690*
Ro 15: 7 accepted you, **in order to b** praise to God. *G1650*
1Co 3:13 because the Day *will* **b** it **to light**. *G1317*
1Co 4: 5 He *will* **b to light** what is hidden in *G5894*
1Co 8: 8 But food *does* not **b** us **near** to God; we *G4225*
1Co 14: 6 unless *I* **b** you some revelation or *G3281*
2Co 8: 6 to **b** also **to completion** this act of grace *G2200*
Eph 1:10 *to* **b unity** to all things in heaven and on *G368*
Eph 6: 4 **b** them **up** in the training and instruction *G1763*
Php 3:21 him *to* **b** everything **under** his **control**, *G5718*
1Th 4:14 we believe that God *will* **b** with Jesus those *G72*
2Th 1:11 his power *he may* **b to fruition** your every *G4444*
1Ti 5:12 Thus *they* **b** judgment **on** *themselves* *G2400*
1Ti 6:15 which God *will* **b about** in his own time *G1259*
2Ti 4:11 Get Mark and **b** him with you, because he is *G72*
2Ti 4:13 **b** the cloak that I left with Carpus at Troas *G5770*
2Ti 4:18 evil attack and *will* **b** me **safely** to his *G5392*
Heb 9:28 but to *b* salvation to those who are waiting AIT
Jas 5:19 someone *should b* that person **back**, AIT
1Pe 3:18 the unrighteous, to **b** you to God. *G4642*
2Pe 2: 2 *will* **b** the way of truth **into disrepute**. *G1059*
2Pe 3:12 That day will **b about** the destruction of *G1328*
2Jn 10 to you and *does* not **b** this teaching, *G5770*
Jude 21 our Lord Jesus Christ to *b* you to eternal life. AIT
Rev 15: 4 fear you, Lord, and **b glory** to your name? *G1519*
Rev 17:16 *They will* **b** her **to ruin** and leave *G2246+4472*
Rev 21:24 kings of the earth *will* **b** their splendor *G5770*

BRINGING (68) [BRING]

Ge 19: 9 *They* **kept b pressure** on Lot and H7210+4394
Ex 6:27 Egypt about **b** the Israelites **out** of Egypt— H3655
Ex 14:11 have you done to us by **b** us **out** of Egypt? H3655
Ex 36: 5 "The people *are* **b** more than enough for H995
Ex 36: 6 so the people were restrained from **b** more, H995
Lev 4: 3 anointed priest sins, **b** guilt on the people H4200
Lev 17: 4 instead of **b** it to the entrance to the tent of H995

Lev 18: 3 in the land of Canaan, where I *am* **b** you. H995
Lev 20:22 the land where I *am* **b** you to live may not H995
Lev 23:37 assemblies for **b** food offerings to the H7928
Nu 14: 3 Why *is* the LORD **b** us to this land only to let H995
Dt 8: 7 For the LORD your God *is* **b** you into a good H995
1Sa 28:15 "Why have you disturbed me by **b** me **up**?" H6590
2Sa 4:10 and thought he was **b good news**, H1413
2Sa 6:15 he and all Israel *were* **b up** the ark of the H6590
2Sa 18:26 king said, "He *must be* **b good news**, too." H1413
2Sa 19:10 do you say nothing about **b** the king **back**?" H8740
2Sa 19:43 we the first to speak of **b back** our king?" H8740
1Ki 1:42 man like you *must be* **b** good **news**." H1413
1Ki 8:32 the guilty by **b down** on their heads what H5989
2Ki 4:42 **b** the man of God twenty loaves of barley H995
1Ch 12:40 Naphtali **came b** food on donkeys, H995
2Ch 6:23 the guilty and **b down** on their heads H5989
2Ch 34:14 While they *were* **b out** the money that H3655
Ne 10:35 responsibility for **b** to the house of the LORD H995
Ne 13:15 on the Sabbath and **b in** grain and loading H995
Ne 13:15 And *they were* **b** all this **into** Jerusalem on H995
Ne 13:16 lived in Jerusalem *were* **b in** fish and all H995
Est 2:20 as she had done when he was **b** her **up**. H594
Ps 104:14 to cultivate—**b forth** food from the earth: H3655
Pr 31:14 the merchant ships, **b** her food from afar. H995
SS 8:10 in his eyes like *one* **b** contentment. H3655
Isa 1:13 Stop **b** meaningless offerings! Your incense H995
Isa 46:13 *I am* **b** my righteousness **near**, it is not far H7928
Isa 60: 9 ships of Tarshish, **b** your children from afar H995
Jer 4: 6 For I *am* **b** disaster from the north, even H995
Jer 5:15 "*I am* **b** a distant nation against you H995
Jer 6:19 I am **b** disaster on this people, the fruit of H995
Jer 17:26 the Negev, **b** burnt offerings and sacrifices H995
Jer 17:26 **b** thank offerings to the house of the H995
Jer 28: 6 **b** the articles of the LORD's house and all
the exiles **back** H8740
Jer 41: 5 **b** grain offerings and incense with them to H995
Jer 43:11 **b** death to those destined for death NDT
Eze 17:12 **b** them *back* with him to Babylon. H995
Eze 22:31 **b down** on their own heads all they have H5989
Eze 27:10 helmets on your walls, **b** you splendor. H5989
Eze 46:20 to avoid **b** them into the outer court and H3655
Da 9:12 against our rulers by **b** on us great disaster. H995
Mt 15:30 came to him, **b** the lame, the blind G2400+3552
Mt 26:62 *is this* **testimony** that these men *are* **b against**
G2909
Mt 27:13 *the* **testimony** *they are* **b against** you?" G2909
Mk 2: 3 men came, **b** to him a paralyzed man G5770
Mk 10:13 *People were* **b** little children **to** Jesus for G4712
Mk 14:60 *this* **testimony** that these men *are* **b against** G2909
Lk 18:15 *People were* also **b** babies to Jesus for G4712
Jn 18:29 "What charges *are you* **b** against this man G5770
Jn 19: 4 *I am* **b** him out to you to let you know that I G72
Jn 19:34 **b** a sudden **flow** of blood and water. G2002
Ac 5:16 **b** their sick and those tormented by G5770
Ac 7:11 all Egypt and Canaan, **b** great suffering, and NDT
Ac 14:15 *We are* **b** you **good news**, telling you to G2294
Ac 17:20 *You are* **b** some strange ideas to our ears G1662
Ac 24: 8 all these **charges** we *are* **b** against him." G2989
Ro 3: 5 That God is unjust *in* **b** his wrath **on** us? G2214
1Ti 5:10 such as **b up children**, showing G5452
Heb 2:10 *In* **b** many sons and daughters to glory, it G72
2Pe 2: 1 them—**b** swift destruction **on** themselves. G2042
2Pe 2:11 on such beings *when* **b** judgment on G5770

BRINGS (83) [BRING]

Ex 13: 5 When the LORD **b** you into the land of the H995
Ex 13:11 "After the LORD **b** you into the land of the H995
Lev 1: 2 anyone among you **b** an offering to the H7928
Lev 2: 1 " 'When anyone **b** a grain offering to the H7928
Lev 4:32 " 'If *someone* **b** a lamb as their sin offering, H995
Lev 7:29 'Anyone *who* **b** a fellowship offering to H7928
Lev 22:21 When anyone **b** from the herd or flock a H7928
Nu 5:18 holds the bitter water that **b a curse**. H826
Nu 5:19 bitter water that **b a curse** not harm you. H826
Nu 5:22 this water that **b a curse** enter your body H826
Nu 5:24 woman drink the bitter water that **b a curse**, H826
Nu 5:24 this water that **b a curse** and causes bitter H826
Nu 5:27 the water that **b a curse** and causes bitter H826
Nu 15: 4 then the *person who* **b** an offering shall H7928
Nu 16:30 But if the LORD **b about** something totally H1343
Dt 6:10 the LORD your God **b** you into the land he H995
Dt 7: 1 the LORD your God **b** you into the land you H995
Dt 33:14 the best the sun **b forth** and the finest the H9311
1Sa 2: 6 "The LORD **b death** and makes alive; he H4637
1Sa 2: 6 *he* **b down** *to* the grave and raises up. H3718
2Sa 23: 4 after rain that **b** grass from the earth. NDT
Job 9:23 When a scourge **b** sudden **death**, he H4637
Job 12:22 of darkness and **b** utter darkness into H3655
Job 22: 4 he rebukes you and **b** charges against you? H995
Job 34:11 *he* **b on** them what their conduct deserves. H5162
Job 37:13 *He* **b** the clouds to punish people, or to H5162
Ps 73:14 every morning **b** new punishments. NDT
Ps 74:12 long ago; *he* **b** salvation on the earth. H7188
Ps 75: 7 *He* **b** one **down**, he exalts H9164
Ps 76:10 your wrath against mankind **b** you **praise**, H3344
Ps 94:20 a throne *that* **b on** misery by its decrees? H3670
Ps 135: 7 with the rain and **b out** the wind from his H3655
Pr 10: 1 A wise son **b joy** *to* his father, but a H8523
Pr 10: 1 a foolish son **b** grief to his mother. NDT
Pr 10:22 The blessing of the LORD **b wealth**, without H6947
Pr 11:29 *Whoever* **b ruin** *on* their family will inherit H6579
Pr 12:14 the work of their hands **b** them **reward**. H8740
Pr 12:18 the tongue of the wise **b** healing. NDT
Pr 13:17 but a trustworthy envoy **b** healing. AIT
Pr 14:23 All hard work **b** a profit, but mere talk H2118
Pr 15: 6 the income of the wicked **b ruin**. H6579
Pr 15:20 A wise son **b joy** *to* his father, but a H8523
Pr 15:21 Folly *b* joy to one who has no sense, but AIT
Pr 15:30 in a messenger's eyes **b joy** *to* the heart, H8523
Pr 16:22 the prudent, but folly **b** punishment to fools. NDT
Pr 17:21 To have a fool for a child **b** grief; there is H4200
Pr 17:25 A foolish son **b** grief to his father and NDT
Pr 19:15 Laziness **b on** deep sleep, and the H5877
Pr 19:26 is a child *who* **b shame** and disgrace. H1017
Pr 21:12 **b** the wicked **to ruin**. H6156+4200+2021+8273
Pr 21:15 it **b** joy to the righteous but terror to NDT
Pr 25:23 Like a north wind *that* **b** unexpected rain H2655
Pr 29: 3 man who loves wisdom **b joy** *to* his father, H8523
Pr 29:23 Pride **b** a person **low**, but the lowly in H9164
Pr 31:12 *She* **b** him good, not harm, all the days of H1694
Isa 40:23 He **b** princes to naught and reduces the H5989
Isa 40:26 He *who* **b out** the starry host one by one H3655
Jer 10:13 with the rain and **b out** the wind from his H3655
Jer 13:16 LORD your God before *he* **b** *the* **darkness**, H3124
Jer 51:16 with the rain and **b out** the wind from his H3655
La 3:32 Though *he* **b grief**, he will show H3324
La 3:51 What I see **b grief** to my soul because of H6618
Eze 22: 3 You city *that* **b** *on* herself doom by H995
Eze 46: 4 offering the prince **b** to the LORD on the H7928
Am 5: 9 the stronghold and **b** the fortified city to H995
Na 1:15 the feet of *one who* **b good news**, who H1413
Mal 2:12 even though *he* **b** an offering to the LORD H5602
Mt 12:35 A good man **b** good things **out** of the G1675
Mt 12:35 an evil man **b** evil things **out** of the evil G1675
Mt 13:52 of a house who **b out** of his storeroom G1675
Lk 6:45 A good man **b** good things **out** of the G4734
Lk 6:45 an evil man **b** evil things **out** of the evil G4734
Jn 2:10 "Everyone **b out** the choice wine first and G5502
Ro 1:16 is the power of God *that* **b** salvation to G1650
Ro 3: 5 **b out** God's righteousness **more clearly**, G5319
Ro 4:15 because the law **b** wrath. And where there G2981
2Co 2:16 an aroma that **b death**; G1666+2505+1650+2505
2Co 2:16 an aroma that **b life**. G1666+2437+1650+2437
2Co 3: 9 glorious is the ministry that *b* **righteousness**! AIT
2Co 7:10 Godly sorrow **b** repentance that leads to G2237
2Co 7:10 no regret, but worldly sorrow **b** death. G2981
Heb 1: 6 when God **b** his firstborn **into** the world G1652
Heb 10:22 heart and with the full assurance *that* **faith** *b*, AIT

BRITTLE (1)

Da 2:42 will be partly strong and partly **b**. A10752

BROAD (13) [BROADENED]

Nu 25: 4 expose them in **b daylight** before the LORD H9087
2Sa 12:11 your wives **in b daylight**.
H4200+6524+2021+9087+2021+2296
2Sa 12:12 thing **in b daylight** before H5584+2021+9087
2Sa 22:37 *You* **provide a b** path for my feet, so that H8143
Ne 3: 8 restored Jerusalem as far as the **B** Wall. H8146
Ne 12:38 past the Tower of the Ovens to the **B** Wall, H8146
Job 37:10 and the **b** waters become frozen. H8145
Ps 18:36 *You* **provide a b** path for my feet, so that H8143
Isa 30:23 day your cattle will graze in **b** meadows. H8146+3338
Isa 33:21 like a place of **b** rivers and streams H8146+3338
Am 8: 9 and darken the earth in **b daylight**. H240+3427
Mt 7:13 wide is the gate and **b** is the road that G2353
2Pe 2:13 of pleasure is to carouse in **b daylight**. G2465

BROADENED (1) [BROAD]

Ps 119:32 for *you have* **b** my understanding. H8143

BROIDED (KJV) ELABORATE

BROILED (1)

Lk 24:42 They gave him a piece of **b** fish, G3966

BROKE (82) [BREAK]

Ex 9:10 festering boils **b out** on people and H7255
Ex 34: 1 that were on the first tablets, which *you* **b**. H8689
Lev 24:10 a **fight b out** in the camp between H5897
Lev 26:13 *I* **b** the bars of your yoke and enabled you H8689
Dt 10: 2 that were on the first tablets, which *you* **b**. H8689
Dt 32:51 is because *both of you* **b faith** with me in H5085
Jos 3:14 the people **b camp** to cross H5825+4946+185
Jdg 6:32 So because Gideon **b down** Baal's altar H5997
Jdg 7:19 their trumpets and **b** the jars that were in H5879
1Sa 11:11 watch of the night *they* **b** into the camp of H995
1Sa 19: 8 Once more war **b out**, and David went out H2118
1Sa 23:28 Then Saul **b off** his pursuit of David H8740+4946
2Sa 23:16 three mighty warriors **b** through the H1324
2Ki 8:21 he rose up and **b through** by night; his H5782
2Ki 14:13 went to Jerusalem and **b down** the wall of H7287
2Ki 18: 4 *He* **b into pieces** the bronze snake Moses H4198
2Ki 19:36 king of Assyria **b camp** and withdrew. H5825
2Ki 23: 8 *He* **b down** the gateway at the entrance of H5997
2Ki 25:10 imperial guard **b down** the walls around H5997
2Ki 25:13 The Babylonians **b up** the bronze pillars H8689
1Ch 11:18 So the Three **b** through the Philistine lines, H1324
1Ch 15:13 LORD our God **b out in anger** against us. H7287
1Ch 20: 4 of time, war **b out** with the Philistines H6641
2Ch 15:16 **b it up** and burned it in the Kidron Valley. H1990
2Ch 21: 9 he rose up and **b through** by night. H5782
2Ch 25:23 him to Jerusalem and **b down** the wall of H7287
2Ch 26: 6 Philistines and **b down** the walls of Gath, H7287
2Ch 26:19 temple, leprosy **b out** on his forehead. H2436
2Ch 34: 4 These *he* **b to pieces** and scattered over H1990
2Ch 36:19 to God's temple and **b down** the wall of H5997
Job 22: 9 empty-handed and **b** the strength of the H1917
Job 29:17 *I* **b** the fangs of the wicked and snatched H8689
Ps 74:13 *you* **b** the heads of the monster in the H8689
Ps 76: 3 There *he* **b** the flashing arrows, the H8689
Ps 78:21 his fire **b out** against Jacob, and H5956
Ps 102:23 In the course of my life *he* **b** my strength H6700
Ps 106:29 and a plague **b out** among them. H7287
Ps 107:14 utter darkness, and **b away** their chains. H5998
Isa 7:17 any since Ephraim **b away** from Judah— H6073
Isa 37:37 king of Assyria **b camp** and withdrew. H5825
Isa 38:13 like a lion *he* **b** all my bones; day and H8689
Jer 2:20 "Long ago *you* **b off** your yoke and tore off H8689
Jer 28:10 the neck of the prophet Jeremiah and **b** it, H8689
Jer 31:32 because they **b** my covenant, though H7296
Jer 39: 8 of the people and **b down** the walls of H5997
Jer 52:14 **b down** all the walls around Jerusalem. H5997
Jer 52:17 The Babylonians **b up** the bronze pillars H8689
Eze 17: 4 *he* **b off** its topmost shoot and carried it H7786
Eze 17:16 oath he despised and whose treaty *he* **b**. H7296
Eze 19: 7 *He* **b down** their strongholds and H8318
Eze 29: 7 *you* **b** and their backs were wrenched. H8689
Eze 44: 7 fat and blood, and *you* **b** my covenant. H7296
Da 2:45 *that* **b** the iron, the bronze, the clay, the silver
and the gold **to pieces** A10182
Zec 11:10 Then I took my staff called Favor and **b** it H1548
Zec 11:14 Then *I* **b** my second staff called Union H1548
Mt 14:19 heaven, he gave thanks and **b** the loaves. G3089
Mt 15:36 *he* **b** them and gave them to the disciples, G3089
Mt 26:26 *he* **b** it and gave it to his disciples G3089
Mt 27:52 the tombs **b open**. The bodies of many G487
Mk 4:37 and the waves **b over** the boat, so that G2095
Mk 5: 4 the chains apart and **b** the irons on his G5341
Mk 6:41 heaven, he gave thanks and **b** the loaves. G2880
Mk 8: 6 *he* **b** them and gave them to his disciples G3089
Mk 8:19 When *I* **b** the five loaves for the five G3089
Mk 8:20 "And when I **b** the seven loaves for the four NDT
Mk 14: 3 *She* **b** the jar and poured the perfume on G5341
Mk 14:22 *he* **b** it and gave it to his disciples G3089
Mk 14:72 And *he* **b down** and wept. G2095
Lk 9:16 to heaven, he gave thanks and **b** them. G2880
Lk 22:19 gave thanks and **b** it, and gave it to G3089
Lk 24:30 **b** it and began to give it to them. G3089
Lk 24:35 recognized by them when *he* **b** the bread. G3082
Jn 19:32 therefore came and **b** the legs of the first G2862
Ac 2:46 *They* **b** bread in their homes and ate G3089
Ac 8: 1 great persecution **b out** against the church G1181
Ac 11:19 persecution that **b out** when Stephen was G1181
Ac 20:11 went upstairs again and **b** bread and ate. G3089
Ac 23: 7 a dispute **b out** between the Pharisees G1181
Ac 27:35 Then *he* **b** it and began to eat G3089
1Co 11:24 had given thanks, *he* **b** it and said, "This G3089
Rev 12: 7 Then war **b out** in heaven. Michael and G1181
Rev 16: 2 festering sores **b out** on the people who G1181

BROKEN (129) [BREAK]

Ge 17:14 from his people; he *has* **b** my covenant." H7296
Ge 38:29 "So this is how *you have* **b out**!" H7287+7288
Ex 21: 8 foreigners, because he *has* **b faith** with her. H953
Lev 6:21 the grain offering **b** *in* pieces as an aroma H9519
Lev 6:28 clay pot the meat is cooked in *must* **be b**; H8689
Lev 11:35 an oven or cooking pot *must* **be b up**. H5997
Lev 13:20 skin disease *that has* **b out** where the boil H7255
Lev 13:25 disease *that has* **b out** in the burn. H7255
Lev 13:39 harmless rash *that has* **b out** on the skin; H7255
Lev 15:12 clay pot that the man touches *must* **be b**, H8689
Nu 15:31 the LORD's word and **b** his commands, H7296
Dt 21: 6 the heifer whose **neck was b** in the valley, H6904
Jdg 6:30 because *he has* **b down** Baal's altar and H5997
1Sa 2: 4 "The bows of the warriors are **b**, but those H3146
1Sa 2:10 those who oppose the LORD *will* **be b**. H3169
1Sa 4:18 His neck **was b** and he died, for he was H8689
1Sa 5: 4 hands *had* **been b off** and were lying H4162
1Sa 14:33 "*You have* **b faith**," he said H953
2Sa 5:20 the LORD *has* **b out** *against* my enemies H7287
2Sa 6: 8 the LORD's wrath *had* **b out** against Uzzah, H7287
2Ki 25: 4 Then the city wall **was b through**, and the H1324
1Ch 13:11 the LORD's wrath *had* **b out** against Uzzah, H7287
1Ch 14:11 God *has* **b out** *against* my enemies by my H7287
2Ch 24: 7 woman Athaliah *had* **b into** the temple of H7287
2Ch 32: 5 all the **b** *sections* of the wall and H7287
Ne 1: 3 The wall of Jerusalem *is* **b down**, and its H7287
Ne 2:13 which *had been* **b down**, and its gates, H7287
Job 2: 8 Job took a **piece of b pottery** and scraped H3084
Job 4:10 the teeth of the great lions **are b**. H5996
Job 4:20 dawn and dusk *they* **are b to pieces**; H4198
Job 7: 5 scabs, my skin *is* **b** and festering. H8090
Job 17: 1 My spirit **is b**, my days are cut short, the H2472
Job 24:20 longer remembered but **are b** like a tree. H8689
Job 30:24 lays a hand on a **b man** when he cries H6505
Job 31:22 the shoulder, *let* it **be b off** at the joint. H8689
Job 31:39 yield without payment or **b** the spirit of its H5870
Job 38:15 their light, and their upraised arm **is b**. H8689
Ps 31:12 I were dead; I have become like **b** pottery. H6
Ps 34:20 all his bones, not one of them *will* **be b**. H8689
Ps 37:15 their own hearts, and their bows *will* **be b**. H8689
Ps 37:17 the power of the wicked *will* **be b**, but H8689
Ps 51:17 is a **b** spirit; a broken and contrite H8689
Ps 51:17 a broken spirit; a **b** and contrite heart you H8689
Ps 69:20 Scorn *has* **b** my heart and has left me H8689
Ps 80:12 Why *have you* **b down** its walls so that all H7287

Ps 89:40 *You have* **b through** all his walls and H7287
Ps 119:126 you to act, LORD; your law *is being* **b**. H7296
Ps 124: 7 the snare *has* **been b**, and we have H8689
Pr 22: 8 the rod they wield in fury *will be* **b**. H3983
Pr 25:19 Like a **b** tooth or a lame foot is reliance H8317
Pr 25:28 whose walls **are b through** is a person H7287
Ecc 4:12 A cord of three strands **is** not quickly **b**. H5998
Ecc 12: 6 the golden bowl *is* **b**; before the H8368
Ecc 12: 6 the spring, and the wheel **b** at the well, H8368
Isa 1:28 But rebels and sinners will both be **b**, and H8691
Isa 5:27 at the waist, not a sandal strap *is* **b**. H5998
Isa 8:15 they will fall and **be b**, they will be snared H8689
Isa 10:27 the yoke *will* **be b** because you have H2472
Isa 14: 5 The LORD *has* **b** the rod of the wicked, the H8689
Isa 14:29 that the rod that struck you *is* **b**; from the H8689
Isa 22: 9 **walls** of the City of David were **b through** H1323
Isa 24: 5 the statutes and **b** the everlasting H7296
Isa 24:19 The earth **is b up**, the earth is split H8318+8318
Isa 27:11 *they* **are b off** and women come and H8689
Isa 33: 8 The treaty *is* **b**, its witnesses are despised H7296
Isa 33:20 never be pulled up, nor any of its ropes **b**. H5998
Isa 58:12 you will be called Repairer of **B** Walls H7288
Isa 59: 5 will die, and *when* one *is* **b**, an adder is H2318
Jer 2:13 cisterns, **b** cisterns that cannot hold water. H8689
Jer 5: 5 accord they too *had* **b off** the yoke and H8689
Jer 11:10 Israel and Judah *have* **b** the covenant I H7296
Jer 11:16 set it on fire, and its branches *will be* **b**. H8318
Jer 22:28 a despised, **b**, pot, an object no one H5879
Jer 23: 9 My heart *is* **b** within me; all my bones H8689
Jer 28:12 prophet Hananiah *had* **b** the yoke off the H8689
Jer 28:13 *You have* **b** a wooden yoke, but in its H8689
Jer 33:21 *can* **be b** and David will no longer have a H7296
Jer 39: 2 eleventh year, the city wall **was b through**. H1324
Jer 48: 4 Moab *will* **be b**; her little ones will cry out. H8689
Jer 48:17 'How **b** *is* the mighty scepter, how H8689
Jer 48:17 the mighty scepter, how **b** the glorious staff! NDT
Jer 48:25 is cut off; her arm **is b**," declares the LORD. H8689
Jer 48:38 for *I have* **b** Moab like a jar that no one H8689
Jer 50:23 How **b** and shattered is the hammer of H1548
Jer 51: 8 Babylon will suddenly fall and **be b**. H8689
Jer 51:30 are set on fire; the bars of her gates **are b**. H8689
Jer 51:56 will be captured, and their bows *will be* **b**. H3169
Jer 52: 7 Then the city wall **was b through**, and the H1324
La 2: 9 their bars *he has* **b** and destroyed. H8689
La 3: 4 my flesh grow old and *has* **b** my bones. H8689
La 3:16 *He has* **b** my teeth with gravel; he has H1756
Eze 6: 6 your incense altars **b down**, and what you H1548
Eze 21: 6 before them with **b** heart and bitter grief H8695
Eze 26: 2 The gate to the nations **is b**, and its doors H8689
Eze 26:10 a city whose walls *have* **been b through**. H1324
Eze 30:21 *I have* **b** the arm of Pharaoh king of Egypt. H8689
Eze 30:22 the good arm as well as the **b** *one*, and H8689
Eze 31:12 its branches *lay* **b** in all the ravines of the H8689
Eze 32:28 *will* **be b** and will lie among the H8689
Da 2:35 the gold *were* all **b to pieces** and A10182
Da 8: 8 of its power the large horn **was b off**, H8689
Da 8:22 replaced the *one that* **was b off** represent H8689
Da 11: 4 his empire *will* **be b up** and parceled out H8689
Da 12: 7 of the holy people *has been* finally **b**, H5879
Hos 6: 7 As at Adam, they *have* **b** the covenant H6296
Hos 8: 1 the people *have* **b** my covenant and H6296
Hos 8: 6 It will be **b in pieces**, that calf of H8646
Joel 1:17 the granaries *have* **been b down**, for the H2238
Am 9:11 I will repair its **b walls** and restore its ruins H7288
Mic 1: 7 All her idols *will* **be b to pieces**; all her H4198
Zec 9:10 Jerusalem, and the battle bow *will* **be b**. H4162
Mt 14:20 basketfuls *of* **b pieces** that were left *G3083*
Mt 15:37 seven basketfuls *of* **b pieces** that were left *G3083*
Mt 21:44 who falls on this stone *will be* **b to pieces**; *G5314*
Mt 24:43 would not have let his house *be* **b into**. *G1482*
Mk 6:43 twelve basketfuls *of* **b pieces** of bread *G3083*
Mk 8: 8 seven basketfuls *of* **b pieces** that were left *G3083*
Lk 8:29 *he had* **b** his chains and had been driven *G1396*
Lk 9:17 basketfuls *of* **b pieces** that were left *G3083*
Lk 12:39 he would not have let his house *be* **b into**. *G1482*
Lk 20:18 falls on that stone *will be* **b to pieces**; *G5314*
Jn 7:23 so that the law of Moses *may* not *be* **b**, *G3395*
Jn 19:31 Pilate to *have* the legs **b** and the bodies *G2862*
Jn 19:36 "Not *one* of his bones *will be* **b**," *G5341*
Ac 27:41 the stern *was* **b to pieces** by the *G3395*
Ro 11:17 If some of the branches *have been* **b off** *G1709*
Ro 11:19 "Branches *were* **b off** so that I could be *G1709*
Ro 11:20 But *they were* **b off** because of unbelief *G1709*
1Ti 5:12 because *they have* **b** their first pledge. *G119*

BROKENHEARTED (4) [HEART]

Ps 34:18 is close to the **b** and saves those H8689+4213
Ps 109:16 the poor and the needy and the **b**. H3874+4222
Ps 147: 3 He heals the **b** and binds up their H8689+4213
Isa 61: 1 He has sent me to bind up the **b** H8689+4213

BROKENNESS (1) [BREAK]

Isa 65:14 anguish of heart and wail in **b** *of* spirit. H8691

BRONZE (160) [BRONZE-TIPPED]

Ge 4:22 forged all kinds of tools out of **b** and iron. H5733
Ex 25: 3 to receive from them: gold, silver and **b**; H5733
Ex 26:11 Then make fifty **b** clasps and put them in H5733
Ex 26:37 And cast five **b** bases for them. H5733
Ex 27: 2 of one piece, and overlay the altar with **b**. H5733
Ex 27: 3 Make all its utensils of **b**—its pots to H5733
Ex 27: 4 a grating for it, a **b** network, and make a H5733
Ex 27: 4 make a **b** ring at each of the four H5733
Ex 27: 6 the altar and overlay them with **b**. H5733
Ex 27:10 posts and twenty **b** bases and with silver H5733
Ex 27:11 posts and twenty **b** bases and with silver H5733
Ex 27:17 silver bands and hooks, and **b** bases. H5733
Ex 27:18 linen five cubits high, and with **b** bases. H5733
Ex 27:19 those for the courtyard, are to be of **b**. H5733
Ex 30:18 "Make a **b** basin, with its bronze stand, for H5733
Ex 30:18 with its **b** stand, for washing. H5733
Ex 31: 4 designs for work in gold, silver and **b**, H5733
Ex 35: 5 the LORD an offering of gold, silver and **b**; H5733
Ex 35:16 the altar of burnt offering with its **b** grating, H5733
Ex 35:16 all its utensils; the **b** basin with its stand; NDT
Ex 35:24 an offering of silver or **b** brought it as an H5733
Ex 35:32 designs for work in gold, silver and **b**, H5733
Ex 36:18 They made fifty **b** clasps to fasten the tent H5733
Ex 36:38 with gold and made their five bases of **b**. H5733
Ex 38: 2 and they overlaid the altar with **b**. H5733
Ex 38: 3 They made all its utensils of **b**—its pots H5733
Ex 38: 4 the altar, a **b** network, to be under its H5733
Ex 38: 5 They cast **b** rings to hold the poles for the NDT
Ex 38: 5 poles for the four corners of the **b** grating. H5733
Ex 38: 6 of acacia wood and overlaid them with **b**. H5733
Ex 38: 8 They made the **b** basin and its bronze H5733
Ex 38: 8 bronze basin and its **b** stand from the H5733
Ex 38:10 with twenty posts and twenty **b** bases, and H5733
Ex 38:11 had twenty posts and twenty **b** bases, H5733
Ex 38:17 The bases for the posts were **b**. The hooks H5733
Ex 38:19 with four posts and four **b** bases. H5733
Ex 38:20 of the surrounding courtyard were **b**. H5733
Ex 38:29 The **b** *from* the wave offering was 70 H5733
Ex 38:30 the **b** altar with its bronze grating and all H5733
Ex 38:30 bronze altar with its **b** grating and all its H5733
Ex 39:39 the **b** altar with its bronze grating, its poles H5733
Ex 39:39 the bronze altar with its **b** grating, its poles H5733
Lev 6:28 if it is cooked in a **b** pot, the pot is to H5733
Lev 26:19 iron and the ground beneath you like **b**. H5703
Nu 4:13 the ashes from the **b** altar and spread a NDT
Nu 16:39 priest collected the **b** censers brought by H5733
Nu 21: 9 So Moses made a **b** snake and put it up H5733
Nu 21: 9 by a snake and looked at the **b** snake, H5733
Nu 31:22 silver, **b**, iron, tin, lead H5733
Dt 28:23 The sky over your head will be **b**, the H5733
Dt 33:25 The bolts of your gates will be iron and **b** H5733
Jos 6:19 the articles of **b** and iron are sacred H5733
Jos 6:24 the articles of **b** and iron into the H5733
Jos 22: 8 **b** and iron, and a great quantity of H5733
Jdg 16:21 Binding him with **b** *shackles*, they set him H5733
1Sa 17: 5 He had a **b** helmet on his head and wore H5733
1Sa 17: 5 of scale armor of **b** weighing five H5733
1Sa 17: 6 on his legs he wore **b** greaves, and a H5733
1Sa 17: 6 a **b** javelin was slung on his back. H5733
1Sa 17:38 armor on him and a **b** helmet on his head H5733
2Sa 8: 8 King David took a great quantity of **b**. H5733
2Sa 8:10 him articles of silver, of gold and of **b**. H5733
2Sa 21:16 whose **b** spearhead weighed three H5733
2Sa 22:35 battle; my arms can bend a bow of **b**. H5703
1Ki 4:13 sixty large walled cities with **b** gate bars); H5733
1Ki 7:14 from Tyre and a skilled craftsman in **b**. H5733
1Ki 7:14 with knowledge to do all kinds of **b** work. H5733
1Ki 7:15 He cast two **b** pillars, each eighteen H5733
1Ki 7:16 two capitals of cast **b** to set on the tops of H5733
1Ki 7:27 He also made ten movable stands of **b** H5733
1Ki 7:30 Each stand had four **b** wheels with bronze H5733
1Ki 7:30 had four bronze wheels with **b** axles, H5733
1Ki 7:38 He then made ten **b** basins, each holding H5733
1Ki 7:45 temple of the LORD were of burnished **b**. H5733
1Ki 7:47 the weight of the **b** was not determined. H5733
1Ki 8:64 because the **b** altar that stood before the H5733
1Ki 14:27 Rehoboam made **b** shields to replace H5733
2Ki 16:14 As for the **b** altar that stood before the H5733
2Ki 16:15 But I will use the **b** altar for seeking H5733
2Ki 16:17 the Sea from the **b** bulls that supported it H5733
2Ki 18: 4 into pieces the **b** snake Moses had made, H5733
2Ki 25: 7 bound him with **b shackles** and took him H5733
2Ki 25:13 The Babylonians broke up the **b** pillars H5733
2Ki 25:13 stands and the **b** Sea that were at the H5733
2Ki 25:13 LORD and they carried the **b** to Babylon. H5733
2Ki 25:14 dishes and all the **b** articles used in the H5733
2Ki 25:16 The **b** *from* the two pillars, the Sea and H5733
2Ki 25:17 The **b** capital on top of one pillar was H5733
2Ki 25:17 pomegranates of **b** all around. H5733
1Ch 15:19 Ethan were to sound the **b** cymbals; H5733
1Ch 18: 8 David took a great quantity of **b**, which H5733
1Ch 18: 8 which Solomon used to make the **b** Sea H5733
1Ch 18: 8 the pillars and various **b** articles. H5733
1Ch 18:10 kinds of articles of gold, of silver and of **b**. H5733
1Ch 22: 3 more **b** than could be weighed. H5733
1Ch 22:14 quantities of **b** and iron too great to be H5733
1Ch 22:16 in gold and silver, **b** and iron—craftsmen H5733
1Ch 29: 2 silver for the silver, **b** for the bronze, iron H5733
1Ch 29: 2 bronze for the **b**, iron for the iron and H5733
1Ch 29: 7 thousand talents of **b** and a hundred H5733
2Ch 1: 5 But the **b** altar that Bezalel son of Uri, the H5733
2Ch 1: 6 went up to the **b** altar before the LORD H5733
2Ch 2: 7 in gold and silver, **b** and iron, and in H5733
2Ch 2:14 in gold and silver, **b** and iron, stone and H5733
2Ch 4: 1 He made a **b** altar twenty cubits long H5733
2Ch 4: 9 the court, and overlaid the doors with **b**. H5733
2Ch 4:16 the temple of the LORD were of polished **b**. H5733
2Ch 4:18 that the weight of the **b** could not be H5733
2Ch 6:13 Now he had made a **b** platform, five cubits H5733
2Ch 7: 7 because the **b** altar he had made could H5733
2Ch 12:10 Rehoboam made **b** shields to replace H5733
2Ch 24:12 workers in iron and **b** to repair the temple. H5733
2Ch 33:11 bound him with **b shackles** and took him H5733
2Ch 36: 6 bound him with **b shackles** to take him to H5733
Ezr 8:27 two fine articles of polished **b**, as H5733
Job 6:12 have the strength of stone? Is my flesh **b**? H5702
Job 37:18 out the skies, hard as a mirror of **cast b**? H4607
Job 40:18 Its bones are tubes of **b**, its limbs like rods H5703
Job 41:27 it treats like straw and **b** like rotten wood. H5703
Ps 18:34 battle; my arms can bend a bow of **b**. H5703
Ps 107:16 breaks down gates of **b** and cuts through H5733
Isa 45: 2 break down gates of **b** and cut through H5703
Isa 48: 4 muscles were iron, your forehead was **b**. H5703
Isa 60:17 Instead of **b** I will bring you gold, and H5733
Isa 60:17 Instead of wood I will bring you **b**, and H5733
Jer 1:18 an iron pillar and a **b** wall to stand H5733
Jer 6:28 They are **b** and iron; they all H5733
Jer 15:12 break iron—iron from the north—or **b**? H5733
Jer 15:20 a fortified wall of **b**; they will fight against H5733
Jer 27:19 about the pillars, the **b** Sea, the movable NDT
Jer 39: 7 bound him with **b shackles** to take him to H5733
Jer 52:11 bound him with **b shackles** and took him H5733
Jer 52:17 The Babylonians broke up the **b** pillars H5733
Jer 52:17 stands and the **b** Sea that were at the H5733
Jer 52:17 LORD and they carried all the **b** to Babylon. H5733
Jer 52:18 dishes and all the **b** articles used in the H5733
Jer 52:20 The **b** *from* the two pillars, the Sea and H5733
Jer 52:20 the Sea and the twelve **b** bulls under it H5733
Jer 52:22 The **b** capital on top of one pillar was five H5733
Jer 52:22 pomegranates of **b** all around. H5733
Eze 1: 7 of a calf and gleamed like burnished **b**. H5733
Eze 9: 2 came in and stood beside the **b** altar. H5733
Eze 27:13 beings and articles of **b** for your wares. H5733
Eze 40: 3 saw a man whose appearance was like **b**; H5733
Da 2:32 arms of silver, its belly and thighs of **b**, A10473
Da 2:35 the clay, the **b**, the silver and the gold A10473
Da 2:39 kingdom, one of **b**, will rule over the A10473
Da 2:45 broke the iron, the **b**, the clay, the silver A10473
Da 4:15 bound with iron and **b**, remain in the A10473
Da 4:23 bound with iron and **b**, in the grass of A10473
Da 5: 4 the gods of gold and silver, of **b**, iron, A10473
Da 5:23 the gods of silver and gold, of **b**, iron, A10473
Da 7:19 with its iron teeth and **b** claws—the A10473
Da 10: 6 legs like the gleam of burnished **b**, H5733
Mic 4:13 I will give you hooves of **b**, and you will H5703
Zec 6: 1 between two mountains—mountains of **b**. H5733
Rev 1:15 His feet were like **b** glowing in a furnace *G5909*
Rev 2:18 fire and whose feet are like **burnished b**. *G5909*
Rev 9:20 of gold, silver, **b**, stone and wood—idols *G5911*
Rev 18:12 of ivory, costly wood, **b**, iron and marble; *G5910*

BRONZE-TIPPED (1) [BRONZE]

Job 20:24 an iron weapon, a **b** arrow pierces him. H5703

BROOCHES (1)

Ex 35:22 jewelry of all kinds: **b**, earrings, rings and H2626

BROOD (9)

Nu 32:14 here you are, a **b** *of* sinners, standing H9551
Job 30: 8 A base and nameless **b**, they were driven H1201
Isa 1: 4 guilt is great, a **b** *of* evildoers, children H2446
Isa 57: 4 Are you not a **b** *of* rebels, the offspring of H3529
Mt 3: 7 "You **b** of vipers! Who *G1165*
Mt 12:34 You **b** of vipers, how can you who are evil *G1165*
Mt 23:33 *You* **b** of vipers! How will *G1165*
Lk 3: 7 to be baptized by him, "*You* **b** of vipers! *G1165*
2Pe 2:14 they are experts in greed—an accursed **b**! *G5451*

BROOK (6) [BROOKS]

2Sa 17:20 "They crossed over the **b**. H4782+4784
1Ki 17: 4 You will drink from the **b**, and I have H5707
1Ki 17: 6 in the evening, and he drank from the **b**. H5707
1Ki 17: 7 Some time later the **b** dried up because H5707
Ps 110: 7 He will drink from a **b** along the way, and H5707
Jer 15:18 You are to me like a deceptive **b**, like a NDT

BROOKS (1) [BROOK]

Dt 8: 7 good land—a land with **b**, streams, H5707+4784

BROOM (4)

1Ki 19: 4 He came to a **b bush**, sat down under it H8413
Job 30: 4 their food was the root of the **b bush**. H8413
Ps 120: 4 with burning coals of the **b bush**. H8413
Isa 14:23 I will sweep her with the **b** *of* destruction," H4748

BROTH (3)

Jdg 6:19 the meat in a basket and its **b** in a pot, H5348
Jdg 6:20 them on this rock, and pour out the **b**." H5348
Isa 65: 4 whose pots hold **b** *of* impure meat; H5348

BROTHER (293) [BROTHER-IN-LAW, BROTHER'S, BROTHERHOOD, BROTHERS]

Ge 4: 2 Later she gave birth to his **b** Abel. H278
Ge 4: 8 Now Cain said to his **b** Abel, "Let's go out H278
Ge 4: 8 Cain attacked his **b** Abel and killed him. H278
Ge 4: 9 LORD said to Cain, "Where is your **b** Abel?" H278
Ge 10:21 whose older **b** was Japheth; Shem H278
Ge 10:25 was divided; his **b** was named Joktan. H278
Ge 14:13 the Amorite, a **b** *of* Eshkol and Aner H278
Ge 20: 5 didn't she also say, 'He is my **b**'? H278
Ge 20:13 say of me, "He is my **b**." ' " H278
Ge 20:16 "I am giving your **b** a thousand shekels of H278

Ge 22:20 she has borne sons to your **b** Nahor: H278
Ge 22:21 firstborn, Buz his **b**, Kemuel (the father of H278
Ge 22:23 these eight sons to Abraham's **b** Nahor. H278
Ge 24:15 who was the wife of Abraham's **b** Nahor. H278
Ge 24:29 Now Rebekah had a **b** named Laban, and H278
Ge 24:48 granddaughter of my master's **b** for his son. H278
Ge 24:53 gave costly gifts to her **b** and to her mother. H278
Ge 24:55 But her **b** and her mother replied, "Let the H278
Ge 25:26 After this, his **b** came out, with his hand H278
Ge 27: 6 I overheard your father say to your **b** Esau, H278
Ge 27:11 "But my **b** Esau is a hairy man while I have H278
Ge 27:23 hands were hairy like those of his **b** Esau; H278
Ge 27:30 presence, his **b** Esau came in from hunting. H278
Ge 27:35 "Your **b** came deceitfully and took your H278
Ge 27:40 live by the sword and you will serve your **b**. H278
Ge 27:41 father are near; then I will kill my **b** Jacob." H278
Ge 27:42 "Your **b** Esau is planning to avenge himself H278
Ge 27:43 Flee at once to my **b** Laban in Harran. H278
Ge 27:45 When your **b** is no longer angry with you H278
Ge 28: 2 the daughters of Laban, your mother's **b**. H278
Ge 28: 5 the Aramean, the **b** *of* Rebekah, who was H278
Ge 32: 3 ahead of him to his **b** Esau in the land of H278
Ge 32: 6 "We went to your **b** Esau, and now he is H278
Ge 32:11 from the hand of my **b** Esau, for I am afraid H278
Ge 32:13 with him he selected a gift for his **b** Esau: H278
Ge 32:17 "When my **b** Esau meets you and asks H278
Ge 33: 3 seven times as he approached his **b**. H278
Ge 33: 9 have plenty, my **b**. Keep what you have H278
Ge 35: 1 when you were fleeing from your **b** Esau." H278
Ge 35: 7 to him when he was fleeing from his **b**. H278
Ge 36: 6 to a land some distance from his **b** Jacob. H278
Ge 37:26 gain if we kill our **b** and cover up his blood H278
Ge 37:27 after all, he is our **b**, our own flesh and H278
Ge 38: 8 to raise up offspring for your **b**. H278
Ge 38: 9 to keep from providing offspring for his **b**. H278
Ge 38:29 back his hand, his **b** came out, and she H278
Ge 38:30 Then his **b**, who had the scarlet thread on H278
Ge 42: 4 Benjamin, Joseph's **b**, with the others, H278
Ge 42:15 place unless your youngest **b** comes here. H278
Ge 42:16 Send one of your number to get your **b**; the H278
Ge 42:20 But you must bring your youngest **b** to me H278
Ge 42:21 we are being punished because of our **b**. H278
Ge 42:34 bring your youngest **b** to me so I will know H278
Ge 42:34 Then I will give your **b** back to you, and you H278
Ge 42:38 his **b** is dead and he is the only one left. H278
Ge 43: 3 my face again unless your **b** is with you. H278
Ge 43: 4 If you will send our **b** along with us, we will H278
Ge 43: 5 my face again unless your **b** is with you. H278
Ge 43: 6 me by telling the man you had another **b**?" H278
Ge 43: 7 'Do you have another **b**?' We simply H278
Ge 43: 7 he would say, 'Bring your **b** down here'?" H278
Ge 43:13 Take your **b** also and go back to the man at H278
Ge 43:14 will let your other **b** and Benjamin come H278
Ge 43:29 he looked about and saw his **b** Benjamin, H278
Ge 43:29 "Is this your youngest **b**, the one you told H278
Ge 43:30 Deeply moved at the sight of his **b**, Joseph H278
Ge 44:19 his servants, 'Do you have a father or a **b**? H278
Ge 44:20 His **b** is dead, and he is the only one of his H278
Ge 44:23 your youngest **b** comes down with you, H278
Ge 44:26 Only if our youngest **b** is with us will we go H278
Ge 44:26 face unless our youngest **b** is with us. H278
Ge 45: 4 he said, "I am your **b** Joseph, the one you H278
Ge 45:12 so can my **b** Benjamin, that it is H278
Ge 45:14 his arms around his **b** Benjamin and wept, H278
Ge 48:19 his younger **b** will be greater than he H278
Ex 4:14 "What about your **b**, Aaron the Levite? H278
Ex 7: 1 your **b** Aaron will be your prophet. H278
Ex 7: 2 your **b** Aaron is to tell Pharaoh to let H278
Ex 28: 1 "Have Aaron your **b** brought to you from H278
Ex 28: 2 garments for your **b** Aaron to give him H278
Ex 28: 4 garments for your **b** Aaron and his sons, H278
Ex 28:41 clothes on your **b** Aaron and his sons, H278
Ex 32:27 each killing his **b** and friend and neighbor. H278
Lev 16: 2 "Tell your **b** Aaron that he is not to come H278
Lev 18:14 dishonor your father's **b** by approaching his H278
Lev 18:16 brother's wife; that would dishonor your **b**. H278
Lev 20:21 an act of impurity; he has dishonored his **b**. H278
Lev 21: 2 father, his son or daughter, his **b**, H278
Nu 6: 7 own father or mother or **b** or sister dies, H278
Nu 20: 8 you and your **b** Aaron gather the H278
Nu 20:14 "This is what your **b** Israel says: You know H278
Nu 27:13 to your people, as your **b** Aaron was, H278
Nu 36: 2 the inheritance of our **b** Zelophehad to his H278
Dt 13: 6 If your **very own b**, or H278+1201+562+3870
Dt 25: 5 Her **husband's b** shall take her and marry H3303
Dt 25: 6 the name of the dead **b** so that his name H278
Dt 25: 7 "My **husband's b** refuses to carry on his H3303
Dt 28:54 on his own **b** or the wife he loves H278
Dt 32:50 just as your **b** Aaron died on Mount Hor H278
Jos 15:17 son of Kenaz, Caleb's **b**, took it; so Caleb H278
Jdg 1:13 son of Kenaz, Caleb's younger **b**, took it; H278
Jdg 3: 9 Caleb's younger **b**, who saved them. H278
Jdg 9:21 because he was afraid of his **b** Abimelek. H278
Jdg 9:24 avenged on their **b** Abimelek and on the H278
1Sa 14: 3 a son of Ichabod's **b** Ahitub son of H278
1Sa 17:28 David's oldest **b**, heard him speaking H278
1Sa 20:29 in the town and my **b** has ordered me to be H278
1Sa 26: 6 of Zeruiah, Joab's **b**, "Who will go down H278
2Sa 1:26 you, Jonathan my **b**; you were very dear H278
2Sa 2:22 How could I look your **b** Joab in the face?" H278
2Sa 3:27 to avenge the blood of his **b** Asahel, Joab H278
2Sa 3:30 Joab and his **b** Abishai murdered Abner H278
2Sa 3:30 he had killed their **b** Asahel in the battle at H278
2Sa 4: 6 Then Rekab and his **b** Baanah slipped H278
2Sa 4: 9 David answered Rekab and his **b** Baanah H278
2Sa 10:10 of Abishai his **b** and deployed them H278
2Sa 13: 3 Jonadab son of Shimeah, David's **b**. H278
2Sa 13: 4 in love with Tamar, my **b** Absalom's sister." H278
2Sa 13: 7 to the house of your **b** Amnon and prepare H278
2Sa 13: 8 Tamar went to the house of her **b** Amnon, H278
2Sa 13:10 brought it to her **b** Amnon in his bedroom. H278
2Sa 13:12 my **b**!" she said to him. "Don't force H278
2Sa 13:20 Her **b** Absalom said to her, "Has that H278
2Sa 13:20 "Has that Amnon, your **b**, been with you? H278
2Sa 13:20 my sister; he is your **b**. Don't take this thing H278
2Sa 13:20 And Tamar lived in her **b** Absalom's house, H278
2Sa 13:26 please let my **b** Amnon come with us." H278
2Sa 13:32 Jonadab son of Shimeah, David's **b**, said, H278
2Sa 14: 7 'Hand over the one who struck his **b** down H278
2Sa 14: 7 death for the life of his **b** whom he killed; H278
2Sa 18: 2 a third under Joab's **b** Abishai son of H278
2Sa 20: 9 "How are you, my **b**?" Then Joab took H278
2Sa 20:10 Then Joab and his **b** Abishai pursued H278
2Sa 21:19 killed the **b** *of* Goliath the Gittite, H278
2Sa 21:21 son of Shimeah, David's **b**, killed him. H278
2Sa 23:18 Abishai the **b** *of* Joab son of Zeruiah was H278
2Sa 23:24 Asahel the **b** *of* Joab, Elhanan son of Dodo H278
1Ki 1:10 the special guard or his **b** Solomon. H278
1Ki 2: 7 by me when I fled from your **b** Absalom. H278
1Ki 2:15 the kingdom has gone to my **b**; for it H278
1Ki 2:21 be given in marriage to your **b** Adonijah." H278
1Ki 2:22 he is my older **b**—yes, for him and for H278
1Ki 9:13 towns are these you have given me, my **b**?" H278
1Ki 13:30 mourned over him and said, "Alas, my **b**!" H278
1Ki 20:32 answered, "Is he still alive? He is my **b**." H278
1Ki 20:33 "Yes, your **b** Ben-Hadad!" they H278
1Ch 1:19 was divided; his **b** was named Joktan. H278
1Ch 2:32 of Jada, Shammai's **b**: Jether and H278
1Ch 2:42 The sons of Caleb the **b** *of* Jerahmeel H278
1Ch 4:11 Shuhah's **b**, was the father of Mehir H278
1Ch 7:16 His **b** was named Sheresh, and his sons H278
1Ch 7:35 The sons of his **b** Helem: Zophah, Imna H278
1Ch 8:39 The sons of his **b** Eshek: Ulam his firstborn H278
1Ch 11:20 Abishai the **b** *of* Joab was chief of the H278
1Ch 11:26 Asahel the **b** *of* Joab, Elhanan son of Dodo H278
1Ch 11:38 Joel the **b** *of* Nathan, Mibhar son of Hagri, H278
1Ch 11:45 son of Shimri, his **b** Joha the Tizite, H278
1Ch 19:11 men under the command of Abishai his **b**, H278
1Ch 19:15 too fled before his **b** Abishai and went H278
1Ch 20: 5 killed Lahmi the **b** *of* Goliath the Gittite, H278
1Ch 20: 7 son of Shimea, David's **b**, killed him. H278
1Ch 24:25 The **b** *of* Micah: Ishiah; from the sons of H278
1Ch 24:31 of the oldest **b** were treated the same H278
1Ch 26:22 Zetham and his **b** Joel. They were in H278
1Ch 27: 7 was Asahel the **b** *of* Joab; his son H278
1Ch 27:18 Elihu, a **b** *of* David; over Issachar H278
2Ch 31:12 and his **b** Shimei was next in rank. H278
2Ch 31:13 assistants of Konaniah and Shimei his **b**. H278
2Ch 36: 4 made Eliakim, a **b** *of* Jehoahaz, king over H278
2Ch 36: 4 took Eliakim's **b** Jehoahaz and carried H278
Ne 7: 2 I put in charge of Jerusalem my **b** Hanani H278
Job 30:29 I have become a **b** of jackals, a companion H278
Ps 35:14 mourning as though for my friend or **b**. H278
Ps 50:20 testify against your **b** and slander your own H278
Pr 17:17 a **b** is born for a time of adversity. H278
Pr 18: 9 slack in his work is **b** to one who destroys. H278
Pr 18:19 A **b** wronged is more unyielding than a H278
Pr 18:24 there is a friend who sticks closer than a **b**. H278
Ecc 4: 8 a man all alone; he had neither son nor **b**. H278
SS 8: 1 If only you were to me like a **b**, who was H278
Isa 19: 2 Egyptian—**b** will fight against brother H408
Isa 19: 2 brother will fight against **b**, neighbor H278
Jer 22:18 will not mourn for him: 'Alas, my **b**! Alas, H278
Eze 18:18 robbed his **b** and did what was wrong H278
Eze 38:21 Every man's sword will be against his **b**. H278
Eze 44:25 son or daughter, **b** or unmarried sister, then H278
Am 1:11 Because he pursued his **b** with a sword H278
Ob 10 of the violence against your **b** Jacob, H278
Ob 12 not gloat over your **b** in the day of his H278
Hag 2:22 riders will fall, each by the sword of his **b**. H278
Mal 1: 2 "Was not Esau Jacob's **b**?" declares the H278
Mt 4:18 Simon called Peter and his **b** Andrew. *G81*
Mt 4:21 James son of Zebedee and his **b** John. *G81*
Mt 5:22 who is angry *with* a **b or sister** will be subject *G81*
Mt 5:22 anyone who says *to* a **b or sister**, 'Raca, *G81*
Mt 5:23 that your **b or sister** has something *G81*
Mt 7: 4 How can you say *to* your **b**, 'Let me take the *G81*
Mt 10: 2 and his **b** Andrew; James son of *G81*
Mt 10: 2 James son of Zebedee, and his **b** John; *G81*
Mt 10:21 "**B** will betray brother to death, and a father *G81*
Mt 10:21 "Brother will betray **b** to death, and a father *G81*
Mt 12:50 in heaven is my **b** and sister and mother." *G81*
Mt 14: 3 because of Herodias, his **b** Philip's wife, *G81*
Mt 17: 1 James and John the **b** of James, and led *G81*
Mt 18:15 "If your **b or sister** sins, go and point out *G81*
Mt 18:21 shall I forgive my **b or sister** who sins against *G81*
Mt 18:35 you forgive your **b or sister** from your heart." *G81*
Mt 22:24 his **b** must marry the widow and raise up *G81*
Mt 22:25 he had no children, he left his wife *to* his **b**. *G81*
Mt 22:26 thing happened to the second and third **b**, NDT
Mk 1:16 saw Simon and his **b** Andrew casting a net *G81*
Mk 1:19 son of Zebedee and his **b** John in a boat, *G81*
Mk 3:17 James son of Zebedee and his **b** John (to *G81*
Mk 3:35 God's will is my **b** and sister and mother *G81*
Mk 5:37 James and John the **b** of James. *G81*
Mk 6: 3 Isn't this Mary's son and the **b** of James *G81*
Mk 6:17 of Herodias, his **b** Philip's wife, whom he *G81*
Mk 12:19 us that if a man's **b** dies and leaves a wife *G81*
Mk 12:19 the widow and raise up offspring *for* his **b**. *G81*
Mk 13:12 "**B** will betray brother to death, and a father *G81*
Mk 13:12 "Brother will betray **b** to death, and a father *G81*
Lk 3: 1 his **b** Philip tetrarch of Iturea and Traconitis *G81*
Lk 6:14 named Peter), his **b** Andrew, James, John, *G81*
Lk 6:42 How can you say *to* your **b**, 'Brother, let me *G81*
Lk 6:42 say to your brother, '**B**, let me take the speck *G81*
Lk 12:13 tell my **b** to divide the inheritance with me." *G81*
Lk 15:27 'Your **b** has come,' he replied, 'and your *G81*
Lk 15:28 "The older **b** became angry and refused to NDT
Lk 15:32 because this **b** of yours was dead and is *G81*
Lk 17: 3 "If your **b or sister** sins against you, rebuke *G81*
Lk 20:28 us that if a man's **b** dies and leaves a wife *G81*
Lk 20:28 the widow and raise up offspring *for* his **b**. *G81*
Jn 1:40 Simon Peter's **b**, was one of the two *G81*
Jn 1:41 did was to find his **b** Simon and tell him, *G81*
Jn 6: 8 Andrew, Simon Peter's **b**, spoke up, *G81*
Jn 11: 2 This Mary, whose **b** Lazarus now lay sick, *G81*
Jn 11:19 Mary to comfort them in the loss of their **b**. *G81*
Jn 11:21 had been here, my **b** would not have died. *G81*
Jn 11:23 Jesus said to her, "Your **b** will rise again." *G81*
Jn 11:32 had been here, my **b** would not have died." *G81*
Ac 9:17 on Saul, he said, "**B** Saul, the Lord—Jesus, *G81*
Ac 12: 2 He had James, the **b** of John, put to death *G81*
Ac 21:20 "You see, **b**, how many thousands of Jews *G81*
Ac 22:13 beside me and said, '**B** Saul, receive your *G81*
Ro 14:10 why do you judge your **b or sister**? Or why *G81*
Ro 14:13 block or obstacle in the way *of* a **b or sister**. *G81*
Ro 14:15 If your **b or sister** is distressed because of *G81*
Ro 14:21 else that will cause your **b or sister** to fall. *G81*
Ro 16:23 our **b** Quartus send you their greetings. *G81*
1Co 1: 1 by the will of God, and our **b** Sosthenes, *G81*
1Co 5:11 who claims to be a **b or sister** but is sexually *G81*
1Co 6: 6 But instead, one **b** takes another to court *G81*
1Co 7:12 If any **b** has a wife who is not a believer *G81*
1Co 7:15 The **b** or the sister is not bound in such *G81*
1Co 8:11 this weak **b or sister**, for whom Christ died *G81*
1Co 8:13 I eat causes my **b or sister** to fall into sin, *G81*
1Co 16:12 Now about our **b** Apollos: I strongly urged *G81*
2Co 1: 1 and Timothy our **b**, To the church of *G81*
2Co 2:13 because I did not find my **b** Titus there. *G81*
2Co 8:18 along with him the **b** who is praised by all *G81*
2Co 8:22 with them our **b** who has often proved *G81*
2Co 12:18 Titus to go to you and I sent our **b** with him. *G81*
Gal 1:19 other apostles—only James, the Lord's **b**. *G81*
Eph 6:21 the dear **b** and faithful servant in the Lord *G81*
Php 2:25 you Epaphroditus, my **b**, co-worker and *G81*
Col 1: 1 Jesus by the will of God, and Timothy our **b**, *G81*
Col 4: 7 He is a dear **b**, a faithful minister and fellow *G81*
Col 4: 9 our faithful and dear **b**, who is one of you. *G81*
1Th 3: 2 who is our **b** and co-worker in God's service *G81*
1Th 4: 6 wrong or take advantage of a **b or sister**. *G81*
Phm 1 Timothy our **b**, To Philemon our dear *G81*
Phm 7 because you, **b**, have refreshed the hearts of *G81*
Phm 16 but better than a slave, as a dear **b**. *G81*
Phm 16 both as a fellow man and as a **b** in the Lord. NDT
Phm 20 I do wish, **b**, that I may have some benefit *G81*
Heb 13:23 you to know that our **b** Timothy has been *G81*
Jas 2:15 Suppose a **b** or a sister is without clothes *G81*
Jas 4:11 speaks against a **b or sister** or judges them *G81*
1Pe 5:12 whom I regard as a faithful **b**, I have written *G81*
2Pe 3:15 just as our dear **b** Paul also wrote you with *G81*
1Jn 2: 9 the light but hates a **b or sister** is still in the *G81*
1Jn 2:10 who loves their **b and sister** lives in the light, *G81*
1Jn 2:11 anyone who hates a **b or sister** is in the *G81*
1Jn 3:10 anyone who does not love their **b and sister**. *G81*
1Jn 3:12 to the evil one and murdered his **b**. *G81*
1Jn 3:15 Anyone who hates a **b or sister** is a murderer *G81*
1Jn 3:17 sees a **b or sister** in need but has no *G81*
1Jn 4:20 to love God yet hates a **b or sister** is a liar. *G81*
1Jn 4:20 For whoever does not love their **b and sister** *G81*
1Jn 4:21 loves God must also love their **b and sister**. *G81*
1Jn 5:16 If you see any **b or sister** commit a sin that *G81*
Jude 1 a servant of Jesus Christ and a **b** of James *G81*
Rev 1: 9 your **b** and companion in the suffering and *G81*

BROTHER'S (23) [BROTHER]

Ge 4: 9 he replied. "Am I my **b** keeper?" H278
Ge 4:10 Your **b** blood cries out to me from the H278
Ge 4:11 to receive your **b** blood from your hand. H278
Ge 4:21 His **b** name was Jubal; he was the father of H278
Ge 27:44 him for a while until your **b** fury subsides. H278
Ge 38: 8 "Sleep with your **b** wife and fulfill your duty H278
Ge 38: 9 so whenever he slept with his **b** wife, he H278
Lev 18:16 not have sexual relations with your **b** wife; H278
Lev 20:21 " 'If a man marries his **b** wife, it is an act of H278
Dt 25: 7 a man does not want to marry his **b wife**, H3304
Dt 25: 7 refuses to carry on his **b** name in Israel. H278
Dt 25: 9 his **b widow** shall go up to him in the H3304
Dt 25: 9 who will not build up his **b** family line." H278
Job 1:13 drinking wine at the oldest **b** house, H278
Job 1:18 drinking wine at the oldest **b** house, H278
Hos 12: 3 In the womb he grasped his **b** heel; as a H278
Mt 7: 3 of sawdust in your **b** eye and pay no *G81*
Mt 7: 5 clearly to remove the speck from your **b** eye. *G81*
Mk 6:18 "It is not lawful for you to have your **b** wife." *G81*
Lk 3:19 to Herodias, his **b** wife, and all the other *G81*
Lk 6:41 of sawdust in your **b** eye and pay no *G81*

Lk 6:42 clearly to remove the speck from your **b** eye. *G81*
1Jn 3:12 actions were evil and his **b** were righteous. *G81*

BROTHER-IN-LAW (4) [BROTHER]

Ge 38: 8 wife and **fulfill** *your* **duty** *to* her **as a b** to H3302
Dt 25: 5 marry her and **fulfill the duty of a b** *to* her. H3302
Dt 25: 7 He will not **fulfill the duty of a b** *to* me." H3302
Jdg 4:11 of Hobab, Moses' **b**, and pitched his tent H3162

BROTHERHOOD (1) [BROTHER]

Am 1: 9 to Edom, disregarding a treaty of **b**, H278

BROTHERS (313) [BROTHER]

Ge 9:22 his father naked and told his two **b** outside. H278
Ge 9:25 The lowest of slaves will he be to his **b**." H278
Ge 16:12 he will live in hostility toward all his **b**." H278
Ge 27:29 Be lord over your **b**, and may the sons of H278
Ge 29: 4 the shepherds, "My **b**, where are you from?" H278
Ge 34:11 Shechem said to Dinah's father and **b**, H278
Ge 34:25 Levi, Dinah's **b**, took their swords and H278
Ge 37: 2 was tending the flocks with his **b**, the sons H278
Ge 37: 4 When his **b** saw that their father loved him H278
Ge 37: 5 when he told it to his **b**, they hated H278
Ge 37: 8 His **b** said to him, "Do you intend to reign H278
Ge 37: 9 had another dream, and he told it to his **b**. H278
Ge 37:10 When he told his father as well as his **b** H278
Ge 37:10 I and your **b** actually come and bow H278
Ge 37:11 His **b** were jealous of him, but his father H278
Ge 37:12 Now his **b** had gone to graze their father's H278
Ge 37:13 your **b** are grazing the flocks near Shechem. H278
Ge 37:14 if all is well with your **b** and with the flocks, H278
Ge 37:16 "I'm looking for my **b**. Can you tell me H278
Ge 37:17 went after his **b** and found them near H278
Ge 37:23 So when Joseph came to his **b**, they H278
Ge 37:26 Judah said to his **b**, "What will we gain if H278
Ge 37:27 our own flesh and blood." His **b** agreed. H278
Ge 37:28 his **b** pulled Joseph up out of the cistern NDT
Ge 37:30 He went back to his **b** and said, "The boy H278
Ge 38: 1 Judah left his **b** and went down to stay with H278
Ge 38:11 thought, "He may die too, just like his **b**." H278
Ge 42: 3 Then ten *of* Joseph's **b** went down to buy H278
Ge 42: 6 So when Joseph's **b** arrived, they bowed H278
Ge 42: 7 As soon as Joseph saw his **b**, he recognized H278
Ge 42: 8 Although Joseph recognized his **b**, they did H278
Ge 42:13 "Your servants were twelve **b**, the sons of H278
Ge 42:19 let one of your **b** stay here in prison H278
Ge 42:28 silver has been returned," he said to his **b**. H278
Ge 42:32 We were twelve **b**, sons of one father. H278
Ge 42:33 Leave one of your **b** here with me, and take H278
Ge 43:32 him by himself, **the b** by themselves H2157S
Ge 44:14 the house when Judah and his **b** came in, H278
Ge 44:33 the boy, and let the boy return with his **b**. H278
Ge 45: 1 when he made himself known to his **b**. H278
Ge 45: 3 Joseph said to his **b**, "I am Joseph! Is my H278
Ge 45: 3 But his **b** were not able to answer him H278
Ge 45: 4 Then Joseph said to his **b**, "Come close to H278
Ge 45:15 And he kissed all his **b** and wept over them H278
Ge 45:15 Afterward his **b** talked with him. H278
Ge 45:16 palace that Joseph's **b** had come, H278
Ge 45:17 said to Joseph, "Tell your **b**, 'Do this: H278
Ge 45:24 Then he sent his **b** away, and as they were H278
Ge 46:31 Joseph said to his **b** and to his father's H278
Ge 46:31 'My **b** and my father's household H278
Ge 47: 1 "My father and **b**, with their flocks and H278
Ge 47: 2 He chose five of his **b** and presented them H278
Ge 47: 3 Pharaoh asked the **b**, "What is your H278
Ge 47: 5 "Your father and your **b** have come to you, H278
Ge 47: 6 your father and your **b** in the best part of H278
Ge 47:11 his father and his **b** in Egypt and gave H278
Ge 47:12 his father and his **b** and all his father's H278
Ge 48: 6 be reckoned under the names of their **b**. H278
Ge 48:22 give one more ridge of land than to your **b**, H278
Ge 49: 5 "Simeon and Levi are **b**—their swords are H278
Ge 49: 8 your **b** will praise you; your hand H278
Ge 49:26 on the brow of the prince among his **b**. H278
Ge 50: 8 household and his **b** and those belonging H278
Ge 50:14 together with his **b** and all the others who H278
Ge 50:15 When Joseph's **b** saw that their father was H278
Ge 50:17 you to forgive your **b** the sins and the H278
Ge 50:18 His **b** then came and threw themselves H278
Ge 50:24 Then Joseph said to his **b**, "I am about to H278
Ex 1: 6 Now Joseph and all his **b** and all that H278
Ex 32:29 you were against your own sons and **b** H278
Lev 21:10 the one among his **b** who has had the H278
Nu 8:26 They may assist their **b** in performing their H278
Nu 20: 3 had died when our **b** fell dead before the H278
Nu 27: 9 no daughter, give his inheritance to his **b**. H278
Nu 27:10 If he has no **b**, give his inheritance to his H278
Nu 27:10 give his inheritance to his father's **b**. H278
Nu 27:11 If his father had no **b**, give his inheritance H278
Dt 1:28 Our **b** have made our hearts melt in fear H278
Dt 25: 5 If **b** are living together and one of them H278
Dt 33: 9 did not recognize his **b** or acknowledge his H278
Dt 33:16 on the brow of the prince among his **b**. H278
Dt 33:24 let him be favored by his **b**, and let him H278
Jos 2:13 mother, my **b** and sisters, and all H278
Jos 2:18 your **b** and all your family into your house. H278
Jos 6:23 her **b and sisters** and all who belonged to H278
Jos 17: 4 inheritance along with the **b** *of* their father, H278
Jdg 8:19 "Those were my **b**, the sons of my own H278
Jdg 9: 1 to his mother's **b** in Shechem and said H278
Jdg 9: 3 When the **b** repeated all this to the H278+562
Jdg 9: 5 on one stone murdered his seventy **b**, H278
Jdg 9:24 who had helped him murder his **b**. H278
Jdg 9:56 to his father by murdering his seventy **b**. H278
Jdg 11: 3 Jephthah fled from his **b** and settled in the H278
Jdg 16:31 Then his **b** and his father's whole family H278
Jdg 21:22 When their fathers or **b** complain to us, we H278
1Sa 16:13 anointed him in the presence of his **b**, H278
1Sa 17:17 of bread for your **b** and hurry to their camp. H278
1Sa 17:18 See how your **b** are and bring back some H278
1Sa 17:22 battle lines and asked his **b** how they were. H278
1Sa 20:29 in your eyes, let me get away to see my **b**. H278
1Sa 22: 1 When his **b** and his father's household H278
1Sa 30:23 my **b**, you must not do that with what H278
2Sa 19:41 "Why did our **b**, the men of Judah, H278
1Ki 1: 9 He invited all his **b**, the king's sons, and all H278
1Ki 12:24 Do not go up to fight against your **b**, the H278
1Ch 4: 9 Jabez was more honorable than his **b**. H278
1Ch 4:27 his **b** did not have many children H278
1Ch 5: 2 the strongest of his **b** and a ruler came H278
2Ch 11:22 of Maakah as crown prince among his **b**, H278
2Ch 21: 2 Jehoram's **b**, the sons of Jehoshaphat, were H278
2Ch 21: 4 he put all his **b** to the sword along with H278
2Ch 21:13 You have also murdered your own **b** H278
2Ch 35: 9 Nethanel, his **b**, and Hashabiah, H278
Ezr 3: 9 his sons and **b** and Kadmiel and his H278
Ezr 3: 9 sons of Henadad and their sons and **b**— H278
Ezr 8:18 Sherebiah's sons and **b**, 18 in all; H278
Ezr 8:19 of Merari, and his **b** and nephews, 20 in all H278
Ezr 8:24 Sherebiah, Hashabiah and ten of their **b**, H278
Ezr 10:18 of Joshua son of Jozadak, and his **b**: H278
Ne 1: 2 one of my **b**, came from Judah with H278
Ne 4:23 Neither I nor my **b** nor my men nor the H278
Ne 5:10 my **b** and my men are also lending H278
Ne 5:14 neither I nor my **b** ate the food allotted to H278
Job 6:15 But my **b** are as undependable as H278
Job 42:11 All his **b** and sisters and everyone who had H278
Job 42:15 them an inheritance along with their **b**. H278
Isa 3: 6 A man will seize *one of* his **b** in his father's H278
Jer 35: 3 his **b** and all his sons—the H278
Hos 2: 1 "Say of your **b**, 'My people,' and of your H278
Hos 13:15 even though he thrives among his **b**. H278
Mic 5: 3 the rest of his **b** return to join the H278
Mt 1: 2 Jacob the father of Judah and his **b**, *G81*
Mt 1:11 of Jeconiah and his **b** at the time of the *G81*
Mt 4:18 of Galilee, he saw two **b**, Simon called Peter *G81*
Mt 4:21 he saw two other **b**, James son of Zebedee *G81*
Mt 12:46 his mother and **b** stood outside *G81*
Mt 12:47 "Your mother and **b** are standing outside *G81*
Mt 12:48 "Who is my mother, and who are my **b**?" *G81*
Mt 12:49 "Here are my mother and my **b**. *G81*
Mt 13:55 name Mary, and aren't his **b** James, Joseph, *G81*
Mt 19:29 who has left houses or **b** or sisters or father *G81*
Mt 20:24 they were indignant with the two **b**. *G81*
Mt 22:25 Now there were seven **b** among us. The first *G81*
Mt 23: 8 you have one Teacher, and you are all **b**. *G81*
Mt 25:40 of the least *of* these **b and sisters** of mine, *G81*
Mt 28:10 Go and tell my **b** to go to Galilee; there they *G81*
Mk 3:31 Then Jesus' mother and **b** arrived. *G81*
Mk 3:32 "Your mother and **b** are outside looking *G81*
Mk 3:33 "Who are my mother and my **b**?" he asked. *G81*
Mk 3:34 said, "Here are my mother and my **b**! *G81*
Mk 10:29 who has left home or **b** or sisters or mother *G81*
Mk 10:30 **b**, sisters, mothers, children and *G81*
Mk 12:20 Now there were seven **b**. The first one *G81*
Lk 8:19 Now Jesus' mother and **b** came to see him *G81*
Lk 8:20 "Your mother and **b** are standing outside *G81*
Lk 8:21 "My mother and **b** are those who hear God's *G81*
Lk 14:12 your friends, your **b or sisters**, your relatives, *G81*
Lk 14:26 wife and children, **b** and sisters—yes, even *G81*
Lk 16:28 I have five **b**. Let him warn them, so that *G81*
Lk 18:29 left home or wife or **b or sisters** or parents *G81*
Lk 20:29 Now there were seven **b**. The first one *G81*
Lk 21:16 even by parents, **b and sisters**, relatives and *G81*
Lk 22:32 you have turned back, strengthen your **b**." *G81*
Jn 2:12 with his mother and **b** and his disciples. *G81*
Jn 7: 3 Jesus' **b** said to him, "Leave Galilee and go *G81*
Jn 7: 5 For even his own **b** did not believe in him. *G81*
Jn 7:10 However, after his **b** had left for the festival *G81*
Jn 20:17 Go instead to my **b** and tell them, 'I am *G81*
Ac 1:14 Mary the mother of Jesus, and with his **b**. *G81*
Ac 1:16 said, "**B and sisters**, the Scripture *G467+81*
Ac 2:37 other apostles, "**B**, what shall we do?" *G467+81*
Ac 6: 3 **B and sisters**, choose seven men from among *G81*
Ac 7: 2 this he replied: "**B** and fathers, listen *G467+81*
Ac 7:13 Joseph told his **b** who he was, and *G81*
Ac 7:26 you are **b**; why do you want to hurt *G81*
Ac 11:12 These six **b** also went with me, and we *G81*
Ac 11:29 to provide help *for* the **b and sisters** living in *G81*
Ac 12:17 the *other* **b and sisters** about this, *G81*
Ac 13:15 "**B**, if you have a word of *G467+81*
Ac 14: 2 poisoned their minds against the **b**. *G81*
Ac 15: 7 "**B**, you know that some time ago God *G467+81*
Ac 15:13 James spoke up. "**B**," he said, "listen *G467+81*
Ac 15:23 elders, your **b**, To the Gentile believers *G81*
Ac 16:40 met with the **b and sisters** and encouraged *G81*
Ac 18:18 Then he left the **b and sisters** and sailed *G81*
Ac 18:27 the **b and sisters** encouraged him and wrote *G81*
Ac 21: 7 we greeted the **b and sisters** and stayed with *G81*
Ac 21:17 the **b and sisters** received us warmly. *G81*
Ac 22: 1 "**B** and fathers, listen now to my *G467+81*
Ac 23: 1 said, "My **b**, I have fulfilled my *G467+81*
Ac 23: 5 Paul replied, "**B**, I did not realize that he *G81*
Ac 23: 6 the Sanhedrin, "My **b**, I am a Pharisee, *G467+81*
Ac 28:14 we found *some* **b and sisters** who invited *G81*
Ac 28:15 The **b and sisters** there had heard that we *G81*
Ac 28:17 "My **b**, although I have done nothing *G467+81*
Ro 1:13 to be unaware, **b and sisters**, that I planned *G81*
Ro 7: 1 Do you not know, **b and sisters**—for I am *G81*
Ro 7: 4 my **b and sisters**, you also died to the *G81*
Ro 8:12 Therefore, **b and sisters**, we have an *G81*
Ro 8:29 be the firstborn among many **b and sisters**. *G81*
Ro 10: 1 **B and sisters**, my heart's desire and prayer to *G81*
Ro 11:25 of this mystery, **b and sisters**, so that you *G81*
Ro 12: 1 I urge you, **b and sisters**, in view of God's *G81*
Ro 15:14 am convinced, my **b and sisters**, that you *G81*
Ro 15:30 I urge you, **b and sisters**, by our Lord Jesus *G81*
Ro 16:14 the other **b and sisters** with them. *G81*
Ro 16:17 I urge you, **b and sisters**, to watch out for *G81*
1Co 1:10 appeal to you, **b and sisters**, in the name of *G81*
1Co 1:11 My **b and sisters**, some from Chloe's *G81*
1Co 1:26 **B and sisters**, think of what you were when *G81*
1Co 2: 1 was with me, **b and sisters**. When I came to *G81*
1Co 3: 1 **B and sisters**, I could not address you as *G81*
1Co 4: 6 **b and sisters**, I have applied these *G81*
1Co 6: 8 and you do this *to* your **b and sisters**. *G81*
1Co 7:24 **B and sisters**, each person, as responsible to *G81*
1Co 7:29 What I mean, **b and sisters**, is that the time *G81*
1Co 9: 5 other apostles and the Lord's **b** and Cephas? *G81*
1Co 10: 1 of the fact, **b and sisters**, that our ancestors *G81*
1Co 11:33 So then, my **b and sisters**, when you gather *G81*
1Co 12: 1 of the Spirit, **b and sisters**, I do not want you *G81*
1Co 14: 6 **b and sisters**, if I come to you and *G81*
1Co 14:20 **B and sisters**, stop thinking like children. *G81*
1Co 14:26 shall we say, **b and sisters**? When you come *G81*
1Co 14:39 Therefore, my **b and sisters**, be eager to *G81*
1Co 15: 1 **b and sisters**, I want to remind you of *G81*
1Co 15: 6 five hundred *of* the **b and sisters** at the same *G81*
1Co 15:50 I declare to you, **b and sisters**, that flesh *G81*
1Co 15:58 my dear **b and sisters**, stand firm. *G81*
1Co 16:11 I am expecting him along with the **b**. *G81*
1Co 16:12 I strongly urged him to go to you with the **b** *G81*
1Co 16:15 the Lord's people. I urge you, **b and sisters**, *G81*
1Co 16:20 All the **b and sisters** here send you greetings *G81*
2Co 1: 8 to be uninformed, **b and sisters**, about the *G81*
2Co 8: 1 And now, **b and sisters**, we want you to *G81*
2Co 8:23 among you; as for our **b**, they are *G81*
2Co 9: 3 But I am sending the **b** in order that our *G81*
2Co 9: 5 necessary to urge the **b** to visit you in *G81*
2Co 11: 9 the **b** who came from Macedonia *G81*
2Co 13:11 **b and sisters**, rejoice! Strive for full *G81*
Gal 1: 2 all the **b and sisters** with me, To the *G81*
Gal 1:11 you to know, **b and sisters**, that the gospel *G81*
Gal 3:15 **B and sisters**, let me take an example from *G81*
Gal 4:12 with you, **b and sisters**, become like me *G81*
Gal 4:28 Now you, **b and sisters**, like Isaac, are *G81*
Gal 4:31 Therefore, **b and sisters**, we are not children *G81*
Gal 5:11 **B and sisters**, if I am still preaching *G81*
Gal 5:13 my **b and sisters**, were called to be free. *G81*
Gal 6: 1 **B and sisters**, if someone is caught in a sin *G81*
Gal 6:18 Jesus Christ be with your spirit, **b and sisters**. *G81*
Eph 6:23 Peace *to* the **b and sisters**, and love with *G81*
Php 1:12 you to know, **b and sisters**, that what has *G81*
Php 1:14 most *of* the **b and sisters** have become *G81*
Php 3: 1 my **b and sisters**, rejoice in the Lord *G81*
Php 3:13 **B and sisters**, I do not consider myself yet to *G81*
Php 3:17 my example, **b and sisters**, and just as you *G81*
Php 4: 1 Therefore, my **b and sisters**, you whom I love *G81*
Php 4: 8 **b and sisters**, whatever is true *G81*
Php 4:21 The **b and sisters** who are with me send *G81*
Col 1: 2 Colossae, the faithful **b and sisters** in Christ: *G81*
Col 4:15 my greetings *to* the **b and sisters** at Laodicea *G81*
1Th 1: 4 For we know, **b and sisters** loved by God *G81*
1Th 2: 1 You know, **b and sisters**, that our visit to you *G81*
1Th 2: 9 you remember, **b and sisters**, our toil and *G81*
1Th 2:14 **b and sisters**, became imitators of *G81*
1Th 2:17 **b and sisters**, when we were orphaned *G81*
1Th 3: 7 Therefore, **b and sisters**, in all our distress *G81*
1Th 4: 1 other matters, **b and sisters**, we instructed *G81*
1Th 4:10 we urge you, **b and sisters**, to do so more *G81*
1Th 4:13 **B and sisters**, we do not want you to be *G81*
1Th 5: 1 **b and sisters**, about times and dates *G81*
1Th 5: 4 **b and sisters**, are not in darkness so *G81*
1Th 5:12 we ask you, **b and sisters**, to acknowledge *G81*
1Th 5:14 we urge you, **b and sisters**, warn those who *G81*
1Th 5:25 **B and sisters**, pray for us. *G81*
1Th 5:27 have this letter read to all the **b and sisters**. *G81*
2Th 1: 3 God for you, **b and sisters**, and rightly so, *G81*
2Th 2: 1 gathered to him, we ask you, **b and sisters**, *G81*
2Th 2:13 God for you, **b and sisters** loved by the Lord *G81*
2Th 2:15 So then, **b and sisters**, stand firm and hold *G81*
2Th 3: 1 other matters, **b and sisters**, pray for us that *G81*
2Th 3: 6 command you, **b and sisters**, to keep away *G81*
2Th 3:13 And as for you, **b and sisters**, never tire of *G81*
1Ti 4: 6 point these things out *to* the **b and sisters**, *G81*
1Ti 5: 1 were your father. Treat younger men as **b**, *G81*
2Ti 4:21 Claudia and all the **b and sisters**. *G81*
Heb 2:11 is not ashamed to call them **b and sisters**. *G81*
Heb 2:12 "I will declare your name *to* my **b and sisters**; *G81*
Heb 3: 1 Therefore, holy **b and sisters**, who share in *G81*
Heb 3:12 See to it, **b and sisters**, that none of you has *G81*
Heb 10:19 Therefore, **b and sisters**, since we have *G81*
Heb 13: 1 on **loving one another as b and sisters**. *G5789*
Heb 13:22 **B and sisters**, I urge you to bear with my *G81*
Jas 1: 2 it pure joy, my **b and sisters**, whenever you *G81*

Jas 1:16 Don't be deceived, my dear **b and sisters**. *G81*
Jas 1:19 My dear **b and sisters**, take note of this *G81*
Jas 2: 1 My **b and sisters**, believers in our glorious *G81*
Jas 2: 5 my dear **b and sisters**: Has not God *G81*
Jas 2:14 good is it, my **b and sisters**, if someone *G81*
Jas 3:10 My **b and sisters**, this should *G81*
Jas 3:12 My **b and sisters**, can a fig tree bear olives, or *G81*
Jas 4:11 **B and sisters**, do not slander one another *G81*
Jas 5: 7 then, **b and sisters**, until the Lord's *G81*
Jas 5: 9 one another, **b and sisters**, or you will be *G81*
Jas 5:10 **B and sisters**, as an example of patience in *G81*
Jas 5:12 Above all, my **b and sisters**, do not swear *G81*
Jas 5:19 My **b and sisters**, if one of you should *G81*
2Pe 1:10 Therefore, my **b and sisters**, make every *G81*
1Jn 3:13 be surprised, my **b and sisters**, if the world *G81*
1Jn 3:16 to lay down our lives for our **b and sisters**. *G81*
3Jn 5 in what you are doing for the **b and sisters**, *G81*
Rev 6:11 servants, their **b and sisters**, were killed just *G81*
Rev 12:10 For the accuser *of* our **b and sisters**, who *G81*
Rev 19:10 you and *with* your **b and sisters** who hold to *G81*

BROUGHT (768) [BRING]

Ge 2:19 *He* **b** them to the man to see what he H995
Ge 2:22 out of the man, and *he* **b** her to the man. H995
Ge 4: 1 the help of the LORD *I have* **b forth** a man." H7865
Ge 4: 3 course of time Cain **b** some of the fruits of H995
Ge 4: 4 And Abel also **b** an offering—fat portions H995
Ge 8: 9 took the dove and **b** it **back** to himself in H995
Ge 14:16 all the goods and **b back** his relative Lot H8740
Ge 14:18 king of Salem **b out** bread and wine. H3655
Ge 15: 7 who **b** you **out** of Ur of the Chaldeans to H3655
Ge 15:10 Abram **b** all these to him, cut them in two H4374
Ge 18: 4 *Let* a little water **be b**, and then you may H4374
Ge 18: 8 *He* then **b** some curds and milk and the H4374
Ge 19:17 As soon as they *had* **b** them out, one of H3655
Ge 19:29 and *he* **b** Lot out of the catastrophe that H8938
Ge 20: 9 wronged you that *you have* **b** such great H995
Ge 20:14 Then Abimelek **b** sheep and cattle and H4374
Ge 21: 6 Sarah said, "God *has* **b** me laughter, and H6913
Ge 21:27 So Abraham **b** sheep and cattle and gave H4374
Ge 24: 7 who **b** me out of my father's household H4374
Ge 24:32 Straw and fodder *were* **b** for the camels H5989
Ge 24:53 Then the servant **b out** gold and silver H3655
Ge 24:67 Isaac **b** her into the tent of his mother Sarah H995
Ge 26:10 and *you would have* **b** guilt upon us." H995
Ge 27:14 got them and **b** them to his mother, H995
Ge 27:25 Jacob **b** it to him and he ate; and he H5602
Ge 27:25 and *he* **b** some wine and he drank. H995
Ge 27:31 some tasty food and **b** it to his father. H995
Ge 27:33 then, that hunted game and **b** it to me? H995
Ge 29:13 kissed him and **b** him to his home, H995
Ge 29:22 So Laban **b together** all the people of the H665
Ge 29:23 took his daughter Leah and **b** her to Jacob, H995
Ge 30:14 which *he* **b** to his mother Leah. H995
Ge 33:11 Please accept the present that **was b** to you H995
Ge 34:30 "*You have* **b trouble** *on* me by making me H6579
Ge 37: 2 he **b** their father a bad report about H995
Ge 38:25 *As* she **was** *being* **b out**, she sent a H3655
Ge 39:14 "this Hebrew *has been* **b** to us to make H995
Ge 39:17 Hebrew slave *you* **b** us came to me to H995
Ge 41:14 he *was* **quickly b** from the dungeon. H8132
Ge 43: 2 eaten all the grain *they had* **b** from Egypt, H995
Ge 43:18 "We **were b** here because of the silver that H995
Ge 43:21 So *we have* **b** it **back** with us. H8740
Ge 43:22 *We have* also **b** additional silver with us to H3718
Ge 43:23 Then *he* **b** Simeon **out** to them. H3655
Ge 43:26 the gifts they had **b** into the house, H928+3338
Ge 44: 8 *We* even **b back** to you from the land of H8740
Ge 46: 7 Jacob **b** with him to Egypt his sons and H995
Ge 46:32 and *they have* **b** *along* their flocks and H995
Ge 47: 7 Then Joseph **b** his father Jacob **in** and H995
Ge 47:14 and he **b** it to Pharaoh's palace. H995
Ge 47:17 So *they* **b** their livestock to Joseph, and he H995
Ge 47:17 And *he* **b** them through that year with H5633
Ge 48:10 So Joseph **b** his sons **close** to him, and H5602
Ge 48:13 right hand, and **b** them **close** to him. H5602
Ex 3:12 When you *have* **b** the people out of Egypt, H3655
Ex 4:29 Moses and Aaron **b together** all the elders H665
Ex 5:22 why *have you* **b trouble** on this people? H8317
Ex 5:23 *he has* **b trouble** on this people H8317
Ex 6: 7 who **b** you **out** from under the yoke of the H3655
Ex 8:12 about the frogs *he had* **b** on Pharaoh. H8492
Ex 9:19 animal that *has* not **been b** in and is H665
Ex 10: 8 Aaron **were b back** to Pharaoh. H8740
Ex 10:13 By morning the wind *had* **b** the locusts; H5951
Ex 12:17 day that *I* **b** your divisions **out** of Egypt. H3655
Ex 12:39 the dough the Israelites *had* **b** from Egypt, H3655
Ex 12:51 the LORD **b** the Israelites **out** of Egypt by H3655
Ex 13: 3 because the LORD **b** you **out** of it with a H3655
Ex 13: 9 For the LORD **b** you **out** of Egypt with his H3655
Ex 13:14 a mighty hand the LORD **b** us **out** of Egypt, H3655
Ex 13:16 that the LORD **b** us **out** of Egypt with his H3655
Ex 14:11 graves in Egypt *that you* **b** us to the desert H4374
Ex 14:20 the night the cloud **b** darkness to the one H2118
Ex 15:19 the LORD **b** the waters of the sea **back** over H8740
Ex 15:26 any of the diseases *I* **b** on the Egyptians, H8492
Ex 16: 3 but *you have* **b** us **out** into this desert to H3655
Ex 16: 6 it was the LORD *who* **b** you **out** of Egypt, H3655
Ex 16:32 the wilderness when I **b** you **out** of Egypt. H3655
Ex 18: 1 how the LORD *had* **b** Israel **out** of Egypt. H3655
Ex 18:12 **b** a burnt offering and other sacrifices to H4374
Ex 18:16 have a dispute, *it is* **b** to me, and I decide H995
Ex 18:26 The difficult cases *they* **b** to Moses, but the H995
Ex 19: 4 you on eagles' wings and **b** you to myself. H995
Ex 19: 8 So Moses **b** their answer **back** to the LORD. H8740
Ex 20: 2 your God, who **b** you **out** of Egypt, out of H3655
Ex 28: 1 "**Have** Aaron your brother **b** to you from H7928
Ex 29:46 who **b** them **out** of Egypt so that I might H3655
Ex 32: 1 fellow Moses who **b** us **up** out of Egypt, H6590
Ex 32: 3 took off their earrings and **b** them to Aaron. H995
Ex 32: 4 Israel, who **b** you **up** out of Egypt. H6590
Ex 32: 7 your people, whom *you* **b up** out of Egypt H6590
Ex 32: 8 Israel, who **b** you **up** out of Egypt. H6590
Ex 32:11 whom *you* **b out** of Egypt with great power H3655
Ex 32:12 'It was with evil intent *that he* **b** them **out** H3655
Ex 32:23 fellow Moses who **b** us **up** out of Egypt, H6590
Ex 33: 1 you and the people *you* **b up** out of Egypt H6590
Ex 35:21 moved them came and **b** an offering to the H995
Ex 35:22 came and **b** gold jewelry of all kinds: H995
Ex 35:23 red or the other durable leather **b** them. H995
Ex 35:24 of silver or bronze **b** it as an offering to the H995
Ex 35:24 acacia wood for any part of the work **b** it. H995
Ex 35:25 with her hands and **b** what she had spun— H995
Ex 35:27 The leaders **b** onyx stones and other gems H995
Ex 35:28 They also **b** spices and olive oil for the light NDT
Ex 35:29 who were willing **b** to the LORD freewill H995
Ex 36: 3 the Israelites *had* **b** to carry out the work H995
Ex 39:33 Then *they* **b** the tabernacle to Moses: the H995
Ex 40:21 Then *he* **b** the ark into the tabernacle and H995
Lev 6:30 offering whose blood **is b** into the tent of H995
Lev 8: 6 Moses **b** Aaron and his sons **forward** and H7928
Lev 8:13 Then he **b** Aaron's sons **forward**, put tunics H7928
Lev 8:24 also **b** Aaron's sons **forward** and put H7928
Lev 9: 9 His sons **b** the blood to him, and he H7928
Lev 9:15 Aaron then **b** the offering that was for the H7928
Lev 9:16 *He* **b** the burnt offering and offered it in H7928
Lev 9:17 *He* also **b** the grain offering, took a H7928
Lev 10:15 that was waved *must be* **b** with the fat H995
Lev 11:45 who **b** you **up** out of Egypt to be your God H6590
Lev 13: 2 *they must* **be b** to Aaron the priest or to H995
Lev 13: 9 skin disease, *they must* **be b** to the priest. H995
Lev 14: 2 cleansing, when *they are* **b** to the priest: H995
Lev 14: 4 yarn and hyssop *be* **b** for the person to be H4374
Lev 16:27 whose blood **was b** into the Most Holy H995
Lev 19:36 LORD your God, who **b** you **out** of Egypt. H3655
Lev 22:33 who **b** you **out** of Egypt to be your God H3655
Lev 23:15 the day you **b** the sheaf of the wave H995
Lev 23:43 shelters when I **b** them **out** of Egypt. H3655
Lev 24:11 with a curse; so *they* **b** him to Moses. H995
Lev 25:38 who **b** you **out** of Egypt to give you the H3655
Lev 25:42 my servants, whom *I* **b out** of Egypt, they H3655
Lev 25:55 are my servants, whom *I* **b out** of Egypt. H3655
Lev 26:13 who **b** you **out** of Egypt so that you would H3655
Lev 26:45 ancestors whom *I* **b out** of Egypt in the H3655
Nu 6:13 They *are to be* **b** to the entrance to the tent H995
Nu 7: 3 *They* **b** as their gifts before the LORD six H995
Nu 7:10 the leaders **b** their offerings for its H7928
Nu 7:12 The *one who* **b** his offering on the first H7928
Nu 7:18 the leader of Issachar, **b** his **offering**. H7928
Nu 7:19 The offering *he* **b** was one silver plate H7928
Nu 7:24 of the people of Zebulun, **b** his offering. NDT
Nu 7:30 of the people of Reuben, **b** his offering. NDT
Nu 7:36 of the people of Simeon, **b** his offering. NDT
Nu 7:42 leader of the people of Gad, **b** his offering. NDT
Nu 7:48 of the people of Ephraim, **b** his offering. NDT
Nu 7:54 of the people of Manasseh, **b** his offering. NDT
Nu 7:60 of the people of Benjamin, **b** his offering. NDT
Nu 7:66 leader of the people of Dan, **b** his offering. NDT
Nu 7:72 of the people of Asher, **b** his offering. NDT
Nu 7:78 of the people of Naphtali, **b** his offering. NDT
Nu 11:11 "Why *have you* **b** *this* **trouble** on your H8317
Nu 11:24 *He* **b together** seventy of their elders and H665
Nu 12:14 seven days; after that *she can* **be b back**." H665
Nu 12:15 did not move on till she *was* **b back**. H665
Nu 14:13 power *you* **b** these people **up** from among H6590
Nu 15:33 him gathering wood **b** him to Moses and H7928
Nu 15:41 who **b** you **out** of Egypt to be your God. H3655
Nu 16: 9 community and **b** you **near** himself to do H7928
Nu 16:10 *He has* **b** you and all your fellow Levites **near** H7928
Nu 16:13 enough that *you have* **b** us **up** out of a H6590
Nu 16:14 *you* haven't **b** us into a land flowing with H995
Nu 16:39 bronze censers **b** *by* those who had been H7928
Nu 17: 9 Then Moses **b out** all the staffs from the H3655
Nu 20:16 sent an angel and **b** us **out** of Egypt. H3655
Nu 21: 5 "Why *have you* **b** us **up** out of Egypt to die H6590
Nu 23: 7 "Balak **b** me from Aram, the king of Moab H5697
Nu 23:11 *I* **b** you to curse my enemies, but you have H4374
Nu 23:22 God **b** them **out** of Egypt; they have the H3655
Nu 24: 8 "God **b** them **out** of Egypt; they have the H3655
Nu 25: 6 Then an Israelite man **b** into the camp a H7928
Nu 27: 5 So Moses **b** their case before the LORD, H7928
Nu 31:12 **b** the captives, spoils and plunder to H995
Nu 31:50 So *we have* **b** as an offering to the LORD H7928
Nu 31:54 of hundreds and **b** it into the tent of H995
Nu 32:17 Israelites until *we have* **b** them to their H995
Nu 33: 4 the LORD *had* **b** judgment on their gods. H6913
Dt 1:25 *they* **b** it **down** to us and reported H3718
Dt 1:27 so *he* **b** us **out** of Egypt to deliver us into H3655
Dt 4:20 LORD took you and **b** you **out** of the H3655
Dt 4:37 *he* **b** you **out** of Egypt by his Presence H3655
Dt 5: 6 your God, who **b** you **out** of Egypt, out of H3655
Dt 5:15 LORD your God **b** you **out** of there with a H3655
Dt 6:12 the LORD, who **b** you **out** of Egypt, out of H3655
Dt 6:21 the LORD **b** us **out** of Egypt with a H3655
Dt 6:23 But *he* **b** us **out** from there to bring us in H3655
Dt 7: 8 ancestors that he **b** you **out** with a mighty H3655
Dt 7:19 with which the LORD your God **b** you **out**. H3655
Dt 8:14 your God, who **b** you **out** of Egypt, out of H3655
Dt 8:15 He **b** you water **out** of hard rock. H3655
Dt 9: 4 "The LORD *has* **b** me here to take H995
Dt 9:12 people whom *you* **b out** of Egypt have H3655
Dt 9:26 great power and **b out** of Egypt with a H3655
Dt 9:28 the country from which *you* **b** us will say H3655
Dt 9:28 *he* **b** them **out** to put them to death in the H3655
Dt 9:29 inheritance that *you* **b out** by your great H3655
Dt 11: 4 and how the LORD **b** lasting **ruin** *on* them. H6
Dt 11:29 the LORD your God *has* **b** you into the land H995
Dt 13: 5 who **b** you **out** of Egypt and redeemed H3655
Dt 13:10 your God, who **b** you **out** of Egypt, out of H3655
Dt 16: 1 month of Aviv he **b** you **out** of Egypt by H3655
Dt 17: 4 *this has* **been b** to your **attention** H5583+2256+9048
Dt 19:12 the town elders, *be* **b back** from the city H4374
Dt 20: 1 LORD your God, who **b** you **up** out of Egypt H6590
Dt 22:21 she *shall be* **b** to the door of her father's H3655
Dt 26: 8 the LORD **b** us **out** of Egypt with a mighty H3655
Dt 26: 9 *He* **b** us to this place and gave us this land H995
Dt 29:25 with them when he **b** them **out** of Egypt. H3655
Dt 29:27 so that *he* **b** on it all the curses written in H995
Dt 31:20 When *I have* **b** them into the land flowing H995
Jos 2:18 unless *you have* **b** your father and H665
Jos 6:23 done the spying went in and **b out** Rahab, H3655
Jos 6:23 *They* **b out** her entire family and put them H3655
Jos 7:23 **b** them to Joshua and all the Israelites H995
Jos 7:25 "Why *have you* **b** *this* **trouble** *on* us? H6579
Jos 8:23 the king of Ai alive and **b** him to Joshua. H7928
Jos 10:23 So *they* **b** the five kings **out** of the cave H3655
Jos 10:24 When they *had* **b** these kings to Joshua H3655
Jos 14: 7 And *I* **b** him **back** a report according to my H8740
Jos 18: 1 The country **was b under** their **control**, H3899
Jos 24: 5 by what I did there, and *I* **b** you **out**. H3655
Jos 24: 6 When *I* **b** your people **out** of Egypt, you H3655
Jos 24: 7 *he* **b** the sea over them and covered them. H995
Jos 24: 8 " '*I* **b** you to the land of the Amorites who H995
Jos 24:17 who **b** us and our parents **up** out of H6590
Jos 24:32 which the Israelites *had* **b up** from Egypt H6590
Jdg 1: 7 *They* **b** him to Jerusalem, and he died H995
Jdg 2: 1 "*I* **b** you **up** out of Egypt and led you into H6590
Jdg 2:12 ancestors, who *had* **b** them **out** of Egypt. H3655
Jdg 5:25 bowl fit for nobles *she* **b** him curdled milk. H7928
Jdg 6: 8 I **b** you **up** out of Egypt, out of the land of H6590
Jdg 6:19 *he* **b** them **out** and offered them to him H3655
Jdg 7:25 the Midianites and **b** the heads of Oreb H995
Jdg 11:35 You *have* **b** me **down** and I am H4156+4156
Jdg 12: 9 sons *he* **b in** thirty young women **as wives** H995
Jdg 16: 8 rulers of the Philistines **b** her seven fresh H6590
Jdg 16:31 *They* **b** him **back** and buried him between H5583
Jdg 18: 3 in there and asked him, "Who **b** you here? H995
Ru 1:21 but the LORD *has* **b** me **back** empty. H8740
Ru 1:21 the Almighty *has* **b misfortune** upon me." H8317
Ru 2:18 Ruth also **b out** and gave her what she H3655
1Sa 1:24 and **b** him *to* the house of the LORD at H995
1Sa 1:25 had been sacrificed, *they* **b** the boy to Eli, H995
1Sa 2:14 Whatever the fork **b up** the priest would H6590
1Sa 4: 4 and *they* **b** back the ark of the covenant of H5951
1Sa 4:17 The *man who* **b the news** replied, "Israel H1413
1Sa 5: 6 *he* **b devastation** *on* them and afflicted H9037
1Sa 5:10 *They have* **b** the ark of the god of Israel **around** H6015
1Sa 6: 9 then the LORD *has* **b** this great disaster on H6913
1Sa 7: 1 *They* **b** it to Abinadab's house on the hill H995
1Sa 8: 8 from the day *I* **b** them **up** out of Egypt H6590
1Sa 9:22 Then Samuel **b** Saul and his servant into H995
1Sa 10:18 'I **b** Israel **up** out of Egypt, and I delivered H6590
1Sa 10:21 Then *he* **b forward** the tribe of Benjamin H7928
1Sa 10:23 They ran and **b** him out, and as he stood H4374
1Sa 10:27 They despised him and **b** him no gifts. H995
1Sa 12: 6 Aaron and **b** your ancestors **up** out of H6590
1Sa 12: 8 *who* **b** your ancestors **out** of Egypt and H3655
1Sa 14:34 So everyone **b** his ox that night and H5602
1Sa 14:45 *he* who *has* **b about** this great deliverance H6913
1Sa 15:15 "The soldiers **b** them from the Amalekites H995
1Sa 15:20 the Amalekites and **b back** Agag their king. H995
1Sa 16:12 So he sent for him and **had** him **b in**. H995
1Sa 17:30 someone else and **b up** the same matter, H606
1Sa 17:54 the Philistine's head and **b** it *to* Jerusalem; H995
1Sa 17:57 Abner took him and **b** him before Saul H995
1Sa 18:27 Philistines and **b back** their foreskins. H995
1Sa 19: 7 He **b** him to Saul, and David was with Saul H995
1Sa 20: 8 for *you have* **b** him into a covenant with H995
1Sa 21: 8 *I* haven't **b** my sword or any other weapon, H4374
1Sa 23: 6 Ahimelek *had* **b** the ephod **down** with H3718
1Sa 25:27 which your servant *has* **b** to my lord, be H995
1Sa 25:31 the LORD your God *has* **b** my lord **success**, H3512
1Sa 25:35 her hand what *she had* **b** him and said, H995
1Sa 25:39 and *has* **b** Nabal's wrongdoing **down** on H8740
1Sa 27:11 a man or woman alive to *be* **b** *to* Gath, H995
1Sa 30: 7 me the ephod." Abiathar **b** it to him, H5602
1Sa 30:11 an Egyptian in a field and **b** him to David. H4374
1Sa 30:19 they had taken. David **b** everything **back**. H8740
2Sa 1: 5 to the young man who **b** him *the* **report**, H5583
2Sa 1:10 on his arm and *have* **b** them here to my H995
2Sa 1:13 to the young man who **b** him *the* **report**, H5583
2Sa 2: 8 son of Saul and **b** him **over** *to* Mahanaim. H6296
2Sa 3:22 from a raid and **b** with them a great deal H995

2Sa 3:26 and *they* **b** him **back** from the cistern at H8740
2Sa 4: 8 *They* **b** the head of Ish-Bosheth to David at H995
2Sa 6: 1 David again **b together** all the able young H665
2Sa 6: 3 on a new cart and **b** it from the house of H5951
2Sa 6:17 *They* **b** the ark of the LORD and set it in its H995
2Sa 7: 6 the day I **b** the Israelites **up** out of Egypt H6590
2Sa 7:18 is my family, that *you have* **b** me this far? H995
2Sa 8: 2 subject to David and **b** him tribute. H5951
2Sa 8: 6 became subject to him and **b** tribute. H5951
2Sa 8: 7 of Hadadezer and **b** them *to* Jerusalem. H995
2Sa 8:10 Joram **b with** him articles of H2118+928+3338
2Sa 9: 5 David **had** him **b** from Lo H8938+2256+4374
2Sa 10:16 Hadadezer **had** Arameans **b** from beyond H3655
2Sa 11:27 was over, David **had** her **b** to his house H665
2Sa 12:31 and **b out** the people who were there H3655
2Sa 13:10 she had prepared and **b** it to her brother H995
2Sa 14: 2 Tekoa and **had** a wise woman **b** from H4374
2Sa 14:13 the king *has* not **b back** his banished H8740
2Sa 14:23 Geshur and **b** Absalom **back** *to* Jerusalem. H995
2Sa 16: 2 king asked Ziba, "Why have you **b** these?" H4200
2Sa 17:28 **b** bedding and bowls and articles of pottery NDT
2Sa 17:28 *They* also **b** wheat and barley, flour and H5602
2Sa 21:13 David **b** the bones of Saul and his son H6590
2Sa 22:20 *He* **b** me **out** into a spacious place; he H3655
2Sa 23:10 The LORD **b about** a great victory that day H6913
2Sa 23:12 the LORD **b about** a great victory. H6913
1Ki 1: 3 a Shunammite, and **b** her to the king. H995
1Ki 1:53 and *they* **b** him **down** from the altar. H3718
1Ki 2:19 *He* **had** a throne **b** for the king's mother H8492
1Ki 2:40 away and **b** the slaves **back** from Gath. H995
1Ki 3: 1 *He* **b** her to the City of David until he H995
1Ki 3:24 So *they* **b** a sword for the king H995
1Ki 4:21 *These* countries **b** tribute and were H5602
1Ki 4:28 *They* also **b** to the proper place their quotas H995
1Ki 7:13 King Solomon sent to Tyre and **b** Huram, H4374
1Ki 7:51 he **b in** the things his father David had H995
1Ki 8: 4 and *they* **b up** the ark of the LORD and the H6590
1Ki 8: 6 The priests then **b** the ark of the LORD's H995
1Ki 8:16 the day *I* **b** my people Israel **out** of Egypt, H3655
1Ki 8:21 ancestors when he **b** them **out** of Egypt." H3655
1Ki 8:51 whom *you* **b out** of Egypt, out of H3655
1Ki 8:53 **b** our ancestors **out** of Egypt. H3655
1Ki 9: 9 who **b** their ancestors **out** of Egypt H3655
1Ki 9: 9 that is why the LORD **b** all this disaster on H995
1Ki 9:28 sailed to Ophir and **b** back 420 talents of H4374
1Ki 10:10 again *were* so many spices **b in** as those H995
1Ki 10:11 Hiram's ships **b** gold from Ophir; and H5951
1Ki 10:11 from there *they* **b** great cargoes of H995
1Ki 10:25 everyone who came **b** a gift—articles of H995
1Ki 11:20 whom Tahpenes **b up** in the royal palace. H1694
1Ki 12:28 Israel, who **b** you **up** out of Egypt. H6590
1Ki 13:20 to the old prophet who *had* **b** him **back**. H8740
1Ki 13:23 prophet who *had* **b** him **back** saddled his H8740
1Ki 13:26 the prophet who *had* **b** him **back** from his H8740
1Ki 13:29 and **b** it **back** to his own city to mourn H8740
1Ki 15:15 *He* **b into** the temple of the LORD the silver H995
1Ki 17: 6 The ravens **b** him bread and meat in the H995
1Ki 17:20 *have you* **b tragedy** even on this widow I H8317
1Ki 18:40 Elijah *had* them **b down** to the H3718
1Ki 21:13 him and **b charges against** Naboth before H6386
1Ki 22: 6 king of Israel **b together** the prophets— H7695
1Ki 22:37 So the king died and *was* **b** *to* Samaria H995
2Ki 2:20 "and put salt in it." So *they* **b** it to him. H4374
2Ki 4: 5 They **b** the jars to her and she kept H5602
2Ki 5:20 by not accepting from him what *he* **b**. H995
2Ki 8: 5 son Elisha *had* **b back to life** came to H2649
2Ki 10: 8 "*They have* **b** the heads of the princes." H995
2Ki 10:18 Jehu **b** all the people **together** and said H7695
2Ki 10:22 So *he* **b out** robes for them. H3655
2Ki 10:26 *They* **b** the sacred stone **out** *of* the temple H3655
2Ki 11: 4 the guards and **had** them **b** to him at the H995
2Ki 11:12 Jehoiada **b out** the king's son and put the H3655
2Ki 11:19 and *together they* **b** the king **down** from H3718
2Ki 12: 4 money that **is b** as sacred offerings *to* the H995
2Ki 12: 4 the money **b** voluntarily *to* the temple. H995
2Ki 12: 9 the money that **was b** *to* the temple of the H995
2Ki 12:10 money that *had* **been b** *into* the temple of H5162
2Ki 12:13 The money **b into** the temple was not H995
2Ki 12:16 sin offerings **was** not **b into** the temple of H995
2Ki 14:20 *He was* **b back** by horse and was buried in H5951
2Ki 16:14 *he* **b** it from the front of the temple H7928
2Ki 17: 7 who *had* **b** them **up** out of Egypt from H6590
2Ki 17:24 The king of Assyria **b** people from Babylon H995
2Ki 17:33 the nations from which they *had been* **b**. H1655
2Ki 17:36 who **b** you **up** out of Egypt with mighty H6590
2Ki 19:25 now *I have* **b** it **to pass**, that you have H995
2Ki 20:20 the tunnel by which *he* **b** water into the city H995
2Ki 22: 4 money that *has* **been b into** the temple of H995
2Ki 23: 8 Josiah **b** all the priests from the towns of H995
2Ki 23:30 Josiah's servants **b** his body in a chariot H995
2Ki 25:20 took them all and **b** them to the king of H2143
1Ch 2: 7 who **b trouble** *on* Israel by violating the H6579
1Ch 9:28 them *when* they *were* **b in** and when H995
1Ch 10:12 of Saul and his sons and **b** them to Jabesh. H995
1Ch 11:14 the LORD **b about** a great **victory**. H3828+9591
1Ch 15:28 So all Israel **b up** the ark of the covenant H6590
1Ch 16: 1 *They* **b** the ark of God and set it inside the H995
1Ch 17: 5 from the day *I* **b** Israel **up** out of Egypt to H6590
1Ch 17:16 is my family, that *you have* **b** me this far? H995
1Ch 18: 2 became subject to him and **b** him tribute. H5951
1Ch 18: 6 became subject to him and **b** him tribute. H5951
1Ch 18: 7 of Hadadezer and **b** them *to* Jerusalem. H995
1Ch 18:10 Hadoram **b** all kinds of articles of gold, of NDT
1Ch 19:16 and **had** Arameans **b** from beyond H3655
1Ch 20: 3 and **b out** the people who were there H3655
1Ch 22: 4 Tyrians *had* **b** large numbers of H995
2Ch 1: 4 Now David *had* **b up** the ark of God from H6590
2Ch 5: 1 he **b in** the things his father David had H995
2Ch 5: 5 and *they* **b up** the ark and the tent of H6590
2Ch 5: 7 The priests then **b** the ark of the LORD's H995
2Ch 6: 5 'Since the day *I* **b** my people **out** of Egypt H3655
2Ch 7:22 ancestors, who **b** them **out** of Egypt, and H3655
2Ch 7:22 that is why *he* **b** all this disaster on them. H995
2Ch 8:11 Solomon **b** Pharaoh's daughter **up** from H6590
2Ch 8:18 sailed to Ophir and **b** back four hundred H4374
2Ch 9:10 the servants of Solomon **b** gold from Ophir; H995
2Ch 9:10 *they* also **b** algumwood and precious H995
2Ch 9:12 he gave her more than *she had* **b** to him. H995
2Ch 9:14 the revenues **b in** *by* merchants and traders H995
2Ch 9:14 of the territories **b** gold and silver to H995
2Ch 9:24 everyone who came **b** a gift—articles of H995
2Ch 15:11 goats from the plunder *they had* **b back**. H995
2Ch 15:18 *He* **b into** the temple of God the silver and H995
2Ch 16: 6 Then King Asa **b** all the men of Judah H4374
2Ch 17: 5 all Judah **b** gifts to Jehoshaphat H5989
2Ch 17:11 Some Philistines **b** Jehoshaphat gifts and H995
2Ch 17:11 as tribute, and the Arabs **b** him flocks: H995
2Ch 18: 5 king of Israel **b together** the prophets— H7695
2Ch 22: 7 God **b about** Ahaziah's downfall. H2118+4946
2Ch 22: 9 He *was* **b** to Jehu and put to death H995
2Ch 23:11 his sons **b out** the king's son and H3655
2Ch 23:20 of the land and **b** the king **down** from the H3718
2Ch 24:10 all the people **b** their contributions H995
2Ch 24:11 Whenever the chest *was* **b in** by the Levites H995
2Ch 24:14 *they* **b** the rest of the money to the king H995
2Ch 25:14 *he* **b back** the gods of the people of Seir. H995
2Ch 25:23 Then Jehoash **b** him *to* Jerusalem and H995
2Ch 25:28 He *was* **b back** by horse and was buried H5951
2Ch 26: 8 The Ammonites **b** tribute to Uzziah, and H5989
2Ch 27: 5 The Ammonites **b** him the same amount H8740
2Ch 28: 5 as prisoners and **b** them *to* Damascus. H995
2Ch 29: 4 *He* **b in** the priests and the Levites H995
2Ch 29:16 *They* **b out** to the courtyard of the LORD's H3655
2Ch 29:21 *They* **b** seven bulls, seven rams, seven male H995
2Ch 29:23 the sin offering *were* **b** before the king H5602
2Ch 29:31 So the assembly **b** sacrifices and thank H995
2Ch 29:31 whose hearts were willing **b** burnt offerings. NDT
2Ch 29:32 offerings the assembly **b** was seventy bulls, H995
2Ch 29:36 at what God *had* **b about** for his people, H3922
2Ch 30:15 and **b** burnt offerings *to* the temple of H995
2Ch 31: 5 *They* **b** a great amount, a tithe of H995
2Ch 31: 6 towns of Judah also **b** a tithe of their herds H995
2Ch 31:12 Then *they* faithfully **b in** the contributions H995
2Ch 32:23 Many **b** offerings to Jerusalem for the LORD H995
2Ch 33:11 So the LORD **b** against them the army H995
2Ch 33:13 so *he* **b** him **back** *to* Jerusalem and to his H8740
2Ch 34: 9 money that *had* **been b into** the temple of H995
2Ch 35:24 his other chariot and **b** him *to* Jerusalem, H2143
2Ch 36:10 sent for him and **b** him to Babylon, H995
2Ch 36:17 *He* **b up** against them the king of the H6590
Ezr 1: 7 King Cyrus **b out** the articles belonging to H3655
Ezr 1: 8 king of Persia **had** them **b** by Mithredath H3655
Ezr 1:11 Sheshbazzar **b** all these **along** with the H6590
Ezr 3: 5 those **b as freewill offerings** to the H5605+5607
Ezr 4: 2 king of Assyria, who **b** us here. H6590
Ezr 5:14 in Jerusalem and **b** to the temple in A10308
Ezr 6: 5 temple in Jerusalem and **b** to Babylon, A10308
Ezr 8:18 our God was on us, *they* **b** us Sherebiah, H995
Ezr 8:20 They also **b** 220 of the temple servants—a NDT
Ne 2: 1 when wine was **b** for him, I took the wine NDT
Ne 8: 2 month Ezra the priest **b** the Law before the H995
Ne 8:16 went out and **b back** branches and built H995
Ne 9: 7 chose Abram and **b** him **out** of Ur of the H3655
Ne 9:15 in their thirst *you* **b** them water from H3655
Ne 9:18 is your god, who **b** you **up** out of Egypt,' H6590
Ne 9:23 and *you* **b** them into the land that you told H995
Ne 12:27 they lived and *were* **b** to Jerusalem to H995
Ne 12:28 musicians also **were b together** from the H665
Ne 13:12 All Judah **b** the tithes of grain, new wine H995
Ne 13:18 so that our God **b** all this calamity on us H995
Ne 13:19 that no load *could be* **b in** on the Sabbath H995
Est 1:17 Queen Vashti to *be* **b** before him, H995
Est 2: 7 whom *he had* **b up** because she had H587
Est 2: 8 many young women **were b** to the citadel H7695
Est 6: 1 of his reign, to *be* **b in** and read to him. H995
Job 4:12 "A word **was secretly b** to me, my ears H1704
Job 14:21 if their offspring *are* **b low**, they do not H7592
Job 15: 7 **Were** *you* **b forth** before the hills? H2655
Job 22:29 When *people are* **b low** and you say, 'Lift H9164
Job 24:24 *they* **are b low** and gathered up like all H4812
Job 42:11 over all the trouble the LORD *had* **b** on him, H995
Ps 18:19 *He* **b** me **out** into a spacious place; he H3655
Ps 20: 8 They *are* **b** *to their* **knees** and fall, but we H4156
Ps 22: 9 Yet you **b** me out of the womb; you made H1631
Ps 30: 3 *You*, LORD, **b** me **up** from the realm of the H6590
Ps 37:33 let them be condemned when **b to trial**. H9149
Ps 38: 6 I am bowed down and **b** very **low**; all day H8820
Ps 44:25 We *are* **b down** to the dust; our bodies cling AIT
Ps 45:14 follow her—*those* **b** to be with her. H995
Ps 46: 8 the desolations *he has* **b** on the earth. H8492
Ps 66:11 *You* **b** us into prison and laid burdens on H995
Ps 66:12 but *you* **b** us to a place of abundance. H3655
Ps 71: 6 you **b** me **forth** from my mother's womb. H1602
Ps 74: 3 all *this* **destruction** the enemy *has* **b** on H8317
Ps 78:16 *he* **b** streams **out** of a rocky crag and H3655
Ps 78:52 But *he* **b** his people **out** like a flock; he H5825
Ps 78:54 And so *he* **b** them to the border of his holy H995
Ps 78:71 from tending the sheep *he* **b** him to be the H995
Ps 81:10 your God, who **b** you **up** out of Egypt. H6590
Ps 90: 2 were born or *you* **b forth** the whole world, H2655
Ps 94:19 within me, your consolation **b** me **joy**. H9130
Ps 105:37 *He* **b out** Israel, laden with silver and gold H3655
Ps 105:40 They asked, and *he* **b** them quail; he fed H995
Ps 105:43 *He* **b out** his people with rejoicing, his H3655
Ps 107:14 *He* **b** them **out** of darkness, the utter H3655
Ps 107:28 and *he* **b** them **out** of their distress. H3655
Ps 107:36 there *he* **b** the hungry **to live**, and they H3782
Ps 116: 6 the unwary; *when I* **was b low**, he saved H1937
Ps 118: 5 the LORD; he **b** me into a spacious place. H6699
Ps 136:11 and **b** Israel **out** from among them His H3655
Ps 136:14 **b** Israel through the midst of it, His H6296
Pr 7:26 Many are the victims *she has* **b down**; her H5877
Pr 8:22 "The LORD **b** me **forth** as the first of his H7865
Pr 11: 5 the wicked *are* **b down** by their own H5877
Pr 14:32 the wicked **are b down**, but even in H1890
Pr 21:27 how much more so *when* **b** with evil intent! H995
SS 3: 4 let him go till *I had* **b** him to my mother's H995
Isa 1: 2 "I reared children and **b** them **up**, but they H8123
Isa 2: 9 So people *will* **be b low** and everyone H8820
Isa 2:11 will be humbled and human pride **b low**; H8820
Isa 2:17 of man *will be* **b low** and human pride H8820
Isa 3: 9 *They have* **b** disaster upon themselves H1694
Isa 5:15 So people *will* **be b low** and everyone H8820
Isa 10:33 will be felled, the tall ones *will be* **b low**. H9164
Isa 14:11 your pomp *has* **been b down** *to* the grave, H3718
Isa 14:15 But *you* **are b down** to the realm of the H3718
Isa 18: 7 gifts *will* **be b** to the LORD Almighty *from* a H3297
Isa 18: 7 the gifts will be **b** to Mount Zion, the place NDT
Isa 23: 4 neither reared sons nor **b up** daughters." H8123
Isa 26:14 You punished them and **b** them **to ruin** H9012
Isa 26:18 *We have* not **b** salvation *to* the earth, and H6913
Isa 29: 4 **B low**, you will speak from the ground H9164
Isa 29:10 The LORD *has* **b** over you a deep sleep: He H5818
Isa 37:26 now *I have* **b** it **to pass**, that you have H995
Isa 43:23 *You have* not **b** me sheep for burnt H995
Isa 44:11 they *will be* **b down to terror** and shame. H7064
Isa 45:10 to a mother, 'What *have you* **b to birth**? H2655
Isa 48: 5 'My images **b** them **about**; my wooden H6913
Isa 49:21 Who **b** these **up**? I was left all H1540
Isa 53: 5 the **punishment** *that* **b** us peace was on him AIT
Isa 60: 5 the wealth on the seas *will* **be b** to you, to H2200
Isa 63:11 where is he *who* **b** them through the sea H6590
Isa 66: 8 a day or a nation **be b forth** in a moment? H3528
Jer 2: 6 who **b** us **up** out of Egypt and led us H6590
Jer 2: 7 *I* **b** you into a fertile land to eat its fruit H995
Jer 2:17 *Have you* not **b** this on yourselves by H6913
Jer 4:18 conduct and actions *have* **b** this on you. H6913
Jer 6:15 *they will* **be b down** when I punish them," H4173
Jer 7:22 For when I **b** your ancestors **out** of Egypt H3655
Jer 8:12 *they will* **be b down** when they are H4173
Jer 10: 9 Hammered silver **is b** from Tarshish and H995
Jer 11: 4 ancestors when I **b** them **out** of Egypt, H3655
Jer 11: 7 the time I **b** your ancestors **up** from Egypt H6590
Jer 11: 8 So *I* **b** on them all the curses of the H995
Jer 16:14 who **b** the Israelites **up** out of Egypt H6590
Jer 16:15 who **b** the Israelites **up** out of the land of H6590
Jer 20: 8 the word of the LORD *has* **b** me insult and H2118
Jer 20:15 be the man who **b** my father **the news**, H1413
Jer 23: 7 who **b** the Israelites **up** out of Egypt H6590
Jer 23: 8 who **b** the descendants of Israel **up** out of H6590
Jer 25: 7 and you have **b** harm to yourselves. NDT
Jer 26:23 *They* **b** Uriah **out** of Egypt and took him to H3655
Jer 27:16 LORD's house *will* **be b back** from Babylon. H8740
Jer 32:21 *You* **b** your people Israel **out** of Egypt with H3655
Jer 32:23 So *you* **b** all this disaster **on** them. H7925
Jer 32:42 As *I have* **b** all this great calamity on this H995
Jer 34:13 ancestors when *I* **b** them **out** of Egypt, H3655
Jer 35: 4 *I* **b** them into the house of the LORD, into the H995
Jer 36:21 Jehudi **b** it from the room of H4374
Jer 37:14 Jeremiah and **b** him to the officials. H995
Jer 37:17 sent for him and **had** him **b** to the palace, H4374
Jer 38:14 the prophet and *had* him **b** to the third H4374
Jer 38:22 king of Judah *will* **be b out** to the officials H3655
Jer 38:23 children *will be* **b out** to the H3655
Jer 40: 3 And now the LORD *has* **b** it **about**; he has H995
Jer 44: 2 the great disaster *I* **b** on Jerusalem and on H995
Jer 50:25 his arsenal and **b out** the weapons of his H3655
Jer 52:26 took them all and **b** them to the king of H2143
La 1: 5 The LORD *has* **b** her **grief** because of her H3324
La 1:12 that the LORD **b** on me in the day of his H3324
La 2: 2 *He has* **b** her kingdom and its princes **down** H5595
La 4: 5 Those **b up** in royal purple now lie on ash H587
Eze 8: 7 Then *he* **b** me to the entrance to the court H995
Eze 8:14 Then *he* **b** me to the entrance of the north H995
Eze 8:16 *He* then **b** me into the inner court of the H995
Eze 9:11 the writing kit at his side **b back** word, H8740
Eze 11: 1 lifted me up and **b** me to the gate of the H995
Eze 11:24 lifted me up and **b** me to the exiles in H995
Eze 12: 7 During the day *I* **b out** my things packed H3655
Eze 13:22 when I *had* **b** them no **grief**, and H3872
Eze 14:22 sons and daughters who *will* **be b out** of it. H3655
Eze 14:22 the disaster *I have* **b** on Jerusalem— H995
Eze 14:22 Jerusalem—every disaster *I have* **b** on it. H995
Eze 17:14 so that the kingdom would be **b low**, unable AIT
Eze 19: 3 *She* **b up** one of her cubs, and he became H6590
Eze 19: 9 him into a cage and **b** him to the king of H995

Eze 20: 9 sake of my name, I **b** them **out** of Egypt. H3655
Eze 20:10 them out of Egypt and **b** them into the H995
Eze 20:14 nations in whose sight *I had* **b** them **out**. H3655
Eze 20:22 nations in whose sight *I had* **b** them **out**. H3655
Eze 20:28 When *I* **b** them into the land I had sworn to H995
Eze 21:24 you people *have* **b to mind** your guilt by H2349
Eze 21:26 be exalted and the exalted *will be* **b low**. H9164
Eze 22: 4 *You have* **b** your days **to a close**, and the H7928
Eze 23:30 *have* **b** this on you, because you lusted H6913
Eze 23:42 drunkards **were b** from the desert along H995
Eze 27: 4 your builders **b** your beauty **to perfection**. H4005
Eze 27:11 they **b** your beauty **to perfection**. H4005
Eze 30:11 nations—*will* **be b in** to destroy the land. H995
Eze 31:15 On the day it *was* **b down** to the realm of H3718
Eze 31:16 of its fall when I **b** it **down** to the realm of H3718
Eze 31:18 Yet *you*, too, *will* **be b down** with the trees H3718
Eze 34: 4 *You have* not **b back** the strays or H8740
Eze 37: 1 and he **b** me **out** by the Spirit of the LORD H3655
Eze 38: 8 They *had* **been b out** from the nations H3655
Eze 39:27 When I *have* **b** them **back** from the nations H8740
Eze 40: 4 for that is why *you have* **been b** here. H995
Eze 40:17 Then *he* **b** me into the outer court. There I H995
Eze 40:28 Then *he* **b** me into the inner court through H995
Eze 40:32 Then *he* **b** me to the inner court on the H995
Eze 40:35 Then *he* **b** me to the north gate and H995
Eze 40:48 *He* **b** me to the portico of the temple and H995
Eze 41: 1 Then the man **b** me to the main hall and H995
Eze 42: 1 the outer court and **b** me to the rooms H995
Eze 43: 1 Then the man **b** me to the gate facing H2143
Eze 43: 5 lifted me up and **b** me into the inner court H995
Eze 44: 1 Then the man **b** me **back** to the outer H8740
Eze 44: 4 Then the man **b** me by way of the north H995
Eze 44: 7 you **b** foreigners uncircumcised in heart H995
Eze 46:19 Then the man **b** me through the entrance H995
Eze 46:21 *He* then **b** me to the outer court and led H3655
Eze 47: 1 The man **b** me **back** to the entrance to the H8740
Eze 47: 2 *He* then **b** me **out** through the north gate H3655
Da 3:13 So these men **were b** before the king, A10085
Da 4: 6 wise men of Babylon *be* **b** before me to A10549
Da 5: 3 So *they* **b in** the gold goblets that had A10085
Da 5:13 So Daniel **was b** before the king, and A10549
Da 5:13 exiles my father the king **b** from Judah? A10085
Da 5:15 enchanters **were b** before me to A10549
Da 5:23 the goblets from his temple **b** to you, A10085
Da 5:26 the days of your reign and **b** it **to an end**. A10719
Da 6:16 and *they* **b** Daniel and threw him into A10085
Da 6:17 A stone **was b** and placed over the A10085
Da 6:18 any entertainment *being* **b** to him. A10549
Da 6:24 accused Daniel *were* **b in** and thrown A10085
Da 9:15 who **b** your people **out** of Egypt with a H3655
Hos 10: 1 spreading vine; *he* **b forth** fruit for himself. H8751
Am 2:10 I **b** you **up** out of Egypt and led you forty H6590
Am 3: 1 the whole family *I* **b up** out of Egypt: H6590
Jnh 2: 6 But *you*, LORD my God, **b** my life **up** from H6590
Mic 4: 6 the exiles and those *I have* **b to grief**. H8317
Mic 6: 4 *I* **b** you **up** out of Egypt and redeemed you H6590
Hag 1: 9 What *you* **b** home, I blew away H995
Zec 10:11 Assyria's pride *will* **be b down** and Egypt's H3718
Mal 1:11 pure offerings *will* **be b** to me, H5602
Mt 4:24 and *people* **b** to him all who were ill with G4712
Mt 8:16 were demon-possessed *were* **b** to him, G4712
Mt 9: 2 *Some men* **b** to him a paralyzed man G4712
Mt 9:32 could not talk *was* **b** to Jesus. G4712
Mt 10:18 On my account *you will be* **b** before G72
Mt 12:20 till *he has* **b** justice **through** to victory. G1675
Mt 12:22 Then *they* **b** him a demon-possessed G4712
Mt 14:11 His head *was* **b in** on a platter and given G5770
Mt 14:35 *People* **b** all their sick to him G4712
Mt 17:16 *I* **b** him to your disciples, but they could G4712
Mt 18:24 ten thousand bags of gold *was* **b** to him. G4712
Mt 19:13 Then *people* **b** little children to Jesus G4712
Mt 21: 7 *They* **b** the donkey and the colt and placed G72
Mt 22:19 paying the tax." They **b** him a denarius, G4712
Mt 25:20 received five bags of gold **b** the other five. G4712
Mk 1:32 after sunset *the people* **b** to Jesus all the G5770
Mk 4:22 is concealed *is* meant to *be* **b** out into the G2262
Mk 6:28 and **b back** his head on a platter. G5770
Mk 7:32 There *some people* **b** to him a man who G5770
Mk 8:22 and *some people* **b** a blind man and G5770
Mk 9:17 "Teacher, *I* **b** you my son, who is G5770
Mk 9:20 So *they* **b** him. When the spirit saw Jesus G5770
Mk 11: 7 *When they* **b** the colt to Jesus and threw G5770
Mk 12:16 They **b** the coin, and he asked them G5770
Mk 13:11 Whenever you are arrested and **b to trial**, do G72
Mk 15:22 *They* **b** Jesus to the place called Golgotha G5770
Lk 1:52 *He has* **b down** rulers from their thrones G2747
Lk 2:27 When the parents **b in** the child Jesus to G1652
Lk 4:16 where he had been **b up**, and on the G5555
Lk 4:40 *the people* **b** to Jesus all who had various G72
Lk 8:17 will not be known or **b out** into the open. G2262
Lk 10:34 **b** him to an inn and took care of him. G72
Lk 12:11 "When you *are* **b** before synagogues G1662
Lk 18:40 ordered the man *to be* **b** to him. G72
Lk 19:35 *They* **b** it to Jesus, threw their cloaks on the G72
Lk 21:12 and *you will be* **b** before kings and G552
Lk 23:14 "*You* **b** me this man as one who was G4712
Jn 1:42 And *he* **b** him to Jesus. Jesus looked at him G72
Jn 4:33 "Could someone *have* **b** him food? G5770
Jn 8: 3 the Pharisees **b in** a woman caught in G72
Jn 9:13 *They* **b** to the Pharisees the man who had G72
Jn 10: 4 When *he has* **b out** all his own, he goes G1675
Jn 17: 4 I *have* **b** you **glory** on earth by finishing G1519
Jn 17:23 so that they may be *b* to **complete** unity. AIT
Jn 18:13 **b** him first to Annas, who was the G72
Jn 18:16 servant girl on duty there and **b** Peter **in**. G1652
Jn 19:13 *he* **b** Jesus out and sat down on the judge's G72
Jn 19:39 Nicodemus **b** a mixture of myrrh and G5770
Ac 4: 7 *They* **had** Peter and John **b** before them G2705
Ac 4:34 sold them, **b** the money from the sales G5770
Ac 4:37 field he owned and **b** the money and put G5770
Ac 5: 2 **b** the rest and put it at the apostles' G5770
Ac 5:15 *people* **b** the sick into the streets and laid G1766
Ac 5:19 the doors of the jail and **b** them **out**. G1974
Ac 5:26 went with his officers and **b** the apostles. G72
Ac 5:27 The apostles *were* **b in** and made to appear G72
Ac 6:12 They seized Stephen and **b** him before the G72
Ac 7:16 *Their bodies were* **b back** to Shechem and G3572
Ac 7:21 took him and **b** him **up** as her own son. G427
Ac 7:41 *They* **b** sacrifices to it and reveled in what G343
Ac 7:45 under Joshua **b** it with them when they G1652
Ac 9:27 took him and **b** him to the apostles. G72
Ac 11:24 number of people *were* **b to** the Lord. G4707
Ac 11:26 when he found him, *he* **b** him to Antioch. G72
Ac 12:17 how the Lord *had* **b** him **out** of prison. G1974
Ac 13: 1 who had been **b up with** Herod the G5343
Ac 13:23 descendants God *has* **b** to Israel the Savior G72
Ac 14:13 **b** bulls and wreaths to the city gates G5770
Ac 15: 2 This **b** Paul and Barnabas *into* sharp G1181
Ac 16:20 *They* **b** them **before** the magistrates and G4642
Ac 16:30 *He* then **b** them out and asked, "Sirs, what G4575
Ac 16:34 The jailer **b** them into his house and set a G343
Ac 17:15 who escorted Paul **b** him to Athens and then G72
Ac 17:19 they took him and **b** him to a meeting of G72
Ac 18:12 attack on Paul and **b** him to the place of G72
Ac 19:19 sorcery **b** their scrolls **together** and burned G5237
Ac 19:24 **b in** a lot of business for the craftsmen G4218
Ac 19:37 *You have* **b** these men here, though they G72
Ac 21:16 accompanied us and **b** us to the home of G72
Ac 21:28 *he has* **b** Greeks **into** the temple and G1652
Ac 21:29 that Paul *had* **b** him **into** the temple.) G1652
Ac 22: 3 in Tarsus of Cilicia, but **b up** in this city. G427
Ac 22:30 Then *he* **b** Paul and had him stand before G2864
Ac 23:28 so *I* **b** him to their Sanhedrin. G2864
Ac 23:31 during the night and **b** him as far as G72
Ac 24: 1 they **b** *their* **charges** against Paul G1872
Ac 24: 2 your foresight *has* **b about** reforms in this G1181
Ac 25: 6 court and ordered *that* Paul *be* **b** before him. G72
Ac 25: 7 *They* **b** many serious charges against him G2965
Ac 25:11 But if *the* **charges b** against me by these G2989
Ac 25:15 of the Jews **b charges** against him and G1872
Ac 25:17 next day and ordered the man *to be* **b in**. G72
Ac 25:23 At the command of Festus, Paul *was* **b in**. G72
Ac 25:26 Therefore *I have* **b** him before all of you G4575
Ro 5:16 followed one sin and **b** condemnation, G1650[S]
Ro 5:16 many trespasses and **b** justification. G1650[S]
Ro 5:20 The law *was* **b in** so that the trespass G4209
Ro 6:13 those who have been **b from** death to life; G1666
Ro 7:10 intended to bring life actually **b** death. G1650
Ro 8:15 Spirit you received **b** about your adoption to NDT
Ro 8:21 to decay and *b* **into** the freedom and AIT
Ro 11:15 For if their rejection **b** reconciliation to the NDT
1Co 14:24 of sin and *are* **b under judgment** by all, G373
2Co 3: 7 Now if the ministry that *b* **death**, which was AIT
2Co 3: 9 ministry that *b* **condemnation** was glorious, AIT
Eph 2:13 were far away *have been* **b** near by the G1181
Col 1:13 of darkness and **b** us into the kingdom of G3496
Col 2:10 in Christ you have been **b to fullness** G4444
1Th 3: 6 from you and *has* **b good news** about your G2294
1Ti 5:19 an elder unless it is *b* **by** two or three AIT
1Ti 6: 7 For *we* **b** nothing **into** the world, and we G1662
2Ti 1:10 and *has* **b** life and immortality **to light** G5894
Titus 1: 3 *now* at his appointed season *he has* **b to light** G5746
Heb 6: 6 *to be* **b back** to repentance. G4099+362
Heb 11: 4 By faith Abel **b** God a better offering than G4712
Heb 13:20 eternal covenant **b back** from the dead our G343
Jas 5:11 have seen what the Lord **finally b about**. G5465
1Pe 1:13 hope on the grace *to be* **b** to you when G5770
2Pe 2: 5 world *when he* **b** the flood **on** its ungodly G2042
Rev 18:17 such great wealth *has been* **b to ruin**! G2246
Rev 18:19 In one hour *she has been* **b to ruin**!' G2246
Rev 21:26 honor of the nations *will be* **b** into it. G5770

BROW (5)
Ge 3:19 By the sweat of your **b** you will eat your H678
Ge 49:26 on the **b** *of* the prince among his brothers. H7721
Dt 33:16 on the **b** *of* the prince among his brothers. H7721
Job 16:15 over my skin and buried my **b** in the dust. H7967
Lk 4:29 took him to the **b** of the hill on which G4059

BROWN (1)
Zec 1: 8 Behind him were red, **b** and white horses. H8601

BROWSE (2) [BROWSES]
SS 4: 5 of a gazelle that **b** among the lilies. H8286
SS 6: 2 to **b** in the gardens and to gather lilies. H8286

BROWSES (2) [BROWSE]
SS 2:16 mine and I am his; he **b** among the lilies. H8286
SS 6: 3 beloved is mine; he **b** among the lilies. H8286

BRUISE (2) [BRUISED, BRUISES]
Ex 21:25 burn, wound for wound, **b** for bruise. H2467
Ex 21:25 burn, wound for wound, bruise for **b**. H2467

BRUISED (5) [BRUISE]
Lev 22:24 the LORD an animal whose testicles *are* **b**, H5080
Ps 105:18 *They* **b** his feet with shackles, his neck H6700
SS 5: 7 They beat me, *they* **b** me; they took away H7205
Isa 42: 3 A **b** reed he will not break, and a H8368
Mt 12:20 A **b** reed he will not break, and a G5341

BRUISES (2) [BRUISE]
Pr 23:29 Who has needless **b**? Who has bloodshot H7206
Isa 30:26 LORD binds up the **b** *of* his people and H8691

BRUIT (KJV) NEWS, REPORT

BRUSH (1) [BRUSHWOOD, UNDERBRUSH]
Job 30: 4 In the **b** they gathered salt herbs, and H8489

BRUSHED (4) [BRUSHING]
Ex 29: 2 loaves without yeast and **b** with olive oil. H5417
Lev 2: 4 made without yeast and **b** with olive oil. H5417
Lev 7:12 loaves made without yeast and **b** with oil, H5417
Nu 6:15 mixed in, and thin loaves **b** with olive oil. H5417

BRUSHING (1) [BRUSHED]
Eze 3:13 the living creatures **b** against each other H5976

BRUSHWOOD (1) [BRUSH, WOOD]
Ac 28: 3 Paul gathered a pile *of* **b** and, as he put it G5866

BRUTAL (2) [BRUTE]
Eze 21:31 I will deliver you into the hands of **b** men H1279
2Ti 3: 3 without self-control, **b**, not lovers of the G466

BRUTALLY (3) [BRUTE]
2Ch 16:10 same time Asa **b oppressed** some of the H8368
Eze 34: 4 You have ruled them harshly and **b**. H928+7266
1Co 4:11 we are in rags, *we are* **b treated**, we are G3139

BRUTE (2) [BRUTAL, BRUTALLY, BRUTES]
Ps 73:22 ignorant; I was a **b beast** before you. H989
Pr 30: 2 Surely I am *only* a **b**, not a man; I do not H1280

BRUTES (1) [BRUTE]
Titus 1:12 are always liars, evil **b**, lazy gluttons." G2563

BUBASTIS (1)
Eze 30:17 men of Heliopolis and **B** will fall by the H7083

BUBBLING (1)
Isa 35: 7 a pool, the thirsty ground **b springs**. H4432+4784

BUCKET (1) [BUCKETS]
Isa 40:15 Surely the nations are like a drop in a **b** H1932

BUCKETS (1) [BUCKET]
Nu 24: 7 Water will flow from their **b**; their seed H1932

BUCKLED (1)
Eph 6:14 *with* the **belt** of truth **b around** your waist G4322

BUCKLER, BUCKLERS (KJV) (LARGE) SHIELD, SHIELDS

BUD (11) [BUDDED, BUDS]
Ex 25:35 One **b** shall be under the first pair of H4117
Ex 25:35 a second **b** under the second pair H4117
Ex 25:35 and a third **b** under the third pair H4117
Ex 37:21 One **b** was under the first pair of branches H4117
Ex 37:21 a second **b** under the second pair H4117
Ex 37:21 and a third **b** under the third pair H4117
Job 14: 9 the scent of water *it will* **b** and put forth H7255
Isa 17:11 plant them, *you* **bring** them to **b**, yet the H7255
Isa 27: 6 Israel *will* **b** and blossom and fill all the H7437
Isa 55:10 the earth and **making** it **b** and flourish, H3528
Hab 3:17 the fig tree *does* not **b** and there are no H7255

BUDDED (6) [BUD]
Ge 40:10 As soon as it **b**, it blossomed, and its H7255
Nu 17: 8 had not only sprouted but *had* **b** H3655+7258
SS 6:11 to see if the vines *had* **b** or the H7255
SS 7:12 to the vineyards to see if the vines *have* **b**, H7255
Eze 7:10 burst forth, the rod *has* **b**, arrogance has H7437
Heb 9: 4 Aaron's staff that *had* **b**, and the stone G1056

BUDS (8) [BUD]
Ex 25:31 **b** and blossoms of one piece with them. H4117
Ex 25:33 flowers with **b** and blossoms are to H4117
Ex 25:34 like almond flowers with **b** and blossoms. H4117
Ex 25:36 The **b** and branches shall all be of one H4117
Ex 37:17 **b** and blossoms of one piece with them. H4117
Ex 37:19 almond flowers with **b** and blossoms were H4117
Ex 37:20 like almond flowers with **b** and blossoms. H4117
Ex 37:22 The **b** and the branches were all of one H4117

BUFFET, BUFFETED (KJV) BEATING, BRUTALLY TREATED, STRUCK, TORMENT

BUFFETED (1)
Mt 14:24 **b** by the waves because the wind was G989

BUILD (147) [BUILDER, BUILDERS, BUILDING, BUILDINGS, BUILDS, BUILT, REBUILD, REBUILDING, REBUILT, WELL-BUILT]
Ge 6:15 This is how *you are to* **b** it: The ark is to be H6913
Ge 11: 4 *let us* **b** ourselves a city, with a H1215
Ge 16: 2 perhaps *I can* **b a family** through her." H1215

Ge 30: 3 me and I too can b a family through her." H1215
Ge 35: 1 settle there, and b an altar there to God H6913
Ge 35: 3 to Bethel, where I will b an altar to God H6913
Ex 20:25 me, do not b it with dressed stones H1215
Ex 27: 1 "B an altar of acacia wood, three cubits H6913
Nu 23: 1 Balaam said, "B me seven altars here H1215
Nu 23:29 Balaam said, "B me seven altars here H1215
Nu 32:16 "We would like to b pens here for our H1215
Nu 32:24 B cities for your women and children, and H1215
Dt 6:10 with large, flourishing cities you did not b, H1215
Dt 8:12 when you b fine houses and settle down, H1215
Dt 16:21 beside the altar you b to the LORD your H6913
Dt 20:20 fruit trees and use them to b siege works H1215
Dt 22: 8 When you b a new house, make a H1215
Dt 25: 9 to the man who will not b up his brother's H1215
Dt 27: 5 B there an altar to the LORD your God, an H1215
Dt 27: 6 B the altar of the LORD your God with H1215
Dt 28:30 You will b a house, but you will not live in H1215
Jos 22:16 from the LORD and b yourselves an altar in H1215
Jos 22:26 'Let us get ready and b an altar—but not H1215
Jos 24:13 you did not toil and cities you did not b; H1215
Jdg 6:26 Then b a proper kind of altar to the LORD H1215
2Sa 7: 5 Are you the one to b me a house to dwell H1215
2Sa 7:13 He is the one who will b a house for my H1215
2Sa 7:27 servant, saying, 'I will b a house for you. H1215
2Sa 24:18 "Go up and b an altar to the LORD on the H7756
2Sa 24:21 answered, "so I can b an altar to the LORD H1215
1Ki 2:36 "B yourself a house in Jerusalem and live H1215
1Ki 5: 3 he could not b a temple for the Name of H1215
1Ki 5: 5 to b a temple for the Name of the LORD my H1215
1Ki 5: 5 in your place will b the temple for my H1215
1Ki 6: 1 he began to b the temple of the LORD. H1215
1Ki 8:17 it in his heart to b a temple for the Name H1215
1Ki 8:18 it in your heart to b a temple for my Name H1215
1Ki 8:19 you are not the one to b the temple, but H1215
1Ki 8:19 he is the one who will b the temple for my H1215
1Ki 9:15 conscripted to b the LORD's temple, H1215
1Ki 9:19 whatever he desired to b in Jerusalem, in H1215
1Ki 11:38 I will b you a dynasty as enduring as the H1215
2Ki 6: 2 and let us b a place there for us to meet." H6913
2Ki 19:32 it with shield or b a siege ramp against it. H9161
1Ch 14: 1 carpenters to b a palace for him. H1215
1Ch 17: 4 You are not the one to b me a house to H1215
1Ch 17:10 to you that the LORD will b a house for you: H1215
1Ch 17:12 He is the one who will b a house for me H1215
1Ch 17:25 servant that you will b a house for him. H1215
1Ch 21:18 David to go up and b an altar to the LORD H7756
1Ch 21:22 threshing floor so I can b an altar to the H1215
1Ch 22: 6 charged him to b a house for the LORD H1215
1Ch 22: 7 it in my heart to b a house for the Name H1215
1Ch 22: 8 You are not to b a house for my Name H1215
1Ch 22:10 He is the one who will b a house for my H1215
1Ch 22:11 you have success and b the house of the H1215
1Ch 22:19 Begin to b the sanctuary of the LORD God H1215
1Ch 28: 2 it in my heart to b a house as a place of H1215
1Ch 28: 2 of our God, and I made plans to b it. H1215
1Ch 28: 3 'You are not to b a house for my Name H1215
1Ch 28: 6 son is the one who will b my house and H1215
1Ch 28:10 LORD has chosen you to b a house as the H1215
1Ch 29:19 to do everything to b the palatial structure H1215
2Ch 2: 1 gave orders to b a temple for the Name H1215
2Ch 2: 3 sent him cedar to b a palace to live in. H1215
2Ch 2: 4 Now I am about to b a temple for the H1215
2Ch 2: 5 "The temple I am going to b will be great, H1215
2Ch 2: 6 But who is able to b a temple for him H1215
2Ch 2: 6 Who then am I to b a temple for him H1215
2Ch 2: 9 because the temple I b must be large H1215
2Ch 2:12 who will b a temple for the LORD and a H1215
2Ch 3: 1 Solomon began to b the temple of the H1215
2Ch 6: 7 it in his heart to b a temple for the Name H1215
2Ch 6: 8 it in your heart to b a temple for my Name H1215
2Ch 6: 9 you are not the one to b the temple, but H1215
2Ch 6: 9 he is the one who will b the temple for my H1215
2Ch 8: 6 whatever he desired to b in Jerusalem, in H1215
2Ch 14: 7 "Let us b up these towns," he said to H1215
2Ch 36:23 appointed me to b a temple for him at H1215
Ezr 1: 2 appointed me to b a temple for him at H1215
Ezr 1: 3 in Judah and b the temple of the LORD H1215
Ezr 1: 5 prepared to go up and b the house of the H1215
Ezr 3: 2 associates began to b the altar of the God H1215
Ezr 4: 2 said, "Let us help you b because, like H1215
Ezr 4: 3 We alone will b it for the LORD, the God of H1215
Ezr 6:14 of the Jews continued to b and prosper A10111
Job 19:12 they b a siege ramp against me and H6148
Job 20:19 he has seized houses he did not b. H1215
Job 30:12 they b their siege ramps against me. H6148
Job 39:27 at your command and b its nest on high? H8123
Ps 28: 5 them down and never b them up again. H1215
Ps 51:18 to b up the walls of Jerusalem. H1215
Pr 24:27 your fields ready; after that, b your house. H1215
Ecc 3: 3 a time to tear down and a time to b, H1215
SS 8: 9 is a wall, we will b towers of silver on her. H1215
Isa 37:33 it with shield or b a siege ramp against it. H9161
Isa 57:14 it will be said: "B up, build up, prepare H6148
Isa 57:14 "Build up, b up, prepare the road H6148
Isa 62:10 way for the people. B up, build up the H6148
Isa 62:10 Build up, b up the highway H6148
Isa 65:21 They will b houses and dwell in them H1215
Isa 65:22 No longer will they b houses and others H1215
Isa 66: 1 Where is the house you will b for me H1215
Jer 1:10 destroy and overthrow, to b and to plant." H1215
Jer 6: 6 down the trees and b siege ramps against H9161
Jer 22:14 'I will b myself a great palace with H1215
Jer 24: 6 I will b them up and not tear them down H1215
Jer 29: 5 "B houses and settle down; plant gardens H1215
Jer 29:28 Therefore b houses and settle down H1215
Jer 31: 4 I will b you up again, and you, Virgin H1215
Jer 31:28 I will watch over them to b and to plant," H1215
Jer 35: 7 Also you must never b houses, sow seed H1215
Jer 42:10 I will b you up and not tear you down H1215
Jer 49:16 Though you b your nest as high as the H1467
Eze 4: 2 works against it, b a ramp up to it, set up H9161
Eze 21:22 to b a ramp and to erect siege works. H9161
Eze 22:30 among them who would b up the wall H1553
Eze 26: 8 b a ramp up to your walls and raise his H9161
Eze 28:26 in safety and will b houses and plant H1215
Da 11:15 will come and b up siege ramps and H9161
Mic 3:10 who b Zion with bloodshed, and H1215
Zep 1:13 Though they b houses, they will not live H1215
Hag 1: 8 bring down timber and b my house, H1215
Zec 5:11 country of Babylonia to b a house for it. H1215
Zec 6:12 from his place and b the temple of the H1215
Zec 6:13 It is he who will b the temple of the LORD H1215
Zec 6:15 will come and help to b the temple of the H1215
Mal 1: 4 Almighty says: "They may b, but I will H1215
Mt 16:18 on this rock I will b my church, and G3868
Mt 23:29 You b tombs for the prophets and G3868
Mt 27:40 destroy the temple and b it in three days, G3868
Mk 14:58 hands and in three days will b another, G3868
Mk 15:29 destroy the temple and b it in three days, G3868
Lk 11:47 because you b tombs for the prophets G3868
Lk 11:48 the prophets, and you b their tombs. G3868
Lk 12:18 tear down my barns and b bigger ones, G3868
Lk 14:28 "Suppose one of you wants to b a tower G3868
Lk 14:30 'This person began to b and wasn't able G3868
Lk 19:43 your enemies will b an embankment G4212
Jn 2:20 "It has taken forty-six years to b this G3868
Ac 7:49 What kind of house will you b for me G3868
Ac 20:32 which can b you up and give you an G3868
Ro 15: 2 neighbors for their good, to b them up. G3869
1Co 3:10 But each one should b with care. G2224
1Co 14:12 try to excel in those that b up the church. G3869
1Th 5:11 one another and b each other up, G3868
Heb 8: 5 when he was about to b the tabernacle: G2200

BUILDER (7) [BUILD]

Isa 62: 5 woman, so will your B marry you; as a H1215
1Co 3:10 I laid a foundation as a wise b, and G802
1Co 3:14 built survives, the b will receive a reward. NDT
1Co 3:15 the b will suffer loss but yet will be saved G899S
Heb 3: 3 just as the b of a house has greater honor G2941
Heb 3: 4 someone, but God is the b of everything. G2941
Heb 11:10 whose architect and b is God. G1321

BUILDERS (14) [BUILD]

2Ki 12:11 of the LORD—the carpenters and b, H1215
2Ki 22: 6 the carpenters, the b and the masons H1215
2Ch 34:11 the carpenters and b to purchase dressed H1215
Ezr 3:10 When the b laid the foundation of the H1215
Ne 4: 5 have thrown insults in the face of the b. H1215
Ne 4:18 each of the b wore his sword at his H1215
Ps 118:22 The stone the b rejected has become the H1215
Ps 127: 1 LORD builds the house, the b labor in vain. H1215
Eze 27: 4 your b brought your beauty to perfection. H1215
Mt 21:42 " 'The stone the b rejected has become G3868
Mk 12:10 " 'The stone the b rejected has become G3868
Lk 20:17 " 'The stone the b rejected has become G3868
Ac 4:11 Jesus is " 'the stone you b rejected, which G3871
1Pe 2: 7 "The stone the b rejected has become the G3868

BUILDING (52) [BUILD]

Ge 4:17 Cain was then b a city, and he named it H1215
Ge 11: 5 the city and the tower the people were b. H1215
Ge 11: 8 all the earth, and they stopped b the city. H1215
Jos 22:19 LORD or against us by b an altar for H1215
Jos 22:29 from him today by b an altar for burnt H1215
1Ki 3: 1 until he finished b his palace and the H1215
1Ki 5:18 timber and stone for the b of the temple. H1215
1Ki 6: 5 he built a structure around the b, H1074
1Ki 6: 7 In b the temple, only blocks dressed at H1215
1Ki 6:12 "As for this temple you are b, if you follow H1215
1Ki 6:38 He had spent seven years b it. H1215
1Ki 9: 1 Solomon had finished b the temple of the H1215
1Ki 15:21 he stopped b Ramah and withdrew to H1215
2Ki 25: 9 Every important b he burned down. H1074
1Ch 22: 2 dressed stone for b the house of God. H1215
1Ch 29:16 we have provided for b you a temple for H1215
2Ch 3: 2 He began b on the second day of the H1215
2Ch 3: 3 Solomon laid for b the temple of God was H1215
2Ch 3: 4 the width of the b and twenty cubits high. H1074
2Ch 16: 5 he stopped b Ramah and abandoned his H1215
2Ch 32: 5 sections of the wall and b towers on it. H6590
Ezr 3: 8 to supervise the b of the house of the LORD H4856
Ezr 4: 1 that the exiles were b a temple for the H1215
Ezr 4: 3 no part with us in b a temple to our God. H1215
Ezr 4: 4 Judah and make them afraid to go on b. H1215
Ezr 5: 4 of those who are constructing this b?" A10112
Ezr 5: 8 The people are b it with large stones A10111
Ezr 6:14 They finished b the temple according to A10111
Ne 3: 1 b as far as the Tower of the Hundred NDT
Ne 4: 3 "What they are b—even a fox H1215
Ne 4:17 who were b the wall. Those who carried H1215
Ne 6: 6 to revolt, and therefore you are b the wall. H1215
Jer 52:13 Every important b he burned down. H1074
Eze 41:12 The b facing the temple courtyard on the H1230
Eze 41:12 The wall of the b was five cubits thick all H1230
Eze 41:13 courtyard and the b with its walls were H1224
Eze 41:15 the length of the b facing the courtyard at H1230
Eze 42: 2 The b whose door faced north was a NDT
Eze 42: 5 on the lower and middle floors of the b. H1230
Mic 7:11 The day for b your walls will come, the H1215
Hab 1:10 by b earthen ramps they capture them. H7392
Lk 6:48 They are like a man b a house, who dug G3868
Lk 17:28 buying and selling, planting and b. G3868
Ro 15:20 so that I would not be b on someone G3868
1Co 3: 9 you are God's field, God's b. G3869
1Co 3:10 wise builder, and someone else is b on it. G2224
2Co 5: 1 we have a b from God, an eternal G3869
2Co 10: 8 Lord gave us for b you up rather than G3869
2Co 13:10 authority the Lord gave me for b you up, G3869
Eph 2:21 In him the whole b is joined together and G3869
Eph 4:29 is helpful for b others up according to G3869
Jude 20 by b yourselves up in your most holy faith G2224

BUILDINGS (12) [BUILD]

1Ki 9:10 during which Solomon built these two b H1074
1Ch 15: 1 David had constructed b for himself in the H1074
1Ch 28:11 portico of the temple, its b, its storerooms, H1074
1Ch 29: 4 the overlaying of the walls of the b, H1074
2Ch 32:28 He also made b to store the harvest of H5016
2Ch 34:11 beams for the b that the kings of H1074
Isa 22:10 You counted the b in Jerusalem and tore H1074
Jer 22:23 who are nestled in cedar b, how you will NDT
Eze 40: 2 south side were some b that looked like a H4445
Mt 24: 1 up to him to call his attention to its b. G3869
Mk 13: 1 massive stones! What magnificent b!" G3869
Mk 13: 2 "Do you see all these great b?" replied G3869

BUILDS (12) [BUILD]

Job 27:18 The house he b is like a moth's cocoon H1215
Ps 127: 1 Unless the LORD b the house, the builders H1215
Ps 147: 2 The LORD b up Jerusalem; he gathers the H1215
Pr 14: 1 The wise woman b her house, but with H1215
Pr 17:19 whoever b a high gate invites destruction. H1467
Jer 22:13 "Woe to him who b his palace by H1215
Am 9: 6 he b his lofty palace in the heavens and H1215
Hab 2: 9 "Woe to him who b his house by unjust H1298
Hab 2:12 "Woe to him who b a city with bloodshed H1215
1Co 3:12 If anyone b on this foundation using gold G2224
1Co 8: 1 But knowledge puffs up while love b up. G3868
Eph 4:16 grows and b itself up in love, as each G3869

BUILT (198) [BUILD]

Ge 8:20 Then Noah b an altar to the LORD and H1215
Ge 10:11 to Assyria, where he b Nineveh, Rehoboth H1215
Ge 12: 7 So he b an altar there to the LORD, who H1215
Ge 12: 8 There he b an altar to the LORD and called H1215
Ge 13: 4 where he had first b an altar. H6913
Ge 13:18 There he b an altar to the LORD. H1215
Ge 22: 9 Abraham b an altar there and arranged H1215
Ge 26:25 Isaac b an altar there and called on the H1215
Ge 33:17 where he b a place for himself and made H1215
Ge 35: 7 There he b an altar, and he called the H1215
Ex 1:11 and they b Pithom and Rameses as store H1215
Ex 17:15 Moses b an altar and called it The LORD is H1215
Ex 24: 4 next morning and b an altar at the foot H1215
Ex 32: 5 he b an altar in front of the calf and H1215
Ex 38: 1 They b the altar of burnt offering of acacia H6913
Nu 13:22 Hebron had been b seven years before H1215
Nu 23:14 there he b seven altars and offered a H1215
Nu 32:34 The Gadites b up Dibon, Ataroth, Aroer, H1215
Nu 32:36 as fortified cities, and b pens for their flocks. NDT
Dt 20: 5 "Has anyone b a new house and not yet H1215
Jos 8:30 Then Joshua b on Mount Ebal an altar to H1215
Jos 8:31 He b it according to what is written in the NDT
Jos 11:13 burn any of the cities b on their mounds— H6641
Jos 19:50 And he b up the town and settled there H1215
Jos 22:10 of Manasseh b an imposing altar H1215
Jos 22:11 heard that they had b the altar on the H1215
Jos 22:23 If we have b our own altar to turn away H1215
Jos 22:28 which our ancestors b, not for burnt H6913
Jdg 1:26 where he b a city and called it Luz H1215
Jdg 6:24 So Gideon b an altar to the LORD there H1215
Jdg 6:28 bull sacrificed on the newly b altar! H1215
Jdg 21: 4 next day the people b an altar and H1215
Ru 4:11 who together b up the family of Israel. H1215
1Sa 7:17 And he b an altar there to the LORD H1215
1Sa 14:35 Then Saul b an altar to the LORD; it was the H1215
2Sa 5: 9 He b up the area around it, from the H1215
2Sa 5:11 and they b a palace for David. H1215
2Sa 7: 7 "Why have you not b me a house of cedar H1215
2Sa 20:15 They b a siege ramp up to the city, and it H9161
2Sa 24:25 David b an altar to the LORD there and H1215
1Ki 3: 2 a temple had not yet been b for the H1215
1Ki 6: 2 that King Solomon b for the LORD was H1215
1Ki 6: 5 inner sanctuary he b a structure around H1215
1Ki 6: 7 at the temple site while it was being b. H1215
1Ki 6: 9 So he b the temple and completed it H1215
1Ki 6:10 And he b the side rooms all along the H1215
1Ki 6:14 So Solomon b the temple and completed H1215
1Ki 6:36 And he b the inner courtyard of three H1215
1Ki 7: 2 He b the Palace of the Forest of Lebanon a H1215
1Ki 7: 7 He b the throne hall, the Hall of Justice H6913
1Ki 8:13 I have indeed b a magnificent H1215+1215
1Ki 8:16 of Israel to have a temple b so that my H1215
1Ki 8:20 and I have b the temple for the Name of H1215

1Ki 8:27 How much less this temple *I have* **b**! H1215
1Ki 8:43 that this house *I have* **b** bears your Name. H1215
1Ki 8:44 the temple *I have* **b** for your Name, H1215
1Ki 8:48 the temple *I have* **b** for your Name; H1215
1Ki 9:3 temple, which *you have* **b**, by putting my H1215
1Ki 9:10 which Solomon **b** these two buildings— H1215
1Ki 9:17 He **b** up Lower Beth Horon, NDT
1Ki 9:24 to the palace Solomon *had* **b** for her, H1215
1Ki 9:25 on the altar *he had* **b** for the LORD, H1215
1Ki 9:26 King Solomon also **b** ships at Ezion Geber H6913
1Ki 10:4 of Solomon and the palace *he had* **b**, H1215
1Ki 11:7 Solomon **b** a high place for Chemosh the H1215
1Ki 11:27 Solomon *had* **b** the terraces and had H1215
1Ki 11:38 enduring as the one *I* **b** for David and will H1215
1Ki 12:25 From there he went out and **b up** Peniel. H1215
1Ki 12:31 Jeroboam **b** shrines on high places and H6913
1Ki 12:33 sacrifices on the altar *he had* **b** at Bethel. H6913
1Ki 15:22 them King Asa **b up** Geba in Benjamin, H1215
1Ki 15:23 all he did and the cities *he* **b**, are they not H1215
1Ki 16:24 talents of silver and **b** a city *on* the hill, H1215
1Ki 16:32 the temple of Baal that *he* **b** in Samaria. H1215
1Ki 18:32 *With* the stones *he* **b** an altar in the name H1215
1Ki 22:39 the palace *he* **b** and adorned with ivory H1215
1Ki 22:48 Now Jehoshaphat **b** a fleet of trading H6913
2Ki 16:11 So Uriah the priest **b** an altar in H1215
2Ki 16:18 canopy that *had been* **b** at the temple H1215
2Ki 17:9 to fortified city *they* **b** themselves high H1215
2Ki 21:4 *He* **b** altars in the temple of the LORD, of H1215
2Ki 21:5 the LORD, *he* **b** altars to all the starry hosts. H1215
2Ki 23:12 altars Manasseh *had* **b** in the two courts H6913
2Ki 23:13 king of Israel *had* **b** for Ashtoreth the H1215
2Ki 23:19 the kings of Israel *had* **b** in the towns of H6913
2Ki 25:1 outside the city and **b** siege works all H1215
1Ch 6:10 in the temple Solomon **b** in Jerusalem), H1215
1Ch 6:32 until Solomon **b** the temple of the LORD in H1215
1Ch 7:24 *who* **b** Lower and Upper Beth Horon as H1215
1Ch 8:12 who **b** Ono and Lod with its surrounding H1215
1Ch 11:8 *He* **b up** the city around it, from the H1215
1Ch 17:6 "Why *have you* not **b** me a house of cedar H1215
1Ch 21:26 David **b** an altar to the LORD there and H1215
1Ch 22:5 the house to *be* **b** for the LORD should H1215
1Ch 22:19 the temple that *will* **be b** for the Name of H1215
2Ch 3:8 *He* **b** the Most Holy Place, its length H6913
2Ch 6:2 I *have* **b** a magnificent temple for you, H1215
2Ch 6:5 of Israel to *have* a temple **b** so that my H1215
2Ch 6:10 and *I have* **b** the temple for the Name of H1215
2Ch 6:18 How much less this temple *I have* **b**! H1215
2Ch 6:33 that this house *I have* **b** bears your Name. H1215
2Ch 6:34 the temple *I have* **b** for your Name, H1215
2Ch 6:38 the temple *I have* **b** for your Name; H1215
2Ch 8:1 which Solomon **b** the temple of the H1215
2Ch 8:4 *He* also **b up** Tadmor in the desert and all H1215
2Ch 8:4 all the store cities *he had* **b** in Hamath. H1215
2Ch 8:11 of David to the palace *he had* **b** for her, H1215
2Ch 8:12 of the LORD that *he had* **b** in front of the H1215
2Ch 9:3 as well as the palace *he had* **b**, H1215
2Ch 11:5 in Jerusalem and **b up** towns for defense H1215
2Ch 14:6 *He* **b up** the fortified cities of Judah, since H1215
2Ch 14:7 on every side." So *they* **b** and prospered. H1215
2Ch 16:6 With them *he* **b up** Geba and Mizpah. H1215
2Ch 17:12 *he* **b** forts and store cities in Judah H1215
2Ch 20:8 lived in it and *have* **b** in it a sanctuary H1215
2Ch 20:36 After these *were* **b** at Ezion Geber, H6913
2Ch 21:11 He *had* also **b** high places on the hills of H6913
2Ch 26:9 Uzziah **b** towers in Jerusalem at the H1215
2Ch 26:10 *He* also **b** towers in the wilderness and H1215
2Ch 27:4 *He* **b** towns in the hill country of Judah H1215
2Ch 28:25 every town in Judah *he* **b** high places to H6913
2Ch 32:5 He **b** another wall outside that one and NDT
2Ch 32:29 *He* **b** villages and acquired great numbers H6913
2Ch 33:4 *He* **b** altars in the temple of the LORD, of H1215
2Ch 33:5 the LORD, *he* **b** altars to all the starry hosts. H1215
2Ch 33:15 as well as all the altars *he had* **b** on the temple H1215
2Ch 33:19 the sites where *he* **b** high places and H1215
2Ch 35:3 Solomon son of David king of Israel **b**. H1215
Ezr 3:3 *they* **b** the altar on its foundation and H3922
Ezr 4:13 know that if this city **is b** and its walls are A10111
Ezr 4:16 king that if this city **is b** and its walls are A10111
Ezr 5:11 the temple that was **b** many years ago, A10111
Ezr 5:11 that a great king of Israel **b** and finished. A10111
Ne 3:2 The men of Jericho **b** the adjoining H1215
Ne 3:2 Zakkur son of Imri **b** next to them. H1215
Ne 8:4 high wooden platform **b** for the occasion. H6913
Ne 8:16 back branches and **b** themselves H6913
Ne 8:17 returned from exile **b** temporary shelters H6913
Ne 12:29 the musicians *had* **b** villages for H1215
Job 3:14 who **b** for themselves places now lying in H1215
Ps 78:69 *He* **b** his sanctuary like the heights, like H1215
Ps 122:3 Jerusalem **is b** like a city that is closely H1215
Pr 9:1 Wisdom *has* **b** her house; she has set up H1215
Pr 24:3 By wisdom a house **is b**, and through H1215
Ecc 2:4 *I* **b** houses for myself and planted H1215
Ecc 9:14 surrounded it and **b** huge siege works H1215
SS 4:4 tower of David, **b** with courses of stone H1215
Isa 5:2 *He* **b** a watchtower in it and cut out a H1215
Isa 22:11 *You* **b** a reservoir between the two walls H6913
Jer 7:31 *They have* **b** the high places of Topheth in H1215
Jer 18:9 kingdom *is to be* **b up** and planted, H1215
Jer 18:15 them walk in byways, on roads not **b up**. H6148
Jer 19:5 *They have* **b** the high places of Baal to H1215
Jer 32:24 the siege ramps *are* **b up** to take the city. H995
Jer 32:31 From the day it *was* **b** until now, this city H1215
Jer 32:35 *They* **b** high places for Baal in the Valley H1215
Jer 35:9 **b** houses to live in or had vineyards H1215
Jer 45:4 overthrow what *I have* **b** and uproot what I H1215
Jer 52:4 outside the city and **b** siege works all H1215
Eze 13:10 when a flimsy wall *is* **b**, they cover it with H1215
Eze 16:24 *you* **b** a mound for yourself and made a H1215
Eze 16:25 every street corner *you* **b** your lofty shrines H1215
Eze 16:31 When you **b** your mounds at every street H1215
Eze 17:17 when ramps *are* **b** and siege works H9161
Eze 41:7 the temple was **b** in ascending stages, NDT
Eze 43:18 blood against the altar when it **is b**: H6913
Eze 46:23 with places for fire **b** all around under the H6913
Da 4:30 the great Babylon I *have* **b** as the royal A10111
Hos 8:11 "Though Ephraim **b many** altars for sin H8049
Hos 8:14 has forgotten their Maker and **b** palaces; H1215
Hos 10:1 fruit increased, *he* **b more** altars; as his H8049
Am 5:11 though *you have* **b** stone mansions H1215
Am 7:7 by a wall that had been **b** true to plumb, NDT
Zec 8:9 be strong so that the temple *may* **be b**. H1215
Zec 9:3 Tyre *has* **b** herself a stronghold; she has H1215
Mt 5:14 A town **b** on a hill cannot be hidden. *G3023*
Mt 7:24 like a wise man who **b** his house on the *G3868*
Mt 7:26 a foolish man who **b** his house on sand. *G3868*
Mt 21:33 dug a winepress in it and **b** a watchtower. *G3868*
Mk 12:1 pit for the winepress and **b** a watchtower. *G3868*
Lk 4:29 brow of the hill on which the town *was* **b**, *G3868*
Lk 6:48 could not shake it, because it *was* well **b**. *G3868*
Lk 6:49 is like a man *who* **b** a house on the *G3868*
Lk 7:5 our nation and *has* **b** our synagogue." *G3868*
Ac 7:47 But it was Solomon *who* **b** a house for him. *G3868*
Ac 17:24 not live in temples **b by human hands**. *G5935*
Ac 28:2 *They* **b** a fire and welcomed us all because *G721*
1Co 3:14 If what *has been* **b** survives, the builder *G2224*
1Co 14:26 be done so that the church may be **b up**. *G3869*
2Co 5:1 house in heaven, **not b by human hands**. *G942*
Eph 2:20 **b on** the foundation of the apostles and *G2224*
Eph 2:22 you too *are being* **b together** to become *G5325*
Eph 4:12 so that the body of Christ may be **b up** *G3869*
Col 2:7 rooted and **b up** in him, strengthened in *G2224*
Heb 3:4 For every house *is* **b** by someone, but God *G2941*
Heb 11:7 in holy fear **b** an ark to save his family. *G2941*
1Pe 2:5 *are being* **b** into a spiritual house to be a *G3868*
1Pe 3:20 days of Noah *while* the ark *was being* **b**. *G2941*

BUKKI (5)

Nu 34:22 **B** son of Jogli, the leader from the tribe of H1321
1Ch 6:5 Abishua the father of **B**, Bukki the father H1321
1Ch 6:5 the father of Bukki, **B** the father of Uzzi, H1321
1Ch 6:51 **B** his son, Uzzi his son, Zerahiah his son, H1321
Ezr 7:4 of Zerahiah, the son of Uzzi, the son of **B**, H1321

BUKKIAH (2)

1Ch 25:4 **B**, Mattaniah, Uzziel, Shubael and H1322
1Ch 25:13 the sixth to **B**, his sons and relatives 12 H1322

BUL (1)

1Ki 6:38 In the eleventh year in the month of **B**, the H1004

BULGES (1) [BULGING]

Job 15:27 with fat and his waist **b with flesh**, H6913+7089

BULGING (1) [BULGES]

Isa 30:13 high wall, cracked and **b**, that collapses H1240

BULL (98) [BULL'S, BULLS]

Ex 21:28 "If a **b** gores a man or woman to death H8802
Ex 21:28 to death, the **b** is to be stoned to death H8802
Ex 21:28 But the owner of the **b** will not be held H8802
Ex 21:29 the **b** has had the habit of goring and the H8802
Ex 21:29 the **b** is to be stoned and its owner also is H8802
Ex 21:31 also applies if the **b** gores a son or daughter NDT
Ex 21:32 If the **b** gores a male or female slave, the H8802
Ex 21:32 and the **b** is to be stoned to death. H8802
Ex 21:35 "If anyone's **b** injures someone else's bull H8802
Ex 21:35 bull injures someone else's **b** and it dies, H8802
Ex 21:36 it was known that the **b** had the habit of H8802
Ex 29:1 Take a young **b** and two rams H1330+7228
Ex 29:3 them along with the **b** and the two rams. H7228
Ex 29:10 "Bring the **b** to the front of the tent of H7228
Ex 29:36 Sacrifice a **b** each day as a sin offering to H7228
Lev 1:5 to slaughter the young **b** before the LORD, H1330
Lev 4:3 the LORD a young **b** without defect H1330+7228
Lev 4:4 He is to present the **b** at the entrance to H7228
Lev 4:8 all the fat from the **b** *of* the sin offering— H7228
Lev 4:11 But the hide of the **b** and all its flesh, as H7228
Lev 4:12 all the rest of the **b**—he must take outside H7228
Lev 4:14 bring a young **b** as a sin offering H1330+7228
Lev 4:15 the **b** shall be slaughtered before the H7228
Lev 4:20 do with this **b** just as he did with the H7228
Lev 4:20 as he did with the **b** *for* the sin offering. H7228
Lev 4:21 he shall take the **b** outside the camp and H7228
Lev 4:21 camp and burn it as he burned the first **b**. H7228
Lev 8:2 anointing oil, the **b** *for* the sin offering H7228
Lev 8:14 then presented the **b** *for* the sin offering, H7228
Lev 8:15 slaughtered the **b** and took some of the NDT
Lev 8:17 But the **b** with its hide and its flesh and its H7228
Lev 9:2 "Take a **b** calf for your sin offering H1201+1330
Lev 16:3 bring a young **b** for a sin offering H1330+7228
Lev 16:6 "Aaron is to offer the **b** for his own sin H7228
Lev 16:11 "Aaron shall bring the **b** for his own sin H7228
Lev 16:11 he is to slaughter the **b** for his own sin H7228
Lev 16:27 The **b** and the goat for the sin offerings H7228
Lev 23:18 defect, one young **b** and two rams. H1330+7228
Nu 7:15 one young **b**, one ram and one H1330+7228
Nu 7:21 one young **b**, one ram and one H1330+7228
Nu 7:27 one young **b**, one ram and one H1330+7228
Nu 7:33 one young **b**, one ram and one H1330+7228
Nu 7:39 one young **b**, one ram and one H1330+7228
Nu 7:45 one young **b**, one ram and one H1330+7228
Nu 7:51 one young **b**, one ram and one H1330+7228
Nu 7:57 one young **b**, one ram and one H1330+7228
Nu 7:63 one young **b**, one ram and one H1330+7228
Nu 7:69 one young **b**, one ram and one H1330+7228
Nu 7:75 one young **b**, one ram and one H1330+7228
Nu 7:81 one young **b**, one ram and one H1330+7228
Nu 8:8 them take a young **b** with its grain H1330+7228
Nu 8:8 a second young **b** for a sin offering. H1330+7228
Nu 15:8 you prepare a young **b** as a burnt offering H1330
Nu 15:9 bring with the **b** a grain offering of H1330
Nu 15:11 Each **b** or ram, each lamb or young goat H8802
Nu 15:24 is to offer a young **b** for a burnt H1330+7228
Nu 23:2 of them offered a **b** and a ram on each H7228
Nu 23:4 each altar I have offered a **b** and a ram." H7228
Nu 23:14 altars and offered a **b** and a ram on each H7228
Nu 23:30 offered a **b** and a ram on each altar. H7228
Nu 28:12 With each **b** there is to be a grain offering H7228
Nu 28:14 With each **b** there is to be a drink offering H7228
Nu 28:20 With each **b** offer a grain offering of H7228
Nu 28:28 With each **b** there is to be a grain offering H7228
Nu 29:2 a burnt offering of one young **b**, H1330+7228
Nu 29:3 With the **b** offer a grain offering of H7228
Nu 29:8 a burnt offering of one young **b**, H1330+7228
Nu 29:9 With the **b** offer a grain offering of H7228
Nu 29:36 consisting of a burnt offering of one **b**, H7228
Nu 29:37 With the **b**, the ram and the lambs, offer H7228
Dt 18:3 the people who sacrifice a **b** or a sheep: H8802
Dt 33:17 In majesty he is like a firstborn **b**; his H8802
Jdg 6:25 "Take the second **b** from your father's H7228
Jdg 6:26 offer the second **b** as a burnt offering." H7228
Jdg 6:28 down and the second **b** sacrificed on the H7228
1Sa 1:24 along with a three-year-old **b**, an ephah H7228
1Sa 1:25 When the **b** had been sacrificed, they H7228
2Sa 6:13 he sacrificed a **b** and a fattened calf. H8802
1Ki 18:23 prepare the other **b** and put it on the H7228
1Ki 18:26 So they took the **b** given them and H7228
1Ki 18:33 cut the **b** into pieces and laid it on the H7228
2Ch 13:9 with a young **b** and seven rams may H1330
Ps 50:9 I have no need of a **b** from your stall or of H7228
Ps 69:31 more than a **b** with its horns and hooves. H7228
Ps 106:20 their glorious God for an image of a **b**, H8802
Isa 34:7 the **b calves** and the great bulls. H7228
Isa 66:3 whoever sacrifices a **b** is like one who kills H8802
Eze 43:19 to give a young **b** as a sin offering H1330+7228
Eze 43:21 You are to take the **b** *for* the sin offering H7228
Eze 43:22 be purified as it was purified with the **b**. H7228
Eze 43:23 to offer a young **b** and a ram from H1330+7228
Eze 43:25 provide a young **b** and a ram from H1330+7228
Eze 45:18 to take a young **b** without defect H1330+7228
Eze 45:22 is to provide a **b** as a sin offering for H7228
Eze 45:24 an ephah for each **b** and an ephah for H7228
Eze 46:6 New Moon he is to offer a young **b**, H1330+7228
Eze 46:7 as a grain offering one ephah with the **b**, H7228
Eze 46:11 grain offering is to be an ephah with a **b**, H7228

BULL'S (9) [BULL]

Ex 29:12 Take some of the **b** blood and put it on H7228
Ex 29:14 But burn the **b** flesh and its hide and its H7228
Lev 4:5 shall take some of the **b** blood and carry it H7228
Lev 4:7 The rest of the **b** blood he shall pour out H7228
Lev 4:15 their hands on the **b** head before the LORD H7228
Lev 4:16 to take some of the **b** blood into the tent H7228
Lev 16:14 to take some of the **b** blood and with his H7228
Lev 16:15 do with it as he did with the **b** blood: H7228
Lev 16:18 take some of the **b** blood and some of the H7228

BULLOCK, BULLOCKS (KJV) BULL, BULLS

BULLS (64) [BULL]

Ge 32:15 forty cows and ten **b**, and twenty female H7228
Ex 24:5 sacrificed **young b** as fellowship H7228
Nu 7:87 burnt offering came to twelve **young b**, H7228
Nu 8:12 to lay their hands on the heads of the **b**, H7228
Nu 23:1 prepare seven **b** and seven rams for H7228
Nu 23:29 prepare seven **b** and seven rams for H7228
Nu 28:11 a burnt offering of two young **b**, H1330+7228
Nu 28:19 of a burnt offering of two young **b**, H1330+7228
Nu 28:27 a burnt offering of two young **b**, H1330+7228
Nu 29:13 burnt offering of thirteen young **b**, H1330+7228
Nu 29:14 each of the thirteen **b** offer a grain H7228
Nu 29:17 second day offer twelve young **b**, H1330+7228
Nu 29:18 With the **b**, rams and lambs, offer their H7228
Nu 29:20 " 'On the third day offer eleven **b**, two H7228
Nu 29:21 With the **b**, rams and lambs, offer their H7228
Nu 29:23 " 'On the fourth day offer ten **b**, two rams H7228
Nu 29:24 With the **b**, rams and lambs, offer their H7228
Nu 29:26 " 'On the fifth day offer nine **b**, two rams H7228
Nu 29:27 With the **b**, rams and lambs, offer their H7228
Nu 29:29 " 'On the sixth day offer eight **b**, two rams H7228
Nu 29:30 With the **b**, rams and lambs, offer their H7228
Nu 29:32 " 'On the seventh day offer seven **b**, two H7228
Nu 29:33 With the **b**, rams and lambs, offer their H7228
1Ki 7:25 The Sea stood on twelve **b**, three facing H1330
1Ki 7:29 were lions, **b** and cherubim—and on H1330
1Ki 7:29 below the lions and **b** were wreaths of H1330
1Ki 7:44 the Sea and the twelve **b** under it; H1330
1Ki 18:23 Get two **b** for us. Let Baal's prophets H7228

1Ki 18:25 "Choose one of the b and prepare it first H7228
2Ki 16:17 Sea from the bronze b that supported it H1330
1Ch 15:26 seven b and seven rams were sacrificed. H7228
1Ch 29:21 a thousand b, a thousand rams and a H7228
2Ch 4: 3 the rim, figures of b encircled it—ten to a H1330
2Ch 4: 3 The b were cast in two rows in one piece H1330
2Ch 4: 4 The Sea stood on twelve b, three facing H1330
2Ch 4:15 the Sea and the twelve b under it; H1330
2Ch 29:21 They brought seven b, seven rams, seven H7228
2Ch 29:22 So they slaughtered the b, and the priests H1330
2Ch 29:32 the assembly brought was seventy b, H1330
2Ch 29:33 to six hundred b and three thousand H1330
2Ch 30:24 a thousand b and seven thousand H7228
2Ch 30:24 them with a thousand b and ten thousand H7228
Ezr 6: 9 is needed—young b, rams, male lambs A10756
Ezr 6:17 house of God they offered a hundred b, A10756
Ezr 7:17 With this money be sure to buy b, rams A10756
Ezr 8:35 twelve b for all Israel, ninety-six rams H7228
Job 21:10 Their b never fail to breed; their cows H8802
Job 42: 8 So now take seven b and seven rams and H7228
Ps 22:12 Many b surround me; strong bulls of H7228
Ps 22:12 strong b of Bashan encircle me. NDT
Ps 50:13 Do I eat the flesh of b or drink the blood of H52
Ps 51:19 then b will be offered on your altar. H7228
Ps 66:15 offering of rams; I will offer b and goats. H1330
Ps 68:30 the herd of b among the calves of the H52
Isa 1:11 in the blood of b and lambs and goats. H7228
Isa 34: 7 with them, the bull calves and the great b. NDT
Jer 50:27 Kill all her young b; let them go down to H7228
Jer 52:20 the Sea and the twelve bronze b under it H1330
Eze 39:18 goats and b—all of them fattened H7228
Eze 45:23 is to provide seven b and seven rams H7228
Hos 12:11 Do they sacrifice b in Gilgal? Their altars H8802
Ac 14:13 brought b and wreaths to the city gates G5436
Heb 9:13 blood of goats and b and the ashes of a G5436
Heb 10: 4 the blood of b and goats to take away G5436

BULRUSH, BULRUSHES (KJV) PAPYRUS, REED

BULWARKS (KJV) CORNER DEFENSES, RAMPARTS, SEIGE WORKS

BUNAH (1)

1Ch 2:25 Ram his firstborn, B, Oren, Ozem and H1007

BUNCH (1)

Ex 12:22 Take a b of hyssop, dip it into the blood in H99

BUNDLE (2) [BUNDLES]

Ru 3:15 measures of barley and placed the b on her. NDT
1Sa 25:29 securely in the b of the living by the H7655

BUNDLES (2) [BUNDLE]

Ru 2:16 her from the b and leave them for her H7395
Mt 13:30 weeds and tie them in b to be burned; G1299

BUNNI (3)

Ne 9: 4 Kadmiel, Shebaniah, B, Sherebiah, Bani H1221
Ne 10:15 B, Azgad, Bebai, H1221
Ne 11:15 the son of Hashabiah, the son of B; H1221

BURDEN (36) [BURDENED, BURDENS, BURDENSOME]

Ge 49:15 his shoulder to the b and submit to forced H6022
Nu 11:11 that you put the b of all these people on H5362
Nu 11:14 people by myself; the b is too heavy for me. NDT
Nu 11:17 They will share the b of the people with H5362
Dt 1: 9 are too heavy a b for me to carry alone. H4202+3523+5951
1Sa 25:31 the staggering b of needless H7050+2256+4842
2Sa 13:25 we would only be a b to you. H3877
2Sa 15:33 "If you go with me, you will be a b to me. H5362
2Sa 19:35 servant be an added b to my lord the king H5362
Ne 5:15 placed a heavy b on the people and took H3877
Job 7:20 Have I become a b to you? H5362
Ps 38: 4 me like a b too heavy to bear. H5362
Ps 81: 6 "I removed the b from their shoulders H6023
Pr 27: 3 Stone is heavy and sand a b, but a fool's H5748
Ecc 1:13 What a heavy b God has laid on H6721+6701
Ecc 3:10 I have seen the b God has laid on H6721+6701
Isa 1:14 They have become a b to me; I am weary H3268
Isa 10:27 In that day their b will be lifted from your H6024
Isa 14:25 his b removed from their shoulders." H6024
Isa 46: 1 are borne by beasts of b. H2651+2256+989
Isa 46: 1 about are burdensome, a b for the weary. H5362
Isa 46: 2 unable to rescue the b, they themselves H5362
Zep 3:18 which is a b and reproach for you. H5368
Mal 1:13 And you say, 'What a b!' and you sniff at it H9430
Mt 11:30 For my yoke is easy and my b is light." G5845
Mt 20:12 who have borne the b of the work and the G983
Ac 15:28 and to us not to b you with anything G2202+983
2Co 11: 9 something, I was not a b to anyone, for G2915
2Co 11: 9 kept myself from being a b to you in any way, G4
2Co 12:13 except that I was never a b to you? G2915
2Co 12:14 third time, and I will not be a b to you G2915
2Co 12:16 that as it may, I have not been a b to you. G2851
1Th 2: 9 in order not to be a b to anyone while we G2096
2Th 3: 8 so that we would not be a b to any of you. G2096
Heb 13:17 will be a joy, not a b, for that would be of G5100
Rev 2:24 'I will not impose any other b on you, G983

BURDENED (7) [BURDEN]

Isa 43:23 I have not b you with grain offerings nor H6268
Isa 43:24 But you have b me with your sins and H6268
Mic 6: 3 How have I b you? Answer me. H4206
Mt 11:28 all you who are weary and b, and I will G5844
2Co 5: 4 we groan and are b, because we do G976
Gal 5: 1 and do not let yourselves be b again by a G1923
1Ti 5:16 not let the church be b with them, G976

BURDENS (7) [BURDEN]

Dt 1:12 problems and your b and your disputes all H5362
Ps 66:11 us into prison and laid b on our backs. H4601
Ps 68:19 to God our Savior, who daily bears our b. H6673
Ps 73: 5 They are free from common human b H6662
Isa 9: 4 you have shattered the yoke that b them H6024
Lk 11:46 load people down with b they can hardly G5845
Gal 6: 2 Carry each other's b, and in this way you G983

BURDENSOME (2) [BURDEN]

Isa 46: 1 The images that are carried about are b H6673
1Jn 5: 3 And his commands are not b, G987

BURIAL (17) [BURY]

Ge 23: 4 property for a b site here so I can bury H7700
Ge 23: 9 the full price as a b site among you." H7700
Ge 23:20 to Abraham by the Hittites as a b site. H7700
Ge 49:30 with the field as a b place from Ephron H7700
Ge 50:13 with the field as a b place from Ephron H7700
Ecc 6: 3 prosperity and does not receive proper b, H7690
Isa 14:20 you will not join them in b, for you have H7690
Jer 22:19 He will have the b of a donkey H7699+7690
Jer 26:23 thrown into the b place of the common H7700
Eze 39:11 day I will give Gog a b place in Israel, H7700
Mt 26:12 my body, she did it to prepare me for b. G1946
Mt 27: 7 potter's field as a b place for foreigners. G5438
Mk 14: 8 my body beforehand to prepare for my b. G1947
Jn 12: 7 save this perfume for the day of my b. G1947
Jn 19:40 was in accordance with Jewish b customs. G1946
Heb 11:22 instructions concerning the b of his bones. NDT
Rev 11: 9 bodies and refuse them b. G5502+1650+3645

BURIED (111) [BURY]

Ge 15:15 in peace and be b at a good old age. H7699
Ge 23:19 Afterward Abraham b his wife Sarah in the H7699
Ge 25: 9 Isaac and Ishmael b him in the cave of H7699
Ge 25:10 There Abraham was b with his wife Sarah. H7699
Ge 35: 4 Jacob b them under the oak at H3243
Ge 35: 8 died and was b under the oak outside H7699
Ge 35:19 So Rachel died and was b on the way to H7699
Ge 35:29 And his sons Esau and Jacob b him. H7699
Ge 47:30 of Egypt and bury me where they are b." H7690
Ge 48: 7 So I b her there beside the road to H7699
Ge 49:31 There Abraham and his wife Sarah were b, H7699
Ge 49:31 there Isaac and his wife Rebekah were b H7699
Ge 49:31 Rebekah were buried, and there I b Leah. H7699
Ge 50:13 land of Canaan and b him in the cave in H7699
Nu 11:34 because there they b the people who had H7699
Nu 20: 1 There Miriam died and was b. H7699
Dt 10: 6 There Aaron died and was b, and Eleazar H7699
Dt 34: 6 He b him in Moab, in the valley opposite H7699
Jos 24:30 And they b him in the land of his H7699
Jos 24:32 were b at Shechem in the tract of land H7699
Jos 24:33 son of Aaron died and was b at Gibeah, H7699
Jdg 2: 9 And they b him in the land of his H7699
Jdg 8:32 a good old age and was b in the tomb of H7699
Jdg 10: 2 then he died, and was b in Shamir. H7699
Jdg 10: 5 When Jair died, he was b in Kamon. H7699
Jdg 12: 7 Gileadite died and was b in a town in H7699
Jdg 12:10 Then Ibzan died and was b in Bethlehem. H7699
Jdg 12:12 Then Elon died and was b in Aijalon in H7699
Jdg 12:15 of Hillel died and was b at Pirathon in H7699
Jdg 16:31 him back and b him between Zorah H7699
Ru 1:17 you die I will die, and there I will be b. H7699
1Sa 25: 1 and they b him at his home in Ramah. H7699
1Sa 28: 3 him and b him in his own town H7699
1Sa 31:13 took their bones and b them under a H7699
2Sa 2: 4 men from Jabesh Gilead who had b Saul, H7699
2Sa 2:32 They took Asahel and b him in his father's H7699
2Sa 3:32 They b Abner in Hebron, and the king H7699
2Sa 4:12 of Ish-Bosheth and b it in Abner's tomb at H7699
2Sa 17:23 So he died and was b in his father's tomb. H7699
2Sa 21:14 They b the bones of Saul and his son H7699
1Ki 2:10 his ancestors and was b in the City of H7699
1Ki 2:34 and he was b at his home out in the H7699
1Ki 11:43 his ancestors and was b in the city of H7699
1Ki 13:22 your body will not be b in the tomb of H995
1Ki 13:31 in the grave where the man of God is b; H7699
1Ki 14:13 to Jeroboam who will be b, H995+448+7700
1Ki 14:18 They b him, and all Israel mourned for H7699
1Ki 14:31 his ancestors and was b with them in the H7699
1Ki 15: 8 his ancestors and was b in the City of H7699
1Ki 15:24 his ancestors and was b with them in the H7699
1Ki 16: 6 with his ancestors and was b in Tirzah. H7699
1Ki 16:28 with his ancestors and was b in Samaria. H7699
1Ki 22:37 brought to Samaria, and they b him there. H7699
1Ki 22:50 his ancestors and was b with them in the H7699
2Ki 8:24 his ancestors and was b with them in the H7699
2Ki 9:28 to Jerusalem and b him with his ancestors H7699
2Ki 10:35 with his ancestors and was b in Samaria. H7699
2Ki 12:21 He died and was b with his ancestors in H7699
2Ki 13: 9 with his ancestors and was b in Samaria. H7699
2Ki 13:13 Jehoash was b in Samaria with the kings H7699
2Ki 13:20 Elisha died and was b. Now Moabite H7699
2Ki 14:16 his ancestors and was b in Samaria with H7699
2Ki 14:20 back by horse and was b in Jerusalem H7699
2Ki 15: 7 his ancestors and was b near them in the H7699
2Ki 15:38 his ancestors and was b with them in the H7699
2Ki 16:20 his ancestors and was b with them in the H7699
2Ki 21:18 his ancestors and was b in his palace H7699
2Ki 21:26 He was b in his tomb in the garden of H7699
2Ki 22:20 and you will be b in peace. H665+448+7700
2Ki 23:30 to Jerusalem and b him in his own tomb. H7699
1Ch 10:12 Then they b their bones under the great H7699
2Ch 9:31 his ancestors and was b in the city of H7699
2Ch 12:16 his ancestors and was b in the City of H7699
2Ch 14: 1 his ancestors and was b in the City of H7699
2Ch 16:14 They b him in the tomb that he had cut H7699
2Ch 21: 1 his ancestors and was b with them in the H7699
2Ch 21:20 and was b in the City of David H7699
2Ch 22: 9 They b him, for they said, "He was a son H7699
2Ch 24:16 He was b with the kings in the City of H7699
2Ch 24:25 So he died and was b in the City of David H7699
2Ch 25:28 back by horse and was b with his H7699
2Ch 26:23 his ancestors and was b near them in a H7699
2Ch 27: 9 his ancestors and was b in the City of H7699
2Ch 28:27 with his ancestors and was b in the city of H7699
2Ch 32:33 his ancestors and was b on the hill where H7699
2Ch 33:20 his ancestors and was b in his palace. H7699
2Ch 34:28 and you will be b in peace. H665+448+7700
2Ch 35:24 He was b in the tombs of his ancestors H7699
Ne 2: 3 city where my ancestors are b lies in ruins, H7700
Ne 2: 5 my ancestors are b so that I can rebuild H7700
Job 16:15 over my skin and b my brow in the dust. H6619
Ps 106:17 Dathan; it b the company of Abiram. H4059
Ecc 8:10 I saw the wicked b—those who used to H7699
Jer 8: 2 They will not be gathered up or b, but will H7699
Jer 16: 4 not be mourned or b but will be like dung H7699
Jer 16: 6 They will not be b or mourned, and no H7699
Jer 20: 6 There you will die and be b, you and all H7699
Jer 25:33 will not be mourned or gathered up or b, H7699
Jer 43:10 throne over these stones I have b here; H3243
Eze 39:11 Gog and all his hordes will be b there. H7699
Mt 14:12 disciples came and took his body and b it. G2507
Lk 16:22 The rich man also died and was b. G2507
Ac 2:29 that the patriarch David died and was b, G2507
Ac 5: 6 his body, and carried him out and b him. G2507
Ac 5: 9 The feet of the men who b your husband G2507
Ac 5:10 carried her out and b her beside her G2507
Ac 8: 2 Godly men b Stephen and mourned G5172
Ac 13:36 he was b with his ancestors and his body G4707
Ro 6: 4 We were therefore b with him through G5313
1Co 15: 4 that he was b, that he was raised on the G2507
Col 2:12 having been b with him in baptism, in G5313

BURIES (2) [BURY]

Pr 19:24 A sluggard b his hand in the dish; he will H3243
Pr 26:15 A sluggard b his hand in the dish; he is H3243

BURN (137) [BURNED, BURNED-OUT, BURNING, BURNS, BURNT]

Ex 3: 2 though the bush was on fire it did not b up. H430
Ex 3: 3 why the bush does not b up. H1277
Ex 12:10 morning, you must b it. H8596+928+2021+836
Ex 21:25 b for burn, wound for wound, bruise for H3918
Ex 21:25 burn for b, wound for wound, bruise for H3918
Ex 29:13 the fat on them, and b them on the altar. H7787
Ex 29:14 But b the bull's flesh and H8596+928+2021+836
Ex 29:18 Then b the entire ram on the altar. It is a H7787
Ex 29:25 from their hands and b them on the altar H7787
Ex 29:34 over till morning, b it up. H8596+928+2021+836
Ex 30: 7 "Aaron must b fragrant incense on the H7787
Ex 30: 8 He must b incense again when he lights H7787
Ex 30: 8 so incense will b regularly before the NDT
Ex 32:10 so that my anger may b against them H3013
Ex 32:11 "why should your anger b against your H3013
Lev 1: 9 the priest is to b all of it on the altar. H7787
Lev 1:13 bring all of them and b them on the altar. H7787
Lev 1:15 wring off the head and b it on the altar H7787
Lev 1:17 then the priest shall b it on the wood H7787
Lev 2: 2 b this as a memorial portion on the H7787
Lev 2: 9 grain offering and b it on the altar as a H7787
Lev 2:11 for you are not to b any yeast or honey in H7787
Lev 2:16 The priest shall b the memorial portion of H7787
Lev 3: 5 Then Aaron's sons are to b it on the altar H7787
Lev 3:11 The priest shall b them on the altar as a H7787
Lev 3:16 The priest shall b them on the altar as a H7787
Lev 4:10 Then the priest shall b them on the altar H7787
Lev 4:12 b it there in a wood fire on the ash H8596
Lev 4:19 all the fat from it and b it on the altar, H7787
Lev 4:21 the camp and b it as he burned the H8596
Lev 4:26 He shall b all the fat on the altar as he H7787
Lev 4:31 the priest shall b it on the altar as an H7787
Lev 4:35 the priest shall b it on the altar on H7787
Lev 5:12 memorial portion and b it on the altar on H7787
Lev 6:12 offering on the fire and b the fat of the H7787
Lev 6:15 b the memorial portion on the altar H7787
Lev 7: 5 The priest shall b them on the altar as a H7787
Lev 7:31 The priest shall b the fat on the altar, but H7787
Lev 8:32 Then b up the rest of the H8596+928+2021+836
Lev 13:24 someone has a b on their skin and a H4805+836
Lev 13:24 spot appears in the raw flesh of the b, H4805
Lev 13:25 disease that has broken out in the b. H4805
Lev 13:28 it is a swelling from the b, and the priest H4805
Lev 13:28 them clean; it is only a scar from the b. H4805
Lev 13:52 He must b the fabric, the woven or knitted H8596
Lev 13:55 B it, no matter which H8596+928+2021+836
Lev 16:25 He shall also b the fat of the sin offering H7787

B

Lev 17: 6 tent of meeting and **b** the fat as an aroma H7787
Nu 5:26 a memorial offering and **b** it on the altar; H7787
Nu 16:40 should come to **b** incense before the H7787
Nu 18:17 against the altar and **b** their fat as a food H7787
Dt 6:15 God and his anger *will* **b** against you, H3013
Dt 7: 4 the LORD's anger *will* **b** against you and H3013
Dt 7: 5 Asherah poles and **b** their idols in the fire H8596
Dt 7:25 of their gods *you are to* **b** in the fire. H8596
Dt 11:17 Then the LORD's anger *will* **b** against you H3013
Dt 12: 3 sacred stones and **b** their Asherah poles H8596
Dt 12:31 *They* even **b** their sons and daughters in the fire **as sacrifices** H8596
Dt 13:16 completely **b** the town H8596+928+2021+836
Dt 29:20 his wrath and zeal *will* **b** against them. H6939
Jos 11: 6 horses and **b** their H8596+928+2021+836
Jos 11:13 Yet Israel *did* not **b** any of the cities built H8596
Jos 23:16 the LORD's anger *will* **b** against you, and H3013
Jdg 12: 1 *We're going to* **b down** H8596+928+2021+836
Jdg 14:15 *we will* **b** you and your father's household **to death** H8596+928+2021+836
1Sa 2:28 up to my altar, to **b** incense, and to wear H7787
1Ki 14:10 *I will* **b up** the house of Jeroboam as one H1277
1Ki 22:43 to offer sacrifices and **b incense** there. H7787
2Ki 12: 3 to offer sacrifices and **b incense** there. H7787
2Ki 14: 4 to offer sacrifices and **b incense** there. H7787
2Ki 15: 4 to offer sacrifices and **b incense** there. H7787
2Ki 15:35 to offer sacrifices and **b incense** there. H7787
2Ki 22:17 my anger *will* **b** against this place and H3675
2Ki 23: 5 kings of Judah *to* **b incense** on the high H7787
1Ch 14:12 David gave orders *to* **b** *them* in the fire. H8596
2Ch 2: 6 as a place to **b sacrifices** before him? H7787
2Ch 4:20 to **b** in front of the inner sanctuary as H1277
2Ch 26:16 of the LORD to **b incense** on the altar of H7787
2Ch 26:18 you, Uzziah, to **b incense** to the LORD. H7787
2Ch 26:18 who have been consecrated to **b incense**. H7787
2Ch 26:19 a censer in his hand *ready* to **b incense**, H7787
2Ch 28:25 high places to **b sacrifices** to other gods H7787
2Ch 29: 7 *They did* not **b** incense or present any H7787
2Ch 29:11 to minister before him and *to* **b incense**." H7787
2Ch 32:12 before one altar and **b sacrifices** on it'? H7787
Ne 10:34 of wood to **b** on the altar of the H1277
Ps 21: 9 *you will* **b** them up as in a blazing H8883S
Ps 79: 5 How long *will* your jealousy **b** like fire? H1277
Ps 89:46 How long *will* your wrath **b** like fire? H1277
Ps 102: 3 my bones **b** like glowing embers. H3081
Isa 1:31 work a spark; both *will* **b** together, with no H1277
Isa 10:17 in a single day *it will* **b** and consume his H1277
Isa 47:14 are like stubble; the fire *will* **b** them **up**. H8596
Isa 57: 5 You **b with lust** among the oaks and H2801
Jer 4: 4 will flare up and **b** like fire because of H1277
Jer 4: 4 have done—**b** with no one to quench it. NDT
Jer 6:29 blow fiercely *to* **b away** the lead with fire, H9462
Jer 7: 9 **b incense** to Baal and follow other gods H7787
Jer 7:20 and *it will* **b** and not be quenched. H1277
Jer 7:31 Valley of Ben Hinnom to **b** their sons and H8596
Jer 11:12 out to the gods to whom they **b incense**, H7787
Jer 11:13 have set up to **b incense** to that shameful H7787
Jer 15:14 will kindle a fire *that will* **b** against you." H3678
Jer 17: 4 kindled my anger, and *it will* **b** forever." H3678
Jer 18:15 *they* **b incense** to worthless idols H7787
Jer 19: 5 places of Baal to **b** their children in the H8596
Jer 21:12 will break out and **b** like fire because of H1277
Jer 21:12 have done—**b** with no one to quench it. NDT
Jer 32:29 it on fire; *they will* **b** it **down**, along with H8596
Jer 33:18 *to* **b** grain offerings and to present H7787
Jer 34: 2 and *he will* **b** it **down**. H8596+928+2021+836
Jer 34:22 take it and **b** it **down**. H8596+928+2021+836
Jer 36:25 urged the king not *to* **b** the scroll, H8596
Jer 37: 8 capture it and **b** it **down**. H8596+928+2021+836
Jer 37:10 out and **b** this city **down**." H8596+928+2021+836
Jer 38:18 and *they will* **b** it **down**; H8596+928+2021+836
Jer 43:12 *he will* **b** their temples and take their H8596
Jer 43:13 and *will* **b down** the H8596+928+2021+836
Jer 44:17 We *will* **b incense** to the Queen of H7787
Jer 44:25 vows we made to **b incense** and pour out H7787
Jer 48:35 high places and **b incense** to their gods," H7787
Eze 5: 2 **b** a third of the hair H1277+928+2021+241
Eze 5: 4 the fire and **b** them **up**. H8596+928+2021+836
Eze 16:41 *They will* **b down** your H8596+928+2021+836
Eze 23:47 and **b down** their houses H8596+928+2021+836
Eze 39: 9 the weapons for fuel and **b** them **up**— H5956
Eze 43:21 the sin offering and **b** it in the designated H8596
Hos 4:13 mountaintops and **b offerings** on the hills, H7787
Am 4: 5 **B** leavened bread as a thank offering and H7787
Am 6:10 out of the house *to* **b** them asks anyone H6251
Na 2:13 "*I will* **b up** your chariots in smoke, and H1277
Mal 4: 1 the day is coming; *it will* **b** like a furnace. H1277
Lk 1: 9 into the temple of the Lord and **b incense**. *G2594*
Lk 3:17 but *he will* **b up** the chaff with *G2876*
1Co 7: 9 it is better to marry than *to* **b with passion**. *G4792*
2Co 11:29 is led into sin, and I *do* not *inwardly* **b**? *G4792*
Rev 17:16 they will eat her flesh and **b** her with fire. *G2876*

BURNED (150) [BURN]

Ge 38:24 "Bring her out and *have her* **b to death**!" H8596
Ge 39:19 your slave treated me," he **b** *with* anger. H3013
Ex 4:14 the LORD's anger **b** against Moses and he H3013
Ex 32:19 his anger **b** and he threw the tablets out H3013
Ex 32:20 the people had made and **b** it in the fire; H8596
Ex 40:27 **b** fragrant incense on it, as the LORD H7787
Lev 4:21 the camp and burn it as *he* **b** the first bull. H8596
Lev 4:26 fat on the altar as he **b** the fat of the NDT
Lev 6:22 share and *is to* **be b** completely. H7787
Lev 6:23 offering of a priest shall be **b** completely; NDT
Lev 6:30 eaten; *it must* **be b up**. H8596+928+2021+836
Lev 7:17 third day *must* **be b up**. H8596+928+2021+836
Lev 7:19 eaten; *it must* **be b up**. H8596+928+2021+836
Lev 8:16 kidneys and their fat, and **b** it on the altar. H7787
Lev 8:17 *he* **b up** outside H8596+928+2021+836
Lev 8:20 He cut the ram into pieces and **b** the head, H7787
Lev 8:21 legs with water and **b** the whole ram on H7787
Lev 8:28 their hands and **b** them on the altar on H7787
Lev 9:10 On the altar *he* **b** the fat, the kidneys and H7787
Lev 9:11 the hide *he* **b up** outside H8596+928+2021+836
Lev 9:13 the head, and *he* **b** them on the altar. H7787
Lev 9:14 the legs and **b** them on top of the H7787
Lev 9:17 took a handful of it and **b** it on the altar in H7787
Lev 9:20 then Aaron **b** the fat on the altar. H7787
Lev 10:16 offering and found that *it had* **been b up**, H8596
Lev 13:52 the article *must* **be b**. H8596+928+2021+836
Lev 13:57 has the mold *must be* **b**. H8596+928+2021+836
Lev 16:27 *are to be* **b up**. H8596+928+2021+836
Lev 19: 6 third day *must* **be b up**. H8596+928+2021+836
Lev 20:14 Both he and they *must be* **b** in the fire, so H8596
Lev 21: 9 her father; *she must* **be b** in the fire. H8596
Nu 11: 1 fire from the LORD **b** among them and H1277
Nu 11: 3 fire from the LORD *had* **b** among them. H1277
Nu 11:33 anger of the LORD **b** against the people, H3013
Nu 12: 9 The anger of the LORD **b** against them H3013
Nu 16:39 by those *who had* **been b to death**, H8596
Nu 19: 5 watches, the heifer *is to be* **b**—its hide, H8596
Nu 19:17 some ashes from the **b** purification H8599
Nu 24:10 Then Balak's anger **b** against Balaam. H3013
Nu 25: 3 And the LORD's anger **b** against them. H3013
Nu 31:10 *They* **b** all the towns H8596+928+2021+836
Nu 32:13 The LORD's anger **b** against Israel and he H3013
Dt 9:21 the calf you had made, and **b** it in the fire. H8596
Dt 29:27 the LORD's anger **b** against this land, H3013
Jos 6:24 Then *they* **b** the whole H8596+928+2021+836
Jos 7: 1 So the LORD's anger **b** against Israel. H3013
Jos 7:25 the rest, *they* **b** them. H8596+928+2021+836
Jos 8:28 So Joshua **b** Ai and made it a permanent H8596
Jos 11: 9 horses and **b** their H8596+928+2021+836
Jos 11:11 and *he* **b** Hazor itself. H8596+928+2021+836
Jos 11:13 mounds—except Hazor, which Joshua **b**. H8596
Jdg 3: 8 The anger of the LORD **b** against Israel so H3013
Jdg 15: 5 *He* **b up** the shocks and standing grain H1277
Jdg 15: 6 **b** her and her father **to death** H8596+928+2021+836
Jdg 18:27 sword and **b down** their H8596+928+2021+836
1Sa 2:15 But even before the fat *was* **b**, the priest's H7787
1Sa 2:16 to him, "*Let* the fat *be* **b** first, and H7787+7787
1Sa 11: 6 upon him, and he **b** with anger. H3013+4394
1Sa 17:28 he **b** *with* anger at him and asked H3013
1Sa 30: 1 attacked Ziklag and **b** it, H8596+928+2021+836
1Sa 30:14 And *we* **b** Ziklag." H8596+928+2021+836
1Sa 31:12 went to Jabesh, where *they* **b** them. H8596
2Sa 6: 7 The LORD's anger **b** against Uzzah because H3013
2Sa 12: 5 David **b** *with* anger against the H3013+4394
2Sa 23: 7 *they* **are b up** where they lie." H8596+928+2021+836+8596
2Sa 24: 1 the anger of the LORD **b** against Israel, H3013
1Ki 3: 3 sacrifices and **b incense** on the high H7787
1Ki 11: 8 *who* **b incense** and offered sacrifices to H7787
1Ki 13: 2 and human bones *will be* **b** on you. H8596
1Ki 15:13 Asa cut it down and **b** it in the Kidron H8596
1Ki 18:38 fire of the LORD fell and **b up** the sacrifice, H430
1Ki 19:21 *He* **b** the plowing equipment **to cook** the H1418
2Ki 10:26 stone out of the temple of Baal and **b** it. H8596
2Ki 13: 3 So the LORD's anger **b** against Israel, and H3013
2Ki 16: 4 sacrifices and **b incense** at the high H7787
2Ki 17:11 At every high place *they* **b incense**, as the H7787
2Ki 17:31 **b** their children in the fire **as sacrifices** to H8596
2Ki 22:17 forsaken me and **b incense** to other gods H7787
2Ki 23: 4 *He* **b** them outside Jerusalem in the fields H8596
2Ki 23: 5 those *who* **b incense** to Baal, to H7787
2Ki 23: 6 Valley outside Jerusalem and **b** it there. H8596
2Ki 23: 8 where the priests *had* **b incense**. H7787
2Ki 23:11 Josiah then **b** the H8596+928+2021+836
2Ki 23:15 *He* **b** the high place and ground it to H8596
2Ki 23:15 to powder, and **b** the Asherah pole also. H8596
2Ki 23:16 removed from them and **b** on the altar to H8596
2Ki 23:20 on the altars and **b** human bones on H8596
2Ki 23:26 which **b** against Judah because of all that H3013
2Ki 25: 9 building *he* **b down**. H8596+928+2021+836
1Ch 13:10 The LORD's anger **b** against Uzzah, and he H3013
2Ch 15:16 broke it up and **b** it in the Kidron Valley. H8596
2Ch 25:14 down to them and **b sacrifices** to them. H7787
2Ch 25:15 The anger of the LORD **b** against Amaziah H3013
2Ch 28: 3 He **b sacrifices** in the Valley of Ben H7787
2Ch 28: 4 sacrifices and **b incense** at the high H7787
2Ch 34: 5 *He* **b** the bones of the priests on their H8596
2Ch 34:25 forsaken me and **b incense** to other gods H7787
2Ch 36:19 *they* **b** all the palaces H8596+928+2021+836
Ne 1: 3 and its gates *have* **been b** with fire." H3675
Ne 2:17 and its gates *have* **been b** with fire." H3675
Ne 4: 2 those heaps of rubble—**b** as they are?" H8596
Est 1:12 king became furious and **b** *with* anger. H1277
Job 1:16 the heavens and **b up** the sheep and the H1277
Ps 39: 3 meditated, the fire **b**; then I spoke with H1277
Ps 74: 7 *They* **b** your sanctuary to H8938+928+2021+836
Ps 74: 8 *They* **b** every place where God was H8596
Ps 80:16 vine is cut down, *it* **is b** with fire; at your H8596
Pr 6:27 into his lap without his clothes **being b**? H8596
Isa 1: 7 desolate, your cities **b** *with* fire; your fields H8596
Isa 24: 6 Therefore earth's inhabitants *are* **b up** H3081
Isa 33:12 The peoples will be **b** *to* ashes; like cut H5386
Isa 43: 2 the fire, *you will* not **be b**; the flames will H3917
Isa 64:11 has been **b** *with* fire, and all that we H8599
Isa 65: 7 "Because *they* **b sacrifices** on the H7787
Jer 2:15 his land; his towns **are b** and deserted. H3675
Jer 19: 4 *they have* **b incense** in it to gods that H7787
Jer 19:13 houses where *they* **b incense** on the roofs H7787
Jer 29:22 whom the king of Babylon **b** in the fire. H7828
Jer 36:23 until the entire scroll *was* **b** in the fire. H9462
Jer 36:27 After the king **b** the scroll containing the H8596
Jer 36:28 which Jehoiakim king of Judah **b up**. H8596
Jer 36:29 You **b** that scroll and said, "Why did you H8596
Jer 36:32 Jehoiakim king of Judah *had* **b** in the fire. H8596
Jer 38:17 city *will* not **be b down**; H8596+928+2021+836
Jer 38:23 and this city *will be* **b down**." H8596+928+2021+836
Jer 44:19 "When we **b incense** to the Queen of H7787
Jer 44:21 to mind the incense **b** in the towns of H7787
Jer 44:23 Because *you have* **b incense** and have H7787
Jer 52:13 building *he* **b down**. H8596+928+2021+836
La 2: 3 *He has* **b** in Jacob like a flaming fire that H1277
Eze 15: 5 useful *when* the fire *has* **b** it and it is H430
Eze 24:11 may be melted and its deposit **b away**. H9462
Da 11:33 fall by the sword or be **b** or captured or H4259
Hos 2:13 the days *she* **b incense** to the Baals; H7787
Hos 11: 2 the Baals and *they* **b incense** to images. H7787
Joel 1:19 flames *have* **b up** all the trees of the H4265
Am 2: 1 Because he **b** to ashes the bones of H8596
Mic 1: 7 all her temple gifts *will* **be b** with fire; H8596
Mt 13:30 weeds and tie them in bundles to *be* **b**; *G2876*
Mt 13:40 the weeds are pulled up and **b** in the fire, *G2876*
Mt 22: 7 those murderers and **b** their city. *G1856*
Jn 5:35 John was a lamp that **b** and gave light *G2794*
Jn 15: 6 are picked up, thrown into the fire and **b**. *G2794*
Ac 19:19 their scrolls together and **b** them publicly. *G2876*
1Co 3:15 If it *is* **b up**, the builder will suffer loss but *G2876*
Heb 6: 8 of being cursed. In the end it will be **b**. *G3011*
Heb 13:11 the bodies *are* **b** outside the camp. *G2876*
Rev 8: 7 A third of the earth *was* **b up**, a third of *G2876*
Rev 8: 7 a third of the trees *were* **b up**, and all the *G2876*
Rev 8: 7 and all the green grass *was* **b up**. *G2876*

BURNED-OUT (1) [BURN]

Jer 51:25 off the cliffs, and make you a **b** mountain. H8599

BURNING (84) [BURN]

Ge 19:24 LORD rained down **b** sulfur on Sodom and H836
Ex 15: 7 You unleashed your **b anger**; it consumed H3019
Ex 27:20 the light so that the lamps *may be* kept **b**. H6590
Ex 27:21 to keep the lamps **b** before the LORD from NDT
Ex 30: 1 an altar of acacia wood for **b** incense. H5230
Lev 1: 8 wood that is **b** on the altar. H6584+2021+836
Lev 1:12 wood that is **b** on the altar. H6584+2021+836
Lev 1:17 wood that is **b** on the altar. H6584+2021+836
Lev 3: 5 that is lying on the **b** wood; H6584+2021+836
Lev 6: 9 the fire *must* **be kept b** on the altar. H3678
Lev 6:12 The fire on the altar *must* **be kept b**; it H3678
Lev 6:13 The fire *must* **be kept b** on the altar H3678
Lev 16:12 take a censer full of **b** coals from the altar H836
Lev 24: 2 that the lamps *may be* **kept b** continually. H6590
Nu 16: 7 tomorrow put **b coals** and incense in H836
Nu 16:18 his censer, put **b coals** and incense in it H836
Nu 16:46 along with **b coals** from the altar, and H836
Nu 19: 6 wool and throw them onto the **b** heifer. H8599
Dt 29:23 land will be a **b waste** *of* salt and sulfur— H8599
Dt 29:24 Why this fierce, **b** anger?" H3034
Dt 33:16 the favor of him who dwelt in the **b** bush. NDT
Jdg 14:19 **B** *with* anger, he returned to his father's H3013
2Sa 14: 7 would put out the only **b coal** I have left, H1625
2Sa 22: 9 from his mouth, **b coals** blazed out of it. H1624
1Ki 9:25 **b incense** before the LORD along with H7787
2Ki 18: 4 the Israelites had been **b incense** to it. H7787
2Ch 2: 4 dedicate it to him for **b** fragrant incense H7787
Job 18: 5 snuffed out; the flame of his fire stops **b**. H5585
Job 18:15 **b sulfur** is scattered over his dwelling. H1730
Job 20:23 God will vent his **b** anger against him H3019
Job 41:20 nostrils as from a boiling pot over **b** reeds. NDT
Ps 11: 6 he will rain fiery coals and **b sulfur**; H1730
Ps 18: 8 from his mouth, **b coals** blazed out of it. H1624
Ps 18:28 **keep** my lamp **b**; my God turns my H239
Ps 118:12 they were consumed as quickly as **b** thorns; H836
Ps 120: 4 with **b coals** *of* the broom bush. H1624
Ps 140:10 May **b coals** fall on them; may they be H1624
Pr 25:22 you will heap **b coals** on his head, and H1624
Isa 9: 5 rolled in blood will be destined for **b**, H8599
Isa 13:13 LORD Almighty, in the day of his **b** anger. H3019
Isa 30:27 with **b** anger and dense clouds of smoke H1277
Isa 30:33 like a stream of **b sulfur**, sets it ablaze. H1730
Isa 33:14 Who of us can dwell with everlasting **b**?" H4611
Isa 34: 9 her dust into **b sulfur**; her land will H1730
Isa 35: 7 The **b sand** will become a pool, the thirsty H9220
Isa 42:25 So he poured out on them his **b** anger H2779
Isa 44:15 It is used as *fuel* for **b**; some of it he takes H1277
Isa 65: 3 in gardens and **b incense** on altars of H7787
Isa 65: 5 in my nostrils, a fire *that keeps* **b** all day. H3678
Jer 1:16 *in* **b incense** to other gods and in H7787
Jer 11:17 aroused my anger by **b incense** to Baal. H7787
Jer 32:29 my anger by **b incense** on the roofs to H7787
Jer 36:22 with a fire **b** in the firepot in front of him. H1277
Jer 44: 3 my anger by **b incense** to and worshiping H7787
Jer 44: 5 stop **b incense** to other gods. H7787

Jer 44: 8 **b incense** to other gods in Egypt H7787
Jer 44:15 their wives *were* **b incense** to other gods, H7787
Jer 44:18 we stopped **b incense** to the Queen of H7787
Eze 1:13 creatures was like **b** coals of fire or like H1277
Eze 10: 2 your hands with **b** coals from among the H836
Eze 36: 5 In my **b** zeal I have spoken against the rest H836
Eze 38:22 hailstones and **b** sulfur on him and on his H836
Hos 7: 4 **b** like an oven whose fire the baker need H1277
Hos 13: 5 in the wilderness, in the land of **b heat**. H9429
Am 4:11 You were like a **b stick** snatched from the H202
Zec 3: 2 Is not this man a **b stick** snatched from the H202
Zec 8: 2 Zion; I am **b** *with* jealousy for her. H2779
Mt 3:12 into the barn and **b up** the chaff with *G2876*
Mk 12:26 in the account of the **b** bush, how God said NDT
Lk 1:10 when the time *for* the **b of incense** came, *G2592*
Lk 12:35 ready for service and *keep* your lamps **b**, *G2794*
Lk 20:37 But in the account of the *b* **bush**, even Moses AIT
Lk 24:32 "Were not our hearts **b** within us while he *G2794*
Jn 21: 9 they saw a **fire of b coals** there with fish on *G471*
Ac 7:30 in the flames of a **b** bush in the desert *G4786*
Ro 12:20 you will heap **b** coals on his head. *G4786*
Heb 12:18 can be touched and *that is* **b** with fire; *G2794*
2Pe 2: 6 Gomorrah *by* **b** them **to ashes**, *G5491*
Rev 14:10 be tormented with **b** sulfur in the *G4786*
Rev 18: 9 shared her luxury see the smoke *of* her **b**, *G4796*
Rev 18:18 When they see the smoke *of* her **b**, they *G4796*
Rev 19:20 thrown alive into the fiery lake of **b** sulfur. *G2794*
Rev 20:10 was thrown into the lake of **b** sulfur *G4786*
Rev 21: 8 be consigned to the fiery lake of **b** sulfur. *G4786*

BURNISHED (4)

1Ki 7:45 the temple of the LORD were of **b** bronze. H5307
Eze 1: 7 of a calf and gleamed like **b** bronze. H7838
Da 10: 6 arms and legs like the gleam of **b** bronze, H7838
Rev 2:18 fire and whose feet are like **b bronze**. *G5909*

BURNS (21) [BURN]

Ex 22: 6 thornbushes so that *it* **b** shocks of grain H430
Lev 16:28 The *man who* **b** them must wash his H8596
Nu 19: 8 The *man who* **b** it must also wash his H8596
Dt 32:22 *one that* **b** down to the realm of the dead H3678
1Ki 14:10 up the house of Jeroboam as *one* **b** dung, H1277
2Ki 22:13 LORD's anger that **b** against us because H3675
Job 19:11 His anger **b** against me; he counts me H3013
Job 30:30 black and peels; my body **b** with fever. H3081
Job 31:12 It is a fire *that* **b** to Destruction; it would H430
Ps 46: 9 the spear; *he* **b** the shields with fire. H8596
SS 8: 6 It **b** like blazing fire, like a H8404
Isa 5:25 the LORD's anger **b** against his people; H3013
Isa 9:18 Surely wickedness **b** like a fire; it H1277
Isa 44:16 Half of the wood *he* **b** in the fire; over it H8596
Isa 66: 3 and *whoever* **b memorial** incense is like H2349
Isa 66:24 the **fire** *that* **b** them will not be quenched AIT
Jer 48:45 midst of Sihon; *it* **b** the foreheads of Moab H430
Eze 15: 4 as fuel and the fire **b** both ends and chars H430
Hos 8: 5 My anger **b** against them. H3013
Hab 1:16 to his net and **b incense** to his dragnet, H7787
Zec 10: 3 "My anger **b** against the shepherds, and I H3013

BURNT (275) [BURN]

Ge 8:20 clean birds, he sacrificed **b offerings** on it. H6592
Ge 22: 2 him there as a **b offering** on a mountain I H6592
Ge 22: 3 had cut enough wood for the **b offering**, H6592
Ge 22: 6 the wood for the **b offering** and placed it H6592
Ge 22: 7 "but where is the lamb for the **b offering**?" H6592
Ge 22: 8 will provide the lamb for the **b offering**, H6592
Ge 22:13 sacrificed it as a **b offering** instead of his H6592
Ex 10:25 sacrifices and **b offerings** to present to the H6592
Ex 18:12 brought a **b offering** and other sacrifices H6592
Ex 20:24 on it your **b offerings** and fellowship H6592
Ex 24: 5 they offered **b offerings** and sacrificed H6592
Ex 29:18 It is a **b offering** to the LORD, a pleasing H6592
Ex 29:25 along with the **b offering** for a pleasing H6592
Ex 29:42 to come this **b offering** is to be made H6592
Ex 30: 9 incense or any **b offering** or grain offering, H6592
Ex 30:28 the altar of **b offering** and all its utensils H6592
Ex 31: 9 the altar of **b offering** and all its utensils H6592
Ex 32: 6 sacrificed **b offerings** and presented H6592
Ex 35:16 the altar of **b offering** with its bronze H6592
Ex 38: 1 the altar of **b offering** *of* acacia wood, H6592
Ex 40: 6 the altar of **b offering** in front of the H6592
Ex 40:10 anoint the altar of **b offering** and all its H6592
Ex 40:29 set the altar of **b offering** near the H6592
Ex 40:29 offered on it **b offerings** and grain H6592
Lev 1: 3 the offering is a **b offering** from the herd, H6592
Lev 1: 4 your hand on the head of the **b offering**, H6592
Lev 1: 6 are to skin the **b offering** and cut it into H6592
Lev 1: 9 It is a **b offering**, a food offering, an H6592
Lev 1:10 the offering is a **b offering** from the flock, H6592
Lev 1:13 It is a **b offering**, a food offering, an H6592
Lev 1:14 to the LORD is a **b offering** of birds, H6592
Lev 1:17 It is a **b offering**, a food offering, an H6592
Lev 3: 5 on top of the **b offering** that is lying on H6592
Lev 4: 7 of the altar of **b offering** at the entrance to H6592
Lev 4:10 shall burn them on the altar of **b offering**. H6592
Lev 4:18 of the altar of **b offering** at the entrance to H6592
Lev 4:24 place where the **b offering** is slaughtered H6592
Lev 4:25 of the altar of **b offering** and pour out the H6592
Lev 4:29 slaughter it at the place of the **b offering**. H6592
Lev 4:30 of the altar of **b offering** and pour out the H6592
Lev 4:33 place where the **b offering** is slaughtered. H6592
Lev 4:34 of the altar of **b offering** and pour out the H6592
Lev 5: 7 sin offering and the other for a **b offering**. H6592
Lev 5:10 the other as a **b offering** in the prescribed H6592
Lev 6: 9 are the regulations for the **b offering**: H6592
Lev 6: 9 The **b offering** is to remain on the altar H6592
Lev 6:10 the ashes of the **b offering** that the fire H6592
Lev 6:12 arrange the **b offering** on the fire and H6592
Lev 6:25 in the place the **b offering** is slaughtered; H6592
Lev 7: 2 place where the **b offering** is slaughtered, H6592
Lev 7: 8 who offers a **b offering** *for* anyone may H6592
Lev 7:37 are the regulations for the **b offering**, the H6592
Lev 8:18 then presented the ram for the **b** *offering*, H6592
Lev 8:21 It was a **b offering**, a pleasing aroma, H6592
Lev 8:28 on top of the **b offering** as an ordination H6592
Lev 9: 2 sin offering and a ram for your **b offering**, H6592
Lev 9: 3 old and without defect—for a **b offering**, H6592
Lev 9: 7 offering and your **b offering** and make H6592
Lev 9:12 Then he slaughtered the **b offering**. H6592
Lev 9:13 handed him the **b offering** piece by piece, H6592
Lev 9:14 them on top of the **b offering** on the altar. H6592
Lev 9:16 He brought the **b offering** and offered it in H6592
Lev 9:17 in addition to the morning's **b offering**. H6592
Lev 9:22 the **b offering** and the fellowship offering H6592
Lev 9:24 consumed the **b offering** and the fat H6592
Lev 10:19 their **b offering** before the LORD, H6592
Lev 12: 6 lamb for a **b offering** and a young pigeon H6592
Lev 12: 8 one for a **b offering** and the other for a sin H6592
Lev 14:13 the **b offering** are slaughtered H6592
Lev 14:19 the priest shall slaughter the **b offering** H6592
Lev 14:22 sin offering and the other for a **b offering**. H6592
Lev 14:31 sin offering and the other as a **b offering**, H6592
Lev 15:15 sin offering and the other for a **b offering**. H6592
Lev 15:30 sin offering and the other for a **b offering**. H6592
Lev 16: 3 a sin offering and a ram for a **b offering**. H6592
Lev 16: 5 a sin offering and a ram for a **b offering**. H6592
Lev 16:24 sacrifice the **b offering** *for* himself and the H6592
Lev 16:24 himself and the **b offering** *for* the people, H6592
Lev 17: 8 them who offers a **b offering** or sacrifice H6592
Lev 22:18 presents a gift for a **b offering** to the LORD H6592
Lev 23:12 sacrifice as a **b offering** to the LORD a lamb H6592
Lev 23:18 They will be a **b offering** to the LORD H6592
Lev 23:37 the **b offerings** and grain offerings H6592
Nu 6:11 the other as a **b offering** to make H6592
Nu 6:14 male lamb without defect for a **b offering**, H6592
Nu 6:16 make the sin offering and the **b offering**. H6592
Nu 7:15 one male lamb a year old for a **b offering**; H6592
Nu 7:21 one male lamb a year old for a **b offering**; H6592
Nu 7:27 one male lamb a year old for a **b offering**; H6592
Nu 7:33 one male lamb a year old for a **b offering**; H6592
Nu 7:39 one male lamb a year old for a **b offering**; H6592
Nu 7:45 one male lamb a year old for a **b offering**; H6592
Nu 7:51 one male lamb a year old for a **b offering**; H6592
Nu 7:57 one male lamb a year old for a **b offering**; H6592
Nu 7:63 one male lamb a year old for a **b offering**; H6592
Nu 7:69 one male lamb a year old for a **b offering**; H6592
Nu 7:75 one male lamb a year old for a **b offering**; H6592
Nu 7:81 one male lamb a year old for a **b offering**; H6592
Nu 7:87 animals for the **b offering** came to twelve H6592
Nu 8:12 to the LORD and the other for a **b offering**, H6592
Nu 10:10 over your **b offerings** and fellowship H6592
Nu 15: 3 LORD—whether **b offerings** or sacrifices H6592
Nu 15: 5 lamb for the **b offering** or the sacrifice H6592
Nu 15: 8 a young bull as a **b offering** or sacrifice, H6592
Nu 15:24 a young bull for a **b offering** as an aroma H6592
Nu 28: 3 as a regular **b offering** each day. H6592
Nu 28: 6 This is the regular **b offering** instituted at H6592
Nu 28:10 This is the **b offering** *for* every Sabbath, in H6592
Nu 28:10 to the regular **b offering** and its drink H6592
Nu 28:11 to the LORD a **b offering** of two young bulls H6592
Nu 28:13 This is for a **b offering**, a pleasing aroma H6592
Nu 28:14 is the monthly **b offering** to be made at H6592
Nu 28:15 Besides the regular **b offering** with its H6592
Nu 28:19 consisting of a **b offering** of two young H6592
Nu 28:23 to the regular morning **b offering**. H6592
Nu 28:24 to the regular **b offering** and its drink H6592
Nu 28:27 Present a **b offering** of two young bulls H6592
Nu 28:31 to the regular **b offering** and its grain H6592
Nu 29: 2 offer a **b offering** of one young bull H6592
Nu 29: 6 daily **b offerings** with their grain H6592
Nu 29: 8 to the LORD a **b offering** of one young bull, H6592
Nu 29:11 the regular **b offering** with its grain H6592
Nu 29:13 consisting of a **b offering** of thirteen H6592
Nu 29:16 to the regular **b offering** with its grain H6592
Nu 29:19 to the regular **b offering** with its grain H6592
Nu 29:22 to the regular **b offering** with its grain H6592
Nu 29:25 to the regular **b offering** with its grain H6592
Nu 29:28 to the regular **b offering** with its grain H6592
Nu 29:31 to the regular **b offering** with its grain H6592
Nu 29:34 to the regular **b offering** with its grain H6592
Nu 29:36 consisting of a **b offering** of one bull, H6592
Nu 29:38 to the regular **b offering** with its grain H6592
Nu 29:39 your **b offerings**, grain offerings, drink H6592
Dt 12: 6 there bring your **b offerings** and sacrifices H6592
Dt 12:11 your **b offerings** and sacrifices, your tithes H6592
Dt 12:13 to sacrifice your **b offerings** anywhere you H6592
Dt 12:27 Present your **b offerings** on the altar of the H6592
Dt 13:16 plunder as a **whole b offering** to the LORD H4003
Dt 27: 6 offer **b offerings** on it to the LORD H6592
Dt 33:10 you and **whole b offerings** on your altar H4003
Jos 8:31 to the LORD **b offerings** and sacrificed H6592
Jos 22:23 LORD and to offer **b offerings** and grain H6592
Jos 22:26 but not for **b offerings** or sacrifices. H6592
Jos 22:27 LORD at his sanctuary with our **b offerings**, H6592
Jos 22:28 not for **b offerings** and sacrifices, but H6592
Jos 22:29 today by building an altar for **b offerings**, H6592
Jdg 6:26 offer the second bull as a **b offering**." H6592
Jdg 11:31 I will sacrifice it as a **b offering**. H6592
Jdg 13:16 But if you prepare a **b offering**, offer it to H6592
Jdg 13:23 have accepted a **b offering** and grain H6592
Jdg 20:26 presented **b offerings** and fellowship H6592
Jdg 21: 4 presented **b offerings** and fellowship H6592
1Sa 6:14 the cows as a **b offering** to the LORD. H6592
1Sa 6:15 Shemesh offered **b offerings** and made H6592
1Sa 7: 9 it *as* a whole **b offering** to the LORD. H6592
1Sa 7:10 Samuel was sacrificing the **b offering**, H6592
1Sa 10: 8 you to sacrifice **b offerings** and fellowship H6592
1Sa 13: 9 "Bring me the **b offering** and the H6592
1Sa 13: 9 And Saul offered up the **b offering**. H6592
1Sa 13:12 So I felt compelled to offer the **b offering**." H6592
1Sa 15:22 LORD delight in **b offerings** and sacrifices H6592
2Sa 6:17 sacrificed **b offerings** and fellowship H6592
2Sa 6:18 sacrificing the **b offerings** and fellowship H6592
2Sa 24:22 Here are oxen for the **b offering**, and here H6592
2Sa 24:24 the LORD my God **b offerings** that cost me H6592
2Sa 24:25 sacrificed **b offerings** and fellowship H6592
1Ki 3: 4 a thousand **b offerings** on that altar. H6592
1Ki 3:15 sacrificed **b offerings** and fellowship H6592
1Ki 8:64 there he offered **b offerings**, grain H6592
1Ki 8:64 was too small to hold the **b offerings**, H6592
1Ki 9:25 sacrificed **b offerings** and fellowship H6592
1Ki 10: 5 the **b offerings** he made at the H6592
2Ki 5:17 again make **b offerings** and sacrifices H6592
2Ki 10:24 went in to make sacrifices and **b offerings**. H6592
2Ki 10:25 Jehu had finished making the **b offering**, H6592
2Ki 16:13 He offered up his **b offering** and grain H6592
2Ki 16:15 the morning **b offering** and the evening H6592
2Ki 16:15 the king's **b offering** and his grain offering H6592
2Ki 16:15 the **b offering** *of* all the people of the H6592
2Ki 16:15 blood of all the **b offerings** and sacrifices. H6592
1Ch 6:49 on the altar of **b offering** and on the altar H6592
1Ch 16: 1 they presented **b offerings** and fellowship H6592
1Ch 16: 2 sacrificing the **b offerings** and fellowship H6592
1Ch 16:40 to present **b offerings** to the LORD on the H6592
1Ch 16:40 LORD on the altar of **b offering** regularly, H6592
1Ch 21:23 I will give the oxen for the **b offerings**, the H6592
1Ch 21:24 sacrifice a **b offering** that costs me H6592
1Ch 21:26 sacrificed **b offerings** and fellowship H6592
1Ch 21:26 fire from heaven on the altar of **b offering**. H6592
1Ch 21:29 the altar of **b offering** were at that H6592
1Ch 22: 1 also the altar of **b offering** for Israel." H6592
1Ch 23:31 whenever **b offerings** were presented H6592
1Ch 29:21 the LORD and presented **b offerings** to him: H6592
2Ch 1: 6 offered a thousand **b offerings** on it. H6592
2Ch 2: 4 for making **b offerings** every morning H6592
2Ch 4: 6 to be used for the **b offerings** were rinsed, H6592
2Ch 7: 1 consumed the **b offering** and the H6592
2Ch 7: 7 there he offered **b offerings** and the fat of H6592
2Ch 7: 7 had made could not hold the **b offerings**, H6592
2Ch 8:12 Solomon sacrificed **b offerings** to the LORD H6592
2Ch 9: 4 robes and the **b offerings** he made at the H6592
2Ch 13:11 they present **b offerings** and fragrant H6592
2Ch 23:18 to present the **b offerings** *of* the LORD as H6592
2Ch 24:14 the service and for the **b offerings**, H6590
2Ch 24:14 **b offerings** were presented continually in H6592
2Ch 29: 7 present any **b offerings** at the sanctuary H6592
2Ch 29:18 the altar of **b offering** with all its utensils H6592
2Ch 29:24 had ordered the **b offering** and the sin H6592
2Ch 29:27 to sacrifice the **b offering** on the altar. H6592
2Ch 29:28 sacrifice of the **b offering** was completed. H6592
2Ch 29:31 hearts were willing brought **b offerings**. H6592
2Ch 29:32 The number of **b offerings** the assembly H6592
2Ch 29:32 all of them for **b offerings** to the LORD. H6592
2Ch 29:34 were too few to skin all the **b offerings**; so H6592
2Ch 29:35 There were **b offerings** in abundance H6592
2Ch 29:35 that accompanied the **b offerings**. H6592
2Ch 30:15 brought **b offerings** to the temple of H6592
2Ch 31: 2 to offer **b offerings** and fellowship H6592
2Ch 31: 3 evening **b offerings** and for the burnt H6592
2Ch 31: 3 for the **b offerings** on the Sabbaths, H6592
2Ch 35:12 set aside the **b offerings** to give them to H6592
2Ch 35:14 were sacrificing the **b offerings** and the fat H6592
2Ch 35:16 the offering of **b offerings** on the altar of H6592
Ezr 3: 2 God of Israel to sacrifice **b offerings** on it, H6592
Ezr 3: 3 sacrificed **b offerings** on it to the LORD, H6592
Ezr 3: 4 number of **b offerings** prescribed for H6592
Ezr 3: 5 they presented the regular **b offerings**, the H6592
Ezr 3: 6 they began to offer **b offerings** to the LORD, H6592
Ezr 6: 9 male lambs for **b offerings** to the God of A10545
Ezr 8:35 sacrificed **b offerings** to the God of H6592
Ezr 8:35 All this was a **b offering** to the LORD. H6592
Ne 10:33 regular grain offerings and **b offerings**; H6592
Job 1: 5 sacrifice a **b offering** for each of them H6592
Job 42: 8 sacrifice a **b offering** for yourselves. H6592
Ps 20: 3 your sacrifices and accept your **b offerings**. H6592
Ps 40: 6 **b offerings** and sin offerings you did not H6592
Ps 50: 8 sacrifices or concerning your **b offerings**, H6592
Ps 51:16 you do not take pleasure in **b offerings**. H6592
Ps 51:19 the righteous, in **b offerings** offered whole H6592
Ps 66:13 your temple with **b offerings** and fulfill my H6592
Isa 1:11 "I have more than enough of **b offerings** H6592
Isa 40:16 its animals enough for **b offerings**. H6592
Isa 43:23 not brought me sheep for **b offerings**, H6592
Isa 56: 7 Their **b offerings** and sacrifices will be H6592
Jer 6:20 Your **b offerings** are not acceptable; your H6592
Jer 7:21 add your **b offerings** to your other H6592

B

Jer 7:22 commands about **b offerings** and H6592
Jer 14:12 though they offer **b offerings** and grain H6592
Jer 17:26 bringing **b offerings** and sacrifices H6592
Jer 33:18 before me continually to offer **b offerings**, H6592
Eze 40:38 where the **b offerings** were washed. H6592
Eze 40:39 on which the **b offerings**, sin offerings H6592
Eze 40:42 tables of dressed stone for the **b offerings**, H6592
Eze 40:42 slaughtering the **b offerings** and the other H6592
Eze 43:18 sacrificing **b offerings** and splashing H6592
Eze 43:24 sacrifice them as a **b offering** to the LORD. H6592
Eze 43:27 to present your **b offerings** and fellowship H6592
Eze 44:11 slaughter the **b offerings** and sacrifices H6592
Eze 45:15 **b offerings** and fellowship offerings to H6592
Eze 45:17 of the prince to provide the **b offerings**, H6592
Eze 45:17 **b offerings** and fellowship offerings to H6592
Eze 45:23 without defect as a **b offering** to the LORD, H6592
Eze 45:25 sin offerings, **b offerings**, grain offerings H6592
Eze 46: 2 to sacrifice his **b offering** and his H6592
Eze 46: 4 **b offering** the prince brings to the LORD H6592
Eze 46:12 whether a **b offering** or fellowship H6592
Eze 46:12 shall offer his **b offering** or his fellowship H6592
Eze 46:13 without defect for a **b offering** to the LORD; H6592
Eze 46:15 by morning for a regular **b offering**. H6592
Hos 6: 6 of God rather than **b offerings**. H6592
Am 5:22 you bring me **b offerings** and grain H6592
Mic 6: 6 Shall I come before him with **b offerings** H6592
Mk 12:33 than all **b offerings** and sacrifices. G3906
Heb 10: 6 *with* **b offerings** and sin offerings you G3906
Heb 10: 8 **b offerings** and sin offerings you did not G3906

BURST (21) [BURSTS]

Ge 7:11 all the springs of the great deep **b forth**, H1324
Ge 27:34 *he* **b** *out with* a loud and bitter cry and H7590
Job 26: 8 the clouds *do* not **b** under their weight. H1324
Job 32:19 like new wineskins **ready to b**. H1324
Job 38: 8 doors when it **b** forth from the womb, H1631
Ps 60: 1 and **b upon** us; you have been angry H7287
Ps 98: 4 the earth, **b** *into* jubilant song with music H7200
Isa 35: 2 *it will* **b into bloom**; it will rejoice H7255+7255
Isa 44:23 **B** *into* song, *you* mountains, you forests H7200
Isa 49:13 you earth; **b** *into* song, *you* mountains! H7200
Isa 52: 9 **B** *into* songs of joy together, you ruins of H7200
Isa 54: 1 bore a child; **b** *into* song, shout for joy H7200
Isa 55:12 hills *will* **b** *into* song before you, H7200
Jer 23:19 the storm of the LORD *will* **b out** in wrath, H3655
Jer 30:23 the storm of the LORD *will* **b out** *in* wrath, H3655
Eze 7:10 Doom *has* **b forth**, the rod has budded H3655
Eze 13:11 and violent winds *will* **b forth**. H1324
Mt 9:17 they do, the skins *will* **b**; the wine will run G4838
Mk 2:22 Otherwise, the wine *will* **b** the skins, and G4838
Lk 5:37 the new wine *will* **b** the skins; the wine G4838
Ac 1:18 *his body* **b open** and all his G3279+3545

BURSTS (1) [BURST]

Job 16:14 **Again and again** *he* **b** upon H7287+7288+7288

BURY (39) [BURIAL, BURIED, BURIES, BURYING]

Ge 23: 4 a burial site here so *I can* **b** my dead." H7699
Ge 23: 6 **B** your dead in the choicest of our tombs H7699
Ge 23: 8 "If you are willing to *let* me **b** my dead H7699
Ge 23:11 the presence of my people. **B** your dead." H7699
Ge 23:13 it from me so *I can* **b** my dead there." H7699
Ge 23:15 that between you and me? **B** your dead." H7699
Ge 47:29 faithfulness. *Do* not **b** me in Egypt, H7699
Ge 47:30 me out of Egypt and **b** me where they are H7699
Ge 49:29 **B** me with my fathers in the cave in the H7699
Ge 50: 5 **b** me in the tomb I dug for myself in the H7699
Ge 50: 5 Now let me go up and **b** my father; then I H7699
Ge 50: 6 "Go up and **b** your father, as he H7699
Ge 50: 7 So Joseph went up to **b** his father. H7699
Ge 50:14 who had gone with him to **b** his father. H7699
Dt 21:23 **Be sure to b** it that same day H7699+7699
1Ki 2:31 Strike him down and **b** him, and so clear H7699
1Ki 11:15 who had gone up to **b** the dead, had H7699
1Ki 13:29 his own city to mourn for him and **b** him. H7699
1Ki 13:31 **b** me in the grave where the man of God H7699
1Ki 14:13 All Israel will mourn for him and **b** him H7699
2Ki 9:10 ground at Jezreel, and no *one will* **b** her. H7699
2Ki 9:34 he said, "and **b** her, for she was a king's H7699
2Ki 9:35 But when they went out to **b** her, they H7699
Job 27:15 The plague *will* **b** those who survive him H7699
Job 40:13 **B** them all in the dust together; shroud H3243
Ps 79: 3 there is no *one to* **b** the dead. H7699
Jer 7:32 for *they will* **b** the dead in Topheth until H7699
Jer 14:16 There will be no *one to* **b** them, their H7699
Jer 19:11 *They will* **b** the dead in Topheth until H7699
Jer 43: 9 stones with you and **b** them in clay in the H3243
La 3:29 *Let him* **b** his face in the dust—there may H5989
Eze 39:13 All the people of the land *will* **b** them H7699
Eze 39:14 *they will* **b** any bodies that are lying on H7699
Eze 39:15 until the gravediggers **b** it in the Valley of H7699
Hos 9: 6 gather them, and Memphis *will* **b** them. H7699
Mt 8:21 first let me go and **b** my father. G2507
Mt 8:22 and let the dead **b** their own dead." G2507
Lk 9:59 first let me go and **b** my father. G2507
Lk 9:60 "Let the dead **b** their own dead, but G2507

BURYING (7) [BURY]

Ge 23: 6 will refuse you his tomb for **b** your dead." H7699
Ge 50:14 After **b** his father, Joseph returned to Egypt H7699
Nu 33: 4 who *were* **b** all their firstborn, whom the H7699
2Sa 2: 5 kindness to Saul your master *by* **b** him. H7699
1Ki 13:31 After **b** him, he said to his sons, "When I H7699

2Ki 13:21 Once *while* some Israelites *were* **b** a man H7699
Eze 39:12 the Israelites *will be* **b** them in order to H7699

BUSH (15) [BUSHES]

Ex 3: 2 to him in flames of fire from within a **b**. H6174
Ex 3: 2 saw that though the **b** was on fire it did H6174
Ex 3: 3 why the **b** does not burn up. H6174
Ex 3: 4 God called to him from within the **b** H6174
Dt 33:16 favor of him who dwelt in the burning **b**. H6174
1Ki 19: 4 He came to a **broom b**, sat down under it H8413
1Ki 19: 5 he lay down under the **b** and fell asleep. H8413
Job 30: 4 their food was the root of the **broom b**. H8413
Ps 120: 4 with burning coals of the **broom b**. H8413
Jer 17: 6 person will be like a **b** in the wastelands; H6899
Jer 48: 6 your lives; become like a **b** in the desert. H6899
Mk 12:26 in the account of the burning **b**, how God G1003
Lk 20:37 But in the account of the *burning* **b**, even G1003
Ac 7:30 in the flames *of* a burning **b** in the desert G1003
Ac 7:35 the angel who appeared to him in the **b**. G1003

BUSHELS (1)

Lk 16: 7 " 'A **thousand b** of wheat,' he G1669+3174

BUSHES (2) [BUSH]

Ge 21:15 she put the boy under one of the **b**. H8489
Job 30: 7 brayed among the **b** and huddled in the H8489

BUSINESS (17)

Ex 22:25 do not treat it like a **b deal**; charge no H5957
Ecc 4: 8 This too is meaningless—a miserable **b**! H6721
Eze 27:12 " 'Tarshish **did b with** you because of your H6086
Eze 27:13 Tubal and Meshek **did b with** you; they H8217
Eze 27:16 " 'Aram **did b with** you because of your H6086
Eze 27:18 " 'Damascus **did b with** you because of H6086
Eze 27:21 customers; *they* **did b with** you in lambs H6086
Da 8:27 I got up and went about the king's **b**. H4856
Zec 8:10 one *could* **go about** *their* **b** H3655+2256+995
Mt 22: 5 one to his field, another to his **b**. G1865
Jn 15:15 does not know his master's **b**. G5515+4472
Ac 19:24 brought in a lot of **b** for the craftsmen G2238
Ac 19:25 we receive a good income from this **b**. G2238
1Co 5:12 **What** *b* is it of mine to judge those outside AIT
1Th 4:11 *You should* **mind** your own **b** and work G4556
Jas 1:11 away even while they **go about** their **b**. G4512
Jas 4:13 a year there, **carry on b** and make money." G1864

BUSY (5)

1Ki 18:27 he is deep in thought, or **b**, or traveling. H8485
1Ki 20:40 While your servant was **b** here and there H6913
Hag 1: 9 while each of you *is* **b** with your own H8132
2Th 3:11 disruptive. *They are* not **b**; they are G2237
Titus 2: 5 pure, to be **b at home**, to be kind, G3877

BUSYBODIES (2)

2Th 3:11 They are not busy; *they are* **b**. G4318
1Ti 5:13 but also **b** who talk nonsense G5827

BUSYBODY (KJV) MEDDLER

BUT (3962) See Index of Articles Etc.

BUTCHERED (4)

1Sa 14:32 they **b** them on the ground and ate them H8821
1Sa 28:24 calf at the house, which *she* **b** at once. H2284
Jer 12: 3 Drag them off like sheep to be **b**! Set H3186
Mt 22: 4 My oxen and fattened cattle *have been* **b** G2604

BUTLER (KJV) CUPBEARER

BUTT (1) [BUTTING]

2Sa 2:23 so Abner thrust the **b** *of* his spear into H339

BUTTER (2)

Ps 55:21 His talk is smooth as **b**, yet war is in his H4717
Pr 30:33 For as churning cream produces **b**, and as H2772

BUTTING (1) [BUTT]

Eze 34:21 **b** all the weak sheep with your horns until H5590

BUTTOCKS (3)

2Sa 10: 4 cut off their garments at the **b**, and sent H9268
1Ch 19: 4 cut off their garments at the **b**, and sent H5156
Isa 20: 4 young and old, with **b** bared—to Egypt's H9268

BUY (54) [BOUGHT, BUYER, BUYER'S, BUYERS, BUYING, BUYS]

Ge 41:57 came to Egypt to **b grain** from Joseph, H8690
Ge 42: 2 Go down there and **b** some for us, so that H8690
Ge 42: 3 brothers went down to **b** grain from Egypt. H8690
Ge 42: 5 were among those who went to **b grain**, H8690
Ge 42: 7 land of Canaan," they replied, "to **b** food." H8690
Ge 42:10 "Your servants have come to **b** food. H8690
Ge 43: 2 "Go back and **b** us a little more food." H8690
Ge 43: 4 we will go down and **b** food for you. H8690
Ge 43:20 came down here the first time to **b** food. H8690
Ge 43:22 additional silver with us to **b** food. H8690
Ge 44:25 'Go back and **b** a little more food.' H8690
Ge 47:19 **B** us and our land in exchange for food H7864
Ge 47:22 *he did* not **b** the land of the priests H7864
Ex 21: 2 "If *you* **b** a Hebrew servant, he is to serve H7864
Lev 25:14 of your own people or **b** land from them, H7864
Lev 25:15 *You are to* **b** from your own people on the H7864
Lev 25:44 around you; from them *you may* **b** slaves. H7864
Lev 25:45 *You may* also **b** some of the temporary H7864

Dt 14:26 *Use* the silver *to* **b** whatever you like: cattle H5989
Dt 28:68 female slaves, but no *one will* **b** you. H7864
Ru 4: 4 suggest that *you* **b** it in the presence H7864
Ru 4: 5 "On the day you **b** the land from Naomi H7864
Ru 4: 8 said to Boaz, "**B** it yourself. H7864
2Sa 24:21 "To **b** your threshing floor," David H7864
Ezr 7:17 With this money be sure *to* **b** bulls, rams A10632
Ne 10:31 *we will* not **b** from them on the Sabbath H4374
Pr 17:16 fools have money in hand to **b** wisdom, H7864
Pr 23:23 **B** the truth and do not sell it—wisdom H7864
Isa 55: 1 who have no money, come, **b** and eat! H8690
Isa 55: 1 **b** wine and milk without money and H8690
Jer 13: 1 "Go and **b** a linen belt and put it around H7864
Jer 19: 1 "Go and **b** a clay jar from a potter H7864
Jer 32: 7 to you and say, '**B** my field at Anathoth H7864
Jer 32: 7 relative it is your right and duty to **b** it. H7864
Jer 32: 8 '**B** my field at Anathoth in the territory of H7864
Jer 32: 8 redeem it and possess it, **b** it for yourself. H7864
Jer 32:25 '**B** the field with silver and have the H7864
La 5: 4 We must **b** the water we drink; our H928+4084
Mt 14:15 to the villages and **b** themselves some food." G60
Mt 25: 9 who sell oil and **b** some for yourselves. G60
Mt 25:10 while they were on their way *to* **b** the oil, G60
Mt 27: 7 they decided *to use* the money *to* **b** the G60
Mt 27:10 and *they used* them *to* **b** the potter's field G1443
Mk 6:36 villages and **b** themselves something to G60
Lk 9:13 unless we go and **b** food for all this crowd." G60
Lk 22:36 have a sword, sell your cloak and **b** one. G60
Jn 4: 8 disciples had gone into the town to **b** food.) G60
Jn 6: 5 "Where *shall we* **b** bread for these people to G60
Jn 6: 7 a year's wages *to b* **enough** bread for each AIT
Jn 13:29 was telling him *to* **b** what was needed for G60
Ac 8:20 you thought *you could* **b** the gift of God G3227
1Co 7:30 were not; those *who* **b** something, as if it G60
Rev 3:18 I counsel you *to* **b** from me gold refined in G60
Rev 13:17 so that they could not **b** or sell unless they G60

BUYER (7) [BUY]

Lev 25:28 the possession of the **b** until the Year of H7864
Lev 25:30 permanently to the **b** and the buyer's H7864
Lev 25:50 They and their **b** are to count the time H7864
Pr 20:14 says the **b**—then goes off and boasts H7864
Isa 24: 2 seller as for **b**, for borrower as for H7864
Eze 7:12 Let not the **b** rejoice nor the seller grieve H7864
Eze 7:13 as long as *both* **b and seller** live. H4392S

BUYER'S (1) [BUY]

Lev 25:30 to the buyer and **the b** descendants. H2257S

BUYERS (1) [BUY]

Zec 11: 5 Their **b** slaughter them and go H7864

BUYING (5) [BUY]

Ge 47:14 in payment for the grain they *were* **b**, H8690
Am 8: 6 **b** the poor with silver and the needy for a H7864
Mt 21:12 drove out all who *were* **b** and selling G4797
Mk 11:15 driving out those *who were* **b** and selling G4797
Lk 17:28 eating and drinking, **b** and selling, planting G60

BUYS (3) [BUY]

Lev 22:11 But if a priest **b** a slave *with* money H7864+7871
Pr 31:16 She considers a field and **b** it; out of her H4374
Rev 18:11 her because no one **b** their cargoes anymore G60

BUZ (3) [BUZITE]

Ge 22:21 Uz the firstborn, **B** his brother, Kemuel (the H998
1Ch 5:14 Jeshishai, the son of Jahdo, the son of **B**. H998
Jer 25:23 **B** and all who are in distant places; H998

BUZI (1)

Eze 1: 3 the son of **B**, by the Kebar River in H1001

BUZITE (2) [BUZ]

Job 32: 2 But Elihu son of Barakel the **B**, of the H1000
Job 32: 6 So Elihu son of Barakel the **B** said: "I am H1000

BY (2348) See Index of Articles Etc.

BYBLOS (4)

Jos 13: 5 the area of **B**; and all Lebanon to the east, H1490
1Ki 5:18 Hiram and **workers from B** cut and H1490
Ps 83: 7 **B**, Ammon and Amalek, Philistia, with the H1489
Eze 27: 9 Veteran craftsmen of **B** were on board as H1488

BYWAYS (1) [WAY]

Jer 18:15 They made them walk in **b**, on roads not H5986

BYWORD (10) [WORD]

Dt 28:37 a **b** and an object of ridicule among all H5442
1Ki 9: 7 will then become a **b** and an object of H5442
2Ch 7:20 I will make it a **b** and an object of ridicule H5442
Job 17: 6 "God has made me a **b** to everyone, H5439
Job 30: 9 in song; I have become a **b** among them. H4863
Ps 44:14 have made us a **b** among the nations; H5442
Jer 24: 9 a reproach and a **b**, a curse and an object H5442
Eze 14: 8 make them an example and a **b**. H5442
Eze 23:10 She became a **b** among women, and H9005
Joel 2:17 object of scorn, a **b** among the nations. H5442

C

CAB (1)
2Ki 6:25 a quarter of a c of seed pods for five H7685

CABBON (NIV84) KABBON

CABUL (NIV84) KABUL

CAESAR (20) [CAESAR'S]
Mt 22:17 it right to pay the imperial tax to C or not?" G2790
Mt 22:21 "So give back to C what is Caesar's G2790
Mk 12:14 it right to pay the imperial tax to C or not? G2790
Mk 12:17 "Give back to C what is Caesar's and to G2790
Lk 2: 1 In those days C Augustus issued a decree G2790
Lk 3: 1 fifteenth year of the reign of Tiberius C— G2790
Lk 20:22 Is it right for us to pay taxes to C or not?" G2790
Lk 20:25 "Then give back to C what is Caesar's G2790
Lk 23: 2 payment of taxes to C and claims to be G2790
Jn 19:12 let this man go, you are no friend of C. G2790
Jn 19:12 who claims to be a king opposes C." G2790
Jn 19:15 "We have no king but C," the chief priests G2790
Ac 25: 8 law or against the temple or against C." G2790
Ac 25:11 to hand me over to them. I appeal to C!" G2790
Ac 25:12 "You have appealed to C. To Caesar you G2790
Ac 25:12 appealed to Caesar. To C you will go!" G2790
Ac 25:21 him held until I could send him to C." G2790
Ac 26:32 been set free if he had not appealed to C." G2790
Ac 27:24 You must stand trial before C; and God G2790
Ac 28:19 I was compelled to make an appeal to C. G2790

CAESAR'S (9) [CAESAR]
Mt 22:21 "C," they replied. Then he said to them G2790
Mt 22:21 "So give back to Caesar what is C, and to G2790
Mk 12:16 And whose inscription?" "C," they replied. G2790
Mk 12:17 to Caesar what is C and to God what is G2790
Lk 20:24 inscription are on it?" "C," they replied. G2790
Lk 20:25 "Then give back to Caesar what is C, and G2790
Ac 17: 7 They are all defying C decrees, saying G2790
Ac 25:10 "I am now standing before C court, where G2790
Php 4:22 those who belong to C household. G2790

CAESAREA (19)
Mt 16:13 Jesus came to the region of C Philippi, G2791
Mk 8:27 went on to the villages around C Philippi. G2791
Ac 8:40 in all the towns until he reached C. G2791
Ac 9:30 took him down to C and sent him off to G2791
Ac 10: 1 At C there was a man named Cornelius, G2791
Ac 10:24 The following day he arrived in C G2791
Ac 11:11 sent to me from C stopped at the house G2791
Ac 12:19 went from Judea to C and stayed there. G2791
Ac 18:22 When he landed at C, he went up to G2791
Ac 21: 8 we reached C and stayed at the house of G2791
Ac 21:16 the disciples from C accompanied us and G2791
Ac 23:23 spearmen to go to C at nine tonight. G2791
Ac 23:33 When the cavalry arrived in C, they G2791
Ac 24: 1 Ananias went down to C with some of the NDT
Ac 25: 1 Festus went up from C to Jerusalem, G2791
Ac 25: 4 "Paul is being held at C, and I myself am G2791
Ac 25: 6 days with them, Festus went down to C. G2791
Ac 25:13 Bernice arrived at C to pay their respects G2791
Ac 25:24 me about him in Jerusalem and here in C, NDT

CAGE (1) [CAGES]
Eze 19: 9 pulled him into a c and brought him to H6050

CAGES (1) [CAGE]
Jer 5:27 Like c full of birds, their houses are full of H3990

CAIAPHAS (9)
Mt 26: 3 of the high priest, whose name was C, G2780
Mt 26:57 Jesus took him to C the high priest, G2780
Lk 3: 2 the high-priesthood of Annas and C, G2780
Jn 11:49 one of them, named C, who was high G2780
Jn 18:13 who was the father-in-law of C, the high G2780
Jn 18:14 C was the one who had advised the G2780
Jn 18:24 sent him bound to C the high priest. G2780
Jn 18:28 took Jesus from C to the palace of the G2780
Ac 4: 6 priest was there, and so were C, John, G2780

CAIN (20)
Ge 4: 1 she became pregnant and gave birth to C. H7803
Ge 4: 2 Abel kept flocks, and C worked the soil. H7803
Ge 4: 3 the course of time C brought some of the H7803
Ge 4: 5 on C and his offering he did not look H7803
Ge 4: 5 So C was very angry, and his face was H7803
Ge 4: 6 Then the LORD said to C, "Why are you H7803
Ge 4: 8 Now C said to his brother Abel, "Let's go H7803
Ge 4: 8 C attacked his brother Abel and killed him H7803
Ge 4: 9 Then the LORD said to C, "Where is your H7803
Ge 4:13 C said to the LORD, "My punishment is H7803
Ge 4:15 anyone who kills C will suffer vengeance H7803
Ge 4:15 LORD put a mark on C so that no one who H7803
Ge 4:16 So C went out from the LORD's presence H7803
Ge 4:17 C made love to his wife, and she became H7803
Ge 4:17 C was then building a city, and he named it NDT
Ge 4:24 If C is avenged seven times, then Lamech H7803
Ge 4:25 child in place of Abel, since C killed him." H7803
Heb 11: 4 brought God a better offering than C did. G2782
1Jn 3:12 Do not be like C, who belonged to the evil G2782
Jude 11 They have taken the way of C; they have G2782

CAINAN (1)
Lk 3:36 the son of C, the son of Arphaxad, the son G2783

CAKE (5) [CAKES]
1Sa 30:12 part of a c of pressed figs and two cakes of H1811
2Sa 6:19 a c of dates and a cake of raisins to each H882
2Sa 6:19 of dates and a c of raisins to each person H862
1Ch 16: 3 a c of dates and a cake of raisins to each H882
1Ch 16: 3 of dates and a c of raisins to each Israelite H862

CAKES (12) [CAKE]
1Sa 25:18 a hundred c of raisins and two hundred H7540
1Sa 25:18 raisins and two hundred c of pressed figs, H1811
1Sa 30:12 a cake of pressed figs and two c of raisins. H7540
2Sa 16: 1 a hundred c of raisins, a hundred H7540
2Sa 16: 1 a hundred c of figs and a skin of wine. H7811
1Ki 14: 3 bread with you, some c and a jar of honey H5926
1Ch 12:40 supplies of flour, fig c, raisin cakes, H1811
1Ch 12:40 of flour, fig cakes, raisin c, wine, olive oil, H7540
Isa 16: 7 grieve for the raisin c of Kir Hareseth. H862
Jer 7:18 the dough and make c to offer to the H3924
Jer 44:19 that we were making c impressed with her H3924
Hos 3: 1 to other gods and love the sacred raisin c." H862

CALAH (2)
Ge 10:11 where he built Nineveh, Rehoboth Ir, C H3996
Ge 10:12 which is between Nineveh and C—which H3996

CALAMITIES (10) [CALAMITY]
Dt 29:22 lands will see the c that have fallen on H4804
Dt 31:17 Many disasters and c will come on them H7650
Dt 31:21 many disasters and c come on them, H7650
Dt 32:23 "I will heap c on them and spend my H8288
1Sa 10:19 saves you out of all your disasters and c. H7650
2Sa 19: 7 you than all the c that have come on H8288
Job 5:19 From six c he will rescue you; in seven no H7650
Pr 24:22 who knows what c they can bring? H7085
Isa 51:19 These double c have come upon you—who NDT
La 3:38 Most High that both c and good things H8288

CALAMITY (27) [CALAMITIES]
2Sa 12:11 household I am going to bring c on you. H8288
2Ch 20: 9 'If c comes upon us, whether the sword of H8288
Ne 13:18 God brought all this c on us and on this H8288
Job 18:12 C is hungry for him; disaster is ready for H224
Job 21:17 How often does c come upon them, the H369
Job 21:30 the wicked are spared from the day of c, H369
Ps 107:39 humbled by oppression, c and sorrow; H8288
Pr 1:26 I will mock when c overtakes you— H7065
Pr 1:27 when c overtakes you like a storm, when H7065
Pr 14:32 When c comes, the wicked are brought H8288
Pr 21:23 their tongues keep themselves from c. H7650
Pr 22: 8 Whoever sows injustice reaps c, and the H224
Pr 24:16 the wicked stumble when c strikes. H8288
Isa 47:11 A c will fall upon you that you cannot H2096
Jer 14:16 I will pour out on them the c they deserve. H8288
Jer 32:42 brought all this great c on this people, H8288
Jer 48:16 Moab is at hand; her c will come quickly. H8288
Eze 6:10 threaten in vain to bring this c on them. H8288
Eze 7:26 C upon calamity will come, and rumor H2096
Eze 7:26 Calamity upon c will come, and rumor H2096
Eze 35: 5 over to the sword at the time of their c, H369
Joel 2:13 and he relents from sending c. H8288
Ob 13 over them in their c in the day of their H8288
Jnh 1: 7 to find out who is responsible for this c." H8288
Jnh 4: 2 a God who relents from sending c. H8288
Mic 2: 3 walk proudly, for it will be a time of c. H8288
Hab 3:16 the day of c to come on the nation H7650

CALAMUS (5)
Ex 30:23 cinnamon, 250 shekels of fragrant c, H7866
SS 4:14 nard and saffron, c and cinnamon, with H7866
Isa 43:24 have not bought any fragrant c for me, H7866
Jer 6:20 from Sheba or sweet c from a distant land H7866
Eze 27:19 your wares: wrought iron, cassia and c. H7866

CALCOL (NIV84) KALKOL

CALCULATE (1) [CALCULATED]
Rev 13:18 Let the person who has insight c the G6028

CALCULATED (2) [CALCULATE]
2Ch 4:18 the weight of the bronze could not be c. H2983
Ac 19:19 When they c the value of the scrolls, the G5248

CALDRON (2) [CALDRONS]
1Sa 2:14 the fork into the pan or kettle or c or pot. H7831
Job 41:31 churn like a boiling c and stirs up the sea H6105

CALDRONS (1) [CALDRON]
2Ch 35:13 c and pans and served them quickly to all H1857

CALEB (33) [CALEB'S, CALEBITE]
Nu 13: 6 the tribe of Judah, C son of Jephunneh; H3979
Nu 13:30 Then C silenced the people before Moses H3979
Nu 14: 6 son of Nun and C son of Jephunneh, H3979
Nu 14:24 But because my servant C has a different H3979
Nu 14:30 except C son of Jephunneh and Joshua H3979
Nu 14:38 son of Nun and C son of Jephunneh H3979
Nu 26:65 was left except C son of Jephunneh and H3979
Nu 32:12 not one except C son of Jephunneh the H3979
Nu 34:19 C son of Jephunneh, from the tribe of H3979
Dt 1:36 except C son of Jephunneh. He will see it H3979
Jos 14: 6 C son of Jephunneh the Kenizzite H3979
Jos 14:13 Then Joshua blessed C son of Jephunneh H3979
Jos 14:14 has belonged to C son of Jephunneh the H3979
Jos 15:13 Joshua gave to C son of Jephunneh a H3979
Jos 15:14 From Hebron C drove out the three H3979
Jos 15:16 And C said, "I will give my daughter Aksah H3979
Jos 15:17 so C gave his daughter Aksah to him in NDT
Jos 15:18 got off her donkey, C asked her, "What H3979
Jos 15:19 So C gave her the upper and lower springs. NDT
Jos 21:12 they had given to C son of Jephunneh as H3979
Jdg 1:12 And C said, "I will give my daughter H3979
Jdg 1:13 so C gave his daughter Aksah to him in NDT
Jdg 1:14 got off her donkey, C asked her, "What H3979
Jdg 1:15 So C gave her the upper and lower H3979
Jdg 1:20 Hebron was given to C, who drove from it H3979
1Sa 30:14 belonging to Judah and the Negev of C. H3979
1Ch 2: 9 to Hezron were: Jerahmeel, Ram and C. H3992
1Ch 2:18 C son of Hezron had children by his wife H3979
1Ch 2:19 When Azubah died, C married Ephrath H3979
1Ch 2:42 The sons of C the brother of Jerahmeel H3979
1Ch 2:50 These were the descendants of C. H3979
1Ch 4:15 The sons of C son of Jephunneh: Iru, Elah H3979
1Ch 6:56 city were given to C son of Jephunneh. H3979

CALEB EPHRATHAH (1) [EPHRATHAH]
1Ch 2:24 After Hezron died in C, Abijah H3980

CALEB'S (6) [CALEB]
Jos 15:17 Othniel son of Kenaz, C brother, took it; so H3979
Jdg 1:13 Othniel son of Kenaz, C younger brother H3979
Jdg 3: 9 son of Kenaz, C younger brother, who H3979
1Ch 2:46 C concubine Ephah was the mother of H3979
1Ch 2:48 C concubine Maakah was the mother of H3979
1Ch 2:49 C daughter was Aksah. H3979

CALEBITE (1) [CALEB]
1Sa 25: 3 mean in his dealings—he was a C. H3982

CALF (33) [CALF-IDOL, CALF-IDOLS, CALVE, CALVED, CALVES]
Ge 18: 7 tender c and gave it to a servant H1201+1330
Ge 18: 8 and milk and the c that had been H1201+1330
Ex 32: 4 it into an idol cast in the shape of a c, H6319
Ex 32: 5 an altar in front of the c and announced, H2257S
Ex 32: 8 an idol cast in the shape of a c. H6319
Ex 32:19 the camp and saw the c and the dancing, H6319
Ex 32:20 And he took the c the people had made H6319
Ex 32:24 threw it into the fire, and out came this c!" H6319
Ex 32:35 what they did with the c Aaron had made. H6319
Lev 9: 2 "Take a bull c for your sin offering and a H6319
Lev 9: 3 a sin offering, a c and a lamb—both a H6319
Lev 9: 8 slaughtered the c as a sin offering for H6319
Lev 22:27 "When a c, a lamb or a goat is born, it is H8802
Dt 9:16 an idol cast in the shape of a c. H6319
Dt 9:21 thing of yours, the c you had made, and H6319
1Sa 28:24 woman had a fattened c at the house, H6319
2Sa 6:13 he sacrificed a bull and a fattened c. H5309
2Ch 11:15 the goat and c idols he had made. H6319
Ne 9:18 themselves an image of a c and said, H6319
Ps 29: 6 He makes Lebanon leap like a c, Sirion H6319
Ps 106:19 Horeb they made a c and worshiped an H6319
Pr 15:17 with love than a fattened c with hatred. H8802
Isa 11: 6 the c and the lion and the yearling H6319
Jer 31:18 'You disciplined me like an unruly c, and I H6319
Jer 34:18 I will treat like the c they cut in two and H6319
Jer 34:19 who walked between the pieces of the c, H6319
Eze 1: 7 were like those of a c and gleamed like H6319
Hos 8: 6 This c—a metalworker has made it; it is not NDT
Hos 8: 6 be broken in pieces, that c of Samaria. H6319
Lk 15:23 Bring the fattened c and kill it. Let's have a G3675
Lk 15:27 killed the fattened c because he has him G3675
Lk 15:30 you kill the fattened c for him! G3675
Ac 7:41 time they made an idol in the form of a c. G3674

CALF-IDOL (2) [CALF, IDOL]
Hos 8: 5 throw out your c! My anger burns against H6319
Hos 10: 5 in Samaria fear for the c of Beth Aven. H6319

CALF-IDOLS (1) [CALF, IDOL]
Hos 13: 2 "They offer human sacrifices! They kiss c!" H6319

CALL (191) [CALLED, CALLING, CALLS, SO-CALLED]
Ge 4:26 people began to c on the name of the H7924
Ge 17:15 you are no longer to c her Sarai H7924+9005
Ge 17:19 and you will c him Isaac. H7924+9005
Ge 24:57 "Let's c the young woman and ask her H7924
Ge 30:13 The women will c me happy." So she H887
Ex 3:15 the name you shall c me from generation H2352
Dt 3: 9 by the Sidonians; the Amorites c it Senir.) H7924
Dt 4:26 I c the heavens and the earth as witnesses H6386
Dt 18:19 I myself will c to account H2011+4946+6640
Dt 30:19 I c the heavens and the earth as witnesses H6386
Dt 31:14 C Joshua and present yourselves at the H7924
Dt 31:28 and c the heavens and the earth to testify H6386
Jos 22:23 may the LORD himself c us to account. H1335
Jdg 8: 1 Why didn't you c us when you went to H7924
Jdg 9:29 say to Abimelek, 'C out your whole army! H3655
Ru 1:20 "Don't c me Naomi," she told them. H7924
Ru 1:20 "C me Mara, because the Almighty has H7924
Ru 1:21 Why c me Naomi? The LORD H7924
1Sa 3: 5 But Eli said, "I did not c; go back and lie H7924
1Sa 3: 6 Eli said, "I did not c; go back and lie H7924
1Sa 12:17 I will c on the LORD to send thunder and H7924

1Sa 20:16 *May* the LORD **c** David's enemies **to account** H1335+4946+3338
1Sa 23:28 That is why *they* **c** this place Sela H7924
2Sa 15: 2 Absalom *would* **c out** to him, "What H7924
1Ki 1:28 King David said, "**C in** Bathsheba." So she H7924
1Ki 1:32 King David said, "**C in** Zadok the priest H7924
1Ki 18:24 Then *you* **c** on the name of your god, and I H7924
1Ki 18:24 and I *will* **c** on the name of the LORD. H7924
1Ki 18:25 **C** on the name of your god, but do not H7924
2Ki 4:12 his servant Gehazi, "**C** the Shunammite." H7924
2Ki 4:15 Then Elisha said, "**C** her." So he called H7924
2Ki 4:36 Gehazi and said, "**C** the Shunammite." H7924
2Ki 5:11 me and stand and **c** on the name of the H7924
2Ki 10:20 "**C** an assembly **in honor of** Baal." H7727+4200
2Ch 24:22 the LORD see this and **c** you **to account**." H2011
Ne 13: 2 hired Balaam to **c a curse down** *on* them. H7837
Job 5: 1 "**C** if you will, but who will answer you? To H7924
Job 13:10 *He would* **surely c** you **to account** if H3519+3519
Job 14:15 *You will* **c** and I will answer you; you will H7924
Job 19: 7 response; though *I* **c for help**, there is no H8775
Job 27:10 *Will they* **c on** God at all times H7924
Ps 3: 4 *I* **c out** to the LORD, and he answers H7924+7754
Ps 4: 1 Answer me when I **c** to you, my righteous H7924
Ps 4: 3 himself; the LORD hears when I **c** to him. H7924
Ps 10:13 to himself, "*He* won't **c** me **to account**"? H2011
Ps 10:15 **c** the evildoer **to account** *for* his H2011
Ps 14: 4 eating bread; *they* never **c on** the LORD. H7924
Ps 17: 6 I **c on** you, my God, for you will answer H7924
Ps 20: 9 victory to the king! Answer us when we **c**! H7924
Ps 27: 7 Hear my voice *when I* **c**, LORD; be merciful H7924
Ps 28: 1 LORD, *I* **c**; you are my Rock, do not H7924
Ps 28: 2 my cry for mercy as I **c** to you **for help**, H8775
Ps 50:15 and **c on** me in the day of trouble; I will H7924
Ps 53: 4 eating bread; *they* never **c on** God. H7924
Ps 55:16 As for me, *I* **c** to God, and the LORD saves H7924
Ps 56: 9 enemies will turn back when *I* **c for help**. H7924
Ps 61: 2 From the ends of the earth *I* **c** to you, I call H7924
Ps 61: 2 I call to you, I **c** as my heart grows faint NDT
Ps 65: 8 evening fades, *you* **c forth songs of joy**. H8264
Ps 72:17 through him, and *they will* **c** him **blessed**. H887
Ps 79: 6 the kingdoms that *do* not **c** on your name; H7924
Ps 80:18 revive us, and *we will* **c** on your name. H7924
Ps 86: 3 Lord, for *I* **c** to you all day long. H7924
Ps 86: 5 abounding in love to all *who* **c** *to* you. H7924
Ps 86: 7 I am in distress, *I* **c** *to* you, because you H7924
Ps 88: 9 *I* **c** *to* you, LORD, every day; I spread out H7924
Ps 89:26 He *will* **c out** *to* me, 'You are my Father H7924
Ps 91:15 *He will* **c on** me, and I will answer him; H7924
Ps 102: 2 ear to me; when *I* **c**, answer me quickly. H7924
Ps 116: 2 ear to me, *I will* **c** *on* him as long as I live. H7924
Ps 116:13 cup of salvation and **c** on the name of the H7924
Ps 116:17 offering to you and **c** on the name of the H7924
Ps 119:145 *I* **c** with all my heart; answer me, LORD H7924
Ps 119:146 *I* **c out** *to* you; save me and I will keep H7924
Ps 120: 1 *I* **c** on the LORD in my distress, and he H7924
Ps 141: 1 *I* **c** *to* you, LORD, come quickly to me; hear H7924
Ps 141: 1 quickly to me; hear me when I **c** to you. H7924
Ps 145:18 The LORD is near to all *who* **c** *on* him, to H7924
Ps 145:18 call on him, to all who **c** *on* him in truth. H7924
Ps 147: 9 for the young ravens when *they* **c**. H7924
Pr 1:24 refuse to listen *when I* **c** and no one pays H7924
Pr 1:28 "Then *they will* **c** to me but I will not H7924
Pr 2: 3 if *you* **c out** for insight and cry aloud for H7924
Pr 8: 1 *Does* not wisdom **c out**? Does not H7924
Pr 8: 4 O people, *I* **c out**; I raise my voice to all H7924
Pr 31:28 Her children arise and **c** her **blessed**; her H887
Ecc 3:15 God *will* **c** the past **to account**. H1335
Isa 5:20 Woe to those *who* **c** evil good and good H606
Isa 7:14 to a son, and *will* **c** him Immanuel. H7924+9005
Isa 8:12 "*Do* not **c** conspiracy everything this people H606
Isa 30: 7 Therefore *I* **c** her Rahab the Do-Nothing H7924
Isa 44: 5 others *will* **c** *themselves* by the name of H7924
Isa 48: 2 *you who* **c yourselves** citizens of the holy H7924
Isa 54: 6 The LORD *will* **c** you **back** as if you were a H7924
Isa 55: 6 may be found; **c** *on* him while he is near. H7924
Isa 58: 5 Is that what *you* **c** a fast, a day acceptable H7924
Isa 58: 9 Then *you will* **c**, and the LORD will answer H7924
Isa 58:13 if *you* **c** the Sabbath a delight and the H7924
Isa 60:14 at your feet and *will* **c** you the City of the H7924
Isa 60:18 but *you will* **c** your walls Salvation and H7924
Isa 62: 4 No longer *will they* **c** you Deserted, or H606
Isa 62: 6 You who **c on** the LORD, give yourselves no H2349
Isa 65: 1 To a nation *that did* not **c** on my name, H7924
Isa 65:24 Before *they* **c** I will answer; while they are H7924
Jer 3:17 At that time *they will* **c** Jerusalem The H7924
Jer 3:19 I thought *you would* **c** me 'Father' and H7924
Jer 7:27 when *you* **c** to them, they will H7924
Jer 7:32 when people *will* no longer **c** *it* Topheth H606
Jer 9:17 **C** for the wailing women to come; send H7924
Jer 10:25 the peoples who *do* not **c** on your name. H7924
Jer 11:14 listen when they **c** to me in the time of H7924
Jer 19: 6 when *people will* no longer **c** this place H7924
Jer 29:12 Then *you will* **c on** me and come and pray H7924
Jer 33: 3 '**C** to me and I will answer you and tell you H7924
Jer 44:21 LORD remember and **c** to mind the incense H6590
Jer 51:50 a distant land, and **c** to mind Jerusalem." H6590
La 3: 8 Even when *I* **c out** or cry for help, he shuts H2410
La 3:21 Yet this I **c to mind** and H8740+448+4213
Eze 9: 1 Then I heard *him* **c out** *in* a loud voice H7924
Eze 36:29 *I will* **c** for the grain and make it plentiful H7924
Eze 39:17 **C out** to every kind of bird and all the wild H606
Da 5:12 **C** *for* Daniel, and he will tell you what A10637
Hos 1: 4 said to Hosea, "**C** him Jezreel H7924+9005
Hos 1: 6 said to Hosea, "**C** her Lo-Ruhamah H7924+9005
Hos 1: 9 the LORD said, "**C** him Lo-Ammi H7924+9005
Hos 2:16 the LORD, "*you will* **c** me 'my husband' H7924
Hos 2:16 *you will* no longer **c** me 'my master. H7924
Hos 11: 7 Even though *they* **c** me God Most High, H7924
Joel 1:14 Declare a holy fast; **c** a sacred assembly H7924
Joel 1:19 *I* **c**, for fire has devoured the H7924
Joel 2:15 declare a holy fast, **c** a sacred assembly. H7924
Jnh 1: 6 Get up and **c** on your god! Maybe H7924
Jnh 3: 8 *Let everyone* **c** urgently on God H7924
Hab 1: 2 *must I* **c for help**, but you do not H8775
Zep 3: 9 that all of them *may* **c** on the name of the H7924
Zec 13: 9 They *will* **c** on my name and I will answer H7924
Mal 3:12 "Then all the nations *will* **c** you **blessed**, for H887
Mal 3:15 But now we **c** the arrogant **blessed** H887
Mt 1:23 and *they will* **c** him G2813+3836+3950
Mt 9:13 For I have not come *to* **c** the righteous G2813
Mt 20: 8 '**C** the workers and pay them their wages G2813
Mt 23: 9 And *do* not **c** anyone on earth 'father,' G2813
Mt 24: 1 up to him *to* **c** his **attention to** its G2109
Mt 24:31 send his angels with a loud **trumpet c**, G4894
Mt 26:53 Do you think I cannot **c on** my Father, and G4151
Mt 26:74 Then he began *to* **c down curses**, and he G2874
Mk 2:17 I have not come *to* **c** the righteous, but G2813
Mk 3:31 outside, they sent someone in *to* **c** him. G2813
Mk 10:18 "Why *do you* **c** me good?" Jesus G3306
Mk 10:49 stopped and said, "**C** him." So they called G5888
Mk 14:71 He began *to* **c down curses**, and he swore G354
Mk 15:12 with the one *you* **c** the king of the Jews?" G3306
Mk 15:18 And they began *to* **c out** to him, "Hail, king G832
Lk 1:13 and *you are to* **c** him John. G2813+3836+3950
Lk 1:31 and *you are to* **c** him Jesus. G2813+3836+3950
Lk 1:48 now on all generations *will* **c** me **blessed**, G3420
Lk 5:32 I have not come *to* **c** the righteous, but G2813
Lk 6:46 "Why *do you* **c** me, 'Lord, Lord,' and do G2813
Lk 9:54 do you want *us to* **c** fire down from G3306
Lk 18:19 "Why *do you* **c** me good?" Jesus G3306
Lk 22:25 over them **c** *themselves* Benefactors. G2813
Jn 4:16 "Go, **c** your husband and come back." G5888
Jn 9:11 "The man they **c** Jesus made some mud G3306
Jn 13:13 "You **c** me 'Teacher' and 'Lord,' and rightly G5888
Jn 15:15 *I* no longer **c** you servants, because a G3306
Ac 2:39 for all whom the Lord our God *will* **c**." G4673
Ac 9:14 priests to arrest all who **c on** your name." G2126
Ac 9:21 Jerusalem *among* those *who* **c on** this G2126
Ac 10:15 "*Do* not **c** anything **impure** that God has G3124
Ac 10:28 shown me that *I should* not **c** anyone G3306
Ac 11: 9 '*Do* not **c** anything **impure** that God has G3124
Ac 24:14 a follower of the Way, which *they* **c** a sect. G3306
Ro 1: 5 apostleship *to* **c** all the Gentiles to the AIT
Ro 2:17 Now you, if *you* **c** *yourself* a Jew; if you G2226
Ro 9:25 "*I will* **c** them 'my people' who are not my G2813
Ro 9:25 I will **c** her 'my loved one' who is not NDT
Ro 10:12 of all and richly blesses all who **c on** him, G2126
Ro 10:14 *can they* **c on** the one they have not G2126
Ro 11:29 God's gifts and his **c** are irrevocable. G3104
1Co 1: 2 everywhere *who* **c on** the name of our G2126
1Co 14: 8 if the trumpet does not sound a clear **c** G5889
2Co 1:23 I **c** God as my witness—and I stake my life G2126
Eph 2:11 by those *who* **c** *themselves* "the G3306
1Th 4: 7 For God *did* not **c** us to be impure, but to G2813
1Th 4:16 archangel and with the **trumpet c** of God, G4894
2Ti 2:22 along with those *who* **c on** the Lord out of G2126
Heb 2:11 is not ashamed *to* **c** them brothers and G2813
Jas 5:14 *Let them* **c** the elders of the church to pray G4673
1Pe 1:17 Since *you* **c on** a Father who judges each G2126
3Jn 10 *I will* **c attention to** what he is doing G5703
Rev 8:13 was flying in midair **c out** in a loud voice: G3306

CALLED (497) [CALL]

Ge 1: 5 God **c** the light "day," and the darkness he H7924
Ge 1: 5 light "day," and the darkness *he* **c** "night." H7924
Ge 1: 8 God **c** the vault "sky." And there was H7924
Ge 1:10 God **c** the dry ground "land," and the H7924
Ge 1:10 and the gathered waters *he* **c** "seas." H7924
Ge 2:19 whatever the man **c** each living creature H7924
Ge 2:23 of my flesh; she *shall* **be c** 'woman,' for H7924
Ge 3: 9 But the LORD God **c** to the man, "Where are H7924
Ge 11: 9 That is why it *was* **c** Babel H7924+9005
Ge 12: 8 altar to the LORD and **c** on the name of the H7924
Ge 13: 4 There Abram **c** on the name of the LORD. H7924
Ge 14:14 *he* **c out** the 318 trained men born in his H8197
Ge 16:14 That is why the well *was* **c** Beer Lahai Roi H7924
Ge 17: 5 No longer *will* you **be c** Abram; your H7924+9005
Ge 19: 5 *They* **c** to Lot, "Where are the men who H7924
Ge 19:22 That is why the town *was* **c** Zoar.) H7924+9005
Ge 20: 9 Then Abimelek **c** Abraham **in** and said H7924
Ge 21:17 the angel of God **c** to Hagar from heaven H7924
Ge 21:31 So that place *was* **c** Beersheba, because H7924
Ge 21:33 there *he* **c** on the name of the LORD H7924
Ge 22:11 angel of the LORD **c out** to him from H7924
Ge 22:14 So Abraham **c** that place The LORD H7924+9005
Ge 22:15 The angel of the LORD **c** to Abraham from H7924
Ge 24:58 So *they* **c** Rebekah and asked her, "Will H7924
Ge 25:30 That is why he *was* also **c** Edom.) H7924+9005
Ge 26:25 an altar there and **c** on the name of the H7924
Ge 26:33 *He* **c** it Shibah, and to this day the name H7924
Ge 27: 1 *he* **c** *for* Esau his older son and said to H7924
Ge 28: 1 So Isaac **c** for Jacob and blessed him H7924
Ge 28:19 *He* **c** that place Bethel, though the H7924+9005
Ge 28:19 though the city used to *be* **c** Luz. H9005
Ge 31:47 Laban **c** it Jegar Sahadutha, and Jacob H7924
Ge 31:47 Jegar Sahadutha, and Jacob **c** it Galeed. H7924
Ge 31:48 That is why it *was* **c** Galeed. H7924+9005
Ge 31:49 It was also **c** Mizpah, because he said, "May NDT
Ge 32:30 So Jacob **c** the place Peniel, saying H7924+9005
Ge 33:17 That is why the place *is* **c** Sukkoth. H7924+9005
Ge 33:20 he set up an altar and **c** it El Elohe Israel. H7924
Ge 35: 7 an altar, and *he* **c** the place El Bethel H7924
Ge 35:10 you *will* no longer **be c** Jacob H7924+9005
Ge 35:15 Jacob **c** the place where God had H7924+9005
Ge 39:14 *she* **c** her household servants. "Look," H7924
Ge 47:29 *he* **c** for his son Joseph and said to him H7924
Ge 48:16 *May* they **be c** by my name and the H7924
Ge 49: 1 Then Jacob **c** for his sons and said H7924
Ge 50:11 near the Jordan *is* **c** Abel Mizraim. H7924+9005
Ex 3: 4 God **c** to him from within the bush H7924
Ex 15:23 That is why the place *is* **c** Marah.) H7924+9005
Ex 16:31 of Israel **c** the bread manna. H7924+9005
Ex 17: 7 And *he* **c** the place Massah and H7924+9005
Ex 17:15 an altar and **c** it The LORD is my H7924+9005
Ex 19: 3 the LORD **c** to him from the mountain H7924
Ex 19:20 of Mount Sinai and **c** Moses to the top of H7924
Ex 24:16 day the LORD **c** to Moses from within H7924
Ex 34:31 But Moses **c** to them; so Aaron and all the H7924
Lev 1: 1 The LORD **c** to Moses and spoke to him H7924
Nu 1:18 and *they* **c** the whole community **together** H7735
Nu 11: 3 So that place *was* **c** Taberah H7924+9005
Nu 13:24 That place *was* **c** the Valley of Eshkol H7924
Nu 32:41 their settlements and **c** them Havvoth Jair. H7924
Nu 32:42 settlements and **c** it Nobah after himself. H7924
Dt 2:11 the Moabites **c** them Emites. H7924
Dt 2:20 the Ammonites **c** them Zamzummites. H7924
Dt 3: 9 Hermon *is* **c** Sirion by the Sidonians; the H7924
Dt 3:14 so that to this day Bashan is **c** Havvoth Jair. NDT
Dt 28:10 will see that you *are* **c** *by* the name of the H7924
Jos 3:16 at a town **c** Adam in the vicinity of Zarethan NDT
Jos 4: 4 So Joshua **c together** the twelve men he H7924
Jos 5: 9 So the place *has been* **c** Gilgal to H7924+9005
Jos 6: 6 Joshua son of Nun **c** the priests and said H7924
Jos 7:26 that place *has been* **c** the Valley of H7924+9005
Jos 8:16 All the men of Ai **were c** to pursue them H2410
Jos 14:15 Hebron used to be **c** Kiriath Arba after H9005
Jos 15:15 living in Debir (formerly **c** Kiriath Sepher). H9005
Jdg 1:10 in Hebron (formerly **c** Kiriath Arba) and H9005
Jdg 1:11 living in Debir (formerly **c** Kiriath Sepher). H9005
Jdg 1:17 Therefore it *was* **c** Hormah. H7924+9005
Jdg 1:23 men to spy out Bethel (formerly **c** Luz), H9005
Jdg 1:26 where he built a city and **c** it Luz H7924+9005
Jdg 2: 5 and *they* **c** that place Bokim. H7924+9005
Jdg 6:24 the LORD there and **c** it The LORD Is Peace. H7924
Jdg 7:15 He returned to the camp of Israel and **c out**, H606
Jdg 7:23 Asher and all Manasseh **were c out**, and H7590
Jdg 7:24 men of Ephraim **were c out** and they H7590
Jdg 9:54 Hurriedly *he* **c** to his armor-bearer, "Draw H7924
Jdg 10: 4 which to this day *are* **c** Havvoth Jair. H7924
Jdg 10:17 Ammonites **were c to arms** and camped H7590
Jdg 12: 1 The Ephraimite forces **were c out**, and H7590
Jdg 12: 2 Ammonites, and *although I* **c**, you didn't H2410
Jdg 12: 4 Jephthah then **c together** the men of H7695
Jdg 15:17 the place *was* **c** Ramath Lehi. H7924
Jdg 15:19 So the spring *was* **c** En Hakkore H7924+9005
Jdg 16: 9 in the room, *she* **c** to him, "Samson, H606
Jdg 16:12 in the room, *she* **c** to him, "Samson, H606
Jdg 16:14 Again *she* **c** to him, "Samson, the H606
Jdg 16:19 *she* **c** for someone to shave off the seven H7924
Jdg 16:20 Then *she* **c**, "Samson, the Philistines are H606
Jdg 16:25 So *they* **c** Samson out of the prison, and H7924
Jdg 18:12 of Kiriath Jearim *is* **c** Mahaneh Dan to this H7924
Jdg 18:22 near Micah **were c together** and overtook H2410
Jdg 18:23 with you that *you* **c out** your men to **fight**?" H2410
Jdg 18:29 Israel—though the city used to be **c** Laish. H9005
1Sa 1: 2 one was **c** Hannah and the other H9005
1Sa 3: 4 Then the LORD **c** Samuel. H7924
1Sa 3: 5 ran to Eli and said, "Here I am; *you* **c** me." H7924
1Sa 3: 6 Again the LORD **c**, "Samuel!" And Samuel H7924
1Sa 3: 6 to Eli and said, "Here I am; *you* **c** me." H7924
1Sa 3: 8 A third time the LORD **c**, "Samuel!" And H7924
1Sa 3: 8 to Eli and said, "Here I am; *you* **c** me." H7924
1Sa 3:16 Eli **c** him and said, "Samuel, my son." H7924
1Sa 5: 8 So *they* **c together** all the H8938+2256+665
1Sa 5:11 So *they* **c together** all the H8938+2256+665
1Sa 6: 2 the Philistines **c** for the priests and the H7924
1Sa 9: 9 the prophet of today used to **be c** a seer.) H7924
1Sa 9:26 Samuel **c** to Saul on the roof H7924
1Sa 12:18 Then Samuel **c** on the LORD, and that H7924
1Sa 14: 4 one was **c** Bozez and the other Seneh. H9005
1Sa 16: 8 Then Jesse **c** Abinadab and had him pass H7924
1Sa 19: 7 So Jonathan **c** David and told him the H7924
1Sa 20:37 Jonathan **c out** after him, "Isn't H7924
1Sa 23: 8 And Saul **c up** all his forces for battle, to H9048
1Sa 24: 8 went out of the cave and **c out** to Saul, H7924
1Sa 26:14 He **c out** to the army and to Abner son of H7924
1Sa 28:15 So *I have* **c** on you to tell me what to do." H7924
1Sa 29: 6 So Achish **c** David and said to him, "As H7924
2Sa 1: 7 saw me, *he* **c out** to me, and I said, H7924
2Sa 1:15 Then David **c** one of his men and said H7924
2Sa 2:16 place in Gibeon *was* **c** Helkath Hazzurim. H7924
2Sa 2:26 Abner **c out** to Joab, "Must the sword H7924
2Sa 5: 9 in the fortress and **c** it the City of David. H7924
2Sa 5:20 So that place *was* **c** Baal Perazim. H7924+9005
2Sa 6: 2 ark of God, which **is c** *by* the Name, the H7924
2Sa 6: 8 to this day that place *is* **c** Perez Uzzah. H7924

2Sa 13:17 *He* **c** his personal servant and said, "Get H7924
2Sa 18:18 it **is c** Absalom's Monument to this H7924
2Sa 18:25 The watchman **c out** to the king and H7924
2Sa 18:26 and he **c** down to the gatekeeper H7924
2Sa 18:28 Then Ahimaaz **c out** to the king, "All is H7924
2Sa 20:16 a wise woman **c** from the city, "Listen H7924
2Sa 22: 4 "*I* **c** *to* the LORD, who is worthy of praise H7924
2Sa 22: 7 "In my distress *I* **c** *to* the LORD; I called out H7924
2Sa 22: 7 I called to the LORD; *I* **c out** to my God. H7924
1Ki 2: 8 who **c down** bitter **curses** *on* me the H7837+7839
1Ki 9:13 And *he* **c** them the Land of Kabul, a name H7924
1Ki 12:20 they sent and **c** him to the assembly and H7924
1Ki 17:10 *He* **c** to her and asked, "Would you bring H7924
1Ki 17:11 was going to get it, *he* **c**, "And bring me, H7924
1Ki 18:26 Then *they* **c** on the name of Baal from H7924
1Ki 20:39 the prophet **c out** to him, "Your servant H7590
1Ki 22: 9 So the king of Israel **c** one of his officials H7924
2Ki 2:24 at them and **c down a curse** *on* them in H7837
2Ki 3:10 "*Has* the LORD **c** us three kings **together** H7924
2Ki 3:13 the LORD *who* **c** us three kings **together** to H7924
2Ki 3:21 could bear arms **was c up** and stationed H7590
2Ki 4:12 Shunammite." So *he* **c** her, and she stood H7924
2Ki 4:15 So *he* **c** her, and she stood in the H7924
2Ki 4:22 *She* **c** her husband and said, "Please H7924
2Ki 7:10 So they went and **c out** to the city H7924
2Ki 9:17 approaching, *he* **c out**, "I see some troops H606
2Ki 9:32 He looked up at the window and **c out** H606
2Ki 11:14 Then Athaliah tore her robes and **c out** H7924
2Ki 18: 4 (It *was* **c** Nehushtan.) H7924
2Ki 18:18 *They* **c** for the king; and Eliakim son of H7924
2Ki 18:28 stood and **c out** in H7924+928+7754+1524
2Ki 20:11 Then the prophet Isaiah **c** on the LORD H7924
2Ki 23: 1 the king **c together** all the H8938+2256+665
1Ch 4:14 It was **c** this because its people were skilled NDT
1Ch 9:23 the LORD—the house **c** the tent of meeting. NDT
1Ch 11: 7 fortress, and so it *was* **c** the City of David. H7924
1Ch 13: 6 cherubim—the ark that **is c** *by* the Name. H7924
1Ch 13:11 to this day that place *is* **c** Perez Uzzah. H7924
1Ch 14:11 So that place *was* **c** Baal Perazim. H7924+9005
1Ch 15: 4 He **c together** the descendants of Aaron H665
1Ch 21:26 *He* **c** on the LORD, and the LORD answered H7924
1Ch 22: 6 Then *he* **c** for his son Solomon and H7924
2Ch 7:14 if my people, who **are c** *by* my name, will H7924
2Ch 14:11 Then Asa **c** to the LORD his God and said H7924
2Ch 18: 8 So the king of Israel **c** one of his officials H7924
2Ch 20:26 This is why it *is* **c** the Valley of H7924+9005
2Ch 24: 5 He **c together** the priests and Levites and H7695
2Ch 25: 5 **c** the people of Judah **together** and H7695
2Ch 32:18 Then *they* **c out** in H7924+928+7754+1524
2Ch 34:29 the king **c together** all the H8938+2256+665
Ezr 2:61 the Gileadite and **was c** by that name). H7924
Ne 5: 7 So *I* **c together** a large meeting to deal H5989
Ne 7:63 the Gileadite and **was c** by that name). H7924
Ne 13:11 Then *I* **c** them **together** and stationed H7695
Ne 13:25 them and **c curses down** *on* them. H7837
Est 4:11 passed since I **was c** to go to the king." H7924
Est 9:26 Therefore these days *were* **c** Purim, from H7924
Job 12: 4 though *I* **c** on God and he answered H7924
Job 31:14 What will I answer when **c to account**? H7212
Ps 18: 3 *I* **c** *to* the LORD, who is worthy of praise H7924
Ps 18: 6 In my distress *I* **c** *to* the LORD; I cried to my H7924
Ps 30: 2 LORD my God, *I* **c** to you **for help**, and you H8775
Ps 30: 8 LORD, *I* **c**; to the Lord I cried for H7924
Ps 31:22 my cry for mercy when I **c** to you **for help**. H8775
Ps 34: 6 This poor man **c**, and the LORD heard him H7924
Ps 81: 7 In your distress *you* **c** and I rescued you, H7924
Ps 99: 6 was among *those who* **c** *on* his name; H7924
Ps 99: 6 *they* **c** on the LORD and he answered them. H7924
Ps 105:16 *He* **c down** famine on the land and H7924
Ps 116: 4 Then *I* **c** on the name of the LORD: "LORD H7924
Ps 138: 3 When *I* **c**, you answered me; you greatly H7924
Pr 16:21 The wise in heart **are c** discerning, and H7924
SS 5: 6 *I* **c** him but he did not answer. H7924
SS 6: 9 young women saw her and **c** her **blessed**; H887
Isa 1:26 Afterward you *will be* **c** the City of H7924
Isa 4: 1 clothes; only *let* us **be c** *by* your name. H7924
Isa 4: 3 in Jerusalem, *will be* **c** holy, all who are H606
Isa 8: 2 *I* **c in** Uriah the priest and Zechariah son of
Jeberekiah **as** reliable **witnesses** H6386+6332
Isa 9: 6 And he *will be* **c** Wonderful H7924+9005
Isa 19:18 One of them *will* **be c** the City of the Sun. H606
Isa 22:12 **c** you on that day to weep and to wail H7924
Isa 31: 4 band of shepherds **is c together** against it, H7924
Isa 32: 5 No longer *will* the fool **be c** noble nor the H7924
Isa 34:12 have nothing there *to be* **c** a kingdom, H7924
Isa 35: 8 be there; it *will* **be c** the Way of Holiness H7924
Isa 36:13 stood and **c out** in H7924+928+7754+1524
Isa 41: 9 the earth, from its farthest corners *I* **c** you. H7924
Isa 42: 6 the LORD, *have* **c** you in righteousness; H7924
Isa 43: 7 everyone who **is c** by my name, whom I H7924
Isa 43:22 "Yet *you have* not **c** *on* me, Jacob, you H7924
Isa 47: 1 No more *will* you *be* **c** tender or delicate. H7924
Isa 47: 5 no more *will* you *be* **c** queen of kingdoms. H7924
Isa 48: 1 you who **are c** by the name of Israel and H7924
Isa 48: 8 you are; you **were c** a rebel from birth. H7924
Isa 48:12 Jacob, Israel, *whom* I *have* **c**: H7924
Isa 48:15 spoken; yes, *I have* **c** him. I will bring H7924
Isa 49: 1 Before I was born the LORD **c** me; from my H7924
Isa 50: 2 *When I* **c**, why was there no one to H7924
Isa 51: 2 When *I* **c** him he was only one man, and I H7924
Isa 54: 5 *he* **is c** the God of all the earth. H7924
Isa 56: 7 my house *will* **be c** a house of prayer H7924
Isa 58:12 you *will be* **c** Repairer of Broken Walls H7924
Isa 61: 3 They *will* **be c** oaks of righteousness, H7924
Isa 61: 6 And you *will* **be c** priests of the LORD, you H7924
Isa 62: 2 you *will* **be c** *by* a new name that the H7924
Isa 62: 4 But you *will* **be c** Hephzibah, and your H7924
Isa 62:12 They *will be* **c** the Holy People, the H7924
Isa 62:12 the LORD; and you *will* **be c** Sought After H7924
Isa 63:19 they *have* not **been c** *by* your name. H7924
Isa 65:12 slaughter; for *I* **c** but you did not answer H7924
Isa 66: 4 For *when I* **c**, no one answered, when I H7924
Jer 3: 4 *Have you* not just **c** to me: 'My Father, my H7924
Jer 6:30 They *are* **c** rejected silver, because the H7924
Jer 7:13 you did not listen; *I* **c** you, but you did not H7924
Jer 11:16 The LORD **c** you a thriving olive tree H7924+9005
Jer 23: 6 This is the name by which he *will be* **c** H7924
Jer 30:17 'because you *are* **c** an outcast, Zion H7924
Jer 33:16 This is the name by which it *will be* **c**: The H7924
Jer 35:17 they did not listen; *I* **c** to them, but they H7924
Jer 36: 4 So Jeremiah **c** Baruch son of Neriah, and H7924
Jer 42: 8 So *he* **c together** Johanan son of Kareah H7924
La 1:19 "*I* **c** to my allies but they betrayed me. H7924
La 2:15 "Is this the city that *was* **c** the perfection of H606
La 3:55 *I* **c** *on* your name, LORD, from the depths of H7924
La 3:57 You came near when *I* **c** you, and you H7924
Eze 9: 3 Then the LORD **c** to the man clothed in H7924
Eze 10:13 I heard the wheels **being c** "the whirling H7924
Eze 20:29 (It **is c** Bamah to this day. H7924+9005
Eze 38: 8 After many days *you will* **be c to arms**. H7212
Eze 39:11 So *it will be* **c** the Valley of Hamon Gog. H7924
Eze 39:16 near a town **c** Hamonah. And so they will H9005
Da 2:26 asked Daniel (also **c** Belteshazzar), A10721
Da 4: 8 He is **c** Belteshazzar, after the name of A10721
Da 4:14 *He* **c** in a loud voice: 'Cut down the tree A10637
Da 4:19 Then Daniel (also **c** Belteshazzar) was A10721
Da 5:12 whom the king **c** Belteshazzar A10682+10721
Da 6:20 he **c** to Daniel in an anguished voice A10237
Da 10: 1 to Daniel (who **was c** Belteshazzar). H7924+9005
Hos 1:10 they *will* **be c** 'children of the living God. H606
Hos 2:23 my love to the one I **c** 'Not my loved one. NDT
Hos 2:23 I will say to those **c** 'Not my people,' 'You NDT
Hos 11: 1 I loved him, and out of Egypt *I* **c** my son. H7924
Hos 11: 2 But the more they *were* **c**, the more they H7924
Jnh 2: 2 "In my distress *I* **c** to the LORD, and he H7924
Jnh 2: 2 deep in the realm of the dead *I* **c for help**, H8775
Hab 3: 9 uncovered your bow, *you* **c** *for* many arrows. H606
Hag 1:11 *I* **c** *for* a drought on the fields and the H7924
Zec 6: 8 Then *he* **c** to me, "Look, those going H2410
Zec 7:13 " 'When *I* **c**, they did not listen; so when H7924
Zec 7:13 did not listen; so *when they* **c**, I would not H7924
Zec 8: 3 Then Jerusalem *will* **be c** the Faithful City H7924
Zec 8: 3 Almighty will be **c** the Holy Mountain." NDT
Zec 11: 7 I took two staffs and **c** one Favor and the H7924
Zec 11:10 Then I took my staff **c** Favor and broke it NDT
Zec 11:14 Then I broke my second staff **c** Union NDT
Mal 1: 4 They *will be* **c** the Wicked Land, a people H7924
Mal 2: 5 this **c** for reverence and he revered me and NDT
Mt 1:16 the mother of Jesus who *is* **c** the Messiah. G3306
Mt 2: 4 *When he had* **c together** all the people's G5251
Mt 2: 7 Then Herod **c** the Magi secretly and found G2813
Mt 2:15 "Out of Egypt *I* **c** my son." G2813
Mt 2:23 he went and lived in a town **c** Nazareth. G3306
Mt 2:23 prophets, that *he would be* **c** a Nazarene. G2813
Mt 4:18 Simon **c** Peter and his brother Andrew. G3306
Mt 4:21 preparing their nets. Jesus **c** them, G2813
Mt 5: 9 they *will be* **c** children of God. G2813
Mt 5:19 others accordingly *will be* **c** least in the G2813
Mt 5:19 these commands *will be* **c** great in the G2813
Mt 10: 1 Jesus **c** his twelve disciples **to** him and G4673
Mt 10: 2 Simon (who *is* **c** Peter) and his brother G3306
Mt 10:25 head of the house *has been* **c** Beelzebul, G2126
Mt 15:10 Jesus **c** the crowd **to** him and said, "Listen G4673
Mt 15:32 Jesus **c** his disciples **to** him and said, "I G4673
Mt 18: 2 *He* **c** a little child **to** him, and placed the G4673
Mt 18:32 "Then the master **c** the servant **in**. G4673
Mt 20:25 Jesus **c** them **together** and said, "You G4673
Mt 20:32 Jesus stopped and **c** them. "What do you G5888
Mt 21:13 " 'My house *will be* **c** a house of prayer G2813
Mt 21:16 infants *you*, Lord, *have* **c forth** *your* praise' G2936
Mt 23: 7 marketplaces and *to be* **c** 'Rabbi' by G2813
Mt 23: 8 "But you *are* not *to be* **c** 'Rabbi,' for you G2813
Mt 23:10 Nor *are you to be* **c** instructors, for you G2813
Mt 25:14 *who* **c** his servants and entrusted his G2813
Mt 26:14 of the Twelve—the *one* **c** Judas Iscariot G3306
Mt 26:36 his disciples to a place **c** Gethsemane, G3306
Mt 27: 8 That is why it *has been* **c** the Field of G2813
Mt 27:17 Barabbas, or Jesus who *is* **c** the Messiah?" G3306
Mt 27:22 with Jesus who *is* **c** the Messiah? G3306
Mt 27:33 They came to a place **c** Golgotha (which G3306
Mk 1:20 Without delay *he* **c** them, and they left G2813
Mk 3:13 a mountainside and **c to** him those he G4673
Mk 3:23 So Jesus **c** them **over to** him and began to G4673
Mk 7:14 Again Jesus **c** the crowd **to** him and said G4673
Mk 8: 1 Jesus **c** his disciples **to** him and said, G4673
Mk 8:34 Then *he* **c** the crowd **to** him along with his G4673
Mk 9:35 Sitting down, Jesus **c** the Twelve and said G5888
Mk 10:42 Jesus **c** them **together** and said, "You G4673
Mk 10:49 So *they* **c** to the blind man G5888
Mk 11:17 'My house *will be* **c** a house of prayer G2813
Mk 14:32 to a place **c** Gethsemane, G4005+3836+3950
Mk 15: 7 A man **c** Barabbas was in prison with the G3306
Mk 15:16 and **c together** the whole company of G5157
Mk 15:22 They brought Jesus to the place **c** Golgotha NDT
Lk 1:32 will be great and *will be* **c** the Son of the G2813
Lk 1:35 one to be born *will be* **c** the Son of God. G2813
Lk 1:60 up and said, "No! *He is to be* **c** John." G2813
Lk 1:76 *will be* **c** a prophet of the Most High G2813
Lk 2:25 was a man in Jerusalem **c** Simeon, G4005+3950
Lk 6:13 *he* **c** his disciples **to** *him* and chose twelve G4715
Lk 6:15 Alphaeus, Simon who *was* **c** the Zealot, G2813
Lk 7:11 Jesus went to a town **c** Nain, and his G2813
Lk 8: 2 Mary (**c** Magdalene) from whom seven G2813
Lk 8: 8 he said this, *he* **c out**, "Whoever has ears G5888
Lk 9: 1 *When* Jesus *had* **c** the Twelve **together** G5157
Lk 9:10 by themselves to a town **c** Bethsaida, G2813
Lk 9:38 A man in the crowd **c out**, "Teacher, I beg G1066
Lk 10:39 She had a sister **c** Mary, who sat at the G2813
Lk 11:27 a woman in the crowd **c out** G2048+5889+3306
Lk 13:12 saw her, *he* **c** her **forward** and said to her G4715
Lk 15:19 I am no longer worthy *to be* **c** your son G2813
Lk 15:21 I am no longer worthy *to be* **c** your son.' G2813
Lk 15:26 So *he* **c** one of the servants and asked him G4673
Lk 16: 2 So *he* **c** him **in** and asked him, 'What is G5888
Lk 16: 5 "So *he* **c in** each one of his master's G4673
Lk 16:24 So he **c** to him, 'Father Abraham, have pity G5888
Lk 17:13 **c out** in a loud voice, "Jesus, Master G3306
Lk 18:16 But Jesus **c** the children **to** him and said G4673
Lk 18:38 *He* **c out**, "Jesus, Son of David, have G1066
Lk 19:13 So *he* **c** ten of his servants and gave them G2813
Lk 19:29 Bethany at the hill **c** the Mount of Olives, G2813
Lk 21:37 night on the hill **c** the Mount of Olives, G2813
Lk 22: 1 of Unleavened Bread, **c** the Passover, was G3306
Lk 22: 3 Satan entered Judas, **c** Iscariot, one of the G2813
Lk 22:47 and the *man who was* **c** Judas, one of G3306
Lk 23:13 Pilate **c together** the chief priests, the G5157
Lk 23:33 When they came to the place **c** the Skull G2813
Lk 23:46 Jesus **c out** with a loud voice, "Father, into G5888
Lk 24:13 them were going to a village **c** Emmaus, G3950
Jn 1:42 You *will be* **c** Cephas" (which, when G2813
Jn 1:48 still under the fig tree before Philip **c** you." G5888
Jn 2: 9 Then he **c** the bridegroom **aside** G5888
Jn 4: 5 So he came to a town in Samaria **c** Sychar G3306
Jn 4:25 know that Messiah" (**c** Christ) "is coming. G3306
Jn 5: 2 which in Aramaic *is* **c** Bethesda and which G2141
Jn 10:35 If *he* **c** them 'gods,' to whom the word of G3306
Jn 11:28 she went back and **c** her sister Mary aside. G5888
Jn 11:43 he had said this, Jesus **c** in a loud voice G3198
Jn 11:47 the Pharisees **c a meeting** of the G5251
Jn 11:54 to a village **c** Ephraim, where he stayed G3306
Jn 12:17 was with him when *he* **c** Lazarus from the G5888
Jn 15:15 Instead, *I have* **c** you friends, for G3306
Jn 19:17 which in Aramaic *is* **c** Golgotha). G3306
Jn 21: 5 He **c out** to them, "Friends, haven't you G3306
Ac 1:12 from the hill **c** the Mount of Olives, G2813
Ac 1:19 so *they* **c** that field in their language G2813
Ac 1:23 Joseph **c** Barsabbas (also known as Justus) G2813
Ac 3: 2 carried to the temple gate **c** Beautiful, G3306
Ac 3:10 sit begging at the temple gate **c** Beautiful, NDT
Ac 3:11 to them in the *place* **c** Solomon's G2813
Ac 4: 9 If we *are being* **c to account** today for an act G373
Ac 4:18 Then *they* **c** them **in** *again* and G2813
Ac 4:36 whom the apostles **c** Barnabas (which G2126
Ac 5:21 *they* **c together** the Sanhedrin G5157
Ac 5:40 *They* **c** the apostles **in** and had them G4673
Ac 6: 9 the Freedmen (*as it was* **c**)—Jews of G3306
Ac 8:10 "This man is *rightly* **c** the Great Power of G2813
Ac 9:10 The Lord **c** to him in a vision G3306
Ac 9:41 Then *he* **c** for the believers, especially the G5888
Ac 10: 5 back a man named Simon who *is* **c** Peter. G2126
Ac 10: 7 Cornelius **c** two of his servants and a G5888
Ac 10:18 *They* **c out**, asking if Simon who was G5888
Ac 10:24 them and *had* **c together** his relatives G5157
Ac 10:32 Send to Joppa for Simon who *is* **c** Peter G2126
Ac 11:13 'Send to Joppa for Simon who *is* **c** Peter. G2126
Ac 11:26 The disciples *were* **c** Christians first at G5976
Ac 12:12 mother of John, also **c** Mark, where many G2126
Ac 12:25 taking with them John, *also* **c** Mark. G2126
Ac 13: 1 Barnabas, Simeon **c** Niger, Lucius of G2813
Ac 13: 2 Saul for the work to which *I have* **c** them." G4673
Ac 13: 9 who was also **c** Paul, filled with the NDT
Ac 14:10 and **c out**, "Stand up on your G3306+3489+5889
Ac 14:12 Barnabas *they* **c** Zeus, and Paul they G2813
Ac 14:12 Paul they **c** Hermes because he was the NDT
Ac 15:22 They chose Judas (**c** Barsabbas) and Silas G2813
Ac 15:37 to take John, also **c** Mark, with them, G2813
Ac 16:10 that God *had* **c** us to preach the G4673
Ac 16:29 The jailer **c for** lights, rushed in and fell G160
Ac 17: 7 that there is another king, one **c** Jesus." NDT
Ac 19:25 *He* **c** them **together**, along with the G5255
Ac 23: 6 others Pharisees, **c out** in the Sanhedrin G3189
Ac 23:17 Then Paul **c** one of the centurions and G4673
Ac 23:23 Then *he* **c** two of his centurions and G4673
Ac 24: 2 *When* Paul *was* **c** *in*, Tertullus presented G2813
Ac 27: 8 came to a place **c** Fair Havens, G2813
Ac 27:14 of hurricane force, **c** the Northeaster G2813
Ac 27:16 to the lee of a small island **c** Cauda, G2813
Ac 28: 1 we found out that the island *was* **c** Malta. G2813
Ac 28:17 days later he **c together** the local Jewish G5157
Ro 1: 1 **c** to be an apostle and set apart for the G3105
Ro 1: 6 Gentiles who are **c** to belong to Jesus G3105
Ro 1: 7 are loved by God and **c** to be his holy G3105
Ro 7: 3 is still alive, *she is* **c** an adulteress. G5976
Ro 8:28 who have been **c** according to his purpose G3105
Ro 8:30 he predestined, *he* also **c**; those he called G2813
Ro 8:30 also called; those *he* **c**, he also justified; G2813

Ro 9:24 even us, whom *he* also **c**, not only from *G2813*
Ro 9:26 there *they will be* **c** 'children of the living *G2813*
1Co 1: 1 **c** to be an apostle of Christ Jesus by the *G3105*
1Co 1: 2 in Christ Jesus and **c** to be his holy people *G3105*
1Co 1: 9 who *has* **c** *you* into fellowship with his *G2813*
1Co 1:24 to those whom God has **c**, both Jews *G3105*
1Co 1:26 think of what you were when you were **c**. *G3104*
1Co 7:15 God *has* **c** us to live in peace. *G2813*
1Co 7:17 assigned to them, just as God *has* **c** them. *G2813*
1Co 7:18 man already circumcised *when he was* **c**? *G2813*
1Co 7:18 a man uncircumcised *when he was* **c**? *G2813*
1Co 7:20 situation they were in *when* God **c** them. *G2813*
1Co 7:21 Were you a slave *when you were* **c**? Don't *G2813*
1Co 7:22 was a slave *when* **c to faith** in the Lord is *G2813*
1Co 7:22 one who was free *when* **c** is Christ's slave. *G2813*
1Co 7:24 situation they were in *when* God **c** them. *G2813*
1Co 15: 9 do not even deserve *to be* **c** an apostle, *G2813*
Gal 1: 6 deserting the *one who* **c** you to live in the *G2813*
Gal 1:15 my mother's womb and **c** me by his grace, *G2813*
Gal 5:13 my brothers and sisters, *were* **c** to be free. *G2813*
Eph 1:18 know the hope to which he has **c** you, *G3104*
Eph 2:11 Gentiles by birth and **c** "uncircumcised" *G3306*
Eph 4: 4 just as *you were* **c** to one hope when you *G2813*
Eph 4: 4 called to one hope when you were **c**; *G3104*
Php 3:14 which God *has* **c** me heavenward in *G3104*
Col 3:15 of one body *you were* **c** to peace. *G2813*
Col 4:11 who *is* **c** Justus, also sends *G3306*
2Th 2: 4 over everything *that is* **c** God or is *G3306*
2Th 2:14 *He* **c** you to this through our gospel, that *G2813*
1Ti 6:12 life to which *you were* **c** when you made *G2813*
1Ti 6:20 ideas *of* what is **falsely c** knowledge, *G6024*
2Ti 1: 9 He has saved us and **c** us to a holy life *G2813*
Heb 3:13 as long as *it is* **c** "Today," so that *G2813*
Heb 5: 4 he receives it *when* **c** by God, just as *G2813*
Heb 9: 2 this *was* **c** the Holy Place. *G3306*
Heb 9: 3 curtain was a room **c** the Most Holy Place, *G3306*
Heb 9:15 that those *who are* **c** may receive the *G2813*
Heb 11: 8 *when* **c** to go to a place he would later *G2813*
Heb 11:16 God is not ashamed *to be* **c** their God, *G2126*
Jas 2:23 and *he was* **c** God's friend. *G2813*
1Pe 1:15 But just as he *who* **c** you is holy, so be holy *G2813*
1Pe 2: 9 the praises of him *who* **c** you out of *G2813*
1Pe 2:21 To this *you were* **c**, because Christ suffered *G2813*
1Pe 3: 6 who obeyed Abraham and **c** him her lord. *G2813*
1Pe 3: 9 because to this *you were* **c** so that you *G2813*
1Pe 5:10 who **c** you to his eternal glory in Christ *G2813*
2Pe 1: 3 knowledge of him *who* **c** us by his own *G2813*
1Jn 3: 1 that *we should be* **c** children of God! *G2813*
Jude 1 *To those who have been* **c**, who *G3105*
Rev 6:10 *They* **c out** in a loud voice, "How long *G3189*
Rev 6:16 *They* **c** to the mountains and the rocks *G3306*
Rev 7: 2 *He* **c out** in a loud voice to the four angels *G3189*
Rev 11: 8 which *is* figuratively **c** Sodom and Egypt *G2813*
Rev 12: 9 that ancient serpent **c** the devil, or Satan, *G2813*
Rev 14:15 out of the temple and **c** in a loud voice to *G3189*
Rev 14:18 from the altar and **c** in a loud voice to him *G5888*
Rev 16:16 place that in Hebrew *is* **c** Armageddon. *G2813*
Rev 17:14 with him will be his **c**, chosen and *G3105*
Rev 19:11 whose rider *is* **c** Faithful and True. *G2813*

CALLING (43) [CALL]

Ex 33: 7 distance away, **c** it the "tent of meeting." H7924
Nu 10: 2 them for **c** the community **together** and H5246
Jdg 6:35 Manasseh, **c** them **to arms**, and also H2410+339
Jdg 12: 1 Ammonites without **c** us to go with you? H7924
1Sa 3: 8 Eli realized that the LORD *was* **c** the boy. H7924
1Sa 3:10 stood there, **c** as at the other times H7924
1Ki 16:24 a city on the hill, **c** it Samaria, after H7924+9005
2Ki 9:23 about and fled, **c out** to Ahaziah H606
2Ki 14: 7 Sela in battle, **c** it Joktheel, the name it H7924
2Ch 30: 5 **c** the people to come to Jerusalem and NDT
Est 5:10 **C together** his friends and H8938+2256+995
Ps 69: 3 I am worn out **c for help**; my throat is H7924
Pr 9:15 **c out** to those who pass by, who go H7924
Isa 6: 3 And *they were* **c** to one another: "Holy H7924
Isa 40: 3 A voice of *one* **c**: "In the wilderness H7924
Isa 41: 2 **c** him in righteousness to his service? H7924
Isa 41: 4 **c forth** the generations from the H7924
Jer 25:29 I *am* **c down** a sword on all who live H7924
Da 8:16 And I heard a man's voice from the Ulai **c** H7924
Hos 7:11 senseless—now **c** *to* Egypt, now H7924
Am 7: 4 The Sovereign LORD *was* **c** for judgment by H7924
Mic 6: 9 The LORD *is* **c** to the city—and to H7754+7924
Mt 3: 3 "A voice *of one* **c** in the wilderness *G1066*
Mt 9:27 men followed him, **c out**, "Have mercy on *G3189*
Mt 11:16 in the marketplaces and **c out** to others: *G4715*
Mt 27:47 there heard this, they said, "He's **c** Elijah." *G5888*
Mk 1: 3 "a voice *of one* **c** in the wilderness *G1066*
Mk 6: 7 **C** the Twelve **to** him, he began to send *G4673*
Mk 10:49 On your feet! *He's* **c** you." *G5888*
Mk 12:43 **C** his disciples **to** him, Jesus said, "Truly I *G4673*
Mk 15:35 they said, "Listen, *he's* **c** Elijah. *G5888*
Lk 3: 4 "A voice *of one* **c** in the wilderness *G1066*
Lk 7:18 him about all these things. **C** two of them, *G4673*
Lk 7:32 the marketplace and **c out** to each other: *G4715*
Jn 1:23 "I am the voice *of one* **c** in the wilderness *G1066*
Jn 5:18 but *he was* even **c** God his own Father *G3306*
Ac 22:16 wash your sins away, **c on** his name. *G2126*
Eph 4: 1 a life worthy of the **c** you have received. *G3104*
2Th 1:11 our God may make you worthy *of* his **c**, *G3104*
Heb 3: 1 who share in the heavenly **c**, fix your *G3104*
Heb 4: 7 set a certain day, **c** it "Today." This he did NDT
Heb 8:13 By **c** this covenant "new," he has made *G3306*
2Pe 1:10 every effort to confirm your **c** and election. *G3104*

CALLOUS (3) [CALLOUSED]

Ps 17:10 They close up their **c hearts**, and their H2693
Ps 73: 7 From their **c hearts** comes iniquity; their H2693
Ps 119:70 hearts are **c** and unfeeling, H3869+2021+2693

CALLOUSED (3) [CALLOUS]

Isa 6:10 **Make** the heart of this people **c**; make H9042
Mt 13:15 For this people's heart *has become* **c**; they *G4266*
Ac 28:27 For this people's heart *has become* **c**; they *G4266*

CALLS (39) [CALL]

Ge 46:33 When Pharaoh **c** you **in** and asks, 'What is H7924
1Sa 3: 9 lie down, and if *he* **c** you, say, 'Speak, H7924
1Sa 26:14 replied, "Who are you *who* **c** to the king?" H7924
Ps 42: 7 Deep **c** to deep in the roar of your H7924
Ps 147: 4 of the stars and **c** them each by name. H7924
Pr 1:20 Out in the open wisdom **c aloud**, she H8264
Pr 9: 3 and *she* **c** from the highest point of the H7924
Isa 8:12 everything this people **c** a conspiracy; H606
Isa 21:11 *Someone* **c** to me from Seir, "Watchman H7924
Isa 40:26 one by one and **c forth** each of them by H7924
Isa 41:25 from the rising sun *who* **c** on my name. H7924
Isa 59: 4 No *one* **c** for justice; no one pleads a case H7924
Isa 64: 7 No *one* **c** on your name or strives to lay H7924
Hos 7: 7 kings fall, and none of them **c** on me. H7924
Joel 2:32 And everyone who **c** on the name of the H7924
Joel 2:32 among the survivors whom the LORD **c**. H7924
Am 5: 8 who **c** for the waters of the sea and pours H7924
Am 9: 6 he **c** for the waters of the sea and pours H7924
Mt 22:43 speaking by the Spirit, **c** him 'Lord'? *G2813*
Mt 22:45 If then David **c** him 'Lord,' how can he be *G2813*
Mk 12:37 David himself **c** him 'Lord.' How then can *G3306*
Lk 15: 6 *he* **c** his friends and neighbors **together** *G5157*
Lk 15: 9 *she* **c** her friends and neighbors **together** *G5157*
Lk 20:37 for *he* **c** the Lord 'the God of Abraham *G3306*
Lk 20:44 David **c** him 'Lord.' How then can he be *G2813*
Jn 10: 3 *He* **c** his own sheep by name and leads *G5888*
Ac 2:21 And everyone who **c on** the name of the *G2126*
Ro 4:17 life to the dead and **c** into being things *G2813*
Ro 9:12 not by works but by him *who* **c**—she was *G2813*
Ro 10:13 "Everyone who **c on** the name of the Lord *G2126*
Gal 4: 6 our hearts, the Spirit *who* **c out**, "Abba, *G3189*
Gal 5: 8 does not come from the *one who* **c** you. *G2813*
1Th 2:12 who **c** you into his kingdom and glory. *G2813*
1Th 5:24 The *one who* **c** you is faithful, and he will *G2813*
Rev 2:20 woman Jezebel, who **c** herself a prophet. *G3306*
Rev 13:10 This **c for** patient endurance and *G1639*
Rev 13:18 This **c for** wisdom. Let the person who has *G1639*
Rev 14:12 This **c for** patient endurance on the part of *G1639*
Rev 17: 9 "This **c** for a mind with wisdom. The seven NDT

CALM (13) [CALMED, CALMNESS, CALMS]

2Ki 11:20 the city *was* **c**, because Athaliah had H9200
2Ch 23:21 the city *was* **c**, because Athaliah had H9200
Ps 107:30 They were glad when *it grew* **c**, and he H9284
Pr 29:11 their rage, but the wise **bring c** in the end. H8656
Isa 7: 4 'Be careful, *keep* **c** and don't be afraid. H9200
Eze 16:42 from you; *I will be* **c** and no longer angry. H9200
Jnh 1:11 do to you *to make* the sea **c down** for us?" H9284
Jnh 1:12 he replied, "and it *will become* **c**. H9284
Jnh 1:15 overboard, and the raging sea *grew* **c**. H6641
Mt 8:26 the waves, and it was completely **c**. *G1132*
Mk 4:39 wind died down and it was completely **c**. *G1132*
Lk 8:24 the storm subsided, and all was **c**. *G1132*
Ac 19:36 you ought *to* **c down** and not do *G2948+5639*

CALMED (2) [CALM]

Ne 8:11 The Levites **c** all the people, saying, "Be H3120
Ps 131: 2 But *I have* **c** and quieted myself, I am like H8750

CALMNESS (1) [CALM]

Ecc 10: 4 your post; **c** can lay great offenses to rest. H5341

CALMS (1) [CALM]

Pr 15:18 the one who is patient **c** a quarrel. H9200

CALNEH (NIV84) KALNEH

CALNO (NIV84) KALNO

CALVARY (KJV) SKULL

CALVE (1) [CALF]

Job 21:10 to breed; their cows **c** and do not miscarry. H7117

CALVED (1) [CALF]

1Sa 6: 7 with two cows *that have* **c** and have never H6402

CALVES (25) [CALF]

Dt 7:13 the **c** *of* your herds and the lambs of your H8715
Dt 28: 4 the **c** *of* your herds and the lambs of your H8715
Dt 28:18 the **c** *of* your herds and the lambs of H8715
Dt 28:51 any **c** *of* your herds or lambs of your H8715
1Sa 6: 7 take their **c** away and pen them up. H1201
1Sa 6:10 them to the cart and penned up their **c**. H1201
1Sa 14:32 sheep, cattle and **c**, they butchered H1201+1330
1Sa 15: 9 cattle, the **fat** *c* and lambs—everything AIT
1Ki 1: 9 cattle and **fattened c** at the Stone of H5309
1Ki 1:19 numbers of cattle, **fattened c**, and sheep, H5309
1Ki 1:25 numbers of cattle, **fattened c**, and sheep. H5309
1Ki 12:28 the king made two golden **c**. H6319
1Ki 12:32 sacrificing to the **c** he had made. H6319
2Ki 10:29 of the golden **c** at Bethel and Dan. H6319
2Ki 17:16 two idols cast in the **shape of c**, H6319
2Ch 13: 8 you the golden **c** that Jeroboam made H6319
Ps 68:30 herd of bulls among the **c** *of* the nations. H6319
Isa 27:10 there the **c** graze, there they lie H6319
Isa 34: 7 with them, the **bull c** and the great bulls. H7228
Jer 46:21 in her ranks are like fattened **c**. H6319
Am 6: 4 You dine on choice lambs and fattened **c**. H6319
Mic 6: 6 with burnt offerings, with **c** a year old? H6319
Mal 4: 2 you will go out and frolic like well-fed **c**. H6319
Heb 9:12 by means of the blood of goats and **c**; *G3675*
Heb 9:19 he took the blood *of* **c**, together with *G3675*

CAME (1204) [COME]

Ge 2: 6 streams **c up** from the earth and H6590
Ge 7: 6 old when the floodwaters **c** on the earth. H2118
Ge 7: 9 female, **c** to Noah and entered the ark H995
Ge 7:10 seven days the floodwaters **c** on the earth. H2118
Ge 7:15 of life in them **c** to Noah and entered H995
Ge 8: 4 month the ark **c to rest** on the mountains H5663
Ge 8:18 So Noah **c out**, together with his sons H3655
Ge 8:19 that moves on land—**c out** of the ark, one H3655
Ge 9:10 all *those that* **c out** *of* the ark with you H3655
Ge 9:18 sons of Noah who **c out** of the ark were H3655
Ge 9:19 from them **c** the people who were NDT
Ge 10:14 from whom the Philistines **c**) and H3655
Ge 11: 5 But the LORD **c down** to see the city and H3718
Ge 11:31 But when *they* **c** to Harran, they settled H995
Ge 12:14 When Abram **c** to Egypt, the Egyptians saw H995
Ge 13: 3 from place to place until he **c** to Bethel, NDT
Ge 14:13 *A man* who had escaped **c** and reported H995
Ge 14:17 the king of Sodom **c out** to meet him in H3655
Ge 15: 1 word of the LORD **c** to Abram in a vision H2118
Ge 15: 4 Then the word of the LORD **c** to him: "This NDT
Ge 15:11 Then birds of prey **c down** on the carcasses H3718
Ge 15:12 a thick and dreadful darkness **c** over him. H5877
Ge 19: 5 "Where are the men who **c** to you tonight? H995
Ge 19: 9 "This fellow **c** here as a foreigner, and now H995
Ge 20: 3 But God **c** to Abimelek in a dream one H995
Ge 24: 5 your son back to the country *you* **c** from?" H3655
Ge 24:15 Rebekah **c out** with her jar on her H3655
Ge 24:16 the spring, filled her jar and **c up** again. H6590
Ge 24:42 "When *I* **c** to the spring today, I said, 'LORD H995
Ge 24:45 my heart, Rebekah **c out**, with her jar on H3655
Ge 25:24 When the time **c** for her to give birth H4848
Ge 25:26 After this, his brother **c out**, with his hand H3655
Ge 25:29 some stew, Esau **c in** from the open country H995
Ge 26:32 day Isaac's servants **c** and told him about H995
Ge 27:30 his brother Esau **c in** from hunting. H995
Ge 27:33 ate it just before *you* **c** and I blessed him— H995
Ge 27:35 "Your brother **c** deceitfully and took your H995
Ge 29: 1 on his journey and **c** to the land of the H2143
Ge 29: 9 with them, Rachel **c** with her father's sheep H995
Ge 29:23 But when evening **c**, he took his daughter H2118
Ge 29:25 When morning **c**, there was Leah! So H2118
Ge 30:16 So when Jacob **c in** from the fields that H995
Ge 30:30 you had before I **c** has increased greatly, NDT
Ge 30:38 in front of the flocks *when they* **c** to drink. H995
Ge 30:38 the flocks were in heat and **c** to drink, H995
Ge 30:43 prosperous and **c** *to* **own** large flocks, AIT
Ge 31:24 Then God **c** to Laban the Aramean in a H995
Ge 31:33 After *he* **c out** of Leah's tent, he entered H3655
Ge 33: 7 Leah and her children **c** and bowed down. H5602
Ge 33: 7 Last of all **c** Joseph and Rachel, and they H5602
Ge 33:18 After Jacob **c** from Paddan Aram, he H995
Ge 34: 5 he did nothing about it until they **c home**. H995
Ge 34:27 The sons of Jacob **c** upon the dead bodies H995
Ge 35: 6 Jacob and all the people with him **c** to Luz H995
Ge 35:27 Jacob **c home** to his father Isaac in Mamre H995
Ge 37:23 So when Joseph **c** to his brothers, they H995
Ge 37:28 So when the Midianite merchants **c by** H6296
Ge 37:35 his sons and daughters **c** to comfort him, H7756
Ge 38:27 When the time **c** for her to give birth H2118
Ge 38:28 on his wrist and said, "This one **c out** first." H3655
Ge 38:29 his hand, his brother **c out**, and she said, H3655
Ge 38:30 had the scarlet thread on his wrist, **c out**. H3655
Ge 39:14 *He* **c** in here to sleep with me, but I H995
Ge 39:16 cloak beside her until his master **c** home. H995
Ge 39:17 slave you brought us **c** to me to make sport H995
Ge 40: 6 When Joseph **c** to them the next morning H995
Ge 41: 2 out of the river *there* **c up** seven cows, H6590
Ge 41: 3 **c up** out of the Nile and stood beside H6590
Ge 41:14 changed his clothes, *he* **c** before Pharaoh. H995
Ge 41:18 out of the river *there* **c up** seven cows, H6590
Ge 41:19 seven other cows **c up**—scrawny and very H6590
Ge 41:20 ate up the seven fat cows that **c** up first. NDT
Ge 41:27 ugly cows that **c up** afterward are seven H6590
Ge 41:50 Before the years of famine **c**, two sons were H995
Ge 41:53 years of abundance in Egypt **c to an end**, H3983
Ge 41:57 And all the world **c** to Egypt to buy grain H995
Ge 42:24 then **c back** and spoke to them again. H8740
Ge 42:29 When *they* **c** to their father Jacob in the H995
Ge 43:20 "*we* **c down** here the first time to H3718+3718
Ge 43:26 When Joseph **c** home, they presented to H995
Ge 43:31 washed his face, *he* **c out** and, controlling H3655
Ge 44:14 house when Judah and his brothers **c** in, H995
Ge 45:25 and **c** to their father Jacob *in* the land H995
Ge 47:15 was gone, all Egypt **c** to Joseph and said H995
Ge 47:18 *they* **c** to him the following year and said H995
Ge 48: 5 you in Egypt before I **c** to you here will be H995
Ge 50:17 When their **message c** to him, Joseph H1819

Ge 50:18 His brothers then **c** and threw themselves H2143
Ex 1: 8 meant nothing, **c to power** in Egypt. H7756
Ex 1:12 so the Egyptians *c to* **dread** the Israelites AIT
Ex 2:16 and *they* **c** to draw water and fill the H995
Ex 2:17 Some shepherds **c along** and drove them H995
Ex 2:17 got up and **c to** their **rescue** and watered H3828
Ex 3: 1 far side of the wilderness and **c** to Horeb, H995
Ex 8: 6 the frogs **c up** and covered the land. H6590
Ex 8:17 ground, gnats **c** on people and animals. H2118
Ex 13: 3 this day, the day *you* **c out** of Egypt, out of H3655
Ex 13: 8 the LORD did for me when I **c out** of Egypt. H3655
Ex 15:23 When *they* **c** to Marah, they could not drink H995
Ex 15:27 Then *they* **c** to Elim, where there were H995
Ex 16: 1 out from Elim and **c** to the Desert of Sin, H995
Ex 16:13 That evening quail **c** and covered the H6590
Ex 16:22 of the community **c** and reported this to H995
Ex 16:35 until they **c** to a land that was settled H995
Ex 17: 8 The Amalekites **c** and attacked the H995
Ex 18: 5 sons and wife, **c** to him in the wilderness H995
Ex 18:12 Aaron **c** with all the elders of Israel to H995
Ex 19: 1 that very day—*they* **c** *to* the Desert of Sinai. H995
Ex 23:15 for in that month *you* **c out** of Egypt. H3655
Ex 32:24 I threw it into the fire, and **out c** this calf!" H3655
Ex 34: 5 Then the LORD **c down** in the cloud and H3718
Ex 34:18 for in that month *you* **c out** of Egypt. H3655
Ex 34:29 When Moses **c down** from Mount Sinai H3718
Ex 34:31 leaders of the community **c back** to him, H8740
Ex 34:32 Afterward all the Israelites **c near** him, and H5602
Ex 34:34 he removed the veil until he **c out**. H3655
Ex 34:34 And when *he* **c out** and told the Israelites H3655
Ex 35:21 whose heart moved them **c** and brought an H995
Ex 35:22 **c** and brought gold jewelry of all kinds: H995
Lev 9: 5 entire assembly **c near** and stood before H7928
Lev 9: 8 So Aaron **c** to the altar and slaughtered H7928
Lev 9:23 When *they* **c out**, they blessed the people; H3655
Lev 9:24 Fire **c out** from the presence of the LORD H3655
Lev 10: 2 So fire **c out** from the presence of the LORD H3655
Lev 10: 5 So *they* **c** and carried them, still in their H7928
Lev 18:30 practiced before you **c** and do not defile NDT
Nu 1: 1 year after the Israelites **c out** of Egypt. H3655
Nu 4:35 fifty years of age who **c** to serve in the work H995
Nu 4:39 fifty years of age who **c** to serve in the work H995
Nu 4:43 fifty years of age who **c** to serve in the work H995
Nu 4:47 fifty years of age who **c** to do the work of H995
Nu 7:87 the burnt offering **c** to twelve young bulls, NDT
Nu 7:88 fellowship offering **c** to twenty-four oxen, NDT
Nu 8:22 the Levites **c** to do their work at the tent of H995
Nu 9: 1 the second year after they **c out** of Egypt. H3655
Nu 9: 6 So *they* **c** to Moses and Aaron that same H7928
Nu 10:12 until the cloud **c to rest** in the Desert of H8905
Nu 10:36 Whenever it **c to rest**, he said, "Return H5663
Nu 11: 9 camp at night, the manna also **c down**. H3718
Nu 11:25 Then the LORD **c down** in the cloud and H3718
Nu 12: 5 Then the LORD **c down** in a pillar of cloud H3718
Nu 13:22 up through the Negev and **c** to Hebron, H995
Nu 13:26 *They* **c back** to Moses and H2143+2256+995
Nu 14:45 that hill country **c down** and attacked H3718
Nu 16: 3 *They* **c as a group** to oppose Moses and H7735
Nu 16:35 And fire **c out** from the LORD and H3655
Nu 20:20 Then Edom **c out** against them with a H3655
Nu 20:22 set out from Kadesh and **c** to Mount Hor. H995
Nu 20:28 Moses and Eleazar **c down** from the H3718
Nu 21: 7 The people **c** to Moses and said, "We H995
Nu 22: 7 When *they* **c** to Balaam, they told him what H995
Nu 22: 9 God **c** to Balaam and asked, "Who are H995
Nu 22:16 *They* **c** to Balaam and said: "This is what H995
Nu 22:20 That night God **c** to Balaam and said H995
Nu 24: 2 tribe by tribe, the Spirit of God **c** on him H2118
Nu 25:18 killed when the plague **c** as a result of that NDT
Nu 26: 4 were the Israelites who **c out** of Egypt: H3655
Nu 27: 1 Milkah and Tirzah. *They* **c forward** H7928
Nu 30:12 pledges that **c from** her lips will stand H4604
Nu 32: 2 So they **c** to Moses and Eleazar the priest H995
Nu 32:11 old or more *when* they **c up** out of Egypt H6590
Nu 32:16 Then *they* **c up** to him and said, "We H5602
Nu 33: 1 the Israelites when *they* **c out** of Egypt by H3655
Nu 33:38 year after the Israelites **c out** of Egypt. H3655
Nu 36: 1 **c** and spoke before Moses and the H7928
Dt 1:22 Then all of you **c** to me and said, "Let us H7928
Dt 1:24 **c** to the Valley of Eshkol and explored H995
Dt 1:44 who lived in those hills **c out** against you; H3655
Dt 1:45 *You* **c back** and wept before the LORD, but H8740
Dt 2:32 all his army **c out** to meet us in battle H3655
Dt 4:11 *You* **c near** and stood at the foot of the H7928
Dt 4:45 gave them when they **c out** of Egypt H3655
Dt 4:46 the Israelites as they **c out** of Egypt. H3655
Dt 5:23 of your tribes and your elders **c** to me. H7928
Dt 10: 5 Then *I* **c back** down the mountain and put the AIT
Dt 23: 4 on your way when you **c out** of Egypt, H3655
Dt 24: 9 along the way after you **c out** of Egypt. H3655
Dt 25:17 along the way when you **c out** of Egypt. H3655
Dt 29: 7 Og king of Bashan **c out** to fight against H3655
Dt 31:14 So Moses and Joshua **c** and presented H2143
Dt 32:44 Moses **c** with Joshua son of Nun and spoke H995
Dt 33: 2 "The LORD **c** from Sinai and dawned over H995
Dt 33: 2 *He* **c** with myriads of holy ones from the H910
Jos 2: 3 out the men who **c** to you and entered H995
Jos 2: 4 the men **c** to me, but I did not know H995
Jos 2:10 Red Sea for you when you **c out** of Egypt, H3655
Jos 2:23 forded the river and **c** to Joshua son of Nun H995
Jos 4:11 the priests **c to the other side** while the H6296
Jos 4:18 And the priests **c up** out of the river H6590
Jos 5: 4 All those who **c out** of Egypt—all the men H3655
Jos 5: 5 All the people that **c out** had been H3655
Jos 6: 1 No one went out and no *one* **c in**. H995
Jos 7:17 The clans of Judah **c forward**, and the H7928
Jos 8:22 in the ambush also **c out** of the city H3655
Jos 9: 2 *they* **c together** to wage war against H7695+3481
Jos 9:17 set out and on the third day **c** to their cities: H995
Jos 10:24 So *they* **c forward** and placed their feet on H7928
Jos 11: 4 They **c out** with all their troops and a large H3655
Jos 11: 7 his whole army **c** against them H995
Jos 15: 7 of En Shemesh and **c** out at En Rogel. H2118
Jos 15: 9 **c** out at the towns of Mount Ephron and H3655
Jos 15:18 One day when she **c** to Othniel, she urged H995
Jos 16: 7 touched Jericho and **c out** at the Jordan. H3655
Jos 18:11 The first lot **c up** for the tribe of Benjamin H6590
Jos 18:14 the western side and **c** out at Kiriath Baal H2118
Jos 18:15 the boundary **c out** at the spring of H3655
Jos 18:19 of Beth Hoglah and **c** out at the northern H2118
Jos 19: 1 The second lot **c out** for the tribe of H3655
Jos 19:10 The third lot **c up** for Zebulun according to H6590
Jos 19:13 *it* **c out** at Rimmon and turned toward H3655
Jos 19:17 The fourth lot **c out** for Issachar according H3655
Jos 19:24 The fifth lot **c out** for the tribe of Asher H3655
Jos 19:29 turned toward Hosah and **c** out at the H2118
Jos 19:32 The sixth lot **c out** for Naphtali according H3655
Jos 19:34 Aznoth Tabor and **c out** at Hukkok. H3655
Jos 19:40 The seventh lot **c out** for the tribe of Dan H3655
Jos 21: 4 The first lot **c out** *for* the Kohathites H3655
Jos 21:19 of Aaron, **c** to thirteen, together NDT
Jos 21:33 towns of the Gershonite clans **c** to thirteen, NDT
Jos 21:40 who were the rest of the Levites, **c** to twelve. NDT
Jos 22:10 When *they* **c** to Geliloth near the Jordan in H995
Jos 24: 6 out of Egypt, *you* **c** to the sea, and the H995
Jos 24:11 you crossed the Jordan and **c** to Jericho. H995
Jdg 1:14 One day when she **c** *to* Othniel, she urged H995
Jdg 3:10 The Spirit of the LORD **c** on him, so that he H2118
Jdg 3:13 to join him, Eglon **c** and attacked Israel H2143
Jdg 3:24 the servants **c** and found the doors of the H995
Jdg 3:31 After Ehud **c** Shamgar son of Anath, who H2118
Jdg 4:22 Just then Barak **c by in pursuit** *of* Sisera H8103
Jdg 5: 8 new leaders when war **c** to the city gates, NDT
Jdg 5:13 "The remnant of the nobles **c down**; the H3718
Jdg 5:13 of the LORD **c down** to me against the H3718
Jdg 5:14 Some **c** from Ephraim, whose roots were in NDT
Jdg 5:14 From Makir captains **c down**, from H3718
Jdg 5:19 "Kings **c**, they fought, the kings of Canaan H995
Jdg 6: 5 They **c up** with their livestock and their H6590
Jdg 6:11 angel of the LORD **c** and sat down under H995
Jdg 6:34 Then the Spirit of the LORD **c on** Gideon H4252
Jdg 7:13 of barley bread **c tumbling** into the H2200
Jdg 8: 4 the pursuit, **c** to the Jordan and crossed it. H995
Jdg 8:15 Then Gideon **c** and said to the men of H995
Jdg 8:26 rings he asked for **c to** seventeen hundred H2118
Jdg 9:35 his troops **c out** from their hiding H7756
Jdg 9:57 of Jotham son of Jerub-Baal **c** on them. H995
Jdg 11:13 "When Israel **c up** out of Egypt, they took H6590
Jdg 11:16 But when they **c up** out of Egypt, Israel H6590
Jdg 11:29 Then the Spirit of the LORD **c** on Jephthah H2118
Jdg 13: 6 told him, "A man of God **c** to me. H995
Jdg 13: 6 I didn't ask him where he **c** from, and he NDT
Jdg 13: 9 the angel of God **c** again to the woman H995
Jdg 13:11 When *he* **c** to the man, he said, "Are you H995
Jdg 14: 5 a young lion **c** roaring **toward** him. H7925
Jdg 14: 6 of the LORD **c powerfully** upon him so that H7502
Jdg 14:19 Spirit of the LORD **c powerfully** upon him. H7502
Jdg 15:14 the Philistines **c toward** him shouting. H7925
Jdg 15:14 Spirit of the LORD **c powerfully** upon him. H7502
Jdg 15:19 hollow place in Lehi, and water **c out** of it. H3655
Jdg 16:30 and **down c** the temple on the rulers and H5877
Jdg 17: 8 On his way *he* **c** to Micah's house in the H995
Jdg 18: 2 of Ephraim and **c** to the house of Micah, NDT
Jdg 18: 7 So the five men left and **c** to Laish, where H995
Jdg 18:13 country of Ephraim and **c** to Micah's house. H995
Jdg 19:16 **c in** from his work in the fields. H995
Jdg 19:22 out the man who **c** to your house so we H995
Jdg 19:30 the day the Israelites **c up** out of Egypt. H6590
Jdg 20: 1 the land of Gilead **c together** as one and H3655
Jdg 20: 4 "I and my concubine **c** to Gibeah in H995
Jdg 20: 5 the men of Gibeah **c** after me and H7756
Jdg 20:14 their towns they **c together** at Gibeah to H665
Jdg 20:21 The Benjamites **c out** of Gibeah and cut H3655
Jdg 20:25 the Benjamites **c out** from Gibeah to H3655
Jdg 20:31 The Benjamites **c out** to meet them and H3655
Jdg 20:42 And the Israelites who **c** out of the towns cut NDT
Jdg 20:48 All the towns they **c across** they set on fire. H5162
Ru 1:19 women went on until they **c** *to* Bethlehem. H995
Ru 2: 6 the Moabite who **c back** from Moab with H8740
Ru 2: 7 *She* **c into** the field and has remained H995
Ru 2:11 your homeland and **c** to live with a H2143
Ru 3:14 know that a woman **c** *to* the threshing floor." H995
Ru 3:16 When Ruth **c** to her mother-in-law, Naomi H995
Ru 4: 1 he had mentioned **c along**. H6296
1Sa 1: 4 Whenever the day **c** for Elkanah to H2118
1Sa 2:14 treated all the Israelites who **c** to Shiloh. H995
1Sa 2:27 Now a man of God **c** to Eli and said to him H995
1Sa 3:10 The LORD **c** and stood there, calling as at H995
1Sa 4: 1 And Samuel's word **c** to all Israel. H2118
1Sa 4: 5 ark of the LORD's covenant **c** into the camp, H995
1Sa 6:14 The cart **c** to the field of Joshua of Beth H995
1Sa 7: 1 men of Kiriath Jearim **c** and took up the ark H995
1Sa 7: 7 of the Philistines **c up** to attack them. H6590
1Sa 8: 4 together and **c** to Samuel at Ramah. H995
1Sa 9:15 Now the day before Saul **c**, the LORD had H995
1Sa 9:25 After *they* **c down** from the high place to H3718
1Sa 10:10 the Spirit of God **c powerfully** upon him H7502
1Sa 11: 4 the messengers **c** *to* Gibeah of Saul and H995
1Sa 11: 6 the Spirit of God **c powerfully** upon him H7502
1Sa 11: 7 people, and *they* **c out together** as one. H3655
1Sa 15: 2 waylaid them as they **c up** from Egypt. H6590
1Sa 15: 6 the Israelites when they **c up** out of Egypt." H6590
1Sa 15:10 Then the word of the LORD **c** to Samuel: H2118
1Sa 15:32 Agag **c** to him in chains H2143
1Sa 16:13 of the LORD **c powerfully** upon David. H7502
1Sa 16:21 David **c** to Saul and entered his service H995
1Sa 16:23 Whenever the spirit from God **c** on Saul H2118
1Sa 17: 4 from Gath, **c out** of the Philistine camp. H3655
1Sa 17:16 the Philistine **c forward** every morning H5602
1Sa 17:28 *you* **c down** only to watch the battle." H3718
1Sa 17:34 When a lion or a bear **c** and carried off a H995
1Sa 18: 6 the women **c out** from all the towns of H3655
1Sa 18:10 evil spirit from God **c forcefully** on Saul. H7502
1Sa 18:19 So when the time **c** for Merab, Saul's H2118
1Sa 19: 9 spirit from the LORD **c** on Saul as he was H2118
1Sa 19:19 **Word c** to Saul: "David is in Naioth at H5583
1Sa 19:20 the Spirit of God **c** on Saul's men, and H2118
1Sa 19:23 But the Spirit of God **c** even on him, and H2118
1Sa 19:23 along prophesying until he **c** to Naioth. H995
1Sa 20:24 when the New Moon feast **c**, the king H2118
1Sa 20:37 When the boy **c** to the place where H995
1Sa 22:11 priests at Nob, and they all **c** to the king. H995
1Sa 23:27 a messenger **c** to Saul, saying, "Come H995
1Sa 24: 3 *He* **c** to the sheep pens along the way; H995
1Sa 25:20 As she **c riding** her donkey into a H8206
1Sa 26:15 Someone **c** to destroy your lord the king H995
1Sa 28: 4 assembled and **c** and set up camp at H995
1Sa 28:21 When the woman **c** to Saul and saw that H995
1Sa 29: 6 From the day you **c** to me until today, H995
1Sa 29: 8 servant from the day *I* **c** to you until now? H2118
1Sa 30: 9 men with him **c** to the Besor Valley, H995
1Sa 30:21 Then David **c** to the two hundred men who H995
1Sa 30:21 *They* **c out** to meet David and the men H3655
1Sa 30:23 hands the raiding party that **c** against us. H995
1Sa 31: 7 And the Philistines **c** and occupied them. H995
1Sa 31: 8 when the Philistines **c** to strip the dead H995
2Sa 1: 2 When he **c** to David, he fell to the ground H995
2Sa 2: 4 Then the men of Judah **c** to Hebron, and H995
2Sa 2:23 the spear **c out** through his back. H3655
2Sa 2:23 man stopped when he **c** to the place where H995
2Sa 2:24 was setting, they **c** to the hill of Ammah H995
2Sa 2:28 all the troops **c to a halt**; they no H6641
2Sa 2:29 the morning hours and **c** *to* Mahanaim. H995
2Sa 3:20 twenty men with him, **c** to David at Hebron H995
2Sa 3:24 Look, Abner **c** to you. Why did you H995
2Sa 3:25 *he* **c** to deceive you and observe your H995
2Sa 3:35 Then they all **c** and urged David to eat H995
2Sa 4: 4 about Saul and Jonathan **c** from Jezreel. H995
2Sa 5: 1 the tribes of Israel **c** to David at Hebron H995
2Sa 5:22 the Philistines **c up** and spread out in H6590
2Sa 6: 6 When *they* **c** to the threshing floor of H995
2Sa 6:20 daughter of Saul **c out** to meet him and H3655
2Sa 7: 4 night the word of the LORD **c** to Nathan, H2118
2Sa 8: 5 of Damascus **c** to help Hadadezer H995
2Sa 9: 6 the son of Saul, **c** to David, he bowed H995
2Sa 10: 2 When David's men **c** *to* the land of the H995
2Sa 10: 8 The Ammonites **c out** and drew up in H3655
2Sa 10:14 the Ammonites and **c** *to* Jerusalem. H995
2Sa 11: 4 *She* **c** to him, and he slept H995
2Sa 11: 7 When Uriah **c** to him, David asked him how H995
2Sa 11:17 men of the city **c out** and fought against H3655
2Sa 11:23 us and **c out** against us in the H3655
2Sa 12: 1 When *he* **c** to him, he said, "There were H995
2Sa 12: 4 "Now a traveler **c** to the rich man, but the H995
2Sa 13: 6 When the king **c** to see him, Amnon said H995
2Sa 13:30 were on their way, the report **c** to David: H995
2Sa 13:36 the king's sons **c in**, wailing loudly. H995
2Sa 14:33 and he **c** in and bowed down with his face H995
2Sa 15: 2 Whenever anyone **c** with a complaint to H2118
2Sa 15: 6 the Israelites who **c** to the king asking for H995
2Sa 15:13 A messenger **c** and told David, "The hearts H995
2Sa 15:20 You **c** only yesterday. And today shall I H995
2Sa 16: 5 clan as Saul's family **c out** from there. H3655
2Sa 16: 5 of Gera, and he cursed *as he* **c out**. H3655+3655
2Sa 16:15 all the men of Israel **c** *to* Jerusalem, H995
2Sa 17: 6 When Hushai **c** to him, Absalom said H995
2Sa 17:20 When Absalom's men **c** to the woman at H995
2Sa 17:27 When David **c** to Mahanaim, Shobi son of H995
2Sa 18:25 And the runner **c** closer and closer. H2143
2Sa 19: 8 in the gateway," they all **c** before him. H995
2Sa 19:25 When *he* **c** *from* Jerusalem to meet the king H995
2Sa 19:31 Gileadite also **c down** from Rogelim to H3718
2Sa 20: 8 rock in Gibeon, Amasa **c** to meet them. H995
2Sa 20:12 saw that all the troops **c to a halt** there. H6641
2Sa 20:12 that everyone who **c** up to Amasa stopped, H995
2Sa 20:15 the troops with Joab **c** and besieged Sheba H995
2Sa 21:17 son of Zeruiah **c to** David's **rescue**; H6468
2Sa 22: 7 he heard my voice; my cry **c** to his ears. NDT
2Sa 22: 9 consuming fire **c** from his mouth, burning NDT
2Sa 22:10 He parted the heavens and **c down**; dark H3718
2Sa 23:13 thirty chief warriors **c** down to David at the H995
2Sa 24: 8 *they* **c back** *to* Jerusalem at the end of nine H995
1Ki 1:28 So *she* **c** into the king's presence and stood H995
1Ki 1:32 When *they* **c** before the king, H995
1Ki 1:53 And Adonijah **c** and bowed down to King H995
1Ki 2: 8 When he **c down** to meet me at the H3718

1Ki 3:16 Now two prostitutes c to the king and stood H995
1Ki 4:27 Solomon and all who c to the king's table H7929
1Ki 4:34 all nations people c to listen to Solomon's H995
1Ki 6: 1 year after the Israelites c out of Egypt, H3655
1Ki 6:11 The word of the LORD c to Solomon: H2118
1Ki 7:14 He c to King Solomon and did all the work H995
1Ki 8: 2 the Israelites c together to King Solomon H7735
1Ki 8: 9 the Israelites after they c out of Egypt. H3655
1Ki 10: 1 she c to test Solomon with hard questions. H995
1Ki 10: 2 she c to Solomon and talked with him H995
1Ki 10: 7 these things until I c and saw with my own H995
1Ki 10:25 everyone who c brought a gift—articles NDT
1Ki 12:22 this word of God c to Shemaiah the man H2118
1Ki 12:30 the people c to worship the one at Bethel H2143
1Ki 13: 1 LORD a man of God c from Judah to Bethel, H995
1Ki 13: 9 drink water or return by the way you c. H2143
1Ki 13:11 whose sons c and told him all that the man H995
1Ki 13:14 you the man of God who c from Judah?" H995
1Ki 13:17 water there or return by the way you c. H2143
1Ki 13:20 the word of the LORD c to the old prophet H2118
1Ki 13:22 You c back and ate bread and drank water H8740
1Ki 16: 1 the word of the LORD c to Jehu son of H2118
1Ki 16: 7 the word of the LORD c through the prophet H2118
1Ki 16:10 Zimri c in, struck him down and killed him H995
1Ki 17: 2 Then the word of the LORD c to Elijah: H2118
1Ki 17: 8 Then the word of the LORD c to him: H2118
1Ki 17:10 When he c to the town gate, a widow was H995
1Ki 18: 1 third year, the word of the LORD c to Elijah: H2118
1Ki 18:30 They c to him, and he repaired the altar H5602
1Ki 18:46 The power of the LORD c on Elijah and H2118
1Ki 19: 3 When he c to Beersheba in Judah, he left H995
1Ki 19: 4 He c to a broom bush, sat down under it H995
1Ki 19: 7 angel of the LORD c back a second time H8740
1Ki 19: 9 And the word of the LORD c to him: "What H606
1Ki 19:12 After the earthquake c a fire, but the LORD NDT
1Ki 19:12 And after the fire c a gentle whisper. NDT
1Ki 19:15 "Go back the way you c, and go to the NDT
1Ki 20: 5 The messengers c again and said, "This H8740
1Ki 20:13 Meanwhile a prophet c to Ahab king of H5602
1Ki 20:22 the prophet c to the king of Israel and H5602
1Ki 20:28 The man of God c up and told the king of H5602
1Ki 20:33 When Ben-Hadad c out, Ahab had him H3655
1Ki 20:39 someone c to me with a captive and H995
1Ki 21: 5 His wife Jezebel c in and asked him, "Why H995
1Ki 21:13 Then two scoundrels c and sat opposite him H995
1Ki 21:17 the word of the LORD c to Elijah the H2118
1Ki 21:28 the word of the LORD c to Elijah the H2118
1Ki 22:21 a spirit c forward, stood before the H3655
2Ki 1: 6 "A man c to meet us," they replied. H6590
2Ki 1: 7 of man was it who c to meet you and told H6590
2Ki 2: 3 prophets at Bethel c out to Elisha and H3655
2Ki 2:23 some boys c out of the town and jeered at H3655
2Ki 2:24 Then two bears c out of the woods and H3655
2Ki 3:15 playing, the hand of the LORD c on Elisha H2118
2Ki 3:24 when the Moabites c to the camp of Israel H995
2Ki 4: 8 So whenever he c by, he stopped there to H6296
2Ki 4:11 One day when Elisha c, he went up to his H995
2Ki 4:25 So she set out and c to the man of God at H995
2Ki 4:27 Gehazi c over to push her away, but the H5602
2Ki 4:36 When she c, he said, "Take H995
2Ki 4:37 She c in, fell at his feet and bowed to the H995
2Ki 4:42 A man c from Baal Shalishah, bringing the H995
2Ki 5:24 When Gehazi c to the hill, he took the H995
2Ki 6:13 The report c back: "He is in H5583
2Ki 6:18 As the enemy c down toward him, Elisha H3718
2Ki 6:33 to them, the messenger c down to him. H3718
2Ki 7:17 when the king c down to his house. H3718
2Ki 8: 3 seven years she c back from the land of H8740
2Ki 8: 5 brought back to life c to appeal to the king NDT
2Ki 9:19 When he c to them he said, "This is what H995
2Ki 10:15 he c upon Jehonadab son of Rekab H5162
2Ki 10:17 When Jehu c to Samaria, he killed all who H995
2Ki 10:21 all the servants of Baal c; not one H995
2Ki 11: 9 off duty—and c to Jehoiada the priest. H995
2Ki 12:10 the royal secretary and the high priest c H6590
2Ki 13:21 the man c to life and stood up on his feet. H2649
2Ki 14: 9 beast in Lebanon c along and trampled H6296
2Ki 15:29 king of Assyria c and took Ijon, H995
2Ki 16:12 When the king c back from Damascus and H995
2Ki 17: 3 king of Assyria c up to attack Hoshea, H6590
2Ki 17:28 exiled from Samaria c to live in Bethel H995
2Ki 18:17 They c up to Jerusalem and stopped at the H995
2Ki 19: 5 When King Hezekiah's officials c to Isaiah, H995
2Ki 19:28 I will make you return by the way you c. H995
2Ki 19:33 By the way that he c he will return; he will H995
2Ki 20: 4 the word of the LORD c to him: H2118
2Ki 20:14 Hezekiah replied. "They c from Babylon." H995
2Ki 21:15 day their ancestors c out of Egypt until this H3655
2Ki 23:17 of the man of God who c from Judah and H995
2Ki 24:11 Nebuchadnezzar himself c up to the city H995
2Ki 25: 8 of the king of Babylon, c to Jerusalem. H995
2Ki 25:23 as governor, they c to Gedaliah at Mizpah H995
2Ki 25:25 c with ten men and assassinated Gedaliah H995
1Ch 1:12 from whom the Philistines c) and H3655
1Ch 2:55 are the Kenites who c from Hammath, H995
1Ch 4:41 names were listed c in the days of H995
1Ch 5: 2 of his brothers and a ruler c from him, NDT
1Ch 6:31 of the LORD after the ark c to rest there. H4955
1Ch 6:60 among the Kohathite clans c to thirteen. NDT
1Ch 7:22 and his relatives c to comfort him. H995
1Ch 10: 7 And the Philistines c and occupied them. H995
1Ch 10: 8 when the Philistines c to strip the dead H995
1Ch 11: 1 All Israel c together to David at Hebron H7695
1Ch 11:15 of the thirty chiefs c down to David to the H3718
1Ch 12: 1 These were the men who c to David at H995
1Ch 12:16 and some men from Judah also c to David H995
1Ch 12:18 Then the Spirit c on Amasai, chief of the H4252
1Ch 12:22 Day after day men c to help David, until he H995
1Ch 12:23 armed for battle who c to David at Hebron H995
1Ch 12:38 They c to Hebron fully determined to make H995
1Ch 12:40 Naphtali c bringing food on donkeys, H995
1Ch 13: 9 When they c to the threshing floor of Kidon, H995
1Ch 17: 3 that night the word of God c to Nathan, H2118
1Ch 18: 5 of Damascus c to help Hadadezer H995
1Ch 19: 2 When David's envoys c to Hanun in the H995
1Ch 19: 5 When someone c and told David about H2143
1Ch 19: 7 who c and camped near Medeba H995
1Ch 19: 9 The Ammonites c out and drew up in H3655
1Ch 21: 4 Israel and then c back to Jerusalem. H995
1Ch 22: 8 But this word of the LORD c to me: 'You H2118
1Ch 27:24 God's wrath c on Israel on account of this H2118
2Ch 5: 3 all the Israelites c together to the king at H7735
2Ch 5:10 the Israelites after they c out of Egypt. H3655
2Ch 7: 1 fire c down from heaven and consumed H3718
2Ch 9: 1 she c to Jerusalem to test him with hard H995
2Ch 9: 1 she c to Solomon and talked with him H995
2Ch 9: 6 they said until I c and saw with my own H995
2Ch 9:24 everyone who c brought a gift—articles NDT
2Ch 11: 2 word of the LORD c to Shemaiah the man H2118
2Ch 11:14 property and c to Judah and H2143
2Ch 12: 3 Cushites that c with him from Egypt, H995
2Ch 12: 4 cities of Judah and c as far as Jerusalem. H995
2Ch 12: 5 prophet Shemaiah c to Rehoboam and to H995
2Ch 12: 7 this word of the LORD c to Shemaiah: H2118
2Ch 14: 9 chariots, and c as far as Mareshah. H995
2Ch 15: 1 The Spirit of God c on Azariah son of H2118
2Ch 16: 7 Hanani the seer c to Asa king of Judah H995
2Ch 18:20 a spirit c forward, stood before the H3655
2Ch 20: 1 of the Meunites c to wage war against H995
2Ch 20: 2 Some people c and told Jehoshaphat, "A H995
2Ch 20: 4 people of Judah c together to seek help H7695
2Ch 20: 4 they c from every town in Judah to seek H995
2Ch 20:10 Israel to invade when they c from Egypt; H995
2Ch 20:14 the Spirit of the LORD c on Jahaziel son of H2118
2Ch 20:24 When the men of Judah c to the place that H995
2Ch 20:29 The fear of God c on all the surrounding H2118
2Ch 21:19 his bowels c out because of the disease H3655
2Ch 22: 1 who c with the Arabs into the camp H995
2Ch 23: 2 When they c to Jerusalem, H995
2Ch 24:17 officials of Judah c and paid homage to H995
2Ch 24:18 God's anger c on Judah and Jerusalem. H2118
2Ch 24:20 the Spirit of God c on Zechariah son of H4252
2Ch 25: 7 But a man of God c to him and said, "Your H995
2Ch 25:18 beast in Lebanon c along and trampled H6296
2Ch 28:20 Tiglath-Pileser king of Assyria c to him, but H995
2Ch 30:18 of the many people who c from Ephraim, NDT
2Ch 31: 8 his officials c and saw the heaps, H995
2Ch 32: 1 king of Assyria c and invaded Judah. H995
2Ch 36:20 until the kingdom of Persia c to power. H4887
Ezr 1:11 the exiles when they c up from Babylon H6590
Ezr 2: 1 of the province who c up from the captivity H6590
Ezr 2:59 The following c up from the towns of Tel H6590
Ezr 3: 1 the seventh month c and the Israelites H5595
Ezr 4: 2 they c to Zerubbabel and to the heads of H5602
Ezr 4:12 that the people who c up to us from you A10513
Ezr 4:24 in Jerusalem c to a standstill until the A10098
Ezr 5:16 "So this Sheshbazzar c and laid the A10085
Ezr 7: 6 this Ezra c up from Babylon. He was a H6590
Ezr 7: 7 also c up to Jerusalem in the seventh year H6590
Ezr 8: 1 with them who c up with me from Babylon H6590
Ezr 9: 1 the leaders c to me and said, "The H5602
Ne 1: 2 c from Judah with some other men H995
Ne 4:12 who lived near them c and told us ten H995
Ne 4:21 the first light of dawn till the stars c out. H3655
Ne 5:17 as well as those who c to us from the H995
Ne 6: 1 When word c to Sanballat, Tobiah H9048
Ne 7: 6 of the province who c up from the captivity H6590
Ne 7:61 The following c up from the towns of Tel H6590
Ne 7:73 the seventh month c and the Israelites H5595
Ne 8: 1 all the people c together as one in the H665
Ne 9:13 "You c down on Mount Sinai; you spoke H3718
Ne 13: 7 and c back to Jerusalem. Here I learned H995
Ne 13:21 that time on they no longer c on the H995
Est 2:12 a young woman's turn c to go in to King H5595
Est 2:15 When the turn c for Esther (the young H5595
Est 4: 3 to which the edict and order of the king c, H5595
Est 4: 4 female attendants c and told her about H995
Est 8: 1 And Mordecai c into the presence of the H995
Est 8:17 every city to which the edict of the king c, H5595
Est 9:15 The Jews in Susa c together on the H7735
Est 9:25 But when the plot c to the king's attention H995
Job 1: 6 One day the angels c to present H995
Job 1: 6 the LORD, and Satan also c with them. H995
Job 1:14 a messenger c to Job and said, "The oxen H995
Job 1:16 another messenger c and said, "The fire of H995
Job 1:17 another messenger c and said, "The H995
Job 1:18 another messenger c and said, "Your H995
Job 1:21 "Naked I c from my mother's womb, and H3655
Job 2: 1 day the angels c to present themselves H995
Job 2: 1 Satan also c with them to present H995
Job 3:11 at birth, and die as I c from the womb? H3655
Job 30:26 I hoped for good, evil c; when I looked H995
Job 30:26 when I looked for light, then c darkness. H995
Job 31:29 gloated over the trouble that c to him— H5162
Job 42:11 known him before c and ate with him in H995
Ps 18: 6 my voice; my cry c before him, into his H995
Ps 18: 8 consuming fire c from his mouth, burning NDT
Ps 18: 9 He parted the heavens and c down; dark H3718
Ps 21: 3 You c to greet him with rich blessings H7709
Ps 33: 9 he spoke, and it c to be; he commanded, H2118
Ps 44:17 All this c upon us, though we had not H995
Ps 51: T the prophet Nathan c to him after David H995
Ps 105:19 till what he foretold c to pass, till the word H995
Ps 105:31 He spoke, and there c swarms of flies, and H995
Ps 105:34 the locusts c, grasshoppers without H995
Ps 106:32 and trouble c to Moses because of them H8317
Ps 106:33 and rash words c from Moses' lips. H1051
Ps 114: 1 When Israel c out of Egypt, Jacob from a H3655
Ps 116: 3 the anguish of the grave c over me; I was H5162
Ps 132: 6 we c upon it in the fields of Jaar: H5162
Ps 139:16 in your book before one of them c to be. NDT
Pr 7:10 Then out c a woman to meet him H7925
Pr 7:15 So I c out to meet you; I looked for you H3655
Pr 8:23 beginning, when the world c to be. H4946+7710
Ecc 2:14 I c to realize that the same fate overtakes AIT
Ecc 4:16 But those who c later were not pleased with NDT
Ecc 9:14 And a powerful king c against it H995
Ecc 12: 7 the dust returns to the ground it c from, H2118
Isa 11:16 was for Israel when they c up from Egypt. H6590
Isa 14:28 This prophecy c in the year King Ahaz H2118
Isa 20: 1 c to Ashdod and attacked and captured it H995
Isa 23: 3 On the great waters c the grain of the Shihor NDT
Isa 26:16 they c to you in their distress; when H7212
Isa 37: 5 When King Hezekiah's officials c to Isaiah, H995
Isa 37:29 I will make you return by the way you c. H995
Isa 37:34 By the way that he c he will return; he will H995
Isa 38: 4 Then the word of the LORD c to Isaiah: H2118
Isa 39: 3 "They c to me from Babylon. H995
Isa 48: 3 then suddenly I acted, and they c to pass. H995
Isa 50: 2 When I c, why was there no one? When I H995
Isa 64: 3 did not expect, you c down, and the H3718
Isa 66: 2 all these things, and so they c into being?" H2118
Jer 1: 2 The word of the LORD c to him in the H2118
Jer 1: 4 The word of the LORD c to me, saying, H2118
Jer 1:11 The word of the LORD c to me: "What do H2118
Jer 1:13 The word of the LORD c to me again H2118
Jer 2: 1 The word of the LORD c to me: H2118
Jer 2: 7 But you c and defiled my land and made H995
Jer 7: 1 is the word that c to Jeremiah from the H2118
Jer 11: 1 is the word that c to Jeremiah from the H2118
Jer 13: 3 word of the LORD c to me a second time: H2118
Jer 13: 8 Then the word of the LORD c to me: H2118
Jer 14: 1 of the LORD that c to Jeremiah concerning AIT
Jer 15:16 When your words c, I ate them; they were H5162
Jer 16: 1 Then the word of the LORD c to me: H2118
Jer 18: 1 is the word that c to Jeremiah from the H2118
Jer 18: 5 Then the word of the LORD c to me. H2118
Jer 21: 1 The word c to Jeremiah from the LORD H2118
Jer 24: 4 Then the word of the LORD c to me: H2118
Jer 25: 1 The word c to Jeremiah concerning all the H2118
Jer 26: 1 king of Judah, this word c from the LORD: H2118
Jer 27: 1 this word c to Jeremiah from the LORD: H2118
Jer 28:12 the word of the LORD c to Jeremiah: H2118
Jer 29:30 Then the word of the LORD c to Jeremiah: H2118
Jer 30: 1 is the word that c to Jeremiah from the H2118
Jer 31:19 repented; after I c to understand, I beat my AIT
Jer 32: 1 is the word that c to Jeremiah from the H2118
Jer 32: 6 "The word of the LORD c to me: H2118
Jer 32: 8 my cousin Hanamel c to me in the H995
Jer 32:23 They c in and took possession of it, but H995
Jer 32:26 Then the word of the LORD c to Jeremiah: H2118
Jer 33: 1 word of the LORD c to him a second time H2118
Jer 33:19 The word of the LORD c to Jeremiah: H2118
Jer 33:23 The word of the LORD c to Jeremiah: H2118
Jer 34: 1 this word c to Jeremiah from the LORD: H2118
Jer 34: 8 The word c to Jeremiah from the LORD H2118
Jer 34:12 Then the word of the LORD c to Jeremiah: H2118
Jer 35: 1 is the word that c to Jeremiah from the H2118
Jer 35:12 Then the word of the LORD c to Jeremiah H2118
Jer 36: 1 this word c to Jeremiah from the LORD: H2118
Jer 36:27 the word of the LORD c to Jeremiah: H2118
Jer 37: 6 the word of the LORD c to Jeremiah the H2118
Jer 39: 3 the king of Babylon c and took seats in the H995
Jer 39:15 the guard, the word of the LORD c to him: H2118
Jer 40: 1 The word c to Jeremiah from the LORD H2118
Jer 40: 8 they c to Gedaliah at Mizpah—Ishmael son H995
Jer 40:12 they all c back to the land of Judah, to H8740
Jer 40:13 in the open country c to Gedaliah at H995
Jer 41: 1 c with ten men to Gedaliah son of Ahikam H995
Jer 41: 5 cut themselves c from Shechem, H995
Jer 42: 7 later the word of the LORD c to Jeremiah. H2118
Jer 43: 8 the word of the LORD c to Jeremiah: H2118
Jer 44: 1 This word c to Jeremiah concerning all H2118
Jer 44:28 remnant of Judah who c to live in Egypt H995
Jer 46: 1 word of the LORD that c to Jeremiah the H2118
Jer 47: 1 word of the LORD that c to Jeremiah the H2118
Jer 49: 9 If grape pickers c to you, would they not H995
Jer 49: 9 If thieves c during the night, would they not NDT
Jer 49:34 word of the LORD that c to Jeremiah the H2118
Jer 52:12 served the king of Babylon, c to Jerusalem. H995
La 3:57 You c near when I called you, and you H7928
Eze 1: 3 the word of the LORD c to Ezekiel the H2118+2118
Eze 1:25 Then there c a voice from above the vault H2118
Eze 2: 2 the Spirit c into me and raised me to my H995
Eze 3:15 I c to the exiles who lived at Tel Aviv near H995
Eze 3:16 seven days the word of the LORD c to me: H2118

Eze 3:24 Then the Spirit **c** into me and raised me to H995
Eze 6: 1 The word of the LORD **c** to me: H2118
Eze 7: 1 The word of the LORD **c** to me: H2118
Eze 8: 1 hand of the Sovereign LORD **c** on me there. H5877
Eze 9: 2 *They* **c in** and stood beside the bronze altar H995
Eze 11: 5 Then the Spirit of the LORD **c** on me, and H5877
Eze 11:14 The word of the LORD **c** to me: H2118
Eze 12: 1 The word of the LORD **c** to me: H2118
Eze 12: 8 the morning the word of the LORD **c** to me: H2118
Eze 12:17 The word of the LORD **c** to me: H2118
Eze 12:21 The word of the LORD **c** to me: H2118
Eze 12:26 The word of the LORD **c** to me: H2118
Eze 13: 1 The word of the LORD **c** to me: H2118
Eze 14: 1 the elders of Israel **c** to me and sat down in H995
Eze 14: 2 Then the word of the LORD **c** to me: H2118
Eze 14:12 The word of the LORD **c** to me: H2118
Eze 15: 1 The word of the LORD **c** to me: H2118
Eze 16: 1 The word of the LORD **c** to me: H2118
Eze 17: 1 The word of the LORD **c** to me: H2118
Eze 17: 3 full plumage of varied colors **c** to Lebanon. H995
Eze 17:11 Then the word of the LORD **c** to me: H2118
Eze 18: 1 The word of the LORD **c** to me: H2118
Eze 19: 8 Then the nations **c** against him, those H5989
Eze 20: 1 the elders of Israel **c** to inquire of the LORD, H995
Eze 20: 2 Then the word of the LORD **c** to me: H2118
Eze 20:45 The word of the LORD **c** to me: H2118
Eze 21: 1 The word of the LORD **c** to me: H2118
Eze 21: 8 The word of the LORD **c** to me: H2118
Eze 21:18 The word of the LORD **c** to me: H2118
Eze 22: 1 The word of the LORD **c** to me: H2118
Eze 22:17 Then the word of the LORD **c** to me: H2118
Eze 22:23 Again the word of the LORD **c** to me: H2118
Eze 23: 1 The word of the LORD **c** to me: H2118
Eze 23:17 Then the Babylonians **c** to her, to the bed of H995
Eze 23:40 messengers for men *who* **c** from far away, H995
Eze 24: 1 tenth day, the word of the LORD **c** to me: H2118
Eze 24:15 The word of the LORD **c** to me: H2118
Eze 24:20 to them, "The word of the LORD **c** to me: H2118
Eze 25: 1 The word of the LORD **c** to me: H2118
Eze 26: 1 the month, the word of the LORD **c** to me: H2118
Eze 27: 1 The word of the LORD **c** to me: H2118
Eze 27: 9 sea and their sailors **c** alongside to trade H2118
Eze 28: 1 The word of the LORD **c** to me: H2118
Eze 28:11 The word of the LORD **c** to me: H2118
Eze 28:20 The word of the LORD **c** to me: H2118
Eze 29: 1 twelfth day, the word of the LORD **c** to me: H2118
Eze 29:17 the first day, the word of the LORD **c** to me: H2118
Eze 30: 1 The word of the LORD **c** to me: H2118
Eze 30:20 seventh day, the word of the LORD **c** to me: H2118
Eze 31: 1 the first day, the word of the LORD **c** to me: H2118
Eze 31:12 nations of the earth **c out** from under its H3718
Eze 32: 1 the first day, the word of the LORD **c** to me: H2118
Eze 32:17 the month, the word of the LORD **c** to me: H2118
Eze 33: 1 The word of the LORD **c** to me: H2118
Eze 33:21 escaped from Jerusalem **c** to me and said, H995
Eze 33:22 before the man **c** to me in the morning H995
Eze 33:23 Then the word of the LORD **c** to me: H2118
Eze 34: 1 The word of the LORD **c** to me: H2118
Eze 35: 1 The word of the LORD **c** to me: H2118
Eze 36:16 Again the word of the LORD **c** to me: H2118
Eze 37: 7 the bones **c together**, bone to bone. H7928
Eze 37:10 *they* **c to life** and stood up on their feet H2649
Eze 37:15 The word of the LORD **c** to me: H2118
Eze 38: 1 The word of the LORD **c** to me: H2118
Eze 43: 3 I had seen when he **c** to destroy the city H995
Da 1: 1 king of Babylon **c** *to* Jerusalem and H995
Da 2: 2 When *they* **c in** and stood before the king H995
Da 3: 8 astrologers **c forward** and denounced A10638
Da 3:26 Meshach and Abednego **c out** of the fire, A10485
Da 4: 7 astrologers and diviners **c**, I told them A10549
Da 4: 8 Daniel **c into** my presence and I told him A10549
Da 4:31 on his lips, a voice **c** from heaven, "This A10484
Da 5: 8 Then all the king's wise men **c in**, but A10549
Da 5:10 his nobles, **c** into the banquet hall. A10549
Da 6:20 When he **c near** the den, he called to A10638
Da 7: 3 from the others, **c up** out of the sea. A10513
Da 7: 8 a little one, *which* **c up** among them A10513
Da 7:20 head and about the other horn that **c up**, A10513
Da 7:22 the Ancient of Days **c** and pronounced A10085
Da 7:22 the time **c** when they possessed the A10413
Da 8: 5 horn between its eyes **c** from the west, H995
Da 8: 6 *It* **c** toward the two-horned ram I had seen H995
Da 8: 9 Out of one of them **c** another horn, which H3655
Da 8:17 As *he* **c** near the place where I was H995
Da 9:21 **c** to me in swift flight about the time of H5595
Da 10: 1 of the message **c** to him in a vision. NDT
Da 10:13 the chief princes, **c** to help me, because I H995
Hos 1: 1 of the LORD that **c** to Hosea son of Beeri H2118
Hos 2:15 as in the day she **c up** out of Egypt. H6590
Hos 9:10 But when they **c** *to* Baal Peor, they H995
Hos 12: 9 LORD your God *ever since* you *c* **out** of Egypt; AIT
Hos 13: 4 LORD your God *ever since* you *c* **out of** Egypt. AIT
Joel 1: 1 word of the LORD that **c** to Joel son of H2118
Ob 5 "If thieves **c** to you, if robbers in the night H995
Ob 5 If grape pickers **c** to you, would they not H995
Jnh 1: 1 The word of the LORD **c** to Jonah son of H2118
Jnh 3: 1 the word of the LORD **c** to Jonah a second H2118
Mic 1: 1 of the LORD that **c** to Micah of Moresheth H2118
Mic 7:15 "As in the days when you **c out** of Egypt, H3655
Hab 3: 3 God **c** from Teman, the Holy One from H995
Hab 3:13 *You* **c out** to deliver your people, to save H3655
Zep 1: 1 of the LORD that **c** to Zephaniah son of H2118
Hag 1: 1 the word of the LORD **c** through the prophet H2118
Hag 1: 3 the word of the LORD **c** through the prophet H2118
Hag 1:14 *They* **c** and began to work on the house of H995
Hag 2: 1 the word of the LORD **c** through the prophet H2118
Hag 2: 5 with you when you **c out** of Egypt. H3655
Hag 2:10 the word of the LORD **c** to the prophet H2118
Hag 2:16 When anyone **c** to a heap of twenty H995
Hag 2:20 word of the LORD **c** to Haggai a second H2118
Zec 1: 1 the word of the LORD **c** to the prophet H2118
Zec 1: 7 the word of the LORD **c** to the prophet H2118
Zec 2: 3 was leaving, another angel **c** to meet him H3655
Zec 4: 8 Then the word of the LORD **c** to me: H2118
Zec 5: 5 speaking to me **c forward** and said to me, H3655
Zec 6: 9 The word of the LORD **c** to me: H2118
Zec 7: 1 the word of the LORD **c** to Zechariah on the H2118
Zec 7: 4 the word of the LORD Almighty **c** to me: H2118
Zec 7: 8 the word of the LORD **c** again to Zechariah: H2118
Zec 8: 1 The word of the LORD Almighty **c** to me. H2118
Zec 8:18 The word of the LORD Almighty **c** to me. H2118
Mt 1:18 the birth of Jesus the Messiah **c about**: G1639
Mt 1:18 before they **c together**, she was found G5302
Mt 2: 1 Magi from the east **c** to Jerusalem G4134
Mt 3: 1 In those days John the Baptist **c** G4134
Mt 3:13 Then Jesus **c** from Galilee to the Jordan G4134
Mt 4: 3 The tempter **c** to him and said, "If you are G4665
Mt 4:11 left him, and angels **c** and attended him. G4665
Mt 5: 1 sat down. His disciples **c** to him, G4665
Mt 7:25 The rain **c down**, the streams rose, and the G2849
Mt 7:27 The rain **c down**, the streams rose, and the G2849
Mt 8: 1 *When* Jesus **c down** from the G2849
Mt 8: 2 A man with leprosy **c** and knelt before him G4665
Mt 8: 5 a centurion **c** to him, asking for G4665
Mt 8:14 *When* Jesus **c** into Peter's house, he saw G2262
Mt 8:16 *When* evening **c**, many who were G1181
Mt 8:19 a teacher of the law **c** to him and said, G4665
Mt 8:24 Suddenly a furious storm **c up** on the lake G1181
Mt 8:32 So they **c out** and went into the pigs, and G2002
Mt 9: 1 crossed over and **c** to his own town. G2262
Mt 9:10 sinners **c** and ate with him and G2262
Mt 9:14 Then John's disciples **c** and asked him G4665
Mt 9:18 a synagogue leader **c** and knelt before G2262
Mt 9:20 twelve years **c up** behind him and G4665
Mt 9:28 the blind men **c** to him, and he asked G4665
Mt 11:18 For John **c** neither eating nor drinking G2262
Mt 11:19 The Son of Man **c** eating and drinking G2262
Mt 12:42 for *she* **c** from the ends of the earth to G2262
Mt 13: 4 the path, and the birds **c** and ate it up. G2262
Mt 13: 6 But *when* the sun **c up**, the plants were G422
Mt 13:10 The disciples **c** to him and asked, "Why G4665
Mt 13:25 his enemy **c** and sowed weeds among the G2262
Mt 13:27 "The owner's servants **c** to him and said G4665
Mt 13:36 His disciples **c to** him and said, "Explain G4665
Mt 14:12 John's disciples **c** and took his body and G4665
Mt 14:15 the disciples **c** to him and said, "This is G4665
Mt 14:29 walked on the water and **c** toward Jesus. G2262
Mt 15: 1 teachers of the law **c to** Jesus from G4665
Mt 15:12 Then the disciples **c** to him and asked G4665
Mt 15:22 woman from that vicinity **c** *to* him, G2002
Mt 15:23 So his disciples **c to** him and urged him G4665
Mt 15:25 The *woman* **c** and knelt before him. G2262
Mt 15:30 Great crowds **c** to him, bringing the lame G4665
Mt 16: 1 Sadducees **c to** Jesus and tested him G4665
Mt 16:13 *When* Jesus **c** to the region of Caesarea G2262
Mt 17: 7 But Jesus **c** and touched them. "Get up," G4665
Mt 17:14 *When they* **c** to the crowd, a man G2262
Mt 17:18 the demon, and *it* **c out** of the boy, and G2002
Mt 17:19 Then the disciples **c to** Jesus in private G4665
Mt 17:22 *When* they **c together** in Galilee, he said G5370
Mt 17:24 temple tax **c** to Peter and asked, G4665
Mt 17:25 *When* Peter **c** into the house, Jesus was G2262
Mt 18: 1 time the disciples **c to** Jesus and asked, G4665
Mt 18:21 Then Peter **c to** Jesus and asked, "Lord G4665
Mt 19: 3 Some Pharisees **c to** him to test him. G4665
Mt 19:16 Just then a man **c up to** Jesus and asked G4665
Mt 20: 8 "*When* evening **c**, the owner of the G1181
Mt 20: 9 in the afternoon **c** and each received a G2262
Mt 20:10 So *when those* **c** who were hired first, they G2262
Mt 20:20 of Zebedee's sons **c to** Jesus with her G4665
Mt 21: 1 Jerusalem and **c** to Bethphage on the G2262
Mt 21:14 the lame **c** to him at the temple, G4665
Mt 21:23 the elders of the people **c to** him. G4665
Mt 21:32 For John **c** to you to show you the way of G2262
Mt 22:11 "But *when* the king **c in** to see the guests G1656
Mt 22:23 no resurrection, **c** to him with a question. G4665
Mt 24: 1 away *when* his disciples **c up to** him to G4665
Mt 24: 3 of Olives, the disciples **c to** him privately. G4665
Mt 24:39 until the flood **c** and took them all away G2262
Mt 25:11 "Later the others also **c**. 'Lord, Lord,' they G2262
Mt 25:22 "The man with two bags of gold also **c** G4665
Mt 25:24 man who had received one bag of gold **c**. G4665
Mt 25:36 I was in prison and you **c** to visit me. G2262
Mt 26: 7 a woman **c to** him with an alabaster jar of G4665
Mt 26:17 the disciples **c to** Jesus and asked G4665
Mt 26:20 *When* evening **c**, Jesus was reclining at G1181
Mt 26:43 *When he* **c back**, he again found them G2262
Mt 26:50 replied, "Do what *you* **c** *for*, friend." Then G4205
Mt 26:60 *though* many false witnesses **c forward**. G4665
Mt 26:60 came forward. Finally two **c forward** G4665
Mt 26:69 the courtyard, and a servant girl **c to** him. G4665
Mt 27:33 *They* **c** to a place called Golgotha (which G2262
Mt 27:45 the afternoon darkness **c** over all the land. G1181
Mt 27:53 *They* **c out** of the tombs after Jesus' G2002
Mt 27:57 *there* **c** a rich man from Arimathea G2262
Mt 28: 2 of the Lord **c down** from heaven and, G2849
Mt 28: 9 They **c to** him, clasped his feet and G4665
Mt 28:13 'His disciples **c** during the night and stole G2262
Mt 28:18 Then Jesus **c to** them and said, "All G4665
Mk 1: 9 At that time Jesus **c** from Nazareth in G2262
Mk 1:11 And a voice **c** from heaven: "You are my G1181
Mk 1:21 when the Sabbath **c**, Jesus went into NDT
Mk 1:26 man violently and **c out** of him with a G2002
Mk 1:40 A man with leprosy **c** to him and begged G2262
Mk 1:45 Yet *the people still* **c** to him from G2262
Mk 2: 3 *Some men* **c**, bringing to him a paralyzed G2262
Mk 2:13 A large crowd **c** to him, and he began to G2262
Mk 2:18 *Some people* **c** and asked Jesus, "How is G2262
Mk 3: 8 many people **c** to him from Judea G2262
Mk 3:13 to him those he wanted, and *they* **c** to him. G599
Mk 3:22 of the law who **c down** from Jerusalem G2849
Mk 4: 4 the path, and the birds **c** and ate it up. G2262
Mk 4: 6 But when the sun **c up**, the plants were G422
Mk 4: 8 *It* **c up**, grew and produced a crop, some G326
Mk 4:35 That day *when* evening **c**, he said to his G1181
Mk 4:37 A furious squall **c up**, and the waves broke G1181
Mk 5: 2 an impure spirit *c* **from** the tombs to meet AIT
Mk 5:13 the impure spirits **c out** and went into the G2002
Mk 5:15 *When they* **c** to Jesus, they saw the man G2262
Mk 5:22 named Jairus, **c**, and when he saw Jesus G2262
Mk 5:27 *she* **c up** behind him in the crowd and G2262
Mk 5:33 **c** and fell at his feet and G2262
Mk 5:35 *some people* **c** from the house of Jairus G2262
Mk 5:38 *When they* **c** to the home of the G2262
Mk 6: 2 *When* the Sabbath **c**, he began to teach in G1181
Mk 6:21 Finally the opportune time **c**. On his G1181
Mk 6:22 *When* the daughter of Herodias **c in** and G1656
Mk 6:29 John's disciples **c** and took his body and G2262
Mk 6:35 late in the day, so his disciples **c** to him. G4665
Mk 7:25 by an impure spirit **c** and fell at his feet. G2262
Mk 8:11 The Pharisees **c** and began to question G2002
Mk 8:22 *They* **c** to Bethsaida, and some people G2262
Mk 9: 7 and a voice **c** from the cloud: G1181
Mk 9:14 *When they* **c** to the other disciples, they G2262
Mk 9:26 convulsed him violently and **c out**. G2002
Mk 9:33 *They* **c** to Capernaum. When he was in G2262
Mk 10: 1 Again crowds of people **c** to him, and as G5233
Mk 10: 2 *Some* Pharisees **c** and tested him by G4665
Mk 10:35 John, the sons of Zebedee, **c to** him. G4702
Mk 10:46 Then *they* **c** to Jericho. As Jesus and his G2262
Mk 10:50 he jumped to his feet and **c** to Jesus. G2262
Mk 11: 1 Jerusalem and *c* **to** Bethphage and Bethany AIT
Mk 11:19 When evening **c**, Jesus and his disciples G1181
Mk 11:27 of the law and the elders **c** to him. G2262
Mk 12:14 *They* **c** to him and said, "Teacher, we G2262
Mk 12:18 no resurrection, **c** to him with a question. G2262
Mk 12:28 teachers of the law **c** and heard them G4665
Mk 12:42 But a poor widow **c** and put in two very G2262
Mk 14: 3 a woman **c** with an alabaster jar of very G2262
Mk 14:17 *When* evening **c**, Jesus arrived with the G1181
Mk 14:40 *When he* **c back**, he again found them G2262
Mk 14:53 the teachers of the law **c together**. G5302
Mk 14:66 of the servant girls of the high priest **c by**. G2262
Mk 15: 8 The crowd **c up** and asked Pilate to do for G326
Mk 15:33 darkness **c** over the whole land until three G1181
Lk 1:10 when the time for the burning of incense **c**, NDT
Lk 1:22 *When he* **c out**, he could not speak to G2002
Lk 1:59 On the eighth day *they* **c** to circumcise the G2262
Lk 2: 6 the time **c** for the baby to be born, G4398
Lk 2:22 When the time **c** for the purification rites G4398
Lk 3: 2 the word of God **c** to John son of G1181
Lk 3:12 Even tax collectors **c** to be baptized G2262
Lk 3:22 And a voice **c** from heaven: "You G1181
Lk 4:22 at the gracious words that **c from** his lips. G1744
Lk 4:35 before them all and **c out** without injuring G2002
Lk 4:41 Moreover, demons **c out** of many people G2002
Lk 4:42 him and *when they* **c** to where he was, G2262
Lk 5: 7 and *they* **c** and filled both boats so full G2262
Lk 5:12 a man **c along** who was covered G2779+2627
Lk 5:15 crowds of people **c** to hear him and to be G5302
Lk 5:18 Some men **c** carrying a paralyzed G2779+2627
Lk 6:13 When morning **c**, he called his disciples to G1181
Lk 6:48 *When* a flood **c**, the torrent struck that G1181
Lk 7: 4 *When* they **c** to Jesus, they pleaded G4134
Lk 7:20 *When* the men **c** to Jesus, they said G4134
Lk 7:33 John the Baptist **c** neither eating bread G2262
Lk 7:34 The Son of Man **c** eating and drinking G2262
Lk 7:37 *so she* **c** there **with** an alabaster jar of G3152
Lk 7:44 see this woman? *I* **c into** your house. G1656
Lk 8: 6 rocky ground, and *when it* **c up**, the plants G5886
Lk 8: 8 *It* **c up** and yielded a crop, a hundred G5886
Lk 8:19 Jesus' mother and brothers **c** to see him, G4134
Lk 8:23 A squall **c down** on the lake, so that the G2849
Lk 8:33 *When* the demons **c out** of the man, they G2002
Lk 8:35 *When they* **c** to Jesus, they found the man G2262
Lk 8:41 **c** and fell at Jesus' feet G2262
Lk 8:44 *She* **c up** behind him and touched the G4665
Lk 8:47 unnoticed, **c** trembling and fell at his feet. G2262
Lk 8:49 someone **c** from the house of Jairus G2262
Lk 9:12 afternoon the Twelve **c to** him and said, G4665
Lk 9:35 A voice **c** from the cloud, saying, "This is G1181
Lk 9:37 *when* they **c down** from the mountain G2982
Lk 10:32 *when he* **c** to the place and saw him G2262
Lk 10:33 as he traveled, **c** where the man was; and G2262
Lk 10:38 he **c to** a village where a woman named G1656
Lk 10:40 *She* **c to** him and asked, "Lord, don't you G2392

Lk 11:31 for she c from the ends of the earth to G2262
Lk 12:51 Do you think I c to bring peace on earth G4134
Lk 13:31 some Pharisees c to Jesus and said to G4665
Lk 14:21 "The servant c back and reported this to G4134
Lk 15:17 "When he c to his senses, he said, 'How G2262
Lk 15:25 When he c near the house, he heard G2262
Lk 16:21 Even the dogs c and licked his sores G2262
Lk 16:22 "The time c when the beggar died and G1181
Lk 17:15 he was healed, c back, praising God in a G5715
Lk 17:27 Then the flood c and destroyed them all G2262
Lk 18:40 When he c near, Jesus asked G1581
Lk 19: 6 So he c down at once and welcomed him G2849
Lk 19:10 For the Son of Man c to seek and to save G2262
Lk 19:16 "The first one c and said, 'Sir, your mina G4134
Lk 19:18 "The second c and said, 'Sir, your mina G2262
Lk 19:20 "Then another servant c and said, 'Sir G2262
Lk 19:23 so that when I c back, I could have G2262
Lk 19:37 When he c near the place where the road G1581
Lk 20: 1 together with the elders, c up to him. G2392
Lk 20:27 resurrection, c to Jesus with a question. G4665
Lk 21:38 the people c early in the morning to hear G3983
Lk 22: 7 Then c the day of Unleavened Bread on G2262
Lk 22:14 When the hour c, Jesus and his apostles G1181
Lk 22:47 While he was still speaking a crowd c up G2627
Lk 23:33 When they c to the place called the Skull G2262
Lk 23:36 The soldiers also c up and mocked him G4665
Lk 23:44 darkness c over the whole land until G1181
Lk 23:51 He c from the Judean town of Arimathea AIT
Lk 24: 9 When they c back from the tomb, they G5715
Lk 24:15 Jesus himself c up and walked along with G1581
Lk 24:23 They c and told us that they had seen a G2262
Jn 1: 7 He c as a witness to testify concerning that G2262
Jn 1: 8 the light; he c only as a witness to the light. NDT
Jn 1:11 He c to that which was his own, but his G2262
Jn 1:14 only Son, who c from the Father, full of AIT
Jn 1:17 grace and truth c through Jesus Christ. G1181
Jn 1:31 the reason I c baptizing with water G2262
Jn 3: 2 He c to Jesus at night and said, "Rabbi G2262
Jn 3:13 except the one who c from heaven— G2849
Jn 3:26 They c to John and said to him, "Rabbi G2262
Jn 4: 5 So he c to a town in Samaria called Sychar G2262
Jn 4: 7 When a Samaritan woman c to draw G2262
Jn 4:30 They c out of the town and made their way G2002
Jn 4:40 So when the Samaritans c to him, they G2262
Jn 6:16 When evening c, his disciples went down G1181
Jn 6:41 "I am the bread that c down from heaven." G2849
Jn 6:42 can he now say, 'I c down from heaven'?" G2849
Jn 6:51 the living bread that c down from heaven. G2849
Jn 6:58 This is the bread that c down from heaven G2849
Jn 8:14 I know where I c from and where I am G2262
Jn 9: 7 went and washed, and c home seeing. G2262
Jn 10:22 Then c the Festival of Dedication at G1181
Jn 10:35 to whom the word of God c—and G1181
Jn 10:41 many people c to him. They said G2262
Jn 11:38 once more deeply moved, c to the tomb. G2262
Jn 11:44 The dead man c out, his hands and feet G2002
Jn 12: 1 the Passover, Jesus c to Bethany, where G2262
Jn 12: 9 found out that Jesus was there and c, G2262
Jn 12:21 They c to Philip, who was from Bethsaida G4665
Jn 12:27 it was for this very reason I c to this hour. G2262
Jn 12:28 Then a voice c from heaven, "I have G2262
Jn 13: 6 He c to Simon Peter, who said to him G2262
Jn 16:27 me and have believed that I c from God. G2002
Jn 16:28 I c from the Father and entered the world G2002
Jn 16:30 makes us believe that you c from God." G2002
Jn 17: 8 They knew with certainty that I c from you G2002
Jn 18: 3 So Judas c to the garden, guiding a G2262
Jn 18:16 to the high priest, c back, spoke to the G2002
Jn 18:29 So Pilate c out to them and asked, "What G2002
Jn 18:37 I was born and c into the world is to G2262
Jn 19: 4 Once more Pilate c out and said to the G2002
Jn 19: 5 When Jesus c out wearing the crown of G2002
Jn 19:32 soldiers therefore c and broke the legs of G2262
Jn 19:33 But when they c to Jesus and found that G2262
Jn 19:38 permission, he c and took the body away. G2262
Jn 20: 2 So she c running to Simon Peter and the G2262
Jn 20: 6 Then Simon Peter c along behind him G2262
Jn 20:19 Jesus c and stood among them and said G2262
Jn 20:24 was not with the disciples when Jesus c. G2262
Jn 20:26 Jesus c and stood among them and said G2262
Jn 21:13 Jesus c, took the bread and gave it to G2262
Ac 2: 1 When the day of Pentecost c, they were G5230
Ac 2: 2 of a violent wind c from heaven and filled G1181
Ac 2: 3 separated and c to rest on each of them. G2767
Ac 2: 6 a crowd c together in bewilderment G5302
Ac 3:11 astonished and c running to them in the G5340
Ac 4: 1 the Sadducees c up to Peter and John G2392
Ac 5: 6 Then some young men c forward, wrapped G482
Ac 5: 7 About three hours later his wife c in, not G1656
Ac 5:10 Then the young men c in and, finding her G1656
Ac 5:25 Then someone c and said, "Look! The G4134
Ac 5:36 were dispersed, and it all c to nothing. G1181
Ac 7:18 Joseph meant nothing, c to power in Egypt. G482
Ac 7:26 The next day Moses c upon two Israelites G3972
Ac 8: 7 impure spirits c out of many, and many G2002
Ac 8:36 they c to some water and the eunuch said, G2262
Ac 8:39 When they c up out of the water, the Spirit G326
Ac 9:26 When he c to Jerusalem, he tried to join G4134
Ac 10: 3 an angel of God, who c to him and said G1656
Ac 10:29 sent for, I c without raising any objection. G2262
Ac 10:44 the Holy Spirit c on all who heard the G2158
Ac 11: 5 four corners, and it c down to where I was. G2262
Ac 11:15 the Holy Spirit c on them as he had come G2158
Ac 11:27 some prophets c down from Jerusalem to G2982
Ac 12:10 second guards and c to the iron gate G2262
Ac 12:11 Then Peter c to himself and said, "Now I G1181
Ac 12:13 named Rhoda c to answer the door. G4665
Ac 13: 6 the whole island until they c to Paphos. NDT
Ac 13:11 mist and darkness c over him, G4406
Ac 14:19 Then some Jews c from Antioch and G2088
Ac 14:24 through Pisidia, they c into Pamphylia, G2262
Ac 15: 1 Certain people c down from Judea to G2982
Ac 15: 4 When they c to Jerusalem, they were G4134
Ac 16: 1 Paul c to Derbe and then to Lystra, where G2918
Ac 16: 7 When they c to the border of Mysia, they G2262
Ac 16:26 flew open, and everyone's chains c loose. G479
Ac 16:39 They c to appease them and escorted G2262
Ac 16:40 After Paul and Silas c out of the prison G2002
Ac 17: 1 Apollonia, they c to Thessalonica G2262
Ac 18: 5 Silas and Timothy c from Macedonia, G2982
Ac 18:24 a native of Alexandria, c to Ephesus. G2918
Ac 19: 6 the Holy Spirit c on them, and they G2262
Ac 19:18 those who believed now c and openly G2262
Ac 19:19 the total c to fifty thousand drachmas. G2351
Ac 20: 7 of the week we c together to break bread. G5251
Ac 20:18 from the first day I c into the province of G2094
Ac 21:10 named Agabus c down from Judea. G2982
Ac 21:30 the people c running from all G1181
Ac 21:33 The commander c up and arrested him G1581
Ac 22: 6 "About noon as I c near Damascus G4513
Ac 22:12 "A man named Ananias c to see me. G2262
Ac 23:27 but I c with my troops and rescued him G2392
Ac 24:17 I c to Jerusalem to bring my people gifts G4134
Ac 24:24 days later Felix c with his wife Drusilla, G4134
Ac 25: 7 When Paul c in, the Jews who had come G4134
Ac 25:17 When they c here with me, I did not delay G5302
Ac 25:23 Bernice c with great pomp and G2262
Ac 27: 8 with difficulty and c to a place called Fair G2262
Ac 27:39 When daylight c, they did not recognize G1181
Ac 28: 9 of the sick on the island c and were cured. G4665
Ac 28:13 The next day the south wind c up, and on G2104
Ac 28:14 a week with them. And so we c to Rome. G2262
Ac 28:23 c in even larger numbers to the place G2262
Ac 28:30 welcomed all who c to see him. G1660
Ro 3:24 the redemption that c by Christ Jesus. AIT
Ro 5:12 in this way death c to all people G1451
Ro 5:15 the gift that c by the grace of the one AIT
Ro 7: 9 when the commandment c, sin sprang G2262
1Co 2: 1 When I c to you, I did not come with G2262
1Co 2: 3 I c to you in weakness with great fear and G1181
1Co 3: 5 through whom you c to believe—as the Lord AIT
1Co 8: 6 whom all things c and for whom we live NDT
1Co 8: 6 whom all things c and through whom we NDT
1Co 11:12 For as woman c from man, so also man is G1666
1Co 15:21 For since death c through a man, the NDT
2Co 2: 3 so that when I c I would not be distressed G2262
2Co 3: 7 in letters on stone, c with glory, so that G1181
2Co 3:11 And if what was transitory c with glory, how AIT
2Co 7: 5 For when we c into Macedonia, we had G2262
2Co 11: 9 the brothers who c from Macedonia G2262
Gal 2:11 When Cephas c to Antioch, I opposed G2262
Gal 2:12 For before certain men c from James, he G2262
Gal 3:24 our guardian until Christ c that we might be NDT
Eph 2:17 He c and preached peace to you who were G2262
1Th 1: 5 because our gospel c to you not simply G1181
1Ti 1:15 Christ Jesus c into the world to save G2262
2Ti 4:16 no one c to my support, but everyone G4134
Heb 7:28 the oath, which c after the law, appointed AIT
Heb 9:11 But when Christ c as high priest of the G4134
Heb 10: 5 Therefore, when Christ c into the world G1656
Heb 11:12 c descendants as numerous as the stars in G1164
2Pe 1:17 the Father when the voice c to him from G5770
2Pe 1:18 heard this voice that c from heaven when G5770
2Pe 1:20 of Scripture c about by the prophet's own G1181
2Pe 3: 5 the heavens c into being and the earth G1639
1Jn 5: 6 This is the one who c by water and blood G2262
3Jn 3 me great joy when some believers c and G2262
Rev 2: 8 the Last, who died and c to life again. G2409
Rev 4: 5 From the throne c flashes of lightning G1744
Rev 6: 4 Then another horse c out, a fiery red one G2002
Rev 8: 3 a golden censer, c and stood at the altar. G2262
Rev 8: 5 on the earth; and there c peals of thunder G1181
Rev 8: 7 and there c hail and fire mixed with blood G1181
Rev 9: 3 smoke locusts c down on the earth and G2002
Rev 9:17 and out of their mouths c fire G1744
Rev 9:18 sulfur that c out of their mouths. G1744
Rev 11:19 And there c flashes of lightning G1181
Rev 14:15 Then another angel c out of the temple G2002
Rev 14:17 Another angel c out of the temple in G2002
Rev 14:18 c from the altar and called in a loud voice G2002
Rev 15: 6 Out of the temple c the seven angels with G2002
Rev 16:13 they c out of the mouth of the dragon AIT
Rev 16:17 and out of the temple c a loud voice from G2002
Rev 16:18 Then there c flashes of lightning G1181
Rev 17: 1 had the seven bowls c and said to me, G2262
Rev 19: 5 Then a voice c from the throne, saying G2002
Rev 20: 4 They c to life and reigned with Christ a G2409
Rev 20: 9 But fire c down from heaven and G2849
Rev 21: 9 the seven last plagues c and said to me, G2262

CAMEL (7) [CAMEL'S, CAMEL-LOADS, CAMELS, CAMELS', SHE-CAMEL]

Ge 24:64 saw Isaac. She got down from her c H1695
Lev 11: 4 The c, though it chews the cud, does not H1695
Dt 14: 7 a divided hoof you may not eat the c, H1695
Mt 19:24 it is easier for a c to go through the eye of G2823
Mt 23:24 You strain out a gnat but swallow a c. G2823
Mk 10:25 It is easier for a c to go through the eye of G2823
Lk 18:25 it is easier for a c to go through the eye of G2823

CAMEL'S (3) [CAMEL]

Ge 31:34 put them inside her c saddle and was H1695
Mt 3: 4 John's clothes were made of c hair, and G2823
Mk 1: 6 John wore clothing made of c hair, with a G2823

CAMEL-LOADS (1) [LOAD]

2Ki 8: 9 him as a gift forty c of all the finest H1695+5362

CAMELS (49) [CAMEL]

Ge 12:16 male and female servants, and c. H1695
Ge 24:10 ten of his master's c loaded with all kinds H1695
Ge 24:11 He had the c kneel down near the well H1695
Ge 24:14 I'll water your c too'—let her be the H1695
Ge 24:19 "I'll draw water for your c too, until they H1695
Ge 24:20 and drew enough for all his c. H1695
Ge 24:22 When the c had finished drinking, the H1695
Ge 24:30 him standing by the c near the spring. H1695
Ge 24:31 prepared the house and a place for the c." H1695
Ge 24:32 to the house, and the c were unloaded. H1695
Ge 24:32 Straw and fodder were brought for the c H1695
Ge 24:35 female servants, and c and donkeys. H1695
Ge 24:44 I'll draw water for your c too," let her H1695
Ge 24:46 said, 'Drink, and I'll water your c too. H1695
Ge 24:46 So I drank, and she watered the c also. H1695
Ge 24:61 mounted the c and went back with H1695
Ge 24:63 as he looked up, he saw c approaching. H1695
Ge 30:43 male servants, and c and donkeys. H1695
Ge 31:17 Jacob put his children and his wives on c, H1695
Ge 32: 7 the flocks and herds and c as well. H1695
Ge 32:15 thirty female c with their young, forty cows H1695
Ge 37:25 Their c were loaded with spices, balm H1695
Ex 9: 3 donkeys and c and on your cattle H1695
Jdg 6: 5 It was impossible to count them or their c H1695
Jdg 7:12 Their c could no more be counted than H1695
1Sa 15: 3 cattle and sheep, c and donkeys. H1695
1Sa 27: 9 cattle, donkeys and c, and clothes. H1695
1Sa 30:17 young men who rode off on c and fled. H1695
1Ki 10: 2 great caravan—with c carrying spices H1695
1Ch 5:21 fifty thousand c, two hundred fifty H1695
1Ch 12:40 food on donkeys, c, mules and oxen. H1695
1Ch 27:30 Obil the Ishmaelite was in charge of the c. H1695
2Ch 9: 1 great caravan—with c carrying spices H1695
2Ch 14:15 off droves of sheep and goats and c. H1695
Ezr 2:67 435 c and 6,720 donkeys. H1695
Ne 7:69 435 c and 6,720 donkeys. H1695
Job 1: 3 three thousand c, five hundred yoke of H1695
Job 1:17 swept down on your c and made off with H1695
Job 42:12 six thousand c, a thousand yoke of H1695
Isa 21: 7 riders on donkeys or riders on c, let him H1695
Isa 30: 6 their treasures on the humps of c, to that H1695
Isa 60: 6 Herds of c will cover your land, young H1695
Isa 60: 6 your land, young c of Midian and Ephah. H1145
Isa 66:20 on mules and c," says the LORD. H4140
Jer 49:29 be carried off with all their goods and c. H1695
Jer 49:32 Their c will become plunder, and their H1695
Eze 25: 5 into a pasture for c and Ammon into a H1695
Zec 14:15 mules, the c and donkeys, and all H1695

CAMELS' (2) [CAMEL]

Jdg 8:21 took the ornaments off their c necks. H1695
Jdg 8:26 the chains that were on their c necks. H1695

CAMP (183) [CAMPED, CAMPING, CAMPS, ENCAMP, ENCAMPED, ENCAMPS]

Ge 32: 2 saw them, he said, "This is the c of God!" H4722
Ge 32:21 he himself spent the night in the c. H4722
Ex 16:13 evening quail came and covered the c, H4722
Ex 16:13 there was a layer of dew around the c. H4722
Ex 19:16 trumpet blast. Everyone in the c trembled. H4722
Ex 19:17 the people out of the c to meet with God, H4722
Ex 29:14 its hide and its intestines outside the c. H4722
Ex 32:17 "There is the sound of war in the c." H4722
Ex 32:19 approached the c and saw the calf and H4722
Ex 32:26 stood at the entrance to the c and said, H4722
Ex 32:27 forth through the c from one end to the H4722
Ex 33: 7 pitch it outside the c some distance away, H4722
Ex 33: 7 go to the tent of meeting outside the c. H4722
Ex 33:11 Then Moses would return to the c, but his H4722
Ex 36: 6 they sent this word throughout the c: H4722
Lev 4:12 must take outside the c to a place H4722
Lev 4:21 the bull outside the c and burn it as he H4722
Lev 6:11 the ashes outside the c to a place that is H4722
Lev 8:17 its intestines he burned up outside the c, H4722
Lev 9:11 the hide he burned up outside the c. H4722
Lev 10: 4 carry your cousins outside the c, away H4722
Lev 10: 5 outside the c, as Moses ordered. H4722
Lev 13:46 live alone; they must live outside the c. H4722
Lev 14: 3 is to go outside the c and examine them. H4722
Lev 14: 8 After this they may come into the c, but H4722
Lev 16:26 afterward he may come into the c. H4722
Lev 16:27 must be taken outside the c; their hides, H4722
Lev 16:28 afterward he may come into the c. H4722
Lev 17: 3 a lamb or a goat in the c or outside of it H4722
Lev 24:10 broke out in the c between him and an H4722
Lev 24:14 "Take the blasphemer outside the c. H4722
Lev 24:23 outside the c and stoned him. H4722
Nu 1:52 them in their own c under their standard H4722

Nu 2: 2 "The Israelites are to c around the tent of H2837
Nu 2: 3 divisions of the c of Judah are to encamp H4722
Nu 2: 5 The tribe of Issachar will c next to them H2837
Nu 2: 9 All the men assigned to the c of Judah H4722
Nu 2:10 divisions of the c of Reuben under their H4722
Nu 2:12 The tribe of Simeon will c next to them H2837
Nu 2:16 All the men assigned to the c of Reuben H4722
Nu 2:17 of meeting and the c of the Levites will H4722
Nu 2:18 divisions of the c of Ephraim under their H4722
Nu 2:24 All the men assigned to the c of Ephraim H4722
Nu 2:25 the divisions of the c of Dan under their H4722
Nu 2:27 The tribe of Asher will c next to them. H2837
Nu 2:31 assigned to the c of Dan number 157,600 H4722
Nu 3:23 Gershonite clans were to c on the west, H2837
Nu 3:29 Kohathite clans were to c on the south H2837
Nu 3:35 they were to c on the north side of the H2837
Nu 3:38 his sons were to c to the east of the H2837
Nu 4: 5 When the c is to move, Aaron and his H4722
Nu 4:15 when the c is ready to move, only H4722
Nu 5: 2 send away from the c anyone who has a H4722
Nu 5: 3 send them outside the c so they will not H4722
Nu 5: 3 the camp so they will not defile their c, H4722
Nu 5: 4 they sent them outside the c. H4722
Nu 9:18 over the tabernacle, they **remained in** c. H2837
Nu 9:22 Israelites would **remain in** c and not set H2837
Nu 10:14 The divisions of the c of Judah went first H4722
Nu 10:18 divisions of the c of Reuben went next, H4722
Nu 10:22 divisions of the c of Ephraim went next, H4722
Nu 10:25 the divisions of the c of Dan set out under H4722
Nu 10:31 You know where we should c in the H2837
Nu 10:34 them by day when they set out from the c. H4722
Nu 11: 1 consumed some of the outskirts of the c. H4722
Nu 11: 9 When the dew settled on the c at night H4722
Nu 11:26 Eldad and Medad, had remained in the c. H4722
Nu 11:26 on them, and they prophesied in the c. H4722
Nu 11:27 Medad are prophesying in the c. H4722
Nu 11:30 the elders of Israel returned to the c. H4722
Nu 11:31 up to two cubits deep all around the c, H4722
Nu 11:32 they spread them out all around the c. H4722
Nu 12:14 Confine her outside the c for seven days H4722
Nu 12:15 was confined outside the c for seven days, H4722
Nu 14:44 of the LORD's covenant moved from the c. H4722
Nu 15:35 assembly must stone him outside the c." H4722
Nu 15:36 took him outside the c and stoned him to H4722
Nu 19: 3 be taken outside the c and slaughtered in H4722
Nu 19: 7 He may then come into the c, but he will H4722
Nu 19: 9 a ceremonially clean place outside the c. H4722
Nu 22:41 he could see the **outskirts** of the Israelite c. AIT
Nu 23:13 see them all but only the **outskirts** of their c. AIT
Nu 25: 6 brought into the c a Midianite woman H2788
Nu 31:12 assembly at their c on the plains of Moab, H4722
Nu 31:13 went to meet them outside the c. H4722
Nu 31:19 killed must stay outside the c seven days. H4722
Nu 31:24 Then you may come into the c." H4722
Dt 1: 7 **Break** c and advance into the hill country H7155
Dt 1:33 places for you to c and to show you the H2837
Dt 2:14 of fighting men had perished from the c, H4722
Dt 2:15 completely eliminated them from the c. H4722
Dt 23:10 he is to go outside the c and stay there. H4722
Dt 23:11 at sunset he may return to the c. H4722
Dt 23:12 a place outside the c where you can go to H4722
Dt 23:14 moves about in your c to protect you and H4722
Dt 23:14 Your c must be holy, so that he will not H4722
Jos 1:11 "Go through the c and tell the people H4722
Jos 3: 2 days the officers went throughout the c, H4722
Jos 3:14 the people **broke** c to cross H5825+4946+185
Jos 4: 8 carried them over with them to their c, H4869
Jos 5: 8 where they were in c until they were H4722
Jos 6:11 the army returned to c and spent the night H4722
Jos 6:14 the city once and returned to the c. H4722
Jos 6:18 you will make the c of Israel liable to H4722
Jos 6:23 them in a place outside the c of Israel. H4722
Jos 8:11 They **set up** c north of Ai, with the valley H2837
Jos 8:13 with the main c to the north of the city H4722
Jos 9: 6 to Joshua in the c at Gilgal and said to H4722
Jos 10: 6 sent word to Joshua in the c at Gilgal: H4722
Jos 10:15 returned with all Israel to the c at Gilgal. H4722
Jos 10:21 safely to Joshua in the c at Makkedah, H4722
Jos 10:43 returned with all Israel to the c at Gilgal. H4722
Jos 11: 5 joined forces and **made** c together at the H2837
Jos 18: 9 returned to Joshua in the c at Shiloh. H4722
Jdg 7: 1 The c of Midian was north of them in the H4722
Jdg 7: 8 Now the c of Midian lay below him in the H4722
Jdg 7: 9 go down against the c, because I am H4722
Jdg 7:10 go down to the c with your servant Purah H4722
Jdg 7:11 you will be encouraged to attack the c." H4722
Jdg 7:11 went down to the outposts of the c. H4722
Jdg 7:13 came tumbling into the Midianite c. H4722
Jdg 7:14 the whole c into his hands. H4722
Jdg 7:15 He returned to the c of Israel and called H4722
Jdg 7:15 has given the Midianite c into your hands." H4722
Jdg 7:17 When I get to the edge of the c, do H4722
Jdg 7:18 from all around the c blow yours and H4722
Jdg 7:19 the edge of the c at the beginning of the H4722
Jdg 7:21 each man held his position around the c, H4722
Jdg 7:22 men throughout the c to turn on each H4722
Jdg 18:12 On their way they **set up** c near Kiriath H2837
Jdg 20:19 got up and **pitched** c near Gibeah. H2837
Jdg 21: 8 had come to the c for the assembly. H4722
Jdg 21:12 took them to the c at Shiloh in Canaan. H4722
1Sa 4: 3 When the soldiers returned to c, the elders H4722
1Sa 4: 5 ark of the LORD's covenant came into the c, H4722
1Sa 4: 6 "What's all this shouting in the Hebrew c?" H4722
1Sa 4: 6 the ark of the LORD had come into the c, H4722
1Sa 4: 7 "A god has come into the c," they said H4722
1Sa 11:11 they broke into the c of the Ammonites H4722
1Sa 13:17 from the Philistine c in three detachments H4722
1Sa 14:15 those in the c and field, and those H4722
1Sa 14:19 in the Philistine c increased more and H4722
1Sa 14:21 up with them to their c went over to the H4722
1Sa 17: 1 They **pitched** c at Ephes Dammim H2837
1Sa 17: 4 from Gath, came out of the Philistine c. H4722
1Sa 17:17 your brothers and hurry to their c. H4722
1Sa 17:20 He reached the c as the army was going H5046
1Sa 17:53 the Philistines, they plundered their c. H4722
1Sa 26: 3 Saul **made** his c beside the road on the H2837
1Sa 26: 5 Saul was lying inside the c, with the army H5046
1Sa 26: 6 will go down into the c with me to Saul?" H4722
1Sa 26: 7 asleep inside the c with his spear stuck in H5046
1Sa 28: 4 came and **set up** c at Shunem, H2837
1Sa 28: 4 gathered all Israel and **set up** c at Gilboa. H2837
2Sa 1: 2 arrived from Saul's c with his clothes torn H4722
2Sa 1: 3 "I have escaped from the Israelite c." H4722
1Ki 16:16 the Israelites in the c heard that Zimri had H2837
1Ki 16:16 over Israel that very day there in the c. H4722
2Ki 3:24 the Moabites came to the c of Israel, H4722
2Ki 6: 8 "I will **set up** my c in such and such a H9381
2Ki 7: 4 let's go over to the c of the Arameans H4722
2Ki 7: 5 up and went to the c of the Arameans. H4722
2Ki 7: 5 When they reached the edge of the c, no H4722
2Ki 7: 7 They left the c as it was and ran for their H4722
2Ki 7: 8 had leprosy reached the edge of the c, H4722
2Ki 7:10 into the Aramean c and no one was there H4722
2Ki 7:12 so they have left the c to hide in the H4722
2Ki 7:16 out and plundered the c of the Arameans. H4722
2Ki 19:35 eighty-five thousand in the Assyrian c. H4722
2Ki 19:36 king of Assyria **broke** c and withdrew. H5825
1Ch 9:18 belonging to the c of the Levites. H4722
2Ch 22: 1 who came with the Arabs into the c, had H4722
2Ch 32:21 officers in the c of the Assyrian king. H4722
Ps 78:28 He made them come down inside their c H4722
Ps 106:16 In the c they grew envious of Moses and H4722
Isa 10:29 say, "We will c **overnight** at Geba. H4869
Isa 21:13 Dedanites, who c in the thickets of Arabia H4328
Isa 37:36 eighty-five thousand in the Assyrian c. H4722
Isa 37:37 king of Assyria **broke** c and withdrew. H5825
Mic 4:10 must leave the city to c in the open field. H8905
Heb 13:11 the bodies are burned outside the c. G4213
Heb 13:13 go to him outside the c, bearing the G4213
Rev 20: 9 surrounded the c of God's people, G4213

CAMPAIGN (4) [CAMPAIGNS]

Jos 10:42 their lands Joshua conquered in one c, H7193
2Sa 11:10 "Haven't you just come from a **military** c? H2006
Eze 29:18 drove his army in a hard c against Tyre; H6275
Eze 29:18 no reward from the c he led against Tyre. H6275

CAMPAIGNS (4) [CAMPAIGN]

1Sa 18:13 **led** the troops **in** their c. H3655+2256+995+4200+7156
1Sa 18:16 he **led** them **in** their c. H3655+2256+995+4200+7156
2Sa 5: 2 one who **led** Israel **on** their **military** c H3655+2256+995
1Ch 11: 2 one who **led** Israel **on** their **military** c H3655+2256+995

CAMPED (78) [CAMP]

Ge 31:25 Laban and his relatives c there too. H9546
Ge 33:18 in Canaan and c within sight of the H2837
Ex 13:20 leaving Sukkoth they c at Etham on the H2837
Ex 14: 9 overtook them as they c by the sea near H2837
Ex 15:27 and they c there near the water. H2837
Ex 17: 1 They c at Rephidim, but there was no H2837
Ex 18: 5 where he was c near the mountain of God H2837
Ex 19: 2 Israel c there in the desert in front of H2837
Nu 21:10 The Israelites moved on and c at Oboth. H2837
Nu 21:11 set out from Oboth and c in Iye Abarim, H2837
Nu 21:12 they moved on and c in the Zered Valley. H2837
Nu 21:13 out from there and c alongside the Arnon, H2837
Nu 22: 1 plains of Moab and c along the Jordan H2837
Nu 33: 5 Israelites left Rameses and c at Sukkoth. H2837
Nu 33: 6 They left Sukkoth and c at Etham, on the H2837
Nu 33: 7 east of Baal Zephon, and c near Migdol. H2837
Nu 33: 8 in the Desert of Etham, they c at Marah. H2837
Nu 33: 9 seventy palm trees, and they c there. H2837
Nu 33:10 They left Elim and c by the Red Sea. H2837
Nu 33:11 left the Red Sea and c in the Desert of Sin H2837
Nu 33:12 left the Desert of Sin and c at Dophkah. H2837
Nu 33:13 They left Dophkah and c at Alush. H2837
Nu 33:14 They left Alush and c at Rephidim, where H2837
Nu 33:15 left Rephidim and c in the Desert of Sinai H2837
Nu 33:16 Desert of Sinai and c at Kibroth Hattaavah H2837
Nu 33:17 left Kibroth Hattaavah and c at Hazeroth. H2837
Nu 33:18 They left Hazeroth and c at Rithmah. H2837
Nu 33:19 They left Rithmah and c at Rimmon Perez. H2837
Nu 33:20 They left Rimmon Perez and c at Libnah. H2837
Nu 33:21 They left Libnah and c at Rissah. H2837
Nu 33:22 They left Rissah and c at Kehelathah. H2837
Nu 33:23 left Kehelathah and c at Mount Shepher. H2837
Nu 33:24 left Mount Shepher and c at Haradah. H2837
Nu 33:25 They left Haradah and c at Makheloth. H2837
Nu 33:26 They left Makheloth and c at Tahath. H2837
Nu 33:27 They left Tahath and c at Terah. H2837
Nu 33:28 They left Terah and c at Mithkah. H2837
Nu 33:29 They left Mithkah and c at Hashmonah. H2837
Nu 33:30 They left Hashmonah and c at Moseroth. H2837
Nu 33:31 They left Moseroth and c at Bene Jaakan. H2837
Nu 33:32 left Bene Jaakan and c at Hor Haggidgad. H2837
Nu 33:33 left Hor Haggidgad and c at Jotbathah. H2837
Nu 33:34 They left Jotbathah and c at Abronah. H2837
Nu 33:35 They left Abronah and c at Ezion Geber. H2837
Nu 33:36 They left Ezion Geber and c at Kadesh, in H2837
Nu 33:37 They left Kadesh and c at Mount Hor, on H2837
Nu 33:41 They left Mount Hor and c at Zalmonah. H2837
Nu 33:42 They left Zalmonah and c at Punon. H2837
Nu 33:43 They left Punon and c at Oboth. H2837
Nu 33:44 They left Oboth and c at Iye Abarim, on H2837
Nu 33:45 They left Iye Abarim and c at Dibon Gad. H2837
Nu 33:46 left Dibon Gad and c at Almon H2837
Nu 33:47 Diblathaim and c in the mountains of H2837
Nu 33:48 of Abarim and c on the plains of Moab H2837
Nu 33:49 plains of Moab they c along the Jordan H2837
Jos 3: 1 where they c before crossing over. H4328
Jos 4:19 up from the Jordan and c at Gilgal on the H2837
Jos 5:10 while c at Gilgal on the plains of Jericho H2837
Jdg 6: 4 They c on the land and ruined the crops H2837
Jdg 6:33 over the Jordan and c in the Valley of H2837
Jdg 7: 1 all his men c at the spring of Harod. H2837
Jdg 10:17 were called to arms and c in Gilead, H2837
Jdg 10:17 the Israelites assembled and c at Mizpah. H2837
Jdg 11:18 c on the other side of the Arnon. H2837
Jdg 15: 9 The Philistines went up and c in Judah H2837
1Sa 4: 1 The Israelites c at Ebenezer, and the H2837
1Sa 13: 5 They went up and c at Mikmash, east of H2837
1Sa 13:16 while the Philistines c at Mikmash. H2837
1Sa 17: 2 assembled and c in the Valley of Elah H2837
1Sa 26: 5 went to the place where Saul had c. H2837
1Sa 29: 1 Israel c by the spring in Jezreel. H2837
2Sa 11:11 my lord's men are c in the open H2837
2Sa 17:26 Absalom c in the land of Gilead. H2837
2Sa 24: 5 the Jordan, they c near Aroer, south of H2837
1Ki 20:27 The Israelites c opposite them like two H2837
1Ki 20:29 For seven days they c opposite each other H2837
1Ch 19: 7 who came and c near Medeba, while H2837
Ezr 8:15 toward Ahava, and we c there three days. H2837

CAMPHIRE (KJV) HENNA

CAMPING (1) [CAMP]

Nu 10: 5 the tribes c on the east are to set out. H2837

CAMPS (13) [CAMP]

Ge 25:16 according to their settlements and c. H3227
Ge 32:10 this Jordan, but now I have become two c. H4722
Nu 2:17 Levites will set out in the middle of the c. H4722
Nu 2:32 All the men in the c, by their divisions H4722
Nu 10: 2 together and for having the c set out. H4722
Nu 10: 6 the c on the south are to set out. H4722
Nu 31:10 had settled, as well as all their c. H3227
Dt 29:11 living in your c who chop your wood and H4722
2Ch 14:15 They also attacked the c of the herders and H185
Eze 4: 2 set up c against it and put battering rams H4722
Eze 25: 4 will set up their c and pitch their tents H3227
Am 4:10 your nostrils with the stench of your c, H4722
Zec 14:15 donkeys, and all the animals in those c. H4722

CAN (738) [CAN'T, CANNOT]

Ge 4:13 "My punishment is more than I c **bear**. AIT
Ge 8:17 so they c **multiply** on the earth and be fruitful AIT
Ge 15: 2 what c you **give** me since I remain childless AIT
Ge 15: 5 the stars—if indeed you c count them." H3523
Ge 15: 8 how c I **know** that I will gain possession of it? AIT
Ge 16: 2 perhaps I c **build a family** through her." AIT
Ge 18: 5 so you c **be refreshed** and then go on your AIT
Ge 18:30 What if only thirty c **be found** there?" He AIT
Ge 18:31 what if only twenty c **be found** there? AIT
Ge 18:32 What if only ten c **be found** there?" He AIT
Ge 19: 2 You c **wash** your feet and spend the night AIT
Ge 19: 5 out to us so that we c **have sex with** them." AIT
Ge 19: 8 and you c **do** what you like with them. AIT
Ge 19:34 with him so we c **preserve** our family line AIT
Ge 20:13 'This is how you c **show** your love to me: AIT
Ge 23: 4 a burial site here so I c **bury** my dead." AIT
Ge 23:13 Accept it from me so I c **bury** my dead there." AIT
Ge 24: 7 before you so that you c **get** a wife for my son AIT
Ge 24:40 so that you c **get** a wife for my son from my AIT
Ge 24:50 we c say nothing to you one way or the H3523
Ge 27: 9 so I c **prepare** some tasty food for your father AIT
Ge 27:21 "Come near so I c **touch** you, my son, AIT
Ge 27:37 So what c I possibly **do** for you, my son AIT
Ge 30: 3 her so that she c **bear children** for me and I AIT
Ge 30: 3 me and I too c **build a family** through her." AIT
Ge 30:15 "he c **sleep with** you tonight in return for your AIT
Ge 30:25 me on my way so I c **go back** to my own AIT
Ge 31:43 Yet what c I **do** today about these daughters AIT
Ge 34:10 You c **settle** among us; the land is open to AIT
Ge 34:21 We c **marry** their daughters and they can AIT
Ge 34:21 marry their daughters and they c **marry** ours. AIT
Ge 37:16 C you **tell** me where they are grazing their AIT
Ge 37:30 "The boy isn't there! Where c I **turn** now?" AIT
Ge 41:15 "I had a dream, and no one c **interpret** it. AIT
Ge 41:15 when you hear a dream you c **interpret** it." AIT
Ge 41:38 asked them, "C we **find** anyone like this man AIT
Ge 42:34 back to you, and you c **trade** in the land. AIT
Ge 43: 9 you c **hold** me personally **responsible** for him. AIT
Ge 44: 1 sacks with as much food as they c carry, H3523

Ge 44:15 man like me *c* **find things out by divination**? AIT
Ge 44:16 "What *c we* **say** to my lord?" Judah replied AIT
Ge 44:16 "What *c we* **say**? How can we prove AIT
Ge 44:16 How *c we* **prove** *our* **innocence**? God has AIT
Ge 44:21 him down to me so *I c* **see** him for myself. AIT
Ge 44:34 How *c I* **go back** to my father if the boy is not AIT
Ge 45:12 "*You c* **see for yourselves**, and so can my AIT
Ge 45:12 yourselves, and so **c** my brother Benjamin NDT
Ge 45:18 land of Egypt and *you c* **enjoy** the fat of the AIT
Ge 47:23 is seed for you so *you c* **plant** the ground. AIT
Ge 49:1 "Gather around so *I c* **tell** you what will AIT
Ex 4:14 I know he *c* **speak well**. He is already AIT
Ex 4:17 in your hand so *you c* **perform** the signs with AIT
Ex 5:11 get your own straw wherever *you c* **find** it, AIT
Ex 10:21 spreads over Egypt—darkness *that c be* **felt**." AIT
Ex 14:16 so that the Israelites *c* **go** through the sea on AIT
Ex 16:32 so *they c* **see** the bread I gave you to eat in AIT
Ex 18:22 the simple cases *they c* **decide** themselves. AIT
Ex 21:19 liable if the other *c* **get up** and walk around AIT
Ex 22:27 What else *c they* **sleep** in? When they AIT
Ex 24:14 anyone involved in a dispute *c* **go** to them." AIT
Ex 28:7 to two of its corners, so *it c* **be fastened**. AIT
Ex 29:29 so that they *c be* **anointed** and ordained in AIT
Ex 32:30 perhaps *I c* **make atonement** for your sin." AIT
Lev 10:10 so that you *c* **distinguish** between the holy AIT
Lev 10:11 so you *c* **teach** the Israelites all the AIT
Lev 13:12 so far as the priest **c** see, it covers all the NDT
Lev 13:37 sore is unchanged so far as the priest **c** see, NDT
Lev 14:22 pigeons, such as they *c* **afford**, one for a sin AIT
Lev 14:30 young pigeons, such as the person *c* **afford**, AIT
Lev 25:27 *they c* then **go back** to their own property. AIT
Lev 25:28 and *they c* then **go back** to their property. AIT
Lev 25:31 They *c* **be** redeemed, and they are to be AIT
Lev 25:35 so *they c continue to* **live** among you. AIT
Lev 25:46 *You c* **bequeath** them to your children as AIT
Lev 25:46 property and *c* **make** them **slaves** for life, AIT
Lev 27:8 to what the one making the vow *c* **afford**. AIT
Lev 27:20 it to someone else, *it c* never **be redeemed**. AIT
Nu 5:8 to whom **restitution** *c be* **made** *for* the wrong, AIT
Nu 6:21 in addition to whatever else they *c* **afford**. AIT
Nu 10:31 in the wilderness, and *you c* **be** our eyes. AIT
Nu 11:13 Where *c* I **get** meat for all these people? They AIT
Nu 12:14 seven days; after that *she c* **be brought back**." AIT
Nu 13:30 of the land, for *we* **c certainly do** it." H3523+3523
Nu 16:21 assembly so *I c* **put an end** *to* them at once." AIT
Nu 16:45 assembly so *I c* **put an end** *to* them at once." AIT
Nu 20:8 so they and their livestock *c* **drink**." AIT
Nu 21:8 anyone who is bitten *c* **look** *at* it and live." AIT
Nu 22:19 night here so that *I c* **find out** what else the AIT
Nu 23:8 How *c I* **curse** those whom God has not AIT
Nu 23:8 How *c I* **denounce** those whom the LORD has AIT
Nu 23:10 Who *c* **count** the dust of Jacob or number AIT
Nu 23:13 me to another place where *you c* **see** them; AIT
Nu 24:23 Who *c* **live** when God does this? AIT
Nu 31:23 else that *c* **withstand** fire must be put AIT
Nu 35:15 has killed another accidentally *c* **flee** there. AIT
Dt 1:12 But how *c I* **bear** your problems and your AIT
Dt 1:28 Where *c we* **go**? Our brothers have made our AIT
Dt 3:24 on earth who *c* **do** the deeds and mighty AIT
Dt 5:24 seen that a person *c* **live** even if God speaks AIT
Dt 7:17 How *c we* drive them out?" H3523
Dt 8:9 rocks are iron and *you c* **dig** copper out of the AIT
Dt 9:2 "Who *c* **stand up** against the Anakites?" AIT
Dt 18:21 "How *c we* **know** when a message has not AIT
Dt 20:19 an ax to them, because *you c* **eat** their fruit. AIT
Dt 22:20 of the young woman's virginity *c* **be found**, AIT
Dt 22:29 *He* **c** never divorce her as long as he lives H3523
Dt 23:12 the camp where *you c* **go** to relieve yourself. AIT
Dt 31:12 so *they c* **listen** and learn to fear the LORD AIT
Dt 31:28 so that *I c* **speak** these words in their hearing AIT
Dt 32:39 and no *one c* **deliver** out of my hand. AIT
Dt 33:14 brings forth and the finest the moon **c** yield; NDT
Jos 7:8 What *c I* **say**, now that Israel has been routed AIT
Jos 9:7 so how *c we* **make** a treaty with you? AIT
Jos 15:18 Caleb asked her, "What **c** I do for you?" NDT
Jos 17:18 though they are strong, *you c* **drive** them **out**." AIT
Jdg 1:14 Caleb asked her, "What **c** I do for you?" NDT
Jdg 6:15 Gideon replied, "but how *c I* **save** Israel? AIT
Jdg 6:31 *he c* **defend** himself when someone breaks AIT
Jdg 7:14 "This **c** be nothing other than the sword of NDT
Jdg 11:6 commander, so *we c* **fight** the Ammonites." AIT
Jdg 14:12 "If *you c* **give** me *the* **answer** within the seven AIT
Jdg 16:5 "*See if you c* **lure** him *into* showing you the AIT
Jdg 16:5 how *we c* **overpower** him so we may AIT
Jdg 16:6 how *you c* **be tied up** and subdued. AIT
Jdg 16:10 Come now, tell me how *you c* **be tied**." AIT
Jdg 16:13 Tell me how *you c* **be tied**." He replied, AIT
Jdg 16:15 she said to him, "How *c you* **say**, 'I love you, AIT
Jdg 16:26 "Put me where I *c* **feel** the pillars that support AIT
Jdg 18:24 How *c you* **ask**, 'What's the matter AIT
Jdg 19:5 with something to eat; then *you c* **go**." AIT
Jdg 19:9 **Early** tomorrow **morning** *you c* **get up** and be AIT
Jdg 19:22 to your house so *we c* **have sex with** him." AIT
Jdg 19:24 and *you c* **use** them and do to them whatever AIT
Jdg 20:10 it *c* **give** them what they deserve for this AIT
Jdg 21:7 "How *c we* **provide** wives for those who are AIT
Ru 1:19 the women exclaimed, "**C** this be Naomi?" NDT
1Sa 2:36 to some priestly office so I *c have* food *to* **eat**."AIT
1Sa 6:20 "Who **c** stand in the presence of the LORD H3523
1Sa 9:7 "If we go, what *c we* **give** the man? AIT
1Sa 10:27 scoundrels said, "How *c* this fellow **save** us?" AIT
1Sa 11:3 us seven days so *we c* **send** messengers AIT
1Sa 11:10 and *you c* **do** to us whatever you like. AIT
1Sa 12:21 *They c* **do** you no **good**, nor can they rescue AIT
1Sa 12:21 you no good, nor *c they* **rescue** you, because AIT
1Sa 14:6 Nothing **c** hinder the LORD from saving NDT
1Sa 16:2 Samuel said, "How *c I* **go**? If Saul hears AIT
1Sa 16:16 to search for someone *who* **c** play the lyre. H3359
1Sa 18:8 What more **c** he get but the kingdom?" NDT
1Sa 20:7 *you c* **be sure** that he is determined to harm AIT
1Sa 21:3 five loaves of bread, or whatever *you c* **find**." AIT
1Sa 25:8 your son David whatever you *c* **find** for them. AIT
1Sa 25:17 Now think it over and see what *you c* **do** AIT
1Sa 25:17 such a wicked man that no *one c* **talk** to him." AIT
1Sa 26:9 Who *c* **lay** a hand on the LORD's anointed AIT
1Sa 27:1 The best thing I **c** do is to escape to the NDT
1Sa 28:2 will see for yourself what your servant *c* **do**." AIT
1Sa 30:15 "*C you* **lead** me **down** to this raiding party?" AIT
2Sa 1:7 called out to me, and I said, '**What c** I **do**? H2180
2Sa 5:6 even the blind and the lame *c* **ward** you **off**." AIT
2Sa 6:9 How *c* the ark of the LORD *ever* **come** to me?" AIT
2Sa 7:10 them so that *they c* **have a home** *of* their own AIT
2Sa 7:20 "What more *c* David **say** to you? For you AIT
2Sa 9:1 house of Saul to whom *I c* **show** kindness AIT
2Sa 9:3 of Saul to whom *I c* **show** God's kindness?" AIT
2Sa 12:18 How *c we* now **tell** him the child is dead AIT
2Sa 12:23 I go on fasting? **C** *I* bring him back again H3523
2Sa 14:19 no one **c** turn to the right or to the left from NDT
2Sa 14:32 'Come here so *I c* **send** you to the king to ask AIT
2Sa 15:34 then *you c* help me *by* **frustrating** AIT
2Sa 16:10 'Curse David,' who *c* **ask**, 'Why do you do AIT
2Sa 17:5 so *we c* **hear** what he has to say as well." AIT
2Sa 19:26 will ride on it, so *I c* **go** with the king. AIT
2Sa 19:35 *C I* **tell the difference** between what is AIT
2Sa 19:35 *C* your servant **taste** what he eats and drinks AIT
2Sa 19:35 *C I* still **hear** the voices of male and female AIT
2Sa 20:16 Tell Joab to come here so *I c* **speak** to him." AIT
2Sa 22:30 With your help *I c* **advance** *against* a troop AIT
2Sa 22:30 against a troop; with my God *I c* **scale** a wall. AIT
2Sa 22:35 battle; my arms *c* **bend** a bow of bronze. AIT
2Sa 24:21 answered, "so I *c* **build** an altar to the LORD AIT
1Ki 1:2 *She c* **lie** beside him so that our lord the king AIT
1Ki 1:12 me advise you how *you c* **save** your own life AIT
1Ki 2:37 the Kidron Valley, *you c* **be sure** you will die AIT
1Ki 2:42 anywhere else, *you c* **be sure** you will die'? AIT
1Ki 5:9 separate them and you *c* **take** them **away**. AIT
1Ki 13:16 nor *c I* **eat** bread or drink water with you in AIT
1Ki 18:5 Maybe *we c* **find** some grass to keep the AIT
1Ki 20:25 chariot—so *we c* **fight** Israel on the plains. AIT
1Ki 22:7 of the LORD here whom *we c* **inquire of**?" AIT
1Ki 22:8 through whom we *c* **inquire of** the LORD, AIT
1Ki 22:14 *I c* **tell** him only what the LORD tells me." AIT
2Ki 2:9 what *c I* **do** for you before I am taken from AIT
2Ki 2:19 well situated, as you *c* **see**, but the water is AIT
2Ki 4:2 replied to her, "How *c I* **help** you? Tell me, AIT
2Ki 4:7 You and your sons *c* **live** on what is left." AIT
2Ki 4:10 Then *he c* **stay** there whenever he comes to AIT
2Ki 4:13 Now what *c be* **done** for you? Can we AIT
2Ki 4:13 *C* we **speak** on your behalf to the king or the AIT
2Ki 4:14 "What *c be* **done** for her?" Elisha asked AIT
2Ki 4:22 so *I c* **go** to the man of God **quickly** and AIT
2Ki 4:43 "How *c I* **set** this before a hundred men?" AIT
2Ki 5:7 *C I* **kill** and bring back to life AIT
2Ki 5:17 as much earth as a pair of mules **c** carry, NDT
2Ki 6:2 where each of *us c* **get** a pole; and let us AIT
2Ki 6:13 ordered, "so *I c* **send** men and capture him." AIT
2Ki 6:20 open the eyes of these men so *they c* **see**." AIT
2Ki 6:27 not help you, where *c I* **get help** for you? AIT
2Ki 8:1 stay for a while wherever *you c*, H1591[S]
2Ki 9:22 "How **c** there be peace," Jehu replied, "as NDT
2Ki 10:4 kings could not resist him, how **c** we?" H6641[S]
2Ki 18:23 horses—if *you c* put riders on them! H3523
2Ki 18:24 How *c you* **repulse** one officer of the least of AIT
2Ki 18:35 How then *c* the LORD **deliver** Jerusalem from AIT
1Ch 13:12 "How *c I ever* **bring** the ark of God to me?" AIT
1Ch 17:9 that *they c* **have a home** *of their own* and no AIT
1Ch 17:18 "What more **c** David say to you for honoring NDT
1Ch 21:22 threshing floor so I *c* **build** an altar to the AIT
2Ch 2:14 of engraving and *c* **execute** any design given AIT
2Ch 2:16 You *c* then **take** them **up** *to* Jerusalem." AIT
2Ch 18:6 of the LORD here whom *we c* **inquire of**?" AIT
2Ch 18:7 through whom we *c* **inquire of** the LORD, AIT
2Ch 18:13 lives, *I c* **tell** him only what my God says." AIT
2Ch 20:6 in your hand, and no one *c* **withstand** you. AIT
2Ch 25:9 "The LORD *c* **give** you much more than that." AIT
2Ch 29:8 scorn, as you *c* **see** with your own eyes. AIT
2Ch 32:14 How then *c* your god deliver you from my H3523
Ezr 9:10 our God, what *c we* **say** after this? For AIT
Ezr 9:15 of it not one of us *c* **stand** in your presence." AIT
Ne 2:2 This **c** be nothing but sadness of heart." NDT
Ne 2:5 my ancestors are buried so that *I c* **rebuild** it." AIT
Ne 4:2 *C they* **bring** the stones **back to life** from AIT
Ne 4:22 so *they c* **serve** us as guards by night and as AIT
Est 8:6 For how *c I* **bear** to see disaster fall on my AIT
Est 8:6 How *c I* **bear** to see the destruction of my AIT
Est 8:8 name and sealed with his ring *c be* **revoked**." AIT
Job 4:2 But who **c** keep from speaking? H3523
Job 4:17 '*C* a mortal *be* more **righteous** than God? Can AIT
Job 4:17 *C* even a strong man *be* more **pure** than his AIT
Job 6:30 *C* my mouth not **discern** malice? AIT
Job 8:11 *C* papyrus **grow tall** where there is no marsh AIT
Job 8:11 *C* reeds **thrive** without water? AIT
Job 9:2 how *c* mere mortals **prove** *their* **innocence** AIT
Job 9:12 snatches away, who *c* **stop** him? Who can say AIT
Job 9:12 Who *c* **say** to him, 'What are AIT
Job 9:14 "How then *c* **I dispute** *with* him? How can I AIT
Job 9:14 *How c I* **find** words to argue with him? AIT
Job 9:19 it is a matter of justice, who *c* **challenge** him? AIT
Job 10:7 that no *one c* **rescue** me from your hand AIT
Job 10:20 away from me so *I c* **have** a moment's **joy** AIT
Job 11:7 "*C you* **fathom** the mysteries of God? Can AIT
Job 11:7 *C you* **probe** the limits of the Almighty AIT
Job 11:8 than the heavens above—what *c you* **do**? AIT
Job 11:8 than the depths below—what *c you* **know**? AIT
Job 11:10 convenes a court, who *c* **oppose** him? AIT
Job 11:12 the witless *c* no more **become wise** than a AIT
Job 11:12 than a wild donkey's colt *c* **be born** human. AIT
Job 13:19 *C* anyone **bring charges** against me? If so, AIT
Job 14:4 Who *c* **bring** what is pure from the impure AIT
Job 17:15 is my hope—who *c* **see** any hope for me? AIT
Job 18:2 Be sensible, and then *we c* **talk**. AIT
Job 21:22 "*C anyone* **teach** knowledge to God, since he AIT
Job 21:34 "So how *c you* **console** me *with* your AIT
Job 22:2 "*C* a man **be of benefit** to God? Can even a AIT
Job 22:2 *C* even a wise person **benefit** him? AIT
Job 22:17 What *c* the Almighty **do** to us?' AIT
Job 23:7 upright *c* **establish** their **innocence** before AIT
Job 23:13 he stands alone, and who *c* **oppose** him? AIT
Job 24:25 who *c* **prove** me **false** and reduce my words AIT
Job 25:3 *C* his forces **be** numbered? On whom does AIT
Job 25:4 How then *c* a mortal *be* **righteous** before God AIT
Job 25:4 How *c* one born of woman *be* **pure**? AIT
Job 26:14 Who then *c* **understand** the thunder of his AIT
Job 28:12 But where *c* wisdom **be found**? Where does AIT
Job 28:15 nor *c* its price **be weighed out** *in* silver. AIT
Job 28:17 Neither gold nor crystal *c* **compare** *with* it, AIT
Job 28:17 nor **c** it be had for jewels of gold. NDT
Job 30:13 'No *one c* **help** him,' they say. AIT
Job 33:5 Answer me then, if *you* **c**; stand up and H3523
Job 33:26 then *that person c* **pray** to God and find favor AIT
Job 34:17 *C someone who* **hates** justice govern? Will AIT
Job 34:22 no utter darkness, where evildoers *c* **hide**. AIT
Job 34:26 their wickedness where *everyone c* **see** them, AIT
Job 34:29 But if he remains silent, who *c* **condemn** him? AIT
Job 34:29 hides his face, who *c* **see** him? Yet he is over AIT
Job 36:29 Who *c* **understand** how he spreads out the AIT
Job 37:18 *c you* join him in **spreading out** the skies AIT
Job 37:21 Now no *one c* **look** *at* the sun, bright as it is AIT
Job 38:20 *C you* **take** them to their places? Do you know AIT
Job 38:31 "*C you* **bind** the chains of the Pleiades? Can AIT
Job 38:31 of the Pleiades? *C you* **loosen** Orion's belt? AIT
Job 38:32 *C you* **bring forth** the constellations in their AIT
Job 38:33 *C you* **set up** God's dominion over the earth AIT
Job 38:34 "*C you* **raise** your voice to the clouds and AIT
Job 38:37 Who *c* **tip over** the water jars of the heavens AIT
Job 39:10 *C you* **hold** it to the furrow with a harness AIT
Job 39:12 *C you* **trust** it to haul in your grain and bring it AIT
Job 40:4 am unworthy—how *c I* **reply** to you? I put my AIT
Job 40:9 like God's, and *c* your voice **thunder** like his? AIT
Job 40:14 to you that your own right hand *c* **save** you. AIT
Job 40:19 its Maker *c* **approach** it with his sword. AIT
Job 40:24 *C anyone* **capture** it by the eyes, or trap it AIT
Job 41:1 "*C you* **pull in** Leviathan with a fishhook or AIT
Job 41:2 *C you* **put** a cord through its nose or pierce its AIT
Job 41:5 *C you* **make a pet** of it like a bird or put it on AIT
Job 41:7 *C you* **fill** its hide with harpoons or its head AIT
Job 41:13 Who *c* **strip off** its outer coat? Who can AIT
Job 41:13 Who *c* **penetrate** its double coat of armor? AIT
Job 41:16 close to the next that no air *c* **pass** between. AIT
Job 42:2 "I know that *you* **c** do all things; no H3523
Job 42:2 all things; no purpose of yours *c* **be thwarted**. AIT
Ps 2:12 his wrath *c* **flare up** in a moment. AIT
Ps 5:7 by your great love, *c* **come into** your house; in AIT
Ps 5:9 Not a *word* from their mouth *c* **be trusted** AIT
Ps 11:1 How then *c you* **say** to me: "Flee like AIT
Ps 11:3 being destroyed, what *c* the righteous **do**?" AIT
Ps 18:29 With your help *I c* **advance** *against* a troop AIT
Ps 18:29 against a troop; with my God *I c* **scale** a wall. AIT
Ps 18:34 battle; my arms *c* **bend** a bow of bronze. AIT
Ps 19:12 But who *c* **discern** their own errors? Forgive AIT
Ps 38:14 not hear, whose mouth **c** offer no reply. NDT
Ps 40:5 None *c* **compare** with you; were I to speak AIT
Ps 42:2 When *c I* **go** and meet with God? AIT
Ps 49:7 No one *c* **redeem** the life of another or give AIT
Ps 49:10 For *all c* **see** that the wise die, that the AIT
Ps 56:4 What *c* mere mortals **do** to me? AIT
Ps 56:11 am not afraid. What *c* man **do** to me? AIT
Ps 58:9 Before your pots *c* **feel** the heat of the thorns AIT
Ps 59:7 as swords, and they think, "Who *c* **hear** us?" AIT
Ps 59:10 my God on whom I **c** rely. God will go NDT
Ps 59:17 are my fortress, my God on whom I **c** rely. NDT
Ps 71:3 to which I *c* always **go**; give the command AIT
Ps 75:6 west or from the desert *c* **exalt** *themselves*. AIT
Ps 76:5 not one of the warriors *c* **lift** his hands. AIT
Ps 76:7 Who *c* **stand** before you when you are angry? AIT
Ps 78:19 "**C** God really spread a table in the H3523
Ps 78:20 abundantly, but **c** *he* also give us bread? H3523
Ps 78:20 *C he* **supply** meat for his people? AIT
Ps 86:8 Lord; no deeds **c** compare with yours. NDT
Ps 89:6 in the skies above *c* **compare** with the LORD? AIT
Ps 89:48 Who *c* **live** and not see death, or who can AIT
Ps 89:48 who *c* **escape** the power of the grave? AIT
Ps 94:20 *C* a corrupt throne *be* **allied with** you—a AIT
Ps 104:5 earth on its foundations; *it c* never **be moved**. AIT
Ps 106:2 Who *c* **proclaim** the mighty acts of the LORD AIT
Ps 115:7 nor *c they* **utter a sound** with their throats. AIT

Ps 118: 6 What c mere mortals do to me? AIT
Ps 119: 9 How c a young person stay on the path of AIT
Ps 119:42 then I c answer anyone who taunts me, for I AIT
Ps 119:165 and nothing c make them stumble. NDT
Ps 129: 6 on the roof, which withers before it c grow; AIT
Ps 130: 4 so that we c, with reverence, serve you. AIT
Ps 137: 4 How c we sing the songs of the LORD while in AIT
Ps 139: 7 Where c I go from your Spirit? Where can I AIT
Ps 139: 7 Where c I flee from your presence AIT
Ps 145: 3 of praise; his greatness no one c fathom. NDT
Ps 147:17 Who c withstand his icy blast? AIT
Pr 1:17 to spread a net where every bird c see it! NDT
Pr 3:15 nothing you desire c compare with her. AIT
Pr 6:26 For a prostitute c be had for a loaf of bread NDT
Pr 6:27 C a man scoop fire into his lap without his AIT
Pr 6:28 C a man walk on hot coals without his feet AIT
Pr 8:11 nothing you desire c compare with her. AIT
Pr 12: 3 No one c be established through wickedness AIT
Pr 14:10 bitterness, and no one else c share its joy. AIT
Pr 18:14 The human spirit c endure in sickness, but a AIT
Pr 18:14 in sickness, but a crushed spirit who c bear? AIT
Pr 20: 6 but a faithful person who c find? AIT
Pr 20: 9 Who c say, "I have kept my heart pure; I am AIT
Pr 20:24 How then c anyone understand their own AIT
Pr 21:22 One who is wise c go up against the city of AIT
Pr 21:30 no plan that c succeed against the LORD. NDT
Pr 23:35 will I wake up so I c find another drink?" AIT
Pr 24:22 who knows what calamities they c bring? NDT
Pr 25: 4 and a silversmith c produce a vessel; AIT
Pr 25:15 Through patience a ruler c be persuaded AIT
Pr 25:15 a gentle tongue c break a bone. AIT
Pr 27: 4 who c stand before jealousy? AIT
Pr 27: 6 Wounds from a friend c be trusted, but an AIT
Pr 27:11 then I c answer anyone who treats me with AIT
Pr 30: 1 "I am weary, God, but I c prevail. AIT
Pr 30:28 a lizard c be caught with the hand, yet it is AIT
Pr 31:10 A wife of noble character who c find? She is AIT
Pr 31:25 dignity; she c laugh at the days to come. AIT
Ecc 1: 8 are wearisome, more than one c say. H3523
Ecc 1:10 Is there anything of which one c say, "Look AIT
Ecc 2:12 What more c the king's successor do than NDT
Ecc 2:24 A person c do nothing better than to eat NDT
Ecc 2:25 without him, who c eat or find enjoyment? AIT
Ecc 3:11 no one c fathom what God has done from AIT
Ecc 3:14 nothing c be added to it and nothing taken AIT
Ecc 3:22 For who c bring them to see what will AIT
Ecc 4:10 of them falls down, one c help the other up. AIT
Ecc 4:11 But how c one keep warm alone? AIT
Ecc 4:12 be overpowered, two c defend themselves. AIT
Ecc 5:15 from their toil that they c carry in their hands. AIT
Ecc 6:10 no one c contend with someone who is H3523
Ecc 6:12 Who c tell them what will happen under the AIT
Ecc 7:13 Who c straighten what he has made H3523
Ecc 7:14 no one c discover anything about their future. AIT
Ecc 7:24 off and most profound—who c discover it? AIT
Ecc 8: 4 is supreme, who c say to him, "What are AIT
Ecc 8: 7 who c tell someone else what is to come? AIT
Ecc 8:17 No one c comprehend what goes on H3523
Ecc 8:17 search it out, no one c discover its meaning. AIT
Ecc 10: 4 calmness c lay great offenses to rest. AIT
Ecc 10:14 who c tell someone else what will happen AIT
Isa 11:15 so that anyone c cross over in sandals. AIT
Isa 14:27 has purposed, and who c thwart him? AIT
Isa 14:27 hand is stretched out, and who c turn it back? AIT
Isa 19:11 How c you say to Pharaoh, "I am one of the AIT
Isa 19:15 There is nothing Egypt c do—head or tail AIT
Isa 20: 6 the king of Assyria! How then c we escape?'" AIT
Isa 22:22 what he opens no one c shut, and what he AIT
Isa 22:22 can shut, and what he shuts no one c open. AIT
Isa 29:11 the scroll to someone who c read, H3359+6219
Isa 29:16 C the pot say to the potter, "You know AIT
Isa 31: 2 Yet he too is wise and c bring disaster; he AIT
Isa 33:14 "Who of us c dwell with the consuming fire AIT
Isa 33:14 Who of us c dwell with everlasting burning?" AIT
Isa 36: 8 horses—if you c put riders on them! H3523
Isa 36: 9 How then c you repulse one officer of the AIT
Isa 36:20 How then c the LORD deliver Jerusalem from AIT
Isa 38:15 But what c I say? He has spoken to me, and AIT
Isa 40:13 Who c fathom the Spirit of the LORD, or AIT
Isa 40:28 his understanding no one c fathom. NDT
Isa 43:13 No one c deliver out of my hand AIT
Isa 43:13 When I act, who c reverse it?" AIT
Isa 44:10 god and casts an idol, which c profit nothing? AIT
Isa 47:15 in their error; there is not one that c save you. AIT
Isa 48:11 How c I let myself be defamed? I will AIT
Isa 49:15 "C a mother forget the baby at her breast AIT
Isa 49:24 C plunder be taken from warriors, or captives AIT
Isa 51:19 have come upon you—who c comfort you?— AIT
Isa 51:19 famine and sword—who c console you? AIT
Isa 64: 5 you were angry. How then c we be saved? AIT
Isa 66: 8 C a country be born in a day or a nation be AIT
Jer 2:23 "How c you say, 'I am not defiled; I have not AIT
Jer 2:24 her craving—in her heat who c restrain her? AIT
Jer 2:28 Let them come if they c save you when you AIT
Jer 2:33 the worst of women c learn from your ways. AIT
Jer 3: 5 how you talk, but you do all the evil you c." H3523
Jer 5: 1 If you c find but one person who deals AIT
Jer 6: 8 your land desolate so no one c live in it." AIT
Jer 6:10 To whom c I speak and give warning? Who AIT
Jer 8: 8 "'How c you say, "We are wise, for we have AIT
Jer 9: 7 what else c I do because of the sin of my AIT
Jer 9:11 the towns of Judah so no one c live there." AIT
Jer 9:12 been instructed by the LORD and c explain it? AIT
Jer 9:12 laid waste like a desert that no one c cross? AIT
Jer 10: 5 they c do no harm nor can they do any good." AIT
Jer 10: 5 they can do no harm nor c they do any good." AIT
Jer 11:15 C consecrated meat avert your punishment AIT
Jer 12: 5 how c you compete with horses? AIT
Jer 13:23 C an Ethiopian change his skin or a leopard AIT
Jer 13:23 Neither c you do good who are H3523
Jer 15:12 "C a man break iron—iron from the north AIT
Jer 17: 9 beyond cure. Who c understand it? AIT
Jer 18: 6 He said, "C I not do with you, Israel, as H3523
Jer 21:13 you who say, "Who c come against us? AIT
Jer 21:13 come against us? Who c enter our refuge?" AIT
Jer 23:24 Who c hide in secret places so that I cannot AIT
Jer 25: 5 and you c stay in the land the LORD gave to AIT
Jer 30: 6 C a man bear children? Then why AIT
Jer 31:37 the heavens above c be measured and the AIT
Jer 33:20 'If you c break my covenant with the day AIT
Jer 33:21 c be broken and David will no longer have a AIT
Jer 34:22 the towns of Judah so no one c live there." AIT
Jer 38: 5 "The king c do nothing to oppose you." H3523
Jer 47: 7 But how c it rest when the LORD has AIT
Jer 48:14 "How c you say, 'We are warriors, men AIT
Jer 49:11 Your widows too c depend on me.'" AIT
Jer 49:19 Who is like me and who c challenge me AIT
Jer 49:19 And what shepherd c stand against me?" AIT
Jer 50:44 Who is like me and who c challenge me AIT
Jer 50:44 And what shepherd c stand against me?" AIT
Jer 51: 8 balm for her pain; perhaps she c be healed. AIT
La 2:13 What c I say for you? With what can I AIT
La 2:13 With what c I compare you, Daughter AIT
La 2:13 To what c I liken you, that I may comfort you AIT
La 2:13 is as deep as the sea. Who c heal you? AIT
La 3:37 Who c speak and have it happen if the Lord AIT
La 3:44 with a cloud so that no prayer c get through. AIT
La 4:15 the nations say, "They c stay here no longer." AIT
La 5: 4 we drink; our wood c be had only at a price. AIT
Eze 14:15 so that no one c pass through it because of AIT
Eze 15: 5 how much less c it be made into something AIT
Eze 31: 2 "'Who c be compared with you in majesty? AIT
Eze 31:18 of Eden c be compared with you in splendor AIT
Eze 33:10 because of them. How then c we live?" AIT
Eze 34:10 the shepherds c no longer feed themselves. AIT
Eze 37: 3 asked me, "Son of man, c these bones live?" AIT
Da 2: 9 I will know that you c interpret it for me." AIT
Da 2:10 no one on earth who c do what the king A10321
Da 2:11 No one c reveal it to the king except the gods AIT
Da 2:25 from Judah who c tell the king what his AIT
Da 2:27 magician or diviner c explain to the king A10321
Da 3:29 no other god c save in this way. A10321
Da 4:18 men in my kingdom c interpret it for me. A10321
Da 4:18 But you c, because the spirit of the holy A10346
Da 4:35 No one c hold back his hand or say to him AIT
Da 5:16 If you c read this writing and tell me A10321
Da 6:15 edict that the king issues c be changed." AIT
Da 10:17 How c I, your servant, talk with you, my H3523
Da 10:17 gone and I c hardly breathe." H5972+4202+8636
Hos 4:16 How then c the LORD pasture them like lambs AIT
Hos 6: 4 "What c I do with you, Ephraim? What can I AIT
Hos 6: 4 What c I do with you, Judah? Your AIT
Hos 11: 8 "How c I give you up, Ephraim? How can I AIT
Hos 11: 8 How c I hand you over, Israel? How AIT
Hos 11: 8 How c I treat you like Admah? How AIT
Hos 11: 8 How c I make you like Zeboyim AIT
Joel 2:11 LORD is great; it is dreadful. Who c endure it? AIT
Am 3: 8 LORD has spoken—who c but prophesy? AIT
Am 7: 2 How c Jacob survive? He is so small! AIT
Am 7: 5 How c Jacob survive? He is so AIT
Ob 3 'Who c bring me down to the ground? AIT
Jnh 1: 6 went to him and said, "How c you sleep? AIT
Mic 5: 8 mangles as it goes, and no one c rescue. AIT
Na 1: 6 Who c withstand his indignation? Who can AIT
Na 1: 6 Who c endure his fierce anger AIT
Na 3: 7 Where c I find anyone to comfort you?" AIT
Na 3:19 Nothing c heal you; your wound is fatal. NDT
Hab 2:15 so that he c gaze on their naked bodies! AIT
Hab 2:19 C it give guidance? It is covered AIT
Mal 3: 2 But who c endure the day of his coming AIT
Mal 3: 2 Who c stand when he appears AIT
Mt 3: 9 And do not think you c say to yourselves, 'We AIT
Mt 3: 9 of these stones God c raise up children G1538
Mt 5:13 its saltiness, how c it be made salty again? AIT
Mt 6:24 "No one c serve two masters. Either you G1538
Mt 6:27 C any one of you by worrying add a single G1538
Mt 7: 4 How c you say to your brother, 'Let me take AIT
Mt 8: 2 if you are willing, you c make me clean." G1538
Mt 9:15 "How c the guests of the bridegroom G1538
Mt 10:28 be afraid of the One who c destroy both G1538
Mt 11:16 "To what c I compare this generation? They AIT
Mt 12:26 How then c his kingdom stand? AIT
Mt 12:29 how c anyone enter a strong man's house G1538
Mt 12:29 Then he c plunder his house. AIT
Mt 12:31 every kind of sin and slander c be forgiven AIT
Mt 12:34 how c you who are evil say anything good G1538
Mt 14:15 so they c go to the villages and buy AIT
Mt 16:26 Or what c anyone give in exchange for their AIT
Mt 17:20 a mustard seed, you c say to this mountain AIT
Mt 19:11 "Not everyone c accept this word, but only AIT
Mt 19:12 The one who c accept this should accept G1538
Mt 19:25 asked, "Who then c be saved? G1538
Mt 20:22 "C you drink the cup I am going to drink?" G1538
Mt 20:22 going to drink?" "We c," they answered. G1538
Mt 21:21 not only c you do what was done to the fig AIT
Mt 21:21 but also you c say to this mountain AIT
Mt 22:45 David calls him 'Lord,' how c he be his son?" AIT
Mk 1:38 the nearby villages—so I c preach there also. AIT
Mk 1:40 "If you are willing, you c make me clean." G1538
Mk 2: 7 Who c forgive sins but God alone? G1538
Mk 2:19 "How c the guests of the bridegroom fast G1538
Mk 3:23 "How c Satan drive out Satan? G1538
Mk 3:27 no one c enter a strong man's house G1538
Mk 3:27 Then he c plunder the strong man's house. AIT
Mk 3:28 people c be forgiven all their sins and every AIT
Mk 4:32 that the birds c perch in its shade. G1538
Mk 5:31 "and yet you c ask, 'Who touched me? AIT
Mk 6:36 away so that they c go to the surrounding AIT
Mk 7:15 outside a person c defile them by going G1538
Mk 7:18 a person from the outside c defile them? G1538
Mk 8: 4 in this remote place c anyone get enough G1538
Mk 8:37 Or what c anyone give in exchange for their AIT
Mk 9:22 But if you c do anything, take pity on us G1538
Mk 9:23 "'If you c'?" said Jesus. "Everything is G1538
Mk 9:29 "This kind c come out only by prayer." G1538
Mk 9:39 miracle in my name c in the next moment G1538
Mk 9:50 its saltiness, how c you make it salty again? AIT
Mk 10:26 to each other, "Who then c be saved?" G1538
Mk 10:38 "C you drink the cup I drink or be baptized G1538
Mk 10:39 "We c," they answered. Jesus said to G1538
Mk 12:37 How then c he be his son?" The large AIT
Mk 14: 7 and you c help them any time you want. G1538
Lk 1:18 asked the angel, "How c I be sure of this? AIT
Lk 3: 8 of these stones God c raise up children G1538
Lk 4: 6 and I c give it to anyone I want to. AIT
Lk 5:12 if you are willing, you c make me clean." G1538
Lk 5:21 Who c forgive sins but God alone? G1538
Lk 5:34 "C you make the friends of the G1538
Lk 6:39 "C the blind lead the blind G1538
Lk 6:42 How c you say to your brother, 'Brother, let G1538
Lk 7:31 c I compare the people of this generation? AIT
Lk 8:16 so that those who come in c see the light. AIT
Lk 9:12 the crowd away so they c go to the AIT
Lk 11:18 against himself, how c his kingdom stand? AIT
Lk 11:46 down with burdens they c hardly carry, G1546
Lk 12: 4 kill the body and after that c do no more. G2400
Lk 12:25 of you by worrying c add a single hour to G1538
Lk 12:36 knocks they c immediately open the door AIT
Lk 13:33 surely no prophet c die outside G1896
Lk 14:34 its saltiness, how c it be made salty again? AIT
Lk 16:10 "Whoever c be trusted with very little can NDT
Lk 16:10 with very little c also be trusted with much, AIT
Lk 16:13 "No one c serve two masters. Either you G1538
Lk 16:26 nor c anyone cross over from there to us. AIT
Lk 17: 6 you c say to this mulberry tree G323
Lk 17:20 God is not something that c be observed, G4191
Lk 18:26 heard this asked, "Who then c be saved?" G1538
Lk 20:36 they c no longer die; for they are like G1538
Lk 20:44 calls him 'Lord.' How then c he be his son?" AIT
Lk 21:30 you c see for yourselves and know that AIT
Lk 23:15 back to us; as you c see, he has G2779+2627
Jn 1:46 C anything good come from there? G1538
Jn 2:18 sign c you show us to prove your authority to AIT
Jn 3: 3 no one c see the kingdom of God unless G1538
Jn 3: 4 "How c someone be born when they are G1538
Jn 3: 5 no one c enter the kingdom of God unless G1538
Jn 3: 9 "How c this be?" Nicodemus asked. G1538
Jn 3:27 "A person c receive only what is given G1538
Jn 3:28 You yourselves c testify that I said, 'I am not AIT
Jn 4: 9 How c you ask me for a drink?" AIT
Jn 4:11 Where c you get this living water? AIT
Jn 4:19 woman said, "I c see that you are a prophet. AIT
Jn 5:19 I tell you, the Son c do nothing by himself G1538
Jn 5:19 he c do only what he sees his Father doing NDT
Jn 5:30 By myself I c do nothing; I judge only as I G1538
Jn 5:44 How c you believe since you accept glory G1538
Jn 6:42 How c he now say, 'I came down from AIT
Jn 6:44 "No one c come to me unless the Father G1538
Jn 6:52 "How c this man give us his flesh to eat?" G1538
Jn 6:60 is a hard teaching. Who c accept it?" G1538
Jn 6:65 told you that no one c come to me unless G1538
Jn 7:23 Now if a boy c be circumcised on the Sabbath AIT
Jn 7:41 "How c the Messiah come from Galilee? AIT
Jn 8:33 How c you say that we shall be set free?" AIT
Jn 8:46 C any of you prove me guilty of sin? If I am AIT
Jn 9: 4 Night is coming, when no one c work. G1538
Jn 9:16 "How c a sinner perform such signs?" G1538
Jn 9:19 How is it that now he c see?" AIT
Jn 9:21 But how he c see now, or who opened his AIT
Jn 9:41 now that you claim you c see, your guilt AIT
Jn 10:21 C a demon open the eyes of the blind?" G1538
Jn 10:29 no one c snatch them out of my Father's G1538
Jn 12:34 so how c you say, 'The Son of Man AIT
Jn 12:40 so they c neither see with their eyes AIT
Jn 14: 5 are going, so how c we know the way?" G1538
Jn 14: 9 seen the Father. How c you say, 'Show us the AIT
Jn 15: 4 No branch c bear fruit by itself; it must G1538
Jn 15: 4 Neither c you bear fruit unless you remain in AIT
Jn 15: 5 apart from me you c do nothing. G1538
Jn 16:10 to the Father, where you c see me no longer; AIT
Jn 16:12 to say to you, more than you c now bear. G1538
Jn 16:30 Now we c see that you know all things and AIT
Ac 2:29 I c tell you confidently that the patriarch G2003
Ac 3:16 has completely healed him, as you c all see. AIT
Ac 8:31 "How c I," he said, "unless someone G1538
Ac 8:33 Who c speak of his descendants AIT

Ac 8:36 What *c* **stand in the way** *of* my being AIT
Ac 10:47 "Surely no one **c** stand in the way of their G1538
Ac 16:36 Now *you c* **leave**. Go in peace. AIT
Ac 19:38 there are proconsuls. *They c* **press charges**. AIT
Ac 20:32 which **c** build you up and give you an G1538
Ac 21:24 so that *they c have* their heads **shaved**. AIT
Ac 22: 5 all the Council *c themselves* **testify**. AIT
Ac 24:11 You **c** easily verify that no more than G1538
Ac 25: 5 *they c* **press charges** against him there." AIT
Ac 26: 5 have known me for a long time and *c* **testify**, AIT
Ac 26:26 with these things, and *I c* **speak** freely to him. AIT
Ac 26:28 such a short time *you c* **persuade** me to be a AIT
Ac 27:10 *I c* **see** that our voyage is going to be AIT
Ro 5:16 Nor **c** the gift of God be compared with the NDT
Ro 6: 2 died to sin; how *c we* **live** in it any longer? AIT
Ro 8: 7 not submit to God's law, nor **c** *it* do so. G1538
Ro 8:31 If God is for us, who **c** be against us? NDT
Ro 10: 2 For *I c* **testify** about them that they are zealous AIT
Ro 10:14 *c they* **call on** the one they have not believed AIT
Ro 10:14 And how *c they* **believe** in the one of whom AIT
Ro 10:14 And how *c they* **hear** without someone AIT
Ro 10:15 And how *c anyone* **preach** unless they are AIT
1Co 1:15 so no one *c* **say** that you were baptized in my AIT
1Co 3:11 For no one **c** lay any foundation other than G1538
1Co 7:21 although if *you* **c** gain your freedom G1538
1Co 7:32 the Lord's affairs—how *he c* **please** the Lord. AIT
1Co 7:33 of this world—how *he c* **please** his wife— AIT
1Co 7:34 this world—how *she c* **please** her husband. AIT
1Co 10:13 you be tempted beyond what *you* **c** **bear**. G1538
1Co 10:13 provide a way out so that *you* **c** endure it. G1538
1Co 12: 3 and no one **c** say, "Jesus is Lord, G1538
1Co 13: 2 of prophecy and *c* **fathom** all mysteries and AIT
1Co 13: 2 if I have a faith that *c* **move** mountains AIT
1Co 14:16 *c someone else*, who is now put in the position of an inquirer, **say** AIT
1Co 14:31 For *you* **c** all prophesy in turn so that G1538
1Co 15:12 how *c* some of you **say** that there is no AIT
1Co 16: 6 so that you *c* **help** me **on** my **journey** AIT
2Co 1: 4 so that we **c** comfort those in any trouble G1538
2Co 1:14 fully that you **c** boast of us just as we NDT
2Co 5:12 so that *you c* **answer** those who take pride in AIT
2Co 6:14 Or what fellowship **c** light have with NDT
2Co 7:16 glad *I c have* complete **confidence** in you. AIT
2Co 8:24 pride in you, so that the churches **c** see it. NDT
2Co 9:11 way so that you **c** be generous on every NDT
2Co 10:16 *so that we c* **preach the gospel** in the regions AIT
Gal 3:15 Just as no one *c* **set aside** or add to a human AIT
Gal 4:15 *I c* **testify** that, if you could have done so, you AIT
Gal 6: 4 Then *they c* **take** pride in themselves alone AIT
Eph 2: 9 not by works, so that no one *c* **boast**. AIT
Eph 5: 5 For of this *you c* **be** sure: No immoral, impure AIT
Eph 6:11 so that you **c** take your stand against the G1538
Eph 6:16 with which *you* **c** extinguish all the G1538
Php 1: 8 God **c** testify how I long for all of you with NDT
Php 1:17 supposing *that they c* **stir up** trouble for me AIT
Php 4:13 *I c* **do** all this through him who gives me G2710
1Th 3: 9 How **c** *we* thank God *enough* for you in G1538
1Ti 3: 5 how *c he* **take care** of God's church? AIT
1Ti 5:16 so that the church *c* **help** those widows who AIT
1Ti 6: 7 the world, and *we* **c** take nothing out of it. G1538
1Ti 6:16 whom no one has seen or **c** see. G1538
Titus 1: 9 so that *he* **c** encourage others by G1543+1639
Titus 2: 4 Then *they c* **urge** the younger women to love AIT
Titus 2:10 to show that they **c** be fully trusted, so NDT
Titus 3:13 *Do* **everything** *you c* to help Zenas the G5081
Heb 10: 1 For this reason *it* **c** never, by the same G1538
Heb 10:11 sacrifices, which **c** never take away sins. G1538
Heb 12:18 to a mountain *that c be* **touched** and that is AIT
Heb 12:27 indicate the removing *of* what *c be* **shaken** AIT
Heb 13: 6 What *c* mere mortals **do** to me?" AIT
Jas 1:21 word planted in you, which **c** save you. G1538
Jas 2:14 has no deeds? **C** such faith save them G1538
Jas 3: 3 them obey us, *we c* **turn** the whole animal. AIT
Jas 3: 8 no human being **c** tame the tongue. G1538
Jas 3:11 *C* both fresh water and salt water **flow** from AIT
Jas 3:12 sisters, **c** a fig tree bear olives G1538
Jas 3:12 Neither **c** a salt spring produce fresh water NDT
1Pe 1: 4 into an inheritance that **c** never perish NDT
1Jn 3:17 how *c* the love of God **be** in that person? AIT
1Jn 4: 2 This is how *you c* **recognize** the Spirit of God AIT
Rev 3: 7 What he opens no one *c* **shut**, and what he AIT
Rev 3: 7 can shut, and what he shuts no one *c* **open**. AIT
Rev 3: 8 you an open door that no one **c** shut. G1538
Rev 3:18 in the fire, so *you c become* **rich**; and white AIT
Rev 3:18 so *you c* **cover** your shameful nakedness AIT
Rev 3:18 salve to put on your eyes, so *you c* **see**. AIT
Rev 6:17 wrath has come, and who **c** withstand it?" G1538
Rev 13: 4 Who **c** wage war against it? G1538

CAN'T (17) [CAN, NOT]

Ge 19:19 But I **c** flee to the mountains; this H3523+4202
Ge 29: 8 "*We* **c**," they replied, "until all the H3523+4202
Ge 34:14 to them, "*We* **c** do such a thing H3523+4202
Ge 34:14 we **c** give our sister to a man who is not NDT
Nu 13:31 "*We* **c** attack those people H3523+4202
Nu 22:38 "But *I* **c** say whatever I please H3523+3523
Jdg 9:54 kill me, **so that** they **c** say, 'A woman H7153
Jdg 14:13 If *you* **c** tell me the answer, you H3523+4202
Jdg 21:18 We **c** give them our daughters as H3523+4202
1Sa 17:29 said David. "**C** I even speak?" H4202
1Sa 29: 8 Why **c** I go and fight against the enemies H4202
Isa 29:11 they will answer, "*I* **c**; it is sealed." H3523+4202
Mt 27:42 they said, "but *he* **c** save himself! G4024+1538
Mk 15:31 they said, "but *he* **c** save himself! G4024+1538
Lk 11: 7 *I* **c** get up and give you anything G4024+1538
Lk 14:20 'I just got married, so *I* **c** come. G4024+1538
Jn 13:37 why **c** *I* follow you now? G4024+1538

CANA (4)

Jn 2: 1 day a wedding took place at **C** in Galilee. G2830
Jn 2:11 Jesus did here in **C** of Galilee was the G2830
Jn 4:46 Once more he visited **C** in Galilee, where G2830
Jn 21: 2 Nathanael from **C** in Galilee, the sons of G2830

CANAAN (86) [CANAANITE, CANAANITES]

Ge 9:18 (Ham was the father of **C**.) H4046
Ge 9:22 the father of **C**, saw his father naked H4046
Ge 9:25 "Cursed be **C**! The lowest of H4046
Ge 9:26 May **C** be the slave of Shem H4046
Ge 9:27 may **C** be the slave of Japheth. H4046
Ge 10: 6 The sons of Ham: Cush, Egypt, Put and **C**. H4046
Ge 10:15 **C** was the father of Sidon his firstborn H4046
Ge 10:19 the borders of **C** reached from Sidon H4050
Ge 11:31 from Ur of the Chaldeans to go to **C**. H824+4046
Ge 12: 5 they set out for the land of **C**, and H4046
Ge 13:12 Abram lived in the land of **C**, while Lot H4046
Ge 16: 3 had been living in **C** ten years, H824+4046
Ge 17: 8 The whole land of **C**, where you now H4046
Ge 23: 2 in the land of **C**, and Abraham went to H4046
Ge 23:19 which is at Hebron) in the land of **C**. H4046
Ge 31:18 to go to his father Isaac in the land of **C**. H4046
Ge 33:18 of Shechem in **C** and camped within H824+4046
Ge 35: 6 that is, Bethel) in the land of **C**. H4046
Ge 36: 2 Esau took his wives from the women of **C** H4046
Ge 36: 5 of Esau, who were born to him in **C**. H824+4046
Ge 36: 6 all the goods he had acquired in **C**, H824+4046
Ge 37: 1 his father had stayed, the land of **C**. H4046
Ge 42: 5 there was famine in the land of **C** also. H4046
Ge 42: 7 "From the land of **C**," they replied, "to buy H4046
Ge 42:13 of one man, who lives in the land of **C**. H4046
Ge 42:29 to their father Jacob in the land of **C**, H4046
Ge 42:32 youngest is now with our father in **C**. H824+4046
Ge 44: 8 you from the land of **C** the silver we found H4046
Ge 45:17 your animals and return to the land of **C**, H4046
Ge 45:25 to their father Jacob in the land of **C**. H4046
Ge 46: 6 possessions they had acquired in **C**. H824+4046
Ge 46:12 Er and Onan had died in the land of **C**). H4046
Ge 46:31 who were living in the land of **C**, have H4046
Ge 47: 1 from the land of **C** and are now in Goshen H4046
Ge 47: 4 is severe in **C** and your servants' H824+4046
Ge 47:13 both Egypt and **C** wasted away H824+4046
Ge 47:14 in Egypt and **C** in payment for the H824+4046
Ge 47:15 people of Egypt and **C** was gone, H824+4046
Ge 48: 3 appeared to me at Luz in the land of **C**, H4046
Ge 48: 7 died in the land of **C** while we were still H4046
Ge 49:30 near Mamre in **C**, which Abraham H824+4046
Ge 50: 5 the tomb I dug for myself in the land of **C**." H4046
Ge 50:13 him to the land of **C** and buried him in H4046
Ex 6: 4 with them to give them the land of **C**, H4046
Ex 15:15 the people of **C** will melt away; H4046
Ex 16:35 until they reached the border of **C**. H824+4046
Lev 14:34 "When you enter the land of **C**, which I am H4046
Lev 18: 3 must not do as they do in the land of **C**, H4046
Lev 25:38 you the land of **C** and to be your God. H4046
Nu 13: 2 "Send some men to explore the land of **C** H4046
Nu 13:17 When Moses sent them to explore **C**, H824+4046
Nu 26:19 sons of Judah, but they died in **C**. H824+4046
Nu 32:30 their possession with you in **C**." H824+4046
Nu 32:32 over before the LORD into **C** armed, H824+4046
Nu 33:40 who lived in the Negev of **C**, heard H824+4046
Nu 33:51 'When you cross the Jordan into **C**, H824+4046
Nu 34: 2 'When you enter **C**, the land that H824+4046
Nu 34:29 to the Israelites in the land of **C**. H4046
Nu 35:10 'When you cross the Jordan into **C**, H824+4046
Nu 35:14 and three in **C** as cities of refuge H824+4046
Dt 32:49 Jericho, and view **C**, the land I am giving H4046
Jos 5:12 that year they ate the produce of **C**. H824+4046
Jos 14: 1 as an inheritance in the land of **C**, H4046
Jos 21: 2 at Shiloh in **C** and said to them, "The H824+4046
Jos 22: 9 at Shiloh in **C** to return to Gilead, H824+4046
Jos 22:10 Geliloth near the Jordan in the land of **C**, H4046
Jos 22:11 on the border of **C** at Geliloth near H824+4046
Jos 22:32 returned to **C** from their meeting H824+4046
Jos 24: 3 him throughout **C** and gave him H824+4046
Jdg 3: 1 had not experienced any of the wars in **C** H4046
Jdg 4: 2 them into the hands of Jabin king of **C**, H4046
Jdg 4:23 Jabin king of **C** before the Israelites H4046
Jdg 4:24 Jabin king of **C** until they destroyed H4046
Jdg 5:19 they fought, the kings of **C** fought. H4046
Jdg 21:12 them to the camp at Shiloh in **C**. H824+4046
1Ch 1: 8 The sons of Ham: Cush, Egypt, Put and **C**. H4046
1Ch 1:13 **C** was the father of Sidon his firstborn H4046
1Ch 16:18 will give the land of **C** as the portion you H4046
Ps 105:11 will give the land of **C** as the portion you H4046
Ps 106:38 whom they sacrificed to the idols of **C** H4046
Ps 135:11 king of Bashan, and all the kings of **C**— H4046
Isa 19:18 the language of **C** and swear allegiance H4046
Ob 20 exiles who are **in C** will possess the land H4050
Zep 2: 5 LORD is against you, **C**, land of the H4046
Ac 7:11 "Then a famine struck all Egypt and **C** G5913
Ac 13:19 he overthrew seven nations in **C**, G1178+5913

CANAANITE (17) [CANAAN]

Ge 10:18 Later the **C** clans scattered H4050
Ge 28: 1 "Do not marry a **C** woman. H4046
Ge 28: 6 "Do not marry a **C** woman," H4046
Ge 28: 8 how displeasing the **C** women were to his H4046
Ge 38: 2 the daughter of a **C** man named Shua. H4050
Ge 46:10 Zohar and Shaul the son of a **C** *woman*. H4050
Ex 6:15 Zohar and Shaul the son of a **C** *woman*. H4050
Nu 21: 1 When the **C** king of Arad, who lived in the H4050
Nu 33:40 The **C** king of Arad, who lived in the H4050
Jos 5: 1 Jordan and all the **C** kings along the coast H4050
Jos 13: 3 all of it counted as **C** though held by the H4050
Jdg 1:32 lived among the **C** inhabitants of the land H4050
Jdg 1:33 too lived among the **C** inhabitants of the H4050
1Ki 9:16 He killed its **C** inhabitants and then gave H4050
1Ch 2: 3 three were born to him by a **C** *woman*, H4050
Zec 14:21 will no longer be a **C** in the house of the H4050
Mt 15:22 A **C** woman from that vicinity came to him G5914

CANAANITES (58) [CANAAN]

Ge 12: 6 At that time the **C** were in the land. H4050
Ge 13: 7 The **C** and Perizzites were also living in H4050
Ge 15:21 Amorites, **C**, Girgashites and Jebusites." H4050
Ge 24: 3 my son from the daughters of the **C**, H4050
Ge 24:37 my son from the daughters of the **C**, H4050
Ge 34:30 me obnoxious to the **C** and Perizzites, H4050
Ge 50:11 When the **C** who lived there saw the H4050
Ex 3: 8 honey—the home of the **C**, Hittites, H4050
Ex 3:17 misery in Egypt into the land of the **C**, H4050
Ex 13: 5 the LORD brings you into the land of the **C**, H4050
Ex 13:11 into the land of the **C** and gives it to you, H4050
Ex 23:23 Hittites, Perizzites, **C**, Hivites and H4050
Ex 23:28 the Hivites, **C** and Hittites out of your way. H4050
Ex 33: 2 an angel before you and drive out the **C**, H4050
Ex 34:11 out before you the Amorites, **C**, Hittites, H4050
Nu 13:29 the **C** live near the sea and along the H4050
Nu 14:25 the Amalekites and the **C** are living in the H4050
Nu 14:43 Amalekites and the **C** will face you there. H4050
Nu 14:45 Amalekites and the **C** who lived in that H4050
Nu 21: 3 Israel's plea and gave the **C** over to them. H4050
Dt 1: 7 to the land of the **C** and to Lebanon, as H4050
Dt 7: 1 Amorites, **C**, Perizzites, Hivites H4050
Dt 11:30 territory of those **C** living in the Arabah H4050
Dt 20:17 the Hittites, Amorites, **C**, Perizzites, Hivites H4050
Jos 3:10 will certainly drive out before you the **C**, H4050
Jos 7: 9 The **C** and the other people of the country H4050
Jos 9: 1 Hittites, Amorites, **C**, Perizzites, Hivites H4050
Jos 11: 3 to the **C** in the east and west; to the H4050
Jos 12: 8 Hittites, Amorites, **C**, Perizzites, Hivites H4050
Jos 13: 4 all the land of the **C**, from Arah of the H4050
Jos 16:10 did not dislodge the **C** living in Gezer; H4050
Jos 16:10 to this day the **C** live among the people of H4050
Jos 17:12 the **C** were determined to live in that H4050
Jos 17:13 they subjected the **C** to forced labor but H4050
Jos 17:16 all the **C** who live in the plain have H4050
Jos 17:18 though the **C** have chariots fitted with iron H4050
Jos 24:11 Amorites, Perizzites, **C**, Hittites H4050
Jdg 1: 1 us is to go up first to fight against the **C**?" H4050
Jdg 1: 3 allotted to us, to fight against the **C**. H4050
Jdg 1: 4 the LORD gave the **C** and Perizzites into H4050
Jdg 1: 5 putting to rout the **C** and Perizzites. H4050
Jdg 1: 9 to fight against the **C** living in the hill H4050
Jdg 1:10 advanced against the **C** living in Hebron H4050
Jdg 1:17 attacked the **C** living in Zephath, H4050
Jdg 1:27 the **C** were determined to live in that H4050
Jdg 1:28 they pressed the **C** into forced labor but H4050
Jdg 1:29 Ephraim drive out the **C** living in Gezer, H4050
Jdg 1:29 the **C** continued to live there among H4050
Jdg 1:30 Zebulun drive out the **C** living in Kitron H4050
Jdg 1:30 Nahalol, so these **C** lived among them NDT
Jdg 3: 3 of the Philistines, all the **C**, the Sidonians, H4050
Jdg 3: 5 The Israelites lived among the **C**, Hittites H4050
2Sa 24: 7 all the towns of the Hivites and **C**. H4050
Ezr 9: 1 practices, like those of the **C**, Hittites, H4050
Ne 9: 8 give to his descendants the land of the **C**, H4050
Ne 9:24 You subdued before them the **C**, who H4050
Ne 9:24 the land; you gave the **C** into their hands H4392S
Eze 16: 3 birth were in the land of the **C**; H4050

CANAL (6) [CANALS]

Ezr 8:15 them at the **c** that flows toward H5643
Ezr 8:21 by the Ahava **C**, I proclaimed a fast H5643
Ezr 8:31 out from the Ahava **C** to go to Jerusalem. H5643
Da 8: 2 in the vision I was beside the Ulai **C**. H67
Da 8: 3 standing beside the **c**, and the horns were H67
Da 8: 6 standing beside the **c** and charged at it in H67

CANALS (3) [CANAL]

Ex 7:19 over the streams and **c**, over the ponds H3284
Ex 8: 5 staff over the streams and **c** and ponds, H3284
Isa 19: 6 The **c** will stink; the streams of Egypt will H5643

CANCEL (4) [CANCELED, CANCELING]

Dt 15: 1 every seven years *you must* **c debts**. H9024+6913
Dt 15: 2 Every creditor *shall* **c** any loan they have H9023
Dt 15: 3 you *must* **c** *any* **debt** your fellow H9023
Ne 10:31 forgo working the land and will **c** all debts. NDT

CANCELED (3) [CANCEL]

Mt 18:27 took pity on him, **c** the debt and let him go. G668
Mt 18:32 '*I* **c** all that debt of yours because you G918
Col 2:14 *having* **c** the charge of our legal G1981

CANCELING (3) [CANCEL]

Dt 15: 2 the LORD's **time for c debts** has been H9024

Dt 15: 9 seventh year, the year for c debts, is near," H9024
Dt 31:10 in the year for c debts, during the Festival H9024

CANDACE (NIV84) KANDAKE

CANDLE (KJV) LAMP

CANDLESTICK, CANDLESTICK (KJV) LAMPSTAND, LAMPSTANDS

CANE (1)

Zec 8: 4 each of them with c in hand because of H5475

CANKER (KJV) GANGRENE

CANKERWORM (KJV) GRASSHOPPERS, LOCUST, LOCUSTS

CANNEH (NIV84) KANNEH

CANNOT (244) [CAN]

Ge 19:22 because *I* c do anything until you H3523+4202
Ge 21:16 she thought, "I c watch the boy die. H440
Ge 31:35 that *I* c stand up in your presence H3523+4202
Ge 32:12 the sand of the sea, which c be counted. H4202
Ge 41:16 "I c do it," Joseph replied to Pharaoh H1187
Ge 44:22 my lord, 'The boy c leave his father H3523+4202
Ge 44:26 But we said, '*We* c go down. Only if H3523+4202
Ge 44:26 *We* c see the man's face unless H3523+4202
Ge 47:18 "We c hide from our lord the fact that H4202
Ex 10: 5 of the ground so that it c be seen. H3523+4202
Ex 18:18 you; *you* c handle it alone. H3523+4202
Ex 19:23 "The people c come up Mount H3523+4202
Ex 33:20 he said, "*you* c see my face, for no H3523+4202
Lev 5: 7 " 'Anyone who c afford a lamb is to bring H4202
Lev 5:11 they c afford two doves or two young H4202
Lev 12: 8 But if she c afford a lamb, she is to bring H4202
Lev 14:21 they are poor and c afford these, they must H401
Lev 14:32 skin disease and who c afford the regular H4202
Lev 27:33 become holy and c be redeemed. H4202
Nu 11:14 I c carry all these people by myself H3523+4202
Nu 23:20 he has blessed, and I c change it. H4202
Nu 31:23 And whatever c withstand fire must be put H4202
Nu 35:33 atonement c be made for the land on H4202
Dt 4:28 which c see or hear or eat or smell. H4202
Dt 14:24 your God and c carry your tithe H3523+4202
Dt 28:27 the itch, from which *you* c be cured. H3523+4202
Dt 28:35 with painful boils that c be cured, H3523+4202
Jos 7:12 why the Israelites c stand against H3523+4202
Jos 7:13 *You* c stand against your enemies H3523+4202
Jos 9:19 and *we* c touch them now. H3523+4202
Jdg 7: 2 I c deliver Midian into their hands, or H4946
Jdg 11:35 a vow to the LORD that *I* c break." H3523+4202
Ru 4: 6 "Then *I* c redeem it because I H3523+4202
Ru 4: 6 You redeem it yourself. *I* c do it." H3523+4202
1Sa 17:39 "*I* c go in these," he said to Saul H3523+4202
2Sa 5: 6 They thought, "David c get in here." H4202
2Sa 14:14 the ground, which c be recovered, so we H4202
1Ki 8:27 even the highest heaven, c contain you. H4202
1Ki 13:16 "*I* c turn back and go with you H3523+4202
1Ki 20: 9 but this demand *I* c meet. H3523+4202
2Ki 18:29 *He* c deliver you from my hand H3523+4202
1Ch 16:30 world is firmly established; it c be moved. H1153
2Ch 2: 6 even the highest heavens, c contain him? H4202
2Ch 6:18 even the highest heavens, c contain you. H4202
Ezr 10:13 rainy season; so we c stand outside. H401+3946
Ezr 10:13 this matter c be taken care of in a day H4202
Ne 4:10 rubble that we c rebuild the wall." H3523+4202
Ne 6: 3 on a great project and c go down. H3523+4202
Est 1:19 Media, which c be repealed, that H4202
Est 6:13 origin, *you* c **stand** against him H3523+4202
Job 5: 9 He performs wonders that c be fathomed H401
Job 5: 9 be fathomed, miracles that c be counted. H401
Job 9:10 He performs wonders that c be fathomed H401
Job 9:10 be fathomed, miracles that c be counted. H401
Job 9:11 he passes me, I c see him; when he H4202
Job 9:11 when he goes by, I c perceive him. H4202
Job 9:35 but as it now stands with me, I c. H4202
Job 10:15 if I am innocent, I c lift my head, for I am H4202
Job 12:14 What he tears down c be rebuilt; those he H4202
Job 12:14 those he imprisons c be released. H4202
Job 14: 5 months and have set limits he c exceed. H4202
Job 19: 8 He has blocked my way so I c pass; he H4202
Job 20:13 though he c bear to let it go and lets it H4202
Job 20:20 craving; he c save himself by his treasure. H4202
Job 22:11 why it is so dark you c see, and why a H4202
Job 28:13 it c be found in the land of the living. H4202
Job 28:15 It c be bought with the finest gold, nor H4202
Job 28:16 It c be bought with the gold of Ophir, with H4202
Job 28:19 The topaz of Cush c compare with it; it H4202
Job 28:19 it c be bought with pure gold. H4202
Job 34:32 Teach me what I c see; if I have done H1187
Job 37:19 we c draw up our case because of our H4202
Job 39:13 though they c compare with the wings and H561
Job 39:24 it c stand still when the trumpet sounds. H4202
Job 41:17 they cling together and c be parted. H4202
Ps 5: 5 The arrogant c stand in your presence H4202
Ps 21:11 devise wicked schemes, they c succeed. H1153
Ps 22:29 those who c keep themselves alive. H4202
Ps 33:17 despite all its great strength it c save. H4202
Ps 38:13 like the deaf, who c hear, like the mute, H4202
Ps 38:13 cannot hear, like the mute, who c speak; H4202
Ps 40:12 have overtaken me, and *I* c see. H4202+3523
Ps 69:23 May their eyes be darkened **so** they c see H4946
Ps 88: 8 I am confined and c escape; H4202
Ps 96:10 firmly established, it c be moved; he will H1153
Ps 104: 9 You set a boundary they c cross; never H1153
Ps 115: 5 They have mouths, but c speak, eyes, but H4202
Ps 115: 5 cannot speak, eyes, but c see. H4202
Ps 115: 6 They have ears, but c hear, noses, but H4202
Ps 115: 6 but cannot hear, noses, but c smell. H4202
Ps 115: 7 They have hands, but c feel, feet, but H4202
Ps 115: 7 but c walk, nor can they utter a H4202
Ps 125: 1 which c be shaken but endures forever. H4202
Ps 129: 7 a reaper c fill his hands with it, nor one H4202
Ps 135:16 They have mouths, but c speak, eyes, but H4202
Ps 135:16 cannot speak, eyes, but c see. H4202
Ps 135:17 They have ears, but c hear, nor is there H4202
Ps 146: 3 in princes, in human beings, who c save. H401
Pr 4:16 For they c rest until they do evil; they are H4202
Pr 12: 3 the righteous c be uprooted. H1153
Pr 13: 8 the poor c respond to threatening H4202
Pr 29:19 Servants c be corrected by mere words H4202
Pr 30:21 trembles, under four *it* c bear up: H4202+3523
Pr 31: 8 up for **those who c speak** *for themselves*, H522
Ecc 1:15 What is crooked c be straightened H3523+4202
Ecc 1:15 what is lacking c be counted. H3523+4202
Ecc 6: 3 if he c enjoy his prosperity and does not H4202
Ecc 8:17 *they* c really comprehend it. H3523+4202
Ecc 11: 5 so you c understand the work of God H4202
SS 8: 7 Many waters c quench love; rivers H3523+4202
SS 8: 7 quench love; rivers c sweep it away. H4202
Isa 1:13 *I* c **bear** your worthless assemblies. H4202+3523
Isa 28:15 sweeps by, it c touch us, for we have H4202
Isa 29:12 to someone *who* c **read**, H4202+3359+6219
Isa 36:14 deceive you. *He* c deliver you! H3523+4202
Isa 38:18 For the grave c praise you, death cannot H4202
Isa 38:18 praise you, death c sing your praise; those NDT
Isa 38:18 who go down to the pit c hope for your H4202
Isa 44:18 their eyes are plastered over *so* they c see, H4946
Isa 44:18 their minds closed *so* they c understand. H4946
Isa 44:20 misleads him; he c save himself, or say, H4202
Isa 45:20 of wood, who pray to gods that c save. H4202
Isa 46: 7 From that spot it c move. Even though H4202
Isa 46: 7 cries out to it, it c answer; it cannot save H4202
Isa 46: 7 answer; it c save them from their troubles. H4202
Isa 47:11 upon you that *you* c ward off with a H3523+4202
Isa 47:11 a catastrophe you c foresee will suddenly H4202
Isa 47:14 They c even save themselves from the H4202
Isa 48: 7 **So** you c say, 'Yes, I knew H7153
Isa 56:10 all mute dogs, *they* c bark; they lie H3523+4202
Isa 57:20 tossing sea, *which* c rest, whose H3523+4202
Isa 58: 4 You c fast as you do today and expect H4202
Isa 59: 6 they c cover themselves with what they H4202
Isa 59:14 in the streets, honesty c enter. H4202+3523
Jer 2:13 cisterns, broken cisterns that c hold water. H4202
Jer 4:19 heart pounds within me, I c keep silent. H4202
Jer 5:22 the sea, an everlasting barrier it c cross. H4202
Jer 5:22 may roll, but *they* c prevail; they may H4202
Jer 5:22 they may roar, but they c cross it. H4202
Jer 6:10 ears are closed so *they* c hear. H3523+4202
Jer 6:11 of the wrath of the LORD, and *I* c hold it in. H4206
Jer 8:17 vipers that c be charmed, and they H401
Jer 10: 5 their idols c speak; they must be H4202
Jer 10: 5 they must be carried because they c walk. H4202
Jer 10:10 trembles; the nations c endure his wrath. H4202
Jer 11:11 on them a disaster *they* c escape. H3523+4202
Jer 14:19 you afflicted us so that we c be healed? H401
Jer 19:11 jar is smashed and c be repaired. H4202+3523
Jer 20: 9 weary of holding it in; indeed, *I* c. H3523+4202
Jer 23:24 hide in secret places so that I c see them?" H4202
Jer 24: 3 the bad ones are so bad they c be eaten." H4202
Jer 24: 8 which are so bad they c be eaten,' says H4202
Jer 29:17 like figs that are so bad they c be eaten. H4202
Jer 46: 6 "The swift c flee nor the strong escape. H440
Jer 46:15 They c stand, for the LORD will push them H4202
Jer 46:23 numerous than locusts, they c be counted. H401
Jer 49:10 so that *he* c conceal himself. H3523+4202
Jer 51: 9 Babylon, but she c be healed; let us leave H4202
La 1:14 the hands of those *I* c withstand. H3523+4202
La 3: 7 He has walled me in so I c escape; he H4202
Eze 3: 6 language, whose words you c understand. H4202
Eze 3:25 be bound so that you c go out among the H4202
Eze 4: 8 ropes so that you c turn from one side to H4202
Eze 12: 6 Cover your face so that you c see the land H4202
Eze 12:12 cover his face so that he c see the land. H4202
Da 5:23 which c see or hear or understand. A10379
Da 6: 8 put it in writing so that it c be altered— A10379
Da 6: 8 Persians, which c be repealed. A10379
Da 6:12 Persians, which c be repealed. A10379
Hos 1:10 which c be measured or counted. H4202
Hos 2: 6 will wall her in so that she c find her way. H4202
Hos 14: 3 Assyria c save us; we will not mount H4202
Am 7:10 The land c bear all his words. H4202+3523
Jnh 4:11 thousand people who c tell their right H4202
Mic 2: 3 people, from which you c save yourselves. H4202
Hab 1:13 on evil; *you* c tolerate wrongdoing. H3523+4202
Hab 2:18 own creation; he makes idols that c **speak**. H522
Mt 5:14 A town built on a hill c be hidden. G4024+1538
Mt 5:36 for *you* c make even one hair white G4024+1538
Mt 6:24 *You* c serve both God and money. G4024+1538
Mt 7:18 A good tree c bear bad fruit, and a G4024+1538
Mt 7:18 bad fruit, **and** a bad tree c bear good fruit. G4028
Mt 10:28 who kill the body but c kill the soul. G3590+1538
Mt 16: 3 but *you* c interpret the signs of the G4024+1538
Mt 26:53 Do you think *I* c call on my Father G4024+1538
Mk 2:19 *They* c, so long as they have him G4024+1538
Mk 3:24 that kingdom c stand. G4024+1538
Mk 3:25 against itself, that house c stand. G4024+1538
Mk 3:26 and is divided, *he* c stand; his end G4024+1538
Lk 12:26 Since *you* c **do** this very little thing G4028+1538
Lk 14:14 Although *they* c repay you, you will G4024+2400
Lk 14:26 *such a person* c be my disciple. G4024+1538
Lk 14:27 and follow me c be my disciple. G4024+1538
Lk 14:33 you have c be my disciples. G4024+1538
Lk 16: 2 because *you* c be manager any G4024+1538
Lk 16:13 *You* c serve both God and money." G4024+1538
Lk 16:26 who want to go from here to you c, G3590+1538
Jn 3: 4 "**Surely** *they* c enter a second time G3590+1538
Jn 3: 8 you c tell where it comes from or G4024
Jn 7: 7 The world c hate you, but it hates G4024+1538
Jn 7:34 and where I am, you c come. G4024+1538
Jn 7:35 this man intend to go that we c find him? G4024
Jn 7:36 and 'Where I am, you c come'?" G4024+1538
Jn 8:21 Where I go, you c come." G4024+1538
Jn 8:22 he says, 'Where I go, you c come'?" G4024+1538
Jn 10:35 Scripture c be set aside— G4024+1538
Jn 13:33 Where I am going, you c come. G4024+1538
Jn 13:36 I am going, *you* c follow now, but G4024+1538
Jn 14:17 The world c accept him, because it G4024+1538
Ac 4:16 a notable sign, and *we* c deny it. G4024+1538
Ac 4:20 *we* c help speaking about what we G4024+1538
Ac 15: 1 taught by Moses, **you** c be saved." G4024+1538
Ac 24:13 **And** they c prove to you the charges G4028+1538
Ac 27:31 stay with the ship, you c be saved." G4024+1538
Ro 6: 9 the dead, he c die **again**; death no longer G4033
Ro 7:18 to do what is good, but I c carry it out. G4024
Ro 8: 8 realm of the flesh c please God. G4024+1538
Ro 11: 6 if by grace, then it c be based on works; if G4033
Ro 11:10 May their eyes be darkened so they c see G3590
1Co 2:14 and c understand them because G4024+1538
1Co 7: 9 But if they c control themselves, they G4024
1Co 9:16 the gospel, I c boast, since I am G4024+1639
1Co 10:21 *You* c drink the cup of the Lord and G4024+1538
1Co 10:21 *you* c have a part in both the Lord's G4024+1538
1Co 12:21 The eye c say to the hand, "I don't G4024+1538
1Co 12:21 And the head c say to the feet, "I don't NDT
1Co 15:50 flesh and blood c inherit the G4024+1538
2Co 1:13 you anything you c read or G247+2445
2Co 4: 4 so that they c see the light of the gospel G3590
2Co 13: 8 For *we* c **do** anything against the G4024+1538
Gal 6: 7 God c be mocked. G4024
1Ti 5:25 are not obvious c remain hidden G4024+1538
2Ti 2:13 faithful, for *he* c disown himself. G4024+1538
Titus 2: 8 soundness of speech that **c be condemned**, G183
Heb 9: 5 But *we* c discuss these things in G4024+1639
Heb 12:27 so that what c be shaken may remain. G3590
Heb 12:28 are receiving a kingdom that **c be shaken**, G810
Jas 1:13 For God c be **tempted** by evil, nor does he G585
Jas 4: 2 You covet but *you* c get what you G4024+1538
1Jn 3: 9 in them; *they* c go on sinning G4024+1538
1Jn 4:20 they have seen, c love God, whom G4024+1538
1Jn 5:18 them safe, and the evil one c harm them. G4024
Rev 2: 2 I know that *you* c tolerate wicked G4024+1538
Rev 9:20 idols that c see or hear or walk. G4046+1538

CANOPY (6)

2Sa 22:12 He made darkness his c around him—the H6109
2Ki 16:18 away the Sabbath c that had been built H4590
Ps 18:11 his covering, his c around him—the dark H6109
Isa 4: 5 over everything the glory will be a c. H2903
Isa 40:22 He stretches out the heavens like a c, and H1988
Jer 43:10 he will spread his **royal** c above them. H9188

CAPABLE (6)

Ex 18:21 But select c men from all the people H2657
Ex 18:25 He chose c men from all Israel and made H2657
1Ch 26: 6 because they were **very** c **men**. H1475+2657
1Ch 26: 8 their relatives were c men with the H2657
1Ch 26:31 and c **men** among the Hebronites H1475+2657
Ezr 8:18 brought us Sherebiah, a c man, from the H8507

CAPERNAUM (16)

Mt 4:13 he went and lived in C, which was by the G3019
Mt 8: 5 When Jesus had entered C, a centurion G3019
Mt 11:23 And you, C, will you be lifted to the G3019
Mt 17:24 After Jesus and his disciples arrived in C G3019
Mk 1:21 They went to C, and when the Sabbath G3019
Mk 2: 1 when Jesus again entered C, the people G3019
Mk 9:33 They came to C. When he was in the G3019
Lk 4:23 what we have heard that you did in C. G3019
Lk 4:31 Then he went down to C, a town in G3019
Lk 7: 1 people who were listening, he entered C. G3019
Lk 10:15 And you, C, will you be lifted to the G3019
Jn 2:12 he went down to C with his mother and G3019
Jn 4:46 royal official whose son lay sick at C. G3019
Jn 6:17 a boat and set off across the lake for C. G3019
Jn 6:24 boats and went to C in search of Jesus. G3019
Jn 6:59 this while teaching in the synagogue in C. G3019

CAPES (1)

Isa 3:22 the fine robes and the c and cloaks, the H5074

CAPHTOR (3) [CAPHTORITES]

Dt 2:23 coming out from C destroyed them and H4116
Jer 47: 4 the remnant from the coasts of C. H4116
Am 9: 7 the Philistines from C and the Arameans H4116

CAPHTORITES (3) [CAPHTOR]
Ge 10:14 from whom the Philistines came) and C. H4118
Dt 2:23 the C coming out from Caphtor destroyed H4118
1Ch 1:12 from whom the Philistines came) and C. H4118

CAPITAL (7) [CAPITALS]
Dt 21:22 guilty of a c offense is put to death H5477+4638
1Ki 7:16 of the pillars; each c was five cubits high. H4196
1Ki 7:17 on top of the pillars, seven for each c. H4196
1Ki 7:18 He did the same for each c. H4196
2Ki 25:17 The bronze c on top of one pillar was H4196
2Ch 3:15 cubits long, each with a c five cubits high. H7633
Jer 52:22 The bronze c on top of one pillar was five H4196

CAPITALS (12) [CAPITAL]
1Ki 7:16 He also made two c of cast bronze to set H4196
1Ki 7:17 chains adorned the c on top of the pillars, H4196
1Ki 7:18 to decorate the c on top of the pillars. H4196
1Ki 7:19 The c on top of the pillars in the portico H4196
1Ki 7:20 On the c of both pillars, above the H4196
1Ki 7:22 The c on top were in the shape of lilies. NDT
1Ki 7:41 the two bowl-shaped c on top of the H4196
1Ki 7:41 the two bowl-shaped c on top of the H4196
1Ki 7:42 the bowl-shaped c on top of the pillars); H4196
2Ch 4:12 the two bowl-shaped c on top of the H4196
2Ch 4:12 the two bowl-shaped c on top of the H4196
2Ch 4:13 the bowl-shaped c on top of the pillars); H4196

CAPPADOCIA (2)
Ac 2:9 Judea and C, Pontus and Asia, G2838
1Pe 1:1 of Pontus, Galatia, C, Asia and Bithynia, G2838

CAPS (4)
Ex 28:40 sashes and c for Aaron's sons to give H4457
Ex 29:9 fasten c on them. Then tie sashes on H4457
Ex 39:28 the linen c and the undergarments H6996+4457
Lev 8:13 around them and fastened c on them, H4457

CAPSTONE (2) [STONE; see also CORNERSTONE]
Zec 4:7 will bring out the c to shouts of 'God H74+8036
Zec 4:10 when they see the chosen c in the hand of H74

CAPTAIN (22) [CAPTAINS]
Ge 37:36 of Pharaoh's officials, the c *of* the guard. H8569
Ge 39:1 officials, the c *of* the guard, bought him H8569
Ge 40:3 custody in the house of the c *of* the guard, H8569
Ge 40:4 The c *of* the guard assigned them to H8569
Ge 41:10 baker in the house of the c *of* the guard. H8569
Ge 41:12 with us, a servant of the c *of* the guard. H8569
1Sa 22:14 c of your bodyguard and highly respected H6233
2Ki 1:9 sent to Elijah a c with his company H8569+2822
2Ki 1:9 The c went up to Elijah, who was sitting on NDT
2Ki 1:10 Elijah answered the c, "If I am a H8569+2822
2Ki 1:10 consumed the c and his men. H2257S
2Ki 1:11 to Elijah another c with his fifty H8569+2822
2Ki 1:11 The c said to him, "Man of God, this is what NDT
2Ki 1:13 king sent a third c with his fifty men H8569+2822
2Ki 1:13 This third c went up and fell on his H8569+2822
Isa 3:3 the c *of* fifty and the man of rank, the H8569
Jer 37:13 Benjamin Gate, the c *of* the guard, whose H1251
Jnh 1:6 The c went to him and said H8042+2021+2480
Ac 4:1 the c of the temple guard and the G5130
Ac 5:24 the c of the temple guard and the chief G5130
Ac 5:26 the c went with his officers and brought G5130
Rev 18:17 "Every sea c, and all who travel by ship G3237

CAPTAINS (4) [CAPTAIN]
Jdg 5:14 From Makir c came down, from Zebulun H2980
1Ki 9:22 his officers, his c, and the commanders of H8957
2Ki 1:14 the first two c and all their men. H8569+2822
2Ch 8:9 commanders of his c, and commanders of H8957

CAPTIVATE (1) [CAPTURE]
Pr 6:25 her beauty or *let her* c you with her eyes. H4374

CAPTIVE (43) [CAPTURE]
Ge 14:14 heard that his relative *had* been taken c, H8647
Nu 24:22 will be destroyed when Ashur takes you c." H8647
Dt 1:39 little ones that you said would be taken c, H1020
Jdg 5:12 Take c your captives, son of H8647
1Sa 30:2 and *had* taken c the women and everyone H8647
1Sa 30:3 wives and sons and daughters taken c. H8647
1Ki 8:46 *who* take them c to their own lands, H8647+8647
1Ki 8:47 of heart in the land where *they* are held c, H8647
1Ki 8:48 land of their enemies who took them c, H8647
1Ki 20:39 someone came to me with a c and said, H408
2Ki 5:2 gone out and *had* taken c a young girl H8647
2Ki 17:27 of the priests *you took* c from Samaria go H1655
2Ki 24:15 took Jehoiachin c to Babylon. H1655
1Ch 3:17 The descendants of Jehoiachin the c H660
1Ch 5:21 also took one hundred thousand people c, NDT
1Ch 9:1 They were taken c to Babylon because of H1655
2Ch 6:36 *who* takes them c to a land far H8647+8647
2Ch 6:37 of heart in the land where *they* are held c, H8647
2Ch 28:8 The men of Israel took c from their fellow H8647
Ezr 2:1 king of Babylon *had* taken c to Babylon H1655
Ne 7:6 king of Babylon *had* taken c H1655
Est 2:6 among those taken c with Jehoiachin king H1655
Ps 69:33 needy and does not despise his c *people*. H659
Ps 106:46 caused all *who* held them c to show them H8647
SS 7:5 tapestry; the king is held c by its tresses. H673
Isa 52:2 on your neck, Daughter Zion, now a c. H8665
Jer 13:17 because the LORD's flock *will* be taken c. H8647
Jer 22:12 in the place where *they have* led him c; H1655
Jer 41:10 of Nethaniah took them c and set out to H8647
Jer 41:14 people Ishmael *had* taken c at Mizpah H8647
Jer 43:12 burn their temples and take their gods c. H8647
Jer 48:7 you too *will* be taken c, and Chemosh H4334
La 1:5 have gone into exile, c before the foe. NDT
Eze 6:9 nations where *they have* been carried c, H8647
Eze 21:23 them of their guilt and take them c. H9530
Eze 21:24 *you will* be taken c. H9530+928+2021+4090
Am 1:6 Because she took c whole communities H1655
Na 3:10 Yet she was taken c and went into exile H1583
Hab 2:5 the nations and takes c all the peoples. H7695
Ac 8:23 that you are full of bitterness and c to sin." G5278
2Co 10:5 and *we* take c every thought to make it G170
Col 2:8 to it *that* no one takes you c G1639+3836+5194
2Ti 2:26 who *has* taken *them* c to do his will. G2436

CAPTIVES (25) [CAPTURE]
Ge 31:26 carried off my daughters like c *in* war. H8647
Nu 21:29 his daughters as c to Sihon king of the H8669
Nu 31:12 brought the c, spoils and plunder to H8660
Nu 31:19 you must purify yourselves and your c. H8660
Dt 21:10 into your hands and *you* take c, H8647+8660
Dt 21:11 notice among the c a beautiful woman H8664
Dt 32:42 the blood of the slain and the c, the H8664
Jdg 5:12 Take captive your c, son of Abinoam.' H8660
Job 3:18 C also enjoy their ease; they no longer H659
Ps 68:18 on high, *you* took many c; you H8647+8660
Isa 10:4 to cringe among the c or fall among the H660
Isa 14:2 *They will* make c of their captors and rule H8647
Isa 14:17 its cities and would not let his c go home?" H659
Isa 20:4 the Egyptian c and Cushite exiles, H8660
Isa 42:7 to free c from prison and to release from H660
Isa 49:9 to say to the c, 'Come out,' and to those in H673
Isa 49:24 warriors, or c be rescued from the fierce? H8660
Isa 49:25 c will be taken from warriors, and H8660
Isa 61:1 freedom for the c and release from H8647
Jer 40:1 among all the c *from* Jerusalem and H1661
Jer 41:10 Ishmael made c of all the rest of the H8647
Eze 12:11 done to them. They will go into exile as c. H8660
Am 1:9 sold whole communities of c to Edom, H1661
2Co 2:14 leads us as c in Christ's triumphal procession G2581
Eph 4:8 *he* took many c and gave gifts to his G169+168

CAPTIVITY (31) [CAPTURE]
Dt 28:41 keep them, because they will go into c. H8660
Jdg 18:30 of Dan until the time of the c *of* the land. H1655
2Ki 25:21 So Judah went into c, away from her H1655
2Ch 6:37 with you in the land of their c and say, H8660
2Ch 6:38 in the land of their c where they were H8660
2Ch 29:9 daughters and our wives are in c. H8660
Ezr 2:1 who came up from the c *of* the exiles, H8660
Ezr 3:8 had returned from the c to Jerusalem) H8660
Ezr 8:35 who had returned from c sacrificed burnt H8660
Ezr 9:7 have been subjected to the sword and c, H8660
Ne 4:4 Give them over as plunder in a land of c. H8664
Ne 7:6 came up from the c *of* the exiles whom H8660
Ps 78:61 He sent the ark of his might into c, his H8660
Ps 144:14 of walls, no going into c, no cry of distress H3448
Isa 46:2 the burden, they themselves go off into c. H8660
Jer 15:2 to starvation; those for c, to captivity. H8660
Jer 15:2 to starvation; those for captivity, to c. H8660
Jer 29:14 the LORD, "and will bring you back from c. H8654
Jer 30:3 Judah back from c and restore them to H8654
Jer 31:23 "When I bring them back from c, the H8654
Jer 33:7 Israel back from c and will rebuild H8654
Jer 43:11 death, c to those destined for captivity H8660
Jer 43:11 captivity to those destined for c, and the H8660
Jer 48:46 taken into exile and your daughters into c. H8664
Jer 52:27 So Judah went into c, away from her H1655
La 2:14 did not expose your sin to ward off your c. H8654
Eze 29:14 bring them back from c and return them to H8654
Eze 30:17 the cities themselves will go into c. H8660
Eze 30:18 and her villages will go into c. H8660
Rev 13:10 "If anyone is to go into c, into captivity they G168
Rev 13:10 is to go into captivity, into c they will go. G168

CAPTORS (6) [CAPTURE]
1Ki 8:47 with you in the land of their c and say, H8647
1Ki 8:50 cause their c to show them mercy; H8647
2Ch 30:9 compassion by their c and will return to H8647
Ps 137:3 there our c asked us for songs, our H8647
Isa 14:2 captives of their c and rule over their H8647
Jer 50:33 All their c hold them fast, refusing to let H8647

CAPTURE (19) [CAPTIVATE, CAPTIVE, CAPTIVES, CAPTIVITY, CAPTORS, CAPTURED, CAPTURES, CAPTURING, RECAPTURE, RECAPTURED]
Dt 20:19 fighting against it to c it, do not destroy its H9530
1Sa 4:21 because of the c *of* the ark of God and the H4374
1Sa 19:14 When Saul sent the men to c David H4374
1Sa 19:20 so he sent men to c him. But when they H4374
1Sa 23:26 in on David and his men to c them, H9530
2Sa 12:28 of the troops and besiege the city and c it. H4334
2Ki 6:13 ordered, "so I can send men and c him." H4374
2Ch 32:18 make them afraid in order to c the city. H4334
Job 40:24 *Can anyone* c it by the eyes, or trap it and H4374
Jer 18:22 have dug a pit to c me and have hidden H4334
Jer 32:3 of the king of Babylon, and *he will* c it. H4334
Jer 32:28 king of Babylon, *who will* c it. H4334
Jer 37:8 this city; *they will* c it and burn it down. H4334
Jer 38:3 army of the king of Babylon, *who will* c it. H4334
Jer 50:46 sound of Babylon's c the earth will H9530
Da 11:15 up siege ramps and *will* c a fortified city. H4334
Hab 1:10 by building earthen ramps *they* c them. H4334
Mt 26:55 come out with swords and clubs *to* c me? G5197
Mk 14:48 come out with swords and clubs *to* c me? G5197

CAPTURED (75) [CAPTURE]
Nu 21:1 the Israelites and c some of them. H8647+8660
Nu 21:25 Israel c all the cities of the Amorites and H4374
Nu 21:32 the Israelites c its surrounding settlements H4334
Nu 31:9 The Israelites c the Midianite women and H8647
Nu 31:26 all the people and animals that were c. H8660
Nu 32:39 c it and drove out the Amorites who were H4334
Nu 32:41 c their settlements and called them H4334
Nu 32:42 And Nobah c Kenath and its surrounding H4334
Dt 2:35 from the towns *we had* c we carried off H4334
Dt 21:13 the clothes she was wearing when c. H8660
Jos 8:19 entered the city and c it and quickly set it H4334
Jos 10:35 *They* c it that same day and put it to the H4334
Jos 11:10 turned back and c Hazor and put its king H4334
Jos 11:17 *He* c all their kings and put them to death. H4334
Jdg 7:25 *They* also c two of the Midianite leaders H4334
Jdg 8:12 he pursued them and c them, routing H4334
Jdg 9:45 the city until *he had* c it and killed its H4334
Jdg 9:50 went to Thebez and besieged it and c it. H4334
Jdg 12:5 The Gileadites c the fords of the Jordan H4334
1Sa 4:11 The ark of God was c, and Eli's two sons H4374
1Sa 4:17 are dead, and the ark of God *has* been c." H4374
1Sa 4:19 the ark of God *had* been c and that her H4374
1Sa 4:22 from Israel, for the ark of God *has* been c." H4374
1Sa 5:1 After the Philistines *had* c the ark of God H4374
1Sa 7:14 that the Philistines *had* c from Israel were H4374
1Sa 30:5 David's two wives *had* been c—Ahinoam H8647
2Sa 5:7 Nevertheless, David c the fortress of Zion H4334
2Sa 8:4 David c a thousand of his chariots, seven H4334
2Sa 12:26 of the Ammonites and c the royal citadel. H4334
2Sa 12:29 went to Rabbah, and attacked and c it. H4334
1Ki 9:16 king of Egypt had attacked and c Gezer. H4334
2Ki 6:22 you kill those *you have* c with your own H8647
2Ki 12:17 Aram went up and attacked Gath and c it. H4334
2Ki 14:7 in the Valley of Salt and c Sela in battle, H9530
2Ki 14:13 king of Israel c Amaziah king of Judah H9530
2Ki 17:6 the king of Assyria c Samaria and H4334
2Ki 18:10 So Samaria was c in Hezekiah's sixth year, H4334
2Ki 18:13 the fortified cities of Judah and c them. H9530
2Ki 25:6 he *was* c. He was taken to the king of H9530
1Ch 2:23 But Geshur and Aram c Havvoth Jair, as H4374
1Ch 11:5 Nevertheless, David c the fortress of Zion H4334
1Ch 18:4 David c a thousand of his chariots, seven H4334
2Ch 8:3 then went to Hamath Zobah and c it. H2616
2Ch 12:4 *he* c the fortified cities of Judah and came H4334
2Ch 15:8 from the towns *he had* c in the hills of H4334
2Ch 17:2 of Ephraim that his father Asa *had* c. H4334
2Ch 22:9 and *his men* c him while he was hiding in H4334
2Ch 25:12 army of Judah also c ten thousand men H8647
2Ch 25:23 king of Israel c Amaziah king of Judah H9530
2Ch 28:18 *They* c and occupied Beth Shemesh H4334
Ne 9:25 *They* c fortified cities and fertile land; they H4334
Isa 8:15 be broken, they will be snared and c." H4334
Isa 13:15 Whoever is c will be thrust through; all H5162
Isa 20:1 came to Ashdod and attacked and c it— H4334
Isa 22:3 *they have* been c without using the bow. H673
Isa 28:13 they will be injured and snared and c. H4334
Isa 36:1 the fortified cities of Judah and c them. H9530
Jer 10:18 distress on them so that *they may be* c." H5162
Jer 34:3 grasp but *will* surely be c and given H9530+9530
Jer 38:23 their hands but *will* be c by the king of H9530
Jer 38:28 the guard until the day Jerusalem was c. H4334
Jer 39:5 *They* c him and took him to H4374
Jer 48:1 Kiriathaim will be disgraced and c; the H4334
Jer 48:41 Kerioth *will* be c and the strongholds H4334
Jer 50:2 say, 'Babylon *will* be c; Bel will be put H4334
Jer 50:9 and from the north *she will* be c. H4334
Jer 50:24 you were found and c because you H9530
Jer 51:31 the king of Babylon that his entire city is c, H4334
Jer 51:41 "How Sheshak *will* be c, the boast of the H4334
Jer 51:56 her warriors *will* be c, and their bows will H4334
Jer 52:9 he *was* c. He was taken to the king of H9530
Da 11:33 the sword or be burned or c or plundered. H8660
Am 4:10 with the sword, along with your c horses. H8660
Zec 14:2 against it; the city *will* be c, the houses H4334
Rev 19:20 But the beast *was* c, and with it the false G4389

CAPTURES (2) [CAPTURE]
Jos 15:16 the man who attacks and c Kiriath Sepher." H4334
Jdg 1:12 the man who attacks and c Kiriath Sepher." H4334

CAPTURING (2) [CAPTURE]
Jdg 11:22 c all of it from the Arnon to the Jabbok H3769
2Ki 16:9 complied by attacking Damascus and c it. H9530

CAR (NIV84) BETH KAR

CARAVAN (3) [CARAVANS]
Ge 37:25 up and saw a c *of* Ishmaelites coming H785
1Ki 10:2 Arriving at Jerusalem with a very great c H2657
2Ch 9:1 Arriving with a very great c—with camels H2657

CARAVANS (3) [CARAVAN]
Job 6:18 C turn aside from their routes; they go off H785
Job 6:19 The c *of* Tema look for water, the traveling H785
Isa 21:13 You c *of* Dedanites, who camp in the H785

CARAWAY (3)
Isa 28:25 does he not sow c and scatter cumin? H7902
Isa 28:27 C is not threshed with a sledge, nor is the H7902
Isa 28:27 over cumin; c is beaten out with a rod H7902

CARBUNCLE, CARBUNCLES (KJV) BERYL, JEWELS

CARCAS (NIV84) KARKAS

CARCASE, CARCASES (KJV) BODIES, BODY, CARCASS, CARCASSES

CARCASS (10) [CARCASSES]
Lev 5: 2 whether the c *of* an unclean animal H5577
Lev 11:26 whoever touches the c of any of them will NDT
Lev 11:37 If a c falls on any seeds that are to be H5577
Lev 11:38 been put on the seed and a c falls on it, H5577
Lev 11:39 who touches its c will be unclean till H5577
Lev 11:40 who eats some of its c must wash their H5577
Lev 11:40 who picks up the c must wash their H5577
Jdg 14: 8 he turned aside to look at the lion's c H5147
Jdg 14: 9 he had taken the honey from the lion's c. H1581
Mt 24:28 Wherever there is a c, there the vultures G4773

CARCASSES (14) [CARCASS]
Ge 15:11 Then birds of prey came down on the c H7007
Lev 11: 8 must not eat their meat or touch their c; H5577
Lev 11:11 you must regard their c as unclean. H5577
Lev 11:24 touches their c will be unclean till H5577
Lev 11:25 picks up one of their c must wash their H5577
Lev 11:27 touches their c will be unclean till H5577
Lev 11:28 who picks up their c must wash their H5577
Lev 11:35 that one of their c falls on becomes H5577
Lev 11:36 who touches one of these c is unclean. H5577
Dt 14: 8 are not to eat their meat or touch their c. H5577
Dt 28:26 Your c will be food for all the birds and the H5577
1Sa 17:46 day I will give the c *of* the Philistine army H7007
Jer 7:33 Then the c *of* this people will become H5577
Jer 19: 7 I will give their c as food to the birds H5577

CARCHEMISH (3)
2Ch 35:20 went up to fight at C on the Euphrates, H4138
Isa 10: 9 'Has not Kalno fared like C? Is not H4138
Jer 46: 2 which was defeated at C on the Euphrates H4138

CARE (100) [CARED, CAREFREE, CAREFUL, CAREFULLY, CARELESSLY, CARES, CARING]
Ge 2:15 Garden of Eden to work it and **take c of** it. H9068
Ge 30:29 how your livestock has fared **under** my c. H907
Ge 30:35 he placed them in the c *of* his sons. H3338
Ge 39:16 He put them in the c *of* his servants, each H3338
Ge 33:13 that I must c **for** the ewes and cows H6584
Ge 39: 4 he entrusted to his c everything he owned H3338
Ge 39: 6 left everything he had in Joseph's c; H3338
Ge 39: 8 he owns he has entrusted to my c. H3338
Ge 39:23 no attention to anything under Joseph's c, H3338
Ge 42:37 Entrust him to my c, and I will bring him H3338
Ex 12: 6 **Take c** of them until the H2118+4200+5466
Lev 6: 2 them or left in their c or about something H3338
Lev 16:21 wilderness in the c *of* someone appointed H3338
Nu 1:50 they *are to* **take c of** it and encamp H9250
Nu 1:53 responsible for the c *of* the tabernacle of H5466
Nu 3: 8 *They are to* **take c of** all the furnishings of H9068
Nu 3:25 were **responsible for** the c *of* the H5466
Nu 3:28 responsible for the c *of* the sanctuary. H9068
Nu 3:31 They were **responsible for** the c *of* the ark H5466
Nu 3:32 *those who were* responsible for the c *of* H9068
Nu 3:36 were appointed to **take c of** the frames of H5466
Nu 3:38 *They were* responsible for the c *of* the H9068
Nu 4: 4 the c of the most holy things. NDT
Nu 18: 4 responsible for the c *of* the tent of H5466
Nu 18: 5 responsible for the c *of* the sanctuary and H5466
Nu 31:30 responsible for the c *of* the LORD's H5466
Nu 31:47 responsible for the c *of* the LORD's H5466
Dt 7:11 Therefore, **take c** to follow the commands H9068
1Sa 17:20 David left the flock **in the c of** a shepherd, H6584
2Sa 15:16 ten concubines to **take c of** the palace. H9068
2Sa 16:21 whom he left to **take c of** the palace. H9068
2Sa 18: 3 to flee, *they* won't c **about** us. H8492+4213+448
2Sa 18: 3 us die, *they* won't c; but you H8492+4213+448
2Sa 19:24 *He had* not **taken c** of his feet or trimmed H6913
2Sa 20: 3 he had left to **take c of** the palace and put H9068
1Ki 1: 2 to serve the king and **take c of** him. H2118+6125
1Ki 1: 4 *she* **took c of** the king and waited H2118+6125
2Ki 9:34 "**Take c** of that cursed woman," he said H7212
1Ch 9:29 were assigned to **take c of** the furnishings H6584
1Ch 9:30 priests **took c of mixing** the spices H8379+5351
1Ch 26:28 things were in the c *of* Shelomith and his H3338
1Ch 27:32 son of Hakmoni **took c of** the king's sons. H6640
2Ch 25:24 that had been **in the c of** Obed-Edom, H6640
2Ch 32:22 *He* **took c of** them on every side H5633
Ezr 10:13 matter cannot be taken c of in a day or two, NDT
Est 2: 3 Let them be placed under the c *of* Hegai H3338
Est 2: 8 of Susa and put under the c *of* Hegai. H3338
Est 2:14 part of the harem to the c *of* Shaashgaz, H3338
Job 3: 4 *may* God above not c **about** it; may H2011
Job 21:21 For what do they c about the families they H2914
Ps 8: 4 human beings that *you* c **for** them? H7212
Ps 37:18 spend their days **under** the LORD's c, H3359
Ps 43: 3 Send me your light and your **faithful c**, let H622
Ps 65: 9 *You* c **for** the land and water it; you enrich H7212
Ps 73:12 are like—always **free of c**, they go on H8929
Ps 88: 5 no more, who are cut off from your c. H3338
Ps 95: 7 of his pasture, the flock **under** his c. H3338
Ps 144: 3 are human beings that *you* c **for** them, H3359
Pr 12:10 The righteous c **for** the needs of their H3359
Pr 29: 7 The righteous c **about** justice for the poor H3359
SS 1: 6 me and made me **take c of** the vineyards; H5757
Isa 13:17 who *do* not c **for** silver and have no H3108
Isa 34:15 and c **for** *her* **young** under the shadow of H1842
Jer 6:20 **What do I c about** incense H4200+4537+2296+4200+3276
Jer 15:15 understand; remember me and c **for** me. H7212
Jer 23: 2 away and *have* not **bestowed c on** them, H7212
Jer 30:14 have forgotten you; *they* c nothing **for** you. H2011
Eze 34: 2 of Israel who *only* **take c of** yourselves! H8286
Eze 34: 2 *Should* not shepherds **take c of** the flock? H8286
Eze 34: 3 but *you do* not **take c of** the flock. H8286
Hos 14: 8 I will answer him and c **for** him. I am like H8800
Am 7:14 I also **took c of** sycamore-fig trees. H1179
Mic 2: 8 robe from those who pass by **without a c**, H1055
Zep 2: 7 The LORD their God *will* c **for** them; he will H7212
Zec 10: 3 the LORD Almighty *will* c **for** his flock H7212
Zec 11:16 over the land *who will* not c **for** the lost, H7212
Mt 10:29 fall to the ground outside your Father's c. NDT
Mt 27:55 Jesus from Galilee *to* c **for** his **needs**. G1354
Mk 4:38 "Teacher, don't you c if we drown? G3508
Mk 5:26 a great deal **under** *the* c *of* many doctors AIT
Lk 10:34 brought him to an inn and **took c of** him. G2150
Lk 10:40 don't you c that my sister has left me to G3508
Lk 13: 7 said to the **man who took c of the vineyard**, G307
Lk 18: 4 I don't fear God or c **what** people **think**, G1956
Jn 21:16 Jesus said, "**Take c of** my sheep." G4477
Ac 13:40 **Take c** *that* what the prophets have said G1063
Ac 24:23 permit his friends *to* **take c of** his **needs**. G5676
1Co 3:10 But each one should build **with c**. G1063+4802
1Co 4: 3 I **c very little** if I am judged G1650+1788+1639
Eph 5:29 they feed and c **for** their body, just as G2499
Php 2:25 whom you sent to **take c of** my needs. G3313
1Th 5:12 *who* c **for** you in the Lord and who G4613
1Ti 3: 5 how *can he* **take c of** God's church?) G2150
1Ti 5:16 who is a believer **has widows** *in her* c, AIT
1Ti 6:20 guard what has been **entrusted to** your c. G4146
Heb 2: 6 of them, a son of man that *you* c **for** him? G2170
1Pe 1:10 searched intently and **with the greatest** c, G2001
1Pe 5: 2 of God's flock that is **under** your c, G1877
Rev 12: 6 where she *might be* **taken c of** for 1,260 G5555
Rev 12:14 where *she would be* **taken c of** for a time G5555

CARED (12) [CARE]
Dt 32:10 He shielded him and c **for** him; he H1067
Ru 4:16 took the child in her arms and c for him. H587
La 2:20 offspring, the children they have c **for**? H3259
La 2:22 those *I* c **for** and reared my enemy has H3254
Eze 34: 8 my flock but c **for** themselves rather H8286
Hos 12:13 up from Egypt, by a prophet *he* c **for** *him*. H9068
Hos 13: 5 I c **for** you in the wilderness, in the land of H3359
Mk 15:41 had followed him and c **for his needs**. G1354
Lk 18: 2 feared God nor c **what** people **thought**. G1956
Jn 12: 6 say this because he c about the poor but G3508
Ac 7:20 For three months he *was* c **for** by his family. G427
1Th 2: 8 so *we* c **for** you. Because we loved you so G3916

CAREFREE (1) [CARE]
Eze 23:42 "The noise of a c crowd was around her H8929

CAREFUL (78) [CARE]
Ge 31:24 "**Be c** not to say anything to Jacob H9068
Ge 31:29 '**Be c** not to say anything to Jacob H9068
Ex 19:12 '*Be* c *that* you do not approach the H9068
Ex 23:13 "*Be* c **to do** everything I have said to you H9068
Ex 34:12 *Be* c not to make a treaty with those who H9068
Ex 34:15 "Be c not to make a treaty with those who NDT
Lev 18: 4 obey my laws and *be* c to follow my H9068
Lev 25:18 my decrees and *be* c to obey my laws, H9068
Lev 26: 3 my decrees and *are* c to obey my H9068
Dt 2: 4 They will be afraid of you, but *be* very c. H9068
Dt 4: 9 Only *be* c, and watch yourselves closely so H9068
Dt 4:23 *Be* c not to forget the covenant of the LORD H9068
Dt 5:32 So *be* c to do what the LORD your God has H9068
Dt 6: 3 and *be* c to obey so that it may go well H9068
Dt 6:12 *be* c that you do not forget the LORD, who H9068
Dt 6:25 And if *we are* c to obey all this law before H9068
Dt 7:12 to these laws and *are* c to follow them, H9068
Dt 8: 1 *Be* c to follow every command I am giving H9068
Dt 8:11 *Be* c that you do not forget the LORD your H9068
Dt 11:16 *Be* c, or you will be enticed to turn away H9068
Dt 12: 1 laws *you must be* c to follow in the H9068
Dt 12:13 *Be* c not to sacrifice your burnt offerings H9068
Dt 12:19 *Be* c not to neglect the Levites as long as H9068
Dt 12:28 *Be* c to obey all these regulations I am H9068
Dt 12:30 *be* c not to be ensnared by inquiring H9068
Dt 15: 5 LORD your God and *are* c to follow all H9068
Dt 15: 9 *Be* c not to harbor this wicked thought H9068
Dt 17:10 *Be* c to do everything they instruct you to H9068
Dt 24: 8 *be* very c to do exactly as the H9068+9068
Jos 1: 7 *Be* c to obey all the law my servant Moses H9068
Jos 1: 8 so that *you may be* c to do everything H9068
Jos 22: 5 But *be* very c to keep the commandment H9068
Jos 23: 6 *be* c to obey all that is written in the Book H9068
Jos 23:11 So *be* very c to love the LORD your God. H9068
1Ki 8:25 your descendants *are* c in all they do to H9068
2Ki 10:31 Yet Jehu *was* not c to keep the law of the H9068
2Ki 17:37 *You must* always *be* c to keep the decrees H9068
2Ki 21: 8 if only *they will be* c to do everything I H9068
1Ch 22:13 have success if *you are* c to observe the H9068
1Ch 28: 8 *Be* c to follow all the commands of the H9068
2Ch 6:16 your descendants *are* c in all they do to H9068
2Ch 33: 8 if only *they will be* c to do everything I H9068
Ezr 4:22 Be c not to neglect this matter. Why let A10224
Job 36:18 *Be* c that no one entices you by riches; do H2778
Ps 45:10 and **pay c attention**: H8011+2256+5742+265
Ps 101: 2 *I will be* c to lead a blameless life H8505
Pr 4:26 **Give c thought** *to* the paths for your feet H7143
Pr 13:24 loves their children *is* c to discipline them. H8838
Pr 21:28 a c **listener** will testify H408+9048
Pr 27:23 your flocks, give c **attention** to your herds; H4213
Isa 7: 4 Say to him, '*Be* c, keep calm and don't be H9068
Jer 17:21 *Be* c not to carry a load on the Sabbath H9068
Jer 17:24 But if *you are* c **to obey** me H9048+9048
Jer 22: 4 For if *you are* c **to carry out** these H6913+6913
Eze 11:20 my decrees and *be* c to keep my laws. H9068
Eze 18:19 right and *has been* c to keep all my H9068
Eze 20:19 my decrees and *be* c to keep my laws. H9068
Eze 20:21 decrees, *they were* not c to keep my laws H9068
Eze 36:27 my decrees and *be* c to keep my laws. H9068
Eze 37:24 follow my laws and *be* c to keep my H9068
Hag 1: 5 "**Give c thought** to your ways. H8492+4222
Hag 1: 7 "**Give c thought** to your ways. H8492+4222
Hag 2:15 " 'Now **give c thought** to this from H8492+4222
Hag 2:18 **give c thought** to the day when the H8492+4222
Hag 2:18 temple was laid. **Give c thought**: H8492+4222
Mt 6: 1 "*Be* c not to practice your righteousness in G4668
Mt 16: 6 "*Be* c," Jesus said to them. "Be on your G3972
Mt 23: 3 So *you must be* c to do everything they tell G5498
Mk 8:15 "*Be* c," Jesus warned them. "Watch out G3972
Lk 21:34 "*Be* c, or your hearts will be weighed G4668
Ro 12:17 *Be* c to do what is right in the eyes of G4629
1Co 8: 9 *Be* c, however, that the exercise of your G1063
1Co 10:12 are standing firm, *be* c that you don't fall! G1063
Eph 5:15 **Be very c**, then, how you live—not as G1063+209
2Ti 4: 2 with great patience and c **instruction**. G1439
Titus 3: 8 have trusted in God *may be* c to devote G5863
Heb 2: 1 We must pay the **most** c attention G4359
Heb 4: 1 *let us be* c that none of you be found to G5828

CAREFULLY (44) [CARE]
Ge 27: 8 **listen** c and do what I tell you: H9048+928+7754
Ex 15:26 "If *you* **listen** c to the LORD your God H9048+9048
Ex 23:22 If *you* **listen** c to what he says and H9048+9048
Dt 4: 6 Observe them c, for this will show your H9068
Dt 4:15 Therefore **watch** yourselves very c, H9068
Dt 11:22 If *you* c **observe** all these H9068+9068
Dt 16:12 in Egypt, and follow c these decrees. H9068
Dt 17:19 his God and follow c all the words of this H9068
Dt 19: 9 because *you* c follow all these laws I H9068
Dt 24: 8 You must follow c what I have H9068
Dt 26:16 c observe them with all your heart and H9068
Dt 28: 1 the LORD your God and c follow all his H9068
Dt 28:13 that I give you this day and c follow them, H9068
Dt 28:15 your God and do not c follow all his H9068
Dt 28:58 If *you do* not c follow all the words of this H9068
Dt 29: 9 C follow the terms of this covenant, so H9068
Dt 31:12 your God and follow c all the words of this H9068
Dt 32:46 children to obey c all the words of this H9068
Jos 8: 4 "**Listen** c. You are to set an H8011
Jdg 6:29 When *they* c **investigated** H2011+2256+1335
2Ch 19: 6 He told them, "**Consider** c what you do H8011
2Ch 19: 7 Judge c, for with the LORD our God there is H9068
Ezr 8:29 Guard them c until you weigh them out in H9068
Ne 10:29 of God and to obey c all the commands, H9068
Job 13:17 **Listen** c *to* what I say; let my words H9048+9048
Job 21: 2 "**Listen** c *to* my words; let this be H9048+9048
Pr 12:26 The righteous **choose** their friends c, but H9365
Eze 3:10 **listen** c and take to heart all H928+265+9048
Eze 40: 4 **look** c and listen closely and H8011+928+6524
Eze 44: 5 "Son of man, **look** c, listen H8011+928+6524
Da 10:11 *you* who are highly esteemed, **consider** c H1067
Mt 2: 8 said, "Go and search c for the child. G209
Mk 4:24 "**Consider** c what you hear," he continued G1063
Lk 1: 3 since I myself have c investigated G209
Lk 4:10 his angels concerning you *to* **guard** you c; G1428
Lk 8:18 Therefore **consider** c how you listen G1063
Lk 9:44 "**Listen** c to what I am G5502+1650+3836+4044
Lk 14: 1 Pharisee, he was *being* c **watched**. G4190
Lk 15: 8 the house and search c until she finds it? G2151
Ac 2:14 explain this to you; **listen** c to what I say. G1969
Ac 5:35 **consider** c what you intend to do to these G4668
Ac 16:23 jailer was commanded to guard them c. G857
Ac 17:23 around and **looked** c **at** your objects of G355
1Co 14:29 the others *should* **weigh** c what is said. G1359

CARELESSLY (1) [CARE]
Lev 5: 4 in any matter one *might* c swear about H1051

CARES (11) [CARE]
Dt 11:12 It is a land the LORD your God c **for**; the H2011
Job 39:16 she c not that her labor was in vain H7065
Ps 55:22 Cast your c on the LORD and he will sustain H3365
Ps 142: 4 I have no refuge; no *one* c **for** my life. H2011
Ecc 5: 3 A dream comes when there are many c H6721
Jer 12:11 there is no one *who* c. H8492+6584+4213
Jer 30:17 an outcast, Zion for whom no *one* c. H2011
Na 1: 7 *He* c **for** those who trust in him, H3359
Jn 10:13 is a hired hand and c nothing for the G3508
1Th 2: 7 Just as a nursing mother c **for** her children, G2499
1Pe 5: 7 your anxiety on him because he c for you. G3508

CARESSED (3) [CARESSING]
Eze 23: 3 were fondled and their virgin bosoms **c**. H6914
Eze 23: 8 **c** her virgin bosom and poured out their H6914
Eze 23:21 Egypt your bosom *was* **c** and your young H6914

CARESSING (1) [CARESSED]
Ge 26: 8 saw Isaac **c** his wife Rebekah. H7464

CARGO (5) [CARGOES]
Eze 27:25 are filled with **heavy** *c* as you sail the sea AIT
Jnh 1: 5 threw the **c** into the sea H3998+889+928+2021+641
Ac 21: 3 where our ship was to unload its **c**. G1203
Ac 27:10 bring great loss to ship and **c**, G5845
Ac 27:18 day they began to **throw the c overboard**. G1678

CARGOES (4) [CARGO]
1Ki 10:11 there they brought **great** *c of* almugwood AIT
Rev 18:11 because no one buys their **c** anymore— G1203
Rev 18:12 **c** of gold, silver, precious stones and G1203
Rev 18:13 **c** of cinnamon and spice, of incense, myrrh NDT

CARING (1) [CARE]
1Ti 5: 4 *to* **put** *their* **religion into practice by c for** G2355

CARITES (2)
2Ki 11: 4 the **C** and the guards and had them H4133
2Ki 11:19 of hundreds, the **C**, the guards and all the H4133

CARMEL (27) [CARMELITE]
Jos 12:22 Kedesh one the king of Jokneam in **C** one H4151
Jos 15:55 **C**, Ziph, Juttah, H4150
Jos 19:26 boundary touched **C** and Shihor Libnath. H4151
1Sa 15:12 he was told, "Saul has gone to **C**. H4150
1Sa 25: 2 who had property there at **C**, was very H4150
1Sa 25: 2 which he was shearing in **C**. H4150
1Sa 25: 5 "Go up to Nabal at **C** and greet him in my H4150
1Sa 25: 7 time they were at **C** nothing of theirs was H4150
1Sa 25:40 His servants went to **C** and said to Abigail H4150
1Sa 27: 3 Ahinoam of Jezreel and Abigail **of C**, the H4153
1Sa 30: 5 Abigail, the widow of Nabal **of C**. H4153
2Sa 2: 2 Abigail, the widow of Nabal **of C**. H4153
2Sa 3: 3 son of Abigail the widow of Nabal **of C**; H4153
1Ki 18:19 all over Israel to meet me on Mount **C**. H4151
1Ki 18:20 assembled the prophets on Mount **C**. H4151
1Ki 18:42 Elijah climbed to the top of **C**, bent H4151
2Ki 2:25 he went on to Mount **C** and from there H4151
2Ki 4:25 came to the man of God at Mount **C**. H4151
1Ch 3: 1 second, Daniel the son of Abigail **of C**; H4153
SS 7: 5 Your head crowns you like Mount **C**. H4151
Isa 33: 9 Bashan and **C** drop their leaves. H4151
Isa 35: 2 the splendor of **C** and Sharon; they will H4151
Jer 46:18 among the mountains, like **C** by the sea. H4151
Jer 50:19 they will graze on **C** and Bashan H4151
Am 1: 2 and the top of **C** withers. H4151
Am 9: 3 they hide themselves on the top of **C**, H4151
Na 1: 4 Bashan and **C** wither and the blossoms of H4151

CARMELITE (2) [CARMEL]
2Sa 23:35 Hezro the **C**, Paarai the Arbite, H4153
1Ch 11:37 Hezro the **C**, Naarai son of Ezbai, H4153

CARMI (NIV84) KARMI

CARMITE (NIV84) KARMITE

CARNAL (KJV) FLESH, MATERIAL, MERE HUMAN, UNSPIRITUAL, WORLDLY

CARNALLY (KJV) SEXUAL RELATIONS, SLEEPS WITH

CARNELIAN (3) See also RUBY
Ex 28:17 The first row shall be **c**, chrysolite and beryl; H138
Ex 39:10 The first row was **c**, chrysolite and beryl; H138
Eze 28:13 **c**, chrysolite and emerald, topaz, onyx and H138

CAROUSE (1) [CAROUSING]
2Pe 2:13 idea of pleasure is to **c** in broad daylight. G5588

CAROUSING (3) [CAROUSE]
Lk 21:34 your hearts will be weighed down with **c**, G3190
Ro 13:13 in the daytime, not *in* **c** and drunkenness G3269
1Pe 4: 3 **c** and detestable idolatry. G4542

CARPENTER (2) [CARPENTER'S, CARPENTERS]
Isa 44:13 The **c** measures with a line and H3093+6770
Mk 6: 3 Isn't this the **c**? Isn't this Mary's son and G5454

CARPENTER'S (1) [CARPENTER]
Mt 13:55 "Isn't this the **c** son? Isn't his mother's G5454

CARPENTERS (8) [CARPENTER]
2Sa 5:11 cedar logs and **c** and stonemasons, H3093+6770
2Ki 12:11 of the LORD—the **c** and builders, H3093+6770
2Ki 22: 6 the **c**, the builders and the masons. H3093
1Ch 14: 1 stonemasons and **c** to build a H3093+6770
1Ch 22:15 masons and **c**, as well as those H6770
2Ch 24:12 hired masons and **c** to restore the LORD's H3093
2Ch 34:11 also gave money to the **c** and builders to H3093
Ezr 3: 7 they gave money to the masons and **c**, H3093

CARPUS (1)
2Ti 4:13 bring the cloak that I left with **C** at Troas G2842

CARRIAGE (2) [CARRIAGES]
SS 3: 7 It is Solomon's **c**, escorted by sixty warriors H4753
SS 3: 9 King Solomon made for himself the **c**; he H712

CARRIAGES (1) [CARRIAGE]
Rev 18:13 horses and **c**; and human beings G4832

CARRIED (149) [CARRY]
Ge 14:12 *They* also **c** off Abram's nephew Lot and H4374
Ge 22: 6 and *he* himself **c** the fire and H4374+928+3338
Ge 31:26 and *you've* **c** off my daughters like H5627
Ge 34:29 *They* **c** off all their wealth and all their H8647
Ge 40:15 *I* **was forcibly c off** from the land of H1704+1704
Ge 50:13 They **c** him to the land of Canaan and H5951
Ex 10:19 up the locusts and **c** them into the Red H9546
Ex 12:34 **c** it on their shoulders in kneading NDT
Ex 19: 4 how *I* **c** you on eagles' wings and H5951
Ex 27: 7 be on two sides of the altar when it *is* **c**. H5951
Ex 34: 4 and *he* **c** the two stone tablets in his H4374
Lev 10: 5 So they came and **c** them, still in their H5951
Nu 10:17 Merarites, *who* **c** it, set out. H5951
Nu 13:23 Two of them **c** it on a pole between them H5951
Dt 1:31 you saw how the LORD your God **c** you, H5951
Dt 2:35 we had captured *we* **c** off for ourselves. H1024
Dt 3: 7 from their cities *we* **c** off for ourselves. H1024
Dt 31: 9 who **c** the ark of the covenant of the LORD H5951
Dt 31:25 to the Levites *who* **c** the ark of the H5951
Dt 33:21 *he* **c** out the LORD's righteous will H6913
Jos 3:15 soon as the priests *who* **c** the ark reached H5951
Jos 3:17 The priests *who* **c** the ark of the covenant H5951
Jos 4: 8 and *they* **c** them **over** with them to their H6296
Jos 4: 9 spot where the priests *who* **c** the ark of the H5951
Jos 4:10 Now the priests *who* **c** the ark remained H5951
Jos 6:11 So *he had* the ark of the LORD **c around** the H6015
Jos 8:33 facing the Levitical priests *who* **c** it. H5951
Jos 11:14 The Israelites **c** off for themselves all the H1024
Jos 22: 3 Israelites but *have* **c** out the mission the H9068
Jdg 3:18 he sent on their way those *who had* **c** it. H5951
Jdg 16: 3 to his shoulders and **c** them to the top of H6590
Jdg 21:23 caught one and **c** her off to be his wife. H5951
Ru 2:18 *She* **c** it back to town, and her H5951
1Sa 5: 2 Then they **c** the ark *into* Dagon's temple H4374
1Sa 15:11 from me and *has* not **c** out my instructions H7756
1Sa 15:13 *I have* **c** out the LORD's instructions. H7756
1Sa 17:34 a bear came and **c** off a sheep from the H5951
1Sa 23: 5 the Philistines and **c** off their livestock. H5627
1Sa 30: 2 but **c** them off as they went on their way. H5627
2Sa 5:21 and David and his men **c** them off. H5951
2Sa 23:16 gate of Bethlehem and **c** it back to David. H5951
1Ki 2:26 because *you* **c** the ark of the Sovereign H5951
1Ki 8: 4 The priests and Levites **c** them **up**, H6590
1Ki 14:26 *He* **c** off the treasures of the temple of the H4374
1Ki 15:22 and *they* **c** away from Ramah the stones H5951
1Ki 16:20 the rebellion *he* **c** out, are they not H8003
1Ki 17:19 **c** him to the upper room where he was H6590
1Ki 17:23 the child and **c** him **down** from the room H3718
2Ki 4:20 had lifted him up and **c** him to his mother, H995
2Ki 5:23 and *they* **c** them ahead of Gehazi. H5951
2Ki 18:12 listened to the commands nor **c** them out. H6913
2Ki 20:17 up until this day, *will* **be c off** to Babylon. H5951
2Ki 23:34 he took Jehoahaz and **c** him off *to* Egypt, H995
2Ki 24:14 *He* **c** all Jerusalem **into exile**: all H1655+1655
2Ki 25:11 of the guard **c into exile** the people who H1655
2Ki 25:13 of the LORD and *they* **c** the bronze to H5951
1Ch 11:18 gate of Bethlehem and **c** it back to David. H5951
1Ch 15:15 And the Levites **c** the ark of God with the H5951
1Ch 18: 7 the gold shields **c by** the officers of H2118+6584
1Ch 23:32 And so the Levites **c** out their H9068
2Ch 5: 5 The Levitical priests **c** them **up**; H6590
2Ch 8:16 All Solomon's work **was c** out, from the H3922
2Ch 12: 9 *he* **c** off the treasures of the temple of the H4374
2Ch 14:13 The men of Judah **c** off a large amount of H5951
2Ch 14:15 of the herders and **c** off droves of sheep H8647
2Ch 16: 6 and *they* **c** away from Ramah the stones H5951
2Ch 21:17 invaded it and **c** off all the goods found in H8647
2Ch 24:12 gave it to *those who* **c** out the work H6913
2Ch 25:13 people and **c** off great quantities H1024
2Ch 28: 8 of plunder, which *they* **c back** to Samaria. H995
2Ch 28:17 attacked Judah and **c** away prisoners, H8647
2Ch 29:16 Levites took it and **c** it out to the Kidron H3655
2Ch 35: 3 It is not to be **c** about on your shoulders H5362
2Ch 35:16 service of the LORD **was c** out for the H3922
2Ch 36: 4 brother Jehoahaz and **c** him off to Egypt. H995
2Ch 36:18 *He* **c** *to* Babylon all the articles from the H995
2Ch 36:20 *He* **c into exile** to Babylon the remnant H1655
Ezr 1: 7 Nebuchadnezzar *had* **c** away from H3655
Ezr 5: 8 The work *is* **being c** on with diligence A10522
Ezr 6:12 *Let it* **be c** out with diligence. A10522
Ezr 6:13 their associates **c** it out with diligence. A10522
Ne 3:17 of Keilah, **c** out **repairs** for his district. H2616
Ne 4:17 Those *who* **c** materials did their H5951+6673
Ne 11:12 associates, *who* **c** on work for the temple H6913
Est 2: 6 who *had* **been c into exile** from Jerusalem H1655
Est 4:17 went away and **c** out all of Esther's H6913
Est 9: 1 commanded by the king was to **be c** out. H6913
Job 10:19 or *had* **been c** straight from the womb to H3297
Job 15:12 Why *has* your heart **c** you **away**, and why H4374
Job 21:32 They **are c** to the grave, and watch is kept H3297
Job 22:16 They **were c** off before their time, their H7855
Ecc 8:11 sentence for a crime is not quickly **c** out, H6913
Isa 8: 4 of Samaria *will* **be c** off by the king of H5951
Isa 39: 6 up until this day, *will* **be c** off to Babylon. H5951
Isa 41: 4 Who has done this and **c** *it* **through** H6913
Isa 46: 1 The **images that are c about** are H5953
Isa 46: 3 and *have* **c** since you were born. H5951
Isa 60: 4 and your daughters **are c** on the hip. H587
Isa 63: 9 lifted them up and **c** them all the days of H5951
Isa 66:12 you will nurse and **be c** on her arm and H5951
Jer 10: 5 *they* **must be c** because they H5951+5951
Jer 13:19 All Judah *will* **be c into exile**, carried H1655
Jer 13:19 be carried into exile, **c** completely **away**. H1655
Jer 24: 1 of Judah *were* **c into exile** from Jerusalem H1655
Jer 27:20 **c** Jehoiachin son of Jehoiakim king of Judah **into exile** H1655
Jer 29: 1 Nebuchadnezzar *had* **c into exile** from H1655
Jer 29: 4 to all those *I* **c into exile** from Jerusalem H1655
Jer 29: 7 of the city to which *I have* **c** you **into exile**. H1655
Jer 29:14 to the place from which *I* **c** you **into exile**." H1655
Jer 35:16 son of Rekab *have* **c** out the command H7756
Jer 39: 9 imperial guard **c into exile** *to* Babylon the H1655
Jer 40: 1 Judah who *were* **being c into exile** to H1655
Jer 40: 7 who *had* not **been c into exile** to H1655
Jer 49:29 their shelters *will be* **c** off with all their H5951
Jer 52:15 of the guard **c into exile** some of the H1655
Jer 52:17 of the LORD and *they* **c** all the bronze to H5951
Jer 52:28 the people Nebuchadnezzar **c into exile**: H1655
Eze 6: 9 nations where *they have* **been c captive**, H8647
Eze 16:16 where *you* **c on** *your* **prostitution**. H2388
Eze 17: 4 its topmost shoot and **c** it **away** to a land of H995
Eze 17:12 to Jerusalem and **c** off her king and her H4374
Eze 17:13 *He* also **c away** the leading men of the H4374
Eze 23:14 "But *she* **c** her prostitution **still further**. H3578
Eze 23:18 When *she* **c on** her prostitution **openly** H1655
Eze 30: 4 her wealth *will be* **c away** and her H4374
Da 1: 2 These *he* **c** off *to* the temple of his god in H995
Da 11:12 When the army **is c** off, the king of the H5951
Hos 10: 6 It *will* **be c** to Assyria as tribute for the H3297
Joel 3: 5 my gold and **c** off my finest treasures H995
Ob 11 aloof while strangers **c** off his wealth and H8647
Na 2: 7 that Nineveh be exiled and **c away**. H6590
Mal 2: 3 sacrifices, and you *will be* **c** off with it. H5951
Mt 14:11 given to the girl, *who* **c** it to her mother. G5770
Mk 2: 3 to him a paralyzed man, **c** by four of them. G149
Mk 6:55 region and **c** the sick on mats **to** wherever G4367
Lk 7:12 a dead person *was being* **c** out—the only G1714
Lk 16:22 died and the angels **c** him to Abraham's G708
Jn 20:15 if you *have* **c** him **away**, tell me G1002
Ac 3: 2 lame from birth *was being* **c** to the temple G1002
Ac 5: 6 his body, and **c** him **out** and buried him. G1766
Ac 5:10 **c** her **out** and buried her beside her G1766
Ac 13:29 When *they had* **c** out all that was written G5464
Ac 21:35 so great he had to *be* **c** by the soldiers. G1002
Ac 23:30 of a plot *to be* **c** out against the man, G1639
Heb 13: 9 *Do* not **be c away** by all kinds of strange G4195
2Pe 1:21 from God *as they were* **c along** by the G5770
2Pe 3:17 so that *you may* not **be c away** by the error G5270
Rev 17: 3 Then the angel **c** me **away** in the Spirit into G708
Rev 21:10 And *he* **c** me **away** in the Spirit to a G708

CARRIERS (7) [CARRY]
Jos 9:21 water **c** in the service of the H8612
Jos 9:23 water **c** for the house of my H8612
Jos 9:27 woodcutters and water **c** for the assembly, H8612
1Ki 5:15 seventy thousand **c** and eighty H5951+6025
2Ch 2: 2 70,000 men as **c** and 80,000 as H6025
2Ch 2:18 70,000 of them to be **c** and 80,000 to be H6025
Eze 27:25 ships of Tarshish *serve as* **c** *for* your wares. H8801

CARRIES (9) [CARRY]
Nu 11:12 my arms, as a nurse **c** an infant, to the H5951
Dt 1:31 as a father **c** his son, all the way you H5951
Dt 32:11 its wings to catch them and **c** them aloft. H5951
Job 23:14 *He* **c** out his decree against me, and H8966
Job 27:21 The east wind **c** him **off**, and he is gone H5951
Isa 40:11 lambs in his arms and **c** them close to his H5951
Isa 44:26 *who* **c** out the words of his servants and H7756
Hag 2:12 If someone **c** consecrated meat in the fold H5951
Heb 13:11 priest **c** the blood of animals **into** the G1662

CARRION (1)
Eze 39: 4 to all kinds of **c birds** and to the H6514+7606

CARRY (126) [CARRIED, CARRIERS, CARRIES, CARRYING]
Ge 44: 1 sacks with as much food as they can **c**, H5951
Ge 45:27 the carts Joseph had sent to **c** him **back**, H5951
Ge 47:30 **c** me out of Egypt and bury me where they H5951
Ge 50:25 then *you must* **c** my bones **up** from H6590
Ex 13:19 then *you must* **c** my bones **up** with H6590
Ex 25:14 the rings on the sides of the ark to **c** it. H5951
Ex 25:28 them with gold and **c** the table with them. H5951
Ex 30: 4 to hold the poles used to **c** it. H5951
Ex 36: 1 ability to know how to **c** out all the work of H6913
Ex 36: 3 had brought to **c** out the work of H6913
Ex 37: 5 the rings on the sides of the ark to **c** it. H5951
Ex 37:27 to hold the poles used to **c** it. H5951
Lev 4: 5 of the bull's blood and **c** it into the tent of H995
Lev 6:11 **c** the ashes outside the camp to a H3655
Lev 10: 4 **c** your cousins outside the camp H5951
Lev 16:22 The goat *will* **c** on itself all their sins to a H5951
Lev 26:14 listen to me and **c** out all these H6913
Lev 26:15 laws and fail *to* **c** out all my commands H6913
Nu 1:50 They *are to* **c** the tabernacle and all its H5951
Nu 4:15 Kohathites are to **c** those things that are H5362

Nu 4:19 to each man his work and what he is to c. H5362
Nu 4:25 They are to c the curtains of the tabernacle H5951
Nu 4:27 as their responsibility all they are to c. H5362
Nu 4:31 they are to c the frames of the tabernacle H5362
Nu 4:32 to each man the specific things he is to c. H5362
Nu 4:49 was assigned his work and told what to c. H5362
Nu 7: 9 because they were to c on their shoulders H5951
Nu 11:12 Why do you tell me to c them in my arms H5951
Nu 11:14 I cannot c all these people by myself; the H5951
Nu 11:17 you so that you will not have to c it alone. H5951
Nu 31: 3 so that they may c out the LORD's H5989
Dt 1: 9 are too heavy a burden for me to c H4202+3523+5951
Dt 10: 8 the tribe of Levi to c the ark of the H5951
Dt 14:24 LORD your God and cannot c your tithe H5951
Dt 25: 6 she bears shall c on the name of H7756+6584
Dt 25: 7 brother refuses to c on his brother's name H7756
Dt 29:11 who chop your wood and c your water. H8612
Jos 3: 8 Tell the priests who c the ark of the H5951
Jos 3:13 soon as the priests who c the ark of the H5951
Jos 4: 3 and c them over with you and put them H6296
Jos 6: 4 Have seven priests c trumpets of rams' H5951
Jos 6: 6 LORD and have seven priests c trumpets in H5951
Jos 8: 2 except that you may c off their plunder H1024
Jos 8:27 But Israel did c off for themselves the H1024
1Sa 3:12 At that time I will c out against Eli H7756
1Sa 20:40 boy and said, "Go, c them back to town." H995
1Sa 21:15 this fellow here to c on like this in front of H8713
1Sa 28:18 not obey the LORD or c out his fierce wrath H6913
2Sa 18:18 no son to c on the memory of my name." H2349
2Sa 24:12 one of them for me to c out against you. H6913
1Ki 1:30 I will surely c out this very day what I swore H6913
1Ki 3: 7 know how to c out my duties. H3655+2256+995
1Ki 18:12 Spirit of the LORD may c you when I leave H5951
1Ki 20: 6 seize everything you value and c it away. H4374
2Ki 4:19 told a servant, "C him to his mother." H5951
2Ki 5:17 as much earth as a pair of mules can c, H5362
1Ch 15: 2 one but the Levites may c the ark of God, H5951
1Ch 15: 2 LORD chose them to c the ark of the LORD H5951
1Ch 21:10 one of them for me to c out against you. H6913
1Ch 23:26 the Levites no longer need to c the H5951
2Ch 20:25 his men went to c off their plunder, H1024
2Ch 24:11 empty the chest and c it back to its place. H5951
2Ch 30:12 unity of mind to c out what the king and H6913
Est 9:13 Susa permission to c out this day's edict H6913
Job 15:30 breath of God's mouth will c him away. H6073
Job 20:28 A flood will c off his house, rushing H1655
Job 24:10 go about naked; they c the sheaves, but H5951
Ps 28: 9 be their shepherd and c them forever. H5951
Ps 37: 7 when they c out their wicked schemes. H6913
Ps 149: 9 to c out the sentence written against them H6913
Ecc 5:15 their toil that they can c in their hands. H2143
Ecc 10:20 a bird in the sky may c your words, H2143
Isa 5:29 seize their prey and c it off with no one to H7117
Isa 10:23 will c out the destruction decreed upon H6913
Isa 13: 3 summoned my warriors to c out my wrath— NDT
Isa 15: 7 stored up they c away over the Ravine H5951
Isa 28:19 As often as it comes it will c you away H4374
Isa 30: 1 "to those who c out plans that are not H6913
Isa 30: 6 the envoys c their riches on donkeys' H5951
Isa 33:23 even the lame will c off plunder. H1024
Isa 45:20 are those who c about idols of wood, H5951
Isa 46: 4 I have made you and I will c you; I will H5951
Isa 46: 7 They lift it to their shoulders and c it; they H6022
Isa 48:14 LORD's chosen ally will c out his purpose H6913
Isa 49:22 in their arms and c your daughters on H5951
Isa 52:11 you who c the articles of the LORD's house. H5951
Isa 57:13 The wind will c all of them off, a mere H5951
Jer 17:21 Be careful not to c a load on the Sabbath H5951
Jer 20: 4 who will c them away to Babylon or put H1655
Jer 20: 5 it away as plunder and c it off to Babylon. H995
Jer 22: 4 For if you are careful to c out these H6913+6913
Jer 43: 3 may kill us or c us into exile to Babylon." H1655
Jer 44:25 'We will certainly c out the vows H6913+6913
Jer 46: 9 men of Cush and Put who c shields, men H9530
Jer 51:12 The LORD will c out his purpose, his decree H2372
Eze 12: 6 they are watching and c them out at dusk. H3655
Eze 25:17 I will c out great vengeance on them and H6913
Eze 29:19 of Babylon, and he will c off its wealth. H5951
Eze 38:13 hordes to loot, to c off silver and gold, to H5951
Eze 39:14 they will c out a more detailed search. H2983
Da 11: 8 and c them off to Egypt. H995+928+2021+8660
Da 11:10 flood and c the battle as far H8740+2256+1741
Hos 5:14 go away; I will c them off, with no one H5951
Hos 11: 9 I will not c out my fierce anger, nor will I H6913
Am 6:10 relative who comes to c the bodies out of H5951
Mic 2: 1 morning's light they c it out because it is H6913
Mt 3:11 whose sandals I am not worthy to c. G1002
Mt 12:29 man's house and c off his possessions G773
Mt 27:32 and they forced him to c the cross. G149
Mk 11:16 anyone to c merchandise through the G1422
Mk 15:21 and they forced him to c the cross. G149
Lk 11:46 down with burdens they can hardly c, G1546
Lk 14:27 And whoever does not c their cross and G1002
Lk 23:26 on him and made him c it behind Jesus G5770
Jn 5:10 Sabbath; the law forbids you to c your mat." G149
Jn 8:44 you want to c out your father's desires G4472
Ac 5: 9 at the door, and they will c you out also." G1766
Ro 7:18 to do what is good, but I cannot c it out. G2981
Ro 9:28 For the Lord will c out his sentence on G4472
2Co 4:10 We always c around in our body the death G4367
2Co 8:19 to accompany us as we c the offering, NDT
Gal 6: 2 C each other's burdens, and in this way G1002
Gal 6: 5 each one should c their own load. G1002
Php 1: 6 in you will c it on to completion until the G2200
Heb 9: 6 into the outer room to c on their ministry. G2200
Jas 4:13 c on business and make money. G1864

CARRYING (52) [CARRY]

Ex 25:27 rim to hold the poles used in c the table. H5951
Ex 37:14 rim to hold the poles used in c the table. H5951
Ex 37:15 The poles for c the table were made of H5951
Ex 38: 7 would be on the sides of the altar for c it. H5951
Nu 4:10 durable leather and put it on a c frame. H4573
Nu 4:12 leather and put them on a c frame. H4573
Nu 4:15 are the Kohathites to come and do the c. H5951
Nu 4:24 Gershonite clans in their c and their other H5362
Nu 4:27 whether c or doing other work H5362
Nu 4:47 work of serving and c the tent of meeting H5362
Nu 10:21 the Kohathites set out, c the holy things. H5951
Dt 27:26 the words of this law by c them out." H6913
Jos 3: 3 the Levitical priests c it, you are to H5951
Jos 3:14 the priests c the ark of the covenant went H5951
Jos 4:16 "Command the priests c the ark of the H5951
Jos 4:18 up out of the river c the ark of the H5951
Jos 6: 8 the seven priests c the seven trumpets H5951
Jos 6:13 The seven priests c the seven trumpets H5951
1Sa 10: 3 One will be c three young goats, another H5951
2Sa 6:13 When those who were c the ark of the LORD H5951
2Sa 15:24 who were with him were c the ark of the H5951
1Ki 8: 7 overshadowed the ark and its c poles. H964
1Ki 10: 2 caravan—with camels c spices, large H5951
1Ki 10:22 years it returned, c gold, silver and ivory, H5951
1Ch 12:24 from Judah, c shield and spear—6,800 H5951
1Ch 12:34 with 37,000 men c shields and spears; H928
1Ch 15:26 the Levites who were c the ark of the H5951
1Ch 15:27 as were all the Levites who were c the ark H5951
1Ch 28: 7 is unswerving in c out my commands and H6913
2Ch 5: 8 the ark and covered the ark and its c poles. H964
2Ch 7:11 had succeeded in c out all he had in H7503
2Ch 9: 1 caravan—with camels c spices, large H5951
2Ch 9:21 years it returned, c gold, silver and ivory, H5951
Ne 6: 3 "I am c on a great project and cannot go H6913
Ne 10:32 We assume the responsibility for c out H6641+6584
Ps 126: 6 who go out weeping, c seed to sow, will H5951
Ps 126: 6 with songs of joy, c sheaves with them. H5951
Jer 17:27 day holy by not c any load as you come H5951
Eze 12: 7 c them on my shoulders while they H5951
Eze 44: 8 Instead of c out your duty in regard to my H9068
Hos 6: 9 to Shechem, c out their wicked schemes. H6913
Mal 3:14 do we gain by c out his requirements H9068
Mk 14:13 a man c a jar of water will meet you. G1002
Lk 5:18 Some men came c a paralyzed man on a G5770
Lk 7:14 up and touched the bier they were c him on, NDT
Lk 22:10 a man c a jar of water will meet you. G1002
Jn 18: 3 They were c torches, lanterns and G3552
Jn 19:17 C his own cross, he went out to the place G1002
Ac 23:31 So the soldiers, c out their orders, took G2848
Ac 27:43 life and kept them from c out their plan. G3266
1Co 16:10 for he is c on the work of the Lord G2237
1Jn 5: 2 by loving God and c out his commands. G4472

CARSHENA (NIV84) KARSHENA

CART (15) [CARTS]

Nu 7: 3 from each leader and a c from every two. H6322
1Sa 6: 7 get a new c ready, with two cows H6322
1Sa 6: 7 Hitch the cows to the c, but take their H6322
1Sa 6: 8 Take the ark of the LORD and put it on the c, H6322
1Sa 6:10 them to the c and penned up their H6322
1Sa 6:11 of the LORD on the c and along with it the H6322
1Sa 6:14 The c came to the field of Joshua of Beth H6322
1Sa 6:14 up the wood of the c and sacrificed the H6322
2Sa 6: 3 ark of God on a new c and brought it from H6322
2Sa 6: 3 sons of Abinadab, were guiding the new c H6322
1Ch 13: 7 God from Abinadab's house on a new c, H6322
Isa 5:18 and wickedness as with c ropes, H6322
Isa 28:27 is the wheel of a c rolled over cumin H6322
Isa 28:28 The wheels of a threshing c may be rolled H6322
Am 2:13 will crush you as a c crushes when loaded H6322

CARTS (9) [CART]

Ge 45:19 Take some c from Egypt for your children H6322
Ge 45:21 Joseph gave them c, as Pharaoh had H6322
Ge 45:27 when he saw the c Joseph had sent to H6322
Ge 46: 5 their wives in the c that Pharaoh had sent H6322
Nu 7: 3 the LORD six covered c and twelve oxen— H6322
Nu 7: 6 So Moses took the c and oxen and gave H6322
Nu 7: 7 He gave two c and four oxen to the H6322
Nu 7: 8 he gave four c and eight oxen to the H6322
Ps 65:11 your c overflow with abundance. H5047

CARVED (17) [CARVES]

Lev 26: 1 do not place a c stone in your land to H5381
Nu 33:52 Destroy all their c images and their cast H5381
1Ki 6:18 cedar, c with gourds and open flowers. H5237
1Ki 6:29 outer rooms, he c cherubim, palm H7844+5237
1Ki 6:32 olive-wood doors he c cherubim, H7844+5237
1Ki 6:35 He c cherubim, palm trees and open H7844
2Ki 21: 7 He took the c Asherah pole he had made H7181
2Ch 3: 7 and he c cherubim on the walls. H7338
Ps 74: 6 smashed all the c paneling with their H7334
Ps 144:12 will be like pillars c to adorn a palace. H2634
Eze 41:18 were c cherubim and palm trees. H6913
Eze 41:19 They were c all around the whole temple. H6913
Eze 41:20 palm trees were c on the wall of the H6913
Eze 41:25 of the main hall were c cherubim and H6913
Eze 41:25 palm trees like those c on the walls, H6913
Eze 41:26 windows with palm trees c on each side. NDT
Hab 2:18 "Of what value is an idol c by a craftsman? H7180

CARVINGS (1) [CARVED]

1Ki 6:35 with gold hammered evenly over the c. H2977

CASE (55) [CASES]

Ex 18:22 have them bring every difficult c to you; H1821
Lev 5:13 the priest, as in the c of the grain offering. H3869
Nu 27: 5 So Moses brought their c before the LORD, H5477
Dt 1:16 whether the c is between two Israelites or NDT
Dt 1:17 Bring me any c too hard for you, and I will H1821
Dt 6:24 be kept alive, as is the c today. H3869
Dt 22:26 This c is like that of someone who attacks H1821
Dt 25: 1 to court and the judges will decide the c, H4392S
Jos 20: 4 gate and state their c before the elders of H1821
2Sa 15: 4 has a complaint or c could come to me H5477
2Sa 20:21 That is not the c. A man named Sheba H1821
1Ki 15: 5 except in the c of Uriah the Hittite. H1821
2Ki 8: 6 an official to her c and said to him, NDT
2Ch 19:10 In every c that comes before you from your H8190
Job 13: 3 the Almighty and to argue my c with God. H3519
Job 13: 8 Will you argue the c for God? H8189
Job 13:18 Now that I have prepared my c, I know I H5477
Job 23: 4 I would state my c before him and fill my H5477
Job 29:16 the needy; I took up the c of the stranger. H8190
Job 33: 5 stand up and argue your c before me. H3656
Job 35:14 that your c is before him and you must H1907
Job 37:19 we cannot draw up our c because of our H6885
Pr 22:23 will take up their c and will exact life for H8190
Pr 23:11 he will take up their c against you. H8190
Isa 1:17 the fatherless; plead the c of the widow. H8189
Isa 1:23 the widow's c does not come before them. H8190
Isa 41:21 "Present your c," says the LORD. "Set forth H8190
Isa 43:26 together; state the c for your innocence. AIT
Isa 59: 4 no one pleads a c with integrity. H9149
Jer 5:28 do not promote the c of the fatherless; H1907
Jer 12: 1 when I bring a c before you. H8189
La 3:58 took up my c; you redeemed my life H8190
Mic 6: 1 plead my c before the mountains H8189
Mic 6: 2 For the LORD has a c against his people H8190
Mic 7: 9 until he pleads my c and upholds my H8190
Lk 13:33 In any c, I must press on today and G4440
Ac 5:38 in the present c I advise you: G3836+3814
Ac 19:40 In that c we would not be able to G4309+4005
Ac 23:15 accurate information about his c. G3836+4309S
Ac 23:30 to present to you their c against him. G3836S
Ac 23:35 "I will hear your c when your accusers get G1358
Ac 24: 2 Tertullus presented his c before Felix G806+2989
Ac 24:22 he said, "I will decide your c." G3836+2848S
Ac 25:14 discussed Paul's c with the king. G3836+2848S
Ac 25:17 I did not delay the c, but convened the court NDT
1Co 5:10 In that c you would have to leave G2075+726
1Co 14: 7 Even in the c of lifeless things that make G3940
2Co 10:14 as would be the c if we had not come to you AIT
Gal 3:15 has been duly established, so it is in this c. NDT
Gal 5:11 In that c the offense of the cross has been G726
2Ti 3: 9 far because, as in the c of those men G1181
Heb 6: 9 are convinced of better things in your c— G4309
Heb 7: 8 In the one c, the tenth is collected G6045+3525
Heb 7: 8 who die; but in the other c, by him who is G1695
Heb 9:16 In the c of a will, it is necessary to prove G3963

CASES (9) [CASE]

Ex 18:22 the simple c they can decide themselves. H1821
Ex 18:26 The difficult c they brought to Moses, but H1821
Ex 22: 9 In all c of illegal possession of an ox, H1821
Ex 22: 9 are to bring their c before the judges. H1821
Dt 17: 8 If c come before your courts that H1821+8191
Dt 21: 5 to decide all c of dispute and assault. H8190
Dt 24: 8 In c of defiling skin diseases, be very careful NDT
Ezr 10:16 month they sat down to investigate the c, H1821
1Co 6: 2 are you not competent to judge trivial c? AIT

CASIPHIA (NIV84) KASIPHIA

CASKS (1)

Eze 27:19 and c of wine from Izal in exchange for H1969.5

CASLUHITES (NIV84) KASLUHITES

CASSIA (3)

Ex 30:24 500 shekels of c—all according to the H7703
Ps 45: 8 are fragrant with myrrh and aloes and c; H7904
Eze 27:19 wrought iron, c and calamus. H7703

CAST (79) [CASTING, CASTS, OUTCAST]

Ex 25:12 C four gold rings for it and fasten them to H3668
Ex 26:37 And c five bronze bases for them H3668
Ex 32: 4 made it into an idol c in the shape of a H5011
Ex 32: 8 themselves an idol c in the shape of a H5011
Ex 36:36 hooks for them and c their four silver H3668
Ex 37: 3 He c four gold rings for it and fastened H3668
Ex 37:13 They c four gold rings for the table and H3668
Ex 38: 5 They c bronze rings to hold the poles for H3668
Ex 38:27 of silver were used to c the bases for the H3668
Lev 16: 8 He is to c lots for the two goats—one lot H5989
Nu 33:52 all their carved images and their c idols, H5011

C

Dt 9:16 yourselves an **idol c** in the shape of a H5011
Jos 18: 6 here to me and *I will* **c** lots for you in H3721
Jos 18: 8 and *I will* **c** lots for you here at Shiloh in H8959
Jos 18:10 Joshua then **c** lots for them in Shiloh in H8959
1Sa 14:42 "**C** the lot between me and Jonathan my H5877
2Sa 23: 6 evil men are all *to* **be c aside** like thorns, H5610
1Ki 7:15 *He* **c** two bronze pillars, each eighteen H7445
1Ki 7:16 two capitals of **c** bronze to set on the H4607
1Ki 7:23 He made the Sea of **c metal**, circular in H4607
1Ki 7:24 The gourds **were c** in two rows in one H3668
1Ki 7:30 supports, **c** *with* wreaths on each side. H3668
1Ki 7:33 spokes and hubs were all of **c metal**. H4607
1Ki 7:37 were all **c in** the same **molds** and were H4607
1Ki 7:46 The king *had* them **c** in clay molds in the H3668
2Ki 17:16 themselves two **idols c** in the shape of H5011
1Ch 24:31 They also **c** lots, just as their relatives the H5877
1Ch 25: 8 as well as student, **c** lots for their duties. H5877
1Ch 26:13 Lots *were* **c** for each gate, according to H5877
1Ch 26:14 Then lots *were* **c** *for* his son Zechariah, H5877
2Ch 4: 2 He made the Sea of **c metal**, circular in H4607
2Ch 4: 3 The bulls **were c** in two rows in one piece H3668
2Ch 4:17 The king *had* them **c** in clay molds in the H3668
Ne 9:18 even when *they* **c** for themselves an H6913
Ne 10:34 *We*—the priests, the Levites and the people—*have* **c** H5877
Ne 11: 1 rest of the people **c** lots to bring one out H5877
Est 3: 7 *was* **c** in the presence of Haman to select H5877
Est 9:24 Jews to destroy them and *had* **c** the pur H5877
Job 6:27 *You would* even **c** lots for the fatherless H5877
Job 37:18 out the skies, hard as a mirror of **c bronze**? H4607
Ps 22:10 From birth *I was* **c** on you; from my H8959
Ps 22:18 among them and **c** lots for my garment. H5877
Ps 50:17 my instruction and **c** my words behind you H8959
Ps 51:11 *Do* not **c** me from your presence or take H8959
Ps 55:22 **C** your cares on the LORD and he will H8959
Ps 71: 9 *Do* not **c** me **away** when I am old; do not H8959
Ps 73:18 slippery ground; *you* **c** them **down** to ruin. H5877
Ps 89:44 to his splendor and **c** his throne to the H4489
Ps 106:19 calf and worshiped an **idol c from metal**. H5011
Pr 1:14 **c** lots with us; we will all share the loot"— H5877
Pr 16:33 The lot **is c** into the lap, but its every H3214
Pr 23: 5 **C** but a glance at riches, and they are H6414
Pr 29:18 people **c off restraint**; but blessed is H7277
Ecc 11:10 from your heart and **c off** the troubles of H6296
Isa 14:12 *You have* **been c down** to the earth, you H1548
Isa 14:19 But you **are c** out of your tomb like a H8959
Isa 19: 8 lament, all *who* **c** hooks into the Nile H8959
Isa 38: 8 I will make the shadow **c** by the sun go back NDT
Isa 57:20 whose waves **c up** mire and mud. H1764
Jer 22:28 **c** into a land they do not know? H8959
Jer 23:39 forget you and **c** you **out** of my presence H5759
La 3:31 For no *one is* **c off** by the Lord forever. H2396
Eze 21:21 *He will* **c lots** with arrows, he will consult H7837
Eze 31:11 according to its wickedness. *I* **c** it **aside**, H1763
Eze 32: 3 throng of people *I will* **c** my net over you, H7298
Joel 3: 3 *They* **c** lots for my people and traded boys H3341
Am 4: 3 and *you will be* **c out** toward Harmon," H8959
Am 5: 7 into bitterness and **c** righteousness to the H5663
Ob 11 his gates and **c** lots for Jerusalem, H3341
Jnh 1: 7 *let us* **c** lots to find out who is responsible H5877
Jnh 1: 7 *They* **c** lots and the lot fell on Jonah. H5877
Mic 5:12 witchcraft and you will no longer **c spells**. H6726
Na 3:10 Lots *were* **c** for her nobles, and all her H3341
Mk 15:24 *they* **c** lots to see what each would get. G965
Jn 19:24 among them and **c** lots for my garment." G965
Ac 1:26 Then *they* **c** lots, and the lot fell to G1443
Ac 26:10 put to death, *I* **c** my vote **against** them. G2965
1Pe 5: 7 **C** all your anxiety **on** him because he cares G2166
Rev 2:22 So *I will* **c** her on a bed of suffering, and I G965

CASTANETS (1)
2Sa 6: 5 before the LORD, with **c**, harps, H6770+1360

CASTAWAY (KJV) DISQUALIFIED

CASTING (8) [CAST]
Jdg 20: 9 up against it in the order *decided by* **c lots**. AIT
1Ch 24: 5 They divided them impartially by **c lots**, for H1598
Pr 18:18 **C** the lot settles disputes and keeps strong NDT
Eze 26: 3 against you, like the sea **c up** its waves. H6590
Mt 4:18 *They were* **c** a net into the lake, for they G965
Mt 27:35 they divided up his clothes *by* **c** lots. G965
Mk 1:16 his brother Andrew **c a net** into the lake, G311
Lk 23:34 And they divided up his clothes *by* **c** lots. G965

CASTLE, CASTLES (KJV) BARRACKS, CAMPS, CITADEL, FORT, FORTRESS, LOCATIONS

CASTOR (1)
Ac 28:11 figurehead *of* the **twin gods C and Pollux**. G1483

CASTS (6) [CAST]
Dt 18:11 or **c spells**, or who is a medium or H2489+2490
Ps 15: 3 to a neighbor, and **c** no slur on others; H5951
Ps 147: 6 the humble but **c** the wicked to the H9164
Isa 26: 5 it to the ground and **c** it **down** to the dust. H5595
Isa 40:19 a metalworker **c** it, and a goldsmith H5818
Isa 44:10 Who shapes a god and **c** an idol, which H5818

CASUALTIES (7)
Jdg 20:31 They began to inflict **c** on the Israelites as H2728
Jdg 20:39 had begun to inflict **c** on the Israelites H2728
2Sa 18: 7 and the **c** that day were great H4487
1Ki 20:29 **inflicted** a hundred thousand **c** *on* the H5782
2Ch 13:17 hundred thousand **c** among Israel's able H2728
2Ch 28: 5 of Israel, who inflicted heavy **c** on him. H4804
Na 3: 3 Many **c**, piles of dead, bodies without H2728

CATASTROPHE (2)
Ge 19:29 brought Lot out of the **c** that overthrew the H2202
Isa 47:11 a **c** you cannot foresee will suddenly H8739

CATCH (18) [CATCHES, CAUGHT]
Ge 44: 4 when *you* **c up** *with* them, say to H5952
Dt 32:11 spreads its wings *to* **c** them and carries H4374
Jos 2: 5 *You may* **c up** *with* them." H5952
Job 9:18 would not let me **c** my breath but would H8740
Job 23: 9 turns to the south, *I* **c** no **glimpse** of him. H8011
Ps 10: 9 He lies in wait to **c** the helpless; he H2642
SS 2:15 **C** for us the foxes, the little foxes that ruin H296
Jer 2:34 though *you did* not **c** them breaking in. H5162
Jer 5:26 like those who set traps *to* **c** people. H4334
Jer 16:16 declares the LORD, "and *they will* **c** them. H1899
Hos 2: 7 will chase after her lovers but not **c** them; H5952
Hos 7:12 hear them flocking together, *I will* **c** them. H3579
Mt 17:27 Take the first fish *you* **c**; open its mouth G326
Mk 12:13 Herodians to Jesus to **c** him in his words. G65
Lk 5: 4 deep water, and let down the nets for a **c**." G62
Lk 5: 9 astonished at the **c** of fish they had taken G62
Lk 11:54 waiting *to* **c** him in something he might G2561
Lk 20:20 They hoped *to* **c** Jesus in something he G2138

CATCHES (5) [CATCH]
Job 5:13 *He* **c** the wise in their craftiness, and the H4334
Job 39:25 *It* **c the scent** *of* battle from afar, the H8193
Ps 10: 9 *he* **c** the helpless and drags them off in H2642
Hab 1:15 up with hooks, *he* **c** them in his net, he H1760
1Co 3:19 "He **c** the wise in their craftiness" G1533

CATERPILLER, CATERPILLERS (KJV) GRASSHOPPER, GRASSHOPPERS, LOCUSTS

CATTLE (79)
Ge 12:16 Abram acquired sheep and **c**, male H1330
Ge 20:14 brought sheep and **c** and male and H1330
Ge 21:27 brought sheep and **c** and gave them to H1330
Ge 24:35 He has given him sheep and **c**, silver and H1330
Ge 32: 5 I have **c** and donkeys, sheep and goats H8802
Ge 47:17 and goats, their **c** and donkeys. H5238+1330
Ex 9: 3 donkeys and camels and on your **c**, sheep H1330
Ex 11: 5 and all the firstborn of the **c** as well. H989
Ex 20:24 your sheep and goats and your **c**. H1330
Ex 22: 1 pay back five *head of* **c** for the ox and H1330
Ex 22:30 Do the same with your **c** and your sheep H8802
Lev 7:23 'Do not eat any of the fat of **c**, sheep or H8802
Lev 22:19 present a male without defect from the **c**, H1330
Lev 26:22 destroy your **c** and make you so few in H989
Nu 22:40 Balak sacrificed **c** and sheep, and gave H1330
Nu 31:28 whether people, **c**, donkeys or sheep. H1330
Nu 31:30 whether people, **c**, donkeys, sheep or H1330
Nu 31:33 72,000 **c**, H1330
Nu 31:38 36,000 **c**, of which the tribute for the LORD H1330
Nu 31:44 36,000 **c**, H1330
Nu 35: 3 pasturelands for the **c** they own and all H989
Dt 11:15 I will provide grass in the fields for your **c** H989
Dt 14:26 **c**, sheep, wine or other fermented drink H1330
Jos 6:21 young and old, **c**, sheep and donkeys. H8802
Jos 7:24 daughters, his **c**, donkeys and sheep, H8802
Jdg 6: 4 neither sheep nor **c** nor donkeys. H8802
1Sa 8:16 the best of your **c** and donkeys he will H1330
1Sa 14:32 taking sheep, **c** and calves, they H1330
1Sa 14:34 'Each of you bring me your **c** and sheep H8802
1Sa 15: 3 infants, **c** and sheep, camels and H8802
1Sa 15: 9 Agag and the best of the sheep and **c**, H1330
1Sa 15:14 What is this lowing of **c** that I hear?" H1330
1Sa 15:15 best of the sheep and **c** to sacrifice to the H1330
1Sa 15:21 took sheep and **c** from the plunder, H1330
1Sa 22:19 infants, and its **c**, donkeys and sheep. H8802
1Sa 27: 9 took sheep and **c**, donkeys and H1330
2Sa 12: 2 had a very large number of sheep and **c**, H1330
2Sa 12: 4 of his own sheep or **c** to prepare a meal H1330
1Ki 1: 9 **c** and fattened calves at the Stone of H1330
1Ki 1:19 He has sacrificed great numbers of **c** H8802
1Ki 1:25 down and sacrificed great numbers of **c**, H8802
1Ki 4:23 ten *head of* stall-fed **c**, twenty of H1330
1Ki 4:23 of pasture-fed **c** and a hundred sheep H1330
1Ki 8: 5 so many sheep and **c** that they could not H1330
1Ki 8:63 thousand **c** and a hundred and H1330
2Ki 3:17 your **c** and your other animals will drink. H5238
1Ch 12:40 olive oil, **c** and sheep, for there was joy in H1330
2Ch 5: 6 so many sheep and **c** that they could not H1330
2Ch 7: 5 thousand *head of* **c** and a hundred and H1330
2Ch 15:11 LORD seven hundred *head of* **c** and seven H1330
2Ch 18: 2 many sheep and **c** for him and the people H1330
2Ch 32:28 stalls for various **kinds of c**, H989+2256+989
2Ch 35: 7 also three thousand **c**—all from the H1330
2Ch 35: 8 Passover offerings and three hundred **c**. H1330
2Ch 35: 9 five hundred *head of* **c** for the Levites. H1330
2Ch 35:12 They did the same with the **c**. H1330
Ne 9:37 over our bodies and our **c** as they please. H989
Ne 10:36 bring the firstborn of our sons and of our **c**, H989
Job 18: 3 are we regarded as **c** and considered H989
Job 36:33 even the **c** make known its approach. H5238
Ps 50:10 is mine, and the **c** on a thousand hills. H989
Ps 78:48 He gave over their **c** to the hail, their H1248
Ps 104:14 He makes grass grow for the **c**, and plants H989
Ps 147: 9 provides food for the **c** and for the young H989
Ps 148:10 wild animals and all **c**, small creatures H989
Isa 7:25 become places where **c** are turned loose H8802
Isa 22:13 slaughtering of **c** and killing of sheep H1330
Isa 30:23 In that day your **c** will graze in broad H5238
Isa 32:20 letting your **c** and donkeys range free. H8802
Isa 63:14 like **c** that go down to the plain, they were H989
Jer 9:10 the lowing of **c** is not heard. H5238
Eze 32:13 will destroy all her **c** from beside abundant H989
Eze 32:13 foot of man or muddied by the hooves of **c**. H989
Joel 1:18 How the **c** moan! The herds mill about H989
Hab 3:17 sheep in the pen and no **c** in the stalls, H1330
Mt 22: 4 My oxen and **fattened c** have been G4990
Jn 2:14 temple courts he found people selling **c**, G1091
Jn 2:15 both sheep and **c**; he scattered the G1091
Rev 18:13 flour and wheat; **c** and sheep; horses and G3229

CAUDA (1)
Ac 27:16 to the lee of a small island called **C**, G3007

CAUGHT (57) [CATCH]
Ge 22:13 in a thicket he saw a ram **c** by its horns. H296
Ge 27:27 When Isaac **c the smell** *of* his H8193+8194
Ge 31:23 seven days and **c up** *with* him in the hill H1815
Ge 39:12 *She* **c** him by his cloak and said, "Come to H9530
Ge 44: 6 When *he* **c up** *with* them, he repeated H5952
Ex 10:19 *which* **c up** the locusts and carried them H5951
Ex 22: 2 "If a thief **is c** breaking in at night and is H5162
Ex 22: 7 the thief, if **c**, must pay back H5162
Nu 5:13 her and she *has* not **been c in the act**), H9530
Nu 11:22 if all the fish in the sea **were c** for them?" H665
Dt 24: 7 If someone **is c** kidnapping a fellow H5162
Jos 7:15 Whoever **is c** with the devoted things shall H4334
Jos 8:22 so that *they were* **c** in the middle H2118
Jdg 1: 6 they chased him and **c** him, and cut off H296
Jdg 8:14 *He* **c** a young man of Sukkoth and H4334
Jdg 15: 4 So he went out and **c** three hundred foxes H4334
Jdg 21:23 each man **c** one and carried her off to be H1608
1Sa 9:17 When Samuel **c sight of** Saul, the LORD H8011
1Sa 15:27 Saul **c hold** of the hem of his robe H2616
2Sa 18: 9 Absalom's hair *got* **c** in the tree. H2616
Job 4:12 brought to me, my ears **c** a whisper of it. H4374
Ps 9:15 their feet **are c** in the net they have H4334
Ps 10: 2 *who* **are c** in the schemes he devises. H9530
Ps 59:12 of their lips, *let them* **be c** in their pride. H4334
Pr 6:31 Yet if *he* **is c**, he must pay sevenfold H5162
Pr 30:28 a lizard *can be* **c** with the hand, yet it is H9530
Ecc 9:12 As fish **are c** in a cruel net, or birds are H296
Isa 13:15 all who **are c** will fall by the sword. H6200
Isa 22: 3 All you *who* **were c** were taken prisoner H5162
Isa 24:18 climbs out of the pit *will* **be c** in a snare. H4334
Isa 51:20 every street corner, like **antelope** *c in* a net. AIT
Jer 2:26 "As a thief is disgraced when *he* **is c**, so H5162
Jer 6:11 both husband and wife *will* **be c** in it, and H4334
Jer 41:12 *They* **c up** *with* him near the great pool in H5162
Jer 48:27 **Was** *she* **c** among thieves, that you shake H5162
Jer 48:44 climbs out of the pit *will* **be c** in a snare; H4334
Jer 50:24 and *you* **were c** before you knew it H4334
La 4:20 our very life breath, **was c** in their traps. H4334
Eze 12:13 him, and *he will* **be c** in my snare; H9530
Eze 17:20 net for him, and *he will* **be c** in my snare. H9530
Am 3: 4 it growl in its den when *it has* **c** nothing? H4334
Am 3: 5 the ground if *it has* not **c** anything? H4334+4334
Mt 13:47 down into the lake and **c** all kinds of fish. G5251
Mt 14:31 Jesus reached out his hand and **c** him. G2138
Lk 5: 5 hard all night and haven't **c** anything. G3284
Lk 5: 6 *they* **c** such a large number of fish that G5168
Jn 8: 3 brought in a woman **c** in adultery. G2898
Jn 8: 4 this woman *was* **c** in the act of adultery. G2898
Jn 21: 3 the boat, but that night *they* **c** nothing. G4389
Jn 21:10 "Bring some of the fish *you have* just **c**." G4389
Ac 27:15 The ship *was* **c** by the storm and could not G5275
2Co 12: 2 fourteen years ago *was* **c up** to the third G773
2Co 12: 4 *was* **c up** to paradise and heard G773
2Co 12:16 crafty fellow that I am, *I* **c** you by trickery! G3284
Gal 6: 1 if someone *is* **c** in a sin, you who G4624
1Th 4:17 alive and are left *will be* **c up** together with G773
2Pe 2:12 born only to be **c** and destroyed, and like G274

CAUL (KJV) LONG LOBE

CAULK (1)
Eze 27: 9 on board as shipwrights *to* **c** your seams. H2616

CAULS (KJV) HEADBANDS

CAUSE (96) [CAUSED, CAUSES, CAUSING]
Ex 20:24 Wherever *I* **c** my name **to be honored**, H2349
Ex 23:33 land or *they will* **c** you **to sin** against me, H2627
Ex 33:19 "I *will* **c** all my goodness **to pass** in front H6296
Nu 5:21 "*may* the LORD **c** you **to become** a curse H5989
Nu 16: 5 he chooses *he will* **c** *to* **come near** him. H7928
Nu 32:15 and *you will be the* **c** of their **destruction**." H8845
Dt 3:28 across and *will* **c** them **to inherit** the land H5706
Dt 10:18 He defends the **c** *of* the fatherless and the H5477
Dt 28:25 The LORD *will* **c** you to be defeated before H5989
Dt 33: 7 With his own hands *he* **defends** his **c**. H8189
Jos 22:25 descendants *might* **c** ours **to stop** fearing H8697
Jdg 6:31 "*Are* you *going to* **plead** Baal's **c**? H8189
1Sa 24:15 May he consider my **c** and uphold it; may H8190
1Sa 25:39 who has upheld my **c** against Nabal for H8190
1Ki 8:45 prayer and their plea, and uphold their **c**. H5477
1Ki 8:49 prayer and their plea, and uphold their **c**. H5477

1Ki 8:50 c their captors to show them mercy; H5989
1Ki 8:59 he may uphold the c of his servant and H5477
1Ki 8:59 his servant and the c of his people Israel H5477
2Ki 2:21 Never again will it c death or make H2118+4946
2Ki 14:10 trouble and c your own downfall and that of AIT
2Ch 6:35 prayer and their plea, and uphold their c. H5477
2Ch 6:39 prayer and their pleas, and uphold their c. H5477
2Ch 20:27 the LORD had given them c to rejoice over H8523
2Ch 25:19 trouble and c your own downfall and that of AIT
Job 5: 8 I would lay my c before him. H1826
Ps 7: 4 ally with evil or without c have robbed my H8200
Ps 7:16 The trouble they c recoils on them; their AIT
Ps 9: 4 For you have upheld my right and my c H1907
Ps 25: 3 on those who are treacherous without c. H8200
Ps 35: 7 their net for me without c and without H2855
Ps 35: 7 cause and without c dug a pit for me H2855
Ps 35:19 over me who are my enemies without c; H9214
Ps 38:19 have become my enemies without c; H2855
Ps 43: 1 plead my c against an unfaithful H8190
Ps 45: 4 forth victoriously in the c of truth, H6584+1821
Ps 69: 4 many are my enemies without c, those H9214
Ps 74:22 defend your c; remember how fools H8190
Ps 82: 3 uphold the c of the poor and the H7405
Ps 109: 3 surround me; they attack me without c. H2855
Ps 115:14 May the LORD c you to flourish, both you H3578
Ps 119:27 C me to understand the way of your H1067
Ps 119:78 put to shame for wronging me without c; H9214
Ps 119:86 for I am being persecuted without c. H9214
Ps 119:154 Defend my c and redeem me; preserve H8190
Ps 119:161 Rulers persecute me without c, but my H2855
Ps 140:12 the poor and upholds the c of the needy. H5477
Ps 146: 7 He upholds the c of the oppressed and H5477
Pr 24:28 testify against your neighbor without c— H2855
Ecc 8: 3 Do not stand up for a bad c, for he will do H1821
Isa 1:17 Take up the c of the fatherless; plead the H9149
Isa 1:23 They do not defend the c of the fatherless; H9149
Isa 16: 5 justice and speeds the c of righteousness. NDT
Isa 30:30 The LORD will c people to hear his H9048
Isa 34: 8 a year of retribution, to uphold Zion's c. H8189
Isa 40:27 the LORD; my c is disregarded by my God"? H5477
Isa 47:12 you will succeed, perhaps you will c terror. H6907
Isa 53:10 will to crush him and c him to suffer, H2703
Isa 58:14 and I will c you to ride in triumph on the H8206
Isa 64: 2 and c the nations to quake before you AIT
Jer 5:28 they do not defend the just c of the poor. H5477
Jer 11:20 for to you I have committed my c. H8190
Jer 20:12 for to you I have committed my c. H8190
Jer 22:16 He defended the c of the poor and needy H1907
Jer 30:13 There is no one to plead your c, no H1907
Jer 40:15 c all the Jews who are gathered around you to be scattered AIT
Jer 50:34 defend their c so that he may bring H8190
Jer 51:36 I will defend your c and avenge you; I will H8190
La 3:52 my enemies without c hunted me like H2855
La 3:59 seen the wrong done to me. Uphold my c! H5477
Eze 14:23 that I have done nothing in it without c, H2855
Eze 32:10 I will c many peoples to be appalled at H9037
Eze 32:12 I will c your hordes to fall by the swords of H5877
Eze 36:10 and I will c many people to live on you H8049
Eze 36:12 I will c people, my people Israel, to live on H2143
Eze 36:15 of the peoples or c your nation to fall, H4173
Da 8:24 He will c astounding devastation and will H8845
Da 8:25 He will c deceit to prosper, and he H928+3338
Mic 7: 9 he pleads my case and upholds my c. H5477
Zep 1: 3 the idols that c the wicked to stumble." H4843
Mt 17:27 "But so that we may not c offense, go to G4997
Mt 18: 7 of the things that c people to stumble! G4998
Lk 2:10 you good news that will c great joy for all G1639
Lk 2:34 child is destined to c the falling and rising G1650
Lk 17: 1 "Things that c people to stumble are G4998
Lk 17: 2 to c one of these little ones to stumble. G4997
Ro 14:21 that will c your brother or sister to fall. G4684
Ro 16:17 watch out for those who c divisions and put NDT
1Co 8:13 so that I will not c them to fall. G4997
1Co 10:32 Do not c anyone to stumble, whether Jews G718
2Co 4:15 people may c thanksgiving to overflow to the AIT
Gal 6:17 From now on, let no one c me trouble, for G4218
Php 4: 3 at my side in the c of the gospel, G1877
2Ti 1:12 Yet this is no c for shame, because I know G2049
Heb 12:15 root grows up to c trouble and defile G1943
Rev 13:15 could speak and c all who refused to G4472

CAUSED (48) [CAUSE]

Ge 2:21 the LORD God c the man to fall into a deep H5877
Ge 5:29 toil of our hands c by the ground the LORD H4946
Jdg 7:22 c the men throughout the camp to turn on H8492
1Ki 11:25 adding to the trouble c by Hadad. H6913
1Ki 14:16 committed and has c Israel to commit." H2627
1Ki 15:26 sin his father had c Israel to commit. H2627
1Ki 15:30 committed and had c Israel to commit, H2627
1Ki 15:34 sin Jeroboam had c Israel to commit. H2627
1Ki 16: 2 and c my people Israel to sin and to H2627
1Ki 16:13 committed and had c Israel to commit, H2627
1Ki 16:19 sin Jeroboam had c Israel to commit. H2627
1Ki 16:26 sin Jeroboam had c Israel to commit, H2627
1Ki 21:22 my anger and have c Israel to sin. H2627
1Ki 22:52 son of Nebat, who c Israel to sin. H2627
2Ki 3: 3 which he had c Israel to commit; he did H2627
2Ki 7: 6 the Lord had c the Arameans to hear the H9048
2Ki 10:29 which he had c Israel to commit—the H2627
2Ki 10:31 which he had c Israel to commit. H2627
2Ki 13: 2 which he had c Israel to commit, and he H2627
2Ki 13: 6 which he had c Israel to commit; they H2627
2Ki 13:11 which he had c Israel to commit; he H2627
2Ki 14:24 which he had c Israel to commit. H2627
2Ki 15: 9 which he had c Israel to commit. H2627
2Ki 15:18 which he had c Israel to commit. H2627
2Ki 15:24 which he had c Israel to commit. H2627
2Ki 15:28 which he had c Israel to commit. H2627
2Ki 17:21 the LORD and c them to commit a great sin H2627
2Ki 21:16 the sin that he had c Judah to commit, H2627
2Ki 23:15 who had c Israel to sin—even that H2627
2Ch 21:11 had c the people of Jerusalem to prostitute themselves H2388
Ezr 6:12 who has c his Name to dwell there A10709
Job 34:28 They c the cry of the poor to come before H995
Ps 106:46 He c all who held them captive to show H5989
Ps 111: 4 He has c his wonders to be remembered H6913
Isa 21: 2 I will bring to an end all the groaning she c NDT
Jer 50: 6 them astray and c them to roam on the H8740
Eze 7:19 for it has c them to stumble into sin. H2118
Eze 32:30 despite the terror c by their power. H4946
Da 1: 9 Now God had c the official to show favor H5989
Am 3: 6 comes to a city, has not the LORD c it? H6913
Mal 2: 8 by your teaching have c many to stumble; H4173
Mal 2: 9 "So I have c you to be despised and H5989
Ac 10:40 on the third day and c him to be seen. G1443
Ac 17: 6 "These men who have c trouble all over G415
2Co 2: 5 If anyone has c grief, he has not so much G3382
2Co 7: 8 Even if I c you sorrow by my letter, I do G3382
Jas 4: 5 longs for the spirit he has c to dwell in us? G3001
2Pe 1: 4 corruption in the world c by evil desires. G1877

CAUSES (33) [CAUSE]

Nu 5:24 brings a curse and c bitter suffering will H4200
Nu 5:27 that brings a curse and c bitter suffering, H4200
2Sa 22:34 he c me to stand on the heights. H6641
2Ch 21:15 until the disease c your bowels to come H4946
Ps 18:33 he c me to stand on the heights. H6641
Pr 10:10 Whoever winks maliciously c grief, and a H5989
Pr 16: 7 he c their enemies to make peace with H8966
Isa 8:14 stone that c people to stumble and a rock H5598
Isa 61:11 come up and a garden c seeds to grow, H7541
Isa 64: 2 fire sets twigs ablaze and c water to boil, H1240
Da 8:13 the rebellion that c desolation, the H9037
Da 9:27 set up an abomination that c desolation, H9037
Da 11:31 set up the abomination that c desolation. H9037
Da 12:11 abomination that c desolation is set up, H9037
Mt 5:29 If your right eye c you to stumble, gouge it G4997
Mt 5:30 And if your right hand c you to stumble G4997
Mt 5:45 He c his sun to rise on the evil and the G422
Mt 13:41 everything that c sin and all who do evil. G4998
Mt 18: 6 If anyone c one of these little ones—those who believe in me—to stumble G4997
Mt 18: 8 If your hand or your foot c you to stumble G4997
Mt 18: 9 And if your eye c you to stumble, gouge it G4997
Mt 24:15 place 'the abomination that c desolation, G2247
Mk 9:42 c one of these little ones—those who believe in me—to stumble G4997
Mk 9:43 If your hand c you to stumble, cut it off. G4997
Mk 9:45 And if your foot c you to stumble, cut it off G4997
Mk 9:47 And if your eye c you to stumble, pluck it G4997
Mk 13:14 that c desolation' standing where AIT
Ro 9:33 stone that c people to stumble and a rock G4682
Ro 14:20 to eat anything that c someone else to G1328
1Co 8:13 I eat c my brother or sister to fall into sin, G4997
Col 2:19 sinews, grows as God c it to grow. G890
Jas 4: 1 What c fights and quarrels among you G4470
1Pe 2: 8 stone that c people to stumble and a rock G4682

CAUSING (4) [CAUSE]

Dt 8: 3 c you to hunger and then feeding you H8279
1Ki 17:20 I am staying with, by c her son to die?" H4637
Ps 105:29 their waters into blood, c their fish to die. H4637
Rev 13:13 even c fire to come down from heaven to G4472

CAVALRY (8)

Ne 2: 9 had also sent army officers and c with me. H7305
Eze 27:14 c horses and mules for your merchandise. H7304
Da 11:40 with chariots and c and a great fleet of H7305
Joel 2: 4 of horses; they gallop along like c. H7305
Na 3: 3 Charging c, flashing swords and glittering H7305
Hab 1: 8 Their c gallops headlong; their horsemen H7305
Ac 23:32 The next day they let the c go on with him G2689
Ac 23:33 When the c arrived in Caesarea, they G4015S

CAVE (35) [CAVERNS, CAVES]

Ge 19:30 He and his two daughters lived in a c. H5117
Ge 23: 9 so he will sell me the c of Machpelah H5117
Ge 23:11 the field, and I give you the c that is in it. H5117
Ge 23:17 both the field and the c in it, and all the H5117
Ge 23:19 his wife Sarah in the c in the field of H5117
Ge 23:20 So the field and the c in it were deeded to H5117
Ge 25: 9 buried him in the c of Machpelah near H5117
Ge 49:29 my fathers in the c in the field of Ephron H5117
Ge 49:30 the c in the field of Machpelah, near H5117
Ge 49:32 The field and the c in it were bought from H5117
Ge 50:13 buried him in the c in the field of H5117
Jos 10:16 fled and hidden in the c at Makkedah. H5117
Jos 10:17 been found hiding in the c at Makkedah, H5117
Jos 10:18 "Roll large rocks up to the mouth of the c H5117
Jos 10:22 the mouth of the c and bring those five H5117
Jos 10:23 they brought the five kings out of the c— H5117
Jos 10:27 them into the c where they had been H5117
Jos 10:27 At the mouth of the c they placed large H5117
Jdg 15: 8 stayed in a c in the rock of Etam. H6186
Jdg 15:11 went down to the c in the rock of Etam H6186
1Sa 22: 1 Gath and escaped to the c of Adullam. H5117
1Sa 24: 3 along the way; a c was there, and Saul H5117
1Sa 24: 3 David and his men were far back in the c. H5117
1Sa 24: 7 And Saul left the c and went his way. H5117
1Sa 24: 8 David went out of the c and called out to H5117
1Sa 24:10 LORD delivered you into my hands in the c. H5117
2Sa 17: 9 he is hidden in a c or at some other place. H7074
2Sa 23:13 came down to David at the c of Adullam, H5117
1Ki 19: 9 There he went into a c and spent the night H5117
1Ki 19:13 went out and stood at the mouth of the c. H5117
1Ch 11:15 to David to the rock at the c of Adullam, H5117
Ps 57: T When he had fled from Saul into the c. H5117
Ps 142: T When he was in the c. A prayer. H5117
Jer 48:28 that makes its nest at the mouth of a c. H7074
Jn 11:38 It was a c with a stone laid across the G5068

CAVERNS (1) [CAVE]

Isa 2:21 They will flee to c in the rocks and to the H5942

CAVES (10) [CAVE]

Jdg 6: 2 in mountain clefts, c and strongholds. H5117
1Sa 13: 6 pressed, they hid in c and thickets, among H5117
1Ki 18: 4 prophets and hidden them in two c, H5117
1Ki 18:13 a hundred of the LORD's prophets in two c, H5117
Isa 2:19 People will flee to c in the rocks and to H5117
Jer 49: 8 hide in deep c, you who live in Dedan NDT
Jer 49:30 Stay in deep c, you who live in Hazor," NDT
Eze 33:27 in strongholds and c will die of a plague. H5117
Heb 11:38 living in c and in holes in the ground. G5068
Rev 6:15 hid in c and among the rocks of the G5068

CEASE (11) [CEASING]

Ge 8:22 winter, day and night will never c. H8697
Job 3:17 There the wicked c from turmoil, and H2532
Ps 46: 9 He makes wars c to the ends of the earth H8697
Ecc 12: 3 when the grinders c because they are few H1060
Isa 16: 4 destruction will c; the aggressor will H3983
Jer 18:18 teaching of the law by the priest will not c, H6
Jer 31:36 "will Israel ever c being a nation before H8697
Jer 47: 6 Return to your sheath; c and be still.' H8089
Eze 5:13 "Then my anger will c and my wrath H3983
Eze 7:26 priestly instruction in the law will c, the H6
1Co 13: 8 are prophecies, they will c; where there G2934

CEASING (2) [CEASE]

Ps 35:15 They slandered me without c. H1957
Jer 14:17 with tears night and day without c; H1949

CEDAR (59) [CEDARS]

Lev 14: 4 that two live clean birds and some c wood, H780
Lev 14: 6 together with the c wood, the scarlet H780
Lev 14:49 he is to take two birds and some c wood, H780
Lev 14:51 Then he is to take the c wood, the hyssop H780
Lev 14:52 the live bird, the c wood, the hyssop and H780
Nu 19: 6 The priest is to take some c wood, hyssop H780
2Sa 5:11 along with c logs and carpenters and H780
2Sa 7: 2 living in a house of c, while the ark of God H780
2Sa 7: 7 "Why have you not built me a house of c?" H780
1Ki 4:33 from the c of Lebanon to the hyssop that H780
1Ki 5: 8 want in providing the c and juniper logs. H780
1Ki 5:10 supplied with all the c and juniper logs he H780
1Ki 6: 9 roofing it with beams and c planks. H780
1Ki 6:10 were attached to the temple by beams of c. H780
1Ki 6:15 He lined its interior walls with c boards H780
1Ki 6:16 of the temple with c boards from floor to H780
1Ki 6:18 The inside of the temple was c, carved with H780
1Ki 6:18 Everything was c; no stone was to be H780
1Ki 6:20 and he also overlaid the altar of c. H780
1Ki 6:36 stone and one course of trimmed c beams. H780
1Ki 7: 2 with four rows of c columns supporting H780
1Ki 7: 2 columns supporting trimmed c beams. H780
1Ki 7: 3 It was roofed with c above the beams that H780
1Ki 7: 7 he covered it with c from floor to ceiling. H780
1Ki 7:11 cut to size, and c beams. H780
1Ki 7:12 stone and one course of trimmed c beams, H780
1Ki 9:11 him with all the c and juniper and gold he H780
1Ki 10:27 c as plentiful as sycamore-fig trees in H780
2Ki 14: 9 sent a message to a c in Lebanon, H780
1Ch 14: 1 to David, along with c logs, stonemasons H780
1Ch 17: 1 living in a house of c, while the ark of the H780
1Ch 17: 6 "Why have you not built me a house of c?" H780
1Ch 22: 4 He also provided more c logs than could be H780
2Ch 1:15 c as plentiful as sycamore-fig trees in H780
2Ch 2: 3 "Send me c logs as you did for my father NDT
2Ch 2: 3 when you sent him c to build a palace to H780
2Ch 2: 8 "Send me also c, juniper and algum logs H780
2Ch 9:27 c as plentiful as sycamore-fig trees in H780
2Ch 25:18 sent a message to a c in Lebanon, H780
Ezr 3: 7 that they would bring c logs by sea from H780
Job 40:17 Its tail sways like a c; the sinews of its H780
Ps 92:12 they will grow like a c of Lebanon; H780
SS 8: 9 we will enclose her with panels of c. H780
Isa 41:19 I will put in the desert the c and the acacia H780
Jer 22: 7 cut up your fine c beams and throw them H780
Jer 22:14 panels it with c and decorates it in red. H780
Jer 22:15 make you a king to have more and more c? H780
Jer 22:23 who are nestled in c buildings, how you H780
Eze 17: 3 Taking hold of the top of a c, H780
Eze 17:22 shoot from the very top of a c and plant it; H780
Eze 17:23 bear fruit and become a splendid c. H780
Eze 27: 5 they took a c from Lebanon to make a mast H780

Eze 31: 3 Consider Assyria, once a **c** in Lebanon, with H780
Eze 31:10 Because the great **c** towered over the thick NDT
Eze 31:17 They too, like **the great c**, had gone H2257s
Hos 14: 5 Like a **c of Lebanon** he will send down his H4248
Hos 14: 6 his fragrance like a **c of Lebanon**. H4248
Zep 2:14 doorways, the **beams of c** will be exposed. H781
Zec 11: 2 you juniper, for the **c** has fallen; the stately H780

CEDARS (19) [CEDAR]
Nu 24: 6 by the LORD, like **c** beside the waters. H780
Jdg 9:15 thornbush and consume the **c** *of* Lebanon! H780
1Ki 5: 6 "So give orders that **c** of Lebanon be cut H780
2Ki 19:23 I have cut down its tallest **c**, the choicest of H780
Ps 29: 5 The voice of the LORD breaks the **c**; H780
Ps 29: 5 the LORD breaks in pieces the **c** *of* Lebanon. H780
Ps 80:10 its shade, the mighty **c** with its branches. H780
Ps 104:16 watered, the **c** *of* Lebanon that he planted. H780
Ps 148: 9 all hills, fruit trees and all **c**, H780
SS 1:17 The beams of our house are **c**; our rafters H780
SS 5:15 appearance is like Lebanon, choice as its **c**. H780
Isa 2:13 all the **c** *of* Lebanon, tall and lofty, and H780
Isa 9:10 but we will replace them with **c**. H780
Isa 14: 8 junipers and the **c** *of* Lebanon gloat over H780
Isa 37:24 I have cut down its tallest **c**, the choicest of H780
Isa 44:14 He cut down **c**, or perhaps took a cypress H780
Eze 31: 8 The **c** in the garden of God could not rival H780
Am 2: 9 they were tall as the **c** and strong as the H780
Zec 11: 1 Lebanon, so that fire may devour your **c**! H780

CEDRON (KJV) KIDRON

CEILING (4)
1Ki 6:15 them from the floor of the temple to the **c**, H6212
1Ki 6:16 boards from floor to **c** to form within the H7815
1Ki 7: 7 he covered it with cedar from floor to **c**. H7771
2Ch 3: 7 He overlaid the **c beams**, doorframes H7771

CELEBRATE (55) [CELEBRATED, CELEBRATING, CELEBRATION, CELEBRATIONS]
Ex 10: 9 because we are to **c** a festival to the LORD." NDT
Ex 12:14 to come *you shall* **c** it as a festival H2510
Ex 12:17 "**C** the Festival of Unleavened Bread H9068
Ex 12:17 **C** this day as a lasting ordinance for the H9068
Ex 12:47 The whole community of Israel *must* **c** it. H6913
Ex 12:48 among you *who wants to* **c** the LORD's H6913
Ex 23:14 times a year *you are to* **c a festival** to me. H2510
Ex 23:15 "**C** the Festival of Unleavened Bread; for H9068
Ex 23:16 "**C** the Festival of Harvest with the firstfruits NDT
Ex 23:16 "**C** the Festival of Ingathering at the end of NDT
Ex 34:18 "**C** the Festival of Unleavened Bread. H9068
Ex 34:22 "**C** the Festival of Weeks with the firstfruits H6913
Lev 23:39 **c** the festival to the LORD for seven days H2510
Lev 23:41 **C** this as a festival to the LORD for seven H2510
Lev 23:41 to come; **c** it in the seventh month. H2510
Nu 9: 2 "*Have* the Israelites **c** the Passover at the H6913
Nu 9: 3 **C** it at the appointed time, at twilight on H6913
Nu 9: 4 told the Israelites to **c** the Passover, H6913
Nu 9: 6 of them could not **c** the Passover on that H6913
Nu 9:10 *they are still to* **c** the LORD's Passover H6913
Nu 9:12 *When they* **c** the Passover, they must H6913
Nu 9:13 not on a journey fails to **c** the Passover, H6913
Nu 9:14 residing among you *is* also *to* **c** the LORD's H6913
Nu 29:12 **C** a festival to the LORD for seven days H2510
Dt 16: 1 month of Aviv and **c** the Passover of the H6913
Dt 16:10 Then **c** the Festival of Weeks to the LORD H6913
Dt 16:13 **C** the Festival of Tabernacles for seven H6913
Dt 16:15 For seven days **c the festival** to the LORD H2510
Jdg 16:23 sacrifice to Dagon their god and to **c**, H8525
2Sa 6:21 people Israel—*I will* **c** before the LORD. H8471
2Ki 23:21 "**C** the Passover to the LORD your God, as it H6913
2Ch 30: 1 in Jerusalem and **c** the Passover to the H6913
2Ch 30: 2 decided to **c** the Passover in the H6913
2Ch 30: 3 had not been able to **c** it at the regular H6913
2Ch 30: 5 to Jerusalem and **c** the Passover to the H6913
2Ch 30:13 in Jerusalem to **c** the Festival of H6913
2Ch 30:23 then agreed to **c** the festival seven more H6913
Ne 8:12 portions of food and to **c** with great joy, H6913
Ne 12:27 to Jerusalem to **c** joyfully the dedication H6913
Est 9:21 to have them **c** annually the fourteenth H6913
Ps 2:11 the LORD with fear and **c** his rule with H1635
Ps 89:16 all day long; *they* **c** your righteousness. H8123
Ps 145: 7 *They* **c** your abundant goodness and H2352
Isa 30:29 sing as on the night you **c** a **holy** festival; H7727
Hos 5: 7 When they **c** their New Moon feasts, he will NDT
Na 1:15 **C** your festivals, Judah, and fulfill your H2510
Zec 14:16 to **c** the Festival of Tabernacles. H2510
Zec 14:18 that do not go up to **c** the Festival of H2510
Zec 14:19 that do not go up to **c** the Festival of H2510
Mt 26:18 *I am going to* **c** the Passover with my G4472
Lk 15:23 calf and kill it. Let's have a feast and **c**. G2370
Lk 15:24 lost and is found.' So they began *to* **c**. G2370
Lk 15:29 a young goat so *I could* **c** with my friends. G2370
Lk 15:32 But we had to **c** and be glad, because this G2370
Rev 11:10 over them and *will* **c** by sending each G2370

CELEBRATED (18) [CELEBRATE]
Jos 5:10 of Jericho, the Israelites **c** the Passover. H6913
1Ki 8:65 They **c** it before the LORD our God for seven NDT
2Ki 23:23 this Passover **was c** to the LORD in H6913
2Ch 7: 9 for *they had* **c** the dedication of the altar H6913
2Ch 30: 5 *It had* not *been* **c** in large numbers H6913
2Ch 30:21 present in Jerusalem **c** the Festival of H6913
2Ch 30:23 so for another seven days *they* **c** joyfully. H6913
2Ch 35: 1 Josiah **c** the Passover to the LORD in H6913
2Ch 35:17 who were present **c** the Passover at that H6913
2Ch 35:18 kings of Israel *had ever* **c** such a Passover H6913
2Ch 35:19 This Passover **was c** in the eighteenth year H6913
Ezr 3: 4 *they* **c** the Festival of Tabernacles with the H6913
Ezr 6:16 **c** the dedication of the house of God with A10522
Ezr 6:19 the first month, the exiles **c** the Passover. H6913
Ezr 6:22 For seven days *they* **c** with joy the Festival H6913
Ne 8:17 the Israelites *had* not **c** it like this. H6913
Ne 8:18 *They* **c** the festival for seven days, and on H6913
Est 9:28 should never fail to be **c** by the Jews— NDT

CELEBRATING (5) [CELEBRATE]
Ex 31:16 **c** it for the generations to come as a H6913
2Sa 6: 5 David and all Israel *were* **c** with all their H8471
1Ch 13: 8 all the Israelites *were* **c** with all their H8471
1Ch 15:29 when she saw King David dancing and **c**, H8471
Est 8:17 the Jews, with feasting and **c**. H3427+3202

CELEBRATION (6) [CELEBRATE]
1Sa 11:15 Saul and all the Israelites **held a** great **c**. H8523
2Ch 35:16 carried out for the **c** *of* the Passover and H6913
Est 8:15 And the city of Susa **held a** joyous **c**. H7412
Est 9:22 joy and their mourning into a day of **c**. H3202
Est 9:23 agreed to continue **the c** they had begun, H889s
Col 2:16 festival, a **New Moon c** or a Sabbath day. G3741

CELEBRATIONS (1) [CELEBRATE]
Hos 2:11 I will stop all her **c**: her yearly festivals H5375

CELESTIAL (2)
2Pe 2:10 are not afraid to heap abuse *on* **c beings**; G1518
Jude 8 authority and heap abuse on **c beings**. G1518

CELL (3)
Jer 37:16 was put into a **vaulted c** in a dungeon, H2844
Ac 12: 7 Lord appeared and a light shone in the **c**. G3862
Ac 16:24 put them in the inner **c** and fastened their G5871

CELLARS (KJV) SUPPLIES, VATS

CEMETERY (1)
2Ch 26:23 near them in a **c** that belonged to H8441+7690

CENCHREAE (2)
Ac 18:18 his hair cut off at **C** because of a vow he G3020
Ro 16: 1 Phoebe, a deacon of the church in **C**. G3020

CENSER (8) [CENSERS]
Lev 16:12 He is to take a **c** full of burning coals from H4746
Nu 16:17 man is to take his **c** and put incense in it H4746
Nu 16:18 So each of them took his **c**, put burning H4746
Nu 16:46 "Take your **c** and put incense in it H4746
2Ch 26:19 who had a **c** in his hand ready to burn H5233
Eze 8:11 Each had a **c** in his hand, and a fragrant H5233
Rev 8: 3 who had a golden **c**, came and stood at G3338
Rev 8: 5 Then the angel took the **c**, filled it with fire G3338

CENSERS (13) [CENSER]
Lev 10: 1 sons Nadab and Abihu took their **c**, H4746
Nu 16: 6 all your followers are to do this: Take **c** H4746
Nu 16:17 incense in it—250 **c** in all—and present it H4746
Nu 16:17 You and Aaron are to present your **c** also." H4746
Nu 16:37 to remove the **c** from the charred remains H4746
Nu 16:37 some distance away, for the **c** are holy— NDT
Nu 16:38 the **c** *of* the men who sinned at the cost of H4746
Nu 16:38 Hammer **the c** into sheets to overlay the H4392s
Nu 16:39 the bronze **c** brought by those who H4746
1Ki 7:50 dishes and **c**; and the gold sockets H4746
2Ki 25:15 guard took away the **c** and sprinkling H4746
2Ch 4:22 dishes and **c**; and the gold doors H4746
Jer 52:19 took away the basins, **c**, sprinkling bowls, H4746

CENSUS (17)
Ex 30:12 "When *you* **take a c** *of* the H5951+906+8031
Ex 38:25 *those of* the community *who* **were counted in the c** H7212
Nu 1: 2 "**Take a c** *of* the whole Israelite H5951+8031
Nu 1:49 **include** them **in the c** of H5951+906+8031
Nu 4: 2 "**Take a c** *of* the Kohathite H5951+906+8031
Nu 4:22 "**Take a c** also *of* the Gershonites by H5951+8031
Nu 14:29 was counted in the **c** and who has H5031
Nu 26: 2 "**Take a c** *of* the whole H5951+906+8031
Nu 26: 4 "Take a **c** of the men twenty years old or NDT
2Sa 24: 1 "Go and **take a c** *of* Israel and Judah." H4948
2Ki 12: 4 the money collected in the **c**, the H6296+408
1Ch 21: 1 incited David to **take a c** *of* Israel. H4948
2Ch 2:17 Solomon **took a c** *of* all the foreigners H6218
2Ch 2:17 the **c** his father David *had taken*; H6222+6218
Lk 2: 1 decree that a **c** *should* **be taken** of the G616
Lk 2: 2 This was the first **c** that took place while G615
Ac 5:37 in the days *of* the **c** and led a band of G615

CENTER (19) [CENTERS, CENTRAL]
Ex 26:28 The **c** crossbar is to extend from end to H9399
Ex 28:32 with an opening for the head in its **c** H9348
Ex 36:33 They made the **c** crossbar so that it H9399
Ex 39:23 an opening in the **c** *of* the robe like the H9348
Nu 35: 5 on the north, with the town in the **c**. H9348
1Ki 7:25 their hindquarters were toward the **c**. H1074
2Ch 4: 4 their hindquarters were toward the **c**. H1074
2Ch 6:13 had placed it in the **c** *of* the outer court. H9348
Eze 1: 4 The **c** *of* the fire looked like glowing H9348
Eze 5: 5 which I have set in the **c** *of* the nations H9348
Eze 38:12 goods, living at the **c** *of* the land. H3179
Eze 48: 8 the sanctuary will be in the **c** *of* it. H9348
Eze 48:10 In the **c** *of* it will be the sanctuary of the H9348
Eze 48:15 The city will be in the **c** *of* it H9348
Eze 48:21 temple sanctuary will be in the **c** *of* them. H9348
Eze 48:22 city will lie in the **c** *of* the area that H9348
Rev 4: 6 In the **c**, around the throne, were four G3545
Rev 5: 6 standing **at the c of** the throne G1877+3545
Rev 7:17 For the Lamb **at the c of** the throne G324+3545

CENTERS (1) [CENTER]
Ge 10:10 The **first** *c of* his kingdom were Babylon, AIT

CENTRAL (2) [CENTER]
Jdg 9:37 are coming down from the **c hill**, H3179+824
Jdg 16:29 toward the two **c** pillars on which the H9348

CENTS (1)
Mk 12:42 small copper coins, worth **only a few c**. G3119

CENTURION (21) [CENTURION'S, CENTURIONS]
Mt 8: 5 Capernaum, a **c** came to him, asking G1672
Mt 8: 8 The **c** replied, "Lord, I do not deserve to G1672
Mt 8:13 Then Jesus said *to* the **c**, "Go! Let it be G1672
Mt 27:54 When the **c** and those with him who were G1672
Mk 15:39 And when the **c**, who stood there in front G3035
Mk 15:44 Summoning the **c**, he asked him if Jesus G3035
Mk 15:45 When he learned from the **c** that it was so G3035
Lk 7: 3 The **c** heard of Jesus and sent some elders NDT
Lk 7: 6 the house when the **c** sent friends to say G1672
Lk 23:47 The **c**, seeing what had happened G1672
Ac 10: 1 a **c** in what was known as the Italian G1672
Ac 10:22 "We have come from Cornelius the **c**. G1672
Ac 22:25 Paul said to the **c** standing there, "Is G1672
Ac 22:26 When the **c** heard this, he went to the G1672
Ac 23:18 The **c** said, "Paul, the prisoner, sent for me NDT
Ac 24:23 He ordered the **c** to keep Paul under guard G1672
Ac 27: 1 were handed over *to* a **c** named Julius, G1672
Ac 27: 6 There the **c** found an Alexandrian ship G1672
Ac 27:11 But the **c**, instead of listening to what Paul G1672
Ac 27:31 Then Paul said *to* the **c** and the soldiers G1672
Ac 27:43 But the **c** wanted to spare Paul's life and G1672

CENTURION'S (1) [CENTURION]
Lk 7: 2 There a **c** servant, whom his master valued G1672

CENTURIONS (2) [CENTURION]
Ac 23:17 Then Paul called one *of* the **c** and said G1672
Ac 23:23 he called two *of* his **c** and ordered them, G1672

CEPHAS (9) [PETER]
Jn 1:42 You will be called **C**" (which, when G3064
1Co 1:12 another, "I follow **C**"; still another, "I G3064
1Co 3:22 Paul or Apollos or **C** or the world or life G3064
1Co 9: 5 apostles and the Lord's brothers and **C**? G3064
1Co 15: 5 that he appeared *to* **C**, and then to G3064
Gal 1:18 acquainted with **C** and stayed with him G3064
Gal 2: 9 **C** and John, those esteemed as G3064
Gal 2:11 When **C** came to Antioch, I opposed him G3064
Gal 2:14 the gospel, I said *to* **C** in front of them all G3064

CEREMONIAL (9) [CEREMONY]
Lev 14: 2 person at the time of their **c cleansing**, H3200
Lev 15:13 to count off seven days for his **c cleansing**; H3200
Mk 7: 3 they give their hands a **c** washing, G4778s
Jn 2: 6 the kind used by the Jews for **c washing** G2752
Jn 3:25 certain Jew over the matter of **c washing**. G2752
Jn 11:55 Jerusalem for their **c cleansing** before the G49
Jn 18:28 to avoid **c uncleanness** they did not G3620
Heb 9:10 of food and drink and various **c washings**— G968
Heb 13: 9 by grace, not *by* **eating** *c* **foods**, which is of AIT

CEREMONIALLY (40) [CEREMONY]
Lev 4:12 take outside the camp to a place **c clean**, H3196
Lev 5: 2 unwittingly touch anything **c unclean** H3238
Lev 6:11 the camp to a place that is **c clean**. H3196
Lev 7:19 touches anything **c unclean** must not be H3238
Lev 7:19 other meat, anyone **c clean** may eat it. H3196
Lev 10:14 Eat them in a **c clean** place; they have H3196
Lev 11: 4 a divided hoof; it is **c unclean** for you. H3238
Lev 12: 2 to a son *will be* **c unclean** for seven days H3237
Lev 12: 7 then *she will be* **c clean** from her flow H3197
Lev 13: 3 *he shall* **pronounce** them **c unclean**. H3237
Lev 14: 8 with water; then *they will be* **c clean**. H3197
Lev 15:28 and after that *she will be* **c clean**. H3197
Lev 15:33 relations with a *woman who is* **c unclean**. H3238
Lev 17:15 and *they will be* **c unclean** till evening H3237
Lev 21: 1 *must* not **make himself c unclean** for H3237
Lev 22: 3 descendants is **c unclean** and yet comes H3240
Lev 27:11 If what they vowed is a **c unclean** animal— H3238
Nu 5: 2 who is **c unclean** because of a dead H3238
Nu 6: 7 *they must* not **make themselves c unclean** H3237
Nu 8: 6 all the Israelites and **make** them **c clean**. H3197
Nu 9: 6 they were **c unclean** on account of a H3238
Nu 9:13 But if anyone who is **c clean** and not on a H3196
Nu 18:11 your household who is **c clean** may eat it. H3196
Nu 18:13 your household who is **c clean** may eat it. H3196
Nu 19: 7 he *will be* **c unclean** till evening. H3237
Nu 19: 9 put them in a **c clean** place outside H3196
Nu 19:18 Then a man who is **c clean** is to take some H3196
Dt 12:15 Both the **c unclean** and the clean may eat H3238
Dt 12:22 Both the **c unclean** and the clean may eat. H3238
Dt 14: 7 a divided hoof; they are **c unclean** for you. H3238

Dt 15:22 Both the c unclean and the clean may eat H3238
1Sa 20:26 to David to make him c unclean— H1194+3196
2Ch 13:11 the bread on the c clean table and light H3196
2Ch 30:17 all *those who* were not c clean and H3196
Ezr 6:20 purified themselves and were all c clean. H3196
Ne 12:30 Levites *had* purified themselves c, H3197
Isa 66:20 the temple of the LORD in c clean vessels. H3196
Eze 22:10 their period, when they are c unclean. H3238
Ac 24:18 *I was* c clean when they found me in the G49
Heb 9:13 *on* those *who are* c unclean sanctify G3124

CEREMONIES (1) [CEREMONY]
Heb 9:21 tabernacle and everything *used in* its c. G3311

CEREMONY (4) [CEREMONIAL, CEREMONIALLY, CEREMONIES]
Ge 50:11 are holding a solemn c of mourning." H65
Ex 12:25 give you as he promised, observe this c. H6275
Ex 12:26 ask you, 'What does this c mean to you? H6275
Ex 13:5 you are to observe this c in this month: H6275

CERTAIN (35) [CERTAINTY, CERTAINLY]
Ge 15:13 "Know for c that for four hundred H3359+3359
Ge 28:11 When he reached a c place, he stopped H2021
Nu 16:1 the son of Levi, and c Reubenites—Dathan NDT
Jos 8:14 in battle at a c place overlooking the H4595
Jdg 13:2 A c man of Zorah, named Manoah, from H285
1Sa 1:1 There was a c man from Ramathaim, H285
1Sa 21:2 told them to meet me at a c place. H7141+532
1Sa 25:2 A c man in Maon, who had property there at NDT
2Sa 12:1 "There were two men in a c town, one rich H285
1Ki 13:11 Now there was a c old prophet living in H285
2Ki 19:7 When he hears a c report, I will make him NDT
2Ch 17:8 With them were c Levites—Shemaiah H2021
Ne 7:73 along with c *of* the people and the rest of H4946
Est 3:8 "There is a c people dispersed among the H285
Isa 37:7 When he hears a c report, I will make him NDT
Da 2:8 "I *am* c that you are A10427+10327+10313
Hos 5:9 the tribes of Israel I proclaim *what is* c. H586
Mt 26:18 "Go into the city to a c *man* and tell him G1265
Mk 15:21 *A* c *man* from Cyrene, Simon, the father of G5516
Lk 7:41 people owed money to *a* c moneylender. G5516
Lk 11:1 One day Jesus was praying in a c place G5516
Lk 12:16 "The ground of a c rich man yielded an G5516
Lk 14:16 "A c man was preparing a great banquet G5516
Lk 18:2 "In a c town there was a judge who G5516
Lk 18:18 A c ruler asked him, "Good teacher, what G5516
Jn 3:25 disciples and *a* c Jew over the matter of AIT
Jn 4:46 And there was a c royal official whose son G5516
Ac 7:16 of Hamor at Shechem *for a* c sum of money. AIT
Ac 15:1 C *people* came down from Judea to G5516
Ac 28:23 They arranged to meet Paul *on a* c day, and AIT
Gal 2:12 For before c *men* came from James, he G5516
1Ti 1:3 you may command c *people* not to teach G5516
1Ti 4:3 order them to abstain from c foods, NDT
Heb 4:7 God again set a c day, calling it "Today." G5516
Jude 4 For c individuals whose condemnation was G5516

CERTAINLY (51) [CERTAIN]
Ge 2:17 when you eat from it *you will* c die." H4637+4637
Ge 3:4 "*You will* not c die," the serpent H4637+4637
Ex 22:3 who steals must c make restitution, H8966+8966
Ex 22:23 cry out to me, *I will* c hear their cry. H9048+9048
Ex 23:33 of their gods will c be a snare to you." H3954
Nu 13:30 of the land, for *we* can c do it." H3523+3523
Nu 22:33 I would c have killed you by now H3954
Nu 27:7 *You* must c give them property as H5989+5989
Dt 4:26 there long but *will* c be destroyed. H9012+9012
Dt 13:9 *You* must c put them to death. H2222+2222
Dt 13:15 *you* must c put to the sword all who H5782+5782
Dt 23:21 your God *will* c demand it of you H2011+2011
Dt 30:18 to you this day that *you will* c be destroyed. H6+6
Dt 31:18 And I *will* c hide my face in that day H6259+6259
Jos 3:10 and that *he will* c drive out before H3769+3769
Jdg 4:9 "C *I will* go with you," said H2143+2143
Jdg 11:10 our witness; we will c do as you say." H561+4202
1Sa 25:28 LORD your God *will* c make a lasting H6913+6913
1Sa 30:8 "*You will* c overtake them and H5952+5952
1Ki 11:11 *I will* most c tear the kingdom away H7973+7973
1Ki 13:32 towns of Samaria *will* c come true." H2118+2118
2Ki 1:4 you are lying on. *You will* c die!' " H4637+4637
2Ki 1:6 you are lying on. *You will* c die!" H4637+4637
2Ki 1:16 you are lying on. *You will* c die!" H4637+4637
2Ki 8:10 and say to him, '*You will* c recover. H2649+2649
2Ki 8:14 told me that *you would* c recover." H2649+2649
Jer 32:4 but *will* c be given into the hands H5989+5989
Jer 36:29 of Babylon *would* c come and destroy H995+995
Jer 38:3 'This city *will* c be given into the H5989+5989
Jer 42:4 "I will c pray to the LORD your God as you H2180
Jer 44:17 *We will* c do everything we said we H6913+6913
Jer 44:25 '*We will* c carry out the vows we H6913+6913
Da 3:24 They replied, "C, Your Majesty." A10327+10002
Hab 2:3 *it will* c come and will not delay. H995+995
Mal 3:15 C evildoers prosper, and even when they H1685
Mt 5:20 you will c not enter the kingdom of G4024+3590
Mt 10:42 that person will c not lose their G4024+3590
Mt 24:34 generation will c not pass away G4024+3590
Mk 9:41 the Messiah will c not lose their G4024+3590
Mk 13:30 generation will c not pass away G4024+3590
Lk 21:32 generation will c not pass away G4024+3590
Lk 22:59 asserted, "C this fellow was with him G2093+237
Ac 21:22 They will c hear that you have come G4122
Ac 28:19 *I* c *did* not intend to bring any charge against AIT
Ro 3:6 C not! If that were so, how could G3590+1181
Ro 6:5 we will c also be united with him in a G247
Ro 7:7 the law sinful? C not! Nevertheless, G3590+1181
1Co 11:22 Shall I praise you? C not in this matter! G4024
Gal 3:21 righteousness would c have come by the G3953
1Th 2:18 we wanted to come to you—c I, Paul, did, G3525
1Th 4:15 will c not precede those who have G4024+3590

CERTAINTY (2) [CERTAIN]
Lk 1:4 that you may know the c of the things you G854
Jn 17:8 They knew with c that I came from you, and G242

CERTIFICATE (7) [CERTIFIED]
Dt 24:1 he writes her a c *of* divorce, gives it to H6219
Dt 24:3 dislikes her and writes her a c *of* divorce, H6219
Isa 50:1 is your mother's c *of* divorce with which I H6219
Jer 3:8 faithless Israel her c *of* divorce and sent H6219
Mt 5:31 his wife must give her a c of divorce. G687
Mt 19:7 man give his wife a c of divorce and send G1046
Mk 10:4 a man to write a c of divorce and send her G1046

CERTIFIED (1) [CERTIFICATE]
Jn 3:33 has accepted it *has* c that God is truthful. G5381

CHAFF (18)
Job 13:25 Will you chase after dry c? H7990
Job 21:18 the wind, like c swept away by a gale? H5161
Job 41:28 make it flee; slingstones are like c to it. H7990
Ps 1:4 They are like c that the wind blows away. H5161
Ps 35:5 May they be like c before the wind, with H5161
Ps 83:13 my God, like c before the wind. H7990
Isa 17:13 driven before the wind like c *on* the hills H5161
Isa 29:5 fine dust, the ruthless hordes like blown c. H5161
Isa 33:11 You conceive c, you give birth to straw H3143
Isa 40:24 a whirlwind sweeps them away like c. H7990
Isa 41:2 his sword, to windblown c with his bow. H7990
Isa 41:15 crush them, and reduce the hills to c. H5161
Jer 13:24 will scatter you like c driven by the desert H7990
Da 2:35 became like c on a threshing floor A10534
Hos 13:3 like c swirling from a threshing floor H5161
Zep 2:2 that day passes like windblown c, H5161
Mt 3:12 burning up the c with unquenchable G949
Lk 3:17 he will burn up the c with unquenchable G949

CHAIN (9) [CHAINED, CHAINS]
Ge 41:42 linen and put a gold c around his neck. H8054
2Ch 3:5 decorated it with palm tree and c designs. H9249
Pr 1:9 your head and a c to adorn your neck. H6736
Da 5:7 have a gold c placed around his A10212
Da 5:16 have a gold c placed around your A10212
Da 5:29 a gold c was placed around his neck A10212
Mk 5:3 could bind him anymore, not even *with a* c. G268
Ac 28:20 hope of Israel that I am bound with this c." G268
Rev 20:1 Abyss and holding in his hand a great c. G268

CHAINED (4) [CHAIN]
Mk 5:4 For he *had* often *been* c hand and G268+1313
Lk 8:29 and *though he was* c hand and foot G1297+268
2Ti 2:9 to the point of being c like a criminal. G1301
2Ti 2:9 like a criminal. But God's word *is* not c. G1313

CHAINS (53) [CHAIN]
Ex 28:14 two braided c *of* pure gold, like a rope H9249
Ex 28:14 and attach the c to the settings. H9249+6310
Ex 28:22 breastpiece make braided c *of* pure gold, H9249
Ex 28:24 Fasten the two gold c to the rings at the H6310
Ex 28:25 the other ends of the c to the two settings, H6310
Ex 39:15 they made braided c of pure gold, H9249
Ex 39:17 fastened the two gold c to the rings at the H6310
Ex 39:18 the other ends of the c to the two settings, H6310
Jdg 8:26 kings of Midian or the c that were on their H6736
1Sa 15:32 Agag came to him *in* c. And he thought, H5051
1Ki 6:21 he extended gold c across the front of H8411
1Ki 7:17 A network of interwoven c adorned H5126+9249
2Ki 23:33 Pharaoh Necho put him in c at Riblah in the H673
2Ch 3:16 He made interwoven c and put them on H9249
2Ch 3:16 attached them to the c. H9249
Job 36:8 But if people are bound in c, held fast by H2414
Job 38:31 "Can you bind the c *of* the Pleiades? Can H5051
Ps 2:3 "Let us break their c and throw off their H4593
Ps 107:10 darkness, prisoners suffering in iron c, H1366
Ps 107:14 the utter darkness, and broke away their c. H4593
Ps 116:16 mother did; you have freed me from my c. H4591
Ecc 7:26 heart is a trap and whose hands are c. H657
Isa 28:22 mocking, or your c will become heavier H4591
Isa 40:19 it with gold and fashions silver c for it. H8416
Isa 45:14 behind you, coming over to you in c. H2414
Isa 52:2 Free yourself from the c *on* your neck H4591
Isa 58:6 to loose the c *of* injustice and untie the H3078
Jer 40:1 Jeremiah bound in c among all the H272
Jer 40:4 I am freeing you from the c on your wrists. H272
La 3:7 escape; he has weighed me down with c. H5733
Eze 7:23 " 'Prepare c! For the land is full of H8408
Na 3:10 her great men were put in c. H8415+2414+928
Mk 5:4 he tore the c apart and broke the irons G268
Lk 8:29 he had broken his c and had been driven G1301
Ac 12:6 soldiers, bound *with* two c, and sentries G268
Ac 12:7 he said, and the c fell off Peter's wrists. G268
Ac 16:26 flew open, and everyone's c came loose. G1301
Ac 21:33 ordered him to be bound *with* two c. G268
Ac 22:29 *he had* put Paul, a Roman citizen, in c G1639+1313
Ac 26:29 become what I am, except for these c." G1301
Eph 6:20 which I am an ambassador in c. G268
Php 1:7 whether I am in c or defending and G1301
Php 1:13 to everyone else that I am *in* c for Christ. G1301
Php 1:14 And *because of* my c, most of the brothers G1301
Php 1:17 can stir up trouble for me while I am *in* c. G1301
Col 4:3 the mystery of Christ, for which *I am* in c. G1313
Col 4:18 Remember my c. Grace be with you G1301
2Ti 1:16 me and was not ashamed *of* my c. G268
Phm 10 who became my son while I was in c. G1301
Phm 13 helping me while I am in c for the gospel. G1301
Heb 11:36 flogging, and even c and imprisonment. G1301
2Pe 2:4 putting them *in* c of darkness to be held G4937
Jude 6 *bound with* everlasting c for judgment on G1301

CHAIR (4)
1Sa 1:9 was sitting on his c by the doorpost of the H4058
1Sa 4:13 Eli sitting on his c *by* the side of the road, H4058
1Sa 4:18 fell backward off his c by the side of the H4058
2Ki 4:10 bed and a table, a c and a lamp for him. H4058

CHALCEDONY (NIV84) AGATE

CHALDEA (2) [CHALDEAN, CHALDEANS]
Eze 23:15 Babylonian chariot officers, natives of C. H4169
Eze 23:16 them and sent messengers to them in C. H4169

CHALDEAN (1) [CHALDEA]
Ezr 5:12 into the hands of Nebuchadnezzar the C, A10373

CHALDEANS (9) [CHALDEA]

CHALDEANS (KJV) BABYLONIANS
Ge 11:28 Haran died in Ur of the C, in the land of H4169
Ge 11:31 set out from Ur of the C to go to Canaan. H4169
Ge 15:7 you out of Ur of the C to give you this land H4169
Ne 9:7 him out of Ur of the C and named him H4169
Job 1:17 "The C formed three raiding parties and H4169
Eze 12:13 the land of the C, but he will not see it, H4169
Eze 23:14 on a wall, figures of C portrayed in red, H4169
Eze 23:23 the Babylonians and all the C, the men of H4169
Ac 7:4 he left the land *of* the C and settled in G5900

CHALDEES (KJV) BABYLONIAN, BABYLONIANS, CHALDEANS

CHALK (NIV84) LIMESTONE

CHALLENGE (5) [CHALLENGED]
2Ki 14:8 the son of Jehu, king of Israel, *with the* c: H606
2Ch 25:17 he sent this c to Jehoash son of Jehoahaz H606
Job 9:19 if it is a matter of justice, who *can* c him? H3585
Jer 49:19 Who is like me and who *can* c me? And H3585
Jer 50:44 Who is like me and who *can* c me? And H3585

CHALLENGED (3) [CHALLENGE]
Jdg 8:1 And *they* c him vigorously. H8189
Jn 8:13 The Pharisees c him, "Here you are G3306
Jn 18:26 Peter had cut off, c him, "Didn't I see you G3306

CHAMBER (5) [CHAMBERS]
2Sa 3:27 Joab took him aside into an inner c, as if H9133
Job 37:9 The tempest comes out from its c, the H2540
Ps 19:5 It is like a bridegroom coming out of his c H2903
Ps 45:13 All glorious is the princess within her c H7163
Joel 2:16 leave his room and the bride her c. H2903

CHAMBERLAIN, CHAMBERLAINS (KJV) EUNUCH, EUNUCHS, OFFICIALS, OFFICERS, SERVANT

CHAMBERS (5) [CHAMBER]
Ezr 8:29 them out in the c *of* the house of the H4384
Ps 104:3 the beams of his upper c on their waters. H6608
Ps 104:13 He waters the mountains from his upper c; H6608
Pr 7:27 the grave, leading down to the c *of* death. H2540
SS 1:4 Let the king bring me into his c. H2540

CHAMELEON (1)
Lev 11:30 the wall lizard, the skink and the c. H9491

CHAMOIS (KJV) MOUNTAIN SHEEP

CHAMPION (4) [CHAMPIONS]
1Sa 17:4 A c named Goliath, who was H408+2021+1227
1Sa 17:23 the Philistine c from Gath H408+2021+1227
Ps 19:5 like a c rejoicing to run his course. H1475
Isa 42:13 The LORD will march out like a c, like a H1475

CHAMPIONS (1) [CHAMPION]
Isa 5:22 drinking wine and c at mixing drinks, H408+2657

CHANAAN (KJV) CANAAN

CHANCE (5)
Jos 8:20 but they had no c to escape H2118+928+3338
1Sa 6:9 struck us but that it happened to us by c." H5247
1Sa 19:2 father Saul *is* looking for a c to kill you. H1335
Ecc 9:11 time and c happen to them all. H7004
Mk 6:31 that *they did* not even have a c to eat, G2320

CHANCELLOR (KJV) COMMANDING OFFICER

CHANGE (31) [CHANGED, CHANGERS, CHANGES, CHANGING]
Ge 35:2 purify yourselves and c your clothes. H2736

C

Ex 13:17 they might c their minds and return to H5714
Nu 23:19 human being, that he should c his mind. H5714
Nu 23:20 to bless; he has blessed, and I cannot c it. H8740
1Sa 15:29 Glory of Israel does not lie or c his mind; H5714
1Sa 15:29 human being, that he should c his mind." H5714
2Sa 14:20 Joab did this to c the present situation. H6015
1Ki 8:47 if they have a c of heart in the land H8740
1Ki 13:33 Jeroboam did not c his evil ways, but H8740
2Ch 6:37 if they have a c of heart in the land H8740
Ezr 6:12 who lifts a hand to c this decree or to A10731
Job 9:27 my complaint, I will c my expression, and H6440
Job 14:20 you c their countenance and send them H9101
Ps 15: 4 when it hurts, and does not c their mind; H4614
Ps 55:19 from of old, who does not c—he will hear H2722
Ps 102:26 Like clothing you will c them and they will H2736
Ps 110: 4 LORD has sworn and will not c his mind: H5714
Jer 7: 5 If you really c your ways and your H3512+3512
Jer 13:16 to utter darkness and c it to deep gloom. H8883
Jer 13:23 Can an Ethiopian c his skin or a leopard H2200
Eze 1:17 the wheels did not c direction as the H6015
Da 2: 9 hoping the situation will c. A10731
Da 7:25 people and try to c the set times and the A10731
Mal 3: 6 "I the LORD do not c. So you, the H9101
Mt 18: 3 unless you c and become like little G5138
Ac 6:14 destroy this place and c the customs Moses G248
Gal 4:20 I could be with you now and c my tone, G248
Heb 7:21 Lord has sworn and will not c his mind: G3564
Heb 12:17 he could not c what he had G3567+5536+2351
Jas 1:17 who does not c like shifting shadows. G4164
Jas 4: 9 C your laughter to mourning and your joy G3573

CHANGED (33) [CHANGE]

Ge 31:41 and you c my wages ten times. H2736
Ge 41:14 When he had shaved and c his clothes H2736
Ex 7:15 hand the staff that was c into a snake. H2200
Ex 7:17 of the Nile, and it will be c into blood. H2200
Ex 7:20 and all the water was c into blood. H2200
Ex 10:19 And the LORD c the wind to a very strong H2200
Ex 14: 5 his officials c their minds about them H2200
Lev 13:55 if the mold has not c its appearance H2200
Nu 32:38 these names were c) and Sibmah. H6015
Jdg 7:19 just after they had c the guard. H7756+7756
1Sa 10: 6 and you will be c into a different person. H2200
1Sa 10: 9 Samuel, God c Saul's heart, and H2200+337
2Sa 12:20 put on lotions and c his clothes, he went H2736
1Ki 2:15 But things c, and the kingdom has gone H6015
2Ki 23:34 Josiah and c Eliakim's name to Jehoiakim H6015
2Ki 24:17 in his place and c his name to Zedekiah. H6015
2Ch 36: 4 and c Eliakim's name to Jehoiakim. H6015
Jer 2:11 Has a nation ever c its gods? (Yet they are H3558
Jer 15: 7 my people, for they have not c their ways. H8740
Jer 34:11 But afterward they c their minds and took H8740
Da 3:19 his attitude toward them c. A10731
Da 4:16 Let his mind be c from that of a man A10731
Da 6:15 edict that the king issues can be c." A10731
Da 6:17 so that Daniel's situation might not be c. A10731
Hos 11: 8 My heart is c within me; all my H2200
Mt 21:29 later he c his mind and went. G3564
Lk 9:29 the appearance of his face c, and G1181+2283
Ac 28: 6 they c their minds and said he was a god. G3554
1Co 15:51 will not all sleep, but we will all be c— G248
1Co 15:52 be raised imperishable, and we will be c. G248
Heb 1:12 like a robe; like a garment they will be c. G248
Heb 7:12 For when the priesthood is c, the law must G3572
Heb 7:12 is changed, the law must be c also. G3557

CHANGERS (3) [CHANGE]

Mt 21:12 the tables of the money c and the G3142
Mk 11:15 the tables of the money c and the G3142
Jn 2:15 the coins of the money c and overturned G3142

CHANGES (3) [CHANGE]

Lev 13:16 If the raw flesh c and turns white, they H8740
Ecc 8: 1 their face and c its hard appearance. H9101
Da 2:21 He c times and seasons; he deposes A10731

CHANGING (3) [CHANGE]

Ge 31: 7 has cheated me by c my wages ten times. H2736
Ezr 6:22 them with joy by c the attitude of the H6015
Jer 2:36 do you go about so much, c your ways? H9101

CHANNEL (1) [CHANNELED, CHANNELS]

Job 38:25 Who cuts a c for the torrents of rain, and a H9498

CHANNELED (1) [CHANNEL]

2Ch 32:30 the Gihon spring and c the water down to H3837

CHANNELS (5) [CHANNEL]

Job 6:17 in the heat vanish from their c. H5226
Pr 21: 1 stream of water that he c toward all who H5742
Isa 8: 7 It will overflow all its c, run over all its H692
Eze 31: 4 base and sent their c to all the trees of H9498
Zec 4: 2 lamps on it, with seven c to the lamps. H4609

CHANT (3)

Eze 32:16 "This is the lament they will c for her. H7801
Eze 32:16 The daughters of the nations will c it; for H7801
Eze 32:16 Egypt and all her hordes they will c it H7801

CHAOS (1)

Isa 34:11 measuring line of c and the plumb line of H9332

CHAPEL (KJV) SANCTUARY

CHAPITER, CHAPITERS (KJV) CAPITAL, CAPITALS, POSTS, TOPS

CHARACTER (7) [CHARACTERS]

Ru 3:11 know that you are a woman of noble c. H2657
Pr 12: 4 A wife of noble c is her husband's crown H2657
Pr 31:10 A wife of noble c who can find? She is H2657
Ac 17:11 Jews were of more noble c than those in G2302
Ro 5: 4 perseverance, c; and character, hope. G1509
Ro 5: 4 perseverance, character; and c, hope. G1509
1Co 15:33 "Bad company corrupts good c." G2456

CHARACTERS (1) [CHARACTER]

Ac 17: 5 rounded up some bad c from the G467

CHARCOAL (1)

Pr 26:21 As c to embers and as wood to fire, so is H7073

CHARGE (160) [CHARGED, CHARGES, CHARGING]

Ge 24: 2 household, the one in c of all that he had H5440
Ge 39: 4 Potiphar put him in c of his household H7212
Ge 39: 5 From the time he put him in c of his H7212
Ge 39: 6 with Joseph in c, he did not concern NDT
Ge 39: 8 "With me in c," he told her, "my master NDT
Ge 39:22 put Joseph in c of all those held H928+3338
Ge 41:33 man and put him in c of the land of Egypt H6584
Ge 41:40 You shall be in c of my palace, and all my H6584
Ge 41:41 "I hereby put you in c of the whole land of H6584
Ge 41:43 Thus he put him in c of the whole land of H6584
Ge 47: 6 put them in c of my own livestock. H8569
Ex 5: 6 drivers and overseers in c of the people: H928
Ex 22:25 treat it like a business deal; c no interest. H8492
Ex 23: 7 to do with a false c and do not put an H1821
Lev 5: 1 up when they hear a public c to testify H460
Nu 1:50 the Levites to be in c of the tabernacle of H6584
Nu 4:16 is to have c of the oil for the light H7213
Nu 4:16 He is to be in c of the entire tabernacle H7213
Nu 7: 2 leaders in c of those who were H6641+6584
Nu 18: 8 "I myself have put you in c of the offerings H5466
Dt 22:20 the c is true and no proof of the young H1821
Dt 23:19 Do not c a fellow Israelite interest H5967+5968
Dt 23:20 You may c a foreigner interest, but not a H5967
2Sa 20:24 Adoniram was in c of forced labor H6584
2Sa 23:23 And David put him in c of his bodyguard. H448
1Ki 2: 1 he gave a c to Solomon his son. H7422
1Ki 4: 5 of Nathan—in c of the district governors H6584
1Ki 4: 6 son of Abda—in c of forced labor. H6584
1Ki 5:14 Adoniram was in c of the forced labor H6584
1Ki 9:23 chief officials in c of Solomon's projects— H6584
1Ki 11:28 he put him in c of the whole labor force of H7212
1Ki 12:18 Adoniram, who was in c of forced labor H6584
2Ki 7:17 had put the officer on whose arm he leaned in c H7212
2Ki 11:15 of a hundred, who were in c of the troops: H7212
2Ki 15: 5 the king's son had c of the palace and H6584
2Ki 25:19 he took the officer in c of the fighting men H7224
2Ki 25:19 who was chief officer in c of conscripting the NDT
1Ch 6:31 men David put in c of the H6641+6584+3338
1Ch 9:11 the official in c of the house of God H5592
1Ch 9:20 of Eleazar was the official in c of the H5592
1Ch 9:23 descendants were in c of guarding the H6584
1Ch 9:27 they had c of the key for opening it H6584
1Ch 9:28 Some of them were in c of the articles H6584
1Ch 9:32 were in c of preparing for every Sabbath H6584
1Ch 11:25 And David put him in c of his bodyguard. H6584
1Ch 15:22 the head Levite was in c of the singing; H6254
1Ch 15:27 who was in c of the singing of the choirs. H8569
1Ch 23: 4 thousand are to be in c of the work of the H5904
1Ch 23:28 to be in c of the courtyards, the side H6584
1Ch 23:29 They were in c of the bread set out on the H4200
1Ch 26:20 Levites were in c of the treasuries of H6584
1Ch 26:22 They were in c of the treasuries of the H6584
1Ch 26:24 was the official in c of the treasuries. H6584
1Ch 26:26 his relatives were in c of all the treasuries H6584
1Ch 26:32 King David put them in c of the H7212
1Ch 27: 2 In c of the first division, for the first month H6584
1Ch 27: 4 In c of the division for the second month H6584
1Ch 27: 6 His son Ammizabad was in c of his division NDT
1Ch 27:25 son of Adiel was in c of the royal H6584
1Ch 27:25 son of Uzziah was in c of the storehouses H6584
1Ch 27:26 son of Kelub was in c of the workers who H6584
1Ch 27:27 the Ramathite was in c of the vineyards. H6584
1Ch 27:27 the Shiphmite was in c of the produce of H6584
1Ch 27:28 the Gederite was in c of the olive and H6584
1Ch 27:28 Joash was in c of the supplies of olive oil H6584
1Ch 27:29 the Sharonite was in c of the herds H6584
1Ch 27:29 son of Adlai was in c of the herds in the H6584
1Ch 27:30 the Ishmaelite was in c of the camels. H6584
1Ch 27:30 the Meronothite was in c of the donkeys. H6584
1Ch 27:31 Jaziz the Hagrite was in c of the flocks. H6584
1Ch 27:31 were the officials in c of King David's H8569
1Ch 28: 1 the officials in c of all the property H8569
1Ch 28: 8 "So now I c you in the sight of all Israel NDT
1Ch 29: 6 the officials in c of the king's work H8569
2Ch 10:18 Adoniram, who was in c of forced labor H6584
2Ch 23:14 of a hundred, who were in c of the troops H7212
2Ch 24:13 The men in c of the work were diligent H6913
2Ch 26:21 Jotham his son had c of the palace and H6584
2Ch 28: 7 Azrikam the officer in c of the palace, and H5592
2Ch 31:12 was the overseer in c of these things, and H6584
2Ch 31:13 Azariah the official in c of the temple of H5592
2Ch 31:14 was in c of the freewill offerings given to H6584
2Ch 34:13 had c of the laborers and supervised all H6584
2Ch 35: 8 the officials in c of God's temple H5592
Ne 7: 2 I put in c of Jerusalem my brother Hanani H7422
Ne 11:11 the official in c of the house of God H5592
Ne 11:16 who had c of the outside work of the H6584
Ne 11:21 Ziha and Gishpa were in c of them. H6584
Ne 12: 8 was in c of the songs of thanksgiving. H6584
Ne 12:44 appointed to be in c of the storerooms H6584
Ne 13: 4 had been put in c of the storerooms of H928
Ne 13:13 I put Shelemiah the priest, Zadok the scribe, and a Levite named Pedaiah in c of the storerooms H732+6584+238
Est 2: 3 eunuch, who is in c of the women; and H9068
Est 2: 8 to Hegai, who had c of the harem. H9068
Est 2:14 king's eunuch who was in c of the H9068
Est 2:15 king's eunuch who was in c of the harem, H9068
Job 34:13 Who put him in c of the whole world? H8492
Ps 69:27 C them with crime upon crime; do not let H5989
Pr 25:10 you and the c against you will stand. H1804
SS 2: 7 I c you by the gazelles and by the does of H8678
SS 3: 5 I c you by the gazelles and by the does of H8678
SS 5: 8 of Jerusalem, I c you—if you find my H8678
SS 5: 9 better than others, that you so c us? H8678
SS 8: 4 of Jerusalem, I c you: Do not arouse or H8678
Isa 3: 6 leader; take c of this heap of ruins!" H9393+3338
Isa 33:18 Where is the officer in c of the towers?" H6221
Jer 15:13 as plunder, without c, because of all your H4697
Jer 20: 1 the official in c of the temple of the LORD H5592
Jer 29:26 of Jehoiada to be in c of the house of the H7224
Jer 40: 7 the land and had put him in c of the men, H7212
Jer 46: 9 C, you horses! Drive furiously, you H6590
Jer 52:25 he took the officer in c of the fighting men H7224
Jer 52:25 who was chief officer in c of conscripting the NDT
Eze 44: 8 you put others in c of my sanctuary. H9068
Eze 44:11 having c of the gates of the temple and H7213
Da 2:48 and placed him in c of all its A10647+10505
Hos 4: 1 the LORD has a c to bring against you H8190
Hos 4: 4 "But let no one bring a c, let no one H8189
Hos 12: 2 The LORD has a c to bring against Judah H8190
Joel 2: 7 They c like warriors; they scale walls like H8132
Mic 6: 2 people; he is lodging a c against Israel. H3519
Zec 3: 6 angel of the LORD gave this c to Joshua: H6386
Zec 3: 7 govern my house and have c of my courts, H9068
Mt 24:45 whom the master has put in c of the G2770
Mt 24:47 he will put him in c of all his possessions. G2770
Mt 25:21 I will put you in c of many things. G2770
Mt 25:23 I will put you in c of many things. G2770
Mt 26:63 "I c you under oath by the living God: G2019
Mt 27:14 not even to a single c—to the great G4839
Mt 27:37 head they placed the written c against him: G162
Mk 3:21 they went to take c of him, for they G3195
Mk 13:34 his house and puts his servants in c, G2026
Mk 15:26 The written notice of the c against him read: G162
Lk 12:42 whom the master puts in c of his servants G2770
Lk 12:44 he will put him in c of all his possessions. G2770
Lk 19:17 in a very small matter, take c of ten cities. G2026
Lk 19:19 answered, 'You take c of five cities. G2062+1181
Lk 23: 4 "I find no basis for a c against this man." G165
Jn 13:29 Since Judas had c of the money, some G2400
Jn 18:38 "I find no basis for a c against him. G162
Jn 19: 4 that I find no basis for a c against him." G162
Jn 19: 6 I find no basis for a c against him. G162
Jn 19:16 So the soldiers took c of Jesus. G4161
Ac 8:27 important official in c of all the treasury of G2093
Ac 23:29 there was no c against him that G1598
Ac 25:18 they did not c him with any of the G162+5770
Ac 28:19 not intend to bring any c against my own G2989
Ro 3: 9 For we have already made the c that Jews G4577
Ro 8:33 Who will bring any c against those whom G1592
1Co 9:18 preaching the gospel I may offer it free of c, G78
2Co 11: 7 the gospel of God to you free of c? G1562
Col 2:14 canceled the c of our legal indebtedness, G5934
1Th 5:27 I c you before the Lord to have this letter G1941
1Ti 5:21 I c you, in the sight of God and Christ G1371
1Ti 6:13 Pilate made the good confession, I c you G4133
2Ti 4: 1 his kingdom, I give you this c: G1371
Titus 1: 6 are not open to the c of being wild and G2990
Phm 18 wrong or owes you anything, c it to me. G1823
Rev 14:18 who had c of the fire, came from G2026
Rev 16: 5 Then I heard the angel in c of the waters say AIT

CHARGED (10) [CHARGE]

Dt 1:16 And I c your judges at that time, "Hear the H7422
Jos 6:20 so everyone c straight in, and they H6590
Jdg 20:33 Israelite ambush c out of its place on the H1631
1Ch 22: 6 his son Solomon and c him to build a H7422
Eze 18:20 of the wicked will be c against them. H6584
Da 8: 4 I watched the ram as it c toward the west H5590
Da 8: 6 beside the canal and c at it in great rage. H8132
Ac 18:13 they c, "is persuading the people to G3306
Ac 19:40 are in danger of being c with rioting G1592
Ro 5:13 sin is not c against anyone's account G1824

CHARGER, CHARGERS (KJV) DISHES, PLATE, PLATE, PLATTER

CHARGES (37) [CHARGE]

1Ki 21:10 him and have them bring c that he has H6386
1Ki 21:13 him and brought c against Naboth before H6386
Ne 5: 6 When I heard their outcry and these c, H1821
Job 4:18 his servants, if he c his angels with error, H8492
Job 10: 2 tell me what c you have against me. H8189

Job 13:19 *Can* anyone **bring c** against me? If so, H8189
Job 22: 4 he rebukes you and brings **c** against you? H5477
Job 23: 6 he *would* not **press c** against me. H8492
Job 24:12 But God **c** no one *with* wrongdoing. H8492
Job 39:21 in its strength, and **c** into the fray. H3655
Ps 50: 8 *I* **bring** no **c** *against* you concerning your H3519
Isa 50: 8 Who then *will* **bring c** against me H8189
Jer 2: 9 "Therefore *I* **bring c** against you again," H8189
Jer 2: 9 "And *I will* **bring c** against your children's H8189
Jer 2:29 "Why *do you* **bring c** against me? You H8189
Jer 25:31 the LORD will bring **c** against the nations; H8190
Da 6: 4 tried to find **grounds for c** against Daniel A10544
Da 6: 5 never find any **basis for c** against this A10544
Hos 4: 4 are like *those who* **bring c** *against* a priest H8189
Mt 12:10 *Looking* for a reason *to* **bring c against** G2989
Lk 23:14 found no basis *for your* **c** against him. G2989
Jn 18:29 "What **c** are you bringing against this G2990
Ac 7: 1 high priest asked Stephen, "Are **these** *c* true?" AIT
Ac 19:38 there are proconsuls. *They can* **press c.** G1592
Ac 24: 1 they **brought** *their* **c** against Paul G1872
Ac 24: 8 all these **c** we *are* **bringing** against him." G2989
Ac 24:13 to you the **c** *they are* now **making** against G2989
Ac 24:19 here before you and **bring c** if they have G2989
Ac 25: 2 **appeared** before him **and presented** *the* **c** G1872
Ac 25: 5 *they can* **press c** against him there." G2989
Ac 25: 7 They brought many serious **c** against him G166
Ac 25: 9 stand trial before me there on **these** *c*?" AIT
Ac 25:11 But if *the* **c brought** against me by these G2989
Ac 25:15 of the Jews **brought c** against him and G1872
Ac 25:16 to defend themselves against the **c.** G1598
Ac 25:20 to Jerusalem and stand trial there on **these** *c.* AIT
Ac 25:27 Rome without specifying the **c** against him." G162

CHARGING (8) [CHARGE]

Ne 5: 7 "You *are* **c** your own people interest!" H5957
Ne 5:10 But let us stop **c interest!** H5391
Ne 5:11 also *the* **interest** you *are* **c** them—one H5957
Job 1:22 Job did not sin *by* **c** God *with* wrongdoing. H5989
Job 15:26 defiantly **c** against him with a thick, strong H8132
Pr 28:15 a roaring lion or a **c** bear is a wicked ruler H9212
Jer 8: 6 their own course like a horse **c** into battle. H8851
Na 3: 3 **C** cavalry, flashing swords and glittering H6590

CHARIOT (67) [CHARIOTEERS, CHARIOTS]

Ge 41:43 He had him ride in a **c** *as* his H5324
Ge 46:29 Joseph had his **c** made ready and went to H5324
Ex 14: 6 So he had his **c** made ready and took his H8207
Jdg 4:15 got down from his **c** and fled on foot. H5324
Jdg 5:28 cried out, 'Why is his **c** so long in coming? H8207
2Sa 8: 4 all but a hundred of the **c horses.** H8207
2Sa 15: 1 himself with a **c** and horses and with H5324
1Ki 4:26 had four thousand stalls for **c** horses, H5323
1Ki 4:28 straw for the **c horses** and the other H8224
1Ki 7:33 The wheels were made like **c** wheels; the H5324
1Ki 10:26 which he kept in the **c** cities and also with H8207
1Ki 10:29 They imported a **c** from Egypt for six H5324
1Ki 12:18 to get into his **c** and escape to Jerusalem H5324
1Ki 18:44 'Hitch up your **c** and go down before the NDT
1Ki 20:25 horse for horse and **c** for chariot—so we H8207
1Ki 20:25 horse for horse and chariot for **c**—so we H8207
1Ki 20:33 Ahab had him come up into his **c.** H5324
1Ki 22:31 had ordered his thirty-two **c** commanders, H8207
1Ki 22:32 When the **c** commanders saw H8207
1Ki 22:33 the **c** commanders saw that he was not the H8207
1Ki 22:34 The king told his **c driver,** "Wheel around H8208
1Ki 22:35 propped up in his **c** facing the Arameans. H5324
1Ki 22:35 from his wound ran onto the floor of the **c,** H8207
1Ki 22:38 They washed the **c** at a pool in Samaria H8207
2Ki 2:11 suddenly a **c** *of* fire and horses of fire H8207
2Ki 5:21 he got down from the **c** to meet him. H5324
2Ki 5:26 the man got down from his **c** to meet you? H5324
2Ki 8:21 surrounded him and his **c** commanders, H8207
2Ki 9:16 Then he **got into** *his* **c** and rode to Jezreel H8206
2Ki 9:21 "Hitch up my **c,**" Joram ordered. H8207
2Ki 9:21 rode out, each in his own **c,** to meet Jehu. H8207
2Ki 9:24 his heart and he slumped down in his **c.** H8207
2Ki 9:25 to Bidkar, his **c officer,** "Pick him up and H8957
2Ki 9:27 wounded him in his **c** on the way up to H5324
2Ki 9:28 His servants **took** him **by c** to Jerusalem H8206
2Ki 10:15 and Jehu helped him up into the **c.** H5324
2Ki 10:16 Then he had him ride along in his **c.** H8207
2Ki 23:30 brought his body **in a c** from Megiddo to H8206
1Ch 18: 4 all but a hundred of the **c horses.** H8207
1Ch 28:18 He also gave him the plan for the **c,** that H5324
2Ch 1:14 which he kept in the **c** cities and also with H8207
2Ch 1:17 They imported a **c** from Egypt for six H5324
2Ch 9:25 which he kept in the **c** cities and also with H8207
2Ch 10:18 to get into his **c** and escape to Jerusalem H5324
2Ch 18:30 of Aram had ordered his **c** commanders, H8207
2Ch 18:31 When the **c** commanders saw H8207
2Ch 18:32 when the **c** commanders saw that he H8207
2Ch 18:33 The king told the **c driver,** "Wheel around H8208
2Ch 18:34 himself up in his **c** facing the Arameans H5324
2Ch 21: 9 surrounded him and his **c** commanders, H8207
2Ch 35:24 So they took him out of his **c,** put him in H5324
2Ch 35:24 put him in his other **c** and brought him to H7228
Ps 76: 6 God of Jacob, both horse and **c** lie still. H8207
Ps 104: 3 makes the clouds his **c** and rides on the H8213
SS 1: 9 to a mare among Pharaoh's **c horses.** H8207
Isa 5:28 like flint, their **c wheels** like a whirlwind. H1649
Isa 21: 9 comes a man in a **c** with a team of horses H8207
Jer 51:21 rider, with you I shatter **c** and driver, H8207
Eze 23:15 of them looked like Babylonian **c officers,** H8957
Eze 23:23 **c officers** and men of high rank H8957
Eze 27:14 of Beth Togarmah exchanged **c horses,** H6061
Mic 1:13 in Lachish, harness fast horses to the **c.** H5324
Zec 6: 2 The first **c** had red horses, the second H5324
Ac 8:28 was sitting in his **c** reading the Book of G761
Ac 8:29 told Philip, "Go to that **c** and stay near it." G761
Ac 8:30 Philip ran up to the **c** and heard the man NDT
Ac 8:38 And he gave orders to stop the **c.** Then both G761

CHARIOTEERS (11) [CHARIOT]

1Sa 13: 5 chariots, six thousand **c,** and soldiers as H7305
2Sa 8: 4 seven thousand **c** and twenty thousand H7305
2Sa 10:18 hundred of their **c** and forty thousand of H8207
1Ki 9:22 the commanders of his chariots and **c.** H7305
1Ch 18: 4 seven thousand **c** and twenty thousand H7305
1Ch 19: 6 hire chariots and **c** from Aram Naharaim, H7305
1Ch 19: 7 hired thirty-two thousand **chariots and c,** H8207
1Ch 19:18 thousand of their **c** and forty thousand of H8207
2Ch 8: 9 commanders of his chariots and **c.** H7305
Isa 22: 6 the quiver, with her **c** and horses; Kir H8207+132
Jer 46: 9 Drive furiously, you **c!** March on, H8207

CHARIOTS (101) [CHARIOT]

Ge 50: 9 **C** and horsemen also went up with him. H8207
Ex 14: 7 He took six hundred of the best **c,** along H8207
Ex 14: 7 along with all the other **c** *of* Egypt, with H8207
Ex 14: 9 all Pharaoh's horses and **c,** horsemen and H8207
Ex 14:17 his army, through his **c** and his horsemen. H8207
Ex 14:18 through Pharaoh, his **c** and his horsemen." H8207
Ex 14:23 Pharaoh's horses and **c** and horsemen H8207
Ex 14:25 the wheels of their **c** so that they had H5324
Ex 14:26 the Egyptians and their **c** and horsemen." H8207
Ex 14:28 back and covered the **c** and horsemen— H8207
Ex 15: 4 Pharaoh's **c** and his army he has hurled H5324
Ex 15:19 **c** and horsemen went into the sea H8207
Dt 11: 4 to its horses and **c,** how he overwhelmed H8207
Dt 20: 1 see horses and **c** and an army greater H8207
Jos 11: 4 a large number of horses and **c**— H8207
Jos 11: 6 to hamstring their horses and burn their **c.**" H5324
Jos 11: 9 their horses and burned their **c.** H5324
Jos 17:16 live in the plain have **c** *fitted with* iron, H8207
Jos 17:18 Canaanites have **c** *fitted with* iron and H8207
Jos 24: 6 pursued them with **c** and horsemen as far H8207
Jdg 1:19 because they had **c** *fitted with* iron. H8207
Jdg 4: 3 nine hundred **c** *fitted with* iron and had H8207
Jdg 4: 7 with his **c** and his troops to the Kishon H8207
Jdg 4:13 his nine hundred **c** *fitted with* iron. H8207
Jdg 4:15 Sisera and all his **c** and army by the sword H8207
Jdg 4:16 Barak pursued the **c** and army as far as H8207
Jdg 5:28 Why is the clatter of his **c** delayed?' H5324
1Sa 8:11 make them serve with his **c** and horses, H5324
1Sa 8:11 and they will run in front of his **c.** H5324
1Sa 8:12 weapons of war and equipment for his **c.** H8207
1Sa 13: 5 with three thousand **c,** six thousand H8207
2Sa 1: 6 with the **c** and their drivers in hot pursuit. H8207
2Sa 8: 4 David captured a thousand of his **c,** seven H8207
1Ki 1: 5 So he got **c** and horses ready, with fifty H8207
1Ki 9:19 the towns for his **c** and for his horses— H8207
1Ki 9:22 the commanders of his **c** and charioteers. H8207
1Ki 10:26 Solomon accumulated **c** and horses; he H8207
1Ki 10:26 fourteen hundred **c** and twelve thousand H8207
1Ki 16: 9 who had command of half his **c,** plotted H8207
1Ki 20: 1 by thirty-two kings with their horses and **c,** H8207
1Ki 20:21 the horses and **c** and inflicted heavy H8207
2Ki 2:12 The **c** and horsemen of Israel! H8207
2Ki 5: 9 with his horses and **c** and stopped at the H8207
2Ki 6:14 he sent horses and **c** and a strong force H8207
2Ki 6:15 with horses and **c** had surrounded the H8207
2Ki 6:17 full of horses and **c** *of* fire all around H8207
2Ki 7: 6 to hear the sound of **c** and horses and a H8207
2Ki 7:14 So they selected two **c** *with* their horses H8207
2Ki 8:21 So Jehoram went to Zair with all his **c.** H8207
2Ki 9:25 you and I *were* **riding** together **in c** behind H8206
2Ki 10: 2 sons with you and you have **c** and horses, H8207
2Ki 13: 7 ten **c** and ten thousand foot soldiers H8207
2Ki 13:14 "The **c** and horsemen of Israel!" H8207
2Ki 18:24 depending on Egypt for **c** and horsemen? H8207
2Ki 19:23 "With my many **c** I have ascended the H8207
2Ki 23:11 then burned the **c** *dedicated to* the sun. H5324
1Ch 18: 4 David captured a thousand of his **c,** seven H8207
1Ch 19: 6 of silver to hire **c** and charioteers from H8207
1Ch 19: 7 thirty-two thousand **c and charioteers,** H8207
2Ch 1:14 Solomon accumulated **c** and horses; he H8207
2Ch 1:14 fourteen hundred **c** and twelve thousand H8207
2Ch 8: 6 all the cities for his **c** and for his horses— H8207
2Ch 8: 9 commanders of his **c** and charioteers. H8207
2Ch 9:25 had four thousand stalls for horses and **c,** H5324
2Ch 12: 3 With twelve hundred **c** and sixty thousand H8207
2Ch 14: 9 upon thousands and three hundred **c,** H5324
2Ch 16: 8 with great numbers of **c** and horsemen? H8207
2Ch 21: 9 went there with his officers and all his **c.** H8207
Ps 20: 7 Some trust in **c** and some in horses, but H8207
Ps 68:17 The **c** *of* God are tens of thousands and H8207
SS 6:12 set me among the royal **c** *of* my people. H5324
Isa 2: 7 is full of horses; there is no end to their **c.** H5324
Isa 21: 7 When he sees **c** *with* teams of horses H8207
Isa 22: 7 Your choicest valleys are full of **c,** and H8207
Isa 22:18 die and there the **c** you were so proud of H5324
Isa 31: 1 the multitude of their **c** and in the great H8207
Isa 36: 9 depending on Egypt for **c** and horsemen? H8207
Isa 37:24 'With my many **c** I have ascended the H8207
Isa 43:17 who drew out the **c** and horses, the army H8207
Isa 66:15 with fire, and his **c** are like a whirlwind H5324
Isa 66:20 on horses, in **c** and wagons, and on mules H8207
Jer 4:13 the clouds, his **c** come like a whirlwind H5324
Jer 17:25 will come riding in **c** and on horses, H8207
Jer 22: 4 of this palace, riding in **c** and on horses H8207
Jer 47: 3 at the noise of enemy **c** and the rumble of H8207
Jer 50:37 her horses and **c** and all the foreigners H8207
Eze 23:24 **c** and wagons and with a throng of H8207
Eze 26: 7 with horses and **c,** with horsemen and a H8207
Eze 26:10 wagons and **c** when he enters your gates H8207
Da 11:40 out against him with **c** and cavalry and a H8207
Joel 2: 5 a noise like that of **c** they leap over the H5324
Mic 5:10 from among you and demolish your **c.** H5324
Na 2: 3 The metal on the **c** flashes on the day H8207
Na 2: 4 The **c** storm through the streets, rushing H8207
Na 2:13 "I will burn up your **c** in smoke, and the H8207
Na 3: 2 of wheels, galloping horses and jolting **c!** H5324
Hab 3: 8 you rode your horses and your **c** to victory? H5324
Hag 2:22 I will overthrow **c** and their drivers; horses H5324
Zec 6: 1 before me were four **c** coming out from H5324
Zec 9:10 will take away the **c** from Ephraim and the H8207
Rev 9: 9 of many horses and **c** rushing into battle. G761

CHARITY (KJV) LOVE

CHARM (2) [CHARMED, CHARMER, CHARMING, CHARMS]

Pr 17: 8 bribe is seen as a **c** by the one who H74+2834
Pr 31:30 **C** is deceptive, and beauty is fleeting; but H2834

CHARMED (2) [CHARM]

Ecc 10:11 If a snake bites before it is **c,** the charmer H4318
Jer 8:17 vipers that cannot be **c,** and they will bite H4318

CHARMER (2) [CHARM]

Ps 58: 5 that will not heed the tune of the **c** H4317
Ecc 10:11 it is charmed, the **c** receives no fee. H1251+4383

CHARMING (2) [CHARM]

Pr 26:25 Though their speech *is* **c,** do not believe H2858
SS 1:16 Oh, how **c!** And our bed is H5833

CHARMS (3) [CHARM]

Isa 3:20 sashes, the perfume bottles and **c,** H4318
Eze 13:18 the women who sew **magic c** on all their H4086
Eze 13:20 I am against your **magic c** with which you H4086

CHARRAN (KJV) HARRAN

CHARRED (4) [CHARS]

Nu 16:37 censers from the **c remains** and scatter the H8599
Jdg 15:14 arms became like **c** flax, H1277+928+2021+836
Eze 15: 5 when the fire has burned it and *it is* **c**? H3081
Eze 24:10 in the spices; and *let* the bones **be c.** H3081

CHARS (1) [CHARRED]

Eze 15: 4 the fire burns both ends and **c** the middle, H3081

CHASE (10) [CHASED, CHASING]

Lev 26: 8 Five of you *will* **c** a hundred, and a H8103
Lev 26: 8 a hundred of you *will* **c** ten thousand H8103
Dt 32:30 How *could* one man **c** a thousand, or two H8103
Job 13:25 windblown leaf? *Will you* **c** *after* dry chaff? H8103
Pr 12:11 but *those who* **c** fantasies have no sense. H8103
Pr 28:19 but *those who* **c** fantasies will have their H8103
Isa 1:23 they all love bribes and **c after** gifts. H8103
Jer 49:19 *I will* **c** Edom from its land in an instant. H8132
Jer 50:44 *I will* **c** Babylon from its land in an instant. H8132
Hos 2: 7 *She will* **c after** her lovers but not catch H8103

CHASED (10) [CHASE]

Dt 1:44 *they* **c** you like a swarm of bees and beat H8103
Jos 7: 5 *They* **c** the Israelites from the city gate as H8103
Jos 8:24 in the wilderness where *they had* **c** them, H8103
Jdg 1: 6 but *they* **c** him and caught him H8103
Jdg 9:40 Abimelek **c** him all the way to the H8103
Jdg 20:43 **c** them and easily overran them in the H8103
2Sa 2:19 He **c** Abner, turning neither to the right H8103
2Ki 9:27 Beth Haggan. Jehu **c** him, shouting, "Kill H8103
Jer 50:17 is a scattered flock that lions *have* **c away.** H5615
La 4:19 *they* **c** us over the mountains and lay in H1944

CHASING (13) [CHASE]

Nu 15:39 yourselves by **c** after the lusts of your H9365
1Sa 17:53 returned from **c** the Philistines, H1944+339
2Sa 2:21 But Asahel would not stop **c** him. H339
2Sa 2:22 warned Asahel, "Stop **c** me! Why should I H339
Ecc 1:14 them are meaningless, a **c after** the wind. H8296
Ecc 1:17 that this, too, is a **c after** the wind. H8301
Ecc 2:11 meaningless, a **c after** the wind; nothing H8296
Ecc 2:17 All of it is meaningless, a **c after** the wind. H8296
Ecc 2:26 too is meaningless, a **c after** the wind. H8296
Ecc 4: 4 too is meaningless, a **c after** the wind. H8296
Ecc 4: 6 handfuls with toil and **c after** the wind. H8296
Ecc 4:16 too is meaningless, a **c after** the wind. H8301
Ecc 6: 9 too is meaningless, a **c after** the wind. H8296

CHASM (1)

Lk 16:26 us and you a great **c** has been set in G5926

CHASTE (KJV) PURE, PURITY

C

CHASTENED (2) [CHASTENS]
Job 33:19 "Or *someone may* **be** c on a bed of pain H3519
Ps 118:18 The LORD *has* c me **severely**, but he H3579+3579

CHASTENS (1) [CHASTENED]
Heb 12: 6 and *he* c everyone he accepts as his son." *G3463*

CHASTISE, CHASTISED, CHASTISEMENT (KJV) CATCH, DISCIPLINE, DISCIPLINED, PUNISH, PUNISHMENT, SCOURGE

CHATTER (2) [CHATTERING]
1Ti 6:20 away from godless c and the opposing *G3032*
2Ti 2:16 Avoid godless c, because those who *G3032*

CHATTERING (2) [CHATTER]
Pr 10: 8 commands, but a c fool comes to ruin. H8557
Pr 10:10 causes grief, and a c fool comes to ruin. H8557

CHEAPER (1)
Jn 2:10 first and then the c wine after the guests *G1781*

CHEAT (3) [CHEATED, CHEATING]
Lev 6: 2 or if *they* c their neighbor, H6943
Mal 1:14 "Cursed is the c who has an acceptable H5792
1Co 6: 8 *you* yourselves c and do wrong, and *G92*

CHEATED (5) [CHEAT]
Ge 31: 7 your father *has* c me by changing my H9438
1Sa 12: 3 Whom *have I* c? Whom have I H6943
1Sa 12: 4 "*You have* not c or oppressed us," they H6943
Lk 19: 8 if *I have* c anybody **out of** anything, *G5193*
1Co 6: 7 rather be wronged? Why not rather *be* c? *G691*

CHEATING (1) [CHEAT]
Am 8: 5 the price and c *with* dishonest scales, H6430

CHEBAR (KJV) KEBAR

CHECK (2) [CHECKED]
Ge 30:33 whenever *you* c on the wages H995+4200+7156
Jas 3: 2 able *to* **keep** their whole body **in** c. *G5902*

CHECKED (3) [CHECK]
2Ki 6:10 the king of Israel c **on** the place H8938+448
Ezr 8:15 When *I* c among the people and the H1067
Ps 106:30 up and intervened, and the plague **was** c. H6806

CHEDORLAOMER (KJV) KEDORLAOMER

CHEEK (7) [CHEEKS]
Job 16:10 they strike my c in scorn and unite H4305
La 3:30 Let him offer his c to one who would strike H4305
Hos 11: 4 like one who lifts a little child to the c, H4305
Mic 5: 1 will strike Israel's ruler on the c with a rod. H4305
Mt 5:39 If anyone slaps you on the right c, turn to *G4965*
Mt 5:39 right cheek, turn to them the other c also. NDT
Lk 6:29 If someone slaps you on one c, turn to *G4965*

CHEEKS (4) [CHEEK]
SS 1:10 Your c are beautiful with earrings, your H4305
SS 5:13 His c are like beds of spice yielding H4305
Isa 50: 6 my c to those who pulled out my beard H4305
La 1: 2 she weeps at night, tears are on her c. H4305

CHEER (2) [CHEERED, CHEERFUL, CHEERFULLY, CHEERING, CHEERS]
1Ki 21: 7 Get up and eat! **C up**. I'll get you H3512+4213
Mk 10:49 to the blind man, "**C up**! On your feet! *G2510*

CHEERED (1) [CHEER]
Php 2:19 that I also *may be* c when I receive news *G2379*

CHEERFUL (4) [CHEER]
Pr 15:13 A happy heart **makes** the face c, but H3512
Pr 15:15 the c heart has a continual feast. H3202
Pr 17:22 A c heart is good medicine, but a crushed H8524
2Co 9: 7 under compulsion, for God loves a c giver. *G2659*

CHEERFULLY (1) [CHEER]
Ro 12: 8 if it is to show mercy, do it c. *G1877+2660*

CHEERING (3) [CHEER]
1Ki 1:45 From there they have gone up c, and the H8524
2Ch 23:12 of the people running and c the king, H2146
Ecc 2: 3 I tried c myself with wine, and embracing H5432

CHEERS (2) [CHEER]
Jdg 9:13 my wine, which c both gods and humans H8523
Pr 12:25 down the heart, but a kind word c it **up**. H8523

CHEESE (2) [CHEESES]
2Sa 17:29 and c *from* cows' milk for David and his H9147
Job 10:10 me out like milk and curdle me like c, H1482

CHEESES (1) [CHEESE]
1Sa 17:18 along these ten c to the H3043+2692

CHELUB (KJV) KELUB

CHELUBAI (KJV) CALEB

CHEMARIMS (KJV) IDOLATROUS

CHEMOSH (8)
Nu 21:29 people of C! He has given up his H4019
Jdg 11:24 you not take what your god C gives you? H4019
1Ki 11: 7 a high place for C the detestable god of H4019
1Ki 11:33 the Sidonians, C the god of the Moabites H4019
2Ki 23:13 the Sidonians, for C the vile god of Moab H4019
Jer 48: 7 be taken captive, and C will go into exile H4019
Jer 48:13 Then Moab will be ashamed of C, as H4019
Jer 48:46 The people of C are destroyed; your sons H4019

CHENAANAH (KJV) KENAANAH

CHENANIAH (KJV) KENANIAH

CHEPHIRAH (KJV) KEPHIRAH

CHERETHIMS, CHERETHITES (KJV) KERETHITES

CHERISH (2) [CHERISHED, CHERISHES]
Ps 83: 3 people; they plot against *those* you c. H7621
Pr 4: 8 C her, and she will exalt you; embrace her H6147

CHERISHED (3) [CHERISH]
Ps 66:18 If *I had* c sin in my heart, the Lord would H8011
Pr 4: 3 still tender, and c by my mother. H3495
Hos 9:16 bear children, I will slay their c offspring." H4718

CHERISHES (1) [CHERISH]
Pr 19: 8 the *one who* c understanding will soon H9068

CHERITH (KJV) KERITH

CHERUB (16) [CHERUBIM]
Ex 25:19 Make one c on one end and the second H4131
Ex 25:19 one end and the second c on the other; H4131
Ex 37: 8 He made one c on one end and the H4131
Ex 37: 8 one end and the second c on the other; H4131
1Ki 6:24 One wing of the first c was five cubits long H4131
1Ki 6:25 The second c also measured ten cubits, for H4131
1Ki 6:26 The height of each c was ten cubits. H4131
1Ki 6:27 The wing of one c touched one wall H4131
2Ch 3:11 One wing of the first c was five cubits long NDT
2Ch 3:11 touched the wing of the other c. H4131
2Ch 3:12 wing of the second c was five cubits long H4131
2Ch 3:12 touched the wing of the first c. H4131
Eze 10:14 One face was that of a c, the second the H4131
Eze 28:14 You were anointed as a guardian c, for so H4131
Eze 28:16 guardian c, from among the fiery H4131
Eze 41:18 with cherubim. Each c had two faces: H4131

CHERUBIM (73) [CHERUB]
Ge 3:24 the Garden of Eden c and a flaming H4131
Ex 25:18 And make two c out of hammered gold at H4131
Ex 25:19 make the c of one piece with the cover H4131
Ex 25:20 The c are to have their wings spread H4131
Ex 25:20 The c are to face each other, looking H4131
Ex 25:22 between the two c that are over the ark H4131
Ex 26: 1 with c woven into them by a skilled worker H4131
Ex 26:31 with c woven into it by a skilled worker. H4131
Ex 36: 8 with c woven into them by expert hands. H4131
Ex 36:35 with c woven into it by a skilled worker. H4131
Ex 37: 7 Then he made two c out of hammered H4131
Ex 37: 9 The c had their wings spread upward H4131
Ex 37: 9 The c faced each other, looking toward H4131
Nu 7:89 between the two c above the atonement H4131
1Sa 4: 4 who is enthroned between the c. H4131
2Sa 6: 2 is enthroned between the c on the ark. H4131
2Sa 22:11 He mounted the c and flew; he soared on H4131
1Ki 6:23 he made a pair of c out of olive wood, H4131
1Ki 6:25 the two c were identical in size and H4131
1Ki 6:27 He placed the c inside the innermost room H4131
1Ki 6:28 He overlaid the c with gold. H4131
1Ki 6:29 he carved c, palm trees and open H4131
1Ki 6:32 on the two olive-wood doors he carved c, H4131
1Ki 6:32 overlaid the c and palm trees with H4131
1Ki 6:35 He carved c, palm trees and open flowers H4131
1Ki 7:29 bulls and c—and on the uprights H4131
1Ki 7:36 He engraved c, lions and palm trees on H4131
1Ki 8: 6 put it beneath the wings of the c. H4131
1Ki 8: 7 The c spread their wings over the place of H4131
2Ki 19:15 enthroned between the c, you alone are H4131
1Ch 13: 6 who is enthroned between the c—the ark H4131
1Ch 28:18 the c of gold that spread their wings and H4131
2Ch 3: 7 with gold, and he carved c on the walls. H4131
2Ch 3:10 a pair of sculptured c and overlaid them H4131
2Ch 3:11 total wingspan of the c was twenty cubits. H4131
2Ch 3:13 The wings of these c extended twenty H4131
2Ch 3:14 yarn and fine linen, with c worked into it. H4131
2Ch 5: 7 put it beneath the wings of the c. H4131
2Ch 5: 8 The c spread their wings over the place of H4131
Ps 18:10 He mounted the c and flew; he soared on H4131
Ps 80: 1 You who sit enthroned between the c H4131
Ps 99: 1 he sits enthroned between the c, let the H4131
Isa 37:16 enthroned between the c, you alone are H4131
Eze 9: 3 God of Israel went up from above the c, H4131
Eze 10: 1 the vault that was over the heads of the c. H4131
Eze 10: 2 "Go in among the wheels beneath the c. H4131
Eze 10: 2 coals from among the c and scatter them H4131
Eze 10: 3 Now the c were standing on the south H4131
Eze 10: 4 rose from above the c and moved to the H4131
Eze 10: 5 of the wings of the c could be heard as far H4131
Eze 10: 6 from among the c," the man went in and H4131
Eze 10: 7 Then one of the c reached out his hand to H4131
Eze 10: 8 the wings of the c could be seen what H4131
Eze 10: 9 I saw beside the c four wheels, one H4131
Eze 10: 9 one beside each of the c; the wheels H4131
Eze 10:11 one of the four directions **the** c faced; H2157S
Eze 10:11 wheels did not turn about as **the** c went. H4392S
Eze 10:11 The c went in whatever direction the head NDT
Eze 10:14 Each of the c had four faces: One face was NDT
Eze 10:15 Then the c rose upward. These were the H4131
Eze 10:16 When the c moved, the wheels beside H4131
Eze 10:16 when the c spread their wings to rise H4131
Eze 10:17 When **the** c stood still, they also stood H4392S
Eze 10:17 and when **the** c rose, they rose with H4392S
Eze 10:18 of the temple and stopped above the c. H4131
Eze 10:19 the c spread their wings and rose from the H4131
Eze 10:20 and I realized that they were c. H4131
Eze 11:22 Then the c, with the wheels beside them H4131
Eze 41:18 were carved c and palm trees. Palm trees H4131
Eze 41:18 Palm trees alternated with c. Each cherub H4131
Eze 41:20 c and palm trees were carved on the wall H4131
Eze 41:25 hall were carved c and palm trees like H4131
Heb 9: 5 Above the ark were the c of the Glory *G5938*

CHESNUT (KJV) PLANE

CHEST (13) [CHESTS]
1Sa 6: 8 in a c beside it put the gold objects H761
1Sa 6:11 along with it the c containing the gold H761
1Sa 6:15 together with the c containing the gold H761
2Ki 12: 9 the priest took a c and bored a hole in its H778
2Ki 12: 9 entrance put into **the** c all the money H9004S
2Ki 12:10 was a large amount of money in the c, H778
2Ch 24: 8 a c was made and placed outside H778
2Ch 24:10 dropping them into the c until it was full. H778
2Ch 24:11 Whenever the c was brought in by the H778
2Ch 24:11 come and empty the c and carry it back to H778
Job 41:24 Its c is hard as rock, hard as a lower H4213
Da 2:32 of pure gold, its c and arms of silver A10249
Rev 1:13 feet and with a golden sash around his c. *G3466*

CHESTS (1) [CHEST]
Rev 15: 6 wore golden sashes around their c. *G5111*

CHEW (7) [CHEWED, CHEWS]
Lev 11: 4 'There are some *that* only c the cud or H6590
Lev 11: 7 a divided hoof, *does* not c the cud; it is H1760
Lev 11:26 divided hoof or *that does* not c the cud is H6590
Dt 14: 7 of *those that* c the cud or that have a H6590
Dt 14: 7 Although they c the cud, they do not have H6590
Dt 14: 8 it has a divided hoof, it does not c the cud. NDT
Eze 23:34 it and drain it dry and c *on* its pieces— H1751

CHEWED (1) [CHEW]
Jnh 4: 7 *which* c the plant so that it withered. H5782

CHEWS (5) [CHEW]
Lev 11: 3 has a divided hoof and *that* c the cud. H6590
Lev 11: 4 The camel, though it c the cud, does not H6590
Lev 11: 5 The hyrax, though it c the cud, does not H6590
Lev 11: 6 The rabbit, though it c the cud, does not H6590
Dt 14: 6 has a divided hoof and that c the cud. H6590

CHICKENS (KJV) CHICKS

CHICKS (2)
Mt 23:37 as a hen gathers her c under her wings *G3800*
Lk 13:34 as a hen gathers her c under her wings *G3799*

CHIDE (KJV) ACCUSE, CHALLENGED, QUARREL, QUARRELED

CHIEF (141) [CHIEFS]
Ge 40: 2 the c cupbearer and the chief baker H8569
Ge 40: 2 the chief cupbearer and the c baker, H8569
Ge 40: 9 So the c cupbearer told Joseph his dream H8569
Ge 40:16 When the c baker saw that Joseph had H8569
Ge 40:20 up the heads of the c cupbearer and the H8569
Ge 40:20 cupbearer and the c baker in the presence H8569
Ge 40:21 He restored the c cupbearer to his position, H8569
Ge 40:22 he impaled the c baker, just as Joseph H8569
Ge 40:23 The c cupbearer, however, did not H8569
Ge 41: 9 Then the c cupbearer said to Pharaoh H8569
Ge 41:10 me and the c baker in the house of H8569
Nu 3:32 The c **leader** *of* the Levites was H5954+5954
Nu 25:15 a tribal c of a Midianite family. H8031
Dt 29:10 your leaders and c **men**, your elders and H8657
Jos 22:14 With him they sent ten of the c *men*, one H5954
1Sa 21: 7 was Doeg the Edomite, Saul's c shepherd. H52
2Sa 23: 8 a Tahkemonite, was c *of* the Three; he H8031
2Sa 23:13 of the thirty c *warriors* came down to H8031
2Sa 23:18 of Joab son of Zeruiah was c *of* the Three. H8031
1Ki 4: 2 And these were his c **officials**: Azariah son H8569
1Ki 4: 4 **commander in** c; Zadok H6584+2021+7372
1Ki 9:23 They were also the c officials in charge of H8569
2Ki 10:11 as well as all his c *men*, his close friends H1524
2Ki 15:25 One of his c **officers**, Pekah son of H8957
2Ki 18:17 his c officer and his field commander with H8042
2Ki 25:18 took as prisoners Seraiah the c priest, H8031
2Ki 25:19 who was c **officer** in charge H8569+2021+7372
1Ch 5: 7 Jeiel the c, Zechariah, H8031
1Ch 5:12 Joel was the c, Shapham the second H8031
1Ch 9:17 their fellow Levites, Shallum their c H8031
1Ch 11:11 a Hakmonite, was c *of* the officers; he H8031
1Ch 11:20 the brother of Joab was c *of* the Three. H8031
1Ch 11:42 Reubenite, who was c of the Reubenites H8031
1Ch 12: 3 Ahiezer their c and Joash the sons of H8031
1Ch 12: 9 Ezer was the c, Obadiah the second in H8031
1Ch 12:18 came on Amasai, c *of* the Thirty, and he H8031

1Ch 16: 5 Asaph was the **c**, and next to him in rank H8031
1Ch 18:17 David's sons were **c officials** at the king's H8037
1Ch 26:31 Jeriah was their **c** according to the H8031
1Ch 27: 3 descendant of Perez and **c** of all the army H8031
1Ch 27: 5 He was **c** and there were 24,000 men in H8031
2Ch 8:10 were also King Solomon's **c** officials— H8569
2Ch 19:11 "Amariah the **c** priest will be over you in H8031
2Ch 24: 6 Jehoiada the **c** priest and said to H8031
2Ch 24:11 the officer of the **c** priest would come and H8031
2Ch 26:20 When Azariah the **c** priest and all the H8031
2Ch 31:10 Azariah the **c** priest, from the family of H8031
Ezr 7: 5 Eleazar, the son of Aaron the **c** priest— H8031
Ne 11: 9 Joel son of Zikri was their **c officer**, and H7224
Ne 11:14 Their **c officer** was Zabdiel son of H7224
Ne 11:22 The **c officer** *of* the Levites in Jerusalem H7224
Job 29: 9 the **c men** refrained from speaking and H8569
Job 29:25 chose the way for them and sat as their **c**; H8031
Isa 33:18 "Where is that **c officer**? Where is the one H6221
Jer 39: 3 Samgar, Nebo-Sarsekim a **c** officer H8042
Jer 39:13 Nebushazban a **c** officer H8042
Jer 52:24 took as prisoners Seraiah the **c** priest, H8031
Jer 52:25 who was **c officer** in charge H8569+2021+7372
Eze 38: 2 Magog, the **c** prince of Meshek and Tubal H8031
Eze 38: 3 Gog, **c** prince of Meshek and Tubal. H8031
Eze 39: 1 Gog, **c** prince of Meshek and Tubal. H8031
Da 1: 3 ordered Ashpenaz, **c** *of* his court officials H8041
Da 1: 7 The **c** official gave them new names: to H8569
Da 1: 8 he asked the **c** official for permission H8569
Da 1:11 to the guard whom the **c** official had H8569
Da 1:18 the **c** official presented them to H8569
Da 4: 9 "Belteshazzar, **c** *of* the magicians, I know A10647
Da 5:11 appointed him **c** *of* the magicians A10647
Da 10:13 Michael, one of the **c** princes, came to H8037
Mt 2: 4 all the people's **c priests** and teachers of *G797*
Mt 16:21 the **c priests** and the teachers of the law *G797*
Mt 20:18 delivered over *to* the **c priests** and the *G797*
Mt 21:15 But when the **c priests** and the teachers of *G797*
Mt 21:23 the **c priests** and the elders of the people *G797*
Mt 21:45 When the **c priests** and the Pharisees *G797*
Mt 26: 3 Then the **c priests** and the elders of the *G797*
Mt 26:14 called Judas Iscariot—went to the **c priests** *G797*
Mt 26:47 sent from the **c priests** and the elders of the *G797*
Mt 26:59 The **c priests** and the whole Sanhedrin *G797*
Mt 27: 1 all the **c priests** and the elders of the *G797*
Mt 27: 3 of silver *to* the **c priests** and the elders. *G797*
Mt 27: 6 The **c priests** picked up the coins and said *G797*
Mt 27:12 accused by the **c priests** and the elders, *G797*
Mt 27:20 But the **c priests** and the elders persuaded *G797*
Mt 27:41 In the same way the **c priests**, the teachers *G797*
Mt 27:62 the **c priests** and the Pharisees went to *G797*
Mt 28:11 reported *to* the **c priests** everything that *G797*
Mt 28:12 When the **c** priests had met with the elders NDT
Mk 8:31 the **c priests** and the teachers of the law *G797*
Mk 10:33 delivered over *to* the **c priests** and the *G797*
Mk 11:18 The **c priests** and the teachers of the law *G797*
Mk 11:27 temple courts, the **c priests**, the teachers of *G797*
Mk 12:12 Then the **c** priests, the teachers of the law NDT
Mk 14: 1 the **c priests** and the teachers of the *G797*
Mk 14:10 went to the **c priests** to betray Jesus to *G797*
Mk 14:43 sent from the **c priests**, the teachers of *G797*
Mk 14:53 and all the **c priests**, the elders and *G797*
Mk 14:55 The **c priests** and the whole Sanhedrin *G797*
Mk 15: 1 the morning, the **c priests**, with the elders, *G797*
Mk 15: 3 The **c priests** accused him of many things. *G797*
Mk 15:10 that the **c priests** had handed Jesus over *G797*
Mk 15:11 But the **c priests** stirred up the crowd to *G797*
Mk 15:31 the same way the **c priests** and the *G797*
Lk 9:22 the **c priests** and the teachers of the law *G797*
Lk 19: 2 he was a **c tax collector** and was wealthy. *G803*
Lk 19:47 But the **c priests**, the teachers of the law *G797*
Lk 20: 1 the **c priests** and the teachers of the law *G797*
Lk 20:19 the law and the **c priests** looked for a way *G797*
Lk 22: 2 the **c priests** and the teachers of the *G797*
Lk 22: 4 And Judas went *to* the **c priests** and the *G797*
Lk 22:52 Then Jesus said to the **c priests**, the officers *G797*
Lk 22:66 both the **c priests** and the teachers of the *G797*
Lk 23: 4 announced to the **c priests** and the crowd, *G797*
Lk 23:10 The **c priests** and the teachers of the law *G797*
Lk 23:13 Pilate called together the **c priests**, the *G797*
Lk 24:20 The **c priests** and our rulers handed him *G797*
Jn 7:32 Then the **c priests** and the Pharisees sent *G797*
Jn 7:45 went back to the **c priests** and the *G797*
Jn 11:47 Then the **c priests** and the Pharisees called *G797*
Jn 11:57 But the **c priests** and the Pharisees had *G797*
Jn 12:10 So the **c priests** made plans to kill Lazarus *G797*
Jn 18: 3 from the **c priests** and the Pharisees *G797*
Jn 18:35 own people and **c priests** handed you over *G797*
Jn 19: 6 As soon as the **c priests** and their officials *G797*
Jn 19:15 king but Caesar," the **c priests** answered. *G797*
Jn 19:21 The **c priests** of the Jews protested to Pilate *G797*
Ac 4:23 all that the **c priests** and the elders had *G797*
Ac 5:24 guard and the **c priests** were at a loss, *G797*
Ac 9:14 authority from the **c priests** to arrest all who *G797*
Ac 9:21 to take them as prisoners to the **c priests**?" *G797*
Ac 14:12 Hermes because he was the **c** speaker. *G2451*
Ac 19:14 of Sceva, a Jewish **c priest**, were doing this. *G797*
Ac 22:30 him and ordered the **c priests** and all the *G797*
Ac 23:14 They went to the **c priests** and the elders *G797*
Ac 25: 2 where the **c priests** and the Jewish leaders *G797*
Ac 25:15 the **c priests** and the elders of the Jews *G797*
Ac 26:10 authority of the **c priests** I put many of the *G797*
Ac 26:12 authority and commission *of* the **c priests**. *G797*
Ac 28: 7 to Publius, the **c** *official* of the island. *G4755*
Eph 2:20 Christ Jesus himself *as* the **c cornerstone**. *G214*
1Pe 5: 4 And when the **C Shepherd** appears, you will *G799*

CHIEFS (25) [CHIEF]

Ge 36:15 These were the **c** *among* Esau's H477
Ge 36:15 firstborn of Esau: **C** Teman, Omar, Zepho H477
Ge 36:16 were the **c** *descended from* Eliphaz in H477
Ge 36:17 of Esau's son Reuel: **C** Nahath, Zerah H477
Ge 36:17 were the **c** *descended from* Reuel in Edom H477
Ge 36:18 wife Oholibamah: **C** Jeush, Jalam and H477
Ge 36:18 were the **c** *descended from* Esau's wife H477
Ge 36:19 that is, Edom), and these were their **c**. H477
Ge 36:21 These sons of Seir in Edom were Horite **c**. H477
Ge 36:29 These were the Horite **c**: Lotan, Shobal H477
Ge 36:30 These were the Horite **c**, according to their H477
Ge 36:40 These were the **c** *descended from* Esau, by H477
Ge 36:43 These were the **c** *of* Edom, according to H477
Ex 15:15 The **c** *of* Edom will be terrified, the leaders H477
Jos 13:21 had defeated him and the Midianite **c**, H5954
1Ki 8: 1 of the tribes and the **c** of the Israelite H5954
1Ch 1:51 The **c** *of* Edom were: Timna, H477
1Ch 1:54 These were the **c** *of* Edom. H477
1Ch 7: 3 Joel and Ishiah. All five of them were **c**. H8031
1Ch 8:28 of families, **c** as listed in their genealogy H8031
1Ch 9:34 families, **c** as listed in their genealogy H8031
1Ch 11:10 These were the **c** *of* David's mighty H8031
1Ch 11:15 Three of the thirty **c** came down to David H8031
1Ch 12:32 Israel should do—200 **c**, with all their H8031
2Ch 5: 2 of the tribes and the **c** of the Israelite H5954

CHILD (125) [CHILD'S, CHILDHOOD, CHILDLESS, CHILDREN, CHILDREN'S, GRANDCHILDREN]

Ge 4:25 granted me another **c** in place of Abel, H2446
Ge 17:17 *Will* Sarah **bear a c** at the age of ninety?" H3528
Ge 18:13 say, '*Will I* really **have a c**, now that I H3528
Ge 21: 8 The **c** grew and was weaned, and on the H3529
Ge 38: 9 But Onan knew that the **c** would not be his; H2446
Ex 2: 2 When she saw that he was a **fine** *c*, she hid AIT
Ex 2: 3 Then she placed the **c** in it and put it H3529
Ex 2:10 When the **c** grew older, she took him to H3529
Jdg 11:34 She was an **only c**. Except for her he H3495
Ru 4:16 Then Naomi took the **c** in her arms and H3529
1Sa 1:27 I prayed for this **c**, and the LORD has H5853
2Sa 12:15 the LORD struck the **c** that Uriah's wife had H3529
2Sa 12:16 David pleaded with God for the **c**. H5853
2Sa 12:18 On the seventh day the **c** died. H3529
2Sa 12:18 afraid to tell him that the **c** was dead, H3529
2Sa 12:18 thought, "While the **c** was still living, he H3529
2Sa 12:18 How can we now tell him the **c** is dead H3529
2Sa 12:19 he realized the **c** was dead. H3529
2Sa 12:19 "Is the **c** dead?" he asked. H3529
2Sa 12:21 While the **c** was alive, you fasted and H3529
2Sa 12:21 now that the **c** is dead, you get up H3529
2Sa 12:22 answered, "While the **c** was still alive, H3529
2Sa 12:22 may be gracious to me and let the **c** live. H3529
1Ki 3: 7 I am only a little **c** and do not know how H5853
1Ki 3:18 The third day after my **c was born**, this H3528
1Ki 3:25 "Cut the living **c** in two and give half to H3529
1Ki 17:23 Elijah picked up the **c** and carried him H3529
2Ki 4:18 The **c** grew, and one day he went out to H3529
2Ki 4:26 husband all right? Is your **c** all right?' " H3529
2Ch 22:11 she hid **the c** from Athaliah so she could H2084S
Job 3:16 away in the ground like a **stillborn c**, H5878
Job 24: 9 The **fatherless c** is snatched from the H3846
Ps 58: 8 like a **stillborn c** that never sees the H5878+851
Ps 131: 2 I am like a **weaned** *c* with its mother AIT
Ps 131: 2 its mother; like a **weaned** *c* I am content. AIT
Pr 17:21 *To* **have a** fool *for a* **c** brings grief; there is H3528
Pr 19:13 A foolish **c** is a father's ruin, and a H1201
Pr 19:26 their mother is a **c** who brings shame and H1201
Pr 22:15 Folly is bound up in the heart of a **c**, but H5853
Pr 23:13 Do not withhold discipline from a **c**; if you H5853
Pr 23:24 The father of a **righteous** *c* has great joy; AIT
Pr 29:15 a **c** left undisciplined disgraces its H5853
Ecc 6: 3 I say that a **stillborn c** is better off than he. H5878
Isa 9: 6 For to us a **c** is born, to us a son is given H3529
Isa 10:19 be so few that a **c** could write them down H5853
Isa 11: 6 together; and a little **c** will lead them. H5853
Isa 11: 8 the **young c** will put its hand into the H1694
Isa 26:18 *We were* **with c**, we writhed in labor, but H2225
Isa 49:15 no compassion on the **c** she has borne? H1201
Isa 54: 1 woman, *you who* never **bore a c**; burst H3528
Isa 65:20 at a hundred will be thought a *mere* **c**; H5853
Isa 66:13 As a mother comforts her **c**, so will I H408
Jer 4:31 a groan as of *one* **bearing** *her* **first c**—the H1144
Jer 20:15 saying, "A **c** is born to you—a son! H1201
Jer 31:20 my dear son, the **c** *in whom* I delight? H3529
Eze 18: 4 the parent as well as the **c**—both alike H1201
Eze 18:20 The **c** will not share the guilt of the parent H1201
Eze 18:20 will the parent share the guilt of the **c**. H1201
Hos 11: 1 "When Israel was a **c**, I loved him, and H5853
Hos 11: 4 like one who lifts a **little c** to the cheek, H6403
Hos 13:13 but he is a **c** without wisdom H1201
Zec 12:10 him as one mourns for an **only c**, H3495
Mt 2: 8 "Go and search carefully for the **c**. *G4086*
Mt 2: 9 it stopped over the place where the **c** was. *G4086*
Mt 2:11 they saw the **c** with his mother Mary *G4086*
Mt 2:13 "take the **c** and his mother and escape to *G4086*
Mt 2:13 is going to search for the **c** to kill him." *G4086*
Mt 2:14 took the **c** and his mother during the night *G4086*
Mt 2:20 take the **c** and his mother and go to the *G4086*
Mt 2:21 took the **c** and his mother and went to the *G4086*
Mt 10:21 a father his **c**; children will rebel *G5451*
Mt 18: 2 He called a **little c** to him, and placed the *G4086*
Mt 18: 2 and placed **the c** among them. *G899S*
Mt 18: 4 position of this **c** is the greatest in the *G4086*
Mt 18: 5 welcomes one such **c** in my name *G4086*
Mt 23:15 them twice as much a **c** of hell as you are. *G5626*
Mk 5:39 The **c** is not dead but asleep. *G4086*
Mk 5:40 with him, and went in where the **c** was. *G4086*
Mk 7:30 home and found her **c** lying on the bed, *G4086*
Mk 9:36 He took a **little c** whom he placed among *G4086*
Mk 9:36 among them. Taking **the c** in his arms, he *G899S*
Mk 10:15 of God like a **little c** will never enter it." *G4086*
Mk 12:21 the widow, but he also died, leaving no **c**. *G5065*
Mk 13:12 betray brother to death, and a father his **c**. *G5451*
Lk 1:36 is going to have a **c** in her old age, *G5626*
Lk 1:42 is the **c** you will **bear**! *G2843+3836+3120*
Lk 1:59 eighth day they came to circumcise the **c**, *G4086*
Lk 1:62 out what he would like to name **the c**. *G899S*
Lk 1:66 "What then is this **c** going to be? *G4086*
Lk 1:76 And you, my **c**, will be called a prophet of *G4086*
Lk 1:80 And the **c** grew and became strong in *G4086*
Lk 2: 5 be married to him and was **expecting a c**. *G1607*
Lk 2:17 what had been told them about this **c**, *G4086*
Lk 2:21 when it was time to circumcise **the c**, he *G899S*
Lk 2:27 brought in the **c** Jesus to do for him *G4086*
Lk 2:34 "**This** *c* is destined to cause the falling and AIT
Lk 2:38 spoke about **the c** to all who were *G899S*
Lk 2:40 And the **c** grew and became strong; he *G4086*
Lk 8:54 her by the hand and said, "My **c**, get up!" *G4090*
Lk 9:38 you to look at my son, for he is my **only c**. *G3666*
Lk 9:47 took a **little c** and had him stand beside *G4086*
Lk 9:48 welcomes this **little c** in my name *G4086*
Lk 14: 5 "If one of you has a **c** or an ox that falls *G5626*
Lk 18:17 of God like a **little c** will never enter it." *G4086*
Jn 4:49 "Sir, come down before my **c** dies. *G4086*
Jn 16:21 A woman **giving birth to a c** has pain *G5503*
Jn 16:21 of her joy that a **c** is born into the world. *G476*
Ac 7: 5 though at that time Abraham had no **c**. *G5451*
Ac 7:20 Moses was born, and he was **no ordinary** *c*. AIT
Ac 13:10 "*You* are a **c** of the devil and an enemy of *G5626*
Ac 26: 4 the way I have lived ever since I was a **c**, *G3744*
1Co 13:11 When I was a **c**, I talked like a child, *G3758*
1Co 13:11 I talked like a **c**, I thought like a *G3758*
1Co 13:11 I thought like a **c**, I reasoned like a *G3758*
1Co 13:11 I thought like a child, I reasoned like a **c**. *G3758*
Gal 4: 7 a slave, but God's **c**; and since you are his *G5626*
Gal 4: 7 since you are his **c**, God has made *G5626*
Gal 4:27 woman, you *who* never **bore a c**; shout *G5503*
Heb 11:23 because they saw he was no ordinary **c** *G4086*
1Jn 3:10 does not do what is right is not God's **c**, *G1666S*
1Jn 5: 1 who loves the father loves his **c** as well. *G1164*
Rev 12: 4 it might devour her **c** the moment he was *G5451*
Rev 12: 5 birth to a son, a **male** *c*, who "will rule all AIT
Rev 12: 5 And her **c** was snatched up to God and to *G5451*
Rev 12:13 woman who had given birth *to* the **male** *c*. AIT

CHILD'S (6) [CHILD]

2Ki 4:30 But the **c** mother said, "As surely as the H5853
Job 33:25 let their flesh be renewed like a **c**; let H5854
Mt 2:20 were trying to take the **c** life are dead." *G4086*
Mk 5:40 he took the **c** father and mother and the *G4086*
Lk 2:33 **The c** father and mother marveled at what *G899S*
Lk 8:51 James, and the **c** father and mother. *G4090*

CHILDBEARING (4) [BEAR]

Ge 3:16 "I will make your pains in **c** very severe H2228
Ge 18:11 was past the **age of c**. H784+3869+2021+851
1Ti 2:15 But women will be saved through **c**—if *G5450*
Heb 11:11 who was past **c age**, was enabled *G2789+2461*

CHILDBIRTH (6) [BEAR]

Ge 35:17 And as she was having great difficulty in **c** H3528
Ex 1:16 *are* **helping** the Hebrew women **during c** H3528
Isa 42:14 But now, like a *woman* **in c**, I cry out, H3528
Hos 13:13 Pains as of a *woman* **in c** come to him H3528
Ro 8:22 groaning *as* **in the pains of c** right up to *G5349*
Gal 4:19 whom *I am* again **in the pains of c** until *G6048*

CHILDHOOD (5) [CHILD]

Ge 8:21 of the human heart is evil from **c**. H5830
Isa 47:12 which you have labored at since **c**. H5830
Isa 47:15 have dealt with and labored with since **c**. H5830
Mk 9:21 been like this?" "From **c**," he answered. *G4085*
1Co 13:11 I put the ways *of* **c** behind me. *G3758*

CHILDLESS (22) [CHILD]

Ge 11:30 Now Sarai was **c** because she was not H6829
Ge 15: 2 me since I remain **c** and the one who will H6884
Ge 25:21 on behalf of his wife, because she was **c**. H6829
Ge 29:31 her to conceive, but Rachel remained **c**. H6829
Lev 20:20 will be held responsible; they will die **c**. H6884
Lev 20:21 dishonored his brother. They will be **c**. H6884
Dt 7:14 none of your *men* or *women* will be **c**, nor H6829
Dt 32:25 In the street the sword *will* **make** them **c** H8897
Jdg 13: 2 had a wife who was **c**, unable to give H6829
Jdg 13: 3 "You are barren and **c**, but you are H4202+3528
1Sa 15:33 "As your sword *has* **made** women **c**, so H8897
1Sa 15:33 so *will* your mother *be* **c** among women." H8897
Job 24:21 prey on the barren and **c** *woman*, H4202+3528
Ps 113: 9 He settles the **c** *woman* in her home as a H6829
Jer 18:21 Let their wives be made **c** and widows; let H8891
Jer 22:30 "Record this man as if **c**, a man who will H6884

C

Eze 5:17 against you, and *they will* **leave** you **c**. H8897
Eze 14:15 country and *they* **leave** it **c** and it becomes H8897
Eze 36:14 devour people or **make** your nation **c**, H8897
Lk 1: 7 But they were **c** because Elizabeth *G4024+5451*
Lk 20:29 The first one married a woman and died **c**. *G866*
Lk 23:29 'Blessed are the **c women**, the wombs *G5096*

CHILDREN (486) [CHILD]

Ge 3:16 with painful labor you will give birth to **c**. H1201
Ge 6: 4 daughters of humans and **had c** by them. H3528
Ge 15: 3 "You have given me no **c**; so a servant in H2446
Ge 16: 1 Abram's wife, *had* **borne** him no **c**. H3528
Ge 16: 2 "The LORD has kept me from **having c**. H3528
Ge 18:19 he will direct his **c** and his household H1201
Ge 19:31 no man around here to **give us c**— H995+6584
Ge 20:17 female slaves so *they could* **have c** again, H3528
Ge 21: 7 to Abraham that Sarah would nurse **c**? H1201
Ge 21:23 with me or my **c** or my descendants. H5769
Ge 29:35 Then she stopped **having c**. H3528
Ge 30: 1 saw that *she was* not **bearing** Jacob any **c**, H3528
Ge 30: 1 she said to Jacob, "Give me **c**, or I'll die!" H1201
Ge 30: 2 who has kept you from *having* **c**?" H7262+1061
Ge 30: 3 her so that *she can* **bear c** for me and I H3528
Ge 30: 9 Leah saw that she had stopped **having c**, H3528
Ge 30:26 Give me my wives and **c**, for whom I have H3529
Ge 31:16 from our father belongs to us and our **c**. H1201
Ge 31:17 Then Jacob put his **c** and his wives on H1201
Ge 31:43 my daughters, the **c** are my children, and H1201
Ge 31:43 the children are my **c**, and the flocks are H1201
Ge 31:43 of mine, or about the **c** they have borne? H1201
Ge 32:11 and also the mothers with their **c**. H1201
Ge 33: 1 so he divided the **c** among Leah, Rachel H3529
Ge 33: 2 the female servants and their **c** in front, H3529
Ge 33: 2 Leah and her **c** next, and Rachel H3529
Ge 33: 5 looked up and saw the women and **c**. H3529
Ge 33: 5 "They are the **c** God has graciously given H3529
Ge 33: 6 servants and their **c** approached and H3529
Ge 33: 7 Leah and her **c** came and bowed down. H3529
Ge 33:13 lord knows that the **c** are tender and that I H3529
Ge 33:14 herds before me and the pace of the **c**, H3529
Ge 34:29 their wealth and all their women and **c**, H3251
Ge 36:25 The **c** *of* Anah: Dishon and Oholibamah H1201
Ge 42:36 to them, "*You have* **deprived** me of my **c**. H8897
Ge 43: 8 we and you and our **c** may live and not H3251
Ge 45:10 your **c** and grandchildren, your flocks H1201
Ge 45:19 carts from Egypt for your **c** and your wives, H3251
Ge 46: 5 Jacob and their **c** and their wives in the H3251
Ge 46:18 These were the **c** born to Jacob *by* Zilpah H1201
Ge 47:12 according to the number of their **c**. H3251
Ge 47:24 your households and your **c**." H3251
Ge 48: 6 Any **c** born to you after them will be yours H4580
Ge 48:11 God has allowed me to see your **c** too." H2446
Ge 50: 8 Only their **c** and their flocks and herds H3251
Ge 50:21 I will provide for you and your **c**." And he H3251
Ge 50:23 saw the third generation of Ephraim's **c**. H1201
Ge 50:23 Also the **c** *of* Makir son of Manasseh were H1201
Ex 10: 2 you may tell your **c** and grandchildren H1201
Ex 10:10 let you go, along with your **women and c**! H3251
Ex 10:24 Even your **women and c** may go with you H3251
Ex 12:26 And when your **c** ask you, 'What does this H1201
Ex 12:37 men on foot, besides **women and c**. H3251
Ex 17: 3 to make us and our **c** and livestock die of H1201
Ex 20: 5 punishing the **c** for the sin of the parents H1201
Ex 21: 4 the woman and her **c** shall belong to her H3529
Ex 21: 5 my wife and **c** and do not want to go H1201
Ex 22:24 will become widows and your **c** fatherless. H1201
Ex 34: 7 he punishes the **c** and their children for H1201
Ex 34: 7 the children and their **c** for the sin of the H1201
Lev 10:14 to you and your **c** as your share of the H1201
Lev 10:15 be the perpetual share for you and your **c**, H1201
Lev 18:21 not give any of your **c** to be sacrificed to H2446
Lev 20: 2 sacrifices any of his **c** to Molek is to be put H2446
Lev 20: 3 by sacrificing his **c** to Molek, he has H2446
Lev 20: 4 sacrifices one of his **c** to Molek and if they H2446
Lev 22:13 divorced, yet has no **c**, and she returns to H2446
Lev 25:41 Then they and their **c** are to be released H1201
Lev 25:46 them to your **c** as inherited property H1201
Lev 25:54 they and their **c** are to be released in the H1201
Lev 26:22 and *they will* **rob** you of your **c** H8897
Nu 5:28 of guilt and *will* **be able to have c**. H2445+2446
Nu 14: 3 Our wives and **c** will be taken as plunder H3251
Nu 14:18 he punishes the **c** for the sin of the H1201
Nu 14:31 As for your **c** that you said would be taken H3251
Nu 14:33 Your **c** will be shepherds here for forty H1201
Nu 16:27 **c** and little ones at the entrances to their H1201
Nu 31: 9 Midianite women and **c** and took all the H3251
Nu 32:16 livestock and cities for our **women and c**. H3251
Nu 32:17 Meanwhile our **women and c** will live in H3251
Nu 32:24 Build cities for your **women and c**, and H3251
Nu 32:26 Our **c** and wives, our flocks and herds will H3251
Dt 1:39 your **c** who do not yet know good from H1201
Dt 2:34 destroyed them—men, women and **c**. H3251
Dt 3: 6 destroying every city—men, women and **c**. H3251
Dt 3:19 your wives, your **c** and your livestock (I H3251
Dt 4: 9 Teach them to your **c** and to their children H1201
Dt 4: 9 to your children and to their **c** after them. H1201
Dt 4:10 in the land and may teach them to their **c**." H1201
Dt 4:25 After you have had **c** and grandchildren H1201
Dt 4:40 with you and your **c** after you and that you H1201
Dt 5: 9 punishing the **c** for the sin of the parents H1201
Dt 5:29 go well with them and their **c** forever! H1201
Dt 6: 2 your **c** and their children after them may H1201
Dt 6: 2 children and their **c** after them may fear H1201
Dt 6: 7 Impress them on your **c**. Talk about them H1201
Dt 7: 4 they will turn your **c** away from following H1201
Dt 11: 2 today that your **c** were not the ones who H1201
Dt 11: 5 It was not your **c** who saw what he did for NDT
Dt 11:19 Teach them to your **c**, talking about them H1201
Dt 11:21 the days of your **c** may be many in the H1201
Dt 12:25 may go well with you and your **c** after you, H1201
Dt 12:28 go well with you and your **c** after you, H1201
Dt 14: 1 You are the **c** of the LORD your God. Do not H1201
Dt 20:14 As for the women, the **c**, the livestock and H3251
Dt 23: 8 third generation of **c** born to them may H1201
Dt 24:16 are not to be put to death for their **c**, H1201
Dt 24:16 **c** put to death for their parents H1201
Dt 28:54 the wife he loves or his surviving **c**, H1201
Dt 28:55 any of the flesh of his **c** that he is eating. H1201
Dt 28:57 from her womb and the **c** she bears. H1201
Dt 29:11 together with your **c** and your wives, and H3251
Dt 29:22 Your **c** who follow you in later generations H1201
Dt 29:29 belong to us and to our **c** forever, H1201
Dt 30: 2 when you and your **c** return to the LORD H1201
Dt 30:19 so that you and your **c** may live H2446
Dt 31:12 women and **c**, and the foreigners H3251
Dt 31:13 Their **c**, who do not know this law, must H1201
Dt 32: 5 They are corrupt and not his **c**; to their H1201
Dt 32:20 perverse generation, **c** who are unfaithful. H1201
Dt 32:46 may command your **c** to obey carefully H1201
Dt 33: 9 his brothers or acknowledge his own **c**, H1201
Jos 1:14 your **c** and your livestock may stay in the H3251
Jos 4: 6 the future, when your **c** ask you, 'What do H1201
Jos 8:35 including the women and **c**, and the H3251
Jos 14: 9 your inheritance and that of your **c** forever, H1201
Jdg 18:21 Putting their **little c**, their livestock and H3251
Jdg 21:10 living there, including the women and **c**. H3251
1Sa 1: 2 Peninnah had **c**, but Hannah had none. H3529
1Sa 2: 5 She who was barren *has* **borne** seven **c** H3528
1Sa 2:20 the LORD give you **c** by this woman to take H2446
1Sa 15: 3 men and women, **c** and infants, cattle H6407
1Sa 22:19 men and women, its **c** and infants, and its H6407
1Sa 30:22 each man may take his wife and **c** and go." H1201
2Sa 5:14 are the names of the **c born** to him there: H3533
2Sa 6:23 of Saul had no **c** to the day of her death H3529
2Sa 12: 3 and it grew up with him and his **c**. H1201
1Ki 11:20 Genubath lived with Pharaoh's own **c**. H1201
1Ki 20: 3 the best of your wives and **c** are mine. H1201
1Ki 20: 5 silver and gold, your wives and your **c**. H1201
1Ki 20: 7 When he sent for my wives and my **c**, my H1201
2Ki 8:12 dash their **little c** to the ground H6407
2Ki 10: 1 elders and to the **guardians of** Ahab's **c**. H587
2Ki 14: 6 Yet he did not put the **c** *of* the assassins to H1201
2Ki 14: 6 are not to be put to death for their **c**, H1201
2Ki 14: 6 **c** put to death for their parents H1201
2Ki 17:31 Sepharvites burned their **c** in the fire as H1201
2Ki 17:41 To this day their **c** and grandchildren H1201
2Ki 19: 3 as when **c** come to the moment of birth H1201
1Ch 2:18 son of Hezron **had c** by his wife Azubah H3528
1Ch 2:30 Seled and Appaim. Seled died without **c**. H1201
1Ch 2:32 Jonathan. Jether died without **c**. H1201
1Ch 3: 5 these were *the* **c born** to him there AIT
1Ch 4:18 These were the **c** *of* Pharaoh's daughter H1201
1Ch 4:27 his brothers did not have many **c**; so H1201
1Ch 6: 3 The **c** *of* Amram: Aaron, Moses and H1201
1Ch 7: 4 battle, for they had many wives and **c**. H1201
1Ch 14: 4 are the names of the **c born** to him there: H3528
1Ch 16:13 of Israel, his chosen ones, the **c** *of* Jacob. H1201
2Ch 20:13 with their wives and **c** and little ones H1201
2Ch 25: 4 Yet he did not put their **c** to death, but H1201
2Ch 25: 4 shall not be put to death for their **c**, H1201
2Ch 25: 4 **c** be put to death for their parents H1201
2Ch 28: 3 Hinnom and sacrificed his **c** in the fire, H1201
2Ch 30: 9 Israelites and your **c** will be shown H1201
2Ch 33: 6 He sacrificed his **c** in the fire in the Valley H1201
Ezr 8:21 him for a safe journey for us and our **c**, H3251
Ezr 9:12 leave it to your **c** as an everlasting H1201
Ezr 10: 1 women and **c**—gathered around him H3529
Ezr 10: 3 send away all these women and their **c**, H3528
Ezr 10:44 some of them had **c** by these wives. H1201
Ne 5: 5 Jews and though our **c** are as good as H1201
Ne 9:23 You made their **c** as numerous as the H1201
Ne 9:24 Their **c** went in and took possession of the H1201
Ne 12:43 The women and **c** also rejoiced. H3529
Ne 13:24 Half of their **c** spoke the language of H1201
Est 3:13 old, women and **c**—on a single day, H3251
Est 8:11 attack them and their women and **c**, H3251
Job 1: 5 "Perhaps my **c** have sinned and cursed H1201
Job 5: 4 His **c** are far from safety, crushed in court H1201
Job 5:25 You will know that your **c** will be many H2446
Job 8: 4 When your **c** sinned against him, he gave H1201
Job 14:21 If their **c** are honored, they do not know it H1201
Job 17: 5 reward, the eyes of their **c** will fail. H1201
Job 20:10 His **c** must make amends to the poor; his H1201
Job 21: 8 They see their **c** established around them H2446
Job 21:11 They send forth their **c** as a flock; their H6396
Job 21:19 the punishment of the wicked for their **c**. H1201
Job 24: 5 the wasteland provides food for their **c**. H5853
Job 27:14 However many his **c**, their fate is the H1201
Job 29: 5 still with me and my **c** were around me, H5853
Job 42:16 he saw his **c** and their children to the H1201
Job 42:16 his children and their **c** to the fourth H1201
Ps 8: 2 the praise of **c** and infants you have H6407
Ps 17:14 may their **c** gorge themselves on it H1201
Ps 34:11 my **c**, listen to me; I will teach you H1201
Ps 37:25 forsaken or their **c** begging bread. H2446
Ps 37:26 lend freely; their **c** will be a blessing. H2446
Ps 69: 8 a stranger to my own mother's **c**; H1201
Ps 69:36 the **c** *of* his servants will inherit it, and H2446
Ps 72: 4 the people and save the **c** *of* the needy; H1201
Ps 73:15 I would have betrayed your **c**. H1887+1201
Ps 78: 5 our ancestors to teach their **c**, H1201
Ps 78: 6 know them, even the **c** yet to be born, and H1201
Ps 78: 6 and they in turn would tell their **c**. H1201
Ps 90:16 to your servants, your splendor to their **c**. H1201
Ps 102:28 The **c** *of* your servants will live in your H1201
Ps 103:13 As a father has compassion on his **c**, so H1201
Ps 103:17 his righteousness with their children's **c**— H1201
Ps 105: 6 his chosen ones, the **c** *of* Jacob. H1201
Ps 109: 9 May his **c** be fatherless and his wife a H1201
Ps 109:10 May his **c** be wandering beggars; may H1201
Ps 109:12 to him or take pity on his **fatherless c**. H3846
Ps 112: 2 Their **c** will be mighty in the land; the H2446
Ps 113: 9 in her home as a happy mother of **c**. H1201
Ps 115:14 cause you to flourish, both you and your **c**. H1201
Ps 127: 3 **C** are a heritage from the LORD, offspring a H1201
Ps 127: 4 of a warrior are **c** *born in* one's youth. H1201
Ps 128: 3 your **c** will be like olive shoots around H1201
Ps 128: 6 May you live to see your children's **c** H1201
Ps 148:12 young men and women, old men and **c**. H5853
Pr 8:32 "Now then, my **c**, listen to me; blessed H1201
Pr 13:22 an inheritance for their children's **c**, H1201
Pr 13:24 Whoever spares the rod hates their **c**, but H1201
Pr 13:24 the one who loves **their c** is careful to H2257S
Pr 14:26 fortress, and for their **c** it will be a refuge. H1201
Pr 17: 6 Children's **c** are a crown to the aged, and H1201
Pr 17: 6 and parents are the pride of their **c**. H1201
Pr 19:18 Discipline your **c**, for in that there is hope H1201
Pr 20: 7 blessed are their **c** after them. H1201
Pr 20:11 Even **small c** are known by their actions H5853
Pr 22: 6 Start **c** off on the way they should go, and H5853
Pr 29:17 Discipline your **c**, and they will give you H1201
Pr 31:28 Her **c** arise and call her blessed; her H1201
Ecc 5:14 that when they have **c** there is nothing left H1201
Ecc 6: 3 A man *may* **have** a hundred **c** and live H3528
Isa 1: 2 "I reared **c** and brought them up, but they H1201
Isa 1: 4 a brood of evildoers, **c** given to corruption! H1201
Isa 3: 4 their officials; **c** will rule over them." H9500
Isa 8:18 and the **c** the LORD has given me. H3529
Isa 13:18 will they look with compassion on **c**. H1201
Isa 14:21 to slaughter his **c** for the sins of their H1201
Isa 28: 9 To *c* **weaned** from their milk, to those just AIT
Isa 29:23 When they see among them their **c**, the H3529
Isa 30: 1 "Woe to the obstinate **c**," declares the H1201
Isa 30: 9 people, deceitful **c**, children unwilling to H1201
Isa 30: 9 **c** unwilling to listen to the LORD's H1201
Isa 37: 3 as when **c** come to the moment of birth H1201
Isa 38:19 parents tell their **c** about your faithfulness. H1201
Isa 43: 5 I will bring your **c** from the east and H2446
Isa 45:11 do you question me about my **c**, or give H1201
Isa 47: 8 never be a widow or suffer the **loss of c**. H8890
Isa 47: 9 on a single day: **loss of c** and widowhood H8890
Isa 48:19 your **c** like its numberless grains H7368+5055
Isa 49:17 Your **c** hasten back, and those who laid H1201
Isa 49:18 all **your c** gather and come to you. H4392S
Isa 49:20 The **c** *born during* your bereavement will H1201
Isa 49:25 contend with you, and your **c** I will save. H1201
Isa 51:18 Among all the **c** she bore there was none H1201
Isa 51:18 among all the **c** she reared there was H1201
Isa 51:20 Your **c** have fainted; they lie at every H1201
Isa 54: 1 more are the **c** *of* the desolate woman H1201
Isa 54:13 All your **c** will be taught by the LORD, and H1201
Isa 57: 3 come here, you **c** *of* a sorceress, you H1201
Isa 57: 5 you sacrifice your **c** in the ravines and H3529
Isa 59:21 on the lips of your **c** and on the lips of H2446
Isa 60: 9 bringing your **c** from afar, with their H1201
Isa 60:14 The **c** *of* your oppressors will come H1201
Isa 63: 8 are my people, **c** who will be true to me"; H1201
Isa 65:23 nor *will they* **bear** doomed to misfortune; H3528
Isa 66: 8 Zion in labor than she gives birth to her **c**. H1201
Jer 2: 9 bring charges against your children's **c**. H1201
Jer 3:19 I treat you like my **c** and give you a H1201
Jer 4:22 They are senseless **c**; they have no H1201
Jer 5: 7 Your **c** have forsaken me and sworn by H1201
Jer 6:11 "Pour it out on the **c** in the street and on H6408
Jer 6:21 Parents and **c** alike will stumble over H1201
Jer 7:18 The **c** gather wood, the fathers light the H1201
Jer 9:21 it has removed the **c** from the streets and H6408
Jer 10:20 My **c** are gone from me and are no more H1201
Jer 13:14 parents and **c** alike, declares the H1201
Jer 17: 2 Even their **c** remember their altars and H1201
Jer 18:21 So give their **c** over to famine; hand them H1201
Jer 19: 5 of Baal to burn their **c** in the fire as H1201
Jer 22:28 Why will he and his **c** be hurled out, cast H2446
Jer 30: 6 *Can* a man **bear c**? Then why do H3528
Jer 30:20 Their **c** will be as in days of old, and their H1201
Jer 31:15 weeping for her **c** and refusing to be H1201
Jer 31:17 "Your **c** will return to their own land H1201
Jer 32:18 sins into the laps of their **c** after them. H1201
Jer 32:39 well for them and for their **c** after them. H1201
Jer 36:31 punish him and his **c** and his attendants H2446
Jer 38:23 "All your wives and **c** will be brought out H1201
Jer 40: 7 women and **c** who were the poorest in the H3251
Jer 41:16 **c** and court officials he had recovered H3251
Jer 43: 6 women, the **c** and the king's daughters. H3251
Jer 44: 7 men and women, the **c** and infants, and H6407
Jer 47: 3 Parents will not turn to help their **c**; their H1201

Jer 49:11 'Leave your **fatherless c**; I will keep them H3846
La 1: 5 Her c have gone into exile, captive before H6408
La 1:16 My c are destitute because the enemy has H1201
La 2:11 because c and infants faint in the streets H6407
La 2:19 your hands to him for the lives of your c, H6408
La 2:20 their offspring, the c they have cared for? H6407
La 4: 2 How the precious c *of* Zion, once worth H1201
La 4: 4 of its mouth; the c beg for bread, but no H6408
La 4:10 women have cooked their own c, H3529
Eze 5:10 in your midst parents will eat their c, H1201
Eze 5:10 their children, and c will eat their parents. H1201
Eze 9: 6 the mothers and c, but do not touch H3251
Eze 16:21 You slaughtered my c and sacrificed them H1201
Eze 16:45 who despised her husband and her c; and H1201
Eze 16:45 who despised their husbands and their c. H1201
Eze 20:18 I said to their c in the wilderness, "Do not H1201
Eze 20:21 " 'But the c rebelled against me: They did H1201
Eze 20:31 the sacrifice of your c in the fire—you H1201
Eze 23:37 they even sacrificed their c, whom they H1201
Eze 23:39 day they sacrificed their c to their idols, H1201
Eze 36:12 will never again **deprive** them of their c. H8897
Eze 36:13 people and **deprive** your nation of *its* c," H8897
Eze 37:25 They and their c and their children's H1201
Eze 37:25 their children's c will live there H1201
Eze 47:22 residing among you and who have c. H1201
Da 6:24 lions' den, along with their wives and c. A10120
Hos 1: 2 promiscuous woman and have c *with* her, H3529
Hos 1:10 they will be called 'c *of* the living God. H1201
Hos 2: 4 I will not show my love to her c, because H1201
Hos 2: 4 because they are the c *of* adultery. H1201
Hos 4: 6 law of your God, I also will ignore your c. H1201
Hos 5: 7 the LORD; they give birth to illegitimate c. H1201
Hos 9:12 Even if they rear c, I will bereave them of H1201
Hos 9:13 will bring out their c to the slayer. H1201
Hos 9:16 Even if *they* **bear** c, I will slay their H3528
Hos 10:14 were dashed to the ground with their c. H1201
Hos 11:10 his c will come trembling from the west. H1201
Joel 1: 3 Tell it to your c, and let your children tell H1201
Joel 1: 3 let your c tell it to their children H1201
Joel 1: 3 let your children tell it to their c, and H1201
Joel 1: 3 their c to the next generation. H1201
Joel 2:16 gather the c, those nursing at the H6408
Am 2:11 from among your c and Nazirites from H1201
Mic 1:16 mourning for the c *in whom* you delight; H1201
Mic 2: 9 away my blessing from their c forever. H6408
Zec 10: 7 Their c will see it and be joyful; their H1201
Zec 10: 9 They and their c will survive, and they will H1201
Mal 4: 6 turn the hearts of the parents to their c, H1201
Mal 4: 6 the hearts of the c to their parents; or H1201
Mt 2:18 Rachel weeping *for* her c and refusing to *G5451*
Mt 3: 9 stones God can raise up c for Abraham. *G5451*
Mt 5: 9 they will be called c of God. *G5626*
Mt 5:45 that you may be c of your Father in heaven. *G5626*
Mt 7:11 know how to give good gifts *to* your c *G5451*
Mt 10:21 c will rebel against their parents and have *G5451*
Mt 11:16 They are like c sitting in the marketplaces *G4086*
Mt 11:25 learned, and revealed them *to* **little** c. *G3758*
Mt 14:21 thousand men, besides women and c. *G4086*
Mt 15:38 thousand men, besides women and c. *G4086*
Mt 17:25 from their own c or from others? *G5626*
Mt 17:26 "Then the c are exempt," Jesus said to *G5626*
Mt 18: 3 you change and become like **little** c, *G4086*
Mt 18:25 his wife and his c and all that he had *G5451*
Mt 19:13 people brought **little** c to Jesus for him *G4086*
Mt 19:14 "Let the **little** c come to me, and do *G4086*
Mt 19:29 mother or wife or c or fields for my sake *G5451*
Mt 21:15 things he did and the c shouting in the *G4090*
Mt 21:16 "Do you hear what these c are saying?" NDT
Mt 21:16 " 'From the lips *of* c and infants you, Lord *G3758*
Mt 22:24 us that if a man dies without having c, *G5451*
Mt 22:25 since he had no c, he left his wife to *G5065*
Mt 23:37 I have longed to gather your c together, *G5451*
Mt 27:25 "His blood is on us and on our c! *G5451*
Mk 7:27 "First let the c eat all they want," he told *G5451*
Mk 9:37 one of these **little** c in my name *G4086*
Mk 10:13 were bringing **little** c to Jesus for him to *G4086*
Mk 10:14 to them, "Let the **little** c come to me, and *G4086*
Mk 10:16 And he took the c in his arms, placed his NDT
Mk 10:24 But Jesus said again, "C, how hard it is to *G5451*
Mk 10:29 mother or father or c or fields for me and *G5451*
Mk 10:30 mothers, c and fields—along with *G5451*
Mk 12:19 brother dies and leaves a wife but no c, *G5451*
Mk 12:20 married and died without leaving *any* c. *G5065*
Mk 12:22 none of the seven left *any* c. Last of all, *G5065*
Mk 13:12 C will rebel against their parents and *G5451*
Lk 1:17 the parents to their c and the disobedient *G5451*
Lk 3: 8 stones God can raise up c for Abraham. *G5451*
Lk 6:35 and you will be c of the Most High *G5626*
Lk 7:32 They are like c sitting in the marketplace *G4086*
Lk 7:35 But wisdom is proved right by all her c." *G5451*
Lk 10:21 learned, and revealed them *to* **little** c. *G3758*
Lk 11: 7 already locked, and my c and I are in bed. *G4086*
Lk 11:13 know how to give good gifts *to* your c *G5451*
Lk 13:34 I have longed to gather your c together, *G5451*
Lk 14:26 mother, wife and c, brothers and *G5451*
Lk 18:16 But Jesus called **the** c to him and said *G899S*
Lk 18:16 said, "Let the **little** c come to me, and *G4086*
Lk 18:29 sisters or parents or c for the sake of the *G5451*
Lk 19:44 ground, you and the c within your walls. *G5451*
Lk 20:28 brother dies and leaves a wife but **no** c, *G866*
Lk 20:31 same way the seven died, leaving no c. *G5451*
Lk 20:36 They are God's c, since they are children *G5626*
Lk 20:36 since they are c of the resurrection. *G5626*
Lk 23:28 me; weep for yourselves and for your c. *G5451*
Jn 1:12 he gave the right to become c of God— *G5451*
Jn 1:13 c born not of natural descent, nor of *G4005S*
Jn 8:39 "If you were Abraham's c," said Jesus *G5451*
Jn 8:41 "We *are* not illegitimate c," they *G1164*
Jn 11:52 nation but also for the scattered c of God, *G5451*
Jn 12:36 so that you may become c of light. *G5626*
Jn 13:33 "My c, I will be with you only a little *G5448*
Ac 2:39 is for you and your c and for all who are *G5451*
Ac 13:26 "Fellow c of Abraham and you *G5626+1169*
Ac 13:33 fulfilled for us, their c, by raising up Jesus. *G5451*
Ac 21: 5 including wives and c, accompanied us *G5451*
Ac 21:21 to circumcise their c or live according to *G5451*
Ro 2:20 a teacher *of* **little** c, because you have *G3758*
Ro 8:14 led by the Spirit of God are the c of God. *G5626*
Ro 8:16 with our spirit that we are God's c. *G5451*
Ro 8:17 Now if we are c, then we are heirs—heirs *G5451*
Ro 8:19 eager expectation *for* the c of God to be *G5626*
Ro 8:21 the freedom and glory *of* the c of God. *G5451*
Ro 9: 7 his descendants are they all Abraham's c. *G5451*
Ro 9: 8 it is not the c by physical descent who are *G5451*
Ro 9: 8 by physical descent who are God's c, *G5451*
Ro 9: 8 it is the c of the promise who are *G5451*
Ro 9:10 c *were* **conceived at the same time** *G1666+1651+3130+2400*
Ro 9:26 they will be called 'c of the living God. *G5626*
1Co 4:14 shame you but to warn you as my dear c. *G5451*
1Co 7:14 Otherwise your c would be unclean, but *G5451*
1Co 14:20 stop thinking *like* c. In regard to evil be *G4086*
2Co 6:13 I speak as *to* my c—open wide your *G5451*
2Co 12:14 c should not have to save up for their *G5451*
2Co 12:14 up for their parents, but parents *for* their c. *G5451*
Gal 3: 7 those who have faith are c of Abraham. *G5626*
Gal 3:26 Jesus you are all c of God through faith, *G5626*
Gal 4:19 My *dear* c, for whom I am again in the *G5451*
Gal 4:24 Mount Sinai and **bears** c who are to be *G1164*
Gal 4:25 because she is in slavery with her c. *G5451*
Gal 4:27 because more are the c of the desolate *G5451*
Gal 4:28 sisters, like Isaac, are c of promise. *G5451*
Gal 4:31 we are not c of the slave woman *G5451*
Eph 5: 1 example, therefore, as dearly loved c *G5451*
Eph 5: 8 you are light in the Lord. Live as c of light *G5451*
Eph 6: 1 C, obey your parents in the Lord, for this is *G5451*
Eph 6: 4 do not exasperate your c; instead, bring *G5451*
Php 2:15 "c of God without fault in a warped and *G5451*
Col 3:20 C, obey your parents in everything, for this *G5451*
Col 3:21 do not embitter your c, or they will *G5451*
1Th 2: 7 we were like **young** c among you. *G3758*
1Th 2: 7 Just as a nursing mother cares for her c, *G5451*
1Th 2:11 of you as a father deals with his own c, *G5451*
1Th 5: 5 You are all c of the light and children of *G5626*
1Th 5: 5 all children of the light and c of the day. *G5626*
1Ti 3: 4 family well and see that his c obey him, *G5451*
1Ti 3:12 must manage his c and his household *G5451*
1Ti 5: 4 But if a widow has c or grandchildren *G5451*
1Ti 5:10 such as **bringing up** c, showing *G5452*
1Ti 5:14 widows to marry, *to* **have** c, to manage *G5449*
Titus 1: 6 a man whose c believe and are not open *G5451*
Titus 2: 4 women to **love** their husbands and c, *G5817*
Heb 2:13 "Here am I, and the c God has given me." *G4086*
Heb 2:14 Since the c have flesh and blood, he too *G4086*
Heb 11:11 enabled *to* **bear** c *G1650+2856+5065+3284*
Heb 12: 7 as discipline; God is treating you as his c. *G5626*
Heb 12: 7 For what c are not disciplined by their *G5626*
1Pe 1:14 As obedient c, do not conform to the evil *G5451*
1Jn 2: 1 My **dear** c, I write this to you so that you *G5448*
1Jn 2:12 writing to you, **dear** c, because your sins *G5448*
1Jn 2:14 I write to you, **dear** c, because you know *G4086*
1Jn 2:18 **Dear** c, this is the last hour; and as you *G4086*
1Jn 2:28 And now, **dear** c, continue in him, so that *G5448*
1Jn 3: 1 that we should be called c of God! *G5451*
1Jn 3: 2 now we are c of God, and what we *G5451*
1Jn 3: 7 **Dear** c, do not let anyone lead you astray *G5448*
1Jn 3:10 we know who the c of God are and who *G5451*
1Jn 3:10 of God are and who the c of the devil are: *G5451*
1Jn 3:18 **Dear** c, let us not love with words or *G5448*
1Jn 4: 4 **dear** c, are from God and have *G5448*
1Jn 5: 2 is how we know that we love the c of God: *G5451*
1Jn 5:19 We know that we are *c* **of** God, and that the AIT
1Jn 5:21 **Dear** c, keep yourselves from idols. *G5448*
2Jn 1 To the lady chosen by God and *to* her c *G5451*
2Jn 4 joy to find some *of* your c walking in the *G5451*
2Jn 13 The c of your sister, who is chosen by God, *G5451*
3Jn 4 than to hear that my c are walking in the *G5451*
Rev 2:23 I will strike her c dead. Then all the *G5451*
Rev 21: 7 I will be their God and they will be my c. *G5626*

CHILDREN'S (12) [CHILD]

Ps 103:17 his righteousness with their c children— H1201
Ps 128: 6 you live to see your c children— H4200+1201
Pr 13:22 leaves an inheritance for their c children, H1201
Pr 17: 6 C children are a crown to the aged, and H1201
Jer 2: 9 will bring charges against your c children. H1201
Jer 31:29 and the c teeth are set on edge. H1201
Eze 16:36 because you gave them your c blood, H1201
Eze 18: 2 and the c teeth are set on edge'? H1201
Eze 37:25 children and their c children will live there H1201
Mt 15:26 not right to take the c bread and toss it to *G5451*
Mk 7:27 not right to take the c bread and toss it to *G5451*
Mk 7:28 dogs under the table eat the c crumbs." *G4086*

CHILION (KJV) KILION

CHIMHAM (KJV) KIMHAM

CHIN (2)

Lev 13:29 woman has a sore on their head or c, H2417
Lev 13:30 a defiling skin disease on the head or c. H2417

CHINNERETH, CHINNEROTH (KJV) GALILEE, KINNERETH

CHIOS (1)

Ac 20:15 we set sail from there and arrived off C. *G5944*

CHIRP (1)

Isa 10:14 flapped a wing, or opened its mouth *to* c. H7627

CHISEL (4) [CHISELED, CHISELING, CHISELS]

Ex 34: 1 "**C out** two stone tablets like the first ones H7180
Dt 10: 1 "**C out** two stone tablets like the first ones H7180
1Ki 6: 7 c or any other iron tool was heard at the H1749
Jer 10: 3 a craftsman shapes it with his c. H5108

CHISELED (2) [CHISEL]

Ex 34: 4 So Moses c **out** two stone tablets like the H7180
Dt 10: 3 acacia wood and c **out** two stone tablets H7180

CHISELING (1) [CHISEL]

Isa 22:16 on the height and c your resting place in H2980

CHISELS (1) [CHISEL]

Isa 44:13 he roughs it out with c and marks it with H5244

CHISLEU (KJV) KISLEV

CHITTIM (KJV) CYPRUS

CHIUN (KJV) PEDESTAL

CHLOE'S (1)

1Co 1:11 some from C household have informed *G5951*

CHOICE (34) [CHOICEST, CHOOSE, CHOOSES, CHOOSING, CHOSE, CHOSEN]

Ge 18: 7 Then he ran to the herd and selected a c H3202
Ge 27: 9 the flock and bring me two c young goats, H3202
Dt 12:11 all the c **possessions** you have vowed H4436
Dt 32:14 with c rams *of* Bashan and the finest H1201
1Sa 2:29 yourselves on the c **parts** *of* every offering H8040
1Ki 4:23 well as deer, gazelles, roebucks and c fowl. H80
1Ch 7:40 heads of families, c *men*, brave warriors H1405
1Ch 21:11 "This is what the LORD says: '**Take** your c: H7691
Ne 5:18 six c sheep and some poultry were H1405
Ne 8:10 "Go and enjoy c **food** and sweet drinks H5460
Job 36:16 comfort of your table laden with c **food**. H2016
Pr 8:10 of silver, knowledge rather than c gold, H1047
Pr 8:19 fine gold; what I yield surpasses c silver. H1047
Pr 10:20 The tongue of the righteous *is* c silver, but H1047
Pr 18: 8 The words of a gossip are like c **morsels** H4269
Pr 21:20 The wise store up c *food* and olive oil, but H2773
Pr 26:22 The words of a gossip are like c **morsels** H4269
SS 4:13 an orchard of pomegranates with c fruits, H4458
SS 4:16 come into his garden and taste its c fruits. H4458
SS 5:15 is like Lebanon, c as its cedars. H1047
Isa 1:22 your c **wine** is diluted with water. H6011
Jer 2:21 planted you like a c **vine** of sound and H8603
Eze 17:21 All his c troops will fall by the sword, and H4436
Eze 20:40 will require your offerings and your c gifts, H8040
Eze 24: 4 of meat, all the c pieces—the leg and the H3202
Eze 34: 3 the wool and slaughter the c *animals*, H1374
Da 1:16 took away their c **food** and the wine they H7329
Da 10: 3 I ate no c food; no meat or wine touched H2776
Am 5:22 Though you bring c fellowship offerings, H5309
Am 6: 4 You dine on c **lambs** and H4946+7366+4119
Zec 11:16 will eat the meat of the c **sheep** H1374
Jn 2:10 brings out the c wine first and then the *G2819*
Ac 15: 7 time ago God **made a** c among you that *G1721*
Ro 8:20 frustration, not **by its own** c, but by the will *G1776*

CHOICEST (12) [CHOICE]

Ge 23: 6 Bury your dead in the c *of* our tombs H4436
Ge 49:11 his colt to the c **branch**; he will wash his H8605
Dt 33:15 with the c **gifts** *of* the ancient mountains H8031
2Ki 19:23 its tallest cedars, the c *of* its junipers. H4435
Job 22:25 will be your gold, the c silver for you. H9361
Job 33:20 their soul loathes the c meal. H9294
Isa 5: 2 of stones and planted it with the c **vines**. H8603
Isa 16: 8 nations have trampled down the c **vines**, H8602
Isa 22: 7 Your c valleys are full of chariots, and H4436
Isa 37:24 its tallest cedars, the c *of* its junipers. H4436
Eze 31:16 trees of Eden, the c and best of Lebanon H4436
Hab 1:16 he lives in luxury and enjoys the c food. H1374

CHOIR (1) [CHOIRS]

Ne 12:38 The second c proceeded in the opposite H9343

CHOIRS (4) [CHOIR]

1Ch 15:27 who was in charge of the singing of the c. H8876
Ne 12:31 I also assigned two large c **to give thanks** H9343
Ne 12:40 The two c **that gave thanks** then took their H9343
Ne 12:42 The c sang under the direction of H8876

CHOKE (3) [CHOKED]

Mt 13:22 the deceitfulness of wealth c the word, *G5231*
Mt 18:28 He grabbed him and *began to* c him. *G4464*

Mk 4:19 other things come in and **c** the word, *G5231*

CHOKED (4) [CHOKE]

Mt 13: 7 which grew up and **c** the plants. *G4464*
Mk 4: 7 which grew up and **c** the plants, so that *G5231*
Lk 8: 7 which grew up with it and **c** the plants. *G678*
Lk 8:14 go on their way *they are* **c** by life's worries *G5231*

CHOLER (KJV) RAGE

CHOOSE (70) [CHOICE]

Ex 12: 5 The animals you **c** must be year-old males H4200
Ex 17: 9 "**C** some of our men and go out to fight H1047
Ex 34:16 *you* **c** some of their daughters **as wives** H4374
Nu 14: 4 "*We should* **c** a leader and go back to H5989
Nu 17: 5 staff belonging to the man *I* **c** will sprout, H1047
Dt 1:13 **C** some wise, understanding and H2035
Dt 7: 7 on you and **c** you because you were H1047
Dt 12: 5 the LORD your God *will* **c** from among all H1047
Dt 12:11 the LORD your God *will* **c** as a dwelling H1047
Dt 12:14 at the place the LORD *will* **c** in one of your H1047
Dt 12:18 at the place the LORD your God *will* **c**— H1047
Dt 12:26 and go to the place the LORD *will* **c**. H1047
Dt 14:23 God at the place *he will* **c** as a dwelling H1047
Dt 14:24 where the LORD *will* **c** to put his Name is H1047
Dt 14:25 go to the place the LORD your God *will* **c**. H1047
Dt 15:20 the LORD your God at the place he *will* **c**. H1047
Dt 16: 2 the place the LORD *will* **c** as a dwelling H1047
Dt 16: 6 in the place he *will* **c** as a dwelling for H1047
Dt 16: 7 it at the place the LORD your God *will* **c**. H1047
Dt 16:11 at the place he *will* **c** as a dwelling for H1047
Dt 16:15 your God at the place the LORD *will* **c**. H1047
Dt 16:16 the LORD your God at the place *he will* **c**: H1047
Dt 17: 8 to the place the LORD your God *will* **c**. H1047
Dt 17:10 they give you at the place the LORD *will* **c**. H1047
Dt 18: 6 earnestness to the place the LORD *will* **c**, H1047
Dt 23:16 they like and in whatever town *they* **c**. H1047
Dt 26: 2 the LORD your God *will* **c** as a dwelling H1047
Dt 30:19 Now **c** life, so that you and your children H1047
Dt 31:11 the LORD your God at the place *he will* **c**, H1047
Jos 3:12 **c** twelve men from the tribes of Israel H4374
Jos 4: 2 "**C** twelve men from among the people H4374
Jos 9:27 of the LORD at the place the LORD *would* **c**. H1047
Jos 24:15 then **c** for yourselves this day whom you H1047
1Sa 17: 8 **C** a man and have him come down to me H1357
2Sa 17: 1 "*I would* **c** twelve thousand men and set H1047
2Sa 24:12 **C** one of them for me to carry out against H1047
1Ki 18:23 *Let* Baal's prophets **c** one for themselves H1047
1Ki 18:25 "**C** one of the bulls and prepare it first H1047
2Ki 10: 3 **c** the best and most worthy of your H8011
2Ki 18:32 trees and honey. **C life** and not death H2649
1Ch 21:10 **C** one of them for me to carry out against H1047
Ps 25:12 instruct them in the ways they should **c**. H1047
Ps 65: 4 Blessed are those *you* **c** and bring near to H1047
Ps 75: 2 You say, "*I* **c** the appointed time; it is I H4374
Ps 78:67 Joseph, *he did* not **c** the tribe of Ephraim; H1047
Pr 1:29 knowledge and *did* not **c** to fear the LORD. H1047
Pr 3:31 not envy the violent or **c** any of their ways. H1047
Pr 8:10 **C** my instruction instead of silver H4374
Pr 12:26 The righteous **c** their friends **carefully**, but H9365
Isa 7:15 to reject the wrong and **c** the right, H1047
Isa 7:16 to reject the wrong and **c** the right, H1047
Isa 14: 1 once again *he will* **c** Israel and will settle H1047
Isa 56: 4 *who* **c** what pleases me and hold fast to H1047
Isa 66: 4 so I also *will* **c** harsh treatment for them H1047
Jer 3:14 *I will* **c** you—one from a town and two H4374
Jer 33:26 my servant and *will* not **c** one of his sons H4374
Eze 33: 2 people of the land **c** one of their men H4374
Hos 8: 4 *they* **c princes** without my approval. H8606
Zec 1:17 will again comfort Zion and **c** Jerusalem. H1047
Zec 2:12 the holy land and *will* again **c** Jerusalem. H1047
Mt 19:12 those who **c to live like eunuchs** for the *G2335*
Jn 15:16 You *did* not **c** me, but I chose you and *G1721*
Ac 1:21 it is necessary to **c** one of the men who have NDT
Ac 6: 3 **c** seven men from among you who are *G2170*
Ac 15:14 God first intervened *to* **c** a people for his *G3284*
Ac 15:22 decided *to* **c** some of their own men and *G1721*
Ac 15:25 So we all agreed *to* **c** some men and *G1721*
2Co 12: 6 Even if *I should* **c** to boast, I would not be *G2527*
Php 1:22 Yet what *shall I* **c**? I do not know! *G145*
1Pe 4: 3 in the past doing what pagans **c** to do— *G1088*

CHOOSES (15) [CHOICE]

Lev 16: 2 to come whenever he **c** into the Most Holy NDT
Nu 16: 5 The man *he* **c** he will cause to come near H1047
Nu 16: 7 The man the LORD **c** will be the one who is H1047
Dt 12:21 the LORD your God **c** to put his Name is too H1047
Dt 17:15 over you a king the LORD your God **c**. H1047
Jos 7:14 The tribe the LORD **c** shall come forward H4334
Jos 7:14 the clan the LORD **c** shall come forward H4334
Jos 7:14 the family the LORD **c** shall come forward H4334
2Sa 15:15 ready to do whatever our lord the king **c**." H1047
Ps 68:16 at the mountain where God **c** to reign H2773
Isa 41:24 worthless; *whoever* **c** you is detestable. H1047
Mt 11:27 those to whom the Son **c** to reveal him. *G1089*
Lk 10:22 those to whom the Son **c** to reveal him." *G1089*
Jn 7:17 Anyone *who* **c** to do the will of God will *G2527*
Jas 4: 4 anyone *who* **c** to be a friend of the world *G1089*

CHOOSING (2) [CHOICE]

1Ki 12:33 a month of his own **c**, he offered sacrifices H968
Ro 9:22 *although* **c** to show his wrath and make *G2527*

CHOP (3) [CHOPPED]

Dt 29:11 in your camps *who* **c** your wood and carry H2634
Jer 46:23 *They will* **c down** her forest," declares the H4162
Mic 3: 3 *who* **c** them **up** like meat for the pan H7298

CHOPPED (1) [CHOP]

1Sa 6:14 The people **c up** the wood of the cart and H1324

CHOR-ASHAN (KJV) BOR ASHAN

CHORAZIN (2)

Mt 11:21 "Woe to you, **C**! Woe to you, Bethsaida *G5960*
Lk 10:13 "Woe to you, **C**! Woe to you, Bethsaida *G5960*

CHOSE (46) [CHOICE]

Ge 6: 2 they married any of them *they* **c**. H1047
Ge 13:11 So Lot **c** for himself the whole plain of the H1047
Ge 47: 2 *He* **c** five of his brothers and presented H4374
Ex 18:25 He **c** capable men from all Israel and H1047
Dt 4:37 your ancestors and **c** their descendants H1047
Dt 10:15 loved them, and *he* **c** you, their H1047
Dt 33:21 *He* **c** the best land for himself; the H8011
Jos 8: 3 He **c** thirty thousand of his best fighting H1047
Jdg 5: 8 God **c** new leaders when war came to the H1047
Jdg 14:11 *they* **c** thirty men to be his companions. H4374
1Sa 2:28 I **c** your ancestor out of all the tribes of H1047
1Sa 13: 2 Saul **c** three thousand men from Israel H1047
1Sa 17:40 **c** five smooth stones from the stream H1047
2Sa 6:21 who **c** me rather than your father or H1047
1Ki 11:34 whom *I* **c** and who obeyed my commands H1047
1Ki 11:36 the city where *I* **c** to put my Name. H1047
2Ki 23:27 Jerusalem, the city *I* **c**, and this temple, H1047
1Ch 15: 2 because the LORD **c** them to carry the ark of H1047
1Ch 28: 4 **c** me from my whole family to be king H1047
1Ch 28: 4 *He* **c** Judah as leader, and from the tribe H1047
1Ch 28: 4 from the tribe of Judah he **c** my family NDT
2Ch 24: 3 Jehoiada **c** two wives for him, and he had H5951
Ne 9: 7 who **c** Abram and brought him out of Ur H1047
Job 29:25 *I* **c** the way for them and sat as their chief H1047
Ps 33:12 the people *he* **c** for his inheritance. H1047
Ps 47: 4 *He* **c** our inheritance for us, the pride of H1047
Ps 78:68 but *he* **c** the tribe of Judah, Mount Zion H1047
Ps 78:70 *He* **c** David his servant and took him from H1047
Isa 65:12 in my sight and **c** what displeases me." H1047
Isa 66: 4 in my sight and **c** what displeases me." H1047
Jer 33:24 LORD has rejected the two kingdoms *he* **c**'? H1047
Eze 20: 5 On the day I **c** Israel, I swore with uplifted H1047
Lk 6:13 his disciples to him and **c** twelve of them, *G1721*
Jn 5:35 you **c** for a time to enjoy his light. *G2527*
Jn 15:16 I **c** you and appointed you so that you *G1721*
Ac 6: 5 *They* **c** Stephen, a man full of faith and of *G1721*
Ac 13:17 of the people of Israel **c** our ancestors; *G1721*
Ac 15:22 They **c** Judas (called Barsabbas) and Silas NDT
Ac 15:40 Paul **c** Silas and left, commended by *G2141*
1Co 1:27 But God **c** the foolish things of the world to *G1721*
1Co 1:27 God **c** the weak things of the world to *G1721*
1Co 1:28 God **c** the lowly things of this world and *G1721*
Eph 1: 4 For *he* **c** us in him before the creation of *G1721*
2Th 2:13 because God **c** you as firstfruits to be saved *G145*
Heb 11:25 *He* **c** to be mistreated along with the *G145*
Jas 1:18 *He* **c** to give us birth through the word of *G1089*

CHOSEN (123) [CHOICE]

Ge 18:19 For *I have* **c** him, so that he will direct his H3359
Ge 24:14 her be the one *you have* **c** for your servant H3519
Ge 24:44 be the one the LORD *has* **c** for my master's H3519
Ex 31: 2 *I have* **c** Bezalel son of Uri H7924+928+9005
Ex 35:30 the LORD *has* **c** Bezalel son of H7924+928+9005
Lev 16:10 But the goat **c** *by* lot as the scapegoat H6590
Dt 7: 6 The LORD your God *has* **c** you out of all the H1047
Dt 14: 2 the LORD *has* **c** you to be his treasured H1047
Dt 18: 5 the LORD your God *has* **c** them and their H1047
Dt 21: 5 the LORD your God *has* **c** them to minister H1047
Jos 7:16 come forward by tribes, and Judah **was c**. H4334
Jos 7:17 came forward, and the Zerahites *were* **c**. H4334
Jos 7:17 forward by families, and Zimri **was c**. H4334
Jos 7:18 son of Zerah, of the tribe of Judah, **was c**. H4334
Jos 24:22 that you *have* **c** to serve the LORD. H1047
Jdg 10:14 Go and cry out to the gods *you have* **c**. H1047
1Sa 8:18 cry out for relief from the king *you have* **c**, H1047
1Sa 10:24 "Do you see the man the LORD *has* **c**? H1047
1Sa 12:13 Now here is the king *you have* **c**, the one H1047
1Sa 16: 1 *I have* **c** one of his sons to be king." H8011
1Sa 16: 8 "The LORD *has* not **c** this one either." H1047
1Sa 16: 9 Samuel said, "Nor *has* the LORD **c** this one."H1047
1Sa 16:10 said to him, "The LORD *has* not **c** these." H1047
2Sa 16:18 the one **c** by the LORD, by these H1047
2Sa 21: 6 at Gibeah of Saul—the LORD's **c** *one*." H1040
1Ki 3: 8 is here among the people *you have* **c**, H1047
1Ki 8:16 *I have* not **c** a city in any tribe of Israel to H1047
1Ki 8:16 but *I have* **c** David to rule my people H1047
1Ki 8:44 toward the city *you have* **c** and the temple H1047
1Ki 8:48 toward the city *you have* **c** and the temple H1047
1Ki 11:13 the sake of Jerusalem, which *I have* **c**." H1047
1Ki 11:32 which *I have* **c** out of all the tribes of H1047
1Ki 14:21 the city the LORD *had* **c** out of all the tribes H1047
2Ki 21: 7 which *I have* **c** out of all the tribes of H1047
1Ch 9:22 those **c** to be gatekeepers at the H1405
1Ch 16:13 of Israel, his **c** *ones*, the children of Jacob. H1040
1Ch 16:41 the rest of those **c** and designated by H1405
1Ch 28: 5 *he has* **c** my son Solomon to sit on the H1047
1Ch 28: 6 my courts, for *I have* **c** him to be my son H1047
1Ch 28:10 the LORD *has* **c** you to build a house as H1047
1Ch 29: 1 the one whom God *has* **c**, is young and H1047
2Ch 6: 5 *I have* not **c** a city in any tribe of Israel to H1047
2Ch 6: 5 nor *have I* **c** anyone to be ruler over my H1047
2Ch 6: 6 But now *I have* **c** Jerusalem for my Name H1047
2Ch 6: 6 and *I have* **c** David to rule my people H1047
2Ch 6:34 this city *you have* **c** and the temple I H1047
2Ch 6:38 toward the city *you have* **c** and toward the H1047
2Ch 7:12 your prayer and *have* **c** this place for H1047
2Ch 7:16 *I have* **c** and consecrated this temple so H1047
2Ch 12:13 the city the LORD *had* **c** out of all the tribes H1047
2Ch 29:11 the LORD *has* **c** you to stand before him H1047
2Ch 33: 7 which *I have* **c** out of all the tribes of H1047
Ne 1: 9 to the place *I have* **c** as a dwelling for H1047
Ps 89: 3 "I have made a covenant with my **c** *one*, H1040
Ps 105: 6 of Abraham, his **c** *ones*, the children of H1040
Ps 105:26 his servant, and Aaron, whom *he had* **c**. H1047
Ps 105:43 rejoicing, his **c** *ones* with shouts of joy H1040
Ps 106: 5 I may enjoy the prosperity of your **c** *ones*, H1040
Ps 106:23 had not Moses, his **c** *one*, stood in the H1040
Ps 119:30 *I have* **c** the way of faithfulness; I have set H1047
Ps 119:173 to help me, for *I have* **c** your precepts. H1047
Ps 132:13 For the LORD *has* **c** Zion, he has desired it H1047
Ps 135: 4 For the LORD *has* **c** Jacob to be his own H1047
Isa 1:29 because of the gardens that *you have* **c**. H1047
Isa 41: 8 whom *I have* **c**, you descendants of H1047
Isa 41: 9 *I have* **c** you and have not rejected you. H1047
Isa 42: 1 I uphold, my **c** *one* in whom I delight H1040
Isa 43:10 "and my servant whom *I have* **c**, so that H1047
Isa 43:20 to give drink to my people, my **c**, H1040
Isa 44: 1 my servant, Israel, whom *I have* **c**. H1047
Isa 44: 2 my servant, Jeshurun, whom *I have* **c**. H1047
Isa 45: 4 of Israel my **c**, I summon you by name H1040
Isa 48:14 The LORD's **c ally** will carry out his purpose H170
Isa 49: 7 the Holy One of Israel, *who has* **c** you." H1047
Isa 58: 5 Is this the kind of fast *I have* **c**, only a day H1047
Isa 58: 6 "Is not this the kind of fasting *I have* **c**: to H1047
Isa 65: 9 mountains; my **c** *people* will inherit them H1040
Isa 65:15 your name for my **c** *ones* to use in their H1040
Isa 65:22 my **c** *ones* will long enjoy the work of their H1040
Isa 66: 3 They *have* **c** their own ways, and they H1047
Jer 49:19 Who *is the* **c** *one* I will appoint for this H1047
Jer 50:44 Who *is the* **c** *one* I will appoint for this H1047
Da 1: 6 those who were **c** were some from Judah NDT
Am 3: 2 "You only *have I* **c** of all the families of H3359
Hag 2:23 signet ring, for *I have* **c** you,' declares the H1047
Zec 3: 2 The LORD, who *has* **c** Jerusalem, rebuke H1047
Zec 4:10 when they see the **c** capstone in the hand H975
Mt 12:18 "Here is my servant whom *I have* **c**, the one *G147*
Mt 22:14 "For many are invited, but few are **c**." *G1723*
Mt 27:15 to release a prisoner **c** by the crowd. *G2527*
Mk 13:20 the elect, whom *he has* **c**, he has *G1721*
Lk 1: 9 *he was* **c by lot**, according to the custom of *G3275*
Lk 9:35 is my Son, whom *I have* **c**; listen to him." *G1721*
Lk 10:42 Mary *has* **c** what is better, and it will not *G1721*
Lk 18: 7 not God bring about justice *for* his **c** *ones*, *G1723*
Lk 23:35 himself if he is God's Messiah, the **C** *One*." *G1723*
Jn 1:34 seen and I testify that this is God's **C** *One*." *G1723*
Jn 6:70 replied, "*Have* I not **c** you, the Twelve *G1721*
Jn 13:18 to all of you; I know those *I have* **c**. *G1721*
Jn 15:19 but I *have* **c** you out of the world. *G1721*
Ac 1: 2 the Holy Spirit to the apostles *he had* **c**. *G1721*
Ac 1:24 Show us which of these two *you have* **c** *G1721*
Ac 9:15 This man is my **c** instrument to proclaim *G1724*
Ac 10:41 by witnesses whom God *had* **already c**— *G4742*
Ac 22:14 of our ancestors *has* **c** you to know his *G4741*
Ro 8:33 charge against *those whom* God has **c**? *G1723*
Ro 11: 5 time there is a remnant **c** by grace. *G1724*
Ro 16:13 Greet Rufus, **c** in the Lord, and his mother *G1723*
2Co 8:19 *he was* **c** by the churches to accompany us *G5936*
Eph 1:11 In him *we were* also **c**, having been *G3103*
Col 1:27 To them God *has* **c** to make known among *G2527*
Col 3:12 as God's **c** *people*, holy and dearly *G1723*
1Th 1: 4 sisters loved by God, that he has **c** you, *G1724*
Jas 2: 5 *Has* not God **c** those who are poor in the *G1721*
1Pe 1: 2 who have been **c** according to the NDT
1Pe 1:20 *He was* **c before** the creation of the world *G4589*
1Pe 2: 4 by humans but **c** by God and precious *G1723*
1Pe 2: 6 in Zion, a **c** and precious cornerstone *G1723*
1Pe 2: 9 But you are a **c** people, a royal priesthood, *G1723*
1Pe 5:13 is in Babylon, **c together** with you, sends *G5293*
2Jn 1 To the lady **c** *by God* and to her children *G1723*
2Jn 13 your sister, who is **c** *by God*, send their *G1723*
Rev 17:14 will be his called, **c** and faithful followers." *G1723*

CHRIST (469) [CHRIST'S, CHRISTIAN, CHRISTIANS, MESSIAH, MESSIAHS]

Jn 1:17 grace and truth came through Jesus **C**. *G5986*
Jn 1:41 have found the Messiah" (that is, the **C**). *G5986*
Jn 4:25 know that Messiah" (called **C**) "is coming. *G5986*
Jn 17: 3 and Jesus **C**, whom you have sent *G5986*
Ac 2:38 in the name of Jesus **C** for the forgiveness *G5986*
Ac 3: 6 In the name of Jesus **C** of Nazareth, walk." *G5986*
Ac 4:10 It is by the name of Jesus **C** of Nazareth *G5986*
Ac 8:12 kingdom of God and the name of Jesus **C**, *G5986*
Ac 9:34 Peter said to him, "Jesus **C** heals you. *G5986*
Ac 10:36 the good news of peace through Jesus **C**, *G5986*
Ac 10:48 they be baptized in the name of Jesus **C**. *G5986*
Ac 11:17 gave us who believed in the Lord Jesus **C**, *G5986*
Ac 15:26 lives for the name of our Lord Jesus **C**. *G5986*
Ac 16:18 the name of Jesus **C** I command you to *G5986*
Ac 24:24 to him as he spoke about faith in **C** Jesus. *G5986*

Ac 28:31 God and taught about the Lord Jesus C— *G5986*
Ro 1: 1 a servant *of* C Jesus, called to be an *G5986*
Ro 1: 4 from the dead: Jesus C our Lord. *G5986*
Ro 1: 6 who are called to belong to Jesus C. *G5986*
Ro 1: 7 God our Father and from the Lord Jesus C. *G5986*
Ro 1: 8 my God through Jesus C for all of you, *G5986*
Ro 2:16 judges people's secrets through Jesus C, *G5986*
Ro 3:22 faith in Jesus C to all who believe. *G5986*
Ro 3:24 the redemption that came by C Jesus. *G5986*
Ro 3:25 God presented C as a sacrifice of *G4005S*
Ro 5: 1 peace with God through our Lord Jesus C, *G5986*
Ro 5: 6 still powerless, C died for the ungodly. *G5986*
Ro 5: 8 While we were still sinners, C died for us. *G5986*
Ro 5:11 boast in God through our Lord Jesus C, *G5986*
Ro 5:15 the one man, Jesus C, overflow to the *G5986*
Ro 5:17 in life through the one man, Jesus C! *G5986*
Ro 5:21 eternal life through Jesus C our Lord. *G5986*
Ro 6: 3 were baptized into C Jesus were baptized *G5986*
Ro 6: 4 just as C was raised from the dead *G5986*
Ro 6: 8 Now if we died with C, we believe that we *G5986*
Ro 6: 9 we know that since C was raised from the *G5986*
Ro 6:11 dead to sin but alive to God in C Jesus. *G5986*
Ro 6:23 of God is eternal life in C Jesus our Lord. *G5986*
Ro 7: 4 died to the law through the body *of* C, *G5986*
Ro 7:25 who delivers me through Jesus C our Lord! *G5986*
Ro 8: 1 those who are in C Jesus, *G5986*
Ro 8: 2 because through C Jesus the law of the *G5986*
Ro 8: 9 if anyone does not have the Spirit *of* C, *G5986*
Ro 8: 9 Spirit of Christ, they do not belong to C. *G899S*
Ro 8:10 But if C is in you, then even though your *G5986*
Ro 8:11 he who raised C from the dead will also *G5986*
Ro 8:17 heirs of God and co-heirs *with* C, if indeed *G5986*
Ro 8:34 C Jesus who died—more than that, who *G5986*
Ro 8:35 Who shall separate us from the love *of* C *G5986*
Ro 8:39 the love of God that is in C Jesus our Lord. *G5986*
Ro 9: 1 I speak the truth in C—I am not lying, my *G5986*
Ro 9: 3 cut off from C for the sake of my *G5986*
Ro 10: 4 C is the culmination of the law so that *G5986*
Ro 10: 6 (that is, to bring C down) *G5986*
Ro 10: 7 that is, to bring C up from the dead). *G5986*
Ro 10:17 is heard through the word *about* C. *G5986*
Ro 12: 5 so in C we, though many, form one body *G5986*
Ro 13:14 clothe yourselves with the Lord Jesus C *G5986*
Ro 14: 9 C died and returned to life so that he *G5986*
Ro 14:15 eating destroy someone for whom C died. *G5986*
Ro 14:18 anyone who serves C in this way is *G5986*
Ro 15: 3 For even C did not please himself but, as it *G5986*
Ro 15: 5 mind toward each other that C Jesus had, *G5986*
Ro 15: 6 the God and Father of our Lord Jesus C. *G5986*
Ro 15: 7 just as C accepted you, in order to *G5986*
Ro 15: 8 For I tell you that C has become a servant *G5986*
Ro 15:16 to be a minister *of* C Jesus to the Gentiles *G5986*
Ro 15:17 Therefore I glory in C Jesus in my service *G5986*
Ro 15:18 anything except what C has accomplished *G5986*
Ro 15:19 I have fully proclaimed the gospel *of* C. *G5986*
Ro 15:20 the gospel where C was not known, *G5986*
Ro 15:29 in the full measure of the blessing *of* C. *G5986*
Ro 15:30 by our Lord Jesus C and by the love of the *G5986*
Ro 16: 3 Aquila, my co-workers in C Jesus. *G5986*
Ro 16: 5 the first convert to C in the province of *G5986*
Ro 16: 7 apostles, and they were in C before I was. *G5986*
Ro 16: 9 our co-worker in C, and my dear friend *G5986*
Ro 16:10 whose fidelity to C has stood the test. *G5986*
Ro 16:16 All the churches *of* C send greetings. *G5986*
Ro 16:18 For such people are not serving our Lord C *G5986*
Ro 16:25 the message I proclaim about Jesus C, in *G5986*
Ro 16:27 God be glory forever through Jesus C! *G5986*
1Co 1: 1 to be an apostle *of* C Jesus by the will of *G5986*
1Co 1: 2 those sanctified in C Jesus and called to *G5986*
1Co 1: 2 call on the name of our Lord Jesus C— *G5986*
1Co 1: 3 from God our Father and the Lord Jesus C. *G5986*
1Co 1: 4 because of his grace given you in C Jesus. *G5986*
1Co 1: 6 our testimony *about* C among you. *G5986*
1Co 1: 7 wait for our Lord Jesus C to be revealed. *G5986*
1Co 1: 8 blameless on the day of our Lord Jesus C. *G5986*
1Co 1: 9 fellowship with his Son, Jesus C our Lord. *G5986*
1Co 1:10 in the name of our Lord Jesus C, that all *G5986*
1Co 1:12 follow Cephas"; still another, "I follow C." *G5986*
1Co 1:13 Is C divided? Was Paul crucified for you *G5986*
1Co 1:17 For C did not send me to baptize, but to *G5986*
1Co 1:17 lest the cross *of* C be emptied of its power. *G5986*
1Co 1:23 we preach C crucified: a stumbling *G5986*
1Co 1:24 C the power of God and the wisdom of *G5986*
1Co 1:30 is because of him that you are in C Jesus, *G5986*
1Co 2: 2 with you except Jesus C and him crucified. *G5986*
1Co 2:16 But we have the mind *of* C. *G5986*
1Co 3: 1 who are still worldly—mere infants in C. *G5986*
1Co 3:11 the one already laid, which is Jesus C. *G5986*
1Co 3:23 you are *of* C, and Christ is of God. *G5986*
1Co 3:23 you are of Christ, and C is of God. *G5986*
1Co 4: 1 as servants *of* C and as those entrusted *G5986*
1Co 4:10 We are fools for C, but you are so wise in *G5986*
1Co 4:10 fools for Christ, but you are so wise in C! *G5986*
1Co 4:15 if you had ten thousand guardians in C, *G5986*
1Co 4:15 in C Jesus I became your father *G5986*
1Co 4:17 remind you of my way of life in C Jesus, *G5986*
1Co 5: 7 For C, our Passover lamb, has been *G5986*
1Co 6:11 of the Lord Jesus C and by the Spirit of *G5986*
1Co 6:15 your bodies are members *of* C himself? *G5986*
1Co 6:15 take the members *of* C and unite them *G5986*
1Co 8: 6 one Lord, Jesus C, through whom all *G5986*
1Co 8:11 sister, for whom C died, is destroyed by *G5986*
1Co 8:12 their weak conscience, you sin against C. *G5986*
1Co 9:12 rather than hinder the gospel *of* C. *G5986*
1Co 10: 4 accompanied them, and that rock was C. *G5986*
1Co 10: 9 We should not test C, as some of them did *G5986*
1Co 10:16 thanks a participation in the blood *of* C? *G5986*
1Co 10:16 we break a participation in the body *of* C? *G5986*
1Co 11: 1 my example, as I follow the example *of* C. *G5986*
1Co 11: 3 to realize that the head of every man is C, *G5986*
1Co 11: 3 woman is man, and the head *of* C is God. *G5986*
1Co 11:29 the body of C eat and drink judgment NDT
1Co 12:12 many parts form one body, so it is *with* C. *G5986*
1Co 12:27 Now you are the body *of* C, and each one *G5986*
1Co 15: 3 that C died for our sins according to the *G5986*
1Co 15:12 it is preached that C has been raised from *G5986*
1Co 15:13 then not even C has been raised. *G5986*
1Co 15:14 And if C has not been raised, our *G5986*
1Co 15:15 God that he raised C from the dead. *G5986*
1Co 15:16 then C has not been raised either. *G5986*
1Co 15:17 And if C has not been raised, your faith is *G5986*
1Co 15:18 also who have fallen asleep in C are lost. *G5986*
1Co 15:19 If only for this life we have hope in C, we *G5986*
1Co 15:20 But C has indeed been raised from the *G5986*
1Co 15:22 so in C all will be made alive. *G5986*
1Co 15:23 C, the firstfruits; then, when he comes *G5986*
1Co 15:27 God himself, who put everything under C. *G899S*
1Co 15:31 as I boast about you in C Jesus our Lord. *G5986*
1Co 15:57 us the victory through our Lord Jesus C. *G5986*
1Co 16:24 My love to all of you in C Jesus. Amen. *G5986*
2Co 1: 1 an apostle *of* C Jesus by the will of God *G5986*
2Co 1: 2 from God our Father and the Lord Jesus C. *G5986*
2Co 1: 3 to the God and Father of our Lord Jesus C, *G5986*
2Co 1: 5 share abundantly in the sufferings *of* C, *G5986*
2Co 1: 5 so also our comfort abounds through C. *G5986*
2Co 1:19 Son of God, Jesus C, who was preached *G5986*
2Co 1:20 God has made, they are "Yes" in C. *G899S*
2Co 1:21 makes both us and you stand firm in C. *G5986*
2Co 2:10 forgiven in the sight *of* C for your sake, *G5986*
2Co 2:12 preach the gospel *of* C and found that the *G5986*
2Co 2:15 pleasing aroma *of* C among those who *G5986*
2Co 2:17 in C we speak before God with sincerity *G5986*
2Co 3: 3 You show that you are a letter *from* C, the *G5986*
2Co 3: 4 we have through C before God. *G5986*
2Co 3:14 because only in C is it taken away. *G5986*
2Co 4: 4 of the gospel that displays the glory *of* C, *G5986*
2Co 4: 5 ourselves, but Jesus C as Lord, and *G5986*
2Co 4: 6 of God's glory displayed in the face *of* C. *G5986*
2Co 5:10 all appear before the judgment seat *of* C, *G5986*
2Co 5:16 Though we once regarded C in this way *G5986*
2Co 5:17 if anyone is in C, the new creation has *G5986*
2Co 5:18 us to himself through C and gave us the *G5986*
2Co 5:19 was reconciling the world to himself in C, *G5986*
2Co 6:15 harmony is there between C and Belial? *G5986*
2Co 8: 9 For you know the grace of our Lord Jesus C *G5986*
2Co 8:23 of the churches and an honor *to* C. *G5986*
2Co 9:13 your confession of the gospel *of* C, *G5986*
2Co 10: 1 By the humility and gentleness *of* C, *G5986*
2Co 10: 5 every thought to make it obedient *to* C. *G5986*
2Co 10: 7 anyone is confident that they belong *to* C, *G5986*
2Co 10: 7 again that we *belong to* C just as much as *G5986*
2Co 10:14 did get as far as you with the gospel *of* C. *G5986*
2Co 11: 2 you to one husband, *to* C, so that I might *G5986*
2Co 11: 3 from your sincere and pure devotion to C. *G5986*
2Co 11:10 As surely as the truth *of* C is in me, nobody *G5986*
2Co 11:13 workers, masquerading as apostles *of* C. *G5986*
2Co 11:23 Are they servants *of* C? (I am out of my *G5986*
2Co 12: 2 I know a man in C who fourteen years ago *G5986*
2Co 12:19 in the sight of God as those in C; *G5986*
2Co 13: 3 proof that C is speaking through *G5986*
2Co 13: 5 Do you not realize that C Jesus is in you *G5986*
2Co 13:14 May the grace of the Lord Jesus C, and *G5986*
Gal 1: 1 but by Jesus C and God the Father *G5986*
Gal 1: 3 from God our Father and the Lord Jesus C, *G5986*
Gal 1: 6 to live in the grace *of* C and are turning to *G5986*
Gal 1: 7 are trying to pervert the gospel *of* C. *G5986*
Gal 1:10 people, I would not be a servant *of* C. *G5986*
Gal 1:12 I received it by revelation from Jesus C. *G5986*
Gal 1:22 to the churches of Judea that are in C. *G5986*
Gal 2: 4 freedom we have in C Jesus and to make *G5986*
Gal 2:16 works of the law, but by faith in Jesus C. *G5986*
Gal 2:16 put our faith in C Jesus that we may be *G5986*
Gal 2:16 justified by faith *in* C and not by the works *G5986*
Gal 2:17 in seeking to be justified in C, we Jews *G5986*
Gal 2:17 doesn't that mean that C promotes sin? *G5986*
Gal 2:20 been crucified with C and I no longer live, *G5986*
Gal 2:20 I no longer live, but C lives in me. *G5986*
Gal 2:21 through the law, C died for nothing!" *G5986*
Gal 3: 1 your very eyes Jesus C was clearly *G5986*
Gal 3:13 C redeemed us from the curse of the law *G5986*
Gal 3:14 come to the Gentiles through C Jesus, *G5986*
Gal 3:16 meaning one person, who is C. *G5986*
Gal 3:22 being given through faith in Jesus C *G5986*
Gal 3:24 our guardian until C came that we might *G5986*
Gal 3:26 So in C Jesus you are all children of God *G5986*
Gal 3:27 who were baptized into C have clothed *G5986*
Gal 3:27 into Christ have clothed yourselves with C. *G5986*
Gal 3:28 female, for you are all one in C Jesus. *G5986*
Gal 3:29 If you *belong to* C, then you are *G5986*
Gal 4:14 angel of God, as if I were C Jesus himself. *G5986*
Gal 4:19 of childbirth until C is formed in you, *G5986*
Gal 5: 1 It is for freedom that C has set us free *G5986*
Gal 5: 2 C will be of no value to you at all. *G5986*
Gal 5: 4 by the law have been alienated from C; *G5986*
Gal 5: 6 For in C Jesus neither circumcision nor *G5986*
Gal 5:24 Those who *belong to* C Jesus have *G5986*
Gal 6: 2 in this way you will fulfill the law *of* C. *G5986*
Gal 6:12 avoid being persecuted for the cross *of* C. *G5986*
Gal 6:14 except in the cross of our Lord Jesus C, *G5986*
Gal 6:18 of our Lord Jesus C be with your spirit, *G5986*
Eph 1: 1 an apostle *of* C Jesus by the will of God *G5986*
Eph 1: 1 people in Ephesus, the faithful in C Jesus: *G5986*
Eph 1: 2 from God our Father and the Lord Jesus C. *G5986*
Eph 1: 3 to the God and Father of our Lord Jesus C, *G5986*
Eph 1: 3 realms with every spiritual blessing in C. *G5986*
Eph 1: 5 adoption to sonship through Jesus C, *G5986*
Eph 1: 9 good pleasure, which he purposed in C, *G899S*
Eph 1:10 things in heaven and on earth under C. *G5986*
Eph 1:12 who were the first to put our hope in C *G5986*
Eph 1:13 were included in C when you heard the *G4005S*
Eph 1:17 asking that the God of our Lord Jesus C, *G5986*
Eph 1:20 when he raised C from the dead and *G5986*
Eph 2: 5 made us alive with C even when we were *G5986*
Eph 2: 6 God raised us up with C and seated us with NDT
Eph 2: 6 him in the heavenly realms in C Jesus, *G5986*
Eph 2: 7 expressed in his kindness to us in C Jesus. *G5986*
Eph 2:10 created in C Jesus to do good works *G5986*
Eph 2:12 at that time you were separate *from* C, *G5986*
Eph 2:13 But now in C Jesus you who once were far *G5986*
Eph 2:13 been brought near by the blood *of* C. *G5986*
Eph 2:20 with C Jesus himself as the chief *G5986*
Eph 3: 1 the prisoner *of* C Jesus for the sake of you *G5986*
Eph 3: 4 my insight into the mystery *of* C, *G5986*
Eph 3: 6 together in the promise in C Jesus. *G5986*
Eph 3: 8 to the Gentiles the boundless riches *of* C, *G5986*
Eph 3:11 that he accomplished in C Jesus our Lord. *G5986*
Eph 3:17 so that C may dwell in your hearts through *G5986*
Eph 3:18 long and high and deep is the love of C, NDT
Eph 3:21 the church and in C Jesus throughout all *G5986*
Eph 4: 7 grace has been given as C apportioned it. *G5986*
Eph 4:11 So C himself gave the apostles, the prophets, NDT
Eph 4:12 so that the body *of* C may be built up *G5986*
Eph 4:13 to the whole measure of the fullness *of* C. *G5986*
Eph 4:15 body of him who is the head, that is, C. *G5986*
Eph 4:21 you heard about C and were taught in *G5986*
Eph 4:32 each other, just as in C God forgave you. *G5986*
Eph 5: 2 just as C loved us and gave himself up *G5986*
Eph 5: 5 in the kingdom *of* C and of God. *G5986*
Eph 5:14 from the dead, and C will shine on you." *G5986*
Eph 5:20 in the name of our Lord Jesus C. *G5986*
Eph 5:21 to one another out of reverence *for* C. *G5986*
Eph 5:23 head of the wife as C is the head of the *G5986*
Eph 5:24 Now as the church submits *to* C, so also *G5986*
Eph 5:25 just as C loved the church and gave *G5986*
Eph 5:29 their body, just as C does the church— *G5986*
Eph 5:32 I am talking about C and the church. *G5986*
Eph 6: 5 of heart, just as you would obey C. *G5986*
Eph 6: 6 but as slaves *of* C, doing the will of *G5986*
Eph 6:23 from God the Father and the Lord Jesus C. *G5986*
Eph 6:24 love our Lord Jesus C with an undying *G5986*
Php 1: 1 Timothy, servants *of* C Jesus, To all God's *G5986*
Php 1: 1 God's holy people in C Jesus at Philippi, *G5986*
Php 1: 2 from God our Father and the Lord Jesus C. *G5986*
Php 1: 6 on to completion until the day *of* C Jesus. *G5986*
Php 1: 8 all of you with the affection *of* C Jesus. *G5986*
Php 1:10 be pure and blameless for the day *of* C, *G5986*
Php 1:11 that comes through Jesus C— *G5986*
Php 1:13 to everyone else that I am in chains for C. *G5986*
Php 1:15 true that some preach C out of envy and *G5986*
Php 1:17 The former preach C out of selfish *G5986*
Php 1:18 from false motives or true, C is preached. *G5986*
Php 1:19 the Spirit of Jesus C what has happened *G5986*
Php 1:20 that now as always C will be exalted in *G5986*
Php 1:21 For to me, to live is C and to die is gain. *G5986*
Php 1:23 I desire to depart and be with C, which is *G5986*
Php 1:26 your boasting in C Jesus will abound on *G5986*
Php 1:27 in a manner worthy of the gospel *of* C. *G5986*
Php 1:29 to you on behalf of C not only to believe *G5986*
Php 2: 1 encouragement from being united with C, *G5986*
Php 2: 5 have the same mindset as C Jesus: *G5986*
Php 2:11 tongue acknowledge that Jesus C is Lord, *G5986*
Php 2:16 to boast on the day *of* C that I did not run *G5986*
Php 2:21 their own interests, not those of Jesus C. *G5986*
Php 2:30 because he almost died for the work *of* C *G5986*
Php 3: 3 who boast in C Jesus, and who put *G5986*
Php 3: 7 me I now consider loss for the sake of C. *G5986*
Php 3: 8 worth of knowing C Jesus my Lord, *G5986*
Php 3: 8 consider them garbage, that I may gain C *G5986*
Php 3: 9 that which is through faith *in* C—the *G5986*
Php 3:10 I want to know C—yes, to know the power *G899S*
Php 3:12 of that for which C Jesus took hold of me. *G5986*
Php 3:14 has called me heavenward in C Jesus. *G5986*
Php 3:18 many live as enemies of the cross *of* C. *G5986*
Php 3:20 a Savior from there, the Lord Jesus C, *G5986*
Php 4: 7 your hearts and your minds in C Jesus. *G5986*
Php 4:19 to the riches of his glory in C Jesus. *G5986*
Php 4:21 Greet all God's people in C Jesus. *G5986*
Php 4:23 of the Lord Jesus C be with your spirit. *G5986*
Col 1: 1 an apostle *of* C Jesus by the will of God *G5986*
Col 1: 2 the faithful brothers and sisters in C: *G5986*
Col 1: 3 the Father of our Lord Jesus C, when we *G5986*
Col 1: 4 of your faith in C Jesus and of the love *G5986*
Col 1: 7 is a faithful minister *of* C on our behalf, *G5986*
Col 1:27 mystery, which is C in you, the hope of *G5986*
Col 1:28 may present everyone fully mature in C. *G5986*
Col 1:29 with all the energy C so powerfully works *G899S*

Col 2: 2 may know the mystery of God, *namely*, C, G5986
Col 2: 5 you are and how firm your faith in C is. G5986
Col 2: 6 just as you received C Jesus as Lord G5986
Col 2: 8 forces of this world rather than on C. G5986
Col 2: 9 For in C all the fullness of the Deity lives G899S
Col 2:10 in C you have been brought to G899S
Col 2:11 put off when you were circumcised *by* C, G5986
Col 2:13 of your flesh, God made you alive with C. G899S
Col 2:17 the reality, however, is found *in* C. G5986
Col 2:20 Since you died with C to the elemental G5986
Col 3: 1 you have been raised with C, set your G5986
Col 3: 1 on things above, where C is, seated at the G5986
Col 3: 3 your life is now hidden with C in God. G5986
Col 3: 4 When C, who is your life, appears, then G5986
Col 3:11 slave or free, but C is all, and is in all. G5986
Col 3:15 Let the peace *of* C rule in your hearts G5986
Col 3:16 Let the message *of* C dwell among you G5986
Col 3:24 It is the Lord C you are serving. G5986
Col 4: 3 so that we may proclaim the mystery *of* C G5986
Col 4:12 is one of you and a servant *of* C Jesus, G5986
1Th 1: 1 in God the Father and the Lord Jesus C: G5986
1Th 1: 3 inspired by hope in our Lord Jesus C. G5986
1Th 2: 6 though as apostles *of* C we could have G5986
1Th 2:14 churches in Judea, which are in C Jesus: G5986
1Th 3: 2 service in spreading the gospel *of* C, G5986
1Th 4:16 and the dead in C will rise first. G5986
1Th 5: 9 salvation through our Lord Jesus C. G5986
1Th 5:18 this is God's will for you in C Jesus. G5986
1Th 5:23 at the coming of our Lord Jesus C. G5986
1Th 5:28 The grace of our Lord Jesus C be with you. G5986
2Th 1: 1 in God our Father and the Lord Jesus C: G5986
2Th 1: 2 from God the Father and the Lord Jesus C. G5986
2Th 1:12 grace of our God and the Lord Jesus C. G5986
2Th 2: 1 of our Lord Jesus C and our being G5986
2Th 2:14 share in the glory of our Lord Jesus C. G5986
2Th 2:16 May our Lord Jesus C himself and God our G5986
2Th 3: 6 In the name of the Lord Jesus C, we G5986
2Th 3:12 in the Lord Jesus C to settle down and G5986
2Th 3:18 grace of our Lord Jesus C be with you all. G5986
1Ti 1: 1 an apostle *of* C Jesus by the command of G5986
1Ti 1: 1 God our Savior and *of* C Jesus our hope, G5986
1Ti 1: 2 from God the Father and C Jesus our Lord. G5986
1Ti 1:12 I thank C Jesus our Lord, who has given G5986
1Ti 1:14 with the faith and love that are in C Jesus. G5986
1Ti 1:15 C Jesus came into the world to save G5986
1Ti 1:16 C Jesus might display his immense G5986
1Ti 2: 5 God and mankind, the man C Jesus, G5986
1Ti 3:13 great assurance in their faith in C Jesus. G5986
1Ti 4: 6 you will be a good minister *of* C Jesus G5986
1Ti 5:11 desires overcome their dedication *to* C, G5986
1Ti 5:21 sight of God and C Jesus and the elect G5986
1Ti 6: 3 of our Lord Jesus C and to godly teaching, G5986
1Ti 6:13 to everything, and *of* C Jesus, who while G5986
1Ti 6:14 until the appearing of our Lord Jesus C, G5986
2Ti 1: 1 an apostle *of* C Jesus by the will of God G5986
2Ti 1: 1 with the promise of life that is in C Jesus, G5986
2Ti 1: 2 from God the Father and C Jesus our Lord. G5986
2Ti 1: 9 grace was given us in C Jesus before the G5986
2Ti 1:10 of our Savior, C Jesus, who has destroyed G5986
2Ti 1:13 teaching, with faith and love in C Jesus. G5986
2Ti 2: 1 be strong in the grace that is in C Jesus. G5986
2Ti 2: 3 suffering, like a good soldier *of* C Jesus. G5986
2Ti 2: 8 Remember Jesus C, raised from the dead G5986
2Ti 2:10 obtain the salvation that is in C Jesus, G5986
2Ti 3:12 to live a godly life in C Jesus will be G5986
2Ti 3:15 wise for salvation through faith in C Jesus. G5986
2Ti 4: 1 In the presence of God and of C Jesus G5986
Titus 1: 1 an apostle of Jesus C to further the faith G5986
Titus 1: 4 God the Father and C Jesus our Savior. G5986
Titus 2:13 of our great God and Savior, Jesus C, G5986
Titus 3: 6 us generously through Jesus C our Savior, G5986
Phm 1 a prisoner *of* C Jesus, and Timothy G5986
Phm 3 from God our Father and the Lord Jesus C. G5986
Phm 6 good thing we share for the sake of C. G5986
Phm 8 although in C I could be bold and order G5986
Phm 9 man and now also a prisoner of C Jesus— G5986
Phm 20 you in the Lord; refresh my heart in C. G5986
Phm 23 my fellow prisoner in C Jesus, sends you G5986
Phm 25 of the Lord Jesus C be with your spirit. G5986
Heb 3: 6 But C is faithful as the Son over God's G5986
Heb 3:14 We have come to share in C, if indeed we G5986
Heb 5: 5 C did not take on himself the glory of G5986
Heb 6: 1 teachings *about* C and be taken forward G5986
Heb 9:11 But when C came as high priest of the G5986
Heb 9:14 will the blood *of* C, who through the G5986
Heb 9:15 For this reason C is the mediator of a new NDT
Heb 9:24 For C did not enter a sanctuary made with G5986
Heb 9:26 Otherwise C would have had to suffer G899S
Heb 9:28 so C was sacrificed once to take away the G5986
Heb 10: 5 Therefore, when C came into the world, he NDT
Heb 10:10 of the body of Jesus C once for all. G5986
Heb 11:26 disgrace *for the sake of* C as of greater G5986
Heb 13: 8 Jesus C is the same yesterday and today G5986
Heb 13:21 through Jesus C, to whom be glory G5986
Jas 1: 1 a servant of God and of the Lord Jesus C G5986
Jas 2: 1 our glorious Lord Jesus C must not show G5986
1Pe 1: 1 an apostle of Jesus C, To God's elect, G5986
1Pe 1: 2 be obedient to Jesus C and sprinkled with G5986
1Pe 1: 3 to the God and Father of our Lord Jesus C! G5986
1Pe 1: 3 the resurrection of Jesus C from the dead, G5986
1Pe 1: 7 glory and honor when Jesus C is revealed. G5986
1Pe 1:11 to which the Spirit *of* C in them was G5986
1Pe 1:13 to you when Jesus C is revealed at his G5986
1Pe 1:19 with the precious blood *of* C, a lamb G5986
1Pe 2: 5 acceptable to God through Jesus C. G5986
1Pe 2:21 were called, because C suffered for you G5986
1Pe 3:15 But in your hearts revere C as Lord. G5986
1Pe 3:16 good behavior in C may be ashamed of G5986
1Pe 3:18 For C also suffered once for sins, the G5986
1Pe 3:21 It saves you by the resurrection of Jesus C, G5986
1Pe 4: 1 Therefore, since C suffered in his body G5986
1Pe 4:11 God may be praised through Jesus C. G5986
1Pe 4:13 as you participate in the sufferings *of* C, G5986
1Pe 4:14 are insulted because of the name *of* C, G5986
1Pe 5:10 who called you to his eternal glory in C G5986
1Pe 5:14 Peace to all of you who are in C. G5986
2Pe 1: 1 a servant and apostle of Jesus C, To those G5986
2Pe 1: 1 God and Savior Jesus C have received a G5986
2Pe 1: 8 in your knowledge of our Lord Jesus C. G5986
2Pe 1:11 kingdom of our Lord and Savior Jesus C. G5986
2Pe 1:14 as our Lord Jesus C has made clear to me. G5986
2Pe 1:16 the coming of our Lord Jesus C in power, G5986
2Pe 2:20 Lord and Savior Jesus C and are again G5986
2Pe 3:18 knowledge of our Lord and Savior Jesus C. G5986
1Jn 1: 3 with the Father and with his Son, Jesus C. G5986
1Jn 2: 1 the Father—Jesus C, the Righteous One. G5986
1Jn 2:22 It is whoever denies that Jesus is the C G5986
1Jn 3: 2 But we know that when C appears, we shall NDT
1Jn 3:16 **Jesus** C laid down his life for us G1697S
1Jn 3:23 name of his Son, Jesus C, and to love one G5986
1Jn 4: 2 that Jesus C has come in the flesh G5986
1Jn 5: 1 that Jesus is the C is born of God, G5986
1Jn 5: 6 who came by water and blood—Jesus C. G5986
1Jn 5:20 who is true by being in his Son Jesus C. G5986
2Jn 3 from God the Father and from Jesus C, G5986
2Jn 7 acknowledge Jesus C as coming in the G5986
2Jn 9 in the teaching *of* C does not have God; G5986
Jude 1 a servant of Jesus C and a brother of G5986
Jude 1 in God the Father and kept for Jesus C: G5986
Jude 4 deny Jesus C our only Sovereign and G5986
Jude 17 the apostles of our Lord Jesus C foretold. G5986
Jude 21 of our Lord Jesus C to bring you to eternal G5986
Jude 25 through Jesus C our Lord, before all G5986
Rev 1: 1 The revelation from Jesus C, which God G5986
Rev 1: 2 word of God and the testimony of Jesus C. G5986
Rev 1: 5 from Jesus C, who is the faithful G5986
Rev 20: 4 life and reigned with C a thousand years. G5986
Rev 20: 6 priests of God and *of* C and will reign with G5986

CHRIST'S (12) [CHRIST]

1Co 7:22 one who was free when called is C slave. G5986
1Co 9:21 free from God's law but am under C law), G5986
2Co 2:14 us as captives in C triumphal procession G5986
2Co 5:14 For C love compels us, because we are G5986
2Co 5:20 We are therefore C ambassadors, as G5986
2Co 5:20 We implore you on C behalf: Be G5986
2Co 12: 9 so that C power may rest on me. G5986
2Co 12:10 That is why, for C sake, I delight in G5986
Col 1:22 reconciled you by C physical body through G899S
Col 1:24 is still lacking in regard to C afflictions, G5986
2Th 3: 5 into God's love and C perseverance. G5986
1Pe 5: 1 a witness of C sufferings who also G5986

CHRISTIAN (2) [CHRIST]

Ac 26:28 time you can persuade me to be a C?" G5985
1Pe 4:16 if you suffer as a C, do not be ashamed, G5985

CHRISTIANS (1) [CHRIST]

Ac 11:26 disciples were called C first at Antioch. G5985

CHRONIC (1)

Lev 13:11 it is a c skin disease and the priest shall H3823

CHRONICLES (1)

Est 6: 1 so he ordered the book of the c, the H2355

CHRYSOLITE (4)

Ex 28:17 first row shall be carnelian, c and beryl; H7077
Ex 39:10 The first row was carnelian, c and beryl; H7077
Eze 28:13 carnelian, c and emerald, topaz, onyx H7077
Rev 21:20 sixth ruby, the seventh c, the eighth beryl, G5994

CHRYSOPRASE (NIV84) TURQUOISE

CHRYSOPRASUS (KJV) TURQUOISE

CHUB (KJV) KUB

CHUN (KJV) KUN

CHURCH (79) [CHURCHES]

Mt 16:18 on this rock I will build my c, and the G1711
Mt 18:17 to listen, tell it *to* the c; and if they refuse G1711
Mt 18:17 if they refuse to listen even *to* the c G1711
Ac 5:11 fear seized the whole c and all who heard G1711
Ac 8: 1 broke out against the c in Jerusalem, G1711
Ac 8: 3 But Saul began to destroy the c. G1711
Ac 9:31 Then the c throughout Judea, Galilee G1711
Ac 11:22 News of this reached the c in Jerusalem G1711
Ac 11:26 Saul met with the c and taught great G1711
Ac 12: 1 arrested some who belonged to the c, G1711
Ac 12: 5 the c was earnestly praying to God for G1711
Ac 13: 1 Now in the c at Antioch there were G1711
Ac 14:23 appointed elders for them in each c and, G1711
Ac 14:27 they gathered the c together and reported G1711
Ac 15: 3 The c sent them on their way, and as they G1711
Ac 15: 4 welcomed by the c and the apostles and G1711
Ac 15:22 with the whole c, decided to choose G1711
Ac 15:30 they gathered the c together and G4436S
Ac 18:22 greeted the c and then went down to G1711
Ac 20:17 sent to Ephesus for the elders *of* the c. G1711
Ac 20:28 Be shepherds *of* the c of God, which he G1711
Ro 16: 1 Phoebe, a deacon *of* the c in Cenchreae. G1711
Ro 16: 5 Greet also the c that meets at their house G1711
Ro 16:23 hospitality I and the whole c here enjoy, G1711
1Co 1: 2 *To* the c of God in Corinth, to those G1711
1Co 4:17 with what I teach everywhere in every c. G1711
1Co 5:12 is it of mine to judge those outside the c? NDT
1Co 6: 4 whose way of life is scorned in the c? G1711
1Co 10:32 whether Jews, Greeks or the c of God— G1711
1Co 11:18 hear that when you come together as a c, G1711
1Co 11:22 do you despise the c of God by G1711
1Co 12:28 has placed in the c first of all apostles G1711
1Co 14: 4 the one who prophesies edifies the c. G1711
1Co 14: 5 interprets, so that the c may be edified. G1711
1Co 14:12 try to excel in those that build up the c. G1711
1Co 14:19 But in the c I would rather speak five G1711
1Co 14:23 So if the whole c comes together and G1711
1Co 14:26 must be done so that the c may be built up. NDT
1Co 14:28 keep quiet in the c and speak to himself G1711
1Co 14:35 disgraceful for a woman to speak in the c. G1711
1Co 15: 9 because I persecuted the c of God. G1711
1Co 16:19 so does the c that meets at their G1711
2Co 1: 1 our brother, *To* the c of God in Corinth G1711
Gal 1:13 I persecuted the c of God and tried to G1711
Eph 1:22 him to be head over everything *for* the c, G1711
Eph 3:10 through the c, the manifold wisdom G1711
Eph 3:21 to him be glory in the c and in Christ Jesus G1711
Eph 5:23 of the wife as Christ is the head *of* the c, G1711
Eph 5:24 Now as the c submits to Christ, so also G1711
Eph 5:25 as Christ loved the c and gave himself up G1711
Eph 5:27 to present her to himself *as* a radiant c, G1711
Eph 5:29 their body, just as Christ does the c— G1711
Eph 5:32 I am talking about Christ and the c. G1711
Php 3: 6 persecuting the c; as for righteousness G1711
Php 4:15 not one c shared with me in the matter of G1711
Col 1:18 of the body, the c; he is the beginning G1711
Col 1:24 the sake of his body, which is the c. G1711
Col 4:15 to Nympha and the c in her house. G1711
Col 4:16 is also read in the c of the Laodiceans G1711
1Th 1: 1 *To* the c of the Thessalonians in God the G1711
2Th 1: 1 *To* the c of the Thessalonians in God our G1711
1Ti 3: 5 how can he take care of God's c? G1711
1Ti 3:15 which is the c of the living God, the G1711
1Ti 5:16 them and not let the c be burdened with G1711
1Ti 5:16 so that the c can help those widows who are NDT
1Ti 5:17 the affairs of the c well are worthy of double NDT
Phm 2 and *to* the c that meets in your home: G1711
Heb 12:23 *to* the c of the firstborn, whose names are G1711
Jas 5:14 call the elders *of* the c to pray over them G1711
3Jn 6 They have told the c about your love G1711
3Jn 9 I wrote *to* the c, but Diotrephes, who loves G1711
3Jn 10 want to do so and puts them out of the c. G1711
Rev 2: 1 "To the angel *of* the c in Ephesus write G1711
Rev 2: 8 "To the angel *of* the c in Smyrna write G1711
Rev 2:12 "To the angel *of* the c in Pergamum write G1711
Rev 2:18 "To the angel *of* the c in Thyatira write G1711
Rev 3: 1 "To the angel *of* the c in Sardis write G1711
Rev 3: 7 "To the angel *of* the c in Philadelphia G1711
Rev 3:14 "To the angel *of* the c in Laodicea write G1711

CHURCHES (35) [CHURCH]

Ac 15:41 Syria and Cilicia, strengthening the c. G1711
Ac 16: 5 So the c were strengthened in the faith G1711
Ro 16: 4 Not only I but all the c of the Gentiles are G1711
Ro 16:16 All the c of Christ send greetings G1711
1Co 7:17 This is the rule I lay down in all the c. G1711
1Co 11:16 no other practice—nor do the c of God. G1711
1Co 14:34 Women should remain silent in the c G1711
1Co 16: 1 Do what I told the Galatian c to do. G1711
1Co 16:19 The c in the province of Asia send you G1711
2Co 8: 1 that God has given the Macedonian c. G1711
2Co 8:18 is praised by all the c for his service to the G1711
2Co 8:19 was chosen by the c to accompany us as G1711
2Co 8:23 representatives *of* the c and an honor to G1711
2Co 8:24 our pride in you, so that the c can see it. G1711
2Co 11: 8 I robbed other c by receiving support from G1711
2Co 11:28 the pressure of my concern for all the c. G1711
2Co 12:13 How were you inferior to the other c G1711
Gal 1: 2 sisters with me, *To* the c in Galatia: G1711
Gal 1:22 unknown *to* the c of Judea that are G1711
1Th 2:14 became imitators *of* God's c in Judea G1711
1Th 2:14 the same things **those** c suffered from the G899S
2Th 1: 4 among God's c we boast about your G1711
Rev 1: 4 *To* the seven c in the province of Asia: G1711
Rev 1:11 what you see and send it *to* the seven c: G1711
Rev 1:20 seven stars are the angels *of* the seven c, G1711
Rev 1:20 the seven lampstands are the seven c. G1711
Rev 2: 7 let them hear what the Spirit says *to* the c. G1711
Rev 2:11 let them hear what the Spirit says *to* the c. G1711
Rev 2:17 let them hear what the Spirit says *to* the c. G1711
Rev 2:23 Then all the c will know that I am he who G1711
Rev 2:29 let them hear what the Spirit says *to* the c. G1711
Rev 3: 6 let them hear what the Spirit says *to* the c. G1711
Rev 3:13 let them hear what the Spirit says *to* the c. G1711
Rev 3:22 let them hear what the Spirit says *to* the c." G1711
Rev 22:16 angel to give you this testimony for the c. G1711

CHURN (1) [CHURNED, CHURNING]
Job 41:31 *It* **makes** the depths **c** like a boiling H8409

CHURNED (1) [CHURN]
Job 26:12 By his power *he* **c up** the sea; by his H8088

CHURNING (5) [CHURN]
Job 30:27 The **c** inside me never stops; days of H8409
Pr 30:33 For as **c** cream produces butter, and as H4790
Eze 32: 2 **c** the water with your feet and muddying H1931
Da 7: 2 four winds of heaven **c up** the great sea. A10137
Hab 3:15 sea with your horses, **c** the great waters. H2816

CHUSHAN-RISHATHAIM (KJV) CUSHAN-RISHATHAIM

CHUZA (1)
Lk 8: 3 Joanna the wife *of* C, the manager of G5966

CIELED (KJV) COVERED, PANELED, PANELS

CILICIA (8)
Ac 6: 9 as well as the **provinces of C** and Asia— G3070
Ac 15:23 Gentile believers in Antioch, Syria and C: G3070
Ac 15:41 He went through Syria and C G3070
Ac 21:39 from Tarsus *in* C, a citizen of no G3070
Ac 22: 3 born in Tarsus *of* C, but brought up in G3070
Ac 23:34 Learning that he was from C, G3070
Ac 27: 5 sea off the coast of C and Pamphylia, G3070
Gal 1:21 Then I went to Syria and C. G3070

CINNAMON (4)
Ex 30:23 shekels) of fragrant **c**, 250 shekels of H7872
Pr 7:17 perfumed my bed with myrrh, aloes and **c**. H7872
SS 4:14 calamus and **c**, with every kind of H7872
Rev 18:13 cargoes *of* **c** and spice, of incense, myrrh G3077

CINNEROTH (KJV) KINNERETH

CIRCLE (4) [CIRCLED, CIRCLING, CIRCUIT, CIRCULAR, CIRCUMFERENCE, ENCIRCLE, ENCIRCLED, ENCIRCLES, ENCIRCLING]
2Sa 5:23 but **c around** behind them and attack H6015
1Ch 14:14 but **c around** them and attack them in H6015
Isa 40:22 sits enthroned above the **c** *of* the earth, H2553
Mk 3:34 at those seated **in a c** around him and G3241

CIRCLED (1) [CIRCLE]
Jos 6:15 that on that day *they* **c** the city seven H6015

CIRCLING (1) [CIRCLE]
Jos 6:11 the LORD carried around the city, **c** it once. H5938

CIRCUIT (2) [CIRCLE]
1Sa 7:16 went *on a* **c** *from* Bethel *to* Gilgal *to* H6015
Ps 19: 6 the heavens and makes its **c** to the other; H9543

CIRCULAR (4) [CIRCLE]
1Ki 7:23 cast metal, **c in shape**, measuring H6318+6017
1Ki 7:31 that had a **c frame** one cubit deep. H4196
1Ki 7:35 there was a **c band** half a cubit H6318+6017
2Ch 4: 2 cast metal, **c in shape**, measuring H6318+6017

CIRCULATED (1)
Mt 28:15 this story *has been* **widely c** among the G1424

CIRCUMCISE (9) [CIRCUMCISED, CIRCUMCISING, CIRCUMCISION]
Dt 10:16 C your hearts, therefore, and do not H4576+6889
Dt 30: 6 The LORD your God *will* **c** your hearts and H4576
Jos 5: 2 flint knives and **c** the Israelites again." H4909
Jer 4: 4 **C yourselves** to the LORD, circumcise your H4576
Jer 4: 4 **c** your hearts, *you* people of Judah H6073+6889
Lk 1:59 the eighth day they came *to* **c** the child, G4362
Lk 2:21 when it was time *to* **c** the child, he was G4362
Jn 7:22 patriarchs), *you* **c** a boy on the Sabbath. G4362
Ac 21:21 telling them not *to* **c** their children or live G4362

CIRCUMCISED (55) [CIRCUMCISE]
Ge 17:10 Every male among you *shall* **be c**. H4576
Ge 17:12 you who is eight days old *must* **be c**, H4576
Ge 17:13 with your money, *they* **must be c**. H4576+4576
Ge 17:14 who *has* not **been c** *in* the flesh H4576+6889
Ge 17:23 and **c** them, as God H4576+1414+6889
Ge 17:24 years old when he **was c**, H4576+1414+6889
Ge 17:26 his son Ishmael **were** *both* **c** on that very H4576
Ge 17:27 bought from a foreigner, **was c** with him. H4576
Ge 21: 4 days old, Abraham **c** him, as God H4576
Ge 34:14 sister to a man who is **not c**. H6889+4200+2257
Ge 34:17 But if you will not agree to **be c**, we'll take H4576
Ge 34:22 only on the condition that our males **be c**, H4576
Ge 34:24 every male in the city **was c**. H4576
Ex 12:44 bought may eat it after *you have* **c** him, H4576
Ex 12:48 *must have* all the males in his household **c** H4576
Lev 12: 3 day the boy *is to* **be c**. H4576+1414+6889
Jos 5: 3 made flint knives and **c** the Israelites at H4576
Jos 5: 5 All the people that came out *had* **been c** H4576
Jos 5: 7 and these were the ones Joshua **c**. H4576
Jos 5: 7 because they *had* not *been* **c** on the way. H4576
Jos 5: 8 And after the whole nation *had* **been c** H4576
Jer 9:25 I will punish all *who are* **c** only in the H4576
Jn 7:23 Now if a boy *can be* **c** on the G4364+3284
Ac 7: 8 father of Isaac and **c** him eight days after G4362
Ac 10:45 The **c** believers who had come with Peter G4364
Ac 11: 2 Jerusalem, the **c** *believers* criticized him G4364
Ac 15: 1 "Unless *you are* **c**, according to the G4362
Ac 15: 5 "The Gentiles must *be* **c** and required to G4362
Ac 16: 3 so *he* **c** him because of the Jews who G4362
Ro 2:25 become as though you had **not** been **c**. G213
Ro 2:26 if those who are **not c** keep the law's G213
Ro 2:26 not be regarded as though they were **c**? G4364
Ro 2:27 The one who is **not c** physically and yet G213
Ro 3:30 who will justify the **c** by faith and the G4364
Ro 4: 9 Is this blessedness only for the **c**, or also G4364
Ro 4:10 Was it after he was **c**, or before? It G1877+4364
Ro 4:11 of all who believe but have **not** been **c**, G213
Ro 4:12 also the father *of* the **c** who not only are G4364
Ro 4:12 who not only are **c** but who also follow in G4364
Ro 4:12 Abraham had **before** he was **c**. G1877+213
1Co 7:18 *Was* a man *already* **c** when he was called G4362
1Co 7:18 when he was called? *He should* not be **c**. G4362
Gal 2: 3 was compelled *to be* **c**, even though he G4362
Gal 2: 7 just as Peter had been *to* the **c**. G4364
Gal 2: 8 at work in Peter as an apostle *to* the **c**, G4364
Gal 2: 9 go to the Gentiles, and they to the **c**. G4364
Gal 5: 2 tell you that if *you let yourselves be* **c** G4362
Gal 5: 3 every man *who lets himself be* **c** that he is G4362
Gal 6:12 the flesh are trying to compel you *to be* **c**. G4362
Gal 6:13 Not even those *who are* **c** keep the law G4362
Gal 6:13 they want you *to be* **c** that they may G4362
Php 3: 5 **c** on the eighth day, of the people of Israel G4364
Col 2:11 In him *you were* also **c** with a circumcision G4362
Col 2:11 was put off when you were **c** by Christ, G4364
Col 3:11 is no Gentile or Jew, **c** or uncircumcised G4364

CIRCUMCISING (1) [CIRCUMCISE]
Ge 34:15 you become like us by **c** all your males. H4576

CIRCUMCISION (21) [CIRCUMCISE]
Ge 17:11 You *are to* **undergo c** H4576+906+1414+6889
Ex 4:26 said "bridegroom of blood," referring to **c**.) H4581
Jn 7:22 because Moses gave you **c** (though G4364
Ac 7: 8 Then he gave Abraham the covenant *of* **c** G4364
Ro 2:25 **C** has value if you observe the law, but if G4364
Ro 2:27 though you have the written code and **c**, G4364
Ro 2:28 is **c** merely outward and physical. G4364
Ro 2:29 **c** is circumcision of the heart G4364
Ro 2:29 circumcision is **c** of the heart, by the NDT
Ro 3: 1 being a Jew, or what value is there *in* **c**? G4364
Ro 4:11 And he received **c** as a sign, a seal of the G4364
1Co 7:19 **C** is nothing and uncircumcision is nothing. G4364
Gal 2:12 of those who belonged to the **c group**. G4364
Gal 5: 6 Christ Jesus neither **c** nor uncircumcision G4364
Gal 5:11 if I am still preaching **c**, why am I still G4364
Gal 6:13 they may boast about your **c** in the flesh. NDT
Gal 6:15 Neither **c** nor uncircumcision means G4364
Eph 2:11 by those who call themselves "the **c**" G4364
Php 3: 3 For it is we who are the **c**, we who serve G4364
Col 2:11 also circumcised *with* a **c** not performed G4364
Titus 1:10 especially those of the **c group**. G4364

CIRCUMFERENCE (2) [CIRCLE]
1Ki 7:15 cubits high and twelve cubits **in c**. H6015+2562
Jer 52:21 cubits high and twelve cubits *in* **c**; H6015+2562

CIRCUMSPECT, CIRCUMSPECTLY (KJV) CAREFUL

CIRCUMSTANCES (8)
1Ch 29:30 the **c** that surrounded him and Israel H6961
Ro 4:10 **Under what c** was it credited? Was G4802+4036
1Co 7:15 brother or the sister is not bound in **such c**; AIT
Php 4:11 I have learned to be content **whatever** *the* **c**. AIT
Col 4: 8 may know about our **c** and that he may G3836
1Th 5:18 give thanks in **all c**; for this is God's will for AIT
Jas 1: 9 Believers **in humble c** ought to take pride G5424
1Pe 1:11 out the time and **c** to **which** the Spirit of AIT

CISTERN (21) [CISTERNS]
Ge 37:22 Throw him into this **c** here in the H1014
Ge 37:24 they took him and threw him into the **c**. H1014
Ge 37:24 The **c** was empty; there was H1014
Ge 37:28 Joseph up out of the **c** and sold him for H1014
Ge 37:29 returned to the **c** and saw that Joseph H1014
Lev 11:36 a **c** *for* collecting water remains clean H1014
1Sa 19:22 Ramah and went to the great **c** at Seku. H1014
2Sa 3:26 they brought him back from the **c** *at* Sirah. H1014
2Ki 18:31 fig tree and drink water from your own **c**, H1014
Pr 5:15 Drink water from your own **c**, running H1014
Isa 30:14 a hearth or scooping water out of a **c**." H1465
Isa 36:16 fig tree and drink water from your own **c**, H1014
Jer 38: 6 put him into the **c** *of* Malkijah, H1014
Jer 38: 6 lowered Jeremiah by ropes into the **c**; H1014
Jer 38: 7 that they had put Jeremiah into the **c**. H1014
Jer 38: 9 They have thrown him into a **c**, where he H1014
Jer 38:10 the prophet out of the **c** before he dies." H1014
Jer 38:11 down with ropes to Jeremiah in the **c**. H1014
Jer 38:13 with the ropes and lifted him out of the **c**. H1014
Jer 41: 7 them and threw them into a **c**. H1014
Jer 41: 9 Now the **c** where he threw all the bodies H1014

CISTERNS (6) [CISTERN]
Ge 37:20 him into one of these **c** and say that a H1014
1Sa 13: 6 among the rocks, and in pits and **c**. H1014
2Ch 26:10 towers in the wilderness and dug many **c**, H1014
Jer 2:13 have dug their own **c**, broken cisterns H1014
Jer 2:13 cisterns, broken **c** that cannot hold water. H1014
Jer 14: 3 they go to the **c** but find no water. H1463

CITADEL (20) [CITADELS]
2Sa 12:26 the Ammonites and captured the royal **c**. H6551
1Ki 16:18 he went into the **c** *of* the royal palace and H810
2Ki 15:25 in the **c** *of* the royal palace at Samaria. H810
Ezr 6: 2 was found in the **c** of Ecbatana in the A10101
Ne 1: 1 while I was in the **c** of Susa, H1072
Ne 2: 8 the gates of the **c** by the temple and H1072
Ne 7: 2 with Hananiah the commander of the **c**, H1072
Est 1: 2 from his royal throne in the **c** *of* Susa, H1072
Est 1: 5 to the greatest who were in the **c** of Susa. H1072
Est 2: 3 women into the harem at the **c** of Susa. H1072
Est 2: 5 there was in the **c** of Susa a Jew of the H1072
Est 2: 8 were brought to the **c** of Susa and put H1072
Est 3:15 the edict was issued in the **c** of Susa. H1072
Est 8:14 the edict was issued in the **c** of Susa. H1072
Est 9: 6 In the **c** of Susa, the Jews killed and H1072
Est 9:11 those killed in the **c** of Susa was reported H1072
Est 9:12 the ten sons of Haman in the **c** of Susa. H1072
Pr 18:19 disputes are like the barred gates of a **c**. H810
Isa 32:14 **c** and watchtower will become a H6755
Da 8: 2 I saw myself in the **c** of Susa in the H1072

CITADELS (4) [CITADEL]
Ps 48: 3 God is in her **c**; he has shown himself to be H810
Ps 48:13 ramparts, view her **c**, that you may tell of H810
Ps 122: 7 your walls and security within your **c**." H810
Isa 34:13 Thorns will overrun her **c**, nettles and H810

CITIES (149) [CITY]
Ge 13:12 Lot lived among the **c** *of* the plain and H6551
Ge 19:25 he overthrew those **c** and the entire plain, H6551
Ge 19:25 destroying all those living in the **c**—and H6551
Ge 19:29 So when God destroyed the **c** *of* the plain H6551
Ge 19:29 that overthrew the **c** where Lot had lived. H6551
Ge 22:17 take possession of the **c** *of* their enemies, H9133
Ge 24:60 offspring possess the **c** *of* their enemies." H9133
Ge 41:35 of Pharaoh, to be kept in the **c** for food. H6551
Ge 41:48 abundance in Egypt and stored it in the **c**. H6551
Ex 1:11 Rameses as store **c** for Pharaoh. H6551
Lev 26:25 When you withdraw into your **c**, I will H6551
Lev 26:31 I will turn your **c** into ruins and lay waste H6551
Lev 26:33 be laid waste, and your **c** will lie in ruins. H6551
Nu 13:28 the **c** are fortified and very large. H6551
Nu 21: 2 our hands, we will totally destroy their **c**." H6551
Nu 21:25 captured all the **c** *of* the Amorites and H6551
Nu 32:16 our livestock and **c** for our women and H6551
Nu 32:17 women and children will live in fortified **c**, H6551
Nu 32:24 Build **c** for your women and children, and H6551
Nu 32:26 herds will remain here in the **c** *of* Gilead. H6551
Nu 32:33 the whole land with its **c** and the territory H6551
Nu 32:36 Beth Nimrah and Beth Haran as fortified **c** H6551
Nu 32:38 They gave names to the **c** they rebuilt. H6551
Nu 35: 6 you give the Levites will be **c** *of* refuge, H6551
Nu 35:11 select some towns to be your **c** *of* refuge H6551
Nu 35:13 six towns you give will be your **c** *of* refuge. H6551
Nu 35:14 three in Canaan as **c** *of* refuge. H6551
Dt 1:28 than we are; the **c** are large, with walls H6551
Dt 3: 4 At that time we took all his **c**. H6551
Dt 3: 4 not one of the sixty **c** that we did not take H6551
Dt 3: 5 All these **c** were fortified with high walls H6551
Dt 3: 7 the plunder from their **c** we carried off H6551
Dt 4:41 set aside three **c** east of the Jordan, H6551
Dt 4:42 into one of these **c** and save their life. H6551
Dt 4:43 The **c** were these: Bezer in the wilderness NDT
Dt 6:10 with large, flourishing **c** you did not build, H6551
Dt 9: 1 with large **c** that have walls up to the sky. H6551
Dt 19: 2 yourselves three **c** in the land the LORD H6551
Dt 19: 3 may flee for refuge to **one of these c**. H9004S
Dt 19: 5 flee to one of these **c** and save his life. H6551
Dt 19: 7 you to set aside for yourselves three **c**. H6551
Dt 19: 9 then you are to set aside three more **c**. H6551
Dt 19:11 then flees to one of these **c**, H6551
Dt 20:15 are to treat all the **c** that are at a distance H6551
Dt 20:16 in the **c** *of* the nations the LORD your God H6551
Dt 28:52 lay siege to all the **c** throughout your land H9133
Dt 28:52 will besiege all the **c** throughout the land H9133
Dt 28:55 on you during the siege of all your **c**. H9133
Dt 28:57 inflict on you during the siege of your **c**. H9133
Jos 9:17 out and on the third day came to their **c**: H6551
Jos 10: 2 like one of the royal **c**; it was larger than H6551
Jos 10:19 the rear and don't let them reach their **c**, H6551
Jos 10:20 managed to reach their fortified **c**. H6551
Jos 11:12 took all these royal **c** and their kings and H6551
Jos 11:13 not burn any of the **c** built on their H6551
Jos 11:14 all the plunder and livestock of these **c**, H6551
Jos 13:31 the royal **c** *of* Og in Bashan). H6551
Jos 14:12 were there and their **c** were large and H6551
Jos 20: 2 the Israelites to designate the **c** *of* refuge, H6551
Jos 20: 4 When they flee to one of these **c**, they are H6551
Jos 20: 9 to these designated **c** and not be killed by H6551
Jos 24:13 you did not toil and **c** you did not build; H6551
2Sa 10:12 our people and the **c** *of* our God. H6551
2Sa 20: 6 he will find fortified **c** and escape from us." H6551
1Ki 4:13 sixty large walled **c** with bronze gate bars); H6551
1Ki 8:37 besieges them in any of their **c**, H824+9133
1Ki 9:19 as all his store **c** and the towns for his H6551
1Ki 10:26 kept in the chariot **c** and also with him in H6551
1Ki 15:23 all he did and the **c** he built, are they not H6551
1Ki 20:34 "I will return the **c** my father took from H6551
1Ki 22:39 with ivory, and the **c** he fortified, are they H6551

C

2Ki 18:13 all the fortified c of Judah and captured H6551
2Ki 19:25 have turned fortified c into piles of stone. H6551
1Ch 19:13 our people and the c of our God. H6551
2Ch 1:14 kept in the chariot c and also with him in H6551
2Ch 6:28 besiege them in any of their c, H824+9133
2Ch 8:4 all the store c he had built in Hamath H6551
2Ch 8:5 Lower Beth Horon as fortified c, H6551
2Ch 8:6 as well as Baalath and all his store c, and H6551
2Ch 8:6 all the c for his chariots and for his H6551
2Ch 9:25 kept in the chariot c and also with him in H6551
2Ch 11:10 These were fortified c in Judah and H6551
2Ch 11:12 and spears in all the c, H6551+2256+6551
2Ch 11:23 Benjamin, and to all the fortified c. H6551
2Ch 12:4 the fortified c of Judah and came as H6551
2Ch 14:6 He built up the fortified c of Judah, since H6551
2Ch 16:4 Abel Maim and all the store c of Naphtali. H6551
2Ch 17:2 in all the fortified c of Judah and put H6551
2Ch 17:12 he built forts and store c in Judah H6551
2Ch 17:19 in the fortified c throughout Judah. H6551
2Ch 19:5 in each of the fortified c of Judah. H6551
2Ch 19:10 you from your people who live in the c— H6551
2Ch 21:3 as well as fortified c in Judah, but he had H6551
2Ch 32:1 He laid siege to the fortified c, thinking to H6551
2Ch 33:14 in all the fortified c in Judah. H6551
Ne 9:25 They captured fortified c and fertile land H6551
Est 9:2 assembled in their c in all the provinces H6551
Ps 9:6 you have uprooted their c; even the H6551
Ps 69:35 will save Zion and rebuild the c of Judah. H6551
Isa 1:7 is desolate, your c burned with fire; your H6551
Isa 6:11 "Until the c lie ruined and without H6551
Isa 14:17 who overthrew its c and would not let his H6551
Isa 14:21 the land and cover the earth with their c. H6551
Isa 17:2 The c of Aroer will be deserted and left to H6551
Isa 17:9 In that day their strong c, which they left H6551
Isa 19:18 In that day five c in Egypt will speak the H6551
Isa 25:3 c of ruthless nations will revere you. H7953
Isa 36:1 all the fortified c of Judah and captured H6551
Isa 37:26 have turned fortified c into piles of stone. H6551
Isa 54:3 nations and settle in their desolate c. H6551
Isa 61:4 will renew the ruined c that have been H6551
Isa 64:10 Your sacred c have become a wasteland H6551
Jer 4:5 Let us flee to the fortified c!' H6551
Jer 4:16 raising a war cry against the c of Judah. H6551
Jer 5:17 destroy the fortified c in which you trust. H6551
Jer 8:14 us flee to the fortified c and perish there! H6551
Jer 13:19 The c in the Negev will be shut up, and H6551
Jer 14:2 "Judah mourns, her c languish; they wail H9133
Jer 34:7 the other c of Judah that were still H6551
Jer 34:7 were the only fortified c left in Judah. H6551
Jer 46:8 I will destroy c and their people. H6551
Jer 48:18 up against you and ruin your fortified c. H4448
Eze 26:19 a desolate city, like c no longer inhabited H6551
Eze 29:12 her c will lie desolate forty years H6551
Eze 29:12 lie desolate forty years among ruined c. H6551
Eze 30:7 their c will lie among ruined cities. H6551
Eze 30:7 their cities will lie among ruined c. H6551
Eze 30:17 the c themselves will go into captivity. NDT
Eze 36:35 of Eden; the c that were lying in ruins H6551
Eze 36:38 So will the ruined c be filled with flocks of H6551
Hos 8:14 send fire on their c that will consume their H6551
Hos 11:6 A sword will flash in their c; it will devour H6551
Hos 11:9 I will not come against their c. H6551
Am 9:14 will rebuild the ruined c and live in them. H6551
Mic 5:11 I will destroy the c of your land and tear H6551
Mic 5:14 Asherah poles when I demolish your c. H6551
Mic 7:12 to you from Assyria and the c of Egypt, H6551
Hab 1:10 They laugh at all fortified c; by building H4448
Hab 2:8 destroyed lands and c and everyone in H7953
Hab 2:17 destroyed lands and c and everyone in H7953
Zep 1:16 against the fortified c and against the H6551
Zep 3:6 Their c are laid waste; they are deserted H6551
Zec 8:20 the inhabitants of many c will yet come, H6551
Lk 19:17 a very small matter, take charge of ten c. G4484
Lk 19:19 answered, 'You take charge of five c.' G4484
Ac 14:6 to the Lycaonian c of Lystra and Derbe G4484
Ac 26:11 I even hunted them down in foreign c. G4484
2Pe 2:6 if he condemned the c of Sodom and G4484
Rev 16:19 and the c of the nations collapsed. G4484

CITIZEN (8) [CITIZENS, CITIZENSHIP]

Lk 15:15 hired himself out to a c of that country, G4489
Ac 21:39 Tarsus in Cilicia, a c of no ordinary city. G4489
Ac 22:25 you to flog a Roman c who hasn't G476+4871
Ac 22:26 he asked. "This man is a Roman c." G4871
Ac 22:27 asked, "Tell me, are you a Roman c?" G4871
Ac 22:28 "But I was born a c," Paul replied. NDT
Ac 22:29 he had put Paul, a Roman c, in chains. G4871
Ac 23:27 I had learned that he is a Roman c. G4871

CITIZENS (24) [CITIZEN]

Nu 21:28 Ar of Moab, the c of Arnon's heights. H1251
Jos 24:11 The c of Jericho fought against you, as H1251
Jdg 9:2 "Ask all the c of Shechem, 'Which is better H1251
Jdg 9:3 repeated all this to the c of Shechem, H1251
Jdg 9:6 Then all the c of Shechem and Beth Millo H1251
Jdg 9:7 "Listen to me, c of Shechem, so that God H1251
Jdg 9:18 king over the c of Shechem because he is H1251
Jdg 9:20 the c of Shechem and Beth Millo H1251
Jdg 9:20 the c of Shechem and Beth Millo H1251
Jdg 9:23 Abimelek and the c of Shechem so that H1251
Jdg 9:24 Abimelek and on the c of Shechem, H1251
Jdg 9:25 to him these c of Shechem set men on H1251
Jdg 9:26 its c put their confidence in him. H1251
Jdg 9:39 Gaal led out the c of Shechem and fought H1251
Jdg 9:46 the c in the tower of Shechem went into H1251
1Sa 23:11 Will the c of Keilah surrender me to him H1251
1Sa 23:12 "Will the c of Keilah surrender me and my H1251
2Sa 21:12 Jonathan from the c of Jabesh Gilead. H1251
Isa 48:2 who call yourselves c of the holy city H4946S
Jer 29:16 your fellow c who did not go with you into H278
Eze 26:17 you and your c; you put your terror H3782
Ac 16:37 even though we are Roman c, and G476+4871
Ac 16:38 heard that Paul and Silas were Roman c, G4871
Eph 2:19 fellow c with God's people and also G5232

CITIZENSHIP (3) [CITIZEN]

Ac 22:28 "I had to pay a lot of money for my c." G4486
Eph 2:12 excluded from c in Israel and foreigners to G4486
Php 3:20 But our c is in heaven. And we eagerly G4487

CITRON (1)

Rev 18:12 every sort of c wood, and articles of G2591

CITY (720) [CITIES, CITY'S]

Ge 4:17 Cain was then building a c, and he H6551
Ge 10:12 Nineveh and Calah—which is the great c. H6551
Ge 11:4 let us build ourselves a c, with a tower H6551
Ge 11:5 came down to see the c and the tower the H6551
Ge 11:8 and they stopped building the c. H6551
Ge 18:24 if there are fifty righteous people in the c? H6551
Ge 18:26 fifty righteous people in the c of Sodom, H6551
Ge 18:28 you destroy the whole c for lack of five H6551
Ge 19:1 Lot was sitting in the gateway of the c. H6042S
Ge 19:4 men from every part of the c of Sodom— H6551
Ge 19:12 anyone else in the c who belongs to you? H6551
Ge 19:14 because the LORD is about to destroy the c!" H6551
Ge 19:15 be swept away when the c is punished." H6551
Ge 19:16 led them safely out of the c, H6551
Ge 23:10 who had come to the gate of his c. H6551
Ge 23:18 who had come to the gate of the c. H6551
Ge 28:19 though the c used to be called Luz. H6551
Ge 33:18 safely at the c of Shechem in Canaan H6551
Ge 33:18 Canaan and camped within sight of the c. H6551
Ge 34:20 to the gate of their c to speak to the men H6551
Ge 34:20 of their city to speak to the men of their c. H6551
Ge 34:24 who went out of the c gate agreed with H6551
Ge 34:24 every male in the c was circumcised. H6551
Ge 34:25 swords and attacked the unsuspecting c, H6551
Ge 34:27 bodies and looted the c where their sister H6551
Ge 34:28 else of theirs in the c and out in the fields H6551
Ge 36:32 king of Edom. His c was named Dinhabah H6551
Ge 36:35 His c was named Avith. H6551
Ge 36:39 His c was named Pau, and his wife's H6551
Ge 41:48 In each c he put the food grown in the H6551
Ge 44:4 gone far from the c when Joseph said to H6551
Ge 44:13 their donkeys and returned to the c. H6551
Ex 9:29 "When I have gone out of the c, I will H6551
Ex 9:33 Moses left Pharaoh and went out of the c. H6551
Lev 25:29 a house in a walled c retains the right of H6551
Lev 25:30 the house in the walled c shall belong H6551
Nu 21:26 Heshbon was the c of Sihon king of the H6551
Nu 21:27 let it be rebuilt; let Sihon's c be restored. H6551
Nu 21:28 Heshbon, a blaze from the c of Sihon. H7953
Nu 24:19 of Jacob and destroy the survivors of the c." H6551
Nu 35:25 accused back to the c of refuge to which H6551
Nu 35:26 the limits of the c of refuge to which they H6551
Nu 35:27 of blood finds them outside the c, H6551
Nu 35:28 must stay in the c of refuge until the H6551
Nu 35:32 who has fled to a c of refuge and so allow H6551
Dt 3:6 of Heshbon, destroying every c—men, H6551
Dt 17:5 evil deed to your c gate and stone that H9133
Dt 19:12 be brought back from the c, and be H9004S
Dt 20:10 When you march up to attack a c, make H6551
Dt 20:12 engage you in battle, lay siege to that c. H2023S
Dt 20:14 the livestock and everything else in the c H6551
Dt 20:19 When you lay siege to a c for a long time H6551
Dt 20:20 works until the c at war with you falls H6551
Dt 28:3 be blessed in the c and blessed in the H6551
Dt 28:16 will be cursed in the c and cursed in the H6551
Dt 34:3 of Jericho, the C of Palms, as far as Zoar H6551
Jos 2:5 when it was time to close the c gate, they H9133
Jos 2:15 house she lived in was part of the c wall. H7815
Jos 6:3 March around the c once with all the H6551
Jos 6:4 march around the c seven times, with the H6551
Jos 6:5 then the wall of the c will collapse and H6551
Jos 6:7 March around the c, with an armed guard H6551
Jos 6:11 the ark of the LORD carried around the c, H6551
Jos 6:14 marched around the c once and returned H6551
Jos 6:15 marched around the c seven times in the H6551
Jos 6:15 on that day they circled the c seven times. H6551
Jos 6:16 For the LORD has given you the c! H6551
Jos 6:17 The c and all that is in it are to be devoted H6551
Jos 6:20 charged straight in, and they took the c. H6551
Jos 6:21 They devoted the c to the LORD and H6551
Jos 6:24 burned the whole c and everything in it, H6551
Jos 6:26 the one who undertakes to rebuild this c, H6551
Jos 7:5 Israelites from the c gate as far as the H9133
Jos 8:1 king of Ai, his people, his c and his land. H6551
Jos 8:2 Set an ambush behind the c." H6551
Jos 8:4 You are to set an ambush behind the c H6551
Jos 8:5 all those with me will advance on the c, H6551
Jos 8:6 until we have lured them away from the c, H6551
Jos 8:7 to rise up from ambush and take the c. H6551
Jos 8:8 When you have taken the c, set it on fire H6551
Jos 8:11 approached the c and arrived in front H6551
Jos 8:11 with the valley between them and the c. H6504S
Jos 8:12 Bethel and Ai, to the west of the c. H6551
Jos 8:13 to the north of the c and the ambush to H6551
Jos 8:14 all the men of the c hurried out early in H6551
Jos 8:14 had been set against him behind the c. H6551
Jos 8:16 Joshua and were lured away from the c. H6551
Jos 8:17 They left the c open and went in pursuit H6551
Jos 8:18 into your hand I will deliver the c." H5626S
Jos 8:18 held out toward the c the javelin that was H6551
Jos 8:19 They entered the c and captured it and H6551
Jos 8:20 saw the smoke of the c rising up into the H6551
Jos 8:21 had taken the c and that smoke was H6551
Jos 8:22 also came out of the c against them, H6551
Jos 8:27 the livestock and plunder of this c, H6551
Jos 8:29 it down at the entrance of the c gate. H6551
Jos 10:2 because Gibeon was an important c, like H6551
Jos 10:28 He put the c and its king to the sword H2023S
Jos 10:30 LORD also gave that c and its king into H2023S
Jos 10:30 The c and everyone in it Joshua put to H2023S
Jos 10:32 The c and everyone in it he put to the H2023S
Jos 10:37 They took the c and put it to the sword H2023S
Jos 10:39 They took the c, its king and its villages H2023S
Jos 11:19 not one c made a treaty of peace with the H6551
Jos 15:8 along the southern slope of the Jebusite c NDT
Jos 15:62 Nibshan, the C of Salt and En Gedi—six H6551
Jos 18:16 slope of the Jebusite c and so to En Rogel. AIT
Jos 18:28 Haeleph, the Jebusite c (that is AIT
Jos 19:29 Ramah and went to the fortified c of Tyre, H6551
Jos 20:4 the entrance of the c gate and state their H6551
Jos 20:4 state their case before the elders of that c. H6551
Jos 20:4 fugitive into their c and provide a place to H6551
Jos 20:6 are to stay in that c until they have stood H6551
Jos 21:12 villages around the c they had given to H6551
Jos 21:13 a c of refuge for one accused of murder), H6551
Jos 21:21 a c of refuge for one accused of murder H6551
Jos 21:27 a c of refuge for one accused of murder H6551
Jos 21:32 a c of refuge for one accused of murder), H6551
Jos 21:38 a c of refuge for one accused of murder), H6551
Jdg 1:8 They put the c to the sword and set it on H6551
Jdg 1:16 went up from the C of Palms with the H6551
Jdg 1:17 Zephath, and they totally destroyed the c. H6551
Jdg 1:18 Ekron—each c with its territory. NDT
Jdg 1:24 coming out of the c and they said to him, H6551
Jdg 1:24 how to get into the c and we will see that H6551
Jdg 1:25 they put the c to the sword but spared H6551
Jdg 1:26 where he built a c and called it Luz, which H6551
Jdg 3:13 they took possession of the C of Palms. H6551
Jdg 5:8 leaders when war came to the c gates, H9133
Jdg 5:11 of the LORD went down to the c gates. H9133
Jdg 9:30 the governor of the c heard what Gaal son H6551
Jdg 9:31 are stirring up the c against you. H6551
Jdg 9:33 at sunrise, advance against the c. H6551
Jdg 9:35 the entrance of the c gate just as H6551
Jdg 9:43 he saw the people coming out of the c, H6551
Jdg 9:44 to a position at the entrance of the c gate. H6551
Jdg 9:45 attack against the c until he had captured H6551
Jdg 9:45 he destroyed the c and scattered salt H6551
Jdg 9:51 Inside the c, however, was a strong tower H6551
Jdg 9:51 all the people of the c—had fled. H6551
Jdg 16:2 lay in wait for him all night at the c gate. H6551
Jdg 16:3 took hold of the doors of the c gate, H6551
Jdg 18:27 with the sword and burned down their c. H6551
Jdg 18:28 The c was in a valley near Beth Rehob H2085S
Jdg 18:28 Danites rebuilt the c and settled there. H6551
Jdg 18:29 though the c used to be called Laish. H6551
Jdg 19:11 let's stop at this c of the Jebusites and H6551
Jdg 19:12 won't go into any c whose people are not H6551
Jdg 19:15 They went and sat in the c square, but no H6551
Jdg 19:17 saw the traveler in the c square, H6551
Jdg 19:22 wicked men of the c surrounded the H6551
Jdg 20:11 together and united as one against the c. H6551
Jdg 20:31 them and were drawn away from the c. H6551
Jdg 20:32 draw them away from the c to the roads." H6551
Jdg 20:37 out and put the whole c to the sword. H6551
Jdg 20:38 up a great cloud of smoke from the c, H6551
Jdg 20:40 column of smoke began to rise from the c, H6551
Jdg 20:40 saw the whole c going up in smoke. H6551
1Sa 5:9 the LORD's hand was against that c H6551
1Sa 5:9 He afflicted the people of the c, both H6551
1Sa 5:11 For death had filled the c with panic H6551
1Sa 5:12 the outcry of the c went up to heaven. H6551
1Sa 15:5 Saul went to the c of Amalek and set an H6551
1Sa 27:5 your servant live in the royal c with you?" H6551
2Sa 5:7 fortress of Zion—which is the C of David. H6551
2Sa 5:9 in the fortress and called it the C of David. H6551
2Sa 6:10 the LORD to be with him in the C of David. H6551
2Sa 6:12 of Obed-Edom to the C of David with H6551
2Sa 6:16 of the LORD was entering the C of David, H6551
2Sa 10:3 only to explore the c and spy it out and H6551
2Sa 10:8 formation at the entrance of their c gate, H9133
2Sa 10:14 fled before Abishai and went inside the c. H6551
2Sa 11:16 So while Joab had the c under siege, he H6551
2Sa 11:17 When the men of the c came out and H6551
2Sa 11:20 'Why did you get so close to the c to fight? H6551
2Sa 11:23 them back to the entrance of the c gate. H9133
2Sa 11:25 the attack against the c and destroy it. H6551
2Sa 12:28 troops and besiege the c and capture it. H6551
2Sa 12:28 Otherwise I will take the c, and it will be H6551
2Sa 12:30 took a great quantity of plunder from the c H6551
2Sa 15:2 the side of the road leading to the c gate. H9133
2Sa 15:14 ruin on us and put the c to the sword." H6551

2Sa 15:17 and they halted at the edge of the c. H1074
2Sa 15:24 all the people had finished leaving the c. H6551
2Sa 15:25 "Take the ark of God back into the c. H6551
2Sa 15:27 Go back to the c with my blessing. H6551
2Sa 15:34 if you return to the c and say to Absalom, H6551
2Sa 15:37 as Absalom was entering the c. H6551
2Sa 17:13 If he withdraws into a c, then all Israel will H6551
2Sa 17:13 then all Israel will bring ropes to that c H6551
2Sa 17:17 could not risk being seen entering the c. H6551
2Sa 18: 3 now for you to give us support from the c." H6551
2Sa 18: 6 army marched out of the c to fight Israel, H8441
2Sa 19: 3 men stole into the c that day as men steal H6551
2Sa 20:15 They built a siege ramp up to the c, and it H6551
2Sa 20:16 a wise woman called from the c, "Listen H6551
2Sa 20:19 are trying to destroy a c that is a mother in H6551
2Sa 20:21 one man, and I'll withdraw from the c." H6551
2Sa 20:22 his men dispersed from the c, each H6551
1Ki 1:41 the meaning of all the noise in the c?" H7953
1Ki 1:45 up cheering, and the c resounds with it. H7953
1Ki 2:10 was buried in the C *of* David. H6551
1Ki 3: 1 He brought her to the C *of* David until he H6551
1Ki 8: 1 LORD's covenant from Zion, the C *of* David. H6551
1Ki 8:16 I have not chosen a c in any tribe of Israel H6551
1Ki 8:44 LORD toward the c you have chosen and H6551
1Ki 8:48 toward the c you have chosen and the H6551
1Ki 9:24 come up from the C *of* David to the H6551
1Ki 11:27 in the wall of the c *of* David his father. H6551
1Ki 11:32 my servant David and the c of Jerusalem, H6551
1Ki 11:36 the c where I chose to put my Name. H6551
1Ki 11:43 was buried in the c *of* David his father. H6551
1Ki 13:25 reported it in the c where the old prophet H6551
1Ki 13:29 it back to his own c to mourn for him and H6551
1Ki 14:11 belonging to Jeroboam who die in the c, H6551
1Ki 14:12 When you set foot in your c, the boy will H6551
1Ki 14:21 the c the LORD had chosen out of all the H6551
1Ki 14:31 was buried with them in the C *of* David. H6551
1Ki 15: 8 was buried in the C *of* David. H6551
1Ki 15:24 with them in the c *of* his father David. H6551
1Ki 16: 4 belonging to Baasha who die in the c, H6551
1Ki 16:18 When Zimri saw that the c was taken, he H6551
1Ki 16:24 talents of silver and built a c on the hill, H6551
1Ki 20: 2 messengers into the c to Ahab king of H6551
1Ki 20:12 So they prepared to attack the c. H6551
1Ki 20:19 marched out of the c with the army H6551
1Ki 20:30 rest of them escaped to the c of Aphek, H6551
1Ki 20:30 fled to the c and hid in an inner H6551
1Ki 21: 8 nobles who lived in Naboth's c with him. H6551
1Ki 21:11 who lived in Naboth's c did as Jezebel H6551
1Ki 21:13 took him outside the c and stoned him to H6551
1Ki 21:24 belonging to Ahab who die in the c, H6551
1Ki 22:26 Amon the ruler of the c and to Joash the H6551
1Ki 22:50 with them in the c *of* David his father. H6551
2Ki 2:19 The people of the c said to Elisha, "Look H6551
2Ki 3:19 every fortified c and every major town. H6551
2Ki 3:27 offered him as a sacrifice on the **c wall**. H2570
2Ki 6:14 They went by night and surrounded the c. H6551
2Ki 6:15 horses and chariots had surrounded the c. H6551
2Ki 6:19 "This is not the road and this is not the c. H6551
2Ki 6:20 After they entered **the c**, Elisha said H9076S
2Ki 6:25 There was a great famine in **the c**; the H9076S
2Ki 7: 3 with leprosy at the entrance of the **c gate**. H9133
2Ki 7: 4 'We'll go into the c'—the famine is there, H6551
2Ki 7:10 called out to the c gatekeepers and told H6551
2Ki 7:12 we will take them alive and get into the c. H6551
2Ki 7:13 five of the horses that are left in **the c**. H2023S
2Ki 8:24 was buried with them in the C *of* David. H6551
2Ki 9:15 anyone slip out of the c to go and tell the H6551
2Ki 9:28 ancestors in his tomb in the C *of* David. H6551
2Ki 10: 2 horses, a fortified c and weapons. H6551
2Ki 10: 5 administrator, the c governor, the elders H6551
2Ki 10: 6 were with the leading men of the c, who H6551
2Ki 10: 8 the entrance of the **c gate** until morning." H9133
2Ki 11:20 rejoiced, and the c was calm, because H6551
2Ki 12:21 with his ancestors in the C *of* David. H6551
2Ki 14:20 with his ancestors, in the C *of* David. H6551
2Ki 15: 7 was buried near them in the C *of* David. H6551
2Ki 15:16 everyone in **the c** and its vicinity, H2023S
2Ki 15:38 was buried with them in the C *of* David, H6551
2Ki 15:38 them in the City of David, the c of his father. NDT
2Ki 16:20 was buried with them in the C *of* David. H6551
2Ki 17: 9 to fortified c they built themselves H6551
2Ki 18: 8 From watchtower to fortified c, he defeated H6551
2Ki 18:30 this c will not be given into the hand of H6551
2Ki 19:32 will not enter this c or shoot an arrow here H6551
2Ki 19:33 he will not enter this c, declares the LORD. H6551
2Ki 19:34 I will defend this c and save it, for my H6551
2Ki 20: 6 you and this c from the hand of the H6551
2Ki 20: 6 I will defend this c for my sake and for the H6551
2Ki 20:20 by which he brought water into the c, H6551
2Ki 23: 8 Gate of Joshua, the c governor, which was H6551
2Ki 23: 8 which was on the left of the c gate. H6551
2Ki 23:17 The people of the c said, "It marks the H6551
2Ki 23:27 reject Jerusalem, the c I chose, and this H6551
2Ki 24:11 himself came up to the c while his officers H6551
2Ki 25: 1 encamped outside **the c** and built siege H2023S
2Ki 25: 2 The c was kept under siege until the H6551
2Ki 25: 3 the famine in the c had become so severe H6551
2Ki 25: 4 Then the c wall was broken through, and H6551
2Ki 25: 4 the Babylonians were surrounding the c. H6551
2Ki 25:11 exile the people who remained in the c, H6551
2Ki 25:19 Of those still in the c, he took the officer in H6551
2Ki 25:19 of the conscripts who were found in the c. H6551
1Ch 1:43 of Beor, whose c was named Dinhabah. H6551
1Ch 1:46 His c was named Avith. H6551
1Ch 1:50 His c was named Pau, and his wife's H6551
1Ch 6:56 villages around the c were given to Caleb H6551
1Ch 6:57 given Hebron (a c *of* refuge), and Libnah H6551
1Ch 6:67 given Shechem (a c *of* refuge), and Gezer, H6551
1Ch 11: 5 fortress of Zion—which is the C *of* David. H6551
1Ch 11: 7 so it was called the C *of* David. H6551
1Ch 11: 8 He built up the c around it, from the H6551
1Ch 11: 8 while Joab restored the rest of the c. H6551
1Ch 13:13 the ark to be with him in the C *of* David. H6551
1Ch 15: 1 buildings for himself in the C *of* David, H6551
1Ch 15:29 of the LORD was entering the C *of* David, H6551
1Ch 19: 9 battle formation at the entrance to their c, H6551
1Ch 19:15 his brother Abishai and went inside the c. H6551
1Ch 20: 2 took a great quantity of plunder from the c H6551
2Ch 5: 2 LORD's covenant from Zion, the C *of* David. H6551
2Ch 6: 5 I have not chosen a c in any tribe of Israel H6551
2Ch 6:34 to you toward this c you have chosen and H6551
2Ch 6:38 toward the c you have chosen and toward H6551
2Ch 8:11 up from the C *of* David to the palace H6551
2Ch 9:31 was buried in the c *of* David his father. H6551
2Ch 12:13 the c the LORD had chosen out of all the H6551
2Ch 12:16 was buried in the C *of* David. H6551
2Ch 14: 1 was buried in the C *of* David. H6551
2Ch 15: 6 crushed by another and *one* c by another, H6551
2Ch 16:14 had cut out for himself in the C *of* David. H6551
2Ch 18:25 Amon the ruler of the c and to Joash the H6551
2Ch 21: 1 was buried with them in the C *of* David. H6551
2Ch 21:20 was buried in the C *of* David, but not H6551
2Ch 23:21 rejoiced, and the c was calm, because H6551
2Ch 24:16 buried with the kings in the C *of* David, H6551
2Ch 24:25 he died and was buried in the C *of* David, H6551
2Ch 25:28 with his ancestors in the C *of* Judah. H6551
2Ch 27: 9 was buried in the C *of* David. H6551
2Ch 28:15 at Jericho, the C *of* Palms, and returned to H6551
2Ch 28:27 was buried in the c of Jerusalem, H6551
2Ch 29:20 Hezekiah gathered the c officials together H6551
2Ch 32: 3 the water from the springs outside the c, H6551
2Ch 32: 5 reinforced the terraces of the C *of* David. H6551
2Ch 32: 6 the square at the c gate and encouraged H6551
2Ch 32:18 them afraid in order to capture the c. H6551
2Ch 32:30 down to the west side of the C *of* David. H6551
2Ch 33:14 he rebuilt the outer wall of the C *of* David, H6551
2Ch 33:15 he threw them out of the c. H6551
2Ch 34: 8 Azaliah and Maaseiah the ruler of the c, H6551
Ezr 4:10 settled in the c of Samaria and A10640
Ezr 4:12 rebuilding that rebellious and wicked c. A10640
Ezr 4:13 know that if this c is built and its walls A10640
Ezr 4:15 will find that this c is a rebellious city, A10640
Ezr 4:15 will find that this city is a rebellious c, A10640
Ezr 4:15 That is why this c was destroyed. A10640
Ezr 4:16 the king that if this c is built and its walls A10640
Ezr 4:19 was found that this c has a long history A10640
Ezr 4:21 so that this c will not be rebuilt until I so A10640
Ne 2: 3 look sad when the c where my ancestors H6551
Ne 2: 5 him send me to the c in Judah where my H6551
Ne 2: 8 the temple and for the c wall and for the H6551
Ne 3:15 the steps going down from the C *of* David. H6551
Ne 7: 4 Now the c was large and spacious, but H6551
Ne 11: 1 Jerusalem, the holy c, while the H6551
Ne 11: 9 was over the New Quarter of the c. H6551
Ne 11:18 The Levites in the holy c totaled 284. H6551
Ne 12:37 up the steps of the C *of* David on the H6551
Ne 13:18 all this calamity on us and on this c? H6551
Est 3:15 but the c *of* Susa was bewildered. H6551
Est 4: 1 went out into the c, wailing loudly H6551
Est 4: 6 open square of the c in front of the king's H6551
Est 6: 9 him on the horse through the c streets, H6551
Est 6:11 him on horseback through the c streets, H6551
Est 8:11 the Jews in every c the right to assemble H6551
Est 8:15 And the c *of* Susa held a joyous H6551
Est 8:17 in every c to which the edict of H6551
Est 9:28 province and in **every c**. H6551+2256+6551
Job 24:12 The groans of the dying rise from the c H6551
Job 29: 7 to the gate of the c and took my seat in H7984
Ps 31:21 of his love when I was in a c under siege. H6551
Ps 45:12 The c *of* Tyre will come with a gift, people H1426
Ps 46: 4 whose streams make glad the c *of* God, H6551
Ps 48: 1 of praise, in the c *of* our God, his holy H6551
Ps 48: 2 is Mount Zion, the c *of* the Great King. H7953
Ps 48: 8 have seen in the c *of* the LORD Almighty, H6551
Ps 48: 8 of the LORD Almighty, in the c *of* our God: H6551
Ps 55: 9 I see violence and strife in the c. H6551
Ps 55:11 Destructive forces are at work in **the c** H2023S
Ps 59: 6 snarling like dogs, and prowl about the c. H6551
Ps 59:14 snarling like dogs, and prowl about the c. H6551
Ps 60: 9 Who will bring me to the fortified c? Who H6551
Ps 87: 1 He has founded his c on the holy mountain. NDT
Ps 87: 3 Glorious things are said of you, c *of* God: H6551
Ps 101: 8 off every evildoer from the c *of* the LORD. H6551
Ps 107: 4 finding no way to a c where they could H6551
Ps 107: 7 by a straight way to a c where they could H6551
Ps 107:36 they founded a c *where* they could settle H6551
Ps 108:10 Who will bring me to the fortified c? Who H6551
Ps 122: 3 is built like a c that is closely compacted H6551
Ps 127: 1 Unless the LORD watches over the c, the H6551
Pr 1:21 at the c gate she makes her speech: H6551
Pr 8: 3 beside the gate leading into the c, at the H7984
Pr 9: 3 she calls from the highest point of the c, H7984
Pr 9:14 on a seat at the highest point of the c, H7984
Pr 10:15 The wealth of the rich is their fortified c H7953
Pr 11:10 prosper, the c rejoices; when the H7953
Pr 11:11 the blessing of the upright a c is exalted, H7984
Pr 16:32 with self-control than one who takes a c. H6551
Pr 18:11 The wealth of the rich is their fortified c H7953
Pr 18:19 is more unyielding than a fortified c; H7953
Pr 21:22 go up against the c *of* the mighty and pull H6551
Pr 25:28 Like a c whose walls are broken through is H6551
Pr 29: 8 Mockers stir up a c, but the wise turn away H7953
Pr 31:23 Her husband is respected at the **c gate** H9133
Pr 31:31 her works bring her praise at the **c gate**. H9133
Ecc 7:19 more powerful than ten rulers in a c. H6551
Ecc 8:10 receive praise in the c where they did this. H6551
Ecc 9:14 There was once a small c with only a few H6551
Ecc 9:15 Now there lived in **that c** a man poor H2023S
Ecc 9:15 and he saved the c by his wisdom. H6551
SS 3: 2 I will get up now and go about the c H6551
SS 3: 3 me as they made their rounds in the c. H6551
SS 5: 7 me as they made their rounds in the c. H6551
Isa 1: 8 in a cucumber field, like a c under siege. H6551
Isa 1:21 See how the faithful c has become a H7953
Isa 1:26 you will be called the C *of* Righteousness, H6551
Isa 1:26 the City of Righteousness, the Faithful C." H7953
Isa 14:31 Howl, you c! Melt away, all you H6551
Isa 17: 1 will no longer be a c but will become a H6551
Isa 17: 3 The fortified c will disappear from Ephraim NDT
Isa 19: 2 against neighbor, c against city, kingdom H6551
Isa 19: 2 neighbor, city against c, kingdom against H6551
Isa 19:18 of them will be called the C *of* the Sun. H6551
Isa 22: 2 commotion, you c *of* tumult and revelry? H7953
Isa 22: 7 horsemen are posted at the **c gates**. H9133
Isa 22: 9 the walls of the C *of* David were broken H6551
Isa 23: 7 Is this your c of revelry, the old, old city NDT
Isa 23: 7 the old, old c, whose feet have taken her H2023S
Isa 23:16 walk through the c, you forgotten H6551
Isa 24:10 The ruined c lies desolate; the entrance H7953
Isa 24:12 The c is left in ruins, its gate is battered to H6551
Isa 25: 2 You have made the c a heap of rubble H6551
Isa 25: 2 the foreigners' stronghold a c no more; it H6551
Isa 26: 1 We have a strong c; God makes salvation H6551
Isa 26: 5 he lays the lofty c low; he levels it to H7953
Isa 27:10 The fortified c stands desolate, an H6551
Isa 28: 1 fertile valley—to that c, the pride of those NDT
Isa 29: 1 Ariel, the c *where* David settled! H7953
Isa 32:13 of merriment and for this c *of* revelry. H7953
Isa 32:14 abandoned, the noisy c deserted; citadel H6551
Isa 32:19 the forest and the c is leveled completely, H6551
Isa 33:20 Look on Zion, the c *of* our festivals; your H7953
Isa 36:15 this c will not be given into the hand of H6551
Isa 37:33 will not enter this c or shoot an arrow here H6551
Isa 37:34 he will not enter this c," declares the LORD. H6551
Isa 37:35 "I will defend this c and save it, for my H6551
Isa 38: 6 you and this c from the hand of the H6551
Isa 38: 6 of the king of Assyria. I will defend this c. H6551
Isa 45:13 He will rebuild my c and set my exiles H6551
Isa 47: 1 a throne, **queen c** *of* the Babylonians. H1426
Isa 47: 5 into darkness, **queen c** *of* the Babylonians H1426
Isa 48: 2 citizens of the holy c and claim to rely on H6551
Isa 52: 1 of splendor, Jerusalem, the holy c. H6551
Isa 54:11 "Afflicted c, lashed by storms and not NDT
Isa 60:14 feet and will call you the C *of* the LORD, H6551
Isa 62:12 Sought After, the C No Longer Deserted. H6551
Isa 66: 6 Hear that uproar from the c, hear that H6551
Jer 1:18 Today I have made you a fortified c, an H6551
Jer 5: 1 seeks the truth, I will forgive **this c**. H2023S
Jer 6: 6 This c must be punished; it is filled with H6551
Jer 8:16 the c and all who live there. H6551
Jer 14:18 if I go into the c, I see the ravages of H6551
Jer 15: 7 winnowing fork at the **c gates** *of* the land. H9133
Jer 17:24 the gates of this c on the Sabbath, H6551
Jer 17:25 the gates of this c with their officials. H6551
Jer 17:25 this c will be inhabited forever. H6551
Jer 19: 8 I will devastate this c and make it an H6551
Jer 19:11 this nation and this c just as this potter's H6551
Jer 19:12 I will make this c like Topheth. H6551
Jer 19:15 to bring on this c and all the villages H6551
Jer 20: 5 all the wealth of this c into the hands of H6551
Jer 21: 4 And I will gather them inside this c. H6551
Jer 21: 6 I will strike down those who live in this c H6551
Jer 21: 7 the people in this c who survive the H6551
Jer 21: 9 Whoever stays in this c will die by the H6551
Jer 21:10 to do this c harm and not good, H6551
Jer 22: 8 will pass by this c and will ask one H6551
Jer 22: 8 the LORD done such a thing to this great c? H6551
Jer 23:39 along with the c I gave to you and your H6551
Jer 25:29 disaster on the c that bears my Name, H6551
Jer 26: 6 like Shiloh and this c a curse among all H6551
Jer 26: 9 like Shiloh and this c will be desolate H6551
Jer 26:11 because he has prophesied against this c. H6551
Jer 26:12 this house and this c all the things you H6551
Jer 26:15 on this c and on those who live H6551
Jer 26:20 things against this c and this land as H6551
Jer 27:17 Why should this c become a ruin? H6551
Jer 27:19 the other articles that are left in this c, H6551
Jer 29: 7 prosperity of the c to which I have H6551
Jer 29:16 all the people who remain in this c, H6551
Jer 30:18 the c will be rebuilt on her ruins H6551
Jer 31:23 you prosperous c, you sacred H5659
Jer 31:38 "when this c will be rebuilt for me from H6551
Jer 31:40 The c will never again be uprooted or NDT
Jer 32: 3 about to give this c into the hands of the H6551
Jer 32:24 the siege ramps are built up to take the c. H6551
Jer 32:24 the c will be given into the hands of the H6551

Jer 32:25 And though the **c** will be given into the H6551
Jer 32:28 about to give this **c** into the hands of the H6551
Jer 32:29 are attacking this **c** will come in and set H6551
Jer 32:31 this **c** has so aroused my anger and wrath H6551
Jer 32:36 "You are saying about this **c**, 'By the H6551
Jer 33: 4 the houses in this **c** and the royal palaces H6551
Jer 33: 5 hide my face from this **c** because of all its H6551
Jer 33: 9 Then this **c** will bring me renown, joy, praise NDT
Jer 34: 2 about to give this **c** into the hands of the H6551
Jer 34:22 and I will bring them back to this **c**. H6551
Jer 37: 8 Babylonians will return and attack this **c**; H6551
Jer 37:10 would come out and burn this **c** down." H6551
Jer 37:12 started to leave **the c** to go to the H3731S
Jer 37:21 day until all the bread in the **c** was gone. H6551
Jer 38: 2 stays in this **c** will die by the sword, H6551
Jer 38: 3 'This **c** will certainly be given into the H6551
Jer 38: 4 the soldiers who are left in this **c**, H6551
Jer 38: 9 there is no longer any bread in the **c**." H6551
Jer 38:17 be spared and this **c** will not be burned H6551
Jer 38:18 this **c** will be given into the hands of the H6551
Jer 38:23 Babylon; and this **c** will be burned down." H6551
Jer 39: 2 the **c** wall was broken through. H6551
Jer 39: 4 they left the **c** at night by way of the king's H6551
Jer 39: 9 the people who remained in the **c**, H6551
Jer 39:16 about to fulfill my words against this **c**— H6551
Jer 41: 7 When they went into the **c**, Ishmael son of H6551
Jer 49:25 Why has the **c** *of* renown not been H6551
Jer 51:31 of Babylon that his entire **c** is captured, H6551
Jer 52: 4 encamped outside **the c** and built siege H2023S
Jer 52: 5 The **c** was kept under siege until the H6551
Jer 52: 6 the famine in the **c** had become so severe H6551
Jer 52: 7 Then the **c** wall was broken through, and H6551
Jer 52: 7 They left the **c** at night through the gate H6551
Jer 52: 7 the Babylonians were surrounding the **c**. H6551
Jer 52:15 people and those who remained in the **c**, H6551
Jer 52:25 Of those still in the **c**, he took the officer in H6551
Jer 52:25 sixty of whom were found in the **c**. H6551
La 1: 1 How deserted lies the **c**, once so full of H6551
La 1:19 perished in the **c** while they searched H6551
La 2:11 infants faint in the streets of the **c**. H7953
La 2:12 like the wounded in the streets of the **c**, H6551
La 2:15 "Is this the **c** that was called the H6551
La 3:51 soul because of all the women of my **c**. H6551
La 5:14 The elders are gone from the **c gate**; the H9133
Eze 4: 1 of you and draw the **c** of Jerusalem on it. H6551
Eze 4: 3 between you and the **c** and turn your face H6551
Eze 5: 2 burn a third of the hair inside the **c**. H6551
Eze 5: 2 strike it with the sword all around **the c**. H2023S
Eze 7:15 those in the **c** will be devoured by famine H6551
Eze 7:23 of bloodshed, and the **c** is full of violence. H6551
Eze 9: 1 appointed to execute judgment on the **c**, H6551
Eze 9: 4 throughout the **c** *of* Jerusalem and put H6551
Eze 9: 5 "Follow him through the **c** and kill H6551
Eze 9: 7 out and began killing throughout the **c**. H6551
Eze 9: 9 of bloodshed and the **c** is full of injustice. H6551
Eze 10: 2 the cherubim and scatter them over the **c**." H6551
Eze 11: 2 evil and giving wicked advice in this **c**. H6551
Eze 11: 3 **This c** is a pot, and we are the meat in it. H2085S
Eze 11: 6 many people in this **c** and filled its streets H6551
Eze 11: 7 there are the meat and **this c** is the pot, H2085S
Eze 11: 9 drive you out of **the c** and deliver you H2023S
Eze 11:11 **This c** will not be a pot for you, nor will H2085S
Eze 11:23 up from within the **c** and stopped above H6551
Eze 17: 4 where he planted it in a **c** *of* traders. H6551
Eze 21:19 where the road branches off to the **c**. H6551
Eze 22: 2 Will you judge this **c** *of* bloodshed? Then H6551
Eze 22: 3 You **c** that brings on herself doom by H6551
Eze 22: 5 mock you, you infamous **c**, full of turmoil. NDT
Eze 22:20 put you inside the **c** and melt you. NDT
Eze 24: 6 " 'Woe to the **c** *of* bloodshed, to the pot H6551
Eze 24: 9 " 'Woe to the **c** *of* bloodshed! I, H6551
Eze 26:10 gates as men enter a **c** whose walls have H6551
Eze 26:17 are destroyed, **c** *of* renown, peopled by H6551
Eze 26:19 When I make you a desolate **c**, like cities H6551
Eze 33:21 came to me and said, "The **c** has fallen!" H6551
Eze 40: 1 the fourteenth year after the fall of the **c**— H6551
Eze 40: 2 were some buildings that looked like a **c**. H6551
Eze 43: 3 came to destroy the **c** and like the visions H6551
Eze 45: 6 " 'You are to give the **c** as its property an H6551
Eze 45: 7 sacred district and the property of the **c**. H6551
Eze 48:15 will be for the common use of the **c**, for H6551
Eze 48:15 The **c** will be in the center of it H6551
Eze 48:17 pastureland for the **c** will be 250 cubits on H6551
Eze 48:18 will supply food for the workers of the **c**. H6551
Eze 48:19 The workers from the **c** who farm it will H6551
Eze 48:20 portion, along with the property of the **c**. H6551
Eze 48:21 the property of the **c** will belong to the H6551
Eze 48:22 the property of the **c** will lie in the center H6551
Eze 48:30 "These will be the exits of the **c** H6551
Eze 48:31 the gates of the **c** will be named after the H6551
Eze 48:35 "And the name of the **c** from that time on H6551
Da 9:16 from Jerusalem, your **c**, your holy hill. H6551
Da 9:18 desolation of the **c** that bears your Name. H6551
Da 9:19 because your **c** and your people bear your H6551
Da 9:24 people and your holy **c** to finish H6551
Da 9:26 come will destroy the **c** and the sanctuary. H6551
Da 11:15 siege ramps and will capture a fortified **c**. H6551
Hos 6: 8 Gilead is a **c** *of* evildoers, stained with H7953
Joel 2: 9 They rush upon the **c**; they run along the H6551
Am 3: 6 When a trumpet sounds in a **c**, do not the H6551
Am 3: 6 When disaster comes to a **c**, has not the H6551
Am 4: 6 stomachs in every **c** and lack of bread in H6551
Am 5: 3 "Your **c** that marches out a thousand H6551
Am 5: 9 brings the **fortified c** to ruin. H4448
Am 6: 8 I will deliver up the **c** and everything in it." H6551
Am 7:17 wife will become a prostitute in the **c**, H6551
Jnh 1: 2 "Go to the great **c** of Nineveh and preach H6551
Jnh 3: 2 "Go to the great **c** *of* Nineveh and H6551
Jnh 3: 3 Now Nineveh was a very large **c**; it took H6551
Jnh 3: 4 began by going a day's journey into the **c**, H6551
Jnh 4: 5 out and sat down at a place east of the **c**. H6551
Jnh 4: 5 to see what would happen to the **c**. H6551
Jnh 4:11 have concern for the great **c** of Nineveh, H6551
Mic 4:10 you must leave the **c** to camp in the open H7953
Mic 5: 1 your troops now, **c** *of* troops, for a siege is H1426
Mic 6: 9 The LORD is calling to the **c**—and to fear H6551
Na 2: 5 They dash to the **c wall**; the protective H2570
Na 3: 1 Woe to the **c** *of* blood, full of lies, full of H6551
Hab 2:12 to him who builds a **c** with bloodshed H6551
Zep 2:15 This is the **c** *of* revelry that lived in safety H6551
Zep 3: 1 Woe to the **c** *of* oppressors, rebellious H6551
Zec 2: 4 will be a **c without walls** because of the H7252
Zec 8: 3 Jerusalem will be called the Faithful **C**, H6551
Zec 8: 5 The **c** streets will be filled with boys and H6551
Zec 8:21 inhabitants of one **c** will go to another and NDT
Zec 14: 2 fight against it; the **c** will be captured, the H6551
Zec 14: 2 Half of the **c** will go into exile, but the rest H6551
Zec 14: 2 of the people will not be taken from the **c**. H6551
Mt 4: 5 him to the holy **c** and had him stand on *G4484*
Mt 5:35 Jerusalem, for it is the **c** of the Great King. *G4484*
Mt 12:25 every **c** or household divided against *G4484*
Mt 21:10 the whole **c** was stirred and asked *G4484*
Mt 21:17 them and went out of the **c** to Bethany, *G4484*
Mt 21:18 as Jesus was on his way back to the **c**, he *G4484*
Mt 22: 7 those murderers and burned their **c**. *G4484*
Mt 26:18 "Go into the **c** to a certain man and tell *G4484*
Mt 27:53 went into the holy **c** and appeared to *G4484*
Mt 28:11 guards went into the **c** and reported to the *G4484*
Mk 10:46 were leaving **the c**, a blind man, *G2637S*
Mk 11:19 Jesus and his disciples went out of the **c**. *G4484*
Mk 14:13 "Go into the **c**, and a man carrying *G4484*
Mk 14:16 went into the **c** and found things just as *G4484*
Lk 19:41 he approached Jerusalem and saw the **c**, *G4484*
Lk 21:21 let those in **the c** get out, and let those *G899S*
Lk 21:21 let those in the country not enter **the c**. *G899S*
Lk 22:10 "As you enter the **c**, a man carrying a jar *G4484*
Lk 23:19 into prison for an insurrection in the **c**, *G4484*
Lk 24:49 stay in the **c** until you have been *G4484*
Jn 19:20 where Jesus was crucified was near the **c**, *G4484*
Ac 1:12 a Sabbath day's walk from **the c**. *G2642S*
Ac 4:27 of Israel in this **c** to conspire against your *G4484*
Ac 7:58 him out of the **c** and began to stone *G4484*
Ac 8: 5 Philip went down to a **c** in Samaria and *G4484*
Ac 8: 8 So there was great joy in that **c**. *G4484*
Ac 8: 9 sorcery in the **c** and amazed all the *G4484*
Ac 9: 6 "Now get up and go into the **c**, and you *G4484*
Ac 9:24 close watch *on* the **c gates** in order to kill *G4783*
Ac 10: 9 on their journey and approaching the **c**, *G4484*
Ac 11: 5 "I was in the **c** of Joppa praying, and in a *G4484*
Ac 12:10 came to the iron gate leading to the **c**. *G4484*
Ac 13:44 almost the whole **c** gathered to hear the *G4484*
Ac 13:50 standing and the leading men *of* the **c**. *G4484*
Ac 14: 4 The people *of* the **c** were divided; some *G4484*
Ac 14:13 whose temple was just outside the **c** *G4484*
Ac 14:13 wreaths to the **c gates** because he and *G4784*
Ac 14:19 Paul and dragged him outside the **c**, *G4484*
Ac 14:20 he got up and went back into the **c**. *G4484*
Ac 14:21 the gospel *in* that **c** and won a large *G4484*
Ac 15:21 been preached in every **c** from the earliest *G4484*
Ac 16:12 colony and the leading **c** of that district of *G4484*
Ac 16:13 we went outside the **c gate** to the river, *G4783*
Ac 16:14 was a woman *from* the **c** of Thyatira *G4484*
Ac 16:20 are throwing our **c** into an uproar *G4484*
Ac 16:39 requesting them to leave the **c**. *G4484*
Ac 17: 5 formed a mob and started a riot *in* the **c**. *G4484*
Ac 17: 6 other believers before the **c officials**, *G4485*
Ac 17: 8 crowd and the **c officials** were thrown into *G4485*
Ac 17:16 to see that the **c** was full of idols. *G4484*
Ac 18:10 because I have many people in this **c**." *G4484*
Ac 19:29 Soon the whole **c** was in an uproar. *G4484*
Ac 19:35 The **c clerk** quieted the crowd and said *G1208*
Ac 19:35 world know that the **c** of Ephesus is the *G4484*
Ac 20:23 know that in every **c** the Holy Spirit warns *G4484*
Ac 21: 5 accompanied us out of the **c**, and there *G4484*
Ac 21:29 the Ephesian in the **c** with Paul and *G4484*
Ac 21:30 The whole **c** was aroused, and the people *G4484*
Ac 21:31 that the whole **c of Jerusalem** was in an *G2642*
Ac 21:39 Tarsus in Cilicia, a citizen *of* no ordinary **c**. *G4484*
Ac 22: 3 Tarsus of Cilicia, but brought up in this **c**. *G4484*
Ac 24:12 the synagogues or anywhere else in the **c**. *G4484*
Ac 25:23 officers and the prominent men *of* the **c**. *G4484*
2Co 11:26 in danger in the **c**, in danger in the *G4484*
2Co 11:32 King Aretas had the **c** of the Damascenes *G4484*
Gal 4:25 corresponds to the present **c of Jerusalem**, *G2642*
Heb 11:10 looking forward to the **c** with foundations, *G4484*
Heb 11:16 for he has prepared a **c** for them. *G4484*
Heb 12:22 to Mount Zion, *to* the **c** of the living God *G4484*
Heb 13:12 outside the **c gate** to make the people *G4783*
Heb 13:14 For here we do not have an enduring **c** *G4484*
Heb 13:14 we are looking for the **c** that is to come. NDT
Jas 4:13 tomorrow we will go to this or that **c**, *G4484*
Rev 2:13 who was put to death **in** your **c**—where Satan AIT
Rev 3:12 my God and the name *of* the **c** of my God, *G4484*
Rev 11: 2 will trample on the holy **c** for 42 months. *G4484*
Rev 11: 8 lie in the public square *of* the great **c**— *G4484*
Rev 11:13 a tenth *of* the **c** collapsed. *G4484*
Rev 14:20 trampled in the winepress outside the **c**, *G4484*
Rev 16:19 The great **c** split into three parts, and the *G4484*
Rev 17:18 you saw is the great **c** that rules over the *G4484*
Rev 18:10 Woe to you, great **c**, you mighty city of *G4484*
Rev 18:10 great city, you mighty **c** of Babylon! *G4484*
Rev 18:16 Woe to you, great **c**, dressed in fine linen *G4484*
Rev 18:18 'Was there ever a **c** like this great city? NDT
Rev 18:18 'Was there ever a city like this great **c**? *G4484*
Rev 18:19 Woe to you, great **c**, where all who had *G4484*
Rev 18:21 violence the great **c** of Babylon will be *G4484*
Rev 20: 9 the camp of God's people, the **c** he loves. *G4484*
Rev 21: 2 I saw the Holy **C**, the new Jerusalem *G4484*
Rev 21:10 showed me the Holy **C**, Jerusalem, *G4484*
Rev 21:14 The wall *of* the **c** had twelve foundations *G4484*
Rev 21:15 a measuring rod of gold to measure the **c**, *G4484*
Rev 21:16 The **c** was laid out like a square, as long *G4484*
Rev 21:16 He measured the **c** with the rod and *G4484*
Rev 21:18 of jasper, and the **c** of pure gold, as pure *G4484*
Rev 21:19 The foundations *of* the **c** walls were *G4484*
Rev 21:21 The great street *of* the **c** was of gold, as *G4484*
Rev 21:22 I did not see a temple in **the c**, because *G899S*
Rev 21:23 The **c** does not need the sun or the moon *G4484*
Rev 22: 2 the middle of the great street *of* **the c**. *G899S*
Rev 22: 3 of God and of the Lamb will be in **the c**, *G899S*
Rev 22:14 may go through the gates into the **c**. *G4484*
Rev 22:19 share in the tree of life and in the Holy **C**, *G4484*

CITY'S (1) [CITY]

Ro 16:23 who is the **c** director of public works *G4484*

CIVILIAN (1)

2Ti 2: 4 soldier gets entangled in **c affairs**, *G1050+4548*

CLAD (2)

Na 2: 3 are red; the warriors *are* **c in scarlet**. H9443
Zep 1: 8 sons and all those **c** *in* foreign clothes. H4252

CLAIM (26) [CLAIMED, CLAIMING, CLAIMS, RECLAIM, RECLAIMED]

1Sa 8: 9 will reign over them will **c as his rights**." H5477S
1Sa 8:11 will reign over you will **c as his rights**: H5477S
2Sa 19:43 so we **have a** greater **c on** David than you H928
Ne 2:20 in Jerusalem or any **c** or historic right to it." H7407
Job 3: 5 *May* gloom and utter darkness **c** it once H1457
Job 41:11 Who **has a c against** me that I must pay H7709
Ps 73: 9 Their mouths **lay c** to heaven, and their H9286
Pr 20: 6 Many **c** to have unfailing love, but a H7924
Pr 25: 6 and *do* not **c** a place among his great H6641
Ecc 8:17 Even if the wise **c** they know, they cannot H606
Isa 48: 2 of the holy city and **c** *to* **rely** on the God of AIT
Jer 23:38 Although *you* **c**, 'This is a message from the H606
Jer 23:38 even though I told you that *you must* not **c** H606
Lk 11:18 I say this because *you* **c** that I drive out *G3306*
Jn 4:20 you Jews **c** that the place where we *G3306*
Jn 8:54 My Father, whom you **c** as your God, is the *G3306*
Jn 9:41 but now that *you* **c** you can see, your *G3306*
Jn 10:33 a mere man, **c to be** God. *G4472+4932*
Ro 3: 8 as some slanderously **c** that we say—"Let *G5774*
2Co 3: 5 competent in ourselves *to* **c** anything for *G3357*
Titus 1:16 *They* **c** to know God, but by their actions *G3933*
1Jn 1: 6 If *we* **c** to have fellowship with him and *G3306*
1Jn 1: 8 If *we* **c** to be without sin, we deceive *G3306*
1Jn 1:10 If *we* **c** we have not sinned, we make him *G3306*
Rev 2: 2 tested those *who* **c to be** apostles *G3306+1571*
Rev 3: 9 who **c** to be Jews though they are *G3306+1571*

CLAIMED (10) [CLAIM]

1Ki 18:10 a nation or kingdom **c** you were not there, H606
Pr 20:21 **c too soon** will not H987+928+2021+8037
Mk 6:15 And still others **c**, "He is a prophet, like *G3306*
Jn 9: 9 Some **c** that he was. Others said, "No, he *G3306*
Jn 19: 7 because *he* **c to be** the Son of God." *G1571+4472*
Jn 19:21 that this man **c** to be king of the Jews." *G3306*
Ac 4:32 No one **c** *that* any of their possessions *G3306*
Ac 25:19 man named Jesus who Paul **c** was alive. *G5763*
Ro 1:22 *Although they* **c** to be wise, they became *G5763*
Ro 6:17 teaching that *has now* **c** *your* **allegiance**. *G4140*

CLAIMING (4) [CLAIM]

Mt 24: 5 come in my name, **c**, 'I am the Messiah, *G3306*
Mk 13: 6 come in my name, **c**, 'I am he,' and will *G3306*
Lk 21: 8 many will come in my name, **c**, 'I am he, *G3306*
Ac 5:36 appeared, **c** to be somebody *G3306+1571*

CLAIMS (10) [CLAIM]

2Sa 15: 3 your **c** are valid and proper, but H1821
2Sa 19:43 Judah pressed their **c** even more forcefully H1821
Jer 23:34 If a prophet or a priest or anyone else **c** H606
Lk 23: 2 to Caesar and **c** to be Messiah, *G3306+1571*
Jn 19:12 Anyone *who* **c to be** a king *G1571+4472*
1Co 5:11 with anyone *who* **c** to be a brother or *G3951*
Jas 2:14 if someone **c** to have faith but has no *G3306*
1Jn 2: 6 Whoever **c** to live in him must live as *G3306*
1Jn 2: 9 Anyone *who* **c** to be in the light but hates *G3306*
1Jn 4:20 Whoever **c** to love God yet hates a brother *G3306*

CLAMOR (2)

Ps 74:23 Do not ignore the **c** *of* your adversaries H7754
Isa 31: 4 by their shouts or disturbed by their **c**— H2162

CLAN (120) [CLANS]

Ge 24:38 go to my father's family and to my own c, H5476
Ge 24:40 my son from my own c and from my H5476
Ge 24:41 when you go to my c, they refuse to give H5476
Ex 6:25 the heads of the Levite families, c by clan. NDT
Ex 6:25 the heads of the Levite families, clan by c. H5476
Lev 25:10 to your family property and to your own c. H5476
Lev 25:47 to a member of the foreigner's c, H5476
Lev 25:49 relative in their c may redeem them. H5476
Nu 2:34 each of them with their c and family. H5476
Nu 26: 5 the Hanokite c; through Pallu, H5476
Nu 26: 5 through Pallu, the Palluite c; H5476
Nu 26: 6 Hezron, the Hezronite c; through Karmi, H5476
Nu 26: 6 through Karmi, the Karmite c. H5476
Nu 26:12 Nemuel, the Nemuelite c; through Jamin, H5476
Nu 26:12 the Jaminite c; through Jakin, H5476
Nu 26:12 through Jakin, the Jakinite c; H5476
Nu 26:13 the Zerahite c; through Shaul, H5476
Nu 26:13 through Shaul, the Shaulite c. H5476
Nu 26:15 Zephon, the Zephonite c; through Haggi, H5476
Nu 26:15 the Haggite c; through Shuni, H5476
Nu 26:15 through Shuni, the Shunite c; H5476
Nu 26:16 the Oznite c; through Eri, the Erite H5476
Nu 26:16 the Oznite clan; through Eri, the Erite c; H5476
Nu 26:17 the Arodite c; through Areli, H5476
Nu 26:17 Arodite clan; through Areli, the Arelite c. H5476
Nu 26:20 Shelah, the Shelanite c; through Perez, H5476
Nu 26:20 the Perezite c; through Zerah, H5476
Nu 26:20 through Zerah, the Zerahite c. H5476
Nu 26:21 Hezron, the Hezronite c; through Hamul, H5476
Nu 26:21 through Hamul, the Hamulite c. H5476
Nu 26:23 the Tolaite c; through Puah, the H5476
Nu 26:23 Tolaite clan; through Puah, the Puite c; H5476
Nu 26:24 Jashub, the Jashubite c; through Shimron, H5476
Nu 26:24 through Shimron, the Shimronite c. H5476
Nu 26:26 the Seredite c; through Elon, H5476
Nu 26:26 the Elonite c; through Jahleel, H5476
Nu 26:26 through Jahleel, the Jahleelite c. H5476
Nu 26:29 the Makirite c (Makir was the father H5476
Nu 26:29 ; through Gilead, the Gileadite c. H5476
Nu 26:30 the Iezerite c; through Helek, H5476
Nu 26:30 through Helek, the Helekite c; H5476
Nu 26:31 the Asrielite c; through Shechem, H5476
Nu 26:31 through Shechem, the Shechemite c; H5476
Nu 26:32 the Shemidaite c; through Hepher, H5476
Nu 26:32 through Hepher, the Hepherite c. H5476
Nu 26:35 the Shuthelahite c; through Beker, H5476
Nu 26:35 the Bekerite c; through Tahan, H5476
Nu 26:35 through Tahan, the Tahanite c. H5476
Nu 26:36 of Shuthelah: through Eran, the Eranite c. H5476
Nu 26:38 the Belaite c; through Ashbel, H5476
Nu 26:38 Ashbel, the Ashbelite c; through Ahiram, H5476
Nu 26:38 through Ahiram, the Ahiramite c; H5476
Nu 26:39 the Shuphamite c; through Hupham, H5476
Nu 26:39 through Hupham, the Huphamite c. H5476
Nu 26:40 the Ardite c; through Naaman, H5476
Nu 26:40 through Naaman, the Naamite c. H5476
Nu 26:42 the Shuhamite c. These were the clans H5476
Nu 26:44 the Imnite c; through Ishvi, H5476
Nu 26:44 the Ishvite c; through Beriah, H5476
Nu 26:44 Ishvite clan; through Beriah, the Beriite c; H5476
Nu 26:45 the Heberite c; through Malkiel, H5476
Nu 26:45 through Malkiel, the Malkielite c. H5476
Nu 26:48 Jahzeel, the Jahzeelite c; through Guni, H5476
Nu 26:48 through Guni, the Gunite c; H5476
Nu 26:49 the Jezerite c; through Shillem, H5476
Nu 26:49 through Shillem, the Shillemite c. H5476
Nu 26:57 the Gershonite c; through Kohath, H5476
Nu 26:57 Kohath, the Kohathite c; through Merari, H5476
Nu 26:57 through Merari, the Merarite c. H5476
Nu 26:58 the Libnite c, the Hebronite clan, the H5476
Nu 26:58 the Hebronite c, the Mahlite clan, H5476
Nu 26:58 the Mahlite c, the Mushite clan, H5476
Nu 26:58 the Mushite c, the Korahite clan. H5476
Nu 26:58 the Mushite clan, the Korahite c. H5476
Nu 27: 4 disappear from his c because he had no H5476
Nu 27:11 inheritance to the nearest relative in his c, H5476
Nu 36: 1 family heads of the c *of* Gilead son of H5476
Nu 36: 6 as they marry within their father's tribal c. H5476
Nu 36: 8 marry someone in her father's tribal c, H5476
Nu 36:12 remained in their father's tribe and c. H5476
Dt 29:18 c or tribe among you today whose heart H5476
Jos 7:14 LORD chooses shall come forward c by clan; NDT
Jos 7:14 chooses shall come forward clan by c; H5476
Jos 7:14 the c the LORD chooses shall come forward H5476
Jos 7:17 He had the c *of* the Zerahites come H5476
Jdg 6:15 My c is the weakest in Manasseh, and I am H548
Jdg 9: 1 them and to all his mother's c, H5476+1074+3
Jdg 9:26 of Ebed moved with his c into Shechem, H278
Jdg 9:31 son of Ebed and his c have come to H278
Jdg 9:41 drove Gaal and his c out of Shechem. H278
Jdg 12: 9 away in marriage to those **outside** his *c*, AIT
Jdg 12: 9 young women as wives from **outside** his *c*. AIT
Jdg 13: 2 Manoah, from the c *of* the Danites, had a H5476
Jdg 17: 7 had been living within the c *of* Judah, H5476
Jdg 18:19 you serve a tribe and c in Israel as priest H5476
Ru 2: 1 a man of standing from the c *of* Elimelek H5476
Ru 2: 3 to Boaz, who was from the c *of* Elimelek. H5476
1Sa 9:21 is not my c the least of all the clans H5476
1Sa 10:21 the tribe of Benjamin, c by clan, and Matri's NDT
1Sa 10:21 of Benjamin, clan by c, and Matri's clan H5476
1Sa 10:21 clan by clan, and Matri's c was taken. H5476
1Sa 18:18 what is my family or my c in Israel H3+5476
1Sa 20: 6 is being made there for his whole c. H5476
2Sa 14: 7 Now the whole c has risen up against your H5476
2Sa 16: 5 a man from the *same* c *as* Saul's family H5476
1Ch 4:27 so their entire c did not become as H5476
1Ch 6:54 of Aaron who were from the Kohathite c, H5476
1Ch 6:62 of Gershon, **c by clan**, were allotted H4200+5476
1Ch 6:62 of Gershon, **clan by c**, were allotted H4200+5476
1Ch 6:63 of Merari, **c by clan**, were allotted H4200+5476
1Ch 6:63 of Merari, **clan by c**, were allotted H4200+5476
1Ch 6:71 From the c *of* the half-tribe of Manasseh H5476
Jer 3:14 one from a town and two from a c—and H5476
Jer 9: 4 your friends; do not trust anyone **in** your c. H278
Zec 9: 7 to our God and become a c in Judah, H477
Zec 12:12 will mourn, **each c** by itself, with H5476+5476
Zec 12:12 the c *of* the house of David and their H5476
Zec 12:12 the c *of* the house of Nathan and their H5476
Zec 12:13 the c *of* the house of Levi and their wives H5476
Zec 12:13 the c *of* Shimei and their wives, H5476

CLANGING (1)

1Co 13: 1 I am only a resounding gong or a c cymbal. *G226*

CLANS (164) [CLAN]

Ge 10: 5 territories by their c within their nations, H5476
Ge 10:18 Later the Canaanite c scattered H5476
Ge 10:20 sons of Ham by their c and languages, H5476
Ge 10:31 sons of Shem by their c and languages, H5476
Ge 10:32 These are the c *of* Noah's sons, according H5476
Ge 36:40 by name, according to their c and regions: H5476
Ex 6:14 These were the c *of* Reuben. H5476
Ex 6:15 These were the c *of* Simeon. H5476
Ex 6:17 sons of Gershon, by c, were Libni and H5476
Ex 6:19 These were the c *of* Levi according to their H5476
Ex 6:24 These were the Korahite c. H5476
Lev 25:41 go back to their own c and to the property H5476
Lev 25:45 members of their c born in your country H5476
Nu 1: 2 community by their c and families, H5476
Nu 1:16 They were the heads of the c *of* Israel. H548
Nu 1:18 their ancestry by their c and families, H5476
Nu 1:20 to the records of their c and families. H5476
Nu 1:22 to the records of their c and families. H5476
Nu 1:24 to the records of their c and families. H5476
Nu 1:26 to the records of their c and families. H5476
Nu 1:28 to the records of their c and families. H5476
Nu 1:30 to the records of their c and families. H5476
Nu 1:32 to the records of their c and families. H5476
Nu 1:34 to the records of their c and families. H5476
Nu 1:36 to the records of their c and families. H5476
Nu 1:38 to the records of their c and families. H5476
Nu 1:40 to the records of their c and families. H5476
Nu 1:42 to the records of their c and families. H5476
Nu 3:15 "Count the Levites by their families and c H5476
Nu 3:18 were the names of the Gershonite c: H5476
Nu 3:19 The Kohathite c: Amram, Izhar, Hebron H5476
Nu 3:20 The Merarite c: Mahli and Mushi. H5476
Nu 3:20 These were the Levite c, according to their H5476
Nu 3:21 belonged the c *of* the Libnites and H5476
Nu 3:21 Shimeites; these were the Gershonite c. H5476
Nu 3:23 The Gershonite c were to camp on the H5476
Nu 3:27 Kohath belonged the c *of* the Amramites, H5476
Nu 3:27 Uzzielites; these were the Kohathite c. H5476
Nu 3:29 The Kohathite c were to camp on the H5476
Nu 3:30 of the Kohathite c was Elizaphan son of H5476
Nu 3:33 belonged the c *of* the Mahlites and H5476
Nu 3:33 the Mushites; these were the Merarite c. H5476
Nu 3:35 of the Merarite c was Zuriel son of H5476
Nu 3:39 by Moses and Aaron according to their c, H5476
Nu 4: 2 of the Levites by their c and families. H5476
Nu 4:18 the Kohathite tribal c are not destroyed H5476
Nu 4:22 of the Gershonites by their families and c. H5476
Nu 4:24 of the Gershonite c in their carrying and H5476
Nu 4:28 of the Gershonite c at the tent of meeting. H5476
Nu 4:29 the Merarites by their c and families. H5476
Nu 4:33 of the Merarite c as they work at the H5476
Nu 4:34 the Kohathites by their c and families. H5476
Nu 4:36 counted by c, were 2,750. H5476
Nu 4:37 in the Kohathite c who served at the tent H5476
Nu 4:38 were counted by their c and families. H5476
Nu 4:40 counted by their c and families, were H5476
Nu 4:41 in the Gershonite c who served at the tent H5476
Nu 4:42 were counted by their c and families. H5476
Nu 4:44 counted by their c, were 3,200. H5476
Nu 4:45 was the total of those in the Merarite c. H5476
Nu 4:46 all the Levites by their c and families. H5476
Nu 10: 4 the heads of the c *of* Israel—are to H548
Nu 26: 7 These were the c *of* Reuben; those H5476
Nu 26:12 descendants of Simeon by their c were: H5476
Nu 26:14 These were the c *of* Simeon; those H5476
Nu 26:15 The descendants of Gad by their c were H5476
Nu 26:18 These were the c *of* Gad; those numbered H5476
Nu 26:20 The descendants of Judah by their c were H5476
Nu 26:22 These were the c *of* Judah; those H5476
Nu 26:23 descendants of Issachar by their c were: H5476
Nu 26:25 These were the c *of* Issachar; those H5476
Nu 26:26 descendants of Zebulun by their c were: H5476
Nu 26:27 These were the c *of* Zebulun; those H5476
Nu 26:28 of Joseph by their c through Manasseh H5476
Nu 26:34 These were the c *of* Manasseh; those H5476
Nu 26:35 the descendants of Ephraim by their c: H5476
Nu 26:37 These were the c *of* Ephraim; those H5476
Nu 26:37 the descendants of Joseph by their c. H5476
Nu 26:38 descendants of Benjamin by their c were: H5476
Nu 26:41 These were the c *of* Benjamin; those H5476
Nu 26:42 were the descendants of Dan by their c: H5476
Nu 26:42 Shuhamite clan. These were the c *of* Dan: H5476
Nu 26:43 All of them were Shuhamite c; and those H5476
Nu 26:44 The descendants of Asher by their c were H5476
Nu 26:47 These were the c *of* Asher; those H5476
Nu 26:48 descendants of Naphtali by their c were: H5476
Nu 26:50 These were the c *of* Naphtali; those H5476
Nu 26:57 the Levites who were counted by their c: H5476
Nu 26:58 These also were Levite c: the Libnite clan H5476
Nu 27: 1 belonged to the c *of* Manasseh son of H5476
Nu 31: 5 were supplied from the c *of* Israel. H548
Nu 33:54 the land by lot, according to your c. H5476
Nu 36: 1 who were from the c *of* the descendants H5476
Nu 36:12 married within the c *of* the descendants of H5476
Jos 7:17 The c *of* Judah came forward, and the H5476
Jos 13:15 to the tribe of Reuben, according to its c: H5476
Jos 13:23 of the Reubenites, according to their c. H5476
Jos 13:24 to the tribe of Gad, according to its c: H5476
Jos 13:28 of the Gadites, according to their c. H5476
Jos 13:29 of Manasseh, according to its c: H5476
Jos 13:31 of the sons of Makir, according to their c. H5476
Jos 14: 1 the heads of the tribal c of Israel allotted to H3
Jos 15: 1 according to its c, extended down to the H5476
Jos 15:12 around the people of Judah by their c. H5476
Jos 15:20 of the tribe of Judah, according to its c: H5476
Jos 16: 5 the territory of Ephraim, according to its c: H5476
Jos 16: 8 tribe of the Ephraimites, according to its c. H5476
Jos 17: 2 of Manasseh—the c *of* Abiezer, Helek, H1201
Jos 17: 2 of Manasseh son of Joseph by their c. H5476
Jos 18:11 the tribe of Benjamin according to its c. H5476
Jos 18:20 inheritance of the c *of* Benjamin on all H5476
Jos 18:21 according to its c, had the following towns H5476
Jos 18:28 was the inheritance of Benjamin for its c. H5476
Jos 19: 1 the tribe of Simeon according to its c. H5476
Jos 19: 8 tribe of the Simeonites, according to its c. H5476
Jos 19:10 lot came up for Zebulun according to its c: H5476
Jos 19:16 inheritance of Zebulun, according to its c. H5476
Jos 19:17 came out for Issachar according to its c. H5476
Jos 19:23 of the tribe of Issachar, according to its c. H5476
Jos 19:24 the tribe of Asher according to its c. H5476
Jos 19:31 of the tribe of Asher, according to its c. H5476
Jos 19:32 came out for Naphtali according to its c: H5476
Jos 19:39 of the tribe of Naphtali, according to its c. H5476
Jos 19:40 out for the tribe of Dan according to its c. H5476
Jos 19:48 of the tribe of Dan, according to its c. H5476
Jos 19:51 the heads of the tribal c of Israel assigned by H3
Jos 21: 4 the Kohathites, according to their c. H5476
Jos 21: 5 ten towns from the c *of* the tribes of H5476
Jos 21: 6 towns from the c *of* the tribes of Issachar H5476
Jos 21: 7 according to their c, received twelve towns H5476
Jos 21:10 were from the Kohathite c of the Levites, H5476
Jos 21:20 rest of the Kohathite c *of* the Levites were H5476
Jos 21:26 were given to the rest of the Kohathite c. H5476
Jos 21:27 The Levite c of the Gershonites were H5476
Jos 21:33 of the Gershonite c came to thirteen, H5476
Jos 21:34 The Merarite c (the rest of the Levites H5476
Jos 21:40 of towns allotted to the Merarite c, H5476
Jos 22:14 of a family division among the Israelite c. H548
Jos 22:21 replied to the heads of the c *of* Israel: H548
Jos 22:30 the heads of the c *of* the Israelites—heard H548
Jdg 21:24 went home to their tribes and c, H5476
1Sa 9:21 the least of all the c *of* the tribe of H5476
1Sa 10:19 before the LORD by your tribes and c." H548
1Sa 23:23 track him down among all the c *of* Judah." H548
1Ch 2:53 the c *of* Kiriath Jearim: the Ithrites H5476
1Ch 2:55 the c *of* scribes who lived at Jabez H5476
1Ch 4: 2 These were the c *of* the Zorathites. H5476
1Ch 4: 8 of the c *of* Aharhel son of Harum H5476
1Ch 4:21 Mareshah and the c *of* the linen workers H5476
1Ch 4:38 above by name were leaders of their c. H5476
1Ch 5: 7 Their relatives by c, listed according to H5476
1Ch 6:19 These are the c *of* the Levites listed H5476
1Ch 6:60 among the Kohathite c came to thirteen. H5476
1Ch 6:61 ten towns from the c *of* half the tribe of H5476
1Ch 6:66 of the Kohathite c were given as their H5476
1Ch 6:70 to the rest of the Kohathite c. H5476
1Ch 7: 5 men belonging to all the c *of* Issachar, H5476
1Ch 12:30 famous in their own c—20,800; H1074+3
Job 31:34 the contempt of the c that I kept silent H5476
Jer 2: 4 descendants of Jacob, all you c *of* Israel. H5476
Mic 5: 2 you are small among the c *of* Judah, H548
Zec 12: 5 Then the c *of* Judah will say in their hearts H477
Zec 12: 6 day I will make the c *of* Judah like a firepot H477
Zec 12:14 all the rest of the c and their wives. H5476

CLAP (7) [CLAPPED, CLAPS]

Job 21: 5 appalled; c your hand over your mouth. H8492
Ps 47: 1 C your hands, all you nations; shout to H9546
Ps 98: 8 *Let* the rivers c their hands, let the H4673
Pr 30:32 you plan evil, c your hand over your mouth! NDT
Isa 55:12 all the trees of the field *will* c their hands. H4673
La 2:15 who pass your way c their hands at you; H6215
Na 3:19 the news about you c their hands at your H9546

CLAPPED (2) [CLAP]

2Ki 11:12 the people c their hands and shouted H5782
Eze 25: 6 Because you *have* c your hands and H4673

CLAPS (2) [CLAP]

Job 27:23 *It* c its hands **in derision** and hisses him H8562

Job 34:37 scornfully he c his hands among us and H6215

CLASH (1)
Ps 150: 5 praise him with the c of cymbals, praise H9049

CLASPED (1) [CLASPS]
Mt 28: 9 c his feet and worshiped him. G3195

CLASPS (7) [CLASPED]
Ex 26: 6 Then make fifty gold c and use them to H7971
Ex 26:11 make fifty bronze c and put them in the H7971
Ex 26:33 the curtain from the c and place the ark of H7971
Ex 35:11 with its tent and its covering, c, frames, H7971
Ex 36:13 they made fifty gold c and used them to H7971
Ex 36:18 They made fifty bronze c to fasten the tent H7971
Ex 39:33 tent and all its furnishings, its c, frames, H7971

CLASSIFY (1)
2Co 10:12 We do not dare to c or compare ourselves G1605

CLATTER (2)
Jdg 5:28 Why is the c of his chariots delayed H7193
Na 3: 2 of whips, the c of wheels H7754+8323

CLAUDA (KJV) CAUDA

CLAUDIA (1)
2Ti 4:21 C and all the brothers and sisters. G3086

CLAUDIUS (3)
Ac 11:28 This happened during the reign of C.) G3087
Ac 18: 2 because C had ordered all Jews to leave G3087
Ac 23:26 C Lysias, To His Excellency, Governor G3087

CLAVE (KJV) CHOPPED, CLUNG, CUT, DRAWN, FOLOWERS, FROZE, HELD, JOIN, OPENED, SPLIT, STAYED

CLAWS (2)
Da 4:33 of an eagle and his nails like the c of a bird. NDT
Da 7:19 with its iron teeth and bronze c—the A10303

CLAY (40)
Lev 6:28 The c pot the meat is cooked in must be H3084
Lev 11:33 If one of them falls into a c pot, everything H3084
Lev 14: 5 birds be killed over fresh water in a c pot. H3084
Lev 14:42 these and take new c and plaster the H6760
Lev 14:50 of the birds over fresh water in a c pot. H3084
Lev 15:12 " 'A c pot that the man touches must be H3084
Nu 5:17 some holy water in a c jar and put some H3084
1Ki 7:46 had them cast in c molds in the plain of H141
2Ch 4:17 had them cast in c molds in the plain of H141
Job 4:19 much more those who live in houses of c, H2817
Job 10: 9 Remember that you molded me like c H2817
Job 13:12 of ashes; your defenses are defenses of c. H2817
Job 27:16 silver like dust and clothes like piles of c, H2817
Job 33: 6 you in God's sight; I too am a piece of c. H2817
Job 38:14 The earth takes shape like c under a seal H2817
Isa 29:16 if the potter were thought to be like the c! H2817
Isa 41:25 as if he were a potter treading the c. H3226
Isa 45: 9 Does the c say to the potter, 'What are H2817
Isa 64: 8 We are the c, you are the potter; we are H2817
Jer 18: 4 was shaping from the c was marred in his H2817
Jer 18: 6 "Like c in the hand of the potter, so are H2817
Jer 19: 1 "Go and buy a c jar from a potter H3084
Jer 32:14 put them in a c jar so they will last a H3084
Jer 43: 9 you and bury them in c in the brick H4879
La 4: 2 are now considered as pots of c, the work H3084
Eze 4: 1 of man, take a block of c, put it in front H4246
Da 2:33 feet partly of iron and partly of baked c. A10279
Da 2:34 its feet of iron and c and smashed them. A10279
Da 2:35 Then the iron, the c, the bronze, the A10279
Da 2:41 were partly of baked c and partly of iron, A10279
Da 2:41 as you saw iron mixed with c. A10279+10298
Da 2:42 As the toes were partly iron and partly c A10279
Da 2:43 saw the iron mixed with baked c, A10279+10298
Da 2:43 any more than iron mixes with c. A10279
Da 2:45 the bronze, the c, the silver and the gold A10279
Na 3:14 Work the c, tread the mortar, repair the H3226
Lk 8:16 hides it in a c jar or puts it under G5007
Ro 9:21 of the same lump of c some pottery for G4384
2Co 4: 7 this treasure in jars of c to show that this G4017
2Ti 2:20 also of wood and c; some are for G4017

CLEAN (123) [CLEANNESS, CLEANSE, CLEANSED, CLEANSING]
Ge 7: 2 you seven pairs of every kind of c animal, H3196
Ge 7: 8 Pairs of c and unclean animals, of birds H3196
Ge 8:20 some of all the c animals and clean H3196
Ge 8:20 some of all the clean animals and c birds, H3196
Ge 20: 5 this with a clear conscience and c hands." H5931
Lev 4:12 the camp to a place ceremonially c, H3196
Lev 6:11 camp to a place that is ceremonially c. H3196
Lev 7:19 anyone ceremonially c may eat it. H3196
Lev 10:10 common, between the unclean and the c, H3196
Lev 10:14 Eat them in a ceremonially c place; they H3196
Lev 11:32 unclean till evening, and then it will be c. H3197
Lev 11:36 a cistern for collecting water remains c H3196
Lev 11:37 that are to be planted, they remain c. H3196
Lev 11:47 between the unclean and the c, H3196
Lev 12: 7 then she will be ceremonially c from H3197
Lev 12: 8 atonement for her, and she will be c. H3197
Lev 13: 6 the priest shall pronounce them c; it is H3197
Lev 13: 6 wash their clothes, and they will be c. H3197
Lev 13: 7 to the priest to be pronounced c, H3200
Lev 13:13 whole body, he shall pronounce them c. H3197
Lev 13:13 Since it has all turned white, they are c. H3196
Lev 13:17 shall pronounce the affected person c; H3197
Lev 13:17 affected person clean; then they will be c. H3196
Lev 13:23 the priest shall pronounce them c. H3197
Lev 13:28 the priest shall pronounce them c; it H3197
Lev 13:34 the priest shall pronounce them c. H3197
Lev 13:34 wash their clothes, and they will be c. H3197
Lev 13:35 in the skin after they are pronounced c, H3200
Lev 13:37 They are c, and the priest shall pronounce H3196
Lev 13:37 the priest shall pronounce them c. H3197
Lev 13:39 has broken out on the skin; they are c. H3196
Lev 13:40 man who has lost his hair and is bald is c. H3196
Lev 13:41 scalp and has a bald forehead, he is c. H3196
Lev 13:58 must be washed again. Then it will be c." H3197
Lev 13:59 for pronouncing them c or unclean. H3197
Lev 14: 4 order that two live c birds and some cedar H3196
Lev 14: 7 disease, and then pronounce them c. H3197
Lev 14: 8 then they will be ceremonially c. H3197
Lev 14: 9 themselves with water, and they will be c. H3197
Lev 14:11 The priest who pronounces them c shall H3197
Lev 14:20 atonement for them, and they will be c. H3197
Lev 14:48 he shall pronounce the house c, because H3197
Lev 14:53 atonement for the house, and it will be c." H3197
Lev 14:57 when something is c or unclean. H3196
Lev 15: 8 the discharge spits on anyone who is c, H3196
Lev 15:13 himself with fresh water, and he will be c. H3197
Lev 15:28 after that she will be ceremonially c. H3197
Lev 16:30 the LORD, you will be c from all your sins. H3197
Lev 17:15 unclean till evening; then they will be c. H3197
Lev 20:25 between c and unclean animals H3196
Lev 20:25 between unclean and c birds. H3196
Lev 22: 7 sun goes down, he will be c, and after H3197
Nu 5:28 impure, but is c, she will be cleared H3196
Nu 8: 6 Israelites and make them ceremonially c. H3197
Nu 9:13 who is ceremonially c and not on a H3196
Nu 18:11 who is ceremonially c may eat it. H3196
Nu 18:13 who is ceremonially c may eat it. H3196
Nu 19: 9 "A man who is c shall gather up the H3196
Nu 19: 9 put them in a ceremonially c place H3196
Nu 19:12 on the seventh day; then they will be c. H3197
Nu 19:12 third and seventh days, they will not be c. H3197
Nu 19:18 a man who is ceremonially c is to take H3196
Nu 19:19 The man who is c is to sprinkle those who H3196
Nu 19:19 and that evening they will be c. H3197
Nu 31:23 put through the fire, and then it will be c. H3197
Nu 31:24 day wash your clothes and you will be c. H3197
Dt 12:15 unclean and the c may eat it. H3196
Dt 12:22 ceremonially unclean and the c may eat. H3196
Dt 14:11 You may eat any c bird. H3196
Dt 14:20 any winged creature that is c you may eat. H3196
Dt 15:22 unclean and the c may eat it, H3196
2Ki 5:14 was restored and became c like that of a H3197
2Ch 13:11 bread on the ceremonially c table and H3196
2Ch 30:17 all those who were not ceremonially c H3196
2Ch 30:19 even if they are not c according to the H3200
Ezr 6:20 themselves and were all ceremonially c. H3196
Job 17: 9 those with c hands will grow stronger. H3196
Job 33: 9 done no wrong; I am c and free from sin. H2899
Job 37:21 the skies after the wind has swept them c. H3197
Ps 24: 4 The one who has c hands and a pure H5929
Ps 51: 7 me with hyssop, and I will be c; wash me, H3197
Pr 20: 9 my heart pure; I am c and without sin"? H3197
Ecc 9: 2 good and the bad, the c and the unclean H3196
Isa 1:16 Wash and make yourselves c. Take your H2342
Isa 66:20 of the LORD in ceremonially c vessels. H3196
Jer 43:12 As a shepherd picks his garment c of lice H6487
Jer 43:12 so he will pick Egypt c and depart. H6487
Eze 16: 4 you washed with water to make you c, H5470
Eze 22:26 between the unclean and the c; H3196
Eze 24:13 you will not be c again until my wrath H3197
Eze 36:25 I will sprinkle c water on you, and you will H3196
Eze 36:25 and you will be c; I will cleanse H3197
Eze 44:23 between the unclean and the c. H3196
Am 7: 2 When they had stripped the land c, I cried H430
Zec 3: 5 Then I said, "Put a c turban on his head." H3196
Zec 3: 5 So they put a c turban on his head and H3196
Mt 8: 2 if you are willing, you can make me c." G2751
Mt 8: 3 "Be c!" Immediately he was G2751
Mt 12:44 unoccupied, swept c and put in order. G4924
Mt 23:25 You c the outside of the cup and dish, but G2751
Mt 23:26 First c the inside of the cup and dish, and G2751
Mt 23:26 and then the outside also will be c. G2754
Mt 27:59 the body, wrapped it in a c linen cloth, G2754
Mk 1:40 "If you are willing, you can make me c." G2751
Mk 1:41 "I am willing," he said. "Be c!" G2751
Mk 7:19 In saying this, Jesus declared all foods c.) G2751
Lk 5:12 if you are willing, you can make me c." G2751
Lk 5:13 "Be c!" And immediately the G2751
Lk 11:25 finds the house swept c and put in order. G4924
Lk 11:39 you Pharisees c the outside of the cup G2751
Lk 11:41 the poor, and everything will be c for you. G2754
Jn 13:10 to wash their feet; their whole body is c. G2754
Jn 13:10 And you are c, though not every one of G2754
Jn 13:11 that was why he said not every one was c. G2754
Jn 15: 3 You are already c because of the word I G2754
Ac 10:15 anything impure that God has made c." G2751
Ac 11: 9 anything impure that God has made c. G2751
Ac 24:18 I was ceremonially c when they found me in G49
Ro 14:20 All food is c, but it is wrong for a person G2754
Heb 9:13 sanctify them so that they are outwardly c. G2755
Rev 15: 6 They were dressed in c, shining linen G2754
Rev 19: 8 bright and c, was given her to wear G2754
Rev 19:14 dressed in fine linen, white and c. G2754

CLEANNESS (5) [CLEAN]
2Sa 22:21 according to the c of my hands he has H1341
2Sa 22:25 according to my c in his sight. H1341
Job 22:30 be delivered through the c of your hands." H1341
Ps 18:20 according to the c of my hands he has H1341
Ps 18:24 according to the c of my hands in his sight H1341

CLEANSE (19) [CLEAN]
Lev 16:19 finger seven times to c it and to H3197
Lev 16:30 atonement will be made for you, to c you. H3197
Ps 51: 2 all my iniquity and c me from my sin. H3197
Ps 51: 7 C me with hyssop, and I will be clean H2627
Isa 4: 4 he will c the bloodstains from Jerusalem H1866
Jer 4:11 my people, but not to winnow or c; H1405
Jer 33: 8 I will c them from all the sin they have H3197
Eze 24:13 Because I tried to c you but you would not H3197
Eze 36:25 I will c you from all your impurities and H3197
Eze 36:33 On the day I c you from all your sins, I will H3197
Eze 37:23 their sinful backsliding, and I will c them. H3197
Eze 39:12 be burying them in order to c the land. H3197
Eze 39:16 And so they will c the land.' H3197
Eze 43:26 to make atonement for the altar and c it; H3197
Zec 13: 1 Jerusalem, to c them from sin and impurity. NDT
Mt 10: 8 raise the dead, c those who have leprosy G2751
2Ti 2:21 Those who c themselves from the latter G1705
Heb 9:14 will the blood of Christ ... c our G2751
Heb 10:22 having our hearts sprinkled to c us from a G4822

CLEANSED (35) [CLEAN]
Lev 14: 4 hyssop be brought for the person to be c. H3197
Lev 14: 7 sprinkle the one to be c of the defiling H3197
Lev 14: 8 "The person to be c must wash their H3197
Lev 14:11 both the one to be c and their offerings H3197
Lev 14:14 lobe of the right ear of the one to be c, H3197
Lev 14:17 lobe of the right ear of the one to be c, H3197
Lev 14:18 on the head of the one to be c and make H3197
Lev 14:19 atonement for the one to be c from their H3197
Lev 14:25 lobe of the right ear of the one to be c, H3197
Lev 14:28 lobe of the right ear of the one to be c, H3197
Lev 14:29 shall put on the head of the one to be c, H3197
Lev 14:31 the LORD on behalf of the one to be c." H3197
Lev 15:13 " 'When a man is c from his discharge, he H3197
Lev 15:28 " 'When she is c from her discharge, she H3197
Lev 22: 4 not eat the sacred offerings until he is c. H3197
Nu 19:19 Those who are being c must wash their NDT
Jos 22:17 this very day we have not c ourselves from H3197
2Ki 5:10 flesh will be restored and you will be c." H3197
2Ki 5:12 Couldn't I wash in them and be c?" So he H3197
2Ki 5:13 when he tells you, 'Wash and be c'!" H3197
Pr 30:12 own eyes and yet are not c of their filth; H8175
Isa 1: 6 not c or bandaged or soothed with olive H2318
Eze 22:24 a land that has not been c or rained on H3197
Eze 24:13 you but you would not be c from your H3197
Eze 44:26 After he is c, he must wait seven days. H3200
Mt 8: 3 Immediately he was c of his leprosy. G2751
Mt 11: 5 those who have leprosy are c, the deaf G2751
Mk 1:42 the leprosy left him and he was c. G2751
Lk 4:27 not one of them was c—only Naaman G2751
Lk 7:22 those who have leprosy are c, the deaf G2751
Lk 17:14 And as they went, they were c. G2751
Lk 17:17 "Were not all ten c? Where are G2751
Heb 9:22 requires that nearly everything be c with G2751
Heb 10: 2 worshipers would have been c once for all G2751
2Pe 1: 9 that they have been c from their past sins. G2752

CLEANSING (20) [CLEAN]
Lev 14: 2 person at the time of their ceremonial c, H3200
Lev 14:23 bring them for their c to the priest at the H3200
Lev 14:32 afford the regular offerings for their c. H3200
Lev 15:13 count off seven days for his ceremonial c; H3200
Nu 6: 9 on the seventh day—the day of their c. H3200
Nu 8: 7 Sprinkle the water of c on them; then H2633
Nu 19: 9 community for use in the water of c; H5614
Nu 19:13 Because the water of c has not been H5614
Nu 19:20 The water of c has not been sprinkled on H5614
Nu 19:21 the water of c must also wash his H5614
Nu 19:21 touches the water of c will be unclean till H5614
Nu 31:23 must also be purified with the water of c. H5614
Job 9:30 with soap and my hands with c powder, H1342
Jer 2:22 soap and use an abundance of c powder, H1383
Eze 39:14 be continually employed in c the land. H3197
Mk 1:44 that Moses commanded for your c, G2752
Lk 5:14 that Moses commanded for your c, G2752
Jn 11:55 Jerusalem for their ceremonial c before the G49
Eph 5:26 c her by the washing with water through G2751
Heb 6: 2 instruction about c rites, the laying on of G968

CLEAR (40) [CLEARED, CLEARLY]
Ge 20: 5 done this with a c conscience and clean H9448
Ge 20: 6 I know you did this with a c conscience H9448
Ex 27:20 to bring you c oil of pressed olives H2341
Lev 24: 2 to bring you c oil of pressed olives H2341
Lev 24:12 of the LORD should be made c to them. H7300
Nu 15:34 because it was not c what should be done H7300
Jos 17:15 into the forest and c land for yourselves H1345
Jos 17:18 C it, and its farthest limits will be yours H1345
2Sa 19: 6 You have made it c today that the H5583
1Ki 2:31 so c me and my whole family of the H6073
Ne 8: 8 making it c and giving the meaning so H7300

Isa 32: 4 stammering tongue will be fluent and c. H7456
Eze 34:18 Is it not enough for you to drink c water H5488
Mt 3:12 his hand, and *he will* c his threshing floor G1351
Lk 3:17 fork is in his hand *to* c his threshing floor G1350
Jn 8:43 Why *is* my language not c *to you*? Because G1182
Ac 24:16 keep my conscience c before God and man G718
1Co 4: 4 My **conscience is** c, but that does G4029+5323
1Co 14: 8 if the trumpet does **not** sound a c call, who G83
1Co 15:27 it is c that this does not include God G1316
2Co 7:11 what **eagerness to** c yourselves, what G665
2Co 11: 6 *We have* **made** *this* perfectly c to you in G5746
Php 1:13 it has become c throughout the whole G5745
Php 3:15 differently, that too God *will* **make** c to you. G636
1Th 3:11 *may* our God and Father himself and our Lord Jesus c G2985
1Ti 3: 9 truths of the faith with a c conscience. G2754
2Ti 1: 3 with a c conscience, as night G2754
2Ti 3: 9 their folly will be c to everyone. G1684
Heb 5:11 but *it is* **hard to make** it c to you G1549+3306
Heb 6:17 *to* **make** the unchanging nature of his purpose very c G2109
Heb 7:14 For it is c that our Lord descended from G4593
Heb 7:15 said is even more c if another priest like G2867
Heb 9: 9 were not able *to* c the conscience of G5457
Heb 13:18 sure that we have a c conscience and G2819
1Pe 3:16 keeping a c conscience, so that those who G19
1Pe 3:21 the pledge of a c conscience toward God G19
2Pe 1:14 as our Lord Jesus Christ *has* **made** c to me. G1317
Rev 4: 6 what looked like a sea of glass, *c* as crystal. AIT
Rev 21:11 precious jewel, like a jasper, **c as crystal**. G3222
Rev 22: 1 the water of life, as c as crystal, flowing G3287

CLEARED (5) [CLEAR]
Nu 5:28 she *will* **be c of guilt** and will be able to H5927
1Sa 14:41 were taken by lot, and the men *were* c. H3655
2Ch 30:14 in Jerusalem and **c away** the incense H6073
Ps 80: 9 *You* c *the* **ground** for it, and it took root H7155
Isa 5: 2 dug it up and c it **of stones** and planted it H6232

CLEARLY (19) [CLEAR]
Ge 26:28 "*We* **saw** c that the LORD was with H8011+8011
Ex 10:10 C you are bent on evil. H3954+8011
Nu 12: 8 I speak face to face, c and not in riddles H5260
Nu 24: 3 the prophecy of one whose eye **sees** c, H9280
Nu 24:15 the prophecy of one whose eye **sees** c, H9280
Dt 27: 8 you shall write very c all the words of this H930
Jos 9:24 servants **were c told** how the LORD H5583+5583
1Sa 2:27 '*Did I* not c **reveal myself** to your H1655+1655
Jer 23:20 to come *you will* **understand** it c. H1067+1069
Mt 7: 5 then *you will* **see** c to remove the G1332
Mk 8:25 was restored, and he saw everything c. G5495
Lk 6:42 then *you will* **see** c to remove the G1332
Jn 16:29 you are speaking c and without G1877+4244
Ro 1:20 divine nature—*have been* **c seen**, being G2775
Ro 3: 5 **brings out** God's righteousness **more c**, G5319
Gal 3: 1 Jesus Christ *was* **c portrayed** as crucified. G4592
Gal 3:11 C no one who relies on the law is justified G1316
Col 4: 4 Pray that I may proclaim it c, as I should. G5746
1Ti 4: 1 The Spirit c says that in later times some G4843

CLEAVE, CLEAVED, CLEAVETH (KJV) ALLY, BOUND, CLING, CLUNG, DIVIDED, HELD, HOLD, OPENED, PIERCES, SPLITS, STICK, STICKS, STUCK, TEAR, UNITE, UNITED

CLEFT (1) [CLEFTS]
Ex 33:22 I will put you in a c *in* the rock and cover H5942

CLEFTS (4) [CLEFT]
Jdg 6: 2 shelters for themselves in **mountain c**, H2215
SS 2:14 My dove in the c *of* the rock, in the hiding H2511
Jer 49:16 you who live in the c *of* the rocks, who H2511
Ob 3 who live in the c *of* the rocks and make H2511

CLEMENCY (KJV) KIND

CLEMENT (1)
Php 4: 3 along with C and the rest of my G3098

CLEOPAS (1)
Lk 24:18 One of them, named C, asked him, "Are G3093

CLERK (1)
Ac 19:35 The **city c** quieted the crowd and said G1208

CLEVER (2) [CLEVERLY, CLEVERNESS]
Isa 3: 3 skilled craftsman and c enchanter. H1067
Isa 5:21 in their own eyes and c in their own sight. H1067

CLEVERLY (2) [CLEVER]
Hos 13: 2 their silver, **c fashioned** images, all of H9312
2Pe 1:16 did not follow **c devised** stories when we G5054

CLEVERNESS (2) [CLEVER]
Pr 23: 4 out to get rich; do not trust your own c. H1069
Isa 25:11 their pride despite the c *of* their hands. H747

CLIFF (5) [CLIFFS]
1Sa 14: 4 the Philistine outpost was a c; H9094+6152
1Sa 14: 5 One c stood to the north toward Mikmash H9094
2Ch 25:12 to the top of a c and threw them down H6152
Job 39:28 It dwells on a c and stays there at night; H6152
Lk 4:29 was built, in order to **throw** him **off the c**. G2889

CLIFFS (3) [CLIFF]
Ps 141: 6 rulers will be thrown down from the c, H6152
Jer 51:25 roll you off the c, and make you a H6152
Eze 38:20 the c will crumble and every wall will fall H4533

CLIMAX (3)
Eze 21:25 time of punishment has reached its c, H7891
Eze 21:29 time of punishment has reached its c. H7891
Eze 35: 5 the time their punishment reached its c, H7891

CLIMB (7) [CLIMBED, CLIMBING, CLIMBS]
Ge 49:22 a spring, whose branches c over a wall. H7575
1Sa 14:10 up to us,' *we will* **c up**, because that H6590
1Sa 14:12 his armor-bearer, "**C up** after me; the LORD H6590
SS 7: 8 "*I will* c the palm tree; I will take H6590
Jer 4:29 the thickets; *some* **c up** among the rocks. H6590
Joel 2: 9 *They* c into the houses; like thieves they H6590
Am 9: 2 Though *they* **c up** *to* the heavens above H6590

CLIMBED (16) [CLIMB]
Dt 32:50 mountain that you *have* c you will die H6590
Dt 34: 1 Then Moses c Mount Nebo from the H6590
Jos 15: 8 From there it c to the top of the hill west H6590
Jdg 9: 7 *he* **c up** on the top of Mount Gerizim and H2143
Jdg 9:51 themselves in and **c up** on the tower roof. H6590
1Sa 14:13 Jonathan **c up**, using his hands and feet H6590
2Sa 17:18 in his courtyard, and *they* **c down** *into* it. H3718
2Sa 17:21 the two c out of the well and went to H6590
1Ki 18:42 but Elijah c to the top of Carmel H6590
Isa 57: 8 your bed, *you* c *into* it and opened it wide H6590
Jer 9:21 Death *has* **c in** through our windows and H6590
Eze 40: 6 *He* c its steps and measured the threshold H6590
Mt 14:32 And *when* they c into the boat, the wind G326
Mk 6:51 Then *he* c into the boat with them, and the G326
Lk 19: 4 So he ran ahead and c a sycamore-fig tree G326
Jn 21:11 So Simon Peter **c back into** the boat and G326

CLIMBING (2) [CLIMB]
2Ch 20:16 They *will be* **c up** by the Pass of Ziz, and H6590
Ne 4: 3 even a fox **c up** on it would break down H6590

CLIMBS (3) [CLIMB]
Isa 24:18 whoever c out of the pit will be caught in H6590
Jer 48:44 whoever c out of the pit will be caught in H6590
Jn 10: 1 by the gate, but **c in** by some other way G326

CLING (11) [CLINGING, CLUNG]
Dt 28:60 that you dreaded, and *they will* c to you. H1815
2Ki 5:27 Naaman's leprosy *will* c to you and to your H1815
Job 8:15 it gives way; *they* c to it, but it does H2616
Job 41:17 *they* **c together** and cannot be parted. H4334
Ps 31: 6 I hate those *who* c *to* worthless idols; as H9068
Ps 44:25 to the dust; our bodies c to the ground. H1815
Ps 63: 8 I c to you; your right hand upholds me. H1815
Ps 137: 6 *May* my tongue c to the roof of my mouth H1815
Jer 8: 5 always turn away? *They* c to deceit; they H2616
Jnh 2: 8 "*Those who* c *to* worthless idols turn away H9068
Ro 12: 9 Hate what is evil; **c to** what is good. G3140

CLINGING (1) [CLING]
1Ki 1:51 King Solomon and *is* c to the horns of the H296

CLIP (1)
Lev 19:27 of your head or **c off** the edges of your H8845

CLOAK (48) [CLOAKS]
Ge 39:12 She caught him by his c and said, "Come to H955
Ge 39:12 But he left his c in her hand and ran out of H955
Ge 39:13 that he had left his c in her hand and had H955
Ge 39:15 he left his c beside me and ran out of the H955
Ge 39:16 She kept his c beside her until his master H955
Ge 39:18 he left his c beside me and ran out of the H955
Ex 4: 6 LORD said, "Put your hand inside your c." H2668
Ex 4: 6 So Moses put his hand into his c, and H2668
Ex 4: 7 "Now put it back into your c," he said. H2668
Ex 4: 7 So Moses put his hand back into his c H2668
Ex 12:11 with your **c tucked into** your **belt** H2520+5516
Ex 22:26 If you take your neighbor's c as a pledge H8515
Ex 22:27 because that c is the only covering your H8529
Dt 22: 3 find their donkey or c or anything else H8529
Dt 22:12 on the four corners of the c you wear. H4064
Dt 24:13 Return their c by sunset so that your H8515
Dt 24:17 take the c *of* the widow as a pledge. H955
1Ki 11:29 met him on the way, wearing a new c. H8515
1Ki 11:30 hold of the new c he was wearing and H8515
1Ki 18:46 **tucking** his **c into** *his* **belt**, he H9113+5516
1Ki 19:13 he pulled his c over his face and went out H168
1Ki 19:19 up to him and threw his c around him. H168
2Ki 2: 8 Elijah took his c, rolled it up and struck the H168
2Ki 2:13 picked up Elijah's c that had fallen from H168
2Ki 2:14 He took the c that had fallen from Elijah H168
2Ki 4:29 "**Tuck** your **c into** your **belt**, take my H2520+5516
2Ki 9: 1 "**Tuck** *your* **c into** your **belt**, take H2520+5516
Ezr 9: 3 I tore my tunic and c, pulled hair from my H5077
Ezr 9: 5 with my tunic and c torn, and fell on my H5077
Ps 109:19 May it be like a c wrapped about him, like H955
Ps 109:29 disgrace and wrapped in shame as in a c. H5077
Pr 21:14 concealed in the c pacifies great wrath. H2668
Pr 30: 4 Who has wrapped up the waters in a c H8529
SS 5: 7 they took away my c, those watchmen of H8100
Isa 3: 6 say, "You have a c, you be our leader; H8529
Isa 59:17 wrapped himself in zeal as in a c. H5077
Mt 9:20 him and touched the edge *of* his c. G2668
Mt 9:21 "If I only touch his c, I will be healed." G2668
Mt 14:36 to let the sick just touch the edge *of* his c, G2668
Mt 24:18 no one in the field go back to get their c. G2668
Mk 5:27 him in the crowd and touched his c, G2668
Mk 6:56 to let them touch even the edge *of* his c, G2668
Mk 10:50 Throwing his c aside, he jumped to his G2668
Mk 13:16 no one in the field go back to get their c. G2668
Lk 8:44 him and touched the edge *of* his c, G2668
Lk 22:36 have a sword, sell your c and buy one. G2668
Ac 12: 8 "Wrap your c around you and follow me," G2668
2Ti 4:13 bring the c that I left with Carpus at Troas G5742

CLOAKS (9) [CLOAK]
2Ki 9:13 quickly took their c and spread them under H955
Isa 3:22 the fine robes and the capes and c, the H4762
Mt 21: 7 placed their c on them for Jesus to G2668
Mt 21: 8 large crowd spread their c on the road, G2668
Mk 11: 7 the colt to Jesus and threw their c over it, G2668
Mk 11: 8 Many people spread their c on the road G2668
Lk 19:35 threw their c on the colt and put Jesus on G2668
Lk 19:36 people spread their c on the road. G2668
Ac 22:23 throwing off their c and flinging dust into G2668

CLODS (2)
Job 38:38 hard and the **c of earth** stick together? H8073
Joel 1:17 The seeds are shriveled beneath the c H4493

CLOPAS (1)
Jn 19:25 Mary the wife *of* C, and Mary Magdalene. G3116

CLOSE (67) [CLOSED, CLOSELY, CLOSER, CLOSES, CLOSEST, CLOSING, ENCLOSE, ENCLOSED]
Ge 13: 8 mine, for we are **c relatives**. H278+408
Ge 27:22 Jacob **went c** to his father Isaac, who H5602
Ge 45: 4 said to his brothers, "**Come c** to me." H5602
Ge 46: 4 And Joseph's own hand *will* c your eyes." H8883
Ge 48:10 So Joseph **brought** his sons c to him, and H5602
Ge 48:13 right hand, and **brought** them c to him. H5602
Ex 25:27 rings are to be **c to** the rim to hold H4200+6645
Ex 28:27 **c to** the seam just above the H4200+6645
Ex 37:14 rings were put **c to** the rim to hold H4200+6645
Ex 39:20 **c to** the seam just above the H4200+6645
Lev 3: 9 fat tail cut off **c to** the backbone, H4200+6645
Lev 14:38 of the house and **c** it **up** for seven days. H6037
Lev 18: 6 approach any **c relative** to have H8638+1414
Lev 18:12 she is your father's **c relative**. H8638
Lev 18:13 because she is your mother's **c relative**. H8638
Lev 18:17 daughter; they are her **c relatives**. H8638
Lev 20: 4 of the community c their eyes when H6623+6623
Lev 20:19 that would dishonor a **c relative**; both H8638
Lev 21: 2 except for a **c relative**, such as his H8638+7940
Nu 5: 8 that person has no **c relative** to whom H1457
Nu 22:25 angel of the LORD, *it* **pressed c** to the wall H4315
Jos 2: 5 when it was time to c the city gate, they H6037
Jdg 16: 9 string snaps when it **comes c** *to* a flame. H8193
Ru 2:20 "That man is our **c relative**; he is one of H7940
Ru 2:23 So Ruth **stayed c** to the women of Boaz to H1815
1Sa 18: 9 that time on Saul **kept a c eye on** David. H6523
2Sa 11:20 'Why *did you* **get so c** to the city to fight? H5602
2Sa 11:21 Why *did you* **get so c** to the wall H5602
2Sa 12:11 give them to **one who is c** to you, H8291
1Ki 21: 1 **c to** the palace of Ahab king of Samaria. H725
1Ki 21: 2 garden, since it is c to my palace. H7940+725
2Ki 10:11 his chief men, his **c friends** and his priests H3359
2Ki 11: 8 Stay **c to** the king wherever he goes." H907
2Ch 23: 7 Stay **c to** the king wherever he goes." H907
Ne 6:10 the temple, and *let us* c the temple doors H6037
Job 13:27 *you* **keep c watch on** all my paths by H9068
Job 33:11 *he* **keeps c watch** *on* all my paths. H9068
Job 41:16 each *is so* c to the next that no air can H5602
Ps 17:10 *They* **c up** their callous hearts, and their H6037
Ps 34:18 The LORD *is* c to the brokenhearted and H7940
Ps 41: 9 Even my **c friend**, someone I trusted H408+8934
Ps 55:13 like myself, my companion, my **c friend**, H3359
Ps 69:15 me up or the pit c its mouth over me. H358
Ps 88:15 I have suffered and *been* **c to death**; H1588
Ps 148:14 of Israel, the people **c to** his **heart**. H7940
Pr 16:28 and a gossip separates **c friends**. H476
Pr 17: 9 repeats the matter separates **c friends**. H476
Pr 28:27 but *those who* c their eyes to them receive H6623
Isa 6:10 make their ears dull and c their eyes. H9129
Isa 40:11 in his arms and carries them c to his heart; H928
Isa 42:23 this or **pay c attention** in H7992+2256+9048
Isa 56: 1 my salvation is c at hand and my H7940
Isa 66: 9 "*Do I* **c up** the womb when I bring to H6806
Jer 30:21 him near and *he will* **come c** to me— H5602
Jer 30:21 he who will devote himself to *be* c to me? H5602
La 3:56 "*Do* not c your ears to my cry for relief." H6623
Eze 22: 4 *You have* **brought** your days **to a c**, and H7928
Joel 2: 1 of the LORD is coming. It is **c at hand**— H7940
Zec 13: 7 against the man who is c *to* me! H6660
Mt 6: 6 c the door and pray to your Father G3091
Lk 20:20 **Keeping a c watch on** him, they sent spies G4190
Lk 21:34 that day *will* c on you suddenly like a G2392
Jn 4:47 heal his son, *who was* c to death. G3516
Ac 8: 6 they all **paid c attention** to what he said. G4668
Ac 9:24 night *they* **kept c watch** on the city G4190
Ac 10:24 called together his relatives and c friends. G5813
Rev 6: 8 Hades was following **c behind** him. G3552

CLOSE-KNIT (1) [KNIT]
Job 40:17 like a cedar; the sinews of its thighs *are* c. H8571

C

CLOSED (16) [CLOSE]

Ge 2:21 ribs and then c up the place with flesh. H6037
Ge 8: 2 floodgates of the heavens had been c, H6126
Lev 14:46 the house while it is c up will be unclean H6037
Nu 16:33 the earth c over them, and they H4059
Jdg 3:22 pull the sword out, and the fat c in over it. H6037
1Sa 1: 5 loved her, and the LORD had c her womb. H6037
1Sa 1: 6 Because the LORD had c Hannah's womb H6037
Ne 4: 7 ahead and that the gaps were being c, H6258
Job 17: 4 You have c their minds to understanding H7621
Ecc 12: 4 doors to the street are c and the sound of H6037
Isa 32: 3 eyes of those who see will no longer be c, H9129
Isa 44:18 their minds c so they cannot understand NDT
Jer 6:10 Their ears are c so they cannot hear H6888
La 3:54 the waters c over my head, and I thought I H7429
Mt 13:15 with their ears, and they have c their eyes. G2826
Ac 28:27 with their ears, and they have c their eyes. G2826

CLOSELY (18) [CLOSE]

Ge 24:21 the man watched her c to learn whether H8617
Ge 43: 7 "The man questioned us c about H8626+8626
Ge 44:30 whose life is c bound up with the boy's H8003
Dt 4: 9 watch yourselves c so that you do not H4394
Ru 3:12 is another who is more c related than I. H7940
2Sa 19:42 this because the king is c related to us. H7940
1Ki 3:21 But when I looked at him c in the morning H1067
Ne 13: 4 He was c associated with Tobiah, H7940
Job 23:11 My feet have c followed his steps; I have H296
Ps 122: 3 like a city that is c compacted together. H2489
Jer 2:10 send to Kedar and observe c; see if there H4394
Eze 40: 4 carefully and listen c and pay H9048+928+265
Eze 44: 5 listen c and give attention to H9048+928+265
Mk 3: 2 so they watched him c to see if he would G4190
Mk 14:67 warming himself, she looked c at him. G1838
Lk 6: 7 so they watched him c to see if he would G4190
Lk 22:56 She looked c at him and said, "This man G867
1Ti 4:16 Watch your life and doctrine c. G2091

CLOSER (7) [CLOSE]

Ex 3: 5 "Do not come any c," God said. "Take off H7928
1Sa 17:41 in front of him, kept coming c to David. H7929
1Sa 17:48 As the Philistine moved c to attack him H7928
2Sa 18:25 runner came c and closer. H2143+2256+7929
2Sa 18:25 runner came closer and c. H2143+2256+7929
Pr 18:24 is a friend who sticks c than a brother. H1816
Ac 7:31 As he went over to get a c look, he heard G2917

CLOSES (1) [CLOSE]

Lk 13:25 owner of the house gets up and c the door, G643

CLOSEST (8) [CLOSE]

Dt 13: 6 your c friend secretly entices you, H8276+889+3869+5883+3870
Est 1:14 were c to the king—Karshena, Shethar H7940
Job 19:14 my c friends have forgotten me. H3359
Ps 31:11 an object of dread to my c friends— H3359
Ps 88: 8 from me my c friends and have made H3359
Ps 88:18 neighbor—darkness is my c friend. H3359
Pr 19: 4 even the c friend of the poor person AIT
Jn 1:18 is in c relationship with the Father, G3146

CLOSET, CLOSETS (KJV) CHAMBER, ROOM, ROOMS

CLOSING (5) [CLOSE]

Lev 23:36 It is the c special assembly; do no regular H6809
Nu 29:35 day hold a c special assembly and do no H6809
1Sa 23:26 his forces were c in on David and his H6496
Ps 77: 4 You kept my eyes from c; I was too H296+9073
Eze 21:14 slaughter, c in on them from every side. H2539

CLOTH (27) [CLOTHS]

Ex 28:31 the robe of the ephod entirely of blue c, H9418
Ex 39:22 the robe of the ephod entirely of blue c— H9418
Lev 11:32 it is made of wood, c, hide or sackcloth. H955
Nu 4: 6 spread a c of solid blue over that and put H955
Nu 4: 7 are to spread a blue c and put on it the H955
Nu 4: 8 They are to spread a scarlet c over them H955
Nu 4: 9 are to take a blue c and cover the H955
Nu 4:11 are to spread a blue c and cover that with H955
Nu 4:12 wrap them in a blue c, cover that with the H955
Nu 4:13 bronze altar and spread a purple c over it. H955
Dt 22:17 shall display the c before the elders of the H8529
1Sa 21: 9 it is wrapped in a c behind the ephod. H8529
2Ki 8:15 But the next day he took a thick c, soaked H4802
Isa 19:10 The workers in c will be dejected, and all H9271
Isa 30:22 away like a menstrual c and say to them H1865
Eze 16:13 linen and costly fabric and embroidered c. H8391
Mt 9:16 one sews a patch of unshrunk c on an old G4820
Mt 27:59 the body, wrapped it in a clean linen c, G4984
Mk 2:21 one sews a patch of unshrunk c on an old G4820
Mk 15:46 So Joseph bought some linen c, took G4984
Lk 19:20 I have kept it laid away in a piece of c. G5051
Lk 23:53 wrapped it in linen c and placed it in a G4984
Jn 11:44 strips of linen, and a c around his face. G5051
Jn 20: 7 as well as the c that had been wrapped G5051
Jn 20: 7 The c was still lying in its place, separate NDT
Ac 16:14 named Lydia, a dealer in purple c. G4527
Rev 18:12 silk and scarlet c; every sort of G4986

CLOTHE (21) [CLOTHED, CLOTHES, CLOTHING]

Job 10:11 c me with skin and flesh and knit me H4252
Job 39:19 strength or c its neck with a flowing mane H4252
Job 40:10 and c yourself in honor and majesty. H4252
Ps 45: 3 c yourself with splendor and majesty. NDT
Ps 73: 6 they c themselves with violence. H6493+8884
Ps 132:16 I will c her priests with salvation, and her H4252
Ps 132:18 I will c his enemies with shame, but his H4252
Isa 22:21 I will c him with your robe and fasten your H4252
Isa 50: 3 I c the heavens with darkness and make H4252
Isa 51: 9 arm of the LORD, c yourself with strength! H4252
Isa 52: 1 Zion, c yourself with strength! H4252
Isa 58: 7 you see the naked, to c them, and not to H4059
Eze 34: 3 c yourselves with the wool and slaughter H4252
Mt 6:30 will he not much more c you—you of little NDT
Mt 25:38 or needing clothes and c you? G4314
Mt 25:43 I needed clothes and you did not c me, G4314
Lk 12:28 how much more will he c you—you of little NDT
Ro 13:14 c yourselves with the Lord Jesus Christ G1907
1Co 15:53 perishable must c itself with the G1907
Col 3:12 c yourselves with compassion G1907
1Pe 5: 5 All of you, c yourselves with humility G1599

CLOTHED (48) [CLOTHE]

Ge 3:21 of skin for Adam and his wife and c them. H4252
Lev 8: 7 c him with the robe and put the ephod on H4252
2Sa 1:24 Saul, who c you in scarlet and finery H4252
1Ch 15:27 Now David was c in a robe of fine linen H4124
1Ch 21:16 David and the elders, c in sackcloth, fell H4059
2Ch 6:41 May your priests, LORD God, be c with H4252
2Ch 28:15 from the plunder they c all who were H4252
Est 4: 2 because no one c in sackcloth was H4230
Job 7: 5 My body is c with worms and scabs, my H4252
Job 8:22 Your enemies will be c in shame, and the H4252
Ps 30:11 removed my sackcloth and c me with joy, H273
Ps 35:26 may all who exalt themselves over me be c with H4252
Ps 65:12 overflow; the hills are c with gladness. H2520
Ps 104: 1 you are c with splendor and majesty. H4252
Ps 109:29 May my accusers be c with disgrace and H4252
Ps 132: 9 May your priests be c with your H4252
Pr 31:21 household; for all of them are c in scarlet. H4229
Pr 31:22 her bed; she is c in fine linen and purple. H4230
Pr 31:25 She is c with strength and dignity; she can H4230
Ecc 9: 8 Always be c in white, and always anoint H955
Isa 61:10 For he has c me with garments of H4252
Eze 7:18 will put on sackcloth and be c with terror. H4059
Eze 7:27 the prince will be c with despair, and the H4252
Eze 9: 2 them was a man c in linen who had a H4229
Eze 9: 3 called to the man c in linen who had the H4229
Eze 10: 2 The LORD said to the man c in linen, "Go in H4229
Eze 16:10 I c you with an embroidered dress and put H4252
Eze 23: 6 c in blue, governors and commanders, all H4229
Eze 26:16 C with terror, they will sit on the ground H4252
Eze 31:15 Because of it I c Lebanon with gloom, and H7722
Da 5: 7 what it means will be c in purple and A10383
Da 5:16 you will be c in purple and have a gold A10383
Da 5:29 Daniel was c in purple, a gold A10383
Da 12: 6 One of them said to the man c in linen H4229
Da 12: 7 The man c in linen, who was above the H4229
Zec 3: 5 clean turban on his head and c him, H4252+955
Zec 6:13 he will be c with majesty and will sit H5951
Mt 25:36 I needed clothes and you c me, I was sick G4314
Lk 24:49 until you have been c with power from on G1907
Jn 19: 2 They c him in a purple robe G4314
1Co 15:54 the perishable has been c with the G1907
2Co 5: 2 longing to be c instead with our heavenly G2086
2Co 5: 3 because when we are c, we will not be G1907
2Co 5: 4 but to be c instead with our heavenly G2086
Gal 3:27 into Christ have c yourselves with Christ. G1907
Rev 11: 3 prophesy for 1,260 days, c in sackcloth." G4314
Rev 12: 1 a woman c with the sun, with the moon G4314
Rev 16:15 the one who stays awake and remains c, G2668

CLOTHES (168) [CLOTHE]

Ge 27:15 took the best c of Esau her older son, H955
Ge 27:27 When Isaac caught the smell of his c, he H955
Ge 28:20 will give me food to eat and c to wear H955
Ge 35: 2 purify yourselves and change your c. H8529
Ge 37:29 that Joseph was not there, he tore his c. H955
Ge 37:34 Then Jacob tore his c, put on sackcloth H8529
Ge 38:14 she took off her widow's c, covered herself H955
Ge 38:19 off her veil and put on her widow's c again. H955
Ge 41:14 When he had shaved and changed his c H8529
Ge 44:13 they tore their c. Then they all loaded H8529
Ge 45:22 shekels of silver and five sets of c. H8529
Ex 19:10 tomorrow. Have them wash their c H8529
Ex 19:14 and they washed their c. H8529
Ex 28:41 After you put these c on your brother H4252
Lev 6:10 The priest shall then put on his linen c H4496
Lev 6:11 he is to take off these c and put on others, H955
Lev 10: 6 become unkempt and do not tear your c, H955
Lev 11:25 up one of their carcasses must wash their c, H955
Lev 11:28 picks up their carcasses must wash their c, H955
Lev 11:40 eats some of its carcass must wash their c, H955
Lev 11:40 who picks up the carcass must wash their c, H955
Lev 13: 6 They must wash their c, and they will be H955
Lev 13:34 They must wash their c, and they will be H955
Lev 13:45 such a defiling disease must wear torn c, H955
Lev 14: 8 person to be cleansed must wash their c, H955
Lev 14: 9 must wash their c and bathe themselves H955
Lev 14:47 eats in the house must wash their c. H955
Lev 15: 5 bed must wash their c and bathe with H955
Lev 15: 6 on must wash their c and bathe with water, H955
Lev 15: 7 must wash their c and bathe with water, H955
Lev 15: 8 must wash their c and bathe with water H955
Lev 15:10 must wash their c and bathe with water, H955
Lev 15:11 must wash their c and bathe with water, H955
Lev 15:13 he must wash his c and bathe himself with H955
Lev 15:21 must wash their c and bathe with water H955
Lev 15:22 must wash their c and bathe with water H955
Lev 15:27 must wash their c and bathe with water H955
Lev 16:26 must wash his c and bathe himself with H955
Lev 16:28 them must wash his c and bathe himself H955
Lev 17:15 must wash their c and bathe with water, H955
Lev 17:16 do not wash their c and bathe themselves, NDT
Lev 21:10 let his hair become unkempt or tear his c. H955
Nu 8: 7 shave their whole bodies and wash their c. H955
Nu 8:21 purified themselves and washed their c. H955
Nu 14: 6 who had explored the land, tore their c H955
Nu 19: 7 priest must wash his c and bathe himself H955
Nu 19: 8 must also wash his c and bathe with water, H955
Nu 19:10 ashes of the heifer must also wash his c, H955
Nu 19:19 must wash their c and bathe with water, H955
Nu 19:21 water of cleansing must also wash his c, H955
Nu 31:24 day wash your c and you will be clean H955
Dt 8: 4 Your c did not wear out and your feet did H8529
Dt 21:13 put aside the c she was wearing when H8529
Dt 22:11 Do not wear c of wool and linen woven H4252
Dt 29: 5 the wilderness, your c did not wear out H8515
Jos 7: 6 Joshua tore his c and fell facedown to H8529
Jos 9: 5 sandals on their feet and wore old c. H8515
Jos 9:13 And our c and sandals are worn out by H8515
Jdg 11:35 he saw her, he tore his c and cried, "Oh no, H955
Jdg 14:12 thirty linen garments and thirty sets of c. H955
Jdg 14:13 thirty linen garments and thirty sets of c." H955
Jdg 14:19 gave their c to those who had H2722
Jdg 17:10 silver a year, your c and your food." H6886+955
Ru 3: 3 perfume, and get dressed in your best c. H8529
1Sa 4:12 to Shiloh with his c torn and dust on his H4496
1Sa 27: 9 cattle, donkeys and camels, and c. H955
1Sa 28: 8 putting on other c, and at night he and two H955
2Sa 1: 2 Saul's camp with his c torn and dust on his H955
2Sa 1:11 with him took hold of their c and tore them. H955
2Sa 3:31 "Tear your c and put on sackcloth and walk H955
2Sa 12:20 put on lotions and changed his c, he went H8529
2Sa 13:31 tore his c and lay down on the ground H955
2Sa 13:31 all his attendants stood by with their c torn. H955
2Sa 14: 2 Dress in mourning c, and don't use any H955
2Sa 19:24 washed his c from the day the king H955
1Ki 21:27 he tore his c, put on sackcloth and H955
2Ki 5:26 this the time to take money or to accept c— H955
2Ki 7: 8 gold and c, and went off and hid H955
2Ki 18:37 Hezekiah, with their c torn, and told him H955
2Ki 19: 1 he tore his c and put on sackcloth and went H955
2Ki 25:29 put aside his prison c and for the rest of his H955
2Ch 28:15 They provided them with c and sandals H4252
Ne 4:23 men nor the guards with me took off our c; H955
Ne 9:21 their c did not wear out nor did their feet H8515
Est 4: 1 he tore his c, put on sackcloth and H955
Est 4: 4 She sent c for him to put on instead of his H955
Job 9:31 pit so that even my c would detest me. H8515
Job 24: 7 Lacking c, they spend the night naked H4230
Job 24:10 Lacking c, they go about naked; they carry H4230
Job 27:16 up silver like dust and c like piles of clay, H4860
Job 37:17 who swelter in your c when the land lies H955
Ps 22:18 They divide my c among them and cast lots H955
Pr 6:27 fire into his lap without his c being burned? H955
Pr 23:21 and drowsiness c them in rags. H4252
Isa 4: 1 eat our own food and provide our own c; H8529
Isa 23:18 the LORD, for abundant food and fine c. H4833
Isa 32:11 Strip off your fine c and wrap H7320+2256+6910
Isa 36:22 Hezekiah, with their c torn, and told him H955
Isa 37: 1 he tore his c and put on sackcloth and went H955
Jer 2:34 On your c is found the lifeblood of the H4053
Jer 36:24 showed no fear, nor did they tear their c. H955
Jer 38:11 rags and worn-out c from there and let H4874
Jer 38:12 rags and worn-out c under your arms to H4874
Jer 41: 5 torn their c and cut themselves came from H955
Jer 52:33 put aside his prison c and for the rest of his H955
Eze 16:13 your c were of fine linen and costly fabric H4860
Eze 16:18 took your embroidered c to put on them, H955
Eze 16:39 will strip you of your c and take your fine H955
Eze 23:26 also strip you of your c and take your fine H955
Eze 42:14 are to put on other c before they go near H955
Eze 44:17 they are to wear linen c; they must not H955
Eze 44:19 they are to take off the c they have been H955
Eze 44:19 put on other c, so that the people are H955
Da 3:21 turbans and other c, were bound and A10382
Zep 1: 8 king's sons and all those clad in foreign c. H4860
Hag 1: 6 have your fill. You put on c, but are not H4252
Zec 3: 3 was dressed in filthy c as he stood before H955
Zec 3: 4 standing before him, "Take off his filthy c." H955
Mt 3: 4 John's c were made of camel's hair, and G1903
Mt 6:25 than food, and the body more than c? G1903
Mt 6:28 "And why do you worry about c? See how G1903
Mt 6:30 If that is how God c the grass of the field G314
Mt 11: 8 A man dressed in fine c? No, G3434
Mt 11: 8 those who wear fine c are in kings' G3434
Mt 17: 2 his c became as white as the light. G2668
Mt 22:11 there who was not wearing wedding c. G1903
Mt 22:12 did you get in here without wedding c, G1903
Mt 25:36 I needed c and you clothed me, I was sick G1218
Mt 25:38 or needing c and clothe you? G1218
Mt 25:43 I needed c and you did not clothe me G1218
Mt 25:44 a stranger or needing c or sick or in G1218
Mt 26:65 Then the high priest tore his c and said G2668
Mt 27:31 off the robe and put his own c on him. G2668

Mt 27:35 they divided up his c by casting lots. G2668
Mt 28: 3 lightning, and his c were white as snow. G1903
Mk 5:28 "If I just touch his c, I will be healed." G2668
Mk 5:30 crowd and asked, "Who touched my c?" G2668
Mk 9: 3 His c became dazzling white, whiter than G2668
Mk 14:63 The high priest tore his c. "Why do we G5945
Mk 15:20 the purple robe and put his own c on him. G2668
Mk 15:24 Dividing up his c, they cast lots to see G2668
Lk 7:25 A man dressed in fine c? No, G2668
Lk 7:25 who wear expensive c and indulge in G2669
Lk 8:27 man had not worn c or lived in a house, G2668
Lk 9:29 his c became as bright as a flash of G2669
Lk 10:30 They **stripped** him **of** his c, beat him and G1694
Lk 12:23 than food, and the body more *than* c. G1903
Lk 12:28 If that is how God c the grass of the field G313
Lk 23:34 And they divided up his c by casting lots. G2668
Lk 24: 4 suddenly two men in c that gleamed like G2264
Jn 11:44 "Take off the grave c and let him go." NDT
Jn 13:12 he put on his c and returned to his place. G2668
Jn 19:23 they took his c, dividing them into G2668
Jn 19:24 "They divided my c among them and cast G2668
Ac 10:30 a man in shining c stood before me G2264
Ac 12: 8 said to him, "**Put** on your c and sandals." G2439
Ac 14:14 they tore their c and rushed out into the G2668
Ac 18: 6 he shook out his c in protest and said to G2668
Ac 22:20 guarding the c of those who were G2668
1Ti 2: 9 hairstyles or gold or pearls or expensive c, G2669
Jas 2: 2 meeting wearing a gold ring and fine c, G2264
Jas 2: 2 a poor man in filthy old c also comes in. G2264
Jas 2: 3 to the man wearing fine c and say, G2264
Jas 2:15 a sister is **without** c and daily food. G1218
Jas 5: 2 has rotted, and moths have eaten your c. G2668
1Pe 3: 3 wearing of gold jewelry or **fine** c. G1906+2668
Rev 3: 4 in Sardis who have not soiled their c. G2668
Rev 3:18 and white c to wear, so you can G2668

CLOTHING (41) [CLOTHE]

Ge 24:53 jewelry and **articles of** c and gave them to H955
Ge 45:22 To each of them he gave new c, but to H8529
Ex 3:22 articles of silver and gold and for c, H8529
Ex 12:34 in kneading troughs wrapped in c. H8529
Ex 12:35 articles of silver and gold and for c. H8529
Ex 21:10 first one of her food, c and marital rights. H4064
Lev 13:47 a defiling mold—any woolen or linen c, H955
Lev 13:59 defiling molds in woolen or linen c, H955
Lev 15:17 Any c or leather that has semen on it must H955
Lev 19:19 " 'Do not wear c woven of two kinds of H955
Dt 10:18 among you, giving them food and c. H8529
Dt 22: 5 A woman must not wear men's c, nor a H3998
Dt 22: 5 a man wear women's c, for the LORD H8529
Jos 22: 8 a great quantity of c—and divide the H8515
Jdg 3:16 he strapped to his right thigh under his c. H4496
2Ki 5: 5 thousand shekels of gold and ten sets of c. H955
2Ki 5:22 them a talent of silver and two sets of c." H955
2Ki 5:23 of silver in two bags, with two sets of c. H955
2Ki 7:15 road strewn with the c and equipment the H955
2Ch 20:25 of equipment and c and also articles of H955
Job 22: 6 you stripped people of their c, leaving H955
Job 29:14 *I* **put on** righteousness **as** *my* c; justice H4252
Job 30:18 great power God becomes like c *to* me; H4230
Job 31:19 I have seen anyone perishing for lack of c, H4230
Ps 102:26 Like c you will change them and they will H4230
Pr 27:26 the lambs will provide you with c, and the H4230
Isa 3: 7 I have no food or c in my house; do not H8529
Isa 3:24 instead of **fine** c, sackcloth; instead H7345
Isa 59: 6 Their cobwebs are useless for c; they H955
Isa 63: 3 my garments, and I stained all my c. H4860
Eze 18: 7 to the hungry and provides c for the naked. H955
Eze 18:16 to the hungry and provides c for the naked. H955
Da 7: 9 His c was as white as snow; the hair of A10382
Zec 14:14 great quantities of gold and silver and c. H955
Mt 7:15 They come to you in sheep's c, but G1903
Mk 1: 6 John **wore** c made of camel's hair G1639+1907
Jn 13: 4 took off his **outer** c, and wrapped a G2668
Ac 9:39 him the robes and *other* c that Dorcas had G2668
Ac 20:33 not coveted anyone's silver or gold or c. G2669
1Ti 6: 8 But if we have food and c, we will be G5004
Jude 23 hating even the c stained by corrupted G5945

CLOTHS (3) [CLOTH]

Eze 16: 4 rubbed with salt or **wrapped in** c. H3156+3156
Lk 2: 7 *She* **wrapped** him **in** c and placed him in G5058
Lk 2:12 find a baby **wrapped in** c and lying in a G5058

CLOUD (97) [CLOUDBURST, CLOUDLESS, CLOUDS, THUNDERCLOUD]

Ex 13:21 them in a pillar of c to guide them on H6727
Ex 13:22 Neither the pillar of c by day nor the pillar H6727
Ex 14:19 The pillar of c also moved from in front H6727
Ex 14:20 the night the c brought darkness to the H6727
Ex 14:24 pillar of fire and c at the Egyptian army H6727
Ex 16:10 the glory of the LORD appearing in the c. H6727
Ex 19: 9 "I am going to come to you in a dense c H6727
Ex 19:16 with a thick c over the mountain, and H6727
Ex 24:15 up on the mountain, the c covered it, H6727
Ex 24:16 For six days the c covered the mountain H6727
Ex 24:16 LORD called to Moses from within the c. H6727
Ex 24:18 Moses entered the c as he went on up the H6727
Ex 33: 9 the pillar of c would come down and stay H6727
Ex 33:10 saw the pillar of c standing at the H6727
Ex 34: 5 came down in the c and stood there with H6727
Ex 40:34 Then the c covered the tent of meeting H6727
Ex 40:35 meeting because the c had settled on it, H6727
Ex 40:36 whenever the c lifted from above the H6727
Ex 40:37 if the c did not lift, they did not set out H6727
Ex 40:38 So the c *of* the LORD was over the H6727
Ex 40:38 and fire was in **the** c by night, in the H2257S
Lev 16: 2 I will appear in the c over the atonement H6727
Nu 9:15 covenant law, was set up, the c covered it. H6727
Nu 9:15 till morning the c above the tabernacle NDT
Nu 9:16 it continued to be; the c covered it, and at H6727
Nu 9:17 Whenever the c lifted from above the tent H6727
Nu 9:17 wherever the c settled, the H6727
Nu 9:18 As long as the c stayed over the H6727
Nu 9:19 When the c remained over the tabernacle H6727
Nu 9:20 Sometimes the c was over the tabernacle H6727
Nu 9:21 Sometimes the c stayed only from evening H6727
Nu 9:21 whenever the c lifted, they set out. H6727
Nu 9:22 Whether the c stayed over the tabernacle H6727
Nu 10:11 the c lifted from above the tabernacle of H6727
Nu 10:12 to place until the c came to rest in the H6727
Nu 10:34 The c *of* the LORD was over them by day H6727
Nu 11:25 came down in the c and spoke with him, H6727
Nu 12: 5 Then the LORD came down in a pillar of c H6727
Nu 12:10 When the c lifted from above the tent H6727
Nu 14:14 that your c stays over them, and H6727
Nu 14:14 them in a pillar of c by day and a pillar of H6727
Nu 16:42 suddenly the c covered it and the glory of H6727
Dt 1:33 in fire by night and in a c by day, to H6727
Dt 5:22 of the fire, the c and the deep darkness H6727
Dt 31:15 LORD appeared at the tent in a pillar of c, H6727
Dt 31:15 the c stood over the entrance to the H6727
Jdg 20:38 send up a great c *of* smoke from the city, H5368
1Ki 8:10 the c filled the temple of the LORD. H6727
1Ki 8:11 not perform their service because of the c, H6727
1Ki 8:12 has said that he would dwell in a **dark** c; H6906
1Ki 18:44 "A c as small as a man's hand is rising H6265
2Ch 5:13 temple of the LORD was filled with the c, H6727
2Ch 5:14 not perform their service because of the c, H6727
2Ch 6: 1 has said that he would dwell in a **dark** c; H6906
Ne 9:12 By day you led them with a pillar of c, and H6727
Ne 9:19 By day the pillar of c did not fail to guide H6727
Job 3: 5 it once more; may a c settle over it; may H6729
Job 7: 9 As a c vanishes and is gone, so one who H6727
Job 30:15 by the wind, my safety vanishes like a c. H6265
Ps 78:14 guided them with the c by day and with H6727
Ps 99: 7 He spoke to them from the pillar of c; they H6727
Ps 105:39 He spread out a c as a covering, and a H6727
Pr 16:15 his favor is like a rain c in spring. H6265
Isa 4: 5 assemble there a c of smoke by day and H6727
Isa 14:31 A c **of smoke** comes from the north, and H6940
Isa 18: 4 like a c *of* dew in the heat of harvest." H6265
Isa 19: 1 LORD rides on a swift c and is coming to H6265
Isa 25: 5 as heat is reduced by the shadow of a c H6265
Isa 44:22 I have swept away your offenses like a c H6265
La 2: 1 *has* **covered** Daughter Zion **with the** c of H6380
La 3:44 yourself with a c so that no prayer can H6727
Eze 1: 4 an immense c with flashing lightning and H6727
Eze 8:11 a fragrant c *of* incense was rising. H6727
Eze 10: 3 went in, and a c filled the inner court. H6727
Eze 10: 4 The c filled the temple, and the court was H6727
Eze 32: 7 I will cover the sun with a c, and the H6727
Eze 38: 9 you will be like a c covering the land. H6727
Eze 38:16 people Israel like a c that covers the land. H6727
Mt 17: 5 speaking, a bright c covered them, and a G3749
Mt 17: 5 a voice from the c said, "This is my G3749
Mk 9: 7 Then a c appeared and covered them G3749
Mk 9: 7 and a voice came from the c: G3749
Lk 9:34 speaking, a c appeared and covered them G3749
Lk 9:34 they were afraid as they entered the c. G3749
Lk 9:35 A voice came from the c, saying, "This is G3749
Lk 12:54 "When you see a c rising in the west G3749
Lk 21:27 of Man coming in a c with power and G3749
Ac 1: 9 and a c hid him from their sight. G3749
1Co 10: 1 were all under the c and that they all G3749
1Co 10: 2 into Moses in the c and in the sea. G3749
Heb 12: 1 surrounded *by* such a great c of witnesses, G3751
Rev 10: 1 He was robed in a c, with a rainbow G3749
Rev 11:12 And they went up to heaven in a c, while G3749
Rev 14:14 there before me was a white c, and G3749
Rev 14:14 seated on the c was one like a son of G3749
Rev 14:15 voice to him who was sitting on the c, G3749
Rev 14:16 was seated on the c swung his sickle over G3749

CLOUDBURST (1) [CLOUD]

Isa 30:30 consuming fire, with c, thunderstorm and H5881

CLOUDLESS (1) [CLOUD]

2Sa 23: 4 morning at sunrise on a c morning, H4202+6265

CLOUDS (65) [CLOUD]

Ge 9:13 I have set my rainbow in the c, and it will H6727
Ge 9:14 Whenever I **bring** c over the earth H6725+6727
Ge 9:14 earth and the rainbow appears in the c, H6727
Ge 9:16 Whenever the rainbow appears in the c, H6727
Dt 4:11 heavens, with black c and deep darkness. H6727
Dt 33:26 to help you and on the c in his majesty. H8836
Jdg 5: 4 poured, the c poured down water. H6265
2Sa 22:10 came down; **dark** c were under his feet. H6906
2Sa 22:12 the dark rain c **of the sky.** H6265+8836
1Ki 18:45 the sky grew black with c, the wind rose, H6265
Job 20: 6 the heavens and his head touches the c, H6265
Job 22:14 **Thick** c veil him, so he does not see us as H6265
Job 26: 8 He wraps up the waters in his c, yet the H6265
Job 26: 8 the c do not burst under their weight. H6727
Job 26: 9 of the full moon, spreading his c over it. H6727
Job 35: 5 see; gaze at the c so high above you. H8836
Job 36:28 the c pour down their moisture and H8836
Job 36:29 can understand how he spreads out the c, H6265
Job 37:11 He loads the c with moisture; he scatters H6265
Job 37:13 He brings **the** c to punish people, or to H2084S
Job 37:15 how God controls the c and makes his H6727
Job 37:16 Do you know how the c hang poised H6265
Job 38: 9 when I made the c its garment and H6727
Job 38:34 your voice to the c and cover yourself with H6265
Job 38:37 Who has the wisdom to count the c? Who H8836
Ps 18: 9 came down; **dark** c were under his feet. H6906
Ps 18:11 the dark rain c **of the sky.** H6265+8836
Ps 18:12 brightness of his presence c advanced, H6265
Ps 68: 4 extol him who rides on the c; rejoice H6265
Ps 77:17 The c poured down water, the heavens H6265
Ps 97: 2 C and thick darkness surround him H6727
Ps 104: 3 He makes the c his chariot and rides on H6265
Ps 135: 7 He makes c rise from the ends of the H5955
Ps 147: 8 He covers the sky with c; he supplies the H6265
Ps 148: 8 hail, snow and c, stormy winds that H7798
Pr 3:20 were divided, and the c let drop the dew. H8836
Pr 8:28 he established the c above and fixed H8836
Pr 25:14 Like c and wind without rain is one who H5955
Ecc 11: 3 If c are full of water, they pour rain on the H6265
Ecc 11: 4 whoever looks at the c will not reap. H6265
Ecc 12: 2 grow dark, and the c return after the rain; H6265
Isa 5: 6 I will command the c not to rain on it." H6265
Isa 5:30 even the sun will be darkened by its c. H6882
Isa 14:14 I will ascend above the tops of the c; I will H6265
Isa 30:27 with burning anger and dense c **of smoke** H5366
Isa 45: 8 righteousness; let the c shower it down. H8836
Isa 60: 8 "Who are these that fly along like c, like H6265
Jer 4:13 He advances like the c, his chariots come H6727
Jer 10:13 he makes c rise from the ends of the earth H5955
Jer 51:16 he makes c rise from the ends of the earth H5955
Eze 1:28 of a rainbow in the c on a rainy day, H6727
Eze 30: 3 is near—a day of c, a time of doom for H6727
Eze 30:18 She will be covered with c, and her H6727
Eze 34:12 scattered on a day of c and darkness. H6727
Da 7:13 of man, coming with the c *of* heaven. A10560
Joel 2: 2 gloom, a day of c and blackness. H6727
Na 1: 3 the storm, and c are the dust of his feet. H6727
Zep 1:15 gloom, a day of c and blackness— H6727
Mt 24:30 Son of Man coming on the c of heaven, G3749
Mt 26:64 One and coming on the c of heaven." G3749
Mk 13:26 of Man coming in c with great power and G3749
Mk 14:62 One and coming on the c of heaven." G3749
1Th 4:17 with them in the c to meet the Lord in the G3749
Jude 12 They are c without rain, blown along by G3749
Rev 1: 7 he is coming with the c," and "every eye G3749

CLOVEN (KJV) DIVIDED, SEPARATED

CLUB (9) [CLUBS]

2Sa 23:21 Benaiah went against him with a c. H8657
1Ch 11:23 Benaiah went against him with a c. H8657
Job 41:29 A c seems to it but a piece of straw; it H9371
Pr 25:18 Like a c or a sword or a sharp arrow is one H5138
Isa 10: 5 in whose hand is the c of my wrath! H4751
Isa 10:15 a c brandish the one who is not wood! H4751
Isa 10:24 you with a rod and lift up a c against you, H4751
Isa 30:32 with his punishing c will be to the music H4751
Jer 51:20 "You are my **war** c, my weapon for battle H5151

CLUBS (6) [CLUB]

Eze 39: 9 and arrows, the **war** c and spears. H5234+3338
Mt 26:47 a large crowd armed with swords and c, G3833
Mt 26:55 out with swords and c to capture me? G3833
Mk 14:43 was a crowd armed with swords and c, G3833
Mk 14:48 out with swords and c to capture me? G3833
Lk 22:52 that you have come with swords and c? G3833

CLUNG (3) [CLING]

Ru 1:14 mother-in-law goodbye, but Ruth c to her. H1815
2Ki 3: 3 Nevertheless *he* c to the sins of Jeroboam H1815
La 1: 9 Her filthiness c **to** her skirts; she did not H928

CLUSTER (5) [CLUSTERS]

Nu 13:23 off a branch bearing a single c *of* grapes. H864
Nu 13:24 because of the c **of grapes** the Israelites cut H864
SS 1:14 beloved is to me a c *of* henna blossoms H864
Isa 65: 8 still found in a c **of grapes** and people say, H864
Mic 7: 1 there is no c **of grapes** to eat, none of the H864

CLUSTERS (5) [CLUSTER]

Ge 40:10 it blossomed, and its c ripened into grapes. H864
Dt 32:32 with poison, and their c *with* bitterness. H864
SS 7: 7 of the palm, and your breasts like c **of fruit.** H864
SS 7: 8 your breasts be like c **of grapes** *on* the vine, H864
Rev 14:18 gather the c **of grapes** from the G1084

CLUTCHES (5)

Job 5:15 he saves them from the c *of* the powerful. H3338
Job 6:23 rescue me from the c *of* the ruthless'? H3338
Job 16:11 thrown me into the c *of* the wicked. H3338
Hab 2: 9 his nest on high to escape the c *of* ruin! H4090
Ac 12:11 me from Herod's c and from everything G5931

CNIDUS (1)

Ac 27: 7 days and had difficulty arriving off C. G3118

CO-HEIRS (1) [INHERIT]
Ro 8:17 heirs of God and **c** with Christ, if indeed *G5169*

CO-WORKER (5) [WORK]
Ro 16: 9 Greet Urbanus, our **c** in Christ, and my *G5301*
Ro 16:21 Timothy, my **c**, sends his greetings to you *G5301*
2Co 8:23 he is my partner and **c** among you; as *G5301*
Php 2:25 my brother, **c** and fellow soldier, who is *G5301*
1Th 3: 2 brother and **c in** God's **service** in *G5301*

CO-WORKERS (5) [WORK]
Ro 16: 3 Priscilla and Aquila, my **c** in Christ Jesus. *G5301*
1Co 3: 9 For we are **c in** God's **service**; you are *G5301*
2Co 6: 1 *As* God's **c** we urge you not to receive *G5300*
Php 4: 3 along with Clement and the rest *of* my **c** *G5301*
Col 4:11 only Jews among my **c** for the kingdom of *G5301*

COAL (2) [COALS]
2Sa 14: 7 put out the only **burning c** I have left, H1625
Isa 6: 6 flew to me with a **live c** in his hand, H8365

COALS (24) [COAL]
Lev 16:12 full of burning **c** from the altar before H1624
Nu 16: 7 tomorrow put **burning c** and incense in H836
Nu 16:18 his censer, put **burning c** and incense in it H836
Nu 16:37 scatter the **c** some distance away, H836
Nu 16:46 along with **burning c** from the altar H836
2Sa 22: 9 from his mouth, **burning c** blazed out of it. H1624
1Ki 19: 6 head was some bread **baked over hot c**, H8363
Job 41:21 Its breath sets **c** ablaze, and flames dart H1624
Ps 11: 6 he will rain fiery **c** and burning sulfur; H7073
Ps 18: 8 from his mouth, **burning c** blazed out of it. H1624
Ps 120: 4 with **burning c** *of* the broom bush. H1624
Ps 140:10 May **burning c** fall on them; may they be H1624
Pr 6:28 Can a man walk on **hot c** without his feet H1624
Pr 25:22 you will heap **burning c** on his head, and H1624
Isa 30:14 will be found for taking **c** from a hearth H836
Isa 44:12 takes a tool and works with it in the **c**; H7073
Isa 44:19 I even baked bread over its **c**, I roasted H1624
Isa 47:14 These are not **c** for warmth; this is not a H1625
Isa 54:16 who fans the **c** into flame and forges a H7073
Eze 1:13 was like burning **c** *of* fire or like torches. H1624
Eze 10: 2 hands with burning **c** from among the H1624
Eze 24:11 the empty pot on the **c** till it becomes hot H1624
Jn 21: 9 they saw a **fire of burning c** there with fish *G471*
Ro 12:20 you will heap burning **c** on his head." *G472*

COARSE (1)
Eph 5: 4 foolish talk or **c joking**, which are out of *G2365*

COAST (14) [COASTAL, COASTLANDS, COASTLINE, COASTS]
Nu 34: 6 will be the **c** of the Mediterranean H1473
Dt 1: 7 in the Negev and along the **c**, to H2572+3542
Jos 5: 1 kings along the **c** heard how the LORD had H3542
Jos 9: 1 along the entire **c** *of* the Mediterranean H2572
Jdg 5:17 remained on the **c** and stayed in H2572+3542
2Ch 8:17 Geber and Elath on the **c** of Edom. H8557+3542
Isa 20: 6 day the people who live on this **c** will say, H362
Jer 47: 7 it to attack Ashkelon and the **c**?" H2572+3542
Eze 25:16 those remaining along the **c**. H2572+3542
Eze 26:16 the princes of the **c** will step down from H3542
Ac 17:14 sent Paul to **the c**, *G2093+3836+2498*
Ac 27: 2 sail for ports **along the c of** the province of *G2848*
Ac 27: 5 the open sea **off the c of** Cilicia and *G2848*
Ac 27: 8 We moved along **the c** with difficulty and *G899S*

COASTAL (1) [COAST]
Lk 6:17 from the **c region** around Tyre and *G4163*

COASTLANDS (9) [COAST]
Jer 25:22 the kings of the **c** across the sea; H362
Jer 31:10 you nations; proclaim it in distant **c**: H362
Eze 26:15 Will not the **c** tremble at the sound of your H362
Eze 26:18 Now the **c** tremble on the day of your fall H362
Eze 27:15 with you, and many **c** were your customers H362
Eze 27:35 All who live in the **c** are appalled at you H362
Eze 39: 6 on those who live in safety in the **c**, H362
Da 11:18 his attention to the **c** and will take many of H362
Da 11:30 Ships of the **western c** will oppose him H4183

COASTLINE (2) [COAST]
Jos 15:12 boundary is the **c** of the Mediterranean H1473
Jos 15:47 of Egypt and the **c** of the Mediterranean H1473

COASTS (5) [COAST]
Jer 2:10 Cross over to the **c** *of* Cyprus and look, send H362
Jer 47: 4 the remnant from the **c** *of* Caphtor. H362
Eze 27: 3 merchant of peoples on many **c**, 'This is H362
Eze 27: 6 wood from the **c** *of* Cyprus they made H362
Eze 27: 7 of blue and purple from the **c** *of* Elishah. H362

COAT (9) [COATED, COATING, COATS]
Ge 6:14 make rooms in it and **c** it with pitch inside H4106
Dt 27: 2 large stones and **c** them with plaster. H8486
Dt 27: 4 you today, and **c** them with plaster. H8486
1Sa 17: 5 wore a **c of scale armor** *of* bronze H9234+7989
1Sa 17:38 He put a **c of armor** on him and a bronze H9234
Job 41:13 Who can strip off its outer **c**? Who can H4230
Job 41:13 Who can penetrate its double **c of armor**? H6246
Mt 5:40 take your shirt, hand over your **c** as well. *G2668*
Lk 6:29 If someone takes your **c**, do not withhold *G2668*

COAT OF MANY COLOURS (KJV) ORNATE ROBE

COATED (1) [COAT]
Ex 2: 3 basket for him and **c** it with tar and pitch. H2814

COATING (1) [COAT]
Pr 26:23 Like a **c** *of* silver dross on earthenware are H7596

COATS (2) [COAT]
2Ch 26:14 helmets, **c of armor**, bows and slingstones H9234
Ac 7:58 witnesses laid their **c** at the feet of a *G2668*

COAX (1)
Jdg 14:15 "**C** your husband *into* explaining the H7331

COBRA (2) [COBRA'S, COBRAS]
Ps 58: 4 like that of a **c** that has stopped its ears H7352
Ps 91:13 You will tread on the lion and the **c**; you H7352

COBRA'S (1) [COBRA]
Isa 11: 8 The infant will play near the **c** den, and H7352

COBRAS (1) [COBRA]
Dt 32:33 of serpents, the deadly poison of **c**. H7352

COBWEBS (1) [WEB]
Isa 59: 6 Their **c** are useless for clothing; they H7770

COCK (KJV) ROOSTER

COCKATRICE, COCKATRICES (KJV) VIPER, VIPER'S, VIPERS

COCKLE (KJV) STINKWEED

COCOON (1)
Job 27:18 The house he builds is like a **moth's c** H6931

CODE (3)
Ro 2:27 you have the **written c** and circumcision, *G1207*
Ro 2:29 by the Spirit, not *by* the **written c**. *G1207*
Ro 7: 6 not in the old way *of* the **written c**. *G1207*

COFFER (KJV) CHEST

COFFIN (1)
Ge 50:26 he was placed in a **c** in Egypt. H778

COHORTS (1)
Job 9:13 even the **c** *of* Rahab cowered at his feet. H6468

COILED (2) [COILING]
2Sa 22: 6 The cords of the grave **c around** me; the H6015
Ps 18: 5 The cords of the grave **c around** me; the H6015

COILING (1) [COILED]
Isa 27: 1 Leviathan the **c** serpent; he will slay H6825

COIN (4) [COINS]
Mt 17:27 mouth and you will find a **four-drachma c**. *G5088*
Mt 22:19 Show me the **c** used for paying the tax." *G3790*
Mk 12:16 They brought the **c**, and he asked them NDT
Lk 15: 9 'Rejoice with me; I have found my lost **c**. *G1534*

COINS (6) [COIN]
Mt 18:28 who owed him a hundred **silver c**. *G1324*
Mt 27: 6 The chief priests picked up the **c** and said *G736*
Mk 12:42 came and put in two **very small copper c**, *G3321*
Lk 15: 8 a woman has ten **silver c** and loses one. *G1534*
Lk 21: 2 widow put in two **very small copper c**. *G3321*
Jn 2:15 he scattered the **c** of the money changers *G3047*

COL-HOZEH (NIV84) KOL-HOZEH

COLD (15)
Ge 8:22 harvest, **c** and heat, summer and H7923
Ge 31:40 me in the daytime and the **c** at night, H7943
Job 24: 7 have nothing to cover themselves in the **c**. H7938
Job 37: 9 its chamber, the **c** from the driving winds. H7938
Pr 25:20 who takes away a garment on a **c** day, H7938
Pr 25:25 Like **c** water to a weary soul is good news H7922
Na 3:17 that settle in the walls on a **c** day— H7938
Zec 14: 6 day there will be neither sunlight nor **c**, H7938
Mt 10:42 gives even a cup *of* **c** water to one of *G6037*
Mt 24:12 wickedness, the love of most *will* **grow c**, *G6038*
Jn 18:18 It was **c**, and the servants and officials *G6036*
Ac 28: 2 us all because it was raining and **c**. *G6036*
2Co 11:27 without food; I have been **c** and naked. *G6036*
Rev 3:15 your deeds, that you are neither **c** nor hot. *G6037*
Rev 3:16 neither hot nor **c**—I am about to spit you *G6037*

COLLAPSE (5) [COLLAPSED, COLLAPSES]
Jos 6: 5 the wall of the city *will* **c** and the army will H5877
Ps 10:10 victims are crushed, *they* **c**; they fall under H8820
Eze 26:18 islands in the sea are terrified at your **c**. H3655
Mt 15:32 away hungry, or *they may* **c** on the way." *G1725*
Mk 8: 3 them home hungry, *they will* **c** on the way *G1725*

COLLAPSED (8) [COLLAPSE]
Jos 6:20 the wall **c**; so everyone charged H5877
Jdg 7:13 such force that the tent overturned and **c**." H5877
1Ki 20:30 where the wall **c** on twenty-seven H5877
Job 1:19 *It* **c** on them and they are dead, and I am H5877
Hab 3: 6 crumbled and the age-old hills **c**— H8820
Lk 6:49 it **c** and its destruction was complete." *G5229*
Rev 11:13 earthquake and a tenth of the city **c**. *G4406*
Rev 16:19 three parts, and the cities of the nations **c**. *G4406*

COLLAPSES (3) [COLLAPSE]
Isa 30:13 and bulging, that **c** suddenly, in an H995+8691
Eze 13:12 When the wall **c**, will people not ask you H5877
Na 2: 6 gates are thrown open and the palace **c**. H4570

COLLAR (3)
Ex 28:32 woven edge like a **c** around this H7023+9389
Ex 39:23 center of the robe like the opening of a **c**, H9389
Ps 133: 2 Aaron's beard, down on the **c** *of* his robe. H7023

COLLECT (13) [COLLECTED, COLLECTING, COLLECTION, COLLECTIONS, COLLECTOR, COLLECTOR'S, COLLECTORS, COLLECTS]
Ge 41:35 *They should* **c** all the food of these good H7695
Nu 3:47 **c** five shekels for each one, according to H4374
2Ki 12: 4 "**C** all the money that is brought as sacred NDT
2Ki 12: 8 agreed that *they would* not **c** any more H4374
2Ch 20:25 plunder that it took three days *to* **c** it. H1024
2Ch 24: 5 towns of Judah and **c** the money due H7695
Ne 10:37 the Levites who **c** *the* **tithes** in all the H6923
Mt 13:30 First **c** the weeds and tie them in bundles *G5198*
Mt 17:25 whom *do* the kings of the earth **c** duty *G3284*
Mt 21:34 his servants to the tenants *to* **c** his fruit. *G3284*
Mk 12: 2 to the tenants to **c** from them some of the *G3284*
Lk 3:13 "Don't **c** any more than you are required *G4556*
Heb 7: 5 become priests *to* **c a tenth** from the *G620*

COLLECTED (15) [COLLECT]
Ge 41:48 Joseph **c** all the food produced in those H7695
Ge 47:14 Joseph **c** all the money that was to be H4377
Nu 3:49 So Moses **c** the redemption money from H4374
Nu 3:50 of the Israelites *he* **c** silver weighing H4374
Nu 16:39 So Eleazar the priest **c** the bronze censers H4374
2Ki 12: 4 of the LORD—the **money** *c in* the census, the AIT
2Ki 22: 4 the doorkeepers *have* **c** from the people. H665
2Ch 24:11 did this regularly and **c** a great amount of H665
2Ch 34: 9 the gatekeepers *had* **c** from the people of H665
Ecc 12:11 their **c sayings** like firmly embedded H1251+670
Zec 14:14 of all the surrounding nations *will* **be c**— H665
Mt 13:48 Then they sat down and **c** the good fish in *G5198*
Lk 19:23 came back, *I* could have **c** it with interest? *G4556*
Heb 7: 6 *yet he* **c a tenth** from Abraham and *G1282*
Heb 7: 8 the tenth *is* **c** by people who die *G3284*

COLLECTING (1) [COLLECT]
Lev 11:36 a cistern for **c** water remains clean, but H5224

COLLECTION (2) [COLLECT]
Isa 57:13 out for help, let your **c** *of idols* save you! H7689
1Co 16: 1 Now about the **c** for the Lord's people: Do *G3356*

COLLECTIONS (1) [COLLECT]
1Co 16: 2 that when I come no **c** will have to be *G3356*

COLLECTOR (8) [COLLECT]
Da 11:20 will send out a **tax c** to maintain the royal H5601
Mt 10: 3 Thomas and Matthew the **tax c**; James *G5467*
Mt 18:17 them as you would a pagan or a **tax c**. *G5467*
Lk 5:27 went out and saw a **tax c** by the name of *G5467*
Lk 18:10 one a Pharisee and the other a **tax c**. *G5467*
Lk 18:11 adulterers—or even like this **tax c**. *G5467*
Lk 18:13 "But the **tax c** stood at a distance. *G5467*
Lk 19: 2 he was a **chief tax c** and was wealthy. *G803*

COLLECTOR'S (2) [COLLECT]
Mt 9: 9 named Matthew sitting at the **tax c booth**. *G5468*
Mk 2:14 son of Alphaeus sitting at the **tax c booth**. *G5468*

COLLECTORS (16) [COLLECT]
Mt 5:46 Are not even the **tax c** doing that? *G5467*
Mt 9:10 many **tax c** and sinners came and ate with *G5467*
Mt 9:11 your teacher eat with **tax c** and sinners?" *G5467*
Mt 11:19 a drunkard, a friend *of* **tax c** and sinners. *G5467*
Mt 17:24 the **c** of the two-drachma temple tax *G3284*
Mt 21:31 the **tax c** and the prostitutes are entering *G5467*
Mt 21:32 but the **tax c** and the prostitutes did. *G5467*
Mk 2:15 many **tax c** and sinners were eating with *G5467*
Mk 2:16 saw him eating with the sinners and **tax c**, *G5467*
Mk 2:16 "Why does he eat with **tax c** and sinners?" *G5467*
Lk 3:12 Even **tax c** came to be baptized. "Teacher," *G5467*
Lk 5:29 a large crowd *of* **tax c** and others were *G5467*
Lk 5:30 you eat and drink with **tax c** and sinners?" *G5467*
Lk 7:29 people, even the **tax c**, when they heard *G5467*
Lk 7:34 a drunkard, a friend *of* **tax c** and sinners. *G5467*
Lk 15: 1 Now the **tax c** and sinners were all *G5467*

COLLECTS (1) [COLLECT]
Heb 7: 9 say that Levi, who **c** the tenth, paid the *G3284*

COLLEGE (KJV) NEW QUARTER

COLONNADE (4) [COLUMN]
1Ki 7: 6 He made a **c** fifty cubits long and H395+6647
Jn 10:23 the temple courts walking in Solomon's **C**. *G5119*
Ac 3:11 to them in the place called Solomon's **C**. *G5119*
Ac 5:12 used to meet together in Solomon's **C**. *G5119*

COLONNADES (1) [COLUMN]
Jn 5: 2 which is surrounded by five **covered c**. *G5119*

COLONY (1)
Ac 16:12 a **Roman c** and the leading city of that *G3149*

COLORED (1) [COLORFUL, COLORS, DARK-COLORED, MULTICOLORED]
Pr 7:16 covered my bed with c linens from Egypt. H2635

COLORFUL (2) [COLORED]
Jdg 5:30 c garments as plunder for Sisera H7389
Jdg 5:30 Sisera, c garments embroidered H7389

COLORS (2) [COLORED]
1Ch 29: 2 stones of various c, and all kinds of H8391
Eze 17: 3 full plumage of varied c came to Lebanon H8391

COLOSSAE (1)
Col 1: 2 To God's holy people in C, the faithful G3145

COLT (15)
Ge 49:11 a vine, his c to the choicest branch H1201+912
Job 11:12 a wild donkey's c can be born human. H6555
Zec 9: 9 on a donkey, on a c, the foal of a donkey. H6555
Mt 21: 2 find a donkey tied there, with her c by her. G4798
Mt 21: 5 a donkey, and on a c, the foal of a donkey G4798
Mt 21: 7 the donkey and the c and placed their G4798
Mk 11: 2 you will find a c tied there, which no G4798
Mk 11: 4 went and found a c outside in the street G4798
Mk 11: 5 "What are you doing, untying that c?" G4798
Mk 11: 7 they brought the c to Jesus and threw G4798
Lk 19:30 you will find a c tied there, which no G4798
Lk 19:33 As they were untying the c, its owners G4798
Lk 19:33 asked them, "Why are you untying the c?" G4798
Lk 19:35 their cloaks on the c and put Jesus on it. G4798
Jn 12:15 king is coming, seated on a donkey's c." G4798

COLUMN (3) [COLONNADE, COLONNADES, COLUMNS]
Jdg 20:40 But when the c of smoke began to rise H6647
SS 3: 6 up from the wilderness like a c of smoke, H9406
Isa 9:18 so that it rolls upward in a c of smoke. H1455

COLUMNS (4) [COLUMN]
1Ki 7: 2 four rows of cedar c supporting trimmed H6647
1Ki 7: 3 above the beams that rested on the c— H6647
Jer 36:23 had read three or four c of the scroll, H1946
Zep 2:14 the screech owl will roost on her c. H4117

COMB (2) [COMBED]
Pr 24:13 honey from the c is sweet to your taste. H5885
Pr 27: 7 One who is full loathes honey from the c H5885

COMBED (1) [COMB]
Isa 19: 9 Those who work with c flax will despair H8591

COME (1474) [CAME, COMES, COMING]
Ge 6:20 along the ground will c to you to be kept H995
Ge 8:16 "C out of the ark, you and your wife and H3655
Ge 9:12 a covenant for all generations to c: H6409
Ge 11: 3 said to each other, "C, let's make bricks H2035
Ge 11: 4 Then they said, "C, let us build ourselves a H2035
Ge 11: 7 C, let us go down and confuse their H2035
Ge 15:14 afterward they will c out with great H3655
Ge 15:16 your descendants will c back here, H8740
Ge 16: 8 of Sarai, where have you c from, and where H995
Ge 17: 6 nations of you, and kings will c from you. H3655
Ge 17: 7 after you for the generations to c, H1887
Ge 17: 9 after you for the generations to c. H1887
Ge 17:12 For the generations to c every male among H1887
Ge 17:16 nations; kings of peoples will c from her." H2118
Ge 18: 5 now that you have c to your servant." H6296
Ge 19: 8 for they have c under the protection of my H995
Ge 22: 5 worship and then we will c back to you." H8740
Ge 23:10 all the Hittites who had c to the gate of his H995
Ge 23:18 all the Hittites who had c to the gate of the H995
Ge 24: 5 is unwilling to c back with me to this H2143
Ge 24: 8 woman is unwilling to c back with you, H2143
Ge 24:31 "C, you who are blessed by the LORD," H995
Ge 24:39 if the woman will not c back with me? H2143
Ge 24:42 success to the journey on which I have c. H2143
Ge 24:62 Now Isaac had c from Beer Lahai Roi, for H995
Ge 25:25 The first to c out was red, and his whole H3655
Ge 26:26 Abimelek had c to him from Gerar H2143
Ge 26:27 asked them, "Why have you c to me, since H995
Ge 27:21 said to Jacob, "C near so I can touch you H5602
Ge 27:26 father Isaac said to him, "C here, my son, H5602
Ge 27:45 I'll send word for you to c back from there. H4374
Ge 31: 4 to Rachel and Leah to c out to the fields NDT
Ge 31:44 C now, let's make a covenant, you and I H2143
Ge 32:11 I am afraid he will c and attack me, and H995
Ge 33:14 of the children, until I c to my lord in Seir." H995
Ge 34: 7 Jacob's sons had c in from the fields as H995
Ge 35: 3 Then c, let us go up to Bethel, where I will H7756
Ge 35:11 a community of nations will c from you, H2118
Ge 37:10 Will your mother and I and your brothers actually c H995+995
Ge 37:13 near Shechem. C, I am going to send H2143
Ge 37:20 "C now, let's kill him and throw him into H2143
Ge 37:27 C, let's sell him to the Ishmaelites and not H2143
Ge 38:16 roadside and said, "C now, let me sleep H2035
Ge 39: 7 and said, "C to bed with me! H8886+6640
Ge 39:12 cloak and said, "C to bed with me!" H8886+6640
Ge 41:36 years of famine that will c upon Egypt, H2118
Ge 42: 4 he was afraid that harm might c to him. H7925
Ge 42: 7 "Where do you c from?" he asked. H995
Ge 42: 9 You have c to see where our land is H995
Ge 42:10 "Your servants have c to buy food. H995
Ge 42:12 "You have c to see where our land is H995
Ge 42:21 that's why this distress has c on us. H995
Ge 43:14 he will let your other brother and Benjamin c back H8938
Ge 44:34 see the misery that would c on my father." H5162
Ge 45: 4 said to his brothers, "C close to me." H5602
Ge 45: 9 C down to me; don't delay H3718
Ge 45:11 because five years of famine are still to c. AIT
Ge 45:16 palace that Joseph's brothers had c, H995
Ge 45:19 your wives, and get your father and c. H995
Ge 46:31 living in the land of Canaan, have c to me. H995
Ge 47: 1 have c from the land of Canaan and are H995
Ge 47: 4 "We have c to live here for a while H995
Ge 47: 5 father and your brothers have c to you, H995
Ge 48: 2 "Your son Joseph has c to you," Israel H995
Ge 49: 1 you what will happen to you in days to c. H344
Ge 49:10 until he to whom it belongs shall c and the H995
Ge 50:24 God will surely c to your aid and H7212+7212
Ge 50:25 "God will surely c to your aid, and H7212+7212
Ex 1:10 C, we must deal shrewdly with them or H2035
Ex 3: 5 "Do not c any closer," God said. "Take off H7928
Ex 3: 8 So I have c down to rescue them from the H3718
Ex 8: 3 They will c up into your palace and your H995
Ex 8: 4 The frogs will c up on you and your people H6590
Ex 8: 5 and make frogs c up on the land of Egypt. H6590
Ex 8: 7 they also made frogs c up on the land of H6590
Ex 11: 8 All these officials of yours will c to me H3718
Ex 12:14 the generations to c you shall H1887
Ex 12:17 lasting ordinance for the generations to c. H1887
Ex 12:42 to honor the LORD for the generations to c. H1887
Ex 13:14 "In days to c, when your son asks you H4737
Ex 13:19 "God will surely c to your aid, and H7212+7212
Ex 16: 1 month after they had c out of Egypt. H3655
Ex 16: 9 community, 'C before the LORD, for H7928
Ex 16:32 keep it for the generations to c, H1887
Ex 16:33 LORD to be kept for the generations to c." H1887
Ex 17: 6 water will c out of it for the people to H3655
Ex 18:15 "Because the people c to me to seek God's H995
Ex 18:18 these people who c to you will only NDT
Ex 19: 9 "I am going to c to you in a dense cloud H995
Ex 19:11 day the LORD will c down on Mount Sinai H3718
Ex 19:23 "The people cannot c up Mount Sinai H6590
Ex 19:24 force their way through to c up to the LORD, H6590
Ex 20:20 God has c to test you, so that the fear of H995
Ex 20:24 be honored, I will c to you and bless you. H995
Ex 23: 4 "If you c across your enemy's ox or donkey H7003
Ex 24: 1 said to Moses, "C up to the LORD, you and H6590
Ex 24: 2 the LORD; the others must not c near. H5602
Ex 24: 2 And the people may not c up with him." H6590
Ex 24:12 "C up to me on the mountain and stay H6590
Ex 24:14 "Wait here for us until we c back to you. H8740
Ex 27:21 the Israelites for the generations to c. H1887
Ex 29:42 "For the generations to c this burnt H1887
Ex 30: 8 before the LORD for the generations to c. H1887
Ex 30:10 sin offering for the generations to c. H1887
Ex 30:12 Then no plague will c on them when you H2118
Ex 30:21 his descendants for the generations to c." H1887
Ex 30:31 anointing oil for the generations to c. H1887
Ex 31:13 me and you for the generations to c, H1887
Ex 31:16 it for the generations to c as a lasting H1887
Ex 32: 1 Aaron and said, "C, make us gods who H7756
Ex 32:26 said, "Whoever is for the LORD, c to me." NDT
Ex 33: 9 pillar of cloud would c down and stay at H3718
Ex 34: 2 morning, and then c up on Mount Sinai. H6590
Ex 34: 3 No one is to c with you or be seen H6590
Ex 34:30 they were afraid to c near him. H5602
Ex 35:10 skilled among you are to c and make H995
Ex 36: 2 who was willing to c and do the work. H7928
Lev 3:17 lasting ordinance for the generations to c, H1887
Lev 5: 2 then they c to realize their guilt; AIT
Lev 6:18 For all generations to c it is his perpetual H1887
Lev 7:36 perpetual share for the generations to c. H1887
Lev 9: 7 "C to the altar and sacrifice your sin H7928
Lev 10: 4 said to them, "C here; carry your H7928
Lev 10: 9 lasting ordinance for the generations to c, H1887
Lev 11:34 to eat that has c into contact with water H995
Lev 14: 8 After this they may c into the camp, but H995
Lev 15:14 two young pigeons and c before the LORD to H995
Lev 16: 2 Aaron that he is not to c whenever he H995
Lev 16:18 "Then he shall c out to the altar that is H3655
Lev 16:24 Then he shall c out and sacrifice the burnt H3655
Lev 16:26 afterward he may c into the camp. H995
Lev 16:28 afterward he may c into the camp. H995
Lev 17: 7 them and for the generations to c. H1887
Lev 21:17 'For the generations to c none of your H1887
Lev 21:17 who has a defect may c near to offer the H7928
Lev 21:18 No man who has any defect may c near H7928
Lev 21:21 has any defect is to c near to present the H5602
Lev 21:21 he must not c near to offer the food of his H5602
Lev 22: 3 'For the generations to c, if any of your H1887
Lev 23:14 lasting ordinance for the generations to c, H1887
Lev 23:21 lasting ordinance for the generations to c, H1887
Lev 23:31 lasting ordinance for the generations to c, H1887
Lev 23:41 lasting ordinance for the generations to c; H1887
Lev 24: 3 lasting ordinance for the generations to c. H1887
Lev 25:25 nearest relative is to c and redeem what H995
Lev 25:44 female slaves are to c from the nations H2118
Nu 4: 3 fifty years of age who c to serve in the work H995
Nu 4:15 only then are the Kohathites to c and do H995
Nu 4:19 not die when they c near the most holy H5602
Nu 4:23 fifty years of age who c to serve in the work H995
Nu 4:30 fifty years of age who c to serve in the work H995
Nu 5:14 of jealousy c over her husband and H6296
Nu 5:30 feelings of jealousy c over a man because H6296
Nu 8:15 they are to c to do their work at the tent of H995
Nu 8:24 years old or more shall c to take part in the H995
Nu 10: 8 you and the generations to c. H1887
Nu 10:29 C with us and we will treat you well, for H2143
Nu 10:32 If you c with us, we will share with you H2143
Nu 11:16 Have them c to the tent of meeting, that H4374
Nu 11:17 I will c down and speak with you there H3718
Nu 11:23 not what I say will c true for you. H7936
Nu 12: 4 Miriam, "C out to the tent of meeting H3655
Nu 13:33 descendants of Anak c from the Nephilim). NDT
Nu 15:14 For the generations to c, whenever a H1887
Nu 15:15 lasting ordinance for the generations to c. H1887
Nu 15:21 Throughout the generations to c you are to H1887
Nu 15:23 continuing through the generations to c— H1887
Nu 15:38 the generations to c you are to H1887
Nu 16: 5 and he will have that person c near him. H7928
Nu 16: 5 he chooses he will cause to c near him. H7928
Nu 16:12 But they said, "We will not c! H6590
Nu 16:14 these men like slaves? No, we will not c!" H6590
Nu 16:27 Dathan and Abiram had c out and were H3655
Nu 16:40 of Aaron should c to burn incense H7928
Nu 16:46 Wrath has c out from the LORD; the plague H3655
Nu 18: 4 no one else may c near where you are H7928
Nu 18:23 lasting ordinance for the generations to c. H1887
Nu 19: 7 He may then c into the camp, but he will H995
Nu 20:14 about all the hardships that have c on us. H5162
Nu 21:27 "C to Heshbon and let it be rebuilt; let H995
Nu 22: 5 "A people has c out of Egypt; they cover H3655
Nu 22: 6 Now c and put a curse on these people H2143
Nu 22:11 'A people that has c out of Egypt covers H3655
Nu 22:11 Now c and put a curse on them for me H2143
Nu 22:14 said, "Balaam refused to c with us." H2143
Nu 22:17 C and put a curse on these people for me." H2143
Nu 22:20 "Since these men have c to summon you H995
Nu 22:32 I have c here to oppose you because your H3655
Nu 22:37 Why didn't you c to me? Am I really H2143
Nu 22:38 I have c to you now," Balaam H995
Nu 23: 3 Perhaps the LORD will c to meet with me H7936
Nu 23: 7 'C,' he said, 'curse Jacob for me; come H2143
Nu 23: 7 'curse Jacob for me; c, denounce Israel. H2143
Nu 23:13 "C with me to another place where you H2143
Nu 23:27 said to Balaam, "C, let me take you to H2143
Nu 24:14 to my people, but c, let me warn you of H2143
Nu 24:14 people will do to your people in days to c." H344
Nu 24:17 A star will c out of Jacob; a scepter will H2005
Nu 24:19 A ruler will c out of Jacob and destroy the NDT
Nu 24:24 Ships will c from the shores of Cyprus; they NDT
Nu 24:24 Ashur and Eber, but they too will c to ruin." H6330
Nu 27:17 to go out and c in before them, one who H995
Nu 27:21 and at his command they will c in. H995
Nu 31:24 Then you may c into the camp." H995
Nu 32:19 our inheritance has c to us on the east side H995
Nu 35:29 you throughout the generations to c, H1887
Dt 1:22 we are to take and the towns we will c to." H995
Dt 2:19 When you c to the Ammonites, do not H7928
Dt 10: 1 the first ones and c up to me on the H6590
Dt 11:10 from which you have c, where you H3655
Dt 14:29 live in your towns may c and eat and be H995
Dt 17: 8 If cases c before your courts that are too NDT
Dt 18:22 of the LORD does not take place or c true, H995
Dt 20: 2 the priest shall c forward and address the H5602
Dt 22: 2 you and keep it until they c looking for it. H2011
Dt 22: 6 If you c across a bird's nest H7925+4200+7156
Dt 23: 4 For they did not c to meet you with bread H7709
Dt 26: 3 LORD your God that I have c to the land the H995
Dt 28: 2 All these blessings will c on you and H995
Dt 28: 6 blessed when you c in and blessed when H995
Dt 28: 7 They will c at you from one direction but H3655
Dt 28:15 all these curses will c on you and overtake H995
Dt 28:19 be cursed when you c in and cursed when H995
Dt 28:20 destroyed and c to sudden ruin because of H6
Dt 28:24 it will c down from the skies until you are H3718
Dt 28:25 You will c at them from one direction but H3655
Dt 28:45 All these curses will c on you. They will H995
Dt 29:22 foreigners who c from distant lands H995
Dt 30: 1 I have set before you c on you and you take H995
Dt 31:17 disasters and calamities will c on them, H5162
Dt 31:17 'Have not these disasters c on us because H5162
Dt 31:21 many disasters and calamities c on them, H5162
Dt 31:29 In days to c, disaster will fall on you H344
Jos 2: 2 of the Israelites have c here tonight to spy H995
Jos 2: 3 because they have c to spy out the whole H995
Jos 2: 4 I did not know where they had c from. NDT
Jos 3: 9 "C here and listen to the words of the LORD H5602
Jos 4:16 the covenant law to c up out of the Jordan H6590
Jos 4:17 the priests, "C up out of the Jordan." H6590
Jos 5:14 of the army of the LORD I have now c." H995
Jos 7:14 LORD chooses shall c forward clan by clan; H7928
Jos 7:14 LORD chooses shall c forward family by H7928
Jos 7:14 LORD chooses shall c forward man by man. H7928
Jos 7:16 Joshua had Israel c forward by tribes, H7928
Jos 7:17 He had the clan of the Zerahites c forward H7928
Jos 7:18 Joshua had his family c forward man by H7928
Jos 8: 5 when the men c out against us, as H3655
Jos 9: 6 "We have c from a distant country H995
Jos 9: 8 "Who are you and where do you c from?" H995
Jos 9: 9 "Your servants have c from a very distant H995
Jos 9:12 it at home on the day we left to c to you. H2143
Jos 10: 4 "C up and help me attack Gibeon," he H6590
Jos 10: 6 C up to us quickly and save us H6590

C

Book	Ref	Context	Number
Jos	10:24	army commanders who *had* **c** with him,	H2143
Jos	10:24	"**C here** and put your feet on the necks of	H7928
Jos	10:33	king of Gezer *had* **c up** to help Lachish,	H6590
Jos	22:19	is defiled, **c over** to the LORD's land	H6296
Jos	22:20	*did* not wrath **c** on the whole community	H2118
Jos	23:15	your God has promised you *have* **c** to you,	H995
Jdg	1: 3	"**C up** with us into the territory allotted to	H6590
Jdg	1:34	allowing them to **c down** into the plain.	H3718
Jdg	4:18	meet Sisera and said to him, "**C**, my lord,	H6073
Jdg	4:18	said to him, "Come, my lord, **c** right in.	H6073
Jdg	4:22	"**C**," she said, "I will show you the man	H2143
Jdg	5:23	because *they did* not **c** to help the LORD	H995
Jdg	6:18	not go away until I **c back** and bring my	H995
Jdg	7:24	"**C down** against the Midianites and seize	H3718
Jdg	8:21	Zalmunna said, "**C**, do it yourself.	H7756
Jdg	9:10	said to the fig tree, '**C** and be our king.	H2143
Jdg	9:12	trees said to the vine, '**C** and be our king.	H2143
Jdg	9:14	said to the thornbush, '**C** and be our king.	H2143
Jdg	9:15	over you, **c** and take refuge in my shade	H995
Jdg	9:15	then *let* fire **c out** of the thornbush and	H3655
Jdg	9:20	*let* fire **c out** from Abimelek and consume	H3655
Jdg	9:20	Beth Millo, and *let* fire **c out** from you, the	H3655
Jdg	9:31	Ebed and his clan *have* **c** to Shechem and	H995
Jdg	9:32	you and your men *should* **c** and lie in wait	H7756
Jdg	9:33	Gaal and his men **c out** against you,	H3655
Jdg	11: 6	"**C**," they said, "be our commander, so we	H2143
Jdg	11: 7	Why *do you* **c** to me now, when you're in	H995
Jdg	11: 8	you now; **c** with us to fight the Ammonites	H2143
Jdg	11:34	*who should* **c out** to meet him but his	H3655
Jdg	12: 3	Now why *have you* **c up** today to fight me?"	H6590
Jdg	13: 8	you *to let* the man of God you sent to us **c**	H995
Jdg	15:10	Judah asked, "Why *have you* **c** to fight us?"	H6590
Jdg	15:10	"*We have* **c** to take Samson prisoner,"	H6590
Jdg	15:12	"*We've* **c** to tie you up and hand you over	H3718
Jdg	16:10	**C now**, tell me how you can be tied	H6964+5528
Jdg	16:18	the Philistines, "**C back** once more; he has	H6590
Jdg	18: 1	because they *had* not yet **c into an**	H5877+928
Jdg	18: 9	They answered, "**C on**, let's attack them	H7756
Jdg	18:19	Don't say a word. **C** with us, and be our	H2143
Jdg	19:11	said to his master, "**C**, let's stop at this city	H2143
Jdg	19:13	He added, "**C**, let's try to reach Gibeah	H2143
Jdg	19:17	are you going? Where *did you* **c** from?"	H995
Jdg	20:41	they realized that disaster *had* **c** on them.	H5595
Jdg	21: 8	from Jabesh Gilead *had* **c** to the camp	H995
Jdg	21:21	women of Shiloh **c out** to join in the	H3655
Ru	1: 6	the LORD *had* **c to the aid of** his people	H7212
Ru	1:11	Why *would you* **c** with me? Am I	H2143
Ru	2:12	whose wings *you have* **c** to take refuge."	H995
Ru	2:14	mealtime Boaz said to her, "**C** over here.	H5602
Ru	4: 1	Boaz said, "**C over** here, my friend, and sit	H6073
Ru	4: 3	"Naomi, who *has* **c back** from Moab, is	H8740
1Sa	2:13	the priest's servant *would* **c** with a	H995
1Sa	2:15	the priest's servant *would* **c** and say to the	H995
1Sa	2:36	in your family line *will* **c** and bow down	H995
1Sa	4: 6	the ark of the LORD *had* **c** into the camp,	H995
1Sa	4: 7	"A god *has* **c** into the camp,	H995
1Sa	4:16	"I *have just* **c** from the battle line	H995
1Sa	6:21	**C down** and take it up to your town."	H3718
1Sa	9: 5	who was with him, "**C**, let's go back,	H2143
1Sa	9: 9	they would say, "**C**, let us go to the	H2143
1Sa	9:10	said to his servant. "**C**, let's go." So they	H2143
1Sa	9:12	Hurry now; *he has* just **c** to our town today	H995
1Sa	10: 6	of the LORD *will* **c powerfully** upon you,	H7502
1Sa	10: 8	I *will* surely **c down** to you to sacrifice	H3718
1Sa	10: 8	wait seven days until I **c** to you and tell you	H995
1Sa	10:20	Samuel **had** all Israel **c forward** by tribes,	H7928
1Sa	10:22	of the LORD, "*Has* the man **c** here yet?"	H995
1Sa	11: 9	They told the messengers who *had* **c**, "Say	H995
1Sa	11:14	said to the people, "**C**, let us go to Gilgal	H2143
1Sa	13: 8	Samuel *did* not **c** to Gilgal, and	H995
1Sa	13:11	that you *did* not **c** at the set time, and	H995
1Sa	13:12	the Philistines *will* **c down** against me at	H3718
1Sa	14: 1	young armor-bearer, "**C**, let's go over to	H2143
1Sa	14: 6	young armor-bearer, "**C**, let's go over to	H2143
1Sa	14: 8	Jonathan said, "**C on, then**; we will cross	H2180
1Sa	14: 9	'Wait there until we **c** to you,' we will stay	H5595
1Sa	14:10	But if they say, '**C up** to us,' we will climb	H6590
1Sa	14:12	"**C up** to us and we'll teach you a lesson."	H6590
1Sa	14:38	therefore said, "**C** here, all you who are	H5602
1Sa	15:25	forgive my sin and **c back** with me, so that	H8740
1Sa	15:30	before Israel; **c back** with me, so that I	H8740
1Sa	16: 2	'*I have* **c** to sacrifice to the LORD.	H995
1Sa	16: 4	They asked, "*Do* you **c** in peace?"	H995
1Sa	16: 5	in peace; *I have* **c** to sacrifice to the LORD.	H995
1Sa	16: 5	yourselves and **c** to the sacrifice with me."	H995
1Sa	16:23	Then **relief** *would* **c** to Saul; he would feel	H8118
1Sa	17: 8	"Why *do you* **c out** and line up for battle?	H3655
1Sa	17: 8	a man and *have him* **c down** to me.	H3718
1Sa	17:28	asked, "Why *have you* **c down** here?	H3718
1Sa	17:43	"Am I a dog, that you **c** at me with sticks?"	H995
1Sa	17:44	"**C** here," he said, "and I'll give your flesh	H2143
1Sa	17:45	"You **c** against me with sword and spear	H995
1Sa	17:45	I **c** against you in the name of the LORD	H995
1Sa	20:11	"**C**," Jonathan said, "let's go out into the	H2143
1Sa	20:21	them here,' then **c**, because, as surely as	H995
1Sa	20:27	"Why hasn't the son of Jesse **c** to the meal	H995
1Sa	20:29	That is why *he has* not **c** to the king's table	H995
1Sa	21:15	*Must* this man **c** into my house?	H995
1Sa	22: 3	"*Would you* let my father and mother **c**	H3655
1Sa	22: 9	saw the son of Jesse **c** to Ahimelek son of	H995
1Sa	23:10	that Saul plans to **c** to Keilah and destroy	H995
1Sa	23:11	*Will* Saul **c down**, as your servant has	H3718
1Sa	23:15	learned that Saul *had* **c out** to take his life	H3655
1Sa	23:20	**c down** whenever it pleases you to do so	H3718
1Sa	23:23	places he uses and **c back** to me with	H8740
1Sa	23:27	came to Saul, saying, "**C** quickly!	H2143
1Sa	24:13	'From evildoers **c** evil deeds,' so my	H3655
1Sa	24:14	whom *has* the king of Israel **c out**?	H3655
1Sa	25: 8	my men, since we **c** at a festive time.	H995
1Sa	25:34	if *you had* not **c** quickly to meet me	H995
1Sa	26:10	or his time *will* **c** and he will die, or	H995
1Sa	26:20	The king of Israel *has* **c out** to look for a	H3655
1Sa	26:21	"I have sinned. **C back**, David my son	H8740
1Sa	26:22	"*Let* one of your young men **c over** and	H6296
1Sa	29:10	your master's servants who *have* **c** with you,	H995
1Sa	30:13	Where do you **c** from?" He said,	NDT
1Sa	31: 4	fellows *will* **c** and run me through	H995
2Sa	1: 3	"Where *have you* **c** from?" David asked him	H995
2Sa	3:13	*Do* not **c into** my **presence**	H8011+906+7156
2Sa	3:13	daughter of Saul when you **c** to see me."	H995
2Sa	3:23	Abner son of Ner *had* **c** to the king and that	H995
2Sa	5: 3	the elders of Israel *had* **c** to King David at	H995
2Sa	5:18	Now the Philistines *had* **c** and spread out in	H995
2Sa	6: 9	"How *can* the ark of the LORD *ever* **c** to me?"	H995
2Sa	10: 5	your beards have grown, and then **c back**."	H8740
2Sa	10:11	me, then *you are to* **c** to my rescue; but	H2118
2Sa	10:11	strong for you, then *I will* **c** to rescue you.	H2143
2Sa	11:10	"Haven't you *just* **c** from a military	H995
2Sa	12: 4	a meal for the traveler who *had* **c** to him.	H995
2Sa	12: 4	prepared it for the one who *had* **c** to him."	H995
2Sa	13: 5	like my sister Tamar *to* **c** and give me	H995
2Sa	13: 6	like my sister Tamar *to* **c** and make some	H995
2Sa	13:11	her and said, "**C** to bed with me, my	H995
2Sa	13:23	he invited all the king's sons to **c** there.	NDT
2Sa	13:24	"Your servant has had shearers **c**.	H2180
2Sa	13:26	please *let* my brother Amnon **c** with us."	H2143
2Sa	13:35	the king's sons *have* **c**; it has happened	H995
2Sa	14:15	"And now *I have* **c** to say this to my lord the	H995
2Sa	14:29	to the king, but Joab refused to **c** to him.	H995
2Sa	14:29	he sent a second time, but he refused to **c**.	H995
2Sa	14:32	'**C** here so I can send you to the king to ask	H995
2Sa	14:32	the king to ask, "Why *have I* **c** from Geshur?	H995
2Sa	15: 4	complaint or case *could* **c** to me and I	H995
2Sa	15:12	David's counselor, to **c** from Giloh, his	NDT
2Sa	15:14	who were with him in Jerusalem, "**C**!	H7756
2Sa	15:19	"Why *should* you **c** along with us?	H2143
2Sa	16: 8	You have **c** to ruin because you are a	NDT
2Sa	18:22	to Joab, "**C what may**, please let	H2118+4537
2Sa	18:23	He said, "**C what may**, I want to run	H2118+4537
2Sa	19: 7	the calamities that *have* **c** on you from your	H995
2Sa	19:15	the men of Judah *had* **c** to Gilgal to go out	H995
2Sa	19:20	today *I have* **c** here as the first from the	H995
2Sa	19:20	of Joseph to **c down** and meet my lord	H3718
2Sa	20: 4	the men of Judah to **c** to me within three	NDT
2Sa	20:16	Tell Joab *to* **c** here so I can speak to him."	H7928
2Sa	22:46	*they* **c trembling** from their strongholds.	H3004
2Sa	24:11	word of the LORD *had* **c** to Gad the prophet	H2118
2Sa	24:13	"*Shall there* **c** on you three years of famine	H995
2Sa	24:21	"Why *has* my lord the king **c** to his servant?"	H995
1Ki	1:14	I *will* **c in** and add my word to what you	H995
1Ki	1:35	he *is to* **c** and sit on my throne and	H995
1Ki	1:42	Adonijah said, "**C in**. A worthy man like	H995
1Ki	1:47	the royal officials *have* **c** to congratulate	H995
1Ki	2:13	asked him, "*Do* you **c** peacefully?"	H995
1Ki	2:15	brother; for *it has* **c** to him from the LORD.	H2118
1Ki	2:30	said to Joab, "The king says, '**C out**!	H3655
1Ki	8:26	*let* your word that you promised your servant David my father **c true**	H586
1Ki	8:31	take an oath and *they* **c** and swear the oath	H995
1Ki	8:37	whatever disaster or disease *may* **c**,	H2118
1Ki	8:41	people Israel but *has* **c** from a distant land	H995
1Ki	8:42	when *they* **c** and pray toward this temple	H995
1Ki	9:24	daughter *had* **c up** from the City of	H6590
1Ki	12: 5	three days and then **c back** to me.	H8740
1Ki	12:12	had said, "**C back** to me in three days."	H8740
1Ki	13: 7	man of God, "**C** home with me for a meal	H995
1Ki	13:10	not return by the way *he had* **c** to Bethel.	H995
1Ki	13:15	said to him, "**C** home with me and eat."	H2143
1Ki	13:21	to the man of God who *had* **c** from Judah,	H995
1Ki	13:32	of Samaria *will* **certainly c true**."	H2118+2118
1Ki	14: 6	the door, he said, "**C in**, wife of Jeroboam.	H995
1Ki	17:18	*Did you* **c** to remind me of my sin and kill	H995
1Ki	18:30	said to all the people, "**C here** to me."	H5602
1Ki	18:31	to whom the word of the LORD *had* **c**	H2118
1Ki	19:20	he said, "and then *I will* **c** with you."	H2143
1Ki	20:18	He said, "If *they have* **c out** for peace	H3655
1Ki	20:18	them alive; if *they have* **c out** for war, take	H3655
1Ki	20:33	Ahab **had** him **c up** into his chariot.	H6590
2Ki	1: 5	he asked them, "Why *have you* **c back**?"	H8740
2Ki	1: 9	"Man of God, the king says, '**C down**!	H3718
2Ki	1:10	*may* fire **c down** from heaven and	H3718
2Ki	1:11	is what the king says, '**C down** at once!	H3718
2Ki	1:12	"*may* fire **c down** from heaven and	H3718
2Ki	3:21	heard that the kings *had* **c** to fight against	H6590
2Ki	5: 8	*Have* the man **c** to me and he will know	H995
2Ki	5:11	that *he would* **surely c out** to me	H3655+3655
2Ki	5:22	of the prophets *have* just **c** to me from the	H995
2Ki	6: 3	"*Won't you* please **c** with your servants?"	H2143
2Ki	7:12	thinking, '*They will* surely **c out**, and then	H3655
2Ki	8: 7	"The man of God *has* **c** all the way up here,"	H995
2Ki	9:11	Why *did* this maniac **c** to you?" "You	H995
2Ki	9:17	meet them and ask, 'Do you **c in peace**?	H8934
2Ki	9:18	what the king says: 'Do you **c in peace**?' "	H8934
2Ki	9:19	what the king says: 'Do you **c in peace**?' "	H8934
2Ki	9:22	he asked, "Have you **c in peace**, Jehu?"	H8934
2Ki	9:31	"Have you **c in peace**, you Zimri,	H8934
2Ki	10: 6	master's sons and **c** to me in Jezreel by	H995
2Ki	10:13	and *we have* **c down** to greet the families	H3718
2Ki	10:16	"**C** with me and see my zeal for the LORD."	H2143
2Ki	10:19	Anyone who **fails to c** will no longer live."	H7212
2Ki	14: 8	with the challenge: "**C**, let us face each	H2143
2Ki	16: 7	**C up** and save me out of the hand of the	H6590
2Ki	18:23	" '**C now**, make a bargain with my	H6964+5528
2Ki	18:25	*have I* **c** to attack and destroy this place	H6590
2Ki	18:31	Make peace with me and **c out** to me	H3655
2Ki	18:32	I **c** and take you to a land like your	H995
2Ki	19: 3	as when children **c** to the moment of birth	H995
2Ki	19:27	you are and *when* you **c** and go and how	H995
2Ki	19:31	For out of Jerusalem *will* **c** a remnant, and	H3655
2Ki	19:32	*He will* not **c before** it with shield or build	H7709
2Ki	20:14	those men say, and where *did they* **c** from?"	H995
2Ki	20:17	The time *will* surely **c** when everything in	H995
2Ki	23:18	of the prophet who *had* **c** from Samaria.	H995
1Ch	9:25	in their villages *had to* **c** from time to time	H995
1Ch	10: 4	uncircumcised fellows *will* **c** and abuse me."	H995
1Ch	11: 3	the elders of Israel *had* **c** to King David at	H995
1Ch	12:17	"If *you have* **c** to me in peace to help me	H995
1Ch	12:17	But if you have **c** to betray me to my	NDT
1Ch	12:31	by name to **c** and make David king—	H995
1Ch	13: 2	towns and pasturelands, *to* **c and join** us.	H7695
1Ch	14: 9	Now the Philistines *had* **c** and raided the	H995
1Ch	16:29	bring an offering and **c** before him.	H995
1Ch	19: 3	Haven't his envoys **c** to you only to explore	H995
1Ch	19: 5	your beards have grown, and then **c back**."	H8740
1Ch	19: 9	the kings who *had* **c** were by themselves	H995
1Ch	23:25	people and *has* **c to dwell** in Jerusalem	H8905
1Ch	29:12	Wealth and honor **c** from you; you are the	NDT
2Ch	6:17	*let* your word that you promised your servant David **c true**	H586
2Ch	6:22	take an oath and *they* **c** and swear the oath	H995
2Ch	6:28	whatever disaster or disease *may* **c**,	H2118
2Ch	6:32	people Israel but *has* **c** from a distant land	H995
2Ch	6:32	when *they* **c** and pray toward this temple	H995
2Ch	6:41	LORD God, and **c** to your resting place, you	NDT
2Ch	10: 5	answered, "**C back** to me in three days."	H8740
2Ch	10:12	had said, "**C back** to me in three days."	H8740
2Ch	14:11	in your name *we have* **c** against this	H995
2Ch	15: 9	large numbers *had* **c over** to him from	H5877
2Ch	19:10	otherwise his wrath *will* **c** on you and your	H2118
2Ch	21:15	the disease causes your bowels *to* **c out**.	H3655
2Ch	24:11	of the chief priest *would* **c** and empty the	H995
2Ch	24:24	the Aramean army *had* **c** with only a few	H995
2Ch	25:10	the troops who *had* **c** to him from Ephraim	H995
2Ch	25:17	king of Israel: "**C**, let us face each other in	H2143
2Ch	28:17	The Edomites *had* again **c** and attacked	H995
2Ch	29:31	**C** and bring sacrifices and thank offerings	H5602
2Ch	30: 1	inviting them to **c** to the temple of the LORD	H995
2Ch	30: 5	calling the people to **c** to Jerusalem and	H995
2Ch	30: 8	**C** to his sanctuary, which he has	H995
2Ch	30:25	the foreigners who *had* **c** from Israel and	H995
2Ch	32: 2	saw that Sennacherib *had* **c** and that he	H995
2Ch	32: 4	"Why *should* the kings of Assyria **c** and find	H995
2Ch	32:26	the LORD's wrath *did* not **c** on them during	H995
Ezr	10:14	*let* everyone in our towns who has married a foreign woman **c**	H995
Ne	2:10	that someone *had* **c** to promote the	H995
Ne	2:17	**C**, let us rebuild the wall of Jerusalem	H2143
Ne	4: 8	all plotted together to **c** and fight against	H995
Ne	6: 2	"**C**, let us meet together in one of the	H2143
Ne	6: 7	back to the king; so **c**, let us meet	H2143
Ne	9:32	the hardship that *has* **c on** us, on our kings	H5162
Est	1:12	command, Queen Vashti refused to **c**.	H995
Est	1:17	brought before him, but *she would* not **c**.	H995
Est	4:14	knows but that *you have* **c** to your royal	H5595
Est	5: 4	"*let* the king, together with Haman, **c** today	H995
Est	5: 8	*let* the king and Haman **c** tomorrow to the	H995
Est	6:13	him—*you will* **surely c to ruin**!"	H5877+5877
Est	9:25	the Jews *should* **c back** onto his own	H8740
Job	1: 7	said to Satan, "Where *have you* **c** from?"	H995
Job	2: 2	said to Satan, "Where *have you* **c** from?"	H995
Job	2:11	about all the troubles that *had* **c** upon him,	H995
Job	3:21	to those who long for death that does not **c**	NDT
Job	3:25	What I feared *has* **c** *upon* me; what I	H910
Job	5:26	You *will* **c** to the grave in full vigor, like	H995
Job	7: 6	and *they* **c to an end** without hope.—	H3983
Job	7:10	*He will* never **c** to his house again; his	H8740
Job	9: 4	Who has resisted him and *c out* **unscathed**?	AIT
Job	10:17	your forces **c** against me wave upon wave.	NDT
Job	10:19	If only *I had* never **c into being**, or	H2118+2118
Job	13:13	let me speak; then *let* **c** to me what may.	H6296
Job	13:16	godless person *would dare* **c** before him!	H995
Job	14:14	hard service I will wait for my renewal *to* **c**.	H995
Job	17:10	"But **c on**, all of you, try again! I will not	H995
Job	20:22	the full force of misery *will* **c** *upon* him.	H995
Job	20:25	out of his liver. Terrors *will* **c** over him;	H2143
Job	21:17	How often *does* calamity **c** upon them, the	H995
Job	21:21	when their allotted months **c to an end**?	H2951
Job	22:21	in this way prosperity *will* **c** *to* you.	H995
Job	23:10	he has tested me, *I will* **c forth** as gold.	H3655
Job	28:20	Where then *does* wisdom **c** from? Where	H995
Job	30:14	amid the ruins *they* **c rolling in**.	H1670
Job	31:40	then *let* briers **c up** instead of wheat and	H3655
Job	33: 3	My words **c** from an upright heart; my lips	NDT
Job	34:23	that they *should* **c** before him for	H2143
Job	34:28	They **caused** the cry of the poor **to c** before	H995
Job	38:11	'This far *you may* **c** and no farther	H995

Ps 5: 7 by your great love, *can* c into your house; in H995
Ps 14: 7 that salvation for Israel would c out of Zion! NDT
Ps 17: 2 *Let* my vindication c from you; may your H3655
Ps 18:45 *they* c trembling from their strongholds. H3004
Ps 22:19 You are my strength; c quickly to help me. H2590
Ps 24: 7 that the King of glory *may* c in. H995
Ps 24: 9 that the King of glory *may* c in. H995
Ps 25: 3 but shame *will* c on those who are H1017
Ps 31: 2 ear to me, c quickly to my rescue; be my H5911
Ps 32: 9 by bit and bridle or they *will* not c to you. H7928
Ps 34:11 C, my children, listen to me; I will teach H2143
Ps 35: 2 shield and armor; arise and c to my aid. H7756
Ps 35:11 Ruthless witnesses c forward; they H7756
Ps 36:11 *May* the foot of the proud not c *against* me H995
Ps 38: 2 and your hand *has* c down on me. H5737
Ps 38:22 C quickly to help me, my Lord and my H2590
Ps 40: 7 "Here I am, *I have* c—it is written about H995
Ps 40:13 LORD; c quickly, LORD, to help me H2590
Ps 45:12 The city of Tyre will c with a gift, people of NDT
Ps 46: 8 C and see what the LORD has done, the H2143
Ps 49: 5 Why should I fear when evil days c, when NDT
Ps 53: 6 that salvation for Israel would c out of Zion! NDT
Ps 65: 2 who answer prayer, to you all people *will* c. H995
Ps 66: 5 C and see what God has done, his H2143
Ps 66: 6 the waters on foot—*c, let us* rejoice in him. AIT
Ps 66:13 *I will* c *to* your temple with burnt offerings H995
Ps 66:16 C and hear, all you who fear God; let me H2143
Ps 68:17 the Lord *has* c from Sinai into his sanctuary. H995
Ps 68:24 *has* c into view, the procession of my H8011
Ps 68:31 Envoys *will* c from Egypt; Cush will submit H910
Ps 69: 1 for the waters *have* c up to my neck. H995
Ps 69: 2 *I have* c into the deep waters; the floods H995
Ps 69:18 C near and rescue me; deliver me H7928
Ps 70: 1 to save me; c quickly, LORD, to help H2590
Ps 70: 5 poor and needy; c quickly to me, O God. H2590
Ps 71:12 my God; c quickly, God, to help me H2590
Ps 71:16 *I will* c and proclaim your mighty acts H995
Ps 71:18 your mighty acts to all *who are to* c. H995
Ps 78:28 *He* made them c down inside their camp H5877
Ps 79: 8 *may* your mercy c quickly to meet us, for H7709
Ps 79:11 *May* the groans of the prisoners c before H995
Ps 80: 2 Awaken your might; c and save us. H2143
Ps 83: 4 "C," they say, "let us destroy them as a H2143
Ps 86: 9 you have made *will* c and worship before H995
Ps 88: 2 *May* my prayer c before you; turn your ear H995
Ps 90:10 Our days may c to seventy years, or eighty, if NDT
Ps 91: 7 your right hand, but *it will* not c near you. H5602
Ps 91:10 no disaster *will* c near your tent. H7928
Ps 95: 1 C, let us sing for joy to the LORD; let us H2143
Ps 95: 2 *Let us* c before him with thanksgiving and H7709
Ps 95: 6 C, let us bow down in worship, let us kneel H995
Ps 96: 8 bring an offering and c into his courts. H995
Ps 100: 2 gladness; c before him with joyful songs. H995
Ps 101: 2 a blameless life—when *will you* c to me? H995
Ps 102: 1 prayer, LORD; *let* my cry for help c to you. H995
Ps 102:13 favor to her; the appointed time *has* c. H995
Ps 106: 4 people, c to my aid when you save them H7212
Ps 106:31 endless generations to c. H1887+2256+1887
Ps 109:17 pronounce a curse—*may it* c back *on* him. H995
Ps 110: 3 your young men will *c to you* like dew from AIT
Ps 112: 5 Good will c to those who are generous and NDT
Ps 112:10 the longings of the wicked *will* c to nothing. H6
Ps 119:13 I recount all the laws *that c from* your mouth. AIT
Ps 119:41 *May* your unfailing love c *to* me, LORD, your H995
Ps 119:77 *Let* your compassion c *to me* that I may live, H995
Ps 119:118 decrees, for their delusions c to nothing. H9214
Ps 119:143 Trouble and distress *have* c upon me, but H5162
Ps 119:169 *May* my cry c before you, LORD; give me H7928
Ps 119:170 *May* my supplication c before you; deliver H995
Ps 121: 1 mountains—where *does* my help c from? H995
Ps 132: 8 and c to your resting place, you and NDT
Ps 141: 1 c quickly to me; hear me when I call H2590
Ps 143: 1 righteousness c to my relief. H6699
Ps 144: 5 heavens, LORD, and c down; touch the H3718
Ps 146: 4 on that very day their plans c to nothing. H6
Pr 1:11 If they say, "C along with us; let's lie in H2143
Pr 2: 6 from his mouth c knowledge and NDT
Pr 3:28 "C back tomorrow and I'll give it to you" H2143
Pr 6:11 poverty *will* c *on* you like a thief and H995
Pr 7:18 C, let's drink deeply of love till morning H2143
Pr 9: 4 "*Let all* who are simple c to my house!" H6073
Pr 9: 5 "C, eat my food and drink the wine I have H2143
Pr 9:16 "*Let all* who are simple c to my house!" H6073
Pr 10:28 but the hopes of the wicked c to nothing. H6
Pr 13: 3 those who speak rashly will c to ruin. NDT
Pr 14: 4 the strength of an ox c abundant harvests. NDT
Pr 17: 8 they think success *will* c at every turn. H8505
Pr 22:16 gives gifts to the rich—both c to poverty. NDT
Pr 24:25 the guilty, and rich blessing *will* c on them. H995
Pr 24:31 thorns *had* c up everywhere, the ground H6590
Pr 24:34 poverty *will* c *on* you like a thief and H995
Pr 25: 7 to say to you, "C up here," than for him H6590
Pr 26: 2 an undeserved curse *does* not c to rest. H995
Pr 30: 4 Who has gone up to heaven and c down H3718
Pr 31:25 dignity; she can laugh at the days to c. H340
Ecc 1: 4 Generations c and generations go, but H2143
Ecc 1: 7 To the place the streams c from, there H2143
Ecc 1:11 even those yet to c will not be H2118
Ecc 2: 1 I said to myself, "C now, I will test you H2143
Ecc 2:16 the days *have* already c when both have H995
Ecc 3:20 the same place; all c from dust, and to H2118
Ecc 4:14 The youth *may have* c from prison to the H3655
Ecc 8: 5 obeys his command *will* c to no harm, H3359
Ecc 8: 7 who can tell someone else what *is to* c? H2118
Ecc 8:10 *those who used to* c and go from the holy H995
Ecc 9:11 does food c to the wise or wealth to the NDT
Ecc 9:12 no one knows when their hour will c: NDT
Ecc 11: 2 know what disaster *may* c upon the land. H2118
Ecc 11: 8 Everything *to* c is meaningless. H995
Ecc 12: 1 the days of trouble c and the years H995
SS 2:10 my darling, my beautiful one, c with me. H2143
SS 2:12 the season of singing *has* c, the cooing of H5595
SS 2:13 c, my darling; my beautiful one H2143
SS 2:13 my darling; my beautiful one, c with me." H2143
SS 3:11 c out, and look, you daughters of Zion H3655
SS 4: 8 C with me from Lebanon, my bride, come NDT
SS 4: 8 my bride, c with me from Lebanon. H995
SS 4:16 north wind, and c, south wind! Blow on H995
SS 4:16 *Let* my beloved c into his garden and taste H995
SS 5: 1 *I have* c into my garden, my sister, my bride H995
SS 6:13 C back, come back, O Shulammite; come H8740
SS 6:13 Come back, c back, O Shulammite; come H8740
SS 6:13 O Shulammite; c back, come back, that H8740
SS 6:13 come back, c back, that we may gaze on H8740
SS 7:11 C, my beloved, let us go to the H2143
SS 8:14 C away, my beloved, and be like a H1368
Isa 1:12 When *you* c to appear before me, who has H995
Isa 1:18 "C now, let us settle the matter," says the H2143
Isa 1:23 the widow's case *does* not c before them. H995
Isa 2: 3 Many peoples *will* c and say, "Come, let H2143
Isa 2: 3 will come and say, "C, let us go up to the H2143
Isa 2: 5 C, descendants of Jacob, let us walk in H2143
Isa 5:19 it approach, *let it* c into view, so we may H995
Isa 5:26 Here *they* c, swiftly and H995
Isa 7:19 They *will* all c and settle in the steep H995
Isa 11: 1 A shoot *will* c up from the stump of Jesse H3655
Isa 13: 5 *They* c from faraway lands, from the ends H995
Isa 13: 6 *it will* c like destruction from the Almighty. H995
Isa 14: 4 How the oppressor *has* c to an end! How H8697
Isa 16: 4 The oppressor *will* c to an end, and H699
Isa 21:12 would ask, then ask; and c back yet again." H910
Isa 21:16 all the splendor of Kedar *will* c to an end. H3983
Isa 23: 1 the land of Cyprus word *has* c to them. H1655
Isa 26: 9 When your judgments c upon the earth, the NDT
Isa 26:18 the people of the world *have* not c to life. H5877
Isa 27: 5 Or else *let them* c *to* me for refuge; let H2616
Isa 27: 6 *In* days *to* c Jacob will take root, Israel will H995
Isa 27:11 off and women c and make fires with H995
Isa 27:13 were exiled in Egypt *will* c and worship the H995
Isa 29: 4 Your voice *will* c ghostlike from the earth H2118
Isa 29: 6 the LORD Almighty *will* c with thunder and H7212
Isa 29:13 "These people c near to me with their H5602
Isa 30: 8 that for the days to c it may be an H340
Isa 31: 4 LORD Almighty *will* c down to do battle on H3718
Isa 32:10 will fail, and the harvest of fruit *will* not c. H995
Isa 34: 1 C near, you nations, and listen; pay H7928
Isa 35: 4 not fear; your God will c, he will come with NDT
Isa 35: 4 God will come, he *will* c *with* vengeance H995
Isa 35: 4 with divine retribution he *will* c to save you." H995
Isa 36: 8 " 'C now, make a bargain with my H6964+5528
Isa 36:10 *have I* c to attack and destroy this land H6590
Isa 36:16 Make peace with me and c out to me H3655
Isa 36:17 I c and take you to a land like your H995
Isa 37: 3 as when children c to the moment of birth H995
Isa 37:28 you are and *when* you c and go and how H995
Isa 37:32 For out of Jerusalem *will* c a remnant, and H3655
Isa 37:33 *He will* not c before it with shield or build H7709
Isa 38:14 am being threatened; Lord, c to my aid!" H6842
Isa 39: 3 those men say, and where *did they* c from?" H995
Isa 39: 6 The time *will* surely c when everything in H995
Isa 41: 1 *Let them* c forward and speak; let us meet H5602
Isa 41: 5 They approach and c forward; H910
Isa 41:22 Or declare to us the *things to* c, H995
Isa 42:23 to this or pay close attention in time to c? H294
Isa 44: 7 ancient people, and *what is yet to* c—yes, H910
Isa 44: 7 to come—yes, let them foretell what *will* c. H995
Isa 44:11 *Let* them all c together and take their H7695
Isa 45:11 Concerning things to c, do you question me H910
Isa 45:14 *they will* c over to you and will be yours H6296
Isa 45:20 "Gather together and c; assemble, you H995
Isa 45:24 raged against him *will* c to him and be put H995
Isa 46:10 ancient times, what *is* still to c. H4202+6913
Isa 47: 9 *They will* c upon you in full measure, in H995
Isa 47:11 Disaster *will* c upon you, and you will not H995
Isa 47:11 cannot foresee *will* suddenly c upon you. H995
Isa 47:13 *Let* your astrologers c forward, those H6641
Isa 48: 1 name of Israel and c from the line of H3655
Isa 48:14 "C together, all of you, and listen: Which H7695
Isa 48:16 "C near me and listen to this: "From the H7928
Isa 49: 9 to the captives, 'C out,' and to those in H3655
Isa 49:12 they *will* c from afar—some from the H995
Isa 49:18 all your children gather and c to you. H995
Isa 49:21 but these—where have they c from? NDT
Isa 51:19 double calamities *have* c upon you— H7925
Isa 52:11 C out from it and be pure, you who carry H3655
Isa 54:14 will be far removed; *it will* not c near you. H7928
Isa 55: 1 "C, all you who are thirsty, come to the H2098
Isa 55: 1 you who are thirsty, c to the waters; and H2143
Isa 55: 1 you who have no money, c, buy and eat! H2143
Isa 55: 1 C, buy wine and milk without money and H2143
Isa 55: 3 Give ear and c to me; listen, that you may H2143
Isa 55: 5 you do not know *will* c running to you, H8132
Isa 55:10 rain and the snow c down from heaven, H3718
Isa 56: 9 C, all *you* beasts of the field, come and H910
Isa 56: 9 you beasts of the field, c and devour, all you NDT
Isa 56:12 "C," each one cries, "let me get wine! Let H910
Isa 57: 3 you—c here, *you* children of a sorceress H7928
Isa 58: 2 seem eager for God to c near them. H7932
Isa 59:19 For *he will* c like a pent-up flood that the H995
Isa 59:20 "The Redeemer *will* c to Zion, to those in H995
Isa 60: 1 for your light *has* c, and the glory of H995
Isa 60: 3 Nations *will* c to your light, and kings to H2143
Isa 60: 4 All assemble and c to you; your sons come H995
Isa 60: 4 your sons c from afar, and your H995
Isa 60: 5 to you the riches of the nations *will* c. H995
Isa 60: 6 And all from Sheba *will* c, bearing gold H995
Isa 60:13 "The glory of Lebanon *will* c to you, the H995
Isa 60:14 your oppressors *will* c bowing before you H2143
Isa 61:11 as the soil makes the sprout c up and a H3655
Isa 63: 4 the year for me to redeem *had* c. H995
Isa 64: 1 you would rend the heavens and c down, H3718
Isa 64: 2 c down to make your name known to your NDT
Isa 64: 5 *You* c to the help of those who gladly do H7003
Isa 65: 5 'Keep away; don't c near me, for I am too H5602
Isa 65:17 be remembered, nor *will they* c to mind. H6590
Isa 66: 7 before the pains c upon her, she delivers H995
Isa 66:18 *am about to* c and gather the people of all H995
Isa 66:18 and *they will* c and see my glory. H995
Isa 66:23 all mankind *will* c and bow down before H995
Jer 1:15 "Their kings *will* c and set up their thrones H995
Jer 1:15 they will c against all her surrounding walls NDT
Jer 2:27 are in trouble, they say, 'C and save us! H7756
Jer 2:28 *Let them* c if they can save you when you H7756
Jer 2:31 are free to roam; *we will* c to you no more'? H995
Jer 3:18 together *they will* c from a northern H995
Jer 3:22 we *will* c to you, for you are the LORD H910
Jer 4: 7 A lion *has* c out of his lair; a destroyer of H6590
Jer 4:13 his chariots c like a whirlwind, his NDT
Jer 5:12 No harm *will* c to us; we will never see H995
Jer 6: 3 with their flocks *will* c against her; H995
Jer 6:23 they c like men in battle formation to attack NDT
Jer 6:26 suddenly the destroyer *will* c upon us. H995
Jer 7: 2 people of Judah who c through these gates H995
Jer 7:10 then c and stand before me in this H995
Jer 8:15 We hoped for peace but no good has c, for NDT
Jer 8:16 *They have* c to devour the land and H995
Jer 9:17 Call for the wailing women *to* c; send for H995
Jer 9:18 *Let them* c quickly and wail over us till our H4554
Jer 13:18 queen mother, "C down from your thrones H9164
Jer 14:19 We hoped for peace but no good has c, for NDT
Jer 16:19 to you the nations *will* c from the ends of H995
Jer 17:20 in Jerusalem who c through these gates. H995
Jer 17:25 on David's throne *will* c through the gates H995
Jer 17:25 their officials will c riding in chariots and NDT
Jer 17:26 *People will* c from the towns of Judah and H995
Jer 17:27 any load as you c through the gates of H995
Jer 18:18 They said, "C, let's make plans against H2143
Jer 18:18 So c, let's attack him with our tongues H2143
Jer 20:18 Why *did I ever* c out of the womb to see H3655
Jer 21:13 you who say, "Who *can* c against us? H5737
Jer 22: 2 your people who c through these gates H995
Jer 22: 4 on David's throne *will* c through the gates H995
Jer 22:23 you will groan when pangs c upon you, H995
Jer 22:27 *You will* never c back to the land you long H8740
Jer 23:17 hearts they say, 'No harm *will* c to you. H995
Jer 23:20 In days to c you will understand it clearly. H344
Jer 25: 3 word of the LORD *has* c to me and I have H2118
Jer 25:34 For your time to be slaughtered *has* c; you H4848
Jer 26: 2 the towns of Judah who c to worship in the H995
Jer 27: 3 the envoys who *have* c *to* Jerusalem to H995
Jer 27:22 they will remain until the day I c *for* them, H7212
Jer 29:10 *I will* c to you and fulfill my good promise H7212
Jer 29:12 you will call on me and c and pray to me, H2143
Jer 30:19 From them *will* c songs of thanksgiving H3655
Jer 30:21 him near and *he will* c close to me— H5602
Jer 30:24 In days to c you will understand this H344
Jer 31: 2 wilderness; I *will* c to give rest to Israel." H2143
Jer 31: 6 hills of Ephraim, 'C, let us go up to Zion, H7756
Jer 31: 9 *They will* c with weeping; they will pray as I H995
Jer 31:12 *They will* c and shout for joy on the heights H995
Jer 32: 7 your uncle *is going to* c to you and say, H995
Jer 32:29 attacking this city *will* c in and set it on fire; H995
Jer 33:20 day and night no *longer* c at their H2118
Jer 35: 2 invite them *to* c to one of the side H995
Jer 35:11 we said, 'C, we must go to Jerusalem to H995
Jer 36: 6 people of Judah who c in from their towns. H995
Jer 36: 9 those *who had* c from the towns of H995
Jer 36:14 which you have read to the people and c." H2143
Jer 36:17 "Tell us, how *did you* c *to* write all this? AIT
Jer 36:29 of Babylon *would* certainly c and H995+995
Jer 37: 4 Now Jeremiah *was free to* c and go among H995
Jer 37:10 *they would* c out and burn this city down." H7756
Jer 38:25 talked with you, and *they* c to you and say H995
Jer 38:27 All the officials *did* c to Jeremiah and H995
Jer 40: 4 C with me to Babylon, if you like, and I will H995
Jer 40: 4 but if you do not want to, then don't c. H995
Jer 40:10 you before the Babylonians who c to us, H995
Jer 41: 6 he said, "C to Gedaliah son of Ahikam." H995
Jer 43: 5 of Judah who *had* c back to live in the H8740
Jer 43:11 *He will* c and attack Egypt, bringing death H995
Jer 44: 8 gods in Egypt, where you *have* c to live? H995
Jer 44:23 this disaster *has* c upon you, as you now H7925
Jer 46:18 "*one will* c who is like Tabor among the H995
Jer 46:22 in force; *they will* c against her with axes H995
Jer 47: 4 For the day *has* c to destroy all the H995
Jer 48: 2 plot her downfall: 'C, let us put an end to H2143

Jer 48: 8 The destroyer will c against every town H995
Jer 48:16 at hand; her calamity will c quickly. H4554+4394
Jer 48:18 "C down from your glory and sit on the H3718
Jer 48:18 destroys Moab will c up against you and H6590
Jer 48:21 Judgment has c to the plateau—to Holon H995
Jer 48:47 restore the fortunes of Moab in days to c," H344
Jer 49:39 restore the fortunes of Elam in days to c," H344
Jer 50: 5 They will c and bind themselves to the LORD H995
Jer 50:26 C against her from afar. Break open her H995
Jer 50:27 For their day has c, the time for them to be H995
Jer 50:31 "for your day has c, the time for you to H995
Jer 50:42 they c like men in battle formation to attack NDT
Jer 51:10 LORD has vindicated us; c, let us tell in Zion H995
Jer 51:13 treasures, your end has c, the time for you H995
Jer 51:33 the time to harvest her will soon c. H995
Jer 51:45 "C out of her, my people! Run for your H3655
Jer 51:47 For the time will surely c when I will punish H995
Jer 51:56 A destroyer will c against Babylon; her H995
Jer 51:60 the disasters that would c upon Babylon— H995
La 1:22 "Let all their wickedness c before you; deal H995
La 3:38 that both calamities and good things c? H3655
La 4:18 our days were numbered, for our end had c. H995
Eze 5: 2 When the days of your siege c to an end H4848
Eze 7: 2 The end has c upon the four corners of the H995
Eze 7: 6 The end has c! The end has come! It has H995
Eze 7: 6 The end has c! It has roused H995
Eze 7: 7 Doom has c upon you, upon you who dwell H995
Eze 7: 7 The time has c! The day is near! H995
Eze 7:12 The time has c! The day has arrived! Let H995
Eze 7:26 Calamity upon calamity will c, and rumor H995
Eze 7:26 the counsel of the elders will c to an end. NDT
Eze 13:11 Rain will c in torrents, and I will send H2118
Eze 14:22 They will c to you, and when you see their H3655
Eze 15: 7 Although they have c out of the fire, the H3655
Eze 16:33 bribing them to c to you from everywhere H995
Eze 20: 3 Have you c to inquire of me? As H995
Eze 21:13 " 'Testing will surely c. And what if even the AIT
Eze 21:20 the sword to c against Rabbah of the H995
Eze 21:22 Into his right hand will c the lot for H2118
Eze 21:25 of Israel, whose day has c, whose time of H995
Eze 21:27 he to whom it rightfully belongs shall c; H995
Eze 21:29 be slain, whose day has c, whose time of H995
Eze 22: 4 to a close, and the end of your years has c. H995
Eze 23:24 They will c against you with weapons H995
Eze 24:14 The time has c for me to act. H995
Eze 24:26 that day a fugitive will c to tell you the H995
Eze 27:36 you have c to a horrible end and will be H2118
Eze 28:18 So I made a fire c out from you, and it H3655
Eze 28:19 you have c to a horrible end and will be H2118
Eze 30: 4 A sword will c against Egypt, and anguish H995
Eze 30: 4 and anguish will c upon Cush. H2118
Eze 30: 9 the day of Egypt's doom, for it is sure to c. H995
Eze 30:18 there her proud strength will c to an end. H8697
Eze 32:11 of the king of Babylon will c against you. H995
Eze 32:21 'They have c down and they lie with the H3718
Eze 33:28 her proud strength will c to an end H8697
Eze 33:30 'C and hear the message that has come H995
Eze 33:30 the message that has c from the LORD. H3655
Eze 33:31 My people c to you, as they usually do, and H995
Eze 35: 7 waste and cut off from it all who c and go. H6296
Eze 36: 8 people Israel, for they will soon c home. H995
Eze 37: 5 breath enter you, and you will c to life. H2649
Eze 37: 6 to you and make flesh c upon you and H6590
Eze 37: 6 put breath in you, and you will c to life. H2649
Eze 37: 9 C, breath, from the four winds and breathe H995
Eze 38:10 that day thoughts will c into your mind H6590
Eze 38:13 will say to you, "Have you c to plunder? H995
Eze 38:15 You will c from your place in the far north H995
Eze 38:16 In days to c, Gog, I will bring you against H344
Eze 39:17 'Assemble and c together from all around H995
Eze 43:19 who c near to minister before me H7940
Eze 44:13 They are not to c near to serve me as H5602
Eze 44:13 me as priests or c near any of my holy H5602
Eze 44:15 are to c near to minister before me H7928
Eze 44:16 they alone are to c near my table to H7928
Eze 46: 8 gateway, and he is to c out the same way. H3655
Eze 46: 9 people of the land c before the LORD at the H995
Eze 48:19 city who farm it will c from all the tribes of NDT
Da 2:28 what will happen in days to c. A10022
Da 2:29 turned to things to c, A10201+10021+10180
Da 3: 2 officials to c to the dedication of A10085
Da 3:26 servants of the Most High God, c out! A10485
Da 3:26 come out! C here!" So Shadrach A10085
Da 7:24 are ten kings who will c from this A10624
Da 9:13 all this disaster has c on us, yet we have H995
Da 9:22 I have now c to give you insight and H3655
Da 9:23 went out, which I have c to tell you, for you H995
Da 9:26 of the ruler who will c will destroy the city H995
Da 9:26 The end will c like a flood: War will NDT
Da 10:12 and I have c in response to them. H995
Da 10:14 Now I have c to explain to you what will H995
Da 10:14 the vision concerns a time yet to c. H6388
Da 10:20 he said, "Do you know why I have c to you? H995
Da 10:20 when I go, the prince of Greece will c; H995
Da 11:15 king of the North will c and build up siege H995
Da 11:17 He will determine to c with the might of his H995
Da 11:27 an end will still c at the appointed time. NDT
Da 11:35 for it will still c at the appointed time. NDT
Da 11:45 Yet he will c to his end, and no one will H995
Hos 1:11 the people of Israel will c together; H7695+3481
Hos 1:11 one leader and will c up out of the land, H6590
Hos 3: 5 They will c trembling to the LORD and to H7064
Hos 4:14 without understanding will c to ruin! H4231
Hos 6: 1 "C, let us return to the LORD. He has torn H2143
Hos 6: 3 he will c to us like the winter rains H995
Hos 9: 4 it will not c into the temple of the LORD. H995
Hos 11: 9 I will not c against their cities H995
Hos 11:10 his children will c trembling from the west. H3006
Hos 11:11 They will c from Egypt, trembling like H4946
Hos 13:13 Pains as of a woman in childbirth c to him H995
Hos 13:13 have the sense to c out of the womb. H6641
Hos 13:15 An east wind from the LORD will c, blowing H995
Joel 1:13 C, spend the night in sackcloth, you who H995
Joel 1:15 it will c like destruction from the Almighty. H995
Joel 2: 2 nor ever will be in ages to c. H1887+2256+1887
Joel 3:11 C quickly, all you nations from every side H995
Joel 3:13 C, trample the grapes, for the winepress is H995
Am 4: 2 "The time will surely c when you will be H995
Am 6: 1 to whom the people of Israel c! H995
Jnh 1: 2 its wickedness has c up before me." H6590
Jnh 1: 7 said to each other, "C, let us cast lots to H2143
Jnh 1: 8 Where do you c from? What is H995
Jnh 1:12 fault that this great storm has c upon you." NDT
Mic 1:11 Those who live in Zaanan will not c out H3655
Mic 1:12 because disaster has c from the LORD H3718
Mic 3: 6 Therefore night will c over you, without NDT
Mic 3:11 No disaster will c upon us." H995
Mic 4: 2 Many nations will c and say, "Come, let H2143
Mic 4: 2 will come and say, "C, let us go up to the H2143
Mic 4: 8 kingship will c to Daughter Jerusalem." H995
Mic 5: 2 out of you will c for me one who will be H3655
Mic 6: 6 With what shall I c before the LORD and H7709
Mic 6: 6 Shall I c before him with burnt offerings H7709
Mic 7: 4 The day God visits you has c, the day your H995
Mic 7:11 The day for building your walls will c, the NDT
Mic 7:12 In that day people will c to you from H995
Mic 7:17 They will c trembling out of their dens H8074
Na 1: 9 an end; trouble will not c a second time. H7756
Na 1:11 has one c forth who plots evil against the H3655
Hab 1: 8 headlong; their horsemen c from afar. H995
Hab 1: 9 they all c intent on violence. Their hordes H995
Hab 2: 3 it will certainly c and will not delay. H995+995
Hab 2:19 who says to wood, 'C to life!' Or to lifeless H7810
Hab 3:16 day of calamity to c on the nation H6590
Zep 3: 7 all my punishments c upon her. H7212
Hag 1: 2 'The time has not yet c to rebuild the LORD's H995
Hag 2: 7 what is desired by all nations will c H995
Zec 1:21 the craftsmen have c to terrify them and H995
Zec 2: 6 "C! Come! Flee from the land of the north," H2098
Zec 2: 6 C! Flee from the land of the north, H2098
Zec 2: 7 "C, Zion! Escape, you who live in H2098
Zec 3: 8 who are men symbolic of things to c: H4603
Zec 6:15 who are far away will c and help to build H995
Zec 8:20 the inhabitants of many cities will yet c, H995
Zec 8:22 powerful nations will c to Jerusalem to H995
Zec 9: 1 of Hadrak and will c to rest on Damascus— NDT
Zec 10: 4 From Judah will c the cornerstone, from H3655
Zec 14: 5 Then the LORD my God will c, and all the H995
Zec 14:21 all who c to sacrifice will take some of H995
Mal 3: 1 Lord you are seeking will c to his temple; H995
Mal 3: 1 whom you desire, will c," says the LORD H995
Mal 3: 5 "So I will c to put you on trial. I will be H7928
Mal 4: 6 else I will c and strike the land with total H995
Mt 2: 2 when it rose and have c to worship him." G2262
Mt 2: 6 out of you will c a ruler who will G2002
Mt 3: 2 the kingdom of heaven has c near." G1581
Mt 3:14 be baptized by you, and do you c to me?" G2262
Mt 4:17 the kingdom of heaven has c near." G1581
Mt 4:19 "C, follow me," Jesus said, "and I will G1307
Mt 5:17 "Do not think that I have c to abolish the G2262
Mt 5:17 I have not c to abolish them but to fulfill G2262
Mt 5:24 to them; then c and offer your gift. G2262
Mt 6:10 your kingdom c, your will be done, on G2262
Mt 7:15 They c to you in sheep's clothing, but G2262
Mt 8: 7 said to him, "Shall I c and heal him?" G2262
Mt 8: 8 not deserve to have you c under my roof. G1656
Mt 8: 9 he goes; and that one, 'C,' and he comes. G2262
Mt 8:11 to you that many will c from the east and G2457
Mt 8:29 "Have you c here to torture us before the G2262
Mt 9:13 For I have not c to call the righteous, but G2262
Mt 9:15 The time will c when the bridegroom will G2262
Mt 9:18 But c and put your hand on her, and she G2262
Mt 10: 7 'The kingdom of heaven has c near.' G1581
Mt 10:34 not suppose that I have c to bring peace G2262
Mt 10:34 I did not c to bring peace G2262
Mt 10:35 For I have c to turn " 'a man against his G2262
Mt 11: 3 "Are you the one who is to c, or should G2262
Mt 11:14 to accept it, he is the Elijah who was to c. G2262
Mt 11:28 "C to me, all you who are weary and G1307
Mt 12:28 then the kingdom of God has c upon you. G5777
Mt 12:32 either in this age or in the age to c. G3516
Mt 13:27 Where then did the weeds c from?' G2400
Mt 13:32 so that the birds c and perch in its G2262
Mt 13:49 The angels will c and separate the wicked G2002
Mt 14:28 replied, "tell me to c to you on the water." G2262
Mt 14:29 "C," he said. Then Peter got down out of G2262
Mt 15:18 But the things that c out of a person's G1744
Mt 15:18 out of a person's mouth c from the heart, G2002
Mt 15:19 For out of the heart c evil thoughts G2002
Mt 16:27 of Man is going to c in his Father's glory G2262
Mt 17:10 of the law say that Elijah must c first?" G2262
Mt 17:12 tell you, Elijah has already c, and they did G2262
Mt 18: 7 Such things must c, but woe to the person G2262
Mt 18: 7 woe to the person through whom they c! G2262
Mt 19:14 "Let the little children c to me, and do not G2262
Mt 19:21 treasure in heaven. Then c, follow me." G1306
Mt 20:28 as the Son of Man did not c to be served, G2262
Mt 21:25 baptism—where did it c from? Was it from G1639
Mt 21:38 'This is the heir. C, let's kill him and take G1307
Mt 22: 3 invited to the banquet to tell them to c, G2813
Mt 22: 3 tell them to come, but they refused to c. G2262
Mt 22: 4 C to the wedding banquet G1307
Mt 22: 8 those I invited did not deserve to c. NDT
Mt 23:35 And so upon you will c all the righteous G2262
Mt 23:36 I tell you, all this will c on this generation. G2457
Mt 24: 5 For many will c in my name, claiming, 'I G2262
Mt 24: 6 must happen, but the end is still to c. G1639
Mt 24:14 to all nations, and then the end will c. G2457
Mt 24:32 its twigs get tender and its leaves c out, G1770
Mt 24:42 do not know on what day your Lord will c. G2262
Mt 24:44 the Son of Man will c at an hour when G2262
Mt 24:50 of that servant will c on a day when he G2457
Mt 25: 6 the bridegroom! C out to meet him!' G2002
Mt 25:21 C and share your master's happiness G1656
Mt 25:23 C and share your master's happiness G1656
Mt 25:34 on his right, 'C, you who are blessed G1307
Mt 26:45 the hour has c, and the Son of Man G1581
Mt 26:55 that you have c out with swords and clubs G2002
Mt 27:40 C down from the cross, if you are the Son G2849
Mt 27:42 Let him c down now from the cross, and G2849
Mt 27:64 his disciples may c and steal the body G2262
Mt 28: 6 C and see the place where he lay G1307
Mk 1:15 "The time has c," he said. "The kingdom G4444
Mk 1:15 "The kingdom of God has c near. Repent G1581
Mk 1:17 "C, follow me," Jesus said, "and I will G1307
Mk 1:24 of Nazareth? Have you c to destroy us? G2262
Mk 1:25 said Jesus sternly. "C out of him!" G2002
Mk 1:38 preach there also. That is why I have c." G2002
Mk 2: 1 the people heard that he had c home. G1639
Mk 2:17 I have not c to call the righteous, but G2262
Mk 2:20 But the time will c when the bridegroom G2262
Mk 3:26 is divided, he cannot stand; his end has c. G2400
Mk 4:19 other things c in and choke the word, G1660
Mk 4:29 the sickle to it, because the harvest has c." G4225
Mk 5: 8 had said to him, "C out of this man, you G2002
Mk 5:23 Please c and put your hands on her so G2262
Mk 6:31 "C with me by yourselves to a quiet place G1307
Mk 7: 1 of the law who had c from Jerusalem G2262
Mk 7: 4 When they c from the marketplace they do AIT
Mk 7:21 that evil thoughts c—sexual G1744
Mk 7:23 All these evils c from inside and defile a G1744
Mk 8: 3 some of them have c a long distance." G2457
Mk 9: 1 the kingdom of God has c with power." G2262
Mk 9:11 of the law say that Elijah must c first?" G2262
Mk 9:12 "To be sure, Elijah does c first, and G2262
Mk 9:13 I tell you, Elijah has c, and they have G2262
Mk 9:25 c out of him and never enter him again." G2002
Mk 9:29 "This kind can c out only by prayer." G2002
Mk 10:14 "Let the little children c to me, and do not G2262
Mk 10:21 treasure in heaven. Then c, follow me." G1306
Mk 10:30 in the age to c eternal life. G2262
Mk 10:45 the Son of Man did not c to be served, G2262
Mk 12: 7 C, let's kill him, and the inheritance will G1307
Mk 12: 9 He will c and kill those tenants and give G2262
Mk 13: 6 Many will c in my name, claiming, 'I am G2262
Mk 13: 7 must happen, but the end is still to c. G4037
Mk 13:28 its twigs get tender and its leaves c out, G1770
Mk 13:33 You do not know when that time will c. G1639
Mk 13:35 the owner of the house will c back— G2262
Mk 14:41 The hour has c. Look, the Son of G2262
Mk 14:48 "that you have c out with swords and G2002
Mk 15:30 c down from the cross and save yourself!" G2849
Mk 15:32 Let this Messiah, this king of Israel, c down G2849
Mk 15:41 other women who had c up with him to G5262
Lk 1:20 which will c true at their appointed time." G4444
Lk 1:35 "The Holy Spirit will c on you, and the G2088
Lk 1:43 the mother of my Lord should c to me? G2262
Lk 1:68 because he has c to his people and G2170
Lk 1:78 the rising sun will c to us from heaven G2170
Lk 3:16 one who is more powerful than I will c, G2262
Lk 4:34 of Nazareth? Have you c to destroy us? G2262
Lk 4:35 "C out of him!" Then the G2002
Lk 4:36 orders to impure spirits and they c out!" G2002
Lk 5: 7 in the other boat to c and help them, G2262
Lk 5:17 They had c from every village of G1639+2262
Lk 5:32 I have not c to call the righteous, but G2262
Lk 5:35 But the time will c when the bridegroom G2262
Lk 6:18 who had c to hear him and to be healed G2262
Lk 7: 3 asking him to c and heal his servant. G2262
Lk 7: 6 not deserve to have you c under my roof. G1656
Lk 7: 7 even consider myself worthy to c to you. G2262
Lk 7: 8 he goes; and that one, 'C,' and he comes. G2262
Lk 7:16 "God has c to help his people." G2170
Lk 7:19 "Are you the one who is to c, or should G2262
Lk 7:20 'Are you the one who is to c, or should we G2262
Lk 8: 2 from whom seven demons had c out; G2002
Lk 8:16 so that those who c in can see the light. G1660
Lk 8:29 the impure spirit to c out of the man. G2002
Lk 8:41 pleading with him to c to his house G1656
Lk 9: 8 the prophets of long ago had c back to life. G482
Lk 9:19 the prophets of long ago has c back to life." G482
Lk 10: 9 'The kingdom of God has c near to you. G1581
Lk 10:11 The kingdom of God has c near.' G1581
Lk 11: 2 hallowed be your name, your kingdom c. G2262
Lk 11: 6 a friend of mine on a journey has c to me G4134
Lk 11:20 then the kingdom of God has c upon you. G5777

Lk 11:33 so that those who c in may see the light. G1660
Lk 12:37 at the table and will c and wait on them. G4216
Lk 12:40 the Son of Man will c at an hour when G2262
Lk 12:46 of that servant will c on a day when he G2457
Lk 12:49 "I have c to bring fire on the earth, and G2262
Lk 13:14 So c and be healed on those days, not on G2262
Lk 13:25 'I don't know you or where you c from. G1639
Lk 13:27 'I don't know you or where you c from. G1639
Lk 13:29 People will c from east and west and north G2457
Lk 14: 9 invited both of you will c and say to you, G2262
Lk 14:17 had been invited, 'C, for everything is now G2262
Lk 14:20 'I just got married, so I can't c. G2262
Lk 14:23 country lanes and compel them to c in, G1656
Lk 15:27 'Your brother has c,' he replied, 'and your G2457
Lk 16:28 so that they will not also c to this place of G2262
Lk 17: 1 cause people to stumble are bound to c, G2262
Lk 17: 1 woe to anyone through whom they c. G2262
Lk 17: 4 seven times c back to you saying 'I G2188
Lk 17: 7 'C along now and sit down to eat'? G4216
Lk 17:20 when the kingdom of God would c, G2262
Lk 18: 5 that she won't eventually c and attack me! G2262
Lk 18:16 "Let the little children c to me, and do not G2262
Lk 18:22 treasure in heaven. Then c, follow me." G1306
Lk 18:30 this age, and in the age to c eternal life." G2262
Lk 19: 5 "Zacchaeus, c down immediately. G2849
Lk 19: 9 "Today salvation has c to this house G1181
Lk 19:13 money to work,' he said, 'until I c back. G2262
Lk 19:43 The days will c upon you when your G2457
Lk 20:16 He will c and kill those tenants and give G2262
Lk 20:35 taking part in the age to c and in the G1697S
Lk 21: 6 the time will c when not one stone will be G2262
Lk 21: 8 For many will c in my name, claiming, 'I G2262
Lk 21: 9 but the end will not c right away. NDT
Lk 21:35 For it will c on all those who live on the G2082
Lk 22:52 the elders, who had c for him, "Am I G4134
Lk 22:52 that you have c with swords and clubs? G2002
Lk 23: 5 in Galilee and has c all the way here." NDT
Lk 23:29 For the time will c when you will say G2262
Lk 23:42 remember me when you c into your G2262
Lk 23:55 women who had c with Jesus from G1639+5302
Jn 1:32 "I saw the Spirit c down from heaven as a G2849
Jn 1:33 see the Spirit c down and remain is the G2849
Jn 1:39 "C," he replied, "and you will see." So G2262
Jn 1:46 Can anything good c from there? G1639
Jn 1:46 Nathanael asked. "C and see," said Philip G2262
Jn 2: 4 Jesus replied. "My hour has not yet c." G2457
Jn 2: 9 He did not realize where it had c from G1639
Jn 3: 2 that you are a teacher who has c from G2262
Jn 3:19 Light has c into the world, but people G2262
Jn 3:20 and will not c into the light for fear that G2262
Jn 4:16 "Go, call your husband and c back." G2262
Jn 4:23 is coming and has now c when the true G1639
Jn 4:29 "C, see a man who told me everything I G1307
Jn 4:47 begged him to c and heal his son, G2849
Jn 4:49 "Sir, c down before my child dies. G2849
Jn 5:25 is coming and has now c when the dead G1639
Jn 5:29 and c out—those who have done what is G1744
Jn 5:40 you refuse to c to me to have life. G2262
Jn 5:43 I have c in my Father's name, and you do G2262
Jn 6:14 is the Prophet who is to c into the world." G2262
Jn 6:15 they intended to c and make him king by G2262
Jn 6:37 All those the Father gives me will c to me G2457
Jn 6:38 For I have c down from heaven not to do G2849
Jn 6:44 "No one can c to me unless the Father G2262
Jn 6:65 you that no one can c to me unless the G2262
Jn 6:69 We have c to believe and to know that you AIT
Jn 7: 8 because my time has not yet fully c." G4444
Jn 7:22 though actually it did not c from Moses G1639
Jn 7:30 on him, because his hour had not yet c. G2262
Jn 7:34 find me; and where I am, you cannot c." G2262
Jn 7:36 find me,' and 'Where I am, you cannot c'?" G2262
Jn 7:37 "Let anyone who is thirsty c to me and G2262
Jn 7:41 "How can the Messiah c from Galilee? G2262
Jn 7:42 say that the Messiah will c from David's G2262
Jn 7:52 that a prophet does not c out of Galilee." G1586
Jn 8:14 have no idea where I c from or where I G2262
Jn 8:20 because his hour had not yet c. G2262
Jn 8:21 Where I go, you cannot c." G2262
Jn 8:22 why he says, 'Where I go, you cannot c'?" G2262
Jn 8:42 love me, for I have c here from God. G2002
Jn 8:42 here from God. I have not c on my own G2262
Jn 9:39 "For judgment I have c into this world, so G2262
Jn 10: 8 All who have c before me are thieves and G2262
Jn 10: 9 They will c in and go out, and find G1656
Jn 10:10 destroy; I have c that they may have life G2262
Jn 11:19 many Jews had c to Martha and Mary G2262
Jn 11:27 the Son of God, who is to c into the world." G2262
Jn 11:33 the Jews who had c along with her also G5302
Jn 11:34 "C and see, Lord," they replied G2262
Jn 11:43 called in a loud voice, "Lazarus, c out!" G1306
Jn 11:45 many of the Jews who had c to visit Mary, G2262
Jn 11:48 then the Romans will c and take away G2262
Jn 12:12 the great crowd that had c for the festival G2262
Jn 12:23 "The hour has c for the Son of Man to be G2262
Jn 12:46 I have c into the world as a light, so that G2262
Jn 12:47 For I did not c to judge the world, but to G2262
Jn 13: 1 knew that the hour had c for him to leave G2262
Jn 13: 3 that he had c from God and was G2002
Jn 13:33 Where I am going, you cannot c. G2262
Jn 14: 3 I will c back and take you to be with me G2262
Jn 14:18 not leave you as orphans; I will c to you. G2262
Jn 14:23 and we will c to them and make our G2262
Jn 14:31 commanded me. "C now; let us leave. G1586
Jn 15:22 If I had not c and spoken to them, they G2262
Jn 16: 7 the Advocate will not c to you; but if I G2262
Jn 16:13 and he will tell you what is yet to c. G2262
Jn 16:21 a child has pain because her time has c; G2262
Jn 16:32 is coming and in fact has c when you will G2262
Jn 17: 1 "Father, the hour has c. Glorify your Son, G2262
Jn 17:10 And glory has c to me through them. G1519
Jn 18:20 the temple, where all the Jews c together. G5302
Jn 19: 9 "Where do you c from?" he asked G1639
Jn 21:12 Jesus said to them, "C and have breakfast." G1307
Ac 1:11 will c back in the same way you have G2262
Ac 2:31 Seeing what was to c, he spoke of the G4632
Ac 3:19 times of refreshing may c from the Lord, G2262
Ac 7: 7 afterward they will c out of that country G2002
Ac 7:34 groaning and have c down to set them G2849
Ac 7:34 set them free. Now c, I will send you back G1306
Ac 8:16 Holy Spirit had not yet c on any of them; G2158
Ac 8:31 he invited Philip to c up and sit with him. G326
Ac 9:12 man named Ananias c and place his G1656
Ac 9:14 And he has c here with authority from the NDT
Ac 9:21 And hasn't he c here to take them as G2262
Ac 9:38 to him and urged him, "Please c at once!" G1451
Ac 10: 4 gifts to the poor have c up as a memorial G326
Ac 10:21 one you're looking for. Why have you c?" G4205
Ac 10:22 "We have c from Cornelius the centurion. NDT
Ac 10:22 told him to ask you to c to his house so G3569
Ac 10:33 immediately, and it was good of you to c. G4134
Ac 10:45 believers who had c with Peter were G5302
Ac 11:15 on them as he had c on us at the beginning NDT
Ac 14:11 "The gods have c down to us in human G2849
Ac 16: 9 "C over to Macedonia and help us." G1329
Ac 16:15 she said, "c and stay at my house. G1656
Ac 16:18 Christ I command you to c out of her!" G2002
Ac 16:34 joy because he had c to believe in God— AIT
Ac 16:37 Let them c themselves and escort us out." G2262
Ac 17: 6 all over the world have now c here, G4205
Ac 18: 2 who had recently c from Italy with his wife G2262
Ac 18:21 promised, "I will c back if it is God's will." G366
Ac 19:13 Paul preaches, I command you to c out." G3991
Ac 20:29 savage wolves will c in among you and G1656
Ac 21:22 They will certainly hear that you have c, G2262
Ac 24:25 self-control and the judgment to c, Felix G3516
Ac 25: 5 Let some of your leaders c with me, and if G5160
Ac 25: 7 the Jews who had c down from Jerusalem G2849
Ac 28:21 of our people who have c from there has G4134
Ro 1:10 way may be opened for me to c to you. G2262
Ro 1:13 that I planned many times to c to you (but G2262
Ro 5:14 who is a pattern of the one to c. G3516
Ro 6:17 you have c to obey from your heart the AIT
Ro 11:11 salvation has c to the Gentiles to make NDT
Ro 11:25 the full number of the Gentiles has c in, G1656
Ro 11:26 "The deliverer will c from Zion; he will G2457
Ro 13:11 The hour has already c for you to wake up NDT
Ro 14:23 that does not c from faith is sin. G1666
Ro 15:29 I know that when I c to you, I will come in G2262
Ro 15:29 I will c in the full measure of the blessing G2262
Ro 15:32 so that I may c to you with joy, by God's G2262
Ro 16:26 all the Gentiles might c to the obedience AIT
1Co 2: 1 I did not c with eloquence or human G2262
1Co 2:14 the things that c from the Spirit of God but AIT
1Co 4:19 But I will c to you very soon, if the Lord is G2262
1Co 4:21 Shall I c to you with a rod of discipline, or G2262
1Co 4:21 shall I c in love and with a gentle spirit? NDT
1Co 7: 5 Then c together again so that Satan will G1639
1Co 10:11 whom the culmination of the ages has c. G2918
1Co 11: 8 For man did not c from woman, but G1639
1Co 11:18 I hear that when you c together as a G5302
1Co 11:20 when you c together, it G5302+2093+3836+899
1Co 11:31 we would not c under such judgment. G3212
1Co 11:34 And when I c I will give further directions G2262
1Co 14: 6 if I c to you and speak in tongues G2262
1Co 14:23 inquirers or unbelievers c in, will they G1656
1Co 14:26 When you c together, each of you has a G5302
1Co 15:24 Then the end will c, when he hands over the NDT
1Co 15:34 C back to your senses as you ought, and G1729
1Co 15:35 With what kind of body will they c?" G2262
1Co 15:36 What you sow does not c to life unless it G2443
1Co 15:46 The spiritual did not c first, but the natural NDT
1Co 15:54 then the saying that is written will c true: G1181
1Co 16: 2 so that when I c no collections will have G2262
1Co 16: 5 Macedonia, I will c to you—for I will G2262
1Co 16:22 let that person be cursed! C, Lord! G3448
2Co 1:14 you will c to understand fully that you can AIT
2Co 1:16 to Macedonia and to c back to you from G2262
2Co 1:22 as a deposit, guaranteeing what is to c. G775
2Co 5: 5 as a deposit, guaranteeing what is to c. G775
2Co 5:17 if anyone is in Christ, the new creation has c: NDT
2Co 6:17 "C out from them and be separate G2002
2Co 9: 4 if any Macedonians c with me and find G2262
2Co 10: 2 I beg you that when I c I may not have to G4205
2Co 10:14 would be the case if we had not c to you, G5657
2Co 12:20 I am afraid that when I c I may not find G2262
2Co 12:21 I am afraid that when I c again my God G2262
2Co 13:10 that when I c I may not have to be harsh G4205
Gal 3:14 given to Abraham might c to the Gentiles G1181
Gal 3:19 Seed to whom the promise referred had c. G2262
Gal 3:21 would certainly have c by the law. G1639
Gal 3:23 until the faith that was to c would be G3516
Gal 3:25 Now that this faith has c, we are no longer G2262
Gal 4: 4 But when the set time had fully c, God G2262
Gal 5: 8 does not c from the one who calls G1666
Eph 1:21 the present age but also in the one to c. G3516
Eph 4:29 Do not let any unwholesome talk c out of G1744
Php 1:27 whether I c and see you or only hear G2262
Php 2:24 in the Lord that I myself will c soon. G2262
Col 1: 6 that has c to you. In the same way, the G4205
Col 2:17 are a shadow of the things that were to c; G3516
1Th 2:16 The wrath of God has c upon them at last. G5777
1Th 2:18 For we wanted to c to you—certainly I G2262
1Th 3: 6 But Timothy has just now c to us from you G2262
1Th 3:11 Lord Jesus clear the way for us to c to you. AIT
1Th 4:16 the Lord himself will c down from heaven, G2849
1Th 5: 2 the day of the Lord will c like a thief in the G2262
1Th 5: 3 destruction will c on them suddenly, as G2392
2Th 2: 2 that the day of the Lord has already c. G1931
2Th 2: 3 that day will not c until the rebellion NDT
1Ti 2: 4 to be saved and to c to a knowledge of G2262
1Ti 3:14 Although I hope to c to you soon, I am G2262
1Ti 4: 2 Such teachings c through hypocritical liars AIT
1Ti 4: 8 both the present life and the life to c. G3516
1Ti 4:13 Until I c, devote yourself to the public G2262
2Ti 2:26 and that they will c to their senses and G392
2Ti 3: 7 never able to c to a knowledge of the G2262
2Ti 4: 3 For the time will c when people will not G1639
2Ti 4: 9 Do your best to c to me quickly, G2262
2Ti 4:13 When you c, bring the cloak that I left with G2262
Titus 3:12 do your best to c to me at Nicopolis G2262
Heb 2: 5 that he has subjected the world to c, G3516
Heb 3:14 We have c to share in Christ, if indeed we G1181
Heb 7:11 was there still need for another priest to c, G482
Heb 7:25 those who c to God through him G4665
Heb 10: 7 me in the scroll—I have c to do your will G2457
Heb 10: 9 "Here I am, I have c to do your will." G2457
Heb 10:37 he who is coming will c and will not delay G2457
Heb 12:18 You have not c to a mountain that can be G4665
Heb 12:22 But you have c to Mount Zion, to the city G4665
Heb 12:22 You have c to thousands upon thousands of NDT
Heb 12:23 You have c to God, the Judge of all, to the NDT
Heb 13:14 we are looking for the city that is to c. G3516
Heb 13:23 If he arrives soon, I will c with him to see you. AIT
Jas 3:10 Out of the same mouth c praise and G2002
Jas 3:15 does not c down from heaven but is G2982
Jas 4: 1 Don't they c from your desires that battle AIT
Jas 4: 8 C near to God and he will come near to G1581
Jas 4: 8 near to God and he will c near to you. G1581
1Pe 1: 7 These have c so that the proven NDT
1Pe 1:10 who spoke of the grace that was to c to you AIT
1Pe 2: 4 As you c to him, the living Stone G4665
1Pe 3: 3 Your beauty should not c from outward G1639
1Pe 4:12 the fiery ordeal that has c on you to test G1181
2Pe 3: 3 that in the last days scoffers will c, G2262
2Pe 3: 9 to perish, but everyone to c to repentance. G6003
2Pe 3:10 But the day of the Lord will c like a thief G2457
1Jn 2: 3 We know that we have c to know him if we AIT
1Jn 2:18 even now many antichrists have c. G1181
1Jn 4: 2 that Jesus Christ has c in the G2262
1Jn 5: 6 He did not c by water only, but by water NDT
1Jn 5:20 the Son of God has c and has given us G2457
3Jn 10 So when I c, I will call attention to what he G2262
Rev 1: 4 who was, and who is to c, and from the G2262
Rev 1: 8 who was, and who is to c, the Almighty." G2262
Rev 2: 5 I will c to you and remove your lampstand G2262
Rev 2:16 I will soon c to you and will fight against G2262
Rev 2:25 to hold on to what you have until I c. G2457
Rev 3: 3 do not wake up, I will c like a thief, and G2457
Rev 3: 3 will not know at what time I will c to you. G2457
Rev 3: 9 I will make them c and fall down at your G2457
Rev 3:10 that is going to c on the whole world to G2262
Rev 3:20 door, I will c in and eat with that person G1656
Rev 4: 1 a trumpet said, "C up here, and I will show G326
Rev 4: 8 Almighty,' who was, and is, and is to c." G2262
Rev 6: 1 creatures say in a voice like thunder, "C!" G2262
Rev 6: 3 I heard the second living creature say, "C!" G2262
Rev 6: 5 I heard the third living creature say, "C!" G2262
Rev 6: 7 voice of the fourth living creature say, "C!" G2262
Rev 6:17 For the great day of their wrath has c, and G2262
Rev 7:13 who are they, and where did they c from?" G2262
Rev 7:14 "These are they who have c out of the G2262
Rev 9:12 woe is past; two other woes are yet to c. G2262
Rev 11:12 from heaven saying to them, "C up here." G326
Rev 11:18 nations were angry, and your wrath has c. G2262
Rev 11:18 The time has c for judging the dead, and NDT
Rev 12:10 "Now have c the salvation and the power G1181
Rev 13:13 causing fire to c down from heaven to the G2849
Rev 14: 7 because the hour of his judgment has c. G2262
Rev 14:15 because the time to reap has c, for the G2262
Rev 15: 4 All nations will c and worship before you G2457
Rev 16:15 I c like a thief! Blessed is the one G2262
Rev 17: 1 said to me, "C, I will show you the G1306
Rev 17: 8 yet will c up out of the Abyss and go to G326
Rev 17: 8 it once was, now is not, and yet will c. G4205
Rev 17:10 the other has not yet c; but when he G2262
Rev 17:10 but when he does c, he must G2262
Rev 18: 4 "'C out of her, my people,' so that you G2002
Rev 18:10 In one hour your doom has c!' G2262
Rev 19: 7 For the wedding of the Lamb has c, and G2262
Rev 19:17 flying in midair, "C, gather together for G1307
Rev 20: 5 rest of the dead did not c to life until the G2409
Rev 21: 9 said to me, "C, I will show you the G1306
Rev 22:17 the bride say, "C!" And let the one G2262
Rev 22:17 one who hears say, "C!" Let the one who G2262
Rev 22:17 Let the one who is thirsty c; and let the G2262
Rev 22:20 I am coming soon." Amen. C, Lord Jesus. G2262

C

COMES (285) [COME]

Ge 24:43 If a young woman c out to draw water H3655
Ge 29: 6 "and here c his daughter Rachel with the H995
Ge 32: 8 thought, "If Esau c and attacks one group H995
Ge 37:19 "Here c that dreamer!" they said to each H995
Ge 37:20 Then we'll see what c of his dreams." H2118
Ge 42:15 place unless your youngest brother c here. H995
Ge 42:38 If harm c to him on the journey you are H7925
Ge 44:23 your youngest brother c down with you, H3718
Ge 44:29 this one from me too and harm c to him, H7936
Ge 47:24 But when the crop c in, give a fifth of it to H9311
Ex 21: 3 If he c alone, he is to go free alone; but if H995
Ex 21: 3 if he has a wife when he c, she is to go NDT
Ex 28:35 Place before the LORD and when he c out, H3655
Ex 29:30 him as priest and c to the tent of meeting H995
Ex 32:34 when the time c for me to punish, NDT
Lev 14:48 "But if the priest c to examine it and H995+995
Lev 16:17 in the Most Holy Place until he c out, H3655
Lev 22: 3 unclean and yet c near the sacred H7928
Lev 25:22 it until the harvest of the ninth year c in. H995
Nu 6: 4 eat anything that c from the grapevine, H6913
Nu 11:20 until it c out of your nostrils and you loathe H3655
Nu 17:13 Anyone who even c near the H7929+7929
Nu 18: 7 Anyone else who c near the sanctuary is H7929
Nu 35:19 when the avenger c upon the murderer H7003
Nu 36: 4 the Year of Jubilee for the Israelites c, H2118
Dt 2: 8 which c up from Elath and Ezion Geber NDT
Dt 8: 3 on every word that c from the mouth H4604
Dt 18: 6 c in all earnestness to the place the H995
Dt 25:11 wife of one of them c to rescue her H7928
Dt 31:11 when all Israel c to appear before the LORD H995
Dt 32:32 Their vine c from the vine of Sodom and NDT
Jos 20: 5 If the avenger of blood c in pursuit, the H8103
Jdg 4:20 "If someone c by and asks you, 'Is anyone H995
Jdg 11:31 whatever c out of the door of my house to H3655
Jdg 11:39 From this c the Israelite tradition H2118
Jdg 13:14 eat anything that c from the grapevine, H3655
Jdg 13:17 we may honor you when your word c true?" H995
Jdg 16: 9 of string snaps when it c close to a flame. H8193
1Sa 8:18 When that day c, you will cry out for relief NDT
1Sa 9: 6 everything he says c true. H995+995
1Sa 9:13 The people will not begin eating until he c, H995
1Sa 11: 3 if no one c to rescue us, we will NDT
1Sa 14:24 be anyone who eats food before evening c, NDT
1Sa 16:16 when the evil spirit from God c on you, H2118
1Sa 17:25 keeps coming out? He c out to defy Israel H6590
2Sa 13: 5 "When your father c to see you, say to him H995
2Sa 15:28 word c from you to inform me H995
2Sa 18:27 the king said. "He c with good news." H995
1Ki 8:37 "When famine or plague c to the land, or H2118
2Ki 4: 9 that this man who often c our way is a H6296
2Ki 4:10 he can stay there whenever he c to us." H995
2Ki 6:32 when the messenger c, shut the door and H995
1Ch 16:33 before the LORD, for he c to judge the earth. H995
1Ch 29:14 Everything c from you, and we have given NDT
1Ch 29:14 have given you only what c from your hand. NDT
1Ch 29:16 your Holy Name c from your hand, NDT
2Ch 6:28 "When famine or plague c to the land, or H2118
2Ch 13: 9 Whoever c to consecrate himself with a H995
2Ch 19:10 In every case that c before you from your H995
2Ch 20: 9 'If calamity c upon us, whether the sword of H995
Job 4: 5 But now trouble c to you, and you are H995
Job 5:14 Darkness c upon them in the daytime; at H7008
Job 5:21 need not fear when destruction c. H995
Job 11:10 "If he c along and confines you in prison H2736
Job 27: 9 to their cry when distress c upon them? H995
Job 28: 5 from which food c, is transformed below H3655
Job 28: 6 lapis lazuli c from its rocks, and its dust NDT
Job 37: 2 to the rumbling that c from his mouth. H3655
Job 37: 4 After that c the sound of his roar; he H8613
Job 37: 9 The tempest c out from its chamber, the H995
Job 37:22 Out of the north he c in golden splendor H910
Job 37:22 splendor; God c in awesome majesty. NDT
Job 38:29 From whose womb c the ice? Who gives H3655
Ps 3: 8 From the LORD c deliverance. May your NDT
Ps 7:16 their violence c down on their own heads. H3718
Ps 22:25 From you c the theme of my praise in the NDT
Ps 30: 5 the night, but rejoicing c in the morning. NDT
Ps 37:39 salvation of the righteous c from the LORD; NDT
Ps 41: 6 When one of them c to see me, he speaks H995
Ps 50: 3 Our God c and will not be silent; a fire H995
Ps 62: 1 finds rest in God; my salvation c from him. NDT
Ps 62: 5 find rest in God; my hope c from him. NDT
Ps 68:20 the Sovereign LORD c escape from death. NDT
Ps 73: 7 From their callous hearts c iniquity; their H3655
Ps 88:13 in the morning my prayer c before you. H7709
Ps 96:13 the LORD, for he c, he comes to judge H995
Ps 96:13 for he comes, he c to judge the earth. H995
Ps 98: 9 before the LORD, for he c to judge the earth. H995
Ps 118:26 Blessed is he who c in the name of the H995
Ps 121: 2 My help c from the LORD, the Maker of NDT
Pr 10: 8 commands, but a chattering fool c to ruin. H4231
Pr 10:10 and a chattering fool c to ruin. H4231
Pr 10:31 From the mouth of the righteous c the fruit of H5649
Pr 11: 2 When pride c, then comes disgrace, but H995
Pr 11: 2 pride comes, then c disgrace, but with H995
Pr 11: 2 comes disgrace, but with humility c wisdom. NDT
Pr 11: 7 all the promise of their power c to nothing. H6
Pr 11:24 another withholds unduly, but c to poverty. NDT
Pr 11:27 but evil c to one who searches for it. H995
Pr 13:18 discipline c to poverty and shame, NDT
Pr 14: 6 knowledge c easily to the discerning. H7837
Pr 14:32 When calamity c, the wicked are brought NDT
Pr 15:33 fear the LORD, and humility c before honor. NDT
Pr 16: 1 from the LORD c the proper answer of the NDT
Pr 18: 3 When wickedness c, so does contempt H995
Pr 18: 3 does contempt, and with shame c reproach. NDT
Pr 18:12 is haughty, but humility c before honor. NDT
Pr 18:17 someone c forward and H995
Pr 18:24 who has unreliable friends soon c to ruin, H8318
Pr 21:16 path of prudence c to rest in the company H5663
Ecc 1:18 For with much wisdom c much sorrow; the NDT
Ecc 2:18 leave them to the one who c after me. H2118
Ecc 5: 3 A dream c when there are many cares, and H995
Ecc 5:15 Everyone c naked from their mother's H3655
Ecc 5:15 and as everyone c, so they depart. H995
Ecc 5:16 As everyone c, so they depart, and what do H995
Ecc 6: 4 It c without meaning, it departs in darkness H995
SS 2: 8 Here he c, leaping across the mountains H995
Isa 10: 3 of reckoning, when disaster c from afar? H995
Isa 14: 8 been laid low, no one c to cut us down." H6590
Isa 14:31 A cloud of smoke c from the north, and H995
Isa 21: 1 the southland, an invader c from the desert H995
Isa 21: 9 here c a man in a chariot with a team of H995
Isa 23: 5 When word c to Egypt, they will be in NDT
Isa 28:19 As often as it c it will carry you away H6296
Isa 28:29 All this also c from the LORD Almighty H3655
Isa 30:23 the food that c from the land will be H9311
Isa 30:27 the Name of the LORD c from afar, with H995
Isa 34: 1 the world, and all that c out of it! H7368
Isa 40:10 the Sovereign LORD c with power, and he H995
Isa 41:25 from the north, and he c—one from the H910
Isa 62:11 to Daughter Zion, 'See, your Savior c! See, H995
Jer 4:12 a wind too strong for that c from me. H995
Jer 10:15 when their judgment c, they will perish. NDT
Jer 17: 6 they will not see prosperity when it c. H995
Jer 17: 8 It does not fear when heat c; its leaves are H995
Jer 27: 7 his grandson until the time for his land c; H995
Jer 28: 9 by the LORD only if his prediction c true." H995
Jer 51:18 when their judgment c, they will perish. NDT
Jer 51:46 the land; one rumor c this year, another the H995
Jer 51:54 "The sound of a cry c from Babylon, the NDT
La 1: 4 no one c to her appointed festivals. H995
Eze 7: 5 Unheard-of disaster! See, it c! H995
Eze 7: 6 It has roused itself against you. See, it c! H995
Eze 7:10 See, it c! Doom has burst H995
Eze 7:25 When terror c, they will seek peace in vain. H995
Eze 12:22 days go by and every vision c to nothing'? H6
Eze 24: 6 out piece by piece in whatever order it c. NDT
Eze 33: 4 the sword c and takes their life, H995
Eze 33: 6 the sword c and takes someone's H995
Eze 33:33 "When all this c true—and it surely will H995
Da 9:25 the ruler, c, there will be seven NDT
Hos 10:12 until he c and showers his righteousness H995
Hos 14: 8 juniper; your fruitfulness c from me." H5162
Joel 2: 2 the mountains a large and mighty army c, NDT
Am 3: 6 When disaster c to a city, has not the LORD H2118
Am 6:10 And if the relative who c to carry the bodies NDT
Jnh 2: 9 I will say, 'Salvation c from the LORD.'" NDT
Mic 1: 3 he c down and treads on the heights of H3718
Mic 2:11 If a liar and deceiver c and says, 'I will H2143
Zep 2: 2 before the LORD's fierce anger c upon you H995
Zep 2: 2 the day of the LORD's wrath c upon you. H995
Zec 9: 9 your king c to you, righteous and H995
Zec 14: 7 When evening c, there will be light H2118
Mal 4: 5 that great and dreadful day of the LORD c. H995
Mt 3:11 But after me c one who is more powerful G2262
Mt 4: 4 on every word that c from the mouth G1744
Mt 5:37 anything beyond this c from the evil one. G1639
Mt 8: 9 he goes; and that one, 'Come,' and he c. G2262
Mt 10:23 towns of Israel before the Son of Man c. G2262
Mt 12:43 "When an impure spirit c out of a person G2002
Mt 13:19 the evil one c and snatches away what G2262
Mt 13:21 When trouble or persecution c because of G1181
Mt 15:11 but what c out of their mouth, that G1744
Mt 16: 2 He replied, "When evening c, you say, 'It G1181
Mt 17:11 Elijah c and will restore all things. G2262
Mt 21: 5 your king c to you, gentle and riding G2262
Mt 21: 9 "Blessed is he who c in the name of the G2262
Mt 21:40 when the owner of the vineyard c, what G2262
Mt 23:39 'Blessed is he who c in the name of the G2262
Mt 24:27 For as lightning that c from the east is G2002
Mt 25:31 "When the Son of Man c in his glory, and G2262
Mt 26:46 Let us go! Here c my betrayer!" G1581
Mt 27:49 Let's see if Elijah c to save him." G2262
Mk 1: 7 "After me c the one more powerful than I G2262
Mk 4:15 Satan c and takes away the word that was G2262
Mk 4:17 persecution c because of the word, G1181
Mk 7:15 it is what c out of a person that defiles G1744
Mk 7:20 "What c out of a person is what defiles G1744
Mk 8:38 of them when he c in his Father's G2262
Mk 11: 9 "Blessed is he who c in the name of the G2262
Mk 13:36 If he c suddenly, do not let him find you G2262
Mk 14:42 Let us go! Here c my betrayer!" G1581
Mk 15:36 Let's see if Elijah c to take him down," G2262
Lk 6:47 As for everyone who c to me and hears my G2262
Lk 7: 8 he goes; and that one, 'Come,' and he c. G2262
Lk 8:12 then the devil c and takes away the G2262
Lk 9:26 of them when he c in his glory and in G2262
Lk 11:24 "When an impure spirit c out of a person G2002
Lk 12:33 where no thief c near and no moth G1581
Lk 12:36 so that when he c and knocks they can G2262
Lk 12:37 master finds them watching when he c. G2262
Lk 12:38 even if he c in the middle of the night G2262
Lk 13:35 'Blessed is he who c in the name of the G2262
Lk 14:10 so that when your host c, he will say to G2262
Lk 14:26 "If anyone c to me and does not hate G2262
Lk 15:30 your property with prostitutes c home, G2262
Lk 17: 7 to the servant when he c in from the field, G1656
Lk 18: 8 However, when the Son of Man c, will he G2262
Lk 19:38 is the king who c in the name of the Lord!" G2262
Lk 22:18 of the vine until the kingdom of God c." G2262
Jn 1:15 'He who c after me has surpassed me G2262
Jn 1:27 He is the one who c after me, the straps of G2262
Jn 1:30 'A man who c after me has surpassed me G2262
Jn 3: 8 cannot tell where it c from or where it is G2262
Jn 3:21 whoever lives by the truth c into the light, G2262
Jn 3:31 The one who c from above is above all G2262
Jn 3:31 The one who c from heaven is above all G2262
Jn 4:25 When he c, he will explain everything to G2262
Jn 5:43 if someone else c in his own name G2262
Jn 5:44 not seek the glory that c from the only God? AIT
Jn 6:33 is the bread that c down from heaven G2849
Jn 6:35 Whoever c to me will never go hungry G2262
Jn 6:37 whoever c to me I will never drive G2262
Jn 6:45 the Father and learned from him c to me. G2262
Jn 6:50 is the bread that c down from heaven, G2849
Jn 7:16 It c from the one who sent me. NDT
Jn 7:17 my teaching c from God or whether G1639
Jn 7:27 when the Messiah c, no one will know G2262
Jn 7:31 "When the Messiah c, will he perform G2262
Jn 9:29 we don't even know where he c from." G1639
Jn 9:30 You don't know where he c from, yet he G1639
Jn 10:10 The thief c only to steal and kill and G2262
Jn 12:13 "Blessed is he who c in the name of the G2262
Jn 14: 6 No one c to the Father except through me. G2262
Jn 14:31 he c so that the world may learn that I NDT
Jn 15:26 "When the Advocate c, whom I will send G2262
Jn 16: 4 that when their time c you will remember G2262
Jn 16: 8 When he c, he will prove the world to be G2262
Jn 16:13 the Spirit of truth, c, he will guide you into G2262
Jn 17: 7 everything you have given me c from you. G1639
Ac 1: 8 power when the Holy Spirit c on you; G2088
Ac 3:16 the faith that c through him that has AIT
Ac 3:21 him until the time c for God to restore NDT
Ac 24:22 "When Lysias the commander c," he said G2849
Ro 1: 5 the obedience that c from faith for his AIT
Ro 4:13 through the righteousness that c by faith. AIT
Ro 4:16 the promise c by faith, so that it may AIT
Ro 10:17 faith c from hearing the message G1666
Ro 16:26 come to the obedience that c from faith— AIT
1Co 4: 5 the appointed time; wait until the Lord c. G2262
1Co 11:12 But everything c from God. G1666
1Co 11:26 you proclaim the Lord's death until he c. G2262
1Co 13:10 when completeness c, what is in part G2262
1Co 14:23 church c together and G5302+2093+3836+899
1Co 14:24 an inquirer c in while everyone is G1656
1Co 14:30 And if a revelation c to someone who is G636
1Co 15:21 of the dead c also through a man. NDT
1Co 15:23 when he c, those who belong to G4242
1Co 16:10 When Timothy c, see to it that he has G2262
2Co 3: 5 ourselves, but our competence c from God. AIT
2Co 3:18 which c from the Lord, who is the Spirit AIT
2Co 11: 4 For if someone c to you and preaches a G2262
Eph 5: 6 things God's wrath c on those who are G2262
Eph 6:13 so that when the day of evil c, you may be AIT
Eph 6:15 readiness that c from the gospel of peace. AIT
Php 1:11 of righteousness that c through Jesus Christ— AIT
Php 3: 9 righteousness of my own that c from the law, AIT
Php 3: 9 righteousness that c from God on the basis of AIT
Col 4:10 about him; if he c to you, welcome him.) G2262
1Th 2:19 the presence of our Lord Jesus when he c? G4242
1Th 3:13 when our Lord Jesus c with all his holy G4242
2Th 1:10 on the day he c to be glorified in his holy G2262
1Ti 1: 5 which c from a pure heart and a good AIT
Heb 11: 6 because anyone who c to him must G4665
Jas 2: 2 Suppose a man c into your meeting G1656
Jas 2: 2 a poor man in filthy old clothes also c in. G1656
Jas 3:13 done in the humility that c from wisdom. AIT
Jas 3:17 But the wisdom that c from heaven is first of NDT
1Jn 2:16 c not from the Father but from the world. G1639
1Jn 2:21 it and because no lie c from the truth. G1639
1Jn 4: 7 us love one another, for love c from God. G1639
2Jn 10 If anyone c to you and does not bring this G2262
Rev 11: 5 fire c from their mouths and devours their G1744
Rev 11: 7 the beast that c up from the Abyss will G326

COMFORT (46) [COMFORTED, COMFORTER, COMFORTERS, COMFORTING, COMFORTS]

Ge 5:29 "He will c us in the labor and painful toil H5714
Ge 37:35 All his sons and daughters came to c him H5714
1Ch 7:22 and his relatives came to c him. H5714
Job 2:11 to go and sympathize with him and c him. H5714
Job 7:13 I think my bed will c me and my couch H5714
Job 16: 5 c from my lips would bring you relief. H5764
Job 36:16 to the c of your table laden with choice H5739
Ps 23: 4 your rod and your staff, they c me. H5714
Ps 71:21 increase my honor and c me once more. H5714
Ps 119:50 My c in my suffering is this: Your promise H5717
Ps 119:52 your ancient laws, and I find c in them. H5714
Ps 119:76 May your unfailing love be my c H5714
Ps 119:82 your promise; I say, "When will you c me?" H5714
Isa 40: 1 C, comfort my people, says your God. H5714
Isa 40: 1 Comfort, c my people, says your God. H5714
Isa 51: 3 The LORD will surely c Zion and will look H5714

Isa 51:19 have come upon you—who can c you?— H5653
Isa 57:18 them and restore c to Israel's mourners, H5719
Isa 61: 2 of our God, to c all who mourn, H5714
Isa 66:13 her child, so will I c you; and you will be H5714
Jer 16: 7 will offer food to c those who mourn for H5714
Jer 31:13 I will give them c and joy instead of H5714
La 1: 2 all her lovers there is no one to c her. H5714
La 1: 9 was astounding; there was none to c her. H5714
La 1:16 No one is near to c me, no one to restore H5714
La 1:17 her hands, but there is no one to c her. H5714
La 1:21 my groaning, but there is no one to c me. H5714
La 2:13 I liken you, that I may c you, Virgin H5714
Eze 16:54 of all you have done in giving them c. H5714
Na 3: 7 Where can I find anyone to c you?" H5714
Zec 1:17 the LORD will again c Zion and choose H5714
Zec 10: 2 dreams that are false, they give c in vain. H5714
Lk 6:24 for you have already received your c. G4155
Jn 11:19 Martha and Mary to c them in the loss of G4170
1Co 14: 3 their strengthening, encouraging and c. G4171
2Co 1: 3 of compassion and the God of all c, G4155
2Co 1: 4 so that we can c those in any trouble with G4151
2Co 1: 4 trouble with the c we ourselves receive G4155
2Co 1: 5 so also our c abounds through Christ. G4155
2Co 1: 6 it is for your c and salvation; if we are G4155
2Co 1: 6 it is for your c, which produces in you G4155
2Co 1: 7 our sufferings, so also you share in our c. G4155
2Co 2: 7 you ought to forgive and c him, so that he G4151
2Co 7: 7 also by the c you had given him. G4155
Php 2: 1 with Christ, if any c from his love, if any G4172
Col 4:11 and they have proved a c to me. G4219

COMFORTED (17) [COMFORT]

Ge 24:67 Isaac was c after his mother's death. H5714
Ge 37:35 to comfort him, but he refused to be c. H5714
2Sa 12:24 Then David c his wife Bathsheba, and he H5714
Job 42:11 They c and consoled him over all the H5653
Ps 77: 2 out untiring hands, and I would not be c. H5714
Ps 86:17 you, LORD, have helped me and c me. H5714
Isa 12: 1 has turned away and you have c me. H5714
Isa 52: 9 the LORD has c his people, he has H5714
Isa 54:11 lashed by storms and not c, I will rebuild H5714
Isa 66:13 and you will be c over Jerusalem. H5714
Jer 31:15 her children and refusing to be c, H5714
Mt 2:18 her children and refusing to be c, G4151
Mt 5: 4 are those who mourn, for they will be c. G4151
Lk 16:25 now he is c here and you are in agony G4151
Ac 20:12 man home alive and were greatly c. G4151
2Co 1: 6 salvation; if we are c, it is for your G4151
2Co 7: 6 the downcast, c us by the coming of Titus, G4151

COMFORTER (KJV) ADVOCATE, COMFORT

COMFORTER (3) [COMFORT]

Ecc 4: 1 they have no c; power was on the H5714
Ecc 4: 1 of their oppressors—and they have no c. H5714
Jer 8:18 You who are my C in sorrow, my heart is H4443

COMFORTERS (2) [COMFORT]

Job 16: 2 like these; you are miserable c, all of you! H5714
Ps 69:20 there was none, for c, but I found none. H5714

COMFORTING (4) [COMFORT]

Isa 66:11 nurse and be satisfied at her c breasts; H9488
Zec 1:13 LORD spoke kind and c words to the angel H5719
Jn 11:31 Mary in the house, c her, noticed how G4170
1Th 2:12 c and urging you to live lives worthy of G4170

COMFORTS (6) [COMFORT]

Job 29:25 his troops; I was like one who c mourners. H5714
Isa 49:13 For the LORD c his people and will have H5714
Isa 51:12 even I, am he who c you. Who are you H5714
Isa 66:13 As a mother c her child, so will I comfort H5714
2Co 1: 4 who c us in all our troubles, so that we can G4151
2Co 7: 6 But God, who c the downcast, comforted G4151

COMING (249) [COME]

Ge 7:17 For forty days the flood kept c on the earth, H2118
Ge 19:15 With the c of dawn, the angels urged Lot H6590
Ge 24:13 the townspeople are c out to draw water. H3655
Ge 24:65 is that man in the field c to meet us?" H2143
Ge 32: 6 and now he is c to meet you, and H2143
Ge 32:18 sent to my lord Esau, and he is c behind us. NDT
Ge 32:20 'Your servant Jacob is c behind us. NDT
Ge 33: 1 was Esau, c with his four hundred men H995
Ge 37:25 a caravan of Ishmaelites c from Gilead. H995
Ge 41:29 of great abundance are c throughout the H995
Ge 41:35 good years that are c and store up the H995
Ex 14:20 c between the armies of Egypt and Israel H995
Ex 18: 6 am c to you with your wife and her two H995
Ex 32: 1 was so long in c down from the mountain, H3718
Nu 12:12 a stillborn infant c from its mother's womb H3655
Nu 21: 1 heard that Israel was c along the road to H995
Nu 22:16 not let anything keep you from c to me, H2143
Nu 22:36 When Balak heard that Balaam was c, he H995
Nu 33:40 of Canaan, heard that the Israelites were c. H995
Dt 2:23 the Caphtorites c out from Caphtor H3655
Jos 18:12 c out at the wilderness of Beth Aven. H2118
Jdg 1:24 the spies saw a man c out of the city and H3655
Jdg 5:28 cried out, 'Why is his chariot so long in c? H995
Jdg 9:36 people are c down from the tops of the H3718
Jdg 9:37 people are c down from the central hill H3718
Jdg 9:37 a company is c from the direction of H995
Jdg 9:43 When he saw the people c out of the city H3655
Ru 4:11 make the woman who is c into your home H995
1Sa 2:31 The time is c when I will cut short your H995
1Sa 9:11 some young women c out to draw water, H3655
1Sa 9:14 c toward them on his way up to the high H3655
1Sa 10: 5 of prophets c down from the high place H3718
1Sa 17:25 "Do you see how this man keeps c out? H6590
1Sa 17:41 front of him, kept c closer to David. H2143+2143
1Sa 25:11 give it to men c from who knows where?" NDT
1Sa 28:13 see a ghostly figure c up out of the earth." H6590
1Sa 28:14 "An old man wearing a robe is c up," H6590
2Sa 13:34 west of him, c down the side of the hill. H2143
2Sa 19:41 all the men of Israel were c to the king H995
2Sa 24:20 the king and his officials c toward him, H6296
1Ki 14: 5 "Jeroboam's wife is c to ask you about her H995
2Ki 4: 1 now his creditor is c to take my two boys H995
2Ki 9:17 he called out, "I see some troops c. NDT
2Ki 9:18 has reached them, but he isn't c back." H8740
2Ki 9:20 reached them, but he isn't c back either. H8740
2Ch 7: 3 saw the fire c down and the glory of the H3718
2Ch 20: 2 "A vast army is c against you from Edom H995
2Ch 20:11 are repaying us by c to drive us out of the H995
Ne 6:10 because men are c to kill you—by H995
Ne 6:10 to kill you—by night they are c to kill you." H995
Ne 6:17 replies from Tobiah kept c to them. H995
Job 36:33 His thunder announces the c storm; even H2257
Ps 19: 5 is like a bridegroom c out of his chamber, H3655
Ps 37:13 at the wicked, for he knows their day is c. H995
Ps 121: 8 will watch over your c and going both now H995
Ecc 10:14 No one knows what is c—who can tell H2118
SS 3: 6 Who is this c up from the wilderness like H6590
SS 4: 2 sheep just shorn, c up from the washing. H6590
SS 6: 6 a flock of sheep c up from the washing. H6590
SS 8: 5 Who is this c up from the wilderness H6590
Isa 13: 9 the day of the LORD is c—a cruel day, with H995
Isa 14: 9 below is all astir to meet you at your c; H995
Isa 19: 1 rides on a swift cloud and is c to Egypt. H995
Isa 21:12 "Morning is c, but also the night. H910
Isa 26:21 the LORD is c out of his dwelling to punish H3655
Isa 30:30 them see his arm c down with raging H5738
Isa 45:14 behind you, c over to you in chains. H6296
Isa 47:13 let them save you from what is c upon you. H995
Isa 63: 1 Who is this c from Edom, from Bozrah, with H995
Isa 66:15 the LORD is c with fire, and his chariots H995
Jer 4:16 'A besieging army is c from a distant land H995
Jer 6:22 an army is c from the land of the north H995
Jer 7:32 So beware, the days are c, declares the LORD H995
Jer 9:25 "The days are c," declares the LORD, "when H995
Jer 10:22 The report is c—a great commotion from H995
Jer 13:20 up and see those who are c from the north. H995
Jer 16:14 "However, the days are c," declares the H995
Jer 19: 6 So beware, the days are c, declares the LORD H995
Jer 23: 5 "The days are c," declares the LORD, "when H995
Jer 23: 7 "So then, the days are c," declares the LORD, H995
Jer 30: 3 The days are c,' declares the LORD, 'when I H995
Jer 31:27 "The days are c," declares the LORD, "when H995
Jer 31:31 "The days are c," declares the LORD, "when H995
Jer 31:38 "The days are c," declares the LORD, "when H995
Jer 33:14 " 'The days are c,' declares the LORD, 'when H995
Jer 46:13 prophet about the c of Nebuchadnezzar H995
Jer 46:20 a gadfly is c against her from the north. H995
Jer 46:21 the day of disaster is c upon them, the H995
Jer 48:12 But days are c," declares the LORD, "when I H995
Jer 49: 2 But the days are c," declares the LORD H995
Jer 49:19 "Like a lion c up from Jordan's thickets to H6590
Jer 50:41 An army is c from the north; a great nation H995
Jer 50:44 Like a lion c up from Jordan's thickets to a H6590
Jer 51:52 "But days are c," declares the LORD, "when I H995
Eze 1: 4 I saw a windstorm c out of the north H995
Eze 9: 2 And I saw six men c from the direction of H995
Eze 21: 7 shall say, 'Because of the news that is c. H995
Eze 21: 7 be wet with urine.' It is c! It will surely take H995
Eze 33: 3 he sees the sword c against the land and H995
Eze 33: 6 sees the sword c and does not blow the H995
Eze 39: 8 It is c! It will surely take place, declares the H995
Eze 43: 2 glory of the God of Israel c from the east. H995
Eze 47: 1 I saw water c out from under the H3655
Eze 47: 1 The water was c down from under the H3718
Da 4:13 a messenger, c down from heaven. A10474
Da 4:23 c down from heaven and saying A10474
Da 7:10 fire was flowing, c out from before him. A10485
Da 7:13 son of man, c with the clouds of heaven. A10085
Da 11:23 After c to an agreement with him, he will H2489
Hos 9: 7 The days of punishment are c, the days of H995
Joel 2: 1 land tremble, for the day of the LORD is c. H995
Joel 2:31 to blood before the c of the great and H995
Am 7: 1 just as the late crops were c up. H6590
Am 8:11 "The days are c," declares the Sovereign H995
Am 9:13 "The days are c," declares the LORD, "when H995
Mic 1: 3 The LORD is c from his dwelling place; he H3655
Hab 2:16 the LORD's right hand is c around to you, H6015
Zep 1:14 LORD is near—near and c quickly. H4554+4394
Zec 1:21 "What are these c to do?" He answered, H995
Zec 2:10 For I am c, and I will live among you," H995
Zec 6: 1 were four chariots c out from between two H3655
Zec 14: 1 A day of the LORD is c, Jerusalem, when H995
Mal 3: 2 But who can endure the day of his c? Who H995
Mal 4: 1 "Surely the day is c; it will burn like a H995
Mal 4: 1 the day that is c will set them on fire," H995
Mt 2:11 On c to the house, they saw the child with G2262
Mt 3: 7 Sadducees c to where he was G2262
Mt 3: 7 Who warned you to flee from the c wrath? G3516
Mt 8:28 men c from the tombs met him. G2002
Mt 13:54 C to his hometown, he began teaching the G2262
Mt 16:28 they see the Son of Man c in his kingdom." G2262
Mt 17: 9 As they were c down the mountain, Jesus G2849
Mt 24: 3 be the sign of your c and of the end of the G4242
Mt 24:27 so will be the c of the Son of Man. G4242
Mt 24:30 see the Son of Man c on the clouds of G2262
Mt 24:37 so it will be at the c of the Son of Man. G4242
Mt 24:39 how it will be at the c of the Son of Man. G4242
Mt 24:43 at what time of night the thief was c, G2262
Mt 25: 5 The bridegroom was a long time in c, and G5988
Mt 26:64 of the Mighty One and c on the clouds of G2262
Mk 1:10 Just as Jesus was c up out of the water, he G326
Mk 6:31 many people were c and going that they G2262
Mk 9: 9 As they were c down the mountain, Jesus G2849
Mk 11:10 "Blessed is the c kingdom of our father G2262
Mk 13:26 see the Son of Man c in clouds with great G2262
Mk 14:62 of the Mighty One and c on the clouds of G2262
Lk 2:38 C up to them at that very moment, she G2392
Lk 3: 7 said to the crowds c out to be baptized by G1744
Lk 3: 7 Who warned you to flee from the c wrath? G3516
Lk 6:19 because power was c from him and G2002
Lk 8: 4 people were c to Jesus from town G2164
Lk 9:42 Even while the boy was c, the demon G4665
Lk 12:39 had known at what hour the thief was c, G2262
Lk 12:45 'My master is taking a long time in c,' G2262
Lk 13: 7 three years now I've been c to look for G2262
Lk 14:31 to oppose the one c against him with G2262
Lk 17:20 "The c of the kingdom of God is not G2262
Lk 17:22 "The time is c when you will long to see G2262
Lk 18: 3 in that town who kept c to him with the G2262
Lk 19: 4 to see him, since Jesus was c that way. G1451
Lk 19:44 not recognize the time of God's c to you." G2175
Lk 21:26 apprehensive of what is c on the world G2088
Lk 21:27 see the Son of Man c in a cloud with G2262
Jn 1: 9 light to everyone was c into the world. G2262
Jn 1:29 day John saw Jesus c toward him and G2262
Jn 3:23 and people were c and being baptized. G4134
Jn 4:15 thirsty and have to keep c here to draw G1451
Jn 4:21 a time is c when you will worship the G2262
Jn 4:23 Yet a time is c and has now come when G2262
Jn 4:25 "I know that Messiah" (called Christ) "is c. G2262
Jn 4:54 Jesus performed after c from Judea to G2262
Jn 5:25 a time is c and has now come when the G2262
Jn 5:28 a time is c when all who are in their G2262
Jn 6: 5 up and saw a great crowd c toward him, G2262
Jn 9: 4 who sent me. Night is c, when no one can G2262
Jn 10:12 So when he sees the wolf c, he abandons G2262
Jn 11:20 When Martha heard that Jesus was c, she G2262
Jn 11:56 Isn't he c to the festival at all? G2262
Jn 12:15 your king is c, seated on a donkey's G2262
Jn 14:28 'I am going away and I am c back to you. G2262
Jn 14:30 for the prince of this world is c. G2262
Jn 16: 2 the time is c when anyone who kills you G2262
Jn 16:25 a time is c when I will no longer use this G2262
Jn 16:32 "A time is c and in fact has come when G2262
Jn 17:11 are still in the world, and I am c to you. G2262
Jn 17:13 "I am c to you now, but I say these things G2262
Ac 2:20 to blood before the c of the great and G2262
Ac 7:52 who predicted the c of the Righteous One. G1803
Ac 9:17 to you on the road as you were c here— G2262
Ac 13:24 Before the c of Jesus, John preached G1658
Ac 13:25 But there is one c after me whose sandals G2262
Ac 19: 4 people to believe in the one c after him, G2262
Ac 21:11 C over to us, he took Paul's belt, tied his G2262
Ac 28:15 sisters there had heard that we were c, NDT
Ro 15:22 I have often been hindered from c to you. G2262
1Co 2: 6 rulers of this age, who are c to nothing. G2934
1Co 4:18 become arrogant, as if I were not c to you. G2262
2Co 7: 6 downcast, comforted us by the c of Titus, G4242
2Co 7: 7 not only by his c but also by the G4242
2Co 8:17 he is c to you with much enthusiasm G2002
Gal 3:23 Before the c of this faith, we were held in G2262
Eph 2: 7 in order that in the c ages he might show G2088
Php 2:17 on the sacrifice and service c from your faith, AIT
Col 3: 6 Because of these, the wrath of God is c. G2262
Col 4: 9 He is c with Onesimus, our faithful and dear NDT
1Th 1:10 who rescues us from the c wrath. G2262
1Th 4:15 who are left until the c of the Lord, will G4242
1Th 5:23 kept blameless at the c of our Lord Jesus G4242
2Th 2: 1 Concerning the c of our Lord Jesus Christ G4242
2Th 2: 8 destroy by the splendor of his c. G4242
2Th 2: 9 The c of the lawless one will be in G4242
1Ti 6:19 as a firm foundation for the c age, G3516
Heb 6: 5 word of God and the powers of the c age G3516
Heb 8: 8 "The days are c, declares the Lord, when I G2262
Heb 10: 1 a shadow of the good things that are c— G3516
Heb 10:37 he who is c will come and will not delay." G2262
Jas 1:17 c down from the Father of the heavenly G2849
Jas 5: 1 because of the misery that is c on you. G2088
Jas 5: 7 brothers and sisters, until the Lord's c. G4242
Jas 5: 8 stand firm, because the Lord's c is near. G4242
1Pe 1: 5 by God's power until the c of the salvation AIT
1Pe 1:13 to you when Jesus Christ is revealed at his c. NDT
2Pe 1:16 we told you about the c of our Lord Jesus G4242
2Pe 3: 4 will say, "Where is this 'c' he promised? G4242
2Pe 3:12 forward to the day of God and speed its c. G4242
1Jn 2:18 as you have heard that the antichrist is c, G2262
1Jn 2:28 unashamed before him at his c. G4242
1Jn 4: 3 you have heard is c and even now is G2262
2Jn 7 Jesus Christ as c in the flesh, G2262
Jude 14 the Lord is c with thousands upon G2262
Rev 1: 7 he is c with the clouds," and "every G2262

Rev 1:16 and **c out** of his mouth *was* a sharp G1744
Rev 3:11 *I am* **c** soon. Hold on to what you have, so G2262
Rev 3:12 which *is* **c down** out of heaven from my G2849
Rev 7: 2 I saw another angel **c up** from the east, G326
Rev 9:13 I heard a voice *c* **from** the four horns of AIT
Rev 10: 1 mighty angel **c down** from heaven. G2849
Rev 11:14 woe has passed; the third woe *is* **c** soon. G2262
Rev 13: 1 And I saw a beast **c** out of the sea. G326
Rev 13:11 I saw a second beast, **c** out of the earth. G326
Rev 18: 1 I saw another angel **c down** from heaven. G2849
Rev 19:15 **C out** of his mouth *is* a sharp sword with G1744
Rev 19:21 with the sword **c out** of the mouth of the G2002
Rev 20: 1 And I saw an angel **c down** out of heaven, G2849
Rev 21: 2 **c down** out of heaven from God G2849
Rev 21:10 **c down** out of heaven from God. G2849
Rev 22: 7 *I am* **c** soon! Blessed is the one G2262
Rev 22:12 *I am* **c** soon! My reward is with me G2262
Rev 22:20 to these things says, "Yes, *I am* **c** soon." G2262

COMMAND (204) [COMMANDED, COMMANDER, COMMANDER-IN-CHIEF, COMMANDER'S, COMMANDERS, COMMANDING, COMMANDMENT, COMMANDMENTS, COMMANDS, SECOND-IN-COMMAND]

Ex 7: 2 You are to say everything *I* **c** you, and your H7422
Ex 27:20 "**C** the Israelites to bring you clear oil of H7422
Ex 34:11 Obey what I **c** you today. I will drive out H7422
Ex 38:21 recorded at Moses' **c** by the Levites under H7023
Lev 6: 9 "**Give** Aaron and his sons *this* **c**: 'These H7422
Lev 10: 1 fire before the LORD, contrary to *his* **c**. H7422
Lev 24: 2 "**C** the Israelites to bring you clear oil of H7422
Nu 3:39 at the LORD's **c** *by* Moses and Aaron H7023
Nu 4:37 according to the LORD's **c** through Moses. H7023
Nu 4:41 counted them according to the LORD's **c**. H7023
Nu 4:45 according to the LORD's **c** through Moses. H7023
Nu 4:49 At the LORD's **c** through Moses, each was H7023
Nu 5: 2 "**C** the Israelites to send away from the H7422
Nu 9:18 At the LORD's **c** the Israelites set out, and at H7023
Nu 9:18 and at his **c** they encamped. H7023
Nu 9:20 at the LORD's **c** they would encamp H7023
Nu 9:20 then at his **c** they would set out. H7023
Nu 9:23 At the LORD's **c** they encamped, and at the H7023
Nu 9:23 at the LORD's **c** they set out. H7023
Nu 9:23 in accordance with his **c** through Moses. H7023
Nu 10:13 first time, at the LORD's **c** through Moses. H7023
Nu 10:14 son of Amminadab was **in c**. H6584+7372
Nu 10:18 Elizur son of Shedeur was **in c**. H6584+7372
Nu 10:22 son of Ammihud was **in c**. H6584+7372
Nu 10:25 son of Ammishaddai was **in c**. H6584+7372
Nu 13: 3 So at the LORD's **c** Moses sent them out H7023
Nu 14:41 "Why are you disobeying the LORD's **c**? H7023
Nu 20:24 you rebelled against my **c** at the waters of H7023
Nu 22:18 to go beyond the **c** *of* the LORD my God. H7023
Nu 23:20 I have received a **c** to bless; he has blessed NDT
Nu 24:13 to go beyond the **c** *of* the LORD—and I H7023
Nu 27:14 you disobeyed my **c** to honor me as holy H7023
Nu 27:21 At his **c** he and the entire community of H7023
Nu 27:21 will go out, and at his **c** they will come in." H7023
Nu 28: 2 "**Give** *this* **c** *to* the Israelites and say to H7422
Nu 31:49 have counted the soldiers under our **c**, H3338
Nu 33: 2 At the LORD's **c** Moses recorded the stages H7023
Nu 33:38 At the LORD's **c** Aaron the priest went up H7023
Nu 34: 2 "**C** the Israelites and say to them: 'When H7422
Nu 35: 2 "**C** the Israelites to give the Levites towns H7422
Nu 36: 5 Then at the LORD's **c** Moses gave this order H7023
Dt 1:26 against the **c** *of* the LORD your God. H7023
Dt 1:43 against the LORD's **c** and in your arrogance H7023
Dt 2:37 accordance with the **c** *of* the LORD our God, H7422
Dt 4: 2 Do not add to what I **c** you and do not H7422
Dt 8: 1 to follow every **c** I am giving you today, H5184
Dt 9:23 against the **c** *of* the LORD your God. H7023
Dt 11:28 from the way that I **c** you today by H7422
Dt 12:11 there you are to bring everything I **c** you: H7422
Dt 12:14 there observe everything I **c** you. H7422
Dt 12:32 See that you do all I **c** you; do not add to H7422
Dt 15:11 Therefore I **c** you to be openhanded H7422
Dt 15:15 That is why I give you this **c** today. H1821
Dt 17: 3 contrary to *my* **c** has worshiped other H7422
Dt 18:18 He will tell them everything *I* **c** him. H7422
Dt 19: 7 This is why I **c** you to set aside for H7422
Dt 19: 9 follow all these laws I **c** you today— H7422
Dt 24:18 That is why I **c** you to do this. H7422
Dt 24:22 That is why I **c** you to do this. H7422
Dt 27: 4 on Mount Ebal, as I **c** you today, and coat H7422
Dt 30: 2 soul according to everything I **c** you today, H7422
Dt 30:16 I **c** you today to love the LORD your God H7422
Dt 31:23 The LORD **gave** *this* **c** *to* Joshua son of Nun: H7422
Dt 31:25 he **gave** *this* **c** *to* the Levites who carried H7422
Dt 32:46 so that *you may* **c** your children to obey H7422
Jos 1:13 "Remember the **c** that Moses the servant H1821
Jos 1:18 whatever *you may* **c** them, will be H7422
Jos 4:16 "**C** the priests carrying the ark of the H7422
Jos 15:13 In accordance with the LORD's **c** to him H7023
Jos 17: 4 of their father, according to the LORD's **c**. H7023
Jos 22: 9 accordance with the **c** *of* the LORD through H7023
Jdg 4:10 thousand men went up **under** his **c**. H928+8079
Jdg 5:15 sent **under** his **c** into the valley. H928+8079
Jdg 9:29 If only this people were under my **c**! Then I H3338
1Sa 13:13 have not kept the **c** the LORD your God H5184
1Sa 13:14 because you have not kept the LORD's **c**." H7422
1Sa 15:24 violated the LORD's **c** and your instructions H7023
1Sa 16:16 *Let* our lord **c** his servants here to search H606
1Sa 18:13 gave him **c** *over* a thousand men, H8569
2Sa 10:10 the men under the **c** *of* Abishai his H3338
2Sa 18: 2 a third under the **c** *of* Joab, a third under H3338
2Sa 20: 7 warriors went out **under the c of** Abishai. H339
1Ki 2:43 to the LORD and obey the **c** I gave you?" H5184
1Ki 5:17 *At* the king's **c** they removed from the H7422
1Ki 9: 4 do all *I* **c** and observe my decrees H7422
1Ki 11:10 Solomon did not keep the LORD's **c**. H7422
1Ki 11:38 If you do whatever *I* **c** you and walk in H7422
1Ki 13:21 have not kept the **c** the LORD your God H5184
1Ki 16: 9 his officials, who had **c** *of* half his chariots H8569
1Ki 18:36 have done all these things at your **c**. H1821
2Ki 24: 3 to Judah according to the LORD's **c**, H7023
1Ch 11: 6 went up first, and so he received the **c**. H8031
1Ch 12: 9 Obadiah the **second in c**, Eliab the third, H9108
1Ch 12:32 with all their relatives under their **c**; H7023
1Ch 19:11 the men under the **c** *of* Abishai his H3338
1Ch 21: 6 because the king's **c** was repulsive to him. H1821
1Ch 21: 7 This **c** was also evil in the sight of God; so H1821
1Ch 22:12 when *he* **puts** you **in c** over Israel, H7422
1Ch 28:21 all the people will obey your every **c**." H1821
2Ch 7:13 **c** locusts to devour the land or send a H7422
2Ch 7:17 father did, and do all *I* **c**, and observe my H7422
2Ch 23: 6 are to observe the LORD's **c** not to enter. H5466
2Ch 24: 8 *At* the king's **c**, a chest was made and H606
2Ch 26:13 Under their **c** was an army of 307,500 men H3338
2Ch 30: 6 At the king's **c**, couriers went throughout H5184
2Ch 35:22 had said at God's **c** but went to fight him H7023
Ezr 6:14 according to the **c** *of* the God of Israel A10302
Est 1: 8 By the king's **c** each guest was allowed to H2017
Est 1:12 the attendants delivered the king's **c**, H1821
Est 1:15 has not obeyed the **c** *of* King Xerxes that H4411
Est 3: 3 "Why do you disobey the king's **c**? H5184
Est 3:15 spurred on by the king's **c**, and the edict H1821
Est 8:14 spurred on by the king's **c**, and the edict H1821
Job 39:27 eagle soar at your **c** and build its nest on H7023
Ps 71: 3 I can always go; **give** *the* **c** to save me, for H7422
Ps 78:23 Yet *he* **gave** *a* **c** *to* the skies above and H7422
Ps 91:11 For *he will* **c** his angels concerning you to H7422
Ps 147:15 He sends his **c** to the earth; his word runs H614
Ps 148: 5 of the LORD, for *at* his **c** they were created, H7422
Pr 6:20 keep your father's **c** and do not forsake H5184
Pr 6:23 For this **c** is a lamp, this teaching is a light H5184
Pr 8:29 so the waters would not overstep his **c**, H7023
Pr 13:13 but whoever respects a **c** is rewarded. H5184
Ecc 8: 2 Obey the king's **c**, I say, because you took H7023
Ecc 8: 5 Whoever obeys his **c** will come to no H5184
Isa 5: 6 *I will* **c** the clouds not to rain on it. H7422
Jer 1: 7 I send you to and say whatever *I* **c** you. H7422
Jer 1:17 up and say to them whatever I **c** you. H7422
Jer 7:23 but *I* **gave** them this **c**: Obey me, and I will H7422
Jer 7:23 Walk in obedience to all *I* **c** you, that it H7422
Jer 7:31 something *I did* not **c**, nor did it H7422
Jer 11: 4 'Obey me and do everything *I* **c** you, and H7422
Jer 19: 5 something *I did* not **c** or mention H7422
Jer 26: 2 Tell them everything *I* **c** you; do not omit H7422
Jer 35: 6 Jehonadab son of Rekab **gave** us *this* **c**: H7422
Jer 35:14 to drink wine and this **c** has been kept. H1821
Jer 35:14 because they obey their forefather's **c**. H5184
Jer 35:16 have carried out the **c** their forefather H5184
Jer 35:18 'You have obeyed the **c** *of* your forefather H5184
Jer 43: 4 disobeyed the LORD's **c** to stay in the land H7754
La 1:18 is righteous, yet I rebelled against his **c**. H7023
Eze 21:22 to **give** *the* **c** to slaughter, to H7337+7023
Eze 38: 7 and **take c** of them. H2118+4200+5464
Da 3:22 The king's **c** was so urgent and the A10418
Da 3:28 defied the king's **c** and were willing to A10418
Da 4:26 *The* **c** to leave the stump of the tree with A10042
Da 5:29 Then *at* Belshazzar's **c**, Daniel was A10042
Da 6:24 *At* the king's **c**, the men who had falsely A10042
Joel 2:11 mighty is the army that obeys his **c**. H1821
Am 6:11 For the LORD *has* **given the c**, and he will H7422
Am 9: 3 there *I will* **c** the serpent to bite them. H7422
Am 9: 4 there *I will* **c** the sword to slay them. H7422
Am 9: 9 "For I *will* **give** *the* **c**, and I will shake the H7422
Na 1:14 The LORD *has* **given a c** concerning you H7422
Mt 4: 6 " '*He will* **c** his angels concerning you G1948
Mt 15: 3 do you break the **c** of God for the sake G1953
Mt 19: 7 "*did* Moses **c** that a man give his wife a G1948
Mk 9:25 he said, "I **c** you, come out of him and G2199
Mk 10: 3 "What *did* Moses **c** you?" he replied. G1948
Lk 4:10 " '*He will* **c** his angels concerning you to G1948
Jn 10:18 This **c** I received from my Father. G1953
Jn 12:50 I know that his **c** leads to eternal life. G1953
Jn 13:34 "A new **c** I give you: Love one another. G1953
Jn 15:12 My **c** is this: Love each other as I have G1953
Jn 15:14 You are my friends if you do what I **c**. G1948
Jn 15:17 This *is* my **c**: Love each other. G1948
Ac 1: 4 eating with them, *he* **gave** them *this* **c**: G4133
Ac 16:18 of Jesus Christ *I* **c** you to come out of G4133
Ac 19:13 whom Paul preaches, *I* **c** you **to come out**." G3991
Ac 25:23 men of the city. *At the* **c** of Festus, Paul G3027
Ro 5:14 those who did not sin *by* **breaking a c**, G4126
Ro 13: 9 and whatever other **c** there may be, are G1953
Ro 13: 9 may be, are summed up in this one **c**: G3364
Ro 16:26 writings by the **c** of the eternal God, G2198
1Co 7: 6 I say this as a concession, not as a **c**. G2198
1Co 7:10 To the married *I* **give** *this* **c** (not I, but the G4133
1Co 7:25 I have no **c** from the Lord, but I give a G2198
1Co 14:37 what I am writing to you is the Lord's **c**. G1953
Gal 5:14 law is fulfilled in keeping this one **c**: G3364
1Th 4:16 heaven, with a **loud c**, with the voice of G3026
2Th 3: 4 will continue to do the things *we* **c**. G4133
2Th 3: 6 Lord Jesus Christ, *we* **c** you, brothers and G4133
2Th 3:12 Such people *we* **c** and urge in the Lord G4133
1Ti 1: 1 Christ Jesus by the **c** of God our Savior G2198
1Ti 1: 3 Ephesus so that *you may* **c** certain people G4133
1Ti 1: 5 The goal *of* this **c** is love, which comes G4132
1Ti 1:18 I am giving you this **c** in keeping with the G4132
1Ti 4:11 **C** and teach these things. G4133
1Ti 6:14 to keep this **c** without spot or blame until G1953
1Ti 6:17 **C** those who are rich in this present world G4133
1Ti 6:18 **C** them to do good, to be rich in good deeds NDT
Titus 1: 3 to me by the **c** of God our Savior, G2198
Heb 9:19 had proclaimed every **c** of the law to all G1953
Heb 11: 3 that the universe was formed *at* God's **c**, G4839
2Pe 2:21 backs on the sacred **c** that was passed on G1953
2Pe 3: 2 prophets and the **c** given by our Lord and G1953
1Jn 2: 7 not writing you a new **c** but an old one, G1953
1Jn 2: 7 This old **c** is the message you have heard G1953
1Jn 2: 8 Yet I am writing you a new **c**; its truth is G1953
1Jn 3:23 And this is his **c**: to believe in the name of G1953
1Jn 4:21 And he has given us this **c**: Anyone who G1953
2Jn 5 writing you a new **c** but one we have had G1953
2Jn 6 beginning, his **c** is that you walk in love. G1953
Rev 3:10 you have kept my **c** to endure patiently, G3364

COMMANDED (268) [COMMAND]

Ge 2:16 And the LORD God **c** the man, "You are free H7422
Ge 3:11 from the tree that *I* **c** you not to eat from?" H7422
Ge 3:17 ate fruit from the tree *about* which *I* **c** you, H7422
Ge 6:22 Noah did everything just as God **c** him. H7422
Ge 7: 5 And Noah did all that the LORD **c** him. H7422
Ge 7: 9 entered the ark, as God *had* **c** Noah. H7422
Ge 7:16 of every living thing, as God *had* **c** Noah. H7422
Ge 21: 4 Abraham circumcised him, as God **c** him. H7422
Ge 28: 1 Then *he* **c** him: "Do not H7422
Ge 28: 6 that when he blessed him *he* **c** him H7422
Ge 45:21 as Pharaoh had **c**, and he also gave H7023
Ge 50:12 So Jacob's sons did as *he had* **c** them: H7422
Ex 4:28 all the signs *he had* **c** him to perform. H7422
Ex 6:13 and *he* **c** them to bring the Israelites out H7422
Ex 7: 6 Aaron did just as the LORD **c** them. H7422
Ex 7:10 to Pharaoh and did just as the LORD **c**. H7422
Ex 7:20 Aaron did just as the LORD *had* **c**. H7422
Ex 12:28 did just what the LORD **c** Moses and Aaron. H7422
Ex 12:50 what the LORD *had* **c** Moses and Aaron. H7422
Ex 16:16 This is what the LORD *has* **c**: 'Everyone is H7422
Ex 16:23 "This is what the LORD **c**: 'Tomorrow is to H1819
Ex 16:24 morning, as Moses **c**, and it did not stink H7422
Ex 16:32 "This is what the LORD *has* **c**: 'Take an H7422
Ex 16:34 As the LORD **c** Moses, Aaron put the H7422
Ex 17: 1 traveling from place to place as the LORD **c**. H7023
Ex 19: 7 all the words the LORD *had* **c** him to speak. H7422
Ex 23:15 eat bread made without yeast, as *I* **c** you. H7422
Ex 29:35 his sons everything *I have* **c** you, H7422
Ex 31: 6 workers to make everything *I have* **c** you: H7422
Ex 31:11 They are to make them just as *I* **c** you." H7422
Ex 32: 8 away from what *I* **c** them and have made H7422
Ex 32:28 The Levites did as Moses **c**, and that day H1821
Ex 34: 4 as the LORD *had* **c** him; and he carried H7422
Ex 34:18 eat bread made without yeast, as *I* **c** you. H7422
Ex 34:34 told the Israelites what *he had* **been c**, H7422
Ex 35: 1 are the things the LORD *has* **c** you to do: H7422
Ex 35: 4 community, "This is what the LORD *has* **c**: H7422
Ex 35:10 come and make everything the LORD *has* **c**: H7422
Ex 35:29 the LORD through Moses *had* **c** them to do. H7422
Ex 36: 1 are to do the work just as the LORD *has* **c**." H7422
Ex 36: 5 doing the work the LORD **c** to be done." H7422
Ex 38:22 made everything the LORD **c** Moses; H7422
Ex 39: 1 garments for Aaron, as the LORD **c** Moses. H7422
Ex 39: 5 finely twisted linen, as the LORD **c** Moses. H7422
Ex 39: 7 the sons of Israel, as the LORD **c** Moses. H7422
Ex 39:21 out from the ephod—as the LORD **c** Moses. H7422
Ex 39:26 worn for ministering, as the LORD **c** Moses. H7422
Ex 39:29 of an embroiderer—as the LORD **c** Moses. H7422
Ex 39:31 it to the turban, as the LORD **c** Moses. H7422
Ex 39:32 did everything just as the LORD **c** Moses. H7422
Ex 39:42 all the work just as the LORD *had* **c** Moses. H7422
Ex 39:43 they had done it just as the LORD *had* **c**. H7422
Ex 40:16 did everything just as the LORD **c** him. H7422
Ex 40:19 covering over the tent, as the LORD **c** him. H7422
Ex 40:21 ark of the covenant law, as the LORD **c** him. H7422
Ex 40:23 on it before the LORD, as the LORD **c** him. H7422
Ex 40:25 lamps before the LORD, as the LORD **c** him. H7422
Ex 40:27 fragrant incense on it, as the LORD **c** him. H7422
Ex 40:29 grain offerings, as the LORD **c** him. H7422
Ex 40:32 the altar, as the LORD **c** Moses. H7422
Lev 7:36 the LORD **c** that the Israelites give this to H7422
Lev 7:38 of Sinai on the day he **c** the Israelites to H7422
Lev 8: 4 Moses did as the LORD **c** him, and the H7422
Lev 8: 5 "This is what the LORD *has* **c** to be done." H7422
Lev 8: 9 on the front of it, as the LORD **c** Moses. H7422
Lev 8:13 caps on them, as the LORD **c** Moses. H7422
Lev 8:17 up outside the camp, as the LORD **c** Moses. H7422
Lev 8:21 to the LORD, as the LORD **c** Moses. H7422
Lev 8:29 as a wave offering, as the LORD **c** Moses. H7422
Lev 8:31 basket of ordination offerings, as *I was* **c**: H7422
Lev 8:34 has been done today *was* **c** by the LORD to H7422
Lev 8:35 will not die; for that is what *I have* **been c**." H7422
Lev 8:36 did everything the LORD **c** through Moses. H7422
Lev 9: 5 took the things Moses **c** to the front of the H7422
Lev 9: 6 "This is what the LORD *has* **c** you to do, so H7422
Lev 9: 7 atonement for them, as the LORD *has* **c**." H7422

Lev 9:10 the sin offering, as the LORD c Moses; H7422
Lev 9:21 the LORD as a wave offering, as Moses c. H7422
Lev 10:13 to the LORD; for so *I have* **been** c. H7422
Lev 10:15 you and your children, as the LORD *has* c." H7422
Lev 10:18 the goat in the sanctuary area, as *I* c." H7422
Lev 16:34 And it was done, as the LORD c Moses. H7422
Lev 17: 2 'This is what the LORD *has* c: H7422
Lev 24:23 The Israelites did as the LORD c Moses. H7422
Nu 1:19 as the LORD c Moses. And so he counted H7422
Nu 1:54 did all this just as the LORD c Moses. H7422
Nu 2:33 the other Israelites, as the LORD c Moses. H7422
Nu 2:34 Israelites did everything the LORD c Moses; H7422
Nu 3:16 as *he* **was** c by the word of the LORD. H7422
Nu 3:42 of the Israelites, as the LORD c him. H7422
Nu 3:51 as he *was* c by the word of the LORD. H7422
Nu 4:49 they were counted, as the LORD c Moses. H7422
Nu 8: 3 the lampstand, just as the LORD c Moses. H7422
Nu 8:20 with the Levites just as the LORD c Moses. H7422
Nu 8:22 with the Levites just as the LORD c Moses. H7422
Nu 9: 5 did everything just as the LORD c Moses. H7422
Nu 15:36 stoned him to death, as the LORD c Moses. H7422
Nu 17:11 Moses did just as the LORD c him. H7422
Nu 19: 2 of the law that the LORD *has* c: H7422
Nu 20: 9 from the LORD's presence, just as *he* c him. H7422
Nu 20:27 Moses did as the LORD c: They went up H7422
Nu 26: 4 years old or more, as the LORD c Moses." H7422
Nu 27:11 law for the Israelites, as the LORD c Moses. H7422
Nu 27:22 Moses did as the LORD c him. H7422
Nu 29:40 told the Israelites all that the LORD c him. H7422
Nu 31: 7 Midian, as the LORD c Moses, and killed H7422
Nu 31:31 Eleazar the priest did as the LORD c Moses. H7422
Nu 31:41 as the LORD's part, as the LORD c Moses. H7422
Nu 31:47 as the LORD c him, and gave them H7422
Nu 34:13 Moses c the Israelites: "Assign this land H7422
Nu 34:29 are the men the LORD c to assign the H7422
Nu 36: 2 "When the LORD c my lord to give the land H7422
Nu 36:10 daughters did as the LORD c Moses. H7422
Dt 1: 3 all that the LORD *had* c him concerning H7422
Dt 1:19 as the LORD our God c us, we set out from H7422
Dt 1:41 go up and fight, as the LORD our God c us." H7422
Dt 3:18 *I* c you at that time: "The LORD your God H7422
Dt 3:21 At that time *I* c Joshua: "You have seen H7422
Dt 4: 5 laws as the LORD my God c me, H7422
Dt 4:13 which *he* c you to follow and then wrote H7422
Dt 5:12 as the LORD your God *has* c you. H7422
Dt 5:15 the LORD your God *has* c you to observe H7422
Dt 5:16 as the LORD your God *has* c you, so that H7422
Dt 5:32 to do what the LORD your God *has* c you; H7422
Dt 5:33 to all that the LORD your God *has* c you, H7422
Dt 6:20 laws the LORD our God *has* c you? H7422
Dt 6:24 The LORD c us to obey all these decrees H7422
Dt 6:25 LORD our God, as *he has* c us, that will be H7422
Dt 9:12 quickly from what *I* c them and have H7422
Dt 9:16 from the way that the LORD *had* c you. H7422
Dt 10: 5 had made, as the LORD c me, and they are H7422
Dt 12:21 given you, as *I have* c you, and in your H7422
Dt 13: 5 the way the LORD your God c you to follow. H7422
Dt 18:20 speak in my name anything *I have* not c, H7422
Dt 20:17 as the LORD your God *has* c you. H7422
Dt 24: 8 must follow carefully what *I have* c them. H7422
Dt 26:13 the widow, according to all you c. H7422+5184
Dt 26:14 my God; I have done everything *you* c me. H7422
Dt 27: 1 the elders of Israel c the people: H7422
Dt 27:11 On the same day Moses c the people: H7422
Dt 29: 1 covenant the LORD c Moses to make with H7422
Dt 31: 5 do to them all that *I have* c you. H5184+7422
Dt 31:10 Then Moses c them: "At the end of every H7422
Dt 31:29 to turn from the way *I have* c you. H7422
Dt 34: 9 him and did what the LORD *had* c Moses. H7422
Jos 1: 9 *Have I* not c you? Be strong and H7422
Jos 1:16 "Whatever *you have* c us we will do H7422
Jos 4: 8 So the Israelites did as Joshua c them H7422
Jos 4:10 the LORD *had* c Joshua was done by H7422
Jos 4:17 So Joshua c the priests, "Come up out of H7422
Jos 6:10 But Joshua *had* c the army, "Do not give a H7422
Jos 6:16 trumpet blast, Joshua c the army, "Shout! H606
Jos 7:11 my covenant, which *I* c them to keep. H7422
Jos 8: 8 Do what the LORD has c. See to it; H1821
Jos 8:31 servant of the LORD *had* c the Israelites. H7422
Jos 8:33 of the LORD *had* formerly c when he gave H7422
Jos 8:35 of all that Moses *had* c that Joshua did H7422
Jos 9:24 the LORD your God *had* c his servant Moses H7422
Jos 10:40 just as the LORD, the God of Israel, *had* c. H7422
Jos 11:12 as Moses the servant of the LORD *had* c. H7422
Jos 11:15 As the LORD c his servant Moses, so Moses H7422
Jos 11:15 so Moses c Joshua, and Joshua H7422
Jos 11:15 undone of all that the LORD c Moses. H7422
Jos 11:20 without mercy, as the LORD *had* c Moses. H7422
Jos 14: 2 as the LORD *had* c through Moses. H7422
Jos 14: 5 the land, just as the LORD *had* c Moses. H7422
Jos 17: 4 "The LORD c Moses to give us an H7422
Jos 19:50 as the LORD had c. They gave him the town H7023
Jos 21: 2 "The LORD c through Moses that you give H7422
Jos 21: 3 as the LORD had c, the Israelites gave H7023
Jos 21: 8 as the LORD *had* c through Moses. H7422
Jos 22: 2 all that Moses the servant of the LORD c, H7422
Jos 22: 2 you have obeyed me in everything *I* c. H7422
Jos 23:16 your God, which *he* c you, and go and H7422
Jdg 13:14 She must do everything *I have* c her." H7422
2Sa 5:25 So David did as the LORD c him, and he H7422
2Sa 7: 7 of their rulers whom *I* c to shepherd my H7422
2Sa 18: 5 The king c Joab, Abishai and Ittai, "Be H7422
2Sa 18:12 hearing the king c you and Abishai and H7422
2Sa 21:14 Benjamin, and did everything the king c. H7422
2Sa 24:19 went up, as the LORD *had* c through Gad. H7422
1Ki 2:31 Then the king c Benaiah, "Do as he says H606
1Ki 11:11 my decrees, which *I* c you, I will most H7422
1Ki 13: 9 For I *was* c by the word of the LORD: 'You H7422
1Ki 18:40 Then Elijah c them, "Seize the prophets of H606
2Ki 7:14 *He* c the drivers, "Go and find out what has H606
2Ki 11: 5 *He* c them, saying, "This is what you are to H7422
2Ki 14: 6 of the Law of Moses where the LORD c: H7422
2Ki 17:13 the entire Law that *I* c your ancestors to H7422
2Ki 17:35 a covenant with the Israelites, *he* c them: H7422
2Ki 18:12 all that Moses the servant of the LORD c. H7422
2Ki 18:36 because the king had c, "Do not answer H5184
2Ki 21: 8 to do everything *I* c them and will keep H7422
1Ch 6:49 all that Moses the servant of God *had* c. H7422
1Ch 14:16 So David did as God c him, and they struck H7422
1Ch 15:15 as Moses *had* c in accordance with the H7422
1Ch 17: 6 of their leaders whom *I* c to shepherd my H7422
1Ch 24:19 as the LORD, the God of Israel, *had* c him. H7422
2Ch 8:13 offerings c *by* Moses for the Sabbaths, H5184
2Ch 8:18 Hiram sent him ships c by his own men, H3338
2Ch 14: 4 *He* c Judah to seek the LORD, the God of H606
2Ch 25: 4 in the Book of Moses, where the LORD c: H7422
2Ch 29:21 The king c the priests, the descendants of H606
2Ch 29:25 this was c by the LORD through his H5184
2Ch 33: 8 to do everything *I* c them concerning all H7422
2Ch 35: 6 doing what the LORD c through Moses." H1821
Ezr 4: 3 as King Cyrus, the king of Persia, c us." H7422
Ne 8: 1 of Moses, which the LORD *had* c *for* Israel. H7422
Ne 8:14 which the LORD *had* c through Moses H7422
Ne 13:22 Then *I* c the Levites to purify themselves H606
Est 1:10 *he* c the seven eunuchs who served him H606
Est 1:17 'King Xerxes c Queen Vashti to be brought H606
Est 3: 2 the king *had* c this concerning him. H7422
Est 6:10 at once," the king c Haman. "Get the robe H606
Est 9: 1 the edict c *by* the king was to be carried H1821
Est 9:14 So the king c that this be done. An edict H606
Ps 17: 4 the violent through *what* your lips have c. H1821
Ps 33: 9 it came to be; he c, and it stood firm. H7422
Ps 78: 5 which *he* c our ancestors to teach their H7422
Ps 106:34 the peoples as the LORD *had* c them, H606
Isa 13: 3 I *have* c those I prepared for battle; I have H7422
Isa 36:21 because the king had c, "Do not answer H5184
Jer 11: 4 the terms *I* c your ancestors when I brought H7422
Jer 11: 8 of the covenant *I had* c them to follow H7422
Jer 17:22 Sabbath day holy, as *I* c your ancestors. H7422
Jer 26: 8 everything the LORD *had* c him to say, H7422
Jer 32:23 they did not do what *you* c them to do. H7422
Jer 32:35 to Molek, though *I* never c—nor did it H7422
Jer 35: 8 forefather Jehonadab son of Rekab c us. H7422
Jer 35:10 everything our forefather Jehonadab c us. H7422
Jer 36:26 the king c Jerahmeel, a son of the H7422
Jer 38:10 Then the king c Ebed-Melek the Cushite H7422
Jer 47: 7 But how can it rest when the LORD *has* c it H7422
Jer 50:21 "Do everything *I have* c you. H7422
Eze 9:11 back word, saying, "I have done as *you* c." H7422
Eze 10: 6 When the LORD c the man in linen, "Take H7422
Eze 12: 7 So I did as *I* **was** c. During the day I H7422
Eze 24:18 The next morning I did as *I had* **been** c. H7422
Eze 37: 7 So I prophesied as *I* **was** c. And as I was H7422
Eze 37:10 So I prophesied as *he* c me, and breath H7422
Da 3: 4 language, this is what you *are* c to do: A10042
Da 3:20 c some of the strongest soldiers in A10042
Da 4: 6 So *I* c that all the wise men of A10682+10302
Am 2:12 drink wine and c the prophets not to H7422
Jnh 2:10 And the LORD c the fish, and it vomited H606
Zec 1: 6 which *I* c my servants the prophets H7422
Mt 1:24 angel of the Lord *had* c him and took G4705
Mt 8: 4 to the priest and offer the gift Moses c, G4705
Mt 27:10 to buy the potter's field, as the Lord c me." G5332
Mt 28:20 them to obey everything *I have* c you. G1948
Mk 1:44 sacrifices that Moses c for your cleansing, G4705
Mk 7:36 Jesus c them not to tell anyone. G1403
Lk 5:14 sacrifices that Moses c for your cleansing, G4705
Lk 8:29 For Jesus *had* c the impure spirit to come G4133
Jn 8: 5 In the Law Moses c us to stone such G1948
Jn 12:49 who sent me c me to say all that G1953+1443
Jn 14:31 do exactly what my Father *has* c me. G1948
Jn 18:11 Jesus c Peter, "Put your sword away! Shall G3306
Ac 4:18 them in again and c them not to speak G4133
Ac 10:33 to everything the Lord *has* c you to tell us." G4705
Ac 10:42 *He* c us to preach to the people and to G4133
Ac 13:47 For this is what the Lord *has* c us: " 'I have G1948
Ac 16:23 the jailer *was* c to guard them G4133
1Co 9:14 the Lord *has* c that those who preach the G1411
Heb 9:20 covenant, which God *has* c you **to keep**." G1948
Heb 12:20 because they could not bear what *was* c G1403
1Jn 3:23 and to love one another as *he* c us. G1443+1953
2Jn 4 in the truth, just as the Father c *us*. G1953+3284

COMMANDER (109) [COMMAND]

Ge 21:22 Phicol the c *of* his forces said to H8569
Ge 21:32 Phicol the c *of* his forces returned to H8569
Ge 26:26 adviser and Phicol the c *of* his forces. H8569
Jos 5:14 "but as c *of* the army of the LORD I have H8569
Jos 5:15 The c *of* the LORD's army replied, "Take off H8569
Jdg 4: 2 the c *of* his army, was based in H8569
Jdg 4: 7 lead Sisera, the c *of* Jabin's army, with H8569
Jdg 11: 6 they said, "be our c, so we can fight the H7903
Jdg 11:11 people made him head and c over them. H7903
1Sa 12: 9 hand of Sisera, the c *of* the army of Hazor H8569
1Sa 14:50 The name of the c *of* Saul's army was H8569
1Sa 17:18 these ten cheeses to the c *of* their unit. H8569
1Sa 17:55 he said to Abner, c *of* the army, "Abner H8569
1Sa 22: 2 around him, and he became their c. H8569
1Sa 26: 5 son of Ner, the c *of* the army, had lain H8569
2Sa 2: 8 son of Ner, the c *of* Saul's army, had H8569
2Sa 3:38 not realize that a c and a great man has H8569
2Sa 10:16 with Shobak the c *of* Hadadezer's army H8569
2Sa 10:18 struck down Shobak the c *of* their army, H8569
2Sa 11:11 my c Joab and my lord's men are H123
2Sa 19:13 if you are not the c *of* my army for life in H8569
2Sa 23:19 He became their c, even though he was H8569
1Ki 1:19 the priest and Joab the c *of* the army, H8569
1Ki 2:32 Abner son of Ner, c *of* Israel's army, and H8569
1Ki 2:32 son of Jether, c *of* Judah's army—were H8569
1Ki 4: 4 Jehoiada—**c in chief**; Zadok H6584+2021+7372
1Ki 11:15 Joab the c *of* the army, who had H8569
1Ki 11:21 that Joab the c *of* the army was also H8569
1Ki 16:16 the c *of* the army, king over H8569
2Ki 4:13 behalf to the king or the c *of* the army? H8569
2Ki 5: 1 Now Naaman was c *of* the army of the H8569
2Ki 9: 5 a message for you, c," he said. "For which H8569
2Ki 9: 5 asked Jehu. "For you, c," he replied. H8569
2Ki 18:17 The king of Assyria sent his **supreme c** H9580
2Ki 18:17 officer and his **field c** with a large army, H8072
2Ki 18:19 The **field c** said to them, "Tell Hezekiah: H8072
2Ki 18:26 Shebna and Joah said to the **field c** H8072
2Ki 18:27 But the c replied, "Was it only to your H8072
2Ki 18:28 Then the c stood and called out in H8072
2Ki 18:37 told him what the **field c** had said. H8072
2Ki 19: 4 God will hear all the words of the **field c**, H8072
2Ki 19: 8 When the **field c** heard that the king of H8072
2Ki 25: 8 Nebuzaradan c *of* the imperial guard H8042
2Ki 25:10 army under the c *of* the imperial guard H8042
2Ki 25:11 Nebuzaradan the c *of* the guard carried H8042
2Ki 25:12 But the c left behind some of the poorest H8042
2Ki 25:15 The c *of* the imperial guard took away the H8042
2Ki 25:18 The c *of* the guard took as prisoners H8042
2Ki 25:20 Nebuzaradan the c took them all and H8042
1Ch 11:21 above the Three and became their c, H8569
1Ch 19:16 with Shophak the c *of* Hadadezer's army H8569
1Ch 19:18 He also killed Shophak the c *of* their army. H8569
1Ch 27: 5 The third army c, for the third month, was H8569
1Ch 27: 8 was the c Shamhuth the Izrahite. H8569
1Ch 27:34 Joab was the c of the royal army. H8569
2Ch 17:14 Adnah the c, with 300,000 H8569
2Ch 17:15 Jehohanan the c, with 280,000; H8569
Ne 7: 2 along with Hananiah the c *of* the citadel H8569
Pr 6: 7 It has no c, no overseer or ruler, H7903
Isa 20: 1 In the year that the **supreme c**, sent by H9580
Isa 36: 2 Assyria sent his **field c** with a large army H8072
Isa 36: 2 When the c stopped at the aqueduct of the NDT
Isa 36: 4 The **field c** said to them, "Tell Hezekiah: H8072
Isa 36:11 Shebna and Joah said to the **field c** H8072
Isa 36:12 But the c replied, "Was it only to your H8072
Isa 36:13 Then the c stood and called out in H8072
Isa 36:22 told him what the **field c** had said. H8072
Isa 37: 4 God will hear the words of the **field c**, H8072
Isa 37: 8 When the **field c** heard that the king of H8072
Isa 55: 4 the peoples, a ruler and c *of* the peoples. H7422
Jer 39: 9 Nebuzaradan c *of* the imperial guard H8042
Jer 39:10 But Nebuzaradan the c *of* the guard left H8042
Jer 39:11 Nebuzaradan c *of* the imperial guard H8042
Jer 39:13 So Nebuzaradan the c *of* the guard H8042
Jer 40: 1 after Nebuzaradan c *of* the imperial guard H8042
Jer 40: 2 When the c *of* the guard found Jeremiah H8042
Jer 40: 5 Then the c gave him provisions and a H8042
Jer 41:10 whom Nebuzaradan c *of* the imperial H8042
Jer 43: 6 whom Nebuzaradan c *of* the imperial H8042
Jer 51:27 Appoint a c against her; send up horses H3261
Jer 52:12 Nebuzaradan c *of* the imperial guard H8042
Jer 52:14 under the c *of* the imperial guard H8042
Jer 52:15 Nebuzaradan the c *of* the guard carried H8042
Jer 52:19 The c *of* the imperial guard took away the H8042
Jer 52:24 The c *of* the guard took as prisoners H8042
Jer 52:26 Nebuzaradan the c took them all and H8042
Jer 52:30 by Nebuzaradan the c *of* the imperial H8042
Da 2:14 When Arioch, the c *of* the king's guard A10647
Da 8:11 be as great as the c *of* the army of the H8569
Da 11:18 a c will put an end to his insolence H7903
Jn 18:12 of soldiers with its c and the Jewish G5941
Ac 21:31 news reached the c of the Roman troops G5941
Ac 21:32 the rioters saw the c and his soldiers, G5941
Ac 21:33 The c came up and arrested him and G5941
Ac 21:34 since **the** c could not get at the truth G8998
Ac 21:37 he asked the c, "May I say something G5941
Ac 22:24 the c ordered that Paul be taken into the G5941
Ac 22:26 he went to the c and reported it. G5941
Ac 22:27 The c went to Paul and asked, "Tell me G5941
Ac 22:28 Then the c said, "I had to pay a lot of G5941
Ac 22:29 The c himself was alarmed when he G5941
Ac 22:30 The c wanted to find out exactly why Paul NDT
Ac 23:10 so violent that the c was afraid Paul G5941
Ac 23:15 petition the c to bring him before G5941
Ac 23:17 "Take this young man to the c; he has G5941
Ac 23:18 So he took him to the c. The centurion G5941
Ac 23:19 The c took the young man by the hand G5941
Ac 23:22 The c dismissed the young man with this G5941
Ac 24:22 "When Lysias the c comes," he said, "I G5941

COMMANDER'S (2) [COMMAND]

Jdg 5:14 from Zebulun those who bear a c staff. H6221

Ac 21:40 After receiving the c permission, Paul G899S

COMMANDER-IN-CHIEF (1) [COMMAND]

1Ch 11: 6 the Jebusites will become c." H8031+2256+8569

COMMANDERS (92) [COMMAND]

Nu 31:14 the c *of* thousands and commanders of H8569
Nu 31:14 of thousands and c *of* hundreds— H8569
Nu 31:48 the c *of* thousands and commanders of H8569
Nu 31:48 of thousands and c *of* hundreds— H8569
Nu 31:52 All the gold from the c *of* thousands and H8569
Nu 31:52 of thousands and c *of* hundreds that H8569
Nu 31:54 the gold from the c *of* thousands and H8569
Nu 31:54 of thousands and c of hundreds and brought NDT
Dt 1:15 c *of* thousands, *of* hundreds, *of* fifties and *of* H8569
Dt 20: 9 they shall appoint c over it. H8569+7372
Jos 10:24 said to the army c who had come with H7903
1Sa 8:12 he will assign to be c *of* thousands and H8569
1Sa 8:12 commanders of thousands and c *of* fifties, H8569
1Sa 18:30 The Philistine c continued to go out to H8569
1Sa 22: 7 he make all of you c *of* thousands and H8569
1Sa 22: 7 of thousands and c *of* hundreds? H8569
1Sa 29: 3 The c *of* the Philistines asked, "What H8569
1Sa 29: 4 But the Philistine c were angry with H8569
1Sa 29: 9 the Philistine c have said, 'He must not H8569
2Sa 10: 3 the Ammonite c said to Hanun their lord H8569
2Sa 18: 1 appointed over them c *of* thousands and H8569
2Sa 18: 1 of thousands and c *of* hundreds. H8569
2Sa 18: 5 concerning Absalom to each of the c. H8569
2Sa 19: 6 clear today that the c and their men mean H8569
2Sa 24: 2 said to Joab and the army c with him, H8569
2Sa 24: 4 overruled Joab and the army c; so they H8569
1Ki 1:25 the c *of* the army and Abiathar the priest. H8569
1Ki 2: 5 what he did to the two c *of* Israel's armies H8569
1Ki 9:22 the c *of* his chariots and charioteers. H8569
1Ki 14:27 these to the c *of* the guard on duty at H8569
1Ki 15:20 Asa and sent the c *of* his forces against H8569
1Ki 20:14 officers under the provincial c will do it. H8569
1Ki 20:15 232 junior officers under the provincial c. H8569
1Ki 20:17 under the provincial c went out first. H8569
1Ki 20:19 under the provincial c marched out of the H8569
1Ki 22:31 Aram had ordered his thirty-two chariot c, H8569
1Ki 22:32 When the chariot c saw Jehoshaphat, they H8569
1Ki 22:33 the chariot c saw that he was not the king H8569
2Ki 8:21 surrounded him and his chariot c, H8569
2Ki 11: 4 sent for the c *of* units of a hundred, H8569
2Ki 11: 9 The c *of* units of a hundred did just as H8569
2Ki 11:10 Then he gave the c the spears and shields H8569
2Ki 11:15 priest ordered the c *of* units of a hundred, H8569
2Ki 11:19 He took with him the c *of* hundreds, the H8569
1Ch 12:14 These Gadites were army c; the least was H8031
1Ch 12:21 warriors, and they were c in his army. H8569
1Ch 13: 1 the c *of* thousands and commanders of H8569
1Ch 13: 1 of thousands and c of hundreds. NDT
1Ch 15:25 of Israel and the c *of* units of a thousand H8569
1Ch 19: 3 the Ammonite c said to Hanun, "Do you H8569
1Ch 21: 2 said to Joab and the c *of* the troops, H8569
1Ch 25: 1 together with the c *of* the army, set apart H8569
1Ch 26:26 families who were the c *of* thousands H8569
1Ch 26:26 of thousands and c of hundreds, NDT
1Ch 26:26 of hundreds, and by the other army c. H8569
1Ch 27: 1 c *of* thousands and commanders of H8569
1Ch 27: 1 of thousands and c of hundreds, NDT
1Ch 28: 1 the c *of* the divisions in the service of the H8569
1Ch 28: 1 the c *of* thousands and commanders of H8569
1Ch 28: 1 of thousands and c *of* hundreds, H8569
1Ch 29: 6 the c *of* thousands and commanders of H8569
1Ch 29: 6 of thousands and c of hundreds, NDT
2Ch 1: 2 to the c *of* thousands and commanders of H8569
2Ch 1: 2 of thousands and c of hundreds, NDT
2Ch 8: 9 his fighting men, c *of* his captains, and H8569
2Ch 8: 9 and c *of* his chariots and charioteers. H8569
2Ch 11:11 their defenses and put c in them, H5592
2Ch 12:10 these to the c *of* the guard on duty at H8569
2Ch 16: 4 Asa and sent the c *of* his forces against H8569
2Ch 17:14 From Judah, c *of* units of 1,000 H8569
2Ch 18:30 king of Aram had ordered his chariot c, H8569
2Ch 18:31 When the chariot c saw Jehoshaphat, they H8569
2Ch 18:32 when the chariot c saw that he was not H8569
2Ch 21: 9 surrounded him and his chariot c, H8569
2Ch 23: 1 covenant with the c *of* units of a hundred H8569
2Ch 23: 9 Then he gave the c *of* units of a hundred H8569
2Ch 23:14 priest sent out the c *of* units of a hundred, H8569
2Ch 23:20 He took with him the c *of* hundreds, the H8569
2Ch 25: 5 to their families to c *of* thousands and H8569
2Ch 25: 5 of thousands and c *of* hundreds for all H8569
2Ch 32:21 fighting men and the c and officers in the H5592
2Ch 33:11 against them the army c of the king of H8569
2Ch 33:14 He stationed military c in all the fortified H8569
Job 39:25 the shout of c and the battle cry. H8569
Isa 10: 8 'Are not my c all kings?' he says. H8569
Isa 31: 9 of the battle standard their c will panic," H8569
Eze 23: 6 governors and c, all of them H6036
Eze 23:12 governors and c, warriors in full dress H6036
Eze 23:23 all of them governors and c, chariot H6036
Da 11: 5 one of his c will become even H8569
Mic 5: 5 them seven shepherds, even eight c, H5817+132
Mk 6:21 officials and **military** c and the leading G5941

COMMANDING (7) [COMMAND]

Dt 30:11 Now what I *am* c you today is not too H7422
Ezr 4: 8 Rehum the c **officer** and A10116+10302
Ezr 4: 9 Rehum the c **officer** and A10116+10302
Ezr 4:17 To Rehum the c **officer** A10116+10302
Ac 23: 3 violate the law *by* c that I be struck!" G3027
2Co 8: 8 *I am* not c you, but I want to G2848+2198+3306
2Ti 2: 4 rather tries to please his c **officer**. G5133

COMMANDMENT (13) [COMMAND]

Jos 22: 5 careful to keep the c and the law that H5184
Mt 22:36 which is the greatest c in the Law? G1953
Mt 22:38 This is the first and greatest c. G1953
Mk 12:31 There is no c greater than these." G1953
Lk 23:56 on the Sabbath in obedience to the c. G1953
Ro 7: 8 seizing the opportunity afforded by the c G1953
Ro 7: 9 but when the c came, sin sprang to G1953
Ro 7:10 I found that the very c that was intended to G1953
Ro 7:11 seizing the opportunity afforded by the c G1953
Ro 7:11 and through **the** c put me to death. G899S
Ro 7:12 law is holy, and the c is holy, righteous G1953
Ro 7:13 so that through the c sin might become G1953
Eph 6: 2 which is the first c with a promise— G1953

COMMANDMENTS (20) [COMMAND]

Ex 20: 6 of those who love me and keep my c. H5184
Ex 24:12 stone with the law and c I have written H5184
Ex 34:28 the words of the covenant—the Ten C. H1821
Dt 4:13 covenant, the Ten C, which he H1821
Dt 5:10 of those who love me and keep my c. H5184
Dt 5:22 These are the c the LORD proclaimed in a H1821
Dt 6: 6 These c that I give you today are to be on H1821
Dt 7: 9 of those who love him and keep his c. H5184
Dt 9:10 them were all the c the LORD proclaimed H1821
Dt 10: 4 the Ten C he had proclaimed to you on H1821
Ne 1: 5 with those who love him and keep his c, H5184
Pr 19:16 Whoever keeps c keeps their life, but H5184
Ecc 12:13 Fear God and keep his c, for this is the H5184
Da 9: 4 with those who love him and keep his c, H5184
Mt 19:17 If you want to enter life, keep the c." G1953
Mt 22:40 the Prophets hang on these two c. G1953
Mk 10:19 You know the c: 'You shall not murder, you G1953
Mk 12:28 asked him, "Of all the c, which is the most G1953
Lk 18:20 You know the c: 'You shall not commit G1953
Ro 13: 9 The c, "You shall not commit adultery," NDT

COMMANDS (184) [COMMAND]

Ge 26: 5 keeping my c, my decrees and my H5184
Ex 8:27 sacrifices to the LORD our God, as *he* c us." H606
Ex 15:26 pay attention to his c and keep all his H5184
Ex 16:28 refuse to keep my c and my instructions? H5184
Ex 18:23 If you do this and God so c, you will be H7422
Ex 25:22 give you all *my* c for the Israelites. H7422
Ex 34:32 and *he* **gave** them all *the* c the LORD had H7422
Lev 4: 2 what is forbidden in any of the LORD's c— H5184
Lev 4:13 what is forbidden in any of the LORD's c, H5184
Lev 4:22 in any of the c *of* the LORD his God, H5184
Lev 4:27 what is forbidden in any of the LORD's c, H5184
Lev 5:17 what is forbidden in any of the LORD's c, H5184
Lev 22:31 "Keep my c and follow them. I am the H5184
Lev 26: 3 my decrees and are careful to obey my c, H5184
Lev 26:14 not listen to me and carry out all these c, H5184
Lev 26:15 fail to carry out all my c and so violate my H5184
Lev 27:34 These are the c the LORD gave Moses at H5184
Nu 9: 8 I find out what the LORD c concerning you."H7422
Nu 15:22 keep any of these c the LORD gave Moses H5184
Nu 15:23 any of the LORD's c to you through him H7422
Nu 15:31 the LORD's word and broken his c, H5184
Nu 15:39 so you will remember all the c *of* the LORD, H5184
Nu 15:40 to obey all my c and will be consecrated H5184
Nu 30: 1 tribes of Israel: "This is what the LORD c: H7422
Nu 32:25 "We your servants will do as our lord c. H7422
Nu 36: 6 This is what the LORD c for Zelophehad's H7422
Nu 36:13 These are the c and regulations the LORD H5184
Dt 4: 2 keep the c *of* the LORD your God that I H5184
Dt 4:40 Keep his decrees and c, which I am giving H5184
Dt 5:29 to fear me and keep all my c always, H5184
Dt 5:31 with me so that I may give you all the c, H5184
Dt 6: 1 These are the c, decrees and laws the H5184
Dt 6: 2 all his decrees and c that I give you, H5184
Dt 6:17 Be sure to keep the c *of* the LORD your God H5184
Dt 7:11 take care to follow the c, decrees and H5184
Dt 8: 2 whether or not you would keep his c. H5184
Dt 8: 6 Observe the c *of* the LORD your God H5184
Dt 8:11 failing to observe his c, his laws and his H5184
Dt 10:13 observe the LORD's c and decrees that I am H5184
Dt 11: 1 his decrees, his laws and his c always. H5184
Dt 11: 8 therefore all the c I am giving you today, H5184
Dt 11:13 faithfully obey the c I am giving you today H5184
Dt 11:22 observe all these c I am giving you to H5184
Dt 11:27 if you obey the c *of* the LORD your God that H5184
Dt 11:28 if you disobey the c *of* the LORD your God H5184
Dt 13: 4 Keep his c and obey him; serve him and H5184
Dt 13:18 by keeping all his c that I am giving you H5184
Dt 15: 5 to follow all these c I am giving you today H5184
Dt 26:13 aside from your c nor have I forgotten H5184
Dt 26:16 The LORD your God c you this day to follow H7422
Dt 26:17 keep his decrees, c and laws—that you H5184
Dt 26:18 that you are to keep all his c. H5184
Dt 27: 1 "Keep all these c that I give you today. H5184
Dt 27:10 God and follow his c and decrees that I H5184
Dt 28: 1 carefully follow all his c I give you today, H5184
Dt 28: 9 if you keep the c *of* the LORD your God H5184
Dt 28:13 pay attention to the c *of* the LORD your God H5184
Dt 28:14 aside from any of the c I give you today, H1821
Dt 28:15 follow all his c and decrees I am giving H5184
Dt 28:45 observe the c and decrees he gave H5184
Dt 30: 8 follow all his c I am giving you today. H5184
Dt 30:10 God and keep his c and decrees that are H5184
Dt 30:16 and to keep his c, decrees and laws; H5184
Jos 22: 5 to keep his c, to hold fast to him H5184
Jdg 2:17 who had been obedient to the LORD's c. H5184
Jdg 3: 4 see whether they would obey the LORD's c, H5184
Jdg 4: 6 "The LORD, the God of Israel, c you: H7422
1Sa 12:14 obey him and do not rebel against his c, H7023
1Sa 12:15 if you rebel against his c, his hand H7023
2Sa 9:11 my lord the king c his servant to do." H7422
1Ki 2: 3 keep his decrees and c, his laws and H5184
1Ki 3:14 keep my decrees and c as David your H5184
1Ki 6:12 laws and keep all my c and obey them, H5184
1Ki 8:58 walk in obedience to him and keep the c, H5184
1Ki 8:61 to live by his decrees and obey his c, as at H5184
1Ki 9: 6 do not observe the c and decrees I have H5184
1Ki 11:34 chose and who obeyed my c and decrees. H5184
1Ki 11:38 in my eyes by obeying my decrees and c, H5184
1Ki 14: 8 who kept my c and followed me with all H5184
1Ki 15: 5 keep any of the LORD's c all the days of his H7422
1Ki 18:18 the LORD's c and have followed H5184
1Ki 20:24 the kings from their c and replace them H5226
2Ki 17:13 Observe my c and decrees, in accordance H5184
2Ki 17:16 forsook all the c *of* the LORD their God H5184
2Ki 17:19 did not keep the c *of* the LORD their God. H5184
2Ki 17:34 the laws and c that the LORD gave the H5184
2Ki 17:37 the laws and c he wrote for you. H5184
2Ki 18: 6 he kept the c the LORD had given Moses. H5184
2Ki 18:12 listened to the c nor carried them out. NDT
2Ki 23: 3 to follow the LORD and keep his c, statutes H5184
1Ch 28: 7 unswerving in carrying out my c and laws, H5184
1Ch 28: 8 to follow all the c *of* the LORD your God, H5184
1Ch 29:19 the wholehearted devotion to keep your c, H5184
2Ch 7:19 the decrees and c I have given you and H5184
2Ch 8:15 from the king's c to the priests or to H5184
2Ch 14: 4 ancestors, and to obey his laws and c. H5184
2Ch 17: 4 father and followed his c rather than the H5184
2Ch 19:10 concerns of the law, c, decrees or H5184
2Ch 24:20 'Why do you disobey the LORD's c? You H5184
2Ch 31:21 in obedience to the law and the c, H5184
2Ch 34:31 to follow the LORD and keep his c, statutes H5184
Ezr 7:11 concerning the c and decrees of the H5184
Ezr 9:10 say after this? For we have forsaken the c H5184
Ezr 9:14 we then break your c again and intermarry H5184
Ezr 10: 3 of those who fear the c *of* our God. H5184
Ne 1: 7 We have not obeyed the c, decrees and H5184
Ne 1: 9 if you return to me and obey my c H5184
Ne 9:13 and decrees and c that are good. H5184
Ne 9:14 them your holy Sabbath and gave them c, H5184
Ne 9:16 stiff-necked, and they did not obey your c. H5184
Ne 9:29 became arrogant and disobeyed your c. H5184
Ne 9:34 pay attention to your c or the statutes you H5184
Ne 10:29 of God and to obey carefully all the c, H5184
Ne 10:32 carrying out the c to give a third of a H5184
Ne 12:45 according to the c *of* David and his son H5184
Job 23:12 I have not departed from the c *of* his lips H5184
Job 36:10 to correction and c them to repent of their H606
Job 36:32 with lightning and c it to strike its mark. H7422
Job 37:12 whole earth to do whatever *he* c them. H7422
Ps 19: 8 The c *of* the LORD are radiant, giving light H5184
Ps 78: 7 not forget his deeds but would keep his c. H5184
Ps 89:31 violate my decrees and fail to keep my c, H5184
Ps 107:11 against God's c and despised the plans H609
Ps 112: 1 the LORD, who find great delight in his c. H5184
Ps 119: 6 put to shame when I consider all your c. H5184
Ps 119:10 my heart; do not let me stray from your c. H5184
Ps 119:19 on earth; do not hide your c from me. H5184
Ps 119:21 are accursed, those who stray from your c. H5184
Ps 119:32 I run in the path of your c, for you have H5184
Ps 119:35 Direct me in the path of your c, for there I H5184
Ps 119:47 I delight in your c because I love them. H5184
Ps 119:48 I reach out for your c, which I love, that I H5184
Ps 119:60 I will hasten and not delay to obey your c. H5184
Ps 119:66 good judgment, for I trust your c. H5184
Ps 119:73 give me understanding to learn your c. H5184
Ps 119:86 All your c are trustworthy; help me, for I H5184
Ps 119:96 I see a limit, but your c are boundless. H5184
Ps 119:98 Your c are always with me and make me H5184
Ps 119:115 that I may keep the c *of* my God! H5184
Ps 119:127 Because I love your c more than gold H5184
Ps 119:131 my mouth and pant, longing for your c. H5184
Ps 119:143 upon me, but your c give me delight. H5184
Ps 119:151 you are near, LORD, and all your c are true.H5184
Ps 119:166 your salvation, LORD, and I follow your c. H5184
Ps 119:172 of your word, for all your c are righteous. H5184
Ps 119:176 servant, for I have not forgotten your c. H5184
Pr 2: 1 my words and store up my c within you, H5184
Pr 3: 1 my teaching, but keep my c in your heart, H5184
Pr 4: 4 your heart; keep my c, and you will live. H5184
Pr 7: 1 my words and store up my c within you. H5184
Pr 7: 2 Keep my c and you will live; guard my H5184
Pr 10: 8 The wise in heart accept c, but a H5184
Isa 48:18 If only you had paid attention to my c H5184
Isa 58: 2 has not forsaken the c *of* its God. H5477
Jer 7:22 *I did* not *just* **give** them c about burnt H7422
Jer 22: 4 For if you are careful to carry out these c H1821
Jer 22: 5 But if you do not obey these c, declares H1821
Da 9: 5 have turned away from your c and laws. H5184
Zep 2: 3 of the land, you who do what he c. H5477
Mt 5:19 one of the least *of* these c and teaches G1953

Mt 5:19 teaches these **c** will be called great in NDT
Mk 7: 8 have let go of the **c** of God and are *G1953*
Mk 7: 9 of setting aside the **c** of God in order to *G1953*
Lk 1: 6 all the Lord's **c** and decrees blamelessly. *G1953*
Lk 8:25 *He* **c** even the winds and the water, and *G2199*
Jn 14:15 "If you love me, keep my **c**. *G1953*
Jn 14:21 Whoever has my **c** and keeps them is the *G1953*
Jn 15:10 If you keep my **c**, you will remain in my *G1953*
Jn 15:10 have kept my Father's **c** and remain in his *G1953*
Ac 17:30 now *he* **c** all people everywhere to *G4133*
1Co 7:19 Keeping God's **c** is what counts. *G1953*
Eph 2:15 flesh the law *with* its **c** and regulations. *G1953*
Col 2:22 based on merely human **c** and teachings. *G1945*
Titus 1:14 myths or *to* the merely human **c** of those *G1953*
1Jn 2: 3 have come to know him if we keep his **c**. *G1953*
1Jn 2: 4 does not do **what** he **c** is a liar, and *G1953*
1Jn 3:22 we keep his **c** and do what pleases *G1953*
1Jn 3:24 The one who keeps God's **c** lives in him *G1953*
1Jn 5: 2 by loving God and carrying out his **c**. *G1953*
1Jn 5: 3 to keep his **c**. And his commands *G1953*
1Jn 5: 3 And his **c** are not burdensome, *G1953*
2Jn 6 that we walk in obedience to his **c**. *G1953*
Rev 12:17 those who keep God's **c** and hold fast their *G1953*
Rev 14:12 of God who keep his **c** and remain faithful *G1953*

COMMEMORATE (4) [COMMEMORATED]

Ex 12:14 "This is a day you are to **c**; for the H2355
Ex 13: 3 said to the people, "**C** this day, the day H2349
Jdg 11:40 go out for four days to **c** the daughter of H9480
2Ch 35:25 female singers **c** Josiah in the laments H606

COMMEMORATED (1) [COMMEMORATE]

Lev 23:24 a sacred assembly **c** *with* trumpet blasts. H2355

COMMEND (8) [COMMENDABLE, COMMENDED, COMMENDS]

Ecc 8:15 So I **c** the enjoyment of life, because there H8655
Ro 16: 1 *I* **c** to you our sister Phoebe, a deacon of *G5319*
2Co 3: 1 Are we beginning *to* **c** ourselves again *G5319*
2Co 4: 2 forth the truth plainly *we* **c** ourselves to *G5319*
2Co 5:12 *We* are not *trying to* **c** ourselves to you *G5319*
2Co 6: 4 as servants of God *we* **c** ourselves in every *G5319*
2Co 10:12 ourselves with some who **c** themselves. *G5319*
1Pe 2:14 do wrong and to **c** those who do right. *G2047*

COMMENDABLE (2) [COMMEND]

1Pe 2:19 For it is **c** if someone bears up under the *G5921*
1Pe 2:20 you endure it, this is **c** before God. *G5921*

COMMENDED (10) [COMMEND]

Ne 11: 2 The people **c** all who volunteered to live H1385
Job 29:11 well of me, and those who saw me **c** me, H6386
Lk 16: 8 "The master **c** the dishonest manager *G2046*
Ac 15:40 **c** by the believers to the grace of the Lord. *G4140*
Ro 13: 3 do what is right and *you will be* **c**. *G2400+2047*
2Co 12:11 I ought *to have been* **c** by you, for I am *G5319*
Heb 11: 2 This is what the ancients *were* **c** for. *G3455*
Heb 11: 4 By faith *he was* **c** as righteous, when God *G3455*
Heb 11: 5 *he was* **c** as one who pleased God. *G3455*
Heb 11:39 These *were* all **c** for their faith, yet none *G3455*

COMMENDS (3) [COMMEND]

Ps 145: 4 One generation **c** your works to another H8655
2Co 10:18 For it is not the *one who* **c** himself who is *G5319*
2Co 10:18 is approved, but the one whom the Lord **c**. *G5319*

COMMISSION (5) [COMMISSIONED, COMMISSIONERS]

Nu 27:19 entire assembly and **c** him in their H7422
Dt 3:28 But **c** Joshua, and encourage and H7422
Dt 31:14 at the tent of meeting, where *I will* **c** him." H7422
Ac 26:12 the authority and **c** of the chief priests. *G2207*
Col 1:25 its servant by the **c** God gave me to *G3873*

COMMISSIONED (1) [COMMISSION]

Nu 27:23 Then he laid his hands on him and **c** him H7422

COMMISSIONERS (2) [COMMISSION]

Ge 41:34 Let Pharaoh appoint **c** over the land to H7224
Est 2: 3 Let the king appoint **c** in every province of H7224

COMMIT (61) [COMMITMENT, COMMITS, COMMITTED, COMMITTING]

Ex 20:14 "*You shall* not **c adultery**. H5537
Lev 6: 3 about any such sin that people *may* **c**— H6913
Nu 18:23 the **responsibility for** *any* **offenses** they *c* AIT
Dt 5:18 "*You shall* not **c adultery**. H5537
1Sa 7: 3 the Ashtoreths and **c** yourselves to the H3922
1Ki 14:16 has committed and *has* **caused** Israel **to c**." H2627
1Ki 15:26 same sin his father *had* **caused** Israel **to c**. H2627
1Ki 15:30 committed and *had* **caused** Israel **to c**, H2627
1Ki 15:34 sin Jeroboam *had* **caused** Israel **to c**. H2627
1Ki 16:13 committed and *had* **caused** Israel **to c**, H2627
1Ki 16:19 sin Jeroboam *had* **caused** Israel **to c**. H2627
1Ki 16:26 sin Jeroboam *had* **caused** Israel **to c**, H2627
1Ki 16:31 it trivial *to* **c** the sins of Jeroboam H2143+928
2Ki 3: 3 which *he had* **caused** Israel **to c**; he did H2627
2Ki 10:29 which *he had* **caused** Israel **to c**—the H2627
2Ki 10:31 which *he had* **caused** Israel **to c**. H2627
2Ki 13: 2 which *he had* **caused** Israel **to c**, and he H2627
2Ki 13: 6 which *he had* **caused** Israel **to c**; they H2627
2Ki 13:11 which *he had* **caused** Israel **to c**; he H2627
2Ki 14:24 of Nebat, which *he had* **caused** Israel **to c**. H2627
2Ki 15: 9 of Nebat, which *he had* **caused** Israel **to c**. H2627
2Ki 15:18 of Nebat, which *he had* **caused** Israel **to c**. H2627
2Ki 15:24 of Nebat, which *he had* **caused** Israel **to c**. H2627
2Ki 15:28 of Nebat, which *he had* **caused** Israel **to c**. H2627
2Ki 17:21 the LORD and **caused** them **to c** a great sin. H2627
2Ki 21:16 the sin that *he had* **caused** Judah **to c**, H2627
Ezr 9:14 with the **peoples** *who c* such detestable AIT
Ne 6:13 me so that *I would* **c a sin** by doing this, H2627
Ps 10:14 The victims **c** *themselves* to you; you are H6440
Ps 31: 5 Into your hands *I* **c** my spirit; deliver me H7212
Ps 36: 4 *they* **c themselves** to a sinful course and H3656
Ps 37: 5 **C** your way to the LORD; trust in him and he H1670
Pr 16: 3 **C** to the LORD whatever you do, and he will H1670
Jer 7: 9 murder, **c adultery** and perjury, burn H5537
Jer 23:14 They **c adultery** and live a lie H5537
Eze 16:38 of *women who* **c adultery** and who shed H5537
Eze 16:51 Samaria *did* not **c** half the sins you did H2627
Eze 18: 7 *He does* not **c robbery** but gives his H1608+1611
Eze 18:16 *He does* not **c robbery** but gives his H1608+1611
Eze 22: 9 at the mountain shrines and **c** lewd acts. H6913
Eze 22:29 practice extortion and **c robbery**; H1608+1610
Eze 23:45 of *women who* **c adultery** and shed H5537
Hos 4:14 daughters-in-law when *they* **c adultery**, H5537
Hos 4:15 **c adultery**, do not let Judah H2388
Mt 5:27 that it was said, '*You shall* not **c adultery**. *G3658*
Mt 19:18 murder, *you shall* not **c adultery**, you shall *G3658*
Mk 10:19 murder, *you shall* not **c adultery**, you shall *G3658*
Lk 18:20 '*You shall* not **c adultery**, you shall not *G3658*
Lk 23:46 "Father, into your hands *I* **c** my spirit." *G4192*
Ac 20:32 "Now *I* **c** you to God and to the word of *G4192*
Ro 2:22 say *that people should* not **c adultery**, *G3658*
Ro 2:22 not commit adultery, *do you* **c adultery**? *G3658*
Ro 13: 9 "*You shall* not **c adultery**," "You shall AIT
1Co 10: 8 *We should* not **c sexual immorality**, as *G4519*
1Th 4: 6 Lord will punish all those who **c** such sins, NDT
Jas 2:11 who said, "*You shall* not **c adultery**," *G3658*
Jas 2:11 If *you do* not **c adultery** but do commit *G3658*
Jas 2:11 do not commit adultery but *do* **c murder**, *G5839*
1Pe 4:19 to God's will should **c** themselves to their *G4192*
1Jn 5:16 brother or sister **c a sin** that does not *G279+281*
Rev 2:22 will make those *who* **c adultery** with her *G3658*

COMMITMENT (1) [COMMIT]

1Co 7:27 Are you free from **such a c**? Do not look *G1222*[S]

COMMITS (16) [COMMIT]

Lev 20:10 " 'If a man **c adultery** with another man's H5537
Pr 6:32 But *a man who* **c adultery** has no H5537+851
Pr 29:22 a hot-tempered person **c** many sins. NDT
Ecc 8:12 a wicked person *who* **c** a hundred crimes H6913
Eze 18:12 and needy. *He* **c robbery**. He does H1608+1611
Eze 18:14 a son who sees all the sins his father **c**, H6913
Eze 18:24 righteousness and **c** sin and does the H6913
Eze 18:26 turns from their righteousness and **c** sin, H6913
Eze 22:11 In you one man **c** a detestable offense H6913
Mt 5:32 who marries a divorced woman **c adultery**. *G3656*
Mt 19: 9 marries another woman **c adultery**." *G3656*
Mk 10:11 another woman **c adultery** against her. *G3656*
Mk 10:12 marries another man, *she* **c adultery**." *G3656*
Lk 16:18 marries another woman **c adultery**, *G3658*
Lk 16:18 who marries a divorced woman **c adultery**. *G3658*
1Co 6:18 other sins a person **c** are outside the body *G4472*

COMMITTED (87) [COMMIT]

Ge 50:17 the wrongs *they* **c** *in treating* you so badly. H1694
Ex 32:30 people, "You *have* **c a** great **sin**. H2627+2631
Ex 32:31 **a** great **sin** these people *have* **c**! H2627+2631
Lev 4: 3 as a sin offering for the sin *he has* **c**. H2627
Lev 4:14 the sin *they* **c** becomes known, the H2627
Lev 4:23 the sin *he has* **c** becomes known, he H2627
Lev 4:28 the sin *they have* **c** becomes known H2627
Lev 4:28 offering for the sin *they* **c** a female goat H2627
Lev 4:35 them for the sin *they have* **c**, H2627
Lev 5: 6 As a penalty for the sin *they have* **c**, they H2627
Lev 5:10 them for the sin *they have* **c**, H2627
Lev 5:13 them for any of these sins *they have* **c**, H2627
Lev 5:18 **wrong** *they have* **c unintentionally**, H8705+8704
Lev 19:22 him before the LORD for the sin *he has* **c**, H2627
Nu 5: 7 must confess the sin *they have* **c**. H6913
Nu 12:11 against us the sin *we have* so foolishly **c**. H2627
Dt 9:18 because of all the sin *you had* **c**, doing H2627
Dt 19:15 crime or offense *they may have* **c**. H2627+2628
Dt 22:26 she has **c** no sin deserving death. NDT
Jdg 20: 6 because *they* **c** this lewd and outrageous H6913
Jdg 20:12 this awful crime that **was c** among you? H2118
1Sa 14:38 let us find out what sin *has been* **c** today. H2118
1Ki 8:50 all the offenses *they have* **c** against you, H7321
1Ki 8:61 may your hearts be **fully c** to the LORD our H8969
1Ki 14:16 the sins Jeroboam *has* **c** and has caused H2627
1Ki 14:22 By the sins *they* **c** they stirred up his H2627
1Ki 15: 3 *He* **c** all the sins his father had done H2143+928
1Ki 15:14 Asa's heart was **fully c** to the LORD all his H8969
1Ki 15:30 the sins Jeroboam *had* **c** and had caused H2627
1Ki 16:13 his son Elah *had* **c** and had caused H2627
1Ki 16:19 because of the sins *he had* **c**, doing evil in H2627
2Ki 21:11 king of Judah *has* **c** these detestable sins. H6913
2Ki 21:17 including the sin *he* **c**, are they not written H2627
2Ch 15:17 Asa's heart was **fully c** to the LORD all his H8969
2Ch 16: 9 those whose hearts are **fully c** to him. H8969
2Ch 34:16 doing everything that *has* **been c** to them. H5989
Ne 1: 6 *we* Israelites, including myself and my father's family, *have* **c** H2627
Ne 9:18 or when *they* **c** awful blasphemies. H6913
Ne 9:26 back to you; *they* **c** awful blasphemies. H6913
Job 13:23 How many wrongs and sins have I **c** H4200
Ps 51: T David *had* **c adultery with** Bathsheba. H995+448
Jer 2:13 "My people *have* **c** two sins: They have H6913
Jer 3: 6 spreading tree and *has* **c adultery** there. H2388
Jer 3: 8 no fear; she also went out and **c adultery**. H2388
Jer 3: 9 the land and **c adultery** with stone and H5537
Jer 5: 7 yet *they* **c adultery** and thronged to the H5537
Jer 11:20 on them, for to you *I have* **c** my cause. H1655
Jer 16:10 What sin *have* we **c** against the LORD our H2627
Jer 20:12 on them, for to you *I have* **c** my cause. H1655
Jer 29:23 *they have* **c adultery** with their neighbors' H5537
Jer 33: 8 all the sin *they have* **c** against me and H2627
Jer 37:18 "What **crime** *have I* **c** against you or your H2627
Jer 41:11 crimes Ishmael son of Nethaniah *had* **c**, H6913
Jer 44: 9 the wickedness **c** by your ancestors and by H6913
Jer 44: 9 the wickedness **c** by you and your wives NDT
Eze 18:21 all the sins *they have* **c** and keeps all my H6913
Eze 18:22 of the offenses *they have* **c** will be H6913
Eze 18:24 of and because of the sins *they have* **c**, H2627
Eze 18:26 of the sin *they have* **c** they will die. H6913
Eze 18:27 wickedness *they have* **c** and does what H6913
Eze 18:28 all the offenses *they have* **c** and turn away H6913
Eze 18:31 yourselves of all the offenses *you have* **c**, H7321
Eze 23:37 for *they have* **c adultery** and blood is on H5537
Eze 23:37 *They* **c adultery** with their idols; they even H5537
Eze 33:16 None of the sins *that person has* **c** will be H2627
Mal 2:11 detestable thing *has* **been c** in Israel and H6913
Mt 5:28 lustfully *has* already **c adultery** with her in *G3658*
Mt 11:27 "All things *have been* **c** to me by my *G4140*
Mt 27:23 What crime *has he* **c**?" asked Pilate. *G4472*
Mk 15: 7 insurrectionists who *had* **c** murder in the *G4472*
Mk 15:14 What crime *has he* **c**?" asked Pilate. *G4472*
Lk 10:22 "All things *have been* **c** to me by my *G4140*
Lk 23:22 What crime *has* this man **c**? I have found *G4472*
Ac 14:23 prayer and fasting, **c** them to the Lord, in *G4192*
Ac 14:26 they had been **c** to the grace of God *G4140*
Ro 1:27 Men **c** shameful acts with other men, and *G2981*
Ro 3:25 left the sins **c beforehand** unpunished— *G4588*
1Co 9:17 I am simply discharging the trust **c to** *me*. *G4409*
2Co 5:19 And *he has* **c** to us the message of *G5502*
Heb 9: 7 *for* the **sins** the people *had* **c in ignorance**. *G52*
Heb 9:15 them free from the sins **c** under the first NDT
1Pe 2:22 "He **c** no sin, and no deceit was found in *G4472*
Jude 15 acts *they have* **c** *in their* **ungodliness**, *G814*
Rev 2:14 to idols and **c sexual immorality**. *G4519*
Rev 17: 2 With her the kings of the earth **c adultery** *G4519*
Rev 18: 3 The kings of the earth **c adultery** with her *G4519*
Rev 18: 9 of the earth who **c adultery** with her and *G4519*

COMMITTING (4) [COMMIT]

1Ki 15:26 ways of his father and **c** the same sin his H928[S]
1Ki 15:34 ways of Jeroboam and **c** the same sin H928[S]
1Ki 16:19 ways of Jeroboam and **c** the same sin H928[S]
1Ki 16:26 **c** the same sin Jeroboam had caused H928[S]

COMMON (26)

Ge 11: 1 world had one language and a **c** speech. H285
Lev 10:10 distinguish between the holy and the **c**, H2687
1Ki 10:27 made silver **as c** in Jerusalem **as** stones, H3869
2Ki 23: 6 over the graves of the **c people**. H1201+6639
2Ch 1:15 gold **as c** in Jerusalem **as** stones, H3869
2Ch 9:27 made silver **as c** in Jerusalem **as** stones, H3869
Ne 7: 5 officials and the **c people** for registration H6639
Ps 73: 5 They are free from *c* **human** burdens; they AIT
Pr 22: 2 Rich and poor **have** *this* **in c**: The LORD is H7008
Pr 29:13 The poor and the oppressor **have** *this* **in c** H7008
Ecc 9: 2 All share a **c** destiny—the righteous and the H285
Isa 5:13 hunger and the **c people** will be parched H2162
Jer 26:23 the burial place of the **c people**.) H1201+6639
Eze 22:26 distinguish between the holy and the **c**; H2687
Eze 42:20 to separate the holy from the **c**. H2687
Eze 44:23 the holy and the **c** and show them how to H2687
Eze 48:15 will be for the **c use** of the city, for H2687
Ac 2:44 were together and had everything **in c**. *G3123*
Ro 9:21 special purposes and some for **c use**? *G871*
1Co 10:13 overtaken you except **what is c to mankind**. *G474*
1Co 12: 7 of the Spirit is given for the **c good**. *G5237*
2Co 6:14 righteousness and wickedness have **in c**? *G3580*
2Co 6:15 a believer have **in c** with an unbeliever? *G3535*
Php 2: 1 his love, if any **c sharing in** the Spirit, if *G3126*
2Ti 2:20 special purposes and some for **c use**. *G871*
Titus 1: 4 my true son in our **c** faith: Grace and *G3123*

COMMONWEALTH (KJV) CITIZENSHIP

COMMOTION (8)

Job 39: 7 It laughs at the **c** *in* the town; it does not H2162
Isa 22: 2 you town so full of **c**, you city of tumult H9583
Jer 3:23 Surely the idolatrous **c** on the hills and H2162
Jer 10:22 a great **c** from the land of the north! H8323
Mk 5:38 Jesus saw a **c**, with people crying *G2573*
Mk 5:39 said to them, "Why *all this* **c** and wailing? *G2572*
Ac 12:18 there was no small **c** among the soldiers *G5431*
Ac 19:40 would not be able to account for this **c**, *G5371*

COMMUNION (KJV) FELLOWSHIP, PARTICIPATION

COMMUNITIES (2) [COMMUNITY]

Am 1: 6 took captive whole **c** and sold them to H1661
Am 1: 9 she sold whole **c of captives** to Edom, H1661

COMMUNITY (87) [COMMUNITIES, COMMUNITY'S]

Ge 28: 3 numbers until you become a **c** *of* peoples. H7736
Ge 35:11 A nation and a **c** *of* nations will come H7736
Ge 48: 4 I will make you a **c** *of* peoples, and I will H7736
Ex 12: 3 Tell the whole **c** *of* Israel that on the tenth H6337
Ex 12: 6 the members of the **c** *of* Israel must H6337
Ex 12:19 in it must be cut off from the **c** *of* Israel. H6337
Ex 12:47 The whole **c** *of* Israel must celebrate it. H6337
Ex 16: 1 The whole Israelite **c** set out from Elim H6337
Ex 16: 2 the desert the whole **c** grumbled against H6337
Ex 16: 9 "Say to the entire Israelite **c**, 'Come H6337
Ex 16:10 was speaking to the whole Israelite **c**, H6337
Ex 16:22 the leaders of the **c** came and reported H6337
Ex 17: 1 The whole Israelite **c** set out from the H6337
Ex 34:31 all the leaders of the **c** came back to him, H6337
Ex 35: 1 the whole Israelite **c** and said to them, H6337
Ex 35: 4 Moses said to the whole Israelite **c**, "This H6337
Ex 35:20 the whole Israelite **c** withdrew from H6337
Ex 38:25 from those of the **c** who were counted in H6337
Lev 4:13 the whole Israelite **c** sins unintentionally H6337
Lev 4:13 even though the **c** is unaware of the H7736
Lev 4:15 The elders of the **c** are to lay their hands H6337
Lev 4:20 the priest will make atonement for **the c**, H2157S
Lev 4:21 This is the sin offering for the **c**. H7736
Lev 4:27 any member of the **c** sins H6639+2021+824
Lev 10: 6 the LORD will be angry with the whole **c**. H6337
Lev 10:17 the guilt of the **c** by making atonement H6337
Lev 16: 5 From the Israelite **c** he is to take two male H6337
Lev 16:17 his household and the whole **c** *of* Israel. H7736
Lev 16:33 the priests and all the members of the **c**. H7736
Lev 20: 2 The members of the **c** are to stone him. H824
Lev 20: 4 If the members of the **c** close their eyes H824
Nu 1: 2 of the whole Israelite **c** by their clans and H6337
Nu 1:16 were the men appointed from the **c**, H6337
Nu 1:18 called the whole **c** together on the first H6337
Nu 1:53 my wrath will not fall on the Israelite **c**. H6337
Nu 3: 7 him and for the whole **c** at the tent of H6337
Nu 4:34 the leaders of the **c** counted the H6337
Nu 8: 9 assemble the whole Israelite **c**. H6337
Nu 8:20 the whole Israelite **c** did with the Levites H6337
Nu 10: 2 them for calling the **c** together and for H6337
Nu 10: 3 the whole **c** is to assemble before you at H6337
Nu 13:26 the whole Israelite **c** at Kadesh in the H6337
Nu 14: 1 the members of the **c** raised their voices H6337
Nu 14:27 will this wicked **c** grumble against me? H6337
Nu 14:35 do these things to this whole wicked **c**, H6337
Nu 14:36 made the whole **c** grumble against H6337
Nu 15:15 The **c** is to have the same rules for you H7736
Nu 15:22 " 'Now if *you as a c* **unintentionally** fail to AIT
Nu 15:24 without the **c** being aware of it, H6337
Nu 15:24 then the whole **c** is to offer a young bull H6337
Nu 15:25 make atonement for the whole Israelite **c**, H6337
Nu 15:26 The whole Israelite **c** and the foreigners H6337
Nu 16: 2 well-known **c** leaders who had been H6337
Nu 16: 3 The whole **c** is holy, every one of them H6337
Nu 16: 9 of the Israelite **c** and brought you near H6337
Nu 16: 9 to stand before the **c** and minister to them H6337
Nu 16:33 they perished and were gone from the **c**. H7736
Nu 16:41 the whole Israelite **c** grumbled against H6337
Nu 19: 9 kept by the Israelite **c** for use in the water H6337
Nu 19:20 they must be cut off from the **c**, because H7736
Nu 20: 1 the whole Israelite **c** arrived at the Desert H6337
Nu 20: 2 Now there was no water for the **c**, and the H6337
Nu 20: 4 you bring the LORD's **c** into this wilderness, H7736
Nu 20: 8 out of the rock for the **c** so they and their H6337
Nu 20:11 and the **c** and their livestock drank. H6337
Nu 20:12 will not bring this **c** into the land I give H7736
Nu 20:22 The whole Israelite **c** set out from Kadesh H6337
Nu 20:27 up Mount Hor in the sight of the whole **c**. H6337
Nu 20:29 when the whole **c** learned that Aaron H6337
Nu 26: 2 of the whole Israelite **c** by families— H6337
Nu 26: 9 Abiram were the **c** officials who H6337
Nu 27:14 when the **c** rebelled at the waters in H6337
Nu 27:16 living things, appoint someone over this **c** H6337
Nu 27:20 so the whole Israelite **c** will obey him. H6337
Nu 27:21 he and the entire **c** of the Israelites will H6337
Nu 31:13 all the leaders of the **c** went to meet them H6337
Nu 31:26 family heads of the **c** are to count all the H6337
Nu 31:27 part in the battle and the rest of the **c**. H6337
Nu 32: 2 the priest and to the leaders of the **c**, H6337
Jos 22:17 though a plague fell on the **c** *of* the LORD! H6337
Jos 22:18 will be angry with the whole **c** *of* Israel. H6337
Jos 22:20 not wrath come on the whole **c** *of* Israel? H6337
Jos 22:30 the priest and the leaders of the **c**— H6337
2Ch 31:18 daughters of the whole **c** listed in these H7736
Pr 6:19 a person who stirs up conflict in the **c**. H278
Jer 30:20 their **c** will be established before me H6337
Ac 25:24 The whole Jewish **c** has petitioned me *G4436*

COMMUNITY'S (1) [COMMUNITY]

Nu 31:43 the **c** half—was 337,500 sheep, H6337

COMPACTED (1)

Ps 122: 3 is built like a city that is **closely c** together. H2489

COMPANIES (8) [COMPANY]

Jdg 7:16 the three hundred men into three **c**, H8031
Jdg 7:20 The three **c** blew the trumpets and H8031
Jdg 9:34 positions near Shechem in four **c**. H8031
Jdg 9:43 them into three **c** and set an ambush in H8031
Jdg 9:44 Abimelek and the **c** with him rushed H8031
Jdg 9:44 Then two **c** attacked those in the fields H8031
2Ki 11: 5 who are in the three **c** that are going on NDT
2Ki 11: 7 are in the other two **c** that normally go off H3338

COMPANION (11) [COMPANIONS]

Jdg 15: 2 he said, "that I gave her to your **c**. H5335
Jdg 15: 6 because his wife was given to his **c**." H5335
1Ki 20:35 the company of the prophets said to his **c**, H8276
Job 30:29 become a brother of jackals, a **c** of owls. H8276
Ps 55:13 a man like myself, my **c**, my close friend, H476
Ps 55:20 **My c** attacks his friends; he violates his H2257S
Pr 13:20 become wise, for a **c** *of* fools suffers harm. H8287
Pr 28: 7 a **c** *of* gluttons disgraces his father. H8287
Pr 29: 3 a **c** *of* prostitutes squanders his wealth H8287
Php 4: 3 I ask you, my true **c**, help these women *G5187*
Rev 1: 9 your brother and **c** in the suffering and *G5171*

COMPANIONS (27) [COMPANION]

Jdg 14:11 they chose thirty men to be his **c**. H5335
Jdg 14:20 was given to *one of* his **c** who had H5335
2Ki 9: 2 him away from his **c** and take him into an H278
Ps 38:11 My friends and **c** avoid me because of my H8276
Ps 45: 7 set you above your **c** by anointing you H2492
Ps 45:14 to the king; her virgin **c** follow her—those H8292
Isa 41: 6 they help each other and say to their **c**, "Be H278
Mt 12: 3 when he and his **c** were hungry? *G3836+3552*
Mt 12: 4 and he and his **c** ate the *G3836+3552*
Mt 26:51 one of Jesus' **c** reached for his *G3836+3552*
Mk 1:36 Simon and his **c** went to look for *G3836+3552*
Mk 2:25 he and his **c** were hungry and *G3836+3552*
Mk 2:26 And he also gave some *to* his **c**." *G3836+5250*
Lk 5: 9 For he and all his **c** were astonished *G3836+5250*
Lk 6: 3 when he and his **c** were hungry? *G3836+3552*
Lk 6: 4 And he also gave some *to* his **c**." *G3836+3552*
Lk 9:32 Peter and his **c** were very sleepy *G3836+5250*
Lk 24:24 Then some *of* our **c** went to the *G3836+5250*
Ac 13:13 Paul and his **c** sailed to Perga in *G3836+4309*
Ac 16: 6 Paul and his **c** traveled throughout the NDT
Ac 17: 1 When Paul and his **c** had passed through NDT
Ac 19:29 Paul's **traveling c** from Macedonia *G5292*
Ac 20:34 own needs and the needs *of* my **c**. *G1639+3552*
Ac 22: 9 My **c** saw the light, but they *G3836+5250+1639*
Ac 22:11 My **c** led me by the hand into Damascus *G5289*
Ac 26:13 around me and my **c**. *G3836+5250+4513*
Heb 1: 9 set you above your **c** by anointing you *G3581*

COMPANY (38) [COMPANIES]

Ge 13: 9 land before you? *Let's* **part c**. If you go to H7233
Ge 13:11 toward the east. The two men **parted c**: H7233
Ge 50: 9 went up with him. It was a very large **c**. H4722
Jdg 9:37 a **c** is coming from the direction of H8031
1Ki 20:35 the LORD one of the **c** *of* the prophets said H1201
2Ki 1: 9 to Elijah a captain with his *c of* **fifty** *men*. AIT
2Ki 2: 3 The **c** *of* the prophets at Bethel came out H1201
2Ki 2: 5 The **c** *of* the prophets at Jericho went up H1201
2Ki 2: 7 Fifty men from the **c** *of* the prophets went H1201
2Ki 2:15 The **c** *of* the prophets from Jericho, who H1201
2Ki 4: 1 of a man from the **c** *of* the prophets cried H1201
2Ki 4:38 While the **c** *of* the prophets was meeting H1201
2Ki 5:22 men from the **c** *of* the prophets have H1201
2Ki 6: 1 The **c** *of* the prophets said to Elisha, "Look H1201
2Ki 9: 1 a man from the **c** *of* the prophets and said H1201
Ezr 2: 2 **in c with** Zerubbabel, Joshua, Nehemiah H6640
Ezr 2:64 The whole **c** numbered 42,360, H7736
Ne 7: 7 **in c with** Zerubbabel, Joshua, Nehemiah H6640
Ne 7:66 The whole **c** numbered 42,360, H7736
Ne 8:17 The whole **c** that had returned from exile H7736
Job 15:34 For the **c** *of* the godless will be barren H6337
Job 34: 8 *He* **keeps c** with evildoers; he H782+4200+2495
Ps 1: 1 that sinners take or sit in the **c** *of* mockers, H4632
Ps 14: 5 God is present in the **c** *of* the righteous. H1887
Ps 106:17 Dathan; it buried the **c** *of* Abiram. H6337
Pr 21:16 comes to rest in the **c** *of* the dead. H7736
Pr 24: 1 the wicked, do not desire their **c**; H2118+907
Jer 15:17 I never sat in the **c** *of* revelers, never H6051
Eze 27:34 wares and all your **c** have gone down with H7736
Ob 20 This **c** of Israelite exiles who are in H2657
Mt 27:27 the whole **c of soldiers** around him. *G5061*
Mk 15:16 called together the whole **c of soldiers**. *G5061*
Lk 2:13 Suddenly a **great c** of the heavenly host *G4436*
Lk 2:44 Thinking he was in their **c**, they traveled *G5322*
Ac 15:39 a sharp disagreement that they **parted c**. *G714*
Ro 15:24 after *I have* **enjoyed** your **c** for a while. *G1855*
Ro 15:32 by God's will, and **in** your **c be refreshed**. *G5265*
1Co 15:33 "Bad **c** corrupts good character." *G3918*

COMPARE (20) [COMPARED, COMPARING, COMPARISON]

Job 28:17 Neither gold nor crystal *can* **c** *with* it, nor H6885
Job 28:19 The topaz of Cush cannot **c with** it; it H6885
Job 39:13 though they cannot **c** with the wings and NDT
Ps 40: 5 None *can* **c** with you; were I to speak and H6885
Ps 86: 8 like you, Lord; no deeds can **c with** yours. H3869
Ps 89: 6 in the skies above *can* **c** with the LORD? H6885
Pr 3:15 nothing you desire *can* **c** with her. H8750
Pr 8:11 nothing you desire *can* **c** with her. H8750
Isa 40:18 then, *will you* **c** God? To what H1948
Isa 40:25 "To whom *will you* **c** me? Or who is my H1948
Isa 46: 5 "With whom *will you* **c** me or count me H1948
La 2:13 With what *can I* **c** you, Daughter H1948
Eze 31: 8 nor *could* the plane trees **c with** its H2118+3869
Da 1:13 Then **c** our appearance with that of the H8011
Mt 11:16 "To what *can I* **c** this generation? They are *G3929*
Lk 7:31 *can I* **c** the people of this generation? *G3929*
Lk 13:18 kingdom of God like? What *shall I* **c** it to? *G3929*
Lk 13:20 "What *shall I* **c** the kingdom of God to? *G3929*
2Co 10:12 dare to classify or **c** ourselves with some *G5173*
2Co 10:12 by themselves and **c** themselves with *G5173*

COMPARED (6) [COMPARE]

Jdg 8: 2 "What have I accomplished **c to** you? H3869
Jdg 8: 3 What was I able to do **c to** you?" At this, H3869
Isa 46: 5 will you liken me that *we may be* **c**? H1948
Eze 31: 2 " 'Who *can be* **c** with *you* in majesty? H1948
Eze 31:18 of Eden *can be* **c** with *you* in splendor H1948
Ro 5:16 the gift of God be **c with** the result of one *G6055*

COMPARING (3) [COMPARE]

Ro 8:18 are not worth **c with** the glory that will be *G4639*
2Co 8: 8 of your love **by c** it **with** the earnestness of *G1328*
Gal 6: 4 without *c* themselves **to** someone else, AIT

COMPARISON (1) [COMPARE]

2Co 3:10 has no glory now **in c with** the *G1877+4047+3836+3538+1641*

COMPASS, COMPASSED, COMPASSETH (KJV)

AROUND, LEDGE, SURROUNDED, WINDS

COMPASSES (1)

Isa 44:13 it out with chisels and marks it with **c**. H4684

COMPASSION (71) [COMPASSIONATE, COMPASSIONS]

Ex 33:19 and *I will* **have c** *on* whom I will have H8163
Ex 33:19 have compassion on whom *I will* **have c**. H8163
Dt 13:17 show you mercy, and *will* **have c** *on* you. H8163
Dt 28:54 among you *will* **have no c** on his H8317+6524
Dt 30: 3 fortunes and **have c** *on* you and gather H8163
2Ki 13:23 to them and **had c** and showed concern H8163
2Ch 30: 9 will be shown **c** by their captors and H8171
Ne 9:19 of your great **c** you did not abandon H8171
Ne 9:27 in your great **c** you gave them H8171
Ne 9:28 in your **c** you delivered them time H8171
Ps 51: 1 according to your great **c** blot out my H8171
Ps 77: 9 Has he in anger withheld his **c**?" H8171
Ps 90:13 long will it be? **Have c** on your servants. H5714
Ps 102:13 You will arise and **have c** *on* Zion, for it is H8163
Ps 103: 4 the pit and crowns you with love and **c**, H8171
Ps 103:13 As a father **has c** on his children, so the H8163
Ps 103:13 so the LORD **has c** on those who fear him H8163
Ps 116: 5 righteous; our God *is* **full of c**. H8163
Ps 119:77 Let your **c** come to me that I may live, for H8171
Ps 119:156 Your **c**, LORD, is great; preserve my life H8171
Ps 135:14 his people and **have c** on his servants. H5714
Ps 145: 9 good to all; he has **c** on all he has made. H8171
Isa 13:18 nor *will* they **look with c** on children H2571+6524
Isa 14: 1 The LORD *will* **have c** *on* Jacob; once again H8163
Isa 27:11 so their Maker *has* no **c** *on* them, and H8163
Isa 30:18 therefore he will rise up to **show** you **c**. H8163
Isa 49:10 *He who* **has c** *on* them will guide them H8163
Isa 49:13 his people and *will have* **c** *on* his afflicted H8163
Isa 49:15 her breast and **have** no **c** *on* the child she H8163
Isa 51: 3 Zion and *will* **look with c** *on* all her ruins; H5714
Isa 54: 7 but with deep **c** I will bring you back. H8171
Isa 54: 8 everlasting kindness *I will* **have c** *on* you," H8163
Isa 54:10 says the LORD, *who* **has c** *on* you. H8163
Isa 60:10 I struck you, in favor *I will* **show** you **c**. H8163
Isa 63: 7 according to his **c** and many kindnesses. H8171
Isa 63:15 Your tenderness and **c** are withheld from H8171
Jer 12:15 I will again **have c** and will bring each of H8163
Jer 13:14 no pity or mercy or **c** to keep me from H8163
Jer 21: 7 he will show them no mercy or pity or **c**. H8163
Jer 30:18 Jacob's tents and **have c** *on* his dwellings; H8163
Jer 31:20 him; *I* **have great c** *for* him, H8163+8163
Jer 33:26 restore their fortunes and **have c** *on* them. H8163
Jer 42:12 I will show you **c** so that he will have H8171
Jer 42:12 so that *he will* **have c** *on* you and restore H8163
La 3:32 brings grief, *he will* **show c**, so great is his H8163
Eze 9: 5 the city and kill, without showing pity or **c**. H2798
Eze 16: 5 you with pity or **had c** *enough* to do any of H2798
Eze 39:25 of Jacob and *will* **have c** *on* all the people H8163
Da 1: 9 the official to show favor and **c** to Daniel, H8171
Hos 2:19 righteousness and justice, in love and **c**. H8171
Hos 11: 8 is changed within me; all my **c** is aroused. H5719
Hos 13:14 is your destruction? "I will have no **c**, H5716
Hos 14: 3 for in you the fatherless **find c**. H8163
Jnh 3: 9 may yet relent and *with* **c** turn from his H5714
Mic 7:19 You will again **have c** *on* us; you will H8163
Zec 7: 9 show mercy and **c** to one another. H8171
Zec 10: 6 restore them because *I* **have c** *on* them. H8163
Mal 3:17 as a father **has c and spares** his son who H2798
Mt 9:36 saw the crowds, *he* **had c** on them *G5072*
Mt 14:14 *he* **had c** on them and healed their sick. *G5072*
Mt 15:32 him and said, "*I* **have c** for these people *G5072*
Mt 20:34 Jesus **had c** on them and touched their *G5072*
Mk 6:34 a large crowd, *he* **had c** on them, because *G5072*
Mk 8: 2 "*I* **have c** for these people; they have *G5072*
Lk 15:20 saw him and *was* **filled with c** for him; *G5072*
Ro 9:15 and *I will* **have c** on whom I have *G3882*
Ro 9:15 I will have compassion on whom *I* **have c**." *G3882*
2Co 1: 3 the Father *of* **c** and the God of all comfort *G3880*
Php 2: 1 in the Spirit, if any tenderness and **c**, *G3880*
Col 3:12 clothe yourselves with **c**, kindness, *G5073+3880*
Jas 5:11 The Lord is **full of c** and mercy. *G4499*

COMPASSIONATE (14) [COMPASSION]
Ex 22:27 they cry out to me, I will hear, for I am **c**. H2843
Ex 34: 6 the LORD, the **c** and gracious God, slow to H8157
2Ch 30: 9 the LORD your God is gracious and **c**. H8157
Ne 9:17 gracious and **c**, slow to anger and H8157
Ps 86:15 are a **c** and gracious God, slow to H8157
Ps 103: 8 The LORD is **c** and gracious, slow to anger H8157
Ps 111: 4 remembered; the LORD is gracious and **c**. H8157
Ps 112: 4 who are gracious and **c** and righteous. H8157
Ps 145: 8 The LORD is gracious and **c**, slow to anger H8157
La 4:10 their own hands **c** women have cooked H8172
Joel 2:13 he is gracious and **c**, slow to anger H8157
Jnh 4: 2 I knew that you are a gracious and **c** God H8157
Eph 4:32 Be kind and **c** to one another, forgiving *G2359*
1Pe 3: 8 love one another, be **c** and humble. *G2359*

COMPASSIONS (1) [COMPASSION]
La 3:22 we are not consumed, for his **c** never fail. H8171

COMPEL (2) [COMPELLED, COMPELS, COMPULSION]
Lk 14:23 country lanes and **c** them to come in, *G337*
Gal 6:12 means of the flesh *are trying to* **c** you to be *G337*

COMPELLED (7) [COMPEL]
1Sa 13:12 So *I* **felt c** to offer the burnt offering." H706
Ezr 4:23 in Jerusalem and **c** them by force to stop A10264
Ac 20:22 "And now, **c** by the Spirit, I am going to *G1313*
Ac 28:19 so *I was* **c** to make an appeal to Caesar. *G337*
1Co 9:16 cannot boast, since I *am* **c** to preach. *G340+2130*
Gal 2: 3 who was with me, *was* **c** to be circumcised *G337*
Jude 3 I felt **c** to write and urge you to contend *G340*

COMPELS (3) [COMPEL]
Ex 3:19 not let you go unless a mighty hand **c** him. H928
Job 32:18 of words, and the spirit within me **c** me; H7439
2Co 5:14 For Christ's love **c** us, because we are *G5309*

COMPENSATE (2) [COMPENSATION]
Ex 21:26 must let the slave go free **to c for** the eye. H9393
Ex 21:27 let the slave go free **to c for** the tooth. H9393

COMPENSATION (1) [COMPENSATE]
Pr 6:35 He will not accept any **c**; he will refuse a H4111

COMPETE (1) [COMPETES, COMPETING]
Jer 12: 5 worn you out, how *can you* **c** with horses? H3013

COMPETENCE (1) [COMPETENT]
2Co 3: 5 ourselves, but our **c** comes from God. *G2654*

COMPETENT (4) [COMPETENCE]
Ro 15:14 with knowledge and **c** to instruct one *G1538*
1Co 6: 2 are you **not c** to judge trivial cases? *G396*
2Co 3: 5 Not that we are **c** in ourselves to claim *G2653*
2Co 3: 6 He *has* **made** us **c** as ministers of a new *G2655*

COMPETES (2) [COMPETE]
1Co 9:25 Everyone who **c in the games** goes into strict *G76*
2Ti 2: 5 anyone *who* **c as an athlete** does not *G123*

COMPETING (1) [COMPETE]
2Ti 2: 5 victor's crown except *by* **c** according to the *G123*

COMPILED (1)
Pr 25: 1 **c** *by* the men of Hezekiah king of Judah: H6980

COMPLACENCY (2) [COMPLACENT]
Pr 1:32 and the **c** *of* fools will destroy them; H8932
Eze 30: 9 me in ships to frighten Cush out of her **c**. H1055

COMPLACENT (4) [COMPLACENCY]
Isa 32: 9 You women *who* are *so* **c**, rise up and H8633
Isa 32:11 Tremble, you **c** *women*; shudder, you H8633
Am 6: 1 Woe to *you who* are **c** in Zion, and to you H8633
Zep 1:12 with lamps and punish those who *are* **c**, H7884

COMPLAIN (7) [COMPLAINED, COMPLAINT, COMPLAINTS]
Jdg 21:22 When their fathers or brothers **c** to us, we H8189
Job 7:11 *I will* **c** in the bitterness of my soul. H8488
Job 33:13 Why *do you* **c** to him that he responds to H8189
Isa 29:24 *those who* **c** will accept instruction." H8087
Isa 40:27 Why *do you* **c**, Jacob? Why do you say H606
Isa 56: 3 And *let* no eunuch **c**, "I am only a H606
La 3:39 Why *should* the living **c** when punished H645

COMPLAINED (4) [COMPLAIN]
Ge 21:25 Then Abraham **c** *to* Abimelek about a H3519
Nu 11: 1 Now the people **c** *about* their hardships in H645
Lk 5:30 belonged to their sect **c** to his disciples, *G1197*
Ac 6: 1 Jews among them **c** against the *G1181+1198*

COMPLAINT (11) [COMPLAIN]
2Sa 15: 2 anyone came with a **c** to be placed before H8190
2Sa 15: 4 everyone who has a **c** or case could come H8190
Job 7:13 comfort me and my couch will ease my **c**, H8490
Job 9:27 'I will forget my **c**, I will change my H8490
Job 10: 1 give free rein to my **c** and speak out in the H8490
Job 21: 4 "Is my **c** directed to a human being? Why H8490
Job 23: 2 "Even today my **c** is bitter; his hand is H8490
Ps 64: 1 as I voice my **c**; protect my life from H8490
Ps 142: 2 I pour out before him my **c**; before him I H8490
Hab 2: 1 what answer I am to give to this **c**. H9350
Ac 18:14 you Jews *were* **making a c** *about* some *G1639S*

COMPLAINTS (2) [COMPLAIN]
Nu 14:27 I have heard the **c** *of* these grumbling H9442
Pr 23:29 Who has **c**? Who has needless H8490

COMPLETE (27) [COMPLETED, COMPLETELY, COMPLETENESS, COMPLETING, COMPLETION]
Ex 5:13 "**C** the work required of you for each day H3983
Dt 16:15 work of your hands, and your joy will be **c**. H421
1Ki 7: 1 *to* **c** the construction of his palace. H3983
2Ki 12:15 workers, because they acted with **c honesty**. H575
Est 2:12 she *had to* **c** twelve months H2118+4946+7891
Zec 4: 9 of this temple; his hands *will* also **c** it. H1298
Mt 23:32 *Go ahead*, then, *and* **c** what your ancestors *G4444*
Lk 6:49 it collapsed and its destruction was **c**." *G3489*
Lk 14:28 to see if you have enough money to **c** it? *G568*
Jn 3:29 That joy is mine, and *it is now* **c**. *G4444*
Jn 15:11 may be in you and that your joy *may be* **c**. *G4444*
Jn 16:24 you will receive, and your joy will be **c**. *G4444*
Jn 17:23 so that they may be *brought* to **c** unity. *G5457*
Ac 20:24 to finish the race and **c** the task the Lord NDT
2Co 7:16 glad I can have **c** confidence in you *G1877+4246*
2Co 8: 7 in **c** earnestness and in the love we have *G4246*
2Co 10: 6 disobedience, once your obedience *is* **c**. *G4444*
Php 2: 2 then **make** my joy **c** by being like-minded *G4444*
Col 2: 2 have the full riches of **c** understanding, *G4443*
Col 4:17 "See to it that *you* **c** the ministry you have *G4444*
Jas 1: 4 its work so that you may be mature and **c**, *G3908*
Jas 2:22 his faith *was* **made c** by what he did. *G5457*
1Jn 1: 4 We write this to **make** our joy **c**. *G1639+4444*
1Jn 2: 5 love for God *is* truly **made c** in them. *G5457*
1Jn 4:12 lives in us and his love is **made c** in us. *G5457*
1Jn 4:17 This is how love *is* **made c** among us so *G5457*
2Jn 12 you face to face, so that our joy may be **c**. *G4444*

COMPLETED (23) [COMPLETE]
Ge 2: 1 the earth **were c** in all their vast H3983
Ge 29:21 My time *is* **c**, and I want to make love to H4848
Ex 39:32 tabernacle, the tent of meeting, *was* **c**. H3983
Lev 8:33 until the days of your ordination *are* **c**, for H4848
Jos 3:17 the whole nation *had* **c** the crossing on H9462
1Ki 6: 9 So he built the temple and **c** it, roofing it H3983
1Ki 6:14 So Solomon built the temple and **c** it. H3983
1Ki 7:22 And so the work on the pillars *was* **c**. H9462
2Ch 29:28 the sacrifice of the burnt offering *was* **c**. H3983
2Ch 36:21 the seventy years *were* **c** in fulfillment of H4848
Ezr 6:15 The temple *was* **c** on the third day of the A10707
Ne 6: 9 too weak for the work, and *it will* not **be c**." H6913
Ne 6:15 So the wall *was* **c** on the twenty-fifth of H8966
Isa 40: 2 to her that her hard service *has been* **c**, H4848
Jer 29:10 "When seventy years *are* **c** for Babylon, H4848
Da 11:36 be successful until the time of wrath *is* **c**, H3983
Da 12: 7 finally broken, all these things *will be* **c**." H3983
Lk 1:23 When his time of service *was* **c**, he *G4398*
Lk 12:50 what constraint I am under until *it is* **c**! *G5464*
Ac 14:26 grace of God for the work *they had now* **c**. *G4444*
Ro 15:28 So *after I have* **c** this task and have made *G2200*
Rev 15: 1 because with them God's wrath *is* **c**. *G5464*
Rev 15: 8 plagues of the seven angels *were* **c**. *G5464*

COMPLETELY (94) [COMPLETE]
Ge 8:14 of the second month the earth *was* **c dry**. H3312
Ge 20:16 all who are with you; you are **c** vindicated." H3972
Ex 11: 1 when he does, he will drive you out **c**. H3986
Ex 17:14 because *I will* **c blot out** the name H4681+4681
Ex 21:19 and **see that** the victim **is c healed**. H8324+8324
Lev 1:17 by the wings, not **dividing** it **c**, and then the H976
Lev 5: 8 its head from its neck, not **dividing** it **c**, H976
Lev 6:22 perpetual share and is to be burned **c**. H4003
Lev 6:23 offering of a priest shall be burned **c**; H4003
Lev 26:44 abhor them so as to **destroy** them **c**, H3983
Nu 21: 3 *They* **c destroyed** them and their towns; so H3049
Dt 2:15 them until he had **c** eliminated them from H9462
Dt 2:34 took all his towns and **c destroyed** them— H3049
Dt 3: 6 *We* **c destroyed** them, as we had done H3049
Dt 12: 2 **Destroy c** all the places on the high H6+6
Dt 13:15 *You must* **destroy** it **c**, both its people and H3049
Dt 13:16 public square and **c** burn the town and all NDT
Dt 20:17 **C destroy** them—the Hittites H3049+3049
Jos 2:10 east of the Jordan, whom *you* **c destroyed**. H3049
Jos 3:16 the Dead Sea) was **c** cut off. H9462
Jos 10:10 **defeated** them **c** at Gibeon H5782+1524+4804
Jos 10:20 Israelites defeated them **c**, H3983+6330+9462
Jos 11:14 to the sword until they **c destroyed** them, H9012
Jos 17:13 labor but *did* not **drive** them **out c**. H3769+3769
Jdg 1:28 labor but never **drove** them **out c**. H3769+3769
1Sa 15: 9 These they were unwilling *to* **destroy c** H3049
1Sa 15:18 'Go and **c destroy** those wicked people H3049
1Sa 15:20 *I* **c destroyed** the Amalekites and brought H3049
2Sa 22:39 *I* **crushed** them **c**, and they H4730+2256+430
1Ki 11: 6 *he* **did** not follow the LORD **c**, as H4848
1Ki 16:26 He followed **c** the ways of Jeroboam son H3972
2Ki 13:17 "You will **c** destroy the Arameans H6330+3983
2Ki 13:19 defeated Aram and **c destroyed** it. H6330+3983
2Ki 19:11 to all the countries, **destroying** them **c**. H3049
2Ki 21:21 He followed **c** the ways of his father H3972
2Ki 22: 2 the LORD and followed **c** the ways of his H3972
1Ch 4:41 who were there and **c destroyed** them, H3049
Job 19:13 my acquaintances are **c** estranged from me. H421
Job 21:23 dies in full vigor, **c** secure and at ease, H3972
Ps 37:28 Wrongdoers will be **c** destroyed H4200+6409
Ps 73:19 they destroyed, **c** swept away by terrors! H9462
Ps 74: 8 in their hearts, "We will crush them **c**!" H3480
Ps 78:59 he was furious; he rejected Israel **c**. H4394
Ps 88:17 me like a flood; they have **c** engulfed me. H3480
Ps 139: 4 word is on my tongue you, LORD, know it **c**. H3972
Isa 10:18 fields it will **c** destroy, H4946+5883+2256+6330+1414
Isa 24: 3 The earth *will* **be c laid waste** and H1327+1327
Isa 32:19 and the city *is* **leveled c**, H9164+928+2021+9168
Isa 37:11 to all the countries, **destroying** them **c**. H3049
Isa 48: 9 back from you, so as not *to* **destroy** you **c**. H4162
Jer 3: 1 *Would* not the land *be* **c defiled** H2866+2866
Jer 4:10 How **c** *you have* **deceived** this H5958+5958
Jer 4:27 though *I will* not **destroy** it **c**. H6913+3986
Jer 5:10 but *do* not **destroy** them **c**. H6913+3986
Jer 5:18 the LORD, "*I will* not **destroy** you **c**. H6913+3986
Jer 10:25 have devoured him **c** and destroyed his H3983
Jer 12:17 *I will* **c uproot** and destroy it, H6004+6004
Jer 13: 7 it was ruined and **c** useless. H4200+2021+3972
Jer 13:10 be like this belt—**c** useless! H4200+2021+3972
Jer 13:19 will be carried into exile, carried **c** away. H8934
Jer 14:19 *Have you* **rejected** Judah **c**? Do you H4415+4415
Jer 25: 9 *I will* **c destroy** them and make them an H3049
Jer 30:11 'Though *I* **c destroy** all the nations H6913+3986
Jer 30:11 scatter you, *I will* not **c destroy** you. H6913+3986
Jer 46:28 "Though *I* **c destroy** all the nations H6913+3986
Jer 46:28 scatter you, *I will* not **c destroy** you. H6913+3986
Jer 50:13 not be inhabited but will be **c** desolate. H3972
Jer 50:21 kill and **c destroy** them," declares H3049
Jer 50:26 **C destroy** her and leave her no remnant H3049
Jer 51: 3 spare her young men; **c destroy** her army. H3049
Eze 10:12 their wings, were **c** full of eyes, as were H6017
Eze 11:13 *Will* you **c destroy** the remnant of H3986+6913
Eze 17:10 *Will* it not **wither c** when the east H3312+3312
Eze 40: 5 saw a wall **c surrounding** the H6017+6017
Da 7:26 and **c destroyed** forever. A10722+10221+10005
Da 8:23 when rebels *have become* **c** wicked, H9462
Hos 10:15 king of Israel *will* **be c destroyed**. H1950+1950
Na 1:15 invade you; they will be **c** destroyed. H3972
Zec 5: 4 will remain in that house and **destroy** it **c**, H3983
Zec 11:17 *May* his arm *be* **c withered**, his H3312+3312
Mt 8:26 winds and the waves, and it was **c** calm. *G3489*
Mt 12:13 So he stretched it out and *it was* **c restored** *G635*
Mk 3: 5 and his hand *was* **c restored**. *G635*
Mk 4:39 the wind died down and it was **c** calm. *G3489*
Mk 5:42 years old). At this they were **c** astonished. *G3489*
Mk 6:51 They were **c** amazed, *G3336+1666+4356*
Lk 6:10 He did so, and his hand *was* **c restored**. *G635*
Ac 3:16 him *that has* **c healed** *G1443+3836+3907+4047*
Ac 3:23 listen to him *will be* **c cut off** from their *G2017*
1Co 6: 7 means you have been **c** defeated already. *G3914*
Eph 4: 2 Be **c** humble and gentle; be patient, *G3552+4246*
Heb 7:25 able to save **c** those who *G1650+3836+4117*
Heb 12: 5 And *have you* **c forgotten** this word of *G1720*
2Pe 1:19 message *as something* **c reliable**, *G1010*

COMPLETENESS (1) [COMPLETE]
1Co 13:10 when **c** comes, what is in part *G5455*

COMPLETING (1) [COMPLETE]
Ac 13:25 As John *was* **c** his work, he said: 'Who do *G4444*

COMPLETION (4) [COMPLETE]
2Ch 8:16 the temple of the LORD was laid until its **c**. H3983
2Co 8: 6 to **bring** also **to c** this act of grace on your *G2200*
2Co 8:11 to do it may be matched by your **c** of it, *G2200*
Php 1: 6 work in you *will* **carry** it **on to c** until the *G2200*

COMPLIED (1) [COMPLY]
2Ki 16: 9 The king of Assyria **c** *by* attacking H9048

COMPLIMENTS (1)
Pr 23: 8 eaten and will have wasted your **c**. H1821+5833

COMPLY (1) [COMPLIED]
Est 3: 4 day they spoke to him but *he* refused *to* **c**. H9048

COMPOSED (1) [COMPOSE]
2Ch 35:25 Jeremiah **c laments** for Josiah, and to this H7801

COMPREHEND (2) [COMPREHENDED, COMPREHENDS]
Ecc 8:17 No one can **c** what goes on under the sun. H5162
Ecc 8:17 claim they know, they cannot *really* **c** it. H5162

COMPREHENDED (1) [COMPREHEND]
Job 38:18 *Have you* **c** the vast expanses of the earth? H1067

COMPREHENDS (1) [COMPREHEND]
Job 28:13 No mortal **c** its worth; it cannot be found H3359

COMPULSION (2) [COMPEL]
1Co 7:37 who is under no **c** but has control over his *G340*
2Co 9: 7 not reluctantly or under **c**, for God loves a *G340*

COMPUTE (1)
Lev 25:52 *they are to* **c** that and pay for their H3108

CONANIAH (NIV84) KONANIAH

CONCEAL (8) [CONCEALED, CONCEALS]
Lev 16:13 of the incense *will* **c** the atonement cover H4059
Job 14:13 me in the grave and **c** me till your anger H6259
Job 27:11 the ways of the Almighty *I will* not **c**. H3948
Job 40:22 The lotuses **c** it in their shadow; the H6114
Ps 40:10 *I do* not **c** your love and your faithfulness H3948

Pr 25: 2 It is the glory of God *to* **c** a matter; to H6259
Isa 26:21 the earth *will* **c** its slain no longer. H4059
Jer 49:10 so that he cannot **c himself**. H2464

CONCEALED (13) [CONCEAL]
Jdg 9:34 by night and **took up c positions** near H741
Job 10:13 "But this is what *you* **c** in your heart, and I H7621
Job 24:15 eye will see me,' and he keeps his face **c**. H6260
Job 28:21 **c** even from the birds in the sky. H6259
Job 31:33 if *I have* **c** my sin as people do, by hiding H4059
Pr 21:14 a bribe **c in** the cloak pacifies great H928
Pr 26:26 Their malice *may be* **c** by deception, but H4059
Isa 49: 2 a polished arrow and **c** me in his quiver. H6259
Jer 16:17 from me, nor **is** their sin **c** from my eyes. H7621
Mt 10:26 there is nothing **c** that will not be G2821
Mk 4:22 whatever is **c** is meant to be brought G649
Lk 8:17 nothing **c** that will not be known or G649
Lk 12: 2 There is nothing **c** that will not be G5158

CONCEALS (3) [CONCEAL]
Pr 10:11 the mouth of the wicked **c** violence. H4059
Pr 10:18 *Whoever* **c** hatred with lying lips and H4059
Pr 28:13 *Whoever* **c** their sins does not prosper, but H4059

CONCEDE (1) [CONCESSION]
Dt 32:31 not like our Rock, as even our enemies **c**. H7130

CONCEIT (3) [CONCEITED]
Isa 16: 6 of her **c**, her pride and her insolence H1452
Jer 48:29 her **c** and the haughtiness of her heart. H1452
Php 2: 3 nothing out of selfish ambition or **vain c**. G3029

CONCEITED (8) [CONCEIT]
1Sa 17:28 I know how **c** you are and how wicked H2295
Ro 11:25 so that you may not be **c**: G1877+1571+5861
Ro 12:16 of low position. Do not be **c**. G5861+4123+1571
2Co 12: 7 in order to keep *me* from *becoming* **c**, G5643
Gal 5:26 Let us not become **c**, provoking and G3030
1Ti 3: 6 or *he may become* **c** and fall under the G5605
1Ti 6: 4 *they are* **c** and understand nothing. G5605
2Ti 3: 4 **c**, lovers of pleasure rather than G5605

CONCEIVE (13) [CONCEIVED, CONCEIVES, CONCEIVING, CONCEPTION]
Ge 11:30 childless because she was not **able to c**. H2263
Ge 29:31 *he* **enabled** her **to c**, but H7337+906+8167
Ge 30:22 to her and **enabled** her **to c**. H7337+906+8167
Nu 11:12 *Did* I **c** all these people? Did I give them H2225
Ru 4:13 the LORD enabled her to **c**, and she gave H2231
Job 15:35 They **c** trouble and give birth to evil; their H2225
Isa 7:14 The virgin will **c** and give birth to a son H2226
Isa 33:11 *You* **c** chaff, you give birth to straw; your H2225
Isa 59: 4 they **c** trouble and give birth to evil. H2225
Mt 1:23 "The virgin *will* **c** and give G1877+1143+2400
Lk 1: 7 because Elizabeth was **not able to c**, G5096
Lk 1:31 *You will* **c** and give birth to a G5197+1877+1143
Lk 1:36 was said to be **unable to c** is in her sixth G5096

CONCEIVED (22) [CONCEIVE]
Ge 16: 4 with Hagar, and *she* **c**. When she knew H2225
Ge 29:33 *She* **c** again, and when she gave birth to H2225
Ge 29:34 Again *she* **c**, and when she gave birth to H2225
Ge 29:35 *She* **c** again, and when she gave birth to H2225
Ge 30: 7 servant Bilhah **c** again and bore Jacob a H2225
Ge 30:19 Leah **c** again and bore Jacob a sixth son. H2225
Ge 38: 4 *She* **c** again and gave birth to a son and H2225
2Sa 11: 5 The woman **c** and sent word to David H2225
Job 3: 3 the night that said, 'A boy is **c**! H2225
Ps 51: 5 sinful from the time my mother **c** me. H3501
SS 3: 4 to the room of the *one who* **c** me. H2225
SS 8: 5 there your mother **c** you, there she who H2473
Isa 8: 3 and *she* **c** and gave birth to a son. H2225
Isa 59:13 uttering lies our hearts *have* **c**. H2225
Hos 1: 3 Diblaim, and *she* **c** and bore him a son. H2225
Hos 1: 6 Gomer **c** again and gave birth to a H2225
Hos 2: 5 unfaithful and *has* **c** them in disgrace. H2225
Mt 1:20 because what *is* **c** in her is from the Holy G1164
Lk 2:21 him before he *was* **c**. G5197+1877+3836+3120
Ro 9:10 **children** *were* **c at the same time**
G1666+1651+3130+2400
1Co 2: 9 and what no human mind *has* **c**"— G2093+326
Jas 1:15 *after* desire *has* **c**, it gives birth to G5197

CONCEIVES (1) [CONCEIVE]
Ps 7:14 is pregnant with evil **c** trouble and gives H2225

CONCEIVING (1) [CONCEIVE]
Ge 20:18 *had* **kept** all **the women** in Abimelek's household
from c H6806+1237+8167+6806

CONCEPTION (1) [CONCEIVE]
Hos 9:11 like a bird—no birth, no pregnancy, no **c**. H2231

CONCERN (19) [CONCERNED, CONCERNING, CONCERNS]
Ge 39: 6 *he did* not **c** *himself with* anything except H3359
Ge 39: 8 master *does* not **c** *himself with* anything H3359
1Sa 23:21 "The LORD bless you for *your* **c** for me. H2798
2Ki 13:23 and **showed c for** them because H7155+448
Job 9:21 I am blameless, *I* **have** no **c for** myself; H3359
Job 19: 4 gone astray, my error remains my **c** alone. H907
Ps 131: 1 *I do* not **c** *myself* with great matters or H2143
Pr 29: 7 the wicked **have** no *such* **c**. H1067+1981
Eze 36:21 **I had c** for my holy name, which the H2798
Jnh 4:11 And *should* I not **have c** for the great city H2571
Ac 18:17 Gallio **showed** no **c** whatever. G3508
1Co 7:32 I would like you to be **free from c**. G291
1Co 12:25 but *that* its parts *should* **have** equal **c** for G3534
2Co 7: 7 deep sorrow, your **ardent c** for me, so that G2419
2Co 7:11 what longing, what **c**, what readiness to G2419
2Co 8:16 heart of Titus the same **c** I have for you. G5082
2Co 11:28 daily the pressure *of* my **c** for all the G3533
Php 2:20 who *will* **show** genuine **c** for your welfare. G3534
Php 4:10 that at last you renewed your **c** for me. G5858

CONCERNED (20) [CONCERN]
Ge 21:11 Abraham greatly because it **c** his son. H128
Ex 2:25 on the Israelites and *was* **c about** them. H3359
Ex 3: 7 and *I am* **c about** their suffering. H3359
Ex 4:31 that the LORD *was* **c about** them and had H7212
1Sa 22: 8 None of you *is* **c** about me or tells me that H2703
2Sa 13:33 *should* not *be* **c about** the H8492+448+4213
1Ch 27: 1 the king in all *that* **c** the army divisions H1821
Ps 142: 4 one at my right hand; no *one is* **c** for me. H5795
Eze 36: 9 I am **c for** you and will look on you with H448
Da 10: 1 Its message was true and it **c** a great war NDT
Jnh 4:10 "You *have been* **c** about this plant H2571
Ro 11:28 **As far as** the gospel **is c**, they are G2848+3525
Ro 11:28 but **as far as** election **is c**, they are G2848
1Co 7:32 An unmarried man *is* **c about** the Lord's G3534
1Co 7:33 But a married man *is* **c about** the affairs of G3534
1Co 7:34 woman or virgin *is* **c about** the Lord's G3534
1Co 7:34 a married woman *is* **c about** the affairs of G3534
1Co 9: 9 Is it **about** oxen *that* God *is* **c**? G3508
Php 4:10 Indeed, *you were* **c**, but you had no G5858
2Ti 3: 8 who, **as far as** the faith **is c**, are G4309

CONCERNING (113) [CONCERN]
Ge 24: 9 swore an oath to him **c** this matter. H6584
Ge 47:26 established it as a law **c** land in Egypt— H6584
Lev 11:46 " 'These are the **regulations** *c* animals, birds AIT
Lev 13:59 These are the **regulations** *c* defiling molds in AIT
Nu 9: 8 I find out what the LORD commands **c** you." H4200
Nu 18:24 That is why I said **c** them: 'They will have H4200
Nu 30:16 the LORD gave Moses **c** relationships NDT
Dt 1: 3 that the LORD had commanded him **c** them. H448
Dt 19: 4 This is the **rule** *c* anyone who kills a person AIT
Dt 32:36 people and relent **c** his servants when he H6584
Dt 33:21 righteous will, and his judgments **c** Israel." H6640
1Sa 25:30 thing he promised **c** him and has H6584
2Sa 1:17 took up this lament **c** Saul and his son H6584
2Sa 3:28 before the LORD **c** the blood of Abner son H4946
2Sa 7:25 you have made **c** your servant and his H6584
2Sa 10: 2 express his sympathy to Hanun **c** his father. H448
2Sa 13:39 he was consoled **c** Amnon's death. H6584
2Sa 18: 5 giving orders **c** Absalom to each of H6584+1821
2Sa 24:16 the LORD relented **c** the disaster and said to H448
1Ki 16: 1 came to Jehu son of Hanani **c** Baasha: H6584
1Ki 21:23 "And also **c** Jezebel the LORD says: 'Dogs H4200
2Ki 19:20 heard your prayer **c** Sennacherib king of H448
2Ki 19:32 is what the LORD says **c** the king of Assyria: H448
2Ki 22:13 with all that is written there **c** us. H6584
2Ki 22:18 God of Israel, says **c** the words you heard: NDT
1Ch 17:23 you have made **c** your servant and his H6584
1Ch 19: 2 his sympathy to Hanun **c** his father. H6584
1Ch 21:15 saw it and relented **c** the disaster and H6584
2Ch 9:29 of Iddo the seer **c** Jeroboam son of Nebat H6584
2Ch 19:11 will be over you in any **matter** *c* the LORD, AIT
2Ch 19:11 will be over you in any **matter** *c* the king, and AIT
2Ch 23: 3 as the LORD promised **c** the descendants of H6584
2Ch 33: 8 I commanded them **c** all the laws, H4200
2Ch 34:26 God of Israel, says **c** the words you heard: NDT
Ezr 6: 3 the king issued a **decree** *c* the temple of God AIT
Ezr 7:11 a man learned in **matters** *c* the commands AIT
Est 3: 2 the king had commanded this **c** him. H4200
Est 9:29 to confirm this second **letter** *c* Purim. AIT
Ps 7: T which he sang to the LORD **c** Cush, H6584+1821
Ps 36: 1 I have a **message from God** in my heart *c* the AIT
Ps 50: 8 no charges against you **c** your sacrifices H6584
Ps 50: 8 your sacrifices or **c** your burnt offerings, NDT
Ps 91:11 command his angels **c** you to guard you H4200
Isa 1: 1 The vision **c** Judah and Jerusalem that H6584
Isa 2: 1 son of Amoz saw **c** Judah and Jerusalem: H6584
Isa 16:13 word the LORD has already spoken **c** Moab. H448
Isa 23:11 He has given an order **c** Phoenicia that her H448
Isa 30: 6 A **prophecy** *c* the animals of the Negev AIT
Isa 32: 6 ungodliness and spread error **c** the LORD; H448
Isa 37:21 have prayed to me **c** Sennacherib king of H448
Isa 37:33 is what the LORD says **c** the king of Assyria: H448
Isa 45:11 **C** things to come, do you question me about NDT
Jer 4:16 this to the nations, proclaim **c** Jerusalem: H6584
Jer 9:10 take up a lament **c** the wilderness H6584
Jer 14: 1 came to Jeremiah **c** the drought: H6584+1821
Jer 23: 9 **C** the prophets: My heart is broken within H4200
Jer 23:15 the LORD Almighty says **c** the prophets: H6584
Jer 25: 1 came to Jeremiah **c** all the people of H6584
Jer 30: 4 words the LORD spoke **c** Israel and Judah: H448
Jer 34: 4 This is what the LORD says **c** you: You will H6584
Jer 36: 2 the words I have spoken to you **c** Israel, H6584
Jer 39:16 against this city—words **c** disaster, not H4200
Jer 42:10 I have relented **c** the disaster I have H448
Jer 44: 1 came to Jeremiah **c** all the Jews living H448
Jer 46: 1 to Jeremiah the prophet **c** the nations: H6584
Jer 46: 2 **C** Egypt: This is the message against the H4200
Jer 47: 1 Jeremiah the prophet **c** the Philistines H448
Jer 48: 1 **C** Moab: This is what the LORD Almighty H4200
Jer 49: 1 **C** the Ammonites: This is what the LORD H4200
Jer 49: 7 **C** Edom: This is what the LORD Almighty H4200
Jer 49:23 **C** Damascus: "Hamath and Arpad are H4200
Jer 49:28 **C** Kedar and the kingdoms of Hazor H4200
Jer 49:34 that came to Jeremiah the prophet **c** Elam, H448
Jer 50: 1 the prophet **c** Babylon and the land H448
Jer 51:60 all that had been recorded **c** Babylon. H448
Eze 7:13 For the vision **c** the whole crowd will not be H448
Eze 19: 1 "Take up a lament **c** the princes of Israel H448
Eze 21:29 Despite false visions **c** you and lying H4200
Eze 26:17 take up a lament **c** you and say to you: H6584
Eze 27: 2 "Son of man, take up a lament **c** Tyre. H6584
Eze 27:32 over you, they will take up a lament **c** you: H6584
Eze 28:12 take up a lament **c** the king of Tyre and H6584
Eze 32: 2 take up a lament **c** Pharaoh king of Egypt H6584
Eze 36: 6 Therefore prophesy **c** the land of Israel H6584
Eze 44: 5 everything I tell you **c** all the regulations H4200
Da 2:18 from the God of heaven **c** this mystery, A10542
Da 8:13 be fulfilled—the vision **c** the daily sacrifice NDT
Am 1: 1 the vision he saw **c** Israel two years before H6584
Am 5: 1 Israel, this lament I take up **c** you: H6584
Mic 1: 1 the vision he saw **c** Samaria and H6584
Na 1: 1 A **prophecy** *c* Nineveh. The book of the vision AIT
Na 1:14 The LORD has given a command **c** you H6584
Zec 12: 1 The word of the LORD **c** Israel. The LORD, H6584
Mal 3:16 in his presence **c** those who feared the H4200
Mt 4: 6 " 'He will command his angels **c** you, and G4309
Lk 2:17 spread the word **c** what had been told G4309
Lk 4:10 command his angels **c** you to guard you G4309
Lk 24:27 was said in all the Scriptures **c** himself. G4309
Jn 1: 7 He came as a witness to testify **c** that light G4309
Jn 1:15 John testified **c** him. He cried out, saying G4309
Jn 5:37 who sent me has himself testified **c** me. G4309
Ac 1:16 spoke long ago through David **c** Judas, G4309
Ac 13:22 God testified *c* **him**: 'I have found David AIT
Ac 24:21 'It is **c** the resurrection of the dead that I G4309
Ac 28:21 not received any letters from Judea **c** you, G4309
Ro 9:27 Isaiah cries out **c** Israel: "Though the G5642
Ro 10: 8 the message *c* **faith** that we proclaim: AIT
Ro 10:21 But **c** Israel he says, "All day long I have G4639
2Th 2: 1 **C** the coming of our Lord Jesus Christ and G5642
1Ti 1:11 to the gospel *c* the **glory** of the blessed God, AIT
Heb 11:22 gave instructions **c** the burial of his G4309
1Pe 1:10 **C** this salvation, the prophets, who spoke G4309
1Jn 1: 1 this we proclaim **c** the Word of life. G4309

CONCERNS (10) [CONCERN]
2Ch 19:10 whether bloodshed or other **c** of the law NDT
Eze 12:10 This **prophecy** *c* the prince in Jerusalem and AIT
Da 8:17 that the vision **c** the time of the end." H4200
Da 8:19 because the vision **c** the appointed time H4200
Da 8:26 up the vision, for it **c** the distant future." H4200
Da 10:14 for the vision **c** a time yet to come. H4200
Mt 16:23 you do not have in mind **the** *c* of God, but AIT
Mt 16:23 concerns of God, but merely human **c**." G3836[S]
Mk 8:33 "You do not have in mind **the** *c* of God, but AIT
Mk 8:33 the concerns of God, but merely human **c**." G3836

CONCESSION (1) [CONCEDE]
1Co 7: 6 I say this as a **c**, not as a command. G5152

CONCISION (KJV) MUTILATORS OF THE FLESH

CONCLUDE (1) [CONCLUDED, CONCLUDES, CONCLUDING, CONCLUSION]
Ro 3: 9 What shall we **c then**? Do we have any G4036

CONCLUDED (2) [CONCLUDE]
Ecc 9: 1 on all this and **c** that the righteous and H1013
Jn 7:26 *Have* the authorities really **c** that he is the G1182

CONCLUDES (1) [CONCLUDE]
Ps 72:20 *This* **c** the prayers of David son of Jesse. H3983

CONCLUDING (1) [CONCLUDE]
Ac 16:10 **c** that God had called us to preach the G5204

CONCLUSION (1) [CONCLUDE]
Ecc 12:13 been heard; here is the **c** *of* the matter: H6067

CONCORD (KJV) HARMONY

CONCOURSE (KJV) CRIES, RIOTING

CONCUBINE (21) [CONCUBINES]
Ge 22:24 His **c**, whose name was Reumah, also had H7108
Ge 35:22 in and slept with his father's **c** Bilhah, H7108
Ge 36:12 son Eliphaz also had a **c** named Timna, H7108
Jdg 8:31 His **c**, who lived in Shechem, also bore H7108
Jdg 19: 1 of Ephraim took a **c** from Bethlehem in H7108
Jdg 19: 9 the man, with his **c** and his servant, got H7108
Jdg 19:10 with his two saddled donkeys and his **c**. H7108
Jdg 19:24 daughter, and his **c**. I will bring them out H7108
Jdg 19:25 So the man took his **c** and sent her H7108
Jdg 19:27 there lay his **c**, fallen in the doorway H7108
Jdg 19:29 he took a knife and cut up his **c**, limb by H7108
Jdg 20: 4 "I and my **c** came to Gibeah in Benjamin H7108
Jdg 20: 5 They raped my **c**, and she died. H7108
Jdg 20: 6 I took my **c**, cut her into pieces and sent H7108
2Sa 3: 7 Now Saul had had a **c** named Rizpah H7108
2Sa 3: 7 "Why did you sleep with my father's **c**?" H7108
2Sa 21:11 daughter Rizpah, Saul's **c**, had done, H7108
1Ch 1:32 born to Keturah, Abraham's **c**: Zimran, H7108

1Ch 2:46 Caleb's **c** Ephah was the mother of Haran H7108
1Ch 2:48 Caleb's **c** Maakah was the mother of H7108
1Ch 7:14 his descendant through his Aramean **c**. H7108

CONCUBINES (17) [CONCUBINE]

Ge 25: 6 to the sons of his **c** and sent them away H7108
2Sa 5:13 David took more **c** and wives in Jerusalem H7108
2Sa 15:16 he left ten **c** to take care of the palace. H7108
2Sa 16:21 with your father's **c** whom he left to take H7108
2Sa 16:22 slept with his father's **c** in the sight of all H7108
2Sa 19: 5 the lives of your wives and **c**. H7108
2Sa 20: 3 he took the ten **c** he had left to take care H7108
1Ki 11: 3 wives of royal birth and three hundred **c**, H7108
1Ch 3: 9 sons of David, besides his sons by his **c**. H7108
2Ch 11:21 more than any of his other wives and **c**. H7108
2Ch 11:21 he had eighteen wives and sixty **c** H7108
Est 2:14 king's eunuch who was in charge of the **c**. H7108
SS 6: 8 may be, and eighty **c**, and virgins beyond H7108
SS 6: 9 blessed; the queens and **c** praised her. H7108
Da 5: 2 his wives and his **c** might drink from A10390
Da 5: 3 his wives and his **c** drank from them. A10390
Da 5:23 your wives and your **c** drank wine from A10390

CONCUPISCENCE (KJV) COVETING, DESIRES, PASSIONATE

CONDEMN (25) [CONDEMNATION, CONDEMNED, CONDEMNING, CONDEMNS, SELF-CONDEMNED]

Job 9:20 innocent, my mouth *would* **c** me; if I were H8399
Job 34:17 *Will you* **c** the just and mighty One? H8399
Job 34:29 remains silent, who *can* **c** him? If he hides H8399
Job 40: 8 *Would you* **c** me to justify yourself? H8399
Ps 94:21 the righteous and **c** the innocent *to* death. H8399
Ps 109: 7 and *may* his prayers **c** him. H2118+4200+2631
Ps 109:31 their lives from *those who would* **c** them. H9149
Isa 50: 9 Who *will* **c** me? They will all H8399
Mt 12:41 judgment with this generation and **c** it; *G2891*
Mt 12:42 judgment with this generation and **c** it; *G2891*
Mt 20:18 *They will* **c** him to death *G2891*
Mk 10:33 *They will* **c** him to death and will hand *G2891*
Lk 6:37 not be judged. *Do* not **c**, and you will not *G2868*
Lk 11:31 the people of this generation and **c** them, *G2891*
Lk 11:32 judgment with this generation and **c** it, *G2891*
Jn 3:17 send his Son into the world to **c** the world, *G3212*
Jn 7:51 "*Does* our law **c** a man without first *G3212*
Jn 8:11 "Then neither *do* I **c** you," Jesus *G2891*
Jn 12:48 I have spoken *will* **c** them at the last *G3212*
Ro 2:27 yet obeys the law *will* **c** you who, *G3212*
Ro 14:22 is the *one who does* not **c** himself by *G3212*
2Co 7: 3 I do not say this to **c** you; I have said *G2892*
1Jn 3:20 If our hearts **c** us, we know that God is *G2861*
1Jn 3:21 if our hearts *do* not **c** us, we have *G2861*
Jude 9 himself dare *to* **c** him for slander *G3213+2214*

CONDEMNATION (8) [CONDEMN]

Eze 33:12 former wickedness *will* not **bring c**. H4173
Ro 3: 8 evil that good may result"? Their **c** is just! *G3210*
Ro 5:16 judgment followed one sin and brought **c**, *G2890*
Ro 5:18 one trespass resulted in **c** for all people, *G2890*
Ro 8: 1 there is now no **c** for those who are in *G2890*
2Co 3: 9 If the ministry that *brought* **c** was glorious *G2892*
2Pe 2: 3 Their **c** has long been hanging over them *G3210*
Jude 4 individuals whose **c** was written about *G3210*

CONDEMNED (34) [CONDEMN]

Dt 17:17 none of the **c things** are to be found H3051
Job 32: 3 no way to refute Job, and yet *had* **c** him. H8399
Ps 34:21 the foes of the righteous *will be* **c**. H870
Ps 34:22 no one who takes refuge in him *will be* **c**. H870
Ps 37:33 the wicked or **let** them **be c** when brought H8399
Ps 79:11 your strong arm preserve *those* **c to** die. H1201
Ps 102:20 prisoners and release *those* **c to** death." H1201
Mt 12: 7 *you* would not have **c** the innocent. *G2868*
Mt 12:37 by your words *you will be* **c**. *G2868*
Mt 23:33 How will you escape being **c** to hell? *G3213*
Mt 27: 3 saw that Jesus *was* **c**, he was seized *G2891*
Mk 14:64 They all **c** him as worthy of death. *G2891*
Mk 16:16 whoever does not believe *will be* **c**. *G2891*
Lk 6:37 condemn, and *you will* not *be* **c**. Forgive, *G2868*
Jn 3:18 Whoever believes in him *is* not **c**, but *G3212*
Jn 3:18 not believe *stands* **c** already because *G3212*
Jn 5:29 have done what is evil will rise to be **c**. *G3213*
Jn 8:10 where are they? *Has* no one **c** you?" *G2891*
Jn 16:11 the prince of this world *now* **stands c**. *G3212*
Ac 25:15 against him and asked that he be **c**. *G2869*
Ro 3: 7 his glory, why *am* I still **c** as a sinner?" *G3212*
Ro 8: 3 And so *he* **c** sin in the flesh, *G2891*
Ro 14:23 But whoever has doubts *is* **c** if they eat *G2891*
1Co 4: 9 like *those* **c to die** in the arena. *G2119*
1Co 11:32 so that *we will* not *be* **finally c** with the *G2891*
Gal 2:11 him to his face, because he stood **c**. *G2861*
Col 2:14 which stood **against** us **and c** us; he has *G5641*
2Th 2:12 so that all *will be* **c** who have not *G3212*
Titus 2: 8 soundness of speech that **cannot be c** *G183*
Heb 11: 7 By his faith *he* **c** the world and became *G2891*
Jas 5: 6 *You have* **c** and murdered the innocent *G2868*
Jas 5:12 Otherwise *you will be* **c**. *G5679+3213+4406*
2Pe 2: 6 *if he* **c** the cities of Sodom and *G2953+2891*
Rev 19: 2 *He has* **c** the great prostitute who *G3212*

CONDEMNING (6) [CONDEMN]

Dt 25: 1 acquitting the innocent and **c** the guilty. H8399
1Ki 8:32 **c** the guilty by bringing down on their H8399
2Ch 6:23 **c** the guilty and bringing down on their H8740
Pr 17:15 Acquitting the guilty and **c** the innocent H8399
Ac 13:27 yet *in* **c** him they fulfilled the words of the *G3212*
Ro 2: 1 judge another, *you are* **c** yourself *G2891*

CONDEMNS (4) [CONDEMN]

Job 15: 6 Your own mouth **c** you, not mine; your H8399
Pr 12: 2 but *he* **c** those who devise wicked H8399
Pr 14:34 exalts a nation, but sin **c** any people. H2875
Ro 8:34 Who then *is the one who* **c**? No one. *G2891*

CONDITION (7) [CONDITIONS]

Ge 34:15 an agreement with you on **one c** only: H2296S
Ge 34:22 people only on **the c** that our males be H2296S
1Sa 11: 2 you only **on the c that** I gouge out H928+2296
Pr 27:23 Be sure you know the **c** *of* your flocks, give H7156
Mt 12:45 And the **final** *c* of that person is worse than AIT
Lk 11:26 And the **final** *c* of that person is worse than AIT
Jn 5: 6 that *he* had been **in this c** for a long *G2400*

CONDITIONS (1) [CONDITION]

Jer 32:11 sealed copy containing the terms and **c**, H2976

CONDUCT (35) [CONDUCTED, SAFE-CONDUCT]

Est 1:17 For the queen's **c** will become known to all H1821
Est 1:18 about the queen's **c** will respond to all H1821
Job 21:31 Who denounces their **c** to their face? Who H2006
Job 34:11 he brings on them what their **c** deserves. H784
Ps 101: 2 *I will* **c the affairs** *of* my house H2143+928+7931
Ps 112: 5 lend freely, *who* **c** their affairs with justice. H3920
Pr 20:11 so is their **c** really pure and upright? H7189
Pr 21: 8 the **c** *of* the innocent is upright. H7189
Ecc 6: 8 how to **c** *themselves* before others H2143
Jer 4:18 "Your own **c** and actions have brought this H2006
Jer 6:15 Are they ashamed of *their* detestable **c** H6913
Jer 8:12 Are they ashamed of *their* detestable **c** H6913
Jer 17:10 to reward each person according to their **c**, H2006
Jer 32:19 according to their **c** and as their deeds H2006
Eze 7: 3 according to your **c** and repay you for all H2006
Eze 7: 4 repay you for your **c** and for the detestable H2006
Eze 7: 8 according to your **c** and repay you for all H2006
Eze 7: 9 repay you for your **c** and for the detestable H2006
Eze 7:27 I will deal with them according to their **c** H2006
Eze 14:22 when you see their **c** and their actions, H2006
Eze 14:23 when you see their **c** and their actions, H2006
Eze 16:27 who were shocked by your lewd **c**. H2006
Eze 20:43 will remember your **c** and all the actions H2006
Eze 24:14 according to your **c** and your actions, H2006
Eze 36:17 they defiled it by their **c** and their actions. H2006
Eze 36:17 Their **c** was like a woman's monthly H2006
Eze 36:19 according to their **c** and their actions. H2006
Eze 36:32 Be ashamed and disgraced for your **c** H2006
Da 6: 4 against Daniel in his **c** of government affairs NDT
Ac 13:18 about forty years *he* **endured** their **c** in the *G5574*
Php 1:27 **c** *yourselves* in a manner worthy of the *G4488*
1Ti 3:15 people ought to **c** *themselves* in God's *G418*
1Ti 4:12 the believers in speech, in **c**, in love, *G419*
2Pe 2: 2 will follow their **depraved c** and will bring *G816*
2Pe 2: 7 distressed by the depraved **c** of the lawless *G419*

CONDUCTED (1) [CONDUCT]

2Co 1:12 that *we have* **c** *ourselves* in the world, *G418*

CONDUIT (KJV) AQUEDUCT, TUNNEL

CONEY (NIV84) HYRAX

CONFECTIONARIES (KJV) PERFUMERS

CONFECTIONS (1)

Eze 27:17 exchanged wheat from Minnith and **c**, H7154

CONFEDERACY (KJV) ALLIES, CONSPIRACY

CONFER (1) [CONFERRED, CONFERRING]

Lk 22:29 And I **c** on you a kingdom, just as my *G1416*

CONFERRED (6) [CONFER]

2Sa 3:17 Abner **c** with the elders of Israel and said H1821
1Ki 1: 7 Adonijah **c** with Joab son of H2118+1821
1Ch 13: 1 David **c** with each of his officers, the H3619
Lk 22:29 kingdom, just as my Father **c** one on me, *G1416*
Ac 4:15 from the Sanhedrin and then **c** together. *G5202*
Ac 25:12 After Festus *had* **c** with his council, he *G5196*

CONFERRING (1) [CONFER]

2Ki 6: 8 After **c** with his officers, he said, "I will set H3619

CONFESS (10) [CONFESSED, CONFESSES, CONFESSING, CONFESSION]

Lev 5: 5 *they must* **c** in what way they have sinned. H3344
Lev 16:21 head of the live goat and **c** over it all the H3344
Lev 26:40 " 'But if *they will* **c** their sins and the sins H3344
Nu 5: 7 and *must* **c** the sin they have committed H3344
Ne 1: 6 *I* **c** the sins we Israelites, including myself H3344
Ps 32: 5 "*I will* **c** my transgressions to the LORD." H3344
Ps 38:18 *I* **c** my iniquity; I am troubled by my sin. H5583
Jn 1:20 He did not fail *to* **c**, but confessed freely, "I *G3933*
Jas 5:16 Therefore **c** your sins to each other and *G2018*
1Jn 1: 9 If *we* **c** our sins, he is faithful and just and *G3933*

CONFESSED (5) [CONFESS]

1Sa 7: 6 On that day they fasted and there *they* **c** H606
Ne 9: 2 in their places and **c** their sins and the H3344
Da 9: 4 I prayed to the LORD my God and **c**: "Lord H3344
Jn 1:20 fail to confess, but **c** *freely*, "I am not the *G3933*
Ac 19:18 came and **openly c** what they *G2018+2779+334*

CONFESSES (2) [CONFESS]

Pr 28:13 the *one who* **c** and renounces them H3344
2Ti 2:19 "Everyone who **c** the name of the Lord *G3951*

CONFESSING (4) [CONFESS]

Ezr 10: 1 While Ezra was praying and **c**, weeping H3344
Da 9:20 **c** my sin and the sin of my people Israel H3344
Mt 3: 6 **C** their sins, they were baptized by him in *G2018*
Mk 1: 5 **C** their sins, they were baptized by him in *G2018*

CONFESSION (4) [CONFESS]

Ne 9: 3 and *spent* another quarter *in* **c** and in H3344
2Co 9:13 that *accompanies* your **c** of the gospel *G3934*
1Ti 6:12 *when you* **made** your good **c** in the *G3933+3934*
1Ti 6:13 before Pontius Pilate made the good **c**, *G3934*

CONFIDANT (3) [CONFIDE]

2Sa 15:37 So Hushai, David's **c**, arrived at Jerusalem H8291
2Sa 16:16 the Arkite, David's **c**, went to Absalom H8291
1Ch 27:33 Hushai the Arkite was the king's **c**. H8276

CONFIDE (1) [CONFIDANT, CONFIDES]

Jdg 16:15 'I love you,' when you won't **c in** me? H4213+907

CONFIDENCE (36) [CONFIDENT, CONFIDENTLY, SELF-CONFIDENCE, SELF-CONFIDENT]

Jdg 9:26 its citizens **put** *their* **c** in him. H1053
2Ki 18:19 On what are you basing this **c** of yours? H1059
2Ch 32: 8 And the people **gained c** from what H6164
2Ch 32:10 On what *are* you **basing** your **c**, that you H1053
Job 4: 6 your piety be your **c** and your blameless H4074
Ps 71: 5 Sovereign LORD, my **c** since my youth. H4440
Pr 3:32 perverse but takes the upright into his **c**. H6051
Pr 11:13 A gossip betrays a **c**, but a trustworthy H6051
Pr 20:19 A gossip betrays a **c**; so avoid anyone H6051
Pr 25: 9 to court, do not betray another's **c**, H6051
Pr 31:11 Her husband **has full c** in her and H1053+4213
Isa 32:17 its effect will be quietness and **c** forever. H1055
Isa 36: 4 On what are you basing this **c** of yours? H1059
Jer 17: 7 who trusts in the LORD, whose **c** is in him. H4440
Jer 49:31 which lives in **c**," declares the LORD, H1055
Eze 29:16 no longer be a **source of c** for the people H4440
Mic 7: 5 not trust a neighbor; **put** no **c** in a friend. H1053
2Co 2: 3 ***I* had c** in all of you, that you would all *G4275*
2Co 3: 4 Such **c** we have through Christ before God. *G4301*
2Co 7:16 I am glad *I can have* complete **c** in you. *G2509*
2Co 8:22 more so *because of* his great **c** in you. *G4301*
Eph 3:12 may approach God with freedom and **c**. *G4301*
Php 3: 3 and *who* **put** no **c** in the flesh— *G4275*
Php 3: 4 though I myself have reasons for such **c**. *G4301*
Php 3: 4 they have reasons *to* **put c** in the flesh, *G4275*
2Th 3: 4 *We* **have c** in the Lord that you are doing *G4275*
Heb 3: 6 we hold firmly to our **c** and the hope in *G4244*
Heb 4:16 approach God's throne of grace with **c**, *G4244*
Heb 10:19 since we have **c** to enter the Most Holy *G4244*
Heb 10:35 So do not throw away your **c**; it will be *G4244*
Heb 11: 1 Now faith is **c** in what we hope for and *G5712*
Heb 13: 6 So we say *with* **c**, "The Lord is my helper; *G2509*
Heb 13:17 **Have c** in your leaders and submit to their *G4275*
1Jn 3:21 not condemn us, we have **c** before God *G4244*
1Jn 4:17 so that we will have **c** on the day of *G4244*
1Jn 5:14 This is the **c** we have in approaching God *G4244*

CONFIDENT (15) [CONFIDENCE]

Job 6:20 because *they had been* **c**; they arrive H1053
Ps 27: 3 out against me, even then I *will be* **c**. H1053
Ps 27:13 *I* remain **c** of this: I will see the goodness H586
Lk 18: 9 To some who *were* **c** of their own *G4275*
2Co 1:15 Because I was **c** of this, I wanted to visit *G4301*
2Co 5: 6 Therefore *we are* always **c** and know that *G2509*
2Co 5: 8 *We are* **c**, I say, and would prefer to be *G2509*
2Co 9: 4 would be ashamed of having been so **c**. *G5712*
2Co 10: 7 If anyone *is* **c** that they belong to Christ *G4275*
Gal 5:10 I *am* **c** in the Lord that you will take no *G4275*
Php 1: 6 *being* **c** of this, that he who began a good *G4275*
Php 1:14 sisters *have become* **c** in the Lord and *G4275*
Php 2:24 And *I am* **c** in the Lord that I myself will *G4275*
Phm 21 **C** of your obedience, I write to you *G4275*
1Jn 2:28 appears we may be **c** and unashamed *G4244*

CONFIDENTLY (2) [CONFIDENCE]

Ac 2:29 I can tell you **c** that the patriarch *G3552+4244*
1Ti 1: 7 are talking about or what *they so* **c affirm**. *G1331*

CONFIDES (1) [CONFIDE]

Ps 25:14 The LORD **c** in those who fear him; he H6051

CONFINE (2) [CONFINED, CONFINEMENT, CONFINES]

Nu 12:14 **C** *her* outside the camp for seven days H6037
2Co 10:13 will **c** our boasting to the sphere of NDT

CONFINED (9) [CONFINE]

Ge 39:20 the place where the king's prisoners **were c**. H673
Ge 40: 3 in the same prison where Joseph **was c**. H673
Ex 21:18 the victim does not die but *is* **c** to bed, H5877
Nu 12:15 So Miriam *was* **c** outside the camp for H6037
Jdg 1:34 The Amorites **c** the Danites to the hill H4315
Ps 88: 8 **I am c** and cannot escape; H3973
Jer 32: 2 the prophet was **c** in the courtyard of the H3973

Jer 33: 1 While Jeremiah **was** still **c** in the H6806
Jer 39:15 Jeremiah had been **c** in the courtyard of H6806

CONFINEMENT (1) [CONFINE]
2Sa 20: 3 They were **kept in c** till the day of their H7674

CONFINES (1) [CONFINE]
Job 11:10 along and **c** you **in prison** and convenes a H6037

C

CONFIRM (7) [CONFIRMED, CONFIRMING, CONFIRMS]
Ge 26: 3 all these lands and *will* **c** the oath I swore H7756
Nu 30:13 Her husband *may* **c** or nullify any vow she H7756
Dt 29:13 to **c** you this day as his people, that he H7756
Est 9:29 with full authority to **c** this second letter H7756
Da 9:27 *He will* **c** a covenant with many for one H1504
Ac 15:27 Judas and Silas *to* **c** by word of mouth what *G550*
2Pe 1:10 every effort *to* **c** your calling and *G1010+4472*

CONFIRMED (12) [CONFIRM]
Dt 4:31 ancestors, which *he* **c** to them **by oath**. H8678
1Ch 16:17 *He* **c** it to Jacob as a decree, to Israel as H6641
2Ch 1: 9 *let* your promise to my father David **be c** H586
Est 9:32 Esther's decree **c** these regulations about H7756
Job 28:27 appraised it; *he* **c** it and tested it. H3922
Ps 105:10 *He* **c** it to Jacob as a decree, to Israel as H6641
Ps 119:106 I have taken an oath and **c** it, that I will H7756
Mk 16:20 worked with them and **c** his word by the *G1011*
Ac 14: 3 who **c** the message of his grace by *G3455*
Ro 15: 8 made to the patriarchs *might be* **c** *G1011*
Heb 2: 3 Lord, *was* **c** to us by those who heard him. *G1011*
Heb 6:17 what was promised, *he* **c** it with an oath. *G3541*

CONFIRMING (3) [CONFIRM]
2Ki 23: 3 thus **c** the words of the covenant written in H7756
1Co 1: 6 God thus **c** our testimony about Christ *G1011*
Php 1: 7 in chains or defending and **c** the gospel, *G1012*

CONFIRMS (5) [CONFIRM]
Nu 30:14 then *he* **c** all her vows or the pledges H7756
Nu 30:14 *He* **c** them by saying nothing to her when H7756
Dt 8:18 and so **c** his covenant, which he H7756
Ro 9: 1 my conscience **c** it through the Holy Spirit *G5210*
Heb 6:16 and the oath **c** what is said and *G1650+1012*

CONFISCATION (2)
Ezr 7:26 banishment, **c** *of* property, or A10562
Heb 10:34 joyfully accepted the **c** of your property, *G771*

CONFLICT (10) [CONFLICTS]
Pr 6:14 deceit in his heart—he always stirs up **c**. H4506
Pr 6:19 a person who stirs up **c** in the community. H4506
Pr 10:12 Hatred stirs up **c**, but love covers over all H4506
Pr 15:18 A hot-tempered person stirs up **c**, but the H4506
Pr 16:28 A perverse person stirs up **c**, and a gossip H4506
Pr 28:25 The greedy stir up **c**, but those who trust H4506
Pr 29:22 An angry person stirs up **c**, and a H4506
Hab 1: 3 before me; there is strife, and **c** abounds. H4506
Gal 5:17 They *are* **in c** with each other, so that you *G512*
Heb 10:32 when you endured *in* a great **c** full of *G124*

CONFLICTS (1) [CONFLICT]
2Co 7: 5 at every turn—**c** on the outside, fears *G3480*

CONFORM (2) [CONFORMED, CONFORMITY, CONFORMS]
Ro 12: 2 *Do* not **c to the pattern** of this world, but *G5372*
1Pe 1:14 *do* not **c to** the evil desires you had when *G5372*

CONFORMED (4) [CONFORM]
Eze 5: 7 *You have* not even **c to** the H6913+3869
Eze 11:12 my laws but *have* **c to** the H6913+3869
Ac 26: 5 that I **c to** the strictest sect of our religion *G2848*
Ro 8:29 predestined to be **c to** the image of his *G5215*

CONFORMITY (1) [CONFORM]
Eph 1:11 out everything **in c with** the purpose of his *G2848*

CONFORMS (1) [CONFORM]
1Ti 1:11 that **c to** the gospel concerning the glory of *G2848*

CONFOUND (1)
Ps 55: 9 confuse the wicked, **c** their words, for I see H7103

CONFRONT (13) [CONFRONTED, CONFRONTING, CONFRONTS]
Ex 7:15 **C** him on the bank of the H5893+4200+7925
Ex 8:20 in the morning and **c** Pharaoh as he goes H3656
Ex 9:13 in the morning, **c** Pharaoh and say to him H3656
Jdg 14: 4 seeking an occasion to **c** the Philistines; H4946
1Sa 12: 7 *I am going to* **c** you **with evidence** before H9149
Job 9:32 that *we might* **c** each other in court. H995
Job 30:27 me never stops; days of suffering **c** me. H7709
Ps 17:13 Rise up, LORD, **c** them, bring them down H7709
Isa 50: 8 Who is my accuser? *Let him* **c** me! H5602
Eze 16: 2 **c** Jerusalem *with* her detestable practices H3359
Eze 20: 4 Then **c** them *with* the detestable practices H3359
Eze 22: 2 Then **c** her *with* all her detestable H3359
Eze 23:36 Then **c** her them *with* their detestable H5583

CONFRONTED (6) [CONFRONT]
2Sa 22: 6 around me; the snares of death **c** me. H7709
2Sa 22:19 *They* **c** me in the day of my disaster, but H7709
2Ch 26:18 *They* **c** King Uzziah and said, "It is H6641+6584
2Ch 28:12 **c** those who were arriving from the H7756+6584
Ps 18: 5 around me; the snares of death **c** me. H7709
Ps 18:18 *They* **c** me in the day of my disaster, but H7709

CONFRONTING (2) [CONFRONT]
Isa 27: 4 If only there were briers and thorns **c** me! NDT
Isa 30:11 and stop **c** us *with* the Holy One of H4946+7156

CONFRONTS (1) [CONFRONT]
Job 31:14 what will I do when God **c** me? What will H7756

CONFUSE (2) [CONFUSED, CONFUSING, CONFUSION]
Ge 11: 7 let us go down and **c** their language so H1176
Ps 55: 9 **c** the wicked, confound their words H1182

CONFUSED (1) [CONFUSE]
Ge 11: 9 there the LORD **c** the language of the H1176

CONFUSING (1) [CONFUSE]
Pr 23:33 your mind will imagine **c things**. H9337

CONFUSION (19) [CONFUSE]
Ex 14: 3 *are* **wandering around** the land in **c**, H1003
Ex 14:24 at the Egyptian army and **threw** it **into c**. H2169
Ex 23:27 of you and **throw into c** every nation H2169
Dt 7:23 **throwing** them **into** great **c** until H2169+4539
Dt 28:20 **c** and rebuke in everything you put your H4539
Dt 28:28 with madness, blindness and **c** *of* mind. H9451
Jos 10:10 The LORD **threw** them **into c** before Israel H2169
1Sa 14:20 They found the Philistines in total **c** H4539
2Sa 18:29 "I saw great **c** just as Joab was about to H2162
Ps 35:26 over my distress be put to shame and **c**; H2917
Ps 40:14 to take my life be put to shame and **c**; H2917
Ps 70: 2 to take my life be put to shame and **c**; H2917
Ps 71:24 harm me have been put to shame and **c**. H2917
Isa 41:29 nothing; their images are but wind and **c**. H9332
Jer 51:34 *he has* **thrown** us **into c**, he has made H2169
Mic 7: 4 Now is the time of your **c**. H4428
Ac 19:32 The assembly was **in c**: Some were *G5177*
Gal 1: 7 people are **throwing** you **into c** and are *G5429*
Gal 5:10 The *one who is* **throwing** you **into c** *G5429*

CONGEALED (1)
Ex 15: 8 the deep waters **c** in the heart of the sea. H7884

CONGRATULATE (3)
2Sa 8:10 to greet him and **c** him on his victory in H1385
1Ki 1:47 have come to **c** our lord King David, H1385
1Ch 18:10 to greet him and **c** him on his victory in H1385

CONGREGATION (3) [CONGREGATIONS]
Ps 26:12 in the **great c** I will praise the LORD. H5220
Ps 68:26 Praise God in the **great c**; praise the LORD H5220
Ac 13:43 When the **c** was dismissed, many of the *G5252*

CONGREGATIONS (1) [CONGREGATION]
1Co 14:33 as in all the **c** of the Lord's people. *G1711*

CONIES (KJV) HYRAX, HYRAXES

CONJURE (1)
Isa 47:11 you will not know how *to* **c** it **away**. H8838

CONNECTED (6) [CONNECTING, CONNECTION]
Lev 3: 3 organs and all the fat that is **c to** them, H6584
Lev 3: 9 organs and all the fat that is **c to** them, H6584
Lev 3:14 organs and all the fat that is **c to** them, H6584
Lev 4: 8 all the fat that is **c to** the internal organs, H6584
Nu 18: 1 bear the **responsibility for offenses** *c with* the AIT
Nu 18: 1 bear the **responsibility for offenses** *c with* the AIT

CONNECTING (2) [CONNECTED]
Ex 28:28 with blue cord, **c** it to the waistband H2118
Ex 39:21 **c** it to the waistband so that the H2118

CONNECTION (3) [CONNECTED]
Nu 18: 7 serve as priests **in c with** everything at the H4200
1Ch 6:49 altar of incense **in c with** all that was H4200
Col 2:19 *They have* lost **c** with the head, from *G3195*

CONQUER (3) [CONQUERED, CONQUEROR, CONQUERORS, CONQUERS, CONQUEST]
Dt 2:31 Now begin *to* **c** and possess his land." H3769
2Ch 32: 1 thinking to **c** them for himself. H1324
Rev 13: 7 against God's holy people and *to* **c** them. *G3771*

CONQUERED (11) [CONQUER]
Ge 14: 7 and *they* **c** the whole territory of the H5782
Nu 24:18 Edom will be **c**; Seir, his enemy, will be H3771
Nu 24:18 his enemy, will be **c**, but Israel will grow H3771
Jos 10:42 their lands Joshua **c** in one campaign, H4334
Jos 12: 6 of the LORD, and the Israelites **c** them. H5782
Jos 12: 7 the Israelites **c** on the west side of H5782
Jos 23: 4 the nations *I* **c**—between the Jordan H4162
1Ki 15:20 *He* **c** Ijon, Dan, Abel Beth Maakah and all H5782
2Ch 16: 4 *They* **c** Ijon, Dan, Abel Maim and all the H5782
2Ch 27: 5 king of the Ammonites and **c** them. H2616+6584
Heb 11:33 who through faith **c** kingdoms *G2865*

CONQUEROR (2) [CONQUER]
Mic 1:15 I will bring a **c** against you who live in H3769
Rev 6: 2 he rode out *as* a **c** bent on conquest. *G3771*

CONQUERORS (1) [CONQUER]
Ro 8:37 things *we are* **more than c** through him *G5664*

CONQUERS (1) [CONQUER]
2Sa 5: 8 "Anyone *who* **c** the Jebusites will have to H5782

CONQUEST (2) [CONQUER]
Am 6:13 who rejoice in the **c** of Lo Debar and say, NDT
Rev 6: 2 he rode out as a conqueror bent on **c**. *G3771*

CONSCIENCE (29) [CONSCIENCE-STRICKEN, CONSCIENCES, CONSCIENTIOUS]
Ge 20: 5 done this with a clear **c** and clean hands." H4222
Ge 20: 6 I know you did this with a clear **c**, and so I H4222
1Sa 25:31 will not have on his **c** the staggering H4213
Job 27: 6 my **c** will not reproach me as long as I live H4222
Ac 23: 1 my duty to God *in* all good **c** to this day." *G5287*
Ac 24:16 always to keep my **c** clear before God *G5287*
Ro 9: 1 my **c** confirms it through the Holy Spirit *G5287*
Ro 13: 5 punishment but also as a matter of **c**. *G5287*
1Co 4: 4 My **c is clear**, but that does not *G4029+5323*
1Co 8: 7 and since their **c** is weak, it is defiled *G5287*
1Co 8:10 For if someone with a weak **c** sees you *G5287*
1Co 8:12 them in this way and wound their weak **c**, *G5287*
1Co 10:25 market without raising questions of **c**, *G5287*
1Co 10:27 before you without raising questions of **c**. *G5287*
1Co 10:28 one who told you and for the sake of **c**. *G5287*
1Co 10:29 I am referring to the other person's **c**, not *G5287*
1Co 10:29 my freedom being judged by another's **c**? *G5287*
2Co 1:12 Our **c** testifies that we have conducted *G5287*
2Co 4: 2 to everyone's **c** in the sight of God. *G5287*
2Co 5:11 and I hope it is also plain to your **c**. *G5287*
1Ti 1: 5 heart and a good **c** and a sincere faith. *G5287*
1Ti 1:19 holding on to faith and a good **c**, which *G5287*
1Ti 3: 9 the deep truths of the faith with a clear **c**. *G5287*
2Ti 1: 3 with a clear **c**, as night and day I *G5287*
Heb 9: 9 not able to clear the **c** of the worshiper. *G5287*
Heb 10:22 us from a guilty **c** and having our bodies *G5287*
Heb 13:18 that we have a clear **c** and desire to live *G5287*
1Pe 3:16 keeping a clear **c**, so that those who speak *G5287*
1Pe 3:21 the pledge *of* a clear **c** toward God. *G5287*

CONSCIENCE-STRICKEN (2) [CONSCIENCE]
1Sa 24: 5 David *was* **c** for having cut off a H5782+4213
2Sa 24:10 David *was* **c** after he had counted H4213+5782

CONSCIENCES (4) [CONSCIENCE]
Ro 2:15 their hearts, their **c** also bearing witness *G5287*
1Ti 4: 2 whose **c** have been seared as with a hot *G5287*
Titus 1:15 both their minds and **c** are corrupted. *G5287*
Heb 9:14 cleanse our **c** from acts that lead to death *G5287*

CONSCIENTIOUS (1) [CONSCIENCE]
2Ch 29:34 had been more **c** in consecrating H3838+4222

CONSCIOUS (2)
Ro 3:20 through the law *we become* **c of** our sin. *G2106*
1Pe 2:19 suffering because they are **c** of God. *G5287*

CONSCRIPTED (5) [CONSCRIPTING, CONSCRIPTS]
1Ki 5:13 King Solomon **c** laborers from all Israel H6590
1Ki 9:15 labor King Solomon **c** to build the LORD's H6590
1Ki 9:21 Solomon **c** the descendants of all these H6590
2Ch 2: 2 He **c** 70,000 men as carriers and 80,000 H6218
2Ch 8: 8 Solomon **c** the descendants of all these H6590

CONSCRIPTING (2) [CONSCRIPTED]
2Ki 25:19 officer in charge of **c** the people of the H7371
Jer 52:25 officer in charge of **c** the people of the H7371

CONSCRIPTS (1) [CONSCRIPTED]
2Ki 25:19 sixty of the **c** who were found in the H408

CONSECRATE (42) [CONSECRATED, CONSECRATING, CONSECRATION, RECONSECRATED]
Ex 13: 2 "**C** to me every firstborn male. The first H7727
Ex 19:10 "Go to the people and **c** them today and H7727
Ex 19:22 the LORD, *must* **c themselves**, or the LORD H7727
Ex 28:38 in the sacred gifts the Israelites **c**, H7727
Ex 28:41 **C** them so they may serve me as priests. H7727
Ex 29: 1 "This is what you are to do to **c** them, so H7727
Ex 29:27 "**C** those parts of the ordination ram that H7727
Ex 29:36 atonement for it, and anoint it to **c** it. H7727
Ex 29:37 make atonement for the altar and **c** it. H7727
Ex 29:44 "So *I will* **c** the tent of meeting and the H7727
Ex 29:44 the altar and *will* **c** Aaron and his H7727
Ex 30:29 *You shall* **c** them so they will be most holy H7727
Ex 30:30 his sons and **c** them so they may H7727
Ex 40: 9 everything in it; **c** it and all its furnishings H7727
Ex 40:10 all its utensils; **c** the altar, and it will H7727
Ex 40:11 Anoint the basin and its stand and **c** them. H7727
Ex 40:13 anoint him and **c** him so he may serve me H7727
Lev 8:11 the basin with its stand, to **c** them. H7727
Lev 8:12 Aaron's head and anointed him to **c** him. H7727
Lev 11:44 LORD your God; **c yourselves** and be holy H7727
Lev 16:19 times to cleanse it and *to* **c** it from the H7727
Lev 20: 7 " '**C yourselves** and be holy, because I am H7727
Lev 22: 2 the sacred offerings the Israelites **c** to me, H7727
Lev 22: 3 offerings that the Israelites **c** to the LORD, H7727
Lev 25:10 **C** the fiftieth year and proclaim liberty H7727
Nu 6:11 same day *they are to* **c** their head *again*. H7727
Nu 11:18 '**C yourselves** in preparation for tomorrow H7727

Jos 3: 5 the people, "C yourselves, for tomorrow H7727
Jos 7:13 c the people. Tell them, 'Consecrate H7727
Jos 7:13 'C yourselves in preparation for tomorrow H7727
Jdg 17: 3 "I solemnly c my silver to the LORD H7727+7727
1Sa 16: 5 C yourselves and come to the sacrifice H7727
1Ch 15:12 Levites are to c yourselves and bring up H7727
1Ch 23:13 to c the most holy things H7727
1Ch 29: 5 to c themselves to the H4848+3338+2257
2Ch 13: 9 comes to c himself with a young H4848+3338
2Ch 29: 5 C yourselves now and consecrate the H7727
2Ch 29: 5 yourselves now and c the temple of the H7727
2Ch 30:17 clean and could not c their lambs to the H7727
2Ch 35: 6 c yourselves and prepare the lambs for H7727
Isa 66:17 "Those who c and purify themselves to go H7727
Joel 2:16 Gather the people, c the assembly; bring H7727

CONSECRATED (58) [CONSECRATE]
Ex 19:14 to the people, he c them, and they H7727
Ex 29:21 his sons and their garments will be c. H7727
Ex 29:43 the place will be c by my glory. H7727
Lev 8:10 everything in it, and so c them. H7727
Lev 8:15 So he c it to make atonement for it. H7727
Lev 8:30 So he c Aaron and his garments and his H7727
Nu 6: 8 of their dedication, they are c to the LORD. H7705
Nu 7: 1 he anointed and c it and all its H7727
Nu 7: 1 He also anointed and c the altar and all H7727
Nu 15:40 my commands and will be c to your God. H7705
Dt 12:26 But take your c things and whatever you H7731
1Sa 7: 1 house on the hill and c Eleazar his son to H7727
1Sa 16: 5 Then he c Jesse and his sons and invited H7727
1Sa 21: 4 there is some c bread here—provided H7731
1Sa 21: 6 So the priest gave him the c bread, since H7731
1Ki 8:64 same day the king c the middle part of H7727
1Ki 9: 3 made before me; I have c this temple H7727
1Ki 9: 7 reject this temple I have c for my Name. H7727
1Ki 13:33 a priest he c for the high H4848+906+3338
1Ch 15:14 Levites c themselves in order to bring H7727
1Ch 28:16 weight of gold for each table for c bread; H5121
2Ch 2: 4 setting out the c bread regularly, and H5121
2Ch 5:11 priests who were there had c themselves, H7727
2Ch 7: 7 Solomon c the middle part of the H7727
2Ch 7:16 I have chosen and c this temple so that H7727
2Ch 7:20 reject this temple I have c for my Name. H7727
2Ch 23: 6 they may enter because they are c, but all H7731
2Ch 26:18 who have been c to burn incense. H7727
2Ch 29:15 their fellow Levites and c themselves, H7727
2Ch 29:17 eight more days they c the temple of the H7727
2Ch 29:18 the table for setting out the c bread H5121
2Ch 29:19 We have prepared and c all the articles H7727
2Ch 29:33 The animals c as sacrifices amounted to H7731
2Ch 29:34 until other priests had been c, H7727
2Ch 30: 3 enough priests had c themselves and the H7727
2Ch 30: 8 to his sanctuary, which he has c forever. H7727
2Ch 30:15 ashamed and c themselves and brought H7727
2Ch 30:17 many in the crowd had not c themselves, H7727
2Ch 30:24 A great number of priests c themselves. H7727
2Ch 31:14 to the LORD and also the c gifts. H7731+7731
2Ch 35: 3 all Israel and who had been c to the LORD: H7705
2Ch 36:14 of the LORD, which he had c in Jerusalem. H7727
Ezr 8:28 as well as these articles are c to the LORD. H7731
Ps 50: 5 "Gather to me this c people, who made a H2883
Ps 106:16 of Aaron, who was c to the LORD. H7705
Jer 11:15 Can c meat avert your punishment H7731
Eze 44:19 that the people are not c through contact H7727
Eze 48:11 This will be for the c priests, the Zadokites H7727
Hos 9:10 they c themselves to that shameful idol H5692
Zep 1: 7 a sacrifice; he has c those he has invited. H7727
Hag 2:12 If someone carries c meat in the fold of H7731
Hag 2:12 olive oil or other food, does it become c? H7727
Mt 12: 4 he and his companions ate the c bread— G4606
Mk 2:26 the house of God and ate the c bread, G4606
Lk 2:23 firstborn male is to be c to the Lord" G41+2813
Lk 6: 4 and taking the c bread, he ate what G4606
1Ti 4: 5 because it is c by the word of God and prayer. G39
Heb 9: 2 lampstand and the table with its c bread; G4606

CONSECRATING (3) [CONSECRATE]
2Ch 29:34 conscientious in c themselves than the H7727
2Ch 31:18 they were faithful in c themselves. H7727+7731
Eze 46:20 into the outer court and c the people." H7727

CONSECRATION (3) [CONSECRATE]
Ex 28: 3 Aaron, for his c, so he may serve me H7727
Ex 29:33 was made for their ordination and c. H7727
2Ch 29:17 They began the c on the first day of the H7727

CONSENT (5) [CONSENTED]
Job 39: 9 "Will the wild ox c to serve you? Will it stay H14
Hos 8: 4 They set up kings without my c; they H4946
Ac 23:21 waiting for your c to their request. G2039
1Co 7: 5 perhaps by mutual c and for a time, G5247
Phm 14 not want to do anything without your c, G1191

CONSENTED (3) [CONSENT]
Mt 3:15 to fulfill all righteousness." Then John c. G918
Lk 22: 6 He c, and watched for an opportunity to G2018
Lk 23:51 who had not c to their decision and G1639+5163

CONSEQUENCES (9) [CONSEQUENTLY]
Nu 5:31 the woman will bear the c of her sin. H6411
Nu 9:13 They will bear the c of their sin. H2628
Nu 18:22 will bear the c of their sin and will die. H2628
Nu 30:15 then he must bear the c of her H5951
Eze 16:58 will bear the c of your lewdness and your H2365
Eze 23:35 must bear the c of your lewdness and H2365
Eze 23:49 bear the c of your sins of idolatry. H2628
Eze 44:10 their idols must bear the c of their sin. H6411
Eze 44:12 that they must bear the c of their sin, H6411

CONSEQUENTLY (4) [CONSEQUENCES]
Ro 5:18 C, just as one trespass resulted in G726+4036
Ro 10:17 C, faith comes from hearing the message G726
Ro 13: 2 C, whoever rebels against the authority is G6063
Eph 2:19 C, you are no longer foreigners and G726+4036

CONSIDER (89) [CONSIDERABLE, CONSIDERATE, CONSIDERED, CONSIDERS, RECONSIDER]
Ex 30:32 sacred, and you are to c it sacred. H2118+4200
Ex 30:37 yourselves; c it holy to the LORD. H2118+4200
Lev 19:23 years you are to c it forbidden; H2118+4200
Lev 21: 8 C them holy, because I the LORD am H2118+4200
Nu 23: 9 apart and do not c themselves one of the H3108
Dt 15:18 Do not c it a hardship to set your H928+6524
Dt 17:20 not c himself better than his H8123+4222
Dt 32: 7 days of old; c the generations long past. H1067
Jdg 5:10 you who walk along the road, c H8488
1Sa 12:24 c what great things he has done for you. H8011
1Sa 16: 7 "Do not c his appearance or his height H5564
1Sa 24:15 May he c my cause and uphold it; may he H8011
1Ki 2: 9 But now, do not c him innocent. You are a H5927
1Ch 28:10 C now, for the LORD has chosen you to H8011
2Ch 19: 6 He told them, "C carefully what you do H8011
Job 4: 7 "C now: Who, being innocent, has ever H2349
Job 13:24 you hide your face and c me your enemy? H3108
Job 23: 5 and c what he would say to me. H1067
Job 37:14 Job; stop and c God's wonders. H1067
Ps 5: 1 Listen to my words, LORD, c my lament. H1067
Ps 8: 3 When I c your heavens, the work of your H8011
Ps 10:14 you c their grief and take it in hand. H5564
Ps 37:37 C the blameless, observe the upright; H9068
Ps 48:13 c well her ramparts, view her H8883+4213
Ps 50:22 "C this, you who forget God, or I will tear H1067
Ps 77:12 I will c all your works and meditate on all H2047
Ps 119: 6 to shame when I c all your commands. H5564
Ps 119:15 on your precepts and c your ways. H5564
Ps 119:128 because I c all your precepts right, H3837
Ps 137: 6 if I do not c Jerusalem my highest joy. H6590
Ps 143: 5 all your works and c what your hands have H8488
Pr 6: 6 you sluggard; c its ways and be wise! H8011
Pr 20:25 rashly and only later to c one's vows. H1329
Ecc 2:12 Then I turned my thoughts to c wisdom H8011
Ecc 7:13 C what God has done: Who can H8011
Ecc 7:14 be happy; but when times are bad, c this: H8011
Isa 41:20 may see and know, may c and understand H8492
Isa 41:22 so that we may c them and know H8492+4213
Isa 47: 7 But you did not c these H8492+6584+4213
Jer 2:19 C then and realize how evil and bitter it is H3359
Jer 2:23 in the valley; c what you have done. H3359
Jer 2:31 of this generation, c the word of the LORD: H8011
Jer 5: 1 look around and c, search through her H3359
Jer 9:17 LORD Almighty says: "C now! Call for the H1067
La 1: 9 to her skirts; she did not c her future. H2349
La 1:11 LORD, and c, for I am despised." H5564
La 2:20 LORD, and c: Whom have you ever H5564
Eze 18:28 Because they c all the offenses they have H8011
Eze 31: 3 C Assyria, once a cedar in Lebanon, with H2180
Eze 43:10 Let them c its perfection, H4499
Eze 47:22 You are to c them as native-born H2118+4200
Da 8:25 and he will c himself superior. H928+4222
Da 9:23 c the word and understand the vision: H1067
Da 10:11 you who are highly esteemed, c carefully H1067
Hag 2:15 c how things were before one stone was laid NDT
Mk 4:24 "C carefully what you hear," he continued G1063
Lk 7: 7 is why I did not even c myself worthy to G546
Lk 8:18 Therefore c carefully how you listen G1063
Lk 12:24 C the ravens: They do not sow or reap G2917
Lk 12:27 "C how the wild flowers grow. They do not G2917
Lk 14:31 he first sit down and c whether he is able G1086
Ac 4:29 c their threats and enable your servants to G2078
Ac 5:35 c carefully what you intend to do to these G4668
Ac 13:46 you reject it and do not c yourselves G3212
Ac 15: 6 and elders met to c this question. G3972+4309
Ac 16:15 "If you c me a believer in the Lord," she G3212
Ac 20:24 However, I c my life worth nothing to me G4472
Ac 26: 2 I c myself fortunate to stand before you G2451
Ac 26: 8 Why should any of you c it incredible that G3212
Ro 8:18 I c that our present sufferings are not G3357
Ro 11:18 do not c yourself to be superior to those G2878
Ro 11:18 If you do, c this: You do not NDT
Ro 11:22 C therefore the kindness and sternness of G2623
1Co 10:18 C the people of Israel: Do not those who G1063
2Co 10: 7 they should c again that we belong to G3357
Php 2: 6 did not c equality with God something to G2451
Php 3: 7 were gains to me I now c loss for the sake G2451
Php 3: 8 I c everything a loss because of the G2451
Php 3: 8 lost all things. I c them garbage, that I G2451
Php 3:13 I do not c myself yet to have taken hold of G3357
1Ti 6: 1 the yoke of slavery should c their masters G2451
Phm 17 So if you c me a partner, welcome him as G2400
Heb 10:24 And let us c how we may spur one another G2917
Heb 12: 3 C him who endured such opposition from G382
Heb 13: 7 C the outcome of their way of life and G355
Jas 1: 2 C it pure joy, my brothers and sisters G2451
Jas 1:26 Those who c themselves religious and G1506
Jas 3: 5 C what a great forest is set on fire by a G2627
Rev 2: 5 C how far you have fallen! Repent and do G3648

CONSIDERABLE (2) [CONSIDER]
Mt 14:24 boat was already a c distance from land, G4498
Ac 14: 3 So Paul and Barnabas spent c time there G2653

CONSIDERATE (4) [CONSIDER]
Titus 3: 2 to be peaceable and c, and always to be G2117
Jas 3:17 then peace-loving, c, submissive, full of G2117
1Pe 2:18 not only to those who are good and c, but G2117
1Pe 3: 7 the same way be c as you live with G2848+1194

CONSIDERED (32) [CONSIDER]
Ge 30:33 that is not dark-colored, will be c stolen." H1704
Lev 17: 4 that person shall be c guilty of bloodshed H3108
Lev 25:31 around them are to be c as belonging to H3108
Dt 2:11 Anakites, they too were c Rephaites, but H3108
Dt 2:20 That too was c a land of the Rephaites H3108
1Sa 26:21 Because you c my life precious today H928+6524
2Sa 4: 2 Benjamin—Beeroth is c part of Benjamin, H3108
1Ki 10:21 because silver was c of little value in H3108
1Ki 16:31 He not only c it trivial to commit the sins H7837
2Ch 9:20 because silver was c of little value in H3108
Ne 13:13 assistant, because they were c trustworthy. H3108
Job 1: 8 Satan, "Have you c my servant Job? H8492+4213
Job 2: 3 Satan, "Have you c my servant Job? H8492+4213
Job 18: 3 as cattle and c stupid in your sight? H3241
Job 34: 6 I am right, I am c a liar; although I am H3941
Ps 44:22 we are c as sheep to be slaughtered. H3108
Ps 119:59 I have c my ways and have turned my H3108
Isa 53: 4 suffering, yet we c him punished by God H3108
Isa 65:20 to reach a hundred will be c accursed. H7837
La 4: 2 weight in gold, are now c as pots of clay H3108
Hos 9: 7 so great, the prophet is c a fool, the inspired NDT
Mt 1:20 But after he had c this, an angel of the G1926
Mt 14: 5 because they c John a prophet. G6055+2400
Lk 20:35 But those who are c worthy of taking part G2921
Lk 22:24 as to which of them was c to be greatest. G1506
Ro 8:36 we are c as sheep to be slaughtered." G3357
2Co 11:12 an opportunity to be c equal with us in G2351
1Ti 1:12 me strength, that he c me trustworthy G2451
Heb 11:11 children because she c him faithful who G2451
Jas 2:21 Was not our father Abraham c righteous G1467
Jas 2:24 that a person is c righteous by what they G1467
Jas 2:25 was not even Rahab the prostitute c righteous G1467

CONSIDERS (6) [CONSIDER]
Job 33:10 found fault with me; he c me his enemy. H3108
Ps 33:15 hearts of all, who c everything they do. H1067
Pr 31:16 She c a field and buys it; out of her H2372
Ro 14: 5 One person c one day more sacred than G3212
Ro 14: 5 than another; another c every day alike. G3212
1Co 2:14 the Spirit of God but c them foolishness, G1639

CONSIGN (1) [CONSIGNED, CONSIGNING]
Eze 32:18 hordes of Egypt and c to the earth below H3718

CONSIGNED (2) [CONSIGN]
Isa 43:28 I c Jacob to destruction and Israel to scorn. H5989
Rev 21: 8 they will be c to the fiery lake of burning G3538

CONSIGNING (2) [CONSIGN]
2Sa 12:31 c them to labor with saws and with iron H8492
1Ch 20: 3 c them to labor with saws and with iron H8492

CONSIST (3) [CONSISTED, CONSISTING, CONSISTS]
Lev 2: 4 in an oven, it is to c of the finest flour: NDT
Eze 45:12 The shekel is to c of twenty gerahs. H2118
Lk 12:15 life does not c in an abundance of G1639

CONSISTED (2) [CONSIST]
Jos 17: 5 Manasseh's share c of ten tracts of land H5877
1Ch 27: 1 Each division c of 24,000 men. NDT

CONSISTING (4) [CONSIST]
Nu 28:19 LORD a food offering c of a burnt offering of NDT
Nu 29:13 LORD a food offering c of a burnt offering of NDT
Nu 29:36 LORD a food offering c of a burnt offering of NDT
Eze 46:14 c of a sixth of an ephah with a third of a hin NDT

CONSISTS (2) [CONSIST]
Eze 45:14 each cor (which c of ten baths or one homer NDT
Eph 5: 9 the fruit of the light c in all goodness G1877

CONSOLATION (4) [CONSOLE]
Job 6:10 Then I would still have this c—my joy in H5717
Job 21: 2 to my words; let this be the c you give me. H9487
Ps 94:19 great within me, your c brought me joy. H9488
Lk 2:25 He was waiting for the c of Israel, and the G4155

CONSOLATIONS (1) [CONSOLE]
Job 15:11 Are God's c not enough for you, words H9487

CONSOLE (4) [CONSOLATION, CONSOLATIONS, CONSOLED]
Job 21:34 "So how can you c me with your nonsense H5714
Isa 22: 4 Do not try to c me over the destruction of H5714
Isa 51:19 famine and sword—who can c you? H5714
Jer 16: 7 will anyone give them a drink to c them. H9488

CONSOLED (6) [CONSOLE]
2Sa 13:39 for he was c concerning Amnon's death. H5714
Job 42:11 They comforted and c him over all the H5714

Eze 14:22 you will be c regarding the disaster I have H5714
Eze 14:23 You will be c when you see their conduct H5714
Eze 31:16 were c in the earth below. H5714
Eze 32:31 will see them and he will be c for all his H5714

CONSORT (1)

Hos 4:14 the men themselves c with harlots and H7233

CONSPICUOUS (1)

Eze 19:11 c for its height and for its many branches. H8011

CONSPIRACY (10) [CONSPIRE]

2Sa 15:12 And so the c gained strength, and H8004
2Ki 15:15 and the c he led, are written H8004+8003
Ps 64: 2 Hide me from the c of the wicked, from H6051
Isa 8:12 "Do not call c everything this people calls H8004
Isa 8:12 everything this people calls a c; H8004
Jer 11: 9 "There is a c among the people of Judah H8004
Eze 22:25 There is a c of her princes within her like a H8004
Am 7:10 "Amos is raising a c against you in the H8003
Ac 9:23 there was a c among the Jews to kill him, G5205
Ac 23:12 some Jews formed a c and bound G5371

CONSPIRATORS (1) [CONSPIRE]

2Sa 15:31 is among the c with Absalom. H8003

CONSPIRE (10) [CONSPIRACY, CONSPIRATORS, CONSPIRED]

Ps 2: 1 Why do the nations c and the peoples H8093
Ps 31:13 They c against me and plot to take my life H3570
Ps 56: 6 They c, they lurk, they watch my steps H1592
Ps 59: 3 Fierce men c against me for no offense H1592
Ps 71:10 those who wait to kill me c together. H3619
Ps 83: 3 With cunning they c against your people H6051
Ps 105:25 hate his people, to c against his servants. H5792
Mic 7: 3 what they desire—they all c together. H6309
Ac 4:27 in this city to c against your holy servant AIT
Ac 5: 9 "How could you c to test the Spirit of the G5244

CONSPIRED (18) [CONSPIRE]

1Sa 22: 8 Is that why you have all c against me? No H8003
1Sa 22:13 "Why have you c against me, you H8003
1Ki 2:28 who had c with Adonijah though not with H5742
2Ki 9:14 the son of Nimshi, c against Joram. H8003
2Ki 10: 9 It was I who c against my master and H8003
2Ki 12:20 His officials c against him and H8003+8004
2Ki 14:19 They c against him in Jerusalem H8003+8004
2Ki 15:10 son of Jabesh c against Zechariah. H8003
2Ki 15:25 Pekah son of Remaliah, c against him. H8003
2Ki 15:30 son of Elah c against Pekah son H8003+8004
2Ki 21:23 Amon's officials c against him and H8003
2Ch 24:25 His officials c against him for murdering H8003
2Ch 24:26 Those who c against him were Zabad H8003
2Ch 25:27 they c against him in Jerusalem H8003+8004
2Ch 33:24 Amon's officials c against him and H8003
Est 2:21 became angry and c to assassinate King H1335
Est 6: 2 who had c to assassinate King Xerxes. H1335
Da 2: 9 You have c to tell me misleading and A10231

CONSTANT (9) [CONSTANTLY]

Nu 17: 5 this c grumbling against you by the H9442+4296
Dt 28:66 You will live in c suspense, filled H4946+5584
Job 33:19 on a bed of pain with c distress in their H7419
Pr 19:13 wife is like the c dripping of a leaky roof. H3265
Isa 51:13 that you live in c terror every day because H9458
Eze 30:16 by storm; Memphis will be in c distress. H3429
Ac 27:33 "you have been in c suspense and have AIT
1Ti 6: 5 and c friction between people of corrupt G1384
Heb 5:14 who by c use have trained themselves to G2011

CONSTANTLY (8) [CONSTANT]

Ps 119:109 Though I c take my life in my hands, H9458
Pr 8:30 Then I was c at his side. I was filled with H586
Isa 52: 5 all day long my name is c blasphemed. H9458
Ac 1:14 They all joined together c in prayer G1639+4674
Ro 1: 9 is my witness how c I remember you G90
2Co 11:26 I have been c on the move. I have been in G4490
2Th 1:11 With this in mind, we c pray for you, that G4121
2Ti 1: 3 as night and day I c remember you in my G89

CONSTELLATIONS (4)

2Ki 23: 5 to the c and to all the starry hosts. H4655
Job 9: 9 the Pleiades and the c of the south. H2540
Job 38:32 you bring forth the c in their seasons or H4666
Isa 13:10 of heaven and their c will not show their H4068

CONSTRAIN, CONSTRAINED, CONSTRAINETH (KJV) COMPEL, COMPELLED, COMPELS, MADE, PERSUADED, URGED

CONSTRAINT (1)

Lk 12:50 what c I am under until it is G5309

CONSTRUCT (1) [CONSTRUCTED, CONSTRUCTING, CONSTRUCTION, CONSTRUCTIVE]

2Ch 20:36 He agreed with him to c a fleet of trading H6913

CONSTRUCTED (3) [CONSTRUCT]

1Ki 9:24 had built for her, he c the terraces. H1215
1Ch 15: 1 After David had c buildings for himself in H6913
Eze 40:17 a pavement that had been c all around H6913

CONSTRUCTING (3) [CONSTRUCT]

Ex 36: 1 out all the work of c the sanctuary are to H6275
Ex 36: 3 to carry out the work of c the sanctuary. H6275
Ezr 5: 4 names of those who are c this building?" A10111

CONSTRUCTION (4) [CONSTRUCT]

1Ki 7: 1 however, to complete the c of his palace. H1215
2Ki 16:10 of the altar, with detailed plans for its c. H5126
Ezr 5:16 present it has been under c but is not A10111
Ezr 6: 8 of the Jews in the c of this house of God: A10111

CONSTRUCTIVE (1) [CONSTRUCT]

1Co 10:23 to do anything"—but not everything is c. G3868

CONSULT (19) [CONSULTATION, CONSULTED, CONSULTING, CONSULTS]

1Sa 28: 8 "C a spirit for me," he said, "and bring up H7876
1Sa 28:16 "Why do you c me, now that the H8626
2Ki 1: 2 to them, "Go and c Baal-Zebub, the H2011+928
2Ki 1: 3 you are going off to c Baal-Zebub, H2011+928
2Ki 1: 6 messengers to c Baal-Zebub, H2011+928
2Ki 1:16 you to c that you have H2011+928+1821
2Ki 1:16 sent messengers to c Baal-Zebub, H2011+928
2Ki 8: 8 C the LORD through him; ask him, 'Will I H2011
2Ch 17: 3 David before him. He did not c the Baals H2011
2Ch 25:15 "Why do you c this people's gods H2011
Est 1:13 the king to c experts in matters H4200+7156
Isa 8:19 someone tells you to c mediums and H2011
Isa 8:19 Why c the dead on behalf of the living H448
Isa 8:20 C God's instruction and the testimony of H4200
Isa 19: 3 they will c the idols and the spirits of the H2011
Isa 40:14 Whom did the LORD c to enlighten him H3619
Eze 21:21 lots with arrows, he will c his idols, he will H8626
Hos 4:12 My people c a wooden idol, and a H8626
Gal 1:16 response was not to c any human being. G4651

CONSULTATION (1) [CONSULT]

1Ch 12:19 because, after c, their rulers sent him H6783

CONSULTED (10) [CONSULT]

1Ki 12: 6 King Rehoboam c the elders who had H3619
1Ki 12: 8 gave him and c the young men who H3619
2Ki 21: 6 and c mediums and spiritists. H6913
1Ch 10:13 of the LORD and even c a medium for H8626
2Ch 10: 6 King Rehoboam c the elders who had H3619
2Ch 10: 8 gave him and c the young men who H3619
2Ch 25:17 Amaziah king of Judah c his advisers, H3619
2Ch 32: 3 he c with his officials and military staff H3619
2Ch 33: 6 and c mediums and spiritists. H6913
Jer 8: 2 they have followed and c and worshiped. H2011

CONSULTING (2) [CONSULT]

2Ch 20:21 After c the people, Jehoshaphat H3619
Isa 30: 2 go down to Egypt without c me; H8626+7023

CONSULTS (2) [CONSULT]

Dt 18:11 is a medium or spiritist or who c the dead. H2011
Eze 14:10 will be as guilty as the one who c him. H2011

CONSUME (36) [CONSUMED, CONSUMES, CONSUMING]

Dt 5:25 This great fire will c us, and we will die if H430
Jdg 9:15 of the thornbush and c the cedars of H430
Jdg 9:20 let fire come out from Abimelek and c you H430
Jdg 9:20 Shechem and Beth Millo, and c Abimelek!" H430
2Ki 1:10 down from heaven and c you and your fifty H430
2Ki 1:12 down from heaven and c you and your fifty H430
Job 5: 5 The hungry c his harvest, taking it even H430
Job 15:34 fire will c the tents of those who love H430
Job 20:26 A fire unfanned will c him and devour what H430
Ps 21: 9 up in his wrath, and his fire will c them. H430
Ps 39:11 their sin, you c their wealth like a moth H4998
Ps 59:13 c them in your wrath, consume them till H3983
Ps 59:13 your wrath, c them till they are no more. H3983
Ecc 5:11 goods increase, so do those who c them. H430
Isa 10:17 day it will burn and c his thorns and his H430
Isa 26:11 let the fire reserved for your enemies c H430
Jer 17:27 of Jerusalem that will c her fortresses. H430
Jer 21:14 in your forests that will c everything around H430
Jer 49:27 it will c the fortresses of Ben-Hadad." H430
Jer 50:32 fire in her towns that will c all who are H430
Eze 15: 7 out of the fire, the fire will yet c them. H430
Eze 20:47 set fire to you, and it will c all your trees H430
Eze 21:28 polished to c and to flash like lightning! H3920
Eze 22:31 wrath on them and c them with my fiery H3983
Hos 8:14 fire on their cities that will c their fortresses." H430
Am 1: 4 house of Hazael that will c the fortresses of H430
Am 1: 7 the walls of Gaza that will c her fortresses. H430
Am 1:10 the walls of Tyre that will c her fortresses." H430
Am 1:12 fire on Teman that will c the fortresses of H430
Am 1:14 walls of Rabbah that will c her fortresses H430
Am 2: 2 fire on Moab that will c the fortresses of H430
Am 2: 5 fire on Judah that will c the fortresses of H430
Na 3:15 There the fire will c you; the sword will cut H430
Zec 12: 6 They will c all the surrounding peoples H430
Jn 2:17 "Zeal for your house will c me." G2983
Heb 10:27 of raging fire that will c the enemies of G2266

CONSUMED (35) [CONSUME]

Ge 31:40 The heat c me in the daytime and the cold H430
Ex 15: 7 your burning anger; it c them like stubble. H430
Lev 6:10 offering that the fire has c on the altar and H430
Lev 9:24 of the LORD and c the burnt offering and H430
Lev 10: 2 from the presence of the LORD and c them, H430
Nu 11: 1 among them and c some of the outskirts H430
Nu 11:33 their teeth and before it could be c, H4162
Nu 16:35 from the LORD and c the 250 men who were H430
Nu 21:28 It c Ar of Moab, the citizens of Arnon's H430
2Ki 1:10 fell from heaven and c the captain and his H430
2Ki 1:12 fell from heaven and c him and his fifty H430
2Ki 1:14 from heaven and c the first two captains H430
2Ch 7: 1 down from heaven and c the burnt offering H430
Ps 31:10 My life is c by anguish and my years by H3983
Ps 37:20 of the field, they will be c, they will go up H3983
Ps 78:63 Fire c their young men, and their young H430
Ps 90: 7 We are c by your anger and terrified by H3983
Ps 106:18 their followers; a flame c the wicked. H4265
Ps 118:12 but they were c as quickly as burning H1980
Ps 119:20 My soul is c with longing for your laws at H1756
Ecc 10:12 gracious, but fools are c by their own lips. H1180
Isa 42:25 did not understand; it c them, but they did H1277
Jer 3:24 shameful gods have c the fruits of our H430
La 3:22 of the LORD's great love we are not c, H9462
La 4:11 a fire in Zion that c her foundations. H430
Eze 19:12 strong branches withered and fire c them. H430
Eze 19:14 one of its main branches and c its fruit. H430
Eze 23:25 those of you who are left will be c by fire. H430
Eze 28:18 out from you, and it c you, and I reduced H430
Na 1:10 their wine; they will be c like dry stubble. H430
Na 3:13 enemies; fire has c the bars of your gates. H430
Zep 1:18 of his jealousy the whole earth will be c, H430
Zep 3: 8 The whole world will be c by the fire of my H430
Zec 9: 4 power on the sea, and she will be c by fire. H430
Rev 18: 8 She will be c by fire, for mighty is the Lord G2876

CONSUMES (8) [CONSUME]

Ps 69: 9 zeal for your house c me, and the H430
Ps 83:14 As fire c the forest or a flame sets the H1277
Ps 97: 3 goes before him and c his foes on every H4265
Isa 9:18 burns like a fire; it c briers and thorns, it H430
Isa 24: 6 Therefore a curse c the earth; its people H430
Isa 33:11 to straw; your breath is a fire that c you. H430
Jer 5:14 a fire and these people the wood it c. H430
La 2: 3 like a flaming fire that c everything around H430

CONSUMING (11) [CONSUME]

Ex 24:17 of the LORD looked like a c fire on top of the H430
Dt 4:24 For the LORD your God is a c fire, a jealous H430
Dt 32:24 c pestilence and deadly plague H4310
Jdg 6:21 from the rock, c the meat and the bread. H430
2Sa 22: 9 his nostrils; c fire came from his mouth H430
Ps 18: 8 his nostrils; c fire came from his mouth H430
Isa 30:27 are full of wrath, and his tongue is a c fire. H430
Isa 30:30 coming down with raging anger and c fire, H430
Isa 33:14 "Who of us can dwell with the c fire? Who H430
Joel 2: 5 like a crackling fire c stubble, like a mighty H430
Heb 12:29 our "God is a c fire. G2914

CONSUMMATE (1)

Mt 1:25 But he did not c their marriage until she G1182

CONSUMMATION (KJV) END

CONSUMPTION (KJV) WASTING DISEASE, DESTRUCTION

CONTACT (3)

Lev 11:34 that has come into c with water from any H6584
Eze 44:19 consecrated through c with their garments. H928
Hag 2:13 "If a person defiled by c with a dead body AIT

CONTAIN (5) [CONTAINED, CONTAINER, CONTAINING, CONTAINS]

1Ki 8:27 even the highest heaven, cannot c you. H3920
2Ch 2: 6 even the highest heavens, cannot c him? H3920
2Ch 6:18 even the highest heavens, cannot c you. H3920
Ecc 8: 8 As no one has power over the wind to c it H3973
2Pe 3:16 His letters c some things that are hard to G1877

CONTAINED (2) [CONTAIN]

Ac 10:12 It c all kinds of four-footed animals G1877+5639
Heb 9: 4 This ark c the gold jar of manna G1877+2400

CONTAINER (1) [CONTAIN]

Nu 19:15 every open c without a lid fastened on H3998

CONTAINING (9) [CONTAIN]

Ex 13: 3 it with a mighty hand. Eat nothing c yeast. H2809
Ex 23:18 to me along with anything c yeast. H2809
Ex 34:25 to me along with anything c yeast, H2809
Lev 8: 2 two rams and the basket c bread made AIT
1Sa 6:11 with it the chest c the gold rats and the NDT
1Sa 6:15 together with the chest c the gold objects H928
Jer 32:11 the sealed copy c the terms and conditions NDT
Jer 36:27 burned the scroll c the words that Baruch NDT
Eze 45:11 the bath c a tenth of a homer and the H5951

CONTAINS (2) [CONTAIN]

Job 28: 6 its rocks, and its dust c nuggets of gold. H4200
Pr 15: 6 The house of the righteous c great treasure NDT

CONTAMINATED (1) [CONTAMINATES]

Lev 14:40 is to order that the c stones be torn out H5596

CONTAMINATES (1) [CONTAMINATED]

2Co 7: 1 from everything that c body and spirit, G3663

CONTEMN, CONTEMNED (KJV) DESPISED, DESPISES, REVILE, SCORNED

CONTEMPLATE (1) [CONTEMPLATING]

2Co 3:18 who with unveiled faces c the Lord's glory G3002

CONTEMPLATING (1) [CONTEMPLATE]

Isa 33:15 shut their eyes against c evil— H8011

CONTEMPT (37) [CONTEMPTIBLE, CONTEMPTUOUS, CONTEMPTUOUSLY]

Lev 22: 9 guilty and die for treating it with c. H2725
Nu 14:11 long will these people treat me with c? H5540
Nu 14:23 No one who has treated me with c will H5540
Nu 16:30 these men have treated the LORD with c." H5540
Dt 17:12 Anyone who shows c for the judge or for H2295
1Sa 2:17 they were treating the LORD's offering with c H5540
1Sa 25:39 against Nabal for treating me with c. H3075
2Sa 12:14 this you have shown utter c for the H5540+5540
2Sa 19:43 Why then do you treat us with c? Weren't H7837
Job 12: 5 who are at ease have c for misfortune as H997
Job 12:21 He pours c on nobles and disarms the H997
Job 31:34 so dreaded the c of the clans that I H997
Ps 31:11 I am the utter c of my neighbors and an H3075
Ps 31:18 with pride and c they speak arrogantly H997
Ps 79: 4 We are objects of c to our neighbors, of H3075
Ps 79:12 seven times the c they have hurled at you, H3075
Ps 107:40 he who pours c on nobles made them H997
Ps 119:22 Remove from me their scorn and c, for I H997
Ps 123: 3 for we have endured no end of c. H997
Ps 123: 4 from the arrogant, of c from the proud. H997
Pr 14:31 the poor shows c for their Maker, H3070
Pr 17: 5 mocks the poor shows c for their Maker; H3070
Pr 18: 3 so does c, and with shame comes H997
Pr 19:16 but whoever shows c for their ways will H1022
Pr 27:11 can answer anyone who treats me with c. H3070
Eze 22: 7 they have treated father and mother with c H7837
Da 12: 2 others to shame and everlasting c. H1994
Hos 12:14 bloodshed and will repay him for his c. H3075
Na 3: 6 I will treat you with c and make you a H5571
Mal 1: 6 "It is you priests who show c for my name H1022
Mal 1: 6 'How have we shown c for your name?' H1022
Ro 2: 4 Or do you show c for the riches of his G2969
Ro 14: 3 everything must not treat with c the one G2024
Ro 14:10 Or why do you treat them with c? For we G2024
1Co 16:11 should treat him with c. Send him G2024
Gal 4:14 you did not treat me with c or scorn. G2024
1Th 5:20 Do not treat prophecies with c G2024

CONTEMPTIBLE (5) [CONTEMPT]

Pr 30:23 a c woman who gets married, and a H8533
Eze 35:12 have heard all the c things you have said H5542
Da 11:21 succeeded by a c person who has not H1022
Mal 1: 7 "By saying that the LORD's table is c. H1022
Mal 1:12 Lord's table is defiled,' and, 'Its food is c.' H1022

CONTEMPTUOUS (1) [CONTEMPT]

Dt 17:13 be afraid, and will not be c again. H2326

CONTEMPTUOUSLY (1) [CONTEMPT]

Mal 1:13 and you sniff at it c," says the LORD H5870

CONTEND (12) [CONTENDED, CONTENDING, CONTENDS, CONTENTIOUS]

Ge 6: 3 "My Spirit will not c with humans forever H1906
Jdg 6:32 that day, saying, "Let Baal c with him." H8189
Ps 35: 1 C, LORD, with those who contend with me H8189
Ps 35: 1 with those who c with me; fight H3742
Ps 35:23 to my defense! C for me, my God and Lord H8190
Ps 127: 5 be put to shame when they c with their H1819
Ecc 6:10 no one can c with someone who is H1906
Isa 27: 8 By warfare and exile you c with her—with H8189
Isa 49:25 I will c with those who contend with you H8189
Isa 49:25 I will contend with those who c with you H3742
Col 1:29 To this end I strenuously c with all the energy G76
Jude 3 write and urge you to c for the faith that G2043

CONTENDED (2) [CONTEND]

Dt 33: 8 you c with him at the waters of Meribah. H8189
Php 4: 3 women since they have c at my side in G5254

CONTENDING (1) [CONTEND]

Col 2: 1 know how hard I am c for you and for those G74

CONTENDS (2) [CONTEND]

Job 40: 2 "Will the one who c with the Almighty H8189
Jer 15:10 with whom the whole land strives and c! H4506

CONTENT (11) [CONTENTED, CONTENTMENT]

Ge 25:27 while Jacob was c to stay at home among H9447
Jos 7: 7 If only we had been c to stay on the other H3283
Ps 131: 2 with its mother; like a weaned child I am c. NDT
Pr 13:25 The righteous eat to their hearts' c, but H8427
Pr 19:23 then one rests c, untouched by H8428
Ecc 4: 8 his eyes were not c with his wealth. H8425
Lk 3:14 accuse people falsely—be c with your pay." G758
Php 4:11 I have learned to be c whatever the G895
Php 4:12 the secret of being c in any and every NDT
1Ti 6: 8 food and clothing, we will be c with that. G758
Heb 13: 5 love of money and be c with what you have G758

CONTENTED (1) [CONTENT]

Da 4: 4 at home in my palace, c and prosperous. A10710

CONTENTIOUS (1) [CONTEND]

1Co 11:16 If anyone wants to be c about this, we G5809

CONTENTMENT (3) [CONTENT]

Job 36:11 days in prosperity and their years in c. H5833
SS 8:10 become in his eyes like one bringing c. H8934
1Ti 6: 6 But godliness with c is great gain. G894

CONTINUAL (3) [CONTINUE]

1Ki 14:30 There was c warfare between H3972+2021+3427
2Ch 12:15 There was c warfare H3972+2021+3427
Pr 15:15 the cheerful heart has a c feast. H9458

CONTINUALLY (26) [CONTINUE]

Ex 28:38 on Aaron's forehead c so that they will be H9458
Lev 24: 2 so that the lamps may be kept burning c. H9458
Lev 24: 3 the LORD from evening till morning, c. H9458
Lev 24: 4 before the LORD must be tended c. H9458
Nu 4: 7 the bread that is c there is to remain on it. H9458
Dt 11:12 the LORD your God are c on it from the H9458
1Ki 10: 8 who c stand before you and hear your H9458
2Ch 9: 7 who c stand before you and hear your H9458
2Ch 24:14 were presented c in the temple of the H9458
Ps 74:23 the uproar of your enemies, which rises c. H9458
Isa 27: 3 the LORD, watch over it; I water it c. H4200+8092
Isa 28:24 planting, does he plow c? H3972+2021+3427
Isa 65: 3 a people who c provoke me to my very H9458
Jer 33:18 before me c to offer burnt H3972+2021+3427
Eze 8:17 with violence and c arouse my anger? H8740
Eze 39:14 People will be c employed in cleansing H9458
Da 6:16 whom you serve c A10089+10753+10002
Da 6:20 whom you serve c, been A10089+10753+10002
Am 1:11 his anger raged c and his fury H4200+6329
Ob 16 so all the nations will drink c; they will H9458
Lk 24:53 And they stayed c at the temple G1328+4246
Col 1: 9 We c ask God to fill you with the knowledge AIT
1Th 1: 2 God for all of you and c mention you in our G90
1Th 2:13 And we also thank God c because, when G90
1Th 5:17 pray c, G90
Heb 13:15 let us c offer to God a sacrifice of G1328+4246

CONTINUE (67) [CONTINUAL, CONTINUALLY, CONTINUED, CONTINUES, CONTINUING, CONTINUOUSLY]

Ge 37:35 "I will c to mourn until I join my son in the NDT
Ex 9: 2 to let them go and c to hold them back, H6388
Ex 33:13 I may know you and c to find favor with you. AIT
Ex 40:15 to a priesthood that will c throughout their H6409
Lev 25:22 the old crop and will c to eat from it until the AIT
Lev 25:35 stranger, so they can c to live among you. AIT
Lev 25:36 so that they may c to live among you. AIT
Lev 26: 5 Your threshing will c until grape harvest H5952
Lev 26: 5 the grape harvest will c until planting, H5952
Lev 26:23 my correction but c to be hostile toward H2143
Lev 26:27 listen to me but c to be hostile toward me H2143
Nu 34: 4 c on to Zin and go south of Kadesh H6296
Nu 34: 9 c to Ziphron and end at Hazar Enan. H3655
Nu 34:11 east side of Ain and c along the slopes H4682
Dt 22:19 She shall c to be his wife; he must not AIT
Jos 13:13 so they c to live among the Israelites to this AIT
Jdg 19:27 house and stepped out to c on his way, H2143
Ru 2:13 "May I c to find favor in your eyes, my lord," AIT
2Sa 7:29 servant, that it may c forever in your sight H2118
1Ki 8:23 your servants who c wholeheartedly in H2143
2Ki 17:41 grandchildren c to do as their ancestors AIT
1Ch 17:27 servant, that it may c forever in your sight H2118
2Ch 6:14 your servants who c wholeheartedly in H2143
Est 9:23 the Jews agreed to c the celebration they H6913
Ps 36:10 C your love to those who know you, your H5432
Ps 72:17 may it c as long as the sun. H5672
Ps 89:36 that his line will c forever and his throne H2118
Jer 3: 5 Will your wrath c forever?' This H9068
Jer 18:12 We will c with our own plans; we will all H2143
Jer 23:26 How long will this c in the hearts of these H3780
Eze 20:31 you c to defile yourselves with all your idols AIT
Eze 21:13 which the sword despises, does not c? H2118
Da 4:27 It may be that then your prosperity will c." A10073
Da 9:26 War will c until the end, and desolations NDT
Da 12:10 but the wicked will c to be wicked. AIT
Hos 4:18 they c their prostitution; their H2388+2388
Mal 2: 4 so that my covenant with Levi may c," H2118
Jn 17:26 and will c to make you known in order that AIT
Ac 13:43 them and urged them to c in the grace of G4693
Ro 1:32 they not only c to do these very things but AIT
Ro 11:22 provided that you c in his kindness. G2152
2Co 1:10 set our hope that he will c to deliver us, G2285
2Co 11: 9 burden to you in any way, and will c to do so. AIT
Gal 2:10 was that we should c to remember the poor, AIT
Gal 3:10 is everyone who does not c to do G1844
Php 1:18 of this I rejoice. Yes, and I will c to rejoice, AIT
Php 1:25 and I will c with all of you for your G4169
Php 2:12 c to work out your salvation with fear and AIT
Col 1:23 if you c in your faith, established and firm G2152
Col 2: 6 Jesus as Lord, c to live your lives in him, AIT
2Th 2: 7 now holds it back will c to do so till he is NDT
2Th 3: 4 you are doing and will c to do the things we AIT
1Ti 2:15 childbearing—if they c in faith, love and G3531
1Ti 5:16 she should c to help them and not let the AIT
2Ti 3:14 c in what you have learned and have G3531
Heb 6:10 have helped his people and c to help them. AIT
Heb 13: 3 C to remember those in prison as if you were AIT
1Pe 4:19 to their faithful Creator and c to do good. G1877
1Jn 2:28 dear children, c in him, so that when he G3531
1Jn 3: 9 No one who is born of God will c to sin AIT
1Jn 5:18 that anyone born of God does not c to sin; AIT
2Jn 9 runs ahead and does not c in the G3531
3Jn 3 to the truth, telling how you c to walk in it. AIT
Rev 22:11 Let the one who does wrong c to do wrong; G2285
Rev 22:11 let the vile person c to be vile; let the one G2285
Rev 22:11 let the one who does right c to do right G2285
Rev 22:11 and let the holy person c to be holy." G2285

CONTINUED (79) [CONTINUE]

Ge 8: 5 The waters c to recede until the H2118+2143
Ge 12: 9 Abram set out and c toward the Negev. H2143
Ge 26:13 his wealth c to grow until he became H2143
Ge 29: 1 Jacob c on his journey and came H5951+8079
Ge 30:36 while Jacob c to tend the rest of Laban's AIT
Ge 42: 2 He c, "I have heard that there is grain in H606
Ex 36: 3 And the people c to bring freewill H6388
Nu 9:16 That is how it c to be; the cloud covered it H9458
Nu 21:16 From there they c on to Beer, the well where NDT
Jos 9:21 They c, "Let them live, but let them be H606
Jos 15: 3 c on to Zin and went over to the south of H6296
Jos 15: 6 to Beth Hoglah and c north of Beth H6296
Jos 15: 7 It c along to the waters of En Shemesh H6296
Jos 15:10 c down to Beth Shemesh and crossed to H3718
Jos 16: 6 c to the Mediterranean Sea. H3655
Jos 17: 9 the boundary c south to the Kanah Ravine H3718
Jos 18:16 It c down the Hinnom Valley along the H3718
Jos 18:17 went to En Shemesh, c to Geliloth, which H3655
Jos 18:18 It c to the northern slope of Beth Arabah H6296
Jos 19:13 Then it c eastward to Gath Hepher and H6296
Jdg 1:29 the Canaanites c to live there among them. AIT
Jdg 14:17 finally told her, because she c to press him. AIT
Jdg 18:31 They c to use the idol Micah had made, all AIT
1Sa 2:26 the boy Samuel c to grow in stature and H2143
1Sa 3:21 The LORD c to appear at Shiloh, and there H3578
1Sa 7:15 Samuel c as Israel's leader all the days of his AIT
1Sa 18:30 Philistine commanders c to go out to battle, AIT
1Sa 30:10 the other four hundred c the pursuit. AIT
2Sa 2:27 the men would have c pursuing them H6590
2Sa 2:29 c through the morning hours and came to H2143
2Sa 15:30 But David c up the Mount of Olives, weeping AIT
2Sa 16:13 David and his men c along the road while H2143
2Sa 20:18 She c, "Long ago they used to say, 'Get H606
1Ki 2:17 So he c, "Please ask King Solomon—he H606
1Ki 3: 6 You have c this great kindness to him H9068
1Ki 5:11 Solomon c to do this for Hiram year after year AIT
1Ki 18:29 and they c their frantic prophesying until the AIT
1Ki 22:19 Micaiah c, "Therefore hear the word of the H606
1Ki 22:43 the people c to offer sacrifices and H6388
2Ki 12: 3 the people c to offer sacrifices and burn H6388
2Ki 13: 6 caused Israel to commit; they c in them. H2143
2Ki 13:11 caused Israel to commit; he c in them. H2143
2Ki 14: 4 the people c to offer sacrifices and burn H6388
2Ki 15: 4 the people c to offer sacrifices and burn H6388
2Ki 15:35 the people c to offer sacrifices and burn H6388
2Ch 12:13 himself firmly in Jerusalem and c as king. AIT
2Ch 18:18 Micaiah c, "Therefore hear the word of the H606
2Ch 27: 2 people, however, c their corrupt practices. H6388
2Ch 29:28 All this c until the sacrifice of the burnt NDT
2Ch 33:17 however, c to sacrifice at the high places H6388
Ezr 6:14 of the Jews c to build and prosper under AIT
Ezr 10: 6 because he c to mourn over the AIT
Ne 4:21 So we c the work with half the men H6913
Ne 5: 9 So I c, "What you are doing is not right H606
Ne 12:37 Gate they c directly up the steps of H6590
Est 2:20 she c to follow Mordecai's instructions as AIT
Job 27: 1 And Job c his discourse: H3578
Job 29: 1 Job c his discourse: H3578
Job 36: 1 Elihu c: H3578
Ps 78:17 But they c to sin against him H3578+6388
Isa 64: 5 But when we c to sin against them, you H6409
Jer 32:20 in Egypt and have c them to this day, NDT
Da 7:11 "Then I c to watch because of the A10201
Da 10:12 Then he c, "Do not be afraid, Daniel. H606
Mk 4:24 what you hear," he c. "With the measure G3306
Mk 7: 9 And he c, "You have a fine way of G3306
Lk 4:24 he c, "no prophet is accepted in his G3306
Lk 15:11 Jesus c: "There was a man who had two G3306
Lk 24:28 Jesus c on as if he were going farther. G4701
Jn 8:23 But he c, "You are from below; I am from G3306
Jn 12:17 him from the dead c to spread the word. AIT
Ac 2:46 Every day they c to meet together in the G4674
Ac 4:33 power the apostles c to testify to the AIT
Ac 12:24 But the word of God c to spread and flourish. AIT
Ac 14: 7 where they c to preach the gospel. G1639
Ac 15:38 Pamphylia and had not c with them in the G5302
Ac 21: 5 time to leave, we left and c on our way. G4513
Ac 21: 7 We c our voyage from Tyre and landed at G1382
Ac 27:20 days and the storm c raging, G4024+3900+2130

CONTINUES (10) [CONTINUE]

Lev 15: 3 Whether it c flowing from his body or is AIT
Lev 15:25 has a discharge that c beyond her period, NDT
Lev 15:26 on while her discharge c will be H3972+3427
Ps 100: 5 his faithfulness c through all generations. NDT
Ps 119:90 Your faithfulness c through all generations NDT
2Co 10:15 Our hope is that, as your faith c to grow, our AIT
1Ti 5: 5 her hope in God and c night and day to G4693
Jas 1:25 gives freedom, and c in it—not forgetting G4169
1Jn 3: 6 No one who c to sin has either seen him AIT
2Jn 9 whoever c in the teaching has both the G3531

CONTINUING (4) [CONTINUE]
Ex 28:29 of decision as a **c** memorial before the H9458
Nu 15:23 the LORD gave them and **c** through the H2134
Ro 13: 8 except the **c** debt to love one another NDT
Heb 7:23 death prevented them from **c in office**; *G4169*

CONTINUOUSLY (1) [CONTINUE]
Lev 6:13 fire must be kept burning on the altar **c**; H9458

CONTRACT (2)
Isa 16:14 as a **servant bound by c** would count them H8502
Isa 21:16 as a **servant bound by c** would count it H8502

CONTRADICT (2)
Lk 21:15 your adversaries will be able to resist or **c**. *G515*
Ac 13:45 *They began to* **c** what Paul was saying *G515*

CONTRARIWISE (KJV) CONTRARY, INSTEAD

CONTRARY (24)
Lev 10: 1 fire before the LORD, **c** *to* his command. H4202
Dt 17: 3 **c to** my command has worshiped H4202
Jos 22:27 **On the c**, it is to be a witness between us H3954
2Ch 30:18 **c to** what was written. H928+4202+3869
Ps 119:85 dig pits to trap me, **c to** your law. H4202+3869
Ac 18:13 to worship God *in ways* **c to** the law." *G4123*
Ro 9: 7 **On the c**, "It is through Isaac that your *G247*
Ro 11:24 and **c to** nature were grafted into a *G4123*
Ro 12:20 **On the c**: "If your enemy is hungry, feed *G247*
Ro 16:17 in your way that are **c to** the teaching you *G4123*
1Co 9:12 **On the c**, we put up with anything rather *G247*
1Co 12:22 **On the c**, those parts of the *G247+4498+3437*
2Co 2:17 **On the c**, in Christ we speak before God *G247*
2Co 4: 2 **On the c**, by setting forth the truth plainly *G247*
2Co 10: 4 **On the c**, they have divine power to *G247*
Gal 2: 7 **On the c**, they recognized that I had *G247+5539*
Gal 3:12 law is not based on faith; **on the c**, it says, *G247*
Gal 5:17 For the flesh desires what is **c to** the Spirit *G2848*
Gal 5:17 and the Spirit what is **c to** the flesh. *G2848*
1Th 2: 4 **On the c**, we speak as those approved by *G247*
2Th 3: 8 **On the c**, we worked night and day *G247*
1Ti 1:10 whatever else *is* **c to** the sound doctrine *G512*
2Ti 1:17 **On the c**, when he was in Rome, he *G247*
1Pe 3: 9 **On the c**, repay evil with blessing *G5539*

CONTRIBUTE (1) [CONTRIBUTED, CONTRIBUTION, CONTRIBUTIONS]
2Ki 15:20 wealthy person had to **c** fifty shekels of H6584

CONTRIBUTED (4) [CONTRIBUTE]
2Ch 31: 3 The king **c** from his own possessions for H4987
2Ch 35: 8 His officials also **c** voluntarily to the H8123
Ne 7:70 of the heads of the families **c** to the work. H5989
Ne 12:47 all Israel **c** the daily portions for the H5989

CONTRIBUTION (7) [CONTRIBUTE]
Ex 29:28 It is the **c** the Israelites are to make to the H9556
Lev 7:14 kind as an offering, a **c** to the LORD; it H9556
Lev 7:32 fellowship offerings to the priest as a **c**. H9556
Ne 10:34 times each year a **c** *of* wood to burn on H7934
Ro 15:26 pleased to make a **c** for the poor among *G3126*
Ro 15:28 made sure that they have received this **c**, *G2843*
Ro 15:31 Judea and that the **c** I take to Jerusalem *G1355*

CONTRIBUTIONS (10) [CONTRIBUTE]
Lev 22:12 she may not eat any of the sacred **c**. H9556
Nu 5: 9 All the sacred **c** the Israelites bring to a H9556
2Ch 24:10 all the people brought their **c** gladly, NDT
2Ch 31:10 began to bring their **c** to the temple of the H9556
2Ch 31:12 Then they faithfully brought in the **c**, tithes H9556
2Ch 31:14 distributing the **c** *made to* the LORD and H9556
Ne 10:39 are to bring their **c** *of* grain, new wine H9556
Ne 12:44 be in charge of the storerooms for the **c**, H9556
Ne 13: 5 as well as the **c** *for* the priests. H9556
Ne 13:31 made provision for **c** *of* wood at H7934

CONTRITE (4)
Ps 51:17 a broken and **c** heart you, God, H1920
Isa 57:15 also with the *one who* is **c** and lowly in H1918
Isa 57:15 the lowly and to revive the heart of the **c**. H1917
Isa 66: 2 those who are humble and **c** *in* spirit, and H5783

CONTROL (21) [CONTROLLED, CONTROLLING, CONTROLS, SELF-CONTROL, SELF-CONTROLLED]
Ge 45: 1 could no longer **c himself** before all his H706
Ex 32:25 Aaron *had let* them **get out of c** and so H7277
Jos 18: 1 The country **was brought under** their **c**, H3899
2Sa 8: 1 Ammah from the **c** *of* the Philistines. H3338
1Ki 11:24 Damascus, where they settled and **took c**. H4887
1Ch 18: 1 villages from the **c** *of* the Philistines. H3338
2Ch 17: 5 LORD established the kingdom under his **c**; H3338
2Ch 25: 3 After the kingdom was firmly **in** his **c**, he H6584
Ecc 2:19 Yet *they will* **have c** over all the fruit of my H8948
Jer 28:14 I will even give him **c** over the wild animals NDT
Da 11:43 *He will* **gain c** of the treasures of gold and H5440
Ro 6:20 you were free *from* the **c** *of* **righteousness**. AIT
1Co 7: 9 But if *they* cannot **c** *themselves*, they *G1603*
1Co 7:37 compulsion but has **c** over his own will, *G2026*
1Co 14:32 of prophets *are* **subject to** *the* **c** of *G5718*
Gal 3:22 locked up everything **under the c of** sin, *G5679*
Php 3:21 him to **bring** everything **under** his **c**, *G5718*
1Th 4: 4 you should learn to **c** your own body in a *G3227*
2Ti 3: 6 into homes and **gain c over** gullible *G170*
1Jn 5:19 world *is* **under the c** of the evil *G1877+3023*
Rev 16: 9 who had **c** over these plagues *G2026*

CONTROLLED (3) [CONTROL]
Jdg 10: 4 They **c** thirty towns in Gilead, which to this H4200
1Ch 2:22 who **c** twenty-three towns in Gilead H2118+4200
Ps 32: 9 *must be* **c** by bit and bridle H1178

CONTROLLING (1) [CONTROL]
Ge 43:31 he came out and, **c himself**, said, "Serve H706

CONTROLS (1) [CONTROL]
Job 37:15 Do you know how God **c** the clouds and H8492

CONTROVERSIAL (1) [CONTROVERSIES]
1Ti 1: 4 things promote **c speculations** rather than *G1700*

CONTROVERSIES (3) [CONTROVERSIAL]
Ac 26: 3 with all the Jewish customs and **c**. *G2427*
1Ti 6: 4 unhealthy interest in **c** and quarrels about *G2428*
Titus 3: 9 But avoid foolish **c** and genealogies and *G2428*

CONVENED (2) [CONVENES]
Ac 25: 6 day *he* **c the court** and *G2767+2093+3836+1037*
Ac 25:17 but **c the court** the next *G2767+2093+3836+1037*

CONVENES (1) [CONVENED]
Job 11:10 confines you in prison and **c a court**, H7735

CONVENIENT (1)
Ac 24:25 When I find it **c**, I will send for you." *G2789*

CONVERSATION (4)
1Sa 19: 7 called David and told him the whole **c**. H1821
Jer 38:24 "Do not let anyone know about this **c**, or H1821
Jer 38:27 no one had heard his **c** with the king. H1821
Col 4: 6 Let your **c** be always full of grace *G3364*

CONVERT (4) [CONVERTED, CONVERTS]
Mt 23:15 travel over land and sea to win a single **c**, *G4670*
Ac 6: 5 Nicolas from Antioch, a **c to Judaism**. *G4670*
Ro 16: 5 who was the **first c** to Christ in the province *G569*
1Ti 3: 6 He must not be a **recent c**, or he may *G3745*

CONVERTED (1) [CONVERT]
Ac 15: 3 they told how the Gentiles had been **c**. *G2189*

CONVERTS (3) [CONVERT]
Ac 2:11 both Jews and **c to Judaism**); Cretans and *G4670*
Ac 13:43 devout **c to Judaism** followed Paul *G4670*
1Co 16:15 of Stephanas were the **first c** in Achaia, *G569*

CONVEY, CONVEYED (KJV) FLOAT, SAFE-CONDUCT, SLIPPED

CONVICT (4) [CONVICTED, CONVICTION, CONVICTIONS]
Dt 19:15 One witness *is* not *enough to* **c** anyone H7756
2Sa 14:13 does he not **c** himself, for the king H872
Pr 24:25 it will go well with those *who* **c** the guilty, H3519
Jude 15 and *to* **c** all of them of all the ungodly *G1794*

CONVICTED (2) [CONVICT]
1Co 14:24 *they are* **c of sin** and are brought under *G1794*
Jas 2: 9 you sin and *are* **c** by the law as *G1794*

CONVICTION (2) [CONVICT]
1Th 1: 5 with the Holy Spirit and deep **c**. *G4443*
Heb 3:14 we hold our original **c** firmly to the very *G5712*

CONVICTIONS (1) [CONVICT]
Jos 14: 7 back a report according to my **c**, H6640+4222

CONVINCED (16) [CONVINCING]
Ge 45:28 And Israel said, "I'm **c**! My son Joseph is H8041
Lk 16:31 *they will* not be **c** even if someone rises *G4275*
Ac 19:26 how this fellow Paul *has* **c** and led astray *G4275*
Ac 26: 9 "I too *was* **c** that I ought to do all that was *G1506*
Ac 26:26 *I am* **c** that none of this has escaped his *G4275*
Ac 28:24 Some *were* **c** by what he said, but others *G4275*
Ro 2:19 if *you are* **c** that you are a guide for the *G4275*
Ro 8:38 For *I am* **c** that neither death nor life *G4275*
Ro 14: 5 Each of them *should be* **fully c** in their *G4442*
Ro 14:14 *I am* **c**, being fully persuaded in the Lord *G3857*
Ro 15:14 I myself *am* **c**, my brothers and sisters *G4275*
2Co 5:14 *because we are* **c** that one died for all *G3212*
Php 1:25 **C** of this, I know that I will remain, and I *G4275*
2Ti 1:12 and *am* **c** that he is able to guard what I *G4275*
2Ti 3:14 you have learned and *have become* **c** *of*, *G4413*
Heb 6: 9 *we are* **c** of better things in your case *G4275*

CONVINCING (1) [CONVINCED]
Ac 1: 3 gave many **c proofs** that he was alive *G5447*

CONVOCATIONS (1)
Isa 1:13 Sabbaths and **c**—I cannot bear H7924+5246

CONVULSED (2) [CONVULSION]
Ps 77:16 you and writhed; the very depths *were* **c**. H8074
Mk 9:26 shrieked, **c** him violently and came out. *G5057*

CONVULSION (2) [CONVULSED, CONVULSIONS]
Mk 9:20 *it* immediately **threw** the boy **into a c**. *G5360*
Lk 9:42 the demon threw him to the ground *in a* **c**. *G5360*

CONVULSIONS (1) [CONVULSION]
Lk 9:39 *it* **throws** him **into c** so that he foams at *G5057*

COOING (1)
SS 2:12 the **c** *of* doves is heard in our land. H7754

COOK (14) [COOKED, COOKING, COOKS]
Ex 23:19 "*Do* not **c** a young goat in its mother's H1418
Ex 29:31 the ordination and **c** the meat in a sacred H1418
Ex 34:26 "*Do* not **c** a young goat in its mother's H1418
Lev 8:31 "**C** the meat at the entrance to the tent of H1418
Dt 14:21 *Do* not **c** a young goat in its mother's milk. H1418
1Sa 9:23 Samuel said to the **c**, "Bring the piece of H3184
1Sa 9:24 So the **c** took up the thigh with what was H3184
1Ki 19:21 *He* **burned** the plowing equipment **to c** H1418
2Ki 4:38 the large pot and **c** some stew for these H1418
Eze 24: 5 bring it to a boil and **c** the bones in it. H1418
Eze 24:10 **C** the meat **well**, mixing in the spices; and H9462
Eze 46:20 where the priests *are to* **c** the guilt H1418
Eze 46:24 at the temple *are to* **c** the sacrifices of the H1418
Zec 14:21 will take some of the pots and **c** in them. H1418

COOKED (7) [COOK]
Lev 2: 7 If your grain offering is **c** in a pan, it is to be NDT
Lev 6:28 clay pot the meat *is* **c** in must be broken; H1418
Lev 6:28 be broken; but if *it is* **c** in a bronze pot H1418
Lev 7: 9 baked in an oven or **c** in a pan or on a H6913
Nu 11: 8 *They* **c** it in a pot or made it into loaves H1418
2Ki 6:29 So *we* **c** my son and ate him. The next day H1418
La 4:10 *With* their own hands compassionate women *have* **c** H1418

COOKING (4) [COOK]
Ge 25:29 Once when Jacob *was* **c** some stew, Esau H2326
Lev 11:35 an oven or **c pot** must be broken up. H3968
Eze 24: 3 " 'Put on the **c pot**; put it on and pour H6105
Zec 14:20 the **c pots** in the LORD's house will be H6105

COOKS (1) [COOK]
1Sa 8:13 to be perfumers and **c** and bakers. H3185

COOL (3) [SNOW-COOLED]
Ge 3: 8 walking in the garden in the **c** *of* the day, H8120
Jer 18:14 Do its **c** waters from distant sources ever H7922
Lk 16:24 tip of his finger in water and **c** my tongue, *G2976*

COOS (KJV) KOS

COPIED (1) [COPY]
Eze 16:47 followed their ways and **c** their detestable H6913

COPIES (2) [COPY]
Jer 32:14 the sealed and **unsealed** *c* of the deed of AIT
Heb 9:23 *for* the **c** of the heavenly things to be *G5682*

COPPER (8)
Dt 8: 9 are iron and you can dig **c** out of the hills. H5733
Job 28: 2 from the earth, and **c** is smelted from ore. H5703
Eze 22:18 dross to me; all of them are the **c**, tin, H5733
Eze 22:20 As silver, **c**, iron, lead and tin are gathered H5733
Eze 24:11 coals till it becomes hot and its **c** glows, H5733
Mt 10: 9 any gold or silver or **c** to take with you in *G5910*
Mk 12:42 came and put in two **very small c coins**, *G3321*
Lk 21: 2 poor widow put in two **very small c coins**. *G3321*

COPPERSMITH (KJV) METALWORKER

COPULATION (KJV) EMISSION, SEMEN

COPY (15) [COPIED, COPIES]
Dt 17:18 write for himself on a scroll a **c** *of* this law, H5467
Jos 8:32 wrote on stones a **c** *of* the law of Moses. H5467
2Ki 11:12 him with a **c of the covenant** and H6343
2Ch 23:11 him with a **c of the covenant** and H6343
Ezr 4:11 This is a **c** *of* the letter they sent him.) A10598
Ezr 4:23 As soon as the **c** *of* the letter of King A10598
Ezr 5: 6 This is a **c** *of* the letter that Tattenai A10598
Ezr 7:11 This is a **c** *of* the letter King Artaxerxes H7306
Est 3:14 A **c** *of* the text of the edict was to be H7358
Est 4: 8 He also gave him a **c** *of* the text of the H7358
Est 8:13 A **c** *of* the text of the edict was to be H7358
Jer 32:11 the **sealed** *c* containing the terms and AIT
Jer 32:11 conditions, as well as the **unsealed** *c*— AIT
Heb 8: 5 sanctuary that is a **c** and shadow of what *G5682*
Heb 9:24 hands that was *only* a **c** of the true one; *G531*

COR (1) [CORS]
Eze 45:14 is a tenth of a bath from each **c** (which H4123

CORAL (2)
Job 28:18 **C** and jasper are not worthy of mention H8029
Eze 27:16 **c** and rubies for your merchandise. H8029

CORBAN (1)
Mk 7:11 used to help their father or mother is **C** *G3167*

CORD (15) [CORDS]
Ge 38:18 "Your seal and its **c**, and the staff in your H7348
Ge 38:25 whose seal and **c** and staff these are." H7348
Ex 28:28 tied to the rings of the ephod with blue **c**, H7348
Ex 28:37 Fasten a blue **c** to it to attach it to the H7348
Ex 39:21 to the rings of the ephod with blue **c**, H7348
Ex 39:31 they fastened a blue **c** to it to attach it to H7348
Nu 15:38 garments, with a blue **c** on each tassel. H7348

Jos 2:18 tied this scarlet **c** in the window H9535+2562
Jos 2:21 And she tied the scarlet **c** in the window. H9535
2Sa 8: 2 measured them off with a **length of c**. H2475
Job 41: 2 Can you put a **c** through its nose or pierce H109
Ecc 4:12 A **c** of three strands is not quickly broken H2562
Ecc 12: 6 before the silver **c** is severed, and the H2475
Eze 16: 4 the day you were born your **c** was not cut, H9219
Eze 40: 3 with a linen **c** and a measuring rod H7348

CORDIAL (1) [CORDIALLY]

Ezr 5: 7 **C greetings**. A10720+10353+10002+10002

CORDIALLY (2) [CORDIAL]

Ps 28: 3 who speak **c** with their neighbors but H8934
Jer 9: 8 they all speak **c** to their neighbors, H8934

CORDS (16) [CORD]

2Sa 22: 6 The **c** *of* the grave coiled around me; the H2475
Est 1: 6 fastened with **c** *of* white linen and purple H2475
Job 4:21 Are not the **c of** their **tent** pulled up, so H3857
Job 36: 8 in chains, held fast by **c** *of* affliction, H2475
Ps 18: 4 The **c** *of* death entangled me; the torrents H2475
Ps 18: 5 The **c** *of* the grave coiled around me; the H2475
Ps 116: 3 The **c** *of* death entangled me, the H2475
Ps 129: 4 has cut me free from the **c** *of* the wicked." H6310
Ps 140: 5 have spread out the **c** of their net and H2475
Pr 5:22 the **c** *of* their sins hold them fast. H2475
Isa 5:18 those who draw sin along with **c** *of* deceit, H2475
Isa 54: 2 lengthen your **c**, strengthen your H4798
Isa 58: 6 of injustice and untie the **c** *of* the yoke, H99
Eze 27:24 rugs with **c** twisted and tightly H2475
Hos 11: 4 I led them with **c** *of* human kindness, with H2475
Jn 2:15 So he made a whip out of **c**, and drove all *G5389*

CORIANDER (2)

Ex 16:31 It was white like **c** seed and tasted like H1512
Nu 11: 7 The manna was like **c** seed and looked H1512

CORINTH (9) [CORINTHIANS]

Ac 18: 1 After this, Paul left Athens and went to **C**. *G3172*
Ac 18:11 So Paul stayed in **C** for a year and a half NDT
Ac 18:12 the Jews of **C** made a united attack on Paul NDT
Ac 18:18 Paul stayed on in **C** for some time. Then he NDT
Ac 19: 1 While Apollos was at **C**, Paul took the *G3172*
1Co 1: 2 To the church of God in **C**, to those *G3172*
2Co 1: 1 To the church of God in **C**, together with *G3172*
2Co 1:23 to spare you that I did not return to **C**. *G3172*
2Ti 4:20 Erastus stayed in **C**, and I left Trophimus *G3172*

CORINTHIANS (2) [CORINTH]

Ac 18: 8 many *of* the **C** who heard Paul *G3171*
2Co 6:11 freely to you, **C**, and opened wide our *G3171*

CORMORANT (2)

Lev 11:17 the little owl, the **c**, the great owl, H8960
Dt 14:17 the desert owl, the osprey, the **c**, H8960

CORN (EARS OF) (KJV) GRAIN (HEADS OF), KERNEL

CORNELIUS (10)

Ac 10: 1 At Caesarea there was a man named **C**, *G3173*
Ac 10: 3 who came to him and said, "**C**! *G3173*
Ac 10: 4 **C** stared at him in fear. "What is it, Lord?" *G3836S*
Ac 10: 7 **C** called two of his servants and a devout NDT
Ac 10:17 the men sent by **C** found out where *G3173*
Ac 10:22 "We have come from **C** the centurion. *G3173*
Ac 10:24 **C** was expecting them and had called *G3173*
Ac 10:25 **C** met him and fell at his feet in reverence *G3173*
Ac 10:30 **C** answered: "Three days ago I was in my *G3173*
Ac 10:31 '**C**, God has heard your prayer *G3173*

CORNER (32) [CORNERS, CORNERSTONE, CORNERSTONES]

Ru 3: 9 "Spread the **c of** your **garment** over me H4053
1Sa 24: 4 unnoticed and cut off a **c** *of* Saul's robe. H4053
1Sa 24: 5 having cut off a **c** *of* his robe. H4053
1Sa 24:11 I cut off the **c** *of* your robe but did not kill H4053
1Ki 7:34 one on each **c**, projecting from the H7157
1Ki 7:39 at the southeast **c** of the temple. H4578
2Ki 14:13 from the Ephraim Gate to the **C** Gate— H7157
2Ch 4:10 Sea on the south side, at the southeast **c**. H4578
2Ch 25:23 from the Ephraim Gate to the **C** Gate— H7157
2Ch 26: 9 built towers in Jerusalem at the **C** Gate, H7157
2Ch 26:15 on the **c defenses** so that soldiers H7157
2Ch 28:24 up altars at every **street c** in Jerusalem. H7157
Ne 3:24 Azariah's house to the angle and the **c**, H7157
Ne 3:31 and as far as the room above the **c**; H7157
Ne 3:32 the room above the **c** and the Sheep Gate H7157
Pr 7: 8 He was going down the street near her **c** H7157
Pr 7:12 now in the squares, at every **c** she lurks.) H7157
Pr 21: 9 Better to live on a **c** *of* the roof than share H7157
Pr 25:24 Better to live on a **c** *of* the roof than share H7157
Isa 51:20 they lie at every street **c**, like antelope H8031
Jer 31:38 from the Tower of Hananel to the **C** Gate. H7157
Jer 31:40 the east as far as the **c** *of* the Horse Gate, H7157
La 2:19 who faint from hunger at every street **c**. H8031
La 4: 1 gems are scattered at every street **c**. H8031
Eze 16: 8 I spread the **c of** my **garment** over you H4053
Eze 16:25 At every street **c** you built your lofty shrines H8031
Eze 16:31 at every street **c** and made your lofty H8031
Eze 46:21 I saw **in each c** another H928+928+5243+5243
Na 3:10 were dashed to pieces at every street **c**. H8031
Zep 1:16 fortified cities and against the **c** towers. H7157
Zec 14:10 the First Gate, to the **C** Gate, and from the H7157
Ac 26:26 his notice, because it was not done in a **c**. *G1224*

CORNERS (36) [CORNER]

Ex 25:26 the table and fasten them to the four **c**, H6991
Ex 26:23 make two frames for the **c** at the far end. H7910
Ex 26:24 At these two **c** they must be double from H5243
Ex 27: 2 Make a horn at each of the four **c**, so that H7157
Ex 27: 4 ring at each of the four **c** *of* the network. H7896
Ex 28: 7 shoulder pieces attached to two of its **c**, H7896
Ex 28:23 fasten them to two **c** *of* the breastpiece. H7896
Ex 28:24 to the rings at the **c** *of* the breastpiece, H7896
Ex 28:26 to the other two **c** *of* the breastpiece on H7896
Ex 36:28 were made for the **c** *of* the tabernacle at H7910
Ex 36:29 At these two **c** the frames were double H5243
Ex 37:13 the table and fastened them to the four **c**, H6991
Ex 38: 2 They made a horn at each of the four **c**, so H7157
Ex 38: 5 poles for the four **c** of the bronze grating. H7921
Ex 39: 4 which were attached to two of its **c**, so it H7896
Ex 39:16 rings to two of the **c** *of* the breastpiece. H7896
Ex 39:17 to the rings at the **c** *of* the breastpiece, H7896
Ex 39:19 to the other two **c** *of* the breastpiece on H7896
Nu 15:38 to make tassels on the **c** *of* your garments, H4053
Dt 22:12 tassels on the four **c** *of* the cloak you wear H4053
Job 1:19 desert and struck the four **c** *of* the house. H7157
Isa 41: 9 of the earth, from its **farthest c** I called you. H721
Eze 7: 2 end has come upon the four **c** *of* the land! H4053
Eze 41:22 two cubits square; its **c**, its base and its H5243
Eze 43:20 on the four **c** *of* the upper ledge and H7157
Eze 45:19 on the four **c** *of* the upper ledge of the H7157
Eze 46:21 court and led me around to its four **c**, H5243
Eze 46:22 In the four **c** *of* the outer court were H5243
Eze 46:22 the courts in the four **c** was the same size. H7910
Zec 9:15 bowl used for sprinkling the **c** *of* the altar. H2312
Mt 6: 5 on the street **c** to be seen by others. *G1224*
Mt 22: 9 So go to the street **c** and invite to the *G1447*
Ac 10:11 sheet being let down to earth by its four **c**. *G794*
Ac 11: 5 being let down from heaven *by* its four **c**, *G794*
Rev 7: 1 angels standing at the four **c** of the earth, *G1224*
Rev 20: 8 the nations in the four **c** of the earth— *G1224*

CORNERSTONE (12) [CORNER, STONE]

Job 38: 6 its footings set, or who laid its **c**— H74+7157
Ps 118:22 rejected has become the **c**; H8031+7157
Isa 28:16 a precious **c** *for* a sure foundation H7157
Jer 51:26 No rock will be taken from you for a **c**, nor H7157
Zec 10: 4 From Judah will come the **c**, from him the H7157
Mt 21:42 rejected has become the **c**; *G3051+1224*
Mk 12:10 rejected has become the **c**; *G3051+1224*
Lk 20:17 rejected has become the **c**'? *G3051+1224*
Ac 4:11 rejected, which has become the **c**. *G3051+1224*
Eph 2:20 with Christ Jesus himself *as* the **chief c**. *G214*
1Pe 2: 6 a chosen and precious **c**, and the one who *G214*
1Pe 2: 7 rejected has become the **c**, *G3051+1224*

CORNERSTONES (1) [CORNER, STONE]

Isa 19:13 the **c** *of* her peoples have led Egypt astray. H7157

CORNET, CORNETS (KJV) HORN, HORNS, SISTRUMS, TRUMPET

CORPSE (5) [CORPSES]

Lev 22: 4 defiled by a **c** or by anyone who has H5883
Nu 19:11 touches a human **c** will be unclean for H4637
Nu 19:13 themselves after touching a human **c**, H4637
Isa 14:19 Like a **c** trampled underfoot, H7007
Mk 9:26 looked so much like a **c** that many said, *G3738*

CORPSES (1) [CORPSE]

Na 3: 3 number, people stumbling over the **c**— H1581

CORRECT (3) [CORRECTED, CORRECTING, CORRECTION, CORRECTLY, CORRECTS]

Job 6:26 Do you mean to **c** what I say, and treat my H3519
Job 40: 2 who contends with the Almighty **c** him? H3574
2Ti 4: 2 out of season; **c**, rebuke and *G1794*

CORRECTED (1) [CORRECT]

Pr 29:19 Servants cannot **be c** by mere words H3579

CORRECTING (1) [CORRECT]

2Ti 3:16 rebuking, **c** and training in righteousness, *G2061*

CORRECTION (17) [CORRECT]

Lev 26:23 these things *you do* not **accept** my **c** but H3579
Job 36:10 them listen to **c** and commands them to H4592
Pr 5:12 hated discipline! How my heart spurned **c**! H9350
Pr 6:23 **c** and instruction are the way to life, H9350
Pr 10:17 whoever ignores **c** leads others astray. H9350
Pr 12: 1 knowledge, but whoever hates **c** is stupid. H9350
Pr 13:18 but whoever heeds **c** is honored. H9350
Pr 15: 5 whoever heeds **c** shows prudence. H9350
Pr 15:10 the path; the one who hates **c** will die. H9350
Pr 15:12 Mockers resent **c**, so they avoid the wise. H3519
Pr 15:31 heeds life-giving **c** will be at home H9350
Pr 15:32 the one who heeds **c** gains understanding H9350
Jer 2:30 your people; they did not respond to **c**. H4592
Jer 5: 3 you crushed them, but they refused **c**. H4592
Jer 7:28 the LORD its God or responded to **c**. H4592
Zep 3: 2 she accepts no **c**. She does not trust H4592
Zep 3: 7 'Surely you will fear me and accept **c**! H4592

CORRECTLY (6) [CORRECT]

Jdg 12: 6 he could not pronounce the word **c**, H4026
Jer 1:12 said to me, "*You have* seen **c**, for I am H3512
Lk 7:43 "You have judged **c**," Jesus said. *G3987*
Lk 10:28 "You have answered **c**," Jesus replied *G3987*
Jn 7:24 appearances, but instead judge **c**." *G1465+3213*
2Ti 2:15 ashamed and *who* **c handles** the word of *G3982*

CORRECTS (2) [CORRECT]

Job 5:17 "Blessed is the one whom God **c**; so do H3519
Pr 9: 7 *Whoever* **c** a mocker invites insults H3579

CORRESPONDING (3) [CORRESPONDS]

1Ch 23: 6 Levites into divisions **c to** the sons of Levi: H4200
2Ch 3: 8 its length **c to** the width of the H6584+7156
Eze 42:12 was parallel to the **c** wall extending H2054

CORRESPONDS (1) [CORRESPONDING]

Gal 4:25 Sinai in Arabia and **c to** the present city of *G5368*

CORRODED (1) [CORROSION]

Jas 5: 3 Your gold and silver *are* **c**. Their corrosion *G2995*

CORROSION (1) [CORRODED]

Jas 5: 3 Their **c** will testify against you and eat *G2675*

CORRUPT (28) [CORRUPTED, CORRUPTION, CORRUPTLY, CORRUPTS]

Ge 6:11 Now the earth *was* **c** in God's sight and H8845
Ge 6:12 God saw *how* **c** the earth *had become*, for H8845
Ex 32: 7 brought up out of Egypt, *have become* **c**. H8845
Dt 4:16 so that *you do* not *become* **c** and make H8845
Dt 4:25 if *you* then *become* **c** and make any kind H8845
Dt 9:12 you brought out of Egypt *have become* **c**. H8845
Dt 31:29 *you are* **sure to become utterly c** H8845+8845
Dt 32: 5 *They are* **c** and not his children; to their H8845
Jdg 2:19 to ways even more **c** than those of their H8845
2Ch 27: 2 however, continued *their* **c practices**. H8845
Job 15:16 who are vile and **c**, who drink up evil like H480
Ps 14: 1 *They are* **c**, their deeds are vile; there is H8845
Ps 14: 3 all *have become* **c**; there is no H480
Ps 53: 1 *They are* **c**, and their ways are vile; there H8845
Ps 53: 3 all *have become* **c**; there is no H480
Ps 94:20 Can a **c** throne be allied with you—a H2095
Pr 4:24 of perversity; keep **c talk** far from your lips. H4299
Pr 6:12 a villain, who goes about with a **c** mouth, H6838
Pr 17:20 *One whose* heart is **c** does not prosper H6836
Pr 19:28 A **c** witness mocks at justice, and the H1175
Jer 2:21 then did you turn against me into a **c**, H6074
Eze 20:44 to your evil ways and your **c** practices, H8845
Da 6: 4 trustworthy and neither **c** nor negligent. A10705
Da 11:32 With flattery *he will* **c** those who have H2866
Hos 5: 3 now turned to prostitution; Israel *is* **c**. H3237
Ac 2:40 "Save yourselves from this **c** generation." *G5021*
1Ti 6: 5 friction between people of **c** mind, *G1425*
2Pe 2:10 those who follow the **c** desire of the flesh *G3622*

CORRUPTED (8) [CORRUPT]

Ge 6:12 all the people on earth *had* **c** their ways. H8845
Eze 28:17 and *you* **c** your wisdom because of your H8845
2Co 7: 2 no one, *we have* **c** no one, we have *G5780*
Eph 4:22 which *is being* **c** by its deceitful desires; *G5780*
Titus 1:15 but *to* those *who are* **c** and do not believe, *G3620*
Titus 1:15 both their minds and consciences *are* **c**. *G3620*
Jude 23 hating even the clothing stained by *c* **flesh**. AIT
Rev 19: 2 the great prostitute who **c** the earth by her *G5780*

CORRUPTION (8) [CORRUPT]

2Ki 23:13 Jerusalem on the south of the Hill of **C**— H5422
Ezr 9:11 is a land polluted by the **c** *of* its peoples. H5614
Job 17:14 if I say to **c**, 'You are my father,' and to H8846
Isa 1: 4 a brood of evildoers, children **given to c**! H8845
Da 6: 4 They could find no **c** in him, because he A10705
Hos 9: 9 They have sunk deep into **c**, as in the H8845
2Pe 1: 4 having escaped the **c** in the world caused *G5785*
2Pe 2:20 they have escaped the **c** of the world by *G3621*

CORRUPTLY (2) [CORRUPT]

Jer 6:28 They are bronze and iron; they all **act c**. H8845
Zep 3: 7 were still eager *to* **act c** in all they did. H8845

CORRUPTS (3) [CORRUPT]

Ecc 7: 7 person into a fool, and a bribe **c** the heart. H6
1Co 15:33 "Bad company **c** good character." *G5780*
Jas 3: 6 It **c** the whole body, sets the whole course *G5071*

CORS (8) [COR]

1Ki 4:22 were thirty **c** *of* the finest flour and H4123
1Ki 4:22 cors of the finest flour and sixty **c** *of* meal, H4123
1Ki 5:11 twenty thousand **c** *of* wheat as food for H4123
2Ch 2:10 twenty thousand **c** of ground wheat H4123
2Ch 2:10 twenty thousand **c** of barley, twenty H4123
2Ch 27: 5 ten thousand **c** of wheat and ten H4123
2Ch 27: 5 cors of wheat and ten thousand **c** of barley. NDT
Ezr 7:22 a hundred **c** of wheat, a hundred A10367

COS (NIV84) KOS

COSAM (1)

Lk 3:28 of Addi, the son *of* **C**, the son of Elmadam *G3272*

COSMETIC (1) [COSMETICS]

2Sa 14: 2 clothes, and don't use any **c lotions**. H9043

COSMETICS (1) [COSMETIC]
Est 2:12 oil of myrrh and six with perfumes and **c**. H9475

COST (14) [COSTLY, COSTS]
Nu 11: 5 the fish we ate in Egypt **at no c**— H2855
Nu 16:38 the men who sinned **at the c of** their lives. H928
Jos 6:26 "**At the c of** his firstborn son he will lay its H928
Jos 6:26 **at the c of** his youngest he will set up its H928
2Sa 24:24 my God burnt offerings that **c** me **nothing**." H2855
1Ki 16:34 its foundations **at the c of** his firstborn son H928
1Ki 16:34 set up its gates **at the c of** his youngest son H928
1Ch 12:19 "It will **c** us our heads if he deserts to his H928
Pr 4: 7 Though it **c** all you have, get H928
Pr 7:23 a snare, little knowing it will **c** him his life. H928
Pr 23: 7 who is always thinking about the **c**. H5883
Isa 55: 1 milk without money and without **c**. H4697
Lk 14:28 estimate the **c** to see if you have G1252
Rev 21: 6 I will give water **without c** from the spring G1562

COSTLY (8) [COST]
Ge 24:53 he also gave **c gifts** to her brother and to H4458
Est 1: 6 mother-of-pearl and other **c stones**. H6090
Ps 49: 8 the ransom for a life *is* **c**, no payment is H3700
Eze 16:10 linen and covered you with **c garments**. H5429
Eze 16:13 fine linen and **c fabric** and embroidered H5429
Da 11:38 with precious stones and **c gifts**. H2776
1Co 3:12 using gold, silver, **c** stones, wood, hay G5508
Rev 18:12 every kind made of ivory, **c** wood, bronze, G5508

COSTS (3) [COST]
1Ch 21:24 a burnt offering that **c** me **nothing**. H2855
Ezr 6: 4 The **c** are to be paid by the royal treasury A10486
Pr 6:31 though *it* **c** *him* all the wealth of his H5989

COUCH (8) [COUCHES]
Ge 49: 4 father's bed, onto my **c** and defiled it. H3661
1Sa 28:23 got up from the ground and sat on the **c**. H4753
2Ki 4:32 there was the boy lying dead on his **c**. H4753
Est 7: 8 was falling on the **c** where Esther was H4753
Job 7:13 comfort me and my **c** will ease my H5435
Ps 6: 6 with weeping and drench my **c** with tears. H6911
Eze 23:41 You sat on an elegant **c**, with a table H4753
Am 3:12 of a bed and a piece of fabric from a **c**." H6911

COUCHES (2) [COUCH]
Est 1: 6 There were **c** *of* gold and silver on a H4753
Am 6: 4 adorned with ivory and lounge on your **c**. H6911

COULD (277) [COULDN'T]
Ge 8: 9 But the dove *c* **find** nowhere to perch because AIT
Ge 13: 6 But the land *c* not **support** them while they AIT
Ge 13:16 so that if anyone **c** count the dust, then H3523
Ge 13:16 the dust, then your offspring *c* **be counted**. AIT
Ge 19:11 blindness so that *they* **c not** find the door. H4206
Ge 20:17 female slaves so *they c* **have children** again, AIT
Ge 27: 1 eyes were so weak that *he c* no longer **see**, AIT
Ge 31:27 so *I c* **send** you **away** with joy and singing to AIT
Ge 31:35 So he searched but *c* not **find** the household AIT
Ge 32:25 the man saw that *he c* not **overpower** him, AIT
Ge 36: 7 they were staying **c** not support them both H3523
Ge 37: 4 they hated him and **c** not speak a kind H3523
Ge 39: 9 How then *c I* **do** such a wicked thing and sin AIT
Ge 41: 8 but no *one c* **interpret** them for him. AIT
Ge 41:21 ate them, no *one c* **tell** that they had done so AIT
Ge 41:24 none of them *c* **explain** it to me. AIT
Ge 42:23 not realize that Joseph *c* **understand** them, AIT
Ge 43:10 delayed, *we c have* gone and **returned** twice." AIT
Ge 43:32 because Egyptians **c** not eat with Hebrews H3523
Ge 45: 1 Then Joseph **c** no longer control himself H3523
Ge 48:10 because of old age, and he **c** hardly see. H3523
Ex 2: 3 But when *she* **c** hide him no longer, she H3523
Ex 7:21 that the Egyptians **c** not drink its water. H3523
Ex 7:24 because *they* **c** not drink the water of the H3523
Ex 8:18 gnats by their secret arts, *they* **c** not. H3523
Ex 9:11 The magicians **c** not stand before Moses H3523
Ex 9:15 For by now *I c have* **stretched out** my hand AIT
Ex 10:23 No one *c* **see** anyone else or move about AIT
Ex 13:21 so that they *c* **travel** by day or night. AIT
Ex 15:23 *they* **c** not drink its water because it was H3523
Ex 39: 4 to two of its corners, so *it c* **be fastened**. AIT
Ex 40:35 Moses **c** not enter the tent of meeting H3523
Nu 9: 6 But some of them **c** not celebrate the H3523
Nu 11:33 their teeth and before *it c* **be consumed**, AIT
Nu 22:18 *I* **c** not do anything great or small to go H3523
Nu 22:41 from there *he c* **see** the outskirts of the AIT
Nu 24:13 *I* **c** not do anything of my own accord H3523
Dt 4:42 who had killed a person *c* **flee** if they had AIT
Dt 4:42 *They c* **flee** into one of these cities and save AIT
Dt 32:30 How *c* one man **chase** a thousand, or two put AIT
Jos 15:63 Judah **c** not dislodge the Jebusites, who H3523
Jos 20: 9 accidentally *c* **flee** to these designated AIT
Jos 22:16 'How **c** *you* **break faith** with the God of Israel AIT
Jos 22:16 How **c** you turn away from the LORD and NDT
Jdg 7:12 Their camels **c** no more be counted than the NDT
Jdg 10:16 And he *c* **bear** Israel's misery **no longer**. AIT
Jdg 12: 6 because he **c** not pronounce the word H3922
Jdg 14:14 For three days *they* **c** not give the answer H3523
Jdg 20:16 each of whom *c* **sling** a stone at a hair and AIT
Jdg 20:42 wilderness, but they *c* **not escape** the battle. AIT
Ru 1:11 more sons, *who c* **become** your husbands? AIT
Ru 3:14 got up before anyone *c be* **recognized** AIT
1Sa 3: 2 becoming so weak that *he* **c** barely see, H3523
1Sa 4:15 eyes had failed so that *he* **c** not see. H3523
1Sa 6: 6 the Israelites out so *they c* **go on** *their* **way**? AIT
1Sa 9: 2 a young man as **c** be found anywhere in NDT
1Sa 13:19 Not a blacksmith *c* **be found** in the whole AIT
1Sa 29: 4 better *c he* **regain** his master's **favor** than by AIT
2Sa 1:10 that after he had fallen *he c* not **survive**. AIT
2Sa 2:22 How *c I* **look** your brother Joab **in the face**?" AIT
2Sa 11:11 *How c* I **go** to my house to eat and drink AIT
2Sa 13:13 Where *c I* **get rid of** my disgrace AIT
2Sa 15: 4 complaint or case *c* **come** to me and I would AIT
2Sa 17:17 for *they* **c** not **risk** being seen entering the H3523
2Sa 22:39 completely, and *they c* not **rise**; they fell AIT
2Sa 24: 9 able-bodied men *who c* **handle** a sword, AIT
1Ki 1: 1 he *c* not *keep* **warm** even when they put AIT
1Ki 5: 3 *he* **c** not build a temple for the Name of H3523
1Ki 8: 5 cattle that *they c* not **be recorded** or counted. AIT
1Ki 8: 8 that their ends *c* **be seen** from the Holy Place AIT
1Ki 8:11 And the priests **c** not perform their service H3523
1Ki 9:21 whom the Israelites **c** not exterminate—to H3523
1Ki 13: 4 shriveled up, so that *he* **c** not pull it back. H3523
1Ki 14: 4 Now Ahijah **c** not see; his sight was gone H3523
1Ki 18:10 he made them swear *they c* not **find** you. AIT
2Ki 3:21 *who c* **bear arms** was called up and stationed AIT
2Ki 4:39 **as many** of its gourds as his garment **c hold** H4850
2Ki 4:40 is death in the pot!" And *they* **c** not eat it. H3523
2Ki 7: 2 floodgates of the heavens, *c* this **happen**?" AIT
2Ki 7:19 floodgates of the heavens, *c* this **happen**?" AIT
2Ki 8:13 "How *c* your servant, a mere dog, **accomplish** AIT
2Ki 10: 4 "If two kings *c* not **resist** him, how can we?" AIT
2Ki 16: 5 but *they* **c** not overpower him. H3523
2Ki 23:10 so no one *c use* it *to* **sacrifice** their son or AIT
2Ki 25:16 of the LORD, was more than **c** be weighed. NDT
1Ch 5: 1 he *c* not **be listed in the genealogical record** AIT
1Ch 5:18 able-bodied men *who c* **handle** shield and AIT
1Ch 5:18 shield and sword, *who c* **use** a bow, and who AIT
1Ch 8:40 were brave warriors *who c* **handle** the bow. AIT
1Ch 21: 5 thousand men *who c* **handle** a sword, AIT
1Ch 21:30 But David **c** not go before it to inquire of H3523
1Ch 22: 3 more bronze than **c** be weighed. NDT
1Ch 22: 4 more cedar logs than **c** be counted, NDT
2Ch 4:18 the weight of the bronze *c* not **be calculated**. AIT
2Ch 5: 6 cattle that *they c* not **be recorded** or counted. AIT
2Ch 5: 9 *c* **be seen** *from* in front of the inner sanctuary AIT
2Ch 5:14 the priests **c** not perform their service H3523
2Ch 7: 2 The priests **c** not enter the temple of the H3523
2Ch 7: 7 altar he had made **c** not hold the burnt H3523
2Ch 14:13 of Cushites fell that they **c** not recover; NDT
2Ch 20:25 of value—more than *they c* **take away**. AIT
2Ch 22:11 the child from Athaliah so *she c* not **kill** him. AIT
2Ch 25:15 which *c* not **save** their own people from your AIT
2Ch 26:15 so that *soldiers c* **shoot** arrows and hurl AIT
2Ch 30:17 clean and *c* not **consecrate** their lambs to the AIT
2Ch 31: 4 Levites so *they c* **devote** *themselves* to the AIT
Ezr 2:59 but *they* **c** not show that their families H3523
Ezr 2:62 they *c* not **find** *them* and so were AIT
Ezr 3:13 No one *c* **distinguish** the sound of the shouts AIT
Ezr 5: 5 stopped until a report *c* **go** to Darius and his AIT
Ezr 5:10 so that *we c* **write down** the names of their AIT
Ne 5: 8 because *they c* **find** nothing to say. AIT
Ne 7:61 but *they* **c** not show that their families H3523
Ne 7:64 they *c* not **find** *them* and so were AIT
Ne 8: 3 women and others *who c* **understand**. AIT
Ne 8: 5 All the people **c** see him because he was NDT
Ne 9:36 our ancestors so they *c* **eat** its fruit and the AIT
Ne 12:43 *The* **sound** of rejoicing in Jerusalem *c* **be heard** AIT
Ne 13:19 that no load *c be* **brought in** on the Sabbath AIT
Est 6: 1 That night the king **c not** sleep; so he H5610
Est 9: 2 No one *c* **stand** against them, because the AIT
Job 2:12 a distance, *they c* hardly **recognize** him; they AIT
Job 4:16 It stopped, but *I c* not **tell** what it was. AIT
Job 6: 2 only my anguish *c* **be weighed** and all my AIT
Job 9: 3 *they c* not **answer** him one time out of a AIT
Job 9:15 I were innocent, *I c* not **answer** him; I could AIT
Job 9:15 *I c* only **plead** with my Judge **for mercy**. AIT
Job 13: 9 *C you* **deceive** him as you might deceive a AIT
Job 15:14 that *they c* **be pure**, or those born AIT
Job 15:14 born of woman, that *they c* **be righteous**? AIT
Job 16: 4 I also *c* **speak** like you, if you were in my AIT
Job 16: 4 *I c* **make fine speeches** against you and AIT
Job 23: 3 to find him; if only *I c* **go** to his dwelling! AIT
Job 31:23 fear of his splendor *I* **c** not **do** such things. H3523
Ps 18:38 I crushed them so that *they* **c** not rise; they H3523
Ps 37:36 though I looked for him, *he c* not **be found**. AIT
Ps 55:12 were insulting me, *I c* **endure** it; if a foe were AIT
Ps 55:12 if a foe were rising against me, *I c* **hide**. AIT
Ps 78:25 he sent them **all** the food they **c eat**. H8427
Ps 78:44 *they c* not **drink** *from* their streams. AIT
Ps 78:64 to the sword, and their widows *c* not **weep**. AIT
Ps 107: 4 finding no way to a city where they **c** settle. NDT
Ps 107: 7 a straight way to a city where they **c** settle. NDT
Ps 107:36 they founded a city where they **c** settle. NDT
Ps 130: 3 kept a record of sins, Lord, who *c* **stand**? AIT
Isa 5: 4 What more *c have been* **done** for my AIT
Isa 7: 1 Jerusalem, but *they* **c** not overpower it. H3523
Isa 10:19 will be so few that a child *c* **write them down**. AIT
Isa 26:16 *they c* **barely whisper a prayer**. AIT
Isa 41:26 the beginning, so *we c* **know**, or beforehand, AIT
Isa 41:26 beforehand, so *we c* **say**, 'He was right'? AIT
Isa 48: 5 announced them to you so that *you c* not **say**, AIT
Jer 24: 2 very bad figs, so bad *they c* not **be eaten**. AIT
Jer 44:22 When the LORD **c** no longer endure your H3523
Jer 47: 4 all survivors *who c* **help** Tyre and Sidon. AIT
Jer 52:20 of the LORD, was more than **c** be weighed. NDT
La 4:12 that enemies and foes *c* **enter** the gates of AIT
La 4:17 we watched for a nation *that c* not **save** us. AIT
La 4:18 at every step, so we *c* not **walk** in our streets. AIT
Eze 10: 5 of the cherubim *c* **be heard** as far away as AIT
Eze 10: 8 of the cherubim *c* **be seen** what looked like AIT
Eze 14:14 they *c* **save** only themselves by their AIT
Eze 14:16 *they c* not **save** their own sons or daughters. AIT
Eze 14:18 *they c* not **save** their own sons or daughters. AIT
Eze 14:20 *they c* **save** neither son nor daughter. AIT
Eze 20:25 good and laws through which *they c* not **live**; AIT
Eze 31: 8 The cedars in the garden of God *c* not **rival** it AIT
Eze 31: 8 nor *c* the junipers **equal** its boughs AIT
Eze 31: 8 nor *c* the plane trees **compare with** its AIT
Eze 31: 8 tree in the garden of God *c* **match** its beauty. AIT
Eze 47: 5 now it was a river that *I* **c** not cross H3523
Eze 47: 5 to swim in—a river that no *one c* **cross**. AIT
Da 1:17 And Daniel *c* **understand** visions and dreams AIT
Da 2: 1 was troubled and he **c** not sleep. H2118+6584
Da 4: 7 the dream, but *they c* not **interpret** it for me. AIT
Da 5: 8 but *they* **c** not read the writing or tell the A10346
Da 5:15 what it means, but *they* **c** not explain it. A10346
Da 6: 4 *They c* **find** no corruption in him, because he AIT
Da 6:18 brought to him. And he **c not** sleep. A10463
Da 8: 4 No animal *c* **stand** against it, and none could AIT
Da 8: 4 against it, and none *c* **rescue** from its power. AIT
Da 8: 7 and none *c* **rescue** the ram from its power. AIT
Hos 10: 3 even if we had a king, what *c he* **do** for us?" AIT
Jnh 1:13 But *they* **c** not, for the sea grew even H3523
Zec 1:21 Judah so that no one *c* **raise** their head, AIT
Zec 8:10 No one *c* **go about** *their* **business** safely AIT
Mt 8:28 so violent that no one **c** pass that way. G2710
Mt 9:32 and **c not talk** was brought to G3273
Mt 12:22 healed him, so that he *c* both **talk** and see. AIT
Mt 12:23 said, "**C** this be the Son of David?" G3614
Mt 15:33 "Where **c** we get enough bread in this NDT
Mt 17:16 to your disciples, but they **c** not heal him." G1538
Mt 18:30 thrown into prison until *he c* **pay** the debt. AIT
Mt 22:10 gathered all the people *they c* **find**, AIT
Mt 22:46 No one **c** say a word in reply, and from G1538
Mt 26: 9 "This perfume **c** *have* been sold at a high G1538
Mt 26:59 against Jesus so that *they c* **put** him **to death**. AIT
Mk 1:45 Jesus **c** no longer enter a town openly G1538
Mk 2: 4 Since *they* **c** not get him to Jesus because G1538
Mk 4:33 to them, as much as *they* **c** understand. G1538
Mk 5: 3 and no one **c** bind him anymore G1538
Mk 6: 5 *He* **c** not do any miracles there, except lay G1538
Mk 7:24 yet *he* **c** not keep his presence secret. G1538
Mk 7:32 a man who was deaf and **c hardly talk**, G3652
Mk 9: 3 than anyone in the world **c** bleach them. G1538
Mk 9:18 to drive out the spirit, but *they* **c** not." G2710
Mk 14: 5 It **c** *have* been sold for more than a year's G1538
Mk 14: 8 She did what *she* **c**. She poured perfume G2400
Mk 14:55 against Jesus so that *they c* **put** him **to death**, AIT
Lk 1:22 he came out, *he* **c** not speak to them. G1538
Lk 5:19 *When they c* not **find** a way to do this AIT
Lk 6:48 torrent struck that house but **c** not shake it, G2710
Lk 8:43 twelve years, but no one **c** heal her. G2710
Lk 8:47 seeing that *she c* not **go unnoticed**, came AIT
Lk 9:40 disciples to drive it out, but *they* **c** not." G1538
Lk 13:11 was bent over and **c** not straighten up at G1538
Lk 15:29 a young goat so *I c* **celebrate** with my friends. AIT
Lk 19: 3 he was short he **c** not see over the G1538
Lk 19:23 **I c have** collected it with interest? G323
Lk 19:48 Yet *they c* not **find** any way to do it, because AIT
Lk 24:45 their minds *so they c* **understand** the AIT
Jn 3: 2 For no one **c** perform the signs you are G1538
Jn 4:29 **C** this be the Messiah?" G3614
Jn 4:33 "**C** someone have brought him food?" G3590
Jn 9:11 So I went and washed, and then *I c* **see**." AIT
Jn 9:33 man were not from God, *he* **c** do nothing." G1538
Jn 11:37 "**C** not he who opened the eyes of the G1538
Jn 12:39 For this reason *they* **c** not believe G1538
Ac 4:14 But *since they c* **see** the man who had been AIT
Ac 4:14 with them, there was nothing *they c* **say**. AIT
Ac 4:21 *They c* not **decide** how to punish them AIT
Ac 5: 9 "**How c** you conspire to test G5515+5516+4022
Ac 6:10 But *they* **c** not stand up against the G2710
Ac 7:11 suffering, and our ancestors *c* not **find** food. AIT
Ac 8:20 you thought *you c* **buy** the gift of God AIT
Ac 9: 8 when he opened his eyes *he c* **see** nothing. AIT
Ac 9:18 fell from Saul's eyes, and *he c* **see again**. AIT
Ac 10:22 his house so that *he c* **hear** what you have to AIT
Ac 11:17 was I to think that I **c** stand in God's way?" G1543
Ac 21:34 and *since* the commander **c** not get at the G1538
Ac 25: 7 against him, but *they* **c** not prove them. G2710
Ac 25:21 him held until *I c* **send** him to Caesar." AIT
Ac 26:32 "This man **c** *have* been set free if he had G1538
Ac 27:15 by the storm and **c** not head into the wind G1538
Ac 27:39 decided to run the ship aground if *they* **c**. G1538
Ac 27:43 He ordered those *who* **c** swim to jump G1538
Ro 3: 6 If that were so, how *c* God **judge** the world? AIT
Ro 9: 3 For *I c* **wish** that I myself were cursed and cut AIT
Ro 11: 8 eyes that *c* not **see** and ears that could not AIT
Ro 11: 8 that could not see and ears that *c* not **hear**, AIT
Ro 11:19 were broken off so that I *c be* **grafted in**." AIT
1Co 3: 1 I **c** not address you as people who live by G1538
2Co 3: 7 so that the Israelites **c** not look steadily at G1538
2Co 7:12 that before God *you c* **see** for yourselves how AIT
Gal 2:21 if righteousness **c** be gained through the NDT
Gal 3:21 if a law had been given that **c** impart life, G1538

Gal 4:15 testify that, if you **c** have done so, you G1543
Gal 4:20 how I wish *I* **c** **be** with you now and change AIT
Php 2:30 the help you yourselves **c not give** me. G5729
1Th 2:6 *even though* as apostles of Christ *we* **c** *have* G1538
1Th 3:1 So *when we* **c stand** it no longer, we thought AIT
1Th 3:5 For this reason, *when* I **c stand** it no longer, AIT
Phm 8 *although* in Christ *I* **c** *be* **bold** and order you AIT
Phm 13 so that *he* **c** take your place *in* **helping** me AIT
Heb 5:7 tears to the *one who* **c** save him from G1538
Heb 7:11 perfection *c have been* **attained** through the AIT
Heb 11:5 "*He* **c** not *be* **found**, because God had taken AIT
Heb 11:19 reasoned that God **c** even raise the dead, G1543
Heb 12:17 tears, *he* **c** not **change** what he had done. AIT
Heb 12:20 because *they* **c** not **bear** what was AIT
Rev 5:3 under the earth **c** open the scroll or G1538
Rev 7:9 a great multitude that no one **c** count, G1538
Rev 13:15 so that the image *c* **speak** and cause all who AIT
Rev 13:17 so that they **c** not buy or sell unless they G1538
Rev 14:3 No one **c** learn the song except the G1538
Rev 15:8 no one **c** enter the temple until the G1538
Rev 16:20 fled away and the mountains *c* not *be* **found**. AIT

COULDN'T (5) [COULD, NOT]

2Ki 5:12 **C** I wash in them and be cleansed?" H4202
Mt 17:19 and asked, "Why **c** we drive it out?" G4024+1538
Mt 26:40 "**C** *you men* keep watch with me G4024+2710
Mk 9:28 privately, "Why **c** we drive it out?" G4024+1538
Mk 14:37 **C you** keep watch for one hour? G4024+2710

COUNCIL (16) [COUNCILS]

Ge 49:6 Let me not enter their **c**, let me not join H6051
Nu 16:2 had been appointed members of the **c**. H4595
Job 15:8 Do you listen in on God's **c**? Do you have H6051
Ps 89:7 In the **c** *of* the holy ones God is greatly H6051
Ps 107:32 praise him in the **c** *of* the elders. H4632
Ps 111:1 all my heart in the **c** *of* the upright and in H6051
Jer 23:18 has stood in the **c** *of* the LORD to see or H6051
Jer 23:22 But if they had stood in my **c**, they would H6051
Eze 13:9 not belong to the **c** *of* my people or be H6051
Mk 15:43 a prominent **member of the C**, who was G1085
Lk 22:66 daybreak the **c of the elders** of the people G4564
Lk 23:50 Joseph, a **member of the C**, a good and G1085
Jn 3:1 *who was a member of* the Jewish **ruling c**. G807
Ac 17:33 Paul left **the C**. G8998
Ac 22:5 priest and all the **C** can themselves testify. G4564
Ac 25:12 After Festus had conferred with his **c**, he G5206

COUNCILS (2) [COUNCIL]

Mt 10:17 over to the **local c** and be flogged in G5284
Mk 13:9 handed over to the **local c** and flogged in G5284

COUNSEL (25) [COUNSELOR, COUNSELORS, COUNSELS]

2Sa 15:31 turn Ahithophel's **c** into foolishness." H6783
1Ki 22:5 of Israel, "First seek the **c** *of* the LORD." H1821
2Ki 18:20 You say you have the **c** and the might H6783
2Ch 18:4 of Israel, "First seek the **c** *of* the LORD." H1821
2Ch 22:5 also followed their **c** when he went with H6783
2Ch 25:16 done this and have not listened to my **c**." H6783
Ezr 10:3 accordance with the **c** *of* my lord and of H6783
Job 12:13 power; **c** and understanding are his. H6783
Job 29:21 expectantly, waiting in silence for my **c**. H6783
Ps 32:8 *I will* **c** you with my loving eye on you. H3619
Ps 73:24 You guide me with your **c**, and afterward H6783
Pr 8:14 **C** and sound judgment are mine; I have H6783
Pr 15:22 Plans fail for lack of **c**, but with many H6051
Pr 22:20 you, sayings of **c** and knowledge, H4600
Isa 11:2 the Spirit of **c** and of might, the Spirit of H6783
Isa 36:5 You say you have **c** and might for war H6783
Isa 41:28 no one among the gods *to* **give c**, no H3446
Isa 45:21 present it—*let them* **take c** together. H3619
Isa 47:13 All the **c** you have *received* has only worn H6783
Jer 18:18 not cease, nor will **c** from the wise, nor H6783
Jer 38:15 Even if *I did* **give** you **c**, you would not H3619
Jer 49:7 Has **c** perished from the prudent H6783
Eze 7:26 the **c** of the elders will come to an end. H6783
1Ti 5:14 So *I* **c** younger widows to marry, to have G1089
Rev 3:18 *I* **c** you to buy from me gold refined in the G5205

COUNSELOR (8) [COUNSEL]

2Sa 15:12 Gilonite, David's **c**, to come from Giloh, H3446
1Ch 26:14 Zechariah, a wise **c**, and the lot for the H3446
1Ch 27:32 David's uncle, was a **c**, a man of insight H3446
1Ch 27:33 Ahithophel was the king's **c**. Hushai the H3446
Isa 3:3 the man of rank, the **c**, skilled craftsman H3446
Isa 9:6 And he will be called Wonderful **C** H3446
Isa 40:13 the LORD, or instruct the LORD as his **c**? H408+6783
Ro 11:34 Or who has been his **c**?" G5207

COUNSELORS (2) [COUNSEL]

Ps 119:24 are my delight; they are my **c**. H408+6783
Isa 19:11 the wise **c** *of* Pharaoh give senseless H3446

COUNSELS (1) [COUNSEL]

Ps 16:7 the LORD, who **c** me; even at night my H3619

COUNT (46) [COUNTED, COUNTING, COUNTLESS, COUNTS]

Ge 13:16 so that if anyone could **c** the dust, then H4948
Ge 15:5 "Look up at the sky and **c** the stars—if H6218
Ge 15:5 count the stars—if indeed you can **c** them." H6218
Ge 16:10 much that *they will be* too numerous *to* **c**." H6218
Ex 30:12 take a census of the Israelites to **c** them, H7212
Lev 15:13 *he is to* **c off** seven days for his H6218
Lev 15:28 her discharge, *she must* **c off** seven days H6218
Lev 23:15 the wave offering, **c off** seven full weeks. H6218
Lev 23:16 **C off** fifty days up to the day after the H6218
Lev 25:8 " '**C off** seven sabbath years—seven times H6218
Lev 25:50 *They* and their buyer *are to* **c** the time from H3108
Nu 1:3 You and Aaron *are to* **c** according to their H7212
Nu 1:49 "*You must* not **c** the tribe of Levi or include H7212
Nu 3:15 "**C** the Levites by their families and clans H7212
Nu 3:15 **C** every male a month old or more." H7212
Nu 3:40 "**C** all the firstborn Israelite males who are H7212
Nu 4:3 **C** all the men from thirty to fifty years of age NDT
Nu 4:23 **C** all the men from thirty to fifty years of H7212
Nu 4:29 "**C** the Merarites by their clans and H7212
Nu 4:30 **C** all the men from thirty to fifty years of H7212
Nu 6:12 The previous days **do not c**, because they H5877
Nu 23:10 Who *can* **c** the dust of Jacob or number H4948
Nu 31:26 the community *are to* **c** all the H5951+906+8031
Dt 16:9 **C off** seven weeks from the time you H6218
Jdg 6:5 was impossible to **c** them or their camels H5031
1Ki 3:8 people, too numerous *to* **c** or number. H6218
1Ch 21:2 "Go and **c** the Israelites from Beersheba H6218
1Ch 27:24 of Zeruiah began to **c** the men but did not H4948
Job 14:16 Surely then *you will* **c** my steps but not H6218
Job 19:15 my female servants **c** me a foreigner; H3108
Job 31:4 he not see my ways and **c** my every step? H6218
Job 38:37 Who has the wisdom *to* **c** the clouds H6218
Job 39:2 *Do you* **c** the months till they bear? Do H6218
Ps 32:2 sin the LORD *does* not **c** against them and H3108
Ps 48:12 about Zion, go around her, **c** her towers, H6218
Ps 49:18 they live *they* **c** themselves **blessed**— H1385
Ps 139:18 *Were I to* **c** them, they would outnumber H6218
Ps 139:22 them; I **c** *them* my enemies. H2118+4200
Isa 16:14 a servant bound by contract would **c** them, NDT
Isa 21:16 as a servant bound by contract would **c** it, all NDT
Isa 46:5 will you compare me or **c** me **equal**? H8750
Eze 33:12 former righteousness *will* **c for** nothing. H5911
Ro 4:8 sin the Lord *will* never **c against** them." G3357
Ro 6:11 **c** yourselves dead to sin but alive to God G3357
Jas 5:11 *we* **c as blessed** those who have G3420
Rev 7:9 was a great multitude that no one could **c**, G749

COUNTED (69) [COUNT]

Ge 13:16 the dust, then your offspring *could* **be c**. H4948
Ge 32:12 the sand of the sea, which cannot be **c**." H6218
Ex 30:12 a ransom for his life at the time he *is* **c**. H7212
Ex 30:13 over to those *already* **c** is to give a half H7212
Ex 38:25 *those of* the community *who* **were c in the census** H7212
Ex 38:26 everyone who had crossed over to those **c**, H7212
Nu 1:19 And so *he* **c** them in the Desert of Sinai H7212
Nu 1:22 serve in the army **were c** and listed by H7212
Nu 1:44 were the *men* **c** by Moses and H7212+7212
Nu 1:45 in Israel's army were **c** according to their H7212
Nu 1:47 however, **was** not **c** along with the others. H7212
Nu 2:32 Israelites, **c** according to their families. H7212
Nu 2:33 **were** not **c** along with the other Israelites H7212
Nu 3:16 So Moses **c** them, as he was commanded H7212
Nu 3:22 month old or more who **were c** was 7,500. H7212
Nu 3:34 month old or more who **were c** was 6,200. H7212
Nu 3:39 number of Levites **c** at the LORD's H7212
Nu 3:42 So Moses **c** all the firstborn of the H7212
Nu 4:34 of the community **c** the Kohathites by their H7212
Nu 4:36 **c** by clans, were 2,750. H7212
Nu 4:37 Moses and Aaron **c** them according to the H7212
Nu 4:38 The Gershonites **were c** by their clans H7212
Nu 4:40 **c** by their clans and families, were 2,630. H7212
Nu 4:41 Moses and Aaron **c** them according to the H7212
Nu 4:42 The Merarites **were c** by their clans and H7212
Nu 4:44 **c** by their clans, were 3,200. H7212
Nu 4:45 Moses and Aaron **c** them according to the H7212
Nu 4:46 the leaders of Israel **c** all the Levites by H7212
Nu 4:49 Thus they **were c**, as the LORD commanded H7212
Nu 7:2 leaders in charge of those *who* **were c**, H7212
Nu 14:29 years old or more *who* **was c** in the census H7212
Nu 26:57 the Levites *who* **were c** by their clans: H7212
Nu 26:62 *They* **were** not **c** along with the other H7212
Nu 26:63 These are the *ones* **c** *by* Moses and H7212
Nu 26:63 the priest when *they* **c** the Israelites on H7212
Nu 26:64 them was among *those* **c** *by* Moses and H7212
Nu 26:64 the priest when *they* **c** the Israelites in H7212
Nu 31:49 servants *have* **c** the soldiers H5951+906+8031
Jos 13:3 *all of it* **c** as Canaanite though held by the H3108
Jdg 7:12 could no more be **c** than the sand on the H5031
Jdg 21:9 For when *they* **c** the people, they found H7212
1Sa 13:15 Saul **c** the men who were with him. H7212
1Sa 18:27 *They* **c out the full number** to the king so H4848
2Sa 2:15 stood up and *were* **c off**— H6296+928+5031
2Sa 24:10 after *he had* **c** the fighting men, H6218
1Ki 8:5 cattle that they could not be recorded or **c**. H4948
2Ki 12:10 **c** the money that had been brought into H4948
1Ch 9:28 they **c** them when they were brought in H5031
1Ch 21:17 I who ordered the fighting men to *be* **c**? H4948
1Ch 22:4 provided more cedar logs than could be **c**, H5031
1Ch 23:3 The Levites thirty years old or more **were c** H6218
1Ch 23:11 so they were **c** as one family with one NDT
1Ch 23:14 the man of God **were c** as part of the H7924
1Ch 23:24 under their names and **c** individually, H5031
1Ch 23:27 the Levites were **c** from those twenty years H5031
2Ch 5:6 cattle that they could not be recorded or **c**. H4948
Ezr 1:8 *who* **c** them **out** to Sheshbazzar the prince H6218
Job 5:9 be fathomed, miracles that cannot be **c**. H5031
Job 9:10 be fathomed, miracles that cannot be **c**. H5031
Ps 41:2 *they are* **c among the blessed** in the land H887
Ps 88:4 *I* **am c** among those who go down to the H3108
Pr 19:20 at the end *you will be* **c among the wise**. H2681
Ecc 1:15 straightened; what is lacking cannot be **c**. H4948
Isa 22:10 *You* **c** the buildings in Jerusalem and tore H6218
Jer 46:23 numerous than locusts, they cannot be **c**. H5031
Hos 1:10 seashore, which cannot be measured or **c**. H6218
Mt 26:15 So they **c out** for him thirty pieces of silver. G2705
Ac 5:41 because *they had been* **c worthy** of G2921
2Th 1:5 a result you *will be* **c worthy** of the G2921

COUNTENANCE (1)

Job 14:20 you change their **c** and send them away. H7156

COUNTERATTACK (1) [ATTACK]

Jdg 20:39 the Israelites *would* **c**. H2200+928+2021+4878

COUNTERATTACKED (1) [ATTACK]

Jdg 20:41 Then the Israelites **c**, and the Benjamites H2200

COUNTERFEIT (1)

1Jn 2:27 not **c**—just as it has taught G6022

COUNTING (4) [COUNT]

Ge 46:26 **not c** his sons' wives H4946+4200+963
Dt 24:15 are poor and *are* **c on** it. H5951+906+5883+448
Jdg 8:26 shekels, **not c** the ornaments H4200+963+4946
2Co 5:19 not **c** people's sins against them. G3357

COUNTLESS (4) [COUNT]

Nu 10:36 Return, LORD, to the **c** thousands of Israel. H8047
Job 21:33 and a **c** throng goes before them. H401+5031
Jer 33:22 *I will* **make** the descendants of David my servant ... as **c** H8049+889+4202+6218
Heb 11:12 stars in the sky and as **c** as the sand on the G410

COUNTRIES (41) [COUNTRY]

Dt 29:16 we passed through the **c** on the way here. H1580
1Ki 4:21 These **c** brought tribute and were Solomon's NDT
2Ki 18:35 the gods of these **c** has been able to save H824
2Ki 19:11 the kings of Assyria have done to all the **c**, H824
2Ch 9:28 imported from Egypt and from all other **c**. H824
Isa 10:14 so I gathered all the **c**; not one flapped a H824
Isa 36:20 all the gods of these **c** have been able to H824
Isa 37:11 the kings of Assyria have done to all the **c**, H824
Jer 16:15 out of all the **c** where he had banished H824
Jer 23:3 my flock out of all the **c** where I have driven H824
Jer 23:8 out of all the **c** where he had banished H824
Jer 27:6 I will give all your **c** into the hands of my H824
Jer 28:8 against many **c** and great kingdoms. H824
Jer 40:11 all the other **c** heard that the king of H824
Jer 40:12 from all the **c** where they had been H5226
Jer 51:28 all their officials, and all the **c** they rule. H824
Eze 5:5 center of the nations, with **c** all around her. H824
Eze 5:6 more than the nations and **c** around her. H824
Eze 11:16 nations and scattered them among the **c**, H824
Eze 11:16 them in the **c** where they have gone. H824
Eze 11:17 you back from the **c** where you have been H824
Eze 12:15 the nations and scatter them through the **c**. H824
Eze 20:23 the nations and scatter them through the **c**, H824
Eze 20:34 gather you from the **c** where you have been H824
Eze 20:41 gather you from the **c** where you have been H824
Eze 22:4 nations and a laughingstock to all the **c**. H824
Eze 22:15 the nations and scatter you through the **c**; H824
Eze 25:7 nations and exterminate you from the **c**. H824
Eze 29:12 the nations and scatter them through the **c**. H824
Eze 30:23 the nations and scatter them through the **c**. H824
Eze 30:26 the nations and scatter them through the **c**. H824
Eze 34:13 the nations and gather them from the **c**, H824
Eze 35:10 two nations and **c** will be ours and we H824
Eze 36:19 they were scattered through the **c**; H824
Eze 36:24 you from all the **c** and bring you back into H824
Eze 39:27 gathered them from the **c** *of* their enemies, H824
Da 9:7 in all the **c** where you have scattered us H824
Da 11:40 He will invade *many* **c** and sweep through H824
Da 11:41 **Many** *c* will fall, but Edom, Moab and the AIT
Da 11:42 He will extend his power over *many* **c**; Egypt H824
Zec 8:7 my people from the **c** *of* the east and the H824

COUNTRY (248) [COUNTRIES, COUNTRYSIDE]

Ge 10:30 toward Sephar, in the eastern **hill c**. H2215
Ge 12:1 "Go from your **c**, your people and H824
Ge 14:6 the Horites in the **hill c** *of* Seir, as far H2215
Ge 15:13 be strangers in a **c** not their own and that H824
Ge 21:23 Show to me and the **c** where you now H824
Ge 24:4 will go to my **c** and my own relatives H824
Ge 24:5 take your son back to the **c** you came from?" H824
Ge 25:27 a man of the **open c**, while Jacob was H8441
Ge 25:29 Esau came in from the **open c**, famished. H8441
Ge 27:3 go out to the **open c** to hunt some H8441
Ge 27:5 Esau left for the **open c** to hunt game H8441
Ge 29:2 There he saw a well in the **open c**, with H8441
Ge 31:21 and headed for the **hill c** *of* Gilead. H2215
Ge 31:23 caught up with him in the **hill c** *of* Gilead. H2215
Ge 31:25 his tent in the **hill c** *of* Gilead when Laban H2215
Ge 31:54 sacrifice there in the **hill c** and invited his H2215
Ge 32:3 Esau in the land of Seir, the **c** *of* Edom. H8441
Ge 32:9 'Go back to your **c** and your relatives H824
Ge 36:8 that is, Edom) settled in the **hill c** *of* Seir. H2215
Ge 36:9 father of the Edomites in the **hill c** *of* Seir. H2215
Ge 36:35 who defeated Midian in the **c** *of* Moab H8441

Ge 41:36 food should be held in reserve for the c, H824
Ge 41:36 so that the c may not be ruined by the H824
Ge 41:56 the famine had spread over the whole c, H824
Ex 1:10 enemies, fight against us and leave the c." H824
Ex 6: 1 mighty hand he will drive them out of his c." H824
Ex 6:11 of Egypt to let the Israelites go out of his c." H824
Ex 7: 2 Pharaoh to let the Israelites go out of his c. H824
Ex 8: 2 send a plague of frogs on your whole c. H1473
Ex 10: 4 I will bring locusts into your c tomorrow. H1473
Ex 10:14 in every area of the c in great numbers. H5213
Ex 11:10 would not let the Israelites go out of his c. H824
Ex 12:33 urged the people to hurry and leave the c. H824
Ex 13:17 them on the road through the Philistine c, H824
Ex 18:27 his way, and Jethro returned to his own c. H824
Lev 25:31 be considered as belonging to the open c. H824
Lev 25:45 members of their clans born in your c, H824
Lev 26: 6 the sword will not pass through your c. H824
Lev 26:34 you are in the c of your enemies; H824
Nu 13:17 through the Negev and on into the hill c. H2215
Nu 13:29 Jebusites and Amorites live in the hill c H2215
Nu 14:40 set out for the highest point in the hill c, H2215
Nu 14:44 up toward the highest point in the hill c, H2215
Nu 14:45 who lived in that hill c came down and H2215
Nu 20:17 Please let us pass through your c. We will H824
Nu 21:22 "Let us pass through your c. We will not H824
Nu 22:13 "Go back to your own c, for the LORD has H824
Dt 1: 7 advance into the hill c of the Amorites; H2215
Dt 1:19 went toward the hill c of the Amorites H2215
Dt 1:20 have reached the hill c of the Amorites, H2215
Dt 1:24 They left and went up into the hill c, and H2215
Dt 1:41 thinking it easy to go up into the hill c. H2215
Dt 1:43 arrogance you marched up into the hill c. H2215
Dt 2: 1 made our way around the hill c of Seir. H2215
Dt 2: 3 your way around this hill c long enough; H2215
Dt 2: 5 given Esau the hill c of Seir as his own. H2215
Dt 2:24 the Amorite, king of Heshbon, and his c. H824
Dt 2:27 "Let us pass through your c. We will stay on H824
Dt 2:31 to deliver Sihon and his c over to you. H824
Dt 3:12 including half the hill c of Gilead H2215
Dt 3:25 the Jordan—that fine hill c and Lebanon." H2215
Dt 9:28 the c from which you brought us will say H824
Dt 11: 3 Pharaoh king of Egypt and to his whole c; H824
Dt 22:25 But if out in the c a man happens to meet H8441
Dt 22:27 man found the young woman out in the c, H8441
Dt 23: 7 you resided as foreigners in their c. H824
Dt 28: 3 blessed in the city and blessed in the c. H8441
Dt 28:16 be cursed in the city and cursed in the c. H8441
Dt 28:24 the rain of your c into dust and powder; H824
Dt 28:40 throughout your c but you will not use H1473
Jos 1: 4 all the Hittite c—to the Mediterranean Sea H824
Jos 2: 9 all who live in this c are melting in fear H824
Jos 7: 9 other people of the c will hear about this H824
Jos 9: 1 the kings in the hill c, in the western H2215
Jos 9: 6 "We have come from a distant c; make a H824
Jos 9: 9 from a very distant c because of the fame H824
Jos 9:11 all those living in our c said to us, H824
Jos 10: 6 kings from the hill c have joined forces H2215
Jos 10:40 including the hill c, the Negev, H2215
Jos 11: 3 Perizzites and Jebusites in the hill c; and H2215
Jos 11:16 the hill c, all the Negev, the whole region H2215
Jos 11:21 destroyed the Anakites from the hill c: H2215
Jos 11:21 from all the hill c of Judah, and from H2215
Jos 11:21 of Judah, and from all the hill c of Israel. H2215
Jos 12: 8 The lands included the hill c, the western H2215
Jos 13:21 allied with Sihon—who lived in that c. H824
Jos 13:25 half the Ammonite c as far as Aroer, H824
Jos 14:12 Now give me this hill c that the LORD H2215
Jos 15:48 In the hill c: Shamir, Jattir, Sokoh, H2215
Jos 16: 1 the desert into the hill c of Bethel. H2215
Jos 17:15 "and if the hill c of Ephraim is too small H2215
Jos 17:16 replied, "The hill c is not enough for us H2215
Jos 17:18 the forested hill c as well. Clear it, and H2215
Jos 18: 1 The c was brought under their control, H824
Jos 18:12 of Jericho and headed west into the hill c, H2215
Jos 19:50 Timnath Serah in the hill c of Ephraim. H2215
Jos 20: 7 in Galilee in the hill c of Naphtali, H2215
Jos 20: 7 Shechem in the hill c of Ephraim, and H2215
Jos 20: 7 that is, Hebron) in the hill c of Judah. H2215
Jos 21:11 pastureland, in the hill c of Judah. H2215
Jos 21:21 In the hill c of Ephraim they were given H2215
Jos 22:33 to devastate the c where the Reubenites H824
Jos 24: 4 I assigned the hill c of Seir to Esau, but H2215
Jos 24:30 at Timnath Serah in the hill c of Ephraim H2215
Jos 24:33 his son Phinehas in the hill c of Ephraim. H2215
Jdg 1: 9 against the Canaanites living in the hill c, H2215
Jdg 1:19 They took possession of the hill c, but H2215
Jdg 1:34 confined the Danites to the hill c, H2215
Jdg 2: 9 at Timnath Heres in the hill c of Ephraim H2215
Jdg 3:27 he blew a trumpet in the hill c of Ephraim, H2215
Jdg 4: 5 Bethel in the hill c of Ephraim, H2215
Jdg 6: 3 other eastern peoples invaded the c. H2257S
Jdg 7:24 throughout the hill c of Ephraim, H2215
Jdg 10: 1 lived in Shamir, in the hill c of Ephraim. H2215
Jdg 11:12 against me that you have attacked my c?" H824
Jdg 11:17 'Give us permission to go through your c,' H824
Jdg 11:18 along the eastern side of the c of Moab, H824
Jdg 11:19 us pass through your c to our own place.' H824
Jdg 11:21 land of the Amorites who lived in that c, H824
Jdg 12:15 Ephraim, in the hill c of the Amalekites. H2215
Jdg 17: 1 named Micah from the hill c of Ephraim H2215
Jdg 17: 8 to Micah's house in the hill c of Ephraim. H2215
Jdg 18: 2 they entered the hill c of Ephraim and H2215
Jdg 18:13 went on to the hill c of Ephraim and came H2215
Jdg 19: 1 area in the hill c of Ephraim took a H2215
Jdg 19:16 an old man from the hill c of Ephraim, H2215
Jdg 19:18 area in the hill c of Ephraim where I H2215
Ru 1: 1 went to live for a while in the c of Moab. H8441
1Sa 1: 1 a Zuphite from the hill c of Ephraim H2215
1Sa 6: 5 of the rats that are destroying the c, H824
1Sa 6:18 the fortified towns with their c villages. H7253
1Sa 9: 4 passed through the hill c of Ephraim and H2215
1Sa 13: 2 at Mikmash and in the hill c of Bethel, H2215
1Sa 14:22 had hidden in the hill c of Ephraim heard H2215
1Sa 14:29 "My father has made trouble for the c. H824
1Sa 27: 5 be assigned to me in one of the c towns, H8441
2Sa 10: 8 were by themselves in the open c. H8441
2Sa 11:11 my lord's men are camped in the open c. H8441
2Sa 19: 9 now he has fled the c to escape from H824
2Sa 20:21 from the hill c of Ephraim, has H2215
1Ki 2:34 he was buried at his home out in the c. H4497
1Ki 4: 8 Ben-Hur—in the hill c of Ephraim; H2215
1Ki 4:19 the c of Sihon king of the Amorites and the H824
1Ki 4:19 the Amorites and the c of Og king of Bashan NDT
1Ki 10: 6 I heard in my own c about your H824
1Ki 10:13 returned with her retinue to her own c. H824
1Ki 11:21 "Let me go, that I may return to my own c." H824
1Ki 11:22 that you want to go back to your own c?" H824
1Ki 11:29 The two of them were alone out in the c, H8441
1Ki 12:25 Shechem in the hill c of Ephraim and H2215
1Ki 14:11 birds will feed on those who die in the c. H8441
1Ki 16: 4 birds will feed on those who die in the c." H8441
1Ki 21:24 birds will feed on those who die in the c." H8441
2Ki 5:22 come to me from the hill c of Ephraim. H2215
2Ki 8: 6 land from the day she left the c until now." H824
2Ki 13:20 raiders used to enter the c every spring. H824
2Ki 17:26 not know what the god of that c requires. H824
2Ki 18:25 me to march against this c and destroy it. H824
2Ki 19: 7 I will make him want to return to his own c H824
2Ki 24: 7 did not march out from his own c again, H824
1Ch 1:46 who defeated Midian in the c of Moab H8441
1Ch 4:42 the sons of Ishi, invaded the hill c of Seir. H2215
1Ch 6:67 In the hill c of Ephraim they were given H2215
1Ch 19: 3 explore and spy out the c and overthrow it?" H824
1Ch 19: 9 come were by themselves in the open c. H8441
2Ch 9: 5 I heard in my own c about your H824
2Ch 9:12 returned with her retinue to her own c. H824
2Ch 13: 4 Zemaraim, in the hill c of Ephraim, and H2215
2Ch 14: 1 in his days the c was at peace for ten H824
2Ch 19: 4 Beersheba to the hill c of Ephraim and H2215
2Ch 27: 4 built towns in the hill c of Judah and forts H2215
Ne 8:15 "Go out into the hill c and bring back H2215
Ne 9:22 They took over the c of Sihon king of H824
Ne 9:22 of Heshbon and the c of Og king of Bashan H824
Ps 78:54 to the hill c his right hand had taken. H2215
Ps 105:31 and gnats throughout their c. H1473
Ps 105:33 fig trees and shattered the trees of their c. H1473
Pr 28: 2 When a c is rebellious, it has many rulers H824
Pr 29: 4 By justice a king gives a c stability, but H824
Isa 1: 7 Your c is desolate, your cities burned with H824
Isa 13: 5 of his wrath—to destroy the whole c. H824
Isa 22:18 like a ball and throw you into a large c. H824
Isa 36:10 me to march against this c and destroy it. H824
Isa 37: 7 I will make him want to return to his own c H824
Isa 63:13 Like a horse in open c, they did not H4497
Isa 66: 8 Can a c be born in a day or a nation be H824
Jer 12: 5 If you stumble in safe c, how will you H824
Jer 12:15 to their own inheritance and their own c. H824
Jer 14:18 If I go into the c, I see those slain by the H8441
Jer 15:13 because of all your sins throughout your c. H1473
Jer 17: 3 because of sin throughout your c. H1473
Jer 17:26 foothills, from the hill c and the Negev H2215
Jer 22:26 mother who gave you birth into another c, H824
Jer 25:11 This whole c will become a desolate H824
Jer 32:44 of Judah and in the towns of the hill c, H2215
Jer 33:13 In the towns of the hill c, of the western H2215
Jer 40: 4 the whole c lies before you; go H824
Jer 40: 7 were still in the open c heard that the H8441
Jer 40:13 still in the open c came to Gedaliah at H8441
Eze 7:15 Those in the c will die by the sword; those H8441
Eze 14:13 if a c sins against me by being unfaithful H824
Eze 14:15 wild beasts through that c and they leave it H824
Eze 14:17 "Or if I bring a sword against that c and say, H824
Eze 21:19 both starting from the same c. H824
Eze 33:27 those out in the c I will give to the wild H8441
Da 11: 9 of the South but will retreat to his own c. H141
Da 11:19 fortresses of his own c but will stumble H824
Da 11:28 will return to his own c with great wealth, H824
Da 11:28 against it and then return to his own c. H824
Hos 12:12 Jacob fled to the c of Aram; Israel served H8441
Am 7:17 and you yourself will die in a pagan c. H141
Jnh 1: 8 What is your c? From what people H824
Zec 5:11 "To the c of Babylonia to build a house H824
Zec 6: 6 black horses is going toward the north c, H824
Zec 6: 8 toward the north c have given my Spirit H824
Mal 1: 3 I have turned his hill c into a wasteland H2215
Mt 2:12 they returned to their c by another route. G6001
Mt 14:35 they sent word to all the surrounding c. G4369
Mk 15:21 was passing by on his way in from the c, and G69
Mk 16:12 of them while they were walking in the c. G69
Lk 1:39 hurried to a town in the hill c of Judea, G3978
Lk 1:65 throughout the hill c of Judea people G3978
Lk 3: 3 He went into all the c around the Jordan G4369
Lk 7:17 throughout Judea and the surrounding c. G4369
Lk 14:23 the roads and c lanes and compel them G5850
Lk 15: 4 ninety-nine in the open c and go after the G2245
Lk 15:13 off for a distant c and there squandered G6001
Lk 15:14 there was a severe famine in that whole c, G6001
Lk 15:15 hired himself out to a citizen of that c, G6001
Lk 19:12 birth went to a distant c to have himself G6001
Lk 21:21 let those in the c not enter the city. G6001
Lk 23:26 who was on his way in from the c, and put G69
Jn 4:44 that a prophet has no honor in his own c.) G4258
Jn 11:55 many went up from the c to Jerusalem G6001
Ac 7: 3 'Leave your c and your people,' God said G1178
Ac 7: 6 will be strangers in a c not their own, G1178
Ac 7: 7 will come out of that c and worship me in NDT
Ac 9:32 As Peter traveled about the c, he went to G4246S
Ac 10:39 he did in the c of the Jews and in G6001
Ac 12:20 they depended on the king's c for their food AIT
Ac 13:17 mighty power he led them out of that c; G899S
Ac 14: 6 Derbe and to the surrounding c, G4369
Ac 26: 4 from the beginning of my life in my own c, G1620
2Co 11:26 in danger in the c, in danger at sea; G2244
Heb 11: 9 land like a stranger in a foreign c; G259
Heb 11:14 that they are looking for a c of their own. G4258
Heb 11:15 had been thinking of the c they had left, G1697S
Heb 11:16 they were longing for a better c—a heavenly NDT

COUNTRYSIDE (15) [COUNTRY]

1Sa 30:16 they were, scattered over the c, eating, H824
2Sa 15:23 The whole c wept aloud as all the people H824
2Sa 18: 8 The battle spread out over the whole c, and H824
1Ki 20:27 while the Arameans covered the c. H824
2Ki 7:12 they have left the camp to hide in the c, H8441
Job 5:10 the earth; he sends water on the c. H2575
SS 7:11 let us go to the c, let us spend the night H8441
Mk 1: 5 The whole Judean c and all the people of G6001
Mk 5:14 ran off and reported this in the town and c, G69
Mk 6:36 go to the surrounding c and villages and buy G69
Mk 6:56 into villages, towns or c—they placed the sick G69
Lk 4:14 about him spread through the whole c. G4369
Lk 8:34 ran off and reported this in the town and c, G69
Lk 9:12 villages and c and find food and G69
Jn 3:22 his disciples went out into the Judean c, G1178

COUNTS (6) [COUNT]

Job 19:11 against me; he c me among his enemies. H3108
Jer 33:13 under the hand of the one who c them, H4948
Jn 6:63 The Spirit gives life; the flesh c for nothing. G6067
1Co 7:19 Keeping God's commands is what c. G247S
Gal 5: 6 The only thing that c is faith expressing G247
Gal 6:15 anything; what c is the new creation. G247

COURAGE (19) [COURAGEOUS, COURAGEOUSLY]

Jos 2:11 fear and everyone's c failed because of H8120
Jos 5: 1 no longer had the c to face the Israelites H8120
2Sa 4: 1 in Hebron, he lost c, and all Israel H8332+3338
2Sa 7:27 servant has found c to pray this prayer to H4213
1Ch 17:25 So your servant has found c to pray to you H5162
2Ch 15: 8 son of Oded the prophet, he took c. H2616
2Ch 19:11 Act with c, and may the LORD be with H2616
Ezr 7:28 I took c and gathered leaders from Israel H2616
Ezr 10: 4 We will support you, so take c and do it." H2616
Ps 107:26 in their peril their c melted away. H5883
Eze 22:14 Will your c endure or your hands be strong H4213
Da 11:25 up his strength and c against the king of H4222
Mt 14:27 immediately said to them: "Take c! It is I. G2510
Mk 6:50 he spoke to them and said, "Take c! G2510
Ac 4:13 When they saw the c of Peter and John G4244
Ac 23:11 Lord stood near Paul and said, "Take c! G2510
Ac 27:22 But now I urge you to keep up your c G2313
Ac 27:25 So keep up your c, men, for I have faith in G2313
Php 1:20 will have sufficient c so that now as G4244

COURAGEOUS (13) [COURAGE]

Dt 31: 6 Be strong and c. Do not be afraid or terrified H599
Dt 31: 7 "Be strong and c, for you must go with H599
Dt 31:23 "Be strong and c, for you will bring the H599
Jos 1: 6 Be strong and c, because you will lead H599
Jos 1: 7 "Be strong and very c. Be careful to obey all H599
Jos 1: 9 Be strong and c. Do not be afraid; H599
Jos 1:18 will be put to death. Only be strong and c!" H599
Jos 10:25 Be strong and c. This is what the LORD H599
1Ch 22:13 Be strong and c. Do not be afraid or H599
1Ch 28:20 "Be strong and c, and do the work. H599
2Ch 26:17 with eighty other c priests of the H1201+2657
2Ch 32: 7 "Be strong and c. Do not be afraid or H599
1Co 16:13 stand firm in the faith; be c; be strong. G437

COURAGEOUSLY (1) [COURAGE]

2Ch 25: 8 Even if you go and fight c in battle, God H2616

COURIER (1) [COURIERS]

Jer 51:31 One c follows another and messenger H8132

COURIERS (6) [COURIER]

2Ch 30: 6 c went throughout Israel and Judah with H8132
2Ch 30:10 The c went from town to town in Ephraim H8132
Est 3:13 Dispatches were sent by c to all the king's H8132
Est 3:15 The c went out, spurred on by the king's H8132
Est 8:10 sent them by mounted c, who rode H8132
Est 8:14 The c, riding the royal horses, went out H8132

COURSE (33) [COURSES]

Ge 4: 3 In the c of time Cain brought some of the H7891
Dt 2:37 the land along the c of the Jabbok nor H5707
Jdg 4: 9 "But because of the c you are taking, the H2006

1Sa 1:20 So in the **c** *of* time Hannah became H9543
1Sa 22:15 of God for him? **Of c not**! Let not the king H2721
2Sa 2: 1 **In the c of time**, David inquired of H339+4027
2Sa 8: 1 **In the c of time**, David defeated the H339+4027
2Sa 10: 1 **In the c of time**, the king of the H339+4027
2Sa 13: 1 **In the c of time**, Amnon son of H339+4027
2Sa 15: 1 **In the c of time**, Absalom H4946+339+4027
2Sa 21:18 **In the c of time**, there was another H339+4027
1Ki 6:36 stone and one **c** *of* trimmed cedar beams. H3215
1Ki 7:12 stone and one **c** *of* trimmed cedar beams, H3215
1Ch 18: 1 **In the c of time**, David defeated the H339+4027
1Ch 19: 1 **In the c of time**, Nahash king of the H339+4027
1Ch 20: 4 **In the c of time**, war broke out with H339+4027
2Ch 21:19 **In the c of time**, at the H4200+3427+4946+3427
Job 1: 5 When a period of feasting *had* **run** *its* **c** H5938
Ps 19: 5 like a champion rejoicing to run his **c**. H784
Ps 36: 4 to a sinful **c** and do not reject what H2006
Ps 102:23 In the **c of** my **life** he broke my strength H2006
Pr 2: 8 he guards the **c** *of* the just and protects H784
Pr 15:21 has understanding keeps a straight **c**. H2143
Pr 16: 9 In their hearts humans plan their **c**, but H2006
Pr 17:23 bribes in secret to pervert the **c** *of* justice. H784
Ecc 1: 6 round it goes, ever returning on its **c**. H6017
Jer 8: 6 pursues their own **c** like a horse charging H5297
Jer 23:10 follow an evil **c** and use their power H5297
Joel 2: 7 all march in line, not swerving from their **c**. H784
Ac 27: 7 *When* the wind *did* not **allow** us **to hold** our **c** G4661
Ro 10:18 Did they not hear? **Of c** they did: "Their G3529
2Co 13: 5 is in you—unless, **of c**, you fail the test? G3614
Jas 3: 6 sets the *whole* **c** of one's life on fire G5580

COURSES (5) [COURSE]

Jdg 5:20 from their **c** they fought against Sisera. H5019
1Ki 6:36 courtyard of three **c** *of* dressed stone and H3215
1Ki 7:12 by a wall of three **c** of dressed stone and H3215
Ezr 6: 4 with three **c** of large stones and one of A10462
SS 4: 4 built with **c of stone**; on it hang a H9444

COURT (92) [COURTS, COURTYARD, COURTYARDS]

Ge 50: 4 Joseph said to Pharaoh's **c**, "If I have H1074
Ge 50: 7 the dignitaries of his **c** and all the H1074
Ex 21:22 husband demands and the **c** allows. H7130
Dt 25: 1 they are to take it to **c** and the judges will H5477
Jdg 4: 5 She **held c** under the Palm of Deborah H3782
1Sa 7:17 and there *he* also **held c** *for* Israel. H9149
1Ki 3:15 Then he gave a feast for all his **c**. H6269
2Ki 20: 4 Before Isaiah had left the middle **c**, the H2958
2Ki 23:11 They were in the **c** near the room of an H7247
1Ch 26:18 As for the **c** to the west, there were four at H7232
1Ch 26:18 four at the road and two at the **c** itself. H7232
2Ch 4: 9 the large **c** and the doors for the court H6478
2Ch 4: 9 the large court and the doors for the **c**, H6478
2Ch 6:13 had placed it in the center of the **outer c**. H6478
Ne 3:25 the upper palace near the **c** *of* the guard. H2958
Est 4:11 the king in the inner **c** without being H2958
Est 5: 1 stood in the inner **c** *of* the palace, H2958
Est 5: 2 he saw Queen Esther standing in the **c**, H2958
Est 6: 4 "Who is in the **c**?" Now Haman had just H2958
Est 6: 4 entered the outer **c** *of* the palace to speak H2958
Est 6: 5 answered, "Haman is standing in the **c**." H2958
Job 5: 4 crushed in **c** without a defender. H9133
Job 9:32 that we might confront each other in **c**. H5477
Job 11:10 confines you in prison and **convenes a c**, H7735
Job 11:19 afraid, and many *will* **c** your **favor**. H2704+7156
Job 31:21 knowing that I had influence in **c**, H9133
Ps 127: 5 they contend with their opponents in **c**. H9133
Pr 22:22 are poor and do not crush the needy in **c**, H9133
Pr 25: 8 do not bring hastily to **c**, for what will you H8190
Pr 25: 9 If *you* **take** your neighbor **to c**, do H8189+8190
Pr 29: 9 If a wise person **goes to c** with a fool, the H9149
Isa 3:13 The LORD takes his place **in c**; he rises to H8189
Isa 29:21 ensnare the defender in **c** and with false H9133
Jer 19:14 stood in the **c** *of* the LORD's temple H2958
Jer 29: 2 the **c officials** and the leaders of Judah H6247
Jer 34:19 Jerusalem, the **c officials**, the priests and H6247
Jer 41:16 children and **c officials** he had recovered H6247
Eze 8: 3 the entrance of the north gate of the inner **c**, NDT
Eze 8: 7 he brought me to the entrance to the **c**. H2958
Eze 8:16 me into the inner **c** *of* the house of the H2958
Eze 10: 3 went in, and a cloud filled the inner **c**. H2958
Eze 10: 4 the **c** was full of the radiance of the H2958
Eze 10: 5 could be heard as far away as the outer **c**, H2958
Eze 40:17 Then he brought me into the outer **c** H2958
Eze 40:17 had been constructed all around the **c**; H2958
Eze 40:19 gateway to the outside of the inner **c**; H2958
Eze 40:20 of the north gate, leading into the outer **c**. H2958
Eze 40:23 a gate to the inner **c** facing the north gate H2958
Eze 40:27 The inner **c** also had a gate facing south H2958
Eze 40:28 me into the inner **c** through the south H2958
Eze 40:30 around the inner **c** were twenty-five cubits NDT
Eze 40:31 Its portico faced the outer **c**; palm trees H2958
Eze 40:32 me to the inner **c** *on* the east side, H2958
Eze 40:34 Its portico faced the outer **c**; palm trees H2958
Eze 40:37 Its portico faced the outer **c**; palm trees H2958
Eze 40:44 within the inner **c**, were two rooms, H2958
Eze 40:47 Then he measured the **c**: It was square H2958
Eze 41:15 sanctuary and the portico facing the **c**, H2958
Eze 42: 1 into the outer **c** and brought me to the H2958
Eze 42: 3 cubits from the inner **c** and in the section H2958
Eze 42: 3 opposite the pavement of the outer **c**, H2958
Eze 42: 7 wall parallel to the rooms and the outer **c**; H2958
Eze 42: 8 next to the outer **c** was fifty cubits long, H2958
Eze 42: 9 side as one enters them from the outer **c**. H2958
Eze 42:10 the length of the wall of the outer **c**, H2958
Eze 42:14 to go into the outer **c** until they leave H2958
Eze 43: 5 me up and brought me into the inner **c**, H2958
Eze 44:17 'When they enter the gates of the inner **c**, H2958
Eze 44:17 gates of the inner **c** or inside the temple. H2958
Eze 44:19 out into the outer **c** where the people are, H2958
Eze 44:21 to drink wine when he enters the inner **c**. H2958
Eze 44:27 goes into the inner **c** of the sanctuary to H2958
Eze 45:19 altar and on the gateposts of the inner **c**. H2958
Eze 46: 1 gate of the inner **c** facing east is to be H2958
Eze 46:20 them into the outer **c** and consecrating H2958
Eze 46:21 me to the outer **c** and led me around to H2958
Eze 46:21 I saw in each corner another **c**. H2958
Eze 46:22 of the outer **c** were enclosed courts H2958
Da 1: 3 chief of his **c officials**, to bring into the H6247
Da 2:49 Daniel himself remained at the royal **c**. A10776
Da 7:10 The **c** was seated, and the books were A10170
Da 7:26 " 'But the **c** will sit, and his power will be A10170
Am 5:10 upholds justice in **c** and detest the one H9133
Mt 5:22 sister, 'Raca,' is answerable *to* the **c**. G5284
Mt 5:25 *with* your **adversary who is taking** you **to c**. G508
Ac 25: 6 day *he* **convened the c** G2767+2093+3836+1037
Ac 25:10 "I am now standing before Caesar's **c** G1037
Ac 25:17 but **convened the c** the G2767+2093+3836+1037
1Co 4: 3 if I am judged by you or by any human **c**; G2465
1Co 6: 6 *one* brother **takes** another **to c** G3552+3212
Jas 2: 6 not the ones who are dragging you into **c**? G3215
Rev 11: 2 But exclude the outer **c**; do not measure it G885

COURTS (60) [COURT]

Dt 17: 8 come before your **c** that are too difficult H9133
2Ki 21: 5 In the two **c** *of* the temple of the LORD, he H2958
2Ki 23:12 had built in the two **c** *of* the temple of the H2958
1Ch 28: 6 one who will build my house and my **c**, H2958
1Ch 28:12 in his mind for the **c** *of* the temple of the H2958
2Ch 33: 5 In both **c** *of* the temple of the LORD, he H2958
Ne 8:16 in the **c** *of* the house of God and in the H2958
Ne 13: 7 a room in the **c** *of* the house of God. H2958
Ps 65: 4 choose and bring near to live in your **c**! H2958
Ps 84: 2 even faints, for the **c** *of* the LORD; my heart H2958
Ps 84:10 is one day in your **c** than a thousand H2958
Ps 92:13 they will flourish in the **c** *of* our God. H2958
Ps 96: 8 bring an offering and come into his **c**. H2958
Ps 100: 4 with thanksgiving and his **c** with praise; H2958
Ps 116:19 in the **c** *of* the house of the LORD—in your H2958
Ps 135: 2 the LORD, in the **c** *of* the house of our God. H2958
Isa 1:12 asked this of you, this trampling of my **c**? H2958
Isa 62: 9 will drink it in the **c** *of* my sanctuary." H2958
Eze 9: 7 the temple and fill the **c** with the slain. H2958
Eze 42: 6 had no pillars, as the **c** had; so they were H2958
Eze 46:22 corners of the outer court were enclosed **c**, H2958
Eze 46:22 *each of the* **c** in the four corners was the H4392S
Eze 46:23 inside of *each of the* four **c** was a ledge H4392S
Am 5:12 deprive the poor of justice in the **c**. H9133
Am 5:15 love good; maintain justice in the **c**. H9133
Zec 3: 7 my house and have charge of my **c**, H2958
Zec 8:16 render true and sound judgment in your **c**; H9133
Mt 21:12 Jesus entered the **temple c** and drove out G2639
Mt 21:15 the children shouting in the **temple c**, G2639
Mt 21:23 Jesus entered the **temple c**, and, while he G2639
Mt 26:55 Every day I sat in the **temple c** teaching G2639
Mk 11:11 Jerusalem and went into the **temple c**. G2639
Mk 11:15 Jesus entered the **temple c** and began G2639
Mk 11:16 carry merchandise through the **temple c**. G2639
Mk 11:27 while Jesus was walking in the **temple c**, G2639
Mk 12:35 While Jesus was teaching in the **temple c**, G2639
Mk 14:49 teaching in the **temple c**, and you did not G2639
Lk 2:27 by the Spirit, he went into the **temple c**. G2639
Lk 2:46 days they found him in the **temple c**, G2639
Lk 19:45 When Jesus entered the **temple c**, he G2639
Lk 20: 1 people in the **temple c** and proclaiming G2639
Lk 22:53 Every day I was with you in the **temple c** G2639
Jn 2:14 In the **temple c** he found people selling G2639
Jn 2:15 drove all from the **temple c**, both G2639
Jn 7:14 Jesus go up to the **temple c** and begin to G2639
Jn 7:28 still teaching in the **temple c**, cried out, G2639
Jn 8: 2 dawn he appeared again in the **temple c**, G2639
Jn 8:20 teaching in the **temple c** near the place G2639
Jn 10:23 Jesus was in the **temple c** walking in G2639
Jn 11:56 they stood in the **temple c** they asked one G2639
Ac 2:46 to meet together in the **temple c**. G2639
Ac 3: 2 beg from those going into the **temple c**. G2639
Ac 3: 8 he went with them into the **temple c**, G2639
Ac 5:20 stand in the **temple c**," he said, "and G2639
Ac 5:21 At daybreak they entered the **temple c**, as G2639
Ac 5:25 are standing in the **temple c** teaching the G2639
Ac 5:42 in the **temple c** and from house to house G2639
Ac 19:38 the **c** are open and there are proconsuls. G61
Ac 24:18 they found me in the **temple c** doing this. G2639
Ac 26:21 seized me in the **temple c** and tried to kill G2639

COURTYARD (74) [COURT]

Ex 27: 9 "Make a **c** *for* the tabernacle. The south H2958
Ex 27:12 "The west end of the **c** shall be fifty cubits H2958
Ex 27:13 the **c** shall also be fifty cubits wide. H2958
Ex 27:16 "For the entrance to the **c**, provide a H2958
Ex 27:17 the posts around the **c** are to have silver H2958
Ex 27:18 The **c** shall be a hundred cubits long and H2958
Ex 27:19 all the tent pegs for it and those for the **c**, H2958
Ex 35:17 the curtains of the **c** with its posts and H2958
Ex 35:17 the curtain for the entrance to the **c**; H2958
Ex 35:18 tent pegs for the tabernacle and for the **c**, H2958
Ex 38: 9 Next they made the **c**. The south side was H2958
Ex 38:15 on the other side of the entrance to the **c**, H2958
Ex 38:16 curtains around the **c** were of finely H2958
Ex 38:17 so all the posts of the **c** had silver bands. H2958
Ex 38:18 the entrance to the **c** was made of blue, H2958
Ex 38:18 like the curtains of the **c**, five cubits high, H2958
Ex 38:20 of the surrounding **c** were bronze. H2958
Ex 38:31 the surrounding **c** and those for its H2958
Ex 38:31 those for the surrounding **c**. H2958
Ex 39:40 the curtains of the **c** with its posts and H2958
Ex 39:40 the curtain for the entrance to the **c** H2958
Ex 39:40 the ropes and tent pegs for **the c**; all the H2023S
Ex 40: 8 Set up the **c** around it and put the curtain H2958
Ex 40: 8 put the curtain at the entrance to the **c**. H2958
Ex 40:33 Moses set up the **c** around the tabernacle H2958
Ex 40:33 put up the curtain at the entrance to the **c**. H2958
Lev 6:16 are to eat it in the **c** *of* the tent of meeting H2958
Lev 6:26 in the **c** *of* the tent of meeting. H2958
Nu 3:26 the curtains of the **c**, the curtain at the H2958
Nu 3:26 at the entrance to the **c** surrounding the H2958
Nu 3:37 of the surrounding **c** with their bases, H2958
Nu 4:26 the curtains of the **c** surrounding the H2958
Nu 4:26 the curtain for the entrance to the **c**, the H2958
Nu 4:32 of the surrounding **c** with their bases, H2958
2Sa 17:18 He had a well in his **c**, and they climbed H2958
1Ki 6:36 he built the inner **c** of three courses of H2958
1Ki 7: 9 to the great **c** and from foundation H2958
1Ki 7:12 The great **c** was surrounded by a wall of H2958
1Ki 7:12 as was the inner **c** *of* the temple of the H2958
1Ki 8:64 middle part of the **c** in front of the temple H2958
2Ch 4: 9 He made the **c** *of* the priests, and the H2958
2Ch 7: 7 middle part of the **c** in front of the temple H2958
2Ch 20: 5 of the LORD in the front of the new **c** H2958
2Ch 24:21 him to death in the **c** *of* the LORD's temple. H2958
2Ch 29:16 brought out to the **c** *of* the LORD's temple H2958
Est 2:11 forth near the **c** *of* the harem to find H2958
Jer 26: 2 Stand in the **c** *of* the LORD's house and H2958
Jer 32: 2 was confined in the **c** *of* the guard in the H2958
Jer 32: 8 came to me in the **c** *of* the guard and said H2958
Jer 32:12 all the Jews sitting in the **c** *of* the guard. H2958
Jer 33: 1 was still confined in the **c** *of* the guard, H2958
Jer 36:10 was in the upper **c** at the entrance of the H2958
Jer 36:20 to the king in the **c** and reported H2958
Jer 37:21 to be placed in the **c** *of* the guard and H2958
Jer 37:21 Jeremiah remained in the **c** *of* the guard. H2958
Jer 38: 6 which was in the **c** *of* the guard. H2958
Jer 38:13 Jeremiah remained in the **c** *of* the guard. H2958
Jer 38:28 remained in the **c** *of* the guard until the H2958
Jer 39:14 Jeremiah taken out of the **c** *of* the guard. H2958
Jer 39:15 had been confined in the **c** *of* the guard, H2958
Eze 40:14 was up to the portico facing the **c**. H2958
Eze 41:12 facing the temple **c** on the west side was H1619
Eze 41:13 the temple **c** and the building with its H1619
Eze 41:14 The width of the temple **c** on the east H1619
Eze 41:15 the building facing the **c** at the rear of the H1619
Eze 42: 1 opposite the temple **c** and opposite the H1619
Eze 42:10 adjoining the temple **c** and opposite the H1619
Eze 42:13 facing the temple **c** are the priests' rooms, H1619
Mt 26:58 right up to the **c** of the high priest. G885
Mt 26:69 Now Peter was sitting out in the **c**, and a G885
Mk 14:54 distance, right into the **c** of the high priest. G885
Mk 14:66 While Peter was below in the **c**, one of the G885
Lk 22:55 in the middle *of* the **c** and had sat down G885
Jn 18:15 he went with Jesus into the high priest's **c**, G885

COURTYARDS (4) [COURT]

Ex 8:13 in the houses, in the **c** and in the fields. H2958
1Ch 23:28 to be in charge of the **c**, the side rooms H2958
2Ch 23: 5 are to be in the **c** *of* the temple of the H2958
Ne 8:16 own roofs, in their **c**, in the courts of the H2958

COUSIN (6) [COUSINS]

Lev 25:49 An uncle or a **c** or any blood H1201+1856
Est 2: 7 Mordecai had a **c** named Hadassah, H1426+1856
Jer 32: 8 my **c** Hanamel came to me in the H1201+1856
Jer 32: 9 Anathoth from my **c** Hanamel and H1201+1856
Jer 32:12 presence of my **c** Hanamel and of H1201+1856
Col 4:10 greetings, as does Mark, the **c** of Barnabas. G463

COUSINS (3) [COUSIN]

Lev 10: 4 carry your **c** outside the camp, away H278
Nu 36:11 married their **c on their father's side**. H1201+1856
1Ch 23:22 only daughters. Their **c**, the sons of Kish H278

COVENANT (342) [COVENANTED, COVENANTS]

Ge 6:18 But I will establish my **c** with you, and you H1382
Ge 9: 9 "I now establish my **c** with you and with H1382
Ge 9:11 I establish my **c** with you: Never again will H1382
Ge 9:12 is the sign of the **c** I am making between H1382
Ge 9:12 with you, a **c** for all generations to come: NDT
Ge 9:13 be the sign of the **c** between me and the H1382
Ge 9:15 I will remember my **c** between me and you H1382
Ge 9:16 the everlasting **c** between God and all H1382
Ge 9:17 is the sign of the **c** I have established H1382
Ge 15:18 the LORD made a **c** with Abram and said H1382
Ge 17: 2 I will make my **c** between me and you H1382
Ge 17: 4 this is my **c** with you: You will be H1382
Ge 17: 7 I will establish my **c** as an everlasting H1382
Ge 17: 7 as an everlasting **c** between me and you H1382
Ge 17: 9 you must keep my **c**, you and your H1382
Ge 17:10 This is my **c** with you and your H1382

C

Ge 17:10 after you, the c you are to keep: H889S
Ge 17:11 be the sign of the c between me and you. H1382
Ge 17:13 My c in your flesh is to be an everlasting H1382
Ge 17:13 in your flesh is to be an everlasting c. H1382
Ge 17:14 off from his people; he has broken my c." H1382
Ge 17:19 I will establish my c with him as an H1382
Ge 17:19 as an everlasting c for his descendants H1382
Ge 17:21 But my c I will establish with Isaac, whom H1382
Ge 31:44 let's make a c, you and I, and let H1382
Ex 2:24 he remembered his c with Abraham, H1382
Ex 6: 4 I also established my c with them to give H1382
Ex 6: 5 enslaving, and I have remembered my c. H1382
Ex 16:34 the manna with the tablets of the c law, H6343
Ex 19: 5 Now if you obey me fully and keep my c H1382
Ex 23:32 Do not make a c with them or with their H1382
Ex 24: 7 took the Book of the C and read it to the H1382
Ex 24: 8 is the blood of the c that the LORD has H1382
Ex 25:16 Then put in the ark the tablets of the c law, H6343
Ex 25:21 the ark the tablets of the c law that I will H6343
Ex 25:22 that are over the ark of the c law, H6343
Ex 26:33 the ark of the c law behind the curtain. H6343
Ex 26:34 on the ark of the c law in the Most Holy H6343
Ex 27:21 curtain that shields the ark of the c law, H6343
Ex 30: 6 curtain that shields the ark of the c law— H6343
Ex 30: 6 that is over the tablets of the c law— H6343
Ex 30:26 the tent of meeting, the ark of the c law, AIT
Ex 30:36 of the ark of the c law in the tent of H6343
Ex 31: 7 the ark of the c law with the atonement H6343
Ex 31:16 the generations to come as a lasting c. H1382
Ex 31:18 he gave him the two tablets of the c law H6343
Ex 32:15 the two tablets of the c law in his hands. H6343
Ex 34:10 "I am making a c with you. Before all H1382
Ex 34:27 words I have made a c with you and with H1382
Ex 34:28 wrote on the tablets the words of the c— H1382
Ex 34:29 the two tablets of the c law in his hands, H6343
Ex 38:21 the tabernacle of the c law, which were H6343
Ex 39:35 the ark of the c law with its poles and the H6343
Ex 40: 3 Place the ark of the c law in it and shield H6343
Ex 40: 5 of the ark of the c law and put the curtain H6343
Ex 40:20 took the tablets of the c law and placed H6343
Ex 40:21 curtain and shielded the ark of the c law, H6343
Lev 2:13 the salt of the c of your God out of your H1382
Lev 16:13 cover above the tablets of the c law, H6343
Lev 24: 3 shields the ark of the c law in the tent of H6343
Lev 24: 8 on behalf of the Israelites, as a lasting c. H1382
Lev 26: 9 numbers, and I will keep my c with you. H1382
Lev 26:15 out all my commands and so violate my c, H1382
Lev 26:25 on you to avenge the breaking of the c. H1382
Lev 26:42 I will remember my c with Jacob and my H1382
Lev 26:42 with Jacob and my c with Isaac and my H1382
Lev 26:42 with Isaac and my c with Abraham, H1382
Lev 26:44 completely, breaking my c with them. H1382
Lev 26:45 I will remember the c with their ancestors H1382
Nu 1:50 in charge of the tabernacle of the c law— H6343
Nu 1:53 tabernacle of the c law so that my wrath H6343
Nu 1:53 the care of the tabernacle of the c law." H6343
Nu 4: 5 curtain and put it over the ark of the c law. H6343
Nu 7:89 atonement cover on the ark of the c law. H6343
Nu 9:15 the tent of the c law, was set up, H6343
Nu 10:11 from above the tabernacle of the c law. H6343
Nu 10:33 The ark of the c of the LORD went before H1382
Nu 14:44 ark of the LORD's c moved from the camp. H1382
Nu 17: 4 of meeting in front of the ark of the c law, H6343
Nu 17: 7 before the LORD in the tent of the c law. H6343
Nu 17:10 staff in front of the ark of the c law, H6343
Nu 18: 2 sons minister before the tent of the c law. H6343
Nu 18:19 It is an everlasting c of salt before the H1382
Nu 25:12 him I am making my c of peace with him. H1382
Nu 25:13 will have a c of a lasting priesthood, H1382
Dt 4:13 He declared to you his c, the Ten H1382
Dt 4:23 not to forget the c of the LORD your God H1382
Dt 4:31 you or forget the c with your ancestors, H1382
Dt 5: 2 LORD our God made a c with us at Horeb. H1382
Dt 5: 3 our ancestors that the LORD made this c, H1382
Dt 7: 9 keeping his c of love to a thousand H1382
Dt 7:12 your God will keep his c of love with you, H1382
Dt 8:18 so confirms his c, which he swore to H1382
Dt 9: 9 the tablets of the c that the LORD had H1382
Dt 9:11 the two stone tablets, the tablets of the c. H1382
Dt 9:15 the two tablets of the c were in my hands. H1382
Dt 10: 8 of Levi to carry the ark of the c of the LORD, H1382
Dt 17: 2 of the LORD your God in violation of his c, H1382
Dt 29: 1 the terms of the c the LORD commanded H1382
Dt 29: 1 in addition to the c he had made with H1382
Dt 29: 9 Carefully follow the terms of this c, so that H1382
Dt 29:12 to enter into a c with the LORD your God, H1382
Dt 29:12 a c the LORD is making with you this day H889S
Dt 29:14 I am making this c, with its oath, not only H1382
Dt 29:21 all the curses of the c written in this Book H1382
Dt 29:25 this people abandoned the c of the LORD, H1382
Dt 29:25 the c he made with them when he H889S
Dt 31: 9 who carried the ark of the c of the LORD H1382
Dt 31:16 me and break the c I made with them. H1382
Dt 31:20 rejecting me and breaking my c. H1382
Dt 31:25 who carried the ark of the c of the LORD: H1382
Dt 31:26 the ark of the c of the LORD your God. H1382
Dt 33: 9 over your word and guarded your c. H1382
Jos 3: 3 see the ark of the c of the LORD your God, H1382
Jos 3: 6 up the ark of the c and pass on ahead of H1382
Jos 3: 8 Tell the priests who carry the ark of the c H1382
Jos 3:11 the ark of the c of the Lord of all the earth H1382
Jos 3:14 the ark of the c went ahead of them. H1382
Jos 3:17 the ark of the c of the LORD stopped in H1382
Jos 4: 7 cut off before the ark of the c of the LORD. H1382
Jos 4: 9 who carried the ark of the c had stood. H1382
Jos 4:16 the ark of the c law to come up out of the H6343
Jos 4:18 river carrying the ark of the c of the LORD. H1382
Jos 6: 6 up the ark of the c of the LORD and have H1382
Jos 6: 8 the ark of the LORD's c followed them. H1382
Jos 7:11 they have violated my c, which I H1382
Jos 7:15 He has violated the c of the LORD and has H1382
Jos 8:33 both sides of the ark of the c of the LORD, H1382
Jos 23:16 If you violate the c of the LORD your God H1382
Jos 24:25 that day Joshua made a c for the people, H1382
Jdg 2: 1 'I will never break my c with you, H1382
Jdg 2: 2 you shall not make a c with the people of H1382
Jdg 2:20 has violated the c I ordained for their H1382
Jdg 20:27 days the ark of the c of God was there, H1382
1Sa 4: 3 bring the ark of the LORD's c from Shiloh, H1382
1Sa 4: 4 back the ark of the c of the LORD Almighty, H1382
1Sa 4: 4 were there with the ark of the c of God. H1382
1Sa 4: 5 ark of the LORD's c came into the camp, H1382
1Sa 18: 3 Jonathan made a c with David because H1382
1Sa 20: 8 him into a c with you before the LORD. H1382
1Sa 20:16 So Jonathan made a c with the house of H4162
1Sa 22: 8 me when my son makes a c with the son H4162
1Sa 23:18 The two of them made a c before the LORD H1382
2Sa 3:21 so that they may make a c with you, and H1382
2Sa 5: 3 the king made a c with them at Hebron H1382
2Sa 7:28 Your c is trustworthy, and you have H1821S
2Sa 15:24 him were carrying the ark of the c of God. H1382
2Sa 16:12 restore to me his c blessing instead of his H3208
2Sa 23: 5 not have made with me an everlasting c, H1382
1Ki 3:15 the ark of the Lord's c and sacrificed burnt H1382
1Ki 6:19 to set the ark of the c of the LORD there. H1382
1Ki 8: 1 bring up the ark of the LORD's c from Zion, H1382
1Ki 8: 6 the ark of the LORD's c to its place in the H1382
1Ki 8: 9 where the LORD made a c with the H4162
1Ki 8:21 in which is the c of the LORD that he made H1382
1Ki 8:23 you who keep your c of love with your H1382
1Ki 11:11 you have not kept my c and my decrees, H1382
1Ki 19:10 The Israelites have rejected your c, torn H1382
1Ki 19:14 The Israelites have rejected your c, torn H1382
2Ki 11: 4 He made a c with them and put them H1382
2Ki 11:12 him with a copy of the c and proclaimed H6343
2Ki 11:17 then made a c between the LORD and H1382
2Ki 11:17 He also made a c between the king and the NDT
2Ki 13:23 them because of his c with Abraham, H1382
2Ki 17:15 his decrees and the c he had made with H1382
2Ki 17:35 the LORD made a c with the Israelites H1382
2Ki 17:38 Do not forget the c I have made with you H1382
2Ki 18:12 had violated his c—all that Moses the H1382
2Ki 23: 2 hearing all the words of the Book of the C, H1382
2Ki 23: 3 renewed the c in the presence of the H1382
2Ki 23: 3 the words of the c written in this book. H1382
2Ki 23: 3 the people pledged themselves to the c. H1382
2Ki 23:21 as it is written in this Book of the C." H1382
1Ch 11: 3 he made a c with them at Hebron before H1382
1Ch 15:25 up the ark of the c of the LORD from the H1382
1Ch 15:26 were carrying the ark of the c of the LORD, H1382
1Ch 15:28 up the ark of the c of the LORD with shouts, H1382
1Ch 15:29 As the ark of the c of the LORD was H1382
1Ch 16: 6 regularly before the ark of the c of God. H1382
1Ch 16:15 He remembers his c forever, the promise H1382
1Ch 16:16 the c he made with Abraham, the oath he H889S
1Ch 16:17 as a decree, to Israel as an everlasting c: H1382
1Ch 16:37 the ark of the c of the LORD to minister H1382
1Ch 17: 1 the ark of the c of the LORD is under a H1382
1Ch 22:19 bring the ark of the c of the LORD and the H1382
1Ch 28: 2 of rest for the ark of the c of the LORD, H1382
1Ch 28:18 overshadow the ark of the c of the LORD. H1382
2Ch 5: 2 bring up the ark of the LORD's c from Zion, H1382
2Ch 5: 7 the ark of the LORD's c to its place in the H1382
2Ch 5:10 where the LORD made a c with the H4162
2Ch 6:11 in which is the c of the LORD that he made H1382
2Ch 6:14 you who keep your c of love with your H1382
2Ch 13: 5 his descendants forever by a c of salt? H1382
2Ch 15:12 They entered into a c to seek the LORD, the H1382
2Ch 21: 7 because of the c the LORD had made with H1382
2Ch 23: 1 He made a c with the commanders of H1382
2Ch 23: 3 assembly made a c with the king at the H1382
2Ch 23:11 him with a copy of the c and proclaimed H6343
2Ch 23:16 Jehoiada then made a c that he, the H1382
2Ch 24: 6 of Israel for the tent of the c law? H6343
2Ch 29:10 Now I intend to make a c with the LORD H1382
2Ch 34:30 hearing all the words of the Book of the C, H1382
2Ch 34:31 renewed the c in the presence of the H1382
2Ch 34:31 the words of the c written in this book. H1382
2Ch 34:32 did this in accordance with the c of God, H1382
Ezr 10: 3 Now let us make a c before our God to H1382
Ne 1: 5 who keeps his c of love with those who H1382
Ne 9: 8 you made a c with him to give to his H1382
Ne 9:32 who keeps his c of love, do not let H1382
Ne 13:29 office and the c of the priesthood and of H1382
Job 5:23 For you will have a c with the stones of H1382
Job 31: 1 "I made a c with my eyes not to look H1382
Ps 25:10 those who keep the demands of his c. H1382
Ps 25:14 fear him; he makes his c known to them. H1382
Ps 44:17 we had not been false to your c. H1382
Ps 50: 5 who made a c with me by sacrifice." H1382
Ps 50:16 recite my laws or take my c on your lips? H1382
Ps 55:20 attacks his friends; he violates his c. H1382
Ps 60: T To the tune of "The Lily of the C." A H6343
Ps 74:20 Have regard for your c, because haunts of H1382
Ps 78:10 did not keep God's c and refused to live H1382
Ps 78:37 they were not faithful to his c. H1382
Ps 80: T To the tune of "The Lilies of the C." Of H6343
Ps 89: 3 "I have made a c with my chosen one H1382
Ps 89:28 and my c with him will never fail. H1382
Ps 89:34 I will not violate my c or alter what my lips H1382
Ps 89:39 renounced the c with your servant and H1382
Ps 103:18 those who keep his c and remember to H1382
Ps 105: 8 He remembers his c forever, the promise H1382
Ps 105: 9 the c he made with Abraham, the oath he H889S
Ps 105:10 as a decree, to Israel as an everlasting c: H1382
Ps 106:45 he remembered his c and out of his great H1382
Ps 111: 5 who fear him; he remembers his c forever. H1382
Ps 111: 9 he ordained his c forever—holy and H1382
Ps 132:12 If your sons keep my c and the statutes I H1382
Pr 2:17 ignored the c she made before God. H1382
Isa 24: 5 the statutes and broken the everlasting c. H1382
Isa 28:15 "We have entered into a c with death H1382
Isa 28:18 Your c with death will be annulled; your H1382
Isa 42: 6 make you to be a c for the people and a H1382
Isa 42:19 Who is blind like the one in c with me H8966
Isa 49: 8 will make you to be a c for the people, H1382
Isa 54:10 be shaken nor my c of peace be removed," H1382
Isa 55: 3 I will make an everlasting c with you, my H1382
Isa 56: 4 what pleases me and hold fast to my c— H1382
Isa 56: 6 desecrating it and who hold fast to my c— H1382
Isa 59:21 this is my c with them," says the H1382
Isa 61: 8 make an everlasting c with them. H1382
Jer 3:16 longer say, 'The ark of the c of the LORD. H1382
Jer 11: 2 to the terms of this c and tell them to the H1382
Jer 11: 3 who does not obey the terms of this c— H1382
Jer 11: 6 to the terms of this c and follow them. H1382
Jer 11: 8 the curses of the c I had commanded H1382
Jer 11:10 Judah have broken the c I made with their H1382
Jer 14:21 Remember your c with us and do not H1382
Jer 22: 9 have forsaken the c of the LORD their God H1382
Jer 31:31 I will make a new c with the people of H1382
Jer 31:32 It will not be like the c I made with their H1382
Jer 31:32 because they broke my c, though I was a H1382
Jer 31:33 "This is the c I will make with the people H1382
Jer 32:40 I will make an everlasting c with them: H1382
Jer 33:20 you can break my c with the day and my H1382
Jer 33:20 with the day and my c with the night, H1382
Jer 33:21 then my c with David my servant—and my H1382
Jer 33:21 my c with the Levites who are priests NDT
Jer 33:25 I have not made my c with day and night H1382
Jer 34: 8 had made a c with all the people H1382
Jer 34:10 who entered into this c agreed that they H1382
Jer 34:13 I made a c with your ancestors when I H1382
Jer 34:15 You even made a c before me in the H1382
Jer 34:18 who have violated my c and have not H1382
Jer 34:18 the terms of the c they made before me, H1382
Jer 50: 5 LORD in an everlasting c that will not be H1382
Eze 16: 8 oath and entered into a c with you, H1382
Eze 16:59 have despised my oath by breaking the c. H1382
Eze 16:60 I will remember the c I made with you in H1382
Eze 16:60 I will establish an everlasting c with you. H1382
Eze 16:61 not on the basis of my c with you. H1382
Eze 16:62 So I will establish my c with you, and you H1382
Eze 17:18 He despised the oath by breaking the c H1382
Eze 17:19 despising my oath and breaking my c. H1382
Eze 20:37 I will bring you into the bond of the c. H1382
Eze 30: 5 the people of the c land will fall by the H1382
Eze 34:25 " 'I will make a c of peace with them and H1382
Eze 37:26 I will make a c of peace with them; it will H1382
Eze 37:26 with them; it will be an everlasting c. H1382
Eze 44: 7 fat and blood, and you broke my c. H1382
Da 9: 4 who keeps his c of love with those who H1382
Da 9:27 He will confirm a c with many for one H1382
Da 11:22 it and a prince of the c will be destroyed. H1382
Da 11:28 his heart will be set against the holy c. H1382
Da 11:30 back and vent his fury against the holy c. H1382
Da 11:30 favor to those who forsake the holy c. H1382
Da 11:32 will corrupt those who have violated the c, H1382
Hos 2:18 that day I will make a c for them with the H1382
Hos 6: 7 they have broken the c; they were H1382
Hos 8: 1 have broken my c and rebelled against H1382
Zec 9:11 because of the blood of my c with you, H1382
Zec 11:10 revoking the c I had made with all the H1382
Mal 2: 4 warning so that my c with Levi may H1382
Mal 2: 5 "My c was with him, a covenant of life H1382
Mal 2: 5 was with him, a c of life and peace, and I NDT
Mal 2: 8 you have violated the c with Levi," says H1382
Mal 2:10 do we profane the c of our ancestors by H1382
Mal 2:14 your partner, the wife of your marriage c. H1382
Mal 3: 1 the messenger of the c, whom you desire, H1382
Mt 26:28 This is my blood of the c, which is poured G1347
Mk 14:24 "This is my blood of the c, which is G1347
Lk 1:72 our ancestors and to remember his holy c, G1347
Lk 22:20 "This cup is the new c in my blood, which G1347
Ac 3:25 the prophets and of the c God made with G1347
Ac 7: 8 he gave Abraham the c of circumcision. G1347
Ac 7:44 the tabernacle of the c law with them in G3457
Ro 11:27 And this is my c with them when I take G1347
1Co 11:25 "This cup is the new c in my blood; do G1347
2Co 3: 6 us competent as ministers of a new c— G1347
2Co 3:14 same veil remains when the old c is read. G1347
Gal 3:15 add to a human c that has been duly G1347
Gal 3:17 not set aside the c previously established G1347
Gal 4:24 One c is from Mount Sinai and bears NDT
Heb 7:22 has become the guarantor of a better c. G1347
Heb 8: 6 to theirs as the c of which he is mediator G1347

Heb 8: 6 since the new c is established on better G4015S
Heb 8: 7 had been nothing wrong with that first c, AIT
Heb 8: 8 I will make a new c with the people of G1347
Heb 8: 9 It will not be like the c I made with their G1347
Heb 8: 9 they did not remain faithful to my c, G1347
Heb 8:10 This is the c I will establish with the G1347
Heb 8:13 By calling this c "new," he has made the NDT
Heb 9: 1 Now the first c had regulations for worship NDT
Heb 9: 4 incense and the gold-covered ark of the c. G1347
Heb 9: 4 budded, and the stone tablets of the c. G1347
Heb 9:15 reason Christ is the mediator of a new c, G1347
Heb 9:15 from the sins committed under the first c. G1347
Heb 9:18 is why even the first c was not put into effect NDT
Heb 9:20 "This is the blood of the c, which God has G1347
Heb 10:16 "This is the c I will make with them after G1347
Heb 10:29 thing the blood of the c that sanctified G1347
Heb 12:24 to Jesus the mediator of a new c, and to G1347
Heb 13:20 the blood of the eternal c brought back G1347
Rev 11:19 his temple was seen the ark of his c. G1347
Rev 15: 5 the tabernacle of the c law—and it was G3457

COVENANTED (2) [COVENANT]

2Ch 7:18 as I c with David your father when I said H4162
Hag 2: 5 'This is what I c with you when you came H4162

COVENANTS (3) [COVENANT]

Ro 9: 4 the divine glory, the c, the receiving of the G1347
Gal 4:24 The women represent two c. G1347
Eph 2:12 foreigners to the c of the promise, G1347

COVER (97) [COVER-UP, COVERED, COVERING, COVERINGS, COVERS, GOLD-COVERED]

Ge 20:16 This is to c the offense against you H4064+6524
Ge 37:26 if we kill our brother and c up his blood? H4059
Ex 10: 5 They will c the face of the ground so that it H4059
Ex 21:33 digs one and fails to c it and an ox or a H4059
Ex 25:17 "Make an atonement c of pure gold—two H4114
Ex 25:18 of hammered gold at the ends of the c. H4114
Ex 25:19 the cherubim of one piece with the c, H4114
Ex 25:20 upward, overshadowing the c with them. H4114
Ex 25:20 to face each other, looking toward the c. H4114
Ex 25:21 Place the c on top of the ark and put in the H4114
Ex 25:22 above the c between the two cherubim H4114
Ex 26:13 the sides of the tabernacle so as to c it. H4059
Ex 26:34 Put the atonement c on the ark of the H4114
Ex 30: 6 before the atonement c that is over the H4114
Ex 31: 7 covenant law with the atonement c on it, H4114
Ex 33:22 in the rock and c you with my hand until I H8503
Ex 35:12 poles and the atonement c and the H4114
Ex 37: 6 He made the atonement c of pure gold H4114
Ex 37: 7 of hammered gold at the ends of the c. H4114
Ex 37: 8 he made them of one piece with the c. H4114
Ex 37: 9 upward, overshadowing the c with them. H4114
Ex 37: 9 faced each other, looking toward the c. H4114
Ex 39:35 law with its poles and the atonement c; H4114
Ex 40:20 to the ark and put the atonement c over it. H4114
Lev 13:45 c the lower part of their face and cry out H6486
Lev 16: 2 in front of the atonement c on the ark, H4114
Lev 16: 2 appear in the cloud over the atonement c. H4114
Lev 16:13 will conceal the atonement c above the H4114
Lev 16:14 sprinkle it on the front of the atonement c; H4114
Lev 16:14 seven times before the atonement c. H4114
Lev 16:15 it on the atonement c and in front of H4114
Lev 17:13 drain out the blood and c it with earth, H4059
Nu 4: 6 Then they are to c the curtain with a H4062+5989
Nu 4: 8 c that with the durable leather and H4059+4832
Nu 4: 9 a blue cloth and c the lampstand that is H4059
Nu 4:11 a blue cloth and c that with the H4059+4832
Nu 4:12 c that with the durable leather and H4059+4832
Nu 7:89 above the atonement c on the ark of the H4114
Nu 22: 5 they c the face of the land and have H4059
Dt 23:13 dig a hole and c up your H2256+8740+4059
Jdg 9:31 Under c he sent messengers to H928+9564
1Ki 18: 6 So they divided the land they were to c H6296
Ne 4: 5 Do not c up their guilt or blot out their sins H4059
Job 14:17 sealed up in a bag; you will c over my sin. H3260
Job 16:18 do not c my blood; may my cry H4059
Job 21:26 lie in the dust, and worms c them both. H4059
Job 24: 7 they have nothing to c themselves in the H4064
Job 37: 8 The animals take c; they remain in their H743
Job 38:34 the clouds and c yourself with a flood of H4059
Ps 10: 9 like a lion in c he lies in wait. He lies in H6108
Ps 17:12 prey, like a fierce lion crouching in c. H5041
Ps 32: 5 sin to you and did not c up my iniquity. H4059
Ps 83:16 C their faces with shame, LORD, so that H4848
Ps 84: 6 the autumn rains also c it with pools. H6486
Ps 91: 4 He will c you with his feathers, and under H6114
Ps 104: 9 never again will they c the earth. H4059
Isa 8: 8 outspread wings will c the breadth of your H4850
Isa 10:31 is in flight; the people of Gebim take c. H6395
Isa 11: 9 of the LORD as the waters c the sea. H4059
Isa 14:11 spread out beneath you and worms c you. H4833
Isa 14:21 the land and c the earth with their H4848+7156
Isa 54: 9 of Noah would never again c the H6296+6584
Isa 59: 6 they cannot c themselves with what they H4059
Isa 60: 6 Herds of camels will c your land, young H4059
Jer 3:25 in our shame, and let our disgrace c us. H4059
Jer 14: 3 despairing, they c their heads. H2902
Jer 14: 4 farmers are dismayed and c their heads. H2902
Jer 46: 8 'I will rise and c the earth; I will H4059
Jer 51:42 over Babylon; its roaring waves will c her. H4059
Eze 12: 6 C your face so that you cannot see the H4059
Eze 12:12 He will c his face so that he cannot see H4059
Eze 13:10 wall is built, they c it with whitewash, H3212
Eze 13:11 tell those who c it with whitewash H3212
Eze 24: 7 on the ground, where the dust would c it. H4059
Eze 24:17 do not c your mustache and beard or eat H6486
Eze 24:22 You will not c your mustache and beard H6486
Eze 26:10 be so many that they will c you with dust. H4059
Eze 26:19 depths over you and its vast waters c you, H4059
Eze 32: 7 I will c the heavens and darken their stars H4059
Eze 32: 7 their stars; I will c the sun with a cloud H4059
Eze 37: 6 flesh come upon you and c you with skin; H7965
Hos 2: 9 my linen, intended to c her naked body. H4059
Hos 10: 8 thistles will grow up and c their altars. H6584
Hos 10: 8 they will say to the mountains, "C us!" H4059
Mic 3: 7 They will all c their faces because there is H6486
Hab 2:14 glory of the LORD as the waters c the sea. H4059
Hab 2:16 and disgrace will c your glory. H6584
Zec 5: 7 Then the c of lead was raised, and there H3971
Zec 5: 8 the basket and pushed its lead c down on it. H74
Lk 23:30 and to the hills, "C us!" ' G2821
1Co 11: 6 For if a woman does not c her head, she G2877
1Co 11: 6 head shaved, then she should c her head. G2877
1Co 11: 7 A man ought not to c his head, since he G2877
1Th 2: 5 did we put on a mask to c up greed G4733
Heb 9: 5 overshadowing the atonement c. G2663
Jas 5:20 from death and c over a multitude of G2821
Rev 3:18 so you can c your shameful G3590+5746

COVER-UP (1) [COVER]

1Pe 2:16 do not use your freedom as a c for evil; G2127

COVERED (108) [COVER]

Ge 7:19 under the entire heavens were c. H4059
Ge 7:20 The waters rose and c the mountains to a H4059
Ge 9:23 in backward and c their father's naked H4059
Ge 24:65 So she took her veil and c herself. H4059
Ge 27:16 She also c his hands and the smooth part of his neck with H4252
Ge 38:14 c herself with a veil to disguise herself H4059
Ge 38:15 was a prostitute, for she had c her face. H4059
Ex 8: 6 the frogs came up and c the land. H4059
Ex 8:21 even the ground will be c with them. H6584
Ex 10:15 They c all the ground until it was black H4059
Ex 10:22 and total darkness c all Egypt for H2118+928
Ex 14:28 water flowed back and c the chariots and H4059
Ex 15: 5 The deep waters have c them; they sank H4059
Ex 15:10 with your breath, and the sea c them. H4059
Ex 16:13 That evening quail came and c the camp H4059
Ex 19:18 Mount Sinai was c with smoke, because H6939
Ex 24:15 went up on the mountain, the cloud c it, H4059
Ex 24:16 For six days the cloud c the mountain, and H4059
Ex 40:34 Then the cloud c the tent of meeting, and H4059
Lev 13:13 if the disease has c their whole body H4059
Nu 7: 3 before the LORD six c carts and twelve oxen H7369
Nu 9:15 covenant law, was set up, the cloud c it. H4059
Nu 9:16 the cloud c it, and at night it looked H4059
Nu 16:42 suddenly the cloud c it and the glory of H4059
Jos 24: 7 he brought the sea over them and c them. H4059
Jdg 4:18 her tent, and she c him with a blanket. H4059
Jdg 4:19 gave him a drink, and c him up. H4059
Jdg 6:39 dry and let the ground be c with dew." H6584
Jdg 6:40 was dry; all the ground was c with dew. H6584
2Sa 15:30 his head was c and he was barefoot. H2902
2Sa 15:30 the people with him c their heads too H2902
2Sa 19: 4 The king c his face and cried aloud, "O my H4286
1Ki 6:15 c the floor of the temple with planks H7596
1Ki 6:21 Solomon c the inside of the temple with H7596
1Ki 6:30 He also c the floors of both the inner and outer rooms of the temple with H7596
1Ki 7: 7 and he c it with cedar from floor to ceiling. H6211
1Ki 10:18 king made a great throne c with ivory and AIT
1Ki 20:27 while the Arameans c the countryside. H4848
2Ki 3:25 a stone on every good field until it was c. H4848
2Ki 18:16 gold with which he had c the doors and H7596
2Ki 23:14 poles and c the sites with human bones. H4848
2Ch 3: 5 with juniper and c it with fine gold and H2902
2Ch 5: 8 place of the ark and c the ark and its H4059
2Ch 9:17 king made a great throne c with ivory and AIT
2Ch 16:14 him on a bier c with spices and various H4848
Est 6:12 rushed home, with his head c in grief, H2902
Est 7: 8 the king's mouth, they c Haman's face. H2902
Job 15:27 "Though his face is c with fat and his H4059
Job 29: 9 and c their mouths with their hands H8492+4200
Ps 32: 1 are forgiven, whose sins are c. H4059
Ps 34: 5 their faces are never c with shame. H2917
Ps 44:15 all day long, and my face is c with shame H4059
Ps 44:19 you c us over with deep darkness. H4059
Ps 65:13 The meadows are c with flocks and the H4252
Ps 71:13 may those who want to harm me be c with H6486
Ps 80:10 The mountains were c with its shade, the H4059
Ps 85: 2 iniquity of your people and c all their sins. H4059
Ps 89:45 you have c him with a mantle of shame. H6486
Ps 104: 6 You c it with the watery depths as with a H4059
Ps 106:11 The waters c their adversaries; not one of H4059
Pr 7:16 I have c my bed with colored linens H8048+5267
Pr 24:31 the ground was c with weeds, and the H4059
Isa 6: 2 With two wings they c their faces, with H4059
Isa 6: 2 with two they c their feet, and with H4059
Isa 7:24 the land will be c with briers and thorns. H3972
Isa 14:19 you are c with the slain, with H4229
Isa 28: 8 All the tables are c with vomit and there H4848
Isa 29:10 the prophets); he has c your heads (the H4059
Isa 30:22 with silver and your images c with gold; H682
Isa 34: 6 bathed in blood, it is c with fat—the H2014
Isa 51:16 in your mouth and c you with the shadow H4059
Jer 48:37 every waist is c with sackcloth. H6584
La 2: 1 has c Daughter Zion with the cloud of H6380
La 3:43 "You have c yourself with anger and H6114
La 3:44 You have c yourself with a cloud so that H6114
Eze 7:18 Every face will be c with shame, and every H448
Eze 13:12 "Where is the whitewash you c it with?" H3212
Eze 13:14 the wall you have c with whitewash and H3212
Eze 13:15 against those who c it with whitewash. H3212
Eze 16: 8 garment over you and c your naked body. H4059
Eze 16:10 fine linen and c you with costly garments. H4059
Eze 24: 8 on the bare rock, so that it would not be c. H4059
Eze 30:18 She will be c with clouds, and her villages H4059
Eze 31:15 the realm of the dead I c the deep springs H4059
Eze 37: 8 flesh appeared on them and skin c them, H7965
Eze 41:16 threshold was c with wood. H8470+6017+6017
Eze 41:16 to the windows, and the windows were c. H4059
Da 9: 7 this day we are c with shame H4200+7156
Da 9: 8 our ancestors are c with shame, H4200+7156
Ob 10 you will be c with shame; you will H4059
Jnh 3: 6 c himself with sackcloth and sat down in H4059
Jnh 3: 8 But let people and animals be c with H4059
Mic 7:10 will see it and will be c with shame, H4059
Hab 2:19 It is c with gold and silver; there is no H9530
Hab 3: 3 His glory c the heavens and his praise H4059
Zec 7:11 their backs and c their ears. H3877+4946+9048
Mt 17: 5 a bright cloud c them, and a voice from G2173
Mk 9: 7 Then a cloud appeared and c them, and G2173
Lk 5:12 man came along who was c with leprosy. G4441
Lk 9:34 a cloud appeared and c them, and they G2173
Lk 16:20 a beggar named Lazarus, c with sores G1815
Jn 5: 2 which is surrounded by five c colonnades. G5119
Ac 7:57 At this they c their ears and, yelling at the G5309
Ro 4: 7 are forgiven, whose sins are c. G2128
1Co 11: 4 with his head c dishonors G2848+2400
Rev 4: 6 creatures, and they were c with eyes, in G1154
Rev 4: 8 six wings and was c with eyes all around, G1154
Rev 17: 3 scarlet beast that was c with blasphemous G1154

COVERING (25) [COVER]

Ge 8:13 then removed the c from the ark and saw H4832
Ex 22:27 that cloak is the only c your neighbor has. H4064
Ex 26:14 Make for the tent a c of ram skins dyed red, H4832
Ex 26:14 over that a c of the other durable H4832
Ex 28:42 linen undergarments as a c for the body, H4059
Ex 35:11 the tabernacle with its tent and its c H4832
Ex 36:19 the tent a c of ram skins dyed red H4832
Ex 36:19 over that a c of the other durable H4832
Ex 39:34 the c of ram skins dyed red and the H4832
Ex 39:34 dyed red and the c of another durable H4832
Ex 40:19 the tabernacle and put the c over the tent, H4832
Nu 4:10 accessories in a c of the durable leather H4832
Nu 4:14 are to spread a c of the durable leather H4062
Nu 4:15 sons have finished c the holy furnishings H4059
Nu 4:25 its c and its outer covering of durable H4832
Nu 4:25 its outer c of durable leather, H4832
1Sa 19:13 c it with a garment and putting some H4059
2Sa 17:19 His wife took a c and spread it out over the H5009
Ps 18:11 He made darkness his c, his canopy H6260
Ps 105:39 He spread out a cloud as a c, and a fire to H5009
Isa 50: 3 with darkness and make sackcloth its c." H4064
Eze 1:11 each had two other wings c its body. H4059
Eze 1:23 and each had two wings c its body. H4059
Eze 38: 9 you will be like a cloud c the land. H4059
1Co 11:15 For long hair is given to her as a c. G4316

COVERINGS (3) [COVER]

Ge 3: 7 together and made c for themselves. H2514
Nu 3:25 its c, the curtain at the H4832
Pr 31:22 She makes c for her bed; she is clothed in H5267

COVERS (19) [COVER]

Ex 22:15 the money paid for the hire c the loss. H995+928
Lev 7: 3 tail and the fat that c the internal organs, H4059
Lev 13:12 it c all the skin of the affected person from H4059
Nu 22:11 come out of Egypt c the face of the land. H4059
1Ki 1: 1 keep warm even when they put c over him. H955
Job 22:11 and why a flood of water c you. H4059
Job 23:17 by the thick darkness that c my face. H4059
Job 26: 9 He c the face of the full moon, spreading H297
Ps 10:11 he c his face and never sees. H6259
Ps 69: 7 scorn for your sake, and shame c my face. H4059
Ps 147: 8 He c the sky with clouds; he supplies the H4059
Pr 10:12 stirs up conflict, but love c over all wrongs. H4059
Pr 17: 9 would foster love c over an offense, H4059
Isa 25: 7 all peoples, the sheet that c all nations; H5819
Isa 60: 2 darkness c the earth and thick darkness is H4059
Jer 51:51 been insulted and shame c our faces, H4059
Eze 38:16 people Israel like a cloud that c the land. H4059
2Co 3:15 Moses is read, a veil c their hearts. G2093+3023
1Pe 4: 8 because love c over a multitude of sins. G2821

COVES (1)

Jdg 5:17 on the coast and stayed in his c. H5153

COVET (9) [COVETED, COVETING]

Ex 20:17 "You shall not c your neighbor's house H2773
Ex 20:17 You shall not c your neighbor's wife, or H2773
Ex 34:24 no one will c your land when you go H2773
Dt 5:21 "You shall not c your neighbor's wife. H2773
Dt 7:25 Do not c the silver and gold on them, and H2773

Mic 2: 2 *They* **c** fields and seize them, and houses H2773
Ro 7: 7 if the law had not said, "*You shall* not **c**." *G2121*
Ro 13: 9 "*You shall* not **c**," and whatever other *G2121*
Jas 4: 2 *You* **c** but you cannot get what you want *G2420*

COVETED (2) [COVET]
Jos 7:21 fifty shekels, *I* **c** them and took them. H2773
Ac 20:33 *I have* not **c** anyone's silver or gold or *G2121*

COVETING (2) [COVET]
Ro 7: 7 not have known what **c** really was if the *G2123*
Ro 7: 8 produced in me every kind of **c**. *G2123*

COW (5) [COWS, COWS']
Lev 22:28 Do not slaughter a **c** or a sheep and its H8802
Nu 18:17 you must not redeem the firstborn of a **c**, H8802
Isa 7:21 keep alive a **young c** and two goats H6320+1330
Isa 11: 7 The **c** will feed with the bear, their young H7239
Eze 4:15 bake your bread over **c** dung instead of H1330

COWARDLY (1) [COWER]
Rev 21: 8 But the **c**, the unbelieving, the vile, the *G1264*

COWER (3) [COWARDLY, COWERED, COWERING]
Dt 33:29 Your enemies *will* **c** before you, and you H3950
2Sa 22:45 foreigners **c** before me; as soon as they H3950
Ps 18:44 foreigners **c** before me; as soon as they H3950

COWERED (1) [COWER]
Job 9:13 even the cohorts of Rahab **c** at his feet. H8820

COWERING (1) [COWER]
Isa 51:14 The **c prisoners** will soon be set free; they H7579

COWS (21) [COW]
Ge 32:15 with their young, forty **c** and ten bulls, and H7239
Ge 33:13 care for the ewes and **c** that are nursing H1330
Ge 41: 2 out of the river there came up seven **c**, H7239
Ge 41: 3 seven other **c**, ugly and gaunt H7239
Ge 41: 4 And the **c** that were ugly and gaunt ate up H7239
Ge 41: 4 gaunt ate up the seven sleek, fat **c**. H7239
Ge 41:18 out of the river there came up seven **c**, H7239
Ge 41:19 seven other **c** came up—scrawny H7239
Ge 41:19 never seen such ugly **c** in all the land of H2179S
Ge 41:20 ugly **c** ate up the seven fat cows that H7239
Ge 41:20 ate up the seven fat **c** that came up first. H7239
Ge 41:26 The seven good **c** are seven years, and the H7239
Ge 41:27 ugly **c** that came up afterward are seven H7239
Dt 15:19 Do not put the firstborn of your **c** to work H8802
1Sa 6: 7 with two **c** that have calved and have H7239
1Sa 6: 7 Hitch the **c** to the cart, but take their H7239
1Sa 6:10 They took two such **c** and hitched them to H7239
1Sa 6:12 Then the **c** went straight up toward Beth H7239
1Sa 6:14 sacrificed the **c** as a burnt offering to H7239
Job 21:10 their **c** calve and do not miscarry. H7239
Am 4: 1 you **c** *of* Bashan on Mount Samaria H7239

COWS' (1) [COW]
2Sa 17:29 cheese from **c** milk for David and his H1330

COZBI (NIV84) KOZBI

COZEBA (NIV84) KOZEBA

CRACK (1) [CRACKED]
Na 3: 2 The **c** *of* whips, the clatter of wheels H7754

CRACKED (6) [CRACK]
Jos 9: 4 sacks and old wineskins, **c** and mended. H1324
Jos 9:13 filled were new, but see how **c** *they are*. H1324
Jdg 9:53 millstone on his head and **c** his skull. H8368
Isa 30:13 a high wall, **c** and bulging, that H7288+5877
Jer 2:16 Tahpanhes *have* **c** your skull. H8318
Jer 14: 4 The ground *is* **c** because there is no rain H3169

CRACKLING (2)
Ecc 7: 6 Like the **c** *of* thorns under the pot, so is H7754
Joel 2: 5 like a **c** fire consuming stubble H7754

CRAFT (1) [CRAFTED, CRAFTINESS, CRAFTS, CRAFTSMAN, CRAFTSMEN, CRAFTY]
1Ch 28:21 person skilled in any **c** will help you in all H6275

CRAFTED (1) [CRAFT]
Nu 31:51 from them the gold—all the **c** articles. H5126

CRAFTINESS (3) [CRAFT]
Job 5:13 He catches the wise in their **c**, and the H6891
1Co 3:19 "He catches the wise in their **c**"; *G4111*
Eph 4:14 by the cunning and **c** of people in their *G4111*

CRAFTS (2) [CRAFT]
Ex 31: 5 in wood, and to engage in all kinds of **c**. H4856
Ex 35:33 to engage in all kinds of **artistic c**. H4742

CRAFTSMAN (6) [CRAFT]
Ex 39: 8 the breastpiece—the work of a **skilled c**. H3110
1Ki 7:14 was from Tyre and a **skilled c** *in* bronze. H3086
Isa 3: 3 counselor, skilled **c** and clever enchanter. H3093
Jer 10: 3 and a **c** shapes it with his chisel. H3093
Jer 10: 9 What the **c** and goldsmith have made is H3093
Hab 2:18 "Of what value is an idol carved by a **c**? Or H3670

CRAFTSMEN (11) [CRAFT]
1Ki 5:18 The **c** *of* Solomon and Hiram and workers H1215
1Ch 22:16 bronze and iron—**c** beyond number. NDT
1Ch 29: 5 for all the work to be done by the **c**. H3093
Isa 44:11 to shame; such **c** are only human beings. H3093
Jer 52:15 with the rest of the **c** and those who had H570
Eze 27: 9 Veteran **c** *of* Byblos were on board as H2682
Hos 13: 2 images, all of them the work of **c**. H3093
Zec 1:20 Then the LORD showed me four **c**. H3093
Zec 1:21 but **the c** have come to terrify them and H465S
Ac 19:24 brought in a lot of business *for* the **c** there. *G5493*
Ac 19:38 his fellow **c** have a grievance against *G5493*

CRAFTY (6) [CRAFT]
Ge 3: 1 serpent was more **c** than any of the wild H6874
1Sa 23:22 They tell me he *is* **very c**. H6891+6891
Job 5:12 He thwarts the plans of the **c**, so that their H6874
Job 15: 5 you adopt the tongue of the **c**. H6874
Pr 7:10 dressed like a prostitute and with **c** intent. H5915
2Co 12:16 **c** *fellow* that I am, I caught you by *G4112*

CRAG (3) [CRAGS]
Dt 32:13 the rock, and with oil from the flinty **c**, H7446
Job 39:28 there at night; a rocky **c** is its stronghold. H9094
Ps 78:16 streams out of a **rocky c** and made water H6152

CRAGS (6) [CRAG]
1Sa 24: 2 his men near the **C** *of* the Wild Goats. H7446
Ps 104:18 the **c** are a refuge for the hyrax. H6152
Pr 30:26 yet they make their home in the **c**; H6152
Isa 2:21 to the overhanging **c** from the fearful H6152
Isa 57: 5 the ravines and under the overhanging **c**. H6152
Am 6:12 Do horses run on the **rocky c**? Does one H6152

CRANE (KJV) SWIFT

CRASH (2)
Zep 1:10 New Quarter, and a loud **c** from the hills. H8691
Mt 7:27 that house, and it fell with a great **c**." *G4774*

CRAVE (8) [CRAVED, CRAVES, CRAVING, CRAVINGS]
Nu 11: 4 with them *began to* **c other food**, H203+9294
Dt 12:20 promised you, and you **c** meat and say, "I H203
Pr 21:10 The wicked **c** evil; their neighbors get no H203
Pr 23: 3 *Do* not **c** his delicacies, for that food is H203
Pr 23: 6 a begrudging host, *do* not **c** his delicacies; H203
Pr 31: 4 kings to drink wine, not for rulers to **c** beer, H197
Mic 7: 1 none of the early figs that I **c**. H203
1Pe 2: 2 Like newborn babies, **c** pure spiritual milk *G2160*

CRAVED (4) [CRAVE]
Nu 11:34 buried the people who *had* **c other food**. H203
Ps 78:18 to the test by demanding the food they **c**. H5883
Ps 78:29 gorged—he had given them **what** they **c**. H9294
Ps 78:30 But before they turned from what they **c** H9294

CRAVES (1) [CRAVE]
Pr 21:26 All day long *he* **c for more**, but the H203+9294

CRAVING (5) [CRAVE]
Job 20:20 "Surely he will have no respite from his **c** H1061
Ps 106:14 In the desert *they* **gave in to** *their* **c** H203+9294
Pr 10: 3 but he thwarts the **c** of the wicked. H2094
Pr 21:25 The **c** *of* a sluggard will be the death of H9294
Jer 2:24 sniffing the wind in her **c**—in her H205+5883

CRAVINGS (2) [CRAVE]
Ps 10: 3 He boasts about the **c** *of* his heart; he H9294
Eph 2: 3 gratifying the **c** of our flesh and following *G2123*

CRAWL (2) [CRAWLING]
Ge 3:14 *You will* **c** on your belly and you will eat H2143
Mic 7:17 like *creatures that* **c** *on* the ground. H2323

CRAWLING (3) [CRAWL]
Lev 22: 5 if he touches any **c thing** that makes him H9238
1Sa 14:11 "The Hebrews *are* **c out** of the holes they H3655
Eze 8:10 walls all kinds of **c things** and unclean H8254

CREAM (3)
Job 20:17 the rivers flowing with honey and **c**. H2772
Job 29: 6 was drenched with **c** and the rock poured H2772
Pr 30:33 For as churning **c** produces butter, and as H2692

CREATE (11) [CREATED, CREATES, CREATING, CREATION, CREATOR]
Ps 51:10 **C** in me a pure heart, O God, and renew a H1343
Isa 4: 5 the LORD *will* **c** over all of Mount Zion H1343
Isa 45: 7 I form the light and **c** darkness, I bring H1343
Isa 45: 7 I bring prosperity and **c** disaster; I, H1343
Isa 45:18 he founded it; *he did* not **c** it to be empty H1343
Isa 65:17 I *will* **c** new heavens and a new earth. H1343
Isa 65:18 glad and rejoice forever in what I *will* **c**, H1343
Isa 65:18 I *will* **c** Jerusalem to be a delight and H1343
Jer 31:22 The LORD *will* **c** a new thing on earth—the H1343
Mal 2:10 *Did* not one God **c** us? Why do H1343
Eph 2:15 His purpose *was to* **c** in himself one new *G3231*

CREATED (47) [CREATE]
Ge 1: 1 the beginning God **c** the heavens and the H1343
Ge 1:21 So God **c** the great creatures of the sea H1343
Ge 1:27 So God **c** mankind in his own image, in H1343
Ge 1:27 in the image of God *he* **c** them; male H1343
Ge 1:27 male and female *he* **c** them. H1343
Ge 2: 4 heavens and the earth when they **were c**, H1343
Ge 5: 1 When God **c** mankind, he made them in H1343
Ge 5: 2 *He* **c** them male and female and blessed H1343
Ge 5: 2 them "Mankind" when they **were c**. H1343
Ge 6: 7 of the earth the human race *I have* **c**— H1343
Dt 4:32 from the day God **c** human beings on the H1343
Ps 89:12 You **c** the north and the south; Tabor and H1343
Ps 89:47 For what futility *you have* **c** all humanity! H1343
Ps 102:18 that a people **not yet c** may praise the H1343
Ps 104:30 your Spirit, *they* **are c**, and you renew H1343
Ps 139:13 For you **c** my inmost being; you knit me H7865
Ps 148: 5 the LORD, for at his command *they* **were c**, H1343
Ecc 7:29 God **c** mankind upright, but they have H6913
Isa 40:26 to the heavens: Who **c** all these? He who H1343
Isa 41:20 that the Holy One of Israel *has* **c** it. H1343
Isa 43: 1 what the LORD says—*he who* **c** you, Jacob, H1343
Isa 43: 7 by my name, whom *I* **c** for my glory, whom H1343
Isa 45: 8 flourish with it; I, the LORD, *have* **c** it. H1343
Isa 45:12 who made the earth and **c** mankind on it. H1343
Isa 45:18 the LORD says—*he who* **c** the heavens, he H1343
Isa 48: 7 *They* **are c** now, and not long ago; you H1343
Isa 54:16 it is I *who* **c** the blacksmith who fans the H1343
Isa 54:16 And it is I *who have* **c** the destroyer to H1343
Isa 57:16 because of me—the very people I *have* **c**. H6913
Eze 21:30 In the place where *you* **were c**, in the land H1343
Eze 28:13 on the day you **were c** they were prepared. H1343
Eze 28:15 from the day you **were c** till wickedness H1343
Mk 13:19 beginning, when God **c** the world, until *G3231*
Ro 1:25 served **c things** rather than the *G3232*
1Co 11: 9 neither *was* man **c** for woman, but woman *G3231*
Eph 2:10 **c** in Christ Jesus to do good works *G3231*
Eph 3: 9 was kept hidden in God, who **c** all things. *G3231*
Eph 4:24 **c** to be like God in true righteousness *G3231*
Col 1:16 For in him all things *were* **c**: things in *G3231*
Col 1:16 all things *have been* **c** through him and *G3231*
1Ti 4: 3 which God **c** to be received with *G3231*
1Ti 4: 4 For everything God **c** is good, and nothing *G3233*
Heb 12:27 **c** *things*—so that what cannot be *G4472*
Jas 1:18 we might be a kind of firstfruits *of all* he **c**. *G3233*
Rev 4:11 power, for you **c** all things, and by *G3231*
Rev 4:11 by your will *they were* **c** and have their *G3231*
Rev 10: 6 who **c** the heavens and all that is in them *G3231*

CREATES (1) [CREATE]
Am 4:13 the mountains, *who* **c** the wind, and who H1343

CREATING (2) [CREATE]
Ge 2: 3 from all the work *of* **c** that he had done. H1343
Isa 57:19 **c** praise on their lips. Peace, peace, to H1343

CREATION (26) [CREATE]
Ps 96:13 Let all **c** rejoice before the LORD, for he NDT
Hab 2:18 the one who makes it trusts in his own **c**; H3671
Mt 13:35 things hidden since the **c** of the world." *G2856*
Mt 25:34 prepared for you since the **c** of the world. *G2856*
Mk 10: 6 at the beginning *of* **c** God 'made them *G3232*
Mk 16:15 the world and preach the gospel to all **c**. *G3232*
Jn 17:24 you loved me before the **c** of the world. *G2856*
Ro 1:20 For since the **c** of the world God's invisible *G3232*
Ro 8:19 For the **c** waits in eager expectation for the *G3232*
Ro 8:20 For the **c** was subjected to frustration, not *G3232*
Ro 8:21 that the **c** itself will be liberated from its *G3232*
Ro 8:22 know that the whole **c** has been groaning *G3232*
Ro 8:39 anything else *in all* **c**, will be able to *G3232*
2Co 5:17 if anyone is in Christ, the new **c** has come: *G3232*
Gal 6:15 anything; what counts is the new **c**. *G3232*
Eph 1: 4 us in him before the **c** of the world to be *G2856*
Col 1:15 the invisible God, the firstborn *over* all **c**. *G3232*
Heb 4: 3 been finished since the **c** of the world. *G2856*
Heb 4:13 Nothing *in all* **c** is hidden from God's sight. *G3232*
Heb 9:11 that is to say, is not a *part of* this **c**. *G3232*
Heb 9:26 suffer many times since the **c** of the world. *G2856*
1Pe 1:20 He was chosen before the **c** of the world *G2856*
2Pe 3: 4 on as it has since the beginning *of* **c**." *G3232*
Rev 3:14 true witness, the ruler of God's **c**. *G3232*
Rev 13: 8 who was slain from the **c** of the world. *G2856*
Rev 17: 8 book of life from the **c** of the world will be *G2856*

CREATOR (12) [CREATE]
Ge 14:19 by God Most High, **C** *of* heaven and earth. H7865
Ge 14:22 God Most High, **C** *of* heaven and earth, H7865
Dt 32: 6 your Father, your **C**, who made you and H7865
Ecc 12: 1 Remember your **C** in the days of your H1343
Isa 27:11 and their **C** shows them no favor. H3670
Isa 40:28 the **C** *of* the ends of the earth. H1343
Isa 42: 5 the LORD says—the **C** *of* the heavens, who H1343
Isa 43:15 your Holy One, Israel's **C**, your King." H1343
Mt 19: 4 the beginning the **C** 'made them male *G3231*
Ro 1:25 served created things rather than the **C**— *G3231*
Col 3:10 in knowledge in the image *of* its **C**. *G3231*
1Pe 4:19 themselves *to* their faithful **C** and *G3234*

CREATURE (38) [CREATURES]
Ge 1:28 over every **living c** that moves on the H2651
Ge 2:19 whatever the man called each living **c**, H5883
Ge 6:17 every **c** that has the breath of life in it. NDT
Ge 6:20 kind of **c that moves** *along* the ground H8254
Ge 7: 4 of the earth every **living c** I have made." H3685
Ge 7:14 every **c** that moves along the ground H8254
Ge 8:17 out every kind of living **c** that is with you— H1414
Ge 9: 2 on every **c** that moves along the ground H889S
Ge 9:10 with every living **c** that was with you H5883
Ge 9:10 the ark with you—every **living c** *on* earth. H2651
Ge 9:12 me and you and every living **c** with you, H5883
Lev 5: 2 unclean **c that moves along the ground**) H9238

Lev 7:21 unclean c that moves along the ground— H9238
Lev 11:41 " 'Every c that moves along the ground is H9238
Lev 11:42 are not to eat any c that moves along the H9238
Lev 11:44 unclean by any c that moves along the H9238
Lev 11:46 the water and every c that moves along H5883
Lev 17:11 For the life of a c is in the blood, and I H1414
Lev 17:14 because the life of every c is its blood H1414
Lev 17:14 "You must not eat the blood of any c H1414
Lev 17:14 because the life of every c is its blood H1414
Dt 4:18 like any c that moves along the ground H8253
Dt 14:20 But any winged c that is clean you may eat H6416
Job 12:10 is the life of every c and the breath of all H2644
Job 14:15 will long for the c your hands have made. H5126
Job 41:33 on earth is its equal—a c without fear. H6913
Ps 136:25 He gives food to every c. His love endures H1414
Ps 145:21 Let every c praise his holy name for ever H1414
Eze 1:11 wing touching that of the c on either side; H408S
Eze 1:15 ground beside each c with its four faces. H2651
Eze 38:20 every c that moves along the ground H8254
Da 4:12 in its branches; from it every c was fed. A10125
Col 1:23 been proclaimed to every c under heaven, G3232
Rev 4:7 The first living c was like a lion, the G2442
Rev 5:13 Then I heard every c in heaven and on G3233
Rev 6:3 I heard the second living c say, "Come!" G2442
Rev 6:5 I heard the third living c say, "Come!" G2442
Rev 6:7 I heard the voice of the fourth living c say G2442

CREATURES (78) [CREATURE]

Ge 1:20 "Let the water teem with living c, and let H5883
Ge 1:21 the great c of the sea and every living H9490
Ge 1:24 land produce living c according to their H5883
Ge 1:24 the c that move along the ground H8254
Ge 1:25 all the c that move along the ground H8254
Ge 1:26 over all the c that move along the H8254
Ge 1:30 sky and all the c that move along the H8253
Ge 6:7 the c that move along the ground— H8254
Ge 6:19 are to bring into the ark two of all living c, H1414
Ge 7:8 of birds and of all c that move along the H889S
Ge 7:15 Pairs of all c that have the breath of life in H1414
Ge 7:21 all the c that swarm over the earth H9238
Ge 7:23 animals and the c that move along the H8254
Ge 8:17 all the c that move along the ground H8254
Ge 8:19 all the c that move along the ground H8254
Ge 8:21 And never again will I destroy all living c H2645
Ge 9:15 me and you and all living c of every kind. H5883
Ge 9:16 God and all living c of every kind on the H5883
Lev 11:9 " 'Of all the c living in the water of the H889S
Lev 11:10 But all c in the seas or streams that do not NDT
Lev 11:10 all the other living c in the water— H5883
Lev 11:43 Do not defile yourselves by any of these c H9238
Lev 11:47 between living c that may be eaten and H2651
Dt 14:9 Of all the c living in the water, you may H889S
Ps 74:14 gave it as food to the c of the desert. H7470
Ps 104:24 made them all; the earth is full of your c. H7871
Ps 104:25 spacious, teeming with c beyond number H8254
Ps 104:27 All c look to you to give them their food H4392S
Ps 148:7 you great sea c and all ocean depths, H9490
Ps 148:10 all cattle, small c and flying birds, H8254
Pr 30:25 Ants are c of little strength, yet they store H6639
Pr 30:26 hyraxes are c of little power, yet they H6639
Isa 13:21 But desert c will lie there, jackals will fill H7470
Isa 23:13 have made it a place for desert c; H7470
Isa 34:14 Desert c will meet with hyenas, and wild H7470
Isa 34:14 there the night c will also lie down and H4327
Jer 50:39 "So desert c and hyenas will live there H7470
Eze 1:5 the fire was what looked like four living c. H2651
Eze 1:13 of the living c was like burning H2651
Eze 1:13 Fire moved back and forth among the c; it H2651
Eze 1:14 The c sped back and forth like flashes of H2651
Eze 1:15 As I looked at the living c, I saw a wheel H2651
Eze 1:17 in any one of the four directions the c faced; NDT
Eze 1:17 did not change direction as the c went. H5527S
Eze 1:19 When the living c moved, the wheels H2651
Eze 1:19 when the living c rose from the H2651
Eze 1:20 the spirit of the living c was in the wheels. H2651
Eze 1:21 When the c moved, they also moved H4392S
Eze 1:21 also moved; when the c stood still, they H4392S
Eze 1:21 when the c rose from the ground H4392S
Eze 1:21 the spirit of the living c was in the wheels. H2651
Eze 1:22 the heads of the living c was what looked H2651
Eze 1:24 When the c moved, I heard the sound of H4392S
Eze 3:13 the wings of the living c brushing against H2651
Eze 10:15 These were the living c I had seen by the H2651
Eze 10:17 the spirit of the living c was in them. H2651
Eze 10:20 These were the living c I had seen H2651
Eze 47:9 Swarms of living c will live wherever the H5883
Hos 2:18 sky and the c that move along the ground. H8254
Mic 7:17 like a snake, like c that crawl on the ground. AIT
Hab 1:14 the sea, like the sea c that have no ruler. H8254
Zep 2:14 herds will lie down there, c of every kind. H2651
Jas 3:7 reptiles and sea c are being tamed and G1879
2Pe 2:12 animals, c of instinct, born only to be G5879
Rev 4:6 were four living c, and they were G2442
Rev 4:8 Each of the four living c had six wings and G2442
Rev 4:9 Whenever the living c give glory, honor G2442
Rev 5:6 by the four living c and the elders. G2442
Rev 5:8 the four living c and the twenty-four G2442
Rev 5:11 the throne and the living c and the elders. G2442
Rev 5:14 The four living c said, "Amen," and the G2442
Rev 6:1 one of the four living c say in a voice like G2442
Rev 6:6 like a voice among the four living c, G2442
Rev 7:11 around the elders and the four living c. G2442
Rev 8:9 a third of the living c in the sea died, and G3233
Rev 14:3 before the four living c and the elders. G2442
Rev 15:7 one of the four living c gave to the seven G2442
Rev 19:4 elders and the four living c fell down and G2442

CREDIT (7) [ACCREDITED, CREDITED, CREDITOR, CREDITORS, CREDITS]

Lev 7:18 It will not be reckoned to their c, for it has H3108
Est 2:22 it to the king, giving c to Mordecai. H928+9005
Lk 6:32 those who love you, what c is that to you? G5921
Lk 6:33 are good to you, what c is that to you? G5921
Lk 6:34 expect repayment, what c is that to you? G5921
Ro 4:24 to whom God will c righteousness—for us G3357
1Pe 2:20 But how is it to your c if you receive a G3094

CREDITED (15) [CREDIT]

Ge 15:6 and he c it to him as righteousness. H3108
1Sa 18:8 "They have c David with tens of H5989
Ps 106:31 This was c to him as righteousness for H3108
Eze 18:20 of the righteous will be c to them, H6584
Ro 4:3 and it was c to him as righteousness." G3357
Ro 4:4 wages are not c as a gift but as an G3357
Ro 4:5 ungodly, their faith is c as righteousness. G3357
Ro 4:9 saying that Abraham's faith was c to him G3357
Ro 4:10 Under what circumstances was it c? Was it G3357
Ro 4:11 that righteousness might be c to them. G3357
Ro 4:22 This is why "it was c to him as G3357
Ro 4:23 The words "it was c to him" were written G3357
Gal 3:6 and it was c to him as righteousness." G3357
Php 4:17 I desire is that more be c to your account. G4429
Jas 2:23 and it was c to him as righteousness," G3357

CREDITOR (4) [CREDIT]

Dt 15:2 Every c shall cancel any H1251+5408+3338+2257
2Ki 4:1 But now his c is coming to take my two H5957
Ps 109:11 May a c seize all he has; may strangers H5957
Isa 24:2 borrower as for lender, for debtor as for c. H5957

CREDITORS (2) [CREDIT]

Isa 50:1 Or to which of my c did I sell you H5957
Hab 2:7 Will not your c suddenly arise? Will they H5967

CREDITS (1) [CREDIT]

Ro 4:6 one to whom God c righteousness apart G3357

CREPT (2)

1Sa 24:4 Then David c up unnoticed and cut off a H7756
Hab 3:16 at the sound; decay c into my bones, and H995

CRESCENS (1)

2Ti 4:10 C has gone to Galatia, and Titus to G3206

CRESCENT (1)

Isa 3:18 bangles and headbands and c necklaces, H8448

CREST (2)

Est 6:8 one with a royal c placed on its head. H4195
SS 4:8 Descend from the c of Amana, from the H8031

CRETANS (2) [CRETE]

Ac 2:11 C and Arabs—we hear them declaring G3205
Titus 1:12 "C are always liars, evil brutes, lazy G3205

CRETE (5) [CRETANS, CRETE'S]

Ac 27:7 we sailed to the lee of C, opposite G3207
Ac 27:12 This was a harbor in C, facing both G3207
Ac 27:13 anchor and sailed along the shore of C. G3207
Ac 27:21 have taken my advice not to sail from C; G3207
Titus 1:5 reason I left you in C was that you might G3207

CRETE'S (1) [CRETE]

Titus 1:12 One of C own prophets has said it G899S

CRETES, CRETIANS (KJV) CRETANS

CREVICE (1) [CREVICES]

Jer 13:4 hide it there in a c in the rocks. H5932

CREVICES (2) [CREVICE]

Isa 7:19 the steep ravines and in the c in the rocks, H5932
Jer 16:16 hill and from the c of the rocks. H5932

CRIB (KJV) MANGER

CRICKET (1)

Lev 11:22 kind of locust, katydid, c or grasshopper. H3005

CRIED (95) [CRY]

Ge 41:55 famine, the people c to Pharaoh for food. H7590
Ge 45:1 attendants, and he c out, "Have everyone H7924
Ex 2:23 groaned in their slavery and c out, H2410
Ex 8:12 Moses c out to the LORD about the frogs he H7590
Ex 14:10 They were terrified and c out to the LORD. H7590
Ex 15:25 Then Moses c out to the LORD, and the H7590
Ex 17:4 Then Moses c out to the LORD, "What am I H7590
Nu 11:2 When the people c out to Moses, he H7590
Nu 12:13 So Moses c out to the LORD, "Please, God H7590
Nu 16:22 Moses and Aaron fell facedown and c out, H606
Nu 20:16 when we c out to the LORD, he heard H7590
Dt 26:7 Then we c out to the LORD, the God of our H7590
Jos 24:7 But they c to the LORD for help, and he put H7590
Jdg 3:9 But when they c out to the LORD, he raised H2410
Jdg 3:15 Again the Israelites c out to the LORD, and H2410
Jdg 4:3 twenty years, they c to the LORD for help. H7590
Jdg 5:28 behind the lattice she c out, 'Why is his H3291
Jdg 6:6 that they c out to the LORD for help. H2410
Jdg 6:7 When the Israelites c out to the LORD H2410
Jdg 10:10 Then the Israelites c out to the LORD, "We H2410
Jdg 10:12 oppressed you and you c to me for help, H7590
Jdg 11:35 saw her, he tore his clothes and c, "Oh no, H606
Jdg 14:17 She c the whole seven days of the feast H1134
Jdg 15:18 was very thirsty, he c out to the LORD, H7924
Jdg 21:3 God of Israel," they c, "why has this H606
1Sa 5:10 the people of Ekron c out, "They have H2410
1Sa 7:9 He c out to the LORD on Israel's behalf H2410
1Sa 12:8 they c to the LORD for help, and the H2410
1Sa 12:10 They c out to the LORD and said, 'We have H2410
1Sa 15:11 and he c out to the LORD all that night. H2410
1Sa 28:12 she c out at the top of her voice and said H2410
2Sa 19:4 The king covered his face and c aloud, "O H2410
2Sa 22:42 They c for help, but there was no one to H8775
1Ki 13:2 word of the LORD he c out against the altar H7924
1Ki 13:4 the man of God c out against the altar H7924
1Ki 13:21 He c out to the man of God who had come H7924
1Ki 17:20 Then he c out to the LORD, "LORD my God H7924
1Ki 17:21 the boy three times and c out to the LORD, H7924
1Ki 18:39 they fell prostrate and c, "The LORD— H606
1Ki 22:32 attack him, but when Jehoshaphat c out, H2410
2Ki 2:12 Elisha saw this and c out, "My father! My H7590
2Ki 4:1 company of the prophets c out to Elisha, H7590
2Ki 4:40 began to eat it, they c out, "Man of God, H7590
2Ki 6:5 he c out. "It was borrowed H7590
2Ki 6:26 on the wall, a woman c to him, "Help me, H7590
2Ki 13:14 he c. "The chariots and H606
1Ch 4:10 Jabez c out to the God of Israel, "Oh, that H7924
1Ch 5:20 because they c out to him during the H2410
2Ch 13:14 Then they c out to the LORD. H7590
2Ch 18:31 but Jehoshaphat c out, and the LORD H2410
2Ch 32:20 Isaiah son of Amoz c out in prayer to H2410
Ne 9:4 They c out with loud voices to the LORD H2410
Ne 9:27 they were oppressed they c out to you. H7590
Ne 9:28 And when they c out to you again, you H2410
Job 29:12 because I rescued the poor who c for help, H8775
Ps 18:6 called to the LORD; I c to my God for help. H8775
Ps 18:41 They c for help, but there was no one to H8775
Ps 22:5 To you they c out and were saved; in you H2410
Ps 30:8 I called; to the Lord I c for mercy: H2858
Ps 31:17 for I have c out to you; but let the H7924
Ps 66:17 I c out to him with my mouth; his praise H7924
Ps 77:1 I c out to God for help; I cried out H7590+7754
Ps 77:1 to God for help; I c out to God to hear me. H7754
Ps 107:6 Then they c out to the LORD in their trouble H7590
Ps 107:13 Then they c to the LORD in their trouble H2410
Ps 107:19 Then they c to the LORD in their trouble H2410
Ps 107:28 Then they c out to the LORD in their trouble H7590
Ps 118:5 When hard pressed, I c to the LORD; he H7924
Ps 137:7 "Tear it down," they c, "tear it down to its H606
Isa 6:5 I c. "I am ruined! For I am a H606
Isa 38:14 I c like a swift or thrush, I moaned like a H7627
Eze 11:13 I fell facedown and c out in a loud voice, H2410
Am 7:2 the land clean, I c out, "Sovereign LORD, H606
Am 7:5 Then I c out, "Sovereign LORD, I beg you H606
Jnh 1:5 afraid and each c out to his own god. H2410
Jnh 1:14 Then they c out to the LORD, "Please, LORD H7924
Mt 14:26 "It's a ghost," they said, and c out in fear. G3189
Mt 14:30 beginning to sink, c out, "Lord, save me!" G3189
Mt 27:46 the afternoon Jesus c out in a loud voice, G331
Mt 27:50 And when Jesus had c out again in a G3189
Mk 1:23 was possessed by an impure spirit c out, G371
Mk 3:11 they fell down before him and c out, "You G3189
Mk 6:49 they thought he was a ghost. They c out, G371
Mk 15:34 the afternoon Jesus c out in a loud voice, G1066
Lk 4:33 He c out at the top of his voice G371
Lk 8:28 he saw Jesus, he c out and fell at his feet G371
Jn 1:15 He c out, saying, "This is the one I spoke G3189
Jn 7:28 teaching in the temple courts, c out, "Yes, G3189
Jn 12:44 Then Jesus c out, "Whoever believes in G3189
Jn 20:16 turned toward him and c out in Aramaic, G3306
Ac 7:60 fell on his knees and c out, G3189+5889+3489
Rev 7:10 And they c out in a loud voice: "Salvation G3189
Rev 12:2 was pregnant and c out in pain as she G3189
Rev 19:4 seated on the throne. And they c: "Amen, G3306
Rev 19:17 who c in a loud voice to all the birds G3189

CRIES (26) [CRY]

Ge 4:10 Your brother's blood c out to me from the H7590
Nu 16:34 At their c, all the Israelites around them H7754
Job 30:24 broken man when he c for help in his H8780
Job 31:38 "if my land c out against me and all its H2410
Ps 9:12 he does not ignore the c of the afflicted. H7591
Ps 22:1 saving me, so far from my c of anguish? H1821
Ps 47:1 all you nations; shout to God with c of joy. H7754
Pr 1:21 on top of the wall she c out, at the city H7924
Pr 8:3 into the city, at the entrance, she c aloud: H8264
Isa 5:7 righteousness, but heard c of distress. H7591
Isa 15:5 My heart c out over Moab; her fugitives H2410
Isa 26:17 to give birth writhes and c out in her pain, H2410
Isa 46:7 Even though someone c out to it, it H7590
Isa 56:12 each one c, "let me get wine! Let NDT
Jer 30:5 the LORD says: " 'C of fear are heard H7754
Jer 46:12 of your shame; your c will fill the earth. H7424
Jer 48:3 C of anguish arise from Horonaim H7754+7591
Jer 48:3 Horonaim, c of great havoc and destruction. NDT
Jer 48:5 anguished c over the destruction H7591
Hos 8:2 Israel c out to me, 'Our God, we H2410
Am 1:14 her fortresses amid war c on the day of H9558
Am 2:2 great tumult amid war c and the blast of H9558

Am 5:16 in all the streets and c of anguish in every H606
Ro 9:27 Isaiah c out concerning Israel: "Though G3189
Heb 5: 7 with fervent c and tears to the one G3199
Jas 5: 4 The c of the harvesters have reached the G1068

CRIME (18) [CRIMES, CRIMINAL, CRIMINALS]

Ge 31:36 "What is my c?" he asked Laban. H7322
Dt 19:15 accused of any c or offense they may H6411
Dt 19:16 takes the stand to accuse someone of a c, H6240
Dt 25: 2 with the number of lashes the c deserves, H8402
Jdg 9:24 in order that the c *against* Jerub-Baal's H2805
Jdg 20:12 "What about this **awful** c that was H8288
1Sa 20: 1 What is my c? How have I H6411
Ezr 6:11 And for **this** *c* their house is to be made a AIT
Ps 69:27 Charge them with c upon crime; do not let H6411
Ps 69:27 Charge them with crime upon c; do not let H6411
Ecc 8:11 the sentence for a c is not quickly H5126+8288
Jer 37:18 "What c *have I* **committed** against you H2627
Mt 27:23 What c has he committed?" asked G2805
Mk 15:14 What c has he committed?" asked G2805
Lk 23:22 What c has this man committed? G2805
Ac 18:14 about some misdemeanor or serious c, G4815
Ac 24:20 should state what c they found in me when G93
Ac 28:18 I was not guilty of any c **deserving** death. G162

CRIMES (6) [CRIME]

Ecc 8:12 commits a hundred c may live a long time H8273
Jer 18:23 Do not forgive their c or blot out their sins H6411
Jer 41:11 him heard about all the c Ishmael son of H8288
Hos 7: 1 exposed and the c *of* Samaria revealed. H8288
Ac 25:18 not charge him *with* any *of* the c I had G4505
Rev 18: 5 to heaven, and God has remembered her c. G93

CRIMINAL (4) [CRIME]

Lk 23:40 But the other c rebuked him. "Don't you fear NDT
Jn 18:30 "If he were not a c," they replied G2805+4472
2Ti 2: 9 to the point of being chained like a c. G2806
1Pe 4:15 a murderer or thief or *any other kind of* c, G2804

CRIMINALS (4) [CRIME]

1Ki 1:21 my son Solomon will be treated as c." H2629
Lk 23:32 Two other men, *both* c, were also led out G2806
Lk 23:33 along with the c—one on his right, G2806
Lk 23:39 One *of* the c who hung there hurled G2806

CRIMSON (5)

2Ch 2: 7 in purple, c and blue yarn, and H4147
2Ch 2:14 purple and blue and c yarn and fine linen H4147
2Ch 3:14 of blue, purple and c yarn and fine linen H4147
Isa 1:18 though they are red as c, they shall be H9355
Isa 63: 1 from Bozrah, with his garments **stained** c? H2808

CRINGE (3)

Ps 66: 3 power that your enemies c before you. H3950
Ps 81:15 who hate the LORD *would* c before him, H3950
Isa 10: 4 will remain but *to* c among the captives H4156

CRIPPLED (8)

Lev 21:19 no man with a c foot or hand, H8691
Mt 15:30 the blind, the c, the mute and many G3245
Mt 15:31 mute speaking, the c made well, the G3245
Mt 18: 8 enter life maimed or c than to have two G6000
Mk 9:45 you to enter life c than to have two feet G6000
Lk 13:11 was there *who had been* c by a spirit G2400+819
Lk 14:13 invite the poor, the c, the lame, the blind, G401
Lk 14:21 bring in the poor, the c, the blind and the G401

CRISIS (1)

1Co 7:26 Because of the present c, I think that it is G340

CRISPUS (2)

Ac 18: 8 C, the synagogue leader, and his entire G3214
1Co 1:14 baptize any of you except C and Gaius, G3214

CRITICAL (1) [CRITICISM]

1Sa 13: 6 their situation was c and that their army H7639

CRITICALLY (1) [CRITICISM]

1Sa 31: 3 overtook him, they wounded him c. H4394

CRITICISM (1) [CRITICAL, CRITICALLY, CRITICIZED]

2Co 8:20 We want to avoid any c of the way we G3699

CRITICIZED (1) [CRITICISM]

Ac 11: 2 the circumcised believers c him G1359

CROCUS (1)

Isa 35: 1 will rejoice and blossom. Like the c, H2483

CROOKED (11)

Dt 32: 5 they are a warped and c generation. H7350
Ps 125: 5 those who turn to c **ways** the LORD will H6824
Pr 2:15 whose paths are c and who are devious in H6836
Pr 8: 8 are just; none of them *is* c or perverse. H7349
Pr 10: 9 but *whoever* **takes** c paths will be found H6835
Ecc 1:15 *What* **is** c cannot be straightened; what is H6430
Ecc 7:13 Who can straighten what *he has* **made** c? H6430
Isa 59: 8 *They have* **turned** them *into* c roads; no H6835
La 3: 9 blocks of stone; *he has* **made** my paths c. H6390
Lk 3: 5 The c *roads* shall become straight, the G5021
Php 2:15 fault in a warped and c generation." G1406

CROP (15) [CROPS]

Ge 47:24 But when the c **comes in**, give a fifth of it H9311
Lev 1:16 He is to remove the c and the feathers H5263
Lev 25:22 eat from the old c and will continue to H9311
Isa 5: 2 Then he looked for a c of good grapes H6913
Hab 3:17 though the olive c fails and the fields H5126
Mt 13: 8 where it produced a c—a hundred, G2843
Mt 13:23 This is the one *who* **produces a c**, yielding G2844
Mt 21:41 him his share *of* the c at harvest time." G2843
Mk 4: 8 grew and produced a c, some multiplying G2843
Mk 4:20 accept it, and **produce a c**—some thirty G2844
Lk 8: 8 It came up and yielded a c, a hundred G2843
Lk 8:15 retain it, and by persevering **produce a c**. G2844
Jn 4:36 a wage and harvests a c for eternal life, G2843
Heb 6: 7 it and that produces a c useful to those G1083
Jas 5: 7 waits for the land to yield its valuable c, G2843

CROPS (46) [CROP]

Ge 4:12 ground, it will no longer yield its c for you. H3946
Ge 26:12 Isaac **planted** c in that land and the same H2445
Ex 23:10 are to sow your fields and harvest the c, H9311
Ex 23:16 the firstfruits of the c you sow in your field. H5126
Ex 23:16 when you gather in your c from the field. H5126
Lev 23:39 after you have gathered the c *of* the land H9311
Lev 25: 3 prune your vineyards and gather their c. H9311
Lev 25:15 the number of years left for **harvesting** c. H9311
Lev 25:16 being sold to you is the number of c. H9311
Lev 25:20 year if we do not plant or harvest our c?" H9311
Lev 26: 4 ground will yield its c and the trees their H3292
Lev 26:20 because your soil will not yield its c, nor H3292
Dt 7:13 of your womb, the c *of* your land—your H7262
Dt 22: 9 not only the c you plant but also the fruit H4852
Dt 28: 4 the c *of* your land and the young of H7262
Dt 28:11 your livestock and the c *of* your ground— H7262
Dt 28:18 be cursed, and the c *of* your land, and the H7262
Dt 28:42 over all your trees and the c *of* your land. H7262
Dt 28:51 livestock and the c *of* your land until you H7262
Dt 30: 9 of your livestock and the c *of* your land. H7262
Jdg 6: 3 Whenever the Israelites **planted** *their* c H2445
Jdg 6: 4 land and ruined the c all the way to Gaza H3292
2Sa 9:10 to farm the land for him and bring in the c, NDT
Ne 10:35 the firstfruits of our c and of every fruit tree. H141
Ne 10:37 we will bring a tithe of our c to the Levites, H141
Job 31: 8 I have sown, and may my c be uprooted. H7368
Ps 65:10 you soften it with showers and bless its c. H7542
Ps 72:16 May the c flourish like Lebanon and H7262S
Ps 78:46 He gave their c to the grasshopper, their H3292
Pr 3: 9 with the firstfruits of all your c; H9311
Pr 10: 5 *He who* **gathers** c in summer is a prudent H112
Pr 28: 3 poor is like a driving rain that leaves no c. H4312
Jer 7:20 of the field and on the c *of* your land— H7262
Jer 35: 9 to live in or had vineyards, fields or c. H2446
Eze 34:27 their fruit and the ground will yield its c; H3292
Eze 34:29 them a **land** renowned **for** its c, H4760
Eze 36:30 the fruit of the trees and the c *of* the field, H9482
Am 7: 1 just as the **late** c were coming up. H4381
Hag 1:10 withheld their dew and the earth its c. H3292
Zec 8:12 the ground will produce its c, and the H3292
Mal 3:11 pests from devouring your c, H7262+2021+141
Lk 12:17 I have no place to store my c.' G2843
Ac 14:17 rain from heaven and c in their seasons; G2845
2Ti 2: 6 be the first to receive a share *of* the c. G2843
Jas 5:18 gave rain, and the earth produced its c. G2843
Rev 22: 2 bearing twelve **c of fruit**, yielding its fruit G2843

CROSS (90) [ACROSS, CROSSED, CROSSES, CROSSING, CROSSINGS]

Ex 30:14 All who **c over**, those twenty years old or H6296
Nu 32: 5 *Do* not **make** us c the Jordan. H6296
Nu 32:21 you who are armed c **over** the Jordan H6296
Nu 32:27 *will* c **over** to fight before the LORD H6296
Nu 32:29 c **over** the Jordan with you before the LORD, H6296
Nu 32:30 But if *they do* not c **over** with you armed H6296
Nu 32:32 We *will* c **over** before the LORD *into* Canaan H6296
Nu 33:51 'When you c the Jordan into Canaan, H6296
Nu 34: 4 c south of Scorpion Pass, continue on to H6015
Nu 35:10 'When you c the Jordan into Canaan, H6296
Dt 2:13 "Now get up and c the Zered Valley." H6296
Dt 2:24 "Set out now and c the Arnon Gorge. H6296
Dt 2:29 until *we* c the Jordan into the land the H6296
Dt 3:18 *must* c **over** ahead of the other Israelites. H6296
Dt 3:27 since *you are* not *going to* c this Jordan. H6296
Dt 4:21 swore that I *would* not c the Jordan and H6296
Dt 4:22 in this land; I *will* not c the Jordan; but H6296
Dt 4:22 you *are about to* c **over** and take H6296
Dt 9: 1 You *are* now *about to* c the Jordan to go H6296
Dt 11:31 You *are about to* c the Jordan to enter H6296
Dt 12:10 But *you will* c the Jordan and settle in the H6296
Dt 30:13 "Who *will* c the sea to get it and proclaim H6296
Dt 31: 2 said to me, '*You shall* not c the Jordan. H6296
Dt 31: 3 your God himself *will* c **over** ahead of you. H6296
Dt 31: 3 Joshua also *will* c **over** ahead of you, as H6296
Dt 34: 4 your eyes, but *you will* not c **over** into it." H6296
Jos 1: 2 get ready *to* c the Jordan River into the H6296
Jos 1:11 days from now you *will* c the Jordan here H6296
Jos 1:14 *must* c **over** ahead of your fellow Israelites H6296
Jos 3:14 the people broke camp *to* c the Jordan, H6296
Jdg 3:28 to Moab; they allowed no one to c **over**. H6296
Jdg 12: 5 Ephraim said, "*Let me* c **over**," the men of H6296
1Sa 14: 4 Jonathan intended to c to reach the H6296
1Sa 14: 8 we *will* c **over** toward them and let them H6296
1Sa 30:10 them were too exhausted *to* c the valley, H6296
2Sa 17:16 **c over without fail**, or the H6296+6296
2Sa 17:21 "Set out and c the river at once H6296
2Sa 19:31 down from Rogelim *to* c the Jordan with H6296
2Sa 19:33 "**C over** with me and stay with me in H6296
2Sa 19:36 Your servant *will* c **over** the Jordan with the H6296
2Sa 19:37 *Let him* c **over** with my lord the king H6296
2Sa 19:38 "Kimham *shall* c **over** with me, and I H6296
1Ki 2:37 The day you leave and c the Kidron Valley H6296
Ps 104: 9 You set a boundary *they* cannot c; never H6296
Isa 11:15 so that *anyone can* c **over** in sandals. H2005
Isa 23: 6 **C over** to Tarshish; wail, *you* people of the H6296
Isa 23:12 c **over** *to* Cyprus; even there you will H6296
Isa 51:10 sea so that the redeemed *might* c **over**? H6296
Jer 2:10 **C over** *to* the coasts of Cyprus and look H6296
Jer 5:22 the sea, an everlasting barrier *it* cannot c. H6296
Jer 5:22 they may roar, but *they* cannot c it. H6296
Jer 9:12 laid waste like a desert that no *one can* c? H6296
Jer 41:10 set out to c **over** to the Ammonites. H6296
Eze 33:28 desolate so that no *one will* c them. H6296
Eze 47: 5 now it was a river that I could not c H6296
Eze 47: 5 to swim in—a river that no *one could* c. H6296
Mt 8:18 he gave orders *to* c to the other side of the G599
Mt 10:38 not take up their c and follow me is not G5089
Mt 16:24 take up their c and follow me. G5089
Mt 27:32 and they forced him to carry the c. G5089
Mt 27:40 Come down from the c, if you are the Son G5089
Mt 27:42 Let him come down now from the c, and G5089
Mk 8:34 take up their c and follow me. G5089
Mk 15:21 country, and they forced him to carry the c. G5089
Mk 15:30 come down from the c and save yourself!" G5089
Mk 15:32 come down now from the c, that we may G5089
Lk 9:23 take up their c daily and follow me. G5089
Lk 14:27 not carry their c and follow me cannot G5089
Lk 16:26 nor *can anyone* c **over** from there to us. G1385
Lk 23:26 put the c on him and made him carry G5089
Jn 19:17 Carrying his own c, he went out to the G5089
Jn 19:19 a notice prepared and fastened to the c. G5089
Jn 19:25 Near the c of Jesus stood his mother, his G5089
Ac 2:23 put him to death *by* **nailing** him **to** *the* c. G4699
Ac 5:30 whom you killed by hanging him on a c. G3833
Ac 10:39 They killed him by hanging him on a c, G3833
Ac 13:29 him down from the c and laid him in a G3833
1Co 1:17 lest the c of Christ be emptied of its power G5089
1Co 1:18 For the message *of* the c is foolishness to G5089
Gal 5:11 case the offense *of* the c has been G5089
Gal 6:12 avoid being persecuted *for* the c of Christ. G5089
Gal 6:14 boast except in the c of our Lord Jesus G5089
Eph 2:16 both of them to God through the c, G5089
Php 2: 8 obedient to death—even death *on* a c! G5089
Php 3:18 many live as enemies *of* the c of Christ. G5089
Col 1:20 peace through his blood, *shed on* the c. G5089
Col 2:14 he has taken it away, nailing it to the c. G5089
Col 2:15 of them, triumphing over them by **the** c. G899S
Heb 12: 2 the joy set before him he endured the c, G5089
1Pe 2:24 in his body on the c, so that we might die G3833

CROSS-EXAMINED (1) [EXAMINE]

Ac 12:19 *he* c the guards and ordered that they be G373

CROSS-EXAMINES (1) [EXAMINE]

Pr 18:17 until someone comes forward and c. H2983

CROSSBAR (2) [CROSSBARS]

Ex 26:28 The center c is to extend from end to end H1378
Ex 36:33 They made the center c so that it extended H1378

CROSSBARS (12) [CROSSBAR]

Ex 26:26 "Also make c *of* acacia wood: five for the H1378
Ex 26:29 gold and make gold rings to hold the c. H1378
Ex 26:29 Also overlay the c with gold. H1378
Ex 35:11 frames, c, posts and bases; H1378
Ex 36:31 They also made c *of* acacia wood: five H1378
Ex 36:34 gold and made gold rings to hold the c. H1378
Ex 36:34 They also overlaid the c with gold. H1378
Ex 39:33 its clasps, frames, c, posts and bases; H1378
Ex 40:18 inserted the c and set up the posts. H1378
Nu 3:36 the frames of the tabernacle, its c, posts, H1378
Nu 4:31 of the tabernacle, its c, posts and bases, H1378
Jer 27: 2 yoke out of straps and c and put it on your H4574

CROSSED (59) [CROSS]

Ge 31:21 fled with all he had, c the Euphrates River H6296
Ge 32:10 I had only my staff *when I* c this Jordan H6296
Ge 32:22 his eleven sons and c the ford of the H6296
Ex 38:26 everyone who *had* c **over** to those counted H6296
Dt 2:13 the Zered Valley." So *we* c the valley. H6296
Dt 2:14 Barnea until *we* c the Zered Valley. H6296
Dt 27: 2 When *you have* c the Jordan into the land H6296
Dt 27: 3 this law when you *have* c **over** to enter the H6296
Dt 27: 4 And when you *have* c the Jordan, set up H6296
Dt 27:12 When you *have* c the Jordan, these tribes H6296
Jos 3:16 So the people c **over** opposite Jericho. H6296
Jos 4: 7 When it c the Jordan, the waters of the H6296
Jos 4:11 as soon as all of them *had* c, the ark H6296
Jos 4:12 the half-tribe of Manasseh c **over**, H6296
Jos 4:13 armed for battle c **over** before the LORD to H6296
Jos 4:22 'Israel c the Jordan on dry ground.' H6296
Jos 4:23 Jordan before you until you *had* c **over**. H6296
Jos 4:23 dried it up before us until we *had* c **over**. H6296
Jos 5: 1 before the Israelites until they *had* c **over**, H6296
Jos 15: 3 c south of Scorpion Pass, continued on to H3655
Jos 15:10 down to Beth Shemesh and c *to* Timnah. H6296
Jos 16: 2 c **over** to the territory of the Arkites in H6296
Jos 18:13 From there it c to the south slope of Luz H6296
Jos 24:11 " 'Then *you* c the Jordan and came to H6296

Jdg 6:33 joined forces and **c over** the Jordan and H6296
Jdg 8: 4 the pursuit, came to the Jordan and **c** it. H6296
Jdg 10: 9 The Ammonites also **c** the Jordan to fight H6296
Jdg 11:29 *He* **c** Gilead and Manasseh, passed H6296
Jdg 12: 1 called out, and *they* **c over** to Zaphon. H6296
Jdg 12: 3 my life in my hands and **c** over to fight the H6296
1Sa 13: 7 Hebrews even **c** the Jordan *to* the land of H6296
1Sa 26:13 Then David **c over** *to* the other side and H6296
2Sa 2:29 *They* **c** the Jordan, continued through the H6296
2Sa 10:17 **c** the Jordan and went to Helam. H6296
2Sa 15:23 The king also **c** the Kidron Valley, and all H6296
2Sa 17:20 answered them, "*They* **c over** the brook." H6296
2Sa 17:22 people with him set out and **c** the Jordan. H6296
2Sa 17:22 no one was left who *had* not **c** the Jordan. H6296
2Sa 17:24 Absalom **c** the Jordan with all the H6296
2Sa 19:18 *They* **c** *at* the ford to take the king's H6296
2Sa 19:18 When Shimei son of Gera **c** the Jordan H6296
2Sa 19:39 So all the people **c** the Jordan, and then H6296
2Sa 19:39 the Jordan, and then the king **c over**. H6296
2Sa 19:40 When the king **c over** to Gilgal, Kimham H6296
2Sa 19:40 over to Gilgal, Kimham **c** with him. H6296
2Ki 2: 8 the two of them **c over** on dry ground. H6296
2Ki 2: 9 When they *had* **c**, Elijah said to Elisha H6296
2Ki 2:14 to the right and to the left, and he **c over**. H6296
1Ch 12:15 It was they who **c** the Jordan in the first H6296
1Ch 19:17 he gathered all Israel and **c** the Jordan H6296
Mt 9: 1 **c over** and came to his own town. G1385
Mt 14:34 *When they had* **c over**, they landed at G1385
Mk 5:21 *When* Jesus *had* again **c over** by boat to G1385
Mk 6:53 *When they had* **c over**, they landed at G1385
Mk 8:13 back into the boat and **c** to the other side. G599
Jn 5:24 be judged but *has* **c over** from death to G3553
Jn 6: 1 Jesus **c** to the far shore of the Sea of G599
Jn 18: 1 with his disciples and **c** the Kidron Valley. G4305
Ac 20:15 The day after that *we* **c over** to Samos G4125

CROSSES (2) [CROSS]

Ex 30:13 Each *one* who **c over** to those already H6296
Jn 19:31 bodies left on the **c** during the Sabbath, G5089

CROSSING (16) [CROSS]

Ge 48:14 the younger, and **c** his arms, he put his H8506
Nu 32: 7 the Israelites from **c over** into the land the H6296
Dt 4:14 in the land that you *are* **c** the Jordan to H6296
Dt 4:26 the land that you *are* **c** the Jordan to H6296
Dt 6: 1 in the land that you *are* **c** the Jordan to H6296
Dt 11: 8 the land that you *are* **c** the Jordan to H6296
Dt 11:11 But the land you *are* **c** the Jordan to take H6296
Dt 30:18 in the land you *are* **c** the Jordan to enter H6296
Dt 31:13 live in the land you *are* **c** the Jordan to H6296
Dt 32:47 long in the land you *are* **c** the Jordan to H6296
Jos 3: 1 where they camped before **c over**. H6296
Jos 3:17 had completed the **c** on dry ground. H6296
Jos 4: 1 whole nation had finished **c** the Jordan, H6296
2Sa 24: 5 After **c** the Jordan, they camped near H6296
Da 8: 5 **c** the whole earth without touching H6584+7156
Ac 21: 2 We found a ship **c over** to Phoenicia, went G1385

CROSSINGS (1) [CROSS]

Jer 51:32 the **river c** seized, the marshes set on fire H5045

CROSSROADS (2) [ROAD]

Jer 6:16 "Stand at the **c** and look; ask for the H2006
Ob 14 should not wait at the **c** to cut down their H7294

CROUCH (3) [CROUCHES, CROUCHING]

Nu 24: 9 Like a lion *they* **c** and lie down, like a H4156
Job 38:40 when *they* **c** in their dens or lie in wait in H8820
Job 39: 3 *They* **c down** and bring forth their young H4156

CROUCHES (1) [CROUCH]

Ge 49: 9 Like a lion *he* **c** and lies down, like a H4156

CROUCHING (2) [CROUCH]

Ge 4: 7 do what is right, sin *is* **c** at your door; it H8069
Ps 17:12 prey, like a fierce lion **c** in cover. H3782

CROW (1) [CROWED, CROWS]

Jn 18:27 at that moment a rooster *began to* **c**. G5888

CROWD (138) [CROWDED, CROWDING, CROWDS]

Ex 23: 2 "Do not follow the **c** in doing wrong H8041
Ex 23: 2 do not pervert justice by siding with the **c**, H8041
Jdg 6:31 to the hostile **c** around him, H3972+889+6641
2Sa 6:19 each person in the whole **c** *of* Israelites, H2162
2Ch 30:13 A very large **c** of people assembled in H7736
2Ch 30:17 Since many in the **c** had not consecrated H7736
Ezr 10: 1 a large **c** of Israelites—men, H7736
Job 31:34 I so feared the **c** and so dreaded the H2162
Jer 9: 2 all adulterers, a **c** *of* unfaithful people. H6809
Eze 7:11 none of that **c**—none of their wealth H2162
Eze 7:12 for my wrath is on the whole **c**. H2162
Eze 7:13 the whole **c** will not be reversed H2162
Eze 7:14 into battle, for my wrath is on the whole **c**. H2162
Eze 23:42 "The noise of a carefree **c** was around her; H2162
Mt 8:18 When Jesus saw the **c** around him, he G4063
Mt 9: 8 When the **c** saw this, they were filled with G4063
Mt 9:23 saw the noisy **c** and people playing G4063
Mt 9:25 After the **c** had been put outside, he went G4063
Mt 9:33 The **c** was amazed and said, "Nothing G4063
Mt 11: 7 Jesus began to speak *to* the **c** about John: G4063
Mt 12:15 A large **c** followed him, and he healed all G4063
Mt 12:46 While Jesus was still talking *to* the **c**, his G4063
Mt 13:34 all these things *to* the **c** in parables; G4063
Mt 13:36 Then he left the **c** and went into the G4063
Mt 14:14 When Jesus landed and saw a large **c**, he G4063
Mt 14:22 the other side, while he dismissed the **c**. G4063
Mt 15:10 Jesus called the **c** to him and said, "Listen G4063
Mt 15:33 in this remote place to feed such a **c**?" G4063
Mt 15:35 He told the **c** to sit down on the ground. G4063
Mt 15:39 After Jesus had sent the **c** away, he got G4063
Mt 17:14 When they came to the **c**, a man G4063
Mt 20:29 leaving Jericho, a large **c** followed him. G4063
Mt 20:31 The **c** rebuked them and told them to be G4063
Mt 21: 8 A very large **c** spread their cloaks on the G4063
Mt 21:46 they were afraid *of* the **c** because the G4063
Mt 26:47 him was a large **c** armed with swords G4063
Mt 26:55 In that hour Jesus said *to* the **c**, "Am I G4063
Mt 27:15 to release a prisoner chosen *by* the **c**. G4063
Mt 27:17 So when **the c** had gathered, Pilate asked G899S
Mt 27:20 persuaded the **c** to ask for Barabbas G4063
Mt 27:24 washed his hands in front of the **c**. G4063
Mk 2: 4 not get him to Jesus because of the **c**, G4063
Mk 2:13 A large **c** came to him, and he began to G4063
Mk 3: 7 and a large **c** from Galilee followed. G4436
Mk 3: 9 Because of the **c** he told his disciples to G4063
Mk 3:20 and again a **c** gathered, so that he G4063
Mk 3:32 A **c** was sitting around him, and they told G4063
Mk 4: 1 The **c** that gathered around him was so G4063
Mk 4:36 Leaving the **c** behind, they took him along G4063
Mk 5:21 a large **c** gathered around him while he G4063
Mk 5:24 A large **c** followed and pressed around G4063
Mk 5:27 up behind him in the **c** and touched his G4063
Mk 5:30 He turned around in the **c** and asked G4063
Mk 6:34 When Jesus landed and saw a large **c**, he G4063
Mk 6:45 to Bethsaida, while he dismissed the **c**. G4063
Mk 7:14 Again Jesus called the **c** to him and said G4063
Mk 7:17 he had left the **c** and entered the house G4063
Mk 7:33 away from the **c**, Jesus put his G4063
Mk 8: 1 those days another large **c** gathered. G4063
Mk 8: 6 He told the **c** to sit down on the ground G4063
Mk 8:34 Then he called the **c** to him along with G4063
Mk 9:14 they saw a large **c** around them and the G4063
Mk 9:17 A man in the **c** answered, "Teacher, G4063
Mk 9:25 Jesus saw that a **c** was running to the G4063
Mk 10:46 together with a large **c**, were leaving the G4063
Mk 11:18 because the whole **c** was amazed at his G4063
Mk 12:12 But they were afraid *of* the **c**; so they left G4063
Mk 12:37 The large **c** listened to him with delight G4063
Mk 12:41 watched the **c** putting their money G4063
Mk 14:43 With him was a **c** armed with swords and G4063
Mk 15: 8 The **c** came up and asked Pilate to do G4063
Mk 15:11 stirred up the **c** to have Pilate release G4063
Mk 15:15 Wanting to satisfy the **c**, Pilate released G4063
Lk 3:10 "What should we do then?" the **c** asked. G4063
Lk 4:30 right through **the c** and went on his way G899S
Lk 5:19 not find a way to do this because of the **c**, G4063
Lk 5:19 through the tiles into the middle of the **c**, NDT
Lk 5:29 a large **c** of tax collectors and others G4063
Lk 6:17 A large **c** of his disciples was there and a G4063
Lk 7: 9 turning to the **c** following him, he G4063
Lk 7:11 a large **c** went along with him. G4063
Lk 7:12 And a large **c** from the town was with her G4063
Lk 7:24 Jesus began to speak to the **c** about John: G4063
Lk 8: 4 While a large **c** was gathering and G4063
Lk 8:19 not able to get near him because of the **c**. G4063
Lk 8:40 Jesus returned, a **c** welcomed him, for G4063
Lk 9:12 "Send the **c** away so they can go to the G4063
Lk 9:13 unless we go and buy food for all this **c**." G3295
Lk 9:37 from the mountain, a large **c** met him. G4063
Lk 9:38 A man in the **c** called out, "Teacher, I beg G4063
Lk 11:14 been mute spoke, and the **c** was amazed. G4063
Lk 11:27 a woman in the **c** called out, "Blessed G4063
Lk 12: 1 when a **c** of many thousands had G4063
Lk 12:13 Someone in the **c** said to him, "Teacher G4063
Lk 12:54 He said *to* the **c**: "When you see a cloud G4063
Lk 18:36 When he heard the **c** going by, he asked G4063
Lk 19: 3 he was short he could not see over the **c**. G4063
Lk 19:37 the whole **c** of disciples began joyfully to G4436
Lk 19:39 of the Pharisees in the **c** said to Jesus, G4063
Lk 22: 6 over to them when no **c** was present. G4063
Lk 22:47 While he was still speaking a **c** came up G4063
Lk 23: 4 announced to the chief priests and the **c**, G4063
Lk 23:18 But the **whole c** shouted, "Away with this G4101
Jn 5:13 slipped away *into* the **c** that was there. G4063
Jn 6: 2 a great **c of people** followed him G4063
Jn 6: 5 up and saw a great **c** coming toward him, G4063
Jn 6:22 The next day the **c** that had stayed on the G4063
Jn 6:24 Once the **c** realized that neither Jesus nor G4063
Jn 7:20 are demon-possessed," the **c** answered. G4063
Jn 7:31 many in the **c** believed in him. G4063
Jn 7:32 Pharisees heard the **c** whispering such G4063
Jn 12: 9 Meanwhile a large **c** of Jews found out G4063
Jn 12:12 next day the great **c** that had come for the G4063
Jn 12:17 Now the **c** that was with him when he G4063
Jn 12:29 The **c** that was there and heard it said it G4063
Jn 12:34 The **c** spoke up, "We have heard from the G4063
Ac 2: 6 a **c** came together in bewilderment G4436
Ac 2:14 raised his voice and addressed **the c**: G899S
Ac 14:11 When the **c** saw what Paul had done G4063
Ac 14:13 because he and the **c** wanted to offer G4063
Ac 14:14 their clothes and rushed out into the **c**, G4063
Ac 14:18 difficulty keeping the **c** from sacrificing to G4063
Ac 14:19 Antioch and Iconium and won the **c** over. G4063
Ac 16:22 The **c** joined in the attack against Paul G4063
Ac 17: 5 Silas in order to bring them out to the **c**. G1322
Ac 17: 8 the **c** and the city officials were thrown G4063
Ac 18:17 Then **the c** there turned on Sosthenes the G4246S
Ac 19:30 Paul wanted to appear before the **c**, but G1322
Ac 19:33 The Jews in the **c** pushed Alexander to the G4063
Ac 19:35 The city clerk quieted the **c** and said G4063
Ac 21:27 stirred up the whole **c** and seized him, G4063
Ac 21:32 soldiers and ran down to **the c**. G899S
Ac 21:34 Some in the **c** shouted one thing and G4063
Ac 21:36 The **c** that followed kept G4436+3836+3295
Ac 21:40 stood on the steps and motioned *to* the **c**. G3295
Ac 22:22 The **c** listened to Paul until he said this NDT
Ac 24:12 stirring up a **c** in the synagogues or G4063
Ac 24:18 There was no **c** with me, nor was I G4063

CROWDED (4) [CROWD]

Jdg 16:27 Now the temple *was* **c** *with* men and H4848
2Ki 10:21 *They* **c into** the temple of Baal until it was H995
Jer 26: 9 And all the people **c** around Jeremiah in H7735
Da 3:27 royal advisers **c around** them. A10359

CROWDING (4) [CROWD]

Mk 3: 9 him, to keep *the people* from **c** him. G2567
Mk 5:31 "You see the people **c against** you," G5315
Lk 5: 1 the people *were* **c around** him and G2130
Lk 8:45 the people *are* **c** and pressing against you G5309

CROWDS (27) [CROWD]

Mt 4:25 Large **c** from Galilee, the Decapolis G4063
Mt 5: 1 Now when Jesus saw the **c**, he went up G4063
Mt 7:28 the **c** were amazed at his teaching, G4063
Mt 8: 1 the mountainside, large **c** followed him. G4063
Mt 9:36 When he saw the **c**, he had compassion G4063
Mt 13: 2 Such large **c** gathered around him that he G4063
Mt 14:13 the **c** followed him on foot from the towns. G4063
Mt 14:15 Send the **c** away, so they can go to the G4063
Mt 15:30 Great **c** came to him, bringing the lame G4063
Mt 19: 2 Large **c** followed him, and he healed them G4063
Mt 21: 9 The **c** that went ahead of him and those G4063
Mt 21:11 The **c** answered, "This is Jesus, the G4063
Mt 22:33 When the **c** heard this, they were G4063
Mt 23: 1 Then Jesus said *to* the **c** and to his G4063
Mk 10: 1 Again **c of people** came to him, and as G4063
Lk 3: 7 John said *to* the **c** coming out to be G4063
Lk 5:15 so that **c** of people came to hear him and G4498
Lk 8:42 was on his way, the **c** almost crushed him. G4063
Lk 9:11 the **c** learned about it and followed G4063
Lk 9:18 he asked them, "Who do the **c** say I am?" G4063
Lk 11:29 As the **c** increased, Jesus said, "This is a G4063
Lk 14:25 Large **c** were traveling with Jesus, and G4063
Jn 7:12 Among the **c** there was widespread G4063
Ac 5:16 **C** gathered also from the towns around G4436
Ac 8: 6 When the **c** heard Philip and saw the G4063
Ac 13:45 When the Jews saw the **c**, they were filled G4063
Ac 17:13 agitating the **c** and stirring them up. G4063

CROWED (3) [CROW]

Mt 26:74 know the man!" Immediately a rooster **c**. G5888
Mk 14:72 the rooster **c** the second time. G5888
Lk 22:60 Just as he was speaking, the rooster **c**. G5888

CROWN (55) [CROWNED, CROWNS]

Jdg 9: 6 the pillar in Shechem *to* **c** Abimelek king. H4887
2Sa 1:10 And I took the **c** that was on his head H5694
2Sa 12:30 David took the **c** from their king's head H6498
2Ki 11:12 out the king's son and put the **c** on him; H5694
1Ch 20: 2 David took the **c** from the head of their H6498
2Ch 11:22 son of Maakah as **c** prince among his H8031
2Ch 23:11 out the king's son and put the **c** on him; H5694
Est 1:11 wearing her royal **c**, in order to display her H4195
Est 2:17 So he set a royal **c** on her head and made H4195
Est 8:15 a large **c** *of* gold and a purple robe of fine H6498
Job 2: 7 the soles of his feet to the **c of his head**. H7721
Job 19: 9 honor and removed the **c** *from* my head. H6498
Job 31:36 on my shoulder, I would put it on like a **c**. H6498
Ps 21: 3 placed a **c** *of* pure gold on his head H6498
Ps 65:11 *You* **c** the year with your bounty, and your H6497
Ps 89:39 servant and have defiled his **c** in the dust. H5694
Ps 132:18 his head will be adorned with a radiant **c**." H5694
Pr 4: 9 head and present you with a glorious **c**." H6498
Pr 10: 6 Blessings **c** the head of the righteous, but H4200
Pr 12: 4 wife of noble character is her husband's **c**, H6498
Pr 14:24 The wealth of the wise is their **c**, but the H6498
Pr 16:31 Gray hair is a **c** *of* splendor; it is attained H6498
Pr 17: 6 Children's children are a **c** *to* the aged H6498
Pr 27:24 a **c** is not secure for all generations. H5694
SS 3:11 Look on King Solomon wearing a **c**, the H6498
SS 3:11 the **c** with which his mother crowned him on NDT
Isa 28: 5 day the LORD Almighty will be a glorious **c**, H7619
Isa 35:10 singing; everlasting joy will **c** their heads. H6584
Isa 51:11 singing; everlasting joy will **c** their heads. H6584
Isa 61: 3 bestow on them a **c of beauty** instead of H6996
Isa 62: 3 You will be a **c** *of* splendor in the LORD's H6498
La 5:16 The **c** has fallen *from* our head. Woe to H6498
Eze 16:12 your ears and a beautiful **c** on your head. H6498
Eze 21:26 remove the **c**. It will not be as it H6498
Eze 21:27 **The c** will not be restored until he to H2296S
Zec 6:11 Take the silver and gold and make a **c** H6498
Zec 6:14 The **c** will be given to Heldai, Tobijah H6498
Zec 9:16 will sparkle in his land like jewels in a **c**. H5694
Mt 27:29 twisted together a **c** of thorns and set it on G5109
Mk 15:17 twisted together a **c** of thorns and set it on G5109
Jn 19: 2 twisted together a **c** of thorns and put it G5109

Jn 19: 5 came out wearing the c of thorns and the G5109
1Co 9:25 They do it to get a c that will not last, but G5109
1Co 9:25 we do it to get a c that will last forever. NDT
Php 4: 1 long for, my joy and c, stand firm in the G5109
1Th 2:19 the c in which we will glory in the G5109
2Ti 2: 5 *does* not **receive the victor's** c except G5110
2Ti 4: 8 is in store for me the c of righteousness, G5109
Jas 1:12 will receive the c of life that the Lord G5109
1Pe 5: 4 you will receive the c of glory that will G5109
Rev 2:10 I will give you life as your **victor's** c. G5109
Rev 3:11 you have, so that no one will take your c. G5109
Rev 6: 2 he was given a c, and he rode out as G5109
Rev 12: 1 under her feet and a c of twelve stars on G5109
Rev 14:14 a son of man with a c of gold on his head G5109

CROWNED (5) [CROWN]
Ps 8: 5 the angels and c them *with* glory and H6497
Pr 14:18 the prudent *are* c *with* knowledge. H4194
SS 3:11 which his mother c him on the day of his H6497
Heb 2: 7 *you* c them with glory and honor G5110
Heb 2: 9 *now* c with glory and honor because he G5110

CROWNS (13) [CROWN]
Ps 68:21 the hairy c *of* those who go on in their H7721
Ps 103: 4 from the pit and c you *with* love and H6497
Ps 149: 4 his people; *he* c the humble with victory. H6995
SS 7: 5 Your head c you like Mount Carmel. H6584
Isa 23: 8 the **bestower of** c, whose merchants H6497
Jer 13:18 your glorious c will fall from your H6498
Eze 23:42 her sister and beautiful c on their heads. H6498
Rev 4: 4 in white and had c of gold on their heads. G5109
Rev 4:10 They lay their c before the throne and say G5109
Rev 9: 7 heads they wore something like c of gold, G5109
Rev 12: 3 ten horns and seven c on its heads. G1343
Rev 13: 1 with ten c on its horns, and on G1343
Rev 19:12 blazing fire, and on his head are many c. G1343

CROWS (8) [CROW]
Mt 26:34 before the rooster c, you will disown me G5888
Mt 26:75 "Before the rooster c, you will disown me G5888
Mk 13:35 midnight, or **when the rooster** c, or at dawn G231
Mk 14:30 before the rooster c twice you yourself will G5888
Mk 14:72 "Before the rooster c twice you will disown G5888
Lk 22:34 before the rooster c today, you will deny G5888
Lk 22:61 "Before the rooster c today, you will G5888
Jn 13:38 before the rooster c, you will disown me G5888

CRUCIBLE (3)
Ps 12: 6 like silver purified in a c, like gold refined H6612
Pr 17: 3 The c for silver and the furnace for gold H5214
Pr 27:21 The c for silver and the furnace for gold H5214

CRUCIFIED (36) [CRUCIFY]
Mt 20:19 Gentiles to be mocked and flogged and c. G5090
Mt 26: 2 Son of Man will be handed over to *be* c." G5090
Mt 27:26 flogged, and handed him over to *be* c. G5090
Mt 27:35 *When they had* c him, they divided up his G5090
Mt 27:38 Two rebels *were* c with him, one on his G5090
Mt 27:44 the rebels who *were* c **with** him also G5365
Mt 28: 5 that you are looking for Jesus, who *was* c. G5090
Mk 15:15 flogged, and handed him over to *be* c. G5090
Mk 15:24 And *they* c him. Dividing up his clothes G5090
Mk 15:25 was nine in the morning *when they* c him. G5090
Mk 15:27 *They* c two rebels with him, one on his G5090
Mk 15:32 Those c **with** him also heaped insults on G5365
Mk 16: 6 Jesus the Nazarene, who *was* c. G5090
Lk 23:23 they insistently demanded that he *be* c, G5090
Lk 23:33 called the Skull, *they* c him there, along G5090
Lk 24: 7 *be* c and on the third day be raised again. G5090
Lk 24:20 be sentenced to death, and *they* c him; G5090
Jn 19:16 Pilate handed him over to them to *be* c. G5090
Jn 19:18 There *they* c him, and with him two others G5090
Jn 19:20 place where Jesus *was* c was near the city G5090
Jn 19:23 When the soldiers c Jesus, they took his G5090
Jn 19:32 the first man who *had been* c **with** Jesus, G5365
Jn 19:41 At the place where Jesus *was* c, there was G5090
Ac 2:36 this Jesus, whom you c, both Lord and G5090
Ac 4:10 whom you c but whom God raised from G5090
Ro 6: 6 our old self *was* c **with** him so that the G5365
1Co 1:13 Christ divided? *Was* Paul c for you? Were G5090
1Co 1:23 we preach Christ c: a stumbling block G5090
1Co 2: 2 with you except Jesus Christ and him c. G5090
1Co 2: 8 *they* would not have c the Lord of glory. G5090
2Co 13: 4 For to be sure, *he was* c in weakness, yet G5090
Gal 2:20 *I have been* c **with** Christ and I no longer G5365
Gal 3: 1 Jesus Christ was clearly portrayed *as* c. G5090
Gal 5:24 to Christ Jesus *have* c the flesh with its G5090
Gal 6:14 which the world *has been* c to me, G5090
Rev 11: 8 Egypt—where also their Lord *was* c. G5090

CRUCIFY (15) [CRUCIFIED, CRUCIFYING]
Mt 23:34 Some of them you will kill and c; others G5090
Mt 27:22 They all answered, "C him!" G5090
Mt 27:23 But they shouted all the louder, "C him!" G5090
Mt 27:31 Then they led him away to c him. G5090
Mk 15:13 "C him!" they shouted. G5090
Mk 15:14 But they shouted all the louder, "C him!" G5090
Mk 15:20 Then they led him out to c him. G5090
Lk 23:21 they kept shouting, "C him! Crucify him!" G5090
Lk 23:21 they kept shouting, "Crucify him! C him!" G5090
Jn 19: 6 their officials saw him, they shouted, "C! G5090
Jn 19: 6 shouted, "Crucify! C!" But Pilate answered G5090
Jn 19: 6 answered, "You take him and c him. G5090
Jn 19:10 have power either to free you or *to* c you?" G5090
Jn 19:15 Take him away! C him!" "Shall I crucify G5090
Jn 19:15 "*Shall I* c your king?" Pilate G5090

CRUCIFYING (1) [CRUCIFY]
Heb 6: 6 *they are* c the Son of God **all over again** G416

CRUEL (15) [CRUELLY, CRUELTY]
Ge 49: 7 their anger, so fierce, and their fury, so c! H7996
Dt 28:33 have nothing but c oppression all your H8368
Ps 64: 3 like swords and aim c words like deadly H5253
Ps 71: 4 the grasp of those who are evil and c. H2807
Pr 5: 9 to others and your dignity to *one who* is c, H426
Pr 11:17 the c bring ruin on themselves. H426
Pr 12:10 the kindest acts of the wicked are c. H426
Pr 27: 4 Anger is c and fury overwhelming, but who H427
Ecc 9:12 As fish are caught in a c net, or birds are H8273
Isa 13: 9 LORD is coming—a c day, with wrath and H426
Isa 19: 4 Egyptians over to the power of a c master, H7997
Jer 6:23 spear; they are c and show no mercy. H426
Jer 15:21 deliver you from the grasp of the c." H6883
Jer 30:14 would and punished you as would the c, H426
Jer 50:42 spears; they are c and without mercy. H426

CRUELLY (1) [CRUEL]
Jdg 4: 3 with iron and had c oppressed the H928+2622

CRUELTY (1) [CRUEL]
Na 3:19 for who has not felt your endless c? H8288

CRUMBLE (2) [CRUMBLED, CRUMBLES, CRUMBLING]
Lev 2: 6 C it and pour oil on it; it is a grain H7359+7326
Eze 38:20 the cliffs *will* c and every wall will fall to H5877

CRUMBLED (1) [CRUMBLE]
Hab 3: 6 ancient mountains c and the age-old hills H7207

CRUMBLES (1) [CRUMBLE]
Job 14:18 a mountain erodes and c and as a rock is H5570

CRUMBLING (1) [CRUMBLE]
Job 15:28 where no one lives, houses c to rubble. H6963

CRUMBS (2)
Mt 15:27 the dogs eat the c that fall from their G6033
Mk 7:28 dogs under the table eat the children's c." G6033

CRUSE (KJV) BOWL, JAR, JUG

CRUSH (27) [CRUSHED, CRUSHES, CRUSHING]
Ge 3:15 hers; he *will* c your head, and you H8789
Nu 24:17 *He will* c the foreheads of Moab, the H4730
Job 6: 9 that God would be willing *to* c me, to let H1917
Job 9:17 He *would* c me with a storm and multiply H8789
Job 19: 2 will you torment me and c me with words? H1917
Job 24:11 *They* c **olives** among the terraces; they H7414
Job 39:15 unmindful that a foot *may* c them, that H2318
Job 40:12 c the wicked where they stand. H2070
Ps 68:21 Surely God *will* c the heads of his H4730
Ps 72: 4 of the needy; *may he* c the oppressor. H1917
Ps 74: 8 their hearts, "*We will* c them completely!" H3561
Ps 89:23 *I will* c his foes before him and strike H4198
Ps 94: 5 *They* c your people, LORD; they oppress H1917
Ps 110: 5 *he will* c kings on the day of his wrath. H4730
Pr 22:22 they are poor and *do* not c the needy in H1917
Isa 14:25 I *will* c the Assyrian in my land; on my H8689
Isa 41:15 You will thresh the mountains and c them, H1990
Isa 53:10 the LORD's will *to* c him and cause him H1917
Jer 50:17 the last *to* c their **bones** was H6793
La 1:15 an army against me to c my young men. H8689
La 3:34 To c underfoot all prisoners in the land, H1917
Da 2:40 so *it will* c and break all the others. A10182
Da 2:44 *It will* c all those kingdoms and bring A10182
Am 2:13 I *will* c you as a cart crushes when loaded H6421
Am 4: 1 the poor and c the needy and say to H8368
Mic 6:15 you will c grapes but not drink the wine. NDT
Ro 16:20 The God of peace *will* soon c Satan under G5341

CRUSHED (46) [CRUSH]
Lev 2:14 offer c heads of new grain roasted in the H1762
Lev 2:16 portion of the c **grain** and the oil, H1762
Lev 22:24 whose testicles are bruised, c, torn or cut. H4198
Nu 11: 8 ground it in a hand mill or c it in a mortar. H1870
Dt 9:21 Then *I* c it and ground it to powder as fine H4198
Jdg 5:26 She struck Sisera, *she* c his head, she H4735
Jdg 10: 8 who that year shattered and c them. H8368
2Sa 22:38 "I pursued my enemies and c them; I did H9012
2Sa 22:39 *I* c them **completely**, and they H4730+2256+430
2Ch 14:13 *they* **were** c before the LORD and his forces. H8689
2Ch 15: 6 One nation was *being* c by another and H4198
2Ch 34: 7 Asherah poles and c the idols to powder H4198
Job 4:19 who *are* c more readily than a moth! H1917
Job 5: 4 from safety, c in court without a defender. H1917
Job 16:12 he seized me by the neck and c me. H7207
Job 34:25 them in the night and *they are* c. H1917
Ps 10:10 His victims *are* c, they collapse; they fall H1920
Ps 18:38 *I* c them so that they could not rise; they H4730
Ps 34:18 saves *those who* are c *in* spirit. H1918
Ps 38: 8 I am feeble and utterly c; I groan in H1920
Ps 44: 2 *you* c the peoples and made our H8317
Ps 44:19 But *you* c us and made us a haunt for H1920
Ps 51: 8 let the bones *you have* c rejoice. H1920
Ps 74:14 It was you *who* c the heads of Leviathan H8368
Ps 89:10 You c Rahab like one of the slain; with H1917
Pr 17:22 a c spirit dries up the bones. H5779
Pr 18:14 in sickness, but a c spirit who can bear? H5779
Isa 21:10 My people who are c *on* the threshing H4536
Isa 23:12 reveling, Virgin Daughter Sidon, *now* c! H6943
Isa 27: 9 stones to be like limestone c **to pieces**, H5879
Isa 53: 5 transgressions, *he* **was** c for our iniquities H1917
Jer 5: 3 they felt no pain; *you* c them, but they H3983
Jer 8:21 Since my people are c, I am crushed; H8691
Jer 8:21 my people are crushed, *I am* c; I mourn, H8689
Jer 22:20 out from Abarim, for all your allies **are** c. H8689
Eze 30: 8 set fire to Egypt and all her helpers **are** c. H8689
Eze 36: 3 they ravaged and c you from every side so H8635
Da 6:24 overpowered them and c all their bones. A10182
Da 7: 7 *it* c and devoured its victims and A10182
Da 7:19 the beast *that* c and devoured its victims A10182
Hab 3:13 *You* c the leader of the land of H4730
Mal 1: 4 "*Though we have* **been** c, we will H8406
Mt 21:44 anyone on whom it falls *will be* c. G3347
Lk 8:42 was on his way, the crowds *almost* c him. G5231
Lk 20:18 anyone on whom it falls *will be* c. G3347
2Co 4: 8 on every side, but not c; perplexed, G5102

CRUSHES (4) [CRUSH]
Ps 143: 3 pursues me, *he* c me to the ground H1917
Pr 15: 4 but a perverse tongue c the spirit. H8691
Pr 15:13 face cheerful, but heartache c the spirit. H5779
Am 2:13 crush you as a cart c when loaded with H6421

CRUSHING (6) [CRUSH]
Nu 22:25 to the wall, c Balaam's foot against it. H4315
Dt 23: 1 been emasculated by c or cutting may H1918
Ps 110: 6 up the dead and c the rulers of the whole H4730
Isa 3:15 What do you mean by c my people and H1917
Jer 14:17 a grievous wound, a c blow. H2703+4394
Da 7:23 whole earth, trampling it down and c it. A10182

CRUST (1) [ENCRUSTED]
Pr 17: 1 Better a dry c with peace and quiet than a H7326

CRUTCH (1)
2Sa 3:29 who leans on a c or who falls by the H7134

CRY (166) [CRIED, CRIES, CRYING]
Ge 27:34 a loud and bitter c and said to his father H7591
Ex 2:23 their c **for help** because of their H8784
Ex 3: 9 And now the c *of* the Israelites has H7591
Ex 22:23 If you do and *they* c **out** to me, I will H7590+7590
Ex 22:23 cry out to me, I will certainly hear their c. H7591
Ex 22:27 When *they* c **out** to me, I will hear, for I H7590
Lev 13:45 the lower part of their face and c **out**, H7924
Nu 20:16 he heard our c and sent an angel and H7754
Dt 24:15 Otherwise *they may* c to the LORD against H7924
Dt 33: 7 the c *of* Judah; bring him to his H7754
Jos 6:10 the army, "*Do* not **give a war** c, do not H8131
Jdg 10:14 Go and c **out** to the gods you have chosen H2410
1Sa 4:13 happened, the whole town **sent up a** c. H2410
1Sa 8:18 *you will* c **out** for relief from the king you H2410
1Sa 9:16 on my people, for their c has reached me." H7591
1Sa 17:20 to its battle positions, shouting the **war** c. H4878
2Sa 22: 7 he heard my voice; my c came to his ears. H8784
1Ki 8:28 Hear the c and the prayer that your H8262
1Ki 8:52 listen to them whenever they c **out** to you. H7924
1Ki 17:22 The LORD heard Elijah's c, and the boy's H7754
1Ki 22:36 was setting, a c spread through the army: H8262
1Ch 16:35 C **out**, "Save us, God our Savior; gather us H606
2Ch 6:19 Hear the c and the prayer that your H8262
2Ch 13:12 will sound the **battle** c against you. H9558
2Ch 13:15 the men of Judah **raised the battle** c H8131
2Ch 13:15 At the **sound of** their **battle** c, God routed H8131
2Ch 20: 9 your Name and *will* c **out** to you in our H2410
Ne 9: 9 in Egypt; you heard their c at the Red Sea. H2411
Job 16:18 my blood; may my c never be laid to rest! H2411
Job 19: 7 "Though *I* c, 'Violence!' I get no response H7590
Job 24:12 the souls of the wounded c **out for help**. H8775
Job 27: 9 God listen to their c when distress comes H7591
Job 30:20 "*I* c **out** to you, God, but you do not H8775
Job 30:28 I stand up in the assembly and c **for help**. H8775
Job 34:28 They caused the c *of* the poor to come H7591
Job 34:28 so that he heard the c *of* the needy. H7591
Job 35: 9 "*People* c **out** under a load of oppression H2410
Job 35:12 answer when *people* c **out** because of the H7590
Job 36:13 he fetters them, *they do* not c **for help**. H8775
Job 38:41 when its young c **out** to God and wander H8775
Job 39:25 the shout of commanders and the **battle** c. H9558
Ps 5: 2 Hear my c **for help**, my King and H7754+8776
Ps 6: 9 The LORD has heard my c **for mercy**; the H9382
Ps 10:17 encourage them, and you listen to their c, NDT
Ps 17: 1 LORD, my plea is just; listen to my c. H8262
Ps 18: 6 heard my voice; my c came before him H8784
Ps 22: 2 My God, *I* c **out** by day, but you do not H7924
Ps 22:24 him but has listened to his c **for help**. H8775
Ps 28: 2 Hear my c **for mercy** as I call to you H7754+9384
Ps 28: 6 he has heard my c **for mercy**. H7754+9384
Ps 29: 9 And in his temple all c, "Glory!" H606
Ps 31:22 you heard my c **for mercy** when I H7754+9384
Ps 34:15 his ears are attentive to their c; H8784
Ps 34:17 The righteous c **out**, and the LORD hears H7590
Ps 39:12 listen to my c **for help**; do not be deaf H8784
Ps 40: 1 the LORD; he turned to me and heard my c. H8784
Ps 55:17 morning and noon *I* c **out** in distress, and H2159
Ps 57: 2 *I* c **out** to God Most High, to God, who H7924
Ps 61: 1 Hear my c, O God; listen to my prayer. H8262
Ps 72:12 For he will deliver the needy *who* c **out** H8775

Ps 84: 2 heart and my flesh **c out** for the living God H8264
Ps 86: 6 listen to my **c for mercy**. H7754+9384
Ps 88: 1 saves me; day and night *I* **c out** to you. H7590
Ps 88: 2 come before you; turn your ear to my **c**. H8262
Ps 88:13 But **I c** to you **for help**, LORD; in the H8775
Ps 102: 1 let my **c for help** come to you. H8784
Ps 106:44 of their distress when he heard their **c**; H8262
Ps 116: 1 heard my voice; he heard my **c for mercy**. H9384
Ps 119:147 I rise before dawn and **c for help**; I have H8775
Ps 119:169 May my **c** come before you, LORD; give H8262
Ps 130: 1 Out of the depths *I* **c** *to* you, LORD; H7924
Ps 130: 2 ears be attentive to my **c for mercy**. H7754+9384
Ps 140: 6 Hear, LORD, my **c for mercy**. H7754+9384
Ps 142: 1 *I* **c** aloud to the LORD; I lift up my voice to H2410
Ps 142: 5 *I* **c** to you, LORD; I say, "You are my refuge H2410
Ps 142: 6 Listen to my **c**, for I am in desperate need H8262
Ps 143: 1 listen to my **c for mercy**; in your H9384
Ps 144:14 captivity, no **c of distress** in our streets. H7424
Ps 145:19 fear him; he hears their **c** and saves them. H8784
Pr 2: 3 insight and **c aloud** for H5989+7754
Pr 21:13 their ears to the **c** *of* the poor will also cry H2411
Pr 21:13 cry of the poor *will* also **c out** and not be H7924
Pr 30:15 they **c**. "There are three things that NDT
Isa 3: 7 But in that day *he will* **c out** H5951+4200+606
Isa 8: 9 **Raise the war c**, *you* nations, and be H8131
Isa 10:30 **C out**, Daughter Gallim! Listen H7412+7754
Isa 15: 4 Heshbon and Elealeh **c out**, their voices H2410
Isa 15: 4 Therefore the armed men of Moab **c out** H8131
Isa 19:20 When *they* **c out** to the LORD because of H7590
Isa 24:11 In the streets they **c out** for wine; all joy H7424
Isa 30:19 he will be when you **c for help**! H7754+2410
Isa 33: 7 their brave men **c aloud** in the streets; the H7590
Isa 40: 6 A voice says, "**C out**." And I said, "What H7924
Isa 40: 6 And I said, "What *shall I* **c**?" "All people H7924
Isa 42: 2 He will not shout or **c out**, or raise his H9048
Isa 42:13 a shout *he will* **raise the battle c** and will H7658
Isa 42:14 in childbirth, *I* **c out**, I gasp and pant. H7184
Isa 57:13 When you **c out for help**, let your H2410
Isa 58: 9 answer; *you will* **c for help**, and he will H8775
Isa 65:14 you *will* **c out** from anguish of heart H7590
Jer 3:21 A **c** is heard on the barren heights, the H7754
Jer 4: 5 throughout the land!' **C** aloud and say H7924
Jer 4:16 raising a **war c** against the cities of Judah. H7754
Jer 4:19 of the trumpet; I have heard the battle **c**. H9558
Jer 4:31 I hear a **c** as of a woman in labor, a groan H7754
Jer 4:31 the **c** *of* Daughter Zion gasping for breath H7754
Jer 8:19 Listen to the **c** *of* my people from a land H8784
Jer 11:11 Although *they* **c out** to me, I will not listen H2410
Jer 11:12 will go and **c out** to the gods to whom H2410
Jer 12: 6 they *have* **raised** a loud **c** against you. H7924
Jer 14: 2 and a **c** goes up *from* Jerusalem. H7424
Jer 14:12 I will not listen to their **c**; though they H8262
Jer 18:22 Let a **c** be heard from their houses when H2411
Jer 20: 8 *I* **c out** proclaiming violence and H2410
Jer 20:16 in the morning, a **battle c** at noon. H9558
Jer 22:20 "Go up to Lebanon and **c out**, let your H7590
Jer 22:20 heard in Bashan, **c out** from Abarim, for H7590
Jer 25:36 Hear the **c** *of* the shepherds, the wailing H7591
Jer 30:15 Why *do you* **c out** over your wound, your H2410
Jer 31: 6 be a day *when* watchmen **c out** on the H7924
Jer 47: 2 The people *will* **c out**; all who dwell in H2410
Jer 48: 4 be broken; her little ones *will* **c out**. H9048+2411
Jer 48:20 Wail and **c out**! Announce by the H2410
Jer 48:31 for all Moab *I* **c out**, I moan for the H2410
Jer 48:34 "The sound of their **c** rises from Heshbon H2411
Jer 49: 2 sound the battle **c** against Rabbah of the H9558
Jer 49: 3 **C out**, *you* inhabitants of Rabbah H7590
Jer 49:21 their **c** will resound to the Red Sea. H7591+7754
Jer 50:46 its **c** will resound among the nations. H2411
Jer 51:54 "The sound of a **c** comes from Babylon H2411
La 2:18 The hearts of the people **c out** to the Lord H7590
La 2:19 **c out** in the night, as the watches of H8264
La 3: 8 Even when I call out or **c for help**, he H8775
La 3:56 "Do not close your ears to my **c** for relief." H8784
La 4:15 *people* **c** to them. "Away! H7924
Eze 6:11 stamp your feet and **c out** "Alas! H606
Eze 21:12 **C out** and wail, son of man, for it is H2410
Eze 21:22 to sound the **battle c**, to set battering H9558
Eze 27:28 will quake when your sailors **c out**. H7754+2411
Eze 27:30 raise their voice and **c** bitterly over you; H2410
Hos 5: 8 **Raise the battle c** in Beth Aven; lead on H8131
Hos 7:14 *They do* not **c out** to me from their hearts H2410
Joel 1:14 the LORD your God, and **c out** to the LORD. H2410
Jnh 2: 2 I called for help, and you listened to my **c**. H7754
Mic 3: 4 Then *they will* **c out** to the LORD, but he H2410
Mic 4: 9 Why *do you* now **c aloud**—have H8131+8275
Na 2: 8 they **c**, but no one turns back. NDT
Hab 1: 2 do not listen? Or **c out** to you, "Violence!" H2410
Hab 2:11 The stones of the wall *will* **c out**, and the H2410
Zep 1:10 "a **c** will go up from the Fish Gate H7754+7591
Zep 1:14 The **c** *on* the day of the LORD is bitter; the H7754
Zep 1:14 the Mighty Warrior **shouts** *his* **battle c**. H7658
Zep 1:16 a day of trumpet and **battle c** against the H9558
Mt 12:19 He will not quarrel or **c out**; no one will G3198
Mt 25: 6 "At midnight the **c** rang out: 'Here's the G3199
Mk 5: 5 the hills he would **c out** and cut himself G3189
Mk 15:37 With a loud **c**, Jesus breathed his last. G5889
Lk 7:13 went out to her and he said, "Don't **c**." G3081
Lk 7:32 we sang a dirge, and *you did* not **c**. G3081
Lk 18: 7 who **c out** to him day and night? G1066
Lk 19:40 "if they keep quiet, the stones *will* **c out**." G3189
Ro 8:15 And by him *we* **c**, "Abba, Father." G3189
Gal 4:27 shout for joy and **c aloud**, you who were G1066
Rev 18:10 her torment, they will stand far off and **c**: G3306
Rev 18:16 and **c out**: " 'Woe! Woe to you, great city G3306
Rev 18:19 with weeping and mourning **c out**: G3189

CRYING (20) [CRY]

Ge 21:17 God heard the boy **c**, and the angel of H7754
Ge 21:17 God has heard the boy **c** as he lies there. H7754
Ex 2: 6 saw the baby. He *was* **c**, and she felt sorry H1134
Ex 3: 7 I have heard them **c out** because of their H7591
Ex 5: 8 that is why they *are* **c out**, 'Let us go and H7590
Ex 14:15 said to Moses, "Why *are you* **c out** to me? H7590
Jdg 7:21 all the Midianites ran, **c out** as they fled. H8131
1Sa 7: 8 "Do not stop **c out** to the LORD our God H2410
Isa 22: 5 down walls and of **c out** to the mountains. H8779
Isa 65:19 of weeping and of **c** will be heard in it no H2411
Eze 9: 8 I fell facedown, **c out**, "Alas, Sovereign H2410
Mt 15:22 that vicinity came to him, **c out**, "Lord, G3189
Mt 15:23 her away, for *she keeps* **c out** after us." G3189
Mk 5:38 with *people* **c** and wailing loudly. G3081
Jn 20:11 Now Mary stood outside the tomb **c**. G3081
Jn 20:13 "Woman, why *are you* **c**?" "They have G3081
Jn 20:15 "Woman, why *are you* **c**? Who is it you G3081
Ac 9:39 **c** and showing him the robes and other G3081
Jas 5: 4 mowed your fields *are* **c out** against you. G3189
Rev 21: 4 no more death' or mourning or **c** or pain, G3199

CRYSTAL (5)

Job 28:17 Neither gold nor **c** can compare with it H2343
Eze 1:22 sparkling like **c**, and awesome. H7943
Rev 4: 6 what looked like a sea of glass, clear as **c**. G3223
Rev 21:11 precious jewel, like a jasper, **clear as c**. G3222
Rev 22: 1 as clear as **c**, flowing from the G3223

CUB (2) [CUBS]

Ge 49: 9 You are a lion's **c**, Judah; you return from H1594
Dt 33:22 "Dan is a lion's **c**, springing out of Bashan H1594

CUBIT (39) [CUBITS]

Ge 6:16 the roof an opening *one* **c** high all around. H564
Ex 25:10 a half cubits long, a **c** and a half wide, and H564
Ex 25:10 a half wide, and a **c** and a half high. H564
Ex 25:17 a half cubits long and a **c** and a half wide. H564
Ex 25:23 a **c** wide and a cubit and a half high. H564
Ex 25:23 a cubit wide and a **c** and a half high. H564
Ex 26:13 curtains will be a **c** longer on both sides; H564
Ex 26:16 be ten cubits long and a **c** and a half wide, H564
Ex 30: 2 It is to be square, a **c** long and a cubit wide H564
Ex 30: 2 a cubit long and a **c** wide, and two cubits H564
Ex 36:21 ten cubits long and a **c** and a half wide, H564
Ex 37: 1 a half cubits long, a **c** and a half wide, and H564
Ex 37: 1 a half wide, and a **c** and a half high. H564
Ex 37: 6 a half cubits long and a **c** and a half wide. H564
Ex 37:10 a **c** wide and a cubit and a half high. H564
Ex 37:10 a cubit wide and a **c** and a half high. H564
Ex 37:25 a **c** long and a cubit wide and two cubits H564
Ex 37:25 a cubit long and a **c** wide and two cubits H564
Jdg 3:16 a double-edged sword **about a c** long, H1688
1Ki 7:24 gourds encircled it—ten to a **c**. H564
1Ki 7:31 that had a circular frame one **c** deep. H564
1Ki 7:31 its basework it measured a **c** and a half. H564
1Ki 7:32 diameter of each wheel was a **c** and a half. H564
1Ki 7:35 there was a circular band half a **c** deep. H564
2Ch 3: 3 using the **c** of the old standard). H564
2Ch 4: 3 figures of bulls encircled it—ten to a **c**. H564
Eze 40: 5 each of which was a **c** and a handbreadth. H564
Eze 40:12 front of each alcove was a wall one **c** high, H564
Eze 40:42 burnt offerings, each a **c** and a half long, H564
Eze 40:42 a **c** and a half wide and a cubit high. H564
Eze 40:42 a cubit and a half wide and a **c** high. H564
Eze 43:13 that **c** being a cubit and a handbreadth: H564
Eze 43:13 that cubit being a **c** and a handbreadth: H564
Eze 43:13 Its gutter is a **c** deep and a cubit wide, with H564
Eze 43:13 Its gutter is a cubit deep and a **c** wide, with H564
Eze 43:14 two cubits high, and the ledge is a **c** wide. H564
Eze 43:14 and that ledge is also a **c** wide. H564
Eze 43:17 altar is a gutter of *one* **c** with a rim of half a H564
Eze 43:17 a gutter of one cubit with a rim of half a **c**. H564

CUBITS (245) [CUBIT]

Ge 6:15 The ark is to be three hundred **c** long, fifty H564
Ge 6:15 fifty **c** wide and thirty cubits high. H564
Ge 6:15 fifty cubits wide and thirty **c** high. H564
Ge 7:20 to a depth of more than fifteen **c**. H564
Ex 25:10 acacia wood—*two* and a half **c** long, H564
Ex 25:17 *two* and a half **c** long and a cubit and a half H564
Ex 25:23 of acacia wood—*two* **c** long, a cubit wide H564
Ex 26: 2 twenty-eight **c** long and four cubits wide. H564
Ex 26: 2 twenty-eight cubits long and four **c** wide. H564
Ex 26: 8 thirty **c** long and four cubits wide. H564
Ex 26: 8 thirty cubits long and four **c** wide. H564
Ex 26:16 frame is to be ten **c** long and a cubit and a H564
Ex 27: 1 of acacia wood, three **c** high; it is to be H564
Ex 27: 1 be square, five **c** long and five cubits wide. H564
Ex 27: 1 be square, five cubits long and five **c** wide. H564
Ex 27: 9 shall be a hundred **c** long and is to have H564
Ex 27:11 also be a hundred **c** long and is to have NDT
Ex 27:12 shall be fifty **c** wide and have curtains, H564
Ex 27:13 the courtyard shall also be fifty **c** wide. H564
Ex 27:14 Curtains fifteen **c** long are to be on one side H564
Ex 27:15 curtains fifteen **c** long are to be on the NDT
Ex 27:16 provide a curtain twenty **c** long, of blue, H564
Ex 27:18 shall be a hundred **c** long and fifty cubits H564
Ex 27:18 be a hundred cubits long and fifty **c** wide, NDT
Ex 27:18 curtains of finely twisted linen five **c** high, H564
Ex 30: 2 a cubit wide, and *two* **c** high—its horns of H564
Ex 36: 9 twenty-eight **c** long and four cubits wide. H564
Ex 36: 9 twenty-eight cubits long and four **c** wide. H564
Ex 36:15 thirty **c** long and four cubits wide. H564
Ex 36:15 thirty cubits long and four **c** wide. H564
Ex 36:21 Each frame was ten **c** long and a cubit and H564
Ex 37: 1 acacia wood—*two* and a half **c** long, H564
Ex 37: 6 *two* and a half **c** long and a cubit and a half H564
Ex 37:10 of acacia wood—*two* **c** long, a cubit wide H564
Ex 37:25 long and a cubit wide and *two* **c** high— H564
Ex 38: 1 of acacia wood, three **c** high; it was square, H564
Ex 38: 1 five **c** long and five cubits wide. H564
Ex 38: 1 five cubits long and five **c** wide. H564
Ex 38: 9 side was a hundred **c** long and had H564
Ex 38:11 was also a hundred **c** long and had twenty H564
Ex 38:12 west end was fifty **c** wide and had curtains, H564
Ex 38:13 toward the sunrise, was also fifty **c** wide. H564
Ex 38:14 Curtains fifteen **c** long were on one side of H564
Ex 38:15 curtains fifteen **c** long were on the H564
Ex 38:18 It was twenty **c** long and, like the curtains H564
Ex 38:18 the curtains of the courtyard, five **c** high, H564
Nu 11:31 them up to *two* **c** deep all around the H564
Nu 35: 4 extend a thousand **c** from the town wall. H564
Nu 35: 5 measure two thousand **c** on the east side H564
Dt 3:11 was more than nine **c** long and four cubits H564
Dt 3:11 than nine cubits long and four **c** wide. H564
Jos 3: 4 about two thousand **c** between you and the H564
1Sa 17: 4 His height was six **c** and a span. H564
1Ki 6: 2 Solomon built for the LORD was sixty **c** long, H564
1Ki 6: 3 that is twenty **c**, and projected ten H564
1Ki 6: 3 projected ten **c** from the front of the H564
1Ki 6: 6 The lowest floor was five **c** wide, the middle H564
1Ki 6: 6 the middle floor six **c** and the third floor H564
1Ki 6:10 The height of each was five **c**, and they H564
1Ki 6:16 He partitioned off twenty **c** at the rear of the H564
1Ki 6:17 hall in front of this room was forty **c** long. H564
1Ki 6:20 The inner sanctuary was twenty **c** long H564
1Ki 6:23 out of olive wood, each ten **c** high. H564
1Ki 6:24 One wing of the first cherub was five **c** long H564
1Ki 6:24 the other wing five **c**—ten cubits from H564
1Ki 6:24 five cubits—ten **c** from wing tip to wing tip. H564
1Ki 6:25 The second cherub also measured ten **c**, for H564
1Ki 6:26 The height of each cherub was ten **c**. H564
1Ki 7: 2 of the Forest of Lebanon a hundred **c** long, H564
1Ki 7: 6 a colonnade fifty **c** long and thirty wide. H564
1Ki 7:10 some measuring ten **c** and some eight. H564
1Ki 7:15 each eighteen **c** high and twelve cubits in H564
1Ki 7:15 cubits high and twelve **c** in circumference. H564
1Ki 7:16 of the pillars; each capital was five **c** high. H564
1Ki 7:19 were in the shape of lilies, four **c** high. H564
1Ki 7:23 measuring ten **c** from rim to rim and five H564
1Ki 7:23 ten cubits from rim to rim and five **c** high. H564
1Ki 7:23 took a line of thirty **c** to measure around it. H564
1Ki 7:27 each was four **c** long, four wide and H564
1Ki 7:38 forty baths and measuring four **c** across, H564
2Ki 14:13 a section about four hundred **c** long. H564
2Ki 25:17 Each pillar was eighteen **c** high. The bronze H564
2Ki 25:17 one pillar was three **c** high and was H564
1Ch 11:23 down an Egyptian who was five **c** tall. H564
2Ch 3: 3 of God was sixty **c** long and twenty cubits H564
2Ch 3: 3 was sixty cubits long and twenty **c** wide H564
2Ch 3: 4 temple was twenty **c** long across the width H564
2Ch 3: 4 width of the building and twenty **c** high. H564
2Ch 3: 8 twenty **c** long and twenty cubits wide. H564
2Ch 3: 8 twenty cubits long and twenty **c** wide. H564
2Ch 3:11 wingspan of the cherubim was twenty **c**. H564
2Ch 3:11 first cherub was five **c** long and touched the H564
2Ch 3:11 other wing, also five **c** long, touched the H564
2Ch 3:12 cherub was five **c** long and touched the H564
2Ch 3:12 other wing, also five **c** long, touched the H564
2Ch 3:13 of these cherubim extended twenty **c**. H564
2Ch 3:15 which together were thirty-five **c** long, each H564
2Ch 3:15 cubits long, each with a capital five **c** high. H564
2Ch 4: 1 He made a bronze altar twenty **c** long H564
2Ch 4: 1 twenty **c** wide and ten cubits high. H564
2Ch 4: 1 twenty cubits wide and ten **c** high. H564
2Ch 4: 2 measuring ten **c** from rim to rim and five H564
2Ch 4: 2 ten cubits from rim to rim and five **c** high. H564
2Ch 4: 2 took a line of thirty **c** to measure around it. H564
2Ch 6:13 bronze platform, five **c** long, five cubits H564
2Ch 6:13 five **c** wide and three cubits high H564
2Ch 6:13 five cubits wide and three **c** high, and had H564
2Ch 25:23 a section about four hundred **c** long. H564
Ezr 6: 3 It is to be sixty **c** high and sixty cubits A10039
Ezr 6: 3 is to be sixty cubits high and sixty **c** wide, A10039
Ne 3:13 repaired a thousand **c** of the wall as far as H564
Est 5:14 reaching to a height of fifty **c**, and ask the H564
Est 7: 9 to a height of fifty **c** stands by Haman's H564
Jer 52:21 pillar was eighteen **c** high and twelve H564
Jer 52:21 cubits high and twelve **c** in circumference; H564
Jer 52:22 one pillar was five **c** high and was H564
Eze 40: 5 rod in the man's hand was six **long c**, H564
Eze 40: 7 walls between the alcoves were five **c** thick. H564
Eze 40: 9 it was eight **c** deep and its jambs were two H564
Eze 40: 9 cubits deep and its jambs were two **c** thick. H564
Eze 40:11 it was ten **c** and its length was thirteen H564
Eze 40:11 ten cubits and its length was thirteen **c**. H564
Eze 40:12 and the alcoves were six **c** square. H564
Eze 40:13 was twenty-five **c** from one parapet H564
Eze 40:14 around the inside of the gateway—sixty **c**. H564

Eze 40:15 to the far end of its portico was fifty **c**. H564
Eze 40:19 it was a hundred **c** on the east side as well H564
Eze 40:21 It was fifty **c** long and twenty-five cubits H564
Eze 40:21 was fifty cubits long and twenty-five **c** wide. H564
Eze 40:23 to the opposite one; it was a hundred **c**. H564
Eze 40:25 It was fifty **c** long and twenty-five cubits H564
Eze 40:25 was fifty cubits long and twenty-five **c** wide. H564
Eze 40:27 gate on the south side; it was a hundred **c**. H564
Eze 40:29 It was fifty **c** long and twenty-five cubits H564
Eze 40:29 was fifty cubits long and twenty-five **c** wide. H564
Eze 40:30 were twenty-five **c** wide and five cubits H564
Eze 40:30 twenty-five cubits wide and five **c** deep.) H564
Eze 40:33 It was fifty **c** long and twenty-five cubits H564
Eze 40:33 was fifty cubits long and twenty-five **c** wide. H564
Eze 40:36 It was fifty **c** long and twenty-five cubits H564
Eze 40:36 was fifty cubits long and twenty-five **c** wide. H564
Eze 40:47 a hundred **c** long and a hundred cubits H564
Eze 40:47 hundred cubits long and a hundred **c** wide. H564
Eze 40:48 they were five **c** wide on either side. H564
Eze 40:48 entrance was fourteen **c** and its projecting H564
Eze 40:48 walls were three **c** wide on either side. H564
Eze 40:49 The portico was twenty **c** wide, and twelve H564
Eze 40:49 and twelve **c** from front to back. H564
Eze 41: 1 width of the jambs was six **c** on each side. H564
Eze 41: 2 The entrance was ten **c** wide, and the H564
Eze 41: 2 walls on each side of it were five **c** wide. H564
Eze 41: 2 it was forty **c** long and twenty cubits wide. H564
Eze 41: 2 it was forty cubits long and twenty **c** wide. H564
Eze 41: 3 of the entrance; each was two **c** wide. H564
Eze 41: 3 The entrance was six **c** wide, and the H564
Eze 41: 3 walls on each side of it were seven **c** wide. H564
Eze 41: 4 it was twenty **c**, and its width was H564
Eze 41: 4 its width was twenty **c** across the end of the H564
Eze 41: 5 the temple; it was six **c** thick, and each side H564
Eze 41: 5 room around the temple was four **c** wide. H564
Eze 41: 8 It was the length of the rod, six long **c**. H564
Eze 41: 9 wall of the side rooms was five **c** thick. H564
Eze 41:10 rooms was twenty **c** wide all around the H564
Eze 41:11 the open area was five **c** wide all around. H564
Eze 41:12 on the west side was seventy **c** wide. H564
Eze 41:12 of the building was five **c** thick all around, H564
Eze 41:12 all around, and its length was ninety **c**. H564
Eze 41:13 it was a hundred **c** long, and the temple H564
Eze 41:13 with its walls were also a hundred **c** long. H564
Eze 41:14 the front of the temple, was a hundred **c**. H564
Eze 41:15 galleries on each side; it was a hundred **c**. H564
Eze 41:22 a wooden altar three **c** high and two cubits H564
Eze 41:22 altar three cubits high and two **c** square; H564
Eze 42: 2 north was a hundred **c** long and fifty cubits H564
Eze 42: 2 was a hundred cubits long and fifty **c** wide. H564
Eze 42: 3 in the section twenty **c** from the inner court NDT
Eze 42: 4 passageway ten **c** wide and a hundred H564
Eze 42: 4 ten cubits wide and a hundred **c** long. H564
Eze 42: 7 it extended in front of the rooms for fifty **c**. H564
Eze 42: 8 side next to the outer court was fifty **c** long, H564
Eze 42: 8 the sanctuary was a hundred **c** long. H564
Eze 42:16 the measuring rod; it was five hundred **c**. H564
Eze 42:17 it was five hundred **c** by the measuring rod. H564
Eze 42:18 it was five hundred **c** by the measuring rod. H564
Eze 42:19 it was five hundred **c** by the measuring rod. H564
Eze 42:20 five hundred **c** long and five hundred cubits NDT
Eze 42:20 cubits long and five hundred **c** wide, NDT
Eze 43:13 the measurements of the altar in **long c**, H564
Eze 43:14 that goes around the altar it is two **c** high, H564
Eze 43:14 that goes around the altar it is four **c** high, H564
Eze 43:15 the altar hearth is four **c** high, and four H564
Eze 43:16 twelve **c** long and twelve cubits wide. NDT
Eze 43:16 twelve cubits long and twelve **c** wide. NDT
Eze 43:17 fourteen **c** long and fourteen cubits wide. NDT
Eze 43:17 fourteen cubits long and fourteen **c** wide. NDT
Eze 45: 1 25,000 **c** long and 20,000 cubits wide NDT
Eze 45: 1 25,000 cubits long and 20,000 **c** wide; the NDT
Eze 45: 2 a section 500 **c** square is to be for the NDT
Eze 45: 2 with 50 **c** around it for open land. H564
Eze 45: 3 off a section 25,000 **c** long and 10,000 NDT
Eze 45: 3 25,000 cubits long and 10,000 **c** wide. NDT
Eze 45: 5 An area 25,000 **c** long and 10,000 cubits NDT
Eze 45: 5 long and 10,000 **c** wide will belong to NDT
Eze 45: 6 an area 5,000 **c** wide and 25,000 cubits NDT
Eze 45: 6 area 5,000 cubits wide and 25,000 **c** long, NDT
Eze 46:22 forty **c** long and thirty cubits wide NDT
Eze 46:22 forty cubits long and thirty **c** wide; each of NDT
Eze 47: 3 off a thousand **c** and then led me through H564
Eze 47: 4 off another thousand **c** and led me through NDT
Eze 48: 8 It will be 25,000 **c** wide, and its length from NDT
Eze 48: 9 LORD will be 25,000 **c** long and 10,000 NDT
Eze 48: 9 be 25,000 cubits long and 10,000 **c** wide. NDT
Eze 48:10 It will be 25,000 **c** long on the north side NDT
Eze 48:10 north side, 10,000 **c** wide on the west side NDT
Eze 48:10 10,000 **c** wide on the east side and 25,000 NDT
Eze 48:10 east side and 25,000 **c** long on the south NDT
Eze 48:13 an allotment 25,000 **c** long and 10,000 NDT
Eze 48:13 25,000 cubits long and 10,000 **c** wide. NDT
Eze 48:13 length will be 25,000 **c** and its width 10,000 NDT
Eze 48:13 will be 25,000 cubits and its width 10,000 **c**. NDT
Eze 48:15 5,000 **c** wide and 25,000 cubits long NDT
Eze 48:15 5,000 cubits wide and 25,000 **c** long, will NDT
Eze 48:16 the north side 4,500 **c**, the south side 4,500 NDT
Eze 48:16 the south side 4,500 **c**, the east side 4,500 NDT
Eze 48:16 the east side 4,500 **c**, and the west side NDT
Eze 48:16 4,500 cubits, and the west side 4,500 **c**. NDT
Eze 48:17 the city will be 250 **c** on the north, NDT
Eze 48:17 on the north, 250 **c** on the south, 250 cubits NDT
Eze 48:17 on the south, 250 **c** on the east, and 250 NDT
Eze 48:17 cubits on the east, and 250 **c** on the west. NDT
Eze 48:18 will be 10,000 **c** on the east side and NDT
Eze 48:18 the east side and 10,000 **c** on the west side. NDT
Eze 48:20 will be a square, 25,000 **c** on each side. NDT
Eze 48:21 from the 25,000 **c** of the sacred portion to NDT
Eze 48:21 from the 25,000 **c** to the western border. NDT
Eze 48:30 on the north side, which is 4,500 **c** long, NDT
Eze 48:32 which is 4,500 **c** long, will be three NDT
Eze 48:33 which measures 4,500 **c**, will be three gates NDT
Eze 48:34 which is 4,500 **c** long, will be three NDT
Eze 48:35 "The distance all around will be 18,000 **c** NDT
Da 3: 1 of gold, sixty **c** high and six cubits wide A10039
Da 3: 1 sixty cubits high and six **c** wide, and set A10039
Zec 5: 2 twenty **c** long and ten cubits wide. H564
Zec 5: 2 twenty cubits long and ten **c** wide. H564
Rev 21:17 measurement, and it was 144 **c** thick. *G4388*

CUBS (11) [CUB]

2Sa 17: 8 as fierce as a wild bear **robbed of** her **c**. H8891
Job 4:11 the **c** *of* the lioness are scattered. H1201
Job 38:32 seasons or lead out the Bear with its **c**? H1201
Pr 17:12 a bear robbed of her **c** than a fool bent on H408
Jer 51:38 like young lions, they growl like lion **c**. H1596
Eze 19: 2 lay down among them and reared her **c**. H1594
Eze 19: 3 She brought up one of her **c**, and he H1594
Eze 19: 5 took another of her **c** and made him a H1594
Hos 13: 8 Like a bear **robbed of** *her* **c**, I will attack H8891
Na 2:11 and the **c**, with nothing to fear H1594+793
Na 2:12 killed enough for his **c** and strangled the H1596

CUCKOW (KJV) GULL

CUCUMBER (2) [CUCUMBERS]

Isa 1: 8 like a hut in a **c field**, like a city under H5252
Jer 10: 5 Like a scarecrow in a **c field**, their idols H5252

CUCUMBERS (1) [CUCUMBER]

Nu 11: 5 in Egypt at no cost—also the **c**, melons, H7991

CUD (11)

Lev 11: 3 has a divided hoof and that chews the **c**. H1742
Lev 11: 4 that only chew the **c** or only have a H1742
Lev 11: 4 though it chews the **c**, does not have a H1742
Lev 11: 5 though it chews the **c**, does not have a H1742
Lev 11: 6 though it chews the **c**, does not have a H1742
Lev 11: 7 does not chew the **c**; it is unclean for you. H1742
Lev 11:26 does not chew the **c** is unclean for you; H1742
Dt 14: 6 has a divided hoof and that chews the **c**. H1742
Dt 14: 7 those that chew the **c** or that have a H1742
Dt 14: 7 Although they chew the **c**, they do not H1742
Dt 14: 8 a divided hoof, it does not chew the **c**. H1742

CULMINATION (3)

Ro 10: 4 Christ is the **c** of the law so that there may *G5465*
1Co 10:11 on whom the **c** of the ages has come. *G5465*
Heb 9:26 once for all at the **c** of the ages to do *G5333*

CULTIVATE (2) [CULTIVATED]

Dt 28:39 plant vineyards and **c** them but you will H6268
Ps 104:14 plants for people to **c**—bringing forth H6275

CULTIVATED (5) [CULTIVATE]

Isa 5: 6 neither pruned nor **c**, and briers and H6371
Isa 7:25 As for all the hills *once* **c** by the hoe, you H6371
Jer 13:21 over you those you **c** as your special allies H4340
Eze 36:34 The desolate land *will* **be c** instead of H6268
Ro 11:24 to nature were grafted into a **c olive tree**, *G2814*

CUMBERED, CUMBERETH (KJV) DISTRACTED, USE

CUMBERSOME (1)

Mt 23: 4 **c** loads and put them on other people's *G1546*

CUMI (KJV) KOUM

CUMIN (4)

Isa 28:25 does he not sow caraway and scatter **c**? H4021
Isa 28:27 is the wheel of a cart rolled over **c** H4021
Isa 28:27 beaten out with a rod, and **c** with a stick. H4021
Mt 23:23 a tenth of your spices—mint, dill and **c**. *G3248*

CUN (NIV84) KUN

CUNNING (4)

Ps 64: 6 Surely the human mind and heart are **c**. H6678
Ps 83: 3 *With* **c** *they* conspire against your people H6891
2Co 11: 3 as Eve was deceived by the serpent's **c**, *G4111*
Eph 4:14 of teaching and by the **c** and craftiness of *G3235*

CUP (66) [CUPPED, CUPS]

Ge 40:11 Pharaoh's **c** was in my hand, and I took H3926
Ge 40:11 them into Pharaoh's **c** and put the cup in H3926
Ge 40:11 Pharaoh's cup and put the **c** in his hand." H3926
Ge 40:13 you will put Pharaoh's **c** in his hand H3926
Ge 40:21 once again put the **c** into Pharaoh's hand H3926
Ge 44: 2 Then put my **c**, the silver one, in the H1483
Ge 44: 5 Isn't this **the c** my master drinks from and H889S
Ge 44:12 And the **c** was found in Benjamin's sack. H1483
Ge 44:16 the one who was found to have the **c**." H1483
Ge 44:17 found to have the **c** will become my slave. H1483
2Sa 12: 3 drank from his **c** and even slept in his H3926
1Ki 7:26 its rim was like the rim of a **c**, like a H3926
2Ch 4: 5 its rim was like the rim of a **c**, like a H3926
Job 21:20 let them drink the **c** of the wrath of the NDT
Ps 16: 5 you alone are my portion and my **c**; you H3926
Ps 23: 5 anoint my head with oil; my **c** overflows. H3926
Ps 75: 8 of the LORD is a **c** full of foaming wine H3926
Ps 116:13 I will lift up the **c** *of* salvation and call on H3926
Pr 23:31 when it sparkles in the **c**, when it goes H3926
Isa 51:17 the hand of the LORD the **c** *of* his wrath, H3926
Isa 51:22 out of your hand the **c** that made you H3926
Isa 51:22 you stagger; from that **c**, the goblet of my NDT
Jer 25:15 my hand this **c** *filled with* the wine of my H3926
Jer 25:17 So I took the **c** from the LORD's hand and H3926
Jer 25:28 refuse to take the **c** from your hand and H3926
Jer 49:12 do not deserve to drink the **c** must drink it, H3926
Jer 51: 7 Babylon was a gold **c** in the LORD's hand H3926
La 4:21 But to you also the **c** will be passed; you H3926
Eze 23:31 so I will put her **c** into your hand. H3926
Eze 23:32 "You will drink your sister's **c**, a cup large H3926
Eze 23:32 your sister's cup, a **c** large and deep; it will NDT
Eze 23:33 sorrow, the **c** *of* ruin and desolation H3926
Eze 23:33 desolation, the **c** *of* your sister Samaria. H3926
Hab 2:16 The **c** *from* the LORD's right hand is coming H3926
Zec 12: 2 to make Jerusalem a **c** *that sends* all the H6195
Mt 10:42 anyone gives even a **c** of cold water to *G4539*
Mt 20:22 "Can you drink the **c** I am going to drink?" *G4539*
Mt 20:23 "You will indeed drink *from* my **c**, but to *G4539*
Mt 23:25 You clean the outside *of* the **c** and dish *G4539*
Mt 23:26 First clean the inside *of* the **c** and dish *G4539*
Mt 26:27 Then he took a **c**, and when he had given *G4539*
Mt 26:39 is possible, may this **c** be taken from me. *G4539*
Mt 26:42 not possible for this **c** to be taken away NDT
Mk 9:41 anyone *who* **gives** you a **c** of water *G4540+4539*
Mk 10:38 "Can you drink the **c** I drink or be baptized *G4539*
Mk 10:39 "You will drink the **c** I drink and be *G4539*
Mk 14:23 Then he took a **c**, and when he had given *G4539*
Mk 14:36 Take this **c** from me. Yet not what *G4539*
Lk 11:39 clean the outside *of* the **c** and dish, *G4539*
Lk 22:17 After taking the **c**, he gave thanks and *G4539*
Lk 22:20 after the supper he took the **c**, saying, *G4539*
Lk 22:20 "This **c** is the new covenant in my blood *G4539*
Lk 22:42 take this **c** from me; yet not my *G4539*
Jn 18:11 Shall I not drink the **c** the Father has given *G4539*
1Co 10:16 Is not the **c** of thanksgiving for which we *G4539*
1Co 10:21 You cannot drink the **c** of the Lord and the *G4539*
1Co 10:21 cup of the Lord and the **c** of demons too; *G4539*
1Co 11:25 after supper he took the **c**, saying, *G4539*
1Co 11:25 "This **c** is the new covenant in my blood *G4539*
1Co 11:26 you eat this bread and drink this **c**, *G4539*
1Co 11:27 the bread or drinks the **c** of the Lord in an *G4539*
1Co 11:28 they eat of the bread and drink from the **c**. *G4539*
Rev 14:10 full strength into the **c** of his wrath. *G4539*
Rev 16:19 gave her the **c** filled with the wine *G4539*
Rev 17: 4 She held a golden **c** in her hand, filled *G4539*
Rev 18: 6 Pour her a double portion from her own **c**. *G4539*

CUPBEARER (10) [BEAR]

Ge 40: 1 the **c** and the baker *of* the king of Egypt H5482
Ge 40: 2 officials, the chief **c** and the chief baker, H5482
Ge 40: 5 the **c** and the baker of the king of Egypt H5482
Ge 40: 9 So the chief **c** told Joseph his dream. H5482
Ge 40:13 as you used to do when you were his **c**. H5482
Ge 40:20 heads of the chief **c** and the chief baker in H5482
Ge 40:21 He restored the chief **c** to his position, so H5482
Ge 40:23 The chief **c**, however, did not remember H5482
Ge 41: 9 Then the chief **c** said to Pharaoh, "Today I H5482
Ne 1:11 I was **c** to the king. H5482

CUPBEARERS (2) [BEAR]

1Ki 10: 5 in their robes, his **c**, and the burnt H5482
2Ch 9: 4 the **c** in their robes and the burnt offerings H5482

CUPPED (1) [CUP]

Jdg 7: 6 of them drank from **c** hands, H448+7023

CUPS (8) [CUP]

Ex 25:31 make its **flowerlike c**, buds and H1483
Ex 25:33 Three **c** shaped like almond flowers with H1483
Ex 25:34 there are to be four **c** shaped like almond H1483
Ex 37:17 made its **flowerlike c**, buds and H1483
Ex 37:19 Three **c** shaped like almond flowers with H1483
Ex 37:20 were four **c** shaped like almond H1483
Jer 35: 5 full of wine and *some* **c** before the H3926
Mk 7: 4 such as the washing *of* **c**, pitchers and *G4539*

CURDLE (1) [CURDS]

Job 10:10 me out like milk and **c** me like cheese, H7884

CURDLED (1) [CURDS]

Jdg 5:25 bowl fit for nobles she brought him **c milk**. H2772

CURDS (7) [CURDLE, CURDLED]

Ge 18: 8 He then brought *some* **c** and milk and the H2772
Dt 32:14 with **c** and milk from herd and flock and H2772
2Sa 17:29 honey and **c**, sheep, and cheese from H2772
Isa 7:15 He will be eating **c** and honey when he H2772
Isa 7:22 the milk they give, there will be **c** to eat. H2772
Isa 7:22 remain in the land will eat **c** and honey. H2772
Eze 34: 3 You eat the **c**, clothe yourselves with the H2692

CURE (8) [CURED]

2Ki 5: 3 *He would* **c** him of his leprosy. H665
2Ki 5: 6 to you so that *you may* **c** him of his leprosy." H665
2Ki 5:11 hand over the spot and **c** me *of* my leprosy. H665

Jer 3:22 people; *I will* c you *of* backsliding. H8324
Jer 17: 9 is deceitful above all things and **beyond c**. H631
Jer 30:15 over your wound, your pain that has **no c**? H631
Hos 5:13 But he is not able to c you, not able to H8324
Lk 9: 1 to drive out all demons and *to* c diseases, *G2543*

CURED (10) [CURE]

Dt 28:27 the itch, from which you cannot **be c**. H8324
Dt 28:35 legs with painful boils that cannot **be c**, H8324
2Ki 5: 7 send someone to me to *be* c of his leprosy? H665
Lk 6:18 Those troubled by impure spirits *were* c, *G2543*
Lk 7:21 that very time Jesus c many who had *G2543*
Lk 8: 2 women who had been c of evil spirits *G2543*
Lk 8:36 the demon-possessed man *had been* c. *G5392*
Jn 5: 9 At once the man was c; he picked up his *G5618*
Ac 19:12 their illnesses *were* c and the evil *G557*
Ac 28: 9 of the sick on the island came and *were* c. *G2543*

CURRENT (3) [CURRENTS]

Ge 23:16 **according to the weight** c among the H6296
1Ki 10:28 purchased them from Kue at the **c price**. H4697
2Ch 1:16 purchased them from Kue at the **c price**. H4697

CURRENTS (1) [CURRENT]

Jnh 2: 3 of the seas, and the c swirled about me H5643

CURRY (2)

Pr 19: 6 Many **c favor with** a ruler, and H2704+7156
Col 3:22 their eye is on you and to c their **favor**, *G473*

CURSE (101) [ACCURSED, CURSED, CURSES, CURSING]

Ge 4:11 Now you *are* **under a c** and driven from the H826
Ge 8:21 "Never again *will I* c the ground because H7837
Ge 12: 3 whoever curses you *I will* c; and all H826
Ge 27:12 would bring down a c on myself rather H7839
Ge 27:13 said to him, "My son, let the c fall on me. H7839
Ge 27:29 May *those who* c you be cursed and those H826
Ex 22:28 not blaspheme God or c the ruler of your H826
Lev 19:14 " '*Do* not c the deaf or put a stumbling H7837
Lev 24:11 woman blasphemed the Name with a c; H7837
Nu 5:18 holds the bitter water that **brings a c**. H826
Nu 5:19 bitter water that **brings a c** not harm you. H826
Nu 5:21 *is to* **put** the woman under this c H460+8678+8652
Nu 5:21 to become a c among your H460+2256+8652
Nu 5:22 this water that **brings a c** enter your body H826
Nu 5:24 drink the bitter water that **brings a c**, H826
Nu 5:24 this water that **brings a c** and causes bitter H826
Nu 5:27 the water that **brings a c** and causes bitter H826
Nu 5:27 will miscarry, and she will become a c. H460
Nu 22: 6 Now come and **put a c on** these people H826
Nu 22: 6 is blessed, and whoever *you* c is cursed." H826
Nu 22:11 Now come and **put a c on** them for me H7686
Nu 22:12 *You must* not **put a c on** those people H826
Nu 22:17 Come and **put a c on** these people for me." H7686
Nu 23: 7 he said, 'c Jacob for me; come H826
Nu 23: 8 How *can I* c those whom God has not H7686
Nu 23:11 I brought you to c my enemies, but you H7686
Nu 23:13 And from there, c them for me." H7686
Nu 23:25 "Neither c them **at all** nor bless H7686+7686
Nu 23:27 will please God *to let you* c them for me H7686
Nu 24: 9 be blessed and *those who* c you be cursed!" H826
Nu 24:10 "I summoned you to c my enemies, but H7686
Dt 11:26 before you today a blessing and a c— H7839
Dt 11:28 the c if you disobey the commands of the H7839
Dt 21:23 who is hung on a pole is *under* God's c. H7839
Dt 23: 4 Aram Naharaim to **pronounce a c on** you. H7837
Dt 23: 5 turned the c into a blessing for H7839
Jos 9:23 You *are* now **under a c**: You will never be H826
Jos 24: 9 Balaam son of Beor to **put a c on** you. H7837
Jdg 5:23 'C Meroz,' said the angel of the LORD H826
Jdg 5:23 'C its people **bitterly**, because they H826+826
Jdg 9:57 The c *of* Jotham son of Jerub-Baal came H7839
Jdg 17: 2 about which I heard you **utter a c**— H457
2Sa 16: 9 "Why *should* this dead dog c my lord the H7837
2Sa 16:10 LORD said to him, 'C David,' who can ask, H7837
2Sa 16:11 Leave him alone; *let* him c, for the LORD H7837
2Sa 16:12 covenant blessing instead of his c today." H7839
2Ki 2:24 at them and **called down a c** *on* them in H7837
2Ki 22:19 would become a c and be laid waste— H7839
Ne 10:29 themselves with a c and an oath to follow H460
Ne 13: 2 hired Balaam to **call a c down** *on* them. H7837
Ne 13: 2 however, turned the c into a blessing.) H7839
Job 1:11 and *he will* surely c you to your face." H1385
Job 2: 5 and *he will* surely c you to your face." H1385
Job 2: 9 your integrity? C God and die!" H1385S
Job 3: 8 May *those who* c days curse that day, those H826
Job 3: 8 *May* those who curse days c that day H7686
Job 31:30 to sin by invoking a c against their life— H460
Ps 62: 4 they bless, but in their hearts *they* c. H7837
Ps 102: 8 rail against me **use** my **name as a c**. H8678+928
Ps 109:17 He loved to pronounce a c—may it come H7839
Ps 109:28 *While* they c, may you bless; may those H7837
Pr 3:33 The LORD's c is on the house of the wicked, H4423
Pr 11:26 People c the one who hoards grain, but H7686
Pr 26: 2 an undeserved c does not come to rest. H7839
Pr 27:14 in the morning, it will be taken as a c. H7839
Pr 30:10 their master, or *they will* c you, and you H7837
Pr 30:11 "There are those *who* c their fathers and H7837
Ecc 10:20 thoughts, or c the rich in your bedroom H7837
Isa 8:21 upward, *will* c their king and their God. H7837
Isa 24: 6 Therefore a c consumes the earth; its H460
Jer 23:10 because of the c the land lies parched H460
Jer 24: 9 a byword, a c and an object of ridicule H7839
Jer 25:18 horror and scorn, a c—as they are today; H7839
Jer 26: 6 this city a c among all the nations H7839
Jer 29:18 of the earth, a c and an object of horror H460
Jer 29:22 Judah who are in Babylon will use this c: H7839
Jer 42:18 You will be a c and an object of horror, H460
Jer 42:18 of horror, a c and an object of reproach H7839
Jer 44: 8 make yourselves a c and an object of H7839
Jer 44:12 They will become a c and an object of H460
Jer 44:12 of horror, a c and an object of reproach. H7839
Jer 44:22 your land became a c and a desolate H7839
Jer 48:10 "A c *on* anyone who is lax in doing the H826
Jer 48:10 A c *on* anyone who keeps their sword from H826
Jer 49:13 "that Bozrah will become a ruin and a c H7839
La 3:65 their hearts, and may your c be on them! H9297
Zec 5: 3 "This is the c that is going out over the H460
Zec 8:13 have been a c among the nations H7839
Mal 2: 2 "I will send a c on you, and I will curse H4423
Mal 2: 2 a curse on you, and *I will* c your blessings. H826
Mal 3: 9 You *are* under a c—your whole H826+4423
Lk 6:28 bless those *who* c you, pray for those who *G2933*
Jn 7:49 nothing of the law—there is a c **on** them." *G2063*
Ro 12:14 who persecute you; bless and *do* not c. *G2933*
Gal 1: 8 let them be **under God's c**! *G353*
Gal 1: 9 you accepted, let them be **under God's c**! *G353*
Gal 3:10 rely on the works of the law are under a c, *G2932*
Gal 3:13 redeemed us from the c of the law by *G2932*
Gal 3:13 curse of the law by becoming a c for us, *G2932*
Jas 3: 9 with it *we* c human beings, who *G2933*
Rev 22: 3 No longer will there be any c. The throne *G2873*

CURSED (65) [CURSE]

Ge 3:14 "C *are* you above all livestock and all wild H826
Ge 3:17 "C *is* the ground because of you H826
Ge 5:29 hands caused by the ground the LORD *has* c." H826
Ge 9:25 "C *be* Canaan! The lowest of slaves H826
Ge 27:29 *May* those who curse you **be c** and those H826
Ge 49: 7 C *be* their anger, so fierce, and their fury H826
Lev 20: 9 Because *they have* c their father or mother H7837
Nu 22: 6 is blessed, and whoever you curse *is* c." H826
Nu 23: 8 can I curse those whom God *has* not c? H7686
Nu 24: 9 be blessed and those who curse you **be c**!" H826
Dt 27:15 "C *is* anyone who makes an idol—a thing H826
Dt 27:16 "C *is* anyone who dishonors their father H826
Dt 27:17 "C *is* anyone who moves their neighbor's H826
Dt 27:18 "C *is* anyone who leads the blind astray on H826
Dt 27:19 "C *is* anyone who withholds justice from H826
Dt 27:20 "C *is* anyone who sleeps with his father's H826
Dt 27:21 "C *is* anyone who has sexual relations with H826
Dt 27:22 "C *is* anyone who sleeps with his sister, the H826
Dt 27:23 "C *is* anyone who sleeps with his H826
Dt 27:24 "C *is* anyone who kills their neighbor H826
Dt 27:25 "C *is* anyone who accepts a bribe to kill an H826
Dt 27:26 "C *is* anyone who does not uphold the H826
Dt 28:16 You *will* **be c** in the city and cursed in the H826
Dt 28:16 be cursed in the city and c in the country. H826
Dt 28:17 basket and your kneading trough *will* **be c**. H826
Dt 28:18 The fruit of your womb *will* **be c**, and the H826
Dt 28:19 You *will* **be c** when you come in and cursed H826
Dt 28:19 when you come in and c when you go out. H826
Jos 6:26 "C before the LORD is the one who H826
Jdg 9:27 eating and drinking, *they* c Abimelek. H7837
Jdg 21:18 'C **be** anyone who gives a wife to a H826
1Sa 14:24 "C *be* anyone who eats food before H826
1Sa 14:28 'C *be* anyone who eats food today! H826
1Sa 17:43 And the Philistine c David by his gods. H7837
1Sa 26:19 *may* they **be c** before the LORD! H826
2Sa 16: 5 son of Gera, and *he* c as he came out. H7837
2Sa 16: 7 As he c, Shimei said, "Get out, get out H7837
2Sa 19:21 death for this? *He* c the LORD's anointed." H7837
1Ki 21:10 charges that he *has* c both God and the H1385
1Ki 21:13 "Naboth *has* c both God and the king." H1385
2Ki 9:34 "Take care of that c *woman*," he said, "and H826
Job 1: 5 have sinned and c God in their hearts." H1385
Job 3: 1 his mouth and c the day of his birth H7837
Job 5: 3 taking root, but suddenly his house *was* c. H7686
Job 24:18 their portion of the land **is c**, so that no H7837
Pr 24:24 *will be* c *by* peoples and denounced by H7686
Ecc 7:22 many times *you* yourself *have* c others. H7837
Jer 11: 3 'C *is* the one who does not obey the terms H826
Jer 17: 5 "C *is* the one who trusts in man, who draws H826
Jer 20:14 C *be* the day I was born! May the day my H826
Jer 20:15 C *be* the man who brought my father the H826
Mal 1:14 "C *is* the cheat who has an acceptable male H826
Mal 2: 2 *I have already* c them, because you H826
Mt 25:41 from me, you *who are* c, into the eternal *G2933*
Mk 11:21 The fig tree *you* c has withered!" *G2933*
Ro 9: 3 that I myself were c and cut off from Christ *G353*
1Co 4:12 *When we are* c, we bless; when we are *G3366*
1Co 12: 3 God says, "Jesus be c," and no one can say *G353*
1Co 16:22 does not love the Lord, let that person be c! *G353*
Gal 3:10 "C is everyone who does not continue to *G2129*
Gal 3:13 "C is everyone who is hung on a pole." *G2129*
Heb 6: 8 is worthless and is in danger of being c. *G2932*
Rev 16: 9 intense heat and *they* c the name of God, *G1059*
Rev 16:11 c the God of heaven because of their *G1059*
Rev 16:21 And they c God on account of the plague *G1059*

CURSES (32) [CURSE]

Ge 12: 3 bless you, and *whoever* c you I will curse H7837
Ex 21:17 "*Anyone who* c their father or mother is to H7837
Lev 20: 9 " '*Anyone who* c their father or mother is H7837
Lev 24:15 '*Anyone who* c their God will be held H7837
Nu 5:23 is to write these c on a scroll and then H460
Dt 11:29 the blessings, and on Mount Ebal the c. H7839
Dt 27:13 stand on Mount Ebal to **pronounce** c: H7839
Dt 28:15 all these c will come on you and overtake H7839
Dt 28:20 The LORD will send on you c, confusion H4423
Dt 28:45 All these c will come on you. They will H7839
Dt 29:20 All the c written in this book will fall on H460
Dt 29:21 according to all the c *of* the covenant H460
Dt 29:27 brought on it all the c written in this book. H7839
Dt 30: 1 these blessings and c I have set before H7839
Dt 30: 7 will put all these c on your enemies who H460
Dt 30:19 you life and death, blessings and c. H7839
Jos 8:34 the blessings and the c—just as it is H7839
1Ki 2: 8 who **called down** bitter c *on* me the H7837+7839
2Ch 34:24 all the c written in the book that has been H460
Ne 13:25 them and **called** c **down** *on* them. H7837
Ps 37:22 the land, but *those* he c will be destroyed. H7837
Ps 59:12 For the c and lies they utter, H460
Pr 20:20 If *someone* c their father or mother, their H7837
Pr 28:27 close their eyes to them receive many c. H4423
Isa 65:15 my chosen ones to use in their c; H8652
Jer 11: 8 on them all the c *of* the covenant I had H1821
Jer 15:10 lent nor borrowed, yet everyone c me. H7837
Da 9:11 "Therefore the c and sworn judgments H460
Mt 15: 4 mother' and 'Anyone *who* c their father *G2800*
Mt 26:74 Then he began *to* **call down** c, and he *G2874*
Mk 7:10 'Anyone *who* c their father or mother is to *G2800*
Mk 14:71 He began *to* **call down** c, and he swore to *G354*

CURSING (7) [CURSE]

2Sa 16:10 If *he is* c because the LORD said to him H7837
2Sa 16:13 c as he went and throwing stones at him H7837
Ps 109:18 He wore c as his garment; it entered into H7839
Ecc 7:21 or you may hear your servant c you— H7837
Hos 4: 2 There is only c, lying and murder, stealing H457
Ro 3:14 "Their mouths are full of c and bitterness." *G725*
Jas 3:10 Out of the same mouth come praise and c *G2932*

CURTAIN (63) [CURTAINS]

Ex 26: 4 along the edge of the end c in one set, H3749
Ex 26: 4 the same with the end c in the other set. H3749
Ex 26: 5 fifty loops on one c and fifty loops on the H3749
Ex 26: 5 fifty loops on the end c of the other set, H3749
Ex 26: 9 Fold the sixth c double at the front of the H3749
Ex 26:10 the edge of the end c in one set and also H3749
Ex 26:10 the edge of the end c *in* the other set. H3749
Ex 26:12 the half c that is left over is to hang down H3749
Ex 26:31 "Make a c *of* blue, purple and scarlet yarn H7267
Ex 26:33 Hang the c from the clasps and place the H7267
Ex 26:33 the ark of the covenant law behind the c. H7267
Ex 26:33 The c will separate the Holy Place from H7267
Ex 26:35 table outside the c on the north side of H7267
Ex 26:36 the entrance to the tent make a c of blue, H5009
Ex 26:37 gold hooks for this c and five posts of H5009
Ex 27:16 courtyard, provide a c twenty cubits long H5009
Ex 27:21 outside the c that shields the ark of the H7267
Ex 30: 6 altar in front of the c that shields the ark H7267
Ex 35:12 atonement cover and the c that shields it; H7267
Ex 35:15 the c *for* the doorway at the entrance to H5009
Ex 35:17 the c *for* the entrance to the courtyard; H5009
Ex 36:11 along the edge of the end c in one set, H3749
Ex 36:11 was done with the end c in the other set. H3749
Ex 36:12 fifty loops on one c and fifty loops on the H3749
Ex 36:12 fifty loops on the end c of the other set, H3749
Ex 36:17 the edge of the end c in one set and also H3749
Ex 36:17 the edge of the end c in the other set. H3749
Ex 36:35 They made the c of blue, purple and H7267
Ex 36:37 to the tent they made a c *of* blue, H5009
Ex 38:18 The c *for* the entrance to the courtyard H5009
Ex 38:27 the bases for the sanctuary and for the c— H7267
Ex 39:34 durable leather and the shielding c; H7267
Ex 39:38 the c *for* the entrance to the tent H5009
Ex 39:40 the c for the entrance to the courtyard; H5009
Ex 40: 3 law in it and shield the ark with the c. H7267
Ex 40: 5 law and put the c *at* the entrance to the H5009
Ex 40: 8 it and put the c *at* the entrance to the H5009
Ex 40:21 hung the shielding c and shielded the ark H7267
Ex 40:22 north side of the tabernacle outside the c H7267
Ex 40:26 in the tent of meeting in front of the c H7267
Ex 40:28 Then he put up the c *at* the entrance to H5009
Ex 40:33 put up the c *at* the entrance to the H5009
Lev 4: 6 the LORD, in front of the c *of* the sanctuary. H7267
Lev 4:17 the LORD seven times in front of the c. H7267
Lev 16: 2 Holy Place behind the c in front of the H7267
Lev 16:12 incense and take them behind the c. H7267
Lev 16:15 blood behind the c and do with it as he H7267
Lev 21:23 must not go near the c or approach the H7267
Lev 24: 3 Outside the c *that shields* the ark of the H7267
Nu 3:25 the c *at* the entrance to the tent of H5009
Nu 3:26 the c *at* the entrance to the courtyard H5009
Nu 3:31 in ministering, the c, and everything H5009
Nu 4: 5 down the shielding c and put it over the H7267
Nu 4: 6 they are to cover **the c** with a durable H2257S
Nu 4:26 the c *for* the entrance to the courtyard H5009
Nu 18: 7 everything at the altar and inside the c. H7267
2Ch 3:14 He made the c *of* blue, purple and H7267
Mt 27:51 At that moment the c of the temple was *G2925*
Mk 15:38 The c of the temple was torn in two from *G2925*
Lk 23:45 And the c of the temple was torn in two. *G2925*
Heb 6:19 It enters the inner sanctuary *behind* the c, *G2925*
Heb 9: 3 Behind the second c was a room called *G2925*

C

Heb 10:20 living way opened for us through the c, G2925

CURTAINS (36) [CURTAIN]

Ex 26: 1 tabernacle with ten c *of* finely twisted H3749
Ex 26: 2 All the c are to be the same size H3749
Ex 26: 3 Join five of the c together, and do the H3749
Ex 26: 6 them to fasten the c together so that the H3749
Ex 26: 7 "Make c *of* goat hair for the tent over the H3749
Ex 26: 8 All eleven c are to be the same size H3749
Ex 26: 9 Join five of the c together into one set H3749
Ex 26:12 As for the additional length of the tent c H3749
Ex 26:13 The tent c will be a cubit longer on both H3749
Ex 27: 9 long and is to have c of finely twisted H7846
Ex 27:11 be a hundred cubits long and is to have c, H7846
Ex 27:12 shall be fifty cubits wide and have c, H7846
Ex 27:14 C fifteen cubits long are to be on one side H7846
Ex 27:15 c fifteen cubits long are to be on the H7846
Ex 27:18 with c of finely twisted linen five cubits high NDT
Ex 35:17 the c *of* the courtyard with its posts and H7846
Ex 36: 8 tabernacle with ten c *of* finely twisted H3749
Ex 36: 9 All the c were the same size H3749
Ex 36:10 joined five of the c together and did the H3749
Ex 36:13 to fasten the *two sets of* c together so that H3749
Ex 36:14 They made c *of* goat hair for the tent over H3749
Ex 36:15 All eleven c were the same size—thirty H3749
Ex 36:16 joined five of the c into one set and the H3749
Ex 38: 9 cubits long and had c *of* finely twisted H7846
Ex 38:12 west end was fifty cubits wide and had c, H7846
Ex 38:14 C fifteen cubits long were on one side of H7846
Ex 38:15 c fifteen cubits long were on the other H7846
Ex 38:16 All the c around the courtyard were of H7846
Ex 38:18 long and, like the c *of* the courtyard, five H7846
Ex 39:40 the c *of* the courtyard with its posts and H7846
Nu 3:26 the c *of* the courtyard, the curtain at the H7846
Nu 4:25 They are to carry the c *of* the tabernacle H3749
Nu 4:25 the c *for* the entrance to the tent of H5009
Nu 4:26 the c *of* the courtyard surrounding the H7846
SS 1: 5 tents of Kedar, like the **tent c** *of* Solomon. H3749
Isa 54: 2 stretch your tent c wide, do not hold back; H3749

CURVED (4)

Jos 15: 3 up to Addar and c **around** to Karka. H6015
Jos 15:10 Then it c westward from Baalah to Mount H6015
Jos 16: 6 on the north it c eastward to Taanath H6015
Jos 18:17 *It* then c north, went to En Shemesh H9305

CUSH (29) [CUSHITE, CUSHITES]

Ge 2:13 it winds through the entire land of C. H3932
Ge 10: 6 The sons of Ham: C, Egypt, Put and H3932
Ge 10: 7 The sons of C: Seba, Havilah, Sabtah H3932
Ge 10: 8 C was the father of Nimrod, who became H3932
2Ki 19: 9 the king of C, was marching out to H3932
1Ch 1: 8 The sons of Ham: C, Egypt, Put and H3932
1Ch 1: 9 The sons of C: Seba, Havilah, Sabta H3932
1Ch 1:10 C was the father of Nimrod, who became H3932
Est 1: 1 127 provinces stretching from India to C: H3932
Est 8: 9 127 provinces stretching from India to C. H3932
Job 28:19 The topaz of C cannot compare with it; it H3932
Ps 7: T which he sang to the LORD concerning C, H3933
Ps 68:31 from Egypt; C will submit herself to God. H3932
Ps 87: 4 Tyre, along with C—and will say H3932
Isa 11:11 Upper Egypt, from C, from Elam, from H3932
Isa 18: 1 of whirring wings along the rivers of C, H3932
Isa 20: 3 as a sign and portent against Egypt and C, H3932
Isa 20: 5 Those who trusted in C and boasted in H3932
Isa 37: 9 the king of C, was marching out to H3932
Isa 43: 3 your ransom, C and Seba in your stead. H3932
Isa 45:14 of Egypt and the merchandise of C, H3932
Jer 46: 9 men of C and Put who carry shields H3932
Eze 29:10 to Aswan, as far as the border of C. H3932
Eze 30: 4 and anguish will come upon C. H3932
Eze 30: 5 C and Libya, Lydia and all Arabia, Kub H3932
Eze 30: 9 in ships to frighten C out of her H3932
Eze 38: 5 C and Put will be with them, all H3932
Na 3: 9 C and Egypt were her boundless strength H3932
Zep 3:10 beyond the rivers of C my worshipers, H3932

CUSHAN (1)

Hab 3: 7 I saw the tents of C in distress, the H3936

CUSHAN-RISHATHAIM (2)

Jdg 3: 8 into the hands of C king of Aram H3937
Jdg 3:10 The LORD gave C king of Aram into the H3937

CUSHI (2)

Jer 36:14 Shelemiah, the son of C, to say to Baruch, H3935
Zep 1: 1 the LORD that came to Zephaniah son of C, H3935

CUSHION (1)

Mk 4:38 sleeping on a c. The disciples woke G4676

CUSHITE (15) [CUSH]

Nu 12: 1 talk against Moses because of his C wife, H3934
Nu 12: 1 his Cushite wife, for he had married a C. H3934
2Sa 18:21 Then Joab said to a C, "Go, tell the king H3934
2Sa 18:21 The C bowed down before Joab and ran H3934
2Sa 18:22 please let me run behind the C. H3934
2Sa 18:23 ran by way of the plain and outran the C. H3934
2Sa 18:31 Then the C arrived and said, "My lord the H3934
2Sa 18:32 The king asked the C, "Is the young man H3934
2Sa 18:32 The C replied, "May the enemies of my H3934
2Ch 14: 9 Zerah the C marched out against them H3934
Isa 20: 4 the Egyptian captives and C exiles, H3932
Jer 38: 7 But Ebed-Melek, a C, an official in the H3934
Jer 38:10 the king commanded Ebed-Melek the C, H3934
Jer 38:12 Ebed-Melek the C said to Jeremiah, "Put H3934
Jer 39:16 "Go and tell Ebed-Melek the C, 'This is H3934

CUSHITES (9) [CUSH]

2Ch 12: 3 Sukkites and C that came with him from H3934
2Ch 14:12 struck down the C before Asa and Judah H3934
2Ch 14:12 before Asa and Judah. The C fled, H3934
2Ch 14:13 a great number of C fell that they could H3934
2Ch 16: 8 Were not the C and Libyans a mighty army H3934
2Ch 21:16 of the Arabs who lived near the C. H3934
Da 11:43 with the Libyans and C in submission. H3934
Am 9: 7 Israelites the same to me as the C?" H1201+3934
Zep 2:12 "You C, too, will be slain by my sword." H3934

CUSTODY (8)

Ge 40: 3 put them in c *in* the house of the H5464
Ge 40: 4 After they had been in c for some time, H5464
Ge 40: 7 who were in c with him *in* his master's H5464
Ge 42:17 And he put them all in c for three days. H5464
Lev 24:12 They put him in c until the will of the LORD H5464
Nu 15:34 they kept him in c, because it was not H5464
1Ch 29: 8 of the LORD in the c *of* Jehiel the H3338
Gal 3:23 this faith, *we were* **held in** c under the law G5864

CUSTOM (18) [ACCUSTOMED, CUSTOMARY, CUSTOMS]

CUSTOM (KJV) DUTY, REVENUE

Ge 19:31 us children—as is the c all over the earth. H2006
Ge 29:26 "*It is* not our c here to give the H4027+6913
Jdg 8:24 **It was the** c **of** the Ishmaelites to wear H3954
1Ki 18:28 as was their c, until their blood H5477
2Ki 11:14 standing by the pillar, as the c was. H5477
Est 9:27 on themselves *to* **establish the** c that they H7756
Job 1: 5 in their hearts." This *was* Job's regular c. H6913
Mt 27:15 Now *it was* the governor's c at the festival G1665
Mk 10: 1 and as *was* his c, he taught them. G1665
Mk 15: 6 Now *it was the* c at the festival *to* **release** a AIT
Lk 1: 9 according to the c of the priesthood, to G1621
Lk 2:27 do for him what the c of the Law required, G1616
Lk 2:42 went up to the festival, according to the c. G1621
Lk 4:16 he went into the synagogue, as was his c. G1665
Jn 18:39 But it is your c for me to release to you one G5311
Ac 15: 1 *according to* the c taught by Moses G1621
Ac 17: 2 As was his c, Paul went into the G1665
Ac 25:16 it is not the Roman c to hand over anyone G1621

CUSTOMARY (6) [CUSTOM]

Jdg 14:10 held a feast, as *was* c *for* young men. H6913
1Sa 20:25 sat in his c place by the H7193+7193+3869+928
Est 1:13 Since it was c *for* the king to H4027+1821
Eze 24:17 beard or eat the *c* food *of* **mourners**. AIT
Eze 24:22 beard or eat the *c* food *of* **mourners**. AIT
Mk 14:12 when *it was c to* **sacrifice** the Passover lamb AIT

CUSTOMERS (2)

Eze 27:15 and many coastlands were your c H6088+3338
Eze 27:21 the princes of Kedar were your c; H6086+3338

CUSTOMS (13) [CUSTOM]

Lev 18:30 of the detestable c that were practiced H2978
Lev 20:23 live according to the c *of* the nations I am H2978
2Ki 17:33 accordance with the c *of* the nations from H5477
Est 3: 8 Their c are different from those of all H2017
Ps 106:35 with the nations and adopted their c. H5126
Isa 2: 6 like the Philistines and **embrace** pagan c. H8562
Jn 19:40 was in accordance with Jewish burial c. G1621
Ac 6:14 change the c Moses handed down to G1621
Ac 16:21 by advocating c unlawful for us Romans to G1621
Ac 21:21 their children or live *according to* our c. G1621
Ac 26: 3 with all the Jewish c and controversies. G1621
Ac 28:17 people or against the c of our ancestors, G1621
Gal 2:14 that you force Gentiles *to* **follow Jewish** c? G2678

CUT (255) [CUTS, CUTTER, CUTTING, FRESH-CUT]

Ge 15:10 c them in two and arranged the halves H1439
Ge 15:10 the birds, however, *he did* not c **in half**. H1439
Ge 17:14 in the flesh, *will* **be** c **off** from his people H4162
Ge 22: 3 When *he had* c enough wood for the H1324
Ex 4:25 c **off** her son's foreskin and touched H4162
Ex 12:15 the seventh *must* **be** c **off** from Israel. H4162
Ex 12:19 with yeast in it *must* **be** c **off** from the H4162
Ex 29:17 C the ram into pieces and wash the H5983
Ex 30:33 than a priest *must* **be** c **off** from their H4162
Ex 30:38 its fragrance *must* **be** c **off** from their H4162
Ex 31: 5 to c and set stones, to work in wood, and H3098
Ex 31:14 work on that day *must* **be** c **off** from their H4162
Ex 34:13 sacred stones and c **down** their Asherah H4162
Ex 35:33 to c and set stones, to work in wood and to H3098
Ex 39: 3 sheets of gold and c strands to be worked H7915
Lev 1: 6 skin the burnt offering and c it into pieces. H5983
Lev 1:12 *You are to* c it into pieces, and the priest H5983
Lev 3: 9 the entire fat tail c **off** close to the H6073
Lev 7:20 they *must* **be** c **off** from their people. H4162
Lev 7:21 to the LORD *must* **be** c **off** from their people H4162
Lev 7:25 to the LORD *must* **be** c **off** from their people H4162
Lev 7:27 who eats blood *must* **be** c **off** from their H4162
Lev 8:20 *He* c the ram into pieces and burned the H5983
Lev 17: 4 shed blood and *must* **be** c **off** from their H4162
Lev 17: 9 it to the LORD *must* **be** c **off** from the H4162
Lev 17:10 and *I will* c them **off** from the people. H4162
Lev 17:14 anyone who eats it *must* **be** c **off**. H4162
Lev 18:29 such persons *must* **be** c **off** from their H4162
Lev 19: 8 they *must* **be** c **off** from their people. H4162
Lev 19:27 " '*Do* not c the **hair** at the sides of your H5938
Lev 19:28 " '*Do* not c your bodies for the H8582+5989
Lev 20: 3 against him and *will* c him **off** from his H4162
Lev 20: 5 his family and *will* c them **off** from their H4162
Lev 20: 6 and *I will* c them **off** from their people. H4162
Lev 20:18 Both of them *are to* **be** c **off** from their H4162
Lev 21: 5 of their beards or c their bodies. H8581+8583
Lev 22: 3 that person *must* **be** c **off** from my H4162
Lev 22:24 testicles are bruised, crushed, torn or c. H4162
Lev 23:29 on that day *must* **be** c **off** from their H4162
Lev 26:26 When I c **off** your supply of bread, ten H8689
Lev 26:30 c **down** your incense altars and pile your H4162
Nu 9:13 they *must* **be** c **off** from their people for H4162
Nu 13:23 *they* c **off** a branch bearing a single H4162
Nu 13:24 cluster of grapes the Israelites c **off** there. H4162
Nu 15:30 the LORD and *must* **be** c **off** from the H4162
Nu 15:31 they **must surely be** c **off**; their guilt H4162+4162
Nu 19:13 They *must* **be** c **off** from Israel H4162
Nu 19:20 they *must* **be** c **off** from the community H4162
Dt 7: 5 c **down** their Asherah poles and burn their H1548
Dt 12: 3 c **down** the idols of their gods and wipe H1548
Dt 12:29 LORD your God *will* c **off** before you the H4162
Dt 14: 1 *Do* not c **yourselves** or shave the front of H1517
Dt 19: 5 the forest with his neighbor to c wood, H2634
Dt 20:19 *Do* not c them **down**. H4162
Dt 20:20 *you may* c **down** trees that you know are H4162
Dt 25:12 *you shall* c **off** her hand. Show her no pity. H7915
Jos 3:13 downstream *will* **be** c **off** and stand up in H4162
Jos 3:16 the Dead Sea) **was** completely c **off**. H4162
Jos 4: 7 of the Jordan **was** c **off** before the ark of H4162
Jos 4: 7 the waters of the Jordan **were** c **off**. H4162
Jos 8:22 Israel c them **down**, leaving them neither H5782
Jos 10:10 Beth Horon and c them **down** all the way H5782
Jdg 1: 6 and c **off** his thumbs and big toes. H7915
Jdg 1: 7 thumbs and big toes c **off** have picked up H7915
Jdg 6:25 to Baal and c **down** the Asherah pole H4162
Jdg 6:26 of the Asherah pole that *you* c **down**, H4162
Jdg 6:28 pole beside it c **down** and the second bull H4162
Jdg 6:30 Baal's altar and c **down** the Asherah pole H4162
Jdg 9:48 He took an ax and c **off** some branches H4162
Jdg 9:49 So all the men c branches and followed H4162
Jdg 19:29 he took a knife and c **up** his concubine H5983
Jdg 20: 6 c her **into pieces** and sent one piece to H5983
Jdg 20:21 out of Gibeah and c **down** twenty-two H8845
Jdg 20:25 *they* c **down** another eighteen thousand H8845
Jdg 20:42 came out of the towns c them **down** there. H8845
Jdg 20:45 the Israelites c **down** five thousand men H6618
Jdg 21: 6 "Today one tribe *is* c **off** from Israel," H1548
1Sa 2:31 is coming when *I will* c **short** your strength H1548
1Sa 2:33 one of you that *I do* not c **off** from serving H4162
1Sa 11: 7 of oxen, c them **into pieces**, and sent the H5983
1Sa 17:46 I'll strike you down and c **off** your head. H6073
1Sa 17:51 *he* c **off** his head with the sword. H4162
1Sa 20:15 and *do* not ever c **off** your kindness from H4162
1Sa 20:15 even when the LORD *has* c **off** every one of H4162
1Sa 24: 4 up unnoticed and c **off** a corner of Saul's H4162
1Sa 24: 5 *having* c **off** a corner of his robe. H4162
1Sa 24:11 *I* c **off** the corner of your robe but did not H4162
1Sa 28: 9 *He has* c **off** the mediums and spiritists H4162
1Sa 31: 9 *They* c **off** his head and stripped off his H4162
2Sa 4: 7 killed him, *they* c **off** his head. H6073
2Sa 4:12 *They* c **off** their hands and feet and hung H7915
2Sa 7: 9 and *I have* c **off** all your enemies from H4162
2Sa 10: 4 c **off** their garments at the buttocks H4162
2Sa 14:16 of the man *who is trying to* c **off** both me H9012
2Sa 14:26 Whenever he c *the* **hair** *of* his head—he H1662
2Sa 14:26 he used to c *his* **hair** once a year because H1662
2Sa 16: 9 Let me go over and c **off** his head." H6073
2Sa 20:22 and *they* c **off** the head of Sheba son of H4162
1Ki 3:25 "C the living child in two and give half to H1615
1Ki 3:26 I nor you shall have him. C him **in two**!" H1615
1Ki 5: 6 orders that cedars of Lebanon *be* c for me. H4162
1Ki 5:18 workers from Byblos c and prepared the H7180
1Ki 7: 9 of high-grade stone c to size and H1607
1Ki 7:11 high-grade stones, c to size, and cedar H1607
1Ki 9: 7 then *I will* c **off** Israel from the land I have H4162
1Ki 14:10 *I will* c **off** from Jeroboam every last male H4162
1Ki 14:14 king over Israel who *will* c **off** the family of H4162
1Ki 15:13 Asa c it **down** and burned it in the Kidron H4162
1Ki 18:23 and *let them* c it **into pieces** and put it on H5983
1Ki 18:33 c the bull **into pieces** and laid it on the H5983
1Ki 21:21 descendants and c **off** from Ahab every H4162
2Ki 3:19 *You will* c **down** every good tree, stop up H5877
2Ki 3:25 the springs and c **down** every good tree. H5877
2Ki 4:39 *he* c them **up** into the pot of stew H7114
2Ki 6: 4 to the Jordan and *began to* c **down** trees. H1615
2Ki 6: 6 Elisha c a stick and threw it there H7892
2Ki 6:32 is sending someone to c **off** my head? H6073
2Ki 9: 8 *I will* c **off** from Ahab every last male in H4162
2Ki 10:25 So *they* c them **down** with the sword H5782
2Ki 16:17 King Ahaz c **off** the side panels and H7915
2Ki 18: 4 sacred stones and c **down** the Asherah H4162
2Ki 19: 7 there *I will* **have** him c **down** with the H5877
2Ki 19:23 *I have* c **down** its tallest cedars, the H4162
2Ki 23:14 sacred stones and c **down** the Asherah H4162
2Ki 24:13 and c **up** the gold articles that Solomon H7915
1Ch 17: 8 and *I have* c **off** all your enemies from H4162
1Ch 19: 4 c **off** their garments at the buttocks H4162
2Ch 2:10 the woodsmen *who* c the timber, twenty H4162

2Ch 2:16 we will c all the logs from Lebanon H4162
2Ch 14: 3 sacred stones and c down the Asherah H1548
2Ch 15:16 Asa c it down, broke it up and burned it in H4162
2Ch 16:14 the tomb that he had c out for himself in H4125
2Ch 28:24 the temple of God and c them in pieces. H7915
2Ch 31: 1 sacred stones and c down the Asherah H1548
2Ch 32:21 blood, c him down with the sword. H5877
2Ch 34: 4 he c to pieces the incense altars that were H1548
2Ch 34: 7 to powder and c to pieces all the incense H1548
Job 6: 9 to let loose his hand and c off my life! H1298
Job 14: 7 If it is c down, it will sprout again, and its H4162
Job 17: 1 my days are c short, the grave H2403
Job 24:24 they are c off like heads of grain. H4909
Job 26:12 by his wisdom he c Rahab to pieces. H4730
Job 27: 8 have the godless when they are c off, H1298
Job 28: 4 Far from human dwellings they c a shaft H7287
Ps 31:22 alarm I said, "I am c off from your sight!" H1746
Ps 74: 5 men wielding axes to c through a thicket of NDT
Ps 75:10 "I will c off the horns of all the wicked H1548
Ps 80:16 Your vine is c down, it is burned with fire H4065
Ps 88: 5 no more, who are c off from your care. H1615
Ps 89:45 You have c short the days of his youth H7918
Ps 101: 8 I will c off every evildoer from the city of H4162
Ps 102:23 he broke my strength; he c short my days. H7918
Ps 109:13 May his descendants be c off, their names H4162
Ps 118:10 in the name of the LORD I c them down. H4577
Ps 118:11 in the name of the LORD I c them down. H4577
Ps 118:12 in the name of the LORD I c them down. H4577
Ps 129: 4 he has c me free from the cords of the H7915
Pr 2:22 the wicked will be c off from the land H4162
Pr 10:27 the years of the wicked are c short. H7918
Pr 23:18 you, and your hope will not be c off. H4162
Pr 24:14 you, and your hope will not be c off. H4162
Isa 5: 2 in it and c out a winepress as well H2933
Isa 6:13 oak leave stumps when they are c down, H8961
Isa 7:20 private parts, and to c off your beard also. H6200
Isa 9:14 So the LORD will c off from Israel both H4162
Isa 10:34 He will c down the forest thickets with an H5937
Isa 14: 8 laid low, no one comes to c us down." H4162
Isa 15: 2 head is shaved and every beard c off. H1757
Isa 18: 5 he will c off the shoots with pruning H4162
Isa 18: 5 and c down and take away the spreading H9372
Isa 22:16 gave you permission to c out a grave for H2933
Isa 22:25 the load hanging on it will be c down." H4162
Isa 29:20 who have an eye for evil will be c down— H4162
Isa 33:12 like c thornbushes they will be set ablaze." H4065
Isa 37: 7 there I will have him c down with the H5877
Isa 37:24 I have c down its tallest cedars, the H4162
Isa 38:12 and he has c me off from the loom H1298
Isa 44:14 He c down cedars, or perhaps took a H4162
Isa 45: 2 of bronze and c through bars of iron. H1548
Isa 51: 1 rock from which you were c and to the H2933
Isa 51: 9 Was it not you who c Rahab to pieces H2933
Isa 53: 8 For he was c off from the land of the living H1615
Jer 6: 6 "C down the trees and build siege ramps H4162
Jer 7:29 " 'C off your hair and throw it away; take H1605
Jer 9:22 open field, like c grain behind the reaper H6658
Jer 10: 3 worthless; they c a tree out of the forest H4162
Jer 11:19 let us c him off from the land of the living H4162
Jer 16: 6 no one will c themselves or shave H1517
Jer 22: 7 and they will c up your fine cedar beams H4162
Jer 34:18 treat like the calf they c in two and then H4162
Jer 36:23 the king c them off with a scribe's knife H7973
Jer 41: 5 their clothes and c themselves came from H1517
Jer 46:22 her with axes, like men who c down trees. H2634
Jer 47: 5 the plain, how long will you c yourselves? H1517
Jer 48:25 Moab's horn is c off; her arm is broken," H1548
Jer 48:37 head is shaved and every beard c off; H1757
Jer 50:16 C off from Babylon the sower, and the H4162
La 2: 3 In fierce anger he has c off every horn of H1548
Eze 4:16 I am about to c off the food supply in H8689
Eze 5:16 famine upon you and c off your supply of H8689
Eze 14:13 my hand against it to c off its food supply H8689
Eze 16: 4 day you were born your cord was not c, H4162
Eze 21: 3 its sheath and c off from you both the H4162
Eze 21: 4 Because I am going to c off the righteous H4162
Eze 23:25 They will c off your noses and your ears H6073
Eze 23:47 stone them and c them down with their H1345
Eze 31:12 of foreign nations c it down and left it. H4162
Eze 35: 7 a desolate waste and c off from it all who H4162
Eze 37:11 up and our hope is gone; we are c off. H1615
Eze 39:10 from the fields or c it from the forests, H2634
Da 2: 5 I will have you c into pieces and your A10522
Da 2:34 watching, a rock was c out, but not by A10140
Da 2:45 vision of the rock c out of a mountain, A10140
Da 3:29 Abednego be c into pieces and A10522
Da 4:14 'C down the tree and trim off its A10134
Da 4:23 'C down the tree and destroy it A10134
Hos 6: 5 Therefore I c you in pieces with my H2933
Joel 1: 9 drink offerings are c off from the house of H4162
Joel 1:16 Has not the food been c off before our H4162
Am 3:14 of the altar will be c off and fall to the H1548
Ob 9 mountains will be c down in the slaughter H4162
Ob 14 at the crossroads to c down their fugitives, H4162
Na 3:15 the sword will c you down—they will H4162
Zec 11: 2 the dense forest has been c down! H3718
Mt 3:10 good fruit will be c down and thrown into G1716
Mt 5:30 you to stumble, c it off and throw it away. G1716
Mt 7:19 bear good fruit is c down and thrown into G1716
Mt 18: 8 you to stumble, c it off and throw it away. G1716
Mt 21: 8 while others c branches from the trees G3164
Mt 24:22 "If those days had not been c short, no G3143
Mt 24:51 He will c him to pieces and assign him a G1497
Mt 27:60 new tomb that he had c out of the rock. G3300
Mk 5: 5 would cry out and c himself with stones. G2888
Mk 9:43 you to stumble, c it off. It is better for you G644
Mk 9:45 if your foot causes you to stumble, c it off. G644
Mk 11: 8 spread branches they had c in the fields. G3164
Mk 13:20 "If the Lord had not c short those days, no G3143
Mk 15:46 placed it in a tomb c out of rock. G1639+3300
Lk 3: 9 good fruit will be c down and thrown into G1716
Lk 12:46 He will c him to pieces and assign him a G1497
Lk 13: 7 C it down! Why should it use G1716
Lk 13: 9 next year, fine! If not, then c it down.' " G1716
Lk 23:53 cloth and placed it in a tomb c in the rock, G3292
Jn 18:26 of the man whose ear Peter had c off, G644
Ac 2:37 they were c to the heart and said to Peter G2920
Ac 3:23 to him will be completely c off from their G2017
Ac 18:18 he had his hair c off at Cenchreae G3025
Ac 27:32 So the soldiers c the ropes that held the G644
Ro 9: 3 were cursed and c off from Christ for the G608
Ro 11:22 Otherwise, you also will be c off. G1716
Ro 11:24 if you were c out of an olive tree that is G1716
1Co 11: 6 she might as well have her hair c off; but G3025
1Co 11: 6 a woman to have her hair c off or her G3025
2Co 11:12 order to c the ground from under those G1716
Gal 5: 7 Who c in on you to keep you from G1601

CUTH, CUTHAH (KJV, NIV84) KUTHAH

CUTS (3) [CUT]

Job 38:25 Who c a channel for the torrents of rain H7103
Ps 107:16 of bronze and c through bars of iron. H1548
Jn 15: 2 He c off every branch in me that bears no G149

CUTTER (1) [CUT]

Ex 28:11 stones the way a gem c engraves a seal. H3093

CUTTING (11) [CUT]

Dt 23: 1 by crushing or c may enter the H4162+9163
2Ki 6: 5 As one of them was c down a tree, the H5877
2Ch 2: 8 your servants are skilled in c timber there. H4162
Ps 78:31 c down the young men of Israel. H4156
Pr 26: 6 of a fool is like c off one's feet or drinking H7894
Jer 44: 7 on yourselves by c off from Judah the men H4162
Mt 26:51 the servant of the high priest, c off his ear. G904
Mk 14:47 the servant of the high priest, c off his ear. G904
Lk 22:50 servant of the high priest, c off his right ear. G904
Jn 18:10 the high priest's servant, c off his right ear. G644
Ac 27:40 C loose the anchors, they left them in the G4311

CUZA (NIV84) CHUZA

CYCLE (1)

Isa 29: 1 to year and let your c of festivals go on. H5938

CYMBAL (1) [CYMBALS]

1Co 13: 1 only a resounding gong or a clanging c. G3247

CYMBALS (16) [CYMBAL]

2Sa 6: 5 lyres, timbrels, sistrums and c. H7529
1Ch 13: 8 with harps, lyres, timbrels, c and trumpets. H5199
1Ch 15:16 musical instruments: lyres, harps and c. H5199
1Ch 15:19 Ethan were to sound the bronze c; H5199
1Ch 15:28 trumpets, and of c, and the playing of H5199
1Ch 16: 5 harps, Asaph was to sound the c, H5199
1Ch 16:42 of the trumpets and c and for the playing H5199
1Ch 25: 1 accompanied by harps, lyres and c. H5199
1Ch 25: 6 of the LORD, with c, lyres and harps, H5199
2Ch 5:12 dressed in fine linen and playing c, harps H5199
2Ch 5:13 by trumpets, c and other instruments H5199
2Ch 29:25 Levites in the temple of the LORD with c, H5199
Ezr 3:10 sons of Asaph) with c, took their places to H5199
Ne 12:27 of thanksgiving and with the music of c, H5199
Ps 150: 5 praise him with the clash of c, praise him H7529
Ps 150: 5 of cymbals, praise him with resounding c. H7529

CYPRESS (5)

Ge 6:14 So make yourself an ark of c wood; make H1729
Isa 41:19 the wasteland, the fir and the c together, H9309
Isa 44:14 down cedars, or perhaps took a c or oak. H9560
Isa 60:13 the fir and the c together, to adorn my H9309
Eze 27: 6 of c wood from the coasts of Cyprus they H9309

CYPRUS (13)

Nu 24:24 Ships will come from the shores of C; they H4183
Isa 23: 1 From the land of C word has come to H4183
Isa 23:12 cross over to C; even there you will H4183
Jer 2:10 Cross over to the coasts of C and look H4183
Eze 27: 6 from the coasts of C they made your deck, H4183
Ac 4:36 Joseph, a Levite from C, whom the G3250
Ac 11:19 as far as Phoenicia, C and Antioch G3251
Ac 11:20 however, men from C and Cyrene, went to G3250
Ac 13: 4 to Seleucia and sailed from there to C. G3251
Ac 15:39 Barnabas took Mark and sailed for C, G3251
Ac 21: 3 After sighting C and passing to the south G3251
Ac 21:16 He was a man from C and one of the G3250
Ac 27: 4 passed to the lee of C because the winds G3251

CYRENE (7)

Mt 27:32 they met a man from C, named Simon, G3254
Mk 15:21 A certain man from C, Simon, the father G3254
Lk 23:26 they seized Simon from C, who was on his G3254
Ac 2:10 Egypt and the parts of Libya near C G3255
Ac 6: 9 Jews of C and Alexandria as well as the G3254
Ac 11:20 men from Cyprus and C, went to Antioch G3254
Ac 13: 1 called Niger, Lucius of C, Manaen G3254

CYRENIAN, CYRENIANS (KJV) CYRENE

CYRENIUS (KJV) QUIRINIUS

CYRUS (23)

2Ch 36:22 In the first year of C king of Persia, in H3931
2Ch 36:22 moved the heart of C king of Persia to H3931
2Ch 36:23 "This is what C king of Persia says: " 'The H3931
Ezr 1: 1 In the first year of C king of Persia, in H3931
Ezr 1: 1 moved the heart of C king of Persia to H3931
Ezr 1: 2 "This is what C king of Persia says: " 'The H3931
Ezr 1: 7 King C brought out the articles belonging H3931
Ezr 1: 8 C king of Persia had them brought by H3931
Ezr 3: 7 as authorized by C king of Persia. H3931
Ezr 4: 3 of Israel, as King C, the king of Persia, H3931
Ezr 4: 5 the entire reign of C king of Persia and H3931
Ezr 5:13 in the first year of C king of Babylon A10350
Ezr 5:13 King C issued a decree to rebuild this A10350
Ezr 5:14 Then King C gave them to a man named A10350
Ezr 5:17 to see if King C did in fact issue a A10350
Ezr 6: 3 In the first year of King C, the king issued A10350
Ezr 6:14 the God of Israel and the decrees of C, A10350
Isa 44:28 who says of C, 'He is my shepherd and H3931
Isa 45: 1 to his anointed, to C, whose right hand I H3931
Isa 45:13 I will raise up C in my righteousness: H2084S
Da 1:21 there until the first year of King C. H3931
Da 6:28 of Darius and the reign of C the Persian. A10350
Da 10: 1 In the third year of C king of Persia, H3931

D

DABBESHETH (1)

Jos 19:11 to Maralah, touched D, and extended to H1833

DABERATH (3)

Jos 19:12 Tabor and went on to D and up to Japhia. H1829
Jos 21:28 from the tribe of Issachar, Kishion, D, H1829
1Ch 6:72 tribe of Issachar they received Kedesh, D, H1829

DAGGER (3)

2Sa 2:16 head and thrust his d into his opponent's H2995
2Sa 20: 8 his waist was a belt with a d in its sheath. H2995
2Sa 20:10 his guard against the d in Joab's hand, H2995

DAGON (8) [BETH DAGON, DAGON'S]

Jdg 16:23 a great sacrifice to D their god and to H1837
1Sa 5: 2 into Dagon's temple and set it beside D. H1837
1Sa 5: 3 next day, there was D, fallen on his face H1837
1Sa 5: 3 They took D and put him back in his place H1837
1Sa 5: 4 they rose, there was D, fallen on his face H1837
1Sa 5: 5 the priests of D nor any others who H1837
1Sa 5: 7 hand is heavy on us and on D our god." H1837
1Ch 10:10 hung up his head in the temple of D. H1837

DAGON'S (2) [DAGON]

1Sa 5: 2 carried the ark into D temple and set it H1837
1Sa 5: 5 any others who enter D temple at Ashdod H1837

DAILY (30) [DAY]

Nu 29: 6 to the monthly and d burnt offerings with H9458
1Ki 4:22 Solomon's d provisions were H4200+3427+285
2Ch 8:13 to the d requirement for H3427+928+3427
2Ch 31:16 perform the d duties of H3427+928+3427+2257
Ezr 6: 9 given them d without A10317+10089+10317
Ne 11:23 regulated their d activity. H3427+928+3427
Ne 12:47 the d portions for H1821+3427+928+3427
Job 3:24 For sighing has become my d food H4200+7156
Job 23:12 of his mouth more than my d bread. H2976
Ps 68:19 Savior, who d bears our burdens. H3427+3427
Pr 8:34 to me, watching d at my doors H3427+3427
Pr 30: 8 give me only my d bread. H4312+2976
Eze 43:25 a male goat d for a sin H4200+2021+3427
Da 1: 5 them a d amount of food H3427+928+3427
Da 8:11 it took away the d sacrifice from the LORD H9458
Da 8:12 people and the d sacrifice were given H9458
Da 8:13 the vision concerning the d sacrifice, the H9458
Da 11:31 fortress and will abolish the d sacrifice. H9458
Da 12:11 time that the d sacrifice is abolished and H9458
Mt 6:11 Give us today our d bread. G2157
Lk 9:23 up their cross d and follow me. G2848+2465
Lk 11: 3 Give us each day our d bread. G2157
Ac 2:47 to their number d those who were G2848+2465
Ac 6: 1 overlooked in the d distribution of food. G2766
Ac 16: 5 in the faith and grew d in numbers. G2848+2465
Ac 19: 9 had discussions d in the lecture G2848+2465
2Co 11:28 I face d the pressure of my concern G2848+2465
1Th 4:12 so that your d life may win the respect of G4344
Heb 3:13 encourage one another d, G2848+1667+2465
Jas 2:15 a sister is without clothes and d food. G2390

DAINTY (KJV) CHOICEST, DELICACIES, LUXURY

DALE (KJV) VALLEY

DALMANUTHA (1)

Mk 8:10 his disciples and went to the region of D. G1236

DALMATIA (1)

2Ti 4:10 has gone to Galatia, and Titus to D. G1237

DALPHON (1)
Est 9: 7 also killed Parshandatha, **D**, Aspatha, H1943

DAM (1)
Pr 17:14 Starting a quarrel is like breaching a **d**; so H4784

DAMAGE (4) [DAMAGED]
2Ki 12: 5 to repair whatever **d** is found *in* the temple." H981
2Ki 12: 7 you repairing the **d** *done to* the temple? H981
Ac 27:21 have spared yourselves this **d** and loss. *G5615*
Rev 6: 6 and *do* not **d** the oil and the wine! *G92*

DAMAGED (1) [DAMAGE]
Lev 21:20 festering or running sores or **d** testicles. H5293

DAMARIS (1)
Ac 17:34 also a woman named **D**, and a number of *G1240*

DAMASCENES (1) [DAMASCUS]
2Co 11:32 had the city of the **D** guarded in order *G1241*

DAMASCUS (58) [DAMASCENES]
Ge 14:15 them as far as Hobah, north of **D**. H1966
Ge 15: 2 who will inherit my estate is Eliezer *of* **D**?" H1966
2Sa 8: 5 When the Arameans of **D** came to help H1966
2Sa 8: 6 garrisons in the Aramean kingdom of **D**, H1966
1Ki 11:24 they went to **D**, where they settled H1966
1Ki 15:18 the king of Aram, who was ruling in **D**. H1966
1Ki 19:15 way you came, and go to the Desert of **D**. H1966
1Ki 20:34 may set up your own market areas in **D**, H1966
2Ki 5:12 Pharpar, the rivers of **D**, better than all the H1966
2Ki 8: 7 Elisha went to **D**, and Ben-Hadad king of H1966
2Ki 8: 9 camel-loads of all the finest wares of **D**. H1966
2Ki 14:28 recovered for Israel both **D** and Hamath, H1966
2Ki 16: 9 complied by attacking **D** and capturing it. H1966
2Ki 16:10 Then King Ahaz went to **D** to meet H1877
2Ki 16:10 He saw an altar in **D** and sent to Uriah H1966
2Ki 16:11 Ahaz had sent from **D** and finished it H1966
2Ki 16:12 king came back from **D** and saw the altar, H1966
1Ch 18: 5 When the Arameans of **D** came to help H2008
1Ch 18: 6 garrisons in the Aramean kingdom of **D**, H2008
2Ch 16: 2 king of Aram, who was ruling in **D**. H2008
2Ch 24:23 sent all the plunder to their king in **D**. H2008
2Ch 28: 5 as prisoners and brought them to **D**. H2008
2Ch 28:23 He offered sacrifices to the gods of **D**, who H2008
SS 7: 4 the tower of Lebanon looking toward **D**. H1966
Isa 7: 8 the head of Aram is **D**, and the head H1966
Isa 7: 8 the head of **D** is only Rezin. H1966
Isa 8: 4 the wealth of **D** and the plunder of H1966
Isa 10: 9 Hamath like Arpad, and Samaria like **D**? H1966
Isa 17: 1 A prophecy against **D**: "See, Damascus H1966
Isa 17: 1 **D** will no longer be a city but will become H1966
Isa 17: 3 royal power from **D**; the remnant of H1966
Jer 49:23 Concerning **D**: "Hamath and Arpad are H1966
Jer 49:24 **D** has become feeble, she has turned to H1966
Jer 49:27 "I will set fire to the walls of **D**; it will H1966
Eze 27:18 " '**D** did business with you because of H1966
Eze 47:16 on the border between **D** and Hamath), H1966
Eze 47:17 along the northern border of **D**, with the H1966
Eze 47:18 boundary will run between Hauran and **D**, H1966
Eze 48: 1 northern border of **D** next to Hamath will H1966
Am 1: 3 "For three sins of **D**, even for four, I will H1966
Am 1: 5 I will break down the gate of **D**; I will H1966
Am 5:27 I will send you into exile beyond **D**," H1966
Zec 9: 1 of Hadrak and will come to rest on **D**— H1966
Ac 9: 2 him for letters to the synagogues in **D**, *G1242*
Ac 9: 3 As he neared **D** on his journey, suddenly a *G1242*
Ac 9: 8 So they led him by the hand into **D**. *G1242*
Ac 9:10 In **D** there was a disciple named Ananias *G1242*
Ac 9:19 spent several days with the disciples in **D**. *G1242*
Ac 9:22 the Jews living in **D** by proving that Jesus *G1242*
Ac 9:27 how in **D** he had preached fearlessly *G1242*
Ac 22: 5 letters from them to their associates in **D**, *G1242*
Ac 22: 6 "About noon as I came near **D**, suddenly *G1242*
Ac 22:10 'and go into **D**. There you will be *G1242*
Ac 22:11 companions led me by the hand into **D**, *G1242*
Ac 26:12 I was going to **D** with the authority and *G1242*
Ac 26:20 First to those in **D**, then to those in *G1242*
2Co 11:32 In **D** the governor under King Aretas had *G1242*
Gal 1:17 I went into Arabia. Later I returned to **D**. *G1242*

DAMMIM See EPHES DAMMIM, PAS DAMMIM

DAMNATION (KJV) CONDEMNATION, CONDEMNED, DESTRUCTION, JUDGMENT, PUNISHED, SIN

DAMPNESS (1)
SS 5: 2 with dew, my hair with the **d** *of* the night." H8268

DAMSEL, DAMSEL'S, DAMSELS (KJV) ATTENDANTS, CHILD, CHILD'S, FEMALE SERVANTS, FEMALE SLAVE, (SERVANT) GIRL, VIRGIN, (YOUNG) WOMAN, (YOUNG) WOMAN'S, YOUNG WOMEN

DAN (59) [DAN JAAN, DANITE, DANITES, MAHANEH DAN]
Ge 14:14 went in pursuit as far as **D**. H1969
Ge 30: 6 Because of this she named him **D**. H1968
Ge 35:25 Rachel's servant Bilhah: **D** and Naphtali. H1968
Ge 46:23 The son of **D**: Hushim. H1968
Ge 49:16 "**D** will provide justice for his people as H1968
Ge 49:17 **D** will be a snake by the roadside, a viper H1968
Ex 1: 4 **D** and Naphtali; Gad and Asher. H1968
Ex 31: 6 Ahisamak, of the tribe of **D**, to help him. H1968
Ex 35:34 of the tribe of **D**, the ability to teach H1968
Ex 38:23 of the tribe of **D**—an engraver and H1968
Nu 1:12 from **D**, Ahiezer son of Ammishaddai; H1968
Nu 1:38 From the descendants of **D**: All the men H1968
Nu 1:39 number from the tribe of **D** was 62,700. H1968
Nu 2:25 of the camp of **D** under their standard. H1968
Nu 2:25 of the people of **D** is Ahiezer son of H1968
Nu 2:31 to the camp of **D** number 157,600. H1968
Nu 7:66 the leader of the people of **D**, brought his H1968
Nu 10:25 of the camp of **D** set out under H1201+1968
Nu 13:12 from the tribe of **D**, Ammiel son of H1968
Nu 26:42 were the descendants of **D** by their clans: H1968
Nu 26:42 These were the clans of **D**: H1968
Nu 34:22 the leader from the tribe of **D**; H1201+1968
Dt 27:13 Asher, Zebulun, **D** and Naphtali. H1968
Dt 33:22 About **D** he said: "Dan is a lion's cub H1968
Dt 33:22 "**D** is a lion's cub, springing out of Bashan H1968
Dt 34: 1 him the whole land—from Gilead to **D**, H1968
Jos 19:40 the tribe of **D** according to its H1201+1968
Jos 19:47 Leshem and named it **D** after their H1969
Jos 19:48 the inheritance of the tribe of **D**, H1201+1968
Jos 21: 5 of Ephraim, **D** and half of Manasseh. H1968
Jos 21:23 from the tribe of **D** they received Eltekeh, H1968
Jdg 5:17 And **D**, why did he linger by H1968
Jdg 18:29 They named it **D** after their ancestor Dan H1969
Jdg 18:29 They named it Dan after their ancestor **D** H1968
Jdg 18:30 the tribe of **D** until the time of the H1974
Jdg 20: 1 Then all Israel from **D** to Beersheba and H1969
1Sa 3:20 And all Israel from **D** to Beersheba H1969
2Sa 3:10 Israel and Judah from **D** to Beersheba." H1969
2Sa 17:11 Let all Israel, from **D** to Beersheba—as H1969
2Sa 24: 2 tribes of Israel from **D** to Beersheba and H1969
2Sa 24:15 of the people from **D** to Beersheba died. H1969
1Ki 4:25 Israel, from **D** to Beersheba, lived in H1969
1Ki 12:29 he set up in Bethel, and the other in **D**. H1969
1Ki 12:30 went as far as **D** to worship the other. H1969
1Ki 15:20 He conquered Ijon, **D**, Abel Beth Maakah H1969
2Ki 10:29 of the golden calves at Bethel and **D**. H1969
1Ch 2: 2 **D**, Joseph, Benjamin, Naphtali, Gad and H1968
1Ch 12:35 from **D**, ready for battle—28,600; H1974
1Ch 21: 2 count the Israelites from Beersheba to **D**. H1969
1Ch 27:22 over **D**: Azarel son of Jeroham. H1968
2Ch 2:14 mother was from **D** and whose father was H1968
2Ch 16: 4 conquered Ijon, **D**, Abel Maim and all H1969
2Ch 30: 5 from Beersheba to **D**, calling the people H1969
Jer 4:15 A voice is announcing from **D** H1969
Jer 8:16 of the enemy's horses is heard from **D**; H1969
Eze 48: 1 northern frontier, **D** will have one portion H1968
Eze 48: 2 border the territory of **D** from east to west. H1968
Eze 48:32 the gate of Benjamin and the gate of **D**. H1968
Am 8:14 as your god lives, **D**,' or, 'As surely as the H1969

DAN JAAN (1) [DAN]
2Sa 24: 6 on to **D** and around toward H1970

DANCE (7) [DANCED, DANCES, DANCING]
Job 21:11 as a flock; their little ones **d about**. H8376
Ecc 3: 4 a time to mourn and a time *to* **d**, H8376
SS 6:13 Shulammite as on the **d** *of* Mahanaim? H4703
Jer 31: 4 timbrels and go out to **d** *with* the joyful. H4688
Jer 31:13 Then young women will **d** and be glad H4688
Mt 11:17 you, and *you did* not **d**; we sang a *G4004*
Lk 7:32 you, and *you did* not **d**; we sang a *G4004*

DANCED (4) [DANCE]
1Sa 18: 7 As they **d**, they sang: "Saul has slain his H8471
1Ki 18:26 And *they* **d** around the altar they had H7174
Mt 14: 6 daughter of Herodias **d** for the guests *G4004*
Mk 6:22 the daughter of Herodias came in and **d**, *G4004*

DANCES (2) [DANCE]
1Sa 21:11 Isn't he the one they sing about in their **d** H4703
1Sa 29: 5 this the David they sang about in their **d**: H4703

DANCING (14) [DANCE]
Ex 15:20 women followed her, with timbrels and **d**. H4703
Ex 32:19 the camp and saw the calf and the **d**, H4703
Jdg 11:34 his daughter, **d** to the sound of timbrels! H4703
Jdg 21:21 of Shiloh come out to join in the **d**, H4703
Jdg 21:23 While the *young women were* **d**, each H2565
1Sa 18: 6 to meet King Saul with singing and **d**, H4703
2Sa 6:14 David *was* **d** before the LORD with all his H4159
2Sa 6:16 King David leaping and **d** before the LORD, H4159
1Ch 15:29 she saw King David **d** and celebrating, H8376
Ps 30:11 You turned my wailing into **d**; you H4688
Ps 149: 3 his name with **d** and make music to H4688
Ps 150: 4 praise him with timbrel and **d**, praise him H4688
La 5:15 our hearts; our **d** has turned to mourning. H4688
Lk 15:25 near the house, he heard music and **d**. *G5962*

DANDLED (1)
Isa 66:12 be carried on her arm and **d** on her knees. H9130

DANGER (18) [DANGEROUS, DANGERS, ENDANGER, ENDANGERED, ENDANGERS]
1Sa 20:21 the LORD lives, you are safe; there is no **d**. H1821
Pr 22: 3 The prudent see **d** and take refuge, but H8288
Pr 27:12 The prudent see **d** and take refuge, but H8288
Jer 49:31 gates nor bars; its people live **far from d**. H970
Mt 5:22 will be **in d** of the fire of hell. *G1944*
Lk 8:23 swamped, and *they were* **in great d**. *G3073*
Ac 19:27 *There is* **d** not only that our trade will lose *G3073*
Ac 19:40 *we are* **in d** of being charged with rioting *G3073*
Ro 8:35 famine or nakedness or **d** or sword? *G3074*
2Co 11:26 I have been *in* **d** from rivers, in danger *G3074*
2Co 11:26 in danger from rivers, *in* **d** from bandits, in *G3074*
2Co 11:26 from bandits, *in* **d** from my fellow Jews *G3074*
2Co 11:26 my fellow Jews, *in* **d** from Gentiles; in *G3074*
2Co 11:26 danger from Gentiles; *in* **d** in the city, in *G3074*
2Co 11:26 danger in the city, *in* **d** in the country, in *G3074*
2Co 11:26 in the country, *in* **d** at sea; and in danger *G3074*
2Co 11:26 and *in* **d** from false believers. *G3074*
Heb 6: 8 is worthless and is **in d of** being cursed. *G1584*

DANGEROUS (1) [DANGER]
Ac 27: 9 had already become **d** because by now it *G2195*

DANGERS (1) [DANGER]
Ecc 12: 5 afraid of heights and of **d** in the streets; H3152

DANGLE (1)
Job 28: 4 far from other people *they* **d** and sway. H1938

DANIEL (76) [DANIEL'S]
1Ch 3: 1 second, **D** the son of Abigail of Carmel H1975
Ezr 8: 2 of Ithamar, **D**; of the descendants of H1975
Ne 10: 6 **D**, Ginnethon, Baruch, H1975
Eze 14:14 three men—Noah, **D** and Job—were in it H1975
Eze 14:20 even if Noah, **D** and Job were in it, they H1975
Eze 28: 3 Are you wiser than **D**? Is no secret hidden H1975
Da 1: 6 some from Judah: **D**, Hananiah, Mishael H1975
Da 1: 7 to **D**, the name Belteshazzar; to Hananiah H1975
Da 1: 8 But **D** resolved not to defile himself with H1975
Da 1: 9 to show favor and compassion to **D**, H1975
Da 1:10 the official told **D**, "I am afraid of my H1975
Da 1:11 **D** then said to the guard whom the chief H1975
Da 1:11 the chief official had appointed over **D**, H1975
Da 1:17 And **D** could understand visions and H1975
Da 1:19 he found none equal to **D**, Hananiah H1975
Da 1:21 And **D** remained there until the first year H1975
Da 2:13 were sent to look for **D** and his friends to A10181
Da 2:14 **D** spoke to him with wisdom and tact. A10181
Da 2:15 Arioch then explained the matter to **D**. A10181
Da 2:16 **D** went in to the king and asked for time A10181
Da 2:17 Then **D** returned to his house and A10181
Da 2:19 mystery was revealed to **D** in a vision. A10181
Da 2:19 Then **D** praised the God of heaven A10181
Da 2:24 Then **D** went to Arioch, whom the king A10181
Da 2:25 Arioch took **D** to the king at once and A10181
Da 2:26 The king asked **D** (also called A10181
Da 2:27 **D** replied, "No wise man, enchanter A10181
Da 2:46 prostrate before **D** and paid him honor A10181
Da 2:47 The king said to **D**, "Surely your God is A10181
Da 2:48 the king placed **D** in a high position A10181
Da 2:49 while **D** himself remained at the royal A10181
Da 4: 8 **D** came into my presence and I told him A10181
Da 4:19 Then **D** (also called Belteshazzar) was A10181
Da 5:12 He did this because **D**, whom the king A10181
Da 5:12 Call for **D**, and he will tell you what the A10181
Da 5:13 So **D** was brought before the king, and A10181
Da 5:13 "Are you **D**, one of the exiles my A10181
Da 5:17 Then **D** answered the king, "You may A10181
Da 5:29 command, **D** was clothed in purple A10181
Da 6: 2 over them, one of whom was **D**. A10181
Da 6: 3 Now **D** so distinguished himself among A10181
Da 6: 4 charges against **D** in his conduct of A10181
Da 6: 5 against this man **D** unless it has A10181
Da 6:10 Now when **D** learned that the decree A10181
Da 6:11 a group and found **D** praying and asking A10181
Da 6:13 said to the king, "**D**, who is one of the A10181
Da 6:14 determined to rescue **D** and made every A10181
Da 6:16 they brought **D** and threw him into A10181
Da 6:16 The king said to **D**, "May your God A10181
Da 6:20 he called to **D** in an anguished voice A10181
Da 6:20 an anguished voice, "**D**, servant of the A10181
Da 6:21 **D** answered, "May the king live forever! A10181
Da 6:23 gave orders to lift **D** out of the den. A10181
Da 6:23 And when **D** was lifted from the den, no A10181
Da 6:24 falsely accused **D** were brought in and A10181
Da 6:26 must fear and reverence the God of **D**. A10181
Da 6:27 He has rescued **D** from the power of the A10181
Da 6:28 So **D** prospered during the reign of A10181
Da 7: 1 king of Babylon, **D** had a dream, and A10181
Da 7: 2 **D** said: "In my vision at night I looked A10181
Da 7:15 **D**, was troubled in spirit, and the A10181
Da 7:28 **D**, was deeply troubled by my thoughts A10181
Da 8: 1 Belshazzar's reign, I, **D**, had a vision, after H1975
Da 8:15 While I, **D**, was watching the vision and H1975
Da 8:27 **D**, was worn out. I lay exhausted for H1975
Da 9: 2 of his reign, I, **D**, understood from the H1975
Da 9:22 said to me, "**D**, I have now come to H1975
Da 10: 1 a revelation was given to **D** (who was H1975
Da 10: 2 At that time I, **D**, mourned for three weeks H1975
Da 10: 7 **D**, was the only one who saw the vision H1975
Da 10:11 He said, "**D**, you who are highly esteemed, H1975
Da 10:12 "Do not be afraid, **D**. Since the first day H1975
Da 12: 4 **D**, roll up and seal the words of H1975
Da 12: 5 **D**, looked, and there before me H1975
Da 12: 9 "Go your way, **D**, because the words are H1975
Mt 24:15 spoken of through the prophet **D**—let the *G1248*

DANIEL'S (2) [DANIEL]
Da 2:49 at **D** request the king appointed A10181
Da 6:17 so that **D** situation might not be A10089+10181

DANITE (1) [DAN]
Lev 24:11 the daughter of Dibri the **D**.) H4200+4751+1968

DANITES (16) [DAN]
Jos 19:47 territory of the **D** was lost to them, H1201+1968
Jdg 1:34 confined the **D** to the hill country, H1201+1968
Jdg 13: 2 from the clan of the **D**, had a wife who H1974
Jdg 18: 1 the tribe of the **D** was seeking a place H1974
Jdg 18: 2 So the **D** sent five of their leading H1201+1968
Jdg 18: 2 These men represented all the **D**. H5476S
Jdg 18: 8 Eshtaol, their **fellow D** asked them, "How H278
Jdg 18:11 Then six hundred men of the **D** H5476+1974
Jdg 18:14 out the land of Laish said to their **fellow D**, H278
Jdg 18:16 The six hundred **D**, armed for battle, H1201+1968
Jdg 18:22 called together and overtook the **D**. H1201+1968
Jdg 18:23 the **D** turned and said to Micah H1201+1968
Jdg 18:25 The **D** answered, "Don't argue with H1201+1968
Jdg 18:26 So the **D** went their way, and Micah, H1201+1968
Jdg 18:28 The **D** rebuilt the city and settled there NDT
Jdg 18:30 There the **D** set up for themselves H1201+1968

DANNAH (1)
Jos 15:49 **D**, Kiriath Sannah (that is, Debir), H1972

DAPPLED (2)
Zec 6: 3 the fourth **d**—all of them powerful. H1353
Zec 6: 6 the one with the **d** horses toward the H1353

DARDA (2)
1Ki 4:31 Heman, Kalkol and **D**, the sons of Mahol. H1997
1Ch 2: 6 Heman, Kalkol and **D**—five in all. H1997

DARE (12) [DARED, DARES, DARING]
2Sa 3:11 Ish-Bosheth *did* not **d** to say another word H3523
Job 13:16 no godless person *would* **d come** before him! AIT
Pr 29:24 they are put under oath and *d* not **testify**. AIT
Jn 9:34 steeped in sin at birth; *how d* you **lecture** us!" AIT
Ac 7:32 trembled with fear and *did* not **d** to look. G5528
Ac 23: 4 "*How d you* **insult** God's high priest! AIT
Ro 5: 7 person someone *might* possibly **d** to die. G5528
1Co 6: 1 *do you* **d** to take it before the ungodly G5528
2Co 10:12 *We do* not **d** to classify or compare G5528
2Co 11:21 as a fool—I also **d** *to boast about.* G5528
Php 1:14 in the Lord and **d** all the more to proclaim G5528
Jude 9 *did* not *himself* **d** to condemn him for G5528

DARED (7) [DARE]
Est 7: 5 the man who *has* **d** to do such a H4848+4213
Mt 22:46 that day on no one **d** to ask him any more G5528
Mk 12:34 from then on no one **d** ask him any more G5528
Lk 20:40 And no *one* **d** to ask him any more G5528
Jn 21:12 None of the disciples **d** ask him, "Who G5528
Ac 5:13 No one else **d** join them, even though G5528
1Th 2: 2 the help of our God *we* **d** to tell you his G4245

DARES (6) [DARE]
Ge 49: 9 like a lioness—who *d to* **rouse** him? AIT
Nu 24: 9 like a lioness—who *d to* **rouse** them? AIT
Job 41:14 Who *d* **open** the doors of its mouth, ringed AIT
La 4:14 with blood that no *one* **d** to touch their H3523
Zec 4:10 "Who **d despise** the day of small things H996
2Co 11:21 Whatever anyone else **d** *to boast about* G5528

DARICS (6)
1Ch 29: 7 talents and ten thousand **d** of gold, H163
Ezr 2:69 the treasury for this work 61,000 **d** of gold, H2007
Ezr 8:27 20 bowls of gold valued at 1,000 **d**, and H163
Ne 7:70 gave to the treasury 1,000 **d** of gold, H2007
Ne 7:71 the work 20,000 **d** of gold and 2,200 H2007
Ne 7:72 rest of the people was 20,000 **d** of gold, H2007

DARING (1) [DARE]
Job 32: 6 was fearful, **not d** to tell you what I know. H3707

DARIUS (26)
Ezr 4: 5 down to the reign of **D** king of Persia. H2003
Ezr 4:24 year of the reign of **D** king of Persia. A10184
Ezr 5: 5 a report could go to **D** and his written A10184
Ezr 5: 6 of Trans-Euphrates, sent to King **D**. A10184
Ezr 5: 7 To King **D**: Cordial greetings. A10184
Ezr 6: 1 King **D** then issued an order, and they A10184
Ezr 6:12 in Jerusalem. I **D** have decreed it. A10184
Ezr 6:13 because of the decree King **D** had sent A10184
Ezr 6:14 decrees of Cyrus, **D** and Artaxerxes, kings A10184
Ezr 6:15 in the sixth year of the reign of King **D**. A10184
Ne 12:22 recorded in the reign of **D** the Persian. H2003
Da 5:31 **D** the Mede took over the kingdom A10184
Da 6: 1 It pleased **D** to appoint 120 satraps to A10184
Da 6: 6 king and said: "May King **D** live forever! A10184
Da 6: 9 So King **D** put the decree in writing. A10184
Da 6:15 went as a group to King **D** and said to him, NDT
Da 6:25 Then King **D** wrote to all the nations A10184
Da 6:28 during the reign of **D** and the reign of A10184
Da 9: 1 In the first year of **D** son of Xerxes (a H2003
Da 11: 1 And in the first year of **D** the Mede, I took H2003
Hag 1: 1 In the second year of King **D**, on the first H2003
Hag 1:15 In the second year of King **D**, H2003
Hag 2:10 in the second year of **D**, the word of the H2003
Zec 1: 1 the eighth month of the second year of **D**, H2003
Zec 1: 7 in the second year of **D**, the word of the H2003
Zec 7: 1 In the fourth year of King **D**, the word of H2003

DARK (38) [DARK-COLORED, DARKEN, DARKENED, DARKENING, DARKENS, DARKER, DARKEST, DARKNESS, PITCH-DARK]
Dt 28:29 grope about like a blind person in the **d**. H696
2Sa 22:10 came down; **d clouds** were under his feet. H6906
2Sa 22:12 around him—the **d** rain clouds of the sky. H3128
1Ki 8:12 has said that he would dwell in a **d cloud**; H6906
2Ch 6: 1 has said that he would dwell in a **d cloud**; H6906
Job 3: 9 *May* its morning stars *become* **d**; may it H3124
Job 16:16 with weeping, **d shadows** ring my eyes; H7516
Job 18: 6 The light in his tent *becomes* **d**; the lamp H3124
Job 22:11 why it is so **d** you cannot see, and why a H3125
Job 24:16 In the **d**, thieves break into houses, but by H3125
Ps 18: 9 came down; **d clouds** were under his feet. H6906
Ps 18:11 around him—the **d** rain clouds of the sky. H3128
Ps 35: 6 may their path be **d** and slippery, with the H3125
Ps 74:20 of violence fill the **d places** *of* the land. H4743
Ps 105:28 He sent darkness and **made** the land **d** H3124
Ps 139:12 even the darkness *will* not *be* **d** to you H3124
Pr 2:13 left the straight paths to walk in **d** ways, H3125
Pr 7: 9 was fading, as the **d** of night set in. H413+696
Ecc 12: 2 light and the moon and the stars *grow* **d**, H3124
SS 1: 5 **D** am I, yet lovely, daughters of Jerusalem H8839
SS 1: 5 of Jerusalem, **d** like the tents of Kedar NDT
SS 1: 6 Do not stare at me because I am **d** H8842
Isa 50:10 Let the one who walks in the **d**, who has H3128
Jer 4:28 mourn and the heavens above *grow* **d**, H7722
Eze 30:18 **D** *will be* the day at Tahpanhes when I H3124
Mic 3: 6 prophets, and the day *will* **go d** for them. H7722
Mt 10:27 What I tell you in the **d**, speak in the G5028
Mk 1:35 the morning, **while it was still d**, Jesus got G1939
Lk 11:36 no part of it **d**, it will be just as full G5027
Lk 12: 3 have said in the **d** will be heard in the G5028
Jn 6:17 By now it was **d**, and Jesus had not yet G5028
Jn 12:35 walks in the **d** does not know where G5028
Jn 20: 1 while it was still **d**, Mary Magdalene went G5028
Ro 2:19 a light for those who are in the **d**, G5030
Eph 6:12 the powers of this **d** world and against the G5030
2Pe 1:19 as to a light shining in a **d** place, until the G903
Rev 8:12 the stars, so that a third of them **turned d**. G5029
Rev 9:17 were fiery red, **d blue**, and yellow as G5610

DARK-COLORED (4) [DARK, COLORED]
Ge 30:32 every **d** lamb and every spotted or H2569
Ge 30:33 any lamb that is not **d**, will be H2569
Ge 30:35 and all the **d** lambs, and he placed H2569
Ge 30:40 the streaked and **d** animals that belonged H2569

DARKEN (3) [DARK]
Eze 32: 7 I will cover the heavens and **d** their stars; H7722
Eze 32: 8 lights in the heavens *I will* **d** over you; H7722
Am 8: 9 go down at noon and **d** the earth in broad H3124

DARKENED (13) [DARK]
Job 6:16 *when* **d** by thawing ice and swollen with H7722
Ps 69:23 *May* their eyes *be* **d** so they cannot see H3124
SS 1: 6 I am dark, because I *am* **d** *by* the sun. H8812
Isa 5:30 distress; even the sun *will be* **d** by clouds. H3124
Isa 13:10 The rising sun *will be* **d** and the moon H3124
Joel 2:10 the sun and moon *are* **d**, and the stars no H7722
Joel 3:15 The sun and moon *will be* **d**, and the H7722
Mt 24:29 distress of those days " 'the sun *will be* **d**, G5029
Mk 13:24 " 'the sun *will be* **d**, and the moon will G5029
Ro 1:21 futile and their foolish hearts *were* **d**. G5029
Ro 11:10 *May* their eyes *be* **d** so they cannot see G5029
Eph 4:18 They are **d** in their understanding and G5031
Rev 9: 2 The sun and sky *were* **d** by the smoke G5031

DARKENING (1) [DARK]
Jer 13:16 before your feet stumble on the **d** hills. H5974

DARKENS (1) [DARK]
Am 5: 8 midnight into dawn and **d** day *into* night, H3124

DARKER (1) [DARK]
Ge 49:12 His eyes will be **d** than wine, his teeth H2679

DARKEST (2) [DARK]
Ps 23: 4 Even though I walk through the **d** valley, H7516
Ps 88: 6 put me in the lowest pit, in the **d** depths. H4743

DARKNESS (166) [DARK]
Ge 1: 2 **d** was over the surface of the deep H3125
Ge 1: 4 he separated the light from the **d**. H3125
Ge 1: 5 light "day," and the **d** he called "night." H3125
Ge 1:18 the night, and to separate light from **d**. H3125
Ge 15:12 a thick and dreadful **d** came over him. H3128
Ge 15:17 When the sun had set and **d** had fallen, H6602
Ex 10:21 the sky so that **d** spreads over Egypt— H3125
Ex 10:21 spreads over Egypt—**d** that can be felt." H3125
Ex 10:22 and **total d** covered all Egypt for H3125+696
Ex 14:20 the cloud brought **d** to the one side and H3125
Ex 20:21 approached the **thick d** where God was. H6906
Dt 4:11 heavens, with black clouds and **deep d**. H6906
Dt 5:22 the cloud and the **deep d**; and he added H6906
Dt 5:23 When you heard the voice out of the **d** H3125
Jos 24: 7 he put **d** between you and the H4419
1Sa 2: 9 wicked will be silenced in the **place of d**. H3125
2Sa 22:12 He made **d** his canopy around him—the H3125
2Sa 22:29 my lamp; the LORD turns my **d** into light. H3125
Job 3: 4 may it turn to **d**; may God above not H3125
Job 3: 5 May gloom and **utter d** claim it once more H7516
Job 3: 6 That night—may **thick d** seize it; may it not H694
Job 5:14 **D** comes upon them in the daytime; at H3125
Job 10:21 to the land of gloom and **utter d**, H7516
Job 10:22 deepest night, of **utter d** and disorder H7516
Job 10:22 disorder, where even the light is like **d**." H694
Job 11:17 **d** will become like morning. H9507
Job 12:22 the deep things of **d** and brings utter H3125
Job 12:22 darkness and brings **utter d** into the light. H7516
Job 12:25 They grope in **d** with no light; he makes H3125
Job 15:22 He despairs of escaping the **realm of d** H3125
Job 15:23 he knows the day of **d** is at hand. H3125
Job 15:30 He will not escape the **d**; a flame will H3125
Job 17:12 into day; in the face of the **d** light is near. H3125
Job 17:13 if I spread out my bed in the **realm of d**, H3125
Job 18:18 light into the **realm of d** and is banished H3125
Job 19: 8 he has shrouded my paths in **d**. H3125
Job 20:26 total **d** lies in wait for his treasures. A fire H3125
Job 22:13 Does he judge through such **d**? H6906
Job 23:17 Yet I am not silenced by the **d**, by the H3125
Job 23:17 darkness, by the **thick d** that covers my face. H694
Job 24:17 they make friends with the terrors of **d**. H7516
Job 26:10 a boundary between light and **d**. H3125
Job 28: 3 Mortals put an end to the **d**; they search H3125
Job 28: 3 farthest recesses for ore in the blackest **d**. H694
Job 29: 3 head and by his light I walked through **d**! H3125
Job 30:26 when I looked for light, then came **d**. H694
Job 34:22 deep shadow, no **utter d**, where evildoers H7516
Job 37:19 draw up our case because of our **d**. H3125
Job 38: 9 its garment and wrapped it in **thick d**, H6906
Job 38:17 you seen the gates of the **deepest d**? H7516
Job 38:19 abode of light? And where does **d** reside? H3125
Ps 18:11 He made **d** his covering, his canopy H3125
Ps 18:28 burning; my God turns my **d** into light. H3125
Ps 44:19 you covered us over with **deep d**. H7516
Ps 82: 5 They walk about in **d**; all the foundations H3128
Ps 88:12 Are your wonders known in the *place of* **d** H3125
Ps 88:18 neighbor—**d** is my closest friend. H4743
Ps 91: 6 the pestilence that stalks in the **d**, nor H694
Ps 97: 2 Clouds and **thick d** surround him H6906
Ps 104:20 You bring **d**, it becomes night, and all the H3125
Ps 105:28 He sent **d** and made the land dark—for H3125
Ps 107:10 Some sat in **d**, in utter darkness, prisoners H3125
Ps 107:10 sat in darkness, in **utter d**, prisoners H7516
Ps 107:14 He brought them out of **d**, the utter H3125
Ps 107:14 of darkness, the **utter d**, and broke away H7516
Ps 112: 4 Even in **d** light dawns for the upright, for H3125
Ps 139:11 "Surely the **d** will hide me and the light H3125
Ps 139:12 even the **d** will not be dark to you; the H3125
Ps 139:12 shine like the day, for **d** is as light to you. H3128
Ps 143: 3 me dwell in the **d** like those long dead. H4743
Pr 4:19 But the way of the wicked is like **deep d** H696
Pr 20:20 lamp will be snuffed out in **pitch d**. H854+3125
Ecc 2:13 than folly, just as light is better than **d**. H3125
Ecc 2:14 while the fool walks in the **d**; but I came H3125
Ecc 5:17 All their days they eat in **d**, with great H3125
Ecc 6: 4 it departs in **d**, and in darkness its H3125
Ecc 6: 4 darkness, and in **d** its name is shrouded. H3125
Ecc 11: 8 But let them remember the days of **d**, for H3125
Isa 5:20 who put **d** for light and light for darkness H3125
Isa 5:20 who put darkness for light and light for **d** H3125
Isa 5:30 there is only **d** and distress; even H3125
Isa 8:22 see only distress and **d** and fearful gloom, H3128
Isa 8:22 and they will be thrust into **utter d**. H696
Isa 9: 2 people walking in **d** have seen a great H3125
Isa 9: 2 in the land of **deep d** a light has dawned. H7516
Isa 29:15 who do their work in **d** and think, "Who H4743
Isa 29:18 out of gloom and **d** the eyes of the H3125
Isa 42: 7 from the dungeon those who sit in **d**. H3125
Isa 42:16 I will turn the **d** into light before them H4743
Isa 45: 7 I form the light and create **d**, I bring H3125
Isa 45:19 from somewhere in a land of **d**; I have not H3125
Isa 47: 5 "Sit in silence, go into **d**, queen city of the H3125
Isa 49: 9 'Come out,' and to those in **d**, 'Be free! H3125
Isa 50: 3 the heavens with **d** and make sackcloth its H7725
Isa 58:10 then your light will rise in the **d**, and your H3125
Isa 59: 9 look for light, but all is **d**; for brightness, H3125
Isa 60: 2 **d** covers the earth and thick darkness is H3125
Isa 60: 2 the earth and **thick d** is over the peoples H6906
Isa 61: 1 the captives and **release from d** for the H7223
Jer 2: 6 a land of drought and **utter d**, a land H7516
Jer 2:31 a desert to Israel or a land of **great d**? H4420
Jer 13:16 the LORD your God before *he* **brings** *the* **d**, H3124
Jer 13:16 he will turn it to **utter d** and change it to H7516
Jer 23:12 will be banished to **d** and there they will H696
La 3: 2 made me walk in **d** rather than light; H3125
La 3: 6 made me dwell in **d** like those long dead H4743
Eze 8:12 the elders of Israel are doing in the **d**, H3125
Eze 32: 8 over you; I will bring **d** over your land H3125
Eze 34:12 were scattered on a day of clouds and **d**. H6906
Da 2:22 he knows what lies in **d**, and light dwells A10286
Joel 2: 2 a day of **d** and gloom, a day of clouds H3125
Joel 2:31 will be turned to **d** and the moon to blood H3125
Am 4:13 who turns dawn to **d**, and treads on the H6547
Am 5:18 That day will be **d**, not light. H3125
Am 5:20 Will not the day of the LORD be **d**, not light H3125
Mic 3: 6 without visions, and **d**, without divination. H3127
Mic 7: 8 I sit in **d**, the LORD will be my light. H3125
Na 1: 8 he will pursue his foes into the **realm of d**. H3125
Zep 1:15 ruin, a day of **d** and gloom, a day of H3125
Zec 14: 6 will be neither sunlight nor cold, **frosty d**. H7885
Mt 4:16 the people living in **d** have seen a great G5030
Mt 6:23 your whole body will be **full of d**. G5027

Mt 6:23 If then the light within you is **d**, how great G5030
Mt 6:23 you is darkness, how great is that **d**! G5030
Mt 8:12 outside, into the **d**, where there will be G5030
Mt 22:13 outside, into the **d**, where there will be G5030
Mt 25:30 outside, into the **d**, where there will be G5030
Mt 27:45 in the afternoon **d** came over all the land G5030
Mk 15:33 **d** came over the whole land until three in G5030
Lk 1:79 on those living in **d** and in the shadow of G5030
Lk 11:34 are unhealthy, your body also is **full of d**. G5027
Lk 11:35 then, that the light within you is not **d**. G5030
Lk 22:53 But this is your hour—when **d** reigns." G5030
Lk 23:44 **d** came over the whole land until G5030
Jn 1: 5 The light shines in the **d**, and the darkness G5028
Jn 1: 5 darkness, and the **d** has not overcome it. G5028
Jn 3:19 people loved **d** instead of light G5030
Jn 8:12 Whoever follows me will never walk in **d** G5028
Jn 12:35 have the light, before **d** overtakes you. G5028
Jn 12:46 one who believes in me should stay in **d**. G5028
Ac 2:20 will be turned to **d** and the moon to blood G5030
Ac 13:11 Immediately mist and **d** came over him G5030
Ac 26:18 their eyes and turn them from **d** to light, G5030
Ro 13:12 put aside the deeds *of* **d** and put on the G5030
1Co 4: 5 what is hidden *in* **d** and will expose the G5030
2Co 4: 6 "Let light shine out of **d**," made his light G5030
2Co 6:14 Or what fellowship can light have with **d**? G5030
Eph 5: 8 For you were once **d**, but now you are G5030
Eph 5:11 to do with the fruitless deeds *of* **d**, G5030
Col 1:13 from the dominion *of* **d** and brought us G5030
1Th 5: 4 are not in **d** so that this day should G5030
1Th 5: 5 We do not belong to the night or to the **d** G5030
Heb 12:18 burning with fire; *to* **d**, gloom and storm; G1190
1Pe 2: 9 who called you out of **d** into his wonderful G5030
2Pe 2: 4 putting them in chains *of* **d** to be held G2432
2Pe 2:17 Blackest **d** is reserved for them. G5030
1Jn 1: 5 God is light; in him there is no **d** at all. G5028
1Jn 1: 6 fellowship with him and yet walk in the **d**, G5030
1Jn 2: 8 because the **d** is passing and the true G5028
1Jn 2: 9 hates a brother or sister is still in the **d**. G5028
1Jn 2:11 sister is in the **d** and walks around in G5028
1Jn 2:11 the darkness and walks around in the **d**. G5028
1Jn 2:11 because the **d** has blinded them. G5028
Jude 6 these he has kept in **d**, bound with G2432
Jude 13 whom blackest **d** has been reserved G5030
Rev 16:10 its kingdom was **plunged into d**. G5031

DARKON (2)
Ezr 2:56 **D**, Giddel, H2010
Ne 7:58 **D**, Giddel, H2010

DARLING (9)
SS 1: 9 I liken you, my **d**, to a mare among H8299
SS 1:15 you are, my **d**! Oh, how beautiful! H8299
SS 2: 2 among thorns is my **d** among the young H8299
SS 2:10 "Arise, my **d**, my beautiful one H8299
SS 2:13 come, my **d**; my beautiful one H8299
SS 4: 1 you are, my **d**! Oh, how beautiful! H8299
SS 4: 7 beautiful, my **d**; there is no flaw in you H8299
SS 5: 2 my sister, my **d**, my dove, my H8299
SS 6: 4 as Tirzah, my **d**, as lovely as Jerusalem H8299

DART (3) [DARTING]

DART, DARTS (KJV) ARROW, ARROWS, CLUB, JAVELINS, WEAPONS
Job 41:21 and flames **d** from its mouth. H3655
Job 41:26 does the spear or the **d** or the javelin. H5025
Na 2: 4 torches; *they* **d about** like lightning. H8132

DARTING (4) [DART]
Pr 7:23 his liver, like a bird **d** into a snare, little H4554
Pr 26: 2 Like a fluttering sparrow or a **d** swallow H6414
Isa 14:29 its fruit will be a **d**, venomous serpent. H6414
Isa 30: 6 of adders and **d** snakes, the envoys carry H6414

DASH (6) [DASHED, DASHES]
Jdg 20:37 in ambush **made** a sudden **d** into Gibeah, H7320
2Ki 8:12 **d** their little children **to the ground**, and H8187
Ps 2: 9 *you will* **d** them **to pieces** like pottery." H5879
Na 2: 5 *They* **d** to the city wall; the protective H4554
Lk 19:44 *They will* **d** you **to the ground**, you and the G1610
Rev 2:27 scepter and *will* **d** *them* **to pieces** like G5341

DASHED (7) [DASH]
2Ch 25:12 them down so that all **were d to pieces**. H1324
Ps 119:116 I will live; *do* not **let** my hopes **be d**. H1017
Isa 13:16 infants *will* **be d to pieces** before their H8187
Hos 10:14 mothers **were d to the ground** with their H8187
Hos 13:16 their little ones *will* **be d to the ground** H8187
Na 3:10 Her infants **were d to pieces** at every H8187
Ac 27:29 Fearing that *we would be* **d** against the G1738

DASHES (1) [DASH]
Ps 137: 9 your infants and **d** them against the rocks. H5879

DATE (3) [DATES]
Eze 24: 2 "Son of man, record this **d**, this very date H3427
Eze 24: 2 this date, this very **d**, because the king of H3427
Ac 21:26 to give notice *of the d* **when** the days of AIT

DATES (4) [DATE]
2Sa 6:19 a **cake of d** and a cake of raisins to each H882
1Ch 16: 3 a **cake of d** and a cake of raisins to each H882
Ac 1: 7 to know the times or **d** the Father has set G2789
1Th 5: 1 about times and **d** we do not need to G2789

DATHAN (10)
Nu 16: 1 certain Reubenites—**D** and Abiram, sons H2018
Nu 16:12 Then Moses summoned **D** and Abiram H2018
Nu 16:24 from the tents of Korah, **D** and Abiram. H2018
Nu 16:25 Moses got up and went to **D** and Abiram H2018
Nu 16:27 from the tents of Korah, **D** and Abiram. H2018
Nu 16:27 **D** and Abiram had come out and were H2018
Nu 26: 9 of Eliab were Nemuel, **D** and Abiram. H2018
Nu 26: 9 The same **D** and Abiram were the H2018
Dt 11: 6 what he did to **D** and Abiram, sons of H2018
Ps 106:17 The earth opened up and swallowed **D**; it H2018

DAUB, DAUBED (KJV) COATED, COVER, COVERED

DAUGHTER (277) [DAUGHTER'S, DAUGHTER-IN-LAW, DAUGHTERS, DAUGHTERS-IN-LAW, GRANDDAUGHTER, GRANDDAUGHTERS]
Ge 11:29 she was the **d** *of* Haran, the father H1426
Ge 19:31 One day the **older** *d* said to the younger, "Our AIT
Ge 19:33 the **older** *d* went in and slept with him. AIT
Ge 19:34 The next day the **older** *d* said to the younger AIT
Ge 19:35 the **younger** *d* went in and slept with AIT
Ge 19:37 The **older** *d* had a son, and she named him AIT
Ge 19:38 The **younger** *d* also had a son, and she AIT
Ge 20:12 the **d** *of* my father though not *of* my H1426
Ge 24:15 She *was the* **d** of Bethuel son of Milkah H3528
Ge 24:23 he asked, "Whose **d** are you? Please tell H1426
Ge 24:24 "I am the **d** *of* Bethuel, the son that H1426
Ge 24:47 asked her, 'Whose **d** are you?' "She said, H1426
Ge 24:47 "She said, 'The **d** *of* Bethuel son of Nahor H1426
Ge 25:20 he married Rebekah **d** *of* Bethuel the H1426
Ge 26:34 he married Judith **d** *of* Beeri the Hittite H1426
Ge 26:34 also Basemath **d** *of* Elon the Hittite. H1426
Ge 28: 9 sister of Nebaioth and **d** *of* Ishmael son of H1426
Ge 29: 6 "and here comes his **d** Rachel with the H1426
Ge 29:10 Jacob saw Rachel **d** *of* his uncle Laban, H1426
Ge 29:18 years in return for your younger **d** Rachel." H1426
Ge 29:23 he took his **d** Leah and brought her to H1426
Ge 29:24 servant Zilpah to his **d** as her attendant. H1426
Ge 29:26 here to give the **younger** *d* in marriage AIT
Ge 29:28 Laban gave him his **d** Rachel to be his H1426
Ge 29:29 servant Bilhah to his **d** Rachel as her H1426
Ge 30:21 gave birth to a **d** and named her Dinah H1426
Ge 34: 1 the **d** Leah had borne to Jacob H1426
Ge 34: 3 His heart was drawn to Dinah **d** *of* Jacob H1426
Ge 34: 5 Jacob heard that his **d** Dinah had been H1426
Ge 34: 7 in Israel by sleeping with Jacob's **d**— H1426
Ge 34: 8 son Shechem has his heart set on your **d**. H1426
Ge 34:19 because he was delighted with Jacob's **d**. H1426
Ge 36: 2 Adah **d** *of* Elon the Hittite, and H1426
Ge 36: 2 Oholibamah **d** *of* Anah and H1426
Ge 36: 3 also Basemath **d** *of* Ishmael and sister of H1426
Ge 36:14 Esau's wife Oholibamah **d** *of* Anah and H1426
Ge 36:18 from Esau's wife Oholibamah **d** *of* Anah. H1426
Ge 36:25 Dishon and Oholibamah **d** *of* Anah. H1426
Ge 36:39 wife's name was Mehetabel **d** *of* Matred, H1426
Ge 36:39 daughter of Matred, the **d** *of* Me-Zahab. H1426
Ge 38: 2 Judah met the **d** *of* a Canaanite man H1426
Ge 38:12 time Judah's wife, the **d** *of* Shua, died. H1426
Ge 41:45 gave him Asenath **d** *of* Potiphera, H1426
Ge 41:50 born to Joseph by Asenath **d** *of* Potiphera, H1426
Ge 46:15 in Paddan Aram, besides his **d** Dinah. H1426
Ge 46:18 whom Laban had given to his **d** Leah H1426
Ge 46:20 born to Joseph by Asenath **d** *of* Potiphera, H1426
Ge 46:25 whom Laban had given to his **d** Rachel H1426
Ex 2: 5 Then Pharaoh's **d** went down to the Nile H1426
Ex 2: 7 Then his sister asked Pharaoh's **d**, "Shall I H1426
Ex 2: 9 Pharaoh's **d** said to her, "Take this baby H1426
Ex 2:10 him to Pharaoh's **d** and he became her H1426
Ex 2:21 who gave his **d** Zipporah to Moses in H1426
Ex 6:23 **d** *of* Amminadab and sister of Nahshon H1426
Ex 20:10 nor your son or **d**, nor your male or H1426
Ex 21: 7 "If a man sells his **d** as a servant, she is H1426
Ex 21: 9 he must grant her the rights of a **d**. H1426
Ex 21:31 also applies if the bull gores a son or **d**. H1426
Lev 12: 5 If she gives birth to a **d**, for two weeks the H5922
Lev 12: 6 of her purification for a son or **d** are over, H1426
Lev 18: 9 either your father's **d** or your mother's H1426
Lev 18: 9 your father's daughter or your mother's **d**, H1426
Lev 18:10 with your son's **d** or your daughter's H1426
Lev 18:10 your son's daughter or your daughter's **d**; H1426
Lev 18:11 relations with the **d** *of* your father's wife, H1426
Lev 18:17 relations with both a woman and her **d**. H1426
Lev 18:17 with either her son's **d** or her daughter's H1426
Lev 18:17 her son's daughter or her daughter's **d**; H1426
Lev 19:29 " 'Do not degrade your **d** by making her a H1426
Lev 20:17 the **d** *of* either his father or his mother H1426
Lev 21: 2 mother or father, his son or **d**, his brother, H1426
Lev 21: 9 " 'If a priest's **d** defiles herself by H1426
Lev 22:12 If a priest's **d** marries anyone other than a H1426
Lev 22:13 But if a priest's **d** becomes a widow or is H1426
Lev 24:11 was Shelomith, the **d** *of* Dibri the Danite.) H1426
Nu 25:15 who was put to death was Kozbi **d** *of* Zur, H1426
Nu 25:18 sister Kozbi, the **d** *of* a Midianite leader H1426
Nu 26:46 Asher had a **d** named Serah.) H1426
Nu 27: 8 give his inheritance to his **d**. H1426
Nu 27: 9 If he has no **d**, give his inheritance to his H1426
Nu 30:16 father and his young **d** still living at home H1426
Nu 36: 8 Every **d** who inherits land in any Israelite H1426
Dt 5:14 nor your son or **d**, nor your male or H1426
Dt 13: 6 your son or **d**, or the wife you love, H1426
Dt 18:10 who sacrifices their son or **d** in the fire, H1426
Dt 22:16 "I gave my **d** in marriage to this man H1426
Dt 22:17 'I did not find your **d** to be a virgin.' H1426
Dt 27:22 the **d** *of* his father or the daughter of his H1426
Dt 27:22 of his father or the **d** *of* his mother." H1426
Dt 28:56 husband she loves and her own son or **d** H1426
Jos 15:16 "I will give my **d** Aksah in marriage to the H1426
Jos 15:17 so Caleb gave his **d** Aksah to him in H1426
Jdg 1:12 "I will give my **d** Aksah in marriage to the H1426
Jdg 1:13 so Caleb gave his **d** Aksah to him in H1426
Jdg 11:34 should come out to meet him but his **d**, H1426
Jdg 11:34 Except for her he had neither son nor **d**. H1426
Jdg 11:35 tore his clothes and cried, "Oh no, my **d**! H1426
Jdg 11:40 to commemorate the **d** *of* Jephthah the H1426
Jdg 19:24 here is my virgin **d**, and his concubine. H1426
Jdg 21: 1 one of us will give his **d** in marriage to a H1426
Ru 2: 2 Naomi said to her, "Go ahead, my **d**." H1426
Ru 2: 8 said to Ruth, "My **d**, listen to me. H1426
Ru 2:22 be good for you, my **d**, to go with the H1426
Ru 3: 1 said to her, "My **d**, I must find a home H1426
Ru 3:10 LORD bless you, my **d**," he replied. H1426
Ru 3:11 And now, my **d**, don't be afraid. I will do H1426
Ru 3:16 Naomi asked, "How did it go, my **d**?" H1426
Ru 3:18 my **d**, until you find out what H1426
1Sa 14:49 The name of his older **d** was Merab, and H1426
1Sa 14:50 wife's name was Ahinoam **d** *of* Ahimaaz. H1426
1Sa 17:25 also give him his **d** in marriage and will H1426
1Sa 18:17 said to David, "Here is my older **d** Merab. H1426
1Sa 18:19 Merab, Saul's **d**, to be given to David, H1426
1Sa 18:20 Now Saul's **d** Michal was in love with H1426
1Sa 18:27 Saul gave him his **d** Michal in marriage. H1426
1Sa 18:28 David and that his **d** Michal loved David, H1426
1Sa 25:44 But Saul had given his **d** Michal, David's H1426
2Sa 3: 3 the son of Maakah **d** *of* Talmai king of H1426
2Sa 3: 7 a concubine named Rizpah **d** *of* Aiah. H1426
2Sa 3:13 you bring Michal **d** *of* Saul when you H1426
2Sa 6:16 Michal **d** *of* Saul watched from a window. H1426
2Sa 6:20 Michal **d** *of* Saul came out to meet him H1426
2Sa 6:23 And Michal **d** *of* Saul had no children to H1426
2Sa 11: 3 the **d** *of* Eliam and the wife of Uriah the H1426
2Sa 12: 3 slept in his arms. It was like a **d** to him. H1426
2Sa 14:27 Three sons and a **d** were born to Absalom H1426
2Sa 17:25 the **d** *of* Nahash and sister of Zeruiah the H1426
2Sa 21: 8 the two sons of Aiah's **d** Rizpah, whom H1426
2Sa 21: 8 with the five sons of Saul's **d** Merab, H1426
2Sa 21:10 Rizpah **d** *of* Aiah took sackcloth and H1426
2Sa 21:11 David was told what Aiah's **d** Rizpah, H1426
1Ki 3: 1 Pharaoh king of Egypt and married his **d**. H1426
1Ki 4:11 he was married to Taphath **d** *of* Solomon); H1426
1Ki 4:15 he had married Basemath **d** *of* Solomon); H1426
1Ki 7: 8 a palace like this hall for Pharaoh's **d**, H1426
1Ki 9:16 then gave it as a wedding gift to his **d**, H1426
1Ki 9:24 After Pharaoh's **d** had come up from the H1426
1Ki 11: 1 foreign women besides Pharaoh's **d**— H1426
1Ki 15: 2 name was Maakah **d** *of* Abishalom. H1426
1Ki 15:10 name was Maakah **d** *of* Abishalom. H1426
1Ki 16:31 married Jezebel **d** *of* Ethbaal king of the H1426
1Ki 22:42 mother's name was Azubah **d** *of* Shilhi. H1426
2Ki 8:18 had done, for he married a **d** *of* Ahab. H1426
2Ki 9:34 "and bury her, for she was a king's **d**." H1426
2Ki 11: 2 the **d** *of* King Jehoram and sister of H1426
2Ki 14: 9 'Give your **d** to my son in marriage. H1426
2Ki 15:33 mother's name was Jerusha **d** *of* Zadok. H1426
2Ki 18: 2 name was Abijah **d** *of* Zechariah. H1426
2Ki 19:21 " 'Virgin **D** Zion despises you and mocks H1426
2Ki 19:21 **D** Jerusalem tosses her head as you flee H1426
2Ki 21:19 name was Meshullemeth **d** *of* Haruz; H1426
2Ki 22: 1 mother's name was Jedidah **d** *of* Adaiah; H1426
2Ki 23:10 sacrifice their son or **d** in the fire to Molek. H1426
2Ki 23:31 name was Hamutal **d** *of* Jeremiah; H1426
2Ki 23:36 name was Zebidah **d** *of* Pedaiah; H1426
2Ki 24: 8 name was Nehushta **d** *of* Elnathan; H1426
2Ki 24:18 name was Hamutal **d** *of* Jeremiah; H1426
1Ch 1:50 wife's name was Mehetabel **d** *of* Matred, H1426
1Ch 1:50 daughter of Matred, the **d** *of* Me-Zahab. H1426
1Ch 2: 3 by a Canaanite woman, the **d** *of* Shua. H1426
1Ch 2:21 married the **d** *of* Makir the father of H1426
1Ch 2:35 Sheshan gave his **d** in marriage to his H1426
1Ch 2:49 Caleb's **d** was Aksah. H1426
1Ch 3: 2 the son of Maakah **d** *of* Talmai king of H1426
1Ch 3: 5 four were by Bathsheba **d** *of* Ammiel. H1426
1Ch 4:18 were the children of Pharaoh's **d** Bithiah, H1426
1Ch 7:24 His **d** was Sheerah, who built Lower and H1426
1Ch 15:29 Michal **d** *of* Saul watched from a window. H1426
2Ch 8:11 brought Pharaoh's **d** up from the City of H1426
2Ch 11:18 who was the **d** *of* David's son Jerimoth H1426
2Ch 11:18 of Abihail, the **d** *of* Jesse's son Eliab. H1426
2Ch 11:20 Then he married Maakah **d** *of* Absalom H1426
2Ch 11:21 loved Maakah **d** *of* Absalom more than H1426
2Ch 13: 2 was Maakah, a **d** *of* Uriel of Gibeah. H1426
2Ch 20:31 mother's name was Azubah **d** *of* Shilhi. H1426
2Ch 21: 6 had done, for he married a **d** *of* Ahab. H1426
2Ch 22:11 But Jehosheba, the **d** *of* King Jehoram H1426
2Ch 22:11 the **d** *of* King Jehoram and wife of the H1426
2Ch 25:18 'Give your **d** to my son in marriage. H1426
2Ch 27: 1 mother's name was Jerusha **d** *of* Zadok. H1426
2Ch 29: 1 name was Abijah **d** *of* Zechariah. H1426
Ezr 2:61 man who had married a **d** *of* Barzillai the H1426
Ne 6:18 had married the **d** *of* Meshullam son of H1426
Ne 7:63 man who had married a **d** *of* Barzillai the H1426
Est 2: 7 her as his own **d** when her father and H1426

Est 2:15 had adopted, the **d** *of* his uncle Abihail H1426
Est 9:29 So Queen Esther, **d** *of* Abihail, along with H1426
Job 42:14 The first **d** he named Jemimah, the second NDT
Ps 9:14 your praises in the gates of **D** Zion, H1426
Ps 45:10 **d**, and pay careful attention: Forget H1426
Ps 137: 8 **D** Babylon, doomed to destruction, happy H1426
SS 6: 9 is unique, the only **d** of her mother, the H2085S
SS 7: 1 beautiful your sandaled feet, O prince's **d**! H1426
Isa 1: 8 **D** Zion is left like a shelter in a vineyard H1426
Isa 10:30 **D** Gallim! Listen, Laishah! Poor H1426
Isa 10:32 shake their fist at the mount of **D** Zion, H1426
Isa 16: 1 across the desert, to the mount of **D** Zion. H1426
Isa 23:10 do along the Nile, **D** Tarshish, for you no H1426
Isa 23:12 reveling, Virgin **D** Sidon, now crushed! H1426
Isa 37:22 "Virgin **D** Zion despises and mocks you H1426
Isa 37:22 **D** Jerusalem tosses her head as you flee H1426
Isa 47: 1 sit in the dust, Virgin **D** Babylon; sit on the H1426
Isa 52: 2 on your neck, **D** Zion, now a captive. H1426
Isa 62:11 "Say to **D** Zion, 'See, your H1426
Jer 4:31 the cry of **D** Zion gasping for breath H1426
Jer 6: 2 I will destroy **D** Zion, so beautiful and H1426
Jer 6:23 in battle formation to attack you, **D** Zion." H1426
Jer 14:17 ceasing; for the Virgin **D**, my people, H1426
Jer 31:22 long will you wander, unfaithful **D** Israel? H1426
Jer 46:11 to Gilead and get balm, Virgin **D** Egypt. H1426
Jer 46:24 **D** Egypt will be put to shame, given into H1426
Jer 48:18 you inhabitants of **D** Dibon, for the one H1426
Jer 49: 4 Unfaithful **D** Ammon, you trust in your H1426
Jer 50:42 battle formation to attack you, **D** Babylon. H1426
Jer 51:33 "**D** Babylon is like a threshing floor at the H1426
Jer 52: 1 name was Hamutal **d** *of* Jeremiah; H1426
La 1: 6 the splendor has departed from **D** Zion. H1426
La 1:15 the Lord has trampled Virgin **D** Judah. H1426
La 2: 1 Lord has covered **D** Zion with the cloud H1426
La 2: 2 torn down the strongholds of **D** Judah. H1426
La 2: 4 his wrath like fire on the tent of **D** Zion. H1426
La 2: 5 mourning and lamentation for **D** Judah. H1426
La 2: 8 to tear down the wall around **D** Zion. H1426
La 2:10 The elders of **D** Zion sit on the ground in H1426
La 2:13 what can I compare you, **D** Jerusalem? H1426
La 2:13 that I may comfort you, Virgin **D** Zion? H1426
La 2:15 shake their heads at **D** Jerusalem: H1426
La 2:18 You walls of **D** Zion, let your tears flow H1426
La 4:21 be glad, **D** Edom, you who live H1426
La 4:22 punishment will end, **D** Zion; he will not H1426
La 4:22 punish your sin, **D** Edom, and expose your H1426
Eze 14:20 they could save neither son nor **d**. H1426
Eze 16:44 proverb about you: "Like mother, like **d**." H1426
Eze 16:45 You are a true **d** *of* your mother, who H1426
Eze 22:11 violates his sister, his own father's **d**. H1426
Eze 44:25 mother, son or **d**, brother or unmarried H1426
Da 11: 6 The **d** *of* the king of the South will go to H1426
Da 11:17 he will give him a **d** in marriage in order H1426
Hos 1: 3 So he married Gomer **d** *of* Diblaim, and H1426
Hos 1: 6 conceived again and gave birth to a **d**. H1426
Mic 1:13 You are where the sin of **D** Zion began H1426
Mic 4: 8 the flock, stronghold of **D** Zion, the former H1426
Mic 4: 8 kingship will come to **D** Jerusalem." H1426
Mic 4:10 Writhe in agony, **D** Zion, like a woman in H1426
Mic 4:13 "Rise and thresh, **D** Zion, for I will give H1426
Mic 7: 6 his father, a **d** rises up against her mother H1426
Zep 3:14 **D** Zion; shout aloud, Israel! Be glad H1426
Zep 3:14 rejoice with all your heart, **D** Jerusalem! H1426
Zec 2: 7 Escape, you who live in **D** Babylon!" H1426
Zec 2:10 "Shout and be glad, **D** Zion. For I am H1426
Zec 9: 9 Rejoice greatly, **D** Zion! Shout, Daughter H1426
Zec 9: 9 Shout, **D** Jerusalem! See, your H1426
Mt 9:18 before him and said, "My **d** has just died. *G2588*
Mt 9:22 "Take heart, **d**," he said, "your faith has *G2588*
Mt 10:35 his father, a **d** against her mother, *G2588*
Mt 10:37 loves their son or **d** more than me is not *G2588*
Mt 14: 6 birthday the **d** of Herodias danced *G2588*
Mt 15:22 My **d** is demon-possessed and suffering *G2588*
Mt 15:28 And her **d** was healed at that moment *G2588*
Mt 21: 5 "Say *to* **D** Zion, 'See, your king comes to *G2588*
Mk 5:23 earnestly with him, "My **little d** is dying. *G2589*
Mk 5:34 He said to her, "**D**, your faith has healed *G2588*
Mk 5:35 "Your **d** is dead," they said *G2588*
Mk 6:22 When the **d** of Herodias came in and *G2588*
Mk 7:25 a woman whose **little d** was possessed by *G2589*
Mk 7:26 Jesus to drive the demon out of her **d**. *G2588*
Mk 7:29 you may go; the demon has left your **d**." *G2588*
Lk 2:36 the **d** of Penuel, of the tribe of *G2588*
Lk 8:42 because his only **d**, a girl of about twelve *G2588*
Lk 8:48 Then he said to her, "**D**, your faith has *G2588*
Lk 8:49 "Your **d** is dead," he said *G2588*
Lk 12:53 mother against **d** and daughter against *G2588*
Lk 12:53 against daughter and **d** against mother, *G2588*
Lk 13:16 not this woman, a **d** of Abraham, whom *G2588*
Jn 12:15 "Do not be afraid, **D** Zion; see, your king *G2588*
Ac 7:21 Pharaoh's **d** took him and brought him up *G2588*
Heb 11:24 to be known as the son *of* Pharaoh's **d**. *G2588*

DAUGHTER'S (5) [DAUGHTER]

Ge 29:27 Finish **this** *d* bridal week; then we will give AIT
Lev 18:10 your son's daughter or your **d** daughter; H1426
Lev 18:17 her son's daughter or her **d** daughter; H1426
Dt 22:17 But here is the proof of my **d** virginity." H1426
2Sa 14:27 **His d** name was Tamar, and she H2023S

DAUGHTER-IN-LAW (17) [DAUGHTER]

Ge 11:31 son of Haran, and his **d** Sarai, the wife of H3987
Ge 38:11 Judah then said to his **d** Tamar, "Live as a H3987
Ge 38:16 Not realizing that she was his **d**, he went H3987
Ge 38:24 "Your **d** Tamar is guilty of prostitution H3987
Lev 18:15 'Do not have sexual relations with your **d**. H3987
Lev 20:12 " 'If a man has sexual relations with his **d** H3987
Ru 1:22 Ruth the Moabite, her **d**, arriving in H3987
Ru 2:20 Naomi said to her **d**. "He has not H3987
Ru 2:22 Naomi said to Ruth her **d**, "It will be good H3987
Ru 4:15 For your **d**, who loves you and who is H3987
1Sa 4:19 His **d**, the wife of Phinehas, was pregnant H3987
1Ch 2: 4 Judah's **d** Tamar bore Perez and Zerah to H3987
Eze 22:11 another shamefully defiles his **d**, and H3987
Mic 7: 6 mother, a **d** against her mother-in-law H3987
Mt 10:35 mother, a **d** against her mother-in-law— *G3811*
Lk 12:53 against **d** and daughter-in-law *G3811*
Lk 12:53 daughter-in-law and **d** against *G3811*

DAUGHTERS (216) [DAUGHTER]

Ge 5: 4 lived 800 years and had other sons and **d**. H1426
Ge 5: 7 lived 807 years and had other sons and **d**. H1426
Ge 5:10 lived 815 years and had other sons and **d**. H1426
Ge 5:13 lived 840 years and had other sons and **d**. H1426
Ge 5:16 lived 830 years and had other sons and **d**. H1426
Ge 5:19 lived 800 years and had other sons and **d**. H1426
Ge 5:22 God 300 years and had other sons and **d**. H1426
Ge 5:26 lived 782 years and had other sons and **d**. H1426
Ge 5:30 lived 595 years and had other sons and **d**. H1426
Ge 6: 1 on the earth and **d** were born to them, H1426
Ge 6: 2 of God saw that the **d** *of* humans were H1426
Ge 6: 4 of God went to the **d** *of* humans and had H1426
Ge 11:11 lived 500 years and had other sons and **d**. H1426
Ge 11:13 lived 403 years and had other sons and **d**. H1426
Ge 11:15 lived 403 years and had other sons and **d**. H1426
Ge 11:17 lived 430 years and had other sons and **d**. H1426
Ge 11:19 lived 209 years and had other sons and **d**. H1426
Ge 11:21 lived 207 years and had other sons and **d**. H1426
Ge 11:23 lived 200 years and had other sons and **d**. H1426
Ge 11:25 lived 119 years and had other sons and **d**. H1426
Ge 19: 8 I have two **d** who have never slept with a H1426
Ge 19:12 sons-in-law, sons or **d**, or anyone else in H1426
Ge 19:14 who were pledged to marry his **d**. H1426
Ge 19:15 your wife and your two **d** who are here, H1426
Ge 19:16 wife and of his two **d** and led them safely H1426
Ge 19:30 Lot and his two **d** left Zoar and settled in H1426
Ge 19:30 He and his two **d** lived in a cave. H1426
Ge 19:36 So both of Lot's **d** became pregnant by H1426
Ge 24: 3 my son from the **d** *of* the Canaanites, H1426
Ge 24:13 the **d** *of* the townspeople are coming H1426
Ge 24:37 my son from the **d** *of* the Canaanites, H1426
Ge 28: 2 from among the **d** *of* Laban, your mother's H1426
Ge 29:16 Now Laban had two **d**; the name of the H1426
Ge 31:26 carried off my **d** like captives in war. H1426
Ge 31:28 kiss my grandchildren and my **d** goodbye. H1426
Ge 31:31 you would take your **d** away from me by H1426
Ge 31:41 years for your two **d** and six years for your H1426
Ge 31:43 "The women are my **d**, the children are H1426
Ge 31:43 can I do today about these **d** *of* mine, H1426
Ge 31:50 If you mistreat my **d** or if you take any H1426
Ge 31:50 if you take any wives besides my **d**, H1426
Ge 31:55 his **d** and blessed them. H1426
Ge 34: 9 give us your **d** and take our daughters H1426
Ge 34: 9 daughters and take our **d** for yourselves. H1426
Ge 34:16 we will give you our **d** and take your H1426
Ge 34:16 daughters and take your **d** for ourselves. H1426
Ge 34:21 We can marry their **d** and they can marry H1426
Ge 36: 6 wives and sons and **d** and all the H1426
Ge 37:35 All his sons and **d** came to comfort him H1426
Ge 46: 7 grandsons and his **d** and granddaughters H1426
Ge 46:15 These sons and **d** *of* his were thirty-three H1426
Ex 2:16 Now a priest of Midian had seven **d**, and H1426
Ex 2:20 Reuel asked his **d**. "Why did you leave H1426
Ex 3:22 which you will put on your sons and **d**. H1426
Ex 6:25 of Aaron married one of the **d** *of* Putiel, H1426
Ex 10: 9 with our sons and our **d**, and with our H1426
Ex 21: 4 him a wife and she bears him sons or **d**, H1426
Ex 32: 2 your sons and your **d** are wearing, and H1426
Ex 34:16 choose some of their **d** as wives for your H1426
Ex 34:16 your sons and those **d** prostitute H1426
Lev 10:14 your sons and your **d** may eat the breast H1426
Lev 26:29 flesh of your sons and the flesh of your **d**. H1426
Nu 18:11 your sons and **d** as your perpetual H1426
Nu 18:19 your sons and **d** as your perpetual H1426
Nu 21:29 as fugitives and his **d** as captives to Sihon H1426
Nu 26:33 he had only **d**, whose names were H1426
Nu 27: 1 The **d** *of* Zelophehad son of Hepher, the H1426
Nu 27: 1 The names of the **d** were Mahlah, Noah H1426
Nu 27: 7 "What Zelophehad's **d** are saying is right H1426
Nu 36: 2 of our brother Zelophehad to his **d**. H1426
Nu 36: 6 the LORD commands for Zelophehad's **d**: H1426
Nu 36:10 So Zelophehad's **d** did as the LORD H1426
Nu 36:11 Zelophehad's **d**—Mahlah, Tirzah, Hoglah H1426
Dt 7: 3 Do not give your **d** to their sons or take H1426
Dt 7: 3 to their sons or take their **d** for your sons, H1426
Dt 12:12 your sons and **d**, your male and H1426
Dt 12:18 your sons and **d**, your male and H1426
Dt 12:31 even burn their sons and **d** in the fire as H1426
Dt 16:11 your sons and **d**, your male and H1426
Dt 16:14 your sons and **d**, your male and H1426
Dt 28:32 Your sons and **d** will be given to another H1426
Dt 28:41 will have sons and **d** but you will not keep H1426
Dt 28:53 of the sons and **d** the LORD your God has H1426
Dt 32:19 he was angered by his sons and **d**. H1426
Jos 7:24 his sons and **d**, his cattle, donkeys H1426
Jos 17: 3 had no sons but only **d**, whose names H1426
Jos 17: 6 because the **d** *of* the tribe of Manasseh H1426
Jdg 3: 6 They took their **d** in marriage and gave H1426
Jdg 3: 6 gave their own **d** to their sons, H1426
Jdg 12: 9 He had thirty sons and thirty **d**. He gave H1426
Jdg 12: 9 He gave his **d** away in marriage to those NDT
Jdg 21: 7 not to give them any of our **d in marriage**? H1426
Jdg 21:18 We can't give them our **d** as wives, since H1426
Jdg 21:22 because you did not give your **d** to them. NDT
Ru 1:11 "Return home, my **d**. Why would you H1426
Ru 1:12 Return home, my **d**; I am too old to have H1426
Ru 1:13 No, my **d**. It is more bitter for H1426
1Sa 1: 4 wife Peninnah and to all her sons and **d**. H1426
1Sa 2:21 she gave birth to three sons and two **d**. H1426
1Sa 8:13 He will take your **d** to be perfumers and H1426
1Sa 30: 3 their wives and sons and **d** taken captive. H1426
1Sa 30: 6 bitter in spirit because of his sons and **d**. H1426
2Sa 1:20 lest the **d** *of* the Philistines be glad H1426
2Sa 1:20 lest the **d** *of* the uncircumcised rejoice. H1426
2Sa 1:24 "**D** *of* Israel, weep for Saul, who clothed H1426
2Sa 5:13 more sons and **d** were born to him. H1426
2Sa 13:18 of garment the virgin **d** *of* the king wore. H1426
2Sa 19: 5 of your sons and **d** and the lives of your H1426
2Ki 17:17 They sacrificed their sons and **d** in the fire H1426
1Ch 2:34 had no sons—only **d**. He had an Egyptian H1426
1Ch 4:27 Shimei had sixteen sons and six **d**, but his H1426
1Ch 7:15 was named Zelophehad, who had only **d**. H1426
1Ch 14: 3 became the father of more sons and **d**. H1426
1Ch 23:22 he had only **d**. Their cousins, H1426
1Ch 25: 5 gave Heman fourteen sons and three **d**.) H1426
2Ch 11:21 concubines, twenty-eight sons and sixty **d**. H1426
2Ch 13:21 had twenty-two sons and sixteen **d**. H1426
2Ch 24: 3 wives for him, and he had sons and **d**. H1426
2Ch 28: 8 two hundred thousand wives, sons and **d**. H1426
2Ch 29: 9 why our sons and **d** and our wives are in H1426
2Ch 31:18 the sons and **d** of the whole H1426
Ezr 9: 2 taken some of their **d** as wives for H1426
Ezr 9:12 do not give your **d** in marriage to their H1426
Ezr 9:12 to their sons or take their **d** for your sons. H1426
Ne 3:12 the next section with the help of his **d**. H1426
Ne 4:14 your sons and your **d**, your wives and your H1426
Ne 5: 2 "We and our sons and **d** are numerous; in H1426
Ne 5: 5 have to subject our sons and **d** to slavery. H1426
Ne 5: 5 Some of our **d** have already been H1426
Ne 10:28 all their sons and **d** who are able to H1426
Ne 10:30 not to give our **d** in marriage to the H1426
Ne 10:30 around us or take their **d** for our sons. H1426
Ne 13:25 are not to give your **d** in marriage to their H1426
Ne 13:25 are you to take their **d** in marriage for your H1426
Job 1: 2 He had seven sons and three **d**, H1426
Job 1:13 when Job's sons and **d** were feasting and H1426
Job 1:18 "Your sons and **d** were feasting and H1426
Job 42:13 And he also had seven sons and three **d**. H1426
Job 42:15 found women as beautiful as Job's **d**, H1426
Ps 45: 9 **D** *of* kings are among your honored H1426
Ps 106:37 their sons and their **d** to false gods. H1426
Ps 106:38 the blood of their sons and **d**, whom they H1426
Ps 144:12 our **d** will be like pillars carved to H1426
Pr 30:15 "The leech has two **d**. 'Give! Give!' they H1426
SS 1: 5 lovely, **d** *of* Jerusalem, dark like the H1426
SS 2: 7 **D** *of* Jerusalem, I charge you by the H1426
SS 3: 5 **D** *of* Jerusalem, I charge you by the H1426
SS 3:10 interior inlaid with love. **D** *of* Jerusalem, H1426
SS 3:11 and look, you **d** *of* Zion. Look on King H1426
SS 5: 8 **D** *of* Jerusalem, I charge you—if you find H1426
SS 5:16 beloved, this is my friend, **d** *of* Jerusalem. H1426
SS 8: 4 **D** *of* Jerusalem, I charge you: Do not H1426
Isa 23: 4 neither reared sons nor brought up **d**." H1435
Isa 32: 9 listen to me; you **d** who feel secure, hear H1426
Isa 32:11 shudder, you **d** who feel secure! NDT
Isa 43: 6 from afar and my **d** from the ends of the H1426
Isa 49:22 their arms and carry your **d** on their hips. H1426
Isa 56: 5 a name better than sons and **d**; H1426
Isa 60: 4 and your **d** are carried on the hip. H1426
Jer 3:24 their flocks and herds, their sons and **d**. H1426
Jer 5:17 devour your sons and **d**; they will devour H1426
Jer 7:31 to burn their sons and **d** in the fire— H1426
Jer 9:20 Teach your **d** how to wail; teach one H1426
Jer 11:22 by the sword, their sons and **d** by famine. H1426
Jer 14:16 their wives, their sons and their **d**. H1426
Jer 16: 2 marry and have sons or **d** in this place." H1426
Jer 16: 3 about the sons and **d** born in this land H1426
Jer 19: 9 them eat the flesh of their sons and **d**, H1426
Jer 29: 6 Marry and have sons and **d**; find wives H1426
Jer 29: 6 your sons and give your **d** in marriage, H1426
Jer 29: 6 so that they too may have sons and **d**. H1426
Jer 32:35 to sacrifice their sons and **d** to Molek, H1426
Jer 35: 8 our sons and **d** have ever drunk wine H1426
Jer 41:10 the king's **d** along with all the others who H1426
Jer 43: 6 the women, the children and the king's **d**. H1426
Jer 48:46 taken into exile and your **d** into captivity. H1426
Eze 13:17 face against the **d** *of* your people who H1426
Eze 14:16 they could not save their own sons or **d**. H1426
Eze 14:18 they could not save their own sons or **d**. H1426
Eze 14:22 sons and **d** who will be brought out of it. H1426
Eze 16:20 took your sons and **d** whom you bore to H1426
Eze 16:27 of your enemies, the **d** *of* the Philistines H1426
Eze 16:46 who lived to the north of you with her **d** H1426
Eze 16:46 who lived to the south of you with her **d** H1426
Eze 16:48 Sodom and her **d** never did what you H1426
Eze 16:48 never did what you and your **d** have done. H1426

Eze 16:49 She and her **d** were arrogant, overfed H1426
Eze 16:53 of Sodom and her **d** and of Samaria and H1426
Eze 16:53 her daughters and of Samaria and her **d**, H1426
Eze 16:55 Sodom with her **d** and Samaria with her H1426
Eze 16:55 her daughters and Samaria with her **d**, H1426
Eze 16:55 you and your **d** will return to what you H1426
Eze 16:57 now scorned by the **d** *of* Edom and all her H1426
Eze 16:57 neighbors and the **d** *of* the Philistines— H1426
Eze 16:61 I will give them to you as **d**, but not on H1426
Eze 23: 2 were two women, **d** *of* the same mother. H1426
Eze 23: 4 were mine and gave birth to sons and **d**. H1426
Eze 23:10 away her sons and **d** and killed her with H1426
Eze 23:25 They will take away your sons and **d**, and H1426
Eze 23:47 kill their sons and **d** and burn down their H1426
Eze 24:21 The sons and **d** you left behind will fall by H1426
Eze 24:25 and their sons and **d** as well— H1426
Eze 32:16 The **d** *of* the nations will chant it; for H1426
Eze 32:18 both her and the **d** *of* mighty nations, H1426
Hos 4:13 Therefore your **d** turn to prostitution and H1426
Hos 4:14 "I will not punish your **d** when they turn to H1426
Joel 2:28 Your sons and **d** will prophesy, your old H1426
Joel 3: 8 sell your sons and **d** to the people of H1426
Am 7:17 your sons and **d** will fall by the sword. H1426
Lk 23:28 said to them, "**D** of Jerusalem, do not *G2588*
Ac 2:17 Your sons and **d** will prophesy, your young *G2588*
Ac 21: 9 He had four unmarried **d** who prophesied. *G2588*
2Co 6:18 you will be my sons and **d**, says the *G2588*
Heb 2:10 In bringing many **sons and d** to glory, it *G5626*
Heb 12: 8 not legitimate, not *true* **sons and d** at all. *G5626*
1Pe 3: 6 You are her **d** if you do what is right and *G5451*

DAUGHTERS-IN-LAW (5) [DAUGHTER]

Ru 1: 6 she and her **d** prepared to return home H3987
Ru 1: 7 With her two **d** she left the place where H3987
Ru 1: 8 Then Naomi said to her two **d**, "Go back H3987
Hos 4:13 turn to prostitution and your **d** to adultery. H3987
Hos 4:14 your **d** when they commit adultery H3987

DAVID (1009) [DAVID'S]

Ru 4:17 was the father of Jesse, the father of **D**. H1858
Ru 4:22 father of Jesse, and Jesse the father of **D**. H1858
1Sa 16:13 Spirit of the LORD came powerfully upon **D**. H1858
1Sa 16:19 "Send me your son **D**, who is with the H1858
1Sa 16:20 sent them with his son **D** to Saul. H1858
1Sa 16:21 **D** came to Saul and entered his service H1858
1Sa 16:21 **D** became one of his armor-bearers. NDT
1Sa 16:22 "Allow **D** to remain in my service H1858
1Sa 16:23 **D** would take up his lyre and play. H1858
1Sa 17:12 Now **D** was the son of an Ephrathite H1858
1Sa 17:14 **D** was the youngest. The three oldest H1858
1Sa 17:15 **D** went back and forth from Saul to H1858
1Sa 17:17 Now Jesse said to his son **D**, "Take this H1858
1Sa 17:20 Early in the morning **D** left the flock in the H1858
1Sa 17:22 **D** left his things with the keeper of H1858
1Sa 17:23 his usual defiance, and **D** heard it. H1858
1Sa 17:26 **D** asked the men standing near him H1858
1Sa 17:29 said **D**. "Can't I even speak H1858
1Sa 17:31 What **D** said was overheard and reported H1858
1Sa 17:32 **D** said to Saul, "Let no one lose heart on H1858
1Sa 17:34 But **D** said to Saul, "Your servant has H1858
1Sa 17:37 Saul said to **D**, "Go, and the LORD be with H1858
1Sa 17:38 Then Saul dressed **D** in his own tunic. H1858
1Sa 17:39 **D** fastened on his sword over the tunic H1858
1Sa 17:41 in front of him, kept coming closer to **D**. H1858
1Sa 17:42 He looked **D** over and saw that he was H1858
1Sa 17:43 He said to **D**, "Am I a dog, that you come H1858
1Sa 17:43 And the Philistine cursed **D** by his gods. H1858
1Sa 17:45 **D** said to the Philistine, "You come H1858
1Sa 17:48 **D** ran quickly toward the battle line to H1858
1Sa 17:50 So **D** triumphed over the Philistine with a H1858
1Sa 17:51 **D** ran and stood over him. He took hold of H1858
1Sa 17:54 **D** took the Philistine's head and brought H1858
1Sa 17:55 As Saul watched **D** going out to meet the H1858
1Sa 17:57 As soon as **D** returned from killing the H1858
1Sa 17:57 with **D** still holding the Philistine's head. H2257S
1Sa 17:58 **D** said, "I am the son of your servant H1858
1Sa 18: 1 After **D** had finished talking with Saul H2257S
1Sa 18: 1 Jonathan became one in spirit with **D** H1858
1Sa 18: 2 that day Saul kept **D** with him and did H2084S
1Sa 18: 3 a covenant with **D** because he loved him H1858
1Sa 18: 4 the robe he was wearing and gave it to **D**, H1858
1Sa 18: 5 **D** was so successful that Saul gave him a H1858
1Sa 18: 6 returning home after **D** had killed the H1858
1Sa 18: 7 thousands, and **D** his tens of thousands." H1858
1Sa 18: 8 "They have credited **D** with tens of H1858
1Sa 18: 9 that time on Saul kept a close eye on **D**. H1858
1Sa 18:10 in his house, while **D** was playing the lyre H1858
1Sa 18:11 saying to himself, "I'll pin **D** to the wall." H1858
1Sa 18:11 But **D** eluded him twice. H1858
1Sa 18:12 Saul was afraid of **D**, because the LORD H1858
1Sa 18:12 the LORD was with **D** but had departed H2257S
1Sa 18:13 So he sent **D** away from him and gave H2084S
1Sa 18:13 **D** led the troops in their campaigns. NDT
1Sa 18:16 But all Israel and Judah loved **D**, because H1858
1Sa 18:17 Saul said to **D**, "Here is my older H1858
1Sa 18:18 But **D** said to Saul, "Who am I, and what H1858
1Sa 18:19 to be given to **D**, she was given in H1858
1Sa 18:20 daughter Michal was in love with **D**, H1858
1Sa 18:21 So Saul said to **D**, "Now you have a H1858
1Sa 18:22 "Speak to **D** privately and say, 'Look, the H1858
1Sa 18:23 They repeated these words to **D**. H1858
1Sa 18:23 But **D** said, "Do you think it is a small H1858
1Sa 18:24 Saul's servants told him what **D** had said, H1858
1Sa 18:25 replied, "Say to **D**, 'The king wants no H1858
1Sa 18:25 plan was to have **D** fall by the hands of H1858
1Sa 18:26 When the attendants told **D** these things H1858
1Sa 18:27 **D** took his men with him and went out H1858
1Sa 18:27 to the king so that **D** might become the H1858
1Sa 18:28 the LORD was with **D** and that his daughter H1858
1Sa 18:28 that his daughter Michal loved **D**, H2084S
1Sa 18:30 **D** met with more success than the rest of H1858
1Sa 19: 1 Jonathan and all the attendants to kill **D**. H1858
1Sa 19: 1 But Jonathan had taken a great liking to **D** H1858
1Sa 19: 4 spoke well of **D** to Saul his father and H1858
1Sa 19: 4 not the king do wrong to his servant **D**; H1858
1Sa 19: 5 an innocent man like **D** by killing him H1858
1Sa 19: 6 as the LORD lives, **D** will not be put to death." NDT
1Sa 19: 7 So Jonathan called **D** and told him the H1858
1Sa 19: 7 to Saul, and **D** was with Saul as before. H1858
1Sa 19: 8 **D** went out and fought the Philistines. H1858
1Sa 19: 9 While **D** was playing the lyre, H1858
1Sa 19:10 **D** eluded him as Saul drove the spear H1858
1Sa 19:10 That night **D** made good his escape H1858
1Sa 19:12 So Michal let **D** down through a window H1858
1Sa 19:14 When Saul sent the men to capture **D** H1858
1Sa 19:15 the men back to see **D** and told them, H1858
1Sa 19:18 When **D** had fled and made his escape H1858
1Sa 19:19 came to Saul: "**D** is in Naioth at Ramah"; H1858
1Sa 19:22 he asked, "Where are Samuel and **D**?" H1858
1Sa 20: 1 Then **D** fled from Naioth at Ramah and H1858
1Sa 20: 3 But **D** took an oath and said, "Your father H1858
1Sa 20: 4 Jonathan said to **D**, "Whatever you want H1858
1Sa 20: 5 So **D** said, "Look, tomorrow is the New H1858
1Sa 20: 6 '**D** earnestly asked my permission to hurry H1858
1Sa 20:10 **D** asked, "Who will tell me if your father H1858
1Sa 20:12 Then Jonathan said to **D**, "I swear by the H1858
1Sa 20:16 made a covenant with the house of **D**, H1858
1Sa 20:17 And Jonathan had **D** reaffirm his oath out H1858
1Sa 20:18 Then Jonathan said to **D**, "Tomorrow is H2257S
1Sa 20:24 So **D** hid in the field, and when the New H1858
1Sa 20:26 must have happened to **D** to make him H2085S
1Sa 20:28 "**D** earnestly asked me for permission to H1858
1Sa 20:33 knew that his father intended to kill **D**. H1858
1Sa 20:34 at his father's shameful treatment of **D**. H1858
1Sa 20:35 out to the field for his meeting with **D**. H1858
1Sa 20:39 about all this; only Jonathan and **D** knew.) H1858
1Sa 20:41 **D** got up from the south side of the stone H1858
1Sa 20:41 wept together—but **D** wept the most. H1858
1Sa 20:42 Jonathan said to **D**, "Go in peace, for we H1858
1Sa 20:42 Then **D** left, and Jonathan went back to NDT
1Sa 21: 1 **D** went to Nob, to Ahimelek the priest H1858
1Sa 21: 2 **D** answered Ahimelek the priest, "The H1858
1Sa 21: 4 But the priest answered **D**, "I don't have H1858
1Sa 21: 5 **D** replied, "Indeed women have been H1858
1Sa 21: 8 **D** asked Ahimelek, "Don't you have a H1858
1Sa 21: 9 **D** said, "There is none like it; give it to H1858
1Sa 21:10 That day **D** fled from Saul and went to H1858
1Sa 21:11 "Isn't this **D**, the king of the land? H1858
1Sa 21:11 thousands, and **D** his tens of thousands'?" H1858
1Sa 21:12 **D** took these words to heart and was very H1858
1Sa 22: 1 **D** left Gath and escaped to the cave of H1858
1Sa 22: 3 From there **D** went to Mizpah in Moab H1858
1Sa 22: 4 with him as long as **D** was in the H1858
1Sa 22: 5 But the prophet Gad said to **D**, "Do not H1858
1Sa 22: 5 So **D** left and went to the forest of Hereth. H1858
1Sa 22: 6 Now Saul heard that **D** and his men had H1858
1Sa 22:14 "Who of all your servants is as loyal as **D** H1858
1Sa 22:17 because they too have sided with **D**. H1858
1Sa 22:20 Abiathar, escaped and fled to join **D**. H1858
1Sa 22:21 He told **D** that Saul had killed the priests H1858
1Sa 22:22 Then **D** said to Abiathar, "That day, when H1858
1Sa 23: 1 When **D** was told, "Look, the Philistines H1858
1Sa 23: 4 Once again **D** inquired of the LORD, and H1858
1Sa 23: 5 So **D** and his men went to Keilah, fought H1858
1Sa 23: 6 with him when he fled to **D** at Keilah.) H1858
1Sa 23: 7 Saul was told that **D** had gone to Keilah H1858
1Sa 23: 7 **D** has imprisoned himself by entering a NDT
1Sa 23: 8 to Keilah to besiege **D** and his men. H1858
1Sa 23: 9 When **D** learned that Saul was plotting H1858
1Sa 23:10 **D** said, "LORD, God of Israel, your servant H1858
1Sa 23:12 Again **D** asked, "Will the citizens of H1858
1Sa 23:13 So **D** and his men, about six hundred in H1858
1Sa 23:13 Saul was told that **D** had escaped from H1858
1Sa 23:14 **D** stayed in the wilderness strongholds H1858
1Sa 23:14 God did not give **D** into his hands. H2257S
1Sa 23:15 While **D** was at Horesh in the Desert of H1858
1Sa 23:16 Jonathan went to **D** at Horesh and helped H1858
1Sa 23:18 went home, but **D** remained at Horesh. H1858
1Sa 23:19 "Is not **D** hiding among us in the H1858
1Sa 23:22 Find out where **D** usually goes and who H2257S
1Sa 23:24 Now **D** and his men were in the Desert of H1858
1Sa 23:25 the search, and when **D** was told about it H1858
1Sa 23:25 into the Desert of Maon in pursuit of **D**. H1858
1Sa 23:26 **D** and his men were on the other H1858
1Sa 23:26 were closing in on **D** and his men to H1858
1Sa 23:28 off his pursuit of **D** and went to meet the H1858
1Sa 23:29 And **D** went up from there and lived in the H1858
1Sa 24: 1 was told, "**D** is in the Desert of En Gedi." H1858
1Sa 24: 2 set out to look for **D** and his men near the H1858
1Sa 24: 3 **D** and his men were far back in the cave H1858
1Sa 24: 4 Then **D** crept up unnoticed and cut off a H1858
1Sa 24: 5 **D** was conscience-stricken for having cut H1858
1Sa 24: 7 With these words **D** sharply rebuked his H1858
1Sa 24: 8 Then **D** went out of the cave and called H1858
1Sa 24: 8 **D** bowed down and prostrated himself H1858
1Sa 24: 9 men say, '**D** is bent on harming you'? H1858
1Sa 24:16 When **D** finished saying this, Saul asked H1858
1Sa 24:16 Saul asked, "Is that your voice, **D** my son?" H1858
1Sa 24:22 So **D** gave his oath to Saul. Then Saul H1858
1Sa 24:22 **D** and his men went up to the H1858
1Sa 25: 1 Then **D** moved down into the Desert of H1858
1Sa 25: 4 While **D** was in the wilderness, he heard H1858
1Sa 25: 8 your son **D** whatever you can find H1858
1Sa 25:10 David's servants, "Who is this **D**? H1858
1Sa 25:13 **D** said to his men, "Each of you strap on H1858
1Sa 25:13 they did, and **D** strapped his on as well. H1858
1Sa 25:13 About four hundred men went up with **D** H1858
1Sa 25:14 "**D** sent messengers from the wilderness H1858
1Sa 25:20 there were **D** and his men descending H1858
1Sa 25:21 **D** had just said, "It's been useless—all my H1858
1Sa 25:22 May God deal with **D**, be it ever so H1858
1Sa 25:23 When Abigail saw **D**, she quickly got off H1858
1Sa 25:23 bowed down before **D** with her face to the H1858
1Sa 25:32 **D** said to Abigail, "Praise be to the LORD H1858
1Sa 25:35 Then **D** accepted from her hand what she H1858
1Sa 25:39 When **D** heard that Nabal was dead, he H1858
1Sa 25:39 Then **D** sent word to Abigail, asking her H1858
1Sa 25:40 "**D** has sent us to you to take you to H1858
1Sa 25:43 **D** had also married Ahinoam of Jezreel H1858
1Sa 26: 1 "Is not **D** hiding on the hill of Hakilah H1858
1Sa 26: 2 Israelite troops, to search there for **D**. H1858
1Sa 26: 3 Jeshimon, but **D** stayed in the wilderness. H1858
1Sa 26: 5 Then **D** set out and went to the place H1858
1Sa 26: 6 **D** then asked Ahimelek the Hittite and H1858
1Sa 26: 7 So **D** and Abishai went to the army by H1858
1Sa 26: 8 Abishai said to **D**, "Today God has H1858
1Sa 26: 9 But **D** said to Abishai, "Don't destroy him H1858
1Sa 26:12 So **D** took the spear and water jug near H1858
1Sa 26:13 Then **D** crossed over to the other side H1858
1Sa 26:15 **D** said, "You're a man, aren't you? And H1858
1Sa 26:17 said, "Is that your voice, **D** my son? H1858
1Sa 26:17 David my son?" **D** replied, "Yes it is, my H1858
1Sa 26:21 Come back, **D** my son. H1858
1Sa 26:22 the king's spear," **D** answered. "Let one of H1858
1Sa 26:25 Then Saul said to **D**, "May you be blessed H1858
1Sa 26:25 you be blessed, **D** my son; you will do H1858
1Sa 26:25 So **D** went on his way, and Saul returned H1858
1Sa 27: 1 But **D** thought to himself, "One of these H1858
1Sa 27: 2 So **D** and the six hundred men with him H1858
1Sa 27: 3 **D** and his men settled in Gath with Achish. H1858
1Sa 27: 3 family with him, and **D** had his two wives: H1858
1Sa 27: 4 Saul was told that **D** had fled to Gath, H1858
1Sa 27: 5 Then **D** said to Achish, "If I have found H1858
1Sa 27: 7 **D** lived in Philistine territory a year and H1858
1Sa 27: 8 Now **D** and his men went up and raided H1858
1Sa 27: 9 Whenever **D** attacked an area, he did not H1858
1Sa 27:10 **D** would say, "Against the Negev of H1858
1Sa 27:11 inform on us and say, 'This is what **D** did. H1858
1Sa 27:12 Achish trusted **D** and said to himself, "He H1858
1Sa 28: 1 Achish said to **D**, "You must understand H1858
1Sa 28: 2 **D** said, "Then you will see for yourself H1858
1Sa 28:17 given it to one of your neighbors—to **D**. H1858
1Sa 29: 2 **D** and his men were marching at the rear H1858
1Sa 29: 3 replied, "Is this not **D**, who was an officer H1858
1Sa 29: 5 Isn't this the **D** they sang about in their H1858
1Sa 29: 5 thousands, and **D** his tens of thousands'?" H1858
1Sa 29: 6 So Achish called **D** and said to him, "As H1858
1Sa 29: 8 asked **D**. "What have you H1858
1Sa 29:11 So **D** and his men got up early in the H1858
1Sa 30: 1 **D** and his men reached Ziklag on the H1858
1Sa 30: 3 When **D** and his men reached Ziklag H1858
1Sa 30: 4 So **D** and his men wept aloud until they H1858
1Sa 30: 6 **D** was greatly distressed because the men H1858
1Sa 30: 6 But **D** found strength in the LORD his God H1858
1Sa 30: 7 Then **D** said to Abiathar the priest, the H1858
1Sa 30: 8 **D** inquired of the LORD, "Shall I pursue H1858
1Sa 30: 9 **D** and the six hundred men with him H1858
1Sa 30:10 **D** and the other four hundred H1858
1Sa 30:11 Egyptian in a field and brought him to **D**. H1858
1Sa 30:13 **D** asked him, "Who do you belong to H1858
1Sa 30:15 **D** asked him, "Can you lead me down to H1858
1Sa 30:16 He led **D** down, and there they were H2084S
1Sa 30:17 **D** fought them from dusk until the evening H1858
1Sa 30:18 **D** recovered everything the Amalekites H1858
1Sa 30:19 they had taken. **D** brought everything back H1858
1Sa 30:21 Then **D** came to the two hundred men H1858
1Sa 30:21 came out to meet **D** and the men with H1858
1Sa 30:21 As **D** and his men approached, he asked H1858
1Sa 30:23 **D** replied, "No, my brothers, you must not H1858
1Sa 30:25 **D** made this a statute and ordinance for NDT
1Sa 30:26 When **D** reached Ziklag, he sent some of H1858
1Sa 30:27 **D** sent it to those who were in Bethel NDT
2Sa 1: 1 **D** returned from striking down the H1858
2Sa 1: 2 When he came to **D**, he fell to the ground H1858
2Sa 1: 3 have you come from?" **D** asked him. H1858
2Sa 1: 4 "What happened?" **D** asked. "Tell me." H1858
2Sa 1: 5 Then **D** said to the young man who H1858
2Sa 1:11 Then **D** and all the men with him took H1858
2Sa 1:13 **D** said to the young man who brought H1858
2Sa 1:14 **D** asked him, "Why weren't you afraid to H1858
2Sa 1:15 Then **D** called one of his men and said H1858
2Sa 1:16 For **D** had said to him, "Your blood be on H1858
2Sa 1:17 **D** took up this lament concerning Saul H1858
2Sa 2: 1 the course of time, **D** inquired of the LORD. H1858
2Sa 2: 1 **D** asked, "Where shall I go? H1858
2Sa 2: 2 So **D** went up there with his two wives H1858

2Sa 2: 3 **D** also took the men who were with him H1858
2Sa 2: 4 there they anointed **D** king over the tribe H1858
2Sa 2: 4 When **D** was told that it was the men H1858
2Sa 2:10 of Judah, however, remained loyal to **D**. H1858
2Sa 2:11 The length of time **D** was king in Hebron H1858
2Sa 2:15 Ish-Bosheth son of Saul, and twelve for **D**. H1858
2Sa 3: 1 the house of **D** lasted a long time. H1858
2Sa 3: 1 **D** grew stronger and stronger, while the H1858
2Sa 3: 2 Sons were born to **D** in Hebron: His H1858
2Sa 3: 5 These were born to **D** in Hebron. H1858
2Sa 3: 6 the house of Saul and the house of **D**, H1858
2Sa 3: 8 I haven't handed you over to **D**. H1858
2Sa 3: 9 if I do not do for **D** what the LORD H1858
2Sa 3:12 messengers on his behalf to say to **D**, H1858
2Sa 3:13 said **D**. "I will make an agreement NDT
2Sa 3:14 Then **D** sent messengers to Ish-Bosheth H1858
2Sa 3:17 you have wanted to make **D** your king. H1858
2Sa 3:18 For the LORD promised **D**, 'By my servant H1858
2Sa 3:18 'By my servant **D** I will rescue my people H1858
2Sa 3:19 to Hebron to tell **D** everything that Israel H1858
2Sa 3:20 with him, came to **D** at Hebron, David H1858
2Sa 3:20 **D** prepared a feast for him and his men. H1858
2Sa 3:21 Then Abner said to **D**, "Let me go at once H1858
2Sa 3:21 So **D** sent Abner away, and he went in H1858
2Sa 3:22 Abner was no longer with **D** in Hebron, H1858
2Sa 3:22 in Hebron, because **D** had sent him away NDT
2Sa 3:26 Joab then left **D** and sent messengers H1858
2Sa 3:26 the cistern at Sirah. But **D** did not know it. H1858
2Sa 3:28 when **D** heard about this, he said H1858
2Sa 3:31 Then **D** said to Joab and all the people H1858
2Sa 3:31 King **D** himself walked behind the bier H1858
2Sa 3:35 all came and urged **D** to eat something H1858
2Sa 3:35 was still day; but **D** took an oath, saying, H1858
2Sa 4: 8 of Ish-Bosheth to **D** at Hebron and said to H1858
2Sa 4: 9 **D** answered Rekab and his brother H1858
2Sa 4:12 So **D** gave an order to his men, and they H1858
2Sa 5: 1 of Israel came to **D** at Hebron and said, H1858
2Sa 5: 3 of Israel had come to King **D** at Hebron, H1858
2Sa 5: 3 they anointed **D** king over Israel. H1858
2Sa 5: 4 **D** was thirty years old when he became H1858
2Sa 5: 6 The Jebusites said to **D**, "You will not get H1858
2Sa 5: 6 They thought, "**D** cannot get in here." H1858
2Sa 5: 7 **D** captured the fortress of Zion H1858
2Sa 5: 7 fortress of Zion—which is the City of **D**. H1858
2Sa 5: 8 On that day **D** had said, "Anyone who H1858
2Sa 5: 9 **D** then took up residence in the fortress H1858
2Sa 5: 9 in the fortress and called it the City of **D**. H1858
2Sa 5:11 Now Hiram king of Tyre sent envoys to **D** H1858
2Sa 5:11 they built a palace for **D**. H1858
2Sa 5:12 Then **D** knew that the LORD had H1858
2Sa 5:13 **D** took more concubines and wives in H1858
2Sa 5:17 heard that **D** had been anointed king H1858
2Sa 5:17 **D** heard about it and went down to H1858
2Sa 5:19 so **D** inquired of the LORD, "Shall I go and H1858
2Sa 5:20 So **D** went to Baal Perazim, and there he H1858
2Sa 5:21 **D** and his men carried them off. H1858
2Sa 5:23 so **D** inquired of the LORD, and he H1858
2Sa 5:25 So **D** did as the LORD commanded him H1858
2Sa 6: 1 **D** again brought together all the able H1858
2Sa 6: 5 **D** and all Israel were celebrating with all H1858
2Sa 6: 8 Then **D** was angry because the LORD's H1858
2Sa 6: 9 **D** was afraid of the LORD that day and said, H1858
2Sa 6:10 of the LORD to be with him in the City of **D**. H1858
2Sa 6:12 Now King **D** was told, "The LORD has H1858
2Sa 6:12 So **D** went to bring up the ark of God from H1858
2Sa 6:12 to the City of **D** with rejoicing. H1858
2Sa 6:14 **D** was dancing before the LORD with all his H1858
2Sa 6:16 ark of the LORD was entering the City of **D**, H1858
2Sa 6:16 when she saw King **D** leaping and H1858
2Sa 6:17 inside the tent that **D** had pitched for it, H1858
2Sa 6:17 **D** sacrificed burnt offerings and H1858
2Sa 6:20 When **D** returned home to bless his H1858
2Sa 6:21 **D** said to Michal, "It was before the LORD H1858
2Sa 7: 5 "Go and tell my servant **D**, 'This is what H1858
2Sa 7: 8 tell my servant **D**, 'This is what the H1858
2Sa 7:17 Nathan reported to **D** all the words of this H1858
2Sa 7:18 Then King **D** went in and sat before the H1858
2Sa 7:20 "What more can **D** say to you? For you H1858
2Sa 7:26 of your servant **D** will be established H1858
2Sa 8: 1 **D** defeated the Philistines and subdued H1858
2Sa 8: 2 **D** also defeated the Moabites. He made NDT
2Sa 8: 2 became subject to **D** and brought him H1858
2Sa 8: 3 **D** defeated Hadadezer son of Rehob H1858
2Sa 8: 4 **D** captured a thousand of his chariots H1858
2Sa 8: 5 **D** struck down twenty-two thousand of H1858
2Sa 8: 6 LORD gave **D** victory wherever he went. H1858
2Sa 8: 7 **D** took the gold shields that belonged to H1858
2Sa 8: 8 King **D** took a great quantity of bronze. H1858
2Sa 8: 9 of Hamath heard that **D** had defeated the H1858
2Sa 8:10 his son Joram to King **D** to greet him and H1858
2Sa 8:11 King **D** dedicated these articles to the H1858
2Sa 8:13 And **D** became famous after he returned H1858
2Sa 8:14 all the Edomites became subject to **D**. H1858
2Sa 8:14 LORD gave **D** victory wherever he went. H1858
2Sa 8:15 **D** reigned over all Israel, doing what was H1858
2Sa 9: 1 **D** asked, "Is there anyone still left of the H1858
2Sa 9: 2 They summoned him to appear before **D** H1858
2Sa 9: 5 So King **D** had him brought from Lo Debar H1858
2Sa 9: 6 of Saul, came to **D**, he bowed down to H1858
2Sa 9: 6 to pay him honor. **D** said, "Mephibosheth!" H1858
2Sa 9: 7 **D** said to him, "for I will surely show you H1858
2Sa 10: 2 **D** thought, "I will show kindness to Hanun H1858
2Sa 10: 2 So **D** sent a delegation to express his H1858
2Sa 10: 3 "Do you think **D** is honoring your father by H1858
2Sa 10: 3 Hasn't **D** sent them to you only to explore H1858
2Sa 10: 5 When **D** was told about this, he sent H1858
2Sa 10: 6 that they had become obnoxious to **D**, H1858
2Sa 10: 7 **D** sent Joab out with the entire army of H1858
2Sa 10:17 When **D** was told of this, he gathered all H1858
2Sa 10:17 battle lines to meet **D** and fought against H1858
2Sa 10:18 **D** killed seven hundred of their H1858
2Sa 11: 1 **D** sent Joab out with the king's men and H1858
2Sa 11: 1 But **D** remained in Jerusalem H1858
2Sa 11: 2 One evening **D** got up from his bed and H1858
2Sa 11: 3 **D** sent someone to find out about her H1858
2Sa 11: 4 Then **D** sent messengers to get her. H1858
2Sa 11: 5 The woman conceived and sent word to **D** H1858
2Sa 11: 6 So **D** sent this word to Joab: "Send me H1858
2Sa 11: 6 And Joab sent him to **D**. H1858
2Sa 11: 7 came to him, **D** asked him how Joab was H1858
2Sa 11: 8 Then **D** said to Uriah, "Go down to your H1858
2Sa 11:10 **D** was told, "Uriah did not go home." H1858
2Sa 11:11 Uriah said to **D**, "The ark and Israel and H1858
2Sa 11:12 Then **D** said to him, "Stay here one more H1858
2Sa 11:13 drank with him, and **D** made him drunk. NDT
2Sa 11:14 In the morning **D** wrote a letter to Joab H1858
2Sa 11:18 Joab sent **D** a full account of the battle. H1858
2Sa 11:22 he arrived he told **D** everything Joab had H1858
2Sa 11:23 The messenger said to **D**, "The men H1858
2Sa 11:25 **D** told the messenger, "Say this to Joab H1858
2Sa 11:27 was over, **D** had her brought to his house H1858
2Sa 11:27 But the thing **D** had done displeased the H1858
2Sa 12: 1 The LORD sent Nathan to **D**. H1858
2Sa 12: 5 **D** burned with anger against the man H1858
2Sa 12: 7 Then Nathan said to **D**, "You are the man! H1858
2Sa 12:13 Then **D** said to Nathan, "I have sinned H1858
2Sa 12:15 the child that Uriah's wife had borne to **D**, H1858
2Sa 12:16 **D** pleaded with God for the child. H1858
2Sa 12:19 **D** noticed that his attendants were H1858
2Sa 12:20 Then **D** got up from the ground. H1858
2Sa 12:24 Then **D** comforted his wife Bathsheba H1858
2Sa 12:27 Joab then sent messengers to **D**, saying, "I H1858
2Sa 12:29 So **D** mustered the entire army and went H1858
2Sa 12:30 **D** took the crown from their king's head, and NDT
2Sa 12:30 **D** took a great quantity of plunder from the NDT
2Sa 12:31 **D** did this to all the Ammonite towns H1858
2Sa 13: 1 Amnon son of **D** fell in love with Tamar H1858
2Sa 13: 1 the beautiful sister of Absalom son of **D**. H1858
2Sa 13: 7 **D** sent word to Tamar at the palace: "Go H1858
2Sa 13:21 When King **D** heard all this, he was H1858
2Sa 13:30 were on their way, the report came to **D**: H1858
2Sa 13:37 But King **D** mourned many days for his son NDT
2Sa 13:39 And King **D** longed to go to Absalom, for H1858
2Sa 15:13 A messenger came and told **D**, "The H1858
2Sa 15:14 Then **D** said to all his officials who were H1858
2Sa 15:22 **D** said to Ittai, "Go ahead, march on." H1858
2Sa 15:30 But **D** continued up the Mount of Olives H1858
2Sa 15:31 Now **D** had been told, "Ahithophel is H1858
2Sa 15:31 So **D** prayed, "LORD, turn Ahithophel's H1858
2Sa 15:32 When **D** arrived at the summit, where H1858
2Sa 15:33 **D** said to him, "If you go with me, you will H1858
2Sa 16: 1 When **D** had gone a short distance H1858
2Sa 16: 5 As King **D** approached Bahurim, a man H1858
2Sa 16: 6 He pelted **D** and all the king's officials H1858
2Sa 16:10 LORD said to him, 'Curse **D**,' who can ask, H1858
2Sa 16:11 **D** then said to Abishai and all his officials H1858
2Sa 16:13 So **D** and his men continued along the H1858
2Sa 16:23 That was how both **D** and Absalom H1858
2Sa 17: 1 men and set out tonight in pursuit of **D**. H1858
2Sa 17:16 Now send a message at once and tell **D** H1858
2Sa 17:17 they were to go and tell King **D**, for H1858
2Sa 17:21 out of the well and went to inform King **D**. H1858
2Sa 17:22 So **D** and all the people with him set out H1858
2Sa 17:24 **D** went to Mahanaim, and Absalom H1858
2Sa 17:27 When **D** came to Mahanaim, Shobi son H1858
2Sa 17:29 from cows' milk for **D** and his people to H1858
2Sa 18: 1 **D** mustered the men who were with him H1858
2Sa 18: 2 **D** sent out his troops, a third under the H1858
2Sa 18:24 While **D** was sitting between the inner H1858
2Sa 19:11 King **D** sent this message to Zadok and H1858
2Sa 19:16 with the men of Judah to meet King **D**. H1858
2Sa 19:22 **D** replied, "What does this have to do H1858
2Sa 19:43 have a greater claim on **D** than you have. H1858
2Sa 20: 1 "We have no share in **D**, no part in H1858
2Sa 20: 2 of Israel deserted **D** to follow Sheba son H1858
2Sa 20: 3 When **D** returned to his palace in H1858
2Sa 20: 6 **D** said to Abishai, "Now Sheba son of H1858
2Sa 20:11 whoever is for **D**, let him follow Joab!" H1858
2Sa 20:21 up his hand against the king, against **D**. H1858
2Sa 21: 1 During the reign of **D**, there was a famine H1858
2Sa 21: 1 so **D** sought the face of the LORD. H1858
2Sa 21: 3 **D** asked the Gibeonites, "What shall I do H1858
2Sa 21: 4 do you want me to do for you?" **D** asked. NDT
2Sa 21: 7 the LORD between **D** and Jonathan son of H1858
2Sa 21:11 When **D** was told what Aiah's daughter H1858
2Sa 21:13 **D** brought the bones of Saul and his son NDT
2Sa 21:15 **D** went down with his men to fight H1858
2Sa 21:16 with a new sword, said he would kill **D**. H1858
2Sa 21:22 they fell at the hands of **D** and his men. H1858
2Sa 22: 1 **D** sang to the LORD the words of this song H1858
2Sa 22:51 to **D** and his descendants forever. H1858
2Sa 23: 1 These are the last words of **D**: "The H1858
2Sa 23: 1 "The inspired utterance of **D** son of Jesse H1858
2Sa 23: 9 he was with **D** when they taunted the H1858
2Sa 23:13 warriors came down to **D** at the cave of H1858
2Sa 23:14 At that time **D** was in the stronghold, and H1858
2Sa 23:15 **D** longed for water and said, "Oh, that H1858
2Sa 23:16 of Bethlehem and carried it back to **D**. H1858
2Sa 23:17 And **D** would not drink it NDT
2Sa 23:23 And **D** put him in charge of his bodyguard H1858
2Sa 24: 1 he incited **D** against them, saying, H1858
2Sa 24:10 **D** was conscience-stricken after he had H1858
2Sa 24:11 Before **D** got up the next morning, the H1858
2Sa 24:12 "Go and tell **D**, 'This is what the LORD says H1858
2Sa 24:13 So Gad went to **D** and said to him, "Shall H1858
2Sa 24:14 **D** said to Gad, "I am in deep distress. H1858
2Sa 24:17 When **D** saw the angel who was striking H1858
2Sa 24:18 that day Gad went to **D** and said to him, H1858
2Sa 24:19 So **D** went up, as the LORD had H1858
2Sa 24:21 **D** answered, "so I can build an altar to H1858
2Sa 24:22 Araunah said to **D**, "Let my lord the king H1858
2Sa 24:24 So **D** bought the threshing floor and the H1858
2Sa 24:25 **D** built an altar to the LORD there and H1858
1Ki 1: 1 When King **D** was very old, he could not H1858
1Ki 1:11 our lord **D** knows nothing about it? H1858
1Ki 1:13 Go in to King **D** and say to him, 'My lord H1858
1Ki 1:28 Then King **D** said, "Call in Bathsheba." H1858
1Ki 1:31 "May my lord King **D** live forever! H1858
1Ki 1:32 King **D** said, "Call in Zadok the priest H1858
1Ki 1:37 greater than the throne of my lord King **D**!" H1858
1Ki 1:43 "Our lord King **D** has made Solomon king. H1858
1Ki 1:47 come to congratulate our lord King **D**, H1858
1Ki 2: 1 When the time drew near for **D** to die, he H1858
1Ki 2:10 Then **D** rested with his ancestors and was H1858
1Ki 2:10 ancestors and was buried in the City of **D**. H1858
1Ki 2:12 Solomon sat on the throne of his father **D**, H1858
1Ki 2:24 throne of my father **D** and has founded a H1858
1Ki 2:26 LORD before my father **D** and shared all my H1858
1Ki 2:32 without my father **D** knowing it he H1858
1Ki 2:33 But on **D** and his descendants, his house H1858
1Ki 2:44 all the wrong you did to my father **D**. H1858
1Ki 3: 1 her to the City of **D** until he finished H1858
1Ki 3: 3 the instructions given him by his father **D**, H1858
1Ki 3: 6 your servant, my father **D**, because he was H1858
1Ki 3: 7 your servant king in place of my father **D**. H1858
1Ki 3:14 commands as **D** your father did, H1858
1Ki 5: 1 been anointed king to succeed his father **D**, NDT
1Ki 5: 1 had always been on friendly terms with **D**. H1858
1Ki 5: 3 waged against my father **D** from all sides, H1858
1Ki 5: 5 as the LORD told my father **D**, when he H1858
1Ki 5: 7 he has given **D** a wise son to rule over H1858
1Ki 6:12 you the promise I gave to **D** your father. H1858
1Ki 7:51 in the things his father **D** had dedicated— H1858
1Ki 8: 1 LORD's covenant from Zion, the City of **D**. H1858
1Ki 8:15 with his own mouth to my father **D**. H1858
1Ki 8:16 I have chosen **D** to rule my people H1858
1Ki 8:17 "My father **D** had it in his heart to build a H1858
1Ki 8:18 But the LORD said to my father **D**, 'You did H1858
1Ki 8:20 I have succeeded **D** my father and now I H1858
1Ki 8:24 your promise to your servant **D** my father; H1858
1Ki 8:25 keep for your servant **D** my father the H1858
1Ki 8:26 your servant **D** my father come true. H1858
1Ki 8:66 done for his servant **D** and his people H1858
1Ki 9: 4 uprightness, as **D** your father did, and H1858
1Ki 9: 5 as I promised **D** your father when I said H1858
1Ki 9:24 up from the City of **D** to the palace H1858
1Ki 11: 4 as the heart of **D** his father had been. H1858
1Ki 11: 6 completely, as **D** his father had done. H1858
1Ki 11:12 the sake of **D** your father, I will not do H1858
1Ki 11:13 tribe for the sake of **D** my servant and H1858
1Ki 11:15 Earlier when **D** was fighting with Edom H1858
1Ki 11:21 Hadad heard that **D** rested with his H1858
1Ki 11:24 When **D** destroyed Zobah's army, Rezon H1858
1Ki 11:27 gap in the wall of the city of **D** his father. H1858
1Ki 11:32 the sake of my servant **D** and the city of H1858
1Ki 11:33 kept my decrees and laws as **D** H1858
1Ki 11:34 of his life for the sake of **D** my servant, H1858
1Ki 11:36 to his son so that **D** my servant may H1858
1Ki 11:38 commands, as **D** my servant did, H1858
1Ki 11:38 as the one I built for **D** and will give Israel H1858
1Ki 11:43 was buried in the city of **D** his father. H1858
1Ki 12:16 "What share do we have in **D**, what part H1858
1Ki 12:16 after your own house, **D**!" So the Israelites H1858
1Ki 12:19 against the house of **D** to this day. H1858
1Ki 12:20 Judah remained loyal to the house of **D**. H1858
1Ki 12:26 will now likely revert to the house of **D**. H1858
1Ki 13: 2 Josiah will be born to the house of **D**. H1858
1Ki 14: 8 from the house of **D** and gave it to you, H1858
1Ki 14: 8 you have not been like my servant **D** H1858
1Ki 14:31 was buried with them in the City of **D**. H1858
1Ki 15: 3 as the heart of **D** his forefather had been. H1858
1Ki 15: 5 For **D** had done what was right in the eyes H1858
1Ki 15: 8 ancestors and was buried in the City of **D**. H1858
1Ki 15:11 of the LORD, as his father **D** had done. H1858
1Ki 15:24 with them in the city of his father **D**. H1858
1Ki 22:50 with them in the city of **D** his father. H1858
2Ki 8:19 the sake of his servant **D**, the LORD was H1858
2Ki 8:19 a lamp for **D** and his descendants H2257S
2Ki 8:24 was buried with them in the City of **D**. H1858
2Ki 9:28 his ancestors in his tomb in the City of **D**. H1858
2Ki 11:10 belonged to King **D** and that were in the H1858
2Ki 12:21 buried with his ancestors in the City of **D**. H1858
2Ki 14: 3 but not as his father **D** had done. H1858
2Ki 14:20 with his ancestors, in the City of **D**. H1858
2Ki 15: 7 was buried near them in the City of **D**. H1858
2Ki 15:38 was buried with them in the City of **D**, H1858

2Ki 16: 2 Unlike **D** his father, he did not do what H1858
2Ki 16:20 was buried with them in the City of **D**. H1858
2Ki 17:21 he tore Israel away from the house of **D**, H1858
2Ki 18: 3 of the LORD, just as his father **D** had done. H1858
2Ki 19:34 my sake and for the sake of **D** my servant. H1858
2Ki 20: 5 the LORD, the God of your father **D**, says: H1858
2Ki 20: 6 my sake and for the sake of my servant **D**. H1858
2Ki 21: 7 the LORD had said to **D** and to his son H1858
2Ki 22: 2 completely the ways of his father **D**, H1858
1Ch 2:15 the sixth Ozem and the seventh **D**. H1858
1Ch 3: 1 were the sons of **D** born to him in Hebron: H1858
1Ch 3: 4 These six were born to **D** in Hebron H2257S
1Ch 3: 4 **D** reigned in Jerusalem thirty-three years NDT
1Ch 3: 9 All these were the sons of **D**, besides his H1858
1Ch 4:31 were their towns until the reign of **D**. H1858
1Ch 6:31 These are the men **D** put in charge of the H1858
1Ch 7: 2 During the reign of **D**, the descendants of H1858
1Ch 9:22 of trust by **D** and Samuel the seer. H1858
1Ch 10:14 the kingdom over to **D** son of Jesse. H1858
1Ch 11: 1 came together to **D** at Hebron and said, H1858
1Ch 11: 3 of Israel had come to King **D** at Hebron, H1858
1Ch 11: 3 they anointed **D** king over Israel, as H1858
1Ch 11: 4 **D** and all the Israelites marched to H1858
1Ch 11: 5 said to **D**, "You will not get in here." H1858
1Ch 11: 5 **D** captured the fortress of Zion H1858
1Ch 11: 5 fortress of Zion—which is the City of **D**. H1858
1Ch 11: 6 **D** had said, "Whoever leads the attack on H1858
1Ch 11: 7 **D** then took up residence in the fortress H1858
1Ch 11: 7 fortress, and so it was called the City of **D**. H1858
1Ch 11: 9 And **D** became more and more powerful H1858
1Ch 11:13 He was with **D** at Pas Dammim when the H1858
1Ch 11:15 chiefs came down to **D** to the rock at the H1858
1Ch 11:16 At that time **D** was in the stronghold, and H1858
1Ch 11:17 **D** longed for water and said, "Oh, that H1858
1Ch 11:18 of Bethlehem and carried it back to **D**. H1858
1Ch 11:19 lives to bring it back, **D** would not drink it. NDT
1Ch 11:25 And **D** put him in charge of his bodyguard H1858
1Ch 12: 1 were the men who came to **D** at Ziklag, H1858
1Ch 12: 8 Gadites defected to **D** at his stronghold in H1858
1Ch 12:16 Judah also came to **D** in his stronghold. H1858
1Ch 12:17 **D** went out to meet them and said to them H1858
1Ch 12:18 "We are yours, **D**! We are with you, H1858
1Ch 12:18 So **D** received them and made them H1858
1Ch 12:19 defected to **D** when he went with H1858
1Ch 12:20 When **D** went to Ziklag, these were the H2257S
1Ch 12:21 They helped **D** against raiding bands, for H1858
1Ch 12:22 Day after day men came to help **D**, until H1858
1Ch 12:23 battle who came to **D** at Hebron to turn H1858
1Ch 12:31 by name to come and make **D** king— H1858
1Ch 12:33 of weapon, to help **D** with undivided loyalty NDT
1Ch 12:38 determined to make **D** king over all Israel. H1858
1Ch 12:38 were also of one mind to make **D** king. H1858
1Ch 12:39 The men spent three days there with **D** H1858
1Ch 13: 1 **D** conferred with each of his officers, the H1858
1Ch 13: 5 So **D** assembled all Israel, from the H1858
1Ch 13: 6 **D** and all Israel went to Baalah of Judah H1858
1Ch 13: 8 **D** and all the Israelites were celebrating H1858
1Ch 13:11 Then **D** was angry because the LORD's H1858
1Ch 13:12 **D** was afraid of God that day and asked H1858
1Ch 13:13 the ark to be with him in the City of **D**. H1858
1Ch 14: 1 Hiram king of Tyre sent messengers to **D**, H1858
1Ch 14: 2 And **D** knew that the LORD had established H1858
1Ch 14: 3 In Jerusalem **D** took more wives and H1858
1Ch 14: 8 heard that **D** had been anointed king H1858
1Ch 14: 8 **D** heard about it and went out to H1858
1Ch 14:10 so **D** inquired of God: "Shall I go and H1858
1Ch 14:11 So **D** and his men went up to Baal H1858
1Ch 14:12 **D** gave orders to burn them in the fire H1858
1Ch 14:14 so **D** inquired of God again, and God H1858
1Ch 14:16 So **D** did as God commanded him, and H1858
1Ch 15: 1 After **D** had constructed buildings for NDT
1Ch 15: 1 buildings for himself in the City of **D**, H1858
1Ch 15: 2 Then **D** said, "No one but the Levites may H1858
1Ch 15: 3 **D** assembled all Israel in Jerusalem to H1858
1Ch 15:11 Then **D** summoned Zadok and Abiathar H1858
1Ch 15:16 **D** told the leaders of the Levites to H1858
1Ch 15:25 So **D** and the elders of Israel and the H1858
1Ch 15:27 Now **D** was clothed in a robe of fine linen H1858
1Ch 15:27 **D** also wore a linen ephod. H1858
1Ch 15:29 of the LORD was entering the City of **D**, H1858
1Ch 15:29 And when she saw King **D** dancing and H1858
1Ch 16: 1 it inside the tent that **D** had pitched for it, H1858
1Ch 16: 2 After **D** had finished sacrificing the burnt H1858
1Ch 16: 7 That day **D** first appointed Asaph and his H1858
1Ch 16:37 **D** left Asaph and his associates before the NDT
1Ch 16:39 **D** left Zadok the priest and his fellow priests NDT
1Ch 16:43 **D** returned home to bless his family. H1858
1Ch 17: 1 After **D** was settled in his palace, he said H1858
1Ch 17: 2 Nathan replied to **D**, "Whatever you have H1858
1Ch 17: 4 "Go and tell my servant **D**, 'This is what H1858
1Ch 17: 7 tell my servant **D**, 'This is what the H1858
1Ch 17:15 Nathan reported to **D** all the words of this H1858
1Ch 17:16 Then King **D** went in and sat before the H1858
1Ch 17:18 "What more can **D** say to you for honoring H1858
1Ch 17:24 of your servant **D** will be established H1858
1Ch 18: 1 **D** defeated the Philistines and subdued H1858
1Ch 18: 2 **D** also defeated the Moabites, and they H1858
1Ch 18: 3 **D** defeated Hadadezer king of Zobah H1858
1Ch 18: 4 **D** captured a thousand of his chariots H1858
1Ch 18: 5 **D** struck down twenty-two thousand of H1858
1Ch 18: 6 The LORD gave **D** victory wherever he went H1858
1Ch 18: 7 **D** took the gold shields carried by the H1858
1Ch 18: 8 **D** took a great quantity of bronze H1858
1Ch 18: 9 of Hamath heard that **D** had defeated the H1858
1Ch 18:10 son Hadoram to King **D** to greet him and H1858
1Ch 18:11 King **D** dedicated these articles to the H1858
1Ch 18:13 all the Edomites became subject to **D**. H1858
1Ch 18:13 The LORD gave **D** victory wherever he went H1858
1Ch 18:14 **D** reigned over all Israel, doing what was H1858
1Ch 19: 2 **D** thought, "I will show kindness to Hanun H1858
1Ch 19: 2 So **D** sent a delegation to express his H1858
1Ch 19: 3 "Do you think **D** is honoring your father by H1858
1Ch 19: 5 came and told **D** about the men, H1858
1Ch 19: 6 that they had become obnoxious to **D**, H1858
1Ch 19: 8 **D** sent Joab out with the entire army of H1858
1Ch 19:17 When **D** was told of this, he gathered all H1858
1Ch 19:17 **D** formed his lines to meet the Arameans H1858
1Ch 19:18 **D** killed seven thousand of their H1858
1Ch 19:19 made peace with **D** and became subject H1858
1Ch 20: 1 but **D** remained in Jerusalem. H1858
1Ch 20: 2 **D** took the crown from the head of their H1858
1Ch 20: 3 **D** did this to all the Ammonite towns H1858
1Ch 20: 3 Then **D** and his entire army returned to H1858
1Ch 20: 8 they fell at the hands of **D** and his men. H1858
1Ch 21: 1 Israel and incited **D** to take a census of H1858
1Ch 21: 2 So **D** said to Joab and the commanders of H1858
1Ch 21: 5 the number of the fighting men to **D**: H1858
1Ch 21: 8 Then **D** said to God, "I have sinned H1858
1Ch 21:10 "Go and tell **D**, 'This is what the LORD says H1858
1Ch 21:11 So Gad went to **D** and said to him, "This H1858
1Ch 21:13 **D** said to Gad, "I am in deep distress. H1858
1Ch 21:16 **D** looked up and saw the angel of the H1858
1Ch 21:16 Then **D** and the elders, clothed in H1858
1Ch 21:17 **D** said to God, "Was it not I who ordered H1858
1Ch 21:18 ordered Gad to tell **D** to go up and build H1858
1Ch 21:19 So **D** went up in obedience to the word H1858
1Ch 21:21 Then **D** approached, and when Araunah H1858
1Ch 21:21 bowed down before **D** with his face to the H1858
1Ch 21:22 **D** said to him, "Let me have the site of H1858
1Ch 21:23 Araunah said to **D**, "Take it! Let my lord H1858
1Ch 21:24 But King **D** replied to Araunah, "No, H1858
1Ch 21:25 So **D** paid Araunah six hundred shekels of H1858
1Ch 21:26 **D** built an altar to the LORD there and H1858
1Ch 21:28 when **D** saw that the LORD had answered H1858
1Ch 21:30 But **D** could not go before it to inquire of H1858
1Ch 22: 1 Then **D** said, "The house of the LORD God H1858
1Ch 22: 2 So **D** gave orders to assemble the H1858
1Ch 22: 4 had brought large numbers of them to **D**. H1858
1Ch 22: 5 **D** said, "My son Solomon is young and H1858
1Ch 22: 5 So **D** made extensive preparations before H1858
1Ch 22: 7 **D** said to Solomon: "My son, I had it in my H1858
1Ch 22:17 Then **D** ordered all the leaders of Israel to H1858
1Ch 23: 1 When **D** was old and full of years, he H1858
1Ch 23: 4 **D** said, "Of these, twenty-four thousand are NDT
1Ch 23: 6 **D** separated the Levites into divisions H1858
1Ch 23:25 For **D** had said, "Since the LORD, the God H1858
1Ch 23:27 According to the last instructions of **D**, the H1858
1Ch 24: 3 **D** separated them into divisions for their H1858
1Ch 24:31 in the presence of King **D** and of Zadok H1858
1Ch 25: 1 **D**, together with the commanders of the H1858
1Ch 26:26 the things dedicated by King **D**, H1858
1Ch 26:32 King **D** put them in charge of the H1858
1Ch 27:18 a brother of **D**; over Issachar: Omri H1858
1Ch 27:23 **D** did not take the number of the men H1858
1Ch 27:24 in the book of the annals of King **D**. H1858
1Ch 28: 1 **D** summoned all the officials of Israel to H1858
1Ch 28: 2 King **D** rose to his feet and said: "Listen to H1858
1Ch 28:11 Then **D** gave his son Solomon the plans H1858
1Ch 28:19 **D** said, "I have in writing as a result of the NDT
1Ch 28:20 **D** also said to Solomon his son, "Be H1858
1Ch 29: 1 Then King **D** said to the whole assembly H1858
1Ch 29: 9 **D** the king also rejoiced greatly H1858
1Ch 29:10 **D** praised the LORD in the presence of the H1858
1Ch 29:20 Then **D** said to the whole assembly H1858
1Ch 29:22 Solomon son of **D** as king a second time, H1858
1Ch 29:23 the LORD as king in place of his father **D**. H1858
1Ch 29:26 **D** son of Jesse was king over all Israel. H1858
2Ch 1: 1 Solomon son of **D** established himself H1858
2Ch 1: 4 Now **D** had brought up the ark of God from H1858
2Ch 1: 8 great kindness to **D** my father and have H1858
2Ch 1: 9 your promise to my father **D** be confirmed, H1858
2Ch 2: 3 did for my father **D** when you sent him H1858
2Ch 2: 7 workers, whom my father **D** provided. H1858
2Ch 2:12 He has given King **D** a wise son H1858
2Ch 2:14 with those of my lord, **D** your father. H1858
2Ch 2:17 after the census his father **D** had taken H1858
2Ch 3: 1 the LORD had appeared to his father **D**. H1858
2Ch 3: 1 the Jebusite, the place provided by **D**. H1858
2Ch 5: 1 in the things his father **D** had dedicated— H1858
2Ch 5: 2 LORD's covenant from Zion, the City of **D**. H1858
2Ch 6: 4 promised with his mouth to my father **D**. H1858
2Ch 6: 6 I have chosen **D** to rule my people H1858
2Ch 6: 7 "My father **D** had it in his heart to build a H1858
2Ch 6: 8 But the LORD said to my father **D**, 'You did H1858
2Ch 6:10 I have succeeded **D** my father and now I H1858
2Ch 6:15 your promise to your servant **D** my father; H1858
2Ch 6:16 keep for your servant **D** my father the H1858
2Ch 6:17 you promised your servant **D** come true. H1858
2Ch 6:42 the great love promised to **D** your servant." H1858
2Ch 7: 6 which King **D** had made for praising the H1858
2Ch 7:10 LORD had done for **D** and Solomon and H1858
2Ch 7:17 before me faithfully as **D** your father did, H1858
2Ch 7:18 as I covenanted with **D** your father when I H1858
2Ch 8:11 up from the City of **D** to the palace he had H1858
2Ch 8:11 not live in the palace of **D** king of Israel, H1858
2Ch 8:14 with the ordinance of his father **D**, H1858
2Ch 8:14 this was what **D** the man of God had H1858
2Ch 9:31 was buried in the city of **D** his father. H1858
2Ch 10:16 "What share do we have in **D**, what part H1858
2Ch 10:16 after your own house, **D**!" So all the H1858
2Ch 10:19 against the house of **D** to this day. H1858
2Ch 11:17 the ways of **D** and Solomon during H1858
2Ch 12:16 ancestors and was buried in the City of **D**. H1858
2Ch 13: 5 of Israel to **D** and his descendants H1858
2Ch 13: 6 an official of Solomon son of **D**, rebelled H1858
2Ch 14: 1 ancestors and was buried in the City of **D**. H1858
2Ch 16:14 he had cut out for himself in the City of **D**. H1858
2Ch 17: 3 the ways of his father **D** before him. H1858
2Ch 21: 1 was buried with them in the City of **D**. H1858
2Ch 21: 7 the covenant the LORD had made with **D**, H1858
2Ch 21: 7 was not willing to destroy the house of **D**. H1858
2Ch 21:12 the LORD, the God of your father **D**, says: H1858
2Ch 21:20 was buried in the City of **D**, but not in H1858
2Ch 23: 3 concerning the descendants of **D**. H1858
2Ch 23: 9 belonged to King **D** and that were in the H1858
2Ch 23:18 to whom **D** had made assignments in the H1858
2Ch 23:18 rejoicing and singing, as **D** had ordered. H1858
2Ch 24:16 was buried with the kings in the City of **D**, H1858
2Ch 24:25 he died and was buried in the City of **D**, H1858
2Ch 27: 9 ancestors and was buried in the City of **D**. H1858
2Ch 28: 1 Unlike **D** his father, he did not do what H1858
2Ch 29: 2 of the LORD, just as his father **D** had done. H1858
2Ch 29:25 way prescribed by **D** and Gad the king's H1858
2Ch 29:27 the instruments of **D** king of Israel. H1858
2Ch 29:30 with the words of **D** and of Asaph the seer H1858
2Ch 30:26 of Solomon son of **D** king of Israel there H1858
2Ch 32: 5 reinforced the terraces of the City of **D**. H1858
2Ch 32:30 down to the west side of the City of **D**. H1858
2Ch 33: 7 which God had said to **D** and to his son H1858
2Ch 33:14 he rebuilt the outer wall of the City of **D**, H1858
2Ch 34: 2 followed the ways of his father **D**, H1858
2Ch 34: 3 he began to seek the God of his father **D**. H1858
2Ch 35: 3 that Solomon son of **D** king of Israel built. H1858
2Ch 35: 4 written by **D** king of Israel and by H1858
2Ch 35:15 were in the places prescribed by **D**, Asaph H1858
Ezr 3:10 the LORD, as prescribed by **D** king of Israel. H1858
Ezr 8: 2 of the descendants of **D**, Hattush H1858
Ezr 8:20 a body that **D** and the officials had H1858
Ne 3:15 the steps going down from the City of **D**. H1858
Ne 3:16 up to a point opposite the tombs of **D**, H1858
Ne 12:24 as prescribed by **D** the man of God. H1858
Ne 12:36 prescribed by **D** the man of God. H1858
Ne 12:37 steps of the City of **D** on the ascent to the H1858
Ne 12:45 to the commands of **D** and his son H1858
Ne 12:46 in the days of **D** and Asaph, there H1858
Ps 3: T A psalm of **D**. When he fled from his son H1858
Ps 4: T With stringed instruments. A psalm of **D**. H1858
Ps 5: T For pipes. A psalm of **D**. H1858
Ps 6: T According to sheminith. A psalm of **D**. H1858
Ps 7: T A shiggaion of **D**, which he sang to the H1858
Ps 8: T According to gittith. A psalm of **D**. H1858
Ps 9: T of "The Death of the Son." A psalm of **D**. H1858
Ps 11: T For the director of music. Of **D**. H1858
Ps 12: T According to sheminith. A psalm of **D**. H1858
Ps 13: T For the director of music. A psalm of **D**. H1858
Ps 14: T For the director of music. Of **D**. H1858
Ps 15: T A psalm of **D**. H1858
Ps 16: T A miktam of **D**. H1858
Ps 17: T A prayer of **D**. H1858
Ps 18: T Of **D** the servant of the LORD H1858
Ps 18:50 to **D** and to his descendants forever. H1858
Ps 19: T For the director of music. A psalm of **D**. H1858
Ps 20: T For the director of music. A psalm of **D**. H1858
Ps 21: T For the director of music. A psalm of **D**. H1858
Ps 22: T "The Doe of the Morning." A psalm of **D**. H1858
Ps 23: T A psalm of **D**. H1858
Ps 24: T Of **D**. A psalm. H1858
Ps 25: T Of **D**. H1858
Ps 26: T Of **D**. H1858
Ps 27: T Of **D**. H1858
Ps 28: T Of **D**. H1858
Ps 29: T A psalm of **D**. H1858
Ps 30: T For the dedication of the temple. Of **D**. H1858
Ps 31: T For the director of music. A psalm of **D**. H1858
Ps 32: T Of **D**. A maskil. H1858
Ps 34: T Of **D**. When he pretended to be insane H1858
Ps 35: T Of **D**. H1858
Ps 36: T Of **D** the servant of the LORD H1858
Ps 37: T Of **D**. H1858
Ps 38: T A psalm of **D**. A petition. H1858
Ps 39: T For Jeduthun. A psalm of **D**. H1858
Ps 40: T For the director of music. Of **D**. A psalm. H1858
Ps 41: T For the director of music. A psalm of **D**. H1858
Ps 51: T A psalm of **D**. When the prophet H1858
Ps 51: T came to him after **D** had committed adultery NDT
Ps 52: T A maskil of **D**. When Doeg the H1858
Ps 52: T "**D** has gone to the house of Ahimelek." H1858
Ps 53: T According to mahalath. A maskil of **D**. H1858
Ps 54: T A maskil of **D**. When the Ziphites had H1858
Ps 54: T said, "Is not **D** hiding among us? H1858
Ps 55: T With stringed instruments. A maskil of **D**. H1858
Ps 56: T Dove on Distant Oaks." Of **D**. A miktam. H1858
Ps 57: T tune of "Do Not Destroy." Of **D**. A miktam. H1858
Ps 58: T tune of "Do Not Destroy." Of **D**. A miktam. H1858
Ps 59: T tune of "Do Not Destroy." Of **D**. A miktam. H1858
Ps 60: T A miktam of **D**. For teaching. H1858

Ps 61: T With stringed instruments. Of **D**. H1858
Ps 62: T For Jeduthun. A psalm of **D**. H1858
Ps 63: T A psalm of **D**. When he was in the Desert H1858
Ps 64: T For the director of music. A psalm of **D**. H1858
Ps 65: T director of music. A psalm of **D**. A song. H1858
Ps 68: T director of music. Of **D**. A psalm. A song. H1858
Ps 69: T To the tune of "Lilies." Of **D**. H1858
Ps 70: T For the director of music. Of **D**. A petition. H1858
Ps 72:20 concludes the prayers of **D** son of Jesse. H1858
Ps 78:70 He chose **D** his servant and took him from H1858
Ps 78:72 And **D** shepherded them with integrity of NDT
Ps 86: T A prayer of **D**. H1858
Ps 89: 3 I have sworn to **D** my servant, H1858
Ps 89:20 I have found **D** my servant; with my sacred H1858
Ps 89:35 by my holiness—and I will not lie to **D**— H1858
Ps 89:49 which in your faithfulness you swore to **D**? H1858
Ps 101: T Of **D**. A psalm. H1858
Ps 103: T Of **D**. H1858
Ps 108: T A psalm of **D**. H1858
Ps 109: T For the director of music. Of **D**. A psalm. H1858
Ps 110: T Of **D**. A psalm. H1858
Ps 122: T A song of ascents. Of **D**. H1858
Ps 122: 5 judgment, the thrones of the house of **D**. H1858
Ps 124: T A song of ascents. Of **D**. H1858
Ps 131: T A song of ascents. Of **D**. H1858
Ps 132: 1 remember **D** and all his self-denial. H1858
Ps 132:10 For the sake of your servant **D**, do not H1858
Ps 132:11 The LORD swore an oath to **D**, a sure oath H1858
Ps 132:17 a horn grow for **D** and set up a lamp H1858
Ps 133: T A song of ascents. Of **D**. H1858
Ps 138: T Of **D**. H1858
Ps 139: T For the director of music. Of **D**. A psalm. H1858
Ps 140: T For the director of music. A psalm of **D**. H1858
Ps 141: T A psalm of **D**. H1858
Ps 142: T A maskil of **D**. When he was in the cave H1858
Ps 143: T A psalm of **D**. H1858
Ps 144: T Of **D**. H1858
Ps 144:10 to kings, who delivers his servant **D**. H1858
Ps 145: T A psalm of praise. Of **D**. H1858
Pr 1: 1 The proverbs of Solomon son of **D**, king of H1858
Ecc 1: 1 the Teacher, son of **D**, king in Jerusalem: H1858
SS 4: 4 Your neck is like the tower of **D**, built with H1858
Isa 7: 2 Now the house of **D** was told, "Aram has H1858
Isa 7:13 Isaiah said, "Hear now, you house of **D**! H1858
Isa 16: 5 one from the house of **D**—one who in H1858
Isa 22: 9 walls of the City of **D** were broken through H1858
Isa 22:22 on his shoulder the key to the house of **D**; H1858
Isa 29: 1 Ariel, Ariel, the city where **D** settled! H1858
Isa 37:35 my sake and for the sake of **D** my servant!" H1858
Isa 38: 5 the LORD, the God of your father **D**, says: H1858
Isa 55: 3 with you, my faithful love promised to **D**. H1858
Jer 21:12 is what the LORD says to you, house of **D**: H1858
Jer 22:30 sit on the throne of **D** or rule anymore in H1858
Jer 23: 5 I will raise up for **D** a righteous Branch, H1858
Jer 30: 9 serve the LORD their God and **D** their king, H1858
Jer 33:17 '**D** will never fail to have a man to sit on H1858
Jer 33:21 then my covenant with **D** my servant—and H1858
Jer 33:21 can be broken and **D** will no longer have H2257S
Jer 33:22 the descendants of **D** my servant and the H1858
Jer 33:26 of Jacob and **D** my servant and will not H1858
Jer 36:30 will have no one to sit on the throne of **D**; H1858
Eze 34:23 shepherd, my servant **D**, and he will tend H1858
Eze 34:24 my servant **D** will be prince among H1858
Eze 37:24 " 'My servant **D** will be king over them H1858
Eze 37:25 **D** my servant will be their prince H1858
Hos 3: 5 seek the LORD their God and **D** their king. H1858
Am 6: 5 on your harps like **D** and improvise on H1858
Zec 12: 7 of the house of **D** and of Jerusalem's H1858
Zec 12: 8 the feeblest among them will be like **D**, H1858
Zec 12: 8 the house of **D** will be like God, like H1858
Zec 12:10 out on the house of **D** and the inhabitants H1858
Zec 12:12 the clan of the house of **D** and their wives, H1858
Zec 13: 1 to the house of **D** and the inhabitants of H1858
Mt 1: 1 of Jesus the Messiah the son *of* **D**, *G1253*
Mt 1: 6 Jesse the father of King **D**. David was *G1253*
Mt 1: 6 **D** was the father of Solomon, whose *G1253*
Mt 1:17 generations in all from Abraham to **D**, *G1253*
Mt 1:17 fourteen from **D** to the exile to Babylon *G1253*
Mt 1:20 "Joseph son *of* **D**, do not be afraid *G1253*
Mt 9:27 calling out, "Have mercy on us, Son *of* **D**!" *G1253*
Mt 12: 3 you read what **D** did when he and his *G1253*
Mt 12:23 said, "Could this be the Son *of* **D**? *G1253*
Mt 15:22 "Lord, Son *of* **D**, have mercy on me! *G1253*
Mt 20:30 Son *of* **D**, have mercy on us! *G1253*
Mt 20:31 "Lord, Son *of* **D**, have mercy on us! *G1253*
Mt 21: 9 shouted, "Hosanna to the Son *of* **D**!" *G1253*
Mt 21:15 "Hosanna to the Son *of* **D**," they were *G1253*
Mt 22:42 "The son *of* **D**," they replied. *G1253*
Mt 22:43 "How is it then that **D**, speaking by the *G1253*
Mt 22:45 If then **D** calls him 'Lord,' how can he be *G1253*
Mk 2:25 never read what **D** did when he and his *G1253*
Mk 10:47 Son *of* **D**, have mercy on me *G1253*
Mk 10:48 the more, "Son *of* **D**, have mercy on me *G1253*
Mk 11:10 is the coming kingdom of our father **D**!" *G1253*
Mk 12:35 law say that the Messiah is the son *of* **D**? *G1253*
Mk 12:36 **D** himself, speaking by the Holy Spirit *G1253*
Mk 12:37 **D** himself calls him 'Lord.' How then can *G1253*
Lk 1:27 a man named Joseph, a descendant *of* **D**. *G1253*
Lk 1:32 will give him the throne *of* his father **D**, *G1253*
Lk 1:69 us in the house *of* his servant **D** *G1253*
Lk 2: 4 to Bethlehem the town *of* **D**, because he *G1253*
Lk 2: 4 he belonged to the house and line *of* **D**. *G1253*
Lk 2:11 Today in the town *of* **D** a Savior has been *G1253*
Lk 3:31 the son of Nathan, the son *of* **D**, *G1253*
Lk 6: 3 never read what **D** did when he and his *G1253*
Lk 18:38 "Jesus, Son *of* **D**, have mercy on me!" *G1253*
Lk 18:39 the more, "Son *of* **D**, have mercy on me *G1253*
Lk 20:41 is it said that the Messiah is the son *of* **D**? *G1253*
Lk 20:42 **D** himself declares in the Book of Psalms *G1253*
Lk 20:44 **D** calls him 'Lord.' How then can he be *G1253*
Jn 7:42 from Bethlehem, the town where **D** lived?" *G1253*
Ac 1:16 long ago through **D** concerning Judas, *G1253*
Ac 2:25 **D** said about him: " 'I saw the Lord always *G1253*
Ac 2:29 that the patriarch **D** died and was buried, *G1253*
Ac 2:34 For **D** did not ascend to heaven, and yet *G1253*
Ac 4:25 the mouth of your servant, our father **D**: *G1253*
Ac 7:45 remained in the land until the time *of* **D**, *G1253*
Ac 13:22 After removing Saul, he made **D** their king. *G1253*
Ac 13:22 'I have found **D** son of Jesse, a man after *G1253*
Ac 13:34 holy and sure blessings promised *to* **D**. *G1253*
Ac 13:36 "Now when **D** had served God's purpose *G1253*
Ro 1: 3 to his earthly life was a descendant of **D**, *G1253*
Ro 4: 6 **D** says the same thing when he speaks of *G1253*
Ro 11: 9 And **D** says: "May their table become a *G1253*
2Ti 2: 8 raised from the dead, descended from **D**. *G1253*
Heb 4: 7 a long time later he spoke through **D**, *G1253*
Heb 11:32 about **D** and Samuel and the prophets *G1253*
Rev 3: 7 is holy and true, who holds the key *of* **D**. *G1253*
Rev 5: 5 of Judah, the Root *of* **D**, has triumphed. *G1253*
Rev 22:16 I am the Root and the Offspring *of* **D**, and *G1253*

DAVID'S (83) [DAVID]

1Sa 17:28 When Eliab, **D** oldest brother, heard him H2257S
1Sa 19:11 Saul sent men to **D** house to watch it and H1858
1Sa 19:11 But Michal, **D** wife, warned him, "If you H1858
1Sa 20:15 cut off every one of **D** enemies from the H1858
1Sa 20:16 "May the LORD call **D** enemies to account." H1858
1Sa 20:25 sat next to Saul, but **D** place was empty. H1858
1Sa 20:27 of the month, **D** place was empty again. H1858
1Sa 23: 3 But **D** men said to him, "Here in Judah H1858
1Sa 25: 9 When **D** men arrived, they gave Nabal H1858
1Sa 25: 9 they gave Nabal this message in **D** name. H1858
1Sa 25:10 Nabal answered **D** servants, "Who is this H1858
1Sa 25:12 **D** men turned around and went back H1858
1Sa 25:42 went with **D** messengers and became his H1858
1Sa 25:44 his daughter Michal, **D** wife, to Paltiel son H1858
1Sa 26:17 Saul recognized **D** voice and said, "Is that H1858
1Sa 30: 5 **D** two wives had been captured H1858
1Sa 30:20 other livestock, saying, "This is **D** plunder." H1858
1Sa 30:22 troublemakers among **D** followers said, H1858
2Sa 2:13 son of Zeruiah and **D** men went out and H1858
2Sa 2:17 the Israelites were defeated by **D** men. H1858
2Sa 2:30 nineteen of **D** men were found missing. H1858
2Sa 2:31 But **D** men had killed three hundred and H1858
2Sa 3: 5 the sixth, Ithream the son of **D** wife Eglah. H1858
2Sa 3:10 of Saul and establish **D** throne over Israel H1858
2Sa 3:22 Just then **D** men and Joab returned from H1858
2Sa 5: 8 'lame and blind' who are **D** enemies." H1858
2Sa 8:18 Pelethites; and **D** sons were priests. H1858
2Sa 9:11 Mephibosheth ate at **D** table like one of H2257S
2Sa 10: 2 When **D** men came to the land of the H1858
2Sa 10: 4 So Hanun seized **D** envoys, shaved off half H1858
2Sa 11:13 At **D** invitation, he ate and drank with him H1858
2Sa 11:17 some of the men in **D** army fell; moreover H1858
2Sa 12:18 **D** attendants were afraid to tell him that H1858
2Sa 13: 3 Jonadab son of Shimeah, **D** brother. H1858
2Sa 13:32 Jonadab son of Shimeah, **D** brother, said, H1858
2Sa 15:12 the Gilonite, **D** counselor, to come from H1858
2Sa 15:37 So Hushai, **D** confidant, arrived at H1858
2Sa 16: 6 special guard were on **D** right and left. H2257S
2Sa 16:16 Hushai the Arkite, **D** confidant, went to H1858
2Sa 18: 6 **D** army marched out of the city to fight H2021S
2Sa 18: 7 Israel's troops were routed by **D** men, H1858
2Sa 18: 9 Now Absalom happened to meet **D** men H1858
2Sa 20:26 Ira the Jairite was **D** priest. H4200+1858
2Sa 21:17 son of Zeruiah came to **D** rescue; H2257S
2Sa 21:17 Then **D** men swore to him, saying, "Never H1858
2Sa 21:21 son of Shimeah, **D** brother, killed him. H1858
2Sa 23: 8 the names of **D** mighty warriors: H4200+1858
2Sa 24:11 had come to Gad the prophet, **D** seer: H1858
1Ki 1: 8 and Rei and **D** special guard did H4200+1858
1Ki 1:38 had Solomon mount King **D** mule, H1858
1Ki 2:45 **D** throne will remain secure before H1858
1Ki 11:39 I will humble **D** descendants because of H1858
1Ki 15: 4 **D** sake the LORD his God gave him a H1858
1Ch 11:10 the chiefs of **D** mighty warriors— H4200+1858
1Ch 11:11 this is the list of **D** mighty warriors H4200+1858
1Ch 14:17 So **D** fame spread throughout every land H1858
1Ch 18:17 **D** sons were chief officials at the H1858
1Ch 19: 2 When **D** envoys came to Hanun in the H1858
1Ch 19: 4 So Hanun seized **D** envoys, shaved them H1858
1Ch 20: 2 stones—and it was placed on **D** head. H1858
1Ch 20: 7 son of Shimea, **D** brother, killed him. H1858
1Ch 21: 9 The LORD said to Gad, **D** seer, H1858
1Ch 26:31 the fortieth year of **D** reign a search was H1858
1Ch 27:31 in charge of King **D** property. H4200+1858
1Ch 27:32 Jonathan, **D** uncle, was a counselor, H1858
1Ch 29:24 as well as all of King **D** sons, pledged H1858
1Ch 29:29 As for the events of King **D** reign, from H1858
2Ch 11:18 the daughter of **D** son Jerimoth and of H1858
2Ch 13: 8 which is in the hands of **D** descendants. H1858
2Ch 29:26 Levites stood ready with **D** instruments, H1858
2Ch 32:33 where the tombs of **D** descendants are. H1858
Ne 12:37 above the site of **D** palace to the Water H1858
Ps 59: T sent men to watch **D** house in order to H2021S
Isa 9: 7 He will reign on **D** throne and over his H1858
Jer 13:13 the kings who sit on **D** throne, H4200+1858
Jer 17:25 then kings who sit on **D** throne will come H1858
Jer 22: 2 of Judah, you who sit on **D** throne—you, H1858
Jer 22: 4 who sit on **D** throne will come H4200+1858
Jer 29:16 the king who sits on **D** throne and all the H1858
Jer 33:15 a righteous Branch sprout from **D line**; H1858
Am 9:11 that day "I will restore **D** fallen shelter— H1858
Jn 7:42 will come from **D** descendants and from *G1253*
Ac 15:16 this I will return and rebuild **D** fallen tent. *G1253*

DAWN (33) [DAWNED, DAWNS]

Ge 19:15 With the coming of **d**, the angels urged H8840
Jdg 16: 2 saying, "At **d** we'll kill him." H240+2021+1332
Jdg 19:25 the night, and at **d** they let her go. H8840
1Sa 14:36 night and plunder them till **d**, H240+1332+2021
Ne 4:21 from the **first light of d** till the stars H6590+8840
Job 3: 9 in vain and not see the first rays of **d**, H8840
Job 4:20 Between **d** and dusk they are broken to H1332
Job 7: 4 night drags on, and I toss and turn until **d**. H5974
Job 38:12 to the morning, or shown the **d** its place, H8840
Job 41:18 of light; its eyes are like the rays of **d**. H8840
Ps 37: 6 your righteous reward shine like the **d**, H240
Ps 57: 8 harp and lyre! I will awaken the **d**. H8840
Ps 108: 2 harp and lyre! I will awaken the **d**. H8840
Ps 119:147 I rise before **d** and cry for help; I have put H5974
Ps 139: 9 If I rise on the wings of the **d**, if I settle on H8840
SS 6:10 Who is this that appears like the **d**, fair as H8840
Isa 8:20 to this word, they have no **light of d**. H8840
Isa 14:12 from heaven, morning star, son of the **d**! H8840
Isa 38:13 I waited patiently till **d**, but like a lion he H1332
Isa 58: 8 Then your light will break forth like the **d** H8840
Isa 60: 3 kings to the brightness of your **d**. H2437
Isa 62: 1 till her vindication shines out like the **d** H5586
Da 6:19 At the first light of **d**, the king got up A10740
Joel 2: 2 Like **d** spreading across the mountains a H8840
Am 4:13 to mankind, who turns **d** to darkness, and H8840
Am 5: 8 turns midnight into **d** and darkens day H1332
Jnh 4: 7 But at **d** the next day God provided a worm H8840
Mt 14:25 **Shortly before d** Jesus *G5480+5871+3836+3816*
Mt 28: 1 Sabbath, *at* **d** on the first day of the week *G2216*
Mk 6:48 **Shortly before d** he went *G4309+5480+5871+3836+3816*
Mk 13:35 when the rooster crows, or **at d**. *G4745*
Jn 8: 2 *At* **d** he appeared again in the temple *G3986*
Ac 27:33 Just before **d** Paul urged *G2465+3516+1181*

DAWNED (5) [DAWN]

Ge 44: 3 *As* morning **d**, the men were sent on their H239
Dt 33: 2 from Sinai and **d** over them from Seir H2436
Isa 9: 2 the land of deep darkness a light *has* **d**. H5585
Mt 4:16 land of the shadow of death a light *has* **d**." *G422*
Ac 12:12 *When this had* **d** on him, he went to the *G5328*

DAWNS (4) [DAWN]

Ps 65: 8 your wonders; **where** morning **d**, where H4604
Ps 112: 4 Even in darkness light **d** for the upright H2436
Hos 10:15 When that **day d**, the king of Israel will be H8840
2Pe 1:19 until the day **d** and the morning star rises *G1419*

DAY (1421) [DAILY, DAY'S, DAYBREAK, DAYLIGHT, DAYS, DAYTIME, EVERYDAY, MIDDAY, SEVEN-DAY, THREE-DAY]

Ge 1: 5 God called the light "**d**," and the darkness H3427
Ge 1: 5 there was morning—the first **d**. H3427
Ge 1: 8 there was morning—the second **d**. H3427
Ge 1:13 there was morning—the third **d**. H3427
Ge 1:14 the sky to separate the **d** from the night, H3427
Ge 1:16 light to govern the **d** and the lesser light H3427
Ge 1:18 to govern the **d** and the night, and to H3427
Ge 1:19 there was morning—the fourth **d**. H3427
Ge 1:23 there was morning—the fifth **d**. H3427
Ge 1:31 there was morning—the sixth **d**. H3427
Ge 2: 2 By the seventh **d** God had finished the H3427
Ge 2: 2 so on the seventh **d** he rested from all his H3427
Ge 2: 3 blessed the seventh **d** and made it holy, H3427
Ge 3: 8 walking in the garden in the cool of the **d**, H3427
Ge 7:11 on the seventeenth **d** of the second H3427
Ge 7:11 on that **d** all the springs of the great deep H3427
Ge 7:13 On that very **d** Noah and his sons, Shem H3427
Ge 8: 4 on the seventeenth **d** of the seventh H3427
Ge 8: 5 on the first **d** of the tenth month the NDT
Ge 8:13 By the first **d** of the first month of Noah's six NDT
Ge 8:14 the twenty-seventh **d** of the second month H3427
Ge 8:22 winter, **d** and night will never cease." H3427
Ge 15:18 On that **d** the LORD made a covenant with H3427
Ge 17:23 On that very **d** Abraham took his son H3427
Ge 17:26 were both circumcised on that very **d**. H3427
Ge 18: 1 entrance to his tent in the heat of the **d**. H3427
Ge 19:31 **One d** the older daughter said to the H2256
Ge 19:34 The **next d** the older daughter said to the H4740
Ge 21: 8 on the **d** Isaac was weaned Abraham H3427
Ge 22: 4 On the third **d** Abraham looked up and H3427
Ge 22:14 And to this **d** it is said, "On the mountain H3427
Ge 26:32 That **d** Isaac's servants came and told him H3427
Ge 26:33 to this **d** the name of the town has H3427
Ge 27: 2 man and don't know the **d** *of* my death. H3427
Ge 27:45 Why should I lose both of you *in* one **d**?" H3427
Ge 30:35 That same **d** he removed all the male H3427
Ge 31:22 On the third **d** Laban was told that Jacob H3427
Ge 31:39 me for whatever was stolen by **d** or night. H3427

Ge 32:32 Therefore to this **d** the Israelites do not eat H3427
Ge 33:13 If they are driven hard just one **d**, all the H3427
Ge 33:16 So that **d** Esau started on his way back to H3427
Ge 35: 3 answered me in the **d** *of* my distress and H3427
Ge 35:20 to this **d** that pillar marks Rachel's H3427
Ge 39:10 though she spoke to Joseph **d** *after* day, H3427
Ge 39:10 though she spoke to Joseph day after **d**, H3427
Ge 39:11 One **d** he went into the house to attend to H3427
Ge 40:20 Now the third **d** was Pharaoh's birthday H3427
Ge 42:18 On the third **d**, Joseph said to them, "Do H3427
Ge 48:15 been my shepherd all my life to this **d**, H3427
Ge 48:20 He blessed them that **d** and said, "In your H3427
Ex 2:11 One **d**, after Moses had grown up, he H3427
Ex 2:13 The next **d** he went out and saw two H3427
Ex 5: 6 That same **d** Pharaoh gave this order to H3427
Ex 5:13 of you **for each d**, H1821+3427+928+3427
Ex 5:19 of you **for each d**. H1821+3427+928+3427
Ex 8:22 " 'But on that **d** I will deal differently with H3427
Ex 9: 6 And the **next d** the LORD did it: All the H4740
Ex 9:18 from the **d** it was founded till now. H3427
Ex 10: 6 ever seen from the **d** they settled in this H3427
Ex 10:13 the land all that **d** and all that night. H3427
Ex 10:28 The **d** you see my face you will die." H3427
Ex 12: 3 that on the tenth **d** of this month each man NDT
Ex 12: 6 them until the fourteenth **d** of the month, H3427
Ex 12:14 "This is a **d** you are to commemorate; for H3427
Ex 12:15 On the first **d** remove the yeast from your H3427
Ex 12:15 in it from the first **d** through the seventh H3427
Ex 12:16 On the first **d** hold a sacred assembly, and H3427
Ex 12:16 another one on the seventh **d**. H3427
Ex 12:17 it was on this very **d** that I brought your H3427
Ex 12:17 Celebrate this **d** as a lasting ordinance H3427
Ex 12:18 of the fourteenth **d** until the evening of H3427
Ex 12:18 day until the evening of the twenty-first **d**. H3427
Ex 12:41 430 years, to the very **d**, all the LORD's H3427
Ex 12:51 And on that very **d** the LORD brought the H3427
Ex 13: 3 "Commemorate this **d**, the day you came H3427
Ex 13: 3 this day, **the d** you came out of Egypt H889S
Ex 13: 6 on the seventh **d** hold a festival to H3427
Ex 13: 8 On that **d** tell your son, 'I do this because H3427
Ex 13:21 **By d** the LORD went ahead of them in a H3429
Ex 13:21 so that they could travel **by d** or night. H3429
Ex 13:22 the pillar of cloud **by d** nor the pillar of H3429
Ex 14:30 That **d** the LORD saved Israel from the H3427
Ex 16: 1 on the fifteenth **d** of the second month H3427
Ex 16: 4 are to go out each **d** and gather enough NDT
Ex 16: 4 day and gather enough for **that d**. H3427+3427
Ex 16: 5 On the sixth **d** they are to prepare what H3427
Ex 16:22 On the sixth **d**, they gathered twice as H3427
Ex 16:23 'Tomorrow is to be a **d of sabbath rest**, H8702
Ex 16:26 but on the seventh **d**, the Sabbath, H3427
Ex 16:27 went out on the seventh **d** to gather it, H3427
Ex 16:29 is why on the sixth **d** he gives you bread H3427
Ex 16:29 is to stay where they are on the seventh **d**; H3427
Ex 16:30 So the people rested on the seventh **d**. H3427
Ex 18:13 The **next d** Moses took his seat to serve as H4740
Ex 19: 1 On the first **d** of the third month after the NDT
Ex 19: 1 Egypt—on that very **d**—they came to the H3427
Ex 19:11 be ready by the third **d**, because on H3427
Ex 19:11 because on that **d** the LORD will come H3427
Ex 19:15 "Prepare yourselves for the third **d**. H3427
Ex 19:16 morning of the third **d** there was thunder H3427
Ex 20: 8 the Sabbath **d** by keeping it holy. H3427
Ex 20:10 the seventh **d** is a sabbath to the LORD H3427
Ex 20:11 in them, but he rested on the seventh **d**. H3427
Ex 20:11 blessed the Sabbath **d** and made it holy. H3427
Ex 21:21 if the slave recovers after a **d** or two, H3427
Ex 22:30 give them to me on the eighth **d**. H3427
Ex 23:12 on the seventh **d** do not work, so that H3427
Ex 24:16 on the seventh **d** the LORD called to H3427
Ex 29:36 Sacrifice a bull each **d** as a sin offering to H3427
Ex 29:38 are to offer on the altar regularly each **d**: H3427
Ex 31:14 do any work on **that d** must be cut off H2023S
Ex 31:15 the seventh **d** is a day of sabbath rest H3427
Ex 31:15 seventh day is a **d of sabbath rest**, H8701+8702
Ex 31:15 work on the Sabbath **d** is to be put to H3427
Ex 31:17 on the seventh **d** he rested and was H3427
Ex 32: 6 So the **next d** the people rose early and H4740
Ex 32:28 that **d** about three thousand of the H3427
Ex 32:29 brothers, and he has blessed you this **d**." H3427
Ex 32:30 The **next d** Moses said to the people H4740
Ex 34:21 on the seventh **d** you shall rest; even H3427
Ex 35: 2 the seventh **d** shall be your holy day H3427
Ex 35: 2 the seventh day shall be your holy **d**, NDT
Ex 35: 2 a **d of sabbath rest** to the LORD. H8701+8702
Ex 35: 3 any of your dwellings on the Sabbath **d**." H3427
Ex 40: 2 meeting, on the first **d** *of* the first month. H3427
Ex 40:17 was set up on the first **d** of the first month in NDT
Ex 40:37 they did not set out—until the **d** it lifted. H3427
Ex 40:38 of the LORD was over the tabernacle **by d**, H3429
Lev 6: 5 to the owner on the **d** they present their H3427
Lev 6:20 bring to the LORD on the **d** he is anointed: H3427
Lev 7:15 must be eaten on the **d** it is offered; H3427
Lev 7:16 shall be eaten on the **d** they offer it, H3427
Lev 7:16 left over may be eaten on the **next d**. H4740
Lev 7:17 over till the third **d** must be burned up. H3427
Lev 7:18 fellowship offering is eaten on the third **d**, H3427
Lev 7:35 his sons on the **d** they were presented H3427
Lev 7:36 On the **d** they were anointed, the LORD H3427
Lev 7:38 of Sinai on the **d** he commanded the H3427
Lev 8:35 the tent of meeting **d** and night for seven H3429
Lev 9: 1 On the eighth **d** Moses summoned Aaron H3427
Lev 12: 3 On the eighth **d** the boy is to be H3427
Lev 13: 5 On the seventh **d** the priest is to examine H3427
Lev 13: 6 On the seventh **d** the priest is to examine H3427
Lev 13:27 On the seventh **d** the priest is to examine H3427
Lev 13:32 On the seventh **d** the priest is to examine H3427
Lev 13:34 On the seventh **d** the priest is to examine H3427
Lev 13:51 On the seventh **d** he is to examine it, and H3427
Lev 14: 9 On the seventh **d** they must shave off all H3427
Lev 14:10 "On the eighth **d** they must bring two H3427
Lev 14:23 "On the eighth **d** they must bring them H3427
Lev 14:39 On the seventh **d** the priest shall return to H3427
Lev 15:14 On the eighth **d** he must take two doves H3427
Lev 15:29 On the eighth **d** she must take two doves H3427
Lev 16:29 On the tenth **d** of the seventh month you NDT
Lev 16:30 because on this **d** atonement will be H3427
Lev 16:31 It is a **d of sabbath rest**, and you H8701+8702
Lev 19: 6 shall be eaten on the **d** you sacrifice it H3427
Lev 19: 6 the day you sacrifice it or on the **next d**; H4740
Lev 19: 6 over until the third **d** must be burned up. H3427
Lev 19: 7 If any of it is eaten on the third **d**, it is H3427
Lev 22:27 From the eighth **d** on, it will be H3427
Lev 22:28 a sheep and its young on the same **d**. H3427
Lev 22:30 It must be eaten that same **d**; leave none H3427
Lev 23: 3 the seventh **d** is a day of sabbath rest H3427
Lev 23: 3 seventh day is a **d of sabbath rest**, H8701+8702
Lev 23: 3 day of sabbath rest, a **d** of sacred assembly. NDT
Lev 23: 5 on the fourteenth **d** of the first month. NDT
Lev 23: 6 On the fifteenth **d** of that month the LORD's H3427
Lev 23: 7 On the first **d** hold a sacred assembly and H3427
Lev 23: 8 And on the seventh **d** hold a sacred H3427
Lev 23:11 is to wave it on the **d after** the Sabbath. H4740
Lev 23:12 On the **d** you wave the sheaf, you must H3427
Lev 23:14 until the very **d** you bring this offering to H3427
Lev 23:15 " 'From the **d after** the Sabbath, the day H4740
Lev 23:15 the **d** you brought the sheaf of the wave H3427
Lev 23:16 days up to the **d after** the seventh H4740
Lev 23:21 On that same **d** you are to proclaim a H3427
Lev 23:24 'On the first **d** of the seventh month you are NDT
Lev 23:24 you are to have a **d of sabbath rest**, H8702
Lev 23:27 "The tenth **d** of this seventh month is the NDT
Lev 23:27 seventh month is the **D** *of* Atonement. H3427
Lev 23:28 Do not do any work on that **d**, because it is H3427
Lev 23:28 because it is the **D** *of* Atonement, when H3427
Lev 23:29 themselves on that **d** must be cut off from H3427
Lev 23:30 anyone who does any work on that **d**. H3427
Lev 23:32 It is a **d of sabbath rest** for you, and H8701+8702
Lev 23:32 evening of the ninth **d** of the month until NDT
Lev 23:34 'On the fifteenth **d** of the seventh month H3427
Lev 23:35 The first **d** is a sacred assembly; do no H3427
Lev 23:36 on the eighth **d** hold a sacred H3427
Lev 23:37 offerings required for **each d**. H3427+928+3427
Lev 23:39 with the fifteenth **d** of the seventh month, H3427
Lev 23:39 the first **d** is a day of sabbath rest H3427
Lev 23:39 the first day is a **d of sabbath rest**, and the H8702
Lev 23:39 the eighth **d** also is a day of sabbath H3427
Lev 23:39 the eighth day also is a **d of sabbath rest**. H8702
Lev 23:40 On the first **d** you are to take branches H3427
Lev 25: 9 on the tenth **d** of the seventh month; NDT
Lev 25: 9 on the **D** *of* Atonement sound the trumpet H3427
Lev 27:23 its value on that **d** as something holy to H3427
Nu 1: 1 of Sinai on the first **d** of the second month NDT
Nu 1:18 together on the first **d** of the second month. NDT
Nu 6: 9 must shave their head on the seventh **d**— H3427
Nu 6: 9 the seventh day—the **d** *of* their cleansing. H3427
Nu 6:10 Then on the eighth **d** they must bring two H3427
Nu 6:11 That same **d** they are to consecrate their H3427
Nu 7:11 "**Each d** one leader is to H4200+2021+3427+4200+2021+3427
Nu 7:12 offering on the first **d** was Nahshon son of H3427
Nu 7:18 On the second **d** Nethanel son of Zuar H3427
Nu 7:24 On the third **d**, Eliab son of Helon, the H3427
Nu 7:30 On the fourth **d** Elizur son of Shedeur, the H3427
Nu 7:36 On the fifth **d** Shelumiel son of H3427
Nu 7:42 On the sixth **d** Eliasaph son of Deuel, the H3427
Nu 7:48 On the seventh **d** Elishama son of H3427
Nu 7:54 On the eighth **d** Gamaliel son of H3427
Nu 7:60 On the ninth **d** Abidan son of Gideoni H3427
Nu 7:66 On the tenth **d** Ahiezer son of H3427
Nu 7:72 On the eleventh **d** Pagiel son of Okran H3427
Nu 7:78 On the twelfth **d** Ahira son of Enan, the H3427
Nu 9: 3 twilight on the fourteenth **d** of this month, H3427
Nu 9: 5 on the fourteenth **d** of the first month. H3427
Nu 9: 6 the Passover on that **d** because they were H3427
Nu 9: 6 came to Moses and Aaron that same **d** H3427
Nu 9:11 on the fourteenth **d** of the second month H3427
Nu 9:15 On the **d** the tabernacle, the tent of the H3427
Nu 9:21 Whether **by d** or by night, whenever the H3429
Nu 10:11 On the twentieth **d** of the second month of NDT
Nu 10:34 was over them **by d** when they set out H3429
Nu 11:19 You will not eat it *for* just one **d**, or two H3427
Nu 11:32 All that **d** and night and all the next day H3427
Nu 11:32 all the **next d** the people went out H3427
Nu 14:14 in a pillar of cloud **by d** and a pillar of fire H3429
Nu 15:23 from the **d** the LORD gave them and H3427
Nu 15:32 found gathering wood on the Sabbath **d**. H3427
Nu 16:41 The **next d** the whole Israelite community H4740
Nu 17: 8 The **next d** Moses entered the tent and H4740
Nu 19:12 water on the third **d** and on the seventh H3427
Nu 19:12 on the third day and on the seventh **d**; H3427
Nu 19:19 on the seventh **d** he is to purify them. H3427
Nu 22:30 which you have always ridden, to this **d**? H3427
Nu 28: 3 as a regular burnt offering each **d**. H3427
Nu 28: 9 " 'On the Sabbath **d**, make an offering of H3427
Nu 28:16 " 'On the fourteenth **d** of the first month H3427
Nu 28:17 On the fifteenth **d** of this month there is to H3427
Nu 28:18 On the first **d** hold a sacred assembly and H3427
Nu 28:24 food offering every **d** for seven days as an H3427
Nu 28:25 On the seventh **d** hold a sacred assembly H3427
Nu 28:26 " 'On the **d** *of* firstfruits, when you present H3427
Nu 29: 1 " 'On the first **d** of the seventh month hold a NDT
Nu 29: 1 It is a **d** for you to sound the trumpets H3427
Nu 29: 7 " 'On the tenth **d** of this seventh month hold NDT
Nu 29:12 " 'On the fifteenth **d** of the seventh month, H3427
Nu 29:17 " 'On the second **d** offer twelve young H3427
Nu 29:20 " 'On the third **d** offer eleven bulls, two H3427
Nu 29:23 " 'On the fourth **d** offer ten bulls, two rams H3427
Nu 29:26 " 'On the fifth **d** offer nine bulls, two rams H3427
Nu 29:29 " 'On the sixth **d** offer eight bulls, two H3427
Nu 29:32 " 'On the seventh **d** offer seven bulls, two H3427
Nu 29:35 " 'On the eighth **d** hold a closing special H3427
Nu 30:14 says nothing to her about it from **d** to day, H3427
Nu 30:14 says nothing to her about it from day to **d**, H3427
Nu 31:24 On the seventh **d** wash your clothes and H3427
Nu 32:10 was aroused that **d** and he swore this H3427
Nu 33: 3 on the fifteenth **d** of the first month, H3427
Nu 33: 3 the first month, the **d after** the Passover. H4740
Nu 33:38 he died on the first **d** of the fifth month of NDT
Dt 1: 3 on the first **d** of the eleventh month NDT
Dt 1:33 in fire by night and in a cloud **by d**, to H3429
Dt 2:22 out and have lived in their place to this **d**. H3427
Dt 2:25 This very **d** I will begin to put the terror H3427
Dt 3:14 so that to this **d** Bashan is called Havvoth H3427
Dt 4:10 Remember the **d** you stood before the LORD H3427
Dt 4:15 form of any kind the **d** the LORD spoke to H3427
Dt 4:26 against you this **d** that you will quickly H3427
Dt 4:32 from the **d** God created human beings on H3427
Dt 4:39 take to heart this **d** that the LORD is God H3427
Dt 5:12 "Observe the Sabbath **d** by keeping it holy H3427
Dt 5:14 the seventh **d** is a sabbath to the LORD H3427
Dt 5:15 you to observe the Sabbath **d**. H3427
Dt 8:11 his decrees that I am giving you this **d**. H3427
Dt 9: 7 From the **d** you left Egypt until you arrived H3427
Dt 9:10 out of the fire, on the **d** *of* the assembly. H3427
Dt 10: 4 out of the fire, on the **d** *of* the assembly. H3427
Dt 16: 4 of the first **d** remain until morning H3427
Dt 16: 8 on the seventh **d** hold an assembly to H3427
Dt 18:16 at Horeb on the **d** *of* the assembly when H3427
Dt 21:23 Be sure to bury it that same **d**, because H3427
Dt 24:15 them their wages each **d** before sunset, H3427
Dt 26:16 God commands you this **d** to follow these H3427
Dt 26:17 have declared this **d** that the LORD is your H3427
Dt 26:18 LORD has declared this **d** that you are his H3427
Dt 27:11 On the same **d** Moses commanded the H3427
Dt 28:13 that I give you this **d** and carefully follow H3427
Dt 28:29 **d after day** you will be H3972+2021+3427
Dt 28:29 **day after d** you will be H3972+2021+3427
Dt 28:32 them **d after day**, H3972+2021+3427
Dt 28:32 them **day after d**, H3972+2021+3427
Dt 28:66 filled with dread both night and **d**, never H3429
Dt 29: 4 But to this **d** the LORD has not given you a H3427
Dt 29:12 with you this **d** and sealing with an H3427
Dt 29:13 to confirm you this **d** as his people, that he H3427
Dt 30:18 I declare to you this **d** that you will H3427
Dt 30:19 This **d** I call the heavens and the earth as H3427
Dt 31:14 "Now the **d** *of* your death is near. H3427
Dt 31:17 And in that **d** I will become angry with H3427
Dt 31:17 and in that **d** they will ask, 'Have H3427
Dt 31:18 hide my face in that **d** because of all their H3427
Dt 31:22 down this song that **d** and taught it to the H3427
Dt 32:35 their **d** *of* disaster is near and their doom H3427
Dt 32:46 I have solemnly declared to you this **d**, H3427
Dt 32:48 On that same **d** the LORD told Moses, H3427
Dt 33:12 he shields him all **d** *long*, and the one H3427
Dt 34: 6 to this **d** no one knows where his H3427
Jos 1: 8 meditate on it **d** and night, so that H3429
Jos 4: 9 And they are there to this **d**. H3427
Jos 4:14 That **d** the LORD exalted Joshua in the H3427
Jos 4:19 On the tenth **d** of the first month the people NDT
Jos 5: 9 the place has been called Gilgal to this **d**. H3427
Jos 5:10 evening of the fourteenth **d** of the month, H3427
Jos 5:11 The **d after** the Passover, that very day H4740
Jos 5:11 Passover, that very **d**, they ate some of the H3427
Jos 5:12 manna stopped the **d after** they ate this H4740
Jos 6: 4 On the seventh **d**, march around the city H3427
Jos 6:10 say a word until the **d** I tell you to shout. H3427
Jos 6:14 So on the second **d** they marched around H3427
Jos 6:15 On the seventh **d**, they got up at daybreak H3427
Jos 6:15 except that on that **d** they circled the city H3427
Jos 6:25 she lives among the Israelites to this **d**. H3427
Jos 7:26 pile of rocks, which remains to this **d**. H3427
Jos 8:25 thousand men and women fell that **d**— H3427
Jos 8:28 heap of ruins, a desolate place to this **d**. H3427
Jos 8:29 of rocks over it, which remains to this **d**. H3427
Jos 9:12 it at home on the **d** we left to come to you H3427
Jos 9:17 out and on the third **d** came to their cities: H3427
Jos 9:27 That **d** he made the Gibeonites H3427
Jos 9:27 And that is what they are to this **d**. H3427
Jos 10:12 On the **d** the LORD gave the Amorites over H3427
Jos 10:13 delayed going down about a full **d**. H3427
Jos 10:14 There has never been a **d** like it before H3427
Jos 10:14 a **d** when the LORD listened to a human NDT
Jos 10:27 large rocks, which are there to this **d**. H3427
Jos 10:28 That **d** Joshua took Makkedah. He put the H3427
Jos 10:32 Joshua took it on the second **d**. H3427

Jos 10:35 captured it that same **d** and put it to the H3427
Jos 13:13 to live among the Israelites to this **d**. H3427
Jos 14: 9 So on that **d** Moses swore to me, 'The H3427
Jos 14:11 strong today as the **d** Moses sent me out; H3427
Jos 14:12 country that the LORD promised me that **d**. H3427
Jos 15:18 **One d** when she came to Othniel H2256+2118
Jos 15:63 to this **d** the Jebusites live there with the H3427
Jos 16:10 to this **d** the Canaanites live among the H3427
Jos 22: 3 to this very **d**—you have not H3427
Jos 22:17 Up to this very **d** we have not cleansed H3427
Jos 22:22 to the LORD, do not spare us this **d**. H3427
Jos 22:24 it for fear that **some d** your descendants H4737
Jos 23: 9 to this **d** no one has been able to H3427
Jos 24:15 yourselves this **d** whom you will serve, H3427
Jos 24:25 On that **d** Joshua made a covenant for the H3427
Jdg 1:14 **One d** when she came to Othniel H2256+2118
Jdg 1:21 to this **d** the Jebusites live there with the H3427
Jdg 1:26 called it Luz, which is its name to this **d**. H3427
Jdg 3:30 That **d** Moab was made subject to Israel H3427
Jdg 4:14 This is the **d** the LORD has given Sisera H3427
Jdg 4:23 On that **d** God subdued Jabin king of H3427
Jdg 5: 1 On that **d** Deborah and Barak son of H3427
Jdg 6:24 To this **d** it stands in Ophrah of the H3427
Jdg 6:32 gave him the name Jerub-Baal that **d**, H3427
Jdg 6:38 Gideon rose early the **next d**; he H4740
Jdg 9: 8 One **d** the trees went out to anoint a king NDT
Jdg 9:42 The **next d** the people of Shechem went H4740
Jdg 9:45 All that **d** Abimelek pressed his attack H3427
Jdg 10: 4 which to this **d** are called Havvoth Jair. H3427
Jdg 11:27 the dispute this **d** between the Israelites H3427
Jdg 13: 7 from the womb until the **d** *of* his death. H3427
Jdg 13:10 man who appeared to me the other **d**!" H3427
Jdg 14:15 On the fourth **d**, they said to Samson's H3427
Jdg 14:17 So on the seventh **d** he finally told her H3427
Jdg 14:18 on the seventh **d** the men of the town H3427
Jdg 16: 1 **One d** Samson went to Gaza, where he H2256
Jdg 16:16 him **d after day** until he H3972+2021+3427
Jdg 16:16 him **day after d** until he H3972+2021+3427
Jdg 18:12 Jearim is called Mahaneh Dan to this **d**. H3427
Jdg 19: 5 On the fourth **d** they got up early and he H3427
Jdg 19: 8 On the morning of the fifth **d**, when he H3427
Jdg 19: 9 the night here; the **d** is nearly over. H3427
Jdg 19:11 near Jebus and the **d** was almost gone, H3427
Jdg 19:30 not since the **d** the Israelites came up out H3427
Jdg 20:21 Israelites on the battlefield that **d**. H3427
Jdg 20:22 they had stationed themselves the first **d**. H3427
Jdg 20:24 drew near to Benjamin the second **d**. H3427
Jdg 20:26 They fasted that **d** until evening and H3427
Jdg 20:30 on the third **d** and took up positions H3427
Jdg 20:35 on that **d** the Israelites struck down H3427
Jdg 20:46 On that **d** twenty-five thousand Benjamite H3427
Jdg 21: 4 Early the **next d** the people built an altar H4740
Ru 3: 1 **One d** Ruth's mother-in-law Naomi said H2256
Ru 4: 5 "On the **d** you buy the land from Naomi H3427
Ru 4:14 who this **d** has not left you without a H3427
1Sa 1: 4 Whenever the **d** came for Elkanah to H3427
1Sa 2:34 to you—they will both die on the same **d**. H3427
1Sa 4:12 That same **d** a Benjamite ran from the H3427
1Sa 4:16 the battle line; I fled from it this very **d**." H3427
1Sa 5: 3 people of Ashdod rose early the **next d**, H4740
1Sa 5: 5 That is why to this **d** neither the priests of H3427
1Sa 6:15 On that **d** the people of Beth Shemesh H3427
1Sa 6:16 then returned that same **d** to Ekron. H3427
1Sa 6:18 is a witness to this **d** in the field of Joshua H3427
1Sa 7: 6 On that **d** they fasted and there they H3427
1Sa 7:10 But that **d** the LORD thundered with loud H3427
1Sa 8: 8 have done from the **d** I brought them up H3427
1Sa 8: 8 brought them up out of Egypt until this **d**, H3427
1Sa 8:18 When that **d** comes, you will cry out for H3427
1Sa 8:18 the LORD will not answer you in that **d**." H3427
1Sa 9:15 Now the **d** before Saul came, the LORD H3427
1Sa 9:24 And Saul dined with Samuel that **d**. H3427
1Sa 10: 9 all these signs were fulfilled that **d**. H3427
1Sa 11:11 The **next d** Saul separated his men into H4740
1Sa 11:11 slaughtered them until the heat of the **d**. H3427
1Sa 11:13 this **d** the LORD has rescued Israel. H3427
1Sa 12: 2 your leader from my youth until this **d**. H3427
1Sa 12: 5 also his anointed is witness this **d** H3427
1Sa 12:18 that same **d** the LORD sent thunder H3427
1Sa 13:22 So on the **d** *of* the battle not a soldier H3427
1Sa 14: 1 One **d** Jonathan son of Saul said to his H3427
1Sa 14:23 So on that **d** the LORD saved Israel, and the H3427
1Sa 14:24 Now the Israelites were in distress that **d** H3427
1Sa 14:31 That **d**, after the Israelites had struck H3427
1Sa 14:37 But God did not answer him that **d**. H3427
1Sa 15:35 Until the **d** Samuel died, he did not go to H3427
1Sa 16:13 from that **d** on the Spirit of the LORD H3427
1Sa 17:10 "This **d** I defy the armies of Israel! H3427
1Sa 17:46 This **d** the LORD will deliver you into my H3427
1Sa 17:46 This very **d** I will give the carcasses of the H3427
1Sa 18: 2 From that **d** Saul kept David with him and H3427
1Sa 18:10 The **next d** an evil spirit from God came H4740
1Sa 19:24 He lay naked all that **d** and all that night H3427
1Sa 20: 5 until the evening of the **d after tomorrow**. H8958
1Sa 20:12 father by this time the **d after** tomorrow! H8958
1Sa 20:19 **The d after tomorrow**, toward evening, go H8992
1Sa 20:26 Saul said nothing that **d**, for he thought H3427
1Sa 20:27 But the **next d**, the second day of the H4740
1Sa 20:27 next day, the second **d** of the month NDT
1Sa 20:34 on that second **d** *of* the feast he did not H3427
1Sa 21: 6 by hot bread on the **d** it was taken away. H3427
1Sa 21: 7 one of Saul's servants was there that **d**, H3427
1Sa 21:10 That **d** David fled from Saul and went to H3427
1Sa 22:15 Was that **d** the first time I inquired of God H3427
1Sa 22:18 That **d** he killed eighty-five men who H3427
1Sa 22:22 to Abiathar, "That **d**, when Doeg the H3427
1Sa 23:14 **D after day** Saul searched H3972+2021+3427
1Sa 23:14 **Day after d** Saul searched H3972+2021+3427
1Sa 24: 4 "This is the **d** the LORD spoke of when he H3427
1Sa 24:10 This **d** you have seen with your own eyes H3427
1Sa 25:16 Night and **d** they were a wall around us H3429
1Sa 25:33 from bloodshed this **d** and from avenging H3427
1Sa 27: 6 So on that **d** Achish gave him Ziklag, and H3427
1Sa 28:20 nothing all that **d** and all that night. H3427
1Sa 29: 3 from the **d** he left Saul until now H3427
1Sa 29: 6 From the **d** you came to me until today, H3427
1Sa 29: 8 your servant from the **d** I came to you until H3427
1Sa 30: 1 his men reached Ziklag on the third **d**. H3427
1Sa 30:17 from dusk until the evening of the **next d**, H4740
1Sa 30:25 ordinance for Israel from that **d** to this. H3427
1Sa 31: 6 all his men died together that same **d**. H3427
1Sa 31: 8 The **next d**, when the Philistines came to H4740
2Sa 1: 2 On the third **d** a man arrived from Saul's H3427
2Sa 2:17 The battle that **d** was very fierce, and H3427
2Sa 3: 8 This very **d** I am loyal to the house of your H3427
2Sa 3:35 to eat something while it was still **d**; H3427
2Sa 3:37 So on that **d** all the people there and all H3427
2Sa 3:38 a great man has fallen in Israel this **d**? H3427
2Sa 4: 3 have resided there as foreigners to this **d**. H3427
2Sa 4: 5 in the heat of the **d** while he was taking H3427
2Sa 4: 8 This **d** the LORD has avenged my lord the H3427
2Sa 5: 8 On that **d** David had said, "Anyone who H3427
2Sa 6: 8 to this **d** that place is called Perez H3427
2Sa 6: 9 was afraid of the LORD that **d** and said, H3427
2Sa 6:23 had no children to the **d** *of* her death. H3427
2Sa 7: 6 in a house from the **d** I brought the H3427
2Sa 7: 6 the Israelites up out of Egypt to this **d**. H3427
2Sa 11:12 "Stay here one more **d**, and tomorrow I H3427
2Sa 11:12 in Jerusalem that **d** and the next. H3427
2Sa 12:18 On the seventh **d** the child died. H3427
2Sa 13:32 ever since the **d** Amnon raped his sister H3427
2Sa 18: 7 the casualties that **d** were great H3427
2Sa 18: 8 up more men that **d** than the sword. H3427
2Sa 18:18 is called Absalom's Monument to this **d**. H3427
2Sa 19: 2 army the victory that **d** was turned into H3427
2Sa 19: 2 because on that **d** the troops heard it said, H3427
2Sa 19: 3 into the city that **d** as men steal in who H3427
2Sa 19:19 did wrong on the **d** my lord the king left H3427
2Sa 19:24 his clothes from the **d** the king left until H3427
2Sa 19:24 the king left until the **d** he returned safely. H3427
2Sa 20: 3 in confinement till the **d** *of* their death, H3427
2Sa 21:10 birds touch them **by d** or the wild animals H3429
2Sa 22:19 confronted me in the **d** *of* my disaster, H3427
2Sa 23:10 LORD brought about a great victory that **d**. H3427
2Sa 23:20 into a pit on a snowy **d** and killed a lion. H3427
2Sa 24:18 On that **d** Gad went to David and said to H3427
1Ki 1:30 carry out this very **d** what I swore to you by H3427
1Ki 2: 8 curses on me the **d** I went to Mahanaim. H3427
1Ki 2:37 The **d** you leave and cross the Kidron H3427
1Ki 2:42 'On the **d** you leave to go anywhere else H3427
1Ki 3: 6 him a son to sit on his throne this very **d**. H3427
1Ki 3:18 The third **d** after my child was born, this H3427
1Ki 8:16 'Since the **d** I brought my people Israel H3427
1Ki 8:28 servant is praying in your presence this **d**. H3427
1Ki 8:29 be open toward this temple night and **d**, H3427
1Ki 8:59 be near to the LORD our God **d** and night H3429
1Ki 8:64 On that same **d** the king consecrated the H3427
1Ki 8:66 On the following **d** he sent the people H3427
1Ki 9:13 of Kabul, a name they have to this **d**. H3427
1Ki 9:21 to serve as slave labor, as it is to this **d**. H3427
1Ki 10:12 never been imported or seen since that **d**.) H3427
1Ki 12:19 against the house of David to this **d**. H3427
1Ki 12:32 on the fifteenth **d** of the eighth month, H3427
1Ki 12:33 On the fifteenth **d** of the eighth month, H3427
1Ki 13: 3 That same **d** the man of God gave a sign H3427
1Ki 13:11 the man of God had done there that **d**. H3427
1Ki 16:16 over Israel that very **d** there in the camp. H3427
1Ki 17:14 not run dry until the **d** the LORD sends rain H3427
1Ki 17:15 So there was food **every d** for Elijah and H3427
1Ki 20:29 on the seventh **d** the battle was H3427
1Ki 20:29 on the Aramean foot soldiers in one **d**. H3427
1Ki 21: 9 "Proclaim a **d of fasting** and seat Naboth H7427
1Ki 21:29 I will not bring this disaster in his **d**, but I H3427
1Ki 22:25 will find out on the **d** you go to hide in an H3427
1Ki 22:35 **All d long** the battle raged, H928+2021+3427+2021+2085
2Ki 2:22 And the water has remained pure to this **d**, H3427
2Ki 4: 8 One **d** Elisha went to Shunem. H3427
2Ki 4:11 One **d** when Elisha came, he went up to H3427
2Ki 4:18 and one **d** he went out to his father H3427
2Ki 6:29 The next **d** I said to her, 'Give up your son H3427
2Ki 7: 9 This is a **d** *of* good news and we are H3427
2Ki 8: 6 her land from the **d** she left the country H3427
2Ki 8:15 But the **next d** he took a thick cloth, soaked H4740
2Ki 8:22 To this **d** Edom has been in rebellion H3427
2Ki 10:27 people have used it for a latrine to this **d**. H3427
2Ki 13:23 To **this d** he has been unwilling to destroy H6964
2Ki 14: 7 it Joktheel, the name it has to this **d**. H3427
2Ki 15: 5 the king with leprosy until the **d** he died, H3427
2Ki 16: 6 into Elath and have lived there to this **d**. H3427
2Ki 17:34 To this **d** they persist in their former H3427
2Ki 17:41 To this **d** their children and grandchildren H3427
2Ki 19: 3 This **d** is a day of distress and rebuke and H3427
2Ki 19: 3 This day is a **d** *of* distress and rebuke and H3427
2Ki 19:37 **One d**, while he was worshiping in H2118+2256
2Ki 20: 5 On the third **d** from now you will go up to H3427
2Ki 20: 8 of the LORD on the third **d** from now?" H3427
2Ki 20:17 predecessors have stored up until this **d**, H3427
2Ki 21:15 my anger from the **d** their ancestors came H3427
2Ki 21:15 ancestors came out of Egypt until this **d**." H3427
2Ki 25: 1 on the tenth **d** of the tenth month NDT
2Ki 25: 3 By the ninth **d** of the fourth month the NDT
2Ki 25: 8 On the seventh **d** of the fifth month, in the NDT
2Ki 25:27 the twenty-seventh **d** of the twelfth month. NDT
2Ki 25:30 **D by day** the king gave Jehoiachin H1821+3427+928+3427+2257
2Ki 25:30 **Day by d** the king gave Jehoiachin H1821+3427+928+3427+2257
1Ch 4:41 destroyed them, as is evident to this **d**. H3427
1Ch 4:43 they have lived there to this **d**. H3427
1Ch 5:26 river of Gozan, where they are to this **d**. H3427
1Ch 9:33 were responsible for the work **d** and night. H3429
1Ch 10: 8 The **next d**, when the Philistines came to H4740
1Ch 11:22 into a pit on a snowy **d** and killed a lion. H3427
1Ch 12:22 **D** after day men came to help David, until H3427
1Ch 12:22 Day after **d** men came to help David, until H3427
1Ch 13:11 to this **d** that place is called Perez H3427
1Ch 13:12 David was afraid of God that **d** and asked H3427
1Ch 16: 7 That **d** David first appointed Asaph and H3427
1Ch 16:23 proclaim his salvation **d** after day. H3427
1Ch 16:23 proclaim his salvation day after **d**. H3427
1Ch 17: 5 in a house from the **d** I brought Israel up H3427
1Ch 17: 5 I brought Israel up out of Egypt to this **d**. H3427
1Ch 26:17 There were six Levites a **d** on the east, four H3427
1Ch 26:17 day on the east, four a **d** on the north, four a NDT
1Ch 26:17 four a **d** on the south and two at a time at H3427
1Ch 29:21 The next **d** they made sacrifices to the H3427
1Ch 29:22 joy in the presence of the LORD that **d**. H3427
2Ch 3: 2 on the second **d** of the second month in NDT
2Ch 6: 5 'Since the **d** I brought my people out of H3427
2Ch 6:20 be open toward this temple **d** and night, H3429
2Ch 7: 9 On the eighth **d** they held an assembly, for H3427
2Ch 7:10 On the twenty-third **d** of the seventh H3427
2Ch 8: 8 to serve as slave labor, as it is to this **d**. H3427
2Ch 8:16 from the **d** the foundation of the temple H3427
2Ch 9:20 considered of little value in Solomon's **d**. H3427
2Ch 10:19 against the house of David to this **d**. H3427
2Ch 18:24 will find out on the **d** you go to hide in an H3427
2Ch 18:34 **All d long** the battle raged, H928+2021+3427+2021+2085
2Ch 20:26 On the fourth **d** they assembled in the H3427
2Ch 20:26 it is called the Valley of Berakah to this **d**. H3427
2Ch 21:10 To this **d** Edom has been in rebellion H3427
2Ch 26:21 Uzziah had leprosy until the **d** he died. H3427
2Ch 28: 6 In one **d** Pekah son of Remaliah killed a H3427
2Ch 29:17 consecration on the first **d** of the first month, NDT
2Ch 29:17 by the eighth **d** of the month they H3427
2Ch 29:17 on the sixteenth **d** of the first month. H3427
2Ch 30:15 on the fourteenth **d** of the second month. NDT
2Ch 30:21 the LORD **every d** with H3427+928+3427
2Ch 35: 1 on the fourteenth **d** of the first month. NDT
2Ch 35:25 to this **d** all the male and female H3427
Ezr 3: 4 prescribed for **each d**. H3427+928+3427
Ezr 3: 6 On the first **d** of the seventh month they H3427
Ezr 5:16 From **that d** to the present it has been H10008S
Ezr 6:15 on the third **d** of the month Adar, A10317
Ezr 6:19 On the fourteenth **d** of the first month, the NDT
Ezr 7: 9 Babylon on the first **d** of the first month, NDT
Ezr 7: 9 Jerusalem on the first **d** of the fifth month, NDT
Ezr 8:31 On the twelfth **d** of the first month we set NDT
Ezr 8:33 On the fourth **d**, in the house of our God H3427
Ezr 9:15 We are left this **d** as a remnant. H3427
Ezr 10: 9 And on the twentieth **d** of the ninth month NDT
Ezr 10:13 cannot be taken care of in a **d** or two, H3427
Ezr 10:16 On the first **d** of the tenth month they sat H3427
Ezr 10:17 by the first **d** of the first month they H3427
Ne 1: 6 is praying before you **d** and night for your H3429
Ne 4: 2 Will they finish in a **d**? Can they bring the H3427
Ne 4: 9 posted a guard **d** and night to meet H3429
Ne 4:16 From that **d** on, half of my men did the H3427
Ne 4:22 us as guards by night and as workers *by* **d**." H3427
Ne 5:18 Each **d** one ox, six choice sheep and some H3427
Ne 6:10 **One d** I went to the house of Shemaiah H2256
Ne 8: 2 So on the first **d** of the seventh month H3427
Ne 8: 9 "This **d** is holy to the LORD your God. H3427
Ne 8:10 This **d** is holy to our Lord H3427
Ne 8:11 "Be still, for this is a holy **d**. H3427
Ne 8:13 On the second **d** of the month, the heads H3427
Ne 8:17 days of Joshua son of Nun until that **d**, H3427
Ne 8:18 **D** after day, from the first day to the last H3427
Ne 8:18 Day after **d**, from the first day to the last H3427
Ne 8:18 from the first **d** to the last, Ezra read H3427
Ne 8:18 on the eighth **d**, in accordance with H3427
Ne 9: 1 the twenty-fourth **d** of the same month, H3427
Ne 9: 3 the LORD their God *for* a quarter of the **d**, H3427
Ne 9:10 yourself, which remains to this **d**. H3427
Ne 9:12 **By d** you led them with a pillar of cloud H3429
Ne 9:19 **By d** the pillar of cloud did not fail to H928+3429
Ne 10:31 them on the Sabbath or on any holy **d**. H3427
Ne 12:43 And on that **d** they offered great sacrifices H3427
Ne 13: 1 On that **d** the Book of Moses was read H3427
Ne 13:15 them against selling food on that **d**. H3427
Ne 13:17 are doing—desecrating the Sabbath **d**? H3427
Ne 13:19 could be brought in on the Sabbath **d**. H3427
Ne 13:22 gates in order to keep the Sabbath **d** holy. H3427
Est 1:10 On the seventh **d**, when King Xerxes was H3427

D

Est 1:18 This very **d** the Persian and Median H3427
Est 2:11 **Every d** he walked back H3972+3427+2256+3427
Est 3:4 **D** after day they spoke to him but he H3427
Est 3:4 Day after **d** they spoke to him but he H3427
Est 3:7 Haman to **select a d** and H4946+3427+4200+3427
Est 3:12 on the thirteenth **d** of the first month the H3427
Est 3:13 on a single **d**, the thirteenth day H3427
Est 3:13 the thirteenth **d** of the twelfth month NDT
Est 3:14 so they would be ready for that **d**. H3427
Est 4:16 not eat or drink for three days, night or **d**. H3427
Est 5:1 On the third **d** Esther put on her royal H3427
Est 5:9 Haman went out that **d** happy and in high H3427
Est 7:2 they were drinking wine on the second **d**, H3427
Est 8:1 That same **d** King Xerxes gave Queen H3427
Est 8:9 on the twenty-third **d** of the third month, the NDT
Est 8:12 The **d** appointed for the Jews to do this in H3427
Est 8:12 was the thirteenth **d** of the twelfth month, NDT
Est 8:13 be ready on that **d** to avenge themselves H3427
Est 9:1 On the thirteenth **d** of the twelfth month H3427
Est 9:1 On this **d** the enemies of the Jews had H3427
Est 9:11 was reported to the king that same **d**. H3427
Est 9:15 on the fourteenth **d** of the month of Adar, H3427
Est 9:17 on the thirteenth **d** of the month of Adar, H3427
Est 9:17 made it a **d** *of* feasting and joy. H3427
Est 9:18 made it a **d** *of* feasting and joy. H3427
Est 9:19 month of Adar as a **d** *of* joy and feasting, H3427
Est 9:19 a **d** for giving presents to each other. H3427
Est 9:22 their mourning into a **d** *of* celebration. H3427
Job 1:6 One **d** the angels came to present H3427
Job 1:13 One **d** when Job's sons and daughters H3427
Job 2:1 On another **d** the angels came to present H3427
Job 3:1 his mouth and cursed the **d** *of* his birth. H3427
Job 3:3 "May the **d** *of* my birth perish, and the H3427
Job 3:4 That **d**—may it turn to darkness; may God H3427
Job 3:8 May those who curse days curse that **d** H2084S
Job 3:16 like an infant who never saw the **light of d**? H240
Job 15:23 he knows the **d** *of* darkness is at hand. H3427
Job 17:12 turn night into **d**; in the face of the H3427
Job 20:28 rushing waters on the **d** *of* God's wrath. H3427
Job 21:30 wicked are spared from the **d** *of* calamity, H3427
Job 21:30 they are delivered from the **d** *of* wrath? H3427
Job 24:16 houses, but **by d** they shut themselves in H3429
Ps 1:2 who meditates on his law **d** and night. H3429
Ps 7:11 a God who displays his wrath every **d**. H3427
Ps 13:2 thoughts and **d after day** have sorrow in H3429
Ps 13:2 thoughts and **day after d** have sorrow in H3429
Ps 18:18 confronted me in the **d** *of* my disaster, H3427
Ps 19:2 **D** after day they pour forth speech; night H3427
Ps 19:2 Day after **d** they pour forth speech; night H3427
Ps 22:2 My God, I cry out **by d**, but you do not H3429
Ps 25:5 and my hope is in you all **d** *long*. H3427
Ps 27:5 For in the **d** *of* trouble he will keep me H3427
Ps 32:3 away through my groaning all **d** *long*. H3427
Ps 32:4 For **d** and night your hand was heavy on H3429
Ps 35:28 righteousness, your praises all **d** *long*. H3427
Ps 37:13 for he knows their **d** is coming. H3427
Ps 38:6 very low; all **d** *long* I go about mourning. H3427
Ps 38:12 my ruin; all **d** *long* they scheme and lie. H3427
Ps 42:3 My tears have been my food **d** and night H3429
Ps 42:3 while people say to me all **d** *long* H3427
Ps 42:8 **By d** the LORD directs his love, at night his H3429
Ps 42:10 saying to me all **d** *long*, "Where is your H3427
Ps 44:8 In God we make our boast all **d** *long*, and H3427
Ps 44:15 I live in disgrace all **d** *long*, and my face H3427
Ps 44:22 Yet for your sake we face death all **d** *long* H3427
Ps 46:5 God will help her at **break of d**. H7155+1332
Ps 50:15 call on me in the **d** *of* trouble; I will H3427
Ps 52:1 Why do you boast all **d** *long*, you who are H3427
Ps 55:10 **D** and night they prowl about on its walls H3429
Ps 56:1 all **d** *long* they press their attack. H3427
Ps 56:2 My adversaries pursue me all **d** *long*; in H3427
Ps 56:5 All **d** *long* they twist my words; all their H3427
Ps 61:8 your name and fulfill my vows **d** *after* day. H3427
Ps 61:8 your name and fulfill my vows day after **d**. H3427
Ps 71:8 declaring your splendor all **d** *long*. H3427
Ps 71:15 of your saving acts all **d** *long*—though I H3427
Ps 71:17 to **this d** I declare your marvelous H2178S
Ps 71:24 will tell of your righteous acts all **d** *long*, H3427
Ps 72:15 pray for him and bless him all **d** *long*. H3427
Ps 73:14 All **d** *long* I have been afflicted, and every H3427
Ps 74:16 The **d** is yours, and yours also the night H3427
Ps 74:22 remember how fools mock you all **d** *long*. H3427
Ps 78:9 with bows, turned back on the **d** *of* battle; H3427
Ps 78:14 them with the cloud **by d** and with light H3429
Ps 78:42 the **d** he redeemed them from the H3427
Ps 78:43 **the d** he displayed his signs in Egypt, his H889S
Ps 81:3 the moon is full, on the **d** *of* our festival; H3427
Ps 84:10 Better is *one* **d** in your courts than a H3427
Ps 86:3 Lord, for I call to you all **d** *long*. H3427
Ps 88:1 saves me; **d** and night I cry out to you. H3427
Ps 88:9 every **d**; I spread out my hands to H3427
Ps 88:17 All **d** *long* they surround me like a flood H3427
Ps 89:16 They rejoice in your name all **d** *long*; they H3427
Ps 90:4 sight are like a **d** that has just gone H3427+919
Ps 91:5 of night, nor the arrow that flies **by d**, H3429
Ps 92:T A song. For the Sabbath **d**. H3427
Ps 95:8 as you did that **d** *at* Massah in the H3427
Ps 96:2 proclaim his salvation **d** after day. H3427
Ps 96:2 proclaim his salvation day after **d**. H3427
Ps 102:8 All **d** *long* my enemies taunt me; those H3427
Ps 110:3 troops will be willing on your **d** *of* battle. H3427
Ps 110:5 he will crush kings on the **d** *of* his wrath. H3427
Ps 118:24 The LORD has done it this very **d**; let us H3427
Ps 119:91 Your laws endure to this **d**, for all things H3427
Ps 119:97 love your law! I meditate on it all **d** *long*. H3427
Ps 119:164 Seven times a **d** I praise you for your H3427
Ps 121:6 the sun will not harm you **by d**, nor the H3429
Ps 136:8 the sun to govern the **d**, His love endures H3427
Ps 137:7 the Edomites did on the **d** Jerusalem fell. H3427
Ps 139:12 the night will shine like the **d**, for H3427
Ps 140:2 in their hearts and stir up war every **d**. H3427
Ps 140:7 you shield my head in the **d** *of* battle. H3427
Ps 145:2 Every **d** I will praise you and extol your H3427
Ps 146:4 on that very **d** their plans come to nothing. H3427
Pr 4:18 shining ever brighter till the full light of **d**. H3427
Pr 7:9 at twilight, as the **d** was fading, as the H3427
Pr 8:30 I was filled with delight **d** *after* day H3427
Pr 8:30 I was filled with delight day after **d** H3427
Pr 11:4 Wealth is worthless in the **d** *of* wrath, but H3427
Pr 16:4 even the wicked for a **d** *of* disaster. H3427
Pr 21:26 All **d** *long* he craves for more, but the H3427
Pr 21:31 horse is made ready for the **d** *of* battle, H3427
Pr 25:20 who takes away a garment on a cold **d**, H3427
Pr 27:1 you do not know what a **d** may bring. H3427
Ecc 7:1 the **d** *of* death better than the day of H3427
Ecc 7:1 the day of death better than the **d** *of* birth. H3427
Ecc 8:16 people getting no sleep **d** or night— H3427
SS 2:17 Until the **d** breaks and the shadows flee H3427
SS 3:11 crowned him on the **d** *of* his wedding, H3427
SS 3:11 of his wedding, the **d** his heart rejoiced. H3427
SS 4:6 Until the **d** breaks and the shadows flee, H3427
SS 8:8 our sister on the **d** she is spoken for? H3427
Isa 2:11 the LORD alone will be exalted in that **d**. H3427
Isa 2:12 LORD Almighty has a **d** in store for all the H3427
Isa 2:17 the LORD alone will be exalted in that **d**, H3427
Isa 2:20 In that **d** people will throw away to the H3427
Isa 3:7 But in that **d** he will cry out, "I have no H3427
Isa 3:18 In that **d** the Lord will snatch away their H3427
Isa 4:1 In that **d** seven women will take hold of H3427
Isa 4:2 In that **d** the Branch of the LORD will be H3427
Isa 4:5 a cloud of smoke **by d** and a glow of H3429
Isa 4:6 shelter and shade from the heat of the **d**, H3429
Isa 5:30 In that **d** they will roar over it like the H3427
Isa 7:18 In that **d** the LORD will whistle for flies H3427
Isa 7:20 In that **d** the Lord will use a razor hired H3427
Isa 7:21 In that **d**, a person will keep alive a young H3427
Isa 7:23 In that **d**, in every place where there were H3427
Isa 9:4 For as in the **d** *of* Midian's defeat, you H3427
Isa 9:14 both palm branch and reed *in* a single **d**; H3427
Isa 10:3 What will you do on the **d** *of* reckoning H3427
Isa 10:17 in a single **d** it will burn and consume his H3427
Isa 10:20 In that **d** the remnant of Israel, the H3427
Isa 10:27 In that **d** their burden will be lifted from H3427
Isa 10:32 This **d** they will halt at Nob; they will H3427
Isa 11:10 In that **d** the Root of Jesse will stand as a H3427
Isa 11:11 In that **d** the Lord will reach out his hand a H3427
Isa 12:1 In that **d** you will say: "I will praise you H3427
Isa 12:4 In that **d** you will say: "Give praise to the H3427
Isa 13:6 for the **d** *of* the LORD is near; it will H3427
Isa 13:9 the **d** *of* the LORD is coming—a cruel H3427
Isa 13:9 is coming—a cruel **d**, with wrath and fierce NDT
Isa 13:13 Almighty, in the **d** *of* his burning anger. H3427
Isa 14:3 On the **d** the LORD gives you relief from H3427
Isa 17:4 "In that **d** the glory of Jacob will fade; the H3427
Isa 17:7 In that **d** people will look to their Maker H3427
Isa 17:9 In that **d** their strong cities, which they left H3427
Isa 17:11 though on the **d** you set them out, you H3427
Isa 17:11 be as nothing in the **d** *of* disease and H3427
Isa 19:16 In that **d** the Egyptians will become H3427
Isa 19:18 In that **d** five cities in Egypt will speak the H3427
Isa 19:19 In that **d** there will be an altar to the LORD H3427
Isa 19:21 in that **d** they will acknowledge the H3427
Isa 19:23 In that **d** there will be a highway from H3427
Isa 19:24 In that **d** Israel will be the third, along with H3427
Isa 20:6 In that **d** the people who live on this coast H3427
Isa 21:8 shouted, "**D after day**, my lord, H9458+3429
Isa 21:8 shouted, "**Day after d**, my lord, H9458+3429
Isa 22:5 has a **d** *of* tumult and trampling and terror H3427
Isa 22:5 a **d** of battering down walls and of crying NDT
Isa 22:8 you looked in that **d** to the weapons in H3427
Isa 22:12 called you on that **d** to weep and to wail H3427
Isa 22:14 "**Till** your dying *d* this sin will not be atoned AIT
Isa 22:20 "In that **d** I will summon my servant H3427
Isa 22:25 "In that **d**," declares the LORD Almighty H3427
Isa 24:21 In that **d** the LORD will punish the powers H3427
Isa 25:9 In that **d** they will say, "Surely this is our H3427
Isa 26:1 In that **d** this song will be sung in the H3427
Isa 27:1 In that **d**, the LORD will punish with his H3427
Isa 27:2 In that **d**—"Sing about a fruitful vineyard: H3427
Isa 27:3 I guard it **d** and night so that no one may H3427
Isa 27:8 her out, as on a **d** the east wind blows. H3427
Isa 27:12 In that **d** the LORD will thresh from the H3427
Isa 27:13 And in that **d** a great trumpet will sound H3427
Isa 28:5 In that **d** the LORD Almighty will be a H3427
Isa 28:19 after morning, by **d** and by night, it will H3427
Isa 29:18 In that **d** the deaf will hear the words of H3427
Isa 30:23 In that **d** your cattle will graze in broad H3427
Isa 30:25 In the **d** *of* great slaughter, when the H3427
Isa 31:7 For in that **d** every one of you will reject H3427
Isa 34:8 For the LORD has a **d** *of* vengeance, a year H3427
Isa 34:10 It will not be quenched night or **d**; its H3429
Isa 37:3 This **d** is a day of distress and rebuke and H3427
Isa 37:3 This day is a **d** *of* distress and rebuke and H3427
Isa 37:38 **One d**, while he was worshiping in H2256+2118
Isa 38:12 **d** and night you made an end of me. H3427
Isa 38:13 **d** and night you made an end of me. H3427
Isa 39:6 predecessors have stored up until this **d**, H3427
Isa 47:9 overtake you in a moment, on a single **d**: H3427
Isa 49:8 in the **d** *of* salvation I will help you H3427
Isa 51:13 terror every **d** because of the wrath H3427
Isa 52:5 "And all **d** *long* my name is constantly H3427
Isa 52:6 therefore in that **d** they will know that it is H3427
Isa 58:2 For **d** *after* day they seek me out; they H3427
Isa 58:2 For day after **d** they seek me out; they H3427
Isa 58:3 "Yet on the **d** *of* your fasting, you do as H3427
Isa 58:5 only a **d** *for* people to humble themselves H3427
Isa 58:5 you call a fast, a **d** acceptable to the LORD? H3427
Isa 58:13 from doing as you please on my holy **d**, H3427
Isa 58:13 a delight and the LORD's holy **d** honorable, NDT
Isa 60:11 will never be shut, **d** or night, so that H3429
Isa 60:19 The sun will no more be your light **by d** H3429
Isa 61:2 LORD's favor and the **d** *of* vengeance of our H3427
Isa 62:6 they will never be silent **d** or night. H3427
Isa 63:4 It was for me the **d** *of* vengeance; the year H3427
Isa 65:2 All **d** *long* I have held out my hands to an H3427
Isa 65:5 my nostrils, a fire that keeps burning all **d**. H3427
Isa 66:8 country be born in a **d** or a nation be H3427
Jer 3:25 our youth till this **d** we have not obeyed H3427
Jer 4:9 "In that **d**," declares the LORD, "the king H3427
Jer 7:25 until now, **d after day**, again and again H3427
Jer 7:25 until now, **day after d**, again and again H3427
Jer 9:1 I would weep **d** and night for the slain of H3429
Jer 12:3 Set them apart for the **d** *of* slaughter! H3427
Jer 14:17 with tears night and **d** without ceasing; H3429
Jer 15:9 Her sun will set while it is still **d**; she will H3429
Jer 16:13 you will serve other gods **d** and night, H3429
Jer 17:16 know I have not desired the **d** *of* despair. H3427
Jer 17:17 you are my refuge in the **d** *of* disaster. H3427
Jer 17:18 Bring on them the **d** *of* disaster; destroy H3427
Jer 17:21 load on the Sabbath **d** or bring it through H3427
Jer 17:22 keep the Sabbath **d** holy, as I H3427
Jer 17:24 keep the Sabbath **d** holy by not doing H3427
Jer 17:27 to keep the Sabbath **d** holy by not carrying H3427
Jer 17:27 the gates of Jerusalem on the Sabbath **d**, H3427
Jer 18:17 not my face in the **d** *of* their disaster." H3427
Jer 20:3 The **next d**, when Pashhur released him H4740
Jer 20:7 I am ridiculed all **d** *long*; everyone mocks H3427
Jer 20:8 me insult and reproach all **d** *long*. H3427
Jer 20:14 Cursed be the **d** I was born! May the day H3427
Jer 20:14 May the **d** my mother bore me not be H3427
Jer 25:3 of Amon king of Judah until this very **d**— H3427
Jer 27:22 will remain until the **d** I come for them, H3427
Jer 30:7 How awful that **d** will be! No other will be H3427
Jer 30:8 " 'In that **d**,' declares the LORD Almighty, 'I H3427
Jer 31:6 There will be a **d** when watchmen cry out H3427
Jer 31:35 he who appoints the sun to shine **by d** H3429
Jer 32:20 Egypt and have continued them to this **d**, H3427
Jer 32:31 From the **d** it was built until now, this city H3427
Jer 33:20 covenant with the **d** and my covenant with H3427
Jer 33:20 so that **d** and night no longer come at H3429
Jer 33:25 made my covenant with **d** and night and H3429
Jer 35:14 To this **d** they do not drink wine, because H3427
Jer 36:6 of the LORD on a **d** *of* fasting and read to H3427
Jer 36:30 to the heat by **d** and the frost by night H3427
Jer 37:21 of the bakers **each d** until all H4200+2021+3427
Jer 38:28 the guard until the **d** Jerusalem was H3427
Jer 39:2 And on the ninth **d** of the fourth month of NDT
Jer 39:17 But I will rescue you on that **d**, declares H3427
Jer 41:4 The **d** after Gedaliah's assassination H3427
Jer 44:10 To this **d** they have not humbled H3427
Jer 46:10 But that **d** belongs to the Lord, the LORD H3427
Jer 46:10 the LORD Almighty—a **d** *of* vengeance, for H3427
Jer 46:21 the **d** *of* disaster is coming upon them H3427
Jer 47:4 For the **d** has come to destroy all the H3427
Jer 48:41 In that **d** the hearts of Moab's warriors will H3427
Jer 49:22 In that **d** the hearts of Edom's warriors will H3427
Jer 49:26 all her soldiers will be silenced in that **d**," H3427
Jer 50:27 For their **d** has come, the time for them to H3427
Jer 50:30 all her soldiers will be silenced in that **d**," H3427
Jer 50:31 Almighty, "for your **d** has come, the time H3427
Jer 51:2 her on every side in the **d** *of* her disaster. H3427
Jer 52:4 on the tenth **d** of the tenth month NDT
Jer 52:6 By the ninth **d** of the fourth month the NDT
Jer 52:11 put him in prison till the **d** *of* his death. H3427
Jer 52:12 On the tenth **d** of the fifth month, in the NDT
Jer 52:31 on the twenty-fifth **d** of the twelfth month NDT
Jer 52:34 **D by day** the king of H1821+3427+928+3427
Jer 52:34 **Day by d** the king of H1821+3427+928+3427
Jer 52:34 as long as he lived, till the **d** *of* his death. H3427
La 1:12 on me in the **d** *of* his fierce anger? H3427
La 1:13 made me desolate, faint all the **d** *long*. H3427
La 1:21 May you bring the **d** you have announced H3427
La 2:1 his footstool in the **d** *of* his anger. H3427
La 2:7 of the LORD as on the **d** *of* an appointed H3427
La 2:16 This is the **d** we have waited for; we have H3427
La 2:18 let your tears flow like a river **d** and night H3429
La 2:21 have slain them in the **d** *of* your anger; H3427
La 2:22 "As you summon to a feast **d**, so you H3427
La 2:22 In the **d** *of* the LORD's anger no one H3427
La 3:3 against me again and again, all **d** *long*. H3427
La 3:14 people; they mock me in song all **d** *long*. H3427
La 3:62 whisper and mutter against me all **d** *long*. H3427
Eze 1:1 in the fourth month on the fifth **d**, while I NDT
Eze 1:28 of a rainbow in the clouds on a rainy **d**, H3427
Eze 2:3 been in revolt against me to this very **d**. H3427
Eze 4:6 assigned you 40 days, a **d** for each year. H3427

Eze 4:10 of food to eat each **d** and eat it at set H3427
Eze 7: 7 time has come! The **d** is near! There is H3427
Eze 7:10 the **d**! See, it comes! Doom has H3427
Eze 7:12 time has come! The **d** has arrived! Let not H3427
Eze 7:19 deliver them in the **d** *of* the LORD's wrath. H3427
Eze 8: 1 in the sixth month on the fifth **d**, while I was NDT
Eze 12: 7 **During the d** I brought out my things H3429
Eze 13: 5 firm in the battle on the **d** *of* the LORD. H3427
Eze 16: 4 On the **d** you were born your cord was not H3427
Eze 16: 5 on the **d** you were born you were H3427
Eze 16:56 your sister Sodom in the **d** *of* your pride, H3427
Eze 20: 1 in the fifth month on the tenth **d**, some of NDT
Eze 20: 5 On the **d** I chose Israel, I swore with H3427
Eze 20: 6 On that **d** I swore to them that I would H3427
Eze 20:29 (It is called Bamah to this **d**.) H3427
Eze 20:31 yourselves with all your idols to this **d**. H3427
Eze 21:25 of Israel, whose **d** has come, whose time H3427
Eze 21:29 to be slain, whose **d** has come, whose H3427
Eze 22:14 hands be strong in the **d** I deal with you? H3427
Eze 22:24 cleansed or rained on in the **d** *of* wrath. H3427
Eze 23:39 On the very **d** they sacrificed their children H3427
Eze 24: 1 in the tenth month on the tenth **d**, the word NDT
Eze 24: 2 has laid siege to Jerusalem this very **d**. H3427
Eze 24:25 on the **d** I take away their stronghold H3427
Eze 24:26 on that **d** a fugitive will come to tell you H3427
Eze 26: 1 on the first **d** of the month, the word of NDT
Eze 26:18 coastlands tremble *on* the **d** *of* your fall; H3427
Eze 27:27 of the sea on the **d** *of* your shipwreck. H3427
Eze 28:13 on the **d** you were created they were H3427
Eze 28:15 your ways from the **d** you were created till H3427
Eze 29: 1 in the tenth month on the twelfth **d**, the NDT
Eze 29:17 in the first month on the first **d**, the word of NDT
Eze 29:21 "On that **d** I will make a horn grow for the H3427
Eze 30: 2 " 'Wail and say, "Alas for that **d**!" H3427
Eze 30: 3 For the **d** is near, the day of the LORD is H3427
Eze 30: 3 the day is near, the **d** of the LORD is near H3427
Eze 30: 3 the LORD is near—a **d** *of* clouds, a time of H3427
Eze 30: 9 " 'On that **d** messengers will go out from H3427
Eze 30: 9 hold of them on the **d** *of* Egypt's doom, H3427
Eze 30:18 Dark will be the **d** at Tahpanhes when I H3427
Eze 30:20 in the first month on the seventh **d**, the word NDT
Eze 31: 1 in the third month on the first **d**, the word of NDT
Eze 31:15 On the **d** it was brought down to the H3427
Eze 32: 1 in the twelfth month on the first **d**, the word NDT
Eze 32:10 On the **d** *of* your downfall each of them H3427
Eze 32:17 on the fifteenth **d** of the month, the word NDT
Eze 33:21 in the tenth month on the fifth **d**, a man NDT
Eze 34:12 were scattered on a **d** *of* clouds and H3427
Eze 36:33 On the **d** I cleanse you from all your sins, H3427
Eze 38:10 On that **d** thoughts will come into your H3427
Eze 38:14 In that **d**, when my people Israel are H3427
Eze 38:18 This is what will happen in that **d**: When H3427
Eze 39: 8 This is the **d** I have spoken of. H3427
Eze 39:11 " 'On that **d** I will give Gog a burial place H3427
Eze 39:13 the **d** I display my glory will be a H3427
Eze 39:13 my glory will be a memorable **d** for them, NDT
Eze 39:22 From that **d** forward the people of Israel H3427
Eze 40: 1 on that very **d** the hand of the LORD was on H3427
Eze 43:22 "On the second **d** you are to offer a male H3427
Eze 43:27 from the eighth **d** on, the priests are H3427
Eze 44:27 On the **d** he goes into the inner court of H3427
Eze 45:18 month on the first **d** you are to take a young NDT
Eze 45:20 same on the seventh **d** of the month for NDT
Eze 45:21 on the fourteenth **d** you are to observe the H3427
Eze 45:22 On that **d** the prince is to provide a bull as H3427
Eze 45:23 Every **d** *during* the seven days of the H3427
Eze 45:25 in the seventh month on the fifteenth **d**, H3427
Eze 46: 1 on the Sabbath **d** and on the day of H3427
Eze 46: 1 day and on the **d** *of* the New Moon it is to H3427
Eze 46: 4 LORD on the Sabbath **d** is to be six male H3427
Eze 46: 6 On the **d** *of* the New Moon he is to offer a H3427
Eze 46:12 offerings as he does on the Sabbath **d**. H3427
Eze 46:13 " '**Every d** you are to provide H4200+2021+3427
Da 6:10 Three times a **d** he got down on his A10317
Da 6:13 He still prays three times a **d**." A10317
Da 9: 7 this **d** we are covered with shame H3427
Da 9:15 yourself a name that endures to this **d**, H3427
Da 10: 4 On the twenty-fourth **d** of the first month H3427
Da 10:12 Since the first **d** that you set your mind to H3427
Hos 1: 5 In that **d** I will break Israel's bow in the H3427
Hos 1:11 the land, for great will be the **d** *of* Jezreel. H3427
Hos 2: 3 her as bare as on the **d** she was born; H3427
Hos 2:15 as in the **d** she came up out of Egypt. H3427
Hos 2:16 "In that **d**," declares the LORD, "you will H3427
Hos 2:18 In that **d** I will make a covenant for them H3427
Hos 2:21 "In that **d** I will respond," declares the H3427
Hos 4: 5 You stumble **d** and night, and the H3427
Hos 5: 9 will be laid waste on the **d** *of* reckoning. H3427
Hos 6: 2 revive us; on the third **d** he will restore us H3427
Hos 7: 5 On the **d** *of* the festival of our king the H3427
Hos 9: 5 will you do on the **d** *of* your appointed H3427
Hos 10:14 devastated Beth Arbel on the **d** *of* battle, H3427
Hos 10:15 When that **d dawns**, the king of Israel will H8840
Hos 12: 1 the east wind all **d** and multiplies lies H3427
Joel 1:15 Alas for that **d**! For the day of the LORD is H3427
Joel 1:15 For the **d** *of* the LORD is near; it will come H3427
Joel 2: 1 tremble, for the **d** *of* the LORD is coming. H3427
Joel 2: 2 a **d** *of* darkness and gloom, a day of H3427
Joel 2: 2 gloom, a **d** *of* clouds and blackness. H3427
Joel 2:11 his command. The **d** *of* the LORD is great H3427
Joel 2:31 of the great and dreadful **d** *of* the LORD. H3427
Joel 3:14 For the **d** *of* the LORD is near in the valley H3427
Joel 3:18 "In that **d** the mountains will drip new H3427
Am 1:14 amid war cries on the **d** *of* battle, H3427
Am 1:14 amid violent winds on a stormy **d**. H3427
Am 2:16 bravest warriors will flee naked on that **d**," H3427
Am 3:14 "On the **d** I punish Israel for her sins, I will H3427
Am 5: 8 into dawn and darkens **d** into night, H3427
Am 5:18 Woe to you who long for the **d** *of* the LORD! H3427
Am 5:18 Why do you long for the **d** *of* the LORD H3427
Am 5:18 day of the LORD? That **d** will be darkness, NDT
Am 5:20 Will not the **d** *of* the LORD be darkness, not H3427
Am 6: 3 You put off the **d** *of* disaster and bring H3427
Am 8: 3 "In that **d**," declares the Sovereign LORD H3427
Am 8: 9 "In that **d**," declares the Sovereign LORD, "I H3427
Am 8:10 only son and the end of it like a bitter **d**. H3427
Am 8:13 "In that **d** "the lovely young women and H3427
Am 9:11 "In that **d** "I will restore David's fallen H3427
Ob 8 "In that **d**," declares the LORD, "will I not H3427
Ob 11 On the **d** you stood aloof while strangers H3427
Ob 12 your brother in the **d** *of* his misfortune, H3427
Ob 12 of Judah in the **d** *of* their destruction, H3427
Ob 12 boast so much in the **d** *of* their trouble. H3427
Ob 13 of my people in the **d** *of* their disaster, H3427
Ob 13 in their calamity in the **d** *of* their disaster, H3427
Ob 13 their wealth in the **d** *of* their disaster. H3427
Ob 14 their survivors in the **d** *of* their trouble. H3427
Ob 15 "The **d** *of* the LORD is near for all nations H3427
Jnh 4: 7 But at dawn the **next d** God provided a H4740
Mic 2: 4 In that **d** people will ridicule you; they will H3427
Mic 3: 6 prophets, and the **d** will go dark for them. H3427
Mic 4: 6 "In that **d**," declares the LORD, "I will H3427
Mic 4: 7 in Mount Zion from **that d** and forever. H6964
Mic 5:10 "In that **d**," declares the LORD, "I will H3427
Mic 7: 4 The **d** God visits you has come, the day H3427
Mic 7: 4 the **d** your watchmen sound the alarm. NDT
Mic 7:11 The **d** for building your walls will come H3427
Mic 7:11 the **d** for extending your boundaries. H3427
Mic 7:12 In that **d** people will come to you from H3427
Na 2: 3 flashes on the **d** they are made ready; H3427
Na 3:17 that settle in the walls on a cold **d**— H3427
Hab 3: 2 Repeat them in our **d**, in our time make H9102
Hab 3:16 patiently for the **d** *of* calamity to come on H3427
Zep 1: 7 for the **d** *of* the LORD is near. H3427
Zep 1: 8 "On the **d** *of* the LORD's sacrifice I will H3427
Zep 1: 9 On that **d** I will punish all who avoid H3427
Zep 1:10 "On that **d**," declares the LORD, "a cry will H3427
Zep 1:14 The great **d** *of* the LORD is near—near H3427
Zep 1:14 The cry on the **d** *of* the LORD is bitter; the H3427
Zep 1:15 That **d** will be a day of wrath—a day of H3427
Zep 1:15 That day will be a **d** *of* wrath—a day of H3427
Zep 1:15 day of wrath—a **d** *of* distress and anguish H3427
Zep 1:15 anguish, a **d** *of* trouble and ruin, H3427
Zep 1:15 ruin, a **d** *of* darkness and gloom H3427
Zep 1:15 gloom, a **d** *of* clouds and blackness H3427
Zep 1:16 a **d** *of* trumpet and battle cry against the H3427
Zep 1:18 to save them on the **d** *of* the LORD's wrath." H3427
Zep 2: 2 effect and that **d** passes like windblown H3427
Zep 2: 2 before the **d** *of* the LORD's wrath comes H3427
Zep 2: 3 be sheltered on the **d** *of* the LORD's anger. H3427
Zep 3: 5 and every **new d** he does not fail H240
Zep 3: 8 "for the **d** I will stand up to testify. H3427
Zep 3:11 On that **d** you, Jerusalem, will not be put H3427
Zep 3:16 On that **d** they will say to Jerusalem, "Do H3427
Hag 1: 1 on the first **d** of the sixth month H3427
Hag 1:15 on the twenty-fourth **d** of the sixth month H3427
Hag 2: 1 on the twenty-first **d** of the seventh month NDT
Hag 2:10 On the twenty-fourth **d** of the ninth month NDT
Hag 2:15 careful thought to this from this **d** on— H3427
Hag 2:18 'From this **d** on, from this twenty-fourth H3427
Hag 2:18 this twenty-fourth **d** of the ninth month, H3427
Hag 2:18 thought to the **d** when the foundation of H3427
Hag 2:19 " 'From this **d** on I will bless you.' " H3427
Hag 2:20 time on the twenty-fourth **d** of the month: NDT
Hag 2:23 " 'On that **d**,' declares the LORD Almighty H3427
Zec 1: 7 On the twenty-fourth **d** of the eleventh H3427
Zec 2:11 the LORD in that **d** and will become my H3427
Zec 3: 9 remove the sin of this land in a single **d**. H3427
Zec 3:10 " 'In that **d** each of you will invite your H3427
Zec 4:10 "Who dares despise the **d** *of* small things H3427
Zec 6:10 Go the same **d** to the house of Josiah son H3427
Zec 7: 1 on the fourth **d** of the ninth month, NDT
Zec 9:16 his people on that **d** as a shepherd saves H3427
Zec 11:11 It was revoked on that **d**, and so the H3427
Zec 12: 3 On that **d**, when all the nations of the H3427
Zec 12: 4 On that **d** I will strike every horse with H3427
Zec 12: 6 "On that **d** I will make the clans of Judah H3427
Zec 12: 8 On that **d** the LORD will shield those who H3427
Zec 12: 9 On that **d** I will set out to destroy all the H3427
Zec 12:11 On that **d** the weeping in Jerusalem will H3427
Zec 13: 1 "On that **d** a fountain will be opened to H3427
Zec 13: 2 "On that **d**, I will banish the names of the H3427
Zec 13: 4 "On that **d** every prophet will be ashamed H3427
Zec 14: 1 A **d** of the LORD is coming, Jerusalem H3427
Zec 14: 3 nations, as he fights on a **d** *of* battle. H3427
Zec 14: 4 On that **d** his feet will stand on the Mount H3427
Zec 14: 6 On that **d** there will be neither sunlight H3427
Zec 14: 7 It will be a unique **d**—a day known only to H3427
Zec 14: 7 a unique day—a **d** known only to the LORD NDT
Zec 14: 7 with no distinction between **d** and night. H3427
Zec 14: 8 On that **d** living water will flow out from H3427
Zec 14: 9 On that **d** there will be one LORD, and his H3427
Zec 14:13 On that **d** people will be stricken by the H3427
Zec 14:20 On that **d** HOLY TO THE LORD will be H3427
Zec 14:21 And on that **d** there will no longer be a H3427
Mal 3: 2 But who can endure the **d** *of* his coming H3427
Mal 3:17 "On the **d** when I act," says the LORD H3427
Mal 4: 1 "Surely the **d** is coming; it will burn like a H3427
Mal 4: 1 the **d** that is coming will set them on H3427
Mal 4: 3 the soles of your feet on the **d** when I act," H3427
Mal 4: 5 great and dreadful **d** *of* the LORD comes. H3427
Mt 6:34 Each **d** has enough trouble of its own. *G2465*
Mt 7:22 Many will say to me on that **d**, 'Lord, Lord *G2465*
Mt 10:15 Gomorrah on the **d** of judgment than *G2465*
Mt 11:22 Sidon on the **d** of judgment than for *G2465*
Mt 11:23 Sodom, it would have remained to this **d**. *G4958*
Mt 11:24 Sodom on the **d** of judgment than for *G2465*
Mt 12:36 give account on the **d** of judgment for *G2465*
Mt 13: 1 That same **d** Jesus went out of the house *G2465*
Mt 16:21 be killed and *on* the third **d** be raised to *G2465*
Mt 17:23 and *on* the third **d** he will be raised to life." *G2465*
Mt 20: 2 them a denarius *for* the **d** and sent them *G2465*
Mt 20: 6 standing here all **d** long doing nothing? *G2465*
Mt 20:12 burden of the work and the heat *of* the **d**. *G2465*
Mt 20:19 On the third **d** he will be raised to life!" *G2465*
Mt 22:23 That same **d** the Sadducees, who say *G2465*
Mt 22:46 from that **d** on no one dared to ask *G2465*
Mt 24:36 "But about that **d** or hour no one knows *G2465*
Mt 24:38 up to the **d** Noah entered the ark; *G2465*
Mt 24:42 not know on what **d** your Lord will come *G2465*
Mt 24:50 will come on a **d** when he does not *G2465*
Mt 25:13 you do not know the **d** or the hour. *G2465*
Mt 26:17 *On* the **first** *d* of the Festival of Unleavened AIT
Mt 26:29 now on until that **d** when I drink it new *G2465*
Mt 26:55 **Every d** I sat in the temple courts *G2848+2465*
Mt 27: 8 been called the Field of Blood to **this d**. *G4958*
Mt 27:62 The **next d**, the one after Preparation Day *G2069*
Mt 27:62 the one after **Preparation D**, the chief *G4187*
Mt 27:64 tomb to be made secure until the third **d**. *G2465*
Mt 28: 1 at dawn on the **first** *d* of the week, Mary AIT
Mt 28:15 among the Jews to **this very d**. *G4958+2465*
Mk 2:20 from them, and on that **d** they will fast. *G2465*
Mk 4:27 Night and **d**, whether he sleeps or gets up *G2465*
Mk 4:35 That **d** when evening came, he said to his *G2465*
Mk 5: 5 Night and **d** among the tombs and in the *G2465*
Mk 6:35 By this time it was **late in the d**, so *G6052+4498*
Mk 11:12 The **next d** as they were leaving Bethany *G2069*
Mk 13:32 "But about that **d** or hour no one knows *G2465*
Mk 14:12 *On* the first **d** of the Festival of *G2465*
Mk 14:25 the vine until that **d** when I drink it new in *G2465*
Mk 14:49 **Every d** I was with you, teaching in *G2848+2465*
Mk 15:42 It was **Preparation D** (that is, the day *G4187*
Mk 15:42 **the d before the Sabbath**). *G4640*
Mk 16: 2 Very early *on* the **first** *d* of the week, just after AIT
Mk 16: 9 Jesus rose early *on* the **first** *d* of the week, AIT
Lk 1:20 able to speak until the **d** this happens, *G2465*
Lk 1:59 On the eighth **d** they came to circumcise *G2465*
Lk 2:21 *On* the eighth **d**, when it was time to *G2465*
Lk 2:37 the temple but worshiped night and **d**, *G2465*
Lk 2:44 in their company, they traveled on *for* a **d**. *G2465*
Lk 4:16 on the Sabbath **d** he went into the *G2465*
Lk 5: 1 **One d** as Jesus was standing by *G1181+1254*
Lk 5:17 One **d** Jesus was teaching, and Pharisees *G2465*
Lk 6:23 "Rejoice in that **d** and leap for joy *G2465*
Lk 8:22 One **d** Jesus said to his disciples, "Let us *G2465*
Lk 9:22 be killed and *on* the third **d** be raised to *G2465*
Lk 9:37 The next **d**, when they came down from *G2465*
Lk 10:12 bearable on that **d** for Sodom than for *G2465*
Lk 10:35 The **next d** he took out two denarii and *G892*
Lk 11: 1 **One d** Jesus was praying in a *G2779+1181*
Lk 11: 3 Give us each **d** our daily bread. *G2465*
Lk 12:46 will come on a **d** when he does not *G2465*
Lk 13:16 be set free *on* the Sabbath **d** from what *G2465*
Lk 13:32 on the third **d** I will reach my goal. NDT
Lk 13:33 on today and tomorrow and the **next d**— *G2400*
Lk 14: 5 ox that falls into a well on the Sabbath **d**, *G2465*
Lk 16:19 fine linen and lived in luxury every **d**. *G2465*
Lk 17: 4 you seven times *in* a **d** and seven times *G2465*
Lk 17:24 For the Son of Man in his **d** will be like the *G2465*
Lk 17:27 marriage up to the **d** Noah entered the *G2465*
Lk 17:29 But the **d** Lot left Sodom, fire and sulfur *G2465*
Lk 17:30 be just like this *on* the **d** the Son of Man *G2465*
Lk 17:31 On that **d** no one who is on the housetop *G2465*
Lk 18: 7 who cry out to him **d** and night? *G2465*
Lk 18:33 *On* the third **d** he will rise again. *G2465*
Lk 19:42 only known on this **d** what would bring *G2465*
Lk 19:47 Every **d** he was teaching at the temple *G2465*
Lk 20: 1 One **d** as Jesus was teaching the people *G2465*
Lk 21:34 that **d** will close on you suddenly like *G2465*
Lk 21:37 Each **d** Jesus was teaching at the temple *G2465*
Lk 22: 7 Then came the **d** of Unleavened Bread on *G2465*
Lk 22:53 Every **d** I was with you in the temple courts, *G2465*
Lk 23:12 That **d** Herod and Pilate became friends *G2465*
Lk 23:54 It was Preparation **D**, and the Sabbath was *G2465*
Lk 24: 1 *On* the **first** *d* of the week, very early in the AIT
Lk 24: 7 crucified and on the third **d** be raised *G2465*
Lk 24:13 Now that same **d** two of them were going *G2465*
Lk 24:21 it is the third **d** since all this took place. *G2465*
Lk 24:29 it is nearly evening; the **d** is almost over." *G2465*
Lk 24:46 rise from the dead *on* the third **d**, *G2465*
Jn 1:29 The **next d** John saw Jesus coming toward *G2069*
Jn 1:35 The **next d** John was there again with two *G2069*
Jn 1:39 staying, and they spent that **d** with him. *G2465*
Jn 1:43 The **next d** Jesus decided to leave for *G2069*
Jn 2: 1 *On* the third **d** a wedding took place at *G2465*
Jn 5: 9 The **d** on which this took place was a *G2465*

Jn 5:17 Father is always at his work to **this very d**, *G785*
Jn 6:22 The **next d** the crowd that had stayed on *G2069*
Jn 6:39 given me, but raise them up at the last **d**. *G2465*
Jn 6:40 and I will raise them up at the last **d**." *G2465*
Jn 6:44 I will raise them up at the last **d**. *G2465*
Jn 6:54 and I will raise them up at the last **d**. *G2465*
Jn 7:37 On the last and greatest **d** of the festival *G2465*
Jn 8:56 rejoiced at the thought of seeing my **d**; *G2465*
Jn 9: 4 As long as it is **d**, we must do the works of *G2465*
Jn 9:14 Now the **d** on which Jesus had made the *G2465*
Jn 11:24 rise again in the resurrection at the last **d**." *G2465*
Jn 11:53 So from that **d** on they plotted to take his *G2465*
Jn 12: 7 save this perfume for the **d** of my burial. *G2465*
Jn 12:12 The **next d** the great crowd that had come *G2069*
Jn 12:48 spoken will condemn them at the last **d**. *G2465*
Jn 14:20 On that **d** you will realize that I am in my *G2465*
Jn 16:23 In that **d** you will no longer ask me *G2465*
Jn 16:26 In that **d** you will ask in my name. I am not *G2465*
Jn 19:14 It was the **d of Preparation** of the Passover *G4187*
Jn 19:31 Now it was the **d of Preparation**, and the *G4187*
Jn 19:31 the next **d** was to be a special *G2465*
Jn 19:42 the Jewish **d of Preparation** and since the *G4187*
Jn 20: 1 Early *on* the **first** *d* of the week, while it was AIT
Jn 20:19 On the evening of that first **d** of the week *G2465*
Ac 1: 2 the **d** he was taken up to heaven *G2465*
Ac 2: 1 When the **d** of Pentecost came, they were *G2465*
Ac 2:20 coming *of* the great and glorious **d** of the *G2465*
Ac 2:29 was buried, and his tomb is here to this **d**. *G2465*
Ac 2:41 were added to their number that **d**. *G2465*
Ac 2:46 **Every d** they continued to meet *G2848+2465*
Ac 3: 1 **One d** Peter and John were going up to *G1254*
Ac 3: 2 he was put every **d** to beg from those *G2465*
Ac 4: 3 they put them in jail until the **next d**. *G892*
Ac 4: 5 The **next d** the rulers, the elders and the *G892*
Ac 5:42 **D after day**, in the temple courts *G4246+2465*
Ac 5:42 **Day after d**, in the temple courts *G4246+2465*
Ac 7:26 The next **d** Moses came upon two *G2465*
Ac 8: 1 On that **d** a great persecution broke out *G2465*
Ac 9:24 **D** and night they kept close watch on the *G2465*
Ac 10: 3 One **d** at about three in the afternoon he NDT
Ac 10: 9 About noon the **following d** as they were *G2069*
Ac 10:23 The **next d** Peter started out with them *G2069*
Ac 10:24 The **following d** he arrived in Caesarea *G2069*
Ac 10:40 dead on the third **d** and caused him to be *G2465*
Ac 12:21 *On* the appointed **d** Herod, wearing his *G2465*
Ac 14:20 The **next d** he and Barnabas left for Derbe *G2069*
Ac 16:11 the **next d** we went on to Neapolis. *G2079*
Ac 17:11 the Scriptures every **d** to see if what Paul *G2465*
Ac 17:17 **d by day** with those *G2848+4246+2465*
Ac 17:17 **day by d** with those *G2848+4246+2465*
Ac 17:31 For he has set a **d** when he will judge the *G2465*
Ac 19:15 One **d** the evil spirit answered them, "Jesus I NDT
Ac 20: 7 On the **first** *d* of the week we came together AIT
Ac 20: 7 because he intended to leave the **next d** *G2069*
Ac 20:15 The **next d** we set sail from there and *G2079*
Ac 20:15 The **d after that** we crossed over to *G2283*[S]
Ac 20:15 on the following **d** arrived at Miletus. NDT
Ac 20:16 if possible, *by* the **d** of Pentecost. *G2465*
Ac 20:18 from the first **d** I came into the province of *G2465*
Ac 20:31 each of you night and **d** with tears. *G2465*
Ac 21: 1 The **next** *d* we went to Rhodes and from AIT
Ac 21: 7 sisters and stayed with them *for* a **d**. *G2465*
Ac 21: 8 Leaving the **next d**, we reached Caesarea *G2069*
Ac 21:18 The **next d** Paul and the rest of us went to *G2079*
Ac 21:26 The next **d** Paul took the men and *G2465*
Ac 22:30 So the **next d** he released him and *G2069*
Ac 23: 1 to God in all good conscience to this **d**." *G2465*
Ac 23:32 The **next d** they let the cavalry go on with *G2069*
Ac 25: 6 The **next d** he convened the court and *G2069*
Ac 25:17 the court the **next** *d* and ordered the man AIT
Ac 25:23 The **next d** Agrippa and Bernice came *G2069*
Ac 26: 7 as they earnestly serve God **d** and night. *G2465*
Ac 26:22 But God has helped me to this very **d**; so I *G2465*
Ac 27: 3 The **next** *d* we landed at Sidon; and Julius AIT
Ac 27: 9 by now it was after the **D of Atonement**. *G3763*
Ac 27:18 the storm that the **next** *d* they began to throw AIT
Ac 27:19 *On* the **third** *d*, they threw the ship's tackle AIT
Ac 28:13 The next **d** the south wind came up, and *G2465*
Ac 28:13 and **on the following d** we reached *G1308*
Ac 28:23 arranged to meet Paul *on* a *certain* **d**, *G2465*
Ro 2: 5 against yourself for the **d** of God's wrath, *G2465*
Ro 2:16 will take place on the **d** when God judges *G2465*
Ro 8:36 "For your sake we face death all **d** long *G2465*
Ro 10:21 "All **d** long I have held out my hands to a *G2465*
Ro 11: 8 that could not hear, to this **very d**." *G4958+2465*
Ro 13:12 night is nearly over; the **d** is almost here. *G2465*
Ro 14: 5 person considers *one* **d** more sacred than *G2465*
Ro 14: 5 another; another considers every **d** alike. *G2465*
Ro 14: 6 Whoever regards one **d** as special does so *G2465*
1Co 1: 8 be blameless on the **d** of our Lord Jesus *G2465*
1Co 3:13 because the **D** will bring it to light. *G2465*
1Co 5: 5 spirit may be saved on the **d** of the Lord. *G2465*
1Co 10: 8 and *in* one **d** twenty-three thousand of *G2465*
1Co 15: 4 he was raised *on* the third **d** according to *G2465*
1Co 15:31 I face death every **d**—yes, just as surely as *G2465*
1Co 16: 2 *On* the **first** *d* of every week, each one of you AIT
2Co 1:14 boast of you in the **d** of the Lord Jesus. *G2465*
2Co 3:14 to **this d** the same veil *G3836+4958+2465*
2Co 3:15 Even to **this d** when Moses is read, a veil *G4958*
2Co 4:16 inwardly we are being renewed **d** by day. *G2465*
2Co 4:16 inwardly we are being renewed day by **d**. *G2465*
2Co 6: 2 in the **d** of salvation I helped you. *G2465*
2Co 6: 2 of God's favor, now is the **d** of salvation. *G2465*
2Co 11:25 I spent **a night and a d** in the open sea, *G3819*
Eph 4:30 you were sealed for the **d** of redemption. *G2465*
Eph 6:13 so that when the **d** of evil comes, you *G2465*
Php 1: 5 in the gospel from the first **d** until now, *G2465*
Php 1: 6 to completion until the **d** of Christ Jesus. *G2465*
Php 1:10 be pure and blameless for the **d** of Christ, *G2465*
Php 2:16 able to boast on the **d** of Christ that I did *G2465*
Php 3: 5 circumcised **on the eighth d**, of the people *G3892*
Col 1: 6 among you since the **d** you heard it and *G2465*
Col 1: 9 since the **d** we heard about you *G2465*
Col 2:16 a New Moon celebration or a **Sabbath d**. *G4879*
1Th 2: 9 we worked night and **d** in order not to be *G2465*
1Th 3:10 Night and **d** we pray most earnestly that *G2465*
1Th 5: 2 very well that the **d** of the Lord will come *G2465*
1Th 5: 4 darkness so that this **d** should surprise you *G2465*
1Th 5: 5 children of the light and children *of* the **d**. *G2465*
1Th 5: 8 But since we belong to the **d**, let us be *G2465*
2Th 1:10 on the **d** he comes to be glorified in his *G2465*
2Th 2: 2 asserting that the **d** of the Lord has already *G2465*
2Th 2: 3 that **d** will not come until the rebellion NDT
2Th 3: 8 we worked night and **d**, laboring and *G2465*
1Ti 5: 5 continues night and **d** to pray and to ask *G2465*
2Ti 1: 3 as night and **d** I constantly remember you *G2465*
2Ti 1:12 what I have entrusted to him until that **d**. *G2465*
2Ti 1:18 he will find mercy from the Lord on that **d**! *G2465*
2Ti 4: 8 will award to me on that **d**—and not only *G2465*
Heb 4: 4 spoken about the **seventh** *d* in these words: AIT
Heb 4: 4 "On the seventh **d** God rested from all his *G2465*
Heb 4: 7 God again set a certain **d**, calling it *G2465*
Heb 4: 8 not have spoken later about another **d**. *G2465*
Heb 7:27 need to offer sacrifices **d after day**, *G2848+2465*
Heb 7:27 need to offer sacrifices **day after d**, *G2848+2465*
Heb 10:11 **D after day** every priest stands and *G2848+2465*
Heb 10:11 **Day after d** every priest stands and *G2848+2465*
Heb 10:25 the more as you see the **D** approaching. *G2465*
Jas 5: 5 fattened yourselves in the **d** of slaughter. *G2465*
1Pe 2:12 glorify God on the **d** he visits us. *G2465*
2Pe 1:19 until the **d** dawns and the morning star *G2465*
2Pe 2: 8 living among them **d** after day, was *G2465*
2Pe 2: 8 living among them day after **d**, was *G2465*
2Pe 2: 9 punishment on the **d** of judgment. *G2465*
2Pe 3: 7 being kept for the **d** of judgment and *G2465*
2Pe 3: 8 With the Lord a **d** is like a thousand years *G2465*
2Pe 3: 8 and a thousand years are like a **d**. *G2465*
2Pe 3:10 But the **d** of the Lord will come like a thief. *G2465*
2Pe 3:12 look forward to the **d** of God and speed its *G2465*
2Pe 3:12 **That d** will bring about the destruction of *G4005*[S]
1Jn 4:17 have confidence on the **d** of judgment: *G2465*
Jude 6 chains for judgment *on* the great **D**. *G2465*
Rev 1:10 On the Lord's **D** I was in the Spirit, and I *G2465*
Rev 4: 8 **D** and night they never stop saying *G2465*
Rev 6:17 For the great **d** of their wrath has come *G2465*
Rev 7:15 of God and serve him **d** and night in his *G2465*
Rev 8:12 A third *of* the **d** was without light, and *G2465*
Rev 9:15 this very hour and **d** and month and year *G2465*
Rev 12:10 accuses them before our God **d** and night, *G2465*
Rev 14:11 There will be no rest **d** or night for those *G2465*
Rev 16:14 the battle *on* the great **d** of God *G2465*
Rev 18: 8 Therefore in one **d** her plagues will *G2465*
Rev 20:10 will be tormented **d** and night for ever *G2465*
Rev 21:25 *On* no **d** will its gates ever be shut, for *G2465*

DAY'S (10) [DAY]

Nu 11:31 as far as a **d** walk in any direction. H3427
1Ki 8:59 Israel according to **each d** need, H3427+3427
1Ki 19: 4 while he himself went a **d** journey into the H3427
1Ch 16:37 according to **each d** H3427+928+3427+2257
2Ch 8:14 to **each d** requirement H3427+928+3427
Est 9:13 to carry out this **d** edict tomorrow also, H3427
Jnh 3: 4 began by going a **d** journey into the city H3427
Ac 1:12 **a Sabbath d walk from** *G1584+4879+2400+3847*
Rev 6: 6 "Two pounds of wheat *for* **a d wages**, and *G1324*
Rev 6: 6 six pounds of barley *for* **a d wages** *G1324*

DAYBREAK (15) [DAY]

Ge 32:24 and a man wrestled with him till **d**. H8840
Ge 32:26 "Let me go, for it is **d**." But Jacob replied, H8840
Ex 14:27 and at **d** the sea went back to its H7155+1332
Jos 6:15 got up at **d** and marched H6590+2021+8840
Jdg 19:26 At **d** the woman went back to H7155+2021+1332
1Sa 9:26 They rose about **d**, and H6590+2021+8840
1Sa 25:34 have been left alive by **d**." H240+2021+1332
1Sa 25:36 him nothing at all until **d**. H240+2021+1332
2Sa 2:32 all night and arrived at Hebron *by* **d**. H239
2Sa 17:22 By **d**, no one was left who H1332+2021+240
Ne 8: 3 He read it aloud from **d** till noon as he H240
Lk 4:42 *At* **d**, Jesus went out to a *G1181+2465+2002*
Lk 12:38 in the middle of the night or toward **d**. *G5569*
Lk 22:66 At **d** the council of the elders of the *G1181+2465*
Ac 5:21 At **d** they entered the temple courts, as *G3986*

DAYLIGHT (17) [DAY, LIGHT]

Nu 25: 4 expose them in **broad d** before the LORD, H9087
Jdg 19:26 fell down at the door and lay there until **d**. H240
2Sa 12:11 your wives **in broad d**. H4200+6524+2021+9087+2021+2296
2Sa 12:12 this thing **in broad d** before H5584+2021+9087
2Ki 7: 9 If we wait until **d**, punishment H240+2021+1332
Job 3: 9 may it wait for **d** in vain and not see the H240
Job 24:14 When **d** is gone, the murderer rises up H240
Jer 6: 4 the **d** is fading, and the shadows of H3427
Am 8: 9 and darken the earth in **broad d**. H240+3427
Mt 10:27 speak in the **d**; what is whispered in *G5890*
Lk 12: 3 said in the dark will be heard in the **d**, *G5890*
Jn 11: 9 "Are there not twelve hours *of* **d**? *G2465*
Ac 16:35 When it was **d**, the magistrates sent their *G2465*
Ac 20:11 After talking until **d**, he left. *G879*
Ac 27:29 anchors from the stern and prayed *for* **d**. *G2465*
Ac 27:39 When **d** came, they did not recognize the *G2465*
2Pe 2:13 idea of pleasure is to carouse in **broad d**. *G2465*

DAYS (622) [DAY]

Ge 1:14 to mark sacred times, and **d** and years, H3427
Ge 3:14 you will eat dust all the **d** *of* your life. H3427
Ge 3:17 will eat food from it all the **d** *of* your life. H3427
Ge 6: 3 their **d** will be a hundred and twenty years H3427
Ge 6: 4 Nephilim were on the earth in those **d**— H3427
Ge 7: 4 Seven **d** from now I will send rain on the H3427
Ge 7: 4 on the earth for forty **d** and forty nights, H3427
Ge 7:10 And after the seven **d** the floodwaters H3427
Ge 7:12 fell on the earth forty **d** and forty nights. H3427
Ge 7:17 For forty **d** the flood kept coming on the H3427
Ge 7:24 the earth for a hundred and fifty **d**. H3427
Ge 8: 3 hundred and fifty **d** the water had gone H3427
Ge 8: 6 After forty **d** Noah opened a window he H3427
Ge 8:10 waited seven more **d** and again sent out H3427
Ge 8:12 waited seven more **d** and sent the dove H3427
Ge 17:12 among you who is eight **d** old must be H3427
Ge 21: 4 When his son Isaac was eight **d** old H3427
Ge 24:55 young woman remain with us ten **d** or so; H3427
Ge 27:41 "The **d** *of* mourning for my father are near; H3427
Ge 29:20 like only a few **d** to him because of his H3427
Ge 31:23 Jacob for seven **d** and caught up with him H3427
Ge 34:25 Three **d** later, while all of them were still H3427
Ge 37:34 mourned for his son many **d**. H3427
Ge 40:12 "The three branches are three **d**. H3427
Ge 40:13 Within three **d** Pharaoh will lift up your H3427
Ge 40:18 "The three baskets are three **d**. H3427
Ge 40:19 Within three **d** Pharaoh will lift off your H3427
Ge 42:17 And he put them all in custody for three **d**. H3427
Ge 49: 1 you what will happen to you in **d** to come. H3427
Ge 50: 3 taking a full forty **d**, for that was the time H3427
Ge 50: 3 the Egyptians mourned for him seventy **d**. H3427
Ge 50: 4 When the **d** *of* mourning had passed H3427
Ex 7:25 Seven **d** passed after the LORD struck the H3427
Ex 10:22 darkness covered all Egypt *for* three **d**. H3427
Ex 10:23 anyone else or move about *for* three **d**. H3427
Ex 12:15 *For* seven **d** you are to eat bread made H3427
Ex 12:16 Do no work at all on **these d**, except to H2157[S]
Ex 12:19 *For* seven **d** no yeast is to be found in your H3427
Ex 13: 6 *For* seven **d** eat bread made without yeast H3427
Ex 13: 7 unleavened bread *during* those seven **d**; H3427
Ex 13:14 "*In* **d to come**, when your son asks you H4737
Ex 15:22 *For* three **d** they traveled in the desert H3427
Ex 16: 5 as they gather *on* the **other d**." H3427+3427
Ex 16:26 Six **d** you are to gather it, but on the H3427
Ex 16:29 the sixth day he gives you bread *for two* **d**. H3427
Ex 20: 9 Six **d** you shall labor and do all your work, H3427
Ex 20:11 For *in* six **d** the LORD made the heavens H3427
Ex 22:30 them stay with their mothers *for* seven **d**, H3427
Ex 23:12 "Six **d** do your work, but on the seventh H3427
Ex 23:15 *for* seven **d** eat bread made without yeast H3427
Ex 24:16 *For* six **d** the cloud covered the mountain H3427
Ex 24:18 on the mountain forty **d** and forty nights. H3427
Ex 29:30 in the Holy Place is to wear them seven **d**. H3427
Ex 29:35 taking seven **d** to ordain them. H3427
Ex 29:37 *For* seven **d** make atonement for the altar H3427
Ex 31:15 *For* six **d** work is to be done, but the H3427
Ex 31:17 for *in* six **d** the LORD made the heavens H3427
Ex 34:18 *For* seven **d** eat bread made without yeast, H3427
Ex 34:21 "Six **d** you shall labor, but on the seventh H3427
Ex 34:28 with the LORD forty **d** and forty nights H3427
Ex 35: 2 *For* six **d**, work is to be done, but the H3427
Lev 8:33 to the tent of meeting *for* seven **d**, H3427
Lev 8:33 until the **d** *of* your ordination are H3427
Lev 8:33 your ordination will last seven **d**. H3427
Lev 8:35 day and night *for* seven **d** and do what H3427
Lev 12: 2 will be ceremonially unclean *for* seven **d**, H3427
Lev 12: 4 wait thirty-three **d** to be purified from H3427
Lev 12: 4 sanctuary until the **d** *of* her purification H3427
Lev 12: 5 must wait sixty-six **d** to be purified from H3427
Lev 12: 6 " 'When the **d** *of* her purification for a son H3427
Lev 13: 4 to isolate the affected person *for* seven **d**. H3427
Lev 13: 5 he is to isolate them *for* another seven **d**. H3427
Lev 13:21 the priest is to isolate them *for* seven **d**. H3427
Lev 13:26 the priest is to isolate them *for* seven **d**. H3427
Lev 13:31 to isolate the affected person *for* seven **d**. H3427
Lev 13:33 is to keep them isolated another seven **d**. H3427
Lev 13:50 area and isolate the article *for* seven **d**. H3427
Lev 13:54 he is to isolate it *for* another seven **d**. H3427
Lev 14: 8 must stay outside their tent *for* seven **d**. H3427
Lev 14:38 of the house and close it up *for* seven **d**. H3427
Lev 15:13 is to count off seven **d** for his ceremonial H3427
Lev 15:19 of her monthly period will last seven **d**, H3427
Lev 15:24 he will be unclean *for* seven **d**; any bed H3427
Lev 15:25 of blood *for* many **d** at a time other H3427
Lev 15:25 discharge, just as in the **d** *of* her period. H3427
Lev 15:28 she must count off seven **d**, and after that H3427
Lev 22:27 it is to remain with its mother *for* seven **d**. H3427
Lev 23: 3 " 'There are six **d** when you may work, but H3427
Lev 23: 6 *for* seven **d** you must eat bread made H3427
Lev 23: 8 *For* seven **d** present a food offering to the H3427
Lev 23:16 Count off fifty **d** up to the day after the H3427

Lev 23:34 and it lasts *for* seven d. H3427
Lev 23:36 *For* seven d present food offerings to the H3427
Lev 23:39 the festival to the LORD *for* seven d; H3427
Lev 23:40 before the LORD your God *for* seven d. H3427
Lev 23:41 festival to the LORD *for* seven d each year. H3427
Lev 23:42 Live in temporary shelters *for* seven d: All H3427
Nu 6:12 The previous d do not count, because H3427
Nu 9:20 was over the tabernacle only a few d; H3427
Nu 9:22 the tabernacle *for two* d or a month or a H3427
Nu 10:33 of the LORD and traveled for three d. H3427
Nu 10:33 before them *during* those three d to find H3427
Nu 11:19 eat it for just one day, or *two* d, or five, H3427
Nu 11:19 or two days, or five, ten or twenty d, H3427
Nu 12:14 not have been in disgrace *for* seven d? H3427
Nu 12:14 Confine her outside the camp *for* seven d H3427
Nu 12:15 confined outside the camp *for* seven d, H3427
Nu 13:25 At the end of forty d they returned from H3427
Nu 14:34 each of the forty d you explored the land H3427
Nu 19:11 corpse will be unclean *for* seven d. H3427
Nu 19:12 themselves on the third and seventh d, H3427
Nu 19:14 who is in it will be unclean *for* seven d, H3427
Nu 19:16 a grave, will be unclean *for* seven d. H3427
Nu 19:19 are unclean on the third and seventh d, H3427
Nu 20:29 all the Israelites mourned for him thirty d. H3427
Nu 24:14 will do to your people in d to come." H3427
Nu 28:17 *for* seven d eat bread made without yeast. H3427
Nu 28:24 every day *for* seven d as an aroma H3427
Nu 29:12 a festival to the LORD *for* seven d. H3427
Nu 31:19 must stay outside the camp seven d. H3427
Nu 31:19 the third and seventh d you must purify H3427
Nu 33: 8 had traveled *for* three d in the Desert of H3427
Dt 1: 2 It takes eleven d to go from Horeb to H3427
Dt 1:46 And so you stayed in Kadesh many d—all H3427
Dt 4:30 then in later d you will return to the LORD H3427
Dt 4:32 Ask now about the former d, long before H3427
Dt 5:13 Six d you shall labor and do all your work, H3427
Dt 5:33 prolong your d in the land that you H3427
Dt 9: 9 on the mountain forty d and forty nights; H3427
Dt 9:11 At the end of the forty d and forty nights H3427
Dt 9:18 the LORD *for* forty d and forty nights; H3427
Dt 9:25 the LORD those forty d and forty nights H3427
Dt 10:10 on the mountain forty d and forty nights, H3427
Dt 11:21 so that your d and the days of your H3427
Dt 11:21 your days and the d *of* your children may H3427
Dt 11:21 as many as the d that the heavens are H3427
Dt 16: 3 but *for* seven d eat unleavened bread H3427
Dt 16: 3 so that all the d *of* your life you may H3427
Dt 16: 4 possession in all your land *for* seven d. H3427
Dt 16: 8 *For* six d eat unleavened bread and on the H3427
Dt 16:13 of Tabernacles *for* seven d after you have H3427
Dt 16:15 *For* seven d celebrate the festival to the H3427
Dt 17:19 is to read it all the d *of* his life so that he H3427
Dt 28:33 nothing but cruel oppression all your d. H3427
Dt 31:29 In d to come, disaster will fall on you H3427
Dt 32: 7 Remember the d of old; consider the H3427
Dt 33:25 your strength will equal your d. H3427
Dt 34: 8 Moses in the plains of Moab thirty d, H3427
Jos 1: 5 to stand against you all the d *of* your life. H3427
Jos 1:11 Three d from now you will cross the H3427
Jos 2:16 yourselves there three d until they return, H3427
Jos 2:22 into the hills and stayed there three d, H3427
Jos 3: 2 After three d the officers went throughout H3427
Jos 4:14 stood in awe of him all the d *of* his life, H3427
Jos 6: 3 with all the armed men. Do this *for* six d. H3427
Jos 6:14 They did this *for* six d. H3427
Jos 9:16 Three d after they made the treaty with H3427
Jdg 5: 6 "In the d *of* Shamgar son of Anath, in the H3427
Jdg 5: 6 of Anath, in the d *of* Jael, the highways H3427
Jdg 11:40 Israel go out *for* four d to commemorate H3427
Jdg 14:12 answer *within* the seven d *of* the feast, H3427
Jdg 14:14 *For* three d they could not give the answer. H3427
Jdg 14:17 She cried the whole seven d of the feast H3427
Jdg 15:20 twenty years in the d *of* the Philistines. H3427
Jdg 17: 6 In those d Israel had no king; everyone did H3427
Jdg 18: 1 In those d Israel had no king. H3427
Jdg 18: 1 And in those d the tribe of the Danites H3427
Jdg 19: 1 In those d Israel had no king. H3427
Jdg 19: 4 so he remained with him three d, eating H3427
Jdg 20:27 In those d the ark of the covenant of God H3427
Jdg 21:25 In those d Israel had no king; everyone H3427
Ru 1: 1 In the d *when* the judges ruled, there was H3427
1Sa 1:11 him to the LORD *for* all the d *of* his life, H3427
1Sa 3: 1 In those d the word of the LORD was rare H3427
1Sa 7:15 as Israel's leader all the d *of* his life. H3427
1Sa 9:20 As for the donkeys you lost three d ago, do H3427
1Sa 10: 8 you must wait seven d until I come to you H3427
1Sa 11: 3 "Give us seven d so we can send H3427
1Sa 13: 8 He waited seven d, the time set by H3427
1Sa 14:52 All the d *of* Saul there was bitter war with H3427
1Sa 17:16 *For* forty d the Philistine came forward H3427
1Sa 18:29 he remained his enemy the rest of his d. H3427
1Sa 25:10 breaking away from their masters these d. H3427
1Sa 25:38 About ten d later, the LORD struck Nabal H3427
1Sa 27: 1 "One of these d I will be destroyed by the H3427
1Sa 28: 1 In those d the Philistines gathered their H3427
1Sa 30:12 drunk any water *for* three d and three H3427
1Sa 30:13 me when I became ill three d ago. H3427
1Sa 31:13 tree at Jabesh, and they fasted seven d. H3427
2Sa 1: 1 Amalekites and stayed in Ziklag two d. H3427
2Sa 7:12 When your d are over and you rest with H3427
2Sa 13:37 King David mourned many d for his son. H3427
2Sa 14: 2 who has spent many d grieving for the H3427
2Sa 16:23 Now in those d the advice Ahithophel H3427
2Sa 20: 4 of Judah to come to me *within* three d, H3427
2Sa 21: 9 to death during the first d *of* the harvest, H3427
2Sa 24: 8 at the end of nine months and twenty d. H3427
2Sa 24:13 Or three d of plague in your land H3427
1Ki 8:65 our God for seven d and seven days more, H3427
1Ki 8:65 our God for seven days and seven d more, H3427
1Ki 8:65 seven days more, fourteen d in all. H3427
1Ki 10:21 considered of little value in Solomon's d. H3427
1Ki 11:34 him ruler all the d *of* his life for the sake H3427
1Ki 12: 5 "Go away for three d and then come back H3427
1Ki 12:12 Three d later Jeroboam and all the H3427
1Ki 12:12 had said, "Come back to me in three d." H3427
1Ki 15: 5 LORD's commands all the d *of* his life— H3427
1Ki 16:15 of Judah, Zimri reigned in Tirzah seven d. H3427
1Ki 19: 8 he traveled forty d and forty nights until H3427
1Ki 20:29 *For* seven d they camped opposite each H3427
1Ki 21:29 bring it on his house in the d *of* his son." H3427
2Ki 2:17 who searched *for* three d but did not find H3427
2Ki 3: 9 After a roundabout march of seven d, the H3427
2Ki 10:32 In those d the LORD began to reduce the H3427
2Ki 15:37 In those d the LORD began to send Rezin H3427
2Ki 19:25 In d of old I planned it; now I have H3427
2Ki 20: 1 In those d Hezekiah became ill and was H3427
2Ki 23:22 Neither in the d *of* the judges who led H3427
2Ki 23:22 Israel nor in the d *of* the kings of Israel H3427
1Ch 4:41 listed came in the d *of* Hezekiah king of H3427
1Ch 7:22 father Ephraim mourned for them many d, H3427
1Ch 10:12 tree in Jabesh, and they fasted seven d. H3427
1Ch 12:39 The men spent three d there with David H3427
1Ch 17:11 When your d are over and you go to be H3427
1Ch 21:12 or three d of the sword of the LORD H3427
1Ch 21:12 sword of the LORD—d of plague in the land NDT
1Ch 29:15 Our d on earth are like a shadow, without H3427
2Ch 7: 8 the festival at that time *for* seven d, H3427
2Ch 7: 9 of the altar *for* seven d and the festival H3427
2Ch 7: 9 days and the festival *for* seven d more. H3427
2Ch 10: 5 answered, "Come back to me in three d." H3427
2Ch 10:12 Three d later Jeroboam and all the H3427
2Ch 10:12 had said, "Come back to me in three d." H3427
2Ch 14: 1 in his d the country was at peace for H3427
2Ch 15: 5 In those d it was not safe to travel about H6961
2Ch 20:25 plunder that it took three d to collect it. H3427
2Ch 26: 5 He sought God during the d *of* Zechariah H3427
2Ch 29:17 For eight more d they consecrated the H3427
2Ch 30:21 Unleavened Bread *for* seven d with great H3427
2Ch 30:22 *For* the seven d they ate their assigned H3427
2Ch 30:23 to celebrate the festival seven more d; H3427
2Ch 30:23 so *for* another seven d they celebrated H3427
2Ch 30:26 since the d *of* Solomon son of David H3427
2Ch 32:24 In those d Hezekiah became ill and was H3427
2Ch 32:26 come on them during the d *of* Hezekiah. H3427
2Ch 35:17 Festival of Unleavened Bread *for* seven d. H3427
2Ch 35:18 Israel since the d *of* the prophet Samuel H3427
2Ch 36: 9 in Jerusalem three months and ten d. H3427
Ezr 4: 7 And in the d *of* Artaxerxes king of Persia H3427
Ezr 6:22 *For* seven d they celebrated with joy the H3427
Ezr 8:15 and we camped there three d. H3427
Ezr 8:32 in Jerusalem, where we rested three d. H3427
Ezr 9: 7 From the d *of* our ancestors until now, our H3427
Ezr 10: 8 appear within three d would forfeit all his H3427
Ezr 10: 9 Within the three d, all the men of Judah H3427
Ne 1: 4 *For some* d I mourned and fasted and H3427
Ne 2:11 Jerusalem, and after staying there three d H3427
Ne 5:18 every ten d an abundant supply of H3427
Ne 6:15 on the twenty-fifth of Elul, in fifty-two d. H3427
Ne 6:17 in those d the nobles of Judah were H3427
Ne 8:17 From the d *of* Joshua son of Nun until that H3427
Ne 8:18 They celebrated the festival *for* seven d H3427
Ne 9:32 from the d *of* the kings of Assyria until H3427
Ne 12: 7 their associates in the d *of* Joshua. H3427
Ne 12:12 In the d *of* Joiakim, these were the heads H3427
Ne 12:22 heads of the Levites in the d *of* Eliashib, H3427
Ne 12:26 They served in the d *of* Joiakim son of H3427
Ne 12:26 in the d *of* Nehemiah the governor H3427
Ne 12:46 For long ago, in the d *of* David and Asaph H3427
Ne 12:47 So in the d *of* Zerubbabel and of H3427
Ne 13:15 In those d I saw people in Judah treading H3427
Ne 13:23 in those d I saw men of Judah who had H3427
Est 1: 4 *For* a full 180 d he displayed the vast H3427
Est 1: 5 When these d were over, the king gave a H3427
Est 1: 5 banquet, lasting seven d, in the enclosed H3427
Est 4:11 But thirty d have passed since I was called H3427
Est 4:16 Do not eat or drink *for* three d, night or H3427
Est 9:21 fifteenth d of the month of Adar H3427
Est 9:22 them to observe the d as days of H4392S
Est 9:22 observe the days as d *of* feasting and joy H3427
Est 9:26 Therefore these d were called Purim, from H3427
Est 9:27 fail observe these two d every year, H3427
Est 9:28 These d should be remembered and H3427
Est 9:28 And these d *of* Purim should never fail to H3427
Est 9:28 nor *should* the memory of these d die out H4392S
Est 9:31 to establish these d *of* Purim at their H3427
Job 2:13 ground with him *for* seven d and seven H3427
Job 3: 6 included among the d *of* the year nor be H3427
Job 3: 8 May those who curse d curse that day H3427
Job 7: 1 Are not their d like those of hired laborers H3427
Job 7: 6 "My d are swifter than a weaver's shuttle H3427
Job 7:16 Let me alone; my d have no meaning. H3427
Job 8: 9 our d on earth are but a shadow. H3427
Job 9:25 "My d are swifter than a runner; they fly H3427
Job 10: 5 Are your d like those of a mortal or your H3427
Job 10:20 Are not my few d almost over? Turn away H3427
Job 14: 1 woman, are of few d and full of trouble. H3427
Job 14: 5 A person's d are determined; you have H3427
Job 14:14 All the d *of* my hard service I will wait H3427
Job 15:20 All his d the wicked man suffers torment H3427
Job 17: 1 My spirit is broken, my d are cut short, the H3427
Job 17:11 My d have passed, my plans are shattered H3427
Job 24: 1 who know him look in vain for such d? H3427
Job 29: 2 for the d when God watched over me, H3427
Job 29: 4 for the d when I was in my prime H3427
Job 29:18 my d as numerous as the grains of sand. H3427
Job 30:16 my life ebbs away; d *of* suffering grip me. H3427
Job 30:27 never stops; d *of* suffering confront me. H3427
Job 33:25 be restored as in the d *of* their youth'— H3427
Job 36:11 the rest of their d in prosperity and their H3427
Job 38:23 times of trouble, for d *of* war and battle? H3427
Ps 21: 4 it to him—length of d, for ever and ever. H3427
Ps 23: 6 love will follow me all the d *of* my life, H3427
Ps 25:13 They *will* spend *their* d in prosperity, and H4328
Ps 27: 4 the house of the LORD all the d *of* my life, H3427
Ps 34:12 life and desires to see *many* good d, H3427
Ps 37:18 spend their d under the LORD's care H3427
Ps 37:19 in d *of* famine they will enjoy plenty. H3427
Ps 39: 4 my life's end and the number of my d; let H3427
Ps 39: 5 You have made my d a mere H3427
Ps 44: 1 have told us what you did in their d, H3427
Ps 44: 1 what you did in their days, in d long ago. H3427
Ps 49: 5 Why should I fear when evil d come H3427
Ps 55:23 deceitful will not live out half their d. H3427
Ps 61: 6 Increase the d of the king's life, his years H3427
Ps 72: 7 In his d may the righteous flourish and H3427
Ps 77: 5 I thought about the former d, the years of H3427
Ps 78:33 So he ended their d in futility and their H3427
Ps 89:45 You have cut short the d *of* his youth; you H3427
Ps 90: 9 All our d pass away under your wrath; we H3427
Ps 90:10 Our d may come to seventy years H3427+9102
Ps 90:12 Teach us to number our d, that we may H3427
Ps 90:14 we may sing for joy and be glad all our d. H3427
Ps 90:15 Make us glad *for* as many d as you have H3427
Ps 93: 5 holiness adorns your house for endless d. H3427
Ps 94:13 you grant them relief from d *of* trouble, till H3427
Ps 102: 3 For my d vanish like smoke; my bones H3427
Ps 102:11 My d are like the evening shadow; H3427
Ps 102:23 he broke my strength; he cut short my d. H3427
Ps 102:24 in the midst of my d; your years go on H3427
Ps 109: 8 May his d be few; may another take his H3427
Ps 128: 5 of Jerusalem all the d *of* your life. H3427
Ps 139:16 all the d ordained for me were written in H3427
Ps 143: 5 I remember the d of long ago; I meditate H3427
Ps 144: 4 their d are like a fleeting shadow. H3427
Pr 9:11 For through wisdom your d will be many H3427
Pr 15:15 All the d *of* the oppressed are wretched H3427
Pr 31:12 him good, not harm, all the d *of* her life. H3427
Pr 31:25 she can laugh at the d to come. H3427
Ecc 2: 3 heavens during the few d *of* their lives. H3427
Ecc 2:16 the d have already come when both have H3427
Ecc 2:23 All their d their work is grief and pain H3427
Ecc 5:17 All their d they eat in darkness, with great H3427
Ecc 5:18 sun during the few d *of* life God has given H3427
Ecc 5:20 They seldom reflect on the d *of* their life H3427
Ecc 6:12 few and meaningless d they pass through H3427
Ecc 7:10 "Why were the old d better than these?" H3427
Ecc 8:13 their d will not lengthen like a H3427
Ecc 8:15 in their toil all the d *of* the life God has H3427
Ecc 9: 9 all the d *of* this meaningless life that God H3427
Ecc 9: 9 under the sun—all your meaningless d. H3427
Ecc 11: 1 after many d you may receive a return. H3427
Ecc 11: 8 But let them remember the d *of* darkness H3427
Ecc 11: 9 heart give you joy in the d *of* your youth. H3427
Ecc 12: 1 your Creator in the d *of* your youth, H3427
Ecc 12: 1 before the d *of* trouble come and the H3427
Isa 1:26 I will restore your leaders as in d of old H8037
Isa 2: 2 In the last d the mountain of the LORD's H3427
Isa 13:22 at hand, and her d will not be prolonged. H3427
Isa 24:22 in prison and be punished after many d. H3427
Isa 27: 6 In d to come Jacob will take root, Israel will NDT
Isa 30: 8 that for the d to come it may be an H3427
Isa 30:26 like the light of seven *full* d, when the H3427
Isa 37:26 In d of old I planned it; now I have H3427
Isa 38: 1 In those d Hezekiah became ill and was H3427
Isa 38:20 instruments all the d *of* our lives in the H3427
Isa 43:13 from ancient d I am he. No one can H3427
Isa 51: 9 as in d gone by, as in generations H3427
Isa 53:10 will see his offspring and prolong his d, H3427
Isa 54: 9 "To me this is like the d *of* Noah, when I H3427
Isa 60:20 and your d *of* sorrow will end. H3427
Isa 63: 9 them up and carried them all the d of old. H3427
Isa 63:11 Then his people recalled the d of old, the H3427
Isa 63:11 days of old, the d of Moses and his people NDT
Isa 65:20 be in it an infant who lives but a *few* d, H3427
Isa 65:22 For as the d *of* a tree, so will be the days H3427
Isa 65:22 so will be the d *of* my people; my H3427
Jer 2:32 have forgotten me, d without number. H3427
Jer 3:16 In those d, when your numbers have H3427
Jer 3:18 In those d the people of Judah will join H3427
Jer 5:18 "Yet even in those d," declares the LORD H3427
Jer 7:32 So beware, the d are coming, declares the H3427
Jer 9:25 "The d are coming," declares the LORD H3427
Jer 13: 6 Many d later the LORD said to me, "Go H3427
Jer 16: 9 your eyes and in your d I will bring an end H3427
Jer 16:14 "However, the d are coming," declares H3427
Jer 19: 6 So beware, the d are coming, declares the H3427

D

Jer 20:18 sorrow and to end my **d** in shame? H3427
Jer 23: 5 "The **d** are coming," declares the LORD H3427
Jer 23: 6 In his **d** Judah will be saved and Israel H3427
Jer 23: 7 "So then, the **d** are coming," declares the H3427
Jer 23:20 In **d** to come you will understand it clearly. H3427
Jer 26:18 prophesied in the **d** *of* Hezekiah king of H3427
Jer 30: 3 The **d** are coming,' declares the LORD H3427
Jer 30:20 Their children will be as in **d of old**, and H7710
Jer 30:24 In **d** to come you will understand this H3427
Jer 31:27 "The **d** are coming," declares the LORD H3427
Jer 31:29 "In those **d** people will no longer say, 'The H3427
Jer 31:31 "The **d** are coming," declares the LORD H3427
Jer 31:38 "The **d** are coming," declares the LORD H3427
Jer 33:14 " 'The **d** are coming,' declares the LORD H3427
Jer 33:15 " 'In those **d** and at that time I will make H3427
Jer 33:16 In those **d** Judah will be saved and H3427
Jer 42: 7 Ten **d** later the word of the LORD came to H3427
Jer 48:12 But **d** are coming," declares the LORD H3427
Jer 48:47 restore the fortunes of Moab in **d** to come," H3427
Jer 49: 2 But the **d** are coming," declares the LORD H3427
Jer 49:39 restore the fortunes of Elam in **d** to come," H3427
Jer 50: 4 "In those **d**, at that time," declares the H3427
Jer 50:20 In those **d**, at that time," declares the LORD H3427
Jer 51:52 "But **d** are coming," declares the LORD H3427
La 1: 7 In the **d** *of* her affliction and wandering H3427
La 1: 7 the treasures that were hers in **d** of old. H3427
La 4:18 end was near, our **d** were numbered, for H3427
La 5:21 that we may return; renew our **d** as of old H3427
Eze 3:15 I sat among them *for* seven **d**—deeply H3427
Eze 3:16 At the end of seven **d** the word of the LORD H3427
Eze 4: 4 their sin *for* the number of **d** you lie on H3427
Eze 4: 5 the same number of **d** as the years of H3427
Eze 4: 5 So *for* 390 **d** you will bear the sin of the H3427
Eze 4: 6 I have assigned you 40 **d**, a day for each H3427
Eze 4: 8 you have finished the **d** *of* your siege. H3427
Eze 4: 9 it during the 390 **d** you lie on your side. H3427
Eze 5: 2 When the **d** *of* your siege come to an end H3427
Eze 12:22 'The **d** go by and every vision comes to H3427
Eze 12:23 'The **d** are near when every vision will be H3427
Eze 12:25 For in your **d**, you rebellious people, I will H3427
Eze 16:22 you did not remember the **d** *of* your youth, H3427
Eze 16:43 did not remember the **d** *of* your youth H3427
Eze 16:60 I made with you in the **d** *of* your youth, H3427
Eze 22: 4 You have brought your **d** to a close, and H3427
Eze 23:19 as she recalled the **d** *of* her youth, H3427
Eze 38: 8 After many **d** you will be called to arms. H3427
Eze 38:16 In **d** to come, Gog, I will bring you against H3427
Eze 38:17 I spoke of in former **d** by my servants the H3427
Eze 43:25 "*For* seven **d** you are to provide a male H3427
Eze 43:26 *For* seven **d** they are to make atonement H3427
Eze 43:27 At the end of these **d**, from the eighth day H3427
Eze 44:26 After he is cleansed, he must wait seven **d**. H3427
Eze 45:21 a festival lasting seven **d**, during which H3427
Eze 45:23 during the seven **d** *of* the festival he is H3427
Eze 45:25 " 'During the seven **d** of the festival H3427
Eze 46: 1 east is to be shut on the six working **d**, H3427
Da 1:12 "Please test your servants *for* ten **d**: Give H3427
Da 1:14 agreed to this and tested them *for* ten **d**. H3427
Da 1:15 the end of the ten **d** they looked healthier H3427
Da 2:28 what will happen in **d** to come. A10317
Da 5:26 God has numbered the **d** of your reign and NDT
Da 6: 7 human being during the next thirty **d**, A10317
Da 6:12 the next thirty **d** anyone who prays to A10317
Da 7: 9 the Ancient of **D** took his seat. A10317
Da 7:13 the Ancient of **D** and was led into his A10317
Da 7:22 the Ancient of **D** came and pronounced A10317
Da 8:27 I lay exhausted *for several* **d**. Then I got H3427
Da 10:13 kingdom resisted me twenty-one **d**. H3427
Da 11: 6 In those **d** she will be betrayed, together H6961
Da 12:11 is set up, there will be 1,290 **d**. H3427
Da 12:12 and reaches the end of the 1,335 **d**. H3427
Da 12:13 then at the end of the **d** you will rise to H3427
Hos 2:11 New Moons, her **Sabbath d**—all her H8701
Hos 2:13 punish her for the **d** she burned incense H3427
Hos 2:15 she will respond as in the **d** *of* her youth, H3427
Hos 3: 3 "You are to live with me many **d**; you H3427
Hos 3: 4 will live many **d** without king or prince, H3427
Hos 3: 5 the LORD and to his blessings in the last **d**. H3427
Hos 6: 2 After *two* **d** he will revive us; on the third H3427
Hos 9: 5 festivals, on the feast **d** *of* the LORD? H3427
Hos 9: 7 The **d** *of* punishment are coming, the H3427
Hos 9: 7 coming, the **d** *of* reckoning are at hand. H3427
Hos 9: 9 into corruption, as in the **d** *of* Gibeah. H3427
Hos 10: 9 "Since the **d** *of* Gibeah, you have sinned H3427
Hos 12: 9 as in the **d** *of* your appointed festivals. H3427
Joel 1: 2 ever happened in your **d** or in the days of H3427
Joel 1: 2 in your days or in the **d** *of* your ancestors? H3427
Joel 2:29 I will pour out my Spirit in those **d**. H3427
Joel 3: 1 "In those **d** and at that time, when I H3427
Am 8:11 "The **d** are coming," declares the H3427
Am 9:13 "The **d** are coming," declares the LORD H3427
Jnh 1:17 belly of the fish three **d** and three nights. H3427
Jnh 3: 3 large city; it took three **d** to go through it. H3427
Jnh 3: 4 "Forty more **d** and Nineveh will be H3427
Mic 4: 1 In the last **d** the mountain of the LORD's H3427
Mic 7:14 in Bashan and Gilead as in **d** long ago. H3427
Mic 7:15 "As in the **d** *when* you came out of Egypt H3427
Mic 7:20 on oath to our ancestors in **d** long ago. H3427
Hab 1: 5 something in your **d** that you would never H3427
Zec 8:23 "In those **d** ten people from all languages H3427
Zec 14: 5 earthquake in the **d** *of* Uzziah king of H3427
Mal 3: 4 to the LORD, as in **d** gone by, as in former H3427
Mt 3: 1 In those **d** John the Baptist came G2465
Mt 4: 2 After fasting forty **d** and forty nights, he G2465
Mt 11:12 From the **d** of John the Baptist until now G2465
Mt 12:40 as Jonah was three **d** and three nights in G2465
Mt 12:40 of Man will be three **d** and three nights in G2465
Mt 15:32 been with me three **d** and have nothing G2465
Mt 17: 1 After six **d** Jesus took with him Peter G2465
Mt 23:30 'If we had lived in the **d** of our ancestors G2465
Mt 24:19 it will be in those **d** for pregnant women G2465
Mt 24:22 "If those **d** had not been cut short, no one G2465
Mt 24:22 of the elect those **d** will be shortened. G2465
Mt 24:29 after the distress *of* those **d** " 'the sun will G2465
Mt 24:37 As it was in the **d** of Noah, so it will be at G2465
Mt 24:38 For in the **d** before the flood, people were G2465
Mt 26: 2 the Passover is two **d** away—and the Son G2465
Mt 26:61 temple of God and rebuild it in three **d**. G2465
Mt 27:40 destroy the temple and build it in three **d**, G2465
Mt 27:63 'After three **d** I will rise again. G2465
Mk 1:13 he was in the wilderness forty **d** G2465
Mk 2: 1 **A few d later**, when Jesus again G1328+2465
Mk 2:26 **In the d of** Abiathar the high priest, he G2093
Mk 8: 1 During those **d** another large crowd G2465
Mk 8: 2 been with me three **d** and have nothing G2465
Mk 8:31 be killed and after three **d** rise again. G2465
Mk 9: 2 After six **d** Jesus took Peter, James and G2465
Mk 9:31 will kill him, and after three **d** he will rise." G2465
Mk 10:34 Three **d** later he will rise." G2465
Mk 13:17 it will be in those **d** for pregnant women G2465
Mk 13:19 because those will be **d** of distress G2465
Mk 13:20 "If the Lord had not cut short those **d**, no G2465
Mk 13:24 "But in those **d**, following that distress, G2465
Mk 14: 1 Unleavened Bread were only two **d** away, G2465
Mk 14:58 hands and in three **d** will build another, G2465
Mk 15:29 destroy the temple and build it in three **d**, G2465
Lk 1:25 "In these **d** he has shown his favor and G2465
Lk 1:75 righteousness before him all our **d**. G2465
Lk 2: 1 In those **d** Caesar Augustus issued a G2465
Lk 2:46 After three **d** they found him in the temple G2465
Lk 4: 2 where *for* forty **d** he was tempted by the G2465
Lk 4: 2 He ate nothing during those **d**, and at the G2465
Lk 5:35 taken from them; in those **d** they will fast." G2465
Lk 6:12 One of those **d** Jesus went out to a G2465
Lk 9:28 About eight **d** after Jesus said this, he G2465
Lk 13:14 to the people, "There are six **d** for work. G2465
Lk 13:14 So come and be healed on those **d**, not on NDT
Lk 17:22 long to see one *of* the **d** of the Son of G2465
Lk 17:26 "Just as it was in the **d** of Noah, so also G2465
Lk 17:26 also will it be in the **d** of the Son of Man. G2465
Lk 17:28 "It was the same in the **d** of Lot. G2465
Lk 19:43 The **d** will come upon you when your G2465
Lk 21:23 it will be in those **d** for pregnant women G2465
Lk 24:18 that have happened there in these **d**?" G2465
Jn 2:12 There they stayed *for* a few **d**. G2465
Jn 2:19 I will raise it again in three **d**. G2465
Jn 2:20 you are going to raise it in three **d**?" G2465
Jn 4:40 to stay with them, and he stayed two **d**. G2465
Jn 4:43 After the two **d** he left for Galilee. G2465
Jn 10:40 had been baptizing **in the early d**. G3836+4754
Jn 11: 6 he stayed where he was two more **d**, G2465
Jn 11:17 had already been in the tomb *for* four **d**. G2465
Jn 11:39 a bad odor, for he has been there **four d**." G5479
Jn 12: 1 Six **d** before the Passover, Jesus came to G2465
Ac 1: 3 over a period *of* forty **d** and spoke about G2465
Ac 1: 5 in a few **d** you will be baptized with G2465
Ac 1:15 In those **d** Peter stood up among the G2465
Ac 2:17 " 'In the last **d**, God says, I will pour out G2465
Ac 2:18 I will pour out my Spirit in those **d**, and G2465
Ac 3:24 who have spoken have foretold these **d**. G2465
Ac 5:37 appeared in the **d** of the census and led a G2465
Ac 6: 1 In those **d** when the number of disciples G2465
Ac 7: 8 circumcised him eight **d** *after* his birth. G2465
Ac 9: 9 *For* three **d** he was blind, and did not eat G2465
Ac 9:19 Saul spent several **d** with the disciples in G2465
Ac 9:23 After many **d** had gone by, there was a G2465
Ac 10:30 "Three **d** ago I was in my house praying G2465
Ac 10:48 asked Peter to stay with them *for* a few **d**. G2465
Ac 13:31 for many **d** he was seen by those who G2465
Ac 13:41 something in your **d** that you would never G2465
Ac 16:12 And we stayed there several **d**. G2465
Ac 16:18 She kept this up for many **d**. Finally Paul G2465
Ac 17: 2 on three **Sabbath d** he reasoned with G4879
Ac 20: 6 five **d** later joined the others at Troas G2465
Ac 20: 6 others at Troas, where we stayed seven **d**. G2465
Ac 21: 4 there and stayed with them seven **d**. G2465
Ac 21:10 After we had been there a number of **d**, G2465
Ac 21:26 of the date when the **d** of purification G2465
Ac 21:27 When the seven **d** were nearly over, some G2465
Ac 24: 1 Five **d** later the high priest Ananias went G2465
Ac 24:11 no more than twelve **d** ago I went up to G2465
Ac 24:24 Several **d** later Felix came with his wife G2465
Ac 25: 1 Three **d** after arriving in the province G2465
Ac 25: 6 After spending eight or ten **d** with them G2465
Ac 25:13 A few **d** later King Agrippa and Bernice G2465
Ac 25:14 Since they were spending many **d** there G2465
Ac 27: 7 headway for many **d** and had difficulty G2465
Ac 27:20 appeared for many **d** and the storm G2465
Ac 27:33 "For **the last** fourteen **d**," he said G4958+2465
Ac 28: 7 us generous hospitality *for* three **d**. G2465
Ac 28:12 in at Syracuse and stayed there three **d**. G2465
Ac 28:17 Three **d** later he called together the local G2465
Gal 1:18 Cephas and stayed with him fifteen **d**. G2465
Gal 4:10 are observing *special* **d** and months and G2465
Eph 5:16 every opportunity, because the **d** are evil. G2465
Php 4:15 in the **early d** of your acquaintance with the G794
2Ti 3: 1 There will be terrible times in the last **d**. G2465
Heb 1: 2 in these last **d** he has spoken to us by G2465
Heb 5: 7 During the **d** of Jesus' life on earth, he G2465
Heb 7: 3 without beginning *of* **d** or end of life G2465
Heb 8: 8 "The **d** are coming, declares the Lord G2465
Heb 10:32 those earlier **d** after you had received G2465
Heb 11:30 had marched around them for seven **d**. G2465
Jas 5: 3 You have hoarded wealth in the last **d**. G2465
1Pe 3:10 life and see good **d** must keep their G2465
1Pe 3:20 patiently in the **d** of Noah while the ark G2465
2Pe 3: 3 that in the last **d** scoffers will come, G2465
Rev 2:10 you will suffer persecution *for* ten **d**. G2465
Rev 2:13 not even in the **d** of Antipas, my G2465
Rev 9: 6 During those **d** people will seek death G2465
Rev 10: 7 But in the **d** when the seventh angel is G2465
Rev 11: 3 they will prophesy *for* 1,260 **d** G2465
Rev 11: 9 *For* three and a half **d** some from every G2465
Rev 11:11 the three and a half **d** the breath of life G2465
Rev 12: 6 she might be taken care of *for* 1,260 **d**. G2465

DAYSMAN (KJV) MEDIATE

DAYSPRING (KJV) MORNING, RISING SUN

DAYTIME (7) [DAY]

Ge 31:40 consumed me in the **d** and the cold at H3427
Jdg 6:27 he did it at night rather than **in the d**. H3429
Job 5:14 Darkness comes upon them **in the d**; at H3429
Eze 12: 3 your belongings for exile and **in the d**, H3429
Eze 12: 4 **During the d**, while they watch, bring out H3429
Jn 11: 9 who walks in the **d** will not stumble, G2465
Ro 13:13 decently, as in the **d**, not in carousing G2465

DAZZLING (2)

Da 2:31 an enormous, **d** statue, awesome in A10228
Mk 9: 3 His clothes became **d** white, whiter G5118+3336

DEACON (2) [DEACONS]

Ro 16: 1 Phoebe, a **d** of the church in Cenchreae. G1356
1Ti 3:12 A **d** must be faithful to his wife and must G1356

DEACONS (3) [DEACON]

Php 1: 1 together with the overseers and **d**: G1356
1Ti 3: 8 same way, **d** are to be worthy of respect G1356
1Ti 3:10 against them, *let them* **serve as d**. G1354

DEAD (357) [DIE]

Ge 14: 3 of Siddim (that is, the **D** Sea Valley). H4875S
Ge 20: 3 "You *are* **as good as d** because of the H4637
Ge 23: 3 from beside his **d** *wife* and spoke to the H4637
Ge 23: 4 a burial site here so I can bury my **d**." H4637
Ge 23: 6 Bury your **d** in the choicest of our tombs H4637
Ge 23: 6 refuse you his tomb for burying your **d**." H4637
Ge 23: 8 "If you are willing to let me bury my **d** H4637
Ge 23:11 the presence of my people. Bury your **d**." H4637
Ge 23:13 it from me so I can bury my **d** there." H4637
Ge 23:15 that between you and me? Bury your **d**." H4637
Ge 34:27 came upon the **d bodies** and looted the H2728
Ge 42:38 his brother *is* **d** and he is the only one left. H4637
Ge 44:20 His brother *is* **d**, and he is the only one of H4637
Ge 50:15 brothers saw that their father *was* **d**, H4637
Ex 4:19 all those who wanted to kill you *are* **d**." H4637
Ex 12:30 was not a house without *someone* **d**. H4637
Ex 14:30 saw the Egyptians *lying* **d** on the shore. H4637
Ex 21:34 loss and take the **d** *animal* in exchange. H4637
Ex 21:35 the money and the **d** *animal* equally. H4637
Ex 21:36 take the **d** *animal* in exchange. H4637
Lev 7:24 The fat of an **animal found d** or torn by H5577
Lev 11:31 them when they *are* **d** will be unclean till H4637
Lev 14:51 into the blood of the **d** bird and the fresh H8821
Lev 17:15 who eats **anything found d** or torn by wild H5577
Lev 19:28 your bodies for the **d** or put tattoo marks H5883
Lev 21:11 not enter a place where there is a **d** body. H4637
Lev 22: 8 must not eat **anything found d** or torn by H5577
Lev 26:30 pile your **d bodies** on the lifeless H7007
Nu 5: 2 unclean because of a **d body**. H5883
Nu 6: 6 the Nazirite must not go near a **d** body. H4637
Nu 6:11 by being in the presence of the **d body**. H5883
Nu 9: 6 unclean on account of a **d** body. H5883
Nu 9: 7 become unclean because of a **d** body, H5883
Nu 9:10 because of a **d body** or are away on a H5883
Nu 16:30 go down alive into the **realm of the d**, H8619
Nu 16:33 went down alive into the **realm of the d**, H8619
Nu 16:48 He stood between the living and the **d** H4637
Nu 20: 3 when our brothers **fell d** before the LORD! H1588
Nu 34: 3 east from the southern end of the **D** Sea, H4875S
Nu 34:12 along the Jordan and end at the **D** Sea. H4875S
Dt 3:17 the **D** Sea), below the slopes of H4875S
Dt 4:49 as far as the **D Sea**, below the H3542+6858
Dt 14: 1 shave the front of your heads for the **d**, H4637
Dt 14:21 Do not eat anything you find **already d** H5577
Dt 18:11 medium or spiritist or who consults the **d**. H4637
Dt 25: 6 on the name of the **d** brother so that his H4637
Dt 26:14 have I offered any of it to the **d**. H4637
Dt 32:22 burns down to the **realm of the d** below. H8619
Jos 1: 2 "Moses my servant *is* **d**. Now then, you H4637
Jos 3:16 the **D** Sea) was completely H4875S
Jos 12: 3 Arabah (that is, the **D** Sea), to Beth H4875S
Jos 15: 2 bay at the southern end of the **D** Sea, H4875S
Jos 15: 5 boundary is the **D** Sea as far as the H4875S
Jos 18:19 out at the northern bay of the **D** Sea, H4875S

Jdg 3:25 they saw their lord fallen to the floor, **d**. H4637
Jdg 4: 1 eyes of the LORD, now that Ehud *was* **d**. H4637
Jdg 4:22 with the tent peg through his temple—**d**. H4637
Jdg 5:27 where he sank, there he fell—**d**. H8720
Jdg 9:55 the Israelites saw that Abimelek *was* **d**, H4637
Ru 1: 8 kindness to your **d** *husbands* and to me. H4637
Ru 2:20 his kindness to the living and the **d**." H4637
Ru 4: 5 the Moabite, the **d** *man's* widow, in order H4637
Ru 4: 5 the name of the **d** with his property." H4637
Ru 4:10 the name of the **d** with his property, H4637
1Sa 4:17 Phinehas, *are* **d**, and the ark of God H4637
1Sa 4:19 father-in-law and her husband *were* **d**, H4637
1Sa 17:51 the Philistines saw that their hero *was* **d**, H4637
1Sa 17:52 Their **d** were strewn along the Shaaraim H2728
1Sa 24:14 Who are you pursuing? A **d** dog? A flea? H4637
1Sa 25:39 When David heard that Nabal *was* **d**, he H4637
1Sa 28: 3 Now Samuel *was* **d**, and all Israel had H4637
1Sa 31: 1 and many fell **d** on Mount Gilboa. H2728
1Sa 31: 5 the armor-bearer saw that Saul *was* **d**, H4637
1Sa 31: 8 when the Philistines came to strip the **d** H2728
2Sa 1: 4 And Saul and his son Jonathan *are* **d**." H4637
2Sa 1: 5 that Saul and his son Jonathan *are* **d**?" H4637
2Sa 2: 7 Saul your master *is* **d**, and the people H4637
2Sa 4:10 told me, 'Saul *is* **d**,' and thought he was H4637
2Sa 9: 8 that you should notice a **d** dog like me?" H4637
2Sa 11:21 your servant Uriah the Hittite *is* **d**. H4637
2Sa 11:24 your servant Uriah the Hittite *is* **d**. H4637
2Sa 11:26 wife heard that her husband *was* **d**, H4637
2Sa 12:18 afraid to tell him that the child *was* **d**, H4637
2Sa 12:18 How can we now tell him the child *is* **d** H4637
2Sa 12:19 he realized the child *was* **d**. H4637
2Sa 12:19 "*Is* the child **d**?" he asked. H4637
2Sa 12:19 "Yes," they replied, "*he is* **d**." H4637
2Sa 12:21 now that the child *is* **d**, you get up H4637
2Sa 12:23 But now that *he is* **d**, why should I go on H4637
2Sa 13:32 killed all the princes; only Amnon *is* **d**. H4637
2Sa 13:33 the report that all the king's sons *are* **d**. H4637
2Sa 13:33 king's sons are dead. Only Amnon *is* **d**." H4637
2Sa 14: 2 has spent many days grieving for the **d**. H4637
2Sa 14: 5 "I am a widow; my husband *is* **d**. H4637
2Sa 16: 9 "Why should this **d** dog curse my lord the H4637
2Sa 18:20 do so today, because the king's son *is* **d**." H4637
2Sa 19: 6 were alive today and all of us *were* **d**. H4637
2Sa 23:10 returned to Eleazar, but only to **strip the d**. H7320
1Ki 3:20 her breast and put her **d** son by my breast. H4637
1Ki 3:21 I got up to nurse my son—and *he was* **d**! H4637
1Ki 3:22 living one is my son; the **d** *one* is yours." H4637
1Ki 3:22 The **d** *one* is yours; the living one is H4637
1Ki 3:23 'My son is alive and your son *is* **d**,' while H4637
1Ki 3:23 Your son *is* **d** and mine is alive.' H4637
1Ki 11:15 who had gone up to bury the **d**, had struck H2728
1Ki 11:21 the commander of the army *was* also **d**. H4637
1Ki 21:15 He is no longer alive, but **d**." H4637
1Ki 21:16 When Ahab heard that Naboth *was* **d**, he H4637
2Ki 4: 1 "Your servant my husband *is* **d**, and you H4637
2Ki 4:32 there was the boy lying **d** on his couch. H4637
2Ki 8: 5 king how Elisha had restored the **d** to life, H4637
2Ki 11: 1 of Ahaziah saw that her son *was* **d**, H4637
2Ki 14:25 from Lebo Hamath to the **D Sea**, H3542+6858
2Ki 19:35 morning—there were all the **d** bodies! H4637
1Ch 10: 1 and many fell **d** on Mount Gilboa. H2728
1Ch 10: 5 the armor-bearer saw that Saul *was* **d**, H4637
1Ch 10: 8 when the Philistines came to strip the **d** H2728
1Ch 21:14 seventy thousand men of Israel **fell d**. H5877
2Ch 20: 2 from Edom, from the other side of the *D* **Sea**. AIT
2Ch 20:24 they saw only **d bodies** lying on the H7007
2Ch 22:10 of Ahaziah saw that her son *was* **d**, H4637
Job 1:19 It collapsed on them and *they are* **d**, and I H4637
Job 26: 5 "The **d** are in deep anguish, those H8327
Job 26: 6 The **realm of the d** is naked before God H8619
Ps 6: 5 Among the **d** no one proclaims your H4638
Ps 9:17 The wicked go down to the **realm of the d**, H8619
Ps 16:10 not abandon me to the **realm of the d**, H8619
Ps 30: 3 brought me up from the **realm of the d** H8619
Ps 31:12 as though I *were* **d**; H4637+4946+4213
Ps 31:17 be silent in the **realm of the d**. H8619
Ps 49:15 will redeem me from the **realm of the d**; H8619
Ps 55:15 them go down alive to the **realm of the d**, H8619
Ps 79: 2 have left the **d bodies** *of* your servants as H5577
Ps 79: 3 there is no one to bury the **d**. NDT
Ps 86:13 from the depths, from the **realm of the d**. H8619
Ps 88: 5 I am set apart with the **d**, like the slain H4637
Ps 88:10 Do you show your wonders to the **d**? Do H4637
Ps 110: 6 heaping up the **d** and crushing the rulers H1581
Ps 115:17 It is not the **d** who praise the LORD, those H4637
Ps 143: 3 dwell in the darkness like *those* long **d**. H4637
Pr 2:18 death and her paths to the **spirits of the d**. H8327
Pr 9:18 little do they know that the **d** are there, H8327
Pr 9:18 her guests are deep in the **realm of the d**. H8619
Pr 15:24 from going down to the **realm of the d**. H8619
Pr 21:16 comes to rest in the company of the **d**. H8327
Ecc 4: 2 And I declared that the **d**, who had H4637
Ecc 9: 3 they live, and afterward they join the **d**. H4637
Ecc 9: 4 even a live dog is better off than a **d** lion! H4637
Ecc 9: 5 they will die, but the **d** know nothing; they H4637
Ecc 9:10 in the **realm of the d**, where you are H8619
Ecc 10: 1 As **d** flies give perfume a bad smell, so a H4638
Isa 5:25 the **d bodies** are like refuse in the H5577
Isa 8:19 Why consult the **d** on behalf of the living H4637
Isa 14: 9 The **realm of the d** below is all astir to H8619
Isa 14:15 are brought down to the **realm of the d**, H8619
Isa 19: 3 consult the idols and the **spirits of the d**, H356
Isa 26:14 *They are now* **d**, they live no more; their H4637
Isa 26:19 But your **d** will live, LORD; their bodies will H4637
Isa 26:19 morning; the earth will give birth to her **d**. H8327
Isa 28:15 with the **realm of the d** we have made an H8619
Isa 28:18 with the **realm of the d** will not stand. H8619
Isa 34: 3 thrown out, their **d bodies** will stink; the H7007
Isa 37:36 morning—there were all the **d** bodies! H4637
Isa 57: 9 you descended to the *very* **realm of the d**! H8619
Isa 59:10 among the strong, we *are* like the **d**. H4637
Isa 66:24 look on the **d bodies** *of* those who H7007
Jer 7:32 they will bury the **d** in Topheth until there NDT
Jer 9:22 " '**D bodies** will lie like dung on the H5577+132
Jer 16: 4 their **d bodies** will become food for H5577
Jer 16: 6 themselves or shave their head for **the d**. H2157S
Jer 16: 7 to comfort those who mourn for the **d**— H4637
Jer 19:11 They will bury the **d** in Topheth until there is NDT
Jer 22:10 Do not weep for the **d** king or mourn his H4637
Jer 31:40 valley where **d bodies** and ashes are H7007
Jer 33: 5 filled with the **d bodies** *of* the people I H7007
Jer 34:20 Their **d bodies** will become food for the H5577
Jer 41: 9 son of Nethaniah filled it with the **d**. H2728
La 3: 6 me dwell in darkness like *those* long **d**. H4637
Eze 4:14 never eaten **anything found d** or torn by H5577
Eze 6: 5 I will lay the **d bodies** *of* the Israelites in H7007
Eze 11: 6 in this city and filled its streets with the **d**. H2728
Eze 24:17 do not mourn for the **d**. Keep your turban H4637
Eze 31:14 who go down to the **realm of the d**. H1014
Eze 31:15 down to the **realm of the d** I covered the H8619
Eze 31:16 it down to the **realm of the d** to be with H8619
Eze 31:17 had gone down to the **realm of the d**, to H8619
Eze 32:21 From within the **realm of the d** the mighty H8619
Eze 32:27 went down to the **realm of the d** with their H8619
Eze 44:25 defile himself by going near a **d** person; H4637
Eze 44:25 if the **d** person was his father or mother NDT
Eze 44:31 animal, **found d** or torn by wild animals. H5577
Eze 47: 8 into the Arabah, where it enters the *D* **Sea**. AIT
Eze 47:18 to the **D** Sea and as far as Tamar. H7719S
Joel 2:20 will drown in the **D** Sea and its western H7719S
Am 1: 8 till the last of the Philistines *are* **d**," says the H6
Jnh 2: 2 deep in the **realm of the d** I called for H8619
Jnh 4: 9 "And I'm so angry I wish I were **d**." H4638
Na 3: 3 casualties, piles of **d**, bodies without H7007
Hag 2:13 by contact with a **d body** touches one of H5883
Zec 14: 8 half of it east to the *D* **Sea** and half of it west AIT
Mt 2:20 were trying to take the child's life *are* **d**." *G2569*
Mt 8:22 and let the **d** bury their own dead. *G3738*
Mt 8:22 and let the dead bury their own **d**. *G3738*
Mt 9:24 The girl *is* not **d** but asleep." But *G633*
Mt 10: 8 the sick, raise the **d**, cleanse those who *G3738*
Mt 11: 5 the deaf hear, the **d** are raised, and the *G3738*
Mt 14: 2 John the Baptist; he has risen from the **d**! *G3738*
Mt 17: 9 Son of Man has been raised from the **d**." *G3738*
Mt 22:31 But about the resurrection *of* the **d**—have *G3738*
Mt 22:32 He is not the God *of* the **d** but of the *G3738*
Mt 23:27 full of the bones *of* the **d** and everything *G3738*
Mt 27:64 that he has been raised from the **d**. *G3738*
Mt 28: 4 that they shook and became like **d** *men*. *G3738*
Mt 28: 7 has risen from the **d** and is going ahead *G3738*
Mk 5:35 "Your daughter *is* **d**," they said. *G633*
Mk 5:39 The child *is* not **d** but asleep." *G633*
Mk 6:14 the Baptist has been raised from the **d**, *G3738*
Mk 6:16 I beheaded, *has been* **raised from the d**!" *G1586*
Mk 9: 9 until the Son of Man had risen from the **d**. *G3738*
Mk 9:10 discussing what "rising from the **d**" meant *G3738*
Mk 9:26 much like a corpse that many said, "*He's* **d**." *G633*
Mk 12:25 When the **d** rise, they will neither marry *G3738*
Mk 12:26 Now about the **d** rising—have you not *G3738*
Mk 12:27 He is not the God *of* the **d**, but of the *G3738*
Mk 15:44 surprised to hear that *he was* already **d**. *G2569*
Lk 7:12 a **d** *person* was being carried out *G2569*
Lk 7:15 The **d** *man* sat up and began to talk, and *G3738*
Lk 7:22 the deaf hear, the **d** are raised, and the *G3738*
Lk 8:49 "Your daughter *is* **d**," he said. *G2569*
Lk 8:52 "*She is* not **d** but asleep." *G633*
Lk 8:53 laughed at him, knowing that *she was* **d**. *G633*
Lk 9: 7 that John had been raised from the **d**, *G3738*
Lk 9:60 "Let the **d** bury their own dead *G3738*
Lk 9:60 "Let the dead bury their own **d**, but you go *G3738*
Lk 10:30 him and went away, leaving him **half d**. *G2467*
Lk 15:24 this son of mine was **d** and is alive again; *G3738*
Lk 15:32 brother of yours was **d** and is alive again; *G3738*
Lk 16:30 'but if someone from the **d** goes to them *G3738*
Lk 16:31 even if someone rises from the **d**. *G3738*
Lk 17:37 "Where there is a **d body**, there the *G5393*
Lk 20:35 resurrection from the **d** will neither marry *G3738*
Lk 20:37 even Moses showed that the **d** rise, for he *G3738*
Lk 20:38 He is not the God *of* the **d**, but of the *G3738*
Lk 24: 5 do you look for the living among the **d**? *G3738*
Lk 24:46 suffer and rise from the **d** on the third day, *G3738*
Jn 2:22 After he was raised from the **d**, his *G3738*
Jn 5:21 Father raises the **d** and gives them life, *G3738*
Jn 5:25 now come when the **d** will hear the voice *G3738*
Jn 11:14 So then he told them plainly, "Lazarus *is* **d**, *G633*
Jn 11:39 the sister *of* the **d** *man*, "by this time *G5462*
Jn 11:44 The **d** *man* came out, his hands and feet *G2569*
Jn 12: 1 whom Jesus had raised from the **d**. *G3738*
Jn 12: 9 Lazarus, whom he had raised from the **d**. *G3738*
Jn 12:17 raised him from the **d** continued to spread *G3738*
Jn 19:33 to Jesus and found *that* he was already **d**, *G2569*
Jn 20: 9 Scripture that Jesus had to rise from the **d**.) *G3738*
Jn 21:14 disciples after he was raised from the **d**. *G3738*
Ac 2:24 But God **raised** him **from the d**, freeing him *G482*
Ac 2:27 will not abandon me to the **realm of the d**, *G87*
Ac 2:31 was not abandoned to the **realm of the d**, *G87*
Ac 3:15 but God raised him from the **d**. *G3738*
Ac 4: 2 in Jesus the resurrection of the **d**. *G3738*
Ac 4:10 crucified but whom God raised from the **d**, *G3738*
Ac 5:10 finding her **d**, carried her out and *G3738*
Ac 5:30 of our ancestors **raised** Jesus **from the d**— *G1586*
Ac 9:40 Turning toward the **d** *woman*, he said *G5393*
Ac 10:40 God **raised** him **from the d** on the third *G1586*
Ac 10:41 drank with him after he rose from the **d**. *G3738*
Ac 10:42 as judge of the living and the **d**. *G3738*
Ac 13:30 But God raised him from the **d**, *G3738*
Ac 13:34 raised him from the **d** so that he will *G3738*
Ac 13:37 whom God **raised from the d** did not see *G1586*
Ac 14:19 him outside the city, thinking he *was* **d**. *G2569*
Ac 17: 3 Messiah had to suffer and rise from the **d**. *G3738*
Ac 17:31 this to everyone by raising him from the **d**." *G3738*
Ac 17:32 they heard about the resurrection *of* the **d**, *G3738*
Ac 20: 9 from the third story and was picked up **d**. *G3738*
Ac 23: 6 of the hope of the resurrection *of* the **d**." *G3738*
Ac 24:21 the resurrection *of* the **d** that I am on trial *G3738*
Ac 25:19 about a **d** *man* named Jesus who *G2569*
Ac 26: 8 it incredible that God raises the **d**? *G3738*
Ac 26:23 as the first to rise from the **d**, would bring *G3738*
Ac 28: 6 him to swell up or suddenly fall **d**; *G3738*
Ro 1: 4 in power by his resurrection *from* the **d**: *G3738*
Ro 4:17 God who gives life *to* the **d** and calls into *G3738*
Ro 4:19 the fact that his body *was* **as good as d**— *G3739*
Ro 4:19 and that Sarah's womb was also **d**. *G3740*
Ro 4:24 him who raised Jesus our Lord from the **d**. *G3738*
Ro 6: 4 was raised from the **d** through the glory of *G3738*
Ro 6: 9 that since Christ was raised from the **d**, *G3738*
Ro 6:11 count yourselves **d** to sin but alive to God *G3738*
Ro 7: 4 to him who was raised from the **d**, in *G3738*
Ro 7: 8 For apart from the law, sin was **d**. *G3738*
Ro 8:11 raised Jesus from the **d** is living in you, *G3738*
Ro 8:11 Christ from the **d** will also give life to *G3738*
Ro 10: 7 that is, to bring Christ up from the **d**). *G3738*
Ro 10: 9 your heart that God raised him from the **d**, *G3738*
Ro 11:15 their acceptance be but life from the **d**? *G3738*
Ro 14: 9 be the Lord *of* both the **d** and the living. *G3738*
1Co 6:14 his power God **raised** the Lord **from the d**, *G1586*
1Co 15:12 that Christ has been raised from the **d**, *G3738*
1Co 15:12 say that there is no resurrection *of* the **d**? *G3738*
1Co 15:13 If there is no resurrection *of* the **d**, then not *G3738*
1Co 15:15 God that *he* **raised** Christ **from the d**. *G1586*
1Co 15:15 raise him if in fact the **d** are not raised. *G3738*
1Co 15:16 For if the **d** are not raised, then Christ has *G3738*
1Co 15:20 Christ has indeed been raised from the **d**, *G3738*
1Co 15:21 the resurrection *of* the **d** comes also *G3738*
1Co 15:29 will those do who are baptized for the **d**? *G3738*
1Co 15:29 If the **d** are not raised at all, why are *G3738*
1Co 15:32 If the **d** are not raised, "Let us eat and *G3738*
1Co 15:35 someone will ask, "How are the **d** raised? *G3738*
1Co 15:42 So will it be with the resurrection *of* the **d** *G3738*
1Co 15:52 the **d** will be raised imperishable *G3738*
2Co 1: 9 ourselves but on God, who raises the **d**. *G3738*
2Co 4:14 *one who* **raised** the Lord Jesus **from the d** *G1586*
Gal 1: 1 the Father, who raised him from the **d**— *G3738*
Eph 1:20 Christ from the **d** and seated him at his *G3738*
Eph 2: 1 you were **d** in your transgressions and sins *G3738*
Eph 2: 5 even when we were **d** in transgressions— *G3738*
Eph 5:14 rise from the **d**, and Christ will shine *G3738*
Php 3:11 attaining to the resurrection from the **d**. *G3738*
Col 1:18 the firstborn from *among* the **d**, *G3738*
Col 2:12 who raised him from the **d**. *G3738*
Col 2:13 When you were **d** in your sins and in the *G3738*
1Th 1:10 whom he raised from the **d**—Jesus, *G3738*
1Th 4:16 and the **d** in Christ will rise first. *G3738*
1Ti 5: 6 lives for pleasure *is* **d** even while she lives *G2569*
2Ti 2: 8 raised from the **d**, descended from David. *G3738*
2Ti 4: 1 who will judge the living and the **d**, and *G3738*
Heb 6: 2 the resurrection *of* the **d**, and eternal *G3738*
Heb 11: 4 faith Abel still speaks, *even though he is* **d**. *G633*
Heb 11:12 one man, and *he as good as* **d**, came *G3739*
Heb 11:19 reasoned that God could even raise the **d**, *G3738*
Heb 11:35 Women received back their **d**, raised to *G3738*
Heb 13:20 brought back from the **d** our Lord Jesus, *G3738*
Jas 2:17 if it is not accompanied by action, is **d**. *G3738*
Jas 2:26 As the body without the spirit is **d**, so faith *G3738*
Jas 2:26 spirit is dead, so faith without deeds is **d**. *G3738*
1Pe 1: 3 the resurrection of Jesus Christ from the **d**, *G3738*
1Pe 1:21 raised him from the **d** and glorified him, *G3738*
1Pe 4: 5 is ready to judge the living and the **d**. *G3738*
1Pe 4: 6 preached even *to those who are now* **d**, *G3738*
Jude 12 without fruit and uprooted—twice **d**. *G633*
Rev 1: 5 the firstborn *from* the **d**, and the ruler of *G3738*
Rev 1:17 I saw him, I fell at his feet as though **d**. *G3738*
Rev 1:18 am the Living One; I was **d**, and now look, *G3738*
Rev 2:23 *I will* **strike** her children **d** *G650+1877+2505*
Rev 3: 1 a reputation of being alive, but you are **d**. *G3738*
Rev 11:18 The time has come for judging the **d**, and *G3738*
Rev 14:13 Blessed are the **d** who die in the Lord *G3738*
Rev 16: 3 turned into blood like that *of* a **d** *person*, *G3738*
Rev 20: 5 The rest *of* the **d** did not come to life until *G3738*
Rev 20:12 And I saw the **d**, great and small, standing *G3738*
Rev 20:12 The **d** were judged according to what they *G3738*
Rev 20:13 The sea gave up the **d** that were in it, and *G3738*
Rev 20:13 Hades gave up the **d** that were in them, *G3738*

DEADLY (15) [DIE]

Ex 10:17 God to take this **d plague** away from me." H4638

D

Dt 32:24 consuming pestilence and **d** plague; I will H5321
Dt 32:33 venom of serpents, the **d** poison of cobras. H425
Ps 7:13 He has prepared his **d** weapons; he H4638
Ps 64: 3 swords and aim cruel words like *d* **arrows**. AIT
Ps 91: 3 fowler's snare and from the **d** pestilence. H2095
Ps 144:10 his servant David. From the **d** sword H8273
Pr 21: 6 tongue is a fleeting vapor and a **d** snare. H4638
Jer 9: 8 Their tongue is a **d** arrow; it speaks H8821
Jer 16: 4 "They will die of **d** diseases. They will not H4926
Eze 5:16 shoot at you with my **d** and destructive H8273
Eze 9: 2 each with a **d** weapon in his hand. H5150
Mk 16:18 when they drink **d poison**, it will not G2503
2Co 1:10 He has delivered us from such a **d peril** G2505
Jas 3: 8 It is a restless evil, full of **d** poison. G2504

D

DEAF (19)

Ex 4:11 Who makes them **d** or mute? Who gives H3094
Lev 19:14 " 'Do not curse the **d** or put a stumbling H3094
Dt 1:45 weeping and **turned a d ear** to you. H4202+263
Ps 28: 1 are my Rock, *do* not **turn a d ear** to me. H3087
Ps 38:13 I am like the **d**, who cannot hear, like the H3094
Ps 39:12 cry for help; *do* not *be* **d** to my weeping. H3087
Ps 83: 1 *do* not **turn a d ear**, do not stand H3087
Pr 28: 9 anyone turns a **d** ear *to* my H4946+9048
Isa 29:18 In that day the **d** will hear the words of H3094
Isa 35: 5 opened and the ears of the **d** unstopped. H3094
Isa 42:18 you **d**; look, you blind, and see! H3094
Isa 42:19 servant, and **d** like the messenger I send? H3094
Isa 43: 8 are blind, who have ears but are **d**. H3094
Mic 7:16 mouths and their ears *will become* **d**. H3087
Mt 11: 5 are cleansed, the **d** hear, the dead are G3273
Mk 7:32 to him a **man who was d** and could G3273
Mk 7:37 "He even makes the **d** hear and the mute G3273
Mk 9:25 "You **d** and mute spirit," he said, "I G3273
Lk 7:22 are cleansed, the **d** hear, the dead are G3273

DEAL (51) [DEALER, DEALING, DEALINGS, DEALS, DEALT]

Ge 21:23 God that *you will* not **d falsely** with me H9213
Ex 1:10 *we must* **d shrewdly** with them or they will H2681
Ex 8:22 that day *I will* **d differently** *with* the land H7111
Ex 22:25 do not treat it like a **business d**; charge no H5957
Ru 1:17 *May* the LORD **d** with me, be it ever so H6913
1Sa 3:17 *May* God **d** with you, be it ever so severely H6913
1Sa 14:44 Saul said, "*May* God **d** with me, be it ever H6913
1Sa 20:13 harm you, *may* the LORD **d** with Jonathan H6913
1Sa 24: 4 into your hands *for you to* **d** with as you H6913
1Sa 25:22 *May* God **d** with David, be it ever so H6913
2Sa 3: 9 *May* God **d** with Abner, be it ever so H6913
2Sa 3:22 brought with them a **great d** of plunder. H8041
2Sa 3:35 "*May* God **d** with me, be it ever so H6913
2Sa 19:13 *May* God **d** with me, be it ever so severely, H6913
1Ki 2: 6 **D with** him according to your wisdom, but H6913
1Ki 2:23 "*May* God **d** with me, be it ever so H6913
1Ki 8:39 **d** with everyone according to all they do H5989
1Ki 19: 2 "*May* the gods **d with** me, be it H6913
1Ki 20:10 "*May* the gods **d** with me, be it ever so H6913
2Ki 6:31 He said, "*May* God **d** with me, be it ever H6913
2Ch 6:30 **d** with everyone according to all they H5989
2Ch 12:15 of Iddo the seer *that* **d with genealogies**? H3509
2Ch 28: 8 They also took a **great d** of plunder, which H8041
Ne 5: 7 together a large meeting to **d with** them H6584
Ne 9:24 the land, to **d** with them as they pleased. H6913
Job 42: 8 his prayer and not **d** with you according to H6913
Ps 119:124 **D** with your servant according to your H6913
Isa 10:11 *shall I* not **d** with Jerusalem and her H6913
Isa 23:17 of seventy years, the LORD *will* **d** *with* Tyre. H7212
Jer 2: 8 *Those who* **d** with the law did not know H9530
Jer 7: 5 your actions and **d** with each other H6913+6913
Jer 18:23 **d** with them in the time of your anger. H6913
Jer 24: 8 'so *will I* **d** with Zedekiah king of Judah H5989
Jer 32: 5 where he will remain until I **d** *with* him H7212
La 1:22 **d** with them as you have dealt with me H6618
Eze 7:27 *I will* **d with** them according to their H6913
Eze 8:18 Therefore I *will* **d with** them in anger; I will H6913
Eze 16:59 *I will* **d with** you as you deserve, because H6913
Eze 20:44 when I **d** with you for my name's sake H6913
Eze 22:14 hands be strong in the day I **d** with you? H6913
Eze 23:25 and *they will* **d** with you in fury. H6913
Eze 23:29 *They will* **d** with you in hatred and take H6913
Eze 25:14 and *they will* **d** with Edom in accordance H6913
Eze 31:11 *for him to* **d** with according to its H6913+6913
Zep 3:19 At that time I *will* **d** with all who H6913
Zec 8:11 But now I will not **d** with the remnant of this NDT
Mt 27:19 I have suffered a **great d** today in a dream G4498
Mk 5:26 She had suffered a **great d** under the care G4498
Ac 16:16 She earned a **great d** of money for her G4498
2Ti 4:14 metalworker did me a **great d** *of* harm. G4498
Heb 5: 2 He is able *to* **d gently with** those who are G3584

DEALER (1) [DEAL]

Ac 16:14 Thyatira named Lydia, a **d in purple cloth**. G4527

DEALING (4) [DEAL]

Ezr 10:17 they finished **d with** all the men who H928
Lk 16: 8 are more shrewd **in d with** their own kind G1650
2Co 13: 3 He is not weak **in d with** you, but is G1650
2Co 13: 4 we will live with him **in** our **d with** you. G1650

DEALINGS (2) [DEAL]

1Sa 25: 3 husband was surly and mean in his **d**— H5095
2Ki 22: 7 because they *are* honest in *their* **d**." H6913

DEALS (3) [DEAL]

Dt 25:16 these things, anyone *who* **d** dishonestly. H6913
Jer 5: 1 one person *who* **d** honestly and seeks H6913
1Th 2:11 of you as a father **d** with his own children, NDT

DEALT (11) [DEAL]

Ex 10: 2 grandchildren how *I* **d harshly** with the H6618
1Sa 6: 6 When Israel's god **d harshly** with them H6618
1Sa 6:19 of the heavy blow the LORD *had* **d** them. H5782
2Sa 22:21 "The LORD *has* **d with** me according to my H1694
Ps 18:20 The LORD *has* **d with** me according to my H1694
Isa 10:11 her images as *I* **d** with Samaria and H6913
Isa 47:15 these *you have* **d with** and labored with H3333
La 1:22 with them as *you have* **d** with me because H6618
Eze 39:24 *I* **d** with them according to their H6913
Ac 7:19 He **d treacherously** with our people and G2947
1Th 2:11 For you know that we **d** with each of you as a NDT

DEAR (61) [DEARER, DEARLY]

2Sa 1:26 my brother; *you were* very **d** to me. H5838
Ps 102:14 For her stones *are* **d** to your servants; her H8354
Jer 31:20 Is not Ephraim my **d** son, the child in H3692
Ac 15:25 to you with our **d friends** Barnabas and Paul G28
Ro 12:19 take revenge, my **d friends**, but leave room G28
Ro 16: 5 Greet my **d friend** Epenetus, who was the G28
Ro 16: 8 Greet Ampliatus, my **d friend** in the Lord. G28
Ro 16: 9 co-worker in Christ, and my **d friend** Stachys. G28
Ro 16:12 Greet my **d friend** Persis, another woman G28
1Co 4:14 shame you but to warn you as my **d** children. G28
1Co 10:14 Therefore, my **d friends**, flee from idolatry. G28
1Co 15:58 Therefore, my **d** brothers and sisters, stand G28
2Co 7: 1 have these promises, **d friends**, let us purify G28
2Co 12:19 everything we do, **d friends**, is for your G28
Gal 4:19 My *d* **children**, for whom I am again in the AIT
Eph 6:21 the **d** brother and faithful servant in the Lord G28
Php 2:12 Therefore, my **d friends**, as you have always G28
Php 4: 1 stand firm in the Lord in this way, **d friends**! G28
Col 1: 7 it from Epaphras, our **d** fellow servant, who G28
Col 4: 7 He is a **d** brother, a faithful minister and G28
Col 4: 9 our faithful and **d** brother, who is one of you G28
Col 4:14 Our **d friend** Luke, the doctor, and Demas G28
1Ti 6: 2 their masters are **d** to them as fellow G28
2Ti 1: 2 To Timothy, my **d** son: Grace, mercy and G28
Phm 1 To Philemon our **d friend** and fellow worker G28
Phm 16 but better than a slave, as a **d** brother. G28
Phm 16 He is very **d** to me but even dearer to you NDT
Heb 6: 9 speak like this, **d friends**, we are convinced G28
Jas 1:16 Don't be deceived, my **d** brothers and sisters. G28
Jas 1:19 My **d** brothers and sisters, take note of this G28
Jas 2: 5 my **d** brothers and sisters: Has not G28
1Pe 2:11 **D friends**, I urge you, as foreigners and G28
1Pe 4:12 *D* **friends**, do not be surprised at the fiery AIT
2Pe 3: 1 **D friends**, this is now my second letter to you G28
2Pe 3: 8 this one thing, **d friends**: With the Lord a day G28
2Pe 3:14 So then, **d friends**, since you are looking G28
2Pe 3:15 just as our **d** brother Paul also wrote you G28
2Pe 3:17 Therefore, **d friends**, since you have been G28
1Jn 2: 1 My **d children**, I write this to you so that G5448
1Jn 2: 7 **D friends**, I am not writing you a new G28
1Jn 2:12 writing to you, **d children**, because your G5448
1Jn 2:14 I write to you, **d children**, because you G4086
1Jn 2:18 **D children**, this is the last hour; and as G4086
1Jn 2:28 And now, **d children**, continue in him, so G5448
1Jn 3: 2 **D friends**, now we are children of God, and G28
1Jn 3: 7 **D children**, do not let anyone lead you G5448
1Jn 3:18 **D children**, let us not love with words or G5448
1Jn 3:21 **D friends**, if our hearts do not condemn us G28
1Jn 4: 1 **D friends**, do not believe every spirit, but test G28
1Jn 4: 4 **d children**, are from God and have G5448
1Jn 4: 7 **D friends**, let us love one another, for love G28
1Jn 4:11 **D friends**, since God so loved us, we also G28
1Jn 5:21 **D children**, keep yourselves from idols. G5448
2Jn 5 And now, **d lady**, I am not writing you a G3257
3Jn 1 The elder, To my **d friend** Gaius, whom I G28
3Jn 2 **D friend**, I pray that you may enjoy good G28
3Jn 5 **D friend**, you are faithful in what you are G28
3Jn 11 **D friend**, do not imitate what is evil but what G28
Jude 3 **D friends**, although I was very eager to write G28
Jude 17 **d friends**, remember what the apostles G28
Jude 20 **d friends**, by building yourselves up G28

DEARER (1) [DEAR]

Phm 16 He is very dear to me but even **d** to you NDT

DEARLY (3) [DEAR]

Hos 4:18 their rulers **d** love shameful ways. H170
Eph 5: 1 example, therefore, as **d loved** children G28
Col 3:12 holy and **d loved**, clothe yourselves G26

DEARTH (KJV) DROUGHT, FAMINE

DEATH (457) [DIE]

Ge 24:67 Isaac was comforted **after** his mother's *d*. AIT
Ge 25:11 After Abraham's **d**, God blessed his son H4638
Ge 26:11 his wife *shall* **surely be put to d**." H4637+4637
Ge 27: 2 old man and don't know the day of my **d**. H4638
Ge 38: 7 the LORD's sight; so the LORD **put** him **to d**. H4637
Ge 38:10 so the LORD **put** him **to d** also. H4637
Ge 38:24 "Bring her out and *have her* **burned to d**!" H8596
Ge 42:37 "*You may* **put** both of my sons **to d** if I do H4637
Ex 16: 3 desert to starve this entire assembly *to* **d**." H4637
Ex 19:12 the mountain *is to* **be put to d**. H4637+4637
Ex 21:12 with a fatal blow *is to be* **put to d**. H4637+4637
Ex 21:14 is to be taken from my altar and **put to d**. H4637
Ex 21:15 father or mother *is to be* **put to d**. H4637+4637
Ex 21:16 kidnaps someone *is to be* **put to d**, H4637+4637
Ex 21:17 father or mother *is to be* **put to d**. H4637+4637
Ex 21:28 "If a bull gores a man or woman *to* **d**, the H4637
Ex 21:28 the bull *is to* **be stoned to d**, and H6232+6232
Ex 21:29 its owner also *is to be* **put to d**. H4637
Ex 21:32 and the bull *is to* **be stoned to d**. H6232
Ex 22:19 with an animal *is to be* **put to d**. H4637+4637
Ex 23: 7 *do* not **put** an innocent or honest person **to d** H2222
Ex 31:14 who desecrates it *is to be* **put to d**; H4637+4637
Ex 31:15 the Sabbath day *is to be* **put to d**. H4637+4637
Ex 35: 2 does any work on it *is to be* **put to d**. H4637
Lev 16: 1 to Moses after the **d** *of* the two sons of H4638
Lev 19:20 Yet *they are* not **to be put to d**, because H4637
Lev 20: 2 children to Molek *is to be* **put to d**. H4637+4637
Lev 20: 4 to Molek and if *they* fail to **put him to d**, H4637
Lev 20: 9 father or mother *is to* **be put to d**. H4637+4637
Lev 20:10 the adulteress *are to* **be put to d**. H4637+4637
Lev 20:11 and the woman *are to* **be put to d**; H4637+4637
Lev 20:12 both of them *are to* **be put to d**. H4637+4637
Lev 20:13 *They are to* **be put to d**; their blood H4637+4637
Lev 20:15 animal, *he is to* **be put to d**, and H4637+4637
Lev 20:16 *They are to* **be put to d**; their blood H4637+4637
Lev 20:27 among you **must be put to d**. H4637+4637
Lev 24:16 name of the LORD *is to* **be put to d**. H4637+4637
Lev 24:16 the Name *they are to* **be put to d**. H4637
Lev 24:17 of a human being *is to* **be put to d**. H4637+4637
Lev 24:21 kills a human being *is to* **be put to d**. H4637
Lev 27:29 ransomed; *they are to* **be put to d**. H4637+4637
Nu 1:51 else who approaches it *is to* **be put to d**. H4637
Nu 3:10 the sanctuary *is to* **be put to d**. H4637
Nu 3:38 the sanctuary *was to* **be put to d**. H4637
Nu 14:15 If *you* **put** all these people **to d**, leaving H4637
Nu 15:36 outside the camp and stoned him *to* **d**, H4637
Nu 16:29 men die a natural **d** and suffer the fate of H4638
Nu 16:39 by those *who had* **been burned to d**, H8596
Nu 18: 7 near the sanctuary *is to* **be put to d**." H4637
Nu 19:16 *someone who has* **died a natural d**, H4637
Nu 19:18 anyone *who has* **died a natural d**. H4637
Nu 23:10 Let me die the **d** *of* the righteous, and H4638
Nu 25: 5 "Each of *you must* **put to d** those of your H2222
Nu 25:15 woman who **was put to d** was Kozbi H5782
Nu 35:16 the murderer **is to be put to d**. H4637+4637
Nu 35:17 the murderer **is to be put to d**. H4637+4637
Nu 35:18 the murderer **is to be put to d**. H4637+4637
Nu 35:19 of blood *shall* **put** the murderer **to d**; H4637
Nu 35:19 the avenger *shall* **put** the murderer **to d**. H4637
Nu 35:21 that person **is to be put to d**; that H4637+4637
Nu 35:21 of blood *shall* **put** the murderer **to d** when H4637
Nu 35:25 stay there until the **d** *of* the high priest, H4637
Nu 35:28 city of refuge until the **d** *of* the high priest; H4638
Nu 35:28 only after the **d** *of* the high priest may H4638
Nu 35:30 a person *is to be* **put to d** as a murderer H8357
Nu 35:30 But no one *is to be* **put to d** on the H4637
Nu 35:31 *They are to* **be put to d**. H4637+4637
Nu 35:32 own land before the **d** *of* the high priest. H4638
Dt 9:28 them out to **put** them **to d** in the H4637
Dt 13: 5 dreamer *must* **be put to d** for inciting H4637
Dt 13: 9 *You* **must certainly put** them **to d** H2222+2222
Dt 13: 9 must be the first in **putting** them **to d**, H4637
Dt 13:10 Stone them *to* **d**, because they tried to turn H4637
Dt 17: 5 your city gate and stone that person *to* **d**. H4637
Dt 17: 6 three witnesses a person *is to* **be put to d**, H4637
Dt 17: 6 no *one is to* **be put to d** on the H4637
Dt 17: 7 be the first in **putting** that person **to d**, H4637
Dt 17:12 to the LORD your God *is to* **be put to d**. H4637
Dt 18:20 the name of other gods, *is to* **be put to d**." H4637
Dt 19: 6 him even though he is not deserving of **d**, H4638
Dt 21:21 the men of his town are to stone him *to* **d**. H4637
Dt 21:22 capital offense is **put to d** and their body H4637
Dt 22:21 the men of her town shall stone her *to* **d**. H4637
Dt 22:24 gate of that town and stone them *to* **d**— H4637
Dt 22:26 she has committed no sin deserving **d**. H4638
Dt 24:16 Parents *are* not **to be put to d** for their H4637
Dt 24:16 children **put to d** for their parents H4637
Dt 30:15 life and prosperity, **d** and destruction. H4638
Dt 30:19 you that I have set before you life and **d**, H4638
Dt 31:14 to Moses, "Now the day of your **d** is near. H4637
Dt 31:29 I know that after my **d** you are sure to H4638
Dt 32:39 **I put to d** and I bring to life, I have H4637
Dt 33: 1 pronounced on the Israelites before his **d**. H4638
Jos 1: 1 After the **d** *of* Moses the servant of the H4638
Jos 1:18 you may command them, *will* **be put to d**. H4637
Jos 2:13 and that you will save us from **d**. H4638
Jos 10:26 **put** the kings **to d** and H5782+2256+4637
Jos 11:17 kings and **put** them **to d**. H5782+2256+4637
Jos 20: 6 until the **d** *of* the high priest who H4638
Jdg 1: 1 After the **d** *of* Joshua, the Israelites asked H4638
Jdg 6:31 him *shall* **be put to d** by morning! H4637
Jdg 13: 7 God from the womb until the day of his **d**. H4638
Jdg 14:15 *we will* **burn** you and your father's household **to d** H8596+928+2021+836
Jdg 15: 6 **burned** her and her father **to d** H8596+928+2021+836
Jdg 16:16 day after day until he was sick to **d** of it. H4637
Jdg 20:13 so that *we may* **put** them **to d** and purge H4637
Jdg 21: 5 LORD at Mizpah *was to* **be put to d**. H4637+4637
Ru 1:17 severely, if even **d** separates you and me." H4638
Ru 2:11 since the **d** *of* your husband— H4638
1Sa 2: 6 "The LORD **brings d** and makes alive; he H4637

1Sa 2:25 it was the LORD's will to **put** them **to d**. H4637
1Sa 5:11 For **d** had filled the city with panic; God's H4638
1Sa 6:19 **putting** seventy of them **to d** because they H5782
1Sa 11:12 over to us so that *we may* **put** them **to d**." H4637
1Sa 11:13 "No one *will* **be put to d** today, for H4637
1Sa 14:45 Jonathan, and *he was* not **put to d**. H4637
1Sa 15: 3 not spare them; **put to d** men and women H4637
1Sa 15:32 "Surely the bitterness of **d** is past. H4638
1Sa 15:33 And Samuel **put** Agag **to d** before the H9119
1Sa 19: 6 the LORD lives, David *will* not **be put to d**." H4637
1Sa 20: 3 there is only a step between me and **d**." H4638
1Sa 20:32 "Why *should he* **be put to d**? What has he H4637
1Sa 22:22 responsible for the **d** *of* your whole family. H5883
1Sa 28: 9 set a trap for my life to **bring about** my **d**?" H4637
2Sa 1: 1 After the **d** *of* Saul, David returned from H4638
2Sa 1: 9 I'm in the **throes of d**, but I'm still H8688
2Sa 1:23 admired, and in **d** they were not parted. H4638
2Sa 4:10 I seized him and **put** him **to d** in Ziklag. H2222
2Sa 6:23 Saul had no children to the day of her **d**. H4638
2Sa 8: 2 Every two lengths of them *were* **put to d** H4637
2Sa 13:39 he was consoled concerning Amnon's **d**. H4637
2Sa 14: 7 so that *we may* **put** him **to d** for the life of H4637
2Sa 14:32 guilty of anything, *let him* **put** me **to d**." H4637
2Sa 15:21 whether it means life or **d**, there will your H4638
2Sa 17: 3 The **d** of the man you seek will mean the NDT
2Sa 19:21 "Shouldn't Shimei **be put to d** for this? H4637
2Sa 19:22 *Should* anyone **be put to d** in Israel today? H4637
2Sa 19:28 deserved nothing but **d** from my lord the H4638
2Sa 20: 3 kept in confinement till the day of their **d**, H4637
2Sa 21: 1 it is because *he* **put** the Gibeonites **to d**." H4637
2Sa 21: 4 have the right to **put** anyone in Israel *to* **d**." H4637
2Sa 21: 9 they **were put to d** during the first days of H4637
2Sa 22: 5 The waves of **d** swirled about me; the H4638
2Sa 22: 6 the snares of **d** confronted me. H4638
1Ki 1:51 that *he will* not **put** his servant **to d** with H4637
1Ki 2: 8 '*I will* not **put** you **to d** by the sword H4637
1Ki 2:24 Adonijah *shall* **be put to d** today! H4637
1Ki 2:26 but *I will* not **put** you **to d** now H4637
1Ki 3:11 have asked for the **d** *of* your enemies but H5883
1Ki 11:40 and stayed there until Solomon's **d**. H4638
1Ki 12:18 but all Israel stoned him *to* **d**. H4637
1Ki 18: 9 your servant over to Ahab to *be* **put to d**? H4637
1Ki 19:10 and **put** your prophets **to d** with the sword. H2222
1Ki 19:14 and **put** your prophets **to d** with the sword. H2222
1Ki 19:17 Jehu *will* **put to d** any who escape the H4637
1Ki 19:17 Elisha *will* **put to d** any who escape H4637
1Ki 21:10 Then take him out and stone him *to* **d**." H4637
1Ki 21:13 him outside the city and stoned him *to* **d**. H4637
1Ki 21:14 "Naboth has been stoned *to* **d**." H4637
1Ki 21:15 heard that Naboth had been stoned *to* **d**, H4637
1Ki 22:20 Ramoth Gilead and **going to** *his* **d** there? H5877
2Ki 1: 1 After Ahab's **d**, Moab rebelled against H4638
2Ki 2:21 again will it cause **d** or make the land H4638
2Ki 4:40 "Man of God, there is **d** in the pot! H4638
2Ki 11: 8 approaches your ranks *is to* **be put to d**. H4637
2Ki 11:15 "*She must* not **be put to d** in the temple H4637
2Ki 11:16 grounds, and there *she* **was put to d**. H4637
2Ki 14: 6 *he did* not **put** the children of the assassins **to d** H4637
2Ki 14: 6 "Parents *are* not *to* **be put to d** for their H4637
2Ki 14: 6 children **put to d** for their parents H4637
2Ki 14:17 fifteen years after the **d** *of* Jehoash son of H4638
2Ki 16: 9 its inhabitants to Kir and **put** Rezin **to d**. H4637
2Ki 18:32 Choose life and not **d**! "Do not listen to H4637
2Ki 19:35 LORD went out and **put to d** a hundred H5782
2Ki 20: 1 became ill and was at the point of **d**. H4637
1Ch 2: 3 the LORD's sight; so the LORD **put** him **to d**. H4637
1Ch 10:14 So the LORD **put** him **to d** and turned the H4637
1Ch 22: 5 made extensive preparations before his **d**. H4638
2Ch 1:11 nor for the **d** *of* your enemies, and H5883
2Ch 10:18 but the Israelites stoned him *to* **d**. H4637
2Ch 15:13 of Israel, *were to* **be put to d**, whether H4637
2Ch 18:19 Ramoth Gilead and **going to** *his* **d** there? H5877
2Ch 22: 4 after his father's **d** they became his H4638
2Ch 22: 9 He was brought to Jehu and **put to d** H4637
2Ch 23: 7 who enters the temple *is to* **be put to d**. H4637
2Ch 23:14 "*Do* not **put** her **to d** *at* the temple of the H4637
2Ch 23:15 grounds, and there *they* **put** her **to d**. H4637
2Ch 24:17 After the **d** *of* Jehoiada, the officials of H4638
2Ch 24:21 the king *they* **stoned** him **to d** in the H8083+74
2Ch 25: 4 Yet *he did* not **put** their children **to d**, but H4637
2Ch 25: 4 "Parents *shall* not *be* **put** *to* **d** for their H4637
2Ch 25: 4 children *be put to* **d** for their parents H4637
2Ch 25:25 fifteen years after the **d** *of* Jehoash son of H4638
2Ch 32:24 became ill and was at the point of **d**. H4637
Ezr 7:26 the king must surely be punished by **d**, A10409
Est 4:11 that they *be* **put to d** unless the king H4637
Est 9:15 and *they* **put to d** in Susa three hundred H2222
Job 3:21 those who long for **d** that does not come, H4638
Job 5:20 In famine he will deliver you from **d**, and H4638
Job 7:15 so that I prefer strangling and **d**, rather H4638
Job 9:23 When a scourge **brings** sudden **d**, he H4637
Job 17:16 Will it go down to the gates of **d**? Will we H8619
Job 28:22 Destruction and **D** say, "Only a rumor of it H4638
Job 30:23 I know you will bring me down to **d**, to the H4638
Job 33:22 and their life to the **messengers of d**. H4637
Job 38:17 Have the gates of **d** been shown to you H4638
Ps 9: T To the tune of "The **D** of the Son." A H4637
Ps 9:13 mercy and lift me up from the gates of **d**, H4638
Ps 13: 3 Give light to my eyes, or I will sleep in **d**, H4638
Ps 18: 4 The cords of **d** entangled me; the torrents H4638
Ps 18: 5 the snares of **d** confronted me. H4638
Ps 22:15 of my mouth; you lay me in the dust of **d**. H4638
Ps 33:19 deliver them from **d** and keep them alive H4638
Ps 37:32 righteous, intent on **putting** them **to d**; H4637
Ps 44:22 Yet for your sake *we* **face d** all day long H2222
Ps 49:14 destined to die; **d** will be their shepherd H4638
Ps 55: 4 the terrors of **d** have fallen on me. H4638
Ps 55:15 Let **d** take my enemies by surprise; let H4638
Ps 56:13 delivered me from **d** and my feet from H4638
Ps 68:20 the Sovereign LORD comes escape from **d**. H4638
Ps 72:13 the needy and save the needy from **d**. H5883
Ps 78:31 *he* **put to d** the sturdiest among them H2222
Ps 78:50 not spare them from **d** but gave them over H4638
Ps 88: 3 with troubles and my life draws near to **d**. H8619
Ps 88:15 youth I have suffered and *been* **close to d**; H1588
Ps 89:48 Who can live and not see **d**, or who can H4638
Ps 90: 5 sweep people away in the **sleep of d**— H9104
Ps 94:17 soon have dwelt in the **silence of d**. H1872
Ps 94:21 righteous and condemn the innocent to **d**. H1947
Ps 102:20 release those condemned to **d**. H9456
Ps 107:18 all food and drew near the gates of **d**. H4638
Ps 109:16 hounded to **d** the poor and the needy H4637
Ps 116: 3 The cords of **d** entangled me, the anguish H4638
Ps 116: 8 have delivered me from **d**, my eyes from H4638
Ps 116:15 of the LORD is the **d** of his faithful servants H4638
Ps 118:18 he has not given me over to **d**. H4638
Ps 141: 8 I take refuge—*do* not **give** me **over to d**. H6867
Pr 2:18 house leads down to **d** and her paths to H4638
Pr 5: 5 Her feet go down to **d**; her steps lead H4638
Pr 7:27 leading down to the chambers of **d**. H4638
Pr 8:36 harm themselves; all who hate me love **d**." H4638
Pr 10: 2 but righteousness delivers from **d**. H4638
Pr 10:16 the earnings of the wicked are **sin and d**. H2633
Pr 11: 4 but righteousness delivers from **d**. H4638
Pr 11:19 but whoever pursues evil finds **d**. H4638
Pr 13:14 turning a person from the snares of **d**. H4638
Pr 14:12 to be right, but in the end it leads to **d**. H4638
Pr 14:27 turning a person from the snares of **d**. H4638
Pr 14:32 even in **d** the righteous seek refuge in H4638
Pr 15:11 **D** and Destruction lie open before the H8619
Pr 16:14 A king's wrath is a messenger of **d**, but H4638
Pr 16:25 to be right, but in the end it leads to **d**. H4638
Pr 17:11 the messenger of **d** will be sent against H426
Pr 18:21 The tongue has the power of life and **d** H4638
Pr 19:18 do not be a willing party to their **d**. H4637
Pr 21:25 craving of a sluggard *will be the* **d** *of* him, H4637
Pr 23:14 them with the rod and save them from **d**. H8619
Pr 24:11 Rescue those being led away to **d**; hold H4638
Pr 26:18 a maniac shooting flaming arrows of **d** H4638
Pr 27:20 **D** and Destruction are never satisfied, and H8619
Ecc 7: 1 the day of **d** better than the day of H4638
Ecc 7: 2 feasting, for **d** is the destiny of everyone H2085s
Ecc 7:26 more bitter than **d** the woman who is a H4638
Ecc 8: 8 no one has power over the time of their **d**. H4638
SS 8: 6 love is as strong as **d**, its jealousy H4638
Isa 5:14 Therefore **D** expands its jaws, opening H8619
Isa 25: 8 he will swallow up **d** forever. H4638
Isa 28:15 "We have entered into a covenant with **d** H4638
Isa 28:18 Your covenant with **d** will be annulled H4638
Isa 37:36 LORD went out and **put to d** a hundred H5782
Isa 38: 1 became ill and was at the point of **d**. H4637
Isa 38:10 the gates of **d** and be robbed of the H8619
Isa 38:18 praise you, **d** cannot sing your praise H4638
Isa 53: 9 with the rich in his **d**, though he had H4638
Isa 53:12 because he poured out his life unto **d** H4638
Isa 57: 2 into peace; they find rest as they **lie in d**. H5435
Isa 65:15 the Sovereign LORD *will* **put** you **to d**, but H4637
Jer 8: 3 of this evil nation will prefer **d** to life, H4638
Jer 9:21 **D** has climbed in through our windows H4638
Jer 15: 2 " 'Those destined for **d**, to death; those H4638
Jer 15: 2 death, to **d**; those for the sword, H4638
Jer 18:21 let their men be **put to d**, their H2222+4638
Jer 21: 8 you the way of life and the way of **d**. H4638
Jer 26:11 should be sentenced to **d** because he has H4638
Jer 26:15 that if you **put** me **to d**, you will bring the H4637
Jer 26:16 "This man should not be sentenced to **d**! H4638
Jer 26:19 *Did* Hezekiah king of Judah or anyone else in Judah **put** him **to d** H4637+4637
Jer 26:21 the king was determined *to* **put** him **to d**. H4637
Jer 26:24 handed over to the people to *be* **put to d**. H4637
Jer 29:21 and *he will* **put** them **to d** before your very H5782
Jer 38: 4 to the king, "This man *should* **be put to d**. H4637
Jer 38: 9 where *he will* starve *to* **d** when there is no H4637
Jer 43:11 bringing **d** to those destined for death H4638
Jer 43:11 bringing death to those destined for **d** H4638
Jer 52:11 he put him in prison till the day of his **d**. H4638
Jer 52:34 as long as he lived, till the day of his **d**. H4638
La 1:20 sword bereaves; inside, there is only **d**. H4638
Eze 18:13 things, *he is to* **be put to d**; his H4637+4637
Eze 18:23 I take any pleasure in the **d** *of* the wicked? H4638
Eze 18:32 For I take no pleasure in the **d** *of* anyone H4638
Eze 28: 8 you will die a violent **d** in the heart of the H4926
Eze 28:10 You will die the **d** *of* the uncircumcised at H4638
Eze 31:14 they are all destined for **d**, for the earth H4638
Eze 33:11 I take no pleasure in the **d** *of* the wicked H4638
Eze 43: 7 funeral offerings for their kings at their **d**. H4638
Da 2:13 was issued *to* **put** the wise men to **d**, A10625
Da 2:13 Daniel and his friends to **put them to d**. A10625
Da 2:14 had gone out to **put to d** the wise men A10625
Da 5:19 Those the king wanted to put to **d**, he put to NDT
Da 5:19 put to death, *he* **put to d**; those he A10625
Da 9:26 Anointed One *will* **be put to d** and will H4162
Hos 13:14 of the grave; I will redeem them from **d**. H4638
Hos 13:14 Where, O **d**, are your plagues H4638
Hab 2: 5 as the grave and like **d** is never satisfied, H4638
Mt 2:15 where he stayed until the **d** of Herod. G5463
Mt 4:16 land of the shadow *of* **d** a light has G2505
Mt 10:21 "Brother will betray brother to **d**, and a G2505
Mt 10:21 their parents and **have** them **put to d**. G2506
Mt 15: 4 father or mother *is to be* **put to d**. G2505+5462
Mt 16:28 here will not taste **d** before they see the G2505
Mt 20:18 They will condemn him *to* **d** G2505
Mt 24: 9 handed over to *be* persecuted and **put to d**, G650
Mt 26:38 with sorrow to the point of **d**. G2505
Mt 26:59 Jesus so that *they could* **put** him **to d**. G2506
Mt 26:66 "He is worthy *of* **d**," they answered. G2505
Mk 7:10 father or mother *is to be* **put to d**. G2505+5462
Mk 9: 1 here will not taste **d** before they see that G2505
Mk 10:33 will condemn him *to* **d** and will hand him G2505
Mk 13:12 "Brother will betray brother to **d**, and a G2505
Mk 13:12 their parents and *have* them **put to d**. G2506
Mk 14:34 with sorrow to the point of **d**, G2505
Mk 14:55 Jesus so that *they could* **put** him **to d**, G2506
Mk 14:64 They all condemned him as worthy *of* **d**. G2505
Lk 1:79 living in darkness and in the shadow *of* **d**, G2505
Lk 9:27 here will not taste **d** before they see the G2505
Lk 15:17 food to spare, and here I *am* starving *to* **d**! G660
Lk 21:16 and *they will* **put** some of you **to d**. G2506
Lk 22:33 ready to go with you to prison and to **d**." G2505
Lk 23:15 he has done nothing to deserve **d**. G2505
Lk 23:22 in him no **grounds for the d penalty**. G165+2505
Lk 24:20 handed him over to be sentenced *to* **d**, G2505
Jn 4:47 heal his son, who was close to **d**. G633
Jn 5:24 judged but has crossed over from **d** to life. G2505
Jn 8:51 whoever obeys my word will never see **d**." G2505
Jn 8:52 obeys your word will never taste **d**. G2505
Jn 11: 4 "This sickness will not end in **d**. G2505
Jn 11:13 Jesus had been speaking of his **d**, but his G2505
Jn 12:33 to show the kind of **d** he was going to die. G2505
Jn 18:32 about the kind of **d** he was going to die. G2505
Jn 21:19 the kind of **d** *by which* Peter would glorify G2505
Ac 2:23 *you*, with the help of wicked men, **put** him **to d** G359
Ac 2:24 freeing him from the agony *of* **d**, because G2505
Ac 2:24 it was impossible for **d** to keep its hold on G899s
Ac 5:33 were furious and wanted *to* **put** them **to d**. G359
Ac 7: 4 After the **d** *of* his father, God sent him to G633
Ac 12: 2 *He had* James, the brother of John, **put to d** G359
Ac 13:28 found no proper ground *for* **a d sentence**, G2505
Ac 22: 4 the followers of this Way to their **d**, G2505
Ac 23:29 him that deserved **d** or imprisonment. G2505
Ac 25:11 I am guilty of doing anything deserving **d**, G2505
Ac 25:25 he had done nothing deserving *of* **d**, G2505
Ac 26:10 and *when* they *were* **put to d**, I cast my G359
Ac 26:31 anything that deserves **d** or imprisonment." G2505
Ac 28:18 I was not guilty of any crime deserving **d**. G2505
Ro 1:32 that those who do such things deserve **d**, G2505
Ro 4:25 He *was* **delivered over to d** for our sins G4140
Ro 5:10 to him through the **d** of his Son, G2505
Ro 5:12 one man, and **d** through sin, and in G2505
Ro 5:12 and in this way **d** came to all people G2505
Ro 5:14 **d** reigned from the time of Adam to the G2505
Ro 5:17 **d** reigned through that one man G2505
Ro 5:21 just as sin reigned in **d**, so also grace G2505
Ro 6: 3 into Christ Jesus were baptized into his **d**? G2505
Ro 6: 4 him through baptism into **d** in order that, G2505
Ro 6: 5 have been united with him in a **d** like his, G2505
Ro 6: 9 **d** no longer has mastery over him. G2505
Ro 6:10 The **d** he died, he died to sin once for all; G4005s
Ro 6:13 who have been brought from **d** to life; G3738
Ro 6:16 which leads to **d**, or to obedience, G2505
Ro 6:21 Those things result in **d**! G2505
Ro 6:23 For the wages of sin is **d**, but the gift of G2505
Ro 7: 5 at work in us, so that we bore fruit *for* **d**. G2505
Ro 7:10 intended to bring life actually brought **d**. G2505
Ro 7:11 through the commandment **put** me **to d**. G650
Ro 7:13 which is good, then, become **d** to me? G2505
Ro 7:13 it used what is good to bring about my **d** G2505
Ro 7:24 me from this body that is *subject to* **d**? G2505
Ro 8: 2 has set you free from the law of sin and **d**. G2505
Ro 8: 6 The mind governed by the flesh is **d**, but G2505
Ro 8:10 your body is **subject to d** because of sin, G3738
Ro 8:13 by the Spirit *you* **put to d** the misdeeds of G2506
Ro 8:36 "For your sake *we* **face d** all day long; we G2506
Ro 8:38 For I am convinced that neither **d** nor life G2505
1Co 3:22 the world or life or **d** or the present or the G2505
1Co 11:26 you proclaim the Lord's **d** until he comes. G2505
1Co 15:21 For since **d** came through a man, the G2505
1Co 15:26 The last enemy to be destroyed is **d**. G2505
1Co 15:31 *I* **face d** every day—yes, just as surely as I G633
1Co 15:54 "**D** has been swallowed up in victory." G2505
1Co 15:55 "Where, *O* **d**, is your victory? Where, G2505
1Co 15:55 is your victory? Where, *O* **d**, is your sting?" G2505
1Co 15:56 The sting *of* **d** is sin, and the power of sin G2505
2Co 1: 9 we felt we had received the sentence *of* **d**. G2505
2Co 2:16 an aroma that **brings d**; G1666+2505+1650+2505
2Co 3: 7 Now if the ministry that *brought* **d**, which G2505
2Co 4:10 carry around in our body the **d** of Jesus, G3740
2Co 4:11 being given over to **d** for Jesus' sake, G2505
2Co 4:12 So then, **d** is at work in us, but life is at G2505
2Co 7:10 no regret, but worldly sorrow brings **d**. G2505
2Co 11:23 been exposed to **d** again and again. G2505
Eph 2:16 by which *he* **put to d** their hostility. G650
Php 1:20 in my body, whether by life or by **d**. G2505
Php 2: 8 himself by becoming obedient to **d**— G2505

Php 2: 8 obedient to death—even **d** on a cross! *G2505*
Php 3:10 his sufferings, becoming like him *in* his **d**, *G2505*
Col 1:22 body through **d** to present you holy *G2505*
Col 3: 5 **Put to d**, therefore, whatever belongs to *G3739*
1Th 4:13 uninformed about those *who* **sleep in d**, *G3121*
2Ti 1:10 who has destroyed **d** and has brought life *G2505*
Heb 2: 9 glory and honor because he suffered **d**, *G2505*
Heb 2: 9 of God he might taste **d** for everyone. *G2505*
Heb 2:14 so that by his **d** he might break the *G2505*
Heb 2:14 power of him who holds the power *of* **d**— *G2505*
Heb 2:15 were held in slavery by their fear *of* **d**. *G2505*
Heb 5: 7 to the one who could save him from **d**, *G2505*
Heb 6: 1 of repentance from acts *that lead to* **d**, *G3738*
Heb 7:23 since **d** prevented them from continuing *G2505*
Heb 9:14 our consciences from acts *that lead to* **d**, *G3738*
Heb 9:16 to prove the **d** of the one who made it *G2505*
Heb 11: 5 this life, so that he did not experience **d**: *G2505*
Heb 11:19 he did receive Isaac back **from d**. *G3854S*
Heb 11:37 *They were* **put to d by stoning**; they were *G3342*
Heb 12:20 the mountain, *it must be* **stoned to d**." *G3344*
Jas 1:15 when it is full-grown, gives birth to **d**. *G2505*
Jas 5:20 will save them from **d** and cover over a *G2505*
1Pe 3:18 *He was* **put to d** in the body but made *G2506*
1Jn 3:14 know that we have passed from **d** to life, *G2505*
1Jn 3:14 Anyone who does not love remains in **d**. *G2505*
1Jn 5:16 commit a sin that does not lead to **d**, *G2505*
1Jn 5:16 to those whose sin does not lead to **d**. *G2505*
1Jn 5:16 There is a sin that leads to **d**. I am not *G2505*
1Jn 5:17 there is sin that does not lead to **d**. *G2505*
Rev 1:18 And I hold the keys *of* **d** and Hades. *G2505*
Rev 2:10 even to the point of **d**, and I will give you *G2505*
Rev 2:11 will not be hurt at all by the second **d**. *G2505*
Rev 2:13 witness, who *was* **put to d** in your city *G650*
Rev 6: 8 Its rider was named **D**, and Hades was *G2505*
Rev 9: 6 people will seek **d** but will not find it; *G2505*
Rev 9: 6 will long to die, but **d** will elude them. *G2505*
Rev 12:11 their lives so much as to shrink from **d**. *G2505*
Rev 18: 8 will overtake her: **d**, mourning and famine *G2505*
Rev 20: 6 The second **d** has no power over them *G2505*
Rev 20:13 **d** and Hades gave up the dead that *G2505*
Rev 20:14 Then **d** and Hades were thrown into the *G2505*
Rev 20:14 The lake of fire is the second **d**. *G2505*
Rev 21: 4 There will be no more **d**' or mourning *G2505*
Rev 21: 8 of burning sulfur. This is the second **d**." *G2505*

DEATH'S (1) [DIE]
Job 18:13 of his skin; **d** firstborn devours his limbs. H4638

DEATHLY (2) [DIE]
Jer 30: 6 woman in labor, every face turned **d pale**? H3766
Da 10: 8 my face turned **d pale** and I was helpless. H5422

DEATHS (1) [DIE]
1Sa 4:21 ark of God and the **d** of her father-in-law NDT

DEBAR See LO DEBAR

DEBATE (3) [DEBATED, DEBATING]
Ac 15: 2 into sharp dispute and **d** with them. *G2428*
Ac 17:18 Stoic philosophers *began to* **d with** him. *G5202*
Ac 18:28 *he* vigorously **refuted** his Jewish opponents **in** public **d** *G1352*

DEBATED (1) [DEBATE]
Ac 9:29 He talked and **d** with the Hellenistic Jews *G5184*

DEBATING (1) [DEBATE]
Mk 12:28 of the law came and heard them **d**. *G5184*

DEBAUCHERY (5)
Ro 13:13 not in sexual immorality and **d**, not in *G816*
2Co 12:21 sexual sin and **d** in which they have *G816*
Gal 5:19 sexual immorality, impurity and **d**; *G816*
Eph 5:18 drunk on wine, which leads to **d**. *G861*
1Pe 4: 3 pagans choose to do—living in **d**, lust, *G816*

DEBIR (12) [KIRIATH SANNAH]
Jos 10: 3 king of Lachish and **D** king of Eglon. H1809
Jos 10:38 with him turned around and attacked **D**. H1810
Jos 10:39 They did to **D** and its king as they had H1810
Jos 11:21 from Hebron, **D** and Anab, from all the H1810
Jos 12:13 the king of **D** one the king of Geder one H1810
Jos 13:26 from Mahanaim to the territory of **D**; H1810
Jos 15: 7 then went up to **D** from the Valley of H1810
Jos 15:15 marched against the people living in **D** H1810
Jos 15:49 Dannah, Kiriath Sannah (that is, **D**), H1810
Jos 21:15 Holon, **D**, H1810
Jdg 1:11 advanced against the people living in **D** H1810
1Ch 6:58 Hilen, **D**, H1810

DEBORAH (11)
Ge 35: 8 Now **D**, Rebekah's nurse, died and was H1806
Jdg 4: 4 Now **D**, a prophet, the wife of Lappidoth H1806
Jdg 4: 5 under the Palm of **D** between Ramah H1806
Jdg 4: 9 go with you," said **D**. "But because of the NDT
Jdg 4: 9 So **D** went with Barak to Kedesh. H1806
Jdg 4:10 his command. **D** also went up with him H1806
Jdg 4:14 Then **D** said to Barak, "Go! This is the day H1806
Jdg 5: 1 On that day **D** and Barak son of Abinoam H1806
Jdg 5: 7 held back until I, **D**, arose, until I arose, H1806
Jdg 5:12 wake up, **D**! Wake up, wake up, H1806
Jdg 5:15 The princes of Issachar were with **D**; yes H1806

DEBT (11) [DEBTOR, DEBTORS, DEBTS, INDEBTEDNESS]
Dt 15: 3 you *must* **cancel** *any* **d** your fellow H9023
Dt 24: 6 *Do* not **take** a pair of millstones—not even the upper one—**as security for a d** H2471
1Sa 22: 2 in distress or **in d** or discontented H5957+4200
Job 24: 9 the infant of the poor *is* **seized for a d**. H2471
Mt 18:25 all that he had be sold *to* **repay** *the* **d**. *G625*
Mt 18:27 on him, canceled the **d** and let him go. *G1245*
Mt 18:30 into prison until he could pay the **d**. *G4053*
Mt 18:32 'I canceled all that **d** of yours because you *G4051*
Lk 7:43 the one who had the bigger **d** forgiven." NDT
Ro 13: 8 *Let* no **d remain outstanding**, except the *G4053*
Ro 13: 8 except the continuing **d** to love one another NDT

DEBTOR (1) [DEBT]
Isa 24: 2 as for lender, for **d** as for creditor. H5957+928

DEBTORS (2) [DEBT]
Mt 6:12 our debts, as we also have forgiven our **d**. *G4050*
Lk 16: 5 he called in each one *of* his master's **d**. *G5971*

DEBTS (9) [DEBT]
Dt 15: 1 seven years *you must* **cancel d**. H9024+6913
Dt 15: 2 the LORD's **time for canceling d** has been H9024
Dt 15: 9 the year for **canceling d**, is near, H9024
Dt 31:10 in the year for **canceling d**, during the H9024
2Ki 4: 7 he said, "Go, sell the oil and pay your **d**. H5963
Ne 10:31 the land and will cancel all **d**. H5391+3338
Pr 22:26 hands in pledge or puts up security for **d**; H5394
Mt 6:12 And forgive us our **d**, as we also have *G4052*
Lk 7:42 pay him back, so he forgave the **d** of both. NDT

DECAPOLIS (3)
Mt 4:25 crowds from Galilee, the **D**, Jerusalem, *G1279*
Mk 5:20 to tell in the **D** how much Jesus had *G1279*
Mk 7:31 of Galilee and into the region *of* the **D**. *G1279*

DECAY (13) [DECAYED]
Ps 16:10 will you let your faithful one see **d**. H8846
Ps 49: 9 they should live on forever and not see **d**. H8846
Ps 49:14 Their forms *will* **d** in the grave, far from H1162
Ps 55:23 bring down the wicked into the pit of **d**; H8846
Pr 12: 4 a disgraceful wife is like **d** in his bones. H8373
Isa 5:24 so their roots will **d** and their flowers blow H5215
Hab 3:16 at the sound; **d** crept into my bones H8373
Ac 2:27 you will not let your holy one see **d**. *G1426*
Ac 2:31 realm of the dead, nor did his body see **d**. *G1426*
Ac 13:34 dead so that he will never be subject to **d**. *G1426*
Ac 13:35 " 'You will not let your holy one see **d**.' *G1426*
Ac 13:37 God raised from the dead did not see **d**. *G1426*
Ro 8:21 from its bondage *to* **d** and brought into *G5785*

DECAYED (2) [DECAY]
Jer 49: 7 from the prudent? *Has* their wisdom **d**? H6244
Ac 13:36 with his ancestors and his body **d**. *G3972+1426*

DECEASE, DECEASED (KJV) DEAD, DIED, DEPARTURE

DECEIT (28) [DECEIVE]
Job 15:35 give birth to evil; their womb fashions **d**." H5327
Job 31: 5 falsehood or my foot has hurried after **d**— H5327
Ps 32: 2 against them and in whose spirit is no **d**. H8245
Ps 50:19 evil and harness your tongue to **d**. H5327
Ps 52: 2 You who practice **d**, your tongue plots H8245
Ps 101: 7 No one who practices **d** will dwell in my H8245
Pr 6:14 who plots evil with **d** in his heart—he H9337
Pr 12:20 **D** is in the hearts of those who plot evil H5327
Pr 26:24 their lips, but in their hearts they harbor **d**. H5327
Isa 5:18 those who draw sin along with cords of **d**, H8736
Isa 30:12 relied on oppression and depended on **d** H4279
Isa 53: 9 no violence, nor was any **d** in his mouth. H5327
Jer 5:27 their houses are full of **d**; they have H5327
Jer 6:13 prophets and priests alike, all practice **d**. H9214
Jer 8: 5 They cling to **d**; they refuse to H9567
Jer 8:10 prophets and priests alike, all practice **d**. H9214
Jer 9: 6 in their **d** they refuse to acknowledge me," H5327
Da 8:25 He will cause **d** to prosper, and he will H5327
Hos 7: 1 They practice **d**, thieves break into houses, H9214
Hos 11:12 surrounded me with lies, Israel with **d**. H5327
Zep 1: 9 temple of their gods with violence and **d**. H5327
Mk 7:22 adultery, greed, malice, **d**, lewdness, envy *G1515*
Jn 1:47 truly is an Israelite in whom there is no **d**." *G1515*
Ac 13:10 You are full of all kinds of **d** and trickery *G1515*
Ro 1:29 full of envy, murder, strife, **d** and malice. *G1515*
Ro 3:13 are open graves; their tongues **practice d**." *G1514*
1Pe 2: 1 rid yourselves of all malice and all **d** *G1515*
1Pe 2:22 and no **d** was found in his mouth. *G1515*

DECEITFUL (25) [DECEIVE]
Ps 5: 6 The bloodthirsty and **d** you, LORD H5327+408
Ps 17: 1 my prayer—it does not rise from **d** lips. H5327
Ps 26: 4 I do not sit with the **d**, nor do I H8736+5493
Ps 36: 3 words of their mouths are wicked and **d**; H5327
Ps 43: 1 me from those who are **d** and wicked. H5327
Ps 52: 4 love every harmful word, you **d** tongue! H5327
Ps 55:23 bloodthirsty and **d** will not live out H5327+408
Ps 109: 2 who are wicked and **d** have opened their H5327
Ps 119:29 Keep me from **d** ways; be gracious to me H9214
Ps 120: 2 from lying lips and from **d** tongues. H8245
Ps 120: 3 what more besides, you **d** tongue? H8245
Ps 144: 8 are full of lies, whose right hands are **d**. H9214
Ps 144:11 are full of lies, whose right hands are **d**. H9214
Pr 12: 5 are just, but the advice of the wicked is **d**. H5327
Pr 14:25 saves lives, but a false witness is **d**. H5327
Pr 17: 4 A wicked person listens to **d** lips; a liar H224
Isa 30: 9 are rebellious people, **d** children, children H3952
Jer 17: 9 The heart is **d** above all things and H6815
Hos 10: 2 Their heart *is* **d**, and now they must bear H2744
Zep 3:13 A **d** tongue will not be found in their H9567
2Co 11:13 are false apostles, **d** workers *G1513*
Eph 4:14 craftiness of people in their **d** scheming. *G4415*
Eph 4:22 which is being corrupted by its **d** desires; *G573*
1Pe 3:10 from evil and their lips from **d** speech. *G1515*
Rev 21:27 anyone who does what is shameful or **d**, *G6022*

DECEITFULLY (8) [DECEIVE]
Ge 27:35 "Your brother came and took your H928+5327
Ge 34:13 sons replied **d** as they spoke to H928+5327
Ex 8:29 *let* Pharaoh *be sure that he does* not **act d** H9438
Job 13: 7 God's behalf? Will you speak **d** for him? H8245
Jer 9: 8 tongue is a deadly arrow; it speaks **d**. H5327
Da 11:23 he will act **d**, and with only a few H5327
Mic 6:12 are liars and their tongues speak **d**. H8245
Zec 10: 2 The idols speak **d**, diviners see visions that H224

DECEITFULNESS (3) [DECEIVE]
Mt 13:22 of this life and the **d** of wealth choke the *G573*
Mk 4:19 the **d** of wealth and the desires for other *G573*
Heb 3:13 none of you may be hardened *by* sin's **d**. *G573*

DECEIVE (33) [DECEIT, DECEITFUL, DECEITFULLY, DECEITFULNESS, DECEIVED, DECEIVER, DECEIVERS, DECEIVES, DECEIVING, DECEPTION, DECEPTIVE, DECEPTIVELY]
Ge 31:27 Why did you run off secretly and **d** me H1704
Lev 19:11 " '*Do* not **d** one another. H9213
Jos 9:22 said, "Why *did you* **d** us by saying H8228
1Sa 19:17 "Why *did you* **d** me like this and send my H8228
2Sa 3:25 he came to **d** you and observe your H7331
2Ki 18:29 *Do* not **let** Hezekiah **d** you. H5958
2Ki 19:10 *Do* not **let** the god you depend on **d** you H5958
2Ch 32:15 Now *do* not *let* Hezekiah **d** you and H5958
Job 13: 9 *Could you* **d** him as you might deceive a H9438
Job 13: 9 you deceive him as you *might* **d** a mortal? H9438
Job 15:31 *Let him* not **d himself** by trusting what is H9494
Pr 14: 5 An honest witness *does* not **d**, but a false H3941
Isa 36:14 *Do* not *let* Hezekiah **d** you. H5958
Isa 37:10 god you depend on **d** you when he says, H5958
Jer 29: 8 *Do* not *let* the prophets and diviners among you **d** H5958
Jer 37: 9 *Do* not **d** yourselves, thinking, 'The H5958
Ob 7 your friends *will* **d** and overpower you H5958
Zec 13: 4 a prophet's garment of hair in order to **d**. H3950
Mt 24: 5 'I am the Messiah,' and *will* **d** many. *G4414*
Mt 24:11 prophets will appear and **d** many people. *G4414*
Mt 24:24 perform great signs and wonders to **d**, *G4414*
Mk 13: 6 claiming, 'I am he,' and *will* **d** many. *G4414*
Mk 13:22 perform signs and wonders to **d**, *G675*
Ro 16:18 talk and flattery *they* **d** the minds of naive *G1987*
1Co 3:18 Do not **d** yourselves. If any of you think *G1987*
Gal 6: 3 when they are not, *they* **d** themselves. *G5854*
Eph 5: 6 *Let* no one **d** you with empty words, for *G572*
Col 2: 4 this so that no one *may* **d** you by *G4165*
2Th 2: 3 Don't *let* anyone **d** you in any way, for that *G1987*
Jas 1:22 listen to the word, and so **d** yourselves. *G4165*
Jas 1:26 a tight rein on their tongues **d** themselves, *G572*
1Jn 1: 8 *we* **d** ourselves and the truth is not in us. *G4414*
Rev 20: 8 will go out *to* **d** the nations in the four *G4414*

DECEIVED (28) [DECEIVE]
Ge 3:13 "The serpent **d** me, and I ate. H5958
Ge 29:25 didn't I? Why *have you* **d** me?" H8228
Ge 31:20 Jacob **d** Laban the Aramean by not H1704+4213
Ge 31:26 *You've* **d** me, and you've carried off H1704+4222
Nu 25:18 when they **d** you in the Peor H5792+928+5793
1Sa 28:12 said to Saul, "Why *have you* **d** me? H8228
Job 12:16 insight; both **d** and deceiver are his. H8704
Isa 19:13 the leaders of Memphis **are d**; the H5958
Jer 4:10 How **completely** *you have* **d** this H5958+5958
Jer 20: 7 *You* **d** me, LORD, and I was deceived; you H7331
Jer 20: 7 and I **was d**; you overpowered me H7331
Jer 20:10 "Perhaps *he will* **be d**; then we will H7331
Jer 49:16 the pride of your heart *have* **d** you, H5958
Hos 7:11 is like a dove, **easily d** and senseless H7331
Ob 3 The pride of your heart *has* **d** you, you H5958
Lk 21: 8 "Watch out *that you are* not **d**. For many *G4414*
Jn 7:47 "You mean *he has* **d** you also?" the *G4414*
Ro 7:11 the commandment, **d** me, and through *G1987*
1Co 6: 9 kingdom of God? *Do* not *be* **d**: Neither the *G4414*
2Co 11: 3 that just as Eve *was* **d** by the serpent's *G1987*
Gal 6: 7 *Do* not *be* **d**: God cannot be mocked. *G4414*
1Ti 2:14 And Adam was not *the one* **d**; it was the *G572*
1Ti 2:14 *it was* the woman who *was* **d** and became *G1987*
2Ti 3:13 bad to worse, deceiving and *being* **d**. *G4414*
Titus 3: 3 **d** and enslaved by all kinds of passions *G4414*
Jas 1:16 Don't *be* **d**, my dear brothers and sisters. *G4414*
Rev 13:14 *it* **d** the inhabitants of the earth. *G4414*
Rev 20:10 And the devil, who **d** them, was thrown *G4414*

DECEIVER (5) [DECEIVE]
Job 12:16 insight; both deceived and **d** are his. H8706
Jer 9: 4 For every one of them *is a* **d**, and H6810+6810
Mic 2:11 If a liar and **d** comes and says, 'I will H9214

Mt 27:63 that while he was still alive that **d** said, G4418
2Jn 7 such person is the **d** and the antichrist. G4418

DECEIVERS (3) [DECEIVE]

Job 11:11 Surely he recognizes **d**; and when H5493+8736
Ps 49: 5 days come, when wicked **d** surround me— H6812
2Jn 7 I say this because many **d**, who do not G4418

DECEIVES (6) [DECEIVE]

Pr 26:19 is one *who* **d** their neighbor and says, "I H8228
Jer 9: 5 Friend **d** friend, and no one speaks the H9438
Mt 24: 4 "Watch out *that* no one **d** you. G4414
Mk 13: 5 "Watch out that no one **d** you. G4414
Jn 7:12 Others replied, "No, *he* **d** the people." G4414
2Th 2:10 ways that wickedness **d** those who are G573

DECEIVING (8) [DECEIVE]

Lev 6: 2 to the LORD *by* **d** a neighbor about H3950
1Ki 22:22 will go out and be a **d** spirit in the mouths H9214
1Ki 22:23 the LORD has put a **d** spirit in the mouths H9214
2Ch 18:21 " 'I will go and be a **d** spirit in the mouths H9214
2Ch 18:22 the LORD has put a **d** spirit in the mouths H9214
1Ti 4: 1 the faith and follow **d** spirits and things G4418
2Ti 3:13 from bad to worse, **d** and being deceived. G4414
Rev 20: 3 to keep *him* from **d** the nations anymore G4414

DECENCY (1) [DECENTLY]

1Ti 2: 9 dress modestly, with **d** and propriety G133

DECENTLY (1) [DECENCY]

Ro 13:13 Let us behave **d**, as in the daytime, not in G2361

DECEPTION (9) [DECEIVE]

Ps 12: 2 with their lips but **harbor d** in their hearts. H1819
Pr 14: 8 to their ways, but the folly of fools is **d**. H5327
Pr 26:26 Their malice may be concealed by **d**, but H5396
Jer 3:23 on the hills and mountains is a **d**; H9214
Jer 9: 6 You live in the midst of **d**; in their deceit H5327
Hos 10:13 reaped evil, you have eaten the fruit of **d**. H3951
Mt 27:64 This last **d** will be worse than the first." G4415
2Co 4: 2 we do not use **d**, nor do we distort G4111
Titus 1:10 full of meaningless talk and **d**, especially G5855

DECEPTIVE (8) [DECEIVE]

Pr 11:18 A wicked person earns **d** wages, but the H9214
Pr 23: 3 not crave his delicacies, for that food is **d**. H3942
Pr 31:30 Charm is **d**, and beauty is fleeting; but a H9214
Jer 7: 4 Do not trust in **d** words and say, "This is H9214
Jer 7: 8 you are trusting in **d** words that are H9214
Jer 15:18 You are to me like a **d** brook, like a spring H423
Mic 1:14 of Akzib will prove **d** to the kings of Israel. H423
Col 2: 8 captive through hollow and **d** philosophy, G573

DECEPTIVELY (1) [DECEIVE]

2Ki 10:19 Jehu was acting **d** in order to destroy H928+6817

DECIDE (16) [DECIDED, DECISION, DECISIONS]

Ex 18:16 and *I* **d** between the parties and inform H9149
Ex 18:22 the simple cases *they can* **d** themselves. H9149
Ex 33: 5 ornaments and *I will* **d** what to do with H3359
Dt 21: 5 LORD and to **d** all cases of H2118+6584+7023
Dt 25: 1 it to court and *the* **judges** *will* **d** the case, H9149
Jdg 11:27 *Let* the LORD, the Judge, **d** *the* **dispute** this H9149
1Sa 24:15 the LORD be our judge and **d** between us. H9149
2Sa 24:13 think it over and **d** how I should answer H8011
1Ch 21:12 **d** how I should answer the one who sent H8011
Job 22:28 What *you* **d** *on* will be done, and light H1615
Job 34:33 You *must* **d**, not I; so tell me what you H1047
Isa 11: 3 or **d** by what he hears with his ears; H3519
Eze 44:24 serve as judges and **d** it according to my H9149
Jn 19:24 "*Let's* **d by lot** who will get it. G3275
Ac 4:21 *They could* not **d** how to punish them G2351
Ac 24:22 he said, "*I will* **d** your case. G1336

DECIDED (32) [DECIDE]

Ge 41:32 that the matter *has* **been firmly d** by God, H3922
Ex 18:26 the simple ones *they* **d** themselves. H9149
Jdg 4: 5 went up to her to have their **disputes d**. H5477
Jdg 20: 7 up and tell me **what** you have **d to do**." H6783
Jdg 20: 9 go up against it in the order *d by casting* **lots**. AIT
2Ch 24: 4 later Joash **d** to restore the H2118+6640+4213
2Ch 30: 2 assembly in Jerusalem **d** to celebrate the H3619
2Ch 30: 5 *They* **d** to send a proclamation H6641+1821
Est 7: 7 that the king *had already* **d** his fate, H3983
Jer 4:28 not relent, *I have* **d** and will not turn back." H2372
Da 2: 5 astrologers, "This is what I have firmly **d**: A10418
Da 2: 8 realize that this is what I have firmly **d**: A10418
Zep 3: 8 I have **d** to assemble the nations, to H5477
Mt 27: 7 So *they* **d** to use the money to buy G5206+3284
Lk 1: 3 I too **d** to write an orderly account for you G1506
Lk 23:24 So Pilate **d** to grant their demand. G2137
Jn 1:43 The next day Jesus **d** to leave for Galilee G2527
Jn 9:22 who already *had* **d** that anyone who G5338
Ac 3:13 Pilate, *though* he *had* **d** to let him go. G3212
Ac 4:28 will *had* **d beforehand** should G4633
Ac 7:23 he **d** to visit his own G326+2093+3836+2840
Ac 11:29 **d** to provide help for the brothers and G3988
Ac 15:22 **d** to choose some of their own men and G1506
Ac 19:21 Paul **d** to go to G5502+1877+3836+4460
Ac 20: 3 *he* **d** to go back through G1181+1191
Ac 20:16 Paul *had* **d** to sail past Ephesus to avoid G3212
Ac 25:25 to the Emperor *I* **d** to send him to Rome. G3212
Ac 27: 1 When *it was* **d** that we would sail for Italy G3212
Ac 27:12 the majority **d** that we should sail G5502+1087
Ac 27:39 where *they* **d** to run the ship aground if G1086
2Co 9: 7 should give what *you have* **d** in your heart G4576
Titus 3:12 because *I have* **d** to winter there. G3212

DECIMATED (1)

2Sa 21: 5 us so that *we have* **been d** and have no H9012

DECISION (13) [DECIDE]

Ex 28:29 on the breastpiece of **d** as a continuing H5477
2Sa 15: 2 to be placed before the king for a **d**, H5477
Ezr 5:17 let the king send us his **d** in this matter. A10668
Ezr 10: 8 accordance with the **d** *of* the officials and H6783
Pr 16:33 the lap, but its every **d** is from the LORD. H5477
Isa 16: 3 "Render a **d**. Make your shadow H7131
Da 4:17 " 'The **d** is announced by messengers A10601
Joel 3:14 multitudes in the valley of **d**! For the day H3025
Joel 3:14 day of the LORD is near in the valley of **d**. H3025
Lk 23:51 had not consented *to* their **d** and action. G1087
Jn 1:13 of human **d** or a husband's will G2525
Ac 21:25 written to them *our* **d** that they should G3212
Ac 25:21 to be held over for the Emperor's **d**, G1338

DECISIONS (10) [DECIDE]

Ex 28:15 "Fashion a breastpiece for **making d**—the H5477
Ex 28:30 bear the **means of making d** *for* the H5477
Nu 27:21 *who will* **obtain d** for him by inquiring of H8626
Dt 17:10 act according to the **d** they give you at the H1821
Dt 17:11 they teach you and the **d** they give you. H5477
Isa 11: 4 with justice *he will* **give d** for the poor of H3519
Isa 28: 7 they stumble when **rendering d**. H7133
Isa 58: 2 They ask me for just **d** and seem eager H5477
Jn 8:16 But if I do judge, my **d** are true, because I G3213
Ac 16: 4 they delivered the **d** reached by the G1504

DECK (2) [DECKED, DECKS]

DECK, DECKEDST, DECKEST (KJV) ADORN, ADORNED, ADORNS, COVERED, DRESS, GAUDY, GLITTERING, PUT ON

Eze 27: 6 they made your **d**, *adorned with* ivory. H7983
Jnh 1: 5 Jonah had gone **below d**, H3752+2021+6208

DECKED (1) [DECK]

Hos 2:13 *she* **d** herself *with* rings and jewelry H6335

DECKS (1) [DECK]

Ge 6:16 the ark and make lower, middle and **upper** *d*. AIT

DECLARE (46) [DECLARED, DECLARES, DECLARING]

Ex 22: 9 whom the judges **d guilty** must pay back H8399
Dt 5: 1 decrees and laws I **d** in your hearing H1819
Dt 5: 5 the LORD and you to **d** to you the word of H5583
Dt 21: 7 and *they shall* **d**: "Our hands did not shed H6699
Dt 26: 3 "*I* **d** today to the LORD your God that I have H5583
Dt 26: 5 Then *you shall* **d** before the LORD your God H6699
Dt 30:18 *I* **d** to you this day that you will certainly be H5583
1Ki 1:36 *May* the LORD, the God of my lord the king, so **d** H606
2Ki 9: 3 flask and pour the oil on his head and **d**, H606
1Ch 16:24 **D** his glory among the nations, his H6218
1Ch 17:10 " '*I* **d** to you that the LORD will build a H5583
Job 10: 2 *Do* not **d** me **guilty**, but tell me what H8399
Job 34:34 "Men of understanding **d**, wise men who NDT
Ps 5:10 **D** them **guilty**, O God! Let their intrigues be H870
Ps 9:14 that *I may* **d** your praises in the gates of H6218
Ps 19: 1 The heavens **d** the glory of God; the skies H6218
Ps 22:22 *I will* **d** your name to my people; in the H6218
Ps 40: 5 your deeds, they would be too many *to* **d**. H6218
Ps 51:15 and my mouth *will* **d** your praise. H5583
Ps 71:17 to this day *I* **d** your marvelous deeds. H5583
Ps 71:18 till *I* **d** your power to the next generation H5583
Ps 75: 9 As for me, *I will* **d** this forever; I will sing H5583
Ps 89: 2 *I will* **d** that your love stands firm forever H606
Ps 96: 3 **D** his glory among the nations, his H6218
Ps 106: 2 acts of the LORD or fully **d** his praise? H9048
Isa 41:22 Or **d** *to* us the things to come, H9048
Isa 42: 9 new things I **d**; before they spring H5583
Isa 44: 7 *Let him* **d** and lay out before me what has H5583
Isa 45:19 the LORD, speak the truth; I **d** what is right. H5583
Isa 45:21 **D** what is to be, present it—let them take H5583
Isa 58: 1 **D** to my people their rebellion and to the H5583
Jer 23:31 who wag their own tongues and yet **d**, H5535
Eze 38:19 zeal and fiery wrath *I* **d** that at that time H1819
Da 4:17 the holy ones **d** the verdict, so that the A10397
Joel 1:14 **D** *a* **holy** fast; call a sacred assembly H7727
Joel 2:15 trumpet in Zion, **d** a **holy** fast, call a H7727
Mic 3: 8 might, to **d** to Jacob his transgression H5583
Ac 20:26 *I* **d** to you today that I am innocent of the G3458
Ro 10: 9 If *you* **d** with your mouth, "Jesus is Lord," G3933
1Co 2: 7 *we* **d** God's wisdom, a mystery that G3281
1Co 15:50 *I* **d** to you, brothers and sisters, that flesh G5774
Gal 5: 3 Again *I* **d** to every man who lets himself G3458
Eph 6:20 Pray that I *may* **d** it fearlessly, as I G3281
Heb 2:12 "*I will* **d** your name to my brothers and G550
1Pe 2: 9 that *you may* **d** the praises of him who G1972
1Jn 1: 5 we have heard from him and **d** to you: G334

DECLARED (43) [DECLARE]

Nu 14:17 strength be displayed, just as *you have* **d**: H1819
Dt 4:13 *He* **d** to you his covenant, the Ten H5583
Dt 26:17 *You have* **d** this day that the LORD is your H606
Dt 26:18 And the LORD *has* **d** this day that you are his H606
Dt 26:19 He has **d** that he will set you in praise, fame NDT
Dt 32:46 all the words I *have* **solemnly d** to you this H6386
1Ki 1:24 "*Have* you, my lord the king, **d** that H606
1Ki 8:53 just as *you* **d** through your servant Moses H1819
1Ki 13: 3 "This is the sign the LORD *has* **d**: The altar H1819
1Ki 13:32 For the message *he* **d** by the word of the H7924
1Ki 22:11 Kenaanah had made iron horns and *he* **d**, H606
1Ki 22:28 Micaiah **d**, "If you ever return safely, the H606
1Ki 22:38 his blood, as the word of the LORD *had* **d**. H1819
2Ki 9: 6 poured the oil on Jehu's head and **d**, H606
2Ki 13:17 Elisha **d**. "You will completely H606
2Ki 24:13 As the LORD *had* **d**, Nebuchadnezzar H1819
2Ch 18:10 iron horns, and *he* **d**, "This is what the H606
2Ch 18:27 Micaiah **d**, "If you ever return safely, the H606
Job 15:18 what the wise *have* **d**, hiding nothing H5583
Ps 88:11 **Is** your love **d** in the grave, your H6218
Ps 95:11 So *I* **d on oath** in my anger, 'They shall H8678
Ps 102:21 name of the LORD *will be* **d** in Zion and his H6218
Ecc 4: 2 And I **d** that the dead, who had already H8655
Isa 5: 9 The LORD Almighty has **d** in my hearing NDT
Isa 45:21 long ago, *who* **d** it from the distant past? H5583
Mt 26:35 But Peter **d**, "Even if I have to die with you G3306
Mt 26:61 **d**, "This fellow said, 'I am able to G3306
Mk 7:19 In saying this, Jesus **d** all foods **clean**.) G2751
Mk 10:20 he **d**, "all these I have kept since I was a G5774
Mk 12:36 himself, speaking by the Holy Spirit, **d**: G3306
Mk 14:29 Peter **d**, "Even if all fall away, I will not." G5774
Jn 1:49 Then Nathanael **d**, "Rabbi, you are the Son G646
Jn 4:26 Then Jesus **d**, "I, the one speaking to you G3306
Jn 6:35 Then Jesus **d**, "I am the bread of life G3306
Jn 8:11 neither do I condemn you," Jesus **d**. G3306
Ac 20:21 *I have* **d** to both Jews and Greeks that they G1371
Ac 25:12 Festus had conferred with his council, *he* **d**: G646
Ro 2:13 obey the law *who will be* **d righteous**. G1467
Ro 3:20 no one *will be* **d righteous** in God's sight G1467
Heb 3:11 So *I* **d on oath** in my anger, 'They shall G3923
Heb 4: 3 God has said, "So *I* **d on oath** in my anger G3923
Heb 7: 8 other case, *by him who is* **d** to be living. G3455
Heb 7:17 For *it is* **d**: "You are a priest forever, in the G3455

DECLARES (373) [DECLARE]

Ge 22:16 "I swear by myself, **d** the LORD, that H5536
Ex 21: 5 "But if the servant **d**, 'I love my master H606+606
Nu 14:28 'As surely as I live, **d** the LORD, I will do to H5536
1Sa 2:30 the God of Israel, **d**: 'I promised that H5536
1Sa 2:30 But now the LORD **d**: 'Far be it from me! H5536
2Sa 7:11 " 'The LORD **d** to you that the LORD himself H5583
2Ki 9:26 blood of his sons, **d** the LORD, and I will H5536
2Ki 9:26 it on this plot of ground, **d** the LORD. H5536
2Ki 19:33 he will not enter this city, **d** the LORD. H5536
2Ki 22:19 I also have heard you, **d** the LORD. H5536
2Ch 34:27 presence, I have heard you, **d** the LORD. H5536
Isa 1:24 Almighty, the Mighty One of Israel, **d**: H5536
Isa 3:15 faces of the poor?" **d** the Lord, the LORD H5536
Isa 14:22 up against them," **d** the LORD Almighty. H5536
Isa 14:22 offspring and descendants," **d** the LORD. H5536
Isa 14:23 of destruction," **d** the LORD Almighty. H5536
Isa 17: 3 of the Israelites," **d** the LORD Almighty. H5536
Isa 17: 6 fruitful boughs," **d** the LORD, the God of H5536
Isa 19: 4 will rule over them," **d** the Lord, the LORD H5536
Isa 22:25 **d** the LORD Almighty, "the peg driven into H5536
Isa 30: 1 **d** the LORD, "to those who carry out plans H5536
Isa 31: 9 will panic," **d** the LORD, whose fire is H5536
Isa 37:34 he will not enter this city," **d** the LORD. H5536
Isa 41:14 myself will help you," **d** the LORD, your H5536
Isa 43:10 **d** the LORD, "and my servant whom I have H5536
Isa 43:12 are my witnesses," **d** the LORD, "that I am H5536
Isa 49:18 **d** the LORD, "you will wear them all as H5536
Isa 52: 5 what do I have here?" **d** the LORD. "For my H5536
Isa 52: 5 those who rule them mock," **d** the LORD. H5536
Isa 54:17 is their vindication from me," **d** the LORD. H5536
Isa 55: 8 are your ways my ways," **d** the LORD. H5536
Isa 56: 8 The Sovereign LORD **d**—he who gathers H5536
Isa 59:20 who repent of their sins," **d** the LORD. H5536
Isa 66: 2 came into being?" **d** the LORD. "These are H5536
Isa 66:17 with the one they follow," **d** the LORD. H5536
Isa 66:22 **d** the LORD, "so will your name and H5536
Jer 1: 8 with you and will rescue you," **d** the LORD. H5536
Jer 1:15 of the northern kingdoms," **d** the LORD. H5536
Jer 1:19 with you and will rescue you," **d** the LORD. H5536
Jer 2: 3 disaster overtook them,' " **d** the LORD. H5536
Jer 2: 9 charges against you again," **d** the LORD. H5536
Jer 2:12 shudder with great horror," **d** the LORD. H5536
Jer 2:19 have no awe of me," **d** the Lord, the LORD H5536
Jer 2:22 is still before me," **d** the Sovereign LORD. H5536
Jer 2:29 have all rebelled against me," **d** the LORD. H5536
Jer 3: 1 would you now return to me?" **d** the LORD. H5536
Jer 3:10 but only in pretense," **d** the LORD. H5536
Jer 3:12 faithless Israel,' **d** the LORD, 'I will frown H5536
Jer 3:12 I am faithful,' **d** the LORD, 'I will not be H5536
Jer 3:13 have not obeyed me,' " **d** the LORD. H5536
Jer 3:14 faithless people," **d** the LORD, "for I am H5536
Jer 3:16 greatly in the land," **d** the LORD, "people H5536
Jer 3:20 have been unfaithful to me," **d** the LORD. H5536
Jer 4: 1 will return, then return to me," **d** the LORD. H5536
Jer 4: 9 **d** the LORD, "the king and the officials will H5536
Jer 4:17 has rebelled against me,' " **d** the LORD. H5536
Jer 5: 9 them for this?" **d** the LORD. "Should I H5536
Jer 5:11 been utterly unfaithful to me," **d** the LORD. H5536
Jer 5:15 **d** the LORD, "I am bringing a distant H5536
Jer 5:18 **d** the LORD, "I will not destroy you H5536
Jer 5:22 you not fear me?" **d** the LORD. "Should you H5536

Jer 5:29 them for this?" **d** the LORD. "Should I H5536
Jer 6:12 those who live in the land," **d** the LORD. H5536
Jer 7:11 But I have been watching! **d** the LORD. H5536
Jer 7:13 all these things, **d** the LORD, I spoke to H5536
Jer 7:19 they are provoking? **d** the LORD. H5536
Jer 7:30 have done evil in my eyes, **d** the LORD. H5536
Jer 7:32 the days are coming, **d** the LORD, when H5536
Jer 8: 1 " 'At that time, **d** the LORD, the bones of H5536
Jer 8: 3 prefer death to life, **d** the LORD Almighty. H5536
Jer 8:13 'I will take away their harvest, **d** the LORD. H5536
Jer 8:17 they will bite you," **d** the LORD. H5536
Jer 9: 3 they do not acknowledge me," **d** the LORD. H5536
Jer 9: 6 refuse to acknowledge me," **d** the LORD. H5536
Jer 9: 9 them for this?" **d** the LORD. "Should I H5536
Jer 9:22 "This is what the LORD **d**: " 'Dead bodies H5536
Jer 9:24 for in these I delight," **d** the LORD. H5536
Jer 9:25 **d** the LORD, "when I will punish all who H5536
Jer 12:17 uproot and destroy it," **d** the LORD. H5536
Jer 13:11 of Judah to me,' **d** the LORD, 'to be my H5536
Jer 13:14 parents and children alike, **d** the LORD. H5536
Jer 13:25 **d** the LORD, "because you have forgotten H5536
Jer 15: 3 **d** the LORD, "the sword to kill and the H5536
Jer 15: 6 have rejected me," **d** the LORD. "You keep H5536
Jer 15: 9 sword before their enemies," **d** the LORD. H5536
Jer 15:20 you to rescue and save you," **d** the LORD. H5536
Jer 16: 5 my pity from this people," **d** the LORD. H5536
Jer 16:11 ancestors forsook me,' **d** the LORD, 'and H5536
Jer 16:14 **d** the LORD, "when it will no longer be H5536
Jer 16:16 many fishermen," **d** the LORD, "and they H5536
Jer 17:24 careful to obey me, **d** the LORD, and bring H5536
Jer 18: 6 as this potter does?" **d** the LORD. "Like clay H5536
Jer 19: 6 the days are coming, **d** the LORD, when H5536
Jer 19:12 to those who live here, **d** the LORD. H5536
Jer 21: 7 After that, **d** the LORD, I will give Zedekiah H5536
Jer 21:10 this city harm and not good, **d** the LORD. H5536
Jer 21:13 the rocky plateau, **d** the LORD—you who H5536
Jer 21:14 you as your deeds deserve, **d** the LORD. H5536
Jer 22: 5 these commands, **d** the LORD, I swear by H5536
Jer 22:16 what it means to know me?" **d** the LORD. H5536
Jer 22:24 surely as I live," **d** the LORD, "even if you H5536
Jer 23: 1 the sheep of my pasture!" **d** the LORD. H5536
Jer 23: 2 the evil you have done," **d** the LORD. H5536
Jer 23: 4 will any be missing," **d** the LORD. H5536
Jer 23: 5 **d** the LORD, "when I will raise up for H5536
Jer 23: 7 **d** the LORD, "when people will no longer H5536
Jer 23:11 I find their wickedness," **d** the LORD. H5536
Jer 23:12 in the year they are punished," **d** the LORD. H5536
Jer 23:23 only a God nearby," **d** the LORD, "and not H5536
Jer 23:24 I cannot see them?" **d** the LORD. "Do not I H5536
Jer 23:24 not I fill heaven and earth?" **d** the LORD. H5536
Jer 23:28 has straw to do with grain?" **d** the LORD. H5536
Jer 23:29 **d** the LORD, "and like a hammer that H5536
Jer 23:30 **d** the LORD, "I am against the prophets H5536
Jer 23:31 **d** the LORD, "I am against the prophets H5536
Jer 23:31 own tongues and yet declare, 'The LORD **d**. H5536
Jer 23:32 who prophesy false dreams," **d** the LORD. H5536
Jer 23:32 these people in the least," **d** the LORD. H5536
Jer 23:33 I will forsake you, **d** the LORD.' H5536
Jer 25: 7 **d** the LORD, "and you have aroused my H5536
Jer 25: 9 **d** the LORD, "and I will bring them against H5536
Jer 25:12 **d** the LORD, "and will make it desolate H5536
Jer 25:29 live on the earth, **d** the LORD Almighty. H5536
Jer 25:31 put the wicked to the sword,' " **d** the LORD. H5536
Jer 27: 8 famine and plague, **d** the LORD, until I H5536
Jer 27:11 land to till it and to live there, **d** the LORD." H5536
Jer 27:15 have not sent them,' **d** the LORD. 'They are H5536
Jer 27:22 until the day I come for them,' **d** the LORD. H5536
Jer 28: 4 went to Babylon,' **d** the LORD, 'for I will H5536
Jer 29: 9 I have not sent them," **d** the LORD. H5536
Jer 29:11 **d** the LORD, "plans to prosper you and not H5536
Jer 29:14 **d** the LORD, "and will bring you back from H5536
Jer 29:14 **d** the LORD, "and will bring you back to H5536
Jer 29:19 **d** the LORD, "words that I sent to them H5536
Jer 29:19 have not listened either," **d** the LORD. H5536
Jer 29:23 it and am a witness to it," **d** the LORD. H5536
Jer 29:32 do for my people, **d** the LORD, because he H5536
Jer 30: 3 The days are coming,' **d** the LORD, 'when I H5536
Jer 30: 8 " 'In that day,' **d** the LORD Almighty, 'I will H5536
Jer 30:10 do not be dismayed, Israel,' **d** the LORD. H5536
Jer 30:11 with you and will save you,' **d** the LORD. H5536
Jer 30:17 heal your wounds,' **d** the LORD, 'because H5536
Jer 30:21 himself to be close to me?' **d** the LORD. H5536
Jer 31: 1 **d** the LORD, "I will be the God of all the H5536
Jer 31:14 will be filled with my bounty," **d** the LORD. H5536
Jer 31:16 your work will be rewarded," **d** the LORD. H5536
Jer 31:17 is hope for your descendants," **d** the LORD. H5536
Jer 31:20 great compassion for him," **d** the LORD. H5536
Jer 31:27 **d** the LORD, "when I will plant the H5536
Jer 31:28 them to build and to plant," **d** the LORD. H5536
Jer 31:31 **d** the LORD, "when I will make a new H5536
Jer 31:32 I was a husband to them," **d** the LORD. H5536
Jer 31:33 of Israel after that time," **d** the LORD. H5536
Jer 31:34 least of them to the greatest," **d** the LORD. H5536
Jer 31:36 **d** the LORD, "will Israel ever cease being H5536
Jer 31:37 of all they have done," **d** the LORD. H5536
Jer 31:38 **d** the LORD, "when this city will be rebuilt H5536
Jer 32: 5 remain until I deal with him, **d** the LORD. H5536
Jer 32:30 what their hands have made, **d** the LORD. H5536
Jer 32:44 I will restore their fortunes, **d** the LORD." H5536
Jer 33:14 days are coming,' **d** the LORD, 'when I will H5536
Jer 34: 5 I myself make this promise, **d** the LORD.' " H5536
Jer 34:17 'freedom' for you, **d** the LORD—'freedom' H5536
Jer 34:22 to give the order, **d** the LORD, and I will H5536
Jer 35:13 a lesson and obey my words?' **d** the LORD. H5536
Jer 39:17 you on that day, **d** the LORD; you will not H5536
Jer 39:18 because you trust in me, **d** the LORD. H5536
Jer 42:11 not be afraid of him, **d** the LORD, for I am H5536
Jer 44:29 you in this place,' **d** the LORD, 'so that you H5536
Jer 45: 5 on all people, **d** the LORD, but wherever H5536
Jer 46: 5 there is terror on every side," **d** the LORD. H5536
Jer 46:18 **d** the King, whose name is the LORD H5536
Jer 46:23 chop down her forest," **d** the LORD, "dense H5536
Jer 46:26 be inhabited as in times past," **d** the LORD. H5536
Jer 46:28 my servant, for I am with you," **d** the LORD. H5536
Jer 48:12 **d** the LORD, "when I will send men who H5536
Jer 48:15 **d** the King, whose name is the LORD H5536
Jer 48:25 is cut off; her arm is broken," **d** the LORD. H5536
Jer 48:30 **d** the LORD, "and her boasts accomplish H5536
Jer 48:35 burn incense to their gods," **d** the LORD. H5536
Jer 48:38 like a jar that no one wants," **d** the LORD. H5536
Jer 48:43 you people of Moab," **d** the LORD. H5536
Jer 48:44 the year of her punishment," **d** the LORD. H5536
Jer 48:47 of Moab in days to come," **d** the LORD. H5536
Jer 49: 2 **d** the LORD, "when I will sound the battle H5536
Jer 49: 5 all those around you," **d** the Lord, the LORD H5536
Jer 49: 6 fortunes of the Ammonites," **d** the LORD. H5536
Jer 49:13 **d** the LORD, "that Bozrah will become a H5536
Jer 49:16 there I will bring you down," **d** the LORD. H5536
Jer 49:26 silenced in that day," **d** the LORD Almighty. H5536
Jer 49:30 you who live in Hazor," **d** the LORD. H5536
Jer 49:31 **d** the LORD, "a nation that has neither H5536
Jer 49:32 on them from every side," **d** the LORD. H5536
Jer 49:37 even my fierce anger," **d** the LORD. H5536
Jer 49:38 destroy her king and officials," **d** the LORD. H5536
Jer 49:39 of Elam in days to come," **d** the LORD. H5536
Jer 50: 4 **d** the LORD, "the people of Israel and the H5536
Jer 50:10 her will have their fill," **d** the LORD. H5536
Jer 50:20 **d** the LORD, "search will be made for H5536
Jer 50:21 completely destroy them," **d** the LORD. H5536
Jer 50:30 will be silenced in that day," **d** the LORD. H5536
Jer 50:31 you arrogant one," **d** the Lord, the LORD H5536
Jer 50:35 **d** the LORD—"against those who live in H5536
Jer 50:40 neighboring towns," **d** the LORD, "so no H5536
Jer 51:24 they have done in Zion," **d** the LORD. H5536
Jer 51:25 who destroy the whole earth," **d** the LORD. H5536
Jer 51:26 you will be desolate forever," **d** the LORD. H5536
Jer 51:39 sleep forever and not awake," **d** the LORD. H5536
Jer 51:48 destroyers will attack her," **d** the LORD. H5536
Jer 51:52 days are coming," **d** the LORD, "when I will H5536
Jer 51:53 send destroyers against her," **d** the LORD. H5536
Jer 51:57 **d** the King, whose name is the LORD H5536
Eze 5:11 as surely as I live, **d** the Sovereign LORD H5536
Eze 11: 8 bring against you, **d** the Sovereign LORD. H5536
Eze 11:21 they have done, **d** the Sovereign LORD." H5536
Eze 12:25 whatever I say, **d** the Sovereign LORD. H5536
Eze 12:28 say will be fulfilled, **d** the Sovereign LORD. H5536
Eze 13: 6 they say, "The LORD **d**," and expect him to H5536
Eze 13: 7 you say, "The LORD **d**," though I have not H5536
Eze 13: 8 I am against you, **d** the Sovereign LORD. H5536
Eze 13:16 there was no peace, **d** the Sovereign LORD." H5536
Eze 14:11 I will be their God, **d** the Sovereign LORD. H5536
Eze 14:14 their righteousness, **d** the Sovereign LORD. H5536
Eze 14:16 as surely as I live, **d** the Sovereign LORD H5536
Eze 14:18 as surely as I live, **d** the Sovereign LORD H5536
Eze 14:20 as surely as I live, **d** the Sovereign LORD H5536
Eze 14:23 in it without cause, **d** the Sovereign LORD." H5536
Eze 15: 8 been unfaithful, **d** the Sovereign LORD." H5536
Eze 16: 8 a covenant with you, **d** the Sovereign LORD H5536
Eze 16:14 your beauty perfect, **d** the Sovereign LORD. H5536
Eze 16:19 is what happened, **d** the Sovereign LORD. H5536
Eze 16:23 Woe to you, **d** the Sovereign LORD H5536
Eze 16:30 fury against you, **d** the Sovereign LORD H5536
Eze 16:43 you have done, **d** the Sovereign LORD. H5536
Eze 16:48 As surely as I live, **d** the Sovereign LORD H5536
Eze 16:58 your detestable practices, **d** the LORD. H5536
Eze 16:63 of your humiliation, **d** the Sovereign LORD. H5536
Eze 17:16 'As surely as I live, **d** the Sovereign LORD H5536
Eze 18: 3 "As surely as I live, **d** the Sovereign LORD H5536
Eze 18: 9 he will surely live, **d** the Sovereign LORD. H5536
Eze 18:23 death of the wicked? **d** the Sovereign LORD H5536
Eze 18:30 to your own ways, **d** the Sovereign LORD. H5536
Eze 18:32 death of anyone, **d** the Sovereign LORD. H5536
Eze 20: 3 you inquire of me, **d** the Sovereign LORD. H5536
Eze 20:31 As surely as I live, **d** the Sovereign LORD, H5536
Eze 20:33 As surely as I live, **d** the Sovereign LORD, H5536
Eze 20:36 so I will judge you, **d** the Sovereign LORD. H5536
Eze 20:40 mountain of Israel, **d** the Sovereign LORD H5536
Eze 20:44 you people of Israel, **d** the Sovereign LORD. H5536
Eze 21: 7 surely take place, **d** the Sovereign LORD." H5536
Eze 21:13 does not continue? **d** the Sovereign LORD.' H5536
Eze 22:12 have forgotten me, **d** the Sovereign LORD. H5536
Eze 22:31 all they have done, **d** the Sovereign LORD." H5536
Eze 23:34 I have spoken, **d** the Sovereign LORD. H5536
Eze 24:14 your actions, **d** the Sovereign LORD. H5536
Eze 25:14 my vengeance, **d** the Sovereign LORD. H5536
Eze 26: 5 I have spoken, **d** the Sovereign LORD. H5536
Eze 26:14 LORD have spoken, **d** the Sovereign LORD. H5536
Eze 26:21 again be found, **d** the Sovereign LORD." H5536
Eze 28:10 I have spoken, **d** the Sovereign LORD.' " H5536
Eze 29:20 army did it for me, **d** the Sovereign LORD. H5536
Eze 30: 6 sword within her, **d** the Sovereign LORD. H5536
Eze 31:18 all his hordes, **d** the Sovereign LORD. H5536
Eze 32: 8 over your land, **d** the Sovereign LORD. H5536
Eze 32:14 flow like oil, **d** the Sovereign LORD. H5536
Eze 32:16 they will chant it, **d** the Sovereign LORD." H5536
Eze 32:31 killed by the sword, **d** the Sovereign LORD. H5536
Eze 32:32 killed by the sword, **d** the Sovereign LORD." H5536
Eze 33:11 'As surely as I live, **d** the Sovereign LORD, H5536
Eze 34: 8 As surely as I live, **d** the Sovereign LORD H5536
Eze 34:15 them lie down, **d** the Sovereign LORD. H5536
Eze 34:30 are my people, **d** the Sovereign LORD. H5536
Eze 34:31 I am your God, **d** the Sovereign LORD. H5536
Eze 35: 6 as surely as I live, **d** the Sovereign LORD, H5536
Eze 35:11 as surely as I live, **d** the Sovereign LORD, H5536
Eze 36:14 nation childless, **d** the Sovereign LORD. H5536
Eze 36:15 your nation to fall, **d** the Sovereign LORD. H5536
Eze 36:23 that I am the LORD, **d** the Sovereign LORD H5536
Eze 36:32 this for your sake, **d** the Sovereign LORD. H5536
Eze 37:14 spoken, and I have done it, **d** the LORD. H5536
Eze 38:18 will be aroused, **d** the Sovereign LORD. H5536
Eze 38:21 all my mountains, **d** the Sovereign LORD. H5536
Eze 39: 5 I have spoken, **d** the Sovereign LORD. H5536
Eze 39: 8 surely take place, **d** the Sovereign LORD. H5536
Eze 39:10 who looted them, **d** the Sovereign LORD. H5536
Eze 39:13 day for them, **d** the Sovereign LORD. H5536
Eze 39:20 of every kind,' **d** the Sovereign LORD. H5536
Eze 39:29 the people of Israel, **d** the Sovereign LORD." H5536
Eze 43:19 minister before me, **d** the Sovereign LORD. H5536
Eze 43:27 I will accept you, **d** the Sovereign LORD." H5536
Eze 44:12 of their sin, **d** the Sovereign LORD. H5536
Eze 44:15 of fat and blood, **d** the Sovereign LORD. H5536
Eze 44:27 offering for himself, **d** the Sovereign LORD. H5536
Eze 45: 9 my people, **d** the Sovereign LORD. H5536
Eze 45:15 the people, **d** the Sovereign LORD. H5536
Eze 47:23 their inheritance," **d** the Sovereign LORD. H5536
Eze 48:29 be their portions," **d** the Sovereign LORD. H5536
Hos 2:13 her lovers, but me she forgot," **d** the LORD. H5536
Hos 2:16 **d** the LORD, "you will call me 'my H5536
Hos 2:21 day I will respond," **d** the LORD—"I will H5536
Hos 11:11 settle them in their homes," **d** the LORD. H5536
Joel 2:12 **d** the LORD, "return to me with all your H5536
Am 2:11 not true, people of Israel?" **d** the LORD. H5536
Am 2:16 will flee naked on that day," **d** the LORD. H5536
Am 3:10 **d** the LORD, "who store up in their H5536
Am 3:13 of Jacob," **d** the Lord, the LORD God H5536
Am 3:15 will be demolished," **d** the LORD. H5536
Am 4: 3 be cast out toward Harmon," **d** the LORD. H5536
Am 4: 5 you love to do," **d** the Sovereign LORD. H5536
Am 4: 6 you have not returned to me," **d** the LORD. H5536
Am 4: 8 you have not returned to me," **d** the LORD. H5536
Am 4: 9 you have not returned to me," **d** the LORD. H5536
Am 4:10 you have not returned to me," **d** the LORD. H5536
Am 4:11 you have not returned to me," **d** the LORD. H5536
Am 6: 8 by himself—the LORD God Almighty **d**: H5536
Am 6:14 the LORD God Almighty **d**, "I will stir up H5536
Am 8: 3 **d** the Sovereign LORD, "the songs in the H5536
Am 8: 9 **d** the Sovereign LORD, "I will make the H5536
Am 8:11 **d** the Sovereign LORD, "when I will send a H5536
Am 9: 7 as the Cushites?" **d** the LORD. "Did I not H5536
Am 9: 8 the descendants of Jacob," **d** the LORD. H5536
Am 9:12 that bear my name," **d** the LORD, who will H5536
Am 9:13 **d** the LORD, "when the reaper will be H5536
Ob 4 there I will bring you down," **d** the LORD. H5536
Ob 8 **d** the LORD, "will I not destroy the wise H5536
Mic 4: 6 "In that day," **d** the LORD, "I will gather the H5536
Mic 5:10 **d** the LORD, "I will destroy your horses H5536
Na 2:13 "I am against you," **d** the LORD Almighty H5536
Na 3: 5 "I am against you," **d** the LORD Almighty H5536
Zep 1: 2 from the face of the earth," **d** the LORD. H5536
Zep 1: 3 on the face of the earth," **d** the LORD, H5536
Zep 1:10 **d** the LORD, "a cry will go up from the Fish H5536
Zep 2: 9 as surely as I live," **d** the LORD Almighty H5536
Zep 3: 8 **d** the LORD, "for the day I will stand up to H5536
Hag 1: 9 **d** the LORD Almighty. "Because of H5536
Hag 1:13 "I am with you," **d** the LORD. H5536
Hag 2: 4 now be strong, Zerubbabel,' **d** the LORD. H5536
Hag 2: 4 people of the land,' **d** the LORD, 'and work. H5536
Hag 2: 4 For I am with you,' **d** the LORD Almighty. H5536
Hag 2: 8 the gold is mine,' **d** the LORD Almighty. H5536
Hag 2: 9 I will grant peace,' **d** the LORD Almighty." H5536
Hag 2:14 this nation in my sight,' **d** the LORD. H5536
Hag 2:17 you did not return to me,' **d** the LORD. H5536
Hag 2:23 " 'On that day,' **d** the LORD Almighty, H5536
Hag 2:23 son of Shealtiel,' **d** the LORD, 'and I will H5536
Hag 2:23 I have chosen you,' **d** the LORD Almighty." H5536
Zec 1: 3 'Return to me,' **d** the LORD Almighty, 'and H5536
Zec 1: 4 listen or pay attention to me, **d** the LORD. H5536
Zec 1:16 out over Jerusalem,' **d** the LORD Almighty. H5536
Zec 2: 5 of fire around it,' **d** the LORD, 'and I will be H5536
Zec 2: 6 **d** the LORD, "for I have scattered you to H5536
Zec 2: 6 to the four winds of heaven," **d** the LORD. H5536
Zec 2:10 I will live among you," **d** the LORD. H5536
Zec 3:10 vine and fig tree,' **d** the LORD Almighty." H5536
Zec 5: 4 The LORD Almighty **d**, 'I will send it out H5536
Zec 8: 6 marvelous to me?" **d** the LORD Almighty. H5536
Zec 8:11 as I did in the past," **d** the LORD Almighty. H5536
Zec 8:17 swear falsely. I hate all this," **d** the LORD. H5536
Zec 10:12 name they will live securely," **d** the LORD. H5536
Zec 11: 6 on the people of the land," **d** the LORD. H5536
Zec 12: 1 forms the human spirit within a person, **d**: H5536
Zec 12: 4 its rider with madness," **d** the LORD. H5536
Zec 13: 2 no more," **d** the LORD Almighty. H5536
Zec 13: 7 who is close to me!" **d** the LORD Almighty H5536
Zec 13: 8 **d** the LORD, "two-thirds will be struck H5536
Mal 1: 2 Jacob's brother?" **d** the LORD. "Yet I have H5536
Mt 15: 5 say that if anyone **d** *that* what might have *G3306*

Mk 7:11 say that if anyone **d** that what might have *G3306*
Lk 20:42 David himself **d** in the Book of Psalms: *G3306*
Ro 2:16 secrets through Jesus Christ, **as** my gospel *d.* AIT
Heb 8: 8 days are coming, **d** the Lord, when I will *G3306*
Heb 8: 9 I turned away from them, **d** the Lord. *G3306*
Heb 8:10 of Israel after that time, **d** the Lord. *G3306*

DECLARING (4) [DECLARE]

Ps 22:31 his righteousness, **d** to a people yet unborn: NDT
Ps 71: 8 your praise, **d** your splendor all day long. NDT
Jer 50:28 from Babylon **d** in Zion how the LORD H5583
Ac 2:11 we hear them **d** the wonders of God in our *G3281*

DECLINED (1)

Ac 18:20 spend more time with them, *he* **d**. *G4024+2153*

DECORATE (2) [DECORATED, DECORATES, DECORATING, DECORATIONS, DECORATIVE]

1Ki 7:18 each network to **d** the capitals on top of H4059
Mt 23:29 the prophets and **d** the graves of the *G3175*

DECORATED (10) [DECORATE]

Dt 3:11 His **bed** was *d with* iron and was more than AIT
2Ki 25:17 cubits high and was **d with** a network and H6584
2Ch 3: 5 with fine gold and **d** it *with* palm tree H6590
SS 5:14 is like polished ivory **d** *with* lapis lazuli. H6634
Jer 52:22 cubits high and was **d with** a network and H6584
Eze 40:16 projecting walls were **d with** palm trees. H448
Eze 40:31 palm trees **d** its jambs, and eight H448
Eze 40:34 palm trees **d** the jambs on either side H448
Eze 40:37 palm trees **d** the jambs on either side H448
Rev 21:19 of the city walls *were* **d** with every kind of *G3175*

DECORATES (1) [DECORATE]

Jer 22:14 panels it with cedar and **d** it in red. H5417

DECORATING (4) [DECORATE]

1Ki 7:41 sets of network **d** the two bowl-shaped H4059
1Ki 7:42 each network **d** the bowl-shaped H4059
2Ch 4:12 sets of network **d** the two bowl-shaped H4059
2Ch 4:13 **d** the bowl-shaped capitals on top of the H4059

DECORATIONS (2) [DECORATE]

Eze 40:22 portico and its **palm tree d** had the same H9474
Eze 40:26 it had **palm tree d** on the faces of the H9474

DECORATIVE (1) [DECORATE]

Lev 8: 7 fastened the ephod with a **d waistband,** H3109

DECREASE (2) [DECREASED]

Lev 25:16 years are few, *you are to* **d** the price H5070
Jer 29: 6 Increase in number there; *do* not **d**. H5070

DECREASED (2) [DECREASE]

Ps 107:39 Then *their* **numbers d**, and they were H5070
Jer 30:19 numbers, and *they will* not *be* **d**; I will H5070

DECREE (43) [DECREED, DECREES]

2Sa 7:19 this **d**, Sovereign LORD, is *for* a mere H9368
1Ch 16:17 He confirmed it to Jacob as a **d**, to Israel H2976
Ezr 5:13 King Cyrus issued a **d** to rebuild this A10302
Ezr 5:17 did in fact issue a **d** to rebuild this house A10302
Ezr 6: 3 king issued a **d** *concerning* the temple of A10302
Ezr 6: 8 I hereby **d** what you are to do A10682+10302
Ezr 6:11 I **d** that if anyone defies this A10682+10302
Ezr 6:12 a hand to change this **d** or to destroy this NDT
Ezr 6:13 because of the **d** King Darius had sent NDT
Ezr 7:13 Now I **d** that any of the Israelites A10682+10302
Ezr 7:21 **d** that all the treasurers of A10682+10302
Est 1:19 him issue a royal **d** and let it be written H1821
Est 3: 9 the king, *let a* **d be issued** to destroy them H4180
Est 8: 8 Now write another **d** in the king's name in NDT
Est 9:32 Esther's **d** confirmed these regulations H4411
Job 23:14 He carries out his **d** *against* me, and H2976
Job 28:26 when he made a **d** for the rain and a path H2976
Ps 2: 7 I will proclaim the LORD's **d**: He said to me, H2976
Ps 7: 6 Awake, my God; **d** justice. H7422
Ps 81: 4 this is a **d** for Israel, an ordinance of the H2976
Ps 105:10 He confirmed it to Jacob as a **d**, to Israel H2976
Ps 138: 2 so exalted your **solemn d** that it surpasses H614
Ps 148: 6 he issued a **d** that will never pass away. H2976
Jer 51:12 *his* **d** against the people of Babylon. H1819
Da 2:13 So the **d** was issued to put the wise men A10186
Da 2:15 "Why did the king issue such a harsh **d**?" A10186
Da 3:10 has issued a **d** that everyone who A10302
Da 3:29 Therefore I **d** that the people of A10682+10302
Da 4:24 this is the **d** the Most High has A10141
Da 6: 7 enforce the **d** that anyone who prays A10057
Da 6: 8 issue the **d** and put it in writing so that it A10057
Da 6: 9 So King Darius put the **d** in writing. A10057
Da 6:10 learned that the **d** had been published, A10375
Da 6:12 king and spoke to him about his royal **d**: A10057
Da 6:12 you not publish a **d** that during the next A10057
Da 6:12 king answered, "The **d** stands—in A10418
Da 6:13 Majesty, or to the **d** you put in writing. A10057
Da 6:15 Persians no **d** or edict that the A10057
Da 6:26 "I issue a **d** that in every part of my A10302
Jnh 3: 7 "By the **d** *of* the king and his nobles H3248
Zep 2: 2 before the **d** takes effect and that day H2976
Lk 2: 1 Augustus issued a **d** that a census should *G1504*
Ro 1:32 know God's **righteous d** that those who *G1468*

DECREED (26) [DECREE]

1Ki 22:23 The LORD *has* **d** disaster for you." H1819
2Ki 8: 1 because the LORD *has* **d** a famine in the H7924
2Ch 18:22 The LORD *has* **d** disaster for you." H1819
Ezr 6:12 I Darius *have* **d** it. Let it be A10682+10302
Est 2: 1 had done and what *he had* **d** about her. H1615
Est 9:31 Jew and Queen Esther *had* **d** for them, H7756
Job 14: 5 you have **d** the number of his months and H907
Ps 78: 5 *He* **d** statutes for Jacob and established H7756
Ps 138: 4 when they hear **what** you have **d.** H609+7023
Pr 31: 5 they drink and forget *what has* **been d**, H2980
Isa 10:22 Destruction *has* **been d**, overwhelming H3076
Isa 10:23 out the destruction **d** upon the whole land H3076
Isa 28:22 me of the destruction **d** against the whole H3076
Jer 11:17 who planted you, *has* **d** disaster for you H1819
Jer 13:25 the portion I have **d** *for* you," declares the H4496
Jer 16:10 'Why *has* the LORD **d** such a great disaster H1819
Jer 40: 2 "The LORD your God **d** this disaster for this H1819
La 1:17 The LORD *has* **d** for Jacob that his H7422
La 2:17 fulfilled his word, which *he* **d** long ago. H7422
La 3:37 have it happen if the Lord *has* not **d** it? H7422
Da 4:31 heaven, "This is what *is* **d** for you, King A10042
Da 9:24 "Seventy 'sevens' **are d** for your people H3155
Da 9:26 the end, and desolations *have* **been d**. H3076
Da 9:27 until the end *that* **is d** is poured out on H3076
Na 2: 7 *It is* **d** that Nineveh be exiled and carried H5893
Lk 22:22 The Son of Man will go as it *has been* **d** *G3988*

DECREES (138) [DECREE]

Ge 26: 5 my commands, my **d** and my instructions." H2978
Ex 15:26 to his commands and keep all his **d,** H2976
Ex 18:16 inform them of God's **d** and instructions." H2976
Ex 18:20 Teach them his **d** and instructions, and H2976
Lev 10:11 the Israelites all the **d** the LORD has given H2976
Lev 18: 4 my laws and be careful to follow my **d.** H2978
Lev 18: 5 Keep my **d** and laws, for the person who H2978
Lev 18:26 But you must keep my **d** and my laws. H2978
Lev 19:19 " 'Keep my **d.** " 'Do not mate different H2978
Lev 19:37 " 'Keep all my **d** and all my laws and H2978
Lev 20: 8 Keep my **d** and follow them. I am the LORD H2978
Lev 20:22 " 'Keep all my **d** and laws and follow H2978
Lev 25:18 " 'Follow my **d** and be careful to obey my H2978
Lev 26: 3 " 'If you follow my **d** and are careful to H2978
Lev 26:15 if you reject my **d** and abhor my laws H2978
Lev 26:43 they rejected my laws and abhorred my **d.** H2978
Lev 26:46 These are the **d**, the laws and the H2976
Dt 4: 1 hear the **d** and laws I am about to teach H2976
Dt 4: 5 I have taught you **d** and laws as the LORD H2976
Dt 4: 6 who will hear about all these **d** and say H2976
Dt 4: 8 have such righteous **d** and laws as this H2976
Dt 4:14 to teach you the **d** and laws you are to H2976
Dt 4:40 Keep his **d** and commands, which I am H2976
Dt 4:45 **d** and laws Moses gave them when they H2976
Dt 5: 1 the **d** and laws I declare in your hearing H2976
Dt 5:31 **d** and laws you are to teach them to H2976
Dt 6: 1 **d** and laws the LORD your God directed me H2976
Dt 6: 2 by keeping all his **d** and commands that I H2978
Dt 6:17 the stipulations and **d** he has given you. H2976
Dt 6:20 **d** and laws the LORD our God has H2976
Dt 6:24 us to obey all these **d** and to fear the LORD H2976
Dt 7:11 commands, **d** and laws I give you today. H2976
Dt 8:11 his laws and his **d** that I am giving you H2978
Dt 10:13 LORD's commands and **d** that I am giving H2978
Dt 11: 1 his requirements, his **d**, his laws and his H2978
Dt 11:32 you obey all the **d** and laws I am setting H2976
Dt 12: 1 These are the **d** and laws you must be H2976
Dt 16:12 in Egypt, and follow carefully these **d.** H2976
Dt 17:19 all the words of this law and these **d** H2976
Dt 26:16 you this day to follow these **d** and laws; H2976
Dt 26:17 that you will keep his **d**, commands and H2976
Dt 27:10 his commands and **d** that I give you today H2976
Dt 28:15 all his commands and **d** I am giving you H2978
Dt 28:45 the commands and **d** he gave you. H2978
Dt 30:10 his commands and **d** that are written in H2978
Dt 30:16 keep his commands, **d** and laws; then you H2978
Jos 24:25 he reaffirmed for them **d** and laws. H2976
2Sa 22:23 I have not turned away from his **d.** H2978
1Ki 2: 3 and keep his **d** and commands, his H2978
1Ki 3:14 to me and keep my **d** and commands as H2976
1Ki 6:12 if you follow my **d**, observe my laws and H2978
1Ki 8:58 **d** and laws he gave our ancestors. H2976
1Ki 8:61 to live by his **d** and obey his commands H2976
1Ki 9: 4 I command and observe my **d** and laws, H2976
1Ki 9: 6 the commands and **d** I have given you H2978
1Ki 11:11 you have not kept my covenant and my **d,** H2978
1Ki 11:33 my eyes, nor kept my **d** and laws as David H2978
1Ki 11:34 who obeyed my commands and **d.** H2978
1Ki 11:38 my eyes by obeying my **d** and commands, H2978
2Ki 17:13 Observe my commands and **d**, in H2978
2Ki 17:15 They rejected his **d** and the covenant he H2976
2Ki 17:34 LORD nor adhere to the **d** and regulations, H2978
2Ki 17:37 be careful to keep the **d** and regulations, H2976
2Ki 23: 3 statutes and **d** with all his heart and all H2978
1Ch 22:13 to observe the **d** and laws that the LORD H2976
1Ch 29:19 statutes and **d** and to do everything to H2976
2Ch 7:17 I command, and observe my **d** and laws, H2976
2Ch 7:19 forsake the **d** and commands I have H2978
2Ch 19:10 commands, **d** or regulations—you are to H2976
2Ch 33: 8 **d** and regulations given through Moses." H2976
2Ch 34:31 statutes and **d** with all his heart and all H2976
Ezr 6:14 of the God of Israel and the **d** *of* Cyrus, A10302
Ezr 7:10 to teaching its **d** and laws in Israel. H2976
Ezr 7:11 the commands and **d** *of* the LORD for Israel H2976
Ne 1: 7 **d** and laws you gave your servant Moses. H2976
Ne 9:13 **d** and commands that are good. H2976
Ne 9:14 **d** and laws through your servant Moses. H2976
Ne 10:29 regulations and **d** *of* the LORD our Lord. H2976
Ps 18:22 I have not turned away from his **d.** H2978
Ps 19: 9 The **d** *of* the LORD are firm, and all of them H5477
Ps 44: 4 my God, *who* **d** victories for Jacob. H7422
Ps 89:31 if they violate my **d** and fail to keep my H2978
Ps 94:20 a throne that brings on misery by its **d**? H2976
Ps 99: 7 kept his statutes and the **d** he gave them. H2976
Ps 119: 5 my ways were steadfast in obeying your **d**! H2976
Ps 119: 8 I will obey your **d**; do not utterly forsake H2976
Ps 119:12 Praise be to you, LORD; teach me your **d.** H2976
Ps 119:16 I delight in your **d**; I will not neglect your H2978
Ps 119:23 your servant will meditate on your **d.** H2976
Ps 119:26 you answered me; teach me your **d.** H2976
Ps 119:33 the way of your **d**, that I may follow it H2976
Ps 119:48 that I may meditate on your **d.** H2976
Ps 119:54 Your **d** are the theme of my song H2976
Ps 119:64 with your love, LORD; teach me your **d.** H2976
Ps 119:68 what you do is good; teach me your **d.** H2976
Ps 119:71 to be afflicted so that I might learn your **d.** H2976
Ps 119:80 May I wholeheartedly follow your **d**, that I H2976
Ps 119:83 in the smoke, I do not forget your **d.** H2976
Ps 119:112 is set on keeping your **d** to the very end. H2976
Ps 119:117 I will always have regard for your **d.** H2976
Ps 119:118 You reject all who stray from your **d**, for H2976
Ps 119:124 to your love and teach me your **d.** H2976
Ps 119:135 on your servant and teach me your **d.** H2976
Ps 119:145 answer me, LORD, and I will obey your **d.** H2976
Ps 119:155 for they do not seek out your **d.** H2976
Ps 119:171 with praise, for you teach me your **d.** H2976
Ps 147:19 word to Jacob, his laws and **d** to Israel. H2976
Pr 8:15 reign and rulers **issue d** that are just; H2980
Isa 10: 1 to *those who* **issue** oppressive **d**, H4180+4180
Jer 31:35 who **d** the moon and stars to shine by H2978
Jer 31:36 "Only if these **d** vanish from my sight," H2976
Jer 44:10 my law and the **d** I set before you and H2978
Jer 44:23 his law or his **d** or his stipulations, H2978
Eze 5: 6 against my laws and **d** more than the H2978
Eze 5: 6 my laws and has not followed my **d.** H2978
Eze 5: 7 have not followed my **d** or kept my laws. H2978
Eze 11:12 not followed my **d** or kept my laws but H2976
Eze 11:20 they will follow my **d** and be careful to H2978
Eze 18: 9 He follows my **d** and faithfully keeps my H2978
Eze 18:17 He keeps my laws and follows my **d.** H2978
Eze 18:19 has been careful to keep all my **d,** H2978
Eze 18:21 keeps all my **d** and does what is just H2978
Eze 20:11 I gave them my **d** and made known to H2978
Eze 20:13 did not follow my **d** but rejected my laws H2978
Eze 20:16 did not follow my **d** and desecrated my H2978
Eze 20:19 follow my **d** and be careful to keep my H2978
Eze 20:21 They did not follow my **d**, they were not H2978
Eze 20:24 had rejected my **d** and desecrated my H2978
Eze 33:15 follow the **d** *that give* life, and do no H2978
Eze 36:27 move you to follow my **d** and be careful to H2976
Eze 37:24 my laws and be careful to keep my **d.** H2978
Eze 44:24 keep my laws and my **d** for all my H2978
Am 2: 4 law of the LORD and have not kept his **d,** H2976
Zec 1: 6 But did not my words and my **d**, which I H2976
Mal 3: 7 turned away from my **d** and have not kept H2976
Mal 4: 4 the **d** and laws I gave him at Horeb for all H2976
Lk 1: 6 the Lord's commands and **d** blamelessly. *G1468*
Ac 17: 7 They are all defying Caesar's **d**, saying *G1504*

DEDAN (10) [DEDANITES]

Ge 10: 7 The sons of Raamah: Sheba and **D.** H1847
Ge 25: 3 Jokshan was the father of Sheba and **D** H1847
Ge 25: 3 the descendants of **D** were the Ashurites H1847
1Ch 1: 9 The sons of Raamah: Sheba and **D.** H1847
1Ch 1:32 The sons of Jokshan: Sheba and **D.** H1847
Jer 25:23 **D**, Tema, Buz and all who are in distant H1847
Jer 49: 8 you who live in **D**, for I will bring H1847
Eze 25:13 from Teman to **D** they will fall by the H1847
Eze 27:20 " '**D** traded in saddle blankets with you. H1847
Eze 38:13 Sheba and **D** and the merchants of H1847

DEDANITES (1) [DEDAN]

Isa 21:13 You caravans of **D**, who camp in the H1848

DEDICATE (7) [DEDICATED, DEDICATES, DEDICATION, REDEDICATE]

Lev 27: 2 anyone **makes a special vow to d** a H7098+5624
Lev 27:17 If *they* **d** a field during the Year of Jubilee H7727
Lev 27:18 But if *they* **d** a field after the Jubilee, the H7727
Lev 27:26 however, *may* **d** the firstborn of an animal H7727
2Ch 2: 4 LORD my God and to **d** it to him for burning H7727
Pr 20:25 It is a trap to **d** something rashly and only H7731
Eze 43:26 and cleanse it; thus *they will* **d** it. H4848+3338

DEDICATED (31) [DEDICATE]

Lev 21:12 he has been **d** *by* the anointing oil H5694
Lev 27: 8 **the person being d** is to be presented to H2257
Nu 18: 6 **d** to the LORD to do the work at the tent of H5989
Jdg 13: 5 boy is to be a **Nazirite**, *d to* God from the AIT
Jdg 16:17 I have been a **Nazirite** *d to* God from my AIT
2Sa 8:11 King David **d** these articles to the LORD, as H7727
2Sa 8:12 He also **d** the plunder taken from NDT
1Ki 7:51 in the **things** his father David had **d**— H7731
1Ki 8:63 all the Israelites **d** the temple of the LORD H2852
1Ki 15:15 the articles that he and his father had **d.** H7731
2Ki 12:18 the sacred objects **d** *by* his predecessors— H7727
2Ki 12:18 the **gifts** he himself had **d** and all the H7731

2Ki 23:11 that the kings of Judah *had* **d** to the sun. H5989
2Ki 23:11 Josiah then burned the **chariots** *d to* the sun. AIT
1Ch 18:11 King David **d** these articles to the LORD, as H7727
1Ch 26:20 of God and the treasures for the **d things**. H7731
1Ch 26:26 treasures for the things **d** *by* King David, H7727
1Ch 26:27 taken in battle *they* **d** for the repair of the H7727
1Ch 26:28 And everything **d** *by* Samuel the seer and H7727
1Ch 26:28 all the other **d** *things* were in the care H7727
1Ch 28:12 for the treasures for the **d things**. H7731
2Ch 5: 1 in the **things** his father David had **d**— H7731
2Ch 7: 5 all the people **d** the temple of God. H2852
2Ch 15:18 the articles that he and his father had **d**. H7731
2Ch 29:31 "*You have* now **d** yourselves to the H4848+3338
2Ch 30:21 with resounding instruments **d to** the LORD. H4200
2Ch 31: 6 of the holy things **d** to the LORD their God, H7727
2Ch 31:12 in the contributions, tithes and **d gifts**. H7731
Ne 3: 1 They **d** it and set its doors in place H7727
Ne 3: 1 the Hundred, which *they* **d**, and as far as H7727
Lk 21: 5 beautiful stones and *with* **gifts d to God**. *G356*

DEDICATES (5) [DEDICATE]

Lev 27:14 " 'If anyone **d** their house as something H7727
Lev 27:15 If the *one who* **d** their house wishes to H7727
Lev 27:16 " 'If anyone **d** to the LORD part of their H7727
Lev 27:19 If the *one who* **d** the field wishes to H7727
Lev 27:22 " 'If *anyone* **d** to the LORD a field they have H7727

DEDICATION (26) [DEDICATE]

Nu 6: 2 a vow of **d** to the LORD as a Nazirite, H5687
Nu 6: 5 until the period of *their* **d** to the LORD is H5693
Nu 6: 6 the period of their **d** to the LORD, H5693
Nu 6: 7 the **symbol of** their **d** *to* God is on H5694
Nu 6: 8 Throughout the period of their **d**, they are H5694
Nu 6: 9 defiling the hair that symbolizes their **d**, H5694
Nu 6:12 the same period of **d** and must bring a H5694
Nu 6:12 became defiled during their **period of d**. H5694
Nu 6:13 Nazirite when the period of their **d** is over. H5694
Nu 6:18 shave off the hair that symbolizes their **d**. H5694
Nu 6:19 off the hair that symbolizes their **d**, H5694
Nu 6:21 to the LORD in accordance with their **d**, H5694
Nu 7:10 offerings for its **d** and presented them H2853
Nu 7:11 to bring his offering for the **d** *of* the altar." H2853
Nu 7:84 **offerings** of the Israelite leaders **for** the **d** *of*H2853
Nu 7:88 were the **offerings for** the **d** *of* the altar H2853
2Ch 7: 9 had celebrated the **d** *of* the altar for seven H2853
Ezr 6:16 celebrated the **d** *of* the house of God A10273
Ezr 6:17 For the **d** *of* this house of God they A10273
Ne 12:27 At the **d** *of* the wall of Jerusalem, the H2853
Ne 12:27 to celebrate joyfully the **d** with songs of H2853
Ps 30: T For the **d** *of* the temple. Of David H2853
Da 3: 2 to come to the **d** *of* the image he had A10273
Da 3: 3 assembled for the **d** *of* the image that A10273
Jn 10:22 Then came the **Festival of D** at Jerusalem *G1589*
1Ti 5:11 *their* **sensual desires overcome** *their* **d** to *G2952*

DEED (13) [DEEDED, DEEDS]

Dt 17: 5 has done this evil **d** to your city gate and H1821
Ecc 3:17 every activity, a time to judge every **d**." H5126
Ecc 12:14 For God will bring every **d** into judgment H5126
Jer 32:10 I signed and sealed the **d**, had it H6219
Jer 32:11 I took the **d** *of* purchase—the sealed copy H6219
Jer 32:12 I gave this **d** to Baruch son of Neriah H6219
Jer 32:12 who had signed the **d** and of all the Jews H6219
Jer 32:14 unsealed copies of the **d** *of* purchase, H6219
Jer 32:16 I had given the **d** *of* purchase to Baruch H6219
Lk 24:19 in word and **d** before God and all *G2240*
Col 3:17 whether in word or **d**, do it all in the *G2240*
2Th 1:11 your every **d** prompted by faith. *G2240*
2Th 2:17 strengthen you in every good **d** and word. *G2240*

DEEDED (2) [DEED]

Ge 23:17 within the borders of the field—*was* **d** H7756
Ge 23:20 the cave in it *were* **d** to Abraham by the H7756

DEEDS (118) [DEED]

Dt 3:24 who can do the **d** and mighty works you H5126
Dt 4:34 by great and **awesome d**, like all the H4616
Dt 34:12 the awesome **d** that Moses did in the H1524
1Sa 2: 3 who knows, and by him **d** are weighed. H6613
1Sa 2:23 the people about these wicked **d** *of* yours. H1821
1Sa 24:13 'From evildoers come **evil d**,' so my hand H8400
2Sa 3:39 repay the evildoer according to his **evil d**!" H8288
1Ch 16:24 his **marvelous** *d* among all peoples. AIT
Ezr 9:13 is a result of our evil **d** and our great guilt, H5126
Ne 6:19 to me his **good d** and then telling H3208
Job 34:25 Because he takes note of their **d**, he H5042
Ps 9: 1 my heart; I will tell of all your **wonderful** *d*. AIT
Ps 14: 1 are corrupt, their **d** are vile; there is no H6613
Ps 26: 7 praise and telling of all your **wonderful** *d*. AIT
Ps 28: 4 Repay them for their **d** and for their evil H7189
Ps 28: 5 no regard for the **d** *of* the LORD and what H7190
Ps 40: 5 were I to speak and tell of your **d**, they NDT
Ps 45: 4 let your right hand achieve **awesome** *d*. AIT
Ps 65: 5 answer us with awesome and **righteous d**, H7406
Ps 66: 3 "How awesome are your **d**! So great is H5126
Ps 66: 5 has done, his awesome **d** for mankind! H6613
Ps 71:15 My mouth will tell of your **righteous d**, of H7407
Ps 71:16 I will proclaim your **righteous d**, yours H7407
Ps 71:17 to this day I declare your **marvelous** *d*. AIT
Ps 72:18 God of Israel, who alone does **marvelous** *d*. AIT
Ps 73:28 LORD my refuge; I will tell of all your **d**. H4856
Ps 75: 1 people tell of your **wonderful** *d*. AIT
Ps 77:11 I will remember the **d** *of* the LORD; yes, H5095
Ps 77:12 works and meditate on all your **mighty d**." H6613
Ps 78: 4 generation the **praiseworthy d** *of* the LORD, H9335
Ps 78: 7 would not forget his **d** but would keep his H5095
Ps 86: 8 Lord; no **d** can compare with yours. H5126
Ps 86:10 For you are great and do **marvelous** *d*; you AIT
Ps 88:12 your **righteous d** in the land of oblivion? H7407
Ps 90:16 May your **d** be shown to your servants H7189
Ps 92: 4 For you make me glad by your **d**, LORD; H7189
Ps 96: 3 his **marvelous** *d* among all peoples. AIT
Ps 103: 7 to Moses, his **d** to the people of Israel: H6613
Ps 106:22 land of Ham and **awesome** *d* by the Red Sea AIT
Ps 106:29 the LORD's anger by their **wicked d**, H5095
Ps 106:39 by their **d** they prostituted themselves. H5095
Ps 107: 8 love and his **wonderful** *d* for mankind, AIT
Ps 107:15 love and his **wonderful** *d* for mankind, AIT
Ps 107:21 love and his **wonderful** *d* for mankind. AIT
Ps 107:24 of the LORD, his **wonderful** *d* in the deep. AIT
Ps 107:31 love and his **wonderful** *d* for mankind. AIT
Ps 107:43 ponder the **loving d** *of* the LORD. H2876
Ps 111: 3 Glorious and majestic are his **d**, and his H7189
Ps 119:27 that I may meditate on your **wonderful d**. H7098
Ps 141: 4 take part in wicked **d** along with those H6613
Ps 141: 5 will still be against the **d of evildoers**. H8288
Ps 145: 6 works—and I will proclaim your **great d**. H1525
Pr 5:22 The **evil d** *of* the wicked ensnare them H6411
Pr 8:22 the first of his works, before his **d** of old; H5148
Isa 1:16 Take your evil **d** out of my sight; stop H5095
Isa 3: 8 their words and **d** are against the LORD H5095
Isa 3:10 they will enjoy the fruit of their **d**. H5095
Isa 5:12 they have no regard for the **d** *of* the LORD, H7189
Isa 32: 8 noble plans, and by **noble** *d* they stand. AIT
Isa 41:29 Their **d** amount to nothing; their images H5126
Isa 59: 6 Their **d** are evil deeds, and acts of H5126
Isa 59: 6 Their deeds are evil **d**, and acts of H5126
Isa 63: 7 the *d for which* he is to be **praised** AIT
Isa 65: 7 laps the full payment for their former **d**." H7190
Jer 5:28 Their evil **d** have no limit; they do not H1821
Jer 17:10 according to what their **d** deserve. H5095
Jer 21:14 I will punish you as your **d** deserve H5095
Jer 23:22 from their evil ways and from their evil **d**. H5095
Jer 25:14 according to their **d** and the work of their H7189
Jer 32:19 are your purposes and mighty are your **d**. H6614
Jer 32:19 to their conduct and as their **d** deserve. H5095
Jer 32:44 silver, and **d** will be signed, sealed H6219
Jer 48: 7 Since you trust in your **d** and riches, you H5126
Jer 50:29 Repay her for her **d**; do to her as she has H7189
Eze 22:28 whitewash these **d** for them by false NDT
Eze 36:31 remember your evil ways and wicked **d**, H5095
Hos 4: 9 their ways and repay them for their **d**. H5095
Hos 5: 4 "Their **d** do not permit them to return to H5095
Hos 7: 2 realize that I remember all their **evil d**. H8288
Hos 9:15 Because of their sinful **d**, I will drive them H5095
Hos 12: 2 ways and repay him according to his **d**. H5095
Ob 15 your **d** will return upon your own head. H1691
Mic 7:13 of its inhabitants, as the result of their **d**. H5095
Hab 3: 2 your fame; I stand in awe of your **d**, LORD. H7189
Mt 5:16 they may see your good **d** and glorify your *G2240*
Mt 11: 2 heard about the **d** of the Messiah, he sent *G2240*
Mt 11:19 But wisdom is proved right by her **d**." *G2240*
Lk 1:51 He has performed **mighty d** with his arm *G3197*
Lk 23:41 we are getting what *our* **d** deserve. *G4556*
Jn 3:19 instead of light because their **d** were evil. *G2240*
Jn 3:20 light for fear that their **d** will be exposed. *G2240*
Ac 26:20 demonstrate their repentance *by* their **d**. *G2240*
Ro 13:12 let us put aside the **d** of darkness and put *G2240*
Eph 5:11 to do with the fruitless **d** of darkness, *G2240*
1Ti 2:10 with good **d**, appropriate for women *G2240*
1Ti 5:10 is well known for her good **d**, such as *G2240*
1Ti 5:10 devoting herself *to* all kinds of good **d**. *G2240*
1Ti 5:25 In the same way, good **d** are obvious, and *G2240*
1Ti 6:18 to be rich in good **d**, and to be generous *G2240*
Heb 10:24 one another on toward love and good **d**, *G2240*
Jas 2:14 claims to have faith but has no **d**? *G2240*
Jas 2:18 will say, "You have faith; I have **d**. *G2240*
Jas 2:18 Show me your faith without **d**, and I will *G2240*
Jas 2:18 I will show you my faith by my **d**. *G2240*
Jas 2:20 evidence that faith without **d** is useless? *G2240*
Jas 2:26 spirit is dead, so faith without **d** is dead. *G2240*
Jas 3:13 *by* **d** done in the humility that comes from *G2240*
1Pe 2:12 may see your good **d** and glorify God on *G2240*
2Pe 2: 8 soul *by* the lawless **d** he saw and *G2240*
Rev 2: 2 I know your **d**, your hard work and your *G2240*
Rev 2:19 I know your **d**, your love and faith, your *G2240*
Rev 2:23 will repay each of you according to your **d**. *G2240*
Rev 3: 1 I know your **d**; you have a reputation of *G2240*
Rev 3: 2 I have found your **d** unfinished in the *G2240*
Rev 3: 8 I know your **d**. See, I have placed before *G2240*
Rev 3:15 I know your **d**, that you are neither cold *G2240*
Rev 14:13 their labor, for their **d** will follow them." *G2240*
Rev 15: 3 "Great and marvelous are your **d**, Lord *G2240*

DEEP (105) [ANKLE-DEEP, DEEPENING, DEEPER, DEEPEST, DEEPLY, DEPTH, DEPTHS]

Ge 1: 2 darkness was over the surface of the **d** H9333
Ge 2:21 caused the man to fall into a **d sleep**; H9554
Ge 7:11 all the springs of the great **d** burst forth, H9333
Ge 8: 2 the springs of the **d** and the floodgates of H9333
Ge 15:12 Abram fell into a **d sleep**, and a thick H9554
Ge 49:25 blessings of the **d springs** below H9333
Ex 15: 5 The **d waters** have covered them; they H9333
Ex 15: 8 the **d waters** congealed in the heart of the H9333
Lev 13: 3 the sore appears to be more than skin **d**, H6678
Lev 13: 4 to be more than skin **d** and the hair in it H6678
Lev 13:20 to be more than skin **d** and the hair in it H9166
Lev 13:21 it is not more than skin **d** and has faded, H9166
Lev 13:25 it appears to be more than skin **d**, it H6678
Lev 13:26 it is not more than skin **d** and has faded, H9166
Lev 13:30 to be more than skin **d** and the hair in it is H6678
Lev 13:31 to be more than skin **d** and there is no H6678
Lev 13:32 it does not appear to be more than skin **d**, H6678
Lev 13:34 appears to be no more than skin **d**, H6678
Nu 11:31 two cubits **d** all around H6584+7156+2021+824
Dt 4:11 with black clouds and **d darkness**. H6906
Dt 5:22 the cloud and the **d darkness**; and he H6906
Dt 8: 7 and **d springs** gushing out into the valleys H9333
Dt 33:13 with the **d waters** that lie below; H9333
1Sa 1:10 *In* her **d anguish** Hannah prayed to H5253+5883
1Sa 26:12 the LORD had put them into a **d sleep**. H9554
2Sa 22:17 hold of me; he drew me out of **d** waters. H8041
2Sa 24:14 said to Gad, "I am in **d** distress. Let us fall H4394
1Ki 7:31 had a circular frame one cubit **d**. H5087+2025
1Ki 7:35 there was a circular band half a cubit **d**. H7757
1Ki 18:27 Perhaps he is **d in thought**, or busy, or H8490
1Ch 21:13 "I am in **d** distress. Let me fall H4394
Job 4:13 the night, when **d sleep** falls on people, H9554
Job 7:12 or the **monster of the d**, that you put H9490
Job 12:22 He reveals the **d** *things* of darkness and H6678
Job 26: 5 "The dead *are* **in d anguish**, those H2655
Job 28:14 The **d** says, "It is not in me"; the sea says H9333
Job 33:15 when **d sleep** falls on people as they H9554
Job 34:22 There is no **d shadow**, no utter darkness H3125
Job 38:16 sea or walked in the recesses of the **d**? H9333
Job 38:30 when the surface of the **d** is frozen? H9333
Job 41:32 one would think the **d** had white hair. H9333
Ps 6: 3 My soul *is* in **d** anguish. How long, LORD H4394
Ps 18:16 hold of me; he drew me out of **d** waters. H8041
Ps 33: 7 into jars; he puts the **d** into storehouses. H9333
Ps 36: 6 mountains, your justice like the great **d**. H9333
Ps 42: 7 **D** calls to deep in the roar of your H9333
Ps 42: 7 Deep calls to **d** in the roar of your H9333
Ps 44:19 you covered us over with **d darkness**. H7516
Ps 69: 2 I have come into the **d** waters; the floods H5099
Ps 69:14 those who hate me, from the **d** waters. H5099
Ps 107:24 of the LORD, his wonderful deeds in the **d**. H5185
Pr 4:19 the way of the wicked is like **d darkness**; H696
Pr 8:27 out the horizon on the face of the **d**, H9333
Pr 8:28 fixed securely the fountains of the **d**, H9333
Pr 9:18 that her guests are **d** in the realm of the H6679
Pr 18: 4 The words of the mouth are **d** waters, but H6678
Pr 19:15 Laziness brings on **d sleep**, and the H9554
Pr 20: 5 purposes of a person's heart are **d** waters, H6678
Pr 22:14 mouth of an adulterous woman is a **d** pit; H6678
Pr 23:27 an adulterous woman is a **d** pit, and a H6678
Pr 25: 3 the heavens are high and the earth is **d**, H6679
Pr 25:27 to search out matters that are *too* **d**. H3883
Isa 9: 2 in the land of **d darkness** a light has H7516
Isa 29:10 has brought over you a **d sleep**: H8120+9554
Isa 30:33 Its fire pit *has been* **made d** and wide H6676
Isa 44:27 who says to the **watery d**, 'Be dry, and I H7425
Isa 51:10 the waters of the great **d**, who made a H9333
Isa 54: 7 with **d** compassion I will bring you H1524
Isa 59: 9 brightness, but we walk in **d shadows**. H696
Jer 13:16 utter darkness and change it to **d gloom**. H6906
Jer 49: 8 flee, hide in **d** caves, you who live in H6676
Jer 49:30 Stay in **d** caves, you who live in Hazor," H6676
La 2:13 Your wound is as **d** as the sea. H1524
Eze 23:32 a cup large and **d**; it will bring scorn H6678
Eze 31: 4 nourished it, **d springs** made it grow tall H9333
Eze 31:15 I covered the **d springs** with mourning H9333
Eze 40: 6 threshold of the gate; it was one rod **d**. H8145
Eze 40: 7 the portico facing the temple was one rod **d**. NDT
Eze 40: 9 it was eight cubits **d** and its jambs were two NDT
Eze 40:30 twenty-five cubits wide and five cubits **d**.) H8145
Eze 43:13 Its gutter is a cubit **d** and a cubit wide, with NDT
Eze 47: 5 had risen and was **d enough to swim in**— H8467
Da 2:22 He reveals **d** and hidden things; he A10555
Da 8:18 *I was* **in a d sleep**, with my face H8101
Da 10: 9 **I fell into a d sleep**, my face to the H8101
Hos 9: 9 *They have* **sunk d** *into* corruption, as in H6676
Am 7: 4 dried up the great **d** and devoured the H9333
Jnh 1: 5 where he lay down and **fell into a d sleep**. H8101
Jnh 2: 2 From **d** *in* the realm of the dead I called H1061
Jnh 2: 5 threatened me, *the* **d** surrounded me H9333
Hab 3:10 the **d** roared and lifted its waves on high. H9333
Mk 7:34 to heaven and *with a* **d sigh** said to him, *G5100*
Lk 5: 4 "Put out into **d** *water*, and let down the *G958*
Lk 6:48 who dug **down d** and laid the foundation *G959*
Jn 4:11 nothing to draw with and the well is **d**. *G960*
Ac 20: 9 was sinking into a **d** sleep as Paul talked *G960*
Ac 27:28 was **a hundred and twenty feet d**. *G3976+1633*
Ac 27:28 and found it was **ninety feet d**. *G3976+1278*
Ro 10: 7 "or 'Who will descend into the **d**?' " (that is *G12*
1Co 2:10 all things, even the **d** *things* of God. *G958*
2Co 7: 7 longing for me, your **d sorrow**, your ardent *G3851*
Eph 3:18 long and high and **d** is the love of Christ *G958*
1Th 1: 5 with the Holy Spirit and **d** conviction. *G4498*
1Ti 3: 9 keep hold of the **d truths** of the faith with *G3696*
Rev 2:24 not learned Satan's so-called **d** *secrets*, *G960*

DEEPENING (1) [DEEP]

Phm 6 effective in **d** your **understanding** of every *G2106*

DEEPER (2) [DEEP]

Lev 14:37 that appear to be **d** than the surface of H9166

Job 11: 8 They are d than the depths below—what H6678

DEEPEST (3) [DEEP]

Job 10:22 to the land of **d night**, of utter H6547+4017+694
Job 38:17 you seen the gates of the **d darkness**? H7516
Isa 7:11 whether in the d depths or in the highest H6676

DEEPLY (17) [DEEP]

Ge 6: 6 the earth, and his heart **was d troubled**. H6772
Ge 43:30 **D moved** at the sight of his brother H4023+8171
1Sa 1:15 "I am a woman who is **d troubled**. H7997+8120
1Ki 3:26 was alive *was* **d moved** *out of* love for her H4023
Ps 73:16 all this, it troubled me **d** H6662+928+6524
Pr 7:18 *let's* **drink d** *of* love till morning H8115
Isa 66:11 *you will* **drink d** and delight in her H5209
Eze 3:15 them for seven days—**d distressed**. H9037
Da 7:28 was d troubled by my thoughts A10678
Mk 3: 5 **d distressed** at their stubborn hearts G5200
Mk 8:12 He **sighed d** and said, "Why G417+3836+4460
Mk 14:33 he began *to be* **d distressed** and G1701
Jn 11:33 he *was* **d moved** in spirit and troubled. G1839
Jn 11:38 once more **d moved**, came to the G1839
Ac 8: 2 buried Stephen and mourned **d** for him. G3489
1Pe 1:22 love one another **d**, from the heart. G1757
1Pe 4: 8 love each other **d**, because love covers G1756

DEER (14)

Dt 12:15 as if it were gazelle or d, according to the H385
Dt 12:22 Eat them as you would gazelle or d. H385
Dt 14: 5 the d, the gazelle, the roe deer, the wild H385
Dt 14: 5 the gazelle, the **roe d**, the wild goat, the H3502
Dt 15:22 clean may eat it, as if it were gazelle or d. H385
2Sa 22:34 He makes my feet like the feet of a d; he H387
1Ki 4:23 sheep and goats, as well as d, gazelles, H385
Ps 18:33 He makes my feet like the feet of a d; he H387
Ps 42: 1 As the d pants for streams of water, so my H385
Pr 5:19 a graceful d—may her breasts H3607
Pr 7:22 slaughter, like a d stepping into a noose H385
Isa 35: 6 Then will the lame leap like a d, and the H385
La 1: 6 Her princes are like d that find no pasture H385
Hab 3:19 he makes my feet like the feet of a d, he H387

DEFAMED (1)

Isa 48:11 How *can* I *let* myself **be d**? I will not H2725

DEFEAT (9) [DEFEATED, DEFEATING]

Ex 32:18 it is not the sound of d; it is the sound of H2711
Nu 22: 6 then I will be able *to* d them and drive H5782
Jdg 2:15 of the LORD was against them to d them, H8288
1Sa 4: 3 "Why *did* the LORD **bring d on** us today H5597
2Ki 13:19 But now *you will* d it only three times." H5782
Ps 92:11 My eyes have seen the d of my adversaries NDT
Isa 9: 4 For as in the day of Midian's d, you have NDT
Jer 37:10 Even if *you were to* d the entire H5782
Heb 7: 1 returning from the d of the kings and G3158

DEFEATED (53) [DEFEAT]

Ge 14: 5 with him went out and d the Rephaites in H5782
Ge 36:35 who d Midian in the country of Moab H5782
Lev 26:17 you so that *you will* **be d** by your enemies; H5597
Nu 14:42 *You will* **be d** by your enemies, H5597
Dt 1: 4 This was after he *had* d Sihon king of the H5782
Dt 1: 4 at Edrei had d Og king of Bashan, who NDT
Dt 1:42 *You will* **be d** by your enemies H5597
Dt 4:46 in Heshbon and *was* d *by* Moses and the H5782
Dt 7: 2 them over to you and *you have* d them, H5782
Dt 28: 7 rise up against you *will* **be d** before you. H5597
Dt 28:25 LORD will cause you *to* **be d** before your H5597
Dt 29: 7 out to fight against us, but *we* d them. H5782
Jos 10:10 **d** them **completely** at H5782+1524+4804
Jos 10:20 the Israelites **d** them H5782+1524+4394+4804
Jos 10:33 Lachish, but Joshua d him and his army H5782
Jos 11: 8 *They* d them and pursued them all the H5782
Jos 12: 1 whom the Israelites *had* d and whose H5782
Jos 13:12 Moses *had* d them and taken over their H5782
Jos 13:21 Moses *had* d him and the Midianite H5782
Jdg 1:10 Kiriath Arba) and d Sheshai, Ahiman and H5782
Jdg 11:21 army into Israel's hands, and *they* d them. H5782
Jdg 20:35 The LORD d Benjamin before Israel, and on H5597
1Sa 4: 2 Israel **was d** by the Philistines H5597
1Sa 4:10 the Israelites **were d** and every man H5597
1Sa 14:48 He fought valiantly and d the Amalekites H5782
2Sa 2:17 the Israelites **were d** by David's men. H5597
2Sa 5:20 to Baal Perazim, and there he d them. H5782
2Sa 8: 1 David **d** the Philistines and subdued them H5782
2Sa 8: 2 David also **d** the Moabites. H5782
2Sa 8: 3 David **d** Hadadezer son of Rehob H5782
2Sa 8: 9 heard that David *had* **d** the entire army of H5782
1Ki 8:33 people Israel **have been d** by an enemy H5597
2Ki 13:19 then *you would have* **d** Aram and H5782
2Ki 13:25 Three times Jehoash d him, and so he H5782
2Ki 14: 7 He was the *one who* d ten thousand H5782
2Ki 14:10 *You have* **indeed d** Edom and now H5782+5782
2Ki 18: 8 to fortified city, he d the Philistines, as far H5782
1Ch 1:46 who d Midian in the country of Moab H5782
1Ch 5:10 the Hagrites, *who were* d at their hands H5877
1Ch 14:11 up to Baal Perazim, and there *he* d them. H5782
1Ch 18: 1 David d the Philistines and subdued them H5782
1Ch 18: 2 David also d the Moabites, and they H5782
1Ch 18: 3 David d Hadadezer king of Zobah H5782
1Ch 18: 9 heard that David *had* d the entire army of H5782
2Ch 6:24 people Israel *have* **been d** by an enemy H5597
2Ch 20:22 were invading Judah, and *they* **were d**. H5597
2Ch 25:19 You say to yourself that *you have* **d** Edom H5782
2Ch 28: 5 The Arameans **d** him and took many of H5782
2Ch 28:23 of Damascus, who *had* **d** him; for he H5782
Jer 46: 2 **d** at Carchemish on the Euphrates River *by* H5782
Jer 46: 5 they are retreating, their warriors **are d**. H4198
Da 11:11 a large army, but it *will* **be d**. H5989+928+3338
1Co 6: 7 you have been completely **d** already. G2488

DEFEATING (4) [DEFEAT]

Ge 14:17 returned from d Kedorlaomer and the H5782
Jdg 20:32 were saying, "We *are* d them as before," H5597
Jdg 20:39 "We *are* d them as in the first H5597+5597
Da 7:21 war against the holy people and d them, A10321

DEFECT (58) [DEFECTED, DEFECTS]

Ex 12: 5 choose must be year-old males **without d**, H9459
Ex 29: 1 a young bull and two rams **without d**. H9459
Lev 1: 3 you are to offer a male **without d**. H9459
Lev 1:10 you are to offer a male **without d**. H9459
Lev 3: 1 before the LORD an animal **without d**. H9459
Lev 3: 6 are to offer a male or female **without d**. H9459
Lev 4: 3 LORD a young bull **without d** as a sin H9459
Lev 4:23 as his offering a male goat **without d**. H9459
Lev 4:28 they committed a female goat **without d**. H9459
Lev 4:32 they are to bring a female **without d**. H9459
Lev 5:15 one **without d** and of the proper value in H9459
Lev 5:18 one **without d** and of the proper value. H9459
Lev 6: 6 one **without d** and of the proper value. H9459
Lev 9: 2 offering, *both* **without d**, and present H9459
Lev 9: 3 both a year old and **without d**—for a burnt H9459
Lev 14:10 a year old, each **without d**, along with H9459
Lev 21:17 who has a **d** may come near to H4583
Lev 21:18 No man who has any **d** may come near H4583
Lev 21:20 who has any eye **d**, or who has H9319
Lev 21:21 priest who has any **d** is to come near to H4583
Lev 21:21 He has a **d**; he must not come near to H4583
Lev 21:23 because of his **d**, he must not go near H4583
Lev 22:19 present a male **without d** from the cattle, H9459
Lev 22:20 Do not bring anything with a **d**, because it H4583
Lev 22:21 it must be **without d** or blemish to be H9459
Lev 23:12 to the LORD a lamb a year old **without d**, H9459
Lev 23:18 each a year old and **without d**, one young H9459
Nu 6:14 year-old male lamb **without d** for a burnt H9459
Nu 6:14 year-old ewe lamb **without d** for a sin H9459
Nu 6:14 a ram **without d** for a fellowship offering, H9459
Nu 19: 2 you a red heifer **without d** or blemish and H9459
Nu 28: 3 two lambs a year old **without d**, as a H9459
Nu 28: 9 of two lambs a year old **without d**, H9459
Nu 28:11 male lambs a year old, *all* **without d**. H9459
Nu 28:19 male lambs a year old, *all* **without d**. H9459
Nu 28:31 Be sure the animals are **without d**. H9459
Nu 29: 2 male lambs a year old, *all* **without d**. H9459
Nu 29: 8 male lambs a year old, *all* **without d**. H9459
Nu 29:13 male lambs a year old, *all* **without d**. H9459
Nu 29:17 male lambs a year old, *all* **without d**. H9459
Nu 29:20 male lambs a year old, *all* **without d**. H9459
Nu 29:23 male lambs a year old, *all* **without d**. H9459
Nu 29:26 male lambs a year old, *all* **without d**. H9459
Nu 29:29 male lambs a year old, *all* **without d**. H9459
Nu 29:32 male lambs a year old, *all* **without d**. H9459
Nu 29:36 male lambs a year old, *all* **without d**. H9459
Dt 15:21 If an animal has a **d**, is lame or blind, or H4583
Dt 17: 1 ox or a sheep that has any **d** or flaw in it, H4583
Eze 43:22 offer a male goat **without d** for a sin H9459
Eze 43:23 a ram from the flock, both **without d**. H9459
Eze 43:25 a ram from the flock, *both* **without d**. H9459
Eze 45:18 take a young bull **without d** and purify the H9459
Eze 45:23 seven rams **without d** as a burnt H9459
Eze 46: 4 six male lambs and a ram, *all* **without d**. H9459
Eze 46: 6 six lambs and a ram, *all* **without d**. H9459
Eze 46:13 a year-old lamb **without d** for a burnt H9459
Da 1: 4 young men without any **physical d** H4583
1Pe 1:19 of Christ, a lamb without blemish or **d**. G834

DEFECTED (3) [DEFECT]

1Ch 12: 8 Some Gadites d to David at his stronghold H976
1Ch 12:19 tribe of Manasseh d to David when he H5877
1Ch 12:20 were *the men* of Manasseh *who* d to him: H5877

DEFECTS (1) [DEFECT]

Lev 22:25 because they are deformed and have **d**. H4583

DEFEND (23) [DEFENDED, DEFENDER, DEFENDERS, DEFENDING, DEFENDS, DEFENSE, DEFENSES]

Jdg 6:31 *he can* **d** himself when someone breaks H8189
2Ki 19:34 *I will* d this city and save it, for my sake H1713
2Ki 20: 6 *I will* d this city for my sake and for the H1713
Job 13:15 *I will* surely d my ways to his face. H3519
Ps 12: 4 own lips will d us—who is lord over us?" H907
Ps 72: 4 *May he* d the afflicted among the people H8189
Ps 74:22 and d your cause; remember how H8189
Ps 82: 2 "How long *will you* d the unjust and show H9149
Ps 82: 3 **D** the weak and the fatherless; uphold the H9149
Ps 119:154 **D** my cause and redeem me; preserve my H8189
Pr 31: 9 **d** the **rights** *of* the poor and needy. H1906
Ecc 4:12 two *can* **d** *themselves*. H6641+5584
Isa 1:17 **D** the oppressed. Take up the H886
Isa 1:23 *They do* not **d the cause** *of* the fatherless H9149
Isa 37:35 "*I will* d this city and save it, for my sake H1713
Isa 38: 6 of the king of Assyria. *I will* d this city. H1713
Jer 5:28 *they do* not d the just cause of the poor. H9149
Jer 50:34 *He will* **vigorously** d their cause so H8189+8189
Jer 51:36 I *will* d your cause and avenge you H8189
Da 3:16 to d ourselves *before* you in A10754+10601
Lk 12:11 about how *you will* d *yourselves* or what G664
Lk 21:14 beforehand *how you will* d *yourselves*. G664
Ac 25:16 had an opportunity to d themselves against G665

DEFENDED (3) [DEFEND]

2Sa 23:12 *He* d it and struck the Philistines down H5911
1Ch 11:14 *They* d it and struck the Philistines down H5911
Jer 22:16 *He* d the cause of the poor and needy H1906

DEFENDER (7) [DEFEND]

Ex 22: 2 **the d** is not guilty of bloodshed; H2257S
Ex 22: 3 sunrise, **the d** is guilty of bloodshed. H2257S
Job 5: 4 from safety, crushed in court without a **d**. H5911
Ps 68: 5 to the fatherless, a **d** *of* widows, is God in H1908
Pr 23:11 their **D** is strong; he will take up their H1457
Isa 19:20 he will send them a savior and **d**, and he H8189
Isa 29:21 who ensnare the **d** in court and with false H3519

DEFENDERS (1) [DEFEND]

2Sa 11:16 where he knew the **strongest d** were. H408+2657

DEFENDING (5) [DEFEND]

2Ki 9:14 all Israel had been d Ramoth Gilead H9068
Ps 10:18 d the fatherless and the oppressed, so H9149
Ro 2:15 them and at other times even d them.) G664
2Co 12:19 that *we have been* d *ourselves* to you? G664
Php 1: 7 I am in chains or d and confirming the G665

DEFENDS (3) [DEFEND]

Dt 10:18 *He* d the cause of the fatherless and the H6913
Dt 33: 7 With his own hands *he* d his **cause**. H8189
Isa 51:22 LORD says, your God, *who* d his people: H8189

DEFENSE (20) [DEFEND]

Ex 15: 2 "The LORD is my strength and my d; he has H2380
2Ch 11: 5 built up towns for d in Judah: H5190
Job 31:35 I sign now my d—let the Almighty answer NDT
Ps 35:23 rise to my d! Contend for me, my H5477
Ps 118:14 The LORD is my strength and my d; he has H2380
Isa 12: 2 is my strength and my d; he has become H2380
Jer 41: 9 part of his **d against** Baasha king H7156+4946
Na 3: 8 The river was her d, the waters her wall. H2658
Jn 5:17 **In** *his* **d** Jesus **said** to them, "My Father is G646
Ac 7:24 so *he* **went to** his **d** and avenged him by G310
Ac 19:33 in order to **make a d** before the people. G664
Ac 22: 1 "Brothers and fathers, listen now *to* my **d**." G665
Ac 24:10 over this nation; so *I* gladly **make** my **d**. G664
Ac 25: 8 Then Paul **made** *his* **d**: "I have done G664
Ac 26: 1 motioned with his hand and *began his* **d**: G664
Ac 26: 2 you today as *I* **make** *my* **d** against all the G664
Ac 26:24 At this point Festus interrupted Paul's **d** G664
1Co 9: 3 This is my **d** to those who sit in judgment G665
Php 1:16 that I am put here for the **d** of the gospel. G665
2Ti 4:16 At my first **d**, no one came to my support G665

DEFENSES (7) [DEFEND]

2Ch 11:11 strengthened their d and put commanders H5193
2Ch 26:15 on the **corner d** so that soldiers H7157
Job 13:12 of ashes; your d are defenses of clay. H1462
Job 13:12 of ashes; your defenses are d *of* clay. H1462
Isa 22: 8 The Lord stripped away the d *of* Judah H5009
Joel 2: 8 They plunge through d without breaking H8939
Na 3:14 water for the siege, strengthen your d! H4448

DEFERENCE (1) [DEFERRED]

2Ki 16:18 the LORD, **in d to** the king of Assyria. H4946+7156

DEFERRED (1) [DEFERENCE]

Pr 13:12 Hope d makes the heart sick, but a H5432

DEFIANCE (1) [DEFY]

1Sa 17:23 from his lines and shouted his usual d, H1821

DEFIANT (2) [DEFY]

Pr 7:11 She is unruly and d, her feet never stay at H6253
Jude 15 of all the d words ungodly sinners G5017

DEFIANTLY (4) [DEFY]

Nu 15:30 'But anyone who **sins d**, H6913+928+3338+8123
Nu 33: 3 marched out **d** in full view of H928+3338+8123
Job 15:26 **d** charging against him with a thick H928+7418
Ps 75: 5 heaven; do not speak **so d**. H928+6981+7418

DEFIED (9) [DEFY]

1Sa 17:36 because *he has* d the armies of the living H3070
1Sa 17:45 of the armies of Israel, whom *you have* **d**. H3070
1Ki 13:21 '*You have* d the word of the LORD and H5286
1Ki 13:26 the man of God who d the word of the H5286
Isa 65: 7 on the mountains and d me on the hills, H3070
Jer 48:26 her drunk, for *she has* d the LORD. H1540+6584
Jer 48:42 a nation because *she* d the LORD. H1540+6584
Jer 50:29 For *she has* d the LORD, the Holy One of H2326
Da 3:28 in him and d the king's command A10731

DEFIES (1) [DEFY]

Ezr 6:11 I decree that if anyone d this edict, A10731

DEFILE (40) [DEFILED, DEFILEMENT, DEFILES, DEFILING]

Ex 20:25 *you will* d it if you use a tool on it. H2725
Lev 11:43 *Do* not d yourselves by any of these H9210
Lev 18:20 neighbor's wife and d *yourself* with her. H3237
Lev 18:23 with an animal and d *yourself* with it. H3237

Lev 18:24 " '*Do* not d yourselves in any of these H3237
Lev 18:28 And if you d the land, it will vomit you out H3237
Lev 18:30 came and *do* not d yourselves with them. H3237
Lev 20:25 *Do* not d yourselves by any animal or bird H9210
Lev 21: 4 to him by marriage, and so d himself. H2725
Lev 21:15 so that *he will* not d his offspring among H2725
Nu 5: 3 the camp so *they will* not d their camp, H3237
Nu 18:32 then *you will* not d the holy offerings of H2725
Nu 19:13 *they* d the LORD's tabernacle. H3237
Nu 35:34 *Do* not d the land where you live and H3237
2Ki 23:16 from them and burned on the altar *to* d it, H3237
Eze 7:21 to the wicked of the earth, *who will* d it. H2725
Eze 7:22 They will enter it and *will* d it. H2725
Eze 9: 7 "D the temple and fill the courts with the H3237
Eze 14:11 nor *will they* d themselves anymore with H3237
Eze 18: 6 *He does* not d his neighbor's wife or have H3237
Eze 18:15 *He does* not d his neighbor's wife H3237
Eze 20: 7 and *do* not d yourselves with the idols of H3237
Eze 20:18 their laws or d yourselves with their idols. H3237
Eze 20:30 *Will* you d yourselves the way your H3237
Eze 20:31 you *continue to* d yourselves with all your H3237
Eze 37:23 *They will* no longer d themselves with H3237
Eze 43: 7 of Israel *will* never again d my holy name H3237
Eze 44:25 " 'A priest *must* not d *himself* by going H3237
Eze 44:25 unmarried sister, then *he may* d himself. H3237
Da 1: 8 resolved not *to* d himself with the royal H1458
Da 1: 8 permission not *to* d himself this way. H1458
Mt 15:11 into someone's mouth *does* not d them, G3124
Mt 15:18 come from the heart, and these d them. G3124
Mt 15:20 These are what d a person; but eating G3124
Mt 15:20 with unwashed hands *does* not d them." G3124
Mk 7:15 a person can d them by going into G3124
Mk 7:18 a person from the outside can d them? G3124
Mk 7:23 evils come from inside and d a person." G3124
Heb 12:15 grows up to cause trouble and d many. G3620
Rev 14: 4 are those *who did* not d *themselves* with G3662

DEFILED (67) [DEFILE]
Ge 34: 5 that his daughter Dinah *had been* d, H3237
Ge 34:13 Because their sister Dinah *had been* d H3237
Ge 34:27 the city where their sister *had been* d. H3237
Ge 49: 4 your father's bed, onto my couch and d it. H2725
Lev 18:24 going to drive out before you became d. H3237
Lev 18:25 Even the land *was* d; so I punished it for H3237
Lev 18:27 land before you, and the land *became* d. H3237
Lev 19:31 out spiritists, for you *will be* d by them. H3237
Lev 20: 3 *he has* d my sanctuary and profaned my H3237
Lev 21: 7 must not marry women d *by* prostitution H2729
Lev 21:14 woman, or a *woman* d *by* prostitution, but H2729
Lev 22: 4 he touches something d *by* a corpse or by H3238
Nu 6:12 because *they became* d during their H3237
Nu 19:20 because *they have* d the sanctuary of the H3237
Dt 22: 9 also the fruit of the vineyard *will be* d. H7727
Dt 24: 4 to marry her again after *she has* been d. H3237
Jos 22:19 If the land you possess is d, come over to H3238
1Ch 5: 1 when he d his father's marriage bed H2725
Ne 13:29 because they d the priestly office and the H1459
Job 31: 7 or if my hands *have been* d, H1815+4583
Ps 74: 7 *they* d the dwelling place of your Name. H2725
Ps 79: 1 inheritance; *they have* d your holy temple H3237
Ps 89:39 your servant and *have* d his crown in the H2725
Ps 106:39 *They* d *themselves* by what they did; by H3237
Isa 24: 5 The earth is d by its people; they have H2866
Isa 52: 1 uncircumcised and d will not enter you H3238
Jer 2: 7 But you came and d my land and made H3237
Jer 2:23 can you say, '*I am* not d; I have not run H3237
Jer 3: 1 *Would* not the land *be* completely d H2866+2866
Jer 3: 2 *You have* d the land with your prostitution H2866
Jer 3: 9 *she* d the land and committed adultery H2866
Jer 7:30 house that bears my Name and *have* d it. H3237
Jer 16:18 because they *have* d my land with the H2725
Jer 19:13 kings of Judah will be d like this place, H3238
Jer 32:34 the house that bears my Name and d it. H3237
La 4:14 *They* are *so* d with blood that no one H1458
Eze 4:13 of Israel will eat d food among the H3238
Eze 4:14 *I have* never d myself. H3237
Eze 5:11 because *you have* d my sanctuary with all H3237
Eze 20:26 *I* d them through their gifts—the sacrifice H3237
Eze 20:43 actions by which *you have* d yourselves, H3237
Eze 22: 4 shed and *have become* d by the idols H3237
Eze 22:16 When *you have* been d in the eyes of the H2725
Eze 23: 7 the Assyrians and d herself with all the H3237
Eze 23:13 I saw that *she* too d herself; both of them H3237
Eze 23:17 bed of love, and in their lust *they* d her. H3237
Eze 23:17 After *she had been* d by them, she turned H3237
Eze 23:30 the nations and d yourself with their idols. H3237
Eze 23:38 that same time *they* d my sanctuary and H3237
Eze 36:17 *they* d it by their conduct and their actions. H3237
Eze 36:18 land and because *they had* d it with their H3237
Eze 43: 8 *they* d my holy name by their detestable H3237
Hos 6:10 is given to prostitution, Israel *is* d. H3237
Mic 2:10 resting place, because *it is* d, it is ruined, H3237
Mic 4:11 They say, "*Let her be* d, let our eyes gloat H2866
Zep 3: 1 to the city of oppressors, rebellious and d! H1458
Hag 2:13 "If a *person* d *by contact with* a dead body H3238
Hag 2:13 one of these things, *does it become* d?" H3237
Hag 2:13 the priests replied, "*it becomes* d." H3237
Hag 2:14 they do and whatever they offer there is d. H3238
Mal 1: 7 "By offering d food on my altar. "But you H1458
Mal 1: 7 you ask, 'How *have we* d you?' "By saying H1458
Mal 1:12 it by saying, 'The Lord's table *is* d,' and, H1458
Mk 7: 2 eating food with hands that were d, G3123
Mk 7: 5 instead of eating their food with d hands?" G3123
Ac 21:28 into the temple and d this holy place." G3124
1Co 8: 7 since their conscience is weak, *it is* d. G3662

DEFILEMENT (1) [DEFILE]
2Ch 29: 5 Remove *all* d from the sanctuary H5614

DEFILES (8) [DEFILE]
Lev 21: 9 priest's daughter d herself by becoming a H2725
Eze 18:11 *He* d his neighbor's wife H3237
Eze 22: 3 in her midst and d herself by making H3237
Eze 22:11 another shamefully d his daughter-in-law, H3237
Eze 33:26 each of you d his neighbor's wife. H3237
Mt 15:11 out of their mouth, that *is what* d them." G3124
Mk 7:15 what comes out of a person that d them." G3124
Mk 7:20 comes out of a person is what d them. G3124

DEFILING (37) [DEFILE]
Lev 13: 2 on their skin that may be a d skin disease, H5596
Lev 13: 3 than skin deep, it is a d skin disease. H5596
Lev 13: 8 them unclean; it is a d skin disease. H7669
Lev 13: 9 "When anyone has a d skin disease, they H5596
Lev 13:15 flesh is unclean; they have a d disease. H7669
Lev 13:20 It is a d skin disease that has broken out H5596
Lev 13:22 them unclean; it is a d disease. H5596
Lev 13:25 it is a d disease that has broken out in the H7669
Lev 13:25 them unclean; it is a d skin disease. H5596
Lev 13:27 them unclean; it is a d skin disease. H5596
Lev 13:30 it is a d skin disease *on* the head H5999+7669
Lev 13:42 it is a d disease breaking out on his head H7669
Lev 13:43 is reddish-white like a d skin disease, H7669
Lev 13:45 "Anyone with such a d disease must wear H5596
Lev 13:47 any fabric that is spoiled with a d mold— H7669
Lev 13:49 it is a d mold and must be shown to the H7669
Lev 13:51 it is a persistent d mold; the article is H7669
Lev 13:52 because the d mold is persistent, the H7669
Lev 13:59 concerning d molds in woolen or H5596
Lev 14: 3 have been healed of their d skin disease, H5596
Lev 14: 7 the one to be cleansed of the d disease, H7669
Lev 14:32 anyone who has a d skin disease and H5596
Lev 14:35 that looks like a d mold in my house. H5596
Lev 14:43 "If the d mold reappears in the house H5596
Lev 14:44 it is a persistent d mold; the house is H7669
Lev 14:48 house clean, because the d mold is gone. H5596
Lev 14:54 are the regulations for any d skin disease, H5596
Lev 14:55 for d molds *in* fabric or in a house, H7669
Lev 14:57 d skin diseases and defiling molds. H7669
Lev 14:57 defiling skin diseases and d molds. H7669
Lev 15:31 uncleanness for d my dwelling place, H3237
Lev 22: 4 of Aaron *has a* d skin disease or a bodily H7665
Nu 5: 2 anyone *who* has a d skin disease or a H7665
Nu 6: 9 thus d the hair that symbolizes their H3237
Nu 12:10 saw that *she* had a d skin disease, H7665
Dt 24: 8 In cases of d skin diseases, be very careful H7669
2Ch 36:14 of the nations and d the temple of the H3237

DEFINITE (2) [DEFINITELY]
1Sa 23:23 come back to me with d information. H3922
Ac 25:26 But I have nothing d to write to His Majesty G855

DEFINITELY (2) [DEFINITE]
1Sa 23:10 your servant *has* heard d that Saul H9048+9048
1Sa 26: 4 and learned that Saul had d arrived. H448+3922

DEFORMED (3) [FORM]
Lev 21:18 who is blind or lame, disfigured or d; H8594
Lev 22:23 an ox or a sheep *that is* d or stunted, H8594
Lev 22:25 because they are d and have defects. H5426

DEFRAUD (5) [FRAUD]
Lev 19:13 " '*Do* not d or rob your neighbor. " '*Do* not H6943
Hos 12: 7 uses dishonest scales and loves to d. H6943
Mic 2: 2 *They* d people *of* their homes, they rob H6943
Mal 3: 5 against *those who* d laborers *of* their H6943
Mk 10:19 false testimony, *you shall* not d, honor your G691

DEFY (3) [DEFIANCE, DEFIANT, DEFIANTLY, DEFIED, DEFIES, DEFYING]
1Sa 17:10 "This day I d the armies of Israel! H3070
1Sa 17:25 He comes out to d Israel. The king H3070
1Sa 17:26 Philistine that *he should* d the armies of H3070

DEFYING (2) [DEFY]
Isa 3: 8 against the LORD, d his glorious presence. H5286
Ac 17: 7 They are all d Caesar's decrees G595+4556

DEGRADE (1) [DEGRADED, DEGRADING]
Lev 19:29 " '*Do* not d your daughter by making her a H2725

DEGRADED (2) [DEGRADE]
Dt 25: 3 your fellow Israelite *will* be d in your eyes. H7829
Eze 16:25 built your lofty shrines and d your beauty, H9493

DEGRADING (1) [DEGRADE]
Ro 1:24 to sexual impurity *for* the d of their bodies G869

DEGREE, DEGREES (KJV) ASCENTS, CIRCUMSTANCES, EXALTED, HIGHBORN, HUMBLE, LOWBORN, STANDING, STEPS

DEITY (1)
Col 2: 9 all the fullness *of* the D lives in bodily G2540

DEJECTED (2)
Ge 40: 6 next morning, he saw that they *were* d. H2407
Isa 19:10 The workers in cloth will be d, and all the H1917

DELAIAH (7)
1Ch 3:24 Johanan, D and Anani—seven in H1933
1Ch 24:18 the twenty-third to D and the H1934
Ezr 2:60 The descendants of D, Tobiah and H1933
Ne 6:10 went to the house of Shemaiah son of D, H1933
Ne 7:62 the descendants of D, Tobiah and H1933
Jer 36:12 the secretary, D son of Shemaiah H1934
Jer 36:25 D and Gemariah urged the king not to H1934

DELAY (15) [DELAYED]
Ge 45: 9 Come down to me; don't d. H6641
2Ki 9: 3 Then open the door and run; don't d!" H2675
Ps 40:17 my deliverer; you are my God, *do* not d. H336
Ps 70: 5 my help and my deliverer; LORD, *do* not d. H336
Ps 119:60 will hasten and not d to obey your H4538
Ecc 5: 4 make a vow to God, *do* not d to fulfill it. H336
Isa 48: 9 For my own name's sake *I* d my wrath; for H799
Jer 4: 6 Flee for safety without d! For I am bringing H6641
Eze 12:25 and it shall be fulfilled without d. H5432
Da 9:19 my God, *do* not d, because your city and H336
Hab 2: 3 it will certainly come and *will* not d. H336
Mk 1:20 Without d he called them, and they left G2317
Ac 25:17 with me, *I did* not d the case, but G332+4472
Heb 10:37 who is coming will come and *will* not d." G5988
Rev 10: 6 and said, "There will be no more d! G5989

DELAYED (6) [DELAY]
Ge 43:10 if *we had* not d, we could have H4538
Jos 10:13 of the sky and d going down about a H4202+237
Jdg 5:28 Why *is* the clatter of his chariots d?' H336
Isa 46:13 far away; and my salvation *will* not *be* d. H336
Eze 12:28 None of my words *will* be d any longer H5432
1Ti 3:15 if *I am* d, you will know how people ought G1094

DELEGATION (5)
Jos 9: 4 They went *as a* d whose donkeys were H7493
2Sa 10: 2 David sent a d to express his H928+3338+6269
1Ch 19: 2 So David sent a d to express his sympathy H4855
Lk 14:32 he will send a d while the other is still a G4561
Lk 19:14 hated him and sent a d after him to say, G4561

DELIBERATE (1) [DELIBERATELY]
Ac 2:23 over to you by God's d plan and G3988

DELIBERATELY (3) [DELIBERATE]
Ex 21:14 schemes and kills someone d, H928+6893
Heb 10:26 If we d keep on sinning after we have G1731
2Pe 3: 5 But they d forget that long ago by God's G2527

DELICACIES (6) [DELICATE]
Ge 49:20 will be rich; he will provide d *fit for* a king. H5052
Ps 141: 4 are evildoers; do not let me eat their d. H4982
Pr 23: 3 Do not crave his d, for that food is H4761
Pr 23: 6 of a begrudging host, do not crave his d; H4761
Jer 51:34 us and filled his stomach with our d, H6358
La 4: 5 Those who once ate d are destitute in the H5052

DELICACY (1) [DELICATE]
SS 7:13 at our door is every d, both new and H4458

DELICATE (2) [DELICACIES, DELICACY]
Isa 47: 1 No more will you be called tender or d. H6697
Jer 6: 2 Daughter Zion, so beautiful and d. H6695

DELICIOUS (1)
Pr 9:17 water is sweet; food eaten in secret is d!" H5838

DELIGHT (68) [DELIGHTED, DELIGHTFUL, DELIGHTING, DELIGHTS]
Lev 26:31 and *I will* take no d in the pleasing aroma H8193
Dt 30: 9 The LORD *will* again d in you and make H8464
1Sa 2: 1 my enemies, for *I* d in your deliverance. H8523
1Sa 15:22 "Does the LORD d in burnt offerings and H2914
Ne 1:11 of your servants who d in revering your H2913
Job 22:26 Surely then *you will* find d in the Almighty H6695
Job 27:10 *Will they* find d in the Almighty? Will they H6695
Ps 1: 2 whose d is in the law of the LORD, and H2914
Ps 16: 3 are the noble ones in whom is all my d." H2914
Ps 35: 9 rejoice in the LORD and d in his salvation. H8464
Ps 35:27 May *those who* d in my vindication shout H2913
Ps 37: 4 Take d in the LORD, and he will give you H6695
Ps 43: 4 the altar of God, to God, my joy and my d. H1637
Ps 51:16 *You do* not d in sacrifice, or I would bring H2911
Ps 51:19 Then *you will* d in the sacrifices of the H2911
Ps 62: 4 from my lofty place; *they* take d in lies. H8354
Ps 68:30 Scatter the nations *who* d in war. H2911
Ps 111: 2 they are pondered by all *who* d *in* them. H2913
Ps 112: 1 *who* find great d in his commands. H2911
Ps 119:16 *I* d in your decrees; I will not neglect your H9130
Ps 119:24 Your statutes are my d; they are my H9141
Ps 119:35 path of your commands, for there *I* find d. H2911
Ps 119:47 for *I* d in your commands because I love H9130
Ps 119:70 callous and unfeeling, but I d *in* your law. H9130
Ps 119:77 to me that I may live, for your law is my d. H9141
Ps 119:92 If your law had not been my d, I would H9141
Ps 119:143 upon me, but your commands give me d. H9141
Ps 119:174 salvation, LORD, and your law gives me d. H9141
Ps 147:10 nor *his* d in the legs of the warrior H8354
Ps 149: 4 For the LORD takes d in his people; he H8354

Pr 1:22 How long *will* mockers **d in** mockery and H2773
Pr 2:14 who **d in** doing wrong and rejoice in the H8524
Pr 8:30 I was **filled with d** day after day, rejoicing H9141
Pr 18:2 in understanding but **d** in airing their own NDT
Pr 23:26 your heart and *let* your eyes **d** *in* my ways, H8354
Ecc 2:10 My heart *took* **d** in all my labor, and this H8524
SS 1:4 We rejoice and **d** in you; we will praise H8523
SS 2:3 *I* **d** to sit in his shade, and his fruit is H2773
Isa 11:3 he *will* **d** in the fear of the LORD. H8193
Isa 13:17 not care for silver and **have** no **d** in gold. H2911
Isa 32:14 the **d** *of* donkeys, a pasture H5375
Isa 42:1 my chosen one **in** whom I **d**; I will put my H8354
Isa 55:2 and you *will* **d** in the richest of fare. H6695
Isa 58:13 call the Sabbath a **d** and the LORD's holy H6696
Isa 61:10 *I* **d greatly** in the LORD; my soul H8464+8464
Isa 62:4 the LORD *will* **take d** in you, and your H2911
Isa 65:18 Jerusalem to be a **d** and its people a joy. H1638
Isa 65:19 over Jerusalem and **take d** in my people; H8464
Isa 66:3 and they **d** in their abominations; H2911
Isa 66:11 will drink deeply and **d** in her overflowing H6695
Jer 9:24 for in these *I* **d**," declares the LORD. H2911
Jer 15:16 they were my joy and my heart's **d**, for I H8525
Jer 31:20 my dear son, the child in whom I **d**? H9141
Jer 49:25 been abandoned, the town in which I **d**? H5375
Eze 24:16 to take away from you the **d** *of* your eyes. H4718
Eze 24:21 you take pride, the **d** *of* your eyes, the H4718
Eze 24:25 joy and glory, the **d** *of* their eyes, their H4718
Hos 7:3 "*They* **d** the king with their wickedness H8523
Mic 1:16 mourning for the children in whom you **d**; H9503
Mic 7:18 stay angry forever but **d** to show mercy. H2911
Zep 3:17 *He will* **take great d** in you; in H8464+928+8525
Mt 12:18 in whom I **d**; I will put my Spirit G2305
Mk 12:37 The large crowd listened to him **with d**. G2452
Lk 1:14 He will be a joy and **d** to you, and many will G21
Ro 7:22 For in my inner being *I* **d** in God's law; G5310
1Co 13:6 Love *does* not **d** in evil but rejoices with G5897
2Co 12:10 Christ's sake, *I* **d** in weaknesses, in G2305
Col 2:5 you in spirit and **d** to see how disciplined G5897

DELIGHTED (16) [DELIGHT]
Ge 34:19 because *he was* **d** with Jacob's daughter. H2911
Ex 18:9 Jethro *was* **d** to hear about all the good H2525
Dt 30:9 prosperous, just as *he* **d** in your ancestors H8464
2Sa 22:20 he rescued me because *he* **d** in me. H2911
1Ki 10:9 who *has* **d** in you and placed you on the H2911
2Ch 9:8 who *has* **d** in you and placed you on his H2911
Est 5:14 This suggestion **d** Haman, and he had H3512
Ps 18:19 he rescued me because *he* **d** in me. H2911
Isa 1:29 of the sacred oaks *in* which *you have* **d**; H2773
Isa 5:7 the people of Judah are the vines he **d** *in*. H9141
Mk 14:11 They *were* **d** to hear this and promised to G5897
Lk 13:17 the people *were* **d** with all the G5897
Lk 22:5 *They were* **d** and agreed to give him G5897
2Co 7:13 *we were* especially **d** to see how happy G5897
1Th 2:8 *we were* **d** to share with you not only the G2305
2Th 2:12 the truth but *have* **d in** wickedness. G2305

DELIGHTFUL (4) [DELIGHT]
Ps 16:6 surely I have a **d** inheritance. H9182
SS 1:2 your love is more **d** than wine. H3202
SS 4:10 How **d** *is* your love, my sister, my bride H3636
Mal 3:12 yours will be a **d** land," says the LORD H2914

DELIGHTING (1) [DELIGHT]
Pr 8:31 in his whole world and **d** in mankind. H9141

DELIGHTS (19) [DELIGHT]
Est 6:6 be done for the man the king **d** to honor?" H2911
Est 6:7 "For the man the king **d** to honor, H2911
Est 6:9 them robe the man the king **d** to honor, H2911
Est 6:9 is done for the man the king **d** to honor! H2911
Est 6:11 is done for the man the king **d** to honor!" H2911
Ps 22:8 Let him deliver him, since *he* **d** in him." H2911
Ps 35:27 who **d** in the well-being of his servant." H2913
Ps 36:8 you give them drink from your river of **d**. H6358
Ps 37:23 firm the steps of the one *who* **d in** him; H2911
Ps 147:11 the LORD **d in** those who fear him, who put H8354
Pr 3:12 he loves, as a father the son *he* **d in**. H8354
Pr 10:23 a person of understanding **d** in wisdom. NDT
Pr 11:20 he **d** *in* those whose ways are H8356
Pr 12:22 he **d** *in* people who are trustworthy. H8356
Pr 14:35 A king **d** in a wise servant, but a shameful H8356
Pr 29:17 they will bring you the **d** you desire. H5052
Ecc 2:8 a harem as well—the **d of a** man's **heart**. H9503
SS 7:6 how pleasing, my love, with your **d**! H9503
Col 2:18 Do not let anyone *who* **d** in false humility G2527

DELILAH (7)
Jdg 16:4 in the Valley of Sorek whose name was **D**. H1935
Jdg 16:6 So **D** said to Samson, "Tell me the secret H1935
Jdg 16:10 Then **D** said to Samson, "You have made H1935
Jdg 16:12 So **D** took new ropes and tied him with H1935
Jdg 16:13 **D** then said to Samson, "All this time you H1935
Jdg 16:13 **D** took the seven braids of his head NDT
Jdg 16:18 When **D** saw that he had told her H1935

DELIVER (111) [DELIVERANCE, DELIVERED, DELIVERER, DELIVERERS, DELIVERING, DELIVERS, DELIVERY]
Nu 21:2 "If *you will* **d** these people into our H5989+5989
Dt 1:27 us out of Egypt to **d** us into the hands of H5989
Dt 2:31 begun *to* **d** Sihon and his country **over** to H5989
Dt 7:23 the LORD your God *will* **d** them **over** to you, H5989
Dt 23:14 protect you and to **d** your enemies to you. H5989
Dt 31:5 The LORD *will* **d** them to you, and you must H5989
Dt 32:39 and no *one can* **d** out of my hand. H5911
Jos 7:7 the Jordan to **d** us into the hands of H5989
Jos 8:18 for into your hand *I will* **d** the city. H5989
Jdg 4:9 the LORD *will* **d** Sisera into the hands of H4835
Jdg 7:2 I cannot **d** Midian into their hands, or H5989
1Sa 4:8 Who *will* **d** us from the hand of these H5911
1Sa 7:3 and *he will* **d** you out of the hand of the H5911
1Sa 9:16 *he will* **d** them from the hand of the H3828
1Sa 12:10 But now **d** us from the hands of our H5911
1Sa 17:46 This day the LORD *will* **d** you into my hands H6037
1Sa 26:24 value my life and **d** me from all trouble." H5911
1Sa 28:19 The LORD *will* **d** both Israel and you into H5989
2Sa 5:19 *Will you* **d** them into my hands? H5989
2Sa 5:19 for *I will* **surely d** the Philistines H5989+5989
2Sa 14:16 king will agree to **d** his servant from the H5911
1Ki 20:28 *I will* **d** this vast army into your hands H5989
2Ki 3:10 together only to **d** us into the hands of H5989
2Ki 3:13 kings together to **d** us into the hands of H5989
2Ki 3:18 *he will* also **d** Moab into your hands. H5989
2Ki 17:39 it is he *who will* **d** you from the hand of H5911
2Ki 18:29 He cannot **d** you from my hand. H5911
2Ki 18:30 'The LORD *will* **surely d** us; this city H5911+5911
2Ki 18:32 you when he says, 'The LORD *will* **d** us. H5911
2Ki 18:35 How then *can* the LORD **d** Jerusalem from H5911
2Ki 19:3 birth and there is no strength to **d** them. H4256
2Ki 19:12 *Did* the gods of the nations that were destroyed by my predecessors **d** H5911
2Ki 19:19 LORD our God, **d** us from his hand, so that H3828
2Ki 20:6 And *I will* **d** you and this city from the H5911
1Ch 14:10 *Will you* **d** them into my hands? H5989
1Ch 14:10 "Go, *I will* **d** them into your hands. H5989
1Ch 16:35 gather us and **d** us from the nations H5911
2Ch 25:20 so worked that *he might* **d** them into the H5989
2Ch 32:13 nations ever able to **d** their land from my H5911
2Ch 32:14 then can your god **d** you from my hand? H5911
2Ch 32:15 has been able to **d** his people from my H5911
2Ch 32:15 much less *will* your god **d** you from my H5911
Ezr 7:19 **D** to the God of Jerusalem all the A10719
Job 5:20 In famine *he will* **d** you from death, and H7009
Job 6:23 **d** me from the hand of the enemy, rescue H4880
Job 22:30 *He will* **d** even one who is not innocent H4880
Ps 3:2 are saying of me, "God *will* not **d** him." H3802
Ps 3:7 **D** me, my God! Strike all my H3828
Ps 6:4 and **d** me; save me because of your H2740
Ps 7:1 save and **d** me from all who pursue me, H5911
Ps 22:8 LORD rescue him. *Let him* **d** him, since he H5911
Ps 22:20 **D** me from the sword, my precious life H5911
Ps 25:22 **D** Israel, O God, from all their troubles! H7009
Ps 26:11 **d** me and be merciful to me. H7009
Ps 31:1 put to shame; **d** me in your righteousness. H7117
Ps 31:5 your hands I commit my spirit; **d** me, LORD, H7009
Ps 31:15 **d** me from the hands of my enemies H5911
Ps 33:19 to **d** them from death and keep them H5911
Ps 50:15 day of trouble; *I will* **d** you, and you will H2740
Ps 51:14 **D** me from the guilt of bloodshed, O God H5911
Ps 59:1 **D** me from my enemies, O God; be my H5911
Ps 59:2 **D** me from evildoers and save me from H5911
Ps 69:14 me sink; **d** *me* from those who hate me H5911
Ps 69:18 rescue me; **d** me because of my foes. H7009
Ps 71:2 rescue me and **d** me; turn your ear to me H7117
Ps 71:4 **D** me, my God, from the hand of the H7117
Ps 72:12 For *he will* **d** the needy who cry out, the H5911
Ps 79:9 **d** us and forgive our sins for your name's H5911
Ps 82:4 **d** them from the hand of the wicked. H5911
Ps 91:15 in trouble, *I will* **d** him and honor him. H2740
Ps 109:21 out of the goodness of your love, **d** me. H5911
Ps 119:153 Look on my suffering and **d** me, for I H2740
Ps 119:170 **d** me according to your promise. H5911
Ps 144:7 **d** me and rescue me from the mighty H7198
Ps 144:11 **d** me; rescue me from the hands of H7198
Isa 31:5 he will shield it and **d** it, he will 'pass H5911
Isa 36:14 Hezekiah deceive you. He cannot **d** you! H5911
Isa 36:15 'The LORD *will* **surely d** us; this city H5911+5911
Isa 36:18 you when he says, 'The LORD *will* **d** us. H5911
Isa 36:20 How then *can* the LORD **d** Jerusalem from H5911
Isa 37:3 birth and there is no strength to **d** them. H4256
Isa 37:12 *Did* the gods of the nations that were destroyed by my predecessors **d** H5911
Isa 37:20 LORD our God, **d** us from his hand, so that H3828
Isa 38:6 And *I will* **d** you and this city from the H5911
Isa 43:13 No *one can* **d** out of my hand H5911
Isa 50:2 Was my arm too short to **d** you? Do I lack H7014
Jer 15:11 "Surely *I will* **d** you for a good purpose H9223
Jer 15:21 of the wicked and **d** you from the grasp of H7009
Jer 20:5 *I will* **d** all the wealth of this city into the H5989
Jer 22:25 *I will* **d** you into the hands of those H928+5989
Jer 29:21 "*I will* **d** them into the hands of H5989
Jer 31:11 For the LORD *will* **d** Jacob and redeem H7009
Jer 34:20 *I will* **d** into the hands of their enemies H5989
Jer 34:21 "*I will* **d** Zedekiah king of Judah and his H5989
Jer 42:11 will save you and **d** you from his hands. H5911
Jer 44:30 '*I am going to* **d** Pharaoh Hophra king of H5989
Eze 7:19 will not be able to **d** them in the day of H5911
Eze 11:9 out of the city and **d** you into the hands of H5989
Eze 16:39 Then *I will* **d** you into the hands of your H5989
Eze 21:31 *I will* **d** you into the hands of brutal men H5989
Eze 23:28 I *am about to* **d** you into the hands of H5989
Da 3:17 the God we serve is able to **d** us from it A10706
Da 3:17 and *he will* **d** us from Your Majesty's A10706
Hos 13:14 "*I will* **d** this people from the power of the H7009
Am 6:8 *I will* **d up** the city and everything in it." H6037
Mic 5:6 *He will* **d** us from the Assyrians when they H5911
Hab 3:13 You came out to **d** your people, to save H3829
Mt 6:13 temptation, but **d** us from the evil one. G4861
Mt 26:15 willing to give me if I **d** him **over** to you?" G4140
2Co 1:10 a deadly peril, and *he will* **d** us *again*. G4861
2Co 1:10 set our hope that *he will* continue to **d** us, G4861

DELIVERANCE (20) [DELIVER]
Ge 45:7 earth and to save your lives by a great **d**. H7129
Ge 49:18 "I look for your **d**, LORD. H3802
Ex 14:13 you will see the **d** the LORD will bring H3802
1Sa 2:1 over my enemies, for I delight in your **d**. H3802
1Sa 14:45 has brought about this great **d** in Israel? H3802
2Ch 12:7 destroy them but will soon give them **d**. H7129
2Ch 20:17 firm and see the **d** the LORD will give you H3802
Est 4:14 relief and **d** for the Jews will arise from H2208
Job 13:16 this will turn out for my **d**, for no godless H3802
Ps 3:8 From the LORD comes **d**. May your blessing H3802
Ps 32:7 trouble and surround me with songs of **d**. H7119
Ps 33:17 A horse is a vain hope for **d**; despite all H9591
Ps 78:22 did not believe in God or trust in his **d**. H3802
Isa 20:6 we fled to for help and **d** from the king of H5911
Isa 45:24 'In the LORD alone are **d** and strength. H7407
Isa 45:25 of Israel *will* **find d** in the LORD and will H7405
Isa 59:11 find none; for **d**, but it is far away. H3802
Joel 2:32 Zion and in Jerusalem there will be **d**, H7129
Ob 17 But on Mount Zion will be **d**; it will be H7129
Php 1:19 happened to me will turn out for my **d**. G5401

DELIVERED (89) [DELIVER]
Ge 14:20 who **d** your enemies into your hand." H4481
Ge 48:16 the Angel who *has* **d** me from all harm H1457
Nu 21:34 for *I have* **d** him into your hands H5989
Dt 2:33 the LORD our God **d** him **over** to us and we H5989
Dt 3:2 for *I have* **d** him into your hands H5989
Dt 7:2 LORD your God *has* **d** them **over** to you H5989
Jos 6:2 *I have* **d** Jericho into your hands H5989
Jos 8:1 For *I have* **d** into your hands the king of Ai, H5989
Jos 24:10 again, and *I* **d** you out of his hand. H5911
Jdg 6:9 And I **d** you from the hand of all your NDT
Jdg 13:1 so the LORD **d** them into the hands of the H5989
Jdg 16:23 "Our god *has* **d** Samson, our H5989
Jdg 16:24 "Our god *has* **d** our enemy into our hands H5989
1Sa 7:14 Israel **d** the neighboring territory from H5911
1Sa 10:18 and *I* **d** you from the power of Egypt and H5911
1Sa 12:11 and *he* **d** you from the hands of your H5911
1Sa 23:7 he said, "God *has* **d** him into my hands H5796
1Sa 24:10 eyes how the LORD **d** you into my hands in H5989
1Sa 24:18 did to me; the LORD **d** me into your hands H6037
1Sa 26:8 "Today God *has* **d** your enemy into your H6037
1Sa 26:23 The LORD **d** you into my hands today, but I H5989
1Sa 30:23 has protected us and **d** into our hands the H5989
2Sa 4:9 who *has* **d** me out of every trouble H7009
2Sa 12:7 and I **d** you from the hand of Saul. H5911
2Sa 18:28 *He has* **d up** those who lifted their hands H6037
2Sa 19:9 "The king **d** us from the hand of our H5911
2Sa 22:1 song when the LORD **d** him from the hand H5911
2Sa 22:44 "*You have* **d** me from the attacks of the H7117
1Ki 1:29 who *has* **d** me out of every trouble, H7009
1Ki 9:28 which *they* **d** to King Solomon. H995
2Ki 17:13 to obey and that *I* **d** to you through my H8938
2Ki 18:33 *Has* the god of any nation **ever d** H5911+5911
2Ki 19:11 them completely. And *will* you **be d**? H5911
1Ch 5:20 God **d** the Hagrites and all their H5989
2Ch 8:18 which *they* **d** to King Solomon. H995
2Ch 13:16 and God **d** them into their hands. H5989
2Ch 16:8 on the LORD, *he* **d** them into your hand. H5989
2Ch 24:24 the LORD **d** into their hands a much larger H5989
2Ch 28:5 the LORD his God **d** him into the hands of H5989
Ezr 8:36 *They* also **d** the king's orders to the royal H5989
Ne 9:27 So *you* **d** them into the hands of their H5989
Ne 9:28 in your compassion *you* **d** them time after H5911
Est 1:12 the attendants **d** the king's H928+3338
Job 21:30 that *they* **are d** from the day of wrath? H3297
Job 22:30 *who will* **be d** through the cleanness of H4880
Job 23:7 there *I would* **be d** forever from my H7117
Job 33:28 God *has* **d** me from going down to the pit H7009
Ps 18:T song when the LORD **d** him from the hand H5911
Ps 18:43 *You have* **d** me from the attacks of the H7117
Ps 22:4 their trust; they trusted and *you* **d** them. H7117
Ps 34:4 answered me; *he* **d** me from all my fears. H5911
Ps 54:7 *You have* **d** me from all my troubles, and H5911
Ps 56:13 For *you have* **d** me from death and my H5911
Ps 60:5 right hand, that those you love *may* **be d**. H2740
Ps 71:23 I sing praise to you—I whom *you have* **d**. H7009
Ps 86:13 *you have* **d** me from the depths H5911
Ps 106:43 Many times *he* **d** them, but they were H5911
Ps 107:6 trouble, and *he* **d** them from their distress. H5911
Ps 108:6 right hand, that those you love *may* **be d**. H2740
Ps 116:8 *have* **d** me from death, my eyes from H2740
Ps 119:117 Uphold me, and *I will* **be d**; I will always H3828
Isa 1:27 Zion *will* **be d** with justice, her penitent H7009
Isa 36:18 *Have* the gods of any nations *ever* **d** their H5911
Isa 37:11 them completely. And *will* you **be d**? H5911
Jer 37:17 "*you will* **be d** into the hands of the king H5989
Eze 23:9 "Therefore *I* **d** her into the hands of her H5989
Eze 35:5 and **d** the Israelites **over** to the sword H5599
Da 1:2 And the Lord **d** Jehoiakim king of Judah H5989
Da 7:25 The holy people *will* **be d** into his hands A10314
Da 11:41 of Ammon *will* **be d** from his hand. H4880
Da 12:1 is found written in the book—*will* **be d**. H4880

Mt 17:22 of Man is going to *be* **d** into the hands of *G4140*
Mt 20:18 the Son of Man *will be* **d over** to the chief *G4140*
Mt 26:45 the Son of Man *is* **d** into the hands of *G4140*
Mk 9:31 Son of Man *is going to be* **d** into the *G4140*
Mk 10:33 the Son of Man *will be* **d over** to the chief *G4140*
Mk 14:41 the Son of Man *is* **d** into the hands of *G4140*
Lk 9:44 of Man is going to *be* **d** into the hands of *G4140*
Lk 18:32 *He will be* **d over** to the Gentiles. They will *G4140*
Lk 24: 7 Son of Man must *be* **d over** to the hands *G4140*
Ac 12:21 throne and **d a public address** to the *G1319*
Ac 15:30 the church together and **d** the letter. *G2113*
Ac 16: 4 *they* **d** the decisions reached by the *G4140*
Ac 23:33 *they* **d** the letter to the governor and *G347*
Ro 4:25 He *was* **d over to death** for our sins and *G4140*
2Co 1:10 He *has* **d** us from such a deadly peril, and *G4861*
2Th 3: 2 And pray that *we may be* **d** from wicked *G4861*
2Ti 4:17 And *I was* **d** from the lion's mouth. *G4861*
Jude 5 the Lord at one time **d** his people out of *G5392*

DELIVERER (11) [DELIVER]

Jdg 3: 9 he raised up for them a **d**, Othniel son of H4635
Jdg 3:15 to the LORD, and he gave them a **d**—Ehud, H4635
2Sa 22: 2 LORD is my rock, my fortress and my **d**; H7117
2Ki 13: 5 The LORD provided a **d** for Israel, and they H4635
Ps 18: 2 my fortress and my **d**; my God is my rock, H7117
Ps 40:17 You are my help and my **d**; you are my H7117
Ps 70: 5 You are my help and my **d**; LORD, do not H7117
Ps 140: 7 my strong **d**, you shield my head in H3802
Ps 144: 2 my stronghold and my **d**, my shield, H7117
Ac 7:35 to be their ruler and **d** by God himself, *G3392*
Ro 11:26 "The **d** will come from Zion; he will turn *G4861*

DELIVERERS (2) [DELIVER]

Ne 9:27 your great compassion you gave them **d**, H4635
Ob 21 **D** will go up on Mount Zion to govern the H4635

DELIVERING (5) [DELIVER]

Jdg 13: 5 take the lead in **d** Israel from the hands H3828
1Sa 14:48 **d** Israel from the hands of those who had H5911
1Sa 24:15 he vindicate me by **d** me from your hand." NDT
2Sa 18:19 vindicated him *by d* him **from** the hand of his AIT
2Sa 18:31 you today *by d* you **from** the hand of all who AIT

DELIVERS (16) [DELIVER]

Dt 20:13 the LORD your God **d** it into your hand, H5989
Dt 21:10 the LORD your God **d** them into your hands H5989
Job 36:15 those who suffer *he* **d** in their suffering; H2740
Ps 34: 7 those who fear him, and *he* **d** them. H2740
Ps 34:17 *he* **d** them from all their troubles. H5911
Ps 34:19 the LORD **d** him from them all; H5911
Ps 37:40 The LORD helps them and **d** them; he H7117
Ps 37:40 *he* **d** them from the wicked and saves H7117
Ps 41: 1 the LORD **d** them in times of trouble. H4880
Ps 97:10 faithful ones and **d** them from the hand of H5911
Ps 144:10 victory to kings, who **d** his servant David. H7198
Pr 10: 2 but righteousness **d** from death. H5911
Pr 11: 4 of wrath, but righteousness **d** from death. H5911
Pr 11: 6 The righteousness of the upright **d** them H5911
Isa 66: 7 the pains come upon her, *she* **d** a son. H4880
Ro 7:25 who **d** me through Jesus Christ our Lord! NDT

DELIVERY (4) [DELIVER]

Ex 1:16 women during childbirth on the **d stool**, H78
1Sa 4:19 was pregnant and **near the time of d**. H3528
Isa 66: 9 to the moment of birth and not **give d**?" H3528
Isa 66: 9 I close up the womb when I **bring to d**?" H3528

DELTA (1)

Isa 7:18 flies from the Nile **d** in Egypt and for bees H7895

DELUDED (3) [DELUSION]

Pr 28:11 is poor and discerning sees how **d** they are. NDT
Isa 44:20 feeds on ashes; a **d** heart misleads him H9438
Rev 19:20 With these signs *he had* **d** those who had *G4414*

DELUGED (1)

2Pe 3: 6 world of that time *was* **d** and destroyed. *G2885*

DELUSION (1) [DELUDED, DELUSIONS]

2Th 2:11 sends them a powerful **d** so that they will *G4415*

DELUSIONS (4) [DELUSION]

Ps 4: 2 long will you love **d** and seek false gods? H8198
Ps 119:118 your decrees, for their **d** come to nothing. H9567
Jer 14:14 idolatries and the **d** *of* their own minds. H9567
Jer 23:26 who prophesy the **d** *of* their own minds? H9567

DEMAND (15) [DEMANDED, DEMANDING, DEMANDS]

Ge 9: 5 lifeblood *I will* surely **d an accounting**. H2011
Ge 9: 5 *I will* **d an accounting** from every animal H2011
Ge 9: 5 *I will* **d an accounting** for the life of H2011
Dt 23:21 your God *will* **certainly d** it of you H2011+2011
2Sa 3:13 But I **d** one thing of you: Do not H8626
2Sa 4:11 *should I* not now **d** his blood from your H1335
2Sa 21: 4 "We have no right to **d** silver or gold from NDT
1Ki 20: 5 'I sent to **d** your silver and gold, your wives H606
1Ki 20: 9 the first time, but this **d** I cannot meet. H1821
2Ki 18:14 and I will pay whatever *you* **d** of me." H5989
Ne 5:12 "And *we will* not **d** anything more from H1335
Job 17: 3 the pledge you **d**. Who else will put H6640
Lk 6:30 takes what belongs to you, *do* not **d** it **back**. *G555*
Lk 23:24 So Pilate decided to grant their **d**. *G161*

1Co 1:22 Jews **d** signs and Greeks look for wisdom, *G160*

DEMANDED (16) [DEMAND]

Ge 31:39 And *you* **d payment** from me *for* whatever H1335
Ex 21:30 However, if payment **is d**, the owner may H8883
Ex 21:30 his life by the payment of whatever **is d**. H8883
Jdg 6:30 The people of the town **d** of Joash, "Bring H606
1Ki 20: 9 servant will do all *you* **d** the first time, H8938
2Ki 6:11 He summoned his officers and **d of** them H606
2Ki 23:35 Necho the silver and gold he **d**. H6584+7023
Ne 5:18 *I* never **d** the food allotted to the governor, H1335
Job 22: 6 *You* **d security** *from* your relatives for no H2471
Ps 137: 3 our tormentors **d** songs of joy; they NDT
Mt 18:28 'Pay back what you owe me!' *he* **d**. *G3306*
Lk 12:20 This very night your life *will be* **d** from you *G555*
Lk 12:48 given much, much *will be* **d**; and from the *G2426*
Lk 22:64 They blindfolded him and **d**, "Prophesy *G2089*
Lk 23:23 they insistently **d** that he be crucified, *G160*
Jn 18:22 way you answer the high priest?" *he* **d**. *G3306*

DEMANDING (4) [DEMAND]

Ex 5:14 they had appointed, **d**, "Why haven't you H606
2Sa 3:14 son of Saul, **d**, "Give me my wife Michal H606
Ps 78:18 God to the test by **d** the food they craved. H8626
2Co 13: 3 since *you are* **d** proof that Christ is *G2426*

DEMANDS (6) [DEMAND]

Ex 21:22 the woman's husband **d** and the court H8883
1Ki 20: 8 "Don't listen to him or **agree to** his **d**." H14
Ne 5:18 because the **d** were heavy on these H6275
Ps 25:10 those who keep the **d** of his covenant. H6343
Isa 43:23 offerings nor wearied you with **d** for incense. NDT
Mic 7: 3 doing evil; the ruler **d** gifts, the judge H8626

DEMAS (3)

Col 4:14 the doctor, and **D** send greetings. *G1318*
2Ti 4:10 **D**, because he loved this world, has *G1318*
Phm 24 Aristarchus, **D** and Luke, my fellow *G1318*

DEMETRIUS (3)

Ac 19:24 A silversmith named **D**, who made silver *G1320*
Ac 19:38 **D** and his fellow craftsmen have a *G1320*
3Jn 12 **D** is well spoken of by everyone—and *G1320*

DEMOLISH (11) [DEMOLISHED]

Ex 23:24 *You* **must d** them and break their H2238+2238
Nu 33:52 cast idols, and **d** all their high places. H9012
Jer 43:13 the sun in Egypt *he will* **d** the sacred H8689
Eze 26: 9 your walls and **d** your towers with his H5997
Eze 26:12 down your walls and **d** your fine houses H5997
Hos 10: 2 The LORD *will* **d** their altars and destroy H6904
Mic 5:10 horses from among you and **d** your chariots. H6
Mic 5:14 your Asherah poles when *I* **d** your cities. H9012
Mal 1: 4 may build, but I *will* **d**. They will be called H2238
2Co 10: 4 they have divine power to **d** strongholds. *G2746*
2Co 10: 5 *We* **d** arguments and every pretension that *G2747*

DEMOLISHED (11) [DEMOLISH]

Nu 21:30 *We have* **d** them as far as Nophah, which H9037
Jdg 6:28 was Baal's altar, **d**, with the Asherah pole H5997
2Ki 10:27 *They* **d** the sacred stone of Baal and tore H5997
2Ki 23:15 even that altar and high place *he* **d**. H5997
2Ch 33: 3 high places his father Hezekiah *had* **d**; H5997
Jer 31:40 The city will never again be uprooted or **d**." H2238
Eze 6: 4 Your altars *will* **be d** and your incense H9037
Eze 6: 6 will be laid waste and the high places **d**, H9037
Am 3:15 be destroyed and the mansions *will be* **d**," H6066
Zep 1:13 wealth will be plundered, their houses **d**. H9039
Zep 3: 6 destroyed nations; their strongholds **are d**. H9037

DEMON (16) [DEMON-POSSESSED, DEMONIC, DEMONS]

Mt 9:33 And when the **d** was driven out, the man *G1228*
Mt 11:18 drinking, and they say, 'He has a **d**. *G1228*
Mt 17:18 Jesus rebuked the **d**, and it came out of *G1228*
Mk 7:26 Jesus to drive the **d** out of her daughter. *G1228*
Mk 7:29 you may go; the **d** has left your daughter." *G1228*
Mk 7:30 child lying on the bed, and the **d** gone. *G1228*
Lk 4:33 there was a man possessed by a **d**, *G1228*
Lk 4:35 Then the **d** threw the man down before *G1228*
Lk 7:33 drinking wine, and you say, 'He has a **d**. *G1228*
Lk 8:29 been driven by the **d** into solitary places. *G1228*
Lk 9:42 the **d** threw him to the ground in a *G1228*
Lk 11:14 Jesus was driving out a **d** that was mute *G1228*
Lk 11:14 When the **d** left, the man who had been *G1228*
Jn 8:49 "I am not possessed by a **d**," said Jesus *G1228*
Jn 10:21 the sayings *of a man* **possessed by a d**. *G1227*
Jn 10:21 Can a **d** open the eyes of the blind?" *G1228*

DEMON-POSSESSED (17) [DEMON, POSSESS]

Mt 4:24 severe pain, the **d**, those having seizures, *G1227*
Mt 8:16 many *who were* **d** were brought to him *G1227*
Mt 8:28 two **d** *men* coming from the tombs met *G1227*
Mt 8:33 what had happened *to* the **d** *men*. *G1227*
Mt 9:32 a man *who was* **d** and could not talk was *G1227*
Mt 12:22 brought him a **d** *man* who was blind and *G1227*
Mt 15:22 My daughter *is* **d** and suffering terribly." *G1227*
Mk 1:32 brought to Jesus all the sick and **d**. *G1227*
Mk 5:16 what had happened *to* the **d** *man*— *G1227*
Mk 5:18 the *man who had been* **d** begged to go *G1227*
Lk 8:27 he was met by a **d** man from the *G2400+1228*
Lk 8:36 people how the **d** *man* had been cured. *G1227*
Jn 7:20 "*You are* **d**," the crowd answered *G1228+2400*
Jn 8:48 that you are a Samaritan and **d**?" *G1228+2400*
Jn 8:52 "Now we know that *you are* **d**! *G1228+2400*
Jn 10:20 "*He is* **d** and raving mad. *G1228+2400*
Ac 19:13 over those *who were* **d**. *G2400+3836+4460+3836+4505*

DEMONIC (2) [DEMON]

Jas 3:15 from heaven but is earthly, unspiritual, **d**. *G1229*
Rev 16:14 They are **d** spirits that perform signs, and *G1228*

DEMONS (46) [DEMON]

Mt 7:22 your name drive out **d** and in your name *G1228*
Mt 8:31 The **d** begged Jesus, "If you drive us out *G1230*
Mt 9:34 "It is by the prince *of* **d** that he drives out *G1228*
Mt 9:34 the prince of demons that he drives out **d**." *G1228*
Mt 10: 8 those who have leprosy, drive out **d**. *G1228*
Mt 12:24 Beelzebul, the prince *of* **d**, that this fellow *G1228*
Mt 12:24 of demons, that this fellow drives out **d**." *G1228*
Mt 12:27 And if I drive out **d** by Beelzebul, by whom *G1228*
Mt 12:28 it is by the Spirit of God that I drive out **d**, *G1228*
Mk 1:34 He also drove out many **d**, but he would *G1228*
Mk 1:34 would not let the **d** speak because they *G1228*
Mk 1:39 in their synagogues and driving out **d**. *G1228*
Mk 3:15 to have authority to drive out **d**. *G1228*
Mk 3:22 By the prince *of* **d** he is driving out *G1228*
Mk 3:22 the prince of demons he is driving out **d**." *G1228*
Mk 5:12 The **d** begged Jesus, "Send us among the NDT
Mk 5:15 had been **possessed by** the legion of **d**, *G1227*
Mk 6:13 drove out many **d** and anointed many *G1228*
Mk 9:38 driving out **d** in your name and we *G1228*
Mk 16: 9 out of whom he had driven seven **d**. *G1228*
Mk 16:17 In my name they will drive out **d**; they will *G1228*
Lk 4:41 Moreover, **d** came out of many people *G1228*
Lk 8: 2 from whom seven **d** had come out; *G1228*
Lk 8:30 because many **d** had gone into him. *G1228*
Lk 8:32 The **d** begged Jesus to let them go into the NDT
Lk 8:33 When the **d** came out of the man, they *G1228*
Lk 8:35 the man from whom the **d** had gone out, *G1228*
Lk 8:38 man from whom the **d** had gone out *G1228*
Lk 9: 1 to drive out all **d** and to cure diseases, *G1228*
Lk 9:49 driving out **d** in your name and we *G1228*
Lk 10:17 even the **d** submit to us in your name." *G1228*
Lk 11:15 the prince *of* **d**, he is driving out *G1228*
Lk 11:15 the prince of demons, he is driving out **d**." *G1228*
Lk 11:18 you claim that I drive out **d** by Beelzebul. *G1228*
Lk 11:19 Now if I drive out **d** by Beelzebul, by whom *G1228*
Lk 11:20 But if I drive out **d** by the finger of God *G1228*
Lk 13:32 keep on driving out **d** and healing people *G1228*
Ro 8:38 neither angels nor **d**, neither the present *G794*
1Co 10:20 the sacrifices of pagans are offered *to* **d**, *G1228*
1Co 10:20 do not want you to be participants with **d**. *G1228*
1Co 10:21 the cup of the Lord and the cup *of* **d** too; *G1228*
1Co 10:21 both the Lord's table and the table *of* **d**. *G1228*
1Ti 4: 1 deceiving spirits and things taught *by* **d**. *G1228*
Jas 2:19 Even the **d** believe that—and *G1228*
Rev 9:20 they did not stop worshiping **d**, and idols *G1228*
Rev 18: 2 become a dwelling *for* **d** and a haunt *G1228*

DEMONSTRATE (3) [DEMONSTRATES, DEMONSTRATING, DEMONSTRATION]

Ac 26:20 turn to God and **d** their repentance *G545+4556*
Ro 3:25 He did this to **d** his righteousness *G1893*
Ro 3:26 he did it to **d** his righteousness at the *G1893*

DEMONSTRATES (1) [DEMONSTRATE]

Ro 5: 8 But God **d** his own love for us in this *G5319*

DEMONSTRATING (1) [DEMONSTRATE]

2Co 12:12 I persevered *in* **d** among you the marks of *G2981*

DEMONSTRATION (1) [DEMONSTRATE]

1Co 2: 4 but with a **d** of the Spirit's power, *G618*

DEN (17) [DENS]

Isa 11: 8 The infant will play near the cobra's **d** H2987
Jer 7:11 my Name, become a **d** *of* robbers to you? H5117
Da 6: 7 shall be thrown into the lions' **d**. A10129
Da 6:12 would be thrown into the lions' **d**?" A10129
Da 6:16 Daniel and threw him into the lions' **d**. A10129
Da 6:17 placed over the mouth of the **d**, A10129
Da 6:19 king got up and hurried to the lions' **d**. A10129
Da 6:20 When he came near the **d**, he called to A10129
Da 6:23 gave orders to lift Daniel out of the **d**. A10129
Da 6:23 And when Daniel was lifted from the **d** A10129
Da 6:24 brought in and thrown into the lions' **d**, A10129
Da 6:24 before they reached the floor of the **d**, A10129
Am 3: 4 Does it growl in its **d** when it has caught H5104
Na 2:11 Where now is the lions' **d**, the place H5061
Mt 21:13 you are making it 'a **d** of robbers. *G5068*
Mk 11:17 But you have made it 'a **d** of robbers.'" *G5068*
Lk 19:46 you have made it 'a **d** of robbers.' *G5068*

DENARII (2) [DENARIUS]

Lk 7:41 One owed him five hundred **d**, and the *G1324*
Lk 10:35 day he took out two **d** and gave them to *G1324*

DENARIUS (7) [DENARII]

Mt 20: 2 to pay them a **d** for the day and sent *G1324*
Mt 20: 9 afternoon came and each received a **d**. *G1324*
Mt 20:10 But each one of them also received a **d**. *G1324*
Mt 20:13 Didn't you agree to work *for* a **d**? *G1324*
Mt 22:19 paying the tax." They brought him a **d**, *G1324*
Mk 12:15 "Bring me a **d** and let me look at it." *G1324*

Lk 20:24 "Show me a **d**. Whose image and G1324

DENIED (17) [DENY]
Job 6:10 that *I had* not **d** the words of the Holy One H3948
Job 27: 2 as God lives, *who has* **d** me justice, the H6073
Job 31:13 "If *I have* **d** justice *to* any of my servants H4415
Job 31:16 "If *I have* **d** the desires of the poor or let H4979
Job 38:15 The wicked **are d** their light, and their H4979
Ecc 2:10 *I* **d** *myself* nothing my eyes desired; H724
Ecc 5: 8 justice and rights **d**, do not be H1609
Mt 26:70 But he **d** it before them all. "I don't know G766
Mt 26:72 *He* **d** it again, with an oath: "I don't know G766
Mk 14:68 But he **d** it. "I don't know or understand G766
Mk 14:70 Again he **d** it. After a little while, those G766
Lk 8:45 *When they* all **d** it, Peter said, "Master, the G766
Lk 22:57 But he **d** it. "Woman, I don't know him," G766
Jn 18:25 He **d** it, saying, "I am not." G766
Jn 18:27 Again Peter **d** it, and at that moment a G766
1Ti 5: 8 *has* **d** the faith and is worse than an G766
Rev 3: 8 kept my word and *have* not **d** my name. G766

DENIES (3) [DENY]
Job 34: 5 'I am innocent, but God **d** me justice. H6073
1Jn 2:22 It is whoever **d** that Jesus is the Christ G766
1Jn 2:23 No one who **d** the Son has the Father G766

DENOUNCE (5) [DENOUNCED, DENOUNCES]
Nu 23: 7 'curse Jacob for me; come, **d** Israel. H2404
Nu 23: 8 How *can I* **d** those whom the LORD has not H2404
Jer 20:10 on every side! **D** him! Let's denounce H5583
Jer 20:10 Denounce him! *Let's* **d** him!" All my H5583
Mt 11:20 Then Jesus began *to* **d** the towns in which G3943

DENOUNCED (4) [DENOUNCE]
Nu 23: 8 those whom the LORD *has* not **d**? H2404
Pr 24:24 be cursed by peoples and **d** *by* nations. H2404
Da 3: 8 came forward and **d** the Jews. A10030+10642
1Co 10:30 why *am I* **d** because of something I thank G1059

DENOUNCES (2) [DENOUNCE]
Job 17: 5 If *anyone* **d** their friends for reward, the H5583
Job 21:31 Who **d** their conduct to their face? Who H5583

DENS (8) [DEN]
Job 37: 8 animals take cover; they remain in their **d**. H5104
Job 38:40 they crouch in their **d** or lie in wait in a H5104
Ps 104:22 they return and lie down in their **d**. H5104
SS 4: 8 from the lions' **d** and the mountain H5104
Mic 7:17 They will come trembling out of their **d** H4995
Na 2:12 lairs with the kill and his **d** with the prey. H5104
Mt 8:20 "Foxes have **d** and birds have nests G5887
Lk 9:58 "Foxes have **d** and birds have nests G5887

DENSE (6)
Ge 19:28 he saw **d smoke** rising *from* the land H7798
Ex 8:24 **D** swarms of flies poured into Pharaoh's H3878
Ex 19: 9 "I am going to come to you in a **d** cloud H6295
Isa 30:27 burning anger and **d** clouds of smoke; H3880
Jer 46:23 declares the LORD, "**d** though *it be*. H4202+2983
Zec 11: 2 Bashan; the **d** forest has been cut down! H1293

DENY (20) [DENIED, DENIES, DENYING, SELF-DENIAL]
Ex 23: 6 "*Do* not **d** justice to your poor people in H5742
Lev 16:29 seventh month *you must* **d** yourselves H6700
Lev 16:31 and *you must* **d** yourselves; it H6700
Lev 23:27 Hold a sacred assembly and **d** yourselves H6700
Lev 23:29 Those who *do* not **d themselves** on that H6700
Lev 23:32 rest for you, and *you must* **d** yourselves. H6700
Nu 29: 7 *You must* **d** yourselves and do no work. H6700
Nu 30:13 makes or any sworn pledge to **d** herself. H6700
Job 27: 5 the right; till I die, *I will* not **d** my integrity. H6073
Isa 5:23 a bribe, but **d** justice to the innocent. H6073
La 3:35 to **d** people their rights before the Most H5742
Am 2: 7 dust of the ground and **d** justice to the H5742
Mt 16:24 to be my disciple *must* **d** themselves and G565
Mk 8:34 to be my disciple *must* **d** themselves and G565
Lk 9:23 to be my disciple *must* **d** themselves and G766
Lk 22:34 *you will* **d** three times that you know me." G565
Ac 4:16 a notable sign, and we cannot **d** it. G766
Titus 1:16 know God, but by their actions *they* **d** him. G766
Jas 3:14 do not boast about it or **d** the truth. G6017
Jude 4 immorality and **d** Jesus Christ our only G766

DENYING (4) [DENY]
Eze 22:29 mistreat the foreigner, **d** them justice. H4202
2Ti 3: 5 having a form of godliness but **d** its power G766
2Pe 2: 1 even **d** the sovereign Lord who bought G766
1Jn 2:22 is the antichrist—**d** the Father and the Son. G766

DEPART (13) [DEPARTED, DEPARTS, DEPARTURE]
Ge 49:10 The scepter *will* not **d** from Judah, nor the H6073
2Sa 12:10 the sword *will* never **d** from your house H6073
Job 1:21 my mother's womb, and naked *I will* **d**. H8740
Ps 39:13 life again before *I* **d** and am no more." H2143
Ecc 5:15 and as everyone comes, so *they* **d**. H8740
Ecc 5:16 so *they* **d**, and what do they H2143
Isa 49:17 those who laid you waste **d** from you. H3655
Isa 52:11 **D**, depart, go out from there! Touch no H6073
Isa 52:11 **d**, go out from there! Touch no H6073
Isa 59:21 is on you, will not **d** from you, and my words NDT
Jer 43:12 so he will pick Egypt clean and **d**. H3655
Mt 25:41 those on his left, '**D** from me, you who are G4513
Php 1:23 I desire to **d** and be with Christ, which is G386

DEPARTED (16) [DEPART]
Jos 2:21 them away, and *they* **d**. And she tied the H2143
1Sa 4:21 "The Glory *has* **d** from Israel" H1655
1Sa 4:22 She said, "The Glory *has* **d** from Israel, for H1655
1Sa 16:14 the Spirit of the LORD *had* **d** from Saul, H6073
1Sa 18:12 LORD was with David but *had* **d** from Saul. H6073
1Sa 28:15 against me, and God *has* **d** from me. H6073
1Sa 28:16 now that the LORD *has* **d** from you and H6073
Job 23:12 *I have* not **d** *from* the commands of his H4631
Ps 119:102 *I have* not **d** from your laws, for you H6073
Isa 14: 9 it rouses the **spirits of the d** to greet you H8327
La 1: 6 All the splendor *has* **d** from Daughter H3655
Eze 10:18 the glory of the LORD **d** from over the H3655
Jn 4:50 The man took Jesus at his word and **d**. G4513
1Ti 1: 6 Some *have* **d** from these and have turned to G846
1Ti 6:21 in so doing *have* **d** from the faith. G846
2Ti 2:18 who *have* **d** from the truth. They say that the G846

DEPARTS (2) [DEPART]
Ps 146: 4 *When* their spirit **d**, they return to the H3655
Ecc 6: 4 without meaning, *it* **d** in darkness, and in H2143

DEPARTURE (6) [DEPART]
Dt 16: 3 remember the time of your **d** from Egypt. H3655
Dt 16: 6 on the anniversary of your **d** from Egypt. H3655
SS 5: 6 My heart sank at his **d**. I looked for him H1818
Lk 9:31 They spoke *about* his **d**, which he was G2016
2Ti 4: 6 offering, and the time *for* my **d** is near. G385
2Pe 1:15 to see that after my **d** you will always be G2016

DEPEND (9) [DEPENDED, DEPENDENT, DEPENDING, DEPENDS]
2Ki 18:21 king of Egypt to all who **d** on him. H1053
2Ki 19:10 let the god you **d** on deceive you when H1053
Ps 62: 7 My salvation and my honor **d on** God; he H6584
Isa 36: 6 king of Egypt to all who **d** on him. H1053
Isa 37:10 *Do* not **let** the god you **d** on deceive you H1053
Jer 49:11 Your widows too *can* **d** on me.'" H1053
Mic 5: 7 which do not wait for anyone or **d** on man. H3498
Ro 4:14 For if those who **d on** the law are heirs G1666
Ro 9:16 therefore, *d on* human **desire** or effort, but on AIT

DEPENDED (3) [DEPEND]
Isa 30:12 relied on oppression and **d** on deceit, H9128
Hos 10:13 Because *you have* **d** on your own strength H1053
Ac 12:20 because they **d on** the king's country for G608

DEPENDENT (2) [DEPEND]
Lev 21: 3 sister who is **d** on him since she has no H7940
1Th 4:12 so that *you will* not *be* **d on** G5970+2400

DEPENDING (8) [DEPEND]
2Ki 18:20 On whom *are you* **d**, that you rebel H1053
2Ki 18:21 I know *you are* **d** on Egypt, that H1053
2Ki 18:22 "*We are* **d** on the LORD our God" H1053
2Ki 18:24 even though *you are* **d** on Egypt for H1053
Isa 36: 5 On whom *are you* **d**, that you rebel H1053
Isa 36: 6 I know *you are* **d** on Egypt, that H1053
Isa 36: 7 "*We are* **d** on the LORD our God" H1053
Isa 36: 9 even though *you are* **d** on Egypt for H1053

DEPENDS (4) [DEPEND]
Ro 12:18 If it is possible, *as far as* it **d on** you, live at G1666
Gal 3:18 For if the inheritance **d on** the law, then it G1666
Gal 3:18 then it no longer **d on** the promise; but G1666
Col 2: 8 which **d on** human tradition and the G2848

DEPLOYED (5)
1Sa 4: 2 The Philistines **d** *their* **forces** to meet Israel H6885
2Sa 10: 9 troops in Israel and **d** them against the H6885
2Sa 10:10 his brother and **d** them against the H6885
1Ch 19:10 troops in Israel and **d** them against the H6885
1Ch 19:11 and *they were* **d** against the Ammonites. H6885

DEPORTED (11)
2Ki 15:29 of Naphtali, and **d** the people to Assyria. H1655
2Ki 16: 9 *He* **d** its inhabitants to Kir and put Rezin H1655
2Ki 17: 6 captured Samaria and **d** the Israelites to H1655
2Ki 17:26 "The people *you* **d** and resettled in the H1655
2Ki 18:11 The king of Assyria **d** Israel to Assyria and H1655
2Ki 24:16 of Babylon also **d** to Babylon the H995+1583
1Ch 6:15 Jozadak *was* **d** when the LORD sent Judah H2143
1Ch 8: 6 living in Geba and *were* **d** to Manahath: H1655
1Ch 8: 7 who **d** them and who was the father of H1655
Ezr 4:10 Ashurbanipal **d** and settled in the A10144
Ezr 5:12 this temple and **d** the people to Babylon A10144

DEPOSE (1) [DEPOSED, DEPOSES]
Isa 22:19 *I will* **d** you from your office, and you will H2074

DEPOSED (3) [DEPOSE]
1Ki 15:13 *He* even **d** his grandmother Maakah from H6073
2Ch 15:16 King Asa also **d** his grandmother Maakah H6073
Da 5:20 *he* **was d** from his royal throne and A10474

DEPOSES (1) [DEPOSE]
Da 2:21 *he* **d** kings and raises up others. A10528

DEPOSIT (10) [DEPOSITED]
Ezr 5:15 go and **d** them in the temple A10474
Eze 24: 6 now encrusted, whose **d** will not go away! H2689
Eze 24:11 may be melted and its **d** burned away. H2689
Eze 24:12 its heavy **d** has not been removed H2689
Mt 25:27 should have **put** my money **on d** with the G965
Lk 19:23 Why then didn't you put my money on **d** G5544
2Co 1:22 as a **d**, **guaranteeing what is to come**. G775
2Co 5: 5 *as* a **d**, **guaranteeing what is to come**. G775
Eph 1:14 who is a **d guaranteeing** our inheritance G775
2Ti 1:14 the good **d** *that was* **entrusted** to you— G4146

DEPOSITED (2) [DEPOSIT]
1Sa 10:25 down on a scroll and **d** it before the LORD. H5663
Ezr 6: 5 they *are to be* **d** in the house of God. A10474

DEPRAVED (6) [DEPRAVITY]
Eze 16:47 your ways *you* soon *became* more **d** than H8845
Eze 23:11 prostitution *she was* more **d** than her H8845
Ro 1:28 so God gave them over to a **d** mind, so that G99
2Ti 3: 8 *They are* men *of* **d** minds, who, as far as G2967
2Pe 2: 2 will follow their **d conduct** and will bring G816
2Pe 2: 7 was distressed by the **d** conduct of the G816

DEPRAVITY (2) [DEPRAVED]
Ro 1:29 kind of wickedness, evil, greed and **d**. G2798
2Pe 2:19 while they themselves are slaves *of* **d**—for G5785

DEPRESSIONS (1)
Lev 14:37 greenish or reddish **d** that appear to be H9206

DEPRIVE (13) [DEPRIVED, DEPRIVES, DEPRIVING]
Ex 21:10 *he must* not **d** the first one *of* her food H1757
Dt 24:17 *Do* not **d** the foreigner or the fatherless *of* H5742
Pr 18: 5 to the wicked and so **d** the innocent of H5742
Pr 31: 5 and **d** all the oppressed *of* their rights. H9101
Isa 10: 2 to **d** the poor of their rights and withhold H5742
Isa 29:21 with false testimony **d** the innocent of H5742
La 3:36 to **d** them of justice—would not the Lord H6430
Eze 36:12 will never again **d** them **of** their **children**. H8897
Eze 36:13 people and **d** your nation **of** *its* **children**," H8897
Am 5:12 bribes and **d** the poor **of justice** in the H5742
Mal 3: 5 and **d** the foreigners among you **of justice**, H5742
1Co 7: 5 *Do* not **d** each other except perhaps by G691
1Co 9:15 than allow anyone *to* **d** me of this boast. G3033

DEPRIVED (6) [DEPRIVE]
Ge 42:36 to them, "*You have* **d** me **of** my **children**. H8897
Ps 19: 6 to the other; nothing **is d** of its warmth. H6259
Jer 5:25 these away; your sins *have* **d** you of good. H4979
La 3:17 I *have been* **d** of peace; I have forgotten H2396
Mic 7:16 see and be ashamed, **d of** all their power. H4946
Ac 8:33 In his humiliation he *was* **d of** justice. G149

DEPRIVES (1) [DEPRIVE]
Job 12:24 *He* **d** the leaders of the earth *of* their H6073

DEPRIVING (1) [DEPRIVE]
Ecc 4: 8 "and why *am* I **d** myself of enjoyment?" H2893

DEPTH (6) [DEEP]
Ge 7:20 to a **d** *of* more than H2025+4200+5087
La 3:60 You have seen the **d** *of* their vengeance H3972
Ro 8:39 neither height nor **d**, nor anything else in G958
Ro 11:33 the **d** of the riches of the wisdom and G958
2Co 2: 4 to let you know the **d** of my love for you. G4359
Php 1: 9 more in knowledge and **d** of insight, G4246

DEPTHS (39) [DEEP]
Ex 15: 5 they sank to the **d** like a stone. H5185
Ne 9:11 you hurled their pursuers into the **d** H5185
Job 11: 8 They are deeper than the **d below**—what H8619
Job 36:30 about him, bathing the **d** *of* the sea. H9247
Job 41:31 It makes the **d** churn like a boiling caldron H5185
Ps 30: 1 for *you* **lifted** me **out of the d** and did not H1926
Ps 63: 9 they will go down to the **d** *of* the earth. H9397
Ps 68:22 I will bring them from the **d** *of* the sea, H5185
Ps 69: 2 I sink in the miry **d**, where there is no H5185
Ps 69:15 engulf me or the **d** swallow me up or the H5185
Ps 71:20 from the **d** *of* the earth you will again H9333
Ps 77:16 writhed; the very **d** were convulsed. H9333
Ps 86:13 you have delivered me from the **d**, from H9397
Ps 88: 6 put me in the lowest pit, in the darkest **d**. H5185
Ps 95: 4 In his hand are the **d** *of* the earth, and the H4736
Ps 104: 6 it with the **watery d** as with a garment; H9333
Ps 106: 9 them through the **d** as through a desert. H9333
Ps 107:26 to the heavens and went down to the **d**; H9333
Ps 130: 1 Out of the **d** I cry to you, LORD; H5099
Ps 135: 6 on the earth, in the seas and all their **d**. H9333
Ps 139: 8 if I make my bed in the **d**, you are there. H8619
Ps 139:15 was woven together in the **d** *of* the earth. H9397
Ps 148: 7 you great sea creatures and all **ocean d**, H9333
Pr 3:20 his knowledge the **watery d** were divided, H9333
Pr 8:24 When there were no **watery d**, I was given H9333
Isa 7:11 whether in the deepest **d** or in the highest H8619
Isa 14:15 the realm of the dead, to the **d** *of* the pit. H3752
Isa 29:15 Woe to those *who* **go to great d** to hide H6676
Isa 51:10 made a road in the **d** *of* the sea so that H5099
Isa 63:13 who led them through the **d**? Like a horse H9333
La 3:55 on your name, LORD, from the **d** of the pit. H9397
Eze 26:19 when I bring the **ocean d** over you and its H9333
Eze 27:34 by the sea in the **d** *of* the waters; H5099
Eze 32:23 graves are in the **d** *of* the pit and her army H3752
Am 9: 2 Though they dig down to the **d below** H8619
Jnh 2: 3 You hurled me into the **d**, into the very H5185
Mic 7:19 all our iniquities into the **d** *of* the sea. H5185
Zec 10:11 subdued and all the **d** *of* the Nile will dry H5185
Mt 18: 6 to be drowned in the **d** of the sea. G4283

DEPUTY (1)

DEPUTY, DEPUTIES (KJV) GOVERNORS, PROVICIAL GOVERNOR, PROCONSUL, PROCONSULS
Jdg 9:28 Jerub-Baal's son, and isn't Zebul his **d**? H7224

DERBE (4)
Ac 14: 6 cities of Lystra and **D** and to the *G1292*
Ac 14:20 The next day he and Barnabas left for **D**. *G1292*
Ac 16: 1 Paul came to **D** and then to Lystra, where *G1292*
Ac 20: 4 Gaius **from D**, Timothy also, *G1291*

DERIDE, DERIDED (KJV) LAUGH, SNEERED, SNEERING

DERIDES (1) [DERISION]
Pr 11:12 *Whoever* **d** their neighbor has no sense H996

DERISION (6) [DERIDES]
Job 27:23 *It* **claps** its hands **in d** and hisses him out H8562
Ps 44:13 the scorn and **d** of those around us. H7841
Ps 79: 4 of scorn and **d** to those around us. H7841
Ps 80: 6 have made us an **object of d** to our H4954
Eze 23:32 it will bring scorn and **d**, for it holds so H4353
Mic 6:16 you over to ruin and your people to **d**; H9240

DERIVES (1)
Eph 3:15 family in heaven and on earth **d** *its* **name**. *G3951*

DESCEND (7) [DESCENDANT, DESCENDANTS, DESCENDED, DESCENDING, DESCENDS, DESCENT]
Dt 32: 2 fall like rain and my words **d** like dew, H5688
Job 17:16 *Will we* **d** together into the dust? H5737
Ps 49:17 their splendor *will* not **d** with them. H3718
SS 4: 8 **D** from the crest of Amana, from the top H8801
Isa 5:14 into it *will* **d** their nobles and masses with H3718
Isa 14:19 *those who* **d** to the stones of the pit. H3718
Ro 10: 7 "or 'Who *will* **d** into the deep?' " (that is *G2849*

DESCENDANT (26) [DESCEND]
Lev 6:18 Any male **d** of Aaron may eat it. H1201
Lev 21:21 No **d** *of* Aaron the priest who has any H2446
Lev 22: 4 " 'If a **d** *of* Aaron has a H408+4946+2446
Nu 16:40 no one except a **d** *of* Aaron should come H2446
Nu 26:59 was Jochebed, a **d** *of* Levi, who was born H1426
Nu 32:41 a **d** *of* Manasseh, captured their H1201
Dt 3:14 a **d** *of* Manasseh, took the whole H1201
2Sa 14: 7 neither name nor **d** on the face of the H8642
1Ch 7:14 Asriel *was his* **d** *through* his Aramean H3528
1Ch 7:15 Another **d** was named Zelophehad, who NDT
1Ch 9: 4 the son of Bani, a **d** *of* Perez son of Judah. H1201
1Ch 24: 3 the help of Zadok a **d** *of* Eleazar and H1201
1Ch 24: 3 of Eleazar and Ahimelek a **d** *of* Ithamar, H1201
1Ch 26:24 Shubael, a **d** *of* Gershom son of Moses H1201
1Ch 27: 3 He was a **d** *of* Perez and chief of all the H1201
2Ch 20:14 a Levite and **d** *of* Asaph, as he stood in H1201
Ezr 5: 1 the prophet, a **d** *of* Iddo, prophesied to A10120
Ezr 6:14 the prophet and Zechariah, a **d** *of* Iddo. A10120
Ne 11: 4 the son of Mahalalel, a **d** *of* Perez; H1201
Ne 11: 5 the son of Zechariah, a **d** *of* Shelah. H1201
Jer 33:21 will no longer have a **d** to reign on his H1201
Jer 35:19 will never fail to have a **d** to serve me. H408
Lk 1: 5 was also a **d** of Aaron. *G1666+3836+2588*
Lk 1:27 man named Joseph, a **d** of David. *G1666+3875*
Ro 1: 3 who as to his earthly life was a **d** of David, *G5065*
Ro 11: 1 Israelite myself, a **d** of Abraham, from the *G5065*

DESCENDANTS (387) [DESCEND]
Ge 9: 9 with you and with your **d** after you H2446
Ge 15:13 hundred years your **d** will be strangers in H2446
Ge 15:16 generation your **d** will come back here, NDT
Ge 15:18 said, "To your **d** I give this land, from H2446
Ge 16:10 "I will increase your **d** so much that they H2446
Ge 17: 7 me and you and your **d** after you for the H2446
Ge 17: 7 your God and the God of your **d** after you. H2446
Ge 17: 8 possession to you and your **d** after you; H2446
Ge 17: 9 you and your **d** after you for the H2446
Ge 17:10 covenant with you and your **d** after you, H2446
Ge 17:19 everlasting covenant for his **d** after him. H2446
Ge 21:23 falsely with me or my children or my **d**. H5781
Ge 22:17 you and make your **d** as numerous as the H2446
Ge 22:17 Your **d** will take possession of the cities of H2446
Ge 25: 3 the **d** *of* Dedan were the Ashurites H1201
Ge 25: 4 All these were **d** *of* Keturah. H1201
Ge 25:18 His **d** settled in the area from Havilah to NDT
Ge 26: 3 For to you and your **d** I will give all these H2446
Ge 26: 4 I will make your **d** as numerous as the H2446
Ge 26:24 the number of your **d** for the sake of my H2446
Ge 28: 4 he give you and your **d** the blessing given H2446
Ge 28:13 give you and your **d** the land on which H2446
Ge 28:14 Your **d** will be like the dust of the earth H2446
Ge 32:12 will make your **d** like the sand of the H2446
Ge 35:11 and kings will be among your **d**. H4946+2743S
Ge 35:12 I will give this land to your **d** after you." H2446
Ge 36:15 These were the chiefs among Esau's **d** H1201
Ge 46: 8 Jacob and his **d**) who went to Egypt: H1201
Ge 46:26 *those who were* his **direct d**, not H3655+3751
Ge 48: 4 everlasting possession to your **d** after you. H2446
Ge 48:19 his **d** will become a group of nations." H2446
Ex 1: 5 The **d** *of* Jacob numbered H5883+3655+3751
Ex 12:24 as a lasting ordinance for you and your **d**. H1201
Ex 19: 3 are to say to the **d** *of* Jacob and what you H1074
Ex 28:43 a lasting ordinance for Aaron and his **d**. H2446
Ex 29:29 will belong to his **d** so that they can be H1201
Ex 30:21 Aaron and his **d** for the generations to H2446
Ex 32:13 'I will make your **d** as numerous as the H2446
Ex 32:13 I will give your **d** all this land I H2446
Ex 33: 1 Jacob, saying, 'I will give it to your **d**. H2446
Lev 21:17 come none of your **d** who has a defect H2446
Lev 22: 3 if any of your **d** is ceremonially unclean H2446
Lev 23:43 so your **d** will know that I had the Israelites H1887
Lev 25:30 to the buyer and the buyer's **d**. H1887
Nu 1:20 From the **d** *of* Reuben the firstborn son of H1201
Nu 1:22 From the **d** *of* Simeon: All the men twenty H1201
Nu 1:24 From the **d** *of* Gad: All the men twenty H1201
Nu 1:26 From the **d** *of* Judah: All the men twenty H1201
Nu 1:28 From the **d** *of* Issachar: All the men twenty H1201
Nu 1:30 From the **d** *of* Zebulun: All the men H1201
Nu 1:32 From the **d** *of* Ephraim: All the H1201
Nu 1:34 From the **d** *of* Manasseh: All the men H1201
Nu 1:36 From the **d** *of* Benjamin: All the men H1201
Nu 1:38 From the **d** *of* Dan: All the men twenty H1201
Nu 1:40 From the **d** *of* Asher: All the men twenty H1201
Nu 1:42 From the **d** *of* Naphtali: All the men H1201
Nu 9:10 any of you or your **d** are unclean because H1887
Nu 13:22 Sheshai and Talmai, the **d** *of* Anak, lived. H3535
Nu 13:28 We even saw **d** *of* Anak there. H3535
Nu 13:33 the **d** *of* Anak come from the Nephilim). H1201
Nu 14:24 land he went to, and his **d** will inherit it. H2446
Nu 25:13 He and his **d** will have a covenant of a H2446
Nu 26: 5 The **d** *of* Reuben, the firstborn son of H1201
Nu 26:12 The **d** *of* Simeon by their clans were H1201
Nu 26:15 The **d** *of* Gad by their clans were: through H1201
Nu 26:20 The **d** *of* Judah by their clans were H1201
Nu 26:21 The **d** *of* Perez were: through Hezron, the H1201
Nu 26:23 The **d** *of* Issachar by their clans were H1201
Nu 26:26 The **d** *of* Zebulun by their clans were H1201
Nu 26:28 The **d** *of* Joseph by their clans through H1201
Nu 26:29 The **d** *of* Manasseh: through Makir, the H1201
Nu 26:30 These were the **d** *of* Gilead: through Iezer, H1201
Nu 26:35 These were the **d** *of* Ephraim by their H1201
Nu 26:36 These were the **d** *of* Shuthelah: through H1201
Nu 26:37 These were the **d** *of* Joseph by their clans H1201
Nu 26:38 The **d** *of* Benjamin by their clans were H1201
Nu 26:40 The **d** *of* Bela through Ard and Naaman H1201
Nu 26:42 These were the **d** *of* Dan by their clans H1201
Nu 26:44 The **d** *of* Asher by their clans were H1201
Nu 26:45 through the **d** *of* Beriah: through H1201
Nu 26:48 The **d** *of* Naphtali by their clans were H1201
Nu 32:39 The **d** *of* Makir son of Manasseh went to H1201
Nu 32:40 the Makirites, the **d** *of* Manasseh, and H1201
Nu 36: 1 were from the clans of the **d** *of* Joseph, H1201
Nu 36: 5 the tribe of the **d** *of* Joseph is saying is H1201
Nu 36:12 the clans of the **d** *of* Manasseh son of H1201
Dt 1: 8 Jacob—and to their **d** after them. H2446
Dt 1:36 will give him and his **d** the land he set his H1201
Dt 2: 4 the territory of your relatives the **d** *of* Esau, H1201
Dt 2: 8 went on past our relatives the **d** *of* Esau, H1201
Dt 2: 9 given Ar to the **d** *of* Lot as a possession H1201
Dt 2:12 but the **d** *of* Esau drove them out. H1201
Dt 2:19 given it as a possession to the **d** *of* Lot." H1201
Dt 2:22 LORD had done the same for the **d** *of* Esau, H1201
Dt 2:29 as the **d** *of* Esau, who live in Seir, and the H1201
Dt 4:37 ancestors and chose their **d** after them, H2446
Dt 10:15 he chose you, their **d**, above all the H2446
Dt 11: 9 your ancestors to give to them and their **d**, H2446
Dt 17:20 Then he and his **d** will reign a long time H1201
Dt 18: 5 chosen them and their **d** out of all your H1201
Dt 23: 2 any of **their d** may enter the H2257S
Dt 23: 3 Moabite or any of **their d** may enter the H2157S
Dt 28:46 a wonder to you and your **d** forever. H2446
Dt 28:59 send fearful plagues on you and your **d**, H2446
Dt 30: 6 your hearts and the hearts of your **d**, H2446
Dt 31:21 because it will not be forgotten by their **d**. H2446
Dt 34: 4 Jacob when I said, 'I will give it to your **d**. H2446
Jos 4:21 the future when your **d** ask their parents, H1201
Jos 13:29 to half the family of the **d** *of* Manasseh H1201
Jos 13:31 This was for the **d** *of* Makir son of H1201
Jos 14: 4 Joseph's **d** had become two tribes H1201
Jos 16: 4 Ephraim, the **d** *of* Joseph, received H1201
Jos 17: 2 are the other male **d** *of* Manasseh son of H1201
Jos 17: 6 to the rest of the **d** *of* Manasseh. H1201
Jos 21: 4 Levites who were **d** *of* Aaron the priest H1201
Jos 21: 5 The rest of Kohath's **d** were allotted ten H1201
Jos 21: 6 The **d** *of* Gershon were allotted thirteen H1201
Jos 21: 7 The **d** *of* Merari, according to their clans H1201
Jos 21:10 assigned to the **d** *of* Aaron who were from H1201
Jos 21:13 So to the **d** *of* Aaron the priest they gave H1201
Jos 21:19 the priests, the **d** *of* Aaron, came to H1201
Jos 22:24 that some day your **d** might say to ours, H1201
Jos 22:25 So your **d** might cause ours to stop H1201
Jos 22:27 in the future your **d** will not be able to say H1201
Jos 22:28 say this to us, or to our **d**, we will answer: H1887
Jos 24: 3 Canaan and gave him many **d**. H2446
Jos 24:32 became the inheritance of Joseph's **d**. H1201
Jdg 1:16 The **d** *of* Moses' father-in-law, the Kenite H1201
Jdg 3: 2 warfare to the **d** *of* the Israelites who H1887
Jdg 4:11 the other Kenites, the **d** *of* Hobab, Moses' H1201
1Sa 2:33 and all your **d** will die in the prime H5270+1074
1Sa 20:42 between your **d** and my descendants H2446
1Sa 20:42 your descendants and my **d** forever. H2446
1Sa 24:21 will not kill off my **d** or wipe out my name H2446
2Sa 19:28 All my grandfather's **d** deserved nothing H1074
2Sa 21: 6 seven of his male **d** be given to us to be H1201
2Sa 21:16 one of the **d** *of* Rapha, whose bronze H3535
2Sa 21:18 killed Saph, one of the **d** *of* Rapha. H3535
2Sa 21:22 These four *were* **d** of Rapha in Gath, and H3528
2Sa 22:51 his anointed, to David and his **d** forever." H2446
1Ki 2: 4 'If your **d** watch how they live, and if they H1201
1Ki 2:33 on the head of Joab and his **d** forever. H2446
1Ki 2:33 But on David and his **d**, his house and his H2446
1Ki 8:25 if only your **d** are careful in all they do to H1201
1Ki 9: 6 "But if you or your **d** turn away from me H1201
1Ki 9:21 conscripted the **d** *of* all these peoples H1201
1Ki 11:39 I will humble David's **d** because of this H2446
1Ki 21:21 I will wipe out your **d** and cut off from Ahab H339
2Ki 5:27 will cling to you and to your **d** forever." H2446
2Ki 8:19 a lamp for David and his **d** forever. H1201
2Ki 10:30 your **d** will sit on the throne of Israel to H1201
2Ki 15:12 "Your **d** will sit on the throne of Israel to H1201
2Ki 17:34 that the LORD gave the **d** *of* Jacob, H1201
2Ki 20:18 And some of your **d**, your own flesh and H1201
1Ch 1:29 These were their **d**: Nebaioth the firstborn H9352
1Ch 1:33 All these were **d** *of* Keturah. H1201
1Ch 2:23 All these were **d** *of* Makir the father of H1201
1Ch 2:33 These were the **d** *of* Jerahmeel. H1201
1Ch 2:50 These were the **d** *of* Caleb. H1201
1Ch 2:52 The **d** of Shobal the father of Kiriath H1201
1Ch 2:54 The **d** *of* Salma: Bethlehem, the H1201
1Ch 3:17 The **d** *of* Jehoiachin the captive: Shealtiel H1201
1Ch 3:21 The **d** *of* Hananiah: Pelatiah and H1201
1Ch 3:22 The **d** *of* Shekaniah: Shemaiah and his H1201
1Ch 4: 1 The **d** *of* Judah: Perez, Hezron, Karmi, Hur H1201
1Ch 4: 4 These were the **d** *of* Hur, the firstborn of H1201
1Ch 4: 6 These were the **d** *of* Naarah. H1201
1Ch 4:20 The **d** *of* Ishi: Zoheth and H1201
1Ch 4:24 The **d** *of* Simeon: Nemuel, Jamin, Jarib H1201
1Ch 4:26 The **d** *of* Mishma: Hammuel his son H1201
1Ch 5: 4 The **d** *of* Joel: Shemaiah his son, Gog his H1201
1Ch 6:22 The **d** *of* Kohath: Amminadab his son H1201
1Ch 6:25 The **d** *of* Elkanah: Amasai, Ahimoth, H1201
1Ch 6:29 The **d** *of* Merari: Mahli, Libni his son H1201
1Ch 6:49 But Aaron and his **d** were the ones who H1201
1Ch 6:50 These were the **d** *of* Aaron: Eleazar his H1201
1Ch 6:54 assigned to the **d** *of* Aaron who were from H1201
1Ch 6:57 So the **d** *of* Aaron were given Hebron (a H1201
1Ch 6:61 The rest of Kohath's **d** were allotted ten H1201
1Ch 6:62 The **d** *of* Gershon, clan by clan, were H1201
1Ch 6:63 The **d** *of* Merari, clan by clan, were H1201
1Ch 7: 2 the **d** of Tola listed as fighting men in their NDT
1Ch 7:12 Shuppites and Huppites were the **d** *of* Ir, H1201
1Ch 7:12 and the Hushites the **d** *of* Aher. H1201
1Ch 7:13 Jezer and Shillem—the **d** *of* Bilhah. H1201
1Ch 7:14 The **d** *of* Manasseh: Asriel was his H1201
1Ch 7:20 The **d** *of* Ephraim: Shuthelah, Bered his H1201
1Ch 7:29 The **d** *of* Joseph son of Israel lived in H1201
1Ch 7:40 All these were **d** *of* Asher—heads of H1201
1Ch 8: 6 These were the **d** *of* Ehud, who were H1201
1Ch 8:40 All these were the **d** *of* Benjamin. H1201
1Ch 9:23 They and their **d** were in charge of H1201
1Ch 15: 4 He called together the **d** *of* Aaron and the H1201
1Ch 15: 5 From the **d** *of* Kohath, Uriel the leader H1201
1Ch 15: 6 from the **d** *of* Merari, Asaiah the leader H1201
1Ch 15: 7 from the **d** *of* Gershon, Joel the leader H1201
1Ch 15: 8 from the **d** *of* Elizaphan, Shemaiah the H1201
1Ch 15: 9 from the **d** *of* Hebron, Eliel the leader H1201
1Ch 15:10 from the **d** *of* Uzziel, Amminadab the H1201
1Ch 16:13 his servants, the **d** *of* Israel, his chosen H2446
1Ch 20: 4 one of the **d** *of* the Rephaites, and H3535
1Ch 20: 8 These *were* **d** of Rapha in Gath, and they H3528
1Ch 23:13 set apart, he and his **d** forever, to H1201
1Ch 23:16 The **d** *of* Gershom: Shubael was the first. H1201
1Ch 23:17 The **d** *of* Eliezer: Rehabiah was the first H1201
1Ch 23:24 These were the **d** *of* Levi by their families H1201
1Ch 23:28 was to help Aaron's **d** in the service of the H1201
1Ch 23:32 under their relatives the **d** *of* Aaron, for H1201
1Ch 24: 1 were the divisions of the **d** *of* Aaron: H1201
1Ch 24: 4 among Eleazar's **d** than among Ithamar's, H1201
1Ch 24: 4 from Eleazar's **d** and eight heads of H1201
1Ch 24: 4 eight heads of families from Ithamar's **d**. H1201
1Ch 24: 5 of God among the **d** *of* both Eleazar and H1201
1Ch 24:20 As for the rest of the **d** *of* Levi: from the H1201
1Ch 24:31 just as their relatives the **d** *of* Aaron did H1201
1Ch 26: 8 All these were **d** *of* Obed-Edom; they H1201
1Ch 26: 8 to do the work—**d** of Obed-Edom, 62 in all NDT
1Ch 26:19 who were **d** *of* Korah and Merari. H1201
1Ch 26:21 The **d** *of* Ladan, who were Gershonites H1201
1Ch 28: 8 it on as an inheritance to your **d** forever. H1201
2Ch 6:16 if only your **d** are careful in all they do to H1201
2Ch 8: 8 conscripted the **d** of all these people H1201
2Ch 13: 5 to David and his **d** forever by a covenant H1201
2Ch 13: 8 which is in the hands of David's **d**. H1201
2Ch 20: 7 it forever to the **d** *of* Abraham your friend? H2446
2Ch 21: 7 a lamp for him and his **d** forever. H1201
2Ch 23: 3 LORD promised concerning the **d** *of* David. H1201
2Ch 26:18 the priests, the **d** *of* Aaron, who have H1201
2Ch 29:13 from the **d** *of* Elizaphan, Shimri and Jeiel H1201
2Ch 29:13 Jeiel; from the **d** *of* Asaph, Zechariah H1201
2Ch 29:14 from the **d** *of* Heman, Jehiel and Shimei H1201
2Ch 29:14 Shimei; from the **d** *of* Jeduthun H1201
2Ch 29:21 the priests, the **d** *of* Aaron, to offer these H1201
2Ch 31:19 the priests, the **d** *of* Aaron, who lived on H1201
2Ch 32:33 the hill where the tombs of David's **d** are. H1201
2Ch 35:14 the priests, the **d** *of* Aaron, were H1201
2Ch 35:15 The musicians, the **d** *of* Asaph, were in H1201
Ezr 2: 3 the **d** *of* Parosh 2,172 H1201
Ezr 2:36 the **d** *of* Jedaiah (through the family of H1201

Ezr 2:40 the **d** *of* Jeshua and Kadmiel (of the line H1201
Ezr 2:41 The musicians: the **d** *of* Asaph 128 H1201
Ezr 2:42 the **d** *of* Shallum, Ater, Talmon, Akkub H1201
Ezr 2:43 temple servants: the **d** *of* Ziha, Hasupha H1201
Ezr 2:55 The **d** *of* the servants of Solomon: the H1201
Ezr 2:55 the **d** *of* Sotai, Hassophereth H1201
Ezr 2:58 servants and the **d** *of* the servants of H1201
Ezr 2:60 The **d** *of* Delaiah, Tobiah and Nekoda H1201
Ezr 2:61 The **d** *of* Hobaiah, Hakkoz and Barzillai (a H1201
Ezr 3: 9 his sons (**d** *of* Hodaviah) and the H1201
Ezr 8: 2 of the **d** *of* Phinehas, Gershom; of the H1201
Ezr 8: 2 Gershom; of the **d** *of* Ithamar, Daniel; of H1201
Ezr 8: 2 of the **d** *of* David, Hattush H1201
Ezr 8: 3 of the **d** *of* Shekaniah; of the descendants H1201
Ezr 8: 3 Shekaniah; of the **d** *of* Parosh, Zechariah, H1201
Ezr 8: 4 of the **d** *of* Pahath-Moab, Eliehoenai son H1201
Ezr 8: 5 of the **d** *of* Zattu, Shekaniah son of H1201
Ezr 8: 6 of the **d** *of* Adin, Ebed son of Jonathan H1201
Ezr 8: 7 of the **d** *of* Elam, Jeshaiah son of H1201
Ezr 8: 8 of the **d** *of* Shephatiah, Zebadiah son of H1201
Ezr 8: 9 of the **d** *of* Joab, Obadiah son of Jehiel H1201
Ezr 8:10 of the **d** *of* Bani, Shelomith son of H1201
Ezr 8:11 of the **d** *of* Bebai, Zechariah son of Bebai H1201
Ezr 8:12 of the **d** *of* Azgad, Johanan son of H1201
Ezr 8:13 of the **d** *of* Adonikam, the last ones H1201
Ezr 8:14 of the **d** *of* Bigvai, Uthai and Zakkur, and H1201
Ezr 8:18 from the **d** *of* Mahli son of Levi H1201
Ezr 8:19 with Jeshaiah from the **d** *of* Merari, H1201
Ezr 10: 2 one of the **d** *of* Elam, said to Ezra, H1201
Ezr 10:18 Among the **d** *of* the priests, the following H1201
Ezr 10:18 From the **d** *of* Joshua son of Jozadak, and H1201
Ezr 10:20 From the **d** *of* Immer: Hanani and H1201
Ezr 10:21 From the **d** *of* Harim: Maaseiah, Elijah H1201
Ezr 10:22 From the **d** *of* Pashhur: Elioenai H1201
Ezr 10:25 From the **d** *of* Parosh: Ramiah, H1201
Ezr 10:26 From the **d** *of* Elam: Mattaniah, Zechariah, H1201
Ezr 10:27 From the **d** *of* Zattu: Elioenai, Eliashib H1201
Ezr 10:28 From the **d** *of* Bebai: Jehohanan H1201
Ezr 10:29 From the **d** *of* Bani: Meshullam, Malluk H1201
Ezr 10:30 From the **d** *of* Pahath-Moab: Adna, Kelal H1201
Ezr 10:31 From the **d** *of* Harim: Eliezer, Ishijah H1201
Ezr 10:33 From the **d** *of* Hashum: Mattenai H1201
Ezr 10:34 From the **d** *of* Bani: Maadai, Amram, Uel, H1201
Ezr 10:38 From the **d** *of* Binnui: Shimei, H1201
Ezr 10:43 From the **d** *of* Nebo: Jeiel, Mattithiah H1201
Ne 7: 8 the **d** *of* Parosh 2,172 H1201
Ne 7:39 the **d** *of* Jedaiah (through the family of H1201
Ne 7:43 the **d** *of* Jeshua (through Kadmiel through H1201
Ne 7:44 The musicians: the **d** *of* Asaph 148 H1201
Ne 7:45 the **d** *of* Shallum, Ater, Talmon, Akkub H1201
Ne 7:46 temple servants: the **d** *of* Ziha, Hasupha H1201
Ne 7:57 The **d** *of* the servants of Solomon: the H1201
Ne 7:57 the **d** *of* Sotai, Sophereth H1201
Ne 7:60 servants and the **d** *of* the servants of H1201
Ne 7:62 the **d** *of* Delaiah, Tobiah and Nekoda H1201
Ne 7:63 the **d** *of* Hobaiah, Hakkoz and Barzillai (a H1201
Ne 9: 8 with him to give to his **d** the land of the H2446
Ne 11: 3 servants and **d** *of* Solomon's servants H1201
Ne 11: 4 From the **d** *of* Judah: Athaiah son of H1201
Ne 11: 6 The **d** *of* Perez who lived in Jerusalem H1201
Ne 11: 7 From the **d** *of* Benjamin: Sallu son of H1201
Ne 11:22 Uzzi was one of Asaph's **d**, who were the H1201
Ne 11:24 one of the **d** *of* Zerah son of Judah H1201
Ne 11:31 The **d** *of* the Benjamites from Geba lived H1201
Ne 12:23 heads among the **d** *of* Levi up to the time H1201
Ne 12:47 set aside the portion for the **d** *of* Aaron. H1201
Est 9:27 that they and their **d** and all who join H2446
Est 9:28 of these days die out among their **d**. H2446
Est 9:31 themselves and their **d** in regard to their H2446
Job 5:25 your **d** like the grass of the earth. H7368
Job 18:19 has no offspring or **d** among his people, H5781
Ps 18:50 anointed, to David and to his **d** forever. H2446
Ps 21:10 You will destroy their **d** from the earth H7262
Ps 22:23 All you **d** *of* Jacob, honor him H2446
Ps 22:23 Revere him, all you **d** *of* Israel! H2446
Ps 25:13 their **d** will inherit the land. H2446
Ps 77:15 your people, the **d** *of* Jacob and Joseph. H1201
Ps 78: 4 We will not hide them from their **d**; we H1201
Ps 83: 8 has joined them to reinforce Lot's **d**. H1201
Ps 102:28 their **d** will be established before you." H2446
Ps 105: 6 his servants, the **d** *of* Abraham, his H2446
Ps 106:27 make their **d** fall among the nations and H2446
Ps 109:13 May his **d** be cut off, their names blotted H344
Ps 132:11 "One of your own **d** I will place on H7262+1061
Isa 2: 5 **d** *of* Jacob, let us walk in the light H1074
Isa 2: 6 abandoned your people, the **d** *of* Jacob. H1074
Isa 8:17 who is hiding his face from the **d** *of* Jacob. H1074
Isa 14: 1 join them and unite with the **d** *of* Jacob. H1074
Isa 14:22 her offspring and **d**," declares the LORD. H5781
Isa 29:22 Abraham, says to the **d** *of* Jacob: H1074
Isa 39: 7 And some of your **d**, your own flesh and H1201
Isa 41: 8 chosen, you **d** *of* Abraham my friend, H2446
Isa 44: 3 your offspring, and my blessing on your **d**. H7368
Isa 45:19 I have not said to Jacob's **d**, 'Seek me in H2446
Isa 45:25 But all the **d** *of* Israel will find deliverance H2446
Isa 46: 3 "Listen to me, you **d** *of* Jacob, all the H1074
Isa 48: 1 you **d** *of* Jacob, you who are H1074
Isa 48:19 Your **d** would have been like the sand H2446
Isa 54: 3 your **d** will dispossess nations and settle H2446
Isa 58: 1 rebellion and to the **d** *of* Jacob their sins. H1074
Isa 59:21 your children and on the lips of their **d**— H2446
Isa 61: 9 Their **d** will be known among the nations H2446
Isa 65: 9 I will bring forth **d** from Jacob, and from H2446
Isa 65:23 by the LORD, they and their **d** with them. H7368
Isa 66:22 "so will your name and **d** endure. H2446
Jer 2: 4 of the LORD, you **d** *of* Jacob, all you clans H1074
Jer 5:20 this to the **d** *of* Jacob and proclaim H1074
Jer 23: 8 who brought the **d** *of* Israel up out of the H2446
Jer 29:32 Shemaiah the Nehelamite and his **d**. H2446
Jer 30:10 your **d** from the land of their exile. H2446
Jer 31:17 So there is hope for your **d**," declares the H344
Jer 31:37 will I reject all the **d** *of* Israel because of H2446
Jer 33:22 I will make the **d** *of* David my servant and H2446
Jer 33:26 I will reject the **d** *of* Jacob and David my H2446
Jer 33:26 of his sons to rule over the **d** *of* Abraham, H2446
Jer 35: 6 you nor your **d** must ever drink wine. H1201
Jer 35:14 of Rekab ordered his **d** not to drink wine H1201
Jer 35:16 The **d** *of* Jehonadab son of Rekab have H1201
Jer 46:27 your **d** from the land of their exile. H2446
Eze 20: 5 hand to the **d** *of* Jacob and revealed H2446
Eze 44:15 who are **d** *of* Zadok and who guarded my H1201
Eze 46:16 it will also belong to his **d**; it is to be their H1201
Da 11: 4 It will not go to his **d**, nor will it have the H344
Am 3:13 this and testify against the **d** *of* Jacob," H1074
Am 7:16 stop preaching against the **d** *of* Isaac. H1074
Am 9: 8 Yet I will not totally destroy the **d** *of* Jacob," H1074
Mic 2: 7 You **d** *of* Jacob, should it be said, "Does H1074
Na 1:14 "*You will* **have** no **d** to bear your name H2445
Mal 2: 3 "Because of you I will rebuke your **d**; I will H2446
Mal 3: 6 So you, the **d** *of* Jacob, are not H1201
Mt 23:31 that you are the **d** of those who murdered *G5626*
Lk 1:33 he will reign over Jacob's **d** forever *G3875*
Lk 1:55 to Abraham and his **d** forever, just as he *G5065*
Jn 7:42 come from David's **d** and from Bethlehem *G5065*
Jn 8:33 "We are Abraham's **d** and have never *G5065*
Jn 8:37 I know that you are Abraham's **d**. *G5065*
Ac 2:30 one of his **d** on his throne. *G2843+3836+4019*
Ac 7: 5 him that he and his **d** after him would *G5065*
Ac 7: 6 hundred years your **d** will be strangers in *G5065*
Ac 8:33 Who can speak of his **d**? For his life was *G1155*
Ac 13:23 "From this man's **d** God has brought to *G5065*
Ro 9: 7 because they are his **d** are they all *G5065*
Ro 9:29 "Unless the Lord Almighty had left us **d** *G5065*
2Co 11:22 Are they Abraham's **d**? So am I. *G5065*
Heb 2:16 is not angels he helps, but Abraham's **d**. *G5065*
Heb 6:14 bless you and **give** you **many d**." *G4437+4437*
Heb 7: 5 law requires the **d** of Levi who become *G5626*
Heb 11:12 **came d** as numerous as the stars in the *G1164*

DESCENDED (25) [DESCEND]

Ge 36:16 These were the **chiefs** *d from* Eliphaz in AIT
Ge 36:17 These were the **chiefs** *d from* Reuel in Edom AIT
Ge 36:18 These were the **chiefs** *d from* Esau's wife AIT
Ge 36:40 These were the **chiefs** *d from* Esau, by name AIT
Ex 19:18 because the LORD **d** on it in fire. H3718
Ex 19:20 The LORD **d** to the top of Mount Sinai and H3718
Jos 16: 3 **d** westward to the territory of the H3718
2Sa 21:20 He also **was d** from Rapha. H3528
1Ki 18:31 one for each of the tribes **d** *from* Jacob, to H1201
1Ch 2:53 From these **d** the Zorathites and H3655
1Ch 20: 6 He also **was d** from Rapha. H3528
2Ch 34:12 Obadiah, Levites **d** from Merari, and H1201
2Ch 34:12 Meshullam, **d** from Kohath. H1201
Ezr 2:59 that their families were **d** from Israel: H2446
Ne 7:61 that their families were **d** from Israel: H2446
Ne 10:38 A priest **d** *from* Aaron is to accompany the H1201
Isa 57: 9 *you* **d** to the very realm of the dead! H9164
Lk 3:22 the Holy Spirit **d** on him in bodily form *G2849*
Ac 23: 6 I am a Pharisee, **d from** Pharisees. *G5626*
Ro 9: 6 For not all who are **d from** Israel are Israel. *G1666*
Eph 4: 9 mean except that *he* also **d** to the lower *G2849*
Eph 4:10 He *who* **d** is the very one who ascended *G2849*
2Ti 2: 8 raised from the dead, **d from** David. *G1666+5065*
Heb 7: 5 *they also are* **d from** *G2002+1666+3836+4019*
Heb 7:14 For it is clear that our Lord **d** from Judah *G422*

DESCENDING (7) [DESCEND]

Ge 28:12 of God were ascending and **d** on it. H3718
1Sa 25:20 were David and his men **d** toward her, H3718
SS 4: 1 like a flock of goats **d** from the hills of H1683
SS 6: 5 hair is like a flock of goats **d** from Gilead. H1683
Mt 3:16 he saw the Spirit of God **d** like a dove *G2849*
Mk 1:10 open and the Spirit **d** on him like a dove. *G2849*
Jn 1:51 God ascending and **d** on' the Son of Man." *G2849*

DESCENDS (1) [DESCEND]

Isa 34: 5 *it* **d** in judgment on Edom, the H3718

DESCENT (8) [DESCEND]

Ge 10:32 according to their **lines of d**, within their H9352
Ne 9: 2 Those of Israelite **d** had separated H2446
Ne 13: 3 from Israel all who were **of foreign d**. H6850
Eze 44:22 virgins of Israelite **d** or widows of priests. H2446
Da 9: 1 Xerxes (a Mede by **d**), who was made H2446
Jn 1:13 children born not of **natural d**, nor of human *G135*
Ro 9: 8 the children **by physical d** who are God's *G4922*
Heb 7: 6 however, *did* not **trace** *his* **d** from Levi, yet *G1156*

DESCRIBE (2) [DESCRIBED, DESCRIPTION, DESCRIPTIONS]

Eze 43:10 **d** the temple *to* the people of Israel H5583
Mk 4:30 or what parable *shall we* **use** *to* **d** it? *G5502*

DESCRIBED (4) [DESCRIBE]

Ac 12:17 them to be quiet and **d** how the Lord had *G1455*
Ac 15:14 Simon *has* **d** to us how God first *G2007*
Rev 22:18 to that person the plagues **d** in this scroll. *G1211*
Rev 22:19 in the Holy City, which *are* **d** in this scroll. *G1211*

DESCRIPTION (3) [DESCRIBE]

Jos 18: 4 a survey of the land and *to* **write a d** *of* it, H4180
Jos 18: 8 a survey of the land and **write a d** *of* it. H4180
Jos 18: 9 *They* **wrote** its **d** on a scroll, town by town H4180

DESCRIPTIONS (1) [DESCRIBE]

Jos 18: 6 After you *have* **written d** *of* the seven parts H4180

DESECRATE (10) [DESECRATED, DESECRATES, DESECRATING]

Lev 21:12 leave the sanctuary of his God or **d** it H2725
Lev 21:23 the altar, and so **d** my sanctuary. H2725
Lev 22:15 The priests *must* not **d** the sacred offerings H2725
Dt 21:23 *You must* not **d** the land the LORD your H3237
Isa 30:22 Then *you will* **d** your idols overlaid with H3237
Eze 7:22 robbers *will* **d** the place I treasure. H2725
Eze 24:21 I *am about to* **d** my sanctuary—the H2725
Da 11:31 forces will rise up *to* **d** the temple fortress H2725
Mt 12: 5 duty in the temple **d** the Sabbath and *G1014*
Ac 24: 6 even tried *to* **d** the temple; so we *G1014*

DESECRATED (17) [DESECRATE]

Lev 19: 8 because *they have* **d** what is holy to H2725
2Ki 23: 8 the towns of Judah and **d** the high places, H3237
2Ki 23:10 *He* **d** Topheth, which was in the Valley of H3237
2Ki 23:13 The king also **d** the high places that were H3237
Ps 106:38 the land *was* **d** by their blood. H2866
Isa 47: 6 with my people and **d** my inheritance; H2725
Eze 7:24 and their sanctuaries *will* **be d**. H2725
Eze 20:13 will live—and *they* utterly **d** my Sabbaths. H2725
Eze 20:16 follow my decrees and **d** my Sabbaths. H2725
Eze 20:21 live by them," and *they* **d** my Sabbaths. H2725
Eze 20:24 rejected my decrees and **d** my Sabbaths, H2725
Eze 22: 8 my holy things and **d** my Sabbaths. H2725
Eze 23:38 defiled my sanctuary and **d** my Sabbaths. H2725
Eze 23:39 they entered my sanctuary and **d** it. H2725
Eze 25: 3 my sanctuary when *it* **was d** and over the H2725
Eze 28:18 trade you *have* **d** your sanctuaries. H2725
Mal 2:11 Judah *has* **d** the sanctuary the LORD loves H2725

DESECRATES (1) [DESECRATE]

Ex 31:14 *Anyone who* **d** it is to be put to death H2725

DESECRATING (5) [DESECRATE]

Ne 13:17 thing you are doing—**d** the Sabbath day? H2725
Ne 13:18 wrath against Israel by **d** the Sabbath." H2725
Isa 56: 2 who keeps the Sabbath without **d** it, and H2725
Isa 56: 6 the Sabbath without **d** it and who hold H2725
Eze 44: 7 **d** my temple while you offered me food H2725

DESERT (153) [DESERTED, DESERTING, DESERTS]

Ge 14: 6 as far as El Paran near the **d**. H4497
Ge 16: 7 LORD found Hagar near a spring in the **d**; H4497
Ge 21:14 way and wandered in the **D** *of* Beersheba. H4497
Ge 21:20 He lived in the **d** and became an archer H4497
Ge 21:21 While he was living in the **D** *of* Paran, his H4497
Ge 36:24 hot springs in the **d** while he was grazing H4497
Ex 13:18 around by the **d** road toward the Red H4497
Ex 13:20 camped at Etham on the edge of the **d**. H4497
Ex 14: 3 land in confusion, hemmed in by the **d**. H4497
Ex 14:11 Egypt that you brought us to the **d** to die? H4497
Ex 14:12 serve the Egyptians than to die in the **d**!" H4497
Ex 15:22 Red Sea and they went into the **D** *of* Shur. H4497
Ex 15:22 they traveled in the **d** without finding H4497
Ex 16: 1 out from Elim and came to the **D** *of* Sin, H4497
Ex 16: 2 In the **d** the whole community grumbled H4497
Ex 16: 3 us out into this **d** to starve this entire H4497
Ex 16:10 they looked toward the **d**, and there was H4497
Ex 16:14 on the ground appeared on the **d** floor. H4497
Ex 17: 1 community set out from the **D** *of* Sin, H4497
Ex 19: 1 very day—they came to the **D** *of* Sinai. H4497
Ex 19: 2 they entered the **D** *of* Sinai, and Israel H4497
Ex 19: 2 camped there in the **d** in front of the H4497
Ex 23:31 from the **d** to the Euphrates River. H4497
Lev 7:38 Mount Sinai in the **D** *of* Sinai on the day H4497
Lev 11:18 the white owl, the **d owl**, the osprey, H7684
Nu 1: 1 of meeting in the **D** *of* Sinai on the first H4497
Nu 1:19 And so he counted them in the **D** *of* Sinai: H4497
Nu 3: 4 fire before him in the **D** *of* Sinai. H4497
Nu 3:14 The LORD said to Moses in the **D** *of* Sinai, H4497
Nu 9: 1 to Moses in the **D** *of* Sinai in the first H4497
Nu 9: 5 they did so in the **D** *of* Sinai at twilight on H4497
Nu 10:12 set out from the **D** *of* Sinai and traveled H4497
Nu 10:12 the cloud came to rest in the **D** *of* Paran. H4497
Nu 12:16 encamped in the **D** *of* Paran. H4497
Nu 13: 3 Moses sent them out from the **D** *of* Paran. H4497
Nu 13:21 the land from the **D** *of* Zin as far as Rehob H4497
Nu 13:26 community at Kadesh in the **D** *of* Paran. H4497
Nu 14:25 set out toward the **d** along the route to H4497
Nu 20: 1 community arrived at the **D** *of* Zin, H4497
Nu 26:64 counted the Israelites in the **D** *of* Sinai. H4497
Nu 27:14 rebelled at the waters in the **D** *of* Zin, H4497
Nu 27:14 of Meribah Kadesh, in the **D** *of* Zin.) H4497
Nu 33: 6 camped at Etham, on the edge of the **d**. H4497
Nu 33: 8 passed through the sea into the **d**, H4497
Nu 33: 8 traveled for three days in the **D** *of* Etham, H4497
Nu 33:11 the Red Sea and camped in the **D** *of* Sin. H4497
Nu 33:12 They left the **D** *of* Sin and camped at H4497
Nu 33:15 Rephidim and camped in the **D** *of* Sinai. H4497

Nu 33:16 They left the **D** *of* Sinai and camped at H4497
Nu 33:36 camped at Kadesh, in the **D** *of* Zin. H4497
Nu 34: 3 include some of the **D** *of* Zin along the H4497
Dt 1:40 set out toward the **d** along the route to H4497
Dt 2: 8 traveled along the **d** road of Moab. H4497
Dt 2:26 From the **D** *of* Kedemoth I sent H4497
Dt 11:24 will extend from the **d** to Lebanon, H4497
Dt 14:17 the **d owl**, the osprey, the cormorant, H7684
Dt 32:10 In a **d** land he found him, in a barren H4497
Dt 32:51 Kadesh in the **D** *of* Zin and because you H4497
Jos 1: 4 will extend from the **d** to Lebanon, H4497
Jos 15: 1 to the **D** *of* Zin in the extreme south. H4497
Jos 16: 1 there through the **d** into the hill country H4497
Jdg 1:16 inhabitants of the **D** *of* Judah in the H4497
Jdg 8: 7 tear your flesh with **d** thorns and briers." H4497
Jdg 8:16 punishing them with **d** thorns and briers. H4497
Jdg 11:22 the Jabbok and from the **d** to the Jordan. H4497
1Sa 23:14 in the hills of the **D** *of* Ziph. H4497
1Sa 23:15 David was at Horesh in the **D** *of* Ziph, H4497
1Sa 23:24 his men were in the **D** *of* Maon, H4497
1Sa 23:25 to the rock and stayed in the **D** *of* Maon. H4497
1Sa 23:25 he went into the **D** *of* Maon in pursuit of H4497
1Sa 24: 1 he was told, "David is in the **D** *of* En Gedi." H4497
1Sa 25: 1 David moved down into the **D** *of* Paran. H4497
1Sa 26: 2 So Saul went down to the **D** *of* Ziph, with H4497
1Ki 9:18 Tadmor in the **d**, within his land, H4497
1Ki 19:15 you came, and go to the **D** *of* Damascus. H4497
2Ki 3: 8 "Through the **D** *of* Edom," he answered H4497
1Ch 5: 9 to the edge of the **d** that extends to the H4497
2Ch 8: 4 built up Tadmor in the **d** and all the store H4497
2Ch 20:16 at the end of the gorge in the **D** *of* Jeruel. H4497
2Ch 20:20 the morning they left for the **D** *of* Tekoa. H4497
2Ch 20:24 that overlooks the **d** and looked toward H4497
Ne 9:17 Therefore *you did* not **d** them, H6440
Job 1:19 swept in from the **d** and struck the four H4497
Job 24: 5 Like wild donkeys in the **d**, the poor go H4497
Job 38:26 where no one lives, an uninhabited **d**, H4497
Ps 29: 8 The voice of the LORD shakes the **d**; the H4497
Ps 29: 8 the LORD shakes the **D** *of* Kadesh. H4497
Ps 55: 7 I would flee far away and stay in the **d**; H4497
Ps 63: T When he was in the **D** *of* Judah. H4497
Ps 72: 9 May the **d tribes** bow before him and his H7470
Ps 74:14 gave it as food to the **creatures of the d**. H7470
Ps 75: 6 west or from the **d** can exalt themselves H4497
Ps 102: 6 I am like a **d** owl, like an owl among the H4497
Ps 105:41 gushed out; it flowed like a river in the **d**. H7480
Ps 106: 9 them through the depths as through a **d**. H4497
Ps 106:14 In the **d** they gave in to their craving; in H4497
Ps 107: 4 Some wandered in **d** wastelands, finding H4497
Ps 107:33 He turned rivers into a **d**, flowing springs H4497
Ps 107:35 He turned the **d** into pools of water and H4497
Pr 21:19 Better to live in a **d** than with a H824+4497
Isa 13:21 But **d creatures** will lie there, jackals will H7470
Isa 16: 1 from Sela, across the **d**, to the mount of H4497
Isa 16: 8 reached Jazer and spread toward the **d**. H4497
Isa 21: 1 A prophecy against the **D** *by* the Sea: Like H4497
Isa 21: 1 an invader comes from the **d**, from a land H4497
Isa 23:13 have made it a place for **d creatures**; H7470
Isa 25: 5 like the heat of the **d**. You silence the H7481
Isa 32: 2 of water in the **d** and the shadow of a H7481
Isa 32:15 on high, and the **d** becomes a fertile field H4497
Isa 32:16 The LORD's justice will dwell in the **d**, his H4497
Isa 34:11 The **d owl** and screech owl will possess it H7684
Isa 34:14 **D creatures** will meet with hyenas, and H7470
Isa 35: 1 The **d** and the parched land will be glad H4497
Isa 35: 6 in the wilderness and streams in the **d**. H6858
Isa 40: 3 make straight in the **d** a highway for our H6858
Isa 41:18 I will turn the **d** into pools of water, and H4497
Isa 41:19 I will put in the **d** the cedar and the H4497
Isa 49:10 will the **d heat** or the sun beat down H9220
Isa 50: 2 I turn rivers into a **d**; their fish rot for lack H4497
Jer 2:24 a wild donkey accustomed to the **d** H4497
Jer 2:31 "Have I been a **d** to Israel or a land of H4497
Jer 3: 2 lovers, sat like a nomad in the **d**. H4497
Jer 4:11 barren heights in the **d** blows toward my H4497
Jer 4:26 the fruitful land was a **d**; all its towns H4497
Jer 5: 6 a wolf from the **d** will ravage them, H6858
Jer 9: 2 that I had in the **d** a lodging place for H4497
Jer 9:12 laid waste like a **d** that no one can cross H4497
Jer 12:12 heights in the **d** destroyers will swarm H4497
Jer 13:24 scatter you like chaff driven by the **d** wind. H4497
Jer 17: 6 will dwell in the parched places of the **d**, H4497
Jer 17:11 their riches *will* **d** them, and in the H6440
Jer 48: 6 your lives; become like a bush in the **d**. H4497
Jer 50:12 nations—a wilderness, a dry land, a **d**. H6858
Jer 50:39 "So **d creatures** and hyenas will live there H7470
Jer 51:43 desolate, a dry and **d** land, a land where H6858
La 4: 3 become heartless like ostriches in the **d**. H4497
La 4:19 mountains and lay in wait for us in the **d**. H4497
La 5: 9 of our lives because of the sword in the **d**. H4497
Eze 6:14 a desolate waste from the **d** to Diblah— H4497
Eze 19:13 Now it is planted in the **d**, in a dry and H4497
Eze 23:42 brought from the **d** along with men from H4497
Eze 29: 5 I will leave you in the **d**, you and all the H4497
Hos 2: 3 I will make her like a **d**, turn her into a H4497
Hos 9:10 it was like finding grapes in the **d**; when I H4497
Hos 13:15 blowing in from the **d**; his spring will fail H4497
Joel 2: 3 behind them, a **d** waste—nothing H4497
Joel 3:19 be desolate, Edom a **d** waste, because of H4497
Hab 1: 9 advance like a **d wind** and gather H7708
Zep 2:13 Nineveh utterly desolate and dry as the **d**. H4497
Zep 2:14 The **d owl** and the screech owl will roost H7684
Mal 1: 3 left his inheritance to the **d** jackals." H4497
Ac 7:30 a burning bush in the **d** near Mount Sinai. *G2245*
Ac 8:26 to the road—the **d** road—that goes down *G2245*

DESERTED (36) [DESERT]

Lev 26:22 few in number that your roads *will be* **d**. H9037
Lev 26:43 For the land *will be* **d** by them and will H6440
Dt 32:18 *You* **d** the Rock, who fathered you; you H8861
Jos 22: 3 *you have* not **d** your fellow Israelites but H6440
2Sa 20: 2 men of Israel **d** David to H6590+4946+339
2Ki 25:11 those who *had* **d** to the king of H5877
Ps 69:25 May their place be **d**; let there be no one H9037
Isa 6:11 houses are left **d** and the fields H4946+401+132
Isa 17: 2 cities of Aroer *will be* **d** and left to flocks H6440
Isa 32:14 the noisy city **d**; citadel and watchtower H6440
Isa 33: 8 The highways *are* **d**, no travelers are on H9037
Isa 54: 6 as if you were a wife **d** and distressed in H6440
Isa 62: 4 No longer will they call you **D**, or name H6440
Isa 62:12 called Sought After, the City No *Longer* **D**. H6440
Jer 2:15 his towns are burned and **d**. H4946+1172+3782
Jer 4:29 All the towns *are* **d**; no one lives in H6440
Jer 26: 9 city will be desolate and **d**?" H4946+401+3782
Jer 33:10 the streets of Jerusalem that *are* **d**, H9037
Jer 38:22 in the mud; your friends *have* **d** you. H6047+294
Jer 44: 2 Today they *lie* **d** and in ruins H401+3782
Jer 52:15 those who *had* **d** to the king of H5877
La 1: 1 How **d** lies the city, once so full of people H970
Eze 14: 5 who *have* all **d** me for their idols. H2319
Eze 36: 4 ruins and the **d** towns that have been H6440
Hos 4:10 because *they have* **d** the LORD to give H6440
Am 5: 2 never to rise again, **d** in her own land H5759
Zep 3: 6 *I have* **left** their streets **d**, with no one H2990
Zep 3: 6 waste; they are **d** and empty. H4946+1172+408
Zec 9: 5 her king and Ashkelon *will be* **d**. H3782+4202
Mt 26:56 Then all the disciples **d** him and fled. *G918*
Mk 14:50 Then everyone **d** him and fled. *G918*
Ac 1:20 " 'May his place be **d**; let there be no one *G2245*
Ac 15:38 *because* he *had* **d** them in Pamphylia and *G923*
2Ti 1:15 everyone in the province of Asia *has* **d** me, *G695*
2Ti 4:10 *has* **d** me and has gone to Thessalonica. *G1593*
2Ti 4:16 came to my support, but everyone **d** me. *G1593*

DESERTING (3) [DESERT]

Jer 37:13 said, "You *are* **d** to the Babylonians!" H5877
Jer 37:14 "*I am* not **d** to the Babylonians. H5877
Gal 1: 6 that *you are* so quickly **d** the one who *G3572*

DESERTS (8) [DESERT]

1Ch 12:19 cost us our heads *if* **he d** to his master H5877
Pr 19: 4 closest friend of the poor person **d** them. H7233
Isa 48:21 thirst when he led them through the **d**; H2999
Isa 51: 3 he will make her **d** like Eden, her H4497
Jer 2: 6 through a land of **d** and ravines, a land of H6858
Jer 14: 5 the doe in the field **d** her newborn fawn H6440
Zec 11:17 the worthless shepherd, *who* **d** the flock! H6440
Heb 11:38 They wandered in **d** and mountains *G2244*

DESERVE (28) [DESERVED, DESERVES, DESERVING]

Ge 40:15 done nothing *to d being* **put** in a dungeon." AIT
Lev 26:21 seven times over, **as** your sins **d**. H3869
Jdg 20:10 can give them **what** they **d for** this H3869
1Ki 2:26 You **d** to die, but I will not put you to death H408
Ps 28: 4 bring back on them **what** they **d**. H1691
Ps 94: 2 pay back to the proud **what** they **d**. H1691
Ps 103:10 does not treat **us** as our sins **d** or repay us H5646
Ecc 8:14 who get **what** the wicked **d**, H3869+5126
Ecc 8:14 who get **what** the righteous **d**. H3869+5126
Isa 66: 6 the LORD repaying his enemies *all* they **d**. H1691
Jer 14:16 I will pour out on them the **calamity** they *d*. AIT
Jer 17:10 conduct, according to **what** their deeds **d**." H7262
Jer 21:14 I will punish you as your deeds **d** H7262
Jer 32:19 to their conduct and as their deeds **d**. H7262
Jer 49:12 "If those who do not **d** to drink the cup H5477
La 3:64 Pay them back **what** they **d**, LORD, for what H1691
Eze 16:59 I will deal with you as *you* **d**, because you H6913
Zec 1: 6 done to us **what** our ways and practices **d**, H3869
Mt 8: 8 *I do* not **d** to have you come under *G1639+2653*
Mt 22: 8 those I invited did not **d** to come. *G545*
Lk 7: 6 for *I do* not **d** to have you come *G2653+1639*
Lk 23:15 can see, he has done nothing *to* **d** death. *G545*
Lk 23:41 for we are getting what our deeds **d**. *G545*
Ro 1:32 those who do such things **d** death, *G545+1639*
1Co 15: 9 do not even **d** to be called an apostle *G2653*
1Co 16:18 yours also. Such men *d* **recognition**. AIT
2Co 11:15 Their end will be **what** their actions **d**. *G2848*
Rev 16: 6 given them blood to drink **as** *they* **d**." *G545+1639*

DESERVED (4) [DESERVE]

2Sa 19:28 descendants **d** nothing but death from my H408
Ezr 9:13 us less **than** our sins **d** and have given H4946
Job 33:27 what is right, but I *did* not **get what** I **d**. H8750
Ac 23:29 against him that **d** death or imprisonment. *G545*

DESERVES (13) [DESERVE]

Nu 35:31 the life of a murderer, who **d** to die. H8401
Dt 25: 2 If the guilty person **d** to be beaten, the H1201
Dt 25: 2 the number of lashes the crime **d**, H3869+1896
Jdg 9:16 Have you treated him as he **d**? H1691+3338
Job 34:11 he brings on them **what** their conduct **d**. H3869
Jer 51: 6 vengeance; he will repay her **what** she **d**. H1691
Lk 7: 4 "This man **d** to have you do this *G545+1639*
Lk 10: 7 they give you, for the worker **d** his wages. *G545*
Ac 26:31 doing anything that **d** death or *G545*
1Ti 1:15 a trustworthy saying that **d** full acceptance: *G545*
1Ti 4: 9 a trustworthy saying that **d** full acceptance. *G545*
1Ti 5:18 the grain," and "The worker **d** his wages." *G545*
Heb 10:29 do you think *someone* **d** to be punished *G546*

DESERVING (8) [DESERVE]

Dt 19: 6 kill him even though he is not **d** *of* death, H5477
Dt 22:26 she has committed no **sin** *d* death. AIT
Mt 10:13 If the home is **d**, let your peace rest on it; if *G545*
Lk 12:48 know and does *things* **d** punishment will *G545*
Ac 25:11 I am guilty of doing anything **d** death, I do *G545*
Ac 25:25 I found he had done nothing **d** of death *G545*
Ac 28:18 I was not guilty of any **crime d** death. *G162*
Eph 2: 3 the rest, we were by nature **d of** wrath. *G5451*

DESIGN (7) [DESIGNER, DESIGNERS, DESIGNS]

1Ki 7: 8 set farther back, was similar in **d**. H5126
2Ch 2:14 can execute any **d** given to him. H4742
2Ch 24:13 according to its **original d** and reinforced H5504
Eze 43:11 known to them the **d** *of* the temple— H7451
Eze 43:11 its whole **d** and all its regulations and H7451
Eze 43:11 may be faithful to its **d** and follow all its H7451
Ac 17:29 an image made by human **d** and skill. *G1927*

DESIGNATE (3) [DESIGNATED]

Ex 21:13 they are to flee to a place *I will* **d**. H8492
Dt 23:12 **D** a place outside the camp where you H2118
Jos 20: 2 "Tell the Israelites *to* **d** the cities of refuge H5989

DESIGNATED (14) [DESIGNATE]

Jos 20: 8 *they* **d** Bezer in the wilderness on the H5989
Jos 20: 9 could flee to these **d** cities and not be H4597
2Sa 24:15 that morning until the end of the time **d**, H4595
1Ch 12:31 **d** by name to come and make David king H5918
1Ch 16:41 of those chosen and **d** by name to give H5918
1Ch 28:14 He **d** the weight of gold for all the gold NDT
2Ch 28:15 The men **d** by name took the prisoners H5918
2Ch 31:19 men **were d** by name to distribute H5918
Ezr 10:16 family division, and all of them **d** by name. NDT
Ne 13:31 contributions of wood at **d** times, H2374
Est 9:31 these days of Purim at their **d times**, H2375
Eze 43:21 burn it in the **d part** *of* the temple area H5152
Lk 6:13 twelve of them, whom *he* also **d** apostles: *G3951*
Heb 5:10 and *was* **d** by God to be high priest in the *G4641*

DESIGNER (1) [DESIGN]

Ex 38:23 an engraver and **d**, and an embroiderer H3110

DESIGNERS (2) [DESIGN]

Ex 35:35 work as engravers, **d**, embroiderers in H3110
Ex 35:35 all of them skilled workers and **d**. H3110+4742

DESIGNS (3) [DESIGN]

Ex 31: 4 to make **artistic d** for work in gold, silver H4742
Ex 35:32 to make **artistic d** for work in gold, silver H4742
2Ch 3: 5 decorated it with **palm tree** and chain **d**. H9474

DESIRABLE (2) [DESIRE]

Ge 3: 6 to the eye, and also **d** for gaining wisdom H2773
Pr 22: 1 A good name *is* more **d** than great riches H1047

DESIRE (60) [DESIRABLE, DESIRED, DESIRES]

Ge 3:16 Your **d** will be for your husband, and he H9592
Dt 5:21 *You shall* not **set** *your* **d on** your neighbor's H203
1Sa 9:20 And to whom is all the **d** *of* Israel turned H2775
2Sa 19:38 And anything *you* **d** from me I will do H1047
2Sa 23: 5 my salvation and grant me my every **d**. H2914
2Ki 9:15 Jehu said, "If you **d** to make me king H5883
1Ch 28: 9 understands every **d** and every thought. H3671
2Ch 1:11 this is your heart's **d** and you have not H6640
2Ch 9: 8 Israel and his **d** to uphold them forever NDT
Job 13: 3 But I **d** to speak to the Almighty and to H2911
Job 21:14 *We* **have** no **d** to know your ways. H2911
Ps 10:17 hear the **d** *of* the afflicted; you H9294
Ps 20: 4 May he give you the **d** *of* your heart and H3869
Ps 21: 2 him his heart's **d** and have not withheld H9294
Ps 27:12 Do not turn me over to the **d** *of* my foes H5883
Ps 40: 6 Sacrifice and offering *you did* not **d**—but H2911
Ps 40: 8 *I* **d** to do your will, my God; your law is H2911
Ps 40:14 may *all who* **d** my ruin be turned back in H2913
Ps 41: 2 not give them over to the **d** *of* their foes. H5883
Ps 70: 2 may *all who* **d** my ruin be turned back in H2913
Ps 73:25 And earth has nothing *I* **d** besides you. H2911
Pr 3:15 nothing you **d** can compare with her. H2914
Pr 8:11 nothing you **d** can compare with her. H2914
Pr 10:24 *what* the righteous **d** will be granted. H9294
Pr 11:23 The **d** *of* the righteous ends only in good H9294
Pr 12:12 The wicked **d** the stronghold of evildoers H2773
Pr 19: 2 **D** without knowledge is not good—how H5883
Pr 24: 1 envy the wicked, *do* not **d** their company; H203
Pr 29:17 they will bring you the delights you **d**. H5883
Ecc 6: 2 so that they lack nothing their hearts **d**, but H203
Ecc 12: 5 drags itself along and **d** no longer is stirred. H37
SS 6:12 my **d** set me among the royal chariots of H5883
SS 7:10 to my beloved, and his **d** is for me. H9592
Isa 26: 8 name and renown are the **d** *of* our hearts. H9294
Isa 53: 2 in his appearance that *we should* **d** him. H2773
Isa 55:11 will accomplish what *I* **d** and achieve the H2911
Eze 24:25 their heart's **d**, and their sons and H5362
Hos 6: 6 For *I* **d** mercy, not sacrifice, and H2911
Mic 7: 3 the powerful dictate what they **d**—they H2094
Mal 3: 1 of the covenant, whom you **d**, will come," H2913
Mt 9:13 what this means: '*I* **d** mercy, not sacrifice.' *G2527*

Mt 12: 7 these words mean, 'I d mercy, not G2527
Ro 7:18 For I have the d to do what is good, but I G2527
Ro 9:16 therefore, depend on human d or effort G2527
Ro 10: 1 my heart's d and prayer to God for the G2306
1Co 12:31 Now eagerly d the greater gifts. And yet I G2420
1Co 14: 1 the way of love and eagerly d gifts of the G2420
2Co 8:10 to give but also to have the d to do so. G2527
2Co 8:13 Our d is not that others might be relieved NDT
Php 1:23 I d to depart and be with Christ G2123+2400
Php 4:17 Not that I d your gifts; what I desire is that G2118
Php 4:17 what I d is that more be credited to your G2118
2Th 1:11 fruition your every d for goodness and G2306
Heb 10: 5 "Sacrifice and offering you did not d, but G2527
Heb 10: 8 offerings and sin offerings you did not d, G2527
Heb 13:18 conscience and d to live honorably in G2527
Jas 1:14 away by their own evil d and enticed. G2123
Jas 1:15 after d has conceived, it gives birth G2123
Jas 4: 2 You d but do not have, so you kill. G2121
2Pe 2:10 who follow the corrupt d of the flesh and G2123

DESIRED (14) [DESIRE]

1Ki 9: 1 had achieved all he had d to do, H2911+3139
1Ki 9:19 whatever he d to build in Jerusalem H3139+3137
1Ki 10:13 queen of Sheba all she d and asked for, H2914
2Ch 8: 6 whatever he d to build in Jerusalem H3137+3139
2Ch 9:12 queen of Sheba all she d and asked for; H2914
Ps 51: 6 Yet you d faithfulness even in the womb H2911
Ps 107:30 he guided them to their d haven. H2914
Ps 132:13 chosen Zion, he has d it for his dwelling H203
Ps 132:14 here I will sit enthroned, for I have d it. H203
Ecc 2:10 I denied myself nothing my eyes d; H8626
Jer 17:16 you know I have not d the day of despair. H203
Da 11:37 his ancestors or for the one d by women, H2775
Hag 2: 7 and what is d by all nations will come H2775
Lk 22:15 "I have eagerly d to eat this G2123+2121

DESIRES (51) [DESIRE]

Ge 4: 7 at your door; it d to have you, but you H9592
Ge 41:16 God will give Pharaoh the answer he d." H8934
2Sa 3:21 that you may rule over all that your heart d." H203
2Sa 14:14 But that is not what God d; rather H5951+5883
1Ki 11:37 you will rule over all that your heart d H203
1Ch 29:18 keep these d and thoughts in the hearts H3671
Job 17:11 plans are shattered. Yet the d of my heart H4626
Job 31:16 I have denied the d of the poor or let the H2914
Ps 34:12 you loves life and d to see many good days H170
Ps 37: 4 he will give you the d of your heart. H5399
Ps 103: 5 who satisfies your d with good things so H6344
Ps 140: 8 Do not grant the wicked their d, LORD; do H4397
Ps 145:16 hand and satisfy the d of every living H8356
Ps 145:19 He fulfills the d of those who fear him; he H8356
Pr 11: 6 the unfaithful are trapped by evil d. H2094
Pr 13: 4 the d of the diligent are fully satisfied. H5883
Pr 19:22 What a person d is unfailing love; better H9294
SS 2: 7 Do not arouse or awaken love until it so d. H2911
SS 3: 5 Do not arouse or awaken love until it so d. H2911
SS 8: 4 Do not arouse or awaken love until it so d. H2911
Hab 2: 4 is puffed up; his d are not upright—but H5883
Mk 4:19 of wealth and the d for other things come G2123
Jn 8:44 you want to carry out your father's d. G2123
Ro 1:24 them over in the sinful d of their hearts to G2123
Ro 6:12 mortal body so that you obey its evil d. G2123
Ro 8: 5 have their minds set on what the flesh d; G3836S
Ro 8: 5 their minds set on what the Spirit d. G3836S
Ro 13:14 about how to gratify the d of the flesh. G2123
Gal 5:16 you will not gratify the d of the flesh. G2123
Gal 5:17 For the flesh d what is contrary to the Spirit, G2121
Gal 5:24 crucified the flesh with its passions and d. G2123
Eph 2: 3 flesh and following its d and thoughts. G2525
Eph 4:22 which is being corrupted by its deceitful d; G2123
Col 3: 5 impurity, lust, evil d and greed, which is G2123
1Ti 3: 1 aspires to be an overseer d a noble task. G2121
1Ti 5:11 their sensual d overcome their dedication G2952
1Ti 6: 9 foolish and harmful d that plunge people G2123
2Ti 2:22 Flee the evil d of youth and pursue G2123
2Ti 3: 6 sins and are swayed by all kinds of evil d, G2123
2Ti 4: 3 to suit their own d, they will gather G2123
Jas 1:20 not produce the righteousness that God d. AIT
Jas 4: 1 they come from your d that battle within G2454
1Pe 1:14 conform to the evil d you had when you G2123
1Pe 2:11 to abstain from sinful d, which wage war G2123
1Pe 4: 2 rest of their earthly lives for evil human d, G2123
2Pe 1: 4 corruption in the world caused by evil d. G2123
2Pe 2:18 by appealing to the lustful d of the flesh G2123
2Pe 3: 3 scoffing and following their own evil d. G2123
1Jn 2:17 The world and its d pass away, but G2123
Jude 16 they follow their own evil d; they boast G2123
Jude 18 who will follow their own ungodly d." G2123

DESOLATE (84) [DESOLATION, DESOLATIONS]

Ge 47:19 and that the land may not become d." H9037
Ex 23:29 land would become d and the wild H9039
Lev 26:34 all the time that it lies d and you are in H9037
Lev 26:35 All the time that it lies d, the land will H9037
Lev 26:43 its sabbaths while it lies d without them. H9037
Jos 8:28 heap of ruins, a d place to this day. H9039
2Sa 13:20 her brother Absalom's house, a d woman. H9037
Job 30: 3 the parched land in d wastelands at night H8739
Job 38:27 to satisfy a d wasteland and make it H8739
Isa 1: 7 Your country is d, your cities burned with H9039
Isa 5: 9 "Surely the great houses will become d H9014
Isa 13: 9 to make the land d and destroy the H9014
Isa 24:10 The ruined city lies d; the entrance to H8689
Isa 27:10 The fortified city stands d, an abandoned H970
Isa 34:10 From generation to generation it will lie d; H2990
Isa 49: 8 land and to reassign its d inheritances, H9037
Isa 49:19 were ruined and made d and your land H9037
Isa 54: 1 children of the d woman than of her who H9037
Isa 54: 3 nations and settle in their d cities. H9037
Isa 62: 4 call you Deserted, or name your land D. H9039
Jer 6: 8 make your land d so no one can live H9039
Jer 7:34 of Jerusalem, for the land will become d. H2999
Jer 9:10 They are d and untraveled, and the H5898
Jer 10:22 It will make the towns of Judah d, a haunt H9039
Jer 12:10 turn my pleasant field into a d wasteland. H9039
Jer 12:11 parched and d before me; the whole H9038
Jer 25:11 whole country will become a d wasteland, H2999
Jer 25:12 the LORD, "and will make it d forever. H9039
Jer 25:38 land will become d because of the sword H9014
Jer 26: 9 this city will be d and deserted? H2990
Jer 32:43 you say, 'It is a d waste, without people H9039
Jer 33:10 "It is a d waste, without people or H2992
Jer 33:12 d and without people or animals H2992
Jer 44: 6 made them the d ruins they are today H2999
Jer 44:22 became a curse and a d waste without H2999
Jer 48: 9 her towns will become d, with no one to H9014
Jer 49:33 a haunt of jackals, a d place forever. H9039
Jer 50:13 not be inhabited but will be completely d. H9039
Jer 50:23 How d is Babylon among the nations H9014
Jer 51:26 you will be d forever," declares the H9039
Jer 51:41 How d Babylon will be among the nations H9014
Jer 51:43 Her towns will be d, a dry and desert land, H9014
Jer 51:62 animals will live in it; it will be d forever. H9039
La 1: 4 All her gateways are d, her priests groan H9037
La 1:13 He made me d, faint all the day H9037
La 5:18 Mount Zion, which lies d, with jackals H9037
Eze 6:14 make the land a d waste from the H9039
Eze 12:20 will be laid waste and the land will be d. H9039
Eze 14:15 it becomes d so that no one can pass H9039
Eze 14:16 would be saved, but the land would be d. H9039
Eze 15: 8 I will make the land d because they have H9039
Eze 26:19 When I make you a d city, like cities no H2990
Eze 29: 9 Egypt will become a d wasteland. H9039
Eze 29:10 Egypt a ruin and a d waste from Migdol to H9039
Eze 29:12 the land of Egypt d among devastated H9039
Eze 29:12 her cities will lie d forty years among H9039
Eze 30: 7 " 'They will be d among desolate lands H9037
Eze 30: 7 " 'They will be desolate among d lands H9037
Eze 32:15 When I make Egypt d and strip the land H9039
Eze 33:28 I will make the land a d waste, and her H9039
Eze 33:28 of Israel will become d so that no one H9037
Eze 33:29 made the land a d waste because of all H9039
Eze 35: 3 against you and make you a d waste. H9039
Eze 35: 4 your towns into ruins and you will be d. H9039
Eze 35: 7 make Mount Seir a d waste and cut off H9040
Eze 35: 9 I will make you d forever; your towns will H9039
Eze 35:14 whole earth rejoices, I will make you d. H9039
Eze 35:15 when the inheritance of Israel became d, H9037
Eze 35:15 You will be d, Mount Seir, you and all of H9039
Eze 36: 4 to the d ruins and the deserted towns that H9037
Eze 36:34 The d land will be cultivated instead of H9037
Eze 36:34 instead of lying d in the sight of all who H9039
Eze 36:35 were lying in ruins, d and destroyed, are H9037
Eze 36:36 have replanted what was d. H9037
Eze 38: 8 of Israel, which had long been d. H2999
Da 9:17 look with favor on your d sanctuary. H9038
Joel 3:19 But Egypt will be d, Edom a desert waste H9039
Mic 7:13 The earth will become d because of its H9039
Zep 2:13 leaving Nineveh utterly d and dry as the H9039
Zec 7:14 left behind them was so d that no one H9037
Zec 7:14 is how they made the pleasant land d. H9014
Mt 23:38 your house is left to you d. G2245
Lk 13:35 your house is left to you d. I tell you, you G2245
Gal 4:27 the children of the d woman than of her G2245

DESOLATION (14) [DESOLATE]

2Ch 36:21 all the time of its d it rested, until the H9014
Isa 17: 9 undergrowth. And all will be d. H9039
Isa 34:11 line of chaos and the plumb line of d. H983
Isa 64:10 even Zion is a wasteland, Jerusalem a d. H9039
Eze 23:33 the cup of ruin and d, the cup of your H9039
Da 8:13 the rebellion that causes d, the surrender H9037
Da 9: 2 that the d of Jerusalem would last seventy H2999
Da 9:18 eyes and see the d of the city that bears H9037
Da 9:27 will set up an abomination that causes d, H9037
Da 11:31 will set up the abomination that causes d. H9037
Da 12:11 the abomination that causes d is set up, H9037
Mt 24:15 place 'the abomination that causes d, G2247
Mk 13:14 that causes d' standing where G2247
Lk 21:20 by armies, you will know that its d is near. G2247

DESOLATIONS (2) [DESOLATE]

Ps 46: 8 the d he has brought on the earth. H9014
Da 9:26 until the end, and d have been decreed. H9037

DESPAIR (13) [DESPAIRED, DESPAIRING, DESPAIRS]

Ge 35:17 said to her, "Don't d, for you have another H3707
1Sa 4:20 her said, "Don't d; you have given birth to H3707
Job 9:23 he mocks the d of the innocent. H5000
Ps 88:15 I have borne your terrors and am in d. H7041
Ecc 2:20 So my heart began to d over all my H3286
Isa 19: 9 Those who work with combed flax will d H1017
Isa 61: 3 garment of praise instead of a spirit of d. H3910
Jer 17:16 you know I have not desired the day of d. H631
Eze 4:16 in anxiety and drink rationed water in d, H9041
Eze 7:27 the prince will be clothed with d, and the H9039
Eze 12:19 food in anxiety and drink their water in d, H9041
Joel 1:11 D, you farmers, wail, you vine growers H1017
2Co 4: 8 not crushed; perplexed, but not in d; G1989

DESPAIRED (1) [DESPAIR]

2Co 1: 8 to endure, so that we d of life itself. G1989

DESPAIRING (2) [DESPAIR]

Dt 28:65 eyes weary with longing, and a d heart. H1792
Jer 14: 3 unfilled; dismayed and d, they cover their H4007

DESPAIRS (1) [DESPAIR]

Job 15:22 He d of escaping the realm of H4202+586

DESPERATE (5)

2Sa 12:18 child is dead? He may do something d." H8288
Job 6:26 what I say, and treat my d words as wind? H3286
Ps 60: 3 You have shown your people d times; you H7997
Ps 79: 8 quickly to meet us, for we are in d need. H4394
Ps 142: 6 for I am in d need; rescue me from H4394

DESPISE (39) [DESPISED, DESPISES, DESPISING]

Ge 16: 4 she began to d her mistress. H7837+928+6524
Dt 23: 7 Do not d an Edomite, for the Edomites H9493
Dt 23: 7 Do not d an Egyptian, because you H9493
1Sa 2:30 but those who d me will be disdained. H1022
2Sa 12: 9 Why did you d the word of the LORD by H1022
Est 1:17 and so they will d their H1022+928+6524
Job 5:17 so do not d the discipline of the Almighty. H4415
Job 7:16 I d my life; I would not live forever. Let me H4415
Job 9:21 no concern for myself; I d my own life. H4415
Job 42: 6 Therefore I d myself and repent in dust H4415
Ps 51:17 contrite heart you, God, will not d. H1022
Ps 69:33 the needy and does not d his captive H1022
Ps 73:20 Lord, you will d them as fantasies. H1022
Ps 102:17 of the destitute; he will not d their plea. H1022
Pr 1: 7 fools d wisdom and instruction. H996
Pr 3:11 My son, do not d the LORD's discipline H4415
Pr 6:30 People do not d a thief if he steals to H996
Pr 14: 2 but those who d him are devious in their H1022
Pr 14:21 It is a sin to d one's neighbor, but blessed H996
Pr 15:32 who disregard discipline d themselves, H4415
Pr 23:22 and do not d your mother when she is old. H996
SS 8: 1 I would kiss you, and no one would d me. H996
Isa 60:14 all who d you will bow down at your feet H5540
Jer 4:30 Your lovers d you; they want to kill H4415
Jer 14:19 Do you d Zion? Why have H1718
Jer 14:21 For the sake of your name do not d us; do H5540
Jer 23:17 They keep saying to those who d me H5540
Jer 33:24 So they d my people and no longer H5540
La 1: 8 All who honored her d her, for they have H2361
Eze 16:57 all those around you who d you. H8764
Am 5:21 "I hate, I d your religious festivals; your H4415
Mic 3: 9 who d justice and distort all that is right; H9493
Zec 4:10 "Who dares d the day of small things H996
Mt 6:24 be devoted to the one and d the other. G2969
Mt 18:10 "See that you do not d one of these little G2969
Lk 16:13 be devoted to the one and d the other. G2969
1Co 11:22 Or do you d the church of God by G2969
Titus 2:15 Do not let anyone d you. G4368
2Pe 2:10 corrupt desire of the flesh and d authority. G2969

DESPISED (37) [DESPISE]

Ge 25:34 got up and left. So Esau d his birthright. H1022
Nu 15:31 Because they have d the LORD's word and H1022
1Sa 10:27 They d him and brought him no gifts H1022
1Sa 15: 9 everything that was d and weak they H1022
1Sa 17:42 health and handsome, and he d him. H1022
2Sa 1:21 For there the shield of the mighty was d H1718
2Sa 6:16 before the LORD, she d him in her heart. H1022
2Sa 12:10 because you d me and took the wife of H1022
1Ch 15:29 celebrating, she d him in her heart. H1022
2Ch 36:16 d his words and scoffed at his prophets H1022
Ne 4: 4 our God, for we are d. Turn their insults H999
Ps 22: 6 scorned by everyone, d by the people. H1022
Ps 22:24 For he has not d or scorned the suffering H1022
Ps 53: 5 you put them to shame, for God d them. H4415
Ps 106:24 Then they d the pleasant land; they did H4415
Ps 107:11 God's commands and d the plans of the H5540
Ps 119:141 Though I am lowly and d, I do not forget H1022
Pr 12: 8 one with a warped mind is d. H997
Ecc 9:16 But the poor man's wisdom is d, and his H1022
Isa 16:14 all her many people will be d, H7829
Isa 33: 8 its witnesses are d, no one is respected H4415
Isa 49: 7 to him who was d and abhorred by the H1022
Isa 53: 3 He was d and rejected by mankind, H1022
Isa 53: 3 whom people hide their faces he was d, H1022
Jer 22:28 Is this man Jehoiachin a d, broken pot, an H1022
Jer 49:15 small among the nations, d by mankind. H1022
La 1:11 LORD, and consider, for I am d." H2361
Eze 16: 5 on the day you were born you were d. H1719
Eze 16:45 who d her husband and her children H1718
Eze 16:45 who d their husbands and their children. H1718
Eze 16:59 because you have d my oath by breaking H1022
Eze 17:16 whose oath he d and whose treaty he H1022
Eze 17:18 He d the oath by breaking the covenant H1022
Eze 22: 8 You have d my holy things and desecrated H1022
Ob 2 among the nations; you will be utterly d. H1022
Mal 2: 9 I have caused you to be d and humiliated H1022
1Co 1:28 things of this world and the d things— G2024

DESPISES (8) [DESPISE]
Ge 16: 5 she is pregnant, she d *me*. H7837+928+6524
2Ki 19:21 Daughter Zion d you and mocks you. H996
Job 36: 5 "God is mighty, but d no one; he is H4415
Ps 15: 4 *who* d a vile person but H1022+928+6524
Pr 15:20 his father, but a foolish man d his mother. H1022
Isa 37:22 "Virgin Daughter Zion d and mocks you H996
Eze 21:10 The sword d every such stick. H4415
Eze 21:13 which the sword d, does not continue? H4415

DESPISING (1) [DESPISE]
Eze 17:19 will repay him for d my oath and breaking H1022

DESPITE (9)

DESPITE, DESPITEFUL, DESPITEFULLY (KJV) INSOLENT, INSULTED, MALICE, MISTREAT, PERSECUTE, TRAMPLED
Ezr 3: 3 D their fear of the peoples around them H3954
Ps 33:17 d all its great strength it cannot save. H928
Ps 49:12 d their wealth, do not endure; they H928
Ecc 8:17 D all their efforts to search it H928+8611+4200
Isa 25:11 bring down their pride d the cleverness of H6640
Eze 21:29 D false visions concerning you and lying H928
Eze 32:29 all her princes; d their power, they are H928
Eze 32:30 the slain in disgrace d the terror caused by H928
Hos 7:10 d all this he does not return to the LORD H928

DESPOIL (1) [SPOIL]
Jer 30:16 make spoil of you *I will* d. H5989+4200+1020

DESTINATION (1)
2Sa 16:14 with him arrived at their d exhausted. NDT

DESTINE (1) [DESTINED, DESTINY, PREDESTINED]
Isa 65:12 *I will* d you for the sword, and all of you H4948

DESTINED (13) [DESTINE]
Ps 49:14 They are like sheep and *are* d to die H9286
Isa 9: 5 rolled in blood will be d for burning, H4200
Jer 15: 2 " 'Those d for death, to death; those for H4200
Jer 43:11 bringing death to those d for death H4200
Jer 43:11 captivity to those d for captivity, and the H4200
Jer 43:11 the sword to those d for the sword. H4200
Eze 31:14 a height; they *are* all d for death, for the H5989
Lk 2:34 "This child *is* d to cause the falling and *G3023*
1Co 2: 7 hidden and that God d for our glory *G4633*
Col 2:22 things that are all d to perish with use, *G1650*
1Th 3: 3 know quite well that *we are* d for them. *G3023*
Heb 9:27 Just as people *are* d to die once, and after *G641*
1Pe 2: 8 which is also what *they were* d for. *G5502*

DESTINY (7) [DESTINE]
Job 8:13 Such is the d *of* all who forget God; so H784
Ps 73:17 then I understood their final d. H344
Ecc 7: 2 death is the d *of* everyone; the living H6067
Ecc 9: 2 All share a common d—the righteous and H5247
Ecc 9: 3 The same d overtakes all. H5247
Isa 65:11 fill bowls of mixed wine for D, H4972
Php 3:19 Their d is destruction, their god is their *G5465*

DESTITUTE (8)
Ge 45:11 all who belong to you *will become* d. H3769
Job 20:19 has oppressed the poor and left them d; H6440
Ps 102:17 He will respond to the prayer of the d; he H6899
Pr 31: 8 the rights of all *who* are d. H1201+2710
Isa 3:26 lament and mourn; d, she will sit on the H5927
La 1:16 My children are d because the enemy has H9037
La 4: 5 once ate delicacies *are* d in the streets. H9037
Heb 11:37 goatskins, d, persecuted and *G5728*

DESTROY (252) [DESTROYED, DESTROYER, DESTROYERS, DESTROYING, DESTROYS, DESTRUCTION, DESTRUCTIVE]
Ge 6:13 I *am* surely *going to* d both them and the H8845
Ge 6:17 on the earth to d all life under the H8845
Ge 8:21 And never again *will I* d all living H5782
Ge 9:11 again will there be a flood to d the earth." H8845
Ge 9:15 the waters become a flood to d all life. H8845
Ge 18:28 *Will you* d the whole city for lack of five H8845
Ge 18:28 forty-five there," he said, "*I will* not d it." H8845
Ge 18:31 "For the sake of twenty, *I will* not d it." H8845
Ge 18:32 "For the sake of ten, *I will* not d it. H8845
Ge 19:13 because we *are going to* d this place. H8845
Ge 19:13 is so great that he has sent us to d it." H8845
Ge 19:14 because the LORD *is about to* d the city!" H8845
Ge 20: 4 "Lord, *will you* d an innocent nation? H2222
Ex 15: 9 draw my sword and my hand *will* d them. H3769
Ex 32:10 burn against them and that *I may* d them. H3983
Ex 33: 3 people and *I might* d you on the way." H3983
Ex 33: 5 you even for a moment, *I might* d you. H3983
Lev 23:30 *I will* d from among their people anyone who H6
Lev 26:16 fever *that will* d your sight and H3983
Lev 26:22 d your cattle and make you so few in H4162
Lev 26:30 *I will* d your high places, cut down your H9012
Lev 26:44 abhor them so as to d them completely, H3983
Nu 14:12 them down with a plague and d them, H3769
Nu 21: 2 our hands, *we will* totally d their cities." H3049
Nu 24:19 come out of Jacob and d the survivors of the H6
Nu 33:52 D all their carved images and their cast idols H6
Dt 1:27 us into the hands of the Amorites to d us. H9012
Dt 4:31 he will not abandon or d you or forget the H8845
Dt 6:15 and *he will* d you from the face of the H9012
Dt 7: 2 then *you* must d them totally. H3049+3049
Dt 7: 4 burn against you and *will* quickly d you. H9012
Dt 7:16 *You must* d all the peoples the LORD your H430
Dt 7:24 to stand up against you; you *will* d them. H9012
Dt 9: 3 He *will* d them; he will subdue them H9012
Dt 9: 8 so that he was angry enough to d you. H9012
Dt 9:14 so that *I may* d them and blot out their H9012
Dt 9:19 he was angry enough with you to d you. H9012
Dt 9:20 was angry enough with Aaron to d him, H9012
Dt 9:25 the LORD had said *he would* d you. H9012
Dt 9:26 "Sovereign LORD, *do* not d your people H8845
Dt 10:10 this time also. It was not his will *to* d you. H8845
Dt 12: 2 D completely all the places on the high H6+6
Dt 13:15 *You must* d it completely, both its people H3049
Dt 20:17 Completely d them—the Hittites H3049+3049
Dt 20:19 *do* not d its trees by putting an ax to them, H8845
Dt 28:63 so it will please him to ruin and d you. H9012
Dt 31: 3 He *will* d these nations before you, and H9012
Dt 33:27 enemies before you, saying, 'D them! H9012
Jos 7: 7 us into the hands of the Amorites to d us? H6
Jos 7:12 anymore unless *you* d whatever among H9012
Jos 11:20 so that *he might* d them totally H3049
1Sa 2:33 I will spare only to d your sight and sap H3983
1Sa 15: 3 Amalekites and totally d all that belongs H3049
1Sa 15: 6 so that *I do* not d you along with H665
1Sa 15: 9 they were unwilling *to* d completely, H3049
1Sa 15:18 'Go and completely d those wicked H3049
1Sa 23:10 come to Keilah and d the town on H8845
1Sa 26: 9 to Abishai, "Don't d him! Who can lay a H8845
1Sa 26:15 Someone came to d your lord the king. H8845
2Sa 1:14 to lift your hand to d the LORD's anointed?" H8845
2Sa 11:25 Press the attack against the city and d it.' H2238
2Sa 20:19 You are trying to d a city that is a mother H4637
2Sa 20:20 "Far be it from me to swallow up or d! H8845
2Sa 24:16 stretched out his hand to d Jerusalem, H8845
2Ki 8:19 the LORD was not willing to d Judah. H8845
2Ki 9: 7 *You are to* d the house of Ahab your H5782
2Ki 10:19 deceptively in order to d the servants of Baal. H6
2Ki 11: 1 she proceeded *to* d the whole royal family. H6
2Ki 13:17 "*You will* completely d the Arameans at H5782
2Ki 13:23 has been unwilling *to* d them or banish H8845
2Ki 18:25 I come to attack and d this place without H8845
2Ki 18:25 me to march against this country and d it. H8845
2Ki 24: 2 Ammonite raiders against him to d Judah, H6
1Ch 21:15 And God sent an angel to d Jerusalem H8845
2Ch 12: 7 *I will* not d them but will soon give them H8845
2Ch 20:10 away from them and *did* not d them. H9012
2Ch 20:23 from Mount Seir to d and annihilate them H3049
2Ch 20:23 from Seir, they helped to d one another. H8845
2Ch 20:37 the LORD *will* d what you have made." H7287
2Ch 21: 7 was not willing to d the house of David. H8845
2Ch 22: 7 had anointed to d the house of Ahab. H4162
2Ch 22:10 she proceeded *to* d the whole royal family H1818
2Ch 25:16 "I know that God has determined to d you, H8845
2Ch 35:21 who is with me, or *he will* d you. H8845
Ezr 6:12 this decree or to d this temple in A10243
Ezr 9:14 you not be angry enough with us *to* d us, H3983
Est 3: 6 looked for a way to d all Mordecai's H9012
Est 3: 9 let a decree be issued to d them, and I will H6
Est 3:13 the king's provinces with the order to d, H9012
Est 8: 5 devised and wrote to d the Jews in all the H6
Est 8:11 themselves; to d, kill and annihilate H9012
Est 9: 2 to attack those determined to d them. H8288
Est 9:24 against the Jews to d them and had cast the H6
Job 10: 8 Will you now turn and d me? H1180
Job 14:19 wash away the soil, so *you* d a person's hope. H6
Ps 5: 6 *you* d those who tell lies. The bloodthirsty H6
Ps 17: 9 from the wicked who *are* out to d me H8720
Ps 21:10 *You will* d their descendants from the earth H6
Ps 54: 5 slander me; in your faithfulness d them. H7551
Ps 57: T To the tune of "*Do* Not D." Of David. H8845
Ps 58: T To the tune of "*Do* Not D." Of David. H8845
Ps 59: T To the tune of "*Do* Not D." Of David. H8845
Ps 69: 4 without cause, *those who* seek to d me. H7551
Ps 73:27 *you* d all who are unfaithful to you. H7551
Ps 74:11 the folds of your garment and d them! H3983
Ps 75: T To the tune of "*Do* Not D." A psalm of H8845
Ps 78:38 their iniquities and *did* not d them. H8845
Ps 83: 4 they say, "*let us* d them as a nation, so H3948
Ps 94:23 them for their sins and d them for their H7551
Ps 94:23 wickedness; the LORD our God *will* d them. H7551
Ps 106:23 So he said *he would* d them—had not H9012
Ps 106:34 *They did* not d the peoples as the LORD H9012
Ps 119:95 The wicked are waiting to d me, but I will H6
Ps 143:12 silence my enemies; d all my foes, for I am H6
Ps 145:20 love him, but all the wicked *he will* d. H9012
Pr 1:32 the complacency of fools *will* d them; H6
Pr 11: 9 mouths the godless d their neighbors, H8845
Ecc 5: 6 at what you say and d the work of your H2472
Ecc 7:16 neither be overwise—why d yourself? H9037
Isa 10: 7 his purpose is to d, to put an end to many H9012
Isa 10:18 fertile fields *it will* completely d, H3983
Isa 11: 9 will neither harm nor d on all my holy H8845
Isa 13: 5 of his wrath—to d the whole country. H2472
Isa 13: 9 land desolate and d the sinners within it H9012
Isa 14:30 But your root *I will* d by famine; it will slay H4637
Isa 25: 7 this mountain *he will* d the shroud that H1180
Isa 32: 7 up evil schemes to d the poor with lies, H2472
Isa 34: 2 *He will* totally d them, he will give them H3049
Isa 36:10 I come to attack and d this land without H8845
Isa 36:10 me to march against this country and d it. H8845
Isa 48: 9 from you, so as not *to* d you completely. H4162
Isa 65: 8 people say, 'Don't d it, there is still a H8845
Isa 65: 8 of my servants; *I will* not d them all. H8845
Isa 65:25 will neither harm nor d on all my holy H8845
Jer 1:10 tear down, to d and overthrow, to build H6
Jer 4:27 though *I will* not d it completely. H6913+3986
Jer 5:10 but *do* not d them completely. H6913+3986
Jer 5:17 With the sword *they will* d the fortified H8406
Jer 5:18 "*I will* not d you completely. H6913+3986
Jer 6: 2 *I will* d Daughter Zion, so beautiful and H1950
Jer 6: 5 let us attack at night and d her fortresses!" H8845
Jer 11:19 "*Let us* d the tree and its fruit; let H8845
Jer 12:17 I will completely uproot and d it," declares H6
Jer 14:12 Instead, I *will* d them with the sword H3983
Jer 15: 3 the wild animals to devour and d. H8845
Jer 15: 6 So I will reach out and d you; I am tired of H8845
Jer 17:18 disaster; d them *with* double destruction. H8689
Jer 19: 9 so hard against them *to* d them. H1335+5883
Jer 21:10 king of Babylon, and *he will* d it with fire. H8596
Jer 25: 9 *I will* completely d them and make them H3049
Jer 27: 8 declares the LORD, until I d it by his hand. H9462
Jer 30:11 'Though *I* completely d all the H6913+3986
Jer 30:11 *I will* not completely d you. H6913+3986
Jer 31:28 to overthrow, d and bring disaster, so I H6
Jer 36:29 certainly come and d this land and wipe H8845
Jer 44: 8 You *will* d yourselves and make H4162
Jer 44:11 bring disaster on you and to d all Judah. H4162
Jer 46: 8 the earth; *I will* d cities and their people. H6
Jer 46:28 "Though *I* completely d all the H6913+3986
Jer 46:28 *I will* not completely d you. H6913+3986
Jer 47: 4 the day has come to d all the Philistines H8720
Jer 47: 4 The LORD *is about to* d the Philistines, the H8720
Jer 49:28 attack Kedar and d the people of the H8720
Jer 49:38 my throne in Elam and d her king and H6
Jer 50:21 kill and completely d them," declares H3049
Jer 50:26 Completely d her and leave her no H3049
Jer 51: 3 her young men; completely d her army. H3049
Jer 51:11 because his purpose is to d Babylon. H8845
Jer 51:20 I shatter nations, with you *I* d kingdoms, H8845
Jer 51:25 mountain, you who d the whole earth," H8845
Jer 51:55 The LORD *will* d Babylon; he will silence H8720
Jer 51:62 you have said you *will* d this place, so H4162
La 3:66 them in anger and d them from under the H9012
Eze 5:16 arrows of famine, I will shoot to d you. H8845
Eze 6: 3 against you, and *I will* d your high places. H6
Eze 9: 8 *Are* you *going to* d the entire remnant of H8845
Eze 11:13 *Will* you completely d the remnant H3986+6913
Eze 14: 9 against him and d him from among my H9012
Eze 16:39 your mounds and d your lofty shrines. H5997
Eze 17:17 siege works erected to d many lives. H4162
Eze 20:13 my wrath on them and d them in the H3983
Eze 20:17 with pity and *did* not d them or put an H8845
Eze 22:30 of the land so I *would* not *have to* d it, H8845
Eze 25: 7 *I will* d you, and you will know that I am H9012
Eze 25:15 with ancient hostility sought to d Judah, H5422
Eze 25:16 the Kerethites and d those remaining along H6
Eze 26: 4 *They will* d the walls of Tyre and pull H8845
Eze 30:11 nations—will be brought in to d the land. H8845
Eze 30:13 " '*I will* d the idols and put an end to the H6
Eze 32:13 *I will* d all her cattle from beside abundant H6
Eze 34:16 the sleek and the strong *I will* d. H9012
Eze 43: 3 seen when he came to d the city and like H8845
Da 4:23 'Cut down the tree and d it, but leave A10243
Da 8:24 *He will* d those who are mighty, the holy H8845
Da 8:25 *he will* d many and take his stand against H8845
Da 9:26 ruler who will come *will* d the city and the H8845
Da 11:16 Land and will have the power to d it. H3986
Da 11:26 from the king's provisions *will try to* d him; H8689
Da 11:44 in a great rage to d and annihilate many. H9012
Hos 4: 5 So *I will* d your mother— H1950
Hos 10: 2 their altars and d their sacred stones. H8720
Am 1: 5 *I will* d the king who is in the Valley of H4162
Am 1: 8 *I will* d the king of Ashdod and the one H4162
Am 2: 3 *I will* d her ruler and kill all her officials H4162
Am 3:14 her sins, *I will* d the altars of Bethel H7212
Am 9: 8 *I will* d it from the face of the earth H9012
Am 9: 8 Yet *I will* not totally d the H9012+9012
Ob 8 the LORD, "*will I* not d the wise men of Edom H6
Ob 18 they will set him on fire and d him. H430
Mic 1: 7 with fire; *I will* d all her images. H9039+8492
Mic 5:10 "*I will* d your horses from among you and H4162
Mic 5:11 *I will* d the cities of your land and tear H4162
Mic 5:12 *I will* d your witchcraft and you will no H4162
Mic 5:13 *I will* d your idols and your sacred stones H4162
Mic 6:13 I have begun *to* d you, to ruin you H5782
Na 1:14 *I will* d the images and idols that are in H4162
Zep 1: 3 "When *I* d all mankind on the face of the H4162
Zep 1: 4 *I will* d every remnant of Baal worship in H4162
Zep 2: 5 "*I will* d you, and none will be H6
Zep 2:13 out his hand against the north and d Assyria, H6
Zec 5: 4 remain in that house and d it completely, H3983
Zec 9: 4 her possessions and d her power on the H5782
Zec 9:15 *They will* d and overcome with slingstones H430
Zec 12: 9 day I will set out to d all the nations that H9012
Mt 6:19 where moths and vermin d, and where *G906*
Mt 6:20 where moths and vermin *do* not d, and *G906*
Mt 10:28 of the One who can d both soul and body *G660*
Mt 26:61 'I am able *to* d the temple of God and *G2907*
Mt 27:40 "You who are going to d the temple and *G2907*
Mk 1:24 Have you come *to* d us? I know who you *G660*
Mk 14:58 '*I will* d this temple made with human *G2907*
Mk 15:29 You *who are going to* d the temple and *G2907*
Lk 4:34 Have you come *to* d us? I know who you *G660*

Lk 6: 9 do good or to do evil, to save life or to d it?" G660
Lk 9:54 us to call fire down from heaven to d them?" G384
Jn 2:19 answered them, "D this temple, and I G3395
Jn 10:10 The thief comes only to steal and kill and d G660
Ac 6:14 Jesus of Nazareth will d this place and G2907
Ac 8: 3 But Saul began to d the church. G3381
Ro 14:15 Do not by your eating d someone for whom G660
Ro 14:20 Do not d the work of God for the sake of G2907
1Co 1:19 "I will d the wisdom of the wise; the G660
1Co 3:17 God's temple, God will d that person; for G5780
1Co 6:13 food, and God will d them both. G2934
Gal 1:13 the church of God and tried to d it. G4514
Gal 1:23 preaching the faith he once tried to d." G4514
2Th 2: 8 of his mouth and d by the splendor of his G2934
2Ti 2:18 taken place, and they d the faith of some. G426
Jas 4:12 the one who is able to save and d. G660
1Jn 3: 8 God appeared was to d the devil's work. G3395
Jude 10 as irrational animals do—will d them. G5780
Rev 11:18 for destroying those who d the earth." G1425

DESTROYED (221) [DESTROY]

Ge 9:11 Never again will all life be d by the H4162
Ge 13:10 before the LORD d Sodom and Gomorrah.) H8845
Ge 19:29 So when God d the cities of the plain, he H8845
Ge 34:30 attack me, I and my household will be d." H9012
Ex 9:31 The flax and barley were d, since the H5782
Ex 9:32 however, were not d, because they ripen H5782
Ex 22:20 to any god other than the LORD must be d. H3049
Lev 10: 6 mourn for those the LORD has d by fire. H8596
Nu 4:18 See that the Kohathite tribal clans are not d H4162
Nu 21: 3 They completely d them and their towns H3049
Nu 21:29 You are d, people of Chemosh! He has H6
Nu 21:30 dominion has been d all the way to H6
Nu 24:22 you Kenites will be d when Ashur takes H1278
Dt 2:12 They d the Horites from before them and H9012
Dt 2:21 The LORD d them from before the H9012
Dt 2:22 when he d the Horites from before them. H9012
Dt 2:23 out from Caphtor d them and settled in H9012
Dt 2:34 all his towns and completely d them— H3049
Dt 3: 6 We completely d them, as we had done H3049
Dt 4: 3 The LORD your God d from among you H9012
Dt 4:26 there long but will certainly be d. H9012+9012
Dt 7:23 them into great confusion until they are d. H9012
Dt 8:19 against you today that you will surely be d. H6+6
Dt 8:20 Like the nations the LORD d before you, so you H6
Dt 8:20 so you will be d for not obeying the LORD your H6
Dt 12:30 after they have been d before you, be H9012
Dt 19: 1 the LORD your God has d the nations H4162
Dt 28:20 until you are d and come to sudden ruin H9012
Dt 28:21 diseases until he has d you from the land H3983
Dt 28:24 come down from the skies until you are d. H9012
Dt 28:45 you and overtake you until you are d, H9012
Dt 28:48 iron yoke on your neck until he has d you. H9012
Dt 28:51 the crops of your land until you are d. H9012
Dt 28:61 in this Book of the Law, until you are d. H9012
Dt 30:18 to you this day that you will certainly be d. H6+6
Dt 31: 4 whom he d along with their land. H9012
Dt 31:17 my face from them, and they will be d. H430
Jos 2:10 of the Jordan, whom you completely d. H3049
Jos 6:21 They devoted the city to the LORD and d H3049
Jos 7:15 with the devoted things shall be d by fire, H8596
Jos 8:26 his javelin until he had d all who lived in H3049
Jos 10: 1 that Joshua had taken Ai and totally d it, H3049
Jos 10:28 to the sword and totally d everyone in it. H3049
Jos 10:35 it to the sword and totally d everyone in it, H3049
Jos 10:37 they totally d it and everyone in it. H3049
Jos 10:39 Everyone in it they totally d. They left no H3049
Jos 10:40 He totally d all who breathed, just as the H3049
Jos 11:11 They totally d them, not sparing anyone H3049
Jos 11:12 He totally d them, as Moses the servant of H3049
Jos 11:14 to the sword until they completely d them, H9012
Jos 11:21 Joshua went and d the Anakites from H4162
Jos 11:21 Joshua totally d them and their towns H3049
Jos 23:15 the LORD your God has d you from this H9012
Jos 24: 8 I d them from before you, and you took H9012
Jdg 1:17 in Zephath, and they totally d the city. H3049
Jdg 4:24 Jabin king of Canaan until they d him. H4162
Jdg 9:45 Then he d the city and scattered salt over H5997
Jdg 21:16 "With the women of Benjamin d, how H9012
1Sa 15: 8 all his people he totally d with the sword. H3049
1Sa 15: 9 was despised and weak they totally d. H3049
1Sa 15:15 LORD your God, but we totally d the rest." H3049
1Sa 15:20 I completely d the Amalekites and H3049
1Sa 27: 1 of these days I will be d by the hand of H6200
1Sa 30: 3 they found it d by fire and their wives and H8596
2Sa 11: 1 They d the Ammonites and besieged H8845
2Sa 14:11 destruction, so that my son will not be d." H9012
2Sa 21: 5 "As for the man who d us and plotted H3983
2Sa 22:38 I did not turn back till they were d. H3983
2Sa 22:41 turn their backs in flight, and I d my foes. H7551
1Ki 11:16 until they had d all the men in Edom. H4162
1Ki 11:24 When David d Zobah's army, Rezon H2222
1Ki 15:29 that breathed, but d them all, according H9012
1Ki 16: 7 of Jeroboam—and also because he d it. H5782
1Ki 16:12 So Zimri d the whole family of Baasha, in H9012
1Ki 22:11 will gore the Arameans until they are d. H3983
2Ki 3:25 They d the towns, and each man threw a H2238
2Ki 10:17 of Ahab's family; he d them, according to H9012
2Ki 10:28 So Jehu d Baal worship in Israel. H9012
2Ki 13: 7 the king of Aram had d the rest and made H6
2Ki 13:19 Aram and completely d it. H6330+3983
2Ki 19:12 nations that were d by my predecessors H8845
2Ki 19:18 thrown their gods into the fire and d them, H6
2Ki 21: 3 the high places his father Hezekiah had d; H6
2Ki 21: 9 the nations the LORD had d before the H9012
1Ch 4:41 who were there and completely d them, H3049
1Ch 5:25 the land, whom God had d before them. H9012
2Ch 8: 8 whom the Israelites had not d—to serve as H3983
2Ch 12:12 turned from him, and he was not totally d. H8845
2Ch 14:14 They d all the villages around Gerar, for H5782
2Ch 18:10 will gore the Arameans until they are d. H3983
2Ch 31: 1 They d the high places and the altars H5997
2Ch 31: 1 After they had d all of them, the Israelites H3983
2Ch 32:14 that my predecessors d has been able to H3049
2Ch 33: 9 the nations the LORD had d before the H9012
2Ch 36:19 all the palaces and d everything of value H8845
Ezr 4:15 That is why this city was d. A10281
Ezr 5:12 who d this temple and deported the A10520
Ne 2: 3 in ruins, and its gates have been d by fire?" H430
Ne 2:13 its gates, which had been d by fire. H430
Est 7: 4 I and my people have been sold to be d, H9012
Est 9: 6 the Jews killed and d five hundred men. H6
Est 9:12 Jews have killed and d five hundred men H6
Job 4: 7 Where were the upright ever d? H3948
Job 19:26 And after my skin has been d, yet in my H5937
Job 22:20 'Surely our foes are d, and fire devours H3948
Ps 9: 5 have rebuked the nations and d the wicked; H6
Ps 11: 3 When the foundations are being d, what H2238
Ps 18:37 I did not turn back till they were d. H3983
Ps 18:40 turn their backs in flight, and I d my foes. H7551
Ps 37: 9 For those who are evil will be d, but those H4162
Ps 37:22 the land, but those he curses will be d. H4162
Ps 37:28 Wrongdoers will be completely d; the H9012
Ps 37:34 when the wicked are d, you will see it. H4162
Ps 37:38 But all sinners will be d; there will be no H9012
Ps 48: 7 You d them like ships of Tarshish H8689
Ps 63: 9 Those who want to kill me will be d; they H8739
Ps 73:19 How suddenly are they d, completely H9014
Ps 78:47 He d their vines with hail and their H2222
Ps 88:16 swept over me; your terrors have d me. H7551
Ps 92: 7 evildoers flourish, they will be d forever. H9012
Ps 105:16 on the land and d all their supplies of H8689
Pr 6:15 he will suddenly be d—without H8689
Pr 11: 3 the unfaithful are d by their duplicity. H8720
Pr 11:11 by the mouth of the wicked it is d. H2238
Pr 14:11 The house of the wicked will be d, but the H9012
Pr 29: 1 after many rebukes will suddenly be d— H8689
Isa 5: 5 and it will be d; I will break down H1278
Isa 11:13 Judah's enemies will be d; Ephraim H4162
Isa 14:20 for you have d your land and killed your H8845
Isa 15: 1 Ar in Moab is ruined, d in a night! Kir in H8720
Isa 15: 1 Kir in Moab is ruined, d in a night! H8720
Isa 23: 1 For Tyre is d and left without house or H8720
Isa 23:11 Phoenicia that her fortresses be d. H9012
Isa 23:14 you ships of Tarshish; your fortress is d! H8720
Isa 33: 1 destroyer, you who have not been d! H8720
Isa 33: 1 destroying, you will be d; when you stop H8720
Isa 34: 5 on Edom, the people I have totally d. H3051
Isa 37:12 nations that were d by my predecessors H8845
Isa 37:19 thrown their gods into the fire and d them, H6
Isa 48:19 be blotted out nor d from before me." H9012
Jer 4:20 In an instant my tents are d, my shelter in H8720
Jer 10:20 My tent is d; all its ropes are snapped. H8720
Jer 10:25 him completely and d his homeland. H9037
Jer 18: 7 kingdom is to be uprooted, torn down and d, H6
Jer 24:10 them until they are d from the land I gave H9462
Jer 44:27 by sword and famine until they are all d. H3983
Jer 48: 8 valley will be ruined and the plateau d, H9012
Jer 48:15 Moab will be d and her towns invaded H8720
Jer 48:20 Announce by the Arnon that Moab is d. H8720
Jer 48:42 Moab will be d as a nation because she H9012
Jer 48:46 The people of Chemosh are d; your sons are H6
Jer 49: 3 Heshbon, for Ai is d! Cry out, you H8720
Jer 49:10 His armed men are d, also his allies and H8720
Jer 51: 6 Do not be d because of her sins H1959
Jer 51:13 end has come, the time for you to be d. H1299
La 2: 5 up all her palaces and d her strongholds. H8845
La 2: 6 a garden; he has d his place of meeting. H8845
La 2: 9 the ground; their bars he has broken and d. H6
La 2:11 on the ground because my people are d, H8691
La 2:22 I cared for and reared my enemy has d." H3983
La 3:48 from my eyes because my people are d. H8691
La 4:10 their food when my people were d. H8691
Eze 13:14 When it falls, you will be d in it; and you H3983
Eze 26:17 " 'How you are d, city of renown, peopled by H6
Eze 36:35 desolate and d, are now fortified H2238
Eze 36:36 have rebuilt what was d and have H2238
Eze 43: 8 So I d them in my anger. H430
Da 2:44 set up a kingdom that will never be d, A10243
Da 6:26 his kingdom will not be d, his dominion A10243
Da 7:11 slain and its body d and thrown into the A10005
Da 7:14 his kingdom is one that will never be d. A10243
Da 7:26 and completely d forever A10722+10221+10005
Da 8:25 Yet he will be d, but not by H8689
Da 11:20 however, he will be d, yet not in anger H8689
Da 11:22 it and a prince of the covenant will be d. H8689
Hos 4: 6 my people are d from lack of knowledge H1950
Hos 10: 7 Samaria's king will be d, swept away like H1950
Hos 10: 8 The high places of wickedness will be d H9012
Hos 10:15 king of Israel will be completely d. H1950+1950
Hos 13: 9 "You are d, Israel, because you are H8845
Joel 1:10 is dried up; the grain is d, the new wine is H8720
Joel 1:11 because the harvest of the field is d. H6
Am 2: 9 "Yet I d the Amorites before them, though H9012
Am 2: 9 I d their fruit above and their roots below H9012
Am 3:15 with ivory will be d and the mansions H6
Am 7: 9 places of Isaac will be d and the H9037
Ob 10 covered with shame; you will be d forever. H4162
Mic 5: 9 your enemies, and all your foes will be d. H4162
Na 1:12 numerous, they will be d and pass away. H1605
Na 1:15 invade you; they will be completely d. H4162
Hab 2: 8 you have d lands and cities and everyone H2805
Hab 2:17 you have d lands and cities and everyone H2805
Zep 1:11 all who trade with silver will be d. H4162
Zep 3: 6 "I have d nations; their strongholds are H4162
Zep 3: 7 Then her place of refuge would not be d H4162
Zec 11: 3 of the shepherds; their rich pastures are d! H8720
Zec 14:11 will be inhabited; never again will it be d. H3051
Mal 3: 6 the descendants of Jacob, are not d. H3983
Mt 22: 7 sent his army and d those murderers and G660
Lk 17:27 Then the flood came and d them all. G660
Lk 17:29 rained down from heaven and d them all. G660
Ac 27:22 of you will be lost; only the ship will be d. NDT
1Co 8:11 whom Christ died, is d by your knowledge. G660
1Co 15:24 the Father after he has d all dominion, G2934
1Co 15:26 The last enemy to be d is death. G2934
2Co 4: 9 not abandoned; struck down, but not d. G660
2Co 5: 1 that if the earthly tent we live in is d, G2907
Gal 2:18 If I rebuild what I d, then I really would be G2907
Gal 5:15 watch out or you will be d by each other. G384
Eph 2:14 the two groups one and has d the barrier, G3395
Php 1:28 This is a sign to them that they will be d G724
2Ti 1:10 who has d death and has brought life G2934
Heb 10:39 to those who shrink back and are d, G1650+724
Jas 1:11 its blossom falls and its beauty is d. G660
2Pe 2:12 born only to be caught and d, and like G5785
2Pe 3: 6 the world of that time was deluged and d. G660
2Pe 3:10 the elements will be d by fire, and the G3395
2Pe 3:11 Since everything will be d in this way G3395
Jude 5 later d those who did not believe. G660
Jude 11 they have been d in Korah's rebellion. G660
Rev 8: 9 sea died, and a third of the ships were d. G1425

DESTROYER (13) [DESTROY]

Ex 12:23 will not permit the d to enter your houses H5422
Isa 16: 4 stay with you; be their shelter from the d." H8720
Isa 33: 1 Woe to you, d, you who have not been H8720
Isa 54:16 I who have created the d to wreak havoc; H5422
Jer 4: 7 out of his lair; a d of nations has set out. H5422
Jer 6:26 suddenly the d will come upon us. H8720
Jer 15: 8 I will bring a d against the mothers H8720
Jer 48: 8 The d will come against every town, and H8720
Jer 48:32 The d has fallen on your ripened fruit H8720
Jer 51: 1 up the spirit of a d against Babylon and H5422
Jer 51:56 A d will come against Babylon; her H8720
Heb 11:28 so that the d of the firstborn would not G3905
Rev 9:11 in Greek is Apollyon (that is, D). NDT

DESTROYERS (6) [DESTROY]

Jer 12:12 barren heights in the desert d will swarm, H8720
Jer 15: 3 "I will send four kinds of d against them," NDT
Jer 22: 7 I will send d against you, each man with H5422
Jer 51:48 out of the north d will attack her, H8720
Jer 51:53 I will send d against her," declares H8720
Na 2: 2 though d have laid them waste and have H1327

DESTROYING (22) [DESTROY]

Ge 19:25 he overthrew those cities and the entire plain, d H2200
Dt 3: 6 king of Heshbon, d every city—men, H3049
1Sa 6: 5 of the rats that are d the country, H8845
2Ki 19:11 to all the countries, d them completely. H3049
1Ch 21:15 said to the angel who was d the people, H8845
Est 9: 5 the sword, killing and d them, and they did H12
Job 30:13 break up my road; they succeed in d me. H2095
Ps 52: 7 great wealth and grew strong by d others!" H2095
Ps 78:49 hostility—a band of d angels. H8273
Ps 106:23 before him to keep his wrath from d them. H8845
Isa 33: 1 When you stop d, you will be destroyed H8720
Isa 37:11 to all the countries, d them completely. H3049
Jer 13:14 compassion to keep me from d them. H8845
Jer 23: 1 to the shepherds who are d and scattering the H6
Jer 25:36 of the flock, for the LORD is d their pasture. H8720
Jer 51:25 am against you, you d mountain, you who H8845
La 2: 8 did not withhold his hand from d. H1180
Am 4: 9 vineyards, d them with blight and mildew. NDT
Hab 1:17 d nations without mercy? H2222
Lk 9:39 It scarcely ever leaves him and is d him. G5341
1Co 10:10 and were killed by the d angel. G3904
Rev 11:18 and for d those who destroy the earth." G1425

DESTROYS (13) [DESTROY]

Ex 21:26 slave in the eye and d it must let the H8845
Job 9:22 'He d both the blameless and the wicked. H3983
Job 12:23 nations great, and d them; he enlarges H6
Ps 91: 6 the plague that d at midday. H8720
Pr 6:32 has no sense; whoever does so d himself. H8845
Pr 18: 9 in his work is brother to one who d. H1251+5422
Pr 28:24 "It's not wrong," is partner to one who d. H5422
Ecc 9:18 weapons of war, but one sinner d much good. H6
Jer 48:18 the one who d Moab will come up H8720
Am 5: 9 a blinding flash he d the stronghold and H8719
Zep 2:11 to them when he d all the gods of the H8135
Lk 12:33 no thief comes near and no moth d. G1425
1Co 3:17 If anyone d God's temple, God will destroy G5780

DESTRUCTION (95) [DESTROY]

Lev 27:29 " 'No person **devoted to d** may be H3049+3051
Nu 24:20 nations, but their end will be **utter d**." H6330+7
Nu 32:15 and *you will be the* **cause** of their **d**." H8845
Dt 7:10 who hate him he will repay to their face by **d**; H6
Dt 7:26 like it, will be **set apart for d**. H3051
Dt 7:26 utterly detest it, for it is **set apart for d**. H3051
Dt 29:23 will be like the **d** *of* Sodom and Gomorrah H4550
Dt 30:15 today life and prosperity, death and **d**. H8273
Jos 6:18 *you will* not **bring about** *your own* **d** by H3049
Jos 6:18 of Israel liable to **d** and bring trouble on it H3051
Jos 7:12 they have been made liable to **d**. H3051
Jos 7:12 whatever among you is **devoted to d**. H3051
2Sa 14:11 avenger of blood from adding to the **d**, H8845
2Sa 22: 5 the torrents of **d** overwhelmed me. H1175
1Ki 13:34 downfall and to its **d** from the face of the H9012
Est 4: 7 into the royal treasury for *the* **d** of the Jews. H6
Est 8: 6 How can I bear to see the **d** *of* my family?" H13
Est 9:24 that is, the lot) for their ruin and **d**. H6
Job 5:21 tongue, and need not fear when **d** comes. H8719
Job 5:22 You will laugh at **d** and famine, and need H8719
Job 21:20 Let their own eyes see their **d**; let them H3957
Job 26: 6 dead is naked before God; **D** lies uncovered. H11
Job 28:22 **D** and Death say, "Only a rumor of it has H11
Job 31:12 It is a fire that burns to **D**; it would have H11
Job 31:23 For I dreaded **d** *from* God, and for fear of H369
Ps 1: 6 the way of the wicked **leads to d**. H6
Ps 2:12 will be angry and your way *will* **lead to** *your* **d**, H6
Ps 18: 4 the torrents of **d** overwhelmed me. H1175
Ps 52: 2 your tongue plots **d**; it is like a sharpened H2095
Ps 74: 3 all *this* **d** the enemy *has* **brought** on the H8317
Ps 88:11 declared in the grave, your faithfulness in **D**? H11
Ps 137: 8 Babylon, **doomed to d**, happy is the one H8720
Pr 13:15 the way of the unfaithful leads to their **d**. H369
Pr 15:11 Death and **D** lie open before the LORD—how H11
Pr 16:18 Pride goes before **d**, a haughty spirit H8691
Pr 17:19 whoever builds a high gate invites **d**. H8691
Pr 24:22 those two will send sudden **d** on them H369
Pr 27:20 Death and **D** are never satisfied, and neither H9
Isa 10:22 **D** has been decreed, overwhelming and H4001
Isa 10:23 will carry out the **d** decreed upon the H3986
Isa 10:25 my wrath will be directed to their **d**." H9318
Isa 13: 6 it will come like **d** from the Almighty. H8719
Isa 14:23 I will sweep her with the broom of **d**," H9012
Isa 15: 5 the road to Horonaim they lament their **d**. H8691
Isa 16: 4 will come to an end, and **d** will cease; the H8719
Isa 22: 4 try to console me over the **d** *of* my people." H8719
Isa 28:22 has told me of the **d** decreed against the H3986
Isa 30:28 He shakes the nations in the sieve of **d** H8736
Isa 38:17 In your love you kept me from the pit of **d** H1172
Isa 43:28 I consigned Jacob to **d** and Israel to scorn. H3051
Isa 51:13 wrath of the oppressor, who is bent on **d**? H8845
Isa 51:19 ruin and **d**, famine and sword—who H8691
Isa 60:18 nor ruin or **d** within your borders H8691
Jer 4: 6 disaster from the north, even terrible **d**." H8691
Jer 6: 1 looms out of the north, even terrible **d**. H8691
Jer 6: 7 Violence and **d** resound in her; her H8719
Jer 15: 7 I will bring bereavement and **d** *on* my people H6
Jer 17:18 of disaster; destroy them with double **d**. H8695
Jer 20: 8 I cry out proclaiming violence and **d**. H8719
Jer 48: 3 Horonaim, cries of great havoc and **d**. H8691
Jer 48: 5 anguished cries over the **d** are heard. H8691
Jer 50:22 battle is in the land, the noise of great **d**! H8691
Jer 51:54 the sound of great **d** from the land of the H8691
La 1: 7 looked at her and laughed at her **d**. H5404
La 3:47 suffered terror and pitfalls, ruin and **d**." H8691
Eze 21:31 the hands of brutal men, men skilled in **d**. H5422
Eze 32: 9 I bring about your **d** among the nations, H8691
Hos 7:13 **D** to them, because they have rebelled H8719
Hos 8: 4 make idols for themselves to *their own* **d**. H4162
Hos 9: 6 Even if they escape from **d**, Egypt will H8719
Hos 13:14 O grave, is your **d**? "I will have no H7776
Joel 1:15 it will come like **d** from the Almighty. H8719
Ob 12 over the people of Judah in the day of their **d**, H6
Jnh 3:10 bring on them the **d** he had threatened. H8288
Hab 1: 3 **D** and violence are before me; there is H8719
Hab 2:17 and your **d** *of* animals will terrify you. H8719
Mal 4: 6 will come and strike the land with **total d**." H3051
Mt 7:13 gate and broad is the road that leads to **d**, *G724*
Lk 6:49 it collapsed and its **d** was complete." *G4837*
Jn 17:12 the one doomed to **d** so that Scripture *G724*
Ro 9:22 the objects of his wrath—prepared for **d**? *G724*
1Co 5: 5 man over to Satan for the **d** of the flesh, *G3897*
Gal 6: 8 from the flesh will reap **d**; whoever sows *G5785*
Php 3:19 Their destiny is **d**, their god is their stomach, *G724*
1Th 5: 3 **d** will come on them suddenly, as labor *G3897*
2Th 1: 9 be punished *with* everlasting **d** and shut *G3897*
2Th 2: 3 is revealed, the man *doomed to* **d**. *G724*
1Ti 6: 9 desires that plunge people into ruin and **d**. *G724*
2Pe 2: 1 bringing swift **d** on themselves. *G724*
2Pe 2: 3 and their **d** has not been sleeping. *G724*
2Pe 3: 7 the day of judgment and **d** of the ungodly. *G724*
2Pe 3:12 That day *will* bring about *the* **d** of the *G3395*
2Pe 3:16 they do the other Scriptures, to their own **d**. *G724*
Rev 17: 8 come up out of the Abyss and go to its **d**. *G724*
Rev 17:11 belongs to the seven and is going to his **d**. *G724*

DESTRUCTIVE (7) [DESTROY]

Ex 12:13 No **d** plague will touch you when I strike H5422
Ps 55:11 **D forces** are at work in the city; threats H2095
Pr 17: 4 a liar pays attention to a **d** tongue. H2095
Isa 28: 2 Like a hailstorm and a **d** wind, like a H7776
Eze 5:16 with my deadly and **d** arrows of famine, H5422
Eze 13:13 torrents of rain will fall with **d** fury. H3986
2Pe 2: 1 They will secretly introduce **d** heresies *G724*

DETACHMENT (4) [DETACHMENTS]

1Sa 13:23 Now a **d** *of* Philistines had gone out to H5163
Jn 18: 3 guiding a **d of soldiers** and some officials *G5061*
Jn 18:12 Then the **d of soldiers** with its commander *G5061*
Ac 23:23 "Get ready a *d of* two hundred **soldiers** AIT

DETACHMENTS (1) [DETACHMENT]

1Sa 13:17 out from the Philistine camp in three **d**. H8031

DETAIL (3) [DETAILED, DETAILS]

Ac 21:19 and reported **in d** what God *G2848+1651+1667*
Col 2:18 *Such a person* also **goes into great d** *G1836*
Heb 9: 5 we cannot discuss these things in **d** now. *G3538*

DETAILED (2) [DETAIL]

2Ki 16:10 the altar, with **d** plans for its construction. H3972
Eze 39:14 *they will* **carry out a more d search**. H2983

DETAILS (3) [DETAIL]

1Ki 6:38 was finished in all its **d** according to its H1821
1Ch 28:19 me to understand all the **d** *of* the plan." H4856
1Ch 29:30 together with the **d** *of* his reign and power H3972

DETAIN (2) [DETAINED]

Ge 24:56 said to them, "*Do* not **d** me, now that the H336
Jdg 13:16 "Even though *you* **d** me, I will not eat H6806

DETAINED (2) [DETAIN]

1Sa 21: 7 was there that day, **d** before the LORD; he H6806
Da 10:13 because I **was d** there with the king of H3855

DETECT (3)

Job 39:29 it looks for food; its eyes **d** it from afar. H5564
Ps 36: 2 too much to **d** or hate their sin. H5162
Ob 7 will set a trap for you, but you will not **d** it. H9312

DETER (1) [DETRIMENT]

Mt 3:14 But John *tried to* **d** him, saying, "I need to *G1361*

DETERMINATE (KJV) DELIBERATE

DETERMINE (9) [DETERMINED, DETERMINES]

Ex 12: 4 *You are to* **d** the **amount** *of* lamb **needed** H4082
Ex 22: 8 they must **d** whether the owner of the NDT
Lev 14:57 to **d** when something is clean or unclean H3723
Lev 25:27 *they are to* **d the value** *for* the years since H3108
Lev 27:18 the priest *will* **d** the value according to the H3108
Lev 27:23 the priest *will* **d** its value up to the Year of H3108
Dt 19: 3 **D** the distances involved and divide into H3922
Ne 10:34 have cast lots to **d** when each of our families NDT
Da 11:17 *He will* **d** to come with the might of H8492+7156

DETERMINED (32) [DETERMINE]

Jos 17:12 the Canaanites *were* **d** to live in that H3283
Jdg 1:27 the Canaanites *were* **d** to live in that H3283
Jdg 1:35 And the Amorites *were* **d** also to hold out H3283
Ru 1:18 realized that Ruth *was* **d** to go with her, H599
1Sa 20: 7 you can be sure that he *is* **d** to harm me. H3983
1Sa 20: 9 inkling that my father *was* **d** to harm you, H3983
2Sa 17:14 For the LORD *had* **d** to frustrate the good H7422
1Ki 7:47 the weight of the bronze **was** not **d**. H2983
1Ki 20:42 have set free a man I had **d should die**. H3051
2Ki 12:11 When the **amount** *had* **been d**, they gave H9419
1Ch 12:38 to Hebron **fully d** to make H928+4222+8969
2Ch 25:16 "I know that God *has* **d** to destroy you H3619
Est 9: 2 Xerxes to attack *those* **d** *to* destroy them. H1335
Job 14: 5 A person's days *are* **d**; you have decreed H3076
Ecc 7:23 I said, "*I am* **d** *to be* **wise**"—but this was AIT
Isa 14:26 This is the plan **d** for the whole world; this H3619
Jer 21:10 *I have* **d** to do this city harm and not H8492+7156
Jer 26:21 the king *was* **d** to put him to death. H1335
Jer 42:15 'If you *are* **d** to go to Egypt H8492+7156+8492
Jer 42:17 all who *are* **d** to go to Egypt to H8492+7156
Jer 44:11 *I am* **d** to bring disaster on you and H8492+7156
Jer 44:12 of Judah who *were* **d** to go to Egypt H8492+7156
La 2: 8 The LORD **d** to tear down the wall around H3108
Da 6:14 *he was* **d** to rescue Daniel and A10682+10104
Da 11:36 for *what has* **been d** must take place. H3076
Hos 11: 7 My people *are* **d** to turn from me. H9428
Hab 2:13 LORD Almighty **d** that the people's H4946+907
Zec 1: 6 practices deserve, just as *he* **d** to do. H2372
Zec 8:14 "Just as *I had* **d** to bring disaster on you H2372
Zec 8:15 "so now *I have* **d** to do good again to H2372
Ac 5:28 your teaching and *are* **d** to make us guilty *G1089*
1Co 15:38 But God gives it a body as *he has* **d**, and *G2527*

DETERMINES (2) [DETERMINE]

Ps 147: 4 *He* **d** the number of the stars and calls H4948
1Co 12:11 distributes them to each one, just as *he* **d**. *G1089*

DETEST (15) [DETESTABLE, DETESTED, DETESTS]

Nu 21: 5 And we **d** this miserable food! H7762
Dt 7:26 Regard it as vile and **utterly d** it, for H9493+9493
Job 9:31 pit so that even my clothes *would* **d** me. H9493
Job 19:19 All my intimate friends **d** me; those I love H9493
Job 30:10 *They* **d** me and keep their distance; they H9493
Ps 5: 6 bloodthirsty and deceitful *you*, LORD, **d**. H9493
Ps 119:163 I hate and **d** falsehood but I love your law. H9493
Pr 8: 7 what is true, for my lips **d** wickedness. H9359
Pr 13:19 to the soul, but fools **d** turning from evil. H9359
Pr 16:12 Kings **d** wrongdoing, for a throne is H9359
Pr 24: 9 of folly are sin, and people **d** a mocker. H9359
Pr 29:27 The righteous **d** the dishonest; the wicked H9359
Pr 29:27 the dishonest; the wicked **d** the upright. H9359
Am 5:10 justice in court and **d** the one who tells H9493
Am 6: 8 the pride of Jacob and **d** his fortresses; H8533

DETESTABLE (106) [DETEST]

Ge 43:32 with Hebrews, for that is **d** to Egyptians. H9359
Ge 46:34 all shepherds are **d** *to* the Egyptians." H9359
Ex 8:26 LORD our God would be **d** *to* the Egyptians. H9359
Ex 8:26 we offer sacrifices that are **d** in their eyes, H9359
Lev 18:22 man as one does with a woman; that is **d**. H9359
Lev 18:26 you must not do any of these **d things**, H9359
Lev 18:29 who does any of these **d things**— H9359
Lev 18:30 not follow any of the **d** customs that were H9359
Lev 20:13 both of them have done **what** is **d**. H9359
Dt 7:25 for it is **d** *to* the LORD your God. H9359
Dt 7:26 Do not bring a **d thing** into your house H9359
Dt 12:31 do all kinds of **d things** the LORD hates. H9359
Dt 13:14 proved that this **d thing** has been done H9359
Dt 14: 3 Do not eat any **d thing**. H9359
Dt 17: 1 flaw in it, for that would be **d** *to* him. H9359
Dt 17: 4 proved that this **d thing** has been done in H9359
Dt 18: 9 to imitate the **d ways** *of* the nations there. H9359
Dt 18:12 who does these things is **d** *to* the LORD; H9359
Dt 18:12 of these same **d practices** the LORD your H9359
Dt 20:18 you to follow all the **d things** they do in H9359
Dt 24: 4 That would be **d** in the eyes of the LORD H9359
Dt 27:15 makes an idol—a **thing d** *to* the LORD, the H9359
Dt 29:17 among them their **d images** and idols of H9199
Dt 32:16 gods and angered him with their **d idols**. H9359
1Ki 11: 5 Molek the **d god** *of* the Ammonites. H9199
1Ki 11: 7 place for Chemosh the **d god** *of* Moab, H9199
1Ki 11: 7 Molek the **d god** *of* the Ammonites. H9199
1Ki 14:24 in all the **d practices** *of* the nations the H9359
2Ki 16: 3 engaging in the **d practices** *of* the nations H9359
2Ki 21: 2 following the **d practices** *of* the nations H9359
2Ki 21:11 king of Judah has committed these **d sins**. H9359
2Ki 23:13 for Molek the **d god** *of* the people of H9359
2Ki 23:24 all the other **d things** seen in Judah H9199
2Ch 15: 8 He removed the **d idols** from the whole H9199
2Ch 28: 3 engaging in the **d practices** *of* the nations H9359
2Ch 33: 2 following the **d practices** *of* the nations H9359
2Ch 34:33 removed all the **d idols** from all the H9359
2Ch 36: 8 the **d things** he did and all that was found H9359
2Ch 36:14 all the **d practices** *of* the nations and H9359
Ezr 9: 1 peoples with their **d practices**, H9359
Ezr 9:11 By their **d practices** they have filled it with H9359
Ezr 9:14 the peoples who commit such **d practices**? H9359
Pr 6:16 the LORD hates, seven that are **d** *to* him: H9359
Pr 21:27 The sacrifice of the wicked is **d**—how H9359
Pr 28: 9 to my instruction, even their prayers are **d**. H9359
Isa 1:13 Your incense is **d** to me. New Moons, H9359
Isa 41:24 worthless; whoever chooses you is **d**. H9359
Isa 44:19 Shall I make a **d thing** from what is left H9359
Jer 2: 7 my land and made my inheritance **d**. H9359
Jer 4: 1 "If you put your **d idols** out of my sight H9199
Jer 6:15 Are they ashamed of their **d** conduct? No H9359
Jer 7:10 are safe"—safe to do all these **d things**? H9359
Jer 7:30 have set up their **d idols** in the house that H9199
Jer 8:12 Are they ashamed of their **d** conduct? No H9359
Jer 13:27 I have seen your **d acts** on the hills and in H9199
Jer 16:18 filled my inheritance with their **d idols**." H9359
Jer 32:35 should do such a **d thing** and so make H9359
Jer 44: 4 'Do not do this **d** thing that I hate! H9359
Jer 44:22 wicked actions and the **d things** you did, H9359
Eze 5: 9 Because of all your **d idols**, I will do to you H9359
Eze 5:11 with all your vile images and **d practices**, H9359
Eze 6: 9 have done and for all their **d practices**. H9359
Eze 6:11 wicked and **d practices** *of* the people of H9359
Eze 7: 3 repay you for all your **d practices**. H9359
Eze 7: 4 for the **d practices** among you. H9359
Eze 7: 8 repay you for all your **d practices**. H9359
Eze 7: 9 for the **d practices** among you. H9359
Eze 7:20 jewelry and used it to make their **d** idols. H9359
Eze 8: 6 the utterly **d things** the Israelites are doing H9359
Eze 8: 6 you will see **things** *that* are even more **d**." H9359
Eze 8: 9 the wicked and **d things** they are doing H9359
Eze 8:13 them doing **things** *that* are even more **d**." H9359
Eze 8:15 will see **things** *that* are even more **d** than H9359
Eze 8:17 of Judah to do the **d things** they are doing H9359
Eze 9: 4 over all the **d things** that are done in H9359
Eze 11:18 remove all its vile images and **d idols**. H9359
Eze 11:21 devoted to their vile images and **d idols**, H9359
Eze 12:16 may acknowledge all their **d practices**. H9359
Eze 14: 6 idols and renounce all your **d practices**! H9359
Eze 16: 2 confront Jerusalem with her **d practices** H9359
Eze 16:22 In all your **d practices** and your prostitution H9359
Eze 16:36 because of all your **d** idols, and H9359
Eze 16:43 lewdness to all your other **d practices**? H9359
Eze 16:47 their ways and copied their **d practices**, H9359
Eze 16:50 were haughty and did **d things** before me. H9359
Eze 16:51 You have done more **d things** than they H9359
Eze 16:58 of your lewdness and your **d practices**, H9359
Eze 18:12 He looks to the idols. He does **d things**. H9359
Eze 18:13 Because he has done all these **d things** H9359
Eze 18:24 does the same **d things** the wicked person H9359
Eze 20: 4 them with the **d practices** *of* their H9359
Eze 22: 2 Then confront her with all her **d practices** H9359
Eze 22:11 one man commits a **d offense** with his H9359
Eze 23:36 Then confront them with their **d practices**, H9359

Eze 33:26 you do **d things**, and each of you H9359
Eze 33:29 of all the **d things** they have done. H9359
Eze 36:31 yourselves for your sins and **d practices**. H9359
Eze 43: 8 defiled my holy name by their **d practices**. H9359
Eze 44: 6 Enough of your **d practices**, people of H9359
Eze 44: 7 In addition to all your other **d practices** H9359
Eze 44:13 must bear the shame of their **d practices**. H9359
Mal 2:11 A **d thing** has been committed in Israel H9359
Lk 16:15 people value highly is **d** in God's sight. *G1007*
Titus 1:16 They are **d**, disobedient and unfit for *G1008*
1Pe 4: 3 carousing and **d** idolatry. *G116*
Rev 18: 2 a haunt for every unclean and **d** animal. *G3631*

DETESTED (1) [DETEST]
Zec 11: 8 The flock **d** me, and I grew weary H1041

DETESTS (14) [DETEST]
Dt 22: 5 the LORD your God **d** anyone who does this H9359
Dt 23:18 because the LORD your God **d** them both. H9359
Dt 25:16 For the LORD your God **d** anyone who does H9359
Pr 3:32 For the LORD **d** the perverse but takes the H9359
Pr 11: 1 The LORD **d** dishonest scales, but accurate H9359
Pr 11:20 The LORD **d** those whose hearts are H9359
Pr 12:22 The LORD **d** lying lips, but he delights in H9359
Pr 15: 8 The LORD **d** the sacrifice of the wicked, but H9359
Pr 15: 9 The LORD **d** the way of the wicked, but he H9359
Pr 15:26 The LORD **d** the thoughts of the wicked, but H9359
Pr 16: 5 The LORD **d** all the proud of heart. H9359
Pr 17:15 the innocent—the LORD **d** them both. H9359
Pr 20:10 measures—the LORD **d** them both. H9359
Pr 20:23 The LORD **d** differing weights, and H9359

DETHRONED (1) [THRONE]
2Ch 36: 3 The king of Egypt **d** him in Jerusalem and H6073

DETRIMENT (1) [DETER]
Ezr 4:22 to the **d** *of* the royal interests? A10472

DEUEL (5)
Nu 1:14 from Gad, Eliasaph son of **D**; H1979
Nu 2:14 of the people of Gad is Eliasaph son of **D**. H1979
Nu 7:42 On the sixth day Eliasaph son of **D**, the H1979
Nu 7:47 This was the offering of Eliasaph son of **D**. H1979
Nu 10:20 Eliasaph son of **D** was over the H1979

DEVASTATE (7) [DEVASTATED, DEVASTATION]
Jos 22:33 war against them to **d** the country where H8845
Job 12:15 if he lets them loose, *they* **d** the land. H2200
Isa 24: 1 is going to lay waste the earth and **d** it; H1191
Jer 19: 8 I will **d** this city and make it an object of NDT
Jer 51: 2 Babylon to winnow her and *to* **d** her land; H1327
Hos 11: 9 fierce anger, nor will I **d** Ephraim again. H8845
Zec 11: 6 *They will* **d** the land, and I will not rescue H4198

DEVASTATED (13) [DEVASTATE]
Jdg 11:33 *He* **d** twenty towns from H5782+1524+4394+4804
Jdg 11:35 You have brought me down and I am **d**. H6579
Job 16: 7 me out; *you have* **d** my entire household. H9037
Ps 78:45 devoured them, and frogs that **d** them. H8845
Ps 79: 7 devoured Jacob and **d** his homeland. H9037
Isa 61: 4 ruins and restore the *places* long **d**; H9037
Isa 61: 4 cities *that have been* **d** *for* generations. H9037
Jer 4:30 are you doing, you **d** *one*? Why dress H8720
Eze 6: 6 so that your altars will be laid waste and **d** H870
Eze 19: 7 down their strongholds and **d** their towns. H2990
Eze 29:12 land of Egypt desolate among **d** lands, H9037
Hos 10:14 so that all your fortresses *will* **be d**—as H8720
Hos 10:14 as Shalman **d** Beth Arbel on the day of H8720

DEVASTATION (2) [DEVASTATE]
1Sa 5: 6 *he* **brought d** *on* them and afflicted them H9037
Da 8:24 *He will* **cause** astounding **d** and will H8845

DEVELOPED (2)
Eze 16: 7 You grew and **d** and entered puberty H1540
Jn 3:25 An argument **d** between some of John's *G1181*

DEVIATE (1)
2Ch 8:15 *They did* not **d** *from* the king's commands H6073

DEVICES (2) [DEVISE]
2Ch 26:15 Jerusalem he made **d** invented for use on H3115
Ps 81:12 stubborn hearts to follow their own **d**. H4600

DEVIL (32) [DEVIL'S]

DEVIL, DEVILS (KJV) DEMON, DEMON-POSSESSED, DEMONS, FALSE GODS, GOAT IDOLS
Mt 4: 1 the wilderness to be tempted by the **d**. *G1333*
Mt 4: 5 Then the **d** took him to the holy city and *G1333*
Mt 4: 8 the **d** took him to a very high mountain *G1333*
Mt 4:11 Then the **d** left him, and angels came *G1333*
Mt 13:39 the enemy who sows them is the **d** *G1333*
Mt 25:41 fire prepared *for* the **d** and his angels. *G1333*
Lk 4: 2 forty days he was tempted by the **d**. *G1333*
Lk 4: 3 The **d** said to him, "If you are the Son of *G1333*
Lk 4: 5 The **d** led him up to a high place and *G1333*
Lk 4: 9 The **d** led him to Jerusalem and had him NDT
Lk 4:13 When the **d** had finished all this tempting *G1333*
Lk 8:12 then the **d** comes and takes away the *G1333*
Jn 6:70 the Twelve? Yet one of you is a **d**!" *G1333*
Jn 8:44 to your father, the **d**, and you want to carry *G1333*
Jn 13: 2 the **d** had already prompted Judas *G1333*
Ac 10:38 all who were under the power of the **d**, *G1333*
Ac 13:10 "You are a child *of* the **d** and an enemy of *G1333*
Eph 4:27 do not give the **d** a foothold. *G1333*
1Ti 3: 6 fall under the *same* judgment *as* the **d**. *G1333*
2Ti 2:26 senses and escape from the trap *of* the **d**, *G1333*
Heb 2:14 the power of death—that is, the **d**— *G1333*
Jas 4: 7 Resist the **d**, and he will flee from *G1333*
1Pe 5: 8 Your enemy the **d** prowls around like a *G1333*
1Jn 3: 8 one who does what is sinful is of the **d**, *G1333*
1Jn 3: 8 because the **d** has been sinning from the *G1333*
1Jn 3:10 are and who the children *of* the **d** are: *G1333*
Jude 9 was disputing *with* the **d** about the body *G1333*
Rev 2:10 the **d** will put some of you in prison to test *G1333*
Rev 12: 9 that ancient serpent called the **d**, or Satan, *G1333*
Rev 12:12 because the **d** has gone down to you! *G1333*
Rev 20: 2 ancient serpent, who is the **d**, or Satan, *G1333*
Rev 20:10 And the **d**, who deceived them, was *G1333*

DEVIL'S (3) [DEVIL]
Eph 6:11 take your stand against the **d** schemes. *G1333*
1Ti 3: 7 not fall into disgrace and into the **d** trap. *G1333*
1Jn 3: 8 God appeared was to destroy the **d** work. *G1333*

DEVIOUS (5) [DEVISE]
2Sa 22:27 to the **d** you show yourself shrewd. H6836
Ps 18:26 to the **d** you show yourself shrewd. H6836
Pr 2:15 are crooked and *who are* **d** in their ways. H4279
Pr 14: 2 who despise him *are* **d** *in* their ways. H4279
Pr 21: 8 The way of the guilty is **d**, but the conduct H2203

DEVISE (9) [DEVICES, DEVISED, DEVISES, DEVISING]
Ps 21:11 evil against you and **d** wicked schemes, H3108
Ps 35:20 **d** false accusations against those who H3108
Ps 58: 2 in your heart *you* **d** injustice, and your H7188
Ps 119:150 *Those who* **d** wicked schemes are near H8103
Ps 140: 2 who **d** evil **plans** in their hearts and stir up H3108
Ps 140: 4 the violent, who **d ways** to trip my feet. H3108
Pr 12: 2 he condemns **those** *who d* wicked schemes AIT
Isa 8:10 **D** your strategy, but it will be thwarted H6418
Eze 38:10 your mind and *you will* **d** an evil scheme. H3108

DEVISED (9) [DEVISE]
2Sa 14:13 "Why then *have you* **d** a thing like this H3108
Est 8: 3 which *he had* **d** against the Jews. H3108
Est 8: 5 **d** and wrote to destroy the Jews in all the H4742
Est 9:25 scheme Haman *had* **d** against the Jews H3108
Ps 64: 6 say, "We have **d** a perfect plan! H2924
Jer 49:30 against you; *he has* **d** a plan against you. H3108
Da 11:25 stand because of the plots **d** against him. H3108
Mt 28:12 had met with the elders and **d** a plan, *G3284*
2Pe 1:16 did not follow **cleverly d** stories when we *G5054*

DEVISES (5) [DEVISE]
2Sa 14:14 *he* **d** ways so that a banished person does H3108
Ps 10: 2 who are caught in the schemes *he* **d**. H3108
Pr 6:18 a heart *that* **d** wicked schemes, feet that H3086
Pr 14:17 the **one** *who d* evil schemes is hated. AIT
Na 1:11 evil against the LORD and **d** wicked **plans**. H3619

DEVISING (1) [DEVISE]
Jer 18:11 disaster for you and **d** a plan against you. H3108

DEVOTE (11) [DEVOTED, DEVOTES, DEVOTING, DEVOTION, DEVOUT]
1Ch 22:19 Now **d** your heart and soul to seeking the H5989
2Ch 31: 4 Levites so *they could* **d** *themselves* to the H2616
Job 11:13 "Yet if you **d** your heart to him and stretch H3922
Jer 30:21 who is he who *will* **d** himself to be H6842
Mic 4:13 *You will* **d** their ill-gotten gains to the H3049
1Co 7: 5 so that *you may* **d** *yourselves* **to** prayer. *G5390*
Col 4: 2 **D** *yourselves* to prayer, being watchful *G4674*
1Ti 1: 4 or *to* **d** *themselves* to myths and endless *G4668*
1Ti 4:13 **d** *yourself* **to** the public reading of *G4668*
Titus 3: 8 be careful *to* **d** *themselves* **to** doing what *G4613*
Titus 3:14 must learn *to* **d** *themselves* to doing what *G4613*

DEVOTED (34) [DEVOTE]
Lev 27:21 like a field **d** to the LORD; it will H3051
Lev 27:28 everything so **d** is most holy to the LORD. H3051
Lev 27:29 'No person **d to destruction** may be H3049+3051
Nu 18:14 in Israel that is **d to the** LORD is yours. H3051
Jos 6:17 all that is in it are to be **d** to the LORD. H3051
Jos 6:18 But keep away from the **d things**, so that H3051
Jos 6:21 *They* **d** the city to the LORD **and destroyed** H3049
Jos 7: 1 were unfaithful in regard to the **d things**; H3051
Jos 7:11 They have taken some of the **d things** H3051
Jos 7:12 whatever among you is **d to destruction**. H3051
Jos 7:13 There are **d things** among you H3051
Jos 7:15 is caught with the **d things** shall be H3051
Jos 22:20 was unfaithful in regard to the **d things**, H3051
1Sa 15:21 the best of what was **d to God**, in order to H3051
1Ki 11: 4 his heart was not **fully d** to the LORD his H8969
1Ki 15: 3 his heart was not **fully d** to the LORD his H8969
1Ch 2: 7 by violating the ban on taking **d things**. H3051
2Ch 17: 6 His heart *was* **d** to the ways of the LORD H1467
Ezr 7:10 For Ezra *had* **d** himself to the study and H3922
Ne 5:16 Instead, *I* **d** *myself* to the work on this wall H2616
Eze 11:21 whose hearts *are* **d** to their vile images H2143
Eze 20:16 For their hearts *were* **d** to their idols. H2143+339
Eze 44:29 everything in Israel **d** to the LORD will H3051
Mt 6:24 or *you will be* **d** to the one and despise the *G504*
Mt 15: 5 to help their father or mother is '**d to God**, *G1565*
Mk 7:11 mother is Corban (that is, **d to God**)— *G1565*
Lk 16:13 or *you will be* **d** to the one and despise the *G504*
Ac 2:42 *They* **d** *themselves* **to** the apostles' *G1639+4674*
Ac 18: 5 Paul **d** *himself* **exclusively** to preaching *G5309*
Ro 12:10 *Be* **d** to one another in love. Honor one *G5816*
1Co 7:34 Her aim is to be **d to the Lord** in both body *G41*
1Co 16:15 and *they have* **d** themselves to the service *G5435*
2Co 7:12 see for yourselves *how* **d** to us you are. *G5082*
1Ti 6: 2 believers and *are* **d to** the welfare of their *G514*

DEVOTES (1) [DEVOTE]
Lev 27:28 that a person owns and **d** to the LORD— H3049

DEVOTING (1) [DEVOTE]
1Ti 5:10 in trouble and **d** *herself* to all kinds of *G2051*

D

DEVOTION (11) [DEVOTE]
2Ki 20: 3 and with **wholehearted d** and have H4222+8969
1Ch 28: 9 him with **wholehearted d** and with H4213+8969
1Ch 29: 3 in my **d** to the temple of my God I now H8354
1Ch 29:19 the **wholehearted d** to keep H4222+8969
2Ch 32:32 reign and his **acts of d** are written in the H2876
2Ch 35:26 reign and his **acts of d** in accordance with H2876
Job 15: 4 undermine piety and hinder **d** to God. H8491
Isa 38: 3 and with **wholehearted d** and have H4213+8969
Jer 2: 2 " 'I remember the **d** *of* your youth, how as H2876
1Co 7:35 in a right way *in* undivided **d** to the Lord. *G2339*
2Co 11: 3 from your **sincere** and pure **d** to Christ. *G605*

DEVOUR (56) [DEVOURED, DEVOURING, DEVOURS]
Ex 10: 5 *They will* **d** what little you have left after H430
Ex 10:12 over the land and **d** everything growing in H430
Lev 26:38 the land of your enemies *will* **d** you. H430
Nu 14: 9 of the land, because we will **d** them. H4312
Nu 24: 8 *They* **d** hostile nations and break their H430
Dt 28:38 will harvest little, because locusts *will* **d** it. H2887
Dt 28:51 *They will* **d** the young of your livestock and H430
Dt 32:22 *It will* **d** the earth and its harvests and set H430
2Sa 2:26 out to Joab, "*Must* the sword **d** forever? H430
1Ki 21:23 'Dogs *will* **d** Jezebel by the wall of Jezreel H430
2Ki 9:10 dogs *will* **d** her on the plot of ground at H430
2Ki 9:36 at Jezreel dogs *will* **d** Jezebel's flesh. H430
2Ch 7:13 command locusts to **d** the land or send a H430
Job 20:21 Nothing is left for him to **d**; his prosperity H430
Job 20:26 will consume him and **d** what is left in his H8286
Ps 14: 4 *They* **d** my people as though eating bread H430
Ps 27: 2 the wicked advance against me to **d** me, H430
Ps 53: 4 *They* **d** my people as though eating bread H430
Pr 30:14 are set with knives to **d** the poor from the H430
Isa 9:20 On the right *they will* **d**, but still be hungry H1616
Isa 31: 8 a sword, not of mortals, *will* **d** them. H430
Isa 51: 8 a garment; the worm *will* **d** them like wool. H430
Isa 56: 9 the field, come and **d**, all you beasts of the H430
Jer 5:17 *They will* **d** your harvests and food, devour H430
Jer 5:17 food, **d** your sons and daughters H430
Jer 5:17 daughters; *they will* **d** your flocks and herds H430
Jer 5:17 flocks and herds, **d** your vines and fig trees. H430
Jer 8:16 They have come *to* **d** the land and H430
Jer 12: 9 gather all the wild beasts; bring them to **d**. H433
Jer 12:12 sword of the LORD *will* **d** from one end of H430
Jer 15: 3 the wild animals to **d** and destroy. H430
Jer 30:16 " 'But all *who* **d** you will be devoured; all H430
Jer 46:10 The sword *will* **d** till it is satisfied, till it has H430
Jer 50:17 The first *to* **d** them was the king of Assyria H430
Eze 22:25 tearing its prey; *they* **d** people, take H430
Eze 34:28 the nations, nor *will* wild animals **d** them. H430
Eze 35:12 waste and have been given over to us to **d**." H433
Eze 36:13 "You **d** people and deprive your nation of H430
Eze 36:14 therefore *you will* no longer **d** people or H430
Da 7:23 kingdoms and *will* **d** the whole earth, A10030
Hos 2:12 a thicket, and wild animals *will* **d** them. H430
Hos 5: 7 New Moon feasts, *he will* **d** their fields. H430
Hos 7: 7 are hot as an oven; *they* **d** their rulers. H430
Hos 11: 6 *it will* **d** their false prophets and put an H3983
Hos 13: 8 like a lion *I will* **d** them—a wild H430
Am 5: 6 like a fire; *it will* **d** them, and Bethel H430
Na 2:13 the sword *will* **d** your young lions. H430
Na 3:15 *they will* **d** you like a swarm of locusts. H430
Hab 1: 8 They fly like an eagle swooping to **d**; H430
Hab 3:14 as though about to **d** the wretched who H430
Zec 11: 1 Lebanon, so that fire *may* **d** your cedars! H430
Mk 12:40 They **d** widows' houses and for a show *G2983*
Lk 20:47 They **d** widows' houses and for a show *G2983*
Gal 5:15 If you bite and **d** each other, watch out *G2983*
1Pe 5: 8 a roaring lion looking for someone *to* **d**. *G2927*
Rev 12: 4 so that *it might* **d** her child the moment *G2983*

DEVOURED (27) [DEVOUR]
Ge 37:20 say that a ferocious animal **d** him. H430
Ge 37:33 Some ferocious animal *has* **d** him. H430
Ex 10:15 *They* **d** all that was left after the hail H430
Nu 26:10 died when the fire **d** the 250 men. H430
Job 31:39 if *I have* **d** its yield without payment or H430
Ps 44:11 gave us up to be **d** like sheep and have H4407
Ps 78:45 He sent swarms of flies that **d** them, and H430
Ps 79: 7 for *they have* **d** Jacob and devastated his H430
Isa 1:20 resist and rebel, *you will* **be d** *by* the sword." H430
Isa 9:12 from the west *have* **d** Israel with open H430
Isa 49:19 and *those who* **d** you will be far away. H1180
Jer 2: 3 his harvest; all *who* **d** her were held guilty H430
Jer 2:30 Your sword *has* **d** your prophets like a H430
Jer 10:25 For *they have* **d** Jacob; they have devoured H430
Jer 10:25 *they have* **d** him completely and destroyed H430
Jer 30:16 " 'But all who devour you *will* **be d**; all your H430
Jer 50: 7 Whoever found them **d** them; their H430

Jer 51:34 "Nebuchadnezzar king of Babylon *has* **d** us H430
Eze 7:15 in the city *will be* **d** *by* famine and plague H430
Eze 33:27 I will give to the wild animals to *be* **d**, H430
Da 7: 7 it crushed and **d** its victims and trampled A10030
Da 7:19 beast that crushed and **d** its victims and A10030
Joel 1:19 fire *has* **d** the pastures in the wilderness H430
Joel 1:20 dried up and fire *has* **d** the pastures in the H430
Am 4: 9 Locusts **d** your fig and olive trees, yet you H430
Am 7: 4 it dried up the great deep and **d** the land. H430
Rev 20: 9 fire came down from heaven and **d** them. *G2983*

DEVOURING (3) [DEVOUR]

Dt 9: 3 who goes across ahead of you like a **d** fire. H430
Isa 29: 6 tempest and flames of a **d** fire. H430
Mal 3:11 I will prevent pests from **d** your crops, and H8845

DEVOURS (11) [DEVOUR]

Ge 49:27 in the morning *he* **d** the prey, in the H430
Nu 13:32 "The land we explored **d** those living in it. H430
Nu 23:24 that does not rest till *it* **d** its prey and drinks H430
Dt 32:42 drunk with blood, while my sword **d** flesh: H430
2Sa 11:25 the sword **d** one as well as another. H430
Job 18:13 of his skin; death's firstborn **d** his limbs. H430
Job 22:20 foes are destroyed, and fire **d** their wealth. H430
Ps 50: 3 not be silent; a fire **d** before him, and H430
Jer 46:14 for the sword **d** those around you. H430
Joel 2: 3 Before them fire **d**, behind them a flame H430
Rev 11: 5 from their mouths and **d** their enemies. *G2983*

DEVOUT (7) [DEVOTE]

1Ki 18: 3 Obadiah was a **d** believer in the LORD. H4394
Isa 57: 1 it to heart; the **d** are taken away H2876+408
Lk 2:25 called Simeon, who was righteous and **d**. *G2327*
Ac 10: 2 all his family were **d** and God-fearing; *G2356*
Ac 10: 7 his servants and a **d** soldier who was one *G2356*
Ac 13:43 of the Jews and **d** converts to Judaism *G4936*
Ac 22:12 He was a **d** observer of the law and highly *G2327*

DEW (36)

Ge 27:28 give you heaven's **d** and earth's richness H3228
Ge 27:39 away from the **d** *of* heaven above. H3228
Ex 16:13 there was a layer of **d** around the camp. H3228
Ex 16:14 When the **d** was gone, thin flakes like frost H3228
Nu 11: 9 When the **d** settled on the camp at night H3228
Dt 32: 2 fall like rain and my words descend like **d**, H3228
Dt 33:13 with the precious **d** from heaven above H3228
Dt 33:28 new wine, where the heavens drop **d**. H3228
Jdg 6:37 If there is **d** only on the fleece and all the H3228
Jdg 6:38 the fleece and wrung out the **d**— H3228
Jdg 6:39 dry and let the ground be covered with **d**." H3228
Jdg 6:40 all the ground was covered with **d**. H3228
2Sa 1:21 may you have neither **d** nor rain, may no H3228
2Sa 17:12 will fall on him as **d** settles on the ground H3228
1Ki 17: 1 there will be neither **d** nor rain in the next H3228
Job 29:19 the **d** will lie all night on my H3228
Job 38:28 Who fathers the drops of **d**? H3228
Ps 110: 3 will come to you like **d** from the morning's H3228
Ps 133: 3 It is as if the **d** *of* Hermon were falling on H3228
Pr 3:20 divided, and the clouds let drop the **d**. H3228
Pr 19:12 but his favor is like **d** on the grass. H3228
SS 5: 2 My head is drenched with **d**, my hair with H3228
Isa 18: 4 like a cloud of **d** in the heat of harvest." H3228
Isa 26:19 your **d** is like the dew of the morning H3228
Isa 26:19 your dew is like the **d** *of* the morning; the H3228
Da 4:15 him be drenched with the **d** *of* heaven, A10299
Da 4:23 him be drenched with the **d** *of* heaven; A10299
Da 4:25 be drenched with the **d** *of* heaven. A10299
Da 4:33 drenched with the **d** *of* heaven until his A10299
Da 5:21 was drenched with the **d** *of* heaven, A10299
Hos 6: 4 like the early **d** that disappears. H3228
Hos 13: 3 like the early **d** that disappears, like H3228
Hos 14: 5 I will be like the **d** to Israel; he will H3228
Mic 5: 7 of many peoples like **d** from the LORD, H3228
Hag 1:10 have withheld their **d** and the earth its H3228
Zec 8:12 and the heavens will drop their **d**. H3228

DIADEM (1)

Isa 62: 3 a royal **d** in the hand of your God. H7565

DIAMETER (1)

1Ki 7:32 The **d** *of* each wheel was a cubit and a H7757

DIAMOND (KJV) EMERALD, FLINT

DIANA (KJV) ARTEMIS

DIBLAH (1)

Eze 6:14 a desolate waste from the desert to **D**— H1812

DIBLAIM (1)

Hos 1: 3 So he married Gomer daughter of **D**, and H1813

DIBLATHAIM See ALMON DIBLATHAIM, BETH DIBLATHAIM

DIBON (9) [DIBON GAD]

Nu 21:30 has been destroyed all the way to **D**. H1897
Nu 32: 3 "Ataroth, **D**, Jazer, Nimrah, Heshbon H1897
Nu 32:34 The Gadites built up **D**, Ataroth, Aroer, H1897
Jos 13: 9 the whole plateau of Medeba as far as **D**, H1897
Jos 13:17 the plateau, including **D**, Bamoth Baal, H1897
Ne 11:25 settlements, in **D** and its settlements, in H1897
Isa 15: 2 **D** goes up to its temple, to its high places H1897
Jer 48:18 you inhabitants of Daughter **D**, for the H1897
Jer 48:22 to **D**, Nebo and Beth Diblathaim, H1897

DIBON GAD (2) [DIBON, GAD]

Nu 33:45 left Iye Abarim and camped at **D**. H1898
Nu 33:46 They left **D** and camped at Almon H1898

DIBRI (1)

Lev 24:11 Shelomith, the daughter of **D** the Danite.) H1828

DICTATE (2) [DICTATED, DICTATION, EDICT]

Jer 36:17 write all this? Did Jeremiah **d** it?" H4946+7023
Mic 7: 3 the powerful **d** what they desire H1819

DICTATED (5) [DICTATE]

Jer 36: 4 while Jeremiah **d** all the words the H4946+7023
Jer 36: 6 of the LORD that you wrote as I **d**. H4946+7023
Jer 36:18 "he **d** all these words to me H7924+4946+7023
Jer 36:32 as Jeremiah **d**, Baruch wrote on it all H7023
Jer 45: 1 the prophet **d** in the fourth year H4946+7023

DICTATION (1) [DICTATE]

Jer 36:27 Baruch had written *at* Jeremiah's **d**, H4946+7023

DID (1312) [DO]

Ge 3: 1 the woman, "*D* God really **say**, 'You must not AIT
Ge 3: 3 God *d* **say**, 'You must not eat fruit from AIT
Ge 4: 5 his offering *he d* not **look with favor**. AIT
Ge 6:22 Noah **d** everything just as God H6913
Ge 7: 5 And Noah **d** all that the LORD commanded H6913
Ge 8:12 out again, but this time *it d* not **return** to him. AIT
Ge 12:19 Why *d you* **say**, 'She is my sister,' so that I AIT
Ge 15:10 the birds, however, *he d* not **cut in half**. AIT
Ge 18:13 Abraham, "Why *d* Sarah **laugh** and say, 'Will AIT
Ge 18:15 so she lied and said, "*I d* not **laugh**. AIT
Ge 18:15 But he said, "Yes, *you d* **laugh**." AIT
Ge 19: 3 so strongly that *they d* **go** with him and AIT
Ge 20: 5 *D* he not **say** to me, 'She is my sister,' and AIT
Ge 20: 6 I know *you* **d** this with a clear conscience H6913
Ge 20: 6 That is why *I d* not **let** you touch her. AIT
Ge 21: 1 the LORD **d** for Sarah what he had H6913
Ge 21:26 You *d* not **tell** me, and I heard about it only AIT
Ge 26: 5 obeyed me and **d** everything I required H9068
Ge 26: 9 Why *d you* **say**, 'She is my sister'? AIT
Ge 26:29 just as *we d* not **harm** you but always treated AIT
Ge 27:20 "How *d you* **find** it so quickly, my AIT
Ge 27:23 *He d* not **recognize** him, for his hands were AIT
Ge 27:45 with you and forgets what *you* **d** to him, H6913
Ge 29:28 And Jacob **d** so. He finished the week H6913
Ge 30:40 himself and *d* not **put** them with Laban's AIT
Ge 31:27 Why *d you* **run off** secretly and deceive me AIT
Ge 31:30 But why *d you* **steal** my gods?" AIT
Ge 31:32 Now Jacob *d* not **know** that Rachel had AIT
Ge 31:39 *I d* not **bring** you animals torn by wild beasts AIT
Ge 34: 5 so he **d nothing** *about* it until they came H3087
Ge 38:10 What *he* **d** was wicked in the LORD's sight H6913
Ge 38:20 back from the woman, but *he d* not **find** her. AIT
Ge 38:23 After all, *I d* **send** her this young goat, but AIT
Ge 38:26 And *he d* not **sleep with** her again. AIT
Ge 39: 3 LORD gave him success in everything **he d**, H6913
Ge 39: 6 *he d* not **concern** *himself with* anything AIT
Ge 39:23 gave him success in whatever he **d**. H6913
Ge 40:23 however, *d* not **remember** Joseph; he forgot AIT
Ge 42: 4 But Jacob *d* not **send** Benjamin, Joseph's AIT
Ge 42: 8 his brothers, they *d* not **recognize** him. AIT
Ge 42:23 They *d* not **realize** that Joseph could AIT
Ge 43: 6 "Why *d you* **bring** *this* **trouble** on me by AIT
Ge 43:17 The man **d** as Joseph told him and took H6913
Ge 44: 2 his grain." And *he* **d** as Joseph said. H6913
Ge 45:21 So the sons of Israel **d** this. Joseph gave H6913
Ge 45:26 Jacob was stunned; *he d* not **believe** them. AIT
Ge 46:34 from our boyhood on, just as our fathers **d**. NDT
Ge 47:22 However, *he d* not **buy** the land of the priests AIT
Ge 47:22 That is why *they d* not **sell** their land. AIT
Ge 47:26 of the priests that *d* not **become** Pharaoh's. AIT
Ge 50:12 So Jacob's sons **d** as he had commanded H6913
Ge 50:15 us back for all the wrongs *we* **d** *to* him?" H1694
Ex 1:17 feared God and *d* not **do** what the king of AIT
Ex 2:14 "What I **d** must have become known." NDT
Ex 2:20 "Why *d you* **leave** him? Invite him AIT
Ex 3: 2 though the bush was on fire it *d* not **burn up**. AIT
Ex 4: 1 me and say, 'The LORD *d* not **appear** to you'?" AIT
Ex 6: 3 *I d* not **make myself fully known** to them AIT
Ex 6: 9 but *they d* not **listen** to him because of their AIT
Ex 7: 6 Moses and Aaron *d* just as the LORD H6913
Ex 7:10 went to Pharaoh and **d** just as the LORD H6913
Ex 7:11 magicians also **d** the same things by H6913
Ex 7:20 Moses and Aaron **d** just as the LORD had H6913
Ex 7:22 Egyptian magicians **d** the same things by H6913
Ex 7:23 his palace, and *d* not **take** even this *to* heart. AIT
Ex 8: 7 But the magicians **d** the same things by H6913
Ex 8:13 And the LORD **d** what Moses asked. H6913
Ex 8:17 *They* **d** this, and when Aaron stretched out H6913
Ex 8:24 And the LORD **d** this. Dense swarms of flies H6913
Ex 8:31 the LORD **d** what Moses asked. H6913
Ex 9: 6 And the next day the LORD **d** it: All the H6913
Ex 9:26 The only place *it* **d** not hail was the land H2118
Ex 12:28 The Israelites **d** just what the LORD H6913
Ex 12:35 The Israelites **d** as Moses instructed and H6913
Ex 12:39 of Egypt and *d* not **have time** to prepare food AIT
Ex 12:50 All the Israelites **d** just what the LORD had H6913
Ex 13: 8 of what the LORD **d** for me when I came H6913
Ex 13:17 God *d* not **lead** them *on* the road through the AIT
Ex 14: 4 I am the LORD." So the Israelites **d** this. H6913
Ex 16:15 For *they d* not **know** what it was AIT
Ex 16:17 The Israelites **d** as they were told; some H6913
Ex 16:18 who gathered much *d* not **have too much**, AIT
Ex 16:18 one who gathered little *d* not **have too little**. AIT
Ex 16:24 and *it d* not **stink** or get maggots in it. AIT
Ex 17: 3 "Why *d you* **bring** us **up** out of Egypt to make AIT
Ex 17: 6 So Moses **d** this in the sight of the elders H6913
Ex 18:11 he **d** this to those who had treated Israel NDT
Ex 18:24 father-in-law and **d** everything he said. H6913
Ex 19: 4 yourselves have seen what *I* **d** to Egypt, H6913
Ex 21:36 the owner *d* not **keep** it **penned up**, the AIT
Ex 22:11 that the neighbor *d* not **lay** hands on the AIT
Ex 24:11 But God *d* not **raise** his hand against these AIT
Ex 32:14 Then the LORD **relented and d not** bring on H5714
Ex 32:21 "What *d* these people **do** to you, that AIT
Ex 32:28 The Levites **d** as Moses commanded, and H6913
Ex 32:35 of what *they* **d** *with* the calf Aaron H6913
Ex 33:11 aide Joshua son of Nun *d* not **leave** the tent. AIT
Ex 36:10 and **d the same** *with* the H2489+285+448+285S
Ex 39:32 The Israelites **d** everything just as the LORD H6913
Ex 40:16 Moses **d** everything just as the LORD H6913
Ex 40:37 if the cloud *d* not **lift**, they did not set out AIT
Ex 40:37 did not lift, *they d* not **set out**—until the day AIT
Lev 4:20 this bull just as *he* **d** with the bull for the H6913
Lev 6: 7 any of the things *they* **d** that made them H6913
Lev 8: 4 Moses **d** as the LORD commanded him, and H6913
Lev 8:36 Aaron and his sons **d** everything the LORD H6913
Lev 9:15 a sin offering as he **d** with the first one. NDT
Lev 10: 7 So *they* **d** as Moses said. H6913
Lev 16:15 do with it as *he* **d** with the bull's H6913
Lev 20:23 Because *they* **d** all these things, H6913
Lev 24:23 The Israelites **d** as the LORD commanded H6913
Lev 26:35 will have the rest *it d* not **have** during the AIT
Nu 1:54 The Israelites **d** all this just as the LORD H6913
Nu 2:34 So the Israelites **d** everything the LORD H6913
Nu 5: 4 The Israelites **d** so; they sent them outside H6913
Nu 5: 4 They **d** just as the LORD had instructed H6913
Nu 7: 9 But Moses *d* not **give** any to the Kohathites AIT
Nu 8: 3 Aaron **d** so; he set up the lamps so that H6913
Nu 8:20 Israelite community **d** with the Levites just H6913
Nu 8:22 *They* **d** with the Levites just as the LORD H6913
Nu 9: 5 and *they* **d so** in the H6913+906+2021+7175S
Nu 9: 5 The Israelites **d** everything just as the LORD H6913
Nu 9:19 obeyed the LORD's order and *d* not **set out**. AIT
Nu 11:12 *D* I **conceive** all these people? Did I give AIT
Nu 11:12 *D* I **give** them **birth**? Why do you AIT
Nu 11:20 saying, "Why *d we ever* **leave** Egypt? AIT
Nu 11:25 they prophesied—but *d* not **do** *so* **again**. AIT
Nu 11:26 the elders, but *d* not **go out** to the tent. AIT
Nu 12:15 the people *d* not **move on** till she was AIT
Nu 16:47 So Aaron **d** as Moses said, and ran into H4374
Nu 17:11 Moses **d** just as the LORD commanded him. H6913
Nu 20: 4 Why *d you* **bring** the LORD's community into AIT
Nu 20: 5 Why *d you* **bring** us **up** out of Egypt to this AIT
Nu 20:12 "Because *you d* not **trust** in me enough to AIT
Nu 20:27 Moses **d** as the LORD commanded: They H6913
Nu 21:34 Do to him what *you* **d** to Sihon king of the H6913
Nu 22:34 *I d* not **realize** you were standing in the road AIT
Nu 22:37 "*D I* not **send** you an **urgent** summons? AIT
Nu 23: 2 Balak **d** as Balaam said, and the two of H6913
Nu 23:17 Balak asked him, "What *d* the LORD **say**?" AIT
Nu 23:26 "*D I* not **tell** you I must do whatever the LORD AIT
Nu 23:30 Balak **d** as Balaam had said, and offered a H6913
Nu 24: 1 *he d* not **resort to** divination as at other times, AIT
Nu 24:12 "*D I* not **tell** the messengers you sent me, AIT
Nu 25:11 *I d* not **put an end** *to* them in my zeal. AIT
Nu 26:11 The line of Korah, however, *d* not **die out**. AIT
Nu 27:22 Moses **d** as the LORD commanded him. H6913
Nu 31:31 Eleazar the priest **d** as the LORD H6913
Nu 32: 8 is what your fathers **d** when I sent them H6913
Nu 36:10 daughters **d** as the LORD commanded H6913
Dt 1:30 will fight for you, as *he* **d** for you in Egypt H6913
Dt 1:32 you *d* not **trust** in the LORD your God AIT
Dt 2:12 just as Israel **d** in the land the LORD gave H6913
Dt 2:29 who live in Ar, **d** for us—until we cross the H6913
Dt 2:37 *you d* not **encroach** on any of the land of the AIT
Dt 3: 2 Do to him what *you* **d** to Sihon king of the H6913
Dt 3: 4 sixty cities that *we d* not **take** from them— AIT
Dt 4: 3 own eyes what the LORD **d** at Baal Peor. H6913
Dt 4:34 the LORD your God **d** for you in Egypt H6913
Dt 5: 5 of the fire and *d* not **go up** the mountain.) AIT
Dt 6:10 with large, flourishing cities *you d* not **build**, AIT
Dt 6:11 all kinds of good things *you d* not **provide**, AIT
Dt 6:11 wells *you d* not **dig**, and vineyards AIT
Dt 6:11 vineyards and olive groves *you d* not **plant**— AIT
Dt 6:16 your God to the test as *you* **d** at Massah. H5814S
Dt 7: 7 The LORD *d* not **set** *his* **affection** on you and AIT
Dt 7:18 the LORD your God **d** to Pharaoh and to all H6913
Dt 8: 4 Your clothes *d* not **wear out** and your feet did AIT
Dt 8: 4 out and your feet *d* not **swell** during these AIT
Dt 9:23 *You d* not **trust** him or obey him AIT
Dt 10:10 forty nights, as I **d** the first time, and the NDT
Dt 11: 3 the **things** he **d** in the heart of H5126
Dt 11: 4 what *he* **d** to the Egyptian army, to its H6913
Dt 11: 5 children who saw what *he* **d** for you in the H6913
Dt 11: 6 what *he* **d** to Dathan and Abiram H6913
Dt 19: 6 since he **d** it to his neighbor without malice NDT
Dt 21: 7 "Our hands *d* not **shed** this blood, nor did our AIT
Dt 21: 7 shed this blood, nor *d* our eyes **see** it done. AIT
Dt 22:14 *I d* not **find** proof of her virginity, AIT
Dt 22:17 '*I d* not **find** your daughter to be a virgin. AIT
Dt 22:24 she was in a town and *d* not **scream for help**, AIT

Dt 23: 4 For they d not come to meet you with bread AIT
Dt 24: 9 the LORD your God d to Miriam along the H6913
Dt 25:17 what the Amalekites d to you along the H6913
Dt 28:45 because you d not obey the LORD your God AIT
Dt 28:47 Because you d not serve the LORD your God AIT
Dt 28:62 because you d not obey the LORD your God. AIT
Dt 29: 2 all that the LORD d in Egypt to Pharaoh, H6913
Dt 29: 5 your clothes d not wear out, nor did the AIT
Dt 29: 5 wear out, nor d the sandals on your feet. H1162S
Dt 29: 6 I d this so that you might know that I am the NDT
Dt 29:26 to them, gods they d not know, gods he had AIT
Dt 31: 4 do to them what he d to Sihon and Og, H6913
Dt 32:17 appeared, gods your ancestors d not fear. AIT
Dt 32:51 you d not uphold my holiness among AIT
Dt 33: 9 He d not recognize his brothers or AIT
Dt 34: 9 listened to him and d what the LORD had H6913
Dt 34:11 who d all those signs and wonders the LORD NDT
Dt 34:12 deeds that Moses d in the sight of all H6913
Jos 2: 4 but I d not know where they had come from. AIT
Jos 2:10 of Egypt, and what you d to Sihon and Og H6913
Jos 4: 8 So the Israelites d as Joshua commanded H6913
Jos 4:23 The LORD your God d to the Jordan what he NDT
Jos 4:24 He d this so that all the peoples of the earth NDT
Jos 5: 4 Now this is why he d so: All those who H4576S
Jos 5:15 are standing is holy." And Joshua d so. H6913
Jos 6:14 They d this for six days. H6913
Jos 7: 6 The elders of Israel d the same, and NDT
Jos 7: 7 why d you ever bring this people across the AIT
Jos 8: 2 Ai and its king as you d to Jericho and its H6913
Jos 8: 5 out against us, as they d before, we will flee NDT
Jos 8: 6 are running away from us as they d before. NDT
Jos 8:14 But he d not know that an ambush had been AIT
Jos 8:17 in Ai or Bethel who d not go after Israel. AIT
Jos 8:19 As soon as he d this, the H5742+3338+2257S
Jos 8:26 For Joshua d not draw back the hand that AIT
Jos 8:27 But Israel d carry off for themselves the AIT
Jos 8:35 that Joshua d not read to the whole AIT
Jos 9: 9 reports of him: all that he d in Egypt, H6913
Jos 9:10 all that he d to the two kings of the H6913
Jos 9:14 their provisions but d not inquire of the LORD. AIT
Jos 9:18 But the Israelites d not attack them, because AIT
Jos 9:22 said, "Why d you deceive us by saying AIT
Jos 9:24 because of you, and that is why we d this. H6913
Jos 9:26 from the Israelites, and they d not kill them. AIT
Jos 10:28 And he d to the king of Makkedah as he H6913
Jos 10:30 And he d to its king as he had done to H6913
Jos 10:39 They d to Debir and its king as they had H6913
Jos 11: 9 Joshua d to them as the LORD had directed H6913
Jos 11:13 Yet Israel d not burn any of the cities built on AIT
Jos 11:15 Joshua, and Joshua d it; he left nothing H6913
Jos 11:22 only in Gaza, Gath and Ashdod d any survive. AIT
Jos 13:13 the Israelites d not drive out the people of AIT
Jos 16:10 They d not dislodge the Canaanites living in AIT
Jos 17:13 labor but d not drive them out completely. AIT
Jos 22:20 d not wrath come on the whole community of AIT
Jos 22:24 We d it for fear that some day your H6913
Jos 24: 5 I afflicted the Egyptians by what I d there, H6913
Jos 24: 7 your own eyes what I d to the Egyptians. H6913
Jos 24:11 fought against you, as d also the Amorites NDT
Jos 24:12 You d not do it with your own sword and NDT
Jos 24:13 a land on which you d not toil and cities you AIT
Jos 24:13 you did not toil and cities you d not build; AIT
Jos 24:13 olive groves that you d not plant. AIT
Jdg 1: 7 has paid me back for what I d to them." H6913
Jdg 1:21 however, d not drive out the Jebusites, who AIT
Jdg 1:27 But Manasseh d not drive out the people of AIT
Jdg 1:29 Nor d Ephraim drive out the Canaanites living AIT
Jdg 1:30 Neither d Zebulun drive out the Canaanites AIT
Jdg 1:30 Zebulun d subject them to forced labor. AIT
Jdg 1:31 Nor d Asher drive out those living in Akko AIT
Jdg 1:32 the land because they d not drive them out. AIT
Jdg 1:33 Neither d Naphtali drive out those living in AIT
Jdg 2:11 Then the Israelites d evil in the eyes of the H6913
Jdg 2:22 LORD and walk in it as their ancestors d." H9068S
Jdg 2:23 he d not drive them out at once by giving AIT
Jdg 3: 2 he d this only to teach warfare to the NDT
Jdg 3: 7 The Israelites d evil in the eyes of the H6913
Jdg 3:12 Again the Israelites d evil in the eyes of H6913
Jdg 3:12 because they d this evil the LORD gave H6913
Jdg 3:22 Ehud d not pull the sword out, and the fat AIT
Jdg 3:25 when he d not open the doors of the AIT
Jdg 4: 1 Again the Israelites d evil in the eyes of H6913
Jdg 5:16 Why d you stay among the sheep pens to AIT
Jdg 5:17 And Dan, why d he linger by the ships AIT
Jdg 5:18 so d Naphtali on the terraced fields. NDT
Jdg 5:23 because they d not come to help the LORD AIT
Jdg 6: 1 The Israelites d evil in the eyes of the H6913
Jdg 6: 4 way to Gaza and d not spare a living thing AIT
Jdg 6:13 'D not the LORD bring us up out of Egypt? AIT
Jdg 6:20 pour out the broth." And Gideon d so. H6913
Jdg 6:27 of his servants and d as the LORD told him. H6913
Jdg 6:27 he d it at night rather than in the daytime. H6913
Jdg 6:29 each other, "Who d this?" When they H6913
Jdg 6:29 they were told, "Gideon son of Joash d it." H6913
Jdg 6:40 That night God d so. Only the fleece was H6913
Jdg 8:18 "What kind of men d you kill at Tabor?" AIT
Jdg 8:20 But Jether d not draw his sword, because he AIT
Jdg 8:28 the Israelites and d not raise its head again. AIT
Jdg 8:34 and d not remember the LORD their God, who AIT
Jdg 9:24 God d this in order that the crime against NDT
Jdg 10: 6 Again the Israelites d evil in the eyes of H6913
Jdg 10:12 help, d I not save you from their hands? AIT
Jdg 11:15 Israel d not take the land of Moab or the AIT
Jdg 11:18 They d not enter the territory of Moab, for the AIT
Jdg 11:20 d not trust Israel to pass through his territory. AIT
Jdg 11:25 D he ever quarrel with Israel or fight with AIT
Jdg 11:39 and he d to her as he had vowed. H6913
Jdg 12: 1 "Why d you go to fight the Ammonites AIT
Jdg 13: 1 Again the Israelites d evil in the eyes of H6913
Jdg 13:16 Manoah d not realize that it was the angel of AIT
Jdg 13:19 And the LORD d an amazing thing while H6913
Jdg 13:21 the LORD d not show himself again to AIT
Jdg 14: 4 His parents d not know that this was from the AIT
Jdg 14: 9 But he d not tell them that he had taken the AIT
Jdg 14:15 D you invite us here to steal our property?" AIT
Jdg 15: 6 "Who d this?" they were told, H6913
Jdg 15:10 answered, "to do to him as he d to us." H6913
Jdg 15:11 "I merely d to them what they did to me." H6913
Jdg 15:11 "I merely did to them what they d to me." H6913
Jdg 16:20 But he d not know that the LORD had left him. AIT
Jdg 17: 6 had no king; everyone d as they saw fit. H6913
Jdg 18: 8 asked them, "How d you find things?" NDT
Jdg 19:17 are you going? Where d you come from?" AIT
Jdg 20:34 the Benjamites d not realize how near AIT
Jdg 21:22 because we d not get wives for them during AIT
Jdg 21:22 oath because you d not give your daughters AIT
Jdg 21:23 So that is what the Benjamites d. H6913
Jdg 21:25 had no king; everyone d as they saw fit. H6913
Ru 2:11 to live with a people you d not know before. AIT
Ru 2:19 asked her, "Where d you glean today? AIT
Ru 2:19 Where d you work? Blessed be the AIT
Ru 3: 6 to the threshing floor and d everything her H6913
Ru 3:15 When she d so, he poured into it six H296S
Ru 3:16 "How d it go, my daughter? H4769+905
Ru 4: 2 town and said, "Sit here," and they d so. H3782S
1Sa 1:22 Hannah d not go. She said to her husband AIT
1Sa 2:25 however, d not listen to their father's rebuke AIT
1Sa 2:27 'D I not clearly reveal myself to your AIT
1Sa 3: 5 But Eli said, "I d not call; go back and lie AIT
1Sa 3: 6 Eli said, "I d not call; go back and lie AIT
1Sa 3: 7 Now Samuel d not yet know the LORD: The AIT
1Sa 4: 3 "Why d the LORD bring defeat on us today AIT
1Sa 4:20 But she d not respond or pay any attention. AIT
1Sa 5:12 Those who d not die were afflicted with AIT
1Sa 6: 6 and Pharaoh d? H3877+906+4213+4392S
1Sa 6: 6 d they not send the Israelites out so they AIT
1Sa 6:10 So they d this. They took two such cows H6913
1Sa 6:12 they d not turn to the right or to the left. AIT
1Sa 8: 3 But his sons d not follow his ways. AIT
1Sa 9: 4 around Shalisha, but they d not find them. AIT
1Sa 9: 4 of Benjamin, but they d not find them. AIT
1Sa 9:27 the servant d so—"but you stay H6296S
1Sa 10:16 But he d not tell his uncle what Samuel had AIT
1Sa 12:17 what an evil thing you d in the eyes of the H6913
1Sa 13: 8 Samuel d not come to Gilgal, and AIT
1Sa 13:11 that you d not come at the set time, and AIT
1Sa 14: 1 But he d not tell his father. AIT
1Sa 14:17 When they d, it was Jonathan and his H7212S
1Sa 14:37 But God d not answer him that day. AIT
1Sa 14:45 for he d this today with God's help." H6913
1Sa 15: 2 Amalekites for what they d to Israel when H6913
1Sa 15:17 d you not become the head of the tribes of NDT
1Sa 15:19 Why d you not obey the LORD? Why did you AIT
1Sa 15:19 Why d you pounce on the plunder and do AIT
1Sa 15:20 "But I d obey the LORD," Saul said. "I went on AIT
1Sa 15:35 Samuel died, he d not go to see Saul again AIT
1Sa 16: 4 Samuel d what the LORD said. When he H6913
1Sa 17:28 And with whom d you leave those few sheep AIT
1Sa 18: 2 with him and d not let him return home AIT
1Sa 18:10 the lyre, as he usually d. H3869+3427+928+3427
1Sa 18:14 In everything he d he had great success H2006
1Sa 18:30 as often as they d, David met with H3655S
1Sa 19:17 "Why d you deceive me like this and send AIT
1Sa 20:34 on that second day of the feast he d not eat AIT
1Sa 22:17 knew he was fleeing, yet they d not tell me." AIT
1Sa 23:13 had escaped from Keilah, he d not go there. AIT
1Sa 23:14 God d not give David into his hands. AIT
1Sa 24: 7 his men and d not allow them to attack AIT
1Sa 24:11 off the corner of your robe but d not kill you. AIT
1Sa 24:18 now told me about the good you d to me; H6913
1Sa 24:18 me into your hands, but you d not kill me. AIT
1Sa 25: 7 we d not mistreat them, and the AIT
1Sa 25:13 So they d, and David H2520+906+2995S
1Sa 25:15 They d not mistreat us, and the whole time AIT
1Sa 25:19 But she d not tell her husband Nabal AIT
1Sa 25:25 I d not see the men my lord sent. AIT
1Sa 26:12 saw or knew about it, nor d anyone wake up. AIT
1Sa 26:16 because you d not guard your master AIT
1Sa 27: 9 he d not leave a man or woman alive, but AIT
1Sa 27:10 "Where d you go raiding today? AIT
1Sa 27:11 He d not leave a man or woman alive to be AIT
1Sa 27:11 on us and say, 'This is what David d. H6913
1Sa 28: 6 the LORD d not answer him by dreams or AIT
1Sa 28:18 Because you d not obey the LORD or carry out AIT
1Sa 28:21 in my hands and d what you told me to H9048
1Sa 30:22 "Because they d not go out with us, we AIT
2Sa 1:22 the bow of Jonathan d not turn back, the AIT
2Sa 1:22 the sword of Saul d not return unsatisfied. AIT
2Sa 2:28 pursued Israel, nor d they fight anymore. AIT
2Sa 3: 7 "Why d you sleep with my father's concubine AIT
2Sa 3:11 Ish-Bosheth d not dare to say another word to AIT
2Sa 3:24 Why d you let him go? Now he is AIT
2Sa 3:26 the cistern at Sirah. But David d not know it. AIT
2Sa 3:36 everything the king d pleased them. H6913
2Sa 5:25 So David d as the LORD commanded him H6913
2Sa 7: 7 d I ever say to any of their rulers whom I AIT
2Sa 7:10 them anymore, as they d at the beginning NDT
2Sa 11: 9 servants and d not go down to his house. AIT
2Sa 11:10 was told, "Uriah d not go home." So he AIT
2Sa 11:13 his master's servants; he d not go home. AIT
2Sa 11:20 'Why d you get so close to the city to fight? AIT
2Sa 11:21 Why d you get so close to the wall?' AIT
2Sa 12: 5 LORD lives, the man who d this must die! H6913
2Sa 12: 6 because he d such a thing and had no H6913
2Sa 12: 9 Why d you despise the word of the LORD by AIT
2Sa 12:12 You d it in secret, but I will do this thing in H6913
2Sa 12:31 David d this to all the Ammonite towns H6913
2Sa 13:29 So Absalom's men d to Amnon what H6913
2Sa 14:20 Your servant Joab d this to change the H6913
2Sa 14:24 his own house and d not see the face of the AIT
2Sa 14:31 Then Joab d go to Absalom's house, and he AIT
2Sa 19:19 how your servant d wrong on the day my H6390
2Sa 19:41 d our brothers, the men of Judah, steal the king away AIT
2Sa 19:42 "We d this because the king is closely NDT
2Sa 20: 6 Bikri will do us more harm than Absalom d. NDT
2Sa 21:10 she d not let the birds touch them by day AIT
2Sa 21:14 d everything the king commanded. H6913
2Sa 22:38 I d not turn back till they were destroyed. AIT
2Sa 22:42 to the LORD, but he d not answer. AIT
2Sa 22:44 People I d not know now serve me, AIT
1Ki 1: 8 special guard d not join Adonijah. H2118
1Ki 1:10 but he d not invite Nathan the prophet or AIT
1Ki 1:13 the king, d you not swear to me your servant: AIT
1Ki 1:26 your servant Solomon he d not invite. AIT
1Ki 2: 5 know what Joab son of Zeruiah d to me— H6913
1Ki 2: 5 what he d to the two commanders of H6913
1Ki 2:42 "D I not make you swear by the LORD and AIT
1Ki 2:43 Why then d you not keep your oath to the AIT
1Ki 2:44 all the wrong you d to my father David. H6913
1Ki 3:14 commands as David your father d, H2143S
1Ki 7:14 to King Solomon and d all the work H6913
1Ki 7:18 He d the same for each capital H6913
1Ki 8:18 'You d well to have it in your heart to H3201
1Ki 9: 4 as David your father d, and do all I H2143S
1Ki 9:22 But Solomon d not make slaves of any of the AIT
1Ki 9:23 officials supervising those who d the work. H6913
1Ki 10: 7 But I d not believe these things until I came AIT
1Ki 11: 6 So Solomon d evil in the eyes of the LORD H6913
1Ki 11: 6 he d not follow the LORD completely, as H4848
1Ki 11: 8 He d the same for all his foreign wives H6913
1Ki 11:10 Solomon d not keep the LORD's command. AIT
1Ki 11:28 saw how well the young man d his work, H6913
1Ki 11:33 laws as David, Solomon's father, d. NDT
1Ki 11:38 as David my servant d, I will be with you. H6913
1Ki 11:41 all he d and the wisdom he displayed H6913
1Ki 12:15 So the king d not listen to the people, for this AIT
1Ki 12:32 This he d in Bethel, sacrificing to the H6913
1Ki 13:10 another road and d not return by the way he AIT
1Ki 13:12 father asked them, "Which way d he go?" AIT
1Ki 13:27 the donkey for me," and they d so. H2502S
1Ki 13:33 Jeroboam d not change his evil ways AIT
1Ki 14: 4 So Jeroboam's wife d what he said and H6913
1Ki 14:22 Judah d evil in the eyes of the LORD. H6913
1Ki 14:29 and all he d, are they not written in H6913
1Ki 15: 7 and all he d, are they not written H6913
1Ki 15:11 Asa d what was right in the eyes of the H6913
1Ki 15:14 Although he d not remove the high places AIT
1Ki 15:23 all he d and the cities he built H6913
1Ki 15:26 He d evil in the eyes of the LORD, following H6913
1Ki 15:29 He d not leave Jeroboam anyone that AIT
1Ki 15:31 and all he d, are they not written H6913
1Ki 15:34 He d evil in the eyes of the LORD, H6913
1Ki 16: 5 what he d and his achievements H6913
1Ki 16: 7 his anger by the things he d, H5126+3338
1Ki 16:11 He d not spare a single male, whether AIT
1Ki 16:14 and all he d, are they not written H6913
1Ki 16:25 But Omri d evil in the eyes of the LORD H6913
1Ki 16:27 what he d and the things he achieved H6913
1Ki 16:30 Ahab son of Omri d more evil in the eyes H6913
1Ki 16:33 Asherah pole and d more to arouse the H6913
1Ki 16:33 than d all the kings of Israel before him. NDT
1Ki 17: 5 So he d what the LORD had told him. H6913
1Ki 17:15 She went away and d as Elijah had told H6913
1Ki 17:16 not used up and the jug of oil d not run dry, AIT
1Ki 17:18 D you come to remind me of my sin and kill AIT
1Ki 18:13 what I d while Jezebel was killing the H6913
1Ki 18:34 it again," he said, and they d it again. H9101
1Ki 18:34 he ordered, and they d it the third time. H8992
1Ki 20: 7 my silver and my gold, I d not refuse him." AIT
1Ki 20:34 in Damascus, as my father d in Samaria." H8492S
1Ki 21:11 in Naboth's city d as Jezebel directed in H6913
1Ki 22:24 way d the spirit from the LORD go when he AIT
1Ki 22:39 including all he d, the palace he built H6913
1Ki 22:43 of his father Asa and d not stray from them; AIT
1Ki 22:43 he d what was right in the eyes of the H6913
1Ki 22:52 He d evil in the eyes of the LORD, because H6913
2Ki 1:18 and what he d, are they not written H6913
2Ki 2:17 searched for three days but d not find him. AIT
2Ki 3: 2 He d evil in the eyes of the LORD, but not H6913
2Ki 3: 3 to commit; he d not turn away from them. AIT
2Ki 3:14 if I d not have respect for the presence of AIT
2Ki 4:28 "D I ask you for a son, my lord?" she said AIT
2Ki 4:36 And he d. When she came, H7924S
2Ki 6: 6 "Where d it fall?" When he showed AIT
2Ki 8:14 "What d Elisha say to you? AIT

2Ki 8:18 *He* **d** evil in the eyes of the LORD H6913
2Ki 8:23 and all *he* **d**, are they not written in H6913
2Ki 8:27 house of Ahab and **d** evil in the eyes of H6913
2Ki 9:11 Why *d* this maniac **come** to you?" "You AIT
2Ki 10:15 So *he* **d**, and Jehu helped H5989+3338+2257S
2Ki 10:29 he *d* not **turn away** from the sins of Jeroboam AIT
2Ki 10:31 *He d* not **turn away** from the sins of AIT
2Ki 10:34 of Jehu's reign, all *he* **d**, and all his H6913
2Ki 11:9 units of a hundred **d** just as Jehoiada the H6913
2Ki 12:2 Joash **d** what was right in the eyes of the H6913
2Ki 12:15 *They d* not **require an accounting** *from* those AIT
2Ki 12:19 of Joash, and all *he* **d**, are they not H6913
2Ki 13:2 *He* **d** evil in the eyes of the LORD by H6913
2Ki 13:2 and *he d* not **turn away** from them. AIT
2Ki 13:6 But *they d* not **turn away** from the sins of the AIT
2Ki 13:8 Jehoahaz, all *he* **d** and his achievements H6913
2Ki 13:11 *He* **d** evil in the eyes of the LORD and did H6913
2Ki 13:11 of the LORD and *d* not **turn away** from any of AIT
2Ki 13:12 Jehoash, all *he* **d** and his achievements H6913
2Ki 13:15 arrows," and *he* **d so**. H4374+8008+2256+2932S
2Ki 14:3 *He* **d** what was right in the eyes of the LORD H6913
2Ki 14:6 *he d* not **put** the children of the assassins **to death** AIT
2Ki 14:15 Jehoash, what *he* **d** and his achievements H6913
2Ki 14:24 *He* **d** evil in the eyes of the LORD and did H6913
2Ki 14:24 of the LORD and *d* not **turn away** from any of AIT
2Ki 14:28 all *he* **d**, and his military H6913
2Ki 15:3 *He* **d** what was right in the eyes of the LORD H6913
2Ki 15:6 and all *he* **d**, are they not written in H6913
2Ki 15:9 *He* **d** evil in the eyes of the LORD, as his H6913
2Ki 15:9 *He d* not **turn away** from the sins of AIT
2Ki 15:18 *He* **d** evil in the eyes of the LORD. H6913
2Ki 15:18 entire reign *he d* not **turn away** from the sins AIT
2Ki 15:21 and all *he* **d**, are they not written in H6913
2Ki 15:24 Pekahiah **d** evil in the eyes of the LORD. H6913
2Ki 15:24 *He d* not **turn away** from the sins of AIT
2Ki 15:26 and all *he* **d**, are written in the H6913
2Ki 15:28 *He* **d** evil in the eyes of the LORD. He did H6913
2Ki 15:28 *He d* not **turn away** from the sins of AIT
2Ki 15:31 and all *he* **d**, are they not written H6913
2Ki 15:34 *He* **d** what was right in the eyes of the LORD H6913
2Ki 15:36 and what *he* **d**, are they not written H6913
2Ki 16:2 *he d* not **do** what was right in the eyes of the AIT
2Ki 16:16 And Uriah the priest **d** just as King Ahaz H6913
2Ki 16:19 of Ahaz, and what *he* **d**, are they not H6913
2Ki 17:2 *He* **d** evil in the eyes of the LORD, but not H6913
2Ki 17:9 The Israelites **secretly d** things against the H2901
2Ki 17:11 *They* **d** wicked things that aroused the H6913
2Ki 17:14 who *d* not **trust** in the LORD their God. AIT
2Ki 17:19 even Judah *d* not **keep** the commands of AIT
2Ki 17:22 of Jeroboam and *d* not **turn away** from them AIT
2Ki 17:25 lived there, *they d* not **worship** the LORD; so AIT
2Ki 17:41 continue to do as their ancestors **d**. H6913
2Ki 18:3 *He* **d** what was right in the eyes of the LORD H6913
2Ki 18:6 fast to the LORD and *d* not **stop** following him; AIT
2Ki 18:7 the king of Assyria and *d* not **serve** him. AIT
2Ki 19:12 *D* the gods of the nations that were destroyed by my predecessors **deliver** AIT
2Ki 20:7 *They* **d so** and applied it to the boil H4374S
2Ki 20:13 his kingdom that Hezekiah *d* not **show** them. AIT
2Ki 20:14 "What *d* those men **say**, and where AIT
2Ki 20:14 those men say, and where *d they* **come** from?" AIT
2Ki 20:15 "What *d they* **see** in your palace? AIT
2Ki 20:15 among my treasures that *I d* not **show** them." AIT
2Ki 21:2 *He* **d** evil in the eyes of the LORD, following H6913
2Ki 21:6 He **d** much evil in the eyes of the LORD H6913
2Ki 21:9 But *the people d* not **listen**. Manasseh led AIT
2Ki 21:9 so that they **d** more evil than the nations H6913
2Ki 21:16 so that they **d** evil in the eyes of the LORD. H6913
2Ki 21:17 and all *he* **d**, including the sin he H6913
2Ki 21:20 *He* **d** evil in the eyes of the LORD, as his H6913
2Ki 21:22 and *d* not **walk** in obedience to him. AIT
2Ki 21:25 and what *he* **d**, are they not written H6913
2Ki 22:2 *He* **d** what was right in the eyes of the LORD H6913
2Ki 23:5 *He* **d away with** the idolatrous priests H8697
2Ki 23:7 where women **d weaving** for H755+1428
2Ki 23:9 of the high places *d* not **serve** at the altar of AIT
2Ki 23:24 This he **d** to fulfill the requirements of the NDT
2Ki 23:25 like him who turned to the LORD as he **d**— NDT
2Ki 23:26 the LORD *d* not **turn away** from the heat of his AIT
2Ki 23:28 and all *he* **d**, are they not written H6913
2Ki 23:32 *He* **d** evil in the eyes of the LORD, just as H6913
2Ki 23:37 And *he* **d** evil in the eyes of the LORD, just H6913
2Ki 24:5 and all *he* **d**, are they not written in H6913
2Ki 24:7 king of Egypt *d* not **march out** from his own AIT
2Ki 24:9 *He* **d** evil in the eyes of the LORD, just as H6913
2Ki 24:19 *He* **d** evil in the eyes of the LORD, just as H6913
2Ki 25:27 He **d** this on the twenty-seventh day of the NDT
1Ch 4:27 his brothers **d** not have many children NDT
1Ch 4:27 entire clan *d* not *become* as **numerous** as the AIT
1Ch 10:13 *he d* not **keep** the word of the LORD and even AIT
1Ch 10:14 and *d* not **inquire of** the LORD. So the LORD AIT
1Ch 12:19 *He and his men d* not **help** the Philistines AIT
1Ch 13:3 for *we d* not **inquire of** it during the reign of AIT
1Ch 13:13 He *d* not **take** the ark to be with him in the AIT
1Ch 14:16 So David **d** as God commanded him, and H6913
1Ch 15:13 **d** not bring it up the first time that the LORD NDT
1Ch 15:13 *We d* not **inquire of** him *about* how to do it AIT
1Ch 17:6 *d I ever* **say** *to* any of their leaders whom I AIT
1Ch 17:9 them anymore, as they **d** at the beginning NDT
1Ch 20:3 David **d** this to all the Ammonite towns H6913
1Ch 21:6 *d* not include Levi and Benjamin *in the* **numbering** AIT
1Ch 23:11 Jeush and Beriah *d* not **have many** sons AIT
1Ch 24:2 Nadab and Abihu died before their father **d**, NDT
1Ch 24:31 their relatives the descendants of Aaron **d**, NDT
1Ch 27:23 David *d* not **take** the number of the men AIT
1Ch 27:24 began to count the men but *d* not **finish**. AIT
2Ch 2:3 me cedar logs as *you* **d** for my father H6913
2Ch 6:8 '*You* **d well** to have it in your heart to H3201
2Ch 7:6 as **d** the Levites with the LORD's musical NDT
2Ch 7:17 me faithfully as David your father **d**, H2143S
2Ch 8:9 But Solomon *d* not **make** slaves of the AIT
2Ch 8:15 *They d* not **deviate** *from* the king's commands AIT
2Ch 9:6 But *I d* not **believe** what they said until I came AIT
2Ch 10:15 So the king *d* not **listen** to the people, for this AIT
2Ch 12:14 *He* **d** evil because he had not set his heart H6913
2Ch 13:20 Jeroboam *d* not **regain** power during the time AIT
2Ch 13:22 **what** he **d** and what he said H2006
2Ch 14:2 Asa **d** what was good and right in the H6913
2Ch 15:17 Although *he d* not **remove** the high places AIT
2Ch 16:12 his illness *he d* not **seek help** *from* the LORD, AIT
2Ch 17:3 David before him. *He d* not **consult** the Baals AIT
2Ch 17:10 so that *they d* not **go to war** against AIT
2Ch 18:23 way *d* the spirit from the LORD **go** when he AIT
2Ch 20:7 *d* you not **drive out** the inhabitants of this AIT
2Ch 20:10 away from them and *d* not **destroy** them. AIT
2Ch 20:32 of his father Asa and *d* not **stray** from them; AIT
2Ch 20:32 *he* **d** what was right in the eyes of the H6913
2Ch 21:6 *He* **d** evil in the eyes of the LORD H6913
2Ch 21:13 themselves, just as the house of Ahab **d**. H2388S
2Ch 22:4 *He* **d** evil in the eyes of the LORD, as the H6913
2Ch 23:8 the men of Judah **d** just as Jehoiada the H6913
2Ch 24:2 Joash **d** what was right in the eyes of the H6913
2Ch 24:5 But the Levites *d* not **act at once**. AIT
2Ch 24:11 *They* **d** this regularly and collected a great H6913
2Ch 24:22 King Joash *d* not **remember** the kindness AIT
2Ch 25:2 *He* **d** what was right in the eyes of the LORD H6913
2Ch 25:4 Yet *he d* not **put** their children **to death**, but AIT
2Ch 26:4 *He* **d** what was right in the eyes of the LORD H6913
2Ch 27:2 *He* **d** what was right in the eyes of the LORD H6913
2Ch 27:2 unlike him *he d* not **enter** the temple of AIT
2Ch 27:3 the LORD and **d** extensive **work** on the wall H1215
2Ch 27:7 all his wars and the other **things** he **d**, H2006
2Ch 28:1 *he d* not **do** what was right in the eyes of the AIT
2Ch 28:21 the king of Assyria, but that **d** not help him. NDT
2Ch 29:2 *He* **d** what was right in the eyes of the LORD H6913
2Ch 29:6 *they* **d** evil in the eyes of the LORD our God H6913
2Ch 29:7 *They d* not **burn** incense or present any burnt AIT
2Ch 31:20 is what Hezekiah **d** throughout Judah, H6913
2Ch 32:12 *D* not Hezekiah himself **remove** this god's AIT
2Ch 32:17 the other lands *d* not **rescue** their people AIT
2Ch 32:19 of Jerusalem as they **d** about the gods of NDT
2Ch 32:25 proud and he *d* not **respond** to the kindness AIT
2Ch 32:26 of his heart, as **d** the people of Jerusalem NDT
2Ch 32:26 the LORD's wrath *d* not **come** on them during AIT
2Ch 33:2 *He* **d** evil in the eyes of the LORD, following H6913
2Ch 33:6 He **d** much evil in the eyes of the LORD H6913
2Ch 33:9 so that they **d** more evil than the nations H6913
2Ch 33:22 *He* **d** evil in the eyes of the LORD, as his H6913
2Ch 33:23 *he d* not **humble himself** before the LORD AIT
2Ch 34:2 *He* **d** what was right in the eyes of the LORD H6913
2Ch 34:32 people of Jerusalem **d** this in accordance H6913
2Ch 34:33 as he lived, *they d* not **fail** to follow the LORD AIT
2Ch 35:12 They **d** the same with the cattle NDT
2Ch 35:15 at each gate *d* not *need to* **leave** their posts, AIT
2Ch 35:18 celebrated such a Passover as **d** Josiah, H6913
2Ch 36:5 *He* **d** evil in the eyes of the LORD his God H6913
2Ch 36:8 detestable things *he* **d** and all that was H6913
2Ch 36:9 *He* **d** evil in the eyes of the LORD H6913
2Ch 36:12 *He* **d** evil in the eyes of the LORD his God H6913
2Ch 36:12 his God and *d* not **humble himself** before AIT
2Ch 36:17 and *d* not **spare** young men or young women, AIT
Ezr 5:17 see if King Cyrus *d* in fact **issue** a decree to AIT
Ezr 10:16 So the exiles **d** as was proposed. Ezra the H6913
Ne 2:16 The officials *d* not **know** where I had gone AIT
Ne 4:16 half of my men **d** the work, while the H6913
Ne 4:17 carried materials **d** their work with one H6913
Ne 5:13 And the people **d** as they had promised. H6913
Ne 5:15 out of reverence for God I *d* not **act** like that. AIT
Ne 5:16 there for the work; *we d* not **acquire** any land. AIT
Ne 9:16 and *they d* not **obey** your commands. AIT
Ne 9:17 Therefore *you d* not **desert** them, AIT
Ne 9:19 compassion you *d* not **abandon** them in the AIT
Ne 9:19 the pillar of cloud *d* not **fail** to guide them on AIT
Ne 9:20 *You d* not **withhold** your manna from their AIT
Ne 9:21 their clothes *d* not **wear out** nor did their feet AIT
Ne 9:21 wear out nor *d* their feet *become* **swollen**. AIT
Ne 9:28 they again **d** what was evil in your sight. H6913
Ne 9:31 great mercy *you d* not **put** an end *to* them AIT
Ne 9:34 our ancestors *d* not **follow** your law; AIT
Ne 9:34 *they d* not **pay attention** to your commands AIT
Ne 9:35 *they d* not **serve** you or turn from their evil AIT
Ne 12:40 the house of God; so **d** I, together with half NDT
Ne 12:45 as **d** also the musicians and gatekeepers NDT
Ne 13:24 and *d* not **know how** to speak the language AIT
Est 1:21 so the king **d** as Memukan proposed. H6913
Est 9:5 and *they* **d** what they pleased to those H6913
Est 9:10 But *they d* not **lay** their hands on the plunder. AIT
Est 9:15 but *they d* not **lay** their hands on the plunder. AIT
Est 9:16 of them but *d* not **lay** their hands on the AIT
Job 1:22 Job *d* not **sin** by charging God with AIT
Job 2:10 In all this, Job *d* not **sin** in what he said. AIT
Job 3:10 for *it d* not **shut** the doors of the womb *on* me AIT
Job 3:11 "Why *d I* not **perish** at birth, and die as I AIT
Job 10:10 *D you* not **pour** me **out** like milk and curdle AIT
Job 10:18 "Why then *d you* **bring** me **out** of the womb AIT
Job 20:19 he has seized houses *he d* not **build**. AIT
Job 31:15 *D* not he who made me in the womb **make** AIT
Job 31:15 *D* not the same one **form** us both within our AIT
Job 31:20 their hearts *d* not **bless** me for warming AIT
Job 33:27 what is right, but I *d* not **get what I deserved**. AIT
Job 39:17 God *d* **not endow** her *with* wisdom or give AIT
Job 42:3 Surely I spoke of things *I d* not **understand** AIT
Job 42:9 the Naamathite **d** what the LORD told H6913
Ps 18:37 *I d* not **turn back** till they were destroyed. AIT
Ps 18:41 to the LORD, but *he d* not **answer**. AIT
Ps 18:43 People *I d* not **know** now serve me, AIT
Ps 30:1 and *d* not **let** my enemies **gloat** over me. AIT
Ps 32:5 my sin to you and *d* not **cover up** my iniquity. AIT
Ps 40:6 Sacrifice and offering *you d* not **desire**—but AIT
Ps 40:6 offerings and sin offerings *you d* not **require**. AIT
Ps 44:1 have told us what *you* **d** in their days, H7188
Ps 44:3 nor *d* their arm **bring** them **victory**; it was AIT
Ps 50:21 *When you* **d** these things and I kept silent, H6913
Ps 52:7 now is the man *who d* not **make** God his AIT
Ps 69:4 I am forced to restore what *I d* not **steal**. AIT
Ps 78:10 *they d* not **keep** God's covenant and refused AIT
Ps 78:12 *He* **d** miracles in the sight of their H6913
Ps 78:22 for *they d* not **believe** in God or trust in his AIT
Ps 78:32 in spite of his wonders, *they d* not **believe**. AIT
Ps 78:38 their iniquities and *d* not **destroy** them. AIT
Ps 78:38 his anger and *d* not **stir up** his full wrath. AIT
Ps 78:42 *They d* not **remember** his power—the day he AIT
Ps 78:50 *he d* not **spare** them from death but gave AIT
Ps 78:56 the Most High; *they d* not **keep** his statutes. AIT
Ps 78:67 *he d* not **choose** the tribe of Ephraim; AIT
Ps 83:9 Do to them as you **d** to Midian, as you did NDT
Ps 83:9 as you **d** to Sisera and Jabin at the river NDT
Ps 86:16 because I serve you just as my mother **d**. NDT
Ps 95:8 not harden your hearts as you **d** at Meribah, NDT
Ps 95:8 as you **d** that day at Massah in the NDT
Ps 95:9 tried me, though they had seen **what I d**. H7189
Ps 106:6 even as our ancestors **d**; we have done NDT
Ps 106:7 *they d* not **remember** your many kindnesses AIT
Ps 106:13 he had done and *d* not **wait** for his plan to AIT
Ps 106:24 *they d* not **believe** his promise. AIT
Ps 106:25 in their tents and *d* not **obey** the LORD. AIT
Ps 106:34 *They d* not **destroy** the peoples as the LORD AIT
Ps 106:39 They defiled themselves by **what** they **d** H5126
Ps 107:38 and *he d* not **let** their herds **diminish**. AIT
Ps 114:5 Why, Jordan, *d you* **turn** back? AIT
Ps 114:6 mountains, *d you* **leap** like rams, you AIT
Ps 116:16 I serve you **just as my mother d**; you have H563S
Ps 137:7 what the Edomites **d** on the day Jerusalem NDT
Pr 1:29 knowledge and *d* not **choose** to fear the LORD. AIT
Pr 24:29 I'll pay them back for what they **d**. H7189
Ecc 8:10 praise in the city where *they* **d** this. H6913
SS 3:1 I looked for him but *d* not **find** him. AIT
SS 3:2 So I looked for him but *d* not **find** him. AIT
SS 5:6 I looked for him but *d* not **find** him. I called AIT
SS 5:6 I called him but *he d* not **answer**. AIT
SS 6:1 Which way *d* your beloved **turn**, that we may AIT
Isa 5:4 good grapes, why *d it* **yield** only bad? AIT
Isa 10:24 lift up a club against you, as Egypt **d**. NDT
Isa 10:26 his staff over the waters, as he **d** in Egypt. NDT
Isa 20:2 And *he* **d** so, going around stripped and H6913
Isa 22:2 killed by the sword, nor *d they* **die** *in* battle. AIT
Isa 22:11 but *you d* not **look** to the One who made it AIT
Isa 28:21 LORD will rise up as he **d** at Mount Perazim, NDT
Isa 29:16 formed it, "*You d* not **make** me"? AIT
Isa 37:12 *D* the gods of the nations that were destroyed by my predecessors **deliver** AIT
Isa 39:2 his kingdom that Hezekiah *d* not **show** them. AIT
Isa 39:3 "What *d* those men **say**, and where AIT
Isa 39:3 those men say, and where *d they* **come** from?" AIT
Isa 39:4 "What *d they* **see** in your palace? AIT
Isa 39:4 among my treasures that *I d* not **show** them." AIT
Isa 40:14 Whom *d* the LORD **consult** to enlighten him AIT
Isa 42:24 not follow his ways; *they d* not **obey** his law. AIT
Isa 42:25 yet *they d* not **understand**; it AIT
Isa 42:25 but *they d* not **take** it to heart. AIT
Isa 44:8 *D I* not **proclaim** this and foretell it long ago AIT
Isa 45:18 he founded it; *he d* not **create** it to be empty AIT
Isa 47:7 But *you d* not **consider** these things or reflect AIT
Isa 48:21 *They d* not **thirst** when he led them through AIT
Isa 50:1 Or to which of my creditors *d I* **sell** you AIT
Isa 50:6 *I d* not **hide** my face from mocking and AIT
Isa 53:7 afflicted, yet *he d* not **open** his mouth; he AIT
Isa 53:7 is silent, so *he d* not **open** his mouth. AIT
Isa 57:10 of your strength, and so *you d* not **faint**. AIT
Isa 63:13 a horse in open country, *they d* not **stumble**; AIT
Isa 64:3 For when you **d** awesome things that we H6913
Isa 64:3 did awesome things that *we d* not **expect**, AIT
Isa 65:1 myself to *those who d* not **ask** for me; AIT
Isa 65:1 I was found by *those who d* not **seek** me. AIT
Isa 65:1 To a nation *that d* not **call** on my name, AIT
Isa 65:12 I called but *you d* not **answer**, I spoke but AIT
Isa 65:12 did not answer, I spoke but *you d* not **listen**. AIT
Isa 65:12 *You* **d** evil in my sight and chose what H6913
Isa 66:4 *They* **d** evil in my sight and chose what H6913
Jer 2:5 "What fault *d* your ancestors **find** in me, that AIT
Jer 2:6 *They d* not **ask**, 'Where is the LORD, who AIT
Jer 2:8 The priests *d* not **ask**, 'Where is the LORD?' AIT
Jer 2:8 Those who deal with the law *d* not **know** me; AIT

Jer 2:21 How then *d you* **turn** against me **into** a AIT
Jer 2:30 your people; *they d* not **respond to** correction. AIT
Jer 2:34 though *you d* not **catch** them breaking in. AIT
Jer 3: 7 she would return to me but *she* **d** not, H8740S
Jer 3:10 sister Judah *d* not **return** to me with all her AIT
Jer 7:12 see what *I* **d** to it because of the H6913
Jer 7:13 again, but *you d* not **listen**; I called you, AIT
Jer 7:13 not listen; I called you, but *you d* not **answer**. AIT
Jer 7:14 what *I* **d** to Shiloh I will now do to the H6913
Jer 7:15 just as *I* **d** all your fellow Israelites H8959S
Jer 7:22 *I d* not *just* **give** them **commands** about burnt AIT
Jer 7:24 But *they d* not **listen** or pay attention; instead AIT
Jer 7:26 But *they d* not **listen** to me or pay attention AIT
Jer 7:26 stiff-necked and **d** more **evil** than their H8317
Jer 7:31 something *I d* not **command**, nor did it AIT
Jer 7:31 I did not command, nor *d it* **enter** my mind. AIT
Jer 10:11 who *d* not **make** the heavens and the earth AIT
Jer 11: 8 But *they d* not **listen** or pay attention; instead AIT
Jer 11: 8 them to follow but that *they d* not **keep**. AIT
Jer 11:19 *I d* not **realize** that they had plotted against AIT
Jer 14:15 *I d* not **send** them, yet they are saying, 'No AIT
Jer 15: 4 of Hezekiah king of Judah **d** in Jerusalem. H6913
Jer 16:11 They forsook me and *d* not **keep** my law. AIT
Jer 16:19 worthless idols *that* **d** them no **good**. H3603
Jer 17:11 that hatches eggs *it d* not **lay** are those who AIT
Jer 17:23 Yet *they d* not **listen** or pay attention; they AIT
Jer 19: 5 something *I d* not **command** or mention AIT
Jer 19: 5 mention, nor *d it* **enter** my mind. AIT
Jer 20:17 For *he d* not **kill** me in the womb, with my AIT
Jer 20:18 Why *d I ever* **come out** of the womb to see AIT
Jer 22:15 *D* not your father **have food and** drink AIT
Jer 22:15 *He* **d** what was right and just, so all went H6913
Jer 23:21 *I d* not **send** these prophets, yet they have AIT
Jer 23:21 their message; *I d* not **speak** to them, yet AIT
Jer 23:32 yet I *d* not **send** or appoint them. AIT
Jer 25: 7 "But *you d* not **listen** to me," declares the AIT
Jer 26:19 *D* Hezekiah king of Judah or anyone else in Judah **put** him **to death** AIT
Jer 26:19 *D* not Hezekiah **fear** the LORD and seek his AIT
Jer 26:19 *d* not the LORD **relent, so that** he *did* **not bring** AIT
Jer 26:19 *did* not the LORD **relent, so that** he *d* **not bring** AIT
Jer 26:20 this city and this land as Jeremiah **d**. NDT
Jer 27:20 king of Babylon *d* not **take away** when he AIT
Jer 29:16 fellow citizens who *d* not **go** with you into AIT
Jer 29:23 have uttered lies—which *I d* not **authorize**. AIT
Jer 29:31 even though I *d* not **send** him, and has AIT
Jer 32:23 but *they d* not **obey** you or follow your law AIT
Jer 32:23 *they d* not **do** what you commanded them to AIT
Jer 32:35 commanded—nor *d it* **enter** my mind—that AIT
Jer 34:14 *d* not **listen** to me or pay attention to me. AIT
Jer 34:15 you repented and **d** what is right in my H6913
Jer 35:17 to them, but *they d* not **listen**; I called to AIT
Jer 35:17 I called to them, but *they d* not **answer**. AIT
Jer 36: 8 son of Neriah **d** everything Jeremiah H6913
Jer 36:17 "Tell us, how *d you come to* **write** all this? AIT
Jer 36:17 to write all this? **D** Jeremiah dictate it?" NDT
Jer 36:24 showed no fear, nor *d they* **tear** their clothes. AIT
Jer 36:29 "Why *d you* **write** on it that the king of AIT
Jer 38:12 arms to pad the ropes." Jeremiah **d** so, H6913
Jer 38:15 Even if *I d* **give** you **counsel**, you would not AIT
Jer 38:27 All the officials *d* **come** to Jeremiah and AIT
Jer 40: 3 sinned against the LORD and *d* not **obey** him. AIT
Jer 40:14 Gedaliah son of Ahikam *d* not **believe** them. AIT
Jer 41: 8 let them alone and *d* not **kill** them with the AIT
Jer 44: 5 But *they d* not **listen** or pay attention; they did AIT
Jer 44: 5 they *d* not **turn** from their wickedness or stop AIT
Jer 44:17 our officials **d** in the towns of Judah H6913
Jer 44:19 **d** not our husbands know that we were NDT
Jer 44:21 "*D* not the LORD **remember** and call to mind AIT
Jer 44:22 actions and the detestable things *you* **d**, H6913
Jer 48:11 So she tastes **as** she **d**, and her aroma is H6641S
Jer 52: 2 *He* **d** evil in the eyes of the LORD, just as H6913
La 1: 9 to her skirts; *she d* not **consider** her future. AIT
La 2: 8 line and *d* not **withhold** his hand from AIT
La 2:14 *they d* not **expose** your sin to ward off your AIT
La 4:12 The kings of the earth *d* not **believe**, nor did AIT
La 4:12 **d** any of the peoples of the world NDT
Eze 1: 9 *they d* not **turn** as they moved. AIT
Eze 1:17 the wheels *d* not **change direction** as the AIT
Eze 3:20 Since *you d* not **warn** them, they will die AIT
Eze 3:20 righteous things *that person* **d** will not be H6913
Eze 6:10 *I d* not **threaten** in vain to bring this calamity AIT
Eze 10:11 the wheels *d* not **turn about** as the cherubim AIT
Eze 10:16 the wheels *d* not **leave** their side. AIT
Eze 12: 7 So *I* **d** as I was commanded. During the H6913
Eze 12: 9 *d* not the Israelites, that rebellious **people** AIT
Eze 16:22 prostitution *you d* not **remember** the days of AIT
Eze 16:43 " 'Because *you d* not **remember** the days of AIT
Eze 16:43 *D you* not **add** lewdness to all your other AIT
Eze 16:48 her daughters never **d** what you and your H6913
Eze 16:49 *they d* not **help** the poor and needy. AIT
Eze 16:50 were haughty and **d** detestable things H6913
Eze 16:50 Therefore *I* **d away with** them as you have H6073
Eze 16:51 Samaria *d* not **commit** half the sins you did AIT
Eze 16:51 Samaria did not commit half the sins you **d** NDT
Eze 17:18 hand in pledge and yet **d** all these things, H6913
Eze 18:18 his brother and **d** what was wrong among H6913
Eze 20: 8 they *d* not **get rid of** the vile images they had AIT
Eze 20: 8 eyes on, nor *d they* **forsake** the idols of Egypt. AIT
Eze 20: 9 *I* **d** it to keep my name from being H6913
Eze 20:13 *They d* not **follow** my decrees but rejected my AIT
Eze 20:14 sake of my name *I* **d** what would keep it H6913
Eze 20:16 my laws and *d* not **follow** my decrees and AIT
Eze 20:17 with pity and *d* not **destroy** them or put an AIT
Eze 20:21 *They d* not **follow** my decrees, they were not AIT
Eze 20:22 sake of my name *I* **d** what would keep it H6913
Eze 20:30 the way your ancestors **d** and lust after their NDT
Eze 23: 8 *She d* not **give up** the prostitution she began AIT
Eze 23:39 That is what *they* **d** in my house. H6913
Eze 24: 7 the bare rock; *she d* not **pour** it on the ground AIT
Eze 24:18 The next morning *I* **d** as I had been H6913
Eze 27:12 " 'Tarshish **d business with** you because H6086
Eze 27:13 Tubal and Meshek **d business with** you H8217
Eze 27:16 " 'Aram **d business with** you because of H6086
Eze 27:18 " 'Damascus **d business with** you because H6086
Eze 27:21 *they* **d business with** you in lambs H6086
Eze 29:20 because *he and his army* **d** it for me, H6913
Eze 33: 5 of the trumpet but *d* not **heed the warning**, AIT
Eze 34: 8 my shepherds *d* not **search for** my flock but AIT
Eze 35: 6 Since *you d* not **hate** bloodshed, bloodshed AIT
Eze 40:36 as **d** its alcoves, its projecting walls and its NDT
Eze 48:11 serving me and *d* not **go astray** as the Levites AIT
Eze 48:11 as the Levites **d** when the Israelites H9494S
Da 2:15 "Why **d** the king issue such a harsh decree?" NDT
Da 5:12 He **d** this because Daniel, whom the king NDT
Da 5:23 But *you d* not **honor** the God who holds in his AIT
Da 6:12 "*D you* not **publish** a decree that during the AIT
Da 8: 4 *It* **d** as it pleased and became great H6913
Da 8:12 It prospered in everything *it* **d**, and truth H6913
Da 9:14 The LORD **d not hesitate** to bring the H9193
Da 10: 7 those who were with me *d* not **see** it, but AIT
Da 11:24 neither his fathers nor his forefathers **d**. H6913
Da 12: 8 but *I d* not **understand**. So I asked AIT
Hos 10: 3 no king because *we d* not **revere** the LORD. AIT
Hos 11: 3 but *they d* not **realize** it was I who healed AIT
Joel 3: 2 on trial for what they **d** to my inheritance, NDT
Am 4: 8 town for water but *d* not **get enough** to drink, AIT
Am 4:10 "I sent plagues among you as I **d** to Egypt. NDT
Am 5:25 "*D you* **bring** me sacrifices and offerings AIT
Am 6:13 "*D we* not **take** Karnaim by our own strength? AIT
Am 9: 7 "*D I* not **bring** Israel **up** from Egypt, the AIT
Jnh 1:13 the men *d their best to* **row** back to land. AIT
Jnh 3:10 When God saw **what** they **d** and how they H5126
Jnh 3:10 he relented and *d* not **bring** on them the AIT
Jnh 4:10 though *you d* not **tend** it or make it grow. AIT
Hab 3: 8 **D** you rage against the sea when you rode NDT
Zep 3: 7 still eager to act corruptly in all they **d**. H6613
Hag 2:17 yet you **d** not return to me,' NDT
Zec 1: 6 *d* not my words and my decrees, ..., **overtake** AIT
Zec 7:13 *they d* not **listen**; so when they AIT
Zec 8:11 remnant of this people as I **d** in the past," NDT
Mal 2:10 *D* not one God **create** us? Why do AIT
Mt 1:19 yet *d* not **want** to expose her to public AIT
Mt 1:24 *he* **d** what the angel of the Lord had *G4472*
Mt 1:25 But *he d* not **consummate** *their* **marriage** AIT
Mt 7:22 *d we* not **prophesy** in your name and in your AIT
Mt 7:25 that house; yet *it d* not **fall**, because it had its AIT
Mt 9:19 went with him, and so **d** his disciples. NDT
Mt 10:34 *I d* not **come** to bring peace, but AIT
Mt 11: 7 "What *d you* **go out** into the wilderness to AIT
Mt 11: 8 what *d you* **go out** to see? A man AIT
Mt 11: 9 Then what *d you* **go out** to see? A prophet AIT
Mt 11:17 you, and *you d* not **dance**; we sang a AIT
Mt 11:17 we sang a dirge, and *you d* not **mourn**. AIT
Mt 11:20 been performed, because *they d* not **repent**. AIT
Mt 12: 3 you read what David **d** when he and his *G4472*
Mt 13: 5 rocky places, where *it d* not **have** much soil. AIT
Mt 13:17 longed to see what you see but *d* not **see** it, AIT
Mt 13:17 to hear what you hear but *d* not **hear** it. AIT
Mt 13:27 Where then *d* the weeds **come** from?' AIT
Mt 13:28 " 'An enemy **d** this,' he replied. *G4472*
Mt 13:34 *he d* not **say** anything to them without using AIT
Mt 13:54 "Where **d** this man get this wisdom and NDT
Mt 13:56 Where then **d** this man get all these things?" NDT
Mt 13:58 And *he d* not **do** many miracles there AIT
Mt 14:31 of little faith," he said, "why *d you* **doubt**?" AIT
Mt 15:23 Jesus *d* not **answer** a word. So his disciples AIT
Mt 17:12 and *they d* not **recognize** him, but AIT
Mt 18:13 about the ninety-nine that *d* not **wander off**. AIT
Mt 19: 7 "*d* Moses **command** that a man give his wife AIT
Mt 20: 5 in the afternoon and **d** the same thing. *G4472*
Mt 20:28 as the Son of Man *d* not **come** to be served, AIT
Mt 21: 6 The disciples went and **d** as Jesus had *G4472*
Mt 21:15 wonderful things *he* **d** and the children *G4472*
Mt 21:20 "How *d* the fig tree **wither** so quickly? AIT
Mt 21:25 baptism—where *d it* **come** from? Was it from AIT
Mt 21:30 He answered, 'I will, sir,' but *he d* not **go**. AIT
Mt 21:31 "Which of the two **d** what his father *G4472*
Mt 21:32 and *you d* not **believe** him, but the tax AIT
Mt 21:32 the tax collectors and the prostitutes **d**. *G4409S*
Mt 21:32 saw this, *you d* not **repent** and believe him. AIT
Mt 22: 8 those I invited **d** not deserve to come. *G1639*
Mt 22:12 'How *d you* **get in** here without wedding AIT
Mt 25: 3 their lamps but *d* not **take** any oil with them. AIT
Mt 25:37 when *d we* **see** you hungry and feed you AIT
Mt 25:38 When *d we* **see** you a stranger and invite you AIT
Mt 25:39 When *d we* **see** you sick or in prison and go AIT
Mt 25:40 whatever *you* **d** for one of the least of *G4472*
Mt 25:40 brothers and sisters of mine, *you* **d** for me. *G4472*
Mt 25:43 I was a stranger and *you d* not **invite** me **in**, AIT
Mt 25:43 I needed clothes and *you d* not **clothe** me, AIT
Mt 25:43 in prison and *you d* not **look after** me. AIT
Mt 25:44 when *d we* **see** you hungry or thirsty or a AIT
Mt 25:44 sick or in prison, and *d* not **help** you? AIT
Mt 25:45 whatever *you d* not **do** for one of the least of AIT
Mt 25:45 of the least of these, *you d* not **do** for me. AIT
Mt 26:12 my body, she **d** it to prepare me for burial. NDT
Mt 26:19 So the disciples **d** as Jesus had directed *G4472*
Mt 26:55 courts teaching, and *you d* not **arrest** me. AIT
Mt 26:60 But *they d* not **find** any, though many false AIT
Mt 28:15 took the money and **d** as they were *G4472*
Mk 2:25 never read what David **d** when he and his *G4472*
Mk 4: 5 rocky places, where *it d* not **have** much soil. AIT
Mk 4: 7 the plants, so that *they d* not **bear** grain. AIT
Mk 4:34 *He d* not **say** anything to them without using AIT
Mk 5:19 Jesus *d* not **let** him, but said, "Go home to AIT
Mk 5:37 *He d* not **let** anyone follow him except Peter AIT
Mk 6: 2 "Where **d** this man get these things?" NDT
Mk 6:17 He **d** this because of Herodias, his brother NDT
Mk 6:26 dinner guests, *he d* not **want** to refuse her. AIT
Mk 6:31 that *they d* not even **have a chance** to eat, AIT
Mk 7:24 a house and *d* not **want** anyone to know it; AIT
Mk 7:36 But the more *he* **d so**, the more they kept *G1403S*
Mk 8: 6 distribute to the people, and **they d so**. *G4192S*
Mk 8:19 many basketfuls of pieces *d you* **pick up**?" AIT
Mk 8:20 many basketfuls of pieces *d you* **pick up**?" AIT
Mk 9: 6 *He d* not **know** what to say, they were so AIT
Mk 9:30 Jesus *d* not **want** anyone to know where they AIT
Mk 9:32 But they *d* **not understand** what he meant AIT
Mk 10: 3 "What *d* Moses **command** you?" he replied. AIT
Mk 10:45 the Son of Man *d* not **come** to be served, AIT
Mk 14: 8 *She* **d** what she could. She poured *G4472*
Mk 14:40 *They d* not **know** what to say to him AIT
Mk 14:49 the temple courts, and *you d* not **arrest** me. AIT
Mk 14:55 put him to death, but *they d* not **find** any. AIT
Mk 14:56 but their statements **d** not agree. *G1639*
Mk 14:59 Yet even then their testimony **d** not agree. *G1639*
Mk 15: 8 Pilate to do for them what he usually **d**. NDT
Mk 15:23 wine mixed with myrrh, but *he d* not **take** it. AIT
Mk 16:11 that she had seen him, *they d* **not believe** it. AIT
Mk 16:13 but *they d* not **believe** them either. AIT
Lk 1:20 because *you d* not **believe** my words, which AIT
Lk 2:45 *When they d* not **find** him, they went back to AIT
Lk 2:50 they *d* not **understand** what he was saying AIT
Lk 4:23 we have heard *that you* **d** in Capernaum. *G1181*
Lk 6: 3 never read what David **d** when he and his *G4472*
Lk 6:10 He **d** *so*, and his hand was completely *G4472*
Lk 7: 7 why *I d* not even **consider** myself **worthy** to AIT
Lk 7:24 "What *d you* **go out** into the wilderness to AIT
Lk 7:25 what *d you* **go out** to see? A man AIT
Lk 7:26 But what *d you* **go out** to see? A prophet? Yes AIT
Lk 7:32 you, and *you d* not **dance**; we sang a AIT
Lk 7:32 we sang a dirge, and *you d* not **cry**. AIT
Lk 7:44 *You d* not **give** me any water for my feet, but AIT
Lk 7:45 *You d* not **give** me a kiss, but this woman AIT
Lk 7:46 *You d* not **put** oil **on** my head, but she has AIT
Lk 8:51 *he d* not **let** anyone go in with him except AIT
Lk 9:15 The disciples **d** so, and everyone sat down. *G4472*
Lk 9:33 (*He d* not **know** what he was saying. AIT
Lk 9:36 to themselves and *d* not **tell** anyone at that AIT
Lk 9:43 was marveling at all that Jesus **d**, *G4472*
Lk 9:45 But they *d* **not understand** what this meant. AIT
Lk 9:45 so that *they d* not **grasp** it, and they AIT
Lk 9:53 but *the people there d* not **welcome** him AIT
Lk 10:24 wanted to see what you see but *d* not **see** it, AIT
Lk 10:24 to hear what you hear but *d* not **hear** it." AIT
Lk 11:38 that Jesus *d* not first **wash** before the meal. AIT
Lk 11:40 *D* not the one who made the outside **make** AIT
Lk 11:48 that you approve of what your ancestors **d**; *G2240*
Lk 13: 6 went to look for fruit on it but *d* not **find** any. AIT
Lk 17: 9 servant because *he* **d** what he was told *G4472*
Lk 18:34 The disciples *d* not **understand** any of this. AIT
Lk 18:34 and *they d* not **know** what he was talking AIT
Lk 19:21 take out what *you d* not **put in** and reap what AIT
Lk 19:21 did not put in and reap what *you d* not **sow**. AIT
Lk 19:22 You knew, **d** you, that I am a hard man NDT
Lk 19:22 taking out what *I d* not **put in**, and reaping AIT
Lk 19:22 did not put in, and reaping what *I d* not **sow**? AIT
Lk 19:27 of mine who *d* not **want** me to be king over AIT
Lk 19:44 because *you d* not **recognize** the time of AIT
Lk 22:35 bag or sandals, *d you* **lack** anything? AIT
Lk 22:53 and *you d* not **lay** a hand on me. AIT
Lk 24: 3 *they d* not **find** the body of the Lord Jesus. AIT
Lk 24:11 But *they d* **not believe** the women, because AIT
Lk 24:24 women had said, but *they d* not **see** Jesus." AIT
Lk 24:26 *D* not the Messiah **have** to suffer these things AIT
Lk 24:41 And *while* they still *d* **not believe** it because AIT
Jn 1:10 through him, the world *d* not **recognize** him. AIT
Jn 1:11 was his own, but his own *d* not **receive** him. AIT
Jn 1:12 Yet to all *who d* **receive** him, to those who AIT
Jn 1:20 *He d* not **fail** to confess, but confessed freely AIT
Jn 1:31 *I* myself *d* not **know** him, but the reason I AIT
Jn 1:33 And *I* myself *d* not **know** him, but the one AIT
Jn 1:41 The first thing Andrew **d** was to find his NDT
Jn 2: 8 the master of the banquet." They **d so**, *G5770S*
Jn 2: 9 *He d* not **realize** where it had come from AIT
Jn 2:11 What Jesus **d** here in Cana of Galilee was *G4472*
Jn 2:25 *He d* not **need** any testimony about mankind AIT
Jn 3:17 For God *d* not **send** his Son into the world to AIT
Jn 4:12 as **d** also his sons and his livestock? NDT
Jn 4:29 a man who told me everything *I ever* **d**. *G4472*
Jn 4:39 "He told me everything *I ever* **d**." *G4472*
Jn 6:11 as they wanted. He **d** the same with the fish NDT
Jn 6:25 asked him, "Rabbi, when *d you* **get** here?" AIT

Jn 6:64 which of them *d* not **believe** and who would AIT
Jn 7: 1 *He d* not **want** to go about in Judea because AIT
Jn 7: 5 even his own brothers *d* not **believe** in him. AIT
Jn 7:14 the festival *d* Jesus **go up** to the temple AIT
Jn 7:15 "How *d* this man **get** *such* **learning** without AIT
Jn 7:21 said to them, "*I* **d** one miracle, and you G4472
Jn 7:22 though actually *it d* not **come** from Moses, but AIT
Jn 7:36 What *d he* **mean** when he said, 'You will look AIT
Jn 8:27 *They d* not **understand** that he was telling AIT
Jn 8:39 "then you would do what Abraham **d**. G2240
Jn 8:40 Abraham *d* not **do** such things. AIT
Jn 8:52 Abraham died and so **d** the prophets, yet NDT
Jn 8:53 He died, and so **d** the prophets. G633S
Jn 8:55 If I said *I* **d** not, I would be a liar like you, G3857S
Jn 9:18 They *still d* not **believe** that he had been AIT
Jn 9:26 asked him, "What *d he* **do** to you? How did AIT
Jn 9:26 How *d he* **open** your eyes?" AIT
Jn 9:27 "I have told you already and *you d* not **listen**. AIT
Jn 10: 6 the Pharisees *d* not **understand** what he was AIT
Jn 10:25 Jesus answered, "*I d* **tell** you, but you do not AIT
Jn 11:40 "*D I* not **tell** you that if you believe AIT
Jn 11:45 had seen what Jesus **d**, believed in G4472
Jn 11:51 *He d* not **say** this on his own, but as high AIT
Jn 12: 6 *He d* not **say** this because he cared about the AIT
Jn 12:16 At first his disciples *d* not **understand** all this AIT
Jn 12:16 was glorified *d they* **realize** that these things AIT
Jn 12:47 For *I d* not **come** to judge the world, but to AIT
Jn 12:49 For *I d* not **speak** on my own, but the Father AIT
Jn 15:16 You *d* not **choose** me, but I chose you and AIT
Jn 15:24 among them the works no one else **d**, G4472
Jn 16: 4 *I d* not **tell** you this from the beginning AIT
Jn 18:23 if I spoke the truth, why *d you* **strike** me?" AIT
Jn 18:28 uncleanness they *d* not **enter** the palace, AIT
Jn 18:34 "or *d* others **talk** to you about me? AIT
Jn 19:24 So this is what the soldiers **d**. G4472
Jn 19:31 the Jewish leaders **d** not want the bodies NDT
Jn 19:33 was already dead, *they d* not **break** his legs. AIT
Jn 20: 5 the strips of linen lying there but *d* not **go in**. AIT
Jn 20: 9 *They* still *d* not **understand** from Scripture AIT
Jn 20:14 but *she d* not **realize** that it was Jesus. AIT
Jn 21: 4 the disciples *d* not **realize** that it was AIT
Jn 21: 6 When *they* **d**, they were unable to haul G965S
Jn 21:13 it to them, and **d** the same with the fish. NDT
Jn 21:23 But Jesus *d* not **say** that he would not die; he AIT
Jn 21:25 Jesus **d** many other things as well. If every G4472
Ac 2:22 which God **d** among you through him G4472
Ac 2:31 realm of the dead, nor *d* his body **see** decay. AIT
Ac 2:34 For David *d* not **ascend** to heaven, and yet he AIT
Ac 3: 4 straight at him, as **d** John. Then Peter said, NDT
Ac 3:17 you acted in ignorance, as **d** your leaders. NDT
Ac 4: 7 "By what power or what name *d you* **do** this?" AIT
Ac 4:28 *They* **d** what your power and will had G4472
Ac 5:22 at the jail, the officers *d* not **find** them there. AIT
Ac 5:26 They **d** not use force, because they feared NDT
Ac 7:25 him to rescue them, but they **d** not. G5317S
Ac 7:32 trembled with fear and *d* not **dare** to look. AIT
Ac 7:42 " '*D you* **bring** me sacrifices and offerings AIT
Ac 7:52 a prophet your ancestors *d* not **persecute**? AIT
Ac 8:32 shearer is silent, so *he d* not **open** his mouth. AIT
Ac 8:39 the eunuch *d* not **see** him again, but AIT
Ac 9: 7 they heard the sound but *d* not **see** anyone. AIT
Ac 9: 9 was blind, and *d* not **eat** or drink anything. AIT
Ac 10:39 of everything *he* **d** in the country of the G4472
Ac 11:30 This *they* **d**, sending their gift to the elders G4472
Ac 12: 8 And Peter **d** so. "Wrap your G4472
Ac 12:19 search made for him and *d* not **find** him, AIT
Ac 12:23 because Herod *d* not **give** praise to God, an AIT
Ac 13:27 their rulers *d* **not recognize** Jesus, AIT
Ac 13:37 God raised from the dead *d* not **see** decay. AIT
Ac 15: 8 the Holy Spirit to them, just as he **d** to us. NDT
Ac 15: 9 *He d* not **discriminate** between us and them AIT
Ac 15:38 Paul *d* not **think it wise** to take him AIT
Ac 17: 4 as **d** a large number of God-fearing Greeks NDT
Ac 17: 6 But *when they d* not **find** them, they dragged AIT
Ac 17:12 as **d** also a number of prominent Greek NDT
Ac 17:27 God **d** this so that they would seek him and NDT
Ac 19: 2 "*D you* **receive** the Holy Spirit when you AIT
Ac 19: 3 "Then what **baptism** *d you* receive? AIT
Ac 19:11 God **d** extraordinary miracles through Paul G4472
Ac 19:32 of the people *d* not even **know** why they were AIT
Ac 20:35 In everything I **d**, I showed you that by this NDT
Ac 22: 9 but *they d* not **understand** the voice of him AIT
Ac 23: 5 *I d* not **realize** that he was the high priest AIT
Ac 24:12 My accusers *d* not **find** me arguing with AIT
Ac 25:17 here with me, *I d* not **delay** the case, but AIT
Ac 25:18 *they d* not **charge** him with any of the crimes AIT
Ac 26:10 And that is just what *I* **d** in Jerusalem. G4472
Ac 27: 7 *When* the wind *d* not **allow** us **to hold** our **course** AIT
Ac 27:39 *they d* not **recognize** the land, but AIT
Ac 28:19 *I certainly d* not **intend** to bring any charge AIT
Ro 1:28 just as *they d* not **think it worthwhile** to retain AIT
Ro 3:25 He **d** this to demonstrate his righteousness NDT
Ro 3:26 he **d** it to demonstrate his righteousness at NDT
Ro 4:20 Yet *he d* not **waver** through unbelief AIT
Ro 5:14 even over those *who d* not **sin** by breaking a AIT
Ro 5:14 a command, as **d** Adam, who is a pattern NDT
Ro 5:15 *d* God's grace and the gift that came by the grace of the one man, Jesus Christ, **overflow** AIT
Ro 6:21 What benefit *d you* **reap** at that time from the AIT
Ro 7:13 *D* that which is good, then, **become** death to AIT
Ro 8: 3 God **d** by sending his own Son in the NDT
Ro 8:32 *He* who *d* not **spare** his own Son, but gave AIT
Ro 9:20 formed it, 'Why *d you* **make** me like this? AIT
Ro 9:23 What if he **d** this to make the riches of his NDT
Ro 9:30 the Gentiles, who *d* not **pursue** righteousness AIT
Ro 10: 3 Since *they d* not **know** the righteousness of AIT
Ro 10: 3 *they d* not **submit** to God's righteousness. AIT
Ro 10:18 *D they* not **hear**? Of course they did AIT
Ro 10:18 Of course they **d**: "Their voice has NDT
Ro 10:19 *D* Israel not **understand**? First AIT
Ro 10:20 "I was found by those *who d* not **seek** me; AIT
Ro 10:20 myself to those *who d* not **ask for** me." AIT
Ro 11: 1 *D* God **reject** his people? By no AIT
Ro 11: 2 God *d* not **reject** his people, whom he AIT
Ro 11: 7 Israel sought so earnestly *they d* not **obtain**. AIT
Ro 11: 7 The elect among them **d**, but the others G2209S
Ro 11:11 *D they* **stumble** so as to fall beyond recovery AIT
Ro 11:21 For if God *d* not **spare** the natural branches AIT
Ro 15: 3 For even Christ *d* not **please** himself but, as it AIT
1Co 1:14 I thank God that *I d* not **baptize** any of you AIT
1Co 1:17 For Christ *d* not **send** me to baptize, but to AIT
1Co 1:21 world through its wisdom *d* not **know** him, AIT
1Co 2: 1 *I d* not **come** with eloquence or human AIT
1Co 4: 7 What do you have that *you d* not **receive** AIT
1Co 4: 7 And if *you d* **receive** it, why do you boast as AIT
1Co 4: 7 why do you boast as though *you* **d** not? G3284S
1Co 7:30 who mourn, as if *they* **d** not; those who G3081S
1Co 9:12 But *we d* not **use** this right. AIT
1Co 10: 6 our hearts on evil things as they **d**. G2121S
1Co 10: 8 as some of them **d**—and in one day G4519S
1Co 10: 9 as some of them **d**—and were killed by G4279S
1Co 10:10 as some of them **d**—and were killed by G1197
1Co 11: 8 For man *d* not **come** from woman, but woman AIT
1Co 14:36 Or *d* the word of God **originate** with you? Or AIT
1Co 15:15 But *he d* not **raise** him if in fact the dead are AIT
1Co 15:46 The spiritual **d** not come first, but the natural, NDT
2Co 1:23 to spare you *that I d* not **return** to Corinth. AIT
2Co 2: 3 I wrote **as** *I* **d**, so that when I came I G4047+899
2Co 2:13 *because* I *d* not **find** my brother Titus there. AIT
2Co 7: 8 Though *I d* **regret** it—I see that my letter hurt AIT
2Co 7:12 account of the *one who* **d** the **wrong** nor on G92
2Co 8:15 who gathered much *d* not **have too much**, AIT
2Co 8:15 one who gathered little *d* not **have too little**." AIT
2Co 10:14 for *we d* **get** as far as you with the gospel of AIT
2Co 12:17 *D I* **exploit** you through any of the men I sent AIT
2Co 12:18 Titus *d* not **exploit** you, did he? Did AIT
2Co 12:18 did not exploit you, **d** he? Did we not walk NDT
2Co 12:18 *D we* not **walk** in the same footsteps by the AIT
Gal 1:12 I *d* not **receive** it from any man, nor was I AIT
Gal 1:17 *I d* not **go up** to Jerusalem to see those who AIT
Gal 2: 5 *We d* not **give in** to them for a moment, so AIT
Gal 3: 2 *D you* **receive** the Spirit by the works of the AIT
Gal 4: 8 Formerly, *when you d* not **know** God, you AIT
Gal 4:12 I became like you. *You* **d** me no **wrong**. G92
Gal 4:14 *you d* not **treat** me **with contempt** or scorn. AIT
Gal 5:21 I warn you, as *I* **d before**, that those who G4625S
Php 2: 6 *d* not **consider** equality with God something AIT
Php 2:16 day of Christ that *I d* not **run** or labor in vain. AIT
1Th 2: 5 **d** we put on a mask to cover up greed NDT
1Th 2:18 certainly I, Paul, **d**, again and again—but NDT
1Th 4: 7 For God *d* not **call** us to be impure, but to live AIT
1Th 5: 9 For God *d* not **appoint** us to suffer wrath but AIT
2Th 3: 8 nor *d we* **eat** anyone's food without paying AIT
2Th 3: 9 We **d** this, not because we do not have the NDT
2Ti 1: 3 as my ancestors **d**, with a clear NDT
2Ti 4:14 the metalworker **d** me a great deal of G1892
Phm 14 But *I d* not **want** to do anything without your AIT
Heb 1: 5 For to which of the angels *d* God ever **say** AIT
Heb 1:13 To which of the angels *d* God ever **say**, "Sit AIT
Heb 3: 8 harden your hearts as you **d** in the rebellion, NDT
Heb 3: 9 though for forty years they saw **what I d**. G2240
Heb 3:15 harden your hearts as you **d** in the rebellion." NDT
Heb 3:18 And to whom *d* God **swear** that they would AIT
Heb 4: 2 just as they **d**; but the message they NDT
Heb 4: 2 *because they d* not **share** the faith of those AIT
Heb 4: 6 to them *d* not **go in** because of their AIT
Heb 4: 7 This he **d** when a long time later he spoke NDT
Heb 4:10 from their works, just as God **d** from his. NDT
Heb 4:15 every way, just as we are—yet he **d** not sin. NDT
Heb 5: 5 Christ *d* not **take** on himself *the* **glory** of AIT
Heb 6:18 God **d** this so that, by two unchangeable NDT
Heb 7: 6 however, *d* not **trace** *his* **descent** from Levi AIT
Heb 8: 9 because they *d* not **remain faithful** to my AIT
Heb 9:12 He **d** not enter by means of the blood of NDT
Heb 9:24 For Christ *d* not **enter** a sanctuary made with AIT
Heb 9:25 Nor **d** he enter heaven to offer himself again NDT
Heb 10: 5 "Sacrifice and offering *you d* not **desire**, but a AIT
Heb 10: 8 offerings and sin offerings *you d* not **desire**, AIT
Heb 11: 4 brought God a better offering than Cain **d**. NDT
Heb 11: 5 so that *he d* not **experience** death: AIT
Heb 11: 8 *even though he d* not **know** where he was AIT
Heb 11: 9 he lived in tents, as **d** Isaac and Jacob, who NDT
Heb 11:13 *They d* not **receive** the things promised; they AIT
Heb 11:19 speaking *he d* **receive** Isaac **back** from death AIT
Heb 12:25 If they *d* not **escape** when they refused him AIT
Jas 2:21 righteous for *what* he **d** when he offered G2240
Jas 2:22 faith was made complete by what he **d**. G2240
Jas 2:25 righteous for **what** she **d** when she gave G2240
Jas 5:17 and *it d* not **rain** on the land for three and a AIT
1Pe 2:23 insults at him, *he d* not **retaliate**; when he AIT
2Pe 1:16 For *we d* not **follow** cleverly devised stories AIT
2Pe 2: 4 For if God *d* not **spare** angels when they AIT
2Pe 2: 5 if *he d* not **spare** the ancient world when he AIT
1Jn 2: 6 to live in him must live as Jesus **d**. G4344S
1Jn 2:19 but *they* **d** not really belong to us. G1639
1Jn 3: 1 does not know us is that *it d* not **know** him. AIT
1Jn 3:12 And why *d he* **murder** him? Because AIT
1Jn 5: 6 He **d** not come by water only, but by water NDT
Jude 5 later destroyed those *who d* not **believe**. AIT
Jude 6 the angels who *d* not **keep** their positions AIT
Jude 9 *d* not *himself* **dare** to condemn him for AIT
Rev 2: 5 Repent and do the *things* you **d** at first. G2240
Rev 2:13 *You d* not **renounce** your faith in me, not AIT
Rev 2:19 you are now doing more than you **d** at first. NDT
Rev 7:13 who are they, and where *d they* **come** from?" AIT
Rev 9: 4 those people who *d* not **have** the seal of God AIT
Rev 9:20 these plagues *still d* not **repent** of the work of AIT
Rev 9:20 *they d* not stop **worshiping** demons AIT
Rev 9:21 Nor *d they* **repent** of their murders, their AIT
Rev 12:11 *they d* not **love** their lives so much as to AIT
Rev 14: 4 are those *who d* not **defile** *themselves* with AIT
Rev 20: 5 rest of the dead *d* not **come to life** until the AIT
Rev 21:22 *I d* not **see** a temple in the city, because the AIT

DIDN'T (43) [DO, NOT]

Ge 12:18 "Why **d** you tell me she was your wife? H4202
Ge 20: 5 is my sister,' and *d* she also **say**, 'He is my AIT
Ge 29:25 served you for Rachel, **d** I? Why have you H4202
Ge 31:27 Why **d** you tell me, so I could send you H4202
Ge 31:28 You **d** even let me kiss my grandchildren H4202
Ge 38:22 back to Judah and said, "I **d** find her. H4202
Ge 38:23 her this young goat, but you **d** find her." H4202
Ge 42:22 "**D** I tell you not to sin against the boy? H4202
Ex 14:12 **D** we say to you in Egypt, 'Leave us alone H4202
Lev 10:17 "Why **d** you eat the sin offering in the H4202
Nu 22:37 Why **d** you come to me? Am H4202
Jdg 8: 1 Why **d** you call us when you went to fight H1194
Jdg 11: 7 "**D** you hate me and drive me from my H4202
Jdg 11:26 Why **d** you retake them during that time H4202
Jdg 12: 2 I called, you **d** save me out of their hands. H4202
Jdg 13: 6 I **d** ask him where he came from, and he H4202
Jdg 13: 6 came from, and he **d** tell me his name. H4202
1Sa 26:15 Why **d** you guard your lord the king H4202
2Sa 11:10 Why **d** you go home?" H4202
2Sa 11:20 **D** you know they would shoot arrows from H4202
2Sa 11:21 **D** a woman drop an upper millstone on H4202
2Sa 16:17 he's your friend, why **d** you go with him?" H4202
2Sa 18:11 Why **d** you strike him to the ground right H4202
2Sa 19:25 king asked him, "Why **d** you go with me H4202
1Ki 22:18 "**D** I tell you that he never prophesies H4202
2Ki 2:18 he said to them, "**D** I tell you not to go?" H4202
2Ki 4:28 "**D** I tell you, 'Don't raise my H4202
2Ki 5:25 "Your servant **d** go anywhere," Gehazi H4202
2Ch 13: 9 But **d** you drive out the priests of the LORD H4202
2Ch 18:17 "**D** I tell you that he never prophesies H4202
Ne 13:18 **D** your ancestors do the same things, so H4202
Mt 13:27 **d** you sow good seed in your field? G4049
Mt 16: 7 "It is because we **d** bring any bread." G4024
Mt 20:13 **D** you agree to work for a denarius? G4049
Mt 21:25 he will ask, 'Then why **d** you believe him? G4024
Mk 11:31 he will ask, 'Then why **d** you believe him? G4024
Lk 2:49 "**D** you know I had to be in my Father's G4024
Lk 19:23 Why then **d** you put my money on deposit G4024
Lk 20: 5 he will ask, 'Why **d** you believe him? G4024
Lk 24:23 **d** find his body. They came and told us G3590
Jn 7:45 asked them, "Why **d** you bring him in?" G4024
Jn 18:26 "**D** I see you with him in the garden?" G4024
Ac 5: 4 **D** it belong to you before it was sold? And G4049

DIDYMUS (3)

Jn 11:16 Thomas (also known as **D**) said to G1441
Jn 20:24 Thomas (also known as **D**), one of the G1441
Jn 21: 2 Thomas (also known as **D**), Nathanael G1441

DIE (304) [DEAD, DEADLY, DEATH, DEATH'S, DEATHLY, DEATHS, DIED, DIES, DYING]

Ge 2:17 you eat from it *you will* **certainly d**." H4637+4637
Ge 3: 3 you must not touch it, or *you will* **d**. H4637
Ge 3: 4 "*You will* not **certainly d**," the H4637+4637
Ge 19:19 this disaster will overtake me, and *I'll* **d**. H4637
Ge 20: 7 and all who belong to you *will* **d**." H4637+4637
Ge 21:16 she thought, "I cannot watch the boy **d**." H4638
Ge 25:32 I am about to **d**," Esau said. H4637
Ge 27: 4 I may give you my blessing before *I* **d**." H4637
Ge 27: 7 in the presence of the LORD before I **d**. H4638
Ge 30: 1 said to Jacob, "Give me children, or I'll **d**!" H4637
Ge 33:13 hard just one day, all the animals *will* **d**. H4637
Ge 38:11 he thought, "He may **d** too, just like his H4637
Ge 42: 2 so that we may live and not **d**. H4637
Ge 42:20 may be verified and that you *may* not **d**." H4637
Ge 43: 8 you and our children may live and not **d**. H4637
Ge 44: 9 found to have it, *he will* **d**; and the rest of H4637
Ge 44:22 if he leaves him, his father *will* **d**. H4637
Ge 44:31 boy isn't there, *he will* **d**. Your servants H4637
Ge 45:28 I will go and see him before *I* **d**." H4637
Ge 46:30 Joseph, "Now *I am* **ready to d**, since I H4637
Ge 47:15 Why *should we* **d** before your eyes H4637
Ge 47:19 us seed so that we may live and not **d**, H4637
Ge 47:29 When the time drew near for Israel to **d** H4637
Ge 48:21 to Joseph, "*I am about to* **d**, but God will H4637
Ge 50: 5 said, "*I am about to* **d**; bury me in the H4637
Ge 50:24 said to his brothers, "*I am about to* **d**. H4637
Ex 7:18 The fish in the Nile *will* **d**, and the river H4637
Ex 9: 4 animal belonging to the Israelites *will* **d**. H4637
Ex 9:19 is still out in the field, and *they will* **d**. H4637

Ex 10:28 The day you see my face *you will* **d**." H4637
Ex 11: 5 Every firstborn son in Egypt *will* **d**, from H4637
Ex 12:33 otherwise," they said, "*we will* all **d**!" H4637
Ex 14:11 that you brought us to the desert to **d**? H4637
Ex 14:12 the Egyptians than *to* **d** in the desert!" H4637
Ex 17: 3 **make** us and our children and livestock **d** H4637
Ex 20:19 do not have God speak to us or *we will* **d**." H4637
Ex 21:18 the victim *does* not **d** but is confined H4637
Ex 28:35 when he comes out, so that *he will* not **d**. H4637
Ex 28:43 so that they will not incur guilt and **d**. H4637
Ex 30:20 wash with water so that *they will* not **d**. H4637
Ex 30:21 hands and feet so that *they will* not **d**. H4637
Lev 8:35 LORD requires, so *you will* not **d**; for that is H4637
Lev 10: 6 or *you will* **d** and the LORD will be angry H4637
Lev 10: 7 to the tent of meeting or *you will* **d**, H4637
Lev 10: 9 go into the tent of meeting, or *you will* **d**. H4637
Lev 15:31 so *they will* not **d** in their uncleanness H4637
Lev 16: 2 cover on the ark, or else *he will* **d**. H4637
Lev 16:13 of the covenant law, so that *he will* not **d**. H4637
Lev 20:20 be held responsible; *they will* **d** childless. H4637
Lev 21: 1 unclean for any of his people who **d**, H5883
Lev 22: 9 become guilty and **d** for treating it with H4637
Nu 4:15 not touch the holy things or *they will* **d**. H4637
Nu 4:19 may live and not **d** when they come near H4637
Nu 4:20 even for a moment, or *they will* **d**. H4637
Nu 14:35 end in this wilderness; here *they will* **d**." H4637
Nu 15:35 said to Moses, "The man **must d**. H4637+4637
Nu 16:29 If these men **d** a natural death and suffer H4637
Nu 17:10 against me, so that *they will* not **d**." H4637
Nu 17:12 said to Moses, "*We will* **d**! We are lost, H1588
Nu 17:13 near the tabernacle of the LORD *will* **d**. H4637
Nu 17:13 the LORD will die. Are we all *going to* **d**?" H1588
Nu 18: 3 Otherwise both they and you *will* **d**. H4637
Nu 18:22 the consequences of their sin and *will* **d**. H4637
Nu 18:32 of the Israelites, and *you will* not **d**. H4637
Nu 20: 4 that we and our livestock *should* **d** here? H4637
Nu 20:26 gathered to his people; *he will* **d** there." H4637
Nu 21: 5 us up out of Egypt to **d** in the wilderness? H4637
Nu 23:10 *Let* me **d** the death of the righteous, and H4637
Nu 26:11 The line of Korah, however, *did* not **d out**. H4637
Nu 26:65 Israelites *they would* **surely d** in the H4637+4637
Nu 35:12 accused of murder *may* not **d** before they H4637
Nu 35:20 at them intentionally so that *they* **d** H4637
Nu 35:23 to kill them, and *they* **d**, then since that H4637
Nu 35:31 the life of a murderer, who deserves to **d**. H4637
Dt 4:22 I *will* **d** in this land; I will not cross the H4637
Dt 5:25 But now, why *should we* **d**? This great fire H4637
Dt 5:25 and *we will* **d** if we hear the voice of the H4637
Dt 18:16 see this great fire anymore, or *we will* **d**." H4637
Dt 19:12 handed over to the avenger of blood *to* **d**. H4637
Dt 20: 5 or *he may* **d** in battle and someone else H4637
Dt 20: 6 or *he may* **d** in battle and someone else H4637
Dt 20: 7 or *he may* **d** in battle and someone else H4637
Dt 22:22 slept with her and the woman *must* **d**. H4637
Dt 22:25 only the man who has done this *shall* **d**. H4637
Dt 24: 7 them as a slave, the kidnapper *must* **d**. H4637
Dt 24:16 their parents; each *will* **d** for their own sin. H4637
Dt 31:27 how much more will you rebel after I **d**! H4638
Dt 32:50 have climbed *you will* **d** and be gathered H4637
Dt 33: 6 "Let Reuben live and not **d**, nor his H4637
Jdg 6:23 not be afraid. *You are* not *going to* **d**." H4637
Jdg 6:30 *He must* **d**, because he has broken down H4637
Jdg 13:22 "*We are* **doomed to d**!" he said to H4637+4637
Jdg 15:18 *Must I* now **d** of thirst and fall into the H4637
Jdg 16:30 "*Let* me **d** with the Philistines! H4637
Ru 1:17 Where *you* **d** I will die, and there I will be H4637
Ru 1:17 Where you die *I will* **d**, and there I will be H4637
1Sa 2:33 all your descendants *will* **d** in the prime of H4637
1Sa 2:34 to you—they *will* both **d** on the same day. H4637
1Sa 5:12 Those who *did* not **d** were afflicted with H4637
1Sa 12:19 your servants so that *we will* not **d**, H4637
1Sa 14:39 with my son Jonathan, *he* **must d**." H4637+4637
1Sa 14:43 the end of my staff. And now I *must* **d**!" H4637
1Sa 14:44 severely, if *you do* not **d**, Jonathan." H4637+4637
1Sa 14:45 to Saul, "*Should* Jonathan **d**—he who has H4637
1Sa 20: 2 "*You are* not *going to* **d**! Look, H4637
1Sa 20:31 to bring him to me, for he **must d**!" H1201+4638
1Sa 22:16 "*You will* **surely d**, Ahimelek, H4637+4637
1Sa 26:10 his time will come and *he will* **d**, or he H4637
1Sa 26:16 you and your men must **d**, because you H4638
2Sa 3:33 Abner have died as the lawless **d**? H4638
2Sa 11:15 from him so he will be struck down and **d**." H4637
2Sa 12: 5 LORD lives, the man who did this must **d**! H4638
2Sa 12:13 away your sin. *You are* not *going to* **d**. H4637
2Sa 12:14 the LORD, the son born to you *will* **d**."H4637+4637
2Sa 14:14 cannot be recovered, so we **must d**. H4637+4637
2Sa 18: 3 Even if half of us **d**, they won't care; but H4637
2Sa 19:23 the king said to Shimei, "*You shall* not **d**." H4637
2Sa 19:37 that *I may* **d** in my own town near the H4637
1Ki 1:52 if evil is found in him, *he will* **d**. H4637
1Ki 2: 1 When the time drew near for David to **d** H4637
1Ki 2:26 You deserve to **d**, but I will not put you to H4638
1Ki 2:30 he answered, "No, *I will* **d** here." Benaiah H4637
1Ki 2:37 you can be sure *you will* **d**; your H4637+4637
1Ki 2:42 you can be sure *you will* **d**'? H4637+4637
1Ki 13:31 to his sons, "When I **d**, bury me in the H4638
1Ki 14:11 belonging to Jeroboam *who* **d** in the city, H4637
1Ki 14:11 will feed on those *who* **d** in the country. H4637
1Ki 14:12 you set foot in your city, the boy *will* **d**. H4637
1Ki 16: 4 belonging to Baasha *who* **d** in the city, H4637
1Ki 16: 4 will feed on those *who* **d** in the country." H4637
1Ki 17:12 my son, that we may eat it—and **d**." H4637

1Ki 17:20 am staying with, by **causing** her son **to d**?" H4637
1Ki 19: 4 under it and prayed that he *might* **d**. H4637
1Ki 20:42 free a man I had **determined should d**. H3051
1Ki 21:24 belonging to Ahab *who* **d** in the city, H4637
1Ki 21:24 will feed on those *who* **d** in the country." H4637
2Ki 1: 4 are lying on. *You will* **certainly d**!' " H4637+4637
2Ki 1: 6 *You will* **certainly d**!" ' " H4637+4637
2Ki 1:16 are lying on. *You will* **certainly d**!" H4637+4637
2Ki 7: 3 to each other, "Why stay here until we **d**? H4637
2Ki 7: 4 the famine is there, and *we will* **d**. H4637
2Ki 7: 4 if we stay here, *we will* **d**. So let's go over H4637
2Ki 7: 4 we live; if they kill us, then *we* **d**. H4637
2Ki 8:10 to me that *he will* **in fact d**. H4637+4637
2Ki 14: 6 their parents; each *will* **d** for their own sin." H4637
2Ki 20: 1 because you *are going to* **d**; you will not H4637
2Ch 25: 4 their parents; each *will* **d** for their own sin." H4637
2Ch 32:11 to let you **d** of hunger and thirst. H4637
Est 9:28 memory of these days **d out** among their H6066
Job 2: 9 your integrity? Curse God and **d**!" H4637
Job 3:11 at birth, and **d** as I came from the womb? H1588
Job 4:21 pulled up, so that *they* **d** without wisdom? H4637
Job 12: 2 who matter, and wisdom *will* **d** with you! H4637
Job 13:19 If so, I will be silent and **d**. H1588
Job 14: 8 in the ground and its stump **d** in the soil, H4637
Job 27: 5 are in the right; till *I* **d**, I will not deny my H1588
Job 29:18 "I thought, '*I will* **d** in my own house, my H1588
Job 34:20 *They* **d** in an instant, in the middle of the H4637
Job 36:12 by the sword and **d** without knowledge. H1588
Job 36:14 They **d** in their youth, among male H4637
Ps 37: 2 like green plants *they will* soon **d away**. H5570
Ps 41: 5 "When *will he* **d** and his name perish?" H4637
Ps 49:10 For all can see that the wise **d**, that the H4637
Ps 49:14 They are like sheep and are destined to **d**; H8619
Ps 49:17 will take nothing with them when they **d**, H4638
Ps 79:11 arm preserve those condemned to **d**. H9456
Ps 82: 7 But *you will* **d** like mere mortals; you will H4637
Ps 104:29 their breath, *they* **d** and return to the dust. H1588
Ps 105:29 waters into blood, **causing** their fish **to d**. H4637
Ps 118:17 *I will* not **d** but live, and will proclaim H4637
Pr 5:23 For lack of discipline they *will* **d**, led astray H4637
Pr 10:21 but fools **d** for lack of sense. H4637
Pr 11: 7 Hopes placed in mortals **d** with them; all H4638
Pr 15:10 the one who hates correction *will* **d**. H4637
Pr 19:16 shows contempt for their ways *will* **d**. H4637
Pr 23:13 punish them with the rod, *they will* not **d**. H4637
Pr 30: 7 LORD; do not refuse me before *I* **d**: H4637
Ecc 2:16 Like the fool, the wise too *must* **d**! H4637
Ecc 3: 2 a time to be born and a time to **d**, a time H4637
Ecc 7:17 not be a fool—why **d** before your time? H4637
Ecc 9: 5 For the living know that *they will* **d**, but H4637
Isa 5:13 of high rank *will* **d** *of* hunger and the H4637
Isa 22: 2 by the sword, nor *did they* **d** in battle. H4637
Isa 22:13 drink," you say, "for tomorrow *we* **d**!" H4637
Isa 22:18 There *you will* **d** and there the chariots H4637
Isa 38: 1 because you *are going to* **d**; you will not H4637
Isa 50: 2 fish rot for lack of water and **d** of thirst. H4637
Isa 51: 6 a garment and its inhabitants **d** like flies. H4637
Isa 51:14 set free; *they will* not **d** in their dungeon H4637
Isa 59: 5 Whoever eats their eggs *will* **d**, and when H4637
Isa 66:24 the worms that eat them *will* not **d**, the H4637
Jer 11:21 of the LORD or *you will* **d** by our hands"— H4637
Jer 11:22 Their young men *will* **d** by the sword, their H4637
Jer 16: 4 "*They will* **d** *of* deadly diseases. They will H4637
Jer 16: 6 "Both high and low *will* **d** in this land H4637
Jer 20: 6 There *you will* **d** and be buried, you and H4637
Jer 21: 6 and *they will* **d** of a terrible plague. H4637
Jer 21: 9 stays in this city *will* **d** by the sword, H4637
Jer 22:12 *He will* **d** in the place where they have led H4637
Jer 22:26 you was born, and there *you both will* **d**. H4637
Jer 26: 8 seized him and said, "*You* **must d**! H4637+4637
Jer 27:13 Why *will* you and your people **d** by the H4637
Jer 28:16 This very year you *are going to* **d**, because H4637
Jer 31:30 Instead, everyone *will* **d** for their own sin H4637
Jer 34: 4 *You will* not **d** by the sword; H4637
Jer 34: 5 *you will* **d** peacefully. As people made a H4637
Jer 37:20 of Jonathan the secretary, or *I will* **d** there." H4637
Jer 38: 2 stays in this city *will* **d** by the sword, H4637
Jer 38:24 about this conversation, or *you may* **d**. H4637
Jer 38:26 me back to Jonathan's house to **d** there. H4637
Jer 42:16 you into Egypt, and there *you will* **d**. H4637
Jer 42:17 Egypt to settle there *will* **d** by the sword, H4637
Jer 42:22 *You will* **d** by the sword, famine and H4637
Jer 44:12 will fall by the sword or **d** from famine. H9462
Jer 44:12 greatest, *they will* **d** by sword or famine. H4637
La 4: 9 are better off than *those who* **d** *of* famine; H2728
Eze 3:18 person, '*You will* **surely d**,' and you H4637+4637
Eze 3:18 that wicked person *will* **d** for their sin, and H4637
Eze 3:19 their evil ways, they *will* **d** for their sin; but H4637
Eze 3:20 stumbling block before them, they *will* **d**. H4637
Eze 3:20 not warn them, *they will* **d** for their sin. H4637
Eze 5:12 of your people *will* **d** of the plague or H4637
Eze 6:12 One who is far away *will* **d** of the plague H4637
Eze 6:12 survives and is spared *will* **d** of famine. H4637
Eze 7:15 Those in the country *will* **d** by the sword H4637
Eze 12:13 he will not see it, and there *he will* **d**. H4637
Eze 17:16 Sovereign LORD, *he shall* **d** in Babylon, in H4637
Eze 18: 4 The one who sins is the one *who will* **d**. H4637
Eze 18:17 He *will* not **d** for his father's sin; he will H4637
Eze 18:18 But his father *will* **d** for his own sin H4637
Eze 18:20 The one who sins is the one *who will* **d** H4637
Eze 18:21 that person will surely live; *they will* not **d**. H4637
Eze 18:24 the sins they have committed, *they will* **d**. H4637

Eze 18:26 commits sin, *they will* **d** for it; because H4637
Eze 18:26 the sin they have committed *they will* **d**. H4637
Eze 18:28 that person will surely live; *they will* not **d**. H4637
Eze 18:31 Why *will you* **d**, people of H4637
Eze 28: 8 and *you will* **d** a violent death in the heart H4637
Eze 28:10 *You will* **d** the death of the uncircumcised H4637
Eze 33: 8 person, *you will* **surely d**,' and you H4637+4637
Eze 33: 8 that wicked person *will* **d** for their sin, and H4637
Eze 33: 9 do not do so, they *will* **d** for their sin H4637
Eze 33:11 Why *will you* **d**, people of Israel H4637
Eze 33:13 *they will* **d** for the evil they have done. H4637
Eze 33:14 person, '*You will* **surely d**,' but they H4637+4637
Eze 33:15 that person will surely live; *they will* not **d**. H4637
Eze 33:18 does evil, *they will* **d** for it. H4637
Eze 33:27 strongholds and caves *will* **d** of a plague. H4637
Am 6: 9 are left in one house, *they* too *will* **d**. H4637
Am 7:11 " 'Jeroboam *will* **d** by the sword, and H4637
Am 7:17 and *you* yourself *will* **d** in a pagan country. H4637
Am 9:10 among my people *will* **d** by the sword, H4637
Jnh 1:14 *do not let us* **d** for taking this man's life. H6
Jnh 4: 3 for it is better for me to **d** than to live." H4638
Jnh 4: 8 He wanted to **d**, and said, "It would be H4637
Jnh 4: 8 would be better for me to **d** than to live." H4638
Hab 1:12 my Holy One, *you will* never **d**. H4637
Zec 11: 9 your shepherd. *Let* the dying **d**, and the H4637
Zec 13: 3 to them, '*You must* **d**, because you H2649+4202
Mt 26:35 "Even if I have to **d** with you, I will never *G633*
Mt 26:52 all who draw the sword *will* **d** by the sword. *G660*
Mk 9:48 where " 'the worms that eat them *do not* **d**, *G5462*
Mk 14:31 "Even if I have to **d with** you, I will never *G5271*
Lk 2:26 Spirit *that he would* not **d** before *G3972+2505*
Lk 7: 2 valued highly, was sick and about to **d**. *G5462*
Lk 13:33 surely no prophet can **d** outside Jerusalem! *G660*
Lk 20:36 they can no longer **d**; for they are like *G633*
Jn 6:50 heaven, which anyone may eat and not **d**. *G633*
Jn 8:21 will look for me, and *you will* **d** in your sin. *G633*
Jn 8:24 I told you that *you would* **d** in your sins; if *G633*
Jn 8:24 that I am he, *you will indeed* **d** in your sins." *G633*
Jn 11:16 "Let us also go, that we *may* **d** with him." *G633*
Jn 11:25 in me will live, even though *they* **d**; *G633*
Jn 11:26 lives by believing in me *will* never **d**. *G633*
Jn 11:50 you that one man **d** for the people than *G633*
Jn 11:51 that Jesus would **d** for the Jewish nation, *G633*
Jn 12:33 show the kind of death he was going to **d**. *G633*
Jn 18:32 about the kind of death he was going to **d**. *G633*
Jn 19: 7 according to that law he must **d** *G633*
Jn 21:23 the believers that this disciple *would* not **d**. *G633*
Jn 21:23 But Jesus did not say that *he would* not **d** *G633*
Ac 7:19 babies so that *they would* **d**. *G3590+2441*
Ac 21:13 also *to* **d** in Jerusalem for the name of *G633*
Ac 25:11 deserving death, I do not refuse *to* **d**. *G633*
Ro 5: 7 Very rarely *will* anyone **d** for a righteous *G633*
Ro 5: 7 person someone might possibly dare *to* **d**. *G633*
Ro 6: 9 from the dead, *he* cannot **d** again; death *G633*
Ro 8:13 to the flesh, you will **d**; but if by the Spirit *G633*
Ro 14: 8 the Lord; and if *we* **d**, we die for the *G633*
Ro 14: 8 the Lord; and if we die, *we* **d** for the Lord. *G633*
Ro 14: 8 whether we live or **d**, we belong to the Lord *G633*
1Co 4: 9 like *those* **condemned to d** in the arena. *G2119*
1Co 9:15 I *would* rather **d** than allow anyone to *G633*
1Co 15:22 For as in Adam all **d**, so in Christ all will be *G633*
1Co 15:32 "Let us eat and drink, for tomorrow *we* **d**." *G633*
2Co 7: 3 hearts that we would live or **d with** you. *G5271*
Php 1:21 For to me, to live is Christ and *to* **d** is gain. *G633*
Heb 7: 8 the tenth is collected *by* people *who* **d**; but *G633*
Heb 9:27 Just as people are destined *to* **d** once, and *G633*
1Pe 2:24 so that *we might* **d** to sins and live for *G614*
Rev 3: 2 Strengthen what remains and is about to **d** *G633*
Rev 9: 6 they will long to **d**, but death will elude *G633*
Rev 11: 5 anyone who wants to harm them must **d**. *G650*
Rev 14:13 are the dead who **d** in the Lord from now *G633*

DIED (256) [DIE]

Ge 5: 5 lived a total of 930 years, and then *he* **d**. H4637
Ge 5: 8 lived a total of 912 years, and then *he* **d**. H4637
Ge 5:11 lived a total of 905 years, and then *he* **d**. H4637
Ge 5:14 lived a total of 910 years, and then *he* **d**. H4637
Ge 5:17 lived a total of 895 years, and then *he* **d**. H4637
Ge 5:20 lived a total of 962 years, and then *he* **d**. H4637
Ge 5:27 lived a total of 969 years, and then *he* **d**. H4637
Ge 5:31 lived a total of 777 years, and then *he* **d**. H4637
Ge 7:22 that had the breath of life in its nostrils **d**. H4637
Ge 9:29 lived a total of 950 years, and then *he* **d**. H4637
Ge 11:28 still alive, Haran **d** in Ur of the Chaldeans H4637
Ge 11:32 Terah lived 205 years, and he **d** in Harran. H4637
Ge 23: 2 She **d** at Kiriath Arba (that is, Hebron) in H4637
Ge 25: 8 his last and **d** at a good old age, H4637
Ge 25:17 He breathed his last and **d**, and he was H4637
Ge 26:18 had stopped up after Abraham **d**, H4638
Ge 35: 8 **d** and was buried under the oak outside H4637
Ge 35:19 So Rachel **d** and was buried on the way to H4637
Ge 35:29 his last and **d** and was gathered to H4637
Ge 36:33 When Bela **d**, Jobab son of Zerah from H4637
Ge 36:34 When Jobab **d**, Husham from the land of H4637
Ge 36:35 When Husham **d**, Hadad son of Bedad H4637
Ge 36:36 When Hadad **d**, Samlah from Masrekah H4637
Ge 36:37 When Samlah **d**, Shaul from Rehoboth on H4637
Ge 36:38 When Shaul **d**, Baal-Hanan son of Akbor H4637
Ge 36:39 When Baal-Hanan son of Akbor **d**, Hadad H4637
Ge 38:12 Judah's wife, the daughter of Shua, **d**. H4637
Ge 46:12 Er and Onan *had* **d** in the land of H4637
Ge 48: 7 to my sorrow Rachel **d** in the land of H4637

Ge 50:16 father left these instructions before he **d**: H4638
Ge 50:26 So Joseph **d** at the age of a hundred and H4637
Ex 1: 6 all his brothers and all that generation **d**, H4637
Ex 2:23 that long period, the king of Egypt **d**. H4637
Ex 7:21 The fish in the Nile **d**, and the river H4637
Ex 8:13 The frogs **d** in the houses, in the H4637
Ex 9: 6 All the livestock of the Egyptians **d**, but H4637
Ex 9: 6 one animal belonging to the Israelites **d**. H4637
Ex 9: 7 one of the animals of the Israelites *had* **d**. H4637
Ex 16: 3 "If only we *had* **d** by the LORD's hand in H4637
Ex 32:28 about three thousand of the people **d**. H5877
Lev 10: 2 and *they* **d** before the LORD. H4637
Lev 16: 1 two sons of Aaron *who* **d** when they H4637
Nu 3: 4 **d** before the LORD when they made an H4637
Nu 11: 2 he prayed to the LORD and the fire **d down**. H9205
Nu 14: 2 said to them, "If only *we had* **d** in Egypt! H4637
Nu 14:37 the land *were* **struck down and d** of a H4637
Nu 16:49 But 14,700 *people* **d** from the plague, in H4637
Nu 16:49 to those *who had* **d** because of Korah H4637
Nu 19:16 *someone who has* **d a natural death**, H4637
Nu 19:18 anyone *who has* **d a natural death**. H4637
Nu 20: 1 There Miriam **d** and was buried. H4637
Nu 20: 3 "If only *we had* **d** when our brothers fell H1588
Nu 20:28 And Aaron **d** there on top of the H4637
Nu 20:29 community learned that Aaron *had* **d**, H1588
Nu 21: 6 they bit the people and many Israelites **d**. H4637
Nu 25: 9 those *who* **d** in the plague numbered H4637
Nu 26:10 whose followers **d** when the fire devoured H4637
Nu 26:19 were sons of Judah, but *they* **d** in Canaan. H4637
Nu 26:61 Nadab and Abihu **d** when they made an H4637
Nu 27: 3 "Our father **d** in the wilderness. He was H4637
Nu 27: 3 but *he* **d** for his own sin and left no sons. H4637
Nu 33:38 where *he* **d** on the first day of the fifth H4637
Nu 33:39 years old when he **d** on Mount Hor. H4637
Dt 2:16 fighting men among the people *had* **d**, H4637
Dt 10: 6 There Aaron **d** and was buried, and H4637
Dt 32:50 your brother Aaron **d** on Mount Hor and H4637
Dt 34: 5 the servant of the LORD **d** there in Moab, H4637
Dt 34: 7 hundred and twenty years old when he **d**, H4637
Jos 5: 4 **d** in the wilderness on the way after H4637
Jos 5: 6 military age when they left Egypt *had* **d**, H9462
Jos 10:11 more of them **d** from the hail than H4637
Jos 22:20 He was not the only one *who* **d** for his sin H1588
Jos 24:29 **d** at the age of a hundred and ten. H4637
Jos 24:33 Eleazar son of Aaron **d** and was buried at H4637
Jdg 1: 7 him to Jerusalem, and *he* **d** there. H4637
Jdg 2: 8 **d** at the age of a hundred and ten. H4637
Jdg 2:19 But when the judge **d**, the people returned H4638
Jdg 2:21 any of the nations Joshua left when *he* **d**. H4637
Jdg 3:11 forty years, until Othniel son of Kenaz **d**. H4637
Jdg 4:21 his temple into the ground, and *he* **d**. H4637
Jdg 8:32 Gideon son of Joash **d** at a good old age H4637
Jdg 8:33 No sooner *had* Gideon **d** than the H4637
Jdg 9:49 a thousand men and women, also **d**. H4637
Jdg 9:54 So his servant ran him through, and *he* **d**. H4637
Jdg 10: 2 then *he* **d**, and was buried in H4637
Jdg 10: 5 When Jair **d**, he was buried in Kamon. H4637
Jdg 12: 7 the Gileadite **d** and was buried in a H4637
Jdg 12:10 Then Ibzan **d** and was buried in H4637
Jdg 12:12 Then Elon **d** and was buried in Aijalon in H4637
Jdg 12:15 Abdon son of Hillel **d** and was buried at H4637
Jdg 16:30 many more when he **d** than while he H4638
Jdg 20: 5 They raped my concubine, and *she* **d**. H4637
Ru 1: 3 Naomi's husband, **d**, and she was left H4637
Ru 1: 5 both Mahlon and Kilion also **d**, and H4637
1Sa 4:11 Eli's two sons, Hophni and Phinehas, **d**. H4637
1Sa 4:18 His neck was broken and *he* **d**, for he was H4637
1Sa 15:35 Until the day Samuel **d**, he did not go to H4638
1Sa 25: 1 Now Samuel **d**, and all Israel assembled H4637
1Sa 25:38 days later, the LORD struck Nabal and *he* **d**. H4637
1Sa 31: 5 he too fell on his sword and **d** with him. H4637
1Sa 31: 6 all his men **d** together that same day. H4637
1Sa 31: 7 fled and that Saul and his sons *had* **d**, H4637
2Sa 1: 4 "Many of them fell and **d**. And Saul and H4637
2Sa 1:15 So he struck him down, and *he* **d**. H4637
2Sa 2:23 He fell there and **d** on the spot. And every H4637
2Sa 2:23 the place where Asahel had fallen and **d**. H4637
2Sa 3:27 stabbed him in the stomach, and *he* **d**. H4637
2Sa 3:33 "*Should* Abner *have* **d** as the lawless die H4637
2Sa 4: 1 Saul heard that Abner *had* **d** in Hebron, H4637
2Sa 6: 7 and *he* **d** there beside the ark of God. H4637
2Sa 10: 1 the king of the Ammonites **d**, and his son H4637
2Sa 10:18 commander of their army, and *he* **d** there. H4637
2Sa 11:17 army fell; moreover, Uriah the Hittite **d**. H4637
2Sa 11:21 from the wall, so that *he* **d** in Thebez? H4637
2Sa 11:24 the wall, and some of the king's men **d**. H4637
2Sa 12:18 On the seventh day the child **d**. H4637
2Sa 17:23 So *he* **d** and was buried in his father's H4637
2Sa 18:33 If only I *had* **d** instead of you—O Absalom H4637
2Sa 19:10 anointed to rule over us, *has* **d** in battle. H4637
2Sa 20:10 Amasa **d**. Then Joab and his H4637
2Sa 24:15 of the people from Dan to Beersheba **d**. H4637
1Ki 2:25 he struck down Adonijah and *he* **d**. H4637
1Ki 2:46 out and struck Shimei down and *he* **d**. H4637
1Ki 3:19 this woman's son **d** because she lay on H4637
1Ki 14:17 the threshold of the house, the boy **d**. H4637
1Ki 16:18 the palace on fire around him. So *he* **d**, H4637
1Ki 16:22 So Tibni **d** and Omri became king H4637
1Ki 22:35 of the chariot, and that evening *he* **d**. H4637
1Ki 22:37 So the king **d** and was brought to Samaria H4637
2Ki 1:17 So *he* **d**, according to the word of the LORD H4637
2Ki 3: 5 But after Ahab **d**, the king of Moab H4638
2Ki 4:20 sat on her lap until noon, and then *he* **d**. H4637
2Ki 7:17 in the gateway, and *he* **d**, just as the man H4637
2Ki 7:20 trampled him in the gateway, and *he* **d**. H4637
2Ki 8:15 it over the king's face, so that *he* **d**. H4637
2Ki 9:27 he escaped to Megiddo and **d** there. H4637
2Ki 12:21 *He* **d** and was buried with his ancestors in H4637
2Ki 13:14 suffering from the illness from which *he* **d**. H4637
2Ki 13:20 Elisha **d** and was buried. Now Moabite H4637
2Ki 13:24 Hazael king of Aram **d**, and Ben-Hadad H4637
2Ki 15: 5 the king with leprosy until the day he **d**, H4637
2Ki 23:34 carried him off to Egypt, and there *he* **d**. H4637
1Ch 1:44 When Bela **d**, Jobab son of Zerah from H4637
1Ch 1:45 When Jobab **d**, Husham from the land of H4637
1Ch 1:46 When Husham **d**, Hadad son of Bedad H4637
1Ch 1:47 When Hadad **d**, Samlah from Masrekah H4637
1Ch 1:48 When Samlah **d**, Shaul from Rehoboth on H4637
1Ch 1:49 When Shaul **d**, Baal-Hanan son of Akbor H4637
1Ch 1:50 When Baal-Hanan **d**, Hadad succeeded H4637
1Ch 1:51 Hadad also **d**. The chiefs of Edom were H4637
1Ch 2:19 When Azubah **d**, Caleb married Ephrath H4637
1Ch 2:24 After Hezron **d** in Caleb Ephrathah H4638
1Ch 2:30 Seled **d** without children. H4637
1Ch 2:32 Jonathan. Jether **d** without children. H4637
1Ch 10: 5 was dead, he too fell on his sword and **d**. H4637
1Ch 10: 6 So Saul and his three sons **d**, and all his H4637
1Ch 10: 6 sons died, and all his house **d** together. H4637
1Ch 10: 7 fled and that Saul and his sons *had* **d**, H4637
1Ch 10:13 Saul **d** because he was unfaithful to the H4637
1Ch 13:10 So *he* **d** there before God. H4637
1Ch 19: 1 Nahash king of the Ammonites **d**, and his H4637
1Ch 23:22 Eleazar **d** without having sons: he had H4637
1Ch 24: 2 But Nadab and Abihu **d** before their father H4637
1Ch 29:28 *He* **d** at a good old age, having enjoyed H4637
2Ch 13:20 And the LORD struck him down and *he* **d**. H4637
2Ch 16:13 year of his reign Asa **d** and rested with his H4637
2Ch 18:34 until evening. Then at sunset *he* **d**. H4637
2Ch 21:19 of the disease, and *he* **d** in great pain. H4637
2Ch 24:15 and *he* **d** at the age of a hundred and H4637
2Ch 24:25 So *he* **d** and was buried in the City of H4637
2Ch 26:21 Uzziah had leprosy until the day *he* **d**. H4638
2Ch 32:33 of Jerusalem honored him when he **d**. H4637
2Ch 35:24 brought him to Jerusalem, where *he* **d**. H4637
Est 2: 7 daughter when her father and mother **d**. H4638
Job 10:18 *I wish I had* **d** before any eye saw me. H1588
Job 42:17 And so Job **d**, an old man and full of years H4637
Ecc 4: 2 the dead, who *had* already **d**, are happier H4637
Isa 6: 1 In the year that King Uzziah **d**, I saw the H4638
Isa 14:28 prophecy came in the year King Ahaz **d**: H4638
Jer 28:17 that same year, Hananiah the prophet **d**. H4637
Eze 11:13 prophesying, Pelatiah son of Benaiah **d**. H4637
Eze 13:19 those who *should* not *have* **d** and have H4637
Eze 24:18 morning, and in the evening my wife **d**. H4637
Hos 13: 1 he became guilty of Baal worship and **d**. H4637
Jnh 4:10 It sprang up overnight and **d** overnight. H6
Mt 2:19 *After* Herod **d**, an angel of the Lord *G5462*
Mt 8:32 bank into the lake and **d** in the water. *G633*
Mt 9:18 him and said, "My daughter *has* just **d**. *G5462*
Mt 14:32 climbed into the boat, the wind **d down**. *G3156*
Mt 22:25 The first one married and **d**, and since he *G5462*
Mt 22:27 the woman **d**. *G633*
Mt 27:52 holy people who *had* **d** were raised to life *G3121*
Mk 4:39 Then the wind **d down** and it was *G3156*
Mk 6:51 the boat with them, and the wind **d down**. *G3156*
Mk 12:20 first one married and **d** without leaving any *G633*
Mk 12:21 the widow, but *he* also **d**, leaving no child. *G633*
Mk 12:22 Last of all, the woman **d** too. *G633*
Mk 15:39 in front of Jesus, saw how *he* **d**, he said, *G1743*
Mk 15:44 he asked him if Jesus *had* already **d**. *G633*
Lk 13: 4 Or those eighteen who **d** when the tower in *G650*
Lk 16:22 time came *when* the beggar **d** and the *G633*
Lk 16:22 The rich man also **d** and was buried. *G633*
Lk 20:29 first one married a woman and **d** childless. *G633*
Lk 20:31 in the same way the seven **d**, leaving *G633*
Lk 20:32 the woman **d** too. *G633*
Jn 6:49 the manna in the wilderness, yet *they* **d**. *G633*
Jn 6:58 Your ancestors ate manna and **d**, but *G633*
Jn 8:52 Abraham **d** and so did the prophets, yet *G633*
Jn 8:53 our father Abraham? He **d**, and so did the *G633*
Jn 11:21 been here, my brother would not have **d**. *G633*
Jn 11:32 been here, my brother would not have **d**." *G633*
Jn 18:14 would be good *if* one man **d** for the people *G633*
Ac 2:29 that the patriarch David **d** and was buried, *G5462*
Ac 5: 5 Ananias heard this, he fell down and **d**. *G1775*
Ac 5:10 moment she fell down at his feet and **d**. *G1775*
Ac 7:15 to Egypt, where he and our ancestors **d**. *G5462*
Ac 9:37 About that time she became sick and **d** *G633*
Ac 12:23 and he was eaten by worms and **d**. *G1775*
Ro 5: 6 still powerless, Christ **d** for the ungodly. *G633*
Ro 5: 8 While we were still sinners, Christ **d** for us. *G633*
Ro 5:15 For if the many **d** by the trespass of the one *G633*
Ro 6: 2 *We* are those who *have* **d** to sin; how can *G633*
Ro 6: 7 because anyone who *has* **d** has been set *G633*
Ro 6: 8 Now if *we* **d** with Christ, we believe that we *G633*
Ro 6:10 The death *he* **d**, he died to sin once for all *G633*
Ro 6:10 The death he died, *he* **d** to sin once for all *G633*
Ro 7: 4 you also **d** to the law through the body of *G2506*
Ro 7: 9 sin sprang to life and I **d**. *G633*
Ro 8:34 Christ Jesus who **d**—more than that, who *G633*
Ro 14: 9 Christ **d** and returned to life so that he *G633*
Ro 14:15 eating destroy someone for whom Christ **d**. *G633*
1Co 8:11 whom Christ **d**, is destroyed by your *G633*
1Co 10: 8 one day twenty-three thousand *of them* **d**. *G4406*
1Co 15: 3 that Christ **d** for our sins according to the *G633*
2Co 5:14 we are convinced that one **d** for all, *G633*
2Co 5:14 that one died for all, and therefore all **d**. *G633*
2Co 5:15 And *he* **d** for all, that those who live should *G633*
2Co 5:15 for him *who* **d** for them and was *G633*
Gal 2:19 "For through the law I **d** to the law so that I *G633*
Gal 2:21 through the law, Christ **d** for nothing!" *G633*
Php 2:27 and almost **d**. But God had mercy *G2505*
Php 2:30 because he almost **d** for the work of Christ *G2505*
Col 2:20 Since *you* **d** with Christ to the elemental *G633*
Col 3: 3 For *you* **d**, and your life is now hidden with *G633*
1Th 4:14 For we believe that Jesus **d** and rose again *G633*
1Th 5:10 He **d** for us so that, whether we are awake *G633*
2Ti 2:11 If *we* **d with** him, we will also live with *G5271*
Heb 9:15 *now that he has* **d** as a ransom to *G2505+1181*
Heb 9:17 force only when somebody has **d**; *G2093+3738*
Heb 10:28 the law of Moses **d** without mercy on the *G633*
Heb 11:13 were still living by faith *when they* **d**. *G633*
2Pe 3: 4 Ever since our ancestors **d**, everything *G3121*
Rev 2: 8 who **d** and came to life again. *G1181+3738*
Rev 8: 9 a third of the living creatures in the sea **d** *G633*
Rev 8:11 many people **d** from the waters that *G633*
Rev 16: 3 and every living thing in the sea **d**. *G633*

DIES (34) [DIE]

Ge 27:10 he may give you his blessing before he **d**." H4638
Ex 21:20 punished if the slave **d** as a direct result, H4637
Ex 21:35 bull injures someone else's bull and *it* **d**, H4637
Ex 22:10 safekeeping and *it* **d** or is injured or is H4637
Ex 22:14 it is injured or **d** while the owner is H4637
Lev 11:32 When one of them **d** and falls on H4637
Lev 11:39 an animal that you are allowed to eat **d**, H4637
Nu 6: 7 own father or mother or brother or sister **d**, H4637
Nu 6: 9 " 'If someone **d** suddenly in the Nazirite's H4637
Nu 19:14 that applies when a person **d** in a tent: H4637
Nu 27: 8 Israelites, 'If a man **d** and leaves no son H4637
Nu 35:21 another with their fist so that *the other* **d**, H4637
Dt 24: 3 sends her from his house, or if he **d**, H4637
Dt 25: 5 one of them **d** without a son, H4637
Job 14:10 But a man **d** and is laid low; he breathes H4637
Job 14:14 If someone **d**, will they live again? All the H4637
Job 21:23 One person **d** in full vigor, completely H4637
Job 21:25 Another **d** in bitterness of soul, never H4637
Pr 26:20 without a gossip a quarrel **d down**. H9284
Ecc 3:19 As one **d**, so dies the other H4638
Ecc 3:19 As one dies, so **d** the other. All have H4638
Isa 65:20 the *one who* **d** at a hundred will be H4637
Jer 38:10 the prophet out of the cistern before *he* **d**." H4637
Mt 22:24 told us that if a man **d** without having *G633*
Mk 12:19 if a man's brother **d** and leaves a wife but *G633*
Lk 20:28 if a man's brother **d** and leaves a wife but *G633*
Jn 4:49 "Sir, come down before my child **d**. *G633*
Jn 12:24 a kernel of wheat falls to the ground and **d**, *G633*
Jn 12:24 a single seed. But if *it* **d**, it produces many *G633*
Ro 7: 2 if her husband **d**, she is released from *G633*
Ro 7: 3 But if her husband **d**, she is released from *G633*
Ro 14: 7 none of us **d** for ourselves alone. *G633*
1Co 7:39 But if her husband **d**, she is free to marry *G3121*
1Co 15:36 you sow does not come to life unless *it* **d**. *G633*

DIFFERENCE (7) [DIFFERENT]

2Sa 19:35 *Can I* **tell the d** between what is H3359
2Ch 12: 8 so that *they may* **learn the d between** H3359
Eze 22:26 there is no **d between** the unclean and H1068
Eze 44:23 my people **the d between** the holy and H1068
Ro 3:22 There is no **d** between Jew and Gentile, *G1405*
Ro 10:12 For there is no **d** between Jew and Gentile *G1405*
Gal 2: 6 whatever they were **makes** no **d** to me *G1422*

DIFFERENCES (1) [DIFFERENT]

1Co 11:19 there have to be **d** among you to show *G146*

DIFFERENT (26) [DIFFERENCE, DIFFERENCES, DIFFERENTLY, DIFFERING, DIFFERS]

Lev 19:19 " 'Do not mate **d kinds** *of* animals. " 'Do H3977
Nu 14:24 servant Caleb has a **d** spirit and follows me H337
1Sa 10: 6 you will be changed into a **d** person. H337
Est 1: 7 of gold, each one **d** from the other, and H9101
Est 3: 8 Their customs *are* **d** from those of all H9101
Eze 15: 2 the wood of a vine **d from** that of a branch H4946
Da 7: 3 great beasts, each **d** from the others A10731
Da 7: 7 It *was* **d** from all the former beasts, and A10731
Da 7:19 which was **d** from all the others and A10731
Da 7:23 *It will be* **d** from all the other kingdoms A10731
Da 7:24 king will arise, **d** from the earlier ones A10731
Da 11:29 the **outcome** will be **d** *from* what it H4202+3869
Mk 16:12 appeared in a **d** form to two of them *G2283*
Ro 12: 6 We have **d** gifts, according to the grace *G1427*
1Co 4: 7 For who **makes** you **d** from anyone else *G1359*
1Co 12: 4 There are **d kinds** of gifts, but the same *G1348*
1Co 12: 5 There are **d kinds** of service, but the same *G1348*
1Co 12: 6 There are **d kinds** of working, but in all of *G1348*
1Co 12:10 to another speaking in **d kinds** *of* tongues *G1169*
1Co 12:28 of guidance, and *of* **d kinds** of tongues. *G1169*
2Co 11: 4 if you receive a **d** spirit **from** the Spirit you *G2283*
2Co 11: 4 a **d** gospel **from** the one you accepted *G2283*
Gal 1: 6 of Christ and are turning to a **d** gospel— *G2283*
Gal 4: 1 heir is underage, *he is* no **d** from a slave *G1422*
Heb 7:13 things are said belonged to a **d** tribe, *G2283*
Jas 2:25 spies and sent them off in a **d** direction? *G2283*

DIFFERENTLY (2) [DIFFERENT]

Ex 8:22 on that day *I will* **deal d** *with* the land of H7111

Php 3:15 And if on some point you think **d**, that too G2284

DIFFERING (5) [DIFFERENT]
Dt 25:13 not have **two d weights** in your H74+2256+74
Dt 25:14 have **two d measures** in your H406+2256+406
Pr 20:10 **D weights** and differing measures H74+2256+74
Pr 20:10 weights and **d measures**— H406+2256+406
Pr 20:23 The LORD detests **d weights**, and H74+2256+74

DIFFERS (1) [DIFFERENT]
1Co 15:41 another; and star **d** from star in splendor. G1422

DIFFICULT (11) [DIFFICULTIES, DIFFICULTY]
Ge 47:9 My years have been few and **d**, and they H8273
Ex 18:22 have them bring every **d** case to you H1524
Ex 18:26 The **d** cases they brought to Moses, but H7997
Dt 17:8 your courts *that are* too **d** for you to judge H7098
Dt 30:11 you today *is* not too **d** for you or beyond H7098
2Ki 2:10 "You have asked a **d** *thing*," Elijah said H7996
Da 2:11 What the king asks is **too d**. No one can A10330
Da 4:9 is in you, and no mystery is *too* **d** for you. A10048
Da 5:12 explain riddles and solve **d problems**. A10626
Da 5:16 interpretations and to solve **d problems**. A10626
Ac 15:19 *that we should* not **make it d** for the G4214

DIFFICULTIES (1) [DIFFICULT]
2Co 12:10 in hardships, in persecutions, *in* **d**. G5103

DIFFICULTY (6) [DIFFICULT]
Ge 35:16 began to give birth and *had* **great d**. H7996
Ge 35:17 And as she *was* **having great d** in H7996
Ex 14:25 of their chariots so that they had **d** driving. H3881
Ac 14:18 they had **d** keeping the crowd from G3660
Ac 27:7 many days and had **d** arriving off Cnidus. G3660
Ac 27:8 along the coast **with d** and came to a G3660

DIG (10) [DIGGING, DIGS, DUG, GRAVEDIGGERS]
Dt 6:11 wells *you did* not **d**, and vineyards H2933
Dt 8:9 are iron and *you can* **d** copper out of the H2933
Dt 23:13 equipment have **something to d with**, H3845
Dt 23:13 **d a hole** and cover up your excrement. H2916
Ps 119:85 The arrogant **d** pits to trap me, contrary to H4125
Eze 8:8 "Son of man, now **d** into the wall. H3168
Eze 12:5 **d** through the wall and take your H3168
Am 9:2 Though *they* **d down** to the depths below H3168
Lk 13:8 and *I'll* **d** around it and fertilize it. G4999
Lk 16:3 I'm not strong enough *to* **d**, and I'm G4999

DIGGING (1) [DIG]
Mk 2:4 roof above Jesus *by* **d through** it and then G2021

DIGNITARIES (4) [DIGNITY]
Ge 50:7 the **d** *of* his court and all the dignitaries of H2418
Ge 50:7 of his court and all the **d** *of* Egypt— H2418
Isa 9:15 the elders and **d** are the head, the H5951+7156
Isa 43:28 So I disgraced the **d** *of* your temple; H8569

DIGNITY (5) [DIGNITARIES]
Ex 28:2 brother Aaron to give him **d** and honor. H3883
Ex 28:40 Aaron's sons to give them **d** and honor. H3883
Job 30:15 my **d** is driven away as by the wind H5619
Pr 5:9 to others and your **d** to one who is cruel, H9102.5
Pr 31:25 She is clothed with strength and **d**; she H2077

DIGS (4) [DIG]
Ex 21:33 uncovers a pit or **d** one and fails to cover H4125
Ps 7:15 *Whoever* **d** a hole and scoops it out falls H4125
Pr 26:27 *Whoever* **d** a pit will fall into it; if H4125
Ecc 10:8 *Whoever* **d** a pit may fall into it; whoever H2916

DIKLAH (2)
Ge 10:27 Hadoram, Uzal, **D**, H1989
1Ch 1:21 Hadoram, Uzal, **D**, H1989

DILEAN (1)
Jos 15:38 **D**, Mizpah, Joktheel, H1939

DILIGENCE (6) [DILIGENT]
Ezr 5:8 being carried on *with* **d** and is making A10056
Ezr 6:12 Let it be carried out **with d**. A10056
Ezr 6:13 their associates carried it out **with d**. A10056
Ezr 7:21 are to provide **with d** whatever Ezra the A10056
Ezr 7:23 let it be done **with d** for the temple of A10012
Heb 6:11 you to show this same **d** to the very end, G5082

DILIGENT (7) [DILIGENCE, DILIGENTLY]
2Ch 24:13 The men in charge of the work *were* **d** H6913
Pr 10:4 poverty, but **d** hands bring wealth. H3026
Pr 12:24 **D** hands will rule, but laziness ends in H3026
Pr 12:27 the **d** feed on the riches of the hunt. H3026
Pr 13:4 the desires of the **d** are fully satisfied. H3026
Pr 21:5 The plans of the **d** lead to profit as surely H3026
1Ti 4:15 **Be d** in these matters; give yourself wholly G1639

DILIGENTLY (3) [DILIGENT]
Zec 6:15 if *you* **d obey** the LORD H9048+928+7754+9048
Jn 5:39 *You* **study** the Scriptures **d** because you G2236
Ro 12:8 it is to lead, do it **d**; if it is to show G1877+5082

DILL (1)
Mt 23:23 a tenth of your spices—mint, **d** and cumin. G464

DILUTED (1)
Isa 1:22 your choice wine *is* **d** with water. H4543

DIM (4)
Job 17:7 My eyes *have* **grown d** with grief; my H3908
Ps 88:9 my eyes *are* **d** with grief. I call to you, LORD H1790
Ecc 12:3 looking through the windows *grow* **d**; H3124
La 5:17 because of these things our eyes *grow* **d** H3124

DIMENSIONS (2)
Job 38:5 Who marked off its **d**? Surely you know H4924
Eze 42:11 length and width, with similar exits and **d**. H5477

DIMINISH (1)
Ps 107:38 and *he did* not **let** their herds **d**. H5070

DIMNAH (1)
Jos 21:35 **D** and Nahalal, together with their H1962

DIMON (2)
Isa 15:9 The waters of **D** are full of blood, but I H1904
Isa 15:9 I will bring still more upon **D**—a lion H1904

DIMONAH (1)
Jos 15:22 **D**, Adadah, H1905

DIN (1)
Jer 51:55 he will silence her **noisy d**. H7754+1524

DINAH (7) [DINAH'S]
Ge 30:21 birth to a daughter and named her **D**. H1909
Ge 34:1 Now **D**, the daughter Leah had borne to H1909
Ge 34:3 heart was drawn to **D** daughter of Jacob; H1909
Ge 34:5 that his daughter **D** had been defiled, H1909
Ge 34:13 Because their sister **D** had been defiled H1909
Ge 34:26 the sword and took **D** from Shechem's H1909
Ge 46:15 in Paddan Aram, besides his daughter **D**. H1909

DINAH'S (2) [DINAH]
Ge 34:11 Shechem said to **D** father and brothers, H2023S
Ge 34:25 Simeon and Levi, **D** brothers, took their H1909

DINAITES (KJV) JUDGES

DINE (3) [DINED, DINNER]
1Sa 20:5 and I *am* **supposed to d** with H3782+3782+430
Pr 23:1 When you sit to **d** with a ruler, note well H4310
Am 6:4 *You* **d on** choice lambs and fattened calves. H430

DINED (1) [DINE]
1Sa 9:24 And Saul **d** with Samuel that day H430

DINHABAH (2)
Ge 36:32 king of Edom. His city was named **D**. H1973
1Ch 1:43 son of Beor, whose city was named **D**. H1973

DINNER (9) [DINE]
Mt 9:10 *While* Jesus *was* **having d** at Matthew's G367
Mt 14:9 because of his oaths and his **d guests** G5263
Mt 22:4 been invited that I have prepared my **d**: G756
Mk 2:15 *While* Jesus was **having d** at Levi's house G2879
Mk 6:22 she pleased Herod and his **d guests**. G5263
Mk 6:26 because of his oaths and his **d guests** G367
Lk 7:36 invited Jesus to **have d** with him, G2266
Lk 14:12 "When you give a luncheon or **d**, do not G1270
Jn 12:2 Here a **d** was given in Jesus' honor G1270

DIONYSIUS (1)
Ac 17:34 Among them was **D**, a member of the G1477

DIOTREPHES (1)
3Jn 9 to the church, but **D**, who loves to be first, G1485

DIP (10) [DIPPED, DIPPING, DIPS]
Ex 12:22 **d** it into the blood in the basin and put H3188
Lev 4:6 He *is to* **d** his finger into the blood and H3188
Lev 4:17 He *shall* **d** his finger into the blood and H3188
Lev 14:6 He is then to take the live bird and **d** it H3188
Lev 14:16 **d** his right forefinger into the oil in his H3188
Lev 14:51 **d** them into the blood of the dead bird H3188
Nu 19:18 **d** it in the water and sprinkle the tent and H3188
Ru 2:14 Have some bread and **d** it in the wine H3188
Ps 58:10 when *they* **d** their feet in the blood of the H8175
Lk 16:24 send Lazarus to **d** the tip of his finger G970

DIPPED (7) [DIP]
Ge 37:31 a goat and **d** the robe in the blood. H3188
Lev 9:9 and *he* **d** his finger into the blood and put H3188
1Sa 14:27 was in his hand and **d** it into the H3188
2Ki 5:14 went down and **d** *himself* in the Jordan H3188
Mt 26:23 "The *one who has* **d** his hand into the G1835
Jn 13:26 piece of bread *when I have* **d** it in the dish." G970
Rev 19:13 He is dressed in a robe **d** in blood, and his G970

DIPPING (1) [DIP]
Jn 13:26 **d** the piece of bread, he gave it to G970

DIPS (1) [DIP]
Mk 14:20 "one *who* **d** bread into the bowl with me. G1835

DIRE (3)
Dt 28:48 in nakedness and **d** poverty, you will serve H3972
Dt 28:57 For in her **d** need she intends to eat them H3972
Isa 21:2 A **d** vision has been shown to me: The H7997

DIRECT (11) [DIRECTED, DIRECTING, DIRECTION, DIRECTIONS, DIRECTIVES, DIRECTLY, DIRECTOR, DIRECTORS, DIRECTS]
Ge 18:19 so that *he will* **d** his children and his H7422
Ge 46:26 *those who were* his **d descendants** H3655+3751
Ex 21:20 if the slave dies **as a d result**, H9393+3338
2Ch 34:12 Over them to **d** them were Jahath and H5904
Ps 119:35 **D** me in the path of your commands, for H2005
Ps 119:133 **D** my footsteps according to your word; H3922
Jer 10:23 it is not for them *to* **d** their steps. H3922
Eze 23:25 *I will* **d** my jealous anger against you, and H5989
Eze 26:9 *He will* **d** the blows of his battering rams H5989
2Th 3:5 *May* the Lord **d** your hearts into God's love G2985
1Ti 5:17 The elders *who* **d** *the* **affairs** of the church G4613

DIRECTED (27) [DIRECT]
Ge 24:51 of your master's son, as the LORD *has* **d**." H1819
Ge 45:19 "You **are** also **d** to tell them, 'Do this H7422
Ge 47:11 the district of Rameses, as Pharaoh **d**. H7422
Ge 50:2 Then Joseph **d** the physicians in his H7422
Nu 16:40 as the LORD **d** him through Moses. H1819
Dt 2:1 to the Red Sea, as the LORD *had* **d** me. H1819
Dt 4:14 And the LORD **d** me at that time to teach H7422
Dt 6:1 the LORD your God **d** me to teach you to H7422
Jos 4:10 the people, just as Moses *had* **d** Joshua. H7422
Jos 4:12 of the Israelites, as Moses *had* **d** them. H1819
Jos 11:9 Joshua did to them as the LORD *had* **d**: He H606
Jos 11:23 just as the LORD *had* **d** Moses, and he H1819
1Sa 17:20 loaded up and set out, as Jesse *had* **d**. H7422
1Ki 5:16 supervised the project and **d** the workers. H8097
1Ki 17:4 and *I have* **d** the ravens to supply you with H7422
1Ki 17:9 *I have* **d** a widow there to supply you with H7422
1Ki 21:11 city did as Jezebel **d** in the letters she had H8938
Job 21:4 "Is my complaint **d to** a human being H4200
Pr 20:24 A person's steps are **d by** the LORD. H4946
Isa 10:25 my wrath will be **d to** their destruction." H6584
Jer 13:2 as the LORD **d**, and put it around my H1821
Mt 14:19 And *he* **d** the people to sit down on the G3027
Mt 26:19 did as Jesus *had* **d** them and prepared G5332
Mk 6:39 Then Jesus **d** them to have all the people G2199
Ac 7:44 It had been made as God **d** Moses G1411
Ac 22:24 *He* **d** that he be flogged and interrogated G3306
Titus 1:5 appoint elders in every town, as I **d** you. G1411

DIRECTING (1) [DIRECT]
1Ch 15:21 play the harps, **d** according to sheminith. H5904

DIRECTION (25) [DIRECT]
Ex 38:21 Levites under the **d** *of* Ithamar son of H3338
Nu 4:27 be done under the **d** *of* Aaron and his H7023
Nu 4:28 are to be under the **d** *of* Ithamar son of H3338
Nu 4:33 of meeting under the **d** *of* Ithamar son of H3338
Nu 7:8 were all under the **d** *of* Ithamar son of H3338
Nu 11:31 far as a day's walk **in any d**. H3907+2256+3907
Dt 28:7 at you from one **d** but flee from you in H2006
Dt 28:25 at them from one **d** but flee from them in H2006
Jos 8:20 chance to escape **in any d**; H2178+2256+2178
Jdg 9:37 is coming from the **d** *of* the diviners' tree." H2006
Jdg 20:42 the Israelites in the **d** *of* the wilderness, H2006
2Sa 13:34 "I see men in the **d** *of* Horonaim, on the H2006
1Ki 18:6 Ahab going in one **d** and Obadiah in H2006
2Ki 3:20 it was—water flowing from the **d** *of* Edom! H2006
2Ch 26:11 the officer under the **d** *of* Hananiah, H3338
2Ch 34:4 **Under** his **d** the altars of the Baals H4200+7156
Ezr 5:8 is making rapid progress under their **d**. A10311
Ne 12:38 second choir proceeded in the **opposite d**. H4578
Ne 12:42 The choirs sang under the **d** of Jezrahiah. H7224
Job 37:12 At his **d** they swirl around over the face of H9374
Pr 7:8 walking along in the **d** *of* her house H2006
Eze 1:17 the wheels *did* not **change d** as the H6015
Eze 9:2 men coming from the **d** *of* the upper gate, H2006
Eze 10:11 went in whatever **d** the head faced, H5226
Jas 2:25 spies and sent them off *in* a different **d**? G3847

DIRECTIONS (6) [DIRECT]
Ge 46:28 of him to Joseph to **get d** to Goshen. H3723
1Sa 14:16 saw the army melting away **in all d**. H2151
Eze 1:17 any one of the four **d** the creatures faced; H8063
Eze 10:11 any one of the four **d** the cherubim faced; H8063
Ac 21:30 the people came **running from all d**. G5282
1Co 11:34 And when I come *I will* **give** further **d**. G1411

DIRECTIVES (1) [DIRECT]
1Co 11:17 *In* the following **d** I have no praise for you, G4133

DIRECTLY (8) [DIRECT]
Ge 30:38 would be **d in front of** the flocks H4200+5790
Ex 14:2 **d opposite** Baal Zephon. H5790+4200+7156
Lev 25:12 eat only what is taken **d from** the fields. H4946
1Ch 14:14 answered him, "*Do* not **go d** after them H6590
Ne 12:37 Gate they continued **d** up the steps of the H5584
Pr 4:25 straight ahead; **fix** your gaze **d** before you. H3837
Lk 20:17 Jesus **looked d at** them and asked, "Then G1838
Ac 14:9 Paul **looked d at** him, saw that he had faith G867

DIRECTOR (58) [DIRECT]
Ne 11:17 the **d** who led in thanksgiving and prayer H8031
Ps 4:T For the **d of music**. With stringed H5904
Ps 5:T For the **d of music**. For pipes. A psalm of H5904
Ps 6:T For the **d of music**. With stringed H5904
Ps 8:T For the **d of music**. According to gittith. H5904
Ps 9:T For the **d** *of* **music**. To the tune of "The H5904

Ps 11: T For the **d of music**. Of David. H5904
Ps 12: T For the **d of music**. According to sheminith H5904
Ps 13: T For the **d of music**. A psalm of David. H5904
Ps 14: T For the **d of music**. Of David. H5904
Ps 18: T For the **d of music**. Of David the servant of H5904
Ps 19: T For the **d of music**. A psalm of David. H5904
Ps 20: T For the **d of music**. A psalm of David. H5904
Ps 21: T For the **d of music**. A psalm of David. H5904
Ps 22: T For the **d of music**. To the tune of "The H5904
Ps 31: T For the **d of music**. A psalm of David. H5904
Ps 36: T For the **d of music**. Of David the servant of H5904
Ps 39: T For the **d of music**. For Jeduthun. A psalm H5904
Ps 40: T For the **d of music**. Of David. A psalm. H5904
Ps 41: T For the **d of music**. A psalm of David. H5904
Ps 42: T For the **d of music**. A maskil of the Sons of H5904
Ps 44: T For the **d of music**. Of the Sons of Korah H5904
Ps 45: T For the **d of music**. To the tune of "Lilies." H5904
Ps 46: T For the **d of music**. Of the Sons of Korah H5904
Ps 47: T For the **d of music**. Of the Sons of Korah H5904
Ps 49: T For the **d of music**. Of the Sons of Korah H5904
Ps 51: T For the **d of music**. A psalm of David H5904
Ps 52: T For the **d of music**. A maskil of David H5904
Ps 53: T For the **d of music**. According to mahalath. H5904
Ps 54: T For the **d of music**. With stringed H5904
Ps 55: T For the **d of music**. With stringed H5904
Ps 56: T For the **d of music**. To the tune of "A Dove H5904
Ps 57: T For the **d of music**. To the tune of "Do Not H5904
Ps 58: T For the **d of music**. To the tune of "Do Not H5904
Ps 59: T For the **d of music**. To the tune of "Do Not H5904
Ps 60: T For the **d of music**. To the tune of "The H5904
Ps 61: T For the **d of music**. With stringed H5904
Ps 62: T For the **d of music**. For Jeduthun. A psalm H5904
Ps 64: T For the **d of music**. A psalm of David. H5904
Ps 65: T For the **d of music**. A psalm of David. H5904
Ps 66: T For the **d of music**. A song. A psalm. H5904
Ps 67: T For the **d of music**. With stringed H5904
Ps 68: T For the **d of music**. Of David. H5904
Ps 69: T For the **d of music**. To the tune of "Lilies." H5904
Ps 70: T For the **d of music**. Of David. A petition. H5904
Ps 75: T For the **d of music**. To the tune of "Do Not H5904
Ps 76: T For the **d of music**. With stringed H5904
Ps 77: T For the **d of music**. For Jeduthun. H5904
Ps 80: T For the **d of music**. To the tune of "The H5904
Ps 81: T For the **d of music**. According to gittith. H5904
Ps 84: T For the **d of music**. According to gittith. H5904
Ps 85: T For the **d of music**. Of the Sons of Korah H5904
Ps 88: T For the **d of music**. According to H5904
Ps 109: T For the **d of music**. Of David. A psalm. H5904
Ps 139: T For the **d of music**. Of David. A psalm. H5904
Ps 140: T For the **d of music**. A psalm of David. H5904
Hab 3:19 For the **d of music**. On my stringed H5904
Ro 16:23 who is the city's **d of public works**, *G3874*

DIRECTORS (1) [DIRECT]
Ne 12:46 there had been **d** *for* the musicians and H8031

DIRECTS (2) [DIRECT]
Ps 42: 8 By day the LORD **d** his love, at night his H7422
Isa 48:17 *who* **d** you in the way you should go. H2005

DIRGE (2)
Mt 11:17 did not dance; *we* **sang a d**, and you did *G2577*
Lk 7:32 did not dance; *we* **sang a d**, and you did *G2577*

DIRT (3)
2Sa 16:13 stones at him and showering him with **d**. H6760
Zec 9: 3 and gold like the **d** *of* the streets. H3226
1Pe 3:21 not the removal *of* **d** from the body but the *G4866*

DISABLED (3) [ABLE]
2Sa 4: 4 hurried to leave, he fell and **became d**. H7174
Jn 5: 3 a great number *of* **d people** used to lie— *G820*
Heb 12:13 so that the lame *may* not *be* **d**, but rather *G1762*

DISAGREED (1) [AGREE, DISAGREEMENT]
Ac 28:25 *They* **d** among themselves and *G851+1639*

DISAGREEMENT (1) [AGREE, DISAGREED]
Ac 15:39 They had such a **sharp d** that they parted *G4237*

DISALLOW, DISALLOWED (KJV) FORBID, FORBIDS, FORBIDDEN, REJECTED

DISANNUL, DISANNULLED, DISANNULLING (KJV) ANNULLED, DISCREDIT, SET ASIDE, THWART

DISAPPEAR (10) [DISAPPEARED, DISAPPEARS]
Nu 27: 4 Why *should* our father's name **d** from his H1757
Ru 4:10 that his name *will* not **d** from among his H4162
Isa 2:18 the idols *will* totally **d**. H2736
Isa 17: 3 The fortified city *will* **d** from Ephraim, and H8697
Isa 29:20 the mockers *will* **d**, and all who have H3983
Mt 5:18 until heaven and earth **d**, not the smallest *G4216*
Mt 5:18 *will* by any means **d** from the Law until *G4216*
Lk 16:17 heaven and earth *to* **d** than for the least *G4216*
Heb 8:13 what is obsolete and outdated will soon **d**. *G907*
2Pe 3:10 The heavens *will* **d** with a roar; the *G4216*

DISAPPEARED (3) [DISAPPEAR]
Jdg 6:21 And the angel of the LORD **d**. H2143+4946+6524
1Ki 20:40 was busy here and there, the man **d**." H401
Lk 24:31 and he **d from** their **sight**. *G908+1181*

DISAPPEARS (3) [DISAPPEAR]
Hos 6: 4 morning mist, like the early dew *that* **d**. H2143
Hos 13: 3 like the early dew *that* **d**, like chaff H2143
1Co 13:10 completeness comes, what is in part **d**. *G2934*

DISAPPOINTED (3)
Job 6:20 confident; they arrive there, only *to be* **d**. H2917
Isa 49:23 those who hope in me *will* not *be* **d**." H1017
Jer 2:36 *You will be* **d** by Egypt as you were by H1017

DISAPPROVE (1)
Pr 24:18 will see and **d** and turn his H8317+928+6524

DISARMED (1) [DISARMS]
Col 2:15 And *having* **d** the powers and authorities *G588*

DISARMS (1) [DISARMED]
Job 12:21 on nobles and **d** the mighty. H8332+4653

DISASTER (122) [DISASTERS, DISASTROUS]
Ge 19:19 the mountains; this **d** will overtake me H8288
Ex 32:12 relent and do not bring **d** on your people. H8288
Ex 32:14 on his people the **d** he had threatened. H8288
Dt 28:61 kind of sickness and **d** not recorded in this H4804
Dt 29:19 *they will* **bring d** *on* the watered land as H6200
Dt 29:21 them out from all the tribes of Israel for **d**, H8288
Dt 31:29 **d** will fall on you because you will do evil H8288
Dt 32:35 their day of **d** is near and their doom H369
Jos 24:20 he will turn and **bring d** on you and make H8317
Jdg 20:34 did not realize how near **d** was. H8288
Jdg 20:41 they realized that **d** had come on them. H8288
1Sa 6: 9 the LORD has brought this great **d** on us. H8288
1Sa 25:17 because **d** is hanging over our master H8288
2Sa 17:14 in order to bring **d** on Absalom. H8288
2Sa 22:19 They confronted me in the day of my **d**, but H369
2Sa 24:16 concerning the **d** and said to the angel H8288
1Ki 5: 4 and there is no adversary or **d**. H7004+8273
1Ki 8:37 whatever **d** or disease may come, H5596
1Ki 9: 9 is why the LORD brought all this **d** on them. H8288
1Ki 14:10 I am going to bring **d** on the house of H8288
1Ki 21:21 'I am going to bring **d** on you. I will wipe H8288
1Ki 21:29 I will not bring this **d** in his day, but I will H8288
1Ki 22:23 The LORD has decreed **d** for you." H8288
2Ki 6:33 The king said, "This **d** is from the LORD H8288
2Ki 21:12 going to bring such **d** on Jerusalem and H8288
2Ki 22:16 I am going to bring **d** on this place and its H8288
2Ki 22:20 will not see all the **d** I am going to bring H8288
1Ch 21:15 concerning the **d** and said to the angel H8288
2Ch 6:28 whatever **d** or disease may come, H5596
2Ch 7:22 that is why he brought all this **d** on them. H8288
2Ch 18:22 The LORD has decreed **d** for you." H8288
2Ch 34:24 I am going to bring **d** on this place and its H8288
2Ch 34:28 will not see all the **d** I am going to bring H8288
Est 8: 6 can I bear to see **d** fall on my people? H8288
Job 18:12 **d** is ready for him when he falls. H369
Job 31: 3 the wicked, **d** for those who do wrong? H5798
Ps 18:18 They confronted me in the day of my **d**, but H369
Ps 37:19 In times of **d** they will not wither; in days H8288
Ps 57: 1 of your wings until the **d** has passed. H2095
Ps 91:10 no **d** will come near your tent. H5596
Ps 140:11 in the land; may **d** hunt down the violent. H8273
Pr 1:26 I in turn will laugh when **d** *strikes* you; I will H369
Pr 1:27 when **d** sweeps over you like a whirlwind H369
Pr 3:25 no fear of sudden **d** or of the ruin that H7065
Pr 6:15 Therefore **d** will overtake him in an instant H369
Pr 16: 4 even the wicked for a day of **d**. H8288
Pr 17: 5 whoever gloats over **d** will not go H369
Pr 27:10 your relative's house when **d** strikes you— H369
Ecc 11: 2 do not know what **d** may come upon the H8288
Isa 3: 9 They have brought **d** upon themselves. H8288
Isa 3:11 Woe to the wicked! **D** is upon them! They H8273
Isa 10: 3 of reckoning, when **d** comes from afar? H8739
Isa 31: 2 Yet he too is wise and can bring **d**; he H8273
Isa 45: 7 I bring prosperity and create **d**; I, H8273
Isa 47:11 **D** will come upon you, and you will not H8288
Jer 1:14 "From the north **d** will be poured out on H8288
Jer 2: 3 were held guilty, and **d** overtook them,'" H8288
Jer 4: 6 For I am bringing **d** from the north, even H8288
Jer 4:15 proclaiming **d** from the hills of Ephraim. H224
Jer 4:20 **D** follows disaster; the whole land lies in H8691
Jer 4:20 Disaster follows **d**; the whole land lies in H8691
Jer 6: 1 For **d** looms out of the north, even terrible H8288
Jer 6:19 I am bringing **d** on this people, the fruit of H8288
Jer 11:11 bring on them a **d** they cannot escape. H8288
Jer 11:12 will not help them at all when **d** strikes. H8288
Jer 11:17 has decreed **d** for you, because the H8288
Jer 11:23 because I will bring **d** on the people of H8288
Jer 15:11 with you in times of **d** and times of H8288
Jer 16:10 LORD decreed such a great **d** against us? H8288
Jer 17:17 you are my refuge in the day of **d**. H8288
Jer 17:18 Bring on them the day of **d**; destroy them H8288
Jer 18: 8 not inflict on it the **d** I had planned. H8288
Jer 18:11 I am preparing a **d** for you and devising a H8288
Jer 18:17 back and not my face in the day of their **d**." H369
Jer 19: 3 I am going to bring a **d** on this place that H8288
Jer 19:15 around it every **d** I pronounced against H8288
Jer 23:12 I will bring **d** on them in the year they are H8288
Jer 25:29 I am beginning to **bring d** on the city that H8317
Jer 25:32 **D** is spreading from nation to nation; H8288
Jer 26: 3 inflict on them the **d** I was planning H8288
Jer 26:13 not bring the **d** he has pronounced H8288
Jer 26:19 he did not bring the **d** he pronounced H8288
Jer 26:19 about to bring a terrible **d** on ourselves!" H8288
Jer 28: 8 **d** and plague against many countries H8288
Jer 31:28 destroy and **bring d**, so I will watch over H8317
Jer 32:23 So you brought all this **d** on them. H8288
Jer 35:17 in Jerusalem every **d** I pronounced H8288
Jer 36: 3 hear about every **d** I plan to inflict on H8288
Jer 36:31 of Judah every **d** I pronounced against H8288
Jer 39:16 words concerning **d**, not prosperity. H8288
Jer 40: 2 your God decreed this **d** for this place. H8288
Jer 42:10 concerning the **d** I have inflicted on you H8288
Jer 42:17 escape the **d** I will bring on them. H8288
Jer 44: 2 You saw the great **d** I brought on H8288
Jer 44: 7 Why bring such great **d** on yourselves by H8288
Jer 44:11 determined to bring **d** on you and to H8288
Jer 44:23 stipulations, this **d** has come upon you, as H8288
Jer 45: 5 For I will bring **d** on all people, declares H8288
Jer 46:21 the day of **d** is coming upon them H369
Jer 49: 8 I will bring **d** on Esau at the time when I H369
Jer 49:32 places and will bring **d** on them from every H369
Jer 49:37 I will bring **d** on them, even my H8288
Jer 51: 2 her on every side in the day of her **d**. H8288
Jer 51:64 more because of the **d** I will bring on her. H8288
Eze 7: 5 "'**D**! Unheard-of disaster! H8288
Eze 7: 5 Unheard-of **d**! See, it comes! H8288
Eze 14:22 regarding the **d** I have brought on H8288
Eze 14:22 Jerusalem—every **d** I have brought on it. H889S
Da 9:12 our rulers by bringing on us great **d**. H8288
Da 9:13 of Moses, all this **d** has come on us, yet H8288
Da 9:14 LORD did not hesitate to bring the **d** on us, H8288
Am 3: 6 When **d** comes to a city, has not the LORD H8288
Am 6: 3 put off the day of **d** and bring near a reign H8273
Am 9:10 who say, '**D** will not overtake or meet us. H8288
Ob 5 in the night—oh, what a **d awaits** *you*!— H1950
Ob 13 gates of my people in the day of their **d**, H369
Ob 13 them in their calamity in the day of their **d**, H369
Ob 13 seize their wealth in the day of their **d**. H369
Mic 1:12 because **d** has come from the LORD H8273
Mic 2: 3 "I am planning **d** against this people H8288
Mic 3:11 LORD among us? No **d** will come upon us." H8288
Zec 8:14 had determined to **bring d** on you and H8317

DISASTERS (6) [DISASTER]
Dt 28:59 harsh and prolonged **d**, and severe and H4804
Dt 31:17 Many **d** and calamities will come on them H8288
Dt 31:17 'Have not these **d** come on us because H8288
Dt 31:21 And when many **d** and calamities come H8288
1Sa 10:19 saves you out of all your **d** and calamities. H8288
Jer 51:60 about all the **d** that would come upon H8288

DISASTROUS (1) [DISASTER]
Ac 27:10 is going to be **d** and bring great loss *G5615*

DISCARD (1) [DISCARDED]
Ps 119:119 the wicked of the earth *you* **d** like dross; H8697

DISCARDED (1) [DISCARD]
Ps 102:26 you will change them and *they will be* **d**. H2736

DISCERN (6) [DISCERNED, DISCERNING, DISCERNMENT]
Dt 32:29 understand this and **d** what their end will H1067
Job 6:30 *Can* my mouth not **d** malice? H1067
Job 34: 4 *Let us* **d** for ourselves what is right; let us H1047
Ps 19:12 But who *can* **d** their own errors? Forgive H1067
Ps 139: 3 *You* **d** my going out and my lying down H2431
Php 1:10 so that you *may be able to* **d** what is best *G1507*

DISCERNED (1) [DISCERN]
1Co 2:14 them because *they are* **d** only through the *G373*

DISCERNING (23) [DISCERN]
Ge 41:33 Pharaoh look for a **d** and wise man and H1067
Ge 41:39 there is no *one so* **d** and wise as you. H1067
2Sa 14:17 like an angel of God in **d** good and evil. H9048
1Ki 3: 9 give your servant a **d** heart to govern your H9048
1Ki 3:12 I will give you a wise and **d** heart, so that H1067
Pr 1: 5 learning, and let the **d** get guidance— H1067
Pr 8: 9 To the **d** all of them are right; they are H1067
Pr 10:13 Wisdom is found on the lips of the **d**, but H1067
Pr 14: 6 knowledge comes easily to the **d**. H1067
Pr 14:33 in the heart of the **d** and even among H1067
Pr 15:14 The **d** heart seeks knowledge, but the H1067
Pr 16:21 The wise in heart are called **d**, and H1067
Pr 17:10 rebuke impresses a **d** *person* more than a H1067
Pr 17:24 A **d** *person* keeps wisdom in view, but a H1067
Pr 17:28 and **d** if they hold their tongues. H1067
Pr 18:15 The heart of the **d** acquires knowledge H1067
Pr 19:25 rebuke the **d**, and they will gain H1067
Pr 28: 7 A **d** son heeds instruction, but a H1067
Pr 28:11 one who is poor and **d** sees how deluded H1067
Da 2:21 wise and knowledge to the **d**. A10313+10100
Hos 14: 9 Who *is* **d**? Let them H1067
1Co 11:29 eat and drink without **d** the body of Christ *G1359*
1Co 11:31 But if *we were more* **d** with regard to *G1359*

DISCERNMENT (6) [DISCERN]
Dt 32:28 without sense, there is no **d** in them. H9312
1Ki 3:11 of your enemies but for **d** in administering H1067
2Ch 2:12 endowed with intelligence and **d**, who H1069
Job 12:20 advisers and takes away the **d** *of* elders. H3248
Ps 119:125 **give** me **d** that I may understand your H1067
Pr 28: 2 a ruler *with* **d** and knowledge H1067

DISCHARGE (21) [DISCHARGED, DISCHARGING]
Lev 15: 2 'When any man has an **unusual** bodily **d** H2307
Lev 15: 2 bodily discharge, such a **d** is unclean. H2308
Lev 15: 3 This is how his **d** will bring about H2308
Lev 15: 4 " 'Any bed the *man with a* **d** lies on will H2307
Lev 15: 6 that the *man with a* **d** sat on must wash H2307
Lev 15: 7 touches the *man who has a* **d** must wash H2307
Lev 15: 8 " 'If the *man with the* **d** spits on anyone H2307
Lev 15:11 " 'Anyone the *man with a* **d** touches H2307
Lev 15:13 " 'When a man is cleansed from his **d**, he H2308
Lev 15:15 the LORD for the man because of his **d**. H2308
Lev 15:25 a woman **has a d** *of* blood for H2307+2308
Lev 15:25 monthly period or *has a* **d** that continues H2307
Lev 15:25 unclean as long as she has the **d**, H2308+3240
Lev 15:26 she lies on while her **d** continues will be H2308
Lev 15:28 " 'When she is cleansed from her **d**, she H2308
Lev 15:30 the LORD for the uncleanness of her **d**. H2308
Lev 15:32 are the regulations for a *man with a* **d**, H2307
Lev 15:33 a man or a woman *with a* **d** H2307+2308
Lev 22: 4 has a defiling skin disease or a **bodily d**, H2307
Nu 5: 2 a defiling skin disease or a **d** of any kind, H2307
2Ti 4: 5 **d all the duties** of your ministry. *G4442*

DISCHARGED (2) [DISCHARGE]
Jdg 3:22 sank in after the blade, and his bowels **d**. H3655
Ecc 8: 8 As no one is **d** in time of war, so H5449

DISCHARGING (1) [DISCHARGE]
1Co 9:17 I am simply **d** the trust committed to me. NDT

DISCIPLE (32) [DISCIPLES, DISCIPLES']
Isa 19:11 of the wise men, a **d** *of* the ancient kings"? H1201
Mt 8:21 Another **d** said to him, "Lord, first let me *G3412*
Mt 10:42 to one of these little ones who is my **d**, *G3412*
Mt 13:52 of the law *who has* **become a d** in the *G3411*
Mt 16:24 wants *to* **be** my **d** must deny *G3958+2262*
Mt 27:57 who *had* himself **become a d** of Jesus. *G3411*
Mk 8:34 wants *to* **be** my **d** must deny *G3958+199*
Lk 9:23 wants *to* **be** my **d** must deny *G3958+2262*
Lk 14:26 own life—such a person cannot be my **d**. *G3412*
Lk 14:27 their cross and follow me cannot be my **d**. *G3412*
Jn 9:28 at him and said, "You are this fellow's **d**! *G3412*
Jn 13:23 One of them, the **d** whom Jesus loved, was NDT
Jn 13:24 Simon Peter motioned to this **d** and said NDT
Jn 18:15 Peter and another **d** were following Jesus. *G3412*
Jn 18:15 Because this **d** was known to the high *G3412*
Jn 18:16 The other **d**, who was known to the high *G3412*
Jn 19:26 the **d** whom he loved standing *G3412*
Jn 19:27 and *to* the **d**, "Here is your mother." From *G3412*
Jn 19:27 time on, this **d** took her into his home. *G3412*
Jn 19:38 Now Joseph was a **d** of Jesus, but secretly *G3412*
Jn 20: 2 running to Simon Peter and the other **d**, *G3412*
Jn 20: 3 Peter and the other **d** started for the tomb. *G3412*
Jn 20: 4 the other **d** outran Peter and reached *G3412*
Jn 20: 8 Finally the other **d**, who had reached the *G3412*
Jn 21: 7 Then the **d** whom Jesus loved said to *G3412*
Jn 21:20 saw that the **d** whom Jesus loved was *G3412*
Jn 21:23 the believers that this **d** would not die. *G3412*
Jn 21:24 This is the **d** who testifies to these things *G3412*
Ac 9:10 Damascus there was a **d** named Ananias. *G3412*
Ac 9:26 not believing that he really was a **d**. *G3412*
Ac 9:36 In Joppa there was a **d** named Tabitha (in *G3413*
Ac 16: 1 to Lystra, where a **d** named Timothy lived *G3412*

DISCIPLES (266) [DISCIPLE]
Isa 8:16 seal up God's instruction among my **d**. H4341
Mt 5: 1 sat down. His **d** came to him, *G3412*
Mt 8:23 got into the boat and his **d** followed him. *G3412*
Mt 8:25 The **d** went and woke him, saying, "Lord NDT
Mt 9:10 sinners came and ate with him and his **d**. *G3412*
Mt 9:11 they asked his **d**, "Why does your *G3412*
Mt 9:14 Then John's **d** came and asked him *G3412*
Mt 9:14 fast often, but your **d** do not fast? *G3412*
Mt 9:19 up and went with him, and so did his **d**. *G3412*
Mt 9:37 Then he said *to* his **d**, "The harvest is *G3412*
Mt 10: 1 called his twelve **d** to him and gave them *G3412*
Mt 11: 1 had finished instructing his twelve **d**, *G3412*
Mt 11: 2 the deeds of the Messiah, he sent his **d** *G3412*
Mt 11: 7 As **John's d** were leaving, Jesus began *G4047s*
Mt 12: 1 His **d** were hungry and began to pick *G3412*
Mt 12: 2 Your **d** are doing what is unlawful on the *G3412*
Mt 12:49 Pointing to his **d**, he said, "Here are my *G3412*
Mt 13:10 The **d** came to him and asked, "Why do *G3412*
Mt 13:36 His **d** came to him and said, "Explain to *G3412*
Mt 14:12 John's **d** came and took his body and *G3412*
Mt 14:15 approached, the **d** came to him and said *G3412*
Mt 14:19 Then he gave them *to* the **d**, and the *G3412*
Mt 14:19 the **d** gave them to the people. *G3412*
Mt 14:20 the **d** picked up twelve basketfuls of NDT
Mt 14:22 Jesus made the **d** get into the boat and *G3412*
Mt 14:26 When the **d** saw him walking on the lake *G3412*
Mt 15: 2 "Why do your **d** break the tradition of the *G3412*
Mt 15:12 Then the **d** came to him and asked, "Do *G3412*
Mt 15:23 So his **d** came to him and urged him *G3412*
Mt 15:32 Jesus called his **d** to him and said, "I *G3412*
Mt 15:33 His **d** answered, "Where could we get *G3412*
Mt 15:36 he broke them and gave them *to* the **d** *G3412*
Mt 15:37 Afterward the **d** picked up seven basketfuls NDT
Mt 16: 5 across the lake, the **d** forgot to take bread. *G3412*
Mt 16:13 he asked his **d**, "Who do people say *G3412*
Mt 16:20 Then he ordered his **d** not to tell anyone *G3412*
Mt 16:21 began to explain *to* his **d** that he must go *G3412*
Mt 16:24 Then Jesus said *to* his **d**, "Whoever wants *G3412*
Mt 17: 6 When the **d** heard this, they fell facedown *G3412*
Mt 17:10 The **d** asked him, "Why then do the *G3412*
Mt 17:13 Then the **d** understood that he was talking *G3412*
Mt 17:16 I brought him *to* your **d**, but they could not *G3412*
Mt 17:19 Then the **d** came to Jesus in private and *G3412*
Mt 17:23 And the **d** were filled with grief. NDT
Mt 17:24 After **Jesus and his d** arrived in *G899s*
Mt 18: 1 At that time the **d** came to Jesus and *G3412*
Mt 19:10 The **d** said to him, "If this is the situation *G3412*
Mt 19:13 pray for them. But the **d** rebuked them. *G3412*
Mt 19:23 Then Jesus said *to* his **d**, "Truly I tell you *G3412*
Mt 19:25 When the **d** heard this, they were greatly *G3412*
Mt 20:29 As **Jesus and his d** were leaving Jericho *G899s*
Mt 21: 1 on the Mount of Olives, Jesus sent two **d**, *G3412*
Mt 21: 6 The **d** went and did as Jesus had *G3412*
Mt 21:20 When the **d** saw this, they were amazed *G3412*
Mt 22:16 They sent their **d** to him along with the *G3412*
Mt 23: 1 Jesus said to the crowds and *to* his **d**: *G3412*
Mt 24: 1 away when his **d** came up to him to *G3412*
Mt 24: 3 of Olives, the **d** came to him privately. *G3412*
Mt 26: 1 saying all these things, he said *to* his **d**, *G3412*
Mt 26: 8 When the **d** saw this, they were indignant. *G3412*
Mt 26:17 the **d** came to Jesus and asked *G3412*
Mt 26:18 the Passover with my **d** at your house. *G3412*
Mt 26:19 So the **d** did as Jesus had directed them *G3412*
Mt 26:26 he broke it and gave it *to* his **d**, saying, *G3412*
Mt 26:35 And all the other **d** said the same. *G3412*
Mt 26:36 Jesus went with his **d** to a place called *G3412*
Mt 26:40 he returned to his **d** and found them *G3412*
Mt 26:45 he returned to the **d** and said to them, *G3412*
Mt 26:56 Then all the **d** deserted him and fled. *G3412*
Mt 27:64 his **d** may come and steal the body and *G3412*
Mt 28: 7 Then go quickly and tell his **d**: 'He has *G3412*
Mt 28: 8 filled with joy, and ran to tell his **d**. *G3412*
Mt 28:13 'His **d** came during the night and stole *G3412*
Mt 28:16 Then the eleven **d** went to Galilee, to the *G3412*
Mt 28:19 Therefore go and **make d** of all nations *G3411*
Mk 2:15 sinners were eating with him and his **d**, *G3412*
Mk 2:16 tax collectors, they asked his **d**: *G3412*
Mk 2:18 Now John's **d** and the Pharisees were *G3412*
Mk 2:18 is it that John's **d** and the disciples of *G3412*
Mk 2:18 disciples and the **d** of the Pharisees are *G3412*
Mk 2:23 as his **d** walked along, they *G3412*
Mk 3: 7 Jesus withdrew with his **d** to the lake, and *G3412*
Mk 3: 9 crowd he told his **d** to have a small boat *G3412*
Mk 3:20 so that **he and his d** were not even able *G899s*
Mk 4:34 But when he was alone *with* his own **d** *G3412*
Mk 4:35 he said *to* **his d**, "Let us go over to *G899s*
Mk 4:38 The **d** woke him and said to him, "Teacher NDT
Mk 4:40 He said *to* **his d**, "Why are you so afraid *G899s*
Mk 5:31 against you," his **d** answered, "and yet *G3412*
Mk 5:40 mother and the **d** who were with him, NDT
Mk 6: 1 to his hometown, accompanied by his **d**. *G3412*
Mk 6:29 John's **d** came and took his body and laid *G3412*
Mk 6:35 was late in the day, so his **d** came to him. *G3412*
Mk 6:41 he gave them *to* his **d** to distribute to *G3412*
Mk 6:43 the **d** picked up twelve basketfuls of NDT
Mk 6:45 Jesus made his **d** get into the boat and *G3412*
Mk 6:48 He saw **the d** straining at the oars *G899s*
Mk 7: 2 saw some *of* his **d** eating food with *G3412*
Mk 7: 5 "Why don't your **d** live according to the *G3412*
Mk 7:17 his **d** asked him about this parable. *G3412*
Mk 8: 1 Jesus called his **d** to him and said, *G3412*
Mk 8: 4 His **d** answered, "But where in this remote *G3412*
Mk 8: 6 gave them *to* his **d** to distribute to *G3412*
Mk 8: 7 them also and told the **d** to distribute them. NDT
Mk 8: 8 Afterward the **d** picked up seven basketfuls NDT
Mk 8:10 the boat with his **d** and went to the region *G3412*
Mk 8:14 The **d** had forgotten to bring bread, except NDT
Mk 8:27 Jesus and his **d** went on to the villages *G3412*
Mk 8:33 when Jesus turned and looked at his **d**, *G3412*
Mk 8:34 crowd to him along with his **d** and said: *G3412*
Mk 9:14 When they came to the other **d**, they saw *G3412*
Mk 9:18 I asked your **d** to drive out the spirit, but *G3412*
Mk 9:28 gone indoors, his **d** asked him privately *G3412*
Mk 9:31 because he was teaching his **d**. He said to *G3412*
Mk 10:10 the **d** asked Jesus about this. *G3412*
Mk 10:13 hands on them, but the **d** rebuked them. *G3412*
Mk 10:23 Jesus looked around and said *to* his **d** *G3412*
Mk 10:24 The **d** were amazed at his words. *G3412*
Mk 10:26 **The d** were even more amazed, and *G3836s*
Mk 10:32 the way, and the **d** were astonished, while NDT
Mk 10:46 As Jesus and his **d**, together with a large *G3412*
Mk 11: 1 Mount of Olives, Jesus sent two *of* his **d**, *G3412*
Mk 11:14 And his **d** heard him say it. *G3412*
Mk 11:19 Jesus and his **d** went out of the city. NDT
Mk 12:43 Calling his **d** to him, Jesus said, "Truly I *G3412*
Mk 13: 1 the temple, one *of* his **d** said to him *G3412*
Mk 14:12 Jesus' **d** asked him, "Where do *G3412*
Mk 14:13 So he sent two *of* his **d**, telling them, "Go *G3412*
Mk 14:14 where I may eat the Passover with my **d**? *G3412*
Mk 14:16 The **d** left, went into the city and found *G3412*
Mk 14:22 he broke it and gave it *to his* **d**, saying, *G899s*
Mk 14:32 Jesus said *to* his **d**, "Sit here while I *G3412*
Mk 14:37 he returned to his **d** and found them NDT
Mk 16: 7 tell his **d** and Peter, 'He is going *G3412*
Mk 16:20 Then **the d** went out and preached *G1697s*
Lk 5:30 to their sect complained to his **d**, *G3412*
Lk 5:33 said to him, "John's **d** often fast and pray *G3412*
Lk 5:33 and so do the **d** of the Pharisees, but NDT
Lk 6: 1 his **d** began to pick some heads of *G3412*
Lk 6:13 he called his **d** to him and chose twelve *G3412*
Lk 6:17 A large crowd *of* his **d** was there and a *G3412*
Lk 6:20 Looking at his **d**, he said: "Blessed are *G3412*
Lk 7:11 his **d** and a large crowd went along *G3412*
Lk 7:18 John's **d** told him about all these things *G3412*
Lk 8: 9 His **d** asked him what this parable meant. *G3412*
Lk 8:22 One day Jesus said to his **d**, "Let us go *G3412*
Lk 8:24 The **d** went and woke him, saying, "Master NDT
Lk 8:25 he asked **his d**. In fear and *G899s*
Lk 9:14 But he said to his **d**, "Have them sit down *G3412*
Lk 9:15 The **d** did so, and everyone sat down. NDT
Lk 9:16 he gave them *to* the **d** to distribute to *G3412*
Lk 9:17 the **d** picked up twelve basketfuls of NDT
Lk 9:18 in private and his **d** were with him, *G3412*
Lk 9:36 **The d** kept this to themselves and did not *G899s*
Lk 9:40 I begged your **d** to drive it out, but they *G3412*
Lk 9:43 at all that Jesus did, he said to his **d**, *G3412*
Lk 9:46 started among **the d** as to which of them *G899s*
Lk 9:54 When the **d** James and John saw this *G3412*
Lk 9:56 Then *he and his d* **went** to another village. AIT
Lk 10:23 Then he turned to his **d** and said privately, *G3412*
Lk 10:38 As **Jesus and his d** were on their way, he *G899s*
Lk 11: 1 he finished, one *of* his **d** said to him *G3412*
Lk 11: 1 teach us to pray, just as John taught his **d**." *G3412*
Lk 12: 1 Jesus began to speak first to his **d**, saying: *G3412*
Lk 12:22 Then Jesus said to his **d**: "Therefore I tell *G3412*
Lk 14:33 up everything you have cannot be my **d**. *G3412*
Lk 16: 1 Jesus told his **d**: "There was a rich man *G3412*
Lk 17: 1 Jesus said to his **d**: "Things that cause *G3412*
Lk 17:22 Then he said to his **d**, "The time is *G3412*
Lk 18: 1 Then Jesus told **his d** a parable to show *G899s*
Lk 18:15 When the **d** saw this, they *G3412*
Lk 18:34 **The d** did not understand any of this. *G899s*
Lk 19:29 he sent two *of* his **d**, saying to them, *G3412*
Lk 19:37 the whole crowd *of* **d** began joyfully to *G3412*
Lk 19:39 said to Jesus, "Teacher, rebuke your **d**!" *G3412*
Lk 20:45 were listening, Jesus said *to* his **d**, *G3412*
Lk 21: 5 Some of his **d** were remarking about how NDT
Lk 22:11 where I may eat the Passover with my **d**? *G3412*
Lk 22:38 **The d** said, "See, Lord, here are two *G3836s*
Lk 22:39 Mount of Olives, and his **d** followed him. *G3412*
Lk 22:45 rose from prayer and went back to the **d**, *G3412*
Jn 1:35 John was there again with two of his **d**. *G3412*
Jn 1:37 When the two **d** heard him say this, they *G3412*
Jn 2: 2 Jesus and his **d** had also been invited *G3412*
Jn 2:11 his glory; and his **d** believed in him. *G3412*
Jn 2:12 with his mother and brothers and his **d**. *G3412*
Jn 2:17 His **d** remembered that it is written: "Zeal *G3412*
Jn 2:22 his **d** recalled what he had said. *G3412*
Jn 3:22 Jesus and his **d** went out into the Judean *G3412*
Jn 3:25 some of John's **d** and a certain Jew over *G3412*
Jn 4: 1 baptizing more **d** than John— *G3412*
Jn 4: 2 it was not Jesus who baptized, but his **d**. *G3412*
Jn 4: 8 His **d** had gone into the town to buy food.) *G3412*
Jn 4:27 Just then his **d** returned and were *G3412*
Jn 4:31 Meanwhile his **d** urged him, "Rabbi, eat *G3412*
Jn 4:33 Then his **d** said to each other, "Could *G3412*
Jn 6: 3 a mountainside and sat down with his **d**. *G3412*
Jn 6: 8 Another of his **d**, Andrew, Simon Peter's *G3412*
Jn 6:12 he said *to* his **d**, "Gather the *G3412*
Jn 6:16 his **d** went down to the lake *G3412*
Jn 6:22 that Jesus had not entered it with his **d**, *G3412*
Jn 6:24 that neither Jesus nor his **d** were there, *G3412*
Jn 6:60 many of his **d** said, "This is a hard *G3412*
Jn 6:61 Aware that his **d** were grumbling about *G3412*
Jn 6:66 time many of his **d** turned back and no *G3412*
Jn 7: 3 so that your **d** there may see the works *G3412*
Jn 8:31 hold to my teaching, you are really my **d**. *G3412*
Jn 9: 2 His **d** asked him, "Rabbi, who sinned, this *G3412*
Jn 9:27 Do you want to become his **d** too?" *G3412*
Jn 9:28 this fellow's disciple! We are **d** of Moses! *G3412*
Jn 11: 7 then he said *to* his **d**, "Let us go back *G3412*
Jn 11:12 His **d** replied, "Lord, if he sleeps, he will *G3412*
Jn 11:13 but **his d** thought he meant natural *G1697s*
Jn 11:16 said *to* the **rest of** *the* **d**, "Let us also *G5209*
Jn 11:54 Ephraim, where he stayed with his **d**. *G3412*
Jn 12: 4 But one *of* his **d**, Judas Iscariot, who was *G3412*
Jn 12:16 At first his **d** did not understand all this *G3412*
Jn 13:22 His **d** stared at one another, at a loss to *G3412*
Jn 13:35 this everyone will know that you are my **d**, *G3412*
Jn 15: 8 showing yourselves to be my **d**. *G3412*
Jn 16:17 some of his **d** said to one another *G3412*
Jn 16:29 Then Jesus' **d** said, "Now you are *G3412*
Jn 18: 1 Jesus left with his **d** and crossed the *G3412*
Jn 18: 1 a garden, and he and his **d** went into it. *G3412*
Jn 18: 2 Jesus had often met there with his **d**. *G3412*
Jn 18:17 "You aren't one of this man's **d** too, are *G3412*
Jn 18:19 Jesus about his **d** and his teaching. *G3412*
Jn 18:25 "You aren't one of his **d** too, are you?" *G3412*
Jn 20:10 Then the **d** went back to where they were *G3412*
Jn 20:18 Magdalene went *to* the **d** with the news: *G3412*
Jn 20:19 the week, when the **d** were together, with *G3412*
Jn 20:20 The **d** were overjoyed when they saw the *G3412*
Jn 20:24 was not with **the d** when Jesus came. *G899s*
Jn 20:25 So the other **d** told him, "We have seen *G3412*
Jn 20:26 A week later his **d** were in the house *G3412*
Jn 20:30 many other signs in the presence of his **d**, *G3412*
Jn 21: 1 Afterward Jesus appeared again to his **d** *G3412*
Jn 21: 2 Zebedee, and two other **d** were together. *G3412*
Jn 21: 4 the **d** did not realize that it was Jesus. *G3412*
Jn 21: 8 The other **d** followed in the boat, towing *G3412*
Jn 21:12 None *of* the **d** dared ask him, "Who are *G3412*

Jn 21:14 time Jesus appeared *to* his **d** after he was G3412
Ac 6: 1 when the number *of* **d** was increasing, G3412
Ac 6: 2 gathered all the **d** together and said, G3412
Ac 6: 7 The number *of* **d** in Jerusalem increased G3412
Ac 9: 1 murderous threats against the Lord's **d**. G3412
Ac 9:19 several days with the **d** in Damascus. G3412
Ac 9:26 he tried to join the **d**, but they were all G3412
Ac 9:38 so when the **d** heard that Peter was in G3412
Ac 11:26 The **d** were called Christians first at G3412
Ac 11:29 The **d**, as each one was able, decided to G3412
Ac 13:52 And the **d** were filled with joy and with the G3412
Ac 14:20 But after the **d** had gathered around him G3412
Ac 14:21 in that city and **won** a large number of **d**. G3411
Ac 14:22 strengthening the **d** and encouraging G3412
Ac 14:28 they stayed there a long time with the **d**. G3412
Ac 18:23 Phrygia, strengthening all the **d**. G3412
Ac 18:27 him and wrote *to* the **d** there to welcome G3412
Ac 19: 1 There he found some **d** G3412
Ac 19: 9 He took the **d** with him and had G3412
Ac 19:30 the crowd, but the **d** would not let him. G3412
Ac 20: 1 Paul sent for the **d** and, after encouraging G3412
Ac 20:30 truth in order to draw away **d** after them. G3412
Ac 21: 4 We sought out the **d** there and stayed with G3412
Ac 21:16 *Some of* the **d** from Caesarea G3412
Ac 21:16 a man from Cyprus and one of the early **d**. G3412

DISCIPLES' (1) [DISCIPLE]

Jn 13: 5 into a basin and began to wash his **d** feet, G3412

DISCIPLINE (35) [DISCIPLINED, DISCIPLINES, SELF-DISCIPLINE]

Dt 4:36 he made you hear his voice to **d** you. H3579
Dt 11: 2 experienced the **d** *of* the LORD your God: H4592
Dt 21:18 will not listen to them when *they* **d** him, H3579
Job 5:17 so do not despise the **d** *of* the Almighty. H4592
Ps 6: 1 me in your anger or **d** me in your wrath. H3579
Ps 38: 1 me in your anger or **d** me in your wrath. H3579
Ps 39:11 When *you* rebuke and **d** anyone for their H3579
Ps 94:12 Blessed is the one *you* **d**, LORD, the one H3579
Pr 3:11 do not despise the LORD's **d**, and do not H4592
Pr 5:12 "How I hated **d**! How my heart H4592
Pr 5:23 For lack of **d** they will die, led astray by H4592
Pr 10:17 Whoever heeds **d** shows the way to life H4592
Pr 12: 1 Whoever loves **d** loves knowledge, but H4592
Pr 13:18 Whoever disregards **d** comes to poverty H4592
Pr 13:24 loves their children is careful to **d** them. H4592
Pr 15: 5 A fool spurns a parent's **d**, but whoever H4592
Pr 15:10 Stern **d** awaits anyone who leaves the H4592
Pr 15:32 who disregard **d** despise themselves, H4592
Pr 19:18 **D** your children, for in that there is hope H3579
Pr 19:20 Listen to advice and accept **d**, and at the H4592
Pr 22:15 the rod of **d** will drive it far away. H4592
Pr 23:13 Do not withhold **d** from a child; if you H4592
Pr 29:17 **D** your children, and they will give you H3579
Jer 10:24 **D** me, LORD, but only in due measure H3579
Jer 17:23 would not listen or respond to **d**. H4592
Jer 30:11 *I will* **d** you but only in due measure; I will H3579
Jer 32:33 they would not listen or respond to **d**. H4592
Jer 46:28 *I will* **d** you but only in due measure; I will H3579
Hos 5: 2 I will **d** all of them. H4592
1Co 4:21 Shall I come to you with a **rod of d**, or G4811
Heb 12: 5 do not make light of the Lord's **d**, and do G4082
Heb 12: 7 Endure hardship as **d**; God is treating you G4082
Heb 12: 8 everyone undergoes **d**—then you are G4005S
Heb 12:11 No **d** seems pleasant at the time, but G4082
Rev 3:19 Those whom I love I rebuke and **d**. G4084

DISCIPLINED (10) [DISCIPLINE]

Isa 26:16 distress; when you **d** them, they could H4592
Jer 31:18 '*You* **d** me like an unruly calf, and I have H3579
Jer 31:18 me like an unruly calf, and *I have* **been d**. H3579
1Co 11:32 *we are being* **d** so that we will not be G4084
Col 2: 5 delight to see *how* **d** you are and how G5423
Titus 1: 8 who is self-controlled, upright, holy and **d**. G1604
Heb 12: 7 For what children *are* not **d** by their father G4084
Heb 12: 8 If you are not **d**—and everyone undergoes G4082
Heb 12: 9 human fathers who **d** us and we G4083
Heb 12:10 They **d** us for a little while as they thought G4084

DISCIPLINES (6) [DISCIPLINE]

Dt 8: 5 in your heart that as a man **d** his son, H3579
Dt 8: 5 his son, so the LORD your God **d** you. H3579
Ps 94:10 Does he *who* **d** nations not punish? Does H3579
Pr 3:12 because the LORD **d** those he loves, as a H3519
Heb 12: 6 because the Lord **d** the one he loves, and G4084
Heb 12:10 thought best; but God **d** us for our good, in NDT

DISCLOSE (2) [DISCLOSED]

Job 11: 6 **d** to you the secrets of wisdom, for H5583
Isa 26:21 The earth *will* **d** the blood shed on it; the H1655

DISCLOSED (6) [DISCLOSE]

Mt 10:26 is nothing concealed that *will* not be **d**, G636
Mk 4:22 For whatever is hidden *is* meant to *be* **d** G5746
Lk 8:17 there is nothing hidden that will not be **d**, G5745
Lk 12: 2 is nothing concealed that *will* not *be* **d**, G636
Col 1:26 but *is* now **d** to the Lord's people. G5746
Heb 9: 8 *that* the way into the Most Holy Place *had* not yet *been* **d** G5746

DISCOMFITED, DISCOMFITURE (KJV) BEAT, CONFUSION, FORCED LABOR, OVERCAME, PANIC, ROUTED, ROUTING

DISCOMFORT (1)

Jnh 4: 6 to give shade for his head to ease his **d**, H8288

DISCONTENTED (1)

1Sa 22: 2 in debt or **d** gathered around H5253+5883

DISCORD (3)

Est 1:18 There will be no end of disrespect and **d**. H7912
2Co 12:20 I fear that there may be **d**, jealousy, fits of G2251
Gal 5:20 witchcraft; hatred, **d**, jealousy, fits of rage G2251

DISCOURAGE (2) [DISCOURAGED, DISCOURAGEMENT, DISCOURAGING]

Nu 32: 7 Why *do you* **d** the Israelites from H5648+4213
Ezr 4: 4 them *set out to* **d** the people H8332+3338

DISCOURAGED (15) [DISCOURAGE]

Nu 32: 9 *they* **d** the Israelites from entering H5648+4213
Dt 1:21 Do not be afraid; *do not be* **d**." H3169
Dt 31: 8 Do not be afraid; *do not be* **d**." H3169
Jos 1: 9 Do not be afraid; *do not be* **d**, for the LORD H3169
Jos 8: 1 to Joshua, "Do not be afraid; *do not be* **d**. H3169
Jos 10:25 to them, "Do not be afraid; *do not be* **d**. H3169
1Ch 22:13 courageous. Do not be afraid or **d**. H3169
1Ch 28:20 Do not be afraid or **d**, for the LORD God H3169
2Ch 20:15 'Do not be afraid or **d** because of this vast H3169
2Ch 20:17 not be afraid; *do not be* **d**. Go out to face H3169
2Ch 32: 7 Do not be afraid or **d** because of the king H3169
Job 4: 5 and *you are* **d**; it strikes you, H4206
Isa 42: 4 will not falter or *be* **d** till he establishes H8368
Eph 3:13 not *to be* **d** because of my sufferings for G1591
Col 3:21 your children, or *they will become* **d**. G126

DISCOURAGEMENT (1) [DISCOURAGE]

Ex 6: 9 because of their **d** and harsh labor. H7919+8120

DISCOURAGING (1) [DISCOURAGE]

Jer 38: 4 He *is* **d** the soldiers who are left in H8332+3338

DISCOURSE (2)

Job 27: 1 And Job continued his **d**: H5442
Job 29: 1 Job continued his **d**: H5442

DISCOVER (5) [DISCOVERED]

Ecc 7:14 no one *can* **d** anything *about* their future. H5162
Ecc 7:24 far off and most profound—who *can* **d** it? H5162
Ecc 7:27 thing to another to **d** the scheme of things H5162
Ecc 8:17 search it out, no one *can* **d** *its* **meaning**. H5162
2Co 13: 6 And I trust that *you will* **d** that we have not G1182

DISCOVERED (11) [DISCOVER]

Ge 26:19 in the valley and **d** a well of fresh water H5162
Ge 36:24 This is the Anah who **d** the hot springs in H5162
Dt 22:28 be married and rapes her and *they are* **d**, H5162
Jdg 16: 9 So the secret of his strength **was** not **d**. H3359
Jdg 21: 8 They **d** that no one from Jabesh Gilead H2180
1Sa 22: 6 that David and his men *had* **been d**. H3359
2Ki 17: 4 the king of Assyria **d** that Hoshea was a H5162
2Ki 23:24 the priest *had* **d** *in* the temple of the H5162
Ps 44:21 *would* not God *have* **d** it, since he knows H2983
Ecc 7:27 says the Teacher, "this is what *I have* **d**: H5162
Ro 4: 1 *that* Abraham, our forefather according to the flesh, **d** G2351

DISCREDIT (2) [DISCREDITED]

Ne 6:13 they would give me a bad name to **d** me. H3070
Job 40: 8 "*Would you* **d** my justice? Would you H7296

DISCREDITED (2) [DISCREDIT]

Ac 19:27 *that* the temple of the great goddess Artemis *will be* **d** G1650+4029+3357
2Co 6: 3 so that our ministry *will* not *be* **d**. G3699

DISCREETLY (1) [DISCRETION]

Pr 26:16 eyes than seven people who answer **d**. H3248

DISCRETION (7) [DISCREETLY]

1Ch 22:12 the LORD give you **d** and understanding H8507
Pr 1: 4 knowledge and **d** to the young— H4659
Pr 2:11 **D** will protect you, and understanding will H4659
Pr 3:21 preserve sound judgment and **d**; H4659
Pr 5: 2 you may maintain **d** and your lips may H4659
Pr 8:12 prudence; I possess knowledge and **d**. H4659
Pr 11:22 is a beautiful woman who shows no **d**. H3248

DISCRIMINATE (1) [DISCRIMINATED]

Ac 15: 9 *He did* not **d** between us and them, for he G1359

DISCRIMINATED (1) [DISCRIMINATE]

Jas 2: 4 *have you* not **d** among yourselves and G1359

DISCUSS (2) [DISCUSSED, DISCUSSING, DISCUSSION, DISCUSSIONS]

Lk 6:11 were furious and *began to* **d** with one G1362
Heb 9: 5 But we cannot **d** these things in detail G3306

DISCUSSED (9) [DISCUSS]

1Sa 20:23 And about the matter you and I **d** H1819
Mt 16: 7 They **d** this among themselves and said G1368
Mt 21:25 They **d** it among themselves and said, "If G1368
Mk 8:16 *They* **d** this with one another and said, "It G1368
Mk 11:31 *They* **d** it among themselves and said, "If G1368
Lk 20: 5 They **d** it among themselves and said, "If G5199
Lk 22: 4 temple guard and **d** with them how he G5196
Lk 24:15 As they talked and **d** these things with G5184
Ac 25:14 Festus **d** Paul's case with the king. G423

DISCUSSING (2) [DISCUSS]

Mk 9:10 themselves, **d** what "rising from the dead G5184
Lk 24:17 "What *are you* **d** together as you walk G506

DISCUSSION (3) [DISCUSS]

Mt 16: 8 Aware of their **d**, Jesus asked, "You of little NDT
Mk 8:17 Aware of their **d**, Jesus asked them: "Why NDT
Ac 15: 7 After much **d**, Peter got up and addressed G2428

DISCUSSIONS (1) [DISCUSS]

Ac 19: 9 with him and **had d** daily in the lecture G1363

DISDAINED (3) [DISDAINFUL]

1Sa 2:30 those who despise me *will be* **d**. H7837
Job 30: 1 whose fathers *I would have* **d** to put with H4415
Jer 30:19 bring them honor, and *they will* not *be* **d**. H7592

DISDAINFUL (1) [DISDAINED]

Pr 30:13 ever so haughty, whose glances *are* so **d**; H5951

DISEASE (42) [DISEASED, DISEASES]

Lev 13: 2 on their skin that may be a defiling **skin d**, H7669
Lev 13: 3 than skin deep, it is a defiling **skin d**. H7669
Lev 13: 8 them unclean; it is a **defiling skin d**. H7669
Lev 13: 9 "When anyone has a defiling **skin d**, they H7669
Lev 13:11 it is a chronic **skin d** and the priest shall H7669
Lev 13:12 "If the **d** breaks out all over their skin and H7669
Lev 13:13 if the **d** has covered their whole body H7669
Lev 13:15 flesh is unclean; they have a **defiling d**. H7669
Lev 13:20 It is a defiling **skin d** that has broken out H7669
Lev 13:22 them unclean; it is a **defiling d**. H5596
Lev 13:25 it is a **defiling d** that has broken out in the H7669
Lev 13:25 them unclean; it is a defiling **skin d**. H7669
Lev 13:27 them unclean; it is a defiling **skin d**. H7669
Lev 13:30 it is a **defiling skin d** *on* the head H5999+7669
Lev 13:42 it is a **defiling d** breaking out on his head H7669
Lev 13:43 is reddish-white like a **defiling** skin **d**, H7669
Lev 13:45 "Anyone *with* such a defiling **d** must wear H7665
Lev 13:46 as they have the **d** they remain unclean. H5596
Lev 14: 3 have been healed of their defiling **skin d**, H7669
Lev 14: 7 the one to be cleansed of the **defiling d**, H7669
Lev 14:32 who has a defiling **skin d** and who cannot H7669
Lev 14:54 are the regulations for any defiling **skin d**, H7669
Lev 22: 4 of Aaron *has a* **defiling skin d** or a bodily H7665
Nu 5: 2 anyone *who* **has a defiling skin d** or a H7665
Nu 12:10 saw that *she* **had a defiling skin d**, H7665
Dt 7:15 The LORD will keep you free from every **d** H2716
Dt 28:22 The LORD will strike you with **wasting d** H8831
1Ki 8:37 whatever disaster or **d** may come, H4701
2Ch 6:28 whatever disaster or **d** may come, H4701
2Ch 16:12 reign Asa *was* **afflicted with a d** in his feet H2688
2Ch 16:12 Though his **d** was severe, even in his H2716
2Ch 21:15 very ill with a lingering **d** *of* the bowels, H4700
2Ch 21:15 until the **d** causes your bowels to come H2716
2Ch 21:18 with an incurable **d** of the bowels. H2716
2Ch 21:19 his bowels came out because of the **d** H2716
Ps 41: 8 "A vile **d** has afflicted him; he will never H1821
Ps 106:15 but sent a **wasting d** among them. H8137
Isa 10:16 will send a **wasting d** upon his sturdy H8137
Isa 17:11 in the day of **d** and incurable pain. H5710
Mt 4:23 healing every **d** and sickness among G3798
Mt 9:35 healing every **d** and sickness. G3798
Mt 10: 1 spirits and to heal every **d** and sickness. G3798

DISEASED (5) [DISEASE]

Lev 13:44 the man *is* **d** and is unclean. The priest H7665
Lev 14: 2 regulations for any **d** *person* at the time of H7665
1Ki 15:23 his old age, however, his feet *became* **d**. H2703
Mal 1: 8 When you sacrifice lame or **d** *animals*, is H2703
Mal 1:13 lame or **d** *animals* and offer them as H2703

DISEASES (19) [DISEASE]

Ge 12:17 inflicted serious **d** on Pharaoh and his H5596
Ex 15:26 bring on you any of the **d** I brought on the H4701
Lev 14:57 **defiling skin d and defiling molds**. H7669
Lev 26:16 **wasting d** and fever that will destroy your H8831
Dt 7:15 on you the horrible **d** you knew *in* Egypt, H4504
Dt 24: 8 In cases of defiling **skin d**, be very careful H5596
Dt 28:21 will plague you with **d** until he has H1822
Dt 28:60 bring on you all the **d** *of* Egypt that you H4504
Dt 29:22 on the land and the **d** with which the LORD H9377
Ps 103: 3 forgives all your sins and heals all your **d**, H9377
Jer 16: 4 "They will die of deadly **d**. They will not H9377
Mt 4:24 to him all who were ill *with* various **d**, G3798
Mt 8:17 "He took up our infirmities and bore our **d**." G3798
Mk 1:34 healed many who had various **d**. G2809+3798
Mk 3:10 so that those with **d** were pushing forward G3465
Lk 6:18 to hear him and to be healed of their **d**. G3798
Lk 7:21 very time Jesus cured many who had **d**, G3798
Lk 8: 2 who had been cured of evil spirits and **d**: G819
Lk 9: 1 to drive out all demons and to cure **d**, G3798

DISFIGURE (1) [DISFIGURED]

Mt 6:16 for *they* **d** their faces to show others they G906

DISFIGURED (2) [DISFIGURE]

Lev 21:18 who is blind or lame, **d** or deformed; H3050
Isa 52:14 his appearance *was* so **d** beyond that of H5425

DISGRACE (56) [DISGRACED, DISGRACEFUL, DISGRACES]

Ge 30:23 son and said, "God has taken away my **d**." H3075
Ge 34:14 not circumcised. That would be a **d** to us. H3075
Lev 20:17 they have sexual relations, it is a **d**. H2875
Nu 12:14 *would she* not *have* **been in d** for seven H4007
1Sa 11: 2 one of you and so bring **d** on all Israel." H3075
1Sa 17:26 Philistine and removes this **d** from Israel? H3075
2Sa 13:13 Where could I get rid of my **d**? And what H3075
2Ki 19: 3 day is a day of distress and rebuke and **d**, H5541
2Ch 32:21 he withdrew to his own land in **d**. H1425+7156
Ne 1: 3 in the province are in great trouble and **d**. H3075
Ne 2:17 Jerusalem, and we will no longer be *in* **d**." H3075
Ps 35:26 over me be clothed with shame and **d**. H4009
Ps 40:14 who desire my ruin be turned back *in* **d**. H4007
Ps 44:15 I live in **d** all day long, and my face is H4009
Ps 52: 1 you who are a **d** *in the eyes of* God? H2875
Ps 70: 2 who desire my ruin be turned back **in d**. H4007
Ps 71:13 to harm me be covered with scorn and **d**. H4009
Ps 74:21 Do not let the oppressed retreat *in* **d**; may H4007
Ps 83:17 dismayed; may they perish *in* **d**. H2917
Ps 109:29 be clothed with **d** and wrapped in shame H4009
Ps 119:39 Take away the **d** I dread, for your laws are H3075
Pr 6:33 Blows and **d** are his lot, and his shame H7830
Pr 11: 2 then comes **d**, but with humility H7830
Pr 19:26 is a child who brings shame and **d**. H2917
Isa 4: 1 called by your name. Take away our **d**!" H3075
Isa 22:18 of will become a **d** *to* your master's house H7830
Isa 25: 8 remove his people's **d** from all the earth. H3075
Isa 30: 3 Egypt's shade will bring you **d**. H4009
Isa 30: 5 advantage, but only shame and **d**. H3075
Isa 37: 3 day is a day of distress and rebuke and **d**, H5541
Isa 45:16 disgraced; they will go off into **d** together. H4009
Isa 54: 4 put to shame. *Do* not **fear d**; you will not H4007
Isa 61: 7 instead of **d** you will rejoice in your H4009
Jer 3:25 in our shame, and let our **d** cover us. H4009
Jer 23:40 I will bring on you everlasting **d** H3075
Jer 31:19 because I bore the **d** *of* my youth. H3075
La 3:30 strike him, and let him be filled with **d**. H3075
La 5: 1 has happened to us; look, and see our **d**. H3075
Eze 16:52 Bear your **d**, for you have furnished some H4009
Eze 16:52 be ashamed and bear your **d**, for you H4009
Eze 16:54 you may bear your **d** and be ashamed of H4009
Eze 28:16 So *I* **drove** you **in d** from the mount of God H2725
Eze 32:30 down with the slain *in* **d** despite the terror H1017
Eze 36:30 suffer **d** among the nations *because of* H3075
Hos 2: 5 unfaithful and has conceived them *in* **d**. H1017
Mic 2: 6 about these things; **d** will not overtake us." H4009
Hab 2:16 around to you, and **d** will cover your glory. H7814
Mt 1:19 did not want *to* **expose** her **to public d**, *G1258*
Lk 1:25 taken away my **d** among the people." *G3945*
Ac 5:41 counted worthy *of* **suffering d** for the Name. *G869*
1Co 11: 6 if it is a **d** for a woman to have her hair *G156*
1Co 11:14 if a man has long hair, it is a **d** to him, *G871*
1Ti 3: 7 he will not fall into **d** and into the devil's *G3944*
Heb 6: 6 again and **subjecting** him **to public d**. *G4136*
Heb 11:26 He regarded **d** for the sake of Christ as of *G3944*
Heb 13:13 outside the camp, bearing the **d** he bore. *G3944*

DISGRACED (25) [DISGRACE]

2Sa 13:22 Amnon because *he had* **d** his sister H6700
Ezr 9: 6 "I am too ashamed and **d**, my God, to lift H4007
Ps 35: 4 *May* those who seek my life *be* **d** and put H1017
Ps 69: 6 *may* those who hope in you not *be* **d** H1017
Ps 69:19 how I am scorned, **d**, and shamed; all my H1425
Isa 1:29 *you will be* **d** because of the gardens that H2917
Isa 41:11 you will surely be ashamed and **d**; H4007
Isa 43:28 So *I* **d** the dignitaries of your temple; H2725
Isa 45:16 of idols will be put to shame and **d**; H4007
Isa 45:17 you will never be put to shame or **d**, to H4007
Isa 50: 7 Sovereign LORD helps me, *I will* not **be d**. H4007
Jer 2:26 "As a thief is **d** when he is caught, so the H1425
Jer 2:26 so the people of Israel *are* **d**—they, H1017
Jer 15: 9 is still day; *she will be* **d** and humiliated. H1017
Jer 20:11 They will fail and *be* thoroughly **d**; their H1017
Jer 22:22 be ashamed and **d** because of all your H4007
Jer 48: 1 Kiriathaim *will* **be d** and captured; the H1017
Jer 48: 1 the stronghold *will* **be d** and shattered. H1017
Jer 48:20 Moab *is* **d**, for she is shattered. Wail and H1017
Jer 50:12 she who gave you birth *will be* **d**. H2917
Jer 51:47 her whole land *will be* **d** and her slain H1017
Jer 51:51 "*We are* **d**, for we have been insulted H1017
Eze 36:32 Be ashamed and **d** for your conduct H4007
Hos 10: 6 Ephraim *will be* **d**; Israel will be H1423+4374
Mic 3: 7 seers will be ashamed and the diviners **d**. H2917

DISGRACEFUL (5) [DISGRACE]

Pr 10: 5 he who sleeps during harvest *is* a **d** son. H1017
Pr 12: 4 a **d** wife is like decay in his bones. H1017
Pr 17: 2 will rule over a **d** son and will share the H1017
Hos 4: 7 their glorious God for *something* **d**. H7830
1Co 14:35 it is **d** for a woman to speak in the *G156*

DISGRACES (3) [DISGRACE]

Lev 21: 9 a prostitute, she **d** her father; she must be H2725
Pr 28: 7 a companion of gluttons **d** his father. H4007
Pr 29:15 a child left undisciplined **d** its mother. H1017

DISGUISE (5) [DISGUISED]

Ge 38:14 covered herself with a veil *to* **d herself** H6634
1Ki 14: 2 **d yourself**, so you won't be H9101
1Ki 22:30 "I will enter the battle **in d**, but you wear H2924
2Ch 18:29 "I will enter the battle **in d**, but you wear H2924
Pr 26:24 Enemies **d themselves** with their lips, but H5795

DISGUISED (5) [DISGUISE]

1Sa 28: 8 So Saul **d himself**, putting on other H2924
1Ki 20:38 *He* **d himself** with his headband down H2924
1Ki 22:30 the king of Israel **d himself** and went into H2924
2Ch 18:29 the king of Israel **d himself** and went into H2924
2Ch 35:22 but **d himself** to engage him in battle. H2924

DISGUST (4) [DISGUSTED]

Eze 23:17 by them, she **turned away** from them **in d**. H3697
Eze 23:18 I **turned away** from her **in d**, just as I H3697
Eze 23:22 those you **turned away** from **in d**, and I H5936
Eze 23:28 to those you **turned away** from **in d**. H5936

DISGUSTED (1) [DISGUST]

Ge 27:46 "*I'm* **d** with living because of these Hittite H7762

DISH (21) [DISHES]

Nu 7:14 one gold **d** weighing ten shekels, filled H4090
Nu 7:20 one gold **d** weighing ten shekels, filled H4090
Nu 7:26 one gold **d** weighing ten shekels, filled H4090
Nu 7:32 one gold **d** weighing ten shekels, filled H4090
Nu 7:38 one gold **d** weighing ten shekels, filled H4090
Nu 7:44 one gold **d** weighing ten shekels, filled H4090
Nu 7:50 one gold **d** weighing ten shekels, filled H4090
Nu 7:56 one gold **d** weighing ten shekels, filled H4090
Nu 7:62 one gold **d** weighing ten shekels, filled H4090
Nu 7:68 one gold **d** weighing ten shekels, filled H4090
Nu 7:74 one gold **d** weighing ten shekels, filled H4090
Nu 7:80 one gold **d** weighing ten shekels, filled H4090
2Ki 21:13 will wipe out Jerusalem as one wipes a **d**, H7505
1Ch 28:17 of gold for **each** gold **d**; H4094+2256+4094
1Ch 28:17 of silver for **each** silver **d**; H4094+2256+4094
Pr 19:24 A sluggard buries his hand in the **d**; he H7505
Pr 26:15 A sluggard buries his hand in the **d**; he is H7505
Mt 23:25 You clean the outside of the cup and **d** *G4243*
Mt 23:26 First clean the inside of the cup and **d**, *G4243*
Lk 11:39 clean the outside of the cup and **d**, *G4402*
Jn 13:26 of bread when I have dipped it in the **d**." NDT

DISHAN (5)

Ge 36:21 Dishon, Ezer and **D**. These sons of Seir in H1915
Ge 36:28 The sons of **D**: Uz and Aran. H1915
Ge 36:30 Dishon, Ezer and Dishan. These were the H1915
1Ch 1:38 Zibeon, Anah, Dishon, Ezer and **D**. H1915
1Ch 1:42 The sons of **D**: Uz and Aran. H1914

DISHEARTENED (4) [HEART]

Dt 20: 8 *will* not *become* **d** too. H5022+906+4222
Jer 49:23 heard bad news. *They are* **d**, troubled like H4570
Eze 13:22 Because you **d** the righteous with H3874+4213
1Th 5:14 encourage the **d**, help the weak, *G3901*

DISHES (15) [DISH]

Ex 25:29 And make its plates and **d** of pure gold, as H4090
Ex 37:16 its plates and **d** and bowls and its pitchers H4090
Nu 4: 7 put on it the plates, **d** and bowls, and the H4090
Nu 7:84 silver sprinkling bowls and twelve gold **d**. H4090
Nu 7:85 the silver **d** weighed two thousand four H3998
Nu 7:86 The twelve gold **d** filled with incense H4090
Nu 7:86 the gold **d** weighed a hundred and twenty H4090
1Ki 7:50 sprinkling bowls, **d** and censers; and the H4090
2Ki 25:14 **d** and all the bronze articles used in the H4090
2Ch 4:22 sprinkling bowls, **d** and censers; and the H4090
2Ch 24:14 also **d** and other objects of gold and H4090
Ezr 1: 9 gold **d** 30 silver dishes 1,000 silver pans 29 H113
Ezr 1: 9 gold dishes 30 silver **d** 1,000 silver pans 29 H113
Jer 52:18 **d** and all the bronze articles used in the H4090
Jer 52:19 **d** and bowls used for drink offerings H4090

DISHON (7)

Ge 36:21 **D**, Ezer and Dishan. These sons of Seir in H1914
Ge 36:25 **D** and Oholibamah daughter of Anah H1914
Ge 36:26 The sons of **D**: Hemdan, Eshban, Ithran H1914
Ge 36:30 **D**, Ezer and Dishan. These were the H1914
1Ch 1:38 Zibeon, Anah, **D**, Ezer and Dishan. H1914
1Ch 1:41 The son of Anah: **D**. The sons of Dishon H1914
1Ch 1:41 The sons of **D**: Hemdan, Eshban H1914

DISHONEST (19) [DISHONESTLY]

Ex 18:21 trustworthy men who hate **d gain**—and H1299
Lev 19:35 " 'Do not use **d** standards when H6404
1Sa 8: 3 turned aside after **d gain** and accepted H1299
Pr 11: 1 The LORD detests **d** scales, but accurate H5327
Pr 13:11 **D** money dwindles away, but whoever H2039
Pr 20:23 weights, and **d** scales do not please him. H5327
Pr 29:27 The righteous detest the **d**; the wicked H6404
Jer 22:17 your heart are set only on **d gain**, H1299
Eze 28:18 By your many sins and **d** trade you have H6404
Hos 12: 7 The merchant uses **d** scales and loves to H5327
Am 8: 5 the price and cheating with **d** scales, H5327
Mic 6:11 Shall I acquit someone with **d** scales, with H8400
Lk 16: 8 commended the **d** manager because he *G94*
Lk 16:10 whoever is **d** with very little will also be *G96*
Lk 16:10 with very little will also be **d** with much. *G96*
1Ti 3: 8 in much wine, and not **pursuing d gain**. *G153*
Titus 1: 7 not violent, not **pursuing d gain**. *G153*
Titus 1:11 to teach—and that for the sake of **d** gain. *G156*
1Pe 5: 2 not **pursuing d gain**, but eager to *G154*

DISHONESTLY (1) [DISHONEST]

Dt 25:16 does these things, anyone who deals **d**. H6404

DISHONOR (17) [DISHONORED, DISHONORS]

Lev 18: 7 *Do* not **d** your father **by having sexual relations with** H1655+6872
Lev 18: 8 father's wife; that would **d** your father. H6872
Lev 18:10 daughter's daughter; that would **d** you. H6872
Lev 18:14 *Do* not **d** your father's brother **by** approaching his wife **to have sexual relations** H1655+6872
Lev 18:16 brother's wife; that would **d** your brother. H6872
Lev 20:19 for *that would* **d** a close relative H6867
Dt 22:30 *he must* not **d** his father's **bed**. H1655+4053
Pr 30: 9 steal, and so **d** the name of my God. H9530
Jer 14:21 despise us; *do* not **d** your glorious throne. H5571
Jer 20:11 disgraced; their **d** will never be forgotten. H4009
La 2: 2 its princes down to the ground *in* **d**. H2725
Eze 22:10 are *those who* **d** their father's **bed**; H1655+6872
Jn 8:49 "but I honor my Father and you **d** me. *G869*
Ro 2:23 the law, *do you* **d** God by breaking the law? *G869*
1Co 13: 5 *It does* not **d** others, it is not self-seeking, it *G858*
1Co 15:43 it is sown in **d**, it is raised in glory; it is sown *G871*
2Co 6: 8 through glory and **d**, bad report and good *G871*

DISHONORED (8) [DISHONOR]

Lev 20:11 father's wife, *he has* **d** his father. H1655+6872
Lev 20:17 *He has* **d** his sister and will be held H1655+6872
Lev 20:20 with his aunt, *he has* **d** his uncle. H1655+6872
Lev 20:21 of impurity; *he has* **d** his brother. H1655+6872
Dt 21:14 treat her as a slave, since *you have* **d** her. H6700
Ezr 4:14 it is not proper for us to see the king **d**, A10571
1Co 4:10 you are strong! You are honored, we are **d**! *G872*
Jas 2: 6 But you *have* **d** the poor. Is it not the rich *G869*

DISHONORS (6) [DISHONOR]

Dt 27:16 "Cursed is *anyone who* **d** their father or H7829
Dt 27:20 for *he* **d** his father's **bed**. H1655+4053
Job 20: 3 I hear a rebuke that **d** me, and my H4009
Mic 7: 6 For a son **d** his father, a daughter rises up H5571
1Co 11: 4 with his head covered **d** his head. *G2875*
1Co 11: 5 with her head uncovered **d** her head— *G2875*

DISILLUSIONMENT (1)

Ps 7:14 evil conceives trouble and gives birth to **d**. H9214

DISLIKES (3)

Dt 22:13 a wife and, after sleeping with her, **d** her H8533
Dt 22:16 in marriage to this man, but *he* **d** her. H8533
Dt 24: 3 her second husband **d** her and writes her H8533

DISLODGE (2)

Jos 15:63 Judah could not **d** the Jebusites, who H3769
Jos 16:10 *They did* not **d** the Canaanites living in H3769

DISLOYAL (1)

Ps 78:57 their ancestors *they were* **d** and faithless, H6047

DISMAY (2) [DISMAYED]

Job 41:22 resides in its neck; **d** goes before it. H1791
Ps 35: 4 who plot my ruin be turned back *in* **d**. H2917

DISMAYED (18) [DISMAY]

1Sa 17:11 all the Israelites *were* **d** and terrified. H3169
2Ki 19:26 drained of power, *are* **d** and put to shame. H3169
Job 4: 5 discouraged; it strikes you, and *you are* **d**. H987
Job 32:15 "*They are* **d** and have no more to say H3169
Ps 30: 7 but when you hid your face, I was **d**. H987
Ps 83:17 May they ever be ashamed and **d**; may H987
Ps 143: 4 faint within me; my heart within me *is* **d**. H9037
Isa 20: 5 boasted in Egypt *will be* **d** and put to H3169
Isa 24:23 The moon *will be* **d**, the sun ashamed; for H2917
Isa 37:27 drained of power, *are* **d** and put to shame. H3169
Isa 41:10 I am with you; *do* not *be* **d**, for I am your H9283
Isa 41:23 so that *we will be* **d** and filled with fear. H9283
Jer 8: 9 put to shame; *they will be* **d** and trapped. H3169
Jer 14: 3 their jars unfilled; **d** and despairing, they H1017
Jer 14: 4 the farmers *are* **d** and cover their heads. H1017
Jer 30:10 Jacob my servant; *do* not *be* **d**, Israel,' H3169
Jer 46:27 Jacob my servant; *do* not *be* **d**, Israel. H3169
Jer 49:23 "Hamath and Arpad *are* **d**, for they have H1017

DISMISS (1) [DISMISSED]

Lk 2:29 *you may* now **d** your servant in peace. *G668*

DISMISSED (10) [DISMISS]

Jos 24:28 Then Joshua **d** the people, each to their H8938
Jdg 2: 6 After Joshua *had* **d** the Israelites, they H8938
1Sa 10:25 Then Samuel **d** the people to go to their H8938
2Ch 25:10 So Amaziah **d** the troops who had come to H976
Mt 14:22 to the other side, while *he* **d** the crowd. *G668*
Mt 14:23 *After he had* **d** them, he went up on a *G668*
Mk 6:45 of him to Bethsaida, while he **d** the crowd. *G668*
Ac 13:43 *When* the congregation *was* **d**, many of *G3395*
Ac 19:41 After he had said this, *he* **d** the assembly. *G668*
Ac 23:22 The commander **d** the young man with this *G668*

DISOBEDIENCE (9) [DISOBEY]

Jos 22:22 this has been in rebellion or **d** to the LORD, H5086
Jer 43: 7 Egypt *in* **d** *to* the LORD H4202+9048+928+7754
Ro 5:19 just as through the **d** of the one man the *G4157*
Ro 11:30 now received mercy *as a result of* their **d**, *G577*
Ro 11:32 everyone over to **d** so that he may have *G577*
2Co 10: 6 we will be ready to punish every **act of d**, *G4157*

Heb 2: 2 every violation and d received its just G4157
Heb 4: 6 to them did not go in because of their d, G577
Heb 4:11 will perish by following their example of d. G577

DISOBEDIENT (15) [DISOBEY]
Ne 9:26 "But they were d and rebelled against you H5286
Lk 1:17 children and the d to the wisdom of the G579
Ac 26:19 I was not d to the vision from heaven. G579
Ro 10:21 out my hands to a d and obstinate people." G578
Ro 11:30 Just as you who were at one time d to God G578
Ro 11:31 so they too have now become d in order G578
Eph 2: 2 who is now at work in those who are d. G577
Eph 5: 6 God's wrath comes on those who are d. G577
Eph 5:12 even to mention what the d do in secret. G899S
2Ti 3: 2 abusive, d to their parents G579
Titus 1: 6 open to the charge of being wild and d. G538
Titus 1:16 d and unfit for doing anything good. G579
Titus 3: 3 we too were foolish, d, deceived and G579
Heb 11:31 was not killed with those who were d. G578
1Pe 3:20 to those who were d long ago when God G578

DISOBEY (6) [DISOBEDIENCE, DISOBEDIENT, DISOBEYED, DISOBEYING, DISOBEYS]
Dt 11:28 the curse if you d the commands of H9048+4202
2Ch 24:20 'Why do you d the LORD's commands H6296
Est 3: 3 "Why do you d the king's command?" H6296
Jer 42:13 and so d the LORD your H1194+9048+928+7754
Ro 1:30 ways of doing evil; they d their parents; G579
1Pe 2: 8 They stumble because they d the message G578

DISOBEYED (8) [DISOBEY]
Nu 14:22 but who d me and H4202+9048+928+7754
Nu 27:14 both of you d my command to honor me H5286
Jdg 2: 2 Yet you have d me H4202+9048+928+7754
Ne 9:29 arrogant and d your commands. H4202+9048
Isa 24: 5 by its people; they have d the laws H6296
Jer 43: 4 all the people d the LORD's H4202+9048
Lk 15:29 slaving for you and never d your orders. G4216
Heb 3:18 never enter his rest if not to those who d? G578

DISOBEYING (1) [DISOBEY]
Nu 14:41 "Why are you d the LORD's command? H6296

DISOBEYS (1) [DISOBEY]
Eze 33:12 'If someone who is righteous d, that H7322

DISORDER (4)
Job 10:22 of utter darkness and d, where H4202+6043
1Co 14:33 For God is not a God of d but of peace—as G189
2Co 12:20 slander, gossip, arrogance and d. G189
Jas 3:16 there you find d and every evil practice. G189

DISOWN (13) [DISOWNED, DISOWNS]
Pr 30: 9 I may have too much and d you and say H3950
Mt 10:33 I will d before my Father in heaven. G766
Mt 26:34 rooster crows, you will d me three times." G565
Mt 26:35 if I have to die with you, I will never d you." G565
Mt 26:75 rooster crows, you will d me three times." G565
Mk 14:30 crows twice you yourself will d me three G565
Mk 14:31 if I have to die with you, I will never d you." G565
Mk 14:72 crows twice you will d me three times." G565
Lk 22:61 crows today, you will d me three times." G565
Jn 13:38 rooster crows, you will d me three times! G766
2Ti 2:12 reign with him. If we d him, he will also G766
2Ti 2:12 If we disown him, he will also d us; G766
2Ti 2:13 remains faithful, for he cannot d himself. G766

DISOWNED (3) [DISOWN]
Lk 12: 9 me before others will be d before the G565
Ac 3:13 to be killed, and you d him before Pilate G766
Ac 3:14 You d the Holy and Righteous One and G766

DISOWNS (3) [DISOWN]
Job 8:18 its spot, that place d it and says, 'I never H3950
Mt 10:33 But whoever d me before others, I will G766
Lk 12: 9 But whoever d me before others will be G766

DISPATCH (1) [DISPATCHED, DISPATCHES]
Isa 10: 6 I d him against a people who anger me H7422

DISPATCHED (1) [DISPATCH]
1Ki 20:17 Now Ben-Hadad had d scouts, who H8938

DISPATCHES (4) [DISPATCH]
Est 1:22 He sent d to all parts of the kingdom, to H6219
Est 3:13 D were sent by couriers to all the king's H6219
Est 8: 5 overruling the d that Haman son of H6219
Est 8:10 sealed the d with the king's signet ring H6219

DISPENSATION (KJV) ADMINISTRATION, COMMISSION, EFFECT, TRUST

DISPENSES (1)
Zep 3: 5 Morning by morning he d his justice, and H5989

DISPERSE (7) [DISPERSED, DISPERSES, DISPERSING]
Ge 49: 7 them in Jacob and d them in Israel. H7046
Eze 12:15 when I d them among the nations and H7046
Eze 20:23 that I would d them among the H7046
Eze 22:15 I will d you among the nations and scatter H7046
Eze 29:12 And I will d the Egyptians among the H7046
Eze 30:23 I will d the Egyptians among the nations H7046
Eze 30:26 I will d the Egyptians among the nations H7046

DISPERSED (6) [DISPERSE]
2Sa 20:22 his men d from the city, each H7046
1Ki 1:49 guests rose in alarm and d. H2143+4200+2006
Est 3: 8 is a certain people d among the peoples H7061
Job 38:24 way to the place where the lightning is d, H2745
Eze 36:19 I d them among the nations, and they H7046
Ac 5:36 all his followers were d, and it all came to G1370

DISPERSES (2) [DISPERSE]
Dt 30: 1 the LORD your God d you among the H5615
Job 12:23 he enlarges nations, and d them. H5697

DISPERSING (1) [DISPERSE]
2Ch 11:23 d some of his sons throughout the districts H7287

DISPLACES (1)
Pr 30:23 a servant who d her mistress. H3769

DISPLAY (14) [DISPLAYED, DISPLAYS]
Dt 22:17 Then her parents shall d the cloth before H7298
Est 1:11 in order to d her beauty to the people H8011
Job 10:16 again d your awesome power against H7098
Ps 22:17 All my bones are on d; people stare and H6218
Ps 77:14 you d your power among the peoples. H3359
Isa 49: 3 in whom I will d my splendor. H6995
Isa 60:21 of my hands, for the d of my splendor. H6995
Isa 61: 3 of the LORD for the d of his splendor. H6995
Eze 28:22 and among you I will d my glory. H3877
Eze 39:13 the day I d my glory will be a H3877
Eze 39:21 "I will d my glory among the nations, and H5989
Ro 9:17 that I might d my power in you and that G1892
1Co 4: 9 to me that God has put us apostles on d at G617
1Ti 1:16 Christ Jesus might d his immense G1892

DISPLAYED (8) [DISPLAY]
Ex 14:31 hand of the LORD d against the Egyptians, H6913
Nu 14:17 "Now may the Lord's strength be d, just as H1540
1Ki 11:41 all he did and the wisdom he d—are they NDT
Est 1: 4 a full 180 days he d the vast wealth of his H8011
Job 26: 3 And what great insight you have d! H3359
Ps 78:43 the day he d his signs in Egypt, his H8492
Jn 9: 3 that the works of God might be d in him. G5746
2Co 4: 6 of God's glory d in the face of Christ. G1877

DISPLAYS (5) [DISPLAY]
Ps 7:11 a God who d his wrath every day. H2404
Pr 14:29 one who is quick-tempered d folly. H8123
Isa 44:23 redeemed Jacob, he d his glory in Israel. H6995
2Co 4: 4 light of the gospel that d the glory of Christ, AIT
2Th 2: 9 use all sorts of d of power through signs G1539

DISPLEASE (3) [DISPLEASED, DISPLEASES, DISPLEASING, DISPLEASURE]
Nu 11:11 have I done to d you H4202+5162+2834+928+6524
1Sa 29: 7 do nothing to d the Philistine H8273+928+6524
1Th 2:15 They d God and are hostile to G3590+743

DISPLEASED (7) [DISPLEASE]
Ge 48:17 on Ephraim's head he was d; H8317+928+6524
Nu 22:34 Now if you are d, I will go H8317+928+6524
1Sa 8: 6 this d Samuel; so he prayed H8317+928+6524
1Sa 18: 8 this refrain d him greatly. H8317+928+6524
2Sa 11:27 David had done d the LORD. H8317+928+6524
Ne 13: 8 I was greatly d and threw all Tobiah's H8317
Isa 59:15 looked and was d that there H8317+928+6524

DISPLEASES (2) [DISPLEASE]
Isa 65:12 in my sight and chose what d me." H4202+2911
Isa 66: 4 in my sight and chose what d me." H4202+2911

DISPLEASING (2) [DISPLEASE]
Ge 28: 8 d the Canaanite women were to H8273+928+6524
Dt 24: 1 who becomes d to him H4202+5162+2834+928+6524

DISPLEASURE (1) [DISPLEASE]
Ps 85: 4 and put away your d toward us. H4088

DISPOSAL (2) [DISPOSED]
Mt 26:53 and he will at once put at my d more than G4225
Ac 5: 4 it was sold, wasn't the money at your d? G2026

DISPOSED (5) [DISPOSAL]
Ex 3:21 favorably d toward this H2834+928+6524
Ex 11: 3 favorably d toward the H2834+928+6524
Ex 12:36 favorably d toward the H2834+928+6524
Dt 31:21 I know what they are d to do, even before H3671
1Sa 20:12 If he is favorably d toward you, will I not H3201

DISPOSSESS (5) [DISPOSSESSING]
Dt 9: 1 Jordan to go in and d nations greater H3769
Dt 11:23 and you will d nations larger and stronger H3769
Dt 12:29 nations you are about to invade and d. H3769
Dt 18:14 The nations you will d listen to those who H3769
Isa 54: 3 your descendants will d nations and settle H3769

DISPOSSESSING (2) [DISPOSSESS]
Dt 12: 2 the nations you are d worship their gods. H3769
Eze 45: 9 Stop d my people, declares the Sovereign H1766

DISPUTABLE (1) [DISPUTE]
Ro 14: 1 without quarreling over d matters. G1360

DISPUTE (17) [DISPUTABLE, DISPUTED, DISPUTES, DISPUTING]
Ex 18:16 Whenever they have a d, it is brought to H1821
Ex 24:14 anyone involved in a d can go to them." H1821
Dt 19:17 involved in the d must stand in the H8190
Dt 21: 5 to decide all cases of d and assault. H8190
Dt 25: 1 When people have a d, they are to take it H8190
Jdg 11:27 Let the LORD, the Judge, decide the d this H9149
Job 9: 3 Though they wished to d with him, they H8189
Job 9:14 "How then can I d with him? How can I H6699
Pr 17:14 so drop the matter before a d breaks out. H8190
Eze 44:24 " 'In any d, the priests are to serve as H8190
Lk 22:24 A d also arose among them as to which G5808
Ac 15: 2 Barnabas into sharp d and debate with G5087
Ac 23: 7 a d broke out between the Pharisees and G5087
Ac 23:10 The d became so violent that the G5087
Ac 25:19 they had some points of d with him about G2427
1Co 6: 1 If any of you has a d with another, do you G4547
1Co 6: 5 you wise enough to judge a d between G1359

DISPUTED (1) [DISPUTE]
Ge 26:20 the well Esek, because they d with him. H6921

DISPUTES (10) [DISPUTE]
Ex 18:19 before God and bring their d to him. H1821
Dt 1:12 your burdens and your d all by myself? H8190
Dt 1:16 "Hear the d between your people and judge NDT
Jdg 4: 5 went up to her to have their d decided. H5477
2Ch 19: 8 the law of the LORD and to settle d. H8190
Pr 18:18 Casting the lot settles d and keeps strong H4506
Pr 18:19 d are like the barred gates of a citadel. H4506
Isa 2: 4 the nations and will settle d for many H3519
Mic 4: 3 many peoples and will settle d for strong H3519
1Co 6: 4 if you have d about such matters G3215

DISPUTING (2) [DISPUTE]
1Ti 2: 8 lifting up holy hands without anger or d. G1369
Jude 9 when he was d with the devil G1359+1363

DISQUALIFIED (1) [DISQUALIFY]
1Co 9:27 to others, I myself will not be d for the prize. G99

DISQUALIFY (1) [DISQUALIFIED]
Col 2:18 Do not let anyone who delights in false humility and the worship of angels d G2857

DISQUIETING (1)
Job 4:13 Amid d dreams in the night, when deep H8546

DISREGARD (3) [DISREGARDED, DISREGARDING, DISREGARDS]
Pr 1:25 since you d all my advice and do not H7277
Pr 8:33 to my instruction and be wise; do not d it. H7277
Pr 15:32 Those who d discipline despise H7277

DISREGARDED (1) [DISREGARD]
Isa 40:27 from the LORD; my cause is d by my God"? H6296

DISREGARDING (1) [DISREGARD]
Am 1: 9 to Edom, d a treaty of brotherhood, H4202+2349

DISREGARDS (1) [DISREGARD]
Pr 13:18 Whoever d discipline comes to poverty H7277

DISREPUTE (1)
2Pe 2: 2 will bring the way of truth into d. G1059

DISRESPECT (2)
Est 1:18 There will be no end of d and discord. H1025
1Ti 6: 2 masters should not show them d just G2969

DISRUPTING (1) [DISRUPTIVE]
Titus 1:11 because they are d whole households by G426

DISRUPTIVE (3) [DISRUPTING]
1Th 5:14 warn those who are idle and d, encourage G864
2Th 3: 6 believer who is idle and d and does not G865
2Th 3:11 hear that some among you are idle and d. G865

DISSEMBLED, DISSEMBLERS, DISSIMULATION (KJV) DISGUISE, FATAL MISTAKE, HYPOCRISY, HYPOCRITES, LIED

DISSENSION (1) [DISSENSIONS]
Ro 13:13 debauchery, not in d and jealousy. G2251

DISSENSIONS (1) [DISSENSION]
Gal 5:20 fits of rage, selfish ambition, d, factions G1496

DISSOLVED (1)
Isa 34: 4 stars in the sky will be d and the heavens H5245

DISSUADE (2) [DISSUADED]
Eze 3:18 speak out to d them from their evil H2302
Eze 33: 8 do not speak out to d them from their H2302

DISSUADED (1) [DISSUADE]
Ac 21:14 When he would not be d, we gave up G4275

DISTAFF (1)
Pr 31:19 hand she holds the d and grasps the H3969

DISTANCE (48) [DISTANT]
Ge 22: 4 looked up and saw the place in the d. H8158

Ge 35:16 were still some d from H3896+2021+824
Ge 36: 6 to a land some d from his brother H4946+7156
Ge 37:18 But they saw him in the d, and before he H8158
Ge 48: 7 on the way, a little d from Ephrath. H3896+824
Ex 2: 4 His sister stood at a d to see what would H8158
Ex 20:18 trembled with fear. They stayed at a d H8158
Ex 20:21 The people remained at a d, while Moses H8158
Ex 24: 1 You are to worship at a d, H8158
Ex 33: 7 it outside the camp some d away, H8178+4946
Nu 2: 2 the tent of meeting some d from it, H5584
Nu 16:37 scatter the coals some d away, H2134
Dt 19: 6 overtake him if the d is too great, and kill H2006
Dt 20:15 cities that are at a d from you and H8158+4394
Dt 21: 2 go out and measure *the* d from the body H4499
Dt 32:52 you will see the land only from a d; you H5584
Jos 3: 4 But keep a d of about two thousand cubits H8158
Jos 3:16 It piled up in a heap a great d away, at a H8178
Jdg 18:22 When they *had* gone some d from H8178
1Sa 26:13 on top of the hill some d away; H4946+8158
2Sa 16: 1 David had gone a short d beyond the H5071
2Sa 18:13 *would have* kept *your* d *from* H3656+4946+5584
2Sa 19:36 over the Jordan with the king for a short d, H5071
2Ki 2: 7 of the prophets went and stood at a d, H8158
2Ki 4:25 When he saw her in the d, the man of H5584
2Ki 5:19 After Naaman had traveled some d, H3896+824
Job 2:12 When they saw him from a d, they could H8158
Job 30:10 They detest me and keep *their* d; they do H8178
Isa 59:14 righteousness stands at a d; truth has H8158
Eze 40:13 the d was twenty-five cubits from one H8145
Eze 40:15 The d from the entrance of the gateway to NDT
Eze 40:19 he measured the d from the inside of H8145
Eze 48:35 "The d all around will be 18,000 cubits NDT
Mt 8:30 Some d from them a large herd of pigs G3426
Mt 14:24 was already a considerable d from land, G5084
Mt 26:58 But Peter followed him at a d, right up to G3427
Mt 27:55 women were there, watching from a d. G3427
Mk 5: 6 When he saw Jesus from a d, he ran and G3427
Mk 8: 3 some of them have come a long d." G3427
Mk 11:13 Seeing in the d a fig tree in leaf, he went G3427
Mk 14:54 Peter followed him at a d, right into the G3427
Mk 15:40 Some women were watching from a d G3427
Lk 17:12 had leprosy met him. They stood at a d G4523
Lk 18:13 "But the tax collector stood at a d. G3427
Lk 22:54 of the high priest. Peter followed at a d. G3427
Lk 23:49 Galilee, stood at a d, watching these G3427
Heb 11:13 saw them and welcomed them from a d, G4523
Rev 14:20 the horses' bridles for a d of 1,600 stadia. G608

DISTANCES (1) [DISTANT]

Dt 19: 3 Determine the d *involved* and divide into H2006

DISTANT (37) [DISTANCE, DISTANCES]

Dt 14:24 that place *is* too d and you H8049+2021+2006
Dt 29:22 who come from d lands will see the H8158
Dt 30: 4 to the most d land *under* the heavens, H7895
Jos 9: 6 "We have come from a d country; make a H8158
Jos 9: 9 come from a very d country because of H8158
1Ki 8:41 has come from a d land because of H8158
2Ki 20:14 "From a d land," Hezekiah H8158
2Ch 6:32 has come from a d land because of H8158
Est 10: 1 the empire, to its d shores. H362+3542
Ps 56: T To the tune of "A Dove on D Oaks." H8158
Ps 72:10 of Tarshish and of d shores bring tribute to H362
Ps 97: 1 the earth be glad; let the d shores rejoice. H8041
Pr 25:25 a weary soul is good news from a d land. H5305
Isa 5:26 lifts up a banner for the d nations, H4946+8158
Isa 8: 9 all you d lands. Prepare for battle, H5305
Isa 39: 3 "From a d land," Hezekiah H8158
Isa 45:21 long ago, who declared it from the d past? H255
Isa 49: 1 islands; hear this, you d nations: H4946+8158
Isa 66:19 to the d islands that have not heard H8158
Jer 4:16 besieging army is coming from a d land, H5305
Jer 5:15 "I am bringing a d nation against H4946+5305
Jer 6:20 Sheba or sweet calamus from a d land? H5305
Jer 9:26 live in the wilderness in d places. H7916+6991
Jer 18:14 cool waters from d sources ever stop H2424
Jer 25:23 Buz and all who are in d places; H7916+6991
Jer 30:10 'I will surely save you out of a d place H8158
Jer 31:10 proclaim it in d coastlands: H4946+5305
Jer 46:27 I will surely save you out of a d place H8158
Jer 49:32 who are in d places and will bring H7916+6991
Jer 51:50 Remember the LORD in a d *land*, and call H8158
Eze 12:27 he prophesies about the d future. H8158
Da 4:22 dominion extends to d parts *of* the earth. A10509
Da 8:26 vision, for it concerns the d future." H3427+8041
Zep 2:11 D nations will bow down to him, all H3972+362
Zec 10: 9 in d lands they will remember me. H5305
Lk 15:13 set off for a d country and there G3431
Lk 19:12 noble birth went to a d country to have G3431

DISTILL (1)

Job 36:27 of water, *which* d as rain to the streams; H2423

DISTINCTION (7) [DISTINCTLY]

Ex 8:23 I will make a d between my people and H7151
Ex 9: 4 But the LORD *will* make a d between the H7111
Ex 11: 7 that the LORD makes a d between Egypt H7111
Lev 20:25 " 'You must therefore make a d between H976
Zec 14: 7 the LORD—*with* no *d between* day and night. AIT
Mal 3:18 again see the d between the righteous H1068
1Co 14: 7 played unless there is a d in the notes? G1405

DISTINCTLY (1) [DISTINCTION]

Ac 10: 3 He d saw an angel of God, who came to G5747

DISTINGUISH (8) [DISTINGUISHED, DISTINGUISHING]

Ex 33:16 What else *will* d me and your people H7111
Lev 10:10 so that you *can* d between the holy and the H976
Lev 11:47 You *must* d between the unclean and the H976
1Ki 3: 9 your people and to d between right and H1067
Ezr 3:13 No one *could* d the sound of the shouts of H5795
Eze 22:26 *they do* not d between the holy and the H976
Eze 44:23 and show them how to d between H3359
Heb 5:14 trained themselves to d good from evil. G1360

DISTINGUISHED (4) [DISTINGUISH]

Nu 22:15 more numerous and more d than the first. H3877
2Sa 6:20 the king of Israel *has* d himself today, H3877
Da 6: 3 Now Daniel so d himself among the A10488
Lk 14: 8 a person more d than you may have G1952

DISTINGUISHING (2) [DISTINGUISH]

1Co 12:10 to another d between spirits, to another G1360
2Th 3:17 which is the d mark in all my letters. G4956

DISTORT (5) [DISTORTED]

Jer 23:36 So *you* d the words of the living God, the H2200
Mic 3: 9 who despise justice and d all that is right; H6835
Ac 20:30 will arise and d the truth in order to G3281+1406
2Co 4: 2 deception, nor *do we* d the word of God. G1516
2Pe 3:16 which ignorant and unstable people d, as G5137

DISTORTED (1) [DISTORT]

Eze 27:35 with horror and their faces *are* d with fear. H8307

DISTRACTED (1)

Lk 10:40 But Martha *was* d by all the preparations G4352

DISTRAUGHT (1)

Ps 55: 2 My thoughts trouble me and *I am* d H2101

DISTRESS (84) [DISTRESSED, DISTRESSES, DISTRESSING]

Ge 32: 7 In great fear and d Jacob divided the H7674
Ge 35: 3 me in the day of my d and who has been H7650
Ge 42:21 that's why this d has come on us. H7650
Dt 4:30 When you are in d and all these things H7639
Jdg 2:15 had sworn to them. They *were* in great d. H7674
Jdg 10: 9 Ephraim; Israel *was* in great d. H7674
1Sa 2:32 you will see d *in* my dwelling H7639
1Sa 14:24 Now the Israelites *were* in d that day H5601
1Sa 22: 2 All those who were in d or in debt or H5186
1Sa 28:15 "I am in great d," Saul said. H7639
2Sa 22: 7 "In my d I called to the LORD; I called out H7639
2Sa 24:14 "I am in deep d. Let us fall into the H7639
2Ki 4:27 She *is* in bitter d, but the LORD has hidden H5352
2Ki 19: 3 This day is a day of d and rebuke and H7650
1Ch 21:13 "I am in deep d. Let me fall into the H7639
2Ch 15: 4 But in their d they turned to the LORD, the H7639
2Ch 15: 6 was troubling them with every kind of d. H7650
2Ch 20: 9 Name and will cry out to you in our d, H7650
2Ch 33:12 In his d he sought the favor of the LORD his H7674
Ne 9:37 cattle as they please. We are in great d. H7650
Est 4: 4 her about Mordecai, she *was* in great d. H2655
Est 7: 4 because no such d would justify H7639
Job 15:24 D and anguish fill him with terror H7639
Job 20:22 of his plenty, d *will* overtake him; the H7674
Job 27: 9 to their cry when d comes upon them? H7650
Job 30:24 man when he cries for help in his d. H7085
Job 33:19 of pain with constant d *in* their bones, H8190
Job 36:16 you from the jaws of d to a spacious place H7639
Job 36:19 sustain you so you would not be in d? H7639
Ps 4: 1 Give me relief from my d; have mercy on H7639
Ps 18: 6 In my d I called to the LORD; I cried to my H7639
Ps 20: 1 the LORD answer you when you are in d; H7650
Ps 25:18 affliction and my d and take away all my H6662
Ps 31: 9 for I am in d; my eyes grow weak H7639
Ps 35:26 who gloat over my d be put to shame H8288
Ps 55:17 morning and noon I cry out in d, and he H8488
Ps 57: 6 net for my feet—I *was* bowed down in d. H4104
Ps 77: 2 When I was *in* d, I sought the Lord; at H7650
Ps 81: 7 In your d you called and I rescued you, H7650
Ps 86: 7 When I am *in* d, I call to you, because H7650
Ps 102: 2 hide your face from me when I am *in* d. H7639
Ps 102: 5 In my d I groan aloud and am reduced to NDT
Ps 106:44 took note of their d when he heard their H7639
Ps 107: 6 he delivered them from their d. H5188
Ps 107:13 trouble, and he saved them from their d. H5188
Ps 107:19 trouble, and he saved them from their d. H5188
Ps 107:28 he brought them out of their d. H5188
Ps 116: 3 over me; I was overcome by d and sorrow. H7650
Ps 119:143 Trouble and d have come upon me, but H5186
Ps 120: 1 I call on the LORD in my d, and he answers H7650
Ps 144:14 into captivity, no cry of d in our streets. H7424
Pr 1:27 when d and trouble overwhelm you. H7650
Isa 5: 7 righteousness, but heard cries of d. H7591
Isa 5:30 there is only darkness and d; even the sun H7639
Isa 8:22 earth and see only d and darkness and H7650
Isa 9: 1 no more gloom for those who were *in* d. H4608
Isa 25: 4 a refuge for the needy in their d, a shelter H7639
Isa 26:16 they came to you in their d; when you H7639
Isa 30: 6 Through a land of hardship and d, of H7442
Isa 33: 2 every morning, our salvation in time of d. H7650
Isa 37: 3 This day is a day of d and rebuke and H7650
Isa 63: 9 In all their d he too was distressed, and H7650
Jer 10:18 *I will* bring d on them so that they may be H7674
Jer 11:14 they call to me in the time of their d. H8288
Jer 14: 8 its Savior in times of d, why are you like a H7650
Jer 15:11 you in times of disaster and times of d. H7650
Jer 16:19 my refuge in time of d, to you the nations H7650
La 1: 3 have overtaken her in the midst of her d. H5210
La 1:21 All my enemies have heard of my d; they H8288
Eze 30:16 by storm; Memphis will be *in* constant d. H7639
Da 12: 1 There will be a time of d such as has not H7650
Jnh 2: 2 "In my d I called to the LORD, and he H7650
Hab 3: 7 I saw the tents of Cushan in d, the H224
Zep 1:15 of wrath—a day of d and anguish, a day H7650
Zep 1:17 "*I will* bring *such* d on all people that they H7674
Mt 24:21 For then there will be great d, unequaled G2568
Mt 24:29 after the d of those days " 'the G2568
Mk 13:19 those will be days *of* d unequaled from G2568
Mk 13:24 following that d, " 'the sun will be G2568
Lk 21:23 There will be great d in the land and wrath G340
Ro 2: 9 will be trouble and d for every human G5103
2Co 2: 4 you out of great d and anguish of heart G2568
1Th 3: 7 in all our d and persecution we were G340
Jas 1:27 widows in their d and to keep oneself G2568

DISTRESSED (23) [DISTRESS]

Ge 21:11 The matter d Abraham H8317+928+6524
Ge 21:12 "*Do* not *be so* d about the H8317+928+6524
Ge 42:21 We saw *how* d he was when he pleaded H7650
Ge 45: 5 *do* not *be* d and do not be angry with H6772
1Sa 30: 6 David *was* greatly d because the men H7674
Ezr 10: 9 greatly d by the occasion and because of H8283
Job 6:20 *They are* d, because they had been H1017
Isa 8:21 D and hungry, they will roam through the H7996
Isa 54: 6 you were a wife deserted and d *in* spirit— H6772
Isa 63: 9 In all their distress he too was d, and the H7639
La 1:20 LORD, how d I am! I am in torment H7639
Eze 3:15 among them for seven days—deeply d. H9037
Da 6:14 heard this, he *was* greatly d; he was A10091
Mt 14: 9 The king *was* d, but because of his oaths G3382
Mk 3: 5 deeply d at their stubborn hearts G5200
Mk 6:26 The king was greatly d, but because of his G4337
Mk 14:33 he began *to be* deeply d and G1701
Ac 17:16 he *was* greatly d to see that the city was G4236
Ro 14:15 brother or sister *is* d because of what you G3382
2Co 1: 6 If *we are* d, it is for your comfort and G2567
2Co 2: 3 I would not be d by those who should G3383
Php 2:26 all of you and *is* d because you heard he G86
2Pe 2: 7 *who was* d by the depraved conduct of the G2930

DISTRESSES (1) [DISTRESS]

2Co 6: 4 endurance; in troubles, hardships and d; G5103

DISTRESSING (1) [DISTRESS]

Ex 33: 4 When the people heard these d words H8273

DISTRIBUTE (10) [DISTRIBUTED, DISTRIBUTES, DISTRIBUTING, DISTRIBUTION]

Nu 33:54 D the land by lot, according to your clans H5706
Nu 33:54 D it according to your ancestral tribes. H5706
2Ch 31:19 designated by name to d portions to every H5989
Eze 47:21 "*You are to* d this land among yourselves H2745
Da 11:24 *He will* d plunder, loot and wealth among H1029
Da 11:39 many people and *will* d the land at a H2745
Mk 6:41 them to his disciples to d to the people. G4192
Mk 8: 6 them to his disciples to d to the people, G4192
Mk 8: 7 also and told the disciples *to* d them. G4192
Lk 9:16 them to the disciples *to* d to the people. G4192

DISTRIBUTED (11) [DISTRIBUTE]

Nu 26:55 Be sure that the land is d by lot. H2745
Nu 26:56 Each inheritance *is to* be d by lot among H2745
Jos 18:10 there he d the land to the Israelites H2745
1Ch 6:60 number of towns d among the Kohathite H928
2Ch 31:16 they d to the males three years old or more NDT
2Ch 31:17 And they d to the priests enrolled by their NDT
Est 2:18 the provinces and d gifts with royal H5989
Jn 6:11 d to those who were seated as much G1344
Ac 4:35 and *it was* d to anyone who had need. G1344
Ro 12: 3 with the faith God *has* d to each of you. G3532
Heb 2: 4 and *by gifts* of the Holy Spirit d according G3536

DISTRIBUTES (3) [DISTRIBUTE]

Isa 34:17 portions; his hand d them by measure. H2745
1Co 12: 4 kinds of gifts, but the same Spirit d them. NDT
1Co 12:11 same Spirit, and *he* d them to each one G1349

DISTRIBUTING (3) [DISTRIBUTE]

2Ch 31:14 d the contributions made to the LORD and H5989
2Ch 31:15 d to their fellow priests according to their H5989
Ne 13:13 responsible for d *the* supplies to their H2745

DISTRIBUTION (1) [DISTRIBUTE]

Ac 6: 1 being overlooked in the daily d *of food*. G1355

DISTRICT (19) [DISTRICTS, HALF-DISTRICT]

Ge 47:11 of the land, the d *of* Rameses, as Pharaoh H824
1Sa 9: 4 They went on into the d *of* Shaalim, but H824
1Sa 9: 5 When they reached the d *of* Zuph, Saul H824
1Ki 4: 5 in charge of the d governors; Zabud son of H5893
1Ki 4: 7 had twelve d governors over all Israel, H5893
1Ki 4:19 He was the only governor over the d. H824
1Ki 4:27 The d governors, each in his month H5893

D

Ezr 5: 8 know that we went to the d of Judah, A10406
Ne 3:14 of Rekab, ruler of the d of Beth Hakkerem. H7135
Ne 3:15 of Kol-Hozeh, ruler of the d of Mizpah. H7135
Ne 3:17 ruler of half the d of Keilah, carried out H7135
Ne 3:17 of Keilah, carried out repairs for his d. H7135
Ecc 5: 8 If you see the poor oppressed in a d, and H4519
Eze 45: 1 the LORD a portion of the land as a sacred d, AIT
Eze 45: 3 In the sacred d, measure off a section H4500
Eze 45: 7 by the sacred d and the property of H9556
Zep 1:11 you who live in the market d; all your H4847
Mt 2:22 a dream, he withdrew to the d of Galilee, G3538
Ac 16:12 the leading city of that d of Macedonia. G3535

D

DISTRICTS (5) [DISTRICT]
Jdg 5:15 In the d of Reuben there was much H7106
Jdg 5:16 In the d of Reuben there was much H7106
1Ch 27:25 of the storehouses in the outlying d, H8441
2Ch 11:13 Levites from all their d throughout Israel H1473
2Ch 11:23 throughout the d of Judah and Benjamin H824

DISTURB (1) [DISTURBANCE, DISTURBED, DISTURBING]
2Ki 23:18 "Don't let anyone d his bones." So H5675

DISTURBANCE (2) [DISTURB]
Ac 19:23 time there arose a great d about the Way. G5431
Ac 24:18 with me, nor was I involved in any d. G2573

DISTURBED (14) [DISTURB]
1Sa 28:15 "Why have you d me by bringing me up?" H8074
2Sa 7:10 a home of their own and no longer be d. H8074
1Ch 17: 9 a home of their own and no longer be d. H8074
Ne 2:10 they were very much d that H8317+8288
Job 20: 2 me to answer because I am greatly d. H2591
Ps 42: 5 you downcast? Why so d within me? Put H2159
Ps 42:11 you downcast? Why so d within me? Put H2159
Ps 43: 5 you downcast? Why so d within me? Put H2159
Isa 31: 4 by their shouts or d by their clamor— H6700
La 1:20 in my heart I am d, for I have been H2200
Da 7:15 that passed through my mind d me. A10097
Mt 2: 3 When King Herod heard this he was d G5429
Ac 4: 2 They were greatly d because the apostles G1387
Ac 15:24 us without our authorization and d you, G5429

DISTURBING (1) [DISTURB]
Est 7: 4 no such distress would justify d the king." H5691

DIVERS, DIVERSE (KJV) COLORFUL, DIFFERING, DIFFERENT, KINDS, ORNATE, SOME, SWARMS, VARIED, VARIOUS

DIVIDE (23) [DIVIDED, DIVIDES, DIVIDING, DIVISION, DIVISIONS, DIVISIVE, SUBDIVISION, SUBDIVISIONS]
Ex 14:16 hand over the sea to d the water so that H1324
Ex 15: 9 I will d the spoils; I will gorge myself on H2745
Ex 21:35 d both the money and the dead animal equally H2936
Nu 31:27 D the spoils equally between the soldiers H2936
Dt 19: 3 involved and d into three parts the land H8992
Dt 31: 7 must d it among them as their inheritance H5706
Jos 13: 7 d it as an inheritance among the nine H2745
Jos 18: 5 You are to d the land into seven parts H2745
Jos 22: 8 d the plunder from your enemies with H2745
2Sa 19:29 I order you and Ziba to d the land." H2745
Job 27:17 and the innocent will d his silver. H2745
Job 41: 6 Will they d it up among the merchants H2936
Ps 22:18 They d my clothes among them and cast H2745
Ps 68:12 the women at home d the plunder. H2745
Isa 7: 6 us tear it apart and d it among ourselves, H1324
Isa 53:12 and he will d the spoils with the strong H2745
Eze 5: 1 take a set of scales and d up the hair. H2745
Eze 47:13 you will d among the twelve tribes of Israel as their inheritance H5706
Eze 47:14 You are to d it equally among them H5706
Mic 2: 5 no one in the assembly of the LORD to d H8959
Lk 12:13 tell my brother to d the inheritance with G3532
Lk 22:17 said, "Take this and d it among you. G1374
Jude 19 These are the people who d you, who G626

DIVIDED (63) [DIVIDE]
Ge 10:25 because in his time the earth was d; his H7103
Ge 14:15 the night Abram d his men to attack H2745
Ge 32: 7 distress Jacob d the people who were H2936
Ge 33: 1 so he d the children among Leah H2936
Ex 14:21 turned it into dry land. The waters were d, H1324
Lev 11: 3 eat any animal that has a d hoof and that H7271
Lev 11: 4 only chew the cud or only have a d hoof, H7271
Lev 11: 4 the cud, does not have a d hoof; it is H7271
Lev 11: 5 the cud, does not have a d hoof; it is H7271
Lev 11: 6 the cud, does not have a d hoof; it is H7271
Lev 11: 7 the pig, though it has a d hoof, does not H7271
Lev 11:26 animal that does not have a d hoof or H7271
Dt 14: 6 eat any animal that has a d hoof and that H7271
Dt 14: 7 the cud or that have a d hoof you may H7271
Dt 14: 7 the cud, they do not have a d hoof; they H7271
Dt 14: 8 although it has a d hoof, it does not H7271
Dt 32: 8 when he d all mankind, he set H7233
Jos 14: 5 So the Israelites d the land, just as the H2745
Jdg 9:43 d them into three companies and set an H2936
1Ki 18: 6 So they d the land they were to cover H2745
2Ki 2: 8 The water d to the right and to the left H2936
2Ki 2:14 the water, it d to the right and to the left H2936
1Ch 1:19 because in his time the earth was d; his H7103
1Ch 24: 4 Ithamar's, and they were d accordingly: H2745
1Ch 24: 5 They d them impartially by casting lots, for H2745
Ne 9:11 You d the sea before them, so that they H1324
Ps 78:13 He d the sea and led them through; he H1324
Ps 136:13 to him who d the Red Sea asunder His H1615
Pr 3:20 his knowledge the watery depths were d, H1324
Isa 18: 2 strange speech, whose land is d by rivers. H1021
Isa 18: 7 whose land is d by rivers—the gifts H1021
Isa 33:23 of spoils will be d and even the lame H2745
Isa 63:12 right hand, who d the waters before them H1324
Eze 37:22 be two nations or be d into two kingdoms. H2936
Da 2:41 so this will be a d kingdom; yet it will A10583
Da 5:28 Your kingdom is d and given to the A10592
Joel 3: 2 among the nations and d up my land. H2745
Am 7:17 Your land will be measured and d up H2745
Mic 2: 4 my people's possession is d up. H4614
Zec 14: 1 will be plundered and d up within H2745
Mt 12:25 "Every kingdom d against itself will be G3532
Mt 12:25 city or household d against itself will not G3532
Mt 12:26 drives out Satan, he is d against himself. G3532
Mt 27:35 they d up his clothes by casting lots. G1374
Mk 3:24 If a kingdom is d against itself, that G3532
Mk 3:25 If a house is d against itself, that house G3532
Mk 3:26 And if Satan opposes himself and is d, he G3532
Mk 6:41 He also d the two fish among them all G3532
Lk 11:17 "Any kingdom d against itself will be G1374
Lk 11:17 and a house d against itself will fall. NDT
Lk 11:18 If Satan is d against himself, how can his G1374
Lk 12:52 five in one family d against each other, G1374
Lk 12:53 They will be d, father against son and son G1374
Lk 15:12 So he d his property between them G1349
Lk 23:34 And they d up his clothes by casting lots. G1374
Jn 7:43 Thus the people were d because of Jesus. G5388
Jn 9:16 perform such signs?" So they were d. G5388
Jn 10:19 who heard these words were again d. G5388
Jn 19:24 "They d my clothes among them and cast G1374
Ac 14: 4 The people of the city were d; some sided G5387
Ac 23: 7 the Sadducees, and the assembly was d. G5387
1Co 1:13 Is Christ d? Was Paul crucified for you G3532
1Co 7:34 his interests are d. An unmarried G3532

DIVIDES (2) [DIVIDE]
Ge 49:27 the prey, in the evening he d the plunder." H2745
Lk 11:22 the man trusted and d up his plunder. G1344

DIVIDING (11) [DIVIDE]
Lev 1:17 not d it completely, and then the H976
Lev 5: 8 its head from its neck, not d it completely, H976
Jos 19:49 they had finished d the land into its H5706
Jos 19:51 And so they finished d the land. H2745
Jdg 5:30 'Are they not finding and d the spoils: H2745
Jdg 7:16 D the three hundred men into three H2936
Isa 9: 3 as warriors rejoice when d the plunder. H2745
Mk 15:24 D up his clothes, they cast lots to see G1374
Jn 19:23 his clothes, d them into four shares, one G4472
Eph 2:14 the barrier, the d wall of hostility, G3546
Heb 4:12 it penetrates even to d soul and spirit G3536

DIVINATION (17) [DIVINATIONS, DIVINE, DIVINER, DIVINER'S, DIVINERS, DIVINERS']
Ge 30:27 I have learned by d that the LORD has H5727
Ge 44: 5 drinks from and also uses for d? H5727+5727
Ge 44:15 like me can find things out by d?" H5727+5727
Lev 19:26 " 'Do not practice d or seek omens. H5727
Nu 22: 7 taking with them the fee for d. H7877
Nu 23:23 There is no d against Jacob, no evil H5728
Nu 24: 1 he did not resort to d as at other times H5728
Dt 18:10 the fire, who practices d or sorcery H7876+7877
Dt 18:14 listen to those who practice sorcery or d. H7876
Jos 13:22 Balaam son of Beor, who practiced d. H7876
1Sa 15:23 For rebellion is like the sin of d, and H7877
2Ki 17:17 They practiced d and sought H7876+7877
2Ki 21: 6 son in the fire, practiced d, sought omens, H6726
2Ch 33: 6 of Ben Hinnom, practiced d and witchcraft H6726
Isa 2: 6 they practice d like the Philistines and H6726
Eze 13:23 see false visions or practice d. H7876+7877
Mic 3: 6 without visions, and darkness, without d. H7876

DIVINATIONS (7) [DIVINATION]
Jer 14:14 to you false visions, d, idolatries and the H7877
Eze 12:24 flattering d among the people of H5241
Eze 13: 6 Their visions are false and their d a lie H7877
Eze 13: 7 visions and uttered lying d when you say, H5241
Eze 13: 9 who see false visions and utter lying d. H7876
Eze 21:29 concerning you and lying d about you, H7876
Eze 22:28 them by false visions and lying d. H7876

DIVINE (9) [DIVINATION]
Isa 35: 4 with d retribution he will come to save you." H466
Ac 17:29 not think that the d being is like gold or G2521
Ac 19:27 will be robbed of her d majesty. G3484
Ro 1:20 his eternal power and d nature—have G2522
Ro 9: 4 sonship; theirs the d glory, the covenants, G1518
2Co 10: 4 they have d power to demolish G2536
Gal 4:23 was born as the result of a d promise. AIT
2Pe 1: 3 His d power has given us everything we G2521
2Pe 1: 4 them you may participate in the d nature, G2521

DIVINER (2) [DIVINATION]
Isa 3: 2 the prophet, the d and the elder, H7876
Da 2:27 magician or d can explain to the king A10140

DIVINER'S (1) [DIVINATION]
Hos 4:12 wooden idol, and a d rod speaks to them. H5234

DIVINERS (9) [DIVINATION]
1Sa 6: 2 called for the priests and the d and said, H7876
Isa 44:25 of false prophets and makes fools of d, H7876
Jer 27: 9 your prophets, your d, your interpreters of H7876
Jer 29: 8 the prophets and d among you deceive H7876
Da 4: 7 astrologers and d came, I told them the A10140
Da 5: 7 the enchanters, astrologers and d. A10140
Da 5:11 enchanters, astrologers and d. A10140
Mic 3: 7 will be ashamed and the d disgraced. H7876
Zec 10: 2 speak deceitfully, d see visions that lie H7876

DIVINERS' (1) [DIVINATION]
Jdg 9:37 is coming from the direction of the d tree." H6726

DIVISION (43) [DIVIDE]
Nu 2: 4 His d numbers 74,600. H7372
Nu 2: 6 His d numbers 54,400. H7372
Nu 2: 8 His d numbers 57,400. H7372
Nu 2:11 His d numbers 46,500. H7372
Nu 2:13 His d numbers 59,300. H7372
Nu 2:15 His d numbers 45,650. H7372
Nu 2:19 His d numbers 40,500. H7372
Nu 2:21 His d numbers 32,200. H7372
Nu 2:23 His d numbers 35,400. H7372
Nu 2:26 His d numbers 62,700. H7372
Nu 2:28 His d numbers 41,500. H7372
Nu 2:30 His d numbers 53,400. H7372
Nu 10:15 of Zuar was over the d of the tribe of H7372
Nu 10:16 Helon was over the d of the tribe of H7372
Nu 10:19 was over the d of the tribe of Simeon, H7372
Nu 10:20 Deuel was over the d of the tribe of Gad. H7372
Nu 10:23 Pedahzur was over the d of the tribe of H7372
Nu 10:24 Gideoni was over the d of the tribe of H7372
Nu 10:26 Okran was over the d of the tribe of Asher, H7372
Nu 10:27 of Enan was over the d of the tribe of H7372
Jos 22:14 head of a family d among the Israelite H1074
1Ch 27: 1 Each d consisted of 24,000 men H4713
1Ch 27: 2 In charge of the first d, for the first month H4713
1Ch 27: 2 There were 24,000 men in his d. H4713
1Ch 27: 4 In charge of the d for the second month H4713
1Ch 27: 4 Ahohite; Mikloth was the leader of his d. H4713
1Ch 27: 4 There were 24,000 men in his d. H4713
1Ch 27: 5 chief and there were 24,000 men in his d. H4713
1Ch 27: 6 son Ammizabad was in charge of his d. H4713
1Ch 27: 7 There were 24,000 men in his d. H4713
1Ch 27: 8 There were 24,000 men in his d. H4713
1Ch 27: 9 There were 24,000 men in his d. H4713
1Ch 27:10 There were 24,000 men in his d. H4713
1Ch 27:11 There were 24,000 men in his d. H4713
1Ch 27:12 There were 24,000 men in his d. H4713
1Ch 27:13 There were 24,000 men in his d. H4713
1Ch 27:14 There were 24,000 men in his d. H4713
1Ch 27:15 There were 24,000 men in his d. H4713
Ezr 10:16 one from each family d, and all of them H1074
Lk 1: 5 who belonged to the priestly d of Abijah G2389
Lk 1: 8 when Zechariah's d was on duty and he G2389
Lk 12:51 peace on earth? No, I tell you, but d. G1375
1Co 12:25 so that there should be no d in the body G5388

DIVISIONS (52) [DIVIDE]
Ge 36:30 according to their d, in the land of Seir. H477
Ex 6:26 the Israelites out of Egypt by their d." H7372
Ex 7: 4 acts of judgment I will bring out my d, H7372
Ex 12:17 very day that I brought your d out of Egypt. H7372
Ex 12:41 to the very day, all the LORD's d left Egypt. H7372
Ex 12:51 the Israelites out of Egypt by their d. H7372
Nu 1: 3 according to their d all the men in Israel H7372
Nu 1:52 The Israelites are to set up their tents by d H7372
Nu 2: 3 the d of the camp of Judah are to encamp H7372
Nu 2: 9 according to their d, number 186,400. H7372
Nu 2:10 south will be the d of the camp of Reuben H7372
Nu 2:16 according to their d, number 151,450. H7372
Nu 2:18 west will be the d of the camp of Ephraim H7372
Nu 2:24 according to their d, number 108,100. H7372
Nu 2:25 the north will be the d of the camp of Dan H7372
Nu 2:32 in the camps, by their d, number 603,550. H7372
Nu 10:14 The d of the camp of Judah went first H7372
Nu 10:18 The d of the camp of Reuben went next H7372
Nu 10:22 The d of the camp of Ephraim went next H7372
Nu 10:25 the d of the camp of Dan set out under H7372
Nu 10:28 of march for the Israelite d as they set out. H7372
Nu 33: 1 out of Egypt by d under the leadership H7372
Jos 11:23 to Israel according to their tribal d. H4713
Jos 12: 7 tribes of Israel according to their tribal d. H4713
Jos 18:10 to the Israelites according to their tribal d. H4713
1Sa 11:11 day Saul separated his men into three d; H8031
1Ch 23: 6 the Levites into d corresponding to the H4713
1Ch 24: 1 These were the d of the descendants of H4713
1Ch 24: 3 David separated them into d for their H2745
1Ch 26: 1 The d of the gatekeepers: From the H4713
1Ch 26:12 These d of the gatekeepers, through their H4713
1Ch 26:19 These were the d of the gatekeepers who H4713
1Ch 27: 1 concerned the army d that were on duty H4713
1Ch 28: 1 commanders of the d in the service of the H4713
1Ch 28:13 instructions for the d of the priests and H4713
1Ch 28:21 The d of the priests and Levites are ready H4713
2Ch 5:11 themselves, regardless of their d. H4713
2Ch 8:14 he appointed the d of the priests for their H4713
2Ch 8:14 the gatekeepers by d for the various gates H4713

2Ch 23: 8 the priest had not released any of the d. H4713
2Ch 26:11 ready to go out by d according to their H1522
2Ch 31: 2 assigned the priests and Levites to d— H4713
2Ch 31:15 to their fellow priests according to their d, H4713
2Ch 31:16 to their responsibilities and their d. H4713
2Ch 31:17 to their responsibilities and their d. H4713
2Ch 35: 4 Prepare yourselves by families in your d H4713
2Ch 35:10 the Levites in their d as the king had H4713
Ezr 6:18 the priests in their d and the Levites in A10585
Ne 11:36 Some of the d of the Levites of Judah H4713
Ro 16:17 those who cause d and put obstacles G1496
1Co 1:10 say and that there be no d among you, G5388
1Co 11:18 a church, there are d among you, and to G5388

DIVISIVE (1) [DIVIDE]
Titus 3:10 Warn a d person once, and then warn them G148

DIVORCE (16) [DIVORCED, DIVORCES]
Dt 22:19 he must not d her as long as he lives. H8938
Dt 22:29 He can never d her as long as he lives H8938
Dt 24: 1 he writes her a certificate of d, gives H4135
Dt 24: 3 her and writes her a certificate of d, H4135
Isa 50: 1 certificate of d with which I sent her H4135
Jer 3: 8 her certificate of d and sent her away H4135
Mt 1:19 disgrace, he had in mind to d her quietly. G668
Mt 5:31 his wife must give her a certificate of d. G687
Mt 19: 3 it lawful for a man to d his wife for any G668
Mt 19: 7 wife a certificate of d and send her away?" G687
Mt 19: 8 permitted you to d your wives because G668
Mk 10: 2 "Is it lawful for a man to d his wife? G668
Mk 10: 4 write a certificate of d and send her away." G687
1Co 7:11 And a husband must not d his wife. G918
1Co 7:12 willing to live with him, he must not d her. G918
1Co 7:13 willing to live with her, she must not d him. G918

DIVORCED (9) [DIVORCE]
Lev 21: 7 by prostitution or d from their husbands, H1763
Lev 21:14 marry a widow, a d woman, or a woman H1763
Lev 22:13 daughter becomes a widow or is d, H1763
Nu 30: 9 by a widow or d woman will be binding H1763
Dt 24: 4 first husband, who d her, is not allowed to H8938
1Ch 8: 8 in Moab after he had d his wives Hushim H8938
Eze 44:22 They must not marry widows or d women H1763
Mt 5:32 who marries a d woman commits adultery. G668
Lk 16:18 marries a d woman commits G668+608+467

DIVORCES (8) [DIVORCE]
Jer 3: 1 "If a man d his wife and she leaves him H8938
Mal 2:16 "The man who hates and d his wife," H8938
Mt 5:31 'Anyone who d his wife must give her a G668
Mt 5:32 But I tell you that anyone who d his wife G668
Mt 19: 9 I tell you that anyone who d his wife, except G668
Mk 10:11 "Anyone who d his wife and marries G668
Mk 10:12 And if she d her husband and marries G668
Lk 16:18 "Anyone who d his wife and marries G668

DIZAHAB (1)
Dt 1: 1 Tophel, Laban, Hazeroth and D. H1903

DIZZINESS (1)
Isa 19:14 LORD has poured into them a spirit of d; H6413

DO (2769) [DID, DIDN'T, DO-NOTHING, DOES, DOESN'T, DOING, DONE, DON'T]
Ge 4: 7 If you d what is right, will you not be H3512
Ge 4: 7 But if you d not d what is right, sin is AIT
Ge 4: 7 But if you do not d what is right, sin is H3512
Ge 11: 6 language they have begun to d this, H6913
Ge 11: 6 nothing they plan to d will be impossible H6913
Ge 15: 1 "D not be afraid, Abram. I am AIT
Ge 16: 6 "D with her whatever you think best." H6913
Ge 18: 3 my lord, d not pass your servant by. AIT
Ge 18: 5 "Very well," they answered, "d as you say." H6913
Ge 18:17 hide from Abraham what I am about to d? H6913
Ge 18:25 Far be it from you to d such a thing—to kill H6913
Ge 18:25 Will not the Judge of all the earth d right?" H6913
Ge 18:29 "For the sake of forty, I will not d it." H6913
Ge 18:30 "I will not d it if I find thirty there. H6913
Ge 19: 7 Don't d this wicked thing. H8317
Ge 19: 8 and you can d what you like with them. H6913
Ge 19: 8 But don't d anything to these men, for H6913
Ge 19:12 said to Lot, "D you have anyone else here NDT
Ge 19:22 because I cannot d anything until you H6913
Ge 20: 7 But if you d not return her, you may be sure AIT
Ge 21:12 "D not be so distressed about the boy and AIT
Ge 21:17 D not be afraid; God has heard the boy AIT
Ge 21:22 "God is with you in everything you d. H6913
Ge 22:12 "D not lay a hand on the boy," he said. AIT
Ge 22:12 "D not do anything to him. AIT
Ge 22:12 "Do not d anything to him. H6913
Ge 24: 6 sure that you d not take my son back there," AIT
Ge 24: 8 Only d not take my son back there." AIT
Ge 24:56 said to them, "D not detain me, now that the AIT
Ge 26: 2 Isaac and said, "D not go down to Egypt; live AIT
Ge 26:24 D not be afraid, for I am with you; I will bless AIT
Ge 26:29 that you will d us no harm, just as we did H6913
Ge 27: 8 listen carefully and d what I tell you: NDT
Ge 27:13 Just d what I say; go and get H9048
Ge 27:37 So what can I possibly d for you, my H6913
Ge 27:38 to his father, "D you have only one blessing NDT
Ge 27:43 Now then, my son, d what I say: Flee at H9048
Ge 28: 1 "D not marry a Canaanite woman. AIT
Ge 28: 6 "D not marry a Canaanite woman, AIT
Ge 29: 5 said to them, "D you know Laban, Nahor's AIT
Ge 30:30 when may I d something for my own H6913
Ge 30:31 "But if you will d this one thing for me, H6913
Ge 31:14 "D we still have any share in the inheritance AIT
Ge 31:16 So d whatever God has told you. H6913
Ge 31:43 Yet what can I d today about these H6913
Ge 32:17 you and asks, 'Who d you belong to, and NDT
Ge 32:29 he replied, "Why d you ask my name?" AIT
Ge 32:32 day the Israelites d not eat the tendon AIT
Ge 33:15 "But why d that?" Jacob asked. NDT
Ge 34:14 to them, "We can't d such a thing; we H6913
Ge 37: 8 said to him, "D you intend to reign over us? AIT
Ge 39: 9 How then could I d such a wicked thing H6913
Ge 40: 7 "Why d you look so sad today? NDT
Ge 40: 8 "D not interpretations belong to God? NDT
Ge 40:13 just as you used to d when you were his H5477
Ge 41:16 "I cannot d it," Joseph replied to Pharaoh NDT
Ge 41:25 to Pharaoh what he is about to d. H6913
Ge 41:28 has shown Pharaoh what he is about to d. H6913
Ge 41:32 decided by God, and God will d it soon. H6913
Ge 41:55 "Go to Joseph and d what he tells you." H6913
Ge 42: 1 "Why d you just keep looking at each other?" AIT
Ge 42: 7 "Where d you come from?" he AIT
Ge 42:18 said to them, "D this and you will live H6913
Ge 42:20 This they proceeded to d. H6913
Ge 42:37 sons to death if I d not bring him back to you. AIT
Ge 43: 7 'D you have another brother?' AIT
Ge 43: 9 If I d not bring him back to you and set him AIT
Ge 43:11 said to them, "If it must be, then d this: H6913
Ge 44: 7 from your servants to d anything like that! H6913
Ge 44:17 "Far be it from me to d such a thing! H6913
Ge 44:18 D not be angry with your servant, though you AIT
Ge 44:19 servants, 'D you have a father or a brother? AIT
Ge 44:32 'If I d not bring him back to you, I will AIT
Ge 44:34 D not let me see the misery that would come AIT
Ge 45: 5 d not be distressed and do not be angry with AIT
Ge 45: 5 distressed and d not be angry with yourselves AIT
Ge 45:17 to Joseph, "Tell your brothers, 'D this: H6913
Ge 45:19 are also directed to tell them, 'D this: H6913
Ge 46: 3 "D not be afraid to go down to Egypt, for I AIT
Ge 47: 9 and they d not equal the years of the AIT
Ge 47:29 faithfulness. D not bury me in Egypt, AIT
Ge 47:30 they are buried." "I will d as you say," H6913
Ge 50: 6 bury your father, as he made you swear to d." AIT
Ex 1:17 feared God and did not d what the king of H6913
Ex 1:17 what the king of Egypt had told them to d; NDT
Ex 3: 5 "D not come any closer," God said. "Take off AIT
Ex 4: 1 "What if they d not believe me or listen to AIT
Ex 4: 8 "If they d not believe you or pay attention to AIT
Ex 4: 9 But if they d not believe these two signs or AIT
Ex 4:15 of you speak and will teach you what to d. H6913
Ex 4:21 wonders I have given you the power to d. NDT
Ex 5: 2 I d not know the LORD and I will not let Israel AIT
Ex 6: 1 you will see what I will d to Pharaoh: H6913
Ex 8:21 If you d not let my people go, I will send AIT
Ex 9: 5 Tomorrow the LORD will d this in the land. H6913
Ex 9:30 your officials still d not fear the LORD God." AIT
Ex 10: 7 D you not yet realize that Egypt is ruined?" AIT
Ex 10:28 Make sure you d not appear before me again AIT
Ex 12: 9 D not eat the meat raw or boiled in water, but AIT
Ex 12:10 D not leave any of it till morning; if some is AIT
Ex 12:16 D no work at all on these days, except to H6913
Ex 12:16 everyone to eat; that is all you may d. H6913
Ex 12:46 D not break any of the bones. AIT
Ex 13: 8 'I d this because of what the LORD did for me NDT
Ex 13:13 but if you d not redeem it, break its AIT
Ex 14:13 answered the people, "D not be afraid. AIT
Ex 15:26 LORD your God and d what is right in his H6913
Ex 17: 2 "Why d you quarrel with me? Why AIT
Ex 17: 2 Why d you put the LORD to the test?" AIT
Ex 17: 4 "What am I to d with these people? H6913
Ex 18:14 Why d you alone sit as judge, while all these AIT
Ex 18:23 If you d this and God so commands, you H6913
Ex 19: 8 "We will d everything the LORD has said." H6913
Ex 19:12 that you d not approach the mountain or AIT
Ex 19:21 so they d not force their way through to see AIT
Ex 20: 9 days you shall labor and d all your work, H6913
Ex 20:10 On it you shall not d any work, neither you H6913
Ex 20:19 But d not have God speak to us or we will die AIT
Ex 20:20 the people, "D not be afraid. God has come AIT
Ex 20:23 D not make any gods to be alongside me; do AIT
Ex 20:23 d not make for yourselves gods of silver or AIT
Ex 20:25 d not build it with dressed stones AIT
Ex 20:26 And d not go up to my altar on steps, or your AIT
Ex 21: 5 wife and children and d not want to go free, AIT
Ex 21: 7 she is not to go free as male servants d. H3655S
Ex 22:18 "D not allow a sorceress to live. AIT
Ex 22:21 "D not mistreat or oppress a foreigner, for AIT
Ex 22:22 "D not take advantage of the widow or the AIT
Ex 22:23 If you d and they cry out to me, H6700+6700S
Ex 22:25 is needy, d not treat it like a business deal AIT
Ex 22:28 "D not blaspheme God or curse the ruler of AIT
Ex 22:29 "D not hold back offerings from your AIT
Ex 22:30 D the same with your cattle and your H6913
Ex 22:31 So d not eat the meat of an animal torn by AIT
Ex 23: 1 "D not spread false reports. Do not help a AIT
Ex 23: 1 D not help a guilty person by being a AIT
Ex 23: 2 "D not follow the crowd in doing wrong AIT
Ex 23: 2 d not pervert justice by siding with the crowd, AIT
Ex 23: 3 and d not show favoritism to a poor person in AIT
Ex 23: 5 under its load, d not leave it there; be H2532
Ex 23: 6 "D not deny justice to your poor people in AIT
Ex 23: 7 Have nothing to d with a false charge and H8178
Ex 23: 7 d not put an innocent or honest person to death AIT
Ex 23: 8 "D not accept a bribe, for a bribe blinds AIT
Ex 23: 9 "D not oppress a foreigner; you yourselves AIT
Ex 23:11 D the same with your vineyard and your H6913
Ex 23:12 "Six days d your work, but on the seventh H6913
Ex 23:12 on the seventh day d not work, so that H8697
Ex 23:13 "Be careful to d everything I have said to H9068
Ex 23:13 D not invoke the names of other gods; do not AIT
Ex 23:13 gods; d not let them be heard on your lips. AIT
Ex 23:15 D this at the appointed time in the month of NDT
Ex 23:18 "D not offer the blood of a sacrifice to me AIT
Ex 23:19 "D not cook a young goat in its mother's milk. AIT
Ex 23:21 D not rebel against him; he will not forgive AIT
Ex 23:22 to what he says and d all that I say, H6913
Ex 23:24 D not bow down before their gods or worship AIT
Ex 23:32 D not make a covenant with them or with AIT
Ex 23:33 D not let them live in your land or they will AIT
Ex 24: 3 "Everything the LORD has said we will d." H6913
Ex 24: 7 "We will d everything the LORD has said H6913
Ex 26: 3 and d the same with the other five. H2489S
Ex 26: 4 d the same with the end curtain in H6913
Ex 29: 1 "This is what you are to d to consecrate H6913
Ex 29:35 "D for Aaron and his sons everything I H6913
Ex 30: 9 D not offer on this altar any other incense AIT
Ex 30: 9 offering, and d not pour a drink offering on it. AIT
Ex 30:32 D not pour it on anyone else's body and do AIT
Ex 30:32 else's body and d not make any other oil AIT
Ex 30:37 D not make any incense with this formula AIT
Ex 31:14 those who d any work on that day must be H6913
Ex 32:12 relent and d not bring disaster on your H5714
Ex 32:21 "What did these people d to you H6913
Ex 32:22 "D not be angry, my lord," Aaron answered AIT
Ex 33: 5 I will decide what to d with you. H6913
Ex 33:15 not go with us, d not send us up from here. AIT
Ex 33:17 "I will d the very thing you have asked H6913
Ex 34:10 all your people I will d wonders never H6913
Ex 34:10 is the work that I, the LORD, will d for you. H6913
Ex 34:14 D not worship any other god, for the LORD AIT
Ex 34:16 they will lead your sons to d the same H2388+339+466+2177S
Ex 34:17 "D not make any idols. AIT
Ex 34:18 D this at the appointed time in the month of NDT
Ex 34:20 but if you d not redeem it, break its AIT
Ex 34:25 "D not offer the blood of a sacrifice to me AIT
Ex 34:25 d not let any of the sacrifice from the Passover Festival remain AIT
Ex 34:26 "D not cook a young goat in its mother's milk. AIT
Ex 35: 1 things the LORD has commanded you to d: H6913
Ex 35: 3 D not light a fire in any of your dwellings on AIT
Ex 35:29 Moses had commanded them to d. H6913
Ex 35:35 them with skill to d all kinds of work as H6913
Ex 36: 1 the sanctuary are to d the work just as the H6913
Ex 36: 2 who was willing to come and d the work. H6913
Ex 36: 7 was more than enough to d all the work. H6913
Lev 2:13 D not leave the salt of the covenant of your AIT
Lev 4:20 d with this bull just as he did with the H6913
Lev 5: 1 sins because they d not speak up when they AIT
Lev 5: 4 oath to d anything, whether good or evil H3512
Lev 5:16 what they have failed to d in regard to H2627
Lev 5:17 even though they d not know it, they are AIT
Lev 7:23 'D not eat any of the fat of cattle, sheep AIT
Lev 8:33 D not leave the entrance to the tent of AIT
Lev 8:35 seven days and d what the LORD H9068
Lev 9: 6 what the LORD has commanded you to d, H6913
Lev 10: 6 "D not let your hair become unkempt and do AIT
Lev 10: 6 become unkempt and d not tear your clothes, AIT
Lev 10: 7 D not leave the entrance to the tent of AIT
Lev 11:10 seas or streams that d not have fins and NDT
Lev 11:43 D not defile yourselves by any of these AIT
Lev 11:43 D not make yourselves unclean by means of AIT
Lev 11:44 D not make yourselves unclean by any AIT
Lev 16:15 the curtain and d with it as he did with H6913
Lev 16:16 He is to d the same for the tent of H6913
Lev 16:29 deny yourselves and not d any work— H6913
Lev 17:16 But if they d not wash their clothes and bathe AIT
Lev 18: 3 You must not d as they do in Egypt, where H6913
Lev 18: 3 You must not do as they d in Egypt, where H5126
Lev 18: 3 and you must not d as they do in the land H6913
Lev 18: 3 not do as they d in the land of Canaan H5126
Lev 18: 3 am bringing you. D not follow their practices. AIT
Lev 18: 7 D not dishonor your father by having sexual relations with AIT
Lev 18: 7 is your mother; d not have relations with her. AIT
Lev 18: 8 'D not have sexual relations with your AIT
Lev 18: 9 'D not have sexual relations with your sister, AIT
Lev 18:10 'D not have sexual relations with your son's AIT
Lev 18:11 'D not have sexual relations with the AIT
Lev 18:12 'D not have sexual relations with your AIT
Lev 18:13 'D not have sexual relations with your AIT
Lev 18:14 D not dishonor your father's brother by approaching his wife to have sexual relations AIT
Lev 18:15 'D not have sexual relations with your AIT
Lev 18:15 son's wife; d not have relations with her. AIT
Lev 18:16 'D not have sexual relations with your AIT
Lev 18:17 'D not have sexual relations with both a AIT
Lev 18:17 D not have sexual relations with either her AIT
Lev 18:18 " 'D not take your wife's sister as a rival wife AIT
Lev 18:19 " 'D not approach a woman to have sexual AIT
Lev 18:20 " 'D not have sexual relations with your AIT
Lev 18:21 " 'D not give any of your children to be AIT

Lev 18:22 " 'D not have sexual relations with a man as AIT
Lev 18:23 " 'D not have sexual relations with an animal AIT
Lev 18:24 " 'D not defile yourselves in any of these AIT
Lev 18:26 among you must not d any of these H6913
Lev 18:30 my requirements and d not follow any of the AIT
Lev 18:30 came and d not defile yourselves with them. AIT
Lev 19: 4 " 'D not turn to idols or make metal gods AIT
Lev 19: 9 d not reap to the very edges of your field AIT
Lev 19:10 D not go over your vineyard a second time AIT
Lev 19:11 " 'D not steal. " 'Do not lie. " 'Do not AIT
Lev 19:11 " 'Do not steal. " 'D not lie. " 'Do not AIT
Lev 19:11 " 'D not deceive one another. AIT
Lev 19:12 " 'D not swear falsely by my name and so AIT
Lev 19:13 " 'D not defraud or rob your neighbor. " 'Do AIT
Lev 19:13 D not hold back the wages of a hired worker overnight AIT
Lev 19:14 " 'D not curse the deaf or put a stumbling AIT
Lev 19:15 " 'D not pervert justice; do not show partiality AIT
Lev 19:15 d not show partiality to the poor or favoritism AIT
Lev 19:16 " 'D not go about spreading slander among AIT
Lev 19:16 D not do anything that endangers your neighbor's life AIT
Lev 19:16 Do not d anything that endangers your neighbor's life H6641+6584+1947
Lev 19:17 " 'D not hate a fellow Israelite in your heart AIT
Lev 19:18 " 'D not seek revenge or bear a grudge AIT
Lev 19:19 " 'D not mate different kinds of animals AIT
Lev 19:19 'D not plant your field with two kinds of seed. AIT
Lev 19:19 " 'D not wear clothing woven of two kinds of AIT
Lev 19:26 " 'D not eat any meat with the blood still in it AIT
Lev 19:26 " 'D not practice divination or seek omens. AIT
Lev 19:27 " 'D not cut the hair at the sides of your head AIT
Lev 19:28 " 'D not cut your bodies for the dead or put AIT
Lev 19:29 " 'D not degrade your daughter by making AIT
Lev 19:31 'D not turn to mediums or seek out spiritists, AIT
Lev 19:33 among you in your land, d not mistreat them. AIT
Lev 19:35 " 'D not use dishonest standards when AIT
Lev 20:19 " 'D not have sexual relations with the sister AIT
Lev 20:25 D not defile yourselves by any animal or bird AIT
Lev 22: 9 way that they d not become guilty and die AIT
Lev 22:20 D not bring anything with a defect, because it AIT
Lev 22:22 D not offer to the LORD the blind, the injured AIT
Lev 22:22 D not place any of these on the altar as a AIT
Lev 22:24 You must not d this in your own land H6913
Lev 22:28 D not slaughter a cow or a sheep and its AIT
Lev 22:32 D not profane my holy name, for I must be AIT
Lev 23: 3 You are not to d any work; wherever you H6913
Lev 23: 7 a sacred assembly and d no regular work. H6913
Lev 23: 8 a sacred assembly and d no regular work. H6913
Lev 23:21 a sacred assembly and d no regular work. H6913
Lev 23:22 d not reap to the very edges of your field AIT
Lev 23:25 D no regular work, but present a food H6913
Lev 23:28 D not do any work on that day, because it is AIT
Lev 23:28 Do not d any work on that day, because it H6913
Lev 23:29 Those who d not deny themselves on that day AIT
Lev 23:31 You shall d no work at all. This is to be a H6913
Lev 23:35 is a sacred assembly; d no regular work. H6913
Lev 23:36 special assembly; d no regular work. H6913
Lev 25: 4 D not sow your fields or prune your vineyards. AIT
Lev 25: 5 D not reap what grows of itself or harvest the AIT
Lev 25:11 d not sow and do not reap what grows of AIT
Lev 25:11 do not sow and d not reap what grows of AIT
Lev 25:14 d not take advantage of each other. AIT
Lev 25:17 D not take advantage of each other, but fear AIT
Lev 25:20 seventh year if we d not plant or harvest our AIT
Lev 25:28 But if they d not acquire the means to repay AIT
Lev 25:36 D not take interest or any profit from them AIT
Lev 25:39 d not make them work as slaves. AIT
Lev 25:43 D not rule over them ruthlessly, but fear your AIT
Lev 25:53 owe service d not rule over them ruthlessly AIT
Lev 26: 1 " 'D not make idols or set up an image or a AIT
Lev 26: 1 and d not place a carved stone in your land AIT
Lev 26:16 then I will d this to you: I will bring on you H6913
Lev 26:23 things you d not accept my correction but AIT
Lev 26:27 in spite of this you still d not listen to me AIT
Lev 27:20 however, they d not redeem the field, or if AIT
Nu 1:51 is to be set up, the Levites shall d it. H7756S
Nu 4:15 the Kohathites to come and d the carrying. AIT
Nu 4:19 near the most holy things, d this for them: H6913
Nu 4:26 The Gershonites are to d all that needs to H6268
Nu 4:47 of age who came to d the work of serving H6268
Nu 6:12 The previous days d not count, because H5877
Nu 8: 7 To purify them, d this: Sprinkle the water H6913
Nu 8:11 may be ready to d the work of the LORD H6268
Nu 8:15 are to come to d their work at the tent of H6268
Nu 8:19 his sons to d the work at the tent H6268
Nu 8:22 the Levites came to d their work at the H6268
Nu 8:26 but they themselves must not d the work. H6268
Nu 9:11 but they are to d it on the fourteenth day H6913
Nu 10:31 "Please d not leave us. You know AIT
Nu 11:12 Why d you tell me to carry them in my arms AIT
Nu 11:15 and d not let me face my own ruin. AIT
Nu 11:25 they prophesied—but did not d so again. H3578
Nu 12:12 D not let her be like a stillborn infant coming AIT
Nu 13:19 What kind of land d they live in? Is it good AIT
Nu 13:19 What kind of towns d they live in? Are they AIT
Nu 13:20 D your best to bring back some of the fruit H2616
Nu 13:30 the land, for we can certainly d it." H3523+3523
Nu 14: 9 Only d not rebel against the LORD. And do not AIT
Nu 14: 9 And d not be afraid of the people of the land AIT
Nu 14: 9 the LORD is with us. D not be afraid of them." AIT
Nu 14:28 I will d to you the very thing I heard you H6913
Nu 14:35 and I will surely d these things to this H6913
Nu 14:42 D not go up, because the LORD is not with you AIT
Nu 15:12 D this for each one, for as many as you H6913
Nu 15:13 who is native-born must d these things in H6913
Nu 15:14 to the LORD, they must d exactly as you do. H6913
Nu 15:14 to the LORD, they must do exactly as you d. H6913
Nu 16: 3 Why then d you set yourselves above the AIT
Nu 16: 6 You, Korah, and all your followers are to d H6913
Nu 16: 9 you near himself to d the work at the H6268
Nu 16:14 D you want to treat these men like slaves AIT
Nu 16:15 said to the LORD, "D not accept their offering. AIT
Nu 16:26 D not touch anything belonging to them, or AIT
Nu 16:28 LORD has sent me to d all these things H6913
Nu 18: 6 to the LORD to d the work at the tent of H6268
Nu 18:21 the work they d while serving at the H6268
Nu 18:23 is the Levites who are to d the work at the H6268
Nu 19:12 But if they d not purify themselves on the AIT
Nu 19:20 who are unclean d not purify themselves, AIT
Nu 21:34 to Moses, "D not be afraid of him, for I have AIT
Nu 21:34 D to him what you did to Sihon king of H6913
Nu 22:12 God said to Balaam, "D not go with them. AIT
Nu 22:16 D not let anything keep you from coming to AIT
Nu 22:17 you handsomely and d whatever you say. H6913
Nu 22:18 I could not d anything great or small to go H6913
Nu 22:20 go with them, but d only what I tell you." H6913
Nu 23: 9 apart and d not consider themselves one of AIT
Nu 23:26 I not tell you I must d whatever the LORD H6913
Nu 24:13 I could not d anything of my own accord H6913
Nu 24:14 what this people will d to your people in H6913
Nu 28:18 a sacred assembly and d no regular work. H6913
Nu 28:25 a sacred assembly and d no regular work. H6913
Nu 28:26 a sacred assembly and d no regular work. H6913
Nu 29: 1 a sacred assembly and d no regular work. H6913
Nu 29: 7 You must deny yourselves and d no work. H6913
Nu 29:12 a sacred assembly and d no regular work. H6913
Nu 29:35 special assembly and d no regular work. H6913
Nu 30: 2 break his word but must d everything he H6913
Nu 32: 5 D not make us cross the Jordan. AIT
Nu 32: 7 Why d you discourage the Israelites from AIT
Nu 32:20 to them, "If you will d this—if you will H6913
Nu 32:23 "But if you fail to d this, you will be H6913
Nu 32:24 but d what you have promised. H6913
Nu 32:25 "We your servants will d as our lord H6913
Nu 32:30 But if they d not cross over with you armed AIT
Nu 32:31 "Your servants will d what the LORD has H6913
Nu 33:55 " 'But if you d not drive out the inhabitants of AIT
Nu 33:56 And then I will d to you what I plan to do H6913
Nu 33:56 I will do to you what I plan to d to them. H6913
Nu 35:31 " 'D not accept a ransom for the life of a AIT
Nu 35:32 " 'D not accept a ransom for anyone who has AIT
Nu 35:33 " 'D not pollute the land where you are AIT
Nu 35:34 D not defile the land where you live and AIT
Dt 1:14 "What you propose to d is good. H6913
Dt 1:17 D not show partiality in judging; hear both AIT
Dt 1:17 D not be afraid of anyone, for judgment AIT
Dt 1:18 time I told you everything you were to d. H6913
Dt 1:21 D not be afraid; do not be AIT
Dt 1:21 Do not be afraid; d not be discouraged." AIT
Dt 1:29 I said to you, "D not be terrified; do not be AIT
Dt 1:29 "Do not be terrified; d not be afraid of them. AIT
Dt 1:39 children who d not yet know good from bad AIT
Dt 1:42 "Tell them, 'D not go up and fight, because I AIT
Dt 2: 5 D not provoke them to war, for I will not give AIT
Dt 2: 9 "D not harass the Moabites or provoke them AIT
Dt 2:19 d not harass them or provoke them to war AIT
Dt 3: 2 said to me, "D not be afraid of him, for I AIT
Dt 3: 2 D to him what you did to Sihon king of H6913
Dt 3:21 The LORD will d the same to all the H6913
Dt 3:22 D not be afraid of them; the LORD your God AIT
Dt 3:24 on earth who can d the deeds and H6913
Dt 3:24 can do the deeds and mighty works you d? NDT
Dt 3:26 "D not speak to me anymore about this AIT
Dt 4: 2 D not add to what I command you and do not AIT
Dt 4: 2 I command you and d not subtract from it, AIT
Dt 4: 9 closely so that you d not forget the things AIT
Dt 4:16 so that you d not become corrupt and make AIT
Dt 4:19 d not be enticed into bowing down to them AIT
Dt 4:23 d not make for yourselves an idol in the form AIT
Dt 5:13 days you shall labor and d all your work, H6913
Dt 5:14 On it you shall not d any work, neither you H6913
Dt 5:14 female servants may rest, as you d. NDT
Dt 5:32 So be careful to d what the LORD your God H6913
Dt 5:32 d not turn aside to the right or to the left. AIT
Dt 6:12 be careful that you d not forget the LORD, who AIT
Dt 6:14 D not follow other gods, the gods of the AIT
Dt 6:16 D not put the LORD your God to the test as AIT
Dt 6:18 D what is right and good in the LORD's H6913
Dt 7: 3 D not intermarry with them. Do not give your AIT
Dt 7: 3 D not give your daughters to their sons or AIT
Dt 7: 5 This is what you are to d to them: Break H6913
Dt 7:16 D not look on them with pity and do not AIT
Dt 7:16 on them with pity and d not serve their gods, AIT
Dt 7:18 But d not be afraid of them; remember well AIT
Dt 7:19 The LORD your God will d the same to all H6913
Dt 7:21 D not be terrified by them, for the LORD your AIT
Dt 7:25 D not covet the silver and gold on them, and AIT
Dt 7:25 gold on them, and d not take it for yourselves AIT
Dt 7:26 D not bring a detestable thing into your AIT
Dt 8:11 Be careful that you d not forget the LORD your AIT
Dt 9: 4 out before you, d not say to yourself, "The AIT
Dt 9:26 "Sovereign LORD, d not destroy your people AIT
Dt 10: 8 blessings in his name, as they still d today. NDT
Dt 10:16 and d not be stiff-necked any longer. AIT
Dt 12: 8 You are not to d as we do here today H6913
Dt 12: 8 You are not to do as we d here today H6913
Dt 12:23 But be sure you d not eat the blood, because AIT
Dt 12:25 D not eat it, so that it may go well with you AIT
Dt 12:30 "How d these nations serve their gods? AIT
Dt 12:30 serve their gods? We will d the same." H6913
Dt 12:31 they d all kinds of detestable things the H6913
Dt 12:32 See that you d all I command you; do not H6913
Dt 12:32 d not add to it or take away from it. AIT
Dt 13: 8 d not yield to them or listen to them. AIT
Dt 13: 8 D not spare them or shield them AIT
Dt 13:11 no one among you will d such an evil H6913
Dt 14: 1 D not cut yourselves or shave the front of AIT
Dt 14: 3 D not eat any detestable thing. AIT
Dt 14: 7 they d not have a divided hoof; they AIT
Dt 14:19 insects are unclean to you; d not eat them. AIT
Dt 14:21 D not eat anything you find already dead AIT
Dt 14:21 D not cook a young goat in its mother's milk. AIT
Dt 14:27 And d not neglect the Levites living in your AIT
Dt 15: 7 d not be hardhearted or tightfisted toward AIT
Dt 15: 9 so that you d not show ill will toward the AIT
Dt 15:10 to them and d so without a grudging H5989S
Dt 15:13 d not send them away empty-handed. AIT
Dt 15:16 "I d not want to leave you," because AIT
Dt 15:17 D the same for your female servant H6913
Dt 15:18 D not consider it a hardship to set your AIT
Dt 15:18 God will bless you in everything you d. H6913
Dt 15:19 D not put the firstborn of your cows to work AIT
Dt 15:19 and d not shear the firstborn of your sheep. AIT
Dt 16: 3 D not eat it with bread made with yeast, but AIT
Dt 16: 4 D not let any of the meat you sacrifice on the evening of the first day remain AIT
Dt 16: 8 to the LORD your God and d no work. H6913
Dt 16:19 D not pervert justice or show partiality. AIT
Dt 16:19 D not accept a bribe, for a bribe blinds the AIT
Dt 16:21 D not set up any wooden Asherah pole AIT
Dt 16:22 and d not erect a sacred stone, for these the AIT
Dt 17: 1 D not sacrifice to the LORD your God an ox AIT
Dt 17:10 Be careful to d everything they instruct you H6913
Dt 17:10 to do everything they instruct you to d. NDT
Dt 17:11 D not turn aside from what they tell you, to AIT
Dt 17:15 D not place a foreigner over you, one who is AIT
Dt 18: 9 d not learn to imitate the detestable ways of AIT
Dt 18:14 your God has not permitted you to d so. H5989
Dt 18:22 presumptuously, so d not be alarmed. AIT
Dt 19:10 D this so that innocent blood will not be NDT
Dt 19:14 D not move your neighbor's boundary stone AIT
Dt 19:19 then d to the false witness as that witness H6913
Dt 19:19 witness intended to d to the other party. H6913
Dt 20: 1 than yours, d not be afraid of them, because AIT
Dt 20: 3 D not be fainthearted or afraid; do not panic AIT
Dt 20: 3 afraid; d not panic or be terrified by them. AIT
Dt 20:15 a distance from you and d not belong to the NDT
Dt 20:16 d not leave alive anything that breathes. AIT
Dt 20:18 detestable things they d in worshiping H6913
Dt 20:19 d not destroy its trees by putting an ax to AIT
Dt 20:19 D not cut them down. Are the trees AIT
Dt 21: 8 and d not hold your people guilty of the AIT
Dt 22: 1 d not ignore it but be sure to take it back to AIT
Dt 22: 2 If they d not live near you or if you do not NDT
Dt 22: 2 near you or if you d not know who owns it, AIT
Dt 22: 3 D the same if you find their donkey or H6913
Dt 22: 3 anything else they have lost. D not ignore it. AIT
Dt 22: 4 ox fallen on the road, d not ignore it. AIT
Dt 22: 6 d not take the mother with the young. AIT
Dt 22: 9 D not plant two kinds of seed in your AIT
Dt 22: 9 your vineyard; if you d, not only the crops NDT
Dt 22:10 D not plow with an ox and a donkey yoked AIT
Dt 22:11 D not wear clothes of wool and linen woven AIT
Dt 22:26 D nothing to the woman; she has H6913
Dt 23: 6 D not seek a treaty of friendship with them as AIT
Dt 23: 7 D not despise an Edomite, for the Edomites AIT
Dt 23: 7 D not despise an Egyptian, because you AIT
Dt 23:15 d not hand them over to their master. AIT
Dt 23:16 town they choose. D not oppress them. AIT
Dt 23:19 D not charge a fellow Israelite interest AIT
Dt 23:21 LORD your God, d not be slow to pay it, for AIT
Dt 23:23 your lips utter you must be sure to d, H6913
Dt 23:24 you want, but d not put any in your basket. AIT
Dt 24: 4 D not bring sin upon the land the LORD your AIT
Dt 24: 6 D not take a pair of millstones—not even the upper one—as security for a debt AIT
Dt 24: 8 be very careful to d exactly as the Levitical H6913
Dt 24:10 d not go into their house to get what is AIT
Dt 24:12 d not go to sleep with their pledge in your AIT
Dt 24:14 D not take advantage of a hired worker who AIT
Dt 24:17 D not deprive the foreigner or the fatherless of AIT
Dt 24:18 That is why I command you to d this. H6913
Dt 24:19 you overlook a sheaf, d not go back to get it. AIT
Dt 24:20 d not go over the branches a second time. AIT
Dt 24:21 your vineyard, d not go over the vines again. AIT
Dt 24:22 That is why I command you to d this. H6913
Dt 25: 4 D not muzzle an ox while it is treading out AIT
Dt 25: 8 in saying, "I d not want to marry her," AIT
Dt 25:13 D not have two differing weights in your bag AIT
Dt 25:14 D not have two differing measures in your AIT
Dt 25:19 of Amalek from under heaven. D not forget! AIT
Dt 27: 5 D not use any iron tool on them AIT
Dt 28:14 D not turn aside from any of the commands I AIT
Dt 28:15 if you d not obey the LORD your God and do AIT

Dt 28:15 your God and *d* not carefully **follow** all his AIT
Dt 28:29 will be unsuccessful in **everything** you **d**; H2006
Dt 28:33 A people that *you d* not **know** will eat what AIT
Dt 28:58 If *you d* not **carefully** follow all the words of AIT
Dt 28:58 *d* not **revere** this glorious and awesome AIT
Dt 29: 9 that you may prosper in everything *you* **d**. H6913
Dt 31: 4 And the LORD *will* **d** to them what he did to H6913
Dt 31: 5 and *you must* **d** to them all that I have H6913
Dt 31: 6 *D* not *be* **afraid** or terrified because of them AIT
Dt 31: 8 forsake you. *D* not *be* **afraid**; do not be AIT
Dt 31: 8 Do not be afraid; *d* not *be* **discouraged**." AIT
Dt 31:13 Their children, who *d* not **know** this law, must AIT
Dt 31:21 I know what they are disposed *to* **d**, even H6913
Dt 31:29 on you because *you will* **d** evil in the sight H6913
Dt 34:11 wonders the LORD sent him to **d** in Egypt— H6913
Jos 1: 7 *d* not **turn** from it to the right or to the left AIT
Jos 1: 8 may be careful to **d** everything written in H6913
Jos 1: 9 *D* not *be* **afraid**; do not be discouraged, for AIT
Jos 1: 9 be afraid; *d* not *be* **discouraged**, for the LORD AIT
Jos 1:16 you have commanded us *we will* **d**, H6913
Jos 3: 4 between you and the ark; *d* not **go near** it." AIT
Jos 3: 5 tomorrow the LORD *will* **d** amazing things H6913
Jos 4: 6 'What **d** these stones mean?' NDT
Jos 4:21 their parents, 'What **d** these stones mean? NDT
Jos 6: 3 all the armed men. **D** this for six days. H6913
Jos 6:10 the army, "*D* not **give a war cry**, do not raise AIT
Jos 6:10 give a war cry, *d* not **raise** your voices, do not AIT
Jos 6:10 *d* not **say** a word until the day I tell you to AIT
Jos 7: 3 to take it and *d* not **weary** the whole army, AIT
Jos 7: 9 What then *will you* **d** for your own great H6913
Jos 7:19 what you have done; *d* not **hide** it from me." AIT
Jos 8: 1 said to Joshua, "*D* not *be* **afraid**; do not be AIT
Jos 8: 1 "Do not be afraid; *d* not *be* **discouraged**. AIT
Jos 8: 2 *You shall* **d** to Ai and its king as you did to H6913
Jos 8: 8 **D** what the LORD has commanded H6913
Jos 9: 8 "Who are you and where *d you* **come** from?" AIT
Jos 9:20 This is what *we will* **d** to them: We will let H6913
Jos 9:25 **D** to us whatever seems good and right to H6913
Jos 10: 6 "*D* not **abandon** your servants AIT
Jos 10: 8 to Joshua, "*D* not *be* **afraid** of them; I have AIT
Jos 10:25 said to them, "*D* not *be* **afraid**; do not be AIT
Jos 10:25 "Do not be afraid; *d* not *be* **discouraged**. AIT
Jos 10:25 is what the LORD *will* **d** to all the enemies H6913
Jos 11: 6 to Joshua, "*D* not *be* **afraid** of them, because AIT
Jos 15:18 Caleb asked her, "What can I **d for** you?" H4200
Jos 15:19 She replied, "**D** me a special favor. H5989
Jos 16:10 are required *to* **d** forced labor. H6268
Jos 18: 7 however, **d** not get a portion among you NDT
Jos 22:19 But *d* not **rebel** against the LORD or against us AIT
Jos 22:22 to the LORD, *d* not **spare** us this day. AIT
Jos 22:24 'What **d** you have to do with the LORD NDT
Jos 22:24 'What do you **have to d with** the LORD, the H4200
Jos 23: 7 *D* not **associate with** these nations that AIT
Jos 23: 7 *d* not **invoke** the names of their gods or AIT
Jos 24:12 You did not **d** it with your own sword and NDT
Jdg 1:14 Caleb asked her, "What can I **d for** you?" H4200
Jdg 1:15 She replied, "**D** me a special favor. H2035
Jdg 6:10 *d* not **worship** the gods of the Amorites AIT
Jdg 6:18 Please *d* not **go away** until I come back and AIT
Jdg 6:23 *D* not *be* **afraid**. You are not going to AIT
Jdg 6:39 said to God, "*D* not *be* **angry** with me. AIT
Jdg 7:17 to the edge of the camp, **d** exactly as I do. H6913
Jdg 7:17 to the edge of the camp, do exactly as *I* **d**. H6913
Jdg 8: 3 What was I able *to* **d** compared to you?" H6913
Jdg 8: 6 "**D** you already have the hands of Zebah NDT
Jdg 8:15 '**D** you already have the hands of Zebah NDT
Jdg 8:21 Zalmunna said, "Come, **d** *it* yourself. H7003S
Jdg 8:24 And he said, "*I d* **have** *one* **request**, that each AIT
Jdg 9:48 **D** what you have seen me do! H6913
Jdg 9:48 Do what you have seen me **d**!" H6913
Jdg 10:15 **D** with us whatever you think best, but H6913
Jdg 11: 7 Why *d you* **come** to me now, when you're in AIT
Jdg 11:10 our witness; *we will* certainly **d** as you say." H6913
Jdg 11:12 "What **d** you have against me that you have NDT
Jdg 11:36 **D** to me just as you promised, now that H6913
Jdg 13: 4 drink and that *you d* not **eat** anything AIT
Jdg 13: 7 drink and *d* not **eat** anything unclean, AIT
Jdg 13:13 "Your wife *must* **d** all that I have told her. H9068
Jdg 13:14 *She must* **d** everything I have commanded H9068
Jdg 13:18 He replied, "Why *d you* **ask** my name? It is AIT
Jdg 15:10 answered, "to **d** to him as he did to us." H6913
Jdg 18: 9 **Aren't** you *going to* **d something** H3120
Jdg 18:14 "*D you* **know** that one of these houses has an AIT
Jdg 18:14 Now you know what *to* **d**." H6913
Jdg 18:24 What else **d** I have? How can you NDT
Jdg 19:23 is my guest, don't **d** this outrageous thing. H6913
Jdg 19:24 can use them and **d** to them whatever you H6913
Jdg 19:24 don't **d** such an outrageous thing. H6913
Jdg 19:30 *We* **must d something**! So speak H6418
Jdg 20: 7 tell me **what** you have **decided to d**." H6783
Jdg 20: 9 But now this is what *we'll* **d** to Gibeah H6913
Jdg 21:11 "This is what *you are to* **d**," they said. H6913
Jdg 21:22 to them, '**D** us **the favor** of helping them H2858
Ru 2:13 though I *d* not **have** the standing of one of AIT
Ru 3: 4 lie down. He will tell you what *to* **d**." H6913
Ru 3: 5 "*I will* **d** whatever you say," Ruth H6913
Ru 3: 6 everything her mother-in-law told her to **d**. NDT
Ru 3:11 don't be afraid. *I will* **d** for you all you ask H6913
Ru 3:13 *he wants to* **d** *his* **duty** as your
guardian-redeemer H1457
Ru 3:13 as surely as the LORD lives I *will* **d** it. H1457S
Ru 4: 4 you will redeem it, **d** so. But if you will H1457S
Ru 4: 4 For no *one* **has the right to d it** except H1457S
Ru 4: 6 You redeem it yourself. I cannot **d** it." H1457S
1Sa 1:16 *D* not **take** your servant **for** a wicked woman; AIT
1Sa 1:23 "**D** what seems best to you," her husband H6913
1Sa 2: 3 "*D* not **keep** talking so proudly or let your AIT
1Sa 2:23 he said to them, "Why *d you* **do** such things? AIT
1Sa 2:23 said to them, "Why *do you* **d** such things? H6913
1Sa 2:29 Why *d you* **scorn** my sacrifice and offering AIT
1Sa 2:29 Why *d you* **honor** your sons more than me by AIT
1Sa 2:33 one of you that *I d* not **cut off** from serving at AIT
1Sa 2:35 *who will* **d** according to what is in my H6913
1Sa 3:11 *I am about to* **d** something in Israel that H6913
1Sa 3:17 "*D* not **hide** it from me. May God AIT
1Sa 3:18 *let him* **d** what is good in his eyes. H6913
1Sa 5: 8 "What *shall we* **d** with the ark of the god H6913
1Sa 6: 2 "What *shall we* **d** with the ark of the LORD? H6913
1Sa 6: 3 *d* not **send** it **back** to him without a gift AIT
1Sa 6: 6 Why *d you* **harden** your hearts as the AIT
1Sa 7: 8 "*D* not **stop** crying out to the LORD our God AIT
1Sa 8: 5 your sons *d* not **follow** your ways; now AIT
1Sa 9: 7 take to the man of God. What **d** we have?" NDT
1Sa 9:20 three days ago, *d* not **worry** about them; they AIT
1Sa 9:21 Why *d you* **say** such a thing to me? AIT
1Sa 10: 2 is asking, "What *shall I* **d** about my son?" H6913
1Sa 10: 7 fulfilled, **d** whatever your hand finds to do H6913
1Sa 10: 7 do whatever your hand finds to **d**, for God is NDT
1Sa 10: 8 to you and tell you what *you are to* **d**." H6913
1Sa 10:24 "*D you* **see** the man the LORD has chosen? AIT
1Sa 11:10 and *you can* **d** to us whatever you like." H6913
1Sa 12:14 obey him and *d* not **rebel** against his AIT
1Sa 12:15 But if *you d* not **obey** the LORD, and if you AIT
1Sa 12:16 thing the LORD *is about to* **d** before your H6913
1Sa 12:20 "*D* not *be* **afraid**," Samuel replied. "You have AIT
1Sa 12:20 this evil; yet *d* not **turn away** from the LORD AIT
1Sa 12:21 *D* not **turn away** after useless idols. They can AIT
1Sa 12:21 *They can* **d** you no **good**, nor can they H3603
1Sa 14: 7 "**D** all that you have in mind," his H6913
1Sa 14:34 *D* not **sin** against the LORD by eating meat AIT
1Sa 14:36 "**D** whatever seems best to you," they H6913
1Sa 14:40 "**D** what seems best to you," they replied. H6913
1Sa 14:44 it ever so severely, if *you d* not **die**, Jonathan." AIT
1Sa 15: 3 *D* not **spare** them; put to death men and AIT
1Sa 15: 6 so that *I d* not **destroy** you along with AIT
1Sa 15:19 on the plunder and **d** evil in the eyes of H6913
1Sa 16: 3 sacrifice, and I will show you what *to* **d**. H6913
1Sa 16: 4 They asked, "*D you* **come** in peace?" AIT
1Sa 16: 7 "*D* not **consider** his appearance or his height AIT
1Sa 17: 8 "Why *d you* **come out** and line up for battle? AIT
1Sa 17:25 "*D you* **see** how this man keeps coming out? AIT
1Sa 18:17 *Let the* Philistines **d that**!"
H2118+928+2257+3338S
1Sa 18:23 "*D* you think *it is* a **small** *matter* to become AIT
1Sa 19: 4 "*Let* not the king **d wrong** to his servant H2627
1Sa 19: 5 Why then *would you* **d wrong** to an H2627
1Sa 20: 2 my father doesn't **d** anything, great or H6913
1Sa 20: 4 "Whatever you want me to **d**, I'll do for you." NDT
1Sa 20: 4 you want me to do, *I'll* **d** for you. H6913
1Sa 20:13 if *I d* not **let you know** and send you away in AIT
1Sa 20:15 and *d* not ever **cut off** your kindness from my AIT
1Sa 21: 3 what *d* you **have on hand**? Give me AIT
1Sa 22: 3 you until I learn what God *will* **d** for me?" H6913
1Sa 22: 5 said to David, "*D* not **stay** in the stronghold. AIT
1Sa 23:20 down whenever it pleases you to **d so**, H3718S
1Sa 24: 6 LORD forbid that *I should* **d** such a thing to H6913
1Sa 24: 9 "Why *d you* **listen** when men say AIT
1Sa 25:17 Now think it over and see what *you can* **d** H6913
1Sa 26:20 Now *d* not *let* my blood **fall** to the ground far AIT
1Sa 26:25 *you will* **d great things** and surely H6913+6913
1Sa 27: 1 The best thing I can **d** is to escape to the NDT
1Sa 28: 2 see for yourself what your servant *can* **d**." H6913
1Sa 28:13 What *d you* **see**?" The woman said AIT
1Sa 28:15 I have called on you to tell me what *to* **d**." H6913
1Sa 28:16 "Why *d you* **consult** me, now that the AIT
1Sa 28:21 in my hands and did what you told me to **d**. NDT
1Sa 29: 7 **d** nothing to displease the Philistine H6913
1Sa 30:13 asked him, "Who **d** you belong to? Where NDT
1Sa 30:13 Where **d** you come from?" He NDT
1Sa 30:23 *you must* not **d** that with what the LORD H6913
1Sa 31: 4 was terrified and **would** not **d** it; H14
2Sa 1: 5 "How *d you* **know** that Saul and his son AIT
2Sa 1: 7 out to me, and I said, '**What can** I **d**? H2180
2Sa 2:14 "**All right**, *let them* **d** *it*," Joab H7756S
2Sa 3: 9 if *I d* not **do** for David what the LORD AIT
2Sa 3: 9 if *I* do not **d** for David what the LORD H6913
2Sa 3:13 *D* not **come into** my **presence** unless you AIT
2Sa 3:18 Now **d** *it*! For the LORD promised David, H6913
2Sa 3:19 of Benjamin **wanted to d**. H3202+928+6524
2Sa 3:38 "*D you* not **realize** that a commander and a AIT
2Sa 5:23 he answered, "*D* not **go straight up**, but circle AIT
2Sa 7: 3 in mind, go ahead and **d** it, for the LORD is H6913
2Sa 7:25 his house. **D** as you promised, H6913
2Sa 9:11 "Your servant *will* **d** whatever my lord the H6913
2Sa 9:11 my lord the king commands his servant to **d**." NDT
2Sa 10: 3 "**D** you think David is honoring your father NDT
2Sa 10:12 The LORD *will* **d** what is good in his sight." H6913
2Sa 11:11 as you live, *I will* not **d** such a thing!" H6913
2Sa 12:12 I *will* **d** this thing in broad daylight H6913
2Sa 12:18 *He may* **d** something desperate. H6913
2Sa 13: 2 impossible for him to **d** anything to her. H6913
2Sa 13: 4 asked Amnon, "Why **d** you, the king's son NDT
2Sa 13:12 done in Israel! Don't **d** this wicked thing. H6913
2Sa 14:19 who instructed me to **d** this and who put all NDT
2Sa 14:21 king said to Joab, "Very well, *I will* **d** it. H6913
2Sa 15:15 servants are **ready to d** whatever our lord H2180
2Sa 15:20 **d not know where I am going**
H2143+6584+889+2143
2Sa 15:26 *let him* **d** to me whatever seems good to H6913
2Sa 15:27 said to Zadok the priest, "*D* you **understand**? AIT
2Sa 16:10 "What does this **have to d with** you, you H4200
2Sa 16:10 who can ask, 'Why *d you* **do** this? AIT
2Sa 16:10 who can ask, 'Why *do you* **d** this? H6913
2Sa 16:20 "Give us your advice. What *should we* **d**?" H6913
2Sa 17: 6 *Should we* **d** what he says? If H6913
2Sa 17:15 the elders of Israel to **d** such and such, NDT
2Sa 17:15 I have advised them to **d** so and so. NDT
2Sa 17:16 '*D* not **spend** the night at the fords in the AIT
2Sa 18: 4 "*I will* **d** whatever seems best to you." H6913
2Sa 18:20 but *you must* not **d so** today H1413S
2Sa 18:22 Joab replied, "My son, why *d* you *want to* **go**? AIT
2Sa 19:10 So why *d* you **say nothing** *about* bringing the AIT
2Sa 19:18 over and to **d** whatever he wished. H6913
2Sa 19:19 *D* not **remember** how your servant did wrong AIT
2Sa 19:22 "What does this **have to d with** you, you H4200
2Sa 19:22 What right **d** you have to interfere NDT
2Sa 19:27 an angel of God; so **d** whatever you wish. H6913
2Sa 19:28 So what right **d** I have to make any more NDT
2Sa 19:37 **D** for him whatever you wish. H6913
2Sa 19:38 I *will* **d** for him whatever you wish. H6913
2Sa 19:38 you desire from me *I will* **d** for you." H6913
2Sa 19:43 Why then *d you* **treat** us **with contempt** AIT
2Sa 20: 6 son of Bikri *will* **d** us more **harm** than H8317
2Sa 20:19 Why *d you want to* **swallow up** the LORD's AIT
2Sa 21: 3 the Gibeonites, "What *shall I* **d** for you? H6913
2Sa 21: 4 **d** we have the right to put anyone in NDT
2Sa 21: 4 "What *d* you **want** me to do for you? AIT
2Sa 21: 4 "What do you want *me to* **d** for you?" H6913
2Sa 22:37 my feet, so that my ankles *d* not **give way**. AIT
2Sa 23:17 "Far be it from me, LORD, *to* **d** this!" H6913
2Sa 24: 3 my lord the king want to **d** such a thing?" NDT
2Sa 24:14 but *d* not *let me* **fall** into human hands." AIT
1Ki 1: 6 by asking, "Why *d you* **behave** as you do?" AIT
1Ki 1: 6 by asking, "Why do you behave as you **d**?" NDT
1Ki 1:18 *you*, my lord the king, *d* not **know about** it. AIT
1Ki 2: 3 **D** this so that you may prosper in all you do NDT
1Ki 2: 3 prosper in all *you* **d** and wherever you H6913
1Ki 2: 6 but *d* not **let** his gray head **go down** *to* the AIT
1Ki 2: 9 *d* not **consider** him **innocent**. AIT
1Ki 2: 9 wisdom; you will know what *to* **d** to him. H6913
1Ki 2:13 asked him, "*D* you **come** peacefully? AIT
1Ki 2:16 to make of you. *D* not **refuse** me." "You may AIT
1Ki 2:20 "*D* not **refuse** me." The king replied AIT
1Ki 2:22 "Why *d you* **request** Abishag the AIT
1Ki 2:31 king commanded Benaiah, "**D** as he says. H6913
1Ki 2:36 live there, but *d* not **go** anywhere else. AIT
1Ki 2:38 Your servant *will* **d** as my lord the king has H6913
1Ki 3: 7 child and *d* not **know how** to carry out my AIT
1Ki 3:12 *I will* **d** what you have asked. I will give H6913
1Ki 3:27 to the first woman. *D* not **kill** him; she is his AIT
1Ki 5: 8 you sent me and *will* **d** all you want in H6913
1Ki 5:11 Solomon *continued to* **d** this for Hiram H5989S
1Ki 7:14 with knowledge to **d** all kinds of bronze H6913
1Ki 8:25 are careful in **all** they **d** to walk before me H2006
1Ki 8:39 deal with everyone according to all they **d**, H2006
1Ki 8:43 **D** whatever the foreigner asks of you, so H6913
1Ki 8:43 fear you, as **d** your own people Israel NDT
1Ki 9: 1 had achieved all he had desired to **d** H6913
1Ki 9: 4 **d** all I command and observe my H6913
1Ki 9: 6 from me and *d* not **observe** the commands AIT
1Ki 11:12 *I will* not **d** it during your lifetime. H6913
1Ki 11:22 Hadad replied, "but **d let** me **go**!" H8938+8938
1Ki 11:33 I will **d** this because they have forsaken me NDT
1Ki 11:38 If *you* **d** whatever I command you and walk H9048
1Ki 11:38 to me and **d** what is right in my H6913
1Ki 12:16 "What share **d** we have in David, what part NDT
1Ki 12:24 *D* not **go up** to fight against your brothers AIT
1Ki 17:13 Go home and **d** as you have said H6913
1Ki 17:18 said to Elijah, "What **d** you have against me NDT
1Ki 18:25 the name of your god, but *d* not **light** the fire." AIT
1Ki 18:34 "**D** *it* **again**," he said, and they did it H9101
1Ki 18:34 "**D** *it* **a third time**," he ordered, and they H8992
1Ki 19: 2 this time tomorrow *I d* not **make** your life like AIT
1Ki 20: 9 'Your servant *will* **d** all you demanded the H6913
1Ki 20:13 '*D you* **see** this vast army? AIT
1Ki 20:14 "But who will **d** this?" asked Ahab. H928
1Ki 20:14 under the provincial commanders will **d** it. H928
1Ki 20:24 **D** this: Remove all the kings from their H6913
1Ki 21:20 have sold yourself to **d** evil in the eyes of H6913
1Ki 21:25 who sold himself to **d** evil in the eyes of H6913
1Ki 22:22 said the LORD. 'Go and **d** it.' H6913
1Ki 22:31 commanders, "*D* not **fight** *with* anyone, small AIT
2Ki 1:15 "Go down with him; *d* not *be* **afraid** of him." AIT
2Ki 2: 3 "*D you* **know** that the LORD is going to take AIT
2Ki 2: 5 "*D you* **know** that the LORD is going to take AIT
2Ki 2: 9 what *can I* **d** for you before I am taken H6913
2Ki 2:16 Elisha replied, "*d* not **send** them." AIT
2Ki 3:13 of Israel, "Why **d** you want to involve me? NDT
2Ki 4: 2 Tell me, what **d** you have in your house?" NDT
2Ki 4:29 if anyone greets you, *d* not **answer**. AIT
2Ki 5:13 prophet had told you to **d** some great thing, NDT
2Ki 6:15 What *shall we* **d**?" the servant H6913
2Ki 6:22 "*D* not **kill** them," he answered. "Would you AIT
2Ki 8: 2 woman proceeded *to* **d** as the man of H6913
2Ki 8:12 I know the harm *you will* **d** to the H6913
2Ki 9:17 meet them and ask, '**D** you come in peace? NDT

2Ki 9:18 what the king says: '**D** you come in peace?' NDT
2Ki 9:18 "What **d** you have to do with peace?" NDT
2Ki 9:18 "What do you **have to d with** peace?" H4200
2Ki 9:19 what the king says: '**D** you come in peace?' NDT
2Ki 9:19 "What **d** you have to do with peace? NDT
2Ki 9:19 "What do you **have to d with** peace? H4200
2Ki 10: 5 servants and *we will* **d** anything you say H6913
2Ki 10: 5 as king; *you* **d** whatever you think best." H6913
2Ki 10:30 to the house of Ahab all I had in mind to **d**, NDT
2Ki 11: 5 saying, "This is what *you are to* **d**: H6913
2Ki 16: 2 *he did* not **d** what was right in the eyes of H6913
2Ki 17:12 the LORD had said, "*You shall* not **d** this." H6913
2Ki 17:15 had ordered them, "*D* not **do** as they do." AIT
2Ki 17:15 had ordered them, "*Do* not **d** as they do." H6913
2Ki 17:15 had ordered them, "Do not do as they **d**." NDT
2Ki 17:17 sold themselves to **d** evil in the eyes of H6913
2Ki 17:26 towns of Samaria *d* not **know** what the god of AIT
2Ki 17:26 the people *d* not **know** what he requires." AIT
2Ki 17:35 "*D* not **worship** any other gods or bow down AIT
2Ki 17:37 he wrote for you. *D* not **worship** other gods. AIT
2Ki 17:38 *D* not **forget** the covenant I have made with AIT
2Ki 17:38 with you, and *d* not **worship** other gods. AIT
2Ki 17:41 grandchildren *continue to* **d** as their H6913
2Ki 18:29 *D* not **let** Hezekiah **deceive** you. AIT
2Ki 18:30 *D* not **let** Hezekiah **persuade** you **to trust** in AIT
2Ki 18:31 "*D* not **listen** to Hezekiah. This is what the AIT
2Ki 18:32 "*D* not **listen** to Hezekiah, for he is AIT
2Ki 18:36 king had commanded, "*D* not **answer** him." AIT
2Ki 19: 6 *D* not *be* **afraid** of what you have heard AIT
2Ki 19:10 *D* not **let** the god you depend on **deceive** you AIT
2Ki 20: 9 to you that the LORD *will* **d** what he has H6913
2Ki 21: 8 will be careful to **d** everything I H6913
2Ki 23:35 In order to **d so**, he taxed the land and H5989S
2Ki 25:24 "*D* not *be* **afraid** of the Babylonian officials," AIT
1Ch 10: 4 was terrified and would not **d** it; NDT
1Ch 11:19 "God forbid that I *should* **d** this!" he said H6913
1Ch 12:32 times and knew what Israel *should* **d**— H6913
1Ch 13: 4 The whole assembly agreed to **d** this H6913
1Ch 14:14 answered him, "*D* not **go directly** after them AIT
1Ch 15:13 of him about how to **d** it in the prescribed NDT
1Ch 16:22 "*D* not **touch** my anointed ones; do my AIT
1Ch 16:22 my anointed ones; *d* my prophets no **harm**." AIT
1Ch 17: 2 you have in mind, **d** it, for God is with you H6913
1Ch 17:23 established forever. **D** as you promised, H6913
1Ch 19: 3 "**D** you think David is honoring your father NDT
1Ch 19:13 The LORD *will* **d** what is good in his sight." H6913
1Ch 21: 3 Why *does* my lord **want to d** this? Why H1335
1Ch 21:13 but *d* not *let me* **fall** into human hands." AIT
1Ch 21:17 **d** not let this plague remain on your NDT
1Ch 21:23 *Let* my lord the king **d** whatever pleases H6913
1Ch 22:13 courageous. *D* not *be* **afraid** or discouraged AIT
1Ch 23:30 They were to **d** the same in the evening NDT
1Ch 26: 8 men with the strength to **d** the work— NDT
1Ch 28:10 the sanctuary. Be strong and **d** *the* **work**." H6913
1Ch 28:20 strong and courageous, and **d** *the* **work**. H6913
1Ch 28:20 *D* not *be* **afraid** or discouraged, for the LORD AIT
1Ch 29:19 decrees and to **d** everything to build H6913
2Ch 6:16 are careful in **all** they **d** to walk before me H2006
2Ch 6:30 with everyone according to all they **d**, H2006
2Ch 6:33 **D** whatever the foreigner asks of you, so H6913
2Ch 6:33 fear you, as **d** your own people Israel NDT
2Ch 6:42 LORD God, *d* not **reject** your anointed one AIT
2Ch 7:11 he had in mind to **d** in the temple of the H6913
2Ch 7:17 your father did, and **d** all I command, and H6913
2Ch 10:16 "What share **d** we have in David, what part NDT
2Ch 11: 4 *D* not **go up** to fight against your fellow AIT
2Ch 13: 9 of your own as the peoples of other lands **d**? NDT
2Ch 13:12 People of Israel, *d* not **fight** against the LORD AIT
2Ch 14:11 *d* not *let* mere mortals **prevail** against you." AIT
2Ch 15: 7 be strong and *d* not **give up**, for your work AIT
2Ch 18:21 said the LORD. 'Go and **d** it.' H6913
2Ch 18:30 commanders, "*D* not **fight** *with* anyone, small AIT
2Ch 19: 6 "Consider carefully what you **d**, because H6913
2Ch 19:10 you and your people. **D** this, and you will H6913
2Ch 19:11 may the LORD be with those who **d** well." NDT
2Ch 20:12 We *d* not **know** what to do, but our eyes are AIT
2Ch 20:12 We do not know what *to* **d**, but our eyes H6913
2Ch 20:15 '*D* not *be* **afraid** or discouraged because of AIT
2Ch 20:17 Jerusalem. *D* not *be* **afraid**; do not be AIT
2Ch 20:17 be afraid; *d* not *be* **discouraged**. Go out to AIT
2Ch 23: 4 Now this is what *you are to* **d**: A third of H6913
2Ch 23:14 "*D* not **put** her **to death** *at* the temple of the AIT
2Ch 24: 5 **D** it **now**." But the Levites H4554
2Ch 24:20 'Why *d* you **disobey** the LORD's commands AIT
2Ch 25:15 "Why *d you* **consult** this people's gods AIT
2Ch 28: 1 *he did* not **d** what was right in the eyes of H6913
2Ch 28:13 *D* you **intend** to add to our sin and guilt AIT
2Ch 29:11 *d* not *be* **negligent** now, for the LORD AIT
2Ch 30: 7 *D* not **be** like your parents and your fellow AIT
2Ch 30: 8 *D* not *be* **stiff-necked**, as your ancestors were AIT
2Ch 32: 7 *D* not *be* **afraid** or discouraged because of AIT
2Ch 32:13 "*D you* not **know** what I and my predecessors AIT
2Ch 32:15 Now *d* not *let* Hezekiah **deceive** you and AIT
2Ch 32:15 *D* not **believe** him, for no god of any nation AIT
2Ch 33: 8 will be careful to **d** everything I H6913
Ezr 6: 7 *D* **not interfere** with the work on this temple AIT
Ezr 6: 8 decree what *you are to* **d** for these elders A10522
Ezr 7:18 Israelites *may* then **d** whatever seems A10522
Ezr 7:25 you are to teach any who *d* not **know** them. AIT
Ezr 9:12 *d* not **give** your daughters **in marriage** to their AIT
Ezr 9:12 *D* not **seek** a treaty of friendship with them at AIT
Ezr 10: 4 will support you, so take courage and **d** it." H6913
Ezr 10: 5 Israel under oath to **d** what had been H6913
Ezr 10:11 the God of your ancestors, and **d** his will. H6913
Ezr 10:12 "You are right! We *must* **d** as you say. H6913
Ne 2:12 had put in my heart to **d** for Jerusalem. H6913
Ne 4: 5 *D* not **cover up** their guilt or blot out their sins AIT
Ne 5:12 more from them. *We will* **d** as you say." H6913
Ne 5:12 take an oath to **d** what they had promised H6913
Ne 7: 2 feared God more than most people **d**. NDT
Ne 8: 9 *D* not **mourn** or weep." For all AIT
Ne 8:10 *D* not **grieve**, for the joy of the LORD is your AIT
Ne 8:11 "Be still, for this is a holy day. *D* not **grieve**." AIT
Ne 9:32 *d* not *let* all this hardship *seem* **trifling** in AIT
Ne 13:14 and *d* not **blot out** what I have so faithfully AIT
Ne 13:18 Didn't your ancestors **d** the same things H6913
Ne 13:21 "Why *d* you **spend the night** by the wall? AIT
Ne 13:21 If *you* **d** *this* **again**, I will arrest H9101
Est 2:10 Mordecai had forbidden her *to* **d so**. H5583S
Est 2:20 just as Mordecai had told her to **d**, NDT
Est 3: 3 "Why *d you* **disobey** the king's command?" AIT
Est 3: 8 and they *d* not **obey** the king's laws AIT
Est 3:11 "and **d** with the people as you please." H6913
Est 4:13 "*D* not **think** that because you are in the AIT
Est 4:16 fast for me. *D* not **eat** or drink for three days AIT
Est 4:16 I and my attendants will fast as you **d** NDT
Est 5: 5 "so that we **may d** what Esther asks." H6913
Est 6:10 robe and the horse and **d** just as you have H6913
Est 6:10 *D* not **neglect** anything you have AIT
Est 7: 5 the man who has dared to **d** such a thing?" H6913
Est 8: 5 with favor and thinks it the right thing to **d**, NDT
Est 8:12 the Jews to **d** this in all the provinces NDT
Job 1:12 on the man himself *d* not **lay** a finger." AIT
Job 5:17 so *d* not **despise** the discipline of the AIT
Job 6:11 "What strength **d** I have, that I should still NDT
Job 6:12 **D** I have the strength of stone? Is my flesh NDT
Job 6:13 **D** I have any power to help myself, now that NDT
Job 6:25 But what *d* your arguments **prove**? AIT
Job 6:26 *D you* **mean** to correct what I say, and treat AIT
Job 6:29 *d* not **be** unjust; reconsider, for my AIT
Job 7: 1 "**D** not mortals have hard service on earth NDT
Job 7:20 I done to you, you who see everything we **d**? NDT
Job 7:21 Why *d you* not **pardon** my offenses and AIT
Job 9:16 *I d* not **believe** he would give me a hearing. AIT
Job 10: 2 *D* not **declare** me **guilty**, but tell me what AIT
Job 10: 4 **D** you have eyes of flesh? Do you see as a NDT
Job 10: 4 *D you* **see** as a mortal sees? AIT
Job 11: 8 the heavens above—what *can you* **d**? H7188
Job 13:14 Why *d I* **put** myself **in jeopardy** and take my AIT
Job 13:24 Why *d you* **hide** your face and consider me AIT
Job 14: 2 like fleeting shadows, *they d* not **endure**. AIT
Job 14: 3 *D you* **fix** your eye on them? Will you bring AIT
Job 14:21 are honored, *they d* not **know** it; if their AIT
Job 14:21 offspring are brought low, *they d* not **see** it. AIT
Job 15: 8 *D you* **listen in** on God's council? Do you AIT
Job 15: 8 *D you* **have a monopoly on** wisdom? AIT
Job 15: 9 What *d you* **know** that we do not know? What AIT
Job 15: 9 What do you know that *we d* not **know**? What AIT
Job 15: 9 What **insights** *d you* **have** that we do not AIT
Job 15: 9 insights do you have that we **d** not have? NDT
Job 15:12 carried you away, and why *d* your eyes **flash**, AIT
Job 16:18 *d* not **cover** my blood; may my cry AIT
Job 19:22 Why *d you* **pursue** me as God does? Will you AIT
Job 21: 7 Why *d* the wicked **live on**, growing old and AIT
Job 21:10 to breed; their cows calve and *d* not **miscarry**. AIT
Job 21:21 For what **d** they care about the families they NDT
Job 22:17 What *can* the Almighty **d** to us?' H7188
Job 23: 8 not there; if I go to the west, *I d* not **find** him. AIT
Job 23: 9 in the north, *I d* not **see** him; when he turns AIT
Job 24:13 *who d* not **know** its ways or stay in its paths. AIT
Job 24:16 *they* **want** nothing **to d with** the light. H3359
Job 26: 8 the clouds *d* not **burst** under their weight. AIT
Job 27:19 wealthy, but *will* **d** so **no more**; when he H665
Job 28: 8 Proud beasts *d* not **set foot on** it, and no lion AIT
Job 30:10 *they d* not **hesitate** to spit in my face. AIT
Job 30:20 God, but *you d* not **answer**; I stand up AIT
Job 31: 3 disaster for *those who* **d** wrong? H7188
Job 31:14 what *will I* **d** when God confronts me H6913
Job 31:23 of his splendor *I* **could** not **d** such things. H3523
Job 31:33 if I have concealed my sin as people **d**, by NDT
Job 32:13 *D* not **say**, 'We have found wisdom; let God AIT
Job 33:13 Why *d you* **complain** to him that he responds AIT
Job 34:10 Far be it from God to **d** evil, from the NDT
Job 34:10 to do evil, from the Almighty to **d** wrong. NDT
Job 34:12 It is unthinkable that God *would* **d wrong** H8399
Job 34:32 if I have done wrong, *I will* not **d** so **again**. H3578
Job 35: 2 "*D you* **think** this is just? You say, 'I am in the AIT
Job 35: 3 is it to me, and what *d I* **gain** by not sinning? AIT
Job 35: 6 sins are many, what *does that* **d** to him? H6913
Job 35: 7 righteous, what *d you* **give** to him, or what AIT
Job 35:14 listen when you say that *you d* not **see** him, AIT
Job 36:12 But if *they d* not **listen**, they will perish by the AIT
Job 36:13 when he fetters them, *they d* not **cry for help**. AIT
Job 36:18 *d* not *let* a large bribe **turn** you **aside**. AIT
Job 36:20 *D* not **long for** the night, to drag people away AIT
Job 37:12 the whole earth to **d** whatever he H7188
Job 37:15 *D you* **know** how God controls the clouds AIT
Job 37:16 *D you* **know** how the clouds hang poised AIT
Job 38:20 *D you* **know** the paths to their dwellings AIT
Job 38:33 *D you* **know** the laws of the heavens? Can AIT
Job 38:35 *D you* **send** the lightning bolts on their way AIT
Job 38:35 *D they* **report** to you, 'Here we AIT
Job 38:39 "*D you* **hunt** the prey for the lioness and AIT
Job 39: 1 "*D you* **know** when the mountain goats give AIT
Job 39: 1 *D you* **watch** when the doe bears her fawn? AIT
Job 39: 2 *D you* **count** the months till they bear? Do AIT
Job 39: 2 *D you* **know** the time they give birth? AIT
Job 39: 4 in the wilds; they leave and *d* not **return**. AIT
Job 39:19 "*D you* **give** the horse its strength or clothe its AIT
Job 39:20 *D you* **make** it **leap** like a locust, striking AIT
Job 40: 9 **D** you have an arm like God's, and can your NDT
Job 41: 8 the struggle and never **d** *it* **again**! H3578
Job 41:28 Arrows *d* not **make** it **flee**; slingstones are AIT
Job 42: 2 "I know that *you* **can d** all things; no H3523
Ps 1: 3 not wither—whatever *they* **d** prospers. H6913
Ps 2: 1 Why *d* the nations **conspire** and the peoples AIT
Ps 4: 4 Tremble and *d* not **sin**; when you are on your AIT
Ps 5: 5 your presence. You hate all *who* **d** wrong; H7188
Ps 6: 1 *d* not **rebuke** me in your anger or discipline AIT
Ps 6: 8 from me, all you *who* **d** evil, for the LORD H7188
Ps 9:19 *d* not *let* mortals **triumph**; let the AIT
Ps 10: 1 LORD, *d you* **stand** far off? Why do you AIT
Ps 10: 1 *Why d you* **hide** *yourself* in times of trouble AIT
Ps 10: 6 "No one will ever **d** me harm." H928S
Ps 10:12 your hand, O God. *D* not **forget** the helpless. AIT
Ps 11: 3 destroyed, what *can* the righteous **d**?" H7188
Ps 14: 4 *D* all *these* **evildoers** know nothing? They AIT
Ps 18:36 my feet, so that my ankles *d* not **give way**. AIT
Ps 22: 2 out by day, but *you d* not **answer**, by night, AIT
Ps 22:11 *D* not *be* **far** from me, for trouble is near AIT
Ps 22:19 LORD, *d* not *be* **far from** me. You are my AIT
Ps 25: 2 *d* not *let me be* **put to shame**, nor let AIT
Ps 25: 7 *D* not **remember** the sins of my youth and my AIT
Ps 25:20 *d* not *let me be* **put to shame**, for I AIT
Ps 26: 4 *I d* not **sit** with the deceitful, nor do I AIT
Ps 26: 4 deceitful, nor *d I* **associate** with hypocrites. AIT
Ps 26: 9 *D* not **take away** my soul along with sinners AIT
Ps 27: 4 thing I ask from the LORD, this only *d I* **seek**: AIT
Ps 27: 9 *D* not **hide** your face from me, do not turn AIT
Ps 27: 9 *d* not **turn** your servant **away** in anger AIT
Ps 27: 9 *D* not **reject** me or forsake me, God my Savior AIT
Ps 27:12 *D* not **turn** me **over** to the desire of my foes AIT
Ps 28: 1 you are my Rock, *d* not **turn a deaf ear** to me. AIT
Ps 28: 3 *D* not **drag** me **away** with the wicked, with AIT
Ps 28: 3 with *those who* **d** evil, who speak H7188
Ps 32: 9 *D* not **be** like the horse or the mule, which AIT
Ps 33:15 who considers everything they **d**. H5126
Ps 34:14 Turn from evil and **d** good; seek peace H6913
Ps 34:16 of the LORD is against *those who* **d** evil, H6913
Ps 35:19 *D* not *let those* **gloat** over me who are my AIT
Ps 35:19 *d* not *let* those who hate me without reason **maliciously wink** AIT
Ps 35:20 *They d* not **speak** peaceably, but devise false AIT
Ps 35:22 have seen this; *d* not *be* **silent**. Do not be far AIT
Ps 35:22 do not be silent. *D* not *be* **far** from me, Lord. AIT
Ps 35:24 LORD my God; *d* not *let them* **gloat** over me. AIT
Ps 35:25 *D* not *let them* **think**, "Aha, just what we AIT
Ps 36: 3 deceitful; they fail to act wisely or **d good**. H3512
Ps 36: 4 sinful course and *d* not **reject** what is wrong. AIT
Ps 37: 1 *D* not **fret** because of those who are evil AIT
Ps 37: 1 evil or be envious of *those who* **d** wrong; H6913
Ps 37: 3 Trust in the LORD and **d** good; dwell in the H6913
Ps 37: 5 to the LORD; trust in him and he *will* **d** this: H6913
Ps 37: 7 *d* not **fret** when people succeed in their ways AIT
Ps 37: 8 turn from wrath; *d* not **fret**—it leads only to AIT
Ps 37:21 The wicked borrow and *d* not **repay**, but the AIT
Ps 37:27 Turn from evil and **d** good; then you will H6913
Ps 37:31 God is in their hearts; their feet *d* not **slip**. AIT
Ps 38: 1 *d* not **rebuke** me in your anger or discipline AIT
Ps 38:16 "*D* not *let them* **gloat** or exalt themselves AIT
Ps 38:20 though I **seek** *only* **to d** what is good. H8103
Ps 38:21 *d* not **forsake** me; do not be far from me AIT
Ps 38:21 forsake me; *d* not *be* **far** from me, my God AIT
Ps 39: 7 Lord, what *d I* **look for**? My hope is in AIT
Ps 39: 8 *d* not **make** me the scorn of fools. AIT
Ps 39:12 my cry for help; *d* not *be* **deaf** to my weeping. AIT
Ps 40: 8 I desire to **d** your will, my God; your law is H6913
Ps 40: 9 the great assembly; *I d* not **seal** my lips, LORD, AIT
Ps 40:10 *I d* not **hide** your righteousness in my heart; AIT
Ps 40:10 *I d* not **conceal** your love and your AIT
Ps 40:11 *D* not **withhold** your mercy from me, LORD AIT
Ps 40:17 my deliverer; you are my God, *d* not **delay**. AIT
Ps 44:23 Why *d you* **sleep**? Rouse yourself AIT
Ps 44:23 Rouse yourself! *D* not **reject** us forever. AIT
Ps 44:24 Why *d you* **hide** your face and forget our AIT
Ps 49:12 their wealth, *d* not **endure**; they are like the AIT
Ps 49:16 *D* not *be* **overawed** when others grow rich AIT
Ps 50:13 *D I* **eat** the flesh of bulls or drink the blood of AIT
Ps 51:11 *D* not **cast** me from your presence or take AIT
Ps 51:16 *You d* not **delight in** sacrifice, or I would AIT
Ps 51:16 *you d* not **take pleasure in** burnt offerings. AIT
Ps 52: 1 Why *d you* **boast** of evil, you mighty hero AIT
Ps 52: 1 Why **d** you boast all day long, you who are NDT
Ps 53: 4 *D all these* evildoers **know** nothing? They AIT
Ps 55: 1 to my prayer, O God, *d* not **ignore** my plea; AIT
Ps 56: 4 What *can* mere mortals **d** to me? H6913
Ps 56: 7 of their wickedness *d* not **let** them **escape**; AIT
Ps 56:11 am not afraid. What *can* man **d** to me? H6913
Ps 57: T To the tune of "*D* Not **Destroy**." Of David. AIT
Ps 58: T To the tune of "*D* Not **Destroy**." Of David. AIT
Ps 58: 1 *D you* rulers indeed **speak** justly? Do you AIT
Ps 58: 1 *D you* **judge** people with equity AIT
Ps 59: T To the tune of "*D* Not **Destroy**." Of David. AIT
Ps 59:11 But *d* not **kill** them, Lord our shield, or my AIT
Ps 62:10 *D* not **trust** in extortion or put vain hope in AIT
Ps 62:10 riches increase, *d* not **set** your heart on them. AIT

Ps 69:14 from the mire, *d* not *let me* **sink**; deliver me AIT
Ps 69:15 *D* not *let* the floodwaters **engulf** me or the AIT
Ps 69:17 *D* not **hide** your face from your servant AIT
Ps 69:27 *d* not *let them* **share** in your salvation. AIT
Ps 70: 5 my help and my deliverer; LORD, *d* not **delay**. AIT
Ps 71: 9 *D* not **cast** me **away** when I am old; do not AIT
Ps 71: 9 *d* not **forsake** me when my strength is gone. AIT
Ps 71:12 *D* not *be* **far** from me, my God; come quickly AIT
Ps 71:18 I am old and gray, *d* not **forsake** me, my God, AIT
Ps 74:11 Why *d you* **hold back** your hand, your right AIT
Ps 74:19 *D* not **hand over** the life of your dove to wild AIT
Ps 74:19 *d* not **forget** the lives of your afflicted people AIT
Ps 74:21 *D* not *let* the oppressed **retreat** in disgrace AIT
Ps 74:23 *D* not **ignore** the clamor of your adversaries AIT
Ps 75: T To the tune of "*D* Not **Destroy**." A psalm of AIT
Ps 75: 4 to the wicked, '*D* not **lift up** your horns. AIT
Ps 75: 5 *D* not **lift** your horns against heaven; do not AIT
Ps 75: 5 against heaven; *d* not **speak** so defiantly. AIT
Ps 79: 6 on the nations that *d* not **acknowledge** you, AIT
Ps 79: 6 the kingdoms that *d* not **call** on your name; AIT
Ps 79: 8 *D* not **hold** against us the sins of past AIT
Ps 83: 1 **d** not remain silent; do not turn a NDT
Ps 83: 1 *d* not **turn a deaf ear**, do not stand AIT
Ps 83: 1 not turn a deaf ear, *d* not **stand aloof**, O God. AIT
Ps 83: 9 **D** to them as you did to Midian, as you H6913
Ps 86:10 For you are great and **d** marvelous deeds H6913
Ps 88:10 *D you* **show** your wonders to the dead? Do AIT
Ps 88:10 *D* their spirits **rise up** and praise you? AIT
Ps 88:14 *d you* **reject** me and hide your face from me? AIT
Ps 89:30 forsake my law and *d* not **follow** my statutes, AIT
Ps 92: 6 Senseless people *d* not **know**, fools do not AIT
Ps 92: 6 people do not know, fools *d* not **understand**, AIT
Ps 95: 8 "*D* not **harden** your hearts as you did at AIT
Ps 101: 3 I hate *what* faithless people **d**; I will have H6913
Ps 101: 4 *I will* **have** nothing **to d with** what is evil. H3359
Ps 102: 2 *D* not **hide** your face from me when I am in AIT
Ps 102:24 "*D* not **take** me **away**, my God, in the midst AIT
Ps 103:20 you mighty ones *who* **d** his bidding, who H6913
Ps 103:21 you his servants *who* **d** his will. H6913
Ps 105:15 "*D* not **touch** my anointed ones; do my AIT
Ps 105:15 anointed ones; **d** my prophets no **harm**." H8317
Ps 106: 3 who act justly, *who* always **d** what is right. H6913
Ps 109: 1 My God, whom I praise, *d* not *remain* **silent**, AIT
Ps 115: 2 Why *d* the nations **say**, "Where is their God?" AIT
Ps 118: 6 What *can mere* mortals **d** to me? H6913
Ps 119: 3 *they* **d** no wrong but follow his ways. H7188
Ps 119: 8 obey your decrees; *d* not utterly **forsake** me. AIT
Ps 119:10 *d* not **let** me **stray** from your commands. AIT
Ps 119:19 *d* not **hide** your commands from me. AIT
Ps 119:31 statutes, LORD; *d* not **let me be put to shame**. AIT
Ps 119:51 unmercifully, but *I d* not **turn** from your law. AIT
Ps 119:65 **D** good to your servant according to your H6913
Ps 119:68 and *what you* **d** *is* **good**; teach me H3512
Ps 119:83 in the smoke, *I d* not **forget** your decrees. AIT
Ps 119:116 I will live; *d* not **let** my hopes **be dashed**. AIT
Ps 119:121 *d* not **leave** me to my oppressors. AIT
Ps 119:122 *d* not *let* the arrogant **oppress** me. AIT
Ps 119:132 as you **always d** to those who love your H5477
Ps 119:141 despised, *I d* not **forget** your precepts. AIT
Ps 119:155 for *they d* not **seek out** your decrees. AIT
Ps 119:158 with loathing, for *they d* not **obey** your word. AIT
Ps 120: 3 What *will he* **d** to you, and what more H5989
Ps 125: 3 righteous *might* **use** their hands **to d** evil. H8938
Ps 125: 4 **d good** to those who are good, to H3512
Ps 131: 1 *I d* not **concern** *myself* with great matters AIT
Ps 132:10 *d* not **reject** your anointed one. AIT
Ps 137: 6 roof of my mouth if *I d* not **remember** you, AIT
Ps 137: 6 if *I d* not **consider** Jerusalem my highest joy. AIT
Ps 138: 8 *d* not **abandon** the works of your hands. AIT
Ps 139:21 *D I* not **hate** those who hate you, LORD, and AIT
Ps 140: 8 *D* not **grant** the wicked their desires, LORD; AIT
Ps 140: 8 LORD; *d* not **let** their plans **succeed**. AIT
Ps 141: 4 **D** not **let** my heart **be drawn** to what is H5742
Ps 141: 4 evildoers; *d* not *let me* **eat** their delicacies. AIT
Ps 141: 8 I take refuge—*d* not **give** me **over to death**. AIT
Ps 143: 2 *D* not **bring** your servant into judgment, for AIT
Ps 143: 7 *D* not **hide** your face from me or I will be like AIT
Ps 143:10 Teach me to **d** your will, for you are my H6913
Ps 146: 3 *D* not **put** *your* **trust** in princes, in human AIT
Ps 147:20 no other nation; *they d* not **know** his laws. AIT
Ps 148: 8 stormy winds *that* **d** his bidding, H6913
Pr 1: 8 instruction and *d* not **forsake** your mother's AIT
Pr 1:10 sinful men entice you, *d* not **give in** *to* them. AIT
Pr 1:15 *d* not **go** along with them, do not set AIT
Pr 1:15 with them, **d not set** foot on their paths; AIT
Pr 1:25 all my advice and *d* not **accept** my rebuke, AIT
Pr 3: 1 My son, *d* not **forget** my teaching, but keep AIT
Pr 3: 7 *D* not **be** wise in your own eyes; fear the LORD AIT
Pr 3:11 My son, *d* not **despise** the LORD's discipline AIT
Pr 3:11 discipline, and *d* not **resent** his rebuke, AIT
Pr 3:21 *d* not **let** wisdom and understanding **out** of AIT
Pr 3:27 *D* not **withhold** good from those to whom it is AIT
Pr 3:28 *D* not **say** to your neighbor, "Come back AIT
Pr 3:29 *D* not **plot** harm against your neighbor, who AIT
Pr 3:30 *D* not **accuse** anyone for no reason—when AIT
Pr 3:31 *D* not **envy** the violent or choose any of their AIT
Pr 4: 2 learning, so *d* not **forsake** my teaching. AIT
Pr 4: 5 *d* **not** forget my words or turn away from AIT
Pr 4: 6 *D* not **forsake** wisdom, and she will protect AIT
Pr 4:13 on to instruction, *d* not **let it go**; guard it well, AIT
Pr 4:14 *D* not **set foot** on the path of the wicked or AIT
Pr 4:15 Avoid it, *d* not **travel** on it; turn from it and go AIT
Pr 4:16 For they cannot rest until *they* **d evil**; they H8317
Pr 4:19 *they d* not **know** what makes them stumble. AIT
Pr 4:21 *D* not **let** *them* **out** of your sight, keep them AIT
Pr 4:23 for **everything you d** flows from it. H2644
Pr 4:27 *D* not **turn** *to* the right or the left; keep your AIT
Pr 5: 7 listen to me; *d* not **turn aside** from what I say. AIT
Pr 5: 8 from her, *d* not **go near** the door of her house AIT
Pr 6: 3 So **d** this, my son, to free yourself, since H6913
Pr 6:20 command and *d* not **forsake** your mother's AIT
Pr 6:25 *D* not **lust** in your heart **after** her beauty or let AIT
Pr 6:30 *People d* not **despise** a thief if he steals to AIT
Pr 7:25 *D* not *let* your heart **turn** to her ways or stray AIT
Pr 8:33 instruction and be wise; *d* not **disregard** it. AIT
Pr 9: 8 *D* not **rebuke** mockers or they will hate you AIT
Pr 9:18 But little *d they* **know** that the dead are there AIT
Pr 10:29 it is the ruin of *those who* **d** evil. H7188
Pr 12:27 The lazy *d* not **roast** any game, but the AIT
Pr 14:22 *D* not those who plot evil **go astray**? But AIT
Pr 15:11 the LORD—how much more **d** human hearts! NDT
Pr 16: 3 Commit to the LORD **whatever** you **d**, and H5126
Pr 19: 7 how much more *d* their friends **avoid** them! AIT
Pr 19:18 *d* not **be a willing party** to their death. AIT
Pr 19:19 and *you will have to* **d** it **again**. H3578+6388
Pr 20: 4 Sluggards *d* not **plow** in season; so at harvest AIT
Pr 20:13 *D* not **love** sleep or you will grow poor; stay AIT
Pr 20:22 *D* not **say**, "I'll pay you back for this wrong!" AIT
Pr 20:23 dishonest scales **d** not please him. NDT
Pr 21: 3 *To* **d** what is right and just is more H6913
Pr 21: 7 for they refuse to **d** what is right. H6913
Pr 22:22 *D* not **exploit** the poor because they are poor AIT
Pr 22:22 they are poor and *d* not **crush** the needy in AIT
Pr 22:24 *D* not **make friends** with a hot-tempered AIT
Pr 22:24 *d* not **associate** with one easily angered AIT
Pr 22:26 *D* not **be** one who shakes hands in pledge AIT
Pr 22:28 *D* not **move** an ancient boundary stone set AIT
Pr 22:29 *D you* **see** someone skilled in their work AIT
Pr 23: 3 *D* not **crave** his delicacies, for that food is AIT
Pr 23: 4 *D* not **wear** *yourself* **out** to get rich; do not AIT
Pr 23: 4 to get rich; *d* not **trust** your own cleverness. AIT
Pr 23: 6 *D* not **eat** the food of a begrudging host, do AIT
Pr 23: 6 a begrudging host, *d* not **crave** his delicacies; AIT
Pr 23: 9 *D* not **speak** to fools, for they will scorn your AIT
Pr 23:10 *D* not **move** an ancient boundary stone or AIT
Pr 23:13 *D* not **withhold** discipline from a child; if you AIT
Pr 23:17 *D* not *let* your heart **envy** sinners, but always AIT
Pr 23:20 *D* not **join** those who drink too much wine AIT
Pr 23:22 and *d* not **despise** your mother when she is AIT
Pr 23:23 Buy the truth and *d* not **sell** it—wisdom AIT
Pr 23:31 *D* not **gaze** *at* wine when it is red, when it AIT
Pr 24: 1 *D* not **envy** the wicked, do not desire their AIT
Pr 24: 1 envy the wicked, *d* not **desire** their company; AIT
Pr 24:15 *D* not **lurk** like a thief near the house of the AIT
Pr 24:15 righteous, *d* not **plunder** their dwelling place AIT
Pr 24:17 *D* not **gloat** when your enemy falls; when AIT
Pr 24:17 they stumble, *d* not *let* your heart **rejoice**, AIT
Pr 24:19 *D* not **fret** because of evildoers or be envious AIT
Pr 24:21 and *d* not **join** with rebellious officials AIT
Pr 24:28 *D* not **testify** against your neighbor without AIT
Pr 24:29 *D* not **say**, "I'll do to them as they have done AIT
Pr 24:29 "*I'll* **d** to them as they have done to me H6913
Pr 25: 6 *D* not **exalt yourself** in the king's presence AIT
Pr 25: 6 and *d* not **claim** a place among his great AIT
Pr 25: 8 *d* not **bring** hastily to court, for what will you AIT
Pr 25: 8 what *will you* **d** in the end if your H6913
Pr 25: 9 *d* not **betray** another's confidence AIT
Pr 26: 4 *D* not **answer** a fool according to his folly, or AIT
Pr 26:12 *D you* **see** a person wise in their own eyes AIT
Pr 26:25 is charming, *d* not **believe** them, for seven AIT
Pr 27: 1 *D* not **boast** about tomorrow, for you do not AIT
Pr 27: 1 for *you d* not **know** what a day may bring. AIT
Pr 27:10 *D* not **forsake** your friend or a friend of your AIT
Pr 27:10 and *d* not **go** *to* your relative's house when AIT
Pr 27:24 riches **d** not endure forever, and a crown NDT
Pr 28: 5 Evildoers *d* not **understand** what is right, but AIT
Pr 28:21 a person *will* **d wrong** for a piece of H7321
Pr 29:20 *D you* **see** someone who speaks in haste AIT
Pr 30: 2 I **d** not have human understanding. NDT
Pr 30: 6 *D* not **add** to his words, or he will rebuke you AIT
Pr 30: 7 of you, LORD; *d* not **refuse** me before I die: AIT
Pr 30:10 "*D* not **slander** a servant to their master, or AIT
Pr 30:11 their fathers and *d* not **bless** their mothers; AIT
Pr 30:18 amazing for me, four *that I d* not **understand**: AIT
Pr 31: 3 *D* not **spend** your strength on women, your AIT
Pr 31:29 "Many women **d** noble things, but you H6913
Ecc 1: 3 What **d** people gain from all their labors at NDT
Ecc 2: 3 good for people *to* **d** under the heavens H6913
Ecc 2:12 the king's successor **d** than what has already NDT
Ecc 2:15 What then **d** I gain by being wise? NDT
Ecc 2:22 What *d* people **get** for all the toil and anxious AIT
Ecc 2:23 even at night their minds *d* not **rest**. AIT
Ecc 2:24 A person can **d** nothing better than to eat NDT
Ecc 3: 9 What **d** workers gain from their toil? NDT
Ecc 3:12 to be happy and to **d** good while they live H6913
Ecc 5: 1 who *d* not **know** that they do wrong. AIT
Ecc 5: 1 who do not know that they **d** wrong. H6913
Ecc 5: 2 *D* not *be* **quick** with your mouth, do not be AIT
Ecc 5: 2 *d* not *be* **hasty** in your heart to utter anything AIT
Ecc 5: 4 make a vow to God, *d* not **delay** to fulfill it. AIT
Ecc 5: 6 *D* not **let** your mouth lead you into sin. AIT
Ecc 5: 6 And *d* not **protest** to the temple messenger AIT
Ecc 5: 8 *d* not *be* **surprised** at such things AIT
Ecc 5:11 increase, so **d** those who consume them. H8045S
Ecc 5:16 and what **d** they gain, since they NDT
Ecc 6: 6 *D* not all **go** to the same place? AIT
Ecc 6: 8 What **d** the poor gain by knowing how to NDT
Ecc 7: 9 *D* not *be* quickly **provoked** in your spirit, for AIT
Ecc 7:10 *D* not **say**, "Why were the old days better AIT
Ecc 7:16 *D* not **be** overrighteous, neither be overwise AIT
Ecc 7:17 *D* not *be* **overwicked**, and do not be a fool AIT
Ecc 7:17 be overwicked, and *d* not **be** a fool—why die AIT
Ecc 7:21 *D* not pay **attention** to every word people say AIT
Ecc 8: 3 *D* not *be* **in a hurry** to leave the king's AIT
Ecc 8: 3 *D* not **stand up** for a bad cause, for he will do AIT
Ecc 8: 3 for *he will* **d** whatever he pleases. H6913
Ecc 8:11 hearts are filled with schemes to **d** wrong. H6913
Ecc 8:13 Yet because the wicked **d** not fear God, it NDT
Ecc 9: 1 the wise and **what** they **d** are in God's H6271
Ecc 9: 2 who offer sacrifices and *those* who **d** not. H2284S
Ecc 9: 7 God has already approved **what** you **d**. H5126
Ecc 9:10 Whatever your hand finds to **d**, do it with H6913
Ecc 9:10 hand finds to do, **d** it with all your might H6913
Ecc 10: 4 rises against you, *d* not **leave** your post AIT
Ecc 10:15 *they d* not **know** the way to town. AIT
Ecc 10:20 *D* not **revile** the king even in your thoughts AIT
Ecc 11: 2 *you d* not **know** what disaster may come AIT
Ecc 11: 5 As you *d* not **know** the path of the wind, or AIT
Ecc 11: 6 for you *d* not **know** which will succeed AIT
Ecc 11: 6 or whether both will **d** equally well. NDT
SS 1: 6 *D* not **stare** *at* me because I am dark AIT
SS 1: 8 If *you d* not **know**, most beautiful of women AIT
SS 2: 7 *D* not **arouse** or awaken love until it so AIT
SS 3: 5 *D* not **arouse** or awaken love until it so AIT
SS 8: 4 *D* not **arouse** or awaken love until it so AIT
SS 8: 8 What *shall we* **d** for our sister on the day H6913
Isa 1: 3 does not know, my people *d* not **understand**." AIT
Isa 1: 5 Why *d you* **persist** *in* rebellion AIT
Isa 1:17 Learn *to* **d right**; seek justice. Defend the H3512
Isa 1:23 *They d* not **defend the cause** *of* the fatherless AIT
Isa 2: 9 everyone humbled—*d* not **forgive** them. AIT
Isa 3: 7 *d* not **make** me the leader of the people." AIT
Isa 3: 9 their sin like Sodom; *they d* not **hide** it. AIT
Isa 3:15 What **d** you mean by crushing my people NDT
Isa 5: 5 you what I *am going to* **d** to my vineyard H6913
Isa 7: 4 *D* not **lose** heart because of these two AIT
Isa 7: 9 If *you d* not **stand firm** in *your* **faith**, you will AIT
Isa 8:12 "*D* not **call** conspiracy everything this people AIT
Isa 8:12 a conspiracy; *d* not **fear** what they fear, and AIT
Isa 8:12 do not fear what they fear, and *d* not **dread** it. AIT
Isa 10: 3 What *will you* **d** on the day of reckoning H6913
Isa 10:24 live in Zion, *d* not *be* **afraid** of the Assyrians AIT
Isa 13:17 who *d* not **care for** silver and have no delight AIT
Isa 14:29 *D* not **rejoice**, all you Philistines, that the rod AIT
Isa 16: 3 Hide the fugitives, *d* not **betray** the refugees. AIT
Isa 19:15 There is nothing Egypt *can* **d**—head or H6913
Isa 22: 4 *D* not **try** to console me over the destruction AIT
Isa 23:10 Till your land as they **d** along the Nile NDT
Isa 24: 9 No longer *d they* **drink** wine with a song; the AIT
Isa 26:10 to the wicked, *they d* not **learn** righteousness AIT
Isa 26:10 on doing evil and *d* not **regard** the majesty of AIT
Isa 26:11 your hand is lifted high, but *they d* not **see** it. AIT
Isa 26:13 but your name alone *d we* **honor**. AIT
Isa 26:14 they live no more; their spirits *d* not **rise**. AIT
Isa 28:10 **D** this, do that, a rule for this, a rule for H7422
Isa 28:10 Do this, **d** that, a rule for this, a rule for H7422
Isa 28:13 **D** this, do that, a rule for this, a rule for H7422
Isa 28:13 Do this, **d** that, a rule for this, a rule for H7422
Isa 28:21 Valley of Gibeon—to **d** his work, his H6913
Isa 29:15 *who* **d** their work in darkness and think H2118
Isa 31: 1 but *d* not **look** to the Holy One of Israel AIT
Isa 31: 4 will come down to **d battle** on Mount Zion H7371
Isa 35: 4 "Be strong, *d* not **fear**; your God will come AIT
Isa 36:14 *D* not **let** Hezekiah **deceive** you. AIT
Isa 36:15 *D* not **let** Hezekiah **persuade** you **to trust** in AIT
Isa 36:16 "*D* not **listen** to Hezekiah. This is what the AIT
Isa 36:18 "*D* not **let** Hezekiah **mislead** you when he AIT
Isa 36:21 king had commanded, "*D* not **answer** him." AIT
Isa 37: 6 *D* not *be* **afraid** of what you have heard AIT
Isa 37:10 *D* not **let** the god you **depend** on deceive you AIT
Isa 38: 7 to you that the LORD *will* **d** what he has H6913
Isa 40: 9 lift it up, *d* not *be* **afraid**; say to the towns of AIT
Isa 40:21 *D you* not **know**? Have you not heard? Has it AIT
Isa 40:24 no sooner *d they* **take root** in the ground AIT
Isa 40:27 Why *d you* **complain**, Jacob? Why do you say, AIT
Isa 40:27 Why *d you* **say**, Israel, "My way is hidden AIT
Isa 40:28 *D you* not **know**? Have you not heard? The AIT
Isa 41:10 So *d* not **fear**, for I am with you; do not be AIT
Isa 41:10 am with you; *d* not *be* **dismayed**, for I am AIT
Isa 41:13 says to you, *D* not **fear**; I will help you. AIT
Isa 41:14 *D* not *be* **afraid**, *you* worm Jacob, little Israel AIT
Isa 41:14 little Israel, **d** not fear, for I myself will help NDT
Isa 41:23 **D** *something*, whether **good** or bad, so H3512
Isa 42:16 These are the things *I will* **d**; I will not H6913
Isa 42:20 your ears are open, but *you d* not **listen**." AIT
Isa 43: 1 "*D* not **fear**, for I have redeemed you; I have AIT
Isa 43: 5 *D* not *be* **afraid**, for I am with you; I will bring AIT
Isa 43: 6 the south, '*D* not **hold** them **back**.' Bring my AIT
Isa 43:18 the former things; *d* not **dwell on** the past. AIT
Isa 43:19 it springs up; *d you* not **perceive** it? I am AIT
Isa 44: 2 *D* not *be* **afraid**, Jacob, my servant, Jeshurun AIT
Isa 44: 8 *D* not **tremble**, do not be afraid. Did I not AIT
Isa 44: 8 Do not tremble, *d* not *be* **afraid**. Did I not AIT
Isa 44:11 People *who* **d that** will be put to shame H2492S
Isa 45: 4 of honor, though *you d* not **acknowledge** me. AIT
Isa 45: 7 disaster; I, the LORD, **d** all these things. H6913

Isa 45:11 *d you* **question** me about my children AIT
Isa 46:10 will stand, and *I will* **d** all that I please. H6913
Isa 46:11 what I have planned, that *I will* **d**. H6913
Isa 48: 8 Well *d I* **know** how treacherous you are; you AIT
Isa 48:11 For my own sake, for my own sake, *I* **d** this. H6913
Isa 50: 2 **D** I lack the strength to rescue you NDT
Isa 51: 7 *D* not **fear** the reproach of mere mortals or be AIT
Isa 52: 5 "And now what **d** I have here?" declares the NDT
Isa 54: 2 curtains wide, *d* not **hold back**; lengthen your AIT
Isa 54: 4 "*D* not *be* **afraid**; you will not be put to AIT
Isa 54: 4 *D* not **fear disgrace**; you will not be AIT
Isa 55: 5 nations you *d* not **know** will come AIT
Isa 55:10 and *d* not **return** to it without watering the AIT
Isa 56: 1 "Maintain justice and **d** what is right, for H6913
Isa 57: 4 At whom *d you* **sneer** and stick out your AIT
Isa 57:11 long been silent that *you d* not **fear** me? AIT
Isa 58: 1 "Shout it aloud, *d* not **hold back**. Raise your AIT
Isa 58: 3 *you* **d** as you please and exploit all your H5162
Isa 58: 4 cannot fast as you **d** today and expect your NDT
Isa 58: 9 "If *you* **d away with** the yoke H6073+4946+9348
Isa 59: 8 The way of peace *they d* not **know**; there is AIT
Isa 60:22 the LORD; in its time *I will* **d** this **swiftly**." H2590
Isa 63:17 *d you* **make** us **wander** from your ways and AIT
Isa 63:17 harden our hearts so we **d** not revere you? NDT
Isa 64: 5 to the help of those who gladly **d** right, H6913
Isa 64: 9 *D* not *be* **angry** beyond measure, LORD; do not AIT
Isa 64: 9 *d* not **remember** our sins forever. AIT
Isa 65: 8 so *will I* **d** in behalf of my servants H6913
Isa 65:16 in the land *will* **d so** by the one true God H1385S
Isa 66: 9 *D I* **bring to the moment of birth** and not AIT
Isa 66: 9 "*D I* **close up** the womb when I bring to AIT
Jer 1: 6 "*I d* not **know how** to speak; I am too AIT
Jer 1: 7 LORD said to me, "*D* not **say**, 'I am too young. AIT
Jer 1: 8 *D* not *be* **afraid** of them, for I am with you AIT
Jer 1:11 "What *d* you **see**, Jeremiah?" "I AIT
Jer 1:13 "What *d* you **see**?" "I see a pot AIT
Jer 1:17 *D* not *be* **terrified** by them, or I will terrify AIT
Jer 2:25 **D not run** until your feet are bare and your H4979
Jer 2:29 "Why *d you* **bring charges** against me? You AIT
Jer 2:31 Why *d* my people **say**, 'We are free to roam AIT
Jer 2:36 Why *d you* **go about** so much, changing your AIT
Jer 3: 5 you talk, but *you* **d** all the evil you can." H6913
Jer 4: 3 ground and *d* not **sow** among thorns. AIT
Jer 4:22 are fools; *they d* not **know** me. They are AIT
Jer 4:22 doing evil; they know not how to **d good**." H3512
Jer 5: 3 **d** not your eyes look for truth? You NDT
Jer 5: 4 for *they d* not **know** the way of the LORD AIT
Jer 5:10 but *d* not **destroy** them **completely**. AIT
Jer 5:10 these people **d** not belong to the LORD. NDT
Jer 5:12 the LORD; they said, "He will **d** nothing! NDT
Jer 5:15 a people whose language *you d* not **know** AIT
Jer 5:15 whose speech *you d* not **understand**. AIT
Jer 5:21 who have eyes but *d* not **see**, who have ears AIT
Jer 5:21 do not see, who have ears but *d* not **hear**: AIT
Jer 5:24 *They d* not **say** to themselves, 'Let us fear the AIT
Jer 5:28 deeds have no limit; *they d* not **seek justice**. AIT
Jer 5:28 *They d* not **promote** the case of the fatherless AIT
Jer 5:28 *they d* not **defend** the just cause of the poor. AIT
Jer 5:31 But what *will you* **d** in the end? H6913
Jer 6:15 *they d* not even **know how** to blush. AIT
Jer 6:20 **What d I care about** incense H4200+4537+2296+4200+3276
Jer 6:20 acceptable; your sacrifices *d* not **please** me." AIT
Jer 6:25 *D* not **go out** *to* the fields or walk on the AIT
Jer 7: 4 *D* not **trust** in deceptive words and say, "This AIT
Jer 7: 6 if *you d* not **oppress** the foreigner, the AIT
Jer 7: 6 the widow and *d* not **shed** innocent blood AIT
Jer 7: 6 if *you d* not **follow** other gods to your AIT
Jer 7:10 safe to **d** all these detestable things? H6913
Jer 7:14 I did to Shiloh *I will now* **d** to the house H6913
Jer 7:16 "So *d* not **pray** for this people nor offer any AIT
Jer 7:16 petition for them; *d* not **plead** with me, for I AIT
Jer 7:17 *D* you not **see** what they are doing in the AIT
Jer 8: 4 fall down, *d they* not **get up**? When someone AIT
Jer 8: 4 someone turns away, *d they* not **return**? AIT
Jer 8: 6 attentively, but *they d* not **say** what is right. AIT
Jer 8: 7 But my people *d* not **know** the requirements AIT
Jer 8: 9 the LORD, what kind of wisdom **d** they have? NDT
Jer 8:12 *they d* not even **know how** to blush. AIT
Jer 9: 3 to another; *they d* not **acknowledge** me," AIT
Jer 9: 4 your friends; *d* not **trust** anyone in your clan. AIT
Jer 9: 7 what else *can I* **d** because of the sin of H6913
Jer 10: 2 "*D* not **learn** the ways of the nations or be AIT
Jer 10: 5 *D* not **fear** them; they can do no harm nor AIT
Jer 10: 5 *they can* **d** no **harm** nor can they do any H8317
Jer 10: 5 can do no harm nor *can* they **d** *any* **good**." H3512
Jer 10:21 are senseless and *d* not **inquire of** the LORD; AIT
Jer 10:21 so *they d* not **prosper** and all their flock is AIT
Jer 10:25 on the nations that *d* not **acknowledge** you, AIT
Jer 10:25 on the peoples who *d* not **call** on your name. AIT
Jer 11: 4 'Obey me and **d** everything I command H6913
Jer 11:14 "*D* not **pray** for this people or offer any plea AIT
Jer 11:21 "*D* not **prophesy** in the name of the LORD AIT
Jer 12: 1 Why *d* all the faithless **live at ease**? AIT
Jer 12: 6 *D* not **trust** them, though they speak well of AIT
Jer 13: 1 your waist, but *d* not **let it touch** water." AIT
Jer 13:15 pay attention, *d* not *be* **arrogant**, for the LORD AIT
Jer 13:17 If *you d* not **listen**, I will weep in secret AIT
Jer 13:23 Neither can you **d good** who are H3512
Jer 14: 7 sins testify against us, **d something**, LORD, H6913
Jer 14: 9 we bear your name; *d* not **forsake** us! AIT
Jer 14:10 love to wander; *they d* not **restrain** their feet. AIT
Jer 14:11 "*D* not **pray** for the well-being of this people. AIT
Jer 14:19 *D* you **despise** Zion? Why have AIT
Jer 14:21 For the sake of your name *d* not **despise** us AIT
Jer 14:21 *d* not **dishonor** your glorious throne. AIT
Jer 14:21 your covenant with us and *d* not **break** it. AIT
Jer 14:22 *D* any of the worthless idols of the nations **bring rain** AIT
Jer 14:22 *D* the skies *themselves* **send down** showers AIT
Jer 15:14 to your enemies in a land *you d* not **know**, AIT
Jer 15:15 *d* not **take** me **away**; think of how AIT
Jer 16: 5 "*D* not **enter** a house where there is a funeral AIT
Jer 16: 5 *d* not **go** to mourn or show sympathy AIT
Jer 16: 8 "And *d* not **enter** a house where there is AIT
Jer 16:20 *D* people **make** their own gods? Yes, but they AIT
Jer 17: 4 to your enemies in a land *you d* not **know**, AIT
Jer 17:17 *D* not **be** a terror to me; you are my refuge in AIT
Jer 17:22 *D* not **bring** a load **out** of your houses or do AIT
Jer 17:22 out of your houses or **d** any work on the H6913
Jer 17:27 But if *you d* not **obey** me to keep the Sabbath AIT
Jer 18: 6 He said, "Can I not **d** with you, Israel, as H6913
Jer 18:10 the **good** I had intended to **d** *for* it. H3208+3512
Jer 18:14 *D* its cool waters from distant sources *ever* **stop** AIT
Jer 18:23 *D* not **forgive** their crimes or blot out their AIT
Jer 19:12 This is what *I will* **d** to this place and to H6913
Jer 21:10 I have determined to **d** this city harm and not NDT
Jer 22: 3 the LORD says: **D** what is just and right H6913
Jer 22: 3 **D** no **wrong** or violence to the foreigner H3561
Jer 22: 3 and *d* not **shed** innocent blood in this place. AIT
Jer 22: 5 But if *you d* not **obey** these commands AIT
Jer 22:10 *D* not **weep** for the dead king or mourn his AIT
Jer 22:28 hurled out, cast into a land *they d* not **know**? AIT
Jer 23: 5 will reign wisely and **d** what is just and H6913
Jer 23:16 "*D* not **listen** to what the prophets are AIT
Jer 23:24 "*D* not I **fill** heaven and earth? AIT
Jer 23:28 For what **has** straw **to d with** grain? H4200
Jer 23:32 *They d* not **benefit** these people **in the least**," AIT
Jer 24: 3 LORD asked me, "What *d* you **see**, Jeremiah?" AIT
Jer 25: 6 *D* not **follow** other gods to serve and worship AIT
Jer 25: 6 *d* not **arouse** my **anger** with what your hands AIT
Jer 26: 2 I command you; *d* not **omit** a word. AIT
Jer 26: 4 If *you d* not **listen** to me and follow my law AIT
Jer 26: 5 if you *d* not **listen** to the words of my AIT
Jer 26: 9 Why *d you* **prophesy** in the LORD's name that AIT
Jer 26:14 **d** with me whatever you think is good H6913
Jer 27: 9 So *d* not **listen** to your prophets, your diviners AIT
Jer 27:14 *D* not **listen** to the words of the prophets who AIT
Jer 27:16 *D* not **listen** to the prophets who say, 'Very AIT
Jer 27:17 *D* not **listen** to them. Serve the king of AIT
Jer 28: 6 *May* the LORD **d** so! May the LORD H6913
Jer 29: 6 Increase in number there; *d* not **decrease**. AIT
Jer 29: 8 *D* not *let* the prophets and diviners among you **deceive** AIT
Jer 29: 8 *D* not **listen** to the dreams you encourage AIT
Jer 29:32 the good things I *will* **d** for my people, H6913
Jer 30: 6 Then why *d I* **see** every strong man with his AIT
Jer 30:10 " 'So *d* not *be* **afraid**, Jacob my servant; do AIT
Jer 30:10 Jacob my servant; *d* not *be* **dismayed**, Israel,' AIT
Jer 30:15 Why *d you* **cry out** over your wound, your AIT
Jer 32: 3 "Why *d* you **prophesy** as you do? AIT
Jer 32: 3 "Why do you prophesy as you **d**? NDT
Jer 32:23 *they did* not **d** what you commanded H6913
Jer 32:23 not do what you commanded them to **d**. H6913
Jer 32:35 that they *should* **d** such a detestable thing H6913
Jer 33: 3 unsearchable things *you d* not **know**. AIT
Jer 33: 9 that hear of all the good things I **d** *for* it; H6913
Jer 33:15 *he will* **d** what is just and right in the land. H6913
Jer 35: 6 they replied, "*We d* not **drink** wine, because AIT
Jer 35:14 To this day *they d* not **drink** wine, because AIT
Jer 35:15 *d* not **follow** other gods to serve them. AIT
Jer 36: 8 Jeremiah the prophet told him to **d**; NDT
Jer 37: 9 *D* not **deceive** yourselves, thinking, 'The AIT
Jer 37:20 *D* not **send** me **back** to the house of AIT
Jer 38: 5 "The king **can d** nothing to oppose you." H3523
Jer 38:14 "*D* not **hide** anything from me. AIT
Jer 38:24 "*D* not *let* anyone **know** about this AIT
Jer 38:25 *d* not **hide** it from us or we will kill you AIT
Jer 39:12 don't harm him but **d** for him whatever he H6913
Jer 40: 4 after you; but if you **d** not want to, then NDT
Jer 40: 9 "*D* not *be* **afraid** to serve the Babylonians," AIT
Jer 40:16 son of Kareah, "Don't **d** such a thing! H6913
Jer 42: 3 we should go and what *we should* **d**." H6913
Jer 42: 5 against us if we *d* not **act** in accordance with AIT
Jer 42:11 *D* not *be* **afraid** of the king of Babylon, whom AIT
Jer 42:11 *D* not *be* **afraid** of him, declares the LORD, for AIT
Jer 42:15 to go to Egypt and *you d* **go** to settle there, AIT
Jer 42:19 the LORD has told you, '*D* not **go** *to* Egypt. AIT
Jer 42:20 tell us everything he says and *we will* **d** it. H6913
Jer 44: 4 '*D* not **do** this detestable thing that I hate! AIT
Jer 44: 4 '*Do* not **d** this detestable thing that I hate! H6913
Jer 44:17 *We will* **certainly d** everything we H6913+6913
Jer 44:25 you said you would **d** when you promised, NDT
Jer 44:25 "*Go ahead* then, **d** what you H6913+6913
Jer 45: 5 things for yourself? *D* not **seek** them. AIT
Jer 46: 5 What *d I* **see**? They are terrified, they are AIT
Jer 46:27 "*D* not *be* **afraid**, Jacob my servant; do not be AIT
Jer 46:27 Jacob my servant; *d* not *be* **dismayed**, Israel. AIT
Jer 46:28 D not *be* **afraid**, Jacob my servant, for I am AIT
Jer 49: 1 Why *d* his people **live** in its towns? AIT
Jer 49: 4 Why *d you* **boast** of your valleys, boast of AIT
Jer 49:12 "If those who **d** not deserve to drink the cup NDT
Jer 49:36 be a nation where Elam's exiles *d* not **go**. AIT
Jer 50: 9 warriors *who d* not **return** empty-handed. AIT
Jer 50:15 **d** to her as she has done to others. H6913
Jer 50:21 "**D** everything I have commanded you H6913
Jer 50:25 Almighty has work to **d** in the land of the NDT
Jer 50:29 her deeds; **d** to her as she has done. H6913
Jer 51: 3 *D* not **spare** her young men; completely AIT
Jer 51: 6 *D* not **be destroyed** because of her sins AIT
Jer 51:46 *D* not **lose** heart or be afraid when rumors AIT
Jer 51:50 escaped the sword, leave and *d* not **linger**! AIT
La 3:56 "*D* not **close** your ears to my cry for relief." AIT
La 3:57 when I called you, and you said, "*D* not **fear**." AIT
La 5:20 Why *d you* always **forget** us? Why do you AIT
La 5:20 Why *d you* **forsake** us so long? AIT
Eze 2: 6 *d* not *be* **afraid** of them or their words. AIT
Eze 2: 6 *D* not *be* **afraid**, though briers and thorns are AIT
Eze 2: 6 *D* not *be* **afraid** of what they say or be AIT
Eze 2: 8 *D* not **rebel** like that rebellious people; open AIT
Eze 3: 9 *D* not *be* **afraid** *of* them or terrified by them AIT
Eze 3:18 and *you d* not **warn** them or speak out to AIT
Eze 3:19 But if you *d* **warn** the wicked person and they AIT
Eze 3:19 wicked person and *they d* not **turn** from their AIT
Eze 3:21 But if you *d* **warn** the righteous person not to AIT
Eze 3:21 person not to sin and they *d* not **sin**, AIT
Eze 5: 9 *I will* **d** to you what I have never done H6913
Eze 5: 9 never done before and *will* never **d** again. H6913
Eze 8: 6 "Son of man, *d you* **see** what they are doing AIT
Eze 8:15 He said to me, "*D you* **see** this, son of man AIT
Eze 8:17 the people of Judah *to* **d** the detestable H6913
Eze 9: 6 *d* not **touch** anyone who has the mark. AIT
Eze 12: 2 eyes to see but *d* not **see** and ears to hear AIT
Eze 12: 2 do not see and ears to hear but *d* not **hear**, AIT
Eze 14: 5 I will **d** this to recapture the hearts of the NDT
Eze 15: 3 *D they* **make** pegs from it to hang things on? AIT
Eze 16: 5 enough to **d** any of these things H6913
Eze 16:30 when you **d** all these things, acting H6913
Eze 17:12 '*D you* not **know** what these things mean? AIT
Eze 17:24 " 'I the LORD have spoken, and *I will* **d** it.' " H6913
Eze 18: 2 "**What d you** people **mean** H4537+4200+4013
Eze 18:14 he sees them, he *does* not **d** such things: H6913
Eze 18:23 *D I* **take any pleasure in** the death of the AIT
Eze 20: 7 and *d* not **defile yourselves** with the idols of AIT
Eze 20:18 "*D* not **follow** the statutes of your parents AIT
Eze 21:24 revealing your sins in all *that* you **d** H6613
Eze 22:14 I the LORD have spoken, and *I will* **d** it. H6913
Eze 22:26 Her priests **d violence** *to* my law and H2803
Eze 22:26 *they d* not **distinguish** between the holy and AIT
Eze 24:16 Yet *d* not **lament** or weep or shed any tears. AIT
Eze 24:17 Groan quietly; **d** not mourn for the dead H6913
Eze 24:17 *d* not **cover** your mustache and beard or eat AIT
Eze 24:19 us what these things **have to d with** us? H4200
Eze 24:22 And *you will* **d** as I have done. You will H6913
Eze 24:24 *you will* **d** just as he has done. H6913
Eze 32:27 But *they d* not **lie** with the fallen warriors of AIT
Eze 33: 8 and *you d* not **speak out** to dissuade them AIT
Eze 33: 9 But if *you d* **warn** the wicked person to turn AIT
Eze 33: 9 to turn from their ways and *they d* not **do so**, AIT
Eze 33: 9 ways and *they do* not **d so**, H8740+4946+2006S
Eze 33:13 trust in their righteousness and **d** evil, H6913
Eze 33:14 from their sin and **d** what is just and right H6913
Eze 33:15 that give life, and **d** no evil—that person H6913
Eze 33:26 on your sword, *you* **d** detestable things H6913
Eze 33:31 as they usually **d**, and sit before you H4427S
Eze 33:31 but *they d* not **put** them **into practice**. AIT
Eze 33:32 your words but *d* not **put** them **into practice**. AIT
Eze 34: 3 animals, but *you d* not **take care** of the flock. AIT
Eze 36:22 of Israel, that I *am going to* **d** these things H6913
Eze 36:36 I the LORD have spoken, and *I will* **d** it.' H6913
Eze 36:37 yield to Israel's plea and **d** this for them: H6913
Eze 45: 9 oppression and **d** what is just and H6913
Eze 45:20 *You are to* **d** the same on the seventh day H6913
Eze 47: 6 "Son of man, *d you* **see** this?" Then he AIT
Da 2: 5 If *you d* not **tell** me what my dream was and AIT
Da 2: 9 If *you d* not **tell** me the dream, there is only AIT
Da 2:10 on earth who can **d** what the king asks! A10252
Da 2:11 they **d** not live among humans. A10029
Da 2:24 "*D* not **execute** the wise men of Babylon. AIT
Da 3: 4 this is what you are commanded to **d**: NDT
Da 3:14 that you *d* not **serve** my gods or worship the AIT
Da 3:15 But if *you d* not **worship** it, you will be thrownAIT
Da 3:16 *we d* not **need** to defend ourselves before AIT
Da 4:19 *d* not *let* the dream or its meaning **alarm** you." AIT
Da 6: 4 were unable to **d so**. A10708+10353+10544S
Da 6: 5 it has **something to d with** the law of A10089
Da 9:18 We *d* not **make** requests of you because we AIT
Da 9:19 my God, *d* not **delay**, because your city and AIT
Da 10:12 he continued, "*D* not *be* **afraid**, Daniel. AIT
Da 10:19 "*D* not *be* **afraid**, *you* who are highly AIT
Da 10:20 "*D you* **know** why I have come to you? AIT
Da 11: 3 with great power and **d** as he pleases. H6913
Da 11:16 The invader *will* **d** as he pleases; no one H6913
Da 11:36 "The king *will* **d** as he pleases. He will H6913
Hos 4:15 adultery, *d* not *let* Judah *become* **guilty**. AIT
Hos 4:15 "*D* not **go** *to* Gilgal; do not go up to Beth AIT
Hos 4:15 not go to Gilgal; *d* not **go up** *to* Beth Aven. AIT
Hos 4:15 And *d* not **swear**, 'As surely as AIT
Hos 5: 4 "Their deeds *d* not **permit** them to return to AIT
Hos 5: 4 their heart; *they d* not **acknowledge** the LORD. AIT
Hos 6: 4 "What *can I* **d** with you, Ephraim? What H6913
Hos 6: 4 What *can I* **d** with you, Judah H6913
Hos 6: 9 a victim, so **d** bands of priests; they NDT
Hos 7: 2 they *d* not **realize** that I remember all AIT
Hos 7:14 *They d* not **cry out** to me from their hearts AIT

Hos 7:16 *They d* not **turn** *to* the Most High; they are AIT
Hos 9: 1 *D* not **rejoice**, Israel; do not be jubilant like AIT
Hos 9: 1 *d* not *be* **jubilant** like the other nations. AIT
Hos 9: 5 What *will you* **d** on the day of your H6913
Hos 10: 3 if we had a king, what *could he* **d** for us?" H6913
Hos 12:11 *D they* **sacrifice** bulls in Gilgal AIT
Hos 14: 8 what more **have I to d with** idols? H4200
Joel 2: 8 *They d* not **jostle** each other; each marches AIT
Joel 2:17 *D* not **make** your inheritance an object of AIT
Joel 2:21 *D* not *be* **afraid**, land of Judah; be glad and AIT
Joel 2:22 *D* not *be* **afraid**, *you* wild animals, for the AIT
Am 3: 3 *D* two **walk** together unless they have agreed AIT
Am 3: 3 together unless they have agreed to **d** so? NDT
Am 3: 6 sounds in a city, *d* not the people **tremble**? AIT
Am 3:10 *"They d* not **know how** to do right," declares AIT
Am 3:10 "They do not know how *to* **d** right, H6913
Am 4: 5 this is what you love to **d**," declares the NDT
Am 4:12 "Therefore this is what *I will* **d** to you H6913
Am 4:12 and because *I will* **d** this to you H6913
Am 5: 5 *d* not **seek** Bethel, do not go to Gilgal, do not AIT
Am 5: 5 do not seek Bethel, *d* not **go** to Gilgal, do not AIT
Am 5: 5 not go to Gilgal, *d* not **journey** *to* Beersheba. AIT
Am 5:18 Why *d you* **long for** the day of the LORD AIT
Am 6: 6 but *you d* not **grieve** over the ruin of Joseph. AIT
Am 6:12 *D* horses **run** on the rocky crags? Does one AIT
Am 7: 8 the LORD asked me, "What *d you* **see**, Amos?" AIT
Am 7:12 bread there and *d your* **prophesying** there. AIT
Am 7:16 You say, " '*D* not **prophesy** against Israel AIT
Am 8: 2 "What *d* you **see**, Amos?" he asked. AIT
Am 8: 4 the needy and **d away with** the poor of H8697
Am 9:12 declares the LORD, *who will* **d** these things. H6913
Jnh 1: 8 What kind of work **d** you do? Where do you NDT
Jnh 1: 8 What kind of work do you **d**? Where do you NDT
Jnh 1: 8 Where *d you* **come** from? What is AIT
Jnh 1:11 "What *should we* **d** to you to make the H6913
Jnh 1:14 *d* not *let us* **die** for taking this man's life. AIT
Jnh 1:14 *D* not **hold** us **accountable** *for* killing an AIT
Jnh 3: 7 *D* not *let* people or animals, herds or flocks, **taste** AIT
Jnh 3: 7 taste anything; *d* not *let them* **eat** or drink. AIT
Mic 2: 1 it out because it is in their power to **d** it. NDT
Mic 2: 6 "*D* not **prophesy**," their prophets say. "Do not AIT
Mic 2: 6 "*D* not **prophesy** about these things; disgrace AIT
Mic 2: 7 Does he **d** such things?" "Do H5095
Mic 2: 7 "*D* not my words **do good** to the one whose AIT
Mic 2: 7 "*Do* not my words **d good** to the one H3512
Mic 4: 9 Why *d you* now **cry aloud**—have you no king AIT
Mic 4:12 But they *d* not **know** the thoughts of the LORD AIT
Mic 4:12 of the LORD; *they d* not **understand** his plan AIT
Mic 5: 7 which *d* not **wait** for anyone or depend on AIT
Mic 7: 5 *D* not **trust** a neighbor; put no confidence in AIT
Mic 7: 8 *D* not **gloat** over me, my enemy! Though I AIT
Mic 7:18 *You d* not **stay** angry forever but delight to AIT
Hab 1: 2 must I call for help, but *you d* not **listen**? AIT
Hab 1: 2 out to you, "Violence!" but *you d* not **save**? AIT
Hab 1: 3 Why *d you* **make** me **look** *at* injustice? Why AIT
Hab 1: 3 Why *d you* **tolerate** wrongdoing AIT
Hab 1: 5 For *I am going to* **d** something in your H7188
Hab 1:13 Why then *d you* **tolerate** the treacherous AIT
Zep 1:12 'The LORD *will d* nothing, either **good** or bad. AIT
Zep 2: 3 the land, *you who* **d** what he commands. H7188
Zep 3: 4 the sanctuary and **d violence** *to* the law. H2803
Zep 3:13 *They will* **d** no wrong; they will tell no lies. H6913
Zep 3:16 they will say to Jerusalem, "*D* not **fear**, Zion; AIT
Zep 3:16 Zion; *d* not *let* your hands **hang limp**. AIT
Hag 2: 5 my Spirit remains among you. *D* not **fear**.' AIT
Hag 2:14 'Whatever they **d** and whatever H5126+3338
Zec 1: 4 *D* not **be** like your ancestors, to whom the AIT
Zec 1: 5 And the prophets, *d they* **live** forever? AIT
Zec 1: 6 deserve, just as he determined to **d**. H6913
Zec 1:21 "What are these coming to **d**?" He H6913
Zec 4: 2 asked me, "What *d you* **see**?" I answered, "I AIT
Zec 4: 5 answered, "*D you* not **know** what these are?" AIT
Zec 4:13 He replied, "*D you* not **know** what these are?" AIT
Zec 5: 2 asked me, "What *d you* **see**?" I answered, "I AIT
Zec 7:10 *D* not **oppress** the widow or the fatherless, the AIT
Zec 7:10 the poor. *D* not **plot** evil *against* each other AIT
Zec 8:13 be a blessing. *D* not *be* **afraid**, but let your AIT
Zec 8:15 have determined to **d good** again to H3512
Zec 8:15 to Jerusalem and Judah. *D* not *be* **afraid**. AIT
Zec 8:16 These are the things *you are to* **d**: Speak H6913
Zec 8:17 *d* not **plot** evil **against** each other, and do not AIT
Zec 8:17 each other, and *d* not **love** to swear falsely. AIT
Zec 11: 5 Their own shepherds *d* not **spare** them. AIT
Zec 14:17 of the earth *d* not **go up** to Jerusalem to AIT
Zec 14:18 Egyptian people *d* not **go up** and take part, AIT
Zec 14:18 the nations that *d* not **go up** to celebrate the AIT
Zec 14:19 the nations that *d* not **go up** to celebrate the AIT
Mal 2: 2 If *you d* not **listen**, and if you do not resolve to AIT
Mal 2: 2 if *you d* not **resolve** to honor my name," AIT
Mal 2:10 **D** we not all have one Father? Did not one NDT
Mal 2:10 Why *d we* **profane** the covenant of our AIT
Mal 2:13 Another thing *you* **d**: You flood the LORD's H6913
Mal 2:15 and *d* not *be* **unfaithful** to the wife of your AIT
Mal 2:16 be on your guard, and *d* not *be* **unfaithful**. AIT
Mal 2:17 "All *who* **d** evil are good in the eyes of H6913
Mal 3: 5 of justice, but *d* not **fear** me," says the LORD AIT
Mal 3: 6 "I the LORD *d* not **change**. So you, the AIT
Mal 3:14 What **d** we gain by carrying out his NDT
Mal 3:18 who serve God and *those* who **d** not. H6268S
Mt 1:20 *d* not *be* **afraid** to take Mary home as your AIT
Mt 3: 9 And *d* not **think** you can say to yourselves AIT
Mt 3:14 be baptized by you, and *d you* **come** to me?" AIT
Mt 3:15 it is proper for us to **d** this to fulfill all NDT
Mt 4: 7 '*D* not **put** the Lord your God **to the test**.' " AIT
Mt 5:15 Neither *d people* **light** a lamp and put it AIT
Mt 5:17 "*D* not **think** that I have come to abolish the AIT
Mt 5:25 **D** it while you are still together on the way NDT
Mt 5:33 long ago, '*D* not **break** *your* **oath**, but fulfill to AIT
Mt 5:34 I tell you, *d* not **swear an oath** at all: either AIT
Mt 5:36 And *d* not **swear** by your head, for you cannot AIT
Mt 5:39 But I tell you, *d* not **resist** an evil person. AIT
Mt 5:42 and *d* not **turn away** from the one who wants AIT
Mt 5:47 *D* not even pagans **do** that? AIT
Mt 5:47 *Do* not even pagans **d** that? G4472
Mt 6: 1 If you **d**, you will have no reward G3590+1145S
Mt 6: 2 *d* not **announce** it **with trumpets**, as AIT
Mt 6: 2 as the hypocrites **d** in the synagogues G4472
Mt 6: 3 *d* not *let* your left hand **know** what your right AIT
Mt 6: 5 when you pray, *d* not **be** like the hypocrites AIT
Mt 6: 7 you pray, *d* not *keep on* **babbling** like pagans AIT
Mt 6: 8 *D* not *be* **like** them, for your Father knows AIT
Mt 6:15 But if *you d* not **forgive** others their sins, your AIT
Mt 6:16 fast, *d* not **look** somber as the hypocrites do AIT
Mt 6:16 do not look somber as the hypocrites **d**, for NDT
Mt 6:19 "*D* not **store up** for yourselves treasures on AIT
Mt 6:20 where moths and vermin *d* not **destroy**, and AIT
Mt 6:20 where thieves *d* not **break in** and steal. AIT
Mt 6:25 I tell you, *d* not **worry about** your life, what AIT
Mt 6:26 *they d* not **sow** or reap or store away in barns AIT
Mt 6:28 "And why *d you* **worry** about clothes? See AIT
Mt 6:28 of the field grow. *They d* not **labor** or spin. AIT
Mt 6:31 So *d* not **worry**, saying, 'What shall we eat?' AIT
Mt 6:34 Therefore *d* not **worry** about tomorrow, for AIT
Mt 7: 1 "*D* not **judge**, or you too will be judged. AIT
Mt 7: 3 "Why *d you* **look at** the speck of sawdust in AIT
Mt 7: 6 "*D* not **give** dogs what is sacred; do not throw AIT
Mt 7: 6 is sacred; *d* not **throw** your pearls to pigs. AIT
Mt 7: 6 **If you d**, they may trample them under G3607
Mt 7:12 **d** to others what you would have them do G4472
Mt 7:12 what you would have them **d** to you, G4472
Mt 7:16 *D people* **pick** grapes from thornbushes, or AIT
Mt 8: 8 *I d* not **deserve** to have you come under my AIT
Mt 8: 9 say to my servant, '**D** this,' and he does it G4472
Mt 8:29 **What d you want with us** G5515+5516+1609+2779+5148
Mt 9: 4 "Why *d you* **entertain** evil **thoughts** in your AIT
Mt 9:14 fast often, but your disciples *d* not **fast**?" AIT
Mt 9:17 Neither *d people* **pour** new wine into old AIT
Mt 9:17 If they **d**, the skins will burst; the G3590+1145S
Mt 9:28 "*D you* **believe** that I am able to do this?" AIT
Mt 9:28 "Do you believe that I am able *to* **d** this?" G4472
Mt 10: 5 "*D* not **go** among the Gentiles or enter any AIT
Mt 10: 9 "*D* not **get** any gold or silver or copper to take AIT
Mt 10:19 *d* not **worry about** what to say or how to say AIT
Mt 10:26 "So *d* not *be* **afraid** of them, for there is AIT
Mt 10:28 *D* not *be* **afraid** of those who kill the body AIT
Mt 10:34 "*D* not **suppose** that I have come to bring AIT
Mt 11:26 this is what you were pleased *to* **d**. G1181+1869
Mt 12: 4 which was not lawful for them *to* **d**, but G2266S
Mt 12:12 it is lawful *to* **d** good on the Sabbath." G4472
Mt 12:27 by whom *d* your people **drive** them **out**? AIT
Mt 13:10 "Why *d you* **speak** to the people in parables?" AIT
Mt 13:13 *they d* not **see**; though hearing AIT
Mt 13:13 hearing, *they d* not **hear** or understand. AIT
Mt 13:28 '*D you* **want** us to go and pull them up? AIT
Mt 13:41 that causes sin and all who **d** evil. G4472
Mt 13:58 And *he did* not **d** many miracles there G4472
Mt 14:16 "*They d* not **need** to go away. AIT
Mt 15: 2 "Why *d* your disciples **break** the tradition of AIT
Mt 15: 3 "And why *d* you **break** the command of God AIT
Mt 15:12 "*D you* **know** that the Pharisees were AIT
Mt 15:32 *I d* not **want** to send them away hungry, or AIT
Mt 15:34 "How many loaves *d you* **have**?" Jesus asked AIT
Mt 16: 9 *D you* still not **understand**? Don't you AIT
Mt 16:13 "Who *d* people **say** the Son of Man is?" AIT
Mt 16:15 he asked. "Who *d you* **say** I am?" AIT
Mt 16:23 *you d* not **have in mind** the concerns of God AIT
Mt 17:10 "Why then *d* the teachers of the law **say** that AIT
Mt 17:25 "What *d you* **think**, Simon?" he AIT
Mt 17:25 whom *d* the kings of the earth **collect** duty AIT
Mt 18:10 "See that *you d* not **despise** one of these AIT
Mt 18:12 "What *d you* **think**? If a man owns a hundred AIT
Mt 19:14 come to me, and *d* not **hinder** them, for the AIT
Mt 19:16 what good thing *must I* **d** to get eternal G4472
Mt 19:17 "Why *d you* **ask** me about what is good?" AIT
Mt 19:20 the young man said. "What *d I* still **lack**?" AIT
Mt 20:15 I have the right *to* **d** what I want with my G4472
Mt 20:32 "What *d you* **want** me to do for you? AIT
Mt 20:32 "What do you want *me to* **d** for you?" G4472
Mt 21:16 "*D you* **hear** what these children are saying?" AIT
Mt 21:21 if you have faith and *d* not **doubt**, not only AIT
Mt 21:21 not only *can you* **d** what was done to the G4472
Mt 21:28 "What *d you* **think**? There was a man who AIT
Mt 21:40 what *will he* **d** to those tenants? G4472
Mt 22:29 are in error *because you d* not **know** the AIT
Mt 22:42 "What *d* you **think** about the Messiah? Whose AIT
Mt 23: 3 you must be careful *to* **d** everything they G4472
Mt 23: 3 But *d* not **do** what they do, for they do not AIT
Mt 23: 3 But *do* not **d** what they do, for they do not G4472
Mt 23: 3 But do not do what they **d**, for they do not G2240
Mt 23: 3 for *they d* not **practice** what they preach. AIT
Mt 23: 5 "Everything they **d** is done for people to G2240
Mt 23: 9 And *d* not **call** anyone on earth 'father,' for AIT
Mt 23:13 *You* yourselves *d* not **enter**, nor will you let AIT
Mt 24: 2 "*D you* **see** all these things?" he asked. "Truly AIT
Mt 24:23 or, 'There he is!' *d* not **believe** it. AIT
Mt 24:26 the wilderness,' *d* not **go out**; or, 'Here he is, AIT
Mt 24:26 in the inner rooms,' *d* not **believe** it. AIT
Mt 24:42 because *you d* not **know** on what day your AIT
Mt 24:44 come at an hour when *you d* not **expect** him. AIT
Mt 25:13 because *you d* not **know** the day or the hour. AIT
Mt 25:45 whatever *you did* not **d** for one of the G4472
Mt 25:45 of the least of these, *you did* not **d** for me. G4472
Mt 26:17 "Where *d you* **want** us to make preparations AIT
Mt 26:50 Jesus replied, "**D** what you came for, friend." NDT
Mt 26:53 *D you* **think** I cannot call on my Father, AIT
Mt 26:65 Why *d we* **need** any more witnesses AIT
Mt 26:66 What *d you* **think**?" "He is worthy of death," AIT
Mt 27:17 "Which one *d you* **want** me to release to you: AIT
Mt 27:19 *have* anything *to d with* that **innocent** *man*, AIT
Mt 27:21 of the two *d you* **want** me to release to AIT
Mt 27:22 "What *shall I* **d**, then, with Jesus who is G4472
Mt 28: 5 to the women, "*D* not *be* **afraid**, for I know AIT
Mt 28:10 said to them, "*D* not *be* **afraid**. Go and tell AIT
Mk 1:24 "**What d** you **want with** us, Jesus of G5515+5516
Mk 3: 4 *to* **d** good or to do evil, to save life or to G4472
Mk 3: 4 to do good or *to* **d evil**, to save life or to G2803
Mk 4:21 "*D you* **bring** *in* a lamp to put it under a bowl AIT
Mk 4:40 are you so afraid? *D you* still **have** no faith?" AIT
Mk 5: 7 "**What d** you **want with** me G5515+5516
Mk 6: 5 He could not **d** any miracles there, except G4472
Mk 6:38 "How many loaves *d you* **have**?" he asked AIT
Mk 7: 3 all the Jews *d* not **eat** unless they give AIT
Mk 7: 4 the marketplace *they d* not **eat** unless they AIT
Mk 7:12 no longer let them **d** anything for their G4472
Mk 7:13 And *you* **d** many things like that. G4472
Mk 8: 5 "How many loaves *d you* **have**?" Jesus asked AIT
Mk 8:17 *D you* still not **see** or understand AIT
Mk 8:18 *D you* **have** eyes but fail to see, and ears AIT
Mk 8:21 said to them, "*D you* still not **understand**?" AIT
Mk 8:23 Jesus asked, "*D you* **see** anything? AIT
Mk 8:27 he asked them, "Who *d* people **say** I am?" AIT
Mk 8:29 "Who *d you* **say** I am?" Peter AIT
Mk 8:33 "*You d* not **have in mind** the concerns of God, AIT
Mk 9:11 "Why *d* the teachers of the law **say** that AIT
Mk 9:22 But if *you* **can d** anything, take pity on us G1538
Mk 9:24 exclaimed, "*I d* **believe**; help me overcome AIT
Mk 9:39 "*D* not **stop** him," Jesus said. "For no one AIT
Mk 9:48 where " 'the worms that eat them *d* not **die** AIT
Mk 10:14 come to me, and *d* not **hinder** them, for the AIT
Mk 10:17 "what *must I* **d** to inherit eternal life?" G4472
Mk 10:18 "Why *d you* **call** me good?" Jesus answered AIT
Mk 10:35 "we want you to **d** for us whatever we ask." G4472
Mk 10:36 "What *d you* **want** me to do for you?" he AIT
Mk 10:36 "What do you want me *to* **d** for you?" G4472
Mk 10:51 "What *d you* **want** me to do for you?" Jesus AIT
Mk 10:51 "What do you want *me to* **d** for you?" G4472
Mk 11:28 "And who gave you authority to **d** this?" G4472
Mk 12: 9 then *will* the owner of the vineyard **d**? G4472
Mk 12:24 error because *you d* not **know** the Scriptures AIT
Mk 12:35 "Why *d* the teachers of the law **say** that the AIT
Mk 13: 2 "*D you* **see** all these great buildings? AIT
Mk 13: 7 wars and rumors of wars, *d* not *be* **alarmed**. AIT
Mk 13:11 *d* not **worry beforehand about** what to say. AIT
Mk 13:21 'Look, there he is!' *d* not **believe** it. AIT
Mk 13:33 *You d* not **know** when that time will come. AIT
Mk 13:35 watch because *you d* not **know** when the AIT
Mk 13:36 suddenly, *d* not *let him* **find** you sleeping. AIT
Mk 14:12 "Where *d you* **want** us to go and make AIT
Mk 14:63 "Why *d we* **need** any more witnesses?" AIT
Mk 14:64 the blasphemy. What *d you* **think**?" They all AIT
Mk 15: 8 up and asked Pilate *to* **d** for them what he G4472
Mk 15: 9 "*D you* **want** me to release to you the king of AIT
Mk 15:12 "What *shall I* **d**, then, with the one you G4472
Lk 1:13 "*D* not *be* **afraid**, Zechariah; your prayer has AIT
Lk 1:30 the angel said to her, "*D* not *be* **afraid**, Mary; AIT
Lk 2:10 said to them, "*D* not *be* **afraid**. I bring you AIT
Lk 2:27 in the child Jesus *to* **d** for him what the G4472
Lk 3: 8 And *d* not **begin** to say to yourselves, 'We AIT
Lk 3:10 "What *should we* **d** then?" the crowd G4472
Lk 3:11 anyone who has food *should* **d** the same." G4472
Lk 3:12 they asked, "what *should we* **d**? G4472
Lk 3:14 asked him, "And what *should* we **d**?" G4472
Lk 4:12 '*D* not **put** the Lord your God **to the test**.' " AIT
Lk 4:23 '**D** here in your hometown what we have G4472
Lk 4:34 **What d** you **want with** us, Jesus of G5515
Lk 5:19 not find a way *to* **d this** because of the G1662S
Lk 5:30 "Why *d you* **eat** and drink with tax collectors AIT
Lk 5:33 and **so** *d* the disciples of the Pharisees AIT
Lk 6: 9 *to* **d good** or to do evil, to save life or to G16
Lk 6: 9 to do good or *to* **d evil**, to save life or to G2803
Lk 6:11 one another what *they* might **d** to Jesus. G4472
Lk 6:27 enemies, **d** good to those who hate you, G4472
Lk 6:29 *d* not **withhold** your shirt from them. AIT
Lk 6:30 what belongs to you, *d* not **demand** it **back**. AIT
Lk 6:31 **D** to others as you would have them do to G4472
Lk 6:31 others as you would have them **d** to you. G4472
Lk 6:33 And if *you* **d good** to those who are good to G16
Lk 6:33 credit is that to you? Even sinners **d** that. G4472
Lk 6:35 your enemies, **d good** to them, and lend G16
Lk 6:37 "*D* not **judge**, and you will not be judged. AIT
Lk 6:37 *D* not **condemn**, and you will not be AIT
Lk 6:41 "Why *d you* **look at** the speck of sawdust in AIT
Lk 6:44 *People d* not **pick** figs from thornbushes, or AIT
Lk 6:46 "Why *d you* **call** me, 'Lord, Lord,' and do not AIT

Lk 6:46 'Lord, Lord,' and *d* not **do** what I say? AIT
Lk 6:46 'Lord, Lord,' and *do not* **d** what I say? G4472
Lk 7: 4 "This man deserves *to have you* **d** this, G4218
Lk 7: 6 for *I d* not **deserve** to have you come under AIT
Lk 7: 8 say to my servant, '**D** this,' and he does it G4472
Lk 7:44 said to Simon, "*D you* **see** this woman? AIT
Lk 8:14 riches and pleasures, and *they d* not **mature**. AIT
Lk 8:28 **"What d** you **want with** me G5515+5516+2779
Lk 9: 5 If people *d* not **welcome** you, leave their town AIT
Lk 9:18 he asked them, "Who *d* the crowds **say** I am?" AIT
Lk 9:20 "Who *d you* **say** I am?" Peter AIT
Lk 9:50 "*D* not **stop** him," Jesus said, "for whoever is AIT
Lk 9:54 *d you* **want** us to call fire down from heaven AIT
Lk 10: 4 *D* not **take** a purse or bag or sandals; and do AIT
Lk 10: 4 sandals; and *d* not **greet** anyone on the road. AIT
Lk 10: 7 *D* not **move around** from house to house AIT
Lk 10:20 *d* not **rejoice** that the spirits submit to you AIT
Lk 10:21 this is what you were pleased *to* **d**. G1181
Lk 10:25 "what *must I* **d** to inherit eternal life?" G4472
Lk 10:26 he replied. "How *d you* **read** it?" AIT
Lk 10:28 Jesus replied. "**D** this and you will live." G4472
Lk 10:36 of these three *d* you **think** was a neighbor to AIT
Lk 10:37 Jesus told him, "Go and **d** likewise." G4472
Lk 10:40 sister has left me *to* **d** *the* **work** by myself? G1354
Lk 11:19 by whom *d* your followers **drive** them **out**? AIT
Lk 12: 4 *d* not *be* **afraid** of those who kill the body AIT
Lk 12: 4 kill the body and after that can **d** no more. G4472
Lk 12:11 *d* not **worry about** how you will defend AIT
Lk 12:17 himself, 'What *shall I* **d**? I have no place G4472
Lk 12:18 'This is what *I'll* **d**. I will tear down G4472
Lk 12:22 I tell you, *d* not **worry about** your life, what AIT
Lk 12:24 *They d* not **sow** or reap, they have no AIT
Lk 12:26 Since *you* **cannot d** this very little G4028+1538
Lk 12:26 little thing, why *d you* **worry** about the rest? AIT
Lk 12:27 *They d* not **labor** or spin. Yet I AIT
Lk 12:29 And *d* not **set** *your* **heart on** what you will eat AIT
Lk 12:29 you will eat or drink; *d* not **worry about** it. AIT
Lk 12:32 "*D* not *be* **afraid**, little flock, for your Father AIT
Lk 12:40 come at an hour when *you d* not **expect** him." AIT
Lk 12:47 get ready or *does* not **d** what the master G4472
Lk 12:51 *D you* **think** I came to bring peace on earth AIT
Lk 13: 2 "*D you* **think** that these Galileans were worse AIT
Lk 13: 4 *d you* **think** they were more guilty than all the AIT
Lk 14: 8 wedding feast, *d* not **take** the place of honor AIT
Lk 14:12 dinner, *d* not **invite** your friends, your AIT
Lk 14:12 rich neighbors; **if you d**, they may invite G3607
Lk 14:33 of you who *d* not **give up** everything you AIT
Lk 15: 7 righteous persons who *d* not **need** to repent. AIT
Lk 16: 3 said to himself, 'What *shall I* **d** *now*? G4472
Lk 16: 4 I know what *I'll* **d** so that, when I lose my G4472
Lk 16: 5 'How much *d you* **owe** my master? AIT
Lk 16: 7 the second, 'And how much *d* you **owe**? AIT
Lk 16:31 'If *they d* not **listen** *to* Moses and the AIT
Lk 17: 9 because he did what *he was* **told to d**? G1411
Lk 17:10 have done everything you *were* **told to d**, G1411
Lk 17:23 *D* not go running off after them. AIT
Lk 18:16 come to me, and *d* not **hinder** them, for the AIT
Lk 18:18 what *must I* **d** to inherit eternal life?" G4472
Lk 18:19 "Why *d you* **call** me good?" Jesus answered AIT
Lk 18:41 "What *d you* **want** me to do for you?" "Lord, AIT
Lk 18:41 "What do you want *me to* **d** for you?" G4472
Lk 19:48 Yet they could not find any way *to* **d** it G4472
Lk 20:13 of the vineyard said, 'What *shall I* **d**? G4472
Lk 20:15 then *will* the owner of the vineyard **d** to G4472
Lk 20:21 that *you d* not **show partiality** but teach AIT
Lk 21: 8 'The time is near.' *D* not **follow** them. AIT
Lk 21: 9 of wars and uprisings, *d* not *be* **frightened**. AIT
Lk 22: 9 "Where *d you* **want** us to prepare for it?" AIT
Lk 22:19 **d** this in remembrance of me. G4472
Lk 22:23 of them it might be who would **d** this. G4556
Lk 22:71 "Why *d we* **need** any more testimony? AIT
Lk 23:28 of Jerusalem, *d* not **weep** for me; weep for AIT
Lk 23:31 For if *people* **d** these things when the tree G4472
Lk 23:34 for *they d* not **know** what they are doing." AIT
Lk 24: 5 "Why *d you* **look for** the living among the AIT
Lk 24:38 why *d* doubts **rise** in your minds? AIT
Lk 24:41 "*D you* **have** anything here to eat? AIT
Jn 1:22 What *d you* **say** about yourself? AIT
Jn 1:25 "Why then *d you* **baptize** if you are not the AIT
Jn 1:26 "but among you stands one you *d* not **know**. AIT
Jn 1:38 following and asked, "What *d you* **want**?" AIT
Jn 1:48 "How *d you* **know** me?" Nathanael asked AIT
Jn 2: 4 **why d** you **involve** me? G5515+5516+2779
Jn 2: 5 to the servants, "**D** whatever he tells you." G4472
Jn 2:18 us to prove your authority to **d** all this?" G4472
Jn 3:10 "and *d you* not **understand** these things? AIT
Jn 3:11 but *still you people d* not **accept** our AIT
Jn 3:12 you of earthly things and *you d* not **believe**; AIT
Jn 4: 9 For Jews *d* not **associate with** Samaritans.) AIT
Jn 4:22 You Samaritans worship what *you d* not **know** AIT
Jn 4:22 we worship what *we d* **know**, for salvation is AIT
Jn 4:27 one asked, "What *d you* **want**?" or "Why are AIT
Jn 4:34 "is to **d** the will of him who sent me and G4472
Jn 5: 6 he asked him, "*D you* **want** to get well?" AIT
Jn 5:19 tell you, the Son can **d** nothing by himself G4472
Jn 5:19 he can **d** only what he sees his Father doing, NDT
Jn 5:28 "*D* not *be* **amazed** at this, for a time is AIT
Jn 5:30 By myself I can **d** nothing; I judge only as I G4472
Jn 5:38 for you *d* not **believe** the one he sent. AIT
Jn 5:41 "*I d* not **accept** glory from human beings, AIT
Jn 5:42 I know that *you d* not **have** the love of God in AIT
Jn 5:43 and *you d* not **accept** me; but if AIT
Jn 5:44 one another but *d* not **seek** the glory that AIT
Jn 5:45 "But *d* not **think** I will accuse you before the AIT
Jn 5:47 But since *you d* not **believe** what he wrote AIT
Jn 6: 6 had in mind what he was going to **d**. G4472
Jn 6:27 *D* not **work** for food that spoils, but for food AIT
Jn 6:28 "What *must we* **d** to do the works God G4472
Jn 6:28 "What must we do to **d** the works God G2237
Jn 6:30 see it and believe you? What *will you* **d**? G2237
Jn 6:36 you have seen me and *still you d* not **believe**. AIT
Jn 6:38 from heaven not to **d** my will but to do the G4472
Jn 6:38 to do my will but to **d** the will of him who NDT
Jn 6:64 Yet there are some of you who *d* not **believe**." AIT
Jn 6:67 "You *d* not **want** to leave too, do you?" AIT
Jn 6:67 want to leave too, **d** you?" Jesus asked the NDT
Jn 7: 3 disciples there may see the works *you* **d**. G4472
Jn 7: 6 is not yet here; for you any time will **d**. G2289
Jn 7:17 Anyone who chooses *to* **d** the will of God G4472
Jn 7:28 he who sent me is true. You *d* not **know** him, AIT
Jn 8: 5 to stone such women. Now what *d* you **say**?" AIT
Jn 8:11 "Then neither *d* I **condemn** you," Jesus AIT
Jn 8:16 But if *I d* **judge**, my decisions are true AIT
Jn 8:19 "*You d* not **know** me or my Father," Jesus AIT
Jn 8:24 in your sins; if *you d* not **believe** that I am he AIT
Jn 8:28 I am he and that *I* **d** nothing on my own G4472
Jn 8:29 for I always **d** what pleases him. G4472
Jn 8:39 "then *you would* **d** what Abraham did. G4472
Jn 8:40 Abraham *did* not **d** such things. G4472
Jn 8:45 I tell the truth, *you d* not **believe** me! AIT
Jn 8:47 The reason *you d* not **hear** is that you do not AIT
Jn 8:47 do not hear is that *you d* not **belong to** God." AIT
Jn 8:53 did the prophets. Who *d* you **think** *you* **are**?" AIT
Jn 8:55 Though *you d* not **know** him, I know him. If I AIT
Jn 8:55 like you, but *I d* **know** him and obey his word. AIT
Jn 9: 4 we must **d** the works of him who sent me. G2237
Jn 9:25 One thing *I d* **know**. I was blind but AIT
Jn 9:26 they asked him, "What *did he* **d** to you? G4472
Jn 9:27 Why *d you* **want** to hear it again AIT
Jn 9:27 *D* you **want** to become his disciples too?" AIT
Jn 9:33 were not from God, he could **d** nothing." G4472
Jn 9:35 "*D you* **believe** in the Son of Man? AIT
Jn 10: 5 him because *they d* not **recognize** a AIT
Jn 10:25 "I did tell you, but *you d* not **believe**. AIT
Jn 10:25 The works I **d** in my Father's name testify G4472
Jn 10:26 you *d* not **believe** because you are not my AIT
Jn 10:32 For which of these *d you* **stone** me?" AIT
Jn 10:36 Why then *d* you **accuse** me *of* blasphemy AIT
Jn 10:37 *D* not **believe** me unless I do the works of my AIT
Jn 10:37 not believe me unless *I* **d** the works of my G4472
Jn 10:38 But if I **d** them, even though you do not G4472
Jn 10:38 I do them, *even though you d* not **believe** me AIT
Jn 11:26 in me will never die. *D you* **believe** this?" AIT
Jn 11:50 *You d* not **realize** that it is better for you that AIT
Jn 11:56 they asked one another, "What *d* you **think**? AIT
Jn 12:15 "*D* not *be* **afraid**, Daughter Zion; see, your AIT
Jn 12:47 not keep them, I *d* not **judge** that person. AIT
Jn 13: 7 "You *d* not **realize** now what I am doing AIT
Jn 13:12 "*D you* **understand** what I have done for AIT
Jn 13:15 example that you *should* **d** as I have done G4472
Jn 13:17 you will be blessed if *you* **d** them. G4472
Jn 13:27 "What *you are about to* **d**, do quickly G4472
Jn 13:27 "What you are about to do, **d** quickly." G4472
Jn 14: 1 "*D* not *let* your hearts *be* **troubled**. AIT
Jn 14: 7 *you d* **know** him and have seen him. AIT
Jn 14:10 words I say to you *I d* not **speak** on my own AIT
Jn 14:12 believes in me *will* **d** the works I have G4472
Jn 14:12 and *they will* **d** even greater things than G4472
Jn 14:13 And *I will* **d** whatever you ask in my name G4472
Jn 14:14 anything in my name, and I *will* **d** it. G4472
Jn 14:22 why *d you* **intend** to show yourself to us and AIT
Jn 14:27 I *d* not **give** to you as the world gives AIT
Jn 14:27 *D* not *let* your hearts *be* **troubled** and do not AIT
Jn 14:27 your hearts be troubled and *d* not *be* **afraid**. AIT
Jn 14:31 I love the Father and **d** exactly what my G4472
Jn 15: 5 apart from me you can **d** nothing. G4472
Jn 15: 6 If you *d* not **remain** in me, you are like a AIT
Jn 15:14 are my friends if *you* **d** what I command. G4472
Jn 15:19 *you d* not **belong to** the world, but I AIT
Jn 15:21 for *they d* not **know** the one who sent me. AIT
Jn 16: 3 *They will* **d** such things because they have G4472
Jn 16: 9 because *people d* not **believe** in me; AIT
Jn 16:30 that *you d* not even **need** to have AIT
Jn 16:31 "*D you* now **believe**?" Jesus replied. AIT
Jn 17: 4 by finishing the work you gave me to **d**. G4472
Jn 18:39 *D you* **want** me to release 'the king of the AIT
Jn 19: 9 "Where *d* you **come** from?" he asked AIT
Jn 19:10 "*D you* refuse *to* **speak** to me?" Pilate said AIT
Jn 19:21 to Pilate, "*D* not **write** 'The King of the Jews AIT
Jn 20:17 Jesus said, "*D* not **hold on** to me, for I have AIT
Jn 20:23 forgiven; if *you d* **not forgive** them, they are AIT
Jn 21:15 son of John, *d you* **love** me more than these?" AIT
Jn 21:16 "Simon son of John, *d you* **love** me? AIT
Jn 21:17 "Simon son of John, *d you* **love** me? AIT
Jn 21:17 asked him the third time, "*D you* **love** me?" AIT
Jn 21:18 lead you where *you d* not **want** to go." AIT
Ac 1: 1 all that Jesus began *to* **d** and to teach G4472
Ac 1: 4 "*D* not **leave** Jerusalem, but wait for the gift AIT
Ac 1:11 "why *d you* **stand** here looking into the sky? AIT
Ac 2:37 apostles, "Brothers, what *shall we* **d**?" G4472
Ac 3: 6 "Silver or gold *I d* not **have**, but what I do AIT
Ac 3: 6 I do not have, but what *I d* **have** I give you. AIT
Ac 3:12 Why *d you* **stare** at us as if by our own power AIT
Ac 4: 7 what power or what name *did* you **d** this?" G4472
Ac 4:16 "What *are we going to* **d** with these men?" G4472
Ac 4:25 " 'Why *d* the nations **rage** and the peoples AIT
Ac 5:35 what you intend *to* **d** to these men. G4556
Ac 7:26 brothers; why *d you want to* **hurt** each other? AIT
Ac 7:60 "Lord, *d* not **hold** this sin against them." AIT
Ac 8:30 "*D you* **understand** what you are reading?" AIT
Ac 9: 4 "Saul, Saul, why *d you* **persecute** me?" AIT
Ac 9: 6 and you will be told what you must **d**." G4472
Ac 10:15 "*D* not **call** anything **impure** that God has AIT
Ac 10:20 *D* not **hesitate** to go with them, for I have AIT
Ac 11: 9 '*D* not **call** anything **impure** that God has AIT
Ac 13:22 he *will* **d** everything I want him to do. G4472
Ac 13:22 he will do everything I want him to **d**. NDT
Ac 13:25 'Who *d you* **suppose** I am? I am not AIT
Ac 13:41 I *am going to* **d** something in your G2237
Ac 13:46 you reject it and *d* not **consider** yourselves AIT
Ac 15:10 why *d you try to* **test** God by putting on the AIT
Ac 15:29 *You will* **d** well to avoid these things G4556
Ac 16:30 "Sirs, what must I **d** to be saved? G4472
Ac 16:37 And now *d they want to* **get rid of** us quietly AIT
Ac 18: 9 "*D* not *be* **afraid**; keep on speaking, do not AIT
Ac 18: 9 be afraid; keep on speaking, *d* not *be* **silent**. AIT
Ac 19:36 to calm down and not **d** anything rash. G4556
Ac 21:22 **What shall we d**? They will G5515+4036+1639
Ac 21:23 so **d** what we tell you. There are four men G4472
Ac 21:37 "*D you* **speak** Greek?" he replied. AIT
Ac 22: 7 Saul! Why *d you* **persecute** me?' AIT
Ac 22:10 " 'What *shall I* **d**, Lord?' I asked. " 'Get up G4472
Ac 22:10 told all that you have been assigned *to* **d**. G4472
Ac 22:26 "What are you going to **d**?" he asked. G4472
Ac 23: 5 '*D* not **speak** evil about the ruler of your AIT
Ac 23:29 the accusation **had to d with** questions G4309
Ac 25: 9 wishing *to* **d** the Jews a favor, said G2960
Ac 25:11 deserving death, *I d* not **refuse** to die. AIT
Ac 26: 9 that I ought *to* **d** all that was possible G4556
Ac 26:14 Saul, why *d you* **persecute** me? AIT
Ac 26:27 King Agrippa, *d you* **believe** the prophets? AIT
Ac 26:27 you believe the prophets? I know *you* **d**." G4409
Ac 26:28 "**D** you think that in such a short time you NDT
Ac 27:24 '*D* not *be* **afraid**, Paul. You must AIT
Ro 1:13 *I d* not **want** you to be unaware, brothers AIT
Ro 1:28 *so that they* **d** what ought not to be done. G4472
Ro 1:32 decree that those *who* **d** such things G4556
Ro 1:32 *they* not only *continue to* **d** these very G4472
Ro 2: 1 who pass judgment **d** the same things. G4556
Ro 2: 2 against those *who* **d** such things is based G4556
Ro 2: 3 on them and yet **d** the same things, G4472
Ro 2: 3 *d you* **think** you will escape God's judgment? AIT
Ro 2: 4 Or *d you* **show contempt** for the riches of his AIT
Ro 2:14 Gentiles, who *d* not **have** the law, do by AIT
Ro 2:14 **d** by nature things required by the law G4472
Ro 2:14 *even though they d* not **have** the law. AIT
Ro 2:21 who teach others, *d you* not **teach** yourself? AIT
Ro 2:21 who preach against stealing, *d you* **steal**? AIT
Ro 2:22 not commit adultery, *d you* **commit adultery**? AIT
Ro 2:22 You who abhor idols, *d you* **rob temples**? AIT
Ro 2:23 *d you* **dishonor** God by breaking the law? AIT
Ro 3: 8 "*Let us* **d** evil that good may result"? G4472
Ro 3: 9 *D we have any* **advantage**? Not at all! AIT
Ro 3:17 the way of peace *they d* not **know**. AIT
Ro 3:31 *D we*, then, **nullify** the law by this faith? Not AIT
Ro 4:21 that God had power *to* **d** what he had G4472
Ro 6:12 Therefore *d* not *let* sin **reign** in your mortal AIT
Ro 6:13 *D* not **offer** any part of yourself to sin as an AIT
Ro 7: 1 *D you* **not know**, brothers and sisters—for I AIT
Ro 7:15 *I d* not **understand** what I do. For what I want AIT
Ro 7:15 I do not understand what *I* **d**. For what I G2981
Ro 7:15 For what I want to **d** I do not do, but what I NDT
Ro 7:15 For what I want to do *I d* not **do**, but what I AIT
Ro 7:15 For what I want to do *I do* not **d**, but what G4556
Ro 7:15 to do I do not do, but what I hate *I* **d**. G4472
Ro 7:16 And if *I* **d** what I do not want to do, I agree G4472
Ro 7:16 And if I do what *I d* not **want** to do, I agree AIT
Ro 7:16 And if I do what I do not want to **d**, I agree NDT
Ro 7:17 it is no longer *I* myself *who* **d** it, but it is G2981
Ro 7:18 For I have the desire to **d** what is good, but I NDT
Ro 7:19 For *I d* not **do** the good I want to do, but the AIT
Ro 7:19 For *I do* not **d** the good I want to do, but G4472
Ro 7:19 For I do not do the good I want to **d**, but the NDT
Ro 7:19 but the evil *I d* not **want** to do—this I AIT
Ro 7:19 the evil I do not want to **d**—this I keep NDT
Ro 7:20 Now if *I* **d** what I do not want to do, it is no G4472
Ro 7:20 Now if I do what *I d* not **want** to do, it is no AIT
Ro 7:20 Now if I do what I do not want to **d**, it is no NDT
Ro 7:20 it is no longer I *who* **d** it, but it is sin G2981
Ro 7:21 Although I want *to* **d** good, evil is right G4472
Ro 8: 3 law was powerless to **d** because it was NDT
Ro 8: 4 who *d* not **live** according to the flesh but AIT
Ro 8: 7 not submit to God's law, nor can it **d** so. NDT
Ro 8: 9 Spirit of Christ, they *d* not **belong to** Christ. AIT
Ro 8:25 But if we hope for what *we d* **not yet have** G1063
Ro 8:26 We *d* not **know** what we ought to pray for AIT
Ro 10: 6 "*D* not **say** in your heart, 'Who will ascend AIT
Ro 11:18 *d* not **consider** *yourself* **to be superior** to AIT
Ro 11:18 other branches. If *you* **d**, consider this G2878S
Ro 11:18 You *d* not **support** the root, but the root AIT
Ro 11:20 by faith. *D* not *be* **arrogant**, but tremble. AIT
Ro 11:23 And if they *d* not **persist** in unbelief, they will AIT
Ro 11:25 *I d* not **want** you to be ignorant of this AIT
Ro 12: 2 *D* not **conform to the pattern** of this world, AIT
Ro 12: 3 *D* not **think of yourself more highly** than you AIT
Ro 12: 4 these members *d* not all **have** the same AIT

Ro 12: 8 if it is to lead, **d** it diligently; if it is to show NDT
Ro 12: 8 if it is to show mercy, **d** it cheerfully. NDT
Ro 12:14 who persecute you; bless and *d* not **curse**. AIT
Ro 12:16 *D* not *be* **proud**, but be willing to associate AIT
Ro 12:16 people of low position. *D* not **be** conceited. AIT
Ro 12:17 *D* not **repay** anyone evil for evil. Be careful to AIT
Ro 12:17 Be careful to **d** what is right in the eyes of NDT
Ro 12:19 *D* not **take revenge**, my dear friends, but AIT
Ro 12:21 *D* not *be* **overcome** by evil, but overcome evil AIT
Ro 13: 2 those *who* **d so** will bring judgment *G468S*
Ro 13: 3 rulers hold no terror for those who **d** right, *G2240*
Ro 13: 3 who do right, but for those who **d** wrong. NDT
Ro 13: 3 *D you* **want** to be free from fear of the one in AIT
Ro 13: 3 Then **d** what is right and you will be *G4472*
Ro 13: 4 But if *you* **d** wrong, be afraid, for rulers do *G4472*
Ro 13: 4 rulers *d* not **bear** the sword for no reason. AIT
Ro 13:11 And **d** this, understanding the present time NDT
Ro 13:14 and *d* not **think about** how to gratify the AIT
Ro 14:10 why *d you* **judge** your brother or sister? AIT
Ro 14:10 Or why *d* you **treat** them **with contempt**? For AIT
Ro 14:15 *D* not by your eating **destroy** someone for AIT
Ro 14:16 *d* not *let* what you know is good
be **spoken of as evil** AIT
Ro 14:19 make every effort to **d** what leads to peace NDT
Ro 14:20 *D* not **destroy** the work of God for the sake of AIT
Ro 14:21 drink wine or to **d** anything else that will NDT
Ro 15:24 I plan to **d** so when I go to Spain. I hope to NDT
Ro 15:27 They were pleased to **d** it, and indeed they NDT
Ro 16:21 his greetings to you, as **d** Lucius, Jason and NDT
1Co 1: 7 Therefore you *d* not **lack** any spiritual gift as AIT
1Co 2: 6 *We d*, however, **speak** a message of wisdom AIT
1Co 3:18 *D* not **deceive** yourselves. If any of you think AIT
1Co 4: 3 indeed, *I d* not even **judge** myself. AIT
1Co 4: 6 "**D** not go beyond what is written. NDT
1Co 4: 7 What *d you* **have** that you did not receive AIT
1Co 4: 7 why *d you* **boast** as though you did not? AIT
1Co 4:15 in Christ, you **d** not have many fathers NDT
1Co 4:21 What *d you* **prefer**? Shall I come to you with a AIT
1Co 5: 1 of a kind that even pagans **d** not tolerate: NDT
1Co 5:11 *D* not even **eat with** such people. AIT
1Co 6: 1 *d you* **dare** to take it before the ungodly for AIT
1Co 6: 2 Or *d you* not **know** that the Lord's people will AIT
1Co 6: 3 *D you* not **know** that we will judge angels AIT
1Co 6: 4 *d you* **ask for a ruling** from those whose way AIT
1Co 6: 8 you yourselves cheat and **d wrong**, and you *G691*
1Co 6: 8 you **d** this to your brothers and sisters. NDT
1Co 6: 9 Or *d you* not **know** that wrongdoers will not AIT
1Co 6: 9 of God? *D* not *be* **deceived**: Neither the AIT
1Co 6:12 "**I have the right** *to d* anything," you say—but AIT
1Co 6:12 "**I have the right** *to d* anything"—but I will AIT
1Co 6:15 *D you* not **know** that your bodies are members AIT
1Co 6:16 *D you* not **know** that he who unites himself AIT
1Co 6:19 *D you* not **know** that your bodies are temples AIT
1Co 7: 5 *D* not **deprive** each other except perhaps by AIT
1Co 7: 8 It is good for them to stay unmarried, as I **d**. NDT
1Co 7:16 How *d you* **know**, wife, whether you will save AIT
1Co 7:16 how *d you* **know**, husband, whether you AIT
1Co 7:21 if you can gain your freedom, **d so**. *G3437+5968*
1Co 7:23 price; *d* not **become** slaves of human beings. AIT
1Co 7:27 *D* not **seek** to be released. AIT
1Co 7:27 such a commitment? *D* not **look for** a wife. AIT
1Co 7:28 But if *you d* **marry**, you have not sinned; AIT
1Co 7:29 have wives should live as if *they* **d** not; *G2400S*
1Co 7:36 ought to marry, *he should* **d** as he wants. *G4472*
1Co 8: 2 something *d* not yet **know** as they ought AIT
1Co 8: 8 we are no worse if *we d* not **eat**, and no AIT
1Co 8: 8 if we do not eat, and no better if *we* **d**. *G2266S*
1Co 9: 5 as **d** the other apostles and the Lord's NDT
1Co 9: 8 *D I* **say** this merely on human authority AIT
1Co 9: 9 "*D* not **muzzle** an ox while it is treading out AIT
1Co 9:10 should *be able to* **d so** in the hope of *G769S*
1Co 9:15 in the hope that *you will* **d** such things *G1181*
1Co 9:16 Woe to me if *I d* not **preach the gospel!** AIT
1Co 9:23 *I* **d** all this for the sake of the gospel, that I *G4472*
1Co 9:24 *D you* not **know** that in a race all the runners AIT
1Co 9:25 They **d** it to get a crown that will not last NDT
1Co 9:25 we **d** it to get a crown that will last NDT
1Co 9:26 Therefore I **d** not **run** like someone running AIT
1Co 9:26 *I d* not **fight** like a boxer beating the air. AIT
1Co 10: 1 For *I d* not **want** you to be ignorant of the fact, AIT
1Co 10: 7 *D* not **be** idolaters, as some of them were; as AIT
1Co 10:10 And *d* not **grumble**, as some of them did AIT
1Co 10:18 **D** not those who eat the sacrifices *G1639*
1Co 10:19 *D I* **mean** then that food sacrificed to an idol AIT
1Co 10:20 and *I d* not **want** you to be participants with AIT
1Co 10:23 "*I* **have the right** *to d* anything," you say—but AIT
1Co 10:23 "*I* **have the right** *to d* anything"—but not AIT
1Co 10:28 then *d* not **eat** it, both for the sake of the AIT
1Co 10:31 you eat or drink or whatever *you d*, *G4472*
1Co 10:31 **d** it all for the glory of God. *G4472*
1Co 10:32 **D** not cause anyone to stumble, whether *G1181*
1Co 11:16 other practice—nor **d** the churches of God. NDT
1Co 11:17 your meetings **d** more harm than good. *G1650*
1Co 11:22 Or *d you* **despise** the church of God by AIT
1Co 11:24 is for you; **d** this in remembrance of me." *G4472*
1Co 11:25 in my blood; **d** this, whenever you *G4472*
1Co 12: 1 *I d* not **want** you to be uninformed. AIT
1Co 12:15 not a hand, *I d* not **belong to** the body," AIT
1Co 12:16 am not an eye, *I d* not **belong to** the body," AIT
1Co 12:29 Are all teachers? **D** all work miracles? NDT
1Co 12:30 *D* all **have** gifts of healing? Do all speak in AIT
1Co 12:30 gifts of healing? *D* all **speak** in tongues? Do AIT
1Co 12:30 Do all speak in tongues? *D* all **interpret**? AIT
1Co 13: 1 of angels, but *d* not **have** love, I am only a AIT
1Co 13: 2 mountains, but *d* not **have** love, I am nothing AIT
1Co 13: 3 I may boast, but *d* not **have** love, I gain AIT
1Co 14:11 If then *I d* not **grasp** the meaning of what AIT
1Co 14:15 So what *shall I* **d**? I will pray with my spirit *G1639*
1Co 14:16 since *they d* not **know** what you are saying? AIT
1Co 14:39 and *d* not **forbid** speaking in tongues. AIT
1Co 15: 9 of the apostles and **d** not even deserve to *G1639*
1Co 15:29 what *will those* **d** who are baptized for the *G4472*
1Co 15:30 why *d we* **endanger** *ourselves* every hour? AIT
1Co 15:33 *D* not *be* **misled**: "Bad company corrupts AIT
1Co 15:37 *you d* not **plant** the body that will be AIT
1Co 16: 1 **D** what I told the Galatian churches to do. *G4472*
1Co 16: 1 Do what *I* **told** the Galatian churches **to d**. *G1411*
1Co 16: 7 For *I d* not **want** to see you now and make AIT
1Co 16:14 **D** everything in love. *G1181*
2Co 1: 8 *We d* not **want** you to be uninformed AIT
2Co 1:13 For *we d* not **write** you anything you cannot AIT
2Co 1:17 Was I fickle *when I* **intended** *to d* this? Or do AIT
2Co 1:17 Or *d I* **make** *my* **plans** in a worldly manner so AIT
2Co 2:17 *we d* not **peddle** the word of God **for profit**. AIT
2Co 3: 1 Or *d we* **need**, like some people, letters of AIT
2Co 4: 1 we have this ministry, *we d* not **lose heart**. AIT
2Co 4: 2 shameful ways; *we d* not **use** deception, nor AIT
2Co 4: 2 deception, nor *d we* **distort** the word of God. AIT
2Co 4:16 Therefore *we d* not **lose heart**. AIT
2Co 5: 4 because *we d* not **wish** to be unclothed but AIT
2Co 5:16 Christ in this way, *we* **d so** no longer. *G1182S*
2Co 6:14 *D* not **be** yoked together with unbelievers. AIT
2Co 6:14 For what **d** righteousness and wickedness NDT
2Co 7: 3 *I d* not **say** this to condemn you; I have said AIT
2Co 7: 8 you sorrow by my letter, *I d* not **regret** it. AIT
2Co 8:10 to give but also to have the desire to **d** so. NDT
2Co 8:11 eager willingness to **d** it may be matched by NDT
2Co 8:21 For we are taking pains to **d** what is right, not NDT
2Co 10: 3 *we d* not **wage war** as the world does. AIT
2Co 10: 7 we belong to Christ just as much as they **d**. NDT
2Co 10: 9 *I d* not want to **seem** to be trying to frighten AIT
2Co 10:12 *We d* not **dare** to classify or compare AIT
2Co 10:15 Neither **d** we go beyond our limits by NDT
2Co 10:16 *For we d* not *want to* **boast** about work AIT
2Co 11: 5 *I d* not **think** I am in the least inferior to those AIT
2Co 11: 6 as a speaker, but I **d** have knowledge. *G4024S*
2Co 11: 9 in any way, and *will continue to* **d so**. *G5498S*
2Co 11:11 Because *I d* not **love** you? God knows I AIT
2Co 11:11 Because I do not love you? God knows I **d**! NDT
2Co 11:16 But if you **d**, then tolerate me just as you *G3590S*
2Co 11:16 so that I *may* **d** a little **boasting**. *G3016*
2Co 11:29 and *I d* not *feel* **weak**? Who is led AIT
2Co 11:29 is led into sin, and I *d* not *inwardly* **burn**? AIT
2Co 12: 2 in the body or out of the body *I d* not **know**— AIT
2Co 12: 3 the body or apart from the body *I d* not **know**, AIT
2Co 12: 6 me than is warranted by what I **d** or say, *G1063*
2Co 12:19 in Christ; and everything we **d**, dear friends, NDT
2Co 13: 5 *D you* not **realize** that Christ Jesus is in you AIT
2Co 13: 7 pray to God *that* you *will* not **d** anything *G4472*
2Co 13: 7 so that you *will d* what is right even *G4472*
2Co 13: 8 For *we* **cannot d** anything against *G4024+1538*
Gal 2:10 thing I had been eager *to d* all along. *G4472*
Gal 2:21 *I d* not **set aside** the grace of God, for if AIT
Gal 3:10 does not continue *to d* everything written *G4472*
Gal 3:17 by God and thus **d away with** the promise. *G2934*
Gal 4: 9 *D you* **wish** to be enslaved by them all over AIT
Gal 5: 1 and *d* not *let yourselves be* **burdened** again AIT
Gal 5:13 But **d** not use your freedom to indulge the NDT
Gal 5:17 so that *you are* not *to* **d** whatever you *G4472*
Gal 6: 7 *D* not *be* **deceived**: God cannot be mocked AIT
Gal 6: 9 we will reap a harvest *if we d* not **give up**. AIT
Gal 6:10 opportunity, *let us* **d** good to all people *G2237*
Gal 6:12 The only reason they **d** this is to avoid being NDT
Eph 2:10 created in Christ Jesus **to** *d* good works AIT
Eph 2:10 God prepared in advance for *us to* **d**. *G4344*
Eph 3:20 him who is able **to d** immeasurably more *G4472*
Eph 4:17 must no longer live as the Gentiles **d**, *G4344S*
Eph 4:26 "In your anger *d* not **sin**": Do not let the sun AIT
Eph 4:26 *D* not *let* the **sun go down** while you are still AIT
Eph 4:27 and *d* not **give** the devil a foothold. AIT
Eph 4:29 *D* not *let* any unwholesome talk **come out** of AIT
Eph 4:30 And *d* not **grieve** the Holy Spirit of God, with AIT
Eph 5: 7 Therefore *d* not **be** partners with them. AIT
Eph 5:11 **Have** nothing **to d with** the fruitless deeds *G5170*
Eph 5:12 mention what the disobedient **d** in secret. *G1181*
Eph 5:17 Therefore *d* not **be** foolish, but understand AIT
Eph 5:18 *D* not *get* **drunk** on wine, which leads to AIT
Eph 5:22 to your own husbands as you **d** to the Lord. NDT
Eph 6: 4 Fathers, *d* not **exasperate** your children AIT
Eph 6: 8 each one for whatever good *they* **d**, *G4472*
Eph 6: 9 **D not** threaten them, since you know that he AIT
Php 1:16 The latter **d** so out of love, knowing that I am NDT
Php 1:22 Yet what shall I choose? *I d* not **know**! AIT
Php 2: 3 **D** nothing out of selfish ambition or vain NDT
Php 2:14 **D** everything without grumbling or *G4472*
Php 3:13 I *d* not **consider** myself yet to have taken hold AIT
Php 3:13 But one thing I **d**: Forgetting what is NDT
Php 3:17 keep your eyes on those who live as we **d**. NDT
Php 4: 6 *D* not *be* **anxious** about anything, but in every AIT
Php 4:13 *I* **can d** all this through him who gives me *G2710*
Col 1:23 and *d* not **move** from the hope held out in AIT
Col 2:16 Therefore *d* not *let* anyone **judge** you by AIT
Col 2:18 *D* not *let* anyone who delights in false humility
and the worship of angels **disqualify** AIT
Col 2:20 to the world, *d you* **submit** to its **rules**: AIT
Col 2:21 "*D* not **handle**! Do not taste! Do not touch!" AIT
Col 2:21 "Do not handle! *D* not **taste**! Do not touch!" AIT
Col 2:21 "Do not handle! Do not taste! *D* not **touch**!" AIT
Col 2:22 which have to **d** with things that are all NDT
Col 3: 9 *D* not **lie** to each other, since you have taken AIT
Col 3:17 And whatever *you* **d**, whether in word or *G4472*
Col 3:17 **d** it all in the name of the Lord Jesus NDT
Col 3:19 your wives and *d* not *be* **harsh** with them. AIT
Col 3:21 Fathers, *d* not **embitter** your children, or they AIT
Col 3:22 in everything; and **d** it, not only when their NDT
Col 3:23 Whatever *you* **d**, work at it with all your *G4472*
1Th 1: 8 Therefore we *d* not **need** to say anything AIT
1Th 4: 1 in the Lord Jesus to **d** *this* **more** and more. *G4355*
1Th 4: 5 lust like the pagans, who *d* not **know** God; AIT
1Th 4: 9 one another *we d* not **need** to write to you AIT
1Th 4:10 *you d* love all of God's family throughout *G4472*
1Th 4:10 sisters, *to* **d** *so* **more** and more, *G4355*
1Th 4:13 *we d* not **want** you to be uninformed about AIT
1Th 4:13 so that *you d* not **grieve** like the rest of AIT
1Th 5: 1 times and dates *we d* not **need** to write to AIT
1Th 5: 5 *We d* not **belong to** the night or to the AIT
1Th 5:15 always **strive to d** what is good for *G1503*
1Th 5:19 *D* not **quench** the Spirit. AIT
1Th 5:20 *D* not **treat** prophecies **with contempt** AIT
1Th 5:24 who calls you is faithful, and he *will* **d** it. *G4472*
2Th 1: 8 punish those *who d* not **know** God and do AIT
2Th 1: 8 not know God and *d* not **obey** the gospel of AIT
2Th 2: 7 back will continue to **d** so till he is taken out NDT
2Th 3: 4 doing and *will continue to* **d** the things *G4472*
2Th 3: 9 not because *we d* not **have** the right to such AIT
2Th 3:14 *D* not **associate** with them, in order that they AIT
2Th 3:15 Yet *d* not **regard** them as an enemy, but warn AIT
1Ti 1: 7 but *they d* not **know** what they are talking AIT
1Ti 2:12 *I d* not **permit** a woman to teach or to assume AIT
1Ti 3: 4 he must **d** so in a manner worthy of full NDT
1Ti 4: 7 **Have nothing to d with** godless myths and *G4148*
1Ti 4:14 *D* not **neglect** your gift, which was given you AIT
1Ti 4:16 in them, because *if you* **d**, you will save *G4472*
1Ti 5: 1 *D* not **rebuke** an older man **harshly**, but AIT
1Ti 5:11 widows, **d not** put them on such a list. *G4148*
1Ti 5:13 And not only **d** they become idlers, but also NDT
1Ti 5:18 "*D* not **muzzle** an ox while it is treading out AIT
1Ti 5:19 *D* not **entertain** an accusation against an AIT
1Ti 5:21 and *to* **d** nothing out of favoritism. *G4472*
1Ti 5:22 **D** not be hasty in the laying on of hands NDT
1Ti 5:22 and *d* not **share in** the sins of others. AIT
1Ti 6:18 Command them *to* **d good**, to be rich in good *G14*
2Ti 1: 8 So *d* not *be* **ashamed** of the testimony about AIT
2Ti 2:15 **D** *your* **best** to present yourself to God as *G5079*
2Ti 2:21 the Master and prepared *to d* any good work. AIT
2Ti 2:23 **Don't have anything to d with** foolish and *G4148*
2Ti 2:26 who has taken them captive *to d* his will. AIT
2Ti 3: 5 **Have nothing to d with** such people. *G706*
2Ti 4: 5 hardship, **d** the work of an evangelist *G4472*
2Ti 4: 9 **D** *your* **best** to come to me quickly, *G5079*
2Ti 4:21 **D** *your* **best** to get here before winter *G5079*
2Ti 4:21 greets you, and so **d** Pudens, Linus, Claudia NDT
Titus 1:15 those who are corrupted and **d** not believe, NDT
Titus 2:14 are his very own, eager to **d** what is good. *G2240*
Titus 2:15 *D* not *let* anyone **despise** you. AIT
Titus 3: 1 to be ready to **d** whatever is good, *G2240*
Titus 3:10 After that, **have nothing to d with** them. *G4148*
Titus 3:12 **d** *your* **best** to come to me at Nicopolis *G5079*
Titus 3:13 *D* **everything** *you* **can** to help Zenas the AIT
Phm 8 order you to **d** what you ought to do, NDT
Phm 8 order you to do what you **ought to d**, *G465*
Phm 14 But I did not want *to* **d** anything without *G4472*
Phm 14 that any favor you **d** would not seem forced NDT
Phm 20 I **d** wish, brother, that I may have some NDT
Phm 21 knowing that *you will* **d** even more than I *G4472*
Phm 24 so **d** Mark, Aristarchus, Demas and Luke, NDT
Heb 2: 1 we have heard, so that *we d* not **drift away**. AIT
Heb 2: 8 Yet at present *we d* not **see** everything AIT
Heb 2: 9 But *we d* **see** Jesus, who was made lower AIT
Heb 3: 8 *d* not **harden** your hearts as you did in the AIT
Heb 3:15 *d* not **harden** your hearts as you did in the AIT
Heb 4: 7 you hear his voice, *d* not **harden** your hearts." AIT
Heb 4:15 For *we d* not **have** a high priest who is unable AIT
Heb 6: 3 And God permitting, *we will* **d** so. *G4472*
Heb 6: 9 the things *that* **have to d with** salvation. *G2400*
Heb 6:12 We **d** not want you to become lazy, but to NDT
Heb 8: 1 *We d* **have** such a high priest, who sat down AIT
Heb 9:26 of the ages to **d away with** sin by the *G120*
Heb 10: 7 I have come *to d* your will, my God. *G4472*
Heb 10: 9 "Here I am, I have come *to* **d** your will." *G4472*
Heb 10:29 more severely *d you* **think** someone deserves AIT
Heb 10:35 So *d* not **throw away** your confidence; it will AIT
Heb 10:39 But we *d* not **belong** to those who shrink back AIT
Heb 11: 1 and assurance about what *we d* not **see**. AIT
Heb 11:29 when the Egyptians tried *to d* so, they AIT
Heb 11:32 I *d* not **have** time to tell about Gideon, Barak AIT
Heb 12: 5 *d* not **make light of** the Lord's discipline AIT
Heb 12: 5 and *d* not **lose heart** when he rebukes you AIT
Heb 12:25 See to it *that you d* not **refuse** him who AIT
Heb 13: 2 *D* not **forget** to show hospitality to strangers AIT
Heb 13: 6 What *can* mere mortals **d** to me?" *G4472*
Heb 13: 9 *D* not *be* **carried away** by all kinds of strange AIT
Heb 13: 9 which is of no benefit *to* those *who* **d so**. *G4344*
Heb 13:14 For here *we d* not **have** an enduring city, but AIT
Heb 13:16 And *d* not **forget** to do good and to share with AIT
Heb 13:16 do not forget to **d good** and to share with *G2343*

Heb 13:17 **D** this so that their work will be a joy, not a NDT
Jas 1: 8 unstable in all they **d**. G3847
Jas 1:22 **D** not merely listen to the word, and so NDT
Jas 1:22 deceive yourselves. **D** what it says. G1181+4475
Jas 1:23 the word but *does* not **d** what it G1639+4475
Jas 1:25 they will be blessed in what they **d**. G4474
Jas 1:26 and *yet d* not **keep a tight rein on** their AIT
Jas 2:11 If *you d* not **commit adultery** but do commit AIT
Jas 2:11 not commit adultery but *d* **commit murder**, AIT
Jas 2:20 *d you* **want** evidence that faith without deeds AIT
Jas 2:24 righteous by **what** they **d** and not by faith G2240
Jas 3:14 *d* not **boast** about it or deny the truth. AIT
Jas 4: 2 You desire but *d* not **have**, so you kill. AIT
Jas 4: 2 *You d* not **have** because you do not ask God AIT
Jas 4: 2 You do not have because you *d* not **ask** God. AIT
Jas 4: 3 *you d* not **receive**, because you AIT
Jas 4: 5 Or *d you* **think** Scripture says without reason AIT
Jas 4:11 sisters, *d* not **slander** one another. AIT
Jas 4:14 you *d* not *even* **know** what will happen AIT
Jas 4:15 Lord's will, we will live and **d** this or that." G4472
Jas 4:17 the good *they ought to* **d** and doesn't G4472
Jas 4:17 good they ought to do and doesn't **d** it, G4472
Jas 5:12 sisters, *d* not **swear**—not by heaven or by AIT
1Pe 1: 8 and *even though you d* not **see** him now AIT
1Pe 1:14 *d* not **conform** to the evil desires you had AIT
1Pe 1:15 called you is holy, so be holy in all you **d**; G419
1Pe 2: 7 But *to those who d* **not believe**, "The stone AIT
1Pe 2:14 him to punish **those who d wrong** and to G2804
1Pe 2:14 wrong and to commend **those who d right**. G18
1Pe 2:16 but *d* not **use** your freedom as a cover-up AIT
1Pe 3: 1 if any *of them d* **not believe** the word AIT
1Pe 3: 6 daughters *if you* **d** *what is* **right** and do not G16
1Pe 3: 6 do what is right and *d* not **give way to** fear. AIT
1Pe 3: 9 *D* not **repay** evil with evil or insult with insult AIT
1Pe 3:11 They must turn from evil and **d** good; they G4472
1Pe 3:12 of the Lord is against *those who* **d** evil." G4472
1Pe 3:13 to harm you if you are **eager to d** good? G2421
1Pe 3:14 "*D* not **fear** their threats; do not be frightened AIT
1Pe 3:14 not fear their threats; *d* not *be* **frightened**." AIT
1Pe 3:15 But **d** this with gentleness and respect NDT
1Pe 4: 2 *they d* not **live** the rest of their earthly lives AIT
1Pe 4: 3 the past doing what pagans choose to **d**— NDT
1Pe 4: 4 are surprised *that* you *d* not **join** them in their AIT
1Pe 4:11 they should **d** so as one who speaks the very NDT
1Pe 4:11 they should **d** so with the strength God NDT
1Pe 4:12 *d* not *be* **surprised** at the fiery ordeal that has AIT
1Pe 4:16 a Christian, *d* not *be* **ashamed**, but praise AIT
1Pe 4:17 outcome be *for* those *who d* **not obey** the AIT
1Pe 4:19 their faithful Creator and continue to **d good**. G17
2Pe 1:10 For *if you* **d** these things, you will never G4472
2Pe 1:19 and *you will* **d** well to pay attention to it G4472
2Pe 2:11 *d* not heap abuse on such beings when NDT
2Pe 2:12 blaspheme in matters *they d* **not understand**. AIT
2Pe 3: 8 But *d* not **forget** this one thing, dear friends AIT
2Pe 3:16 people distort, as they **d** the other Scriptures NDT
1Jn 1: 6 darkness, we lie and *d* not **live out** the truth. AIT
1Jn 2: 4 but *does* not **d** what he commands is a G5498
1Jn 2:11 *They d* not **know** where they are going AIT
1Jn 2:15 *D* not **love** the world or anything in the world AIT
1Jn 2:21 *I d* not **write** to you because you do not know AIT
1Jn 2:21 to you because *you d* not **know** the truth, AIT
1Jn 2:21 because *you d* **know** it and because no AIT
1Jn 2:27 and *you d* not **need** anyone to teach you. AIT
1Jn 3: 7 children, *d* not *let* anyone **lead** you **astray**. AIT
1Jn 3:10 Anyone who *does* not **d** what is right is G4472
1Jn 3:12 **D** not be like Cain, who belonged to the evil NDT
1Jn 3:13 *D* not *be* **surprised**, my brothers and sisters, if AIT
1Jn 3:21 if our hearts *d* not **condemn** us, we have AIT
1Jn 3:22 his commands and **d** what pleases him. G4472
1Jn 4: 1 Dear friends, *d* not **believe** every spirit, but AIT
1Jn 4:18 because fear **has to d with** punishment. G2400
2Jn 7 who *d* not **acknowledge** Jesus Christ as AIT
2Jn 8 Watch out that *you d* not **lose** what we have AIT
2Jn 10 *d* not **take** them into your house or welcome AIT
2Jn 12 but *I d* not **want** to use paper and ink. AIT
3Jn 10 those who want to **d** so and puts them out NDT
3Jn 11 *d* not **imitate** what is evil but what is good. AIT
3Jn 13 but *I d* not **want to** do so with pen and ink. AIT
3Jn 13 I do not want to **d so** with pen and ink. G1211[S]
Jude 10 slander whatever *they d* not **understand**, AIT
Jude 10 very things *they d* **understand** by instinct— AIT
Jude 10 as irrational animals **d**—will destroy them. NDT
Jude 19 natural instincts and *d* not **have** the Spirit. AIT
Rev 1:17 me and said: "*D* not *be* **afraid**. I am the First AIT
Rev 2: 5 Repent and **d** the things you did at first G4472
Rev 2: 5 If *you d* not **repent**, I will come to you and AIT
Rev 2:10 *D* not *be* **afraid** of what you are about to AIT
Rev 2:24 to you who *d* not **hold** to her teaching and AIT
Rev 3: 3 But if *you d* not **wake up**, I will come like a AIT
Rev 3:17 acquired wealth and *d* not **need** a thing. AIT
Rev 3:17 But *you d* not **realize** that you are wretched AIT
Rev 5: 5 one of the elders said to me, "*D* not **weep**! AIT
Rev 6: 6 and *d* not **damage** the oil and the wine!" AIT
Rev 7: 3 "*D* not **harm** the land or the sea or the trees AIT
Rev 10: 4 thunders have said and *d* not **write** it **down**." AIT
Rev 11: 2 the outer court; *d* not **measure** it, because it AIT
Rev 19:10 said to me, "Don't **d that**! I am a fellow G3972[S]
Rev 22: 9 said to me, "Don't **d that**! I am a fellow G3972[S]
Rev 22:10 "*D* not **seal up** the words of the prophecy of AIT
Rev 22:11 *Let* the one who does wrong continue *to* **d wrong** G92
Rev 22:11 *let* the one who does right continue *to* **d** G4472

DO-NOTHING (1) [DO, NOTHING]

Isa 30: 7 Therefore I call her Rahab the **D**. H8700

DOCTOR (4) [DOCTORS]

Mt 9:12 "It is not the healthy who need a **d**, but G2620
Mk 2:17 "It is not the healthy who need a **d**, but G2620
Lk 5:31 "It is not the healthy who need a **d**, but G2620
Col 4:14 dear friend Luke, the **d**, and Demas send G2620

DOCTORS (1) [DOCTOR]

Mk 5:26 the care of many **d** and had spent all she G2620

DOCTRINE (5) [DOCTRINES]

1Ti 1:10 whatever else is contrary to the sound **d** G1436
1Ti 4:16 Watch your life and **d** closely. Persevere in G1436
2Ti 4: 3 people will not put up with sound **d**. G1436
Titus 1: 9 others by sound **d** and refute those who G1436
Titus 2: 1 teach what is appropriate *to* sound **d**. G1436

DOCTRINES (1) [DOCTRINE]

1Ti 1: 3 people not *to* **teach false d** *any longer* G2281

DOCUMENT (1) [DOCUMENTS]

Est 8: 8 no **d** written in the king's name and H4181

DOCUMENTS (1) [DOCUMENT]

Jer 32:14 Take these **d**, both the sealed and H6219

DODAI (3)

2Sa 23: 9 to him was Eleazar son of **D** the Ahohite. H1862
1Ch 11:12 to him was Eleazar son of **D** the Ahohite, H1862
1Ch 27: 4 the second month was **D** the Ahohite; H1862

DODAVAHU (1)

2Ch 20:37 Eliezer son of **D** of Mareshah prophesied H1845

DODO (3)

Jdg 10: 1 of Puah, the son of **D**, rose to save Israel. H1861
2Sa 23:24 Elhanan son of **D** *from* Bethlehem, H1861
1Ch 11:26 Elhanan son of **D** from Bethlehem, H1861

DOE (5)

Ge 49:21 "Naphtali is a **d** set free that bears H387
Job 39: 1 Do you watch when the **d** bears her fawn? H387
Ps 22: T To the tune of "The **D** *of* the Morning." H387
Pr 5:19 A loving **d**, a graceful deer—may her H387
Jer 14: 5 Even the **d** in the field deserts her newborn H387

DOEG (6)

1Sa 21: 7 the LORD; he was **D** the Edomite, Saul's H1795
1Sa 22: 9 But **D** the Edomite, who was standing H1795
1Sa 22:18 The king then ordered **D**, "You turn and H1795
1Sa 22:18 So **D** the Edomite turned and struck them H1795
1Sa 22:22 "That day, when **D** the Edomite was there H1795
Ps 52: T When **D** the Edomite had gone to Saul H1795

DOES (530) [DO]

Ge 31:15 *D* he not **regard** *us as* foreigners? Not only AIT
Ge 39: 8 master *d* not **concern** *himself with* anything AIT
Ge 44: 7 said to him, "Why *d* my lord **say** such things? AIT
Ex 3: 3 strange sight—why the bush *d* not **burn up**." AIT
Ex 8:29 *let* Pharaoh *be sure that he d* not **act deceitfully** AIT
Ex 11: 1 and when he **d**, he will drive you H8938[S]
Ex 12:26 'What **d** this ceremony mean to you? NDT
Ex 13:14 when your son asks you, 'What **d** this mean? NDT
Ex 21: 8 If *she d* **not please** the master who has AIT
Ex 21:11 If *he d* not **provide** her *with* these three things, AIT
Ex 21:18 fist and the victim *d* not **die** but is confined to AIT
Ex 31:15 Whoever **d** any work on the Sabbath day H6913
Ex 33:15 "If your Presence *d* not **go** with us, do not AIT
Ex 34: 7 Yet *he d* not **leave the guilty unpunished**; he AIT
Ex 35: 2 Whoever **d** any work on it is to be put to H6913
Lev 4: 2 unintentionally and **d** what is forbidden in H6913
Lev 4:13 unintentionally and **d** what is forbidden in H6913
Lev 4:22 unintentionally and **d** what is forbidden in H6913
Lev 4:27 unintentionally and **d** what is forbidden in H6913
Lev 5:17 "If anyone sins and **d** what is forbidden in H6913
Lev 11: 4 *d* not *have* a **divided** hoof; it is AIT
Lev 11: 5 *d* not *have* a **divided** hoof; it is AIT
Lev 11: 6 *d* not *have* a **divided** hoof; it is AIT
Lev 11: 7 has a divided hoof, *d* not **chew** the cud; it is AIT
Lev 11:12 in the water that **d** not have fins and scales NDT
Lev 11:26 animal that *d* not *have* a **divided** hoof or that AIT
Lev 11:26 a divided hoof or *that d* not **chew** the cud is AIT
Lev 13: 4 skin is white but **d** not appear to be more NDT
Lev 13: 7 But if the rash *d* **spread** in their skin after they AIT
Lev 13:31 it **d** not seem to be more than skin deep NDT
Lev 13:32 hair in it and it **d** not appear to be more NDT
Lev 13:35 But if the sore *d* **spread** in the skin after they AIT
Lev 13:36 the skin, he *d* not *need to* **look** for yellow hair AIT
Lev 17: 9 and *d* not **bring** it to the entrance to the tent AIT
Lev 18:22 with a man as one **d** with a woman; H5435[S]
Lev 18:29 " 'Everyone who **d** any of these detestable H6913
Lev 20:13 with a man as one **d** *with* a woman, H5435[S]
Lev 23:30 people anyone who **d** any work on that H6913
Lev 27:33 If *anyone d* **make a substitution**, both the AIT
Nu 13:27 and it *d* **flow** *with* milk and honey! AIT
Nu 14:18 Yet *he d* not **leave the guilty unpunished**; he AIT
Nu 23:19 *D* he **speak** and then not act AIT
Nu 23:19 *D he* **promise** and not fulfill? AIT
Nu 23:24 like a lion *that d* not **rest** till it devours its AIT
Nu 24:23 Who can live when God **d** this? H8492
Nu 30:11 says nothing to her and *d* not **forbid** her, AIT
Dt 8: 3 teach you that man *d* not **live** on bread alone AIT
Dt 10:12 what *d* the LORD your God **ask** of you but to AIT
Dt 14: 8 it has a divided hoof, it **d** not chew the cud. NDT
Dt 14:10 But anything that **d** not have fins and scales NDT
Dt 18:12 Anyone *who* **d** these things is detestable H6913
Dt 18:19 account anyone *who d* not **listen** to my words AIT
Dt 18:22 of the LORD *d* not **take place** or come true, AIT
Dt 21:15 firstborn is the son of the wife *he d* **not love**, AIT
Dt 21:16 firstborn, the son of the wife *he d* **not love**. AIT
Dt 21:18 rebellious son who *d* not **obey** his father AIT
Dt 22: 5 LORD your God detests anyone *who* **d** this. H6913
Dt 25: 7 if a man *d* not **want** to marry his brother's AIT
Dt 25:16 God detests anyone *who* **d** these things, H6913
Dt 27:26 is anyone who *d* not **uphold** the words of this AIT
Dt 32: 4 A faithful God who **d** no wrong, upright NDT
Jos 1:18 rebels against your word and *d* not **obey** it, AIT
Jos 5:14 "What **message** *d* my Lord *have* for his AIT
Ru 2: 5 "Who **d** that young woman belong to?" NDT
1Sa 6: 9 But if it **d** not, then we will know that it was NDT
1Sa 11: 7 of anyone who *d* not **follow** Saul and Samuel AIT
1Sa 15:22 "**D** the LORD delight in burnt offerings and NDT
1Sa 15:29 Glory of Israel *d* not **lie** or change his mind AIT
1Sa 16: 7 The LORD **d** not look at the things people NDT
1Sa 22: 8 servant to lie in wait for me, as he **d** today." NDT
1Sa 22:13 me and lies in wait for me, as he **d** today?" NDT
1Sa 24:19 his enemy, *d he* **let** him **get away** unharmed? AIT
1Sa 28:14 "What **d** he look like?" he asked. "An old NDT
2Sa 7:14 When he **d wrong**, I will punish him with H6390
2Sa 14:13 the king says this, **d** he not convict himself NDT
2Sa 14:14 person *d* not *remain* **banished** from him. AIT
2Sa 16:10 king said, "What **d** this have to do with you NDT
2Sa 19:22 "What **d** this have to do with you NDT
2Sa 24: 3 But why *d* my lord the king **want** to do such a AIT
1Ki 2:23 if Adonijah **d** not pay with his life for this NDT
1Ki 8:41 the foreigner who **d** not belong to your NDT
1Ki 8:46 there is no one who *d* not **sin**—and you AIT
2Ki 5: 7 Why *d* this fellow **send** someone to me to be AIT
2Ki 6:27 "If the LORD *d* not **help** you, where can I get AIT
1Ch 21: 3 Why *d* my lord **want to do** this? Why AIT
2Ch 6:32 the foreigner who **d** not belong to your NDT
2Ch 6:36 there is no one who *d* not **sin**—and you AIT
Ezr 7:26 Whoever *d* not **obey** the law of your God AIT
Ne 2: 2 "Why **d** your face look so sad when you are NDT
Ne 5:13 anyone who *d* not **keep** this promise. AIT
Job 1: 9 "*D* Job **fear** God for nothing?" Satan replied. AIT
Job 3:21 to those who long for death that **d** not come, NDT
Job 5: 6 For hardship *d* not **spring** from the soil, nor AIT
Job 5: 6 nor *d* trouble **sprout** from the ground. AIT
Job 6: 5 *D* a wild donkey **bray** when it has grass, or an AIT
Job 7: 9 who goes down to the grave *d* not **return**. AIT
Job 8: 3 *D* God **pervert** justice? Does the Almighty AIT
Job 8: 3 *D* the Almighty **pervert** what is right? AIT
Job 8:15 it gives way; they cling to it, but *it d* not **hold**. AIT
Job 8:20 "Surely God *d* not **reject** one who is AIT
Job 9: 7 He speaks to the sun and *it d* not **shine**; he AIT
Job 9:13 God *d* not **restrain** his anger; even the AIT
Job 10: 3 **D** it please you to oppress me, to spurn the NDT
Job 11:11 when he sees evil, *d he* not **take note**? AIT
Job 12: 3 Who **d** not know all these things? NDT
Job 12: 9 of all these *d* not **know** that the hand of AIT
Job 12:11 *D* not the ear **test** words as the tongue tastes AIT
Job 12:12 **D** not long life bring understanding? NDT
Job 14:12 so he lies down and *d* not **rise**; till the AIT
Job 16: 6 not relieved; and if I refrain, *it d* not **go** away. AIT
Job 18:21 such is the place of *one who d* not **know** God." AIT
Job 19:16 but *he d* not **answer**, though I beg AIT
Job 19:22 Why do you pursue me as God **d**? Will you NDT
Job 21:17 How often *d* calamity **come** upon them, the AIT
Job 22:13 'What *d* God **know**? Does he judge AIT
Job 22:13 *D he* **judge** through such darkness? AIT
Job 22:14 so *he d* not **see** us as he goes about in the AIT
Job 23:13 *He* **d** whatever he pleases. H6913
Job 24: 1 "Why *d* the Almighty not **set** times for AIT
Job 25: 3 On whom *d* his light not **rise**? AIT
Job 27: 9 *D* God **listen** *to* their cry when distress comes AIT
Job 28:12 Where **d** understanding dwell? NDT
Job 28:20 Where then *d* wisdom **come** from? Where AIT
Job 28:20 Where **d** understanding dwell? NDT
Job 31: 4 *D he* not **see** my ways and count my every AIT
Job 33:14 For God *d* **speak**—now one way, now another AIT
Job 33:29 "God **d** all these things to a person H7188
Job 34:19 to princes and *d* not **favor** the rich over the AIT
Job 35: 6 If you sin, how *d that* **affect** him? If your sins AIT
Job 35: 6 If your sins are many, what *d that* **do** to him? AIT
Job 35: 7 or what *d he* **receive** from your hand? AIT
Job 35:12 *He d* not **answer** when people cry out AIT
Job 35:13 God *d* not **listen** *to* their empty plea AIT
Job 35:15 and *he d* not **take** the least **notice** of AIT
Job 36: 6 *He d* not **keep** the wicked **alive** but gives the AIT
Job 36: 7 *He d* not **take** his eyes off the righteous; he AIT
Job 37: 5 *he* **d** great things beyond our H6913
Job 37:23 great righteousness, *he d* not **oppress**. AIT
Job 37:24 for *d he* not **have regard for** all the wise in AIT
Job 38:19 And where **d** darkness reside? NDT
Job 38:28 *D* the rain **have** a father? Who fathers the AIT
Job 39: 7 in the town; *it d* not **hear** a driver's shout. AIT
Job 39:22 of nothing; *it d* not **shy away** from the sword. AIT
Job 39:26 "*D* the hawk **take flight** by your wisdom and AIT
Job 39:27 *D* the eagle **soar** at your command and build AIT
Job 40:23 A raging river *d* not **alarm** it; it is secure AIT
Job 41:26 **d** the spear or the dart or the javelin. NDT

Ps 1: 1 is the one who d not walk in step with the AIT
Ps 1: 3 fruit in season and whose leaf d not wither— AIT
Ps 7:12 If he d not relent, he will sharpen his sword AIT
Ps 9:12 he d not ignore the cries of the afflicted. AIT
Ps 10: 4 In his pride the wicked man d not seek him AIT
Ps 10:13 Why d the wicked man revile God? Why does AIT
Ps 10:13 Why d he say to himself, "He won't call me AIT
Ps 14: 1 are vile; there is no one who d good. H6913
Ps 14: 3 there is no one who d good, not even one H6913
Ps 15: 2 is blameless, who d what is righteous H7188
Ps 15: 3 no slander, who d no wrong to a neighbor H6913
Ps 15: 4 when it hurts, and d not change their mind; AIT
Ps 15: 5 who d not accept a bribe against the AIT
Ps 15: 5 Whoever d these things will never be H6913
Ps 17: 1 my prayer—it d not rise from deceitful lips. NDT
Ps 24: 4 who d not trust in an idol or swear by a false AIT
Ps 32: 2 sin the LORD d not count against them and AIT
Ps 33: 4 is right and true; he is faithful in all he d. H5126
Ps 38:14 I have become like one who d not hear AIT
Ps 40: 4 in the LORD, who d not look to the proud, to AIT
Ps 41: 2 he d not give them over to the desire of their AIT
Ps 41:11 for my enemy d not triumph over me. AIT
Ps 44: 6 in my bow, my sword d not bring me victory; AIT
Ps 53: 1 are vile; there is no one who d good. H6913
Ps 53: 3 there is no one who d good, not even one H6913
Ps 55:19 from of old, who d not change—he will hear AIT
Ps 69:33 the needy and d not despise his captive AIT
Ps 72:18 of Israel, who alone d marvelous deeds. H6913
Ps 73:11 D the Most High know anything? NDT
Ps 74: 1 Why d your anger smolder against the sheep AIT
Ps 78:39 flesh, a passing breeze that d not return. AIT
Ps 84:11 no good thing d he withhold from those AIT
Ps 94: 7 "The LORD d not see; the God of Jacob AIT
Ps 94: 9 D he who fashioned the ear not hear? Does AIT
Ps 94: 9 D he who formed the eye not see? AIT
Ps 94:10 D he who disciplines nations not punish AIT
Ps 94:10 D he who teaches mankind lack knowledge NDT
Ps 103:10 he d not treat us as our sins deserve or repay AIT
Ps 115: 3 is in heaven; he d whatever pleases him. H6913
Ps 121: 1 mountains—where d my help come from? AIT
Ps 135: 6 The LORD d whatever pleases him, in the H6913
Ps 136: 4 to him who alone d great wonders, His H6913
Ps 145:13 in all he promises and faithful in all he d. H5126
Ps 145:17 in all his ways and faithful in all he d. H5126
Pr 5: 6 wander aimlessly, but she d not know it. AIT
Pr 6:32 no sense; whoever d so destroys himself. H6913
Pr 8: 1 D not wisdom call out? Does not AIT
Pr 8: 1 D not understanding raise her voice AIT
Pr 10: 3 The LORD d not let the righteous go hungry AIT
Pr 13: 1 a mocker d not respond to rebukes. AIT
Pr 14: 5 An honest witness d not deceive, but a false AIT
Pr 14:17 A quick-tempered person d foolish things H6913
Pr 16:10 an oracle, and his mouth d not betray justice. AIT
Pr 17:20 One whose heart is corrupt d not prosper AIT
Pr 18: 3 so d contempt, and with H995S
Pr 24:12 d not he who weighs the heart perceive it? AIT
Pr 24:12 D not he who guards your life know it AIT
Pr 26: 2 an undeserved curse d not come to rest. AIT
Pr 28:13 Whoever conceals their sins d not prosper AIT
Pr 29:16 the wicked thrive, so d sin, but the H8049S
Pr 31:18 her lamp d not go out at night. AIT
Pr 31:27 of her household and d not eat the bread of AIT
Ecc 2: 2 And what d pleasure accomplish?" AIT
Ecc 3:14 that everything God d will endure forever; H6913
Ecc 3:14 God d it so that people will fear him. H6913
Ecc 6: 2 God d not grant them the ability to enjoy AIT
Ecc 6: 3 his prosperity and d not receive proper burial, AIT
Ecc 6: 5 it has more rest than d that man— NDT
Ecc 6:11 the meaning, and how d that profit anyone? NDT
Ecc 7:20 no one who d what is right and never sins. H6913
Ecc 9:11 d food come to the wise or wealth to the NDT
SS 2: 7 by the gazelles and by the d of the field: H387
SS 3: 5 by the gazelles and by the d of the field: H387
Isa 1: 3 Israel d not know, my people do not AIT
Isa 1:23 the widow's case d not come before them. AIT
Isa 8:20 If anyone d not speak according to this word AIT
Isa 10:15 D the ax raise itself above the person who AIT
Isa 19:14 they make Egypt stagger in all that she d H5126
Isa 28:24 plows for planting, d he plow continually? NDT
Isa 28:24 D he keep on breaking up and working the AIT
Isa 28:25 d he not sow caraway and scatter cumin? AIT
Isa 28:25 D he not plant wheat in its place, barley in AIT
Isa 28:28 so one d not go on threshing it forever. AIT
Isa 28:28 but one d not use horses to grind grain. AIT
Isa 31: 2 bring disaster; he d not take back his words. AIT
Isa 45: 9 D the clay say to the potter, 'What are you AIT
Isa 45: 9 are you making?' D your work say, 'The NDT
Isa 54:15 If anyone d attack you, it will not be my AIT
Isa 55: 2 and your labor on what d not satisfy? NDT
Isa 56: 2 Blessed is the one who d this—the H6913
Isa 58: 2 were a nation that d what is right and has H6913
Isa 59: 9 and righteousness d not reach us. AIT
Isa 63:16 though Abraham d not know us or Israel AIT
Isa 65:20 an old man who d not live out his years AIT
Jer 2:32 D a young woman forget her jewelry, a bride AIT
Jer 8: 5 Why d Jerusalem always turn away H5904
Jer 11: 3 is the one who d not obey the terms of this AIT
Jer 12: 1 Why d the way of the wicked prosper? Why AIT
Jer 12:17 if any nation d not listen, I will completely AIT
Jer 14:10 So the LORD d not accept them; he will now AIT
Jer 14:22 for you are the one who d all this. H6913
Jer 17: 8 It d not fear when heat comes; its leaves are AIT
Jer 18: 6 I not do with you, Israel, as this potter d?" NDT
Jer 18:10 if it d evil in my sight and does not H6913
Jer 18:10 if it does evil in my sight and d not obey me, AIT
Jer 18:14 D the snow of Lebanon ever vanish from its AIT
Jer 22:15 "D it make you a king to have more and AIT
La 3:33 For he d not willingly bring affliction or grief AIT
Eze 3:20 turns from their righteousness and d evil, H6913
Eze 8:12 'The LORD d not see us; the LORD has AIT
Eze 9: 9 has forsaken the land; the LORD d not see. AIT
Eze 17:15 Will he who d such things escape H6913
Eze 18: 5 is a righteous man who d what is just H6913
Eze 18: 6 He d not eat at the mountain shrines or look AIT
Eze 18: 6 He d not defile his neighbor's wife or have AIT
Eze 18: 7 He d not oppress anyone, but returns what AIT
Eze 18: 7 He d not commit robbery but gives his food AIT
Eze 18: 8 He d not lend to them at interest or take a AIT
Eze 18:10 who sheds blood or d any of these other H6913
Eze 18:12 He d not return what he took in pledge AIT
Eze 18:12 looks to the idols. He d detestable things. H6913
Eze 18:14 he sees them, he d not do such things: AIT
Eze 18:15 "He d not eat at the mountain shrines or look AIT
Eze 18:15 He d not defile his neighbor's wife AIT
Eze 18:16 He d not oppress anyone or require a pledge AIT
Eze 18:16 He d not commit robbery but gives his food AIT
Eze 18:19 'Why d the son not share the guilt of his AIT
Eze 18:21 all my decrees and d what is just and H6913
Eze 18:24 commits sin and d the same detestable H6913
Eze 18:24 detestable things the wicked person d, H6913
Eze 18:27 have committed and d what is just and H6913
Eze 21:13 which the sword despises, d not continue? AIT
Eze 33: 4 trumpet but d not heed the warning and the AIT
Eze 33: 6 sword coming and d not blow the trumpet to AIT
Eze 33:18 turns from their righteousness and d evil, H6913
Eze 33:19 their wickedness and d what is just and H6913
Eze 46:12 offerings as he d on the Sabbath day. H6913
Da 3: 6 Whoever d not fall down and worship will AIT
Da 3:11 that whoever d not fall down and worship AIT
Da 3:18 But even if he d not, we want you to know NDT
Da 4:35 He d as he pleases with the powers of A10522
Da 4:37 everything he d is right and all his A10434
Da 8:24 will succeed in whatever he d. H6913
Da 9:14 our God is righteous in everything he d; H6913
Hos 7: 9 sap his strength, but he d not realize it. AIT
Hos 7: 9 is sprinkled with gray, but he d not notice. AIT
Hos 7:10 despite all this he d not return to the LORD his AIT
Am 3: 4 D a lion roar in the thicket when it has no AIT
Am 3: 4 D it growl in its den when it has caught AIT
Am 3: 5 D a bird swoop down to a trap on the ground AIT
Am 3: 5 D a trap spring up from the ground if it has AIT
Am 3: 7 the Sovereign LORD d nothing without H6913
Am 6:12 D one plow the sea with oxen AIT
Mic 2: 7 it be said, "D the LORD become impatient? AIT
Mic 2: 7 become impatient? D he do such things?" NDT
Mic 6: 8 And what d the LORD require of you? To AIT
Hab 3:17 the fig tree d not bud and there are no AIT
Zep 3: 2 She d not trust in the LORD, she does not draw AIT
Zep 3: 2 in the LORD, she d not draw near to her God. AIT
Zep 3: 5 within her is righteous; he d no wrong. H6913
Zep 3: 5 every new day he d not fail, yet the AIT
Hag 2: 3 How d it look to you now? Does AIT
Hag 2: 3 D it not seem to you like nothing? NDT
Hag 2:12 oil or other food, d it become consecrated? AIT
Hag 2:13 one of these things, d it become defiled?" AIT
Mal 2:12 As for the man who d this, whoever he H6913
Mal 2:15 And what d the one God seek? Godly AIT
Mal 2:16 "d violence to the one he should protect," H4059
Mt 3:10 every tree that d not produce good fruit AIT
Mt 7:19 Every tree that d not bear good fruit is cut AIT
Mt 7:21 only the one who d the will of my G4472
Mt 7:26 mine and d not put them into practice is like AIT
Mt 8: 9 say to my servant, 'Do this,' and he d it." G4472
Mt 9:11 "Why d your teacher eat with tax collectors AIT
Mt 10:38 Whoever d not take up their cross and follow AIT
Mt 11: 6 is anyone who d not stumble on account of AIT
Mt 12:30 whoever d not gather with me scatters. AIT
Mt 12:43 arid places seeking rest and d not find it. AIT
Mt 12:50 For whoever d the will of my Father in G4472
Mt 13:12 Whoever d not have, even what they have AIT
Mt 13:19 about the kingdom and d not understand it, AIT
Mt 15:11 into someone's mouth d not defile them, AIT
Mt 15:20 with unwashed hands d not defile them." AIT
Mt 17:25 he d," he replied. When Peter came NDT
Mt 24:50 on a day when he d not expect him and at AIT
Mt 25:29 Whoever d not have, even what they have AIT
Mk 2: 7 "Why d this fellow talk like that? He's AIT
Mk 2:16 "Why d he eat with tax collectors and sinners AIT
Mk 3:35 Whoever d God's will is my brother and G4472
Mk 4:25 whoever d not have, even what they AIT
Mk 4:27 grows, though he d not know how. AIT
Mk 8:12 "Why d this generation ask for a sign? AIT
Mk 9:12 "To be sure, Elijah d come first, and restores AIT
Mk 9:37 welcomes me d not welcome me but the one AIT
Mk 9:39 "For no one who d a miracle in my name G4472
Mk 11:23 and d not doubt in their heart but believes AIT
Mk 13:14 desolation' standing where it d not belong— AIT
Mk 16:16 whoever d not believe will be AIT
Lk 3: 9 every tree that d not produce good fruit AIT
Lk 6:43 bad fruit, nor d a bad tree bear good fruit. AIT
Lk 6:49 words and d not put them into practice is like AIT
Lk 7: 8 say to my servant, 'Do this,' and he d it." G4472
Lk 7:23 is anyone who d not stumble on account of AIT
Lk 8:18 whoever d not have, even what they AIT
Lk 11:23 whoever d not gather with me scatters. AIT
Lk 11:24 arid places seeking rest and d not find it. AIT
Lk 12:15 life d not consist in an abundance of AIT
Lk 12:46 on a day when he d not expect him and at AIT
Lk 12:47 will and d not get ready or does not do AIT
Lk 12:47 not get ready or d not do what the master AIT
Lk 12:48 But the one who d not know and does things AIT
Lk 12:48 does not know and d things deserving G4472
Lk 12:54 'It's going to rain,' and it d. G1181+4048
Lk 14:26 comes to me and d not hate father and AIT
Lk 14:27 whoever d not carry their cross and follow AIT
Lk 24:18 Jerusalem who d not know the things that AIT
Lk 24:39 a ghost d not have flesh and bones AIT
Jn 3:18 whoever d not believe stands AIT
Jn 3:20 Everyone who d evil hates the light, and G4556
Jn 5:19 whatever the Father d the Son also does. G4472
Jn 5:19 whatever the Father does the Son also d. G4472
Jn 5:20 loves the Son and shows him all he d. G4472
Jn 5:23 Whoever d not honor the Son does not honor AIT
Jn 5:23 not honor the Son d not honor the Father, AIT
Jn 5:38 nor d his word dwell in you, for you do not AIT
Jn 6:61 Jesus said to them, "D this offend you? AIT
Jn 7:18 speaks on their own d so to gain personal NDT
Jn 7:35 "Where d this man intend to go that we AIT
Jn 7:42 D not Scripture say that the Messiah will AIT
Jn 7:46 "No one ever spoke the way this man d," NDT
Jn 7:51 "D our law condemn a man without first AIT
Jn 7:52 that a prophet d not come out of Galilee." AIT
Jn 9:16 not from God, for he d not keep the Sabbath." AIT
Jn 9:31 We know that God d not listen to sinners. AIT
Jn 9:31 listens to the godly person who d his will. G4472
Jn 10: 1 anyone who d not enter the sheep pen by AIT
Jn 10:12 not the shepherd and d not own the sheep. AIT
Jn 12:35 walks in the dark d not know where they are AIT
Jn 12:44 believes in me d not believe in me only, AIT
Jn 12:47 anyone hears my words but d not keep them, AIT
Jn 12:48 who rejects me and d not accept my words; AIT
Jn 13:19 so that when it d happen you will believe AIT
Jn 14:24 Anyone who d not love me will not obey my AIT
Jn 14:29 so that when it d happen you will believe. AIT
Jn 15: 2 every branch that d bear fruit he prunes so AIT
Jn 15:15 because a servant d not know his master's AIT
Jn 16:17 another, "What d he mean by saying, 'In a AIT
Jn 16:18 "What d he mean by 'a little while'? AIT
Jn 17:25 though the world d not know you, I know you, AIT
Ac 2:12 they asked one another, "What d this mean?" AIT
Ac 3:12 why d this surprise you? Why do you AIT
Ac 3:23 Anyone who d not listen to him will be AIT
Ac 7:48 the Most High d not live in houses made by AIT
Ac 10:34 how true it is that God d not show favoritism AIT
Ac 10:35 one who fears him and d what is right. G2237
Ac 13:40 the prophets have said d not happen to you: AIT
Ac 15:17 says the Lord, who d these things'— G4472
Ac 17:24 earth and d not live in temples built by AIT
Ro 2: 9 distress for every human being who d evil: G2981
Ro 2:10 peace for everyone who d good: G2237
Ro 2:11 For God d not show favoritism. AIT
Ro 3:12 there is no one who d good, not even one G4472
Ro 4: 3 What d Scripture say? "Abraham believed AIT
Ro 4: 5 to the one who d not work but trusts God who AIT
Ro 5: 5 And hope d not put us to shame, because AIT
Ro 7:18 For I know that good itself d not dwell in me AIT
Ro 7:20 I who do it, but it is sin living in me that d it. NDT
Ro 8: 7 hostile to God; it d not submit to God's law AIT
Ro 8: 9 And if anyone d not have the Spirit of Christ AIT
Ro 8:15 Spirit you received d not make you slaves, NDT
Ro 9:16 It d not, therefore, depend on human desire NDT
Ro 9:19 "Then why d God still blame us? For who AIT
Ro 9:21 D not the potter have the right to make out of AIT
Ro 10: 5 "The person who d these things will live G4472
Ro 10: 8 But what d it say? "The word is near you; it is AIT
Ro 13:10 Love d no harm to a neighbor. G2237
Ro 14: 3 treat with contempt the one who d not, G2266S
Ro 14: 3 the one who d not eat everything must AIT
Ro 14: 3 must not judge the one who d, G2266S
Ro 14: 6 one day as special d so to the Lord. G5858S
Ro 14: 6 Whoever eats meat d so to the Lord, for G2266S
Ro 14: 6 abstains d so to the Lord and G4024+2266S
Ro 14:22 is the one who d not condemn himself by AIT
Ro 14:23 everything that d not come from faith is NDT
1Co 2:14 without the Spirit d not accept the things that AIT
1Co 4: 4 but that d not make me innocent. AIT
1Co 7: 4 The wife d not have authority over her own AIT
1Co 7: 4 the husband d not have authority over his AIT
1Co 7:11 But if she d, she must remain unmarried G6004S
1Co 7:37 virgin—this man also d the right thing. G4472
1Co 7:38 he who marries the virgin d right, but he G4472
1Co 7:38 but he who d not marry her does better. AIT
1Co 7:38 he who does not marry her d better. G4472
1Co 8: 8 But food d not bring us near to God; we are AIT
1Co 8: 9 of your rights d not become a stumbling AIT
1Co 9: 7 plants a vineyard and d not eat its grapes? AIT
1Co 9: 7 Who tends a flock and d not drink the milk? AIT
1Co 11: 6 For if a woman d not cover her head, she AIT
1Co 11:14 D not the very nature of things teach you that AIT
1Co 13: 4 It d not envy, it does not boast, it is not proud AIT
1Co 13: 4 does not envy, it d not boast, it is not proud. AIT
1Co 13: 5 It d not dishonor others, it is not self-seeking AIT
1Co 13: 6 Love d not delight in evil but rejoices with the AIT
1Co 14: 2 in a tongue d not speak to people but to AIT
1Co 14: 8 if the trumpet d not sound a clear call, who AIT
1Co 15:27 it is clear that this d not include God himself NDT

1Co 15:36 What you sow d not come to life unless it AIT
1Co 15:50 nor d the perishable inherit the imperishable. AIT
1Co 16:19 so d the church that meets at their NDT
1Co 16:22 If anyone d not love the Lord, let that person AIT
2Co 6:15 Or what d a believer have in common with NDT
2Co 8:12 not according to what one d not have. AIT
2Co 10: 3 we do not wage war as the world d. NDT
2Co 11:18 many are boasting in the way the world d, NDT
Gal 2: 6 God d not show favoritism—they AIT
Gal 3: 5 d God give you his Spirit and work miracles AIT
Gal 3:10 is everyone who d not continue to do AIT
Gal 3:12 "The person who d these things will live G4472
Gal 3:16 Scripture d not say "and to seeds," meaning AIT
Gal 3:17 d not set aside the covenant previously AIT
Gal 4:30 But what d Scripture say? "Get rid of the slave AIT
Gal 5: 8 kind of persuasion d not come from the one NDT
Eph 4: 9 What d "he ascended" mean except that he AIT
Eph 4:16 as each part d its work. G1918+1877+3586
Eph 5:29 their body, just as Christ d the church— NDT
Php 1:18 But what d it matter? The important G5515+5516
Col 3:25 Anyone who d wrong will be repaid for their G92
Col 4:10 you his greetings, as d Mark, the cousin of NDT
1Th 2: 3 the appeal we make d not spring from error NDT
1Th 3:12 for everyone else, just as ours d for you. NDT
1Th 4: 8 this instruction d not reject a human being AIT
2Th 3: 6 disruptive and d not live according to the AIT
2Th 3:14 note of anyone who d not obey our AIT
1Ti 3: 5 If anyone d not know how to manage his own AIT
1Ti 5: 8 Anyone who d not provide for their relatives AIT
1Ti 6: 3 otherwise and d not agree to the sound AIT
2Ti 1: 7 the Spirit God gave us d not make us timid, NDT
2Ti 2: 5 athlete d not receive the victor's crown AIT
2Ti 2:15 worker who d not need to be ashamed and AIT
Titus 1: 2 which God, who d not lie, promised before NDT
Heb 7:27 he d not need to offer sacrifices day after day, AIT
Jas 1:13 be tempted by evil, nor d he tempt anyone; AIT
Jas 1:17 who d not change like shifting shadows. G1928
Jas 1:20 human anger d not produce the AIT
Jas 1:23 to the word but d not do what it says is like AIT
Jas 2:16 d nothing about their physical needs G1443
Jas 3:15 d not come down from heaven but is earthly AIT
1Pe 5:13 you her greetings, and so d my son Mark. NDT
2Pe 1: 9 But whoever d not have them is nearsighted AIT
1Jn 2: 1 But if anybody d sin, we have an advocate AIT
1Jn 2: 4 but d not do what he commands is a liar AIT
1Jn 2:17 whoever d the will of God lives forever G4472
1Jn 2:24 If it d, you also will remain in the Son G3531S
1Jn 2:29 that everyone who d what is right has G4472
1Jn 3: 1 reason the world d not know us is that it did AIT
1Jn 3: 7 The one who d what is right is righteous G4472
1Jn 3: 8 The one who d what is sinful is of the G4472
1Jn 3:10 Anyone who d not do what is right is not AIT
1Jn 3:10 is anyone who d not love their brother AIT
1Jn 3:14 Anyone who d not love remains in death. AIT
1Jn 4: 3 spirit that d not acknowledge Jesus is not AIT
1Jn 4: 6 whoever is not from God d not listen to us. AIT
1Jn 4: 8 Whoever d not love does not know God AIT
1Jn 4: 8 Whoever does not love d not know God AIT
1Jn 4:20 For whoever d not love their brother and AIT
1Jn 5:10 Whoever d not believe God has made him AIT
1Jn 5:12 whoever d not have the Son of God does not AIT
1Jn 5:12 not have the Son of God d not have life. AIT
1Jn 5:16 sister commit a sin that d not lead to death, NDT
1Jn 5:16 refer to those whose sin d not lead to death. NDT
1Jn 5:17 there is sin that d not lead to death. NDT
1Jn 5:18 anyone born of God d not continue to sin; AIT
2Jn 9 runs ahead and d not continue in the AIT
2Jn 9 in the teaching of Christ d not have God; AIT
2Jn 10 comes to you and d not bring this teaching, AIT
3Jn 11 Anyone who d what is good is from God G16
3Jn 11 Anyone who d what is evil has not seen G2803
Rev 2:26 who is victorious and d my will to the end, G5498
Rev 17:10 but when he d come, he must remain AIT
Rev 21:23 The city d not need the sun or the moon to AIT
Rev 21:27 will anyone who d what is shameful G4472
Rev 22:11 Let the one who d wrong continue to do G92
Rev 22:11 let the one who d right continue to do G1465

DOESN'T (13) [DO]

1Sa 20: 2 my father d do anything, great or H4202
1Ki 18:12 If I go and tell Ahab and he d find you H4202
Hos 13:13 he d have the sense to come out of the H4202
Mt 17:24 "D your teacher pay the temple tax?" G4024
Mk 7:19 For it d go into their heart but into their G4024
Lk 13:15 D each of you on the Sabbath untie your G4024
Lk 15: 4 D he leave the ninety-nine in the open G4024
Lk 15: 8 D she light a lamp, sweep the house and G4049
Ac 19:35 d all the world know that the city of G1639+4024
1Co 9: 8 D the Law say the same thing G4024
1Co 9:10 he says this for us, d he? Yes, this was NDT
Gal 2:17 d that mean that Christ promotes sin? G727
Jas 4:17 the good they ought to do and d do it, G3590

DOG (12) [DOG'S, DOGS]

Ex 11: 7 the Israelites not a d will bark at any H3978
Jdg 7: 5 their tongues as a d laps from those who H3978
1Sa 17:43 to David, "Am I a d, that you come at me H3978
1Sa 24:14 Who are you pursuing? A dead d? A flea? H3978
2Sa 9: 8 that you should notice a dead d like me?" H3978
2Sa 16: 9 should this dead d curse my lord the H3978
2Ki 8:13 your servant, a mere d, accomplish such a H3978
Job 18:11 him on every side and d his every step. H7046
Pr 26:11 As a d returns to its vomit, so fools repeat H3978
Pr 26:17 Like one who grabs a stray d by the ears is H3978
Ecc 9: 4 even a live d is better off than a dead lion! H3978
2Pe 2:22 "A d returns to its vomit," and, "A sow G3264

DOG'S (2) [DOG]

2Sa 3: 8 answered, "Am I a d head—on Judah's H3978
Isa 66: 3 a lamb is like one who breaks a d neck; H3978

DOGS (28) [DOG]

Ex 22:31 torn by wild beasts; throw it to the d. H3978
Jdg 7: 6 drank from cupped hands, lapping like d. NDT
1Ki 14:11 D will eat those belonging to Jeroboam H3978
1Ki 16: 4 D will eat those belonging to Baasha who H3978
1Ki 21:19 In the place where d licked up Naboth's H3978
1Ki 21:19 Naboth's blood, d will lick up your blood H3978
1Ki 21:23 'D will devour Jezebel by the wall of H3978
1Ki 21:24 "D will eat those belonging to Ahab who H3978
1Ki 22:38 and the d licked up his blood, as the H3978
2Ki 9:10 d will devour her on the plot of ground at H3978
2Ki 9:36 of ground at Jezreel d will devour H3978
Job 30: 1 have disdained to put with my sheep d. H3978
Ps 22:16 D surround me, a pack of villains encircles H3978
Ps 22:20 my precious life from the power of the d. H3978
Ps 59: 6 snarling like d, and prowl about the H3978
Ps 59:14 snarling like d, and prowl about the H3978
Ps 68:23 the tongues of your d have their share." H3978
Isa 56:10 they are all mute d, they cannot bark; H3978
Isa 56:11 They are d with mighty appetites; they H3978
Jer 15: 3 to kill and the d to drag away and the H3978
Mt 7: 6 "Do not give d what is sacred; do not G3264
Mt 15:26 the children's bread and toss it to the d." G3249
Mt 15:27 "Even the d eat the crumbs that fall from G3249
Mk 7:27 the children's bread and toss it to the d." G3249
Mk 7:28 "even the d under the table eat the G3249
Lk 16:21 Even the d came and licked his sores G3264
Php 3: 2 Watch out for those d, those evildoers G3264
Rev 22:15 Outside are the d, those who practice G3264

DOING (184) [DO]

Ge 2: 2 had finished the work he had been d; H6913
Ge 18:19 way of the LORD by d what is right and just H6913
Ge 20:10 "What was your reason for d this? H6913
Ge 31:12 seen all that Laban has been d to you. H6913
Ge 34:19 lost no time in d what they said, because H6913
Ex 18:14 saw all that Moses was d for the people, H6913
Ex 18:14 "What is this you are d for the people? H6913
Ex 18:17 replied, "What you are d is not good. H6913
Ex 23: 2 "Do not follow the crowd in d wrong. AIT
Ex 36: 4 skilled workers who were d all the work on H6913
Ex 36: 4 on the sanctuary left what they were d H6913
Ex 36: 5 more than enough for d the work the LORD H6275
Nu 3: 7 at the tent of meeting by d the work of the H6268
Nu 3: 8 fulfilling the obligations of the Israelites by d H6268
Nu 4:27 whether carrying or d other work, is to be H6275
Nu 22:30 Have I been in the habit of d this to you?" H6913
Dt 4:25 d evil in the eyes of the LORD your God H6913
Dt 9:18 d what was evil in the LORD's sight and so H6913
Dt 12: 8 do here today, everyone d as they see fit, NDT
Dt 12:25 because you will be d what is right in the H6913
Dt 12:28 because you will be d what is good and H6913
Dt 13:18 giving you today and d what is right in his H6913
Dt 17: 2 gives you is found d evil in the eyes of the H6913
Jos 2:14 "If you don't tell what we are d, we will H1821
Jos 2:20 But if you tell what we are d, we will be H1821
Jos 7:10 What are you d down on your face? AIT
Jos 10: 1 d to Ai and its king as he had done to H6913
Jdg 11:27 you are d me wrong by waging war H6913
Jdg 18: 3 What are you d in this place H6913
Jdg 18:18 the priest said to them, "What are you d?" H6913
1Sa 2:22 his sons were d to all Israel and H6913
1Sa 8: 8 serving other gods, so they are d to you. H6913
1Sa 12:25 Yet if you persist in d evil, both you H8317+8317
1Sa 25:39 his servant from d wrong and has brought NDT
2Sa 3:25 find out everything you are d. H6913
2Sa 8:15 d what was just and right for all his H6913
2Sa 12: 9 word of the LORD by d what is evil in his H6913
2Sa 12:14 But because by d this you have shown utter NDT
1Ki 12:24 every one of you, for this is my d. H4946+907
1Ki 14: 8 d only what was right in my eyes. H6913
1Ki 16:19 d evil in the eyes of the LORD and H6913
1Ki 19: 9 "What are you d here, Elijah H4537+4200+3870
1Ki 19:13 "What are you d here H4537+4200+3870
1Ki 22: 3 to us and yet we are d nothing to retake it H3120
2Ki 7: 9 to each other, "What we're d is not right. H6913
1Ch 18:14 d what was just and right for all his H6913
1Ch 21: 8 "I have sinned greatly by d this. H6913
1Ch 21:15 But as the angel was d so, the LORD saw H8845S
2Ch 11: 4 every one of you, for this is my d. H4946+907
2Ch 31: 7 They began d this in the H3569+2021+6894S
2Ch 31:20 d what was good and right and faithful H6913
2Ch 34:16 "Your officials are d everything that has H6913
2Ch 35: 6 d what the LORD commanded through H6913
Ne 2:16 know where I had gone or what I was d, H6913
Ne 2:16 any others who would be d the work. H6913
Ne 2:19 "What is this you are d?" they asked. H6913
Ne 4: 2 he said, "What are those feeble Jews d?" H6913
Ne 5: 9 I continued, "What you are d is not right. H6913
Ne 6:13 me so that I would commit a sin by d this, H6913
Ne 13:17 "What is this wicked thing you are d H6913
Ne 13:27 now that you too are d all this terrible H6913
Est 9:23 d what Mordecai had written to them. NDT
Job 9:12 Who can say to him, 'What are you d?' H6913
Ps 109:16 For he never thought of d a kindness, but H6913
Pr 1: 3 behavior, d what is right and just and fair AIT
Pr 2:14 who delight in d wrong and rejoice in the H6913
Pr 25:22 In d this, you will heap burning coals on H3954
Ecc 8: 4 who can say to him, "What are you d?" H6913
Isa 1:16 evil deeds out of my sight; stop d wrong. H8317
Isa 22:16 What are you d here and H4537+4200+3870
Isa 26:10 uprightness they go on d evil and do not H6401
Isa 38:19 they praise you, as I am d today; parents tell NDT
Isa 43:19 I am d a new thing! Now it springs H6913
Isa 54:15 it will not be my d; whoever attacks H4946+907
Isa 56: 2 and keeps their hands from d any evil." H6913
Isa 58:13 Sabbath and from d as you please on my H6913
Isa 58:13 your own way and not d as you please H5162
Jer 4:22 They are skilled in d evil; they know not H8317
Jer 4:30 What are you d, you devastated one H6913
Jer 7:13 While you were d all these things H6913
Jer 7:17 not see what they are d in the towns of H6913
Jer 11:15 "What is my beloved d in my H4537+4200
Jer 11:18 time he showed me what they were d. H5095
Jer 13:23 do good who are accustomed to d evil. H8317
Jer 17:24 Sabbath day holy by not d any work on it, H6913
Jer 32:40 I will never stop d good to them, and I H3512
Jer 32:41 I will rejoice in d them good and will H3201
Jer 38:20 "Obey the LORD by d what I tell you. NDT
Jer 48:10 curse on anyone who is lax in d the LORD's H6913
Eze 8: 6 do you see what they are d—the utterly H6913
Eze 8: 6 things the Israelites are d here, H6913
Eze 8: 9 detestable things they are d here. H6913
Eze 8:12 the elders of Israel are d in the darkness, H6913
Eze 8:13 "You will see them d things that are even H6913
Eze 8:17 do the detestable things they are d here? H6913
Eze 12: 9 people, ask you, 'What are you d? H6913
Eze 18: 8 his hand from d wrong and judges fairly H6404
Eze 25:12 on Judah and became very guilty by d so, H5933
Eze 33:19 is just and right, they will live by d so. H2157S
Eze 36:32 you to know that I am not d this for your H6913
Da 4:27 Renounce your sins by d what is right, and NDT
Mic 7: 3 Both hands are skilled in d evil; the ruler NDT
Mt 5:46 Are not even the tax collectors d that? G4472
Mt 5:47 people, what are you d more than others? G4472
Mt 6: 3 left hand know what your right hand is d, G4472
Mt 12: 2 Your disciples are d what is unlawful on G4472
Mt 20: 3 standing in the marketplace d nothing. G734
Mt 20: 6 been standing here all day long d nothing? G734
Mt 21:23 "By what authority are you d these things?" G4472
Mt 21:24 you by what authority I am d these things. G4472
Mt 21:27 you by what authority I am d these things. G4472
Mt 24:46 master finds him d so when he returns. G4472
Mk 2:24 why are they d what is unlawful on the G4472
Mk 3: 8 When they heard about all he was d G4472
Mk 11: 3 asks you, 'Why are you d this?' say, G4472
Mk 11: 5 "What are you d, untying that G4472
Mk 11:28 "By what authority are you d these things?" G4472
Mk 11:29 you by what authority I am d these things. G4472
Mk 11:33 you by what authority I am d these things." G4472
Lk 6: 2 "Why are you d what is unlawful on the G4472
Lk 12:43 the master finds d so when he returns. G4472
Lk 13:17 with all the wonderful things he was d. G1181
Lk 20: 2 by what authority you are d these things," G4472
Lk 20: 8 you by what authority I am d these things." G4472
Lk 23:34 they do not know what they are d. G4472
Jn 3: 2 the signs you are d if God were not with G4472
Jn 5:16 because Jesus was d these things on the G4472
Jn 5:19 he can do only what he sees his Father d G4472
Jn 5:36 the very works that I am d—testify that the G4472
Jn 7: 4 Since you are d these things, show G4472
Jn 7:51 him to find out what he has been d?" G4472
Jn 8:38 and you are d what you have heard from G4472
Jn 8:41 You are d the works of your own father." G4472
Jn 13: 7 "You do not realize now what I am d, but G4472
Jn 14:10 the Father, living in me, who is d his work. G4472
Jn 14:12 in me will do the works I have been d, G4472
Ac 5: 4 What made you think of d such a thing? You AIT
Ac 9:36 she was always d good and helping the G2240
Ac 10:38 he went around d good and healing all G2308
Ac 12: 9 idea that what the angel was d was really G1328
Ac 14:15 "Friends, why are you d this? We too are G4472
Ac 15:36 word of the Lord and see how they are d." G2400
Ac 17:21 spent their time d nothing but talking G1650
Ac 19:14 a Jewish chief priest, were d this. G4472
Ac 24:18 they found me in the temple courts d this. NDT
Ac 25:11 I am guilty of d anything deserving death G4556
Ac 26:31 "This man is not d anything that deserves G4556
Ro 1:13 have been prevented from d so until now) NDT
Ro 1:30 they invent ways of d evil; they disobey their AIT
Ro 2: 7 who by persistence in d good seek glory, G2240
Ro 7:19 evil I do not want to do—this I keep on d. G4556
Ro 12:20 In d this, you will heap burning coals on G4472
1Co 5: 2 fellowship the man who has been d this? G4556
1Co 5: 3 Jesus on the one who has been d this. G2981
2Co 11:12 And I will keep on d what I am doing in G4472
2Co 11:12 keep on doing what I am d in order to cut G4472
Gal 6: 9 Let us not become weary in d good, for at G4472
Eph 4:28 d something useful with their own hands G2237
Eph 6: 6 d the will of God from your heart. G4472
Eph 6:21 may know how I am and what I am d. G4556
Col 1: 6 just as it has been d among you since the NDT
1Th 5:11 each other up, just as in fact you are d. G4472
2Th 3: 4 the Lord that you are d and will continue G4472

2Th 3:13 sisters, never tire *of* **d what is good.** G2818
1Ti 6:21 professed and in so **d** have departed from NDT
Titus 1:16 disobedient and unfit for **d** anything good. G2240
Titus 2: 7 set them an example *by* **d** what is good. G2240
Titus 3: 8 to devote themselves to **d** what is good. G2240
Titus 3:14 to devote themselves to **d** what is good, G2240
Heb 10:25 as some are in the habit of **d**, but NDT
Heb 13: 2 by **so d** some people have shown G4047S
Heb 13:21 you with everything good for **d** his will, G4472
Jas 1:25 they have heard, but **d** it—they will be G4475
Jas 2: 8 neighbor as yourself," *you are* **d** right. G4472
1Pe 2:12 though they accuse you of **d wrong**, they G2804
1Pe 2:15 it is God's will *that by* **d good** you should G16
1Pe 2:20 a beating *for* **d wrong** and endure it? G279
1Pe 2:20 But if you suffer *for* **d good** and you endure it G16
1Pe 3:17 to suffer *for* **d good** than for doing evil. G16
1Pe 3:17 to suffer for doing good than *for* **d evil**. G2803
1Pe 4: 3 time in the past **d** what pagans choose to G2981
3Jn 5 you are faithful *in* what *you are* **d** for the G2237
3Jn 10 I will call attention to what he is **d** G2240
Rev 2:19 that you are now **d** more than you did at G2240

DOLE (1)

Lev 26:26 and *they will* **d out** the bread by weight. H8740

DOLEFUL (KJV) JACKALS, MOURNFUL

DOMAIN (2) [DOMINION]

Dt 33:20 "Blessed is he who enlarges Gad's **d**! Gad NDT
Eze 27: 4 Your **d** was on the high seas; your H1473

DOMESTIC (1)

Lev 5: 2 wild or **d**, or of any unclean H989

DOMINION (19) [DOMAIN]

Nu 21:30 **Heshbon's d** has been destroyed all the H3114
Job 25: 2 "**D** and awe belong to God; he H5440
Job 38:33 Can you set up God's **d** over the earth? H5428
Ps 22:28 **d** belongs to the LORD and he rules H4867
Ps 103:22 the LORD, all his works everywhere in his **d**. H4939
Ps 114: 2 became God's sanctuary, Israel his **d**. H4939
Ps 145:13 your **d** endures through all H4939
Da 2:37 has given you **d** and power and might A10424
Da 4: 3 his **d** endures from generation to A10717
Da 4:22 your **d** extends to distant parts of the A10717
Da 4:34 His **d** is an eternal dominion; his A10717
Da 4:34 His dominion is an eternal **d**; his A10717
Da 6:26 not be destroyed, his **d** will never end. A10717
Da 7:14 His **d** is an everlasting dominion that A10717
Da 7:14 is an everlasting **d** that will not pass A10717
Mic 4: 8 the former **d** will be restored to you H4939
1Co 15:24 God the Father after he has destroyed all **d**, G794
Eph 1:21 power and **d**, and every name that G3262
Col 1:13 rescued us from the **d** of darkness and G2026

DOMINIONS (KJV) POWERS, RULERS

DON'T (219) [DO]

Ge 4: 9 brother Abel?" "I **d** know," he replied H4202
Ge 19: 7 my friends. **D** do this wicked thing. H440
Ge 19: 8 But **d** do anything to these men, for they H440
Ge 19:17 **D** look back, and don't stop anywhere in H440
Ge 19:17 and **d** stop anywhere in the plain! H440
Ge 21:26 "I **d** know who has done this. H4202
Ge 27: 2 an old man and **d** know the day of my H4202
Ge 30:31 "**D** give me anything," Jacob H4202
Ge 31:35 said to her father, "**D** be angry, my lord, H440
Ge 35:17 said to her, "**D** despair, for you have H440
Ge 37:22 "**D** shed any blood. Throw him into this H440
Ge 37:22 in the wilderness, but **d** lay a hand on him." H440
Ge 43:22 We **d** know who put our silver in our sacks. H4202
Ge 43:23 "**D** be afraid. Your God, the God H440
Ge 44:15 **D** you know that a man like me can find H4202
Ge 45: 9 Come down to me; **d** delay. H440
Ge 45:24 he said to them, "**D** quarrel on the way!" H440
Ge 50:19 Joseph said to them, "**D** be afraid. Am I in H440
Ge 50:21 **d** be afraid. I will provide for you H440
Ex 5: 8 of bricks as before; **d** reduce the quota. H4202
Ex 9:28 let you go; you **d** have to stay any longer." H4202
Ex 32: 1 we **d** know what has happened to him." H4202
Ex 32:23 we **d** know what has happened to him. H4202
Jos 2: 5 I **d** know which way they went H4202
Jos 2:14 "If you **d** tell what we are doing, we will H4202
Jos 8: 4 behind the city. **D** go very far from it H440
Jos 10:19 But **d** stop; pursue your enemies! Attack H440
Jos 10:19 from the rear and **d** let them reach their H440
Jdg 4: 8 I will go; but if you **d** go with me, I won't H4202
Jdg 4:18 **D** be afraid." So he entered H440
Jdg 14:16 "You hate me! You **d** really love me H4202
Jdg 15:11 "**D** you realize that the Philistines are H4202
Jdg 18: 9 **D** hesitate to go there and take it over. H440
Jdg 18:19 **D say a word.** H8492+3338+6584+7023
Jdg 18:25 Danites answered, "**D** argue with us, or H440
Jdg 19:19 young man with us. We **d** need anything." H401
Jdg 19:20 Only **d** spend the night in the square." H440
Jdg 19:23 said to them, "No, my friends, **d** be so vile. H440
Jdg 19:23 is my guest, **d** do this outrageous thing. H440
Jdg 19:24 this man, **d** do such an outrageous thing." H4202
Ru 1:16 "**D** urge me to leave you or to turn back H440
Ru 1:20 "**D** call me Naomi," she told them. H440
Ru 2: 8 **D** go and glean in another field and don't H440
Ru 2: 8 in another field and **d** go away from here. H4202
Ru 2:15 among the sheaves and **d** reprimand her. H4202
Ru 2:16 them for her to pick up, and **d** rebuke her." H4202
Ru 3: 3 **d** let him know you are there until he H440
Ru 3:11 my daughter, **d** be afraid. I will do H440
Ru 3:17 '**D** go back to your mother-in-law H440
1Sa 1: 8 you weeping? Why **d** you eat? Why are H4202
1Sa 1: 8 **D** I mean more to you than ten sons?" H4202
1Sa 2:16 it over now; if you **d**, I'll take it by force." H4202
1Sa 4:20 attending her said, "**D** despair; you have H440
1Sa 17:55 surely as you live, Your Majesty, I **d** know." H561
1Sa 19:11 "If you **d** run for your life tonight H401
1Sa 20:30 **D** I know that you have sided with the son H4202
1Sa 20:38 **D** stop!" The boy picked up the H440
1Sa 21: 4 "I **d** have any ordinary bread on hand H401
1Sa 21: 8 "**D** you have a spear or a sword here? H403
1Sa 22:23 Stay with me; **d** be afraid. The man who H440
1Sa 23:17 "**D** be afraid," he said. "My father Saul will H440
1Sa 26: 9 said to Abishai, "**D** destroy him! Who can H440
1Sa 28:13 king said to her, "**D** be afraid. What do you H440
1Sa 29: 6 but the rulers **d** approve of you. H4202
2Sa 2:26 **D** you realize that this will end in H4202
2Sa 9: 7 "**D** be afraid," David said to him, "for I will H440
2Sa 11:25 '**D** let this upset you; the sword devours H440
2Sa 13:12 she said to him. "**D** force me! Such a thing H440
2Sa 13:12 be done in Israel! **D** do this wicked thing. H440
2Sa 13:20 is your brother. **D** take this thing to heart." H440
2Sa 13:28 **D** be afraid. Haven't I given H440
2Sa 14: 2 and **d** use any cosmetic lotions. H440
2Sa 14:18 "**D** keep from me the answer to what I am H440
2Sa 18:22 You **d** have any news that will bring you a H401
2Sa 18:29 your servant, but I **d** know what it was." H4202
2Sa 19: 7 I swear by the LORD that if you **d** go out, not H401
2Sa 19:22 **D** I know that today I am king over Israel?" H4202
1Ki 3:26 her the living baby! **D** kill him!" But the H440
1Ki 17:12 she replied, "I **d** have any bread—only a H561
1Ki 17:13 Elijah said to her, "**D** be afraid. Go home H440
1Ki 18:12 I **d** know where the Spirit of the LORD may H4202
1Ki 18:40 prophets of Baal. **D** let anyone get away!" H440
1Ki 20: 8 "**D** listen to him or agree to his demands." H440
1Ki 22: 3 "**D** you know that Ramoth Gilead belongs H2022
2Ki 4: 3 empty jars. **D** ask for just a few. H440
2Ki 4:16 "*Please*, man of God, **d** mislead your H440
2Ki 4:24 **d** slow down for me unless I tell you." H440
2Ki 4:28 "Didn't I tell you, '**D** raise my hopes'?" H4202
2Ki 4:29 **D** greet anyone you meet, and if anyone H4202
2Ki 6:16 "**D** be afraid," the prophet answered H440
2Ki 6:32 "**D** you see how this murderer is sending H2022
2Ki 9: 3 Then open the door and run; **d** delay!" H4202
2Ki 9:15 **d** let anyone slip out of the city to go and H440
2Ki 18:26 **D** speak to us in Hebrew in the hearing of H440
2Ki 23:18 "**D** let anyone disturb his bones. H440
2Ch 13: 5 **D** you know that the LORD, the God of H4202
Ne 4:14 rest of the people, "**D** be afraid of them. H440
Pr 23:35 They beat me, but I **d** feel it! When will I H1153
Isa 7: 4 'Be careful, keep calm and **d** be afraid. H440
Isa 29:12 they will answer, "I **d** know how to read." H4202
Isa 36:11 **D** speak to us in Hebrew in the hearing of H440
Isa 65: 5 'Keep away; **d** come near me, for I am too H440
Isa 65: 8 people say, '**D** destroy it, there is H440
Jer 13:12 '**D** we know that every wineskin should be H4202
Jer 36:19 **D** let anyone know where you are. H440
Jer 39:12 **d** harm him but do for him whatever he H440
Jer 40: 4 if you do not want to, then **d** come. H2532
Jer 40:14 "**D** you know that Baalis king of the H2022
Jer 40:16 son of Kareah, "**D** do such a thing! H440
Jer 41: 8 said to Ishmael, "**D** kill us! We have wheat H440
La 4:15 **D** touch us!" When they flee and H440
Da 5:10 "**D** be alarmed! Don't look so A10031
Da 5:10 "Don't be alarmed! **D** look so pale! A10031
Am 7:13 **D** prophesy anymore at Bethel, because H4202
Mt 8: 4 said to him, "See that you **d** tell **anyone**. G3594
Mt 10:31 So **d** be afraid; you are worth more than G3590
Mt 14:27 "Take courage! It is I. **D** be afraid." G3590
Mt 15: 2 They **d** wash their hands before they eat!" G4024
Mt 15:17 "**D** you see that whatever enters the mouth G4024
Mt 16: 9 **D** you remember the five loaves for the G4028
Mt 16:11 How is it you **d** understand that I was not G4024
Mt 17: 7 "Get up," he said. "**D** be afraid." G3590
Mt 17: 9 "**D** tell **anyone** what you have seen G3594
Mt 20:15 **D** I have the right to do what I want with G4024
Mt 20:22 "You **d** know what you are asking," Jesus G4024
Mt 21:27 "We **d** know." Then he said G4024
Mt 25:12 he replied, 'Truly I tell you, I **d** know you. G4024
Mt 26:22 the other, "**Surely** you **d** mean me, Lord?" G3614
Mt 26:25 said, "**Surely** you **d** mean me, Rabbi?" G3614
Mt 26:70 "I **d** know what you're talking about," G4024
Mt 26:72 with an oath: "I **d** know the man!" G4024
Mt 26:74 he swore to them, "I **d** know the man!" G4024
Mt 27:13 "**D** you hear the testimony they are G4024
Mt 27:19 "**D** have **anything** to do with that innocent G3594
Mk 1:44 "See that you **d** tell this to anyone. But go G3594
Mk 4:13 to them, "**D** you understand this parable? G4024
Mk 4:21 Instead, **d** you put it on its stand? G4024
Mk 4:38 "Teacher, **d** you care if we drown? G4024
Mk 5: 7 In God's name **d** torture me!" G3590
Mk 5:36 Jesus told him, "**D** be afraid; just G3590
Mk 6:50 "Take courage! It is I. **D** be afraid." G3590
Mk 7: 5 "Why **d** your disciples live according to G4024
Mk 7:18 "**D** you see that nothing that enters a G4024
Mk 8:18 fail to hear? And **d** you remember? G4024
Mk 8:26 "**D even** go into the village. G3593
Mk 10:38 "You **d** know what you are asking," Jesus G4024
Mk 11:33 "We **d** know." Jesus said, G4024
Mk 14:19 they said to him, "**Surely** you **d** mean me?" G3614
Mk 14:68 "I **d** know or understand what you're G4046
Mk 14:71 "I **d** know this man you're talking about." G4024
Mk 16: 6 "**D** be alarmed," he said. "You are G3590
Lk 3:13 "**D** collect **any** more than you are required G3594
Lk 3:14 "**D** extort money and don't accuse people G3594
Lk 3:14 "Don't extort money **and d** accuse people G3593
Lk 5:10 said to Simon, "**D** be afraid; from now G3590
Lk 5:14 ordered him, "**D** tell **anyone**, but go, G3594
Lk 7: 6 **d** trouble yourself, for I do not G3590
Lk 7:13 heart went out to her and he said, "**D** cry." G3590
Lk 8:28 Most High God? I beg you, **d** torture me!" G3590
Lk 8:49 "**D** bother the teacher **anymore**." G3600
Lk 8:50 Jesus said to Jairus, "**D** be afraid; just G3590
Lk 10:40 **d** you care that my sister has left me to do G4024
Lk 11: 7 the one inside answers, '**D** bother me. G3590
Lk 12: 7 **D** be afraid; you are worth more than G3590
Lk 12:56 How is it that you **d** know how to interpret G4024
Lk 12:57 "Why **d** you judge for yourselves what is G4024
Lk 13:25 'I **d** know you or where you come from. G4024
Lk 13:27 'I **d** know you or where you come from. G4024
Lk 18: 4 'Even though I **d** fear God or care what G4024
Lk 19:14 'We **d** want this man to be our king. G4024
Lk 20: 7 answered, "We **d** know where it was from." G3590
Lk 22:36 and if you **d** have a sword, sell G3590
Lk 22:57 "Woman, I **d** know him," he said. G4024
Lk 22:60 I **d** know what you're talking about!" G4024
Lk 23:40 "**D** you fear God," he said, "since you are G4028
Jn 4:35 **D** you have a saying, 'It's still four months G4024
Jn 6:20 But he said to them, "It is I; **d** be afraid." G3590
Jn 8:46 telling the truth, why **d** you believe me? G4024
Jn 9:12 they asked him. "I **d** know," he said. G4024
Jn 9:21 or who opened his eyes, we **d** know. G4024
Jn 9:25 "Whether he is a sinner or not, I **d** know. G4024
Jn 9:29 we **d** even know where he comes from." G4024
Jn 9:30 You **d** know where he comes from, yet he G4024
Jn 14: 5 we **d** know where you are going, so G4024
Jn 14: 9 "**D** you know me, Philip, even after I have G4024
Jn 14:10 **D** you believe that I am in the Father, and G4024
Jn 16:18 We **d** understand what he is saying." G4024
Jn 19:10 "**D** you realize I have power either to free G4024
Jn 20: 2 we **d** know where they have put him!" G4024
Jn 20:13 "and I **d** know where they have put him." G4024
Ac 7:40 we **d** know what has happened to him! G4024
Ac 16:28 But Paul shouted, "**D** harm yourself! We G3594
Ac 20:10 arms around him. "**D** be alarmed," he G3590
Ac 23:21 **D** give in to them, because more than forty G3590
Ac 23:22 "**D** tell **anyone** that you have reported this G3594
Ro 6: 3 Or **d** *you* **know** that all of us who were G51
Ro 6:16 **D** you know that when you offer yourselves G4024
Ro 11: 2 **D** you know what Scripture says in the G4024
1Co 1:16 I **d** remember if I baptized anyone else.) G4024
1Co 3:16 **D** you know that you yourselves are God's G4024
1Co 5: 6 **D** you know that a little yeast leavens the G4024
1Co 7:21 **D** let it trouble you—although if you can G3590
1Co 9: 4 **D** we have the right to food and G3590+4024
1Co 9: 5 **D** we have the right to take a G3590+4024
1Co 9:13 **D** you know that those who serve in the G4024
1Co 10:12 standing firm, be careful **that** you **d** fall! G3590
1Co 11:22 **D** you have homes to eat and drink G3590+4024
1Co 12:21 cannot say to the hand, "I **d** need you!" G4024
1Co 12:21 cannot say to the feet, "I **d** need you!" G4024
2Th 2: 3 **D** let anyone deceive you in any way, for G3590
2Th 2: 5 **D** you remember that when I was with you G4024
1Ti 4:12 **D** let **anyone** look down on you because G3594
2Ti 2:23 **D have anything to do with** foolish and G4148
Jas 1:16 **D** be deceived, my dear brothers and G3590
Jas 4: 1 **D** they come from your desires that battle G4024
Jas 4: 4 **d** you know that friendship with the world G4024
Jas 5: 9 **D** grumble against one another, brothers G3590
Rev 19:10 But he said to me, "**D** do that! I am a G3590
Rev 22: 9 But he said to me, "**D** do that! I am a G3590

DONATED (1)

Ezr 8:25 present there *had* **d** *for* the house of our H8123

DONE (551) [DO]

Ge 2: 3 all the work of creating that he *had* **d**. H6913
Ge 3:13 to the woman, "What is this *you have* **d**?" H6913
Ge 3:14 "Because *you have* **d** this, "Cursed H6913
Ge 4:10 LORD said, "What *have you* **d**? Listen! Your H6913
Ge 8:21 I destroy all living creatures, as *I have* **d**. H6913
Ge 9:24 out what his youngest son *had* **d** to him, H6913
Ge 12:18 "What *have you* **d** to me?" he H6913
Ge 18:21 see if *what they have* **d** is as bad as H6913
Ge 20: 5 *I have* **d** this with a clear conscience and H6913
Ge 20: 9 in and said, "What *have you* **d** to us? H6913
Ge 20: 9 *You have* **d** things to me that should H6913
Ge 20: 9 done things to me that *should* never **be d**." H6913
Ge 21:26 "I don't know who *has* **d** this. H6913
Ge 22:16 that because *you have* **d** this and have H6913
Ge 24:66 Then the servant told Isaac all *he had* **d**. H6913
Ge 26:10 "What is this *you have* **d** to us? H6913
Ge 27:19 your firstborn. *I have* **d** as you told me H6913
Ge 28:15 not leave you until *I have* **d** what I have H6913
Ge 29:25 to Laban, "What is this *you have* **d** to me? H6913
Ge 30:26 You know how much work I've **d** *for* you." H6268
Ge 31:26 Laban said to Jacob, "What *have you* **d**? H6913
Ge 31:28 *You have* **d** a foolish thing. H6913
Ge 34: 7 because Shechem *had* **d** an outrageous H6913
Ge 34: 7 daughter—a *thing that should* not **be d**. H6913
Ge 39:22 made responsible for all that *was* **d** there. H6913

D

Ge 40:15 even here I have d nothing to H6913
Ge 41:21 could tell that they had d so; H995+448+7931S
Ge 42:25 After this was d for them, H6913
Ge 42:28 "What is this that God has d to us? H6913
Ge 44: 5 This is a wicked thing you have d.' " H6913
Ge 44:15 said to them, "What is this you have d? H6913
Ge 45: 4 When they had d so, he said, "I am H5602S
Ge 50:20 good to accomplish what is now being d, NDT
Ex 1:18 asked them, "Why have you d this? H6913
Ex 3:16 have seen what has been d to you in H6913
Ex 14: 5 about them and said, "What have we d? H6913
Ex 14:11 What have you d to us by bringing us out H6913
Ex 18: 1 of everything God had d for Moses and H6913
Ex 18: 8 the LORD had d to Pharaoh and the H6913
Ex 18: 9 good things the LORD had d for Israel in H6913
Ex 21:13 if it is not d intentionally, but God H7399
Ex 31:15 For six days work is to be d, but the H6913
Ex 34:10 never before d in any nation in all H1343
Ex 35: 2 six days, work is to be d, but the seventh H6913
Ex 36: 5 the work the LORD commanded to be d." H6913
Ex 36:11 the same was d with the end curtain H6913
Ex 39:42 The Israelites had d all the work just as H6913
Ex 39:43 work and saw that they had d it just as the H6913
Lev 8: 5 is what the LORD has commanded to be d." H6913
Lev 8:34 What has been d today was commanded H6913
Lev 16:34 And it was d, as the LORD commanded H6913
Lev 18:27 all these things were d by the people who H6913
Lev 20:12 What they have d is a perversion; their H6913
Lev 20:13 both of them have d what is detestable. H6913
Nu 4:26 to do all that needs to be d with these H6913
Nu 4:27 is to be d under the direction of Aaron H2118
Nu 5: 7 full restitution for the wrong they have d, AIT
Nu 11:11 What have I d to displease you that you put AIT
Nu 15:24 if this is d unintentionally without the H6913
Nu 15:34 it was not clear what should be d to him. H6913
Nu 22: 2 saw all that Israel had d to the Amorites, H6913
Nu 22:28 "What have I d to you to make you beat H6913
Nu 23:11 said to Balaam, "What have you d to me? H6913
Nu 23:11 you have d nothing but bless H1385+1385
Nu 23:23 Jacob and of Israel, 'See what God has d! H7188
Nu 32:13 of those who had d evil in his sight H6913
Dt 2:22 The LORD had d the same for the H6913
Dt 2:30 give him into your hands, as he has now d. NDT
Dt 3: 6 as we had d with Sihon king of Heshbon H6913
Dt 3:21 the LORD your God has d to these two H6913
Dt 11: 7 saw all these great things the LORD has d. H6913
Dt 13:14 detestable thing has been d among you, H6913
Dt 15: 2 This is how it is to be d: Every creditor shall NDT
Dt 17: 4 this detestable thing has been d in Israel, H6913
Dt 17: 5 man or woman who has d this evil deed H6913
Dt 19:20 again will such an evil thing be d among H6913
Dt 21: 7 shed this blood, nor did our eyes see it d. NDT
Dt 21: 9 since you have d what is right in the eyes H6913
Dt 22:21 She has d an outrageous thing in Israel H6913
Dt 22:25 the man who has d this shall die. H8886+6640S
Dt 25: 9 "This is what is d to the man who will not H6913
Dt 26:14 I have d everything you commanded me. H6913
Dt 28:20 of the evil you have d in forsaking him. H5095
Dt 29:24 "Why has the LORD d this to this land H6913
Dt 32:27 has triumphed; the LORD has not d all this. H7188
Jos 1:15 them rest, as he has d for you, and until NDT
Jos 4:10 commanded Joshua was d by the people, H9462
Jos 4:23 the Jordan what he had d to the Red Sea H6913
Jos 6:23 men who had d the spying went in and AIT
Jos 7:15 of the LORD and has d an outrageous thing H6913
Jos 7:19 Tell me what you have d; do not hide it H6913
Jos 7:20 the God of Israel. This is what I have d: H6913
Jos 9: 3 heard what Joshua had d to Jericho and H6913
Jos 10: 1 Ai and its king as he had d to Jericho H6913
Jos 10:28 of Makkedah as he had d to the king of H6913
Jos 10:30 did to its king as he had d to the king of H6913
Jos 10:32 to the sword, just as he had d to Libnah. H6913
Jos 10:35 just as they had d to Lachish. H6913
Jos 10:39 its king as they had d to Libnah and H6913
Jos 22: 2 "You have d all that Moses the servant of H9068
Jos 23: 3 the LORD your God has d to all these H6913
Jos 24:31 everything the LORD had d for Israel. H6913
Jdg 2: 2 disobeyed me. Why have you d this? H6913
Jdg 2: 7 the great things the LORD had d for Israel. H6913
Jdg 2:10 the LORD nor what he had d for Israel. H6913
Jdg 8:35 of all the good things he had d for them. H6913
Jdg 9:56 that Abimelek had d to his father by H6913
Jdg 14: 6 his father nor his mother what he had d. H6913
Jdg 15:11 What have you d to us?" He H6913
Jdg 18: 4 He told them what Micah had d for him H6913
Jdg 19:30 "Such a thing has never been seen or d H2118
Jdg 20:10 deserve for this outrageous act d in Israel." H6913
Jdg 20:30 as they had d before. H3869+7193+928+7193
Ru 2:11 all about what you have d for your H6913
Ru 2:12 the LORD repay you for what you have d. H7189
Ru 3:16 she told her everything Boaz had d for her H6913
1Sa 2:32 Although good will be d to Israel, no one H3512
1Sa 8: 8 As they have d from the day I brought H6913
1Sa 11: 7 "This is what will be d to the oxen of H6913
1Sa 12: 3 If I have d any of these things, I will make it NDT
1Sa 12:20 "You have d all this evil; yet do not turn H6913
1Sa 12:24 what great things he has d for you. H1540
1Sa 13:11 "What have you d?" asked Samuel. H6913
1Sa 13:13 "You have d a foolish thing," Samuel said H6118
1Sa 14:35 first time he had d this. H1215+4640+4200+3378S
1Sa 14:43 to Jonathan, "Tell me what you have d." H6913
1Sa 17:26 "What will be d for the man who kills this H6913
1Sa 17:27 "This is what will be d for the man who H6913
1Sa 17:29 "Now what have I d?" said David. H6913
1Sa 19: 4 what he has d has benefited you H5126
1Sa 19:18 told him all that Saul had d to him. H6913
1Sa 20: 1 to Jonathan and asked, "What have I d? H6913
1Sa 20:32 What has he d?" Jonathan H6913
1Sa 24:12 'may the LORD avenge the wrongs you have d to AIT
1Sa 26:16 What you have d is not good. As surely as H6913
1Sa 26:18 What have I d, and what wrong am I H6913
1Sa 26:19 however, people have d it, may they be NDT
1Sa 28: 9 "Surely you know what Saul has d. H6913
1Sa 28:17 The LORD has d what he predicted through H6913
1Sa 28:18 the LORD has d this to you today. H6913
1Sa 29: 8 "But what have I d?" asked David. H6913
1Sa 31:11 heard what the Philistines had d to Saul, H6913
2Sa 2: 6 the same favor because you have d this. H6913
2Sa 3:24 to the king and said, "What have you d? H6913
2Sa 7:11 have d ever since the time I appointed NDT
2Sa 7:21 you have d this great thing and made it H6913
2Sa 8:11 as he had d with the silver and gold H7727S
2Sa 11:27 But the thing David had d displeased the H6913
2Sa 13:12 Such a thing should not be d in Israel H6913
2Sa 13:16 than what you have already d to me." H6913
2Sa 21:11 Saul's concubine, had d, H6913
2Sa 24:10 "I have sinned greatly in what I have d. H6913
2Sa 24:10 I have d a very foolish thing." H6118
2Sa 24:17 I, the shepherd, have d wrong. H6390
2Sa 24:17 What have they d? Let your hand H6913
1Ki 1:27 Is this something my lord the king has d H2118
1Ki 7:51 work King Solomon had d for the temple H6913
1Ki 8:25 walk before me faithfully as you have d. H2143S
1Ki 8:32 down on their heads what they have d, H2006
1Ki 8:47 have sinned, we have d wrong, we have H6390
1Ki 8:66 good things the LORD had d for his servant H6913
1Ki 9: 8 'Why has the LORD d such a thing to this H6913
1Ki 11: 6 LORD completely, as David his father had d. NDT
1Ki 11:33 nor d what is right in my eyes H6913
1Ki 13:11 the man of God had d there that H6913+5126
1Ki 14: 9 You have d more evil than all who lived H6913
1Ki 14:22 than those who were before them had d. H6913
1Ki 15: 3 all the sins his father had d before him; H6913
1Ki 15: 5 For David had d what was right in the eyes H6913
1Ki 15:11 eyes of the LORD, as his father David had d. NDT
1Ki 16: 7 of all the evil he had d in the eyes of the H6913
1Ki 18: 9 "What have I d wrong," asked Obadiah H2627
1Ki 18:36 your servant and have d all these things H6913
1Ki 19: 1 everything Elijah had d and how he had H6913
1Ki 19:20 Elijah replied. "What have I d to you?" H6913
1Ki 20:22 your position and see what must be d, H6913
1Ki 22:53 the God of Israel, just as his father had d. H6913
2Ki 1:16 Because you have d this, you will never NDT
2Ki 3: 2 not as his father and mother had d. NDT
2Ki 4:13 Now what can be d for you? Can we H6913
2Ki 4:14 "What can be d for her?" Elisha asked H6913
2Ki 5:13 great thing, would you not have d it? H6913
2Ki 7:12 tell you what the Arameans have d to us. H6913
2Ki 8: 4 about all the great things Elisha has d." H6913
2Ki 8:18 as the house of Ahab had d, for he H6913
2Ki 8:27 as the house of Ahab had d, for he was NDT
2Ki 10:10 The LORD has d what he announced H6913
2Ki 10:30 "Because you have d well in H3201
2Ki 10:30 in my eyes and have d to the house of H6913
2Ki 12: 7 you repairing the damage d to the temple? AIT
2Ki 14: 3 the LORD, but not as his father David had d. NDT
2Ki 15: 3 just as his father Amaziah had d. H6913
2Ki 15: 9 of the LORD, as his predecessors had d. H6913
2Ki 15:34 the LORD, just as his father Uzziah had d. H6913
2Ki 17: 4 king of Assyria, as he had d year by year. NDT
2Ki 17:11 the LORD had driven out before them had d. NDT
2Ki 18: 3 of the LORD, just as his father David had d. H6913
2Ki 18:14 "I have d wrong. H2627
2Ki 19:11 the kings of Assyria have d to all the H6913
2Ki 20: 3 devotion and have d what is good in your H6913
2Ki 21: 3 as Ahab king of Israel had d. H6913
2Ki 21:11 He has d more evil than the Amorites H8317
2Ki 21:15 they have d evil in my eyes and have H6913
2Ki 21:20 of the LORD, as his father Manasseh had d. H6913
2Ki 23:17 of Bethel the very things you have d to it." H6913
2Ki 23:19 Just as he had d at Bethel, Josiah H6913+5126
2Ki 23:26 all that Manasseh had d to arouse his anger. AIT
2Ki 23:32 the LORD, just as his predecessors had d. H6913
2Ki 23:37 the LORD, just as his predecessors had d. H6913
2Ki 24: 3 of the sins of Manasseh and all he had d, H6913
2Ki 24: 9 eyes of the LORD, just as his father had d. H6913
2Ki 24:19 eyes of the LORD, just as Jehoiakim had d. H6913
1Ch 6:49 with all that was d in the Most Holy Place, H4856
1Ch 10:11 heard what the Philistines had d to Saul, H6913
1Ch 16: 8 known among the nations what he has d. H6613
1Ch 16:12 Remember the wonders he has d, his H6913
1Ch 17:10 have d ever since the time I appointed NDT
1Ch 17:19 you have d this great thing and made H6913
1Ch 18:11 as he had d with the silver and gold he had NDT
1Ch 21: 8 I have d a very foolish thing." H6118
1Ch 21:17 the shepherd, have sinned and d wrong. H8317
1Ch 21:17 What have they d? LORD my God, H6913
1Ch 28: 7 laws, as is being d at this time. NDT
1Ch 29: 5 the work to be d by the craftsmen. H928+3338
2Ch 5: 1 the work Solomon had d for the temple of H6913
2Ch 6:16 me according to my law, as you have d. H2143S
2Ch 6:23 down on their heads what they have d, H2006
2Ch 6:37 we have d wrong and acted wickedly' H6390
2Ch 7:10 good things the LORD had d for David and H6913
2Ch 7:21 'Why has the LORD d such a thing to this H6913
2Ch 16: 9 You have d a foolish thing, and from now H6118
2Ch 21: 6 as the house of Ahab had d, for he H6913
2Ch 22: 4 as the house of Ahab had d, for after his NDT
2Ch 24:16 of the good he had d in Israel for God H6913
2Ch 25:16 because you have d this and have not H6913
2Ch 26: 4 just as his father Amaziah had d. H6913
2Ch 27: 2 just as his father Uzziah had d, but unlike H6913
2Ch 29: 2 of the LORD, just as his father David had d. H6913
2Ch 29:36 his people, because it was d so quickly. H2118
2Ch 31:11 the temple of the LORD, and this was d. H3922S
2Ch 32: 1 After all that Hezekiah had so faithfully d H1821
2Ch 32:13 my predecessors have d to all the peoples H6913
2Ch 33:22 of the LORD, as his father Manasseh had d. H6913
Ezr 7:23 let it be d with diligence for the temple A10522
Ezr 9: 1 After these things had been d, the H3983
Ezr 10: 3 Let it be d according to the Law H6913
Ne 5:19 my God, for all I have d for these people. H6913
Ne 6:14 because of what they have d; remember H5126
Ne 6:16 that this work had been d with the help of H6913
Ne 13: 7 evil thing Eliashib had d in providing H6913
Ne 13:14 out what I have so faithfully d for the H6913
Est 1:15 what must be d to Queen Vashti? H6913
Est 1:16 "Queen Vashti has d wrong, not only H6390
Est 2: 1 Vashti and what she had d and what he H6913
Est 2:20 instructions as she had d when he was H2118
Est 4: 1 Mordecai learned of all that had been d, H6913
Est 4:16 When this is d, I will go to the king, even NDT
Est 6: 3 "Nothing has been d for him," his H6913
Est 6: 6 "What should be d for the man the king H6913
Est 6: 9 'This is what is d for the man the king H6913
Est 6:11 "This is what is d for the man the king H6913
Est 9:12 What have they d in the rest of the king's H6913
Est 9:14 So the king commanded that this be d H6913
Job 7:20 what have I d to you, you who H7188
Job 12: 9 know that the hand of the LORD has d this? H6913
Job 21:31 Who repays them for what they have d? H6913
Job 22:28 What you decide on will be d, and light H7756
Job 33: 9 'I am pure, I have d no wrong; I am clean NDT
Job 34:11 He repays everyone for what they have d H7189
Job 34:32 I cannot see; if I have d wrong, I will not H7188
Job 36: 9 he tells them what they have d—that H7189
Job 36:23 or said to him, 'You have d wrong'? H7188
Ps 7: 3 if I have d this and there is guilt on my H6913
Ps 9:11 among the nations what he has d. H6613
Ps 22:31 to a people yet unborn: He has d it! H6913
Ps 28: 4 them for what their hands have d and H5126
Ps 28: 5 of the LORD and what his hands have d, H5126
Ps 39: 9 you are the one who has d this. H6913
Ps 40: 5 are the wonders you have d, the things H6913
Ps 46: 8 Come and see what the LORD has d, the H5149
Ps 51: 4 have I sinned and d what is evil in your H6913
Ps 52: 9 For what you have d I will always praise H6913
Ps 59: 4 I have d no wrong, yet they are ready to NDT
Ps 62:12 everyone according to what they have d." H5126
Ps 64: 9 works of God and ponder what he has d. H5126
Ps 66: 5 Come and see what God has d, his H5149
Ps 66:16 let me tell you what he has d for me. H6913
Ps 68:28 strength, our God, as you have d before. H7188
Ps 71:19 heavens, you who have d great things. H6913
Ps 78: 4 his power, and the wonders he has d. H6913
Ps 78:11 They forgot what he had d, the wonders H6613
Ps 92: 4 I sing for joy at what your hands have d. H5126
Ps 98: 1 new song, for he has d marvelous things H6913
Ps 99: 4 in Jacob you have d what is just and right. H6913
Ps 105: 1 known among the nations what he has d. H6613
Ps 105: 5 Remember the wonders he has d, his H6913
Ps 106: 6 we have d wrong and acted wickedly. H6390
Ps 106:13 soon forgot what he had d and did not H5126
Ps 106:21 who had d great things in Egypt H6913
Ps 109:27 it is your hand, that you, LORD, have d it. H6913
Ps 118:15 LORD's right hand has d mighty things! H6913
Ps 118:16 the LORD's right hand has d mighty things!" H6913
Ps 118:17 will proclaim what the LORD has d. H5126
Ps 118:23 the LORD has d this, and it is marvelous in H2118
Ps 118:24 The LORD has d it this very day; let us H6913
Ps 119:121 I have d what is righteous and just; do not H6913
Ps 126: 2 "The LORD has d great things for them." H6913
Ps 126: 3 The LORD has d great things for us, and we H6913
Ps 137: 8 you according to what you have d to us. H1694
Ps 143: 5 consider what your hands have d. H5126
Ps 147:20 He has d this for no other nation; they do H6913
Pr 3:30 reason—when they have d you no harm. H1694
Pr 19:17 he will reward them for what they have d. H1691
Pr 20:16 hold it in pledge if it is d for an outsider. NDT
Pr 21:15 When justice is d, it brings joy to the H6913
Pr 24:12 everyone according to what they have d? H7189
Pr 24:29 "I'll do to them as they have d to me; I'll H6913
Pr 27:13 hold it in pledge if it is d for an outsider. NDT
Pr 30:20 mouth and says, 'I've d nothing wrong. H7188
Pr 31:31 Honor her for all that her hands have d H7262
Ecc 1: 9 what has been d will be done again H6913
Ecc 1: 9 what has been done will be d again H6913
Ecc 1:13 by wisdom all that is d under the heavens H6913
Ecc 1:14 all the things that are d under the sun; H6913
Ecc 2:11 all that my hands had d and what I had H6913
Ecc 2:12 do than what has already been d? H6913
Ecc 2:17 the work that is d under the sun was H6913
Ecc 3:11 fathom what God has d from beginning to H6913
Ecc 4: 3 the evil that is d under the sun. H5126+6913
Ecc 7:13 Consider what God has d: Who can H5126

Ecc 8: 9 my mind to everything d under the sun. H6913
Ecc 8:16 to observe the labor that is d on earth— H6913
Ecc 8:17 then I saw all that God has d. No one can H5126
Isa 3:11 be paid back for what their hands have d. H1691
Isa 5: 4 What more could have been d for my H6913
Isa 5: 4 done for my vineyard than I have d for it? H6913
Isa 10:13 " 'By the strength of my hand I have d this, H6913
Isa 12: 4 known among the nations what he has d, H6613
Isa 12: 5 to the LORD, for he has d glorious things H6913
Isa 25: 1 faithfulness you have d wonderful things, H6913
Isa 26:12 we have accomplished you have d for us. H7188
Isa 33:13 hear what I have d; you who are H6913
Isa 37:11 the kings of Assyria have d to all the H6913
Isa 38: 3 devotion and have d what is good in your H6913
Isa 38:15 spoken to me, and he himself has d this. H6913
Isa 41: 4 Who has d this and carried it through H7188
Isa 41:20 that the hand of the LORD has d this, that H6913
Isa 44:23 the LORD has d this; shout aloud, H6913
Isa 53: 9 though he had d no violence, nor H6913
Isa 59:18 According to what they have d, so will he H1692
Isa 63: 7 according to all the LORD has d for us H1694
Isa 63: 7 the many good things he has d for Israel H1694
Isa 66:18 of what they have planned and d, H5126
Jer 2:23 in the valley; consider what you have d. H6913
Jer 3: 6 you seen what faithless Israel has d? H6913
Jer 3: 7 that after she had d all this she would H6913
Jer 4: 4 like fire because of the evil you have d— H5095
Jer 5:13 so let what they say be d to them. H6913
Jer 5:19 Why has the LORD our God d all this to us? H6913
Jer 7:30 people of Judah have d evil in my eyes, H6913
Jer 8: 6 their wickedness, saying, "What have I d?" H6913
Jer 11:17 Israel and Judah have d evil and aroused H6913
Jer 16:10 What wrong have we d? What sin have we NDT
Jer 18:13 horrible thing has been d by Virgin Israel. H6913
Jer 21:12 like fire because of the evil you have d— H5095
Jer 22: 8 'Why has the LORD d such a thing to this H6913
Jer 23: 2 on you for the evil you have d, H5095
Jer 26: 3 planning because of the evil they have d. H5095
Jer 29:23 For they have d outrageous things in H6913
Jer 30:15 many sins I have d these things to H6913
Jer 31:37 of Israel because of all they have d," H6913
Jer 32:30 Israel and Judah have d nothing but evil H6913
Jer 32:30 of Israel have d nothing but arouse my NDT
Jer 32:32 provoked me by all the evil they have d— H6913
Jer 35:18 his instructions and have d everything he H6913
Jer 38: 9 in all they have d to Jeremiah the H6913
Jer 40: 3 he has d just as he said he would. H6913
Jer 44: 3 because of the evil they have d. H6913
Jer 44:25 your wives have d what you H4848+928+3338
Jer 50:15 do to her as she has d to others. H6913
Jer 50:29 her for her deeds; do to her as she has d. H6913
Jer 51:10 tell in Zion what the LORD our God has d. H5126
Jer 51:24 all the wrong they have d in Zion, H6913
Jer 51:35 May the violence d to our flesh be on NDT
Jer 52: 2 eyes of the LORD, just as Jehoiakim had d. H6913
La 1:21 distress; they rejoice at what you have d. H6913
La 2:17 The LORD has d what he planned; he has H6913
La 3:59 you have seen the wrong d to me. H6432
La 3:64 for what their hands have d. H5126
Eze 5: 9 to you what I have never d before and will H6913
Eze 6: 9 the evil they have d and for all their H6913
Eze 9: 4 all the detestable things that are d in it." H6913
Eze 9:10 on their own heads what they have d." H2006
Eze 9:11 "I have d as you commanded. H6913
Eze 11:21 on their own heads what they have d, H2006
Eze 12:11 a sign to you.' "As I have d, so it will be H6913
Eze 12:11 I have done, so it will be d to them. H6913
Eze 14:23 you will know that I have d nothing in it H6913
Eze 16:43 down on your head what you have d, H2006
Eze 16:48 did what you and your daughters have d. H6913
Eze 16:51 You have d more detestable things than H8049
Eze 16:51 righteous by all these things you have d. H6913
Eze 16:54 ashamed of all you have d in giving them H6913
Eze 16:63 atonement for you for all you have d, H6913
Eze 18:11 though the father has d none of them): H6913
Eze 18:13 Because he has d all these detestable H6913
Eze 18:19 Since the son has d what is just and right H6913
Eze 18:22 of the righteous things they have d, H6913
Eze 18:24 righteous things that person has d will be H6913
Eze 20:43 yourselves for all the evil you have d. H6913
Eze 21:24 because you have d this, you will be H2349S
Eze 22:31 down on their own heads all they have d, H2006
Eze 23:38 They have also d this to me: At that same H6913
Eze 24:22 And you will do as I have d. You will not H6913
Eze 24:24 a sign to you; you will do just as he has d. H6913
Eze 33:13 that person has d will be remembered; NDT
Eze 33:13 they will die for the evil they have d. H6913
Eze 33:16 They have d what is just and right; they H6913
Eze 33:29 of all the detestable things they have d. H6913
Eze 37:14 have spoken, and I have d it, declares the H6913
Eze 43:11 if they are ashamed of all they have d, H6913
Eze 44:14 temple for all the work that is to be d in it. H6913
Da 4:35 hand or say to him: "What have you d?" A10522
Da 6:10 to his God, just as he had d before. A10522
Da 6:22 Nor have I ever d any wrong before you A10522
Da 9: 5 we have sinned and d wrong. We have H6390
Da 9:12 nothing has ever been d like what has H6913
Da 9:12 done like what has been d to Jerusalem. H6913
Da 9:15 we have sinned, we have d wrong. H8399
Joel 2:20 Surely he has d great things! H6913
Joel 2:21 Surely the LORD has d great things! H6913
Joel 3: 4 you repaying me for something I have d? H1691
Joel 3: 4 on your own heads what you have d. H1691
Joel 3: 7 on your own heads what you have d. H1691
Joel 3:19 because of violence d to the people of Judah AIT
Am 8: 7 "I will never forget anything they have d. H5126
Ob 15 As you have d, it will be done to you; your H6913
Ob 15 As you have done, it will be d to you; your H6913
Jnh 1:10 them and they asked, "What have you d?" H6913
Jnh 1:14 you, LORD, have d as you pleased. H6913
Mic 3: 4 them because of the evil they have d. H5095
Mic 6: 3 "My people, what have I d to you? How H6913
Hab 2:17 The violence you have d to Lebanon will NDT
Zep 3:11 all the wrongs you have d to me, H6613
Zec 1: 6 'The LORD Almighty has d to us what our H6913
Zec 7: 3 fifth month, as I have d for so many years?" H6913
Mt 6: 4 who sees what is d in secret, will reward NDT
Mt 6: 6 who sees what is d in secret, will reward NDT
Mt 6:10 your will be d, on earth as it is in G1181
Mt 6:18 who sees what is d in secret, will reward NDT
Mt 8:13 Let it be d just as you believed it would." G1181
Mt 9:29 "According to your faith let it be d to you"; G1181
Mt 16:27 person according to what they have d. G4552
Mt 17:12 but have d to him everything they wished. G4472
Mt 18:19 it will be d for them by my Father in G1181
Mt 21:21 only can you do what was d to the fig tree, NDT
Mt 21:21 yourself into the sea,' and it will be d. G1181
Mt 21:42 the Lord has d this, and it is G4123+1181
Mt 23: 5 "Everything they do is d for people to see G4472
Mt 25:21 master replied, 'Well d, good and faithful G2292
Mt 25:23 master replied, 'Well d, good and faithful G2292
Mt 26:10 She has d a beautiful thing to me. G2237
Mt 26:13 what she has d will also be told G4472
Mt 26:42 away unless I drink it, may your will be d." G1181
Mk 5:19 them how much the Lord has d for you, G4472
Mk 5:20 Decapolis how much Jesus had d for him. G4472
Mk 5:32 kept looking around to see who had d it. G4472
Mk 6:30 reported to him all they had d and taught. G4472
Mk 7:37 "He has d everything well, G4472
Mk 9:13 and they have d to him everything they G4472
Mk 11:23 they say will happen, it will be d for them. G1639
Mk 12:11 the Lord has d this, and it is G4123+1181
Mk 14: 6 She has d a beautiful thing to me. G2237
Mk 14: 9 what she has d will also be told G4472
Lk 1:25 "The Lord has d this for me," she said. G4472
Lk 1:49 the Mighty One has d great things for G4472
Lk 2:39 Joseph and Mary had d everything G5464
Lk 3:19 all the other evil things he had d, G4472
Lk 5: 6 When they had d so, they caught such a G4472
Lk 8:39 tell how much God has d for you. G4472
Lk 8:39 over town how much Jesus had d for him. G4472
Lk 9:10 they reported to Jesus what they had d. G4472
Lk 14:22 'what you ordered has been d, but there G1181
Lk 17:10 when you have d everything you were told G4472
Lk 17:10 servants; we have only d our duty. G4472
Lk 19:17 " 'Well d, my good servant!' his master G2301
Lk 22:42 from me; yet not my will, but yours be d." G1181
Lk 23:15 he has d nothing to deserve death. G1639+4556
Lk 23:41 But this man has d nothing wrong." G4556
Jn 3:21 that what they have d has been done in G2240
Jn 3:21 have done has been d in the sight of God G2237
Jn 4:38 Others have d the hard work, and you G3159
Jn 4:45 seen all that he had d in Jerusalem at G4472
Jn 5:29 those who have d what is good will rise to G4472
Jn 5:29 those who have d what is evil will G4556
Jn 11:46 told them what Jesus had d. G4472
Jn 12:16 that these things had been d to him. G4472
Jn 13:12 Do you understand what I have d for you? G4472
Jn 13:15 that you should do as I have d for you. G4472
Jn 15: 7 you wish, and it will be d for you. G1181
Jn 15:24 If I had not d among them the works no G4472
Jn 18:35 you over to me. What is it you have d?" G4472
Ac 9:13 all the harm he has d to your holy G4472
Ac 11:23 saw what the grace of God had d, NDT
Ac 14:11 When the crowd saw what Paul had d G4472
Ac 14:27 all that God had d through them and how G4472
Ac 15: 4 everything God had d through them. G4472
Ac 15:12 wonders God had d among the G4472
Ac 19:18 openly confessed what they had d. G4552
Ac 21:14 gave up and said, "The Lord's will be d." G1181
Ac 21:19 in detail what God had d among the G4472
Ac 21:33 who he was and what he had d. G1639+4472
Ac 25: 5 and if the man has d anything wrong G1639
Ac 25: 8 "I have d nothing wrong against the Jewish G279
Ac 25:10 I have not d any wrong to the Jews, as you G92
Ac 25:25 I found he had d nothing deserving of G4556
Ac 26:26 because it was not d in a corner. G4556
Ac 28:17 although I have d nothing against our G4472
Ro 1:28 so that they do what ought not to be d. G2763
Ro 2: 6 person according to what they have d." G2240
Ro 6: 6 body ruled by sin might be d away with, G2934
Ro 9:11 were born or had d anything good or G4556
Ro 15:18 to obey God by what I have said and d— G2240
1Co 14:26 Everything must be d so that the church G1181
1Co 14:40 But everything should be d in a fitting and G1181
1Co 15:28 When he has d this, G5718+899+3836+4246S
2Co 1:12 We have d so, relying not on worldly NDT
2Co 5:10 due us for the things d while in the body, G4556
2Co 7:11 concern, what readiness to see justice d. G1689
2Co 10:15 our limits by boasting of work d by others. AIT
2Co 10:16 to boast about work already d in someone G2289
Gal 4:15 if you could have d so, you would have torn NDT
Eph 2:11 which is d in the body by human hands)— G5935
Eph 6:13 ground, and after you have d everything G2981
2Ti 1: 9 of anything we have d but because of his G2240
2Ti 4:14 The Lord will repay him for what he has d. G2240
Titus 3: 5 not because of righteous things we had d G4472
Phm 18 If he has d you any wrong or owes you G92
Heb 10:36 so that when you have d the will of God, G4472
Heb 12:17 he could not change what he had d. NDT
Jas 3:13 by deeds d in the humility that comes from NDT
1Pe 4: 1 whoever suffers in the body is d with sin. G4264
2Pe 2:13 back with harm for the harm they have d. G92
2Pe 3:10 earth and everything d in it will be laid G2240
Rev 16:11 they refused to repent of what they had d. G2240
Rev 16:17 voice from the throne, saying, "It is d!" G1181
Rev 18: 6 pay her back double for what she has d. G2240
Rev 20:12 to what they had d as recorded in the G2240
Rev 20:13 was judged according to what they had d. G2240
Rev 21: 6 He said to me: "It is d. I am the Alpha G1181
Rev 22:12 according to what they have d. G2240+1639

DONKEY (75) [DONKEY'S, DONKEYS, DONKEYS']

Ge 16:12 He will be a wild d of a man; his hand H7230
Ge 22: 3 Abraham got up and loaded his d. H2789
Ge 22: 5 "Stay here with the d while I and the boy H2789
Ge 42:27 opened his sack to get feed for his d, H2789
Ge 49:11 He will tether his d to a vine, his colt to H6554
Ge 49:14 is a rawboned d lying down among the H2789
Ex 4:20 put them on a d and started back to Egypt. H2789
Ex 13:13 Redeem with a lamb every firstborn d, but H2789
Ex 20:17 servant, his ox or d, or anything that H2789
Ex 21:33 to cover it and an ox or a d falls into it, H2789
Ex 22: 4 whether ox or d or sheep—they must pay H2789
Ex 22: 9 illegal possession of an ox, a d, a sheep, H2789
Ex 22:10 "If anyone gives a d, an ox, a sheep or H2789
Ex 23: 4 your enemy's ox or d wandering off, H2789
Ex 23: 5 If you see the d of someone who hates H2789
Ex 23:12 so that your ox and your d may rest, and H2789
Ex 34:20 Redeem the firstborn d with a lamb, but if H2789
Nu 16:15 have not taken so much as a d from them, H2789
Nu 22:21 saddled his d and went with the Moabite H912
Nu 22:22 Balaam was riding on his d, and his two H912
Nu 22:23 When the d saw the angel of the LORD H912
Nu 22:25 When the d saw the angel of the LORD, it H912
Nu 22:25 foot against it. So he beat the d again. H2023S
Nu 22:27 When the d saw the angel of the LORD, it lay H912
Nu 22:29 Balaam answered the d, "You have made H912
Nu 22:30 The d said to Balaam, "Am I not your own H912
Nu 22:30 "Am I not your own d, which you have H912
Nu 22:32 have you beaten your d these three times? H912
Nu 22:33 The d saw me and turned away from me H912
Dt 5:14 your ox, your d or any of your animals H2789
Dt 5:21 servant, his ox or d, or anything that H2789
Dt 22: 3 if you find their d or cloak or anything H2789
Dt 22: 4 your fellow Israelite's d or ox fallen on the H2789
Dt 22:10 plow with an ox and a d yoked together. H2789
Dt 28:31 Your d will be forcibly taken from you and H2789
Jos 15:18 When she got off her d, Caleb asked her H2789
Jdg 1:14 When she got off her d, Caleb asked her H2789
Jdg 15:15 Finding a fresh jawbone of a d, he H2789
Jdg 19:28 man put her on his d and set out for H2789
1Sa 12: 3 Whose d have I taken? Whom H2789
1Sa 16:20 So Jesse took a d loaded with bread, H2789
1Sa 25:20 she came riding her d into a mountain H2789
1Sa 25:23 quickly got off her d and bowed down H2789
1Sa 25:42 Abigail quickly got on a d and, attended H2789
2Sa 17:23 he saddled his d and set out for his house H2789
2Sa 19:26 'I will have my d saddled and will ride on H2789
1Ki 2:40 he saddled his d and went to Achish at H2789
1Ki 13:13 he said to his sons, "Saddle the d for me." H2789
1Ki 13:13 And when they had saddled the d for him, H2789
1Ki 13:23 brought him back saddled his d for him. H2789
1Ki 13:24 with both the d and the lion standing H2789
1Ki 13:27 "Saddle the d for me," and they did H2789
1Ki 13:28 with the d and the lion standing beside it. H2789
1Ki 13:28 neither eaten the body nor mauled the d. H2789
1Ki 13:29 laid it on the d, and brought it back H2789
2Ki 4:22 of the servants and a d so I can go to the H912
2Ki 4:24 She saddled the d and said to her servant H912
Job 6: 5 Does a wild d bray when it has grass, or H7230
Job 24: 3 away the orphan's d and take the widow's H2789
Job 39: 5 "Who let the wild d go free? Who untied H7230
Pr 26: 3 a bridle for the d, and a rod for the H2789
Isa 1: 3 its master, the d its owner's manger H2789
Jer 2:24 a wild d accustomed to the desert H7241
Jer 22:19 He will have the burial of a d—dragged H2789
Hos 8: 9 to Assyria like a wild d wandering alone. H7230
Zec 9: 9 lowly and riding on a d, on a colt, H2789
Zec 9: 9 on a donkey, on a colt, the foal of a d. H912
Mt 21: 2 at once you will find a d tied there G3952
Mt 21: 5 gentle and riding on a d, and on a colt, G3952
Mt 21: 5 a donkey, and on a colt, the foal of a d. G5689
Mt 21: 7 They brought the d and the colt and G3952
Lk 10:34 Then he put the man on his own d G3229
Lk 13:15 untie your ox or d from the stall and lead G3952
Jn 12:14 Jesus found a young d and sat on it, as it G3942
2Pe 2:16 was rebuked for his wrongdoing by a d— G5689

DONKEY'S (6) [DONKEY]

Nu 22:28 Then the LORD opened the d mouth, and it H912
Jdg 15:16 "With a d jawbone I have made donkeys H2789
Jdg 15:16 With a d jawbone I have killed a H2789
2Ki 6:25 so long that a d head sold for eighty H2789
Job 11:12 wise than a wild d colt can be born H7230
Jn 12:15 your king is coming, seated on a d colt." G3952

D

DONKEYS (71) [DONKEY]

Ge 12:16 cattle, **male** and female **d**, male and H2789
[Ge 12:16 cattle, male and **female d**, male and H912]
Ge 24:35 female servants, and camels and **d**. H2789
Ge 30:43 male servants, and camels and **d**. H2789
Ge 32: 5 I have cattle and **d**, sheep and goats H2789
Ge 32:15 twenty **female d** and ten male donkeys H912
Ge 32:15 twenty female donkeys and ten **male d**. H6555
Ge 34:28 herds and **d** and everything else H2789
Ge 36:24 he was grazing the **d** of his father Zibeon. H2789
Ge 42:26 they loaded their grain on their **d** and left. H2789
Ge 43:18 us and seize us as slaves and take our **d**." H2789
Ge 43:24 their feet and provided fodder for their **d**. H2789
Ge 44: 3 men were sent on their way with their **d**. H2789
Ge 44:13 they all loaded their **d** and returned to the H2789
Ge 45:23 ten **d** loaded with the best things of Egypt, H2789
Ge 45:23 ten **female d** loaded with grain and H912
Ge 47:17 their sheep and goats, their cattle and **d**. H2789
Ex 9: 3 **d** and camels and on your cattle H2789
Nu 31:28 whether people, cattle, **d** or sheep. H2789
Nu 31:30 people, cattle, **d**, sheep or other animals H2789
Nu 31:34 61,000 **d** H2789
Nu 31:39 30,500 **d**, of which the tribute for the LORD H2789
Nu 31:45 30,500 **d** H2789
Jos 6:21 young and old, cattle, sheep and **d**. H2789
Jos 7:24 his cattle, **d** and sheep, his tent and all H2789
Jos 9: 4 a delegation whose **d** were loaded with H2789
Jdg 5:10 "You who ride on white **d**, sitting on your H912
Jdg 6: 4 Israel, neither sheep nor cattle nor **d**. H2789
Jdg 10: 4 who rode thirty **d**. They controlled H6555
Jdg 12:14 thirty grandsons, who rode on seventy **d**. H6555
Jdg 15:16 jawbone I have made **d** of them. H2789+2789
Jdg 19: 3 He had with him his servant and two **d** H2789
Jdg 19:10 with his two saddled **d** and his concubine. H2789
Jdg 19:19 fodder for our **d** and bread and wine H2789
Jdg 19:21 he took him into his house and fed his **d**. H2789
1Sa 8:16 of your cattle and **d** he will take for his H2789
1Sa 9: 3 Now the **d** belonging to Saul's father Kish H912
1Sa 9: 3 with you and go and look for the **d**. H912
1Sa 9: 4 district of Shaalim, but the **d** were not there. NDT
1Sa 9: 5 stop thinking about the **d** and start worrying H912
1Sa 9:20 As for the **d** you lost three days ago, do not H912
1Sa 10: 2 'The **d** you set out to look for have been H912
1Sa 10:14 "Looking for the **d**," he said. "But when we H912
1Sa 10:16 "He assured us that the **d** had been found." H912
1Sa 15: 3 cattle and sheep, camels and **d**. H2789
1Sa 22:19 infants, and its cattle, **d** and sheep. H2789
1Sa 25:18 of pressed figs, and loaded them on **d**. H2789
1Sa 27: 9 took sheep and cattle, **d** and camels, and H2789
2Sa 16: 1 He had a string of **d** saddled and loaded H2789
2Sa 16: 2 "The **d** are for the king's household to H2789
2Ki 7: 7 their tents and their horses and **d**. H2789
2Ki 7:10 only tethered horses and **d**, and the tents H2789
1Ch 5:21 fifty thousand sheep and two thousand **d**. H2789
1Ch 12:40 Naphtali came bringing food on **d**, H2789
1Ch 27:30 the Meronothite was in charge of the **d**. H912
2Ch 28:15 All those who were weak they put on **d** H2789
Ezr 2:67 435 camels and 6,720 **d**. H2789
Ne 7:69 435 camels and 6,720 **d**. H2789
Ne 13:15 bringing in grain and loading it on **d**, H2789
Job 1: 3 hundred yoke of oxen and five hundred **d**, H912
Job 1:14 plowing and the **d** were grazing nearby, H912
Job 24: 5 Like **wild d** in the desert, the poor go H7230
Job 42:12 a thousand yoke of oxen and a thousand **d**. H912
Ps 104:11 of the field; the **wild d** quench their thirst. H7230
Isa 21: 7 of horses, riders on **d** or riders on camels H2789
Isa 30:24 The oxen and **d** that work the soil will eat H6555
Isa 32:14 the delight of **d**, a pasture for flocks, H7230
Isa 32:20 letting your cattle and **d** range free. H2789
Jer 14: 6 **Wild d** stand on the barren heights and H7230
Eze 23:20 were like those of **d** and whose emission H2789
Da 5:21 he lived with the **wild d** and ate grass A10570
Zec 14:15 the camels and **d**, and all the animals H2789

DONKEYS' (1) [DONKEY]

Isa 30: 6 the envoys carry their riches on **d** backs H6555

DOOM (7) [DOOMED]

Dt 32:35 is near and their **d** rushes upon them." H6969
Eze 7: 7 **D** has come upon you, upon you who H7619
Eze 7:10 **D** has burst forth, the rod has budded H7619
Eze 22: 3 brings on herself **d** by shedding blood in H6961
Eze 30: 3 a day of clouds, a time of **d** for the nations. NDT
Eze 30: 9 take hold of them on the day of Egypt's **d**, NDT
Rev 18:10 In one hour your **d** has come!' *G3213*

DOOMED (8) [DOOM]

Jdg 13:22 "*We are* **d to die**!" he said to his H4637+4637
1Sa 4: 8 We're **d**! Who will deliver us from the hand H208
2Ki 7:13 only be like all these Israelites who *are* **d**. H9462
Ps 137: 8 Babylon, **d to destruction**, happy is the H8720
Isa 65:23 will they bear children **d** to misfortune; H4200
Jer 8:14 LORD our God *has* **d** us **to perish** and given H1959
Jn 17:12 lost except the **one d to** destruction so *G5626*
2Th 2: 3 is revealed, the man *d to* **destruction**. AIT

DOOR (71) [DOORFRAME, DOORFRAMES, DOORKEEPER, DOORKEEPERS, DOORPOST, DOORPOSTS, DOORS, DOORWAY, DOORWAYS]

Ge 4: 7 sin is crouching at your **d**; it desires to H7339
Ge 6:16 Put a **d** in the side of the ark and make H7339
Ge 19: 6 to meet them and shut the **d** behind him H1946
Ge 19: 9 moved forward to break down the **d**. H1946
Ge 19:10 Lot back into the house and shut the **d**. H1946
Ge 19:11 the men who were at the **d** *of* the house, H7339
Ge 19:11 so that they could not find the **d**. H7339
Ex 12:22 shall go out of the **d** *of* your house until H7339
Ex 21: 6 take him to the **d** or the doorpost and H1946
Dt 15:17 push it through his earlobe into the **d**, H1946
Dt 22:21 be brought to the **d** *of* her father's house H7339
Jdg 11:31 comes out of the **d** *of* my house to meet H1946
Jdg 19:22 Pounding on the **d**, they shouted to the H1946
Jdg 19:26 fell down at the **d** and lay there until H7339
Jdg 19:27 opened the **d** *of* the house and H1946
2Sa 13:17 out of my sight and bolt the **d** after her." H1946
2Sa 13:18 put her out and bolted the **d** after her. H1946
1Ki 14: 6 heard the sound of her footsteps at the **d**, H7339
2Ki 4: 4 shut the **d** behind you and your H1946
2Ki 4: 5 him and shut the **d** behind her and her H1946
2Ki 4:21 man of God, then shut the **d** and went out. NDT
2Ki 4:33 shut the **d** on the two of them and prayed H1946
2Ki 5: 9 stopped at the **d** of Elisha's house. H7339
2Ki 6:32 shut the **d** and hold it shut against him. H1946
2Ki 9: 3 Then open the **d** and run; don't delay!" H1946
2Ki 9:10 Then he opened the **d** and ran. H1946
Job 31: 9 if I have lurked at my neighbor's **d**, H7339
Job 31:32 my **d** was always open to the traveler— H1946
Ps 141: 3 keep watch over the **d** *of* my lips. H1923
Pr 5: 8 do not go near the **d** *of* her house, H7339
Pr 9:14 She sits at the **d** *of* her house, on a seat H7339
Pr 26:14 As a **d** turns on its hinges, so a sluggard H1946
SS 7:13 fragrance, and at our **d** is every delicacy H7339
SS 8: 9 If she is a **d**, we will enclose her with H1946
Eze 41:24 Each **d** had two leaves—two hinged H1946
Eze 41:24 leaves—two hinged leaves for each **d**. H1946
Eze 42: 2 The building whose **d** faced north was a H7339
Hos 2:15 will make the Valley of Achor a **d** *of* hope. H7339
Mt 6: 6 close the **d** and pray to your Father *G2598*
Mt 7: 7 knock and *the d will be* **opened** to you. AIT
Mt 7: 8 to the one who knocks, *the d will be* **opened**. AIT
Mt 23:13 *You* **shut** *the d* of the kingdom of heaven in AIT
Mt 24:33 you know that it is near, right at the **d**. *G2598*
Mt 25:10 wedding banquet. And the **d** was shut. *G2598*
Mt 25:11 Lord,' they said, 'open the **d** for us!' NDT
Mk 1:33 The whole town gathered at the **d**, *G2598*
Mk 2: 2 not even outside the **d**, and he preached *G2598*
Mk 13:29 you know that it is near, right at the **d**. *G2598*
Mk 13:34 tells the **one at the d** to keep watch. *G2601*
Lk 11: 7 The **d** is already locked, and my children *G2598*
Lk 11: 9 knock and *the d will be* **opened** to you. AIT
Lk 11:10 to the one who knocks, *the d will be* **opened**. AIT
Lk 12:36 knocks *they can* immediately **open** *the d* AIT
Lk 13:24 every effort to enter through the narrow **d**, *G2598*
Lk 13:25 of the house gets up and closes the **d**, *G2598*
Lk 13:25 pleading, 'Sir, open the **d** for us. *G2598*
Jn 18:16 Peter had to wait outside at the **d**. *G2598*
Ac 5: 9 who buried your husband are at the **d**, *G2598*
Ac 12:13 named Rhoda came to answer the **d**. NDT
Ac 12:14 it and exclaimed, "Peter is at the **d**!" *G4784*
Ac 12:16 when they opened the **d** and saw him NDT
Ac 14:27 how he had opened a **d** of faith to the *G2598*
Ac 18: 7 went **next d** to the house of *G5327*
1Co 16: 9 because a great **d** for effective work has *G2598*
2Co 2:12 that the Lord had opened a **d** for me, *G2598*
Col 4: 3 that God may open a **d** for our message *G2598*
Jas 5: 9 The Judge is standing at the **d**! *G2598*
Rev 3: 8 before you an open **d** that no one can *G2598*
Rev 3:20 I stand at the **d** and knock. If anyone *G2598*
Rev 3:20 If anyone hears my voice and opens the **d**, *G2598*
Rev 4: 1 there before me was a **d** standing open in *G2598*

DOORFRAME (3) [DOOR, FRAME]

Ex 12:22 on the top and on both sides of the **d**. H4647
Ex 12:23 top and sides of the **d** and will pass over H4647
Eze 41:21 The main hall had a rectangular **d**, and H4647

DOORFRAMES (5) [DOOR, FRAME]

Ex 12: 7 tops of the **d** of the houses where H4647
Dt 6: 9 Write them on the **d** *of* your houses and H4647
Dt 11:20 Write them on the **d** *of* your houses and H4647
1Ki 6:33 main hall he made **d** out of olive wood H4647
2Ch 3: 7 the ceiling beams, **d**, walls and doors of H6197

DOORKEEPER (2) [DOOR, KEEP]

Ps 84:10 I would rather be *a* **d** in the house of my H6214
Jer 35: 4 of Maaseiah son of Shallum the **d**. H9068+6197

DOORKEEPERS (6) [DOOR, KEEP]

2Ki 22: 4 which the **d** have collected from H9068+6197
2Ki 23: 4 in rank and the **d** to remove from H9068+6197
2Ki 25:18 priest next in rank and the three **d**. H9068+6197
1Ch 15:23 Elkanah were to be **d** for the ark. H8788
1Ch 15:24 Jehiah were also to be **d** for the ark. H8788
Jer 52:24 priest next in rank and the three **d**. H9068+6197

DOORPOST (2) [DOOR, POST]

Ex 21: 6 to the door or the **d** and pierce his ear H4647
1Sa 1: 9 on his chair by the **d** *of* the LORD's house. H4647

DOORPOSTS (6) [DOOR, POST]

2Ki 18:16 the doors and **d** *of* the temple of the H595
Isa 6: 4 of their voices the **d** and thresholds shook H564
Isa 57: 8 your doors and your **d** you have put your H4647
Eze 43: 8 threshold and their **d** beside my doorposts H4647
Eze 43: 8 their doorposts beside my **d**, H4647
Eze 45:19 offering and put it on the **d** *of* the temple, H4647

DOORS (59) [DOOR]

Jdg 3:23 he shut the **d** *of* the upper room behind H1946
Jdg 3:24 came and found the **d** *of* the upper room H1946
Jdg 3:25 when he did not open the **d** *of* the room, H1946
Jdg 16: 3 up and took hold of the **d** *of* the city gate, H1946
1Sa 3:15 then opened the **d** *of* the house of the H1946
1Sa 21:13 making marks on the **d** *of* the gate and H1946
1Ki 6:31 sanctuary he made **d** out of olive wood H1946
1Ki 6:32 the two olive-wood **d** he carved cherubim, H1946
1Ki 6:34 He also made two **d** out of juniper wood H1946
1Ki 7:50 sockets for the **d** *of* the innermost room, H1946
1Ki 7:50 also for the **d** of the main hall of the H1946
2Ki 18:16 he had covered the **d** and doorposts of H1946
1Ch 22: 3 make nails for the **d** *of* the gateways and H1946
2Ch 3: 7 walls and **d** *of* the temple with gold H1946
2Ch 4: 9 the large court and the **d** for the court, H1946
2Ch 4: 9 the court, and overlaid the **d** with bronze. H1946
2Ch 4:22 censers; and the gold **d** *of* the temple: H7339
2Ch 4:22 the inner **d** to the Most Holy Place and H1946
2Ch 4:22 Holy Place and the **d** of the main hall. H1946
2Ch 23: 4 the Sabbath are to keep watch at the **d**, H6197
2Ch 28:24 He shut the **d** *of* the LORD's temple and set H1946
2Ch 29: 3 he opened the **d** *of* the temple of the LORD H1946
2Ch 29: 7 They also shut the **d** *of* the portico and put H1946
Ne 3: 1 They dedicated it and set its **d** in place H1946
Ne 3: 3 beams and put its **d** and bolts and bars in H1946
Ne 3: 6 beams and put its **d** with their bolts and H1946
Ne 3:13 rebuilt it and put its **d** with their bolts and H1946
Ne 3:14 rebuilt it and put its **d** and bolts and bars H1946
Ne 3:15 over and putting its **d** and bolts and bars H1946
Ne 6: 1 time I had not set the **d** in the gates— H1946
Ne 6:10 let us close the temple **d**, because H1946
Ne 7: 1 been rebuilt and I had set the **d** in place, H1946
Ne 7: 3 have them shut the **d** and bar them. H1946
Ne 13:19 I ordered the **d** to be shut and not opened H1946
Job 3:10 did not shut the **d** *of* the womb on me to H1946
Job 38: 8 up the sea behind **d** when it burst forth H1946
Job 38:10 limits for it and set its **d** and bars in place, H1946
Job 41:14 Who dares open the **d** *of* its mouth H1946
Ps 24: 7 lifted up, you ancient **d**, that the King of H7339
Ps 24: 9 them up, you ancient **d**, that the King of H7339
Ps 78:23 above and opened the **d** *of* the heavens; H1946
Pr 8:34 watching daily at my **d**, waiting at my H1946
Ecc 12: 4 when the **d** to the street are closed and H1946
Isa 26:20 your rooms and shut the **d** behind you; H1946
Isa 45: 1 to open **d** before him so that gates will H1946
Isa 57: 8 Behind your **d** and your doorposts you H1946
Eze 26: 2 is broken, and its **d** have swung open to me NDT
Eze 33:30 by the walls and at the **d** *of* the houses, H7339
Eze 41:23 the Most Holy Place had double **d**. H1946
Eze 41:25 And on the **d** *of* the main hall were carved H1946
Eze 42: 4 Their **d** were on the north. H7339
Zec 11: 1 Open your **d**, Lebanon, so that fire may H1946
Mal 1:10 that one of you would shut the temple **d** H1946
Jn 20:19 with the **d** locked for fear of the Jewish *G2598*
Jn 20:26 Though the **d** were locked, Jesus came *G2598*
Ac 5:19 of the Lord opened the **d** of the jail and *G2598*
Ac 5:23 with the guards standing at the **d**; but *G2598*
Ac 16:26 At once all the prison **d** flew open, and *G2598*
Ac 16:27 when he saw the prison **d** open, he *G2598*

DOORWAY (13) [DOOR, WAY]

Ex 12:23 the doorframe and will pass over that **d**, H7339
Ex 35:15 the curtain for the **d** at the entrance to the H7339
Lev 14:38 shall go out the **d** *of* the house and close H7339
Jdg 4:20 "Stand in the **d** *of* the tent," he told her H7339
Jdg 19:27 fallen in the **d** *of* the house, with her H7339
2Ki 4:15 So he called her, and she stood in the **d**. H7339
Est 2:21 of the king's officers who guarded the **d**, H6197
Est 6: 2 of the king's officers who guarded the **d**, H6197
Pr 8:34 daily at my doors, waiting at my **d**. H4647+7339
Eze 8: 8 So I dug into the wall and saw a **d** there. H7339
Eze 40:38 A room with a **d** was by the portico in H7339
Eze 42:12 There was a **d** at the beginning of the H7339
Mk 11: 4 a colt outside in the street, tied at a **d**. *G2598*

DOORWAYS (4) [DOOR, WAY]

1Ki 7: 5 All the **d** had rectangular frames H7339+4647
Eze 42:11 Similar to the **d** on the north H7339
Eze 42:12 were the **d** *of* the rooms on the south H7339
Zep 2:14 rubble will fill the **d**, the beams of cedar H6197

DOPHKAH (2)

Nu 33:12 left the Desert of Sin and camped at **D**. H1986
Nu 33:13 They left **D** and camped at Alush. H1986

DOR (4) [HAMMOTH DOR, NAPHOTH DOR]

Jos 12:23 the king of **D** (in Naphoth Dor) one H1888
Jos 17:11 Ibleam and the people of **D**, Endor, H1799
Jdg 1:27 Shan or Taanach or **D** or Ibleam or H1888
1Ch 7:29 Megiddo and **D**, together with their H1888

DORCAS (2)

Ac 9:36 in Greek her name is **D**); she was always *G1520*
Ac 9:39 other clothing that **D** had made while she *G1520*

DOTE, DOTED (KJV) FOOLS, LUSTED

DOTHAN (3)

Ge 37:17 "I heard them say, 'Let's go to **D**.'" H2019
Ge 37:17 after his brothers and found them near **D**. H2019

2Ki 6:13 The report came back: "He is in **D**." H2019

DOUBLE (25) [DOUBLE-EDGED, DOUBLE-MINDED, DOUBLE-PRONGED, DOUBLY]
Ge 43:12 Take **d** *the amount of* silver with you, for H5467
Ge 43:15 took the gifts and **d** *the amount of* silver, H5467
Ex 22: 4 donkey or sheep—they must pay back **d**. H9109
Ex 22: 7 the thief, if caught, must pay back **d**. H9109
Ex 22: 9 guilty must pay back **d** to the other. H9109
Ex 26: 9 **Fold** the sixth curtain **d** at the front of the H4100
Ex 26:24 they must be **d** from the bottom all H9339
Ex 28:16 long and a span wide—and **folded d**. H4100
Ex 36:29 the frames were **d** from the bottom all the H9339
Ex 39: 9 long and a span wide—and **folded d**. H4100
Dt 21:17 by giving him a **d** share of all he has. H9109
1Sa 1: 5 to Hannah he gave a **d** portion because he H678
2Ki 2: 9 "Let me inherit a **d** portion of your spirit," H9109
Job 41:13 Who can penetrate its **d** coat of armor? H4101
Isa 40: 2 from the LORD's hand **d** for all her sins. H4101
Isa 51:19 These **d** calamities have come upon you H9109
Isa 61: 7 your shame you will receive a **d portion**, H5467
Isa 61: 7 you will inherit a **d portion** in your land, H5467
Jer 16:18 I will repay them **d** for their wickedness H5467
Jer 17:18 disaster; destroy them with **d** destruction. H5467
Eze 41:23 hall and the Most Holy Place had **d** doors. H9109
Hos 10:10 them to put them in bonds for their **d** sin. H9109
1Ti 5:17 of the church well are worthy of **d** honor, *G1487*
Rev 18: 6 pay her back **d** for what she has done. *G1487*
Rev 18: 6 Pour her a **d** *portion* from her own cup. *G1487*

DOUBLE-EDGED (6) [DOUBLE, EDGE]
Jdg 3:16 Ehud had made a **d** sword about a H9109+7023
Ps 149: 6 their mouths and a **d** sword in their hands H7092
Pr 5: 4 she is bitter as gall, sharp as a **d** sword. H7023
Heb 4:12 Sharper than any **d** sword, it penetrates *G1492*
Rev 1:16 out of his mouth was a sharp, **d** sword. *G1492*
Rev 2:12 words of him who has the sharp, **d** sword. *G1492*

DOUBLE-MINDED (3) [DOUBLE, MIND]
Ps 119:113 I hate **d** *people*, but I love your law. H6189
Jas 1: 8 Such a person is **d** and unstable in all they *G1500*
Jas 4: 8 you sinners, and purify your hearts, *you* **d**. *G1500*

DOUBLE-PRONGED (1) [DOUBLE]
Eze 40:43 And **d hooks**, each a handbreadth long H9191

DOUBLY (1) [DOUBLE]
1Ch 11:21 He was **d** honored above the H928+2021+9109

DOUBT (8) [DOUBTED, DOUBTING, DOUBTLESS, DOUBTS]
Mt 14:31 of little faith," he said, "why *did you* **d**?" *G1491*
Mt 21:21 if you have faith and *do* not **d**, not only *G1359*
Mk 11:23 and *does* not **d** in their heart but believes *G1359*
Ac 12:11 "Now I know **without a d** that the Lord has *G242*
1Co 11:19 **No d** there have to be differences among *G1142*
Heb 7: 7 And without **d** the lesser is blessed by the *G517*
Jas 1: 6 you must believe and not **d**, because the *G1359*
Jude 22 Be merciful to those *who* **d**; *G1359*

DOUBTED (1) [DOUBT]
Mt 28:17 they worshiped him; but some **d**. *G1491*

DOUBTING (1) [DOUBT]
Jn 20:27 put it into my side. Stop **d** and believe." *G603*

DOUBTLESS (1) [DOUBT]
Job 12: 2 "**D** you are the only people who matter H597

DOUBTS (3) [DOUBT]
Lk 24:38 why do **d** rise in your minds? *G1369*
Ro 14:23 But whoever **has d** is condemned if they *G1359*
Jas 1: 6 because the *one who* **d** is like a wave of *G1359*

DOUGH (11)
Ex 12:34 people took their **d** before the yeast was H1302
Ex 12:39 *With* the **d** the Israelites had brought from H1302
Ex 12:39 The **d** was without yeast because they had NDT
2Sa 13: 8 She took some **d**, kneaded it, made the H1302
Jer 7:18 women knead the **d** and make cakes to H1302
Hos 7: 4 stir from the kneading of the **d** till it rises. H1302
Mt 13:33 of flour until *it* **worked** all **through the d**." *G2435*
Lk 13:21 of flour until *it* **worked** all **through the d**." *G2435*
Ro 11:16 the **part** *of the d* **offered as firstfruits** is holy AIT
1Co 5: 6 little yeast leavens the whole **batch of d**? *G5878*
Gal 5: 9 yeast works through the whole **batch of d**." *G5878*

DOVE (24) [DOVES]
Ge 8: 8 Then he sent out a **d** to see if the water H3433
Ge 8: 9 But the **d** could find nowhere to perch H3433
Ge 8: 9 his hand and took **the d** and brought it H2023S
Ge 8:10 again sent out the **d** from the ark. H3433
Ge 8:11 When the **d** returned to him in the H3433
Ge 8:12 more days and sent the **d** out again, H3433
Ge 15: 9 along with a **d** and a young pigeon." H9367
Lev 1:14 you are to offer a **d** or a young pigeon. H9367
Lev 12: 6 a young pigeon or a **d** for a sin offering. H9367
Ps 55: 6 that I had the wings of a **d**! I would fly H3433
Ps 56: T To the tune of "A **D** *on* Distant Oaks." H3433
Ps 68:13 the wings of my **d** are sheathed with silver H3433
Ps 74:19 hand over the life of your **d** to wild beasts; H9367
SS 2:14 My **d** in the clefts of the rock, in the hiding H3433
SS 5: 2 my darling, my **d**, my flawless one. H3433
SS 6: 9 my **d**, my perfect one, is unique, the H3433
Isa 38:14 thrush, I moaned like a mourning **d**. H3433
Jer 8: 7 seasons, and the **d**, the swift and the H9367
Jer 48:28 Be like a **d** that makes its nest at the H3433
Hos 7:11 "Ephraim is like a **d**, easily deceived and H3433
Mt 3:16 descending like a **d** and alighting on him. *G4361*
Mk 1:10 the Spirit descending on him like a **d**. *G4361*
Lk 3:22 descended on him in bodily form like a **d**. *G4361*
Jn 1:32 from heaven as a **d** and remain on him. *G4361*

DOVES (23) [DOVE]
Lev 5: 7 is to bring two **d** or two young pigeons H9367
Lev 5:11 cannot afford two **d** or two young pigeons, H9367
Lev 12: 8 she is to bring two **d** or two young H9367
Lev 14:22 two **d** or two young pigeons, such as H9367
Lev 14:30 shall sacrifice the **d** or the young pigeons, H9367
Lev 15:14 he must take two **d** or two young pigeons H9367
Lev 15:29 she must take two **d** or two young pigeons H9367
Nu 6:10 they must bring two **d** or two young H9367
SS 1:15 how beautiful! Your eyes are **d**. H3433
SS 2:12 the cooing of **d** is heard in our land. H9367
SS 4: 1 Your eyes behind your veil are **d**. H3433
SS 5:12 His eyes are like **d** by the water streams H3433
Isa 59:11 like bears; we moan mournfully like **d**. H3433
Isa 60: 8 fly along like clouds, like **d** to their nests? H3433
Eze 7:16 Like **d** *of* the valleys, they will all moan H3433
Hos 11:11 sparrows, from Assyria, fluttering like **d**. H3433
Na 2: 7 slaves moan like **d** and beat on their H3433
Mt 10:16 shrewd as snakes and as innocent as **d**. *G4361*
Mt 21:12 the benches of those selling **d**. *G4361*
Mk 11:15 the benches of those selling **d**, *G4361*
Lk 2:24 "a pair *of* **d** or two young pigeons. *G5583*
Jn 2:14 sheep and **d**, and others sitting at *G4361*
Jn 2:16 To those who sold **d** he said, "Get these *G4361*

DOWN (1213) [DOWNCAST, DOWNFALL, DOWNHEARTED, DOWNPOUR, DOWNSTAIRS, DOWNSTREAM]
Ge 8: 3 fifty days the water *had* **gone d**, H2893
Ge 11: 5 But the LORD **came d** to see the city and H3718
Ge 11: 7 *let us* **go d** and confuse their language so H3718
Ge 12:10 Abram **went d** to Egypt to live there H3718
Ge 15:11 birds of prey **came d** on the carcasses H3718
Ge 18:16 up to leave, *they* **looked d** toward Sodom H9207
Ge 18:21 that *I will* **go d** and see if what they have H3718
Ge 19: 1 meet them and **bowed d** *with* his face to H2556
Ge 19: 9 moved forward to **break d** the door. H8689
Ge 19:24 Then the LORD **rained d** burning sulfur on H4763
Ge 19:28 *He* **looked d** toward Sodom and Gomorrah, H9207
Ge 19:33 of it when she **lay d** or when she got up. H8886
Ge 19:35 of it when she **lay d** or when she got up. H8886
Ge 21:16 she went off and **sat d** about a bowshot H3782
Ge 23: 7 Abraham rose and **bowed d** before the H2556
Ge 23:12 Again Abraham **bowed d** before the H2556
Ge 24:11 *He* **had** the camels **kneel d** near the well H1384
Ge 24:14 'Please **let d** your jar that I may have a H5742
Ge 24:16 *She* **went d** to the spring, filled her jar H3718
Ge 24:26 Then the man **bowed d** and worshiped H7702
Ge 24:45 *She* **went d** to the spring and drew water H3718
Ge 24:48 and *I* **bowed d** and worshiped the LORD. H7702
Ge 24:52 *he* **bowed d** to the ground before the LORD. H2556
Ge 24:64 saw Isaac. *She* **got d** from her camel H5877
Ge 26: 2 Isaac and said, "*Do* not **go d** to Egypt; live H3718
Ge 26: 8 the Philistines **looked d** from a window H9207
Ge 27:12 tricking him and *would* **bring d** a curse on H995
Ge 27:29 serve you and peoples **bow d** to you. H2556
Ge 27:29 and *may* the sons of your mother **bow d** to H2556
Ge 28:11 put it under his head and **lay d to sleep**. H8886
Ge 31:36 have I wronged you that *you* **hunt** me **d**? H1944
Ge 33: 3 on ahead and **bowed d** to the ground H2556
Ge 33: 6 their children approached and **bowed d**. H2556
Ge 33: 7 Leah and her children came and **bowed d**. H2556
Ge 33: 7 Rachel, and *they* too **bowed d**. H2556
Ge 37: 7 gathered around mine and **bowed d** to it." H2556
Ge 37: 9 eleven stars *were* **bowing d** to me. H2556
Ge 37:10 actually come and **bow d** to the ground H2556
Ge 37:25 As *they* **sat d** to eat their meal, they H3782
Ge 37:25 were on their way to **take** them **d** to Egypt. H3718
Ge 38: 1 his brothers and **went d** to stay with a H3718
Ge 38:14 then **sat d** at the entrance to Enaim H3782
Ge 39: 1 Now Joseph *had* **been taken d** to Egypt H3718
Ge 42: 2 **Go d** there and buy some for us, so that H3718
Ge 42: 3 Joseph's brothers **went d** to buy grain H3718
Ge 42: 6 *they* **bowed d** to him *with* their faces to H2556
Ge 42:38 "My son *will* not **go d** there with you H3718
Ge 42:38 *you will* **bring** my gray head **d** to the grave H3718
Ge 43: 4 *we will* **go d** and buy food for you. H3718
Ge 43: 5 send him, *we will* not **go d**, because the H3718
Ge 43: 7 he would say, '**Bring** your brother **d** here'?" H3718
Ge 43:11 and **take** them **d** to the man *as* a gift— H3718
Ge 43:15 They hurried **d** *to* Egypt and presented H3718
Ge 43:20 "*we* **came d** here the first time to H3718+3718
Ge 43:26 and *they* **bowed d** before him to the H2556
Ge 43:28 And *they* **bowed d**, prostrating H7702
Ge 44:21 '**Bring** him **d** to me so I can see him for H3718
Ge 44:23 your youngest brother **comes d** with you, H3718
Ge 44:26 we said, 'We cannot **go d**. Only if our H3718
Ge 44:29 *you will* **bring** my gray head **d** to the grave H3718
Ge 44:31 *will* **bring** the gray head of our father **d** to H3718
Ge 45: 9 **Come d** to me; don't delay H3718
Ge 45:13 And **bring** my father **d** here quickly." H3718
Ge 46: 3 "Do not be afraid *to* **go d** to Egypt, for I H3718
Ge 46: 4 I *will* **go d** to Egypt with you, and I will H3718
Ge 48:12 knees and **bowed d** *with* his face to the H2556
Ge 49: 8 your father's sons *will* **bow d** to you. H2556
Ge 49: 9 Like a lion he crouches and **lies d**, like a H8069
Ge 49:14 donkey **lying d** among the sheep H8069
Ge 50:18 came and **threw** *themselves* **d** before him. H5877
Ex 2: 5 Pharaoh's daughter **went d** to the Nile to H3718
Ex 2:15 live in Midian, where *he* **sat d** by a well. H3782
Ex 3: 8 So *I have* **come d** to rescue them from the H3718
Ex 4:31 *they* **bowed d** and worshiped. H7702
Ex 7: 9 your staff and **throw** it **d** before Pharaoh, H8959
Ex 7:10 Aaron **threw** his staff **d** in front of Pharaoh H8959
Ex 7:12 Each one **threw d** his staff and it became a H8959
Ex 9:23 lightning **flashed d** to the ground. H2143
Ex 9:25 it **beat d** everything growing in the fields H5782
Ex 9:33 the rain no *longer* **poured d** on the land. H5988
Ex 10:14 all Egypt and **settled d** in every area of H5663
Ex 11: 8 **bowing d** before me and saying H2556
Ex 12:12 through Egypt and **strike d** every firstborn H5782
Ex 12:23 through the land to **strike d** the Egyptians, H5597
Ex 12:23 to enter your houses and **strike** you **d**. H5597
Ex 12:27 homes when he **struck d** the Egyptians. H5597
Ex 12:27 Then the people **bowed d** and worshiped. H7702
Ex 12:29 midnight the LORD **struck d** all the firstborn H5782
Ex 14:24 the night the LORD **looked d** from the pillar H9207
Ex 15: 7 of your majesty *you* **threw d** those who H2238
Ex 16: 4 "I *will* **rain d** bread from heaven for you. H4763
Ex 18: 7 and **bowed d** and kissed him. H2556
Ex 19:11 day the LORD *will* **come d** on Mount Sinai H3718
Ex 19:14 After Moses *had* **gone d** the mountain to H3718
Ex 19:21 "**Go d** and warn the people so they do not H3718
Ex 19:24 "**Go d** and bring Aaron up with you. H3718
Ex 19:25 So Moses **went d** to the people and told H3718
Ex 20: 5 *You shall* not **bow d** to them or worship H2556
Ex 23: 5 who hates you **fallen d** under its load, H8069
Ex 23:24 *Do* not **bow d** before their gods or worship H2556
Ex 24: 4 Moses then **wrote d** everything the LORD H4180
Ex 26:12 that is left over *is to* **hang d** at the rear of H6243
Ex 32: 1 was so long in **coming d** from the H3718
Ex 32: 6 Afterward *they* **sat d** to eat and drink and H3782
Ex 32: 7 said to Moses, "Go **d**, because your H3718
Ex 32: 8 *They have* **bowed d** to it and sacrificed to H2556
Ex 32:15 Moses turned and **went d** the mountain H3718
Ex 33: 9 pillar of cloud *would* **come d** and stay at H3718
Ex 34: 5 Then the LORD **came d** in the cloud and H3718
Ex 34:13 **Break d** their altars, smash their sacred H5997
Ex 34:13 sacred stones and **cut d** their Asherah H4162
Ex 34:27 said to Moses, "**Write d** these words, for H4180
Ex 34:29 When Moses **came d** from Mount Sinai H3718
Lev 1:16 the feathers and **throw** them **d** east of the H8959
Lev 9:22 the fellowship offering, *he* **stepped d**. H3718
Lev 14:45 It *must be* **torn d**—its stones, timbers and H5997
Lev 22: 7 When the sun **goes d**, he will be clean, and H995
Lev 26: 1 stone in your land to **bow d** before it. H2556
Lev 26: 6 and *you will* **lie d** and no one will make H8886
Lev 26:19 *I will* **break d** your stubborn pride and H8689
Lev 26:30 **cut d** your incense altars and pile your H4162
Nu 1:51 the Levites *are to* **take** it **d**, and whenever H3718
Nu 3:13 When I **struck d** all the firstborn in Egypt, H5782
Nu 4: 5 sons are to go in and **take d** the shielding H3718
Nu 8:17 When I **struck d** all the firstborn in Egypt, H5782
Nu 10:17 Then the tabernacle **was taken d**, and the H3718
Nu 11: 2 he prayed to the LORD and the fire **died d**. H9205
Nu 11: 9 camp at night, the manna also **came d**. H3718
Nu 11:17 *I will* **come d** and speak with you there H3718
Nu 11:25 Then the LORD **came d** in the cloud and H3718
Nu 12: 5 Then the LORD **came d** in a pillar of cloud H3718
Nu 14:12 *I will* **strike** them **d** with a plague and H5782
Nu 14:37 the land *were* **struck d and died** of a H4637
Nu 14:45 that hill country **came d** and attacked H3718
Nu 14:45 them and **beat** them **d** all the way to H4198
Nu 16:30 and *they* **go d** alive into the realm of the H3718
Nu 16:33 They **went d** alive into the realm of the H3718
Nu 20:15 Our ancestors **went d** into Egypt, and we H3718
Nu 20:28 Moses and Eleazar **came d** from the H3718
Nu 21:35 So *they* **struck** him **d**, together with his H5782
Nu 22:27 of the LORD, *it* **lay d** under Balaam, and H8069
Nu 24: 9 Like a lion they crouch and **lie d**, like a H8886
Nu 25: 2 meal and **bowed d** before these gods. H2556
Nu 33: 4 whom the LORD *had* **struck d** among them H5782
Nu 34:11 *will* **go d** from Shepham *to* Riblah H3718
Nu 34:12 Then the boundary *will* **go d** along the H3718
Dt 1:25 *they* **brought** it **d** to us and reported H3718
Dt 1:44 of bees and **beat** you **d** from Seir all H4198
Dt 2:33 him over to us and *we* **struck** him **d**, H5782
Dt 3: 3 *We* **struck** them **d**, leaving no H5782
Dt 3:16 from Gilead **d to** the Arnon Gorge H6330
Dt 4:19 not be enticed into **bowing d** to them H2556
Dt 5: 9 *You shall* not **bow d** to them or worship H2556
Dt 6: 7 when you **lie d** and when you get up. H8886
Dt 7: 5 **Break d** their altars, smash their sacred H5997
Dt 7: 5 **cut d** their Asherah poles and burn their H1548
Dt 8:12 when you build fine houses and **settle d**, H3782
Dt 8:19 gods and worship and **bow d** to them, H2556
Dt 9:12 the LORD told me, "**Go d** from here at once H3718
Dt 9:15 So I turned and **went d** from the mountain H3718
Dt 9:21 into a stream that **flowed d** the mountain. H3718
Dt 10: 5 Then I came back **d** the mountain and put H3718
Dt 10:22 Your ancestors *who went* **d** into Egypt were H3718
Dt 11:16 worship other gods and **bow d** to them. H2556
Dt 11:19 when you **lie d** and when you get up. H8886
Dt 12: 3 **Break d** their altars, smash their sacred H5997

D

Dt 12: 3 **cut d** the idols of their gods and wipe out H1548
Dt 16: 6 when the sun **goes d**, on the anniversary H995
Dt 17: 3 **bowing d** to them or to the sun or the H2556
Dt 20:19 *Do* not **cut** them **d**. H4162
Dt 20:20 *you may* **cut d** trees that you know are not H4162
Dt 21: 4 and **lead** it **d** to a valley that has not been H3718
Dt 25: 2 the judge *shall* **make** them **lie d** and have H5877
Dt 26: 4 from your hands and **set** it **d** in front of the H5663
Dt 26: 5 and *he* **went d** into Egypt with a few H3718
Dt 26:10 the LORD your God and **bow d** before him. H2556
Dt 26:15 **Look d** from heaven, your holy dwelling H9207
Dt 28:24 *it will* **come d** from the skies until you are H3718
Dt 28:49 like an eagle **swooping d**, a nation whose H1797
Dt 28:52 fortified walls in which you trust **fall d**. H3718
Dt 29:26 other gods and **bowed d** to them, H2556
Dt 30:17 are drawn away *to* **bow d** to other gods H2556
Dt 31: 9 So Moses **wrote d** this law and gave it to H4180
Dt 31:19 "Now **write d** this song and teach it to the H4180
Dt 31:22 So Moses **wrote d** this song that day and H4180
Dt 32:22 one that burns *d* to the realm of the dead AIT
Dt 33: 3 At your feet they all **bow d**, and from you H9413
Dt 33:11 **Strike d** those who rise against him, H4730+5516
Jos 2: 8 Before the spies **lay d** for the night, she H8886
Jos 2:15 So *she* **let** them **d** by a rope through the H3718
Jos 2:18 in the window through which *you* **let us d**, H3718
Jos 2:23 *They* **went d** out of the hills, forded the H3718
Jos 3:16 while the water **flowing d** to the Sea of H3718
Jos 4: 3 over with you and **put** them **d** at the place H5663
Jos 4: 8 to their camp, where *they* **put** them **d**. H5663
Jos 7: 5 quarries and **struck** them **d** on the slopes. H5782
Jos 7:10 What *are* you *doing* **d** on your face? H5877
Jos 8:22 Israel **cut** them **d**, leaving them neither H5782
Jos 8:29 the pole and **throw** it **d** at the entrance H8959
Jos 10:10 Beth Horon and **cut** them **d** all the way to H5782
Jos 10:11 Israel on the **road d** *from* Beth Horon to H4618
Jos 10:11 large hailstones **d** on them, H4946+2021+9028
Jos 10:13 sky and delayed **going d** about a full day. H995
Jos 10:27 the order and *they* **took** them **d** from the H3718
Jos 15: 1 extended **d** to the territory of Edom H448
Jos 15: 9 Ephron and **went d** *toward* Baalah H9305
Jos 15:10 **continued d** *to* Beth Shemesh and crossed H3718
Jos 16: 7 Then *it* **went d** from Janoah to Ataroth H3718
Jos 18:13 **went d** *to* Ataroth Addar on the hill H3718
Jos 18:16 The boundary **went d** to the foot of the H3718
Jos 18:16 *It* **continued d** the Hinnom Valley along H3718
Jos 18:17 and **ran d** *to* the Stone of Bohan son of H3718
Jos 18:18 of Beth Arabah and *on* **d** into the Arabah. H3718
Jos 23: 7 must not serve them or **bow d** to them. H2556
Jos 23:16 serve other gods and **bow d** to them, H2556
Jos 24: 4 Jacob and his family **went d** *to* Egypt. H3718
Jdg 1: 4 and *they* **struck d** ten thousand men at H5782
Jdg 1: 9 Judah **went d** to fight against the H3718
Jdg 1:34 allowing them to **come d** into the plain. H3718
Jdg 2: 2 but *you shall* **break d** their altars. H5997
Jdg 3:27 the Israelites **went d** with him from the H3718
Jdg 3:28 So *they* followed him **d** and took H3718
Jdg 3:29 At that time *they* **struck d** about ten H5782
Jdg 3:31 *who* **struck d** six hundred Philistines with H5782
Jdg 4:14 So Barak **went d** Mount Tabor, with ten H3718
Jdg 4:15 Sisera **got d** from his chariot and fled H3718
Jdg 5: 4 poured, the clouds **poured d** water. H5752
Jdg 5:11 of the LORD **went d** to the city gates. H3718
Jdg 5:13 "The remnant of the nobles **came d**; the H3718
Jdg 5:13 of the LORD **came d** to me against the H3718
Jdg 5:14 From Makir captains **came d**, from H3718
Jdg 6:11 the LORD came and **sat d** under the oak in H3782
Jdg 6:16 and *you will* **strike d** all the Midianites H5782
Jdg 6:25 **Tear d** your father's altar to Baal and cut H2238
Jdg 6:25 altar to Baal and **cut d** the Asherah pole H4162
Jdg 6:26 wood of the Asherah pole that *you* **cut d**, H4162
Jdg 6:28 pole beside it **cut d** and the second bull H4162
Jdg 6:30 because *he has* **broken d** Baal's altar and H5997
Jdg 6:30 Baal's altar and **cut d** the Asherah pole H4162
Jdg 6:31 himself when *someone* **breaks d** his altar." H5997
Jdg 6:32 So because Gideon **broke d** Baal's altar H5997
Jdg 7: 4 **Take** them **d** to the water, and I will thin H3718
Jdg 7: 5 So Gideon **took** the men **d** to the water H3718
Jdg 7: 5 dog laps from those who kneel **d** to drink." H4156
Jdg 7: 6 All the rest **got d** on their knees to drink. H4156
Jdg 7: 9 "Get up, **go d** against the camp, because H3718
Jdg 7:10 **go d** to the camp with your servant Purah H3718
Jdg 7:11 Purah his servant **went d** to the outposts H3718
Jdg 7:15 *he* **bowed d and worshiped.** H2556
Jdg 7:24 "**Come d** against the Midianites and seize H3718
Jdg 8: 9 I return in triumph, *I will* **tear d** this tower." H5997
Jdg 8:14 the young man **wrote d** for him the H4180
Jdg 8:17 *He* also **pulled d** the tower of Peniel and H5997
Jdg 9:36 people *are* **coming d** from the tops of the H3718
Jdg 9:37 people *are* **coming d** from the central hill H3718
Jdg 9:44 those in the fields and **struck** them **d**. H5782
Jdg 11:35 You *have* **brought** me **d** and I am H4156+4156
Jdg 12: 1 *We're going to* **burn d** H8596+928+2021+836
Jdg 12: 4 The Gileadites **struck** them **d** because the H5782
Jdg 14: 1 Samson **went d** to Timnah and saw there H3718
Jdg 14: 5 Samson **went d** to Timnah together with H3718
Jdg 14: 7 Then *he* **went d** and talked with the H3718
Jdg 14:10 Now his father **went d** to see the woman H3718
Jdg 14:19 *He* **went d** *to* Ashkelon, struck down thirty H3718
Jdg 14:19 to Ashkelon, **struck d** thirty of their men H5782
Jdg 15: 8 Then *he* **went d** and stayed in a cave in H3718
Jdg 15:11 men from Judah **went d** to the cave in the H3718
Jdg 15:15 grabbed it and **struck d** a thousand men. H5782
Jdg 16:21 out his eyes and **took** him **d** to Gaza. H3718
Jdg 16:30 and **d came** the temple on the rulers and H5877
Jdg 16:31 father's whole family **went d** to get him. H3718
Jdg 18:27 and **burned d** their H8596+928+2021+836
Jdg 19: 6 So the two of them **sat d** to eat and drink H3782
Jdg 19:26 **fell d** *at* the door and lay there until H5877
Jdg 20:21 out of Gibeah and **cut d** twenty-two H8845
Jdg 20:25 *they* **cut d** another eighteen thousand H8845
Jdg 20:35 the Israelites **struck d** 25,100 Benjamites H8845
Jdg 20:42 came out of the towns **cut** them **d** there. H8845
Jdg 20:45 the Israelites **cut d** five thousand men H6618
Jdg 20:45 far as Gidom and **struck d** two thousand H5782
Ru 2:10 she bowed **d** with her face to the ground. H5877
Ru 2:14 When *she* **sat d** with the harvesters, he H3782
Ru 3: 3 Then **go d** *to* the threshing floor, but don't H3718
Ru 3: 4 When he **lies d**, note the place where he H8886
Ru 3: 4 Then go and uncover his feet and **lie d** H8886
Ru 3: 6 So *she* **went d** *to* the threshing floor and H3718
Ru 3: 7 he went over to **lie d** at the far end of the H8886
Ru 3: 7 uncovered his feet and **lay d**. H8886
Ru 4: 1 the town gate and **sat d** there just as the H3782
Ru 4: 1 "Come over here, my friend, and **sit d**." H3782
Ru 4: 1 So he went over and **sat d**. H3782
1Sa 2: 6 *he* **brings d** *to* the grave and raises up. H3718
1Sa 2:36 line will come and **bow d** before him for a H2556
1Sa 3: 2 barely see, *was* **lying d** in his usual place. H8886
1Sa 3: 3 Samuel *was* **lying d** in the house of H8886
1Sa 3: 5 Eli said, "I did not call; go back and **lie d**." H8886
1Sa 3: 5 lie down." So he went and **lay d**. H8886
1Sa 3: 6 Eli said, "I did not call; go back and **lie d**." H8886
1Sa 3: 9 Samuel, "Go and **lie d**, and if he calls H8886
1Sa 3: 9 So Samuel went and **lay d** in his place. H8886
1Sa 3:15 Samuel **lay d** until morning and then H8886
1Sa 6:15 The Levites **took d** the ark of the LORD H3718
1Sa 6:19 But God **struck d** some of the inhabitants H5782
1Sa 6:21 **Come d** and take it up to your town." H3718
1Sa 9:25 After *they* **came d** from the high place to H3718
1Sa 9:27 *As* they *were* **going d** to the edge of the H3718
1Sa 10: 5 of prophets **coming d** from the high place H3718
1Sa 10: 8 "**Go d** ahead of me *to* Gilgal. I will surely H3718
1Sa 10: 8 I *will* surely **come d** to you to sacrifice H3718
1Sa 10:25 *He* **wrote** them **d** on a scroll and H4180
1Sa 13:12 the Philistines *will* **come d** against me at H3718
1Sa 13:20 So all Israel **went d** *to* the Philistines to H3718
1Sa 14:31 the Israelites *had* **struck d** the Philistines H5782
1Sa 14:36 "*Let us* **go d** and pursue the Philistines by H3718
1Sa 14:37 "*Shall I* **go d** and pursue the Philistines? H3718
1Sa 15:12 has turned and gone on **d** *to* Gilgal." H3718
1Sa 16:11 him; *we will* not **sit d** until he arrives." H6015
1Sa 17: 8 a man and *have him* **come d** to me. H3718
1Sa 17:28 asked, "Why *have you* **come d** here? H3718
1Sa 17:28 *you* **came d** only to watch the battle." H3718
1Sa 17:46 and *I'll* **strike** you **d** and cut off your head. H5782
1Sa 17:50 in his hand *he* **struck d** the Philistine H5782
1Sa 19:12 So Michal **let** David **d** through a window H3718
1Sa 20:24 Moon feast came, the king **sat d** to eat. H3782
1Sa 20:41 the stone and bowed **d** before Jonathan H5877
1Sa 21:13 gate and **letting** saliva **run d** his beard. H3718
1Sa 22: 1 heard about it, *they* **went d** to him there. H3718
1Sa 22:18 "You turn and **strike d** the priests. H7003
1Sa 22:18 the Edomite turned and **struck** them **d**. H7003
1Sa 23: 4 answered him, "**Go d** *to* Keilah, for I am H3718
1Sa 23: 6 Ahimelek *had* **brought** the ephod **d** with H3718
1Sa 23: 8 to **go d** *to* Keilah to besiege David and H3718
1Sa 23:11 *Will* Saul **come d**, as your servant has H3718
1Sa 23:20 **come d** whenever it pleases you to do so H3718
1Sa 23:23 *I will* **track** him **d** among all the clans of H2924
1Sa 23:25 *he* **went d** *to* the rock and stayed in the H3718
1Sa 24: 8 David **bowed d** and prostrated himself H7702
1Sa 24:11 you *are* **hunting** me **d** to take my life. H7399
1Sa 25: 1 Then David **moved d** into the Desert of H3718
1Sa 25:23 donkey and bowed **d** before David with H5877
1Sa 25:39 *has* **brought** Nabal's wrongdoing **d** on H8740
1Sa 25:41 *She* **bowed d** with her face to the ground H2556
1Sa 26: 2 So Saul **went d** to the Desert of Ziph, with H3718
1Sa 26: 5 the commander of the army, *had* **lain d**. H8886
1Sa 26: 6 "Who *will* **go d** into the camp with me to H3718
1Sa 28:14 and *he* **bowed d** and prostrated himself H7702
1Sa 30:15 "*Can you* **lead** me **d** to this raiding party?" H3718
1Sa 30:15 my master, and *I will* **take** you **d** to them." H3718
1Sa 30:16 *He* **led** David **d**, and there they were H3718
1Sa 30:24 as that of him *who* **went d** to the battle. H3718
1Sa 31:12 *They* **took d** the bodies of Saul and his H4374
2Sa 1: 1 returned from **striking d** the Amalekites H5782
2Sa 1:15 of his men and said, "Go, **strike** him **d**!" H7003
2Sa 1:15 So *he* **struck** him **d**, and he died H5782
2Sa 2:13 One group **sat d** on one side of the pool H3782
2Sa 2:16 opponent's side, and *they* **fell d** together. H5877
2Sa 2:22 Why should I strike you **d**? How H824+2025
2Sa 5:17 about it and **went d** to the stronghold H3718
2Sa 5:25 and *he* **struck d** the Philistines all the way H5782
2Sa 6: 7 therefore God **struck** him **d**, and he died H5782
2Sa 8: 2 *He* **made** them **lie d** on the ground and H8886
2Sa 8: 5 David **struck d** twenty-two thousand of H5782
2Sa 8:13 he returned from **striking d** eighteen H5782
2Sa 9: 6 *he* **bowed d** to pay him H5877+6584+7156
2Sa 9: 8 Mephibosheth **bowed d** and said, "What H2556
2Sa 10:18 *He* also **struck d** Shobak the commander H5782
2Sa 11: 8 "**Go d** to your house and wash your feet." H3718
2Sa 11: 9 servants and *did* not **go d** to his house. H3718
2Sa 11:15 from him so *he will* **be struck d** and die." H5782
2Sa 12: 9 *You* **struck d** Uriah the Hittite with the H5782
2Sa 13: 6 So Amnon **lay d** and pretended to be ill H8886
2Sa 13: 8 of her brother Amnon, who *was* **lying d**. H8886
2Sa 13:28 I say to you, '**Strike** Amnon **d**,' then kill H5782
2Sa 13:30 "Absalom *has* **struck d** all the king's sons H5782
2Sa 13:31 tore his clothes and **lay d** on the ground H8886
2Sa 13:34 west of him, coming **d** the side of the hill. H4946
2Sa 14: 7 over the *one who* **struck** his brother **d**, H5782
2Sa 14:33 he came in and **bowed d** with his face to H2556
2Sa 15: 5 approached him to **bow d** before him, H2556
2Sa 15:24 *They* **set d** the ark of God, and Abiathar H3668
2Sa 17: 2 *I would* **strike d** only the king H5782
2Sa 17:13 and *we will* **drag** it **d** to the valley until H6079
2Sa 17:18 his courtyard, and *they* **climbed d** *into* it. H3718
2Sa 18:21 The Cushite **bowed d** before Joab and ran H2556
2Sa 18:26 and he called **d** to the gatekeeper H448
2Sa 18:28 *He* **bowed d** before the king with his face H2556
2Sa 19:16 hurried **d** with the men of Judah to meet H3718
2Sa 19:20 of Joseph to **come d** and meet my lord H3718
2Sa 19:24 grandson, also **went d** to meet the king. H3718
2Sa 19:31 Gileadite also **came d** from Rogelim to H3718
2Sa 20:15 they were battering the wall to **bring** it **d**, H5877
2Sa 21:10 till the rain **poured d** from the heavens on H5988
2Sa 21:12 them after they **struck** Saul **d** on Gilboa.) H5782
2Sa 21:15 David **went d** with his men to fight H3718
2Sa 21:17 *he* **struck** the Philistine **d** and killed him. H5782
2Sa 22:10 He parted the heavens and **came d**; dark H3718
2Sa 22:17 "*He* **reached d** from on high and took H8938
2Sa 23:10 his ground and **struck d** the Philistines H5782
2Sa 23:12 defended it and **struck** the Philistines **d**, H5782
2Sa 23:13 chief warriors came **d** to David at the cave H3718
2Sa 23:20 He **struck d** Moab's two mightiest warriors H5782
2Sa 23:20 He also **went d** into a pit on a snowy day H3718
2Sa 23:21 And he **struck d** a huge Egyptian H5782
2Sa 24:17 the angel who *was* **striking d** the people, H5782
2Sa 24:20 he went out and **bowed d** before the king H2556
1Ki 1:16 Bathsheba **bowed d**, prostrating herself H7702
1Ki 1:25 Today *he has* **gone d** and sacrificed great H3718
1Ki 1:31 Then Bathsheba **bowed d** with her face to H7702
1Ki 1:33 my own mule and **take** him **d** to Gihon. H3718
1Ki 1:38 the Pelethites **went d** and had Solomon H3718
1Ki 1:53 and *they* **brought** him **d** from the altar. H3718
1Ki 1:53 came and **bowed d** to King Solomon, H2556
1Ki 2: 6 but *do* not **let** his gray head **go d** *to* the H3718
1Ki 2: 8 who **called d** bitter **curses** *on* me H7837+7839
1Ki 2: 8 When he **came d** to meet me at the H3718
1Ki 2: 9 **Bring** his gray head **d** *to* the grave in H3718
1Ki 2:19 **bowed d** to her and sat down on his H2556
1Ki 2:19 down to her and **sat d** on his throne. H3782
1Ki 2:19 mother, and *she* **sat d** at his right hand. H3782
1Ki 2:25 and *he* **struck d** Adonijah and he died. H7003
1Ki 2:29 son of Jehoiada, "Go, **strike** him **d**!" H7003
1Ki 2:31 **Strike** him **d** and bury him, and so clear H7003
1Ki 2:34 went up and **struck d** Joab and killed him H7003
1Ki 2:46 went out and **struck** Shimei **d** and he died H7003
1Ki 5: 9 My men *will* **haul** them **d** from Lebanon to H3718
1Ki 8:32 the guilty by **bringing d** on their heads H5989
1Ki 11:15 *had* **struck d** all the men in Edom. H5782
1Ki 15:13 Asa **cut** it **d** and burned it in the Kidron H4162
1Ki 15:27 and he **struck** him **d** at Gibbethon, H5782
1Ki 16:10 **struck** him **d** and killed him in the H5782
1Ki 17:23 the child and **carried** him **d** from the room H3718
1Ki 18: 7 **bowed d to the ground**, and H5877+6584+7156
1Ki 18:30 altar of the LORD, which *had* **been torn d**. H2238
1Ki 18:35 The water **ran d** around the altar and even H2143
1Ki 18:40 Elijah *had* them **brought d** to the H3718
1Ki 18:42 **bent d** to the ground and put his face H1566
1Ki 18:44 up your chariot and **go d** before the rain H3718
1Ki 19: 4 **sat d** under it and prayed that he might H3782
1Ki 19: 5 Then *he* **lay d** under the bush and fell H8886
1Ki 19: 6 He ate and drank and then **lay d** again. H8886
1Ki 19:10 your covenant, **torn d** your altars, and put H2238
1Ki 19:14 your covenant, **torn d** your altars, and put H2238
1Ki 19:18 whose knees *have* not **bowed d** to Baal H4156
1Ki 20:20 each one **struck d** his opponent. H5782
1Ki 20:38 himself with his headband **d** over his eyes. NDT
1Ki 21:16 he got up and **went d** to take possession H3718
1Ki 21:18 "Go **d** to meet Ahab king of Israel, who H3718
1Ki 22: 2 king of Judah **went d** to see the king of H3718
2Ki 1: 9 "Man of God, the king says, '**Come d**! H3718
2Ki 1:10 *may* fire **come d** from heaven and H3718
2Ki 1:11 is what the king says, '**Come d** at once! H3718
2Ki 1:12 "*may* fire **come d** from heaven and H3718
2Ki 1:15 said to Elijah, "**Go d** with him; do not be H3718
2Ki 1:15 Elijah got up and **went d** with him to the H3718
2Ki 2: 2 not leave you." So *they* **went d** *to* Bethel. H3718
2Ki 2:16 him up and **set** him **d** on some mountain H8959
2Ki 2:24 at them and **called d a curse** *on* them in H7837
2Ki 3:12 the king of Edom **went d** to him. H3718
2Ki 3:19 *You will* **cut d** every good tree, stop up all H5877
2Ki 3:25 all the springs and **cut d** every good tree. H5877
2Ki 4:11 he went up to his room and **lay d** there. H8886
2Ki 4:24 don't **slow d** for me unless I H6806+4200+8206
2Ki 5:14 So *he* **went d** and dipped himself in the H3718
2Ki 5:18 of Rimmon to **bow d** and he is leaning H2556
2Ki 5:18 when I **bow d** *in* the temple of Rimmon H2556
2Ki 5:21 *he* **got d** from the chariot to meet him. H5877
2Ki 5:26 you when the man **got d** from his chariot H2200
2Ki 6: 4 to the Jordan and *began to* **cut d** trees. H1615
2Ki 6: 5 As one of them was **cutting d** a tree, the H5877
2Ki 6: 9 because the Arameans are **going d** there." H5741
2Ki 6:18 As the enemy **came d** toward him, Elisha H3718
2Ki 6:33 to them, the messenger **came d** to him. H3718

2Ki 7:17 when the king **came d** to his house. H3718
2Ki 8:29 king of Judah **went d** to Jezreel to see H3718
2Ki 9:16 king of Judah *had* **gone d** to see him. H3718
2Ki 9:24 his heart and *he* **slumped d** in his chariot. H4156
2Ki 9:32 Two or three eunuchs **looked d** at him. H9207
2Ki 9:33 "**Throw** her **d**!" Jehu said. So they threw H9023
2Ki 9:33 So *they* **threw** her **d**, and some of her H9023
2Ki 10:13 and *we have* **come d** to greet the families H3718
2Ki 10:25 So *they* **cut** them **d** with the sword H5782
2Ki 10:27 stone of Baal and **tore d** the temple of H5997
2Ki 11:18 went to the temple of Baal and **tore** it **d**. H5997
2Ki 11:19 and *together they* **brought** the king **d** from H3718
2Ki 12:20 him at Beth Millo, on the **road d** *to* Silla. H3718
2Ki 13:14 king of Israel **went d** to see him and wept H3718
2Ki 14:13 went to Jerusalem and **broke d** the wall of H7287
2Ki 17:16 *They* **bowed d** to all the starry hosts, and H2556
2Ki 17:35 worship any other gods or **bow d** to them, H2556
2Ki 17:36 To him *you shall* **bow d** and to him offer H2556
2Ki 18: 4 sacred stones and **cut d** the Asherah H4162
2Ki 19: 7 there *I will* **have** him **cut d** with the H5877
2Ki 19:23 *I have* **cut d** its tallest cedars, the choicest H4162
2Ki 20:11 the ten steps *it had* **gone d** on the H3718+345
2Ki 21: 3 *He* **bowed d** to all the starry hosts and H2556
2Ki 21:13 wiping it and turning it **upside d**. H6584+7156
2Ki 21:21 had worshiped, and **bowing d** to them. H2556
2Ki 23: 7 *He* also **tore d** the quarters of the male H5997
2Ki 23: 8 *He* **broke d** the gateway at the entrance of H5997
2Ki 23:12 *He* **pulled d** the altars the kings of Judah H5997
2Ki 23:14 sacred stones and **cut d** the Asherah H4162
2Ki 25: 9 building *he* **burned d**. H8596+928+2021+836
2Ki 25:10 imperial guard **broke d** the walls around H5997
2Ki 25:24 "**Settle d** in the land and serve the king of H3782
1Ch 6:32 according to the **regulations** *laid d* for them. AIT
1Ch 7:21 when *they* **went d** to seize their livestock. H3718
1Ch 11:14 defended it and **struck** the Philistines **d**, H5782
1Ch 11:15 of the thirty chiefs **came d** to David to the H3718
1Ch 11:22 He **struck d** Moab's two mightiest warriors H5782
1Ch 11:22 He also **went d** into a pit on a snowy day H3718
1Ch 11:23 And *he* **struck d** an Egyptian who was five H5782
1Ch 13:10 and *he* **struck** him **d** because he had put H5782
1Ch 14:16 and *they* **struck d** the Philistine army H5782
1Ch 18: 5 David **struck d** twenty-two thousand of H5782
1Ch 18:12 son of Zeruiah **struck d** eighteen thousand H5782
1Ch 21:21 floor and **bowed d** before David with H2556
1Ch 29:20 of their fathers; *they* **bowed d**, prostrating H7702
2Ch 2:16 need and *will* **float** them *as* rafts by sea *d* to AIT
2Ch 6:13 and then **knelt d** before the H1384+6584+1386
2Ch 6:23 the guilty and **bringing d** on their heads H5989
2Ch 7: 1 fire **came d** from heaven and consumed H3718
2Ch 7: 3 saw the fire **coming d** and the glory of the H3718
2Ch 13:20 And the LORD **struck** him **d** and he died. H5597
2Ch 14: 3 sacred stones and **cut d** the Asherah H1548
2Ch 14:12 The LORD **struck d** the Cushites before Asa H5597
2Ch 15:16 Asa **cut** it **d**, broke it up and burned it in H4162
2Ch 18: 2 Some years later *he* **went d** to see Ahab in H3718
2Ch 20:16 Tomorrow **march d** against them. They will H3718
2Ch 20:18 Jehoshaphat **bowed d** with his face to the H7702
2Ch 20:18 Jerusalem **fell d** in worship before H5877
2Ch 22: 6 king of Judah **went d** to Jezreel to see H3718
2Ch 23:17 went to the temple of Baal and **tore** it **d**. H5997
2Ch 23:20 the land and **brought** the king **d** from the H3718
2Ch 25:12 and threw them **d** so that all were H4946+8031
2Ch 25:14 **bowed d** to them and burned sacrifices to H2556
2Ch 25:16 Why *be* **struck d**?" So the prophet H5782
2Ch 25:23 him to Jerusalem and **broke d** the wall of H7287
2Ch 26: 6 Philistines and **broke d** the walls of Gath, H7287
2Ch 29:29 present with him **knelt d** and worshiped. H4156
2Ch 29:30 gladness and **bowed d** and worshiped. H7702
2Ch 31: 1 sacred stones and **cut d** the Asherah H1548
2Ch 32:21 flesh and blood, **cut** him **d** with the sword. H5877
2Ch 32:30 the water **d** to the west side of H4200+4752
2Ch 33: 3 *He* **bowed d** to all the starry hosts and H2556
2Ch 34: 4 the altars of the Baals *were* **torn d**; H5997
2Ch 34: 7 *he* **tore d** the altars and the Asherah poles H5997
2Ch 36:19 to God's temple and **broke d** the wall of H5997
Ezr 4: 5 king of Persia and **d** to the reign of Darius H6330
Ezr 5:10 so that *we could* **write d** the names of A10374
Ezr 9: 3 my head and beard and **sat d** appalled. H3782
Ezr 10: 1 and **throwing himself d** before the H5877
Ezr 10:16 the tenth month *they* **sat d** to investigate H3782
Ne 1: 3 The wall of Jerusalem *is* **broken d**, and its H7287
Ne 1: 4 I heard these things, *I* **sat d** and wept. H3782
Ne 2:13 which *had been* **broken d**, and its gates, H7287
Ne 3:15 as far as the steps **going d** from the City of H3718
Ne 4: 3 up on it *would* **break d** their wall of H7287
Ne 6: 3 on a great project and cannot **go d**. H3718
Ne 6: 3 work stop while I leave it and **go d** to you?" H3718
Ne 8: 6 Then *they* **bowed d** and worshiped the H7702
Ne 9:13 "*You* **came d** on Mount Sinai; you spoke H3718
Ne 13: 2 hired Balaam to **call a curse d** *on* them. H7837
Ne 13:25 them and **called curses d** *on* them. H7837
Est 3: 2 the king's gate **knelt d** and paid honor to H4156
Est 3: 2 Mordecai *would* not **kneel d** or pay him H4156
Est 3: 5 Mordecai *would* not **kneel d** or pay him H4156
Est 3:15 The king and Haman **sat d** to drink, but H3782
Est 9: 5 **struck d** all their enemies *with* the H5782+4804
Est 9:32 and *it* **was written d** in the records. H4180
Job 1:17 parties and **swept d** on your camels and H7320
Job 3:13 For now *I would be* **lying d** in peace; H8886
Job 7: 4 When *I* **lie d** I think, 'How long before I H8886
Job 7: 9 so *one who* **goes d** *to* the grave does not H3718
Job 7:21 For *I will* soon **lie d** in the dust; you will H8886
Job 9:26 like eagles **swooping d** on their prey. H3216
Job 11:19 *You will* **lie d**, with no one to make you H8069
Job 12:14 What *he* **tears d** cannot be rebuilt; those H2238
Job 13:26 For *you* **write d** bitter things against me H4180
Job 14: 7 If *it is* **cut d**, it will sprout again, and its H4162
Job 14:12 so he **lies d** and does not rise; till the H8886
Job 17:16 *Will it* **go d** *to* the gates of death? Will we H3718
Job 18: 7 weakened; his own schemes **throw** him **d**. H8959
Job 19:10 *He* **tears** me **d** on every side till I am gone H5997
Job 20:23 against him and **rain d** his blows on him. H4763
Job 21:13 in prosperity and **go d** *to* the grave in H5737
Job 27:19 *He* **lies d** wealthy, but will do so no more H8886
Job 30:23 I know *you will* **bring** me **d** *to* death, to H8740
Job 33:24 'Spare them from **going d** *to* the pit; H3718
Job 33:28 has delivered me from **going d** to the pit, H6296
Job 36:28 the clouds **pour d** *their* **moisture** and H5688
Job 39: 3 *They* **crouch d** and bring forth their young H4156
Job 41: 1 with a fishhook or **tie d** its tongue with a H9205
Job 41:34 *It* **looks d on** all that are haughty; it is king H8011
Ps 3: 5 I **lie d** and sleep; I wake again, because H8886
Ps 4: 8 In peace *I will* **lie d** and sleep, for you H8886
Ps 5: 7 in reverence *I* **bow d** toward your holy H2556
Ps 7:16 their violence **comes d** on their own H3718
Ps 9:17 The wicked **go d** *to* the realm of the dead H8740
Ps 10: 2 the wicked man **hunts d** the weak, H1944
Ps 14: 2 The LORD **looks d** from heaven on all H9207
Ps 17:11 *They have* **tracked** me **d**, they now surround H892
Ps 17:13 confront them, **bring** them **d**; with your H4156
Ps 18: 9 He parted the heavens and **came d**; dark H3718
Ps 18:16 *He* **reached d** from on high and took hold H8938
Ps 22:27 of the nations *will* **bow d** before him, H2556
Ps 22:29 all *who* **go d** *to* the dust will kneel before H3718
Ps 23: 2 *He* **makes** me **lie d** in green pastures, he H8069
Ps 28: 1 I will be like *those who* **go d** *to* the pit. H3718
Ps 28: 5 *he will* **tear** them **d** and never build them H2238
Ps 30: 3 you spared me from **going d** *to* the pit. H3718
Ps 30: 9 if I am silenced, if I **go d** to the pit? H3718
Ps 33:13 From heaven the LORD **looks d** and sees all H5564
Ps 36:12 lie fallen—**thrown d**, not able to rise! H1890
Ps 37:14 bend the bow to **bring d** the poor and H5877
Ps 38: 2 and your hand *has* **come d** on me. H5737
Ps 38: 6 *I am* **bowed d** and brought very low; all H6390
Ps 44:25 We *are brought* **d** to the dust; our bodies H8863
Ps 52: 5 God *will* **bring** you **d** to everlasting **ruin**: H5997
Ps 53: 2 God **looks d** from heaven on all mankind H9207
Ps 55: 3 for *they* **bring d** suffering on me and H4572
Ps 55:15 *let them* **go d** alive *to* the realm of the H3718
Ps 55:23 *will* **bring d** the wicked into the pit of H3718
Ps 56: 7 in your anger, God, **bring** the nations **d**. H3718
Ps 57: 6 my feet—I *was* **bowed d in distress**. H4104
Ps 59:11 your might uproot them and **bring** them **d**. H3718
Ps 60: T returned and **struck d** twelve thousand H5782
Ps 60:12 he *will* **trample d** our enemies. H1008
Ps 62: 3 *Would* all of you **throw** me **d**—this H8132
Ps 63: 9 *they will* **go d** to the depths of the earth. H995
Ps 64: 7 his arrows; they will suddenly be **struck d**. H4804
Ps 66: 4 All the earth **bows d** to you; they sing H2556
Ps 68: 8 the heavens **poured d rain**, before God, H5752
Ps 72:11 *May* all kings **bow d** to him and all H2556
Ps 73:18 slippery ground; *you* **cast** them **d** to ruin. H5877
Ps 75: 7 *He* **brings** one **d**, he exalts H9164
Ps 75: 8 of the earth **drink** it **d** *to* its very dregs. H5172
Ps 77:17 The clouds **poured d** water, the heavens H2442
Ps 78:16 crag and **made** water **flow d** like rivers. H3718
Ps 78:24 *he* **rained d** manna for the people to eat H4763
Ps 78:27 *He* **rained** meat **d** on them like dust, birds H4763
Ps 78:28 *He* **made** them **come d** inside their camp H5877
Ps 78:31 **cutting d** the young men of Israel. H4156
Ps 78:51 *He* **struck d** all the firstborn of Egypt, the H5782
Ps 80:12 Why *have you* **broken d** its walls so that H7287
Ps 80:14 **Look d** from heaven and see H5564
Ps 80:16 Your vine *is* **cut d**, it is burned with fire; at H4065
Ps 85:11 righteousness **looks d** from heaven. H9207
Ps 88: 4 counted among *those who* **go d** *to* the pit; H3718
Ps 89:23 before him and **strike d** his adversaries. H5597
Ps 95: 6 *let us* **bow d** in worship, let us H4156
Ps 102:19 "The LORD **looked d** from his sanctuary on H9207
Ps 104: 8 mountains, *they* **went d** *into* the valleys H3718
Ps 104:19 the sun knows when to **go d**. H4427
Ps 104:22 they return and **lie d** in their dens. H8069
Ps 105:16 *He* **called d** famine on the land and H7924
Ps 105:33 *he* **struck d** their vines and fig trees and H5782
Ps 105:36 Then *he* **struck d** all the firstborn in their H5782
Ps 107:16 for *he* **breaks d** gates of bronze and cuts H8689
Ps 107:26 to the heavens and **went d** *to* the depths; H3718
Ps 108:13 he *will* **trample d** our enemies. H1008
Ps 113: 6 who **stoops d** to look on the heavens and H9164
Ps 115:17 those *who* **go d** *to* the place of silence H3718
Ps 118:10 in the name of the LORD *I* **cut** them **d**. H4577
Ps 118:11 in the name of the LORD *I* **cut** them **d**. H4577
Ps 118:12 in the name of the LORD *I* **cut** them **d**. H4577
Ps 119: 4 You *have* **laid d** precepts that are to be H7422
Ps 119:138 The statutes *you have* **laid d** are righteous H7422
Ps 133: 2 on the head, **running d** on the beard H3718
Ps 133: 2 on the beard, running **d** on Aaron's beard NDT
Ps 133: 2 Aaron's beard, **d** on the collar of his robe. H3718
Ps 135: 8 He **struck d** the firstborn of Egypt, the H5782
Ps 135:10 He **struck d** many nations and killed H5782
Ps 136:10 to *him who* **struck d** the firstborn of Egypt H5782
Ps 136:17 to *him who* **struck d** great kings, His love H5782
Ps 137: 7 "**Tear** it **d**," they cried, "tear it down to its H6867
Ps 137: 7 they cried, "**tear** it **d** to its foundations!" H6867
Ps 138: 2 *I will* **bow d** toward your holy temple and H2556
Ps 139: 3 You discern my going out and my **lying d** H8061
Ps 140:11 *may* disaster **hunt d** the H7421+4200+4511
Ps 141: 6 Their rulers *will* **be thrown d** from the cliffs H9023
Ps 143: 7 I will be like *those who* **go d** *to* the pit. H3718
Ps 144: 5 heavens, LORD, and **come d**; touch the H3718
Ps 144: 7 **Reach d** your hand from on high; deliver H8938
Ps 145:14 who fall and lifts up all who **are bowed d**. H4104
Ps 146: 8 the LORD lifts up *those who* **are bowed d** H4104
Ps 147:17 *He* **hurls d** his hail like pebbles. Who can H8959
Pr 1:12 like *those who* **go d** *to* the pit; H3718
Pr 2:18 Surely her house **leads d** to death and her H8755
Pr 3:24 When *you* **lie d**, you will not be afraid H8886
Pr 3:24 be afraid; when *you* **lie d**, your sleep will H8886
Pr 5: 5 Her feet **go d** *to* death; her steps lead H3718
Pr 7: 6 of my house *I* **looked d** through the H9207
Pr 7: 8 *He* **was going d** the street near her corner H6296
Pr 7:26 Many are the victims *she has* **brought d** H5877
Pr 7:27 **leading d** to the chambers of death. H3718
Pr 11: 5 the wicked *are* **brought d** by their own H5877
Pr 12:25 Anxiety **weighs d** the heart, but a kind H8817
Pr 14: 1 own hands the foolish one **tears** hers **d**. H2238
Pr 14:19 Evildoers *will* **bow d** in the presence of H8820
Pr 14:32 the wicked **are brought d**, but even in H1890
Pr 15:24 keep them from **going d** to the realm of H4752
Pr 15:25 The LORD **tears d** the house of the proud H5815
Pr 16:29 leads them **d** a path that is not good H928
Pr 18: 8 morsels; they **go d** *to* the inmost parts. H3718
Pr 19:28 the mouth of the wicked **gulps d** evil. H1180
Pr 21:20 food and olive oil, but fools gulp **theirs d**. H5647
Pr 21:22 of the mighty and **pull d** the stronghold in H3718
Pr 23:31 in the cup, when *it* **goes d** smoothly! H2143
Pr 26:20 without a gossip a quarrel **dies d**. H9284
Pr 26:22 morsels; they **go d** *to* the inmost parts. H3718
Pr 29: 4 those who are greedy for bribes **tear** it **d**. H2238
Pr 30: 4 Who has gone up to heaven and **come d** H3718
Ecc 3: 3 a time to **tear d** and a time to build H7287
Ecc 3:21 the animal **goes d** into the H3718+4200+4752
Ecc 4:10 If either of *them* **falls d**, one can help the H5877
Ecc 4:11 if two **lie d** *together*, they will keep H8886
Ecc 8: 6 a person may be **weighed d** by misery. H8041
SS 4:15 flowing water **streaming d** from Lebanon. H5688
SS 6: 2 My beloved *has* **gone d** to his garden, to H3718
SS 6:11 *I* **went d** to the grove of nut trees to look H3718
Isa 2: 8 *they* **bow d** to the work of their hands H2556
Isa 5: 5 be destroyed; I *will* **break d** its wall, and it H7287
Isa 5:24 as dry grass **sinks d** *in* the flames, H8332
Isa 5:25 his hand is raised and *he* **strikes** them **d**. H5782
Isa 6:13 oak leave stumps when they are **cut d**, H8961
Isa 9:10 "The bricks *have* **fallen d**, but we will H5877
Isa 10: 6 and to **trample** them **d** like mud in H8492+5330
Isa 10:19 be so few that a child *could* **write** them **d**. H4180
Isa 10:20 rely on *him who* **struck** them **d** but will H5782
Isa 10:26 as when he **struck d** Midian at the rock of H4804
Isa 10:34 *He will* **cut d** the forest thickets with an ax H5937
Isa 11: 6 the leopard *will* **lie d** with the goat H8069
Isa 11: 7 their young *will* **lie d** together, and H8069
Isa 11:14 *They will* **swoop d** on the slopes of H6414
Isa 13:18 Their bows *will* **strike d** the young men H8187
Isa 14: 6 *which* in anger **struck d** peoples *with* H5782
Isa 14: 8 been laid low, no one comes *to* **cut** us **d**." H4162
Isa 14:11 your pomp *has* **been brought d** *to* the H3718
Isa 14:12 *You have* **been cast d** to the earth, you H1548
Isa 14:15 But *you* **are brought d** to the realm of the H3718
Isa 14:25 on my mountains *I will* **trample** him **d**. H1008
Isa 14:30 pasture, and the needy *will* **lie d** in safety. H8069
Isa 16: 8 the nations *have* **trampled d** the choicest H2150
Isa 17: 2 to flocks, *which will* **lie d**, with no one to H8069
Isa 18: 5 and **cut d** and take away the spreading H9372
Isa 22: 5 a day of **battering d** walls and of crying H7982
Isa 22:10 in Jerusalem and **tore d** houses to H5997
Isa 22:25 the load hanging on it *will* **be cut d**." H4162
Isa 23: 9 to **bring d** her pride in all her splendor H2725
Isa 25:10 land as straw **is trampled d** in the manure H1889
Isa 25:11 God *will* **bring d** their pride despite the H9164
Isa 25:12 *He will* **bring d** your high fortified walls H8820
Isa 25:12 *he will* **bring** them **d** to the ground H5595
Isa 26: 5 it to the ground and **casts** it **d** to the dust. H5595
Isa 26: 6 Feet **trample** it **d**—the feet of the H8252
Isa 27: 7 struck her as he **struck d** those who have H4804
Isa 27:10 calves graze, there *they* **lie d**; they strip its H8069
Isa 28:18 sweeps by, you will be **beaten d** by it. H5330
Isa 29:16 You **turn** things **upside d**, as if the potter H2201
Isa 29:20 who have an eye for evil *will* **be cut d**— H4162
Isa 30: 2 who **go d** *to* Egypt without consulting me H3718
Isa 30:30 them see his arm **coming d** with raging H5738
Isa 30:31 Assyria; with his rod *he will* **strike** them **d**. H5782
Isa 31: 1 Woe to those *who* **go d** *to* Egypt for help H3718
Isa 31: 4 LORD Almighty *will* **come d** to do battle on H3718
Isa 34:14 night creatures *will* also **lie d** and find H8089
Isa 37: 7 there *I will* **have** him **cut d** with the H5877
Isa 37:24 *I have* **cut d** its tallest cedars, the choicest H4162
Isa 38: 8 the ten steps *it has* **gone d** on the H3718
Isa 38: 8 went back the ten steps *it had* **gone d**. H3718
Isa 38:12 my house *has* **been pulled d** and taken H5825
Isa 38:18 *those who* **go d** *to* the pit cannot hope H3718
Isa 41: 7 The *other* **nails d** the idol so H2616+928+5021
Isa 42:10 the earth, you *who* **go d** *to* the sea, and H3718
Isa 43:14 to Babylon and **bring d** as fugitives all H3718
Isa 44:11 they *will be* **brought d** *to* **terror** and shame H7064
Isa 44:14 He **cut d** cedars, or perhaps took a cypress H4162
Isa 44:15 he makes an idol and **bows d** to it. H6032

Isa 44:17 his idol; *he* **bows d** to it and worships. H6032
Isa 44:19 *Shall I* **bow d** to a block of wood? H6032
Isa 45: 2 *I will* **break d** gates of bronze and cut H8689
Isa 45: 8 "*You* heavens above, **rain d** my H8319
Isa 45: 8 righteousness; *let* the clouds **shower** it **d**. H5688
Isa 45:14 *They will* **bow d** before you and plead H2556
Isa 46: 1 Bel **bows d**, Nebo stoops low; their idols H4156
Isa 46: 2 They stoop and **bow d** together; unable to H4156
Isa 46: 6 and *they* **bow d** and worship it. H6032
Isa 47: 1 "**Go d**, sit in the dust, Virgin Daughter H3718
Isa 49: 7 princes will see and **bow d**, because of H2556
Isa 49:10 *will* the desert heat or the sun **beat d** *on* H5782
Isa 49:23 *They will* **bow d** before you *with* their faces *to* H2556
Isa 50:11 from my hand: *You will* **lie d** in torment. H8886
Isa 52: 4 "At first my people **went d** *to* Egypt to live H3718
Isa 55:10 rain and the snow **come d** from heaven, H3718
Isa 60:14 who despise you *will* **bow d** at your feet H2556
Isa 63: 3 in my anger and **trod** them **d** in my wrath; H8252
Isa 63:14 like cattle *that* **go d** to the plain, they H3718
Isa 63:15 **Look d** from heaven and see, from your H5564
Isa 63:18 our enemies *have* **trampled d** your H1008
Isa 64: 1 you would rend the heavens and **come d**, H3718
Isa 64: 2 come **d** to make your name known to your NDT
Isa 64: 3 did not expect, *you* **came d**, and the H3718
Isa 66:15 *he will* **bring d** his anger with fury H8740
Isa 66:23 mankind will come and **bow d** before me," H2556
Jer 1: 3 **d to** the fifth month of the eleventh H6330+9462
Jer 1:10 kingdoms to uproot and **tear d**, H5997
Jer 2:20 spreading tree you **lay d** as a prostitute. H7579
Jer 3:25 *Let us* **lie d** in our shame, and let our H8886
Jer 5: 1 "**Go up and d** the streets of Jerusalem H8763
Jer 6: 6 "**Cut d** the trees and build siege ramps H4162
Jer 6:11 the old, *those* **weighed d** *with* years. H4849
Jer 6:15 *they will* **be brought d** when I punish H4173
Jer 8: 4 " 'When *people* **fall d**, do they not get up? H5877
Jer 8:12 *they will* **be brought d** when they are H4173
Jer 12:10 ruin my vineyard and **trample d** my field; H1008
Jer 13:18 queen mother, "**Come d** from your thrones H9164
Jer 14:22 *Do* the skies *themselves* **send d** showers H5989
Jer 15: 8 suddenly *I will* **bring d** on them anguish H5877
Jer 16: 8 is feasting and **sit d** to eat and drink. H3782
Jer 16:16 and *they will* **hunt** them **d** on every H7421
Jer 18: 2 "**Go d** *to* the potter's house, and there I H3718
Jer 18: 3 So *I* **went d** *to* the potter's house, and I H3718
Jer 18: 7 is to be uprooted, **torn d** and destroyed, H5997
Jer 21: 6 *I will* **strike d** those who live in this city H5782
Jer 22: 1 "**Go d** *to* the palace of the king of Judah H3718
Jer 23:19 a whirlwind **swirling d** on the heads of the H2565
Jer 24: 6 I will build them up and not **tear** them **d**; H2238
Jer 25:29 I *am* **calling d** a sword on all who live H7924
Jer 26:23 *who* **had** him **struck d** with a sword and H5782
Jer 29: 5 "Build houses and **settle d**; plant gardens H3782
Jer 29:28 Therefore build houses and **settle d**; plant H3782
Jer 30:23 a driving wind **swirling d** on the heads of H2565
Jer 31:28 I watched over them to uproot and **tear d**, H5997
Jer 32:29 it on fire; *they will* **burn** it **d**, along with H8596
Jer 33: 4 of Judah that *have* **been torn d** to be used H5997
Jer 34: 2 and *he will* **burn** it **d**. H8596+928+2021+836
Jer 34:22 take it and **burn** it **d**. H8596+928+2021+836
Jer 36:12 *he* **went d** to the secretary's room in the H3718
Jer 36:15 They said to him, "**Sit d**, please, and read H3782
Jer 37: 8 capture it and **burn** it **d**. H8596+928+2021+836
Jer 37:10 out and **burn** this city **d**." H8596+928+2021+836
Jer 38: 6 and Jeremiah **sank d** into the mud. H3190
Jer 38:11 from there and **let** them **d** with ropes to H8938
Jer 38:17 city *will* not **be burned d**; H8596+928+2021+836
Jer 38:18 and *they will* **burn** it **d**; H8596+928+2021+836
Jer 38:23 and this city *will be* **burned d**." H8596+928+2021+836
Jer 39: 8 of the people and **broke d** the walls of H5997
Jer 40: 9 "**Settle d** in the land and serve the king of H3782
Jer 41: 2 him got up and **struck d** Gedaliah son of H5782
Jer 42:10 I will build you up and not **tear** you **d**; H2238
Jer 43:13 and *will* **burn d** the H8596+928+2021+836
Jer 46:12 over another; both *will* **fall d** together." H5877
Jer 46:15 for the LORD *will* **push** them **d**. H2074
Jer 46:22 her with axes, like *men who* **cut d** trees. H2634
Jer 46:23 *They will* **chop d** her forest," declares the H4162
Jer 48: 5 on the **road d** *to* Horonaim anguished H4618
Jer 48:15 finest young men *will* **go d** in the H3718
Jer 48:18 "**Come d** from your glory and sit on the H3718
Jer 48:40 An eagle *is* **swooping d**, spreading its H1797
Jer 49:16 from there *I will* **bring** you **d**," declares the H3718
Jer 49:22 An eagle will soar and **swoop d** H1797
Jer 50:15 her towers fall, her walls **are torn d**. H2238
Jer 50:27 *let them* **go d** to the slaughter! H3718
Jer 51: 4 *They will* **fall d** slain in Babylon, fatally H5877
Jer 51:40 "*I will* **bring** them **d** like lambs to the H3718
Jer 52:13 building *he* **burned d**. H8596+928+2021+836
Jer 52:14 **broke d** all the walls around Jerusalem. H5997
La 1:13 high he sent fire, **sent** it **d** into my bones. H3718
La 2: 1 *He has* **hurled d** the splendor of Israel H8959
La 2: 2 in his wrath *he has* **torn d** the strongholds H2238
La 2: 2 *He has* **brought** her kingdom and its princes **d** H5595
La 2: 8 LORD determined to **tear d** the wall around H8845
La 3: 7 *he has* **weighed** me **d** *with* chains. H3877
La 3:50 until the LORD **looks d** from heaven and H9207
Eze 1:27 that from there **d** he looked like fire H4200+4752
Eze 4: 6 finished this, **lie d** again, this time on H8886
Eze 6: 6 your incense altars **broken d**, and what H1548
Eze 8: 2 to be his waist **d** he was like fire, H4200+4752
Eze 8:16 they *were* **bowing d** to the sun in the east. H2556
Eze 9:10 but *I will* **bring d** on their own heads what H5989
Eze 11:21 *I will* **bring d** on their own heads what H5989
Eze 13:11 I will send hailstones **hurtling d**, and H5877
Eze 13:14 *I will* **tear d** the wall you have covered with H2238
Eze 14: 1 came to me and **sat d** in front of me. H3782
Eze 16:39 and *they will* **tear d** your mounds and H2238
Eze 16:41 *They will* **burn d** your H8596+928+2021+836
Eze 16:43 I *will* surely **bring d** on your head what H5989
Eze 17:24 that I the LORD **bring d** the tall tree and H9164
Eze 19: 2 *She* **lay d** among them and reared her H8069
Eze 19: 7 *He* **broke d** their strongholds and H8318
Eze 20: 1 of the LORD, and *they* **sat d** in front of me. H3782
Eze 22:31 **bringing d** on their own heads all they H5989
Eze 23:47 stone them and **cut** them **d** with their H1345
Eze 23:47 and **burn d** their houses H8596+928+2021+836
Eze 26: 4 the walls of Tyre and **pull d** her towers; H2238
Eze 26:12 *they will* **break d** your walls and demolish H2238
Eze 26:16 of the coast *will* **step d** from their thrones H3718
Eze 26:20 then *I will* **bring** you **d** with those who go H3718
Eze 26:20 you down with *those who* **go d** *to* the pit, H3718
Eze 26:20 with *those who* **go d** *to* the pit, and H3718
Eze 27:34 all your company *have* **gone d** with you. H5877
Eze 28: 8 *They will* **bring** you **d** to the pit, and you H3718
Eze 30: 4 carried away and her foundations **torn d**. H2238
Eze 31: 7 its roots **went** *d* to abundant waters. AIT
Eze 31:12 of foreign nations **cut** it **d** and left it. H4162
Eze 31:14 among mortals *who* **go d** *to* the realm of H3718
Eze 31:15 On the day it *was* **brought d** to the realm H3718
Eze 31:16 its fall when I **brought** it **d** to the realm of H3718
Eze 31:16 dead to be with *those who* **go d** *to* the pit. H3718
Eze 31:17 *had* **gone d** to the realm of the dead H3718
Eze 31:18 Yet *you*, too, *will* **be brought d** with the H3718
Eze 32:15 when I **strike d** all who live there H5782
Eze 32:18 along with *those who* **go d** *to* the pit. H3718
Eze 32:19 **Go d** and be laid among the H3718
Eze 32:21 '*They have* **come d** and they lie with the H3718
Eze 32:24 land of the living **went d** uncircumcised to H3718
Eze 32:24 shame with *those who* **go d** *to* the pit. H3718
Eze 32:25 shame with *those who* **go d** *to* the pit; H3718
Eze 32:27 who **went d** *to* the realm of the dead with H3718
Eze 32:29 with *those who* **go d** *to* the pit. H3718
Eze 32:30 *they* **went d** with the slain in disgrace H3718
Eze 32:30 shame with *those who* **go d** *to* the pit. H3718
Eze 33:10 "Our offenses and sins **weigh** us **d**, and H6584
Eze 34:14 There *they will* **lie d** in good grazing land H8069
Eze 34:15 will tend my sheep and **have** them **lie d**, H8069
Eze 34:26 *I will* **send d** showers in season; there will H3718
Eze 38:22 bloodshed; *I will* **pour d** torrents of rain H4763
Eze 43:11 **Write** these **d** before them so that they H4180
Eze 46: 2 *He is to* **bow d in worship** at the threshold H2556
Eze 47: 1 The water *was* **coming d** from under the H3718
Eze 47: 8 region and **goes d** into the Arabah, H3718
Da 3: 5 *you must* **fall d** and worship the image A10484
Da 3: 6 Whoever *does* not **fall d** and worship will A10484
Da 3: 7 every language **fell d** and worshiped the A10484
Da 3:10 kinds of music *must* **fall d** and worship A10484
Da 3:11 that whoever *does* not **fall d** and worship A10484
Da 3:15 if you are ready *to* **fall d** and worship the A10484
Da 4:13 a messenger, **coming d** from heaven. A10474
Da 4:14 '**Cut d** the tree and trim off its branches A10134
Da 4:23 **coming d** from heaven and saying A10474
Da 4:23 saying, '**Cut d** the tree and destroy it A10134
Da 6:10 times a day he **got d** on his knees and A10121
Da 7: 1 *He* **wrote d** the substance of his dream. A10374
Da 7:23 **trampling** it **d** and crushing it. A10165
Da 8:10 and *it* **threw** some of the starry host **d** to H5877
Da 8:11 the LORD, and his sanctuary **was thrown d**. H8959
Hos 2:18 the land, so that all *may* **lie d** in safety. H8886
Hos 7:12 *I will* **pull** them **d** like the birds in the sky. H3718
Hos 11: 4 to the cheek, and *I* **bent d** to feed them. H5742
Hos 14: 5 cedar of Lebanon *he will* **send d** his roots; H5782
Joel 1:17 the granaries *have* **been broken d**, for the H2238
Joel 3: 2 all nations and **bring** them **d** to the Valley H3718
Joel 3:11 assemble there. **Bring d** your warriors H5737
Am 1: 5 *I will* **break d** the gate of Damascus; I will H8689
Am 2: 2 Moab *will* **go d** in great tumult amid war H4637
Am 2: 8 *They* **lie d** beside every altar on garments H5742
Am 3: 5 *Does* a bird **swoop d** to a trap on the H5877
Am 3:11 **pull d** your strongholds and plunder your H3718
Am 3:15 *I will* **tear d** the winter house along with H5782
Am 6: 2 then **go d** *to* Gath in Philistia. H3718
Am 8: 9 "*I will* **make** the sun **go d** at noon and H995
Am 9: 1 **Bring** them **d** on the heads of all the H1298
Am 9: 2 Though *they* **dig d** to the depths below H3168
Am 9: 2 from there *I will* **bring** them **d**. H3718
Am 9: 3 there *I will* **hunt** them **d** and seize them. H2924
Ob 3 'Who *can* **bring** me **d** to the ground?' H3718
Ob 4 from there *I will* **bring** you **d**," declares the H3718
Ob 9 mountains *will* **be cut d** in the slaughter H4162
Ob 14 at the crossroads to **cut d** their fugitives, H4162
Jnh 1: 3 *He* **went d** *to* Joppa, where he found a H3718
Jnh 1: 5 where *he* **lay d** and fell into a deep sleep. H8886
Jnh 1:11 do to you *to make* the sea **calm d** for us?" H9284
Jnh 2: 6 To the roots of the mountains *I* **sank d** H3718
Jnh 3: 6 with sackcloth and **sat d** in the dust. H3782
Jnh 4: 5 had gone out and **sat d** at a place east of H3782
Mic 1: 3 *he* **comes d** and treads on the heights of H3718
Mic 1: 4 like water rushing **d** a slope. H928
Mic 5:11 of your land and **tear d** all your H2238
Mic 5:13 *you will* no longer **bow d** to the work of H2556
Mic 6: 6 the LORD and **bow d** before the exalted H4104
Na 3:15 the sword *will* **cut** you **d**—they will H4162
Na 3:18 slumber; your nobles **lie d** to **rest**. H8905
Hab 2: 2 "**Write d** the revelation and make it plain H4180
Zep 1: 5 *who* **bow d** on the roofs **to worship** the H2556
Zep 1: 5 those *who* **bow d** and swear by the LORD H2556
Zep 2: 7 the evening *they will* **lie d** in the houses H8069
Zep 2:11 Distant nations *will* **bow d** to him, all of H2556
Zep 2:14 Flocks and herds *will* **lie d** there, creatures H8069
Zep 3:13 They will eat and **lie d** and no one will H8069
Hag 1: 8 mountains and **bring d** timber and build H995
Zec 1:21 terrify them and **throw d** these horns of H3343
Zec 5: 8 basket and **pushed** its lead cover **d** on it. H8959
Zec 10:11 pride *will* **be brought d** and Egypt's H3718
Zec 11: 2 Bashan; the dense forest *has been* **cut d**! H3718
Zec 13: 8 "two-thirds *will* **be struck d** and perish; yet H4162
Mt 2:11 and *they* **bowed d** and worshiped him. *G4406*
Mt 3:10 good fruit *will be* **cut d** and thrown into *G1716*
Mt 4: 6 Son of God," he said, "throw yourself **d**. *G3004*
Mt 4: 9 "if you will **bow d** and worship me." *G4406*
Mt 5: 1 he went up on a mountainside and **sat d**. *G2767*
Mt 7:19 bear good fruit *is* **cut d** and thrown into *G1716*
Mt 7:25 The rain **came d**, the streams rose, and *G2849*
Mt 7:27 The rain **came d**, the streams rose, and *G2849*
Mt 8: 1 *When* Jesus **came d** from the *G2849*
Mt 8:32 whole herd rushed **d** the steep bank into *G2848*
Mt 11:23 No, *you will* **go d** to Hades. *G2849*
Mt 13:47 is like a net *that was* **let d** into the lake *G965*
Mt 13:48 Then *they* **sat d** and collected the good *G2767*
Mt 14:19 directed the people *to* **sit d** on the grass. *G369*
Mt 14:29 Then Peter **got d** out of the boat, walked *G2849*
Mt 14:32 climbed into the boat, the wind **died d**. *G3156*
Mt 15:29 he went up on a mountainside and **sat d**. *G2764*
Mt 15:35 He told the crowd *to* **sit d** on the ground. *G404*
Mt 17: 9 *As* they *were* **coming d** the mountain *G2849*
Mt 20:20 her sons and, **kneeling d**, asked a favor of *G4686*
Mt 22:26 third brother, **right on d to** the seventh. *G2401*
Mt 24: 2 on another; every one *will be* **thrown d**." *G2907*
Mt 24:17 *Let* no one on the housetop **go d** to take *G2849*
Mt 26:58 He entered and **sat d** with the guards to *G2764*
Mt 26:74 Then he began *to* **call d curses**, and he *G2874*
Mt 27:36 And **sitting d**, they kept watch over him *G2764*
Mt 27:40 **Come d** from the cross, if you are the Son *G2849*
Mt 27:42 *Let him* **come d** now from the cross, and *G2849*
Mt 28: 2 of the Lord **came d** from heaven and, *G2849*
Mk 1: 7 I am not worthy *to* **stoop d** and untie. *G3252*
Mk 3:11 *they* **fell d before** him and cried out *G4700*
Mk 3:22 of the law who **came d** from Jerusalem *G2849*
Mk 4:39 Then the wind **died d** and it was *G3156*
Mk 5:13 rushed **d** the steep bank into the lake *G2848*
Mk 6:39 them *to* **have** all the people **sit d** in groups *G369*
Mk 6:40 So *they* **sat d** in groups of hundreds and *G404*
Mk 6:51 the boat with them, and the wind **died d**. *G3156*
Mk 7:13 by your tradition that *you have* **handed d**. *G4140*
Mk 7:31 *d* to the Sea of Galilee and into the region of AIT
Mk 8: 6 He told the crowd *to* **sit d** on the ground *G404*
Mk 9: 9 *As* they *were* **coming d** the mountain *G2849*
Mk 9:35 **Sitting d**, Jesus called the Twelve and *G2767*
Mk 12:41 Jesus **sat d** opposite the place where the *G2767*
Mk 13: 2 on another; every one *will be* **thrown d**." *G2907*
Mk 13:15 *Let* no one on the housetop **go d** or enter *G2849*
Mk 14:71 He began *to* **call d curses**, and he swore to *G354*
Mk 14:72 And *he* **broke d** and wept. *G2095*
Mk 15:30 **come d** from the cross and save yourself!" *G2849*
Mk 15:32 *Let* this Messiah, this king of Israel, **come d** *G2849*
Mk 15:36 Let's see if Elijah comes *to* **take** him **d**," *G2747*
Mk 15:46 linen cloth, **took d** the body, wrapped *G2747*
Lk 1: 2 just as *they were* **handed d** to us *by* those *G4140*
Lk 1:52 *He has* **brought d** rulers from their thrones *G2747*
Lk 2:51 Then *he* **went d** to Nazareth with them *G2849*
Lk 3: 9 good fruit *will be* **cut d** and thrown into *G1716*
Lk 4: 9 he said, "throw yourself **d** from here. *G3004*
Lk 4:20 gave it back to the attendant and **sat d**. *G2767*
Lk 4:31 Then *he* **went d** to Capernaum, a town in *G2982*
Lk 4:35 the demon **threw** the man **d** before them *G4849*
Lk 5: 3 Then *he* **sat d** and taught the people from *G2767*
Lk 5: 4 deep water, and **let d** the nets for a catch." *G5899*
Lk 5: 5 because you say so, **I will let d** the nets." *G5899*
Lk 6:17 *He* **went d** with them and stood on a level *G2849*
Lk 6:38 A good measure, **pressed d**, shaken *G4390*
Lk 6:48 who dug **deep** and laid the foundation *G959*
Lk 8:23 A squall **came d** on the lake, so that the *G2849*
Lk 8:33 the herd rushed **d** the steep bank into *G2848*
Lk 9:14 "*Have* them **sit d** in groups of about fifty *G2884*
Lk 9:15 The disciples did so, and everyone **sat d**. *G2884*
Lk 9:37 *when* they **came d** from the mountain *G2982*
Lk 9:54 want us to call fire **d** from heaven to *G2849*
Lk 10:15 No, *you will* **go d** to Hades. *G2849*
Lk 10:30 "A man *was* **going d** from Jerusalem to *G2849*
Lk 10:31 happened *to be* **going d** the same road, *G2849*
Lk 11:46 because *you* **load** people **d** with burdens *G5844*
Lk 12:18 *I will* **tear d** my barns and build bigger *G2747*
Lk 13: 7 **Cut** it **d**! Why should it use *G1716*
Lk 13: 9 fruit next year, fine! If not, then **cut** it **d**.' " *G1716*
Lk 14:28 Won't *you* first **sit d** and estimate the cost *G2767*
Lk 14:31 Won't *he* first **sit d** and consider whether *G2767*
Lk 16: 6 'Take your bill, **sit d** quickly, and make it *G2767*
Lk 17: 7 'Come along now and **sit d to eat**'? *G404*
Lk 17:29 fire and sulfur **rained d** from heaven and *G1101*
Lk 17:31 *should* **go d** to get them. *G2849*
Lk 18: 9 and **looked d** on everyone else, *G2024*
Lk 19: 5 "Zacchaeus, **come d** immediately. *G2849*
Lk 19: 6 So *he* **came d** at once and welcomed him *G2849*

Lk 19:37 near the **place where the road goes d** the G2853
Lk 21: 6 every one of them *will be* **thrown d.**" G2907
Lk 21:34 your hearts *will be* **weighed d** with G976
Lk 22:41 them, **knelt d** and prayed, G5502+3836+1205
Lk 22:55 of the courtyard and *had* **sat d together,** G5154
Lk 22:55 sat down together, Peter **sat d** with them. G2764
Lk 23:53 Then *he* **took** it **d**, wrapped it in linen cloth G2747
Lk 24: 5 fright the women **bowed d** with their faces G3111
Jn 1:32 "I saw the Spirit **come d** from heaven as a G2849
Jn 1:33 see the Spirit **come d** and remain is the G2849
Jn 2:12 After this he **went d** to Capernaum with G2849
Jn 4: 6 was from the journey, **sat d** by the well. G2757
Jn 4:49 "Sir, **come d** before my child dies. G2849
Jn 5: 7 someone else **goes d** ahead of me." G2849
Jn 6: 3 mountainside and **sat d** with his disciples G2764
Jn 6:10 "Have the people **sit d.**" There was plenty G404
Jn 6:10 in that place, and *they* **sat d** (about five G404
Jn 6:16 his disciples **went d** to the lake, G2849
Jn 6:33 is the bread *that* **comes d** from heaven G2849
Jn 6:38 For *I have* **come d** from heaven not to do G2849
Jn 6:41 "I am the bread that **came d** from heaven." G2849
Jn 6:42 can he now say, '*I* **came d** from heaven'?" G2849
Jn 6:50 is the bread that **comes d** from heaven, G2849
Jn 6:51 the living bread that **came d** from heaven. G2849
Jn 6:58 This is the bread that **came d** from heaven. G2849
Jn 8: 2 around him, and *he* **sat d** to teach them. G2767
Jn 8: 6 But Jesus **bent d** and started to write on G3004
Jn 8: 8 Again *he* **stooped d** and wrote on the G2893
Jn 10:11 The good shepherd **lays d** his life for the G5502
Jn 10:15 Father—and *I* **lay d** my life for the sheep. G5502
Jn 10:17 Father loves me is that I **lay d** my life— G5502
Jn 10:18 it from me, but I **lay** it **d** of my own accord. G5502
Jn 10:18 I have authority *to* **lay** it **d** and authority to G5502
Jn 13:37 *I will* **lay d** my life for you. G5502
Jn 13:38 "*Will you really* **lay d** your life for me? G5502
Jn 15:13 to **lay d** one's life for one's friends. G5502
Jn 19:13 Jesus out and **sat d** on the judge's seat G2767
Jn 19:31 the legs broken and the bodies **taken d.** G149
Jn 21:24 to these things and who **wrote** them **d.** G1211
Jn 21:25 If every one of them *were* **written d,** G1211
Ac 5: 5 Ananias heard this, *he* **fell d** and died. G4406
Ac 5:10 At that moment *she* **fell d** at his feet and G4406
Ac 6:14 the customs Moses **handed d** to us." G4140
Ac 7:15 Then Jacob **went d** to Egypt, where he G2849
Ac 7:34 groaning and *have* **come d** to set them G2849
Ac 8: 5 Philip **went d** to a city in Samaria and G2982
Ac 8:26 that **goes d** from Jerusalem to Gaza." G2849
Ac 8:38 the eunuch **went d** into the water and G2849
Ac 9:30 *they* **took** him **d** to Caesarea and sent him G2864
Ac 9:40 then *he* **got d on** his knees and prayed. G5502
Ac 10:11 a large sheet *being* **let d** to earth by its G2768
Ac 10:21 Peter **went d** and said to the men, "I'm G2849
Ac 11: 5 a large sheet *being* **let d** from heaven by G2768
Ac 11: 5 corners, and it came **d** to where I was. G2849
Ac 11:27 some prophets **came d** from Jerusalem to G2982
Ac 12:23 an angel of the Lord **struck** him **d**, and he G4250
Ac 13: 4 **went d** to Seleucia and sailed from there G2982
Ac 13:14 they entered the synagogue and **sat d.** G2767
Ac 13:29 *they* **took** him **d** from the cross and laid G2747
Ac 14:11 "The gods *have* **come d** to us in human G2849
Ac 14:25 the word in Perga, *they* **went d** to Attalia. G2849
Ac 15: 1 Certain people **came d** from Judea to G2982
Ac 15:30 men were sent off and **went d** to Antioch, G2982
Ac 16: 8 passed by Mysia and **went d** to Troas. G2849
Ac 16:13 *We* **sat d** and began to speak to the G2767
Ac 18:22 the church and then **went d** to Antioch. G2849
Ac 19:36 you ought *to* **calm d** and not do G2948+5639
Ac 20:10 Paul **went d**, threw himself on the young G2849
Ac 20:36 he **knelt d** with all of them G5502+3836+1205
Ac 21:10 named Agabus **came d** from Judea. G2982
Ac 21:32 soldiers and **ran d** to the crowd. G2963
Ac 23:10 the troops *to* **go d** and take him away G2849
Ac 24: 1 priest Ananias **went d** to Caesarea with G2849
Ac 25: 6 with them, Festus **went d** to Caesarea. G2849
Ac 25: 7 the Jews *who had* **come d** from Jerusalem G2849
Ac 26:11 that I even hunted them **d** in foreign cities. NDT
Ac 27:14 the Northeaster, **swept d** from the island. G965
Ac 27:30 the sailors **let** the lifeboat **d** into the sea G5899
Ro 10: 6 (that is, *to* **bring** Christ **d**) G2864
Ro 11: 3 killed your prophets and **torn d** your altars; G2940
Ro 16:22 who **wrote d** this letter, greet you G1211
1Co 7:17 This *is* **the rule** *I* **lay d** in all the churches. G1411
1Co 10: 7 "The people **sat d** to eat and drink and G2767
1Co 10:11 examples and *were* **written d** as warnings G1211
1Co 14:25 So *they will* **fall d** and G4406+2093+4725
1Co 14:30 comes to someone *who is* **sitting d,** G2764
2Co 4: 9 not abandoned; **struck d**, but not G2850
2Co 10: 8 building you up rather than **tearing** you **d**, G2746
2Co 13:10 building you up, not for **tearing** you **d.** G2746
Eph 4:26 *Do* not *let* the sun **go d** while you are still G2115
1Th 4:16 the Lord himself *will* **come d** from heaven, G2849
2Th 3:12 Christ to **settle d** and earn the G3552+2484
1Ti 4:12 Don't *let* anyone **look d on** you because G2969
2Ti 3: 6 *who are* **loaded d with** sins and are G5397
Heb 1: 3 *he* **sat d** at the right hand of the Majesty G2767
Heb 8: 1 who **sat d** at the right hand of the throne G2767
Heb 10:12 sins, *he* **sat d** at the right hand of God, G2767
Heb 12: 2 and **sat d** at the right hand of the throne G2767
Jas 1:17 **coming d** from the Father of the heavenly G2849
Jas 3:15 *does* not **come d** from heaven but is G2982
1Pe 1:18 life **handed d** to you **from** your **ancestors,** G4261
1Jn 3:16 Jesus Christ **laid d** his life for us. G5502
1Jn 3:16 And we ought *to* **lay d** our lives for our G5502
Rev 1:13 in a **robe reaching d** to his **feet** and with a G4468
Rev 3: 9 them come and **fall d** at your feet and G4686
Rev 3:12 which *is* **coming d** out of heaven from my G2849
Rev 3:21 was victorious and **sat d** with my Father on G2767
Rev 4:10 twenty-four elders **fall d** before him who G4406
Rev 5: 8 twenty-four elders **fell d** before the Lamb. G4406
Rev 5:14 and the elders **fell d** and worshiped. G4406
Rev 7:11 *They* **fell d** on their faces before the G4406
Rev 7:16 The sun *will* not **beat d** on them,' nor any G4406
Rev 8: 7 and *it was* **hurled d** on the earth. G965
Rev 9: 3 smoke locusts **came d** on the earth and G2002
Rev 10: 1 mighty angel **coming d** from heaven. G2849
Rev 10: 4 thunders have said and *do* not **write** it **d.**" G1211
Rev 12: 9 The great dragon *was* **hurled d**—that G965
Rev 12:10 our God day and night, *has been* **hurled d.** G965
Rev 12:12 because the devil *has* **gone d** to you! G2849
Rev 13:13 causing fire to **come d** from heaven to the G2849
Rev 18: 1 another angel **coming d** from heaven. G2849
Rev 18:21 the great city of Babylon *will be* **thrown d,** G965
Rev 19: 4 living creatures **fell d** and worshiped God, G4406
Rev 19:15 sword with which to **strike d** the nations. G4250
Rev 20: 1 I saw an angel **coming d** out of heaven, G2849
Rev 20: 9 But fire **came d** from heaven and G2849
Rev 21: 2 **coming d** out of heaven from God G2849
Rev 21: 5 Then he said, "**Write** this **d**, for these G1211
Rev 21:10 **coming d** out of heaven from God. G2849
Rev 22: 2 **d** the middle of the great street of the city G1877
Rev 22: 8 *I* **fell d** to worship at the feet of the angel G4406

DOWNCAST (11) [DOWN, CAST]

Ge 4: 5 Cain was very angry, and his face *was* **d.** H5877
Ge 4: 6 "Why are you angry? Why *is* your face **d**? H5877
1Sa 1:18 then her face *was* no longer **d.** H2118+4200
Job 22:29 then he will save the **d.** H8814+6524
Ps 42: 5 my soul, *are you* **d**? Why so H8863
Ps 42: 6 My soul *is* **d** within me; therefore I will H8863
Ps 42:11 my soul, *are you* **d**? Why so H8863
Ps 43: 5 my soul, *are you* **d**? Why so H8863
La 3:20 and my soul *is* **d** within me. H8820
Lk 24:17 They stood still, *their* **faces d.** G5034
2Co 7: 6 who comforts the **d**, comforted us by the G5424

DOWNFALL (16) [DOWN, FALL]

1Ki 13:34 of Jeroboam that **led to** its **d** and to its H3948
2Ki 14:10 trouble and *cause* your own **d** and that of H5877
2Ch 22: 7 to Joram, God brought about Ahaziah's **d.** H9313
2Ch 25:19 trouble and *cause* your own **d** and that of H5877
2Ch 26:16 became powerful, his pride led to his **d.** H8845
2Ch 28:23 But they were his **d** and the downfall of H4173
2Ch 28:23 were his downfall and the **d** of all Israel. NDT
Est 6:13 before whom your **d** has started, is of H5877
Ps 5:10 *Let* their intrigues *be their* **d** H5877
Pr 18:12 Before a **d** the heart is haughty, but H8691
Pr 29:16 but the righteous will see their **d.** H5147
Jer 48: 2 in Heshbon people will plot her **d**: H8288
Eze 18:30 your offenses; then sin will not be your **d.** H4842
Eze 32:10 On the day of your **d** each of them will H5147
Hos 14: 1 Your sins *have been your* **d**! H4173
Mic 7:10 My eyes will see her **d**; even now she will NDT

DOWNHEARTED (1) [DOWN, HEART]

1Sa 1: 8 Why *are* you **d**? Don't I H8317+4222

DOWNPOUR (2) [DOWN, POUR]

Job 37: 6 to the rain shower, 'Be a mighty **d.** H1773+4764
Isa 28: 2 like a driving rain and a **flooding d** H3888+8851

DOWNSTAIRS (1) [DOWN, STAIRS]

Ac 10:20 So get up and **go d.** Do not hesitate to go G2849

DOWNSTREAM (1) [DOWN, STREAM]

Jos 3:13 flowing **d** will be cut H5087+4946+4200+2025

DOWRY (KJV) BRIDE-PRICE, GIFT, PRICE FOR THE BRIDE

DRACHMAS (1) [FOUR-DRACHMA, TWO-DRACHMA]

Ac 19:19 the total came to fifty thousand **d.** G736

DRAG (8) [DRAGGED, DRAGGING, DRAGS]

2Sa 17:13 and *we will* **d** it **down** to the valley until H6079
Job 36:20 to **d** people **away** *from* their homes. H6590
Ps 28: 3 *Do* not **d** me **away** with the wicked, with H5432
Pr 21: 7 violence of the wicked *will* **d** them **away,** H1760
Jer 12: 3 **D** them **off** like sheep to be butchered H5998
Jer 15: 3 the dogs to **d away** and the birds and H6079
Eze 39: 2 I will turn you around and **d** you **along.** H9255
Lk 12:58 your adversary *may* **d** you **off** to the judge, G2955

DRAGGED (14) [DRAG]

2Sa 20:12 *he* **d** him from the road *into* a field and H6015
Jer 22:19 **d away** and thrown outside the gates of H6079
Jer 49:20 The young of the flock *will be* **d away** H6079
Jer 50:45 The young of the flock *will be* **d away** H6079
La 3:11 *he* **d** me *from* the path and mangled me H6073
Eze 32:20 *let* her *be* **d off** with all her hordes. H5432
Jn 21:11 back into the boat and **d** the net ashore. G1816
Ac 7:58 **d** him **out** of the city and began to stone G1675
Ac 8: 3 *he* **d off** both men and women and put G5359
Ac 14:19 stoned Paul and **d** him outside the city G5359
Ac 16:19 Paul and Silas and **d** them into the G1816
Ac 17: 6 *they* **d** Jason and some other believers G5359
Ac 21:30 Seizing Paul, *they* **d** him from the temple G1816
Jas 1:14 is tempted *when they are* **d away** by their G1999

DRAGGING (1) [DRAG]

Jas 2: 6 they not the *ones who are* **d** you into court G1816

DRAGNET (2) [NET]

Hab 1:15 he gathers them up in his **d**; and so he H4823
Hab 1:16 to his net and burns incense to his **d,** H4823

DRAGON, DRAGONS (KJV) COBRA, JACKAL, JACKALS, MONSTER, SEA CREATURES, SERPENT, SERPENTS

DRAGON (14)

Rev 12: 3 an enormous red **d** with seven heads and G1532
Rev 12: 4 The **d** stood in front of the woman who G1532
Rev 12: 7 his angels fought against the **d,** G1532
Rev 12: 7 the **d** and his angels fought back. G1532
Rev 12: 9 The great **d** was hurled down—that G1532
Rev 12:13 When the **d** saw that he had been hurled G1532
Rev 12:16 the river that the **d** had spewed out of his G1532
Rev 12:17 Then the **d** was enraged at the woman G1532
Rev 13: 1 The **d** stood on the shore of the sea. NDT
Rev 13: 2 The **d** gave the beast his power and his G1532
Rev 13: 4 People worshiped the **d** because he had G1532
Rev 13:11 horns like a lamb, but it spoke like a **d.** G1532
Rev 16:13 they came out of the mouth *of* the **d**, out G1532
Rev 20: 2 He seized the **d**, that ancient serpent, who G1532

DRAGS (4) [DRAG]

Job 7: 4 The night **d on**, and I toss and turn until H4499
Job 24:22 But God **d away** the mighty by his power H5432
Ps 10: 9 the helpless and **d** them **off** in his net. H5432
Ecc 12: 5 grasshopper **d itself along** and desire no H6022

DRAIN (2) [DRAINED, DRAINING]

Lev 17:13 may be eaten *must* **d out** the blood and H9161
Eze 23:34 will drink it and **d** it **dry** and chew on its H5172

DRAINED (5) [DRAIN]

Lev 1:15 its blood *shall* **be d out** on the side of the H5172
Lev 5: 9 of the blood *must* **be d out** at the base of H5172
2Ki 19:26 Their people, **d** *of* power, are dismayed H7920
Isa 37:27 Their people, **d** *of* power, are dismayed H7920
Isa 51:17 *you who have* **d** to its **dregs** the H9272+5172

DRAINING (1) [DRAIN]

Na 2: 8 is like a pool whose water *is* **d away.** H5674

DRAMS (KJV) DARICS

DRANK (41) [DRINK]

Ge 9:21 When *he* **d** some of its wine, he became H9272
Ge 24:46 your camels too.' So *I* **d**, and she watered H9272
Ge 24:54 with him ate and **d** and spent the night H9272
Ge 25:34 He ate and **d**, and then got up and H9272
Ge 26:30 a feast for them, and they ate and **d.** H9272
Ge 27:25 and he brought some wine and *he* **d.** H9272
Ge 43:34 So they feasted and **d freely** with him. H8910
Ex 24:11 they saw God, and they ate and **d.** H9272
Nu 20:11 the community and their livestock **d.** H9272
Dt 9: 9 I ate no bread and **d** no water. H9272
Dt 9:18 I ate no bread and **d** no water, because of H9272
Dt 29: 6 You ate no bread and **d** no wine or other H9272
Dt 32:14 *You* **d** the foaming blood of the grape. H9272
Dt 32:38 their sacrifices and **d** the wine of their H9272
Jdg 7: 6 them **d** from cupped hands, **lapping** like H4379
Jdg 15:19 When Samson **d**, his strength returned H9272
2Sa 11:13 he ate and **d** with him, and David H9272
2Sa 12: 3 **d** from his cup and even slept in his arms. H9272
1Ki 4:20 they ate, *they* **d** and they were happy. H9272
1Ki 13:19 with him and ate and **d** in his house. H9272
1Ki 13:22 ate bread and **d** water in the place H9272
1Ki 17: 6 in the evening, and *he* **d** from the brook. H9272
1Ki 19: 6 He ate and **d** and then lay down again H9272
1Ki 19: 8 So he got up and ate and **d.** Strengthened H9272
2Ki 7: 8 entered one of the tents and ate and **d.** H9272
2Ki 9:34 Jehu went in and ate and **d.** "Take care of H9272
1Ch 29:22 They ate and **d** with great joy in the H9272
Ezr 10: 6 he ate no food and **d** no water, because H9272
Job 29:23 showers and **d in** my words as H7196+7023
Jer 51: 7 The nations **d** her wine; therefore they H9272
Da 5: 1 of his nobles and **d** wine with them. A10748
Da 5: 3 wives and his concubines **d** from them. A10748
Da 5: 4 *As they* **d** the wine, they praised the gods A10748
Da 5:23 your concubines **d** wine from them. A10748
Ob 16 Just as *you* **d** on my holy hill, so all the H9272
Mk 14:23 he gave it to them, and *they* all **d** from it. G4403
Lk 13:26 will say, 'We ate and **d** with you, and you G4403
Jn 4:12 gave us the well and **d** from it himself, G4403
Ac 10:41 by us who ate and **d** with him after he rose G5228
1Co 10: 4 **d** the same spiritual drink; for they G4403
1Co 10: 4 for *they* **d** from the spiritual rock that G4403

DRAUGHT (KJV) CATCH, LATRINE, OUT OF THE BODY

DRAW (49) [DRAWING, DRAWN, DRAWS, DREW]

Ge 24:11 the time the *women* go out *to* **d water.** H8612
Ge 24:13 townspeople are coming out to **d** water. H8612
Ge 24:19 she said, "*I'll* **d water** for your camels too H8612
Ge 24:20 ran back to the well to **d** *more* **water,** and H8612

Ge 24:43 comes out to d water and I say to her, H8612
Ge 24:44 and I'll d water for your camels too," H8612
Ex 2:16 they came to d water and fill the H1926
Ex 15: 9 I will d my sword and my hand will H8197
Lev 26:33 the nations and will d out my sword and H8197
Nu 5:15 to d attention to wrongdoing. H2349
Jos 8:26 For Joshua did not d back the hand that H8740
Jdg 8:20 But Jether did not d his sword, because H8990
Jdg 9:54 armor-bearer, "D your sword and kill me H8990
Jdg 20:32 retreat and d them away from the city to H5998
1Sa 9:11 young women coming out to d water, H8612
1Sa 31: 4 "D your sword and run me through H8990
1Ch 10: 4 "D your sword and run me through H8990
Job 33:22 They d near to the pit, and their life to the H7928
Job 37:19 we cannot d up our case because of our H6885
Ps 37:14 The wicked d the sword and bend the H7337
Ps 58: 7 flows away; when they d the bow, let their H2005
Ps 144:14 our oxen will d heavy loads. There will be H6022
Isa 5:18 Woe to those who d sin along with cords H5432
Isa 12: 3 With joy you will d water from the wells of H8612
Jer 46: 9 shields, men of Lydia who d the bow. H2005
Jer 50:14 around Babylon, all you who d the bow. H2005
Jer 50:29 against Babylon, all those who d the bow. H2005
Eze 4: 1 in front of you and d the city of Jerusalem H2980
Eze 21: 3 I will d my sword from its sheath and cut H3655
Eze 28: 7 they will d their swords against your H8197
Eze 30:11 They will d their swords against Egypt H8197
Eze 40:46 only Levites who may d near to the LORD H7929
Eze 45: 4 sanctuary and who d near to minister H7929
Joel 3: 9 Let all the fighting men d near and attack H5602
Na 3:14 D water for the siege, strengthen your H8612
Zep 3: 2 the LORD, she does not d near to her God. H7928
Hag 2:16 went to a wine vat to d fifty measures, H3106
Mt 26:52 "for all who d the sword will die by the G3284
Lk 1: 1 have undertaken to d up an account of the G421
Jn 2: 8 "Now d some out and take it to the master G533
Jn 4: 7 a Samaritan woman came to d water, G533
Jn 4:11 "you have nothing to d with and the well is G534
Jn 4:15 have to keep coming here to d water." G533
Jn 12:32 from the earth, will d all people to myself." G1816
Ac 20:30 the truth in order to d away disciples after G685
Gal 2:12 he began to d back and separate himself G5713
Heb 7:19 is introduced, by which we d near to God. G1581
Heb 10: 1 make perfect those who d near to worship. G4665
Heb 10:22 let us d near to God with a sincere heart G4665

DRAWING (2) [DRAW]

1Sa 17:21 the Philistines were d up their lines facing H6885
Lk 21:28 because your redemption is d near." G1581

DRAWN (22) [DRAW]

Ge 34: 3 His heart was d to Dinah daughter of H1815
Nu 22:23 in the road with a d sword in his hand, H8990
Nu 22:31 standing in the road with his sword d. H8990
Dt 30:17 if you are d away to bow down to H5615
Jos 5:13 in front of him with a d sword in his hand. H8990
Jdg 20:31 meet them and were d away from the city. H5998
1Ch 21:16 with a d sword in his hand extended over H8990
Job 19: 6 wronged me and d his net around me. H5938
Ps 21:12 backs when you aim at them with d bow. H4798
Ps 55:21 soothing than oil, yet they are d swords. H7347
Ps 141: 4 Do not let my heart be d to what is evil so H5742
Isa 21:15 the sword, from the d sword, from the H5759
Jer 31: 3 I have d you with unfailing kindness. H5432
Eze 5: 2 For I will pursue them with d sword. H8197
Eze 5:12 to the winds and pursue with d sword. H8197
Eze 12:14 and I will pursue them with d sword. H8197
Eze 21: 5 that I the LORD have d my sword from its H3655
Eze 21:28 a sword, d for the slaughter, polished to H7337
Eze 32:20 The sword is d; let her be dragged off H5989
Joel 2: 5 like a mighty army d up for battle. H6885
Mic 5: 6 the land of Nimrod with d sword. H7347
Jn 2: 9 the servants who had d the water knew. G533

DRAWS (7) [DRAW]

Job 36:27 "He d up the drops of water, which distill H1758
Ps 88: 3 with troubles and my life d near to death. H5595
Pr 20: 5 one who has insight d them out. H1926
Isa 51: 5 My righteousness d near speedily, my AIT
Jer 17: 5 who d strength from mere flesh and H8492
Jn 4:36 the one who reaps d a wage and harvests G3284
Jn 6:44 unless the Father who sent me d them, G1816

DREAD (20) [DREADED, DREADFUL]

Ge 9: 2 The fear and d of you will fall on all the H3145
Ex 1:12 so the Egyptians came to d the Israelites H7762
Ex 15:16 terror and d will fall on them. H7065
Nu 22: 3 Moab was filled with d because of the H7762
Dt 28:66 suspense, filled with d both night and day H7064
2Ch 29: 8 made them an object of d and horror and H2317
Job 9:28 I still d all my sufferings, for I know you H3336
Job 13:11 Would not the d of him fall on you? H7065
Ps 14: 5 overwhelmed with d, for God H7064+7065
Ps 31:11 an object of d to my closest H7065
Ps 53: 5 overwhelmed with d, where H7064+7065
Ps 53: 5 with dread, where there was nothing to d. H7065
Ps 105:38 because d of Israel had fallen on them. H7065
Ps 119:39 Take away the disgrace I d, for your laws H3336
Pr 10:24 What the wicked d will overtake them H4475
Isa 7:16 of the two kings you d will be laid waste. H7762
Isa 8:12 do not fear what they fear, and do not d it. H6907
Isa 8:13 you are to fear, he is the one you are to d. H6907
Isa 66: 4 them and will bring on them what they d. H4475
Jer 42:16 the famine you d will follow you into H1793

DREADED (8) [DREAD]

Dt 28:60 you all the diseases of Egypt that you d, H3336
Dt 32:27 but I d the taunt of the enemy, lest the H1593
Job 3:25 upon me; what I d has happened to me. H3336
Job 31:23 For I d destruction from God, and for fear H7065
Job 31:34 the crowd and so d the contempt of the H3169
Isa 57:11 "Whom have you so d and feared that H1793
Da 5:19 of every language d and feared him. A10227
Hab 1: 7 They are a feared and d people; they are H3707

DREADFUL (12) [DREAD]

Ge 15:12 a thick and d darkness came over him. H399
Dt 1:19 all that vast and d wilderness that you H3707
Dt 8:15 you through the vast and d wilderness, H3707
Job 6:21 you see something d and are afraid. H3170
Eze 14:21 against Jerusalem my four d judgments— H8273
Joel 2:11 LORD is great; it is d. H4394+3707
Joel 2:31 coming of the great and d day of the LORD. H3707
Mal 4: 5 that great and d day of the LORD comes H3707
Mt 24:19 How d it will be in those days for pregnant G4026
Mk 13:17 How d it will be in those days for pregnant G4026
Lk 21:23 How d it will be in those days for pregnant G4026
Heb 10:31 It is a d thing to fall into the hands of the G5829

DREAM (78) [DREAMED, DREAMER, DREAMING, DREAMS]

Ge 20: 3 to Abimelek in a d one night and said to H2706
Ge 20: 6 Then God said to him in the d, "Yes, H2706
Ge 28:12 He had a d in which he saw a stairway H2731
Ge 31:10 season I once had a d in which I looked H2706
Ge 31:11 The angel of God said to me in the d H2706
Ge 31:24 the Aramean in a d at night and said to H2706
Ge 37: 5 Joseph had a d, and when he told H2731+2706
Ge 37: 6 to them, "Listen to this d I had: H2706+2731
Ge 37: 8 more because of his d and what he had H2706
Ge 37: 9 Then he had another d, and he H2731+2706
Ge 37: 9 he said, "I had another d, and this H2731+2706
Ge 37:10 and said, "What is this d you had? H2706+2731
Ge 40: 5 in prison—had a d the same night H2731+2706
Ge 40: 5 each d had a meaning of its own. H2706
Ge 40: 9 So the chief cupbearer told Joseph his d H2706
Ge 40: 9 "In my d I saw a vine in front of me H2706
Ge 40:16 he said to Joseph, "I too had a d: H2706
Ge 41: 1 full years had passed, Pharaoh had a d: H2731
Ge 41: 5 He fell asleep again and had a second d H2731
Ge 41: 7 Then Pharaoh woke up; it had been a d. H2706
Ge 41:11 Each of us had a d the same night H2731+2706
Ge 41:11 each d had a meaning of its own. H2706
Ge 41:12 each man the interpretation of his d. H2706
Ge 41:15 to Joseph, "I had a d, and no one H2731+2706
Ge 41:15 when you hear a d you can interpret it H2706
Ge 41:17 "In my d I was standing on the bank of H2706
Ge 41:22 "In my d I saw seven heads of grain, full H2706
Ge 41:26 are seven years; it is one and the same d. H2706
Ge 41:32 The reason the d was given to Pharaoh in H2706
Jdg 7:13 just as a man was telling a friend his d. H2706
Jdg 7:13 "I had a d," he was H2731+2706
Jdg 7:15 When Gideon heard the d and its H2706
1Ki 3: 5 to Solomon during the night in a d, H2706
1Ki 3:15 awoke—and he realized it had been a d. H2706
Job 20: 8 Like a d he flies away, no more to be H2706
Job 33:15 In a d, in a vision of the night, when deep H2706
Ps 73:20 They are like a d when one awakes; when H2706
Ecc 5: 3 A d comes when there are many cares H2706
Isa 29: 7 will be as it is with a d, with a vision in H2706
Isa 56:10 they lie around and d, they love to sleep. H2111
Jer 23:25 They say, 'I had a d! I had a dream! H2731
Jer 23:25 They say, 'I had a dream! I had a d!' H2731
Jer 23:28 Let the prophet who has a d recount the H2706
Jer 23:28 prophet who has a dream recount the d, H2706
Da 2: 3 "I have had a d that troubles me H2731+2706
Da 2: 4 Tell your servants the d, and we will A10267
Da 2: 5 not tell me what my d was and interpret A10267
Da 2: 6 But if you tell me the d and explain it A10267
Da 2: 6 So tell me the d and interpret it for me." A10267
Da 2: 7 "Let the king tell his servants the d, and A10267
Da 2: 9 If you do not tell me the d, there is only A10267
Da 2: 9 So then, tell me the d, and I will know A10267
Da 2:16 so that he might interpret the d for him. NDT
Da 2:23 made known to us the d of the king." H10418S
Da 2:24 to the king, and I will interpret his d for him." NDT
Da 2:25 who can tell the king what his d means." NDT
Da 2:26 me what I saw in my d and interpret it?" A10267
Da 2:28 Your d and the visions that passed A10267
Da 2:36 "This was the d, and now we will A10267
Da 2:45 The d is true and its interpretation is A10267
Da 4: 5 I had a d that made me afraid. As I was A10267
Da 4: 6 before me to interpret the d for me. A10267
Da 4: 7 I told them the d, but they could not A10267
Da 4: 8 into my presence and I told him the d. A10267
Da 4: 9 Here is my d; interpret it for A10256+10267
Da 4:18 "This is the d that I, King A10267
Da 4:19 do not let the d or its meaning alarm A10267
Da 4:19 if only the d applied to your enemies A10267
Da 7: 1 Daniel had a d, and visions passed A10267
Da 7: 1 He wrote down the substance of his d. A10267
Joel 2:28 your old men will d dreams, your young H2731
Mt 1:20 the Lord appeared to him in a d and said, G3941
Mt 2:12 been warned in a d not to go back to G3941
Mt 2:13 of the Lord appeared to Joseph in a d. G3941
Mt 2:19 Lord appeared in a d to Joseph in Egypt G3941
Mt 2:22 Having been warned in a d, he withdrew G3941
Mt 27:19 a great deal today in a d because of him." G3941
Ac 2:17 see visions, your old men will d dreams. G1965

DREAMED (2) [DREAM]

Ps 126: 1 of Zion, we were like those who d. H2731
Da 2: 2 astrologers to tell him what he had d. H2706

DREAMER (4) [DREAM]

Ge 37:19 "Here comes that d!" they H1251+2021+2706
Dt 13: 3 to the words of that prophet or d. H2731+2706
Dt 13: 5 That prophet or d must be put to H2731+2706
Dt 13: 5 That prophet or d tried to turn you from the NDT

DREAMING (1) [DREAM]

Ecc 5: 7 Much d and many words are meaningless H2706

DREAMS (26) [DREAM]

Ge 37:20 Then we'll see what comes of his d." H2706
Ge 40: 8 "We both had d," they answered H2731+2706
Ge 40: 8 belong to God? Tell me your d." NDT
Ge 41: 8 Pharaoh told them his d, but no one H2706
Ge 41:12 We told him our d, and he interpreted H2706
Ge 41:25 "The d of Pharaoh are one and the same. H2706
Ge 42: 9 remembered his d about them and H2706+2731
Nu 12: 6 to them in visions, I speak to them in d. H2706
Dt 13: 1 or one who foretells by d, appears H2731+2706
1Sa 28: 6 not answer him by d or Urim or prophets. H2706
1Sa 28:15 answers me, either by prophets or by d. H2706
Job 4:13 Amid disquieting d in the night, when H2612
Job 7:14 you frighten me with d and terrify me with H2706
Isa 29: 8 as when a hungry person d of eating, but H2731
Isa 29: 8 as when a thirsty person d of drinking H2731
Jer 23:27 They think the d they tell one another will H2706
Jer 23:32 I am against those who prophesy false d," H2706
Jer 27: 9 your interpreters of d, your mediums H2706
Jer 29: 8 the d you encourage them to have. H2731+2706
Da 1:17 understand visions and d of all kinds. H2706
Da 2: 1 Nebuchadnezzar had d; his mind H2731+2706
Da 5:12 also the ability to interpret d A10267
Joel 2:28 your old men will dream d, your young H2706
Zec 10: 2 that lie; they tell d that are false, they H2706
Ac 2:17 see visions, your old men will dream d. G1966
Jude 8 on the strength of their d these ungodly G1965

DREGS (4)

Ps 75: 8 of the earth drink it down to its very d. H9069
Isa 51:17 you who have drained to its d the H9272+5172
Jer 48:11 like wine left on its d, not poured from H9069
Zep 1:12 who are like wine left on its d, who think, H9069

DRENCH (4) [DRENCHED]

Ps 6: 6 with weeping and d my couch with tears. H4998
Ps 65:10 You d its furrows and level its ridges; you H8115
Isa 16: 9 Elealeh, I d you with tears! The H8115
Eze 32: 6 I will d the land with your flowing blood H9197

DRENCHED (9) [DRENCH]

Job 24: 8 They are d by mountain rains and hug the H8182
Job 29: 6 when my path was d with cream and the H8175
SS 5: 2 My head is d with dew, my hair with the H4848
Isa 34: 7 Their land will be d with blood, and the H8115
Da 4:15 " 'Let him be d with the dew of heaven A10607
Da 4:23 Let him be d with the dew of heaven; let A10607
Da 4:25 like the ox and be d with the dew of A10607
Da 4:33 His body was d with the dew of heaven A10607
Da 5:21 his body was d with the dew of A10607

DRESS (13) [DRESSED, DRESSING, WELL-DRESSED]

Ex 29: 5 the garments and d Aaron with the tunic, H4252
Ex 29: 8 Bring his sons and d them in tunics H4252
Ex 40:13 Then d Aaron in the sacred garments H4252
Ex 40:14 Bring his sons and d them in tunics. H4252
2Sa 14: 2 D in mourning clothes, and don't use any H4252
Jer 4:30 Why d yourself in scarlet and put on H4252
Jer 6:14 They d the wound of my people as H8324
Jer 8:11 They d the wound of my people as H8324
Eze 16:10 you with an embroidered d and put H8391
Eze 23:12 warriors in full d, mounted horsemen, H4229
Lk 12:37 tell you, he will d himself to serve, will G4322
Jn 21:18 someone else will d you and lead G2439
1Ti 2: 9 I also want the women to d modestly, with G2950

DRESSED (44) [DRESS]

Ge 41:42 He d him in robes of fine linen and put a H4252
Ex 20:25 do not build it with d stones, for you will H1607
Ru 3: 3 perfume, and get d in your best clothes. H8492
1Sa 17:38 Then Saul d David in his own tunic. H4252
1Sa 25:18 skins of wine, five d sheep, five seahs of H6913
1Ki 5:17 a foundation of d stone for the temple. H1607
1Ki 6: 7 only blocks d at the quarry were used H8969
1Ki 6:36 three courses of d stone and one course H1607
1Ki 7:12 three courses of d stone and one course H1607
1Ki 22:10 D in their royal robes, the king of Israel H4252
2Ki 12:12 timber and blocks of d stone for the repair H4732
2Ki 22: 6 purchase timber and d stone to repair the H4732
1Ch 22: 2 to prepare d stone for building the H1607
2Ch 5:12 d in fine linen and playing cymbals H4252
2Ch 18: 9 D in their royal robes, the king of Israel H4252
2Ch 34:11 builders to purchase d stone, H4732
Pr 7:10 d like a prostitute and with crafty intent. H8884
Isa 9:10 we will rebuild with d stone; the fig H1607

Jer 10: 9 have made is then d in blue and purple— H4230
Eze 16:10 I d you in fine linen and covered you with H2502
Eze 40:42 also four tables of d stone for the burnt H1607
Da 10: 5 there before me was a man d in linen, H4229
Zec 3: 3 Now Joshua was d in filthy clothes as he H4252
Mt 6:29 all his splendor was d like one of these. G4314
Mt 11: 8 go out to see? A man d in fine clothes? No, G314
Mk 5:15 sitting there, d and in his right mind; and G2667
Mk 16: 5 they saw a young man d in a white robe G4314
Lk 7:25 go out to see? A man d in fine clothes? No, G314
Lk 8:35 at Jesus' feet, d and in his right mind G2667
Lk 12:27 all his splendor was d like one of these. G4314
Lk 12:35 "Be d ready for service and G3836+4019+4322
Lk 16:19 was a rich man who was d in purple and G1898
Jn 21:18 you were younger you d yourself and went G2439
Ac 1:10 suddenly two men d in white stood G2264
Rev 1:13 d in a robe reaching down to his feet and G1907
Rev 3: 4 will walk with me, d in white, for they are AIT
Rev 3: 5 will, like them, be d in white G4314+1877+2668
Rev 4: 4 They were d in white and G4314+1877+2668
Rev 15: 6 They were d in clean, shining linen and G1907
Rev 17: 4 The woman was d in purple and scarlet G4314
Rev 18:16 great city, d in fine linen, purple and G4314
Rev 19:13 He is d in a robe dipped in blood, and his G4314
Rev 19:14 riding on white horses and d in fine linen G1907
Rev 21: 2 as a bride beautifully d for her husband. G3175

DRESSING (1) [DRESS]

Lk 23:11 D him in an elegant robe, they sent him G4314

DREW (36) [DRAW]

Ge 14: 8 out and d up their battle lines in the H6885
Ge 24:20 and d enough for all his camels. H8612
Ge 24:45 She went down to the spring and d water H8612
Ge 38:29 But when he d back his hand, his brother H8740
Ge 47:29 When the time d near for Israel to die, he H7928
Ge 49:33 to his sons, he d his feet up into the bed H665
Ex 2:10 saying, "I d him out of the water. H5406
Ex 2:19 He even d water for us and H1926+1926
Jdg 3:21 d the sword from his right thigh and H4374
Jdg 20:24 the Israelites d near to Benjamin the H7928
1Sa 7: 6 they d water and poured it out before the H8612
1Sa 7:10 the Philistines d near to engage Israel in H5602
1Sa 17: 2 of Elah and d up their battle line to meet H6885
1Sa 17:51 sword and d it from the sheath. H8990
2Sa 10: 8 out and d up in battle formation at the H6885
2Sa 22:17 hold of me; he d me out of deep waters. H5406
2Sa 23:16 d water from the well near the gate of H8612
1Ki 2: 1 When the time d near for David to die, he H7928
1Ki 22:34 But someone d his bow at random and hit H5432
2Ki 9:24 Then Jehu d his bow and H4848+3338+928
1Ch 11:18 d water from the well near the gate of H8612
1Ch 19: 9 out and d up in battle formation at the H6885
2Ch 13: 3 Jeroboam d up a battle line against him H6885
2Ch 18:31 God d them away from him, H6077
2Ch 18:33 But someone d his bow at random and hit H5432
Ps 18:16 hold of me; he d me out of deep waters. H5406
Ps 107:18 all food and d near the gates of death. H5595
Isa 43:17 who d out the chariots and horses, the H3655
La 3:12 He d his bow and made me the target H2005
Mt 26:51 d it out and struck the servant of the high G685
Mk 14:47 those standing near d his sword and G5060
Jn 18: 6 they d back and fell to G599+1650+3836+3958
Jn 18:10 d it and struck the high priest's servant G1816
Ac 7:17 "As the time d near for God to fulfill his G1581
Ac 16:27 he d his sword and was about to kill G5060
Ac 23:19 man by the hand, d him aside and asked G432

DRIED (27) [DRY]

Ge 8: 7 until the water had d up from the earth. H3312
Ge 8:13 the water had d up from the earth. H2990
Jos 2:10 heard how the LORD d up the water of the H3312
Jos 4:23 the LORD your God d up the Jordan before H3312
Jos 4:23 Red Sea when he d it up before us until H3312
Jos 5: 1 how the LORD had d up the Jordan before H3312
Jdg 16: 7 fresh bowstrings that have not been d, H2990
Jdg 16: 8 fresh bowstrings that had not been d, H2990
1Ki 17: 7 later the brook d up because there had H3312
2Ki 19:24 of my feet I have d up all the streams H2990
Ps 22:15 My mouth is d up like a potsherd, and my H3312
Ps 74:15 streams; you d up the ever-flowing rivers. H3312
Ps 106: 9 the Red Sea, and it d up; he led them H2990
Isa 15: 6 of Nimrim are d up and the grass is H5457
Isa 37:25 of my feet I have d up all the streams H2990
Isa 51:10 Was it not you who d up the sea, the H2990
Jer 48:34 even the waters of Nimrim are d up. H5457
Eze 37:11 'Our bones are d up and our hope is gone H3312
Joel 1:10 are ruined, the ground is d up; the grain is H62
Joel 1:10 the new wine is d up, the olive oil fails. H3312
Joel 1:12 The vine is d up and the fig tree is H3312
Joel 1:12 all the trees of the field—are d up. H3312
Joel 1:17 been broken down, for the grain has d up. H3312
Joel 1:20 streams of water have d up and fire has H3312
Am 4: 7 had rain; another had none and d up. H3312
Am 7: 4 it d up the great deep and devoured the H430
Rev 16:12 its water was d up to prepare the way G3830

DRIES (7) [DRY]

Job 14:11 the water of a lake d up or a riverbed H261
Pr 17:22 a crushed spirit d up the bones. H3312
Isa 24: 4 The earth d up and withers, the world H62
Isa 24: 7 The new wine d up and the vine withers; all H62
Isa 33: 9 The land d up and wastes away, Lebanon is H61

Hos 4: 3 Because of this the land d up, and all who H62
Na 1: 4 He rebukes the sea and d it up; he makes H3312

DRIFT (2)

Ac 27:32 that held the lifeboat and let it d away. G1738
Heb 2: 1 we have heard, so that we do not d away. G4184

DRINK (327) [DRANK, DRINKERS, DRINKING, DRINKS, DRUNK, DRUNKARD, DRUNKARD'S, DRUNKARDS, DRUNKEN, DRUNKENNESS]

Ge 19:32 Let's get our father to d wine and then H9197
Ge 19:33 That night they got their father to d wine H9197
Ge 19:34 Let's get him to d wine again tonight, and H9197
Ge 19:35 So they got their father to d wine that H9197
Ge 21:19 the skin with water and gave the boy a d. H9197
Ge 24:14 let down your jar that I may have a d, H9272
Ge 24:14 and she says, 'D, and I'll water your H9272
Ge 24:18 "D, my lord," she said, and quickly H9272
Ge 24:18 the jar to her hands and gave him a d. H9197
Ge 24:19 After she had given him a d, she said H9197
Ge 24:19 until they have had enough to d. H9272
Ge 24:43 "Please let me d a little water from your H9197
Ge 24:44 if she says to me, "D, and I'll draw water H9272
Ge 24:45 I said to her, 'Please give me a d. H9197
Ge 24:46 shoulder and said, 'D, and I'll water your H9272
Ge 30:38 in front of the flocks when they came to d. H9272
Ge 30:38 the flocks were in heat and came to d, H9272
Ge 35:14 he poured out a d offering on it; he H5821
Ex 7:18 Egyptians will not be able to d its water. H9272
Ex 7:21 that the Egyptians could not d its water. H9272
Ex 7:24 they could not d the water of the river H9272
Ex 15:23 they could not d its water because it was H9272
Ex 15:24 saying, "What are we to d? H9272
Ex 15:25 the water, and the water became fit to d. H5517
Ex 17: 1 there was no water for the people to d. H9272
Ex 17: 2 with Moses and said, "Give us water to d." H9272
Ex 17: 6 will come out of it for the people to d." H9272
Ex 29:40 a quarter of a hin of wine as a d offering. H5821
Ex 29:41 offering and its d offering as in the H5821
Ex 30: 9 do not pour a d offering on it. H5821
Ex 32: 6 sat down to eat and d and got up to H9272
Ex 32:20 on the water and made the Israelites d it. H9197
Ex 37:16 pitchers for the pouring out of d offerings. H5818
Lev 10: 9 your sons are not to d wine or other H9272
Lev 10: 9 wine or other fermented d whenever you H8911
Lev 23:13 its d offering of a quarter of a hin of H5821
Lev 23:18 their grain offerings and d offerings— H5821
Lev 23:37 sacrifices and d offerings required for H5821
Nu 4: 7 the jars for d offerings; the bread that H5821
Nu 5:24 He shall make the woman d the bitter H9197
Nu 5:26 he is to have the woman d the water. H9197
Nu 5:27 When she is made to d the water that H9197
Nu 6: 3 wine and other fermented d and must not H8911
Nu 6: 3 drink and must not d vinegar made from H9272
Nu 6: 3 made from wine or other fermented d. H8911
Nu 6: 3 They must not d grape juice or eat grapes H9272
Nu 6:15 with their grain offerings and d offerings, H5821
Nu 6:17 with its grain offering and d offering. H5821
Nu 6:20 After that, the Nazirite may d wine. H9272
Nu 15: 5 a quarter of a hin of wine as a d offering. H5821
Nu 15: 7 a third of a hin of wine as a d offering. H5821
Nu 15:10 bring half a hin of wine as a d offering. H5821
Nu 15:24 prescribed grain offering and d offering, H5821
Nu 20: 5 And there is no water to d!" H9272
Nu 20: 8 so they and their livestock can d. H9197
Nu 20:17 field or vineyard, or d water from any well. H9272
Nu 20:19 if we or our livestock d any of your water, H9272
Nu 21:22 field or vineyard, or d water from any well. H9272
Nu 28: 7 The accompanying d offering is to be a H5821
Nu 28: 7 of a hin of fermented d with each lamb. H8911
Nu 28: 7 Pour out the d offering to the LORD at the H5821
Nu 28: 8 offering and d offering that you offer in H5821
Nu 28: 9 together with its d offering and a grain H5821
Nu 28:10 regular burnt offering and its d offering. H5821
Nu 28:14 there is to be a d offering of half a hin of H5821
Nu 28:15 regular burnt offering with its d offering, H5821
Nu 28:24 regular burnt offering and its d offering. H5821
Nu 28:31 Offer these together with their d offerings H5821
Nu 29: 6 offerings and d offerings as specified. H5821
Nu 29:11 its grain offering, and their d offerings. H5821
Nu 29:16 with its grain offering and d offering. H5821
Nu 29:18 offerings and d offerings according to the H5821
Nu 29:19 its grain offering, and their d offerings. H5821
Nu 29:21 offerings and d offerings according to the H5821
Nu 29:22 with its grain offering and d offering. H5821
Nu 29:24 offerings and d offerings according to the H5821
Nu 29:25 with its grain offering and d offering. H5821
Nu 29:27 offerings and d offerings according to the H5821
Nu 29:28 with its grain offering and d offering. H5821
Nu 29:30 offerings and d offerings according to the H5821
Nu 29:31 with its grain offering and d offering. H5821
Nu 29:33 offerings and d offerings according to the H5821
Nu 29:34 with its grain offering and d offering. H5821
Nu 29:37 offerings and d offerings according to the H5821
Nu 29:38 with its grain offering and d offering. H5821
Nu 29:39 d offerings and fellowship offerings. H5821
Nu 33:14 there was no water for the people to d. H9272
Dt 2: 6 the food you eat and the water you d. H9272
Dt 2:28 to eat and water to d for their price in H9272
Dt 14:26 wine or other fermented d, or anything H8911
Dt 28:39 them but you will not d the wine or H9272
Dt 29: 6 drank no wine or other fermented d. H8911

Dt 32:38 drank the wine of their d offerings? H5816
Jdg 4:19 a skin of milk, gave him a d, and covered H9197
Jdg 7: 5 dog laps from those who kneel down to d." H9272
Jdg 7: 6 All the rest got down on their knees to d. H9272
Jdg 13: 4 Now see to it that you d no wine or other H9272
Jdg 13: 4 wine or other fermented d and that you H8911
Jdg 13: 7 d no wine or other fermented drink and H9272
Jdg 13: 7 wine or other fermented d and do not eat H8911
Jdg 13:14 d any wine or other fermented drink H9272
Jdg 13:14 wine or other fermented d nor eat H8911
Jdg 19: 6 of them sat down to eat and d together. H9272
Jdg 19:21 they had something to eat and d. H9272
Ru 2: 9 go and get a d from the water jars the H9272
1Sa 30:11 gave him water to d and food to eat— H9197
2Sa 11:11 house to eat and d and make love to my H9272
2Sa 23:15 someone would get me a d of water from H9197
2Sa 23:16 But he refused to d it; instead, he poured H9272
2Sa 23:17 And David would not d it. Such were the H9272
1Ki 13: 8 would I eat bread or d water here. H9272
1Ki 13: 9 must not eat bread or d water or return by H9272
1Ki 13:16 can I eat bread or d water with you in this H9272
1Ki 13:17 not eat bread or d water there or return H9272
1Ki 13:18 so that he may eat bread and d water. H9272
1Ki 13:22 place where he told you not to eat or d. H9272
1Ki 17: 4 You will d from the brook, and I have H9272
1Ki 17:10 a little water in a jar so I may have a d?" H9272
1Ki 18:41 eat and d, for there is the sound of a H9272
1Ki 18:42 So Ahab went off to eat and d, but Elijah H9272
2Ki 3:17 your cattle and your other animals will d. H9272
2Ki 6:22 they may eat and d and then go back to H9272
2Ki 16:13 poured out his d offering, and splashed H5821
2Ki 16:15 their grain offering and their d offering. H5821
2Ki 18:27 own excrement and d their own urine?" H9272
2Ki 18:31 fig tree and d water from your own H9272
1Ch 11:17 someone would get me a d of water from H9197
1Ch 11:18 But he refused to d it; instead, he poured H9272
1Ch 11:19 "Should I d the blood of these men who H9272
1Ch 11:19 lives to bring it back, David would not d it. H9272
1Ch 29:21 together with their d offerings, and other H5821
2Ch 28:15 sandals, food and d, and healing balm. H9197
2Ch 29:35 the d offerings that accompanied H5821
Ezr 3: 7 gave food and d and olive oil to the H5492
Ezr 7:17 with their grain offerings and d offerings, A10483
Ne 8:12 all the people went away to eat and d, H9272
Est 1: 8 was allowed to d with no restrictions, H9276
Est 3:15 The king and Haman sat down to d, but H9272
Est 4:16 Do not eat or d for three days, night or H9272
Job 1: 4 their three sisters to eat and d with them. H9272
Job 15:16 vile and corrupt, who d up evil like water! H9272
Job 21:20 let them d the cup of the wrath of the H9272
Ps 36: 8 you give them d from your river of delights H9197
Ps 50:13 the flesh of bulls or d the blood of goats? H9272
Ps 73:10 turn to them and d up waters in H5172
Ps 75: 8 of the earth d it down to its very dregs. H5172
Ps 78:44 they could not d from their streams. H9272
Ps 80: 5 you have made them d tears by the H9197
Ps 102: 9 as my food and mingle my d with tears H9198
Ps 110: 7 He will d from a brook along the way, and H9272
Pr 4:17 of wickedness and d the wine of violence. H9272
Pr 5:15 D water from your own cistern, running H9272
Pr 7:18 let's d deeply of love till morning H8115
Pr 9: 5 eat my food and d the wine I have mixed. H9272
Pr 23: 7 "Eat and d," he says to you, but his heart H9272
Pr 23:20 Do not join those who d too much wine H6010
Pr 23:35 will I wake up so I can find another d?" H5647s
Pr 25:13 Like a snow-cooled d at harvest H8920+7557
Pr 25:21 if he is thirsty, give him water to d. H9197
Pr 31: 4 it is not for kings to d wine, not for rulers H9272
Pr 31: 5 lest they d and forget what has been H9272
Pr 31: 7 Let them d and forget their poverty and H9272
Ecc 2:24 than to eat and d and find satisfaction H9272
Ecc 3:13 That each of them may eat and d, and H9272
Ecc 5:18 to d and to find satisfaction in their H9272
Ecc 8:15 the sun than to eat and d and be glad. H9272
Ecc 9: 7 d your wine with a joyful heart H9272
SS 5: 1 Eat, friends, and d; drink your fill of H9272
SS 5: 1 friends, and drink; d your fill of love. H8910
SS 8: 2 I would give you spiced wine to d, the H9197
Isa 21: 5 they spread the rugs, they eat, they d! H9272
Isa 22:13 "Let us eat and d," you say, "for tomorrow H9272
Isa 24: 9 No longer do they d wine with a song; the H9272
Isa 36:12 own excrement and d their own urine?" H9272
Isa 36:16 fig tree and d water from your own H9272
Isa 43:20 the wasteland, to give d to my people, my H9197
Isa 51:22 from that cup, the goblet of my wrath, you will never d H9272
Isa 56:12 Let us d our fill of beer! And H6010
Isa 57: 6 have poured out d offerings and offered H5821
Isa 60:16 You will d the milk of nations and be H3567
Isa 62: 8 never again will foreigners d the new H9272
Isa 62: 9 gather the grapes will d it in the courts of H9272
Isa 65:13 my servants will d, but you will go H9272
Isa 66:11 you will d deeply and delight in her H5209
Jer 2:18 why go to Egypt to d water from the Nile? H9272
Jer 2:18 why go to Assyria to d water from the H9272
Jer 7:18 They pour out d offerings to other gods to H5821
Jer 8:14 perish and given us poisoned water to d, H9197
Jer 9:15 eat bitter food and d poisoned water. H9197
Jer 16: 7 nor will anyone give them a d to H9197+3926
Jer 16: 8 is feasting and sit down to eat and d. H9272
Jer 19:13 poured out d offerings to other gods. H5821
Jer 22:15 Did not your father have food and d? He H9272

Jer 23:15 eat bitter food and **d** poisoned water, H9197
Jer 25:15 **make** all the nations to whom I send you **d** H9197
Jer 25:16 When *they* **d** it, they will stagger and go H9272
Jer 25:17 **made** all the nations to whom he sent me **d** H9197
Jer 25:26 of them, the king of Sheshak *will* **d** it too. H9272
Jer 25:27 **D**, get drunk and vomit, and fall to rise no H9272
Jer 25:28 to take the cup from your hand and **d**, H9272
Jer 25:28 LORD Almighty says: *You* **must d** it! H9272+9272
Jer 32:29 by pouring out **d offerings** to other gods. H5821
Jer 35:2 of the LORD and **give** them wine **to d**." H9197
Jer 35:5 said to them, "**D** some wine. H9272
Jer 35:6 they replied, "*We do* not **d** wine, because H9272
Jer 35:6 your descendants *must* ever **d** wine. H9272
Jer 35:14 his descendants not *to* **d** wine and this H9272
Jer 35:14 To this day *they do* not **d** wine, because H9272
Jer 44:17 will pour out **d offerings** to her just as H5821
Jer 44:18 pouring out **d offerings** to her, H5821
Jer 44:19 Heaven and poured out **d offerings** to her, H5821
Jer 44:19 image and pouring out **d offerings** to her?" H5821
Jer 44:25 pour out **d offerings** to the Queen of H5821
Jer 49:12 do not deserve to **d** the cup must drink it H9272
Jer 49:12 deserve to drink the cup **must d** it, H9272+9272
Jer 49:12 not go unpunished, but **must d** it. H9272+9272
Jer 52:19 dishes and **bowls used for d offerings**—all H4984
La 3:15 with bitter herbs and **given** me gall **to d**. H8115
La 5:4 We must buy the water *we* **d**; our wood H9272
Eze 4:11 of a hin of water and **d** it at set times. H9272
Eze 4:16 food in anxiety and **d** rationed water in H9272
Eze 12:18 shudder in fear *as you* **d** your water. H9272
Eze 12:19 food in anxiety and **d** their water in H9272
Eze 20:28 incense and poured out their **d offerings**. H5821
Eze 23:32 "*You will* **d** your sister's cup, a cup large H9272
Eze 23:34 *You will* **d** it and drain it dry and chew on H9272
Eze 25:4 they will eat your fruit and **d** your milk. H9272
Eze 34:18 Is it not enough for *you to* **d** clear water H9272
Eze 34:19 have trampled and **d** what you have H9272
Eze 39:17 There you will eat flesh and **d** blood. H9272
Eze 39:18 of mighty men and **d** the blood of the H9272
Eze 39:19 you are glutted and **d** blood till you are H9272
Eze 44:21 No priest *is to* **d** wine when he enters the H9272
Eze 45:17 offerings and **d offerings** at the festivals, H5821
Da 1:10 who has assigned your food and **d**. H5492
Da 1:12 vegetables to eat and water *to* **d**. H9272
Da 1:16 the wine they were to **d** and gave them H5492
Da 5:2 his concubines *might* **d** from them. A10748
Hos 2:5 wool and my linen, my olive oil and my **d**. H9198
Joel 1:9 offerings and **d offerings** are cut off from H5821
Joel 1:13 offerings and **d offerings** are withheld H5821
Joel 2:14 offerings and **d offerings** for the LORD your H5821
Joel 3:3 prostitutes; they sold girls for wine *to* **d**. H9272
Am 2:8 house of their god *they* **d** wine taken as H9272
Am 2:12 "But *you* **made** the Nazirites **d** wine and H9197
Am 4:8 water but did not get enough *to* **d**, H9272
Am 5:11 lush vineyards, *you will* not **d** their wine. H9272
Am 6:6 *You* **d** wine by the bowlful and use the H9272
Am 9:14 They will plant vineyards and **d** their wine; H9272
Ob 16 so all the nations *will* **d** continually; they H9272
Ob 16 *they will* **d** and drink and be as if they had H9272
Ob 16 they will drink and **d** and be as if they had H4363
Jnh 3:7 taste anything; do not let them eat or **d**. H9272
Mic 6:15 you will crush grapes but not **d** the wine. H9272
Hab 2:15 "Woe to *him who* **gives d** *to* his neighbors H9197
Hab 2:16 **D** and let your nakedness be exposed H9272
Zep 1:13 plant vineyards, *they will* not **d** the wine." H9272
Hag 1:6 have enough. *You* **d**, but never have H9272
Zec 9:15 *They will* **d** and roar as with wine; they H9272
Mt 6:25 what you will eat or **d**; or about your body, G4403
Mt 6:31 or 'What *shall we* **d**?' or 'What shall G4403
Mt 20:22 "Can you **d** the cup I am going to drink?" G4403
Mt 20:22 "Can you drink the cup I am going to **d**?" G4403
Mt 20:23 to them, "*You will* indeed **d** from my cup G4403
Mt 24:49 servants and to eat and **d** with drunkards. G4403
Mt 25:35 thirsty and *you* **gave** me **something to d**, G4540
Mt 25:37 thirsty and **give** you **something to d**? G4540
Mt 25:42 was thirsty and *you* **gave** me nothing **to d**, G4540
Mt 26:27 it to them, saying, "**D** from it, all of *you*. G4403
Mt 26:29 *I will* not **d** from this fruit of the vine from G4403
Mt 26:29 until that day when *I* **d** it new with you in G4403
Mt 26:42 this cup to be taken away unless *I* **d** it, G4403
Mt 27:34 There they offered Jesus wine *to* **d**, mixed G4403
Mt 27:34 but after tasting it, he refused *to* **d** it. G4403
Mt 27:48 it on a staff, and **offered** it to Jesus *to* **d**. G4540
Mk 10:38 "Can you **d** the cup I drink or be baptized G4403
Mk 10:38 you drink the cup I **d** or be baptized with G4403
Mk 10:39 "*You will* **d** the cup I drink and be G4403
Mk 10:39 will drink the cup I **d** and be baptized with G4403
Mk 14:25 *I will* not **d** again from the fruit of the vine G4403
Mk 14:25 until that day when *I* **d** it new in the G4403
Mk 15:36 it on a staff, and **offered** it to Jesus **to d**. G4540
Mk 16:18 and when *they* **d** deadly poison, it G4403
Lk 1:15 never to take wine or *other* **fermented d**, G4975
Lk 5:30 "Why do you eat and **d** with tax collectors G4403
Lk 12:19 Take life easy; eat, **d** and be merry." G4403
Lk 12:29 set your heart on what you will eat or **d**; G4403
Lk 12:45 women, and to eat and **d** and get drunk. G4403
Lk 17:8 ready and wait on me while I eat and **d**; G4403
Lk 17:8 drink; after that you may eat and **d**'? G4403
Lk 22:18 For I tell you *I will* not **d** again from the G4403
Lk 22:30 that you may eat and **d** at my table in my G4403
Jn 2:10 after the guests *have* **had too much to d**; G3499
Jn 4:7 Jesus said to her, "Will you give me a **d**?" G4403
Jn 4:9 How can you ask me for a **d**?" G4403
Jn 4:10 of God and who it is that asks you for a **d**, G4403
Jn 6:53 flesh of the Son of Man and **d** his blood, G4403
Jn 6:55 flesh is real food and my blood is real **d**. G4530
Jn 7:37 anyone who is thirsty come to me and **d**. G4403
Jn 18:11 *Shall I* not **d** the cup the Father has given G4403
Jn 19:30 When he had received the **d**, Jesus said G3954S
Ac 9:9 was blind, and did not eat or **d** anything. G4403
Ac 23:12 oath not to eat or **d** until they had killed G4403
Ac 23:21 an oath not to eat or **d** until they have G4403
Ro 12:20 if he is thirsty, **give** him **something to d**. G4540
Ro 14:21 not to eat meat or **d** wine or to do G4403
1Co 9:4 Don't we have the right to food and **d**? G4403
1Co 9:7 tends a flock and *does* not **d** the milk? G2266
1Co 10:4 drank the same spiritual **d**; for they G4503
1Co 10:7 sat down to eat and **d** and got up to G4403
1Co 10:21 You cannot **d** the cup of the Lord and the G4403
1Co 10:31 whether you eat or **d** or whatever you do, G4403
1Co 11:22 Don't you have homes to eat and **d** in? Or G4403
1Co 11:25 whenever *you* **d** it, in G4403
1Co 11:26 you eat this bread and **d** this cup, G4403
1Co 11:28 they eat of the bread and **d** from the cup. G4403
1Co 11:29 those who eat and **d** without discerning G4403
1Co 11:29 of Christ eat and **d** judgment on G4403
1Co 12:13 and *we were* all **given** the one Spirit **to d**. G4540
1Co 15:32 "Let us eat and **d**, for tomorrow we die." G4403
Php 2:17 if *I am being* **poured out like a d offering** G5064
Col 2:16 anyone judge you by what you eat or **d**, G4530
2Ti 4:6 *am* already *being* **poured out like a d offering** G5064
Heb 9:10 a matter of food and **d** and various G4503
Rev 14:8 which **made** all the nations **d** the G4540
Rev 14:10 *will* **d** the wine of God's fury, which G4403
Rev 16:6 given them blood *to* **d** as they deserve." G4403

DRINKERS (2) [DRINK]
Isa 24:9 with a song; the beer is bitter to its **d**. H9272
Joel 1:5 all you **d** *of* wine; wail because of H9272

DRINKING (38) [DRINK]
Ge 24:22 When the camels had finished **d**, the H9272
Ex 7:24 dug along the Nile to *get* **d** water, H9272
Ex 34:28 nights without eating bread or **d** water. H9272
Jdg 9:27 While they were eating and **d**, they H9272
Jdg 19:4 eating and **d**, and sleeping there. H9272
Ru 3:3 there until he has finished eating and **d**. H9272
Ru 3:7 finished eating and **d** and was in good H9272
1Sa 1:9 they had finished eating and **d** in Shiloh, H9272
1Sa 1:15 *I have* not *been* **d** wine or beer; I was H9272
1Sa 30:16 **d** and reveling because of the great H9272
2Sa 13:28 in high spirits from **d** wine and I say to you, NDT
1Ki 1:25 are eating and **d** with him and saying H9272
1Ki 13:23 man of God had finished eating and **d**, H9272
1Ki 20:12 he and the kings *were* **d** in their tents, H9272
2Ki 6:23 after they had finished eating and **d** H9272
1Ch 12:39 eating and **d**, for their families H9272
Est 5:6 As they were **d** wine, the king again asked H5492
Est 7:2 as they were **d** wine on the second H5492
Job 1:13 were feasting and **d** wine at the oldest H9272
Job 1:18 were feasting and **d** wine at the oldest H9272
Pr 26:6 is like cutting off one's feet or **d** poison. H9272
Isa 5:22 who are heroes at **d** wine and champions H9272
Isa 22:13 of sheep, eating of meat and **d** *of* wine! H9272
Isa 29:8 as when a thirsty person dreams of **d**, but H9272
Da 5:2 While Belshazzar was **d** his wine, he A10302
Zec 7:6 And when you were eating and **d**, were H9272
Mt 11:18 For John came neither eating nor **d**, and G4403
Mt 11:19 The Son of Man came eating and **d**, and G4403
Mt 24:38 people were eating and **d**, marrying and G4403
Lk 5:33 Pharisees, but yours go on eating and **d**." G4403
Lk 5:39 And no one *after* **d** old wine wants the G4403
Lk 7:33 came neither eating bread nor **d** wine, G4403
Lk 7:34 The Son of Man came eating and **d**, and G4403
Lk 10:7 eating and **d** whatever they give you G4403
Lk 17:27 People were eating, **d**, marrying and G4403
Lk 17:28 People were eating and **d**, buying and G4403
Ro 14:17 of God is not a matter of eating and **d**, G4530
1Ti 5:23 Stop **d only water**, and use a little wine G5621

DRINKS (18) [DRINK]
Ge 44:5 the cup my master **d** from and also uses H9272
Nu 23:24 it devours its prey and **d** the blood of its H9272
Dt 11:11 valleys that **d** rain from heaven. H9272
2Sa 19:35 your servant taste what he eats and **d**? H9272
Ne 8:10 "Go and enjoy choice food and sweet **d** H9272
Job 6:4 my spirit **d in** their poison; God's H9272
Job 34:7 anyone like Job, *who* **d** scorn like water? H9272
Isa 5:11 early in the morning to run after their **d**, H8911
Isa 5:22 drinking wine and champions at mixing **d**, H8911
Isa 44:12 strength; *he* **d** no water and grows faint. H9272
Hos 4:18 Even when their **d** are gone, they H6011
Am 4:1 say to your husbands, "Bring us *some* **d**!" H9272
Jn 4:13 "Everyone who **d** this water will be thirsty G4403
Jn 4:14 whoever **d** the water I give them will G4403
Jn 6:54 eats my flesh and **d** my blood has eternal G4403
Jn 6:56 eats my flesh and **d** my blood remains in G4403
1Co 11:27 eats the bread or **d** the cup of the Lord in G4403
Heb 6:7 Land that **d in** the rain often falling on it G4403

DRIP (3) [DRIPPED, DRIPPING]
Pr 5:3 lips of the adulterous woman **d** honey, H5752
Joel 3:18 that day the mountains *will* **d** new wine, H5752
Am 9:13 New wine *will* **d** *from* the mountains and H5752

DRIPPED (1) [DRIP]
SS 5:5 my hands **d** *with* myrrh, my fingers H5752

DRIPPING (3) [DRIP]
Pr 19:13 wife is like the **constant d** *of* a leaky roof. H3265
Pr 27:15 wife is like the **d** *of* a leaky roof in a H3265
SS 5:13 His lips are like lilies **d** *with* myrrh. H5752

DRIVE (91) [DRIVEN, DRIVER, DRIVER'S, DRIVERS, DRIVES, DRIVING, DROVE]
Ex 6:1 my mighty hand *he will* **d** them **out** of his H1763
Ex 11:1 *he will* **d** you **out** completely. H1763+1763
Ex 23:28 the hornet ahead of you *to* **d** the Hivites, H1763
Ex 23:29 But *I will* not **d** them out in a single year H1763
Ex 23:30 Little by little *I will* **d** them out before you H1763
Ex 23:31 and *you will* **d** them out before you. H1763
Ex 33:2 before you and **d out** the Canaanites, H1763
Ex 34:11 *I will* **d out** before you the Amorites H1763
Ex 34:24 *I will* **d out** nations before you and enlarge H3769
Lev 18:24 that I *am going to* **d out** before you H8938
Lev 20:23 nations I *am going to* **d out** before you. H8938
Nu 22:6 defeat them and **d** them **out** of the land. H1763
Nu 22:11 be able to fight them and **d** them **away**. H1763
Nu 33:52 **d out** all the inhabitants of the land before H3769
Nu 33:55 " 'But if *you do* not **d out** the inhabitants H3769
Dt 4:27 the nations to which the LORD *will* **d** you. H5627
Dt 4:38 to **d out** before you nations greater and H3769
Dt 7:17 How can we **d** them **out**?" H3769
Dt 7:22 The LORD your God *will* **d out** those nations H5970
Dt 9:3 And *you will* **d** them **out** and annihilate H3769
Dt 9:4 the LORD *is going to* **d** them **out** before you H3769
Dt 9:5 LORD your God *will* **d** them **out** before you, H3769
Dt 11:23 then the LORD *will* **d out** all these nations H3769
Dt 18:12 the LORD your God *will* **d out** those nations H3769
Dt 28:34 The sights you see will **d** you **mad**. H8713
Dt 28:36 The LORD *will* **d** you and the king you set H2143
Dt 28:37 all the peoples where the LORD *will* **d** you. H5627
Dt 33:27 *He will* **d out** your enemies before you H1763
Jos 3:10 that *he will* **certainly d out** before H3769+3769
Jos 13:6 *I* myself *will* **d** them **out** before the H3769
Jos 13:13 the Israelites *did* not **d out** the people of H3769
Jos 14:12 *I will* **d** them **out** just as he said. H3769
Jos 17:13 but *did* not **d** them **out completely**. H3769+3769
Jos 17:18 they are strong, *you can* **d** them **out**." H3769
Jos 23:5 *He will* **d** them **out** before you, and you H3769
Jos 23:13 God will no longer **d out** these nations H3769
Jdg 1:19 *they were* unable to **d** the people **from** H3769
Jdg 1:21 however, *did* not **d** *out* the Jebusites, who H3769
Jdg 1:27 But Manasseh *did* not **d out** the people of H3769
Jdg 1:29 Nor *did* Ephraim **d out** the Canaanites H3769
Jdg 1:30 Neither *did* Zebulun **d out** the Canaanites H3769
Jdg 1:31 Nor *did* Asher **d out** those living in Akko H3769
Jdg 1:32 the land because *they did* not **d** them **out**. H3769
Jdg 1:33 Neither *did* Naphtali **d out** those living in H3769
Jdg 2:3 '*I will* not **d** them **out** before you H1763
Jdg 2:21 I will no longer **d out** before them any of H3769
Jdg 2:23 *he did* not **d** them **out** at once by giving H3769
Jdg 11:7 you hate me and **d** me from my father's H1763
2Ch 13:9 But didn't *you* **d out** the priests of the LORD H5615
2Ch 20:7 *did* you not **d out** the inhabitants of this H3769
2Ch 20:11 us by coming to **d** us **out** of the H1763
Job 24:3 *They* **d away** the orphan's donkey and H5627
Job 30:22 snatch me up and **d** me before the wind; H8206
Ps 36:11 the hand of the wicked **d** me **away**. H5653
Pr 22:10 **D out** the mocker, and out goes strife H1763
Pr 22:15 the rod of discipline *will* **d** it **far** away. H8178
Isa 22:23 *I will* **d** him like a peg into a firm place; he H9546
Jer 22:22 The wind *will* **d** all your shepherds **away** H8286
Jer 29:18 among all the nations where *I* **d** them. H5615
Jer 46:9 **D furiously**, you charioteers H2147
Jer 49:2 Then Israel *will* **d out** those who drove her H3769
Eze 4:13 among the nations where *I will* **d** them." H5615
Eze 8:6 things that *will* **d** me **far** from my H8178
Eze 11:7 city is the pot, but *I will* **d** you **out** of it. H3655
Eze 11:9 *I will* **d** you **out** of the city and deliver you H3655
Hos 9:15 *I will* **d** them out of my house. H1763
Hos 10:11 *I will* **d** Ephraim, Judah must plow, and H8206
Joel 2:20 "*I will* **d** the northern horde **far** from you H8178
Mic 2:9 *You* **d** the women of my people from their H1763
Mt 7:22 in your name **d out** demons and in G1675
Mt 8:31 "If *you* **d** us **out**, send us into G1675
Mt 10:1 them authority to **d out** impure spirits and G1675
Mt 10:8 those who have leprosy, **d out** demons. G1675
Mt 12:27 And if I **d out** demons by Beelzebul, by G1675
Mt 12:27 by whom *do* your people **d** them **out**? G1675
Mt 12:28 by the Spirit of God that I **d out** demons, G1675
Mt 17:19 asked, "Why couldn't we **d** it **out**? G1675
Mk 3:15 to have authority *to* **d out** demons. G1675
Mk 3:23 "How can Satan **d out** Satan? G1675
Mk 7:26 begged Jesus to **d** the demon **out** of her G1675
Mk 9:18 I asked your disciples to **d out** the spirit G1675
Mk 9:28 him privately, "Why couldn't we **d** it **out**?" G1675
Mk 16:17 In my name *they will* **d out** demons; they G1675
Lk 9:1 authority *to* **d out** all demons and to G2093
Lk 9:40 I begged your disciples to **d** it **out**, but they G1675
Lk 11:18 you claim that I **d out** demons by G1675
Lk 11:19 Now if I **d out** demons by Beelzebul, by G1675
Lk 11:19 by whom *do* your followers **d** them **out**? G1675
Lk 11:20 But if I **d out** demons by the finger of God G1675
Lk 19:45 he began *to* **d out** those who were selling. G1675
Jn 6:37 whoever comes to me *I will* never **d** away. G1675

DRIVEN (49) [DRIVE]
Ge 4:11 are under a curse and d from the ground, H4946
Ge 33:13 If they are d hard just one day, all the H1985
Ex 10:11 Moses and Aaron were d out of Pharaoh's H1763
Ex 12:39 because they had been d out of Egypt H1763
Nu 32:21 until he has d his enemies out before him H3769
Dt 9:4 LORD your God has d them out before you, H2074
Dt 12:29 But when you have d them out and H3769
Dt 19:1 when you have d them out and H3769
Jos 8:15 all Israel let themselves be d back before H5595
Jos 23:9 "The LORD has d out before you great and H3769
Jdg 11:23 has d the Amorites out before his people H3769
1Sa 26:19 They have d me today from my share in H1763
1Ki 14:24 the nations the LORD had d out before the H3769
2Ki 16:3 the nations the LORD had d out before the H3769
2Ki 17:8 nations the LORD had d out before them, H3769
2Ki 17:11 whom the LORD had d out before them H1655
2Ki 21:2 the nations the LORD had d out before the H3769
2Ch 28:3 the nations the LORD had d out before the H3769
2Ch 33:2 the nations the LORD had d out before the H3769
Job 6:13 now that success has been d from me? H5615
Job 18:18 He is d from light into the realm of H2074
Job 30:8 they were d out of the land. H5777
Job 30:15 my dignity is d away as by the wind, my H8103
Ps 109:10 may they be d from their ruined homes. H1763
Isa 17:13 d before the wind like chaff on the hills H8103
Isa 22:25 "the peg d into the firm place will give H9546
Isa 59:14 So justice is d back, and H6047+294
Jer 13:24 scatter you like chaff d by the desert wind. H6296
Jer 23:2 my flock and d them away and have not H5615
Jer 23:3 countries where I have d them and will H5615
Jer 49:5 "Every one of you will be d away, and no H5615
La 3:2 He has d me away and made me walk in H5627
Eze 34:21 your horns until you have d them away, H7046
Da 4:25 You will be d away from people and will A10304
Da 4:32 You will be d away from people and will A10304
Da 4:33 He was d away from people and ate A10304
Da 5:21 He was d away from people and given A10304
Am 9:4 Though they are d into exile by their H2143
Mic 4:7 remnant, those d away a strong nation. H2133
Mt 9:33 And when the demon was d out, the man G1675
Mk 16:9 out of whom he had d seven demons. G1675
Lk 8:29 his chains and had been d by the demon G1785
Jn 12:31 now the prince of this world will be d out. G1675
Ac 27:15 so we gave way to it and were d along. G5770
Ac 27:17 sea anchor and let the ship be d along. G5770
Ac 27:27 we were still being d across the Adriatic G1422
Ac 28:3 d out by the heat, fastened itself G2002
Jas 3:4 are so large and are d by strong winds, G1785
2Pe 2:17 without water and mists d by a storm. G1785

DRIVER (5) [DRIVE]
Ex 15:1 Both horse and d he has hurled into the H8206
Ex 15:21 Both horse and d he has hurled into the H8206
1Ki 22:34 The king told his chariot d, "Wheel H8208
2Ch 18:33 The king told the chariot d, "Wheel H8208
Jer 51:21 rider, with you I shatter chariot and d, H8206

DRIVER'S (2) [DRIVE]
Job 3:18 they no longer hear the slave d shout. H5601
Job 39:7 in the town; it does not hear a d shout. H5601

DRIVERS (8) [DRIVE]
Ex 3:7 them crying out because of their slave d, H5601
Ex 5:6 this order to the slave d and overseers in H5601
Ex 5:10 Then the slave d and the overseers went H5601
Ex 5:13 The slave d kept pressing them, saying H5601
Ex 5:14 And Pharaoh's slave d beat the Israelite H5601
2Sa 1:6 chariots and their d in hot pursuit. H1251+7304
2Ki 7:14 He commanded the d, "Go and find out NDT
Hag 2:22 I will overthrow chariots and their d H8206

DRIVES (11) [DRIVE]
Dt 7:1 to possess and d out before you many H5970
2Ki 9:20 Jehu son of Nimshi—he d like a maniac." H5853
Pr 16:26 works for them; their hunger d them on. H436
Pr 19:26 their father and d out their mother is a H1368
Pr 20:26 he d the threshing wheel over them. H8740
Isa 27:8 with his fierce blast he d her out, as on a H2048
Isa 59:19 flood that the breath of the LORD d along. H5674
Mt 9:34 prince of demons that he d out demons." G1675
Mt 12:24 of demons, that this fellow d out demons." G1675
Mt 12:26 If Satan d out Satan, he is divided against G1675
1Jn 4:18 But perfect love d out fear, because fear G965

DRIVING (24) [DRIVE]
Ge 4:14 Today you are d me from the land, and I H1763
Ex 14:25 their chariots so that they had difficulty d. H5627
2Sa 7:23 wonders by d out nations and their H1763
1Ki 19:19 he himself was d the twelfth pair. H928
2Ki 9:20 The d is like that of Jehu son of Nimshi H4952
2Ki 16:6 Elath for Aram by d out the people of H5970
1Ch 17:21 awesome wonders by d out nations from H1763
Job 37:9 its chamber, the cold from the d winds. H4668
Ps 35:5 with the angel of the LORD d them away; H1890
Pr 28:3 the poor is like a d rain that leaves no H6085
Isa 25:4 of the ruthless is like a storm d against a wall AIT
Isa 28:2 like a d rain and a flooding H2443+4784
Jer 30:23 a d wind swirling down on the heads of H1760
Eze 46:18 of the people, d them off their property. H3561
Mk 1:39 in their synagogues and d out demons. G1675
Mk 3:22 the prince of demons he is d out demons." G1675
Mk 9:38 "we saw someone d out demons in your G1675
Mk 11:15 courts and began d out those who were G1675
Lk 9:49 "we saw someone d out demons in your G1675
Lk 11:14 Jesus was d out a demon that was mute G1675
Lk 11:15 the prince of demons, he is d out demons." G1675
Lk 13:32 'I will keep on d out demons and healing G1675
Ac 19:13 who went around d out evil spirits tried to G2020
Ac 26:24 "Your great learning is d you insane." G4365

DROMEDARIES, DROMEDARY (KJV) CAMEL, CAMELS, HORSES, SHE-CAMEL

DROP (13) [DROPPED, DROPPING, DROPS]
Dt 28:40 use the oil, because the olives will d off. H5970
Dt 33:28 new wine, where the heavens d dew. H6903
2Sa 11:21 Didn't a woman d an upper millstone on H8959
Pr 3:20 divided, and the clouds let d the dew. H8319
Pr 17:14 so d the matter before a dispute breaks H5759
SS 4:11 Your lips d sweetness as the honeycomb H5752
Isa 33:9 Bashan and Carmel d their leaves. H5850
Isa 40:15 Surely the nations are like a d in a bucket H5254
Eze 39:3 hand and make your arrows d from your H5877
Zec 8:12 and the heavens will d their dew. H5989
Mal 3:11 fields will not d their fruit before it is ripe," H8897
Lk 16:17 least stroke of a pen to d out of the Law. G4406
Rev 6:13 as figs d from a fig tree when shaken by a G965

DROPPED (4) [DROP]
Jdg 9:53 a woman d an upper millstone on his H8959
Jdg 15:14 and the bindings d from his hands. H5022
2Sa 20:8 he stepped forward, it d out of its sheath. H5877
Ac 27:29 they d four anchors from the stern and G4849

DROPPING (1) [DROP]
2Ch 24:10 d them into the chest until it was full. H8959

DROPS (4) [DROP]
Nu 35:23 d on them a stone heavy enough to kill H5877
Job 36:27 "He draws up the d of water, which distill H5754
Job 38:28 have a father? Who fathers the d of dew? H103
Lk 22:44 his sweat was like d of blood falling to G2584

DROPSY (NIV84) SWELLING

DROSS (8)
Ps 119:119 the wicked of the earth you discard like d; H6092
Pr 25:4 Remove the d from the silver, and a H6092
Pr 26:23 a coating of silver d on earthenware are H6092
Isa 1:22 Your silver has become d, your choice H6092
Isa 1:25 purge away your d and remove all your H6092
Eze 22:18 people of Israel have become d to me; H6092
Eze 22:18 They are but the d of silver. H6092
Eze 22:19 'Because you have all become d, I will H6092

DROUGHT (8)
Dt 28:22 with scorching heat and d, with blight H2996
Job 12:15 back the waters, there is d; if he lets them H3312
Job 24:19 As heat and d snatch away the melted H7480
Jer 2:6 ravines, a land of d and utter darkness, H7480
Jer 14:1 that came to Jeremiah concerning the d: H1314
Jer 17:8 worries in a year of d and never fails to H1316
Jer 50:38 A d on her waters! They will dry up. H2996
Hag 1:11 I called for a d on the fields and the H2996

DROVE (44) [DRIVE, DROVES]
Ge 3:24 After he d the man out, he placed on the H1763
Ge 15:11 the carcasses, but Abram d them away. H5959
Ge 31:18 and he d all his livestock ahead of him H5627
Ex 2:17 shepherds came along and d them away, H1763
Ex 14:21 the LORD d the sea back with a strong H2143
Nu 11:31 from the LORD and d quail in from the sea. H1577
Nu 21:32 settlements and d out the Amorites who H3769
Nu 25:8 He d the spear into both of them, right H1991
Nu 32:39 captured it and d out the Amorites who H3769
Dt 2:12 the descendants of Esau d them out. H3769
Dt 2:21 who d them out and settled in their place. H3769
Dt 2:22 They d them out and have lived in their H3769
Jos 15:14 From Hebron Caleb d out the three H3769
Jos 24:12 which d them out before you H1763
Jos 24:18 And the LORD d out before us all the H1763
Jdg 1:20 who d from it the three sons of Anak. H3769
Jdg 1:28 never d them out completely. H3769+3769
Jdg 4:21 She d the peg through his temple into the H9546
Jdg 6:9 I d them out before you and gave you H1763
Jdg 9:41 Zebul d Gaal and his clan out of H1763
Jdg 11:2 were grown up, they d Jephthah away. H1763
1Sa 19:10 eluded him as Saul d the spear into the H5782
1Sa 30:20 his men d them ahead of the other H5627
2Sa 11:23 but we d them back to the entrance H2118+6584
1Ki 21:26 the Amorites the LORD d out before Israel.) H3769
1Ch 8:13 in Aijalon and who d out the inhabitants H1368
Ne 13:28 And I d him away from me. H1368
Ps 34:T Abimelek, who d him away, and he left. H1763
Ps 44:2 With your hand you d out the nations H3769
Ps 78:55 He d out nations before them and H1763
Ps 80:8 you d out the nations and planted it. H1763
Jer 49:2 Israel will drive out those who d her out," H3769
Eze 28:16 So I d you in disgrace from the mount of H2725
Eze 29:18 king of Babylon d his army in a hard H6268
Mt 8:16 and he d out the spirits with a word and G1675
Mt 21:12 temple courts and d out all who were G1675
Mk 1:34 He also d out many demons, but he G1675
Mk 6:13 They d out many demons and anointed G1675
Lk 4:29 They got up, d him out of the town, and G1675
Jn 2:15 of cords, and d all from the temple courts G1675
Ac 7:45 from the nations God d out before them. AIT
Ac 18:16 So he d them off. G590
2Co 12:11 made a fool of myself, but you d me to it. G337
1Th 2:15 Jesus and the prophets and also d us out. G1691

DROVES (2) [DROVE]
Ex 12:38 also large d of livestock, both flocks H5238
2Ch 14:15 and carried off d of sheep and H4200+8044

DROWN (4) [DROWNED]
Joel 2:20 its eastern ranks will d in the Dead Sea NDT
Mt 8:25 "Lord, save us! We're going to d!" G660
Mk 4:38 "Teacher, don't you care if we d? G660
Lk 8:24 "Master, Master, we're going to d! G660

DROWNED (6) [DROWN]
Ex 15:4 of Pharaoh's officers are d in the Red Sea. H3190
Job 10:15 I am full of shame and d in my affliction. H8116
Mt 18:6 their neck and to be d in the depths of the G2931
Mk 5:13 the steep bank into the lake and were d. G4464
Lk 8:33 the steep bank into the lake and was d. G678
Heb 11:29 the Egyptians tried to do so, they were d. G2927

DROWSINESS (1) [DROWSY]
Pr 23:21 become poor, and d clothes them in rags. H5671

DROWSY (1) [DROWSINESS]
Mt 25:5 and they all became d and fell asleep. G3818

DRUNK (38) [DRINK]
Ge 9:21 he became d and lay uncovered inside H8910
Lev 11:34 any liquid that is d from such a pot is H9272
Dt 32:42 I will make my arrows d with blood, while H8910
1Sa 1:13 was not heard. Eli thought she was d H8893
1Sa 1:14 "How long are you going to stay d? H8910
1Sa 25:36 He was in high spirits and very d. So she H8893
1Sa 30:12 eaten any food or d any water for three H9272
2Sa 11:13 drank with him, and David made him d. H8910
1Ki 16:9 getting d in the home of Arza H9272+8893
1Ki 20:16 him were in their tents getting d. H9272+8893
2Ki 19:24 in foreign lands and d the water there. H9272
SS 5:1 my honey; I have d my wine and my milk. H9272
Isa 29:9 be sightless; be d, but not from wine, H8910
Isa 34:5 My sword has d its fill in the heavens; see, H8115
Isa 37:25 in foreign lands and d the water there. H9272
Isa 49:26 they will be d on their own blood H8910
Isa 51:17 you who have d from the hand of the LORD H9272
Isa 51:21 afflicted one, made d, but not with wine H8912
Isa 63:6 in my wrath I made them d and poured H8910
Jer 25:27 get d and vomit, and fall to rise no H8910
Jer 35:8 our sons and daughters have ever d wine H9272
Jer 48:26 "Make her d, for she has defied the LORD H8910
Jer 51:7 LORD's hand; she made the whole earth d. H8910
Jer 51:39 set out a feast for them and make them d, H8910
Jer 51:57 I will make her officials and wise men d H8910
La 4:21 passed; you will be d and stripped naked. H8910
Eze 39:19 are glutted and drink blood till you are d. H8913
Na 1:10 among thorns and d from their wine; H6010
Na 3:11 You too will become d; you will go into H8910
Hab 2:15 pouring it from the wineskin till they are d, H8910
Lk 12:45 women, and to eat and drink and get d. G3499
Ac 2:15 These people are not d, as you suppose G3501
1Co 11:21 remains hungry and another gets d. G3501
Eph 5:18 Do not get d on wine, which leads to G3499
1Th 5:7 and those who get d, get drunk at G3499
1Th 5:7 those who get drunk, get d at night. G3501
Rev 17:6 I saw that the woman was d with the G3501
Rev 18:3 all the nations have d the maddening G4403

DRUNKARD (6) [DRINK]
Dt 21:20 He is a glutton and a d." H6010
Isa 19:14 as a d staggers around in his vomit. H8893
Isa 24:20 The earth reels like a d, it sways like a hut H8893
Mt 11:19 'Here is a glutton and a d, a friend of tax G3884
Lk 7:34 'Here is a glutton and a d, a friend of tax G3884
1Co 5:11 an idolater or slanderer, a d or swindler. G3500

DRUNKARD'S (1) [DRINK]
Pr 26:9 a thornbush in a d hand is a proverb in H8893

DRUNKARDS (10) [DRINK]
Job 12:25 no light; he makes them stagger like d. H8893
Ps 69:12 and I am the song of the d. H9272+8911
Ps 107:27 They reeled and staggered like d; they H8893
Pr 23:21 d and gluttons become poor, and H6010
Isa 28:1 the pride of Ephraim's d, to the fading H8893
Isa 28:3 the pride of Ephraim's d, will be trampled H8893
Eze 23:42 d were brought from the desert along with H6010
Joel 1:5 Wake up, you d, and weep! Wail, all you H8893
Mt 24:49 servants and to eat and drink with d. G3501
1Co 6:10 the greedy nor d nor slanderers nor G3500

DRUNKEN (1) [DRINK]
Jer 23:9 I am like a d man, like a strong man H8893

DRUNKENNESS (9) [DRINK]
Ecc 10:17 a proper time—for strength and not for d. H9275
Jer 13:13 am going to fill with d all who live in this H8913
Eze 23:33 You will be filled with d and sorrow, the H8913
Lk 21:34 with carousing, d and the anxieties of life G3494
Ro 13:13 not in carousing and d, not in sexual G3494

Gal 5:21 envy; **d**, orgies, and the like. I warn G3494
1Ti 3: 3 not **given to d**, not violent but gentle, not G4232
Titus 1: 7 not **given to d**, not violent, G4232
1Pe 4: 3 in debauchery, lust, **d**, orgies, carousing G3886

DRUSILLA (1)

Ac 24:24 days later Felix came with his wife **D**, G1537

DRY (78) [DRIED, DRIES, DRYING]

Ge 1: 9 to one place, and let **d ground** appear." H3317
Ge 1:10 God called the **d ground** "land," and the H3317
Ge 7:22 Everything on **d land** that had the breath H3000
Ge 8:13 saw that the surface of the ground *was* **d**. H2990
Ge 8:14 month the earth *was* **completely d**. H3312
Ex 4: 9 from the Nile and pour it on the **d ground**. H3317
Ex 14:16 can go through the sea on **d ground**. H3317
Ex 14:21 strong east wind and turned it into **d land**. H3000
Ex 14:22 went through the sea on **d ground**, H3317
Ex 14:29 went through the sea on **d ground**, H3317
Ex 15:19 walked through the sea on **d ground**. H3317
Lev 7:10 whether mixed with olive oil or **d**, belongs H2992
Dt 29:19 on the watered land as well as the **d**. H7534
Jos 3:17 of the Jordan and stood on **d ground**, H3000
Jos 3:17 had completed the crossing on **d ground**. H3000
Jos 4:18 their feet on the **d ground** than the waters H3000
Jos 4:22 'Israel crossed the Jordan on **d ground**.' H3317
Jos 9: 5 of their food supply was **d** and moldy. H3312
Jos 9:12 But now see how **d** and moldy it is. H3312
Jdg 6:37 only on the fleece and all the ground is **d**, H2996
Jdg 6:39 make the fleece **d** and let the ground H2996
Jdg 6:40 Only the fleece was **d**; all the ground was H2996
1Ki 17:14 the jug of oil *will* not **run d** until the day H2893
1Ki 17:16 used up and the jug of oil *did* not **run d**, H2893
2Ki 2: 8 the two of them crossed over on **d ground**. H3000
Ne 9:11 that they passed through it on **d ground**, H3317
Job 6:17 that stop flowing in the **d** season, and H2427
Job 13:25 Will you chase after **d** chaff? H3313
Job 14:11 up or a riverbed becomes parched and **d**, H3312
Job 18:16 His roots **d up** below and his branches H3312
Job 30: 6 were forced to live in the **d** stream beds, H6877
Ps 58: 9 whether they be green or **d**—the wicked H3019
Ps 63: 1 in a **d** and parched land where there is no H7480
Ps 66: 6 He turned the sea into **d land**, they H3317
Ps 90: 6 but by evening *it is* **d** and withered. H4908
Ps 95: 5 and his hands formed the **d land**. H3318
Pr 17: 1 Better a **d** crust with peace and quiet than H2992
Isa 5:24 up straw and as **d grass** sinks down in the H3143
Isa 11:15 The LORD *will* **d up** the gulf of the Egyptian H2990
Isa 19: 5 The waters of the river *will* **d up**, and the H5980
Isa 19: 5 the riverbed will be parched and **d**. H3312
Isa 19: 6 streams of Egypt will dwindle and **d up**. H2990
Isa 27:11 When its twigs *are* **d**, they are broken off H3312
Isa 42:15 hills and **d up** all their vegetation; H3312
Isa 42:15 turn rivers into islands and **d up** the pools. H3312
Isa 44: 3 streams on the **d ground**; I will pour H3317
Isa 44:27 the watery deep, '*Be* **d**, and I will dry up H2990
Isa 44:27 and *I will* **d up** your streams,' H3312
Isa 50: 2 By a mere rebuke *I* **d up** the sea, I turn H2990
Isa 53: 2 and like a root out of **d** ground. H7480
Isa 56: 3 no eunuch complain, "I am only a **d** tree." H3313
Jer 2:25 your feet are bare and your throat is **d**. H7535
Jer 50:12 a wilderness, a **d land**, a desert. H7480
Jer 50:38 on her waters! *They will* **d up**. For it is a H3312
Jer 51:36 *I will* **d up** her sea and make her springs H2990
Jer 51:36 dry up her sea and **make** her springs **d**. H3312
Jer 51:43 will be desolate, a **d** and desert land, H7480
La 4: 8 their bones; it has become as **d** as a stick. H3313
Eze 17:24 *I* **d up** the green tree and make the dry H3312
Eze 17:24 green tree and make the **d** tree flourish. H3313
Eze 19:13 in the desert, in a **d** and thirsty land. H7480
Eze 20:47 consume all your trees, both green and **d**. H3313
Eze 23:34 will drink it and **drain** it **d** and chew on its H5172
Eze 30:12 *I will* **d up** the waters of the Nile H5989+3000
Eze 37: 2 floor of the valley, bones *that* were very **d**. H3313
Eze 37: 4 say to them, '**D** bones, hear the word H3313
Hos 9:14 that miscarry and breasts *that are* **d**. H7546
Hos 13:15 his spring will fail and his well **d up**. H2990
Am 1: 2 the pastures of the shepherds **d up**, and the H62
Jnh 1: 9 who made the sea and the **d land**." H3317
Jnh 2:10 and it vomited Jonah onto **d land**. H3317
Na 1: 4 dries it up; *he* **makes** all the rivers **run d**. H2990
Na 1:10 they will be consumed like **d** stubble. H3313
Zep 2:13 utterly desolate and **d** as the desert. H7480
Hag 2: 6 the earth, the sea and the **d land**. H3000
Zec 10:11 all the depths of the Nile *will* **d up**. H3312
Lk 23:31 is green, what will happen when it is **d**?" G3831
Heb 11:29 passed through the Red Sea as on **d** land; G3831

DRYING (1) [DRY]

Jn 13: 5 **d** them with the towel that was wrapped G1726

DUE (24) [DULY]

Lev 19:20 freedom, there must be **d punishment**. H1334
Dt 18: 3 This is the **share** *d* the priests from the AIT
Dt 32:35 In **d time** their foot will slip; their day of H6961
1Ch 16:29 Ascribe to the LORD the **glory** *d* his name AIT
2Ch 24: 5 money **d annually** from all Israel, H4946+1896+9102+928+9102
2Ch 31: 4 to give the **portion** *d* the priests and AIT
Job 36:17 are laden with the **judgment** *d* the wicked; AIT
Ps 29: 2 Ascribe to the LORD the **glory** *d* his name AIT
Ps 90:11 wrath is as great as the **fear** *that is* your *d*. AIT
Ps 96: 8 Ascribe to the LORD the **glory** *d* his name AIT
Pr 3:27 withhold good from **those to whom** it is **d**, H1251
Pr 11:31 If the righteous **receive** *their* **d** on earth H8966
Isa 49: 4 Yet *what* is **d** me is in the LORD's hand H5477
Isa 59:18 his foes; he will repay the islands their **d**. H1691
Jer 10: 7 This is your **d**. Among all the wise H3278
Jer 10:24 but only in **d measure**—not in your H5477
Jer 30:11 I will discipline you but only in **d measure**; H5477
Jer 46:28 I will discipline you but only in **d measure**; H5477
Mal 1: 6 where is the **honor** *d* me? If I am a AIT
Mal 1: 6 where is the **respect** *d* me?" says the LORD AIT
Ro 1:27 in themselves the **d** penalty for their error. G1256
2Co 5:10 each of us *may* **receive what is d** us for G3152
Eph 4:18 that is in them **d to** the hardening of their G1328
1Pe 5: 6 that he may lift you up in *d* **time**. AIT

DUG (32) [DIG]

Ge 21:30 my hand as a witness that *I* **d** this well." H2916
Ge 26:15 father's servants *had* **d** in the time of his H2916
Ge 26:18 the wells that *had been* **d** in the time of H2916
Ge 26:19 Isaac's servants **d** in the valley and H2916
Ge 26:21 Then *they* **d** another well, but they H2916
Ge 26:22 moved on from there and **d** another well, H2916
Ge 26:25 his tent, and there his servants **d** a well. H4125
Ge 26:32 told him about the well *they had* **d**. H2916
Ge 50: 5 bury me in the tomb *I* **d** for myself in the H4125
Ex 7:24 And all the Egyptians **d** along the Nile to H2916
Nu 21:18 about the well that the princes **d**, that the H2916
1Ki 18:32 and *he* **d** a trench around it large enough H6913
2Ki 19:24 I *have* **d wells** in foreign lands and drunk H7769
2Ch 26:10 in the wilderness and **d** many cisterns, H2933
Ne 9:25 of good things, wells *already* **d**, vineyards, H2933
Ps 9:15 have fallen into the pit *they have* **d**; H6913
Ps 35: 7 cause and without cause **d** a pit for me, H2916
Ps 57: 6 *They* **d** a pit in my path—but they have H4125
Ps 94:13 of trouble, till a pit **is d** for the wicked. H4125
Isa 5: 2 *He* **d** it **up** and cleared it of stones and H6466
Isa 37:25 I *have* **d wells** in foreign lands and drunk H7769
Jer 2:13 living water, and *have* **d** their own cisterns H2933
Jer 13: 7 went to Perath and **d up** the belt and took H2916
Jer 18:20 Yet *they have* **d** a pit for me H4125
Jer 18:22 for *they have* **d** a pit to capture me and H4125
Eze 8: 8 So *I* **d** into the wall and saw a doorway H3168
Eze 12: 7 Then in the evening *I* **d** through the wall H3168
Eze 12:12 a hole *will be* **d** in the wall for him to H3168
Mt 21:33 **d** a winepress in it and built a watchtower. G4002
Mt 25:18 **d a hole** in the ground and hid his G4002
Mk 12: 1 **d** a pit for the winepress and built a G4002
Lk 6:48 who **d** down deep and laid the G4999

DUKE, DUKES (KJV) CHIEF, CHIEFS

DULCIMER (KJV) PIPE

DULL (8)

Lev 13:39 if the spots are **d** white, it is a H3910
Ecc 10:10 If the ax *is* **d** and its edge unsharpened H7733
Isa 6:10 **make** their ears **d** and close their eyes. H3877
Isa 59: 1 short to save, nor his ear too **d** to hear. H3877
La 4: 1 has lost its luster, the fine gold *become* **d**! H9096
Mt 15:16 "Are you still so **d**?" Jesus asked them. G852
Mk 7:18 "Are you so **d**?" he asked. "Don't you see G852
2Co 3:14 But their minds *were* **made d**, for to this G4800

DULY (1) [DUE]

Gal 3:15 covenant *that has been* **d established**, G3263

DUMAH (4)

Ge 25:14 Mishma, **D**, Massa, H1874
Jos 15:52 **D**, Eshan, H1873
1Ch 1:30 Mishma, **D**, Massa, Hadad, Tema, H1874
Isa 21:11 A prophecy against **D**: Someone calls to H1874

DUMB (KJV) CANNOT SPEAK, MUTE, SILENT, SPEECHLESS

DUMPED (1)

Lev 14:41 that is scraped off **d** into an unclean place H9161

DUNG (15)

1Ki 14:10 the house of Jeroboam as one burns **d**, H1672
2Ki 9:37 body will be like **d** on the ground in the H1961
Ne 2:13 toward the Jackal Well and the **D** Gate, H883
Ne 3:13 cubits of the wall as far as the **D** Gate. H883
Ne 3:14 The **D** Gate was repaired by Malkijah son H883
Ne 12:31 of the wall to the right, toward the **D** Gate. H883
Job 20: 7 like his own **d**; those who have seen H1645
Ps 83:10 Endor and became like **d** on the ground. H1961
Jer 8: 2 will be like **d** lying on the ground. H1961
Jer 9:22 bodies will lie like **d** on the open field, H1961
Jer 16: 4 will be like **d** lying on the ground. H1961
Jer 25:33 will be like **d** lying on the ground. H1961
Eze 4:15 your bread over cow **d** instead of human H7616
Zep 1:17 out like dust and their entrails like **d**. H1672
Mal 2: 3 on your faces the **d** *from* your festival H7302

DUNGEON (7)

Ge 40:15 done nothing to deserve being put in a **d**." H1014
Ge 41:14 he was quickly brought from the **d**. H1014
Ex 12:29 who was in the **d**, and the firstborn H1074+1014
Isa 24:22 together like prisoners bound in a **d**; H1014
Isa 42: 7 release from the **d** those who sit in H1074+3975
Isa 51:14 they will not die in their **d**, nor will they H8846
Jer 37:16 was put into a vaulted cell in a **d**, H1074+1014

DUNGHILL, DUNGHILLS (KJV) ASH HEAP, ASH HEAPS, MANURE, PILE OF RUBBLE, PILES OF RUBBLE

DUPLICITY (2)

Pr 11: 3 the unfaithful are destroyed by their **d**. H6157
Lk 20:23 He saw through their **d** and said to them, G4111

DURA (1)

Da 3: 1 it up on the plain of **D** in the province of A10164

DURABLE (13)

Ex 25: 5 dyed red and another type of **d leather**; H6425
Ex 26:14 over that a covering of the other **d leather**. H6425
Ex 35: 7 dyed red and another type of **d leather**; H6425
Ex 35:23 red or the other **d leather** brought them. H6425
Ex 36:19 over that a covering of the other **d leather**. H6425
Ex 39:34 of another **d leather** and the shielding H6425
Nu 4: 6 are to cover the curtain with a **d** leather, H9391S
Nu 4: 8 cover that with the **d** leather and put the H9391S
Nu 4:10 in a covering of the **d** leather and put it H9391S
Nu 4:11 cover that with the **d** leather and put the H9391S
Nu 4:12 cover that with the **d** leather and put H9391S
Nu 4:14 a covering of the **d** leather and put the H9391S
Nu 4:25 its outer covering of **d leather**, H9391S

DURING (132)

Ge 14:15 *D the* **night** Abram divided his men to attack AIT
Ge 30:14 **D** wheat harvest, Reuben went out H928+3427
Ge 41:34 of the harvest of Egypt **d** the seven years of H928
Ge 41:36 to be used **d** the seven years of famine H4200
Ge 41:47 **D** the seven years of abundance the land H928
Ex 1:16 *are* **helping** the Hebrew women **d childbirth** H3528
Ex 2:23 **D** that long period, the king of Egypt died H928
Ex 12:30 all the Egyptians got up *d* the **night**, AIT
Ex 12:31 *D* the **night** Pharaoh summoned Moses and AIT
Ex 13: 7 Eat unleavened bread *d* those seven **days** AIT
Ex 14:24 **D** the last watch of the night the LORD H928
Ex 23:11 **d** the seventh year let the land lie NDT
Ex 34:21 even **d** the plowing season and harvest you H928
Ex 40:38 sight of all the Israelites **d** all their travels. H928
Lev 12: 2 as she is unclean **d** her monthly period. H3427
Lev 12: 5 the woman will be unclean, as **d** her period. NDT
Lev 15:20 " 'Anything she lies on **d** her period will be H928
Lev 15:26 unclean, as is her bed **d** her monthly period NDT
Lev 15:26 she sits on will be unclean, as **d** her period. NDT
Lev 18:19 have sexual relations **d** the uncleanness of H928
Lev 20:18 with a woman **d** her monthly period, NDT
Lev 25: 6 the land yields **d** the sabbath year will NDT
Lev 25:22 While you plant **d** the eighth year, you will NDT
Lev 25:29 **D that time** the seller may redeem it H3427
Lev 26:35 rest it did not have **d** the sabbaths you H928
Lev 27:17 dedicate a field **d** the Year of Jubilee, H4946
Nu 3: 4 served as priests **d** the lifetime of their H6584
Nu 6: 5 " '*D* the entire **period** *of* their Nazirite vow AIT
Nu 6:12 they became defiled **d** their period of NDT
Nu 10:33 before them *d* those three **days** to find them AIT
Nu 28:14 to be made at each **new moon** *d* the year. AIT
Nu 28:26 of new grain **d** the Festival of Weeks H928
Dt 8: 4 your feet did not swell *d* these forty **years**. AIT
Dt 28:53 your enemy will inflict on you **d** the siege, H928
Dt 28:55 will inflict on you **d** the siege of all your H928
Dt 28:57 will inflict on you **d** the siege of your cities. H928
Dt 29: 5 "*D* the forty **years** that I led you through the AIT
Dt 31:10 **d** the Festival of Tabernacles, H928
Jos 3:15 the Jordan is at flood stage all **d** harvest. H3427
Jos 5: 5 in the wilderness **d** the journey from Egypt H928
Jdg 7: 9 **D** that night the LORD said to Gideon, "Get H928
Jdg 8:28 **D** Gideon's lifetime, the land had peace H928
Jdg 9:32 *d* the **night** you and your men should come AIT
Jdg 11:26 Why didn't you retake them **d** that time? H928
Jdg 16: 2 They made no move **d** the night, saying H3972
Jdg 20: 5 *D* the **night** the men of Gibeah came after me AIT
Jdg 21:22 we did not get wives for them **d** the war. H928
1Sa 11:11 **d** the last watch of the night they broke into H928
1Sa 29: 4 he will turn against us **d** the fighting. H928
2Sa 3: 6 **D** the war between the house of Saul and H928
2Sa 18:18 **D** his lifetime Absalom had taken a pillar H928
2Sa 19:32 the king **d** his stay in Mahanaim, H928
2Sa 21: 1 **D** the reign of David, there was a famine H928
2Sa 21: 9 were put to death **d** the first days of the H928
2Sa 23:13 **D** harvest time, three of the thirty chief H448
1Ki 3: 5 to Solomon *d* the **night** in a dream, AIT
1Ki 3:19 "*D* the **night** this woman's son died because AIT
1Ki 4:25 **D** Solomon's lifetime Judah and Israel H3972
1Ki 9:10 *d* **which** Solomon built these two buildings AIT
1Ki 11:12 your father, I will not do it **d** your lifetime. H928
1Ki 12: 6 served his father Solomon **d** his lifetime. H928
2Ki 15:18 *D* his entire **reign** he did not turn away from AIT
2Ki 24: 1 **D** Jehoiakim's reign, Nebuchadnezzar king H928
1Ch 5:10 **D** Saul's reign they waged war against the H928
1Ch 5:17 records **d** the reigns of Jotham H928
1Ch 5:20 because they cried out to him **d** the battle. H928
1Ch 7: 2 **D** the reign of David, the descendants of H928
1Ch 13: 3 we did not inquire of it **d** the reign of Saul." H928
1Ch 22: 9 grant Israel peace and quiet **d** his reign. H928
2Ch 8: 1 *d* **which** Solomon built the temple of the LORD AIT
2Ch 10: 6 served his father Solomon **d** his lifetime. H928
2Ch 11:17 ways of David and Solomon **d** this time. H4200
2Ch 13:20 did not regain power **d** the time of Abijah. H928
2Ch 14: 6 No one was at war with him **d** those years H928

2Ch 26: 5 He sought God **d** the days of Zechariah H928
2Ch 32:26 not come on them **d** the days of Hezekiah H928
Ezr 4: 5 frustrate their plans **d** the entire reign of NDT
Ezr 7: 1 **d** the reign of Artaxerxes king of Persia H928
Ezr 8: 1 with me from Babylon **d** the reign of King H928
Ne 2:12 I set out *d* the **night** with a few others. AIT
Ne 5: 3 our homes to get grain **d** the famine." H928
Ne 8:14 in temporary shelters **d** the festival of the H928
Est 1: 1 is what happened **d** the time of Xerxes, H928
Est 2:21 **D** the time Mordecai was sitting at the H928
Pr 10: 5 he who sleeps **d** harvest is a H928
Ecc 2: 3 do under the heavens **d** the few days of NDT
Ecc 5:18 labor under the sun **d** the few days of life NDT
Ecc 6:12 **d** the few and meaningless days they pass NDT
Isa 1: 1 son of Amoz saw **d** the reigns of Uzziah, H928
Isa 49:20 The **children** *born d* your bereavement will AIT
Jer 3: 6 **D** the reign of King Josiah, the LORD said to H928
Jer 35: 1 from the LORD **d** the reign of Jehoiakim H928
Jer 49: 9 If thieves came **d** the night, would they not H928
Eze 4: 9 You are to eat it **d** the 390 days you lie on H5031
Eze 12: 4 **D the daytime**, while they watch, bring out H3429
Eze 12: 7 **D the day** I brought out my things packed H3429
Eze 18: 6 sexual relations with a woman *d* her **period**. AIT
Eze 22:10 are those who violate women **d** their period, NDT
Eze 23: 8 when **d** her youth men slept with her H928
Eze 36:38 offerings at Jerusalem **d** her appointed H928
Eze 45:21 **d** which you shall eat bread made without NDT
Eze 45:23 Every **day** *d* the seven days of the festival he AIT
Eze 45:25 " '**D** the seven days of the festival, which H928
Da 2:19 **D** the night the mystery was revealed to A10168
Da 6: 7 god or human being **d** the next thirty A10527
Da 6:12 a decree that **d** the next thirty days A10527
Da 6:28 Daniel prospered **d** the reign of Darius A10089
Hos 1: 1 Hosea son of Beeri **d** the reigns of Uzziah, H928
Hos 1: 1 **d** the reign of Jeroboam son of H928
Mic 1: 1 Micah of Moresheth **d** the reigns of Jotham H928
Zep 1: 1 **d** the reign of Josiah son of Amon king of H928
Zec 1: 8 **D** the night I had a vision, and there before NDT
Mt 2: 1 in Judea, **d** the time of King Herod *G1877*
Mt 2:14 his mother *d* the **night** and left for Egypt, AIT
Mt 26: 5 "But not **d** the festival," they said, "or there *G1877*
Mt 28:13 disciples came *d* the **night** and stole him AIT
Mk 8: 1 **D** those days another large crowd *G1877*
Mk 14: 2 "But not **d** the festival," they said, "or the *G1877*
Lk 3: 2 **d** the high-priesthood of Annas and *G2093*
Lk 4: 2 He ate nothing **d** those days, and at the *G1877*
Jn 19:31 bodies left on the crosses **d** the Sabbath, *G1877*
Ac 5:19 But **d** the night an angel of the Lord *G1328*
Ac 11:27 **D** this time some prophets came down *G1877*
Ac 11:28 This happened **d the reign of** Claudius.) *G2093*
Ac 12: 3 This happened **d** the Festival of *G2465*
Ac 13:17 the people prosper **d** their stay in Egypt; *G1877*
Ac 16: 9 **D** the night Paul had a vision of a man of *G1328*
Ac 23:31 took Paul with them **d** the night and *G1328*
Heb 3: 8 **d** the time of testing in the wilderness *G2848*
Heb 5: 7 **D** the days of Jesus' life on earth, he *G1877*
Rev 9: 6 **D** those days people will seek death but *G1877*
Rev 11: 6 it will not rain *d* the **time** they are AIT

DURST (KJV) DARE, DARED, DARING

DUSK (10)

Jos 2: 5 At **d**, when it was time to close the city H3125
1Sa 30:17 fought them from **d** until the evening of H5974
2Ki 7: 5 At **d** they got up and went to the camp of H5974
2Ki 7: 7 up and fled in the **d** and abandoned their H5974
Job 4:20 Between dawn and **d** they are broken to H6847
Job 24:15 The eye of the adulterer watches for **d**; he H5974
Eze 12: 6 they are watching and carry them out at **d**. H6602
Eze 12: 7 I took my belongings out at **d**, carrying H6602
Eze 12:12 his things on his shoulder at **d** and leave, H6602
Hab 1: 8 than leopards, fiercer than wolves at **d**. H6847

DUST (109)

Ge 2: 7 a man from the **d** of the ground and H6760
Ge 3:14 you will eat **d** all the days of your H6760
Ge 3:19 **d** you are and to dust you will return." H6760
Ge 3:19 dust you are and to **d** you will return." H6760
Ge 13:16 your offspring like the **d** *of* the earth, H6760
Ge 13:16 so that if anyone could count the **d**, then H6760
Ge 18:27 though I am nothing but **d** and ashes, H6760
Ge 28:14 will be like the **d** *of* the earth, H6760
Ex 8:16 your staff and strike the **d** *of* the ground, H6760
Ex 8:16 the land of Egypt the **d** will become gnats." NDT
Ex 8:17 the staff and struck the **d** *of* the ground, H6760
Ex 8:17 All the **d** throughout the land of Egypt H6760
Ex 9: 9 It will become **fine d** over the whole land of H85
Nu 5:17 jar and put some **d** from the tabernacle H6760
Nu 23:10 Who can count the **d** *of* Jacob or number H6760
Dt 9:21 to powder as fine as **d** and threw the dust H6760
Dt 9:21 as dust and threw the **d** into a stream that H6760
Dt 28:24 rain of your country into **d** and powder; H6760
Dt 32:24 the venom of vipers that glide in the **d**. H6760
Jos 7: 6 the same, and sprinkled **d** on their heads. H6760
1Sa 2: 8 the poor from the **d** and lifts the needy H6760
1Sa 4:12 with his clothes torn and **d** on his head. H141
2Sa 1: 2 with his clothes torn and **d** on his head. H141
2Sa 15:32 meet him, his robe torn and **d** on his head. H141
2Sa 22:43 I beat them as fine as the **d** *of* the earth; H6760
1Ki 16: 2 you up from the **d** and appointed you H6760
1Ki 20:10 if enough **d** remains *in* Samaria to give H6760
2Ki 13: 7 made them like the **d** at threshing time. H6760
2Ki 23: 6 scattered the **d** over the graves of the H6760
2Ch 1: 9 are as numerous as the **d** *of* the earth. H6760
Ne 9: 1 sackcloth and putting **d** on their heads. H141
Job 2:12 robes and sprinkled **d** on their heads. H6760
Job 4:19 whose foundations are in the **d**, who are H6760
Job 7:21 For I will soon lie down in the **d**; you will H6760
Job 10: 9 Will you now turn me to **d** again? H6760
Job 16:15 over my skin and buried my brow in the **d**. H6760
Job 17:16 Will we descend together into the **d**?" H6760
Job 20:11 fills his bones will lie with him in the **d**. H6760
Job 21:26 Side by side they lie in the **d**, and worms H6760
Job 22:24 assign your nuggets to the **d**, your H6760
Job 27:16 heaps up silver like **d** and clothes like H6760
Job 28: 6 and its **d** contains nuggets of gold. H6760
Job 30:19 and I am reduced to **d** and ashes. H6760
Job 34:15 mankind would return to the **d**. H6760
Job 38:38 when the **d** becomes hard and the clods H6760
Job 40:13 Bury them all in the **d** together; shroud H6760
Job 42: 6 myself and repent in **d** and ashes. H6760
Ps 7: 5 the ground and make me sleep in the **d**. H6760
Ps 18:42 I beat them as fine as windblown **d**; H6760
Ps 22:15 my mouth; you lay me in the **d** *of* death. H6760
Ps 22:29 who go down to the **d** will kneel before H6760
Ps 30: 9 Will the **d** praise you? Will it H6760
Ps 44:25 We are brought down to the **d**; our bodies H6760
Ps 72: 9 before him and his enemies lick the **d**. H6760
Ps 78:27 He rained meat down on them like **d** H6760
Ps 89:39 have defiled his crown in the **d**. H824
Ps 90: 3 You turn people back to **d**, saying, "Return H1919
Ps 90: 3 saying, "Return to **d**, you mortals." NDT
Ps 102:14 servants; her very **d** moves them to pity. H6760
Ps 103:14 are formed, he remembers that we are **d**. H6760
Ps 104:29 their breath, they die and return to the **d**. H6760
Ps 113: 7 the poor from the **d** and lifts the needy H6760
Ps 119:25 I am laid low in the **d**; preserve my life H6760
Pr 8:26 its fields or any of the **d** *of* the earth. H6760
Ecc 3:20 all come from **d**, and to dust all H6760
Ecc 3:20 all come from dust, and to **d** all return. H6760
Ecc 12: 7 the **d** returns to the ground it came H6760
Isa 5:24 decay and their flowers blow away like **d**; H85
Isa 25:12 them down to the ground, to the very **d**. H6760
Isa 26: 5 to the ground and casts it down to the **d**. H6760
Isa 26:19 who dwell in the **d** wake up and shout H6760
Isa 29: 4 your speech will mumble out of the **d**. H6760
Isa 29: 4 out of the **d** your speech will whisper. H6760
Isa 29: 5 your many enemies will become like fine **d**, H85
Isa 34: 7 and the **d** will be soaked with fat. H6760
Isa 34: 9 turned into pitch, her **d** into burning sulfur H6760
Isa 40:12 Who has held the **d** *of* the earth in a H6760
Isa 40:15 they are regarded as **d** *on* the scales; he H8836
Isa 40:15 the islands as though they were fine **d**. NDT
Isa 41: 2 He turns them to **d** with his sword, to H6760
Isa 47: 1 "Go down, sit in the **d**, Virgin Daughter H6760
Isa 49:23 ground; they will lick the **d** *at* your feet. H6760
Isa 52: 2 Shake off your **d**; rise up, sit enthroned H6760
Isa 65:25 and **d** will be the serpent's food. H6760
Jer 17:13 will be written in the **d** because they have H824
Jer 25:34 shepherds; roll in the **d**, you leaders of the NDT
La 2:10 they have sprinkled **d** on their heads and H6760
La 2:21 old lie together in the **d** of the streets; H824
La 3:16 with gravel; he has trampled me in the **d**. H709
La 3:29 Let him bury his face in the **d**—there may H6760
Eze 24: 7 the ground, where the **d** would cover it. H6760
Eze 26:10 be so many that they will cover you with **d**. H85
Eze 27:30 they will sprinkle **d** on their heads and roll H6760
Da 12: 2 who sleep in the **d** *of* the earth will awake H6760
Am 2: 7 the poor as on the **d** *of* the ground and H6760
Jnh 3: 6 with sackcloth and sat down in the **d**. H709
Mic 1:10 In Beth Ophrah roll in the **d**. H6760
Mic 7:17 They will lick **d** like a snake, like creatures H6760
Na 1: 3 the storm, and clouds are the **d** *of* his feet. H85
Zep 1:17 be poured out like **d** and their entrails like H6760
Zec 9: 3 she has heaped up silver like **d**, and gold H6760
Mt 10:14 town and shake the **d** off your feet. *G3155*
Mk 6:11 place and shake the **d** off your feet as a *G5967*
Lk 9: 5 town and shake the **d** off your feet as a *G3155*
Lk 10:11 'Even the **d** of your town we wipe from our *G3155*
Ac 13:51 So they shook the **d** off their feet as a *G3155*
Ac 22:23 off their cloaks and flinging **d** into the air, *G3155*
1Co 15:47 The first man was of the **d** of the earth; the *G5954*
Rev 18:19 They will throw **d** on their heads, and with *G5967*

DUTIES (23) [DUTY]

Ge 39:11 he went into the house to attend to his **d**, H4856
Nu 3: 7 They are to perform **d** *for* him and for the H5466
Nu 4:28 Their **d** are to be under the direction of H5466
Nu 8:26 in performing their **d** at the tent of H5466
Nu 18: 3 are to perform all the **d** *of* the tent, H5466
1Sa 10:25 to the people the **rights and d** *of* kingship. H5477
1Ki 3: 7 know how *to* **carry out** *my* **d**. H3655+2256+995
1Ch 6:32 They performed their **d** according to the H6275
1Ch 6:48 to all the other **d** *of* the tabernacle, H6275
1Ch 9:25 to time and **share their d** for H6640+465
1Ch 9:33 and **were exempt from** *other* **d** because H7080
1Ch 23:28 performance of *other d* at the house of H6275
1Ch 25: 8 as well as student, cast lots *for* their **d**. H5466
1Ch 26:12 had **d** for ministering in the temple of the H5466
1Ch 26:29 sons were assigned **d** away from the H4856
2Ch 8:14 the divisions of the priests for their **d**, H6275
2Ch 31: 2 according to their **d** as priests or Levites— H6275
2Ch 31:16 to perform the daily **d** of their various H1821
2Ch 35: 2 priests to their **d** and encouraged them H5466
Ne 10:33 for all the **d** *of* the house of our God. H4856
Ne 13:30 assigned them **d**, each to his own H5466
2Ti 4: 5 **discharge all the d** of your ministry. *G4442*
Heb 10:11 priest stands and **performs** *his* **religious d**; *G3310*

DUTY (33) [DUTIES]

Ge 38: 8 **fulfill** *your* **d** *to* her **as a brother-in-law** to H3302
Dt 24: 5 to war or have any other **d** laid on him. H1821
Dt 25: 5 and **fulfill the d of a brother-in-law** *to* her. H3302
Dt 25: 7 not **fulfill the d of a brother-in-law** *to* me." H3302
Ru 3:13 *he wants to* **do** *his* **d** as your **guardian-redeemer** H1457
1Ki 14:27 of the guard **on d** at the entrance to the H9068
2Ki 11: 5 companies *that are* **going on d** *on* the H995
2Ki 11: 7 *that* normally **go off** Sabbath **d** are all H3655
2Ki 11: 9 *those who were* **going on d** *on* the Sabbath H995
2Ki 11: 9 and *those who were* **going off d**— H3655
1Ch 23:28 The **d** *of* the Levites was to help Aaron's H5096
1Ch 27: 1 that *were* **on d** month by H995+2256+3655
2Ch 12:10 of the guard **on d at** the entrance to the H9068
2Ch 23: 4 Levites *who are* **going on d** *on* the H995
2Ch 23: 6 LORD except the priests and Levites **on d**; H9250
2Ch 23: 8 *those who were* **going on d** *on* the Sabbath H995
2Ch 23: 8 and *those who were* **going off d**— H3655
Ezr 4:13 more taxes, tribute or **d** will be paid, and A10208
Ezr 4:20 tribute and **d** were paid to them. A10208
Ezr 7:24 tribute or **d** on any of the priests A10208
Ne 7: 3 While the gatekeepers are *still* **on d**, have H6641
Ecc 12:13 for **this** is *the d of* all mankind. AIT
Jer 32: 7 **as nearest relative** it is your right and **d** to H1460
Eze 44: 8 out your **d** *in regard to* my holy things, H5466
Eze 45:17 It will be **the d** of the prince to provide the H6584
Mt 12: 5 the priests *on* **Sabbath d** in the temple *G4879*
Mt 17:25 kings of the earth collect **d** and taxes— *G5465*
Lk 1: 8 was **on d** and he was *G1877+3836+5423*
Lk 17:10 servants; we have only done *our* **d**. *G4053*
Jn 18:16 spoke *to* the **servant girl on d** there and *G2601*
Ac 23: 1 I *have* **fulfilled** *my* **d** to God in all good *G4488*
Ro 15:16 He gave me the **priestly d** of proclaiming *G2646*
1Co 7: 3 should fulfill his *marital* **d** to his wife, *G4051*

DWARF (1)

Lev 21:20 who is a hunchback or a **d**, or who has H1987

DWELL (81) [DWELLERS, DWELLING, DWELLINGS, DWELLS, DWELT, TENT-DWELLING]

Ex 25: 8 me, and *I will* **d** among them. H8905
Ex 29:45 Then *I will* **d** among the Israelites and be H8905
Ex 29:46 of Egypt so that I *might* **d** among them. H8905
Nu 5: 3 defile their camp, where I **d** among them." H8905
Nu 35:34 the land where you live and where I **d**, H8905
Nu 35:34 the LORD, **d** among the Israelites. H8905
Dt 33:28 Jacob *will* **d** secure in a land of grain and H6410
2Sa 7: 5 you the one to build me a house to **d in**? H3782
1Ki 8:12 has said that he *would* **d** in a dark cloud; H8905
1Ki 8:13 you, a place for you to **d** forever. H3782
1Ki 8:27 "But *will* God really **d** on earth? The H3782
1Ch 17: 4 not the one to build me a house to **d in**. H3782
1Ch 23:25 people and *has* **come to d** in Jerusalem H8905
2Ch 6: 1 has said that he *would* **d** in a dark cloud; H8905
2Ch 6: 2 you, a place for you to **d** forever. H3782
2Ch 6:18 "But *will* God really **d** on earth with H3782
Ezr 6:12 who *has* **caused** his Name to **d** there A10709
Job 11:14 hand and **allow** no evil **to d** in your tent H8905
Job 17: 2 my eyes *must* **d** *on* their hostility. H4328
Job 28:12 Where does understanding **d**? H5226
Job 28:20 Where does understanding **d**? H5226
Ps 4: 8 you alone, LORD, **make** me **d** in safety. H3782
Ps 15: 1 who *may* **d** in your sacred tent? Who H1591
Ps 23: 6 and *I will* **d** in the house of the LORD H3782
Ps 27: 4 that I *may* **d** in the house of the LORD all H3782
Ps 37: 3 **d in** the land and enjoy safe pasture. H8905
Ps 37:27 then *you will* **d** in the land forever. H8905
Ps 37:29 will inherit the land and **d** in it forever. H8905
Ps 39:12 I **d with** you as a foreigner, a stranger, as H6640
Ps 43: 3 holy mountain, to the **place where** you **d**. H5438
Ps 57: 4 *I am forced to* **d** among ravenous beasts— H8886
Ps 61: 4 *I long to* **d** in your tent forever and take H1591
Ps 68:16 where the LORD himself *will* **d** forever? H8905
Ps 68:18 that you, LORD God, *might* **d** there. H8905
Ps 69:25 let there be no *one to* **d** in their tents. H3782
Ps 69:36 those who love his name *will* **d** there. H8905
Ps 84: 4 Blessed are *those who* **d** in your house H3782
Ps 84:10 of my God than **d** in the tents of the H1884
Ps 85: 9 fear him, that his glory *may* **d** in our land. H8905
Ps 101: 6 that they *may* **d** with me; the one H3782
Ps 101: 7 who practices deceit *will* **d** in my house; H3782
Ps 120: 5 Woe to me that *I* **d** *in* Meshek, that I live H1591
Ps 143: 3 *he* **makes** me **d** in the darkness like those H3782
Pr 8:12 wisdom, **d** *together with* prudence; H8905
SS 8:13 You who **d** in the gardens with friends in H3782
Isa 1:21 righteousness *used to* **d** in her—but now H4328
Isa 13:21 there the owls *will* **d**, and there the wild H8905
Isa 26: 5 He humbles *those who* **d** on high, he lays H3782
Isa 26:19 let *those who* **d** in the dust wake up and H8905
Isa 32:16 The LORD's justice *will* **d** in the desert, his H8905
Isa 33:14 "Who of us *can* **d** *with* the consuming fire? H1591
Isa 33:14 Who of us *can* **d** *with* everlasting burning?" H1591
Isa 33:16 they are the *ones who will* **d** on the H8905
Isa 33:24 the sins of those who **d** there will be H3782
Isa 34:17 it forever and **d** there from generation H8905
Isa 38:11 be with *those who now* **d** in this world. H3782
Isa 43:18 the former things; *do* not **d** on the past. H1067

Isa 44:13 in all its glory, that it *may* d in a shrine. H3782
Isa 65:21 They will build houses and d in them H3782
Jer 17: 6 *They will* d in the parched places of the H8905
Jer 47: 2 will cry out; all *who* d in the land will wail H3782
Jer 48:28 your towns and d among the rocks, H8905
Jer 49:18 one will live there; no people *will* d in it. H1591
Jer 49:33 one will live there; no people *will* d in it." H1591
Jer 50:39 will live there, and there the owl *will* d. H3782
Jer 50:40 one will live there; no people *will* d in it. H1591
La 3: 6 *He has* made me d in darkness like those H3782
Eze 7: 7 upon you, upon you *who* d in the land. H3782
Eze 26:20 *I will* make you d in the earth below, as in H3782
Hos 14: 7 *People will* d again in his shade; they will H3782
Joel 3:17 the LORD your God, d in Zion, my holy hill H8905
Zec 8: 3 "I will return to Zion and d in Jerusalem H8905
Jn 5:38 nor *does* his word d in you, for you *G2400+3531*
Ac 1:20 let there be no one *to* d in it,' and, *G2997*
Ro 7:18 I know that good itself *does* not d in me, *G3861*
Eph 3:17 *so that* Christ *may* d in your hearts through *G2997*
Col 1:19 pleased *to have* all his fullness d in him, *G2997*
Col 3:16 *Let* the message of Christ d among you *G1940*
Jas 4: 5 the spirit *he has* caused to d in us? *G3001*
Rev 12:12 you heavens and you *who* d in them! *G5012*
Rev 21: 3 the people, and *he will* d with them. *G5012*

DWELLERS (1) [DWELL]

Isa 5: 3 "Now you d *in* Jerusalem and people of H3782

DWELLING (70) [DWELL]

Ge 27:39 "Your d will be away from the earth's H4632
Ex 15:13 you will guide them to your holy d. H5659
Ex 15:17 you made for your d, the sanctuary, Lord, H3782
Lev 15:31 their uncleanness for defiling my d place, H5438
Lev 26:11 I will put my d place among you, and I will H5438
Nu 24: 5 your tents, Jacob, your d places, Israel! H5438
Nu 24:21 "Your d place is secure, your nest is set in H4632
Dt 12: 5 your tribes to put his Name there for his d. H8905
Dt 12:11 God will choose as a d *for* his Name— H8905
Dt 14:23 place he will choose as a d *for* his Name, H8905
Dt 16: 2 the LORD will choose as a d *for* his Name. H8905
Dt 16: 6 place he will choose as a d *for* his Name. H8905
Dt 16:11 he will choose as a d *for* his Name— H8905
Dt 26: 2 your God will choose as a d *for* his Name H8905
Dt 26:15 heaven, your holy d place, and bless your H5061
1Sa 2:29 offering that I prescribed for my d? H5061
1Sa 2:32 you will see distress in my d H5061
2Sa 7: 6 from place to place with a tent as my d. H5438
2Sa 15:25 let me see it and his d place again. H5659
1Ki 8:30 from heaven, your d place, and when you H3782
1Ki 8:39 from heaven, your d place. Forgive and H3782
1Ki 8:43 from heaven, your d place. Do whatever H3782
1Ki 8:49 then from heaven, your d place, hear their H3782
1Ch 9:19 the entrance to the d *of* the LORD. H4722
1Ch 16:27 strength and joy are in his d place. H5226
1Ch 17: 5 to another, from one d place to another. H5438
2Ch 6:21 from heaven, your d place; and when you H3782
2Ch 6:30 hear from heaven, your d place. Forgive, H3782
2Ch 6:33 from heaven, your d place. Do whatever H3782
2Ch 6:39 then from heaven, your d place, hear their H3782
2Ch 29: 6 from the LORD's d place and turned their H5438
2Ch 30:27 prayer reached heaven, his holy d place. H5061
2Ch 31: 2 sing praises at the gates of the LORD's d. H4722
2Ch 36:15 pity on his people and on his d place. H5061
Ezr 7:15 God of Israel, whose d is in Jerusalem, A10445
Ne 1: 9 place I have chosen as a d *for* my Name. H8905
Job 18:15 burning sulfur is scattered over his d. H5659
Job 18:21 Surely such is the d *of* an evil man; such H5438
Job 23: 3 to find him; if only I could go to his d! H9414
Ps 27: 5 of trouble he will keep me safe in his d; H6108
Ps 31:20 them safe in your d from accusing H6109
Ps 33:14 from his d place he watches all who live H3782
Ps 68: 5 defender of widows, is God in his holy d. H5061
Ps 74: 7 they defiled the d place *of* your Name. H5438
Ps 76: 2 His tent is in Salem, his d place in Zion. H5104
Ps 84: 1 How lovely is your d place, LORD H5438
Ps 90: 1 you have been our d place throughout all H5061
Ps 91: 9 and you make the Most High your d, H5061
Ps 132: 5 the LORD, a d for the Mighty One of Jacob." H5438
Ps 132: 7 "Let us go to his d place, let us worship at H5438
Ps 132:13 he has desired it for his d, saying, H4632
Pr 24:15 righteous, do not plunder their d place; H8070
Isa 18: 4 quiet and will look on from my d place, H4806
Isa 26:21 coming out of his d to punish the people H5226
Isa 32:18 My people will live in peaceful d places H5659
Jer 7:12 where *I* first made a d *for* my Name, H8905
Jer 25:30 thunder from his holy d and roar mightily H5061
La 2: 6 He has laid waste his d like a garden; he H8494
Eze 37:27 My d place will be with them; I will be H5438
Mic 1: 3 The LORD is coming from his d place; he H5226
Zec 2:13 he has roused himself from his holy d." H5061
Jn 1:14 became flesh and made *his* d among us. *G5012*
Ac 7:46 he might provide a d place for the God of *G5013*
2Co 5: 2 to be clothed instead with our heavenly d, *G3863*
2Co 5: 4 to be clothed instead with our heavenly d, NDT
Eph 2:22 to become a d *in which* God *lives* by his *G2999*
Jude 6 authority but abandoned their *proper* d— *G3863*
Rev 13: 6 his name and his d place and those who *G5008*
Rev 18: 2 She has become a d for demons and a *G2999*
Rev 21: 3 God's d place is now among the people *G5008*

DWELLINGS (15) [DWELL]

Ex 35: 3 a fire in any of your d on the Sabbath day." H4632
1Ch 4:41 the Hamites in their d and also the H185
1Ch 5:10 they occupied the d *of* the Hagrites H185
Job 28: 4 Far from *human* d they cut a shaft, in H1591
Job 38:20 Do you know the paths to their d? H1074
Ps 49:11 their d for endless generations H5438
Ps 87: 2 Zion more than all the other d *of* Jacob. H5438
Isa 58:12 Broken Walls, Restorer of Streets with D. H3782
Jer 30:18 tents and have compassion on his d; H5438
Jer 51:30 Her d are set on fire; the bars of her gates H5438
La 2: 2 Lord has swallowed up all the d *of* Jacob; H5661
Hab 1: 6 the whole earth to seize d not their own. H5438
Hab 3: 7 in distress, the d *of* Midian in anguish. H3749
Zec 12: 7 "The LORD will save the d *of* Judah first, so H185
Lk 16: 9 you will be welcomed into eternal d. *G5008*

DWELLS (14) [DWELL]

Job 28:23 way to it and he alone knows where it d, H5226
Job 39:28 *It* d *on* a cliff and stays there at night; H8905
Ps 26: 8 you live, the place where your glory d. H5438
Ps 46: 4 the holy place where the Most High d. H5438
Ps 91: 1 *Whoever* d in the shelter of the Most High H3782
Ps 135:21 from Zion, to *him who* d in Jerusalem. H8905
Isa 8:18 the LORD Almighty, who d on Mount Zion. H8905
Isa 33: 5 LORD is exalted, for *he* d on high; he will H8905
La 1: 3 She d among the nations; she finds no H3782
Da 2:22 lies in darkness, and light d with him. A10742
Joel 3:21 I will not." The LORD d in Zion! H8905
Mt 23:21 swears by it and by the *one who* d in it. *G2997*
1Co 3:16 that God's Spirit d in your midst? *G3861*
2Pe 3:13 a new earth, where righteousness d. *G2997*

DWELT (6) [DWELL]

Dt 33:16 the favor of *him who* d in the burning H8905
2Sa 7: 6 *I have* not d in a house from the day I H3782
1Ch 17: 5 *I have* not d in a house from the day I H3782
Job 29:25 their chief; *I* d as a king among his troops H8905
Ps 74: 2 redeemed—Mount Zion, where *you* d. H8905
Ps 94:17 I *would* soon *have* d in the silence of H8905

DWINDLE (1) [DWINDLES]

Isa 19: 6 the streams of Egypt *will* d and dry up. H1937

DWINDLES (1) [DWINDLE]

Pr 13:11 Dishonest money d away, but whoever H5070

DYED (6)

Ex 25: 5 ram skins d red and another type of durable H131
Ex 26:14 the tent a covering of ram skins d red, H131
Ex 35: 7 ram skins d red and another type of durable H131
Ex 35:23 ram skins d red or the other durable leather H131
Ex 36:19 the tent a covering of ram skins d red, H131
Ex 39:34 of ram skins d red and the covering of H131

DYING (14) [DIE]

Ge 35:18 her last—for *she was* d—she named her H4637
1Sa 4:20 As she *was* d, the women attending her H4637
2Ch 24:22 who said as he lay d, "May the LORD see H4638
Job 11:20 their hope will become a d gasp. H5883
Job 24:12 The groans of the d rise from the city, and H4637
Job 29:13 The *one who was* d blessed me; I made the H6
Isa 22:14 "Till *your* d day this sin will not be atoned H4637
Zec 11: 9 Let the d die, and the perishing H4637
Mk 5:23 with him, "My little daughter *is* d. *G2275+2400*
Lk 8:42 daughter, a girl of about twelve, was d. *G633*
Jn 11:37 the blind man have kept this man from d?" *G633*
Ro 7: 6 But now, *by* d to what once bound us, we *G633*
2Co 6: 9 as unknown; d, and yet we live on; *G633*
Heb 11:21 faith Jacob, *when he was* d, blessed each *G633*

DYNASTY (3)

1Sa 25:28 will certainly make a lasting d for my lord, H1074
1Ki 2:24 has founded a d for me as he H1074
1Ki 11:38 I will build you a d as enduring as the H1074

DYSENTERY (1)

Ac 28: 8 sick in bed, suffering from fever and d. *G1548*

E

EACH (616)

Ge 1:24 the wild animals, e according to its kind." NDT
Ge 2:19 whatever the man called e living creature, H2257
Ge 9: 5 And from e human being, too H408+278+2257
Ge 10: 5 their nations, e with its own language.) H408
Ge 11: 3 They said to e other, "Come, let's make H408
Ge 11: 7 so they will not understand e other. H408
Ge 15: 9 a goat and a ram, e three years old, along NDT
Ge 15:10 arranged the halves opposite e other; H408
Ge 25:22 The babies jostled e other within her, and H8368
Ge 26:31 morning the men swore an oath to e other. H408
Ge 31:49 me when we are away from e other. H408
Ge 32:16 of his servants, e herd by itself, and H6373+6373
Ge 37:19 comes that dreamer!" they said to e other. H408
Ge 40: 5 e of the two men—the cupbearer and the H408
Ge 40: 5 e dream had a meaning of its own. H408
Ge 41:11 E of us had a dream the same H638+2256+2085
Ge 41:11 e dream had a meaning of its own. H408
Ge 41:12 giving *e* man the interpretation of his dream. AIT
Ge 41:48 In e city he put the food grown in the H2021
Ge 42: 1 "Why *do you just keep* looking at e other?" H8011
Ge 42:25 to put e man's silver back in his sack H408
Ge 42:28 they turned to e other trembling and H408
Ge 42:35 there in e man's sack was his pouch of H408
Ge 43:21 opened our sacks and e man's found his H408
Ge 43:33 they looked at e other in astonishment. H408
Ge 44: 1 put *e* man's silver in the mouth of his AIT
Ge 44:11 E of them quickly lowered his sack to the H408
Ge 45:22 To e *of* them he gave new clothing, but to H3972
Ge 49:28 giving e the blessing appropriate to him. H408
Ex 1: 1 went to Egypt with Jacob, e with his family: H408
Ex 5:13 required of you for e day, H1821+3427+928+3427
Ex 5:19 required of you for e day. H1821+3427+928+3427
Ex 7:12 E *one* threw down his staff and it became a H408
Ex 12: 3 day of this month *e* man is to take a lamb AIT
Ex 12: 3 lamb for his family, one for e household. H2021
Ex 12: 4 in accordance with what e *person* will eat. H408
Ex 13:15 womb and redeem e *of* my firstborn sons. H3972
Ex 16: 4 people are to go out e day and gather NDT
Ex 16:15 they said to e other, "What is it? H408
Ex 16:16 an omer for e person you have H1653+5031
Ex 16:21 E morning everyone gathered H928+2021+1332+928+2021+1332
Ex 16:22 two omers for e *person*—and the leaders of H285
Ex 18: 7 They greeted e other and then went into H408
Ex 25:20 The cherubim are to face e other, looking H408
Ex 26: 5 other set, with the loops opposite e other. H851
Ex 26:16 E frame is to be ten cubits long and a cubit H285
Ex 26:17 with two projections set parallel to e other H851
Ex 26:19 two bases for e frame, one under H285
Ex 26:19 each frame, one under e projection. H9109
Ex 26:21 forty silver bases—two under e frame. H285
Ex 26:25 sixteen silver bases—two under e frame. H285
Ex 27: 2 Make a horn at e of the four corners, so that NDT
Ex 27: 4 make a bronze ring at e of the four corners NDT
Ex 28:21 one for e of the names of the sons of Israel NDT
Ex 28:21 e engraved like a seal with the name of H408
Ex 29:36 Sacrifice a bull e day as a sin offering to H4200
Ex 29:38 are to offer on the altar regularly e day: H4200
Ex 30: 4 two on *e of the* opposite sides—to hold the AIT
Ex 30:12 e *one* must pay the LORD a ransom for his H408
Ex 30:13 E one who crosses over to those already H3972
Ex 32:27 'E *man* strap a sword to his side. H408
Ex 32:27 e killing his brother and friend and H408
Ex 33:10 worshiped, e at the entrance to their tent. H408
Ex 34:24 go up three times e year to appear before H2021
Ex 36:12 other set, with the loops opposite e other. H285
Ex 36:21 E frame was ten cubits long and a cubit H285
Ex 36:22 with two projections set parallel to e other H285
Ex 36:24 two bases for e frame, one under H285
Ex 36:24 each frame, one under e projection. H9109
Ex 36:26 forty silver bases—two under e frame. H285
Ex 36:30 sixteen silver bases—two under e frame. H285
Ex 37: 9 The cherubim faced e other, looking H408
Ex 37:27 two on *e of the* opposite sides—to hold the AIT
Ex 38: 2 They made a horn at e of the four corners, so NDT
Ex 38:27 the 100 talents, one talent for e base. H2021
Ex 39:14 one for e of the names of the sons of Israel NDT
Ex 39:14 e engraved like a seal with the name of H408
Lev 7:14 are to bring one of e *kind* as an offering, H3972
Lev 14:10 ewe lamb a year old, e without defect NDT
Lev 19: 3 " 'E of you must respect your mother and H408
Lev 23:18 male lambs, e a year old and without defect NDT
Lev 23:19 offering and two lambs, e a year old, for a NDT
Lev 23:37 offerings required for e day. H3427+928+3427
Lev 23:41 a festival to the LORD for seven days e year. H928
Lev 24: 5 using two-tenths of an ephah for e loaf. H285
Lev 24: 6 in two stacks, six in e stack, on the table H2021
Lev 24: 7 By e stack put some pure incense as a H2021
Lev 25:10 e of you is to return to your family property H408
Lev 25:14 do not take advantage of e other. H408
Lev 25:17 Do not take advantage of e other, but fear H408
Nu 1: 4 One man from e tribe, each of them the H2021
Nu 1: 4 each tribe, e of them the head of his family H408
Nu 1:44 e one representing his family. H408+408
Nu 1:52 e *of them* in their own camp under their H408
Nu 2: 2 e *of them* under their standard and holding H408
Nu 2:17 e in their own place under their standard. H408
Nu 2:34 e *of them* with their clan and family. H408
Nu 3:47 collect five shekels for e one, according to H1653
Nu 4:19 assign to e man his work and what H408
Nu 4:32 Assign to e man the specific things H928+9005
Nu 4:49 e was assigned his work and told H408+408
Nu 7: 3 an ox from e leader and a cart from every H285
Nu 7: 5 them to the Levites as *e* man's work requires." AIT
Nu 7:11 "E day one leader is to bring his offering H4200+2021+3427+4200+2021+3427
Nu 7:13 e filled with the finest flour mixed with H9109
Nu 7:19 e filled with the finest flour mixed with H9109
Nu 7:25 e filled with the finest flour mixed with H9109
Nu 7:31 e filled with the finest flour mixed with H9109
Nu 7:37 e filled with the finest flour mixed with H9109
Nu 7:43 e filled with the finest flour mixed with H9109
Nu 7:49 e filled with the finest flour mixed with H9109
Nu 7:55 e filled with the finest flour mixed with H9109
Nu 7:61 e filled with the finest flour mixed with H9109
Nu 7:67 e filled with the finest flour mixed with H9109
Nu 7:73 e filled with the finest flour mixed with H9109
Nu 7:79 e filled with the finest flour mixed with H9109
Nu 7:85 E silver plate weighed a hundred and thirty H285
Nu 7:85 e sprinkling bowl seventy shekels. H285
Nu 7:86 incense weighed ten shekels e, H2021+4090S
Nu 13: 2 From e ancestral tribe send one of its H3972

Nu 14: 4 And they said to e other, "We should H408
Nu 14:34 one year for e *of* the forty days you H3427S
Nu 15: 5 With e lamb for the burnt offering or the H285
Nu 15:11 E bull or ram, each lamb or young goat, is H285
Nu 15:11 Each bull or ram, e lamb or young goat, is H2021
Nu 15:12 Do this for **e one**, for as many as you H285
Nu 15:38 garments, with a blue cord on e tassel. H2021
Nu 16:17 *E* **man** is to take his censer and put incense in AIT
Nu 16:18 So e *of them* took his censer, put burning H408
Nu 17: 2 one from the leader of e of their ancestral H3972
Nu 17: 2 Write the name of *e* **man** on his staff. AIT
Nu 17: 3 staff for the head of e ancestral tribe. H4392S
Nu 17: 6 one for the leader of e of their ancestral NDT
Nu 17: 9 and *e of the* **leaders** took his own staff. AIT
Nu 23: 2 them offered a bull and a ram on e altar. H2021
Nu 23: 4 on e altar I have offered a bull and a H2021
Nu 23:14 offered a bull and a ram on e altar. H2021
Nu 23:30 offered a bull and a ram on e altar. H2021
Nu 25: 5 "E of you must put to death those of your H408
Nu 26:54 e is to receive its inheritance according to H408
Nu 26:55 What e group inherits will be according to NDT
Nu 26:56 E inheritance is to be distributed by lot H2257
Nu 28: 3 as a regular burnt offering e day. H2021
Nu 28: 7 of a hin of fermented drink with e lamb. H285
Nu 28:12 With e bull there is to be a grain offering of H285
Nu 28:13 with e lamb, a grain offering of a tenth H285
Nu 28:14 With e bull there is to be a drink offering H2021
Nu 28:14 of a hin; and with e lamb, a quarter of a H2021
Nu 28:14 to be made at e new moon during the NDT
Nu 28:20 With e bull offer a grain offering of H2021
Nu 28:21 with e of the seven lambs, one-tenth. H285
Nu 28:28 With e bull there is to be a grain offering of H285
Nu 28:29 with e *of* the seven lambs, one-tenth. H285
Nu 29: 4 with e of the seven lambs, one-tenth. H285
Nu 29:10 with e of the seven lambs, one-tenth. H285
Nu 29:14 With e of the thirteen bulls offer a grain H285
Nu 29:14 flour mixed with oil; with e of the two rams H285
Nu 29:15 with e of the fourteen lambs, one-tenth H285
Nu 31: 4 a thousand men from e *of* the tribes of H3972
Nu 31: 5 a thousand from e tribe, were supplied H2021
Nu 31: 6 a thousand from e tribe, along with H2021
Nu 31:50 LORD the gold articles e of us acquired— H408
Nu 31:53 E soldier had taken plunder for himself. H408
Nu 32:18 to our homes until e *of* the Israelites has H408
Nu 34:18 one leader from e tribe to help assign H285
Nu 35: 8 in proportion to the inheritance of e tribe: H408
Nu 36: 9 e Israelite tribe is to keep the land it H408
Dt 1:13 respected men from e of your tribes, NDT
Dt 1:23 twelve of you, one man from e tribe. H2021
Dt 3:20 e of you may go back to the possession I H408
Dt 14:22 all that your fields produce **e year**. H9102+9102
Dt 15:20 **E year** you and your family are H9102+928+9102
Dt 16:17 E of you must bring a gift in proportion to H408
Dt 16:18 officials for e of your tribes in every NDT
Dt 24:15 Pay them their wages e day before sunset H928
Dt 24:16 their parents; e will die for their own sin. H408
Jos 3:12 from the tribes of Israel, one from e tribe. H2021
Jos 4: 2 from among the people, one from e tribe, NDT
Jos 4: 4 from the Israelites, one from e tribe, NDT
Jos 4: 5 E of you is to take up a stone on his H408
Jos 18: 4 Appoint three men from e tribe. I will send H2021
Jos 18: 4 according to the inheritance of e. H4392
Jos 21:42 E of these **towns** had pasturelands H6551+6551
Jos 22:14 one from e *of* the tribes of Israel H3972
Jos 22:14 e the head of a family division among the H408
Jos 24:28 the people, e to their own inheritance. H408
Jdg 1:18 Ashkelon and Ekron—e city with its territory. NDT
Jdg 2: 6 of the land, e to their own inheritance. H408
Jdg 5:30 a woman or two for e man, colorful H8031
Jdg 6:29 They asked e other, "Who did this?" When H408
Jdg 7:21 While *e* **man** held his position around the AIT
Jdg 7:22 the camp to turn on e other with their H2084
Jdg 8:18 "**e one** with the bearing of a prince." AIT
Jdg 8:24 that e of you give me an earring from your H408
Jdg 8:25 and *e of* **them** threw a ring from his plunder AIT
Jdg 10:18 of the people of Gilead said to e other, H408
Jdg 11:40 that **e year** the young H4946+3427+3427+2025
Jdg 16: 5 E *one* of us will give you eleven hundred H408
Jdg 20: 6 sent one piece to e region of Israel's H3972
Jdg 20:16 e *of* whom could sling a stone at a hair H3972
Jdg 21:21 the vineyards and e of you seize one of H408
Jdg 21:23 e man caught one and carried her H4200+5031S
Jdg 21:24 tribes and clans, e to his own inheritance. H408
Ru 1: 8 "Go back, e of you, to your mother's H851
Ru 1: 9 the LORD grant that e of you will find rest H851
1Sa 2:19 **E year** his mother made H4946+3427+3427+2025
1Sa 6:17 to the LORD—**one** *e* for Ashdod, Gaza, AIT
1Sa 10:11 prophets, they asked e other, "What is this H408
1Sa 14: 4 On e side of the pass H4946+2021+6298
+4946+2296+4946+2021+6298
1Sa 14:20 striking e other with their swords. H408
1Sa 14:34 'E of you bring me your cattle and sheep H408
1Sa 17:10 Give me a man and let us fight **e other**." H3480
1Sa 17:21 up their lines **facing e other**. H7925+5120
1Sa 20:41 Then they kissed e other and wept together H408
1Sa 20:42 with **e other** in the name of H9109+5646
1Sa 25:13 to his men, "E of you strap on your sword!" H408
1Sa 27: 3 *E* **man** had his family with him, and David AIT
1Sa 30: 6 e one was bitter in spirit because of his H3972
1Sa 30:22 *e* **man** may take his wife and children and go AIT
2Sa 2: 3 who were with him, e with his family, and H408
2Sa 2:16 Then *e* **man** grabbed his opponent by the AIT
2Sa 6:19 a cake of raisins to e person in the whole H3972
2Sa 10: 4 shaved off half of *e* **man's** beard, cut off their AIT
2Sa 14: 6 a fight with **e other** in the field, H9109+2157S
2Sa 18: 5 Absalom to e *of* the commanders. H3972
2Sa 20:22 from the city, e returning to his home. H408
2Sa 21:20 with six fingers on e hand and six toes on H2257
2Sa 21:20 on each hand and six toes on e foot— H2257
1Ki 4: 7 E one had to provide supplies for one H2021
1Ki 4:27 district governors, e *in* his month, supplied H408
1Ki 6:10 The height of e was five cubits, and they H2257
1Ki 6:23 out of olive wood, e ten cubits high. H2257
1Ki 6:26 The height of e cherub was ten cubits. H285
1Ki 6:27 wings touched e other in the middle H4053S
1Ki 6:34 e having two leaves that turned in sockets. H285
1Ki 7: 4 sets of three, **facing e other**. H4691+448+4691
1Ki 7: 5 sets of three, **facing e other**. H4691+448+4691
1Ki 7:15 e eighteen cubits high and twelve cubits in H285
1Ki 7:16 of the pillars; e capital was five cubits high. H285
1Ki 7:17 on top of the pillars, seven for e capital. H285
1Ki 7:18 two rows encircling e network to decorate H285
1Ki 7:18 He did the same for e capital. H9108
1Ki 7:27 stands of bronze; e was four cubits long H285
1Ki 7:30 E stand had four bronze wheels with bronze H285
1Ki 7:30 e had a basin resting on four H2157
1Ki 7:30 four supports, cast with wreaths on e side. H408
1Ki 7:32 The diameter of e wheel was a cubit and a H285
1Ki 7:34 E stand had four handles, one on each H285
1Ki 7:34 four handles, one on e corner, projecting H752S
1Ki 7:38 e holding forty baths and measuring four H285
1Ki 7:38 one basin to go on e of the ten stands. H285
1Ki 7:42 of pomegranates for e network decorating H285
1Ki 8:59 Israel according to **e day's** need, H3427+3427
1Ki 10:16 hundred shekels of gold went into e shield. H285
1Ki 10:17 with three minas of gold in e shield. H285
1Ki 10:19 with a lion standing beside e of them. H9109
1Ki 10:20 on the six steps, one at either end of e step. NDT
1Ki 18: 4 two caves, fifty in e, and had supplied them NDT
1Ki 18:13 in two caves, fifty in e, and supplied them NDT
1Ki 18:31 **one for e** *of* the tribes descended H3869+5031
1Ki 20:10 Samaria to give *e of* my men a handful." H3972
1Ki 20:20 and e *one* struck down his opponent. H408
1Ki 20:29 seven days they camped opposite **e other**, H465
1Ki 22:17 Let e *one* go home in peace.' H408
2Ki 3:23 must have fought and slaughtered e other. H408
2Ki 3:25 and *e* **man** threw a stone on every good field AIT
2Ki 4: 4 all the jars, and as e is filled, put it to one H2021
2Ki 6: 2 to the Jordan, where e of us can get a pole. H408
2Ki 7: 3 They said to e other, "Why stay here until H408
2Ki 7: 9 Then they said to e other, "What we're H408
2Ki 9:21 of Judah rode out, e in his own chariot, to H408
2Ki 11: 8 the king, *e of* **you** with weapon in hand. AIT
2Ki 11: 9 E *one* took his men—those who were H408
2Ki 11:11 The guards, e with weapon in hand H408
2Ki 14: 6 their parents; e will die for their own sin." H408
2Ki 14: 8 "Come, *let us* **face e other in battle**." H8011+7156
2Ki 14:11 king of Judah **faced e other** at Beth H8011+7156
2Ki 17:29 **e national group** made its own H1580+1580
2Ki 18:31 Then e of you will eat fruit from your own H408
2Ki 25:17 E pillar was eighteen cubits high. H285
1Ch 9:27 opening it **e morning**.
H4200+2021+1332+4200+2021+1332
1Ch 13: 1 David conferred with e *of* his officers, the H3972
1Ch 16: 3 a cake of raisins to e Israelite man and H3972
1Ch 16:37 according to **e day's** H3427+928+3427+2257
1Ch 16:43 all the people left, e for their own home H408
1Ch 20: 6 with six fingers on e hand and six toes on NDT
1Ch 20: 6 on each hand and six toes on e foot— NDT
1Ch 26:13 Lots were cast for **e gate** H9133+2256+9133
1Ch 27: 1 E division consisted of 24,000 men H285
1Ch 28:15 for **e lampstand** and its H4963+2256+4963
1Ch 28:15 silver for e silver **lampstand** and its H4963+4963
1Ch 28:15 to the use of **e lampstand**; H4963+2256+4963
1Ch 28:16 of gold for **e table** for H8947+2256+8947
1Ch 28:17 of gold for **e** gold **dish**; H4094+2256+4094
1Ch 28:17 of silver for e silver **dish**; H4094+2256+4094
2Ch 3:15 e with a capital five cubits high. H2257
2Ch 4:13 two rows of pomegranates for e network H285
2Ch 8:14 to **e day's** requirement H3427+928+3427
2Ch 9:15 of hammered gold went into e shield. H285
2Ch 9:16 three hundred shekels of gold in e shield. H285
2Ch 9:18 with a lion standing beside e of them. H9109
2Ch 9:19 on the six steps, one at either end of e step. NDT
2Ch 18:16 Let e *one* go home in peace.' H408
2Ch 19: 5 in e *of* the fortified cities of Judah. H3972
2Ch 23: 7 around the king, e with weapon in hand. H408
2Ch 23: 8 E *one* took his men—those who were H408
2Ch 23:10 all the men, e with his weapon in his hand H408
2Ch 25: 4 their parents; e will die for their own sin." H408
2Ch 25:17 "Come, *let us* **face e other in battle**." H8011+7156
2Ch 25:21 king of Judah **faced e other** at Beth H8011+7156
2Ch 31: 2 e of them according to their duties as H408
2Ch 35: 5 of Levites for *e* **subdivision** *of* the families of AIT
2Ch 35:15 at **e gate** did not need H9133+2256+9133
Ezr 2: 1 Jerusalem and Judah, e to their own town, H408
Ezr 3: 4 offerings prescribed for **e day**. H3427+928+3427
Ezr 6:17 one for e of the tribes of Israel. A10433
Ezr 10:14 elders and judges of **e town**, H6551+2256+6551
Ezr 10:16 one from e family division, and H4392
Ezr 10:19 their guilt they e presented a ram from NDT
Ne 3:28 made repairs, e in front of his own house. H408
Ne 4:15 all returned to the wall, e to our own work. H408
Ne 4:18 e of the builders wore his sword at his H408
Ne 4:19 separated from e other along the wall. H408
Ne 4:23 off our clothes; e had his weapon, even H408
Ne 5:18 E day one ox, six choice sheep and some H285
Ne 6: 4 e time I gave them the same answer. NDT
Ne 7: 6 Jerusalem and Judah, e to his own town, H408
Ne 10:32 a third of a shekel **e year** for the service of H2021
Ne 10:34 to determine when e of our families is to NDT
Ne 10:34 set times **e year** a contribution H9102+928+9102
Ne 10:35 the LORD **e year** the firstfruits H9102+928+9102
Ne 11: 3 e on their own property in the various H408
Ne 11:20 of Judah, e on their ancestral property. H408
Ne 13:30 assigned them duties, e to his own task. H408
Est 1: 7 *e* **one** different from the other AIT
Est 1: 8 the king's command e guest was allowed to NDT
Est 1: 8 stewards to serve *e* **man** what he wished. AIT
Est 1:22 to **e province** in its own H4519+2256+4519
Est 1:22 and to **e people** in their own H6639+2256+6639
Est 3:12 script of **e province** and in H4519+2256+4519
Est 3:12 language of **e people** all H6639+2256+6639
Est 8: 9 the script of **e province** and H4519+2256+4519
Est 8: 9 the language of **e people** and H6639+2256+6639
Est 9:19 a day for giving presents to e other. H408
Job 1: 5 sacrifice a burnt offering for e *of* them, H3972
Job 9:32 that we might confront **e other** in court. H3481
Job 41:16 e is so close to the next that no air can H285
Job 42:11 and e *one* gave him a piece of silver and a H408
Ps 64: 5 They encourage **e other** in evil plans H4564S
Ps 84: 7 to strength, till *e* **appears** before God in Zion. AIT
Ps 85:10 righteousness and peace **kiss** *e other*. AIT
Ps 147: 4 of the stars and calls them e by name. H3972
Pr 14:10 *E* **heart** knows its own bitterness, and no one AIT
Ecc 3:13 That e *of* them may eat and drink, and H3972
SS 3: 8 in battle, e with his sword at his side H408
SS 4: 2 up from the washing. E has its twin; not H3972
SS 6: 6 up from the washing. E has its twin, not H3972
SS 8:11 E was to bring for its fruit a thousand H408
Isa 3: 5 People *will* **oppress e other**—man H5601
Isa 6: 2 him were seraphim, e with six wings: With H285
Isa 9:20 E will feed on the flesh of their own H408
Isa 13: 8 They will look aghast at e other, their faces H408
Isa 14:18 the nations lie in state, e in his own tomb. H408
Isa 32: 2 *E* **one** will be like a shelter from the wind AIT
Isa 34:14 wild goats will bleat to **e other** H8276S
Isa 34:15 the falcons will gather, e with its mate. H851
Isa 36:16 Then e *of* you will eat fruit from your own H408
Isa 40:26 by one and calls forth e *of* them by name. H3972
Isa 41: 6 they help e other and say to their H408
Isa 50: 8 Let us face **e other**! Who is my H3480
Isa 53: 6 e of us has turned to our own way H408
Isa 56:12 e one cries, "let me get wine! Let NDT
Isa 58: 4 and *in* **striking** *e other* with wicked fists. AIT
Jer 5: 8 e neighing for another man's wife. H408
Jer 6: 3 around her, e tending his own portion." H408
Jer 7: 5 your actions and deal with e other justly, H408
Jer 8: 6 E pursues their own course like a horse H3972
Jer 12:15 will bring e of them back to their own H408
Jer 17:10 to reward *e* **person** according to their conduct, AIT
Jer 18:11 your evil ways, e *one* of you, and reform H408
Jer 22: 7 against you, *e* **man** with his weapons, and AIT
Jer 23:35 This is what e of you keeps saying to your H408
Jer 23:36 because *e* **one's** word becomes their own AIT
Jer 25: 5 "Turn now, e of you, from your evil ways H408
Jer 26: 3 they will listen and e will turn from their H408
Jer 32:19 you reward *e* **person** according to their AIT
Jer 34:14 'Every seventh year e of you must free any H408
Jer 34:15 E of you proclaimed freedom to your own H408
Jer 34:16 e of you has taken back the male and H408
Jer 35:15 "E of you must turn from your wicked ways H408
Jer 36: 3 they will e turn from their wicked ways H408
Jer 36: 7 the LORD and will e turn from their wicked H408
Jer 36:16 they looked at e other in fear and said to H408
Jer 37:21 of the bakers **e day** until all H4200+2021+3427
Jer 46:16 repeatedly; they will fall over e other. H408
Jer 51: 9 let us leave her and e go to our own land H408
Jer 52:21 E pillar was eighteen cubits high and H285
Jer 52:21 in circumference; e was four fingers thick H2257
Eze 1: 6 e of them had four faces and four wings. H285
Eze 1: 9 E *one* went straight ahead; they did not H408
Eze 1:10 E *of* the four had the face of a human H4392
Eze 1:10 on the right side e had the face of a H5527
Eze 1:10 of an ox; e also had the face of an eagle. H5527
Eze 1:11 They e had two wings spreading out H408
Eze 1:11 e wing touching that of the creature on NDT
Eze 1:11 e had two other wings covering its body. NDT
Eze 1:12 E *one* went straight ahead. H408
Eze 1:15 on the ground beside e creature with its H2021
Eze 1:16 E appeared to be made like a wheel H2157
Eze 1:23 e had two wings covering its body. H408
Eze 3:13 brushing against e other and the sound of H851
Eze 4: 6 assigned you 40 days, a day for e year. H2021
Eze 4:10 of food to eat e day and eat it at set H2021
Eze 4:17 at the sight of e other and will waste H408
Eze 7:16 they will all moan, e for their own sins. H408
Eze 8:11 E had a censer in his hand, and a fragrant H408
Eze 8:12 darkness, e at the shrine of his own idol? H408
Eze 9: 1 on the city, e with a weapon in his hand." H408
Eze 9: 2 e with a deadly weapon in his hand. H408
Eze 10: 9 one beside e of the cherubim; the H285
Eze 10:10 *e* **was** like a wheel intersecting a wheel. AIT
Eze 10:14 E of the cherubim had four faces: One face H285
Eze 10:21 E had four faces and four wings, and under H285
Eze 10:22 the Kebar River. E *one* went straight ahead. H408

Eze 18:30 I will judge e of you according to your own H408
Eze 20: 7 And I said to them, "E of you, get rid of the H408
Eze 22: 6 " 'See how e of the princes of Israel who H408
Eze 32:10 day of your downfall e of them will tremble H408
Eze 33:20 But I will judge e of you according to your H408
Eze 33:26 e of you defiles his neighbor's wife. H408
Eze 33:30 houses, saying to e other, 'Come and H2522
Eze 40: 5 e of which was a cubit and a handbreadth. NDT
Eze 40:10 three alcoves on e side; H4946+7024+2256+4946+7024
Eze 40:10 walls on e side had the H4946+7024+2256+4946+7024
Eze 40:12 In front of e alcove was a wall one cubit H2021
Eze 40:21 three on e side—its H4946+7024+2256+4946+7024
Eze 40:26 walls on e side. H4946+7024+4946+2256+7024
Eze 40:38 by the portico in e of the inner gateways NDT
Eze 40:39 two tables on e side, H4946+7024+2256+4946+7024
Eze 40:42 the burnt offerings, e a cubit and a half long NDT
Eze 40:43 e a handbreadth long NDT
Eze 40:49 pillars on e side of the H4946+7024+2256+4946+7024
Eze 41: 1 was six cubits on e side. H4946+7024+2256+4946+7024
Eze 41: 2 walls on e side of it H4946+7024+2256+4946+7024
Eze 41: 3 of the entrance; e was two cubits wide. NDT
Eze 41: 3 projecting walls on e side of it were seven NDT
Eze 41: 5 e side room around the temple was H2021
Eze 41: 6 one above another, thirty on e level. AIT
Eze 41: 7 at e successive level. H4200+5087+2025+4200+5087+2025
Eze 41:15 its galleries on e side; H4946+7024+2256+4946+7024
Eze 41:18 with cherubim. E cherub had two faces: H2021
Eze 41:24 E door had two leaves—two hinged H9109S
Eze 41:24 two leaves—two hinged leaves for e door. H285
Eze 41:26 trees carved on e side. H4946+7024+2256+4946+7024
Eze 45: 7 land bordering e side of H4946+2296+2256+4946+2296S
Eze 45:13 of an ephah from e homer of wheat and a NDT
Eze 45:13 a sixth of an ephah from e homer of barley. NDT
Eze 45:14 is a tenth of a bath from e cor (which H2021
Eze 45:24 an ephah for e bull and an ephah for H2021
Eze 45:24 each bull and an ephah for e ram, H2021
Eze 45:24 along with a hin of olive oil for e ephah. H2021
Eze 46: 5 along with a hin of olive oil for e ephah. H2021
Eze 46: 7 along with a hin of oil for e ephah. H2021
Eze 46: 9 entered, but e is to go out the opposite gate. AIT
Eze 46:11 along with a hin of oil for e ephah. H2021
Eze 46:21 I saw in e corner another H928+928+5243+5243
Eze 46:22 e of the courts in the four corners was the AIT
Eze 46:23 the inside of e of the four courts was a ledge AIT
Eze 47: 7 of trees on e side of the river. H4946+2296+2256+4946+2296S
Eze 48:20 will be a square, 25,000 cubits on e side. H928
Da 7: 3 great beasts, e different from the others A10154
Da 11:27 will sit at the same table and lie to e other AIT
Joel 2: 8 They do not jostle e other; each marches H408
Joel 2: 8 each other; e marches straight ahead. H1505S
Am 4: 3 You will e go straight out through breaches H851
Jnh 1: 5 were afraid and e cried out to his own H408
Jnh 1: 7 Then the sailors said to e other, "Come, let H408
Mic 7: 2 to shed blood; they hunt e other with nets. H408
Hag 1: 9 while e of you is busy with your own house. H408
Hag 2:22 will fall, e by the sword of his brother. H408
Zec 3:10 " 'In that day e of you will invite your H408
Zec 7:10 Do not plot evil against e other.' H408
Zec 8: 4 e of them with cane in hand because of H408
Zec 8:16 Speak the truth to e other, and render true H408
Zec 8:17 do not plot evil against e other, and do H2084
Zec 12:12 will mourn, e clan by itself, with H5476+5476
Zec 13: 5 E will say, 'I am not a prophet. I am a farmer AIT
Zec 14:13 They will seize e other by the hand and H408
Mal 3:16 who feared the LORD talked with e other, H408
Mt 6:34 E day has enough trouble of its own. G3836
Mt 16:27 he will reward e person according to what G1667
Mt 18:35 Father will treat e of you unless you G1667
Mt 20: 9 afternoon came and e received a denarius. G324
Mt 20:10 But e one of them also received a denarius. G324
Mt 21:38 they said to e other, 'This is the heir. G1571
Mt 24:10 the faith and will betray and hate e other, G253
Mt 25:15 one bag, e according to his ability. G1667
Mk 1:27 all so amazed that they asked e other, G1571
Mk 4:41 They were terrified and asked e other G253
Mk 9:50 yourselves, and be at peace with e other." G253
Mk 10:26 said to e other, "Who then can be G1571
Mk 13:34 in charge, e with their assigned task G1667
Mk 15:24 they cast lots to see what e would get. G5515
Mk 16: 3 they asked e other, "Who will roll the G1571
Lk 4:36 people were amazed and said to e other, G253
Lk 4:40 laying his hands on e one, he healed G1667
Lk 6:44 E tree is recognized by its own fruit G1667
Lk 7:32 the marketplace and calling out to e other: G253
Lk 9:14 them sit down in groups of about fifty e." G324
Lk 11: 3 Give us e day our daily bread. G2848
Lk 12:52 be five in one family divided against e other, AIT
Lk 13:15 Doesn't e of you on the Sabbath untie G1667
Lk 16: 5 "So he called in e one of his master's G1667
Lk 21:37 E day Jesus was teaching at the temple G3836
Lk 21:37 e evening he went out to spend the G3836
Lk 24:14 were talking with e other about everything G253
Lk 24:15 discussed these things with e other, NDT
Lk 24:32 They asked e other, "Were not our hearts G253
Jn 2: 6 e holding from twenty to thirty gallons. G324
Jn 2:25 he knew what was in e person. G3836
Jn 4:33 Then his disciples said to e other, "Could G253
Jn 6: 7 enough bread for e one to have a bite!" G1667
Jn 15:12 Love e other as I have loved you. G253
Jn 15:17 This is my command: Love e other. G253
Jn 16:32 will be scattered, e to your own home. G1667
Jn 19:18 one on e side and Jesus in G1949+2779+1949
Jn 19:23 four shares, one for e of them, with the G1667
Ac 2: 3 and came to rest on e of them. G1651+1667
Ac 2: 6 because e one heard their own language G1667
Ac 2: 8 Then how is it that e of us hears them in G1667
Ac 3:26 bless you by turning e of you from your G1667
Ac 7:26 brothers; why do you want to hurt e other? G253
Ac 11:29 The disciples, as e one was able, decided G1667
Ac 12: 4 guarded by four squads of four soldiers e. G5482
Ac 14:23 elders for them in e church and, G2848
Ac 20:31 stopped warning e of you night and day G1667
Ac 21: 6 After saying goodbye to e other, we went G253
Ac 21:26 would be made for e of them. G1651+1667
Ac 28: 4 they said to e other, "This man must G253
Ro 1:12 encouraged by e other's faith. G1877+253
Ro 2: 6 God "will repay e person according to G1667
Ro 12: 3 the faith God has distributed to e of you. G1667
Ro 12: 4 For just as e of us has one body with many AIT
Ro 12: 5 and e member belongs to G3836+2848+1651
Ro 12: 6 according to the grace given to e of us. AIT
Ro 14: 5 E of them should be fully convinced in G1667
Ro 14:12 e of us will give an account of ourselves G1667
Ro 15: 2 E of us should please our neighbors for G1667
Ro 15: 5 of mind toward e other that Christ Jesus G253
1Co 3: 5 as the Lord has assigned to e his task. G1667
1Co 3: 8 they will e be rewarded according to G1667
1Co 3:10 But e one should build with care G1667
1Co 3:13 fire will test the quality of e person's work. G1667
1Co 4: 5 At that time e will receive their praise G1667
1Co 7: 2 e man should have sexual relations with G1667
1Co 7: 2 and e woman with her own husband. G1667
1Co 7: 5 Do not deprive e other except perhaps by G253
1Co 7: 7 But e of you has your own gift from God G1667
1Co 7:17 e person should live as a believer in G1667
1Co 7:20 E person should remain in the situation G1667
1Co 7:24 sisters, e person, as responsible to G1667
1Co 12: 7 Now to e one the manifestation of the G1667
1Co 12:11 he distributes them to e one, just as G1667
1Co 12:25 should have equal concern for e other. G253
1Co 12:27 of Christ, and e one of you is a part of it. G3517S
1Co 14:26 you come together, e of you has a hymn G1667
1Co 15:23 But e in turn: Christ, the firstfruits; then G1667
1Co 15:38 and to e kind of seed he gives its own G1667
1Co 16: 2 e one of you should set aside a sum of G1667
2Co 5:10 so that e of us may receive what is due us G1667
2Co 9: 7 E of you should give what you have G1667
Gal 5:15 If you bite and devour e other, watch out G253
Gal 5:15 out or you will be destroyed by e other. G253
Gal 5:17 They are in conflict with e other, so that G253
Gal 5:26 conceited, provoking and envying e other. G253
Gal 6: 2 Carry e other's burdens, and in this way you G253
Gal 6: 4 E one should test their own actions. G1667
Gal 6: 5 for e one should carry their own load. G1667
Eph 4: 7 But to e one of us grace has been given G1667
Eph 4:16 up in love, as e part does its work. G1651+1667
Eph 4:25 Therefore e of you must put off falsehood G1667
Eph 4:32 another, forgiving e other, just as in Christ G1571
Eph 5:33 e one of you also must love his wife as he G1667
Eph 6: 8 Lord will reward e one for whatever good G1667
Php 2: 4 your own interests but e of you to the G1667
Col 3: 9 Do not lie to e other, since you have taken G253
Col 3:13 Bear with e other and forgive one another if G253
1Th 2:11 we dealt with e of you as a father G1651+1667
1Th 3:12 overflow for e other and for everyone G253
1Th 4: 4 that e of you should learn to control your G1667
1Th 4: 9 have been taught by God to love e other. G253
1Th 5:11 one another and build e other up, G1651
1Th 5:13 Live in peace with e other. G1571
1Th 5:15 what is good for e other and for everyone G253
Heb 6:11 We want e of you to show this same G1667
Heb 11:21 was dying, blessed e of Joseph's sons G1667
Jas 1:14 but e person is tempted when they are G1667
Jas 5:16 confess your sins to e other and pray for G253
Jas 5:16 other and pray for e other so that you may G253
1Pe 1:17 who judges e person's work impartially, G1667
1Pe 1:22 so that you have sincere love for e other, G5789
1Pe 4: 8 Above all, love e other deeply, because G1571
1Pe 4:10 E of you should use whatever gift you have G1667
1Jn 3:14 from death to life, because we love e other. G81
Rev 2:23 I will repay e of you according to your G1667
Rev 4: 8 E of the four living creatures G1651+2848+1651
Rev 5: 8 E one had a harp and they were holding G1667
Rev 6: 4 the earth and to make people kill e other. G253
Rev 6:11 Then e of them was given a white robe G1667
Rev 11:10 will celebrate by sending e other gifts, G253
Rev 13: 1 on e head a blasphemous name. G899
Rev 16:21 e weighing about a hundred pounds NDT
Rev 20:13 and e person was judged according to G1667
Rev 21:21 e gate made of a single pearl G324+1651+1667
Rev 22: 2 On e side of the river stood G1949+2779+1696
Rev 22:12 I will give to e person according to G1667

EAGER (19) [EAGERLY, EAGERNESS]

2Ch 26:20 Indeed, he himself was e to leave H1894
Pr 28:20 but one e to get rich will not go H237
Pr 28:22 The stingy are e to get rich and are H987
Pr 31:13 wool and flax and works with e hands. H2914
Isa 58: 2 me out; they seem e to know my ways H2911
Isa 58: 2 decisions and seem e for God to come H2911
Zep 3: 7 But they were still e to act corruptly in all H8899
Ro 1:15 That is why I am so e to preach the gospel G4609
Ro 8:19 creation waits in e expectation for the G638
1Co 14:12 Since you are e for gifts of the Spirit, try to G2421
1Co 14:39 sisters, be e to prophesy, and do G2420
2Co 8:11 so that your e willingness to do it may be G4608
Gal 2:10 very thing I had been e to do all along. G5079
Php 2:28 Therefore I am all the more e to send him G5081
1Ti 6:10 Some people, e for money, have G3977
Titus 2:14 are his very own, e to do what is good. G2421
1Pe 3:13 to harm you if you are e to do good? G2421
1Pe 5: 2 pursuing dishonest gain, but e to serve; G4610
Jude 3 although I was very e to write to you G5082

EAGERLY (10) [EAGER]

2Ch 15:15 They sought God e, and he H928+3972+8356
Ps 78:34 seek him; they e turned to him again. H8838
Lk 22:15 "I have e desired to eat this G2123+2121
Ro 8:23 groan inwardly as we wait e for our G587
1Co 1: 7 spiritual gift as you e wait for our Lord G587
1Co 12:31 Now e desire the greater gifts. And yet I G2420
1Co 14: 1 the way of love and e desire gifts of the G2420
Gal 5: 5 through the Spirit we e await by faith the G587
Php 1:20 I e expect and hope that I will in no way be G638
Php 3:20 And we e await a Savior from there, the G587

EAGERNESS (4) [EAGER]

Ac 17:11 message with great e and examined the G4608
2Co 7:11 what e to clear yourselves, what G665
2Co 8:19 Lord himself and to show our e to help. G4608
2Co 9: 2 For I know your e to help, and I have been G4608

EAGLE (21) [EAGLE'S, EAGLES, EAGLES']

Lev 11:13 they are unclean: the e, the vulture, the H5979
Dt 14:12 you may not eat: the e, the vulture, the H5979
Dt 28:49 of the earth, like an e swooping down, H5979
Dt 32:11 like an e that stirs up its nest and hovers H5979
Job 39:27 Does the e soar at your command and H5979
Pr 23: 5 wings and fly off to the sky like an e. H5979
Pr 30:19 the way of an e in the sky, the way of a H5979
Jer 48:40 An e is swooping down, spreading its H5979
Jer 49:22 An e will soar and swoop down H5979
Eze 1:10 of an ox; each also had the face of an e. H5979
Eze 10:14 of a lion, and the fourth the face of an e. H5979
Eze 17: 3 A great e with powerful wings, long H5979
Eze 17: 7 was another great e with powerful wings H5979
Da 4:33 the feathers of an e and his nails like A10495
Da 7: 4 like a lion, and it had the wings of an e. A10495
Hos 8: 1 An e is over the house of the LORD H5979
Ob 4 you soar like the e and make your nest H5979
Hab 1: 8 They fly like an e swooping to devour; H5979
Rev 4: 7 like a man, the fourth was like a flying e. G108
Rev 8:13 I heard an e that was flying in midair call G108
Rev 12:14 was given the two wings of a great e, G108

EAGLE'S (2) [EAGLE]

Ps 103: 5 so that your youth is renewed like the e. H5979
Jer 49:16 you build your nest as high as the e, H5979

EAGLES (5) [EAGLE]

2Sa 1:23 They were swifter than e, they were H5979
Job 9:26 like e swooping down on their prey. H5979
Isa 40:31 They will soar on wings like e; they will H5979
Jer 4:13 a whirlwind, his horses are swifter than e. H5979
La 4:19 pursuers were swifter than e in the sky; H5979

EAGLES' (1) [EAGLE]

Ex 19: 4 how I carried you on e wings and brought H5979

EAR (48) [EARLOBE, EARS]

Ex 21: 6 the doorpost and pierce his e with an awl. H265
Lev 8:23 put it on the lobe of Aaron's right e, H265
Lev 14:14 the lobe of the right e of the one to be H265
Lev 14:17 the lobe of the right e of the one to be H265
Lev 14:25 the lobe of the right e of the one to be H265
Lev 14:28 the lobe of the right e of the one to be H265
Dt 1:45 weeping and turned a deaf e to you. H4202+263
2Ki 19:16 Give e, LORD, and hear; open your H5742+265
Ne 1: 6 let your e be attentive and your eyes open H265
Ne 1:11 let your e be attentive to the prayer of this H265
Job 12:11 Does not the e test words as the tongue H265
Job 34: 3 For the e tests words as the tongue tastes H265
Ps 17: 6 turn your e to me and hear my prayer. H265
Ps 28: 1 are my Rock, do not turn a deaf e to me. H3087
Ps 31: 2 Turn your e to me, come quickly to my H265
Ps 49: 4 I will turn my e to a proverb; with the harp I H265
Ps 71: 2 deliver me; turn your e to me and save me. H265
Ps 83: 1 do not turn a deaf e, do not stand H3087
Ps 88: 2 come before you; turn your e to my cry. H265
Ps 94: 9 Does he who fashioned the e not hear H265
Ps 102: 2 Turn your e to me; when I call, answer me H265
Ps 116: 2 Because he turned his e to me, I will call H265
Pr 2: 2 turning your e to wisdom and applying your H265
Pr 4:20 to what I say; turn your e to my words. H265
Pr 5: 1 wisdom, turn your e to my words of insight H265
Pr 5:13 my teachers or turn my e to my instructions. H265

Pr 22:17 turn your **e** to the sayings of the H265
Pr 25:12 the rebuke of a wise judge to a listening **e**. H265
Pr 28: 9 If anyone turns a deaf **e** to my instruction H265
Ecc 1: 8 of seeing, nor the **e** its fill of hearing. H265
Isa 37:17 **Give e**, LORD, and hear; open your H5742+265
Isa 50: 4 wakens my **e** to listen like one being H265
Isa 55: 3 **Give e** and come to me; listen, that H5742+265
Isa 59: 1 too short to save, nor his **e** too dull to hear. H265
Isa 64: 4 has heard, no **e** *has* **perceived**, no eye has H263
Da 9:18 **Give e**, our God, and hear; open H5742+265
Am 3:12 only two leg bones or a piece of an **e**, H265
Mt 10:27 what is whispered in your **e**, proclaim *G4044*
Mt 26:51 servant of the high priest, cutting off his **e**. *G6065*
Mk 14:47 servant of the high priest, cutting off his **e**. *G6064*
Lk 12: 3 whispered in the **e** in the inner rooms *G4044*
Lk 22:50 of the high priest, cutting off his right **e**. *G4044*
Lk 22:51 he touched the man's **e** and healed him. *G6065*
Jn 18:10 priest's servant, cutting off his right **e**. *G6064*
Jn 18:26 of the man whose **e** Peter had cut off, *G6065*
1Co 2: 9 has seen, what no **e** has heard, and what *G4044*
1Co 12:16 And if the **e** should say, "Because I am not *G4044*
1Co 12:17 If the whole body were an **e**, where would *G198*

EARED, EARING (KJV) PLOWED, PLOWING

EARLIER (17) [EARLY]
Ge 13: 3 Ai where his tent had been **e** H928+2021+9378
Ru 3:10 is greater than that which you showed **e**: H8037
Ru 4: 7 Now in **e times** in Israel, for the H7156
1Ki 11:15 **E** when David was fighting with Edom H2118
1Ch 9:20 **In e times** Phinehas son of Eleazar H4200+7156
Ne 5:15 But the **e** governors—those preceding me H8037
Da 7:24 different from the **e** *ones*; he will subdue A10623
Da 9:21 I had seen in the **e** vision, H928+2021+9378
Zec 1: 4 to whom the **e** prophets proclaimed: H8037
Zec 7: 7 proclaimed through the **e** prophets when H8037
Zec 7:12 sent by his Spirit through the **e** prophets. H8037
Jn 7:50 had gone to Jesus **e** and who was one of *G4728*
Jn 19:39 the man who **e** had visited Jesus at *G3836+4754*
2Co 8: 6 just as *he had* **e made a beginning**, to *G4599*
2Co 12:21 many who *have* **sinned e** and have not *G4579*
2Co 13: 2 spare those *who* **sinned e** or any of the *G4579*
Heb 10:32 Remember those **e** days after you had *G4728*

EARLIEST (1) [EARLY]
Ac 15:21 in every city from the **e** times and is read in *G792*

EARLOBE (1) [EAR]
Dt 15:17 awl and push it through his **e** into the door, H265

EARLY (68) [EARLIER, EARLIEST]
Ge 19: 2 then go on your way **e in the morning**." H8899
Ge 19:27 **E** the next morning Abraham **got up** and H8899
Ge 20: 8 **E** the next morning Abimelek summoned H8899
Ge 21:14 **E** the next morning Abraham took some H8899
Ge 22: 3 **E** the next morning Abraham **got up** and H8899
Ge 26:31 **E** the next morning the men swore an oath H8899
Ge 28:18 **E** the next morning Jacob took the stone H8899
Ge 31:55 **E** the next morning Laban kissed his H8899
Ex 2:18 "Why have you returned *so* **e** today?" H4554
Ex 8:20 "**Get up e** in the morning and confront H8899
Ex 9:13 said to Moses, "**Get up e** in the morning H8899
Ex 24: 4 *He* **got up e** the next morning and built H8899
Ex 32: 6 next day the people **rose e** and sacrificed H8899
Ex 34: 4 went up Mount Sinai **e** in the morning, H8899
Nu 14:40 **E** the next morning they set out for the H8899
Jos 3: 1 **E** in the morning Joshua and all the H8899
Jos 6:12 Joshua **got up e** the next morning and the H8899
Jos 7:16 **E** the next morning Joshua had Israel H8899
Jos 8:10 **E** the next morning Joshua mustered his H8899
Jos 8:14 hurried out **e in the morning** to meet H8899
Jdg 6:38 Gideon **rose e** the next day; he squeezed H8899
Jdg 7: 1 **E in the morning**, Jerub-Baal (that is H8899
Jdg 19: 5 the fourth day *they* **got up e** and he H8899
Jdg 19: 9 **E** tomorrow **morning** *you can* **get up** and H8899
Jdg 21: 4 **E** the next day the people built an altar H8899
1Sa 1:19 **E** the next morning *they* **arose** and H8899
1Sa 5: 3 the people of Ashdod **rose e** the next day, H8899
1Sa 15:12 **E** in the morning Samuel **got up** and went H8899
1Sa 17:20 **E** in the morning David left the flock in H8899
1Sa 29:10 Now **get up e**, along with your master's H8899
1Sa 29:11 his men **got up e** in the morning H8899
2Sa 15: 2 He *would* **get up e** and stand by the side H8899
2Ki 3:22 When *they* **got up e** in the morning, the H8899
2Ki 6:15 got up and went out **e the next morning**, H8899
2Ch 20:20 **E** in the morning they left for the Desert of H8899
2Ch 29:20 **E the next morning** King Hezekiah H8899
Job 1: 5 **E** in the morning he would sacrifice a H8899
Ps 127: 2 In vain you rise **e** and stay up late, toiling H8899
Pr 27:14 blesses their neighbor **e** in the morning, H8899
SS 2:13 The fig tree forms its **e fruit**; the H7001
SS 7:12 *Let us* **go e** to the vineyards to see if the H8899
Isa 5:11 Woe to *those who* **rise e** in the morning H8899
Jer 24: 2 like those that **ripen e**; the other basket H1136
Jer 26: 1 **E** *in* the reign of Jehoiakim son of H928+8040
Jer 27: 1 **E** *in* the reign of Zedekiah son of H928+8040
Jer 28: 1 **e** *in* the reign of Zedekiah king of H928+8040
Jer 28: 8 From **e times** the prophets who preceded H6409
Jer 49:34 **e** in the reign of Zedekiah king of Judah: H8040
Hos 6: 4 like the **e** dew that disappears. H8899
Hos 9:10 was like seeing the **e fruit** on the fig tree. H1136
Hos 13: 3 like the **e** dew that disappears H8899
Mic 7: 1 none of the **e figs** that I crave. H1136
Mt 20: 1 went out **e in the morning** to hire *G275+4745*
Mt 21:18 **E in the morning**, as Jesus was on his way *G4745*
Mt 27: 1 **E in the morning**, all the chief priests and *G4746*
Mk 1:35 Very **e in the morning**, while it was still *G4745*
Mk 15: 1 **Very e in the morning**, the chief *G2317+4745*
Mk 16: 2 Very **e** on the first day of the week, just *G4745*
Mk 16: 9 When Jesus rose **e** on the first day of the *G4745*
Lk 21:38 the people **came e in the morning** to hear *G3983*
Lk 24: 1 **very e in the morning**, the women *G3986*
Lk 24:22 They went to the tomb **e** *this* **morning** *G3984*
Jn 10:40 had been baptizing **in the e days**. *G3836+4754*
Jn 18:28 By now it was **e morning**, and to avoid *G4745*
Jn 20: 1 **E** on the first day of the week, while it was *G4745*
Jn 21: 4 **E in the morning**, Jesus stood on the *G4746*
Ac 21:16 from Cyprus and one of the **e** disciples. *G792*
Php 4:15 in the **e days** of your acquaintance with the *G794*

EARN (5) [EARNED, EARNERS, EARNINGS, EARNS]
Dt 23:19 food or anything else that *may* **e interest**. H5967
Am 7:12 **E** your bread there and do your H430
Hag 1: 6 You **e wages**, only to put them in a H8509+8509
2Th 3:12 to settle down and **e** the food they eat. *G2237*
Rev 18:17 all *who* **e** *their* **living** from the sea *G2237*

EARNED (3) [EARN]
Lk 19:16 said, 'Sir, your mina *has* **e** ten **more**. *G4664*
Lk 19:18 said, 'Sir, your mina *has* **e** five **more**. *G4472*
Ac 16:16 She **e** a great deal of money for her *G4218*

EARNERS (1) [EARN]
Isa 19:10 all the wage **e** will be sick at heart. H6913

EARNEST (1) [EARNESTNESS, EARNESTLY]
Rev 3:19 discipline. So *be* **e** and repent. *G2418*

EARNESTLY (14) [EARNEST]
1Sa 20: 6 'David **e asked** my **permission** to H8626+8626
1Sa 20:28 **e asked** me **for permission** to go H8626+8626
Job 8: 5 But if you *will* **seek** God **e** and plead with H8838
Ps 63: 1 are my God, **e** *I* **seek** you; I thirst for H8838
Hos 5:15 in their misery *they will* **e seek** me." H8838
Mk 5:23 He pleaded **e** with him, "My little *G4498*
Lk 7: 4 they pleaded **e** with him, "This man *G5081*
Lk 22:44 anguish, he prayed **more e**, and his sweat *G1757*
Ac 12: 5 the church was **e** praying to God for *G1757*
Ac 26: 7 as they **e** serve God day and *G1877+1755*
Ro 11: 7 people of Israel **sought so e** they did not *G2118*
1Th 3:10 day we pray **most e** that we may see *G5655*
Heb 11: 6 that he rewards those *who* **e seek** him. *G1699*
Jas 5:17 *He* **prayed e** that it would not rain *G4666+4667*

EARNESTNESS (4) [EARNEST]
Dt 18: 6 and comes in all **e** to the place the H205+5883
2Co 7:11 what **e**, what eagerness to clear *G5082*
2Co 8: 7 *in* complete **e** and in the love we have *G5082*
2Co 8: 8 love by comparing it with the **e** of others. *G5082*

EARNINGS (4) [EARN]
Dt 23:18 must not bring the **e** *of* a female prostitute H924
Pr 10:16 the **e** *of* the wicked are sin and death. H9311
Pr 31:16 out of her **e** she plants a vineyard. H7262+4090
Isa 23:18 Yet her profit and her **e** will be set apart H924

EARNS (1) [EARN]
Pr 11:18 A wicked person **e** deceptive wages, but H6913

EARRING (2) [EARRINGS]
Jdg 8:24 of you give me an **e** *from* your share of H5690
Pr 25:12 Like an **e** *of* gold or an ornament of fine H5690

EARRINGS (9) [EARRING]
Ex 32: 2 "Take off the gold **e** that your wives, your H5690
Ex 32: 3 took off their **e** and brought them to H5690
Ex 35:22 brooches, **e**, rings and ornaments H5690
Nu 31:50 signet rings, **e** and necklaces—to make H6316
Jdg 8:24 custom of the Ishmaelites to wear gold **e**.) H5690
SS 1:10 Your cheeks are beautiful with **e**, your H9366
SS 1:11 We will make you **e** *of* gold, studded with H9366
Isa 3:19 the **e** and bracelets and veils, H5755
Eze 16:12 **e** on your ears and a beautiful crown on H6316

EARS (91) [EAR]
Ge 35: 4 gods they had and the rings in their **e**, H265
Ex 29:20 lobes of the right **e** *of* Aaron and his sons, H265
Lev 8:24 of the blood on the lobes of their right **e**, H265
Dt 29: 4 understands or eyes that see or **e** that hear. H265
1Sa 3:11 that will make the **e** *of* everyone who hears H265
1Sa 15:14 then is this bleating of sheep in my **e**? H265
2Sa 7:22 as we have heard with our own **e**. H265
2Sa 22: 7 he heard my voice; my cry came to his **e**. H265
2Ki 19:28 because your insolence has reached my **e**, H265
2Ki 21:12 Judah that the **e** *of* everyone who H265
1Ch 17:20 as we have heard with our own **e**. H265
2Ch 6:40 eyes be open and your **e** attentive to the H265
2Ch 7:15 will be open and my **e** attentive to the H265
Job 4:12 brought to me, my **e** caught a whisper of it. H265
Job 13: 1 my **e** have heard and understood it. H265
Job 13:17 to what I say; let my words ring in your **e**. H265
Job 15:21 Terrifying sounds fill his **e**; when all seems H265
Job 28:22 "Only a rumor of it has reached our **e**." H265
Job 29:22 no more; my words fell gently on their **e**. NDT
Job 33:16 may speak in their **e** and terrify them with H265
Job 42: 5 My **e** had heard of you but now my eyes H265
Ps 18: 6 my cry came before him, into his **e**. H265
Ps 34:15 his **e** are attentive to their cry H265
Ps 40: 6 not desire—but my **e** you have opened H265
Ps 44: 1 We have heard it with our **e**, O God; our H265
Ps 58: 4 like that of a cobra that has stopped its **e**, H265
Ps 92:11 my **e** have heard the rout of my wicked foes H265
Ps 115: 6 They have **e**, but cannot hear, noses, but H265
Ps 130: 2 Let your **e** be attentive to my cry for mercy. H265
Ps 135:17 They have **e**, but cannot hear, nor is there H265
Pr 18:15 the **e** *of* the wise seek it out. H265
Pr 20:12 **E** that hear and eyes that see—the LORD H265
Pr 21:13 Whoever shuts their **e** to the cry of the poor H265
Pr 23:12 instruction and your **e** to words of H265
Pr 26:17 a stray dog by the **e** is someone who H265
Isa 6:10 make their **e** dull and close their eyes. H265
Isa 6:10 hear with their **e**, understand with H265
Isa 11: 3 decide by what he hears with his **e**; H265
Isa 30:21 your **e** will hear a voice behind you H265
Isa 32: 3 the **e** *of* those who hear will listen. H265
Isa 33:15 who stop their **e** against plots of murder H265
Isa 35: 5 be opened and the **e** *of* the deaf H265
Isa 37:29 because your insolence has reached my **e**, H265
Isa 42:20 no attention; your **e** are open, but you do H265
Isa 43: 8 are blind, who have **e** but are deaf. H265
Isa 48: 8 from of old your **e** have not been open. H265
Isa 50: 5 The Sovereign LORD has opened my **e**; H265
Jer 5:21 do not see, who have **e** but do not hear: H265
Jer 6:10 Their **e** are closed so they cannot hear H265
Jer 9:20 open your **e** to the words of his mouth. H265
Jer 19: 3 that will make the **e** *of* everyone who hears H265
Jer 26:11 You have heard it with your own **e**!" H265
La 3:56 "Do not close your **e** to my cry for relief." H265
Eze 8:18 Although they shout in my **e**, I will not H265
Eze 12: 2 do not see and **e** to hear but do not H265
Eze 16:12 earrings on your **e** and a beautiful crown H265
Eze 23:25 They will cut off your noses and your **e**, and H265
Mic 7:16 their mouths and their **e** will become deaf. H265
Zec 7:11 they turned their backs and covered their **e**. H265
Mt 11:15 Whoever has **e**, let them hear. *G4044*
Mt 13: 9 Whoever has **e**, let them hear. *G4044*
Mt 13:15 they hardly hear *with* their **e**, and they *G4044*
Mt 13:15 their eyes, hear *with* their **e**, understand *G4044*
Mt 13:16 they see, and your **e** because they hear. *G4044*
Mt 13:43 Whoever has **e**, let them hear. *G4044*
Mk 4: 9 "Whoever has **e** to hear, let them *G4044*
Mk 4:23 If anyone has **e** to hear, let them hear." *G4044*
Mk 7:33 Jesus put his fingers into the man's **e**. *G4044*
Mk 7:35 the man's **e** were opened, his *G198*
Mk 8:18 fail to see, and **e** but fail to hear? *G4044*
Lk 1:44 the sound of your greeting reached my **e**, *G4044*
Lk 8: 8 "Whoever has **e** to hear, let them *G4044*
Lk 14:35 "Whoever has **e** to hear, let them *G4044*
Ac 7:51 Your hearts and **e** are still uncircumcised *G4044*
Ac 7:57 At this they covered their **e** and, yelling at *G4044*
Ac 17:20 are bringing some strange ideas to our **e**, *G198*
Ac 28:27 they hardly hear *with* their **e**, and they *G4044*
Ac 28:27 their eyes, hear *with* their **e**, understand *G4044*
Ro 11: 8 could not see and **e** that could not hear, *G4044*
2Ti 4: 3 *to* **say what** their **itching e want to hear** *G3117+198*
2Ti 4: 4 They will turn their **e** away from the truth *G198*
Jas 5: 4 have reached the **e** of the Lord Almighty. *G4044*
1Pe 3:12 the righteous and his **e** are attentive to *G4044*
Rev 2: 7 Whoever has **e**, let them hear what the *G4044*
Rev 2:11 Whoever has **e**, let them hear what the *G4044*
Rev 2:17 Whoever has **e**, let them hear what the *G4044*
Rev 2:29 Whoever has **e**, let them hear what the *G4044*
Rev 3: 6 Whoever has **e**, let them hear what the *G4044*
Rev 3:13 Whoever has **e**, let them hear what the *G4044*
Rev 3:22 Whoever has **e**, let them hear what the *G4044*
Rev 13: 9 Whoever has **e**, let them hear. *G4044*

EARTH (733) [EARTH'S, EARTHEN, EARTHLY]
Ge 1: 1 God created the heavens and the **e**. H824
Ge 1: 2 Now the **e** was formless and empty H824
Ge 1:15 in the vault of the sky to give light on the **e**." H824
Ge 1:17 in the vault of the sky to give light on the **e**, H824
Ge 1:20 birds fly above the **e** across the vault of the H824
Ge 1:22 and let the birds increase on the **e**." H824
Ge 1:28 in number; fill the **e** and subdue it. H824
Ge 1:29 the face of the whole **e** and every tree that H824
Ge 1:30 all the beasts of the **e** and all the birds in H824
Ge 2: 1 the heavens and the **e** were completed in H824
Ge 2: 4 the heavens and the **e** when they were H824
Ge 2: 4 the LORD God made the **e** and the heavens. H824
Ge 2: 5 appeared on the **e** and no plant had H824
Ge 2: 5 sent rain on the **e** and there was no one H824
Ge 2: 6 came up from the **e** and watered the whole H824
Ge 4:12 You will be a restless wanderer on the **e**." H824
Ge 4:14 I will be a restless wanderer on the **e**, and H824
Ge 6: 1 in number on the **e** and daughters were H141
Ge 6: 4 Nephilim were on the **e** in those days— H824
Ge 6: 5 of the human race had become on the **e**, H824
Ge 6: 6 that he had made human beings on the **e**, H824
Ge 6: 7 from the face of the **e** the human race I H141
Ge 6:11 Now the **e** was corrupt in God's sight and H824
Ge 6:12 God saw how corrupt the **e** had become, for H824
Ge 6:12 all the people on **e** had corrupted their H824
Ge 6:13 the **e** is filled with violence because of H824
Ge 6:13 going to destroy both them and the **e**. H824
Ge 6:17 floodwaters on the **e** to destroy all life H824
Ge 6:17 Everything on **e** will perish. H824
Ge 7: 3 their various kinds alive throughout the **e**. H824

E

Ge 7:4 I will send rain on the e for forty days and H824
Ge 7:4 from the face of the e every living creature I H141
Ge 7:6 old when the floodwaters came on the e. H824
Ge 7:10 seven days the floodwaters came on the e. H824
Ge 7:12 And rain fell on the e forty days and forty H824
Ge 7:17 forty days the flood kept coming on the e, H824
Ge 7:17 they lifted the ark high above the e. H824
Ge 7:18 waters rose and increased greatly on the e, H824
Ge 7:19 They rose greatly on the e, and all the high H824
Ge 7:21 all the creatures that swarm over the e, and H824
Ge 7:23 thing on the face of the e was wiped out; H141
Ge 7:23 the birds were wiped from the e. H824
Ge 7:24 waters flooded the e for a hundred and H824
Ge 8:1 he sent a wind over the e, and the H824
Ge 8:3 The water receded steadily from the e. H824
Ge 8:7 the water had dried up from the e. H824
Ge 8:9 was water over all the surface of the e; H824
Ge 8:11 that the water had receded from the e. H824
Ge 8:13 the water had dried up from the e. H824
Ge 8:14 second month the e was completely dry. H824
Ge 8:17 can multiply on the e and be fruitful and H824
Ge 8:22 "As long as the e endures, seedtime and H824
Ge 9:1 increase in number and fill the e. H824
Ge 9:2 of you will fall on all the beasts of the e, H824
Ge 9:7 multiply on the e and increase upon it." H824
Ge 9:10 ark with you—every living creature on e. H824
Ge 9:11 again will there be a flood to destroy the e." H824
Ge 9:13 of the covenant between me and the e. H824
Ge 9:14 bring clouds over the e and the rainbow H824
Ge 9:16 all living creatures of every kind on the e." H824
Ge 9:17 between me and all life on the e. H824
Ge 9:19 who were scattered over the whole e. H824
Ge 10:8 who became a mighty warrior on the e. H824
Ge 10:25 because in his time the e was divided; his H824
Ge 10:32 spread out over the e after the flood. H824
Ge 11:4 be scattered over the face of the whole e." H824
Ge 11:8 scattered them from there over all the e, H824
Ge 11:9 them over the face of the whole e. H824
Ge 12:3 all peoples on e will be blessed H141
Ge 13:16 make your offspring like the dust of the e, H824
Ge 14:19 God Most High, Creator of heaven and e. H824
Ge 14:22 God Most High, Creator of heaven and e, H824
Ge 18:18 all nations on e will be blessed H824
Ge 18:25 Will not the Judge of all the e do right?" H824
Ge 19:31 children—as is the custom all over the e. H824
Ge 22:18 offspring all nations on e will be blessed, H824
Ge 24:3 the God of heaven and the God of e, that H824
Ge 26:4 offspring all nations on e will be blessed, H824
Ge 26:15 stopped up, filling them with e. H6760
Ge 28:12 which he saw a stairway resting on the e, H824
Ge 28:14 descendants will be like the dust of the e, H824
Ge 28:14 All peoples on e will be blessed through H141
Ge 45:7 you a remnant on e and to save your H824
Ge 48:16 may they increase greatly on the e. H824
Ex 9:14 that there is no one like me in all the e. H824
Ex 9:15 that would have wiped you off the e. H824
Ex 9:16 my name might be proclaimed in all the e. H824
Ex 9:29 so you may know that the e is the LORD's. H824
Ex 15:12 and the e swallows your enemies. H824
Ex 19:5 Although the whole e is mine, H824
Ex 20:4 above or on the e beneath or in the H824
Ex 20:11 days the LORD made the heavens and the e, H824
Ex 20:24 " 'Make an altar of e for me and sacrifice H141
Ex 31:17 days the LORD made the heavens and the e, H824
Ex 32:12 to wipe them off the face of the e'? H141
Ex 33:16 all the other people on the face of the e?" H141
Lev 17:13 drain out the blood and cover it with e, H6760
Nu 12:3 than anyone else on the face of the e.) H141
Nu 14:21 as the glory of the LORD fills the whole e, H824
Nu 16:30 the e opens its mouth and swallows H141
Nu 16:32 the e opened its mouth and swallowed H824
Nu 16:33 they owned; the e closed over them, and H824
Nu 16:34 "The e is going to swallow us too! H824
Nu 26:10 The e opened its mouth and swallowed H824
Dt 3:24 in heaven or on e who can do the deeds H824
Dt 4:17 like any animal on e or any bird that flies H824
Dt 4:26 the heavens and the e as witnesses H824
Dt 4:32 day God created human beings on the e; H824
Dt 4:36 On e he showed you his great fire, and you H824
Dt 4:39 God in heaven above and on the e below. H824
Dt 5:8 above or on the e beneath or in the H824
Dt 7:6 on the face of the e to be his people, H141
Dt 10:14 highest heavens, the e and everything in it. H824
Dt 11:6 when the e opened its mouth right in the H824
Dt 11:21 the days that the heavens are above the e. H824
Dt 14:2 Out of all the peoples on the face of the e H141
Dt 28:1 set you high above all the nations on e. H824
Dt 28:10 all the peoples on e will see that you are H824
Dt 28:25 a thing of horror to all the kingdoms on e. H824
Dt 28:49 from the ends of the e, like an eagle H824
Dt 28:64 nations, from one end of the e to the other. H824
Dt 30:19 the heavens and the e as witnesses H824
Dt 31:28 the heavens and the e to testify against H824
Dt 32:1 will speak; hear, you e, the words of my H824
Dt 32:22 It will devour the e and its harvests and set H824
Dt 33:16 the best gifts of the e and its fullness and H824
Dt 33:17 nations, even those at the ends of the e. H824
Jos 2:11 God in heaven above and on the e below. H824
Jos 3:11 of the Lord of all the e will go into the H824
Jos 3:13 the Lord of all the e—set foot in the Jordan, H824
Jos 4:24 the peoples of the e might know that the H824
Jos 7:9 us and wipe out our name from the e. H824
Jos 23:14 "Now I am about to go the way of all the e H824
Jdg 5:4 land of Edom, the e shook, the heavens H824
1Sa 2:8 "For the foundations of the e are the LORD's H824
1Sa 2:10 the LORD will judge the ends of the e. H824
1Sa 20:15 of David's enemies from the face of the e." H141
1Sa 20:31 As long as the son of Jesse lives on this e H141
1Sa 28:13 a ghostly figure coming up out of the e." H824
2Sa 4:11 blood from your hand and rid the e of you!" H824
2Sa 7:9 like the names of the greatest men on e. H824
2Sa 7:23 the one nation on e that God went out to H824
2Sa 14:7 name nor descendant on the face of the e." H141
2Sa 22:8 The e trembled and quaked, the H824
2Sa 22:16 the foundations of the e laid bare at the H9315
2Sa 22:43 I beat them as fine as the dust of the e; H824
2Sa 23:4 after rain that brings grass from the e. H824
1Ki 2:2 "I am about to go the way of all the e," H824
1Ki 8:23 like you in heaven above or on e below— H824
1Ki 8:27 "But will God really dwell on e? The H824
1Ki 8:43 the peoples of the e may know your name H824
1Ki 8:60 the peoples of the e may know that the H824
1Ki 10:23 wisdom than all the other kings of the e. H824
1Ki 13:34 to its destruction from the face of the e. H141
2Ki 5:17 be given as much e as a pair of mules can H141
2Ki 19:15 are God over all the kingdoms of the e. H824
2Ki 19:15 You have made heaven and e. H824
2Ki 19:19 the kingdoms of the e may know that you H824
1Ch 1:10 who became a mighty warrior on e. H824
1Ch 1:19 because in his time the e was divided; his H824
1Ch 16:14 our God; his judgments are in all the e. H824
1Ch 16:23 to the LORD, all the e; proclaim his salvation H824
1Ch 16:30 before him, all the e! The world is firmly H824
1Ch 16:31 let the e be glad; let them say H824
1Ch 16:33 the LORD, for he comes to judge the e. H824
1Ch 17:8 like the names of the greatest men on e. H824
1Ch 17:21 the one nation on e whose God went out to H824
1Ch 21:16 the LORD standing between heaven and e, H824
1Ch 22:8 shed much blood on the e in my sight. H824
1Ch 29:11 everything in heaven and e is yours. H824
1Ch 29:15 Our days on e are like a shadow, without H824
2Ch 1:9 who are as numerous as the dust of the e. H824
2Ch 2:12 the God of Israel, who made heaven and e! H824
2Ch 6:14 is no God like you in heaven or on e— H824
2Ch 6:18 will God really dwell on e with humans? H824
2Ch 6:33 the peoples of the e may know your name H824
2Ch 9:22 wisdom than all the other kings of the e. H824
2Ch 9:23 All the kings of the e sought audience with H824
2Ch 16:9 range throughout the e to strengthen those H824
2Ch 36:23 the kingdoms of the e and he has H824
Ezr 1:2 the kingdoms of the e and he has H824
Ezr 5:11 the servants of the God of heaven and e, A10075
Ne 9:6 their starry host, the e and all that is on it H824
Job 1:7 "From roaming throughout the e, going H824
Job 1:8 There is no one on e like him; he is H824
Job 2:2 "From roaming throughout the e, going H824
Job 2:3 There is no one on e like him; he is H824
Job 3:14 with kings and rulers of the e, who built H824
Job 5:10 He provides rain for the e; he sends water H824
Job 5:25 your descendants like the grass of the e. H824
Job 7:1 "Do not mortals have hard service on e H824
Job 8:9 our days on e are but a shadow. H824
Job 9:6 He shakes the e from its place and makes H824
Job 11:9 is longer than the e and wider than the sea H824
Job 12:8 speak to the e, and it will teach you, or H824
Job 12:24 the leaders of the e of their reason; H824
Job 16:18 "E, do not cover my blood; may my cry H824
Job 18:4 is the e to be abandoned for your sake? H824
Job 18:17 The memory of him perishes from the e; he H824
Job 19:25 that in the end he will stand on the e. H6760
Job 20:4 ever since mankind was placed on the e, H824
Job 20:27 his guilt; the e will rise up against him. H824
Job 26:7 he suspends the e over nothing. H824
Job 28:2 Iron is taken from the e, and copper is H6760
Job 28:5 The e, from which food comes, is H824
Job 28:24 the ends of the e and sees everything H824
Job 34:13 Who appointed him over the e? Who put H824
Job 35:11 the beasts of the e and makes us wiser H824
Job 37:3 heaven and sends it to the ends of the e. H824
Job 37:6 the snow, 'Fall on the e,' and to the rain H824
Job 37:12 face of the **whole** e to do whatever H9315+824
Job 37:13 to water his e and show his love. H824
Job 38:13 it might take the e by the edges and shake H824
Job 38:14 The e takes shape like clay under a seal; its NDT
Job 38:18 comprehended the vast expanses of the e? H824
Job 38:24 the east winds are scattered over the e? H824
Job 38:33 Can you set up God's dominion over the e H824
Job 38:38 hard and the **clods of e** stick together? H8073
Job 41:33 Nothing on e is its equal—a creature H6760
Ps 2:2 The kings of the e rise up and the rulers H824
Ps 2:8 the ends of the e your possession. H824
Ps 2:10 be wise; be warned, you rulers of the e. H824
Ps 8:1 how majestic is your name in all the e! H824
Ps 8:9 how majestic is your name in all the e! H824
Ps 11:4 He observes **everyone on e**; his eyes H1201+132
Ps 18:7 The e trembled and quaked, and the H824
Ps 18:15 the foundations of the e laid bare at your H9315
Ps 19:4 Yet their voice goes out into all the e, their H824
Ps 21:10 will destroy their descendants from the e, H824
Ps 22:27 All the ends of the e will remember and H824
Ps 22:29 All the rich of the e will feast and worship H824
Ps 24:1 The e is the LORD's, and everything in it, the H824
Ps 33:5 the e is full of his unfailing love. H824
Ps 33:8 Let all the e fear the LORD; let all the H824
Ps 33:14 place he watches all who live on e— H824
Ps 34:16 to blot out their name from the e. H824
Ps 46:2 though the e give way and the mountains H824
Ps 46:6 he lifts his voice, the e melts. H824
Ps 46:8 the desolations he has brought on the e. H824
Ps 46:9 He makes wars cease to the ends of the e H824
Ps 46:10 the nations, I will be exalted in the e." H824
Ps 47:2 is awesome, the great King over all the e. H824
Ps 47:7 For God is the King of all the e; sing to him H824
Ps 47:9 the kings of the e belong to God; he is H824
Ps 48:2 the joy of the whole e, like the heights of H824
Ps 48:10 your praise reaches to the ends of the e H824
Ps 50:1 summons the e from the rising of the H824
Ps 50:4 and the e, that he may judge his H824
Ps 57:5 heavens; let your glory be over all the e. H824
Ps 57:11 heavens; let your glory be over all the e. H824
Ps 58:2 your hands mete out violence on the e. H824
Ps 58:11 surely there is a God who judges the e." H824
Ps 59:13 to the ends of the e that God rules over H824
Ps 61:2 From the ends of the e I call to you, I call H824
Ps 63:9 they will go down to the depths of the e. H824
Ps 65:5 of all the ends of the e and of the farthest H824
Ps 65:8 The **whole** e is filled with awe at H3782+7921
Ps 66:1 Shout for joy to God, all the e! H824
Ps 66:4 All the e bows down to you; they sing H824
Ps 67:2 so that your ways may be known on e, your H824
Ps 67:4 with equity and guide the nations of the e. H824
Ps 67:7 so that all the ends of the e will fear him. H824
Ps 68:8 the e shook, the heavens poured down rain H824
Ps 68:32 you kingdoms of the e, sing praise to the H824
Ps 69:34 Let heaven and e praise him, the seas H824
Ps 71:20 the depths of the e you will again bring H824
Ps 72:6 a mown field, like showers watering the e. H824
Ps 72:8 sea and from the River to the ends of the e. H824
Ps 72:19 may the whole e be filled with his glory. H824
Ps 73:9 their tongues take possession of the e. H824
Ps 73:25 And e has nothing I desire besides you. H824
Ps 74:12 long ago; he brings salvation on the e. H824
Ps 74:17 you who set all the boundaries of the e; H824
Ps 75:3 When the e and all its people quake, it is I H824
Ps 75:8 all the wicked of the e drink it down to its H824
Ps 76:12 of rulers; he is feared by the kings of the e. H824
Ps 77:18 up the world; the e trembled and quaked. H824
Ps 78:69 like the e that he established forever. H824
Ps 82:5 all the foundations of the e are shaken. H824
Ps 82:8 judge the e, for all the nations are H824
Ps 83:18 you alone are the Most High over all the e. H824
Ps 85:11 Faithfulness springs forth from the e, and H824
Ps 89:11 yours also the e; you founded the H824
Ps 89:27 the most exalted of the kings of the e. H824
Ps 94:2 Rise up, Judge of the e; pay back to the H824
Ps 95:4 In his hand are the depths of the e, and H824
Ps 96:1 LORD a new song; sing to the LORD, all the e. H824
Ps 96:9 his holiness; tremble before him, all the e. H824
Ps 96:11 let the e be glad; let the sea H824
Ps 96:13 he comes, he comes to judge the e. H824
Ps 97:1 LORD reigns, let the e be glad; let the H824
Ps 97:4 up the world; the e sees and trembles. H824
Ps 97:5 the LORD, before the Lord of all the e. H824
Ps 97:9 are the Most High over all the e; you are H824
Ps 98:3 all the ends of the e have seen the H824
Ps 98:4 joy to the LORD, all the e, burst into jubilant H824
Ps 98:9 the LORD, for he comes to judge the e. H824
Ps 99:1 between the cherubim, let the e shake. H824
Ps 100:1 Shout for joy to the LORD, all the e. H824
Ps 102:15 all the kings of the e will revere your glory. H824
Ps 102:19 on high, from heaven he viewed the e, H824
Ps 102:25 you laid the foundations of the e, H824
Ps 103:11 For as high as the heavens are above the e, H824
Ps 104:5 He set the e on its foundations; it can H824
Ps 104:9 never again will they cover the e. H824
Ps 104:14 cultivate—bringing forth food from the e: H824
Ps 104:24 them all; the e is full of your creatures. H824
Ps 104:32 he who looks at the e, and it trembles, who H824
Ps 104:35 vanish from the e and the wicked be no H824
Ps 105:7 our God; his judgments are in all the e. H824
Ps 106:17 The e opened up and swallowed Dathan H824
Ps 108:5 heavens; let your glory be over all the e. H824
Ps 109:15 that he may blot out their name from the e. H824
Ps 110:6 crushing the rulers of the whole e. H824
Ps 113:6 down to look on the heavens and the e? H824
Ps 114:7 Tremble, e, at the presence of the Lord, at H824
Ps 115:15 by the LORD, the Maker of heaven and e. H824
Ps 115:16 but the e he has given to mankind. H824
Ps 119:19 I am a stranger on e; do not hide your H824
Ps 119:64 The e is filled with your love, LORD; teach H824
Ps 119:87 They almost wiped me from the e, but I H824
Ps 119:90 you established the e, and it endures. H824
Ps 119:119 All the wicked of the e you discard like H824
Ps 121:2 from the LORD, the Maker of heaven and e. H824
Ps 124:8 of the LORD, the Maker of heaven and e. H824
Ps 134:3 he who is the Maker of heaven and e. H824
Ps 135:6 in the heavens and on the e, in the seas H824
Ps 135:7 makes clouds rise from the ends of the e; H824
Ps 136:6 who spread out the e upon the waters, His H824
Ps 138:4 May all the kings of the e praise you, LORD H824
Ps 139:15 was woven together in the depths of the e. H824
Ps 141:7 "As one plows and breaks up the e, so our H824
Ps 146:6 He is the Maker of heaven and e, the sea H824
Ps 147:8 he supplies the e with rain and makes H824
Ps 147:15 He sends his command to the e; his word H824
Ps 148:7 Praise the LORD from the e, you great sea H824

Ps 148:11 kings of the e and all nations, you princes H824
Ps 148:11 all nations, you princes and all rulers on e, H824
Ps 148:13 splendor is above the e and the heavens. H824
Pr 8:16 and nobles—all who rule on e. H824
Pr 8:26 its fields or any of the dust of the e. H9315
Pr 8:29 he marked out the foundations of the e. H824
Pr 11:31 If the righteous receive their due on e, how H824
Pr 17:24 a fool's eyes wander to the ends of the e. H824
Pr 25: 3 As the heavens are high and the e is deep H824
Pr 30: 4 Who has established all the ends of the e H824
Pr 30:14 the poor from the e and the needy from H824
Pr 30:21 "Under three things the e trembles, under H824
Pr 30:24 "Four things on e are small, yet they are H824
Ecc 1: 4 generations go, but the e remains forever. H824
Ecc 3:21 spirit of the animal goes down into the e?" H824
Ecc 5: 2 God is in heaven and you are on e, so let H824
Ecc 7:20 there is no one on e who is righteous, no H824
Ecc 8:14 else meaningless that occurs on e: H824
Ecc 8:16 to observe the labor that is done on e— H824
Ecc 11: 3 are full of water, they pour rain on the e. H824
SS 2:12 Flowers appear on the e; the season of H824
Isa 1: 2 Listen, e! For the LORD has H824
Isa 2:19 his majesty, when he rises to shake the e. H824
Isa 2:21 his majesty, when he rises to shake the e. H824
Isa 5:26 he whistles for those at the ends of the e. H824
Isa 6: 3 Almighty; the whole e is full of his glory." H824
Isa 8:22 will look toward the e and see only distress H824
Isa 11: 4 he will give decisions for the poor of the e. H824
Isa 11: 4 He will strike the e with the rod of his H824
Isa 11: 9 the e will be filled with the knowledge H824
Isa 11:12 of Judah from the four quarters of the e. H824
Isa 13:13 the e will shake from its place at the H824
Isa 14:12 You have been cast down to the e, you H824
Isa 14:16 man who shook the e and made kingdoms H824
Isa 14:21 the land and cover the e with their cities. H9315
Isa 18: 3 you who live on the e, when a banner is H824
Isa 19:24 Egypt and Assyria, a blessing on the e. H824
Isa 23: 8 whose traders are renowned in the e? H824
Isa 23: 9 to humble all who are renowned on the e. H824
Isa 23:17 with all the kingdoms on the face of the e. H141
Isa 24: 1 going to lay waste the e and devastate it; H824
Isa 24: 3 The e will be completely laid waste and H824
Isa 24: 4 The e dries up and withers, the world H824
Isa 24: 4 the heavens languish with the e. H824
Isa 24: 5 The e is defiled by its people; they have H824
Isa 24: 6 Therefore a curse consumes the e; its H824
Isa 24:11 all joyful sounds are banished from the e. H824
Isa 24:13 So will it be on the e and among the H824
Isa 24:16 From the ends of the e we hear singing H824
Isa 24:17 pit and snare await you, people of the e. H824
Isa 24:18 opened, the foundations of the e shake. H824
Isa 24:19 The e is broken up, the earth is split H824
Isa 24:19 is broken up, the e is split asunder, the H824
Isa 24:19 is split asunder, the e is violently shaken. H824
Isa 24:20 The e reels like a drunkard, it sways like a H824
Isa 24:21 above and the kings on the e below. H141
Isa 25: 8 his people's disgrace from all the e. H824
Isa 26: 9 When your judgments come upon the e H824
Isa 26:18 We have not brought salvation to the e H824
Isa 26:19 morning; the e will give birth to her dead. H824
Isa 26:21 to punish the people of the e for their sins. H824
Isa 26:21 The e will disclose the blood shed on it H824
Isa 26:21 the e will conceal its slain no longer. NDT
Isa 29: 4 Your voice will come ghostlike from the e H824
Isa 34: 1 Let the e hear, and all that is in it, the H824
Isa 37:16 are God over all the kingdoms of the e. H824
Isa 37:16 You have made heaven and e. H824
Isa 37:20 the kingdoms of the e may know that you, H824
Isa 40:12 Who has held the dust of the e in a basket H824
Isa 40:21 not understood since the e was founded? H824
Isa 40:22 He sits enthroned above the circle of the e H824
Isa 40:28 the Creator of the ends of the e. H824
Isa 41: 5 seen it and fear; the ends of the e tremble. H824
Isa 41: 9 I took you from the ends of the e, from its H824
Isa 42: 4 discouraged till he establishes justice on e. H824
Isa 42: 5 who spreads out the e with all that springs H824
Isa 42:10 his praise from the ends of the e, you who H824
Isa 43: 6 my daughters from the ends of the e— H824
Isa 44:23 has done this; shout aloud, you e beneath. H824
Isa 44:24 heavens, who spreads out the e by myself, H824
Isa 45: 8 Let the e open wide, let salvation spring up H824
Isa 45:12 is I who made the e and created mankind H824
Isa 45:18 he who fashioned and made the e, he H824
Isa 45:22 all you ends of the e; for I am God, H824
Isa 48:13 My own hand laid the foundations of the e H824
Isa 48:20 Send it out to the ends of the e; say, "The H824
Isa 49: 6 salvation may reach to the ends of the e." H824
Isa 49:13 you e; burst into song, you H824
Isa 51: 6 look at the e beneath; the heavens H824
Isa 51: 6 the e will wear out like a garment and its H824
Isa 51:13 who lays the foundations of the e, H824
Isa 51:16 who laid the foundations of the e, and who H824
Isa 52:10 all the ends of the e will see the salvation H824
Isa 54: 5 he is called the God of all the e. H824
Isa 54: 9 of Noah would never again cover the e. H824
Isa 55: 9 "As the heavens are higher than the e, so H824
Isa 55:10 without watering the e and making it bud H824
Isa 60: 2 darkness covers the e and thick darkness is H824
Isa 62: 7 makes her the praise of the e. H824
Isa 62:11 made proclamation to the ends of the e: H824
Isa 65:17 I will create new heavens and a new e. H824
Isa 66: 1 is my throne, and the e is my footstool. H824
Isa 66:22 heavens and the new e that I make will H824
Jer 4:23 I looked at the e, and it was formless and H824
Jer 4:28 Therefore the e will mourn and the H824
Jer 6:19 you e: I am bringing disaster on this H824
Jer 6:22 is being stirred up from the ends of the e. H824
Jer 9:24 justice and righteousness on e, for in these H824
Jer 10:10 he is angry, the e trembles; the nations H824
Jer 10:11 did not make the heavens and the e, A10077
Jer 10:11 perish from the e and from under the A10075
Jer 10:12 But God made the e by his power; he H824
Jer 10:13 makes clouds rise from the ends of the e. H824
Jer 15: 4 all the kingdoms of the e because of what H824
Jer 16:19 will come from the ends of the e and say, H824
Jer 23:24 "Do not I fill heaven and e?" declares the H824
Jer 24: 9 an offense to all the kingdoms of the e, H824
Jer 25:26 all the kingdoms on the face of the e. H141
Jer 25:29 down a sword on all who live on the e, H824
Jer 25:30 shout against all who live on the e. H824
Jer 25:31 tumult will resound to the ends of the e, H824
Jer 25:32 storm is rising from the ends of the e." H824
Jer 25:33 from one end of the e to the other. H824
Jer 26: 6 city a curse among all the nations of the e. H824
Jer 27: 5 arm I made the e and its people and the H824
Jer 28:16 about to remove you from the face of the e. H141
Jer 29:18 abhorrent to all the kingdoms of the e, H824
Jer 31: 8 gather them from the ends of the e. H824
Jer 31:22 The LORD will create a new thing on e—the H824
Jer 31:37 foundations of the e below be searched H824
Jer 32:17 the heavens and the e by your great power H824
Jer 33: 2 he who made the e, the LORD who H2023S
Jer 33: 9 before all nations on e that hear of all the H824
Jer 33:25 established the laws of heaven and e, H824
Jer 34:17 you abhorrent to all the kingdoms of the e. H824
Jer 44: 8 of reproach among all the nations on e. H824
Jer 45: 4 what I have planted, throughout the e. H824
Jer 46: 8 'I will rise and cover the e; I will destroy H824
Jer 46:12 of your shame; your cries will fill the e. H824
Jer 49:21 At the sound of their fall the e will tremble H824
Jer 50:23 shattered is the hammer of the whole e! H824
Jer 50:41 are being stirred up from the ends of the e. H824
Jer 50:46 of Babylon's capture the e will tremble; H824
Jer 51: 7 LORD's hand; she made the whole e drunk. H824
Jer 51:15 "He made the e by his power; he founded H824
Jer 51:16 makes clouds rise from the ends of the e. H824
Jer 51:25 you who destroy the whole e," declares the H824
Jer 51:41 captured, the boast of the whole e seized! H824
Jer 51:48 Then heaven and e and all that is in them H824
Jer 51:49 the slain in all the e have fallen because H824
La 2: 1 the splendor of Israel from heaven to e; H824
La 2:15 of beauty, the joy of the whole e? H824
La 4:12 The kings of the e did not believe, nor did H824
Eze 7:21 as loot to the wicked of the e, H824
Eze 8: 3 lifted me up between e and heaven and in H824
Eze 26:20 I will make you dwell in the e below, as in H824
Eze 27:33 your wares you enriched the kings of the e. H824
Eze 28:17 So I threw you to the e; I made a spectacle H824
Eze 29: 5 to the beasts of the e and the birds of the H824
Eze 31:12 the nations of the e came out from under H824
Eze 31:14 death, for the e below, among mortals H824
Eze 31:16 were consoled in the e below. H824
Eze 31:18 with the trees of Eden to the e below; H824
Eze 32:18 consign to the e below both her and H824
Eze 32:24 went down uncircumcised to the e below. H824
Eze 34: 6 They were scattered over the whole e, and H824
Eze 35:14 While the whole e rejoices, I will make you H824
Eze 38:20 on the face of the e will tremble at my H141
Eze 39:18 of the princes of the e as if they were rams H824
Da 2:10 is no one on e who can do what the A10309
Da 2:35 a huge mountain and filled the whole e. A10075
Da 2:39 one of bronze, will rule over the whole e. A10075
Da 4: 1 of every language, who live in all the e: A10075
Da 4:11 it was visible to the ends of the e. A10075
Da 4:15 the animals among the plants of the e. A10075
Da 4:17 over all kingdoms on e and gives them A10050S
Da 4:20 touching the sky, visible to the whole e, A10075
Da 4:22 extends to distant parts of the e. A10075
Da 4:25 over all kingdoms on e and gives them A10050S
Da 4:32 over all kingdoms on e and gives them A10050S
Da 4:35 All the peoples of the e are regarded as A10075
Da 4:35 of heaven and the peoples of the e. A10075
Da 5:21 over all kingdoms on e and sets over A10050S
Da 6:25 peoples of every language in all the e: A10075
Da 6:27 wonders in the heavens and on the e. A10075
Da 7:17 are four kings that will rise from the e. A10075
Da 7:23 a fourth kingdom that will appear on e. A10075
Da 7:23 kingdoms and will devour the whole e, A10075
Da 8: 5 crossing the whole e without touching the H824
Da 8:10 host down to the e and trampled on them. H824
Da 12: 2 who sleep in the dust of the e will awake: H141
Hos 2:21 the skies, and they will respond to the e; H824
Hos 2:22 the e will respond to the grain, the H824
Hos 6: 3 like the spring rains that water the e." H824
Joel 2:10 Before them the e shakes, the heavens H824
Joel 2:30 wonders in the heavens and on the e, H824
Joel 3:16 the e and the heavens will tremble. H824
Am 3: 2 have I chosen of all the families of the e; H141
Am 4:13 treads on the heights of the e—the H824
Am 8: 9 noon and darken the e in broad daylight. H824
Am 9: 5 he touches the e and it melts, and all H824
Am 9: 6 heavens and sets its foundation on the e; H824
Am 9: 8 I will destroy it from the face of the e. Yet I H141
Jnh 2: 6 the e beneath barred me in forever. H824
Mic 1: 2 e and all who live in it, that the H824
Mic 1: 3 down and treads on the heights of the e. H824
Mic 4:13 their wealth to the Lord of all the e. H824
Mic 5: 4 greatness will reach to the ends of the e. H824
Mic 6: 2 you everlasting foundations of the e. H824
Mic 7:13 The e will become desolate because of its H824
Na 1: 5 The e trembles at his presence, the world H824
Na 2:13 I will leave you no prey on the e. H824
Hab 1: 6 across the whole e to seize dwellings not H824
Hab 2:14 For the e will be filled with the knowledge H824
Hab 2:20 let all the e be silent before him. H824
Hab 3: 3 the heavens and his praise filled the e. H824
Hab 3: 6 shook the e; he looked, and made H824
Hab 3: 9 many arrows. You split the e with rivers; H824
Hab 3:12 you strode through the e and in anger you H824
Zep 1: 2 away everything from the face of the e," H141
Zep 1: 3 I destroy all mankind on the face of the e," H141
Zep 1:18 his jealousy the whole e will be consumed, H824
Zep 1:18 a sudden end of all who live on the e. H824
Zep 2:11 when he destroys all the gods of the e. H824
Zep 3:20 all the peoples of the e when I restore your H824
Hag 1:10 withheld their dew and the e its crops. H824
Hag 2: 6 once more shake the heavens and the e, H824
Hag 2:21 am going to shake the heavens and the e. H824
Zec 1:10 the LORD has sent to go throughout the e." H824
Zec 1:11 throughout the e and found the whole H824
Zec 4:10 range throughout the e will rejoice when H824
Zec 4:14 are anointed to serve the Lord of all the e." H824
Zec 5: 9 up the basket between heaven and e. H824
Zec 6: 7 they were straining to go throughout the e. H824
Zec 6: 7 "Go throughout the e!" So they went H824
Zec 6: 7 So they went throughout the e. H824
Zec 9:10 sea and from the River to the ends of the e. H824
Zec 12: 1 who lays the foundation of the e, and who H824
Zec 12: 3 the nations of the e are gathered against H824
Zec 14: 9 The LORD will be king over the whole e. H824
Zec 14:17 of the peoples of the e do not go up to H824
Mt 5: 5 are the meek, for they will inherit the e. G1178
Mt 5:13 "You are the salt *of* the e. But if the salt G1178
Mt 5:18 until heaven and e disappear, not the G1178
Mt 5:35 by the e, for it is his footstool; or by G1178
Mt 6:10 your will be done, on e as it is in heaven. G1178
Mt 6:19 not store up for yourselves treasures on e, G1178
Mt 9: 6 of Man has authority on e to forgive sins." G1178
Mt 10:34 that I have come to bring peace to the e. G1178
Mt 11:25 Lord of heaven and e, because you have G1178
Mt 12:40 three nights in the heart *of* the e. G1178
Mt 12:42 came from the ends *of* the e to listen to G1178
Mt 16:19 whatever you bind on e will be bound in G1178
Mt 16:19 whatever you loose on e will be loosed in G1178
Mt 17:25 do the kings *of* the e collect duty and G1178
Mt 18:18 whatever you bind on e will be bound in G1178
Mt 18:18 whatever you loose on e will be loosed in G1178
Mt 18:19 if two of you on e agree about anything G1178
Mt 23: 9 And do not call anyone on e 'father,' for G1178
Mt 23:35 righteous blood that has been shed on e, G1178
Mt 24:30 all the peoples *of* the e will mourn when G1178
Mt 24:35 Heaven and e will pass away, but my G1178
Mt 27:51 top to bottom. The e shook, the rocks split G1178
Mt 28:18 in heaven and on e has been given to me G1178
Mk 2:10 of Man has authority on e to forgive sins." G1178
Mk 4:31 which is the smallest of all seeds on e. G1178
Mk 13:27 from the ends *of* the e to the ends of the G1178
Mk 13:31 Heaven and e will pass away, but my G1178
Lk 2:14 on e peace to those on whom his G1178
Lk 5:24 of Man has authority on e to forgive sins." G1178
Lk 10:21 Lord of heaven and e, because you have G1178
Lk 11:31 came from the ends *of* the e to listen to G1178
Lk 12:49 "I have come to bring fire on the e, and G1178
Lk 12:51 Do you think I came to bring peace on e G1178
Lk 12:56 the appearance *of* the e and the sky. G1178
Lk 16:17 heaven and e to disappear than for G1178
Lk 18: 8 of Man comes, will he find faith on the e?" G1178
Lk 21:25 On the e, nations will be in anguish and G1178
Lk 21:33 Heaven and e will pass away, but my G1178
Lk 21:35 those who live on the face of the whole e. G1178
Jn 3:31 one who is from the e belongs to the G1178
Jn 3:31 who is from the earth belongs to the e, G1178
Jn 3:31 the earth, and speaks as one from the e. G1178
Jn 12:32 when I am lifted up from the e, will draw G1178
Jn 17: 4 brought you glory on e by finishing the G1178
Ac 1: 8 Samaria, and to the ends *of* the e. G1178
Ac 2:19 heavens above and signs on the e below, G1178
Ac 3:25 offspring all peoples *on* e will be blessed. G1178
Ac 4:24 made the heavens and the e and the sea, G1178
Ac 4:26 The kings *of* the e rise up and the rulers G1178
Ac 7:49 is my throne, and the e is my footstool. G1178
Ac 8:33 For his life was taken from the e." G1178
Ac 10:11 being let down to e by its four corners. G1178
Ac 11: 6 it and saw four-footed animals *of* the e, G1178
Ac 13:47 may bring salvation to the ends *of* the e. G1178
Ac 14:15 the heavens and the e and the sea and G1178
Ac 17:24 Lord of heaven and e and does not live in G1178
Ac 17:26 that they should inhabit the whole e; and G1178
Ac 22:22 voices and shouted, "Rid the e of him! G1178
Ro 9:17 name might be proclaimed in all the e." G1178
Ro 9:28 out his sentence on e with speed and G1178
Ro 10:18 "Their voice has gone out into all the e G1178
1Co 4:13 We have become the scum *of* the e, the G3180
1Co 8: 5 whether in heaven or on e (as indeed G1178
1Co 10:26 "The e is the Lord's, and everything in G1178
1Co 15:47 The first man was of the dust *of* the e; the G1178

1Co 15:48 so are those who are **of** the e; and as is *G5954*
Eph 1:10 things in heaven and on e under Christ. *G1178*
Eph 3:15 in heaven and on e derives its name. *G1178*
Eph 6: 3 that you may enjoy long life on the e." *G1178*
Php 2:10 in heaven and **on** e and under the earth, *G2103*
Php 2:10 in heaven and on earth and **under the** e, *G2973*
Col 1:16 things in heaven and on e, visible and *G1178*
Col 1:20 whether things on e or things in heaven *G1178*
Heb 1:10 you laid the foundations *of* the e, and the *G1178*
Heb 5: 7 During the days of Jesus' **life on** e, he *G4922*
Heb 8: 4 If he were on e, he would not be a priest *G1178*
Heb 11:13 they were foreigners and strangers on e. *G1178*
Heb 12:25 they refused him who warned them on e, *G1178*
Heb 12:26 At that time his voice shook the e, but now *G1178*
Heb 12:26 shake not only the e but also the heavens *G1178*
Jas 5: 5 You have lived on e in luxury and *G1178*
Jas 5:12 not by heaven or *by* e or by anything else. *G1178*
Jas 5:18 gave rain, and the e produced its crops. *G1178*
2Pe 3: 5 into being and the e was formed out of *G1178*
2Pe 3: 7 present heavens and e are reserved for *G1178*
2Pe 3:10 the e and everything done in it will *G1178*
2Pe 3:13 forward to a new heaven and a new e, *G1178*
Rev 1: 5 and the ruler of the kings *of* the e. *G1178*
Rev 1: 7 all peoples *on* e "will mourn because *G1178*
Rev 3:10 world to test the inhabitants of the e. *G1178*
Rev 5: 3 one in heaven or on e or under the earth *G1178*
Rev 5: 3 earth or under the e could open the scroll *G1178*
Rev 5: 6 spirits of God sent out into all the e. *G1178*
Rev 5:10 our God, and they will reign on the e." *G1178*
Rev 5:13 in heaven and on e and under the earth *G1178*
Rev 5:13 on earth and under the e and on the sea, *G1178*
Rev 6: 4 peace from the e and to make people *G1178*
Rev 6: 8 over a fourth *of* the e to kill by sword, *G1178*
Rev 6: 8 plague, and by the wild beasts *of* the e. *G1178*
Rev 6:10 inhabitants of the e and avenge our *G1178*
Rev 6:13 the stars in the sky fell to e, as figs *G1178*
Rev 6:15 Then the kings *of* the e, the princes, the *G1178*
Rev 7: 1 standing at the four corners *of* the e, *G1178*
Rev 7: 1 the four winds *of* the e to prevent any *G1178*
Rev 8: 5 hurled it on the e; and there came *G1178*
Rev 8: 7 and it was hurled down on the e. *G1178*
Rev 8: 7 A third *of* the e was burned up, a third of *G1178*
Rev 8:13 Woe to the inhabitants of the e, because *G1178*
Rev 9: 1 star that had fallen from the sky to the e. *G1178*
Rev 9: 3 came down on the e and were given *G1178*
Rev 9: 3 power like that of scorpions *of* the e. *G1178*
Rev 9: 4 to harm the grass *of* the e or any plant *G1178*
Rev 10: 6 that is in them, the e and all that is in it *G1178*
Rev 11: 4 "they stand before the Lord *of* the e." *G1178*
Rev 11: 6 to strike the e with every kind of *G1178*
Rev 11:10 inhabitants of the e will gloat over them *G1178*
Rev 11:10 had tormented those who live on the e. *G1178*
Rev 11:18 destroying those who destroy the e." *G1178*
Rev 12: 4 out of the sky and flung them to the e. *G1178*
Rev 12: 9 He was hurled to the e, and his angels *G1178*
Rev 12:12 But woe *to* the e and the sea, because *G1178*
Rev 12:13 saw that he had been hurled to the e, *G1178*
Rev 12:16 But the e helped the woman by opening *G1178*
Rev 13: 8 All inhabitants of the e will worship the *G1178*
Rev 13:11 saw a second beast, coming out of the e. *G1178*
Rev 13:12 made the e and its inhabitants *G1178*
Rev 13:13 from heaven to the e in full view of the *G1178*
Rev 13:14 it deceived the inhabitants of the e. *G1178*
Rev 14: 3 who had been redeemed from the e. *G1178*
Rev 14: 6 to proclaim to those who live on the e— *G1178*
Rev 14: 7 made the heavens, the e, the sea and the *G1178*
Rev 14:15 has come, for the harvest *of* the e is ripe." *G1178*
Rev 14:16 on the cloud swung his sickle over the e, *G1178*
Rev 14:16 over the earth, and the e was harvested. *G1178*
Rev 14:19 The angel swung his sickle on the e *G1178*
Rev 16: 1 the seven bowls of God's wrath on the e." *G1178*
Rev 16:18 occurred since mankind has been on e, *G1178*
Rev 17: 2 With her the kings *of* the e committed *G1178*
Rev 17: 2 the inhabitants *of* the e were intoxicated *G1178*
Rev 17: 5 of the abominations *of* the e. *G1178*
Rev 17: 8 inhabitants of the e whose names have *G1178*
Rev 17:18 city that rules over the kings *of* the e." *G1178*
Rev 18: 1 the e was illuminated by his splendor *G1178*
Rev 18: 3 The kings *of* the e committed adultery *G1178*
Rev 18: 3 the merchants *of* the e grew rich from *G1178*
Rev 18: 9 "When the kings *of* the e who committed *G1178*
Rev 18:11 "The merchants *of* the e will weep and *G1178*
Rev 18:24 all who have been slaughtered on the e." *G1178*
Rev 19: 2 who corrupted the e by her adulteries. *G1178*
Rev 19:19 the kings *of* the e and their armies *G1178*
Rev 20: 8 the nations in the four corners *of* the e— *G1178*
Rev 20: 9 the breadth *of* the e and surrounded *G1178*
Rev 20:11 The e and the heavens fled from his *G1178*
Rev 21: 1 Then I saw "a new heaven and a new e," *G1178*
Rev 21: 1 heaven and the first e had passed away, *G1178*
Rev 21:24 the kings *of* the e will bring their *G1178*

EARTH'S (6) [EARTH]

Ge 27:28 give you heaven's dew and e richness— H824
Ge 27:39 dwelling will be away from the e richness, H824
Job 38: 4 were you when I laid the e foundation? H824
Pr 3:19 By wisdom the LORD laid the e foundations H824
Isa 24: 6 Therefore e inhabitants are burned up, and H824
Rev 14:18 the clusters of grapes from the e vine, *G1178*

EARTHEN (1) [EARTH, EARTHENWARE]

Hab 1:10 by building **e ramps** they capture them. H6760

EARTHENWARE (1) [EARTHEN]

Pr 26:23 of silver dross on e are fervent lips with an H3084

EARTHLY (17) [EARTH]

Ps 10:18 so that mere e mortals will H4946+2021+824
Jn 3:12 spoken to you *of* e **things** and you do not *G2103*
Ro 1: 3 who as to his e **life** was a descendant of *G4922*
1Co 15:40 heavenly bodies and there are e bodies; *G2103*
1Co 15:40 the splendor *of* the e bodies is *G2103*
1Co 15:48 As was the e *man*, so are those who are of *G5954*
1Co 15:49 we have borne the image *of* the e *man*, *G5954*
2Co 5: 1 For we know that if the e tent we live in is *G2103*
Eph 4: 9 also descended to the lower, e regions? *G1178*
Eph 6: 5 obey your e masters with respect *G2848+4922*
Php 3:19 Their mind is set on e things. *G2103*
Col 3: 2 above, not on e things. *G2093+3836+1178*
Col 3: 5 belongs to your e nature: *G2093+3836+1178*
Col 3:22 obey your e masters in everything *G2848+4922*
Heb 9: 1 worship and also an e sanctuary. *G3176*
Jas 3:15 not come down from heaven but is e, *G2103*
1Pe 4: 2 the rest of their e lives for evil *G1877+4922*

EARTHQUAKE (17) [QUAKE]

1Ki 19:11 After the wind there was an e, but the H8323
1Ki 19:11 earthquake, but the LORD was not in the e. H8323
1Ki 19:12 After the e came a fire, but the LORD was H8323
Isa 29: 6 come with thunder and e and great noise, H8323
Eze 38:19 shall be a great e in the land of Israel. H8323
Am 1: 1 concerning Israel two years before the e, H8323
Zec 14: 5 as you fled from the e in the days of H8323
Mt 27:54 guarding Jesus saw the e and all that had *G4939*
Mt 28: 2 There was a violent e, for an angel of the *G4939*
Ac 16:26 was such a violent e that the foundations *G4939*
Rev 6:12 There was a great e. The sun turned black *G4939*
Rev 8: 5 rumblings, flashes of lightning and an e. *G4939*
Rev 11:13 there was a severe e and a tenth of the *G4939*
Rev 11:13 thousand people were killed in the e, *G4939*
Rev 11:19 of thunder, an e and a severe hailstorm. *G4939*
Rev 16:18 peals of thunder and a severe e. *G4939*
Rev 16:18 No e like it has ever occurred since mankind NDT

EARTHQUAKES (3) [QUAKE]

Mt 24: 7 will be famines and e in various places. *G4939*
Mk 13: 8 There will be e in various places, and *G4939*
Lk 21:11 There will be great e, famines and *G4939*

EASE (10) [EASIER, EASILY, EASY]

Ru 2:13 "*You have* **put** me **at** e by speaking kindly H5714
Job 3:18 Captives also **enjoy** *their* e; they no longer H8631
Job 7:13 me and my couch *will* e my complaint, H5951
Job 12: 5 *Those who* are **at** e have contempt for H8633
Job 21:23 in full vigor, completely secure and **at** e, H8929
Pr 1:33 to me will live in safety and *be* **at** e, H8631
Jer 12: 1 Why *do* all the faithless **live at** e? H8922
Jer 49:31 "Arise and attack a nation **at** e, which H8929
La 1: 5 her masters; her enemies *are* **at** e. H8922
Jnh 4: 6 shade for his head to e his discomfort, H5911

EASIER (7) [EASE]

Mt 9: 5 Which is e: to say, 'Your sins are forgiven,' *G2324*
Mt 19:24 it is e for a camel to go through the eye of *G2324*
Mk 2: 9 Which is e: to say to this paralyzed man *G2324*
Mk 10:25 It is e for a camel to go through the eye of *G2324*
Lk 5:23 Which is e: to say, 'Your sins are forgiven,' *G2324*
Lk 16:17 It is e for heaven and earth to disappear *G2324*
Lk 18:25 it is e for a camel to go through the eye of *G2324*

EASILY (10) [EASE]

Jdg 16: 9 the bowstrings **as** e **as** a piece of H3869+889
Jdg 20:43 chased them and e overran them in the H4957
Pr 14: 6 knowledge **comes** e to the discerning. H7837
Pr 22:24 do not associate with one **e angered**, H2779
Hos 7:11 is like a dove, **e deceived** and senseless H7331
Ac 24:11 You can *e* **verify** that no more than twelve AIT
1Co 13: 5 *it is* not **e angered**, it keeps no *G4236*
2Co 11: 4 accepted, you put up with it e *enough*. *G2822*
2Th 2: 2 not to become e unsettled or alarmed by *G5441*
Heb 12: 1 hinders and the sin that **so e entangles**. *G2342*

EAST (185) [EASTERN, EASTWARD, NORTHEASTER, SOUTHEAST]

Ge 2: 8 LORD God had planted a garden in the e, H7710
Ge 2:14 it runs along the e *side of* Ashur. H7713
Ge 3:24 he placed on the e *side* of the Garden of H7710
Ge 4:16 lived in the land of Nod, e *of* Eden. H7713
Ge 12: 8 on toward the hills e of Bethel and H4946+7710
Ge 12: 8 with Bethel on the west and Ai on the e. H7710
Ge 13:11 of the Jordan and set out toward the e. H7710
Ge 13:14 to the north and south, to the e and west. H7711
Ge 25: 6 from his son Isaac to the land of the e. H7710
Ge 28:14 will spread out to the west and to the e, H7711
Ge 41: 6 thin and scorched by the **e wind**. H7708
Ge 41:23 thin and scorched by the **e wind**. H7708
Ge 41:27 heads of grain scorched by the **e wind**: H7708
Ex 10:13 the LORD made an e wind blow across the H7708
Ex 14:21 back with a strong e wind and turned it H7708
Ex 27:13 On the e end, toward the sunrise H7711+2025
Ex 38:13 The e end, toward the sunrise, was H7711+2025
Lev 1:16 throw them down e *of* the altar H7711+725
Nu 2: 3 On the e, toward the sunrise, the divisions H7711
Nu 3:38 were to camp to the e *of* the tabernacle, H7711
Nu 10: 5 the tribes camping on the e are to set out. H7711
Nu 32:19 come to us on the e side of the Jordan." H4667
Nu 33: 7 Pi Hahiroth, to the e *of* Baal Zephon, and H7156
Nu 34: 3 will start in the e from the southern end of H7711
Nu 34:11 to Riblah on the e *side* of Ain and H7710
Nu 34:11 along the slopes e of the Sea of H7711+2025
Nu 34:15 their inheritance e of the Jordan H7711+2025
Nu 35: 5 two thousand cubits on the e side, H7711
Dt 1: 1 in the wilderness e *of* the Jordan— H928+6298
Dt 1: 5 E *of* the Jordan in the territory of H928+6298
Dt 3: 8 the territory e *of* the Jordan, H928+6298
Dt 3:27 west and north and south and e. H4667+2025
Dt 4:41 three cities e *of* the Jordan, H928+6298+4667+2025+9087
Dt 4:46 near Beth Peor e *of* the Jordan, H928+6298
Dt 4:47 kings e *of* the Jordan. H928+6298+4667+9087
Dt 4:49 the Arabah e *of* the Jordan, H6298+4667+2025
Jos 1:14 Moses gave you e *of* the Jordan, H928+6298
Jos 1:15 the LORD gave you e *of* the Jordan H928+6298
Jos 2:10 of the Amorites e *of* the Jordan, H928+6298
Jos 7: 2 is near Beth Aven to the e of Bethel, H7710
Jos 9:10 of the Amorites e *of* the Jordan— H928+6298
Jos 11: 3 to the Canaanites in the e and west; to the H4667
Jos 11: 8 to the Valley of Mizpah on the e H4667
Jos 12: 1 took over e *of* the Jordan H4667+2025+2021+9087
Jos 13: 3 Shihor River on the e *of* Egypt to the H7156
Jos 13: 5 and all Lebanon to the e H4667+2021+9087
Jos 13: 8 given them e of the H928+6298+4667+2025
Jos 13:27 king of Heshbon (the e side of the Jordan H4667
Jos 13:32 across the Jordan e *of* Jericho. H4667+2025
Jos 14: 3 inheritance e of the Jordan but H4946+6298
Jos 16: 1 Jordan, e of the springs of Jericho H4667+2025
Jos 16: 5 Addar in the e to Upper Beth Horon H4667
Jos 16: 6 passing by it to Janoah on the e. H4667
Jos 17: 5 and Bashan e of the Jordan, H4946+6298
Jos 17: 7 to Mikmethath e *of* Shechem. H6584+7156
Jos 17:10 Asher on the north and Issachar on the e. H4667
Jos 18: 7 inheritance on the e side of the Jordan. H4667
Jos 19:12 It turned e from Sarid toward the H7711+2025
Jos 19:27 It then turned e toward Beth H4667+2021+9087
Jos 19:34 the west and the Jordan on the e. H4667+9087
Jos 20: 8 E of the Jordan (on the other side H4667+2025
Jos 24: 8 Amorites who lived e *of* the Jordan. H928+6298
Jdg 8:11 of the nomads e of Nobah and H4946+7710
Jdg 10: 8 Israelites on the e **side** *of* the Jordan in H6298
Jdg 20:43 in the vicinity of Gibeah on the e. H4667+9087
Jdg 21:19 e of the road that goes H4667+2025+2021+9087
1Sa 13: 5 camped at Mikmash, e *of* Beth Aven. H7713
1Ki 4:30 the wisdom of all the people of the **E**, H7710
1Ki 7:25 facing south and three facing e. H4667+2025
1Ki 11: 7 On a hill e *of* Jerusalem, Solomon H6584+7156
1Ki 17: 3 the Kerith Ravine, e *of* the Jordan. H6584+7156
1Ki 17: 5 Kerith Ravine, e *of* the Jordan, and H6584+7156
2Ki 10:33 e of the Jordan in all the H4667+2021+9087
2Ki 13:17 "Open the e window," he said, and H7711+2025
2Ki 23:13 places that were e *of* Jerusalem on H6584+7156
1Ch 4:39 of Gedor to the e *of* the valley in search of H4667
1Ch 5: 9 To the e they occupied the land up to the H4667
1Ch 5:10 throughout the entire region e of Gilead. H4667
1Ch 6:78 across the Jordan e *of* Jericho they H4667
1Ch 7:28 Naaran to the e, Gezer and its villages H4667
1Ch 9:18 stationed at the King's Gate on the e, H4667
1Ch 9:24 on the four sides: e, west, north and south H4667
1Ch 12:15 in the valleys, to the e and to the west. H4667
1Ch 12:37 from e of the Jordan, from Reuben H6298
1Ch 26:14 The lot for the **E** Gate fell to Shelemiah H4667
1Ch 26:17 There were six Levites a day on the e, four H4667
2Ch 4: 4 facing south and three facing e. H4667+2025
2Ch 5:12 stood on the e *side* of the altar, dressed H4667
2Ch 29: 4 them in the square on the e *side* H4667
2Ch 31:14 keeper of the **E** Gate, was in H4667+2025
Ne 3:26 Gate toward the e and the projecting H4667
Ne 3:29 the guard at the **E** Gate, made repairs. H4667
Ne 12:37 palace to the Water Gate *on* the e. H4667
Job 1: 3 man among all the people of the **E**. H7710
Job 15: 2 fill their belly with the **hot e wind**? H7708
Job 18:20 *those of the* e are seized with horror. H7719
Job 23: 8 "But if I go to the e, he is not there; if I go H7710
Job 27:21 The **e wind** carries him off, and he is H7708
Job 38:24 place where the **e winds** are scattered H7708
Ps 48: 7 ships of Tarshish shattered by an **e wind**. H7708
Ps 75: 6 No one from the e or the west or from the H4604
Ps 78:26 He let loose the **e wind** from the heavens H7708
Ps 103:12 as far as the e is from the west, so far has H4667
Ps 107: 3 the lands, from e and west, from north H4667
Isa 2: 6 They are full of superstitions from the **E** H7710
Isa 9:12 Arameans from the e and Philistines from H7710
Isa 11:14 they will plunder the people to the e. H7710
Isa 24:15 Therefore in the e give glory to the LORD H241
Isa 27: 8 her out, as on a day the **e wind** blows. H7708
Isa 41: 2 "Who has stirred up one from the e H4667
Isa 43: 5 children from the e and gather you from H4667
Isa 46:11 From the e I summon a bird of prey; from H4667
Jer 18:17 Like a wind from the e, I will scatter them H7708
Jer 31:40 Kidron Valley on the e as far as the corner H4667
Jer 49:28 Kedar and destroy the people of the **E**. H7710
Eze 8:16 of the LORD and their faces toward the e, H7711
Eze 8:16 were bowing down to the sun in the e. H7711
Eze 10:19 at the entrance of the e gate of the LORD's H7719
Eze 11: 1 the house of the LORD that faces e. H7708+2025
Eze 11:23 above the mountain e of it. H4946+7710
Eze 17:10 completely when the e wind strikes it— H7708
Eze 19:12 The e wind made it shrivel, it was H7708

Eze 25: 4 to the people of the **E** as a possession. H7710
Eze 25:10 to the people of the **E** as a possession, H7710
Eze 27:26 But the **e** wind will break you to pieces far H7708
Eze 39:11 valley of those who travel **e** *of* the Sea. H7713
Eze 40: 6 he went to the **e** gate. H7156+2006+2021+7708+2025
Eze 40:10 Inside the **e** gate were three H2006+2021+7708
Eze 40:19 cubits on the **e** *side* as well as on the H7708
Eze 40:22 those of the gate facing **e**. H2006+2021+7708
Eze 40:23 the north gate, just as there was on the **e**. H7708
Eze 40:32 me to the inner court on the **e** side, H7708
Eze 41:14 width of the temple courtyard on the **e**, H7708
Eze 42: 9 an entrance on the **e** *side* as one enters H7708
Eze 42:15 led me out by the **e** gate and measured H7708
Eze 42:16 He measured the **e** side with the H7708
Eze 43: 1 me to the gate facing **e**, H2006+2021+7708
Eze 43: 2 of the God of Israel coming from the **e**. H7708
Eze 43: 4 through the gate facing **e**. H2006+2021+7708
Eze 43:17 The steps of the altar face **e**." H7708
Eze 44: 1 the one facing **e**, and it was shut. H7708
Eze 45: 7 side and eastward from the **e** side, H7711+2025
Eze 46: 1 inner court facing **e** is to be shut on the H7708
Eze 46:12 the gate facing **e** is to be opened for him. H7708
Eze 47: 1 the threshold of the temple toward the **e** H7708
Eze 47: 1 the temple faced **e**). The water was H7708
Eze 47: 2 the outside to the outer gate facing **e**, H7708
Eze 47:18 "On the **e** side the boundary will run H7708
Eze 48: 1 its border from the **e** *side* to the west side. H7708
Eze 48: 2 border the territory of Dan from **e** to west. H7708
Eze 48: 3 territory of Asher from **e** to west. H7708+2025
Eze 48: 4 territory of Naphtali from **e** to west. H7708+2025
Eze 48: 5 of Manasseh from **e** to west. H7708+2025
Eze 48: 6 the territory of Ephraim from **e** to west. H7708
Eze 48: 7 the territory of Reuben from **e** to west. H7708
Eze 48: 8 of Judah from **e** to west will be the H7708
Eze 48: 8 its length from **e** to west will equal H7708+2025
Eze 48:10 wide on the **e** *side* and 25,000 cubits H7708
Eze 48:16 4,500 cubits, the **e** side 4,500 cubits, and H7708
Eze 48:17 250 cubits on the **e**, and 250 cubits on H7708
Eze 48:18 cubits on the **e** *side* and 10,000 cubits H7708
Eze 48:23 extend from the **e** side to the west H7708+2025
Eze 48:24 of Benjamin from **e** to west. H7708+2025
Eze 48:25 territory of Simeon from **e** to west. H7708+2025
Eze 48:26 territory of Issachar from **e** to west. H7708+2025
Eze 48:27 territory of Zebulun from **e** to west. H7708+2025
Eze 48:32 "On the **e** side, which is 4,500 H7708+2025
Da 8: 9 to the south and to the **e** and toward the H4667
Da 11:44 But reports from the **e** and the north will H4667
Hos 12: 1 he pursues the **e wind** all day and H7708
Hos 13:15 An **e** wind from the LORD will come H7708
Am 8:12 sea to sea and wander from north to **e**, H4667
Jnh 4: 5 out and sat down at a place **e** of the city. H7710
Jnh 4: 8 God provided a scorching **e** wind, and the H7708
Zec 8: 7 from the countries of the **e** and the west. H4667
Zec 14: 4 of Olives, **e** of Jerusalem H6584+7156+7710
Zec 14: 4 Olives will be split in two from **e** to west, H4667
Zec 14: 8 half of it **e** to the Dead Sea and half of it H7719
Mt 2: 1 Magi from the **e** came to Jerusalem *G424*
Mt 8:11 many will come from the **e** and the west, *G424*
Mt 24:27 that comes from the **e** is visible even in the *G424*
Lk 13:29 will come from **e** and west and north *G424*
Rev 7: 2 angel coming up from the **e**, *G424+2463*
Rev 16:12 the way for the kings from the **E**. *G424+2463*
Rev 21:13 There were three gates on the **e**, three on *G424*

EASTER (KJV) PASSOVER

EASTERN (21) [EAST]

Ge 10:30 toward Sephar, in the **e** hill country. H7710
Ge 25:18 near the *e* **border** *of* Egypt, as you go AIT
Ge 29: 1 came to the land of the **e** peoples. H7710
Nu 23: 7 the king of Moab from the **e** mountains. H7710
Nu 34:10 " 'For your **e** boundary, run a line H7711+2025
Jos 4:19 at Gilgal on the **e** border of Jericho. H4667
Jos 12: 1 all the **e** *side of* the Arabah: H4667+2025
Jos 12: 3 ruled over the **e** Arabah from the H4667+2025
Jos 15: 5 The **e** boundary is the Dead Sea as H7711+2025
Jos 18:20 formed the boundary on the **e** side. H7711+2025
Jdg 6: 3 other **e** peoples invaded the H7710
Jdg 6:33 Amalekites and other **e** peoples joined H7710
Jdg 7:12 all the other **e** peoples had settled in H7710
Jdg 8:10 were left of the armies of the **e** peoples; H7710
Jdg 11:18 passed along the **e** side of the H4667+9087
1Sa 15: 7 to Shur, near the *e* **border** *of* Egypt. H7156
Eze 45: 7 western to the **e** border parallel to H7708+2025
Eze 47: 8 flows toward the **e** region and goes down H7716
Eze 47:18 This will be the **e** boundary. H7708+2025
Eze 48:21 cubits of the sacred portion to the **e** border, NDT
Joel 2:20 its **e ranks** will drown in the Dead Sea H7156

EASTWARD (8) [EAST]

Ge 11: 2 As people moved **e**, they found a H4946+7710
Jos 16: 6 north it curved **e** to Taanath Shiloh, H4667+2025
Jos 19:13 it continued **e** to Gath H7711+2025+4667+2025
1Ki 17: 3 turn **e** and hide in the Kerith H7711+2025
Eze 42:12 to the corresponding wall extending **e**, H7708
Eze 45: 7 the west side and **e** from the east H7708+2025
Eze 47: 3 As the man went **e** with a measuring line H7708
Eze 48:21 It will **extend e** from the 25,000 H7708+2025

EASY (5) [EASE]

Dt 1:41 **thinking it e** to go up into the hill country. H2103
2Ki 3:18 This *is an e thing* in the eyes of the LORD H7837
2Ki 5:20 "My master *was* **too e on** Naaman, this H3104
Mt 11:30 For my yoke is **e** and my burden is light." *G5982*
Lk 12:19 many years. **Take life e**; eat, drink and *G399*

EAT (521) [ATE, EATEN, EATER, EATING, EATS, MANEATER]

Ge 2:16 "*You are* **free to e** from any tree in the H430+430
Ge 2:17 but *you must* not **e** from the tree of the H430
Ge 2:17 when you **e** from it you will certainly die." H430
Ge 3: 1 '*You must* not **e** from any tree in the H430
Ge 3: 2 "*We may* **e** fruit from the trees in the H430
Ge 3: 3 '*You must* not **e** fruit from the tree that is in H430
Ge 3: 5 knows that when you **e** from it your eyes H430
Ge 3:11 tree that I commanded you not *to* **e** from?" H430
Ge 3:14 on your belly and *you will* **e** dust all the H430
Ge 3:17 commanded you, '*You must* not **e** from it,' H430
Ge 3:17 painful toil *you will* **e food** *from* it all the H430
Ge 3:18 and *you will* **e** the plants of the field. H430
Ge 3:19 of your brow *you will* **e** your food until H430
Ge 3:22 take also from the tree of life and **e**, H430
Ge 9: 4 "But *you must* not **e** meat that has its H430
Ge 18: 5 Let me get you **something to e**, so H7326+4312
Ge 24:33 "*I will* not **e** until I have told you what I H430
Ge 27: 4 of tasty food I like and bring it to me *to* **e**, H430
Ge 27: 7 prepare me some tasty food *to* **e**, H430
Ge 27:10 Then take it to your father *to* **e**, so that he H430
Ge 27:19 Please sit up and **e** some of my game, so H430
Ge 27:25 bring me some of your game *to* **e**, so that I H430
Ge 27:31 please sit up and **e** some of my game, so H430
Ge 28:20 will give me food to **e** and clothes to wear H430
Ge 32:32 day the Israelites *do* not **e** the tendon H430
Ge 37:25 As they sat down to **e** their meal, they H430
Ge 40:19 And the birds *will* **e away** your flesh." H430
Ge 43:16 they *are to* **e** with me at noon. H430
Ge 43:25 they had heard that *they were to* **e** there. H430
Ge 43:32 Egyptians could not **e** with Hebrews, H430
Ex 2:20 Invite him *to have* something *to* **e**." H430
Ex 12: 4 accordance with what each person *will* **e**. H430
Ex 12: 7 of the houses where *they* **e** the lambs. H430
Ex 12: 8 That same night *they are to* **e** the meat H430
Ex 12: 9 *Do* not **e** the meat raw or boiled in water H430
Ex 12:11 This is how *you are to* **e** it: *with* your cloak H430
Ex 12:11 staff in your hand. **E** it in haste; it is the H430
Ex 12:15 For seven days *you are to* **e** bread made H430
Ex 12:16 except *to* **prepare food** for everyone **to e** H430
Ex 12:18 In the first month *you are to* **e** bread made H430
Ex 12:20 **E** nothing made with yeast. Wherever you H430
Ex 12:20 you live, *you must* **e** unleavened bread." H430
Ex 12:43 the Passover meal: "No foreigner *may* **e** it. H430
Ex 12:44 you have bought *may* **e** it after you have H430
Ex 12:45 resident or a hired worker *may* not **e** it. H430
Ex 12:48 No uncircumcised male *may* **e** it. H430
Ex 13: 3 a mighty hand. **E** nothing containing yeast. H430
Ex 13: 6 For seven days **e** bread made without yeast H430
Ex 13: 7 **E** unleavened bread during those seven H430
Ex 16: 8 he gives you meat to **e** in the evening and H430
Ex 16:12 'At twilight *you will* **e** meat, and in the H430
Ex 16:15 "It is the bread the LORD has given you to **e**. H433
Ex 16:25 "**E** it today," Moses said, "because today is H430
Ex 16:32 see the bread *I* **gave** you **to e** in the H430
Ex 18:12 the elders of Israel to **e** a meal with Moses' H430
Ex 22:31 So *do* not **e** the meat of an animal torn by H430
Ex 23:11 and the wild animals *may* **e** what is left. H430
Ex 23:15 seven days **e** bread made without yeast H430
Ex 29:32 his sons *are to* **e** the meat of the H430
Ex 29:33 *They are to* **e** these offerings by which H430
Ex 29:33 But no *one* else *may* **e** them, because they H430
Ex 32: 6 they sat down to **e** and drink and got up to H430
Ex 34:15 invite you and *you will* **e** their sacrifices. H430
Ex 34:18 For seven days **e** bread made without yeast, H430
Lev 3:17 live: *You must* not **e** any fat or any blood H430
Lev 6:16 Aaron and his sons *shall* **e** the rest of it, but H430
Lev 6:16 *they are to* **e** it in the courtyard of the tent H430
Lev 6:18 Any male descendant of Aaron *may* **e** it. H430
Lev 6:26 The priest who offers it *shall* **e** it; it is to be H430
Lev 6:29 Any male in a priest's family *may* **e** it; it is H430
Lev 7: 6 Any male in a priest's family *may* **e** it, but it H430
Lev 7:19 anyone ceremonially clean *may* **e** it. H430
Lev 7:23 '*Do* not **e** any of the fat of cattle, sheep H430
Lev 7:24 other purpose, but *you* **must** not **e** it. H430+430
Lev 7:26 *you must* not **e** the blood of any bird or H430
Lev 8:31 tent of meeting and **e** it there with the H430
Lev 8:31 'Aaron and his sons *are to* **e** it.' H430
Lev 10:12 to the LORD and **e** it beside the altar, H430
Lev 10:13 **E** it in the sanctuary area, because it is your H430
Lev 10:14 your daughters *may* **e** the breast that H430
Lev 10:14 **E** them in a ceremonially clean place; they NDT
Lev 10:17 "Why didn't *you* **e** the sin offering in the H430
Lev 11: 2 live on land, these are the ones *you may* **e**: H430
Lev 11: 3 *You may* **e** any animal that has a divided H430
Lev 11: 4 a divided hoof, but *you must* not **e** them. H430
Lev 11: 8 *You must* not **e** their meat or touch their H430
Lev 11: 9 the streams *you may* **e** any that have H430
Lev 11:11 as unclean, *you must* not **e** their meat; you H430
Lev 11:13 as unclean and not **e** because they are H430
Lev 11:21 that walk on all fours that *you may* **e**: H430
Lev 11:22 Of these *you may* **e** any kind of locust H430
Lev 11:34 Any food you *are allowed* **to e** that has H430
Lev 11:39 an animal that you are allowed to **e** dies, H433
Lev 11:42 *You are* not *to* **e** any creature that moves H430
Lev 17:12 "None of you *may* **e** blood, nor may any H430
Lev 17:12 *may* any foreigner residing among you **e** H430
Lev 17:14 "*You must* not **e** the blood of any creature H430
Lev 19:25 But in the fifth year *you may* **e** its fruit. H430
Lev 19:26 " '*Do* not **e** any meat with the blood still in H430
Lev 21:22 *He may* **e** the most holy food of his God, as H430
Lev 22: 4 *he may* not **e** the sacred offerings until he H430
Lev 22: 6 *He must* not **e** any of the sacred offerings H430
Lev 22: 7 after that *he may* **e** the sacred H430
Lev 22: 8 *He must* not **e** anything found dead or torn H430
Lev 22:10 a priest's family *may* **e** the sacred offering, H430
Lev 22:10 *may* the guest of a priest or his hired worker **e** H430
Lev 22:11 born in his household, they *may* **e** his food. H430
Lev 22:12 she *may* not **e** any of the sacred H430
Lev 22:13 in her youth, *she may* **e** her father's food. H430
Lev 22:13 No unauthorized person, however, *may* **e** it. H430
Lev 22:16 by *allowing* them *to* **e** the sacred offerings H430
Lev 23: 6 seven days *you must* **e** bread made H430
Lev 23:14 *You must* not **e** any bread, or roasted or H430
Lev 24: 9 *who are to* **e** it in the sanctuary area H430
Lev 25:12 **e** only what is taken directly from the fields. H430
Lev 25:19 and *you will* **e** your fill and live there in H430
Lev 25:20 "What *will we* **e** in the seventh year if we H430
Lev 25:22 *you will* **e** from the old crop and will H430
Lev 25:22 old crop and *will continue to* **e** *from* it until H430
Lev 26: 5 and *you will* **e** all the food you want and H430
Lev 26:16 because your enemies *will* **e** it. H430
Lev 26:26 bread by weight. *You will* **e**, but you will H430
Lev 26:29 *You will* **e** the flesh of your sons and the H430
Nu 6: 3 not drink grape juice or **e** grapes or raisins. H430
Nu 6: 4 *they must* not **e** anything that comes from H430
Nu 9:11 *They are to* **e** the lamb, together with H430
Nu 11: 4 "If only we **had** meat **to e**! H430
Nu 11:13 keep wailing to me, 'Give us meat *to* **e**! H430
Nu 11:18 tomorrow, when *you will* **e** meat. H430
Nu 11:18 you wailed, "If only we **had** meat **to e**! H430
Nu 11:18 LORD will give you meat, and *you will* **e** it. H430
Nu 11:19 *You will* not **e** it for just one day, or two H430
Nu 11:21 give them meat *to* **e** for a whole month! H430
Nu 15:19 you **e** the food of the land, present a H430
Nu 18:10 **E** it as something most holy; every male H430
Nu 18:10 something most holy; every male *shall* **e** it. H430
Nu 18:11 who is ceremonially clean *may* **e** it. H430
Nu 18:13 who is ceremonially clean *may* **e** it. H430
Nu 18:31 your households *may* **e** the rest of it H430
Nu 28:17 seven days **e** bread made without yeast. H430
Dt 2: 6 silver for the food *you* **e** and the water you H430
Dt 2:28 Sell us food *to* **e** and water to drink for their H430
Dt 4:28 which cannot see or hear or **e** or smell. H430
Dt 6:11 then when *you* **e** and are satisfied, H430
Dt 8:12 Otherwise, when *you* **e** and are satisfied H430
Dt 8:16 He **gave** you manna **to e** in the wilderness H430
Dt 11:15 your cattle, and *you will* **e** and be satisfied. H430
Dt 12: 7 your families *shall* **e** and shall rejoice H430
Dt 12:15 of your towns and **e** as much of the meat H430
Dt 12:15 unclean and the clean *may* **e** it. H430
Dt 12:16 But *you must* not **e** the blood; pour it out on H430
Dt 12:17 You must not **e** in your own towns the tithe H430
Dt 12:18 *you are to* **e** them in the presence of the H430
Dt 12:20 then *you may* **e** as much of it as you want. H430
Dt 12:21 your own towns *you may* **e** as much of H430
Dt 12:22 **E** them as you would gazelle or deer. H430
Dt 12:22 ceremonially unclean and the clean *may* **e**. H430
Dt 12:23 But be sure you *do* not **e** the blood H430
Dt 12:23 and *you must* not **e** the life with the meat. H430
Dt 12:24 *You must* not **e** the blood; pour it out on the H430
Dt 12:25 *Do* not **e** it, so that it may go well with you H430
Dt 12:27 the LORD your God, but *you may* **e** the meat. H430
Dt 14: 3 *Do* not **e** any detestable thing. H430
Dt 14: 4 These are the animals *you may* **e**: the ox H430
Dt 14: 6 *You may* **e** any animal that has a divided H430
Dt 14: 7 a divided hoof *you may* not **e** the camel, H430
Dt 14: 8 *You are* not *to* **e** their meat or touch their H430
Dt 14: 9 *you may* **e** any that has fins and scales. H430
Dt 14:10 not have fins and scales *you may* not **e**; H430
Dt 14:11 *You may* **e** any clean bird. H430
Dt 14:12 But these *you may* not **e**: the eagle, the H430
Dt 14:19 insects are unclean to you; *do* not **e** *them*. H430
Dt 14:20 winged creature that is clean *you may* **e**. H430
Dt 14:21 *Do* not **e** anything you find already dead H430
Dt 14:21 your towns, and *they may* **e** it, or you may H430
Dt 14:23 **E** the tithe of your grain, new wine and H430
Dt 14:26 your household *shall* **e** there in the H430
Dt 14:29 towns may come and **e** and be satisfied, H430
Dt 15:20 you and your family *are to* **e** them in the H430
Dt 15:22 *You are to* **e** it in your own towns. H430
Dt 15:22 unclean and the clean may **e** it, NDT
Dt 15:23 But *you must* not **e** the blood; pour it out on H430
Dt 16: 3 *Do* not **e** it with bread made with yeast, but H430
Dt 16: 3 for seven days **e** unleavened bread, the H430
Dt 16: 7 Roast it and **e** it at the place the LORD your H430
Dt 16: 8 For six days **e** unleavened bread and on the H430
Dt 20:19 ax to them, because *you can* **e** their fruit. H430
Dt 23:24 *you may* **e** all the grapes you want H430
Dt 26:12 so that *they may* **e** in your towns and be H430
Dt 28:31 before your eyes, but *you will* **e** none of it. H430
Dt 28:33 you do not know *will* **e** what your land and H430
Dt 28:39 the grapes, because worms *will* **e** them. H430
Dt 28:53 the siege, *you will* **e** the fruit of the womb H430
Dt 28:57 her dire need *she intends to* **e** them H430
Dt 31:20 when *they* **e** their fill and thrive H430
Jos 24:13 live in them and **e** *from* vineyards and olive H430
Jdg 13: 4 drink and that *you do* not **e** anything H430

E

Jdg 13: 7 drink and *do* not e anything unclean, H430
Jdg 13:14 *She must* not e anything that comes from H430
Jdg 13:14 fermented drink nor e anything unclean. H430
Jdg 13:16 detain me, *I will* not e any of your food. H430
Jdg 14:14 of the eater, **something to e**; out of the H4407
Jdg 19: 5 yourself with **something to e**; H7326+4312
Jdg 19: 6 of them sat down *to* e and drink together. H430
Jdg 19:21 *they had something to* e and drink. H430
1Sa 1: 7 provoked her till she wept and *would* not e. H430
1Sa 1: 8 Why don't *you* e? Why are you H430
1Sa 2:36 some priestly office so I *can have* food *to* e." H430
1Sa 9:13 before he goes up to the high place to e. H430
1Sa 9:13 afterward, those who are invited *will* e. H430
1Sa 9:19 today *you are to* e with me, and in H430
1Sa 9:24 **E**, because it was set aside for you for this H430
1Sa 14:34 slaughter them here and e them. H430
1Sa 20:24 Moon feast came, the king sat down to e. H430
1Sa 20:34 that second day of the feast *he did* not e, H430
1Sa 28:22 you some food so *you may* e and have the H430
1Sa 28:23 "*I will* not e." But his men H430
1Sa 30:11 gave him water to drink and food *to* e— H430
2Sa 3:35 all came and **urged** David **to e** something H1356
2Sa 9: 7 and you *will* always e at my table. H430
2Sa 9:10 of your master, *will* always e at my table." H430
2Sa 11:11 I go to my house to e and drink and make H430
2Sa 12:17 and *he would* not e any food with them. H1356
2Sa 12:21 that the child is dead, you get up and e!" H430
2Sa 13: 5 to come and **give** me something **to e**. H1356
2Sa 13: 5 may watch her and then e it from her hand. H430
2Sa 13: 6 in my sight, so *I may* e from her hand." H1356
2Sa 13: 9 served him the bread, but he refused to e. H430
2Sa 13:10 my bedroom so *I may* e from your hand." H1356
2Sa 13:11 But when she took it to him to e, he H430
2Sa 16: 2 the bread and fruit are for the men to e H430
2Sa 17:29 cows' milk for David and his people to e. H430
2Sa 19:28 a place among *those who* e *at* your table. H430
1Ki 2: 7 them be among *those who* e *at* your table. H430
1Ki 13: 8 nor *would I* e bread or drink water here. H430
1Ki 13: 9 '*You must* not e bread or drink water or H430
1Ki 13:15 said to him, "Come home with me and e." H430
1Ki 13:16 nor *can I* e bread or drink water with you in H430
1Ki 13:17 '*You must* not e bread or drink water there H430
1Ki 13:18 house so that *he may* e bread and drink H430
1Ki 13:22 place where he told you not *to* e or drink. H430
1Ki 14:11 Dogs *will* e those belonging to Jeroboam H430
1Ki 16: 4 Dogs *will* e those belonging to Baasha who H430
1Ki 17:12 my son, that *we may* e it—and die. H430
1Ki 18:19 of Asherah, *who* e *at* Jezebel's table." H430
1Ki 18:41 e and drink, for there is the sound of a H430
1Ki 18:42 So Ahab went off to e and drink, but Elijah H430
1Ki 19: 5 touched him and said, "Get up and e." H430
1Ki 19: 7 said, "Get up and e, for the journey is H430
1Ki 21: 4 He lay on his bed sulking and refused *to* e. H430
1Ki 21: 5 are you so sullen? Why won't you e?" H430
1Ki 21: 7 king over Israel? Get up and e! Cheer up. H430
1Ki 21:24 "Dogs *will* e those belonging to Ahab who H430
2Ki 4: 8 he came by, he stopped there to e. H430
2Ki 4:40 but as they *began to* e it, they cried H430
2Ki 4:40 death in the pot!" And they could not e it. H430
2Ki 4:41 pot and said, "Serve it to the people *to* e." H430
2Ki 4:42 "Give it to the people *to* e," Elisha said. H430
2Ki 4:43 answered, "Give it to the people *to* e. H430
2Ki 4:43 'They *will* e and have some left over H430
2Ki 6:22 them so that *they may* e and drink and H430
2Ki 6:28 'Give up your son so *we may* e him today H430
2Ki 6:28 him today, and tomorrow *we'll* e my son. H430
2Ki 6:29 'Give up your son so *we may* e him,' but H430
2Ki 7: 2 "but *you will* not e any of it! H430
2Ki 7:19 your own eyes, but *you will* not e any of it!" H430
2Ki 18:27 *will have to* e their own excrement and H430
2Ki 18:31 each of you *will* e *fruit from* your own vine H430
2Ki 19:29 "This year you *will* e what grows by itself H430
2Ki 19:29 reap, plant vineyards and e their fruit. H430
2Ki 25: 3 that there was no food for the people to e. NDT
2Ch 31:10 we have had enough *to* e and plenty to H430
Ezr 2:63 ordered them not *to* e any of the most H430
Ezr 9:12 may be strong and e the good things of H430
Ne 5: 2 in order for *us to* e and stay alive, we H430
Ne 7:65 ordered them not *to* e any of the most H430
Ne 8:12 all the people went away to e and drink, H430
Ne 9:36 ancestors so they *could* e its fruit and the H430
Est 4:16 *Do* not e or drink for three days, night or H430
Job 1: 4 their three sisters to e and drink with them. H430
Job 27:14 his offspring will never have enough to e. H4312
Job 31: 8 then *may* others e what I have sown, and H430
Ps 22:26 The poor *will* e and be satisfied; those who H430
Ps 50:13 *Do I* e the flesh of bulls or drink the blood H430
Ps 78:24 he rained down manna for the people to e H430
Ps 78:25 he sent them **all** the food they **could** e. H8427
Ps 102: 4 withered like grass; I forget *to* e my food. H430
Ps 102: 9 For *I* e ashes as my food and mingle my H430
Ps 127: 2 toiling for food *to* e—for he grants sleep H430
Ps 128: 2 *You will* e the fruit of your labor; blessings H430
Ps 141: 4 evildoers; *do* not *let me* e their delicacies. H4310
Pr 1:31 *they will* e the fruit of their ways and be H430
Pr 4:17 *They* e the bread of wickedness and drink H4310
Pr 9: 5 e my food and drink the wine I have H4310
Pr 13:25 The righteous e to their hearts' content, but H430
Pr 18:21 and those who love it *will* e its fruit. H430
Pr 23: 6 *Do* not e the food of a begrudging host H4310
Pr 23: 7 "**E** and drink," he says to you, but his heart H430
Pr 24:13 **E** honey, my son, for it is good; honey from H430
Pr 25:16 If you find honey, e just enough—too H430
Pr 25:21 is hungry, **give** him food **to e**; if he is H430
Pr 25:27 It is not good *to* e too much honey, nor is it H430
Pr 27:18 one who guards a fig tree *will* e its fruit, H430
Pr 30:22 a godless fool who gets plenty to e, H4312
Pr 31:27 her household and *does* not e the bread of H430
Ecc 2:24 nothing better than *to* e and drink and find H430
Ecc 2:25 without him, who *can* e or find enjoyment? H430
Ecc 3:13 That each of them *may* e and drink, and H430
Ecc 5:12 is sweet, whether *they* e little or much, but H430
Ecc 5:17 All their days *they* e in darkness, with great H430
Ecc 5:18 that it is appropriate for a person to e, to H430
Ecc 8:15 the sun than to e and drink and be glad H430
Ecc 9: 7 e your food with gladness, and drink H430
Ecc 10:17 whose princes e at a proper time— H430
SS 5: 1 my wine and my milk. **E**, friends, and drink H430
Isa 1:19 *you will* e the good things of the land; H430
Isa 4: 1 "*We will* e our own food and provide our H430
Isa 7:22 the milk they give, *there will be* curds *to* e. H430
Isa 7:22 remain in the land *will* e curds and honey. H430
Isa 9:20 on the left *they will* e, but not be H430
Isa 11: 7 the lion *will* e straw like the ox. H430
Isa 21: 5 they spread the rugs, they e, they drink! H430
Isa 22:13 "*Let* us e and drink," you say, "for tomorrow H430
Isa 30:24 that work the soil *will* e fodder and mash, H430
Isa 36:12 *will have to* e their own excrement and H430
Isa 36:16 each of you *will* e *fruit from* your own vine H430
Isa 37:30 "This year you *will* e what grows by itself H430
Isa 37:30 reap, plant vineyards and e their fruit. H430
Isa 49:26 *I will* **make** your oppressors e their own H430
Isa 50: 9 like a garment; the moths *will* e them **up**. H430
Isa 51: 8 For the moth *will* e them **up** like a garment H430
Isa 55: 1 you who have no money, come, buy and e! H430
Isa 55: 2 listen to me, and e what is good, and you H430
Isa 62: 9 those who harvest it *will* e it and praise the H430
Isa 65: 4 secret vigil; who e the flesh of pigs, and H430
Isa 65:13 "My servants *will* e, but you will go hungry H430
Isa 65:21 they will plant vineyards and e their fruit. H430
Isa 65:22 others live in them, or plant and others e. H430
Isa 65:25 the lion *will* e straw like the ox H430
Isa 66:17 one who is among *those who* e the flesh of H430
Isa 66:24 the **worms** *that* e them will not die AIT
Jer 2: 7 into a fertile land to e its fruit and rich H430
Jer 7:21 other sacrifices and e the meat *yourselves*! H430
Jer 9:15 *I will* **make** this people e bitter **food** and H430
Jer 16: 8 is feasting and sit down to e and drink. H430
Jer 19: 9 *I will* **make** them e the flesh of their sons H430
Jer 19: 9 and *they will* e one another's flesh H430
Jer 23:15 "*I will* **make** them e bitter **food** and drink H430
Jer 29: 5 plant gardens and e what they produce. H430
Jer 29:28 plant gardens and e what they produce. H430
Jer 52: 6 that there was no food for the people to e. NDT
La 2:20 *Should* women e their offspring, the H430
Eze 2: 8 open your mouth and e what I give you." H430
Eze 3: 1 "Son of man, e what is before you, eat this H430
Eze 3: 1 what is before you, e this scroll; then go H430
Eze 3: 2 my mouth, and *he* **gave** me the scroll **to e**. H430
Eze 3: 3 e this scroll I am giving you and fill your H430
Eze 4: 9 *You are to* e it during the 390 days you lie H430
Eze 4:10 shekels of food *to* e each day and eat it at H430
Eze 4:10 food to eat each day and e it at set times. H430
Eze 4:12 **E** the food as you would a loaf of barley H430
Eze 4:13 people of Israel *will* e defiled food among H430
Eze 4:16 *The people will* e rationed food in anxiety H430
Eze 5:10 in your midst parents *will* e their children, H430
Eze 5:10 children, and children *will* e their parents. H430
Eze 12:18 tremble *as you* e your food, and H430
Eze 12:19 *They will* e their food in anxiety and drink H430
Eze 16:19 olive oil and honey *I* **gave** you **to e**—you H430
Eze 18: 2 " 'The parents e sour grapes, and the H430
Eze 18: 6 *He does* not e at the mountain shrines H430
Eze 18:15 "*He does* not e at the mountain shrines H430
Eze 22: 9 in you are *those who* e at the mountain H430
Eze 24:17 beard or e the customary food of H430
Eze 24:22 beard or e the customary food of H430
Eze 25: 4 they *will* e your fruit and drink your milk. H430
Eze 33:25 Since *you* e meat with the blood still in it H430
Eze 34: 3 *You* e the curds, clothe yourselves with the H430
Eze 39:17 *There you will* e flesh and drink blood. H430
Eze 39:18 *You will* e the flesh of mighty men and H430
Eze 39:19 *you will* e fat till you are glutted and drink H430
Eze 39:20 At my table *you will* e *your* **fill** *of* horses H8425
Eze 42:13 who approach the LORD *will* e the most holy H430
Eze 44: 3 inside the gateway to e in the presence of H430
Eze 44:29 They *will* e the grain offerings, the sin H430
Eze 44:31 The priests *must* not e anything, whether H430
Eze 45:21 during which you *shall* e bread made H430
Da 1:12 vegetables *to* e and water to drink. H430
Da 1:13 of the young men who e the royal food, H430
Da 4:25 you *will* e grass like the ox and be A10301
Da 4:32 animals; you *will* e grass like the ox. A10301
Da 7: 5 was told, 'Get up and e your fill of flesh! A10030
Da 11:26 *Those who* e *from* the king's provisions will H430
Hos 4:10 "*They will* e but not have enough; they will H430
Hos 8:13 and *though they* e the meat, the H430
Hos 9: 3 return to Egypt and e unclean food in H430
Hos 9: 4 mourners; all *who* e them will be unclean. H430
Joel 2:26 *You will* **have plenty to e**, until you H430+430
Am 9:14 they will make gardens and e their fruit. H430
Ob 7 those who e your bread will set a trap for NDT
Jnh 3: 7 taste anything; *do* not *let them* e or drink. H8286
Mic 3: 3 who e my people's flesh, strip off their skin H430
Mic 3: 5 if they **have something to e**, H5966+928+9094
Mic 6:14 You *will* e but not be satisfied; your H430
Mic 7: 1 there is no cluster of grapes to e, none of H430
Zep 3:13 They *will* e and lie down and no one will H8286
Hag 1: 6 harvested little. *You* e, but never have H430
Zec 11: 9 *Let* those who are left e one another's flesh H430
Zec 11:16 but *will* e the meat of the choice sheep H430
Mt 6:25 your life, what *you will* e or drink; or about G2266
Mt 6:31 'What *shall we* e?' or 'What shall G2266
Mt 9:11 "Why *does* your teacher e with tax G2266
Mt 12: 1 to pick some heads of grain and e them. G2266
Mt 14:16 You give them something *to* e." G2266
Mt 15: 2 don't wash their hands before *they* e!" G2266
Mt 15:27 "Even the dogs e the crumbs that fall from G2266
Mt 15:32 me three days and have nothing *to* e. G2266
Mt 24:49 his fellow servants and *to* e and drink with G2266
Mt 25:35 hungry and you gave me something *to* e, G2266
Mt 25:42 hungry and you gave me nothing *to* e, G2266
Mt 26:17 preparations for you *to* e the Passover?" G2266
Mt 26:26 "Take and e; this is my body. G2266
Mk 2:16 "Why *does he* e with tax collectors and G2266
Mk 2:26 which is lawful only for priests *to* e. G2266
Mk 3:20 disciples were not even able *to* e. G788+2266
Mk 5:43 told them to give her something *to* e. G2266
Mk 6:31 that they did not even have a chance *to* e, G2266
Mk 6:36 buy themselves something *to* e. G2266
Mk 6:37 "You give them something *to* e. G2266
Mk 6:37 much on bread and give it to them *to* e?" G2266
Mk 7: 3 all the Jews *do* not e unless they give G2266
Mk 7: 4 the marketplace *they do* not e unless they G2266
Mk 7:27 "First let the children e **all** *they* **want**," G5963
Mk 7:28 dogs under the table e the children's G2266
Mk 8: 1 Since they had nothing *to* e, Jesus called G2266
Mk 8: 2 me three days and have nothing *to* e. G2266
Mk 9:48 where " 'the **worms** *that* e them do not die AIT
Mk 11:14 "*May* no one ever e fruit from you again." G2266
Mk 14:12 preparations for you to e the Passover?" G2266
Mk 14:14 where *I may* e the Passover with my G2266
Lk 5:30 "Why *do you* e and drink with tax G2266
Lk 6: 1 rub them in their hands and e the kernels. G2266
Lk 6: 4 he ate what is lawful only for priests *to* e. G2266
Lk 8:55 told them to give her *something to* e. G2266
Lk 9:13 replied, "You give them *something to* e." G2266
Lk 10: 8 are welcomed, e what is offered to you. G2266
Lk 11:37 a Pharisee invited him to e with him; so he G753
Lk 12:19 Take life easy; e, drink and be merry." G2266
Lk 12:22 your life, what *you will* e; or about your G2266
Lk 12:29 set your heart on what *you will* e or drink; G2266
Lk 12:45 women, and *to* e and drink and get drunk. G2266
Lk 14: 1 when Jesus went *to* e in the house G2266+788
Lk 14:15 is the one *who will* e at the feast in G2266
Lk 16:21 longing *to* e what fell from the rich G5963
Lk 17: 7 'Come along now and **sit down to e**'? G404
Lk 17: 8 ready and wait on me while *I* e and drink; G2266
Lk 17: 8 drink; after that you *may* e and drink'? G2266
Lk 22: 8 preparations for us *to* e the Passover." G2266
Lk 22:11 where *I may* e the Passover with my G2266
Lk 22:15 eagerly desired *to* e this Passover with G2266
Lk 22:16 *I will* not e it again until it finds G2266
Lk 22:30 so that *you may* e and drink at my table in G2266
Lk 24:41 "Do you have anything here *to* e? G1110
Jn 4:31 disciples urged him, "Rabbi, e something." G2266
Jn 4:32 "I have food *to* e that you know nothing G2266
Jn 6: 5 shall we buy bread for these people *to* e?" G2266
Jn 6:12 When *they had all* **had enough to e**, he G1855
Jn 6:31 'He gave them bread from heaven *to* e.'" G2266
Jn 6:50 heaven, which anyone *may* e and not die. G2266
Jn 6:52 "How can this man give us his flesh *to* e?" G2266
Jn 6:53 unless *you* e the flesh of the Son of Man G2266
Jn 18:28 because *they wanted to be able to* e the G2266
Ac 9: 9 and *did* not e or drink anything. G2266
Ac 10:10 hungry and wanted something *to* e, G1174
Ac 10:13 voice told him, "Get up, Peter. Kill and e." G2266
Ac 11: 7 telling me, 'Get up, Peter. Kill and e.' G2266
Ac 23:12 with an oath not *to* e or drink until they G2266
Ac 23:14 a solemn oath not *to* e anything until we G1174
Ac 23:21 taken an oath not *to* e or drink until they G2266
Ac 27:33 dawn Paul urged them all *to* e. G3561+5575
Ac 27:35 Then he broke it and began *to* e. G2266
Ro 14: 2 person's faith allows them *to* e anything, G2266
Ro 14: 3 the *one who does* not e everything G2266
Ro 14:15 sister is distressed because of **what** you e, G1109
Ro 14:20 wrong for a person *to* e anything that G2266
Ro 14:21 It is better not *to* e meat or drink wine or to G2266
Ro 14:23 has doubts is condemned if *they* e, G2266
1Co 5:11 *Do* not even e **with** such people. G5303
1Co 8: 7 to idols *that when they* e sacrificial food G2266
1Co 8: 8 we are no worse if *we do* not e, and no G2266
1Co 8:10 be emboldened to e what is sacrificed to G2266
1Co 8:13 if **what I** e causes my brother or sister to G1109
1Co 8:13 fall into sin, *I will* never e meat again, so G2266
1Co 9: 7 a vineyard and *does* not e its grapes? G2266
1Co 10: 7 people sat down *to* e and drink and got G2266
1Co 10:18 Do not those *who* e the sacrifices G2266
1Co 10:25 **E** anything sold in the meat market G2266
1Co 10:27 e whatever is put before you without G2266
1Co 10:28 then *do* not e it, both for the sake of the G2266
1Co 10:31 So whether *you* e or drink or whatever you G2266
1Co 11:20 it is not the Lord's Supper *you* e, G2266
1Co 11:22 Don't you have homes to e and drink in G2266
1Co 11:26 For whenever *you* e this bread and drink G2266
1Co 11:28 before *they* e of the bread and G2266

1Co 11:29 For those *who* **e** and drink without G2266
1Co 11:29 the body of Christ **e** and drink judgment G2266
1Co 11:33 when you gather to **e**, you should all eat G2266
1Co 11:33 you gather to eat, you should all **e** together. NDT
1Co 11:34 who is hungry *should* **e** something at G2266
1Co 15:32 are not raised, "*Let us* **e** and drink, for G2266
Gal 2:12 James, *he used to* **e with** the Gentiles. G5303
Col 2:16 anyone judge you by *what* you **e** or drink, G1111
2Th 3:8 nor *did we* **e** anyone's food without paying G2266
2Th 3:10 one who is unwilling to work *shall* not **e**." G2266
2Th 3:12 to settle down and earn the food they **e**. G2266
Heb 13:10 at the tabernacle have no right *to* **e**. G2266
Jas 5:3 against you and **e** your flesh like fire. G2266
Rev 2:7 I will give the right *to* **e** from the tree of G2266
Rev 3:20 I will come in and **e** with that person, and G1268
Rev 10:9 "Take it and **e** it. It will turn your G2983
Rev 17:16 *they will* **e** her flesh and burn her with fire. G2266
Rev 19:18 so that *you may* **e** the flesh of kings G2266

EATEN (65) [EAT]

Ge 3:11 *Have you* **e** from the tree that I H430
Ge 6:21 kind of food that *is to* **be e** and store it H430
Ge 14:24 what my men *have* **e** and the share H430
Ge 31:38 nor *have I* **e** rams from your flocks. H430
Ge 31:54 After *they had* **e**, they spent the night there. H430
Ge 43:2 So when *they had* **e** all the grain they had H430
Ex 12:46 "*It must* **be e** inside the house; take none H430
Ex 21:28 to death, and its meat *must* not **be e**. H430
Ex 29:34 *It must* not **be e**, because it is H430
Lev 6:16 but *it is to* **be e** without yeast in the H430
Lev 6:23 be burned completely; *it must* not **be e**." H430
Lev 6:26 *it is to* **be e** in the sanctuary area H430
Lev 6:30 in the Holy Place *must* not **be e**; H430
Lev 7:6 but *it must* **be e** in the sanctuary area H430
Lev 7:15 of thanksgiving *must* **be e** on the day it is H430
Lev 7:16 the sacrifice *shall* **be e** on the day they H430
Lev 7:16 left over *may* **be e** on the next day. H430
Lev 7:18 offering *is* **e** on the third day, H430+430
Lev 7:19 ceremonially unclean *must* not **be e**; H430
Lev 10:18 *you should have* **e** the goat in the H430+430
Lev 10:19 been pleased if *I had* **e** the sin offering H430
Lev 11:41 to be regarded as unclean; it *is* not *to* **be e**. H430
Lev 11:47 creatures that *may* **be e** and those that may H430
Lev 11:47 may be eaten and those that *may* not **be e**. H430
Lev 17:13 bird that *may* **be e** must drain out the H430
Lev 19:6 *It shall* **be e** on the day you sacrifice it or on H430
Lev 19:7 If *any of it* **is e** on the third day, it is H430+430
Lev 19:23 to consider it forbidden; *it must* not **be e**. H430
Lev 22:30 *It must* **be e** that same day; leave none of it H430
Lev 25:7 Whatever the land produces may be **e**. H430
Nu 12:12 mother's womb with its flesh half **e away**." H430
Dt 8:10 When *you have* **e** and are satisfied, praise H430
Dt 26:14 *I have* not **e** any of the sacred portion while H430
Ru 2:18 she had left over after she *had* **e enough**. H8427
1Sa 14:30 been if the men *had* **e** today some of H430+430
1Sa 28:20 for *he had* **e** nothing all that day and all H430
1Sa 30:12 for *he had* not **e** any food or drunk any H430
2Sa 19:42 *Have we* **e** any of the king's **provisions** H430+430
1Ki 13:28 The lion *had* neither **e** the body nor H430
Job 6:6 **Is** tasteless food **e** without salt, or is there H430
Job 13:28 like a garment **e** *by* moths. H430
Pr 9:17 water is sweet; food **e** in secret is delicious!" NDT
Pr 23:8 vomit up the little *you have* **e** and will have H430
Pr 30:17 of the valley, *will be* **e** *by* the vultures. H430
SS 5:1 *I have* **e** my honeycomb and my honey; H430
Jer 24:2 very bad figs, so bad *they could* not **be e**. H430
Jer 24:3 the bad ones are so bad *they* cannot **be e**." H430
Jer 24:8 which are so bad *they* cannot **be e**,' says H430
Jer 29:17 like figs that are so bad *they* cannot **be e**. H430
Jer 31:29 'The parents *have* **e** sour grapes, and H430
Eze 4:14 now *I have* never **e** anything found H430
Hos 10:13 *you have* **e** the fruit of deception. H430
Joel 1:4 swarm has left the great locusts *have* **e**; H430
Joel 1:4 locusts have left the young locusts *have* **e**; H430
Joel 1:4 locusts have left other locusts *have* **e**. H430
Joel 2:25 repay you for the years the locusts *have* **e**— H430
Mk 6:44 number of the men *who had* **e** was five G2266
Jn 6:13 loaves left over *by* those *who had* **e**. G1048
Jn 6:23 place where *the people had* **e** the bread G2266
Ac 10:14 "*I have* never **e** anything impure or G2266
Ac 12:23 and he was **e by worms** and died. G5037
Ac 27:33 without food—*you* haven't **e** anything. G4689
Ac 27:38 *When they had* **e as much as** *they* **wanted** G3170+5575
Jas 5:2 and **moths** *have* **e** your clothes. G4963+1181
Rev 10:10 but when *I had* **e** it, my stomach G2266

EATER (3) [EAT]

Jdg 14:14 He replied, "Out of the **e**, something to eat; H430
Isa 55:10 seed for the sower and bread for the **e**, H430
Na 3:12 the figs fall into the mouth of the **e**. H430

EATING (60) [EAT]

Ge 40:17 the birds *were* **e** them out of the basket H430
Ex 34:28 forty nights without **e** bread or drinking H430
Lev 26:10 *You will still be* **e** last year's harvest when H430
Dt 27:7 **e** them and rejoicing in the presence of the H430
Dt 28:55 any of the flesh of his children that *he is* **e**. H430
Jdg 9:27 While *they were* **e** and drinking, they H430
Jdg 19:4 with him three days, **e** and drinking, and H430
Ru 3:3 there until he has finished **e** and drinking. H430
Ru 3:7 When Boaz *had finished* **e** and drinking H430
1Sa 1:9 Once when *they had* finished **e** and H430
1Sa 9:13 The people *will* not *begin* **e** until he comes H430
1Sa 14:33 against the LORD by **e** meat that has blood H430
1Sa 14:34 against the LORD by **e** meat with blood still H430
1Sa 30:16 over the countryside, **e**, drinking and H430
1Ki 1:25 Right now they *are* **e** and drinking with him H430
1Ki 13:23 man of God had finished **e** and drinking, H430
2Ki 6:23 after *they had finished* **e** and drinking H430
1Ch 12:39 days there with David, **e** and drinking, for H430
Ps 14:4 They devour my people *as though* **e** bread H430
Ps 53:4 They devour my people *as though* **e** bread H430
Isa 7:15 *He will be* **e** curds and honey when he H430
Isa 22:13 of sheep, **e** *of* meat and drinking of wine! H430
Isa 29:8 as when a hungry person dreams of **e**, but H430
Jer 41:1 While *they were* **e** together there, H430
Da 6:18 spent the night **without e** and without A10297
Zec 7:6 And when *you were* **e** and drinking, were H430
Mt 11:18 For John came neither **e** nor drinking, and G2266
Mt 11:19 The Son of Man came **e** and drinking, and G2266
Mt 15:20 **e** with unwashed hands does not G2266
Mt 24:38 people were **e** and drinking G5592
Mt 26:21 And *while* they *were* **e**, he said, "Truly I G2266
Mt 26:26 *While* they *were* **e**, Jesus took bread, and G2266
Mk 2:15 sinners *were* **e with** him and his G5263
Mk 2:16 Pharisees saw *him* **e** with the sinners G2266
Mk 7:2 of his disciples **e** food with hands that G2266
Mk 7:5 the elders instead of **e** their food with G2266
Mk 14:18 While they were reclining at the table **e** G2266
Mk 14:18 will betray me—one *who is* **e** with me." G2266
Mk 14:22 *While* they *were* **e**, Jesus took bread, and G2266
Mk 16:14 appeared to the Eleven *as* they *were* **e**; G367
Lk 5:29 collectors and others were **e** with them. G2879
Lk 5:33 Pharisees, but yours *go on* **e** and drinking." G2266
Lk 7:33 Baptist came neither **e** bread nor drinking G2266
Lk 7:34 The Son of Man came **e** and drinking, and G2266
Lk 7:37 learned that Jesus *was* **e** at the Pharisee's G2879
Lk 10:7 **e** and drinking whatever they give you G2266
Lk 15:16 with the pods that the pigs *were* **e**, G2266
Lk 17:27 *People were* **e**, drinking, marrying and G2266
Lk 17:28 *People were* **e** and drinking, buying and G2266
Jn 21:15 When *they had finished* **e**, Jesus said to G753
Ac 1:4 occasion, *while he was* **e with** them, he G5259
Ro 14:15 Do not *by* your **e** destroy someone for G1109
Ro 14:17 of God is not a *matter of* **e** and drinking, G1111
Ro 14:23 because their **e** is not from faith; and NDT
1Co 8:4 So then, about **e** food sacrificed to idols G1111
1Co 8:10 all your knowledge, **e** in an idol's temple G2879
1Co 11:21 when you *are* **e**, some of you go ahead G2266
Heb 13:9 not *by* **e** *ceremonial* **foods**, which is G1109
Jude 12 **e with** you without the slightest qualm G5307
Rev 2:20 immorality and the **e** of food sacrificed to G2266

EATS (33) [EAT]

Ex 12:15 whoever **e** anything with yeast in it from H430
Ex 12:19 *who* **e** anything with yeast in it must be cut H430
Lev 7:18 the person who **e** any of it will be held H430
Lev 7:20 if anyone who is unclean **e** any meat of the H430
Lev 7:21 then **e** any of the meat of the H430
Lev 7:25 Anyone *who* **e** the fat of an animal from H430
Lev 7:27 Anyone who **e** blood must be cut off from H430
Lev 11:40 Anyone *who* **e** some of its carcass must H430
Lev 14:47 Anyone who sleeps or **e** in the house must H430
Lev 17:10 residing among them who **e** blood, H430
Lev 17:14 its blood; anyone *who* **e** it must be cut off." H430
Lev 17:15 who **e** anything found dead or torn by wild H430
Lev 19:8 *Whoever* **e** it will be held responsible H430
Lev 22:14 " 'Anyone *who* **e** a sacred offering by H430
1Sa 14:24 be anyone who **e** food before evening H430
1Sa 14:28 'Cursed be anyone who **e** food today!' H430
2Sa 19:35 your servant taste what *he* **e** and drinks? H430
Job 18:13 *It* **e away** parts of his skin; death's firstborn H430
Job 39:24 In frenzied excitement *it* **e up** the ground H1686
Ps 106:20 God for an image of a bull, *which* **e** grass. H430
Pr 30:20 *She* **e** and wipes her mouth and says, 'I've H430
Isa 44:16 his meal, he roasts his meat and **e** *his* **fill**. H8425
Isa 59:5 Whoever **e** their eggs will die, and when H430
Jer 31:30 own sin; whoever **e** sour grapes—their own H430
Eze 18:11 "*He* **e** at the mountain shrines. He defiles H430
Lk 15:2 man welcomes sinners and **e with** them." G5303
Jn 6:51 Whoever **e** this bread will live forever G2266
Jn 6:54 Whoever **e** my flesh and drinks my blood G5592
Jn 6:56 Whoever **e** my flesh and drinks my blood G5592
Ro 14:2 whose faith is weak, **e** only vegetables. G2266
Ro 14:3 The *one who* **e** everything must not treat G2266
Ro 14:6 Whoever **e** meat does so to the Lord, for G2266
1Co 11:27 whoever **e** the bread or drinks the cup of G2266

EAVES (1)

1Ki 7:9 great courtyard and from foundation to **e**, H3258

EBAL (7)

Ge 36:23 Manahath, **E**, Shepho and Onam. H6507
Dt 11:29 the blessings, and on Mount **E** the curses. H6506
Dt 27:4 set up these stones on Mount **E**, as I H6506
Dt 27:13 stand on Mount **E** to pronounce curses: H6506
Jos 8:30 built on Mount **E** an altar to the LORD, H6506
Jos 8:33 half of them in front of Mount **E**, H6506
1Ch 1:40 Manahath, **E**, Shepho and Onam H6507

EBB (1) [EBBED, EBBING, EBBS]

La 2:12 as their lives **e away** in their mothers' H9161

EBBED (1) [EBB]

Ps 107:5 hungry and thirsty, and their lives **e away**. H6494

EBBING (1) [EBB]

Jnh 2:7 "When my life *was* **e away**, I remembered H6494

EBBS (1) [EBB]

Job 30:16 "And now my life **e away**; days of H9161

EBED (6)

Jdg 9:26 Now Gaal son of **E** moved with his clan H6270
Jdg 9:28 Then Gaal son of **E** said, "Who is H6270
Jdg 9:30 of the city heard what Gaal son of **E** said, H6270
Jdg 9:31 "Gaal son of **E** and his clan have come to H6270
Jdg 9:35 Now Gaal son of **E** had gone out and was H6270
Ezr 8:6 of Adin, **E** son of Jonathan, and H6270

EBED-MELEK (6)

Jer 38:7 But **E**, a Cushite, an official in the royal H6283
Jer 38:8 **E** went out of the palace and said to him, H6283
Jer 38:10 Then the king commanded **E** the Cushite H6283
Jer 38:11 So **E** took the men with him and went to a H6283
Jer 38:12 **E** the Cushite said to Jeremiah, "Put these H6283
Jer 39:16 "Go and tell **E** the Cushite, 'This is what H6283

EBENEZER (3)

1Sa 4:1 The Israelites camped at **E**, and the H75
1Sa 5:1 ark of God, they took it from **E** to Ashdod. H75
1Sa 7:12 He named it **E**, saying, "Thus far the LORD H75

EBER (16)

Ge 10:21 was the ancestor of all the sons of **E**. H6299
Ge 10:24 of Shelah, and Shelah the father of **E**. H6299
Ge 10:25 Two sons were born to **E**: One was named H6299
Ge 11:14 lived 30 years, he became the father of **E**. H6299
Ge 11:15 And after he became the father of **E** H6299
Ge 11:16 When **E** had lived 34 years, he became H6299
Ge 11:17 **E** lived 430 years and had other sons and H6299
Nu 24:24 they will subdue Ashur and **E**, but they H6299
1Ch 1:18 of Shelah, and Shelah the father of **E**. H6299
1Ch 1:19 Two sons were born to **E**: One was named H6299
1Ch 1:25 **E**, Peleg, Reu, H6299
1Ch 5:13 Jakan, Zia and **E**—seven in all. H6299
1Ch 8:12 **E**, Misham, Shemed (who built Ono and H6299
1Ch 8:22 Ishpan, **E**, Eliel, H6299
Ne 12:20 of Sallu's, Kallai; of Amok's, **E**; H6299
Lk 3:35 of Peleg, the son *of* **E**, the son of Shelah, G1576

EBEZ (1)

Jos 19:20 Rabbith, Kishion, **E**, H82

EBIASAPH (3)

1Ch 6:23 Elkanah his son, **E** his son, Assir his son, H47
1Ch 6:37 son of Assir, the son of **E**, the son of Korah, H47
1Ch 9:19 son of Kore, the son of **E**, the son of Korah, H47

EBONY (1)

Eze 27:15 they paid you with ivory tusks and **e**. H2041

ECBATANA (1)

Ezr 6:2 in the citadel of **E** in the province of A10020

ECHO (2) [ECHOES]

Hab 2:11 the beams of the woodwork *will* **e** it. H6699
Zep 2:14 Their hooting *will* **e** through the windows H8876

ECHOES (1) [ECHO]

Isa 15:8 Their outcry **e along** the border of Moab H5938

EDEN (19) [BETH EDEN]

Ge 2:8 in the east, in **E**; and there he put the H6359
Ge 2:10 A river watering the garden flowed from **E**; H6359
Ge 2:15 him in the Garden of **E** to work it and take H6359
Ge 3:23 from the Garden of **E** to work the ground H6359
Ge 3:24 side of the Garden of **E** cherubim and a H6359
Ge 4:16 lived in the land of Nod, east of **E**. H6359
2Ki 19:12 the people of **E** who were in Tel H6361
2Ch 29:12 Joah son of Zimmah and **E** son of Joah; H6360
2Ch 31:15 **E**, Miniamin, Jeshua, Shemaiah, Amariah H6360
Isa 37:12 the people of **E** who were in Tel H6361
Isa 51:3 he will make her deserts like **E**, her H6359
Eze 27:23 Kanneh and **E** and merchants of Sheba H6361
Eze 28:13 You were in **E**, the garden of God; every H6359
Eze 31:9 of all the trees of **E** in the garden of God. H6359
Eze 31:16 Then all the trees of **E**, the choicest and H6359
Eze 31:18 of the trees of **E** can be compared with H6359
Eze 31:18 with the trees of **E** to the earth below; H6359
Eze 36:35 waste has become like the garden of **E**; H6359
Joel 2:3 them the land is like the garden of **E**, H6359

EDER (5) [MIGDAL EDER]

Jos 15:21 of Edom were: Kabzeel, **E**, Jagur, H6375
1Ch 8:15 Zebadiah, Arad, **E**, H6376
1Ch 23:23 Mahli, **E** and Jerimoth—three in H6374
1Ch 24:30 Mahli, **E** and Jerimoth. H6374

EDGE (35) [DOUBLE-EDGED, EDGES]

Ex 13:20 camped at Etham on the **e** *of* the desert. H7895
Ex 26:4 material along the **e** *of* the end curtain in H8557
Ex 26:10 loops along the **e** *of* the end curtain in H8557
Ex 26:10 also along the **e** *of* the end curtain in H8557
Ex 28:26 on the inside **e** next to the ephod. H8557
Ex 28:32 shall be a woven **e** like a collar around H8557
Ex 36:11 material along the **e** *of* the end curtain in H8557

E

Ex 36:17 loops along the e *of* the end curtain in H8557
Ex 36:17 also along the e *of* the end curtain in H8557
Ex 39:19 on the inside e next to the ephod. H8557
Nu 20:16 Kadesh, a town on the e *of* your territory. H7895
Nu 22:36 the Arnon border, at the e *of* his territory. H7895
Nu 33: 6 camped at Etham, on the e *of* the desert. H7895
Jos 3: 8 'When you reach the e *of* the Jordan's H7895
Jos 3:15 their feet touched the water's e, H7895
Jdg 7:17 When I get to the e *of* the camp, do H7895
Jdg 7:19 with him reached the e *of* the camp at the H7895
1Sa 9:27 were going down to the e *of* the town, H7895
2Sa 15:17 and they halted at the e *of* the city. H5305
2Ki 7: 5 When they reached the e *of* the camp, no H7895
2Ki 7: 8 had leprosy reached the e *of* the camp, H7895
1Ch 5: 9 the land up to the e *of* the desert that H995
Ps 89:43 turned back the e *of* his sword and have H7644
Ecc 10:10 If the ax is dull and its e unsharpened H7156
Jer 31:29 the children's teeth *are* **set on** e. H7733
Jer 31:30 grapes—their own teeth *will be* **set on** e. H7733
Eze 18: 2 the children's teeth *are* **set on** e'? H7733
Eze 43:13 with a rim of one span around the e. H8557
Mt 9:20 him and touched the e of his cloak. G3192
Mt 14:36 to let the sick just touch the e of his cloak, G3192
Mk 4: 1 were along the shore **at** the water's e. G4639
Mk 6:56 to let them touch even the e of his cloak, G3192
Lk 5: 2 He saw **at** the water's e two boats, left G4123
Lk 8:44 him and touched the e of his cloak, G3192
Heb 11:34 escaped the e of the sword; whose G5125

EDGES (5) [EDGE]

Lev 19: 9 not reap to the very e *of* your field or H6991
Lev 19:27 your head or clip off the e *of* your beard. H6991
Lev 21: 5 shave off the e *of* their beards or cut H6991
Lev 23:22 not reap to the very e *of* your field or H6991
Job 38:13 the earth by the e and shake the wicked H4053

EDICT (17) [DICTATE]

Ezr 6:11 I decree that if anyone defies this e, A10601
Est 1:20 Then when the king's e is proclaimed H7330
Est 2: 8 king's order and e had been proclaimed, H2017
Est 3:14 of the text of the e was to be issued as law NDT
Est 3:15 the e was issued in the citadel of H2017
Est 4: 3 to which the e and order of the king H1821
Est 4: 8 of the text of the e for their annihilation, H2017
Est 8:11 The king's e granted the Jews in every city H889S
Est 8:13 of the text of the e was to be issued as law NDT
Est 8:14 the e was issued in the citadel of H2017
Est 8:17 every city to which the e *of* the king came, H2017
Est 9: 1 the e commanded by the king was to be H2017
Est 9:13 to carry out this day's e tomorrow also, H2017
Est 9:14 An e was issued in Susa, and they H2017
Da 6: 7 king should issue an e and enforce the A10628
Da 6:15 no decree or e that the king issues A10628
Heb 11:23 they were not afraid *of* the king's e. G1409

EDIFICATION (1) [EDIFIED, EDIFIES]

Ro 14:19 do what leads to peace and *to* mutual e. G3869

EDIFIED (2) [EDIFICATION]

1Co 14: 5 so that the church *may be* e. G3869+3284
1Co 14:17 thanks well enough, but no one else *is* e. G3868

EDIFIES (2) [EDIFICATION]

1Co 14: 4 who speaks in a tongue e themselves, G3868
1Co 14: 4 the one who prophesies e the church. G3868

EDOM (92) [EDOM'S, EDOMITE, EDOMITES, ESAU]

Ge 25:30 That is why he was also called E.) H121
Ge 32: 3 Esau in the land of Seir, the country of E. H121
Ge 36: 1 of the family line of Esau (that is, E). H121
Ge 36: 8 So Esau (that is, E) settled in the hill H121
Ge 36:16 chiefs descended from Eliphaz in E; H824+121
Ge 36:17 the chiefs descended from Reuel in E; H824+121
Ge 36:19 of Esau (that is, E), and these were their H121
Ge 36:21 sons of Seir in E were Horite chiefs. H824+121
Ge 36:31 who reigned in E before any Israelite H824+121
Ge 36:32 Bela son of Beor became king of E. His city H121
Ge 36:43 These were the chiefs of E, according to H121
Ex 15:15 The chiefs of E will be terrified, the leaders H121
Nu 20:14 messengers from Kadesh to the king of E, H121
Nu 20:18 But E answered: "You may not pass H121
Nu 20:20 Then E came out against them with a large H121
Nu 20:21 Since E refused to let them go through their H121
Nu 20:23 near the border of E, the LORD said to H824+121
Nu 21: 4 route to the Red Sea, to go around E. H824+121
Nu 24:18 E will be conquered; Seir, his enemy, will H121
Nu 33:37 at Mount Hor, on the border of E. H824+121
Nu 34: 3 of the Desert of Zin along the border of E. H121
Jos 15: 1 extended down to the territory of E, to the H121
Jos 15:21 the Negev toward the boundary of E were: H121
Jdg 5: 4 when you marched from the land of E, the H121
Jdg 11:17 Israel sent messengers to the king of E, H121
Jdg 11:17 but the king of E would not listen. H121
Jdg 11:18 skirted the lands of E and Moab, passed H121
1Sa 14:47 the Ammonites, E, the kings of Zobah H121
2Sa 8:12 E and Moab, the Ammonites and the H121
2Sa 8:14 He put garrisons throughout E, and all the H121
1Ki 9:26 which is near Elath in E, on the shore H824+121
1Ki 11:14 the Edomite, from the royal line of E. H121
1Ki 11:15 Earlier when David was fighting with E H121
1Ki 11:15 had struck down all the men in E. H121
1Ki 11:16 they had destroyed all the men in E. H121
1Ki 22:47 There was then no king in E; a provincial H121
2Ki 3: 8 "Through the Desert of E," he answered. H121
2Ki 3: 9 with the king of Judah and the king of E. H121
2Ki 3:12 the king of E went down to him. H121
2Ki 3:20 water flowing from the direction of E! H121
2Ki 3:26 to break through to the king of E, H121
2Ki 8:20 E rebelled against Judah and set up its H121
2Ki 8:22 To this day E has been in rebellion against H121
2Ki 14:10 have indeed defeated E and now you are H121
1Ch 1:43 who reigned in E before any Israelite H824+121
1Ch 1:51 The chiefs of E were: Timna, H121
1Ch 1:54 These were the chiefs of E. H121
1Ch 18:11 E and Moab, the Ammonites and the H121
1Ch 18:13 He put garrisons in E, and all the Edomites H121
2Ch 8:17 Geber and Elath on the coast of E. H824+121
2Ch 20: 2 "A vast army is coming against you from E H121
2Ch 21: 8 E rebelled against Judah and set up its H121
2Ch 21:10 To this day E has been in rebellion against H121
2Ch 25:19 say to yourself that you have defeated E, H121
2Ch 25:20 because they sought the gods of E. H121
Ps 60: 8 is my washbasin, on E I toss my sandal H121
Ps 60: 9 the fortified city? Who will lead me to E? H121
Ps 83: 6 the tents of E and the Ishmaelites, of Moab H121
Ps 108: 9 is my washbasin, on E I toss my sandal H121
Ps 108:10 the fortified city? Who will lead me to E? H121
Isa 11:14 They will subdue E and Moab, and the H121
Isa 34: 5 it descends in judgment on E, the people I H121
Isa 34: 6 a great slaughter in the land of E. H121
Isa 34:11 stretch out over E the measuring line of H2023S
Isa 63: 1 Who is this coming from E, from Bozrah H121
Jer 9:26 Judah, E, Ammon, Moab and all H121
Jer 25:21 E, Moab and Ammon; H121
Jer 27: 3 Then send word to the kings of E, Moab H121
Jer 40:11 E and all the other countries heard that the H121
Jer 49: 7 Concerning E: This is what the LORD H121
Jer 49:17 "E will become an object of horror; all who H121
Jer 49:19 I will chase E from its land in an instant. H5647S
Jer 49:20 hear what the LORD has planned against E H121
La 4:21 be glad, Daughter E, you who live in the H121
La 4:22 your sin, Daughter E, and expose your H121
Eze 16:57 by the daughters of E and all her neighbors H121
Eze 25:12 'Because E took revenge on Judah and H121
Eze 25:13 out my hand against E and kill both man H121
Eze 25:14 take vengeance on E by the hand of my H121
Eze 25:14 they will deal with E in accordance with my H121
Eze 32:29 "E is there, her kings and all her princes H121
Eze 35:15 be desolate, Mount Seir, you and all of E. H121
Eze 36: 5 against all E, for with glee and with H121
Da 11:41 will fall, but E, Moab and the leaders of H121
Joel 3:19 will be desolate, E a desert waste, because H121
Am 1: 6 whole communities and sold them to E, H121
Am 1: 9 sold whole communities of captives to E, H121
Am 1:11 "For three sins of E, even for four, I will not H121
Am 9:12 the remnant of E and all the nations H121
Ob 1 is what the Sovereign LORD says about E— H121
Ob 8 "will I not destroy the wise men of E, those H121
Mal 1: 4 E may say, "Though we have been crushed, H121

EDOM'S (3) [EDOM]

Isa 34: 9 E streams will be turned into pitch, her H2023S
Jer 49:22 that day the hearts of E warriors will be like H121
Am 2: 1 he burned to ashes the bones of E king, H121

EDOMITE (8) [EDOM]

Dt 23: 7 Do not despise an E, for the Edomites are H122
1Sa 21: 7 he was Doeg the E, Saul's chief H122
1Sa 22: 9 But Doeg the E, who was standing with H122
1Sa 22:18 So Doeg the E turned and struck them H122
1Sa 22:22 when Doeg the E was there, I knew he H122
1Ki 11:14 adversary, Hadad the E, from the royal line H122
1Ki 11:17 fled to Egypt with some E officials who had H122
Ps 52: T When Doeg the E had gone to Saul and H122

EDOMITES (16) [EDOM]

Ge 36: 9 the father of the E in the hill country of H121
Ge 36:43 the family line of Esau, the father of the E. H121
Dt 23: 7 an Edomite, for the E are related to you. H2085S
2Sa 8:13 eighteen thousand E in the Valley of Salt. H121
2Sa 8:14 all the E became subject to David. H121
1Ki 11: 1 Moabites, Ammonites, E, Sidonians and H122
2Ki 8:21 The E surrounded him and his chariot H121
2Ki 14: 7 ten thousand E in the Valley of Salt H121
2Ki 16: 6 E then moved into Elath and have lived H122
1Ch 18:12 eighteen thousand E in the Valley of Salt. H121
1Ch 18:13 all the E became subject to David. H121
2Ch 21: 9 The E surrounded him and his chariot H121
2Ch 25:14 Amaziah returned from slaughtering the E, H122
2Ch 28:17 The E had again come and attacked Judah H122
Ps 60: T down twelve thousand E in the Valley of H121
Ps 137: 7 what the E did on the day Jerusalem H1201+121

EDREI (8)

Nu 21:33 marched out to meet them in battle at E. H167
Dt 1: 4 at E had defeated Og king of Bashan H167
Dt 3: 1 army marched out to meet us in battle at E. H167
Dt 3:10 all Bashan as far as Salekah and E H167
Jos 12: 4 who reigned in Ashtaroth and E. H167
Jos 13:12 who had reigned in Ashtaroth and E. H167
Jos 13:31 Ashtaroth and E (the royal cities of Og H167
Jos 19:37 Kedesh, E, En Hazor, H167

EDUCATED (1)

Ac 7:22 Moses *was* e in all the wisdom of the G4084

EFFECT (7) [EFFECTIVE, EFFECTIVELY, EFFECTS]

Job 41:26 The sword that reaches it **has** no e, nor H7756
Isa 32:17 its e will be quietness and confidence H6275
Zep 2: 2 before the decree **takes** e and that day H3528
1Co 15:10 his grace to me was not **without** e. G3031
Eph 1:10 to be **put into** e when the times reach their G3873
Heb 9:17 *it* never **takes** e while the one who made G2710
Heb 9:18 covenant *was* not **put into** e without blood G1590

EFFECTIVE (3) [EFFECT]

1Co 16: 9 a great door *for* e **work** has opened to me, G1921
Phm 6 in the faith may be e in deepening your G1921
Jas 5:16 of a righteous person is powerful and e. G1919

EFFECTIVELY (1) [EFFECT]

Ac 14: 1 There they spoke **so** e that a great number of AIT

EFFECTS (1) [EFFECT]

Ac 28: 5 off into the fire and suffered no **ill** e. G2805

EFFORT (14) [EFFORTS]

Ecc 2:19 into which *I have* **poured** *my* e and skill H6661
Da 6:14 Daniel and **made every** e until sundown A10700
Lk 13:24 "**Make every** e to enter through the narrow G76
Ro 9:16 depend on human desire or e, but on G5556
Ro 14:19 *Let us* therefore **make every** e to do what G1503
Eph 4: 3 **Make every** e to keep the unity of the Spirit G5079
1Th 2:16 *in their* e *to* **keep** us **from** speaking to the AIT
1Th 2:17 longing *we* **made** every e to see you. G5079
Heb 4:11 *Let us*, therefore, **make every** e to enter G5079
Heb 12:14 **Make every** e *to live* in peace with G1503
2Pe 1: 5 make every e to add to your faith G5082
2Pe 1:10 **make every** e to confirm your calling and G5079
2Pe 1:15 And *I will* **make every** e *to see that* after G5079
2Pe 3:14 **make every** e to be found spotless G5079

EFFORTS (5) [EFFORT]

Job 36:19 even all your mighty e sustain you so you H4410
Ecc 8:17 Despite *all their* e to search it out, no one H6661
Eze 24:12 It has frustrated *all* e; its heavy deposit H9303
Eze 29:20 as a reward for *his* e because he and his H6268
Gal 4:11 that somehow *I have* wasted *my* e on you. G3159

EGG (1) [EGGS]

Lk 11:12 Or if he asks for an e, will give him a G6051

EGGS (7) [EGG]

Dt 22: 6 mother is sitting on the young or on the e, H1070
Job 39:14 She lays her e on the ground and lets H1070
Isa 10:14 as people gather abandoned e, so I H1070
Isa 34:15 The owl will nest there and **lay** e, she will H4880
Isa 59: 5 They hatch the e *of* vipers and spin a H1070
Isa 59: 5 Whoever eats their e will die, and when H1070
Jer 17:11 a partridge *that* **hatches** e it did not lay H1842

EGLAH (2)

2Sa 3: 5 Ithream the son of David's wife E. H6321
1Ch 3: 3 the sixth, Ithream, by his wife E. H6321

EGLAIM (1) [EN EGLAIM]

Isa 15: 8 their wailing reaches as far as E, their H104

EGLATH SHELISHIYAH (2)

Isa 15: 5 as far as Zoar, as far as E. H6326
Jer 48:34 as far as Horonaim and E, H6326

EGLON (14)

Jos 10: 3 king of Lachish and Debir king of E. H6324
Jos 10: 5 Jarmuth, Lachish and E—joined forces. H6324
Jos 10:23 Hebron, Jarmuth, Lachish and E. H6324
Jos 10:34 with him moved on from Lachish to E; H6324
Jos 10:36 with him went up from E to Hebron and H6324
Jos 10:37 Just as at E, they totally destroyed it and H6324
Jos 12:12 the king of E one the king of Gezer one H6324
Jos 15:39 Lachish, Bozkath, E, H6324
Jdg 3:12 evil the LORD gave E king of Moab power H6323
Jdg 3:13 to join him, E came and attacked Israel NDT
Jdg 3:14 were subject to E king of Moab for H6323
Jdg 3:15 sent him with tribute to E king of Moab. H6323
Jdg 3:17 presented the tribute to E king of Moab, H6323
Jdg 3:19 Gilgal he himself went back to E and said, NDT

EGYPT (610) [EGYPT'S, EGYPTIAN, EGYPTIAN'S, EGYPTIANS]

Ge 10: 6 Cush, E, Put and Canaan. H5213
Ge 10:13 E was the father of the Ludites, Anamites H5213
Ge 12:10 Abram went down to E to live there for a H5213
Ge 12:11 As he was about to enter E, he said to his H5213
Ge 12:14 When Abram came to E, the Egyptians H5213
Ge 13: 1 So Abram went up from E to the Negev H5213
Ge 13:10 the garden of the LORD, like the land of E. H5213
Ge 15:18 from the Wadi of E to the great river H5213
Ge 21:21 his mother got a wife for him from E. H824+5213
Ge 25:18 near the eastern border of E, as you go H5213
Ge 26: 2 "Do not go down to E; live in the land H5213
Ge 37:25 were on their way to take them down to E. H5213
Ge 37:28 to the Ishmaelites, who took him to E. H5213
Ge 37:36 Midianites sold Joseph in E to Potiphar, H5213
Ge 39: 1 Now Joseph had been taken down to E H5213
Ge 40: 1 baker of the king of E offended their H5213
Ge 40: 1 Egypt offended their master, the king of E. H5213
Ge 40: 5 cupbearer and the baker of the king of E, H5213
Ge 41: 8 all the magicians and wise men of E. H5213

Ge 41:19 seen such ugly cows in all the land of **E**. H5213
Ge 41:29 are coming throughout the land of **E**, H5213
Ge 41:30 the abundance in **E** will be forgotten H824+5213
Ge 41:33 put him in charge of the land of **E**. H5213
Ge 41:34 of the harvest of **E** during the seven H824+5213
Ge 41:36 of famine that will come upon **E**, H824+5213
Ge 41:41 put you in charge of the whole land of **E**." H5213
Ge 41:43 put him in charge of the whole land of **E**. H5213
Ge 41:44 no one will lift hand or foot in all **E**." H824+5213
Ge 41:45 Joseph went throughout the land of **E**. H5213
Ge 41:46 entered the service of Pharaoh king of **E**. H5213
Ge 41:46 presence and traveled throughout **E**. H824+5213
Ge 41:48 of abundance in **E** and stored it in H824+5213
Ge 41:53 of abundance in **E** came to an end, H824+5213
Ge 41:54 in the whole land of **E** there was food. H5213
Ge 41:55 When all **E** began to feel the famine, H824+5213
Ge 41:56 the famine was severe throughout **E**. H824+5213
Ge 41:57 all the world came to **E** to buy grain from H5213
Ge 42: 1 Jacob learned that there was grain in **E**, H5213
Ge 42: 2 "I have heard that there is grain in **E**. H5213
Ge 42: 3 brothers went down to buy grain from **E**. H5213
Ge 43: 2 all the grain they had brought from **E**, H5213
Ge 43:15 They hurried down to **E** and presented H5213
Ge 45: 4 brother Joseph, the one you sold into **E**! H5213
Ge 45: 8 entire household and ruler of all **E**. H824+5213
Ge 45: 9 God has made me lord of all **E**. H5213
Ge 45:13 accorded me in **E** and about everything H5213
Ge 45:18 best of the land of **E** and you can enjoy H5213
Ge 45:19 some carts from **E** for your children H824+5213
Ge 45:20 the best of all **E** will be yours. H824+5213
Ge 45:23 donkeys loaded with the best things of **E**, H5213
Ge 45:25 they went up out of **E** and came to their H5213
Ge 45:26 he is ruler of all **E**." Jacob was H824+5213
Ge 46: 3 "Do not be afraid to go down to **E**, for I H5213
Ge 46: 4 I will go down to **E** with you, and I will H5213
Ge 46: 6 So Jacob and all his offspring went to **E** H5213
Ge 46: 7 brought with him to **E** his sons and H5213
Ge 46: 8 Jacob and his descendants) who went to **E**: H5213
Ge 46:20 In **E**, Manasseh and Ephraim were H824+5213
Ge 46:26 All those who went to **E** with Jacob H5213
Ge 46:27 sons who had been born to Joseph in **E**, H5213
Ge 46:27 which went to **E**, were seventy in all. H5213
Ge 47: 6 the land of **E** is before you; settle your H5213
Ge 47:11 and his brothers in **E** and gave them H824+5213
Ge 47:13 both **E** and Canaan wasted away H824+5213
Ge 47:14 was to be found in **E** and Canaan in H824+5213
Ge 47:15 of the people of **E** and Canaan was H824+5213
Ge 47:15 was gone, all **E** came to Joseph and said H5213
Ge 47:20 bought all the land in **E** for Pharaoh. H5213
Ge 47:21 servitude, from one end of **E** to the other. H5213
Ge 47:26 it as a law concerning land in **E**— H5213
Ge 47:27 settled in **E** in the region of H824+5213
Ge 47:28 Jacob lived in **E** seventeen years H824+5213
Ge 47:29 faithfulness. Do not bury me in **E**, H5213
Ge 47:30 carry me out of **E** and bury me where they H5213
Ge 48: 5 born to you in **E** before I came to H824+5213
Ge 50: 7 court and all the dignitaries of **E**— H824+5213
Ge 50:14 Joseph returned to **E**, together with his H5213
Ge 50:22 Joseph stayed in **E**, along with all his H5213
Ge 50:26 he was placed in a coffin in **E**. H5213
Ex 1: 1 sons of Israel who went to **E** with Jacob, H5213
Ex 1: 5 seventy in all; Joseph was already in **E**. H5213
Ex 1: 8 meant nothing, came to power in **E**. H5213
Ex 1:15 The king of **E** said to the Hebrew H5213
Ex 1:17 do what the king of **E** had told them to do H5213
Ex 1:18 Then the king of **E** summoned the H5213
Ex 2:23 that long period, the king of **E** died. H5213
Ex 3: 7 seen the misery of my people in **E**. H5213
Ex 3:10 to bring my people the Israelites out of **E**." H5213
Ex 3:11 Pharaoh and bring the Israelites out of **E**?" H5213
Ex 3:12 you have brought the people out of **E**, H5213
Ex 3:16 seen what has been done to you in **E**. H5213
Ex 3:17 out of your misery in **E** into the land of the H5213
Ex 3:18 are to go to the king of **E** and say to him, H5213
Ex 3:19 know that the king of **E** will not let you go H5213
Ex 4:18 to my own people in **E** to see if any of H5213
Ex 4:19 Midian, "Go back to **E**, for all those who H5213
Ex 4:20 on a donkey and started back to **E**. H824+5213
Ex 4:21 "When you return to **E**, see that you H5213
Ex 5: 4 But the king of **E** said, "Moses and Aaron H5213
Ex 5:12 scattered all over **E** to gather stubble H5213+824
Ex 6:11 tell Pharaoh king of **E** to let the Israelites H5213
Ex 6:13 the Israelites and Pharaoh king of **E**, H5213
Ex 6:13 them to bring the Israelites out of **E**. H824+5213
Ex 6:26 Israelites out of **E** by their divisions." H824+5213
Ex 6:27 to Pharaoh king of **E** about bringing the H5213
Ex 6:27 about bringing the Israelites out of **E**— H5213
Ex 6:28 when the LORD spoke to Moses in **E**, H824+5213
Ex 6:29 Tell Pharaoh king of **E** everything I tell H5213
Ex 7: 3 multiply my signs and wonders in **E**, H824+5213
Ex 7: 4 will lay my hand on **E** and with mighty H5213
Ex 7: 5 out my hand against **E** and bring the H5213
Ex 7:19 out your hand over the waters of **E**— H5213
Ex 7:19 Blood will be everywhere in **E**, even H824+5213
Ex 7:21 Blood was everywhere in **E**. H824+5213
Ex 8: 5 make frogs come up on the land of **E**. H5213
Ex 8: 6 out his hand over the waters of **E**, H5213
Ex 8: 7 made frogs come up on the land of **E**. H5213
Ex 8:16 the land of **E** the dust will become H5213
Ex 8:17 throughout the land of **E** became gnats. H5213
Ex 8:24 throughout **E** the land was ruined by H824+5213
Ex 9: 4 the livestock of Israel and that of **E**, H5213

Ex 9: 9 fine dust over the whole land of **E**, H5213
Ex 9:18 worst hailstorm that has ever fallen on **E**, H5213
Ex 9:22 sky so that hail will fall all over **E**— H824+5213
Ex 9:22 everything growing in the fields of **E**." H824+5213
Ex 9:23 So the LORD rained hail on the land of **E**; H5213
Ex 9:24 in all the land of **E** since it had become a H5213
Ex 9:25 Throughout **E** hail struck everything H824+5213
Ex 10: 7 Do you not yet realize that **E** is ruined?" H5213
Ex 10:12 out your hand over **E** so that locusts H824+5213
Ex 10:13 Moses stretched out his staff over **E**, H824+5213
Ex 10:14 they invaded all **E** and settled down H824+5213
Ex 10:15 on tree or plant in all the land of **E**. H5213
Ex 10:19 Not a locust was left anywhere in **E**. H1473+5213
Ex 10:21 so that darkness spreads over **E**— H824+5213
Ex 10:22 covered all **E** for three days. H824+5213
Ex 11: 1 one more plague on Pharaoh and on **E**. H5213
Ex 11: 3 highly regarded in **E** by Pharaoh's H824+5213
Ex 11: 4 'About midnight I will go throughout **E**. H5213
Ex 11: 5 Every firstborn son in **E** will die, from H824+5213
Ex 11: 6 will be loud wailing throughout **E**— H824+5213
Ex 11: 7 makes a distinction between **E** and Israel. H5213
Ex 11: 9 my wonders may be multiplied in **E**." H824+5213
Ex 12: 1 LORD said to Moses and Aaron in **E**, H824+5213
Ex 12:12 I will pass through **E** and strike down H824+5213
Ex 12:12 I will bring judgment on all the gods of **E**. H5213
Ex 12:13 will touch you when I strike **E**. H824+5213
Ex 12:17 that I brought your divisions out of **E**. H824+5213
Ex 12:27 the Israelites in **E** and spared our homes H5213
Ex 12:29 struck down all the firstborn in **E**, H824+5213
Ex 12:30 there was loud wailing in **E**, for there H5213
Ex 12:39 dough the Israelites had brought from **E**, H5213
Ex 12:39 been driven out of **E** and did not have H5213
Ex 12:40 Israelite people lived in **E** was 430 years. H5213
Ex 12:41 all the LORD's divisions left **E**. H824+5213
Ex 12:42 that night to bring them out of **E**, H824+5213
Ex 12:51 Israelites out of **E** by their divisions. H824+5213
Ex 13: 3 the day you came out of **E**, out of the land H5213
Ex 13: 8 the LORD did for me when I came out of **E**. H5213
Ex 13: 9 brought you out of **E** with his mighty hand H5213
Ex 13:14 mighty hand the LORD brought us out of **E**, H5213
Ex 13:15 of both people and animals in **E**. H824+5213
Ex 13:16 brought us out of **E** with his mighty hand." H5213
Ex 13:17 might change their minds and return to **E**." H5213
Ex 13:18 went up out of **E** ready for battle. H824+5213
Ex 14: 5 When the king of **E** was told that the H5213
Ex 14: 7 along with all the other chariots of **E**, with H5213
Ex 14: 8 hardened the heart of Pharaoh king of **E**, H5213
Ex 14:11 were no graves in **E** that you brought us to H5213
Ex 14:11 you done to us by bringing us out of **E**? H5213
Ex 14:12 Didn't we say to you in **E**, 'Leave us alone H5213
Ex 14:20 between the armies of **E** and Israel. H5213
Ex 14:25 The LORD is fighting for them against **E**." H5213
Ex 16: 1 month after they had come out of **E**. H824+5213
Ex 16: 3 we had died by the LORD's hand in **E**! H824+5213
Ex 16: 6 the LORD who brought you out of **E**, H824+5213
Ex 16:32 when I brought you out of **E**. H824+5213
Ex 17: 3 bring us up out of **E** to make us and our H5213
Ex 18: 1 how the LORD had brought Israel out of **E**. H5213
Ex 19: 1 month after the Israelites left **E**— H824+5213
Ex 19: 4 'You yourselves have seen what I did to **E** H5213
Ex 20: 2 who brought you out of **E**, out of the H824+5213
Ex 22:21 you were foreigners in **E**. H824+5213
Ex 23: 9 because you were foreigners in **E**. H824+5213
Ex 23:15 for in that month you came out of **E**. H5213
Ex 29:46 them out of **E** so that I might H824+5213
Ex 32: 1 Moses who brought us up out of **E**, H824+5213
Ex 32: 4 who brought you up out of **E**. H824+5213
Ex 32: 7 whom you brought up out of **E**, have H824+5213
Ex 32: 8 who brought you up out of **E**. H824+5213
Ex 32:11 brought out of **E** with great power H824+5213
Ex 32:23 Moses who brought us up out of **E**, H824+5213
Ex 33: 1 the people you brought up out of **E**, H824+5213
Ex 34:18 for in that month you came out of **E**. H5213
Lev 11:45 you up out of **E** to be your God; H824+5213
Lev 18: 3 You must not do as they do in **E** H824+5213
Lev 19:34 you were foreigners in **E**. H824+5213
Lev 19:36 your God, who brought you out of **E**. H824+5213
Lev 22:33 brought you out of **E** to be your God. H824+5213
Lev 23:43 when I brought them out of **E**. H824+5213
Lev 25:38 brought you out of **E** to give you the H824+5213
Lev 25:42 whom I brought out of **E**, they must H824+5213
Lev 25:55 servants, whom I brought out of **E**. H824+5213
Lev 26:13 you out of **E** so that you would H824+5213
Lev 26:45 I brought out of **E** in the sight of the H824+5213
Nu 1: 1 after the Israelites came out of **E**. H824+5213
Nu 3:13 I struck down all the firstborn in **E**, H824+5213
Nu 8:17 I struck down all the firstborn in **E**, H824+5213
Nu 9: 1 year after they came out of **E**. H824+5213
Nu 11: 5 the fish we ate in **E** at no cost— H5213
Nu 11:18 We were better off in **E**!" Now the LORD H5213
Nu 11:20 saying, "Why did we ever leave **E**? H5213
Nu 13:22 been built seven years before Zoan in **E**.) H5213
Nu 14: 2 to them, "If only we had died in **E**! H824+5213
Nu 14: 3 it be better for us to go back to **E**? H5213
Nu 14: 4 should choose a leader and go back to **E**." H5213
Nu 14:19 them from the time they left **E** until now." H5213
Nu 14:22 signs I performed in **E** and in the H5213
Nu 15:41 brought you out of **E** to be your God. H824+5213
Nu 20: 5 bring us up out of **E** to this terrible place H5213
Nu 20:15 Our ancestors went down into **E**, and we H5213
Nu 20:16 sent an angel and brought us out of **E**. H5213
Nu 21: 5 brought us up out of **E** to die in the H5213

Nu 22: 5 "A people has come out of **E**; they cover H5213
Nu 22:11 that has come out of **E** covers the face of H5213
Nu 23:22 God brought them out of **E**; they have the H5213
Nu 24: 8 "God brought them out of **E**; they have H5213
Nu 26: 4 the Israelites who came out of **E**: H824+5213
Nu 26:59 who was born to the Levites in **E**. H5213
Nu 32:11 they came up out of **E** will see the land I H5213
Nu 33: 1 they came out of **E** by divisions H824+5213
Nu 33:38 after the Israelites came out of **E**. H824+5213
Nu 34: 5 join the Wadi of **E** and end at the H5213
Dt 1:27 brought us out of **E** to deliver us into H824+5213
Dt 1:30 as he did for you in **E**, before your very H5213
Dt 4:20 furnace, out of **E**, to be the people of his H5213
Dt 4:34 God did for you in **E** before your very eyes H5213
Dt 4:37 brought you out of **E** by his Presence and H5213
Dt 4:45 gave them when they came out of **E** H5213
Dt 4:46 the Israelites as they came out of **E**. H5213
Dt 5: 6 who brought you out of **E**, out of the H824+5213
Dt 5:15 were slaves in **E** and that the LORD H824+5213
Dt 6:12 who brought you out of **E**, out of the H824+5213
Dt 6:21 "We were slaves of Pharaoh in **E**, but the H5213
Dt 6:21 brought us out of **E** with a mighty hand. H5213
Dt 6:22 on **E** and Pharaoh and his whole H5213
Dt 7: 8 from the power of Pharaoh king of **E**. H5213
Dt 7:15 you the horrible diseases you knew in **E**, H5213
Dt 7:18 LORD your God did to Pharaoh and to all **E**. H5213
Dt 8:14 who brought you out of **E**, out of the H824+5213
Dt 9: 7 the day you left **E** until you arrived H824+5213
Dt 9:12 you brought out of **E** have become corrupt H5213
Dt 9:26 brought out of **E** with a mighty hand. H5213
Dt 10:19 you yourselves were foreigners in **E**. H824+5213
Dt 10:22 who went down into **E** were seventy in all, H5213
Dt 11: 3 the things he did in the heart of **E**, H5213
Dt 11: 3 to Pharaoh king of **E** and to his whole H5213
Dt 11:10 to take over is not like the land of **E**, H5213
Dt 13: 5 you out of **E** and redeemed you H824+5213
Dt 13:10 who brought you out of **E**, out of the H824+5213
Dt 15:15 were slaves in **E** and the LORD your H824+5213
Dt 16: 1 of Aviv he brought you out of **E** by night. H5213
Dt 16: 3 because you left **E** in haste—so that H824+5213
Dt 16: 3 the time of your departure from **E**. H824+5213
Dt 16: 6 the anniversary of your departure from **E**. H5213
Dt 16:12 Remember that you were slaves in **E**, and H5213
Dt 17:16 people return to **E** to get more of them, H5213
Dt 20: 1 who brought you up out of **E**, will be H824+5213
Dt 23: 4 on your way when you came out of **E**, H5213
Dt 24: 9 along the way after you came out of **E**. H5213
Dt 24:18 you were slaves in **E** and the LORD your H5213
Dt 24:22 Remember that you were slaves in **E** H824+5213
Dt 25:17 along the way when you came out of **E**. H5213
Dt 26: 5 he went down into **E** with a few people H5213
Dt 26: 8 brought us out of **E** with a mighty hand H5213
Dt 28:27 you with the boils of **E** and with tumors, H5213
Dt 28:60 all the diseases of **E** that you dreaded, H5213
Dt 28:68 you back in ships to **E** on a journey I said H5213
Dt 29: 2 all that the LORD did in **E** to Pharaoh, H824+5213
Dt 29:16 how we lived in **E** and how we H824+5213
Dt 29:25 when he brought them out of **E**. H824+5213
Dt 34:11 the LORD sent him to do in **E**— H824+5213
Jos 2:10 Red Sea for you when you came out of **E**, H5213
Jos 5: 4 All those who came out of **E**—all the men H5213
Jos 5: 4 the wilderness on the way after leaving **E**. H5213
Jos 5: 5 during the journey from **E** had not. H5213
Jos 5: 6 of military age when they left **E** had died, H5213
Jos 5: 9 rolled away the reproach of **E** from you." H5213
Jos 9: 9 heard reports of him: all that he did in **E**, H5213
Jos 13: 3 River on the east of **E** to the territory of H5213
Jos 15: 4 to Azmon and joined the Wadi of **E**, H5213
Jos 15:47 far as the Wadi of **E** and the coastline of H5213
Jos 24: 4 Jacob and his family went down to **E**. H5213
Jos 24: 6 When I brought your people out of **E**, you H5213
Jos 24:14 beyond the Euphrates River and in **E**, H5213
Jos 24:17 us and our parents up out of **E**, H824+5213
Jos 24:32 the Israelites had brought up from **E**, H5213
Jdg 2: 1 you up out of **E** and led you into the H5213
Jdg 2:12 who had brought them out of **E**. H824+5213
Jdg 6: 8 I brought you up out of **E**, out of the land H5213
Jdg 6:13 'Did not the LORD bring us up out of **E**? H5213
Jdg 11:13 "When Israel came up out of **E**, they took H5213
Jdg 11:16 But when they came up out of **E**, Israel H5213
Jdg 19:30 day the Israelites came up out of **E**. H824+5213
1Sa 2:27 when they were in **E** under Pharaoh? H5213
1Sa 8: 8 I brought them up out of **E** until this day, H5213
1Sa 10:18 'I brought Israel up out of **E**, and I H5213
1Sa 10:18 from the power of **E** and all the kingdoms H5213
1Sa 12: 6 brought your ancestors up out of **E**. H824+5213
1Sa 12: 8 "After Jacob entered **E**, they cried to the H5213
1Sa 12: 8 ancestors out of **E** and settled them in H5213
1Sa 15: 2 waylaid them as they came up from **E**. H5213
1Sa 15: 6 the Israelites when they came up out of **E**." H5213
1Sa 15: 7 to Shur, near the eastern border of **E**. H5213
1Sa 27: 8 in the land extending to Shur and **E**.) H824+5213
2Sa 7: 6 the Israelites up out of **E** to this day. H5213
2Sa 7:23 people, whom you redeemed from **E**? H5213
1Ki 3: 1 with Pharaoh king of **E** and married his H5213
1Ki 4:21 the Philistines, as far as the border of **E**. H5213
1Ki 4:30 greater than all the wisdom of **E**. H5213
1Ki 6: 1 after the Israelites came out of **E**, H824+5213
1Ki 8: 9 Israelites after they came out of **E**. H824+5213
1Ki 8:16 day I brought my people Israel out of **E**, H5213
1Ki 8:21 when he brought them out of **E**." H824+5213
1Ki 8:51 whom you brought out of **E**, out of that H5213

1Ki 8:53 brought our ancestors out of E. H5213
1Ki 8:65 from Lebo Hamath to the Wadi of E. H5213
1Ki 9: 9 who brought their ancestors out of E H824+5213
1Ki 9:16 Pharaoh king of E had attacked and H5213
1Ki 10:28 were imported from E and from Kue— H5213
1Ki 10:29 a chariot from E for six hundred shekels H5213
1Ki 11:17 fled to E with some Edomite officials who H5213
1Ki 11:18 they went to E, to Pharaoh king of H5213
1Ki 11:18 to Pharaoh king of E, who gave Hadad a H5213
1Ki 11:21 While he was in E, Hadad heard that H5213
1Ki 11:40 Jeroboam fled to E, to Shishak the H5213
1Ki 12: 2 he was still in E, where he had fled H5213
1Ki 12: 2 from King Solomon), he returned from E. H5213
1Ki 12:28 who brought you up out of E. H824+5213
1Ki 14:25 Shishak king of E attacked Jerusalem. H5213
2Ki 17: 4 he had sent envoys to So king of E H5213
2Ki 17: 7 them up out of E from under the H824+5213
2Ki 17: 7 under the power of Pharaoh king of E. H5213
2Ki 17:36 you up out of E with mighty power H824+5213
2Ki 18:21 I know you are depending on E, that H5213
2Ki 18:21 is Pharaoh king of E to all who depend on H5213
2Ki 18:24 you are depending on E for chariots and H5213
2Ki 19:24 feet I have dried up all the streams of E." H5191
2Ki 21:15 ancestors came out of E until this day." H5213
2Ki 23:29 Pharaoh Necho king of E went up to the H5213
2Ki 23:34 took Jehoahaz and carried him off to E, H5213
2Ki 24: 7 The king of E did not march out from his H5213
2Ki 24: 7 from the Wadi of E to the Euphrates River. H5213
2Ki 25:26 fled to E for fear of the Babylonians. H5213
1Ch 1: 8 Cush, E, Put and Canaan. H5213
1Ch 1:11 E was the father of the Ludites, Anamites H5213
1Ch 13: 5 the Shihor River in E to Lebo Hamath, H5213
1Ch 17: 5 day I brought Israel up out of E to this day. NDT
1Ch 17:21 people, whom you redeemed from E? H5213
2Ch 1:16 were imported from E and from Kue— H5213
2Ch 1:17 a chariot from E for six hundred shekels H5213
2Ch 5:10 the Israelites after they came out of E. H5213
2Ch 6: 5 day I brought my people out of E, H824+5213
2Ch 7: 8 from Lebo Hamath to the Wadi of E. H5213
2Ch 7:22 who brought them out of E, and H824+5213
2Ch 9:26 the Philistines, as far as the border of E. H5213
2Ch 9:28 were imported from E and from all other H5213
2Ch 10: 2 he was in E, where he had fled H5213
2Ch 10: 2 from King Solomon), he returned from E. H5213
2Ch 12: 2 Shishak king of E attacked Jerusalem in H5213
2Ch 12: 3 Cushites that came with him from E, H5213
2Ch 12: 9 Shishak king of E attacked Jerusalem, H5213
2Ch 20:10 to invade when they came from E; H824+5213
2Ch 26: 8 his fame spread as far as the border of E, H5213
2Ch 35:20 Necho king of E went up to fight at H5213
2Ch 36: 3 The king of E dethroned him in Jerusalem H5213
2Ch 36: 4 The king of E made Eliakim, a brother of H5213
2Ch 36: 4 brother Jehoahaz and carried him off to E. H5213
Ne 9: 9 saw the suffering of our ancestors in E; H5213
Ne 9:18 who brought you up out of E,' or when H5213
Ps 68:31 Envoys will come from E; Cush will submit H5213
Ps 78:12 sight of their ancestors in the land of E, H5213
Ps 78:43 the day he displayed his signs in E, his H5213
Ps 78:51 He struck down all the firstborn of E, the H5213
Ps 80: 8 You transplanted a vine from E; you drove H5213
Ps 81: 5 When God went out against E, he H824+5213
Ps 81:10 who brought you up out of E. H824+5213
Ps 105:23 Then Israel entered E; Jacob resided as a H5213
Ps 105:38 E was glad when they left, because dread H5213
Ps 106: 7 When our ancestors were in E, they gave H5213
Ps 106:21 who had done great things in E, H5213
Ps 114: 1 When Israel came out of E, Jacob from a H5213
Ps 135: 8 He struck down the firstborn of E, the H5213
Ps 135: 9 into your midst, E, against Pharaoh and H5213
Ps 136:10 down the firstborn of E His love endures H5213
Pr 7:16 my bed with colored linens from E. H5213
Isa 7:18 the Nile delta in E and for bees from the H5213
Isa 10:24 lift up a club against you, as E did. H5213
Isa 10:26 his staff over the waters, as he did in E. H5213
Isa 11:11 Assyria, from Lower E, from Upper Egypt H5213
Isa 11:11 Lower Egypt, from Upper E, from Cush, H7356
Isa 11:16 Israel when they came up from E. H824+5213
Isa 19: 1 A prophecy against E: See, the LORD rides H5213
Isa 19: 1 rides on a swift cloud and is coming to E. H5213
Isa 19: 1 The idols of E tremble before him, and H5213
Isa 19: 6 the streams of E will dwindle and dry up. H5191
Isa 19:12 the LORD Almighty has planned against E. H5213
Isa 19:13 of her peoples have led E astray. H5213
Isa 19:14 they make E stagger in all that she does H5213
Isa 19:15 There is nothing E can do—head or tail H5213
Isa 19:18 day five cities in E will speak the H824+5213
Isa 19:19 an altar to the LORD in the heart of E, H824+5213
Isa 19:20 to the LORD Almighty in the land of E. H5213
Isa 19:22 The LORD will strike E with a plague; he H5213
Isa 19:23 there will be a highway from E to Assyria. H5213
Isa 19:23 will go to E and the Egyptians to H5213
Isa 19:24 the third, along with E and Assyria, H5213
Isa 19:25 "Blessed be E my people, Assyria H5213
Isa 20: 3 as a sign and portent against E and Cush, H5213
Isa 20: 5 Cush and boasted in E will be dismayed H5213
Isa 23: 5 When word comes to E, they will be in H5213
Isa 27:12 of the flowing Euphrates to the Wadi of E, H5213
Isa 27:13 who were exiled in E will come and H824+5213
Isa 30: 2 who go down to E without consulting me H5213
Isa 30: 7 to E, whose help is utterly useless H5213
Isa 31: 1 Woe to those who go down to E for help H5213
Isa 36: 6 I know you are depending on E, that H5213
Isa 36: 6 is Pharaoh king of E to all who depend on H5213
Isa 36: 9 you are depending on E for chariots and H5213
Isa 37:25 feet I have dried up all the streams of E. H5191
Isa 43: 3 Savior; I give E for your ransom, Cush H5213
Isa 45:14 "The products of E and the merchandise H5213
Isa 52: 4 "At first my people went down to E to live H5213
Jer 2: 6 us up out of E and led us through H824+5213
Jer 2:18 Now why go to E to drink water from the H5213
Jer 2:36 be disappointed by E as you were by H5213
Jer 7:22 ancestors out of E and spoke to H824+5213
Jer 7:25 time your ancestors left E until now, H824+5213
Jer 9:26 E, Judah, Edom, Ammon, Moab and all H5213
Jer 11: 4 when I brought them out of E, H824+5213
Jer 11: 7 your ancestors up from E until today, H824+5213
Jer 16:14 brought the Israelites up out of E, H824+5213
Jer 23: 7 brought the Israelites up out of E, H824+5213
Jer 24: 8 they remain in this land or live in E. H824+5213
Jer 25:19 Pharaoh king of E, his attendants, his H5213
Jer 26:21 But Uriah heard of it and fled in fear to E. H5213
Jer 26:22 sent Elnathan son of Akbor to E, along H5213
Jer 26:23 Uriah out of E and took him to King H5213
Jer 31:32 by the hand to lead them out of E, H824+5213
Jer 32:20 and wonders in E and have H824+5213
Jer 32:21 people Israel out of E with signs and H824+5213
Jer 34:13 when I brought them out of E, H824+5213
Jer 37: 5 Pharaoh's army had marched out of E, and H5213
Jer 37: 7 will go back to its own land, to E. H5213
Jer 41:17 near Bethlehem on their way to E H5213
Jer 42:14 we will go and live in E, where we H824+5213
Jer 42:15 determined to go to E and you do go to H5213
Jer 42:16 famine you dread will follow you into E, H5213
Jer 42:17 determined to go to E to settle there will H5213
Jer 42:18 be poured out on you when you go to E. H5213
Jer 42:19 the LORD has told you, 'Do not go to E. H5213
Jer 43: 2 'You must not go to E to settle there. H5213
Jer 43: 7 So they entered E in disobedience to H824+5213
Jer 43:11 He will come and attack E, bringing H824+5213
Jer 43:12 set fire to the temples of the gods of E; H5213
Jer 43:12 so he will pick E clean and depart. H824+5213
Jer 43:13 of the sun in E he will demolish the H824+5213
Jer 43:13 burn down the temples of the gods of E. H5213
Jer 44: 1 all the Jews living in Lower E— H824+5213
Jer 44: 1 and Memphis—and in Upper E: H824+7356
Jer 44: 8 burning incense to other gods in E H824+5213
Jer 44:12 to go to E to settle there. H824+5213
Jer 44:12 They will all perish in E; they will H824+5213
Jer 44:13 those who live in E with the sword, H824+5213
Jer 44:14 have gone to live in E will escape H824+5213
Jer 44:15 people living in Lower and Upper E, H824+5213
Jer 44:24 all you people of Judah in E. H824+5213
Jer 44:26 of the LORD, all you Jews living in E: H824+5213
Jer 44:26 living anywhere in E will ever again H824+5213
Jer 44:27 the Jews in E will perish by sword H824+5213
Jer 44:28 of Judah from E will be very few. H824+5213
Jer 44:28 came to live in E will know whose H824+5213
Jer 44:30 Hophra king of E into the hands of his H5213
Jer 46: 2 Concerning E: This is the message H5213
Jer 46: 2 the army of Pharaoh Necho king of E, H5213
Jer 46: 8 E rises like the Nile, like rivers of surging H5213
Jer 46:11 Gilead and get balm, Virgin Daughter E. H5213
Jer 46:13 king of Babylon to attack E: H824+5213
Jer 46:14 "Announce this in E, and proclaim it in H5213
Jer 46:17 'Pharaoh king of E is only a loud noise H5213
Jer 46:19 you who live in E, for Memphis will H1426+5213
Jer 46:20 "E is a beautiful heifer, but a gadfly is H5213
Jer 46:22 E will hiss like a fleeing serpent as the H2023S
Jer 46:24 Daughter E will be put to shame, given H5213
Jer 46:25 Pharaoh, on E and her gods and her kings H5213
Jer 46:26 E will be inhabited as in times past, NDT
La 5: 6 We submitted to E and Assyria to get H5213
Eze 17:15 his envoys to E to get horses and a H5213
Eze 19: 4 They led him with hooks to the land of E. H5213
Eze 20: 5 and revealed myself to them in E. H824+5213
Eze 20: 6 bring them out of E into a land I had H824+5213
Eze 20: 7 not defile yourselves with the idols of E. H5213
Eze 20: 8 nor did they forsake the idols of E. H5213
Eze 20: 8 spend my anger against them in E. H824+5213
Eze 20: 9 my name, I brought them out of E. H824+5213
Eze 20:10 led them out of E and brought them H824+5213
Eze 20:36 in the wilderness of the land of E, H5213
Eze 23: 3 They became prostitutes in E, engaging in H5213
Eze 23: 8 give up the prostitution she began in E, H5213
Eze 23:19 when she was a prostitute in E. H824+5213
Eze 23:21 when in E your bosom was caressed and H5213
Eze 23:27 and prostitution you began in E. H824+5213
Eze 23:27 with longing or remember E anymore. H5213
Eze 27: 7 linen from E was your sail and H5213
Eze 29: 2 Pharaoh king of E and prophesy against H5213
Eze 29: 2 prophesy against him and against all E. H5213
Eze 29: 3 Pharaoh king of E, you great monster H5213
Eze 29: 6 Then all who live in E will know that I am H5213
Eze 29: 9 E will become a desolate wasteland H824+5213
Eze 29:10 make the land of E a ruin and a desolate H5213
Eze 29:12 I will make the land of E desolate among H5213
Eze 29:14 captivity and return them to Upper E, H824+7356
Eze 29:16 E will no longer be a source of confidence NDT
Eze 29:19 am going to give E to H824+5213
Eze 29:20 I have given him E as a reward for H824+5213
Eze 30: 4 A sword will come against E, and anguish H5213
Eze 30: 4 When the slain fall in E, her wealth will H5213
Eze 30: 5 land will fall by the sword along with E. H4392S
Eze 30: 6 " 'The allies of E will fall and her proud H5213
Eze 30: 8 when I set fire to E and all her helpers are H5213
Eze 30:10 an end to the hordes of E by the hand of H5213
Eze 30:11 their swords against E and fill the land H5213
Eze 30:13 No longer will there be a prince in E, H824+5213
Eze 30:14 I will lay waste Upper E, set fire to Zoan H7356
Eze 30:15 the stronghold of E, and wipe out the H5213
Eze 30:16 I will set fire to E; Pelusium will writhe in H5213
Eze 30:18 at Tahpanhes when I break the yoke of E; H5213
Eze 30:19 So I will inflict punishment on E, and they H5213
Eze 30:21 have broken the arm of Pharaoh king of E. H5213
Eze 30:22 I am against Pharaoh king of E. H5213
Eze 30:25 and he brandishes it against E. H824+5213
Eze 31: 2 to Pharaoh king of E and to his hordes: H5213
Eze 32: 2 Pharaoh king of E and say to him: H5213
Eze 32:12 They will shatter the pride of E, and all H5213
Eze 32:15 When I make E desolate and strip H824+5213
Eze 32:16 E and all her hordes they will chant it H5213
Eze 32:18 the hordes of E and consign to the H5213
Eze 32:21 leaders will say of E and her allies, H2257S
Eze 47:19 then along the Wadi *of E* to the AIT
Eze 48:28 then along the Wadi *of E* to the AIT
Da 9:15 people out of E with a mighty hand H824+5213
Da 11: 8 of silver and gold and carry them off to E. H5213
Da 11:42 many countries; E will not escape. H824+5213
Da 11:43 of gold and silver and all the riches of E, H5213
Hos 2:15 as in the day she came up out of E. H824+5213
Hos 7:11 now calling to E, now turning to Assyria. H5213
Hos 7:16 this they will be ridiculed in the land of E. H5213
Hos 8:13 punish their sins: They will return to E. H5213
Hos 9: 3 will return to E and eat unclean food H5213
Hos 9: 6 from destruction, E will gather them, and H5213
Hos 11: 1 I loved him, and out of E I called my son. H5213
Hos 11: 5 they not return to E and will not H824+5213
Hos 11:11 They will come from E, trembling like H5213
Hos 12: 1 with Assyria and sends olive oil to E. H5213
Hos 12: 9 God ever since you came out of E; H824+5213
Hos 12:13 used a prophet to bring Israel up from E, H5213
Hos 13: 4 God ever since you came out of E. H824+5213
Joel 3:19 But E will be desolate, Edom a desert H5213
Am 2:10 you up out of E and led you forty H824+5213
Am 3: 1 whole family I brought up out of E: H824+5213
Am 3: 9 of Ashdod and to the fortresses of E: H824+5213
Am 4:10 "I sent plagues among you as I did to E. H5213
Am 8: 8 stirred up and then sink like the river of E. H5213
Am 9: 5 like the Nile, then sinks like the river of E; H5213
Am 9: 7 "Did I not bring Israel up from E, the H824+5213
Mic 6: 4 you up out of E and redeemed you H824+5213
Mic 7:12 to you from Assyria and the cities of E, H5191
Mic 7:12 even from E to the Euphrates and from H5191
Mic 7:15 in the days when you came out of E, H824+5213
Na 3: 9 Cush and E were her boundless strength H5213
Hag 2: 5 with you when you came out of E. H5213
Zec 10:10 them back from E and gather them H824+5213
Zec 14:19 the punishment of E and the punishment H5213
Mt 2:13 the child and his mother and escape to E. *G131*
Mt 2:14 his mother during the night and left for E, *G131*
Mt 2:15 "Out of E I called my son." *G131*
Mt 2:19 Lord appeared in a dream to Joseph in E *G131*
Ac 2:10 E and the parts of Libya near Cyrene *G131*
Ac 7: 9 of Joseph, they sold him as a slave into E. *G131*
Ac 7:10 to gain the goodwill of Pharaoh king *of* E. *G131*
Ac 7:10 made him ruler over E and all his palace. *G131*
Ac 7:11 "Then a famine struck all E and Canaan *G131*
Ac 7:12 Jacob heard that there was grain in E, *G131*
Ac 7:15 Then Jacob went down to E, where he and *G131*
Ac 7:17 of our people in E had greatly increased. *G131*
Ac 7:18 meant nothing, came to power in E. *G131*
Ac 7:34 seen the oppression of my people in E. *G131*
Ac 7:34 Now come, I will send you back to E.' *G131*
Ac 7:36 He led them out of E and performed NDT
Ac 7:36 performed wonders and signs in E, *G1178+131*
Ac 7:39 him and in their hearts turned back to E. *G131*
Ac 7:40 fellow Moses who led us out of E— *G1178+131*
Ac 13:17 prosper during their stay in E; *G1178+131*
Heb 3:16 Were they not all those Moses led out of E? *G131*
Heb 8: 9 by the hand to lead them out of E, *G1178+131*
Heb 11:22 of the Israelites from E and gave instructions NDT
Heb 11:26 as of greater value than the treasures *of* E, *G131*
Heb 11:27 By faith he left E, not fearing the king's *G131*
Jude 5 time delivered his people out of E, *G1178+131*
Rev 11: 8 which is figuratively called Sodom and E *G131*

EGYPT'S (5) [EGYPT]

Isa 20: 4 with buttocks bared—to E shame. H5213
Isa 30: 2 protection, to E shade for refuge. H5213
Isa 30: 3 E shade will bring you disgrace. H5213
Eze 30: 9 take hold of them on the day of E doom, H5213
Zec 10:11 be brought down and E scepter will pass H5213

EGYPTIAN (35) [EGYPT]

Ge 16: 1 But she had an E slave named Hagar; H5212
Ge 16: 3 his wife took her E slave Hagar and gave H5212
Ge 21: 9 son whom Hagar the E had borne to H5212
Ge 25:12 Hagar the E, bore to Abraham. H5212
Ge 39: 1 an E who was one of Pharaoh's officials H5212
Ge 39: 2 he lived in the house of his E master. H5212
Ge 39: 5 household of the E because of Joseph. H5212
Ex 1:19 "Hebrew women are not like E women H5212
Ex 2:11 He saw an E beating a Hebrew, one H5212+408
Ex 2:12 he killed the E and hid him in the sand. H5212
Ex 2:14 thinking of killing me as you killed the E?" H5212
Ex 2:19 "An E rescued us from the H408+5212

Ex 7:11 the **E** magicians also did the same H5213
Ex 7:22 But the **E** magicians did the same things H5213
Ex 14:24 fire and cloud at the **E** army and threw it H5213
Lev 24:10 mother and an **E** father went out among H5212
Dt 11: 4 what he did to the **E** army, to its horses H5213
Dt 23: 7 Do not despise an **E**, because you resided H5212
1Sa 30:11 They found an **E** in a field and brought H5212
1Sa 30:13 He said, "I am an **E**, the slave of an H5212
2Sa 23:21 And he struck down a huge **E**. H5212
2Sa 23:21 Although the **E** had a spear in his hand H5212
2Ki 7: 6 hired the Hittite and **E** kings to attack us!" H5213
1Ch 2:34 He had an **E** servant named Jarha H5212
1Ch 11:23 he struck down an **E** who was five cubits H5212
1Ch 11:23 Although the **E** had a spear like a H5212
Isa 11:15 The LORD will dry up the gulf of the **E** sea H5213
Isa 19: 2 "I will stir up **E** against Egyptian—brother H5213
Isa 19: 2 "I will stir up Egyptian against **E**—brother H5213
Isa 20: 4 barefoot the **E** captives and Cushite H5213
Zec 14:18 If the **E** people do not go up and take part H5213
Ac 7:24 saw one of them being mistreated by an **E**, NDT
Ac 7:24 defense and avenged him by killing the **E**. *G130*
Ac 7:28 of killing me as you killed the **E** yesterday? *G130*
Ac 21:38 "Aren't you the **E** who started a revolt and *G130*

EGYPTIAN'S (2) [EGYPT]

2Sa 23:21 the spear from the **E** hand and killed him H5212
1Ch 11:23 the spear from the **E** hand and killed him H5212

EGYPTIANS (92) [EGYPT]

Ge 12:12 When the **E** see you, they will say, 'This is H5213
Ge 12:14 the **E** saw that Sarai was a very beautiful H5213
Ge 41:55 Then Pharaoh told all the **E**, "Go to H5213
Ge 41:56 the storehouses and sold grain to the **E**, H5213
Ge 43:32 the **E** who ate with him by H5213
Ge 43:32 because **E** could not eat with Hebrews H5213
Ge 43:32 with Hebrews, for that is detestable to **E**. H5213
Ge 45: 2 he wept so loudly that the **E** heard him, H5213
Ge 46:34 all shepherds are detestable to the **E**." H5213
Ge 47:20 The **E**, one and all, sold their fields H5213
Ge 50: 3 And the **E** mourned for him seventy days. H5213
Ge 50:11 "The **E** are holding a solemn ceremony of H5213
Ex 1:12 so the **E** came to dread the Israelites NDT
Ex 1:14 their harsh labor the **E** worked them NDT
Ex 3: 8 the hand of the **E** and to bring them up H5213
Ex 3: 9 seen the way the **E** are oppressing them. H5213
Ex 3:20 hand and strike the **E** with all the wonders H5213
Ex 3:21 "And I will make the **E** favorably disposed H5213
Ex 3:22 And so you will plunder the **E**." H5213
Ex 6: 5 whom the **E** are enslaving, and I H5213
Ex 6: 6 you out from under the yoke of the **E**. H5213
Ex 6: 7 you out from under the yoke of the **E**. H5213
Ex 7: 5 And the **E** will know that I am the LORD H5213
Ex 7:18 the **E** will not be able to drink its water. H5213
Ex 7:21 so bad that the **E** could not drink its H5213
Ex 7:24 And all the **E** dug along the Nile to get H5213
Ex 8:21 The houses of the **E** will be full of flies H5213
Ex 8:26 our God would be detestable to the **E**. H5213
Ex 9: 6 All the livestock of the **E** died, but not one H5213
Ex 9:11 boils that were on them and on all the **E**. H5213
Ex 10: 2 harshly with the **E** and how I performed H5213
Ex 10: 6 those of all your officials and all the **E**— H5213
Ex 11: 3 The LORD made the **E** favorably disposed H5213
Ex 12:23 through the land to strike down the **E**, H5213
Ex 12:27 our homes when he struck down the **E**. H5213
Ex 12:30 officials and all the **E** got up during the H5213
Ex 12:33 The **E** urged the people to hurry and H5213
Ex 12:35 instructed and asked **the E** for articles of H5213
Ex 12:36 LORD had made the **E** favorably disposed H5213
Ex 12:36 they asked for; so they plundered the **E**. H5213
Ex 14: 4 the **E** will know that I am the LORD. H5213
Ex 14: 9 The **E**—all Pharaoh's horses and chariots H5213
Ex 14:10 there were the **E**, marching after H5213
Ex 14:12 'Leave us alone; let us serve the **E**'? H5213
Ex 14:12 us to serve the **E** than to die in the H5213
Ex 14:13 The **E** you see today you will never see H5213
Ex 14:17 the hearts of the **E** so that they will go in H5213
Ex 14:18 The **E** will know that I am the LORD when I H5213
Ex 14:23 The **E** pursued them, and all Pharaoh's H5213
Ex 14:25 And the **E** said, "Let's get away from the H5213
Ex 14:26 flow back over the **E** and their chariots H5213
Ex 14:27 The **E** were fleeing toward it, and the LORD H5213
Ex 14:30 LORD saved Israel from the hands of the **E**, H5213
Ex 14:30 Israel saw the **E** lying dead on the H5213
Ex 14:31 hand of the LORD displayed against the **E**, H5213
Ex 15:26 any of the diseases I brought on the **E**, H5213
Ex 18: 8 to Pharaoh and the **E** for Israel's sake H5213
Ex 18: 9 in rescuing them from the hand of the **E**. H5213
Ex 18:10 from the hand of the **E** and of Pharaoh, H5213
Ex 18:10 the people from the hand of the **E**. H5213
Ex 32:12 Why should the **E** say, 'It was with evil H5213
Lev 26:13 you would no longer be slaves to **the E**; H2157S
Nu 14:13 to the LORD, "Then the **E** will hear about it! H5213
Nu 20:15 The **E** mistreated us and our ancestors H5213
Nu 33: 3 out defiantly in full view of all the **E**, H5213
Dt 26: 6 But the **E** mistreated us and made us H5213
Jos 24: 5 I afflicted the **E** by what I did there H5213
Jos 24: 6 the **E** pursued them with chariots and H5213
Jos 24: 7 he put darkness between you and the **E**; H5213
Jos 24: 7 with your own eyes what I did to the **E**. H5213
Jdg 6: 9 I rescued you from the hand of the **E**. H5213
Jdg 10:11 LORD replied, "When the **E**, the Amorites, H5213
1Sa 4: 8 the gods who struck the **E** with all kinds of H5213
1Sa 6: 6 your hearts as the **E** and Pharaoh did? H5213
Ezr 9: 1 Ammonites, Moabites, **E** and Amorites. H5212
Ne 9:10 knew how arrogantly the **E** treated them. NDT
Isa 19: 1 the hearts of the **E** melt with fear. H5213
Isa 19: 3 The **E** will lose heart, and I will bring their H5213
Isa 19: 4 I will hand the **E** over to the power of a H5213
Isa 19:16 In that day the **E** will become weaklings H5213
Isa 19:17 land of Judah will bring terror to the **E**; H5213
Isa 19:21 LORD will make himself known to the **E**, H5213
Isa 19:23 will go to Egypt and the **E** to Assyria. H5213
Isa 19:23 The **E** and Assyrians will worship together. H5213
Isa 31: 3 But the **E** are mere mortals and not God H5213
Eze 16:26 engaged in prostitution with the **E**, H1201+5213
Eze 29:12 I will disperse the **E** among the nations H5213
Eze 29:13 I will gather the **E** from the nations where H5213
Eze 30:23 I will disperse the **E** among the nations H5213
Eze 30:26 I will disperse the **E** among the nations H5213
Ac 7:22 all the wisdom *of* the **E** and was powerful *G130*
Heb 11:29 but when the **E** tried to do so, they *G130*

EHI (1)

Ge 46:21 Naaman, **E**, Rosh, Muppim, Huppim H305

EHUD (12)

Jdg 3:15 them a deliverer—**E**, a left-handed man, H179
Jdg 3:16 Now **E** had made a double-edged sword H179
Jdg 3:18 After **E** had presented the tribute, he sent on NDT
Jdg 3:20 **E** then approached him while he was H179
Jdg 3:21 **E** reached with his left hand, drew the H179
Jdg 3:22 **E** did not pull the sword out, and the fat NDT
Jdg 3:23 Then **E** went out to the porch; he shut the H179
Jdg 3:26 While they waited, **E** got away. He passed H179
Jdg 3:31 After **E** came Shamgar son of Anath H2257S
Jdg 4: 1 the eyes of the LORD, now that **E** was dead. H179
1Ch 7:10 Benjamin, **E**, Kenaanah, Zethan H179
1Ch 8: 6 These were the descendants of **E**, who H287

EIGHT (35) [EIGHTH]

Ge 17:12 among you who is **e** days old must be H9046
Ge 21: 4 When his son Isaac was **e** days old H9046
Ge 22:23 Milkah bore these **e** sons to Abraham's H9046
Ex 26:25 So there will be **e** frames and sixteen H9046
Ex 36:30 So there were **e** frames and sixteen silver H9046
Nu 7: 8 gave four carts and **e** oxen to the H9046
Nu 29:29 " 'On the sixth day offer **e** bulls, two rams H9046
Jdg 3: 8 the Israelites were subject for **e** years. H9046
Jdg 12:14 seventy donkeys. He led Israel **e** years. H9046
1Sa 17:12 Jesse had **e** sons, and in Saul's time he H9046
2Sa 23: 8 raised his spear against **e** hundred men, H9046
2Sa 24: 9 In Israel there were **e** hundred thousand H9046
1Ki 7:10 some measuring ten cubits and some **e**. H9046
2Ki 8:17 he reigned in Jerusalem **e** years. H9046
2Ki 22: 1 Josiah was **e** years old when he became H9046
1Ch 24: 4 descendants and **e** heads of families from H9046
2Ch 13: 3 against him with **e** hundred thousand H9046
2Ch 21: 5 he reigned in Jerusalem **e** years. H9046
2Ch 21:20 he reigned in Jerusalem **e** years. H9046
2Ch 29:17 For **e** more days they consecrated the H9046
2Ch 34: 1 Josiah was **e** years old when he became H9046
Ecc 11: 2 in **e**; you do not know what disaster H9046
Jer 41:15 of Nethaniah and **e** *of* his men escaped H9046
Eze 40: 9 it was **e** cubits deep and its jambs were H9046
Eze 40:31 its jambs, and **e** steps led up to it. H9046
Eze 40:34 on either side, and **e** steps led up to it. H9046
Eze 40:37 on either side, and **e** steps led up to it. H9046
Eze 40:41 four on the other—**e** tables in all—on H9046
Mic 5: 5 seven shepherds, even **e** commanders, H9046
Lk 9:28 About **e** days after Jesus said this, he took *G3893*
Lk 16: 7 'Take your bill and make it **e hundred**. *G3837*
Ac 7: 8 circumcised him **e** days after his birth. *G3838*
Ac 9:33 had been bedridden for **e** years. *G3893*
Ac 25: 6 After spending **e** or ten days with them *G3893*
1Pe 3:20 it only a few people, **e** in all, were saved *G3893*

EIGHTEEN (16) [EIGHTEENTH, 18]

Jdg 3:14 to Eglon king of Moab for **e** years. H9046+6926
Jdg 10: 8 For **e** years they oppressed all the H9046+6926
Jdg 20:25 cut down another **e** thousand H9046+6925
Jdg 20:44 **E** thousand Benjamites fell, all of H9046+6925
2Sa 8:13 striking down **e** thousand Edomites H9046+6925
1Ki 7:15 each **e** cubits high and twelve H9046+6926
2Ki 24: 8 Jehoiachin was **e** years old when H9046+6926
2Ki 25:17 Each pillar was **e** cubits high. H9046+6926
1Ch 18:12 struck down **e** thousand Edomites H9046+6925
1Ch 29: 7 **e thousand** talents of H8052+2256+9046+547
2Ch 11:21 he had **e** wives and sixty H9046+6926
2Ch 36: 9 Jehoiachin was **e** years old when H9046+6926
Jer 52:21 Each pillar was **e** cubits high and H9046+6926
Lk 13: 4 Or those **e** who died when the tower in *G1277*
Lk 13:11 had been crippled by a spirit for **e** years. *G1277*
Lk 13:16 kept bound *for* **e** long years, *G1274+2779+3893*

EIGHTEENTH (11) [EIGHTEEN]

1Ki 15: 1 In the **e** year of the reign of H9046+6926
2Ki 3: 1 in Samaria in the **e** year of H9046+6926
2Ki 22: 3 In the **e** year of his reign, King H9046+6926
2Ki 23:23 But in the **e** year of King Josiah, this H9046+6926
1Ch 24:15 to Hezir, the **e** to Happizzez, H9046+6925
1Ch 25:25 the **e** to Hanani, his sons and H9046+6925
2Ch 13: 1 In the **e** year of the reign of H9046+6926
2Ch 34: 8 In the **e** year of Josiah's reign, to H9046+6926
2Ch 35:19 celebrated in the **e** year of Josiah's H9046+6926
Jer 32: 1 which was the **e** year of H9046+6926
Jer 52:29 in Nebuchadnezzar's **e** year, 832 H9046+6926

EIGHTH (35) [EIGHT]

Ex 22:30 but give them to me on the **e** day. H9029
Lev 9: 1 On the **e** day Moses summoned Aaron H9029
Lev 12: 3 On the **e** day the boy is to be circumcised. H9029
Lev 14:10 "On the **e** day they must bring two male H9029
Lev 14:23 "On the **e** day they must bring them for H9029
Lev 15:14 On the **e** day he must take two doves or H9029
Lev 15:29 On the **e** day she must take two doves H9029
Lev 22:27 From the **e** day on, it will be acceptable H9029
Lev 23:36 on the **e** day hold a sacred assembly H9029
Lev 23:39 the **e** day also is a day of sabbath H9029
Lev 25:22 While you plant during the **e** year, you will H9029
Nu 6:10 Then on the **e** day they must bring two H9029
Nu 7:54 On the **e** day Gamaliel son of Pedahzur H9029
Nu 29:35 " 'On the **e** day hold a closing special H9029
1Ki 6:38 month of Bul, the **e** month, the temple H9029
1Ki 12:32 on the fifteenth day of the **e** month, H9029
1Ki 12:33 On the fifteenth day of the **e** month, H9029
2Ki 24:12 In the **e** year of the reign of the king of H9046
1Ch 12:12 Johanan the **e**, Elzabad the ninth, H9029
1Ch 24:10 the seventh to Hakkoz, the **e** to Abijah, H9029
1Ch 25:15 the **e** to Jeshaiah, his sons and relatives H9029
1Ch 26: 5 Issachar the seventh and Peullethai the **e**. H9029
1Ch 27:11 The **e**, for the eighth month, was Sibbekai H9029
1Ch 27:11 The eighth, for the **e** month, was Sibbekai H9029
2Ch 7: 9 On the **e** day they held an assembly, for H9029
2Ch 29:17 by the **e** day of the month they H9046
2Ch 34: 3 In the **e** year of his reign, while he was H9046
Ne 8:18 and on the **e** day, in accordance H9029
Eze 43:27 these days, from the **e** day on, the priests H9029
Zec 1: 1 In the **e** month of the second year of H9029
Lk 1:59 On the **e** day they came to circumcise the *G3838*
Lk 2:21 On the **e** day, when it was time to *G3893*
Php 3: 5 circumcised **on the e day**, of the people of *G3892*
Rev 17:11 once was, and now is not, is an **e** king. *G3838*
Rev 21:20 chrysolite, the **e** beryl, the ninth topaz, *G3838*

EIGHTIETH (1) [EIGHTY]

1Ki 6: 1 In the four hundred and **e** year after the H9046

EIGHTY (15) [EIGHTIETH, 80]

Ge 35:28 Isaac lived a hundred and **e** years. H9046
Ex 7: 7 Moses was **e** years old and Aaron H9046
Jdg 3:30 the land had peace for **e** years. H9046
2Sa 19:32 Now Barzillai *was* very old, **e** years of age H9046
2Sa 19:35 I am now **e** years old. Can I tell the H9046
1Ki 5:15 carriers and **e** thousand stonecutters H9046
1Ki 12:21 a hundred and **e** thousand able young H9046
2Ki 6:25 donkey's head sold for **e** shekels of silver, H9046
2Ki 10:24 Now Jehu had posted **e** men outside with H9046
2Ch 11: 1 a hundred and **e** thousand able young H9046
2Ch 14: 8 two hundred and **e** thousand from H9046
2Ch 26:17 Azariah the priest with **e** other courageous H9046
Ps 90:10 to seventy years, or **e**, if our strength H9046
SS 6: 8 there may be, and **e** concubines, and H9046
Jer 41: 5 **e** men who had shaved off their beards H9046

EIGHTY-FIVE (4)

Jos 14:10 here I am today, **e** years old! H9046+2256+2822
1Sa 22:18 he killed **e** men who wore H9046+2256+2822
2Ki 19:35 hundred and **e** thousand in H9046+2256+2822
Isa 37:36 hundred and **e** thousand in H9046+2256+2822

EIGHTY-FOUR (1)

Lk 2:37 then was a widow until she was **e**. *G3837+5475*

EIGHTY-SIX (1)

Ge 16:16 Abram was **e** years old when H9046+9252+2256

EIGHTY-THREE (1)

Ex 7: 7 old and Aaron **e** when they H9046+2256+8993

EITHER (40)

Ge 31:24 to say anything to Jacob, **e** good or bad." H4946
Ge 31:29 to say anything to Jacob, **e** good or bad. H4946
Lev 1: 2 an animal from **e** the herd **or** the flock. H2256
Lev 1:10 from **e** the sheep **or** the goats, you H196
Lev 2: 4 **e** thick loaves made without yeast and with olive oil mixed in **or** H2256
Lev 18: 9 **e** your father's daughter **or** your mother's H196
Lev 18:17 with **e** her son's daughter **or** her H2256
Lev 20:17 the daughter of **e** his father **or** his mother H196
Lev 20:19 the sister of **e** your mother **or** your father, H2256
Lev 22:18 **e** to fulfill a vow **or** as a freewill offering, H2256
Nu 22:26 room to turn, **e** to the right **or** to the left. H2256
Dt 1:37 also and said, "You shall not enter it, **e**. H1685
Dt 22: 6 the road, **e** in a tree **or** on the ground H196
1Sa 16: 8 "The LORD has not chosen this one **e**." H1685
1Sa 20:27 come to the meal, **e** yesterday or today?" H1685
1Sa 28:15 answers me, **e** by prophets or by dreams. H1685
2Sa 13:22 a word to Amnon, **e** good or bad; he H4946
1Ki 10:20 one **at e end** of each H4946+2296+2256+4946+2296S
2Ki 9:20 reached them, but he isn't coming back **e**. NDT
2Ki 18: 5 kings of Judah, **e** before him **or** after him. H2256
2Ch 9:19 one **at e end** of each H4946+2296+2256+4946+2296S
Ecc 4:10 If **e** *of* them falls down, one can help the H285
Jer 29:19 And you exiles have not listened **e**, NDT
Eze 1:11 wing touching that of the creature on **e** side; NDT

Eze 40:34 the jambs **on e side**, H4946+7024+2256+4946+7024
Eze 40:37 the jambs **on e side**, H4946+7024+2256+4946+7024
Eze 40:48 cubits wide **on e side**. H4946+7024+2256+4946+7024
Eze 40:48 cubits wide **on e side**. H4946+7024+2256+4946+7024
Am 7: 6 "This will not happen e," the Sovereign H1685
Zep 1:12 'The LORD will do nothing, e good or bad. H4202
Mt 5:34 swear an oath at all: e by heaven, for it is *G3612*
Mt 6:24 E you will hate the one and love the other *G2445*
Mt 12:32 e in this age or in the age to come. *G4046*
Mk 16:13 the rest; **but** they did **not** believe them e. *G4028*
Lk 16:13 E you will hate the one and love the other *G2445*
Jn 19:10 I have power e to free you **or** to crucify you *G2779*
Ro 11:21 natural branches, he will **not** spare you e. *G4028*
1Co 15:16 then Christ has **not** been raised e. *G4028*
1Jn 3: 6 to sin has e seen him **or** known him. *G4028*
Rev 3:15 I wish you were e one **or** the other! *G2445*

EKED See BETH EKED

EKER (1)
1Ch 2:27 of Jerahmeel: Maaz, Jamin and E. H6831

EKRON (24)
Jos 13: 3 of Egypt to the territory of E on the north, H6833
Jos 13: 3 Ashkelon, Gath and E; the territory of the H6834
Jos 15:11 It went to the northern slope of E, turned H6833
Jos 15:45 E, with its surrounding settlements and H6833
Jos 15:46 west of E, all that were in the vicinity of H6833
Jos 19:43 Elon, Timnah, E, H6833
Jdg 1:18 Ashkelon and E—each city with its H6833
1Sa 5:10 So they sent the ark of God to E. As the ark H6833
1Sa 5:10 As the ark of God was entering E, the H6833
1Sa 5:10 the **people of** E cried out, "They H6834
1Sa 6:16 this and then returned that same day to E. H6833
1Sa 6:17 Ashdod, Gaza, Ashkelon, Gath and E. H6833
1Sa 7:14 The towns from E to Gath that the H6833
1Sa 17:52 entrance of Gath and to the gates of E. H6833
1Sa 17:52 along the Shaaraim road to Gath and E. H6833
2Ki 1: 2 Baal-Zebub, the god of E, to see if I will H6833
2Ki 1: 3 off to consult Baal-Zebub, the god of E? H6833
2Ki 1: 6 to consult Baal-Zebub, the god of E? H6833
2Ki 1:16 to consult Baal-Zebub, the god of E? H6833
Jer 25:20 of Ashkelon, Gaza, E, and the people left H6833
Am 1: 8 I will turn my hand against E, till the last H6833
Zep 2: 4 Ashdod will be emptied and E uprooted. H6833
Zec 9: 5 writhe in agony, and E too, for her hope H6833
Zec 9: 7 in Judah, and E will be like the Jebusites. H6833

EL See IPHTAH EL, MIGDAL EL

EL BETHEL (1) [BETHEL]
Ge 35: 7 he called the place E, because H450

EL ELOHE ISRAEL (1) [ISRAEL]
Ge 33:20 set up an altar and called it E. H449

EL PARAN (1) [PARAN]
Ge 14: 6 as far as E near the desert. H386

EL-BERITH (1)
Jdg 9:46 into the stronghold of the temple of E. H451

ELA (1)
1Ki 4:18 Shimei son of E—in Benjamin; H452

ELABORATE (2)
1Ti 2: 9 not with **e hairstyles** or gold or pearls or *G4427*
1Pe 3: 3 such as **e hairstyles** and the *G1862+2582*

ELAH (16) [ELAH'S]
Ge 36:41 Oholibamah, E, Pinon, H462
1Sa 17: 2 in the Valley of E and drew up their H463
1Sa 17:19 all the men of Israel in the Valley of E, H463
1Sa 21: 9 whom you killed in the Valley of E, is here; H463
1Ki 16: 6 And E his son succeeded him as king H462
1Ki 16: 8 E son of Baasha became king of Israel H462
1Ki 16: 9 E was in Tirzah at the time, getting H2085S
1Ki 16:13 Baasha and his son E had committed and H462
2Ki 15:30 Then Hoshea son of E conspired against H462
2Ki 17: 1 Hoshea son of E became king of Israel in H462
2Ki 18: 1 third year of Hoshea son of E king of Israel, H462
2Ki 18: 9 year of Hoshea son of E king of Israel, H462
1Ch 1:52 Oholibamah, E, Pinon, H462
1Ch 4:15 of Jephunneh: Iru, E and Naam. The son of H462
1Ch 4:15 Elah and Naam. The son of E: Kenaz. H462
1Ch 9: 8 son of Jeroham; E son of Uzzi, the son of H462

ELAH'S (1) [ELAH]
1Ki 16:14 As for the other events of E reign, and all H462

ELAM (27) [ELAM'S, ELAMITES]
Ge 10:22 The sons of Shem: E, Ashur, Arphaxad H6521
Ge 14: 1 Kedorlaomer king of E and Tidal king of H6520
Ge 14: 9 against Kedorlaomer king of E, Tidal king H6520
1Ch 1:17 The sons of Shem: E, Ashur, Arphaxad H6521
1Ch 8:24 Hananiah, E, Anthothijah, H6521
1Ch 26: 3 E the fifth, Jehohanan the sixth and H6521
Ezr 2: 7 of E 1,254 H6521
Ezr 2:31 of the other E 1,254 H6521
Ezr 8: 7 of the descendants of E, Jeshaiah son of H6521
Ezr 10: 2 one of the descendants of E, said to Ezra, H6521
Ezr 10:26 From the descendants of E: Mattaniah H6521
Ne 7:12 of E 1,254 H6521
Ne 7:34 of the other E 1,254 H6521
Ne 10:14 Pahath-Moab, E, Zattu, Bani, H6521
Ne 12:42 Jehohanan, Malkijah, E and Ezer. H6521
Isa 11:11 from Cush, from E, from Babylonia, from H6520
Isa 21: 2 the looter takes loot. E, attack! Media, lay H6520
Isa 22: 6 E takes up the quiver, with her charioteers H6520
Jer 25:25 all the kings of Zimri, E and Media; H6520
Jer 49:34 to Jeremiah the prophet concerning E, H6520
Jer 49:35 I will break the bow of E, the mainstay of H6520
Jer 49:36 I will bring against E the four winds from H6520
Jer 49:37 I will shatter E before their foes, before H6520
Jer 49:38 set my throne in E and destroy her king H6520
Jer 49:39 restore the fortunes of E in days to come," H6520
Eze 32:24 "E is there, with all her hordes around her H6520
Da 8: 2 in the citadel of Susa in the province of E; H6520

ELAM'S (1) [ELAM]
Jer 49:36 not be a nation where E exiles do not go. H6520

ELAMITES (2) [ELAM]
Ezr 4: 9 Uruk and Babylon, the E of Susa, A10551
Ac 2: 9 Parthians, Medes and E; residents of *G1780*

ELAPSED (1)
1Sa 18:26 So **before** the allotted time e, H4202+4848

ELASAH (2)
Ezr 10:22 Ishmael, Nethanel, Jozabad and E. H543
Jer 29: 3 the letter to E son of Shaphan and to H543

ELATED (1) [ELATION]
1Sa 11: 9 this to the men of Jabesh, *they were* e. H8523

ELATH (7)
Dt 2: 8 which comes up from E and Ezion Geber H397
1Ki 9:26 which is near E in Edom, on the H393
2Ki 14:22 the one who rebuilt E and restored it to H397
2Ki 16: 6 of Aram recovered E for Aram by driving H397
2Ki 16: 6 then moved into E and have lived there to H397
2Ch 8:17 to Ezion Geber and E on the coast of Edom H393
2Ch 26: 2 the one who rebuilt E and restored it to H393

ELATION (1) [ELATED]
Pr 28:12 there is great e; but when the wicked H9514

ELDAAH (2)
Ge 25: 4 were Ephah, Epher, Hanok, Abida and E. H456
1Ch 1:33 Hanok, Abida and E. All these were H456

ELDAD (2)
Nu 11:26 whose names were E and Medad, had H455
Nu 11:27 "E and Medad are prophesying in the H455

ELDER (6) [ELDERLY, ELDERS]
Isa 3: 2 the prophet, the diviner and the e, H2418
1Ti 5:19 against an e unless it is brought *G4565*
Titus 1: 6 An e must be blameless, faithful to his wife NDT
1Pe 5: 1 I appeal *as* a **fellow** e and a witness of *G5236*
2Jn 1 The e, To the lady chosen by God and to *G4565*
3Jn 1 The e, To my dear friend Gaius, whom I *G4565*

ELDERLY (2) [ELDER]
Lev 19:32 respect for the e and revere your God. H2418
2Ch 36:17 men or young women, the e or the infirm. H2418

ELDERS (192) [ELDER]
Ex 3:16 assemble the e *of* Israel and say to them H2418
Ex 3:18 "The e *of* Israel will listen to you. H2418
Ex 3:18 Then you and the e are to go to the king of NDT
Ex 4:29 together all the e *of* the Israelites, H2418
Ex 12:21 summoned all the e *of* Israel and said to H2418
Ex 17: 5 you some of the e *of* Israel and take in H2418
Ex 17: 6 did this in the sight of the e *of* Israel. H2418
Ex 18:12 came with all the e *of* Israel to eat a meal H2418
Ex 19: 7 summoned the e *of* the people and H2418
Ex 24: 1 Abihu, and seventy of the e *of* Israel. H2418
Ex 24: 9 the seventy e *of* Israel went up H2418
Ex 24:14 He said to the e, "Wait here for us until H2418
Lev 4:15 The e *of* the community are to lay their H2418
Lev 9: 1 Aaron and his sons and the e *of* Israel. H2418
Nu 11:16 seventy of Israel's e who are known to you H2418
Nu 11:24 seventy of their e and had them stand H2418
Nu 11:25 was on him and put it on the seventy e. H2418
Nu 11:26 They were listed among the e, but did not NDT
Nu 11:30 Then Moses and the e *of* Israel returned to H2418
Nu 16:25 Abiram, and the e *of* Israel followed him. H2418
Nu 22: 4 The Moabites said to the e *of* Midian H2418
Nu 22: 7 The e *of* Moab and Midian left, taking H2418
Dt 5:23 of your tribes and your e came to me. H2418
Dt 19:12 the killer shall be sent for *by* the town e H2418
Dt 21: 2 your e and judges shall go out and H2418
Dt 21: 3 Then the e *of* the town nearest the body H2418
Dt 21: 6 Then all the e *of* the town nearest the H2418
Dt 21:19 bring him to the e at the gate of his H2418
Dt 21:20 They shall say to the e, "This son of ours is H2418
Dt 22:15 bring to the town e at the gate proof that H2418
Dt 22:16 Her father will say to the e, "I gave my H2418
Dt 22:17 display the cloth before the e *of* the town, H2418
Dt 22:18 the e shall take the man and punish H2418
Dt 25: 7 she shall go to the e at the town gate H2418
Dt 25: 8 Then the e *of* his town shall summon him H2418
Dt 25: 9 go up to him in the presence of the e, H2418
Dt 27: 1 Moses and the e *of* Israel commanded H2418
Dt 29:10 chief men, your e and officials, and H2418
Dt 31: 9 of the LORD, and to all the e *of* Israel. H2418
Dt 31:28 before me all the e *of* your tribes and all H2418
Dt 32: 7 will tell you, your e, and they will explain H2418
Jos 7: 6 The e *of* Israel did the same, and H2418
Jos 8:33 with their e, officials and judges, H2418
Jos 9:11 And our e and all those living in our H2418
Jos 20: 4 state their case before the e *of* that city. H2418
Jos 20: 4 Then the e are to admit the fugitive into NDT
Jos 20: 5 the e must not surrender the fugitive NDT
Jos 23: 2 all Israel—their e, leaders, judges and H2418
Jos 24: 1 He summoned the e, leaders, judges H2418
Jos 24:31 Joshua and of the e who outlived him H2418
Jdg 2: 7 Joshua and of the e who outlived him H2418
Jdg 8:14 officials of Sukkoth, the e *of* the town. H2418
Jdg 8:16 He took the e *of* the town and taught the H2418
Jdg 11: 5 the e *of* Gilead went to get Jephthah from H2418
Jdg 11: 8 The e *of* Gilead said to him H2418
Jdg 11:10 The e *of* Gilead replied, "The LORD is our H2418
Jdg 11:11 So Jephthah went with the e *of* Gilead H2418
Jdg 21:16 And the e *of* the assembly said, "With the H2418
Ru 4: 2 took ten of the e *of* the town and said, H2418
Ru 4: 4 in the presence of the e *of* my people. H2418
Ru 4: 9 announced to the e and all the people, H2418
Ru 4:11 Then the e and all the people at the gate H2418
1Sa 4: 3 to camp, the e *of* Israel asked, "Why H2418
1Sa 8: 4 So all the e *of* Israel gathered together H2418
1Sa 11: 3 The e *of* Jabesh said to him, "Give us H2418
1Sa 15:30 honor me before the e *of* my people and H2418
1Sa 16: 4 the e *of* the town trembled when they met H2418
1Sa 30:26 some of the plunder to the e *of* Judah, H2418
2Sa 3:17 conferred with the e *of* Israel and said, H2418
2Sa 5: 3 When all the e *of* Israel had come to King H2418
2Sa 12:17 The e *of* his household stood beside him H2418
2Sa 17: 4 to Absalom and to all the e *of* Israel. H2418
2Sa 17:15 Absalom and the e *of* Israel to do such H2418
2Sa 19:11 "Ask the e *of* Judah, 'Why should you be H2418
1Ki 8: 1 his presence at Jerusalem the e *of* Israel, H2418
1Ki 8: 3 When all the e *of* Israel had arrived, the H2418
1Ki 12: 6 consulted the e who had served his H2418
1Ki 12: 8 the advice the e gave him and consulted H2418
1Ki 12:13 Rejecting the advice given him by the e, H2418
1Ki 20: 7 summoned all the e *of* the land and said H2418
1Ki 20: 8 The e and the people all answered H2418
1Ki 21: 8 sent them to the e and nobles who lived H2418
1Ki 21:11 So the e and nobles who lived in H2418
2Ki 6:32 and the e were sitting with him. H2418
2Ki 6:32 Elisha said to the e, "Don't you see how H2418
2Ki 10: 1 to the e and to the guardians of Ahab's H2418
2Ki 10: 5 the e and the guardians sent this H2418
2Ki 23: 1 together all the e *of* Judah and Jerusalem H2418
1Ch 11: 3 When all the e *of* Israel had come to King H2418
1Ch 15:25 So David and the e *of* Israel and the H2418
1Ch 21:16 Then David and the e, clothed in H2418
2Ch 5: 2 summoned to Jerusalem the e *of* Israel, H2418
2Ch 5: 4 When all the e *of* Israel had arrived, the H2418
2Ch 10: 6 consulted the e who had served his H2418
2Ch 10: 8 the advice the e gave him and consulted H2418
2Ch 10:13 Rejecting the advice of the e, H2418
2Ch 34:29 together all the e *of* Judah and Jerusalem H2418
Ezr 5: 5 was watching over the e *of* the Jews, A10675
Ezr 5: 9 We questioned the e and asked them A10675
Ezr 6: 7 the Jewish e rebuild this house A10675
Ezr 6: 8 are to do for these e *of* the Jews in the A10675
Ezr 6:14 So the e *of* the Jews continued to build A10675
Ezr 10: 8 with the decision of the officials and e, H2418
Ezr 10:14 along with the e and judges of each town, H2418
Job 12:20 takes away the discernment of e. H2418
Ps 105:22 as he pleased and teach his e wisdom. H2418
Ps 107:32 praise him in the council of the e. H2418
Ps 119:100 I have more understanding than the e, for H2418
Pr 31:23 takes his seat among the e *of* the land. H2418
Isa 3:14 judgment against the e and leaders of his H2418
Isa 9:15 the e and dignitaries are the head, the H2418
Isa 24:23 before its e—with great glory. H2418
Jer 19: 1 along some of the e *of* the people and of H2418
Jer 26:17 Some of the e *of* the land stepped H2418
Jer 29: 1 to the surviving e *among* the exiles and to H2418
La 1:19 My priests and my e perished in the city H2418
La 2:10 The e *of* Daughter Zion sit on the ground H2418
La 4:16 are shown no honor, the e no favor. H2418
La 5:12 by their hands; e are shown no respect. H2418
La 5:14 The e are gone from the city gate; the H2418
Eze 7:26 the counsel of the e will come to an end. H2418
Eze 8: 1 my house and the e *of* Judah were sitting H2418
Eze 8:11 In front of them stood seventy e *of* Israel H2418
Eze 8:12 you seen what the e *of* Israel are doing in H2418
Eze 14: 1 Some of the e *of* Israel came to me and H2418
Eze 20: 1 some of the e *of* Israel came to inquire of H2418
Eze 20: 3 speak to the e *of* Israel and say to them H2418
Joel 1: 2 Hear this, you e; listen, all who live in the H2418
Joel 1:14 Summon the e and all who live in the H2418
Joel 2:16 bring together the e, gather the children, H2418
Mt 15: 2 your disciples break the tradition *of* the e? *G4565*
Mt 16:21 suffer many things at the hands of the e, *G4565*
Mt 21:23 priests and the e of the people came to *G4565*
Mt 26: 3 chief priests and the e of the people *G4565*
Mt 26:47 the chief priests and the e of the people. *G4565*
Mt 26:57 of the law and the e had assembled. *G4565*
Mt 27: 1 priests and the e of the people made *G4565*

Mt 27: 3 of silver to the chief priests and the e. *G4565*
Mt 27:12 accused by the chief priests and the e, *G4565*
Mt 27:20 priests and the e persuaded the crowd *G4565*
Mt 27:41 of the law and the e mocked him. *G4565*
Mt 28:12 had met with the e and devised a plan, *G4565*
Mk 7: 3 washing, holding to the tradition *of* the e. *G4565*
Mk 7: 5 to the tradition *of* the e instead of eating *G4565*
Mk 8:31 many things and be rejected by the e, *G4565*
Mk 11:27 of the law and the e came to him. *G4565*
Mk 12:12 of the law and the e looked for a way to NDT
Mk 14:43 the teachers of the law, and the e. *G4565*
Mk 14:53 the e and the teachers of the law came *G4565*
Mk 15: 1 with the e, the teachers of the *G4565*
Lk 7: 3 of Jesus and sent *some* e of the Jews to *G4565*
Lk 9:22 many things and be rejected by the e, *G4565*
Lk 20: 1 together with the e, came up to him. *G4565*
Lk 22:52 and the e, who had come for him *G4565*
Lk 22:66 daybreak the **council of the** e of the *G4564*
Ac 4: 5 the e and the teachers of the law met in *G4565*
Ac 4: 8 "Rulers and e of the people! *G4565*
Ac 4:23 chief priests and the e had said to them. *G4565*
Ac 5:21 the full **assembly of** the e of Israel—and *G1172*
Ac 6:12 the people and the e and the teachers of *G4565*
Ac 11:30 their gift to the e by Barnabas and Saul. *G4565*
Ac 14:23 Barnabas appointed e for them in each *G4565*
Ac 15: 2 the apostles and e about this question. *G4565*
Ac 15: 4 by the church and the apostles and e, *G4565*
Ac 15: 6 The apostles and e met to consider this *G4565*
Ac 15:22 Then the apostles and e, with the whole *G4565*
Ac 15:23 The apostles and e, your brothers, To the *G4565*
Ac 16: 4 by the apostles and e in Jerusalem for the *G4565*
Ac 20:17 sent to Ephesus for the e of the church. *G4565*
Ac 21:18 to see James, and all the e were present. *G4565*
Ac 23:14 to the chief priests and the e and said, *G4565*
Ac 24: 1 Caesarea with some *of* the e and a lawyer *G4565*
Ac 25:15 priests and the e of the Jews brought *G4565*
1Ti 4:14 when the **body of** e laid their hands *G4564*
1Ti 5:17 The e who direct the affairs of the church *G4565*
1Ti 5:20 But those e who are sinning you are to NDT
Titus 1: 5 unfinished and appoint e in every town, *G4565*
Jas 5:14 Let them call the e of the church to pray *G4565*
1Pe 5: 1 *To* the e among you, I appeal as a fellow *G4565*
1Pe 5: 5 are younger, submit yourselves *to* your e. *G4565*
Rev 4: 4 seated on them were twenty-four e. *G4565*
Rev 4:10 the twenty-four e fall down before him *G4565*
Rev 5: 5 Then one of the e said to me, "Do not *G4565*
Rev 5: 6 by the four living creatures and the e. *G4565*
Rev 5: 8 the twenty-four e fell down before *G4565*
Rev 5:11 throne and the living creatures and the e. *G4565*
Rev 5:14 and the e fell down and worshiped. *G4565*
Rev 7:11 around the e and the four living *G4565*
Rev 7:13 Then one of the e asked me, "These in *G4565*
Rev 11:16 And the twenty-four e, who were seated *G4565*
Rev 14: 3 before the four living creatures and the e. *G4565*
Rev 19: 4 The twenty-four e and the four living *G4565*

ELEAD (1)

1Ch 7:21 Ezer and E were killed by the native-born H537

ELEADAH (1)

1Ch 7:20 Tahath his son, E his son, Tahath his H538

ELEALEH (5)

Nu 32: 3 Nimrah, Heshbon, E, Sebam, Nebo and H542
Nu 32:37 rebuilt Heshbon, E and Kiriathaim, H541
Isa 15: 4 Heshbon and E cry out, their voices are H542
Isa 16: 9 Heshbon and E, I drench you with H542
Jer 48:34 cry rises from Heshbon to E and Jahaz, H542

ELEASAH (4)

1Ch 2:39 the father of Helez, Helez the father of E, H543
1Ch 2:40 E the father of Sismai, Sismai the father of H543
1Ch 8:37 was his son, E his son and Azel his son. H543
1Ch 9:43 was his son, E his son and Azel his son. H543

ELEAZAR (75) [ELEAZAR'S]

Ex 6:23 him Nadab and Abihu, E and Ithamar. H540
Ex 6:25 E son of Aaron married one of the H540
Ex 28: 1 Nadab and Abihu, E and Ithamar, so they H540
Lev 10: 6 said to Aaron and his sons E and Ithamar, H540
Lev 10:12 his remaining sons, E and Ithamar, "Take H540
Lev 10:16 he was angry with E and Ithamar, Aaron's H540
Nu 3: 2 the firstborn and Abihu, E and Ithamar. H540
Nu 3: 4 so E and Ithamar served as priests during H540
Nu 3:32 leader of the Levites was E son of Aaron, H540
Nu 4:16 "E son of Aaron, the priest, is to have H540
Nu 16:37 "Tell E son of Aaron, the priest, to remove H540
Nu 16:39 So E the priest collected the bronze censers H540
Nu 19: 3 Give it to E the priest; it is to be taken H540
Nu 19: 4 Then E the priest is to take some of its H540
Nu 20:25 Get Aaron and his son E and take them up H540
Nu 20:26 garments and put them on his son E, H540
Nu 20:28 garments and put them on his son E. H540
Nu 20:28 Then Moses and E came down from the H540
Nu 25: 7 When Phinehas son of E, the son of Aaron H540
Nu 25:11 "Phinehas son of E, the son of Aaron, the H540
Nu 26: 1 the LORD said to Moses and E son of Aaron, H540
Nu 26: 3 Moses and E the priest spoke with them H540
Nu 26:60 father of Nadab and Abihu, E and Ithamar. H540
Nu 26:63 by Moses and E the priest when they H540
Nu 27: 2 stood before Moses, E the priest, the H540
Nu 27:19 Have him stand before E the priest and the H540
Nu 27:21 He is to stand before E the priest, who will H540
Nu 27:22 had him stand before E the priest and the H540
Nu 31: 6 along with Phinehas son of E, the priest, H540
Nu 31:12 plunder to Moses and E the priest and the H540
Nu 31:13 E the priest and all the leaders of the H540
Nu 31:21 Then E the priest said to the soldiers who H540
Nu 31:26 "You and E the priest and the family heads H540
Nu 31:29 share and give it to E the priest as the H540
Nu 31:31 So Moses and E the priest did as the LORD H540
Nu 31:41 gave the tribute to E the priest as the LORD's H540
Nu 31:51 Moses and E the priest accepted from them H540
Nu 31:52 that Moses and E presented as a gift to NDT
Nu 31:54 Moses and E the priest accepted the gold H540
Nu 32: 2 came to Moses and E the priest and to the H540
Nu 32:28 orders about them to E the priest and H540
Nu 34:17 E the priest and Joshua son of Nun H540
Dt 10: 6 E his son succeeded him as priest. H540
Jos 14: 1 land of Canaan, which E the priest, Joshua H540
Jos 17: 4 They went to E the priest, Joshua son of H540
Jos 19:51 These are the territories that E the priest H540
Jos 21: 1 of the Levites approached E the priest, H540
Jos 22:13 So the Israelites sent Phinehas son of E H540
Jos 22:31 And Phinehas son of E, the priest, said to H540
Jos 22:32 Then Phinehas son of E, the priest, and the H540
Jos 24:33 And E son of Aaron died and was buried at H540
Jdg 20:28 with Phinehas son of E, the son of Aaron H540
1Sa 7: 1 hill and consecrated E his son to guard the H540
2Sa 23: 9 Next to him was E son of Dodai the H540
2Sa 23:10 E stood his ground and struck down H2085S
2Sa 23:10 The troops returned to E, but only to strip H2257S
1Ch 6: 3 Nadab, Abihu, E and Ithamar. H540
1Ch 6: 4 E was the father of Phinehas, Phinehas the H540
1Ch 6:50 E his son, Phinehas his son, Abishua his H540
1Ch 9:20 times Phinehas son of E was the official in H540
1Ch 11:12 Next to him was E son of Dodai the H540
1Ch 23:21 The sons of Mahli: E and Kish. H540
1Ch 23:22 E died without having sons: he had only H540
1Ch 24: 1 Aaron were Nadab, Abihu, E and Ithamar. H540
1Ch 24: 2 so E and Ithamar served as the priests. H540
1Ch 24: 3 Zadok a descendant of E and Ahimelek a H540
1Ch 24: 5 the descendants of both E and Ithamar. H540
1Ch 24: 6 being taken from E and then one from H540
1Ch 24:28 E, who had no sons. H540
Ezr 7: 5 Phinehas, the son of E, the son of Aaron H540
Ezr 8:33 E son of Phinehas was with him, and so H540
Ezr 10:25 Malkijah, Mijamin, E, Malkijah and H540
Ne 12:42 Maaseiah, Shemaiah, E, Uzzi, Jehohanan, H540
Mt 1:15 Elihud the father of E, Eleazar the father *G1789*
Mt 1:15 father of Eleazar, E the father of Matthan *G1789*

ELEAZAR'S (2) [ELEAZAR]

1Ch 24: 4 were found among E descendants than H540
1Ch 24: 4 of families from E descendants and eight H540

ELECT (11) [ELECTION]

Mt 24:22 the sake of the e those days will be *G1723*
Mt 24:24 to deceive, if possible, even the e. *G1723*
Mt 24:31 they will gather his e from the four winds, *G1723*
Mk 13:20 But for the sake of the e, whom he has *G1723*
Mk 13:22 to deceive, if possible, even the e. *G1723*
Mk 13:27 gather his e from the four winds, *G1723*
Ro 11: 7 The e among them did, but the others *G1724*
1Ti 5:21 of God and Christ Jesus and the e angels, *G1723*
2Ti 2:10 I endure everything for the sake of the e, *G1723*
Titus 1: 1 further the faith *of* God's e and their *G1723*
1Pe 1: 1 of Jesus Christ, *To God's* e, exiles *G1723*

ELECTION (3) [ELECT]

Ro 9:11 that God's purpose in e might stand: *G1724*
Ro 11:28 but as far as e is concerned, they *G1724*
2Pe 1:10 every effort to confirm your calling and e. *G1724*

ELEGANT (2)

Eze 23:41 You sat on an e couch, with a table spread H3884
Lk 23:11 Dressing him in an e robe, they sent him *G3287*

ELEMENTAL (3) [ELEMENTARY, ELEMENTS]

Gal 4: 3 under the e **spiritual forces** of the world. *G5122*
Col 2: 8 the e **spiritual forces** of this world *G5122*
Col 2:20 to the e **spiritual forces** of this world *G5122*

ELEMENTARY (2) [ELEMENTAL]

Heb 5:12 you the e **truths** of God's *G5122+3836+794*
Heb 6: 1 us move beyond the e teachings about *G794*

ELEMENTS (2) [ELEMENTAL]

2Pe 3:10 with a roar; the e will be destroyed by fire *G5122*
2Pe 3:12 and the e will melt in the heat. *G5122*

ELEVATE (1) [ELEVATED, ELEVATING]

2Co 11: 7 myself in order to e you by preaching the *G5738*

ELEVATED (1) [ELEVATE]

Est 5:11 him and how *he had* e him above the H5951

ELEVATING (1) [ELEVATE]

Est 3: 1 e him and giving him a seat of honor H5951

ELEVEN (23) [ELEVENTH]

Ge 32:22 servants and his e sons and crossed H285+6925
Ge 37: 9 sun and moon and e stars were H285+6925
Ex 26: 7 over the tabernacle—e altogether. H6954+6926
Ex 26: 8 All e curtains are to be the same H6954+6926
Ex 36:14 over the tabernacle—e altogether. H6954+6926
Ex 36:15 All e curtains were the same size H6954+6926
Nu 29:20 " 'On the third day offer e bulls H6954+6925
Dt 1: 2 It takes e days to go from Horeb to H285+6925
Jos 15:51 Giloh—e towns and their villages. H285+6926
Jdg 16: 5 give you e **hundred** shekels of H547+2256+4395
Jdg 17: 2 "The e **hundred** shekels of H547+2256+4395
Jdg 17: 3 the e **hundred** shekels of H547+2256+4395
2Ki 23:36 he reigned in Jerusalem e years. H285+6926
2Ki 24:18 he reigned in Jerusalem e years. H285+6926
2Ch 36: 5 he reigned in Jerusalem e years. H285+6926
2Ch 36:11 he reigned in Jerusalem e years. H285+6926
Jer 52: 1 he reigned in Jerusalem e years. H285+6926
Mt 28:16 Then the e disciples went to Galilee, to *G1894*
Mk 16:14 Jesus appeared *to* the E as they were *G1894*
Lk 24: 9 all these things *to* the E and to all the *G1894*
Lk 24:33 they found the E and those with them, *G1894*
Ac 1:26 so he was added to the e apostles. *G1894*
Ac 2:14 Then Peter stood up with the E, raised his *G1894*

ELEVENTH (18) [ELEVEN]

Nu 7:72 On the e day Pagiel son of Okran H6954+6925
Dt 1: 3 on the first day of the e month H6954+6925
1Ki 6:38 In the e year in the month of Bul, the H285+6926
2Ki 9:29 In the e year of Joram son of Ahab H285+6926
2Ki 25: 2 siege until the e year of King H6954+6926
1Ch 12:13 the tenth and Makbannai the e. H6954+6925
1Ch 24:12 the e to Eliashib, the twelfth to H6954+6925
1Ch 25:18 the e to Azarel, his sons and H6954+6925
1Ch 27:14 The e, for the eleventh month, was H6954+6925
1Ch 27:14 eleventh, for the e month, was H6954+6925
Jer 1: 3 month of the e year of Zedekiah H6954+6926
Jer 39: 2 fourth month of Zedekiah's e year, H6954+6926
Jer 52: 5 siege until the e year of King H6954+6926
Eze 26: 1 In the e month of the twelfth year H6954+6925
Eze 30:20 In the e year, in the first month on H285+6926
Eze 31: 1 In the e year, in the third month on H285+6926
Zec 1: 7 twenty-fourth day of the e month, H6954+6925
Rev 21:20 tenth turquoise, the e jacinth, and the *G1895*

ELHANAN (4)

2Sa 21:19 E son of Jairthe Bethlehemite killed the H481
2Sa 23:24 of Joab, E son of Dodo from Bethlehem H481
1Ch 11:26 of Joab, E son of Dodo from Bethlehem H481
1Ch 20: 5 E son of Jair killed Lahmi the brother of H481

ELI (35) [ELI'S]

1Sa 1: 3 the two sons of E, were priests of the LORD H6603
1Sa 1: 9 Now E the priest was sitting on his chair H6603
1Sa 1:12 to the LORD, E observed her mouth. H6603
1Sa 1:13 was not heard. E thought she was drunk H6603
1Sa 1:17 E answered, "Go in peace, and may the H6603
1Sa 1:25 sacrificed, they brought the boy to E, H6603
1Sa 2:11 before the LORD under E the priest. H6603
1Sa 2:20 E would bless Elkanah and his wife H6603
1Sa 2:22 Now E, who was very old, heard about H6603
1Sa 2:27 a man of God came to E and said to him, H6603
1Sa 3: 1 ministered before the LORD under E. H6603
1Sa 3: 2 One night E, whose eyes were becoming H6603
1Sa 3: 5 And he ran to E and said, "Here I am; you H6603
1Sa 3: 5 But E said, "I did not call; go back and lie NDT
1Sa 3: 6 Samuel got up and went to E and said, H6603
1Sa 3: 6 "My son," E said, "I did not call; go back NDT
1Sa 3: 8 Samuel got up and went to E and said, H6603
1Sa 3: 8 Then E realized that the LORD was calling H6603
1Sa 3: 9 So E told Samuel, "Go and lie down, and H6603
1Sa 3:12 will carry out against E everything I spoke H6603
1Sa 3:14 Therefore I swore to the house of E, 'The H6603
1Sa 3:15 He was afraid to tell E the vision, H6603
1Sa 3:16 E called him and said, "Samuel, my H6603
1Sa 3:17 it he said to you?" E asked. "Do not hide it NDT
1Sa 3:18 Then E said, "He is the LORD; let him do NDT
1Sa 4:13 there was E sitting on his chair by the side H6603
1Sa 4:14 E heard the outcry and asked, "What is H6603
1Sa 4:14 The man hurried over to E, H6603
1Sa 4:16 He told E, "I have just come from the H6603
1Sa 4:16 it this very day." E asked, "What happened NDT
1Sa 4:18 E fell backward off his chair by the side of NDT
1Sa 14: 3 Phinehas, the son of E, the LORD's priest in H6603
1Ki 2:27 spoken at Shiloh about the house of E. H6603
Mt 27:46 Jesus cried out in a loud voice, "E, Eli, *G2458*
Mt 27:46 a loud voice, "Eli, E, lema sabachthani?" *G2458*

ELI'S (4) [ELI]

1Sa 2:12 E sons were scoundrels; they had no H6603
1Sa 3:14 'The guilt of E house will never be atoned H6603
1Sa 4: 4 And E two sons, Hophni and Phinehas H6603
1Sa 4:11 was captured, and E two sons, Hophni H6603

ELIAB (20)

Nu 1: 9 from Zebulun, E son of Helon; H482
Nu 2: 7 of the people of Zebulun is E son of Helon. H482
Nu 7:24 On the third day, E son of Helon, the H482
Nu 7:29 This was the offering of E son of Helon. H482
Nu 10:16 E son of Helon was over the division of H482
Nu 16: 1 Abiram, sons of E, and On son of H482
Nu 16:12 Dathan and Abiram, the sons of E. H482
Nu 26: 8 The son of Pallu was E, H482
Nu 26: 9 the sons of E were Nemuel, Dathan H482
Dt 11: 6 Abiram, sons of E the Reubenite, when H482
1Sa 16: 6 Samuel saw E and thought, "Surely H482
1Sa 17:13 The firstborn was E; the second, Abinadab H482
1Sa 17:28 When E, David's oldest brother, heard him H482
1Ch 2:13 Jesse was the father of E his firstborn; the H482
1Ch 6:27 E his son, Jeroham his son, Elkanah his H482

1Ch 12: 9 the second in command, **E** the third, H482
1Ch 15:18 Unni, **E**, Benaiah, Maaseiah H482
1Ch 15:20 **E**, Maaseiah and Benaiah were to H482
1Ch 16: 5 Mattithiah, **E**, Benaiah, Obed-Edom H482
2Ch 11:18 of Abihail, the daughter of Jesse's son **E**. H482

ELIADA (4)
2Sa 5:16 Elishama, **E** and Eliphelet. H486
1Ki 11:23 Rezon son of **E**, who had fled from his H486
1Ch 3: 8 Elishama, **E** and Eliphelet—nine in all. H486
2Ch 17:17 **E**, a valiant soldier, with 200,000 men H486

ELIAH (KJV) ELIJAH

ELIAHBA (2)
2Sa 23:32 **E** the Shaalbonite, the sons of Jashen H494
1Ch 11:33 the Baharumite, **E** the Shaalbonite, H494

ELIAKIM (15) [ELIAKIM'S]
2Ki 18:18 **E** son of Hilkiah the palace H509
2Ki 18:26 Then **E** son of Hilkiah, and Shebna and H509
2Ki 18:37 Then **E** son of Hilkiah the palace H509
2Ki 19: 2 He sent **E** the palace administrator, Shebna H509
2Ki 23:34 Pharaoh Necho made **E** son of Josiah king H509
2Ch 36: 4 The king of Egypt made **E**, a brother of H509
Ne 12:41 as the priests—**E**, Maaseiah, Miniamin H509
Isa 22:20 I will summon my servant, **E** son of Hilkiah. H509
Isa 36: 3 **E** son of Hilkiah the palace administrator H509
Isa 36:11 Then **E**, Shebna and Joah said to the field H509
Isa 36:22 Then **E** son of Hilkiah the palace H509
Isa 37: 2 He sent **E** the palace administrator, Shebna H509
Mt 1:13 Abihud the father of **E**, Eliakim the father *G1806*
Mt 1:13 the father of Eliakim, **E** the father of Azor, *G1806*
Lk 3:30 Joseph, the son of Jonam, the son *of* **E**, *G1806*

ELIAKIM'S (3) [ELIAKIM]
2Ki 23:34 changed **E** name to Jehoiakim. H2257S
2Ch 36: 4 changed **E** name to Jehoiakim. H2257S
2Ch 36: 4 But Necho took **E** brother Jehoahaz and H2257S

ELIAM (2)
2Sa 11: 3 the daughter of **E** and the wife of Uriah the H500
2Sa 23:34 **E** son of Ahithophel the Gilonite H500

ELIAS (KJV) ELIJAH

ELIASAPH (6)
Nu 1:14 from Gad, **E** son of Deuel; H498
Nu 2:14 of the people of Gad is **E** son of Deuel. H498
Nu 3:24 of the Gershonites was **E** son of Lael. H498
Nu 7:42 On the sixth day **E** son of Deuel, the leader H498
Nu 7:47 This was the offering of **E** son of Deuel. H498
Nu 10:20 **E** son of Deuel was over the division of H498

ELIASHIB (15) [ELIASHIB'S]
1Ch 3:24 Hodaviah, **E**, Pelaiah, Akkub, Johanan H513
1Ch 24:12 the eleventh to **E**, the twelfth to Jakim, H513
Ezr 10: 6 went to the room of Jehohanan son of **E**. H513
Ezr 10:24 From the musicians: **E**. From the H513
Ezr 10:27 Elioenai, **E**, Mattaniah, Jeremoth, Zabad H513
Ezr 10:36 Meremoth, **E**, H513
Ne 3: 1 **E** the high priest and his fellow priests H513
Ne 3:20 entrance of the house of **E** the high priest. H513
Ne 12:10 Joiakim the father of **E**, Eliashib the father H513
Ne 12:10 father of Eliashib, **E** the father of Joiada, H513
Ne 12:22 family heads of the Levites in the days of **E**, H513
Ne 12:23 of Johanan son of **E** were recorded in the H513
Ne 13: 4 **E** the priest had been put in charge of the H513
Ne 13: 7 about the evil thing **E** had done in H513
Ne 13:28 sons of Joiada son of **E** the high priest was H513

ELIASHIB'S (1) [ELIASHIB]
Ne 3:21 from the entrance of **E** house to the end of H513

ELIATHAH (2)
1Ch 25: 4 Hananiah, Hanani, **E**, Giddalti and H484
1Ch 25:27 the twentieth to **E**, his sons and relatives 12 H517

ELIDAD (1)
Nu 34:21 **E** son of Kislon, from the tribe of Benjamin; H485

ELIEHOENAI (2)
1Ch 26: 3 Jehohanan the sixth and **E** the seventh. H492
Ezr 8: 4 of Pahath-Moab, **E** son of Zerahiah, and H492

ELIEL (10)
1Ch 5:24 Ishi, **E**, Azriel, Jeremiah, Hodaviah H483
1Ch 6:34 of Jeroham, the son of **E**, the son of Toah, H483
1Ch 8:20 Zillethai, **E**, H483
1Ch 8:22 Eber, **E**, H483
1Ch 11:46 **E** the Mahavite, Jeribai and Joshaviah the H483
1Ch 11:47 **E**, Obed and Jaasiel the Mezobaite. H483
1Ch 12:11 Attai the sixth, **E** the seventh, H483
1Ch 15: 9 of Hebron, **E** the leader and 80 relatives; H483
1Ch 15:11 Shemaiah, **E** and Amminadab the Levites. H483
2Ch 31:13 Jerimoth, Jozabad, **E**, Ismakiah, Mahath H483

ELIENAI (1)
1Ch 8:20 **E**, Zillethai, Eliel, H501

ELIEZER (15)
Ge 15: 2 will inherit my estate is **E** of Damascus?" H499
Ex 18: 4 the other was named **E**, for he said H499
1Ch 7: 8 Zemirah, Joash, **E**, Elioenai, Omri H499
1Ch 15:24 Benaiah and **E** the priests were to blow H499
1Ch 23:15 The sons of Moses: Gershom and **E**. H499
1Ch 23:17 The descendants of **E**: Rehabiah was the H499
1Ch 23:17 **E** had no other sons, but the sons of H499
1Ch 26:25 His relatives through **E**: Rehabiah his son H499
1Ch 27:16 over the Reubenites: **E** son of Zikri; over the H499
2Ch 20:37 **E** son of Dodavahu of Mareshah prophesied H499
Ezr 8:16 So I summoned **E**, Ariel, Shemaiah H499
Ezr 10:18 Maaseiah, **E**, Jarib and Gedaliah H499
Ezr 10:23 that is, Kelita), Pethahiah, Judah and **E**. H499
Ezr 10:31 descendants of Harim: **E**, Ishijah, Malkijah H499
Lk 3:29 of Joshua, the son *of* **E**, the son of Jorim, *G1808*

ELIHOREPH (1)
1Ki 4: 3 **E** and Ahijah, sons of Shisha—secretaries H495

ELIHU (10)
1Sa 1: 1 of Jeroham, the son of **E**, the son of Tohu, H491
1Ch 12:20 Jozabad, **E** and Zillethai, leaders of units H491
1Ch 26: 7 his relatives **E** and Semakiah were also H490
1Ch 27:18 **E**, a brother of David; over H490
Job 32: 2 But **E** son of Barakel the Buzite, of the H491
Job 32: 4 Now **E** had waited before speaking to Job H490
Job 32: 6 So **E** son of Barakel the Buzite said: "I am H491
Job 34: 1 Then **E** said: H491
Job 35: 1 Then **E** said: H490
Job 36: 1 **E** continued: H491

ELIHUD (2)
Mt 1:14 the father of Akim, Akim the father of **E**, *G1809*
Mt 1:15 **E** the father of Eleazar, Eleazar the father *G1809*

ELIJAH (111) [ELIJAH'S]
1Ki 17: 1 Now **E** the Tishbite, from Tishbe in Gilead H489
1Ki 17: 2 Then the word of the LORD came to **E**: H2257S
1Ki 17:13 **E** said to her, "Don't be afraid. Go home H489
1Ki 17:15 She went away and did as **E** had told her H489
1Ki 17:15 food every day for **E** and for the woman H2085S
1Ki 17:16 with the word of the LORD spoken by **E**. H489
1Ki 17:18 She said to **E**, "What do you have against H489
1Ki 17:19 "Give me your son," **E** replied. He took him NDT
1Ki 17:23 **E** picked up the child and carried him down H489
1Ki 17:24 Then the woman said to **E**, "Now I know H489
1Ki 18: 1 third year, the word of the LORD came to **E**: H489
1Ki 18: 2 So **E** went to present himself to Ahab. H489
1Ki 18: 7 was walking along, **E** met him. Obadiah H489
1Ki 18: 7 said, "Is it really you, my lord **E**? H489
1Ki 18: 8 "Go tell your master, '**E** is here.' " H489
1Ki 18:11 me to go to my master and say, '**E** is here. H489
1Ki 18:14 me to go to my master and say, '**E** is here. H489
1Ki 18:15 **E** said, "As the LORD Almighty lives, whom H489
1Ki 18:16 told him, and Ahab went to meet **E**. H489
1Ki 18:17 When he saw **E**, he said to him, "Is that you H489
1Ki 18:18 have not made trouble for Israel," **E** replied. NDT
1Ki 18:21 **E** went before the people and said, "How H489
1Ki 18:22 Then **E** said to them, "I am the only one of H489
1Ki 18:25 **E** said to the prophets of Baal, "Choose H489
1Ki 18:27 At noon **E** began to taunt them. "Shout H489
1Ki 18:30 Then **E** said to all the people, "Come here H489
1Ki 18:31 **E** took twelve stones, one for each of the H489
1Ki 18:36 the prophet **E** stepped forward and prayed: H489
1Ki 18:40 Then **E** commanded them, "Seize the H489
1Ki 18:40 **E** had them brought down to the H489
1Ki 18:41 And **E** said to Ahab, "Go, eat and drink, for H489
1Ki 18:42 but **E** climbed to the top of Carmel H489
1Ki 18:43 Seven times **E** said, "Go back." NDT
1Ki 18:44 So **E** said, "Go and tell Ahab, 'Hitch up NDT
1Ki 18:46 The power of the LORD came on **E** and H489
1Ki 19: 1 Jezebel everything **E** had done and how he H489
1Ki 19: 2 So Jezebel sent a messenger to **E** to say H489
1Ki 19: 3 **E** was afraid and ran for his life. When he NDT
1Ki 19: 9 "What are you doing here, **E**?" H489
1Ki 19:13 When **E** heard it, he pulled his cloak over H489
1Ki 19:13 said to him, "What are you doing here, **E**?" H489
1Ki 19:19 So **E** went from there and found Elisha son NDT
1Ki 19:19 **E** went up to him and threw his cloak H489
1Ki 19:20 Elisha then left his oxen and ran after **E** H489
1Ki 19:20 "Go back," **E** replied. "What have I NDT
1Ki 19:21 he set out to follow **E** and became his H489
1Ki 21:17 word of the LORD came to **E** the Tishbite: H489
1Ki 21:20 Ahab said to **E**, "So you have found me H489
1Ki 21:28 word of the LORD came to **E** the Tishbite: H489
2Ki 1: 3 the angel of the LORD said to **E** the Tishbite, H488
2Ki 1: 4 You will certainly die!' " So **E** went. H488
2Ki 1: 8 The king said, "That was **E** the Tishbite." H488
2Ki 1: 9 Then he sent to **E** a captain with his H2257S
2Ki 1: 9 The captain went up to **E**, who was H2257S
2Ki 1:10 **E** answered the captain, "If I am a man of H489
2Ki 1:11 the king sent to **E** another captain with H2257S
2Ki 1:12 **E** replied, "may fire come down from H488
2Ki 1:13 went up and fell on his knees before **E**. H489
2Ki 1:15 The angel of the LORD said to **E**, "Go down H489
2Ki 1:15 So **E** got up and went down with him to the NDT
2Ki 1:17 to the word of the LORD that **E** had spoken. H489
2Ki 2: 1 LORD was about to take **E** up to heaven in a H489
2Ki 2: 1 **E** and Elisha were on their way from Gilgal. H489
2Ki 2: 2 **E** said to Elisha, "Stay here; the LORD has H489
2Ki 2: 4 Then **E** said to him, "Stay here, Elisha; the H489
2Ki 2: 6 Then **E** said to him, "Stay here; the LORD H489
2Ki 2: 7 where **E and Elisha** had stopped H9109+2157S
2Ki 2: 8 **E** took his cloak, rolled it up and struck the H489
2Ki 2: 9 they had crossed, **E** said to Elisha, "Tell H489
2Ki 2:10 **E** said, "yet if you see me when I am taken NDT
2Ki 2:11 **E** went up to heaven in a whirlwind. H489
2Ki 2:14 that had fallen from **E** and struck the water H489
2Ki 2:14 now is the LORD, the God of **E**?" he asked. H489
2Ki 2:15 "The spirit of **E** is resting on Elisha. H489
2Ki 3:11 He used to pour water on the hands of **E**." H489
2Ki 9:36 spoke through his servant **E** the Tishbite: H489
2Ki 10:10 what he announced through his servant **E**." H489
2Ki 10:17 to the word of the LORD spoken to **E**. H489
1Ch 8:27 **E** and Zikri were the sons of Jeroham. H488
2Ch 21:12 received a letter from **E** the prophet, H489
Ezr 10:21 Maaseiah, **E**, Shemaiah, Jehiel and Uzziah H488
Ezr 10:26 Zechariah, Jehiel, Abdi, Jeremoth and **E**. H488
Mal 4: 5 I will send the prophet **E** to you before that H488
Mt 11:14 to accept it, he is the **E** who was to come. *G2460*
Mt 16:14 the Baptist; others say **E**; and still others, *G2460*
Mt 17: 3 appeared before them Moses and **E**, *G2460*
Mt 17: 4 one for you, one for Moses and one *for* **E**." *G2460*
Mt 17:10 of the law say that **E** must come first?" *G2460*
Mt 17:11 **E** comes and will restore all things. *G2460*
Mt 17:12 But I tell you, **E** has already come, and *G2460*
Mt 27:47 heard this, they said, "He's calling **E**." *G2460*
Mt 27:49 Let's see if **E** comes to save him." *G2460*
Mk 6:15 Others said, "He is **E**." And still others *G2460*
Mk 8:28 the Baptist; others say **E**; and still others, *G2460*
Mk 9: 4 appeared before them **E** and Moses, *G2460*
Mk 9: 5 one for you, one for Moses and one *for* **E**." *G2460*
Mk 9:11 of the law say that **E** must come first?" *G2460*
Mk 9:12 "To be sure, **E** does come first, and *G2460*
Mk 9:13 But I tell you, **E** has come, and they have *G2460*
Mk 15:35 they said, "Listen, he's calling **E**. *G2460*
Mk 15:36 Let's see if **E** comes to take him down," *G2460*
Lk 1:17 in the spirit and power *of* **E**, to turn the *G2460*
Lk 4:26 Yet **E** was not sent to any of them, but to a *G2460*
Lk 9: 8 others that **E** had appeared, and still *G2460*
Lk 9:19 the Baptist; others say **E**; and still others, *G2460*
Lk 9:30 Two men, Moses and **E**, appeared in *G2460*
Lk 9:33 one for you, one for Moses and one *for* **E**." *G2460*
Jn 1:21 Are you **E**?" He said, "I am not *G2460*
Jn 1:25 not the Messiah, nor **E**, nor the Prophet?" *G2460*
Ro 11: 2 Scripture says in the *passage about* **E**— *G2460*
Jas 5:17 **E** was a human being, even as we are *G2460*

ELIJAH'S (3) [ELIJAH]
1Ki 17:22 The LORD heard **E** cry, and the boy's life H489
2Ki 2:13 then picked up **E** cloak that had fallen H489
Lk 4:25 were many widows in Israel in **E** time, *G2460*

ELIKA (1)
2Sa 23:25 Shammah the Harodite, **E** the Harodite, H508

ELIM (5) [BEER ELIM]
Ex 15:27 Then they came to **E**, where there were H396
Ex 16: 1 set out from **E** and came to the Desert H396
Ex 16: 1 which is between **E** and Sinai, on the H396
Nu 33: 9 They left Marah and went to **E**, where there H396
Nu 33:10 They left **E** and camped by the Red Sea. H396

ELIMELEK (6)
Ru 1: 2 The man's name was **E**, his wife's name H497
Ru 1: 3 Now **E**, Naomi's husband, died, and she H497
Ru 2: 1 a man of standing from the clan of **E** H497
Ru 2: 3 to Boaz, who was from the clan of **E**. H497
Ru 4: 3 of land that belonged to our relative **E**. H497
Ru 4: 9 bought from Naomi all the property of **E**, H497

ELIMINATE (1) [ELIMINATED]
Dt 7:22 will not be allowed to **e** them all at once, H3983

ELIMINATED (1) [ELIMINATE]
Dt 2:15 until he *had* completely **e** them from the H2169

ELIOENAI (7)
1Ch 3:23 sons of Neariah: **E**, Hizkiah and Azrikam H493
1Ch 3:24 The sons of **E**: Hodaviah, Eliashib, Pelaiah H493
1Ch 4:36 also **E**, Jaakobah, Jeshohaiah, Asaiah H493
1Ch 7: 8 Eliezer, **E**, Omri, Jeremoth, Abijah, H493
Ezr 10:22 **E**, Maaseiah, Ishmael, Nethanel, Jozabad H493
Ezr 10:27 **E**, Eliashib, Mattaniah, Jeremoth, Zabad H493
Ne 12:41 Micaiah, **E**, Zechariah and Hananiah with H493

ELIPHAL (1)
1Ch 11:35 son of Sakar the Hararite, **E** son of Ur, H503

ELIPHAZ (14)
Ge 36: 4 Adah bore **E** to Esau, Basemath bore Reuel H502
Ge 36:10 **E**, the son of Esau's wife Adah, and Reuel H502
Ge 36:11 The sons of **E**: Teman, Omar, Zepho H502
Ge 36:12 Esau's son **E** also had a concubine named H502
Ge 36:15 The sons of **E** the firstborn of Esau H502
Ge 36:16 were the chiefs descended from **E** in Edom; H502
1Ch 1:35 The sons of Esau: **E**, Reuel, Jeush, Jalam H502
1Ch 1:36 The sons of **E**: Teman, Omar, Zepho H502
Job 2:11 Job's three friends, **E** the Temanite, Bildad H502
Job 4: 1 Then **E** the Temanite replied: H502
Job 15: 1 Then **E** the Temanite replied: H502
Job 22: 1 Then **E** the Temanite replied: H502
Job 42: 7 he said to **E** the Temanite, "I am H502
Job 42: 9 So **E** the Temanite, Bildad the Shuhite and H502

ELIPHELEHU (2)
1Ch 15:18 Mattithiah, **E**, Mikneiah, Obed-Edom H504
1Ch 15:21 Mattithiah, **E**, Mikneiah, Obed-Edom H504

ELIPHELET (8)
2Sa 5:16 Elishama, Eliada and **E**. H505

2Sa 23:34 **E** son of Ahasbai the Maakathite, Eliam H505
1Ch 3: 6 There were also Ibhar, Elishua, **E**, H505
1Ch 3: 8 Elishama, Eliada and **E**—nine in all. H505
1Ch 8:39 Jeush the second son and **E** the third. H505
1Ch 14: 7 Elishama, Beeliada and **E**. H505
Ezr 8:13 whose names were **E**, Jeuel and Shemaiah H505
Ezr 10:33 Mattattah, Zabad, **E**, Jeremai, Manasseh H505

ELISEUS (KJV) ELISHA

ELISHA (90) [ELISHA'S]
1Ki 19:16 anoint **E** son of Shaphat from Abel H515
1Ki 19:17 **E** will put to death any who escape the H515
1Ki 19:19 from there and found **E** son of Shaphat. H515
1Ki 19:20 **E** then left his oxen and ran after Elijah. NDT
1Ki 19:21 So **E** left him and went back. He took his NDT
2Ki 2: 1 Elijah and **E** were on their way from Gilgal. H515
2Ki 2: 2 Elijah said to **E**, "Stay here; the LORD has H515
2Ki 2: 2 But **E** said, "As surely as the LORD lives and H515
2Ki 2: 3 at Bethel came out to **E** and asked, H515
2Ki 2: 3 I know," **E** replied, "so be quiet. NDT
2Ki 2: 4 "Stay here, **E**; the LORD has sent me to H515
2Ki 2: 5 at Jericho went up to **E** and asked him, H515
2Ki 2: 7 where **Elijah and E** had stopped H9109+2157S
2Ki 2: 9 had crossed, Elijah said to **E**, "Tell me, H515
2Ki 2: 9 a double portion of your spirit," **E** replied. H515
2Ki 2:12 **E** saw this and cried out, "My father! My H515
2Ki 2:12 And **E** saw him no more. Then he NDT
2Ki 2:13 **E** then picked up Elijah's cloak that had NDT
2Ki 2:15 "The spirit of Elijah is resting on **E**. H515
2Ki 2:16 "No," **E** replied, "do not send NDT
2Ki 2:18 When they returned to **E**, who was H2257S
2Ki 2:19 The people of the city said to **E**, "Look, our H515
2Ki 2:22 according to the word **E** had spoken. H515
2Ki 2:23 From there **E** went up to Bethel. As he was NDT
2Ki 3:11 Israel answered, "**E** son of Shaphat is here. H515
2Ki 3:13 **E** said to the king of Israel, "Why do you H515
2Ki 3:14 **E** said, "As surely as the LORD Almighty H515
2Ki 3:15 playing, the hand of the LORD came on **E** H2257S
2Ki 4: 1 the company of the prophets cried out to **E**, H515
2Ki 4: 2 **E** replied to her, "How can I help you? Tell H515
2Ki 4: 3 **E** said, "Go around and ask all your NDT
2Ki 4: 8 One day **E** went to Shunem. And a H515
2Ki 4:11 One day when **E** came, he went up to his NDT
2Ki 4:13 **E** said to him, "Tell her, 'You have gone to NDT
2Ki 4:14 can be done for her?" **E** asked. Gehazi said, NDT
2Ki 4:15 Then **E** said, "Call her." So he called her NDT
2Ki 4:16 this time next year," **E** said, "you will hold a NDT
2Ki 4:17 gave birth to a son, just as **E** had told her. H515
2Ki 4:29 **E** said to Gehazi, "Tuck your cloak into your NDT
2Ki 4:31 went back to meet **E** and told him, H2257S
2Ki 4:32 When **E** reached the house, there was the H515
2Ki 4:35 **E** turned away and walked back and forth in NDT
2Ki 4:36 **E** summoned Gehazi and said, "Call the NDT
2Ki 4:38 **E** returned to Gilgal and there was a H515
2Ki 4:41 **E** said, "Get some flour." He put it into the NDT
2Ki 4:42 "Give it to the people to eat," **E** said. NDT
2Ki 4:43 But **E** answered, "Give it to the people to NDT
2Ki 5: 8 When **E** the man of God heard that the H515
2Ki 5:10 **E** sent a messenger to say to him, "Go H515
2Ki 5:19 "Go in peace," **E** said. After Naaman had NDT
2Ki 5:20 the servant of **E** the man of God, said H515
2Ki 5:25 before his master, **E** asked him, "Where H515
2Ki 5:26 But **E** said to him, "Was not my spirit with NDT
2Ki 6: 1 The company of the prophets said to **E** H515
2Ki 6: 3 with your servants?" "I will," **E** replied. NDT
2Ki 6: 6 the place, **E** cut a stick and threw it there NDT
2Ki 6:10 Time and again **E** warned the king, so that NDT
2Ki 6:12 of his officers, "but **E**, the prophet who is in H515
2Ki 6:12 And **E** prayed, "Open his eyes, LORD, so that H515
2Ki 6:17 of horses and chariots of fire all around **E**. H515
2Ki 6:18 down toward him, **E** prayed to the LORD H515
2Ki 6:18 struck them with blindness, as **E** had asked. H515
2Ki 6:19 **E** told them, "This is not the road and this H515
2Ki 6:20 entered the city, **E** said, "LORD, open the H515
2Ki 6:21 saw them, he asked **E**, "Shall I kill them, H515
2Ki 6:31 if the head of **E** son of Shaphat remains on H515
2Ki 6:32 Now **E** was sitting in his house, and the H515
2Ki 6:32 before he arrived, **E** said to the elders H2085S
2Ki 7: 1 **E** replied, "Hear the word of the LORD. H515
2Ki 7: 2 own eyes," answered **E**, "but you will not NDT
2Ki 8: 1 Now **E** had said to the woman whose son H515
2Ki 8: 4 me about all the great things **E** has done." H515
2Ki 8: 5 telling the king how **E** had restored the NDT
2Ki 8: 5 woman whose son **E** had brought back to NDT
2Ki 8: 5 this is her son whom **E** restored to life." H515
2Ki 8: 7 **E** went to Damascus, and Ben-Hadad king H515
2Ki 8: 9 Hazael went to meet **E**, taking with him H2257S
2Ki 8:10 **E** answered, "Go and say to him, 'You will H515
2Ki 8:13 will become king of Aram," answered **E**. H515
2Ki 8:14 Then Hazael left **E** and returned to his H515
2Ki 8:14 Ben-Hadad asked, "What did **E** say to you?" H515
2Ki 9: 1 The prophet **E** summoned a man from the H515
2Ki 13:14 Now **E** had been suffering from the illness H515
2Ki 13:15 **E** said, "Get a bow and some arrows," H515
2Ki 13:16 **E** put his hands on the king's hands. H515
2Ki 13:17 **E** said, and he shot. "The LORD's H515
2Ki 13:17 of victory over Aram!" **E** declared. NDT
2Ki 13:18 the king took them. **E** told him, "Strike the NDT
2Ki 13:20 **E** died and was buried. Now Moabite H515
Lk 4:27 with leprosy in the time of **E** the prophet, *G1811*

ELISHA'S (4) [ELISHA]
2Ki 5: 9 stopped at the door of **E** house. H515
2Ki 5:27 Gehazi went from **E** presence and his H2257S
2Ki 13:21 so they threw the man's body into **E** tomb. H515
2Ki 13:21 When the body touched **E** bones, the man H515

ELISHAH (3)
Ge 10: 4 The sons of Javan: **E**, Tarshish, the Kittites H511
1Ch 1: 7 The sons of Javan: **E**, Tarshish, the Kittites H511
Eze 27: 7 of blue and purple from the coasts of **E**. H511

ELISHAMA (16)
Nu 1:10 from Ephraim, **E** son of Ammihud; from H514
Nu 2:18 people of Ephraim is **E** son of Ammihud. H514
Nu 7:48 On the seventh day **E** son of Ammihud, the H514
Nu 7:53 This was the offering of **E** son of Ammihud. H514
Nu 10:22 **E** son of Ammihud was in command. H514
2Sa 5:16 **E**, Eliada and Eliphelet. H514
2Ki 25:25 Nethaniah, the son of **E**, who was of royal H514
1Ch 2:41 of Jekamiah, and Jekamiah the father of **E**. H514
1Ch 3: 8 **E**, Eliada and Eliphelet—nine in all. H514
1Ch 7:26 Ammihud his son, **E** his son, H514
1Ch 14: 7 **E**, Beeliada and Eliphelet. H514
2Ch 17: 8 the priests **E** and Jehoram. H514
Jer 36:12 **E** the secretary, Delaiah son of Shemaiah H514
Jer 36:20 put the scroll in the room of **E** the secretary, H514
Jer 36:21 it from the room of **E** the secretary and read H514
Jer 41: 1 Nethaniah, the son of **E**, who was of royal H514

ELISHAPHAT (1)
2Ch 23: 1 son of Adaiah, and **E** son of Zikri. H516

ELISHEBA (1)
Ex 6:23 Aaron married **E**, daughter of Amminadab H510

ELISHUA (3)
2Sa 5:15 **E**, Nepheg, Japhia, H512
1Ch 3: 6 There were also Ibhar, **E**, Eliphelet, H512
1Ch 14: 5 **E**, Elpelet, H512

ELITE (1)
Eze 23: 7 prostitute to all the **e** *of* the Assyrians H4436

ELIUD (NIV84) ELIHUD

ELIZABETH (10) [ELIZABETH'S]
Lk 1: 5 his wife **E** was also a descendant of *G1810*
Lk 1: 7 were childless because **E** was not able to *G1810*
Lk 1:13 Your wife **E** will bear you a son, and you *G1810*
Lk 1:24 After this his wife **E** became pregnant and *G1810*
Lk 1:36 Even **E** your relative is going to have a *G1810*
Lk 1:40 entered Zechariah's home and greeted **E**. *G1810*
Lk 1:41 When **E** heard Mary's greeting, the baby *G1810*
Lk 1:41 **E** was filled with the Holy Spirit. *G1810*
Lk 1:56 Mary stayed with **E** for about three months *G899S*
Lk 1:57 When it was time *for* **E** to have her baby *G1810*

ELIZABETH'S (1) [ELIZABETH]
Lk 1:26 In the sixth month of **E** pregnancy, God sent NDT

ELIZAPHAN (4)
Nu 3:30 of the Kohathite clans was **E** son of Uzziel. H507
Nu 34:25 **E** son of Parnak, the leader from the tribe H507
1Ch 15: 8 from the descendants of **E**, Shemaiah the H507
2Ch 29:13 from the descendants of **E**, Shimri and H507

ELIZUR (5)
Nu 1: 5 from Reuben, **E** son of Shedeur; H506
Nu 2:10 the people of Reuben is **E** son of Shedeur. H506
Nu 7:30 On the fourth day **E** son of Shedeur, the H506
Nu 7:35 This was the offering of **E** son of Shedeur. H506
Nu 10:18 **E** son of Shedeur was in command. H506

ELKANAH (20)
Ex 6:24 sons of Korah were Assir, **E** and Abiasaph. H555
1Sa 1: 1 whose name was **E** son of Jeroham, the H555
1Sa 1: 4 Whenever the day came for **E** to sacrifice H555
1Sa 1: 8 Her husband **E** would say to her, "Hannah H555
1Sa 1:19 **E** made love to his wife Hannah, and the H555
1Sa 1:21 When her husband **E** went up with all his H555
1Sa 1:23 best to you," her husband **E** told her. H555
1Sa 2:11 Then **E** went home to Ramah, but the boy H555
1Sa 2:20 Eli would bless **E** and his wife, saying, "May H555
1Ch 6:23 **E** his son, Ebiasaph his son, Assir his son, H555
1Ch 6:25 The descendants of **E**: Amasai, Ahimoth, H555
1Ch 6:26 **E** his son, Zophai his son, Nahath his son, H555
1Ch 6:27 **E** his son and Samuel his son. H555
1Ch 6:34 the son of **E**, the son of Jeroham, the son H555
1Ch 6:35 of Zuph, the son of **E**, the son of Mahath, H555
1Ch 6:36 the son of **E**, the son of Joel, the son of H555
1Ch 9:16 son of Asa, the son of **E**, who lived in the H555
1Ch 12: 6 **E**, Ishiah, Azarel, Joezer and Jashobeam H555
1Ch 15:23 Berekiah and **E** were to be doorkeepers H555
2Ch 28: 7 of the palace, and **E**, second to the king. H555

ELKOSHITE (1)
Na 1: 1 The book of the vision of Nahum the **E**. H556

ELLASAR (2)
Ge 14: 1 Arioch king of **E**, Kedorlaomer king of H536
Ge 14: 9 king of Shinar and Arioch king of **E**— H536

ELMADAM (1)
Lk 3:28 son of Cosam, the son of **E**, the son of Er, *G1825*

ELNAAM (1)
1Ch 11:46 Jeribai and Joshaviah the sons of **E** H534

ELNATHAN (7)
2Ki 24: 8 name was Nehushta daughter of **E**; H535
Ezr 8:16 Shemaiah, **E**, Jarib, Elnathan H535
Ezr 8:16 Elnathan, Jarib, **E**, Nathan, Zechariah and H535
Ezr 8:16 Joiarib and **E**, who were men of H535
Jer 26:22 however, sent **E** son of Akbor to Egypt H535
Jer 36:12 son of Shemaiah, **E** son of Akbor H535
Jer 36:25 Even though **E**, Delaiah and Gemariah H535

ELOHE (1)
Ge 33:20 he set up an altar and called it **El E Israel**. H449

ELOI (2)
Mk 15:34 Jesus cried out in a loud voice, "**E**, Eloi, *G1830*
Mk 15:34 a loud voice, "Eloi, **E**, lema sabachthani?" *G1830*

ELON (7) [ELONITE]
Ge 26:34 also Basemath daughter of **E** the Hittite. H390
Ge 36: 2 Adah daughter of **E** the Hittite, and H390
Ge 46:14 sons of Zebulun: Sered, **E** and Jahleel. H472
Nu 26:26 Seredite clan; through **E**, the Elonite clan; H472
Jos 19:43 **E**, Timnah, Ekron, H391
Jdg 12:11 **E** the Zebulunite led Israel ten years. H390
Jdg 12:12 Then **E** died and was buried in Aijalon in H390

ELON BETHHANAN (1)
1Ki 4: 9 Beth Shemesh and **E**; H392

ELONITE (1) [ELON]
Nu 26:26 through Elon, the **E** clan; through Jahleel H533

ELOQUENCE (2) [ELOQUENT]
1Co 1:17 not with wisdom and **e**, lest the cross of *G3364*
1Co 2: 1 not come with **e** or human wisdom *G5667+3364*

ELOQUENT (2) [ELOQUENCE]
Ex 4:10 I have never been **e**, neither in the H408+1821
Pr 17: 7 **E** lips are unsuited to a godless fool H3856

ELPAAL (3)
1Ch 8:11 By Hushim he had Abitub and **E**. H551
1Ch 8:12 The sons of **E**: Eber, Misham, Shemed H551
1Ch 8:18 Izliah and Jobab were the sons of **E**. H551

ELPELET (1)
1Ch 14: 5 Ibhar, Elishua, **E**, H550

ELSE (103) [ELSE'S, ELSEWHERE]
Ge 19:12 "Do you have anyone **e** here H6388
Ge 19:12 anyone **e** in the city who belongs to you? NDT
Ge 34:28 donkeys and **everything e** of theirs in H889
Ex 4:13 Please send **someone e**." H928+3338S
Ex 10:23 No one could see **anyone e** or move about H278S
Ex 22:27 your neighbor has. **What** *e* can they sleep in AIT
Ex 29:33 But no one **e** may eat them, because they H2424
Ex 33:16 What **e** will distinguish me and your people NDT
Ex 36: 6 is to make anything **e** as an offering for H6388
Lev 16: 2 cover on the ark, or **e** he will die. H4202
Lev 27:20 if they have sold it to someone **e**, it can H337
Nu 1:51 **Anyone e** who approaches it is to be put H2424
Nu 3:10 **anyone e** who approaches the sanctuary H2424
Nu 3:38 **Anyone e** who approached the sanctuary H2424
Nu 6:21 in addition to **whatever** *e* they can afford. AIT
Nu 12: 3 humble than anyone **e** on the face of the H132S
Nu 15:14 a foreigner or **anyone** *e* living among you AIT
Nu 18: 4 no one **e** may come near where you H2424
Nu 18: 7 **Anyone e** who comes near the sanctuary H2424
Nu 20:19 want to pass through on foot—nothing **e**." H1821
Nu 22:19 I can find out what **e** the LORD will tell me." H3578
Nu 31:23 anything **e** that can withstand fire must NDT
Dt 20: 5 battle and someone **e** may begin to live in H337
Dt 20: 6 may die in battle and someone **e** enjoy it. H337
Dt 20: 7 die in battle and someone **e** marry her." H337
Dt 20:14 the livestock and everything **e** in the city H889S
Dt 22: 3 donkey or cloak or **anything** *e* they have lost. AIT
Dt 23:19 food or anything **e** that may earn interest. NDT
Jdg 18: 7 had no relationship with anyone **e**. NDT
Jdg 18:24 What **e** do I have? How can H6388
Jdg 18:28 had no relationship with anyone **e**. NDT
Jdg 20:48 the animals and everything **e** they found. NDT
1Sa 9: 2 he was a head taller than anyone **e**. H6639S
1Sa 17:30 turned away to **someone e** and brought up H337
1Sa 30: 2 captive the women and **everyone e** in it, H889
1Sa 30:19 plunder or **anything** *e* they had taken. AIT
2Sa 3:35 if I taste bread or **anything** *e* before the sun AIT
1Ki 2:36 do not go **anywhere e**. H625+2025+2256+625+2025
1Ki 2:42 leave to go **anywhere e**, H625+2025+2256+625+2025
1Ki 4:31 He was wiser than anyone **e**, including H132S
1Ki 14: 5 she *will* **pretend to be someone e**. H5796
Ezr 7:20 And **anything e** needed for the temple A10692
Est 1:19 royal position to **someone e** who is better H8295
Job 17: 3 Who **e** will put up security for me? H2085
Pr 4:23 Above all **e**, guard your heart, for H5464S
Pr 14:10 bitterness, and no *one* **e** can share its joy. H2424
Pr 27: 2 Let **someone e** praise you, and not your H2424
Ecc 3:16 And I saw **something e** under the sun: In H6388
Ecc 8: 7 who can tell **someone e** what is to come H2257S
Ecc 8:14 There is something **e** meaningless that NDT

Ecc 9:11 I have seen **something** e under the sun H8740
Ecc 10:14 who can tell **someone** e what will H2257S
Isa 27: 5 **Or** e let them come to me for refuge; let H196
Jer 9: 7 for **what** e can I do because of the sin of H375
Jer 23:34 a prophet or a priest or **anyone** e claims, H6639S
Jer 26:19 king of Judah or **anyone** *e in* Judah put him AIT
Jer 40: 5 the people, or go **anywhere** *e* you please." AIT
Eze 27:27 and **everyone** e on board will sink H3972+7736
Da 2:30 I have greater wisdom than **anyone** *e* alive, AIT
Da 5:17 give your rewards to **someone** e. A10025
Am 6:10 be hiding there, "Is *anyone* e with you?" H6388
Hag 1:11 the olive oil and **everything** *e* the ground AIT
Mal 4: 6 **or** e I will come and strike the land with H7153
Mt 11: 3 to come, or should we expect **someone** e?" *G2283*
Mk 1:38 "Let us go **somewhere** e—to the nearby *G250*
Lk 7:19 to come, or should we expect **someone** e?" *G257*
Lk 7:20 to come, or should we expect **someone** e? *G257*
Lk 13:31 "Leave this place and go somewhere e. NDT
Lk 18: 9 looked down on **everyone** e, *G3370*
Lk 22:58 A little later **someone** e saw him and said *G2283*
Jn 5: 7 **someone** e goes down ahead of me." *G257*
Jn 5:43 if **someone** e comes in his own name *G257*
Jn 15:24 done among them the works no one e did, *G257*
Jn 21:18 and **someone** e will dress you and lead *G257*
Ac 4:12 Salvation is found in no one e, for there is *G257*
Ac 5:13 No one e dared join them, even though *G3370*
Ac 8:34 talking about, himself or someone e?" *G2283*
Ac 17:25 everyone life and breath and **everything** *e*. AIT
Ac 24:12 the synagogues or **anywhere** e **in** the city. *G2848*
Ro 2: 1 you who pass judgment on someone e, for NDT
Ro 8:39 nor anything e in all creation, will *G2283*
Ro 14:20 anything that causes someone e to stumble. NDT
Ro 14:21 wine or to do anything e that will cause your NDT
1Co 1:16 I don't remember if I baptized anyone e.) *G257*
1Co 3:10 and **someone** e is building on it. *G257*
1Co 4: 7 For who makes you different from anyone e NDT
1Co 7:11 remain unmarried **or** e be reconciled to *G2445*
1Co 14:16 *can someone e*, who is now put in the position of an inquirer, **say** AIT
1Co 14:17 well enough, but no *one* e is edified. *G2283*
1Co 15:37 perhaps of wheat or of something e. *G3370*
2Co 9:13 in sharing with them and with **everyone** *e*. AIT
2Co 11:21 Whatever **anyone** *e* dares to boast about—I AIT
2Co 11:28 **Besides everything** e, I face *G6006+3836+4211*
Gal 6: 4 comparing themselves to **someone** e, *G2283*
Php 1:13 to everyone e that I am in chains *G3370*
Php 2:20 I have **no one** *e* like him, who will show AIT
Php 3: 4 If someone e thinks they have reasons to *G257*
1Th 2: 6 not from you or **anyone** e, even though as *G257*
1Th 3:12 overflow for each other and for **everyone** *e*, AIT
1Th 5:15 is good for each other and for **everyone** *e*. AIT
1Ti 1:10 for whatever e is contrary to the sound *G2283*
Jas 5:12 not by heaven or by earth or by anything e. *G257*
Rev 6:15 the mighty, and **everyone** *e*, both slave and AIT

ELSE'S (9) [ELSE]

Ge 43:34 was five times as much as anyone e. H4392
Ex 21:35 bull injures **someone** e bull and it dies, H8276
Ex 22: 5 stray and they graze in **someone** e field, H337
Ex 30:32 Do not pour it on **anyone** e body and do not H132
Ru 2:22 because in **someone** e field you might be H337
Lk 16:12 been trustworthy with **someone** e property, *G259*
Ro 14: 4 Who are you to judge **someone** e servant *G259*
Ro 15:20 not be building on **someone** e foundation. *G259*
2Co 10:16 work already done in **someone** e territory. *G259*

ELSEWHERE (7) [ELSE, WHERE]

Lev 18: 9 she was born in the same home or e. H2575
2Ch 26: 6 near Ashdod and e among the Philistines NDT
Ezr 4:10 of Samaria and e *in* Trans-Euphrates. A10692
Ezr 4:17 in Samaria and e *in* Trans-Euphrates: A10692
Ps 84:10 is one day in your courts than a thousand e; NDT
Jn 12:39 not believe, because, as Isaiah says e: *G4099*
Ac 13:35 So it is also stated e: " 'You will not let *G2283*

ELTEKEH (2)

Jos 19:44 **E**, Gibbethon, Baalath, H559
Jos 21:23 Also from the tribe of Dan they received **E** H558

ELTEKON (1)

Jos 15:59 Beth Anoth and **E**—six towns and their H560

ELTOLAD (2)

Jos 15:30 **E**, Kesil, Hormah, H557
Jos 19: 4 **E**, Bethul, Hormah, H557

ELUDE (2) [ELUDED]

Job 11:20 and escape *will* e them; their hope H6
Rev 9: 6 will long to die, but death *will* e them. *G5771*

ELUDED (2) [ELUDE]

1Sa 18:11 But David e him twice. H6015+4946+7156
1Sa 19:10 David e him as Saul drove the spear H7080

ELUL (1)

Ne 6:15 was completed on the twenty-fifth of **E**, H469

ELUZAI (1)

1Ch 12: 5 **E**, Jerimoth, Bealiah, Shemariah and H539

ELYMAS (2)

Ac 13: 8 But **E** the sorcerer (for that is what his *G1829*
Ac 13: 9 Holy Spirit, looked straight at **E** and said, *G899S*

ELZABAD (2)

1Ch 12:12 Johanan the eighth, **E** the ninth, H479
1Ch 26: 7 Rephael, Obed and **E**; his relatives Elihu H479

ELZAPHAN (2)

Ex 6:22 sons of Uzziel were Mishael, **E** and Sithri. H553
Lev 10: 4 Moses summoned Mishael and **E**, sons of H553

EMASCULATE (1) [EMASCULATED]

Gal 5:12 I wish *they would go the whole way and* e *themselves* *G644*

EMASCULATED (1) [EMASCULATE]

Dt 23: 1 No *one who has* **been** e *by* crushing or H7205

EMBALM (1) [EMBALMED, EMBALMING]

Ge 50: 2 in his service to e his father Israel. H2846

EMBALMED (2) [EMBALM]

Ge 50: 2 his father Israel. So the physicians e him, H2846
Ge 50:26 And after *they* e him, he was placed in a H2846

EMBALMING (1) [EMBALM]

Ge 50: 3 for that was the time required for e. H2847

EMBANKMENT (1) [BANK]

Lk 19:43 enemies will build an e against you and *G5918*

EMBARRASSED (3) [EMBARRASSMENT]

2Ki 2:17 persisted until *he was* too e to refuse. H1017
2Ki 8:11 him with a fixed gaze until Hazael *was* e. H1017
2Co 7:14 to him about you, and you *have* not e *me*. *G2875*

EMBARRASSMENT (1) [EMBARRASSED]

Jdg 3:25 They waited to the point of e, but when he H1017

EMBEDDED (1)

Ecc 12:11 their collected sayings like **firmly** e nails H5749

EMBERS (2)

Ps 102: 3 like smoke; my bones burn like **glowing** e. H4611
Pr 26:21 As charcoal to e and as wood to fire, so is H1624

EMBITTER (1) [BITTER]

Col 3:21 Fathers, *do* not e your children, or they *G2241*

EMBITTERED (1) [BITTER]

Ps 73:21 my heart was grieved and my spirit e, H9111

EMBLEM (3)

Ex 29: 6 attach the sacred e to the turban. H5694
Ex 39:30 the sacred e, out of pure gold and H5694
Lev 8: 9 gold plate, the sacred e, on the front of it, H5694

EMBODIMENT (1) [BODY]

Ro 2:20 have in the law the e of knowledge and *G3673*

EMBOLDENED (2) [BOLD]

Ps 138: 3 answered me; *you* **greatly** e me. H8104+6437
1Co 8:10 won't *that person be* e to eat what is *G3868*

EMBRACE (6) [EMBRACED, EMBRACES, EMBRACING]

Pr 4: 8 she will exalt you; e her, and she will H2485
Pr 5:20 Why e the bosom of a wayward woman H2485
Ecc 3: 5 a time to e and a time to refrain from H2485
Isa 2: 6 like the Philistines and e pagan **customs**. H8562
Mic 3: 1 rulers of Israel. *Should* you not e justice, H3359
Mic 7: 5 who lies in your e guard the words of H2668

EMBRACED (8) [EMBRACE]

Ge 29:13 *He* e him and kissed him and brought H2485
Ge 33: 4 But Esau ran to meet Jacob and e him; he H2485
Ge 45:14 and Benjamin e him, weeping. H6584+7418
Ge 48:10 his father kissed them and e them. H2485
1Ki 9: 9 out of Egypt, and *have* e other gods H2616
2Ch 7:22 them out of Egypt, and *have* e other gods H2616
Ac 20:37 wept *as they* e him and *G2158+2093+3836+5549*
Heb 11:17 He *who had* e the promises was about to *G346*

EMBRACES (2) [EMBRACE]

SS 2: 6 is under my head, and his right arm e me. H2485
SS 8: 3 is under my head and his right arm e me. H2485

EMBRACING (2) [EMBRACE]

Ecc 2: 3 with wine, and e folly—my mind still H296
Ecc 3: 5 to embrace and a time to refrain from e, H2485

EMBROIDERED (10) [EMBROIDERER, EMBROIDERERS]

Jdg 5:30 colorful garments e, highly embroidered H8391
Jdg 5:30 **highly** e garments for my neck H8391
Ps 45:14 In e **garments** she is led to the king; her H8391
Eze 16:10 you with an e **dress** and put sandals of H8391
Eze 16:13 of fine linen and costly fabric and e **cloth**. H8391
Eze 16:18 And you took your e clothes to put on H8391
Eze 26:16 their robes and take off their e garments. H8391
Eze 27: 7 Fine e linen from Egypt was your sail and H8391
Eze 27:16 purple fabric, e **work**, fine linen, coral H8391
Eze 27:24 e **work** and multicolored rugs with cords H8391

EMBROIDERER (7) [EMBROIDERED]

Ex 26:36 finely twisted linen—the work of an e. H8387
Ex 27:16 the work of an e—with four posts and H8387
Ex 28:39 The sash is to be the work of an e. H8387
Ex 36:37 finely twisted linen—the work of an e; H8387
Ex 38:18 finely twisted linen—the work of an e. H8387
Ex 38:23 designer, and an e in blue, purple and H8387
Ex 39:29 the work of an e—as the LORD H8387

EMBROIDERERS (1) [EMBROIDERED]

Ex 35:35 designers, e in blue, purple and scarlet H8387

EMEK See BETH EMEK, EMEK KEZIZ

EMEK KEZIZ (1)

Jos 18:21 Jericho, Beth Hoglah, **E**, H6681

EMERALD (5)

Ex 28:18 row shall be turquoise, lapis lazuli and e; H3402
Ex 39:11 row was turquoise, lapis lazuli and e; H3402
Eze 28:13 chrysolite and e, topaz, onyx and jasper, H3402
Rev 4: 3 that shone like an e encircled the throne. *G5039*
Rev 21:19 sapphire, the third agate, the fourth e, *G5040*

EMERGE (1)

Da 8:22 four kingdoms *that will* e from his nation H6641

EMERODS (KJV) TUMORS

EMINENT (KJV) LOFTY, MOUND, MOUNDS

EMISSION (6)

Lev 15:16 " 'When a man has an e *of* semen, he H8887
Lev 15:18 a woman and there is an e *of* semen, H8887
Lev 15:32 anyone made unclean by an e *of* semen, H8887
Lev 22: 4 by anyone who has an e *of* semen, H8887
Dt 23:10 men is unclean because of a nocturnal e, H7937
Eze 23:20 of donkeys and whose e was like that of H2444

EMITES (3)

Ge 14: 5 Zuzites in Ham, the **E** in Shaveh Kiriathaim H400
Dt 2:10 The **E** used to live there—a people strong H400
Dt 2:11 Rephaites, but the Moabites called them **E**. H400

EMMANUEL (KJV) IMMANUEL

EMMAUS (1)

Lk 24:13 of them were going to a village called **E**, *G1843*

EMPATHIZE (1)

Heb 4:15 who is unable *to* e **with** our weaknesses, *G5217*

EMPEROR (3) [EMPIRE]

Ac 25:25 made his appeal *to* the **E** I decided to *G4935*
1Pe 2:13 whether *to* the e, as the supreme authority, *G995*
1Pe 2:17 family of believers, fear God, honor the e. *G995*

EMPEROR'S (1) [EMPIRE]

Ac 25:21 appeal to be held over for the **E** decision, *G4935*

EMPHATICALLY (1)

Mk 14:31 But Peter insisted e, "Even if I have to die *G1735*

EMPIRE (4) [EMPEROR, EMPEROR'S, IMPERIAL]

Est 10: 1 Xerxes imposed tribute throughout the e, H824
Jer 34: 1 peoples in the e he ruled were H824
Da 11: 4 his e will be broken up and parceled out H4895
Da 11: 4 because his e will be uprooted and given H4895

EMPLOYED (1)

Eze 39:14 People *will be* continually e in cleansing H976

EMPTIED (5) [EMPTY]

Ge 24:20 So she quickly e her jar into the trough H6867
Lev 14:36 order the house *to be* e before he goes in H7155
Ne 5:13 may such a person be shaken out and e!" H8199
Zep 2: 4 At midday Ashdod *will be* e and Ekron H1763
1Co 1:17 lest the cross of Christ *be* e **of its power**. *G3033*

EMPTIES (1) [EMPTY]

Eze 47: 8 *When* it e into the sea, the salty water H3655

EMPTY (33) [EMPTY-HANDED, EMPTIED, EMPTIES, EMPTYING]

Ge 1: 2 Now the earth was formless and e, darkness H983
Ge 37:24 The cistern was e; there was no water in it H8199
Jdg 7:16 placed trumpets and e jars in the hands H8199
Ru 1:21 but the LORD has brought me back e. H8200
1Sa 20:18 be missed, because your seat *will be* e. H7212
1Sa 20:25 sat next to Saul, but David's place *was* e. H7212
1Sa 20:27 of the month, David's place *was* e again. H7212
2Ki 4: 3 ask all your neighbors for e jars. H8199
2Ki 18:20 but you speak only e **words**. H1821+8557
2Ch 24:11 would come and e the chest and carry H6867
Job 15: 2 person answer with e notions or fill their H8120
Job 26: 7 out the northern skies over e **space**; H9332
Job 35:13 God does not listen to their e **plea**; the H8736
Job 35:16 So Job opens his mouth with e **talk** H2039
Pr 14: 4 the manger is e, but from the H1338
Isa 16: 6 her insolence; but her boasts are e. H4202+4027
Isa 32: 6 the hungry they **leave** e and from the H8197
Isa 36: 5 but you speak only e **words**. H1821+8557
Isa 45:18 he did not create it to be e, but formed it H9332
Isa 55:11 It will not return to me e, but will H8200
Isa 59: 4 They rely on e arguments, they utter lies H9332
Jer 4:23 it was formless and e; and at the H983
Jer 48:12 *they will* e her pitchers and smash her jars H8197
Jer 51:34 into confusion, he has made us an e jar. H8198
Eze 24:11 Then set the e pot on the coals till it H8199
Am 4: 6 "I gave you e **stomachs** in every city H5931+9094

Mic 6:14 be satisfied; your stomach will still be **e**. H3803
Zep 3: 6 they are deserted and **e**. H4946+401+3782
Mt 12:36 judgment for every **e** word they have *G734*
Lk 1:53 good things but has sent the rich away **e**. *G3031*
Eph 5: 6 Let no one deceive you with **e** words, for *G3031*
1Pe 1:18 redeemed from the **e** way of life handed *G3469*
2Pe 2:18 For they mouth **e**, boastful words and, by *G3470*

EMPTY-HANDED (12) [EMPTY, HAND]
Ge 31:42 you would surely have sent me away **e**. H8200
Ex 3:21 so that when you leave you will not go **e**. H8200
Ex 23:15 "No one is to appear before me **e**. H8200
Ex 34:20 "No one is to appear before me **e**. H8200
Dt 15:13 release them, do not send them away **e**. H8200
Dt 16:16 No one should appear before the LORD **e**: H8200
Ru 3:17 'Don't go back to your mother-in-law **e**. H8200
Job 22: 9 you sent widows away **e** and broke the H8200
Jer 50: 9 like skilled warriors who do not return **e**. H8200
Mk 12: 3 beat him and sent him away **e**. *G3031*
Lk 20:10 tenants beat him and sent him away **e**. *G3031*
Lk 20:11 treated shamefully and sent away **e**. *G3031*

EMPTYING (2) [EMPTY]
Ge 42:35 As they were **e** their sacks, there in each H8197
Hab 1:17 *Is he to* keep on **e** his net, destroying H8197

EMULATION, EMULATIONS (KJV) ENVY, JEALOUSY

EN EGLAIM (1) [EGLAIM]
Eze 47:10 from En Gedi to **E** there will be H6536

EN GANNIM (3)
Jos 15:34 Zanoah, **E**, Tappuah, Enam, H6528
Jos 19:21 Remeth, **E**, En Haddah and Beth H6528
Jos 21:29 Jarmuth and **E**, together with H6528

EN GEDI (6) [HAZEZON TAMAR]
Jos 15:62 the City of Salt and **E**—six towns H6527
1Sa 23:29 lived in the strongholds of **E**. H6527
1Sa 24: 1 "David is in the Desert of **E**. H6527
2Ch 20: 2 in Hazezon Tamar" (that is, **E**). H6527
SS 1:14 blossoms from the vineyards of **E**. H6527
Eze 47:10 from **E** to En Eglaim there will be H6527

EN HADDAH (1)
Jos 19:21 En Gannim, **E** and Beth Pazzez. H6532

EN HAKKORE (1)
Jdg 15:19 So the spring was called **E**, and it H6530

EN HAZOR (1) [HAZOR]
Jos 19:37 Kedesh, Edrei, **E**, H6533

EN MISHPAT (1) [KADESH]
Ge 14: 7 they turned back and went to **E** H6535

EN RIMMON (1) [RIMMON]
Ne 11:29 in **E**, in Zorah, in Jarmuth, H6538

EN ROGEL (4)
Jos 15: 7 of En Shemesh and came out at **E**. H6537
Jos 18:16 of the Jebusite city and so to **E**. H6537
2Sa 17:17 Ahimaaz were staying at **E**. H6537
1Ki 1: 9 at the Stone of Zoheleth near **E**. H6537

EN SHEMESH (2)
Jos 15: 7 the waters of **E** and came out at H6539
Jos 18:17 went to **E**, continued to H6539

EN TAPPUAH (1) [TAPPUAH]
Jos 17: 7 include the people living at **E**. H6540

ENABLE (2) [ABLE]
Lk 1:74 *to* **e** us to serve him without fear *G1443*
Ac 4:29 their threats and **e** your servants to speak *G1443*

ENABLED (9) [ABLE]
Ge 29:31 *he* **e** her **to conceive**, but H7337+906+8167
Ge 30:22 to her and **e** her **to conceive**. H7337+906+8167
Lev 26:13 your yoke and **e** you **to walk** with heads H2143
Ru 4:13 the LORD **e** her to conceive, and H5989
1Ch 28:19 and *he* **e** me **to understand** all the details H8505
Jn 6:65 come to me unless the Father *has* **e** them." *G1443*
Ac 2: 4 other tongues as the Spirit **e** them. *G1443+710*
Ac 7:10 gave Joseph wisdom and **e** him to gain the NDT
Heb 11:11 was **e** to bear children because she *G1539*

ENABLES (2) [ABLE]
Hab 3:19 he **e** me **to tread** on the heights. H2005
Php 3:21 by the power that **e** him to bring *G1538*

ENABLING (1) [ABLE]
Ac 14: 3 of his grace *by* **e** them to perform *G1443*

ENACTED (1)
Ps 111: 8 **e** in faithfulness and uprightness. H6913

ENAIM (2)
Ge 38:14 then sat down at the entrance to **E** H6542
Ge 38:21 prostitute who was beside the road at **E**?" H6542

ENAM (1)
Jos 15:34 Zanoah, En Gannim, Tappuah, **E**, H6543

ENAN (5) [HAZAR ENAN]
Nu 1:15 from Naphtali, Ahira son of **E**." H6544
Nu 2:29 the people of Naphtali is Ahira son of **E**. H6544
Nu 7:78 On the twelfth day Ahira son of **E**, the H6544
Nu 7:83 This was the offering of Ahira son of **E**. H6544
Nu 10:27 Ahira son of **E** was over the division of H6544

ENCAMP (10) [CAMP]
Ex 14: 2 to turn back and **e** near Pi Hahiroth, H2837
Ex 14: 2 *They are to* **e** by the sea, directly opposite H2837
Nu 1:50 they are to take care of it and **e** around it. H2837
Nu 2: 3 of the camp of Judah *are to* **e** under their H2837
Nu 2:17 will set out in the same order as *they* **e**, H2837
Nu 9:20 at the LORD's command *they would* **e**, and H2837
Job 19:12 ramp against me and **e** around my tent. H2837
Isa 29: 3 *I will* **e** against you on all sides; I will H2837
Jer 50:29 who draw the bow. **E** all around her; let H2837
Zec 9: 8 But *I will* **e** at my temple to guard it H2837

ENCAMPED (15) [CAMP]
Ge 26:17 away from there and **e** in the Valley of H2837
Nu 2:34 that is the way *they* **e** under their H2837
Nu 9:17 the cloud settled, the Israelites **e**. H2837
Nu 9:18 and at his command *they* **e**. H2837
Nu 9:23 At the LORD's command *they* **e**, and at the H2837
Nu 12:16 left Hazeroth and **e** in the Desert of Paran H2837
Nu 24: 2 looked out and saw Israel **e** tribe by tribe, H8905
Dt 23: 9 When *you are* **e** against your H3655+4722
Jdg 11:20 all his troops and **e** at Jahaz and fought H2837
1Sa 26: 5 the camp, with the army **e** around him. H2837
2Sa 23:13 band of Philistines *was* **e** in the Valley of H2837
1Ki 16:15 The army *was* **e** near Gibbethon, H2837
2Ki 25: 1 *He* **e** outside the city and built siege H2837
1Ch 11:15 band of Philistines *was* **e** in the Valley of H2837
Jer 52: 4 *They* **e** outside the city and built siege H2837

ENCAMPS (1) [CAMP]
Ps 34: 7 angel of the LORD **e** around those who fear H2837

ENCHANTER (4) [ENCHANTERS]
Ps 58: 5 however skillful the **e** *may be*. H2489+2490
Isa 3: 3 counselor, skilled craftsman and clever **e**. H4318
Da 2:10 thing of any magician or **e** or astrologer. A10081
Da 2:27 "No wise man, **e**, magician or diviner A10081

ENCHANTERS (6) [ENCHANTER]
Da 1:20 the magicians and **e** in his whole kingdom. H879
Da 2: 2 summoned the magicians, **e**, sorcerers H879
Da 4: 7 When the magicians, **e**, astrologers and A10081
Da 5: 7 The king summoned the **e**, astrologers A10081
Da 5:11 of the magicians, **e**, astrologers and A10081
Da 5:15 The wise men and **e** were brought before A10081

ENCIRCLE (3) [CIRCLE]
Ps 22:12 strong bulls of Bashan **e** me. H4193
Isa 29: 3 *I will* **e** you *with* towers and set up H7443+6584
Lk 19:43 against you and **e** you and hem you in on *G4333*

ENCIRCLED (6) [CIRCLE]
1Ki 7:24 the rim, gourds **e** it—ten to a cubit. H6015+6017
2Ch 4: 3 figures of bulls **e** it—ten to a H6017+6017+6015
SS 7: 2 Your waist is a mound of wheat **e** by lilies. H6048
Rev 4: 3 that shone like an emerald **e** the throne. *G3239*
Rev 5: 6 **e** by the four living creatures and *G1877+3545*
Rev 5:11 They **e** the throne and the living creatures *G3241*

ENCIRCLES (1) [CIRCLE]
Ps 22:16 a pack of villains **e** me; they pierce my H5938

ENCIRCLING (2) [CIRCLE]
1Ki 7:18 in two rows **e** each network to decorate H6017
2Ch 33:14 of the Fish Gate and **e** the hill of Ophel; H6015

ENCLOSE (1) [CLOSE]
SS 8: 9 *we will* **e** her *with* panels of cedar. H7443

ENCLOSED (3) [CLOSE]
Est 1: 5 in the **e** garden of the king's palace H2958
SS 4:12 you are a spring **e**, a sealed fountain. H3159
Eze 46:22 corners of the outer court were **e** courts, H7788

ENCOUNTER (3)
Ex 23:27 into confusion every nation *you* **e**. H995+928
2Sa 23: 8 hundred men, whom he killed in one **e**. H7193
1Ch 11:11 hundred men, whom he killed in one **e**. H7193

ENCOURAGE (23) [ENCOURAGED, ENCOURAGEMENT, ENCOURAGES, ENCOURAGING, ENCOURAGINGLY]
Dt 1:38 **E** him, because he will lead Israel to H2616
Dt 3:28 Joshua, and **e** and strengthen him H2616
2Sa 11:25 city and destroy it.' Say this *to* **e** Joab." H2616
2Sa 19: 7 Now go out and **e** your men H1819+6584+4213
Job 16: 5 But my mouth *would* **e** you; comfort from H599
Ps 10:17 the afflicted; *you* **e** them, and you H3922+4213
Ps 64: 5 *They* **e** each other in evil plans, they talk H2616
Jer 29: 8 to the **dreams** you **e** them **to have**. H2731+2706
Ac 15:32 said much *to* **e** and strengthen the *G4151*
Ro 12: 8 if it is *to* **e**, then give encouragement; if it *G4151*
2Co 13:11 restoration, **e** *one another*, be of one *G4151*
Eph 6:22 know how we are, and that *he may* **e** you. *G4151*
Col 4: 8 that *he may* **e** your hearts. *G4151*
1Th 3: 2 to strengthen and **e** you in your faith, *G4151*
1Th 4:18 Therefore **e** one another with these words. *G4151*
1Th 5:11 Therefore **e** one another and build each *G4151*
1Th 5:14 idle and disruptive, **e** the disheartened *G4170*
2Th 2:17 **e** your hearts and strengthen you in every *G4151*
2Ti 4: 2 rebuke and **e**—with great patience *G4151*
Titus 1: 9 so that he can **e** others by sound doctrine *G4151*
Titus 2: 6 **e** the young men to be self-controlled. *G4151*
Titus 2:15 **E** and rebuke with all authority *G4151*
Heb 3:13 But **e** one another daily, as long as it is *G4151*

ENCOURAGED (19) [ENCOURAGE]
Jdg 7:11 you *will be* **e** to attack the camp." H2616+3338
Jdg 20:22 But the Israelites **e** one another and again H2616
2Ch 22: 3 his mother **e** him to act wickedly. H3446
2Ch 32: 6 city gate and **e** them with H1819+6584+4222
2Ch 35: 2 to their duties and **e** them in the service H2616
Eze 13:22 and because you **e** the wicked not H2616+3338
Ac 9:31 fear of the Lord and **e** by the Holy Spirit, *G4155*
Ac 11:23 he was glad and **e** them all to remain *G4151*
Ac 16:40 with the brothers and sisters and **e** them. *G4151*
Ac 18:27 sisters **e** him and wrote to the *G4730*
Ac 27:36 They were all **e** and ate some food *G2314*
Ac 28:15 Paul thanked God and *was* **e**. *G3284+2511*
Ro 1:12 *that* you and I *may be* **mutually e** by each *G5220*
1Co 14:31 so that everyone may be instructed and **e**. *G4151*
2Co 7: 4 I am greatly **e**; in all our troubles my joy *G4155*
2Co 7:13 By all this *we are* **e**. In addition to our own *G4151*
Col 2: 2 My goal is that *they may be* **e** in heart *G4151*
1Th 3: 7 persecution *we were* **e** about you *G4151*
Heb 6:18 set before us *may be* greatly **e**. *G4155+2400*

ENCOURAGEMENT (10) [ENCOURAGE]
Ac 4:36 Barnabas (which means "son *of* **e**"), *G4155*
Ac 20: 2 **speaking** many words *of* **e** to the people *G4151*
Ro 12: 8 is to encourage, then give **e**; if it is giving, *G4155*
Ro 15: 4 Scriptures and the **e** they provide we *G4155*
Ro 15: 5 gives endurance and **e** give you the same *G4155*
2Co 7:13 In addition to our own **e**, we were *G4155*
Php 2: 1 if you have any **e** from being united with *G4155*
2Th 2:16 grace gave us eternal **e** and good hope, *G4155*
Phm 7 Your love has given me great joy and **e** *G4155*
Heb 12: 5 forgotten this *word of* **e** that addresses *G4155*

ENCOURAGES (1) [ENCOURAGE]
Isa 41: 7 The metalworker **e** the goldsmith, and the H2616

ENCOURAGING (7) [ENCOURAGE]
Ac 14:22 the disciples and **e** them to remain true to *G4151*
Ac 15:31 read it and were glad for its **e message**. *G4155*
Ac 20: 1 disciples and, *after* **e** them, said goodbye *G4151*
1Co 14: 3 their strengthening, **e** and comfort. *G4155*
1Th 2:12 **e**, comforting and urging you to live lives *G4151*
Heb 10:25 of doing, but **e** one another—and all *G4151*
1Pe 5:12 **e** you and testifying that this is the true *G4151*

ENCOURAGINGLY (1) [ENCOURAGE]
2Ch 30:22 Hezekiah spoke **e** to all the Levites H6584+4213

ENCROACH (2)
Dt 2:37 *you did* not **e** on any of the land of the H7928
Pr 23:10 boundary stone or **e** on the fields of the H995

ENCRUSTED (1) [CRUST]
Eze 24: 6 to the pot now **e**, whose deposit will not H2689

END (274) [ENDED, ENDING, ENDS, ENDLESS, ENDLESSLY]
Ge 6:13 "I am going to put an **e** *to* all people, for H7891
Ge 8: 3 At the **e** *of* the hundred and fifty days the H7895
Ge 23: 9 belongs to him and is at the **e** *of* his field. H7895
Ge 41:53 of abundance in Egypt **came to an e**, H3983
Ge 47:21 from *one* **e** *of* Egypt to the other. H7895+1473
Ex 12:41 At the **e** *of* the 430 years, to the very day H7891
Ex 23:16 of Ingathering at the **e** *of* the year, H3655
Ex 25:19 one cherub on one **e** and the second H7896
Ex 26: 4 the edge of the **e** curtain in one set, H7896
Ex 26: 4 the same with the **e** curtain in the other H7812
Ex 26: 5 fifty loops on the **e** curtain of the other H7895
Ex 26:10 along the edge of the **e** curtain in one set H7812
Ex 26:10 along the edge of the **e** curtain in the other NDT
Ex 26:22 Make six frames for the **far e**, that is, the H3752
Ex 26:22 that is, the west **e** of the tabernacle, NDT
Ex 26:23 two frames for the corners at the **far e**. H3752
Ex 26:27 on the west, at the **far e** *of* the tabernacle. H3752
Ex 26:28 is to extend from **e** to end at the middle H7895
Ex 26:28 extend from end to **e** at the middle of the H7895
Ex 27:12 "The west **e** *of* the courtyard shall be fifty H6991
Ex 27:13 On the east **e**, toward the sunrise, the H6991
Ex 32:27 the camp from *one* **e** to the other, H9133
Ex 36:11 the edge of the **e** curtain in one set, H7896
Ex 36:11 was done with the **e** curtain in the other H7812
Ex 36:12 fifty loops on the **e** curtain of the other H7895
Ex 36:17 along the edge of the **e** curtain in one set H7812
Ex 36:17 along the edge of the **e** curtain in the other NDT
Ex 36:27 They made six frames for the **far e**, that is H3752
Ex 36:27 that is, the west **e** of the tabernacle, NDT
Ex 36:28 the corners of the tabernacle at the **far e**. H3752
Ex 36:32 on the west, at the **far e** *of* the tabernacle. H3752
Ex 36:33 it extended from **e** to end at the middle H7895
Ex 36:33 from end to **e** at the middle of the H7895
Ex 37: 8 one cherub on one **e** and the second H7896
Ex 38:12 The west **e** was fifty cubits wide and had H6991
Ex 38:13 The east **e**, toward the sunrise, was also H6991

Nu 13:25 At the e *of* forty days they returned from H7891
Nu 14:35 *They will* **meet** their e in this wilderness H9462
Nu 16:21 assembly so *I can* **put an e** *to* them at H3983
Nu 16:45 assembly so *I can* **put an e** *to* them at H3983
Nu 17:10 *This will* **put an e** *to* their grumbling H3983
Nu 23:10 and *may* my **final e** be like theirs! H344
Nu 24:20 their e will be utter destruction. H344
Nu 25:11 *I did* not **put an e** *to* them in my zeal. H3983
Nu 34: 3 east from the southern e *of* the Dead Sea, H7895
Nu 34: 5 Wadi of Egypt and e at the H2118+9362
Nu 34: 9 to Ziphron and e *at* Hazar Enan. H2118+9362
Nu 34:12 the Jordan and e *at* the Dead Sea. H2118+9362
Dt 4:32 ask from *one* e *of* the heavens to the H7895
Dt 8:16 you so that in the e it might go well with H344
Dt 9:11 At the e *of* the forty days and forty nights H7891
Dt 11:12 it from the beginning of the year to its e. H344
Dt 13: 7 from one e *of* the land to the other), H7895
Dt 14:28 At the e *of* every three years, bring all the H7895
Dt 15: 1 At the e *of* every seven years you must H7891
Dt 28:64 from one e *of* the earth to the other. H7895
Dt 31:10 "At the e *of* every seven years, in the year H7891
Dt 31:24 the words of this law from beginning to e, H9462
Dt 31:30 from beginning to e in the hearing of the H9462
Dt 32:20 "and see what their e will be; for they are a H344
Dt 32:29 this and discern what their e will be! H344
Jos 13:27 territory up to the e *of* the Sea of Galilee). H7895
Jos 15: 2 bay at the southern e *of* the Dead Sea, H7895
Jos 15: 8 at the northern e *of* the Valley of Rephaim H7895
Jos 24:20 disaster on you and **make an e** *of* you, H3983
Ru 3: 7 to lie down at the **far e** *of* the grain pile. H7895
1Sa 3:12 against his family—from beginning to e. H3983
1Sa 14:27 he reached out the e *of* the staff that was H7895
1Sa 14:43 tasted a little honey with the e *of* my staff. H7895
2Sa 2:26 that *this will* e in H2118+928+2021+340
2Sa 15: 7 At the e *of* four years, Absalom said to H7891
2Sa 24: 8 to Jerusalem at the e *of* nine months and H7895
2Sa 24:15 from that morning **until the e of** the time H6330
1Ki 9:10 At the e *of* twenty years, during which H7895
1Ki 10:20 one **at either e** of each H4946+2296+2256+4946+2296S
2Ki 8: 3 At the e *of* the seven years she came back H7895
2Ki 10:21 until it was full from *one* e to the other. H7023
2Ki 18:10 At the e *of* three years the Assyrians took it H7895
2Ki 21:16 that he filled Jerusalem from e to end— H7023
2Ki 21:16 that he filled Jerusalem from end to e— H7023
2Ki 24:20 and **in the e** he thrust them from his H6330
1Ch 29:29 from beginning to e, they are written in the H340
2Ch 8: 1 At the e *of* twenty years, during which H7891
2Ch 9:19 one **at either e** of each H4946+2296+2256+4946+2296S
2Ch 9:29 from beginning to e, are they not written in H340
2Ch 12:15 from beginning to e, are they not written in H340
2Ch 16:11 from beginning to e, are written in the H340
2Ch 20:16 will find them at the e *of* the gorge in the H6067
2Ch 20:34 from beginning to e, are written in the H340
2Ch 21:19 course of time, at the e of the second year H7891
2Ch 25:26 from beginning to e, are they not written in H340
2Ch 26:22 from beginning to e, are recorded by the H340
2Ch 28:26 from beginning to e, are written in the H340
2Ch 35:27 from beginning to e, are written in the H340
Ezr 9:11 their impurity from *one* e to the other. H7023
Ne 3:21 entrance of Eliashib's house to the e *of* it. H9417
Ne 4:11 will kill them and **put an e** *to* the work." H8697
Ne 9:31 you did not put an e to them or abandon H3986
Est 1:18 There will be **no e** *of* disrespect H3869+1896
Est 8: 3 begged him to **put an e** *to* the evil plan of H6296
Job 4:15 and the hair on my body **stood on e**. H6169
Job 7: 6 and *they* **come to an e** without hope. H3983
Job 16: 3 Will your long-winded speeches never e H7891
Job 18: 2 "When *will you* e these speeches H8492+7874
Job 19:25 that *in* the e he will stand on the earth. H340
Job 21:21 when their allotted months **come to an e**? H2951
Job 28: 3 Mortals put an e to the darkness; they H7891
Ps 7: 9 **Bring to an e** the violence of the wicked H1698
Ps 19: 6 It rises at *one* e *of* the heavens and H7895
Ps 39: 4 my life's e and the number of my days H7891
Ps 48:14 he will be our guide even to the e. H4637
Ps 89:44 *You have* **put an e** to his splendor and H8697
Ps 102:27 the same, and your years *will* never e. H9462
Ps 107:27 they *were* **at their wits' e**. H3972+2683+1182
Ps 112: 8 **in the e** they will look in triumph on H6330+889
Ps 119:33 your decrees, that I may follow it **to the e**. H6813
Ps 119:112 your decrees **to the very e**. H4200+6409+6813
Ps 123: 3 we have endured **no e** *of* contempt. H8041
Ps 123: 4 We have endured **no e** *of* ridicule from H8041
Pr 5: 4 but *in* the e she is bitter as gall, sharp as a H344
Pr 5:11 At the **e of** your **life** you will groan, when H344
Pr 14:12 to be right, but *in* the e it leads to death. H344
Pr 14:13 may ache, and rejoicing may e in grief. H344
Pr 16: 4 works out everything to its **proper e**— H5102
Pr 16:25 to be right, but *in* the e it leads to death. H344
Pr 19:20 at the e you will be counted among H344
Pr 20:21 too soon will not be blessed at the e. H344
Pr 23:32 *In* the e it bites like a snake and poisons H344
Pr 25: 8 will you do in the e if your neighbor puts H344
Pr 28:23 a person will **in the e** gain favor rather H343
Pr 29:11 their rage, but the wise bring calm in the e. H294
Ecc 3:11 what God has done from beginning to e. H6067
Ecc 4: 8 There was no e to his toil, yet his eyes H7891
Ecc 4:16 There was no e to all the people who H7891
Ecc 7: 8 The e *of* a matter is better than its H344
Ecc 10:13 are folly; at the e they are wicked madness H344
Ecc 12:12 Of making many books there is no e, and H7891
Isa 2: 7 gold; there is no e to their treasures. H7897
Isa 2: 7 of horses; there is no e to their chariots. H7897
Isa 7: 3 to meet Ahaz at the e *of* the aqueduct of H7895
Isa 9: 7 government and peace there will be no e. H7891
Isa 10: 7 is to destroy, to **put an e** *to* many nations. H4162
Isa 10:25 against you *will* e and my wrath will H3983
Isa 13:11 *I will* **put an e** *to* the arrogance of the H8697
Isa 14: 4 How the oppressor *has* **come to an e** H8697
Isa 16: 4 The oppressor *will* **come to an e**, and H699
Isa 16:10 for *I have* **put an e** *to* the shouting. H8697
Isa 21: 2 *I will* **bring to an e** all the groaning she H8697
Isa 21:16 the splendor of Kedar *will* **come to an e**. H3983
Isa 23:15 But at the e *of* these seventy years, it will H7891
Isa 23:17 At the e *of* seventy years, the LORD will H7891
Isa 38:12 day and night *you* **made an e** *of* me. H8966
Isa 38:13 day and night *you* **made an e** *of* me. H8966
Isa 46:10 I make known the e from the beginning H344
Isa 60:20 and your days of sorrow *will* e. H8966
Isa 66:17 *they will* **meet** *their* e together with the H6066
Jer 5:31 But what will you do in the e? H344
Jer 7:34 *I will* **bring an e** *to* the sounds of joy and H8697
Jer 9:16 the sword until *I have* **made an e** *of* them." H3983
Jer 12:12 will devour from *one* e *of* the land to the H7895
Jer 16: 9 your days I *will* **bring an e** *to* the sounds H8697
Jer 17:11 in the e they will prove to be fools. H344
Jer 20:18 sorrow and *to* e my days in shame? H3983
Jer 25:33 from *one* e *of* the earth to the other. H7895
Jer 48: 2 *let us* **put an e** to that nation.' H4162
Jer 48:35 In Moab *I will* **put an e** *to* those who H8697
Jer 49:37 the sword until I *have* **made an e** *of* them. H3983
Jer 51:13 in treasures, your e has come, the time H7891
Jer 51:64 The words of Jeremiah e here. H6330
Jer 52: 3 and **in the e** he thrust them from his H6330
La 3:53 *They tried to* e my life in a pit and threw H7551
La 4:18 Our e was near, our days were numbered H7891
La 4:18 days were numbered, for our e had come. H7891
La 4:22 Your punishment *will* e, Daughter Zion H9462
Eze 3:16 At the e *of* seven days the word of the H7895
Eze 5: 2 When the days of your siege **come to an e**, H4848
Eze 7: 2 " 'The e! The end has come H7891
Eze 7: 2 The e has come upon the four corners of H7891
Eze 7: 3 The e is now upon you, and I will unleash H7891
Eze 7: 6 The e has come! The end has come! It H7891
Eze 7: 6 end has come! The e has come! It has H7891
Eze 7:24 *I will* **put an e** *to* the pride of the mighty H8697
Eze 7:26 the counsel of the elders will come to an e. NDT
Eze 12:23 *I am going to* **put an e** *to* this proverb H8697
Eze 20:17 destroy them or put an e to them in the H3986
Eze 22: 4 a close, and the e *of* your years has come. H6961
Eze 22:15 and *I will* **put an e** *to* your uncleanness. H9462
Eze 23:48 "So *I will* **put an e** *to* lewdness in the land H8697
Eze 26:13 *I will* **put an e** *to* your noisy songs, and the H8697
Eze 26:21 bring you to a **horrible e** and you will be H1166
Eze 27:36 have come to a **horrible e** and will be no H1166
Eze 28:19 have come to a **horrible e** and will be no H1166
Eze 29:13 At the e *of* forty years I will gather the H7891
Eze 30:10 " '*I will* **put an e** *to* the hordes of Egypt by H8697
Eze 30:13 the idols and **put an e** *to* the images in H8697
Eze 30:18 her proud strength *will* **come to an e**. H8697
Eze 33:28 her proud strength *will* **come to an e** H8697
Eze 40:15 the gateway to the **far e** of its portico was H7164
Eze 41: 4 cubits across the e *of* the main hall. H7156
Eze 43:27 *At the* e *of* these days, from the eighth day H3983
Eze 46:19 showed me a place at the western e. H3752
Da 1:15 At the e *of* the ten days they looked H7921
Da 1:18 At the e *of* the time set by the king to H7921
Da 2:44 those kingdoms and **bring** them **to an e**, A10508
Da 4:34 At the e *of* that time, I, Nebuchadnezzar A10636
Da 5:26 days of your reign and **brought** it **to an e**. A10719
Da 6:26 dominion will **never e**. A10527+10509+10002
Da 7:28 "This is the e of the matter. I, Daniel A10509
Da 8:17 that the vision concerns the time of the e." H7891
Da 8:19 concerns the appointed time of the e. H7891
Da 9:24 transgression, to **put an e** *to* sin, to atone H9462
Da 9:26 The e will come like a flood H7891
Da 9:26 War will continue until the e, and H7891
Da 9:27 the 'seven' *he will* **put an e** *to* sacrifice H8697
Da 9:27 until the e that is decreed is poured out H3986
Da 11:18 a commander *will* **put an e** *to* his H8697
Da 11:27 because an e will still come at the H7891
Da 11:35 made spotless until the time of the e, H7891
Da 11:40 "At the time of the e the king of the South H7891
Da 11:45 Yet he will come to his e, and no one will H7891
Da 12: 4 words of the scroll until the time of the e. H7891
Da 12: 9 up and sealed until the time of the e. H7891
Da 12:12 and reaches the e of the 1,335 days. NDT
Da 12:13 go your way till the e. You will rest, H7891
Da 12:13 then at the e *of* the days you will rise H7891
Hos 1: 4 and *I will* **put an e** *to* the kingdom of H8697
Hos 11: 6 false prophets and **put an e** to their plans. H430
Am 6: 7 your feasting and lounging *will* e. H6073
Am 8:10 an only son and the e *of* it like a bitter day. H344
Na 1: 8 flood he will make an e of Nineveh; H3986
Na 1: 9 plot against the LORD he will bring to an e; H3986
Hab 2: 3 it speaks of the e and will not prove false. H7891
Zep 1:18 will make a sudden e of all who live on H3986
Zec 9: 6 and *I will* **put an e** *to* the pride of the H4162
Mt 10:22 who stands firm to the e will be saved. G5465
Mt 13:39 The harvest is the e of the age, and the G5333
Mt 13:40 the fire, so it will be at the e of the age. G5333
Mt 13:49 This is how it will be at the e of the age G5333
Mt 21:41 *He will* **bring** those wretches **to a** wretched e G660
Mt 24: 3 of your coming and *of* the e of the age?" G5333
Mt 24: 6 must happen, but the e is still to come. G5465
Mt 24:13 who stands firm to the e will be saved. G5465
Mt 24:14 to all nations, and then the e will come. G5465
Mt 24:31 from *one* e of the heavens to the other. G216
Mt 28:20 with you always, to the **very** e of the age." G5333
Mk 3:26 divided, he cannot stand; his e has come. G5465
Mk 13: 7 must happen, but the e is still to come. G5465
Mk 13:13 who stands firm to the e will be saved. G5465
Lk 1:33 his kingdom will never e. G5465
Lk 4: 2 and *at the* e of them he was hungry. G5334
Lk 17:24 lights up the sky from one e to the other. G5679
Lk 21: 9 but the e will not come right away." G5465
Jn 11: 4 "This sickness will not e **in** death. G4639
Jn 13: 1 were in the world, he loved them to the e. G5465
Ac 21:26 of purification would e and the offering G1741
1Co 1: 8 He will also keep you firm to the e, so that G5465
1Co 4: 9 on display *at* the e *of the procession*, G2274
1Co 15:24 Then the e will come, when he hands over G5465
2Co 3:13 from seeing the e of what was passing G5465
2Co 11:15 Their e will be what their actions deserve. G5465
Col 1:29 To **this** e I strenuously contend with all G4005S
Heb 1:12 the same, and your years *will* never e." G1722
Heb 3:14 our original conviction firmly to the very e. G5465
Heb 6: 8 of being cursed. *In* the e it will be burned G5465
Heb 6:11 to show this same diligence to the **very** e, G5465
Heb 6:16 is said and puts an e to all argument. G4306
Heb 7: 3 without beginning of days or e of life G5465
Heb 11:22 Joseph, *when his* **e was near**, spoke G5462
1Pe 1: 9 you are receiving the e **result** of your faith, G5465
1Pe 4: 7 The e of all things is near. Therefore be G5465
2Pe 2:20 are worse off *at* the e than they were at G2274
Rev 2:26 is victorious and does my will to the e, G5465
Rev 21: 6 the Omega, the Beginning and the **E**. G5465
Rev 22:13 the Last, the Beginning and the **E**. G5465

ENDANGER (2) [DANGER]

Ru 4: 6 it because *I might* e my own estate. H8845
1Co 15:30 why *do we* e *ourselves* every hour? G3073

ENDANGERED (1) [DANGER]

Ecc 10: 9 whoever splits logs *may* **be e** by them. H6124

ENDANGERS (1) [DANGER]

Lev 19:16 *Do* not **do anything that** e your neighbor's **life** H6641+6584+1947

ENDEAVOUR, ENDEAVOURED, ENDEAVOURING, ENDEAVOURS (KJV) MADE EVERY EFFORT, MAKE EVERY EFFORT, READY, WORK

ENDED (17) [END]

Jos 15:11 The boundary e at the sea. H2118+9362
Jos 16: 8 Kanah Ravine and e at the H2118+9362
Jos 17: 9 of the ravine and e at the H2118+9362
Jos 19:14 Hannathon and e at the Valley of H2118+9362
Jos 19:22 Shemesh, and e at the Jordan. H2118+9362
2Ch 31: 1 When all this *had* e, the Israelites who H3983
Job 31:40 The words of Job *are* e. H9462
Job 39: 3 forth their young; their labor pains *are* e. H8938
Ps 78:33 So *he* e their days in futility and their H3983
Pr 10:19 Sin *is* not e by multiplying words, but the H2532
Pr 22:10 out goes strife; quarrels and insults *are* e. H8697
Isa 14: 4 has come to an end! How his fury *has* e! H8697
Jer 8:20 the summer *has* e, and we are not H3983
Am 8: 5 the Sabbath be e that we may market NDT
Ac 20: 1 When the uproar *had* e, Paul sent for the G4264
Rev 20: 3 anymore until the thousand years *were* e. G5464
Rev 20: 5 to life until the thousand years *were* e.) G5464

ENDING (4) [END]

Ge 44:12 with the oldest and e with the youngest. H3983
Jos 15: 4 e at the Mediterranean Sea. H2118+9362
Jos 16: 3 Gezer, e at the Mediterranean Sea. H2118+9362
Jos 19:33 to Lakkum and e *at* the Jordan. H2118+9362

ENDLESS (8) [END]

Job 22: 5 Are not your sins e? H401+7891
Ps 9: 6 **E** ruin has overtaken my enemies H4200+5905
Ps 49:11 dwellings for **e generations**, H1887+2256+1887
Ps 93: 5 holiness adorns your house for e days. H802
Ps 106:31 righteousness for e generations to H6330+6409
Na 2: 9 The supply is e, the wealth from all H401+7897
Na 3:19 for who has not felt your e cruelty? H9458
1Ti 1: 4 themselves to myths and e genealogies. G596

ENDLESSLY (1) [END]

Heb 10: 1 repeated e year after year, G1650+3836+1457

ENDOR (3)

Jos 17:11 the people of Dor, E, Taanach and H6529
1Sa 28: 7 "There is one in E," they said. H6529
Ps 83:10 who perished at E and became like dung H6529

ENDOW (2) [ENDOWED]

Job 39:17 God *did* **not** e her *with* wisdom or give H5960
Ps 72: 1 **E** the king *with* your justice, O God,
the royal son *with* H5989

ENDOWED (5) [ENDOW]

2Ch 2:12 e **with** intelligence and discernment H3359

Ps 89:13 Your arm is **e with** power; your hand is H6640
Isa 48:16 LORD has sent me, **e with** his Spirit. H2256
Isa 55: 5 of Israel, for *he has* **e** you **with splendor**." H6995
Isa 60: 9 of Israel, for *he has* **e** you **with splendor**. H6995

ENDS (65) [END]

Ex 25:18 of hammered gold at the **e** *of* the cover. H7896
Ex 25:19 of one piece with the cover, at the two **e**. H7896
Ex 28:25 the other **e** *of* the chains to the two H7896
Ex 37: 7 of hammered gold at the **e** *of* the cover. H7896
Ex 37: 8 at the two **e** he made them of one piece H7896
Ex 39:18 the other **e** *of* the chains to the two H7896
Dt 28:49 far away, from the **e** *of* the earth, like an H7895
Dt 33:17 nations, even those at the **e** *of* the earth. H700
1Sa 2:10 the LORD will judge the **e** *of* the earth. H700
1Ki 8: 8 so long that their **e** could be seen from H8031
2Ch 5: 9 These poles were so long that their **e** H8031
Job 28:24 he views the **e** *of* the earth and sees H7896
Job 37: 3 heaven and sends it to the **e** *of* the earth. H4053
Ps 2: 8 the **e** *of* the earth your possession. H700
Ps 19: 4 their words to the **e** *of* the world. H7895
Ps 22:27 All the **e** *of* the earth will remember and H700
Ps 46: 9 makes wars cease to the **e** *of* the earth. H7895
Ps 48:10 your praise reaches to the **e** *of* the earth H7898
Ps 59:13 be known to the **e** *of* the earth that God H700
Ps 61: 2 From the **e** *of* the earth I call to you, I call H7895
Ps 65: 5 the hope of all the **e** *of* the earth and of H7898
Ps 67: 7 so that all the **e** *of* the earth will fear him. H700
Ps 72: 8 from the River to the **e** *of* the earth. H700
Ps 98: 3 all the **e** *of* the earth have seen the H700
Ps 135: 7 makes clouds rise from the **e** *of* the earth; H7895
Pr 11:23 The desire of the righteous **e** only in good NDT
Pr 12:24 will rule, but laziness **e** in forced labor. H2118
Pr 17:24 a fool's eyes wander to the **e** *of* the earth. H7895
Pr 18: 1 person pursues **selfish e** and against all H9294
Pr 20:17 one **e up** with a mouth full of gravel. H339
Pr 30: 4 Who has established all the **e** *of* the earth H700
Isa 5:26 he whistles for those at the **e** *of* the earth. H7895
Isa 13: 5 from the **e** *of* the heavens—the H7895
Isa 24:16 From the **e** *of* the earth we hear singing H4053
Isa 40:28 the Creator of the **e** *of* the earth. H7896
Isa 41: 5 it and fear; the **e** *of* the earth tremble. H7896
Isa 41: 9 I took you from the **e** *of* the earth, from its H7896
Isa 42:10 his praise from the **e** *of* the earth, you H7895
Isa 43: 6 my daughters from the **e** *of* the earth— H7895
Isa 45:22 be saved, all you **e** *of* the earth; for I am H700
Isa 48:20 Send it out to the **e** *of* the earth; say, "The H7895
Isa 49: 6 salvation may reach to the **e** *of* the earth." H7895
Isa 52:10 all the **e** *of* the earth will see the H700
Isa 58: 4 Your fasting **e** in quarreling and strife, and NDT
Isa 62:11 made proclamation to the **e** *of* the earth: H7895
Jer 6:22 is being stirred up from the **e** *of* the earth. H3752
Jer 10:13 makes clouds rise from the **e** *of* the earth. H7895
Jer 16:19 will come from the **e** *of* the earth and say, H700
Jer 25:31 tumult will resound to the **e** *of* the earth, H7895
Jer 25:32 storm is rising from the **e** *of* the earth." H3752
Jer 31: 8 gather them from the **e** *of* the earth. H3752
Jer 48:47 Here **e** the judgment on Moab. H6330
Jer 50:41 being stirred up from the **e** *of* the earth. H3752
Jer 51:16 makes clouds rise from the **e** *of* the earth. H7895
Eze 15: 4 the fire burns both **e** and chars the middle H7896
Da 4:11 it was visible to the **e** *of* the earth. A10509
Mic 5: 4 greatness will reach to the **e** *of* the earth. H700
Zec 9:10 from the River to the **e** *of* the earth. H700
Mt 12:42 she came from the **e** of the earth to *G4306*
Mk 13:27 from the **e** of the earth to the ends of the *G216*
Mk 13:27 ends of the earth to the **e** of the heavens. *G216*
Lk 11:31 she came from the **e** of the earth to *G4306*
Ac 1: 8 Samaria, and to the **e** of the earth." *G2274*
Ac 13:47 may bring salvation to the **e** of the earth. *G2274*
Ro 10:18 their words to the **e** of the world. *G4306*

ENDURANCE (12) [ENDURE]

Ro 15: 4 so that through the **e** taught in the *G5705*
Ro 15: 5 the God who gives **e** and encouragement *G5705*
2Co 1: 6 produces in you **patient e** of the same *G5705*
2Co 6: 4 in great **e**; in troubles, hardships and *G5705*
Col 1:11 that you may have great **e** and patience, *G5705*
1Th 1: 3 your **e** inspired by hope in our Lord *G5705*
1Ti 6:11 godliness, faith, love, **e** and gentleness. *G5705*
2Ti 3:10 my purpose, faith, patience, love, **e**, *G5705*
Titus 2: 2 sound in faith, in love and in **e**. *G5705*
Rev 1: 9 kingdom and **patient e** that are ours *G5705*
Rev 13:10 This calls for **patient e** and faithfulness on *G5705*
Rev 14:12 This calls for **patient e** on the part of the *G5705*

ENDURE (42) [ENDURANCE, ENDURED, ENDURES, ENDURING]

1Sa 13:14 But now your kingdom *will* not **e**; the LORD H7756
2Sa 7:16 your kingdom *will* **e** forever before me; H586
Job 14: 2 like fleeting shadows, *they do* not **e**. H6641
Job 15:29 longer be rich and his wealth *will* not **e**, H7756
Job 20:21 him to devour; his prosperity *will* not **e**. H2656
Ps 37:18 and their inheritance *will* **e** forever. H2118
Ps 49:12 their wealth, *do* not **e**; they are like the H4328
Ps 55:12 insulting me, *I could* **e** it; if a foe were H5951
Ps 69: 7 For *I* **e** scorn for your sake, and shame H5951
Ps 69:10 I weep and fast, I *must* **e** scorn; H2118+4200
Ps 72: 5 *May he* **e** as long as the sun, as long as H799
Ps 72:17 *May* his name **e** forever; may it continue H2118
Ps 89:29 throne **as long as** the heavens **e**. H3869+3427
Ps 89:36 his throne **e** before me like the sun NDT
Ps 104:31 *May* the glory of the LORD **e** forever; may H2118
Ps 119:91 Your laws **e** to this day, for all things serve H6641
Pr 12:19 Truthful lips **e** forever, but a lying tongue H3922
Pr 18:14 The human spirit *can* **e** in sickness, but a H3920
Pr 27:24 riches do not **e** forever, and a crown is NDT
Ecc 3:14 that everything God does *will* **e** forever; H2118
Isa 55:13 everlasting sign, *that will* **e forever**." H4202+4162
Isa 56: 5 name that *will* **e forever**. H4202+4162
Isa 66:22 new earth that I make *will* **e** before me," H6641
Isa 66:22 "so *will* your name and descendants **e**. H6641
Jer 10:10 trembles; the nations cannot **e** his wrath. H3920
Jer 10:19 "This is my sickness, and *I must* **e** it." H5951
Jer 44:22 could no longer **e** your wicked actions H5951
Eze 22:14 *Will* your courage **e** or your hands be H6641
Da 2:44 to an end, but *it will* itself **e** forever. A10624
Joel 2:11 LORD is great; it is dreadful. Who *can* **e** it? H3920
Na 1: 6 Who *can* **e** his fierce anger H7756
Mal 3: 2 But who *can* **e** the day of his coming H3920
1Co 4:12 we bless; when we are persecuted, *we* **e** it; *G462*
1Co 10:13 provide a way out so that you can **e** it. *G5722*
2Co 1: 8 far beyond our **ability** *to* **e**, so that we AIT
2Ti 2:10 Therefore *I* **e** everything for the sake of the *G5702*
2Ti 2:12 if *we* **e**, we will also reign with him. If we *G5702*
2Ti 4: 5 all situations, **e hardship**, do the work of *G2802*
Heb 12: 7 **E hardship** as discipline; God is treating *G5702*
1Pe 2:20 a beating for doing wrong and **e** it? *G5702*
1Pe 2:20 if you suffer for doing good and *you* **e** it, *G5702*
Rev 3:10 have kept my command to **e patiently**, *G5705*

ENDURED (8) [ENDURE]

Ps 123: 3 for *we have* **e** no end of contempt. H8425
Ps 123: 4 We *have* **e** no end of ridicule from the H8425
Ac 13:18 about forty years *he* **e** their **conduct** in the *G5574*
2Ti 3:11 Iconium and Lystra, the persecutions *I* **e**. *G5722*
Heb 10:32 when *you* **e** in a great conflict full of *G5702*
Heb 12: 2 For the joy set before him he **e** the cross *G5702*
Heb 12: 3 Consider him *who* **e** such opposition from *G5702*
Rev 2: 3 and *have* **e hardships** for my name, *G1002*

ENDURES (64) [ENDURE]

Ge 8:22 "As long as the earth **e**, seedtime and H3427
1Ch 16:34 the LORD, for he is good; his love **e** forever. NDT
1Ch 16:41 thanks to the LORD, "for his love **e** forever." NDT
2Ch 5:13 "He is good; his love **e** forever." Then the NDT
2Ch 7: 3 saying, "He is good; his love **e** forever." NDT
2Ch 7: 6 he gave thanks, saying, "His love **e** forever." NDT
2Ch 20:21 thanks to the LORD, for his love **e** forever." NDT
Ezr 3:11 his love toward Israel **e** forever." And all the NDT
Ps 90:10 if our strength **e**; yet the best of them H928
Ps 100: 5 For the LORD is good and his love **e** forever NDT
Ps 102:12 your renown **e** through all generations. NDT
Ps 106: 1 the LORD, for he is good; his love **e** forever. NDT
Ps 107: 1 the LORD, for he is good; his love **e** forever. NDT
Ps 111: 3 and his righteousness **e** forever. H6641
Ps 112: 3 houses, and their righteousness **e** forever. H6641
Ps 112: 9 their righteousness **e** forever; their horn H6641
Ps 117: 2 the faithfulness of the LORD **e** forever. NDT
Ps 118: 1 the LORD, for he is good; his love **e** forever. NDT
Ps 118: 2 "His love **e** forever." NDT
Ps 118: 3 house of Aaron say: "His love **e** forever." NDT
Ps 118: 4 who fear the LORD say: "His love **e** forever." NDT
Ps 118:29 the LORD, for he is good; his love **e** forever. NDT
Ps 119:90 you established the earth, and *it* **e**. H6641
Ps 125: 1 which cannot be shaken but **e** forever. H3782
Ps 135:13 Your name, LORD, **e** forever, your renown NDT
Ps 136: 1 the LORD, for he is good. His love **e** forever. NDT
Ps 136: 2 to the God of gods. His love **e** forever. NDT
Ps 136: 3 to the Lord of lords: His love **e** forever. NDT
Ps 136: 4 does great wonders, His love **e** forever. NDT
Ps 136: 5 made the heavens, His love **e** forever. NDT
Ps 136: 6 earth upon the waters, His love **e** forever. NDT
Ps 136: 7 made the great lights—His love **e** forever. NDT
Ps 136: 8 the sun to govern the day, His love **e** forever. NDT
Ps 136: 9 stars to govern the night; His love **e** forever. NDT
Ps 136:10 the firstborn of Egypt His love **e** forever. NDT
Ps 136:11 out from among them His love **e** forever. NDT
Ps 136:12 outstretched arm; His love **e** forever. NDT
Ps 136:13 the Red Sea asunder His love **e** forever. NDT
Ps 136:14 through the midst of it, His love **e** forever. NDT
Ps 136:15 army into the Red Sea; His love **e** forever. NDT
Ps 136:16 through the wilderness; His love **e** forever. NDT
Ps 136:17 struck down great kings, His love **e** forever. NDT
Ps 136:18 killed mighty kings—His love **e** forever. NDT
Ps 136:19 king of the Amorites His love **e** forever. NDT
Ps 136:20 Og king of Bashan—His love **e** forever. NDT
Ps 136:21 land as an inheritance, His love **e** forever. NDT
Ps 136:22 to his servant Israel. His love **e** forever. NDT
Ps 136:23 us in our low estate His love **e** forever. NDT
Ps 136:24 us from our enemies. His love **e** forever. NDT
Ps 136:25 food to every creature. His love **e** forever. NDT
Ps 136:26 to the God of heaven. His love **e** forever. NDT
Ps 138: 8 **e** forever—do not abandon the works NDT
Ps 145:13 your dominion **e** through all NDT
Pr 12:12 evildoers, but the root of the righteous **e**. H5989
Isa 40: 8 but the word of our God **e** forever. H7756
Jer 33:11 the LORD is good; his love **e** forever. NDT
La 5:19 your throne **e** from generation to generation. NDT
Da 4: 3 his dominion **e** from generation to NDT
Da 4:34 his kingdom **e** from generation to NDT
Da 6:26 he is the living God and he **e** forever; A10629
Da 9:15 made for yourself a name that **e** to this day, NDT
Jn 6:27 for food that **e** to eternal life, which *G3531*
2Co 9: 9 to the poor; their righteousness **e** forever." *G3531*
1Pe 1:25 the word of the Lord **e** forever." And *G3531*

ENDURING (7) [ENDURE]

1Ki 11:38 you a dynasty as **e** as the one I built for H586
Ps 19: 9 of the LORD is pure, **e** forever. The decrees H6641
Pr 8:18 riches and honor, **e** wealth and prosperity. H6982
Jer 5:15 an ancient and **e** nation, a people H419
2Th 1: 4 in all the persecutions and trials *you are* **e**. *G462*
Heb 13:14 For here we do not have an **e** city, but we *G3531*
1Pe 1:23 through the living and **e** word of God. *G3531*

ENEMIES (278) [ENEMY]

Ge 14:20 who delivered your **e** into your hand." H7640
Ge 22:17 will take possession of the cities of their **e**, H367
Ge 24:60 your offspring possess the cities of their **e**." H8533
Ge 49: 8 your hand will be on the neck of your **e** H367
Ex 1:10 will join our **e**, fight against us and H8533
Ex 15:12 and the earth swallows **your e**. H4564S
Ex 23:22 be an enemy to your **e** and will oppose H367
Ex 23:27 I will make all your **e** turn their backs and H367
Ex 32:25 so become a laughingstock to their **e**. H7756
Lev 26: 7 You will pursue your **e**, and they will fall by H367
Lev 26: 8 your **e** will fall by the sword before you. H367
Lev 26:16 seed in vain, because your **e** will eat it. H367
Lev 26:17 you so that you will be defeated by your **e**; H367
Lev 26:32 so that your **e** who live there will be H367
Lev 26:34 you are in the country of your **e**; H367
Lev 26:36 in the lands of their **e** that the sound of a H367
Lev 26:37 you will not be able to stand before your **e**. H367
Lev 26:38 nations; the land of your **e** will devour you. H367
Lev 26:39 in the lands of their **e** because of their sins; H367
Lev 26:41 that I sent them into the land of their **e**— H367
Lev 26:44 when they are in the land of their **e**, I will H367
Nu 10: 9 the LORD your God and rescued from your **e**. H367
Nu 10:35 May your **e** be scattered; may your foes flee H367
Nu 14:42 You will be defeated by your **e**, H367
Nu 23:11 I brought you to curse my **e**, but you have H367
Nu 24:10 "I summoned you to curse my **e**, but you H367
Nu 25:17 "**Treat** the Midianites **as e** and kill them. H7675
Nu 25:18 They **treated** you **as e** when they deceived H7675
Nu 32:21 he has driven his **e** out before him— H367
Dt 1:42 You will be defeated by your **e**.'" H367
Dt 6:19 thrusting out all your **e** before you, as the H367
Dt 12:10 rest from all your **e** around you so that you H367
Dt 20: 1 to war against your **e** and see horses and H367
Dt 20: 3 you are going into battle against your **e**. H367
Dt 20: 4 you against your **e** to give you victory." H367
Dt 20:14 the LORD your God gives you from your **e**. H367
Dt 21:10 to war against your **e** and the LORD your H367
Dt 23: 9 When you are encamped against your **e** H367
Dt 23:14 to protect you and to deliver your **e** to you. H367
Dt 25:19 you rest from all the **e** around you in the H367
Dt 28: 7 will grant that the **e** who rise up against H367
Dt 28:25 cause you to be defeated before your **e**. H367
Dt 28:31 Your sheep will be given to your **e**, and no H367
Dt 28:48 you will serve the **e** the LORD sends against H367
Dt 28:68 sale to your **e** as male and female H367
Dt 30: 7 these curses on your **e** who hate and H367
Dt 32:31 is not like our Rock, as even our **e** concede. H367
Dt 32:43 vengeance on his **e** and make atonement H7640
Dt 33:27 He will drive out your **e** before you, saying H367
Dt 33:29 Your **e** will cower before you, and you will H367
Jos 5:13 asked, "Are you for us or for our **e**? H7640
Jos 7: 8 now that Israel has been routed by its **e**? H367
Jos 7:12 the Israelites cannot stand against their **e**; H367
Jos 7:13 stand against your **e** until you remove them H367
Jos 10:13 till the nation avenged itself on its **e**, as it H367
Jos 10:19 pursue your **e**! Attack them from the H367
Jos 10:25 will do to all the **e** you are going to fight." H367
Jos 21:44 Not one of their **e** withstood them; the LORD H367
Jos 21:44 the LORD gave all their **e** into their hands. H367
Jos 22: 8 the plunder from your **e** with your fellow H367
Jos 23: 1 Israel rest from all their **e** around them, H367
Jdg 2:14 them into the hands of their **e** all around, H367
Jdg 2:18 of the hands of their **e** as long as the judge H367
Jdg 5:31 "So may all your **e** perish, LORD! But may all H367
Jdg 8:34 from the hands of all their **e** on every side. H367
Jdg 11:36 that the LORD has avenged you of your **e**, H367
1Sa 2: 1 My mouth boasts over my **e**, for I delight in H367
1Sa 4: 3 with us and save us from the hand of our **e**." H367
1Sa 12:10 But now deliver us from the hands of our **e** H367
1Sa 12:11 from the hands of your **e** all around you, H367
1Sa 14:24 before I have avenged myself on my **e**!" H367
1Sa 14:30 some of the plunder they took from their **e**. H367
1Sa 14:47 he fought against their **e** on every side: H367
1Sa 18:25 foreskins, to take revenge on his **e**. H367
1Sa 20:15 every one of David's **e** from the face of the H367
1Sa 20:16 "May the LORD call David's **e** to account." H367
1Sa 25:26 may your **e** and all who are intent on H367
1Sa 25:29 the lives of your **e** he will hurl away as H367
1Sa 29: 8 fight against the **e** *of* my lord the king?" H367
1Sa 30:26 for you from the plunder of the LORD's **e**." H367
2Sa 3:18 Philistines and from the hand of all their **e**. H367
2Sa 5: 8 and blind' *who are* David's **e**." H8533+5883
2Sa 5:20 has broken out against my **e** before me." H367
2Sa 7: 1 given him rest from all his **e** around him, H367
2Sa 7: 9 I have cut off all your **e** from before you. H367
2Sa 7:11 I will also give you rest from all your **e**. H367
2Sa 18:19 by delivering him from the hand of his **e**." H367
2Sa 18:32 "May the **e** *of* my lord the king and all who H367
2Sa 19: 9 king delivered us from the hand of our **e**; H367

2Sa 22: 1 the hand of all his e and from the hand of H367
2Sa 22: 4 of praise, and have been saved from my e. H367
2Sa 22:38 "I pursued my e and crushed them; I did H367
2Sa 22:41 You made my e turn their backs in flight H367
2Sa 22:49 who sets me free from my e. You exalted H367
2Sa 24:13 of fleeing from your e while they pursue H7640
1Ki 3:11 the death of your e but for discernment H367
1Ki 5: 3 until the LORD put **his** e under his feet. H4392S
1Ki 8:44 your people go to war against their e, H367
1Ki 8:46 with them and give them over to their e, H367
1Ki 8:48 in the land of their e who took them H367
2Ki 17:39 will deliver you from the hand of all your e." H367
2Ki 21:14 give them into the hands of e. H367
2Ki 21:14 will be looted and plundered by all their e; H367
1Ch 12:17 to betray me to my e when my hands are H7640
1Ch 14:11 has broken out against my e by my hand." H367
1Ch 17: 8 I have cut off all your e from before you. H367
1Ch 17:10 I will also subdue all your e. H367
1Ch 21:12 of being swept away before your e, H7640
1Ch 22: 9 give him rest from all his e on every side. H367
2Ch 1:11 for the death of your e, and since you H8533
2Ch 6:28 when e besiege them in any of their H367
2Ch 6:34 your people go to war against their e, H367
2Ch 20:27 given them cause to rejoice over their e. H367
2Ch 20:29 the LORD had fought against the e *of* Israel. H367
2Ch 26:13 force to support the king against his e. H367
Ezr 4: 1 When the e *of* Judah and Benjamin H7640
Ezr 8:22 horsemen to protect us from e on the road, H367
Ezr 8:31 he protected us from e and bandits along H367
Ne 4:11 Also our e said, "Before they know it or H7640
Ne 4:15 When our e heard that we were aware of H367
Ne 5: 9 God to avoid the reproach of our Gentile e? H367
Ne 6: 1 the rest of our e that I had rebuilt the H367
Ne 6:16 When all our e heard about this, all the H367
Ne 9:27 delivered them into the hands of their e, H7640
Ne 9:27 rescued them from the hand of their e. H7640
Ne 9:28 to the hand of their e so that they ruled H367
Est 8:11 to plunder the property of **their** e. H4392S
Est 8:13 that day to avenge themselves on their e. H367
Est 9: 1 On this day the e *of* the Jews had hoped to H367
Est 9: 5 Jews struck down all their e with the sword, H367
Est 9:16 themselves and get relief from their e. H367
Est 9:22 time when the Jews got relief from their e, H367
Job 8:22 Your e will be clothed in shame, and the H8533
Job 19:11 against me; he counts me among his e. H7640
Ps 3: 7 Strike all my e on the jaw; break the teeth H367
Ps 5: 8 in your righteousness because of my e H8806
Ps 6:10 All my e will be overwhelmed with shame H367
Ps 7: 6 rise up against the rage of my e. H7675
Ps 8: 2 established a stronghold against your e, H7675
Ps 9: 3 My e turn back; they stumble and perish H367
Ps 9: 6 Endless ruin has overtaken my e, you have H367
Ps 9:13 see how my e persecute me! Have H8533
Ps 10: 5 are rejected by him; he sneers at all his e. H7675
Ps 17: 9 from my mortal e who surround me. H367
Ps 18: T the hand of all his e and from the hand of H367
Ps 18: 3 and I have been saved from my e. H367
Ps 18:37 I pursued my e and overtook them; I did H367
Ps 18:40 You made my e turn their backs in flight H367
Ps 18:48 who saves me from my e. You exalted me H367
Ps 21: 8 Your hand will lay hold on all your e; your H367
Ps 23: 5 table before me in the presence of my e. H7675
Ps 25: 2 to shame, nor let my e triumph over me. H367
Ps 25:19 how numerous are my e and how fiercely H367
Ps 27: 2 it is my e and my foes who will stumble H7640
Ps 27: 6 be exalted above the e who surround me; H367
Ps 30: 1 depths and did not let my e gloat over me. H367
Ps 31:11 Because of all my e, I am the utter H7675
Ps 31:15 deliver me from the hands of my e, from H367
Ps 35:19 gloat over me *who* are my e without cause; H367
Ps 37:20 Though the LORD's e are like the flowers of H367
Ps 38:19 Many have become my e without cause H367
Ps 41: 5 My e say of me in malice, "When will he H367
Ps 41: 7 All my e whisper together against me H8533
Ps 44: 5 Through you we push back our e; through H7640
Ps 44: 7 you give us victory over our e, you put H7640
Ps 45: 5 arrows pierce the hearts of the king's e; H367
Ps 55:15 Let death take **my** e by surprise; let them H4564S
Ps 56: 1 my God, for my e are in hot pursuit; all H632S
Ps 56: 9 Then my e will turn back when I call for H367
Ps 59: 1 Deliver me from my e, O God; be my H367
Ps 60:12 and he will trample down our e. H7640
Ps 66: 3 is your power that your e cringe before you. H367
Ps 68: 1 God arise, may his e be scattered; may his H367
Ps 68:21 Surely God will crush the heads of his e H367
Ps 69: 4 many are my e without cause, those H367
Ps 69:19 shamed; all my e are before you. H7675
Ps 71:10 For my e speak against me; those who wait H367
Ps 72: 9 bow before him and his e lick the dust. H367
Ps 74:23 the uproar of your e, which rises H7756
Ps 78:53 unafraid; but the sea engulfed their e. H367
Ps 78:66 He beat back his e; he put them to H7640
Ps 80: 6 to our neighbors, and our e mock us. H367
Ps 81:14 I would subdue their e and turn my hand H367
Ps 83: 2 See how your e growl, how your foes rear H367
Ps 86:17 that my e may see it and be put to shame, H8533
Ps 89:10 with your strong arm you scattered your e. H367
Ps 89:42 his foes; you have made all his e rejoice. H367
Ps 89:51 the taunts with which your e, LORD, have H367
Ps 92: 9 For surely your e, LORD, surely your enemies H367
Ps 92: 9 surely your e will perish; all evildoers H367
Ps 102: 8 All day long my e taunt me; those who rail H367
Ps 106:42 Their e oppressed them and subjected H367
Ps 108:13 and he will trample down our e. H7640
Ps 110: 1 I make your e a footstool for your H367
Ps 110: 2 saying, "Rule in the midst of your e!" H367
Ps 118: 7 he is my helper. I look in triumph on my e. H8533
Ps 119:98 with me and make me wiser than my e. H367
Ps 119:139 wears me out, for my e ignore your words. H7640
Ps 132:18 I will clothe his e with shame, but his head H367
Ps 136:24 freed us from our e. His love endures H7640
Ps 139:22 hatred for them; I count them my e. H367
Ps 143: 9 Rescue me from my e, LORD, for I hide H367
Ps 143:12 silence my e; destroy all my foes, H367
Pr 16: 7 he causes their e to make peace with them. H367
Pr 26:24 E disguise themselves with their lips, but H8533
Pr 29:24 accomplices of thieves are their own e; H8533
Isa 1:24 on my foes and avenge myself on my e. H367
Isa 9:11 against them and has spurred their e on. H367
Isa 11:13 and Judah's e will be destroyed H7675
Isa 26:11 the fire reserved for your e consume them. H7640
Isa 29: 5 But your many e will become like fine H2424
Isa 41:12 Though you search for your e, you H408+5194
Isa 42:13 the battle cry and will triumph over his e. H367
Isa 59:18 he repay wrath to his e and retribution to H7640
Isa 62: 8 will I give your grain as food for your e, H367
Isa 63:18 now our e have trampled down your H7640
Isa 64: 2 name known to your e and cause the H7640
Isa 66: 6 of the LORD repaying his e all they deserve. H367
Jer 12: 7 give the one I love into the hands of her e. H367
Jer 15: 9 the survivors to the sword before their e," H367
Jer 15:11 I will make your e plead with you in times H367
Jer 15:14 enslave you to your e in a land you do not H367
Jer 17: 4 enslave you to your e in a land you do not H367
Jer 18:17 I will scatter them before their e; I will H367
Jer 19: 7 make them fall by the sword before their e, H367
Jer 19: 9 flesh because their e will press the siege H367
Jer 20: 4 will see them fall by the sword of their e. H367
Jer 20: 5 of this city into the hands of their e— H367
Jer 21: 7 Babylon and to their e who want to kill H367
Jer 30:16 be devoured; all your e will go into exile. H7640
Jer 34:20 the hands of their e who want to kill them. H367
Jer 34:21 the hands of their e who want to kill them, H367
Jer 44:30 the hands of his e who want to kill him, H367
Jer 50: 7 devoured them; their e said, 'We are not H7640
Jer 51:55 Waves of e will rage like great waters H2157S
La 1: 2 betrayed her; they have become her e. H367
La 1: 5 become her masters; her e are at ease. H367
La 1: 7 Her e looked at her and laughed at her H7640
La 1:21 All my e have heard of my distress; they H367
La 2:16 All your e open their mouths wide against H367
La 3:46 "All our e have opened their mouths wide H367
La 3:52 *Those who* were my e without cause H367
La 3:62 what my e whisper and mutter against me H7756
La 4:12 that e and foes could enter the gates of H367
Eze 16:27 I gave you over to the greed of your e, the H8533
Eze 39:23 them and handed them over to their e, H7640
Eze 39:27 them from the countries of their e, H367
Da 4:19 applied to your e and its meaning to A10686
Am 9: 4 Though they are driven into exile by their e, H367
Mic 4:10 will redeem you out of the hand of your e. H367
Mic 5: 9 will be lifted up in triumph over your e, H7640
Mic 7: 6 a man's e are the members of his own H367
Na 1: 2 his foes and vents his wrath against his e. H367
Na 3:13 gates of your land are wide open to your e; H367
Zec 8:10 their business safely because of their e, H7640
Mt 5:44 love your e and pray for those who *G2398*
Mt 10:36 a man's e will be the members of his own *G2398*
Mt 22:44 hand until I put your e under your feet." *G2398*
Mk 12:36 hand until I put your e under your feet." *G2398*
Lk 1:71 salvation from our e and from the hand of *G2398*
Lk 1:74 to rescue us from the hand *of* our e, and *G2398*
Lk 6:27 Love your e, do good to those who hate *G2398*
Lk 6:35 But love your e, do good to them, and *G2398*
Lk 19:27 But those e of mine who did not want me *G2398*
Lk 19:43 come upon you when your e will build an *G2398*
Lk 20:43 until I make your e a footstool for your *G2398*
Lk 23:12 before this they had been e. *G1877+2397*
Ac 2:35 until I make your e a footstool for your *G2398*
Ro 5:10 while we were God's e, we were *G2398*
Ro 11:28 concerned, they are e for your sake; but as *G2398*
1Co 15:25 until he has put all his e under his feet. *G2398*
Php 3:18 many live *as* e of the cross of Christ. *G2398*
Col 1:21 from God and were e in your minds *G2398*
Heb 1:13 until I make your e a footstool for your *G2398*
Heb 10:13 time he waits for his e to be made his *G2398*
Heb 10:27 fire that will consume the e of God. *G5641*
Rev 11: 5 from their mouths and devours their e. *G2398*
Rev 11:12 in a cloud, while their e looked on. *G2398*

ENEMY (110) [ENEMIES, ENEMY'S, ENMITY]

Ex 15: 6 Your right hand, LORD, shattered the e. H367
Ex 15: 9 The e boasted, 'I will pursue, I will H367
Ex 23:22 *I will be an e to* your enemies and will H366
Lev 26:25 and you will be given into e hands. H367
Nu 10: 9 own land against an e who is oppressing H7640
Nu 24:18 conquered; Seir, his e, will be conquered H367
Nu 35:23 person was not an e and no harm was H367
Dt 28:53 of the suffering your e will inflict on you H367
Dt 28:55 of the suffering your e will inflict on you H367
Dt 28:57 of the suffering your e will inflict on you H367
Dt 32:27 I dreaded the taunt of the e, lest the H367
Dt 32:42 the captives, the heads of the e leaders." H367
Jdg 3:28 has given Moab, your e, into your hands." H367
Jdg 16:23 delivered Samson, our e, into our hands." H367
Jdg 16:24 god has delivered our e into our hands, H367
1Sa 18:29 he remained his e the rest of his days. H367
1Sa 19:17 like this and send my e away so that he H367
1Sa 24: 4 'I will give your e into your hands for you to H367
1Sa 24:19 When a man finds his e, does he let him H367
1Sa 26: 8 God has delivered your e into your hands. H367
1Sa 28:16 departed from you and become your e? H6839
2Sa 4: 8 son of Saul, your e, who tried to kill you. H367
2Sa 22:15 He shot his arrows and scattered **the e** H4392S
2Sa 22:18 He rescued me from my powerful e, from H367
1Ki 8:33 been defeated by an e because they have H367
1Ki 8:37 when an e besieges them in any of their H367
1Ki 21:20 to Elijah, "So you have found me, my e!" H367
2Ki 6:18 As the e came down toward him, Elisha NDT
2Ch 6:24 been defeated by an e because they have H367
2Ch 6:36 with them and give them over to the e, H367
2Ch 25: 8 God will overthrow you before the e, for H367
Est 3:10 the Agagite, the e *of* the Jews. H7675
Est 7: 6 "An adversary and e! This vile Haman!" H367
Est 8: 1 the estate of Haman, the e *of* the Jews. H7675
Est 9:10 son of Hammedatha, the e *of* the Jews. H7675
Est 9:24 the Agagite, the e *of* all the Jews, had H7675
Job 6:23 deliver me from the hand of the e, rescue H7640
Job 13:24 you hide your face and consider me your e? H367
Job 27: 7 "May my e be like the wicked, my adversary H367
Job 33:10 found fault with me; he considers me his e. H367
Ps 7: 5 then let my e pursue and overtake me; let H367
Ps 13: 2 How long will my e triumph over me? H367
Ps 13: 4 my e will say, "I have overcome him," H367
Ps 18:14 He shot his arrows and scattered **the e** H4392
Ps 18:17 He rescued me from my powerful e, from H367
Ps 31: 8 the hands of the e but have set my feet H367
Ps 41:11 for my e does not triumph over me. H367
Ps 42: 9 I go about mourning, oppressed by the e?" H367
Ps 43: 2 I go about mourning, oppressed by the e? H367
Ps 44:10 You made us retreat before the e, and our H7640
Ps 44:16 because of the e, who is bent on H367
Ps 55: 3 because of what my e is saying, because of H367
Ps 55:12 If an e were insulting me, I could endure it H367
Ps 60:11 Give us aid against the e, for human help H7640
Ps 64: 1 protect my life from the threat of the e. H367
Ps 74: 3 this destruction the e has brought on the H367
Ps 74:10 How long will the e mock you, God? Will H7640
Ps 74:18 Remember how the e has mocked you H367
Ps 78:61 his splendor into the hands of the e. H7640
Ps 89:22 The e will not get the better of him; the H367
Ps 106:10 from the hand of the e he redeemed them. H367
Ps 108:12 Give us aid against the e, for human help H7640
Ps 109: 6 Appoint someone evil to oppose my e H2257S
Ps 143: 3 The e pursues me, he crushes me to the H367
Ps 144: 6 Send forth lightning and scatter **the e** H4392S
Pr 24:17 Do not gloat when your e falls; when they H367
Pr 25:21 If your e is hungry, give him food to eat; if H8533
Pr 27: 6 can be trusted, but an e multiplies kisses. H8533
Isa 22: 3 having fled while the e was still far away. NDT
Isa 63:10 became their e and he himself fought H367
Jer 6:25 on the roads, for the e has a sword, and H367
Jer 30:14 struck you as an e would and punished H367
Jer 31:16 "They will return from the land of the e. H367
Jer 44:30 of Babylon, the e who wanted to kill him. H367
Jer 46:22 a fleeing serpent as the e advances in force; NDT
Jer 47: 3 at the noise of e chariots and the rumble H2257S
La 1: 7 When her people fell into e hands, there H7640
La 1: 9 on my affliction, for the e has triumphed." H367
La 1:10 The e laid hands on all her treasures; she H7640
La 1:16 are destitute because the e has prevailed." H367
La 2: 3 his right hand at the approach of the e. H367
La 2: 4 Like an e he has strung his bow; his right H367
La 2: 5 The Lord is like an e; he has swallowed up H367
La 2: 7 of her palaces into the hands of the e; H367
La 2:17 he has let the e gloat over you, he has H367
La 2:22 I cared for and reared my e has destroyed." H367
Eze 36: 2 The e said of you, "Aha! The H367
Hos 8: 3 what is good; an e will pursue him. H367
Am 3:11 "An e will overrun your land, pull down H7640
Mic 2: 8 Lately my people have risen up like an e H367
Mic 7: 8 gloat over me, my e! Though I have fallen H367
Mic 7:10 Then my e will see it and will be covered H367
Na 3:11 go into hiding and seek refuge from the e. H367
Hab 2: 4 the e is puffed up; his desires are not NDT
Zep 3:15 punishment, he has turned back your e. H367
Zec 10: 5 battle trampling their e into the mud of the NDT
Zec 10: 5 they will put the e horsemen to shame. NDT
Mt 5:43 'Love your neighbor and hate your e. *G2398*
Mt 13:25 his e came and sowed weeds among the *G2398*
Mt 13:28 " 'An e did this,' he replied. *G2398+476*
Mt 13:39 the e who sows them is the devil. *G2398*
Lk 10:19 to overcome all the power *of* the e; *G2398*
Ac 13:10 of the devil and an e of everything that is *G2398*
Ro 12:20 "If your e is hungry, feed him; if he is *G2398*
1Co 15:26 The last e to be destroyed is death. *G2398*
Gal 4:16 I now become your e by telling you the *G2398*
2Th 3:15 Yet do not regard them as an e, but warn *G2398*
1Ti 5:14 homes and to give the e no opportunity *G512*
Jas 4: 4 friend of the world becomes an e of God. *G2398*
1Pe 5: 8 Your e the devil prowls around like a *G508*

ENEMY'S (3) [ENEMY]

Ex 23: 4 you come across your e ox or donkey H367
Job 31:29 have rejoiced at my e misfortune or H8533
Jer 8:16 The snorting of **the e** horses is heard H2257S

ENERGY (1)
Col 1:29 contend with *all* the e Christ so powerfully *G1918*

ENFOLDS (1) [FOLD]
Isa 25: 7 will destroy the shroud that e all peoples, H4286

ENFORCE (1) [FORCE]
Da 6: 7 issue an edict and e the decree that A10772

ENGAGE (9) [ENGAGED, ENGAGES, ENGAGING]
Ex 31: 5 in wood, and to e in all kinds of crafts. H6913
Ex 35:33 to work in wood and to e in all kinds of H6913
Dt 2:24 take possession of it and e him *in* battle. H1741
Dt 20:12 to make peace and *they* e you in battle, H6913
1Sa 7:10 Philistines drew near to e Israel in battle. NDT
2Ch 35:22 disguised himself to e him **in battle**. H4309
Jer 11:15 When you e in your wickedness, then you NDT
Da 11:40 the king of the South *will* e him **in battle**, H5590
Hos 4:10 *they will* e **in prostitution** but not flourish H2388

ENGAGED (7) [ENGAGE]
Jdg 12: 2 "I and my people *were* e **in** a great H2118
1Ki 14:24 the people e **in** all the detestable H6913
Eze 16:17 idols and e **in prostitution** with them. H2388
Eze 16:26 *You* e **in prostitution** with the Egyptians H2388
Eze 16:28 *You* e **in prostitution** with the Assyrians too H2388
Eze 23: 5 "Oholah e **in prostitution** while she was H2388
1Co 7:36 honorably toward the virgin he is e to, NDT

ENGAGES (1) [ENGAGE]
Dt 18:10 interprets omens, e **in witchcraft**, H4175

ENGAGING (3) [ENGAGE]
2Ki 16: 3 e **in** the detestable practices of the H3869
2Ch 28: 3 e **in** the detestable practices of the H3869
Eze 23: 3 in Egypt, e **in prostitution** from their youth. H2388

ENGRAFTED (KJV) PLANTED

ENGRAVE (4) [ENGRAVED, ENGRAVER, ENGRAVERS, ENGRAVES, ENGRAVING]
Ex 28: 9 onyx stones and e on them the names H7338
Ex 28:11 **E** the names of the sons of Israel *on* the H7338
Ex 28:36 of pure gold and e on it as on a H7338+7334
Zec 3: 9 one stone, and I *will* e an inscription on it H7338

ENGRAVED (10) [ENGRAVE]
Ex 28:21 each e *like* a seal with the name of one H7334
Ex 32:16 was the writing of God, e on the tablets. H3100
Ex 39: 6 and e them *like* a seal with H7338+7334
Ex 39:14 each e *like* a seal with the name of one H7334
Ex 39:30 out of pure gold and e on it, like an H4180
1Ki 7:36 *He* e cherubim, lions and palm trees on H7338
Job 19:24 an iron tool on lead, or e in rock forever! H2933
Isa 49:16 *I have* e you on the palms of my hands H2980
Jer 17: 1 "Judah's sin *is* e with an iron tool H4180
2Co 3: 7 death, *which was* e in letters on stone *G1963*

ENGRAVER (1) [ENGRAVE]
Ex 38:23 the tribe of Dan—an e and designer, and H3093

ENGRAVERS (1) [ENGRAVE]
Ex 35:35 with skill to do all kinds of work as e, H3093

ENGRAVES (1) [ENGRAVE]
Ex 28:11 two stones the way a gem cutter e a seal. H7334

ENGRAVING (3) [ENGRAVE]
1Ki 7:31 Around its opening there was e. H5237
2Ch 2: 7 and experienced in the **art of** e, to H7338+7334
2Ch 2:14 He *is* **experienced** in all kinds of e H7334+7338

ENGROSSED (1)
1Co 7:31 things of the world, as if not e **in** them. *G2974*

ENGULF (4) [ENGULFED, ENGULFING]
Ps 69: 2 into the deep waters; the floods e me. H8851
Ps 69:15 *Do* not *let* the floodwaters e me or the H8851
Ps 140: 9 *may* the mischief of their lips e them. H4059
Hos 7: 2 Their sins e them; they are always before H6015

ENGULFED (3) [ENGULF]
Ps 78:53 unafraid; but the sea e their enemies. H4059
Ps 88:17 like a flood; *they have* completely e me. H5938
Ps 124: 4 the flood *would have* e us, the torrent H8851

ENGULFING (1) [ENGULF]
Jnh 2: 5 The e waters threatened me, the deep H705

ENHANCES (1)
Ro 3: 7 "If my falsehood e God's truthfulness and *G4355*

ENJOIN, ENJOINED (KJV) COMMANDED, DECREED, PRESCRIBED, ORDER

ENJOY (43) [JOY]
Ge 45:18 land of Egypt and *you can* e the fat of the H430
Ex 30:38 like it to e its **fragrance** must be cut off H8193
Lev 26:34 Then the land *will* e its sabbath years all H8354
Lev 26:34 then the land will rest and e its sabbaths. H8354
Lev 26:43 by them and *will* e its sabbaths while H8354
Nu 14:31 I will bring them in *to* e the land you have H3359
Dt 6: 2 and so that you *may* e **long life**. H799+3427
Dt 20: 6 planted a vineyard and not *begun to* e it? H2725
Dt 20: 6 may die in battle and someone else e it. H2725
Dt 28:30 but *you will* not *even begin to* e its fruit. H2725
Jdg 19: 6 "Please stay tonight and e yourself." H3512
Jdg 19: 9 Stay and e yourself. Early H3512
Ne 8:10 "Go and e choice food and sweet drinks H430
Est 5:14 the king to the banquet and e yourself." H8524
Job 3:18 Captives also e *their* **ease**; they no longer H8631
Job 20:17 *He will* not e the streams, the rivers H8011
Job 20:18 *he will* not e the profit from his trading. H6632
Job 33:28 and I shall live *to* e the light of life. H8011
Ps 37: 3 dwell in the land and e safe **pasture**. H8286
Ps 37:11 the land and e peace and prosperity H6695
Ps 37:19 in days of famine *they will* e **plenty**. H8425
Ps 39:13 that *I may* e **life** *again* before I depart H1158
Ps 106: 5 that I *may* e the prosperity of your chosen H8011
Pr 7:18 till morning; *let's* e **ourselves** with love! H6632
Pr 13: 2 the fruit of their lips people e good things, H430
Pr 28:16 ill-gotten gain *will* e **a long reign**. H799+3427
Ecc 3:22 better for a person than *to* e their work, H8523
Ecc 5:19 the ability to e them, to accept their lot H430
Ecc 6: 2 does not grant them the ability to e them, H430
Ecc 6: 2 enjoy them, and strangers e them instead. H430
Ecc 6: 3 if he cannot e his prosperity and does not H8425
Ecc 6: 6 twice over but fails *to* e his prosperity. H8011
Ecc 9: 9 **E** life with your wife, whom you love, all H8011
Ecc 11: 8 anyone may live, *let them* e them all. H8523
Isa 3:10 for *they will* e the fruit of their deeds. H430
Isa 65:22 my chosen ones *will* **long** e the work of H1162
Jer 31: 5 farmers will plant them and e their fruit. H2725
Jer 33: 6 my people and *will* **let** them e abundant H1655
Jn 5:35 and you chose for a time *to* e his light. *G22*
Ro 16:23 **hospitality** I and the whole church here e, *G3828*
Eph 6: 3 you and that *you may* e long life on the *G1639*
Heb 11:25 of God rather than *to* e the fleeting *G2400*
3Jn 2 I pray *that* you *may* e **good health** and *G5617*

ENJOYABLE (1) [JOY]
2Sa 19:35 between what is e and what is not? H3202

ENJOYED (8) [JOY]
1Ch 29:28 having e **long life**, wealth and H8428+3427
2Ch 36:21 The land e its sabbath rests; all the time H8354
Job 21:25 never *having* e anything good. H430
Ps 55:14 with whom *I once* e **sweet** fellowship at H5517
Ac 7:46 who e God's favor and asked that he *G2351*
Ac 9:31 Samaria e a time of peace and *G2400*
Ac 24: 2 "*We have* e a long period of peace under *G5593*
Ro 15:24 after *I have* e your **company** for a while. *G1855*

ENJOYING (3) [JOY]
Jdg 19:22 *While* they *were* e themselves, some of H3512
Ne 9:35 e your great goodness to them in the NDT
Ac 2:47 praising God and e the favor of all the *G2400*

ENJOYMENT (4) [JOY]
Ecc 2:25 without him, who can eat or **find** e? H2591
Ecc 4: 8 "and why am I depriving myself of e?" H3208
Ecc 8:15 So I commend the e of life, because there H8525
1Ti 6:17 richly provides us with everything for our e. *G656*

ENJOYS (1) [JOY]
Hab 1:16 he lives in luxury and e the choicest food. NDT

ENLARGE (4) [LARGE]
Ex 34:24 nations before you and e your territory, H8143
1Ch 4:10 you would bless me and e my territory! H8049
Isa 54: 2 "**E** the place of your tent, stretch your tent H8143
2Co 9:10 store of seed and *will* e the harvest of your *G889*

ENLARGED (5) [LARGE]
Dt 12:20 the LORD your God *has* e your territory as H8143
Isa 9: 3 *You have* e the nation and increased their H8049
Isa 26:15 *You have* e the nation, LORD; you have H3578
Isa 26:15 the nation, LORD; *you have* e the nation. H3578
Jer 20:17 mother as my grave, her womb e forever. H2226

ENLARGES (3) [LARGE]
Dt 19: 8 If the LORD your God e your territory, as he H8143
Dt 33:20 "Blessed is *he who* e Gad's domain H8143
Job 12:23 destroys them; *he* e nations, and H8848

ENLIGHTEN (1) [LIGHT]
Isa 40:14 Whom did the LORD consult *to* e him, and H1067

ENLIGHTENED (2) [LIGHT]
Eph 1:18 *that* the eyes of your heart *may be* e in *G5894*
Heb 6: 4 *for* those *who have* once *been* e, *G5894*

ENMITY (4) [ENEMY]
Ge 3:15 And I will put e between you and the H368
Nu 35:21 if out of e one person hits another with H368
Nu 35:22 " 'But if without e someone suddenly H368
Jas 4: 4 with the world means e against God? *G2397*

ENOCH (13)
Ge 4:17 she became pregnant and gave birth to **E**. H2840
Ge 4:17 and he named it after his son **E**. H2840
Ge 4:18 To **E** was born Irad, and Irad was the H2840
Ge 5:18 162 years, he became the father of **E**. H2840
Ge 5:19 After he became the father of **E**, Jared H2840
Ge 5:21 When **E** had lived 65 years, he became H2840
Ge 5:22 **E** walked faithfully with God 300 years H2840
Ge 5:23 Altogether, **E** lived a total of 365 years. H2840
Ge 5:24 **E** walked faithfully with God; then he was H2840
1Ch 1: 3 **E**, Methuselah, Lamech, Noah. H2840
Lk 3:37 the son *of* **E**, the son of Jared, *G1970*
Heb 11: 5 By faith **E** was taken from this life, so that *G1970*
Jude 14 **E**, the seventh from Adam, prophesied *G1970*

ENORMOUS (3)
Da 2:31 a large statue—an e, dazzling statue, A10647
Da 4:10 the middle of the land. Its height was e. A10678
Rev 12: 3 an e red dragon with seven heads and *G3489*

ENOS (KJV) ENOSH

ENOSH (8)
Ge 4:26 he named him **E**. At that time people H633
Ge 5: 6 lived 105 years, he became the father of **E**. H633
Ge 5: 7 After he became the father of **E**, Seth lived H633
Ge 5: 9 When **E** had lived 90 years, he became the H633
Ge 5:10 **E** lived 815 years and had other sons and H633
Ge 5:11 Altogether, **E** lived a total of 905 years, and H633
1Ch 1: 1 Adam, Seth, **E**, H633
Lk 3:38 the son *of* **E**, the son of Seth, the son of *G1968*

ENOUGH (101)
Ge 19:20 here is a town **near** *e* to run to, and it is AIT
Ge 22: 3 When he had cut *e* **wood** *for* the burnt AIT
Ge 24:19 camels too, until *they have* **had** e to drink." H3983
Ge 24:20 more water, and drew *e* **for** all his camels. AIT
Ge 30:15 "**Wasn't** it e *that* you took away my H5071
Ge 47:22 Pharaoh and **had food** e *from* the H430
Ex 9:28 for we have had e thunder and hail. H8041
Ex 16: 4 go out each day and gather e for that day. H1821
Ex 23:30 until *you have* **increased** *e* to take possession AIT
Ex 36: 5 bringing more than e *for* doing the work H1896
Ex 36: 7 had was more than e to do all the work. H1896
Lev 25:21 that the land will yield e for three years. H9311
Nu 11:22 *Would* they **have** e if flocks and herds H5162
Nu 11:22 *Would* they **have** e if all the fish in the H5162
Nu 16: 9 **Isn't** it e for you that the God of Israel has H5071
Nu 16:13 **Isn't** it e that you have brought us up out H5071
Nu 20:12 did not trust in me e to honor me as holy in NDT
Nu 35:23 on them a stone **heavy** e to kill them, H8898
Dt 1: 6 "You have stayed **long** e at this mountain. H8041
Dt 2: 3 your way around this hill country **long** e; H8041
Dt 2: 5 their land, not **even** e to put your foot on. H6330
Dt 3:26 "That is e," the LORD said. H8041
Dt 9: 8 wrath so that he *was* **angry** e to destroy you. AIT
Dt 9:19 for *he was* **angry** *e* with you to destroy you. AIT
Dt 9:20 the LORD was angry e with Aaron to H4394
Dt 19:15 One witness *is* not *e to* **convict** anyone AIT
Jos 17:16 "The hill country *is* not e for us, and all H5162
Jos 22:17 Was **not** the sin of Peor e for us? Up to this H5071
Jdg 21:14 But there were not e for all of them. H4027
Ru 2:18 she had left over after she *had* **eaten** e. H8427
1Sa 15:16 "**E**!" Samuel said to Saul. "Let me tell you H8332
2Sa 7:19 as if this *were* **not** e in your sight H6388+7781
2Sa 24:16 angel who was afflicting the people, "**E**! H8041
1Ki 18:32 trench around it **large** e to hold two seahs H3869
1Ki 19: 4 "I have had e, LORD," he said. "Take H8041
1Ki 20:10 if e dust *remains* in Samaria to give each H8563
1Ch 17:17 And as if this *were* **not** e in your sight, my H7781
1Ch 21:15 angel who was destroying the people, "**E**! H8041
2Ch 13: 7 indecisive and not **strong** *e* to resist them. AIT
2Ch 22: 9 house of Ahaziah **powerful** *e* to retain the AIT
2Ch 30: 3 because not e priests had H4200+4537+1896
2Ch 31:10 we *have* **had** e to eat and plenty to spare H8425
Ezr 9:14 you not be angry e with us to destroy us, H6330
Ne 2:14 there was not e room for my mount to NDT
Job 15:11 Are God's consolations **not** e for you H5071
Job 19:22 *Will you* never **get** e of my flesh? H8425
Job 27:14 his offspring *will* never **have** e to eat. H8425
Job 41:10 No *one* is **fierce** *e* to rouse it. Who then is AIT
Ps 49: 8 a life is costly, **no** payment is ever e— H2532
Pr 25:16 find honey, eat **just** e—too much of it, H1896
Pr 30:15 are never satisfied, four that never say, '**E**! H2104
Pr 30:16 with water, and fire, which never says, '**E**! H2104
Ecc 1: 8 The eye never **has** e *of* seeing, nor the H8425
Ecc 5:10 Whoever loves money never **has** e H8425
Isa 1:11 "*I* **have more than** e *of* burnt offerings, of H8425
Isa 7:13 Is it **not** e to try the patience of humans H5071
Isa 7:15 honey when he **knows** *e* to reject the AIT
Isa 7:16 before the boy **knows** *e* to reject the wrong AIT
Isa 40:16 nor its animals e *for* burnt offerings. H1896
Isa 56:11 with mighty appetites; they never have e. H8429
Jer 9:12 Who is **wise** *e* to understand this? Who has AIT
La 5: 6 to Egypt and Assyria to **get** e bread. H8425
Eze 16: 5 with pity or **had compassion** *e* to do any of AIT
Eze 16: 8 at you and saw that you were **old** *e for* love, AIT
Eze 16:20 Was your prostitution **not** e? H5071
Eze 30:21 so that it *may become* **strong** *e* to hold a AIT
Eze 34:18 Is it **not** e for you to feed on the good H5071
Eze 34:18 Is it not e for you to drink clear water NDT
Eze 44: 6 **E** of your detestable practices, people of H8041
Eze 45: 9 You have **gone far** e, princes of H8041
Eze 47: 5 had risen and was **deep** *e* **to swim in**— AIT
Hos 4:10 "They will eat but not **have** e; they will H8425
Joel 2:19 olive oil, *e to* **satisfy** you **fully**; never again AIT
Am 4: 8 town for water but *did* not **get** e to drink, H8425
Na 2:12 The lion killed e *for* his cubs and H1896
Hag 1: 6 You eat, but never **have** e. You drink, H8425
Zec 10:10 and *there will* not be **room** e for them. H5162
Mal 3:10 that there will not be **room** e **to store** it. H1896
Mt 6:34 Each day has e trouble of its own. *G757*
Mt 10:25 It is e for students to be like their teachers *G757*

E

Mt 15:33 “Where could we get e bread in this G5537
Mt 25: 9 ‘there may not be e for both us and you. G758
Mk 5: 4 No one was strong e to subdue him. AIT
Mk 8: 4 place can anyone get e bread to feed them?” AIT
Mk 14:41 E! The hour has come. G600
Lk 14:28 to see if you have e money to complete it? AIT
Lk 16: 3 I'm not strong e to dig, and I'm ashamed to AIT
Lk 22:38 are two swords.” “That's e!” he replied. G2653
Jn 6: 7 a year's wages to buy e bread for each one G758
Jn 6:12 When they had all had e to eat, he said G1855
Jn 14: 8 show us the Father and that will be e for us.” G758
Ac 7: 5 not even e ground to set his foot on. NDT
Ac 24: 4 request that you be kind e to hear us briefly. AIT
Ac 24:25 was afraid and said, “That's e for now! G2400
1Co 6: 5 among you wise e to judge a dispute G1538
1Co 14:17 You are giving thanks well e, but no one G2822
2Co 11: 4 one you accepted, you put up with it easily e. AIT
Php 4:18 full payment and have more than e. G4355
1Th 3: 9 How can we thank God e for you in return AIT
1Pe 4: 3 For you have spent e time in the past doing G757
Rev 12: 8 But he was not strong e, and they lost their AIT

ENRAGED (8) [RAGE]

2Ki 6:11 This e the king of Aram. H6192+4213
2Ch 16:10 he was so e that he put him in prison. H2408
Est 3: 5 down or pay him honor, he was e. H4848+2779
Isa 8:21 famished, they will become e and H7911
Isa 57:17 I was e by their sinful greed; I punished H7911
Eze 16:43 days of your youth but e me with all these H8074
Mt 22: 7 The king was e. He sent his army and G3974
Rev 12:17 Then the dragon was e at the woman and G3974

ENRICH (2) [RICH]

Ps 65: 9 the land and water it; you e it abundantly. H6947
Pr 5:10 wealth and your toil e the house of another H928

ENRICHED (4) [RICH]

Isa 23: 2 of Sidon, whom the seafarers have e. H4848
Eze 27:33 your wares you e the kings of the H6947
1Co 1: 5 For in him you have been e in every way G4457
2Co 9:11 You will be e in every way so that you can G4457

ENROLL (2) [ENROLLED, ENROLLMENT]

2Sa 24: 2 to Beersheba and e the fighting men, H7212
2Sa 24: 4 of the king to e the fighting men of H7212

ENROLLED (1) [ENROLL]

2Ch 31:17 e by their families in the genealogical records H3509

ENROLLMENT (1) [ENROLL]

2Ch 17:14 Their e by families was as follows: From H7213

ENSAMPLE, ENSAMPLES (KJV) EXAMPLE, EXAMPLES, MODEL

ENSLAVE (3) [SLAVE]

Jer 15:14 I will e you to your enemies in a land you H6268
Jer 17: 4 I will e you to your enemies in a land you H6268
Jer 30: 8 no longer will foreigners e them. H6268

ENSLAVED (9) [SLAVE]

Ge 15:13 that they will be e and mistreated H6268
Ne 5: 5 of our daughters have already been e, H3899
Jer 25:14 They themselves will be e by many H6268
Jer 34:11 freed and e them again. H3899+4200+6269+2256+4200+9148
Eze 34:27 from the hands of those who e them. H6268
Na 3: 4 who e nations by her prostitution and H4835
Ac 7: 6 and they will be e and mistreated. G1530
Gal 4: 9 Do you wish to be e by them all over G1526
Titus 3: 3 deceived and e by all kinds of passions G1526

ENSLAVES (1) [SLAVE]

2Co 11:20 put up with anyone who e you or exploits G2871

ENSLAVING (1) [SLAVE]

Ex 6: 5 whom the Egyptians are e, and I have H6268

ENSNARE (7) [SNARE]

Pr 5:22 The evil deeds of the wicked e them; the H4334
Ecc 7:26 will escape her, but the sinner she will e. H4334
Isa 29:21 who e the defender in court and with H7772
Eze 13:18 their heads in order to e people. H7421
Eze 13:18 Will you e the lives of my people but H7421
Eze 13:20 with which you e people like birds and H7421
Eze 13:20 set free the people that you e like birds. H7421

ENSNARED (5) [SNARE]

Dt 7:25 yourselves, or you will be e by it, for it is H3704
Dt 12:30 be careful not to be e by inquiring about H5943
Ps 9:16 the wicked are e by the work of their H3704
Pr 6: 2 you said, e by the words of your mouth. H4334
Pr 22:25 may learn their ways and get yourself e. H4613

ENSURE (1)

Ps 119:122 E your servant's well-being; do not let the H6842

ENTANGLE (1) [ENTANGLED, ENTANGLES]

Ps 35: 8 may the net they hid e them, may H4334

ENTANGLED (5) [ENTANGLE]

Ps 18: 4 The cords of death e me; the torrents of H705
Ps 116: 3 The cords of death e me, the anguish of H705
Na 1:10 They will be e among thorns and drunk H6018
2Ti 2: 4 as a soldier gets e in civilian affairs, G1861
2Pe 2:20 Jesus Christ and are again e in it and are G1861

ENTANGLES (1) [ENTANGLE]

Heb 12: 1 that hinders and the sin that so easily e. G2342

ENTER (170) [ENTERED, ENTERING, ENTERS, ENTRANCE, ENTRANCES, ENTRYWAY, REENTERED]

Ge 6:18 with you, and you will e the ark—you H995+448
Ge 12:11 As he was about to e Egypt, he said to his H995
Ge 34:15 We will e into an agreement with you on H252
Ge 49: 6 Let me not e their council, let me not H995+928
Ex 12:23 the destroyer to e your houses and H995+448
Ex 12:25 When you e the land that the LORD will H995+448
Ex 28:43 them whenever they e the tent of H995+448
Ex 30:20 Whenever they e the tent of meeting H995+448
Ex 40:35 Moses could not e the tent of meeting H995+448
Lev 14:34 “When you e the land of Canaan H995+448
Lev 16: 3 is how Aaron is to e the Most Holy H995+448
Lev 19:23 “ ‘When you e the land and plant any H995+448
Lev 21:11 He must not e a place where there is H995+6584
Lev 23:10 ‘When you e the land I am going to H995+448
Lev 25: 2 ‘When you e the land I am going to H995+448
Nu 5:22 May this water that brings a curse e H995+928
Nu 5:24 causes bitter suffering will e her. H995+928
Nu 5:27 suffering, it will e her, her abdomen H995+928
Nu 14:30 Not one of you will e the land I swore H995+448
Nu 15: 2 ‘After you e the land I am giving you H995+448
Nu 15:18 ‘When you e the land to which I am H995+448
Nu 20:24 He will not e the land I give the H995+448
Nu 34: 2 ‘When you e Canaan, the land that H995+448
Dt 1:37 also and said, “You shall not e it, either. H995
Dt 1:38 your assistant, Joshua son of Nun, will e it. H995
Dt 1:39 know good from bad—they will e the land. H995
Dt 4:21 the Jordan and e the good land the H995+448
Dt 8: 1 increase and may e and possess the H995
Dt 10:11 so that they may e and possess the land I H995
Dt 11:31 cross the Jordan to e and take possession H995
Dt 17:14 When you e the land the LORD your H995+448
Dt 18: 9 When you e the land the LORD your H995+448
Dt 23: 1 cutting may e the assembly of H995+928
Dt 23: 2 descendants may e the assembly of H995+928
Dt 23: 3 descendants may e the assembly of H995+928
Dt 23: 8 born to them may e the assembly of H995+928
Dt 23:24 If you e your neighbor's vineyard, you H995+928
Dt 23:25 If you e your neighbor's grainfield, you H995+928
Dt 27: 3 crossed over to e the land the LORD H995+448
Dt 29:12 here in order to e into a covenant with the H6296
Dt 30:18 are crossing the Jordan to e and possess. H995
Dt 32:52 you will not e the land I am giving to H995+448
Jos 2:18 when we e the land, you have H995+928
Jdg 11:18 They did not e the territory of Moab H995+928
1Sa 5: 5 Dagon nor any others who e Dagon's H995
1Sa 9:13 As soon as you e the town, you will find H995
2Sa 5: 8 lame' will not e the palace. H995+448
1Ki 22:30 “I will e the battle in disguise H995+928
2Ki 11:16 where the horses e the palace grounds, H4427
2Ki 13:20 Moabite raiders used to e the country H995+928
2Ki 19:32 “ ‘He will not e this city or shoot an H995+448
2Ki 19:33 he will return; he will not e this city H995+448
2Ch 7: 2 priests could not e the temple of the H995+448
2Ch 18:29 “I will e the battle in disguise H995+928
2Ch 23: 6 No one is to e the temple of the LORD except H995
2Ch 23: 6 they may e because they are consecrated H995
2Ch 23: 6 are to observe the LORD's command not to e. NDT
2Ch 23:19 one who was in any way unclean might e. H995
2Ch 27: 2 unlike him he did not e the temple of H995+448
2Ch 31:16 all who would e the temple of the H995+4200
Ne 9:23 you told their parents to e and possess. H995
Est 1:19 that Vashti is never again to e the presence H995
Est 4: 2 in sackcloth was allowed to e it. H995+448
Ps 45:15 they e the palace of the king. H995+928
Ps 95:11 my anger, ‘They shall never e my rest. H995+448
Ps 100: 4 E his gates with thanksgiving and his courts H995
Ps 118:19 I will e and give thanks to the LORD. H995+928
Ps 118:20 LORD through which the righteous may e. H995
Ps 132: 3 “I will not e my house or go to my H995+928
Pr 2:10 For wisdom will e your heart, and H995+928
Isa 10:28 They e Aiath; they pass through H995+6584
Isa 13: 2 beckon to them to e the gates of the H995
Isa 26: 2 the gates that the righteous nation may e, H995
Isa 26:20 e your rooms and shut the doors H995+928
Isa 35:10 They will e Zion with singing; everlasting H995
Isa 37:33 “He will not e this city or shoot an H995+448
Isa 37:34 he will return; he will not e this city,” H995+448
Isa 51:11 They will e Zion with singing; everlasting H995
Isa 52: 1 defiled will not e you again. H995+928
Isa 57: 2 Those who walk uprightly e into peace H995
Isa 59:14 stumbled in the streets, honesty cannot e. H995
Jer 3:16 It will never e their minds or be H6590+6584
Jer 7:31 command, nor did it e my mind. H6590+6584
Jer 16: 5 “Do not e a house where there is a funeral H995
Jer 16: 8 “And do not e a house where there is H995
Jer 19: 5 mention, nor did it e my mind. H6590+6584
Jer 21:13 Who can e our refuge?” H995+928
Jer 32:35 nor did it e my mind—that H6590+6584
La 1:10 she saw pagan nations e her sanctuary H995
La 1:10 had forbidden to e your assembly. H995+928
La 4:12 foes could e the gates of H995+928
Eze 7:22 They will e it and will defile it. H995+928
Eze 13: 9 nor will they e the land of Israel. H995+448
Eze 20:38 yet they will not e the land of Israel. H995+448
Eze 26:10 your gates as men e a city whose walls H4427
Eze 37: 5 I will make breath e you, and you will H995+928
Eze 42:14 Once the priests e the holy precincts, they H995
Eze 44: 2 not be opened; no one may e through it. H995
Eze 44: 3 He is to e by way of the portico of the H995
Eze 44: 9 heart and flesh is to e my sanctuary, H995+448
Eze 44:16 They alone are to e my sanctuary; they H995+448
Eze 44:17 “ ‘When they e the gates of the inner H995+448
Eze 46: 2 The prince is to e from the outside through H995
Da 1: 5 they were to e the king's service H6641+4200+7156
Da 11: 7 king of the North and e his fortress; H995+928
Joel 2: 9 like thieves they e through the windows. H995
Zec 5: 4 and it will e the house of the thief H995+448
Mt 5:20 you will certainly not e the kingdom of G1656
Mt 7:13 “E through the narrow gate. For wide is G1656
Mt 7:13 destruction, and many e through it. G1639+1656
Mt 7:21 ‘ will e the kingdom of heaven, but G1656
Mt 10: 5 among the Gentiles or e any town of the G1656
Mt 10:11 Whatever town or village you e, search G1656
Mt 10:12 As you e the home, give it your greeting. G1656
Mt 12:29 how can anyone e a strong man's house G1656
Mt 18: 3 you will never e the kingdom of heaven. G1656
Mt 18: 8 It is better for you to e life maimed or G1656
Mt 18: 9 It is better for you to e life with one eye G1656
Mt 19:17 If you want to e life, keep the G1656
Mt 19:23 someone who is rich to e the kingdom of G1656
Mt 19:24 who is rich to e the kingdom of God G1656
Mt 23:13 You yourselves do not e, nor will you let G1656
Mt 23:13 will you let those e who are trying to. G1656
Mk 1:45 could no longer e a town openly but G1656
Mk 3:27 no one can e a strong man's house G1656
Mk 6:10 Whenever you e a house, stay there until G1656
Mk 9:25 come out of him and never e him again.” G1656
Mk 9:43 It is better for you to e life maimed than G1656
Mk 9:45 It is better for you to e life crippled than to G1656
Mk 9:47 is better for you to e the kingdom of God G1656
Mk 10:15 of God like a little child will never e it.” G1656
Mk 10:23 it is for the rich to e the kingdom of God!” G1656
Mk 10:24 how hard it is to e the kingdom of God! G1656
Mk 10:25 who is rich to e the kingdom of God G1656
Mk 11: 2 and just as you e it, you will find a G1660
Mk 13:15 housetop go down or e the house to take G1656
Lk 9: 4 Whatever house you e, stay there until you G1656
Lk 10: 5 “When you e a house, first say, ‘Peace to G1656
Lk 10: 8 “When you e a town and are welcomed G1656
Lk 10:10 But when you e a town and are not G1656
Lk 13:24 “Make every effort to e through the narrow G1656
Lk 13:24 will try to e and will not be able to. G1656
Lk 18:17 of God like a little child will never e it.” G1656
Lk 18:24 it is for the rich to e the kingdom of God! G1660
Lk 18:25 who is rich to e the kingdom of God G1656
Lk 19:30 ahead of you, and as you e it, you will G1660
Lk 21:21 and let those in the country not e the city. G1656
Lk 22:10 He replied, “As you e the city, a man G1656
Lk 24:26 suffer these things and then e his glory?” G1656
Jn 3: 4 “Surely they cannot e a second time into G1656
Jn 3: 5 no one can e the kingdom of God unless G1656
Jn 10: 1 anyone who does not e the sheep pen by G1656
Jn 18:28 uncleanness they did not e the palace, G1656
Ac 3: 3 When he saw Peter and John about to e G1655
Ac 14:22 many hardships to e the kingdom of God,” G1656
Ac 16: 7 Mysia, they tried to e Bithynia, but G1650+4513
Heb 3:11 in my anger, ‘They shall never e my rest. G1656
Heb 3:18 swear that they would never e his rest G1656
Heb 3:19 So we see that they were not able to e G1656
Heb 4: 3 Now we who have believed e that rest G1656
Heb 4: 3 in my anger, ‘They shall never e my rest. G1656
Heb 4: 5 he says, “They shall never e my rest.” G1656
Heb 4: 6 it still remains for some to e that rest, G1656
Heb 4:11 make every effort to e that rest, so that no G1656
Heb 9:12 He did not e by means of the blood of goats NDT
Heb 9:24 For Christ did not e a sanctuary made with G1656
Heb 9:25 Nor did he e heaven to offer himself again NDT
Heb 10:19 have confidence to e the Most Holy Place G1658
Rev 15: 8 no one could e the temple until the G1656
Rev 21:27 Nothing impure will ever e it, nor will G1656

ENTERED (109) [ENTER]

Ge 7: 7 his sons' wives e the ark to escape H995+448
Ge 7: 9 came to Noah and e the ark, as God had NDT
Ge 7:13 the wives of his three sons, e the ark. H995+448
Ge 7:15 of life in them came to Noah and e the ark. NDT
Ge 19: 3 they did go with him and e his house. H995+448
Ge 31:33 out of Leah's tent, he e Rachel's tent. H995+928
Ge 41:46 when he e the service of H6641+4200+7156
Ex 19: 2 from Rephidim, they e the Desert of Sinai H995
Ex 24:18 Then Moses e the cloud as he H995+928+9348
Ex 33: 8 watching Moses until he e the tent. H995+2025
Ex 34:34 But whenever he e the LORD's presence to H995
Ex 40:32 whenever they e the tent of meeting H995+448
Lev 16:23 put on before he e the Most Holy H995+448
Nu 7:89 When Moses e the tent of meeting to H995+448
Nu 17: 8 next day Moses e the tent and saw H995+448
Dt 26: 1 When you have e the land the LORD H995+448
Jos 2: 1 So they went and e the house of a H995
Jos 2: 3 who came to you and e your house, H995+4200
Jos 8:19 They e the city and captured it and quickly H995
Jdg 4:18 So he e her tent, and she covered H6073+448
Jdg 18: 2 So they e the hill country of Ephraim and H995
Ru 2: 3 e a field and began to glean behind H995+928

1Sa 4:13 When the man e the town and told H995+928
1Sa 12: 8 "After Jacob e Egypt, they cried to the LORD H995+928
1Sa 14:25 The entire army e the woods, and H995+928
1Sa 16:21 to Saul and e his **service**. H6641+4200+7156
1Sa 19:16 But when the men e, there was the idol in H995
1Ki 2:30 So Benaiah e the tent of the LORD and H995+448
2Ki 6:20 After they e the city, Elisha said, "LORD H995
2Ki 7: 8 e one of the tents and ate and drank. H995+448
2Ki 7: 8 They returned and e another tent and H995+448
2Ki 9:31 As Jehu e the gate, she asked, "Have H995+928
2Ki 10:25 out and then e the inner shrine of H2143+6330
1Ch 5:17 these **were e in the genealogical records** H3509
1Ch 24:19 when they e the temple of the H995+4200
1Ch 27:24 the number *was* not e in the book of H6590
2Ch 8:11 the ark of the LORD *has* e are holy." H995+448
2Ch 15:12 *They* e into a covenant to seek the LORD, the H995
2Ch 20:28 *They* e Jerusalem **and went** to the temple H995
2Ch 26:16 e the temple of the LORD to burn H995+448
Est 6: 4 Now Haman *had just* e the outer H995+4200
Est 6: 6 When Haman e, the king asked him H995
Job 3: 6 days of the year nor *be* e in any of the H995
Job 38:22 "*Have you* e the storehouses of the H995+448
Ps 73:17 till *I* e the sanctuary of God; then I H995+448
Ps 105:23 Then Israel e Egypt; Jacob resided as a H995
Ps 109:18 as his garment; *it* e into his body like water H995
Isa 28:15 "*We have* e *into* a covenant with death H4162
Jer 9:21 our windows and *has* e our fortresses; H995+928
Jer 34:10 people who e into this covenant H995
Jer 43: 7 So *they* e Egypt in disobedience to the LORD H995
Jer 51:51 foreigners *have* e the holy places H995+6584
Eze 4:14 impure meat *has ever* e my mouth." H995+928
Eze 16: 7 grew and developed and e puberty. H995+928
Eze 16: 8 my solemn oath and e into a covenant with H995
Eze 23:39 *they* e my sanctuary and desecrated it. H995+448
Eze 37:10 and breath e them; they came to H995+928
Eze 43: 4 glory of the LORD e the temple through H995+448
Eze 44: 2 the God of Israel, *has* e through it. H995
Eze 46: 9 through the gate by which *they* e, H995+928
Da 1:19 so *they* e the king's **service**. H6641+4200+7156
Am 5:19 as though *he* e his house and rested his H995
Ob 11 wealth and foreigners e his gates and cast H995
Mt 8: 5 *When* Jesus *had* e Capernaum, *G1656*
Mt 9:23 When Jesus e the synagogue *G2262+1650*
Mt 12: 4 *He* e the house of God, and he and his *G1656*
Mt 21:10 *When* Jesus e Jerusalem, the whole city *G1656*
Mt 21:12 Jesus e the temple courts and drove out *G1656*
Mt 21:23 Jesus e the temple courts, and *G2262+1650*
Mt 24:38 in marriage, up to the day Noah e the ark; *G1656*
Mt 26:58 *He* e and sat down with the guards to see *G1656*
Mk 2: 1 *when* Jesus again e Capernaum *G1656*
Mk 2:26 *he* e the house of God and ate the *G1656*
Mk 3:20 Then Jesus e a house, and again a *G2262+1650*
Mk 7:17 After *he had* left the crowd and e the *G1656*
Mk 7:24 *He* e a house and did not want anyone to *G1656*
Mk 11:11 Jesus e Jerusalem and went into the *G1656*
Mk 11:15 Jesus e the temple courts and began *G1656*
Mk 16: 5 *As they* e the tomb, they saw a young man *G1656*
Lk 1:40 where *she* e Zechariah's home and *G1656*
Lk 6: 4 *He* e the house of God, and taking the *G1656*
Lk 7: 1 who were listening, *he* e Capernaum. *G1656*
Lk 7:45 from the time *I* e, has not stopped *G1656*
Lk 9:34 they were afraid as they e the cloud. *G1656*
Lk 11:52 *You* yourselves *have* not e, and you have *G1656*
Lk 17:27 in marriage up to the day Noah e the ark. *G1656*
Lk 19: 1 Jesus e Jericho and was passing through. *G1656*
Lk 19:45 *When* Jesus e the temple courts, he *G1656*
Lk 22: 3 Then Satan e Judas, called Iscariot, one of *G1656*
Lk 24: 3 but *when they* e, they did not find the *G1656*
Jn 6:22 that Jesus *had* not e it **with** his disciples *G5291*
Jn 11:30 Now Jesus *had* not yet e the village, but *G2262*
Jn 13:27 Judas took the bread, Satan e into him. *G1656*
Jn 16:28 from the Father and e the world; *G2262+1650*
Ac 5:21 At daybreak *they* e the temple courts, as *G1656*
Ac 9:17 Then Ananias went to the house and e it *G1656*
Ac 10:25 As Peter e the house, Cornelius met him *G1656*
Ac 11: 8 impure or unclean *has* ever e my mouth. *G1656*
Ac 11:12 went with me, and *we* e the man's house. *G1656*
Ac 13:14 the Sabbath *they* e the synagogue *G2262+1650*
Ac 19: 8 Paul e the synagogue and spoke boldly *G1656*
Ac 25:23 great pomp and e the audience room *G1656*
Ro 5:12 just as sin e the world through one man *G1656*
Heb 6:20 forerunner, Jesus, *has* e on our behalf. *G1656*
Heb 9: 6 the priests e regularly into the outer room *G1655*
Heb 9: 7 But only the high priest e the inner room *G1650*
Heb 9:12 but *he* e the Most Holy Place once for all *G1656*
Heb 9:24 of the true one; he e heaven itself, now to *G1650*
Rev 11:11 days the breath of life from God e them, *G1656*

ENTERING (24) [ENTER]

Nu 32: 9 the Israelites from e the land the LORD H995+448
Dt 4: 5 in the land you *are* e to take possession H995
Dt 7: 1 you into the land you *are* e to possess and H995
Dt 11:10 The land you *are* e to take over is not like H995
Dt 11:29 you into the land you *are* e to possess, H995
Dt 23:20 hand to in the land you *are* e to possess. H995
Dt 28:21 you from the land you *are* e to possess. H995
Dt 28:63 from the land you *are* e to possess. H995
Dt 30:16 bless you in the land you *are* e to possess. H995
Dt 31:16 gods of the land they *are* e. H995+928+7931
1Sa 5:10 As the ark of God *was* e Ekron, the people H995
1Sa 9:14 and *as* they *were* e it H995+928+9348
1Sa 23: 7 himself by e a town with gates and H995+928
2Sa 6:16 the ark of the LORD *was* e the City of David, H995
2Sa 15:37 at Jerusalem as Absalom *was* e the city. H995
2Sa 17:17 could not risk being seen e the city. H995+2025
1Ki 15:17 from leaving or e the territory of Asa H995+4200
2Ki 11:19 e by way of the gate of the guards. NDT
1Ch 15:29 of the LORD was e the City of David, H995+6330
2Ch 16: 1 from leaving or e the territory of Asa H995+4200
Ezr 9:11 'The land you *are* e to possess is a land H995
Mt 21:31 *are* e the kingdom of God **ahead** of you. *G4575*
Lk 11:52 you have hindered those *who were* e." *G1656*
Heb 4: 1 since the promise *of* e his rest still stands *G1656*

ENTERS (25) [ENTER]

Ex 28:29 "Whenever Aaron e the Holy Place H995+448
Ex 28:30 heart whenever he e the presence of the H995
Ex 28:35 be heard when he e the Holy Place H995+448
Nu 19:14 Anyone who e the tent and anyone H995+448
2Ki 5:18 When my master e the temple of Rimmon H995
2Ki 12: 9 the right side as one e the temple of the H995
2Ch 23: 7 Anyone *who* e the temple is to be put H995+448
Isa 3:14 The LORD e into judgment against the H995
Eze 26:10 chariots when he e your gates as men H995+928
Eze 42: 9 east side as one e them from the H995+4200
Eze 42:12 eastward, by which *one* e the rooms. H995
Eze 44:21 drink wine when he e the inner court. H995+448
Eze 46: 8 When the prince e, he is to go in through H995
Eze 46: 9 whoever e by the north gate to worship is H995
Eze 46: 9 whoever e by the south gate is to go H995
Eze 47: 8 Arabah, where *it* e the Dead Sea. H995+2025
Mt 15:17 see that whatever e the mouth goes into *G1660*
Mk 7:18 see that nothing *that* e a person from the *G1660*
Mk 14:14 Say to the owner of the house *he* e, 'The *G1656*
Lk 22:10 Follow him to the house that *he* e, *G1660*
Jn 10: 2 The *one who* e by the gate is the *G1656*
Jn 10: 9 whoever e through me will be saved. *G1656*
Heb 4:10 anyone *who* e God's rest also rests *G1656*
Heb 6:19 *It* e the inner sanctuary behind the curtain, *G1656*
Heb 9:25 way the high priest e the Most Holy Place *G1656*

ENTERTAIN (3) [ENTERTAINMENT]

Jdg 16:25 they shouted, "Bring out Samson *to* e us." H8471
Mt 9: 4 "Why *do you* e evil **thoughts** in your *G1926*
1Ti 5:19 *Do* not e an accusation against an elder *G4138*

ENTERTAINMENT (1) [ENTERTAIN]

Da 6:18 without any e being brought to him. A10166

ENTHRALLED (1)

Ps 45:11 *Let* the king *be* e *by* your beauty; honor him H203

ENTHRONED (24) [THRONE]

1Sa 4: 4 *who is* e *between* the cherubim. H3782
2Sa 6: 2 *who is* e *between* the cherubim on the ark H3782
2Ki 19:15 God of Israel, e *between* the cherubim H3782
1Ch 13: 6 the LORD, *who is* e *between* the cherubim H3782
Ps 2: 4 The *One* e in heaven laughs; the Lord H3782
Ps 7: 7 while *you sit* e over them on high. H3782
Ps 9: 4 sitting e as the righteous judge. H4200+4058
Ps 9:11 of the LORD, e *in* Zion; proclaim among H3782
Ps 22: 3 Yet you *are* e as the Holy One; you are H3782
Ps 29:10 The LORD **sits** e over the flood; the LORD is H3782
Ps 29:10 the flood; the LORD *is* e as King forever. H3782
Ps 55:19 *who is* e *from* of old, who does not H3782
Ps 61: 7 *May he be* e in God's presence forever H3782
Ps 80: 1 You *who* **sit** e *between* the cherubim H3782
Ps 99: 1 tremble; *he* **sits** e *between* the cherubim H3782
Ps 102:12 **sit** e forever; your renown endures H3782
Ps 113: 5 LORD our God, the One who **sits** e on high, H3782
Ps 123: 1 eyes to you, to you who **sit** e in heaven. H3782
Ps 132:14 ever and ever; here *I will* **sit** e, for I have H3782
Isa 14:13 *I will* **sit** e on the mount of assembly H3782
Isa 37:16 God of Israel, e *between* the cherubim H3782
Isa 40:22 He **sits** e above the circle of the earth H3782
Isa 52: 2 off your dust; rise up, **sit** e, Jerusalem. H3782
Rev 18: 7 she boasts, '*I* **sit** e as queen. I am not *G2764*

ENTHRONES (1) [THRONE]

Job 36: 7 *he* e them with kings H3782+4200+2021+4058

ENTHUSIASM (2)

2Co 8:17 coming to you *with much* e and on his *G5080*
2Co 9: 2 your e has stirred most of them to *G2419*

ENTICE (7) [ENTICED, ENTICES, ENTICING]

1Ki 22:20 'Who *will* e Ahab *into* attacking Ramoth H7331
1Ki 22:21 before the LORD and said, 'I *will* e him. H7331
2Ch 18:19 'Who *will* e Ahab king of Israel *into* H7331
2Ch 18:20 before the LORD and said, 'I *will* e him. H7331
Pr 1:10 My son, if sinful men e you, do not give in H7331
2Pe 2:18 *they* e people who are just escaping from *G1284*
Rev 2:14 *to* e the Israelites **to sin** so *G965+4998+1967*

ENTICED (9) [ENTICE]

Nu 31:16 Balaam's advice and e the Israelites to be H5034
Dt 4:19 *do* not **be** e *into* bowing down to them H5615
Dt 11:16 you *will be* e to turn away and H7331+4222
2Ki 17:21 Jeroboam e Israel away from following H5615
Job 31: 9 "If my heart *has* **been** e by a woman, or if H7331
Job 31:27 that my heart *was* secretly e and my hand H7331
Eze 14: 9 'And if the prophet **is** e to utter a H7331
Eze 14: 9 I the LORD *have* e that prophet, and I H7331
Jas 1:14 away by their own evil desire and e. *G1284*

ENTICES (3) [ENTICE]

Dt 13: 6 your closest friend secretly e you H6077
Job 36:18 Be careful that no *one* e you by riches; do H6077
Pr 16:29 A violent person e their neighbor and H7331

ENTICING (2) [ENTICE]

1Ki 22:22 " 'You will succeed *in* e him,' said the H7331
2Ch 18:21 " 'You will succeed *in* e him,' said the H7331

ENTIRE (84) [ENTIRELY]

Ge 2:11 it winds through the e land of Havilah H3972
Ge 2:13 it winds through the e land of Cush. H3972
Ge 7:19 mountains under the e heavens were H3972
Ge 19:25 he overthrew those cities and the e plain, H3972
Ge 45: 8 lord of his e household and ruler of all H3972
Ex 14:28 the e army of Pharaoh that had followed H3972
Ex 16: 3 desert to starve this e assembly to death." H3972
Ex 16: 9 "Say to the e Israelite community H3972
Ex 29:18 Then burn the e ram on the altar. It is a H3972
Lev 3: 9 the e fat tail cut off close to the backbone H9459
Lev 8: 3 gather the e assembly at the entrance H3972
Lev 9: 5 the e assembly came near and stood H3972
Lev 19: 2 "Speak to the e assembly of Israel and say H3972
Lev 24:14 and the e assembly is to stone him. H3972
Lev 24:16 The e assembly must stone them H3972
Nu 4:16 to be in charge of the e tabernacle and H3972
Nu 5:30 the LORD and is to apply this e law to her. H3972
Nu 6: 5 " 'During the e period of their Nazirite H3972
Nu 14: 7 said to the e Israelite assembly, "The H3972
Nu 16:19 of the LORD appeared to the e assembly. H3972
Nu 16:22 be angry with the e assembly when only H3972
Nu 21:23 He mustered his e army and marched out H3972
Nu 27:19 the priest and the e assembly and H3972
Nu 27:21 command he and the e community of the H3972
Dt 2:14 that e generation of fighting men had H3972
Jos 6:23 brought out her e family and put them H3972
Jos 8:11 The e force that was with him marched up H3972
Jos 9: 1 along the e coast of the H3972
Jos 10: 7 marched up from Gilgal with his e army, H3972
Jos 11:16 So Joshua took this e land: the hill H3972
Jos 11:23 So Joshua took the e land, just as the H3972
Jos 13:21 the plateau and the e realm of Sihon king H3972
Jos 13:30 Bashan, the e realm of Og king of Bashan H3972
Jos 24:17 protected us on our e journey and among H3972
Jdg 8:12 captured them, routing their e army. H3972
1Sa 14:25 The e army entered the woods, and there H3972
2Sa 6:11 LORD blessed him and his e household. H3972
2Sa 7:17 to David all the words of this e revelation. H3972
2Sa 8: 9 had defeated the e army of Hadadezer, H3972
2Sa 10: 7 Joab out with the e army of fighting men. H3972
2Sa 12:29 David mustered the e army and went to H3972
2Sa 12:31 Then he and his e army returned to H3972
2Sa 15:16 with his e household following him H3972
2Sa 20:14 through the e *region of* the Bikrites, H3972
2Sa 20:23 Joab was over Israel's e army; Benaiah H3972
2Sa 24: 8 After they had gone through the e land H3972
1Ki 8: 5 Solomon and the e assembly of Israel H3972
1Ki 20: 1 king of Aram mustered his e army. H3972
2Ki 6:24 Aram mobilized his e army and marched H3972
2Ki 15:18 During his e reign he did not turn away H3972
2Ki 17: 5 The king of Assyria invaded the e land H3972
2Ki 17:13 accordance with the e Law that I H3972
2Ki 24:16 to Babylon the e *force of* seven thousand H3972
1Ch 4:27 so their e clan did not become as H3972
1Ch 5:10 throughout the e region east of Gilead. H3972
1Ch 17:15 to David all the words of this e revelation. H3972
1Ch 18: 9 had defeated the e army of Hadadezer H3972
1Ch 19: 8 Joab out with the e army of fighting men. H3972
1Ch 20: 3 Then David and his e army returned to H3972
2Ch 5: 6 Solomon and the e assembly of Israel H3972
2Ch 26:14 bows and slingstones for the e army. H3972
2Ch 29:18 have purified the e temple of the LORD, H3972
2Ch 30:25 The e assembly of Judah rejoiced, along H3972
2Ch 34: 9 Ephraim and the e remnant of Israel and H3972
2Ch 35:16 So at that time the e service of the LORD H3972
Ezr 4: 5 plans during the e reign of Cyrus king of H3972
Ezr 8:34 the e weight was recorded at that H3972
Job 16: 7 you have devastated my e household. H3972
Isa 39: 2 his e armory and everything found among H3972
Jer 26:17 said to the e assembly of people, H3972
Jer 36:23 until the e scroll was burned in the fire. H3972
Jer 37:10 were to defeat the e Babylonian army that H3972
Jer 42: 2 to the LORD your God for this e remnant. H3972
Jer 51:31 Babylon that his e city is captured, H4946+7895
Eze 9: 8 going to destroy the e remnant of Israel in H3972
Eze 10:12 Their e bodies, including their backs, their H3972
Eze 45: 1 cubits wide; the e area will be holy. H3972
Eze 48:20 The e portion will be a square, 25,000 H3972
Da 2:48 him ruler over the e province of Babylon A10353
Da 11:17 the might of his e kingdom and will make H3972
Lk 2: 1 should be taken of the e Roman world. *G4246*
Ac 11:28 would spread over the e Roman world. *G3910*
Ac 18: 8 his e household believed in the Lord *G3910*
Gal 5:14 For the e law is fulfilled in keeping this *G4246*

ENTIRELY (5) [ENTIRE]

Ex 28:31 the robe of the ephod e *of* blue cloth, H4003
Ex 39:22 the robe of the ephod e *of* blue cloth— H4003
Jer 30:11 *I will* not **let** you **go** e **unpunished**. H5927+5927
Jer 46:28 *I will* not **let you go** e **unpunished**." H5927+5927
2Co 8: 3 even beyond their ability. **E on their own**, *G882*

ENTRAILS (1)
Zep 1:17 poured out like dust and their **e** like dung. H4302

ENTRANCE (145) [ENTER]
Ge 18: 1 was sitting at the **e** *to* his tent in the heat H7339
Ge 18: 2 he hurried from the **e** *of* his tent to meet H7339
Ge 18:10 Sarah was listening at the **e** *to* the tent, H7339
Ge 38:14 then sat down at the **e** *to* Enaim H7339
Ge 43:19 spoke to him at the **e** *to* the house. H7339
Ex 26:36 "For the **e** *to* the tent make a curtain of H7339
Ex 27:14 cubits long are to be on one side of the **e**, NDT
Ex 27:16 "For the **e** *to* the courtyard, provide a H9133
Ex 29: 4 his sons to the **e** *to* the tent of H7339
Ex 29:11 presence at the **e** *to* the tent of meeting. H7339
Ex 29:32 At the **e** *to* the tent of meeting, Aaron H7339
Ex 29:42 regularly at the **e** *to* the tent of meeting, H7339
Ex 32:26 So he stood at the **e** *to* the camp and said H9133
Ex 33: 9 would come down and stay at the **e**, H7339
Ex 33:10 of cloud standing at the **e** *to* the tent, H7339
Ex 33:10 worshiped, each at the **e** *to* their tent. H7339
Ex 35:15 the doorway at the **e** *to* the tabernacle; H7339
Ex 35:17 the curtain for the **e** *to* the courtyard; H9133
Ex 36:37 For the **e** *to* the tent they made a curtain of H7339
Ex 38: 8 who served at the **e** *to* the tent of meeting H7339
Ex 38:14 cubits long were on one side of the **e**, NDT
Ex 38:15 on the other side of the **e** *to* the courtyard, H9133
Ex 38:18 The curtain for the **e** *to* the courtyard was H9133
Ex 38:30 the bases for the **e** *to* the tent of meeting, H7339
Ex 38:31 those for its **e** and all the tent pegs H9133
Ex 39:38 the curtain for the **e** *to* the tent; H7339
Ex 39:40 the curtain for the **e** *to* the courtyard H9133
Ex 40: 5 put the curtain at the **e** to the tabernacle. H7339
Ex 40: 6 offering in front of the **e** *to* the tabernacle, H7339
Ex 40: 8 put the curtain at the **e** *to* the courtyard. H9133
Ex 40:12 his sons to the **e** *to* the tent of H7339
Ex 40:28 up the curtain at the **e** to the tabernacle. H7339
Ex 40:29 offering near the **e** *to* the tabernacle, H7339
Ex 40:33 up the curtain at the **e** *to* the courtyard. H9133
Lev 1: 3 present it at the **e** *to* the tent of meeting H7339
Lev 1: 5 of the altar at the **e** *to* the tent of meeting H7339
Lev 3: 2 slaughter it at the **e** *to* the tent of meeting H7339
Lev 4: 4 the bull at the **e** *to* the tent of meeting H7339
Lev 4: 7 offering at the **e** *to* the tent of meeting. H7339
Lev 4:18 offering at the **e** *to* the tent of meeting. H7339
Lev 8: 3 assembly at the **e** *to* the tent of meeting." H7339
Lev 8: 4 gathered at the **e** *to* the tent of meeting. H7339
Lev 8:31 the meat at the **e** *to* the tent of meeting H7339
Lev 8:33 Do not leave the **e** *to* the tent of meeting H7339
Lev 8:35 You must stay at the **e** *to* the tent of H7339
Lev 10: 7 Do not leave the **e** *to* the tent of meeting H7339
Lev 12: 6 the priest at the **e** *to* the tent of meeting H7339
Lev 14:11 the LORD at the **e** *to* the tent of meeting. H7339
Lev 14:23 the priest at the **e** *to* the tent of meeting H7339
Lev 15:14 the LORD to the **e** *to* the tent of meeting H7339
Lev 15:29 the priest at the **e** *to* the tent of meeting H7339
Lev 16: 7 the LORD at the **e** *to* the tent of meeting. H7339
Lev 17: 4 bringing it to the **e** *to* the tent of meeting H7339
Lev 17: 5 at the **e** *to* the tent of meeting and H7339
Lev 17: 6 of the LORD at the **e** *to* the tent of meeting H7339
Lev 17: 9 not bring it to the **e** *to* the tent of meeting H7339
Lev 19:21 bring a ram to the **e** *to* the tent of H7339
Nu 3:25 the curtain at the **e** *to* the tent of meeting, H7339
Nu 3:26 the curtain at the **e** *to* the courtyard H7339
Nu 4:25 curtains for the **e** *to* the tent of meeting H7339
Nu 4:26 curtain for the **e** *to* the courtyard, H7339+9133
Nu 6:10 the priest at the **e** *to* the tent of meeting H7339
Nu 6:13 be brought to the **e** *to* the tent of meeting H7339
Nu 6:18 " 'Then at the **e** *to* the tent of meeting H7339
Nu 10: 3 before you at the **e** *to* the tent of meeting. H7339
Nu 11:10 every family wailing at the **e** *to* their tents. H7339
Nu 12: 5 he stood at the **e** *to* the tent and H7339
Nu 16:18 Aaron at the **e** *to* the tent of meeting. H7339
Nu 16:19 to them at the **e** *to* the tent of meeting, H7339
Nu 16:50 to Moses at the **e** *to* the tent of meeting, H7339
Nu 20: 6 the assembly to the **e** *to* the tent of H7339
Nu 25: 6 were weeping at the **e** *to* the tent of H7339
Nu 27: 2 the whole assembly *at* the **e** *to* the tent of H7339
Dt 31:15 the cloud stood over the **e** *to* the tent. H7339
Jos 8:29 throw it down at the **e** *of* the city gate. H7339
Jos 19:51 of the LORD at the **e** *to* the tent of meeting. H7339
Jos 20: 4 are to stand in the **e** *of* the city gate and H7339
Jdg 9:35 was standing at the **e** *of* the city gate just H7339
Jdg 9:40 him all the way to the **e** *of* the gate, H7339
Jdg 9:44 to a position at the **e** *of* the city gate. H7339
Jdg 9:52 he approached the **e** *to* the tower to set it H7339
Jdg 18:16 battle, stood at the **e** *of* the gate. H7339
Jdg 18:17 armed men stood at the **e** *of* the gate. H7339
1Sa 2:22 who served at the **e** *to* the tent of meeting H7339
1Sa 17:52 Philistines to the **e** *of* Gath and to the H995
2Sa 10: 8 battle formation at the **e** *of* their city gate, H7339
2Sa 11: 9 Uriah slept at the **e** to the palace with all H7339
2Sa 11:23 drove them back to the **e** *of* the city gate. H7339
1Ki 6: 8 The **e** to the lowest floor was on the south H7339
1Ki 6:31 For the **e** *to* the inner sanctuary he made H7339
1Ki 6:33 the **e** *to* the main hall he made H7339
1Ki 14:27 guard on duty at the **e** *to* the royal palace. H7339
1Ki 22:10 floor by the **e** *of* the gate of Samaria, H7339
2Ki 7: 3 men with leprosy at the **e** *of* the city gate. H7339
2Ki 10: 8 in two piles at the **e** *of* the city gate until H7339
2Ki 12: 9 who guarded the **e** put into the chest all H6197
2Ki 23: 8 the gateway at the **e** *of* the Gate of H7339
2Ki 23:11 He removed from the **e** *to* the temple of the H995
1Ch 9:19 guarding the **e** to the dwelling of the H4427
1Ch 9:21 the gatekeeper at the **e** to the tent of H7339
1Ch 19: 9 in battle formation at the **e** *to* their city, H7339
2Ch 12:10 guard on duty at the **e** *to* the royal palace. H7339
2Ch 18: 9 floor by the **e** *of* the gate of Samaria, H7339
2Ch 23:13 the king, standing by his pillar at the **e**. H4427
2Ch 23:15 she reached the **e** of the Horse Gate on H4427
2Ch 33:14 as far as the **e** of the Fish Gate and H995
Ne 3:20 from the angle to the **e** *of* the house of H7339
Ne 3:21 from the **e** *of* Eliashib's house to the end H7339
Est 5: 1 his royal throne in the hall, facing the **e**. H7339
Pr 8: 3 the city, at the **e**, she cries aloud: H4427+7339
Isa 24:10 desolate; the **e** *to* every house is barred. H995
Jer 1:15 their thrones in the **e** *of* the gates of H7339
Jer 19: 2 Hinnom, near the **e** *of* the Potsherd Gate. H7339
Jer 26:10 their places at the **e** *of* the New Gate of H7339
Jer 36:10 courtyard at the **e** *of* the New Gate of the H7339
Jer 38:14 brought to the third **e** to the temple of the H4427
Jer 43: 9 pavement at the **e** *to* Pharaoh's palace in H7339
Eze 8: 3 to the **e** *of* the north gate of the inner H7339
Eze 8: 5 in the **e** north of the gate of the altar I H929
Eze 8: 7 Then he brought me to the **e** *to* the court H7339
Eze 8:14 brought me to the **e** of the north gate of H7339
Eze 8:16 there at the **e** *to* the temple, between H7339
Eze 10:19 They stopped at the **e** *of* the east gate of H7339
Eze 11: 1 There at the **e** *of* the gate were H7339
Eze 40:11 the width of the **e** *of* the gateway; H7339
Eze 40:15 distance from the **e** *of* the gateway to the H415
Eze 40:40 the steps at the **e** *of* the north gateway H7339
Eze 40:48 The width of the **e** was fourteen cubits H9133
Eze 41: 2 The **e** was ten cubits wide, and the H7339
Eze 41: 3 measured the jambs of the **e**; H7339
Eze 41: 3 The **e** was six cubits wide, and the H7339
Eze 41:17 the outside of the **e** to the inner sanctuary H7339
Eze 41:20 From the floor to the area above the **e** H7339
Eze 42: 9 lower rooms had an **e** on the east side as H4427
Eze 44: 5 attention to the **e** *to* the temple and all H4427
Eze 46: 3 of the LORD at the **e** *of* that gateway. H7339
Eze 46:19 me through the **e** at the side of the H4427
Eze 47: 1 brought me back to the **e** *to* the temple, H7339
Mt 27:60 in front of the **e** to the tomb and went G2598
Mk 15:46 rolled a stone against the **e** of the tomb. G2598
Mk 16: 3 the stone away from the **e** of the tomb?" G2598
Jn 11:38 was a cave with a stone laid across **the e**. G899S
Jn 20: 1 the stone had been removed from the **e**. G3646S
Ac 12: 6 and sentries stood guard at the **e**. G2598
Ac 12:13 Peter knocked *at* the outer **e**, and a servant G2598

ENTRANCES (4) [ENTER]
Ex 33: 8 rose and stood at the **e** *to* their tents, H7339
Nu 16:27 little ones at the **e** *to* their tents. H7339
Eze 41:11 There were **e** *to* the side rooms from the H7339
Eze 43:11 its exits and **e**—its whole design and all H4569

ENTREAT (3) [ENTREATY]
Zec 7: 2 with their men, to **e** the LORD H2704+906+7156
Zec 8:21 go at once to **e** the LORD and H2704+906+7156
Zec 8:22 LORD Almighty and to **e** him." H2704+906+7156

ENTREATY (2) [ENTREAT]
2Ch 33:13 the LORD **was moved by** his **e** and listened H6983
2Ch 33:19 prayer and how God **was moved by** his **e**, H6983

ENTRUST (5) [TRUST]
Ge 42:37 **E** him to my care, and I will bring him H5989
2Ki 22: 5 *Have them* **e** it to the men appointed to H5989
Ps 143: 8 the way I should go, for to you *I* **e** my life. H5951
Jn 2:24 But Jesus *would* not **e** himself to them, for G4409
2Ti 2: 2 of many witnesses **e** to reliable people G4192

ENTRUSTED (34) [TRUST]
Ge 39: 4 and *he* **e** to his care everything he owned. H5989
Ge 39: 8 everything he owns *he has* **e** to my care. H5989
Lev 6: 2 neighbor about **something e** to them or H7214
Lev 6: 4 what **was e** to them, or the H7214+7212
1Ki 15:18 *He* **e** it to his officials and sent them to H5989
2Ki 22: 7 not account for the money **e** to them, H5989
2Ki 22: 9 of the LORD and *have* **e** it to the workers H5989
1Ch 9:26 were **e with** the responsibility for the H928+575
1Ch 9:31 was **e with** the responsibility for H928+575
2Ch 34:10 Then *they* **e** it to the men appointed to H5989
2Ch 34:17 of the LORD and *have* **e** it to the H5989
Ezr 7:19 all the articles **e** to you for worship in the A10314
Est 2: 8 to the king's palace and **e to** Hegai, H448+3338
Est 6: 9 Then *let* the robe and horse *be* **e** to one of H5989
Jer 13:20 Where is the flock *that* **was e** to you, the H5989
Jer 29: 3 He **e** the letter **to** Elasah son of H928+3338
Mt 25:14 his servants and **e** his wealth to them. G4140
Mt 25:20 he said, '*you* **e** me with five bags of gold. G4140
Mt 25:22 he said, '*you* **e** me with two bags of gold G4140
Lk 12:48 from the one *who has been* **e** with much, G4192
Jn 5:22 but *has* **e** all judgment to the Son, G1443
Ro 3: 2 the Jews *have been* **e with** the very words G4409
1Co 4: 1 of Christ and as *those* **e with** the mysteries G3874
Gal 2: 7 that *I had been* **e with** *the* **task** of G4409
Gal 3:19 angels and **e to** a mediator. G1877+5931
1Th 2: 4 approved by God *to be* **e** with the gospel. G4409
1Ti 1:11 of the blessed God, which he **e** *to* me. G4409
1Ti 6:20 guard what has been **e** to your **care**. G4146
2Ti 1:12 to guard what I have **e** to him until that G4146
2Ti 1:14 the good **deposit** *that was* **e** to you— G4146
Titus 1: 3 the preaching **e** to me by the command of G4409
1Pe 2:23 *he* **e** *himself* to him who judges justly. G4140
1Pe 5: 3 not lording it over those **e** to you, but G3102
Jude 3 the faith *that was* once for all **e** to God's G4140

ENTRYWAY (2) [ENTER]
2Ki 16:18 removed the royal **e** outside the temple of H4427
Mk 14:68 he said, and went out into the **e**. G4580

ENTWINES (1)
Job 8:17 *it* **e** its roots around a pile of rocks and H6018

ENVELOPED (1)
Isa 42:25 It **e** them in flames, yet they did H4946+6017

ENVIED (2) [ENVY]
Ge 26:14 servants that the Philistines **e** him. H7861
Ps 73: 3 For *I* **e** the arrogant when I saw the H7861

ENVIOUS (7) [ENVY]
Dt 32:21 I *will* **make** them **e** by those who are not a H7861
Ps 37: 1 who are evil or *be* **e** of those who do H7861
Ps 106:16 In the camp *they grew* **e** of Moses and of H7861
Pr 24:19 of evildoers or *be* **e** of the wicked, H7861
Mt 20:15 Or are you **e** because I am G3836+4057+4505
Ro 10:19 "I *will* **make** you **e** by those who are not a G4143
Ro 11:11 come to the Gentiles to **make** Israel **e**. G4143

ENVOY (3) [ENVOYS]
Pr 13:17 a trustworthy **e** brings healing. H7495
Jer 49:14 an **e** was sent to the nations to say H7495
Ob 1 An **e** was sent to the nations to say, "Rise H7495

ENVOYS (20) [ENVOY]
2Sa 5:11 Now Hiram king of Tyre sent **e** to David H4855
2Sa 10: 3 your father by sending **e** to you to express H6269
2Sa 10: 4 So Hanun seized David's **e**, shaved off H6269
1Ki 5: 1 he sent his **e** to Solomon, because H6269
2Ki 17: 4 he had sent **e** to So king of Egypt, and H4855
2Ki 20:13 received **the e** and showed them H2157S
1Ch 19: 2 When David's **e** came to Hanun in the H6269
1Ch 19: 3 your father by sending **e** to you to express NDT
1Ch 19: 3 Haven't his **e** come to you only to explore H6269
1Ch 19: 4 So Hanun seized David's **e**, shaved them H6269
2Ch 32:31 But when **e** were sent *by* the rulers of H4885
Ps 68:31 **E** will come from Egypt; Cush will submit H3134
Isa 14:32 shall be given to the **e** *of* that nation? H4855
Isa 18: 2 which sends **e** by sea in papyrus boats H7495
Isa 30: 4 in Zoan and their **e** have arrived in Hanes H4855
Isa 30: 6 the **e** carry their riches on donkeys' backs NDT
Isa 33: 7 the streets; the **e** *of* peace weep bitterly. H4855
Isa 39: 2 Hezekiah received **the e** gladly and H2157S
Jer 27: 3 Sidon through the **e** who have come to H4855
Eze 17:15 him by sending his **e** to Egypt to get H4855

ENVY (19) [ENVIED, ENVIOUS, ENVYING]
Job 5: 2 kills a fool, and **e** slays the simple. H7863
Ps 68:16 why **gaze in e**, *you* rugged mountain, at H8353
Pr 3:31 *Do* not **e** the violent or choose any of their H7861
Pr 14:30 life to the body, but **e** rots the bones. H7863
Pr 23:17 Do not *let* your heart **e** sinners, but always H7861
Pr 24: 1 *Do* not **e** the wicked, do not desire their H7861
Ecc 4: 4 spring from one person's **e** of another. H7863
Eze 31: 9 *the* **e** *of* all the trees of Eden in the H7861
Mk 7:22 deceit, lewdness, **e**, slander G4057+4505
Ro 1:29 They are full *of* **e**, murder, strife, deceit G5784
Ro 11:14 *I may* somehow **arouse** my own people **to e** G4143
1Co 13: 4 *It does* not **e**, it does not boast, it is not G2420
Gal 5:21 **e**; drunkenness, orgies, and the like. G5784
Php 1:15 some preach Christ out of **e** and rivalry, G5784
1Ti 6: 4 quarrels about words that result in **e**, G5784
Titus 3: 3 We lived in malice and **e**, being hated G5784
Jas 3:14 if you harbor bitter **e** and selfish ambition G2419
Jas 3:16 For where you have **e** and selfish ambition, G2419
1Pe 2: 1 hypocrisy, **e**, and slander of every G5784

ENVYING (1) [ENVY]
Gal 5:26 conceited, provoking and **e** each other. G5783

EPAPHRAS (3)
Col 1: 7 You learned it from **E**, our dear fellow G2071
Col 4:12 **E**, who is one of you and a servant of G2071
Phm 23 **E**, my fellow prisoner in Christ Jesus G2071

EPAPHRODITUS (2)
Php 2:25 think it is necessary to send back to you **E**, G2073
Php 4:18 I have received from **E** the gifts you sent. G2073

EPENETUS (1)
Ro 16: 5 Greet my dear friend **E**, who was the first G2045

EPHAH (52)
Ge 25: 4 The sons of Midian were **E**, Epher, Hanok H6549
Ex 16:36 An omer is one-tenth of an **e**. H406
Ex 29:40 lamb offer a tenth of an **e** of the finest flour NDT
Lev 5:11 sin a tenth of an **e** *of* the finest flour for a H406
Lev 6:20 a tenth of an **e** *of* the finest flour as a H406
Lev 14:10 with three-tenths of an **e** of the finest flour NDT
Lev 14:21 with a tenth of an **e** of the finest flour mixed NDT
Lev 19:36 weights, an honest **e** and an honest hin. H406
Lev 23:13 of two-tenths of an **e** of the finest flour NDT
Lev 23:17 of two-tenths of an **e** of the finest flour, NDT
Lev 24: 5 using two-tenths of an **e** for each loaf. NDT
Nu 5:15 of a tenth of an **e** *of* barley flour on her H406
Nu 15: 4 of a tenth of an **e** of the finest flour mixed NDT
Nu 15: 6 of two-tenths of an **e** of the finest flour NDT

Nu 15: 9 of three-tenths of an **e** of the finest flour NDT
Nu 28: 5 of a tenth of an **e** *of* the finest flour mixed H406
Nu 28: 9 of two-tenths of an **e** of the finest flour NDT
Nu 28:12 of three-tenths of an **e** of the finest flour NDT
Nu 28:12 of two-tenths of an **e** of the finest flour NDT
Nu 28:13 of a tenth of an **e** of the finest flour mixed NDT
Nu 28:20 of three-tenths of an **e** of the finest flour NDT
Nu 28:28 of three-tenths of an **e** of the finest flour NDT
Nu 29: 3 of three-tenths of an **e** of the finest flour NDT
Nu 29: 9 of three-tenths of an **e** of the finest flour NDT
Nu 29:14 of three-tenths of an **e** of the finest flour NDT
Jdg 6:19 from an **e** *of* flour he made bread H406
Ru 2:17 gathered, and it amounted to about an **e**. H406
1Sa 1:24 an **e** of flour and a skin of wine H406
1Sa 17:17 "Take this **e** *of* roasted grain and these ten H406
1Ch 1:33 The sons of Midian: **E**, Epher, Hanok H6549
1Ch 2:46 Caleb's concubine **E** was the mother of H6549
1Ch 2:47 Jotham, Geshan, Pelet, **E** and Shaaph. H6549
Isa 5:10 homer of seed will yield only an **e** of grain." H406
Isa 60: 6 your land, young camels of Midian and **E**. H6548
Eze 45:10 an accurate **e** and an accurate bath. H406
Eze 45:11 The **e** and the bath are to be the same size H406
Eze 45:11 of a homer and the **e** a tenth of a homer; H406
Eze 45:13 a sixth of an **e** from each homer of wheat H406
Eze 45:13 a sixth of an **e** from each homer of H406
Eze 45:24 a grain offering an **e** for each bull and an H406
Eze 45:24 ephah for each bull and an **e** for each ram, H406
Eze 45:24 along with a hin of olive oil for each **e**. H406
Eze 46: 5 offering given with the ram is to be an **e**, H406
Eze 46: 5 along with a hin of olive oil for each **e**. H406
Eze 46: 7 as a grain offering *one* **e** with the bull, H406
Eze 46: 7 with the bull, *one* **e** with the ram, and H406
Eze 46: 7 along with a hin of oil for each **e**. H406
Eze 46:11 the grain offering is to be an **e** with a bull H406
Eze 46:11 with a bull, an **e** with a ram, and with H406
Eze 46:11 pleases, along with a hin of oil for each **e**. H406
Eze 46:14 of a sixth of an **e** with a third of a hin of H406
Mic 6:10 and the short **e**, which is accursed? H406

EPHAI (1)

Jer 40: 8 the sons of **E** the Netophathite, and H6550

EPHER (4)

Ge 25: 4 Midian were Ephah, **E**, Hanok, Abida H6761
1Ch 1:33 Ephah, **E**, Hanok, Abida and H6761
1Ch 4:17 Jether, Mered, **E** and Jalon. One of H6761
1Ch 5:24 **E**, Ishi, Eliel, Azriel, Jeremiah, Hodaviah H6761

EPHES DAMMIM (1)

1Sa 17: 1 They pitched camp at **E**, between H702

EPHESIAN (1) [EPHESUS]

Ac 21:29 seen Trophimus the **E** in the city with Paul *G2386*

EPHESIANS (3) [EPHESUS]

Ac 19:28 "Great is Artemis *of* the **E**!" *G2386*
Ac 19:34 "Great is Artemis *of* the **E**!" *G2386*
Ac 19:35 "Fellow **E**, doesn't all the world know that *G2386*

EPHESUS (17) [EPHESIAN, EPHESIANS]

Ac 18:19 They arrived at **E**, where Paul left Priscilla *G2387*
Ac 18:21 it is God's will." Then he set sail from **E**. *G2387*
Ac 18:24 a native of Alexandria, came to **E**. *G2387*
Ac 19: 1 road through the interior and arrived at **E**. *G2387*
Ac 19:17 known to the Jews and Greeks living in **E**, *G2387*
Ac 19:26 of people here *in* **E** and in practically the *G2387*
Ac 19:35 know that the city **of E** is the guardian of *G2386*
Ac 20:16 decided to sail past **E** to avoid spending *G2387*
Ac 20:17 Paul sent to **E** for the elders of the church. *G2387*
1Co 15:32 fought wild beasts in **E** with no more than *G2387*
1Co 16: 8 But I will stay on at **E** until Pentecost, *G2387*
Eph 1: 1 To God's holy people in **E**, the faithful in *G2387*
1Ti 1: 3 stay there in **E** so that you may command *G2387*
2Ti 1:18 in how many ways he helped me in **E**. *G2387*
2Ti 4:12 I sent Tychicus to **E**. *G2387*
Rev 1:11 to **E**, Smyrna, Pergamum, Thyatira, Sardis *G2387*
Rev 2: 1 "To the angel of the church in **E** write *G2387*

EPHLAL (2)

1Ch 2:37 Zabad the father of **E**, Ephlal the father of H697
1Ch 2:37 the father of Ephlal, **E** the father of Obed, H697

EPHOD (50)

Ex 25: 7 to be mounted on the **e** and breastpiece. H680
Ex 28: 4 a breastpiece, an **e**, a robe, a woven tunic H680
Ex 28: 6 "Make the **e** of gold, and of blue, purple H680
Ex 28: 8 of one piece with **the e** and made with H5647S
Ex 28:12 pieces of the **e** as memorial stones for H680
Ex 28:15 of skilled hands. Make it like the **e**: of gold, H680
Ex 28:25 to the shoulder pieces of the **e** at the front. H680
Ex 28:26 on the inside edge next to the **e**. H680
Ex 28:27 of the shoulder pieces on the front of the **e**, H680
Ex 28:27 seam just above the waistband of the **e**. H680
Ex 28:28 be tied to the rings of the **e** with blue cord, H680
Ex 28:28 breastpiece will not swing out from the **e**. H680
Ex 28:31 "Make the robe of the **e** entirely of blue H680
Ex 29: 5 the robe of the **e**, the ephod itself and H680
Ex 29: 5 the ephod, the **e** itself and the breastpiece. H680
Ex 29: 5 Fasten the **e** on him by its skillfully woven H680
Ex 35: 9 to be mounted on the **e** and breastpiece. H680
Ex 35:27 to be mounted on the **e** and breastpiece. H680
Ex 39: 2 They made the **e** of gold, and of blue H680
Ex 39: 4 They made shoulder pieces for **the e** H2257S
Ex 39: 5 of one piece with **the e** and made with H5647S
Ex 39: 7 pieces of the **e** as memorial stones for H680
Ex 39: 8 They made it like the **e**: of gold, H680
Ex 39:18 to the shoulder pieces of the **e** at the front. H680
Ex 39:19 on the inside edge next to the **e**. H680
Ex 39:20 of the shoulder pieces on the front of the **e**, H680
Ex 39:20 seam just above the waistband of the **e**. H680
Ex 39:21 to the rings of the **e** with blue cord, H680
Ex 39:21 would not swing out from the **e**— H680
Ex 39:22 made the robe of the **e** entirely of blue H680
Lev 8: 7 him with the robe and put the **e** on him. H680
Lev 8: 7 He also fastened the **e** with a decorative H680
Nu 34:23 Hanniel son of **E**, the leader from the tribe H681
Jdg 8:27 Gideon made the gold into an **e**, which he H680
Jdg 17: 5 he made an **e** and some household H680
Jdg 18:14 know that one of these houses has an **e**, H680
Jdg 18:17 the **e** and the household gods while the H680
Jdg 18:18 the idol, the **e** and the household gods H680
Jdg 18:20 He took the **e**, the household gods and the H680
1Sa 2:18 before the LORD—a boy wearing a linen **e**. H680
1Sa 2:28 incense, and to wear an **e** in my presence. H680
1Sa 14: 3 whom was Ahijah, who was wearing an **e**. H680
1Sa 21: 9 it is wrapped in a cloth behind the **e**. H680
1Sa 22:18 eighty-five men who wore the linen **e**. H680
1Sa 23: 6 had brought the **e** down with him when he H680
1Sa 23: 9 he said to Abiathar the priest, "Bring the **e**." H680
1Sa 30: 7 the son of Ahimelek, "Bring me the **e**." H680
2Sa 6:14 Wearing a linen **e**, David was dancing H680
1Ch 15:27 David also wore a linen **e**. H680
Hos 3: 4 without **e** or household gods. H680

EPHPHATHA (1)

Mk 7:34 with a deep sigh said to him, "**E**! *G2395*

EPHRAIM (157) [EPHRAIM'S, EPHRAIMITE, EPHRAIMITES]

Ge 41:52 The second son he named **E** and said, "It is H713
Ge 46:20 Manasseh and **E** were born to Joseph by H713
Ge 48: 1 two sons Manasseh and **E** along with him. H713
Ge 48: 5 as mine; **E** and Manasseh will be mine H713
Ge 48:13 **E** on his right toward Israel's left hand and H713
Ge 48:20 'May God make you like **E** and Manasseh.' H713
Ge 48:20 So he put **E** ahead of Manasseh. H713
Nu 1:10 from **E**, Elishama son of Ammihud; from H713
Nu 1:32 From the descendants of **E**: All the men H713
Nu 1:33 The number from the tribe of **E** was 40,500. H713
Nu 2:18 of the camp of **E** under their standard. H713
Nu 2:18 of the people of **E** is Elishama son of H713
Nu 2:24 All the men assigned to the camp of **E** H713
Nu 7:48 the leader of the people of **E**, brought his H713
Nu 10:22 divisions of the camp of **E** went next, H1201+713
Nu 13: 8 from the tribe of **E**, Hoshea son of Nun; H713
Nu 26:28 their clans through Manasseh and **E** were: H713
Nu 26:35 were the descendants of **E** by their clans: H713
Nu 26:37 These were the clans of **E**; those H1201+713
Nu 34:24 from the tribe of **E** son of Joseph; H1201+713
Dt 33:17 Such are the ten thousands of **E**; such are H713
Dt 34: 2 the territory of **E** and Manasseh, all the H713
Jos 14: 4 had become two tribes—Manasseh and **E**. H713
Jos 16: 4 So Manasseh and **E**, the descendants of H713
Jos 16: 5 This was the territory of **E**, according H1201+713
Jos 16:10 among the people of **E** but are required to H713
Jos 17: 9 towns belonging to **E** lying among the H713
Jos 17:10 On the south the land belonged to **E**, on H713
Jos 17:15 if the hill country of **E** is too small for you, H713
Jos 17:17 of Joseph—to **E** and Manasseh—"You H713
Jos 19:50 Timnath Serah in the hill country of **E**. H713
Jos 20: 7 Shechem in the hill country of **E**, and H713
Jos 21: 5 ten towns from the clans of the tribes of **E**, H713
Jos 21:20 were allotted towns from the tribe of **E**: H713
Jos 21:21 In the hill country of **E** they were given H713
Jos 24:30 at Timnath Serah in the hill country of **E** H713
Jos 24:33 to his son Phinehas in the hill country of **E**. H713
Jdg 1:29 Nor did **E** drive out the Canaanites living in H713
Jdg 2: 9 at Timnath Heres in the hill country of **E** H713
Jdg 3:27 he blew a trumpet in the hill country of **E** H713
Jdg 4: 5 Ramah and Bethel in the hill country of **E**, H713
Jdg 5:14 Some came from **E**, whose roots were in H713
Jdg 7:24 throughout the hill country of **E**, H713
Jdg 7:24 So all the men of **E** were called out and H713
Jdg 10: 1 He lived in Shamir, in the hill country of **E**. H713
Jdg 10: 9 Benjamin and **E**; Israel was in H1074+713
Jdg 12: 4 the men of Gilead and fought against **E**. H713
Jdg 12: 4 are renegades from **E** and Manasseh." H713
Jdg 12: 5 the fords of the Jordan leading to **E**, H713
Jdg 12: 5 whenever a survivor of **E** said, "Let me H713
Jdg 12:15 died and was buried at Pirathon in **E**, H824+713
Jdg 17: 1 named Micah from the hill country of **E** H713
Jdg 17: 8 to Micah's house in the hill country of **E**. H713
Jdg 18: 2 the hill country of **E** and came to the house H713
Jdg 18:13 to the hill country of **E** and came to Micah's H713
Jdg 19: 1 the hill country of **E** took a concubine from H713
Jdg 19:16 an old man from the hill country of **E**, H713
Jdg 19:18 area in the hill country of **E** where I live. H713
1Sa 1: 1 a Zuphite from the hill country of **E**, whose H713
1Sa 9: 4 the hill country of **E** and through the area H713
1Sa 14:22 in the hill country of **E** heard that the H713
2Sa 2: 9 and also over **E**, Benjamin and all H713
2Sa 13:23 were at Baal Hazor near the border of **E**, H713
2Sa 18: 6 the battle took place in the forest of **E**. H713
2Sa 20:21 from the hill country of **E**, has lifted up his H713
1Ki 4: 8 Ben-Hur—in the hill country of **E**; H713
1Ki 12:25 in the hill country of **E** and lived there. H713
2Ki 5:22 just come to me from the hill country of **E**. H713
2Ki 14:13 of Jerusalem from the **E** Gate to the Corner H713
1Ch 6:66 as their territory towns from the tribe of **E**. H713
1Ch 6:67 In the hill country of **E** they were given H713
1Ch 7:20 The descendants of **E**: Shuthelah, Bered H713
1Ch 7:22 Their father **E** mourned for them many days H713
1Ch 9: 3 and from **E** and Manasseh who lived H1201+713
1Ch 12:30 from **E**, brave warriors, famous in H1201+713
2Ch 13: 4 in the hill country of **E**, and said, H713
2Ch 15: 8 the towns he had captured in the hills of **E**. H713
2Ch 15: 9 Benjamin and the people from **E**, H713
2Ch 17: 2 in the towns of **E** that his father Asa H713
2Ch 19: 4 the hill country of **E** and turned them back H713
2Ch 25: 7 not with any of the people of **E**. H713
2Ch 25:10 come to him from **E** and sent them home. H713
2Ch 25:23 of Jerusalem from the **E** Gate to the Corner H713
2Ch 28:12 Then some of the leaders in **E** H1201+713
2Ch 30: 1 also wrote letters to **E** and Manasseh, H713
2Ch 30:10 town to town in **E** and Manasseh, H824+713
2Ch 30:18 of the many people who came from **E**, H713
2Ch 31: 1 Benjamin and in **E** and Manasseh. H713
2Ch 34: 6 towns of Manasseh, **E** and Simeon, as far H713
2Ch 34: 9 **E** and the entire remnant of Israel and from H713
Ne 8:16 Water Gate and the one by the Gate of **E**. H713
Ne 12:39 over the Gate of **E**, the Jeshanah Gate, the H713
Ps 60: 7 Manasseh is mine; **E** is my helmet, Judah H713
Ps 78: 9 The men of **E**, though armed with bows H713
Ps 78:67 of Joseph, he did not choose the tribe of **E**; H713
Ps 80: 2 before **E**, Benjamin and Manasseh H713
Ps 108: 8 Manasseh is mine; **E** is my helmet, Judah H713
Isa 7: 2 "Aram has allied itself with **E**"; so the H713
Isa 7: 5 **E** and Remaliah's son have plotted your H713
Isa 7: 8 sixty-five years **E** will be too shattered H713
Isa 7: 9 The head of **E** is Samaria, and the head of H713
Isa 7:17 unlike any since **E** broke away from Judah H713
Isa 9: 9 know it—**E** and the inhabitants of Samaria H713
Isa 9:21 Manasseh will feed on **E**, and Ephraim on H713
Isa 9:21 feed on Ephraim, and **E** on Manasseh H713
Isa 11:13 destroyed; **E** will not be jealous of Judah H713
Isa 11:13 of Judah, nor Judah hostile toward **E**. H713
Isa 17: 3 The fortified city will disappear from **E**, H713
Jer 4:15 proclaiming disaster from the hills of **E**. H713
Jer 7:15 all your fellow Israelites, the people of **E**. H713
Jer 31: 6 when watchmen cry out on the hills of **E**, H713
Jer 31: 9 Israel's father, and **E** is my firstborn son. H713
Jer 31:20 Is not **E** my dear son, the child in whom I H713
Jer 50:19 be satisfied on the hills of **E** and Gilead. H713
Eze 37:16 Joseph (that is, to **E**) and all the Israelites H713
Eze 48: 5 "**E** will have one portion; it will border the H713
Eze 48: 6 border the territory of **E** from east to west. H713
Hos 4:17 **E** is joined to idols; leave him alone! H713
Hos 5: 3 I know all about **E**; Israel is not hidden H713
Hos 5: 3 **E**, you have now turned to prostitution H713
Hos 5: 5 the Israelites, even **E**, stumble in their sin H713
Hos 5: 9 **E** will be laid waste on the day of H713
Hos 5:11 **E** is oppressed, trampled in judgment H713
Hos 5:12 I am like a moth to **E**, like rot to the people H713
Hos 5:13 "When **E** saw his sickness, and Judah his H713
Hos 5:13 Judah his sores, then **E** turned to Assyria H713
Hos 5:14 For I will be like a lion to **E**, like a great H713
Hos 6: 4 can I do with you, **E**? What can I do with H713
Hos 6:10 There **E** is given to prostitution, Israel is H713
Hos 7: 1 the sins of **E** are exposed and the crimes of H713
Hos 7: 8 "**E** mixes with the nations; Ephraim is a flat H713
Hos 7: 8 the nations; **E** is a flat loaf not turned over. H713
Hos 7:11 "**E** is like a dove, easily deceived and H713
Hos 8: 9 **E** has sold herself to lovers. H713
Hos 8:11 "Though **E** built many altars for sin H713
Hos 9: 3 **E** will return to Egypt and eat unclean food H713
Hos 9: 8 is the watchman over **E**, yet snares await H713
Hos 9:13 I have seen **E**, like Tyre, planted in a H713
Hos 9:13 But **E** will bring out their children to the H713
Hos 9:16 **E** is blighted, their root is withered, they H713
Hos 10: 6 **E** will be disgraced; Israel will be ashamed H713
Hos 10:11 **E** is a trained heifer that loves to thresh; so H713
Hos 10:11 I will drive **E**, Judah must plow, and Jacob H713
Hos 11: 3 It was I who taught **E** to walk, taking them H713
Hos 11: 8 can I give you up, **E**? How can I hand you H713
Hos 11: 9 fierce anger, nor will I devastate **E** again. H713
Hos 11:12 **E** has surrounded me with lies, Israel with H713
Hos 12: 1 **E** feeds on the wind; he pursues the east H713
Hos 12: 8 **E** boasts, "I am very rich; I have become H713
Hos 12:14 But **E** has aroused his bitter anger; his Lord H713
Hos 13: 1 When **E** spoke, people trembled; he was H713
Hos 13:12 The guilt of **E** is stored up, his sins are kept H713
Hos 14: 8 **E**, what more have I to do with idols? I will H713
Ob 19 will occupy the fields of **E** and Samaria, H713
Zec 9:10 the chariots from **E** and the warhorses from H713
Zec 9:13 Judah as I bend my bow and fill it with **E**. H713
Jn 11:54 to a village called **E**, where he stayed *G2394*

EPHRAIM'S (11) [EPHRAIM]

Ge 48:14 out his right hand and put it on **E** head, H713
Ge 48:17 his right hand on **E** head he was H713
Ge 48:17 to move it from **E** head to Manasseh's H713
Ge 50:23 saw the third generation of **E** children H713
Jdg 8: 2 the gleanings of **E** grapes better than the H713
Isa 11:13 **E** jealousy will vanish, and Judah's H713
Isa 28: 1 the pride of **E** drunkards, to the H713
Isa 28: 3 the pride of **E** drunkards, will be H713
Jer 31:18 "I have surely heard **E** moaning: 'You H713

Eze 37:19 of Joseph—which is in E hand—and of the H713
Hos 9:11 E glory will fly away like a bird—no birth H713

EPHRAIMITE (7) [EPHRAIM]
Jdg 12: 1 The E forces were called out, and they H713
Jdg 12: 5 men of Gilead asked him, "Are you an E?" H718
1Sa 1: 1 the son of Tohu, the son of Zuph, an E. H718
1Ki 11:26 officials, an E from Zeredah, and his H718
1Ch 27:10 was Helez the Pelonite, an E. H1201+713
1Ch 27:14 was Benaiah the Pirathonite, an E. H1201+713
2Ch 28: 7 an E warrior, killed Maaseiah the H713

EPHRAIMITES (8) [EPHRAIM]
Jos 16: 8 the inheritance of the tribe of the E, H1201+713
Jos 16: 9 set aside for the E within the H1201+713
Jos 17: 8 of Manasseh, belonged to the E.) H1201+713
Jdg 8: 1 Now the E asked Gideon, "Why have H408+713
Jdg 12: 4 struck them down because the E had said, H713
Jdg 12: 6 Forty-two thousand E were killed at H4946+713
1Ch 27:20 over the E: Hoshea son of Azaziah H1201+713
Zec 10: 7 The E will become like warriors, and their H713

EPHRATH (5) [EPHRATHITE, EPHRATHITES]
Ge 35:16 While they were still some distance from E H714
Ge 35:19 died and was buried on the way to E H714
Ge 48: 7 still on the way, a little distance from E. H714
Ge 48: 7 So I buried her there beside the road to E" H714
1Ch 2:19 Caleb married E, who bore him Hur. H715

EPHRATHAH (5) [BETHLEHEM, CALEB EPHRATHAH]
Ru 4:11 you have standing in E and be famous in H716
1Ch 2:50 The sons of Hur the firstborn of E: Shobal H717
1Ch 4: 4 the firstborn of E and father of Bethlehem. H717
Ps 132: 6 We heard it in E, we came upon it in the H716
Mic 5: 2 "But you, Bethlehem E, though you are H716

EPHRATHITE (1) [EPHRATH]
1Sa 17:12 David was the son of an E named Jesse, H718

EPHRATHITES (1) [EPHRATH]
Ru 1: 2 They were E from Bethlehem, Judah H718

EPHRON (10) [EPHRON'S]
Ge 23: 8 intercede with E son of Zohar on my H6766
Ge 23:10 E the Hittite was sitting among his people H6766
Ge 23:13 he said to E in their hearing, "Listen H6766
Ge 23:14 E answered Abraham, H6766
Ge 25: 9 in the field of E son of Zohar the Hittite, H6766
Ge 49:29 in the cave in the field of E the Hittite, H6766
Ge 49:30 field as a burial place from E the Hittite. H6766
Ge 50:13 field as a burial place from E the Hittite. H6766
Jos 15: 9 the towns of Mount E and went down H6767
2Ch 13:19 Jeshanah and E, with their H6767

EPHRON'S (2) [EPHRON]
Ge 23:16 Abraham agreed to E terms and weighed H6766
Ge 23:17 So E field in Machpelah near Mamre H6766

EPICUREAN (1)
Ac 17:18 A group *of* E and Stoic philosophers *G2134*

EPISTLE, EPISTLES (KJV) LETTER, LETTERS

EQUAL (17) [EQUALED, EQUALITY, EQUALLY, EQUITY, EQUIVALENT]
Ge 44:18 though you are e to Pharaoh himself. H4017
Ge 47: 9 and *they do* not e the years of the H5952
Ex 30:34 frankincense, all **in e amounts**, H963+928+963
Dt 33:25 and your strength will e your days. H3869
1Ki 3:13 lifetime you will have no e among kings. H4017
Job 41:33 Nothing on earth is its e—a creature H5444
Isa 40:25 Or who *is my* e?" says the Holy H8750
Isa 46: 5 will you compare me or **count** me e? H8750
Eze 31: 8 nor *could* the junipers e its boughs H1948
Eze 45:12 shekels plus fifteen shekels e one mina. NDT
Eze 48: 8 from east to west will e one of the tribal H3869
Da 1:19 he found none **e to** Daniel H3869
Mt 20:12 you have made them e to us who have *G2698*
Jn 5:18 own Father, making himself e with God. *G2698*
1Co 12:25 parts should have e concern for each *G3836+899*
2Co 2:16 And who is e to such a task? *G2653*
2Co 11:12 to be considered **e with** us in the things *G2777*

EQUALED (2) [EQUAL]
Mt 24:21 until now—and never *to be* e again. *G1181*
Mk 13:19 until now—and never *to be* e again. *G1181*

EQUALITY (3) [EQUAL]
2Co 8:13 hard pressed, but that there might be e. *G2699*
2Co 8:14 will supply what you need. The goal is e, *G2699*
Php 2: 6 did not consider e with God *G3836+1639+2698*

EQUALLY (6) [EQUAL]
Ex 21:35 **divide** both the money and the dead animal e H2936
Lev 7:10 belongs e to all the sons H408+3869+278+2257
Nu 31:27 **Divide** the spoils e between the soldiers H2936
Dt 18: 8 He is to share e in their benefits, even H3869
Ecc 11: 6 or whether both will do e well. H3869+285
Eze 47:14 divide it e **among them**. H408+3869+278+2257

EQUIP (2) [EQUIPMENT, EQUIPPED]
Eph 4:12 to e his people for works of service, so that *G2938*
Heb 13:21 e you with everything good for doing his *G2936*

EQUIPMENT (11) [EQUIP]
Ge 27: 3 Now then, get your e—your quiver and H3998
Nu 3:36 all its e, and everything related to H3998
Nu 4:26 ropes and all the e *used in* the service of H3998
Nu 4:32 all their e and everything related to their H3998
Dt 23:13 As part of your e have something to dig H266
1Sa 8:12 weapons of war and e *for* his chariots. H3998
1Ki 19:21 burned the plowing e to cook the meat H3998
2Ki 7:15 the clothing and e the Arameans had H3998
2Ch 20:25 a great amount of e and clothing and H8214
Ne 13: 9 back into them the e *of* the house of God, H3998
Zec 11:15 "Take again the e *of* a foolish shepherd. H3998

EQUIPPED (4) [EQUIP]
2Ch 14: 8 e *with* large shields and *with* spears H5951
Ne 4:16 while the other half *were* e *with* spears H2616
Da 11:13 he will advance with a huge army fully e. H8214
2Ti 3:17 may be thoroughly e for every good work. *G787*

EQUITY (7) [EQUAL]
Ps 9: 8 judges the peoples with e. H4797
Ps 58: 1 Do you judge people *with* e? H4797
Ps 67: 4 you rule the peoples **with** e and guide the H4793
Ps 75: 2 appointed time; it is I who judge **with** e. H4797
Ps 96:10 he will judge the peoples with e. H4797
Ps 98: 9 in righteousness and the peoples with e. H4797
Ps 99: 4 you have established e; in Jacob you H4797

EQUIVALENT (2) [EQUAL]
Lev 27: 2 a person to the LORD by giving the **e value**, H6886
Eze 45:14 one homer, for ten baths are e to a homer). NDT

ER (10)
Ge 38: 3 gave birth to a son, who was named E. H6841
Ge 38: 6 Judah got a wife for E, his firstborn, and H6841
Ge 38: 7 But E, Judah's firstborn, was wicked in the H6841
Ge 46:12 E, Onan, Shelah, Perez and Zerah (but Er H6841
Ge 46:12 E and Onan had died in the land of H6841
Nu 26:19 E and Onan were sons of Judah, but they H6841
1Ch 2: 3 The sons of Judah: E, Onan and Shelah H6841
1Ch 2: 3 E, Judah's firstborn, was wicked in the H6841
1Ch 4:21 E the father of Lekah, Laadah the father of H6841
Lk 3:28 the son of Elmadam, the son *of* E, *G2474*

ERAN (1) [ERANITE]
Nu 26:36 of Shuthelah: through E, the Eranite clan. H6896

ERANITE (1) [ERAN]
Nu 26:36 of Shuthelah: through Eran, the E clan. H6897

ERASE (1)
Dt 32:26 scatter them and e their name from H8697

ERASTUS (3)
Ac 19:22 helpers, Timothy and E, to Macedonia, *G2235*
Ro 16:23 E, who is the city's director of public works, *G2235*
2Ti 4:20 E stayed in Corinth, and I left Trophimus *G2235*

ERECH (NIV84) URUK

ERECT (3) [ERECTED]
Dt 16:22 and *do* not e a sacred stone, for these the H7756
Eze 4: 2 E siege works against it, build a ramp up H1215
Eze 21:22 to build a ramp and to e siege works. H1215

ERECTED (8) [ERECT]
Ex 40:18 the bases in place, e the frames, inserted H8492
2Sa 18:18 e it in the King's Valley **as a monument** to H5893
1Ki 7:21 *He* e the pillars at the portico of the H7756
2Ki 21: 3 *he* also e altars to Baal and made an H7756
2Ki 23:12 the kings of Judah *had* e on the roof near H6913
2Ch 3:17 *He* e the pillars in the front of the temple H7756
2Ch 33: 3 *he* also e altars to the Baals and made H7756
Eze 17:17 siege works e to destroy many lives H1215

ERI (2) [ERITE]
Ge 46:16 Shuni, Ezbon, E, Arodi and Areli. H6878
Nu 26:16 the Oznite clan; through E, the Erite clan; H6878

ERITE (1) [ERI]
Nu 26:16 the Oznite clan; through Eri, the E clan; H6879

ERODES (1)
Job 14:18 "But as a mountain e and crumbles and H5877

ERRED (1) [ERROR]
Nu 15:28 the LORD for the one who e by sinning H8704

ERROR (13) [ERRED, ERRORS]
Job 4:18 servants, if he charges his angels with e, H9334
Job 19: 4 my e remains my concern alone. H5413
Ecc 10: 5 the sort of e that arises from a ruler: H8705
Isa 32: 6 spread e concerning the LORD; H9360
Isa 47:15 All of them go on in their e; there is not H9494
Mt 22:29 "*You are* in e because you do not know *G4414*
Mk 12:24 "*Are you* not **in** e because you do not *G4414*
Ro 1:27 in themselves the due penalty *for* their e. *G4415*
1Th 2: 3 does not spring from e or impure motives, *G4415*
Jas 5:20 a sinner from the e of their way will save *G4415*
2Pe 2:18 just escaping from those who live in e. *G4415*
2Pe 3:17 be carried away *by* the e of the lawless *G4415*
Jude 11 have rushed for profit *into* Balaam's e; *G4415*

ERRORS (1) [ERROR]
Ps 19:12 But who can discern their own e? Forgive H8709

ESAIAS (KJV) ISAIAH

ESARHADDON (3)
2Ki 19:37 And E his son succeeded him as king H675
Ezr 4: 2 to him since the time of E king of Assyria, H675
Isa 37:38 And E his son succeeded him as king. H675

ESAU (87) [EDOM, ESAU'S]
Ge 25:25 a hairy garment; so they named him E. H6916
Ge 25:27 grew up, and E became a skillful hunter H6916
Ge 25:28 wild game, loved E, but Rebekah loved H6916
Ge 25:29 E came in from the open country H6916
Ge 25:32 I am about to die," E said. "What good is H6916
Ge 25:34 Then Jacob gave E some bread and some H6916
Ge 25:34 up and left. So E despised his birthright H6916
Ge 26:34 When E was forty years old, he married H6916
Ge 27: 1 he called for E his older son and said to H6916
Ge 27: 5 was listening as Isaac spoke to his son E. H6916
Ge 27: 5 When E left for the open country to hunt H6916
Ge 27: 6 your father say to your brother E, H6916
Ge 27:11 "But my brother E is a hairy man while I H6916
Ge 27:15 took the best clothes of E her older son, H6916
Ge 27:19 said to his father, "I am E your firstborn. H6916
Ge 27:21 whether you really are my son E or not." H6916
Ge 27:22 but the hands are the hands of E. H6916
Ge 27:23 were hairy like those of his brother E; H6916
Ge 27:24 "Are you really my son E?" he asked. "I am H6916
Ge 27:30 his brother E came in from hunting. H6916
Ge 27:32 your son," he answered, "your firstborn, E." H6916
Ge 27:34 When E heard his father's words, he burst H6916
Ge 27:36 E said, "Isn't he rightly named Jacob? This NDT
Ge 27:37 Isaac answered E, "I have made him lord H6916
Ge 27:38 E said to his father, "Do you have only H6916
Ge 27:38 me too, my father!" Then E wept aloud. H6916
Ge 27:41 E held a grudge against Jacob because of H6916
Ge 27:42 was told what her older son E had said, H6916
Ge 27:42 "Your brother E is planning to avenge H6916
Ge 28: 5 who was the mother of Jacob and E. H6916
Ge 28: 6 Now E learned that Isaac had blessed H6916
Ge 28: 8 E then realized how displeasing the H6916
Ge 32: 3 of him to his brother E in the land of Seir, H6916
Ge 32: 4 "This is what you are to say to my lord E H6916
Ge 32: 6 "We went to your brother E, and now he H6916
Ge 32: 8 "If E comes and attacks one group H6916
Ge 32:11 from the hand of my brother E, for I am H6916
Ge 32:13 him he selected a gift for his brother E: H6916
Ge 32:17 "When my brother E meets you and asks H6916
Ge 32:18 They are a gift sent to my lord E, and he H6916
Ge 32:19 the same thing to E when you meet him. H6916
Ge 33: 1 Jacob looked up and there was E, coming H6916
Ge 33: 4 But E ran to meet Jacob and embraced H6916
Ge 33: 5 Then E looked up and saw the women and NDT
Ge 33: 8 E asked, "What's the meaning of all these NDT
Ge 33: 9 But E said, "I already have plenty, my H6916
Ge 33:11 And because Jacob insisted, E accepted it. NDT
Ge 33:12 Then E said, "Let us be on our way; I'll NDT
Ge 33:15 E said, "Then let me leave some of my H6916
Ge 33:16 So that day E started on his way back to H6916
Ge 35: 1 you were fleeing from your brother E." H6916
Ge 35:29 And his sons E and Jacob buried him. H6916
Ge 36: 1 This is the account of the family line of E H6916
Ge 36: 2 E took his wives from the women of H6916
Ge 36: 4 Adah bore Eliphaz to E, Basemath bore H6916
Ge 36: 5 These were the sons of E, who were born H6916
Ge 36: 6 E took his wives and sons and daughters H6916
Ge 36: 8 So E (that is, Edom) settled in the hill H6916
Ge 36: 9 of the family line of E the father of the H6916
Ge 36:14 of Zibeon, whom she bore to E: H6916
Ge 36:15 The sons of Eliphaz the firstborn of E H6916
Ge 36:19 These were the sons of E (that is, Edom), H6916
Ge 36:40 These were the chiefs descended from E H6916
Ge 36:43 This is the family line of E, the father of H6916
Dt 2: 4 of your relatives the descendants of E, H6916
Dt 2: 5 I have given E the hill country of Seir as H6916
Dt 2: 8 past our relatives the descendants of E, H6916
Dt 2:12 the descendants of E drove them out. H6916
Dt 2:22 done the same for the descendants of E, H6916
Dt 2:29 as the descendants of E, who live in Seir H6916
Jos 24: 4 to Isaac I gave Jacob and E. H6916
Jos 24: 4 I assigned the hill country of Seir to E, but H6916
1Ch 1:34 The sons of Isaac: E and Israel. H6916
1Ch 1:35 The sons of E: Eliphaz, Reuel, Jeush H6916
Jer 49: 8 will bring disaster on E at the time when I H6916
Jer 49:10 But I will strip E bare; I will uncover his H6916
Ob 6 But how E will be ransacked, his hidden H6916
Ob 8 of understanding in the mountains of E? H6916
Ob 18 Joseph a flame; E will be stubble H1074+6916
Ob 18 There will be no survivors from E." H1074+6916
Ob 19 the Negev will occupy the mountains of E, H6916
Ob 21 Mount Zion to govern the mountains of E. H6916
Mal 1: 2 "Was not E Jacob's brother? H6916
Mal 1: 3 E I have hated, and I have turned his H6916
Ro 9:13 "Jacob I loved, but E I hated." *G2481*
Heb 11:20 blessed Jacob and E in regard to their *G2481*
Heb 12:16 is godless like E, who for a single meal *G2481*

ESAU'S (14) [ESAU]
Ge 25:26 with his hand grasping E heel; so he was H6916
Ge 36:10 These are the names of E sons: Eliphaz H6916

Ge 36:10 Eliphaz, the son of **E** wife Adah, and H6916
Ge 36:10 Reuel, the son of **E** wife Basemath. H6916
Ge 36:12 **E** son Eliphaz also had a concubine H6916
Ge 36:12 These were grandsons of **E** wife Adah. H6916
Ge 36:13 were grandsons of **E** wife Basemath. H6916
Ge 36:14 The sons of **E** wife Oholibamah daughter H6916
Ge 36:15 were the chiefs among **E** descendants: H6916
Ge 36:17 The sons of **E** son Reuel: Chiefs Nahath H6916
Ge 36:17 they were grandsons of **E** wife Basemath. H6916
Ge 36:18 The sons of **E** wife Oholibamah: Chiefs H6916
Ge 36:18 descended from **E** wife Oholibamah H6916
Ob 9 everyone in **E** mountains will be cut H6916

ESCAPE (67) [ESCAPED, ESCAPES, ESCAPING]

Ge 7: 7 entered the ark *to* **e** the waters of H4946+7156
Ge 32: 8 one group, the group that is left may **e**." H7129
Jos 8:20 they had no chance to **e** in any direction; H5674
Jdg 20:42 they *could* **not e** the battle. H1815
1Sa 19:10 David **made good** *his* **e**. H5674+2256+4880
1Sa 19:18 When David had fled and **made** *his* **e**, he H4880
1Sa 27: 1 thing I can do *is to* **e** to the land of H4880+4880
2Sa 15:14 or none of us will **e** from Absalom. H7129
2Sa 19: 9 fled the country to **e from** Absalom; H4946+6584
2Sa 20: 6 he will find fortified cities and **e** *from* us." H5911
1Ki 12:18 to get into his chariot and **e** *to* Jerusalem. H5674
1Ki 19:17 put to death any *who* **e** the sword of H4880
1Ki 19:17 put to death any *who* **e** the sword of Jehu. H4880
2Ki 10:24 of the men I am placing in your hands **e**, H4880
2Ki 10:25 kill them; *let* no one **e**." So they cut H3655
2Ch 10:18 to get into his chariot and **e** *to* Jerusalem. H5674
Est 4:13 house *you* alone of all the Jews *will* **e**. H4880
Job 11:20 wicked will fail, and **e** will elude them H4960
Job 15:30 *He will* not **e** the darkness; a flame will H6073
Ps 56: 7 of their wickedness *do* not **let** them **e**; H7117
Ps 68:20 the Sovereign LORD comes **e** from death. H9362
Ps 88: 8 *I am* confined and cannot **e**; H3655
Ps 89:48 who *can* **e** the power of the H4880+5883
Pr 11: 9 through knowledge the righteous **e**. H2740
Pr 12:13 sinful talk, and so the innocent **e** trouble. H3655
Ecc 7:26 The man who pleases God *will* **e** her, but H4880
Isa 20: 6 the king of Assyria! How then *can* we **e**?' " H4880
Jer 11:11 bring on them a disaster they cannot **e**. H3655
Jer 21: 9 will live; they will **e with** their lives. H4200+8965
Jer 25:35 the leaders of the flock no **place to e**. H7129
Jer 32: 4 king of Judah *will* not **e** the H4880+4946+3338
Jer 34: 3 You *will* not **e** from his grasp but will H4880
Jer 35:11 to Jerusalem to **e** the Babylonian H4946+7156
Jer 38: 2 They will **e with** their lives; they H4200+8965
Jer 38:18 it down; *you* yourself *will* not **e** from them. H4880
Jer 38:23 *You* yourself *will* not **e** from their hands H4880
Jer 39:18 the sword but will **e with** your life, H4200+8965
Jer 41:18 to **e** the Babylonians. They were H4946+7156
Jer 42:17 of them will survive or **e** the disaster I will H7127
Jer 44:14 to live in Egypt will **e** or survive to return H7127
Jer 44:28 *Those who* **e** the sword and return to the H7127
Jer 45: 5 go I will let you **e with** your life. H4200+8965
Jer 46: 6 "The swift cannot flee nor the strong **e**. H4880
Jer 48: 8 against every town, and not a town *will* **e**. H4880
Jer 50:29 around her; let no *one* **e**. Repay her for H7129
La 3: 7 He has walled me in so *I* cannot **e**; he H3655
Eze 6: 8 some of you will **e** the sword when you H7127
Eze 6: 9 captive, *those who* **e** will remember me H7127
Eze 7:16 The fugitives *who* **e** will flee to the H7117
Eze 17:15 *Will he* who does such things **e**? Will he H4880
Eze 17:15 Will he break the treaty and yet **e**? H4880
Eze 17:18 did all these things, *he shall* not **e**. H4880
Da 11:42 over many countries; Egypt will not **e**. H7129
Hos 9: 6 Even if *they* **e** from destruction, Egypt will H2143
Am 2:14 The swift *will* **not e**, the strong will not H6+4960
Am 9: 1 Not one will get away, none *will* **e**. H4880+7127
Hab 2: 9 his nest on high to **e** the clutches of ruin! H5911
Zec 2: 7 **E**, you who live in Daughter Babylon H4880
Mt 2:13 the child and his mother and **e** to Egypt. *G5771*
Mt 23:33 How *will you* **e** being condemned to hell? *G5771*
Lk 21:36 that you may be able *to* **e** all that is about *G1767*
Ac 27:30 In an attempt *to* **e** from the ship, the *G5771*
Ro 2: 3 do you think you *will* **e** God's judgment? *G1767*
1Th 5: 3 a pregnant woman, and *they will* not **e**. *G1767*
2Ti 2:26 to their senses and *e* **from** the trap of the AIT
Heb 2: 3 how *shall* we **e** if we ignore so great a *G1767*
Heb 12:25 If they *did* not **e** when they refused him *G1767*

ESCAPED (39) [ESCAPE]

Ge 14:13 A man who *had* **e** came and reported this H7127
Jdg 3:26 by the stone images and **e** to Seirah. H4880
Jdg 3:29 all vigorous and strong; not one **e**. H4880
Jdg 9: 5 youngest son of Jerub-Baal, **e** by hiding. H3855
1Sa 19:12 through a window, and he fled and **e**. H4880
1Sa 19:17 send my enemy away so that *he* **e**?" H4880
1Sa 22: 1 David left Gath and **e** to the cave of H4880
1Sa 22:20 named Abiathar, **e** and fled to join David. H4880
1Sa 23:13 was told that David *had* **e** from Keilah, H4880
2Sa 1: 3 "*I have* **e** from the Israelite camp. H4880
1Ki 20:20 king of Aram **e** on horseback with some H4880
1Ki 20:30 The rest of them **e** to the city of Aphek H5674
2Ki 9:27 but *he* **e** *to* Megiddo and died there. H5674
2Ki 13: 5 and *they* **e** from the power of Aram. H3655
2Ki 19:37 and they **e** *to* the land of Ararat. H4880
1Ch 4:43 the remaining Amalekites who had **e**, H7129
2Ch 16: 7 of the king of Aram *has* **e** from your hand. H4880
2Ch 20:24 lying on the ground; no one had **e**. H7129
2Ch 30: 6 who have **e** from the hand of the kings of H7129
2Ch 36:20 the remnant, who **e from** the sword, and H4946
Job 1:15 I am the only one *who has* **e** to tell you!" H4880
Job 1:16 I am the only one *who has* **e** to tell you!" H4880
Job 1:17 I am the only one *who has* **e** to tell you!" H4880
Job 1:19 I am the only one *who has* **e** to tell you!" H4880
Job 19:20 *I have* **e** only by the skin of my teeth. H4880
Ps 124: 7 We *have* **e** like a bird from the fowler's H4880
Ps 124: 7 snare has been broken, and we *have* **e**. H4880
Isa 37:38 and they **e** *to* the land of Ararat. H4880
Jer 41:15 eight of his men **e** from Johanan and H4880
Jer 51:50 You *who* have **e** the sword, leave and do H7128
La 2:22 of the LORD's anger no one **e** or survived; H7127
Eze 33:21 a **man who** *had* **e** from Jerusalem came H7127
Jn 10:39 tried to seize him, but *he* **e** their grasp. *G2002*
Ac 16:27 because he thought the prisoners *had* **e**. *G1767*
Ac 26:26 that none of this *has* **e** his **notice**, *G3291*
Ac 28: 4 a murderer; *for though* he **e** from the sea *G1407*
Heb 11:34 the flames, and **e** the edge of the sword *G5771*
2Pe 1: 4 *having* **e** the corruption in the world caused *G709*
2Pe 2:20 If *they have* **e** the corruption of the world by *G709*

ESCAPES (2) [ESCAPE]

Ps 33:16 no warrior **e** by his great strength. H5911
Joel 2: 3 a desert waste—nothing **e** them. H2118+7129

ESCAPING (7) [ESCAPE]

Jdg 9:21 Then Jotham fled, **e** to Beer, and he lived H1368
Job 15:22 He despairs of **e** the realm of darkness H8740
Jer 48:19 Ask the man fleeing and the *woman* **e** H4880
Hos 13: 3 like smoke **e** through a window. NDT
Ac 27:42 any of them from swimming away and **e**. *G1423*
1Co 3:15 though only as one *e* **through** the flames. AIT
2Pe 2:18 people *who are* just **e from** those who *G709*

ESCHEW, ESCHEWED, ESCHEWETH (KJV) SHUNNED, SHUNS, TURN FROM

ESCORT (2) [ESCORTED]

Da 11: 6 with her royal **e** and her father and the H995
Ac 16:37 Let them come themselves and **e** us **out**." *G1974*

ESCORTED (4) [ESCORT]

1Ki 1:38 David's mule, and *they* **e** him to Gihon. H2143
SS 3: 7 carriage, **e by** sixty warriors, the H6017
Ac 16:39 them and **e** them **from** the prison, *G1974*
Ac 17:15 Those *who* **e** Paul brought him to Athens *G2770*

ESEK (1)

Ge 26:20 So he named the well **E**, because they H6922

ESH-BAAL (2) [BAAL]

1Ch 8:33 of Jonathan, Malki-Shua, Abinadab and **E**. H843
1Ch 9:39 of Jonathan, Malki-Shua, Abinadab and **E**. H843

ESHAN (1)

Jos 15:52 Arab, Dumah, **E**, H878

ESHBAN (2)

Ge 36:26 Hemdan, **E**, Ithran and Keran. H841
1Ch 1:41 Hemdan, **E**, Ithran and Keran. H841

ESHCOL (NIV84) ESHKOL

ESHEK (1)

1Ch 8:39 The sons of his brother **E**: Ulam his H6944

ESHKOL (6)

Ge 14:13 a brother of **E** and Aner, all of whom H866
Ge 14:24 who went with me—to Aner, **E** and Mamre. H866
Nu 13:23 When they reached the Valley of **E**, they cut H865
Nu 13:24 called the Valley of **E** because of the H865
Nu 32: 9 up to the Valley of **E** and viewed the land, H865
Dt 1:24 came to the Valley of **E** and explored it. H865

ESHTAOL (7) [ESHTAOLITES]

Jos 15:33 In the western foothills: **E**, Zorah, Ashnah, H900
Jos 19:41 Zorah, **E**, Ir Shemesh, H900
Jdg 13:25 in Mahaneh Dan, between Zorah and **E**. H900
Jdg 16:31 between Zorah and **E** in the tomb of H900
Jdg 18: 2 men from Zorah and **E** to spy out the land H900
Jdg 18: 8 When they returned to Zorah and **E**, their H900
Jdg 18:11 armed for battle, set out from Zorah and **E**. H900

ESHTAOLITES (1) [ESHTAOL]

1Ch 2:53 these descended the Zorathites and **E**. H901

ESHTEMOA (5)

Jos 21:14 Jattir, **E**, H904
1Sa 30:28 to those in Aroer, Siphmoth, **E** H904
1Ch 4:17 Shammai and Ishbah the father of **E**. H904
1Ch 4:19 Keilah the Garmite, and **E** the Maakathite. H904
1Ch 6:57 a city of refuge), and Libnah, Jattir, **E**, H904

ESHTEMOH (1)

Jos 15:50 Anab, **E**, Anim, H903

ESHTERAH See BE ESHTERAH

ESHTON (2)

1Ch 4:11 father of Mehir, who was the father of **E**. H902
1Ch 4:12 **E** was the father of Beth Rapha, Paseah H902

ESLI (1)

Lk 3:25 of Nahum, the son *of* **E**, the son of *G2268*

ESPECIALLY (16) [SPECIAL]

Jos 2: 1 look over the land," he said, "**e** Jericho." H2256
Est 8:10 fast horses **e bred** for the H1201+2021+8247
Ac 9:41 the believers, **e** the widows, and *G2779*
Ac 25:26 before all of you, and **e** before you, King *G3436*
Ac 26: 3 and **e so** because you are well acquainted *G3436*
1Co 14: 1 desire gifts of the Spirit, **e** prophecy. *G3437*
2Co 1:12 the world, and **e** in our relations with you *G4359*
2Co 7:13 we were **e** delighted to see how *G4359+3437*
Gal 6:10 **e** to those who belong to the family of *G3436*
Php 4:22 **e** those who belong to Caesar's *G3436*
1Ti 4:10 of all people, and **e** of those who believe. *G3436*
1Ti 5: 8 relatives, and **e** for their own household *G3436*
1Ti 5:17 **e** those whose work is preaching and *G3436*
2Ti 4:13 and my scrolls, **e** the parchments. *G3436*
Titus 1:10 **e** those of the circumcision group. *G3436*
2Pe 2:10 This is **e** *true* of those who follow the *G3436*

ESPIED, ESPY (KJV) EXPLORE, SAW, SEARCHED OUT, WATCHED

ESPOUSALS, ESPOUSED (KJV) BETROTHED, BRIDE, PLEDGED TO BE MARRIED, PROMISED, WEDDING

ESROM (KJV) HEZRON

ESTABLISH (37) [ESTABLISHED, ESTABLISHES, ESTABLISHING, REESTABLISHED]

Ge 6:18 But *I will* **e** my covenant with you, and you H7756
Ge 9: 9 "I now **e** my covenant with you and with H7756
Ge 9:11 *I* **e** my covenant with you: Never again will H7756
Ge 17: 7 *I will* **e** my covenant as an everlasting H7756
Ge 17:19 *I will* **e** my covenant with him as an H7756
Ge 17:21 But my covenant *I will* **e** with Isaac, whom H7756
Ex 23:31 "*I will* **e** your borders from the Red Sea to H8883
Dt 28: 9 The LORD *will* **e** you as his holy people, as H7756
1Sa 2:35 *I will* firmly **e** his priestly house, and they H1215
2Sa 3:10 house of Saul and **e** David's throne over H7756
2Sa 7:11 that the LORD *himself will* **e** a house for H6913
2Sa 7:12 flesh and blood, and *I will* **e** his kingdom. H3922
2Sa 7:13 and *I will* **e** the throne of his kingdom H3922
1Ki 9: 5 *I will* **e** your royal throne over Israel H7756
1Ch 17:11 your own sons, and *I will* **e** his kingdom. H3922
1Ch 17:12 me, and *I will* **e** his throne forever. H3922
1Ch 22:10 And *I will* **e** the throne of his kingdom H3922
1Ch 28: 7 *I will* **e** his kingdom forever if he is H3922
2Ch 7:18 *I will* **e** your royal throne, as I covenanted H7756
Est 9:27 on themselves *to* **e the custom** that they H7756
Est 9:31 to **e** these days of Purim at their H7756
Job 23: 7 upright *can* **e** their **innocence** before him H3519
Ps 87: 5 and the Most High himself *will* **e** her." H3922
Ps 89: 4 '*I will* **e** your line forever and make your H3922
Ps 89:29 *I will* **e** his line forever, his throne as long H8492
Ps 90:17 rest on us; **e** the work of our hands for us H3922
Ps 90:17 us—yes, **e** the work of our hands. H3922
Pr 16: 3 and he *will* **e** your plans. H3922
Isa 26:12 *you* **e** peace for us; all that we have H9189
Eze 16:60 and *I will* **e** an everlasting covenant with H7756
Eze 16:62 So I *will* **e** my covenant with you, and you H7756
Eze 37:26 *I will* **e** them and increase their numbers H5989
Da 11:16 He *will* **e** *himself* in the Beautiful Land H6641
Ro 10: 3 of God and sought *to* **e** their own, *G2705*
Ro 16:25 to him who is able *to* **e** you in accordance *G5114*
Heb 8:10 is the covenant *I will* **e** with the people of *G1416*
Heb 10: 9 He sets aside the first to **e** the second. *G2705*

ESTABLISHED (82) [ESTABLISH]

Ge 9:17 of the covenant *I have* **e** between me H7756
Ge 47:26 So Joseph **e** it as a law concerning land H8492
Ex 6: 4 *I* also **e** my covenant with them to give H7756
Ex 15:17 the sanctuary, Lord, your hands **e**. H3922
Lev 26:46 that the LORD **e** at Mount Sinai between H5989
Dt 19:15 A matter *must be* **e** by the testimony of H7756
1Sa 13:13 he *would have* **e** your kingdom over Israel H3922
1Sa 20:31 neither you nor your kingdom *will* **be e**. H3922
1Sa 24:20 kingdom of Israel *will be* **e** in your hands. H7756
2Sa 5:12 knew that the LORD *had* **e** him as king over H3922
2Sa 7:16 before me; your throne will be **e** forever. H3922
2Sa 7:24 *You have* **e** your people Israel as your very H3922
2Sa 7:26 your servant David will be **e** in your sight. H3922
1Ki 2:12 his father David, and his rule **was** firmly **e**. H3922
1Ki 2:24 *he* who *has* **e** me securely on the throne of H3922
1Ki 2:46 The kingdom **was** now **e** in Solomon's H3922
1Ch 14: 2 knew that the LORD *had* **e** him as king over H3922
1Ch 16:30 The world **is firmly e**; it cannot be H3922
1Ch 17:14 his throne will be **e** forever. H3922
1Ch 17:23 *let* the promise you have made concerning your servant and his house **be e** H586
1Ch 17:24 so that *it will* **be e** and that your name will H586
1Ch 17:24 of your servant David *will* **be e** before you. H3922
2Ch 1: 1 son of David **e himself firmly** over his H2616
2Ch 12: 1 position as king *was* **e** and he had H3922
2Ch 12:13 Rehoboam **e himself firmly** in Jerusalem H2616
2Ch 17: 5 The LORD **e** the kingdom under his control H3922
2Ch 21: 4 When Jehoram **e** *himself* firmly over his H7756
Ezr 8:20 the officials *had* **e** to assist the H5989
Est 9:31 as *they had* **e** for themselves and H7756
Job 12:19 stripped and overthrows *officials* **long e**. H419
Job 21: 8 They see their children **e** around them H3922
Job 24:22 though *they become* **e**, they have H7756
Job 28:25 When he **e** the force of the wind and H6913

Ps 8: 2 infants *you have* e a stronghold H3569
Ps 9: 7 *he has* e his throne for judgment. H3922
Ps 24: 2 it on the seas and e it on the waters. H3922
Ps 74:16 also the night; you e the sun and moon. H3922
Ps 78: 5 statutes for Jacob and e the law in Israel, H8492
Ps 78:69 heights, like the earth that *he* e forever. H3569
Ps 81: 5 *he* e it as a statute for Joseph. H8492
Ps 89: 2 that *you have* e your faithfulness in H3922
Ps 89:37 *it will* **be** e forever like the moon, the H3922
Ps 93: 1 indeed, the world **is** e, **firm** and secure. H3922
Ps 93: 2 Your throne **was** e long ago; you are from H3922
Ps 96:10 The world **is firmly** e, it cannot be moved; H3922
Ps 99: 4 justice—you *have* e equity; in Jacob H3922
Ps 102:28 their descendants *will be* e before you." H3922
Ps 103:19 The LORD *has* e his throne in heaven, and H3922
Ps 111: 8 *They are* e for ever and ever, enacted in H6164
Ps 119:90 all generations; *you* e the earth, and it H3922
Ps 119:152 your statutes that *you* e them to last H3569
Ps 140:11 *May* slanderers not **be** e in the land; may H3922
Ps 148: 6 and *he* e them for ever and ever—he H6641
Pr 8:28 when he e the clouds above and fixed H599
Pr 12: 3 No one *can* **be** e through wickedness, but H3922
Pr 16:12 a throne is **e** through righteousness. H3922
Pr 20:18 Plans **are** e by seeking advice; so if you H3922
Pr 24: 3 and through understanding *it* **is** e; H3922
Pr 25: 5 his throne *will* **be** e through H3922
Pr 29:14 with fairness, his throne *will* **be** e forever. H3922
Pr 30: 4 Who *has* e all the ends of the earth H7756
Isa 2: 2 temple will **be** e as the highest of the H3922
Isa 14:32 "The LORD *has* e Zion, and in her his H3569
Isa 16: 5 In love a throne *will* **be** e; in faithfulness H3922
Isa 44: 7 happened since I e my ancient people, H8492
Isa 54:14 In righteousness *you will* **be** e: Tyranny H3922
Jer 12:16 then *they will* **be** e among my people. H1215
Jer 30:20 their community *will* **be** e before me H3922
Jer 33: 2 the LORD who formed it and e it—the LORD H3922
Jer 33:25 day and night and e the laws of heaven NDT
Mic 4: 1 temple will be e as the highest of the H3922
Mt 18:16 'every matter *may be* e by the testimony *G2705*
Ro 13: 1 no authority except that which God has e. *G5679*
Ro 13: 1 authorities that exist have been e by God. *G5435*
2Co 13: 1 "Every matter *must be* e by the testimony *G2705*
Gal 3:15 a human covenant *that has been* **duly** e, *G3263*
Gal 3:17 the covenant **previously** e by God and *G4623*
Eph 3:17 pray that you, being rooted and e in love, *G2530*
Col 1:23 in your faith, e and firm, and do not *G2530*
Heb 7:11 given to the people e that priesthood— *G2093*
Heb 8: 6 *since* the new covenant *is* e on better *G3793*
2Pe 1:12 know them and *are* **firmly** e in the truth *G5114*

ESTABLISHES (5) [ESTABLISH]

Job 25: 2 *he* e order in the heights of heaven. H6913
Pr 16: 9 their course, but the LORD e their steps. H3922
Isa 42: 4 be discouraged till *he* e justice on earth. H8492
Isa 62: 7 him no rest till *he* e Jerusalem and makes H3922
Hab 2:12 with bloodshed and e a town by injustice! H3922

ESTABLISHING (1) [ESTABLISH]

Isa 9: 7 e and upholding it with justice and H3922

ESTATE (10)

Ge 15: 2 who will inherit my e is Eliezer of H1074
Ge 31:14 share in the inheritance of our father's e? H1074
Ru 4: 6 it because I might endanger my own e. H5709
Est 8: 1 gave Queen Esther the e *of* Haman, H1074
Est 8: 2 Esther appointed him over Haman's e. H1074
Est 8: 7 I have given his e to Esther, and they H1074
Ps 136:23 us in our **low** e His love endures H9165
Lk 15:12 'Father, give me my share *of* the e. *G4045*
Ac 28: 7 There was an e nearby that belonged to *G6005*
Gal 4: 1 from a slave, although he owns *the* **whole** e. AIT

ESTEEM (4) [ESTEEMED]

Est 10: 3 and **held in high** e by his many fellow H8354
Isa 2:22 in their nostrils. Why **hold** them **in** e? H3108
Isa 53: 3 was despised, and *we* **held** him in low e. H3108
Gal 2: 6 As for those who were **held in high** e *G1506*

ESTEEMED (6) [ESTEEM]

Pr 22: 1 to be e is better than silver or gold. H2834
Da 9:23 come to tell you, for you are **highly** e. H2776
Da 10:11 you who are **highly** e, consider carefully H2776
Da 10:19 be afraid, you who are **highly** e," he said. H2776
Gal 2: 2 meeting privately *with* those **e as leaders** *G1506*
Gal 2: 9 John, those e as pillars, gave me *G1506*

ESTHER (41) [ESTHER'S]

Est 2: 7 who was also known as **E**, had a lovely H676
Est 2: 8 **E** also was taken to the king's palace and H676
Est 2:10 **E** had not revealed her nationality and H676
Est 2:11 harem to find out how **E** was and what was H676
Est 2:15 When the turn came for **E** (the young H676
Est 2:15 And **E** won the favor of everyone who saw H676
Est 2:17 king was attracted to **E** more than to any of H676
Est 2:20 But **E** had kept secret her family background H676
Est 2:22 found out about the plot and told Queen **E**, H676
Est 4: 5 Then **E** summoned Hathak, one of the H676
Est 4: 8 in Susa, to show to **E** and explain it to her H676
Est 4: 9 back and reported to **E** what Mordecai had H676
Est 4:15 Then **E** sent this reply to Mordecai: H676
Est 5: 1 On the third day **E** put on her royal robes H676
Est 5: 2 When he saw Queen **E** standing in the H676
Est 5: 2 So **E** approached and touched the tip of H676
Est 5: 3 "What is it, Queen **E**? What is your request H676
Est 5: 4 the king," replied **E**, "let the king, together H676
Est 5: 5 king said, "so that we may do what **E** asks." H676
Est 5: 5 went to the banquet **E** had prepared. H676
Est 5: 6 the king again asked **E**, "Now what is your H676
Est 5: 7 **E** replied, "My petition and my request is H676
Est 5:12 only person Queen **E** invited to accompany H676
Est 6:14 away to the banquet **E** had prepared. H676
Est 7: 2 again asked, "Queen **E**, what is your H676
Est 7: 3 Then Queen **E** answered, "If I have found H676
Est 7: 5 King Xerxes asked Queen **E**, "Who is he H676
Est 7: 6 **E** said, "An adversary and enemy! This vile H676
Est 7: 7 stayed behind to beg Queen **E** for his life. H676
Est 7: 8 falling on the couch where **E** was reclining. H676
Est 8: 1 Xerxes gave Queen **E** the estate of Haman, H676
Est 8: 1 **E** had told how he was related to her. H676
Est 8: 2 And **E** appointed him over Haman's estate. H676
Est 8: 3 **E** again pleaded with the king, falling at H676
Est 8: 4 the gold scepter to **E** and she arose and H676
Est 8: 7 replied to Queen **E** and to Mordecai the H676
Est 8: 7 I have given his estate to **E**, and they have H676
Est 9:12 The king said to Queen **E**, "The Jews have H676
Est 9:13 **E** answered, "give the Jews in Susa H676
Est 9:29 So Queen **E**, daughter of Abihail, along H676
Est 9:31 the Jew and Queen **E** had decreed for H676

ESTHER'S (6) [ESTHER]

Est 2:18 a great banquet, **E** banquet, for all his H676
Est 4: 4 When **E** eunuchs and female attendants H676
Est 4:12 When **E** words were reported to Mordecai, H676
Est 4:17 away and carried out all of **E** instructions. H676
Est 7: 1 Haman went to Queen **E** banquet, H676
Est 9:32 **E** decree confirmed these regulations about H676

ESTIMATE (1)

Lk 14:28 first sit down and e the cost to see if you *G6028*

ESTRANGED (1) [STRANGE]

Job 19:13 acquaintances *are* completely e from me. H2319

ETAM (5)

Jdg 15: 8 stayed in a cave in the rock of **E**. H6515
Jdg 15:11 cave in the rock of **E** and said to Samson, H6515
1Ch 4: 3 These were the sons of **E**: Jezreel, Ishma H6515
1Ch 4:32 Their surrounding villages were **E**, Ain H6515
2Ch 11: 6 Bethlehem, **E**, Tekoa, H6515

ETERNAL (80) [ETERNITY]

Ge 21:33 on the name of the LORD, the **E** God. H6409
Dt 33:27 The e God is your refuge, and underneath H7710
1Ki 10: 9 of the LORD's e love for Israel, H4200+6409
Ps 16:11 with e pleasures at your right hand. H5905
Ps 111:10 To him belongs e praise. H4200+6329
Ps 119:89 is e; it stands firm in the H4200+6409
Ps 119:160 all your righteous laws are e. H4200+6409
Ecc 12: 5 people go to their e home and mourners H6409
Isa 26: 4 the LORD, the LORD himself, is the Rock e. H6409
Isa 47: 7 'I am forever—the e queen!' But you did H6329
Jer 10:10 true God; he is the living God, the e King. H6409
Da 4: 3 His kingdom is an e kingdom; his A10550
Da 4:34 His dominion is an e dominion; his A10550
Mt 18: 8 hands or two feet and be thrown into e fire. *G173*
Mt 19:16 what good thing must I do to get e life?" *G173*
Mt 19:29 times as much and will inherit e life. *G173*
Mt 25:41 into the e fire prepared for the devil and *G173*
Mt 25:46 "Then they will go away to e punishment *G173*
Mt 25:46 punishment, but the righteous to e life." *G173*
Mk 3:29 be forgiven; they are guilty of an e sin." *G173*
Mk 10:17 he asked, "what must I do to inherit e life?" *G173*
Mk 10:30 in the age to come e life. *G173*
Lk 10:25 he asked, "what must I do to inherit e life?" *G173*
Lk 16: 9 you will be welcomed into e dwellings. *G173*
Lk 18:18 teacher, what must I do to inherit e life?" *G173*
Lk 18:30 in this age, and in the age to come e life." *G173*
Jn 3:15 who believes may have e life in him." *G173*
Jn 3:16 in him shall not perish but have e life. *G173*
Jn 3:36 Whoever believes in the Son has e life, but *G173*
Jn 4:14 them a spring of water welling up to e life." *G173*
Jn 4:36 draws a wage and harvests a crop for e life, *G173*
Jn 5:24 him who sent me has e life and will not be *G173*
Jn 5:39 you think that in them you have e life. *G173*
Jn 6:27 for food that endures to e life, which *G173*
Jn 6:40 Son and believes in him shall have e life, *G173*
Jn 6:47 I tell you, the one who believes has e life. *G173*
Jn 6:54 my flesh and drinks my blood has e life, *G173*
Jn 6:68 You have the words *of* e life. *G173*
Jn 10:28 I give them e life, and they shall never *G173*
Jn 12:25 their life in this world will keep it for e life. *G173*
Jn 12:50 I know that his command leads to e life. *G173*
Jn 17: 2 that he might give e life to all those you *G173*
Jn 17: 3 Now this is e life: that they know you, the *G173*
Ac 13:46 do not consider yourselves worthy of e life, *G173*
Ac 13:48 all who were appointed for e life believed. *G173*
Ro 1:20 qualities—his e power and divine nature *G132*
Ro 2: 7 honor and immortality, he will give e life. *G173*
Ro 5:21 righteousness to bring e life through Jesus *G173*
Ro 6:22 leads to holiness, and the result is e life. *G173*
Ro 6:23 the gift of God is e life in Christ Jesus *G173*
Ro 16:26 writings by the command *of* the e God, *G173*
2Co 4:17 are achieving for us an e glory that far *G173*
2Co 4:18 seen is temporary, but what is unseen is e. *G173*
2Co 5: 1 from God, an e house in heaven, not *G173*
Gal 6: 8 the Spirit, from the Spirit will reap e life. *G173*
Eph 3:11 according to his e purpose that he *G172*
2Th 2:16 by his grace gave us e encouragement *G173*
1Ti 1:16 would believe in him and receive e life. *G173*
1Ti 1:17 Now to the King e, immortal, invisible, the *G172*
1Ti 6:12 Take hold of the e life to which you were *G173*
2Ti 2:10 that is in Christ Jesus, with e glory. *G173*
Titus 1: 2 in the hope of e life, which God, who does *G173*
Titus 3: 7 become heirs having the hope of e life. *G173*
Heb 5: 9 became the source of e salvation for all *G173*
Heb 6: 2 resurrection of the dead, and e judgment. *G173*
Heb 9:12 own blood, thus obtaining e redemption. *G173*
Heb 9:14 who through the e Spirit offered himself *G173*
Heb 9:15 may receive the promised e inheritance— *G173*
Heb 13:20 the blood of the e covenant brought back *G173*
1Pe 5:10 who called you to his e glory in Christ, after *G173*
2Pe 1:11 welcome into the e kingdom of our Lord *G173*
1Jn 1: 2 we proclaim to you the e life, which *G173*
1Jn 2:25 And this is what he promised us—e life. *G173*
1Jn 3:15 that no murderer has e life residing in him. *G173*
1Jn 5:11 God has given us e life, and this life is in *G173*
1Jn 5:13 so that you may know that you have e life. *G173*
1Jn 5:20 He is the true God and e life. *G173*
Jude 7 those who suffer the punishment of e fire. *G173*
Jude 21 our Lord Jesus Christ to bring you to e life. *G173*
Rev 14: 6 he had the e gospel to proclaim to *G173*

ETERNITY (2) [ETERNAL]

Ps 93: 2 established long ago; you are from **all** e. H6409
Ecc 3:11 He has also set e in the human heart; yet H6409

ETH KAZIN (1)

Jos 19:13 eastward to Gath Hepher and **E**; H6962

ETHAM (4)

Ex 13:20 they camped at **E** on the edge of the H918
Nu 33: 6 They left Sukkoth and camped at **E**, on the H918
Nu 33: 7 They left **E**, turned back to Pi Hahiroth, to H918
Nu 33: 8 traveled for three days in the Desert of **E**, H918

ETHAN (8)

1Ki 4:31 including **E** the Ezrahite—wiser H420
1Ch 2: 6 **E**, Heman, Kalkol and Darda—five H420
1Ch 2: 8 The son of **E**: Azariah. H420
1Ch 6:42 the son of **E**, the son of Zimmah, the son of H420
1Ch 6:44 **E** son of Kishi, the son of Abdi, the son of H420
1Ch 15:17 relatives the Merarites, **E** son of Kushaiah; H420
1Ch 15:19 Asaph and **E** were to sound the bronze H420
Ps 89: T A maskil of **E** the Ezrahite. H420

ETHANIM (1)

1Ki 8: 2 the time of the festival in the month of **E**, H923

ETHBAAL (1)

1Ki 16:31 Jezebel daughter of **E** king of the H909

ETHER (2)

Jos 15:42 **E**, Ashan, H6987
Jos 19: 7 Rimmon, **E** and Ashan—four towns and H6987

ETHIOPIA, ETHIOPIAN, ETHIOPIANS (KJV)

CUSH, CUSHITE, CUSHITES

ETHIOPIAN (2) [ETHIOPIANS]

Jer 13:23 Can an **E** change his skin or a leopard its H3934
Ac 8:27 on his way he met an **E** eunuch *G467+134*

ETHIOPIANS (1) [ETHIOPIAN]

Ac 8:27 Kandake (which means "queen *of* the **E**") *G134*

ETHNAN (1)

1Ch 4: 7 The sons of Helah: Zereth, Zohar, **E**, H925

ETHNI (1)

1Ch 6:41 the son of **E**, the son of Zerah, the son of H922

EUBULUS (1)

2Ti 4:21 **E** greets you, and so do Pudens, Linus *G2300*

EUNICE (1)

2Ti 1: 5 Lois and in your mother **E** and, *G2332*

EUNUCH (10) [EUNUCHS]

Est 2: 3 of Hegai, the king's e, who is in charge of H6247
Est 2:14 the king's e who was in charge of the H6247
Est 2:15 the king's e who was in charge of the H6247
Isa 56: 3 And let no e complain, "I am only a dry H6247
Ac 8:27 on his way he met an Ethiopian e, an *G2336*
Ac 8:32 the passage of Scripture the e was reading: NDT
Ac 8:34 The e asked Philip, "Tell me, please, who *G2336*
Ac 8:36 they came to some water and the e said *G2336*
Ac 8:38 both Philip and the e went down into the *G2336*
Ac 8:39 and the e did not see him again *G2336*

EUNUCHS (14) [EUNUCH]

2Ki 9:32 Two or three e looked down at him H6247
2Ki 20:18 they will become e in the palace of the H6247
Est 1:10 the seven e who served him— H6247
Est 1:15 King Xerxes that the e have taken to her." H6247
Est 4: 4 When Esther's e and female attendants H6247
Est 4: 5 one of the king's e assigned to attend her, H6247
Est 6:14 the king's e arrived and hurried Haman H6247
Est 7: 9 Harbona, one of the e attending the king H6247
Isa 39: 7 they will become e in the palace of the H6247
Isa 56: 4 "To the e who keep my Sabbaths, who H6247

Mt 19:12 For there are **e** who were born that way *G2336*
Mt 19:12 there are **e** who have been made *G2336*
Mt 19:12 who *have been* **made e** by others— *G2335*
Mt 19:12 those who **choose to live like e** for the *G2335*

EUODIA (1)

Php 4: 2 I plead with **E** and I plead with Syntyche *G2337*

EUPHRATES (36) [TRANS-EUPHRATES]

Ge 2:14 And the fourth river is the **E**. H7310
Ge 15:18 Wadi of Egypt to the great river, the **E**— H7310
Ge 31:21 crossed the **E River**, and headed for H5643
Ex 23:31 and from the desert to the **E River**. H5643
Nu 22: 5 at Pethor, near the **E River**, in his native H5643
Dt 1: 7 Lebanon, as far as the great river, the **E**. H7310
Dt 11:24 from the **E** River to the Mediterranean H7310
Jos 1: 4 the great river, the **E**—all the Hittite H7310
Jos 24: 2 lived beyond the **E River** and worshiped H5643
Jos 24: 3 the land beyond the **E** and led him H5643
Jos 24:14 beyond the **E River** and in Egypt, H5643
Jos 24:15 gods your ancestors served beyond the **E**, H5643
2Sa 8: 3 to restore his monument at the **E** River. H7310
2Sa 10:16 brought from beyond the **E River**; H5643
1Ki 4:21 kingdoms from the **E River** to the land of H5643
1Ki 4:24 over all the kingdoms west of the **E River**, H5643
1Ki 14:15 scatter them beyond the **E River**, H5643
2Ki 23:29 Egypt went up to the **E** River to help the H7310
2Ki 24: 7 from the Wadi of Egypt to the **E** River. H7310
1Ch 5: 9 of the desert that extends to the **E** River, H7310
1Ch 18: 3 to set up his monument at the **E** River. H7310
1Ch 19:16 brought from beyond the **E River**, H5643
2Ch 9:26 the kings from the **E River** to the land of H5643
2Ch 35:20 went up to fight at Carchemish on the **E**, H7310
Isa 7:20 a razor hired from beyond the **E River**— H5643
Isa 8: 7 them the mighty floodwaters of the **E**— H5643
Isa 11:15 he will sweep his hand over the **E River**. H5643
Isa 27:12 from the flowing **E** to the Wadi of Egypt, H5643S
Jer 2:18 go to Assyria to drink water from the **E**? H5643
Jer 46: 2 at Carchemish on the **E** River by H7310
Jer 46: 6 north by the River **E** they stumble and fall. H7310
Jer 46:10 in the land of the north by the River **E**. H7310
Jer 51:63 tie a stone to it and throw it into the **E**. H7310
Mic 7:12 from Egypt to the **E** and from sea to sea H5643S
Rev 9:14 angels who are bound at the great river **E**." *G2371*
Rev 16:12 poured out his bowl on the great river **E**, *G2371*

EUROCLYDON (KJV) NORTHEASTER

EUTYCHUS (1)

Ac 20: 9 in a window was a young man named **E**, *G2366*

EVANGELIST (2) [EVANGELISTS]

Ac 21: 8 stayed at the house of Philip the **e**, *G2296*
2Ti 4: 5 do the work *of* an **e**, discharge all the *G2296*

EVANGELISTS (1) [EVANGELIST]

Eph 4:11 the prophets, the **e**, the pastors and *G2296*

EVE (4)

Ge 3:20 Adam named his wife **E**, because she H2558
Ge 4: 1 Adam made love to his wife **E**, and she H2558
2Co 11: 3 afraid that just as **E** was deceived by the *G2293*
1Ti 2:13 For Adam was formed first, then **E**. *G2293*

EVEN (571) [EVENLY]

Ge 8:21 **e though** every inclination of the human H3954
Ge 14:23 you, **not e** a thread or the strap of a sandal H561
Ge 31:28 You didn't **e** let me kiss my grandchildren H2256
Ge 31:50 my daughters, **e** though no one is with us NDT
Ge 39:10 to go to bed with her or **e** be with her. NDT
Ge 40:15 **e** here I have done nothing to H1685
Ge 41:21 **But e** after they ate them, no one could H2256
Ge 44: 8 We **e** brought back to you from the land of H2176
Ge 48:14 **e though** Manasseh was the firstborn. H3954
Ex 1:10 or *they will become e more* **numerous** and, AIT
Ex 1:20 increased and became **e more** numerous. H4394
Ex 2:19 He **e** drew water for us and watered the H1685
Ex 7:19 in Egypt, **e** in vessels of wood and stone." H2256
Ex 7:23 and did not take **e** this to heart. H1685
Ex 8:21 **e** the ground will be covered with them. H1685
Ex 9: 7 found that not **e** one of the animals H6330
Ex 10:24 **E** your women and children may go with H1685
Ex 19:22 **E** the priests, who approach the H2256+1685
Ex 33: 5 If I were to go with you **e** for a moment, NDT
Ex 34: 3 not **e** the flocks and herds may graze in H1685
Ex 34:21 **e** during the plowing season and harvest NDT
Lev 4:13 **e though** the community is unaware of H2256
Lev 5: 3 unclean) **e though** they are unaware of it H2256
Lev 5: 4 **e though** they are unaware of it H2256
Lev 5:17 commands, **e though** they do not know it H2256
Lev 13:55 appearance, **e though** it has not spread H2256
Lev 18:25 **E** the land was defiled; so I punished it H2256
Lev 21:11 himself unclean, **e** for his father or mother, NDT
Lev 25:54 " '**E** if someone is not redeemed in any of H2256
Lev 26:17 you will flee **e when** no one is H2256
Lev 26:36 **e though** no one is pursuing them. H2256
Lev 26:37 **e though** no one is pursuing them. H2256
Nu 4:20 at the holy things, **e for** a moment, or they H3869
Nu 5:14 suspects her **e though** she is not H2256
Nu 6: 4 the grapevine, not **e** the seeds or skins. H6330
Nu 6: 7 **E if** their own father or mother or brother H928
Nu 13:28 We **e** saw descendants of Anak H2256+1685
Nu 17:13 Anyone who **e comes near** the H7929+7929
Nu 22:18 "**E if** Balak gave me all the silver and gold H561
Nu 23:10 dust of Jacob or number *e a* **fourth** *of* Israel? AIT
Nu 24:13 '**E if** Balak gave me all the silver and gold H561
Nu 32:14 making the LORD **e** more angry with H6388
Dt 1:28 We **e** saw the Anakites there H1685
Dt 2: 5 not **e enough** to put your foot on. H6330
Dt 2:36 town in the gorge, **e** as far as Gilead, not H2256
Dt 5:24 that a person can live **e** if God speaks with NDT
Dt 7:20 among them until **e** the survivors who H2256
Dt 10:14 the heavens, **e** the highest heavens H2256
Dt 12:31 They **e** burn their sons and H3954+1685
Dt 18: 8 **e though** he has received money H4200+963
Dt 19: 6 kill him **e though** he is not deserving H2256
Dt 23: 2 of the LORD, not **e** in the tenth generation. H1685
Dt 23: 3 of the LORD, not **e** in the tenth generation. H1685
Dt 24: 6 of millstones—not **e** the upper one—as H2256
Dt 28:30 but *you will* not *e begin to* **enjoy** its fruit. AIT
Dt 28:54 **E** the most gentle and sensitive man among NDT
Dt 29:19 **e though** I persist in going my own way," H3954
Dt 30: 4 **E if** you have been banished to the most H561
Dt 31:21 **e** before I bring them into the land I NDT
Dt 32:31 like our Rock, as **e** our enemies concede. H2256
Dt 33:17 nations, **e** those at the ends of the earth. H3481
Jos 22:17 **e though** a plague fell on the community H2256
Jdg 2:19 to ways **e more** corrupt **than** those of their H4946
Jdg 3:22 **E** the handle sank in after the blade, and H1685
Jdg 5: 3 *e* **I**, will sing to the LORD; I will praise the AIT
Jdg 13:16 LORD replied, "**E though** you detain me, H561
Jdg 14:16 "I haven't **e** explained it to my father or H2180
Jdg 15: 3 "This time *I* **have a right to get e** with the H5927
Ru 1:12 **E if** I thought there was still hope for me— H3954
Ru 1:12 **e if** I had a husband tonight and then H1685
Ru 1:17 **if e** death separates you and me. H3954
Ru 2:16 **E** pull out some stalks for her from H2256+1685
Ru 2:21 the Moabite said, "He **e** said to me, 'Stay H3954
1Sa 2:15 But **e** before the fat was burned, the priest's NDT
1Sa 12:12 **e though** the LORD your God was your king. H2256
1Sa 13: 7 Some Hebrews **e** crossed the Jordan to the H2256
1Sa 14:30 of the Philistines have been **e** greater?" H3954
1Sa 14:39 **e** if the guilt lies with my son Jonathan H3954
1Sa 17:29 said David. "Can't I **e** speak?" NDT
1Sa 18: 4 with his tunic, and **e** his sword, his bow H6330
1Sa 19:23 But the Spirit of God came **e** on him, and H1685
1Sa 20:15 not **e** when the LORD has cut off every one H2256
1Sa 21: 5 bodies are holy **e** on missions that are H2256
1Sa 23:17 **E** my father Saul knows this. H2256+1685
1Sa 25:29 **E though** someone is pursuing you to take H2256
2Sa 5: 6 **e** the blind and the lame can ward H3954+561
2Sa 6:22 I will become **e** more undignified than this H6388
2Sa 12: 3 drank from his cup **and e** slept in his arms. H2256
2Sa 12: 8 *I would have* **given** you **e more** H3578+3869+2179+2256+3869+2179
2Sa 17: 9 **E** now, he is hidden in a cave or some H2180
2Sa 17:10 Then **e** the bravest soldier, whose heart is H1685
2Sa 18: 3 **E** if half of us die, they won't care; but you H2256
2Sa 18:12 "**E** if a thousand shekels were weighed H2256
2Sa 19:43 claims **e more** forcefully **than** the men of H4946
2Sa 23:19 **e though** he was not included among H2256
1Ki 1: 1 not keep warm **e when** they put covers H2256
1Ki 1:37 Solomon *to* **make** his throne *e* **greater** than AIT
1Ki 1:42 **E as** he was speaking, Jonathan son of H6388
1Ki 8:27 The heavens, **e** the highest heaven H2256
1Ki 10: 7 **not e** half was told me; in wisdom AIT
1Ki 12:11 you a heavy yoke; I *will* **make** it **e heavier**. H3578
1Ki 12:14 your yoke heavy; I *will* **make** it **e heavier**. H3578
1Ki 12:31 of people, **e though** they were not Levites. H889
1Ki 13: 8 "**E if** you were to give me half your H561
1Ki 13:33 **E** after this, Jeroboam did not change his NDT
1Ki 14:14 **E** now this is beginning to happen. H1685
1Ki 14:24 There were **e** male shrine H2256+1685
1Ki 15:13 He **e** deposed his grandmother H2256+1685
1Ki 17:20 you brought tragedy **e** on this widow I am H1685
1Ki 18:35 around the altar and **e** filled the trench. H1685
1Ki 22:46 who remained there **e after** the reign of his H928
2Ki 5:16 **And e though** Naaman urged him, he H2256
2Ki 7: 2 *e if* the LORD *should* **open** the floodgates of AIT
2Ki 7:19 *e if* the LORD *should* **open** the floodgates of AIT
2Ki 16: 3 kings of Israel and **e** sacrificed his son in H1685
2Ki 17:19 **and e** Judah did not keep the commands H1685
2Ki 17:41 **E while** these people were worshiping the H2256
2Ki 18:24 **e though** you are depending on Egypt H2256
2Ki 23:15 **E** the altar at Bethel, the high H2256+1685
2Ki 23:15 **e** that altar and high place he demolished. H1685
1Ch 10:13 of the LORD and **e** consulted a medium H1685
1Ch 11: 2 In the past, **e** while Saul was king, you H1685
1Ch 11:21 **e though** he was not included among H2256
2Ch 2: 6 since the heavens, **e** the highest heavens H2256
2Ch 6:18 The heavens, **e** the highest heavens H2256
2Ch 9: 6 **not e** half the greatness of your wisdom was AIT
2Ch 10:11 you a heavy yoke; I *will* **make** it **e heavier**. H3578
2Ch 10:14 your yoke heavy; I *will* **make** it **e heavier**. H3578
2Ch 11:14 The Levites **e** abandoned their H3954
2Ch 16:12 **e** in his illness he did not seek H2256+1685
2Ch 24: 7 of God and had used **e** its sacred objects H1685
2Ch 25: 8 **E** if you go and fight courageously in H3954
2Ch 28:22 King Ahaz became **e** more unfaithful to H2256
2Ch 30:19 **e if** they are not clean according to the H2256
Ezr 5:14 He **e** removed from the temple A10221+10059
Ne 1: 9 then **e if** your exiled people are at the H561
Ne 4: 3 **e** a fox climbing up on it would break down H561
Ne 4:23 had his weapon, **e** when he went for water. NDT
Ne 6: 7 have **e** appointed prophets to make H1685
Ne 9: 6 made the heavens, **e** the highest heavens NDT
Ne 9:18 **e** when they cast for themselves an image H677
Ne 9:22 allotting to them **e** the remotest frontiers. NDT
Ne 9:35 **E** while they were in their kingdom H2256
Ne 13:26 **but e** he was led into sin by foreign H1685
Est 4:16 to the king, **e though** it is against the law. H889
Est 5: 3 **E** up to half the kingdom, it will be given NDT
Est 5: 6 is your request? **E** up to half the kingdom NDT
Est 7: 2 is your request? **E** up to half the kingdom NDT
Est 7: 8 "Will he **e** molest the queen while she is H1685
Job 4:17 Can **e** a strong man be more pure than his H561
Job 5: 5 harvest, taking it **e** from among thorns H2256
Job 6:27 You would **e** cast lots for the fatherless H677
Job 7:14 **e then** you frighten me with dreams and H2256
Job 7:19 from me, or let me alone **e** for an instant? NDT
Job 8: 6 **e** now he will rouse himself on your H3954
Job 9:13 **e** the cohorts of Rahab cowered at his feet. NDT
Job 9:16 **E if** I summoned him and he responded, H561
Job 9:20 **E if** I were innocent, my mouth would H561
Job 9:30 **E if** I washed myself with soap and my H561
Job 9:31 a slime pit so that **e** my clothes would NDT
Job 10:15 **E if** I am innocent, I cannot lift my head H2256
Job 10:22 where **e** the light is like darkness. H2256
Job 11: 6 God has **e** forgotten some of your sin. H3954
Job 15: 4 **But** you **e** undermine piety and hinder H677
Job 15:10 on our side, *men e* **older** than your father. AIT
Job 15:15 if **e** the heavens are not pure in his eyes, H2256
Job 16:19 **E** now my witness is in heaven; my H1685
Job 19:18 **E** the little boys scorn me; when I appear H1685
Job 21:22 since he judges **e** the highest? NDT
Job 22: 2 Can **e** a wise person benefit him? H3954
Job 22:30 He will deliver **e** one who is not innocent NDT
Job 23: 2 "**E** today my complaint is bitter; his hand H1685
Job 25: 5 If **e** the moon is not bright and the stars H6330
Job 28:21 concealed **e** from the birds in the sky. H2256
Job 33:29 things to a person—twice, **e** three times— NDT
Job 36:13 resentment; **e when** he fetters them H3954
Job 36:19 Would your wealth **or** *e* all your mighty AIT
Job 36:33 **e** the cattle make known its approach. H677
Ps 9: 6 **e** the memory of them has perished. NDT
Ps 14: 3 is no one who does good, not **e** one. H1685
Ps 15: 4 who keeps an oath *e* **when** it hurts, and does AIT
Ps 16: 7 **e** at night my heart instructs me. H677
Ps 22: 9 me trust in you, **e** at my mother's breast. NDT
Ps 23: 4 **E** though I walk through the darkest valley, H1685
Ps 27: 3 out against me, **e** then I will be confident. NDT
Ps 33:22 **e as** we put our hope in you. H3869+889
Ps 36: 4 **E** on their beds they plot evil; they commit NDT
Ps 38:10 **e** the light has gone from my eyes. H2256
Ps 39: 2 utterly silent, **not** *e* **saying** anything good. AIT
Ps 39: 5 is but a breath, **e** those who seem secure. NDT
Ps 41: 9 **E** my close friend, someone I trusted, one H1685
Ps 48:14 ever; he will be our guide **e** to the end. NDT
Ps 51: 6 Yet you desired faithfulness **e in** the womb AIT
Ps 53: 3 is no one who does good, not **e** one. H1685
Ps 55:18 against me, **e though** many oppose me. H3954
Ps 58: 3 **E** from birth the wicked go astray; from the NDT
Ps 68:13 **E** while you sleep among the sheep pens NDT
Ps 68:18 from people, **e** from the rebellious H2256+677
Ps 71:18 **E** when I am old and gray, do not H2256+1685
Ps 78: 6 know them, **e** the children yet to be born NDT
Ps 78:30 **e** while the food was still in their mouths, NDT
Ps 83: 8 **E** Assyria has joined them to reinforce H1685
Ps 84: 2 My soul yearns, **e** faints, for the H2256+1685
Ps 84: 3 **E** the sparrow has found a home, and the H1685
Ps 106: 6 We have sinned, **e as** our ancestors did H6640
Ps 112: 4 **E** in darkness light dawns for the upright, for NDT
Ps 133: 3 bestows his blessing, **e** life forevermore. NDT
Ps 139:10 **e** there your hand will guide me, your H1685
Ps 139:12 **e** the darkness will not be dark to you; the H1685
Pr 11:24 yet gains **e more**; another H6388
Pr 14:13 **E** in laughter the heart may ache, and H1685
Pr 14:20 poor are shunned **e** by their neighbors, H1685
Pr 14:32 **but e** in death the righteous seek refuge H2256
Pr 14:33 of the discerning **and e** among fools she H2256
Pr 16: 4 **e** the wicked for a day of disaster. H2256+1685
Pr 17:28 **E** fools are thought wise if they keep H1685
Pr 19: 4 **but** *e* the closest friend of the poor person AIT
Pr 19:24 he will not **e** bring it back to his mouth! H1685
Pr 20:11 **E** small children are known by their H1685
Pr 22: 6 **and** *e* when they are old they will not turn AIT
Pr 22:19 be in the LORD, I teach you today, **e** you. H677
Pr 27: 7 to the hungry **e** what is bitter tastes H3972
Pr 28: 9 instruction, **e** their prayers are detestable. H1685
Ecc 1:11 **e** those yet to come will not be H1685
Ecc 2:23 **e** at night their minds do not rest. H1685
Ecc 6: 6 **e** if he lives a thousand years twice over H2256
Ecc 8:17 **E** if the wise claim they know, they H2256+1685
Ecc 9: 4 **e** a live dog is better off than a dead lion! H3954
Ecc 9: 5 and **e** their name is forgotten. H3954
Ecc 10: 3 **E** as fools walk along the road H2256+1685
Ecc 10:20 Do not revile the king **e** in your thoughts H1685
Isa 1:15 from you; **e** when you offer many prayers H1685
Isa 5:30 **e** the sun will be darkened by clouds. H2256
Isa 14: 8 **E** the junipers and the cedars of Lebanon H1685
Isa 23:12 to Cyprus; **e** there you will find no rest." H1685
Isa 26:10 **e** in a land of uprightness they go on doing NDT
Isa 32: 7 **e** when the plea of the needy is just. H2256
Isa 33:23 will be divided and **e** the lame will carry off NDT
Isa 36: 9 **e though** you are depending on Egypt H2256
Isa 40:30 **E** youths grow tired and weary, and young H2256
Isa 43:11 **e** I, am the LORD, and apart from me there NDT

Isa 43:25 **e** I, am he who blots out your NDT
Isa 44:19 used for fuel; I **e** baked bread over its coals H677
Isa 46: 4 **E** to your old age and gray hairs I am he, H2256
Isa 46: 7 **E though** someone cries out to it, it cannot H677
Isa 47: 6 **E** on the aged you laid a very heavy yoke. NDT
Isa 47:14 They cannot **e** save themselves from the NDT
Isa 48:15 **e** I, have spoken; yes, I have called him. NDT
Isa 51:12 **e** I, am he who comforts you. Who are NDT
Isa 56:12 will be like today, or **e far** better." H3856+4394
Isa 64:10 become a wasteland; **e** Zion is a wasteland NDT
Jer 2:33 **E** the worst of women can learn from your H1685
Jer 4: 6 from the north, **e** terrible destruction." H2256
Jer 5:18 "Yet **e** in those days," declares the LORD, "I H1685
Jer 6: 1 out of the north, **e** terrible destruction. H2256
Jer 6:15 they do not **e** know how to blush. H1685
Jer 8: 7 **E** the stork in the sky knows her appointed H1685
Jer 8:12 they do not **e** know how to blush. H2256
Jer 9:26 **and e** the whole house of Israel is H2256
Jer 11:23 Not **e** a remnant will be left to them H2256
Jer 12: 6 own family—**e** they have betrayed you H1685
Jer 12:16 **e as** they once taught my people to H3869+889
Jer 14: 5 **E** the doe in the field deserts her H3954+1685
Jer 15: 1 "**E if** Moses and Samuel were to stand H561
Jer 16: 7 the dead—not **e** for a father or a mother H2256
Jer 17: 2 **E** their children remember their altars H3869
Jer 22:24 declares the LORD, "**e if** you, Jehoiachin H3954
Jer 23:11 **e** in my temple I find their wickedness," H1685
Jer 23:38 **e though** I told you that you must not H2256
Jer 27: 6 I will make **e** the wild animals subject to H1685
Jer 28:14 I will **e** give him control over the wild H1685
Jer 29:31 **e though** I did not send him H2256
Jer 34:15 You **e** made a covenant before me in the H2256
Jer 36:25 **E** though Elnathan, Delaiah and H1685
Jer 37:10 **E** if you were to defeat the entire H3954
Jer 38:15 **E** if I did give you counsel, you would not H2256
Jer 48:34 **e** the waters of Nimrim are dried up. H1685
Jer 49:37 bring disaster on them, **e** my fierce anger," NDT
Jer 51:53 **E if** Babylon ascends to the heavens and H3954
La 3: 8 **E** when I call out or cry for help, he shuts H1685
La 4: 3 **E** jackals offer their breasts to nurse their H1685
Eze 5: 7 You have not **e** conformed to the H2256
Eze 8: 6 see things that are **e more** detestable." H1524
Eze 8:13 doing things that are **e more** detestable." H1524
Eze 8:15 things that are **e more** detestable than H1524
Eze 13: 6 **E though** the LORD has not sent them, they H2256
Eze 14:14 **e if** these three men—Noah, Daniel and H2256
Eze 14:16 **e** if these three men were in it NDT
Eze 14:18 **e if** these three men were in it H2256
Eze 14:20 the Sovereign LORD, **e if** Noah, Daniel H2256
Eze 16:28 were insatiable; **and e after** that, you still H2256
Eze 16:29 **but e** with this you were not H2256+1685
Eze 16:56 You would not **e** mention your sister H2256
Eze 16:57 **E so**, you are now scorned by the H4017
Eze 21:13 And what if **e** the scepter, which the H1685
Eze 21:14 the sword strike twice, **e** three times. It is a NDT
Eze 23:37 they **e** sacrificed their children H2256+1685
Eze 23:40 "They **e** sent messengers for H2256+677+3954
Eze 24:12 deposit has not been removed, not **e** by fire. NDT
Eze 33:12 be allowed to live **e though** they were H928
Eze 35:10 of them," **e though** I the LORD was there H2256
Eze 44: 9 not **e** the foreigners who live among the H3972
Da 2:41 **e as** you saw iron mixed A10353+10619+10168
Da 3:18 But **e if** he does not, we want you to A10213
Da 4:31 **E as** the words were on his lips, a voice A10531
Da 4:36 and **became e greater** A10650+10339+10323
Da 5: 9 Belshazzar became **e more** terrified and A10678
Da 9: 9 **e though** we have rebelled against him; H3954
Da 11: 5 commanders *will become e* **stronger** than he AIT
Da 11:15 **e** their best troops will not have the H2256
Hos 4:18 **E** when their drinks are gone, they continue NDT
Hos 5: 5 the Israelites, **e** Ephraim, stumble in their H2256
Hos 9: 6 **E** if they escape from destruction, Egypt H2180
Hos 9:12 **E** if they rear children, I will bereave them H3954
Hos 9:16 **E** if they bear children, I will slay their H1685
Hos 10: 3 But **e** if we had a king, what could he do NDT
Hos 11: 7 **E though** they call me God Most High, H2256
Hos 11:12 **e** against the faithful Holy One. H2256
Hos 13:15 **e though** he thrives among his brothers H3954
Joel 1:18 **e** the flocks of sheep are suffering. H1685
Joel 1:20 **E** the wild animals pant for you; the H1685
Joel 2:12 "**E** now," declares the LORD, "return H2256+1685
Joel 2:29 **E** on my servants, both men and H2256+1685
Joel 2:32 **e** among the survivors whom the LORD H2256
Am 1: 3 sins of Damascus, **e** for four, I will not H2256
Am 1: 6 three sins of Gaza, **e** for four, I will not H2256
Am 1: 9 "For three sins of Tyre, **e** for four, I will not H2256
Am 1:11 three sins of Edom, **e** for four, I will not H2256
Am 1:13 three sins of Ammon, **e** for four, I will not H2256
Am 2: 1 three sins of Moab, **e** for four, I will not H2256
Am 2: 4 three sins of Judah, **e** for four, I will not H2256
Am 2: 6 three sins of Israel, **e** for four, I will not H2256
Am 2:16 **E** the bravest warriors will flee naked on H2256
Am 5:22 **E** though you bring me burnt offerings H3954
Am 8: 6 selling **e** the sweepings with the wheat. H2256
Jnh 1:13 the sea **grew e wilder** than H6192+2143+2256
Mic 1: 9 gate of my people, **e** to Jerusalem itself. NDT
Mic 1:12 from the LORD, **e** to the gate of Jerusalem. NDT
Mic 5: 5 seven shepherds, **e** eight commanders, H2256
Mic 7: 5 *E* **with** the woman who lies in your embrace AIT
Mic 7:10 **e** now she will be trampled underfoot like NDT
Mic 7:12 **e** from Egypt to the Euphrates and from H2256
Hab 1: 5 you would not believe, **e if** you were told. H3954

Zec 9:12 **e** now I announce that I will restore twice H1685
Mal 1: 5 **e beyond** the borders of Israel! H4946+6584
Mal 2:12 **e though** he brings an offering to the LORD H2256
Mal 3:15 **e** when they put God to the test H1685
Mt 5:36 you cannot make *e* **one** hair white or AIT
Mt 5:46 Are not **e** the tax collectors doing that? G2779
Mt 5:47 Do not **e** pagans do that? G2779
Mt 6:29 Yet I tell you that **not e** Solomon in all his G4028
Mt 8:27 **E** the winds and the waves obey him!" G2779
Mt 10:30 And **e** the very hairs of your head are all G2779
Mt 10:42 And if anyone gives **e** a cup of cold water G3667
Mt 13:12 **e** what they have will be taken from them. G2779
Mt 15:27 "**E** the dogs eat the crumbs that fall from G2779
Mt 18:17 if they refuse to listen **e** to the church G2779
Mt 21:32 And **e** after you saw this, you did not G1254
Mt 24:24 to deceive, if possible, **e** the elect. G2779
Mt 24:27 from the east is visible **e in** the west, G2401
Mt 24:33 **E** so, when you see all these things, you G2779
Mt 24:36 no one knows, **not e** the angels in heaven G4028
Mt 25:29 **e** what they have will be taken from them. G2779
Mt 26:33 "**E if** all fall away on account of you G1623
Mt 26:35 Peter declared, "**E if** I have to die with you G2829
Mt 27:14 made no reply, **not e** to a single charge G4028
Mk 1:27 He **e** gives orders to impure spirits and G2779
Mk 2: 2 was no room left, **not e** outside the door G3593
Mk 2:28 the Son of Man is Lord **e** of the Sabbath." G2779
Mk 3:20 his disciples were **not e** able to eat. G3593
Mk 4:24 it will be measured to you—and **e more.** G4707
Mk 4:25 **e** what they have will be taken from them." G2779
Mk 4:41 **E** the wind and the waves obey him!" G2779
Mk 5: 3 bind him anymore, **not e** with a chain. G4028
Mk 6:31 that they did **not e** have a chance to G4028
Mk 6:56 to let them touch **e** the edge of his cloak G2829
Mk 7:28 "**e** the dogs under the table eat the G2779
Mk 7:37 "He **e** makes the deaf hear and the mute G2779
Mk 8:26 "**Don't e** go into the village. G3593
Mk 10:26 The disciples were **e more** amazed, and G4360
Mk 10:45 For **e** the Son of Man did not come to be G2779
Mk 13:22 wonders to deceive, if possible, **e** the elect. NDT
Mk 13:29 **E** so, when you see these things G2779
Mk 13:32 no one knows, **not e** the angels in heaven G4028
Mk 14:29 Peter declared, "**E** if all fall away, I will G2779
Mk 14:31 emphatically, "**E if** I have to die with you G1569
Mk 14:59 Yet **e** then their testimony did **not** agree. G4028
Lk 1:15 with the Holy Spirit **e before** he is born. G2285
Lk 1:36 **E** Elizabeth your relative is going to G2779+2627
Lk 3:12 **E** tax collectors came to be baptized G2779
Lk 6:32 **E** sinners love those who love them. G2779
Lk 6:33 credit is that to you? **E** sinners do that. G2779
Lk 6:34 **E** sinners lend to sinners, expecting to be G2779
Lk 7: 7 That is why I did **not e** consider myself G4028
Lk 7: 9 I have **not** found such great faith **e** in G4028
Lk 7:29 All the people, **e** the tax collectors, when G2779
Lk 7:49 "Who is this who **e** forgives sins? G2779
Lk 8:18 **e** what they think they have will be taken G2779
Lk 8:25 He commands **e** the winds and the water G2779
Lk 9:42 **E** while the boy was coming, the demon G2285
Lk 10:11 '**E** the dust of your town we wipe from our G2779
Lk 10:17 **e** the demons submit to us in your name." G2779
Lk 11: 8 **e** though he will not get up and give you G2779
Lk 12:27 **not e** Solomon in all his splendor was G4028
Lk 12:38 **e if** he comes in the middle of the night G2829
Lk 14:26 **e** their own life—such a person G2779
Lk 15:29 **Yet** you never gave me **e** a young goat so G2779
Lk 16:21 **E** the dogs came and licked his sores G2779
Lk 16:31 they will **not** be convinced **e** if someone G4028
Lk 17: 4 **E** if they sin against you seven times in a G2779
Lk 18: 4 '**E** though I don't fear God or care what G2779
Lk 18:11 adulterers—or **e** like this tax collector. G2779
Lk 18:13 He would not **e** look up to heaven, but G4028
Lk 19:26 **e** what they have will be taken away. G2779
Lk 19:42 **e** you, had only known on this day G2779
Lk 20:37 **e** Moses showed that the dead rise G2779
Lk 21:16 You will be betrayed **e** by parents, brothers G2779
Lk 21:31 **E** so, when you see these things G2779
Lk 23:35 the rulers **e** sneered at him. G2779
Jn 4:36 **E now** the one who reaps draws a wage G2453
Jn 5:18 he was **e** calling God his own Father G2779
Jn 5:20 he will show him *e* **greater** works than these, AIT
Jn 5:21 **e** so the Son gives life to whom he is G2779
Jn 7: 5 For **e** his own brothers did not believe in G4028
Jn 8:14 answered, "**E if** I testify on my own behalf G2829
Jn 8:30 *E as* he **spoke**, many believed in him. AIT
Jn 9:29 *we* don't *e* **know** where he comes from." AIT
Jn 10:38 I do them, *e though you do* not **believe** me AIT
Jn 11:22 But I know that **e** now God will give you G2779
Jn 11:25 in me will live, **e though** they die; G2829
Jn 12:37 **E** after Jesus had performed so many G1254
Jn 12:42 the same time many **e** among the leaders G2779
Jn 14: 9 **e** after I have been among you such a G2779
Jn 14:12 they will do *e* **greater** *things* than these AIT
Jn 15: 2 he prunes so that it will be *e* **more** fruitful. AIT
Jn 16:30 that you do **not** *e* need to have anyone AIT
Jn 17:16 are not of the world, **e as** I am not of it. G2777
Jn 17:23 have loved them **e as** you have loved me. G2777
Jn 19: 8 Pilate heard this, he was **e more** afraid, G3437
Jn 21:11 **but e** with so many the net was not torn. G2779
Jn 21:25 that **e** the whole world would **not** have G4028
Ac 2:18 **E** on my servants, both men and G2779+1145
Ac 3:20 who has been appointed for you—**e** Jesus. NDT
Ac 5:13 **e though** they were highly regarded by the G247
Ac 7: 5 **not e** enough ground to set his foot on. G4028

Ac 7: 5 *e though at that time* Abraham **had** no child. AIT
Ac 7:52 They **e** killed those who predicted the G2779
Ac 10:45 Spirit had been poured out **e** on Gentiles. G2779
Ac 11:18 **e** to Gentiles God has granted repentance G2779
Ac 13:11 not *e able to* **see** the light of the sun." AIT
Ac 13:41 never believe, **e if** someone told you. G1569
Ac 14:18 **E** with these words, they had difficulty G2779
Ac 15:17 **e** all the Gentiles who bear my name G2779
Ac 16:37 *e though we* **are** Roman citizens AIT
Ac 17:23 I **e** found an altar with this inscription: G2779
Ac 19: 2 we have **not e** heard that there is a Holy G4028
Ac 19:12 so that **e** handkerchiefs and aprons that G2779
Ac 19:31 **E** some of the officials of the province G2779
Ac 19:32 the people did not **e** know why they were G2779
Ac 20:30 **E** from your own number men will arise G2779
Ac 22: 5 I **e** obtained letters from them to their G2779
Ac 22:25 citizen who hasn't **e** been found guilty?" G2779
Ac 24: 6 **and e** tried to desecrate the temple; so we G2779
Ac 26:11 them that I **e** hunted them down in G2779
Ac 28:23 came *in e* **larger** *numbers* to the place AIT
Ro 1:26 **E** their women exchanged natural sexual G5445
Ro 2:14 *e though they do* not **have** the law. AIT
Ro 2:15 them **and** *at other times e* defending AIT
Ro 2:27 **e** though you have the written code and NDT
Ro 3:10 "There is no one righteous, **not e** one; G4028
Ro 3:12 is no one who does good, not **e** one." G2401
Ro 5:14 **e** over those who did not sin by breaking G2779
Ro 8:10 then **e though** your body is subject to G3525
Ro 9:24 **e** us, whom he also called, not only from the NDT
Ro 15: 3 For **e** Christ did not please himself but, as G2779
1Co 2:10 all things, **e** the deep things of God. G2779
1Co 3:15 **e though** only as one escaping through G1254
1Co 4: 3 indeed, I do **not e** judge myself. G4028
1Co 4:15 **E if** you had ten thousand guardians in G1569
1Co 5: 1 of a kind that **e** pagans do **not** tolerate: G4028
1Co 5: 3 **e though** I am not physically G3525+1142
1Co 5:11 Do **not e** eat with such people. G3593
1Co 8: 5 For **e** if there are so-called gods, whether G2779
1Co 9: 2 **E though** I may not be an apostle to others G1623
1Co 10:33 **e as** I try to please everyone in every way G2743
1Co 12:14 **E so** the body is not made up of G2779+1142
1Co 13:12 I shall know fully, **e** as I am fully known. G2779
1Co 14: 7 **E in the case of** lifeless things that make G3940
1Co 14:21 **but e** then they will not listen to me G2779
1Co 15: 9 the apostles and do **not e** deserve to be G4024
1Co 15:13 then **not e** Christ has been raised. G4028
1Co 16: 6 you for a while, or **e** spend the winter, so G2779
2Co 3: 8 ministry of the Spirit be **e** more glorious? G4802
2Co 3:15 **E** to this day when Moses is read, a veil G247
2Co 4: 3 And **e** if our gospel is veiled, it is veiled to G2779
2Co 7: 8 **E** if I caused you sorrow by my letter, I do G2779
2Co 7:12 So **e** though I wrote to you, it was neither G2779
2Co 8: 3 were able, **and e** beyond their ability. G2779
2Co 8:22 now *e* **more** so because of his great AIT
2Co 10: 8 So **e** if I boast somewhat freely about the G5445
2Co 11:20 you **e** put up with anyone who enslaves G1623
2Co 12: 6 **E** if I should choose to boast, I would not G1142
2Co 12:11 "super-apostles," **e** though I am nothing. G2779
2Co 13: 7 do what is right **e** though we may seem to G1254
Gal 1: 8 But **e** if we or an angel from heaven G2779
Gal 2: 3 Yet **not e** Titus, who was with me, was G4028
Gal 2: 3 to be circumcised, *e though he* **was** a Greek. AIT
Gal 2:13 by their hypocrisy **e** Barnabas was led G2779
Gal 4:14 **e** though my illness was a trial to you NDT
Gal 6:13 **Not e** those who are circumcised keep the G4028
Eph 2: 5 alive with Christ **e** when we were dead in G2779
Eph 5: 3 you there must **not** be **e** a hint of sexual G3593
Eph 5:12 It is shameful **e** to mention what the G2779
Php 2: 8 obedient to death—**e** death on a cross! G1254
Php 2:17 But **e** if I am being poured out like a drink G2779
Php 3:18 now tell you again **e** with tears, G2779
Php 4:16 **e** when I was in Thessalonica, you sent G2779
1Th 2: 6 *e though* as apostles of Christ **we** *could have* AIT
2Th 3:10 For **e** when we were with you, we gave you G2779
1Ti 1:13 *E though I* **was** once a blasphemer and a AIT
1Ti 5: 6 lives for pleasure is dead *e while she* **lives**. AIT
1Ti 5:25 **and e** those that are not obvious cannot G2779
1Ti 6: 2 should serve them **e better** because their G3437
2Ti 2: 9 am suffering **e to the point of** being G3588
Phm 16 dear to me but **e** dearer to you, G4531+3437
Phm 21 that you will do **e** more than I ask. G2779
Heb 4:12 it penetrates **e to** dividing soul and spirit G948
Heb 6: 9 **E** though we speak like this, dear friends G2779
Heb 7: 4 **E** the patriarch Abraham gave him a tenth G2779
Heb 7: 5 **e though** they also are descended from G2788
Heb 7: 9 **One might e say** that Levi G6055+2229+3306
Heb 7:15 what we have said is **e** more clear if G2285
Heb 9:18 is why **e** the first covenant was not put G4028
Heb 11: 4 faith Abel still speaks, *e though he is* **dead.** AIT
Heb 11: 8 *e though he did* not **know** where he was AIT
Heb 11:11 And by faith **e** Sarah, who was past G2779
Heb 11:18 **e** though God had said to him, "It is through NDT
Heb 11:19 that God could **e** raise the dead, G2779
Heb 11:35 that they might gain an *e* **better** resurrection. AIT
Heb 11:36 flogging, and **e** chains and imprisonment. G2285
Heb 12:17 **E though** he sought the blessing with G2788
Heb 12:20 "**If e** an animal touches the mountain, it G2829
Jas 1:11 rich will fade away *e* **while** they go about AIT
Jas 2:19 **E** the demons believe that—and G2779
Jas 2:25 was not **e** Rahab the prostitute considered G2779
Jas 4:14 you *do* not *e* **know** what will happen AIT
Jas 5:17 a human being, **e as** we are. He prayed G3926

1Pe 1: 7 which perishes e though refined by fire G1254
1Pe 1: 8 and e though you do not see him now AIT
1Pe 1:12 E angels long to look into these things NDT
1Pe 3:14 But e if you should suffer for what is right G2779
1Pe 4: 6 gospel was preached e to those who are G2779
1Pe 4:15 any other kind of criminal, or e as a meddler. AIT
2Pe 1:12 e though you know them and are firmly G2788
2Pe 2: 1 e denying the sovereign Lord who bought G2779
2Pe 2:11 yet e angels, although they are stronger G3963
1Jn 2:18 e now many antichrists have come. G2779
1Jn 4: 3 heard is coming and e now is already in the AIT
1Jn 5: 4 that has overcome the world, e our faith. NDT
3Jn 2 e as your soul is getting along well. G2777
3Jn 5 sisters, e though they are strangers to you. G2779
3Jn 10 he e refuses to welcome other believers. G4046
3Jn 12 of by everyone—and e by the truth itself. G2779
Jude 9 But e the archangel Michael, when he was G1254
Jude 23 hating e the clothing stained by corrupted G2779
Rev 1: 7 will see him, e those who pierced him"; G2779
Rev 2:10 Be faithful, e to the point of death, and I G948
Rev 2:13 faith in me, not e in the days of Antipas G2779
Rev 4: 8 with eyes all around, e under its wings. G2779
Rev 5: 3 could open the scroll or e look inside it. G4046
Rev 13:13 e causing fire to come down from heaven G2779

EVEN-TEMPERED (1) [TEMPER]

Pr 17:27 whoever has understanding is e. H7922+8120

EVENING (140) [EVENINGS]

Ge 1: 5 And there was e, and there was morning H6847
Ge 1: 8 And there was e, and there was morning H6847
Ge 1:13 And there was e, and there was morning— H6847
Ge 1:19 And there was e, and there was morning— H6847
Ge 1:23 And there was e, and there was morning— H6847
Ge 1:31 And there was e, and there was morning H6847
Ge 8:11 When the dove returned to him in the e H6847
Ge 19: 1 The two angels arrived at Sodom in the e H6847
Ge 24:11 it was toward e, the time the women H6847
Ge 24:63 He went out to the field one e to meditate, H6847
Ge 29:23 But when e came, he took his daughter H6847
Ge 30:16 Jacob came in from the fields that e, H6847
Ge 49:27 the prey, in the e he divides the plunder." H6847
Ex 12:18 from the e of the fourteenth day until the H6847
Ex 12:18 day until the e of the twenty-first day. H6847
Ex 16: 6 "In the e you will know that it was the H6847
Ex 16: 8 meat to eat in the e and all the bread you H6847
Ex 16:13 That e quail came and covered the camp H6847
Ex 18:13 stood around him from morning till e. H6847
Ex 18:14 stand around you from morning till e?" H6847
Ex 27:21 before the LORD from e till morning. H6847
Lev 6:20 half of it in the morning and half in the e. H6847
Lev 11:24 their carcasses will be unclean till e. H6847
Lev 11:25 clothes, and they will be unclean till e. H6847
Lev 11:27 their carcasses will be unclean till e. H6847
Lev 11:28 clothes, and they will be unclean till e. H6847
Lev 11:31 when they are dead will be unclean till e. H6847
Lev 11:32 it will be unclean till e, and then it will be H6847
Lev 11:39 touches its carcass will be unclean till e. H6847
Lev 11:40 clothes, and they will be unclean till e. H6847
Lev 11:40 clothes, and they will be unclean till e. H6847
Lev 14:46 while it is closed up will be unclean till e. H6847
Lev 15: 5 with water, and they will be unclean till e. H6847
Lev 15: 6 with water, and they will be unclean till e. H6847
Lev 15: 7 with water, and they will be unclean till e. H6847
Lev 15: 8 with water, and they will be unclean till e. H6847
Lev 15:10 that were under him will be unclean till e; H6847
Lev 15:10 with water, and they will be unclean till e. H6847
Lev 15:11 with water, and they will be unclean till e. H6847
Lev 15:16 with water, and he will be unclean till e. H6847
Lev 15:17 with water, and it will be unclean till e. H6847
Lev 15:18 with water, and they will be unclean till e. H6847
Lev 15:19 who touches her will be unclean till e. H6847
Lev 15:21 with water, and they will be unclean till e. H6847
Lev 15:22 with water, and they will be unclean till e. H6847
Lev 15:23 touches it, they will be unclean till e. H6847
Lev 15:27 with water, and they will be unclean till e. H6847
Lev 17:15 they will be ceremonially unclean till e; H6847
Lev 22: 6 any such thing will be unclean till e. H6847
Lev 23:32 From the e of the ninth day of the month H6847
Lev 23:32 until the following e you are to observe H6847
Lev 24: 3 lamps before the LORD from e till morning, H6847
Nu 9:15 From e till morning the cloud above the H6847
Nu 9:21 the cloud stayed only from e till morning, H6847
Nu 19: 7 he will be ceremonially unclean till e. H6847
Nu 19: 8 and he too will be unclean till e. H6847
Nu 19:10 clothes, and he too will be unclean till e. H6847
Nu 19:19 with water, and that e they will be clean. H6847
Nu 19:21 water of cleansing will be unclean till e. H6847
Nu 19:22 who touches it becomes unclean till e." H6847
Dt 16: 4 you sacrifice on the e of the first day H6847
Dt 16: 6 you must sacrifice the Passover in the e, H6847
Dt 23:11 But as e approaches he is to wash himself H6847
Dt 28:67 morning you will say, "If only it were e!" H6847
Dt 28:67 and in the e, "If only it were H6847
Jos 5:10 On the e of the fourteenth day of the H6847
Jos 7: 6 the ark of the LORD, remaining there till e. H6847
Jos 8:29 pole and left it there until e. H6961+2021+6847
Jos 10:26 were left hanging on the poles until e. H6847
Jdg 19: 9 said, "Now look, it's almost e. H6845
Jdg 19:16 That e an old man from the hill country of H6847
Jdg 20:23 went up and wept before the LORD until e, H6847
Jdg 20:26 that day until e and presented burnt H6847
Jdg 21: 2 where they sat before God until e, raising H6847
Ru 2:17 So Ruth gleaned in the field until e. H6847
1Sa 14:24 be anyone who eats food before e comes, H6847
1Sa 17:16 every morning and e and took his stand. H6845
1Sa 20: 5 in the field until the e of the day after H6847
1Sa 20:19 after tomorrow, toward e, go to the H3718+4394
1Sa 30:17 from dusk until the e of the next day, H6847
2Sa 1:12 wept and fasted till e for Saul and his son H6847
2Sa 11: 2 One e David got up from his bed and H6847
2Sa 11:13 But in the e Uriah went out to sleep on H6847
1Ki 17: 6 morning and bread and meat in the e, H6847
1Ki 18:29 until the time for the e sacrifice. H6590+4966
1Ki 22:35 floor of the chariot, and that e he died. H6847
2Ki 16:15 burnt offering and the e grain offering, H6847
1Ch 16:40 morning and e, in accordance with H6847
1Ch 23:30 They were to do the same in the e H6847
2Ch 2: 4 every morning and e and on the Sabbaths H6847
2Ch 13:11 morning and e they present H928+2021+6847+928+2021+6847
2Ch 13:11 on the gold lampstand every e. H928+2021+6847+928+2021+6847
2Ch 18:34 in his chariot facing the Arameans until e. H6847
2Ch 31: 3 the morning and e burnt offerings and H6847
Ezr 3: 3 both the morning and e sacrifices. H6847
Ezr 9: 4 I sat there appalled until the e sacrifice. H6847
Ezr 9: 5 at the e sacrifice, I rose from my H6847
Ne 13:19 When e shadows fell on the gates of H7511
Est 2:14 In the e she would go there and in the H6847
Job 7: 2 Like a slave longing for the e shadows, or H7498
Ps 55:17 E, morning and noon I cry out in distress H6847
Ps 59: 6 They return at e, snarling like dogs, and H6847
Ps 59:14 They return at e, snarling like dogs, and H6847
Ps 65: 8 morning dawns, where e fades, you call H6847
Ps 90: 6 up new, but by e it is dry and withered. H6847
Ps 102:11 My days are like the e shadow; I wither H5742
Ps 104:23 go out to their work, to their labor until e. H6847
Ps 109:23 I fade away like an e shadow; I am H5742
Ps 141: 2 up of my hands be like the e sacrifice. H6847
Ecc 11: 6 at e let your hands not be idle H6847
Isa 17:14 In the e, sudden terror! Before the H6847
Jer 6: 4 and the shadows of e grow long. H6847
Eze 12: 4 Then in the e, while they are watching H6847
Eze 12: 7 Then in the e I dug through the wall with H6847
Eze 24:18 the morning, and in the e my wife died. H6847
Eze 33:22 Now the e before the man arrived, the H6847
Eze 46: 2 but the gate will not be shut until e. H6847
Da 9:21 flight about the time of the e sacrifice. H6847
Zep 2: 7 In the e they will lie down in the houses H6847
Zep 3: 3 her rulers are e wolves, who leave H6847
Zec 14: 7 day and night. When e comes, there will H6847
Mt 8:16 When e came, many who were G4068
Mt 14:15 As e approached, the disciples G4068+4070
Mt 16: 2 replied, "When e comes, you say, G4068+4070
Mt 20: 8 "When e came, the owner of the vineyard G4068
Mt 26:20 When e came, Jesus was reclining at the G4068
Mt 27:57 As e approached, there came a rich man G4068
Mk 1:32 That e after sunset the people G4068+1181
Mk 4:35 That day when e came, he said to his G4068
Mk 11:19 When e came, Jesus and his disciples G4067
Mk 13:35 whether in the e, or at midnight, G4067
Mk 14:17 When e came, Jesus arrived with the G4068
Mk 15:42 the Sabbath). So as e approached, G4068
Lk 21:37 each e he went out to spend the G3816
Lk 24:29 for it is nearly e; the day is almost over G2270
Jn 6:16 When e came, his disciples went down to G4068
Jn 13: 2 The e meal was in progress, and the devil G1270
Jn 20:19 On the e of that first day of the week G4068
Ac 4: 3 because it was e, they put them in G2270
Ac 28:23 He witnessed to them from morning till e G2270

EVENINGS (2) [EVENING]

Da 8:14 "It will take 2,300 e and mornings; then H6847
Da 8:26 "The vision of the e and mornings that H6847

EVENLY (1) [EVEN]

1Ki 6:35 them with gold hammered e over the H3837

EVENTS (55)

1Ki 11:41 As for the other e of Solomon's reign—all H1821
1Ki 12:15 this turn of e was from the LORD H6016
1Ki 14:19 The other e of Jeroboam's reign, his wars H1821
1Ki 14:29 As for the other e of Rehoboam's reign H1821
1Ki 15: 7 As for the other e of Abijah's reign, and H1821
1Ki 15:23 As for all the other e of Asa's reign, all H1821
1Ki 15:31 As for the other e of Nadab's reign, and H1821
1Ki 16: 5 As for the other e of Baasha's reign, what H1821
1Ki 16:14 As for the other e of Elah's reign, and all H1821
1Ki 16:20 As for the other e of Zimri's reign, and the H1821
1Ki 16:27 As for the other e of Omri's reign, what he H1821
1Ki 22:39 As for the other e of Ahab's reign H1821
1Ki 22:45 As for the other e of Jehoshaphat's reign H1821
2Ki 1:18 As for all the other e of Ahaziah's reign H1821
2Ki 8:23 As for the other e of Jehoram's reign, and H1821
2Ki 10:34 As for the other e of Jehu's reign, all he H1821
2Ki 12:19 As for the other e of the reign of Joash H1821
2Ki 13: 8 As for the other e of the reign of H1821
2Ki 13:12 As for the other e of the reign of Jehoash H1821
2Ki 14:15 As for the other e of the reign of Jehoash H1821
2Ki 14:18 As for the other e of Amaziah's reign, are H1821
2Ki 14:28 As for the other e of Jeroboam's reign, all H1821
2Ki 15: 6 As for the other e of Azariah's reign, and H1821
2Ki 15:11 The other e of Zechariah's reign are H1821
2Ki 15:15 The other e of Shallum's reign, and the H1821
2Ki 15:21 As for the other e of Menahem's reign H1821
2Ki 15:26 The other e of Pekahiah's reign, and all H1821
2Ki 15:31 As for the other e of Pekah's reign, and H1821
2Ki 15:36 As for the other e of Jotham's reign, and H1821
2Ki 16:19 As for the other e of the reign of Ahaz H1821
2Ki 20:20 As for the other e of Hezekiah's reign, all H1821
2Ki 21:17 As for the other e of Manasseh's reign H1821
2Ki 21:25 As for the other e of Amon's reign, and H1821
2Ki 23:28 As for the other e of Josiah's reign, and H1821
2Ki 24: 5 As for the other e of Jehoiakim's reign H1821
1Ch 29:29 As for the e of King David's reign, from H1821
2Ch 9:29 As for the other e of Solomon's reign H1821
2Ch 10:15 people, for this turn of e was from God, to H5813
2Ch 12:15 As for the e of Rehoboam's reign, from H1821
2Ch 13:22 The other e of Abijah's reign, what he did H1821
2Ch 16:11 The e of Asa's reign, from beginning to H1821
2Ch 20:34 The other e of Jehoshaphat's reign, from H1821
2Ch 25:26 As for the other e of Amaziah's reign, from H1821
2Ch 26:22 The other e of Uzziah's reign, from H1821
2Ch 27: 7 The other e in Jotham's reign, including H1821
2Ch 28:26 The other e of his reign and all his ways H1821
2Ch 32:32 The other e of Hezekiah's reign and his H1821
2Ch 33:18 The other e of Manasseh's reign H1821
2Ch 35:26 The other e of Josiah's reign and his acts H1821
2Ch 35:27 all the e, from beginning to end, are H1821
2Ch 36: 8 The other e of Jehoiakim's reign, the H1821
Est 3: 1 After these e, King Xerxes honored H1821
Est 9:20 Mordecai recorded these e, and he sent H1821
Lk 21:11 and fearful e and great signs from heaven G5831
Ac 5:11 church and all who heard about these e. AIT

EVENTUALLY (2)

Ezr 4:13 be paid, and e the royal revenues will suffer. AIT
Lk 18: 5 that she won't e come and attack G1650+5465

EVER (247) [EVERLASTING, FOREVER, FOREVERMORE]

Ge 24:16 no man had e slept with her. AIT
Ex 5:23 E since I went to Pharaoh to speak in H4946+255
Ex 9:18 worst hailstorm that has e fallen on Egypt, H4202
Ex 10: 6 your ancestors have e seen from the day they AIT
Ex 10:14 plague of locusts, nor will there e be again. AIT
Ex 11: 6 worse than there has e been or ever will be AIT
Ex 11: 6 than there has ever been or e will be again. AIT
Ex 15:18 "The LORD reigns for e and ever. H6409
Ex 15:18 "The LORD reigns for ever and e. H6329
Nu 11:20 saying, "Why did we e leave Egypt? AIT
Nu 14:23 not one of them will e see the land I AIT
Nu 14:23 has treated me with contempt will e see it. AIT
Nu 35:26 accused e goes outside the limits H3655+3655
Dt 4:32 Has anything so great as this e happened, or AIT
Dt 4:32 has anything like it e been heard of? AIT
Dt 4:34 Has any god e tried to take for himself one AIT
Dt 5:26 For what mortal has e heard the voice of H3972
Dt 8:19 If you e forget the LORD your God H8894+8894
Dt 9:24 the LORD e since I have known H4946+3427
Dt 34:12 For no one has e shown the mighty power NDT
Jos 7: 7 why did you e bring this people across the AIT
Jos 7:26 Valley of Achor e since. H6330+2021+3427+2021+2296
Jos 14:14 the Kenizzite e since, H6330+2021+3427+2021+2296
Jos 22:28 we said, 'If they e say this to us, or to H4737
Jdg 11:25 Did he e quarrel with Israel or fight with AIT
Jdg 16:17 "No razor has e been used on my head," AIT
Ru 1:17 deal with me, be it e so severely, if even H3907
1Sa 1:11 and no razor will e be used on his head." AIT
1Sa 2:32 line will e reach old age. H3972+2021+3427
1Sa 3:17 deal with you, be it e so severely, if you H3907
1Sa 14:44 deal with me, be it e so severely, if you H3907
1Sa 20:13 with Jonathan, be it e so severely, if I do H3907
1Sa 20:15 do not e cut off your kindness H6330+6409
1Sa 25:22 deal with David, be it e so severely, if by H3907
1Sa 27: 6 kings of Judah e since. H6330+2021+3427+2021+2296
2Sa 3: 9 with Abner, be it e so severely, if I do not H3907
2Sa 3:35 deal with me, be it e so severely, if I taste H3907
2Sa 6: 9 "How can the ark of the LORD e come to me?" AIT
2Sa 7: 7 did I e say to any of their rulers H1819+1821
2Sa 7:11 have done e since the time I H4946
2Sa 13:32 express intention e since the day Amnon H4946
2Sa 19:13 deal with me, be it e so severely, if you H3907
1Ki 2:23 deal with me, be it e so severely, if H3907
1Ki 3:12 been anyone like you, nor will there e be. H339
1Ki 10:20 like it had e been made for any other AIT
1Ki 19: 2 deal with me, be it e so severely, if by this H3907
1Ki 20:10 deal with me, be it e so severely, if H3907
1Ki 22:28 "If you e return safely, the H8740+8740
2Ki 6:31 deal with me, be it e so severely, if the H3907
2Ki 18:33 Has the god of any nation e delivered H5911+5911
1Ch 13:12 "How can I e bring the ark of God to me?" AIT
1Ch 17: 6 did I e say to any of their leaders whom I AIT
1Ch 17:10 have done e since the time I H4946
1Ch 29:25 such as no king over Israel e had before. H3972
2Ch 1:12 who was before you e had and none after AIT
2Ch 9:11 like them had e been seen in H4200+7156
2Ch 9:19 like it had e been made for any other AIT
2Ch 18:27 "If you e return safely, the H8740+8740
2Ch 32:13 Were the gods of those nations e able H3523+3523
2Ch 35:18 kings of Israel had e celebrated such a AIT
Ne 13: 1 Moabite should e be admitted into H6330+6409

Job 4: 7 innocent, *has e* **perished**? Where were the AIT
Job 4: 7 Where **were** the upright *e* **destroyed**? AIT
Job 6:22 Have I e said, 'Give something on my H3954
Job 15: 7 "Are you the **first** man *e* born? Were you AIT
Job 20: 4 **e since** mankind was placed on the earth H4974
Job 29:20 not fade; the bow *will be* **e new** in my hand. AIT
Job 38:12 "Have you e given orders to the H4946+3427
Ps 5:11 be glad; let them **e** sing for joy. H4200+6409
Ps 9: 5 blotted out their name for **e** and ever. H6409
Ps 9: 5 blotted out their name for ever and **e**. H6329
Ps 10: 6 will **e** shake me. H4200+1887+2256+1887
Ps 10: 6 He swears, "No one will **e** do me harm." NDT
Ps 10:16 The LORD is King **for e** and ever; the H6409
Ps 10:16 The LORD is King for ever and **e**; the H6329
Ps 21: 4 it to him—length of days, **for e** and ever. H6409
Ps 21: 4 it to him—length of days, for ever and **e**. H6329
Ps 25: 3 who hopes in you will **e** be put to shame, H1685
Ps 25:15 My eyes are **e** on the LORD, for only he will H9458
Ps 38:17 about to fall, and my pain is **e** with me. H9458
Ps 45: 6 will last **for e** and ever; a scepter H6409
Ps 45: 6 will last for ever and **e**; a scepter of justice H6329
Ps 45:17 the nations will praise you for **e** and ever. H6409
Ps 45:17 the nations will praise you for ever and **e**. H6329
Ps 48:14 For this God is our God **for e** and ever; he H6409
Ps 48:14 For this God is our God for ever and **e**; he H6329
Ps 49: 8 no payment is **e** enough— H4200+6409
Ps 50: 8 burnt offerings, which are **e** before me. H9458
Ps 52: 8 in God's unfailing love **for e** and ever. H6409
Ps 52: 8 in God's unfailing love for ever and **e**. H6329
Ps 61: 8 Then I will **e** sing in praise of your H4200+6329
Ps 71: 6 my mother's womb. I will **e** praise you. H9458
Ps 72:15 May people **e** pray for him and bless him H9458
Ps 83:17 May they **e** be ashamed and H6330+6329
Ps 84: 4 in your house; they are **e** praising you. H6388
Ps 89:33 from him, nor *will I* **e betray** my faithfulness. AIT
Ps 111: 8 They are established for **e** and ever H6329
Ps 111: 8 are established for ever and **e**, H4200+6409
Ps 119:44 I will always obey your law, for **e** and ever. H6409
Ps 119:44 I will always obey your law, for ever and **e**. H6329
Ps 132:12 sons will sit on your throne for **e and ever**." H6329
Ps 132:12 sons will sit on your throne for **ever and e**." H6329
Ps 132:14 "This is my resting place for **e and ever** H6329
Ps 132:14 "This is my resting place for **ever and e** H6329
Ps 132:16 faithful people *will* **e sing for joy**. H8264+8264
Ps 145: 1 I will praise your name for **e** and ever. H6409
Ps 145: 1 I will praise your name for ever and **e**. H6329
Ps 145: 2 you and extol your name for **e** and ever. H6409
Ps 145: 2 you and extol your name for ever and **e**. H6329
Ps 145:21 praise his holy name for **e** and ever. H6409
Ps 145:21 praise his holy name for ever and **e**. H6329
Ps 148: 6 he established them for **e** and ever H6329
Ps 148: 6 established them for ever and **e**— H4200+6409
Pr 4:18 **shining e brighter** till the full H2143+2256+239
Pr 5:19 may you **e** be intoxicated with her love. H9458
Pr 30:13 those whose eyes are **e so** haughty H4537
Ecc 1: 6 round it goes, *e* **returning** on its course. AIT
Isa 6: 9 " '*Be* **e hearing**, but never H9048+9048
Isa 6: 9 *be* **e seeing**, but never H8011+8011
Isa 34:10 will **e** pass through it **again**. H4200+5905+5905
Isa 36:18 *Have* the gods of any nations *e* **delivered** AIT
Isa 49:16 of my hands; your walls are **e** before me. H9458
Isa 59:12 Our offenses are **e** with us, and we NDT
Isa 66: 8 Who *has e* **heard** *of* such things? Who has AIT
Isa 66: 8 Who *has e* **seen** things like this AIT
Jer 2:10 see if *there has e* **been** anything like this: AIT
Jer 2:11 Has a nation *e* **changed** its gods? (Yet they AIT
Jer 6: 7 her sickness and wounds are **e** before me. H9458
Jer 7: 7 gave your ancestors for **e** and ever. H4946+6409
Jer 7: 7 gave your ancestors for ever and **e**. H6330+6409
Jer 18:13 Who *has e* **heard** anything like this AIT
Jer 18:14 *Does* the snow of Lebanon *e* **vanish** from its AIT
Jer 18:14 *Do* its cool waters from distant sources *e* **stop** AIT
Jer 19: 4 ancestors nor the kings of Judah *e* **knew**, AIT
Jer 20:18 Why *did I e* **come out** of the womb to see AIT
Jer 25: 5 and your ancestors for **e** and ever. H4946+6409
Jer 25: 5 and your ancestors for ever and **e**. H6330+6409
Jer 31:36 "will Israel **e** cease being a H3972+2021+3427
Jer 33:18 nor *will* the Levitical priests *e* **fail to have** a AIT
Jer 35: 6 descendants must **e** drink wine. H6330+6409
Jer 35: 8 and daughters have **e** drunk wine H3972+3427
Jer 44: 3 they nor you nor your ancestors *e* **knew**. AIT
Jer 44:18 But **e since** we stopped burning H4946+255
Jer 44:26 in Egypt will **e again** invoke my name H6388
La 2:20 Whom *have you e* **treated** like this AIT
Eze 4:14 No impure meat *has e* **entered** my mouth." AIT
Eze 15: 3 **Is** wood *e* **taken** from it to make anything AIT
Eze 27:32 "Who was **e** silenced like Tyre, surrounded NDT
Eze 31:14 by the waters *are e to* **tower proudly** on high, AIT
Eze 31:14 so well-watered *are e to* **reach** such a height; AIT
Da 2:10 *has e* **asked** such a thing of any magician AIT
Da 2:20 the name of God for **e** and ever; A10550+10002
Da 2:20 of God for ever and **e**; A10527+10550+10002
Da 6:22 Nor *have I e* **done** any wrong before you AIT
Da 7:18 possess it forever—yes, for **e** and ever. A10550
Da 7:18 it forever—yes, for ever and **e**. A10550+10002
Da 9:12 nothing *has e* **been done** like what has AIT
Da 12: 3 like the stars for **e** and ever. H6409
Da 12: 3 like the stars for ever and **e**. H6329
Hos 12: 9 your God *e since* you *came* **out of** Egypt; AIT
Hos 13: 4 your God *e since* you *came* **out of** Egypt. AIT
Joel 1: 2 *Has* anything like this *e* **happened** in your AIT
Joel 2: 2 times nor **e** *will be* in ages to come. H3578
Mic 4: 5 name of the LORD our God for **e** and ever. H6409
Mic 4: 5 name of the LORD our God for ever and **e**. H6329
Mal 3: 7 **E since** the time of your ancestors H4200+4946
Mt 9:33 "**Nothing** like this has **e** been seen in *G4030*
Mt 13:14 " '*You will be* **e hearing** but never *G198+201*
Mt 13:14 *you will be* **e seeing** but never *G1063+1063*
Mk 4:12 " '*they may be* **e seeing** but never *G1063+1063*
Mk 4:12 and **e hearing** but never *G201+201*
Mk 11: 2 tied there, which no one has **e** ridden. *G4037*
Mk 11:14 "May no one **e** eat fruit from *G1650+3836+172*
Lk 1:37 For no word from God *will e* **fail**. AIT
Lk 9:39 It **scarcely e** leaves him and is destroying *G3653*
Lk 19:30 tied there, which no one has **e** ridden. *G4799*
Jn 1:18 No one has **e** seen God, but the one and *G4799*
Jn 3:13 No one *has e* **gone** into heaven except the AIT
Jn 4:29 see a man who told me everything *I e* **did**. AIT
Jn 4:39 testimony, "He told me everything *I e* **did**." AIT
Jn 7:46 "**No** one **e** spoke the way this man does," *G4030*
Jn 9:32 Nobody has **e** heard of *G1666+3836+172*
Jn 19:41 in which no one had **e** been laid. *G4031*
Ac 7:52 **Was there e** a prophet your ancestors did *G5515*
Ac 11: 8 **Nothing** impure or unclean has **e** entered *G4030*
Ac 20:25 **none** of you ... will **e** see me **again** *G4033+4246*
Ac 26: 4 the way I have lived **e since** I was a child, *G1666*
Ac 28:26 "*You will be* **e hearing** but never *G198+201*
Ac 28:26 *you will be* **e seeing** but never *G1063+1063*
Ro 11:35 "Who *has e* **given** to God, that God should AIT
2Co 7: 7 so that my joy was **greater than e**. *G3437*
Gal 1: 5 to whom be glory for **e** and ever. Amen. *G172*
Gal 1: 5 to whom be glory for ever and **e**. Amen. *G172*
Eph 1:15 *e since* I **heard** about your faith in the Lord AIT
Eph 3:21 throughout all generations, *for* **e** and ever! *G172*
Eph 3:21 throughout all generations, for ever and **e**! *G172*
Eph 5:29 After all, no one **e** hated their own body *G4537*
Php 4:20 our God and Father be glory for **e** and ever. *G172*
Php 4:20 our God and Father be glory for ever and **e**. *G172*
1Ti 1:17 be honor and glory for **e** and ever. *G172*
1Ti 1:17 be honor and glory for ever and **e**. *G172*
2Ti 4:18 To him be glory for **e** and ever. Amen. *G172*
2Ti 4:18 To him be glory for ever and **e**. Amen. *G172*
Heb 1: 5 For to which of the angels did God **e** say *G4537*
Heb 1: 8 will last for **e** and ever; a scepter of *G172*
Heb 1: 8 will last for ever and **e**; a scepter of justice *G172*
Heb 1:13 To which of the angels did God **e** say, "Sit *G4537*
Heb 7:13 one from that tribe *has e* **served at** the altar. AIT
Heb 13:21 to whom be glory for **e** and ever. *G172*
Heb 13:21 to whom be glory for ever and **e**. *G172*
1Pe 4:11 be the glory and the power for **e** and ever. *G172*
1Pe 4:11 be the glory and the power for ever and **e**. *G172*
1Pe 5:11 To him be the power for **e** and ever. Amen. *G172*
1Pe 5:11 To him be the power for ever and **e**. Amen. *G172*
2Pe 3: 4 **E since** our ancestors died *G608+4005*
1Jn 4:12 No one has **e** seen God; but if we love *G4799*
Rev 1: 6 to him be glory and power for **e** and ever! *G172*
Rev 1: 6 to him be glory and power for ever and **e**! *G172*
Rev 1:18 now look, I am alive for **e** and ever! *G172*
Rev 1:18 now look, I am alive for ever and **e**! *G172*
Rev 4: 9 on the throne and who lives for **e** and ever, *G172*
Rev 4: 9 on the throne and who lives for ever and **e**, *G172*
Rev 4:10 worship him who lives for **e** and ever. *G172*
Rev 4:10 worship him who lives for ever and **e**. *G172*
Rev 5:13 honor and glory and power, for **e** and ever!" *G172*
Rev 5:13 honor and glory and power, for ever and **e**!" *G172*
Rev 7:12 strength be to our God for **e** and ever. *G172*
Rev 7:12 strength be to our God for ever and **e**. *G172*
Rev 10: 6 he swore by him who lives for **e** and ever, *G172*
Rev 10: 6 he swore by him who lives for ever and **e**, *G172*
Rev 11:15 Messiah, and he will reign for **e** and ever." *G172*
Rev 11:15 Messiah, and he will reign for ever and **e**." *G172*
Rev 14:11 of their torment will rise for **e** and ever. *G172*
Rev 14:11 of their torment will rise for ever and **e**. *G172*
Rev 15: 7 the wrath of God, who lives for **e** and ever. *G172*
Rev 15: 7 the wrath of God, who lives for ever and **e**. *G172*
Rev 16:18 like it *has e* **occurred** since mankind has AIT
Rev 18:18 '**Was there e** a city like this great *G5515+5516*
Rev 18:22 **No** worker of any trade will **e** *G4246+4024+3590*
Rev 19: 3 The smoke from her goes up for **e** and ever." *G172*
Rev 19: 3 The smoke from her goes up for ever and **e**." *G172*
Rev 20:10 be tormented day and night for **e** and ever. *G172*
Rev 20:10 be tormented day and night for ever and **e**. *G172*
Rev 21:25 On **no** day will its gates **e** be shut *G4024+3590*
Rev 21:27 Nothing impure *will e* **enter** it, nor will AIT
Rev 22: 5 And they will reign for **e** and ever. *G172*
Rev 22: 5 And they will reign for ever and **e**. *G172*

EVER-FLOWING (1) [FLOW]

Ps 74:15 streams; you dried up the **e** rivers. H419

EVER-INCREASING (2) [INCREASE]

Ro 6:19 impurity and *to* **e wickedness**, *G490+1650+490*
2Co 3:18 his image **with e glory**, *G608+1518+1650+1518*

EVER-PRESENT (1) [PRESENT]

Ps 46: 1 and strength, an **e** help in trouble. H5162+4394

EVERLASTING (70) [EVER]

Ge 9:16 it and remember the **e** covenant between H6409
Ge 17: 7 my covenant as an **e** covenant between H6409
Ge 17: 8 I will give as an **e** possession to you and H6409
Ge 17:13 in your flesh is to be an **e** covenant. H6409
Ge 17:19 with him as an **e** covenant for his H6409
Ge 48: 4 give this land as an **e** possession to your H6409
Nu 18:19 It is an **e** covenant of salt before the LORD H6409
Dt 33:15 the fruitfulness of the **e** hills; H6409
Dt 33:27 and underneath are the **e** arms. H6409
2Sa 23: 5 not have made with me an **e** covenant, H6409
1Ch 16:17 as a decree, to Israel as an **e** covenant: H6409
1Ch 16:36 the God of Israel, from **e** to everlasting. H6409
1Ch 16:36 the God of Israel, from everlasting to **e**. H6409
1Ch 29:10 of our father Israel, from **e** to everlasting. H6409
1Ch 29:10 of our father Israel, from everlasting to **e**. H6409
Ezr 9:12 your children as an **e** inheritance. H6409+6330
Ne 9: 5 your God, who is from **e** to everlasting." H6409
Ne 9: 5 your God, who is from everlasting to **e**." H6409
Ps 41:13 the God of Israel, from **e** to everlasting. H6409
Ps 41:13 the God of Israel, from everlasting to **e**. H6409
Ps 52: 5 God will bring you down to **e** ruin: H5905+4200
Ps 74: 3 Turn your steps toward these **e** ruins, all H5905
Ps 78:66 his enemies; he put them to **e** shame. H6409
Ps 90: 2 from **e** to everlasting you are God. H6409
Ps 90: 2 from everlasting to **e** you are God. H6409
Ps 103:17 But from **e** to everlasting the LORD's love is H6409
Ps 103:17 from everlasting to **e** the LORD's love is H6409
Ps 105:10 as a decree, to Israel as an **e** covenant: H6409
Ps 106:48 the God of Israel, from **e** to everlasting. H6409
Ps 106:48 the God of Israel, from everlasting to **e**. H6409
Ps 119:142 righteousness is **e** and your law is H4200+6409
Ps 139:24 way in me, and lead me in the way **e**. H6409
Ps 145:13 Your kingdom is an **e** kingdom H3972+6409
Isa 9: 6 Counselor, Mighty God, **E** Father, Prince of H6329
Isa 24: 5 the statutes and broken the **e** covenant. H6409
Isa 30: 8 to come it may be an **e** witness. H6330+6409
Isa 33:14 Who of us can dwell with **e** burning?" H6409
Isa 35:10 with singing; **e** joy will crown their heads. H6409
Isa 40:28 The LORD is the **e** God, the Creator of the H6409
Isa 45:17 be saved by the LORD with an **e** salvation; H6409
Isa 45:17 be put to shame or disgraced, to ages **e**. H6329
Isa 51:11 with singing; **e** joy will crown their heads. H6409
Isa 54: 8 with **e** kindness I will have H6409
Isa 55: 3 I will make an **e** covenant with you, my H6409
Isa 55:13 LORD's renown, for an **e** sign, that will H6409
Isa 56: 5 I will give them an **e** name that will H6409
Isa 60:15 I will make you the **e** pride and the joy of H6409
Isa 60:19 the LORD will be your **e** light, and your H6409
Isa 60:20 the LORD will be your **e** light, and your H6409
Isa 61: 7 in your land, and **e** joy will be yours. H6409
Isa 61: 8 make an **e** covenant with them H6409
Isa 63:12 to gain for himself **e** renown, H6409
Jer 5:22 the sea, an **e** barrier it cannot cross. H6409
Jer 23:40 I will bring on you **e** disgrace—everlasting H6409
Jer 23:40 **e** shame that will not be forgotten. H6409
Jer 25: 9 object of horror and scorn, and an **e** ruin. H6409
Jer 31: 3 "I have loved you with an **e** love; I have H6409
Jer 32:40 I will make an **e** covenant with them: I will H6409
Jer 50: 5 to the LORD in an **e** covenant that will not H6409
Eze 16:60 I will establish an **e** covenant with you. H6409
Eze 37:26 peace with them; it will be an **e** covenant. H6409
Da 7:14 His dominion is an **e** dominion that will A10550
Da 7:27 His kingdom will be an **e** kingdom, and A10550
Da 9:24 to bring in **e** righteousness, to seal H6409
Da 12: 2 some to **e** life, others to shame and H6409
Da 12: 2 others to shame and **e** contempt. H6409
Mic 6: 2 you **e** foundations of the earth. H419
Hab 1:12 are you not from **e**? My God, my Holy One H7710
2Th 1: 9 be punished with **e** destruction and shut *G173*
Jude 6 bound with **e** chains for judgment on the *G132*

EVERY (613) [EVERYDAY, EVERYONE, EVERYONE'S, EVERYTHING, EVERYWHERE]

Ge 1:21 of the sea and **e** living thing with which H3972
Ge 1:21 **e** winged bird according to its kind. H3972
Ge 1:28 in the sky and over **e** living creature that H3972
Ge 1:29 "I give you **e** seed-bearing plant on the H3972
Ge 1:29 the whole earth and **e** tree that has fruit H3972
Ge 1:30 of life in it—I give **e** green plant for food." H3972
Ge 6: 5 that **e** inclination of the thoughts of H3972
Ge 6:17 **e** creature that has the breath of life in it. NDT
Ge 6:20 Two of **e** kind of bird, of every kind of animal NDT
Ge 6:20 of **e** kind of animal and of every kind of NDT
Ge 6:20 of animal and of **e** kind of creature that H3972
Ge 6:21 You are to take **e** *kind of* food that is to be H3972
Ge 7: 2 you seven pairs of **e** *kind of* clean animal, H3972
Ge 7: 2 one pair of **e** kind of unclean animal NDT
Ge 7: 3 also seven pairs of **e** kind of bird, male NDT
Ge 7: 4 the face of the earth **e** living creature I H3972
Ge 7:14 They had with them **e** wild animal H3972
Ge 7:14 **e** creature that moves along the ground H3972
Ge 7:14 to its kind and **e** bird according to its H3972
Ge 7:16 were male and female of **e** living thing, H3972
Ge 7:21 **E** living thing that moved on land perished H3972
Ge 7:23 **E** living thing on the face of the earth was H3972
Ge 8:17 Bring out **e** *kind of* living creature that is H3972
Ge 8:21 even though **e** inclination of the human NDT
Ge 9: 2 on **e** creature that moves along the H3972
Ge 9: 5 demand an accounting from **e** animal. H3972
Ge 9:10 with **e** living creature that was with H3972
Ge 9:10 ark with you—**e** living creature on earth. H3972
Ge 9:12 me and you and **e** living creature with H3972
Ge 9:15 you and all living creatures of **e** kind. H3972
Ge 9:16 all living creatures of **e** kind on the earth." H3972
Ge 17:10 **E** male among you shall be circumcised. H3972
Ge 17:12 to come **e** male among you who H3972
Ge 17:23 with his money, **e** male in his household H3972
Ge 17:27 And **e** male in Abraham's household H3972
Ge 19: 4 all the men from **e part** of the city of H7895

Ge 24: 1 the LORD had blessed him in **e way**. H3972
Ge 30:32 remove from them e speckled or spotted H3972
Ge 30:32 e dark-colored lamb and every spotted H3972
Ge 30:32 lamb and e spotted or speckled H928
Ge 34:24 e male in the city was circumcised. H3972
Ge 34:25 the unsuspecting city, killing e male. H3972
Ex 1:22 "E Hebrew boy that is born you must H3972
Ex 1:22 throw into the Nile, but let e girl live." H3972
Ex 3:22 *E* **woman** is to ask her neighbor and any AIT
Ex 9:19 the hail will fall on e person and animal H3972
Ex 9:25 growing in the fields and stripped e tree. H3972
Ex 10: 5 including e tree that is growing in your H3972
Ex 10:14 settled down in e area of the country H3972
Ex 11: 5 E firstborn son in Egypt will die, from the H3972
Ex 12:12 Egypt and strike down e firstborn of both H3972
Ex 13: 2 "Consecrate to me e firstborn male. H3972
Ex 13: 2 The first offspring of e womb among the H3972
Ex 13:12 to the LORD the first offspring of e womb. H3972
Ex 13:13 Redeem with a lamb e firstborn donkey H3972
Ex 13:13 Redeem e firstborn among your sons. H3972
Ex 13:15 male offspring of e womb and redeem H3972
Ex 18:22 have them bring e difficult case to you H3972
Ex 23:27 into confusion e nation you encounter H3972
Ex 30: 7 altar **e morning** when he tends
H928+2021+1332+928+2021+1332
Ex 34:19 first offspring of e womb belongs to me, H3972
Ex 35:25 E skilled woman spun with her hands and H3972
Ex 36: 1 Oholiab and e skilled person to whom the H3972
Ex 36: 2 Oholiab and e skilled person to H3972
Lev 2:11 " 'E grain offering you bring to the LORD H3972
Lev 6:12 **E morning** the priest is to add
H928+2021+1332+928+2021+1332
Lev 6:23 E grain offering of a priest shall be burned H3972
Lev 7: 9 E grain offering baked in an oven or H3972
Lev 7:10 e grain offering, whether mixed with H3972
Lev 11:26 " 'E animal that does not have a divided H3972
Lev 11:41 " 'E creature that moves along the ground H3972
Lev 11:46 e living thing that moves about in the H3972
Lev 11:46 in the water and e creature that moves H3972
Lev 17:14 because the life of e creature is its blood H3972
Lev 17:14 because the life of e creature is its blood H3972
Lev 27:25 E value is to be set according to the H3972
Lev 27:32 E tithe of the herd and flock—every tenth H3972
Lev 27:32 e tenth animal that passes under the H3972
Nu 1: 2 families, listing e man by name, one by H3972
Nu 3:12 first male offspring of e Israelite woman. H3972
Nu 3:13 I set apart for myself e firstborn in Israel H3972
Nu 3:15 Count e male a month old or more." H3972
Nu 3:39 including e male a month old or more H3972
Nu 7: 3 ox from each leader and a cart from e two. NDT
Nu 8:16 male offspring from e Israelite woman. H3972
Nu 8:17 E firstborn male in Israel, whether human H3972
Nu 11:10 heard the people of e family wailing at H2257S
Nu 14:29 e *one of* you twenty years old or more who H3972
Nu 16: 3 is holy, e *one of* them, and the H3972
Nu 18:10 something most holy; e male shall eat it. H3972
Nu 18:15 The first offspring of e womb, both human H3972
Nu 18:15 But you must redeem e firstborn son and NDT
Nu 18:15 every firstborn son and e firstborn male of NDT
Nu 19:15 e open container without a lid H3972
Nu 28:10 burnt offering for **e Sabbath**, H8701+928+8701
Nu 28:11 " 'On the first of e month, present to the H4013S
Nu 28:24 the food offering e day for seven days as H4200
Nu 30: 4 all her vows and e pledge by which she H3972
Nu 31: 7 commanded Moses, and killed e man. H3972
Nu 31:17 And kill e woman who has slept with a H3972
Nu 31:18 save for yourselves e girl who has never H3972
Nu 31:20 Purify e garment as well as everything H3972
Nu 31:28 the LORD one out of e five hundred, H2021
Nu 31:30 select one out of e fifty, whether people, H2021
Nu 31:47 selected one out of e fifty people and H2021
Nu 32:27 servants, e man who is armed for battle H3972
Nu 32:29 Reubenites, e man armed for battle H3972
Nu 34:12 your land, with its boundaries **on e side**. H6017
Nu 36: 7 e Israelite shall keep the tribal H408
Nu 36: 8 E daughter who inherits land in any H3972
Nu 36: 8 so that e Israelite will possess the H408
Dt 1:41 So e *one of* you put on his weapons H408
Dt 3: 6 king of Heshbon, destroying e city—men, H3972
Dt 7:15 LORD will keep you free from e disease. H3972
Dt 8: 1 careful to follow e command I am giving H3972
Dt 8: 3 bread alone but on e word that comes H3972
Dt 11: 6 their tents and e living thing that H3972
Dt 11:24 E place where you set your foot will be H3972
Dt 12: 2 on the hills and under e spreading tree H3972
Dt 14:28 At the end of e three years, bring all the NDT
Dt 15: 1 At the end of e seven years you must cancel NDT
Dt 15: 2 E creditor shall cancel any loan they have H3972
Dt 15:19 the LORD your God e firstborn male of H3972
Dt 16:18 of your tribes in e town the LORD your God H3972
Dt 28:61 also bring on you e *kind of* sickness and H3972
Dt 31:10 "At the end of e seven years, in the year NDT
Jos 1: 3 I will give you e place where you set your H3972
Jos 6:21 with the sword e living thing in it— H3972
Jos 8:24 when e *one of* them had been put to H3972
Jos 21:44 The LORD gave them rest on e **side**, just as H6017
Jos 21:45 to Israel failed; e *one* was fulfilled. H3972
Jos 23:14 E promise has been fulfilled; not one has H3972
Jdg 8:34 of all their enemies **on e side**. H4946+6017
Jdg 15: 4 He then fastened a torch to e pair of tails, NDT
Jdg 20:10 take ten men out of e hundred from all H2021
Jdg 21:11 "Kill e male and every woman who is not H3972
Jdg 21:11 every male and e woman who is not a H3972
1Sa 2:29 the choice parts of e offering made by my H3972
1Sa 2:33 *E one* of you that I do not cut off from H408
1Sa 4:10 were defeated and *e* **man** fled to his tent. AIT
1Sa 11: 2 the right eye of e *one of* you and so bring H3972
1Sa 14:47 fought against their enemies **on e side**: H6017
1Sa 17:16 came forward *e* **morning** and evening and AIT
1Sa 20:15 LORD has cut off e *one of* David's enemies H408
1Sa 25:12 When they arrived, they reported e word. H3972
1Sa 25:30 fulfilled for my lord e good thing he H3972
2Sa 2:23 And e *man* stopped when he came to the H3972
2Sa 4: 9 who has delivered me out of e trouble, H3972
2Sa 8: 2 E two lengths of them were put to death NDT
2Sa 20: 1 part in Jesse's son! *E* **man** to his tent, Israel!" AIT
2Sa 23: 5 arranged and secured in e *part*; surely he H3972
2Sa 23: 5 my salvation and grant me my e desire. H3972
1Ki 1:29 who has delivered me out of e trouble, H3972
1Ki 5: 4 LORD my God has given me rest **on e side**, H6017
1Ki 7:36 on the panels, in e available space, with H408
1Ki 8:39 you alone know e human heart), H3972
1Ki 10:22 Once e three years it returned, carrying H4200
1Ki 12:24 Go home, e *one* of you, for this is my doing H408
1Ki 14:10 Jeroboam **e last male** in H8874+928+7815
1Ki 14:23 Asherah poles on e high hill and under H3972
1Ki 14:23 high hill and under e spreading tree. H3972
1Ki 17:15 So there was food **e day** for Elijah and H3427
1Ki 21:21 from Ahab **e last male** in H8874+928+7815
1Ki 22:36 through the army: "*E* **man** to his town. AIT
1Ki 22:36 "Every man to his town. *E* **man** to his land!" AIT
2Ki 3:19 You will overthrow e fortified city and H3972
2Ki 3:19 every fortified city and e major town. H3972
2Ki 3:19 You will cut down e good tree, stop up all H3972
2Ki 3:19 springs, and ruin e good field with stones." H3972
2Ki 3:21 against them; so e *man*, young and old, H3972
2Ki 3:25 man threw a stone on e good field until it H3972
2Ki 3:25 all the springs and cut down e good tree. H3972
2Ki 9: 8 from Ahab **e last male** in H8874+928+7815
2Ki 12: 5 Let e priest receive the money from one of H408
2Ki 13:20 used to enter the country **e spring**. H995+9102
2Ki 14:12 routed by Israel, and *e* **man** fled to his home. AIT
2Ki 15:20 E wealthy person had to contribute fifty H3972
2Ki 16: 4 the hilltops and under e spreading tree. H3972
2Ki 17:10 Asherah poles on e high hill and under H3972
2Ki 17:10 high hill and under e spreading tree. H3972
2Ki 17:11 At e high place they burned incense, as H3972
2Ki 25: 9 E important building he burned down. H3972
1Ch 9:32 preparing *for* **e Sabbath** the bread H8701+8701
1Ch 12:33 prepared for battle with e *type of* weapon, H3972
1Ch 12:37 armed with e *type of* weapon—120,000. H3972
1Ch 14:17 David's fame spread throughout e land, H3972
1Ch 21:12 angel of the LORD ravaging e part of Israel. H3972
1Ch 22: 9 rest from all his enemies **on e side**. H4946+6017
1Ch 22:15 as well as those skilled in e *kind of* work H3972
1Ch 22:18 he not granted you rest **on e side**? H4946+6017
1Ch 23:30 to stand **e morning** to thank
H928+2021+1332+928+2021+1332
1Ch 26:32 of Manasseh for e matter pertaining to H3972
1Ch 28: 9 the LORD searches e heart and H3972
1Ch 28: 9 heart and understands e desire and every H3972
1Ch 28: 9 understands every desire and e thought. NDT
1Ch 28:21 e willing person skilled in any craft H3972
1Ch 28:21 all the people will obey your e command." H3972
2Ch 2: 4 burnt offerings e morning and evening H4200
2Ch 9:21 Once e three years it returned, carrying H4200
2Ch 11: 4 Go home, e *one* of you, for this is my doing H408
2Ch 11:16 Those from e tribe of Israel who set their H3972
2Ch 13:11 **E morning** and evening they present
H928+2021+1332+928+2021+1332
2Ch 13:11 on the gold lampstand **e evening**.
H928+2021+6847+928+2021+6847
2Ch 14: 5 incense altars in e town in Judah, H3972
2Ch 14: 7 and he has given us rest **on e side**." H4946+6017
2Ch 15: 6 was troubling them with e *kind of* distress. H3972
2Ch 15:15 the LORD gave them rest **on e side**. H4946+6017
2Ch 19:10 *In* e case that comes before you from your H3972
2Ch 20: 4 they came from e town in Judah to seek H3972
2Ch 20:30 God had given him rest **on e side**. H4946+6017
2Ch 25:22 routed by Israel, and *e* **man** fled to his home. AIT
2Ch 28: 4 the hilltops and under e spreading tree. H3972
2Ch 28:24 set up altars at e street corner in H3972
2Ch 28:25 In e town in Judah he built high places to H3972
2Ch 30:21 the LORD **e day** with H3427+928+3427
2Ch 31:19 portions to e male among them and to H3972
2Ch 32:22 He took care of them **on e side**. H4946+6017
Ne 4:22 "Have *e* **man** and his helper stay inside AIT
Ne 5:18 e ten days an abundant supply of H1068
Ne 10:31 E seventh year we will forgo working the H2021
Ne 10:35 firstfruits of our crops and of e fruit tree. H3972
Ne 11: 1 to bring one out of e ten of them to live in H2021
Est 1:22 proclaiming that e man should be ruler H3972
Est 2: 3 commissioners in e province of his realm H3972
Est 2:11 **E day** he walked back H3972+3427+2256+3427
Est 3:14 be issued as law in e province and made H3972
Est 3:14 to the people of e nationality so they H3972
Est 4: 3 In e province to which the edict and order H3972
Est 8:11 granted the Jews in e city the right to H3972
Est 8:13 be issued as law in e province and made H3972
Est 8:13 to the people of e nationality so that H3972
Est 8:17 In e province and in every city to which the H3972
Est 8:17 every province and in e city to which the H3972
Est 9:27 fail observe these two days e year, H3972
Est 9:28 observed in e generation by every H3972
Est 9:28 generation by **e family**, H5476+2256+5476
Est 9:28 and in **e province** and in H4519+2256+4519
Est 9:28 every province and in **e city**. H6551+2256+6551
Job 7:18 you examine them e morning and test H4200
Job 7:18 every morning and test them e moment? H4200
Job 12:10 hand is the life of e creature and the H3972
Job 18:11 startle him **on e side** and dog his every H6017
Job 18:11 startle him on every side and dog his *e* **step**. AIT
Job 19:10 tears me down **on e side** till I am gone; H6017
Job 28:21 It is hidden from the eyes of e living thing, H3972
Job 31: 4 he not see my ways and count my e step? H3972
Job 31:37 I would give him an account of my *e* **step**; AIT
Job 34:21 the ways of mortals; he sees their e step. H3972
Ps 3: 6 tens of thousands assail me **on e side**. H6017
Ps 7:11 a God who displays his wrath e day. H3972
Ps 12: 3 all flattering lips and e boastful tongue— NDT
Ps 31:13 whispering, "Terror **on e side**!" H4946+6017
Ps 50:10 e animal of the forest is mine, and the H3972
Ps 50:11 I know e bird in the mountains, and the H3972
Ps 52: 4 You love e harmful word, you deceitful H3972
Ps 73:14 e morning brings new punishments. H4200
Ps 74: 8 They burned e place where God was H3972
Ps 82: 7 mere mortals; you will fall like *e* **other** ruler." AIT
Ps 88: 9 I call to you, LORD, e day; I spread out my H3972
Ps 89:51 they have mocked *e* **step** *of* your anointed AIT
Ps 97: 3 him and consumes his foes **on e side**. H6017
Ps 101: 8 E morning I will put to silence all the H4200
Ps 101: 8 I will cut off e evildoer from the city of the H3972
Ps 105:35 they ate up e green thing in their land H3972
Ps 118:11 They surrounded me **on e side**, but in the H6015
Ps 119:101 kept my feet from e evil path so that I H3972
Ps 119:104 precepts; therefore I hate e wrong path. H3972
Ps 119:128 your precepts right, I hate e wrong path. H3972
Ps 136:25 He gives food to e creature. His love H3972
Ps 140: 2 plans in their hearts and stir up war e day. H3972
Ps 144:13 with **e kind** *of* provision. H4946+2385+448+2385
Ps 145: 2 E day I will praise you and extol your H3972
Ps 145:16 satisfy the desires of e living thing. H3972
Ps 145:21 Let e creature praise his holy name for H3972
Pr 1:17 to spread a net where e bird can see it! H3972
Pr 2: 9 is right and just and fair—e good path. H3972
Pr 7:12 now in the squares, at e corner she lurks.) H3972
Pr 16:33 the lap, but its e decision is from the LORD. H3972
Pr 17: 8 they think success will come at e turn. H3972
Pr 20: 3 avoid strife, but e fool is quick to quarrel. H3972
Pr 30: 5 "E word of God is flawless; he is a shield H3972
Ecc 3: 1 a season for e activity under the H3972
Ecc 3:17 there will be a time for e activity, H3972
Ecc 3:17 every activity, a time to judge e deed." H3972
Ecc 7:21 not pay attention to e word people say, H3972
Ecc 8: 6 a proper time and procedure for e matter, H3972
Ecc 12:14 For God will bring e deed into judgment H3972
Ecc 12:14 judgment, including e hidden thing H3972
SS 4:14 cinnamon, with e *kind of* incense tree H3972
SS 7:13 at our door is e delicacy, both new H3972
Isa 2:15 e lofty tower and every fortified wall, H3972
Isa 2:15 every lofty tower and e fortified wall, H3972
Isa 2:16 e trading ship and every stately vessel. H3972
Isa 2:16 every trading ship and e stately vessel. H3972
Isa 7:23 in e place where there were a thousand H3972
Isa 9: 5 E warrior's boot used in battle and every H3972
Isa 9: 5 used in battle and e garment rolled in NDT
Isa 9:17 wicked, e mouth speaks folly. H3972
Isa 13: 7 go limp, e heart will melt with fear. H3972+632
Isa 15: 2 E head is shaved and every beard cut off. H3972
Isa 15: 2 Every head is shaved and e beard cut off. H3972
Isa 19: 7 E sown field along the Nile will become H3972
Isa 21: 8 the watchtower; e night I stay at my post. H3972
Isa 24:10 the entrance to e house is barred. H3972
Isa 30:25 of water will flow on e high mountain H3972
Isa 30:25 on every high mountain and e lofty hill. H3972
Isa 30:32 E stroke the LORD lays on them with his H3972
Isa 31: 7 For in that day e *one of* you will reject the H408
Isa 32:20 sowing your seed by e stream, and letting H3972
Isa 33: 2 Be our strength e morning, our salvation H4200
Isa 40: 4 E valley shall be raised up, every H3972
Isa 40: 4 raised up, e mountain and hill made low H3972
Isa 45:23 Before me e knee will bow; by me every H3972
Isa 45:23 knee will bow; by me e tongue will swear. H3972
Isa 49: 9 roads and find pasture on e barren hill. H3972
Isa 51:13 in constant terror e day because of the H3972
Isa 51:20 fainted; they lie at e street corner, like H3972
Isa 54:17 you will refute e tongue that accuses H3972
Isa 57: 5 the oaks and under e spreading tree; H3972
Isa 58: 6 set the oppressed free and break e yoke? H3972
Jer 2:20 on e high hill and under every spreading H3972
Jer 2:20 high hill and under e spreading tree you H3972
Jer 3: 6 She has gone up on e high hill and under H3972
Jer 3: 6 high hill and under e spreading tree and H3972
Jer 3:13 to foreign gods under e spreading tree, H3972
Jer 4:25 people; e bird in the sky had flown away. H3972
Jer 4:29 archers e town takes to flight H3972
Jer 6:25 sword, and there is terror **on e side**. H4946+6017
Jer 9: 4 For e *one of* them is a deceiver, and every H3972
Jer 9: 4 is a deceiver, and e friend a slanderer. H3972
Jer 10:14 e goldsmith is shamed by his idols. H3972
Jer 12: 4 the grass in e field be withered? H3972
Jer 13:12 E wineskin should be filled with wine H3972
Jer 13:12 'Don't we know that e wineskin should be H3972
Jer 16:16 hunt them down on e mountain and hill H3972
Jer 19:15 villages around it e disaster I pronounced H3972
Jer 20: 3 you is not Pashhur, but Terror on **E Side**. H6017

E

Jer 20:10 whispering, "Terror on e side! H4946+6017
Jer 21:12 " 'Administer justice e morning; rescue H4200
Jer 30: 6 Then why do I see e strong man with his H3972
Jer 30: 6 in labor, e face turned deathly pale? H3972
Jer 34:14 'E seventh year each of you must H4946+7891
Jer 35:17 living in Jerusalem e disaster I H3972
Jer 36: 3 of Judah hear about e disaster I plan to H3972
Jer 36:31 the people of Judah e disaster I H3972
Jer 46: 5 and there is terror on e side, H4946+6017
Jer 48: 8 The destroyer will come against e town H3972
Jer 48:37 E head is shaved and every beard cut off H3972
Jer 48:37 Every head is shaved and e beard cut off H3972
Jer 48:37 e hand is slashed and every waist is H3972
Jer 48:37 hand is slashed and e waist is covered with NDT
Jer 49: 5 "E *one* of you will be driven away, and no H408
Jer 49:29 shout to them, 'Terror on e side! H4946+6017
Jer 49:32 will bring disaster on them from e side," H3972
Jer 50:15 Shout against her on e side! She H6017
Jer 51: 2 oppose her on e side in the day of H4946+6017
Jer 51:17 e goldsmith is shamed by his idols. H3972
Jer 52:13 E important building he burned down. H3972
La 2: 3 anger he has cut off e horn of Israel. H3972
La 2:19 who faint from hunger at e street corner. H3972
La 2:22 against me terrors on e side. H4946+6017
La 3:23 They are new e morning; great is your H4200
La 4: 1 gems are scattered at e street corner. H3972
La 4:18 People stalked us at *e* step, so we could not AIT
Eze 6:13 on e high hill and on all the H3972
Eze 6:13 under e spreading tree and every leafy H3972
Eze 6:13 every spreading tree and e leafy oak— H3972
Eze 7:17 E hand will go limp; every leg will be wet H3972
Eze 7:17 will go limp; e leg will be wet with urine. H3972
Eze 7:18 E face will be covered with shame, and H3972
Eze 7:18 with shame, and e head will be shaved. H3972
Eze 12:22 'The days go by and e vision comes to H3972
Eze 12:23 'The days are near when e vision will be H3972
Eze 14:22 e disaster I have brought on it. H3972
Eze 16:24 made a lofty shrine in e public square. H3972
Eze 16:25 At e street corner you built your lofty H3972
Eze 16:31 built your mounds at e street corner and H3972
Eze 16:31 your lofty shrines in e public square, H3972
Eze 17:23 Birds *of* e *kind* will nest in it; they will find H3972
Eze 20:26 the sacrifice of e firstborn—that I might H3972
Eze 20:39 serve your idols, e *one* of you! But H408
Eze 20:47 e face from south to north will be H3972
Eze 21: 7 E heart will melt with fear and every hand H3972
Eze 21: 7 will melt with fear and e hand go limp; H3972
Eze 21: 7 e spirit will become faint and every leg H3972
Eze 21: 7 become faint and e leg will be wet with H3972
Eze 21:10 The sword despises e such stick. H3972
Eze 21:14 slaughter, **closing in** on them **from e side**. H2539
Eze 23:22 will bring them against you from e side— H6017
Eze 23:24 against you on e side with large and H6017
Eze 26:16 ground, trembling e moment, appalled at H4200
Eze 27:11 Helek guarded your walls on e side; H6017
Eze 28:13 e precious stone adorned you: H3972
Eze 28:23 the sword against you on e side. H4946+6017
Eze 29:18 e head was rubbed bare and every H3972
Eze 29:18 rubbed bare and e shoulder made raw. H3972
Eze 32:10 them will tremble e moment for his life. H4200
Eze 34: 6 over all the mountains and on e high hill. H3972
Eze 36: 3 crushed you from e side so that you H4946+6017
Eze 38:20 e creature that moves along the ground H3972
Eze 38:20 will crumble and e wall will fall to the H3972
Eze 38:21 *E* **man's** sword will be against his brother. AIT
Eze 39:17 Call out to e kind of bird and all the wild H3972
Eze 39:20 mighty men and soldiers of e *kind*,' H3972
Eze 45:15 is to be taken from e flock of two hundred H2021
Eze 45:23 E day during the seven days of the festival H4200
Eze 46:13 " 'E day you are to provide a H4200+2021+3427
Eze 47:12 E month they will bear fruit, because the H4200
Da 1: 4 showing aptitude for e *kind of* learning H3972
Da 1:20 In e matter of wisdom and understanding H3972
Da 3: 4 "Nations and peoples *of* e **language**, this is AIT
Da 3: 7 peoples *of* e **language** fell down and AIT
Da 4: 1 To the nations and peoples *of* e **language** AIT
Da 4:12 its branches; from it e creature was fed. A10353
Da 5:19 peoples *of* e **language** dreaded and AIT
Da 6:14 Daniel and **made** e **effort** until sundown A10700
Da 6:25 peoples *of* e **language** in all the earth: AIT
Da 6:26 a decree that in e part of my kingdom A10353
Da 7:14 peoples *of* e **language** worshiped him. AIT
Da 11:36 magnify himself above e god and will say H3972
Hos 9: 1 wages of a prostitute at e threshing floor. H3972
Hos 9:12 rear children, I will bereave them of e *one*. H132
Joel 2: 6 nations are in anguish; e face turns pale. H3972
Joel 3:11 all you nations from e side, and H4946+6017
Joel 3:12 to judge all the nations on e side. H4946+6017
Am 2: 8 They lie down beside e altar on garments H3972
Am 4: 4 Bring your sacrifices e morning, your tithes H4200
Am 4: 4 every morning, your tithes e three years. H4200
Am 4: 6 you empty stomachs in e city and lack of H3972
Am 4: 6 in every city and lack of bread in e town, H3972
Am 5:16 cries of anguish in e public square. H3972
Na 2:10 bodies tremble, e face grows pale. H3972
Na 3:10 were dashed to pieces at e street corner. H3972
Zep 1: 4 I will destroy *e* **remnant** *of* Baal worship in AIT
Zep 2:14 will lie down there, creatures of e kind. H3972
Zep 3: 5 and e new day he does not fail H4200
Zep 3:19 praise and honor in e land where they H3972
Zec 5: 3 says on one side, e thief will be banished H3972
Zec 10: 4 from him the battle bow, from him e ruler. H3972
Zec 12: 4 day I will strike e horse with panic and H3972
Zec 13: 4 "On that day e prophet will be ashamed of H408
Zec 14:21 E pot in Jerusalem and Judah will be holy H3972
Mal 1:11 In e place incense and pure offerings will H3972
Mal 4: 1 All the arrogant and e evildoer will be H3972
Mt 3:10 e tree that does not produce good G4246
Mt 4: 4 on e word that comes from the mouth G4246
Mt 4:23 healing e disease and sickness G4246
Mt 7:17 Likewise, e good tree bears good fruit, but G4246
Mt 7:19 E tree that does not bear good fruit is cut G4246
Mt 9:35 kingdom and healing e disease and G4246
Mt 10: 1 spirits and to heal e disease and sickness. G4246
Mt 12:25 "E kingdom divided against itself will be G4246
Mt 12:25 e city or household divided against G4246
Mt 12:31 e *kind of* sin and slander can be forgiven G4246
Mt 12:36 day of judgment for e empty word they G4246
Mt 13:52 "Therefore e teacher of the law who has G4246
Mt 15:13 "E plant that my heavenly Father has not G4246
Mt 18:16 so that 'e matter may be established by G4246
Mt 19: 3 to divorce his wife for **any and** e reason?" G4246
Mt 24: 2 left on another; *e* **one** will be thrown down." AIT
Mt 26:55 **E day** I sat in the temple courts G2848+2465
Mk 3:28 their sins and e slander they utter G4012+1569
Mk 13: 2 left on another; *e* **one** will be thrown down." AIT
Mk 14:49 **E day** I was with you, teaching in G2848+2465
Lk 2:23 "E firstborn male is to be consecrated to G4246
Lk 2:41 E year Jesus' parents went to Jerusalem G2848
Lk 3: 5 E valley shall be filled in, every mountain G4246
Lk 3: 5 filled in, e mountain and hill made low. G4246
Lk 3: 9 e tree that does not produce good G4246
Lk 5:17 They had come from e village of Galilee G4246
Lk 10: 1 two ahead of him to e town and place G4246
Lk 13:24 "**Make** e **effort** to enter through the narrow G76
Lk 16:19 fine linen and lived in luxury e day. G2848
Lk 19:43 encircle you and hem you in **on e side**. G4119
Lk 19:47 E day he was teaching at the temple. G2848
Lk 21: 6 another; *e one of* **them** will be thrown down." AIT
Lk 22:53 E day I was with you in the temple courts G2848
Jn 13:10 you are clean, though not e *one* of you." G4246
Jn 13:11 was why he said not e *one* was clean. G4246
Jn 15: 2 He cuts off e branch in me that bears no G4246
Jn 15: 2 while e branch that does bear fruit he G4246
Jn 21:25 If e one of them were written down, G2848
Ac 2: 5 Jews from e nation under heaven. G4246
Ac 2:38 be baptized, e *one* of you, in the G1667
Ac 2:46 **E day** they continued to meet G2848+2465
Ac 3: 2 where he was put e day to beg from those G2848
Ac 10:35 accepts from e nation the one who G4246
Ac 13:27 of the prophets that are read e Sabbath. G4246
Ac 13:39 who believes is set free from e *sin*, G4246
Ac 15:21 has been preached **in** e city from the G2848
Ac 15:21 is read in the synagogues on e Sabbath." G4246
Ac 17:11 the Scriptures e day to see if what Paul G2848
Ac 17:22 I see that **in** e **way** you are very religious. G4246
Ac 18: 4 E Sabbath he reasoned in the G2848+4246
Ac 20:23 I only know that **in** e city the Holy Spirit G2848
Ac 24: 3 Everywhere and *in* e *way*, most excellent G4118
Ro 1:29 become filled *with* e *kind* of wickedness, G4246
Ro 2: 9 distress for e human being who does G4246
Ro 3: 2 Much in e way! First of all, the Jews have G4246
Ro 3: 4 God be true, and e human being a liar. G4246
Ro 3:19 so that e mouth may be silenced and the G4246
Ro 6:13 offer e part of yourself to him as an G3836
Ro 7: 8 produced in me e *kind of* coveting. G4246
Ro 12: 3 the grace given me I say *to* e *one* of you: G4246
Ro 14: 5 another; another considers e day *alike*. G4246
Ro 14:11 says the Lord, 'e knee will bow before me G4246
Ro 14:11 e tongue will acknowledge God. G4246
Ro 14:19 *Let us* therefore **make e effort** to do what G1503
1Co 1: 5 him you have been enriched in e *way*— G4246
1Co 4:17 with what I teach everywhere in e church. G4246
1Co 10:33 even as I try to please everyone *in* e *way* G4246
1Co 11: 3 to realize that the head of e man is Christ, G4246
1Co 11: 4 E man who prays or prophesies with his G4246
1Co 11: 5 But e woman who prays or prophesies with G4246
1Co 12:18 parts in the body, e one of them, just as G1667
1Co 12:26 If one part suffers, e part suffers with it; if G4246
1Co 12:26 part is honored, e part rejoices with it. G4246
1Co 14: 5 I would like e *one* of you to speak in G4246
1Co 15:30 why do we endanger ourselves e hour? G4246
1Co 15:31 I face death e day—yes, just as surely as I G2848
1Co 16: 2 On the first day of e week, each one of you G2848
2Co 4: 8 We are hard pressed on e *side*, but not G4246
2Co 6: 4 of God we commend ourselves in e *way*: G4246
2Co 7: 5 we were harassed at e *turn*—conflicts G4246
2Co 7:11 At e *point* you have proved yourselves to G4246
2Co 9: 8 you will abound in e good work. G4246
2Co 9:11 be enriched in e *way* so that you can be G4246
2Co 9:11 that you can be generous on e *occasion*, G4246
2Co 10: 5 arguments and e pretension that sets G4246
2Co 10: 5 we take captive e thought to make it G4246
2Co 10: 6 be ready to punish e act of disobedience, G4246
2Co 11: 6 made this perfectly clear to you in e *way*. G4246
2Co 13: 1 "E matter must be established by the G4246
Gal 5: 3 Again I declare *to* e man who lets himself G4246
Eph 1: 3 heavenly realms with e spiritual blessing G4246
Eph 1:21 dominion, and e name that is invoked G4246
Eph 1:23 of him who fills everything in e *way*. G4246
Eph 3:15 from whom e family in heaven and on G4246
Eph 4: 3 **Make e effort** to keep the unity of the Spirit G5079
Eph 4:14 here and there by e wind of teaching and G4246
Eph 4:15 to become *in* **e respect** the mature G3836+4246
Eph 4:16 held together by e supporting ligament, G4246
Eph 4:19 so as to indulge in e *kind of* impurity, G4246
Eph 4:31 slander, along with e *form of* malice. G4246
Eph 5:16 making the most of e opportunity, because G3836
Php 1: 3 I thank my God e *time* I remember you. G4246
Php 1:18 The important thing is that *in* e way G4246
Php 2: 9 gave him the name that is above e name, G4246
Php 2:10 at the name of Jesus e knee should bow, G4246
Php 2:11 e tongue acknowledge that Jesus G4246
Php 4: 6 anything, but in e *situation*, by prayer G4246
Php 4:12 of being content in any and e *situation*, G4246
Col 1:10 of the Lord and please him in e *way*: G4246
Col 1:10 bearing fruit in e good work, growing in G4246
Col 1:23 been proclaimed to e creature under G4246
Col 2:10 He is the head over e power and authority G4246
Col 4: 5 outsiders; make the most of e opportunity. G3836
1Th 2:17 longing we made e effort to see you. G4359
1Th 5:22 reject e kind of evil. G4246
2Th 1:11 to fruition your e desire for goodness G4246
2Th 1:11 goodness and your e deed prompted by NDT
2Th 2:17 strengthen you in e good deed and word. G4246
2Th 3: 6 to keep away from e believer who is idle G4246
2Th 3:16 give you peace at all times and in e way. G4246
2Ti 3:17 be thoroughly equipped for e good work. G4246
2Ti 4:18 will rescue me from e evil attack and will G4246
Titus 1: 5 unfinished and appoint elders **in** e town, G2848
Titus 2:10 so that in e *way* they will make the G4246
Phm 6 understanding of e good thing we share G4246
Heb 2: 2 e violation and disobedience G4246
Heb 2:17 fully human in e *way*, in order that he G4246
Heb 3: 4 For e house is built by someone, but God G4246
Heb 4:11 *Let us*, therefore, **make e effort** to enter G5079
Heb 4:15 one who has been tempted in e *way*, G4246
Heb 5: 1 E high priest is selected from among the G4246
Heb 8: 3 E high priest is appointed to offer both G4246
Heb 9:19 had proclaimed e command of the law G4246
Heb 9:25 the Most Holy Place e year with blood G2848
Heb 10:11 Day after day e priest stands and performs G4246
Heb 12:14 **Make e effort** *to live* in peace with G1503
Heb 13:18 desire to live honorably in e *way*. G4246
Jas 1:17 E good and perfect gift is from above G4246
Jas 3:16 there you find disorder and e evil practice. G4246
1Pe 2: 1 hypocrisy, envy, and slander *of* e *kind*. G4246
1Pe 2:13 the Lord's sake *to* e human authority: G4246
2Pe 1: 5 make e effort to add to your faith G4246
2Pe 1:10 make e effort to confirm your calling and G3437
2Pe 1:15 And *I will* **make e effort** *to see that* after G5079
2Pe 3:14 **make e effort** to be found spotless G5079
1Jn 4: 1 do not believe e spirit, but test the G4246
1Jn 4: 2 E spirit that acknowledges that Jesus G4246
1Jn 4: 3 e spirit that does not acknowledge G4246
Rev 1: 7 and "e eye will see him, even those who G4246
Rev 5: 9 God persons from e tribe and language G4246
Rev 5:13 Then I heard e creature in heaven and on G4246
Rev 6:14 e mountain and island was removed G4246
Rev 7: 9 no one could count, from e nation, tribe, G4246
Rev 7:17 God will wipe away e tear from their eyes. G4246
Rev 11: 6 the earth with e *kind* of plague as often G4246
Rev 11: 9 a half days some from e people, G3836
Rev 13: 7 And it was given authority over e tribe G4246
Rev 14: 6 who live on the earth—to e nation, tribe, G4246
Rev 16: 3 and e living thing in the sea died. G4246
Rev 16:20 E island fled away and the mountains G4246
Rev 18: 2 demons and a haunt for e impure spirit, G4246
Rev 18: 2 a haunt for e unclean bird, a haunt G4246
Rev 18: 2 a haunt for e unclean and detestable G4246
Rev 18:12 scarlet cloth; e *sort* of citron wood G4246
Rev 18:12 and articles *of* e *kind* of ivory G4246
Rev 18:17 "E sea captain, and all who travel by ship G4246
Rev 21: 4 'He will wipe e tear from their eyes. G4246
Rev 21:19 decorated with e *kind of* precious stone. G4246
Rev 22: 2 of fruit, yielding its fruit e month. G2848+1667

EVERYDAY (2) [DAY, EVERY]

Ro 6:19 an example **from e life** because of your G474
Gal 3:15 let me take an example **from e life**. G2848+476

EVERYONE (262) [EVERY, ONE]

Ge 16:12 will be against e and everyone's hand H3972
Ge 21: 6 e who hears about this will laugh H3972
Ge 45: 1 "Have e leave my presence! H3972+408
Ex 12:16 except to prepare food for e to eat H3972+5883
Ex 16:16 'E is to gather as much as they need H408
Ex 16:18 E had gathered just as much as they H408
Ex 16:21 Each morning e gathered as much as they H408
Ex 16:29 E is to stay where they are on the seventh H408
Ex 19:16 E in the camp trembled. H3972+2021+6639
Ex 25: 2 me from e whose heart prompts H3972+408
Ex 35: 5 E *who* is willing is to bring to the LORD an H3972
Ex 35:21 e who was willing and whose H3972+408
Ex 35:23 E who had blue, purple or scarlet H3972+408
Ex 35:24 e who had acacia wood for any part H3972
Ex 38:26 from e who had crossed over to those H3972
Lev 18:29 " 'E who does any of these detestable H3972
Lev 25:13 'In this Year of Jubilee e is to return to their H408
Nu 15:13 " 'E who is native-born must do these H3972
Nu 15:29 the same law applies to e who sins H2021S
Nu 18:11 E in your household *who* is ceremonially H3972
Nu 18:13 E in your household who is ceremonially H3972
Dt 4: 3 among you e who followed H3972+2021+408
Dt 12: 8 we do here today, e doing as they see fit, H408
Jos 6: 5 the army will go up, e straight in. H408

Jos 6:20 wall collapsed; so e charged straight in H6639
Jos 10:28 and totally destroyed e in it. H3972+2021+5883
Jos 10:30 The city and e in it Joshua H3972+2021+5883
Jos 10:32 The city and e in it he put to H3972+2021+5883
Jos 10:35 and totally destroyed e in it, H3972+2021+5883
Jos 10:37 its villages and e in it. H3972+2021+5883
Jos 10:37 destroyed it and e in it. H3972+2021+5883
Jos 10:39 E in it they totally destroyed H3972+5883
Jos 11:11 E in it they put to the sword H3972+2021+5883
Jdg 9:25 to ambush and rob e who passed by, H3972
Jdg 17: 6 Israel had no king; e did as they saw fit. H408
Jdg 19:30 E who saw it was saying to one another H3972
Jdg 21:25 Israel had no king; e did as they saw fit. H408
1Sa 2:36 Then e left in your family line will come H3972
1Sa 3:11 will make the ears of e who hears about it H3972
1Sa 8:22 the Israelites, "E go back to your own town." H408
1Sa 11: 5 he asked, "What is wrong with e?" H6639
1Sa 14:34 So e brought his ox that H3972+2021+6639
1Sa 26:23 The LORD rewards e for their righteousness H408
1Sa 30: 2 taken captive the women and **e else** in it, H889
2Sa 13: 9 "Send e out of here," Amnon H3972+408
2Sa 13: 9 Amnon said. So e left him. H3972+408
2Sa 15: 4 Then e who has a complaint or case H3972+408
2Sa 16:21 the hands of e with you will be more H3972
2Sa 20:12 he realized that e who came up to Amasa H3972
2Sa 20:13 e went on with Joab to pursue H3972+408
1Ki 4:25 e under their own vine and under their own H408
1Ki 8:39 deal with e according to all they do H2021+408
1Ki 10:25 Year after year, e who came brought a gift H408
2Ki 10:11 So Jehu killed e in Jezreel who remained H3972
2Ki 14:26 The LORD had seen how bitterly e in Israel NDT
2Ki 15:16 attacked Tiphsah and e in the city and its H3972
2Ki 21:12 that the ears of e who hears of it will H3972
1Ch 12:15 they put to flight e *living in* the valleys, H3972
2Ch 6:30 and deal with e according to all they H2021+408
2Ch 9:24 Year after year, e who came brought a gift H408
2Ch 29:29 the king and e present with him knelt H3972
2Ch 30:18 "May the LORD, who is good, pardon e H3972
2Ch 34:32 Then he had e in Jerusalem and H3972
Ezr 1: 5 Levites—e whose heart God had moved H3972
Ezr 8:22 hand of our God is on e who looks to him, H3972
Ezr 9: 4 Then e who trembled at the words of the H3972
Ezr 10:14 Then let e in our towns who has married H3972
Est 2:15 Esther won the favor of e who saw her. H3972
Job 17: 6 "God has made me a byword to e, a man H6639
Job 21:33 sweet to them; e follows after them H3972+132
Job 34:11 He repays e for what they have done; he H132
Job 34:26 their wickedness where *e can* **see** them, AIT
Job 37: 7 So that e he has made may know H3972+408
Job 42:11 sisters and e who had known him H3972
Ps 11: 4 He observes **e on earth**; his eyes H1201+132
Ps 12: 2 E lies to their neighbor; they flatter with H408
Ps 22: 6 not a man, scorned by e, despised by the H132
Ps 39: 5 E is but a breath, even those who seem H3972
Ps 39: 6 "Surely e goes around like a mere H408
Ps 39:11 a moth—surely e is but a breath. H3972+132
Ps 53: 3 E has turned away, all have become H3972
Ps 62:12 "You reward e according to what they have H408
Ps 116:11 in my alarm I said, "E is a liar." H3972+2021+132
Pr 19: 6 e is the friend of one who gives gifts. H3972
Pr 24:12 Will he not repay e according to what they H132
Ecc 5:15 *E* **comes** naked from their mother's womb AIT
Ecc 5:15 and as *e* **comes**, so they depart. AIT
Ecc 5:16 As *e* **comes**, so they depart, and what do AIT
Ecc 7: 2 death is the destiny of e H3972+2021+132
Ecc 10: 3 sense and show e how stupid they are H3972
Isa 2: 9 will be brought low and e humbled— H408
Isa 5:15 will be brought low and e humbled, H408
Isa 6:12 the LORD has sent e far away and the land H132
Isa 9:17 widows, for e is ungodly and wicked H3972
Isa 19:17 e to whom Judah is mentioned will be H3972
Isa 30: 5 e will be put to shame because of a H3972
Isa 43: 7 e who is called by my name, whom I H3972
Jer 1: 7 You must go to e I send you to and say H3972
Jer 10:14 E is senseless and without H3972+132
Jer 15:10 lent nor borrowed, yet e curses me. H3972
Jer 17:20 of Judah and e living in Jerusalem H3972
Jer 19: 3 will make the ears of e who hears of it H3972
Jer 20: 7 I am ridiculed all day long; e mocks me. H3972
Jer 31:30 Instead, e will die for their own sin H408
Jer 34: 9 E was to free their Hebrew slaves, both H408
Jer 35:17 on Judah and on e living in Jerusalem H3972
Jer 50:16 of the oppressor let e return to their own H408
Jer 50:16 own people, let e flee to their own land. H408
Jer 51:17 "E is senseless and without H3972+132
Eze 16:44 " 'E who quotes proverbs will quote this H3972
Eze 18: 4 For e belongs to me, the H3972+2021+5883
Eze 20:48 E will see that I the LORD have H3972+1414
Eze 21: 4 against e from south to H3972+1414
Eze 23: 7 with all the idols of e she lusted after. H3972
Eze 27:27 and **e else** on board will sink into H3972+7736
Da 3:10 a decree that e who hears the A10353+10050
Da 11: 2 he will stir up e against the kingdom of H3972
Da 12: 1 e whose name is found written in the book H3972
Joel 2:32 And e who calls on the name of the LORD H3972
Ob 9 e in Esau's mountains will be cut H408
Jnh 3: 8 *Let e* **call** urgently on God. AIT
Mic 4: 4 E will sit under their own vine and under H408
Mic 7: 2 E lies in wait to shed blood; they H3972+4392
Hab 2: 8 lands and cities and e in them. H3972+3782
Hab 2:17 lands and cities and e in them. H3972+3782
Zec 5: 3 e who swears falsely will be banished. H3972
Zec 8:10 I had turned e against their H3972+2021+132
Zec 10: 1 to all people, and plants of the field to e. H408
Zec 11: 6 "I will give e into the hands of their H132+408
Mt 5:15 and it gives light *to* e in the house. G4246
Mt 7: 8 For e who asks receives; the one who G4246
Mt 7:21 "Not e who says to me, 'Lord, Lord,' will G4246
Mt 7:24 "Therefore e who hears these words of G4246
Mt 7:26 But e who hears these words of mine and G4246
Mt 10:22 You will be hated by e because of me, but G4246
Mt 12:36 But I tell you that e will have to give G476
Mt 13:25 But while e was sleeping, his enemy came G476S
Mt 19:11 Jesus replied, "Not e can accept this word G4246
Mt 19:29 And e who has left houses or brothers G4246
Mk 1:37 they exclaimed: "E is looking for you!" G4246
Mk 2:12 This amazed e and they praised God G4246
Mk 3: 3 "Stand up **in front of e**. G1650+3836+3545
Mk 7:14 "Listen to me, e, and understand this G4246
Mk 9:49 E will be salted with fire. G4246
Mk 11:32 e held that John really was a prophet.) G570
Mk 13:13 E will hate you because of me, but the G4246
Mk 13:37 What I say to you, I say *to* e: 'Watch!' " G4246
Mk 14:50 Then e deserted him and fled. G4246
Lk 1:66 E who heard this wondered about it G4246
Lk 2: 3 And e went to their own town to register. G4246
Lk 2:47 E who heard him was amazed at his G4246
Lk 4:15 in their synagogues, and e praised him. G4246
Lk 4:20 The eyes *of* e in the synagogue were G4246
Lk 5:26 E was amazed and gave praise to God G570
Lk 6: 8 up and stand **in front of e**." G1650+3836+3545
Lk 6:26 to you when e speaks well of G4246+3836+476
Lk 6:30 Give *to* e who asks you, and if anyone G4246
Lk 6:40 e who is fully trained will be like their G4246
Lk 6:47 As for e who comes to me and hears my G4246
Lk 9:15 The disciples did so, and e sat down. G570
Lk 9:43 While e was marveling at all that Jesus G4246
Lk 11: 4 we also forgive e who sins against us. G4246
Lk 11:10 For e who asks receives; the one who G4246
Lk 12:10 And e who speaks a word against the Son G4246
Lk 12:41 are you telling this parable to us, or to e?" G4246
Lk 12:48 *From* e who has been given much, much G4246
Lk 14:29 to finish it, e who sees it will ridicule you, G4246
Lk 16:16 e is forcing their way into it. G4246
Lk 18: 9 looked down on **e else**, G3370
Lk 19:26 'I tell you that *to* e who has, more will be G4246
Lk 20:18 E who falls on that stone will be broken to G4246
Lk 21:17 E will hate you because of me. G4246
Jn 1: 9 gives light to e was coming into the G4246+476
Jn 2:10 "E brings out the choice wine first G4246+476
Jn 3: 8 So it is *with* e born of the Spirit." G4246
Jn 3:15 that e who believes may have eternal life G4246
Jn 3:20 E who does evil hates the light, and will G4246
Jn 3:26 he is baptizing, and e is going to him." G4246
Jn 4:13 "E who drinks this water will be thirsty G4246
Jn 6:40 Father's will is that e who looks to the Son G4246
Jn 6:45 E who has heard the Father and learned G4246
Jn 8:34 truly I tell you, e who sins is a slave to sin. G4246
Jn 11:48 him go on like this, e will believe in him G4246
Jn 13:35 By this e will know that you are my G4246
Jn 18:37 E on the side of truth listens to me." G4246
Ac 1:19 E in Jerusalem heard about this, so they G4246
Ac 2:21 And e who calls on the name of the Lord G4246
Ac 2:43 E was filled with awe at the many G4246+6034
Ac 4:16 "E living in Jerusalem knows they have G4246
Ac 8:19 this ability so that e on whom I lay my G1569
Ac 10:43 about him that e who believes in him G4246
Ac 13:39 Through him e who believes is set free G4246
Ac 17:25 he himself gives e life and breath and G4246
Ac 17:31 given proof of this *to* e by raising him G4246
Ac 21:24 Then e will know there is no truth in these G4246
Ac 21:28 man who teaches e everywhere against G4246
Ac 27:44 In this way e reached land safely. G4246
Ro 1:16 that brings salvation *to* e who believes: G4246
Ro 2:10 honor and peace *for* e who does good: G4246
Ro 10: 4 may be righteousness *for* e who believes. G4246
Ro 10:13 "E who calls on the name of the Lord will G4246
Ro 11:32 For God has bound e over to disobedience G4246
Ro 12:17 to do what is right in the eyes of e. G4246+476
Ro 12:18 on you, live at peace with e. G4246+476
Ro 13: 1 Let e be subject to the governing G4246+6034
Ro 13: 7 Give *to* e what you owe them: If you owe G4246
Ro 16:19 E has heard about your obedience, so I G4246
1Co 8: 7 But not e possesses this knowledge G4246
1Co 9:19 I have made myself a slave *to* e, to win as G4246
1Co 9:25 E who competes in the games goes into G4246
1Co 10:33 even as I try to please e in every way. G4246
1Co 11:28 E ought to examine themselves before they G476
1Co 12: 6 all of them and in e it is the same God at G4246
1Co 14:23 comes together and e speaks in tongues, G4246
1Co 14:24 inquirer comes in while e is prophesying, G4246
1Co 14:31 in turn so that e may be instructed and G4246
1Co 16:16 to such people and *to* e who joins in the G4246
2Co 3: 2 on our hearts, known and read by e. G4246+476
2Co 9:13 in sharing with them and with e *else*. G4246
Gal 3:10 "Cursed is e who does not continue to do G4246
Gal 3:13 "Cursed is e who is hung on a pole." G4246
Eph 3: 9 to make plain *to* e the administration G4246
Php 1:13 palace guard and *to* e else that I am in G4246
Php 2:21 For e looks out for their own interests, not G4246
Col 1:28 and teaching e with all wisdom, G4246+476
Col 1:28 we may present e fully mature in G4246+476
Col 4: 6 you may know how to answer e. G1651+1667
1Th 2:15 displease God and are hostile to e G4246+476
1Th 3:12 overflow for each other and for e *else*, G4246
1Th 5:14 help the weak, be patient with e. G4246
1Th 5:15 is good for each other and for e *else*. G4246
2Th 3: 2 evil people, for not e has faith. G4246
1Ti 4:15 to them, so that e may see your progress. G4246
1Ti 5:20 are sinning you are to reprove before e, G4246
2Ti 1:15 You know that e in the province of Asia G4246
2Ti 2:19 "E who confesses the name of the Lord G4246
2Ti 2:24 not be quarrelsome but must be kind to e, G4246
2Ti 3: 9 of those men, their folly will be clear *to* e. G4246
2Ti 3:12 e who wants to live a godly life in Christ G4246
2Ti 4:16 came to my support, but e deserted me. G4246
Titus 3: 2 and always to be gentle toward e. G4246+476
Titus 3: 8 things are excellent and profitable *for* e. G476
Titus 3:15 E with me sends you greetings. Greet G4246
Heb 2: 9 grace of God he might taste death for e. G4246
Heb 12: 6 he chastens e he accepts as his son." G4246
Heb 12: 8 disciplined—and e undergoes discipline G4246
Heb 12:14 to live in peace with e and to be holy; G4246
Jas 1:19 E should be quick to listen, slow to G4246+476
1Pe 2:17 Show proper respect *to* e, love the family G4246
1Pe 3:15 to give an answer *to* e who asks you to G4246
2Pe 3: 9 to perish, but e to come to repentance. G4246
1Jn 2:29 you know that e who does what is right G4246
1Jn 3: 4 E who sins breaks the law; in fact, sin is G4246
1Jn 4: 7 E who loves has been born of God and G4246
1Jn 5: 1 E who believes that Jesus is the Christ is G4246
1Jn 5: 1 e who loves the father loves his child G4246
1Jn 5: 4 e born of God overcomes the world G4246
3Jn 12 Demetrius is well spoken of by e—and G4246
Jude 15 to judge e, and to convict all of them of all G4246
Rev 6:15 the mighty, and e *else*, both slave and G4246
Rev 22:15 the idolaters and e who loves and G4246
Rev 22:18 I warn e who hears the words of the G4246

EVERYONE'S (7) [EVERY, ONE]

Ge 16:12 everyone and e hand against him, H3972
Jos 2:11 melted in fear and e courage failed H928+408
Ecc 6: 7 E toil is for their mouth, yet H3972+2021+132
Lk 1:63 and to e astonishment he wrote G4246
Ac 1:24 you know e heart. Show us which of G4246
Ac 16:26 flew open, and e chains came loose. G4246
2Co 4: 2 ourselves to e conscience in the G4246+476

EVERYTHING (382) [EVERY, THING]

Ge 1:30 ground—e that has the breath of life in it NDT
Ge 6:17 breath of life in it. E on earth will perish. H3972
Ge 6:22 Noah did e just as God commanded him. H3972
Ge 7:14 bird according to its kind, e *with* wings. H3972
Ge 7:22 E on dry land that had the breath of life in H3972
Ge 8:19 all the birds—e that moves on land H3972
Ge 9: 3 E that lives and moves about will be food H3972
Ge 9: 3 you the green plants, I now give you e. H3972
Ge 12:20 on his way, with his wife and e he had. H3972
Ge 13: 1 with his wife and e he had, and Lot went H3972
Ge 14:20 Then Abram gave him a tenth of e. H3972
Ge 21:22 to Abraham, "God is with you in e you do. H3972
Ge 24:36 and he has given him e he owns. H3972
Ge 25: 5 Abraham left e he owned to Isaac. H3972
Ge 26: 5 obeyed me and did e I **required** of him, H5466
Ge 31: 1 "Jacob has taken e our father owned and H3972
Ge 31:34 searched through e *in* the tent but found H3972
Ge 34:28 donkeys and **e else** of theirs in the city H889
Ge 34:29 taking as plunder e in the houses. H3972
Ge 39: 3 the LORD gave him success in e he did, H3972
Ge 39: 4 he entrusted to his care e he owned. H3972
Ge 39: 5 of the LORD was on e Potiphar had, H3972
Ge 39: 6 So Potiphar left e he had in Joseph's care H3972
Ge 39: 8 e he owns he has entrusted to my care. H3972
Ge 42:36 take Benjamin. E is against me!" H3972+5626
Ge 45:13 me in Egypt and about e you have seen. H3972
Ge 45:27 they told him e Joseph had said to H3972+1821
Ge 46:32 their flocks and herds and e they own. H3972
Ge 47: 1 their flocks and herds and e they own, H3972
Ex 4:28 Moses told Aaron e the LORD had sent H3972
Ex 4:30 Aaron told them e the LORD had H3972+1821
Ex 6:29 Tell Pharaoh king of Egypt e I tell you." H3972
Ex 7: 2 You are to say e I command you, and your H3972
Ex 9:19 your livestock and e you have in the field H3972
Ex 9:22 animals and on e growing in the H3972
Ex 9:25 Egypt hail struck e in the fields— H3972
Ex 9:25 it beat down e growing in the fields and H3972
Ex 10:12 the land and devour e growing in the H3972
Ex 10:12 growing in the fields, e left by the hail." H3972
Ex 10:15 e growing in the fields and the fruit on the H3972
Ex 18: 1 heard of e God had done for Moses and H3972
Ex 18: 8 father-in-law about e the LORD had done H3972
Ex 18:24 to his father-in-law and did e he said. H3972
Ex 19: 8 together, "We will do e the LORD has said." H3972
Ex 23:13 "Be careful to do e I have said to you. H3972
Ex 24: 3 "E the LORD has said we will H3972+2021+1821
Ex 24: 4 then wrote down e the LORD had said. H3972
Ex 24: 7 "We will do e the LORD has said; we H3972
Ex 29:35 Aaron and his sons e I have commanded H3972
Ex 31: 6 workers to make e I have commanded you H3972
Ex 35:10 are to come and make e the LORD has H3972
Ex 38:22 made e the LORD commanded Moses H3972
Ex 39:32 The Israelites did e just as the LORD H3972
Ex 40: 9 oil and anoint the tabernacle and e in it; H3972
Ex 40:16 Moses did e just as the LORD commanded H3972
Lev 8:10 anointed the tabernacle and e in it, H3972
Lev 8:36 and his sons did e the LORD H3972+2021+1821

Lev 11:33 falls into a clay pot, e in it will be unclean H3972
Lev 15: 9 " 'E the man sits on when riding will be H3972
Lev 27:28 e so devoted is most holy to the LORD. H3972
Lev 27:30 " 'A tithe of e *from* the land, whether H3972
Nu 1:50 all its furnishings and e belonging to it. H3972
Nu 2:34 the Israelites did e the LORD commanded H3972
Nu 3:26 the ropes—and e related to their use. H3972
Nu 3:31 the curtain, and e *related to* their use. H3972
Nu 3:36 its equipment, and e *related to* their use, H3972
Nu 4:16 of the entire tabernacle and e in it, H3972
Nu 4:32 their equipment and e related to their use H3972
Nu 9: 5 The Israelites did e just as the LORD H3972
Nu 16:30 with e that belongs to them H3972
Nu 16:33 of the dead, with e they owned; the earth H3972
Nu 18: 7 connection with e *at* the altar and H3972+1821
Nu 18:14 "E in Israel that is devoted to the LORD is H3972
Nu 18:29 best and holiest part of e given to you. H3972
Nu 22: 4 horde is going to lick up e around us, H3972
Nu 30: 2 not break his word but must do e he said. H3972
Nu 31:20 as well as e made of leather, H3972+3998
Dt 1:18 I told you e you were to do. H3972+2021+1821
Dt 5:28 people said to you. E they said was good. H3972
Dt 10:14 the highest heavens, the earth and e in it. H3972
Dt 12: 7 shall rejoice in e you have put your H3972
Dt 12:11 there you are to bring e I command you: H3972
Dt 12:14 there observe e I command you. H3972
Dt 12:18 LORD your God in e you put your hand to H3972
Dt 15:10 your work and in e you put your hand to H3972
Dt 15:18 LORD your God will bless you in e you do. H3972
Dt 17:10 Be careful to do e they instruct you to do H3972
Dt 18:18 He will tell them e I command him. H3972
Dt 20:14 the livestock and e else in the city, you H3972
Dt 23: 9 keep away from e impure. H3972+1821
Dt 23:20 may bless you in e you put your hand to H3972
Dt 26:14 I have done e you commanded me. H3972
Dt 28: 8 your barns and on e you put your hand to H3972
Dt 28:20 rebuke in e you put your hand to, H3972
Dt 28:29 You will be unsuccessful in e you **do**; day H2006
Dt 29: 9 so that you may prosper in e you do. H3972
Dt 30: 2 soul according to e I command you today, H3972
Jos 1: 8 you may be careful to do e written in it. H3972
Jos 2:23 of Nun and told him e that had happened H3972
Jos 4:10 Jordan until e the LORD had H3972+2021+1821
Jos 6:24 they burned the whole city and e in it, H3972
Jos 22: 2 you have obeyed me in e I commanded. H3972
Jos 23: 3 yourselves have seen e the LORD your God H3972
Jos 24:31 had experienced e the LORD had H3972+5126
Jdg 13:14 She must do e I have commanded her." H3972
Jdg 14:19 stripped them of e and gave their H2723S
Jdg 16:17 So he told her e. "No razor has H3972+4213
Jdg 16:18 Delilah saw that he had told her e, H3972+4213
Jdg 16:18 back once more; he has told me e." H3972+4213
Jdg 20:48 the animals and e else they found. H3972
Ru 3: 6 floor and did e her mother-in-law told H3972
Ru 3:16 Then she told her e Boaz had done for her H3972
1Sa 2:22 heard about e his sons were doing to all H3972
1Sa 3:12 carry out against Eli e I spoke against his H3972
1Sa 3:18 So Samuel told him e H3972+2021+1821
1Sa 9: 6 respected, and e he says comes true. H3972
1Sa 12: 1 "I have listened to e you said to me and H3972
1Sa 15: 9 fat calves and lambs—e that was good. H3972
1Sa 15: 9 but e that was despised and H3972+2021+4856
1Sa 18:14 In e he did he had great success, because H3972
1Sa 30:18 David recovered e the Amalekites had H3972
1Sa 30:19 David brought e back. H2021+3972
2Sa 3:19 Hebron to tell David e that Israel and the H3972
2Sa 3:25 movements and find out e you are doing." H3972
2Sa 3:36 indeed, e the king did pleased them. H3972
2Sa 6:12 household of Obed-Edom and e he has, H3972
2Sa 9: 9 master's grandson e that belonged to H3972
2Sa 11:22 he told David e Joab had sent him to H3972
2Sa 14:20 he knows e that happens in the land." H3972
2Sa 19:30 "Let him take e, now that my lord H3972
2Sa 21:14 did e the king commanded. H3972
1Ki 6:18 open flowers. E was cedar; no stone H3972
1Ki 14:26 He took e, including all the gold shields H3972
1Ki 19: 1 Ahab told Jezebel e Elijah had done and H3972
1Ki 20: 6 They will seize e you value and carry it H3972
1Ki 22:43 In e he followed the ways of his father Asa H3972
2Ki 4:26 "E is all right," she said. NDT
2Ki 5:21 "Is e all right?" he asked. NDT
2Ki 5:22 "E is all right," Gehazi answered. NDT
2Ki 8: 6 "Give back e that belonged to her H3972
2Ki 9:11 one of them asked him, "Is e all right? NDT
2Ki 14: 3 *In* e he followed the example of his father H3972
2Ki 20:13 his armory and e found among his H3972
2Ki 20:15 "They saw e in my palace," Hezekiah H3972
2Ki 20:17 will surely come when e in your palace, H3972
2Ki 21: 8 be careful to do e I commanded them H3972
2Ki 22:16 according to e written in the book the king H3972
1Ch 13:14 LORD blessed his household and e he had. H3972
1Ch 16:32 let the fields be jubilant, and e in them! H3972
1Ch 16:40 in accordance with e written in the Law of H3972
1Ch 26:28 And e dedicated by Samuel the seer and H3972
1Ch 29: 3 over and above e I have provided for this H3972
1Ch 29:11 e in heaven and earth is yours. H3972
1Ch 29:14 E comes from you, and we have given you H3972
1Ch 29:19 decrees and to do e to build the palatial H3972
2Ch 12: 9 He took e, including the gold shields H3972
2Ch 21:14 your wives and e *that* is yours, with H3972+8214
2Ch 29:16 of the LORD's temple e unclean that they H3972
2Ch 31: 5 brought a great amount, a tithe of e. H3972
2Ch 31:21 In e that he undertook in the service H3972+5126
2Ch 32:30 He succeeded in e he undertook. H3972
2Ch 32:31 test him and to know e that was in his H3972
2Ch 33: 8 will be careful to do e I commanded them H3972
2Ch 34:16 officials are doing e that has been H3972
2Ch 36:19 and destroyed e *of* value there. H3972+3998
Ezr 7: 6 The king had granted him e he asked, for H3972
Ezr 8:34 E was accounted for by number and H3972
Ne 9: 6 You give life to e, and the multitudes of H3972
Ne 13:30 the priests and the Levites of e foreign, H3972
Est 4: 7 Mordecai told him e that had happened to H3972
Est 6:13 all his friends e that had happened H3972
Est 9:26 Because of e written in this letter and H3972
Job 1:10 him and his household and e he has? H3972
Job 1:11 stretch out your hand and strike e he has, H3972
Job 1:12 e he has is in your power, but on H3972
Job 7:20 have I done to you, who see e we do? NDT
Job 28:24 the earth and sees e under the heavens. H3972
Job 33: 1 to my words; pay attention to e I say. H3972
Job 41:11 E under heaven belongs to me H3972
Ps 8: 6 of your hands; you put e under their feet: H3972
Ps 24: 1 earth is the LORD's, and **e in** it, the world, H4850
Ps 33:15 the hearts of all, who considers e they do. H3972
Ps 96:12 be jubilant, and e in them; let all the H3972
Ps 98: 7 Let the sea resound, and **e in** it, the world, H4850
Ps 146: 6 the sea, and e in them—he remains H3972
Ps 150: 6 Let e that has breath praise the LORD H3972
Pr 4:23 your heart, for **e you do** flows from it. H2644
Pr 16: 4 The LORD works out e to its proper end H3972
Ecc 1: 2 "Utterly meaningless! E is meaningless." H3972
Ecc 2:11 toiled to achieve, e was meaningless, H3972
Ecc 3: 1 There is a time for e, and a season for H3972
Ecc 3:11 He has made e beautiful in its time. H3972
Ecc 3:14 I know that e God does will endure forever; H3972
Ecc 3:19 over animals. E is meaningless. H3972
Ecc 8: 9 my mind to e done under the sun H3972+5126
Ecc 9: 3 This is the evil in e that happens under H3972
Ecc 10:19 life merry, and money is the answer for e. H3972
Ecc 11: 8 will be many. E to come is meaningless H3972
Ecc 12: 8 says the Teacher. "E is meaningless!" H3972
Isa 4: 5 over e the glory will be a canopy. H3972
Isa 8:12 not call conspiracy e this people calls a H3972
Isa 39: 2 his entire armory and e found among his H3972
Isa 39: 4 "They saw e in my palace," Hezekiah H3972
Isa 39: 6 will surely come when e in your palace, H3972
Jer 8:16 have come to devour the land and **e in** it, H4850
Jer 11: 4 'Obey me and do e I command you, and H3972
Jer 21:14 forests that will consume e around you. H3972
Jer 26: 2 Tell them e I command you H3972+2021+1821
Jer 26: 8 all the people e the LORD had H3972
Jer 35: 8 We have obeyed e our forefather H3972
Jer 35:10 have fully obeyed e our forefather H3972
Jer 35:18 instructions and have done e he ordered. H3972
Jer 36: 8 son of Neriah did e Jeremiah the prophet H3972
Jer 36:13 told them e he had heard H3972+2021+1821
Jer 36:20 and reported e to him. H3972+2021+1821
Jer 38:27 he told them e the king had ordered H3972
Jer 42: 4 I will tell you e the LORD says H3972+2021+1821
Jer 42: 5 with e the LORD your H3972+2021+1821
Jer 42:20 tell us e he says and we will do it. H3972
Jer 43: 1 e the LORD had sent him to tell H3972+2021+1821+2021+465
Jer 44:17 certainly do e we said we H3972+2021+1821
Jer 47: 2 They will overflow the land and **e in** it H4850
Jer 50:21 "Do e I have commanded you. H3972
La 2: 3 a flaming fire that consumes e **around** it. H6017
Eze 11:25 I told the exiles e the LORD had H3972+1821
Eze 12:19 will be stripped of e in it because of the H4850
Eze 23:29 take away e you have worked for. H3972
Eze 30:12 I will lay waste the land and **e in** it. H4850
Eze 32:15 desolate and strip the land of **e in** it, H4850
Eze 40: 4 pay attention to e I am going to show H3972
Eze 40: 4 Tell the people of Israel e you see." H3972
Eze 41:16 e beyond and including the threshold was NDT
Eze 44: 5 give attention to e I tell you concerning H3972
Eze 44:29 e in Israel devoted to the LORD will H3972
Eze 47: 9 so where the river flows e will live. H3972
Da 2:40 iron breaks and smashes e—and as A10353
Da 4:37 because e he does is right and all his A10353
Da 8:12 It prospered in e it did, and truth was thrown NDT
Da 9:14 our God is righteous in e he does; H3972+5126
Am 6: 8 I will deliver up the city and **e in** it." H4850
Zep 1: 2 "I will sweep away e from the face of the H3972
Hag 1:11 the olive oil and e *else* the ground H889
Mt 5:18 from the Law until e is accomplished. *G4246*
Mt 7:12 So *in* e, do to others what you would have *G4246*
Mt 13:41 out of his kingdom e that causes sin and *G4246*
Mt 13:46 went away and sold e he had and bought *G4246*
Mt 17:12 but have done to him e they wished. *G4012*
Mt 18:26 he begged, 'and I will pay back e. *G4246*
Mt 18:31 told their master e that had happened. *G4246*
Mt 19:27 "We have left e to follow you! *G4246*
Mt 22: 4 have been butchered, and e is ready. *G4246*
Mt 23: 3 careful to do e they tell you. *G4246+4012+1569*
Mt 23: 5 "E they do is done for people to see: They *G4246*
Mt 23:20 by the altar swears by it and by e on it. *G4246*
Mt 23:27 of the bones of the dead and e unclean. *G4246*
Mt 28:11 to the chief priests e that had happened. *G570*
Mt 28:20 them to obey e I have commanded *G4246+4012*
Mk 4:11 those on the outside e is said in parables *G4246*
Mk 4:34 with his own disciples, he explained e. *G4246*
Mk 7:37 "He has done e well," they said. *G4246*
Mk 8:25 sight was restored, and he saw e clearly. *G570*
Mk 9:13 they have done to him e they wished *G4012*
Mk 9:23 "E is possible for one who believes." *G4246*
Mk 10:21 sell e you have and give to the poor *G4012*
Mk 10:28 spoke up, "We have left e to follow you!" *G4246*
Mk 11:11 He looked around *at* e, but since it was *G4246*
Mk 12:44 her poverty, put in e—all she had to live *G4246*
Mk 13:23 I have told you e ahead of time. *G4246*
Mk 14:36 Father," he said, "e is possible for you. *G4246*
Lk 1: 3 investigated e from the beginning, *G4246*
Lk 2:39 Mary had done e required by the Law *G4246*
Lk 5:11 up on shore, left e and followed him. *G4246*
Lk 5:28 Levi got up, left e and followed him. *G4246*
Lk 11:41 to the poor, and e will be clean for you. *G4246*
Lk 14:17 had been invited, 'Come, for *e* is now ready. AIT
Lk 14:33 who do not give up e you have cannot be *G4246*
Lk 15:14 After he had spent e, there was a severe *G4246*
Lk 15:31 are always with me, and e I have is yours. *G4246*
Lk 17:10 when you have done e you were told to *G4246*
Lk 18:22 Sell e you have and give to the poor, and *G4246*
Lk 18:31 e that is written by the prophets *G4246*
Lk 24:14 each other about e that had happened. *G4246*
Lk 24:44 E must be fulfilled that is written about *G4246*
Jn 3:35 the Son and has placed e in his hands. *G4246*
Jn 4:25 When he comes, he will explain e to us." *G570*
Jn 4:29 see a man who told me e I ever did. *G4246*
Jn 4:39 testimony, "He told me e I ever did." *G4246*
Jn 14:26 will remind you *of* e I have said to you *G4246*
Jn 15:15 e that I learned from my Father I have *G4246*
Jn 17: 7 Now they know that e you have given me *G4246*
Jn 19:28 knowing that e had now been finished *G4246*
Ac 2:44 were together and had e in common. *G570*
Ac 3:21 until the time comes for God to restore e, *G4246*
Ac 3:22 must listen to e he tells you. *G4246+4012+323*
Ac 4:24 the earth and the sea, and e in them. *G4246*
Ac 4:32 was their own, but they shared e they had. *G570*
Ac 10: 8 He told them e that had happened and *G570*
Ac 10:33 of God to listen *to* e the Lord has *G4246*
Ac 10:39 "We are witnesses *of* e he did in the *G4246*
Ac 12:11 clutches and from e the Jewish people *G4246*
Ac 13:10 the devil and an enemy *of* e that is right! *G4246*
Ac 13:22 own heart; he will do e I want him to do. *G4246*
Ac 14:15 the earth and the sea and e in them. *G4246*
Ac 15: 4 whom they reported e God had done *G4012*
Ac 17:24 made the world and e in it is the Lord of *G4246*
Ac 17:25 life and breath and e *else*. *G3836+4246*
Ac 20:35 *In* e I did, I showed you that by this kind of *G4246*
Ac 24:14 I believe e that is in accordance with the *G4246*
Ro 14: 3 The one who eats e must not treat with NDT
Ro 14: 3 one who does not eat e must not judge the NDT
Ro 14:23 e that does not come from faith is sin. *G4246*
Ro 15: 4 For e *that* was written in the past was *G4012*
1Co 6:12 you say—but not e is beneficial. *G4246*
1Co 10:23 you say—but not e is beneficial. *G4246*
1Co 10:23 to do anything"—but not e is constructive. *G4246*
1Co 10:26 "The earth is the Lord's, and e in it." *G4445*
1Co 11: 2 remembering me *in* e and for holding *G4246*
1Co 11:12 But e comes from God. *G3836+4246*
1Co 14:26 E must be done so that the church may be *G4246*
1Co 14:40 But e should be done in a fitting and *G4246*
1Co 15:27 For he "has put e under his feet." Now *G4246*
1Co 15:27 Now when it says that "e" has been put *G4246*
1Co 15:27 himself, who put e under Christ. *G3836+4246*
1Co 15:28 to him who put e under him, *G3836+4246*
1Co 16:14 Do e in love. *G4246*
2Co 2: 9 stand the test and be obedient in e. *G4246*
2Co 6:10 having nothing, and yet possessing e. *G4246*
2Co 7: 1 purify ourselves from e that contaminates *G4246*
2Co 7:14 But just as e we said to you was true, so *G4246*
2Co 8: 7 But since you excel in e—in faith, in *G4246*
2Co 11:28 **Besides e else,** I face daily *G6006+3836+4211*
2Co 12:15 So I *will* very gladly **spend** for you e *I* **have** *G1251*
2Co 12:19 in Christ; and e we do, dear friends *G3836+4246*
Gal 3:10 not continue to do e written in the Book of *G4246*
Gal 3:22 has locked up e under the control *G3836+4246*
Eph 1:11 him who works out e in conformity *G3836+4246*
Eph 1:22 him to be head over e for the church, *G4246*
Eph 1:23 of him who fills e in every way. *G3836+4246*
Eph 5:13 But e exposed by the light becomes *G3836+4246*
Eph 5:13 e that is illuminated becomes a light. *G4246*
Eph 5:20 giving thanks to God the Father for e, *G4246*
Eph 5:24 should submit to their husbands in e. *G4246*
Eph 6:13 after you have done e, to stand. *G570*
Eph 6:21 will tell you e, so that you also may *G4246*
Php 2:14 Do e without grumbling or arguing, *G4246*
Php 3: 8 I consider e a loss because of the *G4246*
Php 3:21 him to bring e under his control, *G3836+4246*
Col 1:18 so that in e he might have the supremacy. *G4246*
Col 3:20 obey your parents in e, for this pleases *G4246*
Col 3:22 obey your earthly masters in e; and do it, *G4246*
Col 4: 9 They will tell you e that is happening *G4246*
2Th 2: 4 exalt himself over e that is called God *G4246*
1Ti 3:11 talkers but temperate and trustworthy in e. *G4246*
1Ti 4: 4 For e God created is good, and nothing is *G4246*
1Ti 6:13 who gives life *to* e, and of Christ *G3836+4246*
1Ti 6:17 richly provides us *with* e for our enjoyment *G4246*
2Ti 2:10 Therefore I endure e for the sake of the *G4246*
Titus 2: 7 In e set them an example by doing what is *G4246*
Titus 2: 9 slaves to be subject to their masters in e, *G4246*
Titus 3:13 *Do* e *you* **can** to help Zenas the lawyer *G5081*
Titus 3:13 see that they **have** e they **need**. *G3594+3309*
Heb 2: 8 put e under their feet." In putting *G4246*

Heb 2: 8 In putting e under them, God left G3836+4246
Heb 2: 8 we do not see e subject to them. G3836+4246
Heb 2:10 whom and through whom e exists, G3836+4246
Heb 3: 4 by someone, but God is the builder *of* e. G4246
Heb 4:13 E is uncovered and laid bare before the G4246
Heb 7: 2 Abraham gave him a tenth of e. First G4246
Heb 8: 5 to it that you make e according to the G4246
Heb 9: 6 When e had been arranged like this, the G4047
Heb 9:21 tabernacle and e used in its G4246+3836+5007
Heb 9:22 requires that nearly e be cleansed with G4246
Heb 12: 1 let us throw off e that hinders and the sin G4246
Heb 13:21 equip you with e good for doing his will G4246
2Pe 1: 3 power has given us e we need for a godly G4246
2Pe 3: 4 e goes on as it has since the beginning of G4246
2Pe 3:10 the earth and e done in it will be laid G3836
2Pe 3:11 Since e will be destroyed in this way G4246
1Jn 2:16 For e in the world—the lust of the flesh G4246
1Jn 3:20 greater than our hearts, and he knows e. G4246
Rev 1: 2 who testifies *to* e he saw—that is, the G4012
Rev 21: 5 on the throne said, "I am making e new!" G4246

EVERYWHERE (26) [EVERY, WHERE]

Ge 20:13 E we go, say of me, "He is H3972+2021+5226
Ge 41:57 famine was severe e. H928+3972+2021+824
Ex 7:19 Blood will be e in Egypt, even in vessels H3972
Ex 7:21 not drink its water. Blood was e in Egypt. H3972
Ex 8:18 the gnats were on people and animals e, NDT
Lev 25: 9 the trumpet sounded e on the tenth day of NDT
Ps 103:22 all his works e in his dominion. H3972+5226
Pr 15: 3 The eyes of the LORD are e H928+3972+5226
Pr 24:31 thorns had come up e, the ground was H3972
SS 4:16 garden, that its fragrance *may* **spread** e. H5688
Jer 25:33 that time those slain by the LORD will be e— NDT
Eze 16:33 to come to you from e for your illicit favors H6017
Am 8: 3 many bodies—flung e! Silence!" H3972+5226
Mk 1:45 Yet the people still came to him **from** e. G4119
Mk 16:20 the disciples went out and preached e, G4116
Lk 9: 6 the good news and healing people e. G4116
Ac 8:13 And *he* **followed** Philip e, astonished by G4674
Ac 17:30 now he commands all people e to repent. G4116
Ac 21:28 teaches everyone e against our people G4114
Ac 24: 3 E and in every way, most excellent Felix G4116
Ac 28:22 we know that people e are talking against G4116
1Co 1: 2 with all those e who call on G1877+4246+5536
1Co 4:17 with what I teach e in every church. G4116
2Co 2:14 of the knowledge of him e. G1877+4246+5536
1Th 1: 8 faith in God has become known e. G4246+5536
1Ti 2: 8 I want the men e to pray, G1877+4246+5536

EVI (2)

Nu 31: 8 Among their victims were E, Rekem, Zur H209
Jos 13:21 him and the Midianite chiefs, E, Rekem, H209

EVIDENCE (7) [EVIDENT]

Ex 22:13 bring in the remains as e and shall not be H6332
1Sa 12: 7 *I am going to* **confront** you **with** e before H9149
Mt 26:59 were looking for **false** e against Jesus so G6019
Mk 14:55 were looking for e against Jesus so that G3456
Jn 14:11 at least believe **on the** e **of** the works G1328
2Th 1: 5 All this is e that God's judgment is right G1891
Jas 2:20 do you want e that faith without deeds is G1182

EVIDENT (2) [EVIDENCE, EVIDENTLY]

1Ch 4:41 destroyed them, as is e to this day. NDT
Php 4: 5 *Let* your gentleness *be* e to all. The Lord is G1182

EVIDENTLY (1) [EVIDENT]

Gal 1: 7 E some people are throwing you G1623+3590

EVIL (406) [EVILDOER, EVILDOERS, EVILS]

Ge 2: 9 the tree of the knowledge of good and e. H8273
Ge 2:17 the tree of the knowledge of good and e, H8273
Ge 3: 5 will be like God, knowing good and e." H8273
Ge 3:22 like one of us, knowing good and e. H8273
Ge 6: 5 the human heart was only e all the time. H8273
Ge 8:21 of the human heart is e from childhood. H8273
Ge 44: 4 'Why have you repaid good with e? H8288
Ex 10:10 Clearly you are bent on e. H8288
Ex 32:12 'It was with e **intent** that he brought them H8288
Ex 32:22 know how prone these people are to e. H8273
Lev 5: 4 whether good or e (in any matter one H8317
Nu 23:23 against Jacob, no e **omens** against Israel. H7877
Nu 32:13 those who had done e in his sight was H8273
Dt 1:35 "No one from this e generation shall see H8273
Dt 4:25 doing e in the eyes of the LORD your God H8273
Dt 9:18 doing what was e in the LORD's sight and H8273
Dt 13: 5 You must purge the e from among you. H8273
Dt 13:11 among you will do such an e thing again. H8273
Dt 17: 2 you is found doing e in the eyes of the H8273
Dt 17: 5 who has done this e deed to your city H8273
Dt 17: 7 You must purge the e from among you. H8273
Dt 17:12 You must purge the e from Israel. H8273
Dt 19:19 You must purge the e from among you. H8273
Dt 19:20 again will such an e thing be done H8273
Dt 21:21 You must purge the e from among you H8273
Dt 22:21 You must purge the e from among you. H8273
Dt 22:22 You must purge the e from Israel. H8273
Dt 22:24 You must purge the e from among you. H8273
Dt 24: 7 You must purge the e from among you. H8273
Dt 28:20 ruin because of the e you have done in H8278
Dt 31:29 because you will do e in the sight of the H8273
Jos 23:15 bring on you all the e things he has H8273
Jdg 2:11 Then the Israelites did e in the eyes of the H8273
Jdg 2:19 to give up their e **practices** and stubborn H5095
Jdg 3: 7 The Israelites did e in the eyes of the LORD H8273
Jdg 3:12 the Israelites did e in the eyes of the LORD, H8273
Jdg 3:12 they did this e the LORD gave Eglon H8273
Jdg 4: 1 the Israelites did e in the eyes of the LORD, H8273
Jdg 6: 1 The Israelites did e in the eyes of the LORD H8273
Jdg 10: 6 the Israelites did e in the eyes of the LORD. H8273
Jdg 13: 1 the Israelites did e in the eyes of the LORD, H8273
Jdg 20:13 to death and purge the e from Israel." H8288
1Sa 12:17 realize what an e **thing** you did in the H8288
1Sa 12:19 our other sins the e of asking for a king." H8288
1Sa 12:20 "You have done all this e; yet do not turn H8288
1Sa 12:25 Yet if *you* **persist in doing** e, both H8317+8317
1Sa 15:19 the plunder and do e in the eyes of the H8273
1Sa 15:23 arrogance like the e of idolatry. H224
1Sa 16:14 an e spirit from the LORD tormented H8273
1Sa 16:15 an e spirit from God is tormenting you. H8273
1Sa 16:16 will play when the e spirit from God H8273
1Sa 16:23 and the e spirit would leave him. H8273
1Sa 18:10 The next day an e spirit from God came H8273
1Sa 19: 9 But an e spirit from the LORD came on Saul H8273
1Sa 24:13 'From evildoers come e **deeds**,' so my H8400
1Sa 25:21 He has paid me back e for good. H8288
1Sa 30:22 But all the e men and troublemakers H8273
2Sa 3:39 the evildoer according to his e **deeds**!" H8288
2Sa 12: 9 of the LORD by doing what is e in his eyes? H8273
2Sa 14:17 angel of God in discerning good and e. H8273
2Sa 23: 6 But e **men** are all to be cast aside like H1175
1Ki 1:52 to the ground; but if e is found in him, he H8288
1Ki 11: 6 So Solomon did e in the eyes of the LORD H8273
1Ki 13:33 Jeroboam did not change his e ways, but H8273
1Ki 14: 9 *You have* done more e than all who lived H8317
1Ki 14:22 Judah did e in the eyes of the LORD. H8273
1Ki 15:26 He did e in the eyes of the LORD, following H8273
1Ki 15:34 He did e in the eyes of the LORD, following H8273
1Ki 16: 7 because of all the e he had done in the H8288
1Ki 16:19 doing e in the eyes of the LORD and H8273
1Ki 16:25 But Omri did e in the eyes of the LORD H8273
1Ki 16:30 son of Omri did more e in the eyes of the H8273
1Ki 21:20 sold yourself to do e in the eyes of the H8273
1Ki 21:25 sold himself to do e in the eyes of the H8273
1Ki 22:52 He did e in the eyes of the LORD, because H8273
2Ki 3: 2 He did e in the eyes of the LORD, but not as H8273
2Ki 8:18 He did e in the eyes of the LORD H8273
2Ki 8:27 of Ahab and did e in the eyes of the H8273
2Ki 13: 2 He did e in the eyes of the LORD by H8273
2Ki 13:11 He did e in the eyes of the LORD and did H8273
2Ki 14:24 He did e in the eyes of the LORD and did H8273
2Ki 15: 9 He did e in the eyes of the LORD, as his H8273
2Ki 15:18 He did e in the eyes of the LORD. H8273
2Ki 15:24 Pekahiah did e in the eyes of the LORD. H8273
2Ki 15:28 He did e in the eyes of the LORD. He did H8273
2Ki 17: 2 He did e in the eyes of the LORD, but not H8273
2Ki 17:13 "Turn from your e ways. Observe my H8273
2Ki 17:17 sold themselves to do e in the eyes of the H8273
2Ki 21: 2 He did e in the eyes of the LORD, following H8273
2Ki 21: 6 He did much e in the eyes of the LORD H8273
2Ki 21: 9 that they did more e than the nations the H8273
2Ki 21:11 *He has* **done** more e than the Amorites H8317
2Ki 21:15 they have done e in my eyes and have H8273
2Ki 21:16 so that they did e in the eyes of the LORD. H8273
2Ki 21:20 He did e in the eyes of the LORD, as his H8273
2Ki 23:32 He did e in the eyes of the LORD, just as his H8273
2Ki 23:37 And he did e in the eyes of the LORD, just H8273
2Ki 24: 9 He did e in the eyes of the LORD, just as his H8273
2Ki 24:19 He did e in the eyes of the LORD, just as H8273
1Ch 21: 7 This command *was* also e in the sight of H8317
2Ch 12:14 He did e because he had not set his heart H8273
2Ch 21: 6 He did e in the eyes of the LORD H8273
2Ch 22: 4 He did e in the eyes of the LORD, as the H8273
2Ch 29: 6 they did e in the eyes of the LORD our God H8273
2Ch 33: 2 He did e in the eyes of the LORD, following H8273
2Ch 33: 6 He did much e in the eyes of the LORD H8273
2Ch 33: 9 that they did more e than the nations the H8273
2Ch 33:22 He did e in the eyes of the LORD, as his H8273
2Ch 36: 5 He did e in the eyes of the LORD his God H8273
2Ch 36: 9 He did e in the eyes of the LORD H8273
2Ch 36:12 He did e in the eyes of the LORD his God H8273
Ezr 9:13 us is a result of our e deeds and our great H8273
Ne 9:28 they again did what was e in your sight. H8273
Ne 9:35 not serve you or turn from their e ways. H8273
Ne 13: 7 learned about the e **thing** Eliashib had H8288
Est 8: 3 to put an end to the e plan of Haman the H8288
Est 9:25 orders that the e scheme Haman had H8288
Job 1: 1 upright; he feared God and shunned e. H8273
Job 1: 8 a man who fears God and shuns e." H8273
Job 2: 3 a man who fears God and shuns e. H8273
Job 4: 8 those who plow e and those who sow H224
Job 11:11 when he sees e, does he not take note H224
Job 11:14 hand and allow no e to dwell in your tent, H6406
Job 15:16 corrupt, who drink up e like water! H6406
Job 15:35 They conceive trouble and give birth to e H224
Job 18:21 Surely such is the dwelling of an e **man** H6405
Job 20:12 "Though e is sweet in his mouth and he H8288
Job 28:28 wisdom, and to shun e is understanding." H8273
Job 30:26 I hoped for good, e came; when I looked H8273
Job 34:10 Far be it from God to do e, from the H8400
Job 36:10 commands them to repent of their e. H224
Job 36:21 Beware of turning to e, which you seem to H224
Ps 5: 4 with you, e *people* are not welcome. H8273
Ps 6: 8 all you who do e, for the LORD has H224
Ps 7: 4 repaid my ally with e or without cause H8273
Ps 7:14 is pregnant with e conceives trouble and H224
Ps 10: 7 trouble and e are under his tongue. H224
Ps 17: 3 you will find that *I have* **planned** no e; my H2372
Ps 21:11 Though they plot e against you and H8288
Ps 23: 4 I will fear no e, for you are with me; H8273
Ps 28: 3 with those who do e, who speak cordially H224
Ps 28: 4 them for their deeds and for their e work; H8278
Ps 34:13 your tongue from e and your lips from H8273
Ps 34:14 Turn from e and do good; seek peace H8273
Ps 34:16 of the LORD is against those who do e, H8273
Ps 34:21 E will slay the wicked; the foes of the H8288
Ps 35:12 They repay me e for good and leave me H8288
Ps 36: 4 Even on their beds they plot e; they commit H224
Ps 37: 1 because of those *who are* e or be envious H8317
Ps 37: 8 from wrath; do not fret—it **leads** only **to** e. H8317
Ps 37: 9 For *those who are* e will be destroyed, but H8317
Ps 37:27 Turn from e and do good; then you will H8273
Ps 38:20 repay my good with e lodge accusations H8288
Ps 49: 5 Why should I fear when e days come H8273
Ps 50:19 use your mouth for e and harness your H8288
Ps 51: 4 I sinned and done what is e in your sight; H8273
Ps 52: 1 Why do you boast of e, you mighty hero H8288
Ps 52: 3 You love e rather than good, falsehood H8273
Ps 54: 5 Let e recoil on those who slander me; in H8273
Ps 55:15 for e finds lodging among them. H8288
Ps 64: 5 They encourage each other in e plans H8273
Ps 71: 4 the grasp of *those who* are e and cruel. H6401
Ps 73: 7 their e **imaginations** have no limits. H5381+4222
Ps 97:10 Let those who love the LORD hate e, for he H8273
Ps 101: 4 I will have nothing to do with *what* is e. H8273
Ps 109: 5 They repay me e for good, and hatred H8288
Ps 109: 6 Appoint *someone* e to oppose my enemy H8401
Ps 109:20 my accusers, to those who speak e of me. H8273
Ps 119:101 my feet from every e path so that I might H8273
Ps 125: 3 righteous might use their hands to do e. H6406
Ps 139:20 They speak of you with e **intent**; your H4659
Ps 140: 2 who devise e plans in their hearts and stir H8273
Ps 141: 4 be drawn to what is e so that I take part in H8273
Pr 1:16 their feet rush into e, they are swift to H8273
Pr 2:14 rejoice in the perverseness of e, H8273
Pr 3: 7 your own eyes; fear the LORD and shun e. H8273
Pr 4:16 For they cannot rest until *they* **do** e; they H8317
Pr 4:27 the right or the left; keep your foot from e. H8273
Pr 5:22 The e **deeds** *of* the wicked ensnare them H6411
Pr 6:14 who plots e with deceit in his heart—he H8273
Pr 6:18 feet that are quick to rush into e, H8288
Pr 8:13 To fear the LORD is to hate e; I hate pride H8273
Pr 8:13 e behavior and perverse speech. H8273
Pr 10:29 it is the ruin of those who do e. H224
Pr 11: 6 the unfaithful are trapped by e **desires**. H2094
Pr 11:19 but whoever pursues e finds death. H8288
Pr 11:27 e comes to one who searches for it. H8288
Pr 12:20 Deceit is in the hearts of those who plot e, H8273
Pr 13:19 the soul, but fools detest turning from e. H8273
Pr 14:16 The wise fear the LORD and shun e, but a H8273
Pr 14:17 the one who devises e **schemes** is hated. H4659
Pr 14:22 Do not those who plot e go astray? But H8273
Pr 15:28 the mouth of the wicked gushes e. H8288
Pr 16: 6 through the fear of the LORD e is avoided. H8273
Pr 16:17 The highway of the upright avoids e H8273
Pr 16:27 A scoundrel plots e, and on their lips it is H8288
Pr 16:30 whoever purses their lips is bent on e. H8288
Pr 17:13 E will never leave the house of one who H8288
Pr 17:13 house of one who pays back e for good. H8288
Pr 19:28 the mouth of the wicked gulps down e. H224
Pr 20: 8 he winnows out all e with his eyes. H8273
Pr 20:30 Blows and wounds scrub away e, and H8273
Pr 21:10 The wicked crave e; their neighbors get H8273
Pr 21:27 more so when brought with e **intent**! H2365
Pr 24: 8 Whoever plots e will be known as a H8317
Pr 26:23 are fervent lips with an e heart. H8273
Pr 28:10 the upright along an e path will fall into H8273
Pr 30:32 yourself, or if *you* **plan** e, clap your hand H2372
Ecc 4: 3 has not seen the e that is done under H8273
Ecc 5:13 I have seen a grievous e under the sun H8288
Ecc 5:16 This too is a grievous e: As everyone H8288
Ecc 6: 1 I have seen another e under the sun, and H8288
Ecc 6: 2 This is meaningless, a grievous e. H2716
Ecc 9: 3 This is the e in everything that happens H8273
Ecc 9: 3 are full of e and there is madness in their H8273
Ecc 9:12 so people are trapped by e times that fall H8288
Ecc 10: 5 There is an e I have seen under the sun H8288
Ecc 12:14 hidden thing, whether it is good or e. H8273
Isa 1:16 Take your e deeds out of my sight; stop H8278
Isa 5:20 to those who call e good and good evil, H8273
Isa 5:20 to those who call evil good and good e, H8273
Isa 13:11 I will punish the world for its e, the wicked H8288
Isa 26:10 *they go on* **doing** e and do not H6401
Isa 29:20 who have an eye for e will be cut down— H224
Isa 32: 6 fools speak folly, their hearts are bent on e: H224
Isa 32: 7 they make up e **schemes** to destroy the H2365
Isa 33:15 shut their eyes against contemplating e— H8273
Isa 56: 2 keeps their hands from doing any e." H8273
Isa 57: 1 are taken away to be spared from e. H8288
Isa 59: 4 they conceive trouble and give birth to e. H224
Isa 59: 6 Their deeds are e deeds, and acts of H224
Isa 59: 7 They pursue e schemes; acts of violence H224
Isa 59:15 whoever shuns e becomes a prey. H8273
Isa 65:12 You did e in my sight and chose what H8273
Isa 66: 4 They did e in my sight and chose what H8273
Jer 2:19 then and realize how e and bitter it is H8273
Jer 3: 5 you talk, but you do *all* the e you can." H8273

Jer 3:17 follow the stubbornness of their e hearts. H8273
Jer 4: 4 fire because of the e you have done— H8278
Jer 4:14 wash the e from your heart and be saved. H8288
Jer 4:22 They are skilled in **doing** e; they know not H8317
Jer 5:28 Their e deeds have no limit; they do not H8273
Jer 7:24 the stubborn inclinations of their e hearts. H8273
Jer 7:26 stiff-necked and **did** more e than their H8317
Jer 7:30 people of Judah have done e in my eyes, H8273
Jer 8: 3 the survivors of this e nation will prefer H8273
Jer 11: 8 the stubbornness of their e hearts. H8273
Jer 11:15 many others, works out her e **schemes**? H4659
Jer 11:17 Judah have done e and aroused my H8288
Jer 13:23 do good who are accustomed to **doing** e. H8317
Jer 16:12 stubbornness of your e hearts instead of H8273
Jer 18: 8 if that nation I warned repents of its e H8288
Jer 18:10 if it does e in my sight and does not H8273
Jer 18:11 So turn from your e ways, each one of you, H8273
Jer 18:12 follow the stubbornness of our e hearts. H8273
Jer 18:20 Should good be repaid with e? Yet they H8288
Jer 21:12 fire because of the e you have done— H8278
Jer 23: 2 on you for the e you have done, H8278
Jer 23:10 prophets follow an e course and use their H8288
Jer 23:22 them from their e ways and from their H8273
Jer 23:22 their evil ways and from their e deeds. H8278
Jer 25: 5 from your e ways and your evil practices H8273
Jer 25: 5 from your evil ways and your e practices H8278
Jer 26: 3 each will turn from their e ways. H8273
Jer 26: 3 because of the e they have done. H8278
Jer 32:30 have done nothing but e in my sight from H8273
Jer 32:32 me by all the e they have done— H8288
Jer 44: 3 because of the e they have done. H8288
Jer 52: 2 He did e in the eyes of the LORD, just as H8273
Eze 3:18 them from their e ways in order to save H8401
Eze 3:19 their wickedness or from their e ways, H8401
Eze 3:20 turns from their righteousness and does e, H6404
Eze 6: 9 themselves for the e they have done and H8288
Eze 11: 2 men who are plotting e and giving wicked H224
Eze 13:22 to turn from their e ways and so save their H8273
Eze 20:43 yourselves for all the e you have done. H8288
Eze 20:44 according to your e ways and your corrupt H8288
Eze 30:12 the Nile and sell the land to an e *nation*; H8273
Eze 33:11 Turn from your e ways! Why will you H8273
Eze 33:13 they trust in their righteousness and do e, H6404
Eze 33:13 they will die for the e they have done. H6404
Eze 33:15 give life, and do no e—that person will H6404
Eze 33:18 turns from their righteousness and does e, H6404
Eze 36:31 will remember your e ways and wicked H8273
Eze 38:10 mind and you will devise an e scheme. H8273
Da 11:27 with their hearts bent on e, will sit at the H5334
Hos 7: 2 realize that I remember all their e **deeds**. H8288
Hos 7:15 their arms, but they plot e against me. H8273
Hos 10:13 you have reaped e, you have eaten the H6406
Am 5:13 quiet in such times, for the times are e. H8273
Am 5:14 Seek good, not e, that you may live. H8273
Am 5:15 Hate e, love good; maintain justice in the H8273
Jnh 3: 8 Let them give up their e ways and their H8273
Jnh 3:10 how they turned from their e ways, H8273
Mic 2: 1 to those who plot e on their beds! H8273
Mic 3: 2 you who hate good and love e; who tear H8273
Mic 3: 4 them because of the e they have done. H8317
Mic 7: 3 Both hands are skilled in doing e; the H8273
Na 1:11 forth who plots e against the LORD and H8288
Hab 1:13 Your eyes are too pure to look on e; you H8273
Zec 1: 4 'Turn from your e ways and your evil H8273
Zec 1: 4 from your evil ways and your e practices. H8273
Zec 7:10 Do not plot e against each other.' H8288
Zec 8:17 do not plot e against each other, and do H8288
Mal 2:17 "All who do e are good in the eyes of the H8273
Mt 5:11 say all kinds of e against you because of G4505
Mt 5:37 beyond this comes from the e *one*. G4505
Mt 5:39 do not resist an e *person*. If anyone slaps G4505
Mt 5:45 his sun to rise on the e and the good, G4505
Mt 6:13 temptation, but deliver us from the e *one*. G4505
Mt 7:11 though you are e, know how to give G4505
Mt 9: 4 "Why do you entertain e thoughts in your G4505
Mt 12:34 can you who are e say anything good? G4505
Mt 12:35 an e man brings evil things out of the G4505
Mt 12:35 an evil man brings e *things* out of the evil G4505
Mt 12:35 evil things out of the e stored up in him. G4505
Mt 13:19 the e *one* comes and snatches away what G4505
Mt 13:38 The weeds are the people *of* the e *one*, G4505
Mt 13:41 that causes sin and all who do e. G490
Mt 15:19 For out of the heart come e thoughts G4505
Mt 22:18 knowing their e *intent*, said, "You G4504
Mk 3: 4 to do good or *to* **do** e, to save life or to kill G2803
Mk 7:21 that e thoughts come—sexual G2805
Lk 3:19 all the other e *things* he had done, G4505
Lk 6: 9 to do good or *to* **do** e, to save life or to G2803
Lk 6:22 insult you and reject your name as e, G4505
Lk 6:45 an e *man* brings evil things out of the G4505
Lk 6:45 an evil man brings e *things* out of the evil G4505
Lk 6:45 things out of the e stored up in his heart G4505
Lk 7:21 sicknesses and e spirits, and gave sight G4505
Lk 8: 2 had been cured of e spirits and diseases: G4505
Lk 11:13 though you are e, know how to give G4505
Jn 3:19 of light because their deeds were e. G4505
Jn 3:20 Everyone who does e hates the light, and G5765
Jn 5:29 who have done what is e will rise to be G5765
Jn 7: 7 me because I testify that its works are e. G4505
Jn 17:15 that you protect them from the e *one*. G4505
Ac 19:12 were cured and the e spirits left them. G4505
Ac 19:13 went around **driving out e spirits** tried to G2020
Ac 19:15 One day the e spirit answered them G4505
Ac 19:16 the man who had the e spirit jumped on G4505
Ac 23: 5 'Do not speak e about the ruler of your G2809
Ro 1:29 kind of wickedness, e, greed and G4504
Ro 1:30 they invent *ways of doing* e; they disobey G2805
Ro 2: 8 who reject the truth and follow e, G94
Ro 2: 9 every human being who does e: G2805
Ro 3: 8 "Let us do e that good may result"? G2805
Ro 6:12 mortal body so that you obey its e **desires**. G2123
Ro 7:19 I want to do, but the e I do not want to do G2805
Ro 7:21 want to do good, e is right there with me. G2805
Ro 12: 9 Hate what is e; cling to what is G4505
Ro 12:17 Do not repay anyone e for evil. Be careful G2805
Ro 12:17 Do not repay anyone evil for e. Be careful G2805
Ro 12:21 Do not be overcome by e, but overcome G2805
Ro 12:21 but overcome e with good. G2805
Ro 14:16 *do* not *let* what you know is good
be **spoken of as** e G1059
Ro 16:19 is good, and innocent about what is e. G2805
1Co 10: 6 setting our hearts on e *things* as they did. G2805
1Co 13: 6 does not delight in e but rejoices with the G94
1Co 14:20 *In regard to* e be infants, but in your G2798
Gal 1: 4 sins to rescue us from the present e age, G4505
Eph 5:16 every opportunity, because the days are e. G4505
Eph 6:12 the spiritual forces *of* e in the heavenly G4504
Eph 6:13 so that when the day *of* e comes, you may G4505
Eph 6:16 all the flaming arrows *of* the e *one*. G4505
Col 1:21 in your minds because of your e behavior. G4505
Col 3: 5 e desires and greed, which is idolatry G2805
1Th 5:22 reject every kind *of* e. G4505
2Th 3: 2 be delivered from wicked and e people, G4505
2Th 3: 3 you and protect you from the e *one*. G4505
1Ti 6: 4 in envy, strife, malicious talk, e suspicions G4505
1Ti 6:10 love of money is a root of all kinds *of* e. G2805
2Ti 2:22 Flee the e **desires** of youth and pursue G2123
2Ti 3: 6 are swayed *by* all kinds of e **desires**, G2123
2Ti 4:18 rescue me from every e attack and will G4505
Titus 1:12 are always liars, e, brutes, lazy gluttons." G2805
Heb 5:14 themselves to distinguish good *from* e. G2805
Jas 1:13 For God cannot be tempted *by* e, nor does G2805
Jas 1:14 away by their own e **desire** and enticed. G2123
Jas 1:21 moral filth and the e that is so prevalent G2798
Jas 2: 4 become judges with e thoughts? G4505
Jas 3: 6 a world *of* e among the parts of the body. G94
Jas 3: 8 It is a restless e, full of deadly poison. G2805
Jas 3:16 you find disorder and every e practice. G5765
Jas 4:16 arrogant schemes. All such boasting is e. G4505
1Pe 1:14 conform to the e **desires** you had when G2123
1Pe 2:16 not use your freedom as a cover-up *for* e; G2798
1Pe 3: 9 Do not repay e with evil or insult with G2805
1Pe 3: 9 not repay evil with e or insult with insult G2805
1Pe 3: 9 the contrary, repay e with blessing, because NDT
1Pe 3:10 their tongue from e and their lips from G2805
1Pe 3:11 They must turn from e and do good; they G2805
1Pe 3:12 of the Lord is against those who do e." G2805
1Pe 3:17 to suffer for doing good than *for* **doing** e. G2803
1Pe 4: 2 of their earthly lives *for* e human **desires**, G2123
2Pe 1: 4 in the world caused by e **desires**. G2123
2Pe 3: 3 scoffing and following their own e **desires**. G2123
1Jn 2:13 because you have overcome the e *one*. G4505
1Jn 2:14 and you have overcome the e *one*. G4505
1Jn 3:12 belonged to the e *one* and murdered his G4505
1Jn 3:12 his own actions were e and his brother's G4505
1Jn 5:18 and the e *one* cannot harm them. G4505
1Jn 5:19 world is under the control of the e *one*. G4505
3Jn 11 do not imitate what is e but what is good. G2805
3Jn 11 Anyone *who* **does** *what is* e has not seen G2803
Jude 16 they follow their own e **desires**; they boast G2123

EVIL-MERODACH (NIV84) AWEL-MARDUK

EVILDOER (5) [EVIL]

2Sa 3:39 LORD repay the e according to his H6913+8288
Ps 10:15 call the e to account for his wickedness H8273
Ps 101: 8 will cut off every e from the city of H7188+224
Pr 24:20 the e has no future hope, and the H8273
Mal 4: 1 and every e will be stubble, H8402+6913

EVILDOERS (41) [EVIL]

1Sa 24:13 saying goes, 'From e come evil deeds,' so H8401
Job 8:20 is blameless or strengthen the hands of e. H8317
Job 34: 8 He keeps company with e; he H7188+224
Job 34:22 no utter darkness, where e can hide. H7188+224
Ps 14: 4 *Do* all *these* e know nothing? They H7188+224
Ps 14: 6 You e frustrate the plans of the poor, but the NDT
Ps 26: 5 abhor the assembly of e and refuse to sit H8317
Ps 36:12 See how the e lie fallen—thrown H7188+224
Ps 53: 4 Do all these e know nothing? They devour H224
Ps 59: 2 Deliver me from e and save me from H7188+224
Ps 64: 2 of the wicked, from the plots of e. H7188+224
Ps 92: 7 up like grass and all e flourish, H7188+224
Ps 92: 9 will perish; all e will be scattered. H7188+224
Ps 94: 4 all the e are full of boasting. H7188+224
Ps 94:16 will take a stand for me against e? H7188+224
Ps 119:115 Away from me, you e, that I may keep the H8317
Ps 125: 5 ways the LORD will banish with the e. H7188+224
Ps 140: 1 from e; protect me from the H8273+132
Ps 141: 4 deeds along with those *who are* e; H7188+224
Ps 141: 5 prayer will still be against the **deeds of** e. H8288
Ps 141: 9 me safe from the traps set by e, H7188+224
Pr 4:14 path of the wicked or walk in the way of e. H8273
Pr 12:12 The wicked desire the stronghold of e, but H8273
Pr 12:13 E are trapped by their sinful talk, and so H8273
Pr 14:19 E will bow down in the presence of the H8273
Pr 17:11 E foster rebellion against God; the H8273
Pr 21:15 joy to the righteous but terror to e. H7188+224
Pr 24:19 not fret because of e or be envious of the H8317
Pr 28: 5 E do not understand what is right H8273+408
Pr 29: 6 E are snared by their own sin, but H8273+408
Isa 1: 4 is great, a brood of e, children given to H8317
Isa 31: 2 nation, against those who help e. H7188+224
Jer 23:14 They strengthen the hands of e, so that H8317
Hos 6: 8 Gilead is a city of e, stained with H224+7188
Hos 10: 9 again overtake the e in Gibeah? H1201+6594
Mal 3:15 Certainly e prosper, and even when H8402+6913
Mt 7:23 Away from me, you e!' G2237+3836+490
Lk 13:27 Away from me, all *you* e!' G2239+94
Lk 18:11 people—robbers, e, adulterers—or even G96
Php 3: 2 those e, those mutilators G2805+2239
2Ti 3:13 while e and impostors will go from G4505+476

EVILS (1) [EVIL]

Mk 7:23 All these e come from inside and defile a G4505

EWE (6) [EWES]

Ge 21:28 set apart seven e **lambs** *from* the flock, H3898
Ge 21:29 of these seven e **lambs** you have set apart H3898
Lev 14:10 male lambs and one e **lamb** a year old, H3898
Nu 6:14 a year-old e **lamb** without defect for a sin H3898
2Sa 12: 3 except one little e **lamb** he had bought. H3898
2Sa 12: 4 took the e **lamb** *that belonged to* the poor H3898

EWES (2) [EWE]

Ge 32:14 two hundred e and twenty rams, H8161
Ge 33:13 I must care for the e and cows that are H7366

EXACT (6) [EXACTED, EXACTLY]

Ge 43:21 his silver—the e **weight**—in the mouth of H5486
Est 4: 7 including the e **amount** *of* money Haman H7308
Pr 22:23 take up their case and will e life for life. H7693
Mt 2: 7 and **found out** from them the e time the G208
Jn 4:53 that this was the e time at which Jesus G1697
Heb 1: 3 the e **representation** of his being G5917

EXACTED (3) [EXACT]

2Ki 15:20 Menahem e this money from Israel. H3655
2Ki 18:14 The king of Assyria e from Hezekiah king H8492
2Ki 23:35 land and e the silver and gold *from* the H5601

EXACTLY (10) [EXACT]

Ge 41:13 And things turned out e as he interpreted H4027
Ex 25: 9 furnishings e **like** the H3869+3972+889+4027
Nu 8: 4 was made e **like** the pattern the H3869+4027
Nu 15:14 they must do e **as** you do. H3869+889+4027
Dt 24: 8 careful to do e **as** the Levitical H3869+3972+889
Jdg 7:17 of the camp, do e **as** I do. H3869+889+4027
2Ki 7:20 And that is e what happened to him, for H4027
Ps 50:21 you thought *I* **was** e like you. H2118+2118
Jn 14:31 the Father and do e what my Father has G2777
Ac 22:30 wanted to find out e why Paul was being G855

EXALT (32) [EXALTED, EXALTS]

Ex 15: 2 my father's God, and *I will* e him. H8123
Jos 3: 7 "Today I will begin *to* e you in the eyes of H1540
1Sa 2:10 to his king and e the horn of his anointed H8123
1Ch 25: 5 through the promises of God to e him. H8123
1Ch 29:12 power to e and give strength to H1540
Job 19: 5 indeed *you would* e *yourselves* above me H1540
Ps 30: 1 *I will* e you, LORD, for you lifted me out of H8123
Ps 34: 3 LORD with me; *let us* e his name together. H8123
Ps 35:26 may *all* who e *themselves* over me be H1540
Ps 37:34 *He will* e you to inherit the land; when H8123
Ps 38:16 them gloat or e *themselves* over me when H1540
Ps 75: 6 west or from the desert *can* e *themselves*. H8123
Ps 89:17 strength, and by your favor *you* e our horn. H8123
Ps 99: 5 E the LORD our God and worship at his H8123
Ps 99: 9 E the LORD our God and worship at his H8123
Ps 107:32 *Let them* e him in the assembly of the H8123
Ps 118:28 you are my God, and *I will* e you. H8123
Ps 145: 1 *I will* e you, my God the King; I will praise H8123
Pr 4: 8 Cherish her, and *she will* e you; embrace H8123
Pr 25: 6 *Do* not e **yourself** in the king's presence H2075
Pr 30:32 "If you play the fool and e **yourself**, or if H5951
Isa 24:15 glory to the LORD; e the name of the LORD NDT
Isa 25: 1 *I will* e you and praise your name H8123
Eze 29:15 and *will* never again e **itself** above the H5951
Da 4:37 praise and e and glorify the King of A10659
Da 11:36 *He will* e and magnify **himself** above H8123
Da 11:37 but *will* e **himself** above them all. H1540
Hos 11: 7 Most High, *I will* by no means e them. H8123
Mt 23:12 For those who e themselves will be G5738
Lk 14:11 For all those *who* e themselves will be G5738
Lk 18:14 For all those *who* e themselves will be G5738
2Th 2: 4 will oppose and *will* e *himself* over G5643

EXALTED (66) [EXALT]

Ex 15: 1 sing to the LORD, for *he is* **highly** e. H1448+1448
Ex 15:21 for *he is* **highly** e. Both horse H1448+1448
Nu 24: 7 than Agag; their kingdom *will* **be** e. H5951
Jos 4:14 That day the LORD e Joshua in the sight of H1540
2Sa 5:12 over Israel and *had* e his kingdom for the H5951
2Sa 22:47 be to my Rock! E *be* my God, the Rock, my H8123
2Sa 22:49 *You* e me above my foes; from a violent H8123
2Sa 23: 1 utterance of the man e *by* the Most High, H7756
1Ch 14: 2 his kingdom *had* **been** highly e for the H5951
1Ch 17:17 though I were the **most** e *of* men. H9366+5092

1Ch 29:11 the kingdom; you *are* e as head over all. H5951
1Ch 29:25 The LORD highly e Solomon in the sight of H1540
Ne 9: 5 and *may it* **be** e above all blessing and H8123
Job 24:24 For a little while *they are* e, and then they H8250
Job 36:22 "God *is* e in his power. Who is a teacher H8435
Job 37:23 is beyond our reach and e *in* power; H8438
Ps 18:46 Praise be to my Rock! **E** *be* God my Savior! H8123
Ps 18:48 *You* e me above my foes; from a violent H8123
Ps 21:13 *Be* e in your strength, LORD; we will sing H8123
Ps 27: 6 Then my head *will be* e above the H8123
Ps 35:27 "The LORD *be* e, who delights in the H1540
Ps 46:10 I am God; *I will be* e among the nations H8123
Ps 46:10 the nations, *I will be* e in the earth." H8123
Ps 47: 9 the earth belong to God; *he is* greatly e. H6590
Ps 57: 5 *Be* e, O God, above the heavens; let your H8123
Ps 57:11 *Be* e, O God, above the heavens; let your H8123
Ps 89:13 your hand is strong, your right hand **e**. H8123
Ps 89:24 through my name his horn *will be* e. H8123
Ps 89:27 the **most** e of the kings of the earth. H6609
Ps 89:42 *You have* e the right hand of his foes; you H8123
Ps 92: 8 But you, LORD, are forever **e**. H5294
Ps 92:10 *You have* e my horn like that of a wild ox H8123
Ps 97: 9 all the earth; *you* **are** e far above all gods. H6590
Ps 99: 2 LORD in Zion; he *is* e over all the nations. H8123
Ps 108: 5 *Be* e, O God, above the heavens; let your H8123
Ps 113: 4 The LORD *is* e over all the nations, his H8123
Ps 138: 2 *you have so* e your solemn decree *that* it H1540
Ps 138: 6 Though the LORD *is* e, he looks kindly on H8123
Ps 148:13 his name alone **is** e; his splendor is H8435
Pr 11:11 the blessing of the upright a city *is* e, H8123
Isa 2: 2 the mountains; *it will* **be** e above the hills H5951
Isa 2:11 the LORD alone *will* **be** e in that day. H8435
Isa 2:12 lofty, for all *that* **is** e (and they will be H5951
Isa 2:17 the LORD alone *will* **be** e in that day, H8435
Isa 5:16 the LORD Almighty *will be* e by his justice, H1467
Isa 6: 1 the Lord, high and e, seated on a throne; H5951
Isa 12: 4 and proclaim that his name *is* e. H8435
Isa 33: 5 The LORD **is** e, for he dwells on high; he H8435
Isa 33:10 "Now *will I* **be** e; now will I be H8123
Isa 52:13 will be raised and lifted up and highly **e**. H1467
Isa 57:15 For this is what the high and e One says H5951
Jer 17:12 A glorious throne, e from the beginning H5294
La 2:17 over you, *he has* e the horn of your foes. H8123
Eze 21:26 The lowly *will be* e and the exalted will H1467
Eze 21:26 be exalted and the e will be brought low. H1469
Hos 13: 1 people trembled; he *was* e in Israel. H5951
Mic 4: 1 the mountains; it *will* **be** e above the hills H5951
Mic 6: 6 the LORD and bow down before the e God? H5294
Mt 23:12 those who humble themselves *will be* e. G5738
Lk 14:11 those who humble themselves *will be* e." G5738
Lk 18:14 those who humble themselves *will be* e." G5738
Ac 2:33 **E** to the right hand of God, he has G5738
Ac 5:31 God e him to his own right hand as Prince G5738
Php 1:20 now as always Christ *will be* e in my body, G3486
Php 2: 9 God e him **to the highest place** and gave G5671
Heb 7:26 apart from sinners, e **above** the heavens. G5734

EXALTS (4) [EXALT]

1Sa 2: 7 wealth; he humbles and *he* e. H8123
Job 36: 7 them with kings and e *them* forever. H1467
Ps 75: 7 He brings one down, *he* e another. H8123
Pr 14:34 Righteousness e a nation, but sin H8123

EXAMINE (36) [CROSS-EXAMINED, CROSS-EXAMINES, EXAMINED, EXAMINES, EXAMINING]

Ge 37:32 **E** it **to see** whether it is your son's robe." H5795
Lev 13: 3 The priest *is to* e the sore on the skin, and H8011
Lev 13: 5 On the seventh day the priest *is to* e them H8011
Lev 13: 6 seventh day the priest *is to* e them again, H8011
Lev 13: 8 The priest *is to* e that person, and if the H8011
Lev 13:10 The priest *is to* e them, and if there is a H8011
Lev 13:13 the priest *is to* e them, and if the disease H8011
Lev 13:17 The priest *is to* e them, and if the sores H8011
Lev 13:20 The priest *is to* e it, and if it appears to be H8011
Lev 13:25 the priest *is to* e the spot, and if the hair in H8011
Lev 13:27 seventh day the priest *is to* e that person, H8011
Lev 13:30 the priest *is to* e the sore, and if it appears H8011
Lev 13:32 the seventh day the priest *is to* e the sore, H8011
Lev 13:34 the seventh day the priest *is to* e the sore, H8011
Lev 13:36 the priest *is to* e them, and if he finds that H8011
Lev 13:39 the priest *is to* e them, and if the spots are H8011
Lev 13:43 The priest *is to* e him, and if the swollen H8011
Lev 13:50 The priest *is to* e the affected area and H8011
Lev 13:51 On the seventh day *he is to* e it, and if the H8011
Lev 13:55 the priest *is to* e it *again*, and if the mold H8011
Lev 14: 3 is to go outside the camp and e them. H8011
Lev 14:36 emptied before he goes in to e the mold, H8011
Lev 14:37 *He is to* e the mold on the walls, and if it H8011
Lev 14:44 the priest is to go and e it and, if the mold H8011
Lev 14:48 the priest comes *to* e it and the mold has H8011
Job 7:18 that *you* e them every morning and test H7212
Job 34:23 God *has* no *need to* e people further, that H8492
Ps 11: 4 everyone on earth; his eyes e them. H1043
Ps 17: 3 though *you* e me at night and test me H7212
Ps 26: 2 try me, e my heart and my mind; H7671
Jer 17:10 the LORD search the heart and e the mind, H1043
Jer 20:12 you *who* e the righteous and probe the H1043
La 3:40 *Let us* e our ways and test them, and let H2924
Eze 21:21 will consult his idols, *he will* e the liver. H8011
1Co 11:28 Everyone *ought to* e themselves before G1507
2Co 13: 5 **E** yourselves *to see* whether you are in the G4279

EXAMINED (5) [EXAMINE]

Job 5:27 "*We have* e this, and it is true. So hear it H2983
Job 13: 9 Would it turn out well if *he* e you? Could H2983
Lk 23:14 I *have* e him in your presence and have G373
Ac 17:11 great eagerness and e the Scriptures every G373
Ac 28:18 They e me and wanted to release me G373

EXAMINES (8) [EXAMINE]

Lev 13: 3 When the priest e that person, he shall H8011
Lev 13:21 when the priest e it, there is no white H8011
Lev 13:26 But if the priest e it and there is no white H8011
Lev 13:31 when the priest e the sore, it does not H8011
Lev 13:53 when the priest e it, the mold has not H8011
Lev 13:56 when the priest e it, the mold has faded H8011
Ps 11: 5 The LORD e the righteous, but the wicked H1043
Pr 5:21 view of the LORD, and *he* e all your paths. H7143

EXAMINING (3) [EXAMINE]

Ne 2:13 the Dung Gate, e the walls of Jerusalem H8431
Ne 2:15 so I went up the valley by night, e the wall. H8431
Ac 24: 8 *By* e him yourself you will be able to learn G373

EXAMPLE (21) [EXAMPLES]

2Ki 14: 3 *he* **followed the** e *of* his H6913+3869+6913
Ecc 9:13 saw under the sun **this** *e of* wisdom that AIT
Eze 14: 8 them and make them an e and a byword. H253
Jn 13:15 I have set you an e that you should do as I G5682
Ro 6:19 *I am* **using an** e from everyday life G3306
Ro 7: 2 **For** e, by law a married woman is bound to G1142
1Co 11: 1 **Follow** my e, as I follow the G3629+1181
1Co 11: 1 my example, as I follow the e of Christ. NDT
Gal 3:15 *let me* **take an** e from everyday life. G3306
Eph 5: 1 **Follow** God's e, therefore, as dearly G1181+3629
Php 3:17 **Join together in following** my e G5213+1181
2Th 3: 7 know how you ought to **follow** our e. G3628
1Ti 1:16 patience as an e for those who would G5721
1Ti 4:12 set an e for the believers in speech G5596
Titus 2: 7 set them an e by doing what is good. G5596
Heb 4:11 by following their e of disobedience. G5682
Jas 3: 4 Or **take** ships **as an** e. Although they are G2627
Jas 5:10 *as* an e of patience in the face of G5682
1Pe 2:21 leaving you an e, that you should G5681
2Pe 2: 6 made them an e of what is going to G5682
Jude 7 They serve as an e of those who suffer the G1257

EXAMPLES (3) [EXAMPLE]

1Co 10: 6 these things occurred *as* e to keep us from G5596
1Co 10:11 happened to them *as* e and were written G5595
1Pe 5: 3 entrusted to you, but being e to the flock. G5596

EXASPERATE (1)

Eph 6: 4 Fathers, *do* not e your children; instead G4239

EXCEED (2) [EXCEEDED, EXCEEDINGLY, EXCESSIVE]

Nu 3:46 who e the **number** *of* the Levites, H6369
Job 14: 5 months and have set limits *he* cannot e. H6296

EXCEEDED (4) [EXCEED]

Nu 3:49 from those *who* e the **number** redeemed H6369
1Ki 10: 7 wealth *you have* **far** e the report I H3578
2Ch 9: 6 told me; *you have* **far** e the report I heard. H3578
2Co 8: 5 And they e our expectations: They G4024+2777

EXCEEDINGLY (6) [EXCEED]

Ge 30:43 the man grew e prosperous and H4394+4394
Ex 1: 7 the Israelites *were* e **fruitful**; they H7238
Nu 11:10 The LORD became e angry, and Moses was H4394
Nu 14: 7 through and explored is e good. H4394+4394
2Ch 1: 1 him and made him e great. H4200+5087+2025
Eze 9: 9 of Israel and Judah is e great; H928+4394+4394

EXCEL (4) [EXCELLED, EXCELLENCY, EXCELLENT, EXCELLING]

Ge 49: 4 the waters, *you will* no longer e, for you H3855
1Co 14:12 try to e in those that build up the church. G4355
2Co 8: 7 But since *you* e in everything—in faith, in G4355
2Co 8: 7 see that *you* also e in this grace of giving. G4355

EXCELLED (1) [EXCEL]

Isa 10:10 whose images e those of Jerusalem H4946

EXCELLENCY (1) [EXCEL]

Ac 23:26 Claudius Lysias, *To* His **E**, Governor Felix G3196

EXCELLENT (8) [EXCEL]

Ps 45: 2 *You are the* **most** e of men and your lips H3636
Lk 1: 3 account for you, **most** e Theophilus, G3196
Ac 24: 3 in every way, **most** e Felix, we G3196
Ac 26:25 "I am not insane, **most** e Festus," Paul G3196
1Co 12:31 I will show you the **most** e way. G2848+5651
Php 4: 8 if anything is e or praiseworthy—think G746
1Ti 3:13 served well gain an e standing and great G2819
Titus 3: 8 These things are e and profitable for G2819

EXCELLING (2) [EXCEL]

Ge 49: 3 of my strength, e *in* honor, excelling in H3856
Ge 49: 3 strength, excelling in honor, e *in* power. H3856

EXCEPT (96) [EXCEPTION, EXCEPTIONAL]

Ge 39: 6 with anything e the food he ate. H3954+561
Ge 39: 9 withheld nothing from me e you, H3954+561
Ge 47:18 left for our lord e our bodies and our H1194+561
Ex 8: 9 e *for* those that remain in the Nile." H8370
Ex 12:16 e to prepare food for everyone to eat H421
Lev 13:33 themselves, e **for** the affected area H2256+4202
Lev 21: 2 e for a close relative, such as his H3954+561
Nu 14:30 e Caleb son of Jephunneh and H3954+561
Nu 16:40 that no one e a descendant of H889+4202
Nu 26:65 one of them was left e Caleb son of H3954+561
Nu 32:12 not one e Caleb son of Jephunneh the H1194
Nu 35:33 e by the blood of the one who shed H3954+561
Dt 1:36 e Caleb son of Jephunneh. He will see it H2314
Dt 16: 6 e in the place he will choose as a H3954+561
Jos 6:15 e **that** on that day they circled the city H8370
Jos 8: 2 e **that** you may carry off their plunder and H8370
Jos 11:13 on their mounds—e Hazor, which Joshua H2314
Jos 11:19 **E for** the Hivites living in Gibeon, not one H1194
Jdg 11:34 **E for** her he had neither son nor daughter H4946
Ru 2: 7 till now, e **for** a short rest in the shelter." H2296
Ru 4: 4 For no one has the right to do it e you H2314
1Sa 21: 6 no bread there e the bread of the H3954+561
1Sa 30:17 e four hundred young men who rode H3954+561
2Sa 12: 3 man had nothing e one little ewe H3954+561
2Sa 22:32 And who is the Rock e our God? H4946+1187
1Ki 3: 3 e that he offered sacrifices and burned H8370
1Ki 8: 9 nothing in the ark e the two stone tablets H8370
1Ki 15: 5 his life—e in the case of Uriah the Hittite. H8370
1Ki 17: 1 in the next few years e at my word." H3954+561
1Ki 22:31 small or great, e the king of Israel." H3954+561
2Ki 4: 2 she said, "e a small jar of olive oil." H3954+561
2Ki 5:15 is no God in all the world e in Israel. H3954+561
2Ki 9:35 they found nothing e her skull, her H3954+561
2Ki 13: 7 army of Jehoahaz e fifty horsemen, H3954+561
2Ch 2: 6 e as a place to burn sacrifices before H3954+561
2Ch 5:10 nothing in the ark e the two tablets that H8370
2Ch 18:30 small or great, e the king of Israel." H3954+561
2Ch 21:17 Not a son was left to him e Ahaziah H3954+561
2Ch 23: 6 temple of the LORD e the priests and H3954+561
Ne 2:12 no mounts with me e the one I was H3954+561
Ps 18:31 And who is the Rock e our God? H2314
Ecc 5:11 they to the owners e to feast their H3954+561
Jer 44:14 none will return e a few fugitives." H3954+561
Da 2:11 one can reveal it to the king e the gods, A10386
Da 3:28 worship any god e their own God. A10386
Da 6: 7 next thirty days, e to you, Your Majesty, A10386
Da 6:12 to any god or human being e to you, A10386
Da 10:21 me against them e Michael, H3954+561
Hos 13: 4 no God but me, no Savior e me. H1194
Mt 5:13 e to be thrown out and trampled G1623+3590
Mt 5:32 his wife, e **for** sexual immorality G4211+3364
Mt 11:27 No one knows the Son e the Father, G1623+3590
Mt 11:27 knows the Father e the Son and G1623+3590
Mt 12:39 will be given it e the sign of the G1623+3590
Mt 13:57 without honor e in his own town G1623+3590
Mt 16: 4 will be given it e the sign of Jonah." G1623+3590
Mt 17: 8 they saw no one e Jesus. G1623+3590+3668
Mt 19: 9 divorces his wife, e for sexual immorality G3590
Mt 21:19 nothing on it e leaves. G1623+3590+3667
Mk 5:37 not let anyone follow him e Peter, G1623+3590
Mk 6: 4 without honor e in his own town, G1623+3590
Mk 6: 5 e lay his hands on a few sick G1623+3590
Mk 6: 8 the journey e a staff— G1623+3590+3667
Mk 8:14 e **for** one loaf they had with them G1623+3590
Mk 9: 8 saw anyone with them e Jesus. G247+3668
Mk 10:18 "No one is good—e God alone. G1623+3590
Lk 8:51 let anyone go in with him e Peter, G1623+3590
Lk 10:22 knows who the Son is e the Father, G1623+3590
Lk 10:22 the Father is e the Son and those G1623+3590
Lk 11:29 will be given it e the sign of Jonah. G1623+3590
Lk 17:18 give praise to God e this foreigner?" G1623+3590
Lk 18:19 "No one is good—e God alone. G1623+3590
Jn 3:13 into heaven e the one who came G1623+3590
Jn 6:46 seen the Father e the one who is G1623+3590
Jn 14: 6 comes to the Father e through me. G1623+3590
Jn 17:12 has been lost e the one doomed to G1623+3590
Ac 8: 1 all e the apostles were scattered G4440
Ac 26:29 become what I am, e **for** these chains." G4211
Ro 13: 1 is no authority e that which God G1623+3590
Ro 13: 8 e the continuing debt to love one G1623+3590
Ro 15:18 to speak of anything e what Christ has G4024
1Co 1:14 any of you e Crispus and Gaius, G1623+3590
1Co 2: 2 I was with you e Jesus Christ and G1623+3590
1Co 2:11 person's thoughts e their own spirit G1623+3590
1Co 2:11 thoughts of God e the Spirit of God G1623+3590
1Co 7: 5 each other e perhaps by mutual G1623+3614
1Co 10:13 overtaken you e what is common to G1623+3590
1Co 12: 3 "Jesus is Lord," e by the Holy Spirit. G1623+3590
2Co 12: 5 myself, e about my weaknesses. G1623+3590
2Co 12:13 e that I was never a burden to you? G1623+3590
Gal 6:14 May I never boast e in the cross of G1623+3590
Eph 4: 9 mean e that he also descended to G1623+3590
Php 4:15 of giving and receiving, e you only; G1623+3590
2Ti 2: 5 the victor's crown e by competing G1569+3590
Rev 2:25 e to hold on to what you have until I G4440
Rev 14: 3 learn the song e the 144,000 who G1623+3590

EXCEPTION (2) [EXCEPT]

1Ki 22:13 other prophets **without** e are H285+7023S
2Ch 18:12 other prophets **without** e are H285+7023

EXCEPTIONAL (1) [EXCEPT]

Da 6: 3 the satraps by his e qualities that the A10339

EXCESSIVE (2) [EXCEED]

2Co 2: 7 he will not be overwhelmed *by* e sorrow. G4358

Rev 18: 3 of the earth grew rich from her e luxuries." G1539

EXCHANGE (16) [EXCHANGED, EXCHANGING]

Ge 47:16 "I will sell you food **in e for** your livestock H928
Ge 47:17 he gave them food **in e for** their horses, H928
Ge 47:17 that year with food **in e for** all their H928
Ge 47:19 Buy us and our land **in e for** food, and we H928
Ex 21:34 the loss and **take** the dead animal **in e.** H2118
Ex 21:36 animal, and **take** the dead animal **in e.** H2118
Lev 27:10 *They must* not e it or substitute a good H2736
Dt 14:25 then e your tithe for silver, and take the H5989
1Ki 21: 2 **In e** I will give you a better vineyard or, if H9393
Isa 43: 4 I will give people **in e for** you, nations in H9393
Isa 43: 4 you, nations **in e for** your life. H9393
Eze 27:19 casks of wine from Izal in e for your wares: H5989
Eze 48:14 They must not sell or e any of it. This is H4614
Mt 16:26 Or what can anyone give **in e for** their soul? G498
Mk 8:37 Or what can anyone give **in e for** their soul? G498
2Co 6:13 *As* a fair e—I speak as to my children G521

EXCHANGED (11) [EXCHANGE]

Ps 106:20 *They* e their glorious God for an image of H4614
Jer 2:11 But my people *have* e their glorious God H4614
Eze 27:12 great wealth of goods; *they* e silver, iron, H5989
Eze 27:14 e chariot horses, cavalry horses and mules *for* H5989
Eze 27:16 many products; *they* e turquoise, purple H5989
Eze 27:17 *they* e wheat from Minnith and H5989
Eze 27:22 your merchandise *they* e the finest of all H5989
Hos 4: 7 *they* e their glorious God for something H4614
Ro 1:23 e the glory of the immortal God for G248
Ro 1:25 They e the truth about God for a lie, and G3563
Ro 1:26 Even their women e natural sexual G3563

EXCHANGING (1) [EXCHANGE]

Jn 2:14 others sitting at tables **e money.** G3048

EXCITEMENT (1)

Job 39:24 In frenzied e it eats up the ground; it H8075

EXCLAIM (3) [EXCLAIMED, EXCLAIMING]

Ps 35:10 My whole being *will* e, "Who is like you H606
Jer 46:17 There *they will* e, 'Pharaoh king of Egypt H7924
Rev 18:18 of her burning, *they will* e, 'Was there G3189

EXCLAIMED (11) [EXCLAIM]

Jdg 6:22 it was the angel of the LORD, he e, "Alas, H606
Ru 1:19 of them, and *the women* e, "Can this be H606
2Ki 3:10 e the king of Israel. "Has the LORD H606
Est 7: 8 The king e, "Will he even molest the H606
Mt 27:54 were terrified, and e, "Surely he was the G3306
Mk 1:37 when they found him, *they* e: "Everyone is G3306
Mk 9:24 Immediately the boy's father e, "I do G3189
Lk 1:42 In a loud voice *she* e: "Blessed are you G430
Jn 8:52 At this they e, "Now we know that you are G3306
Ac 8:10 gave him their attention and e, "This man G3306
Ac 12:14 she ran back without opening it and e, G550

EXCLAIMING (1) [EXCLAIM]

1Co 14:25 worship God, e, "God is really among G550

EXCLUDE (4) [EXCLUDED, EXCLUSIVELY]

Isa 56: 3 "The LORD *will* **surely** e me from his H976+976
Isa 66: 5 hate you, and e you because of my name H5612
Lk 6:22 when *they* e you and insult you and reject G928
Rev 11: 2 But e the outer court; do not G1675+2033

EXCLUDED (5) [EXCLUDE]

Ezr 2:62 them and so were **e from** the priesthood H4946
Ne 7:64 them and so were **e from** the priesthood H4946
Ne 13: 3 *they* e from Israel all who were of foreign H976
Ro 3:27 is boasting? *It is* e. Because of what G1710
Eph 2:12 e from citizenship in Israel and foreigners G558

EXCLUSIVELY (1) [EXCLUDE]

Ac 18: 5 Paul **devoted** *himself* e to preaching G5309

EXCREMENT (5)

Dt 23:13 yourself, dig a hole and cover up your e. H7362
2Ki 18:27 to eat their own e and drink their own H2989
Isa 36:12 to eat their own e and drink their own H2989
Eze 4:12 people, using human e for fuel." H1645+7362
Eze 4:15 bread over cow dung instead of human e." H1645

EXCUSE (5) [EXCUSES]

Lk 14:18 I must go and see it. Please e me.' G2400+4148
Lk 14:19 way to try them out. Please e me.' G2400+4148
Jn 15:22 but now they have no e for their sin. G4733
Ro 1:20 been made, so that people are **without e.** G406
Ro 2: 1 therefore, have **no e**, you who pass G406

EXCUSES (1) [EXCUSE]

Lk 14:18 "But they all alike began *to* **make** e. G4148

EXECRATION (KJV) CURSE

EXECUTE (12) [EXECUTED, EXECUTING, EXECUTION, EXECUTIONER]

2Ch 2:14 of engraving and *can* e any design given H3108
Isa 66:16 the LORD *will* e **judgment** *on* all people, H9149
Eze 9: 1 *those who* are **appointed to e judgment** *on* H7213
Eze 11:10 and *I will* e **judgment** *on* you at the H9149
Eze 11:11 *I will* e **judgment** *on* you at the borders of H9149
Eze 17:20 to Babylon and e **judgment** on him there H9149
Eze 20:35 face to face, *I will* e **judgment** upon you. H9149
Eze 38:22 *I will* e **judgment** on him with plague and H9149
Da 2:24 king had appointed to e the wise men of A10005
Da 2:24 "*Do* not e the wise men of Babylon. A10005
Hab 1:12 have appointed them to e judgment; you, NDT
Jn 18:31 "But we have no right *to* e anyone," they G650

EXECUTED (11) [EXECUTE]

2Ki 14: 5 *he* e the officials who had murdered his H5782
2Ki 25:21 the king *had* them e. H5782+2256+4637
2Ch 24:24 their ancestors, judgment *was* e *on* Joash. H6913
2Ch 25: 3 *he* e the officials who had murdered his H2222
Jer 52:27 the king **had** them e. H5782+2256+4637
Da 2:18 his friends *might* not *be* e with the rest A10005
Mt 27: 1 made their plans how to **have** Jesus e. G2506
Mt 27:20 to ask for Barabbas and *to* **have** Jesus e. G660
Lk 23:32 were also led out with him *to* be e. G359
Ac 12:19 the guards and ordered *that they be* e. G552
Ac 13:28 sentence, they asked Pilate *to have* him e. G359

EXECUTING (1) [EXECUTE]

2Ch 22: 8 While Jehu was e **judgment** on the house H9149

EXECUTION (1) [EXECUTE]

Da 2:12 he ordered the e of all the wise men A10005

EXECUTIONER (1) [EXECUTE]

Mk 6:27 immediately sent an e with orders to G5063

EXEMPT (4)

1Sa 17:25 and *will* e his family **from taxes** in H6913+2930
1Ki 15:22 Judah—no one was e—and they carried H5929
1Ch 9:33 and **were** e **from** *other* **duties** because H7080
Mt 17:26 "Then the children are e," Jesus said to G1801

EXERCISE (5) [EXERCISED, EXERCISES, EXERTED]

Mt 20:25 their high officials e **authority over** them. G2980
Mk 10:42 their high officials e **authority over** them. G2980
Lk 22:25 those *who* e **authority over** them call G2027
1Co 8: 9 that the e **of** your **rights** does not become G2026
Rev 13: 5 blasphemies and *to* e its authority for G4472

EXERCISED (2) [EXERCISE]

Da 11: 4 will it have the power *he* e, because H5440
Rev 13:12 *It* e all the authority of the first beast on its G4472

EXERCISES (1) [EXERCISE]

Jer 9:24 that I am the LORD, *who* e kindness, justice H6913

EXERTED (1) [EXERCISE]

Eph 1:20 *he* e when he raised Christ from the dead G1919

EXHAUST (2) [EXHAUSTED, EXHAUSTION]

Jer 51:58 the peoples e *themselves* for nothing, the H3333
Hab 2:13 that the nations e *themselves* for nothing? H3615

EXHAUSTED (13) [EXHAUST]

Jdg 4:21 quietly to him while he lay fast asleep, e. H6545
Jdg 8: 4 e yet keeping up the pursuit H6546
Jdg 8:15 Why should we give bread to your e men H3617
1Sa 14:31 Mikmash to Aijalon, *they were* e. H6545+4394
1Sa 30:10 hundred of them were too e to cross the H7006
1Sa 30:21 men who *had been* too e to follow him H7006
2Sa 16: 2 those who become e in the wilderness." H3617
2Sa 16:14 with him arrived at their destination e. H6546
2Sa 17:29 people have become e and hungry and H6546
2Sa 21:15 against the Philistines, and he *became* e. H6545
Jer 51:30 Their strength *is* e; they have become H5980
Da 8:27 was worn out. *I* **lay** e for several days H2703
Lk 22:45 he found them asleep, *e* **from** sorrow. AIT

EXHAUSTION (1) [EXHAUST]

Pr 6: 3 Go—**to the point of** e—and give your H8332

EXHORT (1) [EXHORTATION, EXHORTED]

1Ti 5: 1 e him as if he were your father. G4151

EXHORTATION (2) [EXHORT]

Ac 13:15 if you have a word *of* e for the people G4155
Heb 13:22 I urge you to bear with my word *of* e, for G4155

EXHORTED (1) [EXHORT]

Lk 3:18 many other words John e the people and G4151

EXILE (79) [EXILED, EXILES]

2Sa 15:19 are a foreigner, an e from your homeland. H1655
2Ki 17:23 *were* **taken** from their homeland **into** e in H1655
2Ki 24:14 *He* **carried** all Jerusalem **into** e: all H1655+1655
2Ki 25:11 of the guard **carried into** e the people H1655
2Ki 25:27 year of the e *of* Jehoiachin king of Judah, H1661
1Ch 5: 6 Tiglath-Pileser king of Assyria **took into** e. H1655
1Ch 5:22 And they occupied the land until the e. H1583
1Ch 5:26 *who* **took** the Reubenites, the Gadites and the half-tribe of Manasseh **into** e H1655
1Ch 6:15 LORD **sent** Judah and Jerusalem **into** e by H1655
2Ch 36:20 *He* **carried into** e to Babylon the remnant H1655
Ezr 6:21 who had returned from the e ate it, H1583
Ne 1: 2 Jewish remnant that had survived the e, H8660
Ne 1: 3 who survived the e and are back in the H8660
Ne 8:17 that had returned from e built temporary H8660
Est 2: 6 who **had been carried into** e from H1655
Isa 5:13 my people *will* **go into** e for lack of H1655
Isa 27: 8 By warfare and e you contend with her H8938
Jer 1: 3 the people of Jerusalem **went into** e. H1655
Jer 13:19 All Judah *will* **be carried into** e, carried H1655
Jer 20: 6 in your house will go into e to Babylon. H8660
Jer 22:22 and your allies will go into e. H8660
Jer 24: 1 of Judah *were* **carried into** e from H1655
Jer 27:20 **carried** Jehoiachin son of Jehoiakim king of Judah **into** e H1655
Jer 29: 1 Nebuchadnezzar *had* **carried into** e from H1655
Jer 29: 2 artisans had gone into e from Jerusalem.) NDT
Jer 29: 4 to all those *I* **carried into** e from H1655
Jer 29: 7 the city to which *I have* **carried** you **into** e. H1655
Jer 29:14 the place from which *I* **carried** you **into** e." H1655
Jer 29:16 citizens who did not go with you into e— H1583
Jer 30:10 your descendants from the land of their e. H8660
Jer 30:16 devoured; all your enemies will go into e. H8660
Jer 39: 9 guard **carried into** e *to* Babylon the H1655
Jer 40: 1 Judah who *were* **being carried into** e to H1655
Jer 40: 7 who *had* not **been carried into** e to H1655
Jer 43: 3 may kill us or **carry** us **into** e *to* Babylon." H1655
Jer 46:19 Pack your belongings for e, you who live H1583
Jer 46:27 your descendants from the land of their e. H8660
Jer 48: 7 Chemosh will go into e, together with H1583
Jer 48:11 jar to another—she has not gone into e. H1583
Jer 48:46 sons are taken into e and your daughters H8660
Jer 49: 3 Molek will go into e, together with his H1583
Jer 52:15 of the guard **carried into** e some of the H1655
Jer 52:28 people Nebuchadnezzar **carried into** e: H1655
Jer 52:30 745 Jews **taken into** e *by* Nebuzaradan H1655
Jer 52:31 year of the e *of* Jehoiachin king of Judah, H1661
La 1: 3 harsh labor, Judah *has* **gone into** e. H1655
La 1: 5 Her children have gone into e, captive H8660
La 1:18 men and young women have gone into e. H8660
La 4:22 Daughter Zion; he will not prolong your e. H1655
Eze 1: 2 fifth year of the e *of* King Jehoiachin— H1661
Eze 3:11 to your people in e and speak to them. H1583
Eze 12: 3 your belongings for e and in the daytime, H1583
Eze 12: 4 bring out your belongings packed for e. H1583
Eze 12: 4 watching, go out like those who go into e. H1583
Eze 12: 7 day I brought out my things packed for e. H1583
Eze 12:11 They will go into e as captives. H1583
Eze 25: 3 people of Judah when they went into e, H1583
Eze 33:21 In the twelfth year of our e, in the tenth H1661
Eze 39:23 people of Israel **went into** e for their sin, H1655
Eze 39:28 though I **sent** them **into** e among the H1655
Eze 40: 1 In the twenty-fifth year of our e, at the H1661
Hos 10: 5 because *it is* **taken** from them **into** e. H1655
Am 1: 5 The people of Aram *will* **go into** e to Kir," H1655
Am 1:15 Her king will go into e, he and his H1583
Am 5: 5 For Gilgal *will* **surely go into** e, and H1655+1655
Am 5:27 Therefore *I will* **send** you **into** e beyond H1655
Am 6: 7 *you will* be among the first to **go into** e H1655+1655
Am 7:11 and Israel *will* **surely go into** e H1655+1655
Am 7:17 And Israel *will* **surely go into** e H1655+1655
Am 9: 4 they are driven into e by their enemies, H8660
Am 9:14 I will bring my people Israel back from e. H8654
Mic 1:16 for *they will* **go** from you **into** e. H1655
Na 3:10 she was taken captive and went into e. H8660
Zec 14: 2 Half of the city will go into e, but the rest H1583
Mt 1:11 brothers at the time of the e to Babylon. G3578
Mt 1:12 After the e to Babylon: Jeconiah was the G3578
Mt 1:17 fourteen from David to the e to Babylon G3578
Mt 1:17 fourteen from the e to the Messiah. G3578
Ac 7:43 Therefore *I will* **send** you **into** e' beyond G3579

EXILED (7) [EXILE]

2Ki 17:28 the priests who *had been* e from Samaria H1655
Ne 1: 9 then even if your e *people* are at the H5615
Isa 27:13 those *who* **were** e in Egypt will H5615
Isa 49:21 barren; I *was* e and rejected. H1655
Jer 22:10 weep bitterly for him *who is* e, because H2143
La 2: 9 her princes are e among the nations, NDT
Na 2: 7 that Nineveh **be** e and carried away. H1655

EXILES (42) [EXILE]

Ezr 1:11 along with the e when they came up H1583
Ezr 2: 1 who came up from the captivity of the e, H1583
Ezr 4: 1 heard that the e were building a H1201+1583
Ezr 6:16 Levites and the rest of the e— A10120+10145
Ezr 6:19 the e celebrated the Passover. H1201+1583
Ezr 6:20 the Passover lamb for all the e, H1201+1583
Ezr 8:35 Then the e who had returned from H1201+1583
Ezr 9: 4 because of this unfaithfulness of the e. H1583
Ezr 10: 6 to mourn over the unfaithfulness of the e. H1583
Ezr 10: 7 all the e to assemble in H1201+1583
Ezr 10: 8 be expelled from the assembly of the e. H1583
Ezr 10:16 So the e did as was proposed. Ezra H1201+1583
Ne 7: 6 captivity of the e whom Nebuchadnezzar H1583
Ps 147: 2 up Jerusalem; he gathers the e *of* Israel. H5615
Isa 11:12 the nations and gather the e *of* Israel; H5615
Isa 20: 4 the Egyptian captives and Cushite e, H1661
Isa 45:13 He will rebuild my city and set my e free H1661
Isa 56: 8 declares—he who gathers the e *of* Israel: H5615
Jer 24: 5 I regard as good the e *from* Judah, whom H1661
Jer 28: 4 all the other e *from* Judah who went H1661
Jer 28: 6 house and all the e back to this place H1583
Jer 29: 1 elders among the e and to the priests, H1583
Jer 29:19 And you e have not listened either, NDT
Jer 29:20 all you e whom I have sent away from H1583
Jer 29:22 all the e *from* Judah who are in Babylon H1661
Jer 29:31 "Send this message to all the e: 'This is H1583
Jer 49:36 be a nation where Elam's e do not go. H5615
Eze 1: 1 I was among the e by the Kebar River, H1583

Eze 3:15 I came to the e who lived at Tel Aviv near H1583
Eze 11:15 of your fellow e and all the other H408+1460
Eze 11:24 brought me to the e in Babylonia in the H1583
Eze 11:25 I told the e everything the LORD had H1583
Da 2:25 man among the e from Judah A10120+10145
Da 5:13 one of the e my father the king A10120+10145
Da 6:13 who is one of the e from Judah A10120+10145
Ob 20 company of Israelite e who are in Canaan H1661
Ob 20 the e *from* Jerusalem who are in H1661
Mic 4:6 I will assemble the e and those I have H5615
Zep 3:19 I will gather the e. I will give them H5615
Zec 6:10 "Take silver and gold from the e Heldai H1583
1Pe 1:1 e scattered throughout the provinces of *G4215*
1Pe 2:11 as foreigners and e, to abstain from *G4215*

EXIST (1) [EXISTS]
Ro 13:1 The authorities *that* e have been *G1639*

EXISTS (4) [EXIST]
Ecc 6:10 Whatever e has already been named H2118
Ecc 7:24 Whatever e is far off and most profound H2118
Heb 2:10 whom and through whom everything e NDT
Heb 11:6 must believe that *he* e and that he *G1639*

EXITS (4)
Eze 42:11 width, with similar e and dimensions. H4604
Eze 43:11 its arrangement, its e and entrances—its H4604
Eze 44:5 the temple and all the e *of* the sanctuary. H4604
Eze 48:30 "These will be the e *of* the city: Beginning H9362

EXODUS (1)
Heb 11:22 spoke about the e of the Israelites from *G2016*

EXPAND (1) [EXPANDS, EXPANSES]
2Co 10:15 of activity among you *will* greatly e, *G3486*

EXPANDS (1) [EXPAND]
Isa 5:14 Therefore Death e its jaws, opening wide H8143

EXPANSES (1) [EXPAND]
Job 38:18 comprehended the **vast** e *of* the earth? H8144

EXPECT (14) [EXPECTANT, EXPECTANTLY, EXPECTATION, EXPECTATIONS, EXPECTED, EXPECTING]
Isa 58:4 e your voice **to be heard** on high. H9048
Isa 64:3 did awesome things that *we did* not e, H7747
Eze 13:6 declares," and e him to fulfill their words. H3498
Mt 11:3 is to come, or *should we* e someone else?" *G4659*
Mt 24:44 come at an hour when *you do* not e him. *G1506*
Mt 24:50 on a day when *he does* not e him and at *G4659*
Lk 6:34 to those from whom *you* e repayment, *G1827*
Lk 7:19 is to come, or *should we* e someone else?" *G4659*
Lk 7:20 is to come, or *should we* e someone else? *G4659*
Lk 12:40 come at an hour when *you do* not e him." *G1506*
Lk 12:46 on a day when *he does* not e him and at *G4659*
2Co 10:2 to be as bold as *I* e to be toward some *G3357*
Php 1:20 I **eagerly** e and hope that I will in no way *G638*
Jas 1:7 That person *should* not e to receive *G3887*

EXPECTANT (1) [EXPECT]
Jer 31:8 the lame, e **mothers** and women in labor H2226

EXPECTANTLY (3) [EXPECT]
Job 29:21 "People listened to me e, waiting in H3498
Ps 5:3 I lay my requests before you and **wait** e. H7595
Lk 3:15 The people *were* **waiting** e and were all *G4659*

EXPECTATION (3) [EXPECT]
Eze 19:5 hope unfulfilled, her e gone, she took H9536
Ro 8:19 creation waits *in* **eager** e for the children *G638*
Heb 10:27 only a fearful e of judgment and of *G1693*

EXPECTATIONS (1) [EXPECT]
2Co 8:5 And they exceeded *our* e: They gave *G1827*

EXPECTED (6) [EXPECT]
Ge 48:11 Joseph, "*I* never e to see your face again H7136
Hag 1:9 "*You* e much, but see, it turned out to be H7155
Mt 20:10 were hired first, *they* e to receive more. *G3787*
Ac 16:13 where *we* e to find a place of prayer. *G3787*
Ac 25:18 charge him with any of the crimes I *had* e. *G5706*
Ac 28:6 The *people* e him to swell up or suddenly *G4659*

EXPECTING (7) [EXPECT]
Lk 2:5 to be married to him and was **e a child.** *G1607*
Lk 6:34 lend to sinners, **e to be** repaid in full. *G2671*
Lk 6:35 to them without **e to get** anything **back**. *G594*
Lk 8:40 welcomed him, for they were all e him. *G4659*
Ac 3:5 attention, e to get something from them. *G4659*
Ac 10:24 Cornelius was e them and had called *G4659*
1Co 16:11 *I am* e him along with the brothers *G1683*

EXPEDIENT (KJV) BENEFICIAL, BEST, BETTER, GAINED, GOOD

EXPEL (1) [EXPELLED]
1Co 5:13 "**E** the wicked person from among you." *G1976*

EXPELLED (5) [EXPEL]
1Sa 28:3 Saul *had* e the mediums and spiritists H6073
1Ki 15:12 *He* e the male shrine prostitutes from the H6296
Ezr 10:8 and *would* himself **be** e from the assembly H976
Eze 28:16 mount of God, and *I* e you, guardian cherub H6
Ac 13:50 Barnabas, and e them from their region. *G1675*

EXPEND (1) [EXPENSE]
2Co 12:15 everything I have and e *myself* **as well**. *G1682*

EXPENSE (2) [EXPEND, EXPENSES, EXPENSIVE]
Lk 10:35 you for any **extra** e *you may* **have**. *G4655*
1Co 9:7 Who serves as a soldier *at* his own e *G4072*

EXPENSES (3) [EXPENSE]
2Ki 12:12 and **met** all *the other* e of restoring the H3655
Ezr 6:8 Their e are to be fully paid out of the A10486
Ac 21:24 in their purification rites and **pay** their e, *G1251*

EXPENSIVE (5) [EXPENSE]
Mt 26:7 with an alabaster jar of **very** e perfume, *G988*
Mk 14:3 with an alabaster jar of **very** e perfume, *G4500*
Lk 7:25 those who wear e clothes and indulge in *G1902*
Jn 12:3 of pure nard, an e perfume; she poured *G4501*
1Ti 2:9 hairstyles or gold or pearls or e clothes, *G4500*

EXPERIENCE (3) [EXPERIENCED]
Jdg 3:2 who *had* not **had** previous battle e): H3359
Job 21:19 so that *they themselves will* e it! H3359
Heb 11:5 from this life, so that *he did* not e death: *G3972*

EXPERIENCED (14) [EXPERIENCE]
Dt 11:2 the ones who saw and e the discipline of H3359
Jos 24:31 him and who *had* e everything the LORD H3359
Jdg 3:1 Israelites who *had* not e any of the wars H3359
2Sa 17:8 your father is an **e fighter**; he will H408+4878
1Ch 12:33 **e soldiers** prepared for battle with H3655+7372
1Ch 12:36 **e soldiers** prepared for battle H3655+7372
2Ch 2:7 blue yarn, and e in the art of engraving H3359
2Ch 2:14 *He is* **e in** all kinds of **engraving** H7334+7338
2Ch 17:13 kept **e fighting men** in H408+4878+1475+2657
Ecc 1:16 I *have* e much of wisdom and knowledge." H8011
SS 3:8 the sword, all e *in* battle, each with his H4340
Ro 11:25 Israel *has* e a hardening in part until the *G1181*
2Co 1:8 about the troubles we e in the province of *G1181*
Gal 3:4 *Have you* e so much in vain—if it really *G4248*

EXPERT (4) [EXPERTS]
Ex 36:8 cherubim woven into them by e **hands**. H3110
Mt 22:35 One of them, an e **in the law**, tested him *G3788*
Lk 10:25 one occasion an e **in the law** stood up to *G3788*
Lk 10:37 **The e in the law** replied, "The one who *G3836*[S]

EXPERTS (7) [EXPERT]
Est 1:13 the king to consult e *in* matters of law H3359
Lk 7:30 the e **in the law** rejected God's *G3788*
Lk 11:45 One *of* the e **in the law** answered him *G3788*
Lk 11:46 "And you e **in the law**, woe *to* you *G3788*
Lk 11:52 "Woe to you e **in the law**, because you *G3788*
Lk 14:3 asked the Pharisees and e **in the law**, *G3788*
2Pe 2:14 unstable; they are e in greed—an *G2840+1214*

EXPIRED (KJV) ELAPSED, END, OVER, PASSED, SPRING

EXPLAIN (19) [EXPLAINED, EXPLAINING, EXPLAINS, EXPLANATION]
Ge 41:24 none of them *could* e it to me. H5583
Dt 32:7 tell you, your elders, and *they will* e to you. H606
Jdg 14:16 he replied, "so *why should I* e it to you?" H5583
1Ki 10:3 was too hard for the king *to* e to her. H5583
2Ch 9:2 nothing was too hard for him *to* e to her. H5583
Est 4:8 to show to Esther and e it to her, and he H5583
Job 15:17 "Listen to me and *I will* e *to* you; let me H2555
Jer 9:12 been instructed by the LORD and *can* e it? H5583
Da 2:6 But if you tell me the dream and e it, you A10600
Da 2:27 diviner can e to the king the mystery A10252
Da 5:12 e riddles and solve difficult problems. A10252
Da 5:15 it means, but they could not e it. A10252+10600
Da 10:14 Now I have come to e *to* you what will H1067
Mt 13:36 "**E** to us the parable of the weeds in the *G1397*
Mt 15:15 Peter said, "**E** the parable to us. *G5851*
Mt 16:21 time on Jesus began *to* e to his disciples *G1259*
Jn 4:25 When he comes, *he will* e everything to us." *G334*
Ac 2:14 in Jerusalem, *let me* e this to you *G1196+1639*
Rev 17:7 I *will* e to you the mystery of the woman *G3306*

EXPLAINED (10) [EXPLAIN]
Jdg 14:16 "*I* haven't even e it to my father or mother," H5583
Jdg 14:17 *She* in turn e the riddle to her people H5583
Jdg 14:19 clothes to *those who had* e the riddle. H5583
1Sa 10:25 Samuel e to the people the rights and H1819
Da 2:15 Arioch then e the matter to Daniel A10313
Da 2:17 to his house and e the matter to his A10313
Zec 1:10 man standing among the myrtle trees e, H6699
Mk 4:34 with his own disciples, *he* e everything. *G2147*
Lk 24:27 *he* e to them **what was said** in all the *G1450*
Ac 18:26 to their home and e to him the way of *G1758*

EXPLAINING (5) [EXPLAIN]
Jdg 14:15 your husband into e the riddle for us, H5583
Isa 28:9 *To* whom *is he* e his message H1067
Ac 17:3 e and proving that the Messiah had to *G1380*
Ac 28:23 till evening, **e about** the kingdom of God *G1758*
1Co 2:13 e spiritual realities with Spirit-taught *G5173*

EXPLAINS (1) [EXPLAIN]
Ac 8:31 he said, "unless someone e it to me?" *G3842*

EXPLANATION (2) [EXPLAIN]
Ecc 8:1 Who knows the e *of* things? A person's H7323
Da 7:23 "*He* **gave** me this e: 'The fourth beast is A10042

EXPLOIT (5) [EXPLOITED, EXPLOITING, EXPLOITS]
Pr 22:22 *Do* not e the poor because they are poor H1608
Isa 58:3 do as you please and e all your workers. H5601
2Co 12:17 *Did I* e you through any of the men I sent *G4430*
2Co 12:18 Titus *did* not e you, did he? Did *G4430*
2Pe 2:3 these teachers *will* e you with fabricated *G1864*

EXPLOITED (1) [EXPLOIT]
2Co 7:2 corrupted no one, *we have* e no one. *G4430*

EXPLOITING (1) [EXPLOIT]
Jas 2:6 Is it not the rich *who are* e you? Are they *G2872*

EXPLOITS (8) [EXPLOIT]
2Sa 23:17 Such *were the* e of the three mighty H6913
2Sa 23:20 fighter from Kabzeel, performed great e. H7189
2Sa 23:22 Such *were the* e *of* Benaiah son of H6913
1Ki 22:45 the things he achieved and *his* **military** e H4309
1Ch 11:19 Such *were the* e *of* the three mighty H6913
1Ch 11:22 fighter from Kabzeel, **performed** great e. H7189
1Ch 11:24 Such *were the* e *of* Benaiah son of H6913
2Co 11:20 who enslaves you or e you or takes *G2983*

EXPLORE (11) [EXPLORED, EXPLORING]
Nu 13:2 "Send some men *to* e the land of Canaan H9365
Nu 13:16 of the men Moses sent to e the land. H9365
Nu 13:17 When Moses sent them to e Canaan, he H9365
Nu 14:36 So the men Moses had sent to e the land H9365
Nu 14:38 Of the men who went to e the land, only H9365
Jos 14:7 me from Kadesh Barnea to e the land. H8078
Jdg 18:2 Eshtaol to spy out the land and e it. H2983
Jdg 18:2 They told them, "Go, e the land." So they H2983
2Sa 10:3 them to you only to e the city and spy it H2983
1Ch 19:3 come to you only to e and spy out the H2983
Ecc 1:13 mind to study and to e by wisdom all that H9365

EXPLORED (7) [EXPLORE]
Nu 13:21 So they went up and e the land from the H9365
Nu 13:32 a bad report about the land *they had* e. H9365
Nu 13:32 "The land *we* e devours those H6296+9365
Nu 14:6 were among those *who had* e the land, H9365
Nu 14:7 passed through and e is exceedingly H9365
Nu 14:34 each of the forty days *you* e the land— H9365
Dt 1:24 came to the Valley of Eshkol and e it. H8078

EXPLORING (1) [EXPLORE]
Nu 13:25 forty days they returned from e the land. H9365

EXPORTED (2)
1Ki 10:29 They also e *them* to all the kings of the H3655
2Ch 1:17 They also e them to all the kings of the H3655

EXPOSE (11) [EXPOSED, EXPOSING]
Nu 25:4 **kill** them **and** e them in broad daylight H3697
Job 20:27 The heavens *will* e his guilt; the earth will H1655
Pr 13:16 act with knowledge, but fools e their folly. H7298
Isa 57:12 I *will* e your righteousness and your works H5583
La 2:14 *they did* not e your sin to ward off your H1655
La 4:22 Daughter Edom, and e your wickedness. H1655
Eze 25:9 therefore I *will* e the flank of Moab H7337
Hos 2:10 So now *I will* e her lewdness before the H1655
Mt 1:19 did not want *to* e her **to public disgrace**, *G1258*
1Co 4:5 in darkness and *will* e the motives of the *G5746*
Eph 5:11 deeds of darkness, but rather e them. *G1794*

EXPOSED (26) [EXPOSE]
Ex 20:26 on steps, or your private parts *may* **be** e. H1655
Lev 20:18 *he has* e the source of her flow H6867
Dt 21:22 to death and their body *is* e on a pole, H9434
Jos 10:26 kings to death and e their bodies on five H9434
2Sa 21:6 to us *to be* **killed and** their bodies e H3697
2Sa 21:9 *who* **killed** them **and** e their bodies on a H3697
2Sa 21:13 of those *who had* **been killed and** e were H3697
2Sa 22:16 valleys of the sea **were** e and the H8011
Ne 4:13 lowest points of the wall at the e **places**, H7460
Est 6:2 there that Mordecai *had* e Bigthana and H5583
Ps 18:15 valleys of the sea **were** e and the H8011
Pr 26:26 their wickedness *will* **be** e in the assembly H1655
Isa 47:3 Your nakedness *will* **be** e and your shame H1655
Jer 8:2 They *will be* e to the sun and the moon H8848
Jer 36:30 be thrown out and e to the heat by day and NDT
Eze 16:36 out your lust and e your naked body in H1655
Eze 23:18 prostitution openly and e her naked body, H1655
Eze 23:29 the shame of your prostitution *will* **be** e. H1655
Hos 7:1 sins of Ephraim *are* e and the crimes of H1655
Hab 2:16 Drink and *let your* **nakedness be** e! The H6887
Zep 2:14 doorways, the beams of cedar *will be* e. H6867
Jn 3:20 light for fear that their deeds *will be* e. *G1794*
2Co 11:23 been e to death again and again. *G1877*
Eph 5:13 But everything e by the light becomes *G1794*
Heb 10:33 Sometimes *you were* **publicly** e to insult *G2518*
Rev 16:15 as not to go naked and *be* shamefully e." *G1063*

EXPOSING (1) [EXPOSE]
Ge 30:37 the bark and e the white inner wood H4741

EXPOUND (2)
Dt 1:5 Moses began *to* e this law, saying: H930
Ps 49:4 a proverb; with the harp *I will* e my riddle: H7337

EXPRESS (7) [EXPRESSED, EXPRESSING, EXPRESSION, EXPRESSIONS]
2Sa 10: 2 a delegation to e his **sympathy** to Hanun H5714
2Sa 10: 3 by sending envoys to you *to* e **sympathy**? H5714
2Sa 13:32 been Absalom's e intention ever H6584+7023
1Ch 19: 2 a delegation to e his **sympathy** *to* Hanun H5714
1Ch 19: 2 of the Ammonites to e **sympathy** *to* him, H5714
1Ch 19: 3 by sending envoys to you *to* e **sympathy**? H5714
Col 4: 8 to you **for the** e **purpose** that G1650+899+4047

EXPRESSED (1) [EXPRESS]
Eph 2: 7 e **in** his kindness to us in Christ Jesus. G1877

EXPRESSING (1) [EXPRESS]
Gal 5: 6 that counts is faith e *itself* through love. G1919

EXPRESSION (2) [EXPRESS]
Lev 7:12 " 'If they offer it as an e **of thankfulness** H9343
Job 9:27 complaint, I will change my e, and smile, H7156

EXPRESSIONS (1) [EXPRESS]
2Co 9:12 overflowing in many e **of thanks** to God. G2374

EXTEND (19) [EXTENDED, EXTENDING, EXTENDS, EXTENSIVE, EXTENT]
Ge 9:27 *May* God e Japheth's **territory**; may H7332
Ge 49:13 ships; his border will e **toward** Sidon. H6584
Ex 25:32 Six branches *are to* e from the sides of the H3655
Ex 26:28 The center crossbar *is to* e from end to end H1368
Nu 35: 4 the Levites will e a thousand cubits H2575+2025
Dt 11:24 Your territory *will* e from the desert to H2118
Jos 1: 4 Your territory *will* e from the desert to H2118
1Ch 11:10 strong support to e it over the whole land, H4887
Ps 109:12 *May no one* e kindness to him or take pity H5432
Ps 110: 2 The LORD *will* e your mighty scepter from H8938
Isa 66:12 "I *will* e peace to her like a river, and the H5742
Eze 45: 7 It will e **westward** from the west H3542+2025
Eze 47:17 The boundary *will* e from the sea to Hazar H2118
Eze 48:21 It will e **eastward** from the 25,000 H7708+2025
Eze 48:23 it will e **from** the east side to the west H4946
Da 11:42 *He will* e his power over many countries H8938
Am 1:13 of Gilead in order to e his borders, H8143
Zec 9:10 His rule will e **from** sea to sea and from H4946
Zec 14: 5 my mountain valley, for it *will* e to Azel. H5595

EXTENDED (16) [EXTEND]
Ex 36:33 crossbar so that *it* e from end to end at H1368
Ex 37:18 Six branches e from the sides of the H3655
Dt 4:48 This land e **from** Aroer on the rim of the H4946
Jos 13: 9 It e **from** Aroer on the rim of the Arnon H4946
Jos 15: 1 its clans, e down to the territory of Edom H2118
Jos 17: 7 territory of Manasseh e from Asher to H2118
Jos 19:11 e to the ravine near Jokneam. H7003
1Ki 6: 3 of the temple e the width of the H6584+7156
1Ki 6:21 and *he* e gold chains across the front of H6296
1Ch 5:16 pasturelands of Sharon as far as they e. H9362
1Ch 21:16 sword in his hand e over Jerusalem. H5742
2Ch 3:13 wings of these cherubim e twenty cubits. H7298
Ezr 7:28 and *who has* e his good favor to me H5742
Est 8: 4 Then the king e the gold scepter to Esther H3804
Isa 26:15 *you have* e all the borders of the land. H8178
Eze 42: 7 it e in front of the rooms for fifty cubits. H802

EXTENDING (11) [EXTEND]
Ex 25:33 all six branches e from the lampstand. H3655
Ex 25:35 pair of branches e from the lampstand, H3655
Ex 37:19 all six branches e from the lampstand. H3655
Ex 37:21 pair of branches e from the lampstand, H3655
Nu 21:13 is in the wilderness e into Amorite H3655
Dt 3:16 gave the territory e **from** Gilead down to H4946
Jos 13:30 The territory e from Mahanaim and H2118
1Sa 27: 8 had lived in the land e to Shur and Egypt.) H995
2Ch 5: 9 that their ends, e **from** the ark, could be H4946
Eze 42:12 to the corresponding wall e eastward, H2006
Mic 7:11 will come, the day *for* e your boundaries. H8178

EXTENDS (6) [EXTEND]
Nu 21:30 as far as Nophah, which e **to** Medeba." H6330
1Ch 5: 9 the desert that e **to** the Euphrates H4200+4946
Est 4:11 unless the king e the gold scepter to H3804
Pr 31:20 arms to the poor and e her hands to the H8938
Da 4:22 your dominion e **to** distant parts of A10378
Lk 1:50 His mercy e *to* those *who* **fear** him, from AIT

EXTENSIVE (3) [EXTEND]
1Ch 22: 5 So David made e preparations H4200+8044
2Ch 27: 3 the LORD and did e work on the wall H4200+8044
Ne 4:19 "The work is e and spread out, and H2221

EXTENT (2) [EXTEND]
1Co 11:18 among you, and *to* some e I believe it. G3538
2Co 2: 5 as he has grieved all of you to *some* e— G3538

EXTERMINATE (2) [EXTERMINATING]
1Ki 9:21 whom the Israelites could not e—to serve H3049
Eze 25: 7 among the nations and e you from the H6

EXTERMINATING (1) [EXTERMINATE]
Jos 11:20 them totally, e them without mercy H9012

EXTERNAL (1)
Heb 9:10 e regulations applying until the time of G4922

EXTINCT (KJV) CUT SHORT, EXTINGUISHED

EXTINGUISH (1) [EXTINGUISHED]
Eph 6:16 with which you can e all the flaming G4931

EXTINGUISHED (2) [EXTINGUISH]
2Sa 21:17 so that the lamp of Israel *will* not *be* e." H3882
Isa 43:17 never to rise again, e, snuffed out like a H1980

EXTOL (13)
1Ch 16: 4 before the ark of the LORD, to e, thank, H2349
Job 36:24 Remember *to* e his work, which people H8434
Ps 34: 1 *I will* e the LORD at all times; his praise H1385
Ps 68: 4 his name, e him who rides on the clouds H6148
Ps 95: 2 thanksgiving and e him with music and H8131
Ps 109:30 With my mouth *I will* greatly e the LORD; H3344
Ps 111: 1 *I will* e the LORD with all my heart in the H3344
Ps 115:18 it is we *who* e the LORD, both now and H1385
Ps 117: 1 all you nations; e him, all *you* peoples. H8655
Ps 145: 2 I will praise you and e your name for ever H2146
Ps 145:10 LORD; your faithful people e you. H1385
Ps 147:12 E the LORD, Jerusalem; praise your God H8655
Ro 15:11 all you Gentiles; *let* all the peoples e him." G2046

EXTORT (2) [EXTORTION]
Eze 22:12 You e unjust gain from your H928+2021+6945
Lk 3:14 "Don't e **money** and don't accuse people G1398

EXTORTION (9) [EXTORT]
Lev 6: 4 they have stolen or **taken by** e, H6943+6945
Ps 62:10 Do not trust in e or put vain hope in H6945
Pr 28:16 A tyrannical ruler practices e, but one who H5131
Ecc 7: 7 E turns a wise person into a fool, and a H6945
Isa 33:15 reject gain from e and keep their hands H5131
Jer 22:17 innocent blood and on oppression and e." H5298
Eze 18:18 because *he* **practiced** e, robbed his H6943+6945
Eze 22:29 of the land **practice** e and commit H6943+6945
Hab 2: 6 goods and makes himself wealthy *by* e! H6294

EXTRA (4)
Mt 10:10 the journey or e shirt or sandals or a G1545
Mk 6: 9 Wear sandals but not an e shirt. G1545
Lk 9: 3 no bag, no bread, no money, no e shirt. G1545
Lk 10:35 you for any e **expense** *you may* **have**. G4655

EXTRAORDINARY (1)
Ac 19:11 God did e miracles through G4024+3836+5593

EXTREME (2) [EXTREMES, EXTREMELY]
Jos 15: 1 to the Desert of Zin in the e south. H7895
2Co 8: 2 joy and their e poverty welled up in G2848+958

EXTREMELY (2) [EXTREME]
Pr 30:24 are small, yet they *are* e **wise**: H2681+2682
Gal 1:14 my people and was e zealous for the G4359

EXTREMES (1) [EXTREME]
Ecc 7:18 Whoever fears God will avoid all e. H4392S

EYE (76) [EYEBROWS, EYED, EYELIDS, EYES]
Ge 2: 9 were pleasing to the e and good for food. H5260
Ge 3: 6 was good for food and pleasing to the e, H6524
Ex 21:24 e for eye, tooth for tooth, hand for hand H6524
Ex 21:24 eye for e, tooth for tooth, hand for hand H6524
Ex 21:26 female slave in the e and destroys it must H6524
Ex 21:26 the slave go free to compensate for the e. H6524
Lev 21:20 who has any e defect, or who has H6524
Lev 24:20 fracture for fracture, e for eye, tooth for H6524
Lev 24:20 fracture, eye for e, tooth for tooth. H6524
Nu 24: 3 the prophecy of one whose e sees clearly, H6524
Nu 24:15 the prophecy of one whose e sees clearly H6524
Dt 19:21 life for life, e for eye, tooth for tooth, hand H6524
Dt 19:21 life for life, eye for e, tooth for tooth, hand H6524
Dt 32:10 he guarded him as the apple of his e, H6524
1Sa 11: 2 I gouge out the right e of every one of you H6524
1Sa 18: 9 that time on Saul **kept a close** e **on** David. H6523
2Ki 9:30 she put on e makeup, arranged her H6524
Ezr 5: 5 But the e *of* their God was watching over A10540
Job 7: 8 The e that now sees me will see me no H6524
Job 10:18 I wish I had died before any e saw me. H6524
Job 14: 3 Do you fix your e on them? Will you bring H6524
Job 20: 9 The e that saw him will not see him H6524
Job 24:15 The e *of* the adulterer watches for dusk H6524
Job 24:15 he thinks, 'No e will see me,' and he H6524
Job 28: 7 hidden path, no falcon's e has seen it. H6524
Ps 17: 8 Keep me as the apple of your e; hide me H6524
Ps 32: 8 I will counsel you with my *loving* e on you. H6524
Ps 35:19 me without reason maliciously wink the e. H6524
Ps 94: 9 Does he who formed the e not see? H6524
Pr 6:13 who winks maliciously with his e, signals H6524
Pr 7: 2 my teachings as the apple of your e. H6524
Pr 16:30 winks with their e is plotting perversity; H6524
Pr 30:17 "The e that mocks a father, that scorns an H6524
Ecc 1: 8 The e never has enough of seeing, nor H6524
Ecc 6: 9 Better what the e sees than the roving of H6524
Isa 29:20 all *who* **have an** e **for** evil will be cut H9193
Isa 64: 4 no e has seen any God besides you H6524
La 2: 4 has slain all who were pleasing to the e; H6524
Eze 23:40 applied e makeup and put on your H6524
Am 9: 4 "I will keep my e on them for harm and H6524
Zec 2: 8 touches you touches the apple of his e— H6524
Zec 11:17 the sword strike his arm and his right e! H6524
Zec 11:17 withered, his right e totally blinded!" H6524
Zec 12: 4 "I will keep a watchful e over Judah, but I H6524
Mt 5:29 If your right e causes you to stumble G4057
Mt 5:38 that it was said, 'E for eye, and tooth for G4057
Mt 5:38 it was said, 'Eye for e, and tooth for tooth. G4057
Mt 6:22 "The e is the lamp of the body. G4057
Mt 7: 3 in your brother's e and pay no attention to G4057
Mt 7: 3 no attention to the plank in your own e? G4057
Mt 7: 4 'Let me take the speck out *of* your e,' G4057
Mt 7: 4 the time there is a plank in your own e? G4057
Mt 7: 5 first take the plank out *of* your own e, and G4057
Mt 7: 5 to remove the speck from your brother's e. G4057
Mt 18: 9 And if your e causes you to stumble G4057
Mt 18: 9 to enter life **with one** e than to have two G3669
Mt 19:24 to go through the e of a needle than for G5585
Mk 9:47 And if your e causes you to stumble, pluck G4057
Mk 9:47 kingdom of God *with* **one** e than to have G3669
Mk 10:25 to go through the e of a needle than for G5584
Lk 6:41 in your brother's e and pay no attention to G4057
Lk 6:41 no attention to the plank in your own e? G4057
Lk 6:42 let me take the speck out of your e,' when G4057
Lk 6:42 fail to see the plank in your own e? G4057
Lk 6:42 first take the plank out of your e, and then G4057
Lk 6:42 to remove the speck from your brother's e. G4057
Lk 11:34 Your e is the lamp of your body. G4057
Lk 18:25 to go through the e of a needle than for G5557
1Co 2: 9 "What no e has seen, what no ear has G4057
1Co 12:16 "Because I am not an e, I do not belong G4057
1Co 12:17 If the whole body were an e, where would G4057
1Co 12:21 The e cannot say to the hand, "I don't G4057
1Co 15:52 in the twinkling *of* an e, at the last G4057
Eph 6: 6 to win their favor when their e **is on** you, G4056
Col 3:22 only when their e **is on** you and to curry G4056
Rev 1: 7 and "every e will see him, even those G4057

EYEBROWS (1) [EYE]
Lev 14: 9 their e and the rest of their hair. H1461+6524

EYED (1) [EYE]
Ecc 5: 8 one official *is* e *by* a higher one, and H9068

EYELIDS (3) [EYE]
Ps 132: 4 no sleep to my eyes or slumber to my e, H6757
Pr 6: 4 sleep to your eyes, no slumber to your e. H6757
Jer 9:18 with tears and water streams from our e. H6757

EYES (518) [EYE]
Ge 3: 5 you eat from it your e will be opened, H6524
Ge 3: 7 Then the e *of* both of them were opened H6524
Ge 6: 8 But Noah found favor in the e *of* the LORD. H6524
Ge 18: 3 "If I have found favor in your e, my lord, H6524
Ge 19:19 Your servant has found favor in your e, H6524
Ge 21:19 God opened her e and she saw a well H6524
Ge 27: 1 was old and his e were so weak that he H6524
Ge 29:17 Leah had weak e, but Rachel had a lovely H6524
Ge 30:27 "If I have found favor in your e, please H6524
Ge 31:40 cold at night, and sleep fled from my e. H6524
Ge 32: 5 to my lord, that I may find favor in your e. H6524
Ge 33: 8 "To find favor in *your* e, my lord," he said H6524
Ge 33:10 "If I have found favor in your e, accept this H6524
Ge 33:15 "Just let me find favor in the e *of* my lord." H6524
Ge 34:11 "Let me find favor in your e, and I will H6524
Ge 39: 4 found favor in his e and became his H6524
Ge 39:21 him favor in the e *of* the prison warden. H6524
Ge 42:24 from them and bound before their e. H6524
Ge 46: 4 And Joseph's own hand will close your e." H6524
Ge 47:15 Why should we die before your e? Our NDT
Ge 47:19 Why should we perish before your e—we H6524
Ge 47:25 "May we find favor in the e *of* our lord; we H6524
Ge 47:29 "If I have found favor in your e, put your H6524
Ge 48:10 Now Israel's e were failing because of old H6524
Ge 49:12 His e will be darker than wine, his teeth H6524
Ge 50: 4 "If I have found favor in your e, speak to H6524
Ex 8:26 sacrifices that are detestable in their e, H6524
Ex 15:26 your God and do what is right in his e, H6524
Ex 34: 9 "if I have found favor in your e, then let H6524
Lev 20: 4 community close their e when that man H6524
Nu 10:31 in the wilderness, and you can be our e. H6524
Nu 11:15 if I have found favor in your e—and do not H6524
Nu 13:33 seemed like grasshoppers in our own e, H6524
Nu 15:39 after the lusts of your own hearts and e. H6524
Nu 20: 8 that rock before their e and it will pour out H6524
Nu 22:31 Then the LORD opened Balaam's e, and H6524
Nu 24: 4 falls prostrate, and whose e are opened: H6524
Nu 24:16 falls prostrate, and whose e are opened: H6524
Nu 25: 6 right before the e *of* Moses and the whole H6524
Nu 27:14 to honor me as holy before their e." H6524
Nu 32: 5 If we have found favor in your e," they said H6524
Nu 33:55 become barbs in your e and thorns in your H6524
Dt 1:30 did for you in Egypt, before your very e, H6524
Dt 3:21 seen with your own e all that the LORD H6524
Dt 3:27 Look at the land with your own e, since H6524
Dt 4: 3 saw with your own e what the LORD did at H6524
Dt 4: 9 the things your e have seen or let them H6524
Dt 4:25 doing evil in the e *of* the LORD your God H6524
Dt 4:34 did for you in Egypt before your very e? H6524
Dt 6:22 Before our e the LORD sent signs and H6524
Dt 7:19 You saw with your own e the great trials H6524
Dt 9:17 breaking them to pieces before your e. H6524
Dt 10:21 wonders you saw with your own e. H6524
Dt 11: 7 But it was your own e that saw all these H6524
Dt 11:12 the e *of* the LORD your God are continually H6524
Dt 12:25 be doing what is right in the e *of* the LORD. H6524
Dt 12:28 right in the e *of* the LORD your God. H6524

Dt 13:18 you today and doing what is right in his e. H6524
Dt 16:19 a bribe blinds the e of the wise and twists H6524
Dt 17: 2 doing evil in the e of the LORD your God in H6524
Dt 21: 7 shed this blood, nor did our e see it done. H6524
Dt 21: 9 done what is right in the e of the LORD. H6524
Dt 24: 4 be detestable **in the e of** the LORD. H4200+7156
Dt 25: 3 Israelite will be degraded in your e. H6524
Dt 28:31 Your ox will be slaughtered before your e H6524
Dt 28:32 will wear out your e watching for them H6524
Dt 28:65 an anxious mind, e weary with longing H6524
Dt 28:67 hearts and the sights that your e will see. H6524
Dt 29: 2 Your e have seen all that the LORD did in H6524
Dt 29: 3 With your own e you saw those great trials, H6524
Dt 29: 4 that understands or e that see or ears that H6524
Dt 34: 4 I have let you see it with your e, but you H6524
Dt 34: 7 his e were not weak nor his strength H6524
Jos 3: 7 begin to exalt you in the e of all Israel, H6524
Jos 23:13 whips on your backs and thorns in your e H6524
Jos 24: 7 You saw with your own e what I did to the H6524
Jos 24:17 performed those great signs before our e. H6524
Jdg 2:11 did evil in the e of the LORD and served H6524
Jdg 3: 7 The Israelites did evil in the e of the LORD H6524
Jdg 3:12 the Israelites did evil in the e of the LORD, H6524
Jdg 4: 1 the Israelites did evil in the e of the LORD, H6524
Jdg 6: 1 The Israelites did evil in the e of the LORD H6524
Jdg 6:17 "If now I have found favor in your e, give H6524
Jdg 10: 6 the Israelites did evil in the e of the LORD. H6524
Jdg 13: 1 the Israelites did evil in the e of the LORD, H6524
Jdg 16:21 gouged out his e and took him down to H6524
Jdg 16:28 revenge on the Philistines for my two e." H6524
Ru 2: 2 behind anyone in whose e I find favor." H6524
Ru 2:10 such favor in your e that you notice me— H6524
Ru 2:13 "May I continue to find favor in your e, my H6524
1Sa 1:18 "May your servant find favor in your e." H6524
1Sa 3: 2 whose e were becoming so weak that he H6524
1Sa 3:18 the LORD; let him do what is good in his e." H6524
1Sa 4:15 years old and whose e had failed so that H6524
1Sa 12: 3 I accepted a bribe to make me shut my e? H6524
1Sa 12:16 the LORD is about to do before your e! H6524
1Sa 12:17 you did in the e of the LORD when you H6524
1Sa 14:27 hand to his mouth, and his e brightened. H6524
1Sa 14:29 See how my e brightened when I tasted a H6524
1Sa 15:17 you were once small in your own e, H6524
1Sa 15:19 plunder and do evil in the e of the LORD?" H6524
1Sa 20: 3 very well that I have found favor in your e, H6524
1Sa 20:29 If I have found favor in your e, let me get H6524
1Sa 24:10 seen with your own e how the LORD H6524
1Sa 27: 5 "If I have found favor in your e, let a place H6524
1Sa 29: 9 as pleasing in my e as an angel of God; H6524
2Sa 6:22 I will be humiliated in my own e. H6524
2Sa 12: 9 of the LORD by doing what is evil in his e? H6524
2Sa 12:11 Before your very e I will take your wives H6524
2Sa 14:22 knows that he has found favor in your e, H6524
2Sa 15:25 If I find favor in the LORD's e, he will bring H6524
2Sa 16: 4 "May I find favor in your e, my lord the H6524
2Sa 22:28 your e are on the haughty to bring H6524
2Sa 24: 3 may the e of my lord the king see it. H6524
1Ki 1:20 lord the king, the e of all Israel are on you H6524
1Ki 1:48 who has allowed my e to see a successor H6524
1Ki 8:29 May your e be open toward this temple H6524
1Ki 8:52 "May your e be open to your servant's H6524
1Ki 9: 3 My e and my heart will always be there H6524
1Ki 10: 7 until I came and saw with my own e. H6524
1Ki 11: 6 So Solomon did evil in the e of the LORD H6524
1Ki 11:33 done what is right in my e, nor kept H6524
1Ki 11:38 what is right in my e by obeying my H6524
1Ki 14: 8 doing only what was right in my e. H6524
1Ki 14:22 Judah did evil in the e of the LORD. H6524
1Ki 15: 5 was right in the e of the LORD and had not H6524
1Ki 15:11 did what was right in the e of the LORD, H6524
1Ki 15:26 He did evil in the e of the LORD, following H6524
1Ki 15:34 He did evil in the e of the LORD, following H6524
1Ki 16: 7 the evil he had done in the e of the LORD, H6524
1Ki 16:19 doing evil in the e of the LORD and H6524
1Ki 16:25 did evil in the e of the LORD and sinned H6524
1Ki 16:30 did more evil in the e of the LORD than any H6524
1Ki 20:38 with his headband down over his e. H6524
1Ki 20:41 quickly removed the headband from his e, H6524
1Ki 21:20 yourself to do evil in the e of the LORD. H6524
1Ki 21:25 himself to do evil in the e of the LORD, H6524
1Ki 22:43 he did what was right in the e of the LORD. H6524
1Ki 22:52 He did evil in the e of the LORD, because H6524
2Ki 3: 2 He did evil in the e of the LORD, but not as H6524
2Ki 3:18 This is an easy thing in the e of the LORD H6524
2Ki 4:34 mouth to mouth, e to eyes, hands to H6524
2Ki 4:34 to mouth, eyes to e, hands to hands. H6524
2Ki 4:35 sneezed seven times and opened his e. H6524
2Ki 6:17 "Open his e, LORD, so that he may H6524
2Ki 6:17 Then the LORD opened the servant's e H6524
2Ki 6:20 open the e of these men so they can see." H6524
2Ki 6:20 the LORD opened their e and they looked, H6524
2Ki 7: 2 "You will see it with your own e, H6524
2Ki 7:19 "You will see it with your own e, but you H6524
2Ki 8:18 He did evil in the e of the LORD. H6524
2Ki 8:27 of Ahab and did evil in the e of the LORD, H6524
2Ki 10:30 what is right in my e and have done to H6524
2Ki 12: 2 what was right in the e of the LORD all the H6524
2Ki 13: 2 He did evil in the e of the LORD by H6524
2Ki 13:11 He did evil in the e of the LORD and did not H6524
2Ki 14: 3 He did what was right in the e of the LORD H6524
2Ki 14:24 He did evil in the e of the LORD and did not H6524
2Ki 15: 3 He did what was right in the e of the LORD H6524
2Ki 15: 9 He did evil in the e of the LORD, as his H6524
2Ki 15:18 He did evil in the e of the LORD. During his H6524
2Ki 15:24 Pekahiah did evil in the e of the LORD. H6524
2Ki 15:28 He did evil in the e of the LORD. He did not H6524
2Ki 15:34 He did what was right in the e of the LORD H6524
2Ki 16: 2 was right in the e of the LORD his God. H6524
2Ki 17: 2 He did evil in the e of the LORD, but not H6524
2Ki 17:17 themselves to do evil in the e of the LORD, H6524
2Ki 18: 3 He did what was right in the e of the LORD H6524
2Ki 19:16 hear; open your e, LORD, and see; H6524
2Ki 19:22 your voice and lifted your e in pride? H6524
2Ki 20: 3 have done what is good in your e. H6524
2Ki 21: 2 He did evil in the e of the LORD, following H6524
2Ki 21: 6 He did much evil in the e of the LORD H6524
2Ki 21:15 done evil in my e and have aroused my H6524
2Ki 21:16 so that they did evil in the e of the LORD. H6524
2Ki 21:20 He did evil in the e of the LORD, as his H6524
2Ki 22: 2 what was right in the e of the LORD and H6524
2Ki 22:20 Your e will not see all the disaster I am H6524
2Ki 23:32 He did evil in the e of the LORD, just as his H6524
2Ki 23:37 And he did evil in the e of the LORD, just as H6524
2Ki 24: 9 He did evil in the e of the LORD, just as his H6524
2Ki 24:19 He did evil in the e of the LORD, just as H6524
2Ki 25: 7 killed the sons of Zedekiah before his e. H6524
2Ki 25: 7 Then they put out his e, bound him with H6524
2Ch 6:20 May your e be open toward this temple H6524
2Ch 6:40 may your e be open and your ears H6524
2Ch 7:15 Now my e will be open and my ears H6524
2Ch 7:16 My e and my heart will always be there H6524
2Ch 9: 6 said until I came and saw with my own e. H6524
2Ch 14: 2 right in the e of the LORD his God. H6524
2Ch 16: 9 For the e of the LORD range throughout the H6524
2Ch 20:12 know what to do, but our e are on you." H6524
2Ch 20:32 he did what was right in the e of the LORD. H6524
2Ch 21: 6 He did evil in the e of the LORD. H6524
2Ch 22: 4 He did evil in the e of the LORD, as the H6524
2Ch 24: 2 what was right in the e of the LORD all the H6524
2Ch 25: 2 He did what was right in the e of the LORD H6524
2Ch 26: 4 He did what was right in the e of the LORD H6524
2Ch 27: 2 He did what was right in the e of the LORD H6524
2Ch 28: 1 not do what was right in the e of the LORD. H6524
2Ch 29: 2 He did what was right in the e of the LORD H6524
2Ch 29: 6 they did evil in the e of the LORD our God H6524
2Ch 29: 8 as you can see with your own e. H6524
2Ch 33: 2 He did evil in the e of the LORD, following H6524
2Ch 33: 6 He did much evil in the e of the LORD H6524
2Ch 33:22 He did evil in the e of the LORD, as his H6524
2Ch 34: 2 what was right in the e of the LORD and H6524
2Ch 34:28 Your e will not see all the disaster I am H6524
2Ch 36: 5 He did evil in the e of the LORD his God. H6524
2Ch 36: 9 He did evil in the e of the LORD. H6524
2Ch 36:12 He did evil in the e of the LORD his God H6524
Ezr 9: 8 gives light to our e and a little relief in H6524
Ne 1: 6 be attentive and your e open to hear the H6524
Ne 9:32 hardship seem trifling **in** your **e**— H4200+7156
Job 3:10 womb on me to hide trouble from my e. H6524
Job 4:16 A form stood before my e, and I heard a H6524
Job 7: 7 my e will never see happiness again. H6524
Job 10: 4 Do you have e of flesh? Do you see as a H6524
Job 11:20 But the e of the wicked will fail, and H6524
Job 13: 1 "My e have seen all this, my ears have H6524
Job 15:12 you away, and why do your e flash, H6524
Job 15:15 if even the heavens are not pure in his e, H6524
Job 16: 9 opponent fastens on me his piercing e. H6524
Job 16:16 with weeping, dark shadows ring my e; H6757
Job 16:20 is my friend as my e pour out tears to God H6524
Job 17: 2 my e must dwell on their hostility. H6524
Job 17: 5 reward, the e of their children will fail. H6524
Job 17: 7 My e have grown dim with grief; my H6524
Job 19:27 I myself will see him with my own e—I H6524
Job 21: 8 their offspring before their e. H6524
Job 21:20 Let their own e see their destruction; let H6524
Job 24:23 of security, but his e are on their ways. H6524
Job 25: 5 bright and the stars are not pure in his e, H6524
Job 27:19 when he opens his e, all is gone. H6524
Job 28:10 the rock; their e see all its treasures. H6524
Job 28:21 is hidden from the e of every living thing, H6524
Job 29:15 I was e to the blind and feet to the lame. H6524
Job 31: 1 a covenant with my e not to look lustfully H6524
Job 31: 7 if my heart has been led by my e, or if my H6524
Job 31:16 the poor or let the e of the widow grow H6524
Job 32: 1 because he was righteous in his own e. H6524
Job 34:21 "His e are on the ways of mortals; he sees H6524
Job 36: 7 He does not take his e off the righteous H6524
Job 39:29 it looks for food; its e detect it from afar. H6524
Job 40:24 Can anyone capture it by the e, or trap it H6524
Job 41:18 of light; its e are like the rays of dawn. H6524
Job 42: 5 of you but now my e have seen you. H6524
Ps 6: 7 My e grow weak with sorrow; they fail H6524
Ps 10: 8 His e *watch* in secret for his victims H6524
Ps 11: 4 everyone on earth; his e examine them. H6757
Ps 13: 3 Give light to my e, or I will sleep in H6524
Ps 16: 8 I keep my e always on the LORD H4200+5584[S]
Ps 17: 2 from you; may your e see what is right. H6524
Ps 17:11 surround me, with e alert, to throw me to H6524
Ps 18:27 bring low those whose e are haughty. H6524
Ps 19: 8 the LORD are radiant, giving light to the e. H6524
Ps 25:15 My e are ever on the LORD, for only he will H6524
Ps 31: 9 in distress; my e grow weak with sorrow H6524
Ps 33:18 But the e of the LORD are on those who H6524
Ps 34:15 The e of the LORD are on the righteous H6524
Ps 35:21 With our own e we have seen it." H6524
Ps 36: 1 There is no fear of God before their e. H6524
Ps 36: 2 In their own e they flatter themselves too H6524
Ps 38:10 even the light has gone from my e. H6524
Ps 52: 1 you who are a **disgrace** *in the e of* God? AIT
Ps 54: 7 my e have looked in triumph on my H6524
Ps 66: 7 by his power, his e watch the nations H6524
Ps 69: 3 throat is parched. My e fail, looking for my H6524
Ps 69:23 May their e be darkened so they cannot H6524
Ps 77: 4 You kept my e from closing; I was too H6524
Ps 79:10 Before our e, make known among the H6524
Ps 88: 9 my e are dim with grief. I call to you, LORD H6524
Ps 91: 8 observe with your e and see the H6524
Ps 92:11 My e have seen the defeat of my H6524
Ps 101: 5 whoever has haughty e and a proud heart, H6524
Ps 101: 6 My e will be on the faithful in the land H6524
Ps 115: 5 cannot speak, e, but cannot see. H6524
Ps 116: 8 me from death, my e from tears, my feet H6524
Ps 118:23 done this, and it is marvelous in our e. H6524
Ps 119:18 Open my e that I may see wonderful H6524
Ps 119:37 Turn my e away from worthless things H6524
Ps 119:82 My e fail, looking for your promise; I say H6524
Ps 119:123 My e fail, looking for your salvation H6524
Ps 119:136 Streams of tears flow from my e, for your H6524
Ps 119:148 My e stay open through the watches of H6524
Ps 121: 1 I lift up my e to the mountains—where H6524
Ps 123: 1 I lift up my e to you, to you who sit H6524
Ps 123: 2 As the e of slaves look to the hand of H6524
Ps 123: 2 as the e of a female slave look to the H6524
Ps 123: 2 mistress, so our e look to the LORD our God H6524
Ps 131: 1 my e are not haughty; I do not H6524
Ps 132: 4 allow no sleep to my e or slumber to my H6524
Ps 135:16 cannot speak, e, but cannot see. H6524
Ps 139:16 Your e saw my unformed body; all the H6524
Ps 141: 8 But my e are fixed on you, Sovereign LORD H6524
Ps 145:15 The e of all look to you, and you give H6524
Pr 3: 7 Do not be wise in your own e; fear the H6524
Pr 4:25 Let your e look straight ahead; fix your H6524
Pr 6: 4 Allow no sleep to your e, no slumber to H6524
Pr 6:17 haughty e, a lying tongue, hands that H6524
Pr 6:25 beauty or let her captivate you with her e. H6757
Pr 10:26 vinegar to the teeth and smoke to the e, H6524
Pr 15: 3 The e of the LORD are everywhere, keeping H6524
Pr 15:30 Light in a messenger's e brings joy to the H6524
Pr 17:24 a fool's e wander to the ends of the H6524
Pr 20: 8 he winnows out all evil with his e. H6524
Pr 20:12 Ears that hear and e that see—the LORD H6524
Pr 21: 4 Haughty e and a proud heart—the H6524
Pr 22:12 The e of the LORD keep watch over H6524
Pr 23:26 heart and let your e delight in my ways, H6524
Pr 23:29 needless bruises? Who has bloodshot e? H6524
Pr 23:33 Your e will see strange sights, and your H6524
Pr 25: 7 What you have seen with your e H6524
Pr 26: 5 his folly, or he will be wise in his own e. H6524
Pr 26:12 Do you see a person wise in their own e H6524
Pr 26:16 is wiser in his own e than seven people H6524
Pr 27:20 never satisfied, and neither are human e. H6524
Pr 28:11 The rich are wise in their own e; one who H6524
Pr 28:27 who close their e to them receive many H6524
Pr 29:13 The LORD gives sight to the e of both. H6524
Pr 30:12 are pure in their own e and yet are not H6524
Pr 30:13 those whose e are ever so haughty H6524
Ecc 2:10 I denied myself nothing my e desired; H6524
Ecc 2:14 The wise have e in their heads, while the H6524
Ecc 4: 8 his e were not content with his wealth. H6524
Ecc 5:11 owners except to feast their e on them? H6524
Ecc 11: 7 it pleases the e to see the sun. H6524
Ecc 11: 9 of your heart and whatever your e see, H6524
SS 1:15 how beautiful! Your e are doves. H6524
SS 4: 1 Your e behind your veil are doves H6524
SS 4: 9 stolen my heart with one glance of your e, H6524
SS 5:12 His e are like doves by the water streams H6524
SS 6: 5 Turn your e from me; they overwhelm me H6524
SS 7: 4 Your e are the pools of Heshbon by the H6524
SS 8:10 I have become in his e like one bringing H6524
Isa 1:15 I hide my e from you; even when H6524
Isa 2:11 The e of the arrogant will be humbled H6524
Isa 3:16 flirting with their e, strutting along with H6524
Isa 5:15 humbled, the e of the arrogant humbled. H6524
Isa 5:21 are wise in their own e and clever in their H6524
Isa 6: 5 and my e have seen the King H6524
Isa 6:10 make their ears dull and close their e. H6524
Isa 6:10 Otherwise they might see with their e H6524
Isa 10:12 of his heart and the haughty look in his e. H6524
Isa 11: 3 will not judge by what he sees with his e, H6524
Isa 13:16 will be dashed to pieces before their e; H6524
Isa 17: 7 Maker and turn their e to the Holy One of H6524
Isa 29:10 He has sealed your e (the prophets); H6524
Isa 29:18 darkness the e of the blind will see. H6524
Isa 30:20 with your own e you will see them. H6524
Isa 32: 3 Then the e of those who see will no H6524
Isa 33:15 shut their e against contemplating H6524
Isa 33:17 Your e will see the king in his beauty and H6524
Isa 33:20 our festivals; your e will see Jerusalem, H6524
Isa 35: 5 Then will the e of the blind be opened H6524
Isa 37:17 hear; open your e, LORD, and see; H6524
Isa 37:23 your voice and lifted your e in pride? H6524
Isa 38: 3 have done what is good in your e. H6524
Isa 38:14 My e grew weak as I looked to the H6524
Isa 40:26 Lift up your e and look to the heavens H6524
Isa 42: 7 to open e that are blind, to free captives H6524
Isa 43: 8 Lead out those who have e but are blind H6524
Isa 44:18 their e are plastered over so they cannot H6524

Isa 49: 5 I am honored in the e *of* the LORD and my H6524
Isa 49:18 Lift up your e and look around; all your H6524
Isa 51: 6 Lift up your e to the heavens, look at the H6524
Isa 52: 8 to Zion, they will see it with their own e. H6524
Isa 59:10 feeling our way like people without e. H6524
Isa 60: 4 "Lift up your e and look about you: All H6524
Isa 65:16 will be forgotten and hidden from my e. H6524
Jer 4:30 Why highlight your e with makeup? You H6524
Jer 5: 3 do not your e look for truth? You H6524
Jer 5:21 people, who have e but do not see, who H6524
Jer 7:30 people of Judah have done evil in my e, H6524
Jer 9: 1 of water and my e a fountain of tears! H6524
Jer 9:18 wail over us till our e overflow with tears H6524
Jer 13:17 of your pride; my e will weep bitterly H6524
Jer 14: 6 like jackals; their e fail for lack of food." H6524
Jer 14:17 " 'Let my e overflow with tears night and H6524
Jer 16: 9 Before your e and in your days I will bring H6524
Jer 16:17 My e are on all their ways; they are not H6524
Jer 16:17 nor is their sin concealed from my e. H6524
Jer 20: 4 with your own e you will see them fall by H6524
Jer 22:17 "But your e and your heart are set only on H6524
Jer 24: 6 My e will watch over them for their good H6524
Jer 29:21 will put them to death before your very e. H6524
Jer 31:16 voice from weeping and your e from tears, H6524
Jer 32: 4 face to face and see him with his own e. H6524
Jer 32:19 Your e are open to the ways of all H6524
Jer 34: 3 see the king of Babylon with your own e, H6524
Jer 39: 6 Zedekiah before his e and also killed all H6524
Jer 39: 7 put out Zedekiah's e and bound him with H6524
Jer 39:16 they will be fulfilled **before** your e. H4200+7156
Jer 51:24 "Before your e I will repay Babylon and all H6524
Jer 52: 2 He did evil in the e *of* the LORD, just as H6524
Jer 52:10 killed the sons of Zedekiah before his e; H6524
Jer 52:11 Then he put out Zedekiah's e, bound him H6524
La 1:16 why I weep and my e overflow with tears. H6524
La 2:11 My e fail from weeping, I am in torment H6524
La 2:18 yourself no relief, your e no rest. H1426+6524
La 3:48 tears flow from my e because my people H6524
La 3:49 My e will flow unceasingly, without relief, H6524
La 4:17 Moreover, our e failed, looking in vain H6524
La 5:17 because of these things our e grow dim H6524
Eze 1:18 all four rims were full of e all around. H6524
Eze 6: 9 and by their e, which have lusted H6524
Eze 10:12 were completely full of e, as were their H6524
Eze 12: 2 They have e to see but do not see and H6524
Eze 20: 7 of the vile images you have set your e on, H6524
Eze 20: 8 of the vile images they had set their e on, H6524
Eze 20: 9 profaned in the e *of* the nations among H6524
Eze 20:14 profaned in the e *of* the nations in whose H6524
Eze 20:22 profaned in the e *of* the nations in whose H6524
Eze 20:24 their e lusted after their parents' idols H6524
Eze 22:16 have been defiled in the e *of* the nations, H6524
Eze 22:26 they shut their e to the keeping of my H6524
Eze 24:16 take away from you the delight of your e. H6524
Eze 24:21 the delight of your e, the object of your H6524
Eze 24:25 the delight of their e, their heart's desire, H6524
Eze 36:23 proved holy through you before their e. H6524
Eze 37:20 Hold before their e the sticks you have H6524
Eze 38:16 proved holy through you before their e. H6524
Da 4:34 raised my e toward heaven, and my A10540
Da 7: 8 This horn had e like the eyes of a A10540
Da 7: 8 had eyes like the e *of* a human being A10540
Da 7:20 others and that had e and a mouth that A10540
Da 8: 5 horn between its e came from the west, H6524
Da 8:21 large horn between its e is the first king. H6524
Da 9:18 open your e and see the desolation of the H6524
Da 10: 6 like lightning, his e like flaming torches H6524
Hos 2:10 her lewdness before the e *of* her lovers; H6524
Joel 1:16 the food been cut off before our very e— H6524
Am 9: 3 they hide from my e at the bottom of the H6524
Am 9: 8 "Surely the e *of* the Sovereign LORD are on H6524
Mic 4:11 her be defiled, let our e gloat over Zion!" H6524
Mic 7:10 My e will see her downfall; even now H6524
Hab 1:13 Your e are too pure to look on evil; you H6524
Zep 3:20 I restore your fortunes before your very e," H6524
Zec 3: 9 There are seven e on that one stone, and H6524
Zec 4:10 since the seven e *of* the LORD that range H6524
Zec 9: 1 the e *of* all people and all the tribes of H6524
Zec 14:12 their feet, their e will rot in their sockets H6524
Mal 1: 5 You will see it with your own e and say H6524
Mal 2:17 who do evil are good in the e *of* the LORD, H6524
Mt 6:22 If your e are healthy, your whole body will *G4057*
Mt 6:23 But if your e are unhealthy, your whole *G4057*
Mt 9:29 Then he touched their e and said *G4057*
Mt 13:15 their ears, and they have closed their e. *G4057*
Mt 13:15 Otherwise they might see *with* their e *G4057*
Mt 13:16 But blessed are your e because they see *G4057*
Mt 18: 9 than to have two e and be thrown into *G4057*
Mt 20:34 compassion on them and touched their e. *G3921*
Mt 21:42 done this, and it is marvelous in our e'? *G4057*
Mt 26:43 sleeping, because their e were heavy. *G4057*
Mk 8:18 Do you have e but fail to see, and ears *G4057*
Mk 8:23 spit on the man's e and put his hands on *G3921*
Mk 8:25 more Jesus put his hands on the man's e. *G4057*
Mk 8:25 Then *his* e *were* **opened**, his sight was *G1332*
Mk 9:47 than to have two e and be thrown into *G4057*
Mk 12:11 done this, and it is marvelous in our e'?" *G4057*
Mk 14:40 sleeping, because their e were heavy. *G4057*
Lk 2:30 For my e have seen your salvation, *G4057*
Lk 4:20 The e of everyone in the synagogue were *G4057*
Lk 10:23 "Blessed are the e that see what you see. *G4057*
Lk 11:34 When your e are healthy, your whole *G4057*
Lk 16:15 who justify yourselves **in the e of** others, *G1967*
Lk 19:42 peace—but now it is hidden from your e. *G4057*
Lk 24:31 Then their e were opened and they *G4057*
Jn 4:35 open your e and look at the fields! *G4057*
Jn 9: 6 with the saliva, and put it on the man's e. *G4057*
Jn 9:10 "How then were your e opened?" they *G4057*
Jn 9:11 made some mud and put it on my e. *G4057*
Jn 9:14 opened the man's e was a Sabbath. *G4057*
Jn 9:15 "He put mud on my e," the man replied *G4057*
Jn 9:17 It was your e he opened." The man *G4057*
Jn 9:21 who opened his e, we don't know. *G4057*
Jn 9:26 he do to you? How did he open your e?" *G4057*
Jn 9:30 he comes from, yet he opened my e. *G4057*
Jn 9:32 of opening the e of a man born blind. *G4057*
Jn 10:21 Can a demon open the e of the blind?" *G4057*
Jn 11:37 he who opened the e of the blind man *G4057*
Jn 12:40 has blinded their e and hardened their *G4057*
Jn 12:40 so they can neither see *with* their e, nor *G4057*
Ac 1: 9 he was taken up **before** their very e, and a *G1063*
Ac 4:19 John replied, "Which is right **in** God's e: *G1967*
Ac 9: 8 when he opened his e he could see *G4057*
Ac 9:18 something like scales fell from Saul's e *G4057*
Ac 9:40 She opened her e, and seeing Peter she *G4057*
Ac 26:18 to open their e and turn them from *G4057*
Ac 28:27 their ears, and they have closed their e. *G4057*
Ac 28:27 Otherwise they might see *with* their e *G4057*
Ro 3:18 "There is no fear of God before their e." *G4057*
Ro 11: 8 e that could not see and ears that could *G4057*
Ro 11:10 May their e be darkened so they cannot *G4057*
Ro 12:17 to do what is right **in the e of** everyone. *G1967*
2Co 4:18 *So* we **fix** our e not **on** what is seen, but on *G5023*
2Co 8:21 not only **in the e of** the Lord but also in *G1967*
2Co 8:21 eyes of the Lord but also **in the e of** man. *G1967*
Gal 3: 1 Before your very e Jesus Christ was clearly *G4057*
Gal 4:15 have torn out your e and given them to *G4057*
Eph 1:18 I pray that the e of your heart may be *G4057*
Php 3:17 **keep** *your* **e on** those who live as we do. *G5023*
Heb 4:13 laid bare *before* the e of him to *G4057*
Heb 12: 2 **fixing** our e on Jesus, the pioneer and *G927*
Jas 2: 5 who are poor *in the e of* the **world** to be rich AIT
1Pe 3:12 For the e of the Lord are on the righteous *G4057*
2Pe 2:14 With e full of adultery, they never stop *G4057*
1Jn 1: 1 which we have seen *with* our e, which we *G4057*
1Jn 2:16 the lust *of* the e, and the pride of *G4057*
Rev 1:14 as snow, and his e were like blazing fire. *G4057*
Rev 2:18 whose e are like blazing fire and whose *G4057*
Rev 3:18 salve to put on your e, so you can see *G4057*
Rev 4: 6 they were covered with e, in front and *G4057*
Rev 4: 8 wings and was covered with e all around, *G4057*
Rev 5: 6 The Lamb had seven horns and seven e *G4057*
Rev 7:17 will wipe away every tear from their e. *G4057*
Rev 19:12 His e are like blazing fire, and on his head *G4057*
Rev 21: 4 'He will wipe every tear from their e. *G4057*

EYEWITNESSES (2) [WITNESS]
Lk 1: 2 from the first were e and servants of the *G898*
2Pe 1:16 in power, but we were e of his majesty. *G2228*

EZBAI (1)
1Ch 11:37 Hezro the Carmelite, Naarai son of E, H256

EZBON (2)
Ge 46:16 Shuni, E, Eri, Arodi and Areli H719
1Ch 7: 7 E, Uzzi, Uzziel, Jerimoth and Iri, heads of H719

EZEKIAS (KJV) HEZEKIAH

EZEKIEL (2)
Eze 1: 3 the word of the LORD came to E the priest H3489
Eze 24:24 E will be a sign to you; you will do just as H3489

EZEL (1) [BETH EZEL]
1Sa 20:19 trouble began, and wait by the stone E. H262

EZEM (3)
Jos 15:29 Baalah, Iyim, E, H6796
Jos 19: 3 Hazar Shual, Balah, E, H6796
1Ch 4:29 Bilhah, E, Tolad, H6796

EZER (10)
Ge 36:21 E and Dishan. These sons of Seir H733
Ge 36:27 The sons of E: Bilhan, Zaavan and Akan. H733
Ge 36:30 E and Dishan. These were the H733
1Ch 1:38 Anah, Dishon, E and Dishan. H733
1Ch 1:42 The sons of E: Bilhan, Zaavan and Akan H733
1Ch 4: 4 of Gedor, and E the father of Hushah. H6470
1Ch 7:21 E and Elead were killed by the H6470
1Ch 12: 9 E was the chief, Obadiah the second in H6470
Ne 3:19 Next to him, E son of Jeshua, ruler of H6470
Ne 12:42 Jehohanan, Malkijah, Elam and E. H6472

EZION GEBER (7) [GEBER]
Nu 33:35 left Abronah and camped at E. H6787
Nu 33:36 They left E and camped at Kadesh H6787
Dt 2: 8 which comes up from Elath and E H6787
1Ki 9:26 King Solomon also built ships at E H6787
1Ki 22:48 set sail—they were wrecked at E. H6787
2Ch 8:17 Solomon went to E and Elath on H6787
2Ch 20:36 After these were built at E, H6787

EZRA (26) [EZRA'S]
Ezr 7: 1 king of Persia, E son of Seraiah, the son H6474
Ezr 7: 6 this E came up from Babylon. He was a H6474
Ezr 7: 8 E arrived in Jerusalem in the fifth month of NDT
Ezr 7:10 For E had devoted himself to the study H6474
Ezr 7:11 King Artaxerxes had given to E the priest, H6474
Ezr 7:12 king of kings, To E the priest, teacher of A10537
Ezr 7:21 with diligence whatever E the priest, A10537
Ezr 7:25 And you, E, in accordance with the A10537
Ezr 10: 1 While E was praying and confessing H6474
Ezr 10: 2 of Elam, said to E, "We have been H6474
Ezr 10: 5 So E rose up and put the leading priests H6474
Ezr 10: 6 Then E withdrew from before the house of H6474
Ezr 10:10 Then E the priest stood up and said to H6474
Ezr 10:16 E the priest selected men who were H6474
Ne 8: 1 They told E the teacher of the Law to H6474
Ne 8: 2 of the seventh month E the priest brought H6474
Ne 8: 4 E the teacher of the Law stood on a high H6474
Ne 8: 5 E opened the book. All the people could H6474
Ne 8: 6 E praised the LORD, the great God; and all H6474
Ne 8: 9 E the priest and teacher of the Law H6474
Ne 8:13 gathered around E the teacher to give H6474
Ne 8:18 E read from the Book of the Law of God. NDT
Ne 12: 1 with Joshua: Seraiah, Jeremiah, E, H6474
Ne 12:26 the governor and of E the priest, H6474
Ne 12:33 along with Azariah, E, Meshullam, H6474
Ne 12:36 E the teacher of the Law led the H6474

EZRA'S (1) [EZRA]
Ne 12:13 of E, Meshullam; of Amariah's H6474

EZRAH (1) [EZRAHITE]
1Ch 4:17 The sons of E: Jether, Mered, Epher and H6477

EZRAHITE (3) [EZRAH]
1Ki 4:31 including Ethan the E—wiser than Heman, H276
Ps 88: T A maskil of Heman the E. H276
Ps 89: T A maskil of Ethan the E. H276

EZRI (1)
1Ch 27:26 E son of Kelub was in charge of the H6479

F

FABLES (KJV) MYTHS, STORIES, TALES

FABRIC (17)
Lev 13:47 "As for any f that is spoiled with a defiling H955
Lev 13:49 if the affected area in the f, the leather, the H955
Lev 13:51 if the mold has spread in the f, the H955
Lev 13:52 He must burn the f, the woven or knitted H955
Lev 13:53 the mold has not spread in the f, the H955
Lev 13:55 which side of **the f** has been spoiled. H2257S
Lev 13:56 he is to tear the spoiled part out of the f H955
Lev 13:57 But if it reappears in the f, in the woven H955
Lev 13:58 Any f, woven or knitted material, or any H955
Lev 14:55 defiling molds in f or in a house, H955
Jdg 16:13 of my head into the f on the loom and H5018
Jdg 16:13 braids of his head, wove them into the f H5018
Jdg 16:14 up the pin and the loom, with the f. H5018
Eze 16:13 of fine linen and **costly** f and embroidered H5429
Eze 27:16 turquoise, purple f, embroidered work, NDT
Eze 27:24 garments, blue f, embroidered work and H1659
Am 3:12 of a bed and a **piece of** f *from* a couch." H1967

FABRICATED (1)
2Pe 2: 3 teachers will exploit you with f stories. *G4422*

FACE (307) [FACED, FACEDOWN, FACES, FACING]
Ge 1:29 plant on the f *of* the whole earth and H7156
Ge 4: 5 was very angry, and his f was downcast. H7156
Ge 4: 6 are you angry? Why is your f downcast? H7156
Ge 6: 7 will wipe from the f *of* the earth the H7156
Ge 7: 4 I will wipe from the f *of* the earth every H7156
Ge 7:23 living thing on the f *of* the earth was H7156
Ge 11: 4 be scattered over the f *of* the whole earth." H7156
Ge 11: 9 them over the f *of* the whole earth. H7156
Ge 19: 1 bowed down with his f to the ground. H678
Ge 30:40 but **made** the rest f the streaked H7156+5989
Ge 32:30 "It is because I saw God f to face, and H7156
Ge 32:30 "It is because I saw God face to f, and H7156
Ge 33:10 For to see your f is like seeing the face of H7156
Ge 33:10 see your face is like seeing the f *of* God, H7156
Ge 38:15 a prostitute, for she had covered her f. H7156
Ge 43: 3 'You will not see my f again unless your H7156
Ge 43: 5 'You will not see my f again unless your H7156
Ge 43:31 After he had washed his f, he came out H7156
Ge 44:23 with you, you will not see my f again. H7156
Ge 44:26 see the man's f unless our youngest H7156
Ge 48:11 "I never expected to see your f again, and H7156
Ge 48:12 bowed down with his f to the ground. H678
Ex 3: 6 Moses hid his f, because he was H7156
Ex 10: 5 They will cover the f *of* the ground so that H6524
Ex 10:28 The day you see my f you will die." H7156
Ex 13:17 God said, "If they f war, they might H8011
Ex 25:20 The cherubim are to f each other, looking H7156
Ex 32:12 to wipe them off the f *of* the earth'? H7156
Ex 33:11 The LORD would speak to Moses f to face H7156
Ex 33:11 The LORD would speak to Moses face to f H7156
Ex 33:16 all the other people on the f *of* the earth?" H7156
Ex 33:20 "you cannot see my f, for no one may see H7156
Ex 33:23 see my back; but my f must not be seen." H7156
Ex 34:29 not aware that his f was radiant H7156+6425
Ex 34:30 saw Moses, his f was radiant, and H7156+6425

Ex 34:33 speaking to them, he put a veil over his f. H7156
Ex 34:35 they saw that his f was radiant H7156+6425
Ex 34:35 the veil back over his f until he went in to H7156
Lev 13:45 cover the lower part of their f and cry out H8559
Lev 17:10 " 'I will set my f against any Israelite or H7156
Lev 20: 3 I myself will set my f against him and will H7156
Lev 20: 5 I myself will set my f against him and his H7156
Lev 20: 6 " 'I will set my f against anyone who turns H7156
Lev 26:17 I will set my f against you so that you will H7156
Nu 6:25 the LORD make his f shine on you and be H7156
Nu 6:26 the LORD turn his f toward you and give H7156
Nu 11:15 and do not let me f my own ruin. H8011
Nu 12: 3 than anyone else on the f of the earth.) H7156
Nu 12: 8 With him I speak f to face, clearly and not H7023
Nu 12: 8 With him I speak face to f, clearly and not H7023
Nu 12:14 "If her father had spit in her f, would she H7156
Nu 14:14 have been seen f to face, that your H6524
Nu 14:14 have been seen face to f, that your cloud H6524
Nu 14:43 the Canaanites will f you there. H4200+7156
Nu 22: 5 they cover the f of the land and have H6524
Nu 22:11 come out of Egypt covers the f of the land. H6524
Nu 24: 1 turned his f toward the wilderness. H7156
Dt 5: 4 The LORD spoke to you f to face out of the H7156
Dt 5: 4 spoke to you face to f out of the fire on H7156
Dt 6:15 he will destroy you from the f of the land. H7156
Dt 7: 6 the peoples on the f of the earth to be his H7156
Dt 7:10 him he will repay to their f by destruction; H7156
Dt 7:10 to repay to their f those who hate him. H7156
Dt 14: 2 of all the peoples on the f of the earth, H7156
Dt 25: 9 sandals, spit in his f and say, "This is H7156
Dt 31:17 I will hide my f from them, and they H7156
Dt 31:18 certainly hide my f in that day because of H7156
Dt 32:20 "I will hide my f from them," he said H7156
Dt 34:10 like Moses, whom the LORD knew f to face, H7156
Dt 34:10 like Moses, whom the LORD knew face to f, H7156
Jos 5: 1 had the courage to f the Israelites. H4946+7156
Jos 7:10 What are you doing down on your f? H7156
Jdg 6:22 I have seen the angel of the LORD f to face!" H7156
Jdg 6:22 I have seen the angel of the LORD face to f!" H7156
Ru 2:10 she bowed down with her f to the ground. H7156
1Sa 1:18 her f was no longer downcast. H7156
1Sa 5: 3 fallen on his f on the ground before the H7156
1Sa 5: 4 fallen on his f on the ground before the H7156
1Sa 20:15 David's enemies from the f of the earth." H7156
1Sa 20:41 three times, with his f to the ground. H678
1Sa 24: 8 prostrated himself with his f to the ground. H678
1Sa 25:23 before David with her f to the ground. H7156
1Sa 25:41 bowed down with her f to the ground and H678
1Sa 28:14 prostrated himself with his f to the ground. H678
2Sa 2:22 could I look your brother Joab in the f H5951+7156+448
2Sa 14: 4 she fell with her f to the ground to pay him H678
2Sa 14: 7 descendant on the f of the earth. H7156
2Sa 14:22 Joab fell with his f to the ground to pay H7156
2Sa 14:24 to his own house; he must not see my f." H7156
2Sa 14:24 house and did not see the f of the king. H7156
2Sa 14:28 in Jerusalem without seeing the king's f. H7156
2Sa 14:32 I want to see the king's f, and if I am H7156
2Sa 14:33 bowed down with his f to the ground H678
2Sa 18:28 the king with his f to the ground and said, H678
2Sa 19: 4 The king covered his f and cried aloud, "O H7156
2Sa 21: 1 so David sought the f of the LORD. H7156
2Sa 24:20 before the king with his f to the ground. H678
1Ki 1:23 king and bowed with his f to the ground. H678
1Ki 1:31 bowed down with her f to the ground, H678
1Ki 13:34 to its destruction from the f of the earth. H7156
1Ki 18:42 ground and put his f between his knees. H7156
1Ki 19:13 his cloak over his f and went out and H7156
1Ki 22:24 went up and slapped Micaiah in the f. H4305
2Ki 4:29 Lay my staff on the boy's f." H7156
2Ki 4:31 on ahead and laid the staff on the boy's f, H7156
2Ki 8:15 it in water and spread it over the king's f, H7156
2Ki 14: 8 "Come, let us f each other in battle." H8011+7156
2Ki 20: 2 Hezekiah turned his f to the wall and H7156
1Ch 16:11 LORD and his strength; seek his f always. H7156
1Ch 21:21 down before David with his f to the ground. H678
2Ch 7:14 pray and seek my f and turn from their H7156
2Ch 18:23 went up and slapped Micaiah in the f. H4305
2Ch 20:12 have no power to f this vast army H4200+7156
2Ch 20:17 Go out to f them tomorrow, and the H4200+7156
2Ch 20:18 bowed down with his f to the ground, H678
2Ch 25:17 "Come, let us f each other in battle." H8011+7156
2Ch 30: 9 He will not turn his f from you if you return H7156
Ezr 9: 6 to lift up my f to you, because our H7156
Ne 2: 2 "Why does your f look so sad when you H7156
Ne 2: 3 Why should my f not look sad when the H7156
Ne 4: 5 insults in the f of the builders. H4200+5584
Est 7: 8 the king's mouth, they covered Haman's f. H7156
Job 1:11 and he will surely curse you to your f." H7156
Job 2: 5 he will surely curse you to your f." H7156
Job 4:15 A spirit glided past my f, and the hair on H7156
Job 6:28 as to look at me. Would I lie to your f? H7156
Job 11:15 you will lift up your f; you will stand firm H7156
Job 13:15 I will surely defend my ways to his f. H7156
Job 13:24 do you hide your f and consider me your H7156
Job 15:27 "Though his f is covered with fat and his H7156
Job 16:16 My f is red with weeping, dark shadows H7156
Job 17: 6 everyone, a man in whose f people spit. H7156
Job 17:12 in the f of the darkness light is near. H7156
Job 21:31 Who denounces their conduct to their f H7156
Job 22:26 the Almighty and will lift up your f to God. H7156
Job 23:17 by the thick darkness that covers my f. H7156
Job 24:15 see me,' and he keeps his f concealed. H7156
Job 26: 9 He covers the f of the full moon H7156
Job 26:10 out the horizon on the f of the waters for a H7156
Job 29:24 the light of my f was precious to them. H7156
Job 30:10 they do not hesitate to spit in my f. H7156
Job 33:26 they will see God's f and shout for joy; he H7156
Job 34:29 If he hides his f, who can see him H7156
Job 37:12 around over the f of the whole earth to H7156
Ps 4: 6 Let the light of your f shine on us. H7156
Ps 10:11 he covers his f and never sees. H7156
Ps 11: 7 he loves justice; the upright will see his f. H7156
Ps 13: 1 How long will you hide your f from me? H7156
Ps 17:15 I will be vindicated and will see your f H7156
Ps 22:24 he has not hidden his f from him but has H7156
Ps 24: 6 seek him, who seek your f, God of Jacob. H7156
Ps 27: 8 heart says of you, "Seek his f!" Your face, H7156
Ps 27: 8 "Seek his face!" Your f, LORD, I will seek. H7156
Ps 27: 9 Do not hide your f from me, do not turn H7156
Ps 30: 7 when you hid your f, I was dismayed. H7156
Ps 31:16 Let your f shine on your servant; save me H7156
Ps 34:16 the f of the LORD is against those who H7156
Ps 44: 3 the light of your f, for you loved them. H7156
Ps 44:15 day long, and my f is covered with shame H7156
Ps 44:22 Yet for your sake we f death all day long H2222
Ps 44:24 Why do you hide your f and forget our H7156
Ps 51: 9 Hide your f from my sins and blot out all H7156
Ps 67: 1 bless us and make his f shine on us— H7156
Ps 69: 7 your sake, and shame covers my f. H7156
Ps 69:17 Do not hide your f from your servant H7156
Ps 80: 3 make your f shine on us, that we H7156
Ps 80: 7 Almighty; make your f shine on us, that H7156
Ps 80:19 Almighty; make your f shine on us, that H7156
Ps 88:14 do you reject me and hide your f from me? H7156
Ps 102: 2 Do not hide your f from me when I am in H7156
Ps 104:29 When you hide your f, they are terrified H7156
Ps 104:30 you renew the f of the ground. H7156
Ps 105: 4 LORD and his strength; seek his f always. H7156
Ps 119:58 I have sought your f with all my heart; be H7156
Ps 119:135 Make your f shine on your servant and H7156
Ps 143: 7 Do not hide your f from me or I will be H7156
Pr 7:13 kissed him and with a brazen f she said: H7156
Pr 8:27 out the horizon on the f of the deep, H7156
Pr 15:13 A happy heart makes the f cheerful, but H7156
Pr 16:15 When a king's f brightens, it means life H7156
Pr 27:19 As water reflects the f, so one's life H7156
Ecc 7: 3 because a sad f is good for the heart. H7156
Ecc 8: 1 brightens their f and changes its hard H7156
SS 2:14 show me your f, let me hear your voice; H5260
SS 2:14 your voice is sweet, and your f is lovely. H5260
Isa 8:17 who is hiding his f from the descendants H7156
Isa 23:17 all the kingdoms on the f of the earth. H7156
Isa 24: 1 he will ruin its f and scatter its inhabitants H7156
Isa 38: 2 Hezekiah turned his f to the wall and H7156
Isa 50: 6 I did not hide my f from mocking and H7156
Isa 50: 7 Therefore have I set my f like flint, and I H7156
Isa 50: 8 Let us f each other! Who is H6641
Isa 54: 8 of anger I hid my f from you for a moment H7156
Isa 57:17 and hid my f in anger, yet they kept NDT
Isa 59: 2 your sins have hidden his f from you, so H7156
Isa 64: 7 you have hidden your f from us and have H7156
Isa 65: 3 who continually provoke me to my very f, H7156
Jer 13:26 your skirts over your f that your shame may H7156
Jer 18:17 my back and not my f in the day of their H7156
Jer 25:26 all the kingdoms on the f of the earth. H7156
Jer 28:16 to remove you from the f of the earth. H7156
Jer 30: 6 in labor, every f turned deathly pale? H7156
Jer 32: 4 will speak with him f to face and see him H7023
Jer 32: 4 with him face to f and see him with his H7023
Jer 33: 5 I will hide my f from this city because of H7156
Jer 34: 3 and he will speak with you f to face. H7023
Jer 34: 3 and he will speak with you face to f. H7023
La 3:29 Let him bury his f in the dust—there may H7023
Eze 1:10 of the four had the f of a human being, H7156
Eze 1:10 on the right side each had the f of a lion, H7156
Eze 1:10 on the left the f of an ox; each also H7156
Eze 1:10 of an ox; each also had the f of an eagle. H7156
Eze 4: 3 you and the city and turn your f toward it. H7156
Eze 4: 7 Turn your f toward the siege of Jerusalem H7156
Eze 6: 2 set your f against the mountains of Israel H7156
Eze 7:18 Every f will be covered with shame, and H7156
Eze 7:22 I will turn my f away from the people, and H7156
Eze 10:14 One f was that of a cherub, the second H7156
Eze 10:14 the second the f of a human being, the H7156
Eze 10:14 the third the f of a lion, and the H7156
Eze 10:14 of a lion, and the fourth the f of an eagle. H7156
Eze 12: 6 Cover your f so that you cannot see the H7156
Eze 12:12 He will cover his f so that he cannot see H7156
Eze 13:17 set your f against the daughters of your H7156
Eze 14: 8 I will set my f against them and make H7156
Eze 15: 7 I will set my f against them. Although they H7156
Eze 15: 7 And when I set my f against them, you H7156
Eze 20:35 the nations and there, f to face, I will H7156
Eze 20:35 there, face to f, I will execute H7156
Eze 20:46 "Son of man, set your f toward the south H7156
Eze 20:47 every f from south to north will be H7156
Eze 21: 2 set your f against Jerusalem and preach H7156
Eze 25: 2 set your f against the Ammonites and H7156
Eze 28:21 "Son of man, set your f against Sidon H7156
Eze 29: 2 set your f against Pharaoh king of Egypt H7156
Eze 35: 2 "Son of man, set your f against Mount Seir H7156
Eze 38: 2 "Son of man, set your f against Gog, of the H7156
Eze 38:20 all the people on the f of the earth will H7156
Eze 39:23 So I hid my f from them and handed them H7156
Eze 39:24 their offenses, and I hid my f from them. H7156
Eze 39:29 I will no longer hide my f from them, for I H7156
Eze 41:19 the f of a human being toward the palm H7156
Eze 41:19 on one side and the f of a lion toward the H7156
Eze 43:17 The steps of the altar f east." H7155
Da 5: 6 His f turned pale and he was so A10228
Da 5: 9 more terrified and his f grew more pale. A10228
Da 7:28 my f turned pale, but I kept the A10228
Da 8:18 in a deep sleep, with my f to the ground. H7156
Da 10: 6 was like topaz, his f like lightning, his H7156
Da 10: 8 my f turned deathly pale and I was H2086
Da 10: 9 fell into a deep sleep, my f to the ground. H7156
Da 10:15 I bowed with my f toward the ground and H7156
Hos 2: 2 look from her f and the unfaithfulness H7156
Hos 5:15 have borne their guilt and seek my f— H7156
Joel 2: 6 nations are in anguish; every f turns pale. H7156
Am 5: 8 pours them out over the f of the land— H7156
Am 9: 6 pours them out over the f of the land— H7156
Am 9: 8 I will destroy it from the f of the earth. H7156
Mic 3: 4 he will hide his f from them because of H7156
Na 2:10 bodies tremble, every f grows pale. H7156
Na 3: 5 "I will lift your skirts over your f. I will H7156
Zep 1: 2 away everything from the f of the earth," H7156
Zep 1: 3 I destroy all mankind on the f of the earth," H7156
Mt 6:17 put oil on your head and wash your f, G4725
Mt 17: 2 His f shone like the sun, and his clothes G4725
Mt 18:10 heaven always see the f of my Father in G4725
Mt 26:39 he fell with his f to the ground and G2093+4725
Mt 26:67 Then they spit in his f and struck him with G4725
Mk 10:22 At this the man's f fell. He went away sad, G5145
Lk 5:12 he fell with his f to the ground and G2093+4725
Lk 9:29 the appearance of his f changed, and his G4725
Lk 21:35 who live on the f of the whole earth. G4725
Jn 11:44 strips of linen, and a cloth around his f. G4071
Jn 18:22 nearby slapped him in the f. G1443+4825
Jn 19: 3 And they slapped him in the f. G1443+4825
Ac 6:15 they saw that his f was like the face of G4725
Ac 6:15 that his face was like the f of an angel. G4725
Ac 16:19 into the marketplace to f the authorities. G2093
Ac 20:38 that they would never see his f again. G4725
Ro 8:36 "For your sake we f death all day long; we G2506
1Co 7:28 those who marry will f many troubles in G2400
1Co 13:12 as in a mirror; then we shall see f to face. G4725
1Co 13:12 as in a mirror; then we shall see face to f. G4725
1Co 15:31 I f death every day—yes, just as surely as I G633
2Co 3: 7 look steadily at the f of Moses because of G4725
2Co 3:13 put a veil over his f to prevent the G4725
2Co 4: 6 of God's glory displayed in the f of Christ. G4725
2Co 10: 1 am "timid" when f to face with you G2848+4725
2Co 10: 1 am "timid" when face to f with you G2848+4725
2Co 11:20 of you or puts on airs or slaps you in the f. G4725
2Co 11:28 I f daily the pressure of my concern for all NDT
Gal 2:11 I opposed him to his f, because he stood G4725
1Th 2: 2 you his gospel in the f of strong G1877
Heb 9:27 to die once, and after that to f judgment, NDT
Jas 1: 2 whenever you f trials of many kinds, G4346
Jas 1:23 who looks at his f in a mirror G4725+3836+1161
Jas 5:10 an example of patience in the f of suffering, AIT
1Pe 3:12 the f of the Lord is against those who G4725
2Jn 12 to visit you and talk with you f to face, G5125
2Jn 12 to visit you and talk with you face to f, G5125
3Jn 14 to see you soon, and we will talk f to face. G5125
3Jn 14 to see you soon, and we will talk face to f. G5125
Rev 1:16 His f was like the sun shining in all its G4071
Rev 4: 7 the third had a f like a man, the fourth G4725
Rev 6:16 hide us from the f of him who sits on G4725
Rev 10: 1 above his head; his f was like the sun G4725
Rev 22: 4 They will see his f, and his name will be G4725

FACED (20) [FACE]

Ex 37: 9 The cherubim f each other, looking H7156
Nu 8: 3 so that they f forward on the H448+4578+7156
2Ki 14:11 king of Judah f each other at Beth H8011+7156
2Ki 23:29 Necho f him and killed him at H8011
2Ch 25:21 king of Judah f each other at Beth H8011+7156
Ne 8: 3 till noon as he f the square before H4200+7156
Eze 1:17 one of the four directions the creatures f; NDT
Eze 10:11 one of the four directions the cherubim f; NDT
Eze 10:11 went in whatever direction the head f, H7155
Eze 40: 9 The portico of the gateway f the temple. H4946
Eze 40:16 the openings all around f inward. H4200
Eze 40:31 Its portico f the outer court; palm trees H448
Eze 40:34 Its portico f the outer court; palm trees H4200
Eze 40:37 Its portico f the outer court; palm trees H4200
Eze 42: 2 whose door f north was a hundred H448+7156
Eze 42: 3 gallery f gallery at the three levels. H448+7156
Eze 47: 1 for the temple f east). The water was H7156
Ac 25:16 before they have f their G2848+4725+2400
Ro 4:19 he f the fact that his body was as good as G2917
Heb 11:36 Some f jeers and flogging, and G4278+3284

FACEDOWN (20) [FACE]

Ge 17: 3 Abram fell f, and God said to him, H6584+7156
Ge 17:17 Abraham fell f; he laughed and H6584+7156
Lev 9:24 they shouted for joy and fell f. H6584+7156
Nu 14: 5 and Aaron fell f in front of the H6584+7156
Nu 16: 4 When Moses heard this, he fell f. H6584+7156
Nu 16:22 and Aaron fell f and cried out, H6584+7156
Nu 16:45 to them at once." And they fell f. H6584+7156
Nu 20: 6 to the tent of meeting and fell f, H6584+7156
Nu 22:31 So he bowed low and fell f. H2556+4200+678

Jos 5:14 Then Joshua fell f to the ground in H448+7156
Jos 7: 6 clothes and fell f to the ground H6584+7156
1Sa 17:49 and he fell f on the ground. H6584+7156
1Ch 21:16 elders, clothed in sackcloth, fell f. H6584+7156
Eze 1:28 I saw it, I fell f, and I heard the H6584+7156
Eze 3:23 by the Kebar River, and I fell f. H6584+7156
Eze 9: 8 I was left alone, I fell f, crying out, H6584+7156
Eze 11:13 Then I fell f and cried out in a loud H6584+7156
Eze 43: 3 seen by the Kebar River, and I fell f. H448+7156
Eze 44: 4 the temple of the LORD, and I fell f. H448+7156
Mt 17: 6 they fell f to the ground, terrified. G2093+4725

FACES (62) [FACE]

Ge 9:23 Their f were turned the other way so that H7156
Ge 42: 6 down to him with their f to the ground. H678
Nu 21:11 wilderness that f Moab toward the H6584+7156
Jos 15: 7 which f the Pass of Adummim south of H5790
Jos 18:17 to Geliloth, which f the Pass of Adummim H5790
Jdg 13:20 his wife fell with their f to the ground. H7156
Jdg 16: 3 to the top of the hill that f Hebron. H6584+7156
1Sa 26: 1 hill of Hakilah, which f Jeshimon?" H6584+7156
1Ki 7: 9 size and smoothed on their inner and outer f. AIT
1Ch 12: 8 Their f were the faces of lions, and they H7156
1Ch 12: 8 Their faces were the f of lions, and they H7156
2Ch 7: 3 on the pavement with their f to the ground, H678
2Ch 29: 6 They turned their f away from the LORD's H7156
Ne 8: 6 the LORD with their f to the ground. H678
Job 40:13 dust together; shroud their f in the grave. H7156
Ps 34: 5 their f are never covered with shame. H7156
Ps 83:16 Cover their f with shame, LORD, so that H7156
Ps 104:15 oil to make their f shine, and bread that H7156
Isa 3: 9 The look on their f testifies against them H7156
Isa 3:15 my people and grinding the f of the poor?" H7156
Isa 6: 2 With two wings they covered their f, with H7156
Isa 13: 8 look aghast at each other, their f aflame. H7156
Isa 25: 8 LORD will wipe away the tears from all f; H7156
Isa 29:22 ashamed; no longer will their f grow pale. H7156
Isa 49:23 down before you with their f to the ground; H678
Isa 53: 3 people hide their f he was despised, H7156
Jer 2:27 turned their backs to me and not their f; H7156
Jer 5: 3 They made their f harder than stone and H7156
Jer 32:33 turned their backs to me and not their f; H7156
Jer 50: 5 the way to Zion and turn their f toward it. H7156
Jer 51:51 been insulted and shame covers our f, H7156
Eze 1: 6 each of them had four f and four wings. H7156
Eze 1: 8 All four of them had f and wings, H7156
Eze 1:10 Their f looked like this: Each of the four H7156
Eze 1:11 Such were their f. They each had two H7156
Eze 1:15 beside each creature with its four f. H7156
Eze 8:16 of the LORD and their f toward the east, H7156
Eze 9: 2 the upper gate, which f north, each with a H7155
Eze 10:14 Each of the cherubim had four f: One face H7156
Eze 10:21 Each had four f and four wings, and under H7156
Eze 10:22 Their f had the same appearance as those H7156
Eze 11: 1 gate of the house of the LORD that f east. H7155
Eze 14: 3 put wicked stumbling blocks before their f. H7156
Eze 14: 4 block before their f and then go to a H7156
Eze 14: 7 block before their f and then go to a H7156
Eze 27:35 with horror and their f are distorted with H7156
Eze 40:10 the f of the projecting walls on each NDT
Eze 40:14 He measured along the f of the projecting NDT
Eze 40:16 The f of the projecting walls were decorated NDT
Eze 40:26 tree decorations on the f of the projecting H448
Eze 41:18 with cherubim. Each cherub had two f: H7156
Mic 3: 7 will all cover their f because there is no H8559
Mal 2: 3 I will smear on your f the dung from your H7156
Mt 6:16 they disfigure their f to show others they G4725
Mt 23:13 of the kingdom of heaven in people's f. G1869
Lk 24: 5 bowed down with their f to the ground, G4725
Lk 24:17 They stood still, their f downcast. G5034
2Co 3:18 who with unveiled f contemplate the G4725
Rev 7:11 fell down on their f before the throne and G2585
Rev 9: 7 and their f resembled human faces. G4725
Rev 9: 7 and their faces resembled human f. G4725
Rev 11:16 fell on their f and worshiped God, G4725

FACING (45) [FACE]

Jos 8:33 f the Levitical priests who carried it. H5584
Jos 18:14 From the hill f Beth Horon on the H6584+7156
Jos 18:16 foot of the hill f the Valley of Ben H6584+7156
Jos 19:46 Jarkon and Rakkon, with the area f Joppa. H4578
1Sa 13:18 the Valley of Zeboyim f the wilderness. H2025
1Sa 17:21 drawing up their lines f each other. H7925+5120
1Sa 26: 3 on the hill of Hakilah f Jeshimon, H6584+7156
1Ki 7: 4 in sets of three, f each other. H4691+448+4691
1Ki 7: 5 in sets of three, f each other. H4691+448+4691
1Ki 7:25 on twelve bulls, three f north, three facing H7155
1Ki 7:25 facing north, three f west, three facing H7155
1Ki 7:25 three f south and three facing east. H7155
1Ki 7:25 three facing south and three f east. H7155
1Ki 22:35 propped up in his chariot f the Arameans. H5790
2Ki 2: 7 f the place where Elijah and Elisha H4946+5584
2Ch 3:13 They stood on their feet, f the main hall. H7156
2Ch 4: 4 on twelve bulls, three f north, three facing H7155
2Ch 4: 4 facing north, three f west, three facing H7155
2Ch 4: 4 three f south and three facing east. H7155
2Ch 4: 4 three facing south and three f east. H7155
2Ch 18:34 up in his chariot f the Arameans until H5790
Ne 3:19 from a point f the ascent to the armory as H5584
Est 5: 1 his royal throne in the hall, f the entrance. H5790
Eze 40: 7 next to the portico f the temple was one H4946
Eze 40:14 was up to the portico f the courtyard. AIT
Eze 40:22 measurements as those of the gate f east. H7156
Eze 40:23 a gate to the inner court f the north gate, H5584
Eze 40:27 The inner court also had a gate f south H2006
Eze 40:44 at the side of the north gate and f south, H7156
Eze 40:44 at the side of the south gate and f north. H7156
Eze 40:45 "The room f south is for the priests who H7156
Eze 40:46 the room f north is for the priests who H7156
Eze 41:12 The building f the temple courtyard H448+7156
Eze 41:15 of the building f the courtyard at the H448+7156
Eze 41:15 inner sanctuary and the portico f the court, AIT
Eze 42:13 and south rooms f the temple H448+7156
Eze 43: 1 the man brought me to the gate f east, H7155
Eze 43: 4 the temple through the gate f east. H7156
Eze 44: 1 the sanctuary, the one f east, and it was H7155
Eze 46: 1 of the inner court f east is to be shut on H7155
Eze 46:12 the gate f east is to be opened for him. H7155
Eze 46:19 of the gate to the sacred rooms f north, H7155
Eze 47: 2 the outside to the outer gate f east, H7155
Ac 20:23 me that prison and hardships are f me. G3531
Ac 27:12 in Crete, f both southwest and northwest. G1063

FACT (35) [FACTS]

Ge 45:26 "Joseph is still alive! In f, he is ruler of all H3954
Ge 47:18 hide from our lord the f that since our money AIT
2Sa 13:15 In f, he hated her more than he had loved H3954
2Ki 8:10 revealed to me that he will in f die." H4637+4637
Ezr 5:17 if King Cyrus did in f issue a decree to A10029
Mk 3:27 In f, no one can enter a strong man's house G247
Mk 7:25 In f, as soon as she heard about him, G247
Mk 12:22 In f, none of the seven left any children G2779
Jn 4: 2 although in f it was not Jesus who G2793
Jn 4:18 The f is, you have had five husbands, and G1142
Jn 9:37 have now seen him; in f, he is the one G2779
Jn 10: 5 follow a stranger; in f, they will run away G247
Jn 16: 2 of the synagogue; in f, the time is coming G247
Jn 16:32 is coming and in f has come when you will AIT
Jn 18:37 In f, the reason I was born and G1650+4047
Ro 4: 2 in f, Abraham was justified by works, he G1142
Ro 4:19 he faced the f that his body was as good G2917
1Co 6: 7 The very f that you have lawsuits among G4022
1Co 10: 1 For I do not want you to be ignorant of the f G51
1Co 12:18 But in f God has placed the parts in the G3815
1Co 15:15 he did not raise him if in f the dead are not G726
2Co 11:20 In f, you even put up with anyone who G1142
1Th 3: 4 In f, when we were with you, we G2779+1142
1Th 4: 1 order to please God, as in f you are living. G2779
1Th 4:10 And in f, you do love all of God's family G2779
1Th 5:11 each other up, just as in f you are doing. G2779
1Ti 5:15 Some have in f already turned away to G1142
2Ti 3:12 In f, everyone who wants to live a godly G2779
Titus 1:15 In f, both their minds and consciences are G247
Heb 5:12 In f, though by this time you ought G2779+1142
Heb 8: 6 But in f the ministry Jesus has received is G3814
Heb 9:22 In f, the law requires that nearly everything G2779
Heb 13:22 for in f I have written to you quite briefly. G2779
1Jn 3: 4 breaks the law; in f, sin is lawlessness. G2779
1Jn 5: 3 In f, this is love for God: to keep his G1142

FACTIONS (2)

1Ki 16:21 the people of Israel were split into two f; AIT
Gal 5:20 fits of rage, selfish ambition, dissensions, f G146

FACTS (1) [FACT]

Ac 19:36 Therefore, since these f are undeniable, you AIT

FADE (8) [FADED, FADES, FADING]

Dt 4: 9 have seen or let them f from your heart H6073
Job 29:20 My glory will not f; the bow will be ever H2543
Ps 109:23 I f away like an evening shadow; I am H2143
Isa 17: 4 "In that day the glory of Jacob will f; the H1937
Na 1: 4 wither and the blossoms of Lebanon f. H581
Jas 1:11 the rich will f away even while they go G3447
1Pe 1: 4 inheritance that can never perish, spoil or f. G278
1Pe 5: 4 the crown of glory that will never f away. G277

FADED (5) [FADE]

Lev 13: 6 if the sore has f and has not spread H3908
Lev 13:21 it is not more than skin deep and has f, H3910
Lev 13:26 if it is not more than skin deep and has f, H3910
Lev 13:28 has not spread in the skin but has f, H3910
Lev 13:56 the mold has f after the article has been H3908

FADES (2) [FADE]

Ps 65: 8 where evening f, you call forth songs NDT
Ecc 12: 4 are closed and the sound of grinding f; H9164

FADING (5) [FADE]

Pr 7: 9 as the day was f, as the dark of night H6847
Isa 1:30 You will be like an oak with f leaves, like H5570
Isa 28: 1 drunkards, to the f flower, his glorious H5570
Isa 28: 4 That f flower, his glorious beauty, set on H5570
Jer 6: 4 the daylight is f, and the shadows of H7155

FAIL (63) [FAILED, FAILING, FAILINGS, FAILS]

Lev 20: 4 to Molek and if they f to put him to death, H1194
Lev 26:15 abhor my laws and f to carry out all my H1194
Nu 15:22 unintentionally f to keep any of these H4202
Nu 19:13 If they f to purify themselves after touching H4202
Nu 32:23 "But if you f to do this, you will be sinning H4202
2Sa 17:16 cross over without f, or the H6296+6296
1Ki 2: 4 you will never f to have a successor H4162+4200
1Ki 8:25 'You shall never f to have a H4162+4200
1Ki 9: 5 'You shall never f to have a H4162+4200
2Ki 10:10 the house of Ahab will f. H5877+824+2025
1Ch 28:20 He will not f you or forsake you until all H8332
2Ch 6:16 'You shall never f to have a H4162+4200
2Ch 7:18 'You shall never f to have a H4162+4200
2Ch 34:33 they did not f to follow the LORD H6073+4946
Ezr 6: 9 must be given them daily without f, A10712
Ne 9:19 pillar of cloud did not f to guide them on H6073
Est 9:27 join them should without f observe these H6296
Est 9:28 days of Purim should never f to be H6296
Job 11:20 But the eyes of the wicked will f, and H3983
Job 14: 7 and its new shoots will not f. H2532
Job 17: 5 reward, the eyes of their children will f. H3983
Job 21:10 Their bulls never f to breed; their cows H1718
Job 41:12 "I will not f to speak of Leviathan's limbs H3087
Ps 6: 7 with sorrow; they f because of all my foes. H6980
Ps 36: 3 deceitful; they f to act wisely or do good. H2532
Ps 69: 3 My eyes f, looking for my God H3983
Ps 73:26 My flesh and my heart may f, but God is H3983
Ps 89:28 my covenant with him will never f. H586
Ps 89:31 my decrees and f to keep my commands, H4202
Ps 119:82 My eyes f, looking for your promise; I say H3983
Ps 119:123 My eyes f, looking for your salvation H3983
Pr 8:36 But those who f to find me harm H2627
Pr 15:22 Plans f for lack of counsel, but with many H7296
Isa 32:10 the grape harvest will f, and the harvest of H3983
Isa 33:16 will be supplied, and water will not f them. H586
Isa 51: 6 last forever, my righteousness will never f. H3169
Isa 58:11 like a spring whose waters never f. H3941
Jer 14: 6 like jackals; their eyes f for lack of food." H3983
Jer 20:11 They will f and be thoroughly H4202+8505
Jer 33:17 'David will never f to have a man H4162+4200
Jer 33:18 will the Levitical priests ever f to have H4162+4200
Jer 35:19 son of Rekab will never f to have a H4162+4200
La 2:11 My eyes f from weeping, I am in torment H3983
La 3:22 consumed, for his compassions never f. H3983
Eze 2: 5 And whether they listen or f to listen—for H2532
Eze 2: 7 whether they listen or f to listen, for they H2532
Eze 3:11 whether they listen or f to listen. H2532
Eze 30: 6 will fall and her proud strength will f. H3718
Eze 47:12 leaves will not wither, nor will their fruit f. H9462
Hos 9: 2 the people; the new wine will f them. H3950
Hos 13:15 his spring will f and his well dry up. H3312
Zep 3: 5 every new day he does not f, yet the H6372
Mk 8:18 Do you have eyes but f to see, and ears G4024
Mk 8:18 fail to see, and ears but f to hear? G4024
Mk 10:30 will f to receive a hundred times as G1569+3590
Lk 1:37 For no word from God will ever f. G104
Lk 6:42 when you yourself f to see the plank in G4024
Lk 12:33 a treasure in heaven that will never f G444
Lk 18:30 will f to receive many times as G4049+3590
Lk 22:32 you, Simon, that your faith may not f. G1722
Jn 1:20 He did not f to confess, but confessed freely, G766
Ac 5:38 activity is of human origin, it will f. G2907
2Co 13: 5 unless, of course, you f the test? G99+1639

FAILED (24) [FAIL]

Lev 5:16 what they have f to do in regard to the H2627
Jos 2:11 courage f because of you, H4202+7756+6388
Jos 21:45 of all the LORD's good promises to Israel f; H5877
Jos 23:14 the LORD your God gave you has f. H5877
Jos 23:14 promise has been fulfilled; not one has f. H5877
Jdg 8:35 They also f to show any loyalty to the H4202
Jdg 21: 5 tribes of Israel has f to assemble before H4202
Jdg 21: 5 that anyone who f to assemble before H4202
Jdg 21: 8 the tribes of Israel f to assemble before H4202
1Sa 3:13 and he f to restrain them. H4202
1Sa 4:15 whose eyes had f so that he could H7756
1Sa 25:37 his heart f him and he became like a H4637
1Ki 8:56 Not one word has f of all the good H5877
1Ki 15: 5 LORD and had not f to keep any of H6073+4946
2Ki 3:26 to the king of Edom, but they f. H4202+3523
Ezr 10: 8 Anyone who f to appear within three days H4202
Ne 9:17 refused to listen and f to remember the H4202
Job 32:15 no more to say; words have f them. H6980+4946
Ps 77: 8 Has his promise f for all time? H1698
La 4:17 Moreover, our eyes f, looking in vain for H3983
Ro 9: 6 It is not as though God's word had f. G1738
2Co 13: 6 discover that we have not f the test. G1639+99
2Co 13: 7 is right even though we may seem to have f. G99
Jas 5: 4 The wages you f to pay the workers who G691

FAILING (3) [FAIL]

Ge 48:10 Now Israel's eyes were f because of old H3877
Dt 8:11 LORD your God, f to observe his commands H1194
1Sa 12:23 sin against the LORD by f to pray for you. H2532

FAILINGS (1) [FAIL]

Ro 15: 1 to bear with the f of the weak and not to G821

FAILS (14) [FAIL]

Ex 21:33 pit or digs one and f to cover it and an ox H4202
Nu 9:13 not on a journey f to celebrate the H2532
2Ki 10:19 Anyone who f to come will no longer live." H7212
Ps 31:10 my strength f because of my affliction H4173
Ps 38:10 pounds, my strength f me; even the light H6440
Ps 40:12 of my head, and my heart f within me. H6440
Ps 143: 7 my spirit f. Do not hide your face H3983
Ecc 6: 6 years twice over but f to enjoy his H4202
Isa 65:20 the one who f to reach a hundred will be H2627
Jer 15:18 deceptive brook, like a spring that f. H4202+586
Jer 17: 8 a year of drought and never f to bear fruit." H4631
Joel 1:10 the new wine is dried up, the olive oil f. H581

Hab 3:17 though the olive crop **f** and the fields H3950
1Co 13: 8 Love never **f**. But where there are G4406

FAINT (30) [FAINTED, FAINTHEARTED, FAINTING, FAINTS]

1Sa 14:28 That is why the men *are* **f**." H6545
Job 23:16 God *has* **made** my heart **f**; the Almighty H8216
Job 26:14 how **f** the whisper we hear of him! H9066
Ps 6: 2 LORD, for I am **f**; heal me, LORD, H583
Ps 61: 2 I call as my heart *grows* **f**; lead me to the H6494
Ps 77: 3 I meditated, and my spirit *grew* **f**. H6494
Ps 142: 3 When my spirit *grows* **f** within me, it is H6494
Ps 143: 4 So my spirit *grows* **f** within me; my heart H6494
Ecc 12: 4 sound of birds, but all their songs *grow* **f**; H8820
SS 2: 5 me with apples, for I *am* **f** *with* love. H2703
SS 5: 8 Tell him I *am* **f** *with* love. H2703
Isa 15: 4 of Moab cry out, and their hearts *are* **f**. H3760
Isa 29: 8 of drinking, but awakens **f** and thirsty still. H6546
Isa 40:31 grow weary, they will walk and not *be* **f**. H3615
Isa 44:12 strength; he drinks no water and *grows* **f**. H3615
Isa 57:10 of your strength, and so *you did* not **f**. H2703
Isa 57:16 then they *would* **f away** because of me H6494
Jer 8:18 in sorrow, my heart is **f** within me. H1868
Jer 15: 9 mother of seven *will grow* **f** and breathe H581
Jer 31:25 refresh the weary and satisfy the **f**." H5883+1790
La 1:13 He made me desolate, **f** all the day long. H1865
La 1:22 My groans are many and my heart is **f**." H1868
La 2:11 children and infants **f** in the streets of the H6494
La 2:12 as they **f** like the wounded in the streets H6494
La 2:19 who **f** from hunger at every street corner. H6488
La 5:17 Because of this our hearts are **f**, because H1865
Eze 21: 7 every spirit *will become* **f** and every leg H3908
Am 8:13 strong young men *will* **f** because of thirst. H6634
Jnh 4: 8 blazed on Jonah's head so that *he grew* **f**. H6634
Lk 21:26 People *will* **f** from terror, apprehensive of G715

FAINTED (1) [FAINT]

Isa 51:20 Your children *have* **f**; they lie at every H6634

FAINTHEARTED (2) [FAINT, HEART]

Dt 20: 3 *Do* not *be* **f** or afraid; do not panic H8216+4222
Dt 20: 8 shall add, "Is anyone afraid or **f**? H8205+4222

FAINTING (1) [FAINT]

Jer 4:31 I *am* **f**; my life is given over to H6545

FAINTS (2) [FAINT]

Ps 84: 2 My soul yearns, even **f**, for the courts of H3983
Ps 119:81 My soul **f with longing** for your salvation H3983

FAIR (9) [FAIRLY, FAIRNESS]

Jdg 9:16 Have you been **f** to Jerub-Baal and his H3208
Job 26:13 By his breath the skies became **f**; his hand H9185
Pr 1: 3 doing what is right and just and **f**; H4797
Pr 2: 9 understand what is right and just and **f**— H4797
SS 6:10 like the dawn, **f** as the moon, bright as H3637
Hos 10:11 so I will put a yoke on her **f** neck. H3206
Mt 16: 2 'It will be **f weather**, for the sky is red G2304
2Co 6:13 As a **f** exchange—I speak as to my children G899
Col 4: 1 your slaves with what is right and **f**, G2699

FAIR HAVENS (1) [FAIR, HAVEN]

Ac 27: 8 called **F**, near the town *of* **Lasea**. G2816

FAIRLY (5) [FAIR]

Lev 19:15 the great, but judge your neighbor **f**. H928+7406
Dt 1:16 between your people and judge **f**, H7406
Dt 16:18 and they shall judge the people **f**. H7406
Pr 31: 9 Speak up and judge **f**; defend the rights H7406
Eze 18: 8 wrong and judges **f** between two parties. H622

FAIRNESS (1) [FAIR]

Pr 29:14 If a king judges the poor with **f**, his throne H622

FAIRS (KJV) MERCHANDISE, PRODUCTS, WARES

FAITH (259) [FAITHFUL, FAITHFULLY, FAITHFULNESS, FAITHLESS]

Ex 21: 8 because he *has* **broken f** with her. H953
Dt 32:51 is because *both of you* **broke f** with me in H5085
Jos 22:16 'How *could you* **break f** with the H5085+5086
Jdg 9:16 honorably and in **good f** by making H9459
Jdg 9:19 honorably and in **good f** toward H9459
1Sa 14:33 "*You have* **broken f**," he said H953
2Ch 20:20 **Have f** in the LORD your God and you will H586
2Ch 20:20 **have f** in his prophets and you will be H586
Isa 7: 9 If *you do* not **stand firm in** *your* **f**, you will H586
Isa 26: 2 nation may enter, the nation that keeps **f**. H574
Mt 6:30 not much more clothe you—you **of little f**? G3899
Mt 8:10 found anyone in Israel with such great **f**. G4411
Mt 8:26 He replied, "*You of* **little f**, why are you so G3899
Mt 9: 2 When Jesus saw their **f**, he said to the G4411
Mt 9:22 he said, "your **f** has healed you. G4411
Mt 9:29 "According to your **f** let it be done to you"; G4411
Mt 13:58 miracles there because of their **lack of f**. G602
Mt 14:31 "You **of little f**," he said, "why did you G3899
Mt 15:28 said to her, "Woman, you have great **f**! G4411
Mt 16: 8 Jesus asked, "You **of little f**, why are you G3899
Mt 17:20 "Because you have *so* **little f**. Truly I tell G3898
Mt 17:20 if you have **f** as small as a mustard seed G4411
Mt 21:21 if you have **f** and do not doubt, not G4411
Mt 24:10 many *will* **turn away from the f** and will G4997
Mk 2: 5 When Jesus saw their **f**, he said to the G4411
Mk 4:40 you so afraid? Do you still have no **f**?" G4411
Mk 5:34 "Daughter, your **f** has healed you. G4411
Mk 6: 6 He was amazed at their **lack of f**. G602
Mk 10:52 said Jesus, "your **f** has healed you." G4411
Mk 11:22 "Have **f** in God," Jesus answered. G4411
Mk 16:14 he rebuked them *for* their **lack of f** and their G602
Lk 5:20 When Jesus saw their **f**, he said, "Friend G4411
Lk 7: 9 have not found such great **f** even in Israel." G4411
Lk 7:50 to the woman, "Your **f** has saved you; go G4411
Lk 8:25 "Where is your **f**?" he asked his disciples G4411
Lk 8:48 "Daughter, your **f** has healed you. G4411
Lk 12:28 more will he clothe you—you **of little f**! G3899
Lk 17: 5 apostles said to the Lord, "Increase our **f**!" G4411
Lk 17: 6 "If you have **f** as small as a mustard seed G4411
Lk 17:19 "Rise and go; your **f** has made you well." G4411
Lk 18: 8 of Man comes, will he find **f** on the earth?" G4411
Lk 18:42 "Receive your sight; your **f** has healed you." G4411
Lk 22:32 you, Simon, that your **f** may not fail. G4411
Jn 12:42 *they would* not **openly acknowledge** *their* **f** G3933
Ac 3:16 By **f** in the name of Jesus, this man whom G4411
Ac 3:16 Jesus' name and the **f** that comes through G4411
Ac 6: 5 a man full *of* **f** and of the Holy Spirit G4411
Ac 6: 7 of priests became obedient *to* the **f**. G4411
Ac 11:24 full of the Holy Spirit and **f**, and a great G4411
Ac 13: 8 tried to turn the proconsul from the **f**. G4411
Ac 14: 9 saw that he had **f** to be healed G4411
Ac 14:22 encouraging them to remain true *to* the **f**. G4411
Ac 14:27 had opened a door *of* **f** to the Gentiles. G4411
Ac 15: 9 them, for he purified their hearts *by* **f**. G4411
Ac 16: 5 were strengthened *in* the **f** and grew daily G4411
Ac 20:21 repentance and have **f** in our Lord Jesus. G4411
Ac 24:24 to him as he spoke about **f** in Christ Jesus. G4411
Ac 26:18 those who are sanctified *by* **f** in me. G4411
Ac 27:25 for **I have f** in God that it will happen just G4409
Ro 1: 5 the obedience *that comes from* **f** for his G4411
Ro 1: 8 because your **f** is being reported all over G4411
Ro 1:12 be mutually encouraged by each other's **f**. G4411
Ro 1:17 that is **by f from first to last**, G1666+4411+1650+4411
Ro 1:17 "The righteous will live by **f**." G4411
Ro 3:22 is given through **f** in Jesus Christ to all G4411
Ro 3:25 of his blood—to be received by **f**. G4411
Ro 3:26 who justifies those who have **f** in Jesus. G4411
Ro 3:27 because of the law that *requires* **f**. G4411
Ro 3:28 person is justified *by* **f** apart from the G4411
Ro 3:30 the circumcised by **f** and the G4411
Ro 3:30 the uncircumcised through that same **f**. G4411
Ro 3:31 nullify the law by this **f**? Not at all! G4411
Ro 4: 5 their **f** is credited as righteousness. G4411
Ro 4: 9 that Abraham's **f** was credited to him G4411
Ro 4:11 that he had *by* **f** while he was still G4411
Ro 4:12 in the footsteps *of* the **f** that our father G4411
Ro 4:13 the righteousness that *comes by* **f**. G4411
Ro 4:14 **f** means nothing and the promise is G4411
Ro 4:16 the promise comes by **f**, so that it may be G4411
Ro 4:16 also to those who have the **f** of Abraham. G4411
Ro 4:19 Without weakening *in* his **f**, he faced the G4411
Ro 4:20 was strengthened *in* his **f** and gave glory G4411
Ro 5: 1 since we have been justified through **f** G4411
Ro 5: 2 have gained access *by* **f** into this grace in G4411
Ro 9:30 obtained it, a righteousness that is by **f**; G4411
Ro 9:32 they pursued it not by **f** but as if it were by G4411
Ro 10: 6 But the righteousness that is by **f** says: "Do G4411
Ro 10: 8 the message *concerning* **f** that we G4411
Ro 10:10 your mouth *that you* **profess** *your* **f** and are G3933
Ro 10:17 **f** comes from hearing the message G4411
Ro 11:20 because of unbelief, and you stand *by* **f**. G4411
Ro 12: 3 accordance with the **f** God has distributed G4411
Ro 12: 6 then prophesy in accordance with your **f**; G4411
Ro 14: 1 Accept the one whose **f** is weak, without G4411
Ro 14: 2 One person's **f** *allows them* to eat G4409
Ro 14: 2 another, whose **f** is weak, eats only NDT
Ro 14:23 because their eating is not from **f**; and G4411
Ro 14:23 that does not come from **f** is sin. G4411
Ro 16:26 to the obedience *that comes from* **f**— G4411
1Co 2: 5 so that your **f** might not rest on human G4411
1Co 7:22 was a slave *when* **called to f** in the Lord is G2813
1Co 12: 9 to another **f** by the same Spirit, to another G4411
1Co 13: 2 if I have a **f** that can move mountains, G4411
1Co 13:13 these three remain: **f**, hope and love. G4411
1Co 15:14 our preaching is useless and so is your **f**. G4411
1Co 15:17 not been raised, your **f** is futile; you are G4411
1Co 16:13 stand firm in the **f**; be courageous; G4411
2Co 1:24 Not that we lord it over your **f**, but we work G4411
2Co 1:24 your joy, because it is *by* **f** you stand firm. G4411
2Co 4:13 Since we have that same spirit *of* **f**, we G4411
2Co 5: 7 For we live by **f**, not by sight. G4411
2Co 8: 7 you excel in everything—*in* **f**, in speech, G4411
2Co 10:15 hope is that, as your **f** continues to grow G4411
2Co 13: 5 yourselves to see whether you are in the **f**; G4411
Gal 1:23 us is now preaching the **f** he once tried to G4411
Gal 2:16 works of the law, but by **f** in Jesus Christ. G4411
Gal 2:16 *have* **put** *our* **f** in Christ Jesus that we may G4409
Gal 2:16 may be justified by **f** in Christ and not by G4411
Gal 2:20 the body, I live by **f** in the Son of God G4411
Gal 3: 7 that those who have **f** are children of G4411
Gal 3: 8 that God would justify the Gentiles by **f**, G4411
Gal 3: 9 So those who rely on **f** are blessed along G4411
Gal 3: 9 along with Abraham, the *man of* **f**. G4412
Gal 3:11 because "the righteous will live by **f**." G4411
Gal 3:12 The law is not based on **f**; on the contrary G4411
Gal 3:14 so that by **f** we might receive the promise G4411
Gal 3:22 being given through **f** in Jesus Christ G4411
Gal 3:23 Before the coming *of* this **f**, we were held G4411
Gal 3:23 locked up until the **f** that was to come G4411
Gal 3:24 came that we might be justified by **f**. G4411
Gal 3:25 Now that this **f** has come, we are no G4411
Gal 3:26 you are all children of God through **f**, G4411
Gal 5: 5 we eagerly await by **f** the righteousness G4411
Gal 5: 6 thing that counts is **f** expressing itself G4411
Eph 1:15 since I heard *about* your **f** in the Lord G4411
Eph 2: 8 been saved, through **f**—and this is not G4411
Eph 3:12 In him and through **f** in him we may G4411
Eph 3:17 Christ may dwell in your hearts through **f**. G4411
Eph 4: 5 one Lord, one **f**, one baptism; G4411
Eph 4:13 we all reach unity *in* the **f** and in the G4411
Eph 6:16 take up the shield *of* **f**, with which you can G4411
Eph 6:23 love with **f** from God the Father and G4411
Php 1:25 of you for your progress and joy *in* the **f**, G4411
Php 1:27 together as one *for* the **f** of the gospel G4411
Php 2:17 sacrifice and service *coming from* your **f**, G4411
Php 3: 9 that which is through **f** in Christ—the G4411
Php 3: 9 that comes from God on the basis of **f**. G4411
Col 1: 4 we have heard *of* your **f** in Christ Jesus G4411
Col 1: 5 the **f** and love that spring from the hope NDT
Col 1:23 if you continue *in* your **f**, established and G4411
Col 2: 5 you are and how firm your **f** in Christ is. G4411
Col 2: 7 strengthened *in* the **f** as you were taught G4411
Col 2:12 him through your **f** in the working of God G4411
1Th 1: 3 God and Father your work *produced by* **f**, G4411
1Th 1: 8 your **f** in God has become known G4411
1Th 3: 2 to strengthen and encourage you in your **f**, G4411
1Th 3: 5 no longer, I sent to find out *about* your **f**. G4411
1Th 3: 6 brought good news *about* your **f** and love. G4411
1Th 3: 7 encouraged about you because of your **f**. G4411
1Th 3:10 again and supply what is lacking *in* your **f**. G4411
1Th 5: 8 putting on **f** and love as a breastplate G4411
2Th 1: 3 because your **f** is growing more and more G4411
2Th 1: 4 your perseverance and **f** in all the G4411
2Th 1:11 your every deed *prompted by* **f**. G4411
2Th 3: 2 evil people, for not everyone has **f**. G4411
1Ti 1: 2 To Timothy my true son in the **f**: Grace G4411
1Ti 1: 4 than advancing God's work—which is by **f**. G4411
1Ti 1: 5 a good conscience and a sincere **f**. G4411
1Ti 1:14 along with the **f** and love that are in Christ G4411
1Ti 1:19 holding on *to* **f** and a good conscience G4411
1Ti 1:19 suffered shipwreck with regard to the **f**. G4411
1Ti 2:15 if they continue in **f**, love and holiness G4411
1Ti 3: 9 of the deep truths *of* the **f** with a clear G4411
1Ti 3:13 great assurance in their **f** in Christ Jesus. G4411
1Ti 4: 1 will abandon the **f** and follow deceiving G4411
1Ti 4: 6 on the truths *of* the **f** and of the good G4411
1Ti 4:12 in conduct, in love, in **f** and in purity. G4411
1Ti 5: 8 has denied the **f** and is worse than an G4411
1Ti 6:10 wandered from the **f** and pierced G4411
1Ti 6:11 godliness, **f**, love, endurance and G4411
1Ti 6:12 Fight the good fight *of* the **f**. Take hold of G4411
1Ti 6:21 in so doing have departed from the **f**. G4411
2Ti 1: 5 I am reminded *of* your sincere **f**, which first G4411
2Ti 1:13 teaching, with **f** and love in Christ Jesus. G4411
2Ti 2:18 and they destroy the **f** of some. G4411
2Ti 2:22 pursue righteousness, **f**, love and peace, G4411
2Ti 3: 8 as far as the **f** is concerned, are G4411
2Ti 3:10 way of life, my purpose, **f**, patience, love, G4411
2Ti 3:15 salvation through **f** in Christ Jesus. G4411
2Ti 4: 7 I have finished the race, I have kept the **f**. G4411
Titus 1: 1 Christ to further the **f** of God's elect and G4411
Titus 1: 4 my true son in our common **f**: Grace and G4411
Titus 1:13 sharply, so that they will be sound in the **f** G4411
Titus 2: 2 sound *in* **f**, in love and in endurance. G4411
Titus 3:15 Greet those who love us in the **f**. Grace be G4411
Phm 5 holy people and your **f** in the Lord Jesus. G4411
Phm 6 with us *in* the **f** may be effective G4411
Heb 4: 2 did not share the **f** of those who obeyed. G4411
Heb 4:14 let us hold firmly *to* the **f** we **profess**. G3934
Heb 6: 1 acts that lead to death, and *of* **f** in God, G4411
Heb 6:12 those who through **f** and patience inherit G4411
Heb 10:22 with the full assurance *that* **f** *brings*, G4411
Heb 10:38 "But my righteous one will live by **f**. G4411
Heb 10:39 but *to those who have* **f** and are saved. G4411
Heb 11: 1 Now **f** is confidence in what we hope for G4411
Heb 11: 3 *By* **f** we understand that the universe was G4411
Heb 11: 4 *By* **f** Abel brought God a better offering G4411
Heb 11: 4 By **f** he was commended as righteous G4005S
Heb 11: 4 And by **f** Abel still speaks, even though G899S
Heb 11: 5 *By* **f** Enoch was taken from this life, so that G4411
Heb 11: 6 And without **f** it is impossible to please G4411
Heb 11: 7 *By* **f** Noah, when warned about things not G4411
Heb 11: 7 By **his f** he condemned the world and G4005S
Heb 11: 7 righteousness that is in keeping with **f**. G4411
Heb 11: 8 *By* **f** Abraham, when called to go to a G4411
Heb 11: 9 *By* **f** he made his home in the promised G4411
Heb 11:11 And *by* **f** even Sarah, who was past G4411
Heb 11:13 were still living by **f** when they died. G4411
Heb 11:17 *By* **f** Abraham, when God tested him G4411
Heb 11:20 *By* **f** Isaac blessed Jacob and Esau in G4411
Heb 11:21 *By* **f** Jacob, when he was dying, blessed G4411
Heb 11:22 *By* **f** Joseph, when his end was near G4411
Heb 11:23 *By* **f** Moses' parents hid him for three G4411
Heb 11:24 *By* **f** Moses, when he had grown up G4411
Heb 11:27 *By* **f** he left Egypt, not fearing the king's G4411
Heb 11:28 *By* **f** he kept the Passover and the G4411
Heb 11:29 *By* **f** the people passed through the Red G4411
Heb 11:30 *By* **f** the walls of Jericho fell, after the G4411

Heb 11:31 *By* **f** the prostitute Rahab, because she G4411
Heb 11:33 who through **f** conquered kingdoms G4411
Heb 11:39 These were all commended for their **f**, yet G4411
Heb 12: 2 on Jesus, the pioneer and perfecter *of* **f**. G4411
Heb 13: 7 of their way of life and imitate their **f**. G4411
Jas 1: 3 that the testing *of* your **f** produces G4411
Jas 2: 5 the world to be rich in **f** and to inherit the G4411
Jas 2:14 claims to have **f** but has no deeds? G4411
Jas 2:14 has no deeds? Can such **f** save them? G4411
Jas 2:17 In the same way, **f** by itself, if it is not G4411
Jas 2:18 will say, "You have **f**; I have deeds." G4411
Jas 2:18 Show me your **f** without deeds, and I will G4411
Jas 2:18 I will show you my **f** by my deeds. G4411
Jas 2:20 you want evidence that **f** without deeds is G4411
Jas 2:22 You see that his **f** and his actions were G4411
Jas 2:22 his **f** was made complete by what he G4411
Jas 2:24 by what they do and not by **f** alone. G4411
Jas 2:26 spirit is dead, so **f** without deeds is dead. G4411
Jas 5:15 And the prayer *offered in* **f** will make the G4411
1Pe 1: 5 who through **f** are shielded by God's G4411
1Pe 1: 7 that the proven genuineness *of* your **f**— G4411
1Pe 1: 9 you are receiving the end result *of* your **f**, G4411
1Pe 1:21 and so your **f** and hope are in God. G4411
1Pe 5: 9 standing firm in the **f**, because you know G4411
2Pe 1: 1 have received a **f** as precious as ours: G4411
2Pe 1: 5 every effort to add to your **f** goodness; G4411
1Jn 5: 4 that has overcome the world, even our **f**. G4411
Jude 3 to contend for the **f** that was once for all G4411
Jude 20 up *in* your most holy **f** and praying G4411
Rev 2:13 You did not renounce your **f** in me, not G4411
Rev 2:19 your love and **f**, your service and G4411

FAITHFUL (114) [FAITH]

Nu 12: 7 my servant Moses; he *is* **f** in all my house. H586
Dt 7: 9 God is God; he is the **f** God, keeping his H586
Dt 32: 4 A **f** God who does no wrong, upright and H575
Dt 33: 8 Urim belong to your **f** servant. H2883
1Sa 2: 9 He will guard the feet of his **f servants** H2883
1Sa 2:35 I will raise up for myself a **f** priest, who will H586
2Sa 20:19 We are the peaceful and **f** *in* Israel. You are H573
2Sa 22:26 "To the **f** you show yourself faithful, to the H2883
2Sa 22:26 "To the faithful *you* **show yourself f**, to the H2874
1Ki 3: 6 because *he was* **f** to you and H2143+928+622
2Ch 6:41 may your **f people** rejoice in your H2883
2Ch 31:18 For they were **f** *in* consecrating themselves H575
2Ch 31:20 good and right and **f** before the LORD his H622
Ne 9: 8 You found his heart **f** to you, and you made H586
Ps 4: 3 has set apart his **f servant** for himself; H2883
Ps 12: 1 for no *one* is **f** anymore; those who H2883
Ps 16:10 will you let your **f** *one* see decay. H2883
Ps 18:25 To the **f** you show yourself faithful, to the H2883
Ps 18:25 To the faithful *you* **show yourself f**, to the H2874
Ps 25:10 LORD are loving and **f** toward those who H622
Ps 30: 4 the LORD, you his **f people**; praise his holy H2883
Ps 31: 5 my spirit; deliver me, LORD, my **f** God. H622
Ps 31:23 the LORD, all his **f people**! The LORD H2883
Ps 32: 6 let all the **f** pray to you while you H2883
Ps 33: 4 LORD is right and true; he is **f** in all he does. H575
Ps 37:28 the just and will not forsake his **f** *ones*. H2883
Ps 43: 3 Send me your light and your **f care**, let H622
Ps 52: 9 you in the presence of your **f people**. H2883
Ps 78: 8 whose spirits *were* not **f** to him. H586
Ps 78:37 *they were* not **f** to his covenant. H586
Ps 85: 8 his people, his **f servants**—but let them H2883
Ps 86: 2 Guard my life, for I am **f** to you; save your H2883
Ps 89:19 in a vision, to your **f** *people* you said: H2883
Ps 89:24 My **f** love will be with him, and through my H575
Ps 89:37 like the moon, the **f** witness in the sky." H586
Ps 97:10 the lives of his **f** *ones* and delivers them H2883
Ps 101: 6 My eyes will be on the **f** *in* the land, that H586
Ps 111: 7 The works of his hands are **f** and just; all H622
Ps 116:15 of the LORD is the death of his **f servants**. H2883
Ps 132: 9 may your **f people** sing for joy. H2883
Ps 132:16 her **f people** will ever sing for joy. H2883
Ps 145:10 praise you, LORD; your **f people** extol you. H2883
Ps 145:13 in all he promises and **f** in all he does. H2883
Ps 145:17 in all his ways and **f** in all he does. H2883
Ps 146: 6 everything in them—he remains **f** forever. H622
Ps 148:14 the praise of all his **f servants**, of Israel, H2883
Ps 149: 1 his praise in the assembly of his **f people**. H2883
Ps 149: 5 Let his **f people** rejoice in this honor and H2883
Ps 149: 9 this is the glory of all his **f people**. H2883
Pr 2: 8 the just and protects the way of his **f** *ones*. H2883
Pr 20: 6 unfailing love, but a **f** person who can find? H574
Pr 28:20 A **f** person will be richly blessed, but one H575
Pr 31:26 **f** instruction is on her tongue. H2876
Isa 1:21 See how the **f** city has become a prostitute H586
Isa 1:26 called the City of Righteousness, the **F** City." H586
Isa 49: 7 of the LORD, who is **f**, the Holy One of Israel H586
Isa 55: 3 with you, my **f** love promised to David. H586
Jer 3:12 no longer, for I am **f**,' declares the LORD, H2883
Jer 42: 5 LORD be a true and **f** witness against us if H586
Eze 43:11 them so that *they may be* **f** *to* its design H9068
Eze 48:11 who *were* **f** *in* serving me and did not go H9068
Hos 11:12 against God, even against the **f** Holy One. H586
Joel 2:23 you the autumn rains because he is **f**. H7407
Mic 7: 2 The **f** have been swept from the land; not H2883
Mic 7:20 You will be **f** to Jacob, and show love to H622
Zec 8: 3 Then Jerusalem will be called the **F** City H622
Zec 8: 8 I will be **f** and righteous to them as H622
Mt 1:19 Joseph her husband was **f to the law**, G1465
Mt 24:45 "Who then is the **f** and wise servant G4412
Mt 25:21 replied, 'Well done, good and **f** servant! G4412
Mt 25:21 You have been **f** with a few things; I will G4412
Mt 25:23 replied, 'Well done, good and **f** servant! G4412
Mt 25:23 You have been **f** with a few things; I will G4412
Lk 12:42 "Who then is the **f** and wise manager G4412
Ro 12:12 in hope, patient in affliction, **f** in prayer. G4674
1Co 1: 9 God is **f**, who has called you into G4412
1Co 4: 2 who have been given a trust must prove **f**. G4412
1Co 4:17 my son whom I love, who is **f** in the Lord. G4412
1Co 10:13 And God is **f**; he will not let you be G4412
2Co 1:18 But as surely as God is **f**, our message to G4412
Eph 1: 1 people in Ephesus, the **f** in Christ Jesus: G4412
Eph 6:21 the dear brother and **f** servant in the Lord G4412
Col 1: 2 the **f** brothers and sisters in Christ: G4412
Col 1: 7 who is a **f** minister of Christ on our behalf G4412
Col 4: 7 a **f** minister and fellow servant in the Lord. G4412
Col 4: 9 with Onesimus, our **f** and dear brother G4412
1Th 5:24 The one who calls you is **f**, and he will do G4412
2Th 3: 3 But the Lord is **f**, and he will strengthen G4412
1Ti 2: 7 a true and **f** teacher of the Gentiles. G237
1Ti 3: 2 reproach, **f to his wife** G1651+1222+467
1Ti 3:12 must be **f to his wife** and G1651+1222+467
1Ti 5: 9 has been **f to her husband**, G1651+467+1222
2Ti 2:13 he remains **f**, for he cannot disown G4412
Titus 1: 6 **f to his wife**, a man G1651+1222+467
Heb 2:17 become a merciful and **f** high priest in G4412
Heb 3: 2 He was **f** to the one who appointed him G4412
Heb 3: 2 just as Moses was **f** in all God's house. NDT
Heb 3: 5 "Moses was **f** as a servant in all God's G4412
Heb 3: 6 But Christ is **f** as the Son over God's house NDT
Heb 8: 9 because they *did* not **remain f** to my G1844
Heb 10:23 we profess, for he who promised is **f**. G4412
Heb 11:11 she considered him **f** who had made the G4412
1Pe 4:10 as **f** stewards of God's grace in its various G2819
1Pe 4:19 themselves to their **f** Creator and continue G4412
1Pe 5:12 whom I regard as a **f** brother, I have G4412
1Jn 1: 9 he is **f** and just and will forgive us our sins G4412
3Jn 5 you are **f** in what you are doing for the G4412
Rev 1: 5 who is the **f** witness, the firstborn G4412
Rev 2:10 Be **f**, even to the point of death, and I will G4412
Rev 2:13 days of Antipas, my **f** witness, who was G4412
Rev 3:14 of the Amen, the **f** and true witness, the G4412
Rev 14:12 his commands and remain **f** to Jesus. G4411
Rev 17:14 will be his called, chosen and **f** *followers*." G4412
Rev 19:11 whose rider is called **F** and True. G4412

FAITHFULLY (24) [FAITH]

Ge 5:22 Enoch **walked f** with God 300 years and H2143
Ge 5:24 Enoch **walked f** with God; then he was no H2143
Ge 6: 9 of his time, and he **walked f** with God. H2143
Ge 17: 1 **walk** before me **f** and be blameless. H2143
Ge 24:40 before whom *I have* **walked f**, will send H2143
Ge 48:15 my fathers Abraham and Isaac **walked f**, H2143
Dt 11:13 So if *you* **f obey** the commands I H9048+9048
Jos 2:14 treat you kindly and **f** when the LORD gives H622
1Sa 12:24 LORD and serve him **f** with all your H928+622
1Ki 2: 4 if they walk **f** before me with all H928+622
1Ki 8:25 they do to **walk** before me **f** as you have H2143
1Ki 9: 4 if *you* **walk** before me **f** with integrity of H2143
2Ki 20: 3 walked before you **f** and with H928+622
2Ch 7:17 if *you* **walk** before me **f** as David your H2143
2Ch 19: 9 "You must serve **f** and wholeheartedly H928+575
2Ch 31:12 Then they **f** brought in the H928+575
2Ch 31:15 assisted him **f** in the towns of the H928+575
2Ch 32: 1 After all that Hezekiah had *so* **f** done H622
2Ch 34:12 The workers labored **f**. Over them to H928+575
Ne 9:33 you have acted **f**, while we acted wickedly. H622
Ne 13:14 out what I have *so* **f** done for the house H2876
Isa 38: 3 walked before you **f** and with H928+622
Jer 23:28 let the one who has my word speak it **f**. H622
Eze 18: 9 my decrees and **f** keeps my laws. H6913+622

FAITHFULNESS (68) [FAITH]

Ge 24:27 his kindness and **f** to my master. H622
Ge 24:49 you will show kindness and **f** to my master, H622
Ge 32:10 all the kindness and **f** you have shown your H622
Ge 47:29 that you will show me kindness and **f**. H622
Ex 34: 6 slow to anger, abounding in love and **f**, H622
Jos 24:14 "Now fear the LORD and serve him with all **f** H622
1Sa 26:23 everyone for their righteousness and **f**. H575
2Sa 2: 6 May the LORD now show you kindness and **f** H622
2Sa 15:20 May the LORD show you kindness and **f**." H622
Ps 26: 3 love and have lived in reliance on your **f**. H622
Ps 30: 9 the dust praise you? Will it proclaim your **f**? H622
Ps 36: 5 reaches to the heavens, your **f** to the skies. H575
Ps 40:10 I speak of your **f** and your saving help. H575
Ps 40:10 your love and your **f** from the great H622
Ps 40:11 may your love and **f** always protect me. H622
Ps 51: 6 Yet you desired **f** even in the womb; you H622
Ps 54: 5 who slander me; in your **f** destroy them. H622
Ps 57: 3 God sends forth his love and his **f**. H622
Ps 57:10 to the heavens; your **f** reaches to the skies. H622
Ps 61: 7 appoint your love and **f** to protect him. H622
Ps 71:22 I will praise you with the harp for your **f**, my H622
Ps 85:10 Love and **f** meet together; righteousness H622
Ps 85:11 **F** springs forth from the earth, and H622
Ps 86:11 that I may rely on your **f**; give me an H622
Ps 86:15 slow to anger, abounding in love and **f**. H622
Ps 88:11 declared in the grave, your **f** in Destruction? H575
Ps 89: 1 mouth I will make your **f** known through all H575
Ps 89: 2 have established your **f** in heaven itself. H575
Ps 89: 5 your **f** too, in the assembly of the holy H575
Ps 89: 8 are mighty, and your **f** surrounds you. H575
Ps 89:14 of your throne; love and **f** go before you. H622
Ps 89:33 love from him, nor will I ever betray my **f**. H575
Ps 89:49 which in your **f** you swore to David? H575
Ps 91: 4 his **f** will be your shield and rampart. H622
Ps 92: 2 love in the morning and your **f** at night, H575
Ps 96:13 in righteousness and the peoples in his **f**. H575
Ps 98: 3 remembered his love and his **f** to Israel; H575
Ps 100: 5 his **f** continues through all generations. H575
Ps 108: 4 the heavens; your **f** reaches to the skies. H622
Ps 111: 8 ever, enacted in **f** and uprightness. H622
Ps 115: 1 be the glory, because of your love and **f**. H622
Ps 117: 2 and the **f** *of* the LORD endures forever. H622
Ps 119:30 I have chosen the way of **f**; I have set my H575
Ps 119:75 that *in* **f** you have afflicted me. H575
Ps 119:90 Your **f** continues through all generations H575
Ps 138: 2 name for your unfailing love and your **f**, H622
Ps 143: 1 in your **f** and righteousness come to my H575
Pr 3: 3 Let love and **f** never leave you; bind them H622
Pr 14:22 who plan what is good find love and **f**. H622
Pr 16: 6 Through love and **f** sin is atoned for H622
Pr 20:28 Love and **f** keep a king safe; through love H622
Isa 11: 5 will be his belt and **f** the sash around his H575
Isa 16: 5 will be established; in **f** a man will sit on it H622
Isa 25: 1 in perfect **f** you have done wonderful H575
Isa 38:18 go down to the pit cannot hope for your **f**. H622
Isa 38:19 parents tell their children about your **f**. H622
Isa 40: 6 all their **f** is like the flowers of the H2876
Isa 42: 3 In **f** he will bring forth justice; H622
Isa 61: 8 In my **f** I will reward my people and make H622
La 3:23 They are new every morning; great is your **f**. H575
Hos 2:20 I will betroth you in **f**, and you will H575
Hos 4: 1 "There is no **f**, no love, no H622
Hab 2: 4 the righteous person will live by his **f**— H575
Mt 23:23 matters of the law—justice, mercy and **f**. G4411
Ro 3: 3 Will their unfaithfulness nullify God's **f**? G4411
Gal 5:22 forbearance, kindness, goodness, **f**, G4411
3Jn 3 came and testified about your **f** *to* the **truth**, AIT
Rev 13:10 endurance and **f** on the part of God's G4411

FAITHLESS (12) [FAITH]

Ps 78:57 their ancestors they were disloyal and **f**, H953
Ps 101: 3 I hate what **f** *people* do; I will have no H6091
Ps 119:158 I look on the **f** with loathing, for they do H953
Pr 14:14 The **f** will be fully repaid for their H6047+4213
Jer 3: 6 "Have you seen what **f** Israel has done? H5412
Jer 3: 8 I gave **f** Israel her certificate of divorce H5412
Jer 3:11 "**F** Israel is more righteous than unfaithful H5412
Jer 3:12 " 'Return, **f** Israel,' declares the LORD, 'I H5412
Jer 3:14 "Return, **f** people," declares the LORD, "for H8743
Jer 3:22 "Return, **f** people; I will cure you of H8743
Jer 12: 1 Why do all the **f** live at ease? H953+954
2Ti 2:13 if *we are* **f**, he remains faithful, for he G601

FALCON (1) [FALCON'S, FALCONS]

Dt 14:13 the red kite, the black kite, any kind of **f**, H1901

FALCON'S (1) [FALCON]

Job 28: 7 that hidden path, no **f** eye has seen it. H370

FALCONS (1) [FALCON]

Isa 34:15 there also the **f** will gather, each H1901

FALL (224) [FALLEN, FALLING, FALLS, FELL, FELLED, FELLING]

Ge 2:21 LORD God **caused** the man **to f** *into* a deep H5877
Ge 9: 2 dread of you *will* **f** on all the beasts H2118
Ge 27:13 said to him, "My son, let the curse **f** on me. NDT
Ex 9:19 because the hail *will* **f** on every person H3718
Ex 9:22 the sky so that hail *will* **f** all over Egypt— H2118
Ex 15:16 terror and dread *will* **f** on them. H5877
Lev 26: 7 and *they will* **f** by the sword before you. H5877
Lev 26: 8 your enemies *will* **f** by the sword H5877
Lev 26:36 the sword, and *they will* **f**, even though no H5877
Nu 1:53 so that my wrath *will* not **f** on the Israelite H2118
Nu 14: 3 to this land only to *let us* **f** by the sword? H5877
Nu 14:29 In this wilderness your bodies *will* **f**—every H5877
Nu 14:32 your bodies *will* **f** in this wilderness. H5877
Nu 14:43 be with you and *you will* **f** by the sword." H5877
Nu 18: 5 so that my wrath *will* not **f** on the H2118
Dt 28:52 fortified walls in which you trust **f down**. H3718
Dt 29:20 curses written in this book *will* **f** on them, H8069
Dt 31:29 disaster *will* **f on** you because you will do H7925
Dt 32: 2 *Let* my teaching **f** like rain and my words H6903
Jos 9:20 that God's wrath *will* not **f** on us for H2118
Jdg 15:18 die of thirst and **f** into the hands of the H5877
1Sa 3:19 and *he* **let** none of Samuel's words **f** to H5877
1Sa 14:45 not a hair of his head *will* **f** to the ground H5877
1Sa 18:25 plan was to **have** David **f** by the hands of H5877
1Sa 26:20 Now *do* not *let* my blood **f** to the ground H5877
2Sa 1:21 may no showers **f** on your terraced fields. NDT
2Sa 3:29 *May* his blood **f** on the head of Joab and H2565
2Sa 14:11 of your son's head *will* **f** to the ground." H5877
2Sa 17:12 we will **f** on him as dew settles on the NDT
2Sa 24:14 *Let us* **f** into the hands of the LORD, for his H5877
2Sa 24:14 but *do* not *let me* **f** into human hands." H5877
2Sa 24:17 *Let* your hand **f** on me and my family." H2118
1Ki 1:52 not a hair of his head *will* **f** to the ground H5877
2Ki 6: 6 "Where *did it* **f**?" When he showed H5877
2Ki 9:18 Jehu replied. "**F** in behind me." H6015+448
2Ki 9:19 to do with peace? **F** in behind me." H6015+448
1Ch 21:13 *Let me* **f** into the hands of the LORD, for his H5877
1Ch 21:13 but *do* not *let me* **f** into human hands." H5877

1Ch 21:17 *let* your hand **f** on me and my family H2118
2Ch 34:11 kings of Judah *had* **allowed to f into ruin**. H8845
Ezr 7:23 Why *should* his wrath **f** on the realm of A10201
Est 8: 6 can I bear to see disaster **f on** my people? H5162
Job 13:11 *Would* not the dread of him **f** on you? H5877
Job 31:22 then *let* my arm **f** from the shoulder, let it H5877
Job 36:28 abundant **showers f** on mankind. H8319
Job 37: 6 says to the snow, '**F** *on* the earth,' and to H2092
Ps 10:10 they collapse; *they* **f** under his strength. H5877
Ps 13: 4 and my foes will rejoice when *I* **f**. H4572
Ps 20: 8 They are brought to their knees and **f**, but H5877
Ps 27: 2 my foes who will stumble and **f**. H5877
Ps 35: 8 entangle them, *may they* **f** into the pit, to H5877
Ps 37:24 he may stumble, *he will* not **f**, for the LORD H3214
Ps 38:17 For I am about to **f**, and my pain is ever H7520
Ps 45: 5 *let* the nations **f** beneath your feet. H5877
Ps 46: 2 the mountains **f** into the heart of the H4572
Ps 46: 5 is within her, *she will* not **f**; God will help H4572
Ps 46: 6 in uproar, kingdoms **f**; he lifts his voice, H4572
Ps 58: 7 they draw the bow, *let* their arrows **f short**. H4908
Ps 69: 9 insults of those who insult you **f** on me. H5877
Ps 82: 7 mortals; *you will* **f** like every other ruler." H5877
Ps 91: 7 A thousand *may* **f** at your side, ten H5877
Ps 106:26 hand that he *would* **make** them **f** in the H5877
Ps 106:27 **make** their descendants **f** among the H5877
Ps 118:13 I was pushed back and *about to* **f**, but the H5877
Ps 140:10 *May* burning coals **f** on them; may they be H4572
Ps 141:10 *Let* the wicked **f** into their own nets, while H5877
Ps 145:14 LORD upholds all who **f** and lifts up all who H5877
Pr 11:28 Those who trust in their riches *will* **f**, but H5877
Pr 16:18 destruction, a haughty spirit before a **f**. H4174
Pr 24:16 though the righteous **f** seven times H5877
Pr 26:27 Whoever digs a pit *will* **f** into it; if H5877
Pr 28:10 along an evil path *will* **f** into their own H5877
Pr 28:18 the *one* whose ways are perverse *will* **f** H5877
Ecc 9:12 by evil times that **f** unexpectedly upon H5877
Ecc 10: 8 Whoever digs a pit *may* **f** into it; whoever H5877
Isa 3:25 Your men *will* **f** by the sword, your warriors H5877
Isa 8:14 to stumble and a rock that **makes** them **f**. H4842
Isa 8:15 will stumble; *they will* **f** and be broken H5877
Isa 9: 8 message against Jacob; *it will* **f** on Israel. H5877
Isa 10: 4 among the captives or **f** among the slain. H5877
Isa 10:34 Lebanon *will* **f** before the Mighty One. H5877
Isa 13:15 all who are caught *will* **f** by the sword. H5877
Isa 22:25 it will be sheared off and *will* **f**, and the H5877
Isa 24:18 flees at the sound of terror *will* **f** into a pit; H5877
Isa 28:13 so that as they go *they will* **f** backward H4173
Isa 30:25 when the towers **f**, streams of water will H5877
Isa 31: 3 those who are helped *will* **f**; all will perish H5877
Isa 31: 8 "Assyria *will* **f** by no human sword; H5877
Isa 31: 9 Their stronghold *will* **f** because of terror H6296
Isa 34: 4 all the starry host *will* **f** like withered H5570
Isa 34: 7 And the wild oxen *will* **f** with them, the H3718
Isa 40: 7 The grass withers and the flowers **f** H5570
Isa 40: 8 The grass withers and the flowers **f**, but H5570
Isa 40:30 and young men **stumble and f**; H4173+4173
Isa 47:11 A calamity *will* **f** upon you that you cannot H5877
Isa 51:23 '**F prostrate** that we may walk on you. H8817
Isa 65:12 all of you *will* **f** in the slaughter H4156
Jer 6:15 So *they will* **f** among the fallen; they will H5877
Jer 8: 4 " 'When *people* **f down**, do they not get H5877
Jer 8:12 So *they will* **f** among the fallen; they will H5877
Jer 13:18 glorious crowns *will* **f** *from* your heads." H3718
Jer 19: 7 *I will* **make** them **f** by the sword before H5877
Jer 20: 4 eyes you will see *them* **f** by the sword of H5877
Jer 23:12 to darkness and there *they will* **f**. H5877
Jer 25:27 **f** to rise no more because of the H5877
Jer 25:34 you *will* **f** like the best of the rams. H5877
Jer 34:17 'freedom' to **f** by the sword, plague NDT
Jer 39:18 *you will* not **f** by the sword but will escape H5877
Jer 44:12 *they will* **f** by the sword or die from famine H5877
Jer 46: 6 by the River Euphrates they stumble and **f**. H5877
Jer 46:12 over another; both *will* **f down** together." H5877
Jer 46:16 repeatedly; *they will* **f** over each other. H5877
Jer 48:16 "The **f** *of* Moab is at hand; her calamity will H369
Jer 48:44 flees from the terror *will* **f** into a pit, H5877
Jer 49:21 At the sound of their **f** the earth will H5877
Jer 49:26 her young men *will* **f** in the streets; all H5877
Jer 50:15 surrenders, her towers **f**, her walls are torn H5877
Jer 50:30 her young men *will* **f** in the streets; all her H5877
Jer 50:32 will stumble and **f** and no one will help H5877
Jer 51: 4 *They will* **f down** slain in Babylon, fatally H5877
Jer 51: 8 Babylon *will* suddenly **f** and be broken H5877
Jer 51:44 And the wall of Babylon *will* **f**. H5877
Jer 51:49 "Babylon *must* **f** because of Israel's slain H5877
Jer 51:64 will bring on her. And *her people will* **f**.' " H3615
La 1: 9 *Her* **f** was astounding; there was none to H3718
Eze 5:12 a third *will* **f** by the sword outside your H5877
Eze 6: 7 Your *people will* **f** slain among you, and H5877
Eze 6:11 of Israel, for *they will* **f** by the sword H5877
Eze 6:12 one who is near *will* **f** by the sword H5877
Eze 11:10 *You will* **f** by the sword, and I will execute H5877
Eze 13:11 it with whitewash that *it is going to* **f**. H5877
Eze 13:13 torrents of rain *will* **f** with destructive H2118
Eze 13:21 and *they will* no longer **f** prey to your H2118
Eze 17:21 All his choice troops *will* **f** by the sword H5877
Eze 23:25 of you who are left *will* **f** by the sword. H5877
Eze 24:21 you left behind *will* **f** by the sword. H5877
Eze 25:13 Teman to Dedan *they will* **f** by the sword. H5877
Eze 26:11 your strong pillars *will* **f** to the ground. H3718
Eze 26:15 coastlands tremble at the sound of your **f**, H5147
Eze 26:18 coastlands tremble on the day of your **f**; H5147
Eze 28:23 The slain *will* **f** within you, with the sword H5877
Eze 29: 5 *You will* **f** on the open field and not be H5877
Eze 30: 4 When the slain **f** in Egypt, her wealth will H5877
Eze 30: 5 the covenant land *will* **f** by the sword H5877
Eze 30: 6 " 'The allies of Egypt *will* **f** and her proud H5877
Eze 30: 6 Migdol to Aswan *they will* **f** by the sword H5877
Eze 30:17 Bubastis *will* **f** by the sword, H5877
Eze 30:22 and **make** the sword **f** from his hand. H5877
Eze 30:25 the arms of Pharaoh *will* **f limp**. H5877
Eze 31:16 at the sound of its **f** when I brought it H5147
Eze 32:12 *I will* **cause** your hordes **to f** by the swords H5877
Eze 32:20 *They will* **f** among those killed by the H5877
Eze 33:27 are left in the ruins *will* **f** by the sword, H5877
Eze 35: 8 killed by the sword *will* **f** on your hills and H5877
Eze 36:15 of the peoples or **cause** your nation **to f**, H4173
Eze 38:20 every wall *will* **f** to the ground. H5877
Eze 39: 4 On the mountains of Israel *you will* **f**, you H5877
Eze 39: 5 *You will* **f** in the open field, for I have H5877
Eze 40: 1 the fourteenth year after the **f** *of* the city— H5782
Eze 44:12 **made** the people of Israel **f** *into* H2118+4200+4842
Da 3: 5 *you must* **f down** and worship the image A10484
Da 3: 6 Whoever *does* not **f down** and worship A10484
Da 3:10 kinds of music *must* **f down** and worship A10484
Da 3:11 whoever *does* not **f down** and worship A10484
Da 3:15 you are ready *to* **f down** and worship the A10484
Da 11:19 of his own country but will stumble and **f**, H5877
Da 11:26 and many *will* **f in battle**. H5877+2728
Da 11:33 a time *they will* **f** by the sword or H4173
Da 11:34 When they **f**, they will receive a little help H4173
Da 11:41 Many countries *will* **f**, but Edom, Moab H4173
Hos 7: 7 All their kings **f**, and none of them calls H5877
Hos 7:16 Their leaders *will* **f** by the sword because H5877
Hos 10: 8 and to the hills, "**F** on us!" H5877
Hos 13:16 *They will* **f** by the sword; their little ones H5877
Am 3:14 altar will be cut off and **f** to the ground. H5877
Am 7:17 sons and daughters *will* **f** by the sword. H5877
Am 8:14 *they will* **f**, never to rise H5877
Na 3:12 the figs **f** into the mouth of the eater. H5877
Na 3:19 news about you clap their hands at your **f**, NDT
Hag 2:22 horses and their riders *will* **f**, each by the H3718
Mt 7:25 that house; yet *it did* not **f**, because it had *G4406*
Mt 10:29 Yet not one of them *will* **f** to the ground *G4406*
Mt 13:21 because of the word, *they* quickly **f away**. *G4997*
Mt 15:14 blind lead the blind, both *will* **f** into a pit." *G4406*
Mt 15:27 eat the crumbs that **f** from their master's *G4406*
Mt 24:29 its light; the stars *will* **f** from the sky, and *G4406*
Mt 26:31 night you *will* all **f away** on account of *G4997*
Mt 26:33 "Even if all **f away** on account of you, *G4997*
Mt 26:41 pray so that *you will* not **f into** temptation. *G1656*
Mk 4:17 because of the word, *they* quickly **f away**. *G4997*
Mk 13:25 the stars *will* **f** from the sky, and the *G1639+4406*
Mk 14:27 "*You will* all **f away**," Jesus told them, "for *G4997*
Mk 14:29 declared, "Even if all **f away**, I will not." *G4997*
Mk 14:38 pray so that *you will* not **f into** temptation *G2262*
Lk 6:39 *Will they* not both **f into** a pit? *G1860*
Lk 8:13 in the time of testing *they* **f away**. *G923*
Lk 10:18 "I saw Satan **f** like lightning from heaven. *G4406*
Lk 11:17 a house divided against itself *will* **f**. *G4406*
Lk 21:24 *They will* **f** by the sword and will be taken *G4406*
Lk 22:40 "Pray *that you will* not **f into** temptation." *G1656*
Lk 22:46 pray so that *you will* not **f into** temptation." *G1656*
Lk 23:30 " 'they will say to the mountains, "**F** on us!"*G4406*
Jn 16: 1 I have told you so that *you will* not **f away**. *G4997*
Ac 5:15 Peter's shadow *might* **f on** some of them *G2173*
Ac 28: 6 him to swell up or suddenly **f** dead; *G2928*
Ro 3:23 all have sinned and **f short** of the glory of *G5728*
Ro 9:33 to stumble and a rock that **makes** them **f**, *G4998*
Ro 11:11 they stumble so as to **f beyond recovery**? *G4406*
Ro 14: 4 servants stand or **f**. And they will stand, *G4406*
Ro 14:21 that *will* **cause** your brother or sister **to f**. *G4684*
1Co 8:13 **causes** my brother or sister **to f into sin**, *G4997*
1Co 8:13 so that *I will* not **cause** them **to f**. *G4997*
1Co 10:12 standing firm, be careful that *you* don't **f**! *G4406*
1Co 14:25 So *they will* **f down** and *G4406+2093+4725*
1Ti 3: 6 conceited and **f under** the same judgment *G1860*
1Ti 3: 7 so that *he will* not **f into** disgrace and into *G1860*
1Ti 6: 9 want to get rich **f into** temptation and a *G1860*
Heb 10:31 a dreadful thing *to* **f into** the hands of the *G1860*
1Pe 1:24 the grass withers and the flowers **f**, *G1738*
1Pe 2: 8 to stumble and a rock that **makes** them **f**." *G4998*
2Pe 3:17 of the lawless and **f from** your secure *G1738*
Rev 3: 9 them come and **f down** at your feet and *G4686*
Rev 4:10 twenty-four elders **f down** before him who *G4406*
Rev 6:16 "**F** on us and hide us from the face of him *G4406*

FALLEN (79) [FALL]

Ge 15:17 When the sun had set and darkness *had* **f**, H2118
Ex 9:18 worst hailstorm that *has* ever **f** on Egypt, H2118
Ex 23: 5 who hates you **f down** under its load, H8069
Lev 19:10 time or pick up the **grapes that have f**. H7261
Dt 22: 4 Israelite's donkey or ox **f** on the road, H5877
Dt 29:22 calamities that have **f** on the land and the NDT
Jos 2: 9 that a great fear of you *has* **f** on us, H5877
Jdg 3:25 There they saw their lord **f** to the floor H5877
Jdg 8:10 twenty thousand swordsmen *had* **f**. H5877
Jdg 19:27 concubine, **f** *in* the doorway of the house H5877
1Sa 5: 3 **f** on his face on the ground before the ark H5877
1Sa 5: 4 **f** on his face on the ground before the ark H5877
1Sa 20:37 the place where Jonathan's arrow *had* **f**, H3721
1Sa 31: 8 his three sons **f** on Mount Gilboa. H5877
2Sa 1:10 I knew that after he *had* **f** he could not H5877
2Sa 1:12 of Israel, because *they had* **f** by the sword. H5877
2Sa 1:19 heights, Israel. How the mighty *have* **f**! H5877
2Sa 1:25 "How the mighty *have* **f** in battle H5877
2Sa 1:27 "How the mighty *have* **f**! The weapons of H5877
2Sa 2:23 the place where Asahel *had* **f** and died. H5877
2Sa 3:38 a great man *has* **f** in Israel this day? H5877
2Ki 1: 2 Now Ahaziah *had* **f** through the lattice of H5877
2Ki 1:14 fire *has* **f** from heaven and consumed the H3718
2Ki 2:13 cloak that *had* **f** from him and went H5877
2Ki 2:14 took the cloak that *had* **f** from Elijah and H5877
1Ch 10: 8 Saul and his sons **f** on Mount Gilboa. H5877
2Ch 14:14 the terror of the LORD *had* **f** on them. H2118
2Ch 29: 8 the anger of the LORD *has* **f** on Judah and H2118
2Ch 29: 9 is why our fathers *have* **f** by the sword H5877
Ps 9:15 The nations *have* **f** into the pit they have H3190
Ps 16: 6 The boundary lines *have* **f** for me in H5877
Ps 36:12 See how the evildoers **lie f**—thrown H5877
Ps 55: 4 the terrors of death *have* **f** on me. H5877
Ps 57: 6 but *they have* **f** into it *themselves*. H5877
Ps 68:14 *it was like* **snow f** on Mount Zalmon. H8919
Ps 105:38 because dread of Israel *had* **f** on them. H5877
Pr 6: 3 since *you have* **f** into your neighbor's hands H995
Isa 9:10 "The bricks *have* **f down**, but we will H5877
Isa 14:12 How *you have* **f** from heaven, morning H5877
Isa 21: 9 'Babylon *has* **f**, has fallen! All H5877
Isa 21: 9 has fallen, *has* **f**! All the images of H5877
Jer 3: 3 withheld, and no spring rains *have* **f**. H2118
Jer 6:15 So they will fall among the **f**; they will be H5877
Jer 8:12 So they will fall among the **f**; they will be H5877
Jer 48:32 The destroyer *has* **f** on your ripened fruit H5877
Jer 51:47 her slain *will* all **lie f** within her. H5877
Jer 51:49 in all the earth *have* **f** because of Babylon H5877
La 2:21 young women *have* **f** by the sword. H5877
La 5:16 The crown *has* **f** from our head. Woe to us H5877
Eze 21:15 may melt with fear and the **f** be many, H4842
Eze 31:13 All the birds settled on the **f** tree, and all H5147
Eze 32:22 all her slain, all who *have* **f** by the sword. H5877
Eze 32:23 land of the living are slain, **f** by the sword. H5877
Eze 32:24 of them are slain, **f** by the sword. All who H5877
Eze 32:27 they do not lie with the **f** warriors of old, H5877
Eze 33:21 came to me and said, "The city *has* **f**!" H5782
Am 5: 2 "**F** *is* Virgin Israel, never to rise again H5877
Am 9:11 that day "I will restore David's **f** shelter— H5877
Mic 7: 8 Though *I have* **f**, I will rise H5877
Zec 11: 2 the cedar *has* **f**; the stately trees H5877
Jn 11:11 "Our friend Lazarus *has* **f asleep**; but I am *G3121*
Ac 15:16 this I will return and rebuild David's **f** tent. *G4406*
Ro 15: 3 of those who insult you *have* **f** on me." *G2158*
1Co 11:30 sick, and a number of you *have* **f asleep**. AIT
1Co 15: 6 still living, though some *have* **f asleep**. *G3121*
1Co 15:18 those also *who have* **f asleep** in Christ are *G3121*
1Co 15:20 the firstfruits *of* those *who have* **f asleep**. *G3121*
Gal 5: 4 from Christ; *you have* **f away from** grace. *G1738*
1Th 4:14 Jesus those *who have* **f asleep** in him. *G3121*
1Th 4:15 not precede those *who have* **f asleep**. *G3121*
Heb 4: 1 none of you be found to *have* **f short** of it. *G5728*
Heb 6: 6 and *who have* **f away**, to have to be brought back *G4178*
Rev 2: 5 Consider how far *you have* **f**! Repent and *G4406*
Rev 9: 1 I saw a star *that had* **f** from the sky to *G4406*
Rev 14: 8 followed and said, " '**F**! Fallen is Babylon *G4406*
Rev 14: 8 **F** is Babylon the Great,' which made all *G4406*
Rev 17:10 Five *have* **f**, one is, the other has not yet *G4406*
Rev 18: 2 voice he shouted: " '**F**! Fallen is Babylon *G4406*
Rev 18: 2 **F** is Babylon the Great!' She has *G4406*

FALLING (14) [FALL]

Ge 8: 2 the rain *had* **stopped f** from the sky. H3973
1Ki 18:45 a heavy rain **started f** and Ahab rode off H2118
Est 7: 8 Haman *was* **f** on the couch where Esther H5877
Est 8: 3 with the king, **f** at his feet and weeping. H5877
Ps 72: 6 May he be like rain **f** on a mown field H3718
Ps 133: 3 the dew of Hermon *were* **f** on Mount Zion. H3718
Isa 3: 8 staggers, Judah *is* **f**; their words and H5877
Mt 13:20 The **seed f** on rocky ground refers to *G5062*
Mt 13:22 The **seed f** among the thorns refers to *G5062*
Mt 13:23 But the **seed f** on good soil refers to *G5062*
Mk 15:19 **F on** their knees, they paid homage to *G5502*
Lk 2:34 to cause the **f** and rising of many in *G4774*
Lk 22:44 was like drops of blood **f** to the ground. *G2849*
Heb 6: 7 in the rain often **f** on it and that produces *G2262*

FALLOW (KJV) UNPLOWED

FALLOWDEER (KJV) ROE DEER, ROEBUCKS

FALLS (42) [FALL]

Ex 21:33 to cover it and an ox or a donkey **f** into it, H5877
Lev 11:32 one of them dies and **f** on something, H5877
Lev 11:33 If one of them **f** into a clay pot, everything H5877
Lev 11:35 of their carcasses **f** on becomes unclean; H5877
Lev 11:37 If a carcass **f** on any seeds that are to be H5877
Lev 11:38 put on the seed and a carcass **f** on it, H5877
Lev 16: 9 bring the goat whose lot **f** to the LORD and H6590
Nu 24: 4 the Almighty, *who* **f prostrate**, and whose H5877
Nu 24:16 the Almighty, *who* **f prostrate**, and whose H5877
Nu 33:54 Whatever **f** to them by lot will be theirs H3655
Dt 20:20 siege works until the city at war with you **f**. H3718
Dt 22: 8 on your house if someone **f** from the roof. H5877
2Sa 3:29 on a crutch or *who* **f** by the sword or who H5877
2Sa 3:34 You fell as *one* **f** before the wicked." H5877
Job 4:13 the night, when deep sleep **f** on people, H5877
Job 9:24 When a land **f** into the hands of the H5989
Job 18:12 disaster is ready for him when he **f**. H7520
Job 33:15 when deep sleep **f** on people as they H5877

F

Ps 7:15 scoops it out f into the pit they have H5877
Pr 11: 8 and *it* f on the wicked instead. H995
Pr 11:14 For lack of guidance a nation f, but victory H5877
Pr 13:17 A wicked messenger f into trouble, but a H5877
Pr 17:20 whose tongue is perverse f into trouble. H5877
Pr 22:14 who is under the LORD's wrath f *into* it. H5877
Pr 24:17 Do not gloat when your enemy f; when H5877
Pr 28:14 whoever hardens their heart f into trouble. H5877
Ecc 4:10 If either of *them* **f down**, one can help the H5877
Ecc 4:10 But pity anyone who f and has no one to H5877
Ecc 11: 3 Whether a tree f to the south or to the H5877
Ecc 11: 3 in the place where it f, there it will lie. H5877
Isa 24:20 it is the guilt of its rebellion that *it* f— H5877
Eze 13:14 When *it* f, you will be destroyed in it; and H5877
Mt 12:11 you has a sheep and it f into a pit on the *G1860*
Mt 17:15 *He* often f into the fire or into the water *G4406*
Mt 21:44 Anyone *who* f on this stone will be broken *G4406*
Mt 21:44 anyone on whom *it* f will be crushed." *G4406*
Lk 14: 5 a child or an ox *that* f into a well on the *G4406*
Lk 20:18 Everyone who f on that stone will be *G4406*
Lk 20:18 anyone on whom *it* f will be crushed." *G4406*
Jn 12:24 a kernel of wheat f to the ground and dies *G4406*
Heb 12:15 See to it *that* no one **f short** of the grace of *G5728*
Jas 1:11 its blossom f and its beauty is destroyed. *G1738*

FALSE (85) [FALSEHOOD, FALSELY]

Ex 20:16 "You shall not give f testimony against H9214
Ex 23: 1 "Do not spread f reports. Do not help a H8736
Ex 23: 7 nothing to do with a f charge and do not H9214
Dt 5:20 "You shall not give f testimony against H8736
Dt 19:18 giving f testimony against a fellow H9214
Dt 19:19 then do to **the f witness** as that witness H2257S
Dt 32:17 They sacrificed to **f gods**, which are not H8717
Job 24:25 who *can* **prove** me f and reduce my words H3941
Job 36: 4 Be assured that my words are not f; one H9214
Job 41: 9 Any hope of subduing it *is* f; the mere H3941
Ps 4: 2 will you love delusions and seek **f gods**? H3942
Ps 24: 4 not trust in an idol or swear by a **f** *god*. H5327
Ps 27:12 for f witnesses rise up against me H9214
Ps 35:20 devise f accusations against those H5327
Ps 40: 4 to those who turn aside to **f gods**. H3942
Ps 44:17 *we had* not *been* f to your covenant. H9213
Ps 106:37 their sons and their daughters to **f gods**. H8717
Pr 6:19 a f witness who pours out lies and a H9214
Pr 12:17 tells the truth, but a f witness tells lies. H9214
Pr 13: 5 The righteous hate what is f, but the H9214
Pr 14: 5 not deceive, but a f witness pours out lies. H9214
Pr 14:25 saves lives, but a f witness is deceitful. H3942
Pr 19: 5 A f witness will not go unpunished, and H9214
Pr 19: 9 A f witness will not go unpunished, and H9214
Pr 21:28 A f witness will perish, but a careful H3942
Pr 25:18 is one who gives f testimony against a H9214
Isa 29:21 in court and with f testimony deprive the H9332
Isa 41:29 they are all f! Their deeds amount to H224
Isa 44:25 the signs of **f prophets** and makes fools H967
Jer 13:25 have forgotten me and trusted in **f gods**. H9214
Jer 14:14 They are prophesying to you f visions H9214
Jer 16:19 ancestors possessed nothing but **f gods**, H9214
Jer 23:16 they **fill** you **with f hopes**. H2038
Jer 23:32 am against those who prophesy f dreams," H9214
Jer 50:36 A sword against her **f prophets**! They will H967
La 2:14 of your prophets were f and worthless; H8736
La 2:14 they gave you were f and misleading. H8736
Eze 12:24 will be no more f visions or flattering H8736
Eze 13: 6 Their visions are f and their divinations a H8736
Eze 13: 7 Have you not seen f visions and uttered H8736
Eze 13: 8 Because of your f words and lying visions H8736
Eze 13: 9 the prophets who see f visions and utter H8736
Eze 13:23 you will no longer see f visions or practice H8736
Eze 21:23 It will seem like a f omen to those who H8736
Eze 21:29 Despite f visions concerning you and lying H8736
Eze 22:28 deeds for them by f visions and lying H8736
Hos 10: 4 take f oaths and make agreements H8736
Hos 11: 6 will devour their **f prophets** and put an end H967
Am 2: 4 they have been led astray by **f gods**, H3942
Mic 6:11 dishonest scales, with a bag of f weights? H5327
Hab 2: 3 it speaks of the end and *will* not **prove f**. H3941
Zec 10: 2 they tell dreams that are f, they give H8736
Mal 2: 6 mouth and nothing f was found on his H6406
Mt 7:15 "Watch out for **f prophets**. They come to *G6021*
Mt 15:19 immorality, theft, **f testimony**, slander. *G6019*
Mt 19:18 not steal, *you shall* not **give f testimole**, *G6018*
Mt 24:11 many **f prophets** will appear and *G6021*
Mt 24:24 For **f messiahs** and false prophets will *G6023*
Mt 24:24 messiahs and **f prophets** will appear and *G6021*
Mt 26:59 were looking for **f evidence** against Jesus *G6019*
Mt 26:60 though many **f witnesses** came forward. *G6020*
Mk 10:19 *you shall* not **give f testimony**, you *G6018*
Mk 13:22 For **f messiahs** and false prophets will *G6023*
Mk 13:22 messiahs and **f prophets** will appear and *G6021*
Mk 14:57 up and **gave** *this* **f testimony** against him *G6018*
Lk 6:26 how their ancestors treated the **f prophets**. *G6021*
Lk 18:20 *you shall* not **give f testimony**, honor *G6018*
Jn 7:18 a man of truth; there is nothing f about him. *G94*
Ac 6:13 They produced f witnesses, who testified *G6014*
Ac 13: 6 sorcerer and **f prophet** named Bar-Jesus, *G6021*
1Co 15:15 then found to be **f witnesses** about God, *G6020*
2Co 11:13 For such people are **f apostles**, deceitful *G6013*
2Co 11:26 and in danger from **f believers**. *G6012*
Gal 2: 4 because some **f believers** had infiltrated *G6012*
Php 1:18 whether *from* **f motives** or true, Christ *G4733*
Col 2:18 who delights in *f* **humility** and the worship of AIT
Col 2:23 their *f* **humility** and their harsh treatment of AIT
1Ti 1: 3 people not *to* **teach f doctrines** *any longer* *G2281*
2Pe 2: 1 there were also **f prophets** among the *G6021*
2Pe 2: 1 just as there will be **f teachers** among you. *G6015*
1Jn 4: 1 because many **f prophets** have gone out *G6021*
Rev 2: 2 are not, and have found them f. *G6014*
Rev 16:13 out of the mouth *of* the **f prophet**. *G6021*
Rev 19:20 with it the **f prophet** who had *G6021*
Rev 20:10 beast and the **f prophet** had been thrown. *G6021*

FALSEHOOD (10) [FALSE]

Job 21:34 Nothing is left of your answers but f!" H5086
Job 31: 5 I have walked with f or my foot has H8736
Ps 52: 3 f rather than speaking the truth. H9214
Ps 119:163 I hate and detest f but I love your law. H9214
Pr 30: 8 Keep f and lies far from me; give me H8736
Isa 28:15 a lie our refuge and f our hiding place." H9214
Ro 3: 7 "If my f enhances God's truthfulness and *G6025*
Eph 4:25 of you must put off f and speak truthfully *G6022*
1Jn 4: 6 the Spirit of truth and the spirit *of* f. *G4415*
Rev 22:15 everyone who loves and practices f. *G6022*

FALSELY (18) [FALSE]

Ge 21:23 God that *you will* not **deal** f with me or my H9213
Lev 6: 3 if they swear f about any such H6584+9214
Lev 6: 5 it was they swore f about. H4200+2021+9214
Lev 19:12 'Do not swear f by my name H4200+2021+9214
Ps 41: 6 to see me, he speaks f, while his heart H8736
Ps 101: 7 no one who speaks f will stand in my H9214
Isa 59: 3 Your lips have spoken f, and your tongue H9214
Jer 5: 2 still they are swearing f." H4200+2021+9214
Jer 8: 8 the scribes has handled it f? H4200+2021+9214
Da 6:24 men who *had* **f accused** Daniel A10030+10642
Hos 7:13 redeem them but they speak about me f. H3942
Zec 5: 3 everyone who **swears** f will be banished. H8678
Zec 5: 4 of anyone who swears f by my name. H9214
Zec 8:17 each other, and do not love to swear f. H9214
Mt 5:11 persecute you and f say all kinds of evil *G6017*
Mk 14:56 Many **testified** f against him, but their *G6018*
Lk 3:14 extort money and don't **accuse** *people* **f**— *G5193*
1Ti 6:20 ideas *of* what is **f called** knowledge, *G6024*

FALTER (2) [FALTERED, FALTERING, FALTERS]

Pr 24:10 If *you* f in a time of trouble, how small is H8332
Isa 42: 4 *he will* not f or be discouraged till he H3908

FALTERED (2) [FALTER]

Ps 26: 1 I have trusted in the LORD and *have* not f. H5048
Ps 105:37 from among their tribes no *one* f. H4173

FALTERING (3) [FALTER]

Ex 6:12 listen to me, since I speak with f lips?" H6888
Ex 6:30 "Since I speak with f lips, why would H6888
Job 4: 4 stumbled; you have strengthened f knees. H4156

FALTERS (1) [FALTER]

Isa 21: 4 My heart f, fear makes me tremble; the H9494

FAME (17) [FAMOUS]

Dt 26:19 f and honor high above all the nations he H9005
Jos 6:27 his f spread throughout the land. H9053
Jos 9: 9 because of the f *of* the LORD your God. H9005
1Ki 4:31 And his f spread to all the surrounding H9005
1Ki 10: 1 heard about the f *of* Solomon and his H9051
1Ch 14:17 So David's f spread throughout every land, H9005
1Ch 22: 5 magnificence and f and splendor in the H9005
2Ch 9: 1 the queen of Sheba heard of Solomon's f, H9051
2Ch 26: 8 his f spread as far as the border of H9005
2Ch 26:15 His f spread far and wide, for he was H9005
Ps 138: 2 solemn decree that it surpasses your f. H9005
Isa 66:19 have not heard of my f or seen my glory. H9051
Jer 48:17 live around her, all who know her f; say, H9005
Eze 16:14 And your f spread among the nations on H9005
Eze 16:15 beauty and used your f to become a H9005
Hos 14: 7 Israel's f will be like the wine of Lebanon. H2352
Hab 3: 2 I have heard of your f; I stand in awe of H9051

FAMILIAR (3)

Ps 139: 3 my lying down; *you are* **f with** all my ways. H6122
Isa 53: 3 a man of suffering, and **f with** pain. H3359
Ac 26:26 The king *is* f with these things, and I can *G2179*

FAMILIES (111) [FAMILY]

Ge 45:18 bring your father and your f back to me. H1074
Ex 1:21 feared God, he gave them f of their own. H1074
Ex 6:14 These were the heads of their f: The H1074+3
Ex 6:25 These were the heads of the Levite f, clan by H3
Ex 12:21 the animals for your f and slaughter the H5476
Nu 1: 2 community by their clans and f, H1074+3
Nu 1:18 their ancestry by their clans and f, H1074+3
Nu 1:20 to the records of their clans and f. H1074+3
Nu 1:22 to the records of their clans and f. H1074+3
Nu 1:24 to the records of their clans and f. H1074+3
Nu 1:26 to the records of their clans and f. H1074+3
Nu 1:28 to the records of their clans and f. H1074+3
Nu 1:30 to the records of their clans and f. H1074+3
Nu 1:32 to the records of their clans and f. H1074+3
Nu 1:34 to the records of their clans and f. H1074+3
Nu 1:36 to the records of their clans and f. H1074+3
Nu 1:38 to the records of their clans and f. H1074+3
Nu 1:40 to the records of their clans and f. H1074+3
Nu 1:42 to the records of their clans and f. H1074+3
Nu 1:45 army were counted according to their f. H1074+3
Nu 2:32 Israelites, counted according to their f. H1074+3
Nu 3:15 "Count the Levites by their f and clans H1074+3
Nu 3:20 the Levite clans, according to their f. H1074+3
Nu 3:24 The leader of the f of the Gershonites H1074+3
Nu 3:30 The leader of the f of the Kohathite H1074+3
Nu 3:35 The leader of the f of the Merarite clans H1074+3
Nu 4: 2 of the Levites by their clans and f. H1074+3
Nu 4:22 of the Gershonites by their f and clans. H1074+3
Nu 4:29 the Merarites by their clans and f. H1074+3
Nu 4:34 the Kohathites by their clans and f. H1074+3
Nu 4:38 were counted by their clans and f. H1074+3
Nu 4:40 counted by their clans and f, were H1074+3
Nu 4:42 were counted by their clans and f. H1074+3
Nu 4:46 all the Levites by their clans and f. H1074+3
Nu 7: 2 the heads of f who were the tribal H1074+3
Nu 26: 2 of the whole Israelite community by f— H1074+3
Nu 34:14 because the f *of* the tribe of Reuben H1074+3
Nu 36: 1 the leaders, the heads of the Israelite f. H3
Dt 12: 7 you and your f shall eat and shall rejoice H1074
Jos 7:17 clan of the Zerahites come forward by f, H1505
Jos 21: 1 the heads of the other tribal f of Israel H3
2Sa 15:22 all his men and the f that were with him. H3251
1Ki 8: 1 of the tribes and the chiefs of the Israelite f, H3
2Ki 10:13 down to greet the f *of* the king and of the H1201
1Ch 4:38 Their f increased greatly, H1074+3
1Ch 5:13 Their relatives, by f, were: Michael H1074+3
1Ch 5:24 These were the heads of their f: Epher H1074+3
1Ch 5:24 famous men, and heads of their f. H1074+3
1Ch 7: 2 Ibsam and Samuel—heads of their f. H1074+3
1Ch 7: 7 Jerimoth and Iri, heads of f—five in all. H1074+3
1Ch 7: 9 the heads of f and 20,200 fighting H1074+3
1Ch 7:11 All these sons of Jediael were heads of f H3
1Ch 7:40 of Asher—heads of f, choice men, H1074+3
1Ch 8: 6 who were heads of f of those living in Geba H3
1Ch 8:10 These were his sons, heads of f. H3
1Ch 8:13 who were heads of f of those living in Aijalon H3
1Ch 8:28 All these were heads of f, chiefs as listed in H3
1Ch 9: 9 All these men were heads of their f. H1074+3
1Ch 9:13 who were heads of f, numbered 1,760. H1074+3
1Ch 9:33 heads of Levite f, stayed in the rooms of H3
1Ch 9:34 All these were heads of Levite f, chiefs as H3
1Ch 12:39 their f had supplied provisions for them. H278
1Ch 15:12 "You are the heads of the Levitical f; you H3
1Ch 16:28 to the LORD, *all you* f *of* nations, ascribe to H5476
1Ch 23: 9 These were the heads of the f of Ladan. H3
1Ch 23:24 the descendants of Levi by their f— H1074+3
1Ch 23:24 the heads of f as they were registered under H3
1Ch 24: 4 sixteen heads of f from Eleazar's H1074+3
1Ch 24: 4 eight heads of f from Ithamar's H1074+3
1Ch 24: 6 the heads of f of the priests and of the H3
1Ch 24:30 were the Levites, according to their f. H1074+3
1Ch 24:31 the heads of f of the priests and of the H3
1Ch 24:31 The f *of* the oldest brother were treated the H3
1Ch 26:13 according to their f, young and old H1074+3
1Ch 26:21 who were heads of f belonging to Ladan H3
1Ch 26:26 by the heads of f who were the commanders H3
1Ch 26:31 to the genealogical records of their f. H3
1Ch 26:32 who were able men and heads of f, and King H3
1Ch 27: 1 the Israelites—heads of f, commanders of H3
1Ch 29: 6 Then the leaders of f, the officers of the tribes H3
2Ch 1: 2 to all the leaders in Israel, the heads of f— H3
2Ch 5: 2 of the tribes and the chiefs of the Israelite f, H3
2Ch 17:14 Their enrollment by f was as follows H1074+3
2Ch 19: 8 heads of Israelite f to administer the law H3
2Ch 23: 2 the heads of Israelite f from all the towns. H3
2Ch 25: 5 according to their f to commanders of H1074+3
2Ch 31:17 enrolled by their f in the genealogical H1074+3
2Ch 35: 4 Prepare yourselves by f in your divisions, H1074+3
2Ch 35: 5 each subdivision of the f of your fellow H1074+3
2Ch 35:12 subdivisions of the f of the people to H1074+3
Ezr 2:59 show that their f were descended from H1074+3
Ezr 2:68 of the heads of the f gave freewill offerings H3
Ezr 4: 2 to the heads of the f and said, H3
Ezr 4: 3 rest of the heads of the f of Israel answered, H3
Ne 4:13 posting them by f, with their swords, H5476
Ne 4:14 fight for your f, your sons and your H278
Ne 7: 5 the common people for **registration by f**. H3509
Ne 7:61 show that their f were descended from H1074+3
Ne 7:70 of the heads of the f contributed to the work. H3
Ne 7:71 of the heads of the f gave to the treasury H3
Ne 8:13 the heads of all the f, along with the priests H3
Ne 10:34 when each of our f is to bring to the H1074+3
Ne 11:13 associates, who were heads of f—242 men; H3
Ne 12:12 these were the heads of the priestly f: H3
Job 21:21 they care about the f they leave behind H1074
Ps 22:27 all the f *of* the nations will bow down H5476
Ps 68: 6 God sets the lonely in f, he leads out the H1074
Ps 96: 7 to the LORD, all you f *of* nations, ascribe to H5476
Ps 107:41 affliction and increased their f like flocks. H5476
Jer 31: 1 "I will be the God of all the f *of* Israel H5476
Am 3: 2 have I chosen of all the f *of* the earth; H5476

FAMILY (203) [FAMILIES]

Ge 5: 1 is the written **account of** Adam's **f line**. H9352
Ge 6: 9 This is the **account of** Noah and his **f** H9352
Ge 7: 1 you and your whole f, because I have H1074
Ge 11:10 This is the **account of** Shem's **f line**. H9352
Ge 11:27 This is the **account of** Terah's **f line**. H9352
Ge 16: 2 perhaps *I can* **build a f** through her." H1215
Ge 19:32 preserve our **f line** through our father." H2446
Ge 19:34 can preserve our **f line** through our father H2446
Ge 24:38 go to my father's f and to my own clan H1074

Ge 24:40 from my own clan and from my father's f. H1074
Ge 25:12 is the **account of the f line** *of* Abraham's H9352
Ge 25:19 is the **account of the f line** *of* Abraham's H9352
Ge 30: 3 me and I too *can* **build a f** through her." H1215
Ge 34:19 was the most honored of all his father's f, H1074
Ge 36: 1 This is the **account of the f line** *of* Esau H9352
Ge 36: 9 is the **account of the f line** *of* Esau the H9352
Ge 36:43 This is the f line of Esau, the father of the NDT
Ge 37: 2 This is the **account** of Jacob's **f line** H9352
Ge 43: 7 us closely about ourselves and our f. H4580
Ge 46:27 the members of Jacob's f, which went to H1074
Ge 50:22 in Egypt, along with all his father's f. H1074
Ex 1: 1 went to Egypt with Jacob, each with his f: H1074
Ex 12: 3 each man is to take a lamb for his f, H1074+3
Lev 6:29 Any male in a priest's f may eat it; it is most NDT
Lev 7: 6 Any male in a priest's f may eat it, but it NDT
Lev 20: 5 against him and his f and will cut them H5476
Lev 22:10 " 'No one **outside a priest's** f may eat the H2424
Lev 25:10 to return to your **f property** and to your own H299
Lev 27:16 to the LORD part of their **f land,** H8441+299
Lev 27:22 which is not part of their **f land,** H8441+299
Lev 27:28 being or an animal or **f land**— H8441+299
Nu 1: 4 each of them the head of his f, is to H1074+3
Nu 1:44 of Israel, each one representing his f. H1074+3
Nu 2: 2 holding the banners of their f. H1074+3
Nu 2:34 each of them with their clan and f. H1074+3
Nu 3: 1 This is the **account of the f** *of* Aaron and H9352
Nu 11:10 the people of every f wailing at the H5476
Nu 18: 1 your sons and your f are to bear the H1074+3
Nu 25:14 of Salu, the leader of a Simeonite f. H1074+3
Nu 25:15 a tribal chief of a Midianite f. H1074+3
Nu 31:26 the priest and the f heads of the community H3
Nu 32:28 son of Nun and to the f heads of the Israelite H3
Nu 36: 1 The f heads of the clan of Gilead son of Makir H3
Dt 15:16 loves you and your f and is well off with H1074
Dt 15:20 year you and your f are to eat them in H1074
Dt 18: 8 money from the sale of **f possessions.** H3
Dt 25: 5 not marry **outside the f.** H2021+2575+2025+2424
Dt 25: 9 who will not build up his brother's **f line.**" H1074
Dt 25:10 in Israel as The F *of* the Unsandaled. H1074
Jos 2:12 that you will show kindness to my f, H1074+3
Jos 2:18 brothers and all your f into your house. H1074+3
Jos 6:23 brought out her entire f and put them in a H5476
Jos 6:25 with her f and all who belonged to her H1074+3
Jos 7:14 chooses shall come forward f by family; NDT
Jos 7:14 chooses shall come forward family by f; H1074
Jos 7:14 the f the LORD chooses shall come H1074
Jos 7:18 Joshua had his f come forward man by H1074
Jos 13:29 to half the f *of* the descendants of H4751
Jos 21: 1 Now the f heads of the Levites approached H3
Jos 22:14 each the head of a f division among the H3
Jos 24: 4 Jacob and his f went down to Egypt. H1201
Jdg 1:25 spared the man and his whole f. H5476
Jdg 4:17 of Hazor and the f *of* Heber the Kenite. H1074
Jdg 6:15 Manasseh, and I am the least in my f." H1074+3
Jdg 6:27 was afraid of his f and the H1074+3
Jdg 8:27 it became a snare to Gideon and his f. H1074
Jdg 8:35 to show any loyalty to the f *of* Jerub-Baal H1074
Jdg 9:16 you been fair to Jerub-Baal and his f? H1074
Jdg 9:18 you have revolted against my father's f. H1074
Jdg 9:19 faith toward Jerub-Baal and his f today? H1074
Jdg 9:28 Serve the f *of* Hamor, Shechem's H408
Jdg 11: 2 going to get any inheritance in our f," H1074+3
Jdg 16:31 his father's whole f went down to get him. H1074
Jdg 18:25 you and your f will lose your lives. H1074
Ru 3: 9 you *are a* **guardian-redeemer of** our f." H1457
Ru 3:12 that I *am a* **guardian-redeemer of** our f, H1457
Ru 4:10 from among his f or from his hometown. H278
Ru 4:11 who together built up the f *of* Israel. H1074
Ru 4:12 woman, may your f be like that of Perez H1074
Ru 4:18 is the **f line** *of* Perez: Perez was H9352
1Sa 1:21 went up with all his f to offer the annual H1074
1Sa 2:27 to your ancestor's f when they were in H1074
1Sa 2:28 gave your ancestor's f all the food H1074
1Sa 2:30 that **members of** your f H1074+2256+1074+3
1Sa 2:32 no one in your **f line** will ever reach old H1074
1Sa 2:36 left in your **f line** will come and bow H1074
1Sa 3:12 Eli everything I spoke against his f— H1074
1Sa 3:13 I would judge his f forever because of the H1074
1Sa 9:20 if not to you and your whole f **line**?" H1074+3
1Sa 17:25 will exempt his f from taxes in H3+1074
1Sa 18: 2 him and did not let him return home to his f. H3
1Sa 18:18 and what is my f or my clan in Israel H2646
1Sa 20:15 not ever cut off your kindness from my f— H1074
1Sa 20:29 because our f is observing a sacrifice in H5476
1Sa 22:11 son of Ahitub and all the men of his f, H3+1074
1Sa 22:15 accuse your servant or any of his father's f, H1074
1Sa 22:16 Ahimelek, you and your whole f." H3+1074
1Sa 22:22 the death of your whole f. H3+1074
1Sa 24:21 wipe out my name from my father's f." H1074
1Sa 27: 3 Each man had his f with him, and David H1074
2Sa 2: 3 each with his f, and they settled in H1074
2Sa 3: 8 of your father Saul and to his f and friends. H278
2Sa 3:29 the head of Joab and on his whole f! H3+1074
2Sa 3:29 May Joab's f never be without someone H1074
2Sa 7:18 and what is my f, that you have H1074
2Sa 9: 9 that belonged to Saul and his f. H1074
2Sa 14: 9 my lord the king pardon me and my f, H3+1074
2Sa 16: 5 same clan as Saul's f came out from there H1074
2Sa 21: 4 demand silver or gold from Saul or his f, H1074
2Sa 24:17 Let your hand fall on me and my f." H1074+3
1Ki 2:31 clear me and my **whole** f of the guilt of H3+1074
1Ki 14:14 Israel who will cut off the f *of* Jeroboam. H1074
1Ki 15:29 to reign, he killed Jeroboam's whole f. H1074
1Ki 16:11 the throne, he killed off Baasha's whole f. H1074
1Ki 16:12 So Zimri destroyed the whole f *of* Baasha H1074
1Ki 17:15 Elijah and for the woman and her f. H1074
1Ki 18:18 "But you and your father's f have. H1074
2Ki 8: 1 "Go away with your f and stay for a while H1074
2Ki 8: 2 She and her f went away and stayed in H1074
2Ki 8:27 he was related by marriage to Ahab's f. H1074
2Ki 10:17 he killed all who were left there of Ahab's f NDT
2Ki 11: 1 proceeded to destroy the whole royal f. H2446
1Ch 5:15 the son of Guni, was head of their f. H1074+3
1Ch 7: 4 According to their f genealogy, they H1074+3
1Ch 7:23 there had been misfortune in his f. H1074
1Ch 9:19 his fellow gatekeepers from his f H1074+3
1Ch 12:27 leader of the **f of Aaron,** with 3,700 men, H195
1Ch 12:28 warrior, with 22 officers from his f; H1074+3
1Ch 13:14 remained with the f *of* Obed-Edom in his H1074
1Ch 16:43 David returned home to bless his f. H1074
1Ch 17:16 and what is my f, that you have H1074
1Ch 21:17 let your hand fall on me and my f, but H1074+3
1Ch 23:11 counted as one f with one assignment H1074+3
1Ch 24: 6 one f being taken from Eleazar and H1074+3
1Ch 26: 6 in their father's f because they were very H1074
1Ch 27:15 the Netophathite, from the f of Othniel. NDT
1Ch 28: 4 me from my whole f to be king over H1074+3
1Ch 28: 4 from the tribe of Judah he chose my f, H1074+3
2Ch 21:13 *members of* your own f, men who H3+1074
2Ch 22:10 the whole royal f of the house of Judah. H2446
2Ch 26:12 The total number of f leaders over the fighting H3
2Ch 31:10 from the f *of* Zadok, answered, H1074
Ezr 1: 5 Then the f heads of Judah and Benjamin H3
Ezr 2:36 of Jedaiah (through the f *of* Jeshua) 973 H1074
Ezr 2:62 These searched for their f records, but H3509
Ezr 3:12 of the older priests and Levites and f heads, H3
Ezr 8: 1 These are the f heads and those registered H3
Ezr 8:29 the Levites and the f heads of Israel. H3
Ezr 10:16 the priest selected men who were f heads, H3
Ezr 10:16 one from each f division, and all of H3
Ne 1: 6 including myself and my father's f, have H1074
Ne 7:39 of Jedaiah (through the f *of* Jeshua) 973 H1074
Ne 7:64 These searched for their f records, but H3509
Ne 12:12 of Seraiah's f, Meraiah; of Jeremiah's NDT
Ne 12:22 The f heads of the Levites in the days of H3
Ne 12:23 The f heads among the descendants of Levi H3
Est 2:10 her nationality and **f background,** H4580
Est 2:20 kept secret her **f background** and H4580
Est 4:14 you and your father's f will perish. H1074
Est 8: 6 can I bear to see the destruction of my f?" H4580
Est 9:28 every generation by **every** f, H5476+2256+5476
Job 19:13 "He has alienated my f from me; my H278
Job 19:17 I am loathsome to my own f. H1201+1061
Job 32: 2 the Buzite, of the f *of* Ram, became very H5476
Ps 69: 8 I am a foreigner to my own f, a stranger to H278
Ps 122: 8 For the sake of my f and friends, I will say H278
Pr 11:29 brings ruin on their f will inherit only wind H1074
Pr 17: 2 will share the inheritance as one of the f. H278
Pr 27:10 Do not forsake your friend or a friend of your f H3
Pr 27:27 milk to feed your f and to nourish your H1074
Pr 31:15 provides food for her f and portions for her H1074
Isa 22:24 All the glory of his f will hang on him H1074+3
Jer 12: 6 **members of** your own f—even they H1074+3
Jer 35: 2 "Go to the Rekabite f and invite them to H1074
Jer 35: 3 all his sons—the whole f *of* the Rekabites. H1074
Jer 35:18 Jeremiah said to the f *of* the Rekabites, H1074
Jer 38:17 be burned down; you and your f will live. H1074
Eze 17:13 member of the royal f and made a treaty H2446
Eze 43:19 to the Levitical priests of the f *of* Zadok, H2446
Da 1: 3 from the royal f and the nobility— H2446
Da 11: 7 "One from her **f line** will arise to H5916+9247
Am 3: 1 against the whole f I brought up out of H5476
Zec 11:14 breaking the **f bond** between Judah and H288
Mk 3:21 When his f heard about this, they *G3836+4123*
Lk 9:61 let me go back and say goodbye to my f." *G3875*
Lk 12:52 will be five in one f divided against each *G3875*
Lk 16:27 send Lazarus to my f, *G3836+3875+3836+4252*
Jn 8:35 a slave has no permanent place in the f, *G3864*
Ac 4: 6 others of the high priest's f. *G1169*
Ac 7:13 Pharaoh learned about Joseph's f. *G1169*
Ac 7:14 sent for his father Jacob and his whole f, *G5149*
Ac 7:20 he was cared for by his f. *G3875+3836+4252*
Ac 10: 2 He and all his f were devout and *G3875*
Gal 6:10 to those *who* **belong to the** f of believers. *G3858*
Eph 3:15 from whom every f in heaven and on earth *G4255*
1Th 4:10 you do love all *of* **God's** f throughout *G3836+81*
1Ti 3: 4 must manage his own f well and see that *G3875*
1Ti 3: 5 does not know how to manage his own f, *G3875*
1Ti 5: 4 caring for their own f and so repaying *G3875*
Heb 2:11 those who are made holy are of the **same** *f.* AIT
Heb 11: 7 in holy fear built an ark to save his f. *G3875*
1Pe 2:17 everyone, love the **f of believers,** fear God, *G82*
1Pe 5: 9 know that the **f of believers** throughout the *G82*

FAMINE (102) [FAMINES]

Ge 12:10 Now there was a f in the land, and Abram H8280
Ge 12:10 a while because the f was severe. H8280
Ge 26: 1 Now there was a f in the land—besides H8280
Ge 26: 1 the previous f in Abraham's time— H8280
Ge 41:27 the east wind: They are seven years of f. H8280
Ge 41:30 seven years of f will follow them. H8280
Ge 41:30 forgotten, and the f will ravage the land. H8280
Ge 41:31 because the f that follows it will be so H8280
Ge 41:36 the seven years of f that will come upon H8280
Ge 41:36 the country may not be ruined by the f." H8280
Ge 41:50 Before the years of f came, two sons were H8280
Ge 41:54 the seven years of f began, just as H8280
Ge 41:54 There was f in all the other lands, but in H8280
Ge 41:55 When all Egypt *began to* **feel the** f, the H8279
Ge 41:56 When the f had spread over the whole H8280
Ge 41:56 the f was severe throughout Egypt. H8280
Ge 41:57 because the f was severe everywhere. H8280
Ge 42: 5 there was f in the land of Canaan also. H8280
Ge 43: 1 Now the f was still severe in the land. H8280
Ge 45: 6 years now there has been f in the land, H8280
Ge 45:11 because five years of f are still to come. H8280
Ge 47: 4 because the f is severe in Canaan and H8280
Ge 47:13 whole region because the f was severe; H8280
Ge 47:13 Canaan wasted away because of the f. H8280
Ge 47:20 because the f was too severe for them. H8280
Dt 32:24 I will send wasting f against them H8280
Ru 1: 1 judges ruled, there was a f in the land. H8280
2Sa 21: 1 there was a f for three successive years H8280
2Sa 24:13 come on you three years of f in your land? H8280
1Ki 8:37 "When f or plague comes to the land, or H8280
1Ki 18: 2 Now the f was severe in Samaria H8280
2Ki 4:38 to Gilgal and there was a f in that region. H8280
2Ki 6:25 There was a great f in the city; the siege H8280
2Ki 7: 4 into the city'—the f is there, and we will H8280
2Ki 8: 1 LORD has decreed a f in the land that will H8280
2Ki 25: 3 the fourth month the f in the city had H8280
1Ch 21:12 three years of f, three months of being H8280
2Ch 6:28 "When f or plague comes to the land, or H8280
2Ch 20: 9 plague or f, we will stand in your H8280
Ne 5: 3 our homes to get grain during the f." H8280
Job 5:20 In f he will deliver you from death, and in H8280
Job 5:22 You will laugh at destruction and f, and H4103
Ps 33:19 from death and keep them alive in f. H8280
Ps 37:19 in days of f they will enjoy plenty. H8282
Ps 105:16 He called down f on the land and H8280
Isa 14:30 But your root I will destroy by f; it will slay H8280
Isa 51:19 destruction, f and sword—who can H8280
Jer 5:12 come to us; we will never see sword or f. H8280
Jer 11:22 the sword, their sons and daughters by f. H8280
Jer 14:12 them with the sword, f and plague." H8280
Jer 14:13 'You will not see the sword or suffer f. H8280
Jer 14:15 'No sword or f will touch this land.' H8280
Jer 14:15 same prophets will perish by sword and f. H8280
Jer 14:16 of Jerusalem because of the f and sword. H8280
Jer 14:18 if I go into the city, I see the ravages of f. H8280
Jer 16: 4 They will perish by sword and f, and their H8280
Jer 18:21 So give their children over to f; hand them H8280
Jer 21: 7 the plague, sword and f, into the hands of H8280
Jer 21: 9 this city will die by the sword, f or plague. H8280
Jer 24:10 f and plague against them until they are H8280
Jer 27: 8 with the sword, f and plague, declares H8280
Jer 27:13 f and plague with which the LORD has H8280
Jer 29:17 f and plague against them and I will H8280
Jer 29:18 f and plague and will make them H8280
Jer 32:24 of the sword, f and plague, the city H8280
Jer 32:36 f and plague it will be given into the H8280
Jer 34:17 to fall by the sword, plague and f. H8280
Jer 38: 2 die by the sword, f or plague, but whoever H8280
Jer 42:16 the f you dread will follow you into H8280
Jer 42:17 die by the sword, f and plague; not one of H8280
Jer 42:22 f and plague in the place where you want H8280
Jer 44:12 they will fall by the sword or die from f. H8280
Jer 44:12 to the greatest, they will die by sword or f. H8280
Jer 44:13 in Egypt with the sword, f and plague, as I H8280
Jer 44:18 have been perishing by sword and f." H8280
Jer 44:27 perish by sword and f until they are all H8280
Jer 52: 6 the fourth month the f in the city had H8280
La 4: 9 are better off than those who die of f; H8280
Eze 5:12 of the plague or perish by f inside you; H8280
Eze 5:16 my deadly and destructive arrows of f, H8280
Eze 5:16 bring more and more f upon you and cut H8280
Eze 5:17 I will send f and wild beasts against you H8280
Eze 6:11 they will fall by the sword, f and plague. H8280
Eze 6:12 who survives and is spared will die of f. H8280
Eze 7:15 is the sword; inside are plague and f. H8280
Eze 7:15 the city will be devoured by f and plague. H8280
Eze 12:16 from the sword, f and plague, so that H8280
Eze 14:13 food supply and send f upon it and kill its H8280
Eze 14:21 sword and f and wild beasts and plague H8280
Eze 34:29 longer be victims of f in the land or bear H8280
Eze 36:29 it plentiful and will not bring f upon you. H8280
Eze 36:30 disgrace among the nations because of f. H8280
Am 8:11 "when I will send a f through the land H8280
Am 8:11 not a f of food or a thirst for water H8280
Am 8:11 a f of hearing the words of the LORD. NDT
Lk 4:25 there was a severe f throughout the land. *G3350*
Lk 15:14 there was a severe f in that whole country *G3350*
Ac 7:11 "Then a f struck all Egypt and Canaan *G3350*
Ac 11:28 that a severe f would spread over the *G3350*
Ro 8:35 persecution or f or nakedness or danger *G3350*
Rev 6: 8 to kill by sword, f and plague, and by the *G3350*
Rev 18: 8 mourning and f. She will be *G3350*

FAMINES (3) [FAMINE]

Mt 24: 7 There will be f and earthquakes in various *G3350*
Mk 13: 8 be earthquakes in various places, and f. *G3350*
Lk 21:11 f and pestilences in various places *G3350*

FAMISHED (3) [FAMISH]

Ge 25:29 Esau came in from the open country, f. H6546

Ge 25:30 me have some of that red stew! I'm **f**!" H6546
Isa 8:21 the land; when *they are* **f**, they will H8279

FAMOUS (11) [FAME]
Ru 4:11 Ephrathah and *be* **f** in Bethlehem. H7924+9005
Ru 4:14 *May* he *become* **f** throughout Israel! H7924+9005
2Sa 8:13 And David **became f** after he H6913+9005
2Sa 23:18 so he became as **f** as the Three. H9005
2Sa 23:22 he too was as **f** as the three mighty H9005
1Ki 1:47 *May* your God **make** Solomon's name more **f** H3512
1Ch 5:24 were brave warriors, **f** men, and heads of H9005
1Ch 11:20 so he became as **f** as the Three. H9005
1Ch 11:24 he too was as **f** as the three mighty H9005
1Ch 12:30 brave warriors, **f** in their own clans H408+9005
Isa 66:19 Libyans and Lydians (**f** as archers), to Tubal NDT

FAN (1) [FANS]
2Ti 1: 6 I remind you *to* **f into flame** the gift of God, *G351*

FANGS (5) [FANG]
Dt 32:24 send against them the **f** *of* wild beasts, H9094
Job 20:16 of serpents; the **f** *of* an adder will kill him. H4383
Job 29:17 I broke the **f** *of* the wicked and snatched H5506
Ps 58: 6 Lord, tear out the **f** *of* those lions! H4922
Joel 1: 6 has the teeth of a lion, the **f** *of* a lioness. H5506

FANS (1) [FAN]
Isa 54:16 blacksmith *who* **f** the coals *into* flame H5870

FANTASIES (3)
Ps 73:20 Lord, you will despise them as **f**. H7513
Pr 12:11 those who chase **f** have no sense. H8199
Pr 28:19 those who chase **f** will have their fill H8199

FAR (248) [AFAR, FAR-OFF, FARAWAY, FARTHER, FARTHEST]
Ge 10:19 from Sidon toward Gerar **as f as** Gaza, H6330
Ge 10:19 Admah and Zeboyim, **as f as** Lasha. H6330
Ge 12: 6 through the land **as f as** the site of the H6330
Ge 14: 6 of Seir, **as f as** El Paran near the desert. H6330
Ge 14:14 went in pursuit **as f as** Dan. H6330
Ge 14:15 pursuing them **as f as** Hobah, north of H6330
Ge 18:25 **F be it** from you to do such a thing—to kill H2721
Ge 18:25 the wicked alike. **F be it** from you! Will not H2721
Ge 44: 4 They had not gone **f** from the city when H8178
Ge 44: 7 **F be it** from your servants to do anything H2721
Ge 44:17 "**F be it** from me to do such a thing! H2721
Ex 1: 9 become **f too numerous** for H8041+2256+6786
Ex 3: 1 the flock to the **f side** *of* the wilderness H339
Ex 8:28 but *you* **must** not go **very f**. H8178+8178
Ex 26:22 Make six frames for the **f end**, that is, the H3752
Ex 26:23 two frames for the corners at the **f end**. H3752
Ex 26:27 the west, at the **f end** *of* the tabernacle. H3752
Ex 36:27 They made six frames for the **f end**, that is H3752
Ex 36:28 the corners of the tabernacle at the **f end**. H3752
Ex 36:32 the west, at the **f end** *of* the tabernacle. H3752
Lev 13:12 skin and, **so f as** the priest can see H4200+3972
Lev 13:37 sore is unchanged **so f as** the priest can H928
Nu 11:31 **as f as** a day's walk in any direction. H3869
Nu 13:21 land from the Desert of Zin **as f as** Rehob, H6330
Nu 16: 3 said to them, "You have **gone too f**! H8041
Nu 16: 7 You Levites have **gone too f**!" H8041
Nu 21:24 Jabbok, but only **as f as** the Ammonites H6330
Nu 21:26 from him all his land **as f as** the Arnon. H6330
Nu 21:30 have demolished them **as f as** Nophah, H6330
Dt 1: 7 to Lebanon, **as f as** the great river H6330
Dt 2:23 Avvites who lived in villages **as f as** Gaza, H6330
Dt 2:36 in the gorge, even **as f as** Gilead, not one H6330
Dt 3: 8 the Arnon Gorge **as f as** Mount Hermon. H6330
Dt 3:10 all Bashan **as f as** Salekah and Edrei H6330
Dt 3:14 region of Argob **as f as** the border of the H6330
Dt 4:49 of the Jordan, **as f as** the Dead Sea H6330
Dt 12:21 to put his Name *is too* **f away** from you, H8178
Dt 13: 7 whether near or **f**, from one end of the H8158
Dt 14:24 will choose to put his Name *is so* **f away**), H8178
Dt 28:49 bring a nation against you from **f away**, H8158
Dt 34: 2 the land of Judah **as f as** the H6330
Dt 34: 3 of Jericho, the City of Palms, **as f as** Zoar. H6330
Jos 7: 5 from the city gate **as f as** the stone H6330
Jos 8: 4 Don't go **very f** from it. All of you H8178
Jos 9: 1 Sea **as f as** Lebanon H448+4578
Jos 13: 4 of the Sidonians **as f as** Aphek and the H6330
Jos 13: 9 whole plateau of Medeba **as f as** Dibon, H6330
Jos 13:11 Hermon and all Bashan **as f as** Salekah— H6330
Jos 13:25 half the Ammonite country **as f as** Aroer, H6330
Jos 15: 5 is the Dead Sea **as f as** the mouth of the H6330
Jos 15:47 **as f as** the Wadi of Egypt and the H6330
Jos 16: 3 of the Japhletites **as f as** the region of H6330
Jos 19: 8 around these towns **as f as** Baalath Beer H6330
Jos 19:10 of their inheritance went **as f as** Sarid. H6330
Jos 19:28 Kanah, **as f as** Greater Sidon. H6330
Jos 22:29 "**F be it** from us to rebel against the LORD H2721
Jos 24: 6 chariots and horsemen **as f as** the Red Sea. NDT
Jos 24:16 "**F be it** from us to forsake the LORD to H2721
Jdg 4:16 chariots and army **as f as** Harosheth H6330
Jdg 7:22 toward Zererah **as f as** the border of Abel H6330
Jdg 7:24 Jordan ahead of them **as f as** Beth Barah." H6330
Jdg 7:24 waters of the Jordan **as f as** Beth Barah. H6330
Jdg 11:33 vicinity of Minnith, **as f as** Abel Keramim. H6330
Jdg 20:45 the Benjamites **as f as** Gidom and struck H6330
Ru 3: 7 to lie down at the **f end** *of* the grain pile. H7895
1Sa 2:30 LORD declares: '**F be it** from me! Those H2721
1Sa 6:12 followed them **as f as** the border of Beth H6330
1Sa 7:12 "**Thus f** the LORD has helped us." H6330+2178
1Sa 12:23 **f be it** from me that I should sin against H2721
1Sa 24: 3 and his men were **f back in** the cave. H928+3752
1Sa 26:20 to the ground **f from** the presence H4946+5584
2Sa 7:18 that you have brought me **this f**? H6330+2151
2Sa 19:15 king returned and went **as f as** the Jordan. H6330
2Sa 20:20 "**F be it** from me!" Joab replied, "Far be it H2721
2Sa 20:20 "**F be it** from me to swallow up or destroy! H2721
2Sa 23:17 "**F be it** from me, LORD, to do this!" he said H2721
1Ki 4:21 the Philistines, **as f as** the border of Egypt. H6330
1Ki 8:46 to their own lands, **f away** or near; H8158
1Ki 10: 7 wealth *you have* **f exceeded** the H3578
1Ki 12:30 at Bethel and went **as f as** Dan to worship H6330
2Ki 7:15 They followed them **as f as** the Jordan H6330
2Ki 18: 8 Philistines, **as f as** Gaza and its territory. H6330
1Ch 4:33 around these towns **as f as** Baalath. H6330
1Ch 5:11 next to them in Bashan, **as f as** Salekah: H6330
1Ch 5:16 of Sharon **as f as** they extended. H6584
1Ch 12:40 their neighbors from **as f away as** Issachar, H6330
1Ch 13: 2 let us send word **f and wide** to the rest of H7287
1Ch 17:16 that you have brought me **this f**? H6330+2151
2Ch 6:36 them captive to a land **f away** or near; H8158
2Ch 9: 6 *you have* **f exceeded** the report I heard. H3578
2Ch 9:26 the Philistines, **as f as** the border of Egypt. H6330
2Ch 12: 4 of Judah and came **as f as** Jerusalem. H6330
2Ch 14: 9 chariots, and came **as f as** Mareshah. H6330
2Ch 14:13 his army pursued them **as f as** Gerar. H6330
2Ch 26: 8 his fame spread **as f as** the border of H6330
2Ch 26:15 fame spread **f and wide**, H6330+4200+4946+8158
2Ch 30:10 Manasseh, **as f as** Zebulun, but H6330
2Ch 33:14 **as f as** the entrance of the Fish Gate and H2256
2Ch 34: 6 Simeon, **as f as** Naphtali, and in H6330
Ezr 3:13 sound was heard **f away**. H6330+4200+4946+8158
Ne 3: 1 building **as f as** the Tower of the Hundred, H6330
Ne 3: 1 and **as f as** the Tower of Hananel. H6330
Ne 3: 8 Jerusalem **as f as** the Broad Wall. H6330
Ne 3:13 cubits of the wall **as f as** the Dung Gate. H6330
Ne 3:15 **as f as** the steps going down from the City H6330
Ne 3:16 **as f as** the artificial pool and the House of H6330
Ne 3:19 ascent to the armory **as f as** the angle of the NDT
Ne 3:31 made repairs **as f as** the house of the H6330
Ne 3:31 and **as f as** the room above the corner H6330
Ne 5: 8 "**As f as possible**, we have bought H3869+1896
Ne 12:39 of the Hundred, **as f as** the Sheep Gate. H6330
Ne 12:43 Jerusalem could be heard **f away**. H4946+8158
Est 4: 2 But he went only **as f as** the king's gate H6330
Est 9:20 the provinces of King Xerxes, near and **f**, H8158
Job 5: 4 His children *are* **f** from safety, crushed in H8178
Job 13:21 **Withdraw** your hand **f** from me, and stop H8178
Job 22:23 If *you* **remove** wickedness **f** from your tent H8178
Job 28: 4 **F from** human dwellings they cut a H4946+6640
Job 28: 4 **f from** other people they dangle and sway. H4946
Job 34:10 **F be it** from God to do evil, from the H2721
Job 38:11 '**This f** you may come and no H6330+7024
Ps 10: 1 do you stand **f off**? Why do you hide H928+8158
Ps 22: 1 Why are you *so* **f** from saving me, so far H8158
Ps 22: 1 saving me, so **f** from my cries of anguish? NDT
Ps 22:11 *Do* not *be* **f** from me, for trouble is near H8178
Ps 22:19 LORD, *do* not *be* **f from** me. You are H8178
Ps 35:22 *Do* not *be* **f** from me, Lord. H8178
Ps 38:11 wounds; my neighbors stay **f away**. H4946+8158
Ps 38:21 forsake me; *do* not *be* **f** from me, my God H8178
Ps 49:14 the grave, **f from** their princely mansions. H4946
Ps 55: 7 *I would* flee **f away** and stay in the desert; H8178
Ps 55: 8 of shelter, **f from** the tempest and storm." H4946
Ps 71:12 *Do* not *be* **f** from me, my God; come H8178
Ps 73:27 *Those who* are **f** *from* you will perish; you H8179
Ps 80:11 Its branches reached **as f as** the Sea, its H6330
Ps 80:11 far as the Sea, its shoots **as f as** the River. H448
Ps 97: 9 you are exalted **f** above all gods. H4394
Ps 101: 4 The perverse of heart *shall be* **f** from me; H6073
Ps 103:12 as **f** as the east *is* from the west, so far H8178
Ps 103:12 *so* **f** *has he* **removed** our transgressions H8178
Ps 109:17 in blessing—*may it be* **f** from him. H8178
Ps 119:150 are near, but *they are* **f** from your law. H8178
Ps 119:155 Salvation is **f** from the wicked, for they do H8158
Ps 139: 9 if I settle on the **f side** *of* the sea, H344
Pr 4:24 **keep** corrupt talk **f** from your lips. H8178
Pr 5: 8 **Keep** *to* a path **f** from her, do not go near H8178
Pr 15:29 The LORD is **f** from the wicked, but he H8158
Pr 22: 5 would preserve their life **stay f** from them. H8178
Pr 22:15 the rod of discipline *will* **drive** it **f** away. H8178
Pr 27:10 a neighbor nearby than a relative **f away**. H8158
Pr 30: 8 **Keep** falsehood and lies **f** from me; give H8178
Pr 31:10 She is worth **f** more than rubies. H8158
Ecc 2: 9 I became greater **by f** than anyone in H3578
Ecc 7:24 Whatever exists is **f off** and most profound H8158
Isa 6:12 the LORD *has* **sent** everyone **f away** and the H8178
Isa 15: 5 her fugitives flee **as f as** Zoar, as far as H6330
Isa 15: 5 as far as Zoar, as **f** as Eglath Shelishiyah. NDT
Isa 15: 8 their wailing reaches **as f as** Eglaim, their H6330
Isa 15: 8 their lamentation as **f** as Beer Elim. NDT
Isa 16: 8 spread out and **went as f as** the sea. H6296
Isa 17:13 he rebukes them they flee **f away**, H4946+5305
Isa 18: 2 feared **f and wide**, H4946+2085+2256+2134
Isa 18: 7 feared **f and wide**, H4946+2085+2256+2134
Isa 22: 3 while the enemy was still **f away**. H4946+8158
Isa 29:13 their lips, but their hearts *are* **f** from me. H8178
Isa 33:13 You *who* are **f away**, hear what I have H8158
Isa 46:12 you who are now **f** from my righteousness. H8158
Isa 46:13 *it is* not **f away**; and my salvation H8178
Isa 49:19 those who devoured you *will be* **f away**. H8178
Isa 54:14 Tyranny *will be* **f** from *you*; you will have H8178
Isa 54:14 Terror will be **f** removed; it will not come NDT
Isa 56:12 will be like today, or **even f** better." H3856+4394
Isa 57: 9 You sent your ambassadors **f away** H4946+8158
Isa 57:19 to those **f** and near," says the H8158
Isa 59: 9 So justice *is* **f** from us, and righteousness H8178
Isa 59:11 find none; for deliverance, but *it is* **f away**. H8178
Jer 2: 5 find in me, that *they* **strayed** *so* **f** from me? H8178
Jer 8:19 the cry of my people from a land **f away**: H5305
Jer 12: 2 always on their lips but **f** from their hearts. H8158
Jer 23:23 the LORD, "and not a God **f away**? H4946+8158
Jer 25:26 the north, near and **f**, one after the other H8158
Jer 27:10 that *will only serve to* **remove** you **f** from H8178
Jer 31:40 Valley on the east **as f as** the corner of the H6330
Jer 43: 7 to the LORD and went **as f as** Tahpanhes. H6330
Jer 48:24 to all the towns of Moab, **f** and near. H8158
Jer 48:32 Your branches spread as **f** as the sea; they NDT
Jer 48:32 far as the sea; they reached **as f as** Jazer. H6330
Jer 48:34 from Zoar **as f as** Horonaim and Eglath H6330
Jer 49:31 its people live **f from danger**. H970
Eze 6:12 One *who* is **f away** will die of the plague H8158
Eze 8: 6 things that *will* **drive** me **f** from my H8178
Eze 10: 5 could be heard **as f away as** the outer H6330
Eze 11:15 Israelites, '*They are* **f away** from the LORD H8178
Eze 11:16 Although *I* **sent** them **f away** among the H8178
Eze 22: 5 those *who* are **f away** will mock you H8158
Eze 23:40 men who came from **f away**, H5305
Eze 27:26 will break you to pieces **f out** *at* sea. H928+4213
Eze 29:10 to Aswan, **as f as** the border of Cush. H6330
Eze 38: 6 Togarmah from the **f** north with all its H3752
Eze 38:15 will come from your place in the **f** north, H3752
Eze 39: 2 bring you from the **f** north and send you H3752
Eze 40:15 the gateway to the **f end** of its portico was H7164
Eze 44:10 " 'The Levites who **went f** from me when H8178
Eze 45: 9 You have **gone f enough**, princes of Israel! H8041
Eze 47:16 as **f** as Hazer Hattikon, which is on the NDT
Eze 47:18 to the Dead Sea and **as f as** Tamar. H2025
Eze 47:19 will run from Tamar **as f as** the waters of H6330
Da 9: 7 both near and **f**, in all the countries H8158
Da 11: 2 who will be **f** richer than all the others. H1524
Da 11:10 carry the battle **as f as** his fortress. H6330
Joel 2:20 "*I will* **drive** the northern horde **f** from you H8178
Joel 3: 6 that *you might* **send** them **f** from their H8178
Joel 3: 8 them to the Sabeans, a nation **f away**." H8158
Ob 20 will possess the land **as f as** Zarephath; H6330
Mic 4: 3 strong nations **f and wide**. H6330+8158
Zec 1:15 they **went too f** with the punishment. H6468
Zec 6:15 *Those who are* **f away** will come and help H8158
Mt 15: 8 their lips, but their hearts are **f** from me. *G4522*
Mk 7: 6 but their hearts *are* **f** from me. *G4522+600*
Mk 12:34 "You are not **f** from the kingdom of God." *G3426*
Lk 7: 6 He was not **f** from the house when the *G3426*
Lk 16:23 looked up and saw Abraham **f away**, *G608+3427*
Jn 6: 1 Jesus crossed to **the f shore** of the Sea of *G4305*
Jn 6: 9 but **how f** will they go among so many?" *G5515*
Jn 21: 8 they were not **f** from shore, about a *G3426*
Ac 2:39 children and for all who are **f off**— *G1650+3426*
Ac 11:19 was killed traveled **as f as** Phoenicia, *G2401*
Ac 17:27 though he is not **f** from any one of us. *G3426*
Ac 22:21 I will send you **f** away to the Gentiles. *G3426*
Ac 23:31 night and brought him **as f as** Antipatris. *G1650*
Ac 28:15 they traveled **as f as** the Forum of *G948*
Ro 11:28 **As f as** the gospel **is concerned** *G2848+3525*
Ro 11:28 but **as f as** election **is concerned**, they *G2848*
Ro 12:18 is possible, *as f as* **it depends on** you, live at AIT
2Co 1: 8 great pressure, *f* **beyond** our ability to endure AIT
2Co 4:17 glory *that* **f outweighs them all** *G2848+5651+1650+5651+983*
2Co 10:14 *We are* **not going too f** in our boasting, as *G2391*
2Co 10:14 we did get **as f as** you with the gospel *G948*
Eph 1:21 **f above** all rule and authority, power and *G5645*
Eph 2:13 you who once were **f away** have been *G3426*
Eph 2:17 to you who were **f away** and peace to *G3426*
Php 1:23 be with Christ, which is better **by f**; *G4498*
2Ti 3: 8 **as f as** the faith **is concerned**, are *G4309*
2Ti 3: 9 But *they will* **not get** very **f** because, as in *G4621*
Rev 2: 5 Consider **how f** you have fallen! Repent *G4470*
Rev 18:10 torment, they will stand **f off** and cry: *G608+3427*
Rev 18:15 their wealth from her will stand **f off**, *G608+3427*
Rev 18:17 living from the sea, will stand **f off**. *G608+3427*

FAR-OFF (2) [FAR]
Isa 23: 7 feet have taken her to settle in **f** lands? H8158
Isa 46:11 bird of prey; from a **f** land, a man to fulfill H5305

FARAWAY (1) [FAR]
Isa 13: 5 They come from **f** lands, from the ends of H5305

FARE (2) [FARED]
Isa 55: 2 you will delight in the **richest of f**. H2016
Jnh 1: 3 After paying the **f**, he went aboard and H8510

FARED (2) [FARE]
Ge 30:29 how your livestock *has* **f** under my care. H2118
Isa 10: 9 'Has not Kalno **f like** Carchemish? Is not H3869

FAREWELL (2)
2Sa 19:39 The king kissed Barzillai and **bid** him **f** H1385
Ac 15:29 You will do well to avoid these things. **F**. *G4874*

FARM (2) [FARMED, FARMER, FARMERS, FARMLANDS]
2Sa 9:10 your servants *are to* **f** the land for him H6268

Eze 48:19 from the city *who* **f** it will come from H6268

FARMED (2) [FARM]

1Ch 27:26 in charge of the workers who **f** the land. H6275
Heb 6: 7 to those for whom *it is* **f** receives the G1175

FARMER (9) [FARM]

Isa 28:24 When a **f** plows for planting, does he H3086
Jer 51:23 with you I shatter **f** and oxen, with you I H438
Zec 13: 5 I am a **f**; the land has been my H408+6268+141
Mt 13: 3 "A **f** went out to sow his seed. G5062
Mk 4: 3 A **f** went out to sow his seed. G5062
Mk 4:14 The **f** sows the word. G5062
Lk 8: 5 "A **f** went out to sow his seed. As he was G5062
2Ti 2: 6 The hardworking **f** should be the first to G1177
Jas 5: 7 See how the **f** waits for the land to yield G1177

FARMERS (8) [FARM]

Jer 14: 4 the **f** are dismayed and cover their heads. H438
Jer 31: 5 the **f** will plant them and enjoy their fruit. H5749
Jer 31:24 **f** and those who move about with their H438
Joel 1:11 Despair, you **f**, wail, you vine growers H438
Am 5:16 The **f** will be summoned to weep and the H438
Mt 21:33 the vineyard *to some* **f** and moved to G1177
Mk 12: 1 the vineyard *to some* **f** and moved to G1177
Lk 20: 9 rented it *to some* **f** and went away for a G1177

FARMLANDS (1) [FARM, LAND]

2Ch 31:19 lived on the **f** *around* their towns H4494+8441

FARTHER (6) [FAR]

1Ki 7: 8 to live, **set f back**, was similar H2958+2021+337
Job 38:11 'This far you may come and no **f**; here is H3578
Mt 26:39 **Going** a little **f**, he fell with his face to the G4601
Mk 1:19 *When he had* **gone** a little **f**, he saw G4581
Mk 14:35 **Going** a little **f**, he fell to the ground and G4601
Lk 24:28 Jesus continued on as if he were going **f**. G4522

FARTHEST (5) [FAR]

Jos 17:18 Clear it, and its **f limits** will be yours H9362
Ne 1: 9 if your exiled people are at the **f** horizon, H7895
Job 28: 3 search out the **f recesses** for ore in H3972+9417
Ps 65: 5 all the ends of the earth and of the **f** seas, H8158
Isa 41: 9 of the earth, from its **f corners** I called you. H721

FARTHING, FARTHINGS (KJV) CENTS, PENNIES, PENNY

FASHION (1) [FASHIONED, FASHIONING, FASHIONS]

Ex 28:15 "**F** a breastpiece for making decisions H6913

FASHIONED (7) [FASHION]

Ex 39: 8 *They* **f** the breastpiece—the work of a H6913
2Ki 19:18 only wood and stone, **f** *by* human hands. H5126
Ps 94: 9 Does he *who* **f** the ear not hear? Does he H5749
Isa 37:19 only wood and stone, **f** *by* human hands. H5126
Isa 45:18 he is God; *he who* **f** and made the earth H3670
Hos 13: 2 from their silver, **cleverly f** images, all of H9312
2Co 5: 5 Now the *one who has* **f** us for this very G2981

FASHIONING (1) [FASHION]

Ex 32: 4 cast in the shape of a calf, **f** it with a tool. H7445

FASHIONS (3) [FASHION]

Job 15:35 give birth to evil; their womb **f** deceit." H3922
Isa 40:19 it with gold and **f** silver chains for it. H7671
Isa 44:15 But *he* also **f** a god and worships it; he H7188

FAST (53) [FASTED, FASTING, FASTS]

Dt 4: 4 all of you who **held f** to the LORD your H1816
Dt 10:20 **Hold f** to him and take your oaths in his H1815
Dt 11:22 obedience to him and to **hold f** to him— H1815
Dt 13: 4 obey him; serve him and **hold f** to him. H1815
Dt 30:20 listen to his voice, and **hold f** to him. H1815
Jos 22: 5 to **hold f** to him and to serve him with all H1815
Jos 23: 8 But *you are to* **hold f** to the LORD your God H1815
Jdg 4:21 went quietly to him while he **lay f asleep**, H8101
1Ki 11: 2 Solomon **held f** to them in love. H1815
1Ki 21:12 They proclaimed a **f** and seated Naboth in H7427
2Ki 18: 6 *He* **held f** to the LORD and did not stop H1815
2Ch 20: 3 and he proclaimed a **f** for all Judah. H7427
Ezr 8:21 I proclaimed a **f**, so that we might H7427
Est 4:16 the Jews who are in Susa, and **f** for me. H7426
Est 4:16 I and my attendants *will* **f** as you do H7426
Est 8:10 who rode **f horses** especially bred for the H8224
Job 18: 9 him by the heel; a snare **holds** him **f**. H2616
Job 36: 8 in chains, **held f** by cords of affliction, H4334
Job 41:17 *They* **are joined f** to one another; they H1815
Ps 69:10 When I weep and **f**, I must endure scorn; H7427
Ps 119:31 *I* **hold f** to your statutes, LORD; do not let H1815
Ps 139:10 guide me, your right hand *will* **hold** me **f**. H296
Pr 3:18 *those who* **hold** her **f** will be blessed. H9461
Pr 5:22 the cords of their sins **hold** *them* **f**. H9461
Isa 56: 2 the person *who* **holds** it **f**, who keeps the H2616
Isa 56: 4 pleases me and **hold f** to my covenant— H2616
Isa 56: 6 it and *who* **hold f** to my covenant— H2616
Isa 58: 4 *You* cannot **f** as you do today and expect H7426
Isa 58: 5 Is this the kind of **f** I have chosen, only a H7427
Isa 58: 5 Is that what you call a **f**, a day acceptable H7427
Jer 14:12 Although *they* **f**, I will not listen to their cry; H7426
Jer 50:33 All their captors **hold** them **f**, refusing to H2616
Joel 1:14 Declare a holy **f**; call a sacred assembly H7427
Joel 2:15 declare a holy **f**, call a sacred H7427
Jnh 3: 5 A **f** was proclaimed, and all of them, from H7427
Mic 1:13 in Lachish, harness **f horses** to the chariot. H8224
Zec 7: 3 "Should I mourn and **f** in the fifth month H5692
Mt 6:16 "When *you* **f**, do not look somber as the G3764
Mt 6:17 But *when* you **f**, put oil on your head and G3764
Mt 9:14 is it that we and the Pharisees **f** often, G3764
Mt 9:14 fast often, but your disciples *do not* **f**?" G3764
Mt 9:15 will be taken from them; then *they will* **f**. G3764
Mk 2:19 of the bridegroom **f** while he is with them G3764
Mk 2:20 from them, and on that day *they will* **f**. G3764
Lk 5:33 "John's disciples often **f** and pray, and so G3764
Lk 5:34 of the bridegroom **f** while he is with them G3764
Lk 5:35 taken from them; in those days *they will* **f**." G3764
Lk 18:12 *I* **f** twice a week and give a tenth of all I G3764
Ac 27:41 The bow **stuck f** and would not move, and G2242
2Th 2:15 stand firm and **hold f** to the teachings we G3195
1Pe 5:12 this is the true grace of God. **Stand f** in it. G2705
Rev 3: 3 received and heard; **hold** it **f**, and repent. G5498
Rev 12:17 commands and **hold f** their testimony G2400

FASTED (15) [FAST]

Jdg 20:26 *They* **f** that day until evening and H7426
1Sa 7: 6 On that day *they* **f** and there they H7426
1Sa 31:13 tree at Jabesh, and *they* **f** seven days. H7426
2Sa 1:12 mourned and wept and **f** till evening for H7426
2Sa 12:16 He **f** and spent the nights lying in H7426+7427
2Sa 12:21 child was alive, *you* **f** and wept, but now H7426
2Sa 12:22 the child was still alive, *I* **f** and wept. H7426
1Ki 21:27 he tore his clothes, put on sackcloth and **f**. H7426
1Ch 10:12 tree in Jabesh, and *they* **f** seven days. H7426
Ezr 8:23 So *we* **f** and petitioned our God about this H7426
Ne 1: 4 days I mourned and **f** and prayed before H7426
Isa 58: 3 'Why *have we* **f**,' they say, 'and you have H7426
Zec 7: 5 'When *you* **f** and mourned in the fifth H7426
Zec 7: 5 was it really *for* me that *you* **f**? H7426+7426
Ac 13: 3 So *after they had* **f** and prayed, they G3764

FASTEN (16) [FASTENED, FASTENS]

Ex 25:12 gold rings for it and **f** them to its four feet, H5989
Ex 25:26 rings for the table and **f** them to the four H5989
Ex 26: 6 clasps and use them *to* **f** the curtains H2489
Ex 26:11 the loops *to* **f** the tent **together** as a unit. H2489
Ex 28:12 **f** them on the shoulder pieces of the H8492
Ex 28:23 gold rings for it and **f** them to two corners H5989
Ex 28:24 **F** the two gold chains to the rings at the H5989
Ex 28:37 **F** a blue cord to it to attach it to the turban H8492
Ex 29: 5 **F** the ephod on him by its skillfully woven H679
Ex 29: 9 **f** caps on them. Then tie sashes on H2502
Ex 36:13 clasps and used them *to* **f** the two sets of H2489
Ex 36:18 clasps to **f** the tent **together** as a unit. H2489
Job 13:27 *You* **f** my feet in shackles; you keep close H8492
Pr 6:21 on your heart; **f** them around your neck. H6698
Isa 22:21 robe and **f** your sash *around* him and H2616
Jer 10: 4 *they* **f** it with hammer and nails so it will H2616

FASTENED (20) [FASTEN]

Ex 28: 7 to two of its corners, so *it can* **be f**. H2489
Ex 37: 3 gold rings for it and **f** them to its four feet, NDT
Ex 37:13 rings for the table and **f** them to the four H5989
Ex 39: 4 to two of its corners, so *it could* **be f**. H2489
Ex 39: 7 Then *they* **f** them on the shoulder pieces H8492
Ex 39:16 **f** the rings to two of the corners of the H5989
Ex 39:17 *They* **f** the two gold chains to the rings at H5989
Ex 39:31 Then *they* **f** a blue cord to it to attach it to H5989
Lev 8: 7 *He* also **f** the ephod with a decorative H2520
Lev 8:13 sashes around them and **f** caps on them, H2502
Nu 19:15 without a lid **f** on it will be unclean. H7348
Jdg 15: 4 *He* then **f** a torch to every pair of tails, H8492
1Sa 17:39 David **f on** his sword over the tunic and H2520
1Sa 31:10 the Ashtoreths and **f** his body to the wall H9546
Est 1: 6 **f** with cords of white linen and purple H296
Eze 24:17 *Keep* your turban **f** and your sandals on H2502
Lk 4:20 everyone in the synagogue were **f on** him. G867
Jn 19:19 had a notice prepared and **f** to the cross. G5502
Ac 16:24 in the inner cell and **f** their feet in the G856
Ac 28: 3 driven out by the heat, **f** *itself* **on** his hand. G2750

FASTENS (2) [FASTEN]

Job 16: 9 my opponent **f** on me his **piercing** eyes. H4323
Job 33:11 *He* **f** my feet in shackles; he keeps close H8492

FASTING (22) [FAST]

2Sa 12:23 that he is dead, why *should* I go on **f**? H7426
1Ki 21: 9 "Proclaim a **day of f** and seat Naboth in a H7427
Ne 9: 1 **f** and wearing sackcloth and putting dust H7427
Est 4: 3 the Jews, with **f**, weeping and wailing H7427
Est 9:31 regard to their times of **f** and lamentation. H7427
Ps 35:13 on sackcloth and humbled myself with **f**. H7427
Ps 109:24 My knees give way from **f**; my body is thin H7427
Isa 58: 3 "Yet on the day of your **f**, you do as you H7427
Isa 58: 4 *Your* **f** ends in quarreling and strife, and H7426
Isa 58: 6 "Is not this the kind of **f** I have chosen: to H7427
Jer 36: 6 the LORD on a day of **f** and read to the H7427
Jer 36: 9 a **time of f** before the LORD was H7427
Da 9: 3 petition, in **f**, and in sackcloth and H7427
Joel 2:12 with **f** and weeping and mourning." H7427
Mt 4: 2 After **f** forty days and forty nights, he was G3764
Mt 6:16 their faces to show others *they are* **f**. G3764
Mt 6:18 not be obvious to others *that you are* **f**, G3764
Mk 2:18 John's disciples and the Pharisees were **f**. G3764
Mk 2:18 the disciples of the Pharisees *are* **f**, G3764
Lk 2:37 worshiped night and day, **f** and praying. G3763
Ac 13: 2 While they were worshiping the Lord and **f**, G3764
Ac 14:23 with prayer and **f**, committed them to G3763

FASTS (1) [FAST]

Zec 8:19 "The **f** *of* the fourth, fifth, seventh and H7427

FAT (93) [FATTENED, FATTENING]

Ge 4: 4 **f portions** from some of the firstborn of his H2693
Ge 41: 2 sleek and **f**, and they grazed H1374+1414
Ge 41: 4 gaunt ate up the seven sleek, **f** cows. H1374
Ge 41:18 up seven cows, **f** and sleek, and H1374+1414
Ge 41:20 ate up the seven **f** cows that came up H1374
Ge 45:18 Egypt and you can enjoy the **f** *of* the land. H2693
Ex 23:18 "The **f** *of* my festival offerings must not be H2693
Ex 29:13 Then take all the **f** on the internal organs H2693
Ex 29:13 both kidneys with the **f** on them, and H2693
Ex 29:22 "Take from this ram the **f**, the fat tail, the H2693
Ex 29:22 this ram the fat, the **f tail**, the fat on the H487
Ex 29:22 the fat tail, the **f** on the internal organs H2693
Ex 29:22 both kidneys with the **f** on them, and the H2693
Lev 1: 8 including the head and the **f**, on the H7022
Lev 1:12 including the head and the **f**, on the H7022
Lev 3: 3 organs and all the **f** that is connected to H2693
Lev 3: 4 both kidneys with the **f** on them near the H2693
Lev 3: 9 its **f**, the entire fat tail cut off close to the H2693
Lev 3: 9 the entire **f tail** cut off close to the H487
Lev 3: 9 organs and all the **f** that is connected to H2693
Lev 3:10 both kidneys with the **f** on them near the H2693
Lev 3:14 organs and all the **f** that is connected to H2693
Lev 3:15 both kidneys with the **f** on them near the H2693
Lev 3:16 a pleasing aroma. All the **f** is the LORD's. H2693
Lev 3:17 You must not eat any **f** or any blood.'" H2693
Lev 4: 8 shall remove all the **f** from the bull of the H2693
Lev 4: 8 all the **f** that is connected to the internal H2693
Lev 4: 9 both kidneys with the **f** on them near the H2693
Lev 4:10 just as the **f** is removed from the ox sacrificed NDT
Lev 4:19 shall remove all the **f** from it and burn it H2693
Lev 4:26 He shall burn all the **f** on the altar as he H2693
Lev 4:26 altar as he burned the **f** *of* the fellowship H2693
Lev 4:31 They shall remove all the **f**, just as the fat H2693
Lev 4:31 just as the **f** is removed from the H2693
Lev 4:35 They shall remove all the **f**, just as the fat H2693
Lev 4:35 just as the **f** is removed from the lamb of H2693
Lev 6:12 the fire and burn the **f** *of* the fellowship H2693
Lev 7: 3 All its **f** shall be offered: the fat tail and H2693
Lev 7: 3 the **f tail** and the fat that covers the internal H487
Lev 7: 3 the fat tail and the **f** that covers the H2693
Lev 7: 4 both kidneys with the **f** on them near the H2693
Lev 7:23 'Do not eat any of the **f** *of* cattle, sheep H2693
Lev 7:24 The **f** *of* an animal found dead or torn by H2693
Lev 7:25 Anyone who eats the **f** of an animal from H2693
Lev 7:30 they are to bring the **f**, together with the H2693
Lev 7:31 The priest shall burn the **f** on the altar, but H2693
Lev 7:33 the blood and the **f** *of* the fellowship H2693
Lev 8:16 also took all the **f** around the internal H2693
Lev 8:16 both kidneys and their **f**, and burned H2693
Lev 8:20 burned the head, the pieces and the **f**. H7022
Lev 8:25 After that, he took the **f**, the fat tail, all the H2693
Lev 8:25 he took the fat, the **f tail**, all the fat around H487
Lev 8:25 all the **f** around the internal organs H2693
Lev 8:25 kidneys and their **f** and the right thigh. H2693
Lev 8:26 put these on the **f portions** and on the H2693
Lev 9:10 On the altar he burned the **f**, the kidneys H2693
Lev 9:19 But the **f portions** of the ox and the ram H2693
Lev 9:19 ox and the ram—the **f tail**, the layer of fat, H487
Lev 9:19 the fat tail, the **layer of f**, the kidneys and H4833
Lev 9:20 then Aaron burned the **f** on the altar. H2693
Lev 9:24 offering and the **f portions** on the altar. H2693
Lev 10:15 brought with the **f portions** *of* the food H2693
Lev 16:25 shall also burn the **f** *of* the sin offering on H2693
Lev 17: 6 burn the **f** as an aroma pleasing H2693
Nu 18:17 altar and burn their **f** as a food offering, H2693
Dt 32:15 Jeshurun **grew f** and kicked; filled with H9042
Dt 32:38 the gods who ate the **f** *of* their sacrifices H2693
Jdg 3:17 king of Moab, who was a very **f** man. H1374
Jdg 3:22 the sword out, and the **f** closed in over it. H2693
1Sa 2:15 But even before the **f** was burned, the H2693
1Sa 2:16 said to him, "Let the **f** be burned first, and H2693
1Sa 15: 9 cattle, the **f** *calves* and lambs H5458
1Sa 15:22 to heed is better than the **f** *of* rams. H2693
1Ki 8:64 grain offerings and the **f** *of* the fellowship H2693
1Ki 8:64 grain offerings and the **f** *of* the fellowship H2693
2Ch 7: 7 burnt offerings and the **f** *of* the fellowship H2693
2Ch 7: 7 the grain offerings and the **f portions**. H2693
2Ch 29:35 together with the **f** *of* the fellowship H2693
2Ch 35:14 offerings and the **f portions** until nightfall. H2693
Job 15:27 face is covered with **f** and his waist bulges H2693
Ps 66:15 I will sacrifice **f animals** to you and an H4671
Isa 1:11 of rams and the **f** *of* fattened animals; H2693
Isa 10:27 be broken because you have grown so **f**. H9043
Isa 17: 4 the **f** *of* his body will waste away. H5458
Isa 34: 6 it is covered with **f**—the blood of lambs H2693
Isa 34: 6 goats, **f** *from* the kidneys of rams. H2693
Isa 34: 7 and the dust will be soaked with **f**. H2693
Isa 43:24 lavished on me the **f** *of* your sacrifices. H2693
Jer 5:28 and *have grown* **f** and sleek. Their evil H9042
Eze 34:20 judge between the **f** sheep and the lean H1374
Eze 39:19 you will eat **f** till you are glutted and drink H2693
Eze 44: 7 offered me food, **f** and blood, and you H2693
Eze 44:15 me to offer sacrifices of **f** and blood, H2693

FATAL (10)

Ex 21:12 a person **with a f blow** is to be put to H4637
Ex 22: 2 breaking in at night and is struck a **f blow**, H4637
Nu 35:16 strikes someone a **f** blow with an iron H4637

Nu 35:17 strikes someone a **f** blow with it, H4637
Nu 35:18 strikes someone a **f** blow with it, H4637
Jer 42:20 that *you* **made a f mistake** H9494+928+5883
Na 3:19 your wound *is* **f**. All who hear the H2703
Rev 13: 3 seemed to have had a **f** wound, *G1650+2505*
Rev 13: 3 the **f** wound had been healed. *G2505*
Rev 13:12 whose **f** wound had been healed. *G2505*

FATALLY (1)

Jer 51: 4 slain in Babylon, **f wounded** in her streets. H1991

FATE (16)

Nu 16:29 death and suffer the **f** *of* all mankind, H7213
Est 7: 7 that the king had already decided his **f**, H8288
Job 12: 5 misfortune as the **f** of those whose feet H5787
Job 18:20 People of the west are appalled at his **f** H3427
Job 20:29 Such is the **f** God allots the wicked, the H2750
Job 21:17 upon them, the **f** God allots in his anger? H2475
Job 27:13 "Here is the **f** God allots to the wicked H2750
Job 27:14 many his children, their **f** is the sword; his NDT
Ps 49:13 This is the **f** *of* those who trust in H2006
Ecc 2:14 that the same **f** overtakes them both. H5247
Ecc 2:15 "The **f** *of* the fool will overtake me also. H5247
Ecc 3:19 Surely the **f** *of* human beings is like that of H5247
Ecc 3:19 animals; the same **f** awaits them both: H5247
Isa 14:16 see you stare at you, they ponder your **f**: NDT
Jer 49:20 their pasture will be appalled **at** their **f**. H6584
Jer 50:45 their pasture will be appalled **at** their **f**. H6584

FATFLESHED (KJV) FAT

FATHER (1081) [FATHER-IN-LAW, FATHER'S, FATHERED, FATHERLESS, FATHERS, FOREFATHER, FOREFATHER'S, FOREFATHERS, GRANDFATHER, GRANDFATHER'S; see also ANCESTOR]

Ge 2:24 is why a man leaves his **f** and mother and is H3
Ge 4:18 and Irad *was the* **f** *of* Mehujael, and H3528
Ge 4:18 Mehujael *was the* **f** *of* Methushael H3528
Ge 4:18 Methushael *was the* **f** *of* Lamech. H3528
Ge 4:20 he was the **f** *of* those who live in tents and H3
Ge 4:21 he was the **f** *of* all who play stringed H3
Ge 5: 6 105 years, *he became the* **f** *of* Enosh. H3528
Ge 5: 7 After he *became the* **f** *of* Enosh, Seth lived H3528
Ge 5: 9 lived 90 years, *he became the* **f** *of* Kenan. H3528
Ge 5:10 After he *became the* **f** *of* Kenan, Enosh H3528
Ge 5:12 70 years, *he became the* **f** *of* Mahalalel. H3528
Ge 5:13 After he *became the* **f** *of* Mahalalel H3528
Ge 5:15 lived 65 years, *he became the* **f** *of* Jared. H3528
Ge 5:16 After he *became the* **f** *of* Jared, Mahalalel H3528
Ge 5:18 162 years, *he became the* **f** *of* Enoch. H3528
Ge 5:19 After he *became the* **f** *of* Enoch, Jared H3528
Ge 5:21 65 years, *he became the* **f** *of* Methuselah. H3528
Ge 5:22 After he *became the* **f** *of* Methuselah H3528
Ge 5:25 187 years, *he became the* **f** *of* Lamech. H3528
Ge 5:26 After he *became the* **f** *of* Lamech H3528
Ge 5:32 years old, *he became the* **f** *of* Shem, Ham H3528
Ge 9:18 (Ham was the **f** *of* Canaan.) H3
Ge 9:22 the **f** *of* Canaan, saw his father naked H3
Ge 9:22 saw his **f** naked and told his two brothers H3
Ge 9:23 way so that they would not see their **f** naked. H3
Ge 10: 8 Cush *was the* **f** *of* Nimrod, who became a H3528
Ge 10:13 Egypt *was the* **f** *of* the Ludites, Anamites H3528
Ge 10:15 *was the* **f** *of* Sidon his firstborn, and *of* the H3528
Ge 10:24 Arphaxad *was the* **f** *of* Shelah, and H3528
Ge 10:24 of Shelah, and Shelah *the* **f** *of* Eber. H3528
Ge 10:26 Joktan *was the* **f** *of* Almodad, Sheleph H3528
Ge 11:10 years old, *he became the* **f** *of* Arphaxad. H3528
Ge 11:11 And after he *became the* **f** *of* Arphaxad H3528
Ge 11:12 35 years, *he became the* **f** *of* Shelah. H3528
Ge 11:13 And after he *became the* **f** *of* Shelah H3528
Ge 11:14 lived 30 years, *he became the* **f** *of* Eber. H3528
Ge 11:15 And after he *became the* **f** *of* Eber, Shelah H3528
Ge 11:16 lived 34 years, *he became the* **f** *of* Peleg. H3528
Ge 11:17 And after he *became the* **f** *of* Peleg, Eber H3528
Ge 11:18 lived 30 years, *he became the* **f** *of* Reu. H3528
Ge 11:19 And after he *became the* **f** *of* Reu, Peleg H3528
Ge 11:20 lived 32 years, *he became the* **f** *of* Serug. H3528
Ge 11:21 And after he *became the* **f** *of* Serug, Reu H3528
Ge 11:22 lived 30 years, *he became the* **f** *of* Nahor. H3528
Ge 11:23 And after he *became the* **f** *of* Nahor, Serug H3528
Ge 11:24 lived 29 years, *he became the* **f** *of* Terah. H3528
Ge 11:25 And after he *became the* **f** *of* Terah, Nahor H3528
Ge 11:26 70 years, *he became the* **f** *of* Abram H3528
Ge 11:27 Terah *became the* **f** *of* Abram, Nahor and H3528
Ge 11:27 And Haran *became the* **f** *of* Lot. H3528
Ge 11:28 While his **f** Terah was still alive, Haran died in H3
Ge 11:29 of Haran, the **f** *of* both Milkah and Iskah. H3
Ge 17: 4 You will be the **f** *of* many nations. H3
Ge 17: 5 I have made you a **f** *of* many nations. H3
Ge 17:20 *He will be the* **f** *of* twelve rulers, and I will H3528
Ge 19:31 to the younger, "Our **f** is old, and there is no H3
Ge 19:32 Let's get our **f** to drink wine and then sleep H3
Ge 19:32 preserve our family line through our **f**." H3
Ge 19:33 That night they got their **f** to drink wine, and H3
Ge 19:34 to the younger, "Last night I slept with my **f**. H3
Ge 19:34 we can preserve our family line through our **f**." H3
Ge 19:35 So they got their **f** to drink wine that night also, H3
Ge 19:36 of Lot's daughters became pregnant by their **f**. H3
Ge 19:37 he is the **f** *of* the Moabites of today. H3
Ge 19:38 he is the **f** *of* the Ammonites of today. H3
Ge 20:12 the daughter of my **f** though not of my mother; H3
Ge 22: 7 Isaac spoke up and said to his **f** Abraham H3
Ge 22: 7 spoke up and said to his father Abraham, "**F**?" H3
Ge 22:21 Buz his brother, Kemuel (the **f** *of* Aram), H3
Ge 22:23 Bethuel *became the* **f** *of* Rebekah. H3528
Ge 25: 3 Jokshan *was the* **f** *of* Sheba and Dedan H3528
Ge 25:19 Abraham *became the* **f** *of* Isaac, H3528
Ge 26: 3 confirm the oath I swore to your **f** Abraham. H3
Ge 26:15 had dug in the time of his **f** Abraham, H3
Ge 26:18 had been dug in the time of his **f** Abraham, H3
Ge 26:18 them the same names his **f** had given them. H3
Ge 26:24 "I am the God of your **f** Abraham. H3
Ge 27: 6 I overheard your **f** say to your brother Esau, H3
Ge 27: 9 so I can prepare some tasty food for your **f** H3
Ge 27:10 Then take it to your **f** to eat, so that he may H3
Ge 27:12 What if my **f** touches me? I would appear to H3
Ge 27:14 some tasty food, just the way his **f** liked it. H3
Ge 27:18 He went to his **f** and said, "My father." "Yes H3
Ge 27:18 to his father and said, "My **f**." "Yes, my son," H3
Ge 27:19 Jacob said to his **f**, "I am Esau your firstborn. H3
Ge 27:22 Jacob went close to his **f** Isaac, who touched H3
Ge 27:26 Then his **f** Isaac said to him, "Come here, my H3
Ge 27:31 some tasty food and brought it to his **f**. H3
Ge 27:31 he said to him, "My **f**, please sit up and eat H3
Ge 27:32 His **f** Isaac asked him, "Who are you?" "I am H3
Ge 27:34 out with a loud and bitter cry and said to his **f**, H3
Ge 27:34 said to his father, "Bless me—me too, my **f**!" H3
Ge 27:38 Esau said to his **f**, "Do you have only one H3
Ge 27:38 "Do you have only one blessing, my **f**? H3
Ge 27:38 Bless me too, my **f**!" Then Esau wept aloud. H3
Ge 27:39 His **f** Isaac answered him, "Your dwelling will H3
Ge 27:41 because of the blessing his **f** had given him. H3
Ge 27:41 "The days of mourning for my **f** are near; then H3
Ge 28: 2 to the house of your mother's **f** Bethuel. H3
Ge 28: 7 Jacob had obeyed his **f** and mother and had H3
Ge 28: 8 the Canaanite women were to his **f** Isaac; H3
Ge 28:13 the God of your **f** Abraham and the God of H3
Ge 29:12 was a relative of her **f** and a son of Rebekah. H3
Ge 29:12 a son of Rebekah. So she ran and told her **f**. H3
Ge 31: 1 taken everything our **f** owned and has gained H3
Ge 31: 1 all this wealth from what belonged to our **f**." H3
Ge 31: 5 the God of my **f** has been with me. H3
Ge 31: 6 I've worked for your **f** with all my strength, H3
Ge 31: 7 your **f** has cheated me by changing my H3
Ge 31:16 took away from our **f** belongs to us and our H3
Ge 31:18 to go to his **f** Isaac in the land of Canaan. H3
Ge 31:29 last night the God of your **f** said to me H3
Ge 31:35 Rachel said to her **f**, "Don't be angry, my lord H3
Ge 31:42 If the God of my **f**, the God of Abraham and H3
Ge 31:53 the God of their **f**, judge between us. H3
Ge 31:53 an oath in the name of the Fear of his **f** Isaac. H3
Ge 32: 9 "O God of my **f** Abraham, God of my H3
Ge 32: 9 my father Abraham, God of my **f** Isaac, LORD, H3
Ge 33:19 sons of Hamor, the **f** *of* Shechem, the plot of H3
Ge 34: 4 And Shechem said to his **f** Hamor, "Get me H3
Ge 34: 6 Then Shechem's **f** Hamor went out to talk H3
Ge 34:11 Then Shechem said to Dinah's **f** and brothers H3
Ge 34:13 as they spoke to Shechem and his **f** Hamor. H3
Ge 35:18 But his **f** named him Benjamin. H3
Ge 35:27 Jacob came home to his **f** Isaac in Mamre H3
Ge 36: 9 line of Esau the **f** *of* the Edomites in the H3
Ge 36:24 he was grazing the donkeys of his **f** Zibeon. H3
Ge 36:43 the family line of Esau, the **f** *of* the Edomites. H3
Ge 37: 1 lived in the land where his **f** had stayed, H3
Ge 37: 2 he brought their **f** a bad report about H3
Ge 37: 4 saw that their **f** loved him more than any H3
Ge 37:10 When he told his **f** as well as his brothers, his H3
Ge 37:10 as his brothers, his **f** rebuked him and said H3
Ge 37:11 but his **f** kept the matter in mind. H3
Ge 37:22 him from them and take him back to his **f**. H3
Ge 37:32 took the ornate robe back to their **f** and said, H3
Ge 37:35 my son in the grave." So his **f** wept for him. H3
Ge 42:13 The youngest is now with our **f**, and one is no H3
Ge 42:29 they came to their **f** Jacob in the land of H3
Ge 42:32 brothers, sons of one **f**. One is no more, H3
Ge 42:32 the youngest is now with our **f** in Canaan. H3
Ge 42:35 When they and their **f** saw the money H3
Ge 42:36 Their **f** Jacob said to them, "You have H3
Ge 42:37 Then Reuben said to his **f**, "You may put both H3
Ge 43: 2 from Egypt, their **f** said to them, "Go back H3
Ge 43: 7 'Is your **f** still living?' he asked H3
Ge 43: 8 Then Judah said to Israel his **f**, "Send the boy H3
Ge 43:11 Then their **f** Israel said to them, "If it must be H3
Ge 43:23 the God of your **f**, has given you treasure H3
Ge 43:27 "How is your aged **f** you told me about? H3
Ge 43:28 "Your servant our **f** is still alive and well." H3
Ge 44:17 The rest of you, go back to your **f** in peace." H3
Ge 44:19 his servants, 'Do you have a **f** or a brother? H3
Ge 44:20 'We have an aged **f**, and there is a young son H3
Ge 44:20 of his mother's sons left, and his **f** loves him. H3
Ge 44:22 'The boy cannot leave his **f**; if he leaves him, H3
Ge 44:22 his father; if he leaves him, his **f** will die. H3
Ge 44:24 When we went back to your servant my **f**, we H3
Ge 44:25 "Then our **f** said, 'Go back and buy a little H3
Ge 44:27 "Your servant my **f** said to us, 'You know that H3
Ge 44:30 with us when I go back to your servant my **f**, H3
Ge 44:30 my father, and if my **f**, whose life is closely NDT
Ge 44:31 the gray head of our **f** down to the grave in H3
Ge 44:32 servant guaranteed the boy's safety to my **f**. H3
Ge 44:32 bear the blame before you, my **f**, all my life! H3
Ge 44:34 How can I go back to my **f** if the boy is not H3
Ge 44:34 me see the misery that would come on my **f**." H3
Ge 45: 3 Is my **f** still living?" But his H3
Ge 45: 8 He made me **f** to Pharaoh, lord of his entire H3
Ge 45: 9 Now hurry back to my **f** and say to him, 'This H3
Ge 45:13 Tell my **f** about all the honor accorded me in H3
Ge 45:13 And bring my **f** down here quickly." H3
Ge 45:18 bring your **f** and your families back to me H3
Ge 45:19 your wives, and get your **f** and come. H3
Ge 45:23 And this is what he sent to his **f**: ten donkeys H3
Ge 45:25 Egypt and came to their **f** Jacob in the land of H3
Ge 45:27 him back, the spirit of their **f** Jacob revived. H3
Ge 46: 1 he offered sacrifices to the God of his **f** Isaac. H3
Ge 46: 3 the God of your **f**," he said. "Do not be H3
Ge 46: 5 sons took their **f** Jacob and their children H3
Ge 46:29 went to Goshen to meet his **f** Israel. H3
Ge 46:29 his arms around **his f** and wept for a H2257S
Ge 47: 1 told Pharaoh, "My **f** and brothers, with H3
Ge 47: 5 "Your **f** and your brothers have come to you H3
Ge 47: 6 settle your **f** and your brothers in the best part H3
Ge 47: 7 Joseph brought his **f** Jacob in and presented H3
Ge 47:11 So Joseph settled his **f** and his brothers in H3
Ge 47:12 also provided his **f** and his brothers and H3
Ge 48: 1 Some time later Joseph was told, "Your **f** is ill." H3
Ge 48: 9 God has given me here," Joseph said to his **f**. H3
Ge 48:10 his **f** kissed them and embraced them. NDT
Ge 48:17 When Joseph saw his **f** placing his right hand H3
Ge 48:18 said to him, "No, my **f**, this one is the firstborn H3
Ge 48:19 But his **f** refused and said, "I know, my son, H3
Ge 49: 2 sons of Jacob; listen to your **f** Israel. H3
Ge 49:28 this is what their **f** said to them when he H3
Ge 50: 1 threw himself on his **f** and wept over him H3
Ge 50: 2 in his service to embalm his **f** Israel. H3
Ge 50: 5 'My **f** made me swear an oath and said, "I am H3
Ge 50: 5 Now let me go up and bury my **f**; then I will H3
Ge 50: 6 "Go up and bury your **f**, as he made you H3
Ge 50: 7 So Joseph went up to bury his **f**. All Pharaoh's H3
Ge 50:10 a seven-day period of mourning for his **f**. H3
Ge 50:14 After burying his **f**, Joseph returned to Egypt H3
Ge 50:14 others who had gone with him to bury his **f**. H3
Ge 50:15 Joseph's brothers saw that their **f** was dead, H3
Ge 50:16 "Your **f** left these instructions before he died: H3
Ge 50:17 the sins of the servants of the God of your **f**." H3
Ex 2:18 When the girls returned to Reuel their **f**, he H3
Ex 3: 6 "I am the God of your **f**, the God of Abraham, H3
Ex 20:12 "Honor your **f** and your mother, so that you H3
Ex 21:15 who attacks their **f** or mother is to be put to H3
Ex 21:17 who curses their **f** or mother is to be put H3
Ex 22:17 If her **f** absolutely refuses to give her to him H3
Ex 40:15 Anoint them just as you anointed their **f**, so H3
Lev 16:32 ordained to succeed his **f** as high priest is to H3
Lev 18: 7 " 'Do not dishonor your **f** by having sexual H3
Lev 18: 8 your father's wife; that would dishonor your **f**. H3
Lev 18:11 father's wife, born to your **f**; she is your sister. H3
Lev 19: 3 " 'Each of you must respect your mother and **f** H3
Lev 20: 9 who curses their **f** or mother is to be put H3
Lev 20: 9 Because they have cursed their **f** or mother H3
Lev 20:11 with his father's wife, he has dishonored his **f**. H3
Lev 20:17 the daughter of either his **f** or his mother, and H3
Lev 20:19 with the sister of either your mother or your **f**, H3
Lev 21: 2 such as his mother or **f**, his son or daughter, H3
Lev 21: 9 she disgraces her **f**; she must be burned in H3
Lev 21:11 himself unclean, even for his **f** or mother, H3
Lev 24:10 an Egyptian **f** went out among the H408
Nu 3: 4 as priests during the lifetime of their **f** Aaron. H3
Nu 6: 7 Even if their own **f** or mother or brother or H3
Nu 12:14 replied to Moses, "If her **f** had spit in her face H3
Nu 26:29 Makir *was the* **f** *of* Gilead); through H3528
Nu 26:60 Aaron *was the* **f** *of* Nadab and Abihu H3528
Nu 27: 3 "Our **f** died in the wilderness. He was not H3
Nu 27:11 If his **f** had no brothers, give his inheritance to H3
Nu 30: 4 her **f** hears about her vow or pledge but H3
Nu 30: 5 But if her **f** forbids her when he hears about it H3
Nu 30: 5 release her because her **f** has forbidden her. H3
Nu 30:16 between a **f** and his young daughter still H3
Dt 1:31 God carried you, as a **f** carries his son, all H408
Dt 5:16 "Honor your **f** and your mother, as the LORD H3
Dt 21:13 mourned her **f** and mother for a full H3
Dt 21:18 who does not obey his **f** and mother and will H3
Dt 21:19 his **f** and mother shall take hold of him and H3
Dt 22:15 then the young woman's **f** and mother shall H3
Dt 22:16 Her **f** will say to the elders, "I gave my H3
Dt 22:19 silver and give them to the young woman's **f**, H3
Dt 22:29 he shall pay her **f** fifty shekels of silver. H3
Dt 26: 5 "My **f** was a wandering Aramean, and he H3
Dt 27:16 is anyone who dishonors their **f** or mother." H3
Dt 27:22 the daughter of his **f** or the daughter of his H3
Dt 32: 6 Is he not your **F**, your Creator, who made you H3
Dt 32: 7 Ask your **f** and he will tell you, your elders H3
Dt 33: 9 He said of his **f** and mother, 'I have no regard H3
Jos 2:13 you will spare the lives of my **f** and mother, H3
Jos 2:18 unless you have brought your **f** and mother, H3
Jos 6:23 brought out Rahab, her **f** and mother, her H3
Jos 15:18 she urged him to ask her **f** for a field. H3
Jos 17: 4 inheritance along with the brothers of their **f**, H3
Jos 24: 2 including Terah the **f** *of* Abraham and Nahor H3
Jos 24: 3 But I took your **f** Abraham from the land H3
Jos 24:32 from the sons of Hamor, the **f** *of* Shechem. H3
Jdg 1:14 she urged him to ask her **f** for a field. H3
Jdg 8:32 in the tomb of his **f** Joash in Ophrah of the H3
Jdg 9:17 Remember that my **f** fought for you and risked H3
Jdg 9:28 of Hamor, Shechem's **f**! Why should we serve H3
Jdg 9:56 had done to his **f** by murdering his seventy H3
Jdg 11: 1 His **f** *was* Gilead; his mother was a H3528
Jdg 11:36 "My **f**," she replied, "you have given your H3
Jdg 11:39 she returned to her **f**, and he did to her as he H3

Jdg 14: 2 he said to his **f** and mother, "I have seen H3
Jdg 14: 3 His **f** and mother replied, "Isn't there an H3
Jdg 14: 3 But Samson said to his **f**, "Get her for me H3
Jdg 14: 5 to Timnah together with his **f** and mother. H3
Jdg 14: 6 he told neither his **f** nor his mother what he H3
Jdg 14:10 Now his **f** went down to see the woman. H3
Jdg 14:16 "I haven't even explained it to my **f** or mother," H3
Jdg 15: 1 But her **f** would not let him go in H3
Jdg 15: 6 went up and burned her and her **f** to death. H3
Jdg 16:31 Eshtaol in the tomb of Manoah his **f**. H3
Jdg 17:10 "Live with me and be my **f** and priest, and I'll H3
Jdg 18:19 Come with us, and be our **f** and priest. H3
Jdg 19: 3 and when her **f** saw him, he gladly H3
Jdg 19: 4 the woman's **f**, prevailed on him to stay; H3
Jdg 19: 5 the woman's **f** said to his son-in-law H3
Jdg 19: 6 Afterward the woman's **f** said, "Please stay H3
Jdg 19: 8 the woman's **f** said, "Refresh yourself H3
Jdg 19: 9 the woman's **f**, said, "Now look, H3
Ru 2:11 how you left your **f** and mother and your H3
Ru 4:17 He was the **f** *of* Jesse, the father of H3
Ru 4:17 He was the father of Jesse, the **f** *of* David. H3
Ru 4:18 Perez *was the* **f** *of* Hezron, H3528
Ru 4:19 Hezron *the* **f** *of* Ram, Ram the father of H3528
Ru 4:19 father of Ram, Ram *the* **f** *of* Amminadab, H3528
Ru 4:20 Amminadab *the* **f** *of* Nahshon, Nahshon H3528
Ru 4:20 of Nahshon, Nahshon *the* **f** *of* Salmon, H3528
Ru 4:21 Salmon *the* **f** *of* Boaz, Boaz the father of H3528
Ru 4:21 the father of Boaz, Boaz *the* **f** *of* Obed, H3528
Ru 4:22 Obed *the* **f** *of* Jesse, and Jesse the father H3528
Ru 4:22 father of Jesse, and Jesse *the* **f** *of* David. H3528
1Sa 9: 3 donkeys belonging to Saul's **f** Kish were lost, H3
1Sa 9: 5 my **f** will stop thinking about the donkeys H3
1Sa 10: 2 And now your **f** has stopped thinking about H3
1Sa 10:12 lived there answered, "And who is their **f**?" H3
1Sa 14: 1 on the other side." But he did not tell his **f**. H3
1Sa 14:27 not heard that his **f** had bound the people H3
1Sa 14:28 "Your **f** bound the army under a strict oath H3
1Sa 14:29 "My **f** has made trouble for the country. H3
1Sa 14:51 Saul's **f** Kish and Abner's father Ner were sons H3
1Sa 14:51 Kish and Abner's **f** Ner were sons of Abiel. H3
1Sa 19: 2 "My **f** Saul is looking for a chance to kill you. H3
1Sa 19: 3 out and stand with my **f** in the field where you H3
1Sa 19: 4 well of David to Saul his **f** and said to him, H3
1Sa 20: 1 How have I wronged your **f**, that he is trying to H3
1Sa 20: 2 my **f** doesn't do anything, great or small, H3
1Sa 20: 3 "Your **f** knows very well that I have found favor H3
1Sa 20: 6 If your **f** misses me at all, tell him, 'David H3
1Sa 20: 8 Why hand me over to your **f**?" H3
1Sa 20: 9 least inkling that my **f** was determined to H3
1Sa 20:10 will tell me if your **f** answers you harshly?" H3
1Sa 20:12 will surely sound out my **f** by this time the day H3
1Sa 20:13 But if my **f** intends to harm you, may the LORD H3
1Sa 20:13 LORD be with you as he has been with my **f**. H3
1Sa 20:32 What has he done?" Jonathan asked his **f**. H3
1Sa 20:33 knew that his **f** intended to kill David H3
1Sa 22: 3 "Would you let my **f** and mother come and H3
1Sa 23:17 "My **f** Saul will not lay a hand on you H3
1Sa 23:17 Even my **f** Saul knows this." H3
1Sa 24:11 my **f**, look at this piece of your robe in my H3
2Sa 3: 8 to the house of your **f** Saul and to his family H3
2Sa 6:21 me rather than your **f** or anyone from his H3
2Sa 7:14 I will be his **f**, and he will be my son. H3
2Sa 9: 7 you kindness for the sake of your **f** Jonathan. H3
2Sa 10: 2 just as his **f** showed kindness to me. H3
2Sa 10: 2 his sympathy to Hanun concerning his **f**. H3
2Sa 10: 3 David is honoring your **f** by sending envoys to H3
2Sa 13: 5 "When your **f** comes to see you, say to him, 'I H3
2Sa 16:19 Just as I served your **f**, so I will serve you." H3
2Sa 16:21 you have made yourself obnoxious to your **f**, H3
2Sa 17: 8 You know your **f** and his men; they are fighters, H3
2Sa 17: 8 your **f** is an experienced fighter; he H3
2Sa 17:10 Israel knows that your **f** is a fighter and that H3
2Sa 19:37 own town near the tomb of my **f** and mother. H3
2Sa 21:14 his son Jonathan in the tomb of Saul's **f** Kish, H3
1Ki 1: 6 His **f** had never rebuked him by asking, "Why H3
1Ki 2:12 So Solomon sat on the throne of his **f** David H3
1Ki 2:24 on the throne of my **f** David and has founded H3
1Ki 2:26 LORD before my **f** David and shared all my H3
1Ki 2:32 because without my **f** David knowing it he H3
1Ki 2:44 heart all the wrong you did to my **f** David. H3
1Ki 3: 3 to the instructions given him by his **f** David, H3
1Ki 3: 6 to your servant, my **f** David, because he was H3
1Ki 3: 7 your servant king in place of my **f** David. H3
1Ki 3:14 decrees and commands as David your **f** did, H3
1Ki 5: 1 been anointed king to succeed his **f** David, H3
1Ki 5: 3 wars waged against my **f** David from all sides, H3
1Ki 5: 5 as the LORD told my **f** David, when he said, H3
1Ki 6:12 you the promise I gave to David your **f**. H3
1Ki 7:14 of Naphtali and whose **f** was from Tyre and a H3
1Ki 7:51 in the things his **f** David had dedicated— H3
1Ki 8:15 promised with his own mouth to my **f** David. H3
1Ki 8:17 "My **f** David had it in his heart to build a H3
1Ki 8:18 But the LORD said to my **f** David, 'You did well H3
1Ki 8:20 succeeded David my **f** and now I sit on the H3
1Ki 8:24 kept your promise to your servant David my **f**; H3
1Ki 8:25 servant David my **f** the promises you made H3
1Ki 8:26 promised your servant David my **f** come true. H3
1Ki 9: 4 as David your **f** did, and do all I command H3
1Ki 9: 5 as I promised David your **f** when I said, 'You H3
1Ki 11: 4 as the heart of David his **f** had been. H3
1Ki 11: 6 the LORD completely, as David his **f** had done. H3
1Ki 11:12 the sake of David your **f**, I will not do it H3
1Ki 11:17 some Edomite officials who had served his **f**. H3
1Ki 11:27 the gap in the wall of the city of David his **f**. H3
1Ki 11:33 decrees and laws as David, Solomon's **f**, did. H3
1Ki 11:43 was buried in the city of David his **f**. H3
1Ki 12: 4 "Your **f** put a heavy yoke on us, but now H3
1Ki 12: 6 who had served his **f** Solomon during his H3
1Ki 12: 9 say to me, 'Lighten the yoke your **f** put on us'?" H3
1Ki 12:10 said to you, 'Your **f** put a heavy yoke on us H3
1Ki 12:11 My **f** laid on you a heavy yoke; I will make it H3
1Ki 12:11 My **f** scourged you with whips; I will scourge H3
1Ki 12:14 men and said, "My **f** made your yoke heavy; H3
1Ki 12:14 My **f** scourged you with whips; I will scourge H3
1Ki 13:11 They also told their **f** what he had said to the H3
1Ki 13:12 Their **f** asked them, "Which way did he go?" H3
1Ki 15: 3 all the sins his **f** had done before him; H3
1Ki 15:11 the eyes of the LORD, as his **f** David had done. H3
1Ki 15:15 the articles that he and his **f** had dedicated. H3
1Ki 15:19 "as there was between my **f** and your father. H3
1Ki 15:19 "as there was between my father and your **f**. H3
1Ki 15:24 buried with them in the city of his **f** David. H3
1Ki 15:26 the ways of his **f** and committing the same H3
1Ki 15:26 the same sin his **f** had caused Israel to NDT
1Ki 19:20 "Let me kiss my **f** and mother goodbye," H3
1Ki 20:34 return the cities my **f** took from your father," H3
1Ki 20:34 return the cities my father took from your **f**," H3
1Ki 20:34 areas in Damascus, as my **f** did in Samaria." H3
1Ki 22:43 the ways of his **f** Asa and did not stray H3
1Ki 22:46 there even after the reign of his **f** Asa. H3
1Ki 22:50 buried with them in the city of David his **f**. H3
1Ki 22:52 followed the ways of his **f** and mother and of H3
1Ki 22:53 the God of Israel, just as his **f** had done. H3
2Ki 2:12 this and cried out, "My **f**! My father! The H3
2Ki 2:12 My **f**! The chariots and horsemen H3
2Ki 3: 2 but not as his **f** and mother had done. H3
2Ki 3: 2 the sacred stone of Baal that his **f** had made. H3
2Ki 3:13 to the prophets of your **f** and the prophets of H3
2Ki 4:18 one day he went out to his **f**, who was H3
2Ki 4:19 He said to his **f**, "My head! My head!" His H3
2Ki 4:19 His **f** told a servant, "Carry him to his NDT
2Ki 5:13 to him and said, "My **f**, if the prophet had told H3
2Ki 6:21 he asked Elisha, "Shall I kill them, my **f**? H3
2Ki 9:25 behind Ahab his **f** when the LORD spoke this H3
2Ki 13:14 see him and wept over him. "My **f**! My father!" H3
2Ki 13:14 "My father! My **f**!" he cried. H3
2Ki 13:25 he had taken in battle from his **f** Jehoahaz. H3
2Ki 14: 3 of the LORD, but not as his **f** David had done. H3
2Ki 14: 3 he followed the example of his **f** Joash. H3
2Ki 14: 5 the officials who had murdered his **f** the king. H3
2Ki 14:21 made him king in place of his **f** Amaziah. H3
2Ki 15: 3 of the LORD, just as his **f** Amaziah had done. H3
2Ki 15:34 of the LORD, just as his **f** Uzziah had done. H3
2Ki 15:38 with them in the City of David, the city of his **f**. H3
2Ki 16: 2 Unlike David his **f**, he did not do what was H3
2Ki 18: 3 eyes of the LORD, just as his **f** David had done. H3
2Ki 20: 5 what the LORD, the God of your **f** David, says: H3
2Ki 21: 3 the high places his **f** Hezekiah had destroyed; H3
2Ki 21:20 eyes of the LORD, as his **f** Manasseh had done. H3
2Ki 21:21 He followed completely the ways of his **f** H3
2Ki 21:21 worshiping the idols his **f** had worshiped, and H3
2Ki 22: 2 followed completely the ways of his **f** David, H3
2Ki 23:30 him and made him king in place of his **f**. H3
2Ki 23:34 king in place of his **f** Josiah and changed H3
2Ki 24: 9 in the eyes of the LORD, just as his **f** had done. H3
1Ch 1:10 Cush *was the* **f** *of* Nimrod, who became a H3528
1Ch 1:11 Egypt *was the* **f** *of* the Ludites, Anamites H3528
1Ch 1:13 *was the* **f** *of* Sidon his firstborn, and *of* the H3528
1Ch 1:18 Arphaxad *was the* **f** *of* Shelah, and H3528
1Ch 1:18 of Shelah, and Shelah *the* **f** *of* Eber. H3528
1Ch 1:20 Joktan *was the* **f** *of* Almodad, Sheleph H3528
1Ch 1:34 Abraham *was the* **f** *of* Isaac. The sons of H3528
1Ch 2:10 Ram *was the* **f** *of* Amminadab, and H3528
1Ch 2:10 Amminadab *the* **f** *of* Nahshon, the H3528
1Ch 2:11 Nahshon *was the* **f** *of* Salmon, Salmon H3528
1Ch 2:11 father of Salmon, Salmon *the* **f** *of* Boaz, H3528
1Ch 2:12 Boaz *the* **f** *of* Obed and Obed the father of H3528
1Ch 2:12 father of Obed and Obed *the* **f** *of* Jesse. H3528
1Ch 2:13 Jesse *was the* **f** *of* Eliab his firstborn; the H3528
1Ch 2:17 of Amasa, whose **f** was Jether the Ishmaelite. H3
1Ch 2:20 Hur *was the* **f** *of* Uri, and Uri the father of H3528
1Ch 2:20 the father of Uri, and Uri *the* **f** *of* Bezalel. H3528
1Ch 2:21 married the daughter of Makir the **f** *of* Gilead. H3
1Ch 2:22 Segub *was the* **f** *of* Jair, who controlled H3528
1Ch 2:23 were descendants of Makir the **f** *of* Gilead. H3
1Ch 2:24 of Hezron bore him Ashhur the **f** *of* Tekoa. H3
1Ch 2:31 who was the **f** *of* Sheshan. H1201S
1Ch 2:31 Sheshan was the **f** *of* Ahlai. H1201S
1Ch 2:36 Attai *was the* **f** *of* Nathan, Nathan the H3528
1Ch 2:36 father of Nathan, Nathan *the* **f** *of* Zabad, H3528
1Ch 2:37 Zabad *the* **f** *of* Ephlal, Ephlal the father of H3528
1Ch 2:37 the father of Ephlal, Ephlal *the* **f** *of* Obed, H3528
1Ch 2:38 Obed *the* **f** *of* Jehu, Jehu the father of H3528
1Ch 2:38 the father of Jehu, Jehu *the* **f** *of* Azariah, H3528
1Ch 2:39 Azariah *the* **f** *of* Helez, Helez the father of H3528
1Ch 2:39 father of Helez, Helez *the* **f** *of* Eleasah, H3528
1Ch 2:40 Eleasah *the* **f** *of* Sismai, Sismai the father H3528
1Ch 2:40 father of Sismai, Sismai *the* **f** *of* Shallum, H3528
1Ch 2:41 Shallum *the* **f** *of* Jekamiah, and Jekamiah H3528
1Ch 2:41 Jekamiah *the* **f** *of* Elishama. H3528
1Ch 2:42 firstborn, who was the **f** *of* Ziph, and his son H3
1Ch 2:42 his son Mareshah, who was the **f** *of* Hebron. H3
1Ch 2:44 Shema *was the* **f** *of* Raham, and Raham H3528
1Ch 2:44 of Raham, and Raham the **f** *of* Jorkeam. H3
1Ch 2:44 Rekem *was the* **f** *of* Shammai. H3528
1Ch 2:45 was Maon, and Maon was the **f** *of* Beth Zur. H3
1Ch 2:46 Haran *was the* **f** *of* Gazez. H3528
1Ch 2:49 birth to Shaaph the **f** *of* Madmannah and to H3
1Ch 2:49 to Sheva the **f** *of* Makbenah and Gibea. H3
1Ch 2:50 Shobal the **f** *of* Kiriath Jearim, H3
1Ch 2:51 Salma the **f** *of* Bethlehem, and Hareph the H3
1Ch 2:51 Bethlehem, and Hareph the **f** *of* Beth Gader. H3
1Ch 2:52 of Shobal the **f** *of* Kiriath Jearim were: H3
1Ch 2:55 came from Hammath, the **f** *of* the Rekabites. H3
1Ch 4: 2 Reaiah son of Shobal *was the* **f** *of* Jahath H3528
1Ch 4: 2 Jahath *the* **f** *of* Ahumai and Lahad. H3528
1Ch 4: 4 Penuel was the **f** *of* Gedor, and Ezer the H3
1Ch 4: 4 the father of Gedor, and Ezer the **f** *of* Hushah. H3
1Ch 4: 4 the firstborn of Ephrathah and **f** *of* Bethlehem. H3
1Ch 4: 5 Ashhur the **f** *of* Tekoa had two wives, Helah H3
1Ch 4: 8 *who was the* **f** *of* Anub and Hazzobebah H3528
1Ch 4:11 brother, *was the* **f** *of* Mehir, who was H3528
1Ch 4:11 the father of Mehir, who was the **f** *of* Eshton. H3
1Ch 4:12 Eshton *was the* **f** *of* Beth Rapha, Paseah H3528
1Ch 4:12 Paseah and Tehinnah the **f** *of* Ir Nahash. H3
1Ch 4:14 Meonothai *was the* **f** *of* Ophrah. H3528
1Ch 4:14 Seraiah *was the* **f** *of* Joab, the father of H3528
1Ch 4:14 was the father of Joab, the **f** *of* Ge Harashim. H3
1Ch 4:17 Shammai and Ishbah the **f** *of* Eshtemoa. H3
1Ch 4:18 of Judah gave birth to Jered the **f** *of* Gedor, H3
1Ch 4:18 of Gedor, Heber the **f** *of* Soko, and Jekuthiel H3
1Ch 4:18 father of Soko, and Jekuthiel the **f** *of* Zanoah.) H3
1Ch 4:19 the **f** *of* Keilah the Garmite, and Eshtemoa H3
1Ch 4:21 Er the **f** *of* Lekah, Laadah the father of H3
1Ch 4:21 Laadah the **f** *of* Mareshah and the clans of H3
1Ch 6: 4 Eleazar *was the* **f** *of* Phinehas, Phinehas H3528
1Ch 6: 4 of Phinehas, Phinehas *the* **f** *of* Abishua, H3528
1Ch 6: 5 Abishua *the* **f** *of* Bukki, Bukki the father of H3528
1Ch 6: 5 the father of Bukki, Bukki *the* **f** *of* Uzzi, H3528
1Ch 6: 6 Uzzi *the* **f** *of* Zerahiah, Zerahiah the father H3528
1Ch 6: 6 of Zerahiah, Zerahiah *the* **f** *of* Meraioth, H3528
1Ch 6: 7 Meraioth *the* **f** *of* Amariah, Amariah the H3528
1Ch 6: 7 of Amariah, Amariah *the* **f** *of* Ahitub, H3528
1Ch 6: 8 Ahitub *the* **f** *of* Zadok, Zadok the father of H3528
1Ch 6: 8 father of Zadok, Zadok *the* **f** *of* Ahimaaz, H3528
1Ch 6: 9 Ahimaaz *the* **f** *of* Azariah, Azariah the H3528
1Ch 6: 9 of Azariah, Azariah *the* **f** *of* Johanan, H3528
1Ch 6:10 Johanan *the* **f** *of* Azariah (it was he who H3528
1Ch 6:11 Azariah *the* **f** *of* Amariah, Amariah the H3528
1Ch 6:11 of Amariah, Amariah *the* **f** *of* Ahitub, H3528
1Ch 6:12 Ahitub *the* **f** *of* Zadok, Zadok the father of H3528
1Ch 6:12 father of Zadok, Zadok *the* **f** *of* Shallum, H3528
1Ch 6:13 Shallum *the* **f** *of* Hilkiah, Hilkiah the H3528
1Ch 6:13 father of Hilkiah, Hilkiah *the* **f** *of* Azariah, H3528
1Ch 6:14 Azariah *the* **f** *of* Seraiah, and Seraiah the H3528
1Ch 6:14 of Seraiah, and Seraiah *the* **f** *of* Jozadak. H3528
1Ch 7:14 She gave birth to Makir the **f** *of* Gilead. H3
1Ch 7:22 Their **f** Ephraim mourned for them many days H3
1Ch 7:31 Heber and Malkiel, who was the **f** *of* Birzaith. H3
1Ch 7:32 Heber *was the* **f** *of* Japhlet, Shomer and H3528
1Ch 8: 1 Benjamin *was the* **f** *of* Bela his firstborn H3528
1Ch 8: 7 them and *who was the* **f** *of* Uzza and H3528
1Ch 8:29 Jeiel the **f** *of* Gibeon lived in Gibeon. H3
1Ch 8:32 Mikloth, *who was the* **f** *of* Shimeah H3528
1Ch 8:33 Ner *was the* **f** *of* Kish, Kish the father of H3528
1Ch 8:33 Kish *the* **f** *of* Saul, and Saul the H3528
1Ch 8:33 of Saul, and Saul *the* **f** *of* Jonathan H3528
1Ch 8:34 Merib-Baal, who *was the* **f** *of* Micah. H3528
1Ch 8:36 Ahaz *was the* **f** *of* Jehoaddah, Jehoaddah H3528
1Ch 8:36 Jehoaddah *was the* **f** *of* Alemeth H3528
1Ch 8:36 Zimri, and Zimri *was the* **f** *of* Moza. H3528
1Ch 8:37 Moza *was the* **f** *of* Binea; Raphah was his H3528
1Ch 9:35 Jeiel the **f** *of* Gibeon lived in Gibeon. H3
1Ch 9:38 Mikloth *was the* **f** *of* Shimeam. H3528
1Ch 9:39 Ner *was the* **f** *of* Kish, Kish the father of H3528
1Ch 9:39 Kish *the* **f** *of* Saul, and Saul the H3528
1Ch 9:39 of Saul, and Saul *the* **f** *of* Jonathan H3528
1Ch 9:40 Merib-Baal, who *was the* **f** *of* Micah. H3528
1Ch 9:42 Ahaz *was the* **f** *of* Jadah, Jadah was the H3528
1Ch 9:42 of Jadah, Jadah *was the* **f** *of* Alemeth H3528
1Ch 9:42 Zimri, and Zimri *was the* **f** *of* Moza. H3528
1Ch 9:43 Moza *was the* **f** *of* Binea; Rephaiah was H3528
1Ch 14: 3 wives and *became the* **f** *of* more sons H3528
1Ch 17:13 I will be his **f**, and he will be my son. H3
1Ch 19: 2 because his **f** showed kindness to me." H3
1Ch 19: 2 his sympathy to Hanun concerning his **f**. H3
1Ch 19: 3 David is honoring your **f** by sending envoys to H3
1Ch 22:10 and I will be his **f**. And I will establish H3
1Ch 24: 2 But Nadab and Abihu died before their **f** did H3
1Ch 25: 3 under the supervision of their **f** Jeduthun, who H3
1Ch 25: 6 the supervision of their **f** for the music of the H3
1Ch 26:10 the firstborn, his **f** had appointed him the first), H3
1Ch 28: 6 chosen him to be my son, and I will be his **f**. H3
1Ch 28: 9 acknowledge the God of your **f**, and serve him H3
1Ch 29:10 the God of our **f** Israel, from everlasting H3
1Ch 29:23 of the LORD as king in place of his **f** David. H3
2Ch 1: 8 kindness to David my **f** and have made me H3
2Ch 1: 9 let your promise to my **f** David be confirmed H3
2Ch 2: 3 logs as you did for my **f** David when you sent H3
2Ch 2: 7 skilled workers, whom my **f** David provided. H3
2Ch 2:14 was from Dan and whose **f** was from Tyre. H3
2Ch 2:14 with those of my lord, David your **f**. H3
2Ch 2:17 after the census his **f** David had taken; and H3
2Ch 3: 1 where the LORD had appeared to his **f** David. H3
2Ch 5: 1 in the things his **f** David had dedicated— H3
2Ch 6: 4 he promised with his mouth to my **f** David. H3

Book	Ref	Context	Number
2Ch	6: 7	“My **f** David had it in his heart to build a	H3
2Ch	6: 8	But the LORD said to my **f** David, ‘You did well	H3
2Ch	6:10	succeeded David my **f** and now I sit on the	H3
2Ch	6:15	kept your promise to your servant David my **f**;	H3
2Ch	6:16	servant David my **f** the promises you made	H3
2Ch	7:17	walk before me faithfully as David your **f** did,	H3
2Ch	7:18	as I covenanted with David your **f** when I said	H3
2Ch	8:14	In keeping with the ordinance of his **f** David	H3
2Ch	9:31	was buried in the city of David his **f**.	H3
2Ch	10: 4	“Your **f** put a heavy yoke on us, but now	H3
2Ch	10: 6	who had served his **f** Solomon during his	H3
2Ch	10: 9	say to me, ‘Lighten the yoke your **f** put on us’?”	H3
2Ch	10:10	said to you, ‘Your **f** put a heavy yoke on us	H3
2Ch	10:11	My **f** laid on you a heavy yoke; I will make it	H3
2Ch	10:11	My **f** scourged you with whips; I will scourge	H3
2Ch	10:14	men and said, “My **f** made your yoke heavy;	H3
2Ch	10:14	My **f** scourged you with whips; I will scourge	H3
2Ch	15:18	the articles that he and his **f** had dedicated.	H3
2Ch	16: 3	“as there was between my **f** and your father.	H3
2Ch	16: 3	“as there was between my father and your **f**.	H3
2Ch	17: 2	towns of Ephraim that his **f** Asa had captured.	H3
2Ch	17: 3	followed the ways of his **f** David before him.	H3
2Ch	17: 4	sought the God of his **f** and followed his	H3
2Ch	20:32	the ways of his **f** Asa and did not stray	H3
2Ch	21: 3	Their **f** had given them many gifts of silver	H3
2Ch	21:12	what the LORD, the God of your **f** David, says:	H3
2Ch	21:12	the ways of your **f** Jehoshaphat or of Asa	H3
2Ch	24:22	kindness Zechariah’s **f** Jehoiada had shown	H3
2Ch	25: 3	the officials who had murdered his **f** the king.	H3
2Ch	26: 1	made him king in place of his **f** Amaziah.	H3
2Ch	26: 4	of the LORD, just as his **f** Amaziah had done.	H3
2Ch	27: 2	of the LORD, just as his **f** Uzziah had done, but	H3
2Ch	28: 1	Unlike David his **f**, he did not do what was	H3
2Ch	29: 2	eyes of the LORD, just as his **f** David had done.	H3
2Ch	33: 3	the high places his **f** Hezekiah had	H3
2Ch	33:22	eyes of the LORD, as his **f** Manasseh had done.	H3
2Ch	33:23	But unlike his **f** Manasseh, he did not humble	H3
2Ch	34: 2	the LORD and followed the ways of his **f** David,	H3
2Ch	34: 3	he began to seek the God of his **f** David.	H3
2Ch	36: 1	made him king in Jerusalem in place of his **f**.	H3
Ne	12:10	Joshua *was the* **f** *of* Joiakim, Joiakim the	H3528
Ne	12:10	Joiakim, Joiakim *the* **f** *of* Eliashib	H3528
Ne	12:10	father of Eliashib, Eliashib the **f** of Joiada,	NDT
Ne	12:11	Joiada *the* **f** *of* Jonathan, and Jonathan	H3528
Ne	12:11	Jonathan, and Jonathan *the* **f** *of* Jaddua.	H3528
Est	2: 7	up because she had neither **f** nor mother.	H3
Est	2: 7	own daughter when her **f** and mother died.	H3
Job	15:10	are on our side, men even older than your **f**.	H3
Job	17:14	to corruption, ‘You are my **f**,’ and to the worm,	H3
Job	29:16	I was a **f** to the needy; I took up the case of	H3
Job	31:18	from my youth I reared them as a **f** would	H3
Job	38:28	Does the rain have a **f**? Who fathers the drops	H3
Job	42:15	their **f** granted them an inheritance along	H3
Ps	2: 7	are my son; today I *have become* your **f**.	H3528
Ps	27:10	Though my **f** and mother forsake me, the LORD	H3
Ps	68: 5	A **f** *to* the fatherless, a defender of widows, is	H3
Ps	89:26	‘You are my **F**, my God, the Rock my	H3
Ps	103:13	As a **f** has compassion on his children, so the	H3
Pr	3:12	those he loves, as a **f** the son he delights in.	H3
Pr	4: 3	For I too was a son to my **f**, still tender, and	H3
Pr	10: 1	A wise son brings joy to his **f**, but a foolish	H3
Pr	15:20	A wise son brings joy to his **f**, but a foolish	H3
Pr	17:25	son brings grief to his **f** and bitterness to the	H3
Pr	19:26	Whoever robs their **f** and drives out their	H3
Pr	20:20	If someone curses their **f** or mother, their	H3
Pr	23:22	Listen to your **f**, who gave you life, and do not	H3
Pr	23:24	The **f** *of* a righteous child has great joy;	H3
Pr	23:25	May your **f** and mother rejoice; may she who	H3
Pr	28: 7	a companion of gluttons disgraces his **f**.	H3
Pr	28:24	Whoever robs their **f** or mother and says, “It’s	H3
Pr	29: 3	A man who loves wisdom brings joy to his **f**	H3
Pr	30:17	“The eye that mocks a **f**, that scorns an aged	H3
Isa	7:17	on the house of your **f** a time unlike any since	H3
Isa	8: 4	boy knows how to say ‘My **f**’ or ‘My mother,	H3
Isa	9: 6	Mighty God, Everlasting **F**, Prince of Peace.	H3
Isa	22:21	He will be a **f** to those who live in Jerusalem	H3
Isa	22:23	become a seat of honor for the house of his **f**.	H3
Isa	38: 5	what the LORD, the God of your **f** David, says:	H3
Isa	43:27	Your first **f** sinned; those I sent to teach you	H3
Isa	45:10	Woe to the one who says to a **f**, ‘What have	H3
Isa	51: 2	look to Abraham, your **f**, and to Sarah, who	H3
Isa	58:14	to feast on the inheritance of your **f** Jacob.”	H3
Isa	63:16	But you are our **F**, though Abraham does not	H3
Isa	63:16	are our **F**, our Redeemer from of old is	H3
Isa	64: 8	LORD, are our **F**. We are the clay, you	H3
Jer	2:27	say to wood, ‘You are my **f**,’ and to stone,	H3
Jer	3: 4	just called to me: ‘My **F**, my friend from my	H3
Jer	3:19	you would call me ‘**F**’ and not turn away from	H3
Jer	16: 7	not even for a **f** or a mother—nor will	H3
Jer	20:15	be the man who brought my **f** the news,	H3
Jer	22:11	who succeeded his **f** as king of Judah but has	H3
Jer	22:15	Did not your **f** have food and drink? He	H3
Jer	31: 9	because I am Israel’s **f**, and Ephraim is my	H3
Eze	16: 3	your **f** was an Amorite and your mother a	H3
Eze	16:45	mother was a Hittite and your **f** an Amorite.	H3
Eze	18:11	though **the f** has done none of them):	H2085S
Eze	18:14	has a son who sees all the sins his **f** commits,	H3
Eze	18:18	But his **f** will die for his own sin, because he	H3
Eze	18:19	‘Why does the son not share the guilt of his **f**?	H3
Eze	22: 7	In you they have treated **f** and mother with	H3
Eze	44:25	if the dead person was his **f** or mother, son	H3
Da	5: 2	his **f** had taken from the	A10003
Da	5:11	In the time of your **f** he was found to	A10003
Da	5:11	Your **f**, King Nebuchadnezzar, appointed	A10003
Da	5:13	one of the exiles my **f** the king brought	A10003
Da	5:18	High God gave your **f** Nebuchadnezzar	A10003
Da	11: 6	royal escort and her **f** and the one who	H3528
Am	2: 7	**F** and son use the same girl and so profane	H3
Mic	7: 6	For a son dishonors his **f**, a daughter rises up	H3
Zec	13: 3	still prophesies, their **f** and mother, to whom	H3
Mal	1: 6	“A son honors his **f**, and a slave his master.	H3
Mal	1: 6	If I am a **f**, where is the honor due	H3
Mal	2:10	Do we not all have one **F**? Did not one God	H3
Mal	3:17	just as a **f** has compassion and spares his	H408
Mt	1: 2	Abraham *was the* **f** *of* Isaac, Isaac the	G1164
Mt	1: 2	of Isaac, Isaac *the* **f** *of* Jacob, Jacob the	G1164
Mt	1: 2	Jacob *the* **f** *of* Judah and his brothers,	G1164
Mt	1: 3	Judah *the* **f** *of* Perez and Zerah, whose	G1164
Mt	1: 3	was Tamar, Perez *the* **f** *of* Hezron, Hezron	G1164
Mt	1: 3	father of Hezron, Hezron *the* **f** *of* Ram,	G1164
Mt	1: 4	Ram *the* **f** *of* Amminadab, Amminadab	G1164
Mt	1: 4	Amminadab *the* **f** *of* Nahshon, Nahshon	G1164
Mt	1: 4	of Nahshon, Nahshon *the* **f** *of* Salmon,	G1164
Mt	1: 5	Salmon *the* **f** *of* Boaz, whose mother was	G1164
Mt	1: 5	was Rahab, Boaz *the* **f** *of* Obed, whose	G1164
Mt	1: 5	mother was Ruth, Obed *the* **f** *of* Jesse,	G1164
Mt	1: 6	Jesse *the* **f** *of* King David. David was	G1164
Mt	1: 6	David *was the* **f** *of* Solomon, whose	G1164
Mt	1: 7	Solomon *the* **f** *of* Rehoboam, Rehoboam	G1164
Mt	1: 7	Rehoboam *the* **f** *of* Abijah, Abijah the	G1164
Mt	1: 7	the father of Abijah, Abijah *the* **f** *of* Asa,	G1164
Mt	1: 8	Asa *the* **f** *of* Jehoshaphat, Jehoshaphat	G1164
Mt	1: 8	Jehoshaphat *the* **f** *of* Jehoram, Jehoram	G1164
Mt	1: 8	of Jehoram, Jehoram *the* **f** *of* Uzziah,	G1164
Mt	1: 9	Uzziah *the* **f** *of* Jotham, Jotham the father	G1164
Mt	1: 9	Jotham, Jotham *the* **f** *of* Ahaz, Ahaz the	G1164
Mt	1: 9	father of Ahaz, Ahaz *the* **f** *of* Hezekiah,	G1164
Mt	1:10	Hezekiah *the* **f** *of* Manasseh, Manasseh	G1164
Mt	1:10	Manasseh *the* **f** *of* Amon, Amon the	G1164
Mt	1:10	father of Amon, Amon *the* **f** *of* Josiah,	G1164
Mt	1:11	Josiah *the* **f** *of* Jeconiah and his	G1164
Mt	1:12	Jeconiah *was the* **f** *of* Shealtiel, Shealtiel	G1164
Mt	1:12	Shealtiel, Shealtiel *the* **f** *of* Zerubbabel,	G1164
Mt	1:13	Zerubbabel *the* **f** *of* Abihud, Abihud the	G1164
Mt	1:13	Abihud, Abihud *the* **f** *of* Eliakim, Eliakim	G1164
Mt	1:13	father of Eliakim, Eliakim *the* **f** *of* Azor,	G1164
Mt	1:14	Azor *the* **f** *of* Zadok, Zadok the father of	G1164
Mt	1:14	of Zadok, Zadok *the* **f** *of* Akim, Akim the	G1164
Mt	1:14	the father of Akim, Akim *the* **f** *of* Elihud,	G1164
Mt	1:15	Elihud *the* **f** *of* Eleazar, Eleazar the father	G1164
Mt	1:15	Eleazar *the* **f** *of* Matthan, Matthan	G1164
Mt	1:15	of Matthan, Matthan *the* **f** *of* Jacob,	G1164
Mt	1:16	Jacob *the* **f** *of* Joseph, the husband of	G1164
Mt	2:22	reigning in Judea in place of his **f** Herod,	G4252
Mt	3: 9	yourselves, ‘We have Abraham *as* our **f**.	G4252
Mt	4:21	They were in a boat with their **f** Zebedee	G4252
Mt	4:22	left the boat and their **f** and followed him.	G4252
Mt	5:16	good deeds and glorify your **F** in heaven.	G4252
Mt	5:45	you may be children *of* your **F** in heaven.	G4252
Mt	5:48	therefore, as your heavenly **F** is perfect.	G4252
Mt	6: 1	have no reward from your **F** in heaven.	G4252
Mt	6: 4	Then your **F**, who sees what is done in	G4252
Mt	6: 6	close the door and pray *to* your **F**, who is	G4252
Mt	6: 6	Then your **F**, who sees what is done in	G4252
Mt	6: 8	your **F** knows what you need before	G4252
Mt	6: 9	“ ‘Our **F** in heaven, hallowed be your	G4252
Mt	6:14	your heavenly **F** will also forgive you.	G4252
Mt	6:15	their sins, your **F** will not forgive your sins.	G4252
Mt	6:18	but only *to* your **F**, who is unseen;	G4252
Mt	6:18	is unseen; and your **F**, who sees what is	G4252
Mt	6:26	yet your heavenly **F** feeds them.	G4252
Mt	6:32	your heavenly **F** knows that you need	G4252
Mt	7:11	more will your **F** in heaven give good	G4252
Mt	7:21	does the will *of* my **F** who is in heaven.	G4252
Mt	8:21	“Lord, first let me go and bury my **f**.”	G4252
Mt	10:20	the Spirit *of* your **F** speaking through	G4252
Mt	10:21	to death, and a **f** his child; children	G4252
Mt	10:32	also acknowledge before my **F** in heaven.	G4252
Mt	10:33	I will disown before my **F** in heaven.	G4252
Mt	10:35	I have come to turn “ ‘a man against his **f**,	G4252
Mt	10:37	who loves their **f** or mother more than me	G4252
Mt	11:25	“I praise you, **F**, Lord of heaven and	G4252
Mt	11:26	**F**, for this is what you were pleased to	G4252
Mt	11:27	have been committed to me by my **F**.	G4252
Mt	11:27	No one knows the Son except the **F**, and	G4252
Mt	11:27	no one knows the **F** except the Son and	G4252
Mt	12:50	does the will *of* my **F** in heaven is my	G4252
Mt	13:43	like the sun in the kingdom *of* their **F**.	G4252
Mt	15: 4	‘Honor your **f** and mother’ and ‘Anyone	G4252
Mt	15: 4	who curses their **f** or mother is to be put	G4252
Mt	15: 5	used to help their **f** or mother is ‘devoted	G4252
Mt	15: 6	are not to ‘honor their **f** or mother’ with it.	G4252
Mt	15:13	that my heavenly **F** has not planted will	G4252
Mt	16:17	flesh and blood, but *by* my **F** in heaven.	G4252
Mt	18:10	always see the face *of* my **F** in heaven.	G4252
Mt	18:14	In the same way your **F** in heaven is not	G4252
Mt	18:19	will be done for them by my **F** in heaven.	G4252
Mt	18:35	is how my heavenly **F** will treat each of	G4252
Mt	19: 5	a man will leave his **f** and mother and be	G4252
Mt	19:19	honor your **f** and mother,’ and ‘love your	G4252
Mt	19:29	brothers or sisters or **f** or mother or wife	G4252
Mt	20:23	whom they have been prepared by my **F**.”	G4252
Mt	21:30	“Then the **f** went to the other son and said	NDT
Mt	21:31	“Which of the two did what his **f** wanted?”	G4252
Mt	23: 9	And do not call anyone on earth ‘**f**,’ for	G4252
Mt	23: 9	you have one **F**, and he is in heaven.	G4252
Mt	24:36	in heaven, nor the Son, but only the **F**.	G4252
Mt	25:34	you who are blessed *by* my **F**; take your	G4252
Mt	26:39	ground and prayed, “My **F**, if it is possible,	G4252
Mt	26:42	time and prayed, “My **F**, if it is not	G4252
Mt	26:53	Do you think I cannot call on my **F**, and he	G4252
Mt	28:19	them in the name *of* the **F** and of the Son	G4252
Mk	1:20	they left their **f** Zebedee in the boat	G4252
Mk	5:40	he took the child’s **f** and mother and the	G4252
Mk	7:10	‘Honor your **f** and mother,’ and,	G4252
Mk	7:10	who curses their **f** or mother is to be put	G4252
Mk	7:11	used to help their **f** or mother is Corban	G4252
Mk	7:12	let them do anything *for* their **f** or mother.	G4252
Mk	9:21	Jesus asked the boy’s **f**, “How long has he	G4252
Mk	9:24	Immediately the boy’s **f** exclaimed, “I do	G4252
Mk	10: 7	a man will leave his **f** and mother and be	G4252
Mk	10:19	not defraud, honor your **f** and mother.	G4252
Mk	10:29	sisters or mother or **f** or children or fields	G4252
Mk	11:10	is the coming kingdom *of* our **f** David!”	G4252
Mk	11:25	so that your **F** in heaven may forgive you	G4252
Mk	13:12	betray brother to death, and a **f** his child.	G4252
Mk	13:32	in heaven, nor the Son, but only the **F**.	G4252
Mk	14:36	**F**,” he said, “everything is possible	G4252
Mk	15:21	the **f** of Alexander and Rufus, was	G4252
Lk	1:32	will give him the throne of his **f** David,	G4252
Lk	1:59	going to name him after his **f** Zechariah,	G4252
Lk	1:62	Then they made signs *to* his **f**, to find out	G4252
Lk	1:67	His **f** Zechariah was filled with the Holy	G4252
Lk	1:73	the oath he swore to our **f** Abraham:	G4252
Lk	2:33	The child’s **f** and mother marveled at	G4252
Lk	2:48	Your **f** and I have been anxiously	G4252
Lk	3: 8	yourselves, ‘We have Abraham *as* our **f**.	G4252
Lk	6:36	Be merciful, just as your **F** is merciful.	G4252
Lk	8:51	James, and the child’s **f** and mother.	G4252
Lk	9:26	in the glory *of* the **F** and of the holy	G4252
Lk	9:42	the boy and gave him back *to* his **f**.	G4252
Lk	9:59	first let me go and bury my **f**.	G4252
Lk	10:21	“I praise you, **F**, Lord of heaven and	G4252
Lk	10:21	**F**, for this is what you were pleased	G4252
Lk	10:22	have been committed to me by my **F**.	G4252
Lk	10:22	one knows who the Son is except the **F**,	G4252
Lk	10:22	no one knows who the **F** is except the Son	G4252
Lk	11: 2	“ ‘**F**, hallowed be your name, your	G4252
Lk	11:13	much more will your **F** in heaven give the	G4252
Lk	12:30	your **F** knows that you need them.	G4252
Lk	12:32	your **F** has been pleased to give you	G4252
Lk	12:53	**f** against son and son against father	G4252
Lk	12:53	father against son and son against **f**	G4252
Lk	14:26	to me and does not hate **f** and mother,	G4252
Lk	15:12	The younger one said *to* his **f**, ‘Father, give	G4252
Lk	15:12	said to his father, ‘**F**, give me my share of	G4252
Lk	15:18	out and go back to my **f** and say to him:	G4252
Lk	15:18	**F**, I have sinned against heaven and	G4252
Lk	15:20	So he got up and went to his **f**. “But while	G4252
Lk	15:20	his **f** saw him and was filled with	G4252
Lk	15:21	son said to him, ‘**F**, I have sinned against	G4252
Lk	15:22	“But the **f** said to his servants, ‘Quick	G4252
Lk	15:27	‘and your **f** has killed the fattened calf	G4252
Lk	15:28	So his **f** went out and pleaded with him.	G4252
Lk	15:29	But he answered his **f**, ‘Look! All these	G4252
Lk	15:31	“ ‘My son,’ **the f** said, ‘you are always	G3836S
Lk	16:24	So he called to him, ‘**F** Abraham, have pity	G4252
Lk	16:27	‘Then I beg you, **f**, send Lazarus to my	G4252
Lk	16:30	**f** Abraham,’ he said, ‘but if	G4252
Lk	18:20	false testimony, honor your **f** and mother.	G4252
Lk	22:29	just as my **F** conferred one on me,	G4252
Lk	22:42	“**F**, if you are willing, take this cup from me	G4252
Lk	23:34	Jesus said, “**F**, forgive them, for they do	G4252
Lk	23:46	out with a loud voice, “**F**, into your hands I	G4252
Lk	24:49	to send you what my **F** has promised;	G4252
Jn	1:14	who came from the **F**, full of grace and	G4252
Jn	1:18	is in closest relationship with the **F**,	G4252
Jn	3:35	The **F** loves the Son and has placed	G4252
Jn	4:12	Are you greater *than* our **f** Jacob, who	G4252
Jn	4:21	you will worship the **F** neither on this	G4252
Jn	4:23	will worship the **F** in the Spirit and in truth	G4252
Jn	4:23	are the kind of worshipers the **F** seeks.	G4252
Jn	4:53	Then the **f** realized that this was the exact	G4252
Jn	5:17	“My **F** is always at his work to this very	G4252
Jn	5:18	he was even calling God his own **F**	G4252
Jn	5:19	he can do only what he sees his **F** doing	G4252
Jn	5:19	because whatever **the F** does the Son	G1697S
Jn	5:20	For the **F** loves the Son and shows him all	G4252
Jn	5:21	For just as the **F** raises the dead and gives	G4252
Jn	5:22	Moreover, the **F** judges no one, but has	G4252
Jn	5:23	honor the Son just as they honor the **F**.	G4252
Jn	5:23	not honor the Son does not honor the **F**,	G4252
Jn	5:26	For as the **F** has life in himself, so he has	G4252
Jn	5:36	the works that the **F** has given me to finish	G4252
Jn	5:36	am doing—testify that the **F** has sent me.	G4252
Jn	5:37	And the **F** who sent me has himself	G4252
Jn	5:45	do not think I will accuse you before the **F**.	G4252
Jn	6:27	For on him God the **F** has placed his seal	G4252
Jn	6:32	it is my **F** who gives you the true bread	G4252
Jn	6:37	All those the **F** gives me will come to me	G4252
Jn	6:42	of Joseph, whose **f** and mother we know?	G4252
Jn	6:44	to me unless the **F** who sent me draws	G4252
Jn	6:45	who has heard the **F** and learned from	G4252
Jn	6:46	No one has seen the **F** except the one who	G4252
Jn	6:46	who is from God; only he has seen the **F**.	G4252
Jn	6:57	Just as the living **F** sent me and I live	G4252

F

Jn 6:57 sent me and I live because of the F, G4252
Jn 6:65 to me unless the F has enabled them." G4252
Jn 8:16 I stand with the F, who sent me. G4252
Jn 8:18 my other witness is the F, who sent me." G4252
Jn 8:19 "Where is your f?" "You do not know G4252
Jn 8:19 "You do not know me or my F," Jesus G4252
Jn 8:19 you knew me, you would know my F also." G4252
Jn 8:27 that he was telling them *about* his F. G4252
Jn 8:28 speak just what the F has taught me. G4252
Jn 8:38 doing what you have heard from your f." G4252
Jn 8:39 "Abraham is our f," they answered. "If you G4252
Jn 8:41 You are doing the works *of* your own f." G4252
Jn 8:41 "The only F we have is God himself." G4252
Jn 8:42 "If God were your F, you would love me, G4252
Jn 8:44 You belong to your f, the devil, and you G4252
Jn 8:44 language, for he is a liar and the f of lies. G4252
Jn 8:49 "but I honor my F and you dishonor me. G4252
Jn 8:53 Are you greater *than* our f Abraham? He G4252
Jn 8:54 My F, whom you claim as your God, is the G4252
Jn 8:56 Your f Abraham rejoiced at the thought of G4252
Jn 10:15 just as the F knows me and I know the G4252
Jn 10:15 the Father knows me and I know the F— G4252
Jn 10:17 The reason my F loves me is that I lay G4252
Jn 10:18 This command I received from my F." G4252
Jn 10:29 My F, who has given them to me, is G4252
Jn 10:30 I and the F are one. G4252
Jn 10:32 shown you many good works from the F. G4252
Jn 10:36 the one whom the F set apart as his very G4252
Jn 10:37 believe me unless I do the works *of* my F. G4252
Jn 10:38 know and understand that the F is in me, G4252
Jn 10:38 that the Father is in me, and I in the F." G4252
Jn 11:41 looked up and said, "F, I thank you that G4252
Jn 12:26 My F will honor the one who serves me G4252
Jn 12:27 what shall I say? 'F, save me from this G4252
Jn 12:28 F, glorify your name!" Then a voice came G4252
Jn 12:49 the F who sent me commanded me to G4252
Jn 12:50 I say is just what the F has told me to say." G4252
Jn 13: 1 him to leave this world and go to the F. G4252
Jn 13: 3 Jesus knew that the F had put all things G4252
Jn 14: 6 No one comes to the F except through me. G4252
Jn 14: 7 know me, you will know my F as well. G4252
Jn 14: 8 show us the F and that will be enough G4252
Jn 14: 9 Anyone who has seen me has seen the F G4252
Jn 14: 9 How can you say, 'Show us the F'? G4252
Jn 14:10 Don't you believe that I am in the F, and G4252
Jn 14:10 am in the Father, and that the F is in me? G4252
Jn 14:10 it is the F, living in me, who is G4252
Jn 14:11 I say that I am in the F and the Father is in G4252
Jn 14:11 that I am in the Father and the F is in me; G4252
Jn 14:12 than these, because I am going to the F. G4252
Jn 14:13 so that the F may be glorified in the Son. G4252
Jn 14:16 And I will ask the F, and he will give you G4252
Jn 14:20 that day you will realize that I am in my F, G4252
Jn 14:21 one who loves me will be loved by my F, G4252
Jn 14:23 My F will love them, and we will come to G4252
Jn 14:24 they *belong to* the F who sent me. G4252
Jn 14:26 whom the F will send in my name G4252
Jn 14:28 would be glad that I am going to the F, G4252
Jn 14:28 to the Father, for the F is greater than I. G4252
Jn 14:31 learn that I love the F and do exactly what G4252
Jn 14:31 exactly what my F has commanded me. G4252
Jn 15: 1 the true vine, and my F is the gardener. G4252
Jn 15: 9 "As the F has loved me, so have I loved G4252
Jn 15:15 I learned from my F I have made known to G4252
Jn 15:16 you ask in my name the F will give you. G4252
Jn 15:23 Whoever hates me hates my F as well. G4252
Jn 15:24 they have hated both me and my F. G4252
Jn 15:26 whom I will send to you from the F—the G4252
Jn 15:26 Spirit of truth who goes out from the F— G4252
Jn 16: 3 because they have not known the F or me. G4252
Jn 16:10 because I am going to the F, where you G4252
Jn 16:15 All that belongs to the F is mine. G4252
Jn 16:17 and 'Because I am going to the F'?" G4252
Jn 16:23 my F will give you whatever you ask in my G4252
Jn 16:25 will tell you plainly about my F. G4252
Jn 16:26 saying that I will ask the F on your behalf. G4252
Jn 16:27 the F himself loves you because you have G4252
Jn 16:28 I came from the F and entered the world G4252
Jn 16:28 leaving the world and going back to the F." G4252
Jn 16:32 Yet I am not alone, for my F is with me. G4252
Jn 17: 1 "F, the hour has come G4252
Jn 17: 5 And now, F, glorify me in your presence G4252
Jn 17:11 Holy F, protect them by the power of your G4252
Jn 17:21 of them may be one, F, just as you are in G4252
Jn 17:24 "F, I want those you have given me to be G4252
Jn 17:25 "Righteous F, though the world does not G4252
Jn 18:11 I not drink the cup the F has given me?" G4252
Jn 20:17 for I have not yet ascended to the F. G4252
Jn 20:17 'I am ascending to my F and your Father G4252
Jn 20:17 'I am ascending to my Father and your F G4252
Jn 20:21 As the F has sent me, I am G4252
Ac 1: 4 wait for the gift my F promised, which G4252
Ac 1: 7 times or dates the F has set by his own G4252
Ac 2:33 has received from the F the promised Holy G4252
Ac 4:25 the mouth of your servant, our f David: G4252
Ac 7: 2 glory appeared *to* our f Abraham while he G4252
Ac 7: 4 After the death of his f, God sent him to G4252
Ac 7: 8 And Abraham *became the* f *of* Isaac and G1164
Ac 7: 8 Later Isaac became the f of Jacob, and NDT
Ac 7: 8 Jacob became the f of the twelve NDT
Ac 7:14 Joseph sent for his f Jacob and his whole G4252
Ac 13:33 are my son; today I *have become* your f. G1164
Ac 16: 1 a believer but whose f was a Greek. G4252
Ac 16: 3 they all knew that his f was a Greek. G4252
Ac 28: 8 His f was sick in bed, suffering from fever G4252
Ro 1: 7 to you from God our F and from the Lord G4252
Ro 4:11 he is the f of all who believe but have not G4252
Ro 4:12 he is then also the f of the circumcised G4252
Ro 4:12 the faith that our f Abraham had before G4252
Ro 4:16 the faith of Abraham. He is the f of us all. G4252
Ro 4:17 "I have made you a f of many nations." G4252
Ro 4:17 He is our f in the sight of God, in whom he NDT
Ro 4:18 so became the f of many nations, G4252
Ro 6: 4 from the dead through the glory *of* the F, G4252
Ro 8:15 And by him we cry, "Abba, F." G4252
Ro 9:10 conceived at the same time by our f Isaac. G4252
Ro 15: 6 glorify the God and F of our Lord Jesus G4252
1Co 1: 3 to you from God our F and the Lord Jesus G4252
1Co 4:15 Christ Jesus I *became* your f through the G1164
1Co 8: 6 is but one God, the F, from whom all G4252
1Co 15:24 kingdom to God the F after he has G4252
2Co 1: 2 to you from God our F and the Lord Jesus G4252
2Co 1: 3 be to the God and F of our Lord Jesus G4252
2Co 1: 3 the F of compassion and the God of all G4252
2Co 6:18 "I will be a F to you, and you will be G4252
2Co 11:31 The God and F of the Lord Jesus, who is to G4252
Gal 1: 1 by Jesus Christ and God the F, who G4252
Gal 1: 3 to you from God our F and the Lord Jesus G4252
Gal 1: 4 according to the will of our God and F, G4252
Gal 4: 2 trustees until the time set *by* his f. G4252
Gal 4: 6 the Spirit who calls out, "Abba, F." G4252
Eph 1: 2 to you from God our F and the Lord Jesus G4252
Eph 1: 3 be to the God and F of our Lord Jesus G4252
Eph 1:17 the glorious F, may give you the G4252
Eph 2:18 both have access to the F by one Spirit. G4252
Eph 3:14 For this reason I kneel before the F, G4252
Eph 4: 6 one God and F of all, who is over all and G4252
Eph 5:20 giving thanks to God the F for everything, G4252
Eph 5:31 a man will leave his f and mother and be G4252
Eph 6: 2 "Honor your f and mother"—which is the G4252
Eph 6:23 faith from God the F and the Lord Jesus G4252
Php 1: 2 to you from God our F and the Lord Jesus G4252
Php 2:11 Christ is Lord, to the glory of God the F. G4252
Php 2:22 because as a son *with* his f he has served G4252
Php 4:20 To our God and F be glory for ever and G4252
Col 1: 2 Grace and peace to you from God our F. G4252
Col 1: 3 thank God, the F of our Lord Jesus Christ G4252
Col 1:12 giving joyful thanks *to* the F, who has G4252
Col 3:17 giving thanks to God the F through him. G4252
1Th 1: 1 in God the F and the Lord Jesus G4252
1Th 1: 3 before our God and F your work produced G4252
1Th 2:11 with each of you as a f deals with his own G4252
1Th 3:11 Now may our God and F himself and our G4252
1Th 3:13 of our God and F when our Lord Jesus G4252
2Th 1: 1 in God our F and the Lord Jesus G4252
2Th 1: 2 to you from God the F and the Lord Jesus G4252
2Th 2:16 Lord Jesus Christ himself and God our F, G4252
1Ti 1: 2 peace from God the F and Christ Jesus our G4252
1Ti 5: 1 exhort him as if he were your f. G4252
2Ti 1: 2 peace from God the F and Christ Jesus our G4252
Titus 1: 4 peace from God the F and Christ Jesus our G4252
Phm 3 to you from God our F and the Lord Jesus G4252
Heb 1: 5 today I *have become* your F"? Or again, G1164
Heb 1: 5 "I will be his F, and he will be my G4252
Heb 5: 5 are my Son; today I *have become* your F." G1164
Heb 7: 3 **Without** f or mother, without genealogy G574
Heb 12: 5 that addresses you as a f addresses his son? NDT
Heb 12: 7 children are not disciplined *by* their f? G4252
Heb 12: 9 should we submit *to* the F of spirits and G4252
Jas 1:17 coming down from the F of the heavenly G4252
Jas 1:27 that God our F accepts as pure and G4252
Jas 2:21 Was not our f Abraham considered G4252
Jas 3: 9 With the tongue we praise our Lord and F G4252
1Pe 1: 2 to the foreknowledge of God the F, G4252
1Pe 1: 3 be to the God and F of our Lord Jesus G4252
1Pe 1:17 Since you call on a F who judges each G4252
2Pe 1:17 glory from God the F when the voice came G4252
1Jn 1: 2 which was with the F and has appeared to G4252
1Jn 1: 3 fellowship is with the F and with his Son, G4252
1Jn 2: 1 we have an advocate with the F—Jesus G4252
1Jn 2:14 dear children, because you know the F. G4252
1Jn 2:15 the world, love *for* the F is not in them. G4252
1Jn 2:16 comes not from the F but from the world. G4252
1Jn 2:22 the antichrist—denying the F and the Son. G4252
1Jn 2:23 No one who denies the Son has the F G4252
1Jn 2:23 acknowledges the Son has the F also. G4252
1Jn 2:24 also will remain in the Son and in the F. G4252
1Jn 3: 1 what great love the F has lavished on us, G4252
1Jn 4:14 testify that the F has sent his Son to G4252
1Jn 5: 1 who loves the f loves his child as G1164
2Jn 3 peace from God the F and from Jesus G4252
2Jn 4 in the truth, just as the F commanded us. G4252
2Jn 9 the teaching has both the F and the Son. G4252
Jude 1 are loved in God the F and kept for Jesus G4252
Rev 1: 6 priests to serve his God and F— G4252
Rev 2:27 just as I have received authority from my F. G4252
Rev 3: 5 that name before my F and his angels. G4252
Rev 3:21 sat down with my F on his throne. G4252

FATHER'S (126) [FATHER]

Ge 9:23 in backward and covered their f naked body. H3
Ge 12: 1 your people and your f household to the land H3
Ge 20:13 God had me wander from my f household, H3
Ge 24: 7 brought me out of my f household and my H3
Ge 24:23 is there room in your f house for us to spend H3
Ge 24:38 go to my f family and to my own clan, and H3
Ge 24:40 son from my own clan and from my f family. H3
Ge 26:15 all the wells that his f servants had dug in the H3
Ge 27:30 Jacob had scarcely left his f presence, his H3
Ge 27:34 When Esau heard his f words, he burst out H3
Ge 28:21 so that I return safely to my f household, then H3
Ge 29: 9 Rachel came with her f sheep, for she H4200+3
Ge 31: 5 "I see that your f attitude toward me is not H3
Ge 31: 9 has taken away your f livestock and has given H3
Ge 31:14 any share in the inheritance of our f estate? H3
Ge 31:19 Rachel stole her f household gods. H4200+3
Ge 31:30 you longed to return to your f household. H3
Ge 34:19 who was the most honored of all his f family H3
Ge 35:22 went in and slept with his f concubine Bilhah, H3
Ge 37: 2 sons of Zilpah, his f wives, and he brought H3
Ge 37:12 gone to graze their f flocks near Shechem, H3
Ge 38:11 as a widow in your f household until my son H3
Ge 38:11 So Tamar went to live in her f household. H3
Ge 41:51 forget all my trouble and all my f household." H3
Ge 46:31 said to his brothers and to his f household, H3
Ge 46:31 'My brothers and my f household, who were H3
Ge 47:12 his brothers and all his f household with food, H3
Ge 48:17 so he took hold of his f hand to move it from H3
Ge 49: 4 you went up onto your f bed, onto my H3
Ge 49: 8 enemies; your f sons will bow down to you. H3
Ge 49:25 because of your f God, who helps you H3
Ge 49:26 Your f blessings are greater than the H3
Ge 50: 8 those belonging to his f household. H3
Ge 50:22 stayed in Egypt, along with all his f family. H3
Ex 2:16 water and fill the troughs to water their f flock. H3
Ex 6:20 Amram married his f **sister** Jochebed, who H1860
Ex 15: 2 I will praise him, my f God, and I will exalt H3
Ex 18: 4 he said, "My f God was my helper; he H3
Lev 18: 8 'Do not have sexual relations with your f wife; H3
Lev 18: 9 either your f daughter or your mother's H3
Lev 18:11 relations with the daughter of your f wife, H3
Lev 18:12 not have sexual relations with your f sister; H3
Lev 18:12 your father's sister; she is your f close relative. H3
Lev 18:14 'Do not dishonor your f brother by H3
Lev 20:11 " 'If a man has sexual relations with his f wife, H3
Lev 22:13 returns to live in her f household as in her H3
Lev 22:13 as in her youth, she may eat her f food. H3
Nu 27: 4 Why should our f name disappear from his H3
Nu 27: 4 Give us property among our f relatives." H3
Nu 27: 7 inheritance among their f relatives and give H3
Nu 27: 7 relatives and give their f inheritance to them. H3
Nu 27:10 brothers, give his inheritance to his f brothers. H3
Nu 30: 3 still living in her f household makes a vow to H3
Nu 36: 6 as long as they marry within their f tribal clan. H3
Nu 36: 8 tribe must marry someone in her f tribal clan, H3
Nu 36:11 married their **cousins on their f side.** H1201+1856
Nu 36:12 inheritance remained in their f tribe and clan. H3
Dt 21:17 That son is the first sign of **his** f strength H2257S
Dt 22:21 to the door of her f house and there the men H3
Dt 22:21 being promiscuous while still in her f house. H3
Dt 22:30 A man is not to marry his f wife; he must not H3
Dt 22:30 father's wife; he must not dishonor his f bed. H3
Dt 27:20 "Cursed is anyone who sleeps with his f wife H3
Dt 27:20 his father's wife, for he dishonors his f bed." H3
Jdg 6:25 "Take the second bull from your f herd, the H3
Jdg 6:25 Tear down your f altar to Baal and cut H3+4200
Jdg 9: 5 He went to his f home in Ophrah and on one H3
Jdg 9:18 today you have revolted against my f family. H3
Jdg 11: 7 you hate me and drive me from my f house? H3
Jdg 14:15 will burn you and your f household to death. H3
Jdg 14:19 Burning with anger, he returned to his f home. H3
Jdg 16:31 his brothers and his f whole family went down H3
1Sa 2:25 did not listen to their f rebuke, for it was the H3
1Sa 17:15 from Saul to tend his f sheep at Bethlehem. H3
1Sa 17:34 servant has been keeping his f sheep. H4200+3
1Sa 20:34 he was grieved at his f shameful treatment of H3
1Sa 22: 1 his brothers and his f household heard about H3
1Sa 22:15 king accuse your servant or any of his f family, H3
1Sa 24:21 wipe out my name from my f family. H3
2Sa 2:32 buried him in his f tomb at Bethlehem. H3
2Sa 3: 7 "Why did you sleep with my f concubine?" H3
2Sa 15:34 I was your f servant in the past, but H3
2Sa 16:21 "Sleep with your f concubines whom he left to H3
2Sa 16:22 he slept with his f concubines in the sight H3
2Sa 17:23 So he died and was buried in his f tomb. H3
1Ki 2:26 father David and shared all my f hardships." H3
1Ki 12:10 'My little finger is thicker than my f waist. H3
1Ki 18:18 "But you and your f family have. You have H3
2Ki 10: 3 master's sons and set him on his f throne. H3
1Ch 5: 1 when he defiled his f marriage bed, his H3
1Ch 26: 6 were leaders in their f family because they H3
1Ch 28: 4 from my f sons he was pleased to make H3
2Ch 10:10 'My little finger is thicker than my f waist. H3
2Ch 21: 4 established himself firmly over his f kingdom, H3
2Ch 22: 4 after his f death they became his advisers H3
Ne 1: 6 including myself and my f family, have H3
Est 4:14 but you and your f family will perish. H3
Ps 45:10 Forget your people and your f house. H3
Pr 1: 8 to your f instruction and do not forsake your H3
Pr 4: 1 my sons, to a f instruction; pay attention and H3
Pr 6:20 keep your f command and do not forsake your H3
Pr 13: 1 A wise son heeds his f instruction, but a H3
Pr 19:13 A foolish child is a f ruin, and a quarrelsome H3
Isa 3: 6 will seize one of his brothers in his f house, H3
Eze 18:17 He will not die for his f sin; he will surely live H3
Eze 22:10 In you are those who dishonor their f bed; in H3

Eze 22:11 another violates his sister, his own f daughter. H3
Mt 10:29 will fall to the ground outside your F care. G4252
Mt 16:27 going to come in his F glory with his G4252
Mt 26:29 I drink it new with you in my F kingdom." G4252
Mk 8:38 he comes in his F glory with the holy G4252
Lk 2:49 you know I had to be in my F house?" G4252
Lk 15:17 'How many *of* my f hired servants have G4252
Jn 2:16 Stop turning my F house into a market!" G4252
Jn 5:43 I have come in my F name, and you do not G4252
Jn 6:40 For my F will is that everyone who looks to G4252
Jn 8:38 you what I have seen in the F presence, G4252
Jn 8:44 you want to carry out your f desires. G4252
Jn 10:25 The works I do in my F name testify about G4252
Jn 10:29 no one can snatch them out of my F hand. G4252
Jn 14: 2 My F house has many rooms; if that were G4252
Jn 15: 8 This is to my F glory, that you bear much G4252
Jn 15:10 as I have kept my F commands and G4252
1Co 5: 1 A man is sleeping with his f wife. G4252
2Jn 3 Jesus Christ, the F Son, will be with us G4252
Rev 14: 1 had his name and his F name written on G4252

FATHER-IN-LAW (24) [FATHER]

Ge 38:13 "Your f is on his way to Timnah to shear H2767
Ge 38:25 brought out, she sent a message to her f. H2767
Ex 3: 1 was tending the flock of Jethro his f, H3162
Ex 4:18 went back to Jethro his f and said to him, H3162
Ex 18: 1 the priest of Midian and f *of* Moses, heard H3162
Ex 18: 2 wife Zipporah, his f Jethro received her H3162
Ex 18: 5 Moses' f, together with Moses' H3162
Ex 18: 6 your f Jethro, am coming to you with H3162
Ex 18: 7 out to meet his f and bowed down and H3162
Ex 18: 8 Moses told his f about everything the LORD H3162
Ex 18:12 Then Jethro, Moses' f, brought a burnt H3162
Ex 18:12 a meal with Moses' f in the presence of H3162
Ex 18:14 When his f saw all that Moses was doing H3162
Ex 18:17 Moses' f replied, "What you are doing is H3162
Ex 18:24 listened to his f and did everything he H3162
Ex 18:27 Then Moses sent his f on his way, and H3162
Nu 10:29 Midianite, Moses' f, "We are setting out H3162
Jdg 1:16 The descendants of Moses' f, the Kenite H3162
Jdg 19: 4 His f, the woman's father, prevailed on H3162
Jdg 19: 7 got up to go, his f persuaded him, so he H3162
Jdg 19: 9 got up to leave, his f, the woman's father H3162
1Sa 4:19 that her f and her husband were H2767
1Sa 4:21 the deaths of her f and her husband. H2767
Jn 18:13 who was the f of Caiaphas, the G4290

FATHERED (1) [FATHER]

Dt 32:18 deserted the Rock, *who* f you; you forgot H3528

FATHERLESS (41) [FATHER]

Ex 22:22 not take advantage of the widow or the f. H3846
Ex 22:24 will become widows and your children f. H3846
Dt 10:18 defends the cause of the f and the widow, H3846
Dt 14:29 the f and the widows who live in your H3846
Dt 16:11 the f and the widows living among you. H3846
Dt 16:14 the f and the widows who live in your H3846
Dt 24:17 deprive the foreigner or the f of justice, H3846
Dt 24:19 the foreigner, the f and the widow, so that H3846
Dt 24:20 the foreigner, the f and the widow. H3846
Dt 24:21 the foreigner, the f and the widow. H3846
Dt 26:12 the foreigner, the f and the widow, so that H3846
Dt 26:13 the foreigner, the f and the widow H3846
Dt 27:19 from the foreigner, the f or the widow." H3846
Job 6:27 cast lots for the f and barter away your H3846
Job 22: 9 broke the strength of the f. H3846
Job 24: 9 The f **child** is snatched from the breast H3846
Job 29:12 the f who had none to assist them. H3846
Job 31:17 to myself, not sharing it with the f— H3846
Job 31:21 if I have raised my hand against the f H3846
Ps 10:14 you are the helper of the f. H3846
Ps 10:18 defending the f and the oppressed, so H3846
Ps 68: 5 A father to the f, a defender of widows, is H3846
Ps 82: 3 Defend the weak and the f; uphold the H3846
Ps 94: 6 the foreigner; they murder the f. H3846
Ps 109: 9 May his children be f and his wife a H3846
Ps 109:12 to him or take pity on his f **children**. H3846
Ps 146: 9 sustains the f and the widow, H3846
Pr 23:10 stone or encroach on the fields of the f, H3846
Isa 1:17 Take up the cause of the f; plead the case H3846
Isa 1:23 They do not defend the cause of the f; the H3846
Isa 9:17 will he pity the f and widows, for H3846
Isa 10: 2 widows their prey and robbing the f. H3846
Jer 5:28 They do not promote the case of the f H3846
Jer 7: 6 the f or the widow and do not shed H3846
Jer 22: 3 the foreigner, the f or the widow, and do H3846
Jer 49:11 'Leave your f **children**; I will keep them H3846
La 5: 3 We have become f, our H3846+2256+401+3
Eze 22: 7 mistreated the f and the widow. H3846
Hos 14: 3 for in you the f find compassion. H3846
Zec 7:10 Do not oppress the widow or the f, the H3846
Mal 3: 5 who oppress the widows and the f, and H3846

FATHERS (49) [FATHER]

Ge 31: 3 to the land of your f and to your relatives, H3
Ge 46:34 from our boyhood on, just as our f did. H3
Ge 47: 3 they replied to Pharaoh, "just as our f were." H3
Ge 47: 9 not equal the years of the pilgrimage of my f." H3
Ge 47:30 when I rest with my f, carry me out of Egypt H3
Ge 48:15 God before whom my f Abraham and Isaac H3
Ge 48:16 the names of my f Abraham and Isaac, H3
Ge 48:21 you and take you back to the land of your f. H3
Ge 49:29 Bury me with my f in the cave in the field of H3
Ex 3:13 'The God of your f has sent me to you,' H3
Ex 3:15 the God of your f—the God of Abraham, H3
Ex 3:16 the God of your f—the God of Abraham, H3
Ex 4: 5 the God of their f—the God of Abraham, H3
Nu 32: 8 This is what your f did when I sent them from H3
Nu 32:14 in the place of your f and making the LORD H3
Dt 1: 8 land the LORD swore he would give to your f— H3
Dt 6:10 brings you into the land he swore to your f, H3
Dt 9: 5 to accomplish what he swore to your f, to H3
Dt 29:13 as he promised you and as he swore to your f, H3
Dt 30:20 years in the land he swore to give to your f, H3
Jdg 21:22 When their f or brothers complain to us, we H3
1Ch 6:19 clans of the Levites listed according to their f: H3
1Ch 29:18 the God of our f Abraham, Isaac and H3
1Ch 29:20 the LORD, the God of their f; they bowed down, H3
2Ch 29: 9 This is why our f have fallen by the sword H3
Job 30: 1 whose f I would have disdained to put with H3
Job 38:28 have a father? Who f the drops of dew? H3528
Ps 45:16 Your sons will take the place of your f; you H3
Ps 109:14 the iniquity of his f be remembered before H3
Pr 23:24 a **man** *who* f a wise **son** rejoices in him. H3528
Pr 30:11 those who curse their f and do not bless their H3
Isa 49:23 Kings will be your **foster** f, and their queens H587
Jer 7:18 gather wood, the f light the fire, and the H3
Jer 16: 3 their mothers and the men who are their f: H3
Da 11:24 what neither his f nor his forefathers did. H3
Lk 11:11 "Which of you f, if your son asks for a fish G4252
Ac 3:13 Jacob, the God *of* our f, has glorified G4252
Ac 3:25 of the covenant God made with your f. G4252
Ac 7: 2 "Brothers and f, listen to me! The God G4252
Ac 7:32 'I am the God *of* your f, the God of G4252
Ac 22: 1 "Brothers and f, listen now to my defense." G4252
1Co 4:15 you do not have many f, for in Christ Jesus G4252
Gal 1:14 zealous for the traditions **of** my f. G4257
Eph 6: 4 F, do not exasperate your children G4252
Col 3:21 F, do not embitter your children, or they G4252
1Ti 1: 9 *for those who* **kill** their f or mothers G4260
Heb 12: 9 have all had human f who disciplined us G4252
1Jn 2:13 I am writing to you, f, because you know G4252
1Jn 2:14 I write to you, f, because you know him G4252

FATHOM (6) [FATHOMED]

Job 11: 7 "*Can you* f the mysteries of God? Can you H5162
Ps 145: 3 of praise; his greatness no one can f. H2984
Ecc 3:11 no one *can* f what God has done from H5162
Isa 40:13 Who *can* f the Spirit of the LORD, H9419
Isa 40:28 his understanding no one can f. H2984
1Co 13: 2 of prophecy and *can* f all mysteries and G3857

FATHOMED (2) [FATHOM]

Job 5: 9 He performs wonders that cannot be f H2984
Job 9:10 He performs wonders that cannot be f H2984

FATLING, FATLINGS (KJV) FAT ANIMALS, FAT CALVES, FATTENED ANIMALS, FATTENED CALF, FATTENED CATTLE, YEARLING

FATTENED (16) [FAT]

Dt 32:14 flock and with f lambs and goats, H2693
1Sa 28:24 The woman had a f calf at the house H5272
2Sa 6:13 six steps, he sacrificed a bull and a **f calf**. H5309
1Ki 1: 9 cattle and **f calves** at the Stone of H5309
1Ki 1:19 numbers of cattle, **f calves**, and sheep, H5309
1Ki 1:25 numbers of cattle, **f calves**, and sheep. H5309
Pr 15:17 with love than a f calf with hatred. H80
Isa 1:11 of rams and the fat of **f animals**; I have no H5309
Jer 46:21 mercenaries in her ranks are like f calves. H5272
Eze 39:18 all of them **f animals** *from* Bashan. H5309
Am 6: 4 You dine on choice lambs and f calves. H5272
Mt 22: 4 My oxen and **f cattle** have been butchered G4990
Lk 15:23 Bring the f calf and kill it. Let's have a G4988
Lk 15:27 father has killed the f calf because he has G4988
Lk 15:30 comes home, you kill the f calf for him! G4988
Jas 5: 5 *You have* f yourselves in the day of G5555

FATTENING (1) [FAT]

1Sa 2:29 sons more than me by f yourselves on the H1344

FAULT (16) [FAULTFINDERS, FAULTLESS, FAULTS, FAULTY]

Ex 5:16 beaten, but *the* f *is with* your own people." H2627
1Sa 14:41 If the f is in me or my son Jonathan H6411
1Sa 14:41 if the men of Israel are **at** f, respond H5647S
1Sa 29: 3 Saul until now, I have found no f in him." H4399
1Sa 29: 6 I have found no f in you, but the rulers H8288
Job 11:15 free of f, you will lift up your face H4583
Job 33:10 Yet God has found f with me; he H9481
Jer 2: 5 "What f did your ancestors find in me H6404
Jer 17: 4 **Through** your own f you will lose the H928
Jnh 1:12 that it is my f that this great H928+8611+4200
Mt 18:15 go and **point out** their f, just G1794
Php 2:15 "children of God **without** f in a warped G320
Heb 8: 8 But God **found** f **with** the people and said G3522
Jas 1: 5 gives generously to all without **finding** f, G3943
Jas 3: 2 Anyone *who is* never **at** f in what they say G4760
Jude 24 glorious presence **without** f and with great G320

FAULTFINDERS (1) [FAULT, FIND]

Jude 16 These people are grumblers and f; they G3523

FAULTLESS (2) [FAULT]

Php 3: 6 as for righteousness based on the law, f. G289
Jas 1:27 our Father accepts as pure and f is this: G299

FAULTS (2) [FAULT]

Job 10: 6 must search out my f and probe after my H6411
Ps 19:12 discern their own errors? Forgive my **hidden** *f*.AIT

FAULTY (2) [FAULT]

Ps 78:57 faithless, as unreliable as a f bow. H8244
Hos 7:16 to the Most High; they are like a f bow. H8244

FAVOR (125) [FAVORABLE, FAVORABLY, FAVORED, FAVORITE, FAVORITISM, FAVORS]

Ge 4: 4 The LORD **looked with** f on Abel and his H9120
Ge 4: 5 his offering *he did* not **look with** f. H9120
Ge 6: 8 But Noah found f in the eyes of the LORD. H2834
Ge 18: 3 "If I have found f in your eyes, my lord, H2834
Ge 19:19 Your servant has found f in your eyes, and H2834
Ge 30:27 "If I have found f in your eyes, please H2834
Ge 32: 5 to my lord, that I may find f in your eyes. H2834
Ge 33: 8 "To find f in your eyes, my lord, H2834
Ge 33:10 "If I have found f in your eyes, accept this H2834
Ge 33:15 "Just let me find f in the eyes of my lord." H2834
Ge 34:11 brothers, "Let me find f in your eyes, and I H2834
Ge 39: 4 Joseph found f in his eyes and became his H2834
Ge 39:21 granted him f in the eyes of the H2834
Ge 47:25 "May we find f in the eyes of our lord; we H2834
Ge 47:29 "If I have found f in your eyes, put H2834
Ge 50: 4 "If I have found f in your eyes, speak to H2834
Ex 32:11 Moses **sought the** f **of** the H2704+906+7156
Ex 33:12 by name and you have found f with me. H2834
Ex 33:13 know you and continue to find f with you. H2834
Ex 34: 9 "if I have found f in your eyes, then let H2834
Lev 26: 9 " '*I will* **look** on you **with** f and make you H7155
Nu 11:15 if I have found f in your eyes—and H2834
Nu 32: 5 If we have found f in your eyes," they said H2834
Dt 33:16 its fullness and the f *of* him who dwelt in H8356
Dt 33:23 is abounding with the f of the LORD and is H8356
Jos 15:19 "Do me a **special** f. Since you have H1388
Jdg 1:15 "Do me a **special** f. Since you have H1388
Jdg 6:17 "If now I have found f in your eyes, give H2834
Jdg 21:22 say to them, '**Do** us **the** f of helping them H2858
Ru 2: 2 behind anyone in whose eyes I find f." H2834
Ru 2:10 have I found such f in your eyes that you H2834
Ru 2:13 "May I continue to find f in your eyes, my H2834
1Sa 1:18 "May your servant find f in your eyes." H2834
1Sa 2:26 grow in stature and *in* f with the LORD and H3202
1Sa 13:12 and *I have* not **sought** the LORD's f. H2704+7156
1Sa 20: 3 very well that I have found f in your eyes, H2834
1Sa 20:29 If I have found f in your eyes, let me get H2834
1Sa 27: 5 "If I have found f in your eyes, let a H2834
1Sa 29: 4 better *could* he **regain** his master's f than H8354
2Sa 2: 6 show you the same f because you have H3208
2Sa 14:22 knows that he has found f in your eyes, H2834
2Sa 15:25 If I find f in the LORD's eyes, he will bring H2834
2Sa 16: 4 "May I find f in your eyes, my lord the king H2834
2Ki 13: 4 Jehoahaz **sought** the LORD's f, H2704+906+7156
2Ch 33:12 distress *he* **sought the** f **of** the H2704+906+7156
Ezr 7:28 has extended his **good** f to me before the H2876
Ne 1:11 today by granting him f in the presence of H8171
Ne 2: 5 if your servant *has* **found** f in his sight, H3512
Ne 5:19 Remember me with f, my God, for all I H3208
Ne 13:31 Remember me with f, my God. H3208
Est 2: 9 She pleased him and won his f H2876
Est 2:15 And Esther won the f of everyone who H2834
Est 2:17 she won his f and approval more H2834
Est 5: 8 king regards me with f and if it pleases H2834
Est 7: 3 "If I have found f with you, Your Majesty, H2834
Est 8: 5 if he regards me with f and thinks it the H2834
Job 11:19 afraid, and many *will* **court** your f. H2704+7156
Job 33:26 can pray to God and **find** f **with** him, H8354
Job 34:19 to princes and *does* not f the rich over the H5795
Ps 5:12 them with your f as with a shield. H8356
Ps 30: 5 only a moment, but his f lasts a lifetime H8356
Ps 45:12 people of wealth *will* **seek** your f. H2704+7156
Ps 69:13 in the time of your f; in your great love, H8356
Ps 77: 7 *Will* he never **show** his f again? H8354
Ps 84: 9 **look with** f *on* your anointed one. H5564+7156
Ps 84:11 the LORD bestows f and honor; no good H2834
Ps 85: 1 *You*, LORD, **showed** f *to* your land; you H8354
Ps 89:17 strength, and by your f you exalt our horn. H8356
Ps 90:17 May the f *of* the Lord our God rest on us H5840
Ps 102:13 it is time to **show** f *to* her; the H2858
Ps 106: 4 when you show f *to* your people, come H8356
Pr 3: 4 Then you will win f and a good name in H2834
Pr 3:34 mockers but shows f to the humble and H2834
Pr 8:35 me find life and receive f from the LORD. H8356
Pr 10:32 lips of the righteous know *what* **finds** f, H8356
Pr 11: 1 accurate weights **find** f *with* him. H8356
Pr 11:27 Whoever seeks good finds f, but evil H8356
Pr 12: 2 Good people obtain f from the LORD, but H8356
Pr 13:15 Good judgment wins f, but the way of the H2834
Pr 16:15 his f is like a rain cloud in spring. H8356
Pr 18:22 what is good and receives f from the LORD. H8356
Pr 19: 6 Many **curry** f **with** a ruler, and H2704+7156
Pr 19:12 but his f is like dew on the grass. H8356
Pr 28:23 will in the end gain f rather than one who H2834
Ecc 9:11 wealth to the brilliant or f to the learned; H2834
Isa 27:11 and their Creator **shows** them no f. H2858
Isa 49: 8 "In the time of my f I will answer you, and H8356
Isa 60:10 in f I will show you compassion. H8356
Isa 61: 2 the year of the LORD's f and the day of H8356
Isa 66: 2 "These are the ones *I* **look on with** f H5564
Jer 16:13 day and night, for I will show you no f. H2850
Jer 26:19 fear the LORD and **seek** his f? H2704+906+7156

Jer 31: 2 the sword will find **f** in the wilderness; H2834
La 4:16 are shown no honor, the elders no **f**. H2858
Eze 36: 9 you and *will* **look** on you **with f**; H7155
Da 1: 9 the official to show **f** and compassion to H2876
Da 7:22 judgment **in f** of the holy people of A10378
Da 9:13 *we have* not **sought the f of** H2704+7156+906
Da 9:17 **look with f** on your desolate H239+7156
Da 11:30 He will return and **show f** to those who H1067
Hos 12: 4 he wept and **begged for** his **f**. H2858
Zec 11: 7 called one **F** and the other Union, H5840
Zec 11:10 Then I took my staff called **F** and broke it H5840
Mal 2:13 because *he* no longer **looks with f** on your H7155
Mt 20:20 kneeling down, asked a **f** of him. *G5516S*
Lk 1:25 these days *he has* **shown** *his* **f** and taken *G2078*
Lk 1:30 Mary; you have found **f** with God. *G5921*
Lk 2:14 earth peace to those *on whom* his **f** *rests*." *G2306*
Lk 2:52 stature, and *in* **f** with God and man. *G5921*
Lk 4:19 to proclaim the year of the Lord's **f**." *G1283*
Jn 5:32 There is another who testifies **in** my **f**, and *G4309*
Ac 2:47 God and enjoying the **f** of all the people. *G5921*
Ac 7:46 who enjoyed God's **f** and asked that he *G5921*
Ac 24:27 Felix wanted to grant a **f** to the Jews, *G5921*
Ac 25: 3 Festus, *as a* **f** *to them*, to have Paul *G160+5921*
Ac 25: 9 wishing to do the Jews a **f**, said to Paul, *G5921*
2Co 1:11 on our behalf *for* the **gracious f** granted us *G5922*
2Co 6: 2 "In the time *of* my **f** I heard you, and *G1283*
2Co 6: 2 now is the time *of* God's **f**, now is the day *G2347*
Eph 6: 6 them not only to **win** their **f** when their eye *G473*
Col 3:22 their eye is on you and to **curry** their **f**, *G473*
Phm 14 so that any **f** you do would not seem forced *G19*
Jas 4: 6 the proud but shows **f** to the humble." *G5921*
1Pe 5: 5 the proud but shows **f** to the humble." *G5921*
Rev 2: 6 But *you* **have** this *in your* **f**: You hate the AIT

FAVORABLE (5) [FAVOR]

Ge 40:16 that Joseph had given a **f** interpretation, H3202
1Sa 25: 8 *be* **f toward** my men, H5162+2834+928+6524
1Ki 12: 7 serve them and give them a **f** answer, H3202
2Ch 10: 7 please them and give them a **f** answer, H3202
Jer 42: 6 Whether it is **f** or unfavorable, we will H3202

FAVORABLY (8) [FAVOR]

Ge 33:10 now that *you have* **received** me **f**. H8354
Ex 3:21 **f disposed toward** this H2834+928+6524
Ex 11: 3 **f disposed toward** the H2834+928+6524
Ex 12:36 **f disposed toward** the H2834+928+6524
1Sa 20:12 If *he is* **f disposed** toward you, will I not H3201
1Ki 22:13 your word agree with theirs, and speak **f**." H3202
2Ch 18:12 your word agree with theirs, and speak **f**." H3202
Ro 15:31 Jerusalem may be **f received** by the Lord's *G2347*

FAVORED (5) [FAVOR]

Dt 33:24 is Asher; let him be **f** *by* his brothers, and H8354
Ps 30: 7 when you **f** me, you made my royal H8356
Eze 32:19 Say to them, '*Are you* **more f** than others H5838
Lk 1:28 "Greetings, *you who are* **highly f**! *G5923*
Lk 1:43 But why am I **so f**, that the mother of my *G4047S*

FAVORITE (1) [FAVOR]

SS 6: 9 her mother, the **f** of the one who bore her. H1338

FAVORITISM (10) [FAVOR]

Ex 23: 3 and *do* not **show f** *to* a poor person in a H2075
Lev 19:15 to the poor or **f** *to* the great, H2075+7156
Ac 10:34 true it is that God *does* not **show f** *G1639+4720*
Ro 2:11 For God *does* not **show f**. *G1639+4721*
Gal 2: 6 God *does* not **show f**—they *G4725+476+3284*
Eph 6: 9 is in heaven, and there is no **f** with him. *G4721*
Col 3:25 repaid for their wrongs, and there is no **f**. *G4721*
1Ti 5:21 partiality, and to do nothing out of **f**. *G4680*
Jas 2: 1 glorious Lord Jesus Christ must not show **f**. *G4721*
Jas 2: 9 But if *you* **show f**, you sin and are *G4719*

FAVORS (5) [FAVOR]

2Sa 20:11 said, "Whoever **f** Joab, and whoever H2911
Jer 3:13 have scattered your **f** to foreign gods H2006
Eze 16:15 You lavished your **f** on anyone who H9373
Eze 16:33 to you from everywhere for your **illicit f**. H9373
Eze 16:34 no *one* **runs after** you **for** your **f**. H2388+339

FAWN (2) [FAWNS]

Job 39: 1 Do you watch when the doe bears her **f**? NDT
Jer 14: 5 field deserts *her* **newborn** *f* because there is AIT

FAWNS (5) [FAWN]

Ge 49:21 is a doe set free that bears beautiful **f**. H611
SS 4: 5 Your breasts are like two **f**, like twin fawns H6762
SS 4: 5 like twin **f** of a gazelle that browse among NDT
SS 7: 3 Your breasts are like two **f**, like twin fawns H6762
SS 7: 3 are like two fawns, like twin **f** of a gazelle. NDT

FEAR (271) [AFRAID, FEARED, FEARFUL, FEARFULLY, FEARING, FEARLESSLY, FEARS, FEARSOME, FRIGHT, FRIGHTEN, FRIGHTENED, FRIGHTENING, GOD-FEARING]

Ge 9: 2 The **f** and dread of you will fall on all the H4616
Ge 20:11 'There is surely no **f** *of* God in this place H3711
Ge 22:12 Now I know that you **f** God, because you H3710
Ge 31:42 the God of Abraham and the **F** *of* Isaac H7065
Ge 31:53 in the name of the **F** *of* his father Isaac. H7065
Ge 32: 7 *In* great **f** and distress Jacob divided the H3707
Ge 42:18 "Do this and you will live, for I **f** God: H3710
Ex 9:30 your officials still *do* not **f** the LORD God." H3707
Ex 18:21 all the people—*men who* **f** God H3710
Ex 20:18 mountain in smoke, they trembled *with* **f**. H3707
Ex 20:20 so that the **f** *of* God will be with you to H3711
Lev 19:14 block in front of the blind, but **f** your God. H3707
Lev 25:17 advantage of each other, but **f** your God. H3707
Lev 25:36 profit from them, but **f** your God, so that H3707
Lev 25:43 rule over them ruthlessly, but **f** your God. H3707
Dt 1:28 brothers have made our hearts **melt in f**. H5022
Dt 2:25 to put the terror and **f** *of* you on all the H3711
Dt 5:29 be inclined to **f** me and keep all my H3707
Dt 6: 2 after them *may* **f** the LORD your God H3707
Dt 6:13 **F** the LORD your God, serve him only and H3707
Dt 6:24 these decrees and to **f** the LORD our God, H3707
Dt 7:19 do the same to all the peoples you now **f**. H3707
Dt 10:12 God ask of you but to **f** the LORD your God, H3707
Dt 10:20 **F** the LORD your God and serve him. H3707
Dt 11:25 put the terror and **f** *of* you on the whole H4616
Dt 25:18 lagging behind; *they had* no **f** *of* God. H3707
Dt 28:10 the name of the LORD, and *they will* **f** you. H3707
Dt 31:12 can listen and learn *to* **f** the LORD your God H3707
Dt 31:13 hear it and learn to **f** the LORD your God as H3707
Dt 32:17 appeared, gods your ancestors *did* not **f**. H8549
Jos 2: 9 land and that a **great f** *of* you has fallen on H399
Jos 2: 9 this country *are* **melting in f** because of H4570
Jos 2:11 our hearts **melted in f** and everyone's H5022
Jos 2:24 the people *are* **melting in f** because of us." H4570
Jos 4:24 so that *you might* always **f** the LORD H3707
Jos 5: 1 their hearts **melted in f** and they no H5022
Jos 7: 5 of the people **melted in f** and became H5022
Jos 14: 8 **made** the hearts of the people **melt in f**. H4998
Jos 22:24 We did it for **f** that some day your H1796
Jos 24:14 "Now **f** the LORD and serve him with all H3707
Jdg 7: 3 who trembles *with* **f** may turn back and H3710
1Sa 12:14 If *you* **f** the LORD and serve and obey him H3707
1Sa 12:24 But *be sure to* **f** the LORD and serve him H3707
1Sa 13: 7 the troops with him *were* **quaking with f**. H3006
1Sa 17:24 the man, they all fled from him *in* great **f**. H3707
1Sa 28:20 **filled with f** because of Samuel's H3707+4394
2Sa 17:10 of a lion, *will* **melt with f**, for all H5022+5022
2Sa 23: 3 when he rules in the **f** *of* God, H3711
1Ki 1:50 But Adonijah, *in* **f** of Solomon, went and H3707
1Ki 8:40 so that *they will* **f** you all the time they H3707
1Ki 8:43 the earth may know your name and **f** you, H3707
2Ki 25:26 fled to Egypt for **f** of the Babylonians. H3707
1Ch 14:17 the LORD made all the nations **f** him. H7065
2Ch 6:31 so that *they will* **f** you and walk in H3707
2Ch 6:33 the earth may know your name and **f** you, H3707
2Ch 12: 5 in Jerusalem **for f** of Shishak, H4946+7156
2Ch 17:10 The **f** *of* the LORD fell on all the kingdoms H7065
2Ch 19: 7 Now let the **f** *of* the LORD be on you. H7065
2Ch 19: 9 wholeheartedly in the **f** *of* the LORD. H3711
2Ch 20:29 The **f** *of* God came on all the surrounding H7065
2Ch 26: 5 who instructed him in the **f** *of* God. H3711
Ezr 3: 3 Despite their **f** of the peoples around them H399
Ezr 10: 3 lord and of those *who* **f** the commands of H3007
Ne 5: 9 you walk in the **f** *of* our God to avoid the H3711
Est 5: 9 neither rose nor **showed f** in his presence, H2316
Est 8:17 became Jews because **f** *of* the Jews had H7065
Est 9: 3 because **f** *of* Mordecai had seized them. H7065
Job 1: 9 "*Does* Job **f** God for nothing?" Satan H3707
Job 4:14 **f** and trembling seized me and made all H7065
Job 5:21 and *need* not **f** when destruction comes. H3707
Job 5:22 famine, and *need* not **f** the wild animals. H3707
Job 6:14 a friend forsakes the **f** *of* the Almighty. H3711
Job 9:35 Then I would speak up without **f** *of* him H3707
Job 11:15 you will stand firm and without **f**. H3707
Job 19:29 *you should* **f** the sword yourselves; for H1593
Job 21: 9 Their homes are safe and free from **f**; the H7065
Job 23:15 when I think of all this, *I* **f** him. H7064
Job 28:28 human race, "The **f** *of* the Lord—that is H3711
Job 31:23 and **for f** of his splendor I could not do H4946
Job 33: 7 No **f** *of* me should alarm you, nor should H399
Job 39:22 It laughs at **f**, afraid of nothing; it does H7065
Job 41:33 earth is its equal—a creature without **f**. H3145
Ps 2:11 Serve the LORD with **f** and celebrate his H3711
Ps 3: 6 *I will* not **f** though tens of thousands H3707
Ps 15: 4 person but honors *those who* **f** the LORD; H3710
Ps 19: 9 The **f** *of* the LORD is pure, enduring forever H3711
Ps 22:23 You *who* **f** the LORD, praise him! All you H3710
Ps 22:25 before *those who* **f** you I will fulfill my H3710
Ps 23: 4 the darkest valley, *I will* **f** no evil, for you H3707
Ps 25:12 are those *who* **f** the LORD? He will H3710
Ps 25:14 The LORD confides in *those who* **f** him; he H3710
Ps 27: 1 light and my salvation—whom *shall I* **f**? H3707
Ps 27: 3 my heart *will* not **f**; though war break H3707
Ps 31:19 you have stored up for *those who* **f** you, H3710
Ps 33: 8 *Let* all the earth **f** the LORD; let all the H3707
Ps 33:18 eyes of the LORD are on *those who* **f** him, H3710
Ps 34: 7 LORD encamps around *those who* **f** him, H3710
Ps 34: 9 **F** the LORD, *you* his holy people, for those H3707
Ps 34: 9 people, for *those who* **f** him lack nothing. H3710
Ps 34:11 I will teach you the **f** *of* the LORD. H3711
Ps 36: 1 There is no **f** *of* God before their eyes. H7065
Ps 40: 3 Many will see and **f** the LORD and put their H3707
Ps 46: 2 Therefore *we will* not **f**, though the earth H3707
Ps 49: 5 Why *should I* **f** when evil days come H3707
Ps 52: 6 The righteous will see and **f**; they will H3707
Ps 55: 5 **F** and trembling have beset me; horror H3711
Ps 55:19 because *they have* no **f** *of* God. H3707
Ps 60: 4 But for *those who* **f** you, you have raised a H3710
Ps 61: 5 the heritage of *those who* **f** your name. H3710
Ps 64: 4 innocent; they shoot suddenly, without **f**. H3707
Ps 64: 9 All people *will* **f**; they will proclaim the H3707
Ps 66:16 hear, all you *who* **f** God; let me tell H3710
Ps 67: 7 so that all the ends of the earth *will* **f** him. H3707
Ps 85: 9 his salvation is near *those who* **f** him, H3710
Ps 86:11 undivided heart, that I *may* **f** your name. H3707
Ps 90:11 wrath is as great as the **f** *that is* your *due*. H3711
Ps 91: 5 *You will* not **f** the terror of night, nor the H3707
Ps 102:15 The nations *will* **f** the name of the LORD H3707
Ps 103:11 so great is his love for *those who* **f** him; H3710
Ps 103:13 LORD has compassion on *those who* **f** him; H3710
Ps 103:17 the LORD's love is with *those who* **f** him, H3710
Ps 111: 5 He provides food for *those who* **f** him; he H3710
Ps 111:10 The **f** *of* the LORD is the beginning of H3711
Ps 112: 1 Blessed are those *who* **f** the LORD, who H3707
Ps 112: 7 *They will* **have** no **f** of bad news; their H3707
Ps 112: 8 are secure, *they will* **have** no **f**; in the end H3707
Ps 115:11 You *who* **f** him, trust in the LORD—he is H3710
Ps 115:13 he will bless *those who* **f** the LORD—small H3710
Ps 118: 4 Let *those who* **f** the LORD say: "His love H3710
Ps 119:63 I am a friend to all who **f** you, to all who H3707
Ps 119:74 May *those who* **f** you rejoice when they H3710
Ps 119:79 May *those who* **f** you turn to me, those H3710
Ps 119:120 My flesh trembles in **f** *of* you; I stand in H7065
Ps 128: 1 Blessed are all *who* **f** the LORD, who walk H3710
Ps 135:20 praise the LORD; you *who* **f** him, praise the H3710
Ps 145:19 He fulfills the desires of *those who* **f** him H3710
Ps 147:11 the LORD delights in *those who* **f** him, who H3710
Pr 1: 7 The **f** *of* the LORD is the beginning of H3711
Pr 1:29 did not choose to **f** the LORD. H3711
Pr 1:33 safety and be at ease, without **f** *of* harm." H7065
Pr 2: 5 will understand the **f** *of* the LORD and find H3711
Pr 3: 7 in your own eyes; **f** the LORD and shun evil. H3707
Pr 3:25 *Have* no **f** of sudden disaster or of the ruin H3707
Pr 8:13 To **f** the LORD is to hate evil; I hate pride H3711
Pr 9:10 The **f** *of* the LORD is the beginning of H3711
Pr 10:27 The **f** *of* the LORD adds length to life, but H3711
Pr 14:16 The wise **f** the LORD and shun evil, but a H3707
Pr 14:27 The **f** *of* the LORD is a fountain of life H3711
Pr 15:16 a little with the **f** *of* the LORD than great H3711
Pr 15:33 Wisdom's instruction is to **f** the LORD, and H3711
Pr 16: 6 through the **f** *of* the LORD evil is avoided. H3711
Pr 19:23 The **f** *of* the LORD leads to life; then one H3711
Pr 22: 4 Humility is the **f** *of* the LORD; its wages are H3711
Pr 23:17 always be zealous for the **f** *of* the LORD. H3711
Pr 24:21 **F** the LORD and the king, my son, and do H3707
Pr 29:25 **F** *of* man will prove to be a snare, but H3010
Pr 31:21 it snows, *she has* no **f** for her household H3707
Ecc 3:14 God does it so that *people will* **f** him. H3707
Ecc 5: 7 words are meaningless. Therefore **f** God. H3707
Ecc 8:12 that it will go better with *those who* **f** God, H3710
Ecc 8:13 Yet because the wicked do not **f** God, it H3710
Ecc 12:13 **F** God and keep his commandments, for H3707
Isa 7:25 no longer go there *for* **f** *of* the briers and H3711
Isa 8:12 a conspiracy; *do* not **f** what they fear, and H3707
Isa 8:12 do not fear *what* they **f**, and do not dread H4616
Isa 8:13 he is the one you are to **f**, he is the one H4616
Isa 11: 2 of the knowledge and **f** *of* the LORD— H3711
Isa 11: 3 he will delight in the **f** *of* the LORD. H3711
Isa 13: 7 will go limp, every heart *will* **melt with f**. H5022
Isa 19: 1 the hearts of the Egyptians **melt with f**. H5022
Isa 19:16 They will shudder *with* **f** at the uplifted H7064
Isa 21: 4 My heart falters, **f** makes me tremble; the H7146
Isa 33: 6 the **f** *of* the LORD is the key to this treasure. H3711
Isa 35: 4 "Be strong, *do* not **f**; your God will come H3707
Isa 41: 5 The islands have seen it and **f**; the ends H3707
Isa 41:10 So *do* not **f**, for I am with you; do not be H3707
Isa 41:13 says to you, *Do* not **f**; I will help you. H3707
Isa 41:14 little Israel, do not **f**, for I myself will help NDT
Isa 41:23 that we will be dismayed and *filled with* **f**. H3707
Isa 43: 1 "*Do* not **f**, for I have redeemed you; I have H3707
Isa 51: 7 *Do* not **f** the reproach of mere mortals H3707
Isa 51:12 Who are you that *you* **f** mere mortals H3707
Isa 54: 4 *Do* not **f disgrace**; you will not be H4007
Isa 54:14 far from you; *you will have* nothing *to* **f**. H3707
Isa 57:11 long been silent that *you do* not **f** me? H3707
Isa 59:19 west, *people will* **f** the name of the LORD H3707
Jer 3: 8 that her unfaithful sister Judah *had* no **f**; H3707
Jer 5:22 *Should you* not **f** me?" declares the LORD H3707
Jer 5:24 to themselves, '*Let us* **f** the LORD our God H3707
Jer 10: 5 *Do* not **f** them; they can do no harm nor H3707
Jer 10: 7 Who *should* not **f** you, King of the nations H3707
Jer 17: 8 *It does* not **f** when heat comes; its leaves H3707
Jer 22:25 those you **f**—Nebuchadnezzar king H3328
Jer 26:19 *Did* not Hezekiah **f** the LORD and seek his H3707
Jer 26:21 But Uriah heard of it and fled *in* **f** to Egypt. H3707
Jer 30: 5 " 'Cries of **f** are heard—terror, not H3010
Jer 32:39 so that they *will* always **f** me and that all H3707
Jer 32:40 I will inspire them to **f** me, so that H3711
Jer 36:16 *they* **looked** at each other **in f** and said to H7064
Jer 36:24 who heard all these words **showed** no **f**, H7064
Jer 39:17 be given into the hands of those you **f**. H3328
Jer 42:11 of the king of Babylon, whom you now **f**. H3710
Jer 42:16 then the sword you **f** will overtake you H3710
La 3:57 I called you, and you said, "*Do* not **f**." H3707
Eze 11: 8 *You* **f** the sword, and the sword is what I H3707
Eze 12:18 shudder in **f** as you drink your water. H1796
Eze 21: 7 Every heart *will* **melt with f** and every H5022
Eze 21:15 that hearts *may* **melt with f** and the fallen H4570
Eze 27:35 horror and their faces *are* **distorted with f**. H8307
Eze 30:13 I will spread **f** throughout the land. H3711
Da 6:26 people must **f** and reverence the A10227
Hos 10: 5 who live in Samaria **f** for the calf-idol of H1593

F

Am 3: 8 roared—who will not f? The Sovereign H3707
Mic 6: 9 to the city—and to f your name is wisdom H3707
Mic 7:17 they will turn in f to the LORD our God and H7064
Na 2:11 and the cubs, with nothing to f? H3006
Zep 3: 7 'Surely you will f me and accept correction H3707
Zep 3:15 with you; never again will you f any harm. H3707
Zep 3:16 will say to Jerusalem, "Do not f, Zion; H3707
Hag 2: 5 my Spirit remains among you. Do not f.' H3707
Zec 9: 5 Ashkelon will see it and f; Gaza will H3707
Mal 3: 5 of justice, but do not f me," says the LORD H3707
Mt 14:26 a ghost," they said, and cried out in f. G5832
Mk 5:33 feet and, trembling with f, told him the G5828
Lk 1:12 he was startled and was gripped with f. G5832
Lk 1:50 His mercy extends to those who f him G5828
Lk 1:74 to enable us to serve him without f G925
Lk 8:25 In f and amazement they asked one G5828
Lk 8:37 because they were overcome with f. G5832
Lk 12: 5 But I will show you whom you should f G5828
Lk 12: 5 F him who, after your body has been G5828
Lk 12: 5 throw you into hell. Yes, I tell you, f him. G5828
Lk 18: 4 'Even though I don't f God or care what G5828
Lk 23:40 "Don't you f God," he said, "since you are G5828
Jn 3:20 into the light for f that their deeds G2671+3590
Jn 7:13 publicly about him for f of the leaders. G5832
Jn 12:42 their faith for f they would be put G2671+3590
Jn 20:19 the doors locked for f of the Jewish G5832
Ac 5: 5 And great f seized all who heard what G5832
Ac 5:11 Great f seized the whole church and all G5832
Ac 7:32 Moses trembled with f and did not G1958+1181
Ac 9:31 Living in the f of the Lord and encouraged G5832
Ac 10: 4 Cornelius stared at him in f. G1873+1181
Ac 19:17 they were all seized with f, and the name G5832
Ro 3:18 "There is no f of God before their eyes." G5832
Ro 8:15 so that you live in f again; rather, G5832
Ro 13: 3 Do you want to be free from f of the one G5828
1Co 2: 3 in weakness with great f and trembling. G5832
1Co 16:10 it that he has nothing to f while he is with G925
2Co 5:11 we know what it is to f the Lord, we try to G5832
2Co 7:15 receiving him with f and trembling. G5832
2Co 12:20 I f that there may be discord, jealousy, fits of NDT
Gal 4:11 I f for you, that somehow I have wasted my G5828
Eph 6: 5 your earthly masters with respect and f, G5571
Php 1:14 the more to proclaim the gospel without f. G925
Php 2:12 out your salvation with f and trembling, G5832
Heb 2:15 were held in slavery by their f of death. G5832
Heb 11: 7 in holy f built an ark to save his family. G2326
Heb 12:21 that Moses said, "I am trembling with f." G1958
1Pe 1:17 your time as foreigners here in reverent f. G5832
1Pe 2:17 family of believers, f God, honor the G5828
1Pe 2:18 in reverent f of God submit G4246+5832
1Pe 3: 6 do what is right and do not give way to f. G4766
1Pe 3:14 "Do not f their threats; do not be G5828
1Jn 4:18 There is no f in love. But perfect love G5832
1Jn 4:18 But perfect love drives out f, because fear G5832
1Jn 4:18 because f has to do with punishment. G5832
Jude 23 mixed with f—hating even the G5832
Rev 14: 7 in a loud voice, "F God and give him glory G5828
Rev 15: 4 Who will not f you, Lord, and bring glory G5828
Rev 19: 5 his servants, you who f him, both great G5828

FEARED (36) [FEAR]

Ex 1:17 f God and did not do what the king of H3707
Ex 1:21 And because the midwives f God, he gave H3707
Ex 9:20 of Pharaoh who f the word of the LORD H3707
Ex 14:31 the people f the LORD and put their trust in H3707
Dt 9:19 I f the anger and wrath of the LORD, for he H3336
Jos 9:24 So we f for our lives because of you, and H3707
1Sa 4:13 because his heart f for the ark of H2118+3007
1Sa 14:26 to his mouth, because they f the oath. H3707
1Ch 16:25 of praise; he is to be f above all gods. H3707
Ne 7: 2 of integrity and f God more than most H3707
Job 1: 1 upright; he f God and shunned evil. H3710
Job 3:25 What I f has come upon me; what I H7064
Job 31:34 because I so f the crowd and so dreaded H6907
Ps 76: 7 It is you alone who are to be f. Who can H3707
Ps 76: 8 the land f and was quiet— H3707
Ps 76:11 lands bring gifts to the One to be f. H4616
Ps 76:12 of rulers; he is f by the kings of the earth. H3707
Ps 89: 7 council of the holy ones God is greatly f; H6907
Ps 96: 4 of praise; he is to be f above all gods. H3707
Ps 119:38 to your servant, so that you may be f. H3711
Isa 18: 2 to a people f far and wide, an aggressive H3707
Isa 18: 7 from a people f far and wide, an H3707
Isa 57:11 you so dreaded and f that you have not H3707
Da 5:19 of every language dreaded and f him. A10167
Jnh 1:16 At this the men greatly f the LORD H3707+3711
Hab 1: 7 They are a f and dreaded people; they are H398
Hag 1:12 had sent him. And the people f the LORD. H3707
Mal 1:14 "and my name is to be f among the H3707
Mal 3:16 Then those who f the LORD talked with H3710
Mal 3:16 concerning those who f the LORD and H3710
Mk 6:20 because Herod f John and protected him G5828
Mk 11:18 to kill him, for they f him, because the G5828
Mk 11:32 (They f the people, for everyone held that G5828
Lk 18: 2 was a judge who neither f God nor cared G5828
Jn 19:38 secretly because he f the Jewish leaders. G5832
Ac 5:26 because they f that the people would G5828

FEARFUL (11) [FEAR]

Lev 26:36 make their hearts so f in the lands of their H5322
Dt 28:59 the LORD will send f plagues on you and H7098
Job 32: 6 that is why I was f, not daring to tell H2324
Isa 2:10 from the f presence of the LORD and H7065
Isa 2:19 from the f presence of the LORD and H7065
Isa 2:21 crags from the f presence of the LORD and H7065
Isa 8:22 only distress and darkness and f gloom, H7442
Isa 32: 4 The f heart will know and understand H4554
Isa 35: 4 say to those with f hearts, "Be strong, do H4554
Lk 21:11 and f events and great signs from heaven. G5831
Heb 10:27 only a f expectation of judgment and G5829

FEARFULLY (1) [FEAR]

Ps 139:14 you because I am f and wonderfully made H3707

FEARING (3) [FEAR]

Jos 22:25 might cause ours to stop f the LORD. H3707
Ac 27:29 F that we would be dashed against the G5828
Heb 11:27 he left Egypt, not f the king's anger; he G5828

FEARLESSLY (3) [FEAR]

Ac 9:27 in Damascus he had preached f in the G4245
Eph 6:19 me so that I will f make known the G1877+4244
Eph 6:20 Pray that I may declare it f, as I should. G4245

FEARS (12) [FEAR]

Job 1: 8 upright, a man who f God and shuns evil." H3710
Job 2: 3 upright, a man who f God and shuns evil. H3710
Ps 34: 4 he delivered me from all my f. H4475
Ps 128: 4 the blessing for the man who f the LORD. H3710
Pr 14: 2 Whoever f the LORD walks uprightly, but H3707
Pr 14:26 Whoever f the LORD has a secure fortress H3711
Pr 31:30 a woman who f the LORD is to be H3710
Ecc 7:18 Whoever f God will avoid all extremes. H3710
Isa 50:10 Who among you f the LORD and obeys the H3710
Ac 10:35 every nation the one who f him and does G5828
2Co 7: 5 conflicts on the outside, f within. G5832
1Jn 4:18 The one who f is not made perfect in love. G5828

FEARSOME (1) [FEAR]

Job 41:14 of its mouth, ringed about with f teeth? H399

FEAST (36) [FEASTED, FEASTING, FEASTS]

Ge 21: 8 was weaned Abraham held a great f. H5492
Ge 26:30 Isaac then made a f for them, and they H5492
Ge 29:22 all the people of the place and gave a f. H5492
Ge 40:20 he gave a f for all his officials. H5492
Dt 33:19 they will f on the abundance of the seas H3567
Jdg 14:10 And there Samson held a f, as was H5492
Jdg 14:12 the answer within the seven days of the f, H5492
Jdg 14:17 She cried the whole seven days of the f H5492
Jdg 14:20 who had attended him at the f. H8287
1Sa 20: 5 tomorrow is the New Moon f, and I am H2544
1Sa 20:18 to David, "Tomorrow is the New Moon f. H2544
1Sa 20:24 when the New Moon f came, the king H2544
1Sa 20:34 that second day of the f he did not eat, H2544S
2Sa 3:20 David prepared a f for him and his men. H5492
1Ki 1:41 him heard it as they were finishing their f. H430
1Ki 3:15 Then he gave a f for all his court. H5492
2Ki 6:23 So he prepared a great f for them H4127+4130
Job 39:30 Its young ones f on blood, and where the H6633
Ps 22:29 All the rich of the earth will f and worship H430
Ps 36: 8 They f on the abundance of your house H8115
Pr 5:10 lest strangers f on your wealth and your H8425
Pr 15:15 the cheerful heart has a continual f. H5492
Ecc 5:11 the owners except to f their eyes on them? H8021
Ecc 10:16 whose princes f in the morning. H430
Ecc 10:19 A f is made for laughter, wine makes life H4312
Isa 25: 6 will prepare a f of rich food for all H5492
Isa 58:14 of the land and to f on the inheritance of H430
Jer 51:39 I will set out a f for them and make them H5492
La 2:22 "As you summon to a f day, so you H4595
Hos 9: 5 festivals, on the f days of the LORD? H2504
Mt 8:11 and will take their places at the f with G369
Lk 13:29 and will take their places at the f in the G369
Lk 14: 8 someone invites you to a wedding f, G1141
Lk 14:15 one who will eat at the f in the kingdom of G756
Lk 15:23 Let's have a f and celebrate. G2266
2Pe 2:13 in their pleasures while they f with you. G5307

FEASTED (1) [FEAST]

Ge 43:34 So they f and drank freely with him H9272

FEASTING (13) [FEAST]

Est 8:17 among the Jews, with f and celebrating. H5492
Est 9:17 rested and made it a day of f and joy. H5492
Est 9:18 rested and made it a day of f and joy. H5492
Est 9:19 the month of Adar as a day of joy and f, H5492
Est 9:22 the days as days of f and joy and giving H5492
Job 1: 5 When a period of f had run its course, Job H5492
Job 1:13 daughters were f and drinking wine H430
Job 1:18 daughters were f and drinking wine H430
Pr 17: 1 peace and quiet than a house full of f, H2285
Ecc 7: 2 of mourning than to go to a house of f, H5492
Jer 16: 8 house where there is f and sit down to eat H5492
Am 6: 7 into exile; your f and lounging will end. H5301
Zec 7: 6 were you not just f for H430+2256+9272

FEASTS (9) [FEAST]

Nu 10:10 festivals and New Moon f— H8031+2544
1Ch 23:31 at the New Moon f and at the appointed H2544
Ne 10:33 at the New Moon f and at the appointed H2544
Job 1: 4 His sons used to hold f in their homes on H5492
Job 24:20 the worm f on them; the wicked are H5517
Isa 1:14 Your New Moon f and your appointed H2544
Eze 46:11 At the f and the appointed festivals, the H2504
Hos 5: 7 When they celebrate their New Moon f H2544
Jude 12 These people are blemishes at your love f G27

FEAT (1)

2Ki 8:13 a mere dog, accomplish such a f?" H1524+1821

FEATHERS (7)

Lev 1:16 the crop and the f and throw them down H5901
Job 39:13 compare with the wings and f of the stork. H5681
Job 39:18 she spreads her f to run, H5257+928+2021+5294
Ps 68:13 sheathed with silver, its f with shining gold." H89
Ps 91: 4 He will cover you with his f, and under his H89
Eze 17: 3 long f and full plumage of varied colors H88
Da 4:33 his hair grew like the f of an eagle and his NDT

FEATURES (2)

1Sa 16:12 had a fine appearance and handsome f. H8024
Job 38:14 its f stand out like those of a garment. NDT

FED (11) [FEED]

Dt 32:13 of the land and f him with the fruit of the H430
Jdg 19:21 took him into his house and f his donkeys. H1176
Ps 80: 5 You have f them with the bread of tears H430
Ps 81:16 But you would be f with the finest of wheat H430
Ps 105:40 he f them well with the bread of heaven. H8425
Da 4:12 its branches; from it every creature was f. A10226
Hos 13: 6 When I f them, they were satisfied; when H5338
Na 2:11 the place where they f their young H5337
Lk 6:25 Woe to you who are well f now, for you G1855
Php 4:12 situation, whether well f or hungry G5963
Jas 2:16 keep warm and well f," but does nothing G5963

FEE (2)

Nu 22: 7 taking with them the f for divination. H7877
Ecc 10:11 it is charmed, the charmer receives no f. H3862

FEEBLE (8) [FEEBLEST]

Ne 4: 2 he said, "What are those f Jews doing? H584
Job 4: 3 how you have strengthened f hands. H8333
Job 26: 2 you have saved the arm that is f! H4202+6437
Ps 38: 8 I am f and utterly crushed; I groan in H7028
Isa 16:14 her survivors will be very few and f." H4202+3888
Isa 35: 3 Strengthen the f hands, steady the knees H8333
Jer 49:24 Damascus has become f, she has turned H8332
Heb 12:12 strengthen your f arms and weak knees. G4223

FEEBLEST (1) [FEEBLE]

Zec 12: 8 so that the f among them will be like H4173

FEED (34) [FED, FEEDING, FEEDS, OVERFED, PASTURE-FED, STALL-FED, WELL-FED]

Ge 42:27 opened his sack to get f for his donkey, H5028
1Ki 14:11 the birds will f on those who die in the H430
1Ki 16: 4 birds will f on those who die in the H430
1Ki 21:24 the birds will f on those who die in the H430
Ps 80:13 and insects from the fields f on it. H8286
Pr 12:27 the diligent f on the riches of the hunt. NDT
Pr 27:27 of goats' milk to f your family and to H4312
Isa 5:17 lambs will f among the ruins of the rich. H430
Isa 9:20 Each will f on the flesh of their own H430
Isa 9:21 Manasseh will f on Ephraim, and Ephraim NDT
Isa 11: 7 The cow will f with the bear, their young H8286
Isa 18: 6 the birds will f on them all summer, the H6584
Isa 49: 9 "They will f beside the roads and find H8286
Isa 61: 6 You will f on the wealth of nations, and in H430
Isa 65:25 The wolf and the lamb will f together H8286
Eze 34:10 shepherds can no longer f themselves. H8286
Eze 34:14 there they will f in a rich pasture on H8286
Eze 34:18 enough for you to f on the good pasture? H8286
Eze 34:19 Must my flock f on what you have trampled H8286
Hos 4: 8 They f on the sins of my people and relish H430
Hos 9: 2 winepresses will not f the people; H8286
Hos 11: 4 to the cheek, and I bent down to f them. H430
Mic 3: 5 who refuses to f them. H5989+6584+7023
Mic 7:14 Let them f in Bashan and Gilead as in H8286
Zec 11:16 heal the injured, or f the healthy, but will H3920
Mt 15:33 in this remote place to f such a crowd?" G5963
Mt 25:37 when did we see you hungry and f you, or G5555
Mk 8: 4 can anyone get enough bread to f them?" G5963
Lk 15:15 who sent him to his fields to f pigs. G1081
Jn 21:15 Jesus said, "F my lambs." G1081
Jn 21:17 that I love you." Jesus said, "F my sheep. G1081
Ro 12:20 your enemy is hungry, f him; if he is thirsty G6039
Eph 5:29 but they f and care for their body G1763
Jude 12 shepherds who f only themselves. G4477

FEEDING (4) [FEED]

Dt 8: 3 you to hunger and then f you with manna, H430
Mt 8:30 from them a large herd of pigs was f. G1081
Mk 5:11 herd of pigs was f on the nearby hillside G1081
Lk 8:32 herd of pigs was f there on the hillside. G1081

FEEDS (8) [FEED]

Job 40:15 with you and which f on grass like an ox. H430
Pr 15:14 the mouth of a fool f on folly. H8286
Isa 44:20 Such a person f on ashes; a deluded H8286
Hos 12: 1 Ephraim f on the wind; he pursues the H8286
Mt 6:26 yet your heavenly Father f them. G5555
Lk 12:24 no storeroom or barn; yet God f them. G5555
Jn 6:57 so the one who f on me will live because G5592
Jn 6:58 whoever f on this bread will live G5592

FEEL (20) [FEELING, FEELINGS, FEELS, FELT, HEARTFELT]

Ge 41:55 When all Egypt *began to* f the famine, the H8279
Jdg 16:26 "Put me where I *can* f the pillars that H4630
1Sa 16:16 God comes on you, and you *will* f better." H3201
1Sa 16:23 to Saul; he *would* f better, and the evil H3201
Job 14:22 *They* f but *the* pain of their own bodies H3872
Ps 58: 9 Before your pots *can* f the heat of the H1067
Ps 115: 7 but cannot f, feet, but cannot walk H4630
Pr 23:35 They beat me, but *I* don't f it! When will I H3359
Isa 32: 9 you daughters *who* f secure, hear what I H1053
Isa 32:10 than a year you *who* f secure will tremble; H1053
Isa 32:11 shudder, you daughters *who* f secure! H1053
Da 8:25 When they f secure, he will destroy many H8932
Da 10:16 my lord, and *I* f very weak. H4202+6806+3946
Da 11:21 the kingdom when its people f secure, H8932
Da 11:24 When the richest provinces f secure, he H8932
Am 6: 1 to *you who* f secure on Mount H1053
Zec 1:15 very angry with the nations that f secure. H8633
2Co 11:29 Who is weak, and *I do* not *f* weak? Who is led AIT
Php 1: 7 It is right for me *to* f this way about all of *G5858*
2Th 3:14 in order that *they may* f ashamed. *G1956*

FEELING (2) [FEEL]

Job 24:23 He may let them rest in a f of security, but H1055
Isa 59:10 f *our* way like people without eyes. H1779

FEELINGS (2) [FEEL]

Nu 5:14 if f *of* jealousy come over her husband H8120
Nu 5:30 when f *of* jealousy come over a man H8120

FEELS (3) [FEEL]

Ex 23: 9 yourselves know how it f to be foreigners, H5883
Pr 14:16 a fool is hotheaded and yet f secure. H1053
1Co 7:36 are too strong and *he f he* ought to marry, AIT

FEET (259) [FOOT]

Ge 18: 4 may all wash your f and rest under this H8079
Ge 19: 2 You can wash your f and spend the night H8079
Ge 24:32 water for him and his men to wash their f. H8079
Ge 43:24 water to wash their f and provided fodder H8079
Ge 49:10 the ruler's staff from between his f H8079
Ge 49:33 to his sons, he drew his f up into the bed H8079
Ex 4:25 foreskin and touched Moses' f with it. H8079
Ex 12:11 your sandals on your f and your staff in H8079
Ex 24:10 Under his f was something like a H8079
Ex 25:12 rings for it and fasten them to its four f, H7193
Ex 29:20 and on the big toes of their right f. H8079
Ex 30:19 wash their hands and f with water from it. H8079
Ex 30:21 wash their hands and f so that they will H8079
Ex 37: 3 rings for it and fastened them to its four f, H7193
Ex 40:31 his sons used it to wash their hands and f. H8079
Lev 8:24 hands and on the big toes of their right f. H8079
Lev 11:42 its belly or walks on all fours or on many f; H8079
Dt 1:36 his descendants the land *he* set *his* f on, H2005
Dt 8: 4 wear out and your f did not swell during H8079
Dt 22: 4 Help the owner get it to its f. H7756+7756
Dt 28:35 from the soles of your f to the top of your H8079
Dt 29: 5 wear out, nor did the sandals on your f. H8079
Dt 33: 3 At your f they all bow down, and from you H8079
Dt 33:24 his brothers, and let him bathe his f in oil. H8079
Jos 3:15 the Jordan and their f touched the water's H8079
Jos 4:18 they set their f on the dry ground H4090+8079
Jos 9: 5 sandals on their f and wore old clothes. H8079
Jos 10:24 here and put your f on the necks of these H8079
Jos 10:24 forward and placed their f on their necks. H8079
Jos 14: 9 land on which your f have walked will be H8079
Jdg 5:27 At her f he sank, he fell; there he lay. H8079
Jdg 5:27 At her f he sank, he fell; where he sank H8079
Jdg 19:21 After they had washed their f, they had H8079
Ru 3: 4 Then go and uncover his f and lie down H5274
Ru 3: 7 uncovered his f and lay down. H5274
Ru 3: 8 there was a woman lying at his f! H5274
Ru 3:14 So she lay at his f until morning, but got H5274
1Sa 2: 9 He will guard the f *of* his faithful servants H8079
1Sa 14:13 using his hands and f, with his H8079
1Sa 25:24 She fell at his f and said: "Pardon your H8079
1Sa 25:41 you and wash the f *of* my lord's servants." H8079
2Sa 3:34 were not bound, your f were not fettered. H8079
2Sa 4: 4 Saul had a son who was lame in *both* f. H8079
2Sa 4:12 off their hands and f and hung the bodies H8079
2Sa 9: 3 a son of Jonathan; he is lame in *both* f." H8079
2Sa 9:13 at the king's table; he was lame in both f. H8079
2Sa 11: 8 "Go down to your house and wash your f." H8079
2Sa 19:24 not taken care of his f or trimmed his H8079
2Sa 22:10 came down; dark clouds were under his f. H8079
2Sa 22:34 He makes my f like the feet of a deer; he H8079
2Sa 22:34 He makes my feet like the f of a deer; he NDT
2Sa 22:37 You provide a broad path for my f, so that H9393
2Sa 22:39 they could not rise; they fell beneath my f. H8079
1Ki 2: 5 around his waist and the sandals on his f. H8079
1Ki 5: 3 LORD put his enemies under his f. H4090+8079
1Ki 15:23 old age, however, his f became diseased. H8079
2Ki 4:27 at the mountain, she took hold of his f. H8079
2Ki 4:37 fell at his f and bowed to the ground. H8079
2Ki 9:35 except her skull, her f and her hands. H8079
2Ki 13:21 man came to life and stood up on his f. H8079
2Ki 19:24 With the soles of my f I have dried up all H7193
2Ki 21: 8 not again make the f *of* the Israelites H8079
1Ch 28: 2 King David rose to his f and said: "Listen H8079
2Ch 3:13 They stood on their f, facing the main hall H8079
2Ch 16:12 Asa was afflicted with a disease in his f. H8079
2Ch 33: 8 not again make the f *of* the Israelites H8079
Ne 9:21 wear out nor did their f become swollen. H8079
Est 8: 3 the king, falling at his f and weeping. H8079
Job 2: 7 from the soles of his f to the crown of his H8079
Job 9:13 the cohorts of Rahab cowered at his f. H9393
Job 12: 5 as the fate of those whose f are slipping. H8079
Job 13:27 You fasten my f in shackles; you keep H8079
Job 13:27 by putting marks on the soles of my f. H8079
Job 18: 8 His f thrust him into a net; he wanders H8079
Job 23:11 My f have closely followed his steps; H8079
Job 28: 4 in places untouched by human f; far from H8079
Job 29: 8 aside and the old men rose to *their* f; H6641
Job 29:15 I was eyes to the blind and f to the lame. H8079
Job 30:12 they lay snares for my f, they build their H8079
Job 33:11 He fastens my f in shackles; he keeps H8079
Ps 8: 6 you put everything under their f: H8079
Ps 9:15 their f are caught in the net they have H8079
Ps 17: 5 to your paths; my f have not stumbled. H7193
Ps 18: 9 came down; dark clouds were under his f. H8079
Ps 18:33 He makes my f like the feet of a deer; he H8079
Ps 18:33 He makes my feet like the f of a deer; he NDT
Ps 18:36 You provide a broad path for my f, so that H9393
Ps 18:38 they could not rise; they fell beneath my f. H8079
Ps 22:16 they pierce my hands and my f. H8079
Ps 25:15 only he will release my f from the snare. H8079
Ps 26:12 My f stand on level ground; in the great H8079
Ps 31: 8 have set my f in a spacious place. H8079
Ps 37:31 God is in their hearts; their f do not slip. H892
Ps 38:16 exalt themselves over me when my f slip." H8079
Ps 40: 2 he set my f on a rock and gave me a firm H8079
Ps 44:18 our f had not strayed from your path. H892
Ps 45: 5 enemies; let the nations fall beneath your f. NDT
Ps 47: 3 nations under us, peoples under our f. H8079
Ps 56:13 me from death and my f from stumbling, H8079
Ps 57: 6 They spread a net for my f—I was bowed H7193
Ps 58:10 when they dip their f in the blood of the H7193
Ps 66: 9 our lives and kept our f from slipping. H8079
Ps 68:23 that your f may wade in the blood of your H8079
Ps 73: 2 But as for me, my f had almost slipped; H8079
Ps 105:18 They bruised his f with shackles, his neck H8079
Ps 110: 1 I make your enemies a footstool for your f." H8079
Ps 115: 7 cannot feel, f, but cannot walk, nor H8079
Ps 116: 8 my eyes from tears, my f from stumbling, H8079
Ps 119:101 I have kept my f from every evil path so H8079
Ps 119:105 Your word is a lamp for my f, a light on H8079
Ps 122: 2 Our f are standing in your gates H8079
Ps 140: 4 the violent, who devise ways to trip my f. H7193
Pr 1:16 their f rush into evil, they are swift to H8079
Pr 4:26 to the paths for your f and be steadfast in H8079
Pr 5: 5 Her f go down to death; her steps lead H8079
Pr 6:13 signals with his f and motions with his H8079
Pr 6:18 schemes, f that are quick to rush into evil, H8079
Pr 6:28 on hot coals without his f being scorched? H8079
Pr 7:11 defiant, her f never stay at home; H8079
Pr 19: 2 how much more will hasty f miss the way! H8079
Pr 26: 6 like cutting off one's f or drinking poison. H8079
Pr 29: 5 neighbors are spreading nets for their f. H7193
SS 5: 3 I have washed my f—must I soil them H8079
SS 7: 1 How beautiful your sandaled f, O prince's H7193
Isa 6: 2 with two they covered their f, and with two H8079
Isa 20: 2 your body and the sandals from your f." H8079
Isa 23: 7 whose f have taken her to settle in far-off H8079
Isa 26: 6 F trample it down—the feet of the H8079
Isa 26: 6 it down—the f *of* the oppressed, the H8079
Isa 37:25 With the soles of my f I have dried up all H7193
Isa 41: 3 by a path his f have not traveled before. H8079
Isa 49:23 ground; they will lick the dust at your f. H8079
Isa 52: 7 mountains are the f *of* those who bring H8079
Isa 58:13 "If you keep your f from breaking the H8079
Isa 59: 7 Their f rush into sin; they are swift to shed H8079
Isa 60:13 I will glorify the place for my f. H8079
Isa 60:14 bow down at your f and will call H4090+8079
Jer 2:25 Do not run until your f are bare and your H8079
Jer 13:16 before your f stumble on the darkening H8079
Jer 14:10 to wander; they do not restrain their f. H8079
Jer 18:22 me and have hidden snares for my f. H8079
Jer 38:22 Your f are sunk in the mud; your friends H8079
La 1:13 spread a net for my f and turned me back. H8079
Eze 1: 7 their f were like those of a calf and H4090+8079
Eze 2: 1 stand up on your f and I will speak to you." H8079
Eze 2: 2 came into me and raised me to my f, H8079
Eze 3:24 came into me and raised me to my f. H8079
Eze 6:11 stamp your f and cry out "Alas! H8079
Eze 24:17 fastened and your sandals on your f; H8079
Eze 24:23 on your heads and your sandals on your f. H8079
Eze 25: 6 clapped your hands and stamped your f, H8079
Eze 32: 2 the water with your f and muddying the H8079
Eze 34:18 the rest of your pasture with your f? H8079
Eze 34:18 Must you also muddy the rest with your f? H8079
Eze 34:19 drink what you have muddied with your f? H8079
Eze 37:10 they came to life and stood up on their f— H8079
Eze 43: 7 throne and the place for the soles of my f. H8079
Da 2:33 its f partly of iron and partly of baked A10655
Da 2:34 the statue on its f of iron and clay and A10655
Da 2:41 as you saw that the f and toes were A10655
Da 3:24 leaped to *his* f in amazement A10624
Da 7: 4 that it stood on *two* f like a human being A10655
Da 8:18 he touched me and raised me to my f. H6642
Na 1: 3 the storm, and clouds are the dust of his f. H8079
Na 1:15 the f *of* one who brings good news H8079
Hab 3:19 he makes my f like the feet of a deer H8079
Hab 3:19 he makes my feet like the f of a deer, he NDT
Zec 14: 4 On that day his f will stand on the Mount H8079
Zec 14:12 rot while they are still standing on their f, H8079
Mal 4: 3 the soles of your f on the day when I act," H8079
Mt 7: 6 they may trample them under their f, and *G4546*
Mt 10:14 town and shake the dust off your f. *G4546*
Mt 15:30 laid them at his f; and he healed *G4546*
Mt 18: 8 two hands or two f and be thrown into *G4546*
Mt 22:44 until I put your enemies under your f." *G4546*
Mt 28: 9 clasped his f and worshiped him. *G4546*
Mk 5: 4 chains apart and broke the irons on his f. *G4267*
Mk 5:22 when he saw Jesus, he fell at his f. *G4546*
Mk 5:33 came and fell at his f and, trembling *G4700*
Mk 6:11 the dust off your f as a testimony against *G4546*
Mk 7:25 by an impure spirit came and fell at his f. *G4546*
Mk 9:27 him by the hand and lifted him to his f, *G1586*
Mk 9:45 than to have two f and be thrown into hell *G4546*
Mk 10:49 "Cheer up! On *your* f! He's calling *G1586*
Mk 10:50 *he* jumped to *his* f and came to Jesus. *G403*
Mk 12:36 until I put your enemies under your f." *G4546*
Lk 1:79 to guide our f into the path of peace." *G4546*
Lk 7:38 As she stood behind him at his f weeping *G4546*
Lk 7:38 she began to wet his f with her tears. *G4546*
Lk 7:44 You did not give me any water for my f *G4546*
Lk 7:44 she wet my f with her tears and wiped *G4546*
Lk 7:45 I entered, has not stopped kissing my f. *G4546*
Lk 7:46 she has poured perfume on my f. *G4546*
Lk 8:28 he cried out and fell at his f, shouting at *G4700*
Lk 8:35 sitting at Jesus' f, dressed and in his *G4546*
Lk 8:41 came and fell at Jesus' f, pleading with *G4546*
Lk 8:47 came trembling and fell at his f. *G4700*
Lk 9: 5 the dust off your f as a testimony against *G4546*
Lk 10:11 we wipe from our f as a warning to you. *G4546*
Lk 10:39 sat at the Lord's f listening to what he *G4546*
Lk 15:22 a ring on his finger and sandals on his f. *G4546*
Lk 17:16 himself at Jesus' f and thanked him— *G4546*
Lk 20:43 I make your enemies a footstool *for* your f." *G4546*
Lk 24:39 Look at my hands and my f. It is I myself *G4546*
Lk 24:40 he showed them his hands and f. *G4546*
Jn 11: 2 on the Lord and wiped his f with her hair.) *G4546*
Jn 11:32 saw him, she fell at his f and said, "Lord, *G4546*
Jn 11:44 his hands and f wrapped with strips of *G4546*
Jn 12: 3 poured it on Jesus' f and wiped his feet *G4546*
Jn 12: 3 Jesus' feet and wiped his f with her hair. *G4546*
Jn 13: 5 basin and began to wash his disciples' f, *G4546*
Jn 13: 6 "Lord, are you going to wash my f?" *G4546*
Jn 13: 8 said Peter, "you shall never wash my f." *G4546*
Jn 13: 9 "not just my f but my hands and my head *G4546*
Jn 13:10 had a bath need only to wash their f; *G4546*
Jn 13:12 When he had finished washing their f, he *G4546*
Jn 13:14 have washed your f, you also should wash *G4546*
Jn 13:14 you also should wash one another's f. *G4546*
Ac 2:35 I make your enemies a footstool *for* your f." *G4546*
Ac 3: 7 instantly the man's f and ankles became *G1000*
Ac 3: 8 He jumped to *his* f and began to walk *G2705*
Ac 4:35 put it at the apostles' f, and it was *G4546*
Ac 4:37 the money and put it at the apostles' f. *G4546*
Ac 5: 2 the rest and put it at the apostles' f. *G4546*
Ac 5: 9 The f of the men who buried your *G4546*
Ac 5:10 moment she fell down at his f and died. *G4546*
Ac 7:58 their coats at the f of a young man named *G4546*
Ac 9:41 her by the hand and helped her to her f. *G482*
Ac 10:25 met him and fell at his f in reverence. *G4546*
Ac 13:51 the dust off their f as a warning to them *G4546*
Ac 14:10 called out, "Stand up on your f!" At that, *G4546*
Ac 16:24 cell and fastened their f in the stocks. *G4546*
Ac 21:11 tied his own hands and f with it and said *G4546*
Ac 26:16 'Now get up and stand on your f. *G4546*
Ac 27:28 was a hundred and twenty f deep. *G3976+1633*
Ac 27:28 and found it was ninety f deep. *G3976+1278*
Ro 3:15 "Their f are swift to shed blood; *G4546*
Ro 10:15 beautiful are the f of those who bring *G4546*
Ro 16:20 peace will soon crush Satan under your f. *G4546*
1Co 12:21 And the head cannot say *to* the f, "I don't *G4546*
1Co 15:25 he has put all his enemies under his f. *G4546*
1Co 15:27 For he "has put everything under his f." *G4546*
Eph 1:22 things under his f and appointed him to *G4546*
Eph 6:15 with your f fitted with the readiness *G4546*
1Ti 5:10 washing the f of the Lord's people *G4546*
Heb 1:13 make your enemies a footstool *for* your f"? *G4546*
Heb 2: 8 put everything under their f." In *G4546*
Heb 12:13 "Make level paths *for* your f," so that the *G4546*
Jas 2: 3 stand there" or "Sit on the floor by my f," *G5711*
Rev 1:13 in a robe reaching down to his f and with *G4468*
Rev 1:15 His f were like bronze glowing in a furnace *G4546*
Rev 1:17 I saw him, I fell at his f as though dead. *G4546*
Rev 2:18 fire and whose f are like burnished *G4546*
Rev 3: 9 fall down at your f and acknowledge that *G4546*
Rev 11:11 they stood on their f, and terror struck *G4546*
Rev 12: 1 the moon under her f and a crown of *G4546*
Rev 13: 2 had f like those of a bear and a *G4546*
Rev 19:10 At this I fell at his f to worship him. *G4546*
Rev 22: 8 to worship at the f of the angel who had *G4546*

FELIX (10)

Ac 23:24 that he may be taken safely to Governor F." *G5772*
Ac 23:26 To His Excellency, Governor F: *G5772*
Ac 24: 2 Tertullus presented his case before F: NDT
Ac 24: 3 most excellent F, we acknowledge *G5772*
Ac 24:22 Then F, who was well acquainted with the *G5772*
Ac 24:24 Several days later F came with his wife *G5772*
Ac 24:25 judgment to come, F was afraid and said *G5772*
Ac 24:27 F was succeeded by Porcius Festus *G5772*

F

Ac 24:27 because F wanted to grant a favor to G5772
Ac 25:14 is a man here whom F left as a prisoner. G5772

FELL (177) [FALL]

Ge 7:12 And rain f on the earth forty days and forty H2118
Ge 14:10 *some of the men* f into them and the rest H5877
Ge 15:12 Abram f *into* a deep sleep, and H5877
Ge 17: 3 Abram f facedown, and God said to him, H5877
Ge 17:17 Abraham f facedown; he laughed and H5877
Ge 35: 5 the terror of God f on the towns all H2118
Ge 41: 5 *He* f **asleep** again and had a second H3822
Ex 9:24 hail f and lightning flashed back and forth H2118
Lev 9:24 they shouted for joy and f facedown. H5877
Nu 14: 5 Moses and Aaron f facedown in front of H5877
Nu 16: 4 When Moses heard this, *he* f facedown. H5877
Nu 16:22 Moses and Aaron f facedown and cried H5877
Nu 16:45 to them at once." And *they* f facedown. H5877
Nu 20: 3 when our brothers f **dead** before the LORD! H1588
Nu 20: 6 to the tent of meeting and f facedown, H5877
Nu 22:31 bowed low and f **facedown**. H2556+4200+678
Dt 9:18 Then once again *I* f **prostrate** before the H5877
Dt 19: 5 as he swings his ax to f a tree, the H4162
Jos 5:14 Then Joshua f facedown to the ground in H5877
Jos 7: 6 tore his clothes and f facedown to the H5877
Jos 8:25 thousand men and women f that day— H5877
Jos 21:10 because the first lot f to them): H2118
Jos 22:17 though a plague f on the community of H2118
Jdg 4:16 all Sisera's troops f by the sword; not H5877
Jdg 5:27 At her feet he sank, *he* f; there he lay. H5877
Jdg 5:27 At her feet he sank, *he* f; where he sank H5877
Jdg 5:27 where he sank, there *he* f—dead. H5877
Jdg 13:20 Manoah and his wife f with their faces to H5877
Jdg 16: 4 *he* f **in love with** a woman in the Valley of H170
Jdg 19:26 f **down** *at* the door and lay there until H5877
Jdg 20:31 that about thirty men f in the open field NDT
Jdg 20:44 Eighteen thousand Benjamites f, all of H5877
Jdg 20:46 thousand Benjamite swordsmen f, H5877
1Sa 4:18 Eli f backward off his chair by the side of H5877
1Sa 11: 7 the terror of the LORD f on the people, H5877
1Sa 14:13 The Philistines f before Jonathan, and his H5877
1Sa 17:49 and *he* f facedown on the ground. H5877
1Sa 25:24 *She* f at his feet and said: "Pardon your H5877
1Sa 28:20 Immediately Saul f full length on the H5877
1Sa 31: 1 and *many* f dead on Mount Gilboa. H5877
1Sa 31: 4 so Saul took his own sword and f on it. H5877
1Sa 31: 5 he too f on his sword and died with him. H5877
2Sa 1: 2 *he* f to the ground to pay him honor. H5877
2Sa 1: 4 "Many of them f and died. And Saul and H5877
2Sa 2:16 and *they* f **down** together. H5877
2Sa 2:23 *He* f there and died on the spot H5877
2Sa 3:34 *You* f as one falls before the wicked." H5877
2Sa 4: 4 to leave, *he* f and became disabled. H5877
2Sa 11:17 some of the men in David's army f H5877
2Sa 13: 1 Amnon son of David f **in love with** Tamar H170
2Sa 14: 4 *she* f with her face to the ground to pay H5877
2Sa 14:22 Joab f with his face to the ground to pay H5877
2Sa 19:18 the Jordan, *he* f **prostrate** before the king H5877
2Sa 21: 9 All seven of them f together; they were H5877
2Sa 21:22 and *they* f at the hands of David and his H5877
2Sa 22:39 could not rise; *they* f beneath my feet. H5877
1Ki 18:38 the fire of the LORD f and burned up the H5877
1Ki 18:39 people saw this, *they* f prostrate and cried H5877
1Ki 19: 5 he lay down under the bush and f **asleep**. H3822
2Ki 1:10 Then fire f from heaven and consumed H3718
2Ki 1:12 Then the fire of God f from heaven and H3718
2Ki 1:13 captain went up and f on his knees before H4156
2Ki 4:37 f at his feet and bowed to the ground. H5877
2Ki 6: 5 the iron axhead f into the water. H5877
1Ch 5:22 many others f slain, because the H5877
1Ch 10: 1 and *many* f dead on Mount Gilboa. H5877
1Ch 10: 4 so Saul took his own sword and f on it. H5877
1Ch 10: 5 was dead, he too f on his sword and died. H5877
1Ch 20: 8 and *they* f at the hands of David and his H5877
1Ch 21:14 seventy thousand men of Israel f **dead**. H5877
1Ch 21:16 clothed in sackcloth, f facedown. H5877
1Ch 24: 7 The first lot f to Jehoiarib, the second to H3655
1Ch 25: 9 which was for Asaph, f to Joseph, his sons H3655
1Ch 26:14 The lot for the East Gate f to Shelemiah H5877
1Ch 26:14 the lot for the North Gate f *to* him. H3655
1Ch 26:15 The lot for the South Gate f to Obed-Edom NDT
1Ch 26:15 the lot for the storehouse f to his sons. NDT
1Ch 26:16 on the upper road f to Shuppim and Hosah. NDT
2Ch 14:13 number of Cushites f that they could not H5877
2Ch 17:10 The fear of the LORD f on all the kingdoms H2118
2Ch 20:18 Jerusalem f **down** in worship before H5877
Ezr 9: 5 f on my knees with my hands spread H4156
Ne 13:19 When **evening shadows** f *on* the gates of H7511
Est 3: 7 And the lot f on the twelfth month, the H5877
Job 1:16 "The fire of God f from the heavens and H5877
Job 1:20 Then *he* f to the ground in worship H5877
Job 29:22 no more; my words f **gently** on their ears. H5752
Ps 18:38 could not rise; *they* f beneath my feet. H5877
Ps 105:44 and *they* f **heir** *to* what others had toiled H3769
Ps 137: 7 the Edomites did on the day Jerusalem f. NDT
La 1: 7 When her people f into enemy hands H5877
Eze 1:28 When I saw it, *I* f facedown, and I heard H5877
Eze 3:23 seen by the Kebar River, and *I* f facedown. H5877
Eze 9: 8 I was left alone, *I* f facedown, crying out, H5877
Eze 11:13 Then *I* f facedown and cried out in a loud H5877
Eze 31:12 Its boughs f on the mountains and in all H5877
Eze 39:23 their enemies, and they all f by the sword. H5877
Eze 43: 3 seen by the Kebar River, and *I* f facedown. H5877
Eze 44: 4 the temple of the LORD, and *I* f facedown. H5877
Da 2:46 King Nebuchadnezzar f prostrate before A10484
Da 3: 7 every language f **down** and worshiped A10484
Da 3:23 firmly tied, f into the blazing furnace. A10484
Da 7:20 before which three of *them* f—the horn A10484
Da 8:17 standing, I was terrified and f prostrate. H5877
Da 10: 9 I f **into a deep sleep**, my face to H8101
Jnh 1: 5 he lay down and f **into a deep sleep**. H8101
Jnh 1: 7 They cast lots and the lot f on Jonah. H5877
Mt 7:27 that house, and *it* f with a great crash." G4406
Mt 13: 4 the seed, some f along the path, and the G4406
Mt 13: 5 Some f on rocky places, where it did not G4406
Mt 13: 7 Other seed f among thorns, which grew up G4406
Mt 13: 8 Still other seed f on good soil, where it G4406
Mt 17: 6 heard this, *they* f facedown to the ground G4406
Mt 18:26 "At this the servant f on his knees before G4406
Mt 18:29 "His fellow servant f to his knees and G4406
Mt 25: 5 they all became drowsy and f **asleep**. G2761
Mt 26:39 *he* f with his face to the ground and G4406
Mk 3:11 *they* f **down before** him and cried out G4700
Mk 4: 4 the seed, some f along the path, and the G4406
Mk 4: 5 Some f on rocky places, where it did not G4406
Mk 4: 7 Other seed f among thorns, which grew up G4406
Mk 4: 8 Still other seed f on good soil. It came up G4406
Mk 5: 6 he ran and f **on** *his* **knees in front of** him. G4686
Mk 5:22 when he saw Jesus, *he* f at his feet. G4406
Mk 5:33 came and f **at** his **feet** and, trembling G4700
Mk 7:25 by an impure spirit came and f at his feet. G4700
Mk 9:20 *He* f to the ground and rolled around G4406
Mk 10:17 up to him and f **on** *his* **knees before** him. G1206
Mk 10:22 At this the man's **face** f. He went away G5145
Mk 14:35 *he* f to the ground and prayed that if G4406
Lk 5: 8 saw this, *he* f **at** Jesus' knees and said G4700
Lk 5:12 *he* f with his face to the ground and G4406
Lk 8: 5 the seed, some f along the path; it was G4406
Lk 8: 6 Some f on rocky ground, and when it came G2928
Lk 8: 7 Other seed f among thorns, which grew up G4406
Lk 8: 8 Still other seed f on good soil. It came up G4406
Lk 8:14 The seed *that* f among thorns stands for G4406
Lk 8:23 As they sailed, *he* f **asleep**. A squall came G934
Lk 8:28 he cried out and f **at** his **feet**, shouting at G4700
Lk 8:41 came and f at Jesus' feet G4406
Lk 8:47 came trembling and f **at** his **feet**. G4700
Lk 10:36 to the *man who* f **into the hands of** G1860
Lk 13: 4 died *when* the tower in Siloam f on them G4406
Lk 16:21 longing to eat what f from the rich man's G4406
Jn 11:32 saw him, *she* f at his feet and said G4406
Jn 18: 6 they drew back and f to the ground. G4406
Ac 1:18 there *he* f **headlong**, his body G4568+1181
Ac 1:26 and the lot f to Matthias; so he was G4406
Ac 5: 5 Ananias heard this, *he* f **down** and died. G4406
Ac 5:10 At that moment *she* f **down** at his feet G4406
Ac 7:60 Then *he* f **on** his knees and cried out G5502
Ac 7:60 When he had said this, *he* f **asleep**. G3121
Ac 9: 4 *He* f to the ground and heard a voice say G4406
Ac 9:18 something like scales f **from** Saul's eyes G674
Ac 10:10 was being prepared, he f into a trance. G1181
Ac 10:25 Cornelius met him and f at his feet in G4406
Ac 12: 7 he said, and the chains f **off** Peter's wrists. G1738
Ac 13:36 generation, *he* f **asleep**; he was buried G3121
Ac 16:29 rushed in and f trembling **before** Paul G4700
Ac 19:35 and *of* her **image, which** f **from heaven**? G1479
Ac 20: 9 *he* f to the ground from the third story G4406
Ac 22: 7 *I* f to the ground and heard a voice say to G4406
Ac 22:17 praying at the temple, I f into a trance G1181
Ac 26:14 We all f to the ground, and I heard a voice G2928
Ro 11:22 sternness to those *who* f, but kindness to G4406
Heb 11:30 By faith the walls of Jericho f, after the G4406
Rev 1:17 I saw him, *I* f at his feet as though dead. G4406
Rev 5: 8 elders f **down** before the Lamb. G4406
Rev 5:14 and the elders f **down** and worshiped. G4406
Rev 6:13 the stars in the sky f to earth, as figs G4406
Rev 7:11 *They* f **down** on their faces before the G4406
Rev 8:10 f from the sky on a third of the rivers and G4406
Rev 11:16 f on their faces and worshiped God G4406
Rev 16:21 about a hundred pounds, f on people. G2849
Rev 19: 4 living creatures f **down** and worshiped G4406
Rev 19:10 At this *I* f at his feet to worship him. G4406
Rev 22: 8 *I* f **down** to worship at the feet of the G4406

FELLED (2) [FALL]

Isa 9:10 the fig trees *have* **been** f, but we will H1548
Isa 10:33 The lofty trees *will* **be** f, the tall ones will H1548

FELLING (1) [FALL]

1Ki 5: 6 no one so skilled in f timber as the H4162

FELLOW (148) [FELLOW'S, FELLOWS, FELLOWSHIP]

Ge 19: 9 "This f came here as a foreigner, and now H285S
Ex 2:13 "Why are you hitting your f Hebrew?" H8276
Ex 32: 1 As for this f Moses who brought us up out H408
Ex 32:23 As for this f Moses who brought us up out H408
Lev 19:17 " 'Do not hate a f **Israelite** in your heart H278
Lev 25:25 'If one of your f **Israelites** becomes poor H278
Lev 25:35 'If any of your f **Israelites** become poor H278
Lev 25:39 'If any of your f **Israelites** become poor H278
Lev 25:46 not rule over your f Israelites ruthlessly. H278
Lev 25:47 any of your f **Israelites** become poor H278
Nu 16:10 you and all your f Levites near himself, H278
Nu 18: 2 Bring your f Levites from your ancestral tribe H278
Nu 18: 6 have selected your f Levites from among H278
Nu 32: 6 "Should your f **Israelites** go to war while H278
Dt 3:20 rest to your f **Israelites** as he has to you, H278
Dt 10: 9 inheritance among their f **Israelites**; H278
Dt 15: 2 any loan they have made to a f **Israelite**. H8276
Dt 15: 3 cancel any debt your f **Israelite** owes you. H278
Dt 15: 7 is poor among your f **Israelites** in any of the H278
Dt 15: 9 among your f **Israelites** and give them H278
Dt 15:11 toward your f **Israelites** who are poor and H278
Dt 17:15 He must be from among your f **Israelites** H278
Dt 17:20 better than his f **Israelites** and turn from the H278
Dt 18: 2 no inheritance among their f **Israelites**; H278
Dt 18: 7 his God like all his f Levites who serve H278
Dt 18:15 me from among you, from your f **Israelites**. H278
Dt 18:18 like you from among their f **Israelites**, H278
Dt 19:18 giving false testimony against a f **Israelite**, H278
Dt 20: 8 home so that his f *soldiers* will not become H278
Dt 22: 1 If you see your f **Israelite's** ox or sheep H278
Dt 22: 4 If you see your f **Israelite's** donkey or ox H278
Dt 23:19 Do not charge a f **Israelite** interest, whether H278
Dt 23:20 not a f **Israelite**, so that the LORD H278
Dt 24: 7 caught kidnapping a f Israelite and treating H278
Dt 24:14 that worker is a f **Israelite** or a foreigner H278
Dt 25: 3 your f **Israelite** will be degraded in your H278
Jos 1:14 must cross over ahead of your f **Israelites**. H278
Jos 14: 8 my f **Israelites** who went up with me H278
Jos 22: 3 deserted your f **Israelites** but have carried H278
Jos 22: 7 of the Jordan along with their f **Israelites**.) H278
Jos 22: 8 from your enemies with your f **Israelites**." H278
Jdg 1: 3 said to the Simeonites their f **Israelites**, H278
Jdg 1:17 Simeonites their f **Israelites** and attacked H278
Jdg 18: 8 Eshtaol, their f **Danites** asked them, "How H278
Jdg 18:14 out the land of Laish said to their f **Danites**, H278
Jdg 20:13 would not listen to their f Israelites. H278
Jdg 20:23 against the Benjamites, our f **Israelites**?" H278
Jdg 20:28 the Benjamites, our f **Israelites**, or not?" H278
Jdg 21: 6 the tribe of Benjamin, their f **Israelites**. H278
1Sa 10:27 scoundrels said, "How can **this** *f* save us?" AIT
1Sa 21:15 you have to bring **this** *f* here to carry on like AIT
2Sa 2:26 your men to stop pursuing their f **Israelites**?" H278
2Sa 6:20 girls of his servants as any **vulgar** *f* would!" AIT
1Ki 22:27 Put **this** *f* in prison and give him nothing AIT
2Ki 5: 7 Why does **this** *f* send someone to me to be AIT
2Ki 9:11 When Jehu went out to his f **officers** H6269+123
2Ki 23: 9 ate unleavened bread with their f priests. H278
1Ch 6:48 Their f Levites were assigned to all the H278
1Ch 9:17 Ahiman and their f **Levites**, Shallum their H278
1Ch 9:19 his f gatekeepers from his family H278
1Ch 9:25 Their f **Levites** in their villages had to come H278
1Ch 9:32 Kohathites, their f **Levites**, were in charge H278
1Ch 15:12 you and your f **Levites** are to consecrate H278
1Ch 15:16 to appoint their f **Levites** as musicians to H278
1Ch 16:39 Zadok the priest and his f priests before the H278
1Ch 26:20 Their f Levites were in charge of the H278
1Ch 28: 2 "Listen to me, my f **Israelites**, my people. H278
2Ch 11: 4 not go up to fight against your f **Israelites**. H278
2Ch 18:26 Put **this** *f* in prison and give him nothing AIT
2Ch 28: 8 from their f **Israelites** who were from H278
2Ch 28:11 Send back your f **Israelites** you have taken H278
2Ch 28:15 them back to their f **Israelites** at Jericho, H278
2Ch 29:15 assembled their f **Levites** and consecrated H278
2Ch 30: 7 be like your parents and your f **Israelites**, H278
2Ch 30: 9 then your f **Israelites** and your children will H278
2Ch 31:15 distributing to their f priests according to H278
2Ch 35: 5 of the families of your f **Israelites**, H278
2Ch 35: 6 prepare the lambs for your f **Israelites**, H278
2Ch 35:15 because their f Levites made the H278
Ezr 3: 2 of Jozadak and his f priests and H278
Ezr 7:18 You and your f **Israelites** may then do A10017
Ezr 8:17 them what to say to Iddo and his f **Levites**, H278
Ne 3: 1 high priest and his f priests went to work H278
Ne 3:18 made by their f **Levites** under Binnui son H278
Ne 5: 1 raised a great outcry against their f Jews. H278
Ne 5: 5 blood as our f **Jews** and though our H278
Ne 5: 8 have bought back our f Jews who were sold H278
Ne 10:29 these now join their f **Israelites** the nobles, H278
Ne 13:13 distributing the supplies to their f **Levites**. H278
Est 10: 3 held in high esteem by his many f **Jews**, H278
Isa 38:11 no longer will I look on my f **man**, or be H132
Jer 7:15 just as I did all your f **Israelites**, the people H278
Jer 29:16 your f **citizens** who did not go with you into H278
Jer 34: 9 no one was to hold a f Hebrew in bondage. H278
Jer 34:14 of you must free any f Hebrews who have H278
Eze 11:15 have said of your f exiles and all the other H278
Mt 9: 3 said to themselves, "**This** *f* is blaspheming!" AIT
Mt 12:24 of demons, that **this** *f* drives out demons." AIT
Mt 18:28 he found one *of* his f **servants** who owed G5281
Mt 18:29 "His f **servant** fell to his knees and G5281
Mt 18:33 had mercy *on* your f **servant** just as I had G5281
Mt 24:49 to beat his f **servants** and to eat and G5281
Mt 26:61 declared, "**This** *f* said, 'I am able to AIT
Mt 26:71 "**This** *f* was with Jesus of Nazareth." AIT
Mk 2: 7 "Why does **this** *f* talk like that? He's AIT
Mk 14:69 standing around, "**This** *f* is one of them." AIT
Lk 5:21 "Who is **this** *f* who speaks blasphemy? AIT
Lk 22:59 "Certainly **this** *f* was with him, for he AIT
Jn 5:12 "Who is this f who told you to pick it up G476
Jn 9:29 to Moses, but *as for* **this** *f*, we don't even AIT
Ac 2:14 "*F* **Jews** and all of you who live in Jerusalem AIT
Ac 2:22 "F Israelites, listen to this: Jesus of G467
Ac 2:29 "F *Israelites*, I can tell you confidently G467+81
Ac 3:12 he said to them: "F Israelites, why does this G467
Ac 3:17 f *Israelites*, I know that you acted in G81
Ac 6:13 "This f never stops speaking against this G476

Ac 7:40 As for this f Moses who led us out of Egypt AIT
Ac 13:16 "F Israelites and you Gentiles who worship G467
Ac 13:26 "F children of Abraham and you G467+81
Ac 19:26 see and hear how this f Paul has convinced AIT
Ac 19:35 "F Ephesians, doesn't all the world know G467
Ac 19:38 and his f craftsmen have a G3836+5250
Ac 21:28 shouting, "F Israelites, help us! This is the G467
Ro 16: 7 my f Jews who have been in prison with G5150
Ro 16:11 Greet Herodion, my f Jew. Greet those in G5150
Ro 16:21 Jason and Sosipater, my f Jews. G5150
2Co 11:26 in danger from my f Jews, in danger from G1169
2Co 12:16 Yet, crafty f that I am, I caught AIT
Eph 2:19 f citizens with God's people and also G5232
Php 2:25 co-worker and f soldier, who is also your G5369
Col 1: 7 Epaphras, our dear f servant, who is a G5281
Col 4: 7 faithful minister and f servant in the Lord. G5281
Col 4:10 My f prisoner Aristarchus sends you his G5257
2Th 3:15 warn them as you would a f believer. G81
1Ti 6: 2 disrespect just because they are f believers. G81
1Ti 6: 2 dear to them as f believers and are G4412
Phm 1 Philemon our dear friend and f worker— G5301
Phm 2 our sister and Archippus our f soldier— G5369
Phm 16 both as a f man and as a brother in the G4922
Phm 23 Epaphras, my f prisoner in Christ Jesus G5257
Phm 24 Demas and Luke, my f workers. G5301
Heb 7: 5 from their f Israelites—even though G81
Jas 3: 1 teachers, my f believers, because you know G81
1Pe 5: 1 I appeal as a f elder and a witness of G5236
Rev 6:11 until the full number of their f servants G5281
Rev 19:10 I am a f servant with you and with your G5281
Rev 22: 9 I am a f servant with you and with your G5281
Rev 22: 9 with you and with your f prophets and with G81

FELLOW'S (2) [FELLOW]

1Sa 25:21 watching over this f property in H2296+4200S
Jn 9:28 at him and said, "You are this f disciple! AIT

FELLOWLABOURER, FELLOWLABOURERS (KJV) CO-WORKER, CO-WORKERS, FELLOW WORKER, FELLOW WORKERS

FELLOWS (2) [FELLOW]

1Sa 31: 4 these uncircumcised f will come and run AIT
1Ch 10: 4 these uncircumcised f will come and AIT

FELLOWSHIP (97) [FELLOW]

Ex 20:24 on it your burnt offerings and f offerings, H8968
Ex 24: 5 young bulls as f offerings to the LORD. H8968
Ex 29:28 to make to the LORD from their f offerings. H8968
Ex 32: 6 burnt offerings and presented f offerings. H8968
Lev 3: 1 " 'If your offering is a f offering, and you H8968
Lev 3: 3 From the f offering you are to bring a food H8968
Lev 3: 6 from the flock as a f offering to the LORD, H8968
Lev 3: 9 From the f offering you are to bring a food H8968
Lev 4:10 from the ox sacrificed as a f offering. H8968
Lev 4:26 altar as he burned the fat of the f offering. H8968
Lev 4:31 as the fat is removed from the f offering, H8968
Lev 4:35 removed from the lamb of the f offering, H8968
Lev 6:12 burn the fat of the f offerings on it. H8968
Lev 7:11 regulations for the f offering anyone may H8968
Lev 7:13 Along with their f offering of thanksgiving H8968
Lev 7:14 the blood of the f offering against the H8968
Lev 7:15 The meat of their f offering of thanksgiving H8968
Lev 7:18 If any meat of the f offering is eaten on H8968
Lev 7:20 eats any meat of the f offering belonging H8968
Lev 7:21 of the meat of the f offering belonging to H8968
Lev 7:29 who brings a f offering to the LORD H8968
Lev 7:32 right thigh of your f offerings to the priest H8968
Lev 7:33 the fat of the f offering shall have the H8968
Lev 7:34 From the f offerings of the Israelites, I have H8968
Lev 7:37 the ordination offering and the f offering, H8968
Lev 9: 4 ox and a ram for a f offering to sacrifice H8968
Lev 9:18 ox and the ram as the f offering for the H8968
Lev 9:22 the burnt offering and the f offering, he H8968
Lev 10:14 as your share of the Israelites' f offerings. H8968
Lev 17: 5 meeting and sacrifice them as f offerings. H8968
Lev 19: 5 you sacrifice a f offering to the LORD, H8968
Lev 22:21 the herd or flock a f offering to the LORD to H8968
Lev 23:19 each a year old, for a f offering. H8968
Nu 6:14 a ram without defect for a f offering, H8968
Nu 6:17 the ram as a f offering to the LORD, H8968
Nu 6:18 that is under the sacrifice of the f offering. H8968
Nu 7:17 a year old to be sacrificed as a f offering. H8968
Nu 7:23 a year old to be sacrificed as a f offering. H8968
Nu 7:29 a year old to be sacrificed as a f offering. H8968
Nu 7:35 a year old to be sacrificed as a f offering. H8968
Nu 7:41 a year old to be sacrificed as a f offering. H8968
Nu 7:47 a year old to be sacrificed as a f offering. H8968
Nu 7:53 a year old to be sacrificed as a f offering. H8968
Nu 7:59 a year old to be sacrificed as a f offering. H8968
Nu 7:65 a year old to be sacrificed as a f offering. H8968
Nu 7:71 a year old to be sacrificed as a f offering. H8968
Nu 7:77 a year old to be sacrificed as a f offering. H8968
Nu 7:83 a year old to be sacrificed as a f offering. H8968
Nu 7:88 sacrifice of the f offering came to H8968
Nu 10:10 over your burnt offerings and f offerings, H8968
Nu 15: 8 a special vow or a f offering to the LORD, H8968
Nu 29:39 offerings, drink offerings and f offerings. H8968
Dt 27: 7 Sacrifice f offerings there, eating them H8968
Jos 8:31 burnt offerings and sacrificed f offerings. H8968
Jos 22:23 to sacrifice f offerings on it, may the H8968
Jos 22:27 burnt offerings, sacrifices and f offerings. H8968
Jdg 20:26 burnt offerings and f offerings to the LORD. H8968
Jdg 21: 4 presented burnt offerings and f offerings. H8968
1Sa 10: 8 to sacrifice burnt offerings and f offerings, H8968
1Sa 11:15 There they sacrificed f offerings before the H8968
1Sa 13: 9 me the burnt offering and the f offerings." H8968
2Sa 6:17 offerings and f offerings before the LORD. H8968
2Sa 6:18 the burnt offerings and f offerings, H8968
2Sa 24:25 sacrificed burnt offerings and f offerings. H8968
1Ki 3:15 sacrificed burnt offerings and f offerings. H8968
1Ki 8:63 a sacrifice of f offerings to the LORD: H8968
1Ki 8:64 offerings and the fat of the f offerings, H8968
1Ki 8:64 offerings and the fat of the f offerings. H8968
1Ki 9:25 offerings and f offerings on the altar he H8968
2Ki 16:13 the blood of his f offerings against the H8968
1Ch 16: 1 burnt offerings and f offerings before God. H8968
1Ch 16: 2 the burnt offerings and f offerings, H8968
1Ch 21:26 sacrificed burnt offerings and f offerings. H8968
2Ch 7: 7 offerings and the fat of the f offerings, H8968
2Ch 29:35 with the fat of the f offerings and the drink H8968
2Ch 30:22 portion and offered f offerings and H8968
2Ch 31: 2 to offer burnt offerings and f offerings, to H8968
2Ch 33:16 LORD and sacrificed f offerings and thank H8968
Ps 55:14 once enjoyed sweet f at the house of God H6051
Pr 7:14 I have food from my f offering at home. H8968
Eze 43:27 offerings and f offerings on the altar. H8968
Eze 45:15 offerings and f offerings to make H8968
Eze 45:17 offerings and f offerings to make H8968
Eze 46: 2 his burnt offering and his f offerings. H8968
Eze 46:12 whether a burnt offering or f offerings—the H8968
Eze 46:12 offering or his f offerings as he does on H8968
Am 5:22 Though you bring choice f offerings, I will H8968
Ac 2:42 to the apostles' teaching and to f, G3126
1Co 1: 9 who has called you into f with his Son G3126
1Co 5: 2 put out of your f the man who has been G3545
2Co 6:14 Or what f can light have with darkness? G3126
2Co 13:14 the f of the Holy Spirit be with you all. G3126
Gal 2: 9 the right hand of f when they recognized G3126
1Jn 1: 3 so that you also may have f with us. G3126
1Jn 1: 3 And our f is with the Father and with his G3126
1Jn 1: 6 If we claim to have f with him and yet walk G3126
1Jn 1: 7 the light, we have f with one another, and G3126

FELLOWWORKERS (KJV) CO-WORKERS

FELT (12) [FEEL]

Ge 2:25 were both naked, and they f no shame. H1017
Ex 2: 6 was crying, and she f sorry for him. H2798
Ex 10:21 over Egypt—darkness that can be f." H5491
1Sa 13:12 So I f compelled to offer the burnt offering." H706
Ps 30: 6 When I f secure, I said, "I will never be H8930
Jer 5: 3 but they f no pain; you crushed H2655
Jer 22:21 I warned you when you f secure, but you H8932
Na 3:19 who has not f your endless cruelty? H6296
Mk 5:29 stopped and she f in her body that G1182
2Co 1: 9 we f we had received the sentence G1877+1571
Heb 10: 2 and would no longer have f guilty for their G2400
Jude 3 I f compelled to write and urge you to G2400

FEMALE (85) [FEMALES]

Ge 1:27 male and f he created them. H5922
Ge 5: 2 them male and f and blessed them. H5922
Ge 6:19 creatures, male and f, to keep them alive H5922
Ge 7: 3 male and f, to keep their various H5922
Ge 7: 9 male and f, came to Noah and entered H5922
Ge 7:16 in were male and f of every living thing, H5922
Ge 12:16 cattle, male and f donkeys, male and H912
Ge 12:16 donkeys, male and f servants, and camels H9148
Ge 20:14 cattle and male and f slaves and gave H9148
Ge 20:17 his wife and his f slaves so they could have H563
Ge 24:35 gold, male and f servants, and H9148
Ge 30:35 all the speckled or spotted f goats (all AIT
Ge 30:43 own large flocks, and f and male servants H9148
Ge 31:33 tent and into the tent of the two f servants, H563
Ge 32: 5 sheep and goats, male and f servants. H9148
Ge 32:14 two hundred f goats and twenty male goats AIT
Ge 32:15 thirty f camels with their young, forty cows H3567
Ge 32:15 twenty f donkeys and ten male H912
Ge 32:22 his two f servants and his eleven sons H9148
Ge 33: 1 Rachel and the two f servants. H9148
Ge 33: 2 He put the f servants and their children in H9148
Ge 33: 6 Then the f servants and their children H9148
Ge 45:23 ten f donkeys loaded with grain and H912
Ex 2: 5 the reeds and sent her f slave to get it. H563
Ex 11: 5 to the firstborn son of the f slave, who is H9148
Ex 20:10 your male or f servant, nor your animals H563
Ex 20:17 or his male or f servant, his ox or H563
Ex 21:20 beats their male or f slave with a rod must H563
Ex 21:26 who hits a male or f slave in the eye and H563
Ex 21:27 the tooth of a male or f slave must let the H563
Ex 21:32 If the bull gores a male or f slave, the H563
Lev 3: 1 whether male or f, you are to present H5922
Lev 3: 6 you are to offer a male or f without defect. H5922
Lev 4:28 they committed a f goat without defect. H5922
Lev 4:32 they are to bring a f without defect. H5922
Lev 5: 6 bring to the LORD a f lamb or goat from the H5922
Lev 19:20 a man sleeps with a f slave who is H851
Lev 25: 6 your male and f servants, and the hired H563
Lev 25:44 " 'Your male and f slaves are to come from H563
Lev 27: 4 a f, set her value at thirty shekels; H5922
Lev 27: 5 twenty shekels and of a f at ten shekels; H5922
Lev 27: 6 of silver and that of a f at three shekels of H5922
Lev 27: 7 fifteen shekels and of a f at ten shekels. H5922
Nu 5: 3 Send away male and f alike; send them H5922
Nu 15:27 person must bring a year-old f goat for a sin AIT
Dt 5:14 your male or f servant, nor your ox, H563
Dt 5:14 so that your male and f servants may rest H563
Dt 5:21 his male or f servant, his ox or H563
Dt 12:12 your male and f servants, and the H563
Dt 12:18 your male and f servants, and the H563
Dt 15:17 Do the same for your f servant. H563
Dt 16:11 your male and f servants, the Levites in H563
Dt 16:14 your male and f servants, and the H563
Dt 23:18 the earnings of a f prostitute or of a male AIT
Dt 28:68 to your enemies as male and f slaves, H9148
Jdg 9:18 the son of his f slave, king over the citizens H563
1Sa 8:16 Your male and f servants and the best of H9148
1Sa 25:42 attended by her five f servants, went with H5855
2Sa 17:17 A f servant was to go and inform them H9148
2Sa 19:35 hear the voices of male and f singers? AIT
2Ki 5:26 flocks and herds, or male and f slaves? H9148
2Ch 35:25 all the male and f singers commemorate AIT
Ezr 2:65 besides their 7,337 male and f slaves; and H563
Ezr 2:65 they also had 200 male and f singers. AIT
Ne 7:67 besides their 7,337 male and f slaves; and H563
Ne 7:67 they also had 245 male and f singers. AIT
Est 2: 9 to her seven f attendants selected from H5855
Est 4: 4 eunuchs and f attendants came and told H5855
Est 7: 4 merely been sold as male and f slaves, H9148
Job 19:15 My guests and my f servants count me a H563
Job 31:13 any of my servants, whether male or f, H563
Ps 123: 2 as the eyes of a f slave look to the hand H9148
Pr 27:27 your family and to nourish your f servants. H5855
Pr 31:15 her family and portions for her f servants. H5855
Ecc 2: 7 I bought male and f slaves and had other H9148
Ecc 2: 8 I acquired male and f singers, and a AIT
Isa 14: 2 make them male and f servants in the H9148
Jer 34: 9 free their Hebrew slaves, both male and f; H9148
Jer 34:10 free their male and f slaves and no longer H9148
Jer 34:16 back the male and f slaves you had set H9148
Na 2: 7 Her f slaves moan like doves and beat on H563
Mt 19: 4 the Creator 'made them male and f, G2559
Mk 10: 6 of creation God 'made them male and f. G2559
Ac 16:16 we were met by a f slave who had a spirit G4087
Gal 3:28 is there male and f, for you are all G2559

FEMALES (1) [FEMALE]

Ge 30:41 Whenever the stronger f were in heat, Jacob AIT

FENCE (1)

Ps 62: 3 down—this leaning wall, this tottering f? H1555

FENCED (KJV) BLOCKED, DUG, FORTIFIED, KNIT, TOOL, WALLS

FERMENTED (10)

Lev 10: 9 wine or other f drink whenever you go H8911
Nu 6: 3 wine and other f drink and must not drink H8911
Nu 6: 3 vinegar made from wine or other f drink. H8911
Nu 28: 7 quarter of a hin of f drink with each lamb. H8911
Dt 14:26 wine or other f drink, or anything you H8911
Dt 29: 6 bread and drank no wine or other f drink. H8911
Jdg 13: 4 no wine or other f drink and that you do H8911
Jdg 13: 7 no wine or other f drink and do not eat H8911
Jdg 13:14 any wine or other f drink nor eat anything H8911
Lk 1:15 He is never to take wine or other f drink G4975

FEROCIOUS (3)

Ge 37:20 say that a f animal devoured him. H8273
Ge 37:33 Some f animal has devoured him H8273
Mt 7:15 clothing, but inwardly they are f wolves. G774

FERTILE (16) [FERTILIZE]

Nu 13:20 How is the soil? Is it f or poor? Are there H9045
2Ch 26:10 vineyards in the hills and in the f lands, H4149
Ne 9:25 They captured fortified cities and f land H9045
Ne 9:35 in the spacious and f land you gave them, H9045
Isa 5: 1 one had a vineyard on a f hillside. H1201+9043
Isa 10:18 of his forests and f fields it will completely H4149
Isa 28: 1 set on the head of a f valley—to that city, H9043
Isa 28: 4 set on the head of a f valley, will be like H9043
Isa 29:17 be turned into a f field and the fertile H4149
Isa 29:17 field and the f field seem like a forest? H4149
Isa 32:15 the desert becomes a f field, and the H4149
Isa 32:15 and the f field seems like a forest. H4149
Isa 32:16 his righteousness live in the f field. H4149
Jer 2: 7 I brought you into a f land to eat its fruit H4149
Eze 17: 5 seedlings of the land and put it in f soil. H2446
Mic 7:14 lives by itself in a forest, in f pasturelands. H4149

FERTILIZE (1) [FERTILE]

Lk 13: 8 and I'll dig around it and f it. G965+3162

FERVENT (2) [FERVOR]

Pr 26:23 on earthenware are f lips with an evil H1944
Heb 5: 7 petitions with f cries and tears to the G2708

FERVOR (2) [FERVENT]

Ac 18:25 he spoke with great f and G2417+3836+4460
Ro 12:11 but keep your spiritual f, serving G2417

FESTAL (1) [FESTIVAL]

Ps 118:27 join in the f procession up to the horns of H2504

FESTER (1) [FESTERING]

Ps 38: 5 My wounds f and are loathsome because H5245

FESTERING (7) [FESTER]

Ex 9: 9 f boils will break out on people and H81
Ex 9:10 f boils broke out on people and animals H81
Lev 21:20 who has f or running sores or damaged H1734
Lev 22:22 anything with warts or f or running sores. H1734
Dt 28:27 with tumors, **f sores** and the itch, from H1734
Job 7: 5 worms and scabs, my skin is broken and f. H4416
Rev 16: 2 f sores broke out on the people who had *G4505*

FESTIVAL (94) [FESTAL, FESTIVALS, FESTIVE]

Ex 5: 1 so that *they may* **hold a f** to me in the H2510
Ex 10: 9 we are to celebrate a f *to* the LORD. H2504
Ex 12:14 you shall celebrate it as a f to the LORD— H2504
Ex 12:17 "Celebrate the **F of Unleavened Bread** H5174
Ex 13: 6 on the seventh day hold a f to the LORD. H2504
Ex 23:14 a year *you are to* **celebrate a f** to me. H2510
Ex 23:15 "Celebrate the F of Unleavened Bread; for H2504
Ex 23:16 "Celebrate the F *of* Harvest with the H2504
Ex 23:16 "Celebrate the F *of* Ingathering at the end H2504
Ex 23:18 "The fat of my **f offerings** must not be kept H2504
Ex 32: 5 "Tomorrow there will be a f to the LORD." H2504
Ex 34:18 "Celebrate the F *of* Unleavened Bread. H2504
Ex 34:22 "Celebrate the F *of* Weeks with the H2504
Ex 34:22 the F *of* Ingathering at the turn of the H2504
Ex 34:25 from the Passover F remain until morning. H2504
Lev 23: 6 month the LORD's F *of* Unleavened Bread H2504
Lev 23:34 month the LORD's F *of* Tabernacles begins, H2504
Lev 23:39 celebrate the f *to* the LORD for seven days H2504
Lev 23:41 Celebrate this as a f to the LORD for seven H2504
Nu 15: 3 vows or freewill offerings or **f offerings**— H4595
Nu 28:17 day of this month there is to be a f; H2504
Nu 28:26 of new grain during the **F of Weeks**, H8651
Nu 29:12 Celebrate a f to the LORD for seven days H2504
Dt 16:10 Then celebrate the F *of* Weeks to the LORD H2504
Dt 16:13 Celebrate the F *of* Tabernacles for seven H2504
Dt 16:14 Be joyful at your f—you, your sons and H2504
Dt 16:15 For seven days **celebrate the** f to the LORD H2510
Dt 16:16 at the F *of* Unleavened Bread, the Festival H2504
Dt 16:16 the F *of* Weeks and the Festival of H2504
Dt 16:16 of Weeks and the F *of* Tabernacles. H2504
Dt 31:10 during the F *of* Tabernacles, H2504
Jdg 9:27 they held a f in the temple of their god. H2136
Jdg 21:19 there is the annual f *of* the LORD in Shiloh H2504
1Ki 8: 2 at the time of the f in the month of H2504
1Ki 8:65 So Solomon observed the f at that time H2504
1Ki 12:32 He instituted a f on the fifteenth day of the H2504
1Ki 12:32 like the f held in Judah, and H2504
1Ki 12:33 So he instituted the f for the Israelites H2504
2Ch 5: 3 at the time of the f in the seventh month. H2504
2Ch 7: 8 Solomon observed the f at that time for H2504
2Ch 7: 9 seven days and the f for seven days more. H2504
2Ch 8:13 festivals—the F *of* Unleavened Bread H2504
2Ch 8:13 the F *of* Weeks and the Festival of H2504
2Ch 8:13 of Weeks and the F *of* Tabernacles. H2504
2Ch 30:13 to celebrate the F *of* Unleavened Bread in H2504
2Ch 30:21 celebrated the F *of* Unleavened Bread H2504
2Ch 30:23 agreed to celebrate the f seven more days; NDT
2Ch 35:17 observed the F *of* Unleavened Bread H2504
Ezr 3: 4 they celebrated the F *of* Tabernacles with H2504
Ezr 6:22 with joy the F *of* Unleavened Bread, H2504
Ne 8:14 shelters during the f of the seventh month H2504
Ne 8:18 They celebrated the f for seven days, and H2504
Ps 81: 3 the moon is full, on the day of our f; H2504
Isa 30:29 as on the night you celebrate a holy f; H2504
La 2: 7 the LORD as on the day of an **appointed f**. H4595
Eze 45:21 the Passover, a f *lasting* seven days H2504
Eze 45:23 the seven days of the f he is to provide H2504
Eze 45:25 " 'During the seven days of the f, which H2504
Hos 7: 5 On the day of the f of our king the princes NDT
Zec 14:16 to celebrate the F *of* Tabernacles. H2504
Zec 14:18 go up to celebrate the F *of* Tabernacles. H2504
Zec 14:19 go up to celebrate the F *of* Tabernacles. H2504
Mal 2: 3 your faces the dung from your **f sacrifices**, H2504
Mt 26: 5 "But not during the f," they said, "or there *G2038*
Mt 26:17 the first day *of* the **F of Unleavened Bread**, *G109*
Mt 27:15 custom at the f to release a prisoner *G2038*
Mk 14: 1 the **F of Unleavened Bread** were only *G109*
Mk 14: 2 "But not during the f," they said, "or the *G2038*
Mk 14:12 the first day *of* the **F of Unleavened Bread**, *G109*
Mk 15: 6 the custom at the f to release a prisoner *G2038*
Lk 2:41 to Jerusalem *for* the F of the Passover. *G2038*
Lk 2:42 they went up to the f, according to the *G2038*
Lk 2:43 After the f was over, while his parents *G2465S*
Lk 22: 1 Now the F of Unleavened Bread, called *G2038*
Jn 2:23 he was in Jerusalem at the Passover F, *G2038*
Jn 4:45 had done in Jerusalem at the **Passover F**, *G2038*
Jn 6: 4 The Jewish Passover F was near. *G2038*
Jn 7: 2 But when the Jewish F of Tabernacles was *G2038*
Jn 7: 8 You go to the f. I am not going up to this *G2038*
Jn 7: 8 I am not going up to this f, because my *G2038*
Jn 7:10 after his brothers had left for the f, he *G2038*
Jn 7:11 Now at the f the Jewish leaders were *G2038*
Jn 7:14 halfway through the f did Jesus go up to *G2038*
Jn 7:37 On the last and greatest day *of* the f *G2038*
Jn 10:22 came the **F of Dedication** at Jerusalem *G1589*
Jn 11:56 Isn't he coming to the f at all?" *G2038*
Jn 12:12 had come for the f heard that Jesus was *G2038*
Jn 12:20 those who went up to worship at the f. *G2038*
Jn 13: 1 It was just before the Passover F. *G2038*
Jn 13:29 him to buy what was needed for the f, *G2038*
Ac 12: 3 during the **F of Unleavened Bread**. *G109*
Ac 20: 6 the **F of Unleavened Bread**, *G2465+3836+109*
1Co 5: 8 Therefore *let us* **keep the F**, not with the *G2037*
Col 2:16 with regard to a **religious f**, a New *G2038*

FESTIVALS (34) [FESTIVAL]

Lev 23: 2 'These are my **appointed f**, the appointed H4595
Lev 23: 2 festivals, the **appointed f** *of* the LORD H4595
Lev 23: 4 " 'These are the LORD's **appointed f**, the H4595
Lev 23:37 " 'These are the LORD's **appointed f**, which H4595
Lev 23:44 the Israelites the **appointed f** *of* the LORD. H4595
Nu 10:10 your **appointed f** and New Moon feasts H4595
Nu 29:39 offer these to the LORD at your **appointed f**: H4595
1Ch 23:31 New Moon feasts and at the **appointed f**. H4595
2Ch 2: 4 at the **appointed f** *of* the LORD our H4595
2Ch 8:13 the New Moons and the three annual f H4595
2Ch 31: 3 at the **appointed f** as written in H4595
Ezr 3: 5 all the **appointed** sacred f *of* the LORD, H4595
Ne 10:33 New Moon feasts and at the **appointed f**; H4595
Isa 1:14 feasts and your **appointed f** I hate with all H4595
Isa 29: 1 year to year and let your cycle of f go on. H2504
Isa 33:20 the city of our f; your eyes will see H4595
La 1: 4 no one comes to her **appointed f**. H4595
La 2: 6 Zion forget her **appointed f** and her H4595
Eze 36:38 at Jerusalem during her **appointed f**. H4595
Eze 44:24 my decrees for all my **appointed f**, H4595
Eze 45:17 grain offerings and drink offerings at the f H2504
Eze 45:17 Sabbaths—at all the **appointed f** *of* Israel. H4595
Eze 46: 9 come before the LORD at the **appointed f**, H4595
Eze 46:11 At the feasts and the **appointed f**, the H4595
Hos 2:11 her **yearly f**, her New Moons, her Sabbath H2504
Hos 2:11 her Sabbath days—all her **appointed f**. H4595
Hos 9: 5 you do on the day of your **appointed f**, H4595
Hos 12: 9 as in the days of your **appointed f**. H4595
Am 5:21 I despise your **religious f**; your assemblies H2504
Am 8:10 I will turn your **religious f** into mourning H2504
Na 1:15 Celebrate your f, Judah, and fulfill your H2504
Zep 3:18 mourn over the loss of your **appointed f**, H4595
Zec 8:19 glad occasions and happy f for Judah. H4595
Jn 5: 1 up to Jerusalem for one of the Jewish f. *G2038*

FESTIVE (2) [FESTIVAL]

1Sa 25: 8 my men, since we come at a f time. H3202
Ps 42: 4 of joy and praise among the f throng. H2510

FESTUS (15) [PORCIUS]

Ac 24:27 Felix was succeeded by Porcius F, but *G5776*
Ac 25: 1 F went up from Caesarea to Jerusalem *G5776*
Ac 25: 3 They requested F, as a favor to them, to *G899S*
Ac 25: 4 F answered, "Paul is being held at *G5776*
Ac 25: 6 days with them, F went down to Caesarea. NDT
Ac 25: 9 F, wishing to do the Jews a favor, said to *G5776*
Ac 25:12 After F had conferred with his council, he *G5776*
Ac 25:13 at Caesarea to pay their respects *to* F. *G5776*
Ac 25:14 F discussed Paul's case with the king. *G5776*
Ac 25:22 Then Agrippa said to F, "I would like to *G5776*
Ac 25:23 At the command *of* F, Paul was brought in *G5776*
Ac 25:24 F said: "King Agrippa, and all who are *G5776*
Ac 26:24 At this point F interrupted Paul's defense *G5776*
Ac 26:25 most excellent F," Paul replied. *G5776*
Ac 26:32 Agrippa said *to* F, "This man could have *G5776*

FETCH, FETCHED, FETCHT (KJV) BRING, BROUGHT, CAPTURE, COME BACK, ESCORT, GET, GOT, SELECTED, TAKE, TOOK

FETTERED (1) [FETTERS]

2Sa 3:34 bound, your feet **were** not f. H5602+4200+5733

FETTERS (2) [FETTERED]

Job 36:13 even when *he* f them, they do not H673
Ps 149: 8 to bind their kings with f, their nobles with H2414

FEVER (11) [FEVERISH]

Lev 26:16 wasting diseases and f that will destroy H7707
Dt 28:22 wasting disease, with f and inflammation H7707
Job 30:30 black and peels; my body burns with f. H2996
Mt 8:14 mother-in-law lying in bed **with a f**. *G4789*
Mt 8:15 He touched her hand and the f left her *G4790*
Mk 1:30 mother-in-law was in bed *with a* f, *G4789*
Mk 1:31 The f left her and she began to wait on *G4790*
Lk 4:38 was suffering *from* a high f, *G4790*
Lk 4:39 So he bent over her and rebuked the f *G4790*
Jn 4:52 at one in the afternoon, the f left him." *G4790*
Ac 28: 8 sick in bed, suffering from f and dysentery. *G4790*

FEVERISH (1) [FEVER]

La 5:10 Our skin is hot as an oven, f from hunger. H2363

FEW (77) [FEWEST]

Ge 29:20 they seemed like **only a f** days to him H285
Ge 34:30 We are f *in* number, and if they join H5493
Ge 47: 9 My years have been f and difficult, and H5071
Lev 25:16 when the years *are* f, you are to H5070
Lev 25:52 If **only a f** years remain until the Year of H5071
Lev 26:22 and **make** you *so* **f in number** that your H5070
Nu 9:20 was over the tabernacle **only a f** days; H5031
Nu 13:18 live there are strong or weak, f or many. H5071
Nu 35: 8 has many, but f from one that has few." H5070
Nu 35: 8 has many, but few from one that has f." H5071
Dt 4:27 and **only a f** *of* you will survive H5493+5031
Dt 26: 5 into Egypt with a f people and lived there H5071
Dt 28:62 the sky will be left but **f in number**, H5493+5071
Dt 33: 6 live and not die, nor his people be f." H5031
Jos 7: 3 whole army, for **only a f** people live there." H5071
Jos 10:20 a f survivors managed to reach their H8586
1Sa 14: 6 from saving, whether by many or by f." H5071
1Sa 17:28 did you leave those f sheep in the H5071
1Ki 17: 1 dew nor rain in the **next** *f* years except at my AIT
1Ki 17:12 I am gathering a f sticks to take home H9109
2Ki 4: 3 empty jars. Don't ask for **just a f**. H5070
1Ch 16:19 When they were but f *in* number, few H5493
1Ch 16:19 few in number, f indeed, and H5071
2Ch 24:24 army had come with **only a f** men, H5203
2Ch 29:34 were **too f** to skin all the burnt offerings H5071
Ne 2:12 I set out during the night with a f others. H5071
Ne 7: 4 there were f people in it, and the H5071
Job 10:20 Are not my f days almost over? Turn away H5071
Job 14: 1 woman, are of f days and full of trouble. H7920
Job 16:22 "Only a f years will pass before I take the H5031
Ps 105:12 When they were but f *in* number, few H5493
Ps 105:12 few in number, f indeed, and H3869+5071
Ps 109: 8 May his days be f; may another take his H5071
Ecc 2: 3 heavens during the f days of their lives. H5031
Ecc 5: 2 you are on earth, so let your words be f. H5071
Ecc 5:18 the sun during the f days of life God has H5031
Ecc 6:12 during the f and meaningless days they H5031
Ecc 9:14 a small city with **only a f** people in it. H5071
Ecc 12: 3 the grinders cease because *they are* f, H5070
Isa 10:19 of his forests will be *so* f that a child could H5031
Isa 16:14 survivors will be **very** f and feeble." H5071+4663
Isa 21:17 archers, the warriors of Kedar, *will be* f." H5070
Isa 24: 6 are burned up, and **very** f are left. H4663+632
Isa 65:20 there be in it an infant who lives but a *f* **days**, AIT
Jer 42: 2 we were once many, now **only a f** are left." H5071
Jer 44:14 live; none will return except a *f* **fugitives**." AIT
Jer 44:28 of Judah from Egypt will be **very f**. H5493+5031
Jer 49: 9 would they not leave a **f grapes**? H6622
Eze 5: 3 But take a f hairs and tuck H5071+928+5031
Eze 5: 4 take a f *of* these and throw them into the H4946
Eze 12:16 But I will spare a f of them from the sword H5031
Eze 13:19 my people for a *f* **handfuls** *of* barley and AIT
Da 11:20 In a f years, however, he will be destroyed H285
Da 11:23 with **only a f** people he will rise to H5071
Ob 5 would they not leave a **f grapes**? H6622
Mt 7:14 road that leads to life, and *only a* f find it. *G3900*
Mt 9:37 harvest is plentiful but the workers are f. *G3900*
Mt 15:34 they replied, "and a f small fish." *G3900*
Mt 22:14 "For many are invited, but f are chosen." *G3900*
Mt 25:21 You have been faithful with a f *things*; *G3900*
Mt 25:23 You have been faithful with a f *things*; *G3900*
Mk 2: 1 **A f days later**, when Jesus again *G1328+2465*
Mk 6: 5 lay his hands on a f sick people and heal *G3900*
Mk 8: 7 They had a f small fish as well; he gave *G3900*
Mk 12:42 small copper coins, worth **only a f cents**. *G3119*
Lk 10: 2 harvest is plentiful, but the workers are f. *G3900*
Lk 10:42 but f *things* are needed—or indeed only *G3900*
Lk 12:48 punishment will be beaten with f blows. *G3900*
Lk 13:23 are only a f *people* going to be saved?" *G3900*
Jn 2:12 There they stayed for a f days. *G4024+4498*
Ac 1: 5 in a f days you will be baptized *G4024+4498*
Ac 10:48 asked Peter to stay with them for a f days. *G5516*
Ac 17: 4 Greeks and quite a f prominent women. *G3900*
Ac 25:13 *A* f days later King Agrippa and Bernice *G5516*
1Pe 3:20 In it *only* a f people, eight in all, were *G3900*
Rev 2:14 I have a f *things* against you: *G3900*
Rev 3: 4 Yet you have a f people in Sardis who *G3900*

FEWEST (1) [FEW]

Dt 7: 7 peoples, for you were the f of all peoples. H5071

FICKLE (1)

2Co 1:17 *Was I* f when I intended to *G3836+1786+5968*

FIDELITY (2)

Ro 1:31 no understanding, **no f**, no love, no mercy. *G853*
Ro 16:10 whose **f to** Christ has stood the test. *G1877*

FIELD (197) [BATTLEFIELD, FIELDS, FIELDSTONES, GRAINFIELD, GRAINFIELDS]

Ge 3:18 and you will eat the plants of the f. H8441
Ge 4: 8 to his brother Abel, "Let's go out to the f." H8441
Ge 4: 8 While they were in the f, Cain attacked H8441
Ge 23: 9 belongs to him and is at the end of his f. H8441
Ge 23:11 I give you the f, and I give you the H8441
Ge 23:13 I will pay the price of the f. Accept it from H8441
Ge 23:17 So Ephron's f in Machpelah near Mamre H8441
Ge 23:17 near Mamre—both the f and the cave in it H8441
Ge 23:17 all the trees within the borders of the f— H8441
Ge 23:19 in the cave in the f *of* Machpelah near H8441
Ge 23:20 So the f and the cave in it were deeded to H8441
Ge 24:63 He went out to the f one evening to H8441
Ge 24:65 is that man in the f coming to meet us?" H8441
Ge 25: 9 in the f *of* Ephron son of Zohar the Hittite, H8441
Ge 25:10 the f Abraham had bought from the H8441
Ge 27:27 is like the smell of a f that the LORD has H8441
Ge 37: 7 of grain out in the f when suddenly my H8441
Ge 39: 5 both in the house and in the f. H8441
Ge 49:29 in the cave in the f *of* Ephron the Hittite, H8441
Ge 49:30 the cave in the f *of* Machpelah, near H8441
Ge 49:30 bought along with the f as a burial place H8441
Ge 49:32 The f and the cave in it were bought from H8441
Ge 50:13 him in the cave in the f *of* Machpelah, H8441
Ge 50:13 bought along with the f as a burial place H8441
Ex 9: 3 terrible plague on your livestock in the f— H8441
Ex 9:19 you have in the f to a place of shelter, H8441
Ex 9:19 been brought in and is still out in the f, H8441

Ex 9:21 LORD left their slaves and livestock in the f. H8441
Ex 22: 5 their livestock in a f or vineyard and lets H8441
Ex 22: 5 stray and they graze in someone else's f, H8441
Ex 22: 5 from the best of their own f or vineyard. H8441
Ex 22: 6 of grain or standing grain or the *whole* f, H8441
Ex 23:16 firstfruits of the crops you sow in your f. H8441
Ex 23:16 when you gather in your crops from the f. H8441
Lev 19: 9 the very edges of your f or gather the H8441
Lev 19:19 " 'Do not plant your f with two kinds of H8441
Lev 23:22 the very edges of your f or gather the H8441
Lev 27:17 If they dedicate a f during the Year of H8441
Lev 27:18 But if they dedicate a f after the Jubilee H8441
Lev 27:19 who dedicates the f wishes to redeem it, H8441
Lev 27:19 and the f will again become theirs. NDT
Lev 27:20 they do not redeem the f, or if they have H8441
Lev 27:21 When the f is released in the Jubilee, it H8441
Lev 27:21 become holy, like a f devoted to the LORD H8441
Lev 27:22 to the LORD a f they have bought, H8441
Lev 27:24 the Year of Jubilee the f will revert to the H8441
Nu 20:17 We will not go through any f or vineyard H8441
Nu 21:22 will not turn aside into any f or vineyard, H8441
Nu 22: 4 as an ox licks up the grass of the f. H8441
Nu 22:23 in his hand, it turned off the road into a f. H8441
Nu 23:14 he took him to the f *of* Zophim on the top H8441
Dt 21: 1 lying in a f in the land the LORD your God H8441
Dt 24:19 harvesting in your f and you overlook a H8441
Dt 28:38 much seed in the f but you will harvest H8441
Jos 15:18 she urged him to ask her father for a f. H8441
Jdg 1:14 she urged him to ask her father for a f. H8441
Jdg 13: 9 to the woman while she was out in the f; H8441
Jdg 20:31 men fell in the **open** f and on the roads— H8441
Ru 2: 3 entered a f and began to glean behind H8441
Ru 2: 3 was working in a f belonging to H2754+8441
Ru 2: 7 She came into the f and has remained here NDT
Ru 2: 8 glean in another f and don't go away H8441
Ru 2: 9 Watch the f where the men are harvesting H8441
Ru 2:17 So Ruth gleaned in the f until evening H8441
Ru 2:22 in someone else's f you might be harmed H8441
1Sa 6:14 The cart came to the f *of* Joshua of Beth H8441
1Sa 6:18 to this day in the f *of* Joshua of Beth H8441
1Sa 14:15 those in the camp and f, and those in the H8441
1Sa 19: 3 with my father in the f where you are. H8441
1Sa 20: 5 go and hide in the f until the evening of H8441
1Sa 20:11 Jonathan said, "let's go out into the f." H8441
1Sa 20:24 So David hid in the f, and when the New H8441
1Sa 20:35 went out to the f for his meeting with H8441
1Sa 30:11 an Egyptian in a f and brought him to H8441
2Sa 14: 6 got into a fight with each other in the f, H8441
2Sa 14:30 Joab's f is next to mine, and he H2754
2Sa 14:30 So Absalom's servants set the f on fire. H2754
2Sa 14:31 "Why have your servants set my f on fire?" H2754
2Sa 20:12 the road into a f and threw a garment H8441
2Sa 23:11 where there was a f full of lentils, H2754+8441
2Sa 23:12 took his stand in the middle of the f. H2754
2Ki 3:19 springs, and ruin every good f with stones." H2754
2Ki 3:25 stone on every good f until it was covered. H2754
2Ki 9:25 on the f *that belonged to* Naboth H2754+8441
2Ki 18:17 officer and his f **commander** with a large H8072
2Ki 18:17 on the road to the Washerman's F. H8441
2Ki 18:19 The f **commander** said to them, "Tell H8072
2Ki 18:26 Joah said to the f **commander**, H8072
2Ki 18:37 told him what the f **commander** had said. H8072
2Ki 19: 4 hear all the words of the f **commander**, H8072
2Ki 19: 8 When the f **commander** heard that the H8072
2Ki 19:26 They are like plants in the f, like tender H8441
1Ch 11:13 where there was a f full of barley, H2754+8441
1Ch 11:14 took their stand in the middle of the f. H2754
Job 5:23 have a covenant with the stones of the f, H8441
Ps 37:20 enemies are like the flowers of the f, H4120
Ps 72: 6 May he be like rain falling on a **mown f** H1600
Ps 72:16 Lebanon and thrive like the grass of the f. H824
Ps 103:15 they flourish like a flower of the f; H8441
Ps 104:11 They give water to all the beasts of the f H8442
Pr 13:23 An **unplowed** f produces food for the poor, H5776
Pr 21: 4 the **unplowed** f *of* the wicked H5776
Pr 24:30 I went past the f *of* a sluggard, past the H8441
Pr 27:26 the goats with the price of a f. H8441
Pr 31:16 She considers a f and buys it; out of her H8441
SS 2: 7 by the gazelles and by the does of the f: H8441
SS 3: 5 by the gazelles and by the does of the f: H8441
Isa 1: 8 like a hut in a **cucumber** f, like a city H5252
Isa 5: 8 to house and join f to field till no space H8441
Isa 5: 8 join field to f till no space is left H8441
Isa 7: 3 on the road to the Launderer's F. H8441
Isa 19: 7 Every **sown** f *along* the Nile will become H4669
Isa 28:25 barley in its plot, and spelt *in* its f? H1474
Isa 29:17 be turned into a **fertile** f and the fertile H4149
Isa 29:17 field and the **fertile** f seem like a forest? H4149
Isa 32:15 the desert becomes a **fertile** f, and H4149
Isa 32:15 and the **fertile** f seems like a forest. H4149
Isa 32:16 his righteousness live in the **fertile** f. H4149
Isa 36: 2 Assyria sent his f **commander** with a large H8072
Isa 36: 2 on the road to the Launderer's F, H8441
Isa 36: 4 The f **commander** said to them, "Tell H8072
Isa 36:11 Joah said to the f **commander**, H8072
Isa 36:22 told him what the f **commander** had said. H8072
Isa 37: 4 will hear the words of the f **commander**, H8072
Isa 37: 8 When the f **commander** heard that the H8072
Isa 37:27 They are like plants in the f, like tender H8441
Isa 40: 6 faithfulness is like the flowers of the f. H8441
Isa 55:12 all the trees of the f will clap their hands. H8441
Isa 56: 9 all you beasts of the f, come and devour, H8442
Jer 4:17 They surround her like men guarding a f H8442
Jer 7:20 on the trees of the f and on the crops of H8441
Jer 9:22 bodies will lie like dung on the open f, H8441
Jer 10: 5 Like a scarecrow in a **cucumber** f, their H5252
Jer 12: 4 the grass in every f be withered? H8441
Jer 12:10 ruin my vineyard and trample down my f; H2754
Jer 12:10 will turn my pleasant f into a desolate H2754
Jer 14: 5 Even the doe in the f deserts her newborn H8441
Jer 26:18 " 'Zion will be plowed like a f, Jerusalem H8441
Jer 32: 7 say, 'Buy my f at Anathoth, because H8441
Jer 32: 8 'Buy my f at Anathoth in the territory of H8441
Jer 32: 9 so I bought the f at Anathoth from my H8441
Jer 32:25 'Buy the f with silver and have the H8441
Jer 41: 8 olive oil and honey, hidden in a f. H8441
La 4: 9 waste away for lack of food from the f. H8442
Eze 16: 5 you were thrown out into the open f, for H8441
Eze 16: 7 I made you grow like a plant of the f. H8441
Eze 29: 5 fall on the open f and not be gathered H8441
Eze 31: 4 their channels to all the trees of the f. H8441
Eze 31: 5 towered higher than all the trees of the f; H8441
Eze 31:15 all the trees of the f withered away. H8441
Eze 32: 4 on the land and hurl you on the open f. H8441
Eze 36:30 the fruit of the trees and the crops of the f, H8441
Eze 38:20 the beasts of the f, every creature that H8441
Eze 39: 5 You will fall in the open f, for I have H7156
Da 2:38 the beasts of the f and the birds in the A10119
Da 4:15 in the ground, in the grass of the f. A10119
Da 4:23 in the grass of the f, while its roots A10119
Hos 2:18 covenant for them with the beasts of the f, H8441
Hos 4: 3 the beasts of the f, the birds in the sky H8441
Hos 10: 4 up like poisonous weeds in a plowed f. H8442
Hos 12:11 will be like piles of stones on a plowed f. H8442
Joel 1:11 because the harvest of the f is destroyed. H8441
Joel 1:12 all the trees of the f—are dried up. H8441
Joel 1:19 have burned up all the trees of the f. H8441
Am 4: 7 One f had rain; another had none and H2754
Mic 3:12 Zion will be plowed like a f, Jerusalem H8441
Mic 4:10 must leave the city to camp in the **open** f. H8441
Zec 10: 1 people, and plants of the f to everyone. H8441
Mt 6:28 See how the flowers *of* the f grow. They do G69
Mt 6:30 If that is how God clothes the grass *of* the f G69
Mt 9:38 to send out workers into his **harvest** f." G2546
Mt 13:24 is like a man who sowed good seed in his f. G69
Mt 13:27 didn't you sow good seed in your f? G69
Mt 13:31 which a man took and planted in his f. G69
Mt 13:36 to us the parable of the weeds *in* the f." G69
Mt 13:38 The f is the world, and the good seed stands G69
Mt 13:44 of heaven is like treasure hidden in a f. G69
Mt 13:44 went and sold all he had and bought that f. G69
Mt 22: 5 went off—one to his f, another to his G69
Mt 24:18 Let no one in the f go back to get their cloak. G69
Mt 24:40 Two men will be in the f; one will be taken G69
Mt 27: 7 to buy the potter's f as a burial place for G69
Mt 27: 8 it has been called the F of Blood to this day. G69
Mt 27:10 they used them to buy the potter's f, as G69
Mk 13:16 Let no one in the f go back to get their cloak. G69
Lk 10: 2 to send out workers into his **harvest** f. G2546
Lk 12:28 If that is how God clothes the grass of the f G69
Lk 14:18 'I have just bought a f, and I must go and G69
Lk 15:25 the older son was in the f. When he came G69
Lk 17: 7 to the servant when he comes in from the f, G69
Lk 17:31 no one in the f should go back for anything. G69
Ac 1:18 Judas bought a f; there he fell headlong, G6005
Ac 1:19 so they called that f in their language G6005
Ac 1:19 language Akeldama, that is, F of Blood.) G6005
Ac 4:37 sold a f he owned and brought the money G69
1Co 3: 9 you are God's f, God's building. G1176
1Pe 1:24 all their glory is like the flowers *of* the f; G5965

FIELDS (106) [FIELD]

Ge 30:14 went out into the f and found some H8441
Ge 30:16 Jacob came in from the f that evening, H8441
Ge 31: 4 to come out to the f where his flocks were. H8441
Ge 34: 5 his sons were in the f with his livestock; so H8441
Ge 34: 7 had come in from the f as soon as they H8441
Ge 34:28 else of theirs in the city and out in the f. H8441
Ge 37:15 wandering around in the f and asked him, H8441
Ge 41:48 put the food grown in the f surrounding it. H8441
Ge 47:20 sold their f, because the famine H8441
Ge 47:24 may keep as seed for the f and as food H8441
Ex 1:14 mortar and with all kinds of work in the f; H8441
Ex 8:13 the houses, in the courtyards and in the f. H8441
Ex 9:22 on everything growing in the f *of* Egypt." H8441
Ex 9:25 Egypt hail struck everything in the f— H8441
Ex 9:25 growing in the f and stripped every tree. H8441
Ex 10: 5 every tree that is growing in your f. H8441
Ex 10:12 devour everything growing in the f, H824
Ex 10:15 growing in the f and the fruit on the H824
Ex 23:10 you are to sow your f and harvest the crops, H824
Lev 14: 7 he is to release the live bird in the open f. H8441
Lev 14:53 live bird in the open f outside the town. H8441
Lev 17: 5 they are now making in the open f. H8441
Lev 25: 3 For six years sow your f, and for six years H8441
Lev 25: 4 Do not sow your f or prune your vineyards. H8441
Lev 25:12 eat only what is taken directly from the f. H8441
Nu 16:14 us an inheritance of f and vineyards. H8441
Dt 11:15 I will provide grass in the f for your cattle H8441
Dt 14:22 tenth of all that your f produce each year. H8441
Dt 32:13 land and fed him with the fruit of the f. H8442
Dt 32:32 of Sodom and from the f *of* Gomorrah. H8727
Jos 8:24 the men of Ai in the f and in the H8441
Jos 21:12 But the f and villages around the city they H8441
Jdg 5:18 so did Naphtali on the terraced f. H8441
Jdg 9:27 had gone out into the f and gathered the H8441
Jdg 9:32 men should come and lie in wait in the f. H8441
Jdg 9:42 the people of Shechem went out to the f, H8441
Jdg 9:43 companies and set an ambush in the f. H8441
Jdg 9:44 those in the f and struck them down. H8441
Jdg 19:16 came in from his work in the f. H8441
Ru 2: 2 "Let me go to the f and pick up the H8441
1Sa 8:14 take the best of your f and vineyards and H8441
1Sa 11: 5 Just then Saul was returning from the f H8441
1Sa 22: 7 of Jesse give all of you f and vineyards? H8441
1Sa 25:15 we were out in the f near them nothing H8441
2Sa 1:21 may no showers fall on your terraced f. H8441
1Ki 2:26 king said, "Go back to your f in Anathoth. H8441
2Ki 4:39 went out into the f to gather herbs and H8441
2Ki 23: 4 Jerusalem in the f *of* the Kidron Valley H8727
2Ki 25:12 of the land to work the vineyards and f. H3320
1Ch 6:56 But the f and villages around the city were H8441
1Ch 16:32 all that is in it; let the f be jubilant, and H8441
2Ch 26:10 people **working** his **f and vineyards** in the H4144
2Ch 31: 5 oil and honey and all that the f produced. H8441
Ne 5: 3 "We are mortgaging our f, our vineyards H8441
Ne 5: 4 pay the king's tax on our f and vineyards. H8441
Ne 5: 5 because our f and our vineyards belong to H8441
Ne 5:11 Give back to them immediately their f H8441
Ne 11:25 As for the villages with their f, some of H8441
Ne 11:30 in Lachish and its f, and in Azekah and its H8441
Ne 12:44 From the f *around* the towns they were to H8441
Ne 13:10 the service had gone back to their own f. H8441
Job 24: 6 gather fodder in the f and glean in the H8441
Ps 50:11 the insects in the f are mine. H8442
Ps 80:13 and insects from the f feed on it. H8442
Ps 96:12 Let the f be jubilant, and everything in H8442
Ps 107:37 They sowed f and planted vineyards that H8441
Ps 132: 6 we came upon it in the f *of* Jaar: H8441
Ps 144:13 thousands, by tens of thousands in our f; H2575
Pr 8:26 the world or its f or any of the dust of H2575
Pr 23:10 encroach on the f *of* the fatherless, H8441
Pr 24:27 work in order and get your f ready; H8441
Ecc 5: 9 the king himself profits from the f. H8441
Isa 1: 7 your f are being stripped by foreigners right H141
Isa 6:11 left deserted and the f ruined and ravaged, H141
Isa 10:18 of his forests and **fertile** f it will H4149
Isa 16: 8 The f *of* Heshbon wither, the vines of H8727
Isa 32:12 Beat your breasts for the pleasant f, for H8441
Isa 61: 5 foreigners will **work** your f and vineyards. H438
Jer 6:12 together with their f and their wives, when H8441
Jer 6:25 not go out to the f or walk on the roads H8441
Jer 8:10 to other men and their f to new owners. H8441
Jer 13:27 detestable acts on the hills and in the f. H8441
Jer 32:15 f and vineyards will again be bought in H8441
Jer 32:43 Once more f will be bought in this land of H8441
Jer 32:44 F will be bought for silver, and deeds will H8441
Jer 35: 9 to live in or had vineyards, f or crops. H8441
Jer 39:10 that time he gave them vineyards and f. H3321
Jer 48:33 are gone from the orchards and f *of* Moab. H824
Jer 52:16 of the land to work the vineyards and f. H3320
Eze 39:10 gather wood from the f or cut it from the H8441
Hos 5: 7 New Moon feasts, he will devour their f. H2750
Joel 1:10 The f are ruined, the ground is dried up H8441
Ob 19 will occupy the f *of* Ephraim and Samaria H8441
Mic 2: 2 They covet f and seize them, and houses H8441
Mic 2: 4 He assigns our f to traitors.' " H8441
Hab 3:17 olive crop fails and the f produce no food, H8727
Hag 1:11 a drought on the f and the mountains, H824
Mal 3:11 the vines in your f will not drop their H8441
Mt 19:29 wife or children or f for my sake will G69
Mk 10:29 father or children or f for me and the gospel G69
Mk 10:30 mothers, children and f—along with G69
Mk 11: 8 others spread branches they had cut in the f. G69
Lk 2: 8 were shepherds living out in the f nearby, G6001
Lk 15:15 who sent him to his f to feed pigs. G69
Jn 4:35 tell you, open your eyes and look at the f! G6001
Jas 5: 4 who mowed your f are crying out against G6001

FIELDSTONES (1) [FIELD, STONE]

Dt 27: 6 LORD your God with f and offer burnt H74+8969

FIERCE (50) [FIERCE-LOOKING, FIERCELY, FIERCER, FIERCEST]

Ge 49: 7 be their anger, so f, and their fury, so H6434
Ex 32:12 Turn from your f anger; relent and do not H3019
Nu 25: 4 so that the LORD's f anger may turn away H3019
Dt 13:17 Then the LORD will turn from his f anger H3019
Dt 29:23 which the LORD overthrew in f anger. H2779
Dt 29:24 Why this f, burning anger?" H1524
Jos 7:26 Then the LORD turned from his f anger H3019
1Sa 20:34 Jonathan got up from the table in f anger H3034
1Sa 28:18 LORD or carry out his f wrath against the H3019
1Sa 31: 3 The fighting *grew* f around Saul, and H3877
2Sa 2:17 The battle that day was very f, and Abner H7997
2Sa 17: 8 and as f as a wild bear robbed of H5253+5883
2Ki 23:26 not turn away from the heat of his f anger, H1524
1Ch 10: 3 The fighting **grew** f around Saul, and H3877
2Ch 28:11 the LORD's f anger rests on you. H3019
2Ch 28:13 and his f anger rests on Israel. H3019
2Ch 29:10 so that his f anger will turn away from us. H3019
2Ch 30: 8 so that his f anger will turn away from you. H3019
Ezr 10:14 until the f anger of our God in this matter H3019
Job 41:10 No *one* is f *enough* to rouse it. Who then is H425
Ps 17:12 prey, like a f **lion** crouching in cover. H4097
Ps 59: 3 F *men* conspire against me for no offense H6434

F

Ps 69:24 on them; let your f anger overtake them. H3019
Ps 85: 3 your wrath and turned from your f anger. H3019
Pr 26:13 in the road, a f lion roaming the streets!" H787
Isa 7: 4 because of the f anger of Rezin and Aram H3034
Isa 13: 9 with wrath and f anger—to make the H3019
Isa 19: 4 and a f king will rule over them, H6434
Isa 27: 1 with his sword—his f, great and powerful H7997
Isa 27: 8 with his f blast he drives her out H7997
Isa 49:24 captives be rescued from the f? H6883
Isa 49:25 plunder retrieved from the f; I will H6883
Jer 4: 8 the f anger of the LORD has not turned H3019
Jer 4:26 ruins before the LORD, before his f anger. H3019
Jer 12:13 harvest because of the LORD's f anger." H3019
Jer 25:37 waste because of the f anger of the LORD. H3019
Jer 25:38 because of the LORD's f anger. H3019
Jer 30:24 The f anger of the LORD will not turn back H3019
Jer 44: 6 Therefore, my f anger was poured out; it H2779
Jer 49:37 on them, even my f anger," declares the H3019
Jer 51:45 Run from the f anger of the LORD. H3019
La 1:12 brought on me in the day of his f anger? H3019
La 2: 3 In f anger he has cut off every horn of H3034
La 2: 6 in his f anger he has spurned both king H2405
La 4:11 his wrath; he has poured out his f anger. H3019
Hos 11: 9 I will not carry out my f anger, nor will I H3019
Jnh 3: 9 turn from his f anger so that we will H3019
Na 1: 6 Who can endure his f anger? His wrath is H3019
Zep 2: 2 before the LORD's f anger comes upon you H3019
Zep 3: 8 out my wrath on them—all my f anger. H3019

FIERCE-LOOKING (2) [FIERCE]

Dt 28:50 a f nation without respect for the H6434+7156
Da 8:23 wicked, a f king, a master of H6434+7156

FIERCELY (4) [FIERCE]

Job 39:21 It paws f, rejoicing in its H928+2021+6677
Ps 25:19 are my enemies and how f they hate me! H2805
Jer 6:29 The bellows blow f to burn away the lead H5723
Lk 11:53 to oppose him f and to besiege him G1267

FIERCER (1) [FIERCE]

Hab 1: 8 than leopards, f than wolves at dusk. H2523

FIERCEST (1) [FIERCE]

2Sa 11:15 Uriah out in front where the fighting is f. H2617

FIERY (14) [FIRE]

Ps 11: 6 the wicked he will rain f coals and burning H836
Eze 21:31 breathe out my f anger against you; H836
Eze 22:20 into a furnace to be melted with a f blast, H836
Eze 22:21 you and I will blow on you with my f wrath, H836
Eze 22:31 them and consume them with my f anger, H836
Eze 28:14 you walked among the f stones. H836
Eze 28:16 guardian cherub, from among the f stones. H836
Eze 38:19 In my zeal and f wrath I declare that at that H836
1Pe 4:12 be surprised *at* the f *ordeal* that has come G4796
Rev 6: 4 horse came out, a f red *one*. Its rider was G4794
Rev 9:17 Their breastplates were f red, dark blue G4791
Rev 10: 1 the sun, and his legs were like f pillars. G4786
Rev 19:20 thrown alive into the f lake of burning G4786
Rev 21: 8 be consigned to the f lake of burning G2794

FIFTEEN (17) [FIFTEENTH]

Ge 7:20 to a depth of more than f cubits. H2822+6926
Ex 27:14 Curtains f cubits long are to be on H2822+6926
Ex 27:15 curtains f cubits long are to be H2822+6926
Ex 38:14 Curtains f cubits long were on one H2822+6926
Ex 38:15 curtains f cubits long were on H2822+6926
Lev 27: 7 of a male at f shekels and of a H2822+6925
Jdg 8:10 a force of about f thousand men, H2822+6925
2Sa 9:10 Now Ziba had f sons and twenty H2822+6925
2Sa 19:17 you and his f sons and twenty servants. H2822+6925
1Ki 7: 3 forty-five beams, f to a row. H2822+6925
2Ki 14:17 of Judah lived for f years after the H2822+6926
2Ki 20: 6 I will add f years to your life. H2822+6926
2Ch 25:25 of Judah lived for f years after the H2822+6926
Isa 38: 5 I will add f years to your life. H2822+6926
Eze 45:12 shekels plus f shekels equal H2822+2256+6927
Hos 3: 2 her for f shekels *of* silver and H2822+6925
Gal 1:18 with Cephas and stayed with him f days. G1278

FIFTEENTH (18) [FIFTEEN]

Ex 16: 1 on the f day of the second month H2822+6925
Lev 23: 6 On the f day of that month the H2822+6925
Lev 23:34 'On the f day of the seventh month H2822+6925
Lev 23:39 with the f day of the seventh H2822+6925
Nu 28:17 On the f day of this month there is H2822+6925
Nu 29:12 " 'On the f day of the seventh H2822+6925
Nu 33: 3 Rameses on the f day of the first H2822+6925
1Ki 12:32 a festival on the f day of the eighth H2822+6925
1Ki 12:33 On the f day of the eighth month, H2822+6925
2Ki 14:23 In the f year of Amaziah son of H2822+6926
1Ch 24:14 the f to Bilgah, the sixteenth to H2822+6925
1Ch 25:22 the f to Jerimoth, his sons and H2822+6925
2Ch 15:10 third month of the f year of Asa's H2822+6926
Est 9:18 and then on the f they rested and H2822+6925
Est 9:21 fourteenth and f days of the month H2822+6925
Eze 32:17 on the f day of the month H2822+6925
Eze 45:25 in the seventh month on the f day, H2822+6925
Lk 3: 1 In the f year of the reign of Tiberius G4298

FIFTH (56) [FIVE]

Ge 1:23 there was morning—the f day. H2797
Ge 30:17 became pregnant and bore Jacob a f son. H2797
Ge 41:34 over the land *to* take a f *of* the harvest of H2821
Ge 47:24 crop comes in, give a f of it to Pharaoh. H2797
Ge 47:26 that a f of the produce belongs to Pharaoh. H2823
Lev 5:16 penalty of a f *of* its *value* and give it all to H2797
Lev 6: 5 add a f *of* the value to it and give it all to H2797
Lev 19:25 But in the f year you may eat its fruit. H2797
Lev 22:14 the offering and add a f *of* the value to it. H2797
Lev 27:13 animal, a f must be added to its value. H2797
Lev 27:15 they must add a f to its value, and the H2797
Lev 27:19 they must add a f to its value, and the H2797
Lev 27:27 its set value, adding a f *of* the value to it. H2797
Lev 27:31 their tithe must add a f *of* the value to it. H2797
Nu 5: 7 add *a* f *of* the value to it and give it all to H2797
Nu 7:36 On the f day Shelumiel son of H2797
Nu 29:26 " 'On the f day offer nine bulls, two rams H2797
Nu 33:38 the first day of the f month of the fortieth H2797
Jos 19:24 The f lot came out for the tribe of Asher H2797
Jdg 19: 8 On the morning of the f day, when he rose H2797
2Sa 3: 4 son of Haggith; the f, Shephatiah the son H2797
1Ki 6:31 wood that were one f *of* the width of the H2797
1Ki 14:25 In the f year of King Rehoboam, Shishak H2797
2Ki 8:16 In the f year of Joram son of Ahab king of H2822
2Ki 25: 8 On the seventh day of the f month, in the H2797
1Ch 2:14 the fourth Nethanel, the f Raddai, H2797
1Ch 3: 3 the f, Shephatiah the son of Abital; and H2797
1Ch 8: 2 Nohah the fourth and Rapha the f. H2797
1Ch 12:10 Mishmannah the fourth, Jeremiah the f, H2797
1Ch 24: 9 the f to Malkijah, the sixth to Mijamin, H2797
1Ch 25:12 the f to Nethaniah, his sons and relatives H2797
1Ch 26: 3 Elam the f, Jehohanan the sixth and H2797
1Ch 26: 4 Sakar the fourth, Nethanel the f, H2797
1Ch 27: 8 The f, for the fifth month, was the H2797
1Ch 27: 8 The fifth, for the f month, was the H2797
2Ch 12: 2 Jerusalem in the f year of King Rehoboam H2797
Ezr 7: 8 in Jerusalem in the f month of the H2797
Ezr 7: 9 Jerusalem on the first day of the f month, H2797
Ne 6: 5 the f time, Sanballat sent his aide H2797
Jer 1: 3 down to the f month of the eleventh year H2797
Jer 28: 1 In the f month of that same year, the H2797
Jer 36: 9 ninth month of the f year of Jehoiakim H2797
Jer 52:12 On the tenth day of the f month, in the H2797
Eze 1: 1 in the fourth month on the f day, while I H2822
Eze 1: 2 On the f of the month—it was the fifth H2822
Eze 1: 2 it was the f year of the exile of King H2797
Eze 8: 1 in the sixth month on the f day, while I H2822
Eze 20: 1 in the f month on the tenth day H2797
Eze 33:21 in the tenth month on the f day, a man H2822
Zec 7: 3 "Should I mourn and fast in the f month H2797
Zec 7: 5 mourned in the f and seventh months H2797
Zec 8:19 fasts of the fourth, f, seventh and tenth H2797
Rev 6: 9 When he opened the f seal, I saw under G4286
Rev 9: 1 The f angel sounded his trumpet, and I G4286
Rev 16:10 The f angel poured out his bowl on the G4286
Rev 21:20 the f onyx, the sixth ruby, the seventh G4286

FIFTIES (5) [FIFTY]

Ex 18:21 over thousands, hundreds, f and tens. H2822
Ex 18:25 over thousands, hundreds, f and tens. H2822
Dt 1:15 of f and of tens and as tribal officials. H2822
1Sa 8:12 of thousands and commanders of f, H2822
Mk 6:40 sat down in groups of hundreds and f. G4299

FIFTIETH (3) [FIFTY]

Lev 25:10 Consecrate the f year and proclaim liberty H2822
Lev 25:11 The f year shall be a jubilee for you; do H2822
2Ki 15:23 In the f year of Azariah king of Judah H2822

FIFTY (85) [FIFTIES, FIFTIETH, 50]

Ge 6:15 f cubits wide and thirty cubits high. H2822
Ge 7:24 the earth for a hundred and f days. H2822
Ge 8: 3 of the hundred and f days the water had H2822
Ge 18:24 What if there are f righteous people in the H2822
Ge 18:24 the sake of the f righteous people in it H2822
Ge 18:26 "If I find f righteous people in the city of H2822
Ge 18:28 of the righteous is five less than f? H2822
Ex 26: 5 Make f loops on one curtain and fifty loops H2822
Ex 26: 5 on one curtain and f loops on the end H2822
Ex 26: 6 Then make f gold clasps and use them to H2822
Ex 26:10 Make f loops along the edge of the end H2822
Ex 26:11 Then make f bronze clasps and put them H2822
Ex 27:12 courtyard shall be f cubits wide and have H2822
Ex 27:13 the courtyard shall also be f cubits wide. H2822
Ex 27:18 a hundred cubits long and f cubits wide, H2822
Ex 36:12 They also made f loops on one curtain H2822
Ex 36:12 on one curtain and f loops on the end H2822
Ex 36:13 Then they made f gold clasps and used H2822
Ex 36:17 Then they made f loops along the edge of H2822
Ex 36:18 They made f bronze clasps to fasten the H2822
Ex 38:12 The west end was f cubits wide and had H2822
Ex 38:13 toward the sunrise, was also f cubits wide. H2822
Lev 23:16 Count off f days up to the day after the H2822
Lev 27: 3 of twenty and sixty at f shekels of silver, H2822
Lev 27:16 f shekels of silver to a homer of barley H2822
Nu 4: 3 men from thirty to f years of age who H2822
Nu 4:23 men from thirty to f years of age who H2822
Nu 4:30 men from thirty to f years of age who H2822
Nu 4:35 men from thirty to f years of age who H2822
Nu 4:39 men from thirty to f years of age who H2822
Nu 4:43 men from thirty to f years of age who H2822
Nu 4:47 men from thirty to f years of age who H2822
Nu 8:25 at the age of f, they must retire from H2822
Nu 31:30 select one out of every f, whether people, H2822
Nu 31:47 one out of every f people and animals, H2822
Dt 22:29 he shall pay her father f shekels of silver H2822
Jos 7:21 a bar of gold weighing f shekels, H2822
2Sa 15: 1 horses and with f men to run ahead of H2822
2Sa 24:24 the oxen and paid f shekels of silver for H2822
1Ki 1: 5 with f men to run ahead of him. H2822
1Ki 7: 2 cubits long, f wide and thirty high H2822
1Ki 7: 6 He made a colonnade f cubits long and H2822
1Ki 10:29 of silver, and a horse for a hundred and f. H2822
1Ki 18: 4 them in two caves, f in each, and had H2822
1Ki 18:13 in two caves, f in each, and supplied H2822
1Ki 18:19 four hundred and f prophets of Baal and H2822
1Ki 18:22 Baal has four hundred and f prophets. H2822
2Ki 1: 9 a captain with his *company of* f *men*. H2822
2Ki 1:10 heaven and consume you and your f *men*!" H2822
2Ki 1:11 to Elijah another captain with his f *men*. H2822
2Ki 1:12 heaven and consume you and your f *men*!" H2822
2Ki 1:12 consumed him and his f *men*. H2822
2Ki 1:13 king sent a third captain with his f *men*. H2822
2Ki 1:13 my life and the lives of these f *men*, H2822
2Ki 2: 7 F men from the company of the prophets H2822
2Ki 2:16 "we your servants have f able men. H2822
2Ki 2:17 And they sent f men, who searched for H2822
2Ki 13: 7 the army of Jehoahaz except f horsemen, H2822
2Ki 15:20 had to contribute f shekels of silver to be H2822
2Ki 15:25 Taking f men of Gilead with him, he H2822
1Ch 5:21 of the Hagrites—f thousand camels, two H2822
1Ch 5:21 two hundred f thousand sheep and two H2822
2Ch 1:17 of silver, and a horse for a hundred and f. H2822
2Ch 3: 9 The gold nails weighed f shekels. H2822
2Ch 8:10 two hundred and f officials supervising the H2822
2Ch 8:18 back four hundred and f talents of gold, H2822
Ne 5:17 a hundred and f Jews and officials ate at H2822
Est 5:14 reaching to a height of f cubits, and ask H2822
Est 7: 9 reaching to a height of f cubits stands by H2822
Isa 3: 3 the captain of f and the man of rank, the H2822
Eze 40:15 to the far end of its portico was f cubits. H2822
Eze 40:21 It was f cubits long and twenty-five cubits H2822
Eze 40:25 It was f cubits long and twenty-five cubits H2822
Eze 40:29 It was f cubits long and twenty-five cubits H2822
Eze 40:33 It was f cubits long and twenty-five cubits H2822
Eze 40:36 It was f cubits long and twenty-five cubits H2822
Eze 42: 2 a hundred cubits long and f cubits wide. H2822
Eze 42: 7 extended in front of the rooms for f cubits. H2822
Eze 42: 8 next to the outer court was f cubits long, H2822
Hag 2:16 went to a wine vat to draw f measures, H2822
Lk 7:41 him five hundred denarii, and the other f. G4299
Lk 9:14 them sit down in groups of about f each." G4299
Lk 16: 6 and make it four hundred and f. G4299
Jn 8:57 "You are not yet f years old," they said to G4299
Ac 19:19 total came to f thousand drachmas. G3689+4297

FIFTY-FIVE (2)

2Ki 21: 1 reigned in Jerusalem f years. H2822+2256+2822
2Ch 33: 1 reigned in Jerusalem f years. H2822+2256+2822

FIFTY-SECOND (1) [FIFTY-TWO]

2Ki 15:27 In the f year of Azariah king H2822+2256+9109

FIFTY-TWO (3) [FIFTY-SECOND, 52]

2Ki 15: 2 in Jerusalem f years. H2822+2256+9109
2Ch 26: 3 in Jerusalem f years. H2822+2256+9109
Ne 6:15 twenty-fifth of Elul, in f days. H2822+2256+9109

FIG (40) [FIGS, SYCAMORE-FIG, SYCAMORE-FIGS]

Ge 3: 7 so they sewed f leaves together and H9300
Dt 8: 8 vines and f trees, pomegranates, H9300
Jdg 9:10 the trees said to the f tree, 'Come and be H9300
Jdg 9:11 "But the f tree replied, 'Should I give up H9300
1Ki 4:25 their own vine and under their own f tree. H9300
2Ki 18:31 your own vine and f tree and drink water H9300
1Ch 12:40 supplies of flour, f cakes, raisin cakes, H1811
Ps 105:33 their vines and f trees and shattered the H9300
Pr 27:18 one who guards a f tree will eat its fruit, H9300
SS 2:13 The f tree forms its early fruit; the H9300
Isa 9:10 the f trees have been felled H9204
Isa 34: 4 the vine, like shriveled figs from the f tree. H9300
Isa 36:16 your own vine and f tree and drink water H9300
Jer 5:17 herds, devour your vines and f trees. H9300
Hos 2:12 I will ruin her vines and her f trees, which H9300
Hos 9:10 like seeing the early fruit on the f tree. H9300
Joel 1: 7 laid waste my vines and ruined my f trees. H9300
Joel 1:12 vine is dried up and the f tree is withered; H9300
Joel 2:22 the f tree and the vine yield their riches. H9300
Am 4: 9 Locusts devoured your f and olive trees H9300
Mic 4: 4 their own vine and under their own f tree, H9300
Na 3:12 fortresses are like f trees with their first H9300
Hab 3:17 Though the f tree does not bud and there H9300
Hag 2:19 the vine and the f tree, the pomegranate H9300
Zec 3:10 neighbor to sit under your vine and f tree, H9300
Mt 21:19 Seeing a f tree by the road, he went up to G5190
Mt 21:20 "How did the f tree wither so quickly?" G5190
Mt 21:21 can you do what was done *to* the f tree, G5190
Mt 24:32 "Now learn this lesson from the f tree: As G5190
Mk 11:13 Seeing in the distance a f tree in leaf, he G5190
Mk 11:20 they saw the f tree withered from the roots G5190
Mk 11:21 The f tree you cursed has withered!" G5190
Mk 13:28 "Now learn this lesson from the f tree: As G5190
Lk 13: 6 "A man had a f tree growing in his G5190
Lk 13: 7 fruit on this f tree and haven't found G5190
Lk 21:29 "Look at the f tree and all the trees. G5190
Jn 1:48 were still under the f tree before Philip G5190
Jn 1:50 I told you I saw you under the f tree. G5190

Jas 3:12 sisters, can a **f tree** bear olives, or a *G5190*
Rev 6:13 as figs drop *from* a **f tree** when shaken by *G3913*

FIGHT (114) [FIGHTER, FIGHTERS, FIGHTING, FIGHTS, FOUGHT]

Ex 1:10 **f** against us and leave the country. H4309
Ex 14:14 The LORD *will* **f** for you; you need only to H4309
Ex 17: 9 our men and go out *to* **f** the Amalekites. H4309
Lev 24:10 a **f broke out** in the camp between H5897
Nu 22:11 I will be able to **f** them and drive them H4309
Nu 32:27 will cross over to **f** before the LORD, just as H4878
Dt 1:30 going before you, *will* **f** for you, as he did H4309
Dt 1:41 We will go up and **f**, as the LORD our God H4309
Dt 1:42 'Do not go up and **f**, because I will not be H4309
Dt 3:22 the LORD your God himself *will* **f** for you." H4309
Dt 20: 4 goes with you to **f** for you against your H4309
Dt 29: 7 king of Bashan came out to **f** against us, H4878
Jos 10:25 do to all the enemies you *are going to* **f**." H4309
Jos 11: 5 the Waters of Merom to **f** against Israel. H4309
Jos 24: 9 of Moab, prepared *to* **f** against Israel, he H4309
Jdg 1: 1 is to go up first to **f** against the H4309
Jdg 1: 3 allotted to us, *to* **f** against the Canaanites. H4309
Jdg 1: 9 Judah went down to **f** against the H4309
Jdg 2:15 Whenever Israel went out to **f**, the hand of NDT
Jdg 5: 7 Villagers in Israel **would not** *f*; they held back AIT
Jdg 8: 1 you call us when you went to **f** Midian?" H4309
Jdg 9:38 men you ridiculed? Go out and **f** them!" H4309
Jdg 10: 9 crossed the Jordan to **f** against Judah, H4309
Jdg 11: 6 commander, so *we can* **f** the Ammonites." H4309
Jdg 11: 8 come with us *to* **f** the Ammonites H4309
Jdg 11: 9 you take me back to **f** the Ammonites H4309
Jdg 11:25 quarrel with Israel or **f** with them? H4309+4309
Jdg 11:32 Jephthah went over to **f** the Ammonites, H4309
Jdg 12: 1 "Why did you go to **f** the Ammonites H4309
Jdg 12: 3 hands and crossed over to **f** the Ammonites, NDT
Jdg 12: 3 why have you come up today to **f** me?" H4309
Jdg 15:10 "Why have you come to **f** us? H6584
Jdg 18:23 you that *you* **called out** your men **to f**?" H2410
Jdg 20:14 Gibeah to **f** against the H3655+4200+2021+4878
Jdg 20:18 is to go up first to **f** against the H4878
Jdg 20:20 went out to **f** the Benjamites and H4878
Jdg 20:23 we go up again to **f** against the H4878
Jdg 20:28 we go up again to **f** against the H4878
1Sa 4: 1 Israelites went out to **f** against the H4878
1Sa 4: 9 they have been to you. Be men, and **f**!" H4309
1Sa 8:20 to go out before us and **f** our battles." H4309
1Sa 13: 5 The Philistines assembled to **f** Israel, with H4309
1Sa 17: 9 If he is able to **f** and kill me, we will H4309
1Sa 17:10 Give me a man and *let us* **f** each other." H4309
1Sa 17:32 Philistine; your servant will go and **f** him." H4309
1Sa 17:33 to go out against this Philistine and **f** him; H4309
1Sa 18:17 serve me bravely and **f** the battles of the H4309
1Sa 25:28 my lord, because you **f** the LORD's battles H4309
1Sa 28: 1 gathered their forces to **f** against Israel. H4309
1Sa 29: 8 Why can't I go and **f** against the enemies H4309
2Sa 2:14 men get up and **f hand to hand** in front of H8471
2Sa 2:28 pursued Israel, nor did they **f** anymore. H4309
2Sa 10:12 and *let us* **f bravely** for our people and the H2616
2Sa 10:13 with him advanced to **f** the Arameans, H4878
2Sa 11:20 'Why did you get so close to the city to **f**? H4309
2Sa 14: 6 *They* **got into a f** *with* each other in the H5897
2Sa 18: 6 army marched out of the city to **f** Israel, H7925
2Sa 21:15 with his men *to* **f** *against* the Philistines, H4309
1Ki 12:24 Do not go up to **f** against your brothers H4309
1Ki 20:23 But if *we* **f** them on the plains, surely we H4309
1Ki 20:25 chariot—so *we can* **f** Israel on the plains. H4309
1Ki 20:26 went up to Aphek to **f** against Israel. H4878
1Ki 22: 4 you go with me to **f** against Ramoth H4878
1Ki 22:31 commanders, "*Do* not **f** *with* anyone H4309
2Ki 3: 7 Will you go with me to **f** against Moab?" H4878
2Ki 3:21 the kings had come to **f** against them; H4309
2Ki 10: 3 Then **f** for your master's house. H4309
2Ki 16: 5 Israel marched up to **f** against Jerusalem H4878
2Ki 19: 9 was marching out to **f** against him. H4309
1Ch 12:19 went with the Philistines to **f** against Saul. H4878
1Ch 19:13 and *let us* **f bravely** for our people and the H2616
1Ch 19:14 with him advanced to **f** the Arameans, H4878
2Ch 11: 4 Do not go up *to* **f** against your fellow H4309
2Ch 13:12 People of Israel, *do* not **f** against the LORD H4309
2Ch 18:30 commanders, "*Do* not **f** *with* anyone H4309
2Ch 20:17 You *will* not *have* to **f** this **battle**. Take up H4309
2Ch 25: 8 Even if you go and **f** courageously in battle H6913
2Ch 32: 8 our God to help us and to **f** our battles." H4309
2Ch 35:20 of Egypt went up to **f** at Carchemish on H4309
2Ch 35:22 went to **f** him on the plain of H4309
Ne 4: 8 together to come and **f** against Jerusalem H4309
Ne 4:14 awesome, and **f** for your families H4309
Ne 4:20 Our God *will* **f** for us!" H4309
Ps 35: 1 **f** against those who fight against me. H4309
Ps 35: 1 fight against *those who* **f** *against* me. H4309
Isa 7: 1 Israel marched up to **f** against Jerusalem, H4878
Isa 19: 2 Egyptian—brother *will* **f** against brother H4309
Isa 29: 7 of all the nations that **f** against Ariel, H7371
Isa 29: 8 all the nations that **f** against Mount Zion. H7371
Isa 37: 9 was marching out to **f** against him. H4309
Jer 1:19 *They will* **f** against you but will not H4309
Jer 15:20 *they will* **f** against you but will not H4309
Jer 21: 4 which you *are* using *to* **f** the king of H4309
Jer 21: 5 *I* myself *will* **f** against you with an H4309
Jer 32: 5 If *you* **f** against the Babylonians, you will H4309
Jer 33: 5 *in the* **f** with the Babylonians: 'They will be H4309
Jer 34:22 *They will* **f** against it, take it and burn it H4309
Jer 41:12 their men and went to **f** Ishmael son of H4309
Da 10:20 Soon I will return to **f** against the prince of H4309
Da 11: 7 *he will* **f** against them and be victorious. H6913
Da 11:11 out in a rage and **f** against the king of the H4309
Zec 10: 5 *They will* **f** because the LORD is with them H4309
Zec 14: 2 the nations to Jerusalem to **f** against it; H4878
Zec 14: 3 LORD will go out and **f** against those H4309
Zec 14:14 Judah too *will* **f** at Jerusalem. The wealth H4309
Jn 18:36 my servants would **f** to prevent my arrest by *G76*
1Co 9:26 *I do* not **f** like a boxer beating the air. *G4782*
2Co 10: 4 The weapons we **f with** are not the *G5127*
1Ti 1:18 recalling them *you may* **f** the battle well, *G5129*
1Ti 6:12 **F** the good fight of the faith. Take hold of the *G76*
1Ti 6:12 Fight the good **f** of the faith. Take hold of the *G74*
2Ti 4: 7 I have fought the good **f**, I have finished the *G74*
Jas 4: 2 get what you want, so you quarrel and **f**. *G4482*
Rev 2:16 come to you and *will* **f** against them with *G4482*

FIGHTER (4) [FIGHT]

2Sa 17: 8 your father is an **experienced f**; he H408+4878
2Sa 17:10 that your father is a **f** and that those with H1475
2Sa 23:20 a **valiant f** from Kabzeel H1201+408+2657
1Ch 11:22 a **valiant f** from Kabzeel H1201+408+2657

FIGHTERS (4) [FIGHT]

Jos 10: 2 than Ai, and all its men were **good f**. H1475
Jdg 20:44 Benjamites fell, all of them **valiant f**. H408+2657
Jdg 20:46 swordsmen fell, all of them **valiant f**. H408+2657
2Sa 17: 8 his men; they are **f**, and as fierce as a H1475

FIGHTING (64) [FIGHT]

Ex 2:13 day he went out and saw two Hebrews **f**. H5897
Ex 14:25 The LORD *is* **f** for them against Egypt." H4309
Ex 21:22 "If people *are* **f** and hit a pregnant H5897
Nu 31:42 Moses set apart from that of the **f** men— H7371
Dt 2:14 entire generation of **f** men had perished H4878
Dt 2:16 the last of these **f** men among the people H4878
Dt 20:19 a long time, **f** against it to capture it H4309
Dt 25:11 If two men *are* **f** and the wife of one of H5897
Jos 1:14 all your **f men**, ready for battle, H2657+1475
Jos 6: 2 along with its king and its **f men**. H2657+1475
Jos 8: 3 of his **best f men** and sent them H2657+1475
Jos 10: 7 including all the **best f men**. H1475+2657
Jos 10:14 Surely the LORD *was* **f** for Israel! H4309
Jdg 11: 4 the Ammonites *were* **f** against Israel, H4309
Jdg 20:34 The **f** was so heavy that the Benjamites H4878
Jdg 21:10 sent twelve thousand **f** men with H1201+2657
1Sa 17:19 Valley of Elah, **f** against the Philistines." H4309
1Sa 23: 1 the Philistines *are* **f** against Keilah and H4309
1Sa 28:15 "The Philistines *are* **f** against me, and H4309
1Sa 29: 4 he will turn against us during the **f**. H4878
1Sa 31: 3 The **f** grew fierce around Saul, and when H4878
2Sa 10: 7 Joab out with the entire army of **f men**. H1475
2Sa 10:14 Joab returned from **f** the Ammonites and H6584
2Sa 11:15 Uriah out in front where the **f** is fiercest. H4878
2Sa 24: 2 Dan to Beersheba and enroll the **f men**, H6639
2Sa 24: 4 of the king to enroll the **f men** *of* Israel. H6639
2Sa 24: 9 the number of the **f men** to the king: H6639
2Sa 24:10 after he had counted the **f men**, H6639
1Ki 9:22 they were his **f** men, his government H4878
1Ki 11:15 Earlier when David *was* **f with** Edom H2118+907
1Ki 22:34 "Wheel around and get me out of the **f**. H4722
2Ki 19: 8 found the king **f** against Libnah. H4309
2Ki 24:14 all the officers and **f men**, and all H1475+2657
2Ki 24:16 the entire force of seven thousand **f** men, H2657
2Ki 25:19 he took the officer in charge of the **f** men H4878
1Ch 5:20 They were helped in **f** them, and God H6584
1Ch 7: 2 of Tola listed as **f men** in their H1475+2657
1Ch 7: 5 who were **f men** belonging to all H1475+2657
1Ch 7: 7 record listed 22,034 **f men**. H1475+2657
1Ch 7: 9 of families and 20,200 **f men**. H1475+2657
1Ch 7:11 were 17,200 **f men** ready to go out H1475+2657
1Ch 10: 3 The **f** grew fierce around Saul, and when H4878
1Ch 12:38 All these were **f** men who volunteered to H4878
1Ch 19: 8 Joab out with the entire army of **f men**. H1475
1Ch 21: 5 the number of the **f men** to David: H6639
1Ch 21:17 I who ordered the **f men** to be counted? H6639
1Ch 28: 1 the warriors and all the brave **f men**. H1475
2Ch 8: 9 they were his **f** men, commanders of H4878
2Ch 13: 3 of four hundred thousand able **f** men, H4878
2Ch 14: 8 All these were **brave f men**. H1475+2657
2Ch 17:13 **experienced f men in** H408+4878+1475+2657
2Ch 17:14 commander, with 300,000 **f men**; H1475+2657
2Ch 18:33 "Wheel around and get me out of the **f**. H4722
2Ch 25: 6 thousand **f men** from Israel for H1475+2657
2Ch 26:12 leaders over the **f men** was 2,600. H1475+2657
2Ch 32:21 all the **f men** and the commanders H1475+2657
Isa 37: 8 found the king **f** against Libnah. H4309
Jer 34: 1 empire he ruled *were* **f** against Jerusalem H4309
Jer 34: 7 king of Babylon *was* **f** against Jerusalem H4309
Jer 51:30 Babylon's warriors have stopped **f**; they H4309
Jer 52:25 he took the officer in charge of the **f** men H4878
Joel 3: 9 Let all the **f** men draw near and attack H4878
Ac 5:39 will only find yourselves **f against God**." *G2534*
Ac 7:26 came upon two Israelites *who were* **f**. *G3481*

FIGHTS (5) [FIGHT]

Jos 23:10 because the LORD your God **f** for you, just H4309
Jdg 6:31 Whoever **f** for him shall be put to death H8189
Isa 30:32 *as he* **f** them in battle *with* the blows of H4309
Zec 14: 3 those nations, as he **f** on a day of battle. H4309
Jas 4: 1 What causes **f** and quarrels among you *G4483*

FIGS (25) [FIG]

Nu 13:23 along with some pomegranates and **f**. H9300
Nu 20: 5 It has no grain or **f**, grapevines or H9300
1Sa 25:18 two hundred **cakes of pressed f**, H1811
1Sa 30:12 part of a **cake of pressed f** and two cakes H1811
2Sa 16: 1 a hundred **cakes of f** and a skin of wine. H7811
2Ki 20: 7 "Prepare a poultice *of* **f**." They did so and H9300
Ne 13:15 **f** and all other kinds of loads. H9300
Isa 28: 4 will be like **f ripe** before harvest—as H1136
Isa 34: 4 the vine, like shriveled **f** from the fig tree. NDT
Isa 38:21 "Prepare a poultice of **f** and apply it to the H9300
Jer 8:13 There will be no **f** on the tree, and their H9300
Jer 24: 1 me two baskets of **f** placed in front of the H9300
Jer 24: 2 One basket had very good **f**, like those that H9300
Jer 24: 2 the other basket had very bad **f**, so bad H9300
Jer 24: 3 "**F**," I answered. "The good H9300
Jer 24: 5 'Like these good **f**, I regard as good the H9300
Jer 24: 8 " 'But like the bad **f**, which are so bad H9300
Jer 29:17 will make them like **f** that are so bad they H9300
Mic 7: 1 none of the **early f** that I crave. H1136
Na 3:12 the **f** fall into the mouth of the eater. NDT
Mt 7:16 from thornbushes, or **f** from thistles? *G5192*
Mk 11:13 because it was not the season *for* **f**. *G5192*
Lk 6:44 People do not pick **f** from thornbushes, or *G5192*
Jas 3:12 fig tree bear olives, or a grapevine bear **f**? *G5192*
Rev 6:13 as **f** drop from a fig tree when shaken by a *G5190*

FIGURATIVELY (3) [FIGURE]

Jn 16:25 "Though I have been speaking **f**, *G1877+4231*
Gal 4:24 These things are *being* **taken f**: The *G251*
Rev 11: 8 which is **f** called Sodom and Egypt *G4462*

FIGURE (7) [FIGURATIVELY, FIGURES]

Ge 29:17 Rachel had a lovely **f** and was beautiful. H9307
1Sa 28:13 "I see a **ghostly f** coming up out of the H466
Est 2: 7 had a lovely **f** and was beautiful. H9307
Eze 1:26 on the throne was a **f** like that of a man. H1952
Eze 8: 2 I looked, and I saw a **f** like that of a man H1952
Jn 7: 4 wants to become a public **f** acts in secret. *G899*
Jn 10: 6 Jesus used this **f of speech**, but the *G4231*

FIGUREHEAD (1) [HEAD]

Ac 28:11 Alexandrian ship *with* the **f** of the twin *G4185*

FIGURES (3) [FIGURE]

2Ch 4: 3 Below the rim, **f** *of* bulls encircled it—ten H1952
Eze 23:14 on a wall, **f** *of* Chaldeans portrayed in red, H7512
Jn 16:29 speaking clearly and without **f of speech**. *G4231*

FILIGREE (6)

Ex 28:11 Then mount the stones in gold **f** settings H5401
Ex 28:13 Make gold **f settings** H5401
Ex 28:20 Mount them in gold **f settings**. H8687
Ex 39: 6 onyx stones in gold **f** settings and H5401
Ex 39:13 They were mounted in gold **f** settings. H5401
Ex 39:16 made two gold **f settings** and two gold H5401

FILL (70) [FILLED, FILLING, FILLS, FULL, FULLNESS, FULLY]

Ge 1:22 in number and **f** the water in the seas, H4848
Ge 1:28 in number; **f** the earth and subdue it. H4848
Ge 9: 1 increase in number and **f** the earth. H4848
Ge 42:25 gave orders *to* **f** their bags *with* grain, H4848
Ge 44: 1 "**F** the men's sacks *with* as much food as H4848
Ex 2:16 to draw water and **f** the troughs to water H4848
Ex 10: 6 *They will* **f** your houses and those of all H4848
Lev 25:19 you will eat your **f** and live there in H8427
Dt 28:67 of the terror that *will* **f** your hearts and the H7064
Dt 31:20 when they eat *their* **f** and thrive, they H8425
1Sa 16: 1 **F** your horn *with* oil and be on your way; H4848
1Ki 18:33 "**F** four large jars *with* water and pour it on H4848
2Ki 3:16 I *will* **f** this valley *with* pools of water H6913
Job 8:21 *He will* yet **f** your mouth *with* laughter H4848
Job 15: 2 notions or **f** their belly *with* the hot east H4848
Job 15:21 Terrifying sounds **f** his ears; when all H928
Job 15:24 Distress and anguish **f** him **with terror** H1286
Job 23: 4 him and **f** my mouth *with* arguments. H4848
Job 41: 7 *Can you* **f** its hide with harpoons or its H4848
Ps 4: 7 **F** my heart *with* joy when their grain and H5989
Ps 16:11 you will **f** me *with* joy in your presence H8427
Ps 17:14 *May* what you have stored up for the wicked **f** H4848
Ps 74:20 haunts of violence **f** the dark places of the H4848
Ps 81:10 Open wide your mouth and *I will* **f** it. H4848
Ps 129: 7 a reaper cannot **f** his hands *with* it, nor H4848
Ps 129: 7 nor one who gathers **f** his arms. NDT
Pr 1:13 things and **f** our houses *with* plunder; H4848
Pr 12:21 the wicked **have** *their* **f** *of* trouble. H4848
Pr 26:25 seven abominations **f** their hearts. H928
Pr 28:19 fantasies *will* **have** *their* **f** *of* poverty. H8425
Ecc 1: 8 of seeing, nor the ear *its* **f** of hearing. H4848
SS 5: 1 and drink; **drink** *your* **f** *of* love. H8910
Isa 13:21 lie there, jackals *will* **f** her houses; there H4848
Isa 27: 6 blossom and **f** all the world *with* fruit. H4848
Isa 33: 5 *he will* **f** Zion *with* his justice and H4848
Isa 34: 5 My sword *has* **drunk its f** in the heavens H8115
Isa 44:16 he roasts his meat and **eats** *his* **f**. H8425
Isa 56:12 *Let us* **drink** *our* **f** *of* beer! And H6010
Isa 65:11 Fortune and **f** bowls of mixed wine H4848
Jer 13:13 *I am going to* **f** *with* drunkenness all who H4848
Jer 23:16 they **f** you **with false hopes**. H2038
Jer 23:24 "*Do* not I **f** heaven and earth? H4848

Jer 46:12 of your shame; your cries will f the earth. H4848
Jer 50:10 all who plunder her will have their f," H8425
Jer 51:14 I will surely f you with troops, as with a H4848
Eze 3: 3 am giving you and f your stomach with it." H4848
Eze 7:19 satisfy their hunger or f their stomachs, H4848
Eze 8:17 Must they also f the land with violence H4848
Eze 9: 7 the temple and f the courts with the slain. H4848
Eze 10: 2 F your hands with burning coals from H4848
Eze 20:26 that I might f them with horror so they H9037
Eze 24: 4 F it with the best of these bones; H4848
Eze 30:11 Egypt and f the land with the slain. H4848
Eze 32: 5 and f the valleys with your remains H4848
Eze 35: 8 I will f your mountains with the slain H4848
Eze 39:20 At my table you will eat your f of horses H8425
Da 7: 5 was told, 'Get up and eat your f of flesh! A10678
Zep 1: 9 who f the temple of their gods with H4848
Zep 2:14 windows, rubble will f the doorways, the H928
Hag 1: 6 but never have your f. You put on H8910
Hag 2: 7 and I will f this house with glory,' H4848
Zec 9:13 as I bend my bow and f it with Ephraim. H4848
Lk 15:16 He longed to f his stomach with the pods G1153
Jn 2: 7 to the servants, "F the jars with water"; G1153
Jn 6:26 you ate the loaves and had your f. G5963
Ac 2:28 you will f me with joy in your presence. G4444
Ro 15:13 May the God of hope f you with all joy G4444
Eph 4:10 heavens, in order to f the whole universe.) G4444
Col 1: 9 ask God to f you with the knowledge of G4444
Col 1:24 and I f up in my flesh what is still lacking in G499

FILLED (183) [FILL]

Ge 6:13 the earth is f with violence because of H4848
Ge 21:19 she went and f the skin with water and H4848
Ge 24:16 the spring, f her jar and came up again. H4848
Ex 1: 7 numerous that the land was f with them. H4848
Ex 16:12 in the morning you will be f with bread. H8425
Ex 31: 3 and I have f him with the Spirit of God H4848
Ex 35:31 and he has f him with the Spirit of God H4848
Ex 35:35 He has f them with skill to do all kinds of H4848
Ex 40:34 the glory of the LORD f the tabernacle. H4848
Ex 40:35 the glory of the LORD f the tabernacle. H4848
Lev 19:29 to prostitution and be f with wickedness. H4848
Nu 7:13 each f with the finest flour mixed with H4849
Nu 7:14 dish weighing ten shekels, f with incense; H4849
Nu 7:19 each f with the finest flour mixed with H4849
Nu 7:20 weighing ten shekels, f with incense; H4849
Nu 7:25 each f with the finest flour mixed with H4849
Nu 7:26 weighing ten shekels, f with incense; H4849
Nu 7:31 each f with the finest flour mixed with H4849
Nu 7:32 weighing ten shekels, f with incense; H4849
Nu 7:37 each f with the finest flour mixed with H4849
Nu 7:38 weighing ten shekels, f with incense; H4849
Nu 7:43 each f with the finest flour mixed with H4849
Nu 7:44 weighing ten shekels, f with incense; H4849
Nu 7:49 each f with the finest flour mixed with H4849
Nu 7:50 weighing ten shekels, f with incense; H4849
Nu 7:55 each f with the finest flour mixed with H4849
Nu 7:56 weighing ten shekels, f with incense; H4849
Nu 7:61 each f with the finest flour mixed with H4849
Nu 7:62 weighing ten shekels, f with incense; H4849
Nu 7:67 each f with the finest flour mixed with H4849
Nu 7:68 weighing ten shekels, f with incense; H4849
Nu 7:73 each f with the finest flour mixed with H4849
Nu 7:74 weighing ten shekels, f with incense; H4849
Nu 7:79 each f with the finest flour mixed with H4849
Nu 7:80 weighing ten shekels, f with incense; H4849
Nu 7:86 gold dishes f with incense weighed H4849
Nu 22: 3 Moab was f with dread because of the H7762
Dt 6:11 houses f with all kinds of good things you H4849
Dt 28:66 suspense, f with dread both night and day H7064
Dt 32:15 fat and kicked; f with food, they became H9042
Dt 32:32 Their grapes are f with poison, and their AIT
Dt 34: 9 Joshua son of Nun was f with the spirit of H4848
Jos 9:13 And these wineskins that we f were new H4848
Ru 2: 9 drink from the water jars the men have f." H8612
1Sa 5:11 death had f the city with H2118+928+3972
1Sa 28: 5 he was afraid; terror f his heart. H3006+4394
1Sa 28:20 f with fear because of Samuel's H3707+4394
1Ki 7:14 Huram was f with wisdom, with H4848
1Ki 8:10 the cloud f the temple of the LORD. H4848
1Ki 8:11 the glory of the LORD f his temple. H4848
1Ki 11:27 the terraces and had f in the gap in the H6037
1Ki 18:35 around the altar and even f the trench. H4848
2Ki 3:17 this valley will be f with water, and H4848
2Ki 3:20 And the land was f with water. H4848
2Ki 4: 4 and as each is f, put it to one side." H4849
2Ki 21:16 blood that he f Jerusalem from end H4848
2Ki 24: 4 For he had f Jerusalem with innocent H4848
2Ch 5:13 temple of the LORD was f with the cloud, H4848
2Ch 5:14 the glory of the LORD f the temple of God. H4848
2Ch 7: 1 the glory of the LORD f the temple. H4848
2Ch 7: 2 the LORD because the glory of the LORD f it. H4848
Ezr 6:22 the LORD had f them with joy by changing H8523
Ezr 9:11 practices they have f it with their H4848
Ne 9:25 of houses f with all kinds of good H4849
Est 5: 9 he was f with rage against Mordecai. H4848
Job 3:15 had gold, who f their houses with silver. H4848
Job 3:22 who are f with gladness and H8524+448+1637
Job 20:23 When he has f his belly, God will vent his H4848
Job 22:18 it was he who f their houses with good H4848
Job 31:31 'Who has not been f with Job's meat? H8425
Ps 5: 9 can be trusted; their heart is f with malice. NDT
Ps 38: 7 My back is f with searing pain; there is no H4848
Ps 48:10 your right hand is f with righteousness. H4848
Ps 65: 4 We are f with the good things of your H8425
Ps 65: 8 The whole earth is f with awe at your H3707
Ps 65: 9 streams of God are f with water to provide H4849
Ps 71: 8 My mouth is f with your praise, declaring H4848
Ps 72:19 may the whole earth be f with his glory. H4848
Ps 80: 9 and it took root and f the land. H4848
Ps 119:64 The earth is f with your love, LORD; teach H4848
Ps 126: 2 were f with laughter, our tongues with H4848
Ps 126: 3 great things for us, and we are f with joy. H8524
Ps 144:13 Our barns will be f with every kind of H4849
Pr 1:31 fruit of their ways and be f with the fruit of H8425
Pr 3:10 then your barns will be f to overflowing H4848
Pr 7:20 He took his purse f with money and will not AIT
Pr 8:30 I was f with delight day after day H9141
Pr 12:14 of their lips people are f with good things, H8425
Pr 13: 4 A sluggard's appetite is never f, but the AIT
Pr 18:20 of their mouth a person's stomach is f; H8425
Pr 24: 4 its rooms are f with rare and beautiful H4848
Ecc 8:11 people's hearts are f with schemes to do H4848
Isa 6: 1 the train of his robe f the temple. H4848
Isa 6: 4 shook and the temple was f with smoke. H4848
Isa 11: 9 the earth will be f with the knowledge H4848
Isa 41:23 so that we will be dismayed and f with fear. AIT
Isa 51:20 They are f with the wrath of the LORD, with H4849
Jer 6: 6 be punished; it is f with oppression. H928+7931
Jer 13:12 Every wineskin should be f with wine.' H4848
Jer 13:12 that every wineskin should be f with wine? H4848
Jer 15:17 on me and you had f me with indignation H4848
Jer 16:18 and have f my inheritance with their H4848
Jer 19: 4 and they have f this place with the blood H4848
Jer 25:15 from my hand this cup f with the wine of my AIT
Jer 31:14 my people will be f with my bounty," H8425
Jer 33: 5 'They will be f with the dead bodies of H4848
Jer 41: 9 son of Nethaniah f it with the dead. H4848
Jer 50: 2 will be put to shame, Marduk f with terror. H3169
Jer 50: 2 put to shame and her idols f with terror. H3169
Jer 50:36 They will be f with terror. H3169
Jer 51:34 swallowed us and f his stomach with our H4848
La 3:15 He has f me with bitter herbs and given H8425
La 3:30 strike him, and let him be f with disgrace. H8425
Eze 10: 3 went in, and a cloud f the inner court. H4848
Eze 10: 4 The cloud f the temple, and the court was H4848
Eze 11: 6 in this city and f its streets with the dead. H4848
Eze 16:30 " 'I am f with fury against you H582+4226
Eze 23:33 You will be f with drunkenness and sorrow H4848
Eze 27:25 You are f with heavy cargo as you sail the H4848
Eze 28:16 trade you were f with violence, H4848
Eze 32: 6 the ravines will be f with your flesh. H4848
Eze 36:38 ruined cities be f with flocks of people. H4849
Eze 43: 5 the glory of the LORD f the temple. H4848
Da 2:35 a huge mountain and f the whole earth. A10416
Da 11:12 South will be f with pride and will H8123+4222
Joel 2:24 The threshing floors will be f with grain H4848
Am 4:10 f your nostrils with the stench of your H6590
Mic 3: 8 But as for me, I am f with power, with the H4848
Na 1: 2 LORD takes vengeance and is f with wrath. H1251
Hab 2:14 For the earth will be f with the knowledge H4848
Hab 2:16 You will be f with shame instead of glory H8425
Hab 3: 3 the heavens and his praise f the earth. H4848
Zec 8: 5 The city streets will be f with boys and girls H4848
Mt 5: 6 thirst for righteousness, for they will be f. G5963
Mt 9: 8 saw this, they were f with awe; and they G5828
Mt 17:23 And the disciples were f with grief. G5379
Mt 22:10 the wedding hall was f with guests. G4398
Mt 27:48 He f it with wine vinegar, put it on a staff G4398
Mt 28: 8 the tomb, afraid yet f with joy, and ran to G3489
Mk 15:36 f a sponge with wine vinegar G1153
Lk 1:15 and he will be f with the Holy Spirit even G4398
Lk 1:41 Elizabeth was f with the Holy Spirit. G4398
Lk 1:53 He has f the hungry with good things but G1855
Lk 1:65 All the neighbors were f with awe G1181+2093
Lk 1:67 father Zechariah was f with the Holy Spirit G4398
Lk 2:40 he was f with wisdom, and G4444
Lk 3: 5 Every valley shall be f in, every mountain G4444
Lk 5: 7 came and f both boats so full that they G4398
Lk 5:26 They were f with awe and said, "We have G4398
Lk 7:16 They were all f with awe and praised God. G3284
Lk 15:20 him and was f with compassion for him; G5072
Jn 2: 7 with water"; so they f them to the brim. G1153
Jn 6:13 gathered them and f twelve baskets with G1153
Jn 12: 3 And the house was f with the fragrance of G4444
Jn 16: 6 you are f with grief because I have said G4444
Ac 2: 2 came from heaven and f the whole house G4444
Ac 2: 4 All of them were f with the Holy Spirit and G4398
Ac 2:43 Everyone was f with awe at the many G1181
Ac 3:10 and they were f with wonder and G4398
Ac 4: 8 Then Peter, f with the Holy Spirit, said to G4398
Ac 4:31 And they were all f with the Holy Spirit G4398
Ac 5: 3 is it that Satan has so f your heart that you G4444
Ac 5:17 of the Sadducees, were f with jealousy. G4398
Ac 5:28 "Yet you have f Jerusalem with your G4444
Ac 9:17 see again and be f with the Holy Spirit." G4398
Ac 13: 9 was also called Paul, f with the Holy Spirit G4398
Ac 13:45 saw the crowds, they were f with jealousy. G4398
Ac 13:52 And the disciples were f with joy and with G4444
Ac 16:34 he was f with joy because he had come to G22
Ro 1:29 They have become f with every kind of G4444
Ro 15:14 f with knowledge and competent to G4444
Eph 3:19 that you may be f to the measure of all the G4444
Eph 5:18 Instead, be f with the Spirit, G4444
Php 1:11 f with the fruit of righteousness that comes G4444
2Ti 1: 4 to see you, so that I may be f with joy. G4444
1Pe 1: 8 are f with an inexpressible and glorious joy G22+5915
Rev 8: 5 took the censer, f it with fire from the altar G1153
Rev 12:12 He is f with fury, because he knows that G2400
Rev 13: 3 whole world was f with wonder and G2513
Rev 15: 7 golden bowls f with the wrath of God, G1154
Rev 15: 8 And the temple was f with smoke from the G1153
Rev 16:19 gave her the cup f with the wine of the fury of AIT
Rev 17: 4 f with abominable things and the filth of G1154

FILLETED, FILLETS (KJV) BANDS

FILLING (3) [FILL]

Ge 26:15 Philistines stopped up, f them with earth. H4848
Eze 44: 4 the glory of the LORD f the temple of the H4848
Na 2:12 f his lairs with the kill and his dens with H4848

FILLS (6) [FILL]

Nu 14:21 as the glory of the LORD f the whole earth, H4848
Job 20:11 The youthful vigor that f his bones will lie H4848
Job 36:32 He f his hands with lightning and H4059
Ps 107: 9 thirsty and f the hungry with good things. H4848
Ac 14:17 plenty of food and f your hearts with joy." NDT
Eph 1:23 the fullness of him who f everything in G4444

FILTH (6) [FILTHINESS, FILTHY]

Pr 30:12 eyes and yet are not cleansed of their f; H7363
Isa 4: 4 wash away the f of the women of Zion H7363
Isa 28: 8 vomit and there is not a spot without f. H7363
Na 3: 6 I will pelt you with f, I will treat you with H9199
Jas 1:21 get rid of all moral f and the evil that is so G4864
Rev 17: 4 things and the f of her adulteries. G176

FILTHINESS (1) [FILTH]

La 1: 9 Her f clung to her skirts; she did not H3240

FILTHY (5) [FILTH]

Isa 64: 6 all our righteous acts are like f rags H6340
Zec 3: 3 was dressed in f clothes as he stood H7364
Zec 3: 4 before him, "Take off his f clothes. H7364
Col 3: 8 slander, and f language from your lips. G155
Jas 2: 2 a poor man in f old clothes also G4865

FINAL (7) [FINALITY, FINALLY]

Nu 23:10 righteous, and may my f end be like theirs!" H344
Ru 4: 7 transfer of property to become f, H7756
Ps 73:17 then I understood their f destiny. H344
Isa 41:22 consider them and know their f outcome. H344
Mt 12:45 And the f condition of that person is G2274
Lk 11:26 And the f condition of that person is G2274
Ac 28:25 after Paul had made this f statement: G1651S

FINALITY (1) [FINAL]

Ro 9:28 his sentence on earth with speed and f." G5334

FINALLY (33) [FINAL]

Nu 10:25 F, as the rear guard for all the units, the H2256
Jdg 9:14 "F all the trees said to the thornbush H2256
Jdg 14:17 So on the seventh day he f told her NDT
1Sa 10:21 F Saul son of Kish was taken H2256
1Sa 19:22 F, he himself left for Ramah and H2256+1685
2Sa 24: 7 F, they went on to Beersheba in the H2256
1Ki 17:17 and worse, and f stopped breathing. H6330+889
1Ki 22:21 F, a spirit came forward, stood before the H2256
2Ch 18:20 F, a spirit came forward, stood before the H2256
Ne 2:15 F, I turned back and reentered through the H2256
Ps 39: 6 up wealth without knowing whose it will f be. AIT
Da 2:40 F, there will be a fourth kingdom, strong A10221
Da 4: 8 F, Daniel came into my A10221+10527+10024
Da 6: 5 F these men said, "We will never find A10008
Da 12: 7 of the holy people has been f broken, H3983
Mt 22:27 F, the woman died. G5731+4246
Mt 26:60 came forward. F two came forward G5731
Mk 6:21 F the opportune time came. On his G2779
Lk 18: 4 But f he said to himself, 'Even G3552+4047
Lk 20:32 F, the woman died too. G5731
Jn 1:22 F they said, "Who are you? Give us an G4036
Jn 7:45 F the temple guards went back to the G4036
Jn 19:16 F Pilate handed him over to them G5538+4036
Jn 20: 8 F the other disciple, who had G5538+4036
Ac 16:18 F Paul became so annoyed that he turned G1254
Ac 20: 2 to the people, and f arrived in Greece, AIT
Ac 27:20 we f gave up all hope of being saved. G3370
1Co 11:32 so that we will not be f condemned with G2891
2Co 13:11 F, brothers and sisters, rejoice! Strive for G3370
Eph 6:10 F, be strong in the Lord and in his G3836+3370
Php 4: 8 F, brothers and sisters, whatever is G3836+3370
Jas 5:11 have seen what the Lord f brought about. G5465
1Pe 3: 8 F, all of you, be like-minded, be G3836+5465

FINANCIAL (1)

1Ti 6: 5 think that godliness is a means to f gain. G4516

FIND (239) [FINDING, FINDS, FOUND]

Ge 8: 9 But the dove could f nowhere to perch H5162
Ge 18:26 "If I f fifty righteous people in the city of H5162
Ge 18:28 "If I f forty-five there," he said, "I will not H5162
Ge 18:30 "I will not do it if I f thirty there." H5162
Ge 19:11 so that they could not f the door. H5162
Ge 27:20 his son, "How did you f it so quickly, my H5162
Ge 31:32 But if you f anyone who has your gods H5162
Ge 31:35 searched but could not f the household H5162
Ge 32: 5 to my lord, that I may f favor in your eyes. H5162

Ge 33: 8 "To f favor in your eyes, my lord," he said H5162
Ge 33:15 "Just let me f favor in the eyes of my lord." H5162
Ge 34:11 brothers, "Let me f favor in your eyes H5162
Ge 38:20 from the woman, but he did not f her. H5162
Ge 38:22 back to Judah and said, "I didn't f her. H5162
Ge 38:23 her this young goat, but you didn't f her." H5162
Ge 41:38 "Can we f anyone like this man H5162
Ge 44:15 me can f things out by divination?" H5727+5727
Ge 47:25 "May we f favor in the eyes of our lord; we H5162
Ex 5:11 get your own straw wherever you can f it, H5162
Ex 16:25 You will not f any of it on the ground H5162
Ex 33:13 know you and continue to f favor with you. H5162
Lev 6: 3 if they f lost property and lie about it, or H5162
Nu 9: 8 "Wait until I f out what the LORD H9048
Nu 10:33 those three days to f them a place to rest. H9365
Nu 22:19 here so that I can f out what else the H3359
Nu 32:23 may be sure that your sin will f you out. H5162
Dt 4:29 you will f him if you seek him with all your H5162
Dt 13: 3 is testing you to f out whether you love H3359
Dt 14:21 Do not eat anything you f already dead. NDT
Dt 22: 3 Do the same if you f their donkey or cloak NDT
Dt 22:14 I did not f proof of her virginity, H5162
Dt 22:17 'I did not f your daughter to be a virgin. H5162
Dt 28:65 Among those nations you will f no repose H8089
Jos 2:16 to the hills so the pursuers will not f you. H7003
Jos 20: 3 may flee there and f protection from the H2118
Jdg 18: 8 asked them, "How did you f things?" H4537
Jdg 18:10 you will f an unsuspecting people H995+448
Ru 1: 9 that each of you will f rest in the home of H5162
Ru 2: 2 behind anyone in whose eyes I f favor." H5162
Ru 2:13 "May I continue to f favor in your eyes, my H5162
Ru 3: 1 "My daughter, I must f a home for you H1335
Ru 3:18 daughter, until you f out what happens. H3359
1Sa 1:18 "May your servant f favor in your eyes." H5162
1Sa 9: 4 around Shalisha, but they did not f them. H5162
1Sa 9: 4 of Benjamin, but they did not f them. H5162
1Sa 9:13 you will f him before he goes up to the H5162
1Sa 9:13 up now; you should f him about this time." H5162
1Sa 14:38 and let us f out what sin has H3359+2256+8011
1Sa 16:17 "F someone who plays well and bring him H8011
1Sa 17:56 "F out whose son this young man is." H8626
1Sa 19: 3 about you and will tell you what I f out." H8011
1Sa 20:21 will send a boy and say, 'Go, f the arrows. H5162
1Sa 20:36 to the boy, "Run and f the arrows I shoot." H5162
1Sa 21: 3 loaves of bread, or whatever you can f." H5162
1Sa 23:16 and helped him f strength in H2616+906+3338
1Sa 23:22 F out where David usually H3359+2256+8011
1Sa 23:23 F out about all the hiding H8011+2256+3359
1Sa 25: 8 son David whatever you can f for them. H5162
1Sa 28: 7 "F me a woman who is a medium H1335
2Sa 3:25 movements and f out everything you are H3359
2Sa 11: 3 David sent someone to f out about her. H2011
2Sa 15:25 If I f favor in the LORD's eyes, he will bring H5162
2Sa 16: 4 "May I f favor in your eyes, my lord the H5162
2Sa 20: 6 or he will f fortified cities and escape from H5162
1Ki 18: 5 Maybe we can f some grass to keep the H5162
1Ki 18:10 he made them swear they could not f you. H5162
1Ki 18:12 If I go and tell Ahab and he doesn't f you H5162
1Ki 22:25 "You will f out on the day you go to hide H8011
2Ki 2:17 searched for three days but did not f him. H5162
2Ki 6:13 f out where he is," the king ordered H8011
2Ki 7:13 let us send them to f out what happened." H8011
2Ki 7:14 "Go and f out what has happened." H8011
2Ch 18:24 "You will f out on the day you go to hide H8011
2Ch 20:16 and you will f them at the end of the H5162
2Ch 32: 4 of Assyria come and f plenty of water?" H5162
Ezr 2:62 they could not f them and so were H5162
Ezr 4:15 In these records you will f that this city is A10708
Ne 5: 8 because they could f nothing to say. H5162
Ne 7:64 they could not f them and so were H5162
Est 2:11 of the harem to f out how Esther was and H3359
Est 4: 5 ordered him to f out what was H3359
Job 5:24 of your property and f nothing missing. H2627
Job 8: 8 generation and f out what their ancestors H3922
Job 9:14 How can I f words to argue with him? H1047
Job 17:10 I will not f a wise man among you. H5162
Job 22:26 Surely then you will f delight in the H6695
Job 23: 3 If only I knew where to f him; if only I H5162
Job 23: 5 I would f out what he would answer me H3359
Job 23: 8 if I go to the west, I do not f him. H1067
Job 27:10 Will they f delight in the Almighty? Will H6695
Job 32:20 I must speak and f relief; I must open my H8118
Job 33:26 can pray to God and f favor with him, H8354
Ps 17: 3 you will f that I have planned no evil H5162
Ps 22: 2 do not answer, by night, but I f no rest. H4200
Ps 62: 5 my soul, f rest in God; my hope comes H1957
Ps 91: 4 under his wings you will f refuge; his H2879
Ps 112: 1 who f great delight in his commands. H2911
Ps 119:35 of your commands, for there I f delight. H2911
Ps 119:52 your ancient laws, and I f comfort in them. H5714
Ps 132: 5 till I f a place for the LORD, a dwelling for H5162
Pr 1:28 they will look for me but will not f me, H5162
Pr 2: 5 of the LORD and f the knowledge of God H5162
Pr 3:13 Blessed are those who f wisdom, those H5162
Pr 4:22 are life to those who f them and health H5162
Pr 8:17 love me, and those who seek me f me. H5162
Pr 8:35 For those who f me find life and receive H5162
Pr 8:35 For those who find me f life and receive H5162
Pr 8:36 But those who fail to f me harm H2627
Pr 11: 1 accurate weights f favor with him. H8356
Pr 14: 7 for you will not f knowledge on their lips. H3359
Pr 14:22 plan what is good f love and faithfulness NDT
Pr 18: 2 Fools f no pleasure in understanding but H2911
Pr 20: 4 so at harvest time they look but f nothing. NDT
Pr 20: 6 but a faithful person who can f? H5162
Pr 23:35 will I wake up so I can f another drink?" H1335
Pr 24:14 If you f it, there is a future hope for you H5162
Pr 25:16 If you f honey, eat just enough—too H5162
Pr 31:10 A wife of noble character who can f? She H5162
Ecc 2: 1 you with pleasure to f out what is good." H8011
Ecc 2:24 to eat and drink and f satisfaction in their H8011
Ecc 2:25 without him, who can eat or f enjoyment? H2591
Ecc 3:13 and f satisfaction in all their toil H8011
Ecc 5:18 to drink and to f satisfaction in their H8011
Ecc 7:26 I f more bitter than death the woman who H5162
Ecc 12: 1 you will say, "I f no pleasure in them"— H4200
Ecc 12:10 Teacher searched to f just the right words, H5162
SS 3: 1 I looked for him but did not f him. H5162
SS 3: 2 So I looked for him but did not f him. H5162
SS 5: 6 I looked for him but did not f him. I called H5162
SS 5: 8 I charge you—if you f my beloved, what H5162
Isa 14:30 The poorest of the poor will f pasture, and H8286
Isa 14:32 in her his afflicted people will f refuge." H2879
Isa 23:12 to Cyprus; even there you will f no rest." H5663
Isa 34:14 also lie down and f for themselves places H5162
Isa 41:12 your enemies, you will not f them. H5162
Isa 45:25 of Israel will f deliverance in the LORD and H7405
Isa 49: 9 beside the roads and f pasture on every NDT
Isa 57: 2 into peace; they f rest as they lie in death. H5663
Isa 58:14 then you will f your joy in the LORD, and I H6695
Isa 59:11 look for justice, but f none; for deliverance, NDT
Jer 2: 5 "What fault did your ancestors f in me H5162
Jer 2:24 themselves; at mating time they will f her. H5162
Jer 5: 1 If you can f but one person who deals H5162
Jer 6:10 offensive to them; they f no pleasure in it. H2911
Jer 6:16 and you will f rest for your souls. H5162
Jer 14: 3 they go to the cisterns but f no water. H5162
Jer 23:11 even in my temple I f their wickedness," H5162
Jer 29: 6 f wives for your sons and give your H4374
Jer 29:13 will seek me and f me when you seek me H5162
Jer 31: 2 who survive the sword will f favor in the H5162
Jer 45: 3 I am worn out with groaning and f no rest. H5162
La 1: 6 Her princes are like deer that f no pasture H5162
La 2: 9 prophets no longer f visions from the LORD. H5162
La 5: 5 at our heels; we are weary and f no rest. H5663
Eze 17:23 they will f shelter in the shade of its H8905
Da 6: 4 the satraps tried to f grounds for charges A10708
Da 6: 4 They could f no corruption in him A10708
Da 6: 5 "We will never f any basis for charges A10708
Hos 2: 6 wall her in so that she cannot f her way. H5162
Hos 2: 7 she will look for them but not f them. H5162
Hos 5: 6 seek the LORD, they will not f him; he has H5162
Hos 12: 8 all my wealth they will not f in me any H5162
Hos 14: 3 in you the fatherless f compassion." H8163
Am 8:12 the word of the LORD, but they will not f it. H5162
Jnh 1: 7 let us cast lots to f out who is responsible H3359
Na 3: 7 Where can I f anyone to comfort you?" H1335
Zep 2: 7 people of Judah; there they will f pasture. H8286
Zec 2: 2 to f out how wide and how long it is." H8011
Mt 2: 8 As soon as you f him, report to me, so G2351
Mt 7: 7 seek and you will f; knock and the G2351
Mt 7:14 leads to life, and only a few f it. G1639+2351
Mt 10:39 loses their life for my sake will f it. G2351
Mt 11:29 in heart, and you will f rest for your souls. G2351
Mt 12:43 arid places seeking rest and does not f it. G2351
Mt 16:25 whoever loses their life for me will f it. G2351
Mt 17:27 its mouth and you will f a four-drachma G2351
Mt 21: 2 at once you will f a donkey tied there G2351
Mt 22: 9 invite to the banquet anyone you f. G2351
Mt 22:10 gathered all the people they could f, G2351
Mt 26:60 But they did not f any, though many false G2351
Mk 11: 2 as you enter it, you will f a colt tied there G2351
Mk 11:13 he went to f out if it had any fruit. G2351
Mk 13:36 suddenly, do not let him f you sleeping. G2351
Mk 14:55 put him to death, but they did not f any. G2351
Lk 1:62 Then they made signs to his father, to f out AIT
Lk 2:12 You will f a baby wrapped in cloths and G2351
Lk 2:45 When they did not f him, they went back G2351
Lk 5:19 When they could not f a way to do this G2351
Lk 9:12 countryside and f food and lodging, G2351
Lk 11: 9 seek and you will f; knock and the G2351
Lk 11:24 arid places seeking rest and does not f it. G2351
Lk 13: 6 to look for fruit on it but did not f any. G2351
Lk 18: 8 Man comes, will he f faith on the earth?" G2351
Lk 19:15 in order to f out what they had gained G1182
Lk 19:30 as you enter it, you will f a colt tied there G2351
Lk 19:48 Yet they could not f any way to do it G2351
Lk 23: 4 "I f no basis for a charge against this man." G2351
Lk 24: 3 they did not f the body of the Lord Jesus. G2351
Lk 24:23 didn't f his body. They came and told G2351
Jn 1:41 thing Andrew did was to f his brother G2351
Jn 4:27 were surprised to f him talking with a G4022
Jn 7:17 do the will of God will f out whether my G1182
Jn 7:34 me, but you will not f me; and where I G2351
Jn 7:35 man intend to go that we cannot f him? G2351
Jn 7:36 me, but you will not f me,' and 'Where G2351
Jn 7:51 hearing him to f out what he has been G1182
Jn 7:52 and you will f that a prophet does not G2623
Jn 10: 9 will come in and go out, and f pasture. G2351
Jn 18:38 "I f no basis for a charge against him. G2351
Jn 19: 4 to let you know that I f no basis for a G2351
Jn 19: 6 I f no basis for a charge against him." G2351
Jn 21: 6 right side of the boat and you will f some." G2351
Ac 5:22 the jail, the officers did not f them there. G2351
Ac 5:39 you will only f yourselves fighting against G2351
Ac 7:11 our ancestors could not f food. G2351
Ac 12:19 search made for him and did not f him, G2351
Ac 16:13 where we expected to f a place of prayer. G1639
Ac 17: 6 But when they did not f them, they G2351
Ac 17:27 perhaps reach out for him and f him, G2351
Ac 22:24 in order to f out why the people were G2105
Ac 22:30 commander wanted to f out exactly why G1182
Ac 23: 9 "We f nothing wrong with this man," G2351
Ac 24:12 My accusers did not f me arguing with G2351
Ac 24:25 You may leave. When I f it convenient, G3561
Ro 7:21 So I f this law at work: Although I want to G2351
1Co 4:19 then I will f out not only how these G1182
2Co 2:13 because I did not f my brother Titus there. G2351
2Co 9: 4 come with me and f you unprepared, G2351
2Co 12:20 when I come I may not f you as I want G2351
2Co 12:20 you may not f me as you want me to G2351
Gal 2:17 we Jews f ourselves also among the G2351
Eph 5:10 and f out what pleases the Lord. G1507
1Th 3: 5 no longer, I sent to f out about your faith. G1182
2Ti 1:18 the Lord grant that he will f mercy from G2351
Heb 4:16 receive mercy and f grace to help us in G2351
Jas 3:16 there you f disorder and every evil practice. NDT
1Pe 1:11 trying to f out the time and circumstances G2236
2Jn 4 me great joy to f some of your children G2351
Rev 9: 6 people will seek death but will not f it; G2351

FINDING (11) [FIND]

Ex 15:22 they traveled in the desert without f water. H5162
Jos 2:22 the road and returned without f them. H5162
Jdg 5:30 'Are they not f and dividing the spoils: H5162
Jdg 15:15 F a fresh jawbone of a donkey, he grabbed H5162
Job 36:26 The number of his years is past f out. H2984
Ps 107: 4 f no way to a city where they could settle. H5162
Ecc 7:28 while I was still searching but not f—I H5162
Hos 9:10 it was like f grapes in the desert NDT
Jn 1:43 to leave for Galilee. F Philip, he said to G2351
Ac 5:10 men came in and, f her dead, carried her G2351
Jas 1: 5 who gives generously to all without f fault, G3943

FINDS (38) [FIND]

Ge 4:14 the earth, and whoever f me will kill me." H5162
Lev 13:36 and if he f that the sore has spread in the AIT
Nu 35:27 the avenger of blood f them outside the H5162
Dt 24: 1 to him because he f something indecent H5162
1Sa 10: 7 do whatever your hand f to do, for God is H5162
1Sa 24:19 When a man f his enemy, does he let him H5162
Job 33:20 their body f food repulsive and their soul H2299
Ps 55:15 of the dead, for evil f lodging among them. NDT
Ps 62: 1 Truly my soul f rest in God; my salvation NDT
Ps 119:162 in your promise like one who f great spoil. H5162
Pr 10:23 A fool f pleasure in wicked schemes, but H4200
Pr 10:32 lips of the righteous know what f favor, H8356
Pr 11:19 but whoever pursues evil f death. H4200
Pr 11:27 Whoever seeks good f favor, but evil H1335
Pr 14: 6 The mocker seeks wisdom and f none, but AIT
Pr 15:23 A person f joy in giving an apt reply—and NDT
Pr 18:22 He who f a wife finds what is good and H5162
Pr 18:22 He who finds a wife f what is good and H5162
Pr 21:21 pursues righteousness and love f life, H5162
Pr 28:13 confesses and renounces them f mercy. H8163
Ecc 9:10 Whatever your hand f to do, do it with all H5162
Isa 38:16 people live; and my spirit f life in them too. NDT
La 1: 3 the nations; she f no resting place. H5162
Mt 7: 8 the one who seeks f; and to the one who G2351
Mt 10:39 Whoever f their life will lose it, and G2351
Mt 12:44 When it arrives, it f the house unoccupied G2351
Mt 18:13 And if he f it, truly I tell you, he is G1181+2351
Mt 24:46 whose master f him doing so when he G2351
Lk 11:10 the one who seeks f; and to the one who G2351
Lk 11:25 it f the house swept clean and put in G2351
Lk 12:37 whose master f them watching when he G2351
Lk 12:38 servants whose master f them ready, G2351
Lk 12:43 whom the master f doing so when he G2351
Lk 15: 4 go after the lost sheep until he f it? G2351
Lk 15: 5 And when he f it, he joyfully puts it on his G2351
Lk 15: 8 house and search carefully until she f it? G2351
Lk 15: 9 And when she f it, she calls her friends G2351
Lk 22:16 it again until it f fulfillment in the G4444

FINE (80) [FINE-LOOKING, FINE-SOUNDING, FINED, FINELY, FINERY, FINES, FINEST]

Ge 41:42 him in robes of f linen and put a gold H9254
Ex 2: 2 When she saw that he was a f child, she H3202
Ex 9: 9 It will become f dust over the whole land of H85
Ex 25: 4 purple and scarlet yarn and f linen; goat H9254
Ex 28: 5 purple and scarlet yarn, and f linen. H9254
Ex 28:39 "Weave the tunic of f linen and make the H9254
Ex 28:39 fine linen and make the turban of f linen. H9254
Ex 30:23 "Take the following f spices: 500 shekels H8031
Ex 35: 6 purple and scarlet yarn and f linen; goat H9254
Ex 35:23 purple or scarlet yarn or f linen, or goat H9254
Ex 35:25 purple or scarlet yarn or f linen. H9254
Ex 35:35 purple and scarlet yarn and f linen, and H9254
Ex 38:23 purple and scarlet yarn and f linen.) H9254
Ex 39: 3 purple and scarlet yarn and f linen—the H9254
Ex 39:27 they made tunics of f linen—the work of a H9254
Ex 39:28 the turban of f linen, the linen caps H9254
Dt 3:25 Jordan—that f hill country and Lebanon." H3202
Dt 8:12 when you build f houses and settle down, H3202
Dt 9:21 it to powder as f as dust and threw the H1990
Dt 22:19 They shall f him a hundred shekels of H6740

1Sa 16:12 with health and had a f appearance and H3637
2Sa 22:43 *I* beat them as f as the dust of the earth; H8835
1Ki 10:18 with ivory and overlaid with f gold. H7059
2Ki 20:13 the spices and the f olive oil—his armory H3202
1Ch 15:27 David was clothed in a robe of f linen, H1009
1Ch 29: 2 all kinds of f stone and marble—all H3701
2Ch 2:14 blue and crimson yarn and f linen. H1009
2Ch 3: 5 covered it with f gold and decorated H3202
2Ch 3: 8 inside with six hundred talents of f gold. H3202
2Ch 3:14 purple and crimson yarn and f linen, with H1009
2Ch 5:12 dressed in f linen and playing cymbals H1009
Ezr 8:27 two f articles of polished bronze H3202
Est 8:15 of gold and a purple robe of f linen. H1009
Job 16: 4 *I could* make f speeches H2488+928+4863
Ps 18:42 *I* beat them as f as windblown dust; H8835
Ps 92:10 a wild ox; f oils have been poured on me. H8316
Pr 8:19 My fruit is better than f gold; what I yield H7058
Pr 17:26 If imposing a f on the innocent is not H6740
Pr 25:12 an ornament of f gold is the rebuke of H4188
Pr 31:22 she is clothed in f linen and purple. H9254
Ecc 7: 1 A good name is better than f perfume H9043
Isa 3:22 the f robes and the capes and cloaks, the H4711
Isa 3:24 instead of f clothing, sackcloth; instead H7345
Isa 5: 9 the f mansions left without H1524+2256+3202
Isa 19: 9 the weavers of f linen will lose hope. H2583
Isa 23:18 the LORD, for abundant food and f clothes. H6971
Isa 29: 5 many enemies will become like f dust, H1987
Isa 32:11 Strip off *your* f clothes and H7320+2256+6910
Isa 39: 2 the spices, the f olive oil—his entire H3202
Isa 40:15 the islands as though they were f dust. H1987
Jer 22: 7 will cut up your f cedar beams and throw H4436
La 4: 1 has lost its luster, the f gold become dull! H3202
Eze 16:10 dress and put sandals *of* f leather on you. H9391
Eze 16:10 I dressed you in f linen and covered you H9254
Eze 16:13 clothes were of f linen and costly fabric H9254
Eze 16:17 You also took the f jewelry I gave you, the H9514
Eze 16:39 take your f jewelry and leave you H9514
Eze 23:26 of your clothes and take your f jewelry. H9514
Eze 26:12 demolish your f houses and throw H2775
Eze 27: 7 F embroidered linen from Egypt was your H9254
Eze 27:16 f linen, coral and rubies H1009
Da 10: 5 with a belt of f gold *from* Uphaz around H4188
Zec 3: 4 your sin, and I will put f garments on you." H4711
Mt 11: 8 A man dressed in f clothes? No, G3434
Mt 11: 8 those who wear f clothes are in kings' G3434
Mt 13:45 is like a merchant looking for f pearls. G2819
Mk 7: 9 "You have a f way of setting aside the G2822
Lk 7:25 A man dressed in f clothes? No, G3434
Lk 13: 9 bears fruit next year, f! If not, then cut it G3525
Lk 16:19 in purple and f linen and lived in luxury G1116
Gal 4:18 It is f to be zealous, provided the purpose G2819
Jas 2: 2 wearing a gold ring and f clothes, G3287
Jas 2: 3 to the man wearing f clothes and say, G3287
1Pe 3: 3 of gold jewelry or f clothes. G1906+2668
Rev 18:12 stones and pearls; f linen, purple, G1115
Rev 18:13 olive oil, *of* f flour and wheat; cattle G4947
Rev 18:16 dressed in f linen, purple and scarlet, G1115
Rev 19: 8 F linen, bright and clean, was given her to G1115
Rev 19: 8 F linen stands for the righteous acts of G1115
Rev 19:14 on white horses and dressed in f linen, G1115

FINE-LOOKING (1) [FINE, LOOK]
1Sa 16:18 He speaks well and is a f man. H9307

FINE-SOUNDING (1) [FINE, SOUND]
Col 2: 4 no one may deceive you by f arguments. G4391

FINED (1) [FINE]
Ex 21:22 the offender must be f whatever H6740+6740

FINELY (22) [FINE]
Ex 26: 1 ten curtains of f twisted linen and blue, H8813
Ex 26:31 scarlet yarn and f twisted linen, H8813
Ex 26:36 scarlet yarn and f twisted linen— H8813
Ex 27: 9 is to have curtains of f twisted linen, H8813
Ex 27:16 scarlet yarn and f twisted linen— H8813
Ex 27:18 with curtains of f twisted linen five cubits H8813
Ex 28: 6 and of f twisted linen—the work of H8813
Ex 28: 8 scarlet yarn, and with f twisted linen. H8813
Ex 28:15 scarlet yarn, and of f twisted linen. H8813
Ex 36: 8 ten curtains of f twisted linen and blue, H8813
Ex 36:35 scarlet yarn and f twisted linen, H8813
Ex 36:37 scarlet yarn and f twisted linen— H8813
Ex 38: 9 long and had curtains of f twisted linen, H8813
Ex 38:16 the courtyard were of f twisted linen. H8813
Ex 38:18 scarlet yarn and f twisted linen— H8813
Ex 39: 2 scarlet yarn, and of f twisted linen. H8813
Ex 39: 5 and with f twisted linen, as the LORD H8813
Ex 39: 8 scarlet yarn, and of f twisted linen. H8813
Ex 39:24 scarlet yarn and f twisted linen around the H8813
Ex 39:28 the undergarments of f twisted linen. H8813
Ex 39:29 was made of f twisted linen and blue, H8813
Lev 16:12 two handfuls of f ground fragrant incense H1987

FINERY (2) [FINE]
2Sa 1:24 who clothed you in scarlet and f, who H6358
Isa 3:18 that day the Lord will snatch away their f: H9514

FINES (1) [FINE]
Am 2: 8 of their god they drink wine taken as f. H6711

FINEST (65) [FINE]
Ge 18: 6 three seahs of the f flour and knead it H6159
Ex 29: 2 And from the f wheat flour make round H6159
Ex 29:40 of an ephah of the f flour mixed with a H6159
Lev 2: 1 their offering is to be of the f flour. H6159
Lev 2: 4 in an oven, it is to consist of the f flour: H6159
Lev 2: 5 is to be made of the f flour mixed with oil, H6159
Lev 2: 7 to be made of the f flour and some olive H6159
Lev 5:11 of an ephah of the f flour for a sin offering H6159
Lev 6:15 a handful of the f flour and some olive oil H6159
Lev 6:20 of an ephah of the f flour as a regular H6159
Lev 7:12 loaves of the f flour well-kneaded and H6159
Lev 14:10 of an ephah of the f flour mixed with olive H6159
Lev 14:21 of an ephah of the f flour mixed with olive H6159
Lev 23:13 of an ephah of the f flour mixed with olive H6159
Lev 23:17 of two-tenths of an ephah of the f flour, H6159
Lev 24: 5 "Take the f flour and bake twelve loaves H6159
Nu 6:15 made with the f flour and without yeast— H6159
Nu 7:13 filled with the f flour mixed with olive H6159
Nu 7:19 filled with the f flour mixed with olive H6159
Nu 7:25 filled with the f flour mixed with olive H6159
Nu 7:31 filled with the f flour mixed with olive H6159
Nu 7:37 filled with the f flour mixed with olive H6159
Nu 7:43 filled with the f flour mixed with olive H6159
Nu 7:49 filled with the f flour mixed with olive H6159
Nu 7:55 filled with the f flour mixed with olive H6159
Nu 7:61 filled with the f flour mixed with olive H6159
Nu 7:67 filled with the f flour mixed with olive H6159
Nu 7:73 filled with the f flour mixed with olive H6159
Nu 7:79 filled with the f flour mixed with olive H6159
Nu 8: 8 offering of the f flour mixed with olive oil H6159
Nu 15: 4 of an ephah of the f flour mixed with a H6159
Nu 15: 6 of an ephah of the f flour mixed with a H6159
Nu 15: 9 an ephah of the f flour mixed with half a H6159
Nu 18:12 "I give you all the f olive oil and all the H2693
Nu 18:12 olive oil and all the f new wine and grain H2693
Nu 28: 5 of an ephah of the f flour mixed with a H6159
Nu 28: 9 of an ephah of the f flour mixed with olive H6159
Nu 28:12 of an ephah of the f flour mixed with oil; H6159
Nu 28:12 of an ephah of the f flour mixed with oil; H6159
Nu 28:13 of an ephah of the f flour mixed with oil. H6159
Nu 28:20 of an ephah of the f flour mixed with oil; H6159
Nu 28:28 of an ephah of the f flour mixed with oil; H6159
Nu 29: 3 of an ephah of the f flour mixed with olive H6159
Nu 29: 9 of an ephah of the f flour mixed with oil; H6159
Nu 29:14 of an ephah of the f flour mixed with oil; H6159
Dt 32:14 of Bashan and the f kernels of wheat. H2693
Dt 33:14 brings forth and the f the moon can yield; H4458
1Ki 4:22 thirty cors of the f flour and sixty cors of H6159
2Ki 7: 1 a seah of the f flour will sell for a shekel H6159
2Ki 7:16 So a seah of the f flour sold for a shekel H6159
2Ki 7:18 a seah of the f flour will sell for a shekel H6159
2Ki 8: 9 of all the f wares *of* Damascus. H3206
2Ki 19:23 remotest parts, the f of its forests. H4149+3623
Job 28:15 It cannot be bought with the f gold, nor H6034
Ps 81:16 But you would be fed with the f *of* wheat H2693
Ps 147:14 satisfies you with the f *of* wheat. H2693
SS 4:14 with myrrh and aloes and all the f spices. H8031
Isa 17:10 though you set out the f plants and plant H5846
Isa 25: 6 the best of meats and the f of wines. H2423
Isa 37:24 heights, the f of its forests. H4149+3623
Jer 48:15 her f young men will go down in the H4436
Eze 16:13 food was honey, olive oil and the f flour. H6159
Eze 27:22 they exchanged the f *of* all kinds of spices H8031
Joel 3: 5 gold and carried off my f treasures to your H3202
Am 6: 6 wine by the bowlful and use the f lotions, H8040

FINGER (31) [FINGERS]
Ge 41:42 signet ring from his f and put it on H3338
Ge 41:42 from his finger and put it on Joseph's f. H3338
Ex 8:19 said to Pharaoh, "This is the f *of* God." H720
Ex 29:12 put it on the horns of the altar with your f, H720
Ex 31:18 tablets of stone inscribed by the f *of* God. H720
Lev 4: 6 He is to dip his f into the blood and sprinkle H720
Lev 4:17 He shall dip his f into the blood and H720
Lev 4:25 sin offering with his f and put it on the H720
Lev 4:30 of the blood with his f and put it on the H720
Lev 4:34 sin offering with his f and put it on the H720
Lev 8:15 with his f he put it on all the horns of H720
Lev 9: 9 he dipped his f into the blood and put H720
Lev 14:16 with his f sprinkle some of it before the H720
Lev 16:14 blood and with his f sprinkle it on the front H720
Lev 16:14 some of it with his f seven times before the H720
Lev 16:19 blood on it with his f seven times to H720
Nu 19: 4 of its blood on his f and sprinkle it seven H720
Dt 9:10 two stone tablets inscribed by the f *of* God. H720
1Ki 12:10 'My little f is thicker than my father's H7782
2Ch 10:10 'My little f is thicker than my father's H7782
Est 3:10 ring from his f and gave it to Haman H3338
Job 1:12 on the man himself do not lay a f. H3338
Isa 58: 9 with the pointing f and malicious talk, H720
Mt 23: 4 are not willing to lift a f to move them. G1235
Lk 11:20 But if I drive out demons by the f of God G1235
Lk 11:46 yourselves will not lift one f to help them. G1235
Lk 15:22 Put a ring on his f and sandals on his feet. G5931
Lk 16:24 to dip the tip *of* his f in water and cool my G1235
Jn 8: 6 started to write on the ground *with* his f. G1235
Jn 20:25 hands and put my f where the nails were G1235
Jn 20:27 Thomas, "Put your f here; see my hands. G1235

FINGERS (14) [FINGER]
2Sa 21:20 huge man with six f *on* each hand and six H720
1Ch 20: 6 a huge man with six f on each hand and H720
Ps 8: 3 the work of your f, the moon and the stars, H720
Ps 144: 1 who trains my hands for war, my f for battle. H720
Pr 6:13 signals with his feet and motions with his f, H720
Pr 7: 3 Bind them on your f; write them on the H720
Pr 31:19 distaff and grasps the spindle with her f. H4090
SS 5: 5 with myrrh, my f with flowing myrrh, on H720
Isa 2: 8 of their hands, to what their f have made. H720
Isa 17: 8 the incense altars their f have made. H720
Isa 59: 3 are stained with blood, your f with guilt. H720
Jer 52:21 each was four f thick, and hollow. H720
Da 5: 5 Suddenly the f of a human hand A10064
Mk 7:33 Jesus put his f into the man's ears. G1235

FINING POT (KJV) CRUCIBLE

FINISH (19) [FINISHED, FINISHING]
Ge 29:27 F this daughter's bridal week; then we will H4848
Ru 2:21 my workers until *they* f harvesting all my H3983
1Ch 27:24 began to count the men but *did* not f. H3983
Ezr 5: 3 you to rebuild this temple and to f it?" A10354
Ezr 5: 9 you to rebuild this temple and to f it?" A10354
Ne 4: 2 offer sacrifices? *Will they* f in a day? Can H3983
Ps 90: 9 your wrath; *we* f our years with a moan. H3983
Jer 51:63 When you f reading this scroll, tie a stone H3983
Da 9:24 your holy city to f transgression, H3974
Mt 10:23 *you will* not f *going through* the towns of G5464
Lk 14:29 lay the foundation and are not able *to* f it, G1754
Lk 14:30 began to build and wasn't able *to* f. G1754
Jn 4:34 will of him who sent me and *to* f his work. G5457
Jn 5:36 works that the Father has given me to f— G5457
Ac 20:24 my only aim is *to* f the race and complete G5457
2Co 8:11 Now f the work, so that your eager G2200
2Co 9: 5 you in advance and f the arrangements G4616
Gal 3: 3 *are you* now *trying to* f by means of the G2200
Jas 1: 4 *Let* perseverance f its work so that G5455+2400

FINISHED (91) [FINISH]
Ge 2: 2 seventh day God *had* f the work he had H3983
Ge 17:22 When *he had* f speaking with Abraham H3983
Ge 18:33 When the LORD *had* f speaking with H3983
Ge 24:15 Before he *had* f praying, Rebekah came H3983
Ge 24:22 When the camels *had* f drinking, the man H3983
Ge 24:45 "Before I f praying in my heart, Rebekah H3983
Ge 27:30 After Isaac f blessing him, and Jacob had H3983
Ge 29:28 *He* f the week with Leah, and then Laban H4848
Ge 49:33 When Jacob *had* f giving instructions to H3983
Ex 31:18 When the LORD f speaking to Moses on H3983
Ex 34:33 When Moses f speaking to them, he put a H3983
Ex 40:33 the courtyard. And so Moses f the work. H3983
Lev 16:20 "When Aaron *has* f making atonement H3983
Nu 4:15 his sons *have* f covering the holy H3983
Nu 7: 1 When Moses f setting up the tabernacle H3983
Nu 16:31 As soon as he f saying all this, the ground H3983
Dt 20: 9 When the officers *have* f speaking to the H3983
Dt 26:12 When *you have* f setting aside a tenth of H3983
Dt 31:24 After Moses f writing in a book the words H3983
Dt 32:45 When Moses f reciting all these words to H3983
Jos 4: 1 the whole nation *had* f crossing the H9462
Jos 8:24 When Israel *had* f killing all the men of H3983
Jos 19:49 When *they had* f dividing the land into its H3983
Jos 19:51 And so *they* f dividing the land. H3983
Jdg 15:17 When he f speaking, he threw away the H3983
Ru 2:23 the barley and wheat harvests *were* f. H3983
Ru 3: 3 are there until he *has* f eating and H3983
Ru 3: 7 When Boaz *had* f eating and drinking and AIT
1Sa 1: 9 Once when they had f eating and drinking H339
1Sa 13:10 Just as he f making the offering, Samuel H3983
1Sa 18: 1 After David *had* f talking with Saul H3983
1Sa 24:16 When David f saying this, Saul asked, "Is H3983
2Sa 6:18 After he *had* f sacrificing the burnt H3983
2Sa 11:19 "When you *have* f giving the king this H3983
2Sa 13:36 As he f speaking, the king's sons came in H3983
2Sa 15:24 until all the people *had* f leaving the city. H9462
1Ki 3: 1 City of David until he f building his palace H3983
1Ki 6:38 the temple *was* f in all its details H3983
1Ki 7:40 So Huram f all the work he had H3983
1Ki 7:51 had done for the temple of the LORD *was* f, H8966
1Ki 8:54 When Solomon *had* f all these prayers H3983
1Ki 9: 1 When Solomon *had* f building the temple H3983
1Ki 13:23 the man of God had f eating and drinking, H339
2Ki 6:23 after *they had* f eating and drinking AIT
2Ki 10:25 As soon as Jehu *had* f making the burnt H3983
2Ki 16:11 from Damascus and f it before King Ahaz H6913
1Ch 16: 2 After David *had* f sacrificing the burnt H3983
1Ch 28:20 the service of the temple of the LORD is f. H3983
2Ch 4:11 So Huram f the work he had undertaken H3983
2Ch 5: 1 had done for the temple of the LORD *was* f, H8966
2Ch 7: 1 When Solomon f praying, fire came down H3983
2Ch 7:11 When Solomon *had* f the temple of the H3983
2Ch 8:16 So the temple of the LORD *was* f. H8966
2Ch 20:23 After they f slaughtering the men from H3983
2Ch 24:14 When they *had* f, they brought the rest of H3983
2Ch 29:29 When the offerings *were* f, the king and H3983
2Ch 29:34 them until the task *was* f and until other H3983
2Ch 31: 7 the third month and f in the seventh H3983
Ezr 5:11 one that a great king of Israel built and f. A10354
Ezr 5:16 been under construction but *is* not yet f." A10719
Ezr 6:14 *They* f building the temple according to A10354
Ezr 10:17 of the first month *they* f dealing with all H3983
Isa 10:12 When the Lord *has* f all his work against H1298
Jer 26: 8 as soon as Jeremiah f telling all the H3983
Jer 43: 1 When Jeremiah *had* f telling the people H3983
Eze 4: 6 "After *you have* f this, lie down again, this H3983
Eze 4: 8 the other until you *have* f the days of your H3983

Eze 42:15 When *he had* **f** measuring what was H3983
Eze 43:23 When you *have* **f** purifying it, you are to H3983
Mt 7:28 When Jesus *had* **f** saying these things G5464
Mt 11: 1 After Jesus *had* **f** instructing his twelve G5464
Mt 13:53 When Jesus *had* **f** these parables, he G5464
Mt 19: 1 When Jesus *had* **f** saying these things, he G5464
Mt 26: 1 When Jesus *had* **f** saying all these things G5464
Lk 4:13 *When* the devil *had* **f** all this tempting, he G5334
Lk 5: 4 When *he had* **f** speaking, he said to G4264
Lk 7: 1 When Jesus *had* **f** saying all this to the G4444
Lk 11: 1 When *he* **f**, one of his disciples said to G4264
Lk 11:37 When Jesus *had* **f speaking**, a Pharisee AIT
Jn 12:36 *When he had* **f speaking**, Jesus left and hid AIT
Jn 13:12 When *he had* **f washing** their feet, he put on AIT
Jn 18: 1 *When he had* **f praying**, Jesus left with his AIT
Jn 19:28 knowing that everything *had* now *been* **f** G5464
Jn 19:30 had received the drink, Jesus said, "*It is* **f**." G5464
Jn 21:15 When *they had* **f eating**, Jesus said to Simon AIT
Ac 12:25 *When* Barnabas and Saul *had* **f** their G4444
Ac 15:13 When they **f**, James spoke up. "Brothers," G4967
Ac 20:36 *When* Paul *had* **f speaking**, he knelt down AIT
2Ti 4: 7 the good fight, *I have* **f** the race, I have G5464
Heb 4: 3 And yet his works *have been* **f** since the G1181
Rev 11: 7 Now when *they have* **f** their testimony, the G5464

FINISHING (3) [FINISH]

1Ki 1:41 him heard it as they *were* **f** their feast. H3983
2Ch 29:17 **f** on the sixteenth day of the first month. H3983
Jn 17: 4 you glory on earth *by* **f** the work you gave G5457

FINS (5)

Lev 11: 9 you may eat any that have **f** and scales. H6181
Lev 11:10 streams that do not have **f** and scales— H6181
Lev 11:12 that does not have **f** and scales is to be H6181
Dt 14: 9 you may eat any that has **f** and scales. H6181
Dt 14:10 that does not have **f** and scales you may H6181

FIR (2) [FIRS]

Isa 41:19 wasteland, the **f** and the cypress together, H9329
Isa 60:13 the juniper, the **f** and the cypress together H9329

FIRE (385) [AFIRE, FIERY, FIRELIGHT, FIREPANS, FIREPOT, FIRES, FIREWOOD]

Ge 22: 6 he himself carried the **f** and the knife. H836
Ge 22: 7 "The **f** and wood are here," Isaac said, "but H836
Ex 3: 2 to him in flames of **f** from within a bush. H836
Ex 3: 2 the bush *was* **on f** it did H1277+928+2021+836
Ex 12: 8 they are to eat the meat roasted over the **f**, H836
Ex 12: 9 but roast it over a **f**—with the head, H836
Ex 13:21 by night in a pillar of **f** to give them light, H836
Ex 13:22 day nor the pillar of **f** by night left its place H836
Ex 14:24 down from the pillar of **f** and cloud at the H836
Ex 19:18 because the LORD descended on it in **f**. H836
Ex 22: 6 "If a **f** breaks out and spreads into H836
Ex 22: 6 one who started the **f** must make H1282
Ex 24:17 like a consuming **f** on top of the mountain. H836
Ex 32:20 people had made and burned it in the **f**; H836
Ex 32:24 I threw it into the **f**, and out came this H836
Ex 35: 3 Do not light a **f** in any of your dwellings on H836
Ex 40:38 and **f** was in the cloud by night H836
Lev 1: 7 the priest are to put **f** on the altar and H836
Lev 1: 7 fire on the altar and arrange wood on the **f**. H836
Lev 2:14 heads of new grain roasted in the **f**. H836
Lev 4:12 burn it there in a wood **f** on the ash heap. H836
Lev 6: 9 the **f** must be kept burning on the altar. H836
Lev 6:10 offering that the **f** has consumed on the H836
Lev 6:12 The **f** on the altar must be kept burning; it H836
Lev 6:12 burnt offering on *the* **f** and burn the fat of H1277
Lev 6:13 The **f** must be kept burning on the altar H836
Lev 9:24 **F** came out from the presence of the LORD H836
Lev 10: 1 censers, put **f** in them and added incense H836
Lev 10: 1 they offered unauthorized **f** before the LORD, H836
Lev 10: 2 So **f** came out from the presence of the LORD H836
Lev 10: 6 those the LORD *has* **destroyed by f**. H8596
Lev 16:13 to put the incense on the **f** before the LORD, H836
Lev 20:14 Both he and they must be burned in the **f** H836
Lev 21: 9 her father; she must be burned in the **f**. H836
Nu 3: 4 with unauthorized **f** before him in the H836
Nu 6:18 the hair and put it in the **f** that is under the H836
Nu 9:15 cloud above the tabernacle looked like **f**. H836
Nu 9:16 covered it, and at night it looked like **f**. H836
Nu 11: 1 Then **f** *from* the LORD burned among them H836
Nu 11: 2 he prayed to the LORD and the **f** died down. H836
Nu 11: 3 because **f** *from* the LORD had burned among H836
Nu 14:14 of cloud by day and a pillar of **f** by night. H836
Nu 16:35 And **f** came out from the LORD and H836
Nu 18: 9 most holy offerings that is kept from the **f**. H836
Nu 21:28 "**F** went out from Heshbon, a blaze from H836
Nu 26:10 died when the **f** devoured the 250 men. H836
Nu 26:61 before the LORD with unauthorized **f**.) H836
Nu 31:23 that can withstand **f** must be put through H836
Nu 31:23 withstand fire must be put through the **f**, H836
Nu 31:23 cannot withstand **f** must be put through H836
Dt 1:33 journey, in **f** by night and in a cloud by day H836
Dt 4:11 while it blazed with **f** to the very heavens, H836
Dt 4:12 Then the LORD spoke to you out of the **f**. H836
Dt 4:15 the LORD spoke to you at Horeb out of the **f**. H836
Dt 4:24 For the LORD your God is a consuming **f**, H836
Dt 4:33 heard the voice of God speaking out of **f**, H836
Dt 4:36 On earth he showed you his great **f**, and H836
Dt 4:36 you heard his words from out of the **f**. H836
Dt 5: 4 face to face out of the **f** on the mountain. H836
Dt 5: 5 were afraid of the **f** and did not go up the H836
Dt 5:22 there on the mountain from out of the **f**, H836
Dt 5:23 while the mountain was ablaze with **f**, all H836
Dt 5:24 we have heard his voice from the **f**. H836
Dt 5:25 This great **f** will consume us, and we will H836
Dt 5:26 voice of the living God speaking out of **f**, H836
Dt 7: 5 Asherah poles and burn their idols in the **f**. H836
Dt 7:25 of their gods you are to burn in the **f**. H836
Dt 9: 3 across ahead of you like a devouring **f**. H836
Dt 9:10 to you on the mountain out of the **f**, H836
Dt 9:15 the mountain while it was ablaze with **f**. H836
Dt 9:21 calf you had made, and burned it in the **f**. H836
Dt 10: 4 mountain, out of the **f**, on the day of the H836
Dt 12: 3 burn their Asherah poles in the **f**; H836
Dt 12:31 daughters in the **f** as sacrifices to their H836
Dt 18:10 sacrifices their son or daughter in the **f**, H836
Dt 18:16 LORD our God nor see this great **f** anymore, H836
Dt 32:22 For a **f** will be kindled by my wrath, one H836
Jos 7:15 the devoted things shall be destroyed by **f**, H836
Jos 8: 8 taken the city, **set it on f**. H3675+928+2021+836
Jos 8:19 it and quickly **set it on f**. H3675+928+2021+836
Jdg 1: 8 put the city to the sword and set it on **f**. H836
Jdg 6:21 **F** flared from the rock, consuming the meat H836
Jdg 9:15 then let **f** come out of the thornbush and H836
Jdg 9:20 let **f** come out from Abimelek and consume H836
Jdg 9:20 Beth Millo, and let **f** come out from you H836
Jdg 9:49 and **set it on f** with the H3675+928+2021+836
Jdg 9:52 the tower to **set it on f**, H8596+928+2021+836
Jdg 20:48 the towns they came across they set on **f**. H836
1Sa 30: 3 found it destroyed by **f** and their wives and H836
2Sa 14:30 Go and **set it on f**." So H3675+836+928+2021
2Sa 14:30 **set** the field **on f**. H3675+836+928+2021
2Sa 14:31 *have* your servants **set** my field **on f** H3675+836+928+2021
2Sa 22: 9 consuming **f** came from his mouth H836
1Ki 9:16 *He had* **set** it **on f**. H8596+928+836+2021
1Ki 16:18 and **set** the palace **on f** H8596+928+2021+836
1Ki 18:23 put it on the wood but not set **f** to it. H836
1Ki 18:23 put it on the wood but not set **f** to it. H836
1Ki 18:24 The god who answers by **f**—he is God." H836
1Ki 18:25 name of your god, but do not light the **f**." H836
1Ki 18:38 Then the **f** *of* the LORD fell and burned up H836
1Ki 19:12 After the earthquake came a **f**, but the LORD H836
1Ki 19:12 came a fire, but the LORD was not in the **f**. H836
1Ki 19:12 And after the **f** came a gentle whisper. H836
2Ki 1:10 may **f** come down from heaven and H836
2Ki 1:10 Then **f** fell from heaven and consumed the H836
2Ki 1:12 "may **f** come down from heaven and H836
2Ki 1:12 Then the **f** *of* God fell from heaven and H836
2Ki 1:14 **f** has fallen from heaven and consumed H836
2Ki 2:11 suddenly a chariot of **f** and horses of fire H836
2Ki 2:11 of fire and horses of **f** appeared and H836
2Ki 6:17 horses and chariots of **f** all around Elisha. H836
2Ki 8:12 "*You will* **set f to** their H8938+928+836+2021
2Ki 16: 3 Israel and even sacrificed his son in the **f**, H836
2Ki 17:17 sacrificed their sons and daughters in the **f**. H836
2Ki 17:31 their children in the **f** as sacrifices to H836
2Ki 19:18 their gods into the **f** and destroyed them, H836
2Ki 21: 6 He sacrificed his own son in the **f**, practiced H836
2Ki 23:10 their son or daughter in the **f** to Molek. H836
2Ki 25: 9 *He* **set f to** the temple of the LORD, the H8596
1Ch 14:12 David gave orders to burn them in the **f**. H836
1Ch 21:26 answered him with **f** from heaven on the H836
2Ch 7: 1 **f** came down from heaven and consumed H836
2Ch 7: 3 Israelites saw the **f** coming down and the H836
2Ch 16:14 they made a huge **f** in his honor. H8599
2Ch 21:19 people made no *funeral* **f** in his honor, H8599
2Ch 28: 3 Hinnom and sacrificed his children in the **f**, H836
2Ch 33: 6 his children in the **f** in the Valley of Ben H836
2Ch 35:13 Passover animals over the **f** as prescribed, H836
2Ch 36:19 *They* **set f to** God's temple and broke H8596
Ne 1: 3 its gates have been burned with **f**. H836
Ne 2: 3 its gates have been destroyed by **f**? H836
Ne 2:13 its gates, which had been destroyed by **f**. H836
Ne 2:17 its gates have been burned with **f**. H836
Ne 9:12 night with a pillar of **f** to give them light on H836
Ne 9:19 the pillar of **f** by night to shine on the H836
Job 1:16 "The **f** *of* God fell from the heavens and H836
Job 15:34 **f** will consume the tents of those who H836
Job 18: 5 the flame of his **f** stops burning. H836
Job 18:15 **F** resides in his tent; burning sulfur is H4442
Job 20:26 A **f** unfanned will consume him and devour H836
Job 22:20 are destroyed, and **f** devours their wealth. H836
Job 28: 5 food comes, is transformed below as by **f**; H836
Job 31:12 It is a **f** that burns to Destruction; it would H836
Job 41:19 from its mouth; sparks of **f** shoot out. H836
Ps 18: 8 consuming **f** came from his mouth H836
Ps 21: 9 in his wrath, and his **f** will consume them. H836
Ps 39: 3 I meditated, the **f** burned; then I spoke H836
Ps 46: 9 the spear; he burns the shields with **f**. H836
Ps 50: 3 will not be silent; a **f** devours before him H836
Ps 66:12 we went through **f** and water, but you H836
Ps 68: 2 as wax melts before the **f**, may the wicked H836
Ps 78:14 by day and with light from the **f** all night. H836
Ps 78:21 was furious; his **f** broke out against Jacob H836
Ps 78:63 **F** consumed their young men, and their H836
Ps 79: 5 How long will your jealousy burn like **f**? H836
Ps 80:16 it is burned with **f**; at your rebuke your H836
Ps 83:14 As **f** consumes the forest or a flame sets H836
Ps 89:46 How long will your wrath burn like **f**? H836
Ps 97: 3 **F** goes before him and consumes his foes H836
Ps 104: 4 his messengers, flames of **f** his servants. H836
Ps 105:39 as a covering, and a **f** to give light at night. H836
Ps 106:18 **F** blazed among their followers; a flame H836
Ps 140:10 may they be thrown into the **f**, into miry pits H836
Pr 6:27 Can a man scoop **f** into his lap without his H836
Pr 16:27 and on their lips it is like a scorching **f**. H836
Pr 26:20 Without wood a **f** goes out; without a H836
Pr 26:21 As charcoal to embers and as wood to **f**, so H836
Pr 30:16 with water, and **f**, which never says, H836
SS 8: 6 It burns like blazing **f**, like a mighty flame. H836
Isa 1: 7 your cities burned with **f**; your fields are H836
Isa 1:31 together, with no *one to* **quench** *the* **f**." H3882
Isa 4: 4 by a spirit of judgment and a spirit of **f**. H1277
Isa 4: 5 by day and a glow of flaming **f** by night; H836
Isa 5:24 as tongues of **f** lick up straw and as dry H836
Isa 9: 5 destined for burning, will be fuel for the **f**. H836
Isa 9:18 Surely wickedness burns like a **f**; it H836
Isa 9:19 the people will be fuel for the **f**; H836
Isa 10:16 under his pomp a **f** will be kindled like a H3679
Isa 10:17 The Light of Israel will become a **f**, their H836
Isa 26:11 let the **f** *reserved for* your enemies H836
Isa 27: 4 them in battle; *I would* **set** them all **on f**. H7455
Isa 29: 6 tempest and flames of a devouring **f**. H836
Isa 30:27 of wrath, and his tongue is a consuming **f**. H836
Isa 30:30 with raging anger and consuming **f**, H4258+836
Isa 30:33 Its **f pit** has been made deep and wide H4509
Isa 30:33 with an abundance of **f** and wood; the H836
Isa 31: 9 the LORD, whose **f** is in Zion, whose H241
Isa 33:11 your breath is a **f** that consumes you. H836
Isa 33:14 of us can dwell with the consuming **f**? H836
Isa 37:19 their gods into the **f** and destroyed them, H836
Isa 43: 2 When you walk through the **f**, you will not H836
Isa 44:15 himself, *he* **kindles a f** and bakes bread. H5956
Isa 44:16 Half of the wood he burns in the **f**; over it H836
Isa 44:16 says, "Ah! I am warm; I see the **f**." H241
Isa 47:14 are like stubble; the **f** will burn them up. H836
Isa 47:14 not coals for warmth; this is not a **f** to sit by. H241
Isa 64: 2 As when **f** sets twigs ablaze and causes H836
Isa 64:11 has been burned with **f**, and all that we H836
Isa 65: 5 my nostrils, a **f** that keeps burning all day. H836
Isa 66:15 the LORD is coming with **f**, and his chariots H836
Isa 66:15 with fury, and his rebuke with flames of **f**. H836
Isa 66:16 For with **f** and with his sword the LORD will H836
Isa 66:24 the **f** *that burns* them will not be quenched H836
Jer 4: 4 flare up and burn like **f** because of the evil H836
Jer 5:14 in your mouth a **f** and these people the H836
Jer 6:29 blow fiercely to burn away the lead with **f**, H836
Jer 7:18 the fathers light the **f**, and the women H836
Jer 7:31 to burn their sons and daughters in the **f**— H836
Jer 11:16 of a mighty storm *he will* **set** it **on f**, H3675+836
Jer 15:14 anger will kindle a **f** that will burn against H836
Jer 17:27 kindle an unquenchable **f** in the gates of H836
Jer 19: 5 their children in the **f** as offerings to Baal— H836
Jer 20: 9 his word is in my heart like a **f**, a fire shut H836
Jer 20: 9 heart like a fire, a **f** shut up in my bones. H1277
Jer 21:10 of Babylon, and he will destroy it with **f**. H836
Jer 21:12 out and burn like **f** because of the evil you H836
Jer 21:14 I will kindle a **f** in your forests that will H836
Jer 22: 7 cedar beams and throw them into the **f**. H836
Jer 23:29 "Is not my word like **f**," declares the LORD H836
Jer 29:22 whom the king of Babylon burned in the **f**. H836
Jer 32:29 come in and **set it on f**; H3675+928+2021+836
Jer 34: 5 people made a **funeral f** *in honor of* your H5386
Jer 34: 5 so *they will* **make a f** in your honor and H8596
Jer 36:22 with a **f** burning *in* the firepot in front of H836
Jer 36:23 the entire scroll was burned in the **f**. H836
Jer 36:32 king of Judah had burned in the **f**. H836
Jer 39: 8 **set f to** the royal H8596+928+2021+836
Jer 43:12 *He will* **set f** to the temples of the H3675+836
Jer 48:45 a **f** has gone out from Heshbon H836
Jer 49: 2 villages *will be* **set on f**. H3675+928+2021+836
Jer 49:27 "*I will* **set f** to the walls of Damascus; H3675+836
Jer 50:32 I will kindle a **f** in her towns that will H836
Jer 51:30 Her dwellings *are* **set on f**; the bars of her H3675
Jer 51:32 the marshes **set on f** H8596+928+2021+836
Jer 51:58 her high gates **set on f**; H3675+928+2021+836
Jer 52:13 *He* **set f to** the temple of the LORD, the H8596
La 1:13 "From on high he sent **f**, sent it down into H836
La 2: 3 in Jacob like a flaming **f** that consumes H836
La 2: 4 out his wrath like **f** on the tent of Daughter H836
La 4:11 He kindled a **f** in Zion that consumed her H836
Eze 1: 4 The center of the **f** looked like glowing H836
Eze 1: 5 in **the f** was what looked like four H2023S
Eze 1:13 was like burning coals of **f** or like torches. H836
Eze 1:13 **F** moved back and forth among the H2085S
Eze 1:27 as if full of **f**, and that from there H836
Eze 1:27 that from there down he looked like **f** H836
Eze 5: 4 throw them into the **f** and burn them up. H836
Eze 5: 4 A **f** will spread from there to all Israel H836
Eze 8: 2 to be his waist down he was like **f**, H836
Eze 10: 6 in linen, "Take **f** from among the wheels H836
Eze 10: 7 out his hand to the **f** that was among them. H836
Eze 15: 4 it is thrown on the **f** as fuel and the fire H836
Eze 15: 4 fire as fuel and the **f** burns both ends and H836
Eze 15: 5 useful when the **f** has burned it and it is H836
Eze 15: 6 the trees of the forest as fuel for the **f**, H836
Eze 15: 7 Although they have come out of the **f**, the H836
Eze 15: 7 out of the fire, the **f** will yet consume them. H836
Eze 19:12 branches withered and **f** consumed them. H836
Eze 19:14 **F** spread from one of its main branches H836
Eze 20:31 the sacrifice of your children in the **f**—you H836
Eze 20:47 I *am about to* **set f** to you, and it will H3675+836
Eze 21:32 You will be fuel for the **f**, your blood will be H836

Eze 23:25 of you who are left will be consumed by **f**. H836
Eze 24:10 So heap on the wood and kindle the **f** H836
Eze 24:12 has not been removed, not even by **f**. H836
Eze 28:18 So I made a **f** come out from you, and it H836
Eze 30: 8 when I set **f** to Egypt and all her helpers H836
Eze 30:14 set **f** to Zoan and inflict punishment on H836
Eze 30:16 I will set **f** to Egypt; Pelusium will writhe in H836
Eze 39: 6 I will send **f** on Magog and on those who H836
Eze 46:23 with **places for f** built all around under the H4453
Da 3:22 the flames of the **f** killed the soldiers A10471
Da 3:24 that we tied up and threw into the **f**?" A10471
Da 3:25 I see four men walking around in the **f** A10471
Da 3:26 Abednego came out of the **f**, A10471
Da 3:27 They saw that the **f** had not harmed their A10471
Da 3:27 there was no smell of **f** on them. A10471
Da 7: 9 His throne was flaming with **f**, and its A10471
Da 7:10 A river of **f** was flowing, coming out from A10471
Da 7:11 destroyed and thrown into the blazing **f**. A10080
Hos 7: 4 like an oven whose **f** the baker need not stir NDT
Hos 7: 6 in the morning it blazes like a flaming **f**. H836
Hos 8:14 But I will send **f** on their cities that will H836
Joel 1:19 **f** has devoured the pastures in the H836
Joel 1:20 have dried up and **f** has devoured the H836
Joel 2: 3 Before them **f** devours, behind them a H836
Joel 2: 5 like a crackling **f** consuming stubble H4258+836
Joel 2:30 blood and **f** and billows of smoke. H836
Am 1: 4 I will send **f** on the house of Hazael that H836
Am 1: 7 I will send **f** on the walls of Gaza that will H836
Am 1:10 I will send **f** on the walls of Tyre that will H836
Am 1:12 I will send **f** on Teman that will consume H836
Am 1:14 *I will* **set f** to the walls of Rabbah H3675+836
Am 2: 2 I will send **f** on Moab that will consume the H836
Am 2: 5 I will send **f** on Judah that will consume H836
Am 4:11 like a burning stick snatched from the **f**, H8599
Am 5: 6 sweep through the tribes of Joseph like a **f**; H836
Am 7: 4 LORD was calling for judgment by **f**; H836
Ob 18 Jacob will be a **f** and Joseph a flame; Esau H836
Ob 18 and *they will* **set** him **on f** and destroy him H1944
Mic 1: 4 like wax before the **f**, like water rushing H836
Mic 1: 7 all her temple gifts will be burned with **f**; H836
Na 1: 6 His wrath is poured out like **f**; the rocks are H836
Na 3:13 **f** has consumed the bars of your gates. H836
Na 3:15 There the **f** will consume you; the sword H836
Hab 2:13 labor is only **fuel for the f**, H928+1896+836
Zep 1:18 In the **f** *of* his jealousy the whole earth will H836
Zep 3: 8 be consumed by the **f** *of* my jealous anger. H836
Zec 2: 5 And I myself will be a wall of **f** around it,' H836
Zec 3: 2 man a burning stick snatched from the **f**?" H836
Zec 9: 4 on the sea, and she will be consumed by **f**. H836
Zec 11: 1 Lebanon, so that **f** may devour your cedars! H836
Zec 13: 9 This third I will put into the **f**; I will refine H836
Mal 3: 2 be like a refiner's **f** or a launderer's soap. H836
Mal 4: 1 the day that is coming *will* **set** them **on f**." H4265
Mt 3:10 will be cut down and thrown into the **f**. G4786
Mt 3:11 will baptize you with the Holy Spirit and **f**. G4786
Mt 3:12 burning up the chaff *with* unquenchable **f**." G4786
Mt 5:22 will be in danger *of* the **f** of hell. G4786
Mt 6:30 today and tomorrow is thrown into the **f**, G3106
Mt 7:19 fruit is cut down and thrown into the **f**. G4786
Mt 13:40 weeds are pulled up and burned *in* the **f**, G4786
Mt 17:15 He often falls into the **f** or into the water. G4786
Mt 18: 8 two feet and be thrown into eternal **f**. G4786
Mt 18: 9 two eyes and be thrown into the **f** of hell. G4786
Mt 25:41 into the eternal **f** prepared for the devil G4786
Mk 9:22 thrown him into **f** or water to kill him. G4786
Mk 9:43 go into hell, where the **f** never goes out. G4786
Mk 9:48 do not die, and the **f** is not quenched. G4786
Mk 9:49 Everyone will be salted *with* **f**. G4786
Mk 14:54 the guards and warmed himself at the **f**. G5890
Lk 3: 9 will be cut down and thrown into the **f**." G4786
Lk 3:16 will baptize you with the Holy Spirit and **f**. G4786
Lk 3:17 burn up the chaff *with* unquenchable **f**." G4786
Lk 9:54 you want us to call **f** down from heaven to G4786
Lk 12:28 tomorrow is thrown into the **f**, how G3106
Lk 12:49 "I have come to bring **f** on the earth, and G4786
Lk 16:24 tongue, because I am in agony in this **f**. G5825
Lk 17:29 **f** and sulfur rained down from heaven G4786
Lk 22:55 there had kindled a **f** in the middle of the G4786
Jn 15: 6 picked up, thrown into the **f** and burned. G4786
Jn 18:18 officials stood *around* a **f** they had made to G471
Jn 21: 9 they saw a **f of burning coals** there with fish G471
Ac 2: 3 to be tongues *of* **f** that separated and G4786
Ac 2:19 blood and **f** and billows of smoke. G4786
Ac 28: 2 They built a **f** and welcomed us all G4787
Ac 28: 3 as he put it on the **f**, a viper, G4787
Ac 28: 5 the snake off into the **f** and suffered no ill G4786
1Co 3:13 It will be revealed with **f**, and the fire will G4786
1Co 3:13 the **f** will test the quality of each G4786
2Th 1: 7 from heaven in blazing **f** with his powerful G4786
Heb 1: 7 and his servants flames *of* **f**. G4786
Heb 10:27 of judgment and *of* raging **f** that will G4786
Heb 12:18 can be touched and that is burning *with* **f**; G4786
Heb 12:29 our "God is a consuming **f**." G4786
Jas 3: 5 a great forest *is* **set on f** by a small spark. G409
Jas 3: 6 The tongue also is a **f**, a world of evil G4786
Jas 3: 6 **sets** the whole course of one's life **on f** G5824
Jas 3: 6 life on fire, and *is itself* **set on f** by hell. G5824
Jas 5: 3 against you and eat your flesh like **f**. G4786
1Pe 1: 7 which perishes even though refined by **f** G4786
2Pe 3: 7 heavens and earth are reserved *for* **f**, G4786
2Pe 3:10 the elements will be destroyed *by* **f**, and G3012
2Pe 3:12 about the destruction of the heavens *by* **f**, G4792
Jude 7 who suffer the punishment *of* eternal **f**. G4786
Jude 23 save others by snatching them from the **f** G4786
Rev 1:14 as snow, and his eyes were like blazing **f**. G4786
Rev 2:18 eyes are like blazing **f** and whose feet are G4786
Rev 3:18 you to buy from me gold refined in the **f**, G4786
Rev 8: 5 filled it with **f** from the altar, and G4786
Rev 8: 7 there came hail and **f** mixed with blood, G4786
Rev 9:17 out of their mouths came **f**, smoke G4786
Rev 9:18 was killed by the three plagues of **f**, G4786
Rev 11: 5 **f** comes from their mouths and devours G4786
Rev 13:13 even causing **f** to come down from G4786
Rev 14:18 who had charge of the **f**, came from the G4786
Rev 15: 2 like a sea of glass glowing *with* **f** and, G4786
Rev 16: 8 sun was allowed to scorch people with **f**. G4786
Rev 17:16 they will eat her flesh and burn her with **f**. G4786
Rev 18: 8 She will be consumed by **f**, for mighty is G4786
Rev 19:12 His eyes are like blazing **f**, and on his G4786
Rev 20: 9 But **f** came down from heaven and G4786
Rev 20:14 Hades were thrown into the lake *of* **f**. G4786
Rev 20:14 The lake *of* **f** is the second death. G4786
Rev 20:15 book of life was thrown into the lake *of* **f**. G4786

FIRELIGHT (1) [FIRE]

Lk 22:56 servant girl saw him seated there in the **f**. G5890

FIREPANS (3) [FIRE]

Ex 27: 3 sprinkling bowls, meat forks and **f**. H4746
Ex 38: 3 sprinkling bowls, meat forks and **f**. H4746
Nu 4:14 at the altar, including the **f**, meat forks, H4746

FIREPOT (4) [FIRE]

Ge 15:17 a smoking **f** with a blazing torch appeared H9486
Jer 36:22 with a fire burning in the **f** in front of him. H279
Jer 36:23 a scribe's knife and threw them into the **f**, H279
Zec 12: 6 of Judah like a **f** in a woodpile, H3963+836

FIRES (5) [FIRE]

Isa 27:11 women come and **make f** *with* them. H239
Isa 40:16 Lebanon is not sufficient for *altar* **f**, nor its H1277
Isa 50:11 all you who light **f** and provide yourselves H836
Isa 50:11 in the light of your **f** and of the torches you H836
Mal 1:10 so that *you would* not **light** useless **f** *on* my H239

FIREWOOD (2) [FIRE]

Lev 6:12 the priest is to add **f** and arrange the H6770
Isa 7: 4 of these two smoldering stubs of **f**— H202

FIRKINS (KJV) GALLONS

FIRM (53) [FIRMLY]

Ex 14:13 **Stand f** and you will see the deliverance H3656
2Ch 20:17 **stand f** and see the deliverance the LORD H6641
Ezr 9: 8 giving us a **f place** in his sanctuary, H3845
Job 11:15 you will stand **f** and without fear. H3668
Job 36: 5 he is mighty, and **f** *in* his purpose. H3946
Job 41:23 tightly joined; *they are* **f** and immovable. H3668
Ps 19: 9 The decrees of the LORD are **f**, and all of H622
Ps 20: 8 knees and fall, but we rise up and **stand f**. H6386
Ps 30: 7 you made my royal mountain stand **f**; but H6437
Ps 33: 9 he commanded, and *it* **stood f**. H6641
Ps 33:11 But the plans of the LORD **stand f** forever H6641
Ps 37:23 The LORD **makes f** the steps of the one H3922
Ps 40: 2 on a rock and **gave** me **a f** place to stand. H3922
Ps 75: 3 people quake, it is I *who* **hold** its pillars **f**. H9419
Ps 89: 2 will declare that your love **stands f** forever, H1215
Ps 89: 4 forever and **make** your throne **f** through all H1215
Ps 93: 1 the world **is established, f** and secure. H3922
Ps 93: 5 **stand f**; holiness adorns your H586+4394
Ps 119:89 is eternal; *it* **stands f** in the heavens. H5893
Pr 10:25 but the righteous **stand f** forever. H3572
Pr 12: 7 the house of the righteous **stands f**. H6641
Isa 7: 9 If *you do* not **stand f in** *your* **faith**, you will H586
Isa 22:17 LORD *is about to* **take f hold** *of* you H6487+6487
Isa 22:23 I will drive him like a peg into a **f** place; he H586
Isa 22:25 peg driven into the **f** place will give way; H586
Eze 13: 5 Israel so that *it will* **stand f** in the battle H6641
Zec 8:23 nations *will* **take f hold** *of* one Jew by H2616
Mt 10:22 the *one who* **stands f** to the end will G5702
Mt 24:13 the *one who* **stands f** to the end will G5702
Mk 13:13 the *one who* **stands f** to the end will G5702
Lk 21:19 **Stand f**, and you will win life. G5705
1Co 1: 8 He *will* also **keep** you **f** to the end, so that G1011
1Co 10:12 if you think you *are* **standing f**, be careful G2705
1Co 15:58 dear brothers and sisters, **stand f**. G1612+1181
1Co 16:13 Be on your guard; **stand f** in the faith; be G5112
2Co 1: 7 And our hope for you is **f**, because we G1010
2Co 1:21 who **makes** both us and you **stand f** in G1011
2Co 1:24 your joy, because it is by faith *you* **stand f**. G2705
Gal 5: 1 **Stand f**, then, and do not let yourselves G5112
Eph 6:14 **Stand f** then, with the belt of truth buckled G2705
Php 1:27 I will know that *you* **stand f** in the one G5112
Php 4: 1 crown, **stand f** in the Lord in this way G5112
Col 1:23 established and **f**, and do not move from G1612
Col 2: 5 you are and *how* **f** your faith in Christ is G5106
Col 4:12 that *you may* **stand f** in all the will of God G2705
1Th 3: 8 since you *are* **standing f** in the Lord. G5112
2Th 2:15 **stand f** and hold fast to the teachings we G5112
1Ti 6:19 themselves as a **f** foundation for the G2819
2Ti 2:19 God's solid foundation **stands f**, sealed G2705
Heb 6:19 as an anchor for the soul, **f** and secure. G855
Jas 5: 8 be patient and **stand f** G5114+3836+2840
1Pe 5: 9 Resist him, **standing f** in the faith, because G5104
1Pe 5:10 you and make you strong, **f** and steadfast. G4964

FIRMAMENT (KJV) HEAVENS, SKIES, VAULT

FIRMLY (22) [FIRM]

Ge 41:32 the matter *has* **been f decided** by God, H3922
1Sa 2:35 I will **f** establish his priestly house, and H586
1Ki 2:12 and his rule was **f** established. H4394
2Ki 14: 5 After the kingdom *was* **f** in his grasp, he H2616
1Ch 16:30 The world **is f established**; it cannot be H3922
2Ch 1: 1 of David **established himself f** over his H2616
2Ch 12:13 Rehoboam **established himself f** in H2616
2Ch 21: 4 established himself **f** over his father's H2616
2Ch 25: 3 After the kingdom *was* **f** in his control, he H2616
Ps 96:10 The world **is f established**, it cannot be H3922
Ecc 12:11 collected sayings like **f embedded** nails— H5749
Da 2: 5 "This is what I have **f** decided: A10014
Da 2: 8 realize that this is what I have **f** decided: A10014
Da 3:23 these three men, **f tied**, fell into the A10366
Da 11:32 who know their God will **f** resist him. H2616
1Co 15: 2 if *you* **hold f** to the word I preached to you. G2988
Php 2:16 *as you* **hold f** to the word of life. G2091
Titus 1: 9 *He must* **hold f** to the trustworthy message G504
Heb 3: 6 if indeed *we* **hold f** to our confidence and G2988
Heb 3:14 our original conviction **f** to the very end. G1010
Heb 4:14 God, *let us* **hold f** to the faith we profess. G3195
2Pe 1:12 them and *are* **f established** in the truth G5114

FIRS (1) [FIR]

SS 1:17 of our house are cedars; our rafters are **f**. H1361

FIRST (374) [FIRSTBORN, FIRSTFRUITS]

Ge 1: 5 there was morning—the **f** day. H285
Ge 2:11 The name of the **f** is the Pishon; it winds H285
Ge 8: 5 on the **f** day of the tenth month the H285
Ge 8:13 By the **f** day of the first month of Noah's six H285
Ge 8:13 the first day of the **f** month of Noah's six H8037
Ge 8:13 month of Noah's six hundred and **f** year, H285
Ge 10:10 The **f** *centers of* his kingdom were Babylon, H8040
Ge 13: 4 where he had **f** built an altar. H8037
Ge 25:25 The **f** to come out was red, and his whole H8037
Ge 25:31 "**F** sell me your birthright." H3869+2021+3427
Ge 25:33 "Swear to me **f**." So he swore an H3869+3427
Ge 38:28 his wrist and said, "This one came out **f**." H8037
Ge 41:20 ate up the seven fat cows that came up **f**. H8037
Ge 43:18 was put back into our sacks the **f time**. H9378
Ge 43:20 came down here the **f time** to buy food. H9378
Ge 49: 3 my might, the **f** *sign of* my strength H8040
Ex 4: 8 believe you or pay attention to the **f** sign, H8037
Ex 12: 2 "This month is to be for you the **f** month H8031
Ex 12: 2 the first month, the **f** month of your year. H8037
Ex 12:15 On the **f** day remove the yeast from your H8037
Ex 12:15 yeast in it from the **f** day through the H8037
Ex 12:16 On the **f** day hold a sacred assembly, and H8037
Ex 12:18 In the **f** month you are to eat bread made H8037
Ex 13: 2 The **f offspring** *of* every womb among the H7081
Ex 13:12 to the LORD the **f offspring** *of* every womb. H7081
Ex 13:15 LORD the **f male offspring** *of* every womb H7081
Ex 19: 1 On the **f** day of the third month after the NDT
Ex 21:10 he must not deprive the **f** one of her food NDT
Ex 25:35 bud shall be under the **f** pair of branches NDT
Ex 28:17 The **f** row shall be carnelian, chrysolite H285
Ex 29:40 With the **f** lamb offer a tenth of an ephah of H285
Ex 34: 1 out two stone tablets like the **f** *ones*, H8037
Ex 34: 1 them the words that were on the **f** tablets, H8037
Ex 34: 4 tablets like the **f** *ones* and went up Mount H8037
Ex 34:19 "The **f offspring** *of* every womb belongs to H7081
Ex 37:21 One bud was under the **f** pair of branches NDT
Ex 39:10 The **f** row was carnelian, chrysolite and H285
Ex 40: 2 of meeting, on the **f** day of the first month. H285
Ex 40: 2 meeting, on the first day of the **f** month. H8037
Ex 40:17 was set up on the **f** day of the first month in H285
Ex 40:17 the first day of the **f** month in the second H8037
Lev 4:21 camp and burn it as he burned the **f** bull. H8037
Lev 5: 8 who shall **f** offer the one for the sin H8037
Lev 9:15 a sin offering as he did with the **f** *one*. H8037
Lev 16: 3 He must **f** bring a young bull for a sin NDT
Lev 23: 5 on the fourteenth day of the **f** month. H8037
Lev 23: 7 On the **f** day hold a sacred assembly and H8037
Lev 23:10 priest a sheaf of the **f** grain you harvest. H8040
Lev 23:24 'On the **f** day of the seventh month you are H285
Lev 23:35 The **f** day is a sacred assembly; do no H8037
Lev 23:39 the **f** day is a day of sabbath rest H8037
Lev 23:40 On the **f** day you are to take branches from H8037
Nu 1: 1 Desert of Sinai on the **f** day of the second H285
Nu 1:18 together on the **f** day of the second month. H285
Nu 2: 9 number 186,400. They will set out **f**. H8037
Nu 3:12 of the **f male offspring** of H1147+7081+8167
Nu 7:12 his offering on the **f** day was Nahshon son H8037
Nu 8:16 the **f male offspring** from every Israelite H1147
Nu 9: 1 of Sinai in the **f** month of the second H8037
Nu 9: 5 on the fourteenth day of the **f** month. H8037
Nu 10:13 They set out, this **f** *time*, at the LORD's H8037
Nu 10:14 The divisions of the camp of Judah went **f**, H8037
Nu 13:20 It was the season for the **f ripe** grapes.) H1137
Nu 15:20 a loaf from the **f** *of* your ground meal and H8040
Nu 15:21 the LORD from the **f** *of* your ground meal. H8040
Nu 18:15 The **f offspring** *of* every womb, both H7081
Nu 20: 1 In the **f** month the whole Israelite H8037
Nu 22:15 more distinguished than **the f**. H465S
Nu 24:20 "Amalek was **f** *among* the nations, but H8040
Nu 28:11 " 'On the **f** *of* every month, present to the H8031
Nu 28:16 fourteenth day of the **f** month the LORD's H8037
Nu 28:18 On the **f** day hold a sacred assembly and H8037

Nu 29: 1 " 'On the f day of the seventh month hold a H285
Nu 33: 3 on the fifteenth day of the f month, H8037
Nu 33:38 where he died on the f day of the fifth H285
Dt 1: 3 on the f day of the eleventh month H285
Dt 10: 1 tablets like the f *ones* and come up to me H8037
Dt 10: 2 the words that were on the f tablets, H8037
Dt 10: 3 out two stone tablets like the f *ones*, H8037
Dt 10:10 as I did the f time, and the LORD H8037
Dt 13: 9 hand must be the f in putting them to H8037
Dt 16: 4 on the evening of the f day remain until H8037
Dt 17: 7 witnesses must be the f in putting that H8037
Dt 18: 4 the f wool from the shearing of your H8040
Dt 21:17 That son is the f sign of his father's H8040
Dt 24: 4 then her f husband, who divorced her, is H8037
Dt 25: 6 The f *son* she bears shall carry on the H1147
Jos 4:19 the tenth day of the f month the people H8037
Jos 18:11 The f lot came up for the tribe of Benjamin NDT
Jos 21: 4 The f lot came out for the Kohathites NDT
Jos 21:10 because the f lot fell to them): H8037
Jdg 1: 1 of us is to go up f to fight against the H9378
Jdg 20:18 us is to go up f to fight H928+2021+9378
Jdg 20:18 replied, "Judah shall go f." H928+2021+9378
Jdg 20:22 they had stationed themselves the f day. H8037
Jdg 20:39 "We are defeating them as in the f battle." H8037
1Sa 2:16 "Let the fat be burned f, and H3869+2021+3427
1Sa 14:14 In that f attack Jonathan and his H8037
1Sa 14:35 it *was the* **f time** he had done this. H2725
1Sa 22:15 *Was* that day *the* **f time** I inquired of God H2725
2Sa 17: 9 he should attack your troops f, H928+2021+9378
2Sa 18:27 to me that the f *one* runs like Ahimaaz H8037
2Sa 19:20 have come here as the f from the tribes of H8037
2Sa 19:43 Weren't we the f to speak of bringing H8037
2Sa 21: 9 to death during the f days of the harvest, H8037
1Ki 3:22 But **the f one** insisted, "No H2296S
1Ki 3:27 "Give the living baby to **the f woman**. H2023S
1Ki 6:24 One wing of the f cherub was five cubits H285
1Ki 17:13 But f make a small loaf of H928+2021+8037
1Ki 18:25 "Choose one of the bulls and prepare it f H8037
1Ki 20: 9 will do all you demanded the f *time*, H8037
1Ki 20:17 the provincial commanders went out f. H8037
1Ki 22: 5 "F seek the counsel of the H3869+2021+3427
2Ki 1:14 consumed the f two captains and all H8037
2Ki 4:42 barley bread baked from the **f ripe grain**, H1137
2Ki 17:25 When they f lived there, they did not H9378
1Ch 6:54 because the f lot was for them): NDT
1Ch 9: 2 Now the f to resettle on their own property H8037
1Ch 11: 6 Joab son of Zeruiah went up f, and so he H8037
1Ch 12:15 the Jordan in the f month when it was H8037
1Ch 15:13 not bring it up the f *time* that the LORD our H8037
1Ch 16: 7 That day David f appointed Asaph and H8031
1Ch 23: 8 Jehiel the f, Zetham and Joel—three in H8031
1Ch 23:11 Jahath was the f and Ziza the second, but H8031
1Ch 23:16 Shubael was the f. H8031
1Ch 23:17 Rehabiah was the f. Eliezer had no other H8031
1Ch 23:18 The sons of Izhar: Shelomith was the f. H8031
1Ch 23:19 Jeriah the f, Amariah the second H8031
1Ch 23:20 Micah the f and Ishiah the second H8031
1Ch 24: 7 The f lot fell to Jehoiarib, the second to H8037
1Ch 24:21 from his sons: Ishiah was the f. H8031
1Ch 24:23 Jeriah the f, Amariah the second H8031
1Ch 25: 9 The f lot, which was for Asaph, fell to H8037
1Ch 26:10 Shimri the f (although he was not the H8031
1Ch 26:10 his father had appointed him the f), H8031
1Ch 27: 2 In charge of the f division, for the first H8037
1Ch 27: 2 division, for the f month, was Jashobeam H8037
1Ch 27: 3 of all the army officers for the f month. H8037
2Ch 3:11 One wing of the f cherub was five cubits NDT
2Ch 3:12 touched the wing of the f cherub. H285
2Ch 18: 4 "F seek the counsel of the H3869+2021+3427
2Ch 29: 3 In the f month of the first year of his reign H8037
2Ch 29: 3 In the first month of the f year of his reign H8037
2Ch 29:17 consecration on the f day of the first month, H285
2Ch 29:17 on the first day of the f month, H8037
2Ch 29:17 on the sixteenth day of the f month. H8037
2Ch 35: 1 on the fourteenth day of the f month. H8037
2Ch 36:22 In the f year of Cyrus king of Persia, in order H285
Ezr 1: 1 In the f year of Cyrus king of Persia, in order H285
Ezr 3: 6 On the f day of the seventh month they H285
Ezr 5:13 in the f year of Cyrus king of Babylon A10248
Ezr 6: 3 In the f year of King Cyrus, the king A10248
Ezr 6:19 On the fourteenth day of the f month, the H8037
Ezr 7: 9 from Babylon on the f day of the first month H285
Ezr 7: 9 Babylon on the first day of the f month, H8037
Ezr 7: 9 in Jerusalem on the f day of the fifth month H285
Ezr 8:31 twelfth day of the f month we set out from H8037
Ezr 10:16 On the f day of the tenth month they sat H285
Ezr 10:17 by the f day of the first month they H285
Ezr 10:17 the first day of the f month they finished H8037
Ne 4:21 from the **f light of dawn** till the H6590+8840
Ne 7: 5 of those who had been the f to return. H8037
Ne 8: 2 So on the f day of the seventh month Ezra H285
Ne 8:18 after day, from the f day to the last, Ezra H8037
Ne 10:37 to the priests, the f *of* our ground meal, of H8040
Est 3: 7 King Xerxes, in the f month, the month of H8037
Est 3:12 the thirteenth day of the f month the royal H8037
Job 3: 9 in vain and not see the **f rays** *of* dawn, H6757
Job 15: 7 "Are you the f man *ever* born? Were you H8037
Job 40:19 It ranks f *among* the works of God, yet its H8040
Job 42:14 The f daughter he named Jemimah, the H285
Pr 8:22 brought me forth as the f *of* his works, H8040
Pr 18:17 In a lawsuit the f to speak seems right H8037
Isa 41: 4 with the f of them and with the last H8037
Isa 41:27 I was the f to tell Zion, 'Look, here they H8037
Isa 43:27 Your f father sinned; those I sent to teach H8037
Isa 44: 6 I am the f and I am the last; apart from H8037
Isa 48:12 I am he; I am the f and I am the last. H8037
Isa 48:16 "From the f announcement I have not H8031
Isa 52: 4 "At f my people went down to Egypt to H8037
Jer 4:31 a groan as of *one* **bearing** *her* **f child** H1144
Jer 7:12 Shiloh where I f made a H928+2021+8037
Jer 25: 1 which was the f year of Nebuchadnezzar H8038
Jer 36:28 it all the words that were on the f scroll, H8037
Jer 50:17 The f to devour them was the king of H8037
Eze 26: 1 twelfth year, on the f day of the month, the H285
Eze 29:17 in the f month on the first day, the H8037
Eze 29:17 in the first month on the f day, the word of H285
Eze 30:20 in the f month on the seventh day H8037
Eze 31: 1 in the third month on the f day, the word of H285
Eze 32: 1 in the twelfth month on the f day, the word H285
Eze 40:21 measurements as those of the f gateway. H8037
Eze 44:30 to give them the f *portion of* your ground H8040
Eze 45:18 In the f month on the first day you are to H8037
Eze 45:18 first month on the f day you are to take a H285
Eze 45:21 " 'In the f month on the fourteenth day H8037
Da 1:21 there until the f year of King Cyrus. H285
Da 6:19 At the **f light** of dawn, the king got up A10459
Da 7: 1 In the f year of Belshazzar king of A10248
Da 7: 4 "The f was like a lion, and it had the A10623
Da 7: 8 three of the f horns were uprooted A10623
Da 8:21 large horn between its eyes is the f king. H8037
Da 9: 1 In the f year of Darius son of Xerxes (a H285
Da 9: 2 in the f year of his reign, I, Daniel H285
Da 10: 4 On the twenty-fourth day of the f month H8037
Da 10:12 Since the f day that you set your mind to H8037
Da 10:21 f I will tell you what is written in the Book NDT
Da 11: 1 And in the f year of Darius the Mede, I took H285
Da 11:13 larger than the f; and after several H8037
Hos 2: 7 'I will go back to my husband as at f, for H8037
Am 6: 7 you will be among the f to go into exile; H8031
Na 3:12 are like fig trees with their **f ripe fruit**; H1137
Hag 1: 1 King Darius, on the f day of the sixth month H285
Zec 6: 2 The f chariot had red horses, the second H8037
Zec 12: 7 LORD will save the dwellings of Judah f, H8037
Zec 14:10 Benjamin Gate to the site of the F Gate, H8037
Mt 5:24 F go and be reconciled to them; then G4754
Mt 6:33 But seek f his kingdom and his G4754
Mt 7: 5 f take the plank out of your own eye G4754
Mt 8:21 f let me go and bury my father. G4754
Mt 10: 2 f, Simon (who is called Peter) and his G4755
Mt 12:29 possessions unless he f ties up the strong G4754
Mt 12:45 of that person is worse *than* the f. G4755
Mt 13:30 F collect the weeds and tie them in G4754
Mt 17:10 law say that Elijah must come f?" G4754+4755
Mt 17:25 into the house, Jesus *was the* f to speak. G4740
Mt 17:27 Take the f fish you catch; open its mouth G4755
Mt 19:30 But many who are f will be last, and many G4755
Mt 19:30 and many who are last will be f. G4755
Mt 20: 8 the last ones hired and going on to the f. G4755
Mt 20:10 So when those came who were hired f G4755
Mt 20:16 "So the last will be f, and the first will be G4755
Mt 20:16 the last will be first, and the f will be last." G4755
Mt 20:27 wants to be f must be your slave— G4755
Mt 21:28 He went to the f and said, 'Son, go and G4755
Mt 21:31 father wanted?" "The f," they answered G4755
Mt 21:36 to them, more *than* the f *time*, and the G4755
Mt 22:25 The f *one* married and died, and since he G4755
Mt 22:38 This is the f and greatest commandment. G4755
Mt 23:26 F clean the inside of the cup and dish G4754
Mt 26:17 *On the* f *day* of the Festival of Unleavened G4755
Mt 27:64 last deception will be worse *than* the f." G4755
Mt 28: 1 at dawn on the f *day* of the week, Mary G1651
Mk 3:27 man's house without f tying him up. G4754
Mk 4:28 soil produces grain—f the stalk, then the G4754
Mk 7:27 "F let the children eat all they want," G4754
Mk 9:11 law say that Elijah must come f?" G4754+4755
Mk 9:12 Elijah does come f, and restores all G4754
Mk 9:35 who wants to be f must be the very last, G4755
Mk 10:31 But many who are f will be last, and the G4755
Mk 10:31 who are first will be last, and the last f." G4755
Mk 10:44 whoever wants to be f must be slave of all G4755
Mk 12:20 The f *one* married and died without G4755
Mk 13:10 And the gospel must f be preached to all G4754
Mk 14:12 On the f day of the Festival of Unleavened G4755
Mk 16: 2 Very early *on the* f *day* of the week, just G1651
Mk 16: 9 Jesus rose early *on the* f *day* of the week, G4755
Mk 16: 9 he appeared f to Mary Magdalene G4754
Lk 1: 2 those who from the f were eyewitnesses G794
Lk 2: 2 This was the f census that took place while G4755
Lk 6:42 hypocrite, f take the plank out of your eye G4754
Lk 9:59 f let me go and bury my father. G4754
Lk 9:61 f let me go back and say goodbye to G4754
Lk 10: 5 you enter a house, f say, 'Peace to this G4754
Lk 11:26 of that person is worse *than* the f. G4755
Lk 11:38 that Jesus did not f wash before the meal. G4754
Lk 12: 1 Jesus began to speak f to his disciples G4754
Lk 13:30 there are those who are last who will be f, G4755
Lk 13:30 who will be first, and f who will be last." G4755
Lk 14:18 The f said, 'I have just bought a field, and G4755
Lk 14:28 Won't you f sit down and estimate the G4754
Lk 14:31 Won't he f sit down and consider whether G4754
Lk 16: 5 He asked the f, 'How much do you owe G4755
Lk 17:25 But f he must suffer many things and be G4754
Lk 19:16 "The f *one* came and said, 'Sir, your mina G4755
Lk 20:29 The f *one* married a woman and died G4755
Lk 21: 9 These things must happen f, but the end G4754
Lk 24: 1 *On the* f *day* of the week, very early in the G1651
Jn 1:41 The f *thing* Andrew did was to find his G4754
Jn 2:10 out the choice wine f and then the G4754
Jn 2:11 of Galilee was the f of the signs through G794
Jn 7:51 a man without f hearing him to find G4754
Jn 8: 7 is without sin be the f to throw a stone at G4755
Jn 8: 9 the older ones f, until only Jesus was G806
Jn 12:16 **At f** his disciples did not G3836+4754
Jn 15:18 keep in mind that it hated me f. G4754
Jn 18:13 brought him f to Annas, who was the G4754
Jn 19:32 broke the legs *of* the f *man* who had been G4755
Jn 20: 1 Early *on* the f *day* of the week, while it G1651
Jn 20: 4 outran Peter and reached the tomb f. G4755
Jn 20: 8 who had reached the tomb f, also went G4755
Jn 20:19 On the evening *of* that f day of the week G1651
Ac 3:26 he sent him f to you to bless you by G4754
Ac 7:12 he sent our forefathers on their f visit. G4754
Ac 11:26 were called Christians f at Antioch. G4759
Ac 12:10 They passed the f and second guards and G4755
Ac 13:46 had to speak the word of God to you f. G4754
Ac 15:14 to us how God f intervened to choose a G4754
Ac 20: 7 On the f *day* of the week we came G1651
Ac 20:18 from the f day I came into the province of G4755
Ac 26:20 F to those in Damascus, then to those in G4754
Ac 26:23 suffer and, as the f to rise from the dead G4755
Ac 27:43 swim to jump overboard f and get to land. G4755
Ro 1: 8 F, I thank my God through Jesus Christ G4754
Ro 1:16 who believes: f to the Jew, then to G4754
Ro 1:17 that is **by faith from f to last**, G1666+4411+1650+4411
Ro 2: 9 being who does evil: f for the Jew, then G4754
Ro 2:10 who does good: f for the Jew, then for G4754
Ro 3: 2 **F of all**, the Jews have been entrusted G4754
Ro 10:19 F, Moses says, "I will make you envious by G4755
Ro 13:11 is nearer now than when *we f* **believed**. AIT
Ro 16: 5 who was the **f convert** to Christ in the G569
1Co 11:18 **In the f place**, I hear that when you come G4754
1Co 12:28 has placed in the church **f of all** apostles, G4754
1Co 14:30 is sitting down, the f speaker should stop. G4755
1Co 15: 3 on to you **as of f importance**: G1877+4755
1Co 15:45 "The f man Adam became a living being"; G4755
1Co 15:46 The spiritual did not come f, but the G4755
1Co 15:47 The f man was of the dust of the earth; the G4755
1Co 16: 2 *On the* f *day* of every week, each one of G1651
1Co 16:15 of Stephanas were the **f converts** in Achaia, G569
2Co 1:15 I wanted to visit you f so that you might G4728
2Co 8: 5 They gave themselves **f of all** to the Lord G4754
2Co 8:10 Last year you *were the* f not only to give G4599
Gal 4:13 an illness that I **f preached** the G3836+4728
Eph 1:12 who *were* **the f to put** our **hope** in Christ G4598
Eph 6: 2 which is the f commandment with a G4755
Php 1: 5 in the gospel from the f day until now, G4755
1Th 4:16 and the dead in Christ will rise f. G4754
1Ti 2: 1 then, f of all, that petitions, prayers G4754
1Ti 2:13 For Adam was formed f, then Eve. G4755
1Ti 3:10 They must f be tested; and then if there is G4754
1Ti 5: 4 these should learn **f of all** to put their G4754
1Ti 5:12 because they have broken their f pledge. G4755
2Ti 1: 5 which f lived in your grandmother Lois G4754
2Ti 2: 6 farmer should be the f to receive a share G4754
2Ti 4:16 At my f defense, no one came to my G4755
Heb 2: 3 which was f announced by the Lord G794
Heb 7: 2 F, the name Melchizedek means "king of G4754
Heb 7:27 day after day, f for his own sins, and G4728
Heb 8: 7 been nothing wrong with that f *covenant*, G4755
Heb 8:13 he has made the f *one* obsolete; and G4755
Heb 9: 1 Now the f covenant had regulations for G4755
Heb 9: 2 In its f *room* were the lampstand and the G4755
Heb 9: 8 as long as the f tabernacle was still G4755
Heb 9:15 the sins committed under the f covenant. G4755
Heb 9:18 This is why even the f covenant was not G4755
Heb 10: 8 **F** he said, "Sacrifices and offerings, burnt G542
Heb 10: 9 He sets aside the f to establish the G4755
Heb 10:15 testifies to us about this. **F** he says: G3552+3836
Jas 3:17 that comes from heaven is f *of all* pure; G4754
1Jn 4:19 We love because he f loved us. G4755
3Jn 9 Diotrephes, who **loves to be f**, will not G5812
Rev 1:17 "Do not be afraid. I am the F and the Last. G4755
Rev 2: 4 You have forsaken the love you had *at* f. G4755
Rev 2: 5 Repent and do the things you did *at* f. G4755
Rev 2: 8 words of him who is the F and the Last, G4755
Rev 2:19 you are now doing more *than* you did *at* f. G4755
Rev 4: 1 And the voice I had f heard speaking to G4755
Rev 4: 7 The f living creature was like a lion, the G4755
Rev 6: 1 the Lamb opened the f of the seven seals. G1651
Rev 8: 7 The f angel sounded his trumpet, and G4755
Rev 9:12 The f woe is past; two other woes are G1651
Rev 13:12 all the authority *of* the f beast on its G4755
Rev 13:12 its inhabitants worship the f beast, G4755
Rev 13:14 power to perform on behalf of the f beast, NDT
Rev 13:15 to give breath to the image of the f beast, NDT
Rev 16: 2 The f angel went and poured out his bowl G4755
Rev 20: 5 This is the f resurrection. G4755
Rev 20: 6 are those who share in the f resurrection. G4755
Rev 21: 1 the f heaven and the first earth had G4755
Rev 21: 1 first heaven and the f earth had passed G4755
Rev 21:19 The f foundation was jasper, the second G4755
Rev 22:13 the Omega, the F and the Last, the G4755

FIRSTBEGOTTEN (KJV) FIRSTBORN

F

FIRSTBORN (132) [FIRST, BEAR]

Ge 4: 4 fat portions from some of the f *of* his flock. H1147
Ge 10:15 Canaan was the father of Sidon his f, and H1147
Ge 22:21 Uz the f, Buz his brother, Kemuel (the H1147
Ge 25:13 Nebaioth the f *of* Ishmael, Kedar, Adbeel H1147
Ge 27:19 "I am Esau your f. I have done as you H1147
Ge 27:32 am your son," he answered, "your f, Esau." H1147
Ge 35:23 Reuben the f *of* Jacob, Simeon, Levi H1147
Ge 36:15 The sons of Eliphaz the f *of* Esau: Chiefs H1147
Ge 38: 6 got a wife for Er, his f, and her name was H1147
Ge 38: 7 Judah's f, was wicked in the LORD's H1147
Ge 41:51 Joseph named his f Manasseh and said H1147
Ge 43:33 their ages, from the f to the youngest; and H1147
Ge 46: 8 went to Egypt: Reuben the f *of* Jacob. H1147
Ge 48:14 even though Manasseh was the f. H1147
Ge 48:18 this one is the f; put your right hand on H1147
Ge 49: 3 "Reuben, you are my f, my might, the first H1147
Ex 4:22 is what the LORD says: Israel is my f son, H1147
Ex 4:23 to let him go; so I will kill your f son. H1147
Ex 6:14 of Reuben the f *son of* Israel were Hanok H1147
Ex 11: 5 Every f *son* in Egypt will die, from the H1147
Ex 11: 5 from the f *son of* Pharaoh, who sits H1147
Ex 11: 5 to the f *son of* the female slave H1147
Ex 11: 5 and all the f *of* the cattle as well. H1147
Ex 12:12 strike down every f of both people and H1147
Ex 12:29 the LORD struck down all the f in Egypt, H1147
Ex 12:29 in Egypt, from the f *of* Pharaoh, who sat H1147
Ex 12:29 the throne, to the f *of* the prisoner, who H1147
Ex 12:29 the f *of* all the livestock as well. H1147
Ex 13: 2 "Consecrate to me every f *male*. The first H1147
Ex 13:12 All the f males *of* your livestock H7081+8715
Ex 13:13 Redeem with a lamb every f donkey, but if H7081
Ex 13:13 Redeem every f among your sons. H1147
Ex 13:15 the LORD killed the f of both people and H1147
Ex 13:15 womb and redeem each of my f sons. H1147
Ex 22:29 "You must give me the f *of* your sons. H1147
Ex 34:19 the f males *of* your livestock, whether *from* H7081
Ex 34:20 Redeem the f donkey with a lamb, but if H7081
Ex 34:20 Redeem all your f sons. "No one is to H1147
Lev 27:26 may dedicate the f of an animal, since H1147
Lev 27:26 the f already **belongs to** the LORD H1144+4200
Nu 1:20 descendants of Reuben the f *son of* Israel: H1147
Nu 3: 2 of Aaron were Nadab the f and Abihu, H1147
Nu 3:13 all the f are mine. When I struck down H1147
Nu 3:13 When I struck down all the f in Egypt, I set H1147
Nu 3:13 I set apart for myself every f in Israel H1147
Nu 3:40 "Count all the f Israelite males who are a H1147
Nu 3:41 me in place of all the f of the Israelites, H1147
Nu 3:41 in place of all the f of the livestock of the H1147
Nu 3:42 Moses counted all the f of the Israelites, H1147
Nu 3:43 The total number of f males a month old H1147
Nu 3:45 the Levites in place of all the f of Israel, H1147
Nu 3:46 To redeem the 273 f Israelites who exceed H1147
Nu 3:50 From the f *of* the Israelites he collected H1147
Nu 8:16 taken them as my own in place of the f, H7082
Nu 8:17 Every f **male** in Israel, whether human H1147
Nu 8:17 When I struck down all the f in Egypt, I set H1147
Nu 8:18 Levites in place of all the f *sons* in Israel. H1147
Nu 18:15 you must redeem every f son and every H1147
Nu 18:15 son and every f **male** *of* unclean animals. H1147
Nu 18:17 "But you must not redeem the f *of* a cow H1147
Nu 26: 5 of Reuben, the f *son of* Israel, were: H1147
Nu 33: 4 who were burying all their f, whom the H1147
Dt 12: 6 the f *of* your herds and flocks. H1147
Dt 12:17 olive oil, or the f *of* your herds and flocks H1147
Dt 14:23 the f *of* your herds and flocks in the H1147
Dt 15:19 LORD your God every f male of your herds H1147
Dt 15:19 Do not put the f *of* your cows to work, and H1147
Dt 15:19 do not shear the f *of* your sheep. H1147
Dt 21:15 bear him sons but the f is the son of the H1147
Dt 21:16 must not **give the rights of the** f *to* the son H1144
Dt 21:16 wife he loves in preference to his actual f, H1147
Dt 21:17 unloved wife as the f by giving him a H1147
Dt 21:17 The right of the f belongs to him. H1148
Dt 33:17 In majesty he is like a f bull; his horns are H1147
Jos 6:26 "At the cost of his f *son* he will lay its H1147
Jos 17: 1 the tribe of Manasseh as Joseph's f, H1147
Jos 17: 1 firstborn, that is, for Makir, Manasseh's f. H1147
1Sa 8: 2 The name of his f was Joel and the name H1147
1Sa 17:13 The f was Eliab; the second, Abinadab H1147
2Sa 3: 2 His f was Amnon the son of Ahinoam of H1147
1Ki 16:34 at the cost of his f *son* Abiram, H1147
2Ki 3:27 Then he took his f son, who was to H1147
1Ch 1:13 Canaan was the father of Sidon his f, and H1147
1Ch 1:29 Nebaioth the f *of* Ishmael, Kedar, Adbeel H1147
1Ch 2: 3 Judah's f, was wicked in the LORD's H1147
1Ch 2:13 Jesse was the father of Eliab his f; the H1147
1Ch 2:25 The sons of Jerahmeel the f *of* Hezron H1147
1Ch 2:25 Ram his f, Bunah, Oren, Ozem and Ahijah H1147
1Ch 2:27 The sons of Ram the f *of* Jerahmeel H1147
1Ch 2:42 Mesha his f, who was the father of Ziph H1147
1Ch 2:50 The sons of Hur the f *of* Ephrathah H1147
1Ch 3: 1 The f was Amnon the son of Ahinoam of H1147
1Ch 3:15 Johanan the f, Jehoiakim the second son H1147
1Ch 4: 4 the f *of* Ephrathah and father of H1147
1Ch 5: 1 The sons of Reuben the f *of* Israel (he was H1147
1Ch 5: 1 he was the f, but when he defiled H1147
1Ch 5: 1 his **rights as** f were given to the sons of H1148
1Ch 5: 2 the **rights of the** f belonged to Joseph)— H1148
1Ch 5: 3 the sons of Reuben the f *of* Israel: Hanok H1147
1Ch 6:28 Joel the f and Abijah the second son H1147
1Ch 8: 1 Benjamin was the father of Bela his f H1147
1Ch 8:30 his f son was Abdon, followed by Zur H1147
1Ch 8:39 Ulam his f, Jeush the second son and H1147
1Ch 9: 5 Asaiah the f and his sons. H1147
1Ch 9:31 the f son of Shallum the Korahite H1147
1Ch 9:36 his f son was Abdon, followed by Zur H1147
1Ch 26: 2 Zechariah the f, Jediael the second H1147
1Ch 26: 4 Shemaiah the f, Jehozabad the second H1147
1Ch 26:10 although he was not the f, his father had H1147
2Ch 21: 3 to Jehoram because he was his f *son*. H1147
Ne 10:36 we will bring the f *of* our sons and of our H1147
Job 18:13 of his skin; death's f devours his limbs. H1147
Ps 78:51 He struck down all the f of Egypt, the H1147
Ps 89:27 And I will appoint him to be my f, the H1147
Ps 105:36 Then he struck down all the f in their land, H1147
Ps 135: 8 He struck down the f *of* Egypt, the firstborn H1147
Ps 135: 8 of Egypt, the f of people and animals. NDT
Ps 136:10 who struck down the f *of* Egypt His love H1147
Jer 31: 9 Israel's father, and Ephraim is my f *son*. H1147
Eze 20:26 the sacrifice of every f—that I might H7081+8167
Mic 6: 7 Shall I offer my f for my transgression, the H1147
Zec 12:10 bitterly for him as one grieves for a f *son*. H1147
Lk 2: 7 she gave birth to her f, a son. *G4758*
Lk 2:23 "Every f male is to be consecrated *G1380+3616*
Ro 8:29 he might be the f among many brothers *G4758*
Col 1:15 the invisible God, the f over all creation. *G4758*
Col 1:18 beginning and the f from among the *G4758*
Heb 1: 6 when God brings his f into the world, he *G4758*
Heb 11:28 that the destroyer *of* the f would not touch *G4758*
Heb 11:28 firstborn would not touch **the f of Israel.** *G899S*
Heb 12:23 to the church *of* the f, whose names are *G4758*
Rev 1: 5 faithful witness, the f from the dead, and *G4758*

FIRSTFRUITS (30) [FIRST]

Ex 23:16 of Harvest with the f *of* the crops you sow H1137
Ex 23:19 "Bring the best of the f *of* your soil to the H1137
Ex 34:22 of Weeks with the f *of* the wheat harvest, H1137
Ex 34:26 "Bring the best of the f *of* your soil to the H1137
Lev 2:12 them to the LORD as an offering of the f, H8040
Lev 2:14 you bring a grain offering of f to the LORD, H1137
Lev 23:17 as a wave offering of f to the LORD. H1137
Lev 23:20 offering, together with the bread of the f. H1137
Nu 18:12 they give the LORD as the **f of** their **harvest**. H8040
Nu 18:13 All the land's f that they bring to the LORD H1137
Nu 28:26 " 'On the day of f, when you present to H1137
Dt 18: 4 You are to give them the f *of* your grain H8040
Dt 26: 2 take some of the f *of* all that you H8040+7262
Dt 26:10 now I bring the f *of* the soil that H8040+7262
2Ch 31: 5 generously gave the f *of* their grain, H8040
Ne 10:35 LORD each year the f *of* our crops and of H1137
Ne 12:44 the contributions, f and tithes. H8040
Ne 13:31 wood at designated times, and for the f. H1137
Ps 78:51 the f *of* manhood in the tents of Ham. H8040
Ps 105:36 in their land, the f of all their manhood. H8040
Pr 3: 9 your wealth, with the f *of* all your crops; H8040
Jer 2: 3 to the LORD, the f *of* his harvest; all who H8040
Eze 44:30 The best of all the f and of all your special H1137
Ro 8:23 who have the f of the Spirit, groan *G569*
Ro 11:16 If the **part** *of the dough* **offered as** f is holy *G569*
1Co 15:20 the f of those who have fallen asleep. *G569*
1Co 15:23 the f; then, when he comes, those *G569*
2Th 2:13 God chose you *as* f to be saved through *G569*
Jas 1:18 we might be a kind of f of all he created. *G569*
Rev 14: 4 mankind and *offered as* f to God and the *G569*

FIRSTLING, FIRSTLINGS (KJV) FIRSTBORN

FISH (67) [FISHERMEN, FISHHOOK, FISHHOOKS, FISHING, FISHNETS]

Ge 1:26 may rule over the f *in* the sea and the H1836
Ge 1:28 Rule over the f *in* the sea and the birds in H1836
Ge 9: 2 on all the f *in* the sea; they are H1834
Ex 7:18 The f in the Nile will die, and the river will H1836
Ex 7:21 The f in the Nile died, and the river H1836
Nu 11: 5 We remember the f we ate in Egypt at no H1836
Nu 11:22 enough if all the f *in* the sea were caught H1834
Dt 4:18 the ground or any f in the waters below. H1836
1Ki 4:33 about animals and birds, reptiles and f. H1834
2Ch 33:14 the entrance of the F Gate and encircling H1834
Ne 3: 3 The F Gate was rebuilt by the sons of H1834
Ne 12:39 Jeshanah Gate, the F Gate, the Tower of H1834
Ne 13:16 were bringing in f and all kinds of H1794
Job 12: 8 or let the f *in* the sea inform you. H1834
Ps 8: 8 in the sky, and the f *in* the sea, all that H1834
Ps 105:29 waters into blood, causing their f to die. H1836
Ecc 9:12 As f are caught in a cruel net, or birds are H1834
Isa 50: 2 their f rot for lack of water and die of thirst. H1836
Eze 29: 4 jaws and make the f *of* your streams stick H1836
Eze 29: 4 with all the f sticking to your scales. H1836
Eze 29: 5 you and all the f *of* your streams. H1836
Eze 38:20 The f *in* the sea, the birds in the sky, the H1834
Eze 47: 9 There will be large numbers of f, because H1836
Eze 47:10 The f will be of many kinds—like the fish H1836
Eze 47:10 like the f *of* the Mediterranean Sea. H1836
Hos 4: 3 in the sky and the f *in* the sea are swept H1834
Jnh 1:17 LORD provided a huge f to swallow Jonah, H1834
Jnh 1:17 in the belly of the f three days and three H1834
Jnh 2: 1 From inside the f Jonah prayed to the LORD H1836
Jnh 2:10 And the LORD commanded the f, and it H1834
Hab 1:14 have made people like the f in the sea, H1834
Zep 1: 3 the birds in the sky and the f *in* the sea— H1834
Zep 1:10 "a cry will go up from the F Gate, wailing H1834
Mt 4:19 "and I will send you out to f for people." *G243*
Mt 7:10 Or if he asks *for* a f, will give him a snake? *G2716*
Mt 12:40 three nights in the belly *of* a **huge** f, *G3063*
Mt 13:47 down into the lake and caught all **kinds** *of* f. AIT
Mt 13:48 sat down and collected the **good** *f* in baskets, AIT
Mt 14:17 here only five loaves of bread and two f," *G2716*
Mt 14:19 loaves and the two f and looking up to *G2716*
Mt 15:34 they replied, "and a few **small** f." *G2715*
Mt 15:36 Then he took the seven loaves and the f *G2716*
Mt 17:27 Take the first f you catch; open its mouth *G2716*
Mk 1:17 I will send you out to f for people." *G1181+243*
Mk 6:38 found out, they said, "Five—and two f." *G2716*
Mk 6:41 loaves and the two f and looking up to *G2716*
Mk 6:41 He also divided the two f among them all. *G2716*
Mk 6:43 of broken pieces of bread and f. *G2716*
Mk 8: 7 They had a few **small** f as well; he gave *G2715*
Lk 5: 6 such a large number *of* f that their nets *G2716*
Lk 5: 9 at the catch *of* f they had taken, *G2716*
Lk 5:10 from now on *you will* f for people." *G1639+2436*
Lk 9:13 have only five loaves of bread and two f— *G2716*
Lk 9:16 loaves and the two f and looking up to *G2716*
Lk 11:11 if your son asks for a f, will give him a *G2716*
Lk 24:42 They gave him a piece *of* broiled f, *G2716*
Jn 6: 9 five small barley loaves and two **small** f, *G4066*
Jn 6:11 He did the same with the f. *G4066*
Jn 21: 3 "I'm going out *to* f," Simon Peter told them *G244*
Jn 21: 5 out to them, "Friends, haven't you any f?" *G4709*
Jn 21: 6 net in because of the large number *of* f. *G2716*
Jn 21: 8 towing the net *full of* f, for they were not *G2716*
Jn 21: 9 a fire of burning coals there with f on it, *G4066*
Jn 21:10 "Bring some of the f you have just caught." *G4066*
Jn 21:11 It was full *of* large f, 153, but even with so *G2716*
Jn 21:13 it to them, and did the same *with* the f. *G4066*
1Co 15:39 another, birds another and f another. *G2716*

FISHERMEN (7) [FISH]

Isa 19: 8 The f will groan and lament, all who cast H1900
Jer 16:16 "But now I will send for many f," declares H1900
Eze 47:10 F will stand along the shore; from En Gedi H1854
Mt 4:18 casting a net into the lake, for they were f. *G243*
Mt 13:48 it was full, *the f* **pulled it up** on the shore. AIT
Mk 1:16 casting a net into the lake, for they were f. *G243*
Lk 5: 2 left there by the f, who were washing their *G243*

FISHHOOK (1) [FISH, HOOK]

Job 41: 1 in Leviathan with a f or tie down its H2676

FISHHOOKS (1) [FISH, HOOK]

Am 4: 2 with hooks, the last of you with f. H1855+6106

FISHING (1) [FISH]

Job 41: 7 with harpoons or its head with f spears? H1834

FISHNETS (2) [FISH, NET]

Eze 26: 5 sea she will become a place to spread f, H3052
Eze 26:14 you will become a place to spread f. H3052

FIST (4) [FISTS, TIGHTFISTED]

Ex 21:18 a stone or with their f and the victim does H114
Nu 35:21 another with their f so that the other dies, H3338
Job 15:25 he shakes his f at God and vaunts H3338
Isa 10:32 they will shake their f at the mount of H3338

FISTS (4) [FIST]

Isa 58: 4 in striking each other with wicked f. H114
Zep 2:15 who pass by her scoff and shake their f. H3338
Mt 26:67 spit in his face and **struck** him **with** *their* f. *G3139*
Mk 14:65 **struck** him **with** *their* f, and said, *G3139*

FIT (15) [FITS, FITTED, FITTING, FITTINGS]

Ge 49:20 he will provide **delicacies** *f for* a king. AIT
Ex 15:25 and the water *became* **f to drink**. H5517
Dt 12: 8 here today, everyone doing as they see f, H3838
Jdg 5:25 in a **bowl** *f for* nobles she brought him AIT
Jdg 17: 6 had no king; everyone did as they saw f. H3838
Jdg 20:17 swordsmen, all of them **f for battle**. H4878+408
Jdg 21:25 had no king; everyone did as they saw f. H3838
2Ki 24:16 strong and f for war, and a thousand H6913
2Ch 25: 5 thousand men **f for military service**, H3655+7372
Isa 54:16 flame and forges a weapon **f for** its work. H4200
Eze 19:11 branches were strong, **f for** a ruler's scepter. H448
Eze 19:14 branch is left on it f for a ruler's scepter. NDT
Lk 9:62 looks back is **f for service** in the kingdom *G2310*
Lk 14:35 It is f neither for the soil nor for the *G2310*
Ac 22:22 "Rid the earth of him! He's not f to live!" *G2763*

FITCHES (KJV) CARAWAY, SPELT

FITS (2) [FIT]

2Co 12:20 jealousy, **f of rage**, selfish ambition *G2596*
Gal 5:20 jealousy, **f of rage**, selfish ambition *G2596*

FITTED (8) [FIT]

Ex 26:24 to the top and f into a single ring H9447+3481
Ex 36:29 to the top and f into a single ring H9447+3481
Jos 17:16 live in the plain have **chariots** *f with* iron, AIT
Jos 17:18 Canaanites have **chariots** *f with* iron and AIT
Jdg 1:19 because they had **chariots** *f with* iron. AIT
Jdg 4: 3 nine hundred **chariots** *f with* iron and had AIT
Jdg 4:13 his nine hundred **chariots** *f with* iron. AIT
Eph 6:15 and *with* your feet f with the readiness that *G5686*

FITTING (7) [FIT]

Ps 33: 1 it is f for the upright to praise him. H5534
Ps 147: 1 how pleasant and f to praise him! H5534

Pr 19:10 It is not **f** for a fool to live in luxury—how H5534
Pr 26: 1 rain in harvest, honor is not **f** for a fool. H5534
1Co 14:40 should be done *in* a **f** and orderly way. *G2361*
Col 3:18 to your husbands, as *is* **f** in the Lord. *G465*
Heb 2:10 to glory, *it was* **f** that God, for whom *G4560*

FITTINGS (1) [FIT]

1Ch 22: 3 the doors of the gateways and for the **f**, H4677

FIVE (212) [FIFTH, FOUR-FIFTHS]

Ge 14: 9 king of Ellasar—four kings against **f**. H2822
Ge 18:28 of the righteous is **f** less than fifty? H2822
Ge 18:28 destroy the whole city for lack of **f** *people*?" H2822
Ge 43:34 portion was **f** times as much as H2822
Ge 45: 6 for the next **f** years there will be no H2822
Ge 45:11 because **f** years of famine are still to H2822
Ge 45:22 shekels of silver and **f** sets of clothes. H2822
Ge 47: 2 He chose **f** of his brothers and presented H2822
Ex 22: 1 it must pay back **f** head of cattle for the H2822
Ex 26: 3 Join **f** *of* the curtains together, and do the H2822
Ex 26: 3 do the same with the other **f**. H2822
Ex 26: 9 Join **f** *of* the curtains into one set H2822
Ex 26:26 **f** for the frames on one side of the H2822
Ex 26:27 **f** for those on the other side, and five for H2822
Ex 26:27 and **f** for the frames on the west H2822
Ex 26:37 this curtain and **f** posts of acacia wood H2822
Ex 26:37 And cast **f** bronze bases for them H2822
Ex 27: 1 **f** cubits long and five cubits wide. H2822
Ex 27: 1 five cubits long and **f** cubits wide. H2822
Ex 27:18 of finely twisted linen **f** cubits high, H2822
Ex 36:10 They joined **f** *of* the curtains together and H2822
Ex 36:10 did the same with the other **f**. H2822
Ex 36:16 They joined **f** *of* the curtains into one set H2822
Ex 36:31 **f** for the frames on one side of the H2822
Ex 36:32 **f** for those on the other side, and five for H2822
Ex 36:32 and **f** for the frames on the west H2822
Ex 36:38 they made **f** posts with hooks for them. H2822
Ex 36:38 gold and made their **f** bases of bronze. H2822
Ex 38: 1 **f** cubits long and five cubits wide. H2822
Ex 38: 1 five cubits long and **f** cubits wide. H2822
Ex 38:18 the curtains of the courtyard, **f** cubits high, H2822
Lev 26: 8 **F** of you will chase a hundred, and a H2822
Lev 27: 5 person between the ages of **f** and twenty, H2822
Lev 27: 6 a person between one month and **f** years, H2822
Lev 27: 6 value of a male at **f** shekels of silver and H2822
Nu 3:47 collect **f** shekels for each one, according to H2822
Nu 7:17 two oxen, **f** rams, five male goats and H2822
Nu 7:17 **f** male goats and five male lambs a year H2822
Nu 7:17 five male goats and **f** male lambs a year H2822
Nu 7:23 two oxen, **f** rams, five male goats and H2822
Nu 7:23 **f** male goats and five male lambs a year H2822
Nu 7:23 five male goats and **f** male lambs a year H2822
Nu 7:29 two oxen, **f** rams, five male goats and H2822
Nu 7:29 **f** male goats and five male lambs a year H2822
Nu 7:29 five male goats and **f** male lambs a year H2822
Nu 7:35 two oxen, **f** rams, five male goats and H2822
Nu 7:35 **f** male goats and five male lambs a year H2822
Nu 7:35 five male goats and **f** male lambs a year H2822
Nu 7:41 two oxen, **f** rams, five male goats and H2822
Nu 7:41 **f** male goats and five male lambs a year H2822
Nu 7:41 five male goats and **f** male lambs a year H2822
Nu 7:47 two oxen, **f** rams, five male goats and H2822
Nu 7:47 **f** male goats and five male lambs a year H2822
Nu 7:47 five male goats and **f** male lambs a year H2822
Nu 7:53 two oxen, **f** rams, five male goats and H2822
Nu 7:53 **f** male goats and five male lambs a year H2822
Nu 7:53 five male goats and **f** male lambs a year H2822
Nu 7:59 two oxen, **f** rams, five male goats and H2822
Nu 7:59 **f** male goats and five male lambs a year H2822
Nu 7:59 five male goats and **f** male lambs a year H2822
Nu 7:65 two oxen, **f** rams, five male goats and H2822
Nu 7:65 **f** male goats and five male lambs a year H2822
Nu 7:65 five male goats and **f** male lambs a year H2822
Nu 7:71 two oxen, **f** rams, five male goats and H2822
Nu 7:71 **f** male goats and five male lambs a year H2822
Nu 7:71 five male goats and **f** male lambs a year H2822
Nu 7:77 two oxen, **f** rams, five male goats and H2822
Nu 7:77 **f** male goats and five male lambs a year H2822
Nu 7:77 five male goats and **f** male lambs a year H2822
Nu 7:83 two oxen, **f** rams, five male goats and H2822
Nu 7:83 **f** male goats and five male lambs a year H2822
Nu 7:83 five male goats and **f** male lambs a year H2822
Nu 11:19 or two days, or **f**, ten or twenty days, H2822
Nu 18:16 redemption price set at **f** shekels *of* silver, H2822
Nu 31: 8 Hur and Reba—the **f** kings of Midian. H2822
Nu 31:28 the LORD one out of every **f** hundred, H2822
Jos 8:12 had taken about **f** thousand men and set H2822
Jos 10: 5 Then the **f** kings of the Amorites—the H2822
Jos 10:16 Now the **f** kings had fled and hidden in H2822
Jos 10:17 was told that the **f** kings had been found H2822
Jos 10:22 cave and bring those **f** kings out to me." H2822
Jos 10:23 So they brought the **f** kings out of the cave H2822
Jos 10:26 exposed their bodies on **f** poles, H2822
Jos 13: 3 though held by the **f** Philistine rulers in H2822
Jdg 3: 3 the **f** rulers of the Philistines, all the H2822
Jdg 18: 2 So the Danites sent **f** *of* their leading men H2822
Jdg 18: 7 So the **f** men left and came to Laish H2822
Jdg 18:14 Then the **f** men who had spied out the H2822
Jdg 18:17 The **f** men who had spied out the land H2822
Jdg 18:18 When **the f men** went into Micah's house H465s
Jdg 20:45 Israelites cut down **f** thousand men along H2822
1Sa 6: 4 replied, "**F** gold tumors and five gold rats H2822
1Sa 6: 4 "Five gold tumors and **f** gold rats H2822
1Sa 6:16 The **f** rulers of the Philistines saw all this H2822
1Sa 6:18 towns belonging to the **f** rulers— H2822
1Sa 17: 5 of bronze weighing **f** thousand shekels; H2822
1Sa 17:40 chose **f** smooth stones from the stream H2822
1Sa 21: 3 Give me **f** loaves of bread, or whatever H2822
1Sa 25:18 two skins of wine, **f** dressed sheep, five H2822
1Sa 25:18 dressed sheep, **f** seahs of roasted grain H2822
1Sa 25:42 attended by her **f** female servants H2822
2Sa 4: 4 He was **f** years old when the news about H2822
2Sa 21: 8 together with the **f** sons of Saul's H2822
2Sa 24: 9 and in Judah **f** hundred thousand. H2822
1Ki 4:32 his songs numbered a thousand and **f**. H2822
1Ki 6: 6 The lowest floor was **f** cubits wide, the H2822
1Ki 6:10 The height of each was **f** cubits, and they H2822
1Ki 6:24 wing of the first cherub was **f** cubits long, H2822
1Ki 6:24 the other wing **f** cubits—ten cubits H2822
1Ki 7:16 the pillars; each capital was **f** cubits high. H2822
1Ki 7:23 cubits from rim to rim and **f** cubits high. H2822
1Ki 7:39 He placed **f** of the stands on the south H2822
1Ki 7:39 side of the temple and **f** on the north. H2822
1Ki 7:49 gold (**f** on the right and five on the left H2822
1Ki 7:49 five on the right and **f** on the left, in front H2822
2Ki 6:25 of a cab of seed pods for **f** shekels. H2822
2Ki 7:13 "Have some men take **f** of the horses that H2822
2Ki 13:19 have struck the ground **f** or six times; H2822
2Ki 25:19 of the fighting men, and **f** royal advisers. H2822
1Ch 2: 4 Zerah to Judah. He had **f** sons in all. H2822
1Ch 2: 6 Heman, Kalkol and Darda—**f** in all. H2822
1Ch 3:20 There were also **f** others: Hashubah, Ohel, H2822
1Ch 4:32 Rimmon, Token and Ashan—**f** towns— H2822
1Ch 4:42 And **f** hundred of these Simeonites, led by H2822
1Ch 7: 3 Joel and Ishiah. All **f** of them were chiefs. H2822
1Ch 7: 7 heads of families—**f** in all. H2822
1Ch 11:23 down an Egyptian who was **f** cubits tall. H2822
1Ch 29: 7 the temple of God **f** thousand talents and H2822
2Ch 3:11 the first cherub was **f** cubits long and H2822
2Ch 3:11 its other wing, also **f** cubits long, touched H2822
2Ch 3:12 the second cherub was **f** cubits long and H2822
2Ch 3:12 its other wing, also **f** cubits long, touched H2822
2Ch 3:15 each with a capital **f** cubits high. H2822
2Ch 4: 2 cubits from rim to rim and **f** cubits high. H2822
2Ch 4: 6 washing and placed **f** on the south side H2822
2Ch 4: 6 five on the south side and **f** on the north. H2822
2Ch 4: 7 **f** on the south side and five on the north. H2822
2Ch 4: 7 five on the south side and **f** on the north. H2822
2Ch 4: 8 **f** on the south side and five on the north. H2822
2Ch 4: 8 five on the south side and **f** on the north. H2822
2Ch 6:13 a bronze platform, **f** cubits long, five H2822
2Ch 6:13 **f** cubits wide and three cubits high H2822
2Ch 13:17 so that there were **f** hundred thousand H2822
2Ch 35: 9 provided **f** thousand Passover offerings H2822
2Ch 35: 9 offerings and **f** hundred head of cattle H2822
Est 9: 6 Jews killed and destroyed **f** hundred men. H2822
Est 9:12 destroyed **f** hundred men and the H2822
Job 1: 3 **f** hundred yoke of oxen and five hundred H2822
Job 1: 3 yoke of oxen and **f** hundred donkeys, H2822
Isa 17: 6 branches, four or **f** on the fruitful boughs," H2822
Isa 19:18 In that day **f** cities in Egypt will speak the H2822
Isa 30:17 at the threat of **f** you will all flee away H2822
Jer 52:22 of one pillar was **f** cubits high and was H2822
Eze 40: 7 between the alcoves were **f** cubits thick. H2822
Eze 40:30 twenty-five cubits wide and **f** cubits deep.) H2822
Eze 40:48 they were **f** cubits wide on either side. H2822
Eze 41: 2 on each side of it were **f** cubits wide. H2822
Eze 41: 9 wall of the side rooms was **f** cubits thick. H2822
Eze 41:11 the open area was **f** cubits wide all H2822
Eze 41:12 of the building was **f** cubits thick all H2822
Eze 42:16 measuring rod; it was **f** hundred cubits. H2822
Eze 42:17 it was **f** hundred cubits by the measuring H2822
Eze 42:18 it was **f** hundred cubits by the measuring H2822
Eze 42:19 it was **f** hundred cubits by the measuring H2822
Eze 42:20 **f** hundred cubits long and five hundred H2822
Eze 42:20 cubits long and **f** hundred cubits wide, H2822
Mt 14:17 "We have here only **f** loaves of bread *G4297*
Mt 14:19 Taking the **f** loaves and the two fish and *G4297*
Mt 14:21 those who ate was about **f thousand** men, *G4295*
Mt 16: 9 you remember the **f** loaves for the five *G4297*
Mt 16: 9 the five loaves *for* the **f thousand**, *G4295*
Mt 20: 6 About **f in the afternoon** he went out and *G1895*
Mt 20: 9 about **f in the afternoon** came and *G1895+6052*
Mt 25: 2 **F** of them were foolish and five were wise. *G4297*
Mt 25: 2 Five of them were foolish and **f** were wise. *G4297*
Mt 25:15 To one he gave **f** bags of gold, to another *G4297*
Mt 25:16 who had received **f** bags of gold went at *G4297*
Mt 25:16 money to work and gained **f** bags more. *G4297*
Mt 25:20 who had received **f** bags of gold brought *G4297*
Mt 25:20 **f**ive bags of gold brought the other **f**. *G4297*
Mt 25:20 'you entrusted me *with* **f** bags of gold. *G4297*
Mt 25:20 See, I have gained **f** more.' *G4297*
Mk 6:38 found out, they said, "**F**—and two fish." *G4297*
Mk 6:41 Taking the **f** loaves and the two fish and *G4297*
Mk 6:44 the men who had eaten was **f thousand**. *G4295*
Mk 8:19 When I broke the **f** loaves for the five *G4297*
Mk 8:19 I broke the five loaves for the **f thousand**, *G4295*
Lk 1:24 pregnant and for **f** months remained in *G4297*
Lk 7:41 One owed him **f hundred** denarii, and the *G4296*
Lk 9:13 "We have only **f** loaves of bread and two *G4297*
Lk 9:14 About **f thousand** men were there.) But he *G4295*
Lk 9:16 Taking the **f** loaves and the two fish and *G4297*
Lk 12: 6 Are not **f** sparrows sold for two pennies *G4297*
Lk 12:52 now on there will be **f** in one family *G4297*
Lk 14:19 'I have just bought **f** yoke of oxen, and I'm *G4297*
Lk 16:28 I have **f** brothers. Let him warn them, so *G4297*
Lk 19:18 'Sir, your mina has earned **f** more.' *G4297*
Lk 19:19 answered, 'You take charge of **f** cities.' *G4297*
Jn 4:18 you have had **f** husbands, and the man *G4297*
Jn 5: 2 is surrounded by **f** covered colonnades. *G4297*
Jn 6: 9 "Here is a boy with **f** small barley loaves *G4297*
Jn 6:10 about **f thousand** men were there). *G4295*
Jn 6:13 with the pieces of the **f** barley loaves left *G4297*
Ac 4: 4 who believed grew to about **f** thousand. *G4297*
Ac 20: 6 **f** days later joined the others at Troas, *G4297*
Ac 24: 1 **F** days later the high priest Ananias went *G4297*
1Co 14:19 I would rather speak **f** intelligible words to *G4297*
1Co 15: 6 appeared *to* more than **f hundred** of the *G4296*
2Co 11:24 **F times** I received from the Jews the forty *G4294*
Rev 9: 5 only to torture them for **f** months. *G4297*
Rev 9:10 power to torment people for **f** months. *G4297*
Rev 17:10 **F** have fallen, one is, the other has not *G4297*

FIX (5) [AFFIXING, FIXED, FIXING]

Dt 11:18 **F** these words of mine in your hearts and H8492
Job 14: 3 *Do you* **f** your eye on them? Will you bring H7219
Pr 4:25 **f** your gaze **directly** before you. H3837
2Co 4:18 *So* we **f** our **eyes** not **on** what is seen, but *G5023*
Heb 3: 1 calling, **f your thoughts on** Jesus, whom *G2917*

FIXED (4) [FIX]

2Ki 8:11 He **stared** *at* him **with a f gaze** H6641+906+7156+2256+8492
Job 38:10 when *I* **f** limits for it and set its doors and H8689
Ps 141: 8 But my eyes are **f on** you, Sovereign LORD H448
Pr 8:28 above and **f securely** the fountains of H6451

FIXING (1) [FIX]

Heb 12: 2 **f** our **eyes on** Jesus, the pioneer and *G927*

FLAG, FLAGS (KJV) REEDS, RUSHES

FLAGSTAFF (1) [STAFF]

Isa 30:17 till you are left like a **f** on a mountaintop H9568

FLAKES (1)

Ex 16:14 thin **f** like frost on the ground appeared H2892

FLAME (16) [AFLAME, FLAMED, FLAMES, FLAMING]

Jdg 13:20 As the **f** blazed up from the altar toward H4258
Jdg 13:20 the angel of the LORD ascended in the **f**. H4258
Jdg 16: 9 of string snaps when it comes close to a **f**. H836
Job 15:30 the darkness; a **f** will wither his shoots H8927
Job 18: 5 snuffed out; the **f** *of* his fire stops burning. H8663
Ps 83:14 the forest or a **f** sets the mountains H4259
Ps 106:18 their followers; a **f** consumed the wicked. H4259
SS 8: 6 It burns like blazing fire, like a **mighty f**. H8928
Isa 10:16 pomp a fire will be kindled like a blazing **f**. H836
Isa 10:17 their Holy One a **f**; in a single day it H4259
Isa 47:14 save themselves from the power of the **f**. H4259
Isa 54:16 fans the coals into **f** and forges a weapon H836
Eze 20:47 The blazing **f** will not be quenched, and H8927
Joel 2: 3 fire devours, behind them a **f** blazes. H4259
Ob 18 Jacob will be a fire and Joseph a **f**; Esau H4259
2Ti 1: 6 I remind you *to* **fan into f** the gift of God, *G351*

FLAMED (1) [FLAME]

Am 1:11 and his fury **f unchecked**, H9068+5905

FLAMES (16) [FLAME]

Ex 3: 2 appeared to him in **f** *of* fire from within a H4225
Job 41:19 **F** stream from its mouth; sparks of fire H4365
Job 41:21 coals ablaze, and **f** dart from its mouth. H4258
Ps 104: 4 his messengers, **f** *of* fire his servants. H4265
Isa 5:24 straw and as dry grass sinks down in the **f**, H4259
Isa 29: 6 tempest and **f** *of* a devouring fire. H4258
Isa 42:25 *It* enveloped them **in f**, yet they did not H4265
Isa 43: 2 be burned; the **f** will not set you ablaze. H4259
Isa 66:15 with fury, and his rebuke with **f** *of* fire. H4258
Jer 51:58 labor is only **fuel for** the **f**." H928+1896+836
Da 3:22 so hot that the **f** of the fire killed the A10695
Joel 1:19 the wilderness and **f** have burned up all H4259
Ac 7:30 to Moses in the **f** of a burning bush in the *G5825*
1Co 3:15 only as one escaping through the **f**. *G4786*
Heb 1: 7 angels spirits, and his servants **f** of fire." *G5825*
Heb 11:34 quenched the fury *of* the **f**, and escaped *G4786*

FLAMING (12) [FLAME]

Ge 3:24 cherubim and a **f** sword flashing back H4267
Ps 7:13 weapons; he makes ready his **f** arrows. H1944
Pr 26:18 Like a maniac shooting **f** arrows of death H2415
Isa 4: 5 by day and a glow of **f** fire by night; H4259
Isa 50:11 fires and provide yourselves with **f torches**, H2338
La 2: 3 in Jacob like a **f** fire that consumes H4259
Da 7: 9 His throne was **f** with fire, and its wheels A10695
Da 10: 6 his eyes like **f** torches, his arms and H836
Hos 7: 6 in the morning it blazes like a **f** fire. H4259
Na 2: 4 They look like **f torches**; they dart about H4365
Zec 12: 6 a woodpile, like a **f** torch among sheaves. H836
Eph 6:16 extinguish all the **f** arrows of the evil one *G4792*

FLANK (2)

Eze 25: 9 therefore I will expose the **f** *of* Moab H4190
Eze 34:21 Because you shove with **f** and shoulder H7396

FLAP (1) [FLAPPED]

Job 39:13 "The wings of the ostrich **f joyfully**, though H6632

FLAPPED (1) [FLAP]
Isa 10:14 the countries; not *one* f a wing, or opened H5610

FLARE (3) [FLARED]
2Sa 11:20 the king's anger *may* **f up**, and he may ask H6590
Ps 2:12 his wrath *can* **f up** in a moment. H1277
Jer 4: 4 my wrath *will* **f up** and burn like fire H3655

FLARED (3) [FLARE]
Jdg 6:21 Fire f from the rock, consuming the meat H6590
1Sa 20:30 Saul's anger **f up** at Jonathan and he said H3013
Ps 124: 3 us alive when their anger f against us; H3013

FLASH (9) [FLASHED, FLASHES, FLASHING]
Job 15:12 carried you away, and why *do* your eyes f, H8141
Job 37:15 the clouds and **makes** his lightning f? H3649
Eze 21:10 the slaughter, polished to **f like lightning**! H1398
Eze 21:28 to consume and to **f like lightning**! H1398
Hos 11: 6 A sword *will* f in their cities; it will devour H2565
Am 5: 9 *With* a **blinding** f he destroys the H1158
Zec 9:14 over them; his arrow *will* f like lightning. H3655
Lk 9:29 became as bright as a **f of lightning**. *G1993*
1Co 15:52 in a f, in the twinkling of an eye, at the last *G875*

FLASHED (7) [FLASH]
Ex 9:23 and lightning **f down** to the ground. H2143
Ex 9:24 lightning **f back and forth**. H4374+928+9348
Ps 77:17 thunder; your arrows **f back and forth**. H2143
Eze 1:13 it was bright, and lightning **f out** of it. H3655
Hab 3: 4 like the sunrise; rays f from his hand, where NDT
Ac 9: 3 a light from heaven **f around** him. *G4313*
Ac 22: 6 a bright light from heaven **f around** me. *G4313*

FLASHES (9) [FLASH]
Job 41:18 Its snorting **throws out** f *of* light; its eyes H2145
Ps 29: 7 of the LORD strikes with f *of* lightning. H4259
Eze 1:14 sped back and forth like **f of lightning**. H1027
Na 2: 3 on the chariots f on the day they are H928+836
Lk 17:24 *which* f and lights up the sky from one end *G848*
Rev 4: 5 From the throne came **f of lightning** *G847*
Rev 8: 5 **f of lightning** and an earthquake. *G847*
Rev 11:19 And there came **f of lightning**, rumblings *G847*
Rev 16:18 Then there came **f of lightning**, rumblings *G847*

FLASHING (7) [FLASH]
Ge 3:24 sword **f back and forth** to guard the H2200
Dt 32:41 when I sharpen my f sword and my hand H1398
Job 39:23 its side, along with the f spear and lance. H4258
Ps 76: 3 There he broke the f arrows, the shields H8404
Eze 1: 4 an immense cloud with f lightning and H4374
Na 3: 3 f swords and glittering spears! H4258
Hab 3:11 at the lightning of your f spear. H5586

FLASK (3)
1Sa 10: 1 Then Samuel took a f *of* olive oil and H7095
2Ki 9: 1 take this f *of* olive oil with you and go to H7095
2Ki 9: 3 Then take the f and pour the oil on his H7095

FLAT (1) [FLATS, FLATTENS]
Hos 7: 8 Ephraim is a **f loaf** not turned over. H6314

FLATS (1) [FLAT]
Job 39: 6 as its home, the **salt** f as its habitat. H4877

FLATTENS (1) [FLAT]
Isa 32:19 Though hail f the forest and the city is H3718

FLATTER (6) [FLATTERING, FLATTERY]
Job 32:21 will show no partiality, nor *will I* f anyone; H4033
Ps 12: 2 they f with their lips but harbor deception H2747
Ps 36: 2 own eyes *they* f themselves *too much* to H2744
Ps 78:36 But then *they would* f him with their H7331
Pr 29: 5 Those *who* f their neighbors are H2744
Jude 16 themselves and f others for their *G2513+4725*

FLATTERING (4) [FLATTER]
Ps 12: 3 the LORD silence all f lips and every H2747
Pr 26:28 those it hurts, and a f mouth works ruin. H2747
Pr 28:23 favor rather than *one who has a* f tongue. H2744
Eze 12:24 false visions or f divinations among the H2747

FLATTERY (4) [FLATTER]
Job 32:22 if I were skilled in f, my Maker would H4033
Da 11:32 With f he will corrupt those who have H2747
Ro 16:18 By smooth talk and f they deceive the *G2330*
1Th 2: 5 You know we never used f, nor did *G3364+3135*

FLAVOR (1)
Job 6: 6 or is there f in the sap of the mallow? H3248

FLAW (3) [FLAWLESS]
Dt 15:21 has any serious f, you must not sacrifice H4583
Dt 17: 1 sheep that has any defect or f in it, H1821+8273
SS 4: 7 beautiful, my darling; there is no f in you. H4583

FLAWLESS (6) [FLAW]
2Sa 22:31 The LORD's word *is* f; he shields all who H7671
Job 11: 4 'My beliefs are f and I am pure in your H2341
Ps 12: 6 And the words of the LORD are f, like silver H3196
Ps 18:30 The LORD's word *is* f; he shields all who H7671
Pr 30: 5 "Every word of God *is* f; he is a shield to H7671
SS 5: 2 my sister, my darling, my dove, my f *one*. H9447

FLAX (6)
Ex 9:31 The f and barley were destroyed, since H7325
Ex 9:31 had headed and the f was in bloom. H7325
Jos 2: 6 under the stalks of f she had laid out on H7324
Jdg 15:14 ropes on his arms became like charred f, H7324
Pr 31:13 selects wool and f and works with eager H7324
Isa 19: 9 who work with combed f will despair, H7324

FLAY, FLAYED (KJV) SKIN, SKINNED, STRIP

FLEA (2)
1Sa 24:14 Who are you pursuing? A dead dog? A f? H7282
1Sa 26:20 of Israel has come out to look for a f— H7282

FLED (120) [FLEE]
Ge 14:10 the kings of Sodom and Gomorrah f, H5674
Ge 14:10 fell into them and the rest f to the hills. H5674
Ge 16: 6 Sarai mistreated Hagar; so *she* f from her. H1368
Ge 31:21 So he f with all he had, crossed the H1368
Ge 31:22 third day Laban was told that Jacob *had* f. H1368
Ge 31:40 cold at night, and sleep f from my eyes. H5610
Ex 2:15 Moses f from Pharaoh and went to H1368
Ex 14: 5 of Egypt was told that the people *had* f, H1368
Nu 16:34 all the Israelites around them f, shouting, H5674
Nu 35:25 back to the city of refuge to which *they* f. H5674
Nu 35:26 limits of the city of refuge to which *they* f H5674
Nu 35:32 a ransom for *anyone who has* f to a city of H5674
Jos 8:15 and *they* f toward the wilderness. H5674
Jos 10:11 As they f before Israel on the road down H5674
Jos 10:16 the five kings *had* f and hidden in the H5674
Jos 20: 6 own home in the town from which *they* f." H5674
Jdg 1: 6 Adoni-Bezek f, but they chased him and H5674
Jdg 4:15 got down from his chariot and f on foot. H5674
Jdg 4:17 meanwhile, f on foot to the tent of Jael H5674
Jdg 7:21 all the Midianites ran, crying out as *they* f. H5674
Jdg 7:22 The army f to Beth Shittah toward Zererah H5674
Jdg 8:12 kings of Midian, f, but he pursued them H5674
Jdg 9:21 Then Jotham f, escaping to Beer, and he H5674
Jdg 9:40 the gate, and many were killed *as they* f. H5674
Jdg 9:51 women—all the people of the city—*had* f. H5674
Jdg 11: 3 So Jephthah f from his brothers and H1368
Jdg 20:42 So *they* f before the Israelites in the H7155
Jdg 20:45 As they turned and f toward the wilderness H5674
Jdg 20:47 of them turned and f into the wilderness H5674
1Sa 4:10 defeated and every man f to his tent. H5674
1Sa 4:16 the battle line; I f from it this very day." H5674
1Sa 4:17 replied, "Israel f before the Philistines H5674
1Sa 17:24 the man, *they* all f from him in great fear. H5674
1Sa 19: 8 with such force that *they* f before him. H5674
1Sa 19:12 through a window, and *he* f and escaped. H1368
1Sa 19:18 When David *had* f and made his escape H1368
1Sa 20: 1 Then David f from Naioth at Ramah and H1368
1Sa 21:10 That day David f from Saul and went to H1368
1Sa 22:20 Abiathar, escaped and f to join David. H1368
1Sa 23: 6 with him when he f to David *at* Keilah.) H1368
1Sa 27: 4 Saul was told that David *had* f *to* Gath, H1368
1Sa 30:17 young men who rode off on camels and f. H5674
1Sa 31: 1 the Israelites f before them, and many H5674
1Sa 31: 7 the Israelite army *had* f and that Saul H5674
1Sa 31: 7 they abandoned their towns and f. H5674
2Sa 1: 4 "The men f from the battle, H5674
2Sa 4: 3 people of Beeroth f to Gittaim and have H1368
2Sa 4: 4 His nurse picked him up and f, but as she H5674
2Sa 10:13 the Arameans, and *they* f before him. H5674
2Sa 10:14 *they* f before Abishai and went inside the H5674
2Sa 10:18 But they f before Israel, and David killed H5674
2Sa 13:29 sons got up, mounted their mules and f. H5674
2Sa 13:34 Meanwhile, Absalom *had* f. Now the man H1368
2Sa 13:37 Absalom f and went to Talmai son of H1368
2Sa 13:38 After Absalom f and went to Geshur, he H1368
2Sa 18:17 all the Israelites f to their homes. H5674
2Sa 19: 8 the Israelites *had* f to their homes. H5674
2Sa 19: 9 But now *he has* f the country to escape H1368
2Sa 23:11 full of lentils, Israel's troops f from them. H5674
1Ki 2: 7 stood by me when I f from your brother H1368
1Ki 2:28 he f to the tent of the LORD and took hold H5674
1Ki 2:29 was told that Joab *had* f to the tent of the H5674
1Ki 11:17 f to Egypt with some Edomite officials H1368
1Ki 11:23 son of Eliada, who *had* f from his master H1368
1Ki 11:40 Jeroboam f to Egypt, to Shishak H1368
1Ki 12: 2 where *he had* f from King Solomon), H1368
1Ki 20:20 the Arameans f, with the Israelites H5674
1Ki 20:30 And Ben-Hadad f to the city and hid in an H5674
2Ki 3:24 rose up and fought them until *they* f. H5674
2Ki 7: 7 So they got up and f in the dusk and H5674
2Ki 8:21 by night; his army, however, **f back** home. H5674
2Ki 9:23 Joram turned about and f, calling out to H5674
2Ki 9:27 *he* **f up** the road to Beth Haggan. H5674
2Ki 14:12 by Israel, and every man f to his home. H5674
2Ki 14:19 in Jerusalem, and *he* f to Lachish, but H5674
2Ki 25: 4 the whole army f at night through the NDT
2Ki 25: 4 *They* f toward the Arabah, H2143
2Ki 25:26 f *to* Egypt for fear of the Babylonians. H995
1Ch 10: 1 the Israelites f before them, and many H5674
1Ch 10: 7 saw that the army *had* f and that Saul H5674
1Ch 10: 7 they abandoned their towns and f. H5674
1Ch 11:13 of barley, the troops f from the Philistines. H5674
1Ch 19:14 the Arameans, and *they* f before him. H5674
1Ch 19:15 they too f before his brother Abishai and H5674
1Ch 19:18 But they f before Israel, and David killed H5674
2Ch 10: 2 where *he had* f from King Solomon), H1368
2Ch 13:16 The Israelites f before Judah, and God H5674
2Ch 14:12 before Asa and Judah. The Cushites f, H5674
2Ch 25:22 by Israel, and every man f to his home. H5674
2Ch 25:27 him in Jerusalem and *he* f to Lachish, H5674
Ps 3: T When he f from his son Absalom. H1368
Ps 48: 5 her and were astounded; *they* f in terror. H2905
Ps 57: T When he *had* f from Saul into the cave. H1368
Ps 104: 7 But at your rebuke the waters f, at the H5674
Ps 114: 3 The sea looked and f, the Jordan turned H5674
Ps 114: 5 sea, that *you* f? Why, Jordan, did H5674
Isa 20: 6 those *we* f *to* for help and deliverance H5674
Isa 22: 3 All your leaders *have* f together; they H5610
Isa 22: 3 *having* f while the enemy was still far H1368
Jer 9:10 The birds *have all* f and the animals are H5610
Jer 26:21 But Uriah heard of it and f in fear *to* Egypt. H1368
Jer 39: 4 soldiers saw them, *they* f; they left the city H1368
Jer 41:15 from Johanan and f to the Ammonites. H2143
Jer 52: 7 broken through, and the whole army f. H1368
Jer 52: 7 *They* f toward the Arabah, H2143
La 1: 6 in weakness *they have* f before the H2143
Da 10: 7 them that *they* f and hid themselves. H1368
Hos 12:12 Jacob f *to* the country of Aram; Israel H1368
Am 5:19 be as though a man f from a lion only to H5674
Zec 14: 5 You will flee as *you* f from the earthquake H5674
Mt 26:56 Then all the disciples deserted him and f. *G5771*
Mk 14:50 Then everyone deserted him and f. *G5771*
Mk 14:52 he f naked, leaving his garment behind. *G5771*
Mk 16: 8 the women went out and f from the tomb. *G5771*
Ac 7:29 Moses heard this, *he* f to Midian, where *G5771*
Ac 14: 6 found out about it and f to the Lycaonian *G2966*
Heb 6:18 we *who have* f to take hold of the hope *G2966*
Rev 12: 6 The woman f into the wilderness to a *G5771*
Rev 16:20 Every island **f away** and the mountains *G5771*
Rev 20:11 the heavens f from his presence, *G5771*

FLEE (92) [FLED, FLEEING, FLEES]
Ge 19:17 one of them said, "F for your lives! H4880
Ge 19:17 F to the mountains or you will be swept H4880
Ge 19:19 But I can't f to the mountains; this disaster H4880
Ge 19:20 it is small. *Let me* f to it—it is very H4880
Ge 19:22 But f there quickly, because I cannot do H4880
Ge 27:43 F at once to my brother Laban in Harran. H1368
Ex 21:13 *they are to* f to a place I will designate. H5674
Lev 26:17 and *you will* f even when no one is H5674
Nu 10:35 be scattered; *may* your foes f before you." H5674
Nu 35: 6 a person who has killed someone *may* f. H5674
Nu 35:11 has killed someone accidentally *may* f. H5674
Nu 35:15 killed another accidentally *can* f there. H5674
Dt 4:42 had killed a person *could* f if they had H5674
Dt 4:42 *They could* f into one of these cities and H5674
Dt 19: 3 kills someone *may* **f for refuge** to one of H5674
Dt 19: 5 That man *may* f to one of these cities H5674
Dt 28: 7 one direction but f from you in seven. H5674
Dt 28:25 one direction but f from them in seven, H5674
Jos 8: 5 as they did before, *we will* f from them. H5674
Jos 8: 6 So when *we* f from them, H5674
Jos 20: 3 unintentionally *may* f there and find H5674
Jos 20: 4 When *they* f to one of these cities, they H5674
Jos 20: 9 accidentally *could* f to these designated H5674
2Sa 15:14 *We must* f, or none of us will escape from H1368
2Sa 17: 2 then all the people with him *will* f. H5674
2Sa 18: 3 go out; if *we are* **forced to** f, they H5674+5674
2Sa 19: 3 are ashamed when they f from battle. H5674
2Ki 19:21 Jerusalem tosses her head as you f. H339
Job 41:28 Arrows *do* not **make** it f; slingstones are H1368
Ps 11: 1 "F like a bird *to* your mountain. H5653
Ps 31:11 those who see me on the street f from me. H5610
Ps 55: 7 I would f far away and stay in the desert; H5610
Ps 68: 1 be scattered; *may* his foes f before him. H5674
Ps 68:12 "Kings and armies **f in haste**; the H5610+5610
Ps 139: 7 Where *can I* f from your presence H1368
Pr 28: 1 The wicked f though no one pursues, but H5674
SS 2:17 Until the day breaks and the shadows f H5674
SS 4: 6 Until the day breaks and the shadows f, H5674
Isa 2:19 *People will* f to caves in the rocks and to H995
Isa 2:21 They *will* f to caverns in the rocks and to H995
Isa 13:14 people, they *will* f to their native land. H5674
Isa 15: 5 her fugitives f as far as Zoar, as far NDT
Isa 17:13 when he rebukes them *they* f far away H5674
Isa 21:15 *They* f from the sword, from the drawn H5610
Isa 30:16 You said, 'No, *we will* f on horses.' H5674
Isa 30:16 Therefore *you will* f! You said, H5674
Isa 30:17 A thousand will f at the threat of one; at the NDT
Isa 30:17 at the threat of five *you will all* **f away**, till H5674
Isa 31: 8 *They will* f before the sword and their H5674
Isa 33: 3 the peoples f; when you rise up, H5610
Isa 35:10 and sorrow and sighing *will* **f away**. H5674
Isa 37:22 Jerusalem tosses her head as you f. H339
Isa 48:20 Leave Babylon, f from the Babylonians H1368
Isa 51:11 and sorrow and sighing *will* **f away**. H5674
Jer 4: 5 *Let us* f to the fortified cities H995
Jer 4: 6 to go to Zion! **F for safety** without delay H6395
Jer 6: 1 "**F for safety**, people of Benjamin! Flee H6395
Jer 6: 1 people of Benjamin! F from Jerusalem NDT
Jer 8:14 *Let us* f to the fortified cities and perish H995
Jer 25:35 The shepherds will have nowhere to f, the H4960
Jer 46: 5 *They* **f in haste** without looking H5674+4960
Jer 46: 6 "The swift cannot f nor the strong escape H5674
Jer 46:21 They too will turn and f together, they will H5674
Jer 48: 6 F! Run for your lives; become like a bush H5674
Jer 49: 8 Turn and f, hide in deep caves, you who H5674
Jer 49:24 she has turned to f and panic has gripped H5674
Jer 49:30 "F quickly away! Stay in deep caves, you H5674

Jer 50: 3 both people and animals *will* **f** away. H5653
Jer 50: 8 "**F** out of Babylon; leave the land of the H5653
Jer 50:16 people, *let* everyone **f** to their own land. H5674
Jer 51: 6 "**F** from Babylon! Run for your lives! H5674
La 4:15 When *they* **f** and wander about, people H5680
Eze 7:16 who escape *will* **f** to the mountains. H2118
Da 4:14 *Let* the animals **f** from under it and the A10469
Am 2:16 bravest warriors *will* **f** naked on that day," H5674
Jnh 1: 3 sailed for Tarshish to **f** from the LORD. NDT
Mic 1:15 The nobles of Israel *will* **f** to Adullam. H995
Na 3: 7 All who see you *will* **f** from you and say H5610
Zec 2: 6 **F** from the land of the north," declares the H5674
Zec 14: 5 *You will* **f** *by* my mountain valley, for it will H5674
Zec 14: 5 *You will* **f** as you fled from the earthquake H5674
Mt 3: 7 Who warned you *to* **f** from the coming G5771
Mt 10:23 are persecuted in one place, **f** to another. G5771
Mt 24:16 then *let* those who are in Judea **f** to the G5771
Mk 13:14 then *let* those who are in Judea **f** to the G5771
Lk 3: 7 Who warned you *to* **f** from the coming G5771
Lk 21:21 Then *let those* who are in Judea **f** to the G5771
1Co 6:18 **F** from sexual immorality. All other sins a G5771
1Co 10:14 Therefore, my dear friends, **f** from idolatry. G5771
1Ti 6:11 man of God, **f** from all this, and pursue G5771
2Ti 2:22 **F** the evil desires of youth and pursue G5771
Jas 4: 7 Resist the devil, and *he will* **f** from you. G5771

FLEECE (7)

Jdg 6:37 I will place a wool **f** on the threshing floor. H1603
Jdg 6:37 is dew only on the **f** and all the ground is H1603
Jdg 6:38 he squeezed the **f** and wrung out the dew H1603
Jdg 6:39 Allow me one more test with the **f**, but H1603
Jdg 6:39 this time make the **f** dry and let the H1603
Jdg 6:40 Only the **f** was dry; all the ground was H1603
Job 31:20 warming them with the **f** *from* my sheep, H1600

FLEEING (13) [FLEE]

Ge 35: 1 to you when you *were* **f** from your brother H1368
Ge 35: 7 to him when he *was* **f** from his brother. H1368
Ex 14:27 The Egyptians *were* **f** toward it, and the H5674
Lev 26:36 They will run as though **f** *from* the sword H4961
Lev 26:37 one another as though **f** from the sword, NDT
Jos 8:20 Israelites who *had been* **f** *toward* the H5674
1Sa 22:17 They knew he *was* **f**, yet they did not tell H1368
2Sa 10:14 realized that the Arameans *were* **f**, H5674
2Sa 24:13 Or three months of **f** from your enemies H5674
1Ch 19:15 realized that the Arameans *were* **f**, H5674
Jer 46:22 will hiss like a **f** serpent as the enemy H2143
Jer 48:19 Ask the *man* **f** and the woman escaping H5674
Jnh 4: 2 is what I tried to forestall by **f** to Tarshish. H1368

FLEES (9) [FLEE]

Dt 19: 4 who kills a person and **f** there for safety— H5674
Dt 19:11 neighbor, and then **f** to one of these cities H5674
Job 20:24 Though *he* **f** from an iron weapon, H1368
Job 27:22 mercy *as he* **f headlong** from its H1368+1368
Pr 27: 8 Like a bird *that* **f** its nest is anyone who H5610
Pr 27: 8 flees its nest is anyone *who* **f** from home. H5610
Isa 10:29 Ramah trembles; Gibeah of Saul **f**. H5674
Isa 24:18 Whoever **f** at the sound of terror will fall H5674
Jer 48:44 "Whoever **f** from the terror will fall into a H5674

FLEET (6) [FLEETING]

1Ki 9:27 to serve in the **f** with Solomon's men. H639
1Ki 10:22 king had a **f of trading ships** at sea H639+9576
1Ki 22:48 built a **f of trading ships** to go to H641+9576
2Ch 9:21 had a **f of trading ships** H641+2143+9576
2Ch 20:36 a **f of trading ships**. H641+4200+2143+9576
Da 11:40 chariots and cavalry and a great **f of ships**. H641

FLEET-FOOTED (2) [FOOT]

2Sa 2:18 Asahel was as **f** as a wild H7824+928+8079
Am 2:15 the **f** soldier will not get away, H7824+928+8079

FLEETING (7) [FLEET]

Job 14: 2 wither away; like **f** shadows, they do not H1368
Ps 39: 4 of my days; let me know how **f** my life is. H2534
Ps 89:47 Remember how **f** is my **life**. H2698
Ps 144: 4 a breath; their days are like a **f** shadow. H6296
Pr 21: 6 a lying tongue is a **f** vapor and a deadly H5622
Pr 31:30 beauty is **f**; but a woman who fears H2039
Heb 11:25 rather than to enjoy the **f** pleasures of sin. G4672

FLESH (171)

Ge 2:21 ribs and then closed up the place with **f**. H1414
Ge 2:23 now bone of my bones and **f** of my flesh; H1414
Ge 2:23 now bone of my bones and flesh of my **f**; H1414
Ge 2:24 to his wife, and they become one **f**. H1414
Ge 15: 4 who is your own **f and blood** will be your H5055
Ge 17:13 My covenant in your **f** is to be an H1414
Ge 17:14 who has not been circumcised in the **f** H1414
Ge 29:14 "You are my own **f** and blood. H1414
Ge 37:27 he is our brother, our own **f and blood**." H1414
Ge 40:19 And the birds will eat away your **f**." H1414
Ex 4: 7 it was restored, like the rest of his **f**. H1414
Ex 29:14 But burn the bull's **f** and its hide and its H1414
Lev 4:11 But the hide of the bull and all its **f**, as H1414
Lev 6:27 touches any of the **f** will become holy, H1414
Lev 8:17 with its hide and its **f** and its intestines he H1414
Lev 9:11 the **f** and the hide he burned up outside H1414
Lev 13:10 white and if there is raw **f** in the swelling, H1414
Lev 13:14 But whenever raw **f** appears on them, they H1414
Lev 13:15 When the priest sees the raw **f**, he shall H1414
Lev 13:15 The raw **f** is unclean; they have a defiling H1414
Lev 13:16 If the raw **f** changes and turns white, they H1414
Lev 13:24 spot appears in the **raw f** *of* the burn, H4695
Lev 16:27 **f** and intestines are to be burned up. H1414
Lev 26:29 You will eat the **f** *of* your sons and the H1414
Lev 26:29 of your sons and the **f** *of* your daughters. H1414
Nu 12:12 mother's womb with its **f** half eaten away." H1414
Nu 19: 5 be burned—its hide, **f**, blood and H1414
Dt 28:53 the **f** *of* the sons and daughters the LORD H1414
Dt 28:55 of them any of the **f** *of* his children that he H1414
Dt 32:42 with blood, while my sword devours **f**: H1414
Jdg 8: 7 I will tear your **f** with desert thorns and H1414
Jdg 9: 2 Remember, I am your **f** and blood." H1414
1Sa 17:44 "and I'll give your **f** to the birds and the H1414
2Sa 1:22 the slain, from the **f** *of* the mighty, the H2693
2Sa 5: 1 said, "We are your own **f** and blood. H1414
2Sa 7:12 your own **f and blood**, and I H3655+4946+5055
2Sa 16:11 my own **f and blood**, is H3655+4946+5055
2Sa 19:12 my relatives, my own **f** and blood. H1414
2Sa 19:13 Amasa, 'Are you not my own **f** and blood? H1414
1Ki 8:19 your own **f and blood**—he is H3655+4946+2743
2Ki 5:10 your **f** will be restored and you will be H1414
2Ki 5:14 his **f** was restored and became clean H1414
2Ki 9:36 at Jezreel dogs will devour Jezebel's **f**. H1414
2Ki 20:18 **your own f and blood** who H3655+4946+3870
1Ch 11: 1 said, "We are your own **f** and blood. H1414
2Ch 6: 9 your own **f and blood**—he is H3655+4946+2743
2Ch 32: 8 With him is only the arm of **f**, but with us H1414
2Ch 32:21 his own **f and blood**, cut him down H5055
Ne 5: 5 are of the same **f and blood** as our fellow H1414
Job 2: 5 out your hand and strike his **f** and bones, H1414
Job 6:12 the strength of stone? Is my **f** bronze? H1414
Job 10: 4 Do you have eyes of **f**? Do you see as a H1414
Job 10:11 me with skin and **f** and knit me together H1414
Job 15:27 with fat and his waist **bulges with f**, H6913+7089
Job 19:22 Will you never get enough of my **f**? H1414
Job 19:26 been destroyed, yet in my **f** I will see God; H1414
Job 33:21 Their **f** wastes away to nothing, and their H1414
Job 33:25 let their **f** be renewed like a child's; let H1414
Job 41:23 The folds of its **f** are tightly joined; they H1414
Ps 50:13 Do I eat the **f** *of* bulls or drink the blood of H1414
Ps 73:26 My **f** and my heart may fail, but God is the H8638
Ps 78:39 He remembered that they were but **f**, H1414
Ps 79: 2 the **f** *of* your own people for the animals H1414
Ps 84: 2 my heart and my **f** cry out for the living H1414
Ps 119:120 My **f** trembles in fear of you; I stand in H1414
Pr 5:11 when your **f** and body are spent. H1414
Isa 9:20 will feed on the **f** *of* their own offspring: H1414
Isa 31: 3 not God; their horses are **f** and not spirit. H1414
Isa 39: 7 **your own f and blood** who H3655+4946+3870
Isa 49:26 will make your oppressors eat their own **f**; H1414
Isa 58: 7 to turn away from your own **f and blood**? H1414
Isa 65: 4 who eat the **f** *of* pigs, and whose H1414
Isa 66:17 who is among those who eat the **f** *of* pigs, H1414
Jer 9:25 all who are circumcised only in the **f**— H6889
Jer 17: 5 strength from *mere* **f** and whose heart H1414
Jer 19: 9 will make them eat the **f** *of* their sons H1414
Jer 19: 9 eat one another's **f** because their H1414
Jer 51:35 the violence done to our **f** be on Babylon," H8638
La 3: 4 made my skin and my **f** grow old and has H6425
Eze 11:19 heart of stone and give them a heart of **f**. H1414
Eze 32: 5 I will spread your **f** on the mountains and H1414
Eze 32: 6 the ravines will be filled with your **f**. NDT
Eze 36:26 heart of stone and give you a heart of **f**. H1414
Eze 37: 6 to you and make **f** come upon you and H1414
Eze 37: 8 tendons and **f** appeared on them and H1414
Eze 39:17 There you will eat **f** and drink blood. H1414
Eze 39:18 You will eat the **f** *of* mighty men and drink H1414
Eze 40:43 The tables were for the **f** *of* the offerings. H1414
Eze 44: 7 in heart and **f** into my sanctuary, H1414
Eze 44: 9 in heart and **f** is to enter my sanctuary, H1414
Da 7: 5 It was told, 'Get up and eat your fill of **f**!' A10125
Mic 3: 2 my people and the **f** from their bones; H8638
Mic 3: 3 who eat my people's **f**, strip off their skin H8638
Mic 3: 3 up like meat for the pan, like **f** for the pot?" H1414
Zec 11: 9 Let those who are left eat one another's **f**." H1414
Zec 14:12 Their **f** will rot while they are still standing H1414
Mt 16:17 was not revealed to you *by* **f** and blood, G4922
Mt 19: 5 his wife, and the two will become one **f**'? G4922
Mt 19: 6 longer two, but one **f**. Therefore what God G4922
Mt 26:41 The spirit is willing, but the **f** is weak." G4922
Mk 10: 8 the two will become one **f**.' So they G4922
Mk 10: 8 So they are no longer two, but one **f**. G4922
Mk 14:38 The spirit is willing, but the **f** is weak." G4922
Lk 24:39 a ghost does not have **f** and bones, as G4922
Jn 1:14 The Word became **f** and made his G4922
Jn 3: 6 **F** gives birth to flesh, but the Spirit gives G4922
Jn 3: 6 Flesh gives birth to **f**, but the Spirit gives G4922
Jn 6:51 This bread is my **f**, which I will give for the G4922
Jn 6:52 "How can this man give us his **f** to eat?" G4922
Jn 6:53 unless you eat the **f** of the Son of Man G4922
Jn 6:54 Whoever eats my **f** and drinks my blood G4922
Jn 6:55 For my **f** is real food and my blood is real G4922
Jn 6:56 Whoever eats my **f** and drinks my blood G4922
Jn 6:63 Spirit gives life; the **f** counts for nothing. G4922
Ro 4: 1 our forefather according to the **f** G4922
Ro 7: 5 For when we were in the realm of the **f** G4922
Ro 8: 3 to do because it was weakened by the **f**, G4922
Ro 8: 3 Son in the likeness *of* sinful **f** to be a sin G4922
Ro 8: 3 And so he condemned sin in the **f**, G4922
Ro 8: 4 live according to the **f** but according to the G4922
Ro 8: 5 according to the **f** have their minds set G4922
Ro 8: 5 their minds set on what the **f** desires; G4922
Ro 8: 6 The mind *governed by* the **f** is death, but G4922
Ro 8: 7 The mind *governed by* the **f** is hostile to G4922
Ro 8: 8 in the realm of the **f** cannot please God. G4922
Ro 8: 9 in the realm of the **f** but are in the realm G4922
Ro 8:12 it is not *to* the **f**, to live according to G4922
Ro 8:13 For if you live according to the **f**, you will G4922
Ro 13:14 about how to gratify the desires *of* the **f**. G4922
1Co 5: 5 over to Satan for the destruction *of* the **f**, G4922
1Co 6:16 it is said, "The two will become one **f**." G4922
1Co 15:39 Not all **f** is the same: People have one G4922
1Co 15:39 People have one kind of **f**, animals have G4922
1Co 15:50 that **f** and blood cannot inherit the G4922
2Co 12: 7 I was given a thorn *in* my **f**, a messenger G4922
Gal 3: 3 you now trying to finish *by means of* the **f**? G4922
Gal 4:23 slave woman was born according to the **f**, G4922
Gal 4:29 born according to the **f** persecuted the son G4922
Gal 5:13 do not use your freedom to indulge the **f**; G4922
Gal 5:16 you will not gratify the desires *of* the **f**. G4922
Gal 5:17 For the **f** desires what is contrary to the G4922
Gal 5:17 the Spirit what is contrary to the **f**. G4922
Gal 5:19 The acts *of* the **f** are obvious: sexual G4922
Gal 5:24 have crucified the **f** with its passions and G4922
Gal 6: 8 Whoever sows to please their **f**, from the G4922
Gal 6: 8 their flesh, from the **f** will reap destruction G4922
Gal 6:12 by means of the **f** are trying to compel G4922
Gal 6:13 boast about your circumcision *in* the **f**. G4922
Eph 2: 3 the cravings *of* our **f** and following its G4922
Eph 2:15 by setting aside in his **f** the law with its G4922
Eph 5:31 his wife, and the two will become one **f**." G4922
Eph 6:12 For our struggle is not against **f** and blood G4922
Php 3: 2 those evildoers, those **mutilators of the f**. G2961
Php 3: 3 who put no confidence in the **f**— G4922
Php 3: 4 have reasons to put confidence in the **f**, G4922
Col 1:24 I fill up in my **f** what is still lacking in G4922
Col 2:11 Your whole self *ruled by* the **f** was put off G4922
Col 2:13 sins and in the uncircumcision *of* your **f**, G4922
1Ti 3:16 He appeared in the **f**, was vindicated by G4922
Heb 2:14 Since the children have **f** and blood, he G4922
Jas 5: 3 testify against you and eat your **f** like fire. G4922
2Pe 2:10 the corrupt desire *of* the **f** and despise G4922
2Pe 2:18 by appealing to the lustful desires *of* the **f**, G4922
1Jn 2:16 the world—the lust *of* the **f**, the lust of the G4922
1Jn 4: 2 Christ has come in the **f** is from God, G4922
2Jn 7 Jesus Christ as coming in the **f**, G4922
Jude 23 even the clothing stained by *corrupted* **f**. G4922
Rev 17:16 they will eat her **f** and burn her with fire. G4922
Rev 19:18 so that you may eat the **f** of kings G4922
Rev 19:18 their riders, and the **f** of all people, free G4922
Rev 19:21 all the birds gorged themselves on their **f**. G4922

FLEW (4) [FLY]

2Sa 22:11 He mounted the cherubim and **f**; he H6414
Ps 18:10 He mounted the cherubim and **f**; he H6414
Isa 6: 6 one of the seraphim **f** to me with a live H6414
Ac 16:26 At once all the prison doors **f open**, and G487

FLIES (15) [FLY]

Ex 8:21 I will send **swarms of f** on you and your H6856
Ex 8:21 houses of the Egyptians will be full of **f**; H6856
Ex 8:22 people live; no **swarms of f** will be there H6856
Ex 8:24 Dense **swarms of f** poured into Pharaoh's H6856
Ex 8:24 Egypt the land was ruined by the **f**. H6856
Ex 8:29 tomorrow the **f** will leave Pharaoh H6856
Ex 8:31 The **f** left Pharaoh and his officials and H6856
Dt 4:17 on earth or any bird that **f** in the air, H6414
Job 20: 8 Like a dream *he* **f away**, no more to be H6414
Ps 78:45 He sent **swarms of f** that devoured them H6856
Ps 91: 5 terror of night, nor the arrow *that* **f** by day, H6414
Ps 105:31 there came **swarms of f**, and gnats H6856
Ecc 10: 1 As dead **f** give perfume a bad smell, so a H2279
Isa 7:18 LORD will whistle for **f** from the Nile delta H2279
Isa 51: 6 a garment and its inhabitants die like **f**. H4031

FLIGHT (14) [FLY]

Lev 26:36 of a windblown leaf *will* **put** them **to f**. H8103
Dt 32:30 two **put** ten thousand **to f**, unless their H5674
2Sa 22:41 You made my enemies turn their backs in **f** NDT
2Ki 7:15 had thrown away in their **headlong f**. H2905
1Ch 12:15 and *they* **put** to **f** everyone living in the H1368
Job 39:26 "*Does* the hawk **take f** by your wisdom and H87
Ps 18:40 You made my enemies turn their backs in **f** NDT
Ps 104: 7 at the sound of your thunder *they* **took to f**; H2905
Isa 10:31 Madmenah *is* in **f**; the people of Gebim H5610
Isa 52:12 But you will not leave in haste or go in **f** H4961
Jer 4:29 archers every town **takes to f**. H1368
Eze 40:49 It was reached by a **f of stairs**, and there H5092
Da 9:21 came to me in **swift f** about the H3618+3616
Mt 24:20 Pray that your **f** will not take place in G5870

FLIMSY (1)

Eze 13:10 because, when a **f wall** is built, they H2666

FLINGING (1) [FLUNG]

Ac 22:23 off their cloaks and **f** dust into the air, G965

FLINT (8) [FLINTY]

Ex 4:25 But Zipporah took a **f knife**, cut off her H7644
Jos 5: 2 "Make **f** knives and circumcise the H7644
Jos 5: 3 So Joshua made **f** knives and circumcised H7644
Isa 5:28 their horses' hooves seem like **f**, their H7641
Isa 50: 7 Therefore have I set my face like **f**, and I H2734
Jer 17: 1 inscribed with a **f** point, on the tablets H9032
Eze 3: 9 like the hardest stone, harder than **f**. H7644

F

Zec 7:12 their hearts **as hard as f** and would not H9032

FLINTY (2) [FLINT]
Dt 32:13 the rock, and with oil from the **f** crag, H2734
Job 28: 9 People assault the **f rock** with their hands H2734

FLIRTING (1)
Isa 3:16 outstretched necks, **f** *with* their eyes H8568

FLOAT (3) [FLOATED]
1Ki 5: 9 I *will* **f** them *as* rafts by sea to the H8492
2Ki 6: 6 threw it there, and **made** the iron **f**. H7429
2Ch 2:16 and *will* **f** them *as* rafts by sea *down* to H995

FLOATED (1) [FLOAT]
Ge 7:18 the ark **f** on the surface of the water. H2143

FLOCK (98) [FLOCKING, FLOCKS]
Ge 4: 4 from some of the firstborn of his **f**. H7366
Ge 21:28 set apart seven ewe lambs from the **f**, H7366
Ge 27: 9 Go out to the **f** and bring me two choice H7366
Ge 30:40 set apart the **young of the f** by themselves H4166
Ge 31:10 goats mating with the **f** were streaked, H7366
Ge 31:12 goats mating with the **f** are streaked, H7366
Ge 38:17 "I'll send you a young goat from my **f**," H7366
Ex 2:16 fill the troughs to water their father's **f**. H7366
Ex 2:17 came to their rescue and watered their **f**. H7366
Ex 2:19 even drew water for us and watered the **f**." H7366
Ex 3: 1 Moses was tending the **f** *of* Jethro his H7366
Ex 3: 1 he led the **f** to the far side of the H7366
Ex 34:19 of your livestock, whether from herd or **f**. H8445
Lev 1: 2 an animal from either the herd or the **f**. H7366
Lev 1:10 the offering is a burnt offering from the **f**, H7366
Lev 3: 6 an animal from the **f** as a fellowship H7366
Lev 5: 6 lamb or goat from the **f** as a sin offering; H7366
Lev 5:15 to the LORD as a penalty a ram from the **f**, H7366
Lev 5:18 priest as a guilt offering a ram from the **f**, H7366
Lev 6: 6 a ram from the **f**, one without defect and H7366
Lev 22:21 from the herd or **f** a fellowship offering H7366
Lev 27:32 Every tithe of the herd and **f**—every tenth H7366
Nu 15: 3 LORD food offerings from the herd or the **f**, H7366
Dt 15:14 Supply them liberally from your **f**, your H7366
Dt 16: 2 your God an **animal from** your **f** or herd at H7366
Dt 32:14 milk from herd and **f** and with fattened H7366
1Sa 17:20 morning David left the **f** in the care of a H7366
1Sa 17:34 came and carried off a sheep from the **f**, H6373
2Sa 7: 8 from tending the **f**, and appointed you H7366
1Ch 17: 7 from tending the **f**, and appointed you H7366
Ezr 10:19 a ram from the **f** as a guilt offering.) H7366
Job 21:11 They send forth their children as a **f**; their H7366
Ps 77:20 your people like a **f** by the hand of Moses H7366
Ps 78:52 But he brought his people out like a **f**; he H7366
Ps 80: 1 of Israel, you who lead Joseph like a **f**. H7366
Ps 95: 7 of his pasture, the **f** under his care. H7366
SS 1: 7 where *you* **graze** *your* **f** and where you rest H8286
SS 4: 1 Your hair is like a **f** *of* goats descending H6373
SS 4: 2 Your teeth are like a **f** *of* sheep just shorn H6373
SS 6: 5 Your hair is like a **f** *of* goats descending H6373
SS 6: 6 teeth are like a **f** *of* sheep coming up from H6373
Isa 40:11 He tends his **f** like a shepherd: He gathers H6373
Isa 63:11 the sea, with the shepherd of his **f**? H7366
Jer 10:21 do not prosper and all their **f** is scattered. H5338
Jer 13:17 because the LORD's **f** will be taken captive. H6373
Jer 13:20 Where is the **f** that was entrusted to you H6373
Jer 23: 2 have scattered my **f** and driven them away H6373
Jer 23: 3 the remnant of my **f** out of all the H7366
Jer 25:34 roll in the dust, you leaders of the **f**. H7366
Jer 25:35 the leaders of the **f** no place to escape. H7366
Jer 25:36 the wailing of the leaders of the **f**, for the H7366
Jer 31:10 will watch over his **f** like a shepherd. H6373
Jer 49:20 The young of the **f** will be dragged away H7366
Jer 50: 8 be like the goats that lead the **f**. H7366
Jer 50:17 is a scattered **f** that lions have chased H8445
Jer 50:45 The young of the **f** will be dragged away H7366
Jer 51:23 with you I shatter shepherd and **f**, with H6373
Eze 24: 5 take the pick of the **f**. Pile wood beneath H7366
Eze 34: 2 Should not shepherds take care of the **f**? H7366
Eze 34: 3 animals, but you do not take care of the **f**. H7366
Eze 34: 8 because my **f** lacks a shepherd and so has H7366
Eze 34: 8 did not search for my **f** but cared for H7366
Eze 34: 8 cared for themselves rather than for my **f**, H7366
Eze 34:10 will hold them accountable for my **f**. H7366
Eze 34:10 from tending the **f** so that the shepherds H7366
Eze 34:10 I will rescue my **f** from their mouths, and it H7366
Eze 34:12 after his scattered **f** when he is with them, H6373
Eze 34:16 I will shepherd **the f** with justice. H5626S
Eze 34:17 " 'As for you, my **f**, this is what the H7366
Eze 34:19 Must my **f** feed on what you have trampled H7366
Eze 34:22 I will save my **f**, and they will no longer be H7366
Eze 43:23 to offer a young bull and a ram from the **f**, H7366
Eze 43:25 a young bull and a ram from the **f**, H7366
Eze 45:15 be taken from every **f** of two hundred from H7366
Am 7:15 me from tending the **f** and said to me, H7366
Mic 2:12 sheep in a pen, like a **f** in its pasture; the H6373
Mic 4: 8 watchtower of the **f**, stronghold of H6373
Mic 5: 4 will stand and **shepherd** *his* **f** in the H8286
Mic 7:14 with your staff, the **f** *of* your inheritance H7366
Zec 9:16 on that day as a shepherd saves his **f**. H7366
Zec 10: 3 the LORD Almighty will care for his **f** H6373
Zec 11: 4 "Shepherd the **f** *marked for* slaughter. H7366
Zec 11: 7 I shepherded the **f** *marked for* slaughter, H7366
Zec 11: 7 particularly the oppressed of the **f**. H7366
Zec 11: 7 the other Union, and I shepherded the **f**. H7366
Zec 11: 8 **The f** detested me, and I grew H5883+4392S
Zec 11:11 oppressed of the **f** who were watching me H7366
Zec 11:17 the worthless shepherd, who deserts the **f**! H7366
Mal 1:14 male in his **f** and vows to give it, H6373
Mt 26:31 the sheep *of* the **f** will be scattered. G4479
Lk 12:32 not be afraid, little **f**, for your Father has G4480
Jn 10:12 Then the wolf attacks **the f** and scatters it. G899S
Jn 10:16 there shall be one **f** and one shepherd. G4479
Ac 20:28 yourselves and all the **f** of which the Holy G4480
Ac 20:29 in among you and will not spare the **f**. G4480
1Co 9: 7 Who tends a **f** and does not drink the milk G4479
1Pe 5: 2 Be shepherds *of* God's **f** that is under your G4480
1Pe 5: 3 but being examples *to* the **f**. G4480

FLOCKING (1) [FLOCK]
Hos 7:12 When I hear them **f together**, I will catch H6337

FLOCKS (102) [FLOCK]
Ge 4: 2 Now Abel kept **f**, and Cain worked the soil H7366
Ge 13: 5 also had **f** and herds and tents. H7366
Ge 26:14 He had so many **f** and herds and H5238+7366
Ge 29: 2 with three **f** *of* sheep lying near it because H6373
Ge 29: 2 near it because the **f** were watered from H6373
Ge 29: 3 When all the **f** were gathered there, the H6373
Ge 29: 7 it is not time for the **f** to be gathered. H5238
Ge 29: 8 "until all the **f** are gathered and the stone H6373
Ge 30:31 go on tending your **f** and watching over H7366
Ge 30:32 go through all your **f** today and remove H7366
Ge 30:36 continued to tend the rest of Laban's **f**. H7366
Ge 30:38 in front of the **f** when they came to drink. H7366
Ge 30:38 When the **f** were in heat and came to H7366
Ge 30:40 he made separate **f** for himself and did H6373
Ge 30:43 prosperous and came to own large **f**, H7366
Ge 31: 4 to come out to the fields where his **f** were. H7366
Ge 31: 8 then all the **f** gave birth to speckled H7366
Ge 31: 8 then all the **f** bore streaked young. H7366
Ge 31:38 have I eaten rams from your **f**. H7366
Ge 31:41 two daughters and six years for your **f**, H7366
Ge 31:43 are my children, and the **f** are my flocks. H7366
Ge 31:43 are my children, and the flocks are my **f**. H7366
Ge 32: 7 the **f** and herds and camels as well. H7366
Ge 33: 8 meaning of all these **f and herds** I met?" H4722
Ge 33:14 pace of the **f and herds** before me and H4856
Ge 34:28 They seized their **f** and herds and donkeys H7366
Ge 37: 2 was tending the **f** with his brothers, the H7366
Ge 37:12 to graze their father's **f** near Shechem, H7366
Ge 37:13 brothers *are* **grazing the f** near Shechem H8286
Ge 37:14 is well with your brothers and with the **f**, H7366
Ge 37:16 you tell me where they *are* **grazing** *their* **f**?" H8286
Ge 45:10 grandchildren, your **f** and herds, and all H7366
Ge 46:32 brought along their **f** and herds and H7366
Ge 47: 1 with their **f** and herds and everything they H7366
Ge 47: 4 your servants' **f** have no pasture. H7366
Ge 50: 8 children and their **f** and herds were left in H7366
Ex 10: 9 with our **f** and herds, because we H7366
Ex 10:24 only leave your **f** and herds behind." H7366
Ex 12:32 Take your **f** and herds, as you have said H7366
Ex 12:38 large droves of livestock, both **f** and herds. H7366
Ex 34: 3 not even the **f** and herds may graze in H7366
Nu 11:22 they have enough if **f** and herds were H7366
Nu 31: 9 Midianite herds, **f** and goods as plunder. H5238
Nu 32: 1 who had very large **herds and f**, saw that H5238
Nu 32:24 pens for your **f**, but do what you have H7366
Nu 32:26 our **f** and herds will remain here in the H5238
Nu 32:36 fortified cities, and built pens for their **f**. H7366
Dt 7:13 the lambs of your **f** in the land he swore H7366
Dt 8:13 your herds and **f** grow large and your H7366
Dt 12: 6 the firstborn of your herds and **f**. H7366
Dt 12:17 the firstborn of your herds and **f**, or H7366
Dt 12:21 from the herds and **f** the LORD has given H7366
Dt 14:23 of your herds and **f** in the presence of the H7366
Dt 15:19 every firstborn male of your herds and **f**. H7366
Dt 28: 4 of your herds and the lambs of your **f**. H7366
Dt 28:18 of your herds and the lambs of your **f**. H7366
Dt 28:51 lambs of your **f** until you are ruined. H7366
Jos 14: 4 with pasturelands for their **f** and herds. H5238
Jdg 5:16 sheep pens to hear the whistling for the **f**? H6373
1Sa 8:17 He will take a tenth of your **f**, and you H7366
1Sa 30:20 He took all the **f** and herds, and his men H7366
1Ki 20:27 opposite them like two **small f** *of* goats, H3105
2Ki 5:26 vineyards, or **f** and herds, or male H7366
1Ch 4:39 the valley in search of pasture for their **f**. H7366
1Ch 4:41 because there was pasture for their **f**. H7366
1Ch 27:31 Jaziz the Hagrite was in charge of the **f** H7366
2Ch 17:11 as tribute, and the Arabs brought him **f**: H7366
2Ch 31: 6 of their herds and **f** and a tithe of the holy H7366
2Ch 32:28 various kinds of cattle, and pens for the **f**. H6373
2Ch 32:29 acquired great numbers of **f** and herds, H7366
Ne 10:36 our herds and of our **f** to the house of our H7366
Job 1:10 so that his **f and herds** are spread H5238
Job 24: 2 they pasture **f** they have stolen. H6373
Ps 8: 7 all **f** and herds, and the animals of the H7556
Ps 65:13 are covered with **f** and the valleys are H7366
Ps 107:41 increased their families like **f**. H7366
Pr 27:23 Be sure you know the condition of your **f** H7366
Ecc 2: 7 owned more herds and **f** than anyone in H7366
SS 1: 7 woman beside the **f** *of* your friends? H6373
Isa 13:20 there no shepherds *will* **rest** *their* **f**. H8069
Isa 17: 2 of Aroer will be deserted and left to **f**, H6373
Isa 32:14 the delight of donkeys, a pasture for **f**, H6373
Isa 60: 7 All Kedar's **f** will be gathered to you, the H7366
Isa 61: 5 Strangers will shepherd your **f**; foreigners H7366
Isa 65:10 Sharon will become a pasture for **f**, and H7366
Jer 3:24 their **f** and herds, their sons H7366
Jer 5:17 they will devour your **f** and herds, devour H7366
Jer 6: 3 Shepherds with their **f** will come against H6373
Jer 31:12 the olive oil, the young of the **f** and herds. H7366
Jer 31:24 those who move about with their **f**. H6373
Jer 33:12 be pastures for shepherds to rest their **f**. H7366
Jer 33:13 **f** will again pass under the hand of the H7366
Jer 49:29 Their tents and their **f** will be taken; their H7366
Eze 36:38 as numerous as the **f** *for* offerings at H7366
Eze 36:38 the ruined cities be filled with **f** *of* people. H7366
Hos 5: 6 they go with their **f** and herds to seek the H7366
Joel 1:18 pasture; even the **f** *of* sheep are suffering. H6373
Jnh 3: 7 animals, herds or **f**, taste anything; H7366
Mic 5: 8 like a young lion among **f** *of* sheep, which H6373
Zep 2: 6 having wells for shepherds and pens for **f**. H7366
Zep 2:14 **F and herds** will lie down there, creatures H6373
Lk 2: 8 keeping watch over their **f** at night. G4479

FLOG (7) [FLOGGED, FLOGGING, FLOGGINGS]
Pr 17:26 surely to **f** honest officials is not right. H5782
Pr 19:25 **F** a mocker, and the simple will learn H5782
Mt 23:34 others *you will* **f** in your synagogues and G3463
Mk 10:34 him and spit on him, **f** him and kill him. G3463
Lk 18:33 *they will* **f** him and kill him. On the third G3463
Ac 22:25 As they stretched him out to **f** him, Paul G2666
Ac 22:25 it legal for you *to* **f** a Roman citizen who G3464

FLOGGED (12) [FLOG]
Dt 25: 2 lie down and **have** them **f** in his presence H5782
Dt 25: 3 the guilty party *is* **f** more than that, H5782+4804
Mt 10:17 local councils and *be* **f** in the synagogues. G3463
Mt 20:19 to be mocked and **f** and crucified. G3463
Mt 27:26 But *he* **had** Jesus **f**, and handed him over G5849
Mk 13: 9 local councils and **f** in the synagogues. G1296
Mk 15:15 *He had* Jesus **f**, and handed him over to G5849
Jn 19: 1 Then Pilate took Jesus and *had* him **f**. G3463
Ac 5:40 called the apostles in and *had* them **f**. G1296
Ac 16:23 *After* they *had been* severely **f**, they G2202+4435
Ac 22:24 directed that he be **f** and interrogated in G3465
2Co 11:23 frequently, been **f** more severely, and G4435

FLOGGING (2) [FLOG]
Ps 89:32 their sin with the rod, their iniquity with **f**; H5596
Heb 11:36 Some faced jeers and **f**, and even chains G3465

FLOGGINGS (1) [FLOG]
2Sa 7:14 by men, with **f** *inflicted by* human hands. H5596

FLOOD (32) [FLOODED, FLOODGATES, FLOODING, FLOODS, FLOODWATERS]
Ge 7: 7 the ark to escape the waters of the **f**. H4429
Ge 7:17 For forty days the **f** kept coming on the H4429
Ge 9:11 all life be destroyed by the waters of a **f**; H4429
Ge 9:11 will there be a **f** to destroy the earth." H4429
Ge 9:15 the waters become a **f** to destroy all life. H4429
Ge 9:28 After the **f** Noah lived 350 years. H4429
Ge 10: 1 who themselves had sons after the **f**. H4429
Ge 10:32 spread out over the earth after the **f**. H4429
Ge 11:10 Two years after the **f**, when Shem was H4429
Jos 3:15 Jordan *is* **at f stage** all H4848+6584+3972+1536
Jos 4:18 and ran **at f stage** as before. H6584+3972+1536
Job 20:28 A **f** will carry off his house, rushing waters H3298
Job 22:11 and why a **f** *of* water covers you. H9180
Job 22:16 their foundations washed away by a **f**. H5643
Job 27:20 Terrors overtake him like a **f**; a tempest H4784
Job 38:34 cover yourself with a **f** *of* water? H9180
Ps 6: 6 All night long *I* **f** my bed with weeping H8466
Ps 29:10 The LORD sits enthroned over the **f**; the H4429
Ps 88:17 All day long they surround me like a **f** H4784
Ps 124: 4 the **f** would have engulfed us, the torrent H4784
Isa 59:19 come like a pent-up **f** that the breath of H5643
Da 9:26 The end will come like a **f**: War will H8852
Da 11:10 like an irresistible **f** and carry the battle as H8851
Da 11:40 sweep through them like *a* **f**. H8851
Hos 5:10 pour out my wrath on them like a **f** of water. NDT
Na 1: 8 an overwhelming **f** he will make an end H8852
Mal 2:13 *You* **f** the LORD's altar *with* tears H4059
Mt 24:38 For in the days before the **f**, people were G2886
Mt 24:39 happen until the **f** came and took them G2886
Lk 6:48 When a **f** came, the torrent struck that G4439
Lk 17:27 Then the **f** came and destroyed them all G2886
2Pe 2: 5 when he brought the **f** on its ungodly G2886

FLOODED (1) [FLOOD]
Ge 7:24 The waters **f** the earth for a hundred and H1504

FLOODGATES (6) [FLOOD]
Ge 7:11 the **f** *of* the heavens were opened. H748
Ge 8: 2 of the deep and the **f** *of* the heavens had H748
2Ki 7: 2 the LORD should open the **f** of the heavens, H748
2Ki 7:19 the LORD should open the **f** of the heavens, H748
Isa 24:18 The **f** of the heavens are opened, the H748
Mal 3:10 not throw open the **f** *of* heaven and pour H748

FLOODING (2) [FLOOD]
Isa 28: 2 a driving rain and a **f downpour**, H3888+8851
Isa 66:12 the wealth of nations like a **f** stream H8851

FLOODS (1) [FLOOD]
Ps 69: 2 into the deep waters; the **f** engulf me. H8673

FLOODWATERS (5) [FLOOD]
Ge 6:17 I am going to bring **f** on the earth to H4429+4784
Ge 7: 6 old when the **f** came on the earth. H4429+4784
Ge 7:10 seven days the **f** came on the earth H4429+4784
Ps 69:15 Do not let the **f** engulf me or the H8673+4784
Isa 8: 7 the mighty **f** *of* the Euphrates— H4784+8041

FLOOR (58) [FLOORS]
Ge 50:10 they reached the **threshing f** *of* Atad, H1755
Ge 50:11 the mourning at the **threshing f** *of* Atad, H1755
Ex 16:14 on the ground appeared on the desert **f**. H7156
Nu 5:17 dust from the tabernacle **f** into the water. H7977
Nu 15:20 it as an offering from the **threshing f**. H1755
Nu 18:27 as grain from the **threshing f** or juice from H1755
Nu 18:30 product of the **threshing f** or the winepress H1755
Dt 15:14 your **threshing f** and your winepress. H1755
Dt 16:13 produce of your **threshing f** and your H1755
Jdg 3:25 There they saw their lord fallen to the **f** H824
Jdg 6:37 place a wool fleece on the **threshing f**. H1755
Ru 3: 2 be winnowing barley on the **threshing f**. H1755
Ru 3: 3 Then go down to the **threshing f**, but H1755
Ru 3: 6 went down to the **threshing f** and did H1755
Ru 3:14 that a woman came to the **threshing f**." H1755
2Sa 6: 6 they came to the **threshing f** *of* Nakon, H1755
2Sa 24:16 then at the **threshing f** *of* Araunah the H1755
2Sa 24:18 the LORD on the **threshing f** *of* Araunah the H1755
2Sa 24:21 "To buy your **threshing f**," David H1755
2Sa 24:24 bought the **threshing f** and the oxen H1755
1Ki 6: 6 The lowest **f** was five cubits wide, the H3666
1Ki 6: 6 the middle **f** six cubits and the third floor NDT
1Ki 6: 6 middle floor six cubits and the third **f** seven. NDT
1Ki 6: 8 to the lowest **f** was on the south side H7521
1Ki 6:15 them from the **f** *of* the temple to the H7977
1Ki 6:15 covered the **f** *of* the temple with H7977
1Ki 6:16 with cedar boards from **f** to ceiling to form H7977
1Ki 7: 7 he covered it with cedar from **f** to ceiling. H7977
1Ki 22:10 thrones at the **threshing f** *by* the entrance H1755
1Ki 22:35 his wound ran onto the **f** *of* the chariot, H2668
2Ki 6:27 From the **threshing f**? From the H1755
1Ch 13: 9 they came to the **threshing f** *of* Kidon, H1755
1Ch 21:15 standing at the **threshing f** *of* Araunah the H1755
1Ch 21:18 the LORD on the **threshing f** *of* Araunah the H1755
1Ch 21:21 he left the **threshing f** and bowed down H1755
1Ch 21:22 the site of your **threshing f** so I can build H1755
1Ch 21:28 him on the **threshing f** *of* Araunah the H1755
2Ch 3: 1 It was on the **threshing f** *of* Araunah the H1755
2Ch 18: 9 thrones at the **threshing f** *by* the entrance H1755
Job 39:12 your grain and bring it to your **threshing f**? H1755
Isa 21:10 who are crushed on the **threshing f**, H1755
Jer 51:33 Babylon is like a **threshing f** at the time it H1755
Eze 37: 2 a great many bones on the **f** *of* the valley, H7156
Eze 41: 7 went up from the **lowest** *f* to the top floor AIT
Eze 41: 7 lowest floor to the **top** *f* through the middle AIT
Eze 41: 7 floor to the top floor through the **middle** *f*. AIT
Eze 41:16 The **f**, the wall up to the windows, and the H824
Eze 41:20 From the **f** to the area above the entrance H824
Eze 42: 6 The rooms *on the* **top** *f* had no pillars, as the AIT
Eze 42: 6 were smaller in **f space** than those on the H824
Da 2:35 chaff on a **threshing f** *in* the summer. A10010
Da 6:24 before they reached the **f** *of* the den, A10076
Hos 9: 1 of a prostitute at every **threshing f**. H1755+1841
Hos 13: 3 like chaff swirling from a **threshing f**, like H1755
Mic 4:12 them like sheaves to the **threshing f**. H1755
Mt 3:12 he will clear his **threshing f**, gathering *G272*
Lk 3:17 to clear his **threshing f** and to gather the *G272*
Jas 2: 3 stand there" or "Sit **on the f by** my **feet**," *G5711*

FLOORS (6) [FLOOR]
1Sa 23: 1 Keilah and are looting the **threshing f**," H1755
1Ki 6:30 He also covered the **f** *of* both the inner H7977
Eze 42: 5 on the lower and **middle** *f* *of* the building. AIT
Eze 42: 6 space than those on the lower and **middle** *f*. AIT
Hos 9: 2 **Threshing f** and winepresses will not feed H1755
Joel 2:24 The **threshing f** will be filled with grain H1755

FLORAL (2) [FLOWER]
1Ki 7:49 the gold **f work** and lamps and tongs H7258
2Ch 4:21 the gold **f work** and lamps and tongs (they H7258

FLOUR (68)
Ge 18: 6 seahs of the finest **f** and knead it and H7854
Ex 29: 2 And from the **finest** wheat **f** make round H6159
Ex 29:40 of an ephah of the **finest f** mixed with a H6159
Lev 2: 1 their offering is to be of the **finest f**. H6159
Lev 2: 2 priest shall take a handful of the **f** and oil, H6159
Lev 2: 4 in an oven, it is to consist of the **finest f**: H6159
Lev 2: 5 to be made of the **finest f** mixed with oil, H6159
Lev 2: 7 to be made of the **finest f** and some olive H6159
Lev 5:11 of an ephah of the **finest f** for a sin H6159
Lev 6:15 a handful of the **finest f** and some olive H6159
Lev 6:20 of an ephah of the **finest f** as a regular H6159
Lev 7:12 loaves of the **finest f** well-kneaded and H6159
Lev 14:10 an ephah of the **finest f** mixed with olive H6159
Lev 14:21 an ephah of the **finest f** mixed with olive H6159
Lev 23:13 an ephah of the **finest f** mixed with olive H6159
Lev 23:17 of two-tenths of an ephah of the **finest f**, H6159
Lev 24: 5 "Take the **finest f** and bake twelve loaves H6159
Nu 5:15 of an ephah of barley **f** on her behalf. H7854
Nu 6:15 made with the **finest f** and without yeast H6159
Nu 7:13 filled with the **finest f** mixed with olive H6159
Nu 7:19 filled with the **finest f** mixed with olive H6159
Nu 7:25 filled with the **finest f** mixed with olive H6159
Nu 7:31 filled with the **finest f** mixed with olive H6159
Nu 7:37 filled with the **finest f** mixed with olive H6159
Nu 7:43 filled with the **finest f** mixed with olive H6159
Nu 7:49 filled with the **finest f** mixed with olive H6159
Nu 7:55 filled with the **finest f** mixed with olive H6159
Nu 7:61 filled with the **finest f** mixed with olive H6159
Nu 7:67 filled with the **finest f** mixed with olive H6159
Nu 7:73 filled with the **finest f** mixed with olive H6159
Nu 7:79 filled with the **finest f** mixed with olive H6159
Nu 8: 8 offering of the **finest f** mixed with olive oil H6159
Nu 15: 4 of an ephah of the **finest f** mixed with a H6159
Nu 15: 6 of an ephah of the **finest f** mixed with a H6159
Nu 15: 9 an ephah of the **finest f** mixed with half a H6159
Nu 28: 5 of an ephah of the **finest f** mixed with a H6159
Nu 28: 9 an ephah of the **finest f** mixed with olive H6159
Nu 28:12 of an ephah of the **finest f** mixed with oil; H6159
Nu 28:12 of an ephah of the **finest f** mixed with oil; H6159
Nu 28:13 of an ephah of the **finest f** mixed with oil. H6159
Nu 28:20 of an ephah of the **finest f** mixed with oil; H6159
Nu 28:28 of an ephah of the **finest f** mixed with oil; H6159
Nu 29: 3 an ephah of the **finest f** mixed with olive H6159
Nu 29: 9 of an ephah of the **finest f** mixed with oil; H6159
Nu 29:14 of an ephah of the **finest f** mixed with oil; H6159
Jdg 6:19 from an ephah of **f** he made bread H7854
1Sa 1:24 an ephah of **f** and a skin of wine H7854
1Sa 28:24 She took *some* **f**, kneaded it and baked H7854
2Sa 17:28 wheat and barley, **f** and roasted grain H7854
1Ki 4:22 thirty cors of the **finest f** and sixty cors of H6159
1Ki 17:12 only a handful of **f** in a jar and a little H7854
1Ki 17:14 'The jar of **f** will not be used up and the H7854
1Ki 17:16 For the jar of **f** was not used up and the H7854
2Ki 4:41 Elisha said, "Get *some* **f**." He put it into H7854
2Ki 7: 1 a seah of the **finest f** will sell for a shekel H6159
2Ki 7:16 So a seah of the **finest f** sold for a shekel H6159
2Ki 7:18 a seah of the **finest f** will sell for a shekel H6159
1Ch 9:29 as well as the **special f** and wine, and the H6159
1Ch 12:40 There were plentiful supplies of **f**, fig H7854
1Ch 23:29 the **special f** for the grain offerings H6159
Isa 47: 2 Take millstones and grind **f**; take off your H7854
Eze 16:13 food was honey, olive oil and the **finest f**. H6159
Eze 16:19 you—the **f**, olive oil and honey H6159
Eze 46:14 a third of a hin of oil to moisten the **f**. H6159
Hos 8: 7 stalk has no head; it will produce no **f**. H7854
Mt 13:33 about sixty pounds *of* **f** until it worked all *G236*
Lk 13:21 about sixty pounds *of* **f** until it worked all *G236*
Rev 18:13 olive oil, *of* **fine f** and wheat; cattle *G4947*

FLOURISH (18) [FLOURISHING]
Ge 26:22 given us room and *we will* **f** in the land." H7238
Job 15:32 he will wither, and his branches *will* not **f**. H8315
Ps 44: 2 the peoples and **made** our ancestors **f**. H8938
Ps 72: 7 In his days *may* the righteous **f** and H7255
Ps 72:16 *May* the crops **f** like Lebanon and thrive H7437
Ps 92: 7 spring up like grass and all evildoers **f**, H7437
Ps 92:12 The righteous *will* **f** like a palm tree, they H7255
Ps 92:13 *they will* **f** in the courts of our God. H7255
Ps 103:15 like grass, *they* **f** like a flower of the field; H7437
Ps 115:14 *May* the LORD **cause** you **to f**, both you H3578
Pr 14:11 the tent of the upright *will* **f**. H7255
Isa 45: 8 spring up, *let* righteousness **f** with it; I, H7541
Isa 55:10 the earth and making it bud and **f**, H7541
Isa 66:14 heart will rejoice and you *will* **f** like grass; H7255
Eze 17:24 up the green tree and **make** the dry tree **f**. H7255
Hos 4:10 they will engage in prostitution but not **f** H7287
Hos 14: 7 in his shade; *they will* **f** like the grain H2649
Ac 12:24 word of God continued to spread and **f**. *G4437*

FLOURISHING (5) [FLOURISH]
Dt 6:10 a land with large, **f** cities you did not build, H3202
Ps 37:35 ruthless man **f** like a luxuriant native H6590
Ps 52: 8 like an olive tree **f** in the house of God; H8316
Ecc 2: 6 I made reservoirs to water groves of **f** trees. H7541
Hos 14: 8 I am like a **f** juniper; your fruitfulness H8316

FLOW (28) [EVER-FLOWING, FLOWED, FLOWING, FLOWS]
Ex 14:26 so that the waters *may* **f back** over the H8740
Lev 12: 7 be ceremonially clean from her **f** *of* blood. H5227
Lev 15:19 has her **regular f** *of* blood, H2307+928+1414
Lev 15:24 with her and her **monthly f** touches him, H5614
Lev 20:18 he has exposed the source of her **f**, and H1947
Nu 13:27 and it *does* **f** *with* milk and honey! H2307
Nu 24: 7 Water *will* **f** from their buckets; their seed H5688
Jos 4: 7 tell them that the **f** *of* the Jordan was cut H4784
Ps 78:16 crag and **made** water **f down** like rivers. H3718
Ps 119:136 Streams of tears **f** *from* my eyes, for your H3718
Ps 147:18 he stirs up his breezes, and the waters **f**. H5688
Ecc 1: 7 All streams **f** into the sea, yet the sea is H2143
Isa 30:25 streams of water will **f** on every high H3298
Isa 41:18 *I will* **make** rivers **f** on barren heights, and H7337
Isa 48:21 *he* **made** water **f** for them from the rock H5688
Jer 48:33 I have stopped the **f** of wine from the NDT
La 2:18 **let** your tears **f** like a river day and night H3718
La 3:48 Streams of tears **f from** my eyes because H3718
La 3:49 My eyes *will* **f** unceasingly, without relief, H5599
Eze 28:23 upon you and make blood **f** in your streets. NDT
Eze 32:14 settle and **make** her streams **f** like oil, H2143
Joel 3:18 and the hills *will* **f** *with* milk; all the H2143
Joel 3:18 A fountain *will* **f out** of the LORD's house H3655
Am 9:13 the mountains and **f** *from* all the hills, H4570
Zec 14: 8 day living water *will* **f out** from Jerusalem, H3655
Jn 7:38 of living water *will* **f** from within them." *G4835*
Jn 19:34 **bringing a** sudden **f** of blood and water. *G2002*
Jas 3:11 *Can* both fresh water and salt water **f** from *G1108*

FLOWED (10) [FLOW]
Ge 2:10 A river watering the garden **f** from Eden H3655
Ex 14:28 The water **f back** and covered the chariots H8740
Dt 9:21 into a stream that **f down** the mountain. H3718
1Ki 18:28 as was their custom, until their blood **f**. H9161
2Ch 32: 4 the stream that **f** through the land. H8851
Ps 78:20 streams **f abundantly**, but can he also H8851
Ps 104: 8 *they* **f over** the mountains, they went H6590
Ps 105:41 gushed out; *it* **f** like a river in the desert. H2143
Eze 31: 4 their streams **f** all around its base and H2143
Rev 14:20 the city, and blood **f out** of the press *G2002*

FLOWER (5) [FLORAL, FLOWERLIKE, FLOWERS]
Ps 103:15 they flourish like a **f** *of* the field; H7488
Isa 18: 5 is gone and the **f** becomes a ripening H5900
Isa 28: 1 to the fading **f**, his glorious beauty, H7488
Isa 28: 4 That fading **f**, his glorious beauty, set on H7491
Jas 1:10 they will pass away like a **wild f**. *G470+5965*

FLOWERLIKE (2) [FLOWER]
Ex 25:31 make its **f cups**, buds and blossoms H1483
Ex 37:17 made its **f cups**, buds and blossoms H1483

FLOWERS (19) [FLOWER]
Ex 25:33 Three cups **shaped like almond f** with H5481
Ex 25:34 four cups **shaped like almond f** with buds H5481
Ex 37:19 Three cups **shaped like almond f** with H5481
Ex 37:20 four cups **shaped like almond f** with buds H5481
1Ki 6:18 was cedar, carved with gourds and open **f**. H7488
1Ki 6:29 carved cherubim, palm trees and open **f**. H7488
1Ki 6:32 palm trees and open **f**, and overlaid the H7488
1Ki 6:35 palm trees and open **f** on them and H7488
Job 14: 2 They spring up like **f** and wither away; like H7488
Ps 37:20 LORD's enemies are like the **f** *of* the field, H3701
SS 2:12 **F** appear on the earth; the season of H5890
Isa 5:24 will decay and their **f** blow away like dust; H7258
Isa 40: 6 their faithfulness is like the **f** *of* the field. H7488
Isa 40: 7 The grass withers and the **f** fall, because H7488
Isa 40: 8 The grass withers and the **f** fall, but the H7488
Mt 6:28 See how the **f** of the field grow *G3211*
Lk 12:27 "Consider how the **wild f** grow. They do *G3211*
1Pe 1:24 all their glory is like the **f** of the field *G470*
1Pe 1:24 the field; the grass withers and the **f** fall, *G470*

FLOWING (44) [FLOW]
Ex 3: 8 a land **f** *with* milk and honey—the H2307
Ex 3:17 Jebusites—a land **f** *with* milk and honey. H2307
Ex 13: 5 give you, a land **f** *with* milk and honey H2307
Ex 33: 3 Go up to the land **f** *with* milk and honey H2307
Lev 15: 3 Whether it *continues* **f** *from* his body or is H8201
Lev 20:24 inheritance, a land **f** *with* milk and honey." H2307
Nu 14: 8 that land, a land **f** *with* milk and honey H2307
Nu 16:13 up out of a land **f** *with* milk and honey to H2307
Nu 16:14 us into a land **f** *with* milk and honey or H2307
Dt 6: 3 greatly in a land **f** *with* milk and honey, H2307
Dt 11: 9 a land **f** *with* milk and honey. H2307
Dt 21: 4 planted and where there is a **f stream**. H419
Dt 26: 9 us this land, a land **f** *with* milk and honey; H2307
Dt 26:15 ancestors, a land **f** *with* milk and honey." H2307
Dt 27: 3 giving you, a land **f** *with* milk and honey H2307
Dt 31:20 them into the land **f** *with* milk and honey, H2307
Jos 3:13 its waters **f** downstream will be cut off H3718
Jos 3:16 the water from upstream stopped **f**. It piled H3718
Jos 3:16 while the water **f down** to the Sea of the H3718
Jos 5: 6 to give us, a land **f** *with* milk and honey. H2307
2Ki 3:20 it was—water **f** from the direction of Edom! H995
2Ki 4: 6 is not a jar left." Then the oil stopped **f**. NDT
Job 6:17 that **stop f** in the dry season, and in H7551
Job 20:17 streams, the **rivers** *f* *with* honey and cream. AIT
Job 39:19 strength or clothe its neck with a **f mane**? H8310
Ps 107:33 desert, **f springs** into thirsty ground H4604+4784
Ps 107:35 the parched ground into **f springs**; H4604+4784
SS 4:15 a well of **f** water streaming down from H2645
SS 5: 5 my fingers with **f** myrrh, on the handles H6296
SS 7: 9 my beloved, **f gently** *over* lips and teeth. H1803
Isa 8: 6 rejected the gently **f** waters of Shiloah H2143
Isa 27:12 will thresh from the **f** Euphrates to the H8673
Isa 44: 4 like poplar trees by **f streams**. H3298+4784
Jer 11: 5 give them a land **f** *with* milk and honey'— H2307
Jer 18:14 waters from distant sources ever stop **f**? H5688
Jer 32:22 ancestors, a land **f** *with* milk and honey. H2307
Eze 20: 6 them, a land **f** *with* milk and honey H2307
Eze 20:15 given them—a land **f** *with* milk and honey H2307
Eze 23:15 their waists and **f** turbans on their heads; H6242
Eze 32: 6 the land with your **f** blood all the way to H7597
Da 7:10 A river of fire *was* **f**, coming out from A10457
Mk 12:38 to walk around in **f robes** and be greeted *G5124*
Lk 20:46 to walk around in **f robes** and love to be *G5124*
Rev 22: 1 **f from** the throne of God and of the Lamb *G1744*

FLOWN (1) [FLY]
Jer 4:25 people; every bird in the sky *had* **f away**. H5610

FLOWS (9) [FLOW]
Ezr 8:15 them at the canal that **f** toward Ahava, H995
Ps 58: 7 Let them vanish like water *that* **f away** H2143
Ps 104:10 the ravines; *it* **f** between the mountains. H2143
Pr 4:23 your heart, for everything you do **f from** it. H9362
Eze 47: 8 "This water **f** toward the eastern region H3655
Eze 47: 9 creatures will live wherever the river **f**. H995

Eze 47: 9 because this water **f** there and makes the H995
Eze 47: 9 so where the river **f** everything will live. H995
Eze 47:12 the water from the sanctuary **f** *to* them. H3655

FLUENT (1)

Isa 32: 4 tongue *will be* **f** and clear. H4554+4200+1819

FLUNG (2) [FLINGING]

Am 8: 3 many bodies—**f** everywhere H8959
Rev 12: 4 stars out of the sky and **f** them to the earth. *G965*

FLUTE (4)

Da 3: 5 you hear the sound of the horn, **f**, zither, A10446
Da 3: 7 heard the sound of the horn, **f**, zither, A10446
Da 3:10 hears the sound of the horn, **f**, zither, A10446
Da 3:15 you hear the sound of the horn, **f**, zither, A10446

FLUTTERING (3)

Pr 26: 2 Like a **f** sparrow or a darting swallow, an H5653
Isa 16: 2 Like **f** birds pushed from the nest, so are H5610
Hos 11:11 like sparrows, from Assyria, **f** like doves. NDT

FLUX (KJV) DYSENTERY

FLY (14) [FLEW, FLIES, FLIGHT, FLOWN, FLYING]

Ge 1:20 and *let* birds **f** above the earth across the H6414
Ex 8:31 officials and his people; not a **f** remained. NDT
Dt 19: 5 the head *may* **f off** and hit his neighbor H5970
Job 5: 7 to trouble as surely as sparks **f** upward. H6414
Job 9:25 *they* **f away** without a glimpse of joy. H1368
Ps 55: 6 *I would* **f away** and be at rest. H6414
Ps 90:10 they quickly pass, and *we* **f away**. H6414
Pr 23: 5 sprout wings and **f off** *to* the sky like an H6414
Isa 60: 8 "Who are these *that* **f along** like clouds H6414
Hos 9:11 Ephraim's glory *will* **f away** like a bird H6414
Na 3:16 they strip the land and then **f away**. H6414
Na 3:17 when the sun appears *they* **f away** H5610
Hab 1: 8 *They* **f** like an eagle swooping to devour H6414
Rev 12:14 so that *she might* **f** to the place prepared *G4375*

FLYING (14) [FLY]

Ge 8: 7 and *it kept* **f** back and forth until the water H3655
Lev 11:20 " 'All **f** insects that walk on all fours are to H6416
Lev 11:21 some **f** insects that walk on all fours that H6416
Lev 11:23 But all other **f** insects that have four legs H6416
Dt 14:19 All **f** insects are unclean to you; do not H6416
Ps 148:10 all cattle, small creatures and **f** birds, H4053
Isa 6: 2 their feet, and with two *they were* **f**. H6414
Hab 3:11 the heavens at the glint of your **f** arrows, H2143
Zec 5: 1 and there before me was a **f** scroll. H6414
Zec 5: 2 I answered, "I see a **f** scroll, twenty cubits H6414
Rev 4: 7 like a man, the fourth was like a **f** eagle. *G4375*
Rev 8:13 I heard an eagle *that was* **f** in midair call *G4375*
Rev 14: 6 Then I saw another angel **f** in midair, and *G4375*
Rev 19:17 in a loud voice to all the birds **f** in midair, *G4375*

FOAL (2)

Zec 9: 9 on a donkey, on a colt, the **f** *of* a donkey. H1201
Mt 21: 5 a donkey, and on a colt, the **f** of a donkey. *G5626*

FOAM (2) [FOAMING, FOAMS]

Job 24:18 "Yet they are **f** on the surface of the water H7824
Ps 46: 3 its waters roar and **f** and the mountains H2812

FOAMING (4) [FOAM]

Dt 32:14 You drank the **f** blood of the grape. H2815
Ps 75: 8 LORD is a cup full of **f** wine mixed with H2812
Mk 9:20 ground and rolled around, **f at the mouth**. *G930*
Jude 13 wild waves of the sea, **f up** their shame *G2072*

FOAMS (2) [FOAM]

Mk 9:18 *He* **f at the mouth**, gnashes his teeth and *G930*
Lk 9:39 so that he **f at the mouth**. *G3552+931*

FODDER (7)

Ge 24:25 "We have plenty of straw and **f**, as well as H5028
Ge 24:32 Straw and **f** were brought for the camels H5028
Ge 43:24 their feet and provided **f** for their donkeys. H5028
Jdg 19:19 have both straw and **f** for our donkeys H5028
Job 6: 5 has grass, or an ox bellow when it has **f**? H1173
Job 24: 6 They gather **f** in the fields and glean in H1173
Isa 30:24 that work the soil will eat **f** and mash, H1173

FOE (10) [FOES]

Ps 7: 4 evil or without cause have robbed my **f**— H7675
Ps 8: 2 enemies, to silence the **f** and the avenger. H367
Ps 55:12 endure it; if a **f** were rising against me H8533
Ps 61: 3 my refuge, a strong tower against the **f**. H367
Ps 74:10 Will the **f** revile your name forever H367
Ps 106:10 He saved them from the hand of the **f** H8533
Ps 107: 2 he redeemed from the hand of the **f**, H7640
La 1: 5 have gone into exile, captive before the **f**. H7640
La 2: 4 Like a **f** he has slain all who were H7640
Hab 1:15 The wicked **f** pulls all of them up with hooks, NDT

FOES (53) [FOE]

Nu 10:35 be scattered; may your **f** flee before you." H8533
Dt 33: 7 Oh, be his help against his **f**!" H7640
Dt 33:11 against him, his **f** till they rise no more." H8533
2Sa 22:18 from my **f**, who were too strong H8533
2Sa 22:41 their backs in flight, and I destroyed my **f**. H8533
2Sa 22:49 You exalted me above my **f**; from a H7756
Job 22:20 'Surely our **f** are destroyed, and fire H7799
Ps 3: 1 how many are my **f**! How many rise up H7640
Ps 6: 7 with sorrow; they fail because of all my **f**. H7675
Ps 13: 4 and my **f** will rejoice when I fall. H7640
Ps 17: 7 those who take refuge in you from their **f**. H7756
Ps 18:17 from my **f**, who were too strong H8533
Ps 18:40 their backs in flight, and I destroyed my **f**. H8533
Ps 18:48 You exalted me above my **f**; from a H7756
Ps 21: 8 enemies; your right hand will seize your **f**. H8533
Ps 27: 2 my enemies and my **f** who will stumble H367
Ps 27:12 Do not turn me over to the desire of my **f** H7640
Ps 34:21 the **f** *of* the righteous will be condemned. H8533
Ps 41: 2 not give them over to the desire of their **f**. H367
Ps 42:10 suffer mortal agony as my **f** taunt me, H7675
Ps 44: 5 through your name we trample our **f**. H7756
Ps 54: 3 **Arrogant f** are attacking me; ruthless H2424
Ps 54: 7 my eyes have looked in triumph on my **f**. H367
Ps 68: 1 be scattered; may his **f** flee before him. H8533
Ps 68:23 your feet may wade in the blood of your **f**, H367
Ps 69:18 rescue me; deliver me because of my **f**. H367
Ps 74: 4 Your **f** roared in the place where you met H7675
Ps 81:14 enemies and turn my hand against their **f**! H7640
Ps 83: 2 how your **f** rear their heads. H8533
Ps 86:14 **Arrogant f** are attacking me, O God H2294
Ps 89:23 I will crush his **f** before him and strike H7640
Ps 89:42 You have exalted the right hand of his **f** H7640
Ps 92:11 ears have heard the rout of my wicked **f**. H7756
Ps 97: 3 him and consumes his **f** on every side. H7640
Ps 105:24 he made them too numerous for their **f**, H7640
Ps 106:41 the nations, and their **f** ruled over them. H8533
Ps 112: 8 end they will look in triumph on their **f**. H7640
Ps 119:157 Many are the **f** who persecute me, but I H7640
Ps 138: 7 out your hand against the anger of my **f**; H367
Ps 143:12 destroy all my **f**, for I am your servant. H7675
Isa 1:24 vent my wrath on my **f** and avenge myself H7640
Isa 9:11 Rezin's **f** against them and has H7640
Isa 59:18 to his enemies and retribution to his **f**; H367
Isa 66:14 servants, but his fury will be shown to his **f**. H367
Jer 46:10 day of vengeance, for vengeance on his **f**. H7640
Jer 49:37 I will shatter Elam before their **f**, before H367
La 1: 5 Her **f** have become her masters; her H7640
La 1:17 Jacob that his neighbors become his **f**; H7640
La 2:17 he has exalted the horn of your **f**. H7640
La 4:12 that enemies and **f** could enter the gates H7640
Mic 5: 9 enemies, and all your **f** will be destroyed. H367
Na 1: 2 vengeance on his **f** and vents his wrath H7640
Na 1: 8 he will pursue his **f** into the realm of H367

FOILS (2)

Ps 33:10 The LORD **f** the plans of the nations; he H7296
Isa 44:25 *who* **f** the signs of false prophets and H7296

FOLD (4) [ENFOLDS, FOLDED, FOLDING, FOLDS]

Ex 26: 9 **F** the sixth curtain **double** at the front of H4100
Ecc 4: 5 Fools **f** their hands and ruin themselves. H2485
Hag 2:12 meat in the **f** *of* their garment, H4053
Hag 2:12 that **f** touches some bread or stew H4053

FOLDED (2) [FOLD]

Ex 28:16 long and a span wide—and **f double**. H4100
Ex 39: 9 long and a span wide—and **f double**. H4100

FOLDING (2) [FOLD]

Pr 6:10 slumber, a little **f** *of* the hands to rest— H2486
Pr 24:33 slumber, a little **f** *of* the hands to rest— H2486

FOLDS (4) [FOLD]

Ne 5:13 I also shook out the **f of** my **robe** and said H2950
Job 41:23 The **f** *of* its flesh are tightly joined; they H5139
Ps 74:11 Take it from the **f** *of* your garment and H7931
Eze 5: 3 tuck them away in the **f of** your **garment**. H4053

FOLIAGE (4)

Eze 19:11 It towered high above the **thick f** H6291
Eze 31: 3 towered on high, its top above the **thick f**. H6291
Eze 31:10 the great cedar towered over the **thick f**, H6291
Eze 31:14 lifting their tops above the **thick f**. H6291

FOLK (KJV) CREATURES, MEN, PEOPLE

FOLLOW (192) [FOLLOWED, FOLLOWER, FOLLOWERS, FOLLOWING, FOLLOWS]

Ge 41:30 seven years of famine *will* **f** them. H7756+339
Ex 11: 8 you and all the people who **f** you! H928+8079
Ex 16: 4 and see whether *they will* **f** my H2143+928
Ex 23: 2 "*Do* not **f** the crowd in doing wrong H2118+339
Ex 23:24 worship them or **f** their practices. H6913+3869
Lev 18: 3 I am bringing you. *Do* not **f** their practices. H2143
Lev 18: 4 my laws and be careful to **f** my decrees. H2143
Lev 18:30 my requirements and *do* not **f** any of the H6913
Lev 19:37 my decrees and all my laws and **f** them. H6913
Lev 20: 5 together with all who **f** him in prostituting H339
Lev 20: 8 Keep my decrees and **f** them. I am the H6913
Lev 20:22 all my decrees and laws and **f** them, H6913
Lev 22:31 "Keep my commands and **f** them. H6913
Lev 25:18 " '**F** my decrees and be careful to obey my H6913
Lev 26: 3 " 'If *you* **f** my decrees and are careful to H2143
Nu 9:12 Passover, they must **f** all the regulations. H3869
Dt 4: 1 **F** them so that you may live and may go H6913
Dt 4: 5 so that you *may* **f** them in the land H6913+4027
Dt 4:13 commanded you to **f** and then wrote them H6913
Dt 4:14 laws you *are to* **f** in the land that you H6913
Dt 5: 1 Learn them and be sure to **f** them. H6913
Dt 5:31 are to teach them *to* **f** in the land I am H6913
Dt 6:14 *Do* not **f** other gods, the gods of the H2143+339
Dt 7:11 take care to **f** the commands, decrees H6913
Dt 7:12 to these laws and are careful *to* **f** them, H6913
Dt 8: 1 Be careful to **f** every command I am giving H6913
Dt 8:19 LORD your God and **f** other gods and H2143+339
Dt 11:22 these commands I am giving you to **f**— H6913
Dt 12: 1 must be careful to **f** in the land that the H6913
Dt 13: 2 prophet says, "*Let us* **f** other gods" H2143+339
Dt 13: 4 It is the LORD your God *you must* **f** H2143+339
Dt 13: 5 LORD your God commanded you to **f**. H2143+928
Dt 15: 5 are careful to **f** all these commands I H6913
Dt 16:12 in Egypt, and **f** carefully these decrees. H6913
Dt 16:20 **F** justice and justice alone, so that you H8103
Dt 17:19 the LORD his God and **f** carefully all the H6913
Dt 19: 9 because you carefully **f** all these laws I H6913
Dt 20:18 will teach you to **f** all the H6913+3869
Dt 24: 8 You *must* **f** carefully what I have H6913
Dt 26:16 you this day to **f** these decrees and laws; H6913
Dt 27:10 LORD your God and **f** his commands and H6913
Dt 28: 1 God and carefully **f** all his commands I H6913
Dt 28:13 I give you this day and carefully **f** them, H6913
Dt 28:15 your God and *do* not carefully **f** all his H6913
Dt 28:58 you do not carefully **f** all the words of this H6913
Dt 29: 9 Carefully **f** the terms of this covenant, so H6913
Dt 29:22 children who **f** you in later H7756+4946+339
Dt 29:29 that we *may* **f** all the words of this law. H6913
Dt 30: 8 obey the LORD and **f** all his commands I H6913
Dt 31:12 the LORD your God and **f** carefully all the H6913
Jos 3: 3 out from your positions and **f** it. H2143+339
Jos 22:27 us and you and the generations that **f**, H339
Jdg 3:28 "**F** me," he ordered, "for the LORD has H8103
Jdg 6:34 summoning the Abiezrites to **f** him. H339
Jdg 7:17 "**F** my **lead**. When I get H6913+4027
Jdg 9: 3 they were inclined to **f** Abimelek, for they H339
Ru 2: 9 harvesting, and **f along** after the women. H2143
1Sa 8: 3 But his sons *did* not **f** his ways. H2143+928
1Sa 8: 5 and your sons *do* not **f** your ways H2143+928
1Sa 11: 7 of anyone who *does* not **f** Saul and H3655+339
1Sa 12:14 reigns over you **f** the LORD your God H2118+339
1Sa 25:19 her servants, "Go on ahead; I'll **f** you." H995+339
1Sa 25:27 given to the men who **f** you. H2143+928+8079
1Sa 30:21 too exhausted *to* **f** him and who H2143+339
2Sa 17: 9 among the troops who **f** Absalom. H339
2Sa 20: 2 deserted David to **f** Sheba son of Bikri. H339
2Sa 20:11 whoever is for David, let him **f** Joab!" H339
1Ki 6:12 are building, if *you* **f** my decrees H2143+928
1Ki 11: 6 the LORD; he did not **f** the LORD completely H339
1Ki 11:10 forbidden Solomon *to* **f** other gods, H2143+339
1Ki 18:21 the LORD is God, **f** him; but if Baal is H2143+339
1Ki 18:21 follow him; but if Baal is God, **f** him." H2143+339
1Ki 19:21 Then he set out *to* **f** Elijah and H2143+339
2Ki 6:19 **F** me, and I will lead you to the man H2143+339
2Ki 23: 3 to **f** the LORD and keep his commands, H2143+339
1Ch 28: 8 Be careful *to* **f** all the commands of the H2011
2Ch 34:31 to **f** the LORD and keep his commands, H2143+339
2Ch 34:33 they did not fail to **f** the LORD, the God of H339
Ne 9:34 our ancestors *did* not **f** your law; H6913
Ne 10:29 and an oath to **f** the Law of God H2143+928
Est 2:20 she *continued to* **f** Mordecai's H6913
Ps 23: 6 goodness and love *will* **f** me all the days H8103
Ps 45:14 her virgin companions **f** her—those H339
Ps 81:12 stubborn hearts *to* **f** their own H2143+928
Ps 81:13 if Israel *would only* **f** my ways, H2143+928
Ps 89:30 my law and *do* not **f** my statutes, H2143+928
Ps 94:15 all the upright in heart will **f** it. H339
Ps 111:10 all *who* **f** his precepts have good H6913
Ps 119: 3 they do no wrong but **f** his ways. H2143+928
Ps 119:33 of your decrees, that *I may* **f** it to the end. H5915
Ps 119:63 who fear you, to *all who* **f** your precepts. H9068
Ps 119:80 *May* I wholeheartedly **f** your decrees H2118+928
Ps 119:106 that I *will* **f** your righteous laws. H9068
Ps 119:166 salvation, LORD, and *I* **f** your commands. H6913
Ecc 1:11 not be remembered by those who **f** them. H340
Ecc 11: 9 **F** the ways of your heart and H2143+928
SS 1: 8 **f** the tracks of the sheep and graze your H3655
Isa 8:11 warning me not *to* **f** the way of this H2143+928
Isa 42:24 For they would not **f** his ways; they H2143+928
Isa 66:17 meet their end together with the one they **f**," NDT
Jer 3:17 No longer *will they* **f** the H2143+339
Jer 7: 6 and if *you do* not **f** other gods to H2143+339
Jer 7: 9 to Baal and **f** other gods you have H2143+339
Jer 11: 6 to the terms of this covenant and **f** them. H6913
Jer 11: 8 commanded them to **f** but that they did H6913
Jer 13:10 who **f** the stubbornness of their H2143+928
Jer 18:12 *we will* all **f** the stubbornness of our evil H6913
Jer 23:10 The prophets **f** an evil course and use H2118
Jer 23:17 And to all *who* **f** the stubbornness H2143+928
Jer 25: 6 *Do* not **f** other gods to serve and H2143+339
Jer 26: 4 do not listen to me and **f** my law, H2143+928
Jer 32:23 they did not obey you or **f** your law; H2143+928
Jer 35:15 *do* not **f** other gods to serve them. H2143+339
Jer 42:16 you dread *will* **f** you *into* Egypt, H1815+339
Eze 9: 5 "**F** him through the city and kill H6296+339
Eze 11:20 Then *they will* **f** my decrees and be H2143+928
Eze 13: 3 prophets who **f** their own spirit and H2143+339
Eze 20:13 *They did* not **f** my decrees but H2143+928
Eze 20:16 my laws and *did* not **f** my decrees H2143+928
Eze 20:18 "*Do* not **f** the statutes of your parents H2143+928
Eze 20:19 **f** my decrees and be careful to keep H2143+928
Eze 20:21 *They did* not **f** my decrees, they were H2143+928
Eze 33:15 stolen, **f** the decrees that give life H2143+928
Eze 36:27 you and move *you to* **f** my decrees H2143+928
Eze 37:24 *They will* **f** my laws and be careful to H2143+928

Eze 43:11 to its design and f all its regulations. H6913
Eze 48: 1 it will f the Hethlon road to Lebo H448+3338
Hos 11:10 *They will* f the LORD; he will roar like H2143+339
Mt 4:19 f me," Jesus said, "and I will send G3958
Mt 8:19 "Teacher, *I will* f you wherever you go." G199
Mt 8:22 But Jesus told him, "F me, and let the dead G199
Mt 9: 9 "F me," he told him, and Matthew got up G199
Mt 10:38 up their cross and f me is not worthy of me. G199
Mt 16:24 take up their cross and f me. G199
Mt 19:21 treasure in heaven. Then come, f me." G199
Mt 19:27 "We have left everything *to* f you! G199
Mk 1:17 f me," Jesus said, "and I will send G3958
Mk 2:14 "F me," Jesus told him, and Levi got up G199
Mk 5:37 He did not let anyone f him except Peter G5258
Mk 8:34 take up their cross and f me. G199
Mk 10:21 treasure in heaven. Then come, f me." G199
Mk 10:28 "We have left everything *to* f you! G199
Mk 14:13 carrying a jar of water will meet you. F him. G199
Lk 5:27 at his tax booth. "F me," Jesus said to him, G199
Lk 9:23 take up their cross daily and f me. G199
Lk 9:57 said to him, "*I will* f you wherever you go." G199
Lk 9:59 to another man, "F me." But he replied, G199
Lk 9:61 another said, "*I will* f you, Lord; but first G199
Lk 14:27 their cross and f me cannot be my G2262+3958
Lk 18:22 treasure in heaven. Then come, f me." G199
Lk 18:28 "We have left all we had *to* f you! G199
Lk 21: 8 'The time is near.' *Do* not f them. G4513+3958
Lk 22:10 F him to the house that he enters, G199
Jn 1:43 Finding Philip, he said to him, "F me." G199
Jn 10: 4 his sheep f him because they know his G199
Jn 10: 5 But *they will* never f a stranger; in fact, they G199
Jn 10:27 to my voice; I know them, and *they* f me. G199
Jn 12:26 Whoever serves me *must* f me; and where I G199
Jn 13:36 I am going, you cannot f now, but you will G199
Jn 13:36 you cannot follow now, but *you will* f later." G199
Jn 13:37 why can't I f you now? I will lay down G199
Jn 21:19 Then he said to him, "F me!" G199
Jn 21:22 what is that to you? You *must* f me." G199
Ac 12: 8 "Wrap your cloak around you and f me," G199
Ro 2: 8 who reject the truth and f evil, G4275
Ro 4:12 who also f in the footsteps of the G5123
1Co 1:12 One of you says, "I f Paul"; another, "I G1639
1Co 1:12 another, "I f Apollos"; another, "I follow NDT
1Co 1:12 another, "I f Cephas"; still another, "I follow NDT
1Co 1:12 "I follow Cephas"; still another, "I f Christ." NDT
1Co 3: 4 For when one says, "I f Paul," and another G1639
1Co 3: 4 another, "I f Apollos," are you not mere NDT
1Co 11: 1 F my **example**, as I follow the G3629+1181
1Co 11: 1 my example, as I f the example of Christ. NDT
1Co 14: 1 F the way of love and eagerly desire gifts G1503
Gal 2:14 you force Gentiles *to* f **Jewish customs**? G2678
Gal 6:16 Peace and mercy to all *who* f this rule—to G5123
Eph 5: 1 F God's **example**, therefore, as G1181+3629
2Th 3: 7 know how you ought to f our **example**. G3628
1Ti 4: 1 the faith and f deceiving spirits and G4668
1Ti 5:15 in fact already turned away to f Satan. G3958
1Pe 1:11 the Messiah and the glories that would f. G3552
1Pe 2:21 example, that *you should* f in his steps. G2051
2Pe 1:16 For *we did* not f cleverly devised stories G1979
2Pe 2: 2 Many *will* f their depraved conduct and G1979
2Pe 2:10 true of those *who* f the corrupt G3958+4513
2Pe 2:15 wandered off *to* f the way of Balaam G1979
Jude 16 *they* f their own evil desires G2848+4513
Jude 18 will be scoffers *who will* f their own G2848+4513
Jude 19 who f **mere natural instincts** and do not G6035
Rev 14: 4 They f the Lamb wherever he goes G199
Rev 14:13 from their labor, for their deeds *will* f them." G199

FOLLOWED (148) [FOLLOW]

Ge 32:19 and all the *others who* f the herds: H2143+339
Ex 14:23 horsemen f them into the sea. H995+339
Ex 14:28 of Pharaoh that *had* f the Israelites H995+339
Ex 15:20 and all the women f her, with H3655+339
Nu 16:25 and the elders of Israel f him. H2143+339
Nu 25: 8 f the Israelite into the tent. H995+339
Nu 31:16 were the ones who f Balaam's advice and H928
Nu 32:11 they have not f me wholeheartedly, H339
Nu 32:12 for they f the LORD wholeheartedly. H339
Dt 1:36 because he f the LORD wholeheartedly." H339
Dt 4: 3 you everyone who f the Baal of Peor, H2143+339
Jos 6: 8 ark of the LORD's covenant f them. H2143+339
Jos 6: 9 and the rear guard f the ark. H2143+339
Jos 6:13 and the rear guard f the ark of the H2143+339
Jos 14: 8 f the LORD my God wholeheartedly. H339
Jos 14: 9 because you have f the LORD my God H339
Jos 14:14 because he f the LORD, the God of H339
Jdg 2:12 *They* f and worshiped various gods H2143+339
Jdg 3:28 So they f him down and took possession of H339
Jdg 5:14 Benjamin was with the people who f you. H339
Jdg 9:49 men cut branches and f Abimelek. H2143+339
Jdg 10: 3 He *was* f by Jair of Gilead, who led H7756+339
Jdg 11: 3 gathered around him and f him. H3655+6640
Jdg 13:11 Manoah got up and f his wife H2143+339
1Sa 6:12 of the Philistines f them as far as the H2143+339
1Sa 14:13 his armor-bearer f and killed behind NDT
1Sa 17:13 oldest sons *had* f Saul to the war: H2143+339
1Sa 17:14 The three oldest f Saul, H2143+339
1Sa 26: 3 he saw that Saul *had* f him there, H995+339
2Sa 17:23 saw that his advice *had* not **been** f, H6913
2Sa 20:14 who gathered together and f him. H995+339
1Ki 11: 5 He f Ashtoreth the goddess of the H2143+339
1Ki 12:14 *he* f the advice of the young men and said, H3869
1Ki 14: 8 my commands and f me with all his H2143+339
1Ki 16: 2 but *you* f the ways of Jeroboam and H2143+928
1Ki 16:26 *He* f completely the ways of H2143+928
1Ki 18:18 commands and *have* f the Baals. H2143+339
1Ki 22:43 In everything *he* f the ways of his H2143+928
1Ki 22:52 because *he* f the ways of his father H2143+928
2Ki 4:30 So he got up and f her. H2143+339
2Ki 7:15 *They* f them as far as the Jordan, and H2143+339
2Ki 8:18 *He* f the ways of the kings of Israel H2143+928
2Ki 8:27 *He* f the ways of the house of Ahab H2143+928
2Ki 14: 3 *he* f **the example** *of* his H6913+3869+6913
2Ki 16: 3 *He* f the ways of the kings of Israel H2143+928
2Ki 17: 8 f the practices of the nations the H2143+928
2Ki 17:15 *They* f worthless idols and H2143+339
2Ki 17:19 *They* f the practices Israel had H2143+928
2Ki 21:21 *He* f completely the ways of his H2143+928
2Ki 22: 2 of the LORD and f completely the H2143+928
1Ch 8:30 firstborn son was Abdon, f **by** Zur, Kish, H2256
1Ch 9:36 firstborn son was Abdon, f **by** Zur, Kish, H2256
2Ch 10:14 *he* f the advice of the young men and said, H3869
2Ch 11:16 f the Levites *to* Jerusalem to offer H995+339
2Ch 17: 3 because *he* f the ways of his H2143+928
2Ch 17: 4 of his father and f his commands H2143+928
2Ch 20:32 *He* f the ways of his father Asa and H2143+928
2Ch 21: 6 *He* f the ways of the kings of Israel H2143+928
2Ch 21:12 '*You have* not f the ways of your H2143+928
2Ch 21:13 But *you have* f the ways of the kings H2143+928
2Ch 22: 3 He too f the ways of the house of H2143+928
2Ch 22: 5 *He* also f their counsel when he went H2143+928
2Ch 26:17 priests of the LORD f him **in**. H995+339
2Ch 28: 2 *He* f the ways of the kings of Israel H2143+928
2Ch 34: 2 of the LORD and f the ways of his H2143+928
Ne 12:32 half the leaders of Judah f them, H2143+339
Ne 12:38 I f them on top of the wall, together with H339
Est 2: 4 appealed to the king, and *he* f it. H6913+4027
Job 23:11 My feet *have* **closely** f his steps; I have kept H296
Pr 7:22 All at once *he* f her like an ox going H2143+339
Ecc 4:15 walked under the sun f the youth, H6640
Jer 2: 2 you loved me and f me through the H2143+339
Jer 2: 5 *They* f worthless idols and became H2143+339
Jer 7:24 *they* f the stubborn inclinations of H2143+928
Jer 8: 2 and which *they have* f and consulted H2143+339
Jer 9:13 have not obeyed me or f my law. H2143+928
Jer 9:14 *they have* f the stubbornness of their H2143+339
Jer 9:14 their hearts; they have f the Baals, as their H339
Jer 11: 8 they f the stubbornness of their evil H2143+928
Jer 11:10 They *have* f other gods to serve H2143+339
Jer 16:11 'and f other gods and served and H2143+339
Jer 35:18 Jehonadab and *have* f all his instructions H9068
Jer 44:10 nor *have they* f my law and the H2143+928
Jer 44:23 not obeyed him or f his law or his H2143+928
Eze 5: 6 my laws and *has* not f my decrees. H2143
Eze 5: 7 around you and *have* not f my decrees H2143
Eze 11:12 for *you have* not f my decrees or kept my H2143
Eze 16:47 *You* not only f their ways and copied H2143+928
Am 2: 4 the gods their ancestors f, H2143+339
Mic 6:16 house; *you have* f their traditions. H2143+928
Hab 3: 5 went before him; pestilence f his steps. H3655
Mal 2: 9 because you *have* not f my ways but have H9068
Mt 4:20 At once they left their nets and f him. G199
Mt 4:22 left the boat and their father and f him. G199
Mt 4:25 the region across the Jordan f him. G199
Mt 8: 1 from the mountainside, large crowds f him. G199
Mt 8:23 got into the boat and his disciples f him. G199
Mt 9: 9 told him, and Matthew got up and f him. G199
Mt 9:27 two blind men f him, calling out, G199
Mt 12:15 A large crowd f him, and he healed all G199
Mt 14:13 the crowds f him on foot from the towns. G199
Mt 19: 2 Large crowds f him, and he healed them G199
Mt 19:28 you who *have* f me will also sit on twelve G199
Mt 20:29 were leaving Jericho, a large crowd f him. G199
Mt 20:34 they received their sight and f him. G199
Mt 21: 9 ahead of him and those *that* f shouted, G199
Mt 26:58 But Peter f him at a distance, right up to the G199
Mt 27:55 They *had* f Jesus from Galilee to care for G199
Mk 1:18 At once they left their nets and f him. G199
Mk 1:20 boat with the hired men and f him. G599+3958
Mk 2:14 Jesus told him, and Levi got up and f him. G199
Mk 2:15 disciples, for there were many *who* f him. G199
Mk 3: 7 the lake, and a large crowd from Galilee f. G199
Mk 5:24 A large crowd f and pressed around him G199
Mk 10:32 astonished, while those *who* f were afraid. G199
Mk 10:52 his sight and f Jesus along the road. G199
Mk 11: 9 who went ahead and those *who* f shouted, G199
Mk 14:54 Peter f him at a distance, right into the G199
Mk 15:41 these women *had* f him and cared for G199
Lk 5:11 up on shore, left everything and f him. G199
Lk 5:28 Levi got up, left everything and f him. G199
Lk 9:11 the crowds learned about it and f him G199
Lk 18:43 he received his sight and f Jesus, G199
Lk 22:39 Mount of Olives, and his disciples f him. G199
Lk 22:54 of the high priest. Peter f at a distance. G199
Lk 23:27 A large number of people f him, including G199
Lk 23:49 the women who *had* f him from Galilee, G5258
Lk 23:55 Jesus from Galilee f Joseph and saw the G2887
Jn 1:37 disciples heard him say this, *they* f Jesus. G199
Jn 1:40 what John had said and *who had* f Jesus. G199
Jn 6: 2 crowd of people f him because they saw G199
Jn 6:66 turned back and no longer f him. G3552+4344
Jn 11:31 up and went out, *they* f her, supposing she G199
Jn 21: 8 The other disciples f in the boat, towing G2262
Ac 8:11 *They* f him because he had amazed them G4668
Ac 8:13 And *he* f Philip **everywhere**, astonished by G4674
Ac 12: 9 Peter f him out of the prison, but he had no G199
Ac 13:43 converts to Judaism f Paul and Barnabas, G199
Ac 16:17 She f Paul and the rest of us, shouting G2887
Ac 21:36 The crowd *that* f kept shouting, "Get rid of G199
Ac 27:11 f **the advice** of the pilot and of the owner G4275
Ro 5:16 The judgment f one sin and brought G1666
Ro 5:16 the gift f many trespasses and brought G1666
Eph 2: 2 used to live when you f the ways of this G2848
1Ti 4: 6 of the good teaching that *you have* f. G4158
Rev 13: 3 was filled with wonder and f the beast. G3958
Rev 14: 8 A second angel f and said, " 'Fallen! Fallen G199
Rev 14: 9 A third angel f them and said in a loud G199

FOLLOWER (2) [FOLLOW]

Ac 24:14 God of our ancestors as a f of the Way, G2848
1Co 4: 6 puffed up in being a f of one of us over G5642

FOLLOWERS (24) [FOLLOW]

Nu 16: 5 Then he said to Korah and all his f: "In the H6337
Nu 16: 6 and all your f are to do this: Take H6337
Nu 16:11 you and all your f have banded together. H6337
Nu 16:16 "You and all your f are to appear before H6337
Nu 16:19 had gathered all his f in opposition to H6337
Nu 16:40 he would become like Korah and his f. H6337
Nu 26: 9 were among Korah's f when they rebelled H6337
Nu 26:10 whose f died when the fire devoured the H6337
Nu 27: 3 He was not among Korah's f, who banded H6337
Jdg 9: 4 scoundrels, *who became* his f. H2143+339
1Sa 30:22 among David's f said, H408+889+2143+6640
1Ki 16:22 But Omri's f proved H2021+6639+889+339
Ne 11: 8 his f, Gabbai and Sallai—928 men. H339
Ps 49:13 of their f, who approve their H339
Ps 106:18 Fire blazed among their f; a flame H6337
Da 11:24 plunder, loot and wealth among **his** f. H2157S
Lk 11:19 by whom do your f drive them out? G5626
Lk 22:49 When Jesus' f saw what was going G3836+4309
Ac 5:36 was killed, all his f were dispersed, and it G4275
Ac 5:37 was killed, and all his f were scattered. G4275
Ac 9:25 But his f took him by night and lowered G3412
Ac 17:34 Some of the people *became* f **of** Paul and G3140
Ac 22: 4 I persecuted the f of this Way to their death NDT
Rev 17:14 him will be his called, chosen and **faithful** *f*." AIT

FOLLOWING (65) [FOLLOW]

Ge 47:18 they came to him the f year and said H9108
Ex 30:23 "Take the f fine spices: 500 shekels of liquid NDT
Lev 20: 6 spiritists to prostitute themselves by f them, H339
Lev 23:32 of the month until the f evening you are to NDT
Nu 32:15 If you turn away from f him, he will again H339
Dt 7: 4 children away from f me to serve other H339
Dt 11:28 command you today by f other gods, H2143+339
Dt 28:14 f other gods and serving them. H2143+339
Jos 18:21 according to its clans, had the f towns: NDT
Jos 21: 3 gave the Levites the f towns and H465S
Jos 21: 9 Simeon they allotted the f towns by name H465S
Jdg 2:19 f other gods and serving and H2143+339
Jdg 4:14 with ten thousand men f him. H339
1Sa 5: 4 But the f morning when they rose, there H4740
2Sa 15:12 and Absalom's f kept on increasing. H6639+907
2Sa 15:16 with his entire household f him; but H928+8079
2Sa 15:17 with all the people f him, and they H928+8079
1Ki 8:66 On the f day he sent the people away H9029S
1Ki 15:26 f the ways of his father and H2143+928
1Ki 15:34 f the ways of Jeroboam and H2143+928
1Ki 16:19 of the LORD and f the ways of H2143+928
2Ki 13: 2 eyes of the LORD *by* f the sins of H2143+339
2Ki 17:21 Israel away from f the LORD and caused H339
2Ki 18: 6 held fast to the LORD and did not stop f him; H339
2Ki 21: 2 f the detestable practices of the nations H3869
1Ch 6:71 The Gershonites received the f: From the NDT
1Ch 6:77 the rest of the Levites) received the f: NDT
2Ch 11:17 f the ways of David and Solomon H2143+928
2Ch 25:27 that Amaziah turned away from f the LORD, H339
2Ch 29:15 king had ordered, f the word of the LORD. H928
2Ch 30:12 had ordered, f the word of the LORD. H928
2Ch 33: 2 f the detestable practices of the nations H3869
2Ch 36:14 f all the detestable practices of the H3869
Ezr 2:59 The f came up from the towns of Tel H465S
Ezr 10:18 *the* f had married foreign women: H5162
Ne 7:61 The f came up from the towns of Tel H465S
Job 34:27 they turned from f him and had no regard H339
Ps 119:14 I rejoice in f your statutes as one rejoices H2006
Isa 66:17 f one who is among those who eat the H339
Jer 2: 8 by Baal, f worthless idols. H2143+339
Jer 3:19 me 'Father' and not turn away from f me. H339
Jer 16:12 how all of you *are* f the H2143+339
Zep 1: 6 who turn back from f the LORD and neither H339
Mt 8:10 he was amazed and said *to* those f him G199
Mt 10: 5 Jesus sent out with **the** f instructions: G899
Mk 13:24 "But in those days, f that distress, " 'the G3552
Mk 14:51 nothing but a linen garment, was f Jesus. G5258
Lk 7: 9 turning *to* the crowd f him, he said, G199
Jn 1:38 Jesus saw them f and asked, "What do G199
Jn 18:15 Peter and another disciple *were* f Jesus. G199
Jn 21:20 the disciple whom Jesus loved *was* f them. G199
Ac 10: 9 About noon the f **day** as they were on G2069
Ac 10:24 The f **day** he arrived in Caesarea G2069
Ac 15:23 With them *they* **sent** *the f* **letter**: The apostles AIT
Ac 15:28 with anything beyond the f requirements: G4047
Ac 20:15 and *on* the f day arrived at Miletus. G2400
Ac 23:11 The f night the Lord stood near Paul and G2079

Ac 28:13 and on the f day we reached Puteoli. G1308
1Co 11:17 In the f directives I have no praise for you G4047
Eph 2: 3 of our flesh and f its desires and thoughts. G4472
Php 3:17 Join together in f my example G5213+1181
Heb 4:11 no one will perish by f their example of G1877
2Pe 3: 3 scoffing and f their own evil desires G2848+4513
Rev 6: 8 and Hades *was* f close behind him. G199
Rev 19:14 The armies of heaven *were* f him, riding on G199

FOLLOWS (16) [FOLLOW]

Ge 41:31 the famine that f it will be so severe. H339+4027
Nu 14:24 a different spirit and f me wholeheartedly, H339
2Ki 11:15 put to the sword anyone *who* f her." H995+339
2Ch 17:14 Their enrollment by families was as f: From H465
2Ch 23:14 put to the sword anyone *who* f her." H995+339
Ezr 4: 8 Jerusalem to Artaxerxes the king as f: A10358
Ezr 5: 7 report they sent him read as f: A10341+10180
Job 21:33 to them; everyone f after them, and a H5432
Jer 4:20 Disaster f disaster; the whole land H7925+6584
Jer 51:31 One courier f another and messenger H7925
Jer 51:31 messenger f messenger to announce H7925
Eze 18: 9 *He* f my decrees and faithfully keeps H2143+928
Eze 18:17 He keeps my laws and f my decrees H2143+928
Hos 4: 2 all bounds, and bloodshed f bloodshed. H5595
Jn 8:12 Whoever f me will never walk in darkness G199
Ac 23:25 He wrote a letter as f: G2400+3836+5596+4047

FOLLY (38) [FOOL]

1Sa 25:25 name means Fool, and f goes with him. H5576
Job 42: 8 not deal with you according to your f. H5576
Ps 38: 5 are loathsome because of my sinful f. H222
Ps 69: 5 know my f; my guilt is not hidden H222
Ps 85: 8 servants—but let them not turn to f. H4074
Pr 5:23 will die, led astray by their own great f. H222
Pr 9:13 F is an unruly woman; she is simple and H4070
Pr 12:23 themselves, but a fool's heart blurts out f. H222
Pr 13:16 with knowledge, but fools expose their f. H222
Pr 14: 8 their ways, but the f *of* fools is deception. H222
Pr 14:18 The simple inherit f, but the prudent are H222
Pr 14:24 is their crown, but the f *of* fools yields folly. H222
Pr 14:24 is their crown, but the folly of fools yields f. H222
Pr 14:29 one who is quick-tempered displays f. H222
Pr 15: 2 the mouth of the fool gushes f. H222
Pr 15:14 the mouth of a fool feeds on f. H222
Pr 15:21 F brings joy to one who has no sense, but H222
Pr 16:22 prudent, but f brings punishment to fools. H222
Pr 17:12 robbed of her cubs than a fool bent on f. H222
Pr 18:13 before listening—that is f and shame. H222
Pr 19: 3 A person's own f leads to their ruin, yet H222
Pr 22:15 F is bound up in the heart of a child, but H222
Pr 24: 9 The schemes of f are sin, and people H222
Pr 26: 4 Do not answer a fool according to his f, or H222
Pr 26: 5 Answer a fool according to his f, or he will H222
Pr 26:11 returns to its vomit, so fools repeat their f. H222
Pr 27:22 you will not remove their f from them. H222
Ecc 1:17 also of madness and f, but I learned H8508
Ecc 2: 3 and embracing f—my mind still H6121
Ecc 2:12 wisdom, and also madness and f. H6121
Ecc 2:13 I saw that wisdom is better than f, just as H6121
Ecc 7:25 of wickedness and the madness of f. H6121
Ecc 10: 1 so a little f outweighs wisdom and honor. H6121
Ecc 10:13 At the beginning their words are f; at the H6121
Isa 9:17 wicked, every mouth speaks f. H5576
Isa 32: 6 For fools speak f, their hearts are bent on H5576
Mk 7:22 lewdness, envy, slander, arrogance and f. G932
2Ti 3: 9 those men, their f will be clear to everyone. G486

FONDLED (2)

Eze 23: 3 land their breasts were f and their virgin H5080
Eze 23:21 was caressed and your young breasts f. H5080

FOOD (382) [FOODS]

Ge 1:29 fruit with seed in it. They will be yours for f. H433
Ge 1:30 of life in it—I give every green plant for f." H433
Ge 2: 9 were pleasing to the eye and good for f. H4407
Ge 3: 6 tree was good for f and pleasing to the H4407
Ge 3:17 painful toil *you will* eat f *from* it all the H430
Ge 3:19 brow you will eat your f until you return to H4312
Ge 6:21 to take every kind of f that is to be eaten H4407
Ge 6:21 store it away as f for you and for them." H433
Ge 9: 3 lives and moves about will be f for you. H433
Ge 14:11 of Sodom and Gomorrah and all their f; H431
Ge 21:14 Abraham took *some* f and a skin of water H4312
Ge 24:33 Then f was set before him, but he said, "I H430
Ge 27: 4 me the kind of tasty f I like and bring it H4761
Ge 27: 7 game and prepare me *some* tasty f to eat, H4761
Ge 27: 9 I can prepare *some* tasty f for your father, H4761
Ge 27:14 she prepared *some* tasty f, just the H4761
Ge 27:17 her son Jacob the tasty f and the bread H4761
Ge 27:31 He too prepared *some* tasty f and brought H4761
Ge 28:20 will give me f to eat and clothes to H4312
Ge 39: 6 himself with anything except the f he ate. H4312
Ge 41:35 collect all the f *of* these good years that H431
Ge 41:35 of Pharaoh, to be kept in the cities for f. H431
Ge 41:36 This f should be held in reserve for the H431
Ge 41:48 collected all the f produced *in* those seven H431
Ge 41:48 each city he put the f *grown in* the fields H431
Ge 41:54 in the whole land of Egypt there was f. H4312
Ge 41:55 famine, the people cried to Pharaoh for f. H4312
Ge 42: 7 land of Canaan," they replied, "to buy f." H431
Ge 42:10 "Your servants have come to buy f. H431
Ge 42:33 take f for your starving households and NDT
Ge 43: 2 "Go back and buy us a little more f. H431
Ge 43: 4 we will go down and buy f for you. H431
Ge 43:20 "we came down here the first time to buy f. H431
Ge 43:22 brought additional silver with us to buy f. H431
Ge 43:31 controlling himself, said, "Serve the f." H4312
Ge 44: 1 sacks with as much f as they can carry, H431
Ge 44:25 'Go back and buy a little more f. H431
Ge 47:12 all his father's household with f, H4312
Ge 47:13 There was no f, however, in the whole H4312
Ge 47:15 came to Joseph and said, "Give us f. H4312
Ge 47:16 "I will sell you f in exchange for your NDT
Ge 47:17 he gave them f in exchange for their H4312
Ge 47:17 that year with f in exchange for all H4312
Ge 47:19 Buy us and our land in exchange for f H4312
Ge 47:22 Pharaoh and had f enough *from* the H430
Ge 47:24 the fields and as f *for* yourselves and your H431
Ge 49:20 "Asher's f will be rich; he will provide H4312
Ex 12:16 except *to* prepare f for everyone to eat; that H430
Ex 12:39 not have time to prepare f for themselves. H7476
Ex 16: 3 pots of meat and ate all the f we wanted, H4312
Ex 21:10 he must not deprive the first one of her f H8638
Ex 23:11 poor among your people *may* get f from it, H430
Ex 23:25 his blessing will be on your f and water. H4312
Ex 29:18 a f offering presented to the LORD. H852
Ex 29:25 the LORD, a f offering presented to the LORD. H852
Ex 29:41 a f offering presented to the LORD. H852
Ex 30:20 by presenting a f offering to the LORD, H852
Lev 1: 9 burnt offering, a f offering, an aroma H852
Lev 1:13 burnt offering, a f offering, an aroma H852
Lev 1:17 burnt offering, a f offering, an aroma H852
Lev 2: 2 on the altar, a f offering, an aroma H852
Lev 2: 3 part of the f offerings *presented to* the LORD. H852
Lev 2: 9 burn it on the altar as a f offering, H852
Lev 2:10 part of the f offerings *presented to* the LORD. H852
Lev 2:11 honey in a f offering presented to the H852
Lev 2:16 as a f offering presented to the LORD. H852
Lev 3: 3 you are to bring a f offering to the LORD: H852
Lev 3: 5 it is a f offering, an aroma pleasing H852
Lev 3: 9 you are to bring a f offering to the LORD: H852
Lev 3:11 the altar as a f offering presented to H4312+852
Lev 3:14 are to present this f offering to the LORD: H852
Lev 3:16 them on the altar as a f offering, H4312+852
Lev 4:35 top of the f offerings *presented to* the LORD. H852
Lev 5:12 top of the f offerings *presented to* the LORD. H852
Lev 6:17 share of the f offerings *presented to* me. H852
Lev 6:18 of the f offerings *presented to* the LORD. H852
Lev 7: 5 on the altar as a f offering presented to the H852
Lev 7:25 from which a f offering may be presented H852
Lev 7:30 are to present the f offering *to* the LORD; H852
Lev 7:35 of the f offerings *presented to* the LORD that H852
Lev 8:21 a f offering presented to the LORD H852
Lev 8:28 a f offering presented to the LORD. H852
Lev 10:12 f offerings prepared without yeast and *presented to* H852
Lev 10:13 of the f offerings *presented to* the LORD; H852
Lev 10:15 with the fat portions of the f offerings, H852
Lev 11:34 Any f you are allowed to eat that has come H431
Lev 21: 6 they present the f offerings to the LORD, H852
Lev 21: 6 to the LORD, the f *of* their God, they are to H4312
Lev 21: 8 because they offer up the f *of* your God. H4312
Lev 21:17 may come near to offer the f *of* his God. H4312
Lev 21:21 near to present the f offerings to the LORD. H852
Lev 21:21 not come near to offer the f *of* his God. H4312
Lev 21:22 He may eat the most holy f *of* his God, as H4312
Lev 21:22 holy food of his God, as well as the holy f; NDT
Lev 22: 7 eat the sacred offerings, for they are his f. H4312
Lev 22:11 born in his household, they may eat his f. H4312
Lev 22:13 as in her youth, she may eat her father's f. H4312
Lev 22:22 on the altar as a f offering presented to the H852
Lev 22:25 offer them as the f *of* your God. H4312
Lev 22:27 as a f offering presented to H7933+852
Lev 23: 8 seven days present a f offering to the LORD. H852
Lev 23:13 olive oil—a f offering presented to the LORD H852
Lev 23:18 drink offerings—a f offering, an aroma H852
Lev 23:25 but present a f offering to the LORD. H852
Lev 23:27 present a f offering to the LORD. H852
Lev 23:36 seven days present f offerings to the LORD, H852
Lev 23:36 present a f offering to the LORD. H852
Lev 23:37 bringing f offerings to the LORD— H852
Lev 24: 7 to be a f offering presented to the H852
Lev 24: 9 of the f offerings *presented to* the LORD." H852
Lev 25: 6 during the sabbath year will be f for you— H433
Lev 25:37 money at interest or sell them f at a profit. H431
Lev 26: 5 you will eat all the f you want and live in H4312
Nu 11: 4 with them *began to* crave other f, H203+9294
Nu 11:34 buried the people who *had* craved other f. H203
Nu 15: 3 to the LORD f offerings from the herd or H852
Nu 15:10 This will be a f offering, an aroma pleasing H852
Nu 15:13 when they present a f offering as an aroma H852
Nu 15:14 you presents a f offering as an aroma H852
Nu 15:19 you eat the f *of* the land, present a H4312
Nu 15:25 LORD for their wrong a f offering and a sin H852
Nu 18:17 the altar and burn their fat as a f offering, H852
Nu 21: 5 And we detest this miserable f!" H4312
Nu 28: 2 at the appointed time my f offerings, H7933+852
Nu 28: 3 'This is the f offering you are to present to H852
Nu 28: 6 a f offering presented to the LORD. H852
Nu 28: 8 This is a f offering, an aroma pleasing to H852
Nu 28:13 a f offering presented to the LORD. H852
Nu 28:19 to the LORD a f offering consisting of a H852
Nu 28:24 way present the f offering every day for H852
Nu 29: 6 They are f offerings presented to the LORD H852
Nu 29:13 to the LORD a f offering consisting of a burnt H852
Nu 29:36 to the LORD a f offering consisting of a burnt H852
Dt 2: 6 in silver for the f you eat and the water H431
Dt 2:28 Sell us f to eat and water to drink for their H431
Dt 10:18 among you, giving them f and clothing. H4312
Dt 18: 1 on the f offerings *presented to* the LORD, H852
Dt 23:19 whether on money or f or anything else H431
Dt 28:26 carcasses will be f for all the birds and H4407
Dt 32:15 fat and kicked; filled with f, they became H9042
Jos 5:12 the day after they ate this f *from* the land; H6289
Jos 9: 5 bread of their f supply was dry and moldy H7474
Jos 13:14 since the f offerings *presented to* the LORD H852
Jdg 13:16 you detain me, I will not eat any of your f. H4312
Jdg 17:10 of silver a year, your clothes and your f." H4695
Ru 1: 6 aid of his people by providing f for them, H4312
1Sa 2: 5 who were full hire themselves out for f, H4312
1Sa 2:28 family all the f offerings *presented by* the H852
1Sa 2:36 priestly office so I can have f to eat." H7326+4312
1Sa 9: 7 give the man? The f in our sacks is gone H4312
1Sa 14:24 be anyone who eats f before evening H4312
1Sa 14:24 So none of the troops tasted f. H4312
1Sa 14:28 'Cursed be anyone who eats f today! H4312
1Sa 28:22 me give you some f so you may eat and H4312
1Sa 30:11 gave him water to drink and f to eat— H4312
1Sa 30:12 he had not eaten *any* f or drunk any water H4312
2Sa 3:29 who falls by the sword or who lacks f." H4312
2Sa 12: 3 It shared his f, drank from his cup and H7326
2Sa 12:17 he would not eat any f with them. H4312
2Sa 12:20 at his request they served him f, and H4312
2Sa 13: 5 Let her prepare the f in my sight so I may H1376
2Sa 13: 7 Amnon and prepare some f for him." H1376
2Sa 13:10 "Bring the f here into my bedroom so I H1376
1Ki 5: 9 my wish by providing f for my royal H4312
1Ki 5:11 cors of wheat as f for his household, H4818
1Ki 10: 5 the f *on* his table, the seating of his H4407
1Ki 11:18 house and land and provided him with f. H4312
1Ki 17: 4 the ravens to supply you with f there." H3870
1Ki 17: 9 a widow there to supply you with f." H3920
1Ki 17:15 So *there was* f every day for Elijah and H430
1Ki 18: 4 had supplied them with f and water.) H4312
1Ki 18:13 supplied them with f and water. H4312
1Ki 19: 8 Strengthened by that f, he traveled forty H428
2Ki 6:22 Set f and water before them so that they H4312
2Ki 25: 3 that there was no f for the people to eat. H4312
1Ch 12:40 Naphtali came bringing f on donkeys, H4312
2Ch 9: 4 the f *on* his table, the seating of his H4407
2Ch 11:11 with supplies of f, olive oil and wine. H4407
2Ch 28:15 clothes and sandals, f and drink, and H430
Ezr 2:63 eat any of the most sacred *f* until there was AIT
Ezr 3: 7 gave f and drink and olive oil to the H4407
Ezr 10: 6 was there, he ate no f and drank no water H4312
Ne 5:14 brothers ate the f *allotted to* the governor. H4312
Ne 5:15 silver from them in addition to f and wine. H4312
Ne 5:18 demanded the f *allotted to* the governor, H4312
Ne 7:65 any of the most sacred f until there H7731+7731
Ne 8:10 "Go and enjoy choice f and sweet drinks H5460
Ne 8:12 to send portions of f and to celebrate with H4950
Ne 13: 2 the Israelites with f and water but had H4312
Ne 13:15 them against selling f on that day. H7474
Est 2: 9 with her beauty treatments and special f. H4950
Est 9:22 joy and giving presents of f to one H4950
Job 3:24 For sighing has become my daily f; my H4312
Job 6: 6 Is tasteless *f* eaten without salt, or is there AIT
Job 6: 7 I refuse to touch it; such f makes me ill. H4312
Job 12:11 the ear test words as the tongue tastes f? H431
Job 15:23 He wanders about for f like a vulture; he H4312
Job 20:14 his f will turn sour in his stomach; it H4312
Job 22: 7 weary and you withheld f from the hungry, H4312
Job 24: 5 the poor go about their labor of foraging f; H3272
Job 24: 5 the wasteland provides f for their children. H4312
Job 28: 5 from which f comes, is transformed H4312
Job 30: 4 their f was the root of the broom bush H4312
Job 33:20 that their body finds f repulsive and their H4312
Job 34: 3 the ear tests words as the tongue tastes f. H430
Job 36:16 comfort of your table laden with choice f. H2016
Job 36:31 the nations and provides f in abundance. H431
Job 38:41 Who provides f for the raven when its H7474
Job 38:41 out to God and wander about for lack of f? H431
Job 39:29 From there it looks for f; its eyes detect it H431
Ps 42: 3 My tears have been my f day and night H4312
Ps 59:15 They wander about for f and howl if not H430
Ps 63:10 to the sword and become f *for* jackals. H4987
Ps 69:21 put gall in my f and gave me vinegar H1362
Ps 74:14 gave it as f to the creatures of the H4407
Ps 78:18 to the test by demanding the f they craved. H431
Ps 78:25 he sent them all the f they could eat. H7476
Ps 78:30 even while the f was still in their mouths, H431
Ps 79: 2 of your servants as f for the birds of the sky H4407
Ps 102: 4 withered like grass; I forget to eat my f. H4312
Ps 102: 9 I eat ashes as my f and mingle my drink H4312
Ps 104:14 cultivate—bringing forth f from the earth: H4312
Ps 104:21 their prey and seek their f from God. H431
Ps 104:27 you to give them their f at the proper time. H431
Ps 105:16 land and destroyed all their supplies of f; H4312
Ps 107:18 They loathed all f and drew near the gates H431
Ps 111: 5 He provides f for those who fear him; he H3272
Ps 127: 2 up late, toiling for f to eat—for he grants H4312
Ps 132:15 provisions; her poor I will satisfy with f. H4312
Ps 136:25 He gives f to every creature. His love H4312
Ps 145:15 you give them their f at the proper time. H431
Ps 146: 7 the oppressed and gives f to the hungry. H4312
Ps 147: 9 He provides f for the cattle and for the H4312
Pr 6: 8 in summer and gathers its f at harvest. H4407

Pr 7:14 I have **f from** my fellowship **offering** at H2285
Pr 9: 5 eat my f and drink the wine I have mixed. H4312
Pr 9:17 is sweet; f eaten in secret is delicious!" H4312
Pr 12: 9 pretend to be somebody and have no f. H4312
Pr 12:11 who work their land will have abundant f, H4312
Pr 13:23 An unplowed field produces f *for* the poor H431
Pr 20:13 stay awake and you will have f to spare. H4312
Pr 20:17 F *gained by* fraud tastes sweet, but one H4312
Pr 21:20 The wise store up **choice** *f* and olive oil, but AIT
Pr 22: 9 they share their f with the poor. H4312
Pr 23: 3 crave his delicacies, for that f is deceptive. H4312
Pr 23: 6 Do not eat the f *of* a begrudging host, do H4312
Pr 25:21 is hungry, give him f to eat; if he is thirsty, H4312
Pr 28:19 who work their land will have abundant f, H4312
Pr 30:25 they store up their f in the summer; H4312
Pr 31:14 merchant ships, bringing her f from afar. H4312
Pr 31:15 she provides f for her family and portions H3272
Ecc 9: 7 eat your f with gladness, and drink H4312
Ecc 9:11 does f come to the wise or wealth to H4312
Isa 3: 1 all supplies of f and all supplies of water, H4312
Isa 3: 7 I have no f or clothing in my house; do H4312
Isa 4: 1 will eat our own f and provide our own H4312
Isa 21:14 who live in Tema, bring f *for* the fugitives. H4312
Isa 23:18 the LORD, for abundant f and fine clothes. H430
Isa 25: 6 prepare a feast of **rich** f for all peoples, H9043
Isa 30:23 the f that comes from the land will be H4312
Isa 58: 7 it not to share your f with the hungry and H4312
Isa 62: 8 I give your grain as f for your enemies, H4407
Isa 65:25 and dust will be the serpent's f. H4312
Jer 5:17 They will devour your harvests and f H4312
Jer 7:33 people will become f for the birds and the H4407
Jer 9:15 I *will* **make** this people **eat** bitter f and H430
Jer 14: 6 like jackals; their eyes fail for lack of f." H6912
Jer 16: 4 bodies will become f for the birds and the H4407
Jer 16: 7 No *one will* **offer** f to comfort those who H7271
Jer 19: 7 their carcasses as f to the birds and the H4407
Jer 22:15 *Did* not your father **have** f and drink H430
Jer 23:15 "I *will* **make** them **eat** bitter f and drink H430
Jer 34:20 bodies will become f for the birds and the H4407
Jer 44:17 we had plenty of f and were well off and H4312
Jer 52: 6 that there was no f for the people to eat. H4312
La 1:11 their treasures for f to keep themselves H431
La 1:19 they searched for f to keep themselves H431
La 4: 9 waste away for lack of f *from* the field. H9482
La 4:10 who became their f when my people were H1356
Eze 4:10 twenty shekels of f to eat each day and H4407
Eze 4:12 **Eat** the f as you would a loaf of barley H5626S
Eze 4:13 will eat defiled f among the nations H4312
Eze 4:16 about to cut off the f supply in Jerusalem. H4312
Eze 4:16 will eat rationed f in anxiety and drink H4312
Eze 4:17 f and water will be scarce. They will be H4312
Eze 5:16 upon you and cut off your supply of f. H4312
Eze 12:18 tremble as you eat your f, and shudder in H4312
Eze 12:19 They will eat their f in anxiety and drink H4312
Eze 14:13 it to cut off its f supply and send famine H4312
Eze 16:13 *Your* f was honey, olive oil and the finest H430
Eze 16:19 Also the f I provided for you—the flour H4312
Eze 16:20 to me and sacrificed them as f to the idols. H430
Eze 18: 7 robbery but gives his f to the hungry and H4312
Eze 18:16 robbery but gives his f to the hungry and H4312
Eze 23:37 whom they bore to me, as f for them. H433
Eze 24:17 beard or eat the customary f of mourners." H4312
Eze 24:22 beard or eat the customary f of mourners. H4312
Eze 29: 5 I will give you as f to the beasts of the H433
Eze 34: 5 scattered they became f for all the wild H433
Eze 34: 8 has become f for all the wild animals H433
Eze 34:10 mouths, and it will no longer be f for them. H433
Eze 39: 4 I will give you as f to all kinds of carrion H433
Eze 44: 7 my temple while you offered me f, H4312
Eze 47:12 fruit will serve for f and their leaves for H4407
Eze 48:18 produce will supply f for the workers of the H4312
Da 1: 5 amount of f and wine *from* the king's H7329
Da 1: 8 defile himself with the royal f and wine, H7329
Da 1:10 who has assigned your f and drink. H4407
Da 1:13 that of the young men who eat the royal f, H7329
Da 1:15 any of the young men who ate the royal f. H7329
Da 1:16 took away their **choice** f and the wine they H7329
Da 4:12 its fruit abundant, and on it was f for all. A10410
Da 4:21 providing f for all, giving shelter A10410
Da 10: 3 I ate no choice f; no meat or wine touched H4312
Hos 2: 5 who give me my f and my water, my wool H4312
Hos 9: 3 return to Egypt and eat unclean f in Assyria. NDT
Hos 9: 4 This f will be for themselves; it will not H4312
Joel 1:16 Has not the f been cut off before our very H431
Am 8:11 not a famine of f or a thirst for water H4312
Hab 1:16 lives in luxury and enjoys the choicest f. H4407
Hab 3:17 olive crop fails and the fields produce no f, H431
Hag 2:12 olive oil or other f, does it become H4407
Zec 9: 7 the **forbidden** f from between their teeth. H9199
Mal 1: 7 "By offering defiled f on my altar. "But you H4312
Mal 1:12 defiled,' and, 'Its f is contemptible. H5762+431
Mal 3:10 that there may be f in my house. H3272
Mt 3: 4 His f was locusts and wild honey *G5575*
Mt 6:25 Is not life more than f, and the body more *G5575*
Mt 14:15 the villages and buy themselves *some* f." *G1109*
Mt 24:45 to give them their f at the proper time? *G5575*
Mk 7: 2 his disciples eating f with hands that were *G788*
Mk 7: 5 of eating their f with defiled hands? *G788*
Lk 3:11 anyone who has f should do the same *G1109*
Lk 9:12 countryside and find f and lodging, *G2169*
Lk 9:13 unless we go and buy f for all this crowd." *G1109*
Lk 11: 6 and I have no f to offer him. *G4005S*
Lk 12:23 For life is more *than* f, and the body more *G5575*
Lk 12:42 give them their f **allowance** at the proper *G4991*
Lk 15:17 my father's hired servants have f to spare, *G788*
Jn 4: 8 disciples had gone into the town to buy f.) *G5575*
Jn 4:32 "I have f to eat that you know nothing *G1111*
Jn 4:33 "Could someone have brought him f?" *G2266*
Jn 4:34 "My f," said Jesus, "is to do the will of *G1109*
Jn 6:27 Do not work *for* f that spoils, but for food *G1111*
Jn 6:27 but *for* f that endures to eternal life *G1111*
Jn 6:55 For my flesh is real f and my blood is real *G1111*
Ac 6: 1 overlooked in the daily **distribution** *of f.* AIT
Ac 7:11 our ancestors could not find f. *G5964*
Ac 9:19 after taking *some* f, he regained his *G5575*
Ac 12:20 on the king's country *for* their f **supply**. *G5555*
Ac 14:17 you with plenty *of* f and fills your hearts *G5575*
Ac 15:20 them to abstain *from f* **polluted** by idols, AIT
Ac 15:29 are to abstain *from* f **sacrificed to idols**, *G1628*
Ac 21:25 should abstain *from* f **sacrificed to idols**, *G1628*
Ac 27:21 After they had gone a long time **without** f *G826*
Ac 27:33 suspense and have gone **without** f— *G827*
Ac 27:34 Now I urge you to take *some* f. You need it *G5575*
Ac 27:36 encouraged and ate *some* f themselves. *G5575*
Ro 14:20 destroy the work of God for the sake of f. *G1109*
Ro 14:20 All f is clean, but it is wrong for a person to NDT
1Co 3: 2 you milk, not **solid** f, for you were not *G1109*
1Co 6:13 "F for the stomach and the stomach for *G1109*
1Co 6:13 the stomach and the stomach *for* f, *G1109*
1Co 8: 1 Now about f **sacrificed to idols**: We know *G1628*
1Co 8: 4 about eating f **sacrificed to idols**: We *G1628*
1Co 8: 7 when they eat sacrificial f they think of it as NDT
1Co 8: 8 But f does not bring us near to God; we *G1109*
1Co 9: 4 Don't we have the right *to* f and drink? *G2266*
1Co 9:13 in the temple **get** *their* f from the temple, *G2266*
1Co 10: 3 They all ate the same spiritual f *G1109*
1Co 10:19 then that f **sacrificed to an idol** is anything *G1628*
2Co 9:10 sower and bread for f will also supply *G1111*
2Co 11:27 thirst and have often **gone without** f; *G3763*
2Th 3: 8 did we eat anyone's f without paying for it. *G788*
2Th 3:12 to settle down and earn the f they eat. *G788*
1Ti 6: 8 But if we have f and clothing, we will be *G1418*
Heb 5:12 all over again. You need milk, not solid f! *G5575*
Heb 5:14 But solid f is for the mature, who by *G5575*
Heb 9:10 are only a matter of f and drink and *G1109*
Jas 2:15 a sister is without clothes and daily f. *G5575*
Rev 2:14 that they ate f **sacrificed to idols** and *G1628*
Rev 2:20 the eating *of* f **sacrificed to idols**. *G1628*

FOODS (4) [FOOD]

Ps 63: 5 as with the **richest of** f; H2693+2256+2016
Mk 7:19 In saying this, Jesus declared all f clean.) *G1109*
1Ti 4: 3 order them to abstain *from* certain f, *G1109*
Heb 13: 9 not *by* **eating** *ceremonial* f, which is *G1109*

FOOL (62) [FOLLY, FOOL'S, FOOLISH, FOOLISHLY, FOOLISHNESS, FOOLS]

Nu 22:29 the donkey, "*You have* **made a** f **of** me! H6618
Jdg 16:10 Samson, "*You have* **made a** f **of** me; you H9438
Jdg 16:13 time *you have been* **making a** f **of** me H9438
Jdg 16:15 third time *you have* **made a** f **of** me and H9438
1Sa 25:25 name—his name means F, and folly goes H5572
1Sa 26:21 Surely *I have* **acted like a** f and have been H6118
Job 5: 2 Resentment kills a f, and envy slays the H211
Job 5: 3 I myself have seen a f taking root, but H211
Ps 14: 1 The f says in his heart, "There is no God." H5572
Ps 53: 1 The f says in his heart, "There is no God." H5572
Pr 10: 8 a chattering f comes to ruin. H211
Pr 10:10 and a chattering f comes to ruin. H211
Pr 10:14 the mouth of a f invites ruin. H211
Pr 10:18 with lying lips and spreads slander is a f. H4067
Pr 10:23 A f finds pleasure in wicked schemes, but H4067
Pr 11:29 and the f will be servant to the wise. H211
Pr 14: 7 Stay away from a f, for you will not H4067+408
Pr 14:16 a f is hotheaded and yet feels secure. H4067
Pr 15: 2 the mouth of the f gushes folly. H4067
Pr 15: 5 A f spurns a parent's discipline, but H211
Pr 15:14 the mouth of a f feeds on folly. H4067
Pr 17: 7 lips are unsuited to a **godless** f— H5572
Pr 17:10 person more than a hundred lashes a f. H4067
Pr 17:12 robbed of her cubs than a f bent on folly. H4067
Pr 17:21 To have a f for a child brings grief; there H4067
Pr 17:21 is no joy for the parent of a **godless** f. H5572
Pr 19: 1 is blameless than a f whose lips are H4067
Pr 19:10 It is not fitting for a f to live in luxury H4067
Pr 20: 3 avoid strife, but every f is quick to quarrel. H211
Pr 26: 1 rain in harvest, honor is not fitting for a f. H4067
Pr 26: 4 Do not answer a f according to his folly, or H4067
Pr 26: 5 Answer a f according to his folly, or he H4067
Pr 26: 6 by the hands of a f is like cutting off one's H4067
Pr 26: 7 is lame is a proverb in the mouth of a f. H4067
Pr 26: 8 in a sling is the giving of honor to a f. H4067
Pr 26: 9 hand is a proverb in the mouth of a f. H4067
Pr 26:10 is one who hires a f or any passer-by. H4067
Pr 26:12 There is more hope for a f than for them. H4067
Pr 27:22 Though you grind a f in a mortar, grinding H211
Pr 29: 9 If a wise person goes to court with a f, the H211
Pr 29: 9 court with a fool, the f rages and scoffs, and NDT
Pr 29:20 There is more hope for a f than for them. H4067
Pr 30:22 a **godless** f who gets plenty to eat H5572
Pr 30:32 "If *you* **play the** f and exalt yourself, or if H5571
Ecc 2:14 while the f walks in the darkness H4067
Ecc 2:15 "The fate of the f will overtake me also. H4067
Ecc 2:16 For the wise, like the f, will not be long H4067
Ecc 2:16 Like the f, the wise too must die H4067
Ecc 5: 3 many words mark the speech of a f. H4067
Ecc 7: 7 Extortion **turns** a wise person **into** a f, and H2147
Ecc 7:17 do not be a f—why die before your H6119
Ecc 10: 2 the right, but the heart of the f to the left. H4067
Isa 32: 5 No longer will the f be called noble nor H5572
Hos 9: 7 the prophet is considered a f, the inspired H211
Mt 5:22 who says, 'You f!' will be in danger *G3704*
Lk 12:20 God said to him, '*You* f! This very night *G933*
2Co 11:16 Let no one take me for a f. But if you do, *G933*
2Co 11:16 then tolerate me just as you would a f, so *G933*
2Co 11:17 not talking as the Lord would, but as a f. *G932*
2Co 11:21 I am speaking as a f—I also dare to boast *G932*
2Co 12: 6 I would not be a f, because I would be *G933*
2Co 12:11 I have made a f of myself, but you drove *G933*

FOOL'S (4) [FOOL]

Pr 12:23 themselves, but a f heart blurts out folly. H4067
Pr 14: 3 A f mouth lashes out with pride, but the H211
Pr 17:24 a f eyes wander to the ends of the H4067
Pr 27: 3 a f provocation is heavier than both. H211

FOOLISH (45) [FOOL]

Ge 31:28 You have done a f *thing*. H6118
Dt 32: 6 repay the LORD, you f and unwise people? H5572
1Sa 13:13 "*You have* **done a** f **thing**," Samuel said H6118
2Sa 24:10 *I have* **done a** very f **thing**." H6118
1Ch 21: 8 *I have* **done a** very f **thing**." H6118
2Ch 16: 9 *You have* **done a** f **thing**, and from now H6118
Job 2:10 replied, "You are talking like a f *woman*. H5572
Ps 49:10 that the f and the senseless also perish H4067
Ps 74:18 how f people have reviled your name. H5572
Pr 8: 5 you who are f, set your hearts on H4067
Pr 10: 1 a f son brings grief to his mother. H4067
Pr 14: 1 her own hands the f *one* tears hers down. H222
Pr 14:17 A quick-tempered person does f *things* H222
Pr 15:20 but a f man despises his mother. H4067
Pr 17:25 A f son brings grief to his father and H4067
Pr 19:13 A f child is a father's ruin, and a H4067
Ecc 2:19 whether that person will be wise or f? H6119
Ecc 4:13 than an old but f king who no longer H4067
Jer 5: 4 only the poor; *they are* f, for they do not H3282
Jer 5:21 Hear this, you f and senseless people H6119
Jer 10: 8 They are all senseless and f; they are H4071
Eze 13: 3 Woe to the f prophets who follow their H5572
Zec 11:15 again the equipment of a f shepherd. H216
Mt 7:26 practice is like a f man who built his *G3704*
Mt 25: 2 Five of them were f and five were wise. *G3704*
Mt 25: 3 The f *ones* took their lamps but did not *G3704*
Mt 25: 8 The f *ones* said to the wise, 'Give us some *G3704*
Lk 11:40 *You* f *people*! Did not the one who made *G933*
Lk 24:25 to them, "**How** f you are *G6043+1639+6042+485*
Ro 1:14 Non-Greeks, both to the wise and the f. *G485*
Ro 1:21 futile and their f hearts were darkened. *G852*
Ro 2:20 an instructor *of* the f, a teacher of little *G933*
1Co 1:20 *Has* not God **made** f the wisdom of the *G3701*
1Co 1:27 But God chose the f *things* of the world to *G3704*
1Co 15:36 *How* f! What you sow does not come to life *G933*
Gal 3: 1 You f Galatians! Who has bewitched you *G485*
Gal 3: 3 Are you so f? After beginning by means of *G485*
Eph 5: 4 there be obscenity, f **talk** or coarse joking *G3703*
Eph 5:17 Therefore do not be f, but understand what *G933*
1Ti 6: 9 a trap and into many f and harmful desires *G485*
2Ti 2:23 anything to do with f and stupid *G3704*
Titus 3: 3 At one time we too were f, disobedient *G485*
Titus 3: 9 But avoid f controversies and genealogies *G3704*
Jas 2:20 You f person, do you want evidence that *G3031*
1Pe 2:15 silence the ignorant talk of f people. *G933*

FOOLISHLY (1) [FOOL]

Nu 12:11 us the sin we have *so* f committed. H3282

FOOLISHNESS (8) [FOOL]

2Sa 15:31 **turn** Ahithophel's counsel **into** f. H6118
1Co 1:18 message of the cross is f to those who are *G3702*
1Co 1:21 pleased through the f of what was *G3702*
1Co 1:23 stumbling block to Jews and f to Gentiles, *G3702*
1Co 1:25 For the f of God is wiser than human *G3704*
1Co 2:14 the Spirit of God but considers them f, *G3702*
1Co 3:19 wisdom of this world is f in God's sight. *G3702*
2Co 11: 1 I hope you will put up with me *in* a little f *G932*

FOOLS (63) [FOOL]

2Sa 13:13 be like one of the **wicked** f in Israel. H5572
Job 12:17 away stripped and **makes** f **of** judges. H2147
Ps 39: 8 do not make me the scorn of f. H5572
Ps 74:22 remember how f mock you all day long. H5572
Ps 92: 6 people do not know, f do not understand, H4067
Ps 94: 8 the people; you f, when will you become H4067
Ps 107:17 *Some* became f through their rebellious H211
Pr 1: 7 f despise wisdom and instruction. H211
Pr 1:22 delight in mockery and f hate knowledge? H4067
Pr 1:32 the complacency of f will destroy them; H4067
Pr 3:35 wise inherit honor, but f get only shame. H4067
Pr 10:21 nourish many, but f die for lack of sense. H211
Pr 12:15 The way of f seems right to them, but the H211
Pr 12:16 F show their annoyance at once, but the H211
Pr 13:16 with knowledge, but f expose their folly. H4067
Pr 13:19 to the soul, but f detest turning from evil. H4067
Pr 13:20 for a companion of f suffers harm. H4067
Pr 14: 8 their ways, but the folly of f is deception. H4067
Pr 14: 9 F mock at making amends for sin, but H211
Pr 14:24 is their crown, but the folly of f yields folly. H4067

F

Pr 14:33 even among **f** she lets herself be H4067
Pr 15: 7 the hearts of **f** are not upright. H4067
Pr 16:22 prudent, but folly brings punishment to **f**. H211
Pr 17:16 Why should **f** have money in hand to buy H4067
Pr 17:28 Even **f** are thought wise if they keep silent H211
Pr 18: 2 **F** find no pleasure in understanding but H4067
Pr 18: 6 The lips of **f** bring them strife, and their H4067
Pr 18: 7 The mouths of **f** are their undoing, and H4067
Pr 19:29 mockers, and beatings for the backs of **f**. H4067
Pr 21:20 and olive oil, but **f** gulp theirs down. H4067+132
Pr 23: 9 Do not speak to **f**, for they will scorn your H4067
Pr 24: 7 Wisdom is too high for **f**; in the assembly H211
Pr 26: 3 the donkey, and a rod for the backs of **f**! H4067
Pr 26:11 returns to its vomit, so **f** repeat their folly. H4067
Pr 28:26 Those who trust in themselves are **f**, but H4067
Pr 29:11 **F** give full vent to their rage, but the wise H4067
Ecc 4: 5 **F** fold their hands and ruin themselves. H4067
Ecc 5: 1 listen rather than to offer the sacrifice of **f**, H4067
Ecc 5: 4 He has no pleasure in **f**; fulfill your vow. H4067
Ecc 6: 8 What advantage have the wise over **f** H4067
Ecc 7: 4 the heart of **f** is in the house of H4067
Ecc 7: 5 wise person than to listen to the song of **f**. H4067
Ecc 7: 6 under the pot, so is the laughter of **f**. H4067
Ecc 7: 9 for anger resides in the lap of **f**. H4067
Ecc 9:17 be heeded than the shouts of a ruler of **f**. H4067
Ecc 10: 3 Even as **f** walk along the road, they lack H6119
Ecc 10: 6 **F** are put in many high positions, while H6120
Ecc 10:12 **f** are consumed by their own lips. H4067
Ecc 10:14 **f** multiply words. No one knows what H6119
Ecc 10:15 The toil of **f** wearies them; they do not H4067
Isa 19:11 The officials of Zoan are nothing but **f**; the H211
Isa 19:13 The officials of Zoan *have* **become f**, the H3282
Isa 32: 6 For **f** speak folly, their hearts are bent on H5572
Isa 35: 8 **wicked f** will not go about on it. H211
Isa 44:25 of false prophets and **makes f** of diviners, H2147
Jer 4:22 "My people are **f**; they do not know me H211
Jer 17:11 in the end they will prove to be **f**. H5572
Jer 50:36 *They will* **become f**. H3282
Mt 23:17 *You* blind **f**! Which is greater: the gold, or *G3704*
Ro 1:22 they claimed to be wise, *they became* **f** *G3701*
1Co 3:18 you should become "**f**" so that you may *G3704*
1Co 4:10 We are **f** for Christ, but you are so wise in *G3704*
2Co 11:19 gladly put up with **f** since you are so wise *G933*

FOOT (82) [BAREFOOT, AFOOT, FEET, FLEET-FOOTED, FOOTHOLD, FOOTINGS, FOOTPRINTS, FOUR-FOOTED, UNDERFOOT]

Ge 41:44 word no one will lift hand or **f** in all Egypt." H8079
Ex 12:37 about six hundred thousand men **on f**, H8081
Ex 19:12 the mountain or touch the **f** *of* it. H7895
Ex 19:17 they stood at the **f** *of* the mountain. H9397
Ex 21:24 tooth for tooth, hand for hand, **f** for foot, H8079
Ex 21:24 tooth for tooth, hand for hand, foot for **f**, H8079
Ex 24: 4 built an altar **at the f** of the mountain H9393
Ex 32:19 them to pieces **at the f** of the mountain. H9393
Lev 8:23 hand and on the big toe of his right **f**. H8079
Lev 13:12 skin of the affected person from head to **f**, H8079
Lev 14:14 hand and on the big toe of their right **f**. H8079
Lev 14:17 hand and on the big toe of their right **f**, H8079
Lev 14:25 hand and on the big toe of their right **f**. H8079
Lev 14:28 hand and on the big toe of their right **f**. H8079
Lev 21:19 no man with a crippled **f** or hand, H8079
Nu 11:21 among six hundred thousand men **on f**, H8081
Nu 20:19 We only want to pass through on **f** H8079
Nu 22:25 to the wall, crushing Balaam's **f** against it. H8079
Dt 2: 5 not even enough to put your **f** on. H4090+8079
Dt 2:28 Only let us pass through on **f**— H8079
Dt 4:11 near and stood **at the f** of the mountain H9393
Dt 11:10 irrigated it by **f** as in a vegetable H8079
Dt 11:24 where you set your **f** will be yours: H4090+8079
Dt 19:21 tooth for tooth, hand for hand, **f** for foot. H8079
Dt 19:21 tooth for tooth, hand for hand, foot for **f**. H8079
Dt 28:56 touch the ground with the sole of her **f**— H8079
Dt 28:65 no resting place for the sole of your **f**. H8079
Dt 32:35 In due time their **f** will slip; their day of H8079
Jos 1: 3 every place where you set your **f**, H4090+8079
Jos 3:13 all the earth—set **f** in the Jordan H4090+8079
Jos 18:16 went down to the **f** *of* the hill facing the H7895
Jdg 4:15 got down from his chariot and fled on **f**. H8079
Jdg 4:17 meanwhile, fled on **f** to the tent of Jael H8079
1Sa 4:10 Israel lost thirty thousand **f soldiers**. H8081
1Sa 15: 4 hundred thousand **f soldiers** and ten H8081
2Sa 8: 4 and twenty thousand **f soldiers**. H408+8081
2Sa 10: 6 Aramean **f soldiers** from Beth Rehob H8081
2Sa 10:18 forty thousand of their **f soldiers**. H8081
2Sa 14:25 to the sole of his **f** there was no blemish H8079
2Sa 21:20 on each hand and six toes on each **f**— H8079
1Ki 14:12 When you set **f** in your city, the boy will H8079
1Ki 20:29 on the Aramean **f soldiers** in one day. H8081
2Ki 13: 7 ten chariots and ten thousand **f soldiers** H8081
1Ch 18: 4 and twenty thousand **f soldiers**. H408+8081
1Ch 19:18 and forty thousand of their **f soldiers**. H408+8081
1Ch 20: 6 on each hand and six toes on each **f**— NDT
Job 28: 8 Proud beasts *do* **not set f on** it, and no H2005
Job 31: 5 with falsehood or my **f** has hurried after H8079
Job 39:15 unmindful that a **f** may crush them, that H8079
Ps 36:11 May the **f** *of* the proud not come against H8079
Ps 66: 6 they passed through the waters on **f** H8079
Ps 91:12 you will not strike your **f** against a stone. H8079
Ps 94:18 When I said, "My **f** is slipping," your H8079
Ps 121: 3 He will not let your **f** slip—he who H8079
Pr 1:15 with them, do not set **f** on their paths; H8079
Pr 3:23 way in safety, and your **f** will not stumble. H8079
Pr 3:26 will keep your **f** from being snared. H8079
Pr 4:14 *Do* **not set f** on the path of the wicked or H995
Pr 4:27 the right or the left; keep your **f** from evil. H8079
Pr 25:17 Seldom set **f** in your neighbor's house H8079
Pr 25:19 broken tooth or a lame **f** is reliance on the H8079
Ecc 10: 7 princes go **on f** like slaves. H6584+2021+824
Isa 1: 6 From the sole of your **f** to the top of your H8079
Jer 12: 5 raced with men on **f** and they have worn H8081
Eze 29:11 The **f** *of* neither man nor beast will pass H8079
Eze 32:13 be stirred by the **f** *of* man or muddied by H8079
Hab 3:13 you stripped him from head to **f**. H3572
Mt 4: 6 you will not strike your **f** against a stone. *G4546*
Mt 14:13 crowds followed him **on f** from the towns. *G4270*
Mt 18: 8 If your hand or your **f** causes you to *G4546*
Mt 22:13 'Tie him hand and **f**, and throw him *G5931*
Mk 5: 4 For he had often been chained hand and **f**, *G4267*
Mk 6:33 them and ran **on f** from all the towns and *G4270*
Mk 9:45 And if your **f** causes you to stumble, cut it *G4546*
Lk 4:11 you will not strike your **f** against a stone. *G4546*
Lk 8:29 chained hand and **f** and kept under guard *G4267*
Jn 20:12 one at the head and the other at the **f**. *G4546*
Ac 7: 5 not even enough ground to set his **f** on. *G4546*
Ac 20:13 because he was **going** there **on f**. *G4269*
1Co 12:15 Now if the **f** should say, "Because I am *G4546*
Rev 10: 2 He planted his right **f** on the sea and his *G4546*
Rev 10: 2 foot on the sea and his left **f** on the land, NDT

FOOTHILLS (20) [HILL]

Dt 1: 7 mountains, in the **western f**, in the Negev H9169
Jos 9: 1 country, in the **western f**, and along the H9169
Jos 10:40 the **western f** and the mountain slopes H9169
Jos 11: 2 in the **western f** and in Naphoth Dor on H9169
Jos 11:16 of Goshen, the **western f**, the Arabah and H9169
Jos 11:16 the mountains of Israel with their **f**, H9169
Jos 12: 8 the hill country, the **western f**, the Arabah, H9169
Jos 15:33 In the **western f**: Eshtaol, Zorah, Ashnah, H9169
Jdg 1: 9 hill country, the Negev and the **western f**. H9169
1Ki 10:27 as plentiful as sycamore-fig trees in the **f**. H9169
1Ch 27:28 sycamore-fig trees in the **western f**. H9169
2Ch 1:15 as plentiful as sycamore-fig trees in the **f**. H9169
2Ch 9:27 as plentiful as sycamore-fig trees in the **f**. H9169
2Ch 26:10 much livestock in the **f** and in the plain. H9169
2Ch 28:18 raided towns in the **f** and in the Negev of H9169
Jer 17:26 territory of Benjamin and the **western f**, H9169
Jer 32:44 country, of the **western f** and of the Negev H9169
Jer 33:13 country, of the **western f** and of the Negev H9169
Ob 19 people from the **f** will possess the H9169
Zec 7: 7 the Negev and the **western f** were settled? H9169

FOOTHOLD (3) [FOOT]

Ps 69: 2 in the miry depths, where there is no **f**. H5097
Ps 73: 2 had almost slipped; I had nearly lost my **f**. H892
Eph 4:27 do not give the devil a **f**. *G5536*

FOOTINGS (1) [FOOT]

Job 38: 6 On what were its **f** set, or who laid its H149

FOOTPRINTS (2) [FOOT]

Ps 77:19 though your **f** were not seen. H6811
Hos 6: 8 a city of evildoers, *stained with* **f** of blood. H6814

FOOTSTEPS (6) [STEP]

1Ki 14: 6 heard the sound of her **f** at the door, H8079
2Ki 6:32 the sound of his master's **f** behind him?" H8079
Ps 119:133 Direct my **f** according to your word; let no H7193
Isa 26: 6 feet of the oppressed, the **f** *of* the poor. H7193
Ro 4:12 who also follow *in* the **f** of the faith that *G2717*
2Co 12:18 we not walk *in* the same **f** by the same *G2717*

FOOTSTOOL (13) [STOOL]

1Ch 28: 2 the LORD, for the **f** *of* our God, and I H2071+8079
2Ch 9:18 and a **f** of gold was attached to it. H3900
Ps 99: 5 LORD our God and worship at his **f**; H2071+8079
Ps 110: 1 I make your enemies a **f** for your feet." H2071
Ps 132: 7 let us worship at his **f**, saying, H2071+8079
Isa 66: 1 is my throne, and the earth is my **f**. H2071+8079
La 2: 1 remembered his **f** in the day of his H2071+8079
Mt 5:35 it is his **f**; or by Jerusalem *G5711+3836+4546*
Lk 20:43 until I make your enemies a **f** for your feet." *G5711*
Ac 2:35 until I make your enemies a **f** for your feet." *G5711*
Ac 7:49 and the earth is my **f**. *G5711+3836+4546*
Heb 1:13 I make your enemies a **f** for your feet"? *G5711*
Heb 10:13 enemies to be made his **f**. *G5711+3836+4546*

FOR (7336) See Index of Articles Etc.

FORAGING (1)

Job 24: 5 the poor go about their labor of **f** food H8838

FORBEARANCE (3)

Ro 2: 4 riches of his kindness, **f** and patience, not *G496*
Ro 3:25 because in his **f** he had left the sins *G496*
Gal 5:22 joy, peace, **f**, kindness, goodness *G3429*

FORBID (8) [FORBIDDEN, FORBIDS]

Nu 30:11 says nothing to her and *does* not **f** her, H5648
1Sa 24: 6 "The LORD **f** that I should do such a thing H2721
1Sa 26:11 But the LORD **f** that I should lay a hand on H2721
1Ki 21: 3 "The LORD **f** that I should give you the H2721
1Ch 11:19 "God **f** that I should do this!" he said H2721
Lk 20:16 heard this, they said, "**God f**!" *G3590+1181S*
1Co 14:39 and *do* not **f** speaking in tongues. *G3266*
1Ti 4: 3 *They* **f** people to marry and order them to *G3266*

FORBIDDEN (14) [FORBID]

Lev 4: 2 and does what *is* **f** in any of the H6913+4202
Lev 4:13 and does what *is* **f** in any of the H6913+4202
Lev 4:22 and does what *is* **f** in any of the H6913+4202
Lev 4:27 and does what *is* **f** in any of the H6913+4202
Lev 5:17 and does what *is* **f** in any of the H6913+4202
Lev 19:23 of fruit tree, **regard** its fruit **as f**. H6887+6889
Lev 19:23 For three years you are to consider it **f**; it H6888
Nu 30: 5 release her because her father *has* **f** her. H5648
Dt 4:23 form of anything the LORD your God *has* **f**. H7422
Dt 23: 2 No **one born of a f marriage** nor any of H4927
1Ki 11:10 Although *he had* **f** Solomon to H7422+1194
Est 2:10 Mordecai *had* **f** her to do so. H7422+4202
La 1:10 those *you had* **f** to enter your H7422+4202
Zec 9: 7 the **f food** from between their teeth. H9199

FORBIDS (3) [FORBID]

Nu 30: 5 But if her father **f** her when he hears about H5648
Nu 30: 8 But if her husband **f** her when he hears H5648
Jn 5:10 **the law f** you to carry your mat." *G4024+2003*

FORCE (33) [ENFORCE, FORCED, FORCEFUL, FORCEFULLY, FORCES, FORCIBLY, FORCING]

Ge 31:31 *you* would **take** your daughters away from me **by f** H1608
Ge 47:26 land in Egypt—**still in f** today—that a fifth H6330
Ex 9:14 I will send the **full f** *of* my plagues against H3972
Ex 19:21 so *they do* not **f** *their* **way through** to see H2238
Ex 19:24 people *must* not **f** *their* **way through** to H2238
Nu 27:11 is to have the **f of law** for the H5477+2978
Nu 35:29 is to have the **f of law** for you H5477+2978
Jos 8:11 The entire **f** that was with him H6639+4878
Jdg 7:13 It struck the tent with **such f** that the tent H5877S
Jdg 8:10 were in Karkor with a **f** of about fifteen H4722
1Sa 2:16 it over now; if you don't, I'll take it by **f**." H2622
1Sa 19: 8 them with such **f** that they fled before H4804
2Sa 5:17 they went up **in full f** to search for him H3972
2Sa 13:12 "Don't **f** me! Such a thing H6700
1Ki 11:28 charge of the whole **labor f** *of* the tribes of H6023
2Ki 6:14 horses and chariots and a strong **f** there. H2657
2Ki 24:16 to Babylon the **entire** *f of* seven thousand AIT
1Ch 14: 8 they went up **in full f** to search for him H3972
2Ch 26:13 a powerful **f** to support the king against H2657
Ezr 4:23 compelled them by **f** to stop. A10013
Job 19:12 His troops advance **in f**; they build a siege H3480
Job 20:22 the full **f** *of* misery will come upon him. H3338
Job 24: 4 and **f** all the poor of the land **into hiding**. H2461
Job 28:25 he established the **f** of the wind and H5486
Jer 46:22 serpent as the enemy advances in **f**; H2657
Ob 7 All your allies *will* **f** you to the border H8938
Jn 6:15 intended to come and make him king *by* **f**, *G773*
Ac 5:26 They did not use **f**, because they feared *G1040*
Ac 23:10 and **take** him away from them by **f** and *G773*
Ac 26:11 and *I tried to* **f** them to blaspheme. *G337*
Ac 27:14 very long, a wind **of hurricane f**, called *G5607*
Gal 2:14 *that you* **f** Gentiles to follow Jewish *G337*
Heb 9:17 because a will is **in f** only when somebody *G1010*

FORCED (27) [FORCE]

Ge 49:15 to the burden and submit to **f labor**. H4989
Ex 1:11 over them to oppress them with **f labor**, H6026
Dt 20:11 be subject to **f labor** and shall work for H4989
Jos 16:10 of Ephraim but are required to do **f labor**. H4989
Jos 17:13 the Canaanites to **f labor** but did not drive H4989
Jdg 1:28 Canaanites into **f labor** but never drove H4989
Jdg 1:30 Zebulun did subject them to **f labor**. H4989
Jdg 1:33 Beth Anath became **f laborers** for them. H4989
Jdg 1:35 they too were pressed into **f labor**. H4989
2Sa 18: 3 go out; if *we are* **f to flee**, they H5674+5674
2Sa 20:24 Adoniram was in charge of **f labor** H4989
1Ki 4: 6 son of Abda—in charge of **f labor**. H4989
1Ki 5:14 Adoniram was in charge of the **f labor**. H4989
1Ki 9:15 is the account of the **f labor** King Solomon H4989
1Ki 12:18 who was in charge of **f labor**, but all Israel H4989
2Ch 10:18 who was in charge of **f labor**, but the H4989
Job 30: 6 They were **f to** live in the dry stream beds H4200
Ps 57: 4 *I am f to* **dwell** among ravenous beasts AIT
Ps 69: 4 *I am* **f to restore** what I did not steal H8740
Pr 12:24 will rule, but laziness ends in **f labor**. H4989
Isa 14: 3 turmoil and from the harsh labor **f** on you, H6268
Isa 31: 8 their young men will be put to **f labor**. H4989
Jer 34:16 *You have* **f** them to become your slaves H3899
Mt 27:32 and *they* **f** him to carry the cross. *G30*
Mk 15:21 the country, and *they* **f** him to carry the cross. *G30*
Phm 14 do would not seem **f** but would be *G2848+340*
Rev 13:16 *It* also **f** all people, great and small, rich *G4472*

FORCEFUL (1) [FORCE]

2Co 10:10 "His letters are weighty and **f**, but in *G2708*

FORCEFULLY (3) [FORCE]

1Sa 18:10 an evil spirit from God **came f** on Saul. H7502
2Sa 19:43 **pressed** their claims even more **f** than H7996
Isa 28: 2 he will throw it **f** to the ground. H928+3338

FORCES (38) [FORCE]

Ge 14: 3 these latter kings **joined f** in the Valley of H2489
Ge 21:22 the commander of his **f** said to Abraham, H7372
Ge 21:32 commander of his **f** returned to the land H7372
Ge 26:26 Phicol the commander of his **f**. H7372
Ge 34:30 and *if they* **join f** against me and attack me, H665
Jos 10: 5 Jarmuth, Lachish and Eglon—**joined f**. H665

Jos 10: 6 the hill country *have* **joined** f against us." H7695
Jos 11: 5 All these kings **joined** f and made camp H3585
Jdg 6:33 peoples **joined** f and crossed H665+3481
Jdg 12: 1 The Ephraimite f were called out, and they H408
1Sa 4: 2 The Philistines **deployed** *their* f to meet H6885
1Sa 14:17 "**Muster** *the* f and see who has left us." H7212
1Sa 17: 1 gathered their f for war and assembled at H4722
1Sa 23: 3 if we go to Keilah against the Philistine f!" H5120
1Sa 23: 8 And Saul called up all his f for battle, to H6639
1Sa 23:26 As Saul and his f were closing in on David H408
1Sa 28: 1 gathered their f to fight against Israel. H4722
1Sa 29: 1 Philistines gathered all their f at Aphek, H4722
1Ki 15:20 commanders of his f against the towns of H2657
1Ch 20: 1 to war, Joab led out the **armed f.** H2657+7372
2Ch 14:13 were crushed before the LORD and his f. H4722
2Ch 16: 4 commanders of his f against the towns of H2657
2Ch 32: 9 Assyria and all his f were laying siege to H4939
Job 10:17 your f come against me wave upon wave. H7372
Job 25: 3 Can his f be numbered? On whom does H1522
Ps 48: 4 When the kings **joined** f, when they H3585
Ps 55:11 **Destructive** f are at work in the city; H2095
Da 11: 7 He will attack the f of the king of the H2657
Da 11:15 The f *of* the South will be powerless to H2432
Da 11:31 "His **armed** f will rise up to desecrate the H2432
Joel 2:11 of his army; his f are beyond number H4722
Zec 9: 8 it against **marauding f.** H6296+2256+8740
Mt 5:41 If anyone f you **to go** one mile, go with them G30
Gal 4: 3 under the **elemental spiritual** f of the G5122
Gal 4: 9 back to those weak and miserable f? G5122
Eph 6:12 world and against the **spiritual** *f* of evil in the AIT
Col 2: 8 the **elemental spiritual** f of this world G5122
Col 2:20 Christ to the **elemental spiritual** f of this G5122

FORCIBLY (2) [FORCE]
Ge 40:15 *I* **was f carried off** from the land of H1704+1704
Dt 28:31 Your donkey *will* **be f taken** from you and H1608

FORCING (2) [FORCE]
Lk 16:16 everyone *is* f *their* **way** into it. G1041
Ac 7:19 our ancestors *by* f them to throw out their G4472

FORD (2) [FORDED, FORDS]
Ge 32:22 sons and crossed the f *of* the Jabbok. H5044
2Sa 19:18 They crossed at the f to take the king's H6302

FORDED (1) [FORD]
Jos 2:23 f the river and came to Joshua son of Nun H6296

FORDS (7) [FORD]
Jos 2: 7 the road that leads to the f of the Jordan, H5045
Jdg 3:28 possession of the f *of* the Jordan that led H5045
Jdg 12: 5 captured the f *of* the Jordan leading to H5045
Jdg 12: 6 him and killed him at the f *of* the Jordan. H5045
2Sa 15:28 I will wait at the f *in* the wilderness until H6302
2Sa 17:16 spend the night at the f *in* the wilderness; H6302
Isa 16: 2 the women of Moab at the f of the Arnon. H5045

FOREFATHER (10) [FATHER]
Nu 26:58 (Kohath *was the* f *of* Amram; H3528
Jos 15:13 Hebron. (Arba was the f *of* Anak.) H3
Jos 21:11 country of Judah. (Arba was the f *of* Anak.) H3
1Ki 15: 3 as the heart of David his f had been. H3
Jer 35: 6 because our f Jehonadab son of Rekab gave H3
Jer 35: 8 obeyed everything our f Jehonadab son of H3
Jer 35:10 everything our f Jehonadab commanded H3
Jer 35:16 carried out the command their f gave them, H3
Jer 35:18 the command of your f Jehonadab and have H3
Ro 4: 1 that Abraham, our f according to the flesh G4635

FOREFATHER'S (1) [FATHER]
Jer 35:14 because they obey their f command. H3

FOREFATHERS (2) [FATHER]
Da 11:24 what neither his fathers nor his f did. H3+3
Ac 7:12 in Egypt, he sent our f on their first visit. G4252

FOREFINGER (2)
Lev 14:16 dip his right f into the oil in his palm, and H720
Lev 14:27 with his right f sprinkle some of the oil H720

FOREHEAD (16) [FOREHEADS]
Ex 13: 9 a reminder **on** your f that this law H1068+6524
Ex 13:16 and a symbol **on** your f that the H1068+6524
Ex 28:38 It will be on Aaron's f, and he will bear H5195
Ex 28:38 It will be on Aaron's f continually so that H5195
Lev 13:41 the front of his scalp and has a **bald** f, H1477
Lev 13:42 reddish-white sore on his bald head or f, H1478
Lev 13:42 disease breaking out on his head or f. H1478
Lev 13:43 sore on his head or f is reddish-white like H1478
1Sa 17:49 slung it and struck the Philistine on the f. H5195
1Sa 17:49 The stone sank into his f, and he fell H5195
2Ch 26:19 LORD's temple, leprosy broke out on his f. H5195
2Ch 26:20 they saw that he had leprosy on his f, so H5195
Isa 48: 4 muscles were iron, your f was bronze. H5195
Eze 3: 9 I will make your f like the hardest stone H5195
Rev 14: 9 its mark on their f or on their hand, G3587
Rev 17: 5 The name written on her f was a mystery G3587

FOREHEADS (11) [FOREHEAD]
Nu 24:17 He will crush the f *of* Moab, the skulls of H6991
Dt 6: 8 hands and bind them **on** your f. H1068+6524
Dt 11:18 hands and bind them **on** your f. H1068+6524
Jer 48:45 it burns the f *of* Moab, the skulls of H6991
Eze 9: 4 put a mark on the f *of* those who grieve H5195
Rev 7: 3 we put a seal on the f of the servants of G3587
Rev 9: 4 did not have the seal of God on their f. G3587
Rev 13:16 a mark on their right hands or on their f, G3587
Rev 14: 1 his Father's name written on their f. G3587
Rev 20: 4 received its mark on their f or their hands. G3587
Rev 22: 4 his face, and his name will be on their f. G3587

FOREIGN (53) [FOREIGNER, FOREIGNER'S, FOREIGNERS, FOREIGNERS']
Ge 35: 2 "Get rid of the f gods you have with you H5797
Ge 35: 4 gave Jacob all the f gods they had and H5797
Ex 2:22 "I have become a foreigner in a f land." H5799
Ex 18: 3 "I have become a foreigner in a f land"; H5799
Dt 31:16 themselves to the f gods of the land they H5797
Dt 32:12 alone led him; no f god was with him. H5797
Dt 32:16 jealous with their f gods and angered him H2424
Jos 24:20 If you forsake the LORD and serve f gods, H5797
Jos 24:23 "throw away the f gods that are among H5797
Jdg 10:16 got rid of the f gods among them and H5797
1Sa 7: 3 rid yourselves of the f gods and the H5797
1Ki 11: 1 loved many f women besides Pharaoh's H5799
1Ki 11: 8 He did the same for all his f wives, who H5799
2Ki 19:24 I have dug wells in f *lands* and drunk the H2424
2Ch 14: 3 He removed the f altars and the high H5797
2Ch 33:15 He got rid of the f gods and removed the H5797
Ezr 9: 7 humiliation at the hand of f kings, H824
Ezr 10: 2 our God by marrying f women from the H5799
Ezr 10:10 you have married f women, adding to H5799
Ezr 10:11 around you and from your f wives. H5799
Ezr 10:14 who has married a f woman come at a set H5799
Ezr 10:17 all the men who had married f women. H5799
Ezr 10:18 the following had married f women: H5799
Ezr 10:44 All these had married f women, and H5799
Ne 13: 3 from Israel all who were of **f descent.** H6850
Ne 13:26 even he was led into sin by f women. H5799
Ne 13:27 to our God by marrying f women? H5799
Ne 13:30 the priests and the Levites of everything f, H5797
Ps 44:20 God or spread out our hands to a f god, H2424
Ps 81: 9 You shall have no f god among you; you H2424
Ps 114: 1 Jacob from a people of **f tongue,** H4357
Ps 137: 4 the songs of the LORD while in a f land? H5797
Isa 28:11 with f lips and strange tongues God will H4353
Isa 37:25 I have dug wells in f *lands* and drunk the H2424
Isa 43:12 and not *some* f god among you. H2424
Jer 2:25 I love f gods, and I must go H2424
Jer 3:13 scattered your favors to f gods under every H2424
Jer 5:19 me and served f gods in your own land, H5797
Jer 8:19 their images, with their worthless f idols?" H5797
Jer 19: 4 me and **made** this a place of f gods; H5796
Jer 25:20 all the **f people** there; all the kings of H6850
Jer 25:24 the kings of the **f people** who live in the H6850
Eze 31:12 the most ruthless of f nations cut it down H2424
Da 11:39 with the help of a f god and will greatly H5797
Hos 8:12 they regarded them as *something* f. H2424
Hos 10: 6 Israel will be ashamed of its *f* **alliances.** AIT
Zep 1: 8 king's sons and all those clad in f clothes. H5799
Hag 2:22 shatter the power of the f kingdoms. H1580
Mal 2:11 by marrying women who worship a f god. H5797
Ac 17:18 "He seems to be advocating f gods." G3828
Ac 26:11 that I even hunted them down in f cities. G2032
Heb 11: 9 promised land like a **stranger in a f country;** G259
Heb 11:34 powerful in battle and routed f armies. G259

FOREIGNER (86) [FOREIGN]
Ge 17: 8 where you now **reside as a f,** I will give as H4472
Ge 17:12 bought with money from a f— H1201+5797
Ge 17:27 his household or bought from a f, H1201+5797
Ge 19: 9 "This fellow came here *as a* f, and now H1591
Ge 21:23 where *you now* **reside as a f** the same H1591
Ge 23: 4 "I am a f and stranger among you. Sell me H1731
Ge 28: 4 of the land where you now **reside as a f,** H4472
Ex 2:22 "I have become a f in a foreign land." H1731
Ex 12:19 anyone, whether f or native-born, who H1731
Ex 12:43 Passover meal: "No f may eat it. H1201+5797
Ex 12:48 "A f residing among you who wants to H1731
Ex 12:49 to the f residing among you. H1731
Ex 18: 3 "I have become a f in a foreign land"; H1731
Ex 20:10 animals, nor any f residing in your towns. H1731
Ex 22:21 "Do not mistreat or oppress a f, for you H1731
Ex 23: 9 "Do not oppress a f; you yourselves know H1731
Ex 23:12 the **f living among** you may be H1731
Lev 16:29 native-born or a f residing among you— H1731
Lev 17: 8 Israelite or any f residing among them H1731
Lev 17:10 Israelite or any f residing among them H1731
Lev 17:12 may any f residing among you eat H1731
Lev 17:13 'Any Israelite or any f residing among you H1731
Lev 17:15 whether native-born or f, who eats H1731
Lev 19:10 Leave them for the poor and the f. H1731
Lev 19:33 " 'When a f resides among you in your H1731
Lev 19:34 The f residing among you must be treated H1731
Lev 20: 2 'Any Israelite or any f residing in Israel H1731
Lev 22:18 an Israelite or a f residing in Israel— H1731
Lev 22:25 the hand of a f and offer them as H1201+5797
Lev 23:22 poor and for the **f residing** *among* you. H1731
Lev 24:16 Whether f or native-born, when they H1731
Lev 24:22 same law for the f and the native-born. H1731
Lev 25:35 help them as you would a f and stranger H1731
Lev 25:47 " 'If a f residing among you becomes rich H1731
Lev 25:47 to the f or to a member of H1731+9369
Nu 9:14 " 'A f residing among you is also to H1731
Nu 9:14 both the f and the native-born. H1731
Nu 15:14 whenever a f or anyone else living among H1731
Nu 15:15 you and for the f residing among you; H1731
Nu 15:15 You and the f shall be the same before H1731
Nu 15:16 to you and to the f residing among you. H1731
Nu 15:29 Israelite or a f residing among you. H1731
Nu 15:30 whether native-born or f, blasphemes the H1731
Dt 1:16 an Israelite and a **f residing** *among* you. H1731
Dt 5:14 animals, nor any **f residing** in your towns H1731
Dt 10:18 loves the **f residing** *among* you H1731
Dt 14:21 You may give it to the f residing in any of H1731
Dt 14:21 or you may sell it to any other f. H5799
Dt 15: 3 You may require payment from a f, but you H5799
Dt 17:15 Do not place a f over you, one who is not H5799
Dt 23:20 You may charge a f interest, but not a H5799
Dt 24:14 Israelite or a **f residing** in one of your H1731
Dt 24:17 Do not deprive the f or the fatherless of H1731
Dt 24:19 Leave it for the f, the fatherless and the H1731
Dt 24:20 Leave what remains for the f, the H1731
Dt 24:21 Leave what remains for the f, the H1731
Dt 26:12 it to the Levite, the f, the fatherless and H1731
Dt 26:13 it to the Levite, the f, the fatherless and H1731
Dt 27:19 anyone who withholds justice from the f, H1731
Jos 20: 9 Israelites or any f residing among them H1731
Ru 2:10 in your eyes that you notice me—a f?" H5799
2Sa 1:13 "I am the son of a f, an Amalekite," H408+1731
2Sa 15:19 You are a f, an exile from your H5799
1Ki 8:41 "As for the f who does not belong to your H5799
1Ki 8:43 Do whatever the f asks of you, so that all H5799
2Ch 6:32 "As for the f who does not belong to your H5799
2Ch 6:33 Do whatever the f asks of you, so that all H5799
Job 19:15 my female servants count me a f; H2424
Ps 39:12 I dwell with you as a f, a stranger, as all H1731
Ps 69: 8 I am a f to my own family, a stranger to H2319
Ps 94: 6 They slay the widow and the f; they H1731
Ps 105:23 Jacob **resided as a f** in the land of Ham. H1591
Ps 146: 9 LORD watches over the f and sustains the H1731
Isa 56: 3 Let no f who is bound to the H1201+2021+5797
Jer 7: 6 if you do not oppress the f, the fatherless H1731
Jer 22: 3 Do no wrong or violence to the f, the H1731
Eze 14: 7 of the Israelites or any f residing in Israel H1731
Eze 22: 7 have oppressed the f and mistreated the H1731
Eze 22:29 the poor and needy and mistreat the f, H1731
Eze 44: 9 No f uncircumcised in heart and H1201+5797
Eze 47:23 In whatever tribe a f resides, there you are H1731
Zec 7:10 widow or the fatherless, the f or the poor. H1731
Lk 17:18 returned to give praise to God except this f?" G254
Ac 7:29 where he settled as a f and had two sons. G4230
1Co 14:11 is saying, I am a f to the speaker, and the G975
1Co 14:11 the speaker, and the speaker is a f to me. G975

FOREIGNER'S (1) [FOREIGN]
Lev 25:47 the foreigner or to a member of the f clan, H1731

FOREIGNERS (70) [FOREIGN]
Ge 31:15 Does he not regard us as f? Not only has H5799
Ex 6: 4 land of Canaan, where they resided *as* f. H1591
Ex 21: 8 He has no right to sell her to f H6639+5799
Ex 22:21 a foreigner, for you were f in Egypt. H1731
Ex 23: 9 you yourselves know how it feels to be f H1731
Ex 23: 9 foreigners, because you were f in Egypt. H1731
Lev 18:26 native-born and the f residing among you H1731
Lev 19:34 them as yourself, for you were f in Egypt. H1731
Lev 25:23 you reside in my land as f and strangers. H1731
Nu 15:26 community and the f residing among H1731
Nu 19:10 for the f residing among them. H1731
Nu 35:15 Israelites and for f residing among them, H1731
Dt 10:19 And you are to love those who are f, for H1731
Dt 10:19 you yourselves were f in Egypt. H1731
Dt 14:29 of their own) and the f, the fatherless and H1731
Dt 16:11 your towns, and the f, the fatherless and H1731
Dt 16:14 the Levites, the f, the fatherless and H1731
Dt 23: 7 because you resided as f in their country. H1731
Dt 26:11 Levites and the **f residing** among you H1731
Dt 28:43 The f who **reside** among you will rise H1731
Dt 29:11 the f living in your camps who chop H1731
Dt 29:22 generations and f who come from distant H5799
Dt 31:12 the **f residing** in your towns—so H1731
Jos 8:33 Both the **f living among** them and the H1731
Jos 8:35 the f who lived among them. H1731
2Sa 4: 3 have resided there *as* f to this day. H1591
2Sa 22:45 f cower before me; as soon as they H1201+5797
1Ch 22: 2 orders to assemble the f residing in Israel, H1731
1Ch 29:15 We are f and strangers in your sight, as H1731
2Ch 2:17 a census of all the **f residing** in Israel, H1731
2Ch 30:25 including the f who had come from Israel H1731
Ne 9: 2 separated themselves from all f. H1201+5797
Job 15:19 was given when no f moved among them): H2424
Ps 18:44 f cower before me; as soon as they H1201+5797
Ps 144: 7 mighty waters, from the hands of f H1201+5797
Ps 144:11 the hands of f whose mouths are H1201+5797
Isa 1: 7 are being stripped by f right before you, H2424
Isa 14: 1 F will join them and unite with the H1731
Isa 25: 5 You silence the uproar of f; as heat is H2424
Isa 56: 6 And f who bind themselves H1201+2021+5797
Isa 60:10 "F will rebuild your walls, and their H1201+5797
Isa 61: 5 f will work your fields and vineyards H1201+5797
Isa 62: 8 never again will f drink the new H1201+5797
Jer 5:19 so now you will serve f in a land not your H2424
Jer 30: 8 no longer will f enslave them. H2424
Jer 50:37 chariots and all the f in her ranks! H6850
Jer 51: 2 I will send f to Babylon to winnow her H2424
Jer 51:51 because f have entered the holy places of H2424
La 5: 2 turned over to strangers, our homes to f. H5799

Eze 7:21 wealth as plunder to f and as loot to the H2424
Eze 11: 9 you into the hands of f and inflict H2424
Eze 28: 7 I am going to bring f against you, the H2424
Eze 28:10 of the uncircumcised at the hands of f. H2424
Eze 30:12 by the hand of f I will lay waste the land H2424
Eze 44: 7 you brought f uncircumcised in H1201+5797
Eze 44: 9 not even the f who live among the H1201+5797
Eze 47:22 for the f residing among you and H1731
Hos 7: 9 F sap his strength, but he does not realize H2424
Hos 8: 7 it to yield grain, f would swallow it up. H2424
Joel 3:17 will be holy; never again will f invade her. H2424
Ob 11 off his wealth and f entered his gates H5799
Mal 3: 5 deprive the f among you of justice H1731
Mt 27: 7 the potter's field as a burial place *for* f. G3828
Ac 17:21 Athenians and the f who lived there spent G3828
1Co 14:21 through the lips *of* f I will speak to G2283
Eph 2:12 in Israel and f to the covenants of the G3828
Eph 2:19 you are no longer f and strangers, but G3828
Heb 11:13 that they were f and strangers on earth. G3828
1Pe 1:17 live out your time *as* f here in reverent G4229
1Pe 2:11 I urge you, as f and exiles, to abstain from G4230

F

FOREIGNERS' (1) [FOREIGN]
Isa 25: 2 the f stronghold a city no more H2424

FOREKNEW (2) [KNOW]
Ro 8:29 For those God f he also predestined to be G4589
Ro 11: 2 his people, whom *he* f. Don't you know G4589

FOREKNOWLEDGE (2) [KNOW]
Ac 2:23 to you by God's deliberate plan and f; G4590
1Pe 1: 2 according to the f of God the Father, G4590

FOREMAN (1) [FOREMEN]
Mt 20: 8 the owner of the vineyard said *to* his f G2208

FOREMEN (3) [FOREMAN]
1Ki 5:16 hundred f who supervised the H8569+5893
2Ch 2: 2 in the hills and 3,600 as f over them. H5904
2Ch 2:18 with 3,600 f over them to keep the people H5904

FOREMOST (2) [MOST]
Jer 31: 7 Jacob; shout for the f *of* the nations. H8031
Am 6: 1 you notable men of the f nation, to whom H8040

FOREORDAINED (KJV) CHOSEN

FOREPART (KJV) BOW, FRONT, INNER

FORERUNNER (1) [RUN]
Heb 6:20 where our f, Jesus, has entered on our G4596

FORESAIL (1) [SAIL]
Ac 27:40 they hoisted the f to the wind and made G784

FORESAW (1) [FORESEE]
Gal 3: 8 Scripture f that God would justify the G4632

FORESEE (1) [FORESAW, FORESIGHT]
Isa 47:11 a catastrophe *you* cannot f will suddenly H3359

FORESIGHT (1) [FORESEE]
Ac 24: 2 your f has brought about reforms in G4630

FORESKIN (1) [FORESKINS]
Ex 4:25 cut off her son's f and touched Moses' H6889

FORESKINS (3) [FORESKIN]
1Sa 18:25 the bride than a hundred Philistine f, H6889
1Sa 18:27 Philistines and brought back their f. H6889
2Sa 3:14 the price of a hundred Philistine f. H6889

FOREST (41) [FORESTED, FORESTS]
Dt 19: 5 man may go into the f with his neighbor H3623
Jos 17:15 go up into the f and clear land for H3623
1Sa 22: 5 So David left and went to the f *of* Hereth. H3623
2Sa 18: 6 the battle took place in the f *of* Ephraim. H3623
2Sa 18: 8 the f swallowed up more men that H3623
2Sa 18:17 into a big pit in the f and piled up a large H3623
1Ki 7: 2 the Palace of the F *of* Lebanon a hundred H3623
1Ki 10:17 them in the Palace of the F *of* Lebanon. H3623
1Ki 10:21 the Palace of the F *of* Lebanon were pure H3623
1Ch 16:33 Let the trees of the f sing, let them sing H3623
2Ch 9:16 them in the Palace of the F *of* Lebanon. H3623
2Ch 9:20 the Palace of the F *of* Lebanon were pure H3623
Ps 50:10 every animal of the f is mine, and the H3623
Ps 80:13 Boars from the f ravage it, and insects H3623
Ps 83:14 As fire consumes the f or a flame sets the H3623
Ps 96:12 let all the trees of the f sing for joy. H3623
Ps 104:20 and all the beasts of the f prowl. H3623
SS 2: 3 the trees of the f is my beloved among H3623
Isa 7: 2 as the trees of the f are shaken by the H3623
Isa 9:18 thorns, it sets the f thickets ablaze, so H3623
Isa 10:34 He will cut down the f thickets with an ax H3623
Isa 22: 8 day to the weapons in the Palace of the F. H3623
Isa 29:17 field and the fertile field seem like a f? H3623
Isa 32:15 and the fertile field seems like a f. H3623
Isa 32:19 hail flattens the f and the city is leveled H3623
Isa 44:14 He let it grow among the trees of the f, or H3623
Isa 56: 9 come and devour, all you beasts of the f! H3623
Jer 5: 6 a lion from the f will attack them, H3623
Jer 10: 3 they cut a tree out of the f, and a H3623
Jer 12: 8 has become to me like a lion in the f. H3623
Jer 46:23 They will chop down her f," declares the H3623
Eze 15: 2 of a branch from any of the trees in the f? H3623
Eze 15: 6 the trees of the f as fuel for the fire, H3623
Eze 17:24 All the trees of the f will know that I the H8441
Eze 20:46 prophesy against the f *of* the southland. H3623
Eze 20:47 Say to the southern f: 'Hear the word of H3623
Eze 31: 3 beautiful branches overshadowing the f; H3091
Mic 5: 8 like a lion among the beasts of the f, like H3623
Mic 7:14 which lives by itself in a f, in fertile H3623
Zec 11: 2 Bashan; the dense f has been cut down! H3623
Jas 3: 5 Consider what a great f is set on fire by a G5627

FORESTALL (1)
Jnh 4: 2 That is what *I tried to* f by fleeing to H7709

FORESTED (1) [FOREST]
Jos 17:18 the f hill country as well. Clear it, and H3623

FORESTS (9) [FOREST]
2Ki 19:23 its remotest parts, the **finest of** its f. H4149+3623
Ps 29: 9 LORD twists the oaks and strips the f bare. H3623
Isa 10:18 The splendor of his f and fertile fields it H3623
Isa 10:19 trees of his f will be so few that a H3623
Isa 37:24 remotest heights, the **finest of** its f. H4149+3623
Isa 44:23 you mountains, you f and all your trees H3623
Jer 21:14 kindle a fire in your f that will consume H3623
Eze 34:25 wilderness and sleep in the f in safety. H3623
Eze 39:10 wood from the fields or cut it from the f, H3623

FORETELL (2) [FORETELLS, FORETOLD]
Isa 44: 7 to come—yes, *let them* f what will come. H5583
Isa 44: 8 Did I not proclaim this and f it long ago H5583

FORETELLS (1) [FORETELL]
Dt 13: 1 or *one who* f **by dreams**, appears H2731+2706

FORETOLD (12) [FORETELL]
2Ki 7:17 as the man of God *had* f when the king H1819
2Ki 23:16 by the man of God who f these things. H7924
Ps 105:19 till **what** he f came to pass, till the word of H1821
Isa 41:26 one told of this, no *one* f it, no one heard H9048
Isa 43: 9 Which of their gods f this and proclaimed H5583
Isa 45:21 Who f this long ago, who declared it from H9048
Isa 48: 3 *I* f the former things long ago, my mouth H5583
Isa 48:14 Which of the idols *has* f these things? The H5583
Isa 52: 6 that day they will know that it is I who f it. H1819
Ac 3:18 fulfilled what *he had* f through all the G4615
Ac 3:24 who have spoken *have* f these days. G2859
Jude 17 the apostles of our Lord Jesus Christ f. G4625

FOREVER (289) [EVER]
Ge 3:22 the tree of life and eat, and live f." H4200+6409
Ge 6: 3 will not contend with humans f, H4200+6409
Ge 13:15 give to you and your offspring f. H6330+6409
Ex 3:15 "This is my name f, the name you H4200+6409
Ex 31:17 between me and the Israelites f, H4200+6409
Ex 32:13 and it will be their inheritance f." H4200+6409
Dt 5:29 well with them and their children f! H4200+6409
Dt 13:16 That town is to remain a ruin f, never to H6409
Dt 28:46 to you and your descendants f. H6330+6409
Dt 29:29 belong to us and to our children f, H6330+6409
Dt 32:40 As surely as I live f, H4200+6409
Jos 4: 7 memorial to the people of Israel f." H6330+6409
Jos 14: 9 and that of your children f, H6330+6409
1Sa 2:30 family would minister before me f. H6330+6409
1Sa 3:13 judge his family f because of the H6330+6409
1Sa 20:23 is witness between you and me f." H6330+6409
1Sa 20:42 and my descendants f." H6330+6409
2Sa 2:26 to Joab, "Must the sword devour f? H4200+5905
2Sa 3:28 my kingdom are f innocent before H6330+6409
2Sa 7:13 the throne of his kingdom f. H6330+6409
2Sa 7:16 kingdom will endure f before me; H6330+6409
2Sa 7:16 your throne will be established f." H6330+6409
2Sa 7:24 people Israel as your very own f, H6330+6409
2Sa 7:25 keep f the promise you have made H6330+6409
2Sa 7:26 so that your name will be great f. H6330+6409
2Sa 7:29 that it may continue f in your sight H4200+6409
2Sa 7:29 of your servant will be blessed f." H4200+6409
2Sa 22:51 to David and his descendants f." H6330+6409
1Ki 1:31 "May my lord King David live f!" H4200+6409
1Ki 2:33 of Joab and his descendants f. H4200+6409
1Ki 2:33 may there be the LORD's peace f." H6330+6409
1Ki 2:45 remain secure before the LORD f." H6330+6409
1Ki 8:13 temple for you, a place for you to dwell f." H6409
1Ki 9: 3 by putting my Name there f. H6330+6409
1Ki 9: 5 your royal throne over Israel f, H4200+6409
1Ki 11:39 because of this, but not f." H3972+2021+3427
2Ki 5:27 to you and to your descendants f." H4200+6409
2Ki 8:19 and his descendants f. H3972+2021+3427
2Ki 21: 7 of Israel, I will put my Name f. H4200+6409
1Ch 15: 2 LORD and to minister before him f." H6330+6409
1Ch 16:15 He remembers his covenant f, the H4200+6409
1Ch 16:34 he is good; his love endures f. H4200+6409
1Ch 16:41 to the LORD, "for his love endures f." H4200+6409
1Ch 17:12 and I will establish his throne f. H6330+6409
1Ch 17:14 house and my kingdom f; H6330+2021+6409
1Ch 17:14 his throne will be established f." H6330+6409
1Ch 17:22 your people Israel your very own f, H6330+6409
1Ch 17:23 and his house be established f. H6330+6409
1Ch 17:24 and that your name will be great f. H6330+6409
1Ch 17:27 that it may continue f in your sight H4200+6409
1Ch 17:27 blessed it, and it will be blessed f." H4200+6409
1Ch 22:10 throne of his kingdom over Israel f.' H6330+6409
1Ch 23:13 he and his descendants f, to H6330+6409
1Ch 23:13 pronounce blessings in his name f. H6330+6409
1Ch 23:25 to dwell in Jerusalem f, H6330+4200+6409
1Ch 28: 4 family to be king over Israel f. H4200+6409
1Ch 28: 7 his kingdom f if he is H6330+4200+6409
1Ch 28: 8 inheritance to your descendants f. H6330+6409
1Ch 28: 9 forsake him, he will reject you f. H4200+6329
1Ch 29:18 in the hearts of your people f, H4200+6409
2Ch 5:13 his love endures f." Then the H4200+6409
2Ch 6: 2 temple for you, a place for you to dwell f." H6409
2Ch 7: 3 "He is good; his love endures f." H4200+6409
2Ch 7: 6 thanks, saying, "His love endures f." H4200+6409
2Ch 7:16 so that my Name may be there f. H6330+6409
2Ch 9: 8 and his desire to uphold them f, H4200+6409
2Ch 13: 5 his descendants f by a covenant of H4200+6409
2Ch 20: 7 and give it f to the descendants H4200+6409
2Ch 20:21 to the LORD, for his love endures f." H4200+6409
2Ch 21: 7 him and his descendants f. H3972+2021+3427
2Ch 30: 8 which he has consecrated f. H4200+6409
2Ch 33: 4 Name will remain in Jerusalem f." H4200+6409
2Ch 33: 7 of Israel, I will put my Name f. H4200+6409
Ezr 3:11 his love toward Israel endures f." H4200+6409
Ne 2: 3 to the king, "May the king live f! H4200+6409
Job 4:20 to pieces; unnoticed, they perish f. H4200+5905
Job 7:16 I would not live f. Let me alone; H4200+6409
Job 19:24 tool on lead, or engraved in rock f! H4200+6329
Job 20: 7 he will perish f, like his own dung H4200+5905
Job 23: 7 be delivered f from my judge. H4200+5905
Job 36: 7 them with kings and exalts them f. H4200+5905
Ps 9: 7 The LORD reigns f; he has H4200+6409
Ps 12: 7 will protect us f from the wicked, H4200+6409
Ps 13: 1 Will you forget me f? How long will you H5905
Ps 18:50 to David and to his descendants f. H6330+6409
Ps 19: 9 fear of the LORD is pure, enduring f. H4200+6329
Ps 22:26 praise him—may your hearts live f! H4200+6329
Ps 23: 6 in the house of the LORD f. H4200+802+3427
Ps 28: 9 shepherd and carry them f. H6330+2021+6409
Ps 29:10 the LORD is enthroned as King f. H4200+6409
Ps 30:12 LORD my God, I will praise you f. H4200+6409
Ps 33:11 the plans of the LORD stand firm f, H4200+6409
Ps 37:18 and their inheritance will endure f. H4200+6409
Ps 37:27 then you will dwell in the land f. H4200+6409
Ps 37:29 inherit the land and dwell in it f. H4200+6329
Ps 41:12 me and set me in your presence f. H4200+6409
Ps 44: 8 and we will praise your name f. H4200+6409
Ps 44:23 Rouse yourself! Do not reject us f. H4200+5905
Ps 45: 2 since God has blessed you f. H4200+6409
Ps 48: 8 God makes her secure f. H6330+6409
Ps 49: 9 should live on f and not see decay. H4200+5905
Ps 49:11 tombs will remain their houses f, H4200+6409
Ps 61: 4 to dwell in your tent f and take refuge in H6409
Ps 61: 7 May he be enthroned in God's presence f H6409
Ps 66: 7 He rules f by his power, his eyes watch H6409
Ps 68:16 where the LORD himself will dwell f? H4200+5905
Ps 69:23 cannot see, and their backs be bent f. H9458
Ps 72:17 May his name endure f; may it H4200+6409
Ps 72:19 Praise be to his glorious name f H4200+6409
Ps 73:26 of my heart and my portion f. H4200+6409
Ps 74: 1 why have you rejected us f? Why H4200+5905
Ps 74:10 Will the foe revile your name f? H4200+5905
Ps 74:19 the lives of your afflicted people f. H4200+5905
Ps 75: 9 I will declare this f; I will sing H4200+6409
Ps 77: 7 "Will the Lord reject f? Will he H4200+6409
Ps 77: 8 Has his unfailing love vanished f H4200+5905
Ps 78:69 like the earth that he established f. H4200+6409
Ps 79: 5 Will you be angry f? How long will H4200+5905
Ps 79:13 will praise you f; from generation H4200+6409
Ps 81:15 and their punishment would last f. H4200+6409
Ps 85: 5 Will you be angry with us f? Will H4200+6409
Ps 86:12 my heart; I will glorify your name f. H4200+6409
Ps 89: 1 I will sing of the LORD's great love f; with H6409
Ps 89: 2 I will declare that your love stands firm f H6409
Ps 89: 4 establish your line f and make your H6330+6409
Ps 89:28 I will maintain my love to him f H4200+6409
Ps 89:29 I will establish his line f, his throne H4200+6329
Ps 89:36 line will continue f and his throne H4200+6409
Ps 89:37 it will be established f like the moon, the H6409
Ps 89:46 Will you hide yourself f? How long H4200+5905
Ps 89:52 Praise be to the LORD f! Amen and H4200+6409
Ps 92: 7 flourish, they will be destroyed f. H6330+6329
Ps 92: 8 But you, LORD, are f exalted. H4200+6409
Ps 100: 5 is good and his love endures f; H4200+6409
Ps 102:12 sit enthroned f; your renown H4200+6409
Ps 103: 9 will he harbor his anger f; H4200+6409
Ps 104:31 May the glory of the LORD endure f H4200+6409
Ps 105: 8 He remembers his covenant f, the H4200+6409
Ps 106: 1 he is good; his love endures f. H4200+6409
Ps 107: 1 he is good; his love endures f. H4200+6409
Ps 109:19 about him, like a belt tied f around him. H9458
Ps 110: 4 "You are a priest f, in the order of H4200+6409
Ps 111: 3 and his righteousness endures f. H4200+6329
Ps 111: 5 he remembers his covenant f. H4200+6409
Ps 111: 9 he ordained his covenant f—holy H4200+6409
Ps 112: 3 and their righteousness endures f. H4200+6329
Ps 112: 6 be shaken; they will be remembered f. H6409
Ps 112: 9 their righteousness endures f; their H4200+6329
Ps 117: 2 faithfulness of the LORD endures f. H4200+6409
Ps 118: 1 he is good; his love endures f. H4200+6409
Ps 118: 2 Let Israel say: "His love endures f." H4200+6409
Ps 118: 3 of Aaron say: "His love endures f." H4200+6409
Ps 118: 4 the LORD say: "His love endures f." H4200+6409
Ps 118:29 he is good; his love endures f. H4200+6409
Ps 119:111 Your statutes are my heritage f H4200+6409
Ps 119:152 that you established them to last f. H4200+6409

Ps 125: 1 cannot be shaken but endures f. H4200+6409
Ps 135:13 endures f, your renown, LORD, H4200+6409
Ps 136: 1 he is good. His love endures f. H4200+6409
Ps 136: 2 God of gods. His love endures f. H4200+6409
Ps 136: 3 Lord of lords: His love endures f. H4200+6409
Ps 136: 4 great wonders, His love endures f. H4200+6409
Ps 136: 5 the heavens, His love endures f. H4200+6409
Ps 136: 6 the waters, His love endures f. H4200+6409
Ps 136: 7 great lights—His love endures f. H4200+6409
Ps 136: 8 govern the day, His love endures f. H4200+6409
Ps 136: 9 the night; His love endures f. H4200+6409
Ps 136:10 of Egypt His love endures f. H4200+6409
Ps 136:11 among them His love endures f. H4200+6409
Ps 136:12 His love endures f. H4200+6409
Ps 136:13 Sea asunder His love endures f. H4200+6409
Ps 136:14 the midst of it, His love endures f. H4200+6409
Ps 136:15 the Red Sea; His love endures f. H4200+6409
Ps 136:16 the wilderness; His love endures f. H4200+6409
Ps 136:17 great kings, His love endures f. H4200+6409
Ps 136:18 mighty kings—His love endures f. H4200+6409
Ps 136:19 of the Amorites His love endures f. H4200+6409
Ps 136:20 of Bashan—His love endures f. H4200+6409
Ps 136:21 an inheritance, His love endures f. H4200+6409
Ps 136:22 servant Israel. His love endures f. H4200+6409
Ps 136:23 our low estate His love endures f. H4200+6409
Ps 136:24 our enemies. His love endures f. H4200+6409
Ps 136:25 every creature. His love endures f. H4200+6409
Ps 136:26 God of heaven. His love endures f. H4200+6409
Ps 138: 8 endures f—do not abandon H4200+6409
Ps 146: 6 in them—he remains faithful f. H4200+6409
Ps 146:10 The LORD reigns f, your God, H4200+6409
Pr 10:25 are gone, but the righteous stand firm f. H6409
Pr 12:19 Truthful lips endure f, but a lying H4200+6329
Pr 27:24 riches do not endure f, and a H4200+6409
Pr 29:14 his throne will be established f. H4200+6329
Ecc 1: 4 but the earth remains f. H4200+6409
Ecc 3:14 everything God does will endure f; H4200+6409
Isa 9: 7 from that time on and f. H6330+6409
Isa 25: 8 he will swallow up death f. H4200+5905
Isa 26: 4 Trust in the LORD f, for the LORD, the H6330+6329
Isa 28:28 one does not go on threshing it f. H4200+5905
Isa 32:14 will become a wasteland f, H6330+6409
Isa 32:17 will be quietness and confidence f. H6330+6409
Isa 34:10 night or day; its smoke will rise f. H4200+6409
Isa 34:17 will possess it f and dwell there H6330+6409
Isa 40: 8 the word of our God endures f." H4200+6409
Isa 47: 7 You said, 'I am f—the eternal H4200+6409
Isa 51: 6 But my salvation will last f, my H4200+6409
Isa 51: 8 But my righteousness will last f, my H4200+6409
Isa 55:13 everlasting sign, *that will* **endure** f." H4202+4162
Isa 56: 5 name that *will* **endure** f. H4202+4162
Isa 57:15 he who lives f, whose name is holy H6329
Isa 57:16 I will not accuse them f, nor will I H4200+6409
Isa 59:21 from this time on and f," says the H6330+6409
Isa 60:21 and they will possess the land f. H4200+6409
Isa 64: 9 do not remember our sins f. H4200+6329
Isa 65:18 be glad and rejoice f in what I will H6330+6329
Jer 3: 5 Will your wrath continue f?' This is H4200+5905
Jer 3:12 the LORD, 'I will not be angry f. H4200+6409
Jer 17: 4 my anger, and it will burn f. H6330+6409
Jer 17:25 and this city will be inhabited f. H4200+6409
Jer 20:17 as my grave, her womb enlarged f. H6409
Jer 25:12 the LORD, "and will make it desolate f. H6409
Jer 33:11 LORD is good; his love endures f." H4200+6409
Jer 49:13 all its towns will be in ruins f. H6409
Jer 49:33 of jackals, a desolate place f. H6330+6409
Jer 51:26 you will be desolate f," declares the H6409
Jer 51:39 laughter—then sleep f and not awake," H6409
Jer 51:57 they will sleep f and not awake, H6409
Jer 51:62 animals will live in it; it will be desolate f. H6409
La 3:31 For no one is cast off by the Lord f. H4200+6409
La 5:19 reign f; your throne endures H4200+6409
Eze 35: 9 I will make you desolate f; your towns will H6409
Eze 37:25 children's children will live there f, H6330+6409
Eze 37:25 my servant will be their prince f. H4200+6409
Eze 37:26 put my sanctuary among them f. H4200+6409
Eze 37:28 my sanctuary is among them f. H4200+6409
Eze 43: 7 I will live among the Israelites f. H4200+6409
Eze 43: 9 and I will live among them f. H4200+6409
Da 2: 4 the king, "May the king live f! A10378+10550
Da 2:44 but it will itself endure f. A10378+10550+10002
Da 3: 9 "May the king live f! A10378+10550
Da 4:34 and glorified him who lives f. A10550+10002
Da 5:10 "May the king live f!" she said. A10378+10550
Da 6: 6 "May King Darius live f! A10378+10550
Da 6:21 answered, "May the king live f! A10378+10550
Da 6:26 the living God and he endures f; A10378+10550
Da 7:18 and will possess it f— A10527+10550+10002
Da 7:26 completely destroyed f. A10527+10509+10002
Da 12: 7 I heard him swear by him who lives f H6409
Hos 2:19 I will betroth you to me f; I will H4200+6409
Joel 3:20 will be inhabited f and Jerusalem H4200+6409
Ob 10 shame; you will be destroyed f. H4200+6409
Jnh 2: 6 the earth beneath barred me in f. H4200+6409
Mic 2: 9 my blessing from their children f. H4200+6409
Mic 4: 7 in Mount Zion from that day and f. H6330+6409
Mic 7:18 do not stay angry f but delight to H4200+6329
Hab 3: 6 hills collapsed—but he marches on f. H6409
Zep 2: 9 weeds and salt pits, a wasteland f. H6330+6409
Zec 1: 5 And the prophets, do they live f? H4200+6409
Lk 1:33 over Jacob's descendants f; G1650+3836+172
Lk 1:55 and his descendants f, G1650+3836+172
Jn 6:51 eats this bread will live f. G1650+3836+172
Jn 6:58 feeds on this bread will live f." G1650+3836+172
Jn 8:35 but a son belongs to it f. G1650+3836+172
Jn 12:34 the Messiah will remain f, G1650+3836+172
Jn 14:16 help you and be with you f— G1650+3836+172
Ro 1:25 the Creator—who is f praised. G1650+3836+172
Ro 9: 5 who is God over all, f praised! G1650+3836+172
Ro 11:10 and their backs be bent f. G1328+4246
Ro 11:36 To him be the glory f! Amen. G1650+3836+172
Ro 16:27 God be glory f through Jesus G1650+3836+172
1Co 9:25 we do it to get a crown **that will last** f. G915
2Co 9: 9 their righteousness endures f." G1650+3836+172
2Co 11:31 who is to be praised f, knows G1650+3836+172
1Th 4:17 And so we will be with the Lord f. G4121
1Ti 5:25 that are not obvious cannot *remain* **hidden** *f*. AIT
1Ti 6:16 To him be honor and might f. Amen. G173
Phm 15 was that you might have him back f— G173
Heb 5: 6 "You are a priest f, in the G1650+3836+172
Heb 6:20 has become a high priest f, G1650+3836+172
Heb 7: 3 he remains a priest f. G1650+3836+1457
Heb 7:17 "You are a priest f, in the G1650+3836+172
Heb 7:21 'You are a priest f.' " G1650+3836+172
Heb 7:24 because Jesus lives f, he G1650+3836+172
Heb 7:28 who has been made perfect f. G1650+3836+172
Heb 10:14 made perfect f those who G1650+3836+1457
Heb 13: 8 yesterday and today and f. G1650+3836+172
1Pe 1:25 word of the Lord endures f." G1650+3836+172
2Pe 3:18 him be glory both now and f! G1650+2465+172
1Jn 2:17 does the will of God lives f. G1650+3836+172
2Jn 2 in us and will be with us f: G1650+3836+172
Jude 13 darkness has been reserved f. G1650+172

FOREVERMORE (7) [EVER]

Ps 113: 2 LORD be praised, both now and f. H6330+6409
Ps 115:18 who extol the LORD, both now and f. H6330+6409
Ps 121: 8 coming and going both now and f. H6330+6409
Ps 125: 2 his people both now and f. H6330+6409
Ps 131: 3 hope in the LORD both now and f. H6330+6409
Ps 133: 3 his blessing, even life f. H6330+2021+6409
Jude 25 all ages, now and f! G1650+4246+3836+172

FOREWARN, FOREWARNED (KJV) SHOW, TOLD BEFORE

FOREWARNED (1) [WARN]

2Pe 3:17 *since* you *have been* f, be on your G4589

FORFEIT (5) [FORFEITING]

Ezr 10: 8 within three days *would* f all his property, H3049
Pr 20: 2 those who anger him f their lives. H2627
Mt 16:26 to gain the whole world, yet f their soul? G2423
Mk 8:36 to gain the whole world, yet f their soul? G2423
Lk 9:25 and yet lose or f their very self? G2423

FORFEITING (1) [FORFEIT]

Hab 2:10 shaming your own house and f your life. H2627

FORGAVE (8) [FORGIVE]

Ps 32: 5 And you f the guilt of my sin. H5951
Ps 65: 3 you f our transgressions. H4105
Ps 78:38 *he* f their iniquities and did not destroy H4105
Ps 85: 2 *You* f the iniquity of your people and H5951
Lk 7:42 to pay him back, so *he* f the debts of both. G5919
Eph 4:32 each other, just as in Christ God f you. G5919
Col 2:13 you alive with Christ. *He* f us all our sins, G5919
Col 3:13 Forgive as the Lord f you. G5919

FORGED (3) [FORGES]

Ge 4:22 *who* f all kinds of tools *out of* bronze and H4323
Isa 54:17 no weapon f against you will prevail, and H3670
Eze 21:15 *It* **is** f to strike like lightning, it is grasped H6913

FORGES (2) [FORGED]

Isa 44:12 *he* f it with the might of his arm. H7188
Isa 54:16 coals into flame and f a weapon fit for its H3655

FORGET (59) [FORGETS, FORGETTING, FORGOT, FORGOTTEN]

Ge 41:51 is because God *has* **made** me f all my H5960
Dt 4: 9 closely so that *you do* not f the things your H8894
Dt 4:23 Be careful not *to* f the covenant of the LORD H8894
Dt 4:31 destroy you or f the covenant with your H8894
Dt 6:12 be careful that *you do* not f the LORD, who H8894
Dt 8:11 Be careful that *you do* not f the LORD your H8894
Dt 8:14 become proud and *you will* f the LORD your H8894
Dt 8:19 If *you* **ever** f the LORD your God and H8894+8894
Dt 9: 7 this and never f how you aroused the H8894
Dt 25:19 of Amalek from under heaven. *Do* not f! H8894
1Sa 1:11 not f your servant but give her a son H8894
2Ki 17:38 *Do* not f the covenant I have made with H8894
Job 8:13 Such is the destiny of all *who* f God; so H8894
Job 9:27 '*I will* f my complaint, I will H8894
Job 11:16 You *will* surely f your trouble, recalling it H8894
Ps 9:17 of the dead, all the nations *that* f God. H8895
Ps 9:18 But God *will* never f the needy; the hope H8894
Ps 10:12 your hand, O God. *Do* not f the helpless. H8894
Ps 13: 1 *Will you* f me forever? How long will H8894
Ps 44:24 you hide your face and f our misery and H8894
Ps 45:10 F your people and your father's house H8894
Ps 50:22 "Consider this, you *who* f God, or I will H8894
Ps 59:11 Lord our shield, or my people *will* f. H8894
Ps 74:19 *do* not f the lives of your afflicted people H8894
Ps 78: 7 trust in God and *would* not f his deeds H8894
Ps 102: 4 withered like grass; *I* f to eat my food. H8894
Ps 103: 2 my soul, and f not all his benefits— H8894
Ps 119:61 bind me with ropes, *I will* not f your law. H8894
Ps 119:83 in the smoke, *I do* not f your decrees. H8894
Ps 119:93 *I will* never f your precepts, for by them H8894
Ps 119:109 my life in my hands, *I will* not f your law. H8894
Ps 119:141 despised, *I do* not f your precepts. H8894
Ps 137: 5 If *I* f you, Jerusalem, may my right hand H8894
Ps 137: 5 Jerusalem, *may* my right hand f its *skill*. H8894
Pr 3: 1 My son, *do* not f my teaching, but keep H8894
Pr 4: 5 do not f my words or turn away from them. H8894
Pr 31: 5 lest they drink and f what has been H8894
Pr 31: 7 Let them drink and f their poverty and H8894
Isa 43:18 "F the former things; do not dwell on H440+2349
Isa 44:21 you are my servant; Israel, I *will* not f *you*. H5960
Isa 49:15 "*Can* a mother f the baby at her breast H8894
Isa 49:15 Though she *may* f, I will not forget H8894
Isa 49:15 Though she may forget, I *will* not f you! H8894
Isa 51:13 that *you* f the LORD your Maker, who H8894
Isa 54: 4 *You will* f the shame of your youth and H8894
Isa 65:11 forsake the LORD and f my holy mountain, H8895
Jer 2:32 *Does* a young woman f her jewelry, H8894
Jer 23:27 another *will* **make** my people f my name, H8894
Jer 23:39 I *will* **surely** f you and cast you out H5960+5960
La 2: 6 The LORD *has* **made** Zion f her appointed H8894
La 5:20 Why *do you* always f us? Why do you H8894
Eze 39:26 *They will* f their shame and all the H5960
Am 8: 7 "*I will* never f anything they have done. H8894
Mic 6:10 *Am I* still *to* f your ill-gotten treasures, you H5960
Heb 6:10 *he will* not f your work and the love you G2140
Heb 13: 2 *Do* not f to show hospitality to strangers G2140
Heb 13:16 And *do* not f to do good and to share with G2140
2Pe 3: 5 But they deliberately f that long ago by G3291
2Pe 3: 8 But *do* not f this one thing, dear friends G3291

FORGETS (4) [FORGET]

Ge 27:45 angry with you and f what you did to him, H8894
Job 24:20 The womb f them, the worm feasts on H8894
Jn 16:21 her baby is born *she* f the anguish G4033+3648
Jas 1:24 immediately f what he looks like. G2140

FORGETTING (3) [FORGET]

Php 3:13 F what is behind and straining toward G2140
Jas 1:25 not f what they have heard G2144
2Pe 1: 9 f that they have been cleansed G3330+3284

FORGIVE (75) [FORGAVE, FORGIVEN, FORGIVENESS, FORGIVES, FORGIVING]

Ge 50:17 I ask you to f your brothers the sins and H5951
Ge 50:17 Now please f the sins of the servants of H5951
Ex 10:17 Now f my sin once more and pray to the H5951
Ex 23:21 against him; *he will* not f your rebellion H5951
Ex 32:32 But now, please f their sin—but if not H5951
Ex 34: 9 people, f our wickedness and our sin H6142
Nu 14:19 your great love, f the sin of these people H6142
Dt 29:20 The LORD will never be willing *to* f them H6142
Jos 24:19 *He will* not f your rebellion and your sins H5951
1Sa 15:25 beg you, f my sin and come back with me H5951
1Sa 25:28 "Please f your servant's presumption. H5951
1Ki 8:30 dwelling place, and when you hear, f. H6142
1Ki 8:34 hear from heaven and f the sin of your H6142
1Ki 8:36 hear from heaven and f the sin of your H6142
1Ki 8:39 F and act; deal with everyone according to H6142
1Ki 8:50 And f your people, who have sinned H6142
1Ki 8:50 f all the offenses they have committed NDT
2Ki 5:18 But *may* the LORD f your servant for this H6142
2Ki 5:18 *may* the LORD f your servant for this." H6142
2Ki 24: 4 and the LORD was not willing *to* f. H6142
2Ch 6:21 dwelling place; and when you hear, f. H6142
2Ch 6:25 hear from heaven and f the sin of your H6142
2Ch 6:27 hear from heaven and f the sin of your H6142
2Ch 6:30 F, and deal with everyone according to all H6142
2Ch 6:39 And f your people, who have sinned H6142
2Ch 7:14 and *I will* f their sin and will heal their H6142
Job 7:21 not pardon my offenses and f my sins? H6296
Ps 19:12 their own errors? F my hidden faults. H5927
Ps 25:11 of your name, LORD, f my iniquity, though H6142
Ps 79: 9 deliver us and f our sins for your name's H4105
Isa 2: 9 everyone humbled—*do* not f them. H5951
Jer 5: 1 seeks the truth, *I will* f this city. H6142
Jer 5: 7 "Why *should I* f you? Your children have H6142
Jer 18:23 *Do* not f their crimes or blot out their sins H4105
Jer 31:34 "For *I will* f their wickedness and will H6142
Jer 33: 8 against me and *will* f all their sins of H6142
Jer 36: 3 then *I will* f their wickedness and their sin." H6142
Jer 50:20 be found, for *I will* f the remnant I spare. H6142
Da 9:19 Lord, f! Lord, hear and act! For H6142
Hos 1: 6 to Israel, that *I should* **at all** f them. H5951+5951
Hos 14: 2 "F all our sins and receive us graciously H5951
Am 7: 2 land clean, I cried out, "Sovereign LORD, f! H6142
Mt 6:12 And f us our debts, as we also have G918
Mt 6:14 For if *you* f other people when they sin G918
Mt 6:14 your heavenly Father *will* also f you. G918
Mt 6:15 But if *you do* not f others their sins, your G918
Mt 6:15 their sins, your Father *will* not f your sins. G918
Mt 9: 6 Son of Man has authority on earth *to* f sins." G918
Mt 18:21 how many times *shall I* f my brother or G918
Mt 18:35 each of you unless *you* f your brother or G918
Mk 2: 7 Who can f sins but God alone?" G918
Mk 2:10 Son of Man has authority on earth *to* f sins." G918
Mk 11:25 against anyone, f them, so that your G918
Mk 11:25 your Father in heaven *may* f you your sins." G918

Lk 5:21 Who can f sins but God alone? G918
Lk 5:24 Son of Man has authority on earth to f sins." G918
Lk 6:37 will not be condemned. F, and you will be G668
Lk 11: 4 F us our sins, for we also forgive everyone G918
Lk 11: 4 we also f everyone who sins against us. G918
Lk 17: 3 rebuke them; and if they repent, f them. G918
Lk 17: 4 to you saying 'I repent,' you must f them." G918
Lk 23:34 f them, for they do not know what G918
Jn 20:23 If you f anyone's sins, their sins are forgiven; G918
Jn 20:23 are forgiven; if you do not f them, they are G3195
Ac 5:31 bring Israel to repentance and f their sins. G912
Ac 8:22 the hope that he may f you for having such G918
2Co 2: 7 instead, you ought to f and comfort him G5919
2Co 2:10 Anyone you f, I also forgive. And what I G5919
2Co 2:10 you forgive, I also f. And what I have NDT
2Co 2:10 if there was anything to f—I have forgiven G5919
2Co 12:13 never a burden to you? F me this wrong! G5919
Col 3:13 with each other and f one another if any G5919
Col 3:13 against someone. F as the Lord forgave you. NDT
Heb 8:12 For I will f their wickedness and will G2664+1639
1Jn 1: 9 faithful and just and will f us our sins and G918

F

FORGIVEN (46) [FORGIVE]

Lev 4:20 the community, and they will be f. H6142
Lev 4:26 the leader's sin, and he will be f. H6142
Lev 4:31 atonement for them, and they will be f. H6142
Lev 4:35 they have committed, and they will be f. H6142
Lev 5:10 they have committed, and they will be f. H6142
Lev 5:13 they have committed, and they will be f. H6142
Lev 5:16 ram as a guilt offering, and they will be f. H6142
Lev 5:18 unintentionally, and they will be f. H6142
Lev 6: 7 they will be f for any of the things H6142
Lev 19:22 he has committed, and his sin will be f. H6142
Nu 14:20 LORD replied, "I have f them, as you asked H6142
Nu 15:25 they will be f, for it was not H6142
Nu 15:26 foreigners residing among them will be f, H6142
Nu 15:28 has been made, that person will be f. H6142
Ps 32: 1 is the one whose transgressions are f, H5951
Isa 33:24 sins of those who dwell there will be f. H5951
La 3:42 sinned and rebelled and you have not f. H6142
Mt 6:12 us our debts, as we also have f our debtors. G918
Mt 9: 2 the man, "Take heart, son; your sins are f." G918
Mt 9: 5 'Your sins are f,' or to say, 'Get up G918
Mt 12:31 every kind of sin and slander can be f, but G918
Mt 12:31 blasphemy against the Spirit will not be f. G918
Mt 12:32 a word against the Son of Man will be f, G918
Mt 12:32 speaks against the Holy Spirit will not be f, G918
Mk 2: 5 to the paralyzed man, "Son, your sins are f." G918
Mk 2: 9 paralyzed man, 'Your sins are f,' or to say, G918
Mk 3:28 people can be f all their sins and every G918
Mk 3:29 the Holy Spirit will never be f; G2400+912
Mk 4:12 otherwise they might turn and be f! G918
Lk 5:20 their faith, he said, "Friend, your sins are f." G918
Lk 5:23 'Your sins are f,' or to say, 'Get up G918
Lk 6:37 be condemned. Forgive, and you will be f. G668
Lk 7:43 the one who had the bigger debt f." G5919
Lk 7:47 her many sins have been f—as her great G918
Lk 7:47 But whoever has been f little loves little." G918
Lk 7:48 Then Jesus said to her, "Your sins are f." G918
Lk 12:10 a word against the Son of Man will be f, G918
Lk 12:10 against the Holy Spirit will not be f. G918
Jn 20:23 their sins are f; if you do not forgive G918
Jn 20:23 if you do not forgive them, they are not f." G3195
Ro 4: 7 are those whose transgressions are f, G918
2Co 2:10 And what I have f—if there was anything G5919
2Co 2:10 I have f in the sight of Christ for your sake NDT
Heb 10:18 And where these have been f, sacrifice G912
Jas 5:15 If they have sinned, they will be f. G918
1Jn 2:12 your sins have been f on account of G918

FORGIVENESS (13) [FORGIVE]

Ps 130: 4 But with you there is f, so that we can H6145
Mt 26:28 is poured out for many for the f of sins. G912
Mk 1: 4 a baptism of repentance for the f of sins. G912
Lk 1:77 of salvation through the f of their sins, G912
Lk 3: 3 a baptism of repentance for the f of sins. G912
Lk 24:47 repentance for the f of sins will be G912
Ac 2:38 name of Jesus Christ for the f of your sins. G912
Ac 10:43 in him receives f of sins through his name G912
Ac 13:38 through Jesus the f of sins is proclaimed G912
Ac 26:18 that they may receive f of sins and a place G912
Eph 1: 7 his blood, the f of sins, in accordance G912
Col 1:14 in whom we have redemption, the f of sins. G912
Heb 9:22 without the shedding of blood there is no f. G912

FORGIVES (3) [FORGIVE]

Ps 103: 3 who f all your sins and heals all your H6142
Mic 7:18 who pardons sin and f the transgression H6296
Lk 7:49 themselves, "Who is this who even f sins?" G918

FORGIVING (7) [FORGIVE]

Ex 34: 7 to thousands, and f wickedness, rebellion H5951
Nu 14:18 abounding in love and f sin and rebellion. H5951
Ne 9:17 But you are a f God, gracious and H6145
Ps 86: 5 are f and good, abounding in love H6143
Ps 99: 8 you were to Israel a f God, though you H5951
Da 9: 9 The Lord our God is merciful and f, even H6145
Eph 4:32 to one another, f each other, just as in G5919

FORGO (1)

Ne 10:31 seventh year we will f working the land H5759

FORGOT (12) [FORGET]

Ge 40:23 did not remember Joseph; he f him. H8894
Dt 32:18 you f the God who gave you birth. H8894
Jdg 3: 7 they f the LORD their God and served the H8894
1Sa 12: 9 "But they f the LORD their God; so he sold H8894
Ps 78:11 They f what he had done, the wonders he H8894
Ps 106:13 But they soon f what he had done and did H8894
Ps 106:21 They f the God who saved them, who had H8894
Jer 23:27 as their ancestors f my name through Baal H8894
Jer 50: 6 mountain and hill and f their own resting H8894
Hos 2:13 her lovers, but me she f," declares the H8894
Hos 13: 6 they became proud; then they f me. H8894
Mt 16: 5 the lake, the disciples f to take bread. G2140

FORGOTTEN (35) [FORGET]

Ge 41:30 Then all the abundance in Egypt will be f H8894
Dt 26:13 your commands nor have I f any of them. H8894
Dt 31:21 because it will not be f by their H8894
Job 11: 6 God has even f some of your sin. H5960
Job 19:14 gone away; my closest friends have f me. H8894
Ps 31:12 I am f as though I were dead; I have H8894
Ps 42: 9 say to God my Rock, "Why have you f me? H8894
Ps 44:17 though we had not f you; we had H8894
Ps 44:20 If we had f the name of our God or spread H8894
Ps 77: 9 Has God f to be merciful? Has he in anger H8894
Ps 119:153 deliver me, for I have not f your law. H8894
Ps 119:176 servant, for I have not f your commands. H8894
Ecc 2:16 already come when both have been f. H8894
Ecc 9: 5 further reward, and even their name is f. H8894
Isa 17:10 You have f God your Savior; you have not H8894
Isa 23:15 At that time Tyre will be f for seventy H8894
Isa 23:16 through the city, you f prostitute; play the H8894
Isa 49:14 LORD has forsaken me, the Lord has f me." H8894
Isa 65:16 past troubles will be f and hidden from H8894
Jer 2:32 Yet my people have f me, days without H8894
Jer 3:21 their ways and have f the LORD their God. H8894
Jer 13:25 "because you have f me and trusted in H8894
Jer 18:15 Yet my people have f me; they burn H8894
Jer 20:11 disgraced; their dishonor will never be f. H8894
Jer 23:40 everlasting shame that will not be f." H8894
Jer 30:14 All your allies have f you; they care H8894
Jer 44: 9 Have you f the wickedness committed by H8894
Jer 50: 5 an everlasting covenant that will not be f. H8894
La 3:17 of peace; I have f what prosperity is. H5960
Eze 22:12 And you have f me, declares the H8894
Eze 23:35 Since you have f me and turned your back H8894
Hos 8:14 Israel has f their Maker and built palaces H8894
Mk 8:14 The disciples had f to bring bread, except G2140
Lk 12: 6 Yet not one of them is f by God. G2140
Heb 12: 5 And have you completely f this word of G1720

FORK (8) [FORKS]

1Sa 2:13 with a three-pronged f in his hand while H4657
1Sa 2:14 would plunge the f into the pan or kettle NDT
1Sa 2:14 Whatever the f brought up the priest H4657
Isa 30:24 mash, spread out with f and shovel. H8181
Jer 15: 7 them with a winnowing f at the city gates H4665
Eze 21:21 of Babylon will stop at the f in the road, H562
Mt 3:12 His winnowing f is in his hand, and he will G4768
Lk 3:17 His winnowing f is in his hand to clear his G4768

FORKS (6) [FORK]

Ex 27: 3 sprinkling bowls, meat f and firepans. H4657
Ex 38: 3 sprinkling bowls, meat f and firepans. H4657
Nu 4:14 the firepans, meat f, shovels and H4657
1Sa 13:21 a shekel for sharpening f and axes and H7849
1Ch 28:17 the weight of pure gold for the f, sprinkling H4657
2Ch 4:16 shovels, meat f and all related articles. H4657

FORM (29) [DEFORMED, FORMATION, FORMED, FORMING, FORMS]

Ex 20: 4 an image in the f of anything in heaven H9454
Nu 12: 8 not in riddles; he sees the f of the LORD. H9454
Dt 4:12 heard the sound of words but saw no f; H9454
Dt 4:15 You saw no f of any kind the day the LORD H9454
Dt 4:23 an idol in the f of anything the LORD your H9454
Dt 5: 8 an image in the f of anything in heaven H9454
1Ki 6:16 floor to ceiling to f within the temple an H1215
Job 4:16 A f stood before my eyes, and I heard a H9454
Job 31:15 Did not the same one f us both within our H3922
Job 41:12 its strength and its graceful f. H6886
Ps 83: 5 together; they f an alliance against you H4162
Isa 44:13 He shapes it in human f, human form in H9322
Isa 44:13 in human form, human f in all its glory, that NDT
Isa 45: 7 I f the light and create darkness, I bring H3670
Isa 52:14 being and his f marred beyond human H9307
Jer 11:16 thriving olive tree with fruit beautiful in f. H9307
Eze 1: 5 In appearance their f was human, H1952
Mk 16:12 in a different f to two of them while G3671
Lk 3:22 descended on him in bodily f like a dove. G1626
Jn 5:37 have never heard his voice nor seen his f, G1626
Ac 7:41 time they made an idol in the f of a calf. G3674
Ac 14:11 gods have come down to us in human f!" G3929
Ro 12: 5 so in Christ we, though many, f one body G1639
1Co 7:31 For this world in its present f is passing G5386
1Co 12:12 all its many parts f one body, so it is G1639
1Co 12:13 by one Spirit so as to f one body— G1650
Eph 4:31 slander, along with every f of malice. AIT
Col 2: 9 the fullness of the Deity lives in bodily f, G5395
2Ti 3: 5 having a f of godliness but denying its G3673

FORMATION (4) [FORM]

2Sa 10: 8 drew up in battle f at the entrance H4878
1Ch 19: 9 drew up in battle f at the entrance H4878
Jer 6:23 come like men in battle f to attack you, H6885
Jer 50:42 come like men in battle f to attack you, H6885

FORMED (44) [FORM]

Ge 2: 7 the LORD God f a man from the dust of the H3670
Ge 2: 8 and there he put the man he had f. H3670
Ge 2:19 Now the LORD God had f out of the ground H3670
Dt 4:16 whether f like a man or a woman H9322
Dt 32: 6 your Creator, who made you and f you? H3922
Jos 18:20 The Jordan f the boundary on the eastern H1487
2Sa 2:25 They f themselves into a group and took H2118
2Sa 10:17 The Arameans f their battle lines to meet H6885
1Ch 19:17 them and f his battle lines opposite them. H6885
1Ch 19:17 David f his lines to meet the Arameans in H6885
Job 1:17 "The Chaldeans f three raiding parties H8492
Ps 65: 6 who f the mountains by your power H3922
Ps 94: 9 Does he who f the eye not see? H3670
Ps 95: 5 he made it, and his hands f the dry land. H3670
Ps 103:14 he knows how we are f, he remembers H3671
Ps 104:26 Leviathan, which you f to frolic there. H3670
Ps 119:73 Your hands made me and f me; give me H3922
Pr 8:23 I was f long ages ago, at the very H5820
Ecc 11: 5 how the body is f in a mother's womb, so NDT
Isa 29:16 Shall what is f say to the one who formed H5126
Isa 29:16 what is formed say to the one who f it, H6913
Isa 43: 1 created you, Jacob, he who f you, Israel: H3670
Isa 43: 7 created for my glory, whom I f and made." H3670
Isa 43:10 Before me no god was f, nor will there be H3670
Isa 43:21 the people I f for myself that they may H3670
Isa 44: 2 he who made you, who f you in the womb H3670
Isa 44:24 your Redeemer, who f you in the womb: H3670
Isa 45:18 it to be empty, but f it to be inhabited H3670
Isa 49: 5 he who f me in the womb to be his H3670
Jer 1: 5 "Before I f you in the womb I knew you H3670
Jer 18: 4 so the potter f it into another pot, shaping H6913
Jer 33: 2 the LORD who f it and established it H3670
Eze 16: 7 Your breasts had f and your hair had H3922
Eze 45: 7 each side of the area f by the sacred district NDT
Eze 48:21 sides of the area f by the sacred portion NDT
Mt 13:26 When the wheat sprouted and f heads G4472
Ac 17: 5 f a mob and started a riot in the city. G4062
Ac 23:12 morning some Jews f a conspiracy and G4472
Ro 9:20 "Shall what is f say to the one who G4420
Ro 9:20 what is formed say to the one who f it, G4421
Gal 4:19 pains of childbirth until Christ is f in you, G3672
1Ti 2:13 For Adam was f first, then Eve. G4421
Heb 11: 3 that the universe was f at God's G2936
2Pe 3: 5 the earth was f out of water and G5319

FORMER (34) [FORMERLY]

Nu 21:26 fought against the f king of Moab and H8037
Dt 4:32 Ask now about the f days, long before H8037
1Ki 16:24 Shemer, the name of the f owner of the hill. NDT
2Ki 17:34 To this day they persist in their f practices H8037
2Ki 17:40 however, but persisted in their f practices. H8037
Ezr 3:12 who had seen the f temple, wept aloud H8037
Job 8: 8 "Ask the f generation and find out what H8037
Job 42:12 part of Job's life more than the f part. H8040
Ps 77: 5 I thought about the f days, the H4946+7710
Ps 89:49 where is your f great love, which in H8037
Ecc 1:11 No one remembers the f generations, and H8037
Isa 33:18 In your thoughts you will ponder the f terror NDT
Isa 41:22 Tell us what the f things were, so that we H8037
Isa 42: 9 the f things have taken place, and H8037
Isa 43: 9 this and proclaimed to us the f things? H8037
Isa 43:18 "Forget the f things; do not dwell on the H8037
Isa 46: 9 Remember the f things, those of long ago; H8037
Isa 48: 3 I foretold the f things long ago, my mouth H8037
Isa 65: 7 laps the full payment for their f deeds." H8037
Isa 65:17 The f things will not be remembered, nor H8037
Eze 33:12 that person's f righteousness will count for NDT
Eze 33:12 that person's f wickedness will not bring NDT
Eze 38:17 the one I spoke of in f days by my servants H7719
Da 7: 7 It was different from all the f beasts, and A10621
Mic 4: 8 the f dominion will be restored to you H8037
Hag 2: 3 is left who saw this house in its f glory? H8037
Hag 2: 9 be greater than the glory of the f house, H8037
Mal 3: 4 the LORD, as in days gone by, as in f years. H7719
Mt 23:23 the latter, without neglecting the f. G2797S
Lk 11:42 the latter without leaving the f undone. G2797S
Ac 1: 1 In my f book, Theophilus, I wrote about G4755
Eph 4:22 with regard to your f way of life, to put off G4728
Php 1:17 The f preach Christ out of selfish G3836+1254
Heb 7:18 The f regulation is set aside because it G4575

FORMERLY (16) [FORMER]

Jos 8:33 the LORD had f commanded H928+2021+8037
Jos 15:15 in Debir (f called Kiriath Sepher). H4200+7156
Jdg 1:10 in Hebron (f called Kiriath Arba H4200+7156
Jdg 1:11 in Debir (f called Kiriath Sepher). H4200+7156
Jdg 1:23 to spy out Bethel (f called Luz), H4200+7156
1Sa 9: 9 F in Israel, if someone went to H4200+7156
1Sa 10:11 who had f known him saw H4946+919+8997
1Ch 4:40 Some Hamites had lived there f. H4200+7156
Ne 13: 5 a large room f used to store the H4200+7156
Eze 33:12 to live even though they were f righteous. NDT
Jn 9: 8 those who had f seen him begging G3836+4728
Gal 1:23 "The man who f persecuted us is now G4537
Gal 4: 8 F, when you did not know God, you were G5538

Eph 2:11 remember that f you who are Gentiles by G4537
Phm 11 F he was useless to you, but now he has G4537
Heb 4: 6 since those who f had the good news G4728

FORMING (3) [FORM]

Isa 30: 1 not mine, f an alliance, but not by H5818+5011
Eze 41: 8 f the foundation of the side rooms. NDT
Zec 14: 4 two from east to west, f a great valley, with NDT

FORMLESS (2)

Ge 1: 2 Now the earth was f and empty, darkness H9332
Jer 4:23 and it was f and empty; and at the H9332

FORMS (9) [FORM]

Ge 41:32 given to Pharaoh *in two* f is that the H7193
Lev 26:30 dead bodies on the lifeless f *of* your idols, H7007
Ps 33:15 he *who* f the hearts of all, who considers H3670
Ps 49:14 Their f will decay in the grave, far from H7451
SS 2:13 The fig tree f its early fruit; the H2845
Jer 16:18 my land with the lifeless f *of* their vile H5577
Am 4:13 *He who* f the mountains, who creates the H3670
Zec 12: 1 and *who* f the human spirit within a H3670
1Pe 4:10 stewards of God's grace *in* its various f. G4476

FORMULA (2)

Ex 30:32 not make any other oil using the same f. H5504
Ex 30:37 any incense with this f for yourselves; H5504

FORNICATION, FORNICATIONS (KJV)

ADULTERIES, ADULTERY, FAVORS, ILLEGITIMATE, PROMISCUITY, PROSTITUTE, PROSTITUTION, SEXUAL IMMORALITY, SEXUAL SIN

FORSAKE (44) [FORSAKEN, FORSAKES, FORSAKING, FORSOOK]

Dt 31: 6 he will never leave you nor f you. H6440
Dt 31: 8 he will never leave you nor f you. H6440
Dt 31:16 *They will* f me and break the covenant I H6440
Dt 31:17 will become angry with them and f them; H6440
Jos 1: 5 with you; I will never leave you nor f you. H6440
Jos 24:16 "Far be it from us *to* f the LORD to serve H6440
Jos 24:20 If *you* f the LORD and serve foreign gods, he H6440
1Ki 8:57 ancestors; may he never leave us nor f us. H5759
2Ki 21:14 *I will* f the remnant of my inheritance and H5759
1Ch 28: 9 but if *you* f him, he will reject H6440
1Ch 28:20 will not fail you or f you until all the work H6440
2Ch 7:19 if you turn away and f the decrees and H6440
2Ch 15: 2 found by you, but if *you* f him, he will H6440
2Ch 15: 2 but if you forsake him, *he will* f you. H6440
Ezr 8:22 his great anger is against all *who* f him." H6440
Ps 27: 9 Do not reject me or f me, God my Savior. H6440
Ps 27:10 Though my father and mother f me, the H6440
Ps 37:28 the just and *will* not f his faithful ones H6440
Ps 38:21 *do* not f me; do not be far from me H6440
Ps 71: 9 *do* not f me when my strength is gone. H6440
Ps 71:18 I am old and gray, *do* not f me, my God, H6440
Ps 89:30 "If his sons f my law and do not follow my H6440
Ps 94:14 his people; *he will* never f his inheritance. H6440
Ps 119: 8 obey your decrees; *do* not utterly f me. H6440
Pr 1: 8 instruction and *do* not f your mother's H5759
Pr 4: 2 sound learning, so *do* not f my teaching. H6440
Pr 4: 6 *Do* not f wisdom, and she will protect you H6440
Pr 6:20 command and *do* not f your mother's H5759
Pr 27:10 *Do* not f your friend or a friend of your H6440
Pr 28: 4 *Those who* f instruction praise the wicked H6440
Isa 1:28 and *those who* f the LORD will perish. H6440
Isa 41:17 *I*, the God of Israel, *will* not f them. H6440
Isa 42:16 are the things I will do; *I will* not f them. H6440
Isa 55: 7 *Let* the wicked f their ways and the H6440
Isa 65:11 "But as for you *who* f the LORD and forget H6440
Jer 2:19 it is for you *when* you f the LORD your God H6440
Jer 12: 7 "*I will* f my house, abandon my H6440
Jer 14: 9 and we bear your name; *do* not f us! H5663
Jer 17:13 all *who* f you will be put to shame. H6440
Jer 23:33 'What message? *I will* f you, declares the H5759
La 5:20 Why *do you* f us so long? H6440
Eze 20: 8 eyes on, nor *did they* f the idols of Egypt. H6440
Da 11:30 show favor to *those who* f the holy H6440
Heb 13: 5 "Never will I leave you; never *will I* f you." G1593

FORSAKEN (41) [FORSAKE]

Jdg 10:13 But you *have* f me and served other gods H6440
1Sa 12:10 *we have* f the LORD and served the Baals H6440
1Ki 9: 9 'Because *they have* f the LORD their God H6440
1Ki 11:33 do this because *they have* f me and H6440
2Ki 22:17 Because *they have* f me and burned H6440
2Ch 7:22 answer, 'Because *they have* f the LORD, the H6440
2Ch 13:10 LORD is our God, and *we have* not f him. H6440
2Ch 13:11 of the LORD our God. But you *have* f him. H6440
2Ch 21:10 because Jehoram *had* f the LORD, the God H6440
2Ch 24:20 Because *you have* f the LORD, he has H6440
2Ch 24:20 you have forsaken the LORD, *he has* f you. H6440
2Ch 24:24 Because Judah *had* f the LORD, the God of H6440
2Ch 28: 6 because Judah *had* f the LORD, the God H6440
2Ch 34:25 Because *they have* f me and burned H6440
Ezr 9: 9 our God *has* not f us in our bondage. H6440
Ezr 9:10 For *we have* f the commands H6440
Ps 9:10 for *you*, LORD, *have* never f those who seek H6440
Ps 22: 1 my God, why *have you* f me? Why are you H6440
Ps 37:25 seen the righteous f or their children H6440
Ps 71:11 They say, "God *has* f him; pursue him H6440
Ps 119:53 of the wicked, *who have* f your law. H6440
Ps 119:87 the earth, but I *have* not f your precepts. H6440
Isa 1: 4 *They have* f the LORD; they have spurned H6440
Isa 6:12 far away and the land is utterly f. H6440
Isa 27:10 settlement, f like the wilderness H6440
Isa 49:14 "The LORD *has* f me, the Lord has H6440
Isa 58: 2 is right and *has* not f the commands of H6440
Isa 60:15 "Although you have been f and hated H6440
Jer 2:13 *They have* f me, the spring of living water H6440
Jer 5: 7 Your children *have* f me and sworn by H6440
Jer 5:19 'As *you have* f me and served foreign H6440
Jer 9:13 "It is because they *have* f my law, which I H6440
Jer 17:13 in the dust because *they have* f the LORD, H6440
Jer 19: 4 For *they have* f me and made this a place H6440
Jer 22: 9 'Because *they have* f the covenant of the H6440
Jer 51: 5 Judah have not been f by their God, H527
Eze 8:12 does not see us; the LORD *has* f the land. H6440
Eze 9: 9 'The LORD *has* f the land; the LORD H6440
Mt 27:46 "My God, my God, why *have you* f me?" G1593
Mk 15:34 "My God, my God, why *have you* f me?" G1593
Rev 2: 4 *You have* f the love you had at first. G918

FORSAKES (1) [FORSAKE]

Job 6:14 kindness from a friend f the fear of the H6440

FORSAKING (6) [FORSAKE]

Dt 28:20 of the evil you have done *in* f him. H6440
Jdg 10:10 f our God and serving the Baals. H6440
1Sa 8: 8 until this day, f me and serving other gods H6440
Isa 57: 8 F me, you uncovered your bed, you H4946+907
Jer 1:16 because of their wickedness *in* f me, H6440
Jer 2:17 this on yourselves *by* f the LORD your God H6440

FORSOOK (8) [FORSAKE]

Jdg 2:12 *They* f the LORD, the God of their ancestors H6440
Jdg 2:13 because *they* f him and served Baal and H6440
Jdg 10: 6 the Israelites f the LORD and no longer H6440
2Ki 17:16 *They* f all the commands of the LORD their H6440
2Ki 21:22 *He* f the LORD, the God of his ancestors H6440
2Ch 29: 6 in the eyes of the LORD our God and f him. H6440
Jer 16:11 'It is because your ancestors f me,' H6440
Jer 16:11 *They* f me and did not keep my law. H6440

FORTH (59)

Ge 3:24 sword flashing back and f to guard the H2200
Ge 4: 1 help of the LORD *I have* brought f a man." H7865
Ge 7:11 all the springs of the great deep burst f, H1324
Ge 8: 7 kept flying back and f until the water had H3655
Ex 9:24 lightning flashed back and f. H4374+928+9348
Ex 32:27 Go back and f through the camp from one H6296
Dt 33: 2 from Seir; *he* shone f from Mount Paran. H3649
Dt 33:14 the best the sun brings f and the finest H9311
1Sa 17:15 David went back and f from Saul to H2143
2Sa 22:13 of his presence bolts of lightning blazed f. H1277
2Ki 4:35 walked back and f in the room H285+2178+2256+285+2178
Est 2:11 Every day he walked back and f near the H2143
Job 1: 7 the earth, going back and f on it. H2143
Job 2: 2 the earth, going back and f on it. H2143
Job 8:10 *Will they* not bring f words from their H3655
Job 14: 9 it will bud and put f shoots like a plant. H6913
Job 15: 7 Were *you* brought f before the hills? H2655
Job 21:11 *They* send f their children as a flock; their H8938
Job 23:10 he has tested me, *I will* come f as gold. H3655
Job 24:14 in the night steals f like a thief. H2118
Job 38: 8 doors when it burst f from the womb, H3655
Job 38:32 *Can you* bring f the constellations in their H3655
Job 39: 3 They crouch down and bring f their young H7114
Ps 19: 2 Day after day *they* pour f speech; night H5580
Ps 45: 4 In your majesty ride f victoriously in the H8206
Ps 50: 2 From Zion, perfect in beauty, God shines f. H3649
Ps 57: 3 God sends f his love and his faithfulness. H8938
Ps 65: 8 evening fades, *you* call f songs of joy. H8264
Ps 71: 6 you brought me f from my mother's womb. H1602
Ps 77:17 thunder; your arrows flashed back and f. H2143
Ps 80: 1 enthroned between the cherubim, shine f H3649
Ps 85:11 Faithfulness springs f from the earth, and H7541
Ps 90: 2 were born or *you* brought f the whole H2655
Ps 94: 1 O God who avenges, shine f. H3649
Ps 104:14 cultivate—bringing f food from the earth: H3655
Ps 144: 6 Send f lightning and scatter the H1397+1398
Pr 8:22 "The LORD brought me f as the first of his H7865
Isa 35: 6 Water *will* gush f in the wilderness and H1324
Isa 40:26 one by one and calls f each of them by H7924
Isa 41: 4 calling f the generations from the H7924
Isa 41:21 says the LORD. "Set f your arguments," H5602
Isa 42: 3 In faithfulness *he will* bring f justice; H3655
Isa 55:12 will go out in joy and be led f in peace; H3297
Isa 58: 8 Then your light *will* break f like the dawn H1324
Isa 65: 9 *I will* bring f descendants from Jacob, and H3655
Isa 66: 8 a nation be brought f in a moment? H3528
Eze 1:13 Fire moved back and f among the H2143
Eze 1:14 The creatures sped back and f like flashes H8351
Eze 7:10 Doom *has* burst f, the rod has budded H3655
Eze 13:11 and violent winds *will* burst f. H1324
Eze 17: 2 set f an allegory and tell it to the H2554
Eze 37: 2 He led me back and f among them H6017+6017
Hos 6: 5 then my judgments go f like the sun. H3655
Hos 10: 1 *he* brought f fruit for himself. H8751
Na 1:11 *has one* come f who plots evil against the H3655
Na 2: 4 rushing back and f through the squares. H9212
Mt 21:16 infants *you*, Lord, *have* called f *your* G2936
2Co 4: 2 *by* setting f the truth plainly we commend G5748
Eph 4:14 tossed back and f by the waves, and G3115

FORTIETH (3) [FORTY]

Nu 33:38 the fifth month of the f year after the H752
Dt 1: 3 In the f year, on the first day of the H752
1Ch 26:31 In the f year of David's reign a search was H752

FORTIFICATIONS (1) [FORTRESS]

2Sa 20:15 the city, and it stood against the outer f. H2658

FORTIFIED (64) [FORTRESS]

Nu 13:19 do they live in? Are they unwalled or f? H4448
Nu 13:28 the cities are f and very large. H1290
Nu 21:24 Ammonites, because their border was f. H6434
Nu 32:17 women and children will live in f cities, H4448
Nu 32:36 Beth Nimrah and Beth Haran as f cities H4448
Dt 3: 5 All these cities were f with high walls and H1290
Dt 28:52 land until the high f walls in which you H1290
Jos 10:20 survivors managed to reach their f cities. H4448
Jos 14:12 there and their cities were large and f, H1290
Jos 19:29 Ramah and went to the f city of Tyre, H4448
Jos 19:35 The f towns were Ziddim, Zer, Hammath H4448
1Sa 6:18 the f towns with their country villages. H4448
2Sa 20: 6 he will find f cities and escape from us." H1290
1Ki 12:25 Then Jeroboam f Shechem in the hill H1215
1Ki 15:17 up against Judah and f Ramah to prevent H1215
1Ki 22:39 the cities *he* f, are they not written H1215
2Ki 3:19 will overthrow every f city and every major H4448
2Ki 8:12 "You will set fire to their f places, kill their H4448
2Ki 10: 2 chariots and horses, a f city and weapons. H4448
2Ki 17: 9 From watchtower to f city they built H4448
2Ki 18: 8 From watchtower to f city, he defeated the H4448
2Ki 18:13 attacked all the f cities of Judah and H1290
2Ki 19:25 that you have turned f cities into piles of H1290
2Ch 8: 5 Horon and Lower Beth Horon as f cities, H5190
2Ch 11:10 These were f cities in Judah and H5193
2Ch 11:23 Benjamin, and to all the f cities. H5193
2Ch 12: 4 he captured the f cities of Judah and came H5193
2Ch 14: 6 He built up the f cities of Judah, since the H5193
2Ch 16: 1 up against Judah and f Ramah to prevent H1215
2Ch 17: 2 troops in all the f cities of Judah and put H1290
2Ch 17:19 he stationed in the f cities throughout H4448
2Ch 19: 5 the land, in each of the f cities of Judah. H1290
2Ch 21: 3 of value, as well as f cities in Judah, but H5193
2Ch 26: 9 at the angle of the wall, and *he* f them. H2616
2Ch 32: 1 He laid siege to the f cities, thinking to H1290
2Ch 33:14 commanders in all the f cities in Judah. H1290
Ne 9:25 They captured f cities and fertile land H1290
Ps 60: 9 Who will bring me to the f city? Who will H5190
Ps 108:10 Who will bring me to the f city? Who will H4448
Pr 10:15 The wealth of the rich is their f city, but H6437
Pr 18:10 The name of the LORD is a f tower; the H6437
Pr 18:11 The wealth of the rich is their f city; they H6437
Pr 18:19 wronged is more unyielding than a f city; H6437
Isa 2:15 every lofty tower and every f wall, H1290
Isa 17: 3 The f city will disappear from Ephraim H4448
Isa 25: 2 a heap of rubble, the f town a ruin, the H1290
Isa 25:12 bring down your high f walls and lay them H4448
Isa 27:10 The f city stands desolate, an abandoned H1290
Isa 36: 1 attacked all the f cities of Judah and H1290
Isa 37:26 that you have turned f cities into piles of H1290
Jer 1:18 Today I have made you a f city, an iron H4448
Jer 4: 5 Let us flee to the f cities!' H4448
Jer 5:17 they will destroy the f cities in which you H4448
Jer 8:14 Let us flee to the f cities and perish there H4448
Jer 15:20 to this people, a f wall of bronze; they H1290
Jer 34: 7 These were the only f cities left in Judah. H4448
Jer 48:18 up against you and ruin your f cities. H4448
Eze 21:20 another against Judah and f Jerusalem. H1290
Eze 36:35 destroyed, are now f and inhabited." H1290
Da 11:15 up siege ramps and will capture a f city. H4448
Hos 8:14 built palaces; Judah has f many towns. H1290
Am 5: 9 stronghold and brings the f city to ruin. H4448
Hab 1:10 They laugh at all f cities; by building H4448
Zep 1:16 cry against the f cities and against the H1290

FORTIFIES (1) [FORTRESS]

Jer 51:53 to the heavens and f her lofty stronghold, H1307

FORTRESS (36) [FORTIFICATIONS, FORTIFIED, FORTIFIES, FORTRESSES, FORTS]

2Sa 5: 7 David captured the f *of* Zion—which is the H5181
2Sa 5: 9 up residence in the f and called it the City H5181
2Sa 22: 2 LORD is my rock, my f and my deliverer; H5181
2Sa 24: 7 they went toward the f *of* Tyre and all the H4448
1Ch 11: 5 David captured the f *of* Zion—which is the H5181
1Ch 11: 7 David then took up residence in the f, and H5171
Ps 18: 2 LORD is my rock, my f and my deliverer; H5181
Ps 28: 8 a f *of* salvation for his anointed one. H5057
Ps 31: 2 of refuge, a strong f to save me. H1074+5181
Ps 31: 3 Since you are my rock and my f, for the H5181
Ps 46: 7 is with us; the God of Jacob is our f. H5369
Ps 46:11 is with us; the God of Jacob is our f. H5369
Ps 48: 3 he has shown himself to be her f. H5369
Ps 59: 1 *be* my f against those who are attacking H8435
Ps 59: 9 I watch for you; you, God, are my f, H5369
Ps 59:16 for you are my f, my refuge in times H5369
Ps 59:17 are my f, my God on whom I can rely H5369
Ps 62: 2 my salvation; he is my f, I will never be H5369
Ps 62: 6 salvation; he is my f, I will not be shaken. H5369
Ps 71: 3 to save me, for you are my rock and my f. H5181
Ps 91: 2 "He is my refuge and my f, my God, H5181
Ps 94:22 But the LORD has become my f, and my H5369
Ps 144: 2 He is my loving God and my f, my H5181

Pr 14:26 Whoever fears the LORD has a secure **f** H6437
Isa 17:10 have not remembered the Rock, your **f**. H5057
Isa 23: 4 and you **f** *of* the sea, for the sea H5057
Isa 23:14 you ships of Tarshish; your **f** is destroyed! H5057
Isa 29: 7 that attack her and her **f** and besiege her H5183
Isa 32:14 The **f** will be abandoned, the noisy city H810
Isa 33:16 whose refuge will be the mountain **f**. H5171
Jer 16:19 my strength and my **f**, my refuge in time H5057
Da 11: 7 of the king of the North and enter his **f**; H5057
Da 11:10 flood and carry the battle as far as his **f**. H5057
Da 11:31 the temple **f** and will abolish the H5057
Na 2: 1 Guard the **f**, watch the road, brace H5193
Zec 9:12 Return to your **f**, you prisoners of hope H1315

FORTRESSES (26) [FORTRESS]

Isa 23:11 Phoenicia that her **f** be destroyed. H5058
Isa 23:13 they stripped its **f** bare and turned it into a H810
Jer 6: 5 let us attack at night and destroy her **f**!" H810
Jer 9:21 our windows and has entered our **f**; H810
Jer 17:27 gates of Jerusalem that will consume her **f**. H810
Jer 49:27 it will consume the **f** *of* Ben-Hadad." H810
Da 11:19 back toward the **f** *of* his own country but H5057
Da 11:24 He will plot the overthrow of **f**—but only H4448
Da 11:38 he will honor a god of **f**; a god unknown H5057
Da 11:39 attack the **mightiest f** with the help H4448+5057
Hos 8:14 fire on their cities that will consume their **f**." H810
Hos 10:14 so that all your **f** will be devastated—as H4448
Am 1: 4 that will consume the **f** *of* Ben-Hadad. H810
Am 1: 7 the walls of Gaza that will consume her **f**. H810
Am 1:10 the walls of Tyre that will consume her **f**." H810
Am 1:12 Teman that will consume the **f** *of* Bozrah." H810
Am 1:14 will consume her **f** amid war cries on the H810
Am 2: 2 on Moab that will consume the **f** *of* Kerioth. H810
Am 2: 5 that will consume the **f** *of* Jerusalem." H810
Am 3: 9 Proclaim to the **f** of Ashdod and to the H810
Am 3: 9 fortresses of Ashdod and to the **f** of Egypt: H810
Am 3:10 "who store up in their **f** what they have H810
Am 3:11 down your strongholds and plunder your **f**." H810
Am 6: 8 "I abhor the pride of Jacob and detest his **f** H810
Mic 5: 5 invade our land and march through our **f**. H810
Na 3:12 All your **f** are like fig trees with their first H4448

FORTS (2) [FORTRESS]

2Ch 17:12 he built **f** and store cities in Judah H1072
2Ch 27: 4 country of Judah and **f** and towers in the H1072

FORTUNATE (1) [FORTUNE]

Ac 26: 2 I consider myself **f** to stand before you *G3421*

FORTUNATUS (1)

1Co 16:17 when Stephanas, **F** and Achaicus arrived *G5847*

FORTUNE (4) [FORTUNATE, FORTUNE-TELLING, FORTUNES]

Ge 30:11 Leah said, "What **good f!**" So she named H1513
Job 31:25 great wealth, the **f** my hands had gained, H3888
Pr 21: 6 A **f** made by a lying tongue is a fleeting H238
Isa 65:11 who spread a table for **F** and fill bowls of H1513

FORTUNE-TELLING (1) [FORTUNE]

Ac 16:16 a great deal of money for her owners *by* **f**. *G3446*

FORTUNES (20) [FORTUNE]

Dt 30: 3 will restore your **f** and have compassion H8654
Job 42:10 LORD restored his **f** and gave him twice as H8654
Ps 85: 1 to your land; you restored the **f** *of* Jacob. H8669
Ps 126: 1 When the LORD restored the **f** *of* Zion, we H8669
Ps 126: 4 Restore our **f**, LORD, like streams in the H8669
Jer 30:18 " 'I will restore the **f** *of* Jacob's tents and H8654
Jer 32:44 because I will restore their **f**, declares the H8654
Jer 33:11 I will restore the **f** *of* the land as they were H8654
Jer 33:26 I will restore their **f** and have compassion H8654
Jer 48:47 I will restore the **f** *of* Moab in days to H8654
Jer 49: 6 I will restore the **f** *of* the Ammonites," H8654
Jer 49:39 I will restore the **f** *of* Elam in days to come H8654
Eze 16:53 I will restore the **f** *of* Sodom and her H8669
Eze 16:53 daughters, and your **f** along with them, H8669
Eze 39:25 now restore the **f** *of* Jacob and will have H8654
Hos 6:11 I would restore the **f** *of* my people, H8654
Joel 3: 1 when I restore the **f** *of* Judah and H8654
Mic 3:11 and her prophets **tell f** for money. H7876
Zep 2: 7 will care for them; he will restore their **f**. H8654
Zep 3:20 when I restore your **f** before your very eyes H8654

FORTY (96) [FORTIETH, 40]

Ge 7: 4 rain on the earth for **f** days and forty nights, H752
Ge 7: 4 rain on the earth for forty days and **f** nights, H752
Ge 7:12 fell on the earth **f** days and forty nights. H752
Ge 7:12 fell on the earth forty days and **f** nights. H752
Ge 7:17 For **f** days the flood kept coming on the H752
Ge 8: 6 After **f** days Noah opened a window he H752
Ge 18:29 "What if only **f** are found there? H752
Ge 18:29 He said, "For the sake of **f**, I will not do it." H752
Ge 25:20 Isaac was **f** years old when he married H752
Ge 26:34 When Esau was **f** years old, he married H752
Ge 32:15 with their young, **f** cows and ten bulls, and H752
Ge 50: 3 taking a full **f** days, for that was the time H752
Ex 16:35 The Israelites ate manna **f** years, until they H752
Ex 24:18 on the mountain **f** days and forty nights. H752
Ex 24:18 on the mountain forty days and **f** nights. H752
Ex 26:19 make **f** silver bases to go under them H752
Ex 26:21 **f** silver bases—two under each frame. H752
Ex 34:28 there with the LORD **f** days and forty nights H752
Ex 34:28 LORD forty days and **f** nights without eating H752
Ex 36:24 made **f** silver bases to go under them H752
Ex 36:26 **f** silver bases—two under each frame. H752
Nu 13:25 At the end of **f** days they returned from H752
Nu 14:33 children will be shepherds here for **f** years, H752
Nu 14:34 For **f** years—one year for each of the forty H752
Nu 14:34 year for each of the **f** days you explored the H752
Nu 32:13 them wander in the wilderness **f** years, H752
Dt 2: 7 These **f** years the LORD your God has been H752
Dt 8: 2 all the way in the wilderness these **f** years, H752
Dt 8: 4 your feet did not swell during these **f** years. H752
Dt 9: 9 on the mountain **f** days and forty nights; H752
Dt 9: 9 on the mountain forty days and **f** nights; H752
Dt 9:11 At the end of the **f** days and forty nights H752
Dt 9:11 At the end of the forty days and **f** nights H752
Dt 9:18 before the LORD for **f** days and forty nights; H752
Dt 9:18 before the LORD for forty days and **f** nights; H752
Dt 9:25 the LORD those **f** days and forty nights H752
Dt 9:25 those forty days and **f** nights because the H752
Dt 10:10 on the mountain **f** days and forty nights, H752
Dt 10:10 on the mountain forty days and **f** nights, H752
Dt 25: 3 judge must not impose more than **f** lashes. H752
Dt 29: 5 "During the **f** years that I led you through H752
Jos 4:13 About **f** thousand armed for battle crossed H752
Jos 5: 6 in the wilderness **f** years until all the men H752
Jos 14: 7 I was **f** years old when Moses the servant of H752
Jdg 3:11 So the land had peace for **f** years, until H752
Jdg 5: 8 was seen among **f** thousand in Israel. H752
Jdg 5:31 Then the land had peace **f** years. H752
Jdg 8:28 lifetime, the land had peace **f** years. H752
Jdg 12:14 He had **f** sons and thirty grandsons, who H752
Jdg 13: 1 into the hands of the Philistines for **f** years. H752
1Sa 4:18 he was heavy. He had led Israel **f** years. H752
1Sa 17:16 For **f** days the Philistine came forward every H752
2Sa 2:10 son of Saul was **f** years old when he H752
2Sa 5: 4 he became king, and he reigned **f** years. H752
2Sa 10:18 their charioteers and **f** thousand of their H752
1Ki 2:11 He had reigned **f** years over Israel—seven H752
1Ki 6:17 hall in front of this room was **f** cubits long. H752
1Ki 7:38 each holding **f** baths and measuring four H752
1Ki 11:42 reigned in Jerusalem over all Israel **f** years. H752
1Ki 19: 8 he traveled **f** days and forty nights until he H752
1Ki 19: 8 forty days and **f** nights until he reached H752
2Ki 8: 9 with him as a gift **f** camel-loads of all the H752
2Ki 12: 1 and he reigned in Jerusalem **f** years. H752
1Ch 19:18 their charioteers and **f** thousand of their H752
1Ch 29:27 He ruled over Israel **f** years—seven in H752
2Ch 9:30 reigned in Jerusalem over all Israel **f** years. H752
2Ch 24: 1 and he reigned in Jerusalem **f** years. H752
Ne 5:15 the people and took **f** shekels of silver from H752
Ne 9:21 For **f** years you sustained them in the H752
Job 42:16 Job lived a hundred and **f** years; he saw his H752
Ps 95:10 For **f** years I was angry with that generation H752
Eze 29:11 through it; no one will live there for **f** years. H752
Eze 29:12 will lie desolate **f** years among ruined H752
Eze 29:13 At the end of **f** years I will gather the H752
Eze 41: 2 it was **f** cubits long and twenty cubits wide. H752
Eze 46:22 **f** cubits long and thirty cubits wide H752
Am 2:10 of Egypt and led you **f** years in the H752
Am 5:25 offerings **f** years in the wilderness, H752
Jnh 3: 4 "**F** more days and Nineveh will be H752
Mt 4: 2 After fasting **f** days and forty nights, he *G5477*
Mt 4: 2 After fasting forty days and **f** nights, he *G5477*
Mk 1:13 he was in the wilderness **f** days, being *G5477*
Lk 4: 2 where for **f** days he was tempted by the *G5477*
Ac 1: 3 over a period of **f** days and spoke about *G5477*
Ac 4:22 miraculously healed was over **f** years old. *G5477*
Ac 7:23 "When Moses was **f years** old, he decided *G5478*
Ac 7:30 "After **f** years had passed, an angel *G5477*
Ac 7:36 at the Red Sea and for **f** years in the *G5477*
Ac 7:42 offerings **f** years in the wilderness, *G5477*
Ac 13:18 *for* about **f years** he endured their *G5478+5989*
Ac 13:21 the tribe of Benjamin, who ruled **f** years. *G5477*
Ac 23:13 More *than* **f** *men* were involved in this plot. *G5477*
Ac 23:21 because more *than* **f** of them are waiting *G5477*
2Co 11:24 from the Jews the **f** *lashes* minus one. *G5477*
Heb 3: 9 though for **f** years they saw what I did. *G5477*
Heb 3:17 And with whom was he angry for **f** years *G5477*

FORTY-EIGHT (2)

Nu 35: 7 must give the Levites **f** towns, H752+2256+9046
Jos 21:41 by the Israelites were **f** in all, H752+2256+9046

FORTY-FIRST (1)

2Ch 16:13 Then in the **f** year of his reign H752+2256+285

FORTY-FIVE (3)

Ge 18:28 "If I find **f** there," he said, "I H752+2256+2822
Jos 14:10 me alive for **f** years since the H752+2256+2822
1Ki 7: 3 the columns—**f** beams H752+2256+2822

FORTY-NINE (1)

Lev 25: 8 amount to a period of **f** years. H752+2256+9596

FORTY-ONE (4)

1Ki 14:21 He was **f** years old when he H752+2256+285
1Ki 15:10 reigned in Jerusalem **f** years. H752+2256+285
2Ki 14:23 and he reigned **f** years. H752+2256+285
2Ch 12:13 He was **f** years old when he H752+2256+285

FORTY-SEVEN (1)

Ge 47:28 his life were a hundred and **f**. H752+2256+8679

FORTY-SIX (1)

Jn 2:20 "It has taken **f** years to build *G5477+2779+1971*

FORTY-TWO (6) [42]

Nu 35: 6 give them **f** other towns. H752+2256+9109
Jdg 12: 6 **F** thousand Ephraimites were H752+2256+9109
1Sa 13: 1 he reigned over Israel **f** years. H752+2256+9109
2Ki 2:24 and mauled **f** of the boys. H752+2256+9109
2Ki 10:14 well of Beth Eked—**f** of them. H752+2256+9109
Rev 13: 5 its authority for **f** months. *G5477+2779+1545*

FORUM (1)

Ac 28:15 traveled as far as the **F** of Appius and the *G5842*

FORWARD (57)

Ge 19: 9 on Lot and **moved f** to break down the H5602
Lev 8: 6 Moses **brought** Aaron and his sons **f** and H7928
Lev 8:13 Then he **brought** Aaron's sons **f**, put tunics H7928
Lev 8:24 Moses also **brought** Aaron's sons **f** and put H7928
Lev 16:20 the altar, *he shall* **bring f** the live goat. H7928
Nu 8: 3 so that they **faced f** *on* the H448+4578+7156
Nu 12: 5 When the two of them **stepped f**, H3655
Nu 27: 1 Hoglah, Milkah and Tirzah. *They* **came f** H7928
Dt 20: 2 the priest *shall* **come f** and address the H5602
Dt 21: 5 The Levitical priests *shall* **step f**, for the H5602
Jos 6: 8 the seven trumpets before the LORD **went f**, H6296
Jos 6:13 priests carrying the seven trumpets **went f**, H2143
Jos 7:14 LORD chooses *shall* **come f** clan by clan; H7928
Jos 7:14 LORD chooses *shall* **come f** family by H7928
Jos 7:14 LORD chooses *shall* **come f** man by man. H7928
Jos 7:16 Joshua **had** Israel **come f** by tribes, H7928
Jos 7:17 The clans of Judah **came f**, and the H7928
Jos 7:17 *He* **had** the clan of the Zerahites **come f** H7928
Jos 7:18 Joshua **had** his family **come f** man by man, H7928
Jos 8:19 quickly from their position and **rushed f**. H8132
Jos 10:24 So *they* **came f** and placed their feet on H7928
Jdg 8:21 So Gideon **stepped f** and killed them H7756
Jdg 9:44 with him **rushed f** to a position at H7320
1Sa 10:20 Samuel **had** all Israel **come f** by tribes, H7928
1Sa 10:21 Then *he* **brought f** the tribe of Benjamin H7928
1Sa 17:16 the Philistine **came f** every morning and H5602
1Sa 17:52 Israel and Judah **surged f** with a shout H7756
2Sa 20: 8 As he **stepped f**, it dropped out of its H3655
1Ki 1: 5 was Haggith, **put himself f** and said, "I H5951
1Ki 18:36 the prophet Elijah **stepped f** and prayed: H5602
1Ki 22:21 a spirit **came f**, stood before the H3655
2Ki 20: 9 *Shall* the shadow **go f** ten steps, or shall it H2143
2Ki 20:10 matter for the shadow to **go f** ten steps," H5742
2Ch 18:20 a spirit **came f**, stood before the H3655
Ps 35:11 Ruthless witnesses **come f**; they question H7756
Pr 18:17 someone **comes** *f* and cross-examines. AIT
Isa 41: 1 *Let them* **come f** and speak; let us meet H5602
Isa 41: 5 earth tremble. They approach and **come f**; H910
Isa 47:13 *Let* your astrologers **come f**, those H6641
Isa 63: 1 **striding f** in the greatness of his strength? H7579
Jer 7:24 They went backward and not **f**. H4200+7156
Jer 26:17 of the land **stepped f** and said to the H7756
Eze 39:22 From that day **f** the people of Israel will H2134
Da 3: 8 some astrologers **came f** and denounced A10638
Zec 5: 5 speaking to me **came f** and said to me, H3655
Mt 26:50 Then *the men* **stepped f**, seized Jesus *G4665*
Mt 26:60 *though* many false witnesses **came f**. *G4665*
Mt 26:60 came forward. Finally two **came f** *G4665*
Mk 3:10 with diseases *were* **pushing f** to touch him *G2158*
Lk 2:38 to all who *were* **looking f** to the *G4657*
Lk 13:12 saw her, *he* **called** her **f** and said to her *G4715*
Ac 5: 6 Then some young men **came f**, wrapped up *G482*
Heb 6: 1 about Christ and be taken **f** to maturity, *G2093*
Heb 11:10 For *he was* **looking f** to the city with *G1683*
2Pe 3:12 *as you* **look f** to the day of God and speed *G4659*
2Pe 3:13 his promise *we are* **looking f** to a new *G4659*
2Pe 3:14 *since you are* **looking f** to this *G4659*

FORWARDNESS (KJV) EARNESTNESS, ENTHUSIASM

FOSTER (3)

Pr 17: 9 *Whoever would* **f** love covers over an H1335
Pr 17:11 Evildoers **f** rebellion against God; the H1335
Isa 49:23 Kings will be your **f fathers**, and their H587

FOUGHT (44) [FIGHT]

Ex 17:10 So Joshua **f** the Amalekites as Moses had H4309
Nu 21:23 When he reached Jahaz, *he* **f** with Israel. H4309
Nu 21:26 who *had* **f** against the former king of H4309
Nu 31: 7 *They* **f** against Midian, as the LORD H7371
Nu 31:28 the soldiers who **f in** the battle, H3655+4200
Nu 31:36 share of those *who* **f in** the battle H3655+928
Jos 10:42 the LORD, the God of Israel, **f** for Israel. H4309
Jos 23: 3 it was the LORD your God who **f** for you. H4309
Jos 24: 8 *They* **f** against you, but I gave them into H4309
Jos 24:11 The citizens of Jericho **f** against you, as H4309
Jdg 1: 5 found Adoni-Bezek and **f** against him, H4309
Jdg 5:19 "Kings came, *they* **f**, the kings of Canaan H4309
Jdg 5:19 they fought, the kings of Canaan **f**. H4309
Jdg 5:20 From the heavens the stars **f**, from their H4309
Jdg 5:20 from their courses *they* **f** against Sisera. H4309
Jdg 9:17 that my father **f** for you and risked his H4309
Jdg 9:39 the citizens of Shechem and **f** Abimelek. H4309
Jdg 11:20 encamped at Jahaz and **f** with Israel. H4309
Jdg 12: 4 the men of Gilead and **f** against Ephraim. H4309
1Sa 4:10 So the Philistines **f**, and the Israelites H4309
1Sa 12: 9 the king of Moab, *who* **f** against them. H4309
1Sa 14:47 *he* **f** against their enemies on every side: H4309

1Sa 14:48 *He* **f** valiantly and defeated the H6913
1Sa 19: 8 David went out and **f** the Philistines. H4309
1Sa 23: 5 **f** the Philistines and carried off their H4309
1Sa 30:17 David **f** them from dusk until the evening H5782
1Sa 31: 1 Now the Philistines **f** against Israel; the H4309
2Sa 10:17 lines to meet David and **f** against him. H4309
2Sa 11:17 of the city came out and **f** against Joab, H4309
2Sa 12:26 Meanwhile Joab **f** against Rabbah of the H4309
2Sa 12:27 "*I have* **f** against Rabbah and taken its H4309
2Ki 3:23 "Those kings **must have f** and H2991+2991
2Ki 3:24 rose up and **f** them until they fled. H5782
1Ch 10: 1 Now the Philistines **f** against Israel; the H4309
1Ch 19:17 in battle, and *they* **f** against him. H4309
1Ch 22: 8 shed much blood and *have* **f** many wars. H6913
2Ch 20:29 heard how the LORD *had* **f** against the H4309
Ps 60: T When he **f** Aram Naharaim and Aram H5897
Isa 63:10 enemy and *he* himself **f** against them. H4309
Zec 14:12 all the nations that **f** against Jerusalem: H7371
1Co 15:32 If *I* **f wild beasts** in Ephesus with no more G2562
2Ti 4: 7 *I have* **f** the good fight, I have finished the G76
Rev 12: 7 his angels **f** against the dragon, G4482
Rev 12: 7 the dragon and his angels **f back**. G4482

FOUL, FOULED, FOULEDST (KJV) IMPURE, MUDDIED, MUDDYING, RED, STORMY, TRAMPLE

FOUND (335) [FIND]

Ge 2:20 But for Adam no suitable helper *was* **f**. H5162
Ge 4:15 so that no one *who* **f** him would kill him H5162
Ge 6: 8 But Noah **f** favor in the eyes of the LORD. H5162
Ge 7: 1 because I *have* **f** you H8011+4200+7156
Ge 9:24 from his wine and **f out** what his youngest H3359
Ge 11: 2 *they* **f** a plain in Shinar and settled there. H5162
Ge 16: 7 angel of the LORD **f** Hagar near a spring H5162
Ge 18: 3 He said, "If *I have* **f** favor in your eyes, my H5162
Ge 18:29 "What if only forty **are f** there? H5162
Ge 18:30 What if only thirty *can* **be f** there?" He H5162
Ge 18:31 what if only twenty *can* **be f** there? H5162
Ge 18:32 What if only ten *can* **be f** there?" He H5162
Ge 19:19 Your servant *has* **f** favor in your eyes, and H5162
Ge 24:30 out to the man and **f** him standing by the H2180
Ge 26:32 They said, "*We've* **f** water!" H5162
Ge 30:14 into the fields and **f** some mandrake H5162
Ge 30:27 said to him, "If *I have* **f** favor in your eyes H5162
Ge 31:33 the two female servants, but *he* **f** nothing. H5162
Ge 31:34 everything in the tent but **f** nothing. H5162
Ge 31:37 what *have you* **f** that belongs to your H5162
Ge 33:10 "If *I have* **f** favor in your eyes, accept this H5162
Ge 37:15 a man **f** him wandering around in the H5162
Ge 37:17 after his brothers and **f** them near Dothan. H5162
Ge 37:32 back to their father and said, "*We* **f** this. H5162
Ge 39: 4 Joseph **f** favor in his eyes and became his H5162
Ge 43:21 our sacks and each of us **f** his silver— H2180
Ge 44: 8 Canaan the silver *we* **f** inside the mouths H5162
Ge 44: 9 If any of your servants **is f** to have *it*, he H5162
Ge 44:10 Whoever **is f** to have *it* will become my H5162
Ge 44:12 And the cup **was f** in Benjamin's sack. H5162
Ge 44:16 the one who **was f** to have the cup." H5162
Ge 44:17 Only the man who **was f** to have the cup H5162
Ge 47:14 the money that *was to* **be f** in Egypt and H5162
Ge 47:29 said to him, "If *I have* **f** favor in your eyes H5162
Ge 50: 4 "If *I have* **f** favor in your eyes H5162
Ex 5:20 *they* **f** Moses and Aaron waiting to meet H7003
Ex 9: 7 investigated and **f** *that* not even one of H2180
Ex 12:19 days no yeast *is to* **be f** in your houses. H5162
Ex 16:27 seventh day to gather it, but *they* **f** none. H5162
Ex 22: 4 the stolen animal **is f** alive in their H5162+5162
Ex 22: 8 But if the thief is not **f**, the owner of the H5162
Ex 33:12 by name and *you have* **f** favor with me. H5162
Ex 34: 9 he said, "if *I have* **f** favor in your eyes H5162
Lev 6: 4 to them, or the lost property *they* **f**, H5162
Lev 7:24 The fat of an **animal f dead** or torn by wild H5577
Lev 10:16 the sin offering and **f** that it had been H2180
Lev 17:15 who eats **anything f dead** or torn by wild H5577
Lev 22: 8 He must not eat **anything f dead** or torn by H5577
Nu 11:15 kill me—if *I have* **f** favor in your eyes H5162
Nu 15:32 a man *was* **f** gathering wood on the H5162
Nu 15:33 Those *who* **f** him gathering wood brought H5162
Nu 23: 6 back to him and **f** him standing beside H2180
Nu 23:17 he went to him and **f** him standing beside H2180
Nu 32: 5 If *we have* **f** favor in your eyes," they said H5162
Dt 13:17 things *are to be* **f** in your hands. H1815
Dt 15: 9 against you, and you will be **f** guilty of sin. NDT
Dt 16: 4 *Let* no yeast **be f** in your possession in all H8011
Dt 17: 2 the LORD gives you **is f** doing evil in the H5162
Dt 18:10 *Let no one* **be f** among you who sacrifices H5162
Dt 21: 1 If *someone* **is f** slain, lying in a field in H5162
Dt 22:20 of the young woman's virginity *can* **be f**, H5162
Dt 22:22 If a man **is f** sleeping with another man's H5162
Dt 22:27 the man **f** the young woman out in the H5162
Dt 32:10 In a desert land *he* **f** him, in a barren and H5162
Jos 10:17 the five kings *had* **been f** hiding in the H5162
Jdg 1: 5 It was there that *they* **f** Adoni-Bezek and H5162
Jdg 3:24 the servants came and **f** the doors of the H8011
Jdg 6:17 replied, "If now *I have* **f** favor in your eyes H5162
Jdg 20:48 the animals and everything else they **f**. H5162
Jdg 21: 9 they **f** that none of the people of Jabesh H2180
Jdg 21:12 *They* **f** among the people living in Jabesh H5162
Ru 2:10 "Why *have I* **f** such favor in your eyes that H5162
1Sa 9: 2 man as could be **f** anywhere in H401+4946s
1Sa 9:20 not worry about them; *they have* **been f**. H5162
1Sa 10: 2 you set out to look for *have* **been f**. H5162
1Sa 10:14 "But when we saw they were not to be **f**, we NDT
1Sa 10:16 assured us that the donkeys *had* **been f**." H5162
1Sa 10:21 they looked for him, *he was* not *to* **be f**. H5162
1Sa 12: 5 that *you have* not **f** anything in my hand." H5162
1Sa 13:19 Not a blacksmith *could* **be f** in the whole H5162
1Sa 14:20 They **f** the Philistines in total confusion H2180
1Sa 20: 3 very well that *I have* **f** favor in your eyes, H5162
1Sa 20:29 If *I have* **f** favor in your eyes, let me get H5162
1Sa 25:28 no wrongdoing **will be f** in you as long H5162
1Sa 27: 5 to Achish, "If *I have* **f** favor in your eyes H5162
1Sa 29: 3 Saul until now, *I have* **f** no fault in him." H5162
1Sa 29: 6 to me until today, *I have* **f** no fault in you H5162
1Sa 29: 8 "What *have you* **f** against your servant H5162
1Sa 30: 3 they **f** it destroyed by fire and their wives H2180
1Sa 30: 6 But David **f strength** in the LORD his God H2616
1Sa 30:11 *They* **f** an Egyptian in a field and brought H5162
1Sa 31: 8 *they* **f** Saul and his three sons fallen on H5162
2Sa 2:30 nineteen of David's men **were f missing**. H7212
2Sa 7:27 So your servant *has* **f** courage to pray this H5162
2Sa 14:22 servant knows that *he has* **f** favor in your H5162
2Sa 17:12 we will attack him wherever *he may* **be f**, H5162
2Sa 17:20 The men searched but **f** no one, so they H5162
1Ki 1: 3 a beautiful young woman and **f** Abishag, H5162
1Ki 1:52 ground; but if evil **is f** in him, he will die." H5162
1Ki 13:14 *He* **f** him sitting under an oak tree and H5162
1Ki 13:28 Then he went out and **f** the body lying on H5162
1Ki 14:13 the God of Israel, *has* **f** anything good. H5162
1Ki 19:19 went from there and **f** Elisha son of H5162
1Ki 20:36 went away, a lion **f** him and killed him. H5162
1Ki 20:37 The prophet **f** another man and said H5162
1Ki 21:20 to Elijah, "So *you have* **f** me, my enemy!" H5162
1Ki 21:20 "*I have* **f** you," he answered, "because H5162
2Ki 4:39 to gather herbs and **f** a wild vine and H5162
2Ki 7:15 they **f** the whole road strewn with the H2180
2Ki 9: 5 he **f** the army officers sitting together. H2180
2Ki 9:35 to bury her, *they* **f** nothing except her skull H5162
2Ki 12: 5 whatever damage **is f** in the temple." H5162
2Ki 12:18 all the gold **f** in the treasuries of the H5162
2Ki 14:14 all the articles **f** *in* the temple of the H5162
2Ki 16: 8 the silver and gold **f** *in* the temple of the H5162
2Ki 18:15 the silver that **was f** *in* the temple of the H5162
2Ki 19: 8 he withdrew and **f** the king fighting H5162
2Ki 20:13 everything **f** among his treasures. H5162
2Ki 22: 8 "*I have* **f** the Book of the Law in the H5162
2Ki 22:13 is written in this book that *has* **been f**. H5162
2Ki 23: 2 which *had* **been f** in the temple of the H5162
2Ki 25:19 of the conscripts who **were f** in the city. H5162
1Ch 4:40 *They* **f** rich, good pasture, and the land H5162
1Ch 10: 8 *they* **f** Saul and his sons fallen on Mount H5162
1Ch 17:25 your servant *has* **f courage** to pray to you H5162
1Ch 20: 2 its weight *was* **f** to be a talent of gold H5162
1Ch 24: 4 of leaders **were f** *among* Eleazar's H5162
1Ch 26:31 the Hebronites **were f** at Jazer in Gilead. H5162
1Ch 28: 9 If you seek him, *he will* **be f** by you; but if H5162
2Ch 2:17 had taken; and *they* **were f** to be 153,600. H5162
2Ch 15: 2 If you seek him, *he will* **be f** by you, but if H5162
2Ch 15: 4 sought him, and *he* **was f** by them. H5162
2Ch 15:15 God eagerly, and *he* **was f** by them. H5162
2Ch 20:25 and *they* **f** among them a great amount of H5162
2Ch 21:17 off all the goods **f** in the king's palace, H5162
2Ch 22: 8 *he* **f** the officials of Judah and the sons of H5162
2Ch 25: 5 old or more and **f** that there were three H5162
2Ch 25:24 all the articles **f** in the temple of God H5162
2Ch 29:16 unclean that *they* **f** in the temple of the H5162
2Ch 34:14 Hilkiah the priest **f** the Book of the Law of H5162
2Ch 34:15 "*I have* **f** the Book of the Law in the H5162
2Ch 34:21 is written in this book that *has* **been f**. H5162
2Ch 34:30 which *had* **been f** in the temple of the H5162
2Ch 36: 8 he did and all that **was f** against him, H5162
Ezr 4:19 and *it was* **f** that this city has a long A10708
Ezr 6: 2 A scroll **was f** in the citadel of Ecbatana A10708
Ezr 8:15 the priests, *I* **f** no Levites there. H5162
Ne 2: 5 if your servant *has* **f favor** in his sight, H3512
Ne 7: 5 *I* **f** the genealogical record of those who H5162
Ne 7: 5 This is what *I* **f** written there: H5162
Ne 8:14 *They* **f** written in the Law, which the LORD H5162
Ne 9: 8 *You* **f** his heart faithful to you, and you H5162
Ne 13: 1 people and there *it* **was f** written that no H5162
Est 2:22 But Mordecai **f out** *about* the plot and told H3359
Est 2:23 report was investigated and **f to be true**, H5162
Est 6: 2 *It* **was f** recorded there that Mordecai had H5162
Est 7: 3 answered, "If *I have* **f** favor with you H5162
Job 9:29 Since I *am already* **f guilty**, why should I AIT
Job 12:12 Is not wisdom **f** among the aged? Does not NDT
Job 20: 8 no more *to be* **f**, banished like a H5162
Job 28:12 But where *can* wisdom **be f**? Where does H5162
Job 28:13 *it* cannot **be f** in the land of the living. H5162
Job 32: 3 because *they had* **f** no way to refute Job H5162
Job 32:13 Do not say, '*We have* **f** wisdom; let God H5162
Job 33:10 Yet God *has* **f** fault with me; he considers H5162
Job 33:24 to the pit; *I have* **f** a ransom for them H5162
Job 42:15 in all the land **were** *there* **f** women as H5162
Ps 10:15 *that would* not otherwise *be* **f out**. H5162
Ps 32: 6 faithful pray to you while you *may* **be f**; H5162
Ps 37:10 though you look for them, they will not be **f**. NDT
Ps 37:36 though I looked for him, *he could* not **be f**. H5162
Ps 69:20 was none, for comforters, but *I* **f** none. H5162
Ps 84: 3 Even the sparrow *has* **f** a home, and the H5162
Ps 89:20 *I have* **f** David my servant; with my sacred H5162
Ps 109: 7 he is tried, *let him be* **f** guilty, and may H3655
Ps 109:17 *He* **f** no **pleasure** in blessing—may it be H2911
Pr 7:15 meet you; I looked for you and *have* **f** you! H5162
Pr 8: 9 upright to *those who have* **f** knowledge. H5162
Pr 10: 9 whoever takes crooked paths *will* **be f out**. H3359
Pr 10:13 Wisdom **is f** on the lips of the discerning H5162
Pr 13:10 wisdom is **f** in those who take advice. NDT
Pr 14: 9 but goodwill is **f** among the upright. NDT
Pr 19: 7 with pleading, they are **nowhere** *to be* **f**. AIT
Pr 30:28 with the hand, yet it is **f** in kings' palaces. NDT
Ecc 7:28 *I* **f** one upright man among a thousand H5162
Ecc 7:29 This only *have I* **f**: God created mankind H5162
SS 3: 3 The watchmen **f** me as they made their H5162
SS 3: 4 I passed them when *I* **f** the one my heart H5162
SS 5: 7 The watchmen **f** me as they made their H5162
SS 8: 1 if *I* **f** you outside, I would kiss you H5162
Isa 30:14 not a fragment *will* **be f** for taking coals H5162
Isa 35: 9 ravenous beast; *they will* not **be f** there. H5162
Isa 37: 8 he withdrew and **f** the king fighting H5162
Isa 39: 2 everything **f** among his treasures. H5162
Isa 51: 3 Joy and gladness *will* **be f** in her H5162
Isa 55: 6 Seek the LORD while he *may* **be f**; call on H5162
Isa 57:10 *You* **f** renewal of your strength, and so H5162
Isa 59:15 Truth is **nowhere to be f**, and whoever H6372
Isa 65: 1 *I* **was f** by those who did not seek me. H5162
Isa 65: 8 "As when juice **is** *still* **f** in a cluster of H5162
Jer 2:34 On your clothes *is* **f** the lifeblood of the H5162
Jer 29:14 *I will* **be f** by you," declares the LORD, "and H5162
Jer 40: 1 He *had* **f** Jeremiah bound in chains H4374
Jer 40: 2 the commander of the guard **f** Jeremiah, H4374
Jer 50: 7 Whoever **f** them devoured them; their H5162
Jer 50:20 of Judah, but none *will* **be f**, for I will H5162
Jer 50:24 *you* **were f** and captured because you H5162
Jer 52:25 the land, sixty of whom **were f** in the city. H5162
Eze 4:14 never eaten **anything f dead** or torn by H5577
Eze 16:37 with whom *you* **f pleasure**, those you H6844
Eze 22:30 not have to destroy it, but *I* **f** no one. H5162
Eze 26:21 but *you will* never again **be f**, declares H5162
Eze 28:15 were created till wickedness **was f** in you. H5162
Eze 44:31 animal, **f dead** or torn by wild animals. H5577
Da 1:19 with them, and he **f** none equal to Daniel H5162
Da 1:20 *he* **f** them ten times better than all the H5162
Da 2:25 "*I have* **f** a man among the exiles from A10708
Da 4:12 Under it the wild animals **f shelter**, and A10300
Da 5:11 of your father he **was f** to have insight A10708
Da 5:12 **was f** to have a keen mind and A10708
Da 5:27 weighed on the scales and **f** wanting. A10708
Da 6:11 as a group and **f** Daniel praying and A10708
Da 6:22 because I **was f** innocent in his sight. A10708
Da 6:23 no wound **was f** on him, because A10708
Da 12: 1 everyone whose name **is f** written in the H5162
Hos 9:10 "When *I* **f** Israel, it was like finding grapes H5162
Hos 12: 4 *He* **f** him at Bethel and talked with him H5162
Jnh 1: 3 where *he* **f** a ship bound for that port. H5162
Mic 1:13 the transgressions of Israel **were f** in you. H5162
Zep 3:13 tongue *will* not **be f** in their mouths. H5162
Zec 1:11 the earth and **f** the whole world at rest H2180
Mal 2: 6 mouth and nothing false **was f** on his lips. H5162
Mt 1:18 *she was* **f** to be pregnant through the Holy G2351
Mt 2: 7 and **f out** from them the **exact** time the G208
Mt 8:10 *I have* not **f** anyone in Israel with such G2351
Mt 13:44 *When* a man **f** it, he hid it again, and G2351
Mt 13:46 *When he* **f** one of great value, he went G2351
Mt 18:28 *he* **f** one of his fellow servants who owed G2351
Mt 20: 6 he went out and **f** still others standing G2351
Mt 21:19 he went up to it but **f** nothing on it except G2351
Mt 26:40 to his disciples and **f** them sleeping. G2351
Mt 26:43 he came back, *he* again **f** them sleeping G2351
Mk 1:37 and *when they* **f** him, they exclaimed G2351
Mk 6:38 *When they* **f out**, they said, "Five—and G1182
Mk 7:30 She went home and **f** her child lying on G2351
Mk 11: 4 They went and **f** a colt outside in the G2351
Mk 11:13 he reached it, *he* **f** nothing but leaves G2351
Mk 14:16 into the city and **f** things just as Jesus G2351
Mk 14:37 to his disciples and **f** them sleeping. G2351
Mk 14:40 he came back, *he* again **f** them sleeping G2351
Lk 1:30 Mary; *you have* **f** favor with God. G2351
Lk 2:16 So they hurried off and **f** Mary and Joseph G461
Lk 2:46 After three days *they* **f** him in the temple G2351
Lk 4:17 *he* **f** the place where it is written: G2351
Lk 7: 9 *I have* not **f** such great faith even in Israel." G2351
Lk 7:10 to the house and **f** the servant well. G2351
Lk 8:35 *they* **f** the man from whom the demons G2351
Lk 9:36 had spoken, *they* **f** that Jesus was alone. G2351
Lk 13: 7 fruit on this fig tree and haven't **f** any. G2351
Lk 15: 6 'Rejoice with me; *I have* **f** my lost sheep. G2351
Lk 15: 9 'Rejoice with me; *I have* **f** my lost coin. G2351
Lk 15:24 is alive again; he was lost and *is* **f**. G2351
Lk 15:32 is alive again; he was lost and *is* **f**. G2351
Lk 19:32 sent ahead went and **f** it just as he had G2351
Lk 22:13 They left and **f** things just as Jesus had G2351
Lk 22:45 to the disciples, *he* **f** them asleep G2351
Lk 23: 2 "*We have* **f** this man subverting our G2351
Lk 23:14 your presence and *have* **f** no basis for your G2351
Lk 23:22 *I have* **f** in him no grounds for the death G2351
Lk 24: 2 *They* **f** the stone rolled away from the G2351
Lk 24:24 to the tomb and **f** it just as the women G2351
Lk 24:33 There *they* **f** the Eleven and those with G2351
Jn 1:41 tell him, "*We have* **f** the Messiah" G2351
Jn 1:45 Philip **f** Nathanael and told him, "We G2351
Jn 1:45 "*We have* **f** the one Moses wrote about in G2351
Jn 2:14 In the temple courts *he* **f** people selling G2351
Jn 5:14 Later Jesus **f** him at the temple and said G2351
Jn 6:25 *When they* **f** him on the other side of the G2351
Jn 9:35 him out, and *when he* **f** him, he said, G2351

Jn 11:17 Jesus **f** that Lazarus had already been in *G2351*
Jn 11:57 that anyone *who* **f out** where Jesus was *G1182*
Jn 12: 9 large crowd of Jews **f out** that Jesus was *G1182*
Jn 12:14 Jesus **f** a young donkey and sat on it, as it *G2351*
Jn 19:33 came to Jesus and **f** that he was already *G3972*
Ac 4:12 Salvation *is* **f** in no one else, for there is *G1639*
Ac 5:23 "*We* **f** the jail securely locked, with the *G2351*
Ac 5:23 we opened them, *we* **f** no one inside." *G2351*
Ac 9: 2 so that if *he* **f** any there who belonged to *G2351*
Ac 9:33 There *he* **f** a man named Aeneas, who *G2351*
Ac 10:17 sent by Cornelius **f out** where Simon's *G1452*
Ac 10:27 went inside and **f** a large gathering of *G2351*
Ac 11:26 and *when he* **f** him, he brought him to *G2351*
Ac 13:22 '*I have* **f** David son of Jesse, a man after *G2351*
Ac 13:28 Though *they* **f** no proper ground for a *G2351*
Ac 14: 6 But *they* **f out** *about* it and fled to the *G5328*
Ac 17:23 *I* even **f** an altar with this inscription: *G2351*
Ac 19: 1 There *he* **f** some disciples *G2351*
Ac 21: 2 *We* **f** a ship crossing over to Phoenicia *G2351*
Ac 22:25 citizen who **hasn't** even **been f guilty**?" *G185*
Ac 23:29 *I* **f** *that* the accusation had to do with *G2351*
Ac 24: 5 "*We have* **f** this man to be a troublemaker *G2351*
Ac 24:18 clean when *they* **f** me in the temple *G2351*
Ac 24:20 state what crime *they* **f** in me when I *G2351*
Ac 25:25 I **f** he had done nothing deserving of *G2898*
Ac 27: 6 There the centurion **f** an Alexandrian ship *G2351*
Ac 27:28 took soundings and **f** that the water was a *G2351*
Ac 27:28 soundings again and **f** it was ninety feet *G2351*
Ac 28: 1 *we* **f out** that the island was called Malta. *G2105*
Ac 28:14 There *we* **f** some brothers and sisters who *G2351*
Ro 7:10 I **f** *that* the very commandment that was *G2351*
Ro 10:20 "*I was* **f** by those who did not seek me *G2351*
1Co 15:15 *we are* then **f** to be false witnesses about *G2351*
2Co 2:12 gospel of Christ and **f** that the Lord had NDT
2Co 5: 3 we are clothed, *we will* not *be* **f** naked. *G2351*
Php 2: 8 And *being* **f** in appearance as a man, he *G2351*
Php 3: 9 and *be* **f** in him, not having a *G2351*
Col 2:17 to come; the reality, however, is **f** in Christ. NDT
2Ti 1:17 he searched hard for me until *he* **f** me. *G2351*
Heb 3: 3 Jesus *has been* **f worthy** of greater honor *G546*
Heb 4: 1 that none of you *be* **f** to have fallen short *G1506*
Heb 8: 8 But God **f fault with** the people and said *G3522*
Heb 11: 5 "*He could* not *be* **f**, because God had *G2351*
Jas 2: 8 If you really keep the royal law *f* **in** Scripture AIT
1Pe 2:22 and no deceit *was* **f** in his mouth. *G2351*
2Pe 3:14 make every effort *to be* **f** spotless *G2351*
Rev 2: 2 are not, and *have* **f** them false. *G2351*
Rev 3: 2 for *I have* **f** your deeds unfinished in the *G2351*
Rev 5: 4 because no one *was* **f** who was worthy to *G2351*
Rev 14: 5 No lie *was* **f** in their mouths; they are *G2351*
Rev 16:20 away and the mountains *could* not *be* **f**. *G2351*
Rev 18:21 will be thrown down, never *to be* **f** again. *G2351*
Rev 18:22 of any trade *will* ever *be* **f** in you again. *G2351*
Rev 18:24 In her *was* **f** the blood of prophets and of *G2351*
Rev 20:15 whose name *was* not **f** written in the *G2351*
Rev 21:16 city with the rod and **f** it to be 12,000 stadia NDT

FOUNDATION (38) [FOUNDATIONS, FOUNDED]

1Ki 5:17 to **provide a f** *of* dressed stone *for* the H3569
1Ki 6:37 **The f** of the temple of the LORD **was laid** in H3569
1Ki 7: 9 to the great courtyard and from **f** to eaves, H4996
2Ch 3: 3 **The f** Solomon **laid** for building the H3569
2Ch 8:16 the **f** *of* the temple of the LORD was **laid** H4586
2Ch 23: 5 the royal palace and a third at the **F** Gate, H3572
Ezr 3: 3 built the altar on its **f** and sacrificed burnt H4807
Ezr 3: 6 the **f** of the LORD's temple *had* not *yet* **been laid** H3569
Ezr 3:10 the builders **laid the f** *of* the temple of H3569
Ezr 3:11 **the f** *of* the house of the LORD **was laid.** H3569
Ezr 3:12 they saw **the f** *of* this temple *being* **laid,** H3569
Job 38: 4 were you when I **laid the** earth's **f**? H3569
Ps 89:14 justice are the **f** *of* your throne; H4806
Ps 97: 2 justice are the **f** *of* his throne. H4806
Isa 28:16 a precious cornerstone for a sure **f**; the H4586
Isa 33: 6 He will be the **sure f** *for* your times, a rich H575
Jer 51:26 any stone for a **f**, for you will be H4589
Eze 13:14 the ground so that its **f** will be laid bare. H3572
Eze 41: 8 around it, forming the **f** *of* the side rooms. H4588
Am 9: 6 in the heavens and sets its **f** on the earth; H99
Hag 2:18 when **the f** of the LORD's temple **was laid.** H3569
Zec 4: 9 Zerubbabel *have* **laid the f** *of* this temple; H3569
Zec 8: 9 present when **the f was laid** *for* the house H3569
Zec 12: 1 the heavens, *who* **lays the f** *of* the earth H3569
Mt 7:25 not fall, because *it had* its **f** on the rock. *G2530*
Lk 6:48 dug down deep and laid the **f** on rock. *G2529*
Lk 6:49 built a house on the ground without a **f**. *G2529*
Lk 14:29 For if you lay the **f** and are not able to *G2529*
Ro 15:20 not be building on someone else's **f**. *G2529*
1Co 3:10 given me, I laid a **f** as a wise builder, and *G2529*
1Co 3:11 no one can lay any **f** other than the one *G2529*
1Co 3:12 If anyone builds on this **f** using gold, silver, *G2529*
Eph 2:20 built on the **f** of the apostles and prophets *G2529*
1Ti 3:15 living God, the pillar and **f** of the truth. *G1613*
1Ti 6:19 themselves *as* a firm **f** for the coming *G2529*
2Ti 2:19 God's solid **f** stands firm, sealed with *G2529*
Heb 6: 1 not laying again the **f** of repentance from *G2529*
Rev 21:19 The first **f** was jasper, the second sapphire *G2529*

FOUNDATIONS (38) [FOUNDATION]

Dt 32:22 set afire the **f** *of* the mountains. H4587
Jos 6:26 cost of his firstborn son *he will* **lay** its **f**; H3569
1Sa 2: 8 "For the **f** *of* the earth are the LORD's; on H5187
2Sa 22: 8 quaked, the **f** *of* the heavens shook H4589
2Sa 22:16 exposed and the **f** *of* the earth laid bare H4589
1Ki 7:10 **The f were laid** *with* large stones of good H3569
1Ki 16:34 *He* **laid** its **f** at the cost of his firstborn son H3569
Ezr 4:12 restoring the walls and repairing the **f**. A10079
Ezr 5:16 came and laid the **f** of the house of God A10079
Ezr 6: 3 to present sacrifices, and let its **f** be laid. A10079
Job 4:19 whose **f** are in the dust, who H3572
Job 22:16 their time, their **f** washed away by a flood. H3572
Ps 11: 3 When the **f** are being destroyed, what can H9268
Ps 18: 7 quaked, and the **f** *of* the mountains shook H4587
Ps 18:15 exposed and the **f** *of* the earth laid bare H4589
Ps 82: 5 darkness; all the **f** *of* the earth are shaken. H4587
Ps 102:25 the beginning *you* **laid the f** *of* the earth, H3569
Ps 104: 5 He set the earth on its **f**; it can never be H4806
Ps 137: 7 it down," they cried, "tear it down to its **f**!" H3572
Pr 3:19 By wisdom the LORD **laid the** earth's **f**, by H3569
Pr 8:29 when he marked out the **f** *of* the earth. H4587
Isa 24:18 are opened, the **f** *of* the earth shake. H4587
Isa 44:28 and of the temple, "*Let its* **f be laid.**" H3569
Isa 48:13 My own hand **laid the f** *of* the earth, and H3569
Isa 51:13 heavens and *who* **lays the f** *of* the earth, H3569
Isa 51:16 in place, *who* **laid the f** *of* the earth, and H3569
Isa 54:11 of turquoise, your **f** with lapis lazuli. H3569
Isa 58:12 ruins and will raise up the age-old **f**; H4587
Jer 31:37 measured and the **f** *of* the earth below be H4587
La 4:11 kindled a fire in Zion that consumed her **f**. H3572
Eze 30: 4 will be carried away and her **f** torn down. H3572
Mic 1: 6 stones into the valley and lay bare her **f**. H3572
Mic 6: 2 you everlasting **f** *of* the earth. H4587
Ac 16:26 earthquake that the **f** of the prison were *G2528*
Heb 1:10 you **laid the f** of the earth, and the *G2530*
Heb 11:10 he was looking forward to the city with **f**, *G2529*
Rev 21:14 The wall of the city had twelve **f**, and on *G2529*
Rev 21:19 The **f** of the city walls were decorated with *G2529*

FOUNDED (11) [FOUNDATION]

Ex 9:18 on Egypt, from the day it **was f** till now. H3569
1Ki 2:24 father David and *has* **f** a dynasty for me as H6913
Ps 24: 2 he **f** it on the seas and established it H3569
Ps 87: 1 He has **f** his city on the holy mountain. H3573
Ps 89:11 you **f** the world and all that is in it. H3569
Ps 94:15 will again be **f on** righteousness, H6330
Ps 107:36 and *they* **f** a city where they could settle. H3922
Isa 40:21 you not understood since the earth was **f**? H4589
Isa 45:18 made the earth, he **f** it; he did not create H3922
Jer 10:12 *he* **f** the world by his wisdom and H3922
Jer 51:15 *he* **f** the world by his wisdom and H3922

FOUNTAIN (15) [FOUNTAINS]

Ne 2:14 on toward the **F** Gate and the King's H6524
Ne 3:15 The **F** Gate was repaired by Shallun son H6524
Ne 12:37 At the **F** Gate they continued directly up H6524
Ps 36: 9 For with you is the **f** *of* life; in your light H5227
Pr 5:18 May your **f** be blessed, and may you H5227
Pr 10:11 The mouth of the righteous is a **f** *of* life H5227
Pr 13:14 The teaching of the wise is a **f** *of* life H5227
Pr 14:27 The fear of the LORD is a **f** *of* life, turning a H5227
Pr 16:22 Prudence is a **f** *of* life to the prudent, but H5227
Pr 18: 4 the **f** *of* wisdom is a rushing stream. H5227
SS 4:12 you are a spring enclosed, a sealed **f**. H1644
SS 4:15 You are a garden **f**, a well of flowing H5078
Jer 9: 1 a spring of water and my eyes a **f** *of* tears! H5227
Joel 3:18 A **f** will flow out of the LORD's house and H5078
Zec 13: 1 "On that day a **f** will be opened to the H5227

FOUNTAINS (2) [FOUNTAIN]

Ps 87: 7 music they will sing, "All my **f** are in you." H5078
Pr 8:28 fixed securely the **f** *of* the deep, H6524

FOUR (229) [FOUR-DRACHMA, FOUR-FIFTHS, FOUR-FOOTED, FOURS, FOURTH]

Ge 2:10 there it was separated into **f** headwaters. H752
Ge 14: 9 Arioch king of Ellasar—**f** kings against five. H752
Ge 14:11 The **f** kings seized all the goods of Sodom NDT
Ge 15:13 certain that for **f** hundred years your H752
Ge 23:15 the land is worth **f** hundred shekels of silver H752
Ge 23:16 **f** hundred shekels of silver, according to the H752
Ge 32: 6 and **f** hundred men are with him. H752
Ge 33: 1 coming with his **f** hundred men; so he H752
Ex 22: 1 cattle for the ox and **f** sheep for the sheep. H752
Ex 25:12 Cast **f** gold rings for it and fasten them to its H752
Ex 25:12 rings for it and fasten them to its **f** feet, H752
Ex 25:26 Make **f** gold rings for the table and fasten H752
Ex 25:26 the table and fasten them to the **f** corners, H752
Ex 25:26 to the four corners, where the **f** legs are. H752
Ex 25:34 there are to be **f** cups shaped like almond H752
Ex 26: 2 twenty-eight cubits long and **f** cubits wide. H752
Ex 26: 8 thirty cubits long and **f** cubits wide. H752
Ex 26:32 with gold hooks on **f** posts of acacia wood H752
Ex 26:32 with gold and standing on **f** silver bases. H752
Ex 27: 2 Make a horn at each of the **f** corners, so that H752
Ex 27: 4 ring at each of the **f** corners of the network. H752
Ex 27:16 embroiderer—with **f** posts and four bases. H752
Ex 27:16 embroiderer—with four posts and **f** bases. H752
Ex 28:17 Then mount **f** rows of precious stones on it H752
Ex 36: 9 twenty-eight cubits long and **f** cubits wide. H752
Ex 36:15 thirty cubits long and **f** cubits wide. H752
Ex 36:36 They made **f** posts of acacia wood for it H752
Ex 36:36 hooks for them and cast their **f** silver bases. H752
Ex 37: 3 He cast **f** gold rings for it and fastened them H752
Ex 37: 3 rings for it and fastened them to its **f** feet, H752
Ex 37:13 They cast **f** gold rings for the table and H752
Ex 37:13 table and fastened them to the **f** corners, H752
Ex 37:13 to the four corners, where the **f** legs were. H752
Ex 37:20 on the lampstand were **f** cups shaped like H752
Ex 38: 2 They made a horn at each of the **f** corners H752
Ex 38: 5 the poles for the **f** corners of the bronze H752
Ex 38:19 with **f** posts and four bronze bases. H752
Ex 38:19 with four posts and **f** bronze bases. H752
Ex 39:10 Then they mounted **f** rows of precious H752
Lev 11:23 insects that have **f** legs you are to regard H752
Nu 7: 7 He gave two carts and **f** oxen to the H752
Nu 7: 8 he gave **f** carts and eight oxen to the H752
Nu 7:85 weighed two thousand **f** hundred shekels, H752
Dt 3:11 than nine cubits long and **f** cubits wide. H752
Dt 22:12 Make tassels on the **f** corners of the cloak H752
Jos 19: 7 Ashan—**f** towns and their villages H752
Jos 21:18 together with their pasturelands—**f** towns. H752
Jos 21:22 together with their pasturelands—**f** towns. H752
Jos 21:24 together with their pasturelands—**f** towns. H752
Jos 21:29 together with their pasturelands—**f** towns; H752
Jos 21:31 together with their pasturelands—**f** towns; H752
Jos 21:35 together with their pasturelands—**f** towns; H752
Jos 21:37 together with their pasturelands—**f** towns; H752
Jos 21:39 with their pasturelands—**f** towns in all. H752
Jdg 9:34 positions near Shechem in **f** companies. H752
Jdg 11:40 of Israel go out for **f** days to commemorate H752
Jdg 19: 2 After she had been there **f** months, H752
Jdg 20: 2 **f** hundred thousand men armed with H752
Jdg 20:17 mustered **f** hundred thousand swordsmen H752
Jdg 20:47 of Rimmon, where they stayed **f** months. H752
Jdg 21:12 in Jabesh Gilead **f** hundred young women H752
1Sa 4: 2 who killed about **f** thousand of them on the H752
1Sa 22: 2 About **f** hundred men were with him H752
1Sa 25:13 About **f** hundred men went up with David H752
1Sa 27: 7 in Philistine territory a year and **f** months. H752
1Sa 30:10 David and the other **f** hundred continued H752
1Sa 30:17 except **f** hundred young men who rode off H752
2Sa 12: 6 He must pay for that lamb **f** *times over* H752
2Sa 15: 7 At the end of **f** years, Absalom said to the H752
2Sa 21:22 These **f** were descendants of Rapha in H752
1Ki 4:26 Solomon had **f** thousand stalls for chariot H752
1Ki 6: 1 In the **f** hundred and eightieth year after H752
1Ki 7: 2 with **f** rows of cedar columns supporting H752
1Ki 7:19 were in the shape of lilies, **f** cubits high. H752
1Ki 7:27 of bronze; each was **f** cubits long, four wide H752
1Ki 7:27 was four cubits long, **f** wide and three high. H752
1Ki 7:30 Each stand had **f** bronze wheels with bronze H752
1Ki 7:30 each had a basin resting on **f** supports H752
1Ki 7:32 The **f** wheels were under the panels, and H752
1Ki 7:34 Each stand had **f** handles, one on each H752
1Ki 7:38 forty baths and measuring **f** cubits across, H752
1Ki 7:42 the **f** hundred pomegranates for the two H752
1Ki 18:19 And bring the **f** hundred and fifty prophets H752
1Ki 18:19 of Baal and the **f** hundred prophets of H752
1Ki 18:22 Baal has **f** hundred and fifty prophets. H752
1Ki 18:33 "Fill **f** large jars with water and pour it on H752
1Ki 22: 6 the prophets—about **f** hundred men—and H752
2Ki 7: 3 Now there were **f** men with leprosy at the H752
2Ki 14:13 a section about **f** hundred cubits long. H752
1Ch 3: 5 These **f** were by Bathsheba daughter of H752
1Ch 7: 1 Puah, Jashub and Shimron—**f** in all. H752
1Ch 9:24 The gatekeepers were on the **f** sides: east H752
1Ch 9:26 But the **f** principal gatekeepers, who were H752
1Ch 21: 5 including **f** hundred and seventy thousand H752
1Ch 21:20 his **f** sons who were with him hid H752
1Ch 23: 5 **F** thousand are to be gatekeepers and four H752
1Ch 23: 5 to be gatekeepers and **f** thousand are to H752
1Ch 23:10 These were the sons of Shimei—**f** in all. H752
1Ch 23:12 Amram, Izhar, Hebron and Uzziel—**f** in all. H752
1Ch 26:17 a day on the east, **f** a day on the north, four H752
1Ch 26:17 **f** a day on the south and two at a time at H752
1Ch 26:18 there were **f** at the road and two at the H752
2Ch 4:13 the **f** hundred pomegranates for the two H752
2Ch 8:18 Ophir and brought back **f** hundred and fifty H752
2Ch 9:25 Solomon had **f** thousand stalls for horses H752
2Ch 13: 3 with an army of **f** hundred thousand able H752
2Ch 18: 5 the prophets—**f** hundred men—and asked H752
2Ch 25:23 a section about **f** hundred cubits long. H752
Ezr 6:17 **f** hundred male lambs and A10065
Ne 6: 4 **F** times they sent me the same message H752
Job 1:19 desert and struck the **f** corners of the house. H752
Pr 30:15 are never satisfied, **f** that never say H752
Pr 30:18 amazing for me, **f** that I do not understand: H752
Pr 30:21 earth trembles, under **f** it cannot bear up: H752
Pr 30:24 "**F** things on earth are small, yet they are H752
Pr 30:29 **f** that move with stately bearing: H752
Isa 11:12 of Judah from the **f** quarters of the earth. H752
Isa 17: 6 branches, **f** or five on the fruitful boughs," H752
Jer 15: 3 "I will send **f** kinds of destroyers against H752
Jer 36:23 had read three or **f** columns of the scroll, H752
Jer 49:36 against Elam the **f** winds from the four H752
Jer 49:36 four winds from the **f** quarters of heaven; H752
Jer 49:36 I will scatter them to the **f** winds, and H3972S
Jer 52:21 circumference; each was **f** fingers thick, and H752
Eze 1: 5 fire was what looked like **f** living creatures. H752
Eze 1: 6 each of them had **f** faces and four wings H752
Eze 1: 6 each of them had four faces and **f** wings. H752
Eze 1: 8 their wings on their **f** sides they had human H752
Eze 1: 8 *All f of* them had faces and wings, H752
Eze 1:10 Each of the **f** had the face of a human H752
Eze 1:15 beside each creature with its **f** faces. H752
Eze 1:16 sparkled like topaz, and *all* **f** looked alike. H752

Eze 1:17 go in any one of the f directions the H752
Eze 1:18 and *all* f rims were full of eyes all around. H752
Eze 7: 2 has come upon the f corners of the land! H752
Eze 10: 9 I saw beside the cherubim f wheels H752
Eze 10:10 appearance, the f *of* them looked alike H752
Eze 10:11 go in any one of the f directions the H752
Eze 10:12 full of eyes, as were their f wheels. H752
Eze 10:14 Each of the cherubim had f faces: One face H752
Eze 10:21 Each had f faces and four wings, and under H752
Eze 10:21 Each had four faces and f wings, and under H752
Eze 14:21 Jerusalem my f dreadful judgments— H752
Eze 37: 9 from the f winds and breathe into these H752
Eze 40:41 So there were f tables on one side of the H752
Eze 40:41 side of the gateway and f on the other— H752
Eze 40:42 There were also f tables of dressed stone H752
Eze 41: 5 room around the temple was f cubits wide. H752
Eze 42:20 So he measured the area on *all* f sides. H752
Eze 43:14 goes around the altar it is f cubits high, H752
Eze 43:15 the altar hearth is f cubits high, and four H752
Eze 43:15 f horns project upward from the hearth. H752
Eze 43:20 put it on the f horns of the altar and H752
Eze 43:20 the altar and on the f corners of the upper H752
Eze 45:19 on the f corners of the upper ledge of the H752
Eze 46:21 court and led me around to its f corners, H752
Eze 46:22 In the f corners of the outer court were H752
Eze 46:22 of the courts in the f corners was the same H752
Eze 46:23 of each of the f courts was a ledge of H752
Da 1:17 To these f young men God gave H752
Da 3:25 I see f men walking around in the fire A10065
Da 7: 2 before me were the f winds of heaven A10065
Da 7: 3 F great beasts, each different from the A10065
Da 7: 6 on its back it had f wings like those of a A10065
Da 7: 6 This beast had f heads, and it was given A10065
Da 7:17 'The f great beasts are four kings that will A10065
Da 7:17 four great beasts are f kings that will rise A10065
Da 8: 8 in its place f prominent horns grew up H752
Da 8: 8 grew up toward the f winds of heaven. H752
Da 8:22 The f horns that replaced the one that was H752
Da 8:22 broken off represent f kingdoms that will H752
Da 11: 4 parceled out toward the f winds of heaven. H752
Am 1: 3 of Damascus, even for f, I will not relent. H752
Am 1: 6 sins of Gaza, even for f, I will not relent. H752
Am 1: 9 sins of Tyre, even for f, I will not relent. H752
Am 1:11 sins of Edom, even for f, I will not relent. H752
Am 1:13 sins of Ammon, even for f, I will not relent. H752
Am 2: 1 sins of Moab, even for f, I will not relent. H752
Am 2: 4 sins of Judah, even for f, I will not relent. H752
Am 2: 6 sins of Israel, even for f, I will not relent. H752
Zec 1:18 and there before me were f horns. H752
Zec 1:20 Then the LORD showed me f craftsmen. H752
Zec 2: 6 scattered you to the f winds of heaven," H752
Zec 6: 1 there before me were f chariots coming out H752
Zec 6: 5 "These are the f spirits of heaven H752
Mt 15:38 of those who ate was f **thousand** men, G5483
Mt 16:10 Or the seven loaves *for* the f **thousand** G5483
Mt 24:31 they will gather his elect from the f winds, G5475
Mk 2: 3 a paralyzed man, carried by f *of them.* G5475
Mk 8: 9 About f **thousand** were present. G5483
Mk 8:20 broke the seven loaves for the f **thousand,** G5483
Mk 13:27 gather his elect from the f winds, G5475
Lk 16: 6 and make it f **hundred and fifty.** G4299
Lk 19: 8 I will pay back f **times** *the amount.* G5487
Jn 1:39 It was about f **in the afternoon.** G6052+1281
Jn 4:35 a saying, 'It's still f **months** until harvest'? G5485
Jn 6:19 had rowed about three or f **miles,** G5084+5558
Jn 11:17 had already been in the tomb for f days. G5475
Jn 11:39 a bad odor, for he has been there f **days.**" G5479
Jn 19:23 dividing them into f shares, one for each G5475
Ac 5:36 about f **hundred** men rallied to him. G5484
Ac 7: 6 'For f **hundred** years your descendants will G5484
Ac 10:11 being let down to earth **by** its f corners. G5475
Ac 11: 5 let down from heaven by its f corners, G5475
Ac 12: 4 over to be guarded *by* f squads of four G5475
Ac 12: 4 guarded by four **squads of** f soldiers **each.** G5482
Ac 21: 9 He had f unmarried daughters who G5475
Ac 21:23 There are f men with us who have made G5475
Ac 21:38 a revolt and led f **thousand** terrorists out G5483
Ac 27:29 they dropped f anchors from the stern G5475
Rev 4: 6 the throne, were f living creatures, and G5475
Rev 4: 8 Each of the f living creatures had six wings G5475
Rev 5: 6 encircled by the f living creatures and the G5475
Rev 5: 8 the f living creatures and the twenty-four G5475
Rev 5:14 The f living creatures said, "Amen," G5475
Rev 6: 1 I heard one of the f living creatures say in G5475
Rev 6: 6 like a voice among the f living creatures, G5475
Rev 7: 1 After this I saw f angels standing at the G5475
Rev 7: 1 standing at the f corners of the earth, G5475
Rev 7: 1 holding back the f winds of the earth to G5475
Rev 7: 2 loud voice to the f angels who had been G5475
Rev 7:11 the elders and the f living creatures. G5475
Rev 9:13 coming from the f horns of the golden G5475
Rev 9:14 "Release the f angels who are bound at G5475
Rev 9:15 And the f angels who had been kept ready G5475
Rev 14: 3 before the f living creatures and G5475
Rev 15: 7 Then one of the f living creatures gave to G5475
Rev 19: 4 elders and the f living creatures fell down G5475
Rev 20: 8 the nations in the f corners of the earth— G5475

FOUR-DRACHMA (1) [DRACHMAS, FOUR]

Mt 17:27 open its mouth and you will find a f **coin.** G5088

FOUR-FIFTHS (1) [FIVE, FOUR]

Ge 47:24 The *other* f you may keep as seed H752+3338

FOUR-FOOTED (2) [FOUR, FOOT]

Ac 10:12 It contained all kinds of f **animals,** as well G5488
Ac 11: 6 into it and saw f **animals** of the earth, G5488

FOURS (4) [FOUR]

Lev 11:20 insects that walk on **all** f are to be regarded H752
Lev 11:21 insects that walk on **all** f that you may eat: H752
Lev 11:27 Of all the animals that walk on **all** f, those H752
Lev 11:42 its belly or walks on **all** f or on many feet; H752

FOURSCORE (KJV) EIGHTY

FOURSQUARE (KJV) SQUARE

FOURTEEN (27) [FOURTEENTH]

Ge 31:41 I worked for you f years for your two H752+6926
Ge 46:22 who were born to Jacob—f in all. H752+6925
Nu 29:13 two rams and f male lambs a year H752+6925
Nu 29:15 with each of the f lambs H752+6925
Nu 29:17 two rams and f male lambs a year H752+6925
Nu 29:20 two rams and f male lambs a year H752+6925
Nu 29:23 two rams and f male lambs a year H752+6925
Nu 29:26 two rams and f male lambs a year H752+6925
Nu 29:29 two rams and f male lambs a year H752+6925
Nu 29:32 two rams and f male lambs a year H752+6925
Jos 15:36 —f towns and their villages. H752+6926
Jos 18:28 Kiriath—f towns and their villages. H752+6926
1Ki 8:65 and seven days more, f days in all. H752+6925
1Ki 10:26 he had f **hundred** H547+2256+752+4395
1Ch 25: 5 God gave Heman f sons and three H752+6925
2Ch 1:14 he had f **hundred** H547+2256+752+4395
2Ch 13:21 He married f wives and had H752+6926
Job 42:12 He had f thousand sheep, six H752+6925
Eze 40:48 of the entrance was f cubits and its H752+6926
Eze 43:17 f cubits long and fourteen cubits H752+6926
Eze 43:17 cubits long and f cubits wide. H752+6926
Mt 1:17 Thus there were f generations in all from G1280
Mt 1:17 f from David to the exile to Babylon G1280
Mt 1:17 f from the exile to the Messiah. G1280
Ac 27:33 "*For* the last f days," he said, "you have G5476
2Co 12: 2 a man in Christ who f years ago was G1280
Gal 2: 1 Then after f years, I went up again to G1280

FOURTEENTH (24) [FOURTEEN]

Ge 14: 5 In the f year, Kedorlaomer and the H752+6926
Ex 12: 6 of them until the f day of the month, H752+6925
Ex 12:18 the evening of the f day until the H752+6925
Lev 23: 5 at twilight on the f day of the first H752+6925
Nu 9: 3 at twilight on the f day of this month, H752+6925
Nu 9: 5 at twilight on the f day of the first H752+6925
Nu 9:11 to do it on the f day of the second H752+6925
Nu 28:16 " 'On the f day of the first month the H752+6925
Jos 5:10 evening of the f day of the month, H752+6925
2Ki 18:13 In the f year of King Hezekiah's H752+6926
1Ch 24:13 to Huppah, the f to Jeshebeab, H752+6925
1Ch 25:21 the f to Mattithiah, his sons and H752+6925
2Ch 30:15 lamb on the f day of the second H752+6925
2Ch 35: 1 slaughtered on the f day of the first H752+6925
Ezr 6:19 On the f day of the first month, the H752+6925
Est 9:15 together on the f day of the month H752+6925
Est 9:17 and on the f they rested and made it H752+6925
Est 9:18 assembled on the thirteenth and f, H752+6925
Est 9:19 observe the f of the month of Adar as H752+6925
Est 9:21 annually the f and fifteenth days of H752+6925
Isa 36: 1 In the f year of King Hezekiah's H752+6926
Eze 40: 1 in the f year after the fall of the city H752+6926
Eze 45:21 first month on the f day you are to H752+6925
Ac 27:27 On the f night we were still being driven G5476

FOURTH (71) [FOUR]

Ge 1:19 there was morning—the f day. H8055
Ge 2:14 And the f river is the Euphrates. H8055
Ge 15:16 *In* the f generation your descendants will H8055
Ex 20: 5 to the third and f **generation** of those who H8067
Ex 28:20 the f row shall be topaz, onyx and jasper H8055
Ex 34: 7 the parents to the third and f **generation.**" H8067
Ex 39:13 the f row was topaz, onyx and jasper. H8055
Lev 19:24 In the f year all its fruit will be holy, an H8055
Nu 7:30 On the f day Elizur son of Shedeur, the H8055
Nu 14:18 the parents to the third and f **generation.** H8067
Nu 23:10 of Jacob or number *even a* f *of* Israel? H8065
Nu 29:23 " 'On the f day offer ten bulls, two rams H8055
Dt 5: 9 to the third and f **generation** of those who H8067
Jos 19:17 The f lot came out for Issachar according H8055
Jdg 14:15 On the f day, they said to Samson's wife H8055
Jdg 19: 5 On the f day they got up early and he H8055
2Sa 3: 4 the f, Adonijah the son of Haggith; the H8055
1Ki 6: 1 in the f year of Solomon's reign over H8055
1Ki 6:33 that were **one** f *of the width of* the hall. H8055
1Ki 6:37 temple of the LORD was laid in the f year, H8055
1Ki 22:41 king of Judah in the f year of Ahab king of H752
2Ki 10:30 on the throne of Israel to the f **generation.**" H8055
2Ki 15:12 on the throne of Israel to the f **generation.**" H8055
2Ki 18: 9 In King Hezekiah's f year, which was the H8055
2Ki 25: 3 the ninth day of the f month the famine in H8055
1Ch 2:14 the f Nethanel, the fifth Raddai, H8055
1Ch 3: 2 king of Geshur; the f, Adonijah the son of H8055
1Ch 3:15 Zedekiah the third, Shallum the f. H8055
1Ch 8: 2 Nohah the f and Rapha the fifth. H8055
1Ch 12:10 Mishmannah the f, Jeremiah the fifth, H8055
1Ch 23:19 Jahaziel the third and Jekameam the f. H8055
1Ch 24: 8 the third to Harim, the f to Seorim, H8055
1Ch 24:23 Jahaziel the third and Jekameam the f. H8055
1Ch 25:11 the f to Izri, his sons and relatives 12 H8055
1Ch 26: 2 Zebadiah the third, Jathniel the f, H8055
1Ch 26: 4 the third, Sakar the f, Nethanel the fifth, H8055
1Ch 26:11 Tabaliah the third and Zechariah the f. H8055
1Ch 27: 7 The f, for the fourth month, was Asahel H8055
1Ch 27: 7 The fourth, for the f month, was Asahel H8055
2Ch 3: 2 the second month in the f year of his reign. H752
2Ch 20:26 On the f day they assembled in the Valley H8055
Ezr 8:33 On the f day, in the house of our God, we H8055
Job 42:16 their children to the f generation. H752
Jer 25: 1 of Judah in the f year of Jehoiakim son H8055
Jer 28: 1 of that same year, the f year, early in the H8055
Jer 36: 1 In the f year of Jehoiakim son of Josiah H8055
Jer 39: 2 the ninth day of the f month of Zedekiah's H8055
Jer 45: 1 dictated in the f year of Jehoiakim son H8055
Jer 46: 2 of Babylon in the f year of Jehoiakim son H8055
Jer 51:59 king of Judah in the f year of his reign. H8055
Jer 52: 6 the ninth day of the f month the famine in H8055
Eze 1: 1 in the f month on the fifth day H8055
Eze 10:14 of a lion, and the f the face of an eagle. H8055
Da 2:40 there will be a f kingdom, strong as iron A10651
Da 3:25 the f looks like a son of the gods. A10651
Da 7: 7 there before me was a f beast A10651
Da 7:19 to know the meaning of the f beast, A10651
Da 7:23 'The f beast is a fourth kingdom that will A10651
Da 7:23 'The fourth beast is a f kingdom that will A10651
Da 11: 2 in Persia, and then a f, who will be far H8055
Zec 6: 3 and the f dappled—all of them H8055
Zec 7: 1 In the f year of King Darius, the word of the H752
Zec 7: 1 to Zechariah on the f day of the ninth H752
Zec 8:19 "The fasts of the f, fifth, seventh and tenth H8055
Rev 4: 7 like a man, the f was like a flying eagle. G5480
Rev 6: 7 When the Lamb opened the f seal, G5480
Rev 6: 7 the voice of the f living creature say, G5480
Rev 6: 8 given power over a f of the earth to kill by G5480
Rev 8:12 The f angel sounded his trumpet, and a G5480
Rev 16: 8 The f angel poured out his bowl on the G5480
Rev 21:19 sapphire, the third agate, the f emerald, G5480

FOWL (1) [FOWLER, FOWLER'S]

1Ki 4:23 as deer, gazelles, roebucks and choice f. H1350

FOWLER (1) [FOWL]

Pr 6: 5 like a bird from the snare of the f. H3687

FOWLER'S (2) [FOWL]

Ps 91: 3 save you from the f snare and from the H3687
Ps 124: 7 have escaped like a bird from the f snare; H3704

FOX (2) [FOXES]

Ne 4: 3 even a f climbing up on it would break H8785
Lk 13:32 "Go tell that f, 'I will keep on G273

FOXES (6) [FOX]

Jdg 15: 4 caught three hundred f and tied them tail H8785
Jdg 15: 5 torches and let the f loose in the standing NDT
SS 2:15 Catch for us the f, the little foxes that ruin H8785
SS 2:15 the little f that ruin the vineyards H8785
Mt 8:20 "F have dens and birds have nests G273
Lk 9:58 "F have dens and birds have nests G273

FRACTURE (2) [FRACTURES]

Lev 24:20 f for fracture, eye for eye, tooth for tooth H8691
Lev 24:20 fracture for f, eye for eye, tooth for tooth H8691

FRACTURES (1) [FRACTURE]

Ps 60: 2 torn it open; mend its f, for it is quaking. H8691

FRAGILE (1)

Job 8:14 What they trust in is f; what they rely on is H3684

FRAGMENT (1)

Isa 30:14 among its pieces not a f will be found H3084

FRAGRANCE (13) [FRAGRANT]

Ex 30:38 incense like it to **enjoy** its f must be cut off H8193
SS 1: 3 Pleasing is the f *of* your perfumes; your H8194
SS 1:12 was at his table, my perfume spread its f. H8194
SS 2:13 the blossoming vines spread their f. H8194
SS 4:10 the f *of* your perfume more than any H8194
SS 4:11 The f *of* your garments is like the H8194
SS 4:11 of your garments is like the f *of* Lebanon. H8194S
SS 4:16 garden, that its f may spread everywhere. H1411
SS 7: 8 the vine, the f *of* your breath like apples, H8194
SS 7:13 The mandrakes send out their f, and at H8194
Isa 3:24 Instead of f there will be a stench; instead H1411
Hos 14: 6 olive tree, his f like a cedar of Lebanon. H8194
Jn 12: 3 was filled with the f of the perfume. G4011

FRAGRANT (28) [FRAGRANCE]

Ex 25: 6 the anointing oil and for the f incense; H6160
Ex 30: 7 "Aaron must burn f incense on the altar H6160
Ex 30:23 250 shekels) of f cinnamon, 250 shekels H1411
Ex 30:23 cinnamon, 250 shekels of f calamus, H1411
Ex 30:25 anointing oil, a f blend, the work of a H5351
Ex 30:34 said to Moses, "Take f **spices**—gum resin, H6160
Ex 30:35 make a f **blend** *of* incense, the work of H8381
Ex 31:11 anointing oil and f incense for the Holy H6160
Ex 35: 8 the anointing oil and for the f incense; H6160
Ex 35:15 the anointing oil and the f incense; the H6160
Ex 35:28 the anointing oil and for the f incense. H6160

F

Ex 37:29 oil and the pure, f incense—the work of a H6160
Ex 39:38 the anointing oil, the f incense, and the H6160
Ex 40:27 burned f incense on it, as the LORD H6160
Lev 4: 7 horns of the altar of f incense that is H6160
Lev 16:12 of finely ground f incense and take them H6160
Nu 4:16 oil for the light, the f incense, the regular H6160
2Ch 2: 4 it to him for burning f incense before him, H6160
2Ch 13:11 burnt offerings and f incense to the LORD. H6160
Ps 45: 8 All your robes are f with myrrh and aloes NDT
Isa 43:24 have not bought *any* f **calamus** for me, H7866
Eze 6:13 they offered f **incense** to all their H8194+5767
Eze 8:11 and a f cloud of incense was rising. H6986
Eze 16:19 offered as f **incense** before them. H8194+5767
Eze 20:28 their f **incense** and poured out H8194+5767
Eze 20:41 you as f **incense** when I bring H8194+5767
Eph 5: 2 up for us as a f offering and *G4011+2380*
Php 4:18 They are a f **offering**, an *G4011+2380*

FRAME (14) [FRAMES]

Ex 26:16 Each f is to be ten cubits long and a cubit H7983
Ex 26:19 two bases for each f, one under each H7983
Ex 26:21 forty silver bases—two under each f. H7983
Ex 26:25 sixteen silver bases—two under each f. H7983
Ex 36:21 Each f was ten cubits long and a cubit H7983
Ex 36:24 two bases for each f, one under each H7983
Ex 36:26 forty silver bases—two under each f. H7983
Ex 36:30 sixteen silver bases—two under each f. H7983
Nu 4:10 durable leather and put it on a **carrying** f. H4573
Nu 4:12 leather and put them on a **carrying** f. H4573
1Ki 7:31 that had a **circular** f one cubit deep. H4196
Job 17: 7 with grief; my whole f is but a shadow. H3674
Ps 139:15 My f was not hidden from you when I was H6798
Isa 58:11 land and will strengthen your f. H6795

FRAMES (29) [FRAME]

Ex 26:15 "Make upright f of acacia wood for the H7983
Ex 26:17 Make all the f *of* the tabernacle in this H7983
Ex 26:18 Make twenty f for the south side of the H7983
Ex 26:20 side of the tabernacle, make twenty f H7983
Ex 26:22 Make six f for the far end, that is, the west H7983
Ex 26:23 make two f for the corners at the far H7983
Ex 26:25 So there will be eight f and sixteen silver H7983
Ex 26:26 five for the f *on* one side of the tabernacle H7983
Ex 26:27 and five for the f on the west, at the H7983
Ex 26:28 from end to end at the middle of the f. H7983
Ex 26:29 Overlay the f with gold and make gold H7983
Ex 35:11 its covering, clasps, f, crossbars, posts H7983
Ex 36:20 They made upright f of acacia wood for H7983
Ex 36:22 They made all the f *of* the tabernacle in H7983
Ex 36:23 They made twenty f for the south side of H7983
Ex 36:25 side of the tabernacle, they made twenty f H7983
Ex 36:27 They made six f for the far end, that is, the H7983
Ex 36:28 two f were made for the corners of the H7983
Ex 36:29 two corners the f were double from the NDT
Ex 36:30 So there were eight f and sixteen silver H7983
Ex 36:31 five for the f *on* one side of the tabernacle H7983
Ex 36:32 and five for the f on the west, at the H7983
Ex 36:33 from end to end at the middle of the f. H7983
Ex 36:34 They overlaid the f with gold and made H7983
Ex 39:33 its clasps, f, crossbars, posts and H7983
Ex 40:18 in place, erected the f, inserted the H7983
Nu 3:36 to take care of the f *of* the tabernacle, H7983
Nu 4:31 they are to carry the f *of* the tabernacle, its H7983
1Ki 7: 5 All the doorways had rectangular f; they H9208

FRANKINCENSE (3) [INCENSE]

Ex 30:34 galbanum—and pure f, all in equal H4247
Mt 2:11 him with gifts of gold, f and myrrh. *G3337*
Rev 18:13 of incense, myrrh and f, of wine and olive *G3337*

FRANKLY (1) [FRANKNESS]

Lev 19:17 **Rebuke** your neighbor f so you will H3519+3519

FRANKNESS (1) [FRANKLY]

2Co 7: 4 I have spoken to you *with* great f; I take *G4244*

FRANTIC (1)

1Ki 18:29 and *they continued their* f **prophesying** H5547

FRAUD (3) [DEFRAUD]

Pr 20:17 Food gained by f tastes sweet, but one H9214
Jer 10:14 The images he makes are a f; they have H9214
Jer 51:17 The images he makes are a f; they have H9214

FRAY (1)

Job 39:21 in its strength, and charges into the f. H5977

FREE (116) [FREED, FREEDMEN, FREEDOM, FREEING, FREELY]

Ge 2:16 "*You are* f **to eat** from any tree in the H430+430
Ge 44:10 the rest of you will be f **from blame**." H5929
Ge 49:21 "Naphtali is a doe **set** f that bears H8938
Ex 6: 6 *I will* f you from being slaves to them, and H5911
Ex 21: 2 he shall go f, without paying H2930
Ex 21: 3 he comes alone, *he is to* **go** f alone; but if H3655
Ex 21: 4 her master, and only the man *shall* **go** f. H3655
Ex 21: 5 wife and children and do not want to go f, H2930
Ex 21: 7 *she is* not *to* **go** f as male servants do. H3655
Ex 21:11 three things, *she is to* **go** f, without any H3655
Ex 21:26 let the slave go f to compensate for the H2930
Ex 21:27 let the slave go f to compensate for the H2930
Nu 32:22 be f **from** your **obligation** to the LORD H5929
Dt 7:15 The LORD *will* **keep** you f from every H6073
Dt 15:12 the seventh year you must let them go f. H2930
Dt 15:18 it a hardship *to* **set** your servant f, H2930+8938
Dt 24: 5 one year he is to be f to stay at home H5929
Dt 32:36 is gone and no one is left, slave or f. H6440
Jdg 16:20 "I'll go out as before and **shake myself** f." H5850
2Sa 22:49 *who* **sets** me f from my enemies. H3655
1Ki 14:10 every last male in Israel—slave or f. H6440
1Ki 20:34 "On the basis of a treaty I *will* **set** you f." H8938
1Ki 20:42 '*You have* **set** f a man I had H8938+4946+3338
1Ki 21:21 Ahab every last male in Israel—slave or f. H6440
2Ki 9: 8 Ahab every last male in Israel—slave or f. H6440
2Ki 14:26 in Israel, whether slave or f, was suffering; H6440
1Ch 4:10 from harm so that I will be f **from** pain." H1194
1Ch 12:17 when my hands are f **from** violence, H4202+928
Job 10: 1 therefore *I will* **give** f **rein** to my complaint H6440
Job 11:15 f **of** fault, you will lift up your face H4946
Job 16:17 my hands have been f **of** violence and my H4202
Job 21: 9 Their homes are safe and f **from** fear; the H4946
Job 33: 9 done no wrong; I am clean and f **from** sin. H4202
Job 36:16 to a spacious place f **from** restriction, H4202
Job 39: 5 "Who let the wild donkey go f? Who H2930
Ps 25:17 of my heart and f me from my anguish. H3655
Ps 31: 4 **Keep** me f from the trap that is set for me H3655
Ps 73: 5 They are f **from** common human burdens H401
Ps 73:12 are like—always f **of care**, they go on H8929
Ps 81: 6 their hands *were* **set** f from the basket. H6296
Ps 105:20 the ruler of peoples **set** him f. H7337
Ps 129: 4 *he has* **cut** me f *from* the cords of the H7915
Ps 142: 7 **Set** me f from my prison, that I may praise H3655
Ps 146: 7 to the hungry. The LORD **sets** prisoners f, H6002
Pr 4:24 **Keep** your mouth f of perversity; keep H6073
Pr 6: 3 my son, *to* f **yourself**, since you have H5911
Pr 6: 5 F **yourself**, like a gazelle from the hand of H5911
Pr 11:21 those who are righteous *will* **go** f. H4880
Pr 19: 5 whoever pours out lies *will* not **go** f. H4880
Isa 32:20 **letting** your cattle and donkeys **range** f H8938+8079
Isa 42: 7 to f captives from prison and to release H3655
Isa 45:13 He will rebuild my city and **set** my exiles f H8938
Isa 49: 9 and to those in darkness, '*Be* f! H1655
Isa 51:14 The cowering prisoners *will* soon **be set** f H7337
Isa 52: 2 F **yourself** *from* the chains on your neck H7337
Isa 58: 6 set the oppressed f and break every yoke H2930
Jer 2:31 people say, '*We are* f *to* **roam**; we will come AIT
Jer 34: 9 Everyone was to f their Hebrew H8938+2930
Jer 34:10 that they *would* f their male and H8938+2930
Jer 34:10 They agreed, and **set** them f. H8938
Jer 34:14 year each of *you must* f any fellow H8938
Jer 34:14 you six years, you must let them go f. H2930
Jer 34:16 slaves you had set f to go where they H2930
Jer 37: 4 Now Jeremiah *was* f *to* **come** and go among AIT
La 5: 8 there is no *one to* f us from their H7293
Eze 13:20 *I will* **set** f the people that you ensnare H8938
Zec 9:11 *I will* f your prisoners from the waterless H8938
Lk 1:64 his mouth was opened and his tongue set f, NDT
Lk 4:18 blind, *to* **set** the oppressed f, *G690+1877+912*
Lk 13:12 "Woman, *you are* **set** f from your infirmity." *G668*
Lk 13:16 *be* **set** f on the Sabbath day from what *G3395*
Jn 8:32 know the truth, and the truth *will* **set** you f." *G1802*
Jn 8:33 How can you say that we shall be **set** f?" *G1801*
Jn 8:36 So if the Son **sets** you f, you will be free *G1802*
Jn 8:36 Son sets you free, you will be f indeed. *G1801*
Jn 19:10 I have power either *to* f you or to crucify you *G668*
Jn 19:12 Pilate tried *to* set Jesus f, but the Jewish *G668*
Ac 7:34 have come down *to* **set** them f. *G1975*
Ac 13:39 who believes *is* **set** f from every sin, *G1467*
Ac 26:32 man could have *been* **set** f if he had not *G668*
Ro 6: 7 who has died *has been* **set** f from sin. *G1467*
Ro 6:18 *You have been* **set** f from sin and have *G1802*
Ro 6:20 you were f from the control of *G1801*
Ro 6:22 But now *that you have been* **set** f from sin *G1802*
Ro 8: 2 who gives life *has* **set** you f from the law *G1802*
Ro 13: 3 Do you want to be f **from** fear of the one *G3590*
1Co 7:22 the one who was f when called is Christ's *G1801*
1Co 7:27 *Are you* f from such a commitment *G3395*
1Co 7:32 I would like you to be f **from concern**. *G291*
1Co 7:39 she is f to marry anyone she wishes *G1801*
1Co 9: 1 Am I not f? Am I not an apostle? Have I *G1801*
1Co 9:18 the gospel I may offer it f **of charge**, *G78*
1Co 9:19 am f **and belong to no one**, *G1801+1666+4246*
1Co 9:21 I am not f **from** God's **law** but am under *G491*
1Co 12:13 Gentiles, slave or f—and we were all *G1801*
2Co 11: 7 the gospel of God to you f **of charge**? *G1562*
Gal 3:28 neither slave nor f, nor is there male and *G1801*
Gal 4:22 woman and the other by the f *woman*. *G1801*
Gal 4:23 his son by the f *woman* was born as the *G1801*
Gal 4:26 But the Jerusalem that is above is f, and *G1801*
Gal 4:30 in the inheritance with the f *woman's* son." *G1801*
Gal 4:31 of the slave woman, but *of* the f *woman*. *G1801*
Gal 5: 1 It is for freedom *that* Christ *has* **set us** f *G1802*
Gal 5:13 brothers and sisters, were called to be f. *G1800*
Eph 6: 8 good they do, whether they are slave or f. *G1801*
Col 1:22 without blemish and f **from accusation**— *G441*
Col 3:11 Scythian, slave or f, but Christ is all, and is *G1801*
Heb 2:15 f those who all their lives were held in *G557*
Heb 9:15 died as a **ransom to set** them f from the *G667*
Heb 13: 5 your lives f **from the love of money** and be *G921*
1Pe 2:16 Live as f *people*, but do not use your *G1801*
Rev 6:15 both slave and f, hid in caves and *G1801*
Rev 13:16 rich and poor, f and slave, to receive a *G1801*
Rev 19:18 flesh of all people, f and slave, great and *G1801*
Rev 20: 3 he must *be* **set** f for a short time. *G3395*
Rev 22:17 who wishes take the f **gift** of the water of *G1562*

FREED (10) [FREE]

Lev 19:20 put to death, because *she had* not **been** f. H2926
Job 3:19 the slaves are f from their owners. H2930
Ps 116:16 *you have* f me from my chains. H7337
Ps 136:24 f us from our enemies. His love H7293
Jer 34:11 the slaves *they had* f and enslaved H8938+2930
Jer 52:31 king of Judah and f him from prison. H3655
Mk 5:29 in her body that *she was* f from her *G2615*
Mk 5:34 Go in peace and be f from your suffering." *G5618*
1Co 7:22 to faith in the Lord is the Lord's f **person**; *G592*
Rev 1: 5 who loves us and *has* f us from our sins by *G3395*

FREEDMEN (1) [FREE]

Ac 6: 9 from members of the Synagogue *of* the F *G3339*

FREEDOM (23) [FREE]

Lev 19:20 has not been ransomed or given her f, H2928
Ps 119:45 I will walk about in f, for I have sought out H8146
Isa 61: 1 to proclaim f for the captives and release H2002
Jer 34: 8 in Jerusalem to proclaim f **for** *the* **slaves**. H2002
Jer 34:15 of you proclaimed f to your own people. H2002
Jer 34:17 not proclaimed f to your own people. H2002
Jer 34:17 So I now proclaim 'f' for you, declares the H2002
Jer 34:17 declares the LORD—'f' to fall by the sword NDT
Eze 46:17 the servant may keep it until the year of f H2002
Lk 4:18 sent me to proclaim f for the prisoners and *G912*
Ac 24:23 to give him some f and permit his *G457*
Ro 8:21 brought into the f and glory of the *G1800*
1Co 7:21 although if you can gain your f, do so. *G1801*
1Co 10:29 For why is my f being judged by another's *G1800*
2Co 3:17 where the Spirit of the Lord is, there is f. *G1800*
Gal 2: 4 ranks to spy on the f we have in Christ *G1800*
Gal 5: 1 It is *for* f that Christ has set us free. *G1800*
Gal 5:13 But do not use your f to indulge the flesh *G1800*
Eph 3:12 may approach God with f and confidence. *G4244*
Jas 1:25 intently into the perfect law that *gives* f, *G1800*
Jas 2:12 to be judged by the law *that gives* f, *G1800*
1Pe 2:16 do not use your f as a cover-up for evil *G1800*
2Pe 2:19 They promise them f, while they *G1800*

FREEING (2) [FREE]

Jer 40: 4 But today *I am* f you from the chains on H7337
Ac 2:24 the dead, f him from the agony of death *G3395*

FREELY (24) [FREE]

Ge 43:34 So they feasted and **drank** f with him. H8910
Dt 15: 8 and f **lend** them whatever H6292+6292
Dt 23:23 you made your vow f to the LORD your God H5607
1Ch 29: 9 for *they had* **given** f and wholeheartedly H5605
Ezr 7:15 his advisers *have* f **given** to the God of A10461
Ps 12: 8 who f **strut** about when what is vile is H2143
Ps 37:26 They are always generous and **lend** f H4278
Ps 112: 5 to those who are generous and **lend** f, H4278
Ps 112: 9 *They have* f **scattered** their gifts to the H7061
Pr 11:24 *One person* **gives** f, yet gains even more H7061
Isa 55: 7 to our God, for *he will* f pardon. H8049
Hos 14: 4 heal their waywardness and love them f, H5607
Mt 10: 8 drive out demons. F you have received *G1562*
Mt 10: 8 Freely you have received; f give. *G1562*
Mk 1:45 Instead he went out and began to talk f *G4498*
Jn 1:20 fail to confess, but **confessed** *f*, "I am not the AIT
Ac 9:28 them and **moved about** f in *G1660+2779+1744*
Ac 26:26 these things, and I can speak f to him. *G4245*
Ro 3:24 all are justified f by his grace through *G1562*
1Co 2:12 may understand what God *has* f **given** us. *G5919*
2Co 6:11 We *have* **spoken** f to you *G3836+5125+487*
2Co 9: 9 "*They have* f **scattered** their gifts to the *G5025*
2Co 10: 8 if I boast somewhat f about the authority *G4358*
Eph 1: 6 which *he has* f **given** us in the One he *G5923*

FREEWILL (22) [WILL]

Ex 35:29 to the LORD f **offerings** for all the work H5607
Ex 36: 3 to bring f **offerings** morning after H5607
Lev 7:16 is the result of a vow or is a f offering, H5607
Lev 22:18 either to fulfill a vow or as a f **offering**, H5607
Lev 22:21 to fulfill a special vow or as a f **offering**, H5607
Lev 22:23 present as a f **offering** an ox or a sheep H5607
Lev 23:38 all the f **offerings** you give to the H5607
Nu 15: 3 special vows or f **offerings** or festival H5607
Nu 29:39 to what you vow and your f **offerings**, H5607
Dt 12: 6 have vowed to give and your f **offerings**, H5607
Dt 12:17 or your f **offerings** or special gifts. H5607
Dt 16:10 God by giving a f **offering** in proportion to H5607
2Ch 31:14 in charge of the f **offerings** *given to* God, H5607
Ezr 1: 4 with f **offerings** for the temple of God H5607
Ezr 1: 6 in addition to all the f **offerings**. H5605
Ezr 2:68 of the families **gave** f **offerings** toward the H5605
Ezr 3: 5 those **brought as** f **offerings** to the H5605+5607
Ezr 7:16 as well as the f **offerings** *of* the people A10461
Ezr 8:28 silver and gold are a f **offering** to the LORD, H5607
Ps 54: 6 I will sacrifice a f **offering** to you; I will H5607
Eze 46:12 prince provides a f **offering** to the LORD— H5607
Am 4: 5 offering and brag about your f **offerings**— H5607

FRENZIED (1)

Job 39:24 In f excitement it eats up the ground; it H8323

FREQUENT (1) [FREQUENTLY]

1Ti 5:23 of your stomach and your f illnesses. *G4781*

FREQUENTLY (2) [FREQUENT]
Ac 24:26 so he sent for him f and talked with him. G4781
2Co 11:23 been in prison **more** f, been flogged more G4359

FRESH (17) [FRESH-CUT, FRESHLY]
Ge 26:19 discovered a well of f water there. H2645
Lev 14: 5 birds be killed over f water in a clay pot. H2645
Lev 14: 6 of the bird that was killed over the f water. H2645
Lev 14:50 one of the birds over f water in a clay pot. H2645
Lev 14:51 blood of the dead bird and the f water, H2645
Lev 14:52 the bird's blood, the f water, the live bird, H2645
Lev 15:13 clothes and bathe himself with f water, H2645
Nu 19:17 into a jar and pour f water over them. H2645
Jdg 15:15 Finding a f jawbone of a donkey, he H3269
Jdg 16: 7 ties me with seven f bowstrings that have H4300
Jdg 16: 8 brought her seven f bowstrings that had H4300
Ps 92:14 in old age, they will stay f and green, H2015
Eze 47: 8 the sea, the salty water there *becomes* f. H8324
Eze 47: 9 flows there and **makes** the salt water f; H8324
Eze 47:11 swamps and marshes *will* not *become* f; H8324
Jas 3:11 Can both f *water* and salt water flow from G1184
Jas 3:12 Neither can a salt spring produce f water. G1184

FRESH-CUT (1) [CUT, FRESH]
Ge 30:37 however, took f branches from poplar H4300

FRESHLY (1) [FRESH]
Ge 8:11 in its beak was a f **plucked** olive leaf! H3273

FRET (4)
Ps 37: 1 *Do* not f because of those who are evil H3013
Ps 37: 7 *do* not f when people succeed in their H3013
Ps 37: 8 turn from wrath; *do* not f—it leads only to H3013
Pr 24:19 *Do* not f because of evildoers or be H3013

FRICTION (1)
1Ti 6: 5 and **constant** f between people of corrupt G1384

FRIEND (63) [FRIENDLY, FRIENDS, FRIENDSHIP]
Ge 38:12 his f Hirah the Adullamite went with H8276
Ge 38:20 the young goat by his f the Adullamite in H8276
Ex 32:27 killing his brother and f and neighbor. H8276
Ex 33:11 Moses face to face, as one speaks to a f. H8276
Dt 13: 6 your **closest** f secretly entices H8276+889+3869+5883+3870
Jdg 7:13 just as a man was telling a f his dream. H8276
Jdg 7:14 His f responded, "This can be nothing H8276
Ru 4: 1 "Come over here, my f, and sit down." H7141+532
2Sa 16:17 "So this is the love you show your f? H8276
2Sa 16:17 If he's your f, why didn't you go H8276
1Ki 16:11 spare a single male, whether relative or f. H8276
2Ch 20: 7 to the descendants of Abraham your f? H170
Job 6:14 kindness from a f forsakes the fear of the H5335
Job 6:27 the fatherless and barter away your f. H8276
Job 16:20 My intercessor is my f as my eyes pour out H8276
Job 16:21 he pleads with God as one pleads for a f. H8276
Ps 35:14 mourning as though for my f or brother. H8276
Ps 41: 9 Even my **close** f, someone I trusted H408+8934
Ps 55:13 like myself, my companion, my **close** f, H3359
Ps 88:18 You have taken from me f and neighbor H170
Ps 88:18 neighbor—darkness is my **closest** f. H3359
Ps 119:63 I am a f to all who fear you, to all who H2492
Pr 17:17 A f loves at all times, and a brother is H8276
Pr 18:24 there is a f who sticks closer than a H170
Pr 19: 4 even the *closest* f *of* the poor person H8276
Pr 19: 6 everyone is the f of one who gives H8276
Pr 22:11 with grace will have the king for a f. H8276
Pr 27: 6 Wounds from a f can be trusted, but an H170
Pr 27: 9 the pleasantness of a f springs from their H8276
Pr 27:10 Do not forsake your f or a friend of your H8276
Pr 27:10 forsake your friend or a f *of* your family, H8276
SS 5:16 my beloved, this is my f, daughters of H8276
Isa 41: 8 you descendants of Abraham my f, H170
Jer 3: 4 'My Father, my f *from* my youth, H476
Jer 9: 4 is a deceiver, and every f a slanderer. H8276
Jer 9: 5 F deceives friend, and no one speaks the H408
Jer 9: 5 Friend deceives f, and no one speaks the H8276
Mic 7: 5 trust a neighbor; put no confidence in a f. H476
Mt 11:19 drunkard, a f of tax collectors and sinners. G5813
Mt 20:13 of them, 'I am not being unfair to you, f. G2279
Mt 22:12 get in here without wedding clothes, f? G2279
Mt 26:50 what you came for, f." Then the men G2279
Lk 5:20 their faith, he said, "F, your sins are G476
Lk 7:34 drunkard, a f of tax collectors and sinners. G5813
Lk 11: 5 "Suppose you have a f, and you go to him G5813
Lk 11: 5 midnight and say, 'F, lend me three G5813
Lk 11: 6 a f of mine on a journey has come to me G5813
Lk 14:10 he will say to you, 'F, move up to a better G5813
Jn 3:29 The f who attends the bridegroom waits G5813
Jn 11:11 tell them, "Our f Lazarus has fallen asleep G5813
Jn 19:12 let this man go, you are no f of Caesar. G5813
Ro 16: 5 Greet my **dear** f Epenetus, who was the first G28
Ro 16: 8 Greet Ampliatus, my **dear** f in the Lord. G28
Ro 16: 9 co-worker in Christ, and my **dear** f Stachys. G28
Ro 16:12 Greet my **dear** f Persis, another woman who G28
Col 4:14 Our **dear** f Luke, the doctor, and Demas send G28
Phm 1 To Philemon our **dear** f and fellow worker— G28
Jas 2:23 and he was called God's f. G5813
Jas 4: 4 who chooses to be a f of the world G5813
3Jn 1 The elder, To my **dear** f Gaius, whom I love G28
3Jn 2 **Dear** f, I pray that you may enjoy good G28
3Jn 5 **Dear** f, you are faithful in what you are G28
3Jn 11 **Dear** f, do not imitate what is evil but what G28

FRIENDLY (2) [FRIEND]
Ge 34:21 "These men are f toward us," they said H8969
1Ki 5: 1 he had always been **on** f **terms** with David. H170

FRIENDS (98) [FRIEND]
Ge 19: 7 said, "No, my f. Don't do this wicked H278
Jdg 11:37 to roam the hills and weep with my f, H8292
Jdg 11:38 She and her f went into the hills and wept H8292
Jdg 19:23 said to them, "No, my f, don't be so vile. H278
1Sa 30:26 elders of Judah, who were his f, saying, H8276
2Sa 3: 8 of your father Saul and to his family and f. H5335
2Ki 10:11 his chief men, his **close** f and his priests H3359
Est 5:10 Calling together his f and Zeresh, his wife, H170
Est 5:14 His wife Zeresh and all his f said to him H170
Est 6:13 his wife and all his f everything that had H170
Job 2:11 When Job's three f, Eliphaz the Temanite, H8276
Job 12: 4 "I have become a laughingstock to my f H8276
Job 17: 5 If anyone denounces their f for reward H8276
Job 19:14 my **closest** f have forgotten me. H3359
Job 19:19 All my intimate f detest me; those I love H5493
Job 19:21 "Have pity on me, my f, have pity, for the H8276
Job 24:17 *they* **make** f **with** the terrors of darkness. H5795
Job 32: 3 He was also angry with the three f H8276
Job 35: 4 like to reply to you and to your f with you. H8276
Job 42: 7 "I am angry with you and your two f H8276
Job 42:10 After Job had prayed for his f, the LORD H8276
Ps 31:11 an object of dread to my **closest** f— H3359
Ps 38:11 My f and companions avoid me because of H170
Ps 55:20 My companion attacks his f; he violates H8934
Ps 88: 8 from me my **closest** f and have made H3359
Ps 122: 8 For the sake of my family and f, I will say H8276
Pr 12:26 The righteous choose their f carefully, but H8276
Pr 14:20 their neighbors, but the rich have many f. H170
Pr 16:28 up conflict, and a gossip separates **close** f. H476
Pr 17: 9 repeats the matter separates **close** f. H476
Pr 18:24 One who has *unreliable* f soon comes to H8276
Pr 19: 4 Wealth attracts many f, but even the H8276
Pr 19: 7 how much more do their f avoid them! H5335
Pr 22:24 *Do* not **make** f with a hot-tempered H8287
SS 1: 7 veiled woman beside the flocks of your f? H2492
SS 5: 1 Eat, f, and drink; drink your H8276
SS 8:13 dwell in the gardens with f in attendance, H2492
Jer 6:21 over them; neighbors and f will perish." H8276
Jer 9: 4 "Beware of your f; do not trust anyone in H8276
Jer 20: 4 you a terror to yourself and to all your f; H170
Jer 20: 6 you and all your f to whom you have H170
Jer 20:10 All my f are waiting for me to slip H632+8934
Jer 23:35 keeps saying to your f and other Israelites: H8276
Jer 38:22 those **trusted** f *of* yours. H408+8934
Jer 38:22 sunk in the mud; your f have deserted you. NDT
La 1: 2 All her f have betrayed her; they have H8276
Da 2:13 Daniel and his f to put them to death A10245
Da 2:17 explained the matter to his f Hananiah, A10245
Da 2:18 so that he and his f might not be A10245
Ob 7 your f will deceive and overpower H408+8934
Zec 13: 6 wounds I was given at the house of my f. H170
Lk 2:44 him among their relatives and f. G1196
Lk 5:34 "Can you make the f of the bridegroom G5626
Lk 7: 6 when the centurion sent f to say to him: G5813
Lk 12: 4 "I tell you, my f, do not be afraid of those G5813
Lk 14:12 do not invite your f, your brothers or sisters G5813
Lk 15: 6 Then he calls his f and neighbors G5813
Lk 15: 9 she calls her f and neighbors together G5813
Lk 15:29 young goat so I could celebrate with my f. G5813
Lk 16: 9 use worldly wealth to gain f for yourselves, G5813
Lk 21:16 relatives and f, and they will put G5813
Lk 23:12 That day Herod and Pilate became f G5813
Jn 15:13 to lay down one's life for one's f. G5813
Jn 15:14 You are my f if you do what I command. G5813
Jn 15:15 I have called you f, for everything that I G5813
Jn 21: 5 called out to them, "F, haven't you any G4086
Ac 10:24 called together his relatives and close f. G338
Ac 13:38 "Therefore, my f, I want you to know G467+81
Ac 14:15 "F, why are you doing this? We too are only G467
Ac 15:25 to you with our **dear** f Barnabas and Paul— G28
Ac 19:25 "You know, my f, that we receive a good G467
Ac 19:31 of the province, f of Paul, sent him a G5813
Ac 24:23 permit his f to take care of his G2625
Ac 27: 3 him to go to his f so they might provide G5813
Ro 12:19 take revenge, my **dear** f, but leave room G28
1Co 10:14 Therefore, my **dear** f, flee from idolatry. G28
2Co 7: 1 we have these promises, **dear** f, let us purify G28
2Co 12:19 everything we do, **dear** f, is for your G28
Php 2:12 Therefore, my **dear** f, as you have always G28
Php 4: 1 stand firm in the Lord in this way, **dear** f! G28
Heb 6: 9 we speak like this, **dear** f, we are convinced G28
1Pe 2:11 **Dear** f, I urge you, as foreigners and exiles G28
1Pe 4:12 *Dear* f, do not be surprised at the fiery G28
2Pe 3: 1 **Dear** f, this is now my second letter to you. G28
2Pe 3: 8 this one thing, **dear** f: With the Lord a day G28
2Pe 3:14 So then, **dear** f, since you are looking G28
2Pe 3:17 Therefore, **dear** f, since you have been G28
1Jn 2: 7 **Dear** f, I am not writing you a new command G28
1Jn 3: 2 **Dear** f, now we are children of God, and G28
1Jn 3:21 **Dear** f, if our hearts do not condemn us, we G28
1Jn 4: 1 **Dear** f, do not believe every spirit, but test G28
1Jn 4: 7 **Dear** f, let us love one another, for love G28
1Jn 4:11 **Dear** f, since God so loved us, we also ought G28
3Jn 14 The f here send their greetings G5813
3Jn 14 their greetings. Greet the f there by name. G5813
Jude 3 **Dear** f, although I was very eager to write to G28
Jude 17 **dear** f, remember what the apostles of G28
Jude 20 **dear** f, by building yourselves up in G28

FRIENDSHIP (8) [FRIEND]
Dt 23: 6 seek a **treaty of** f *with* them H8934+2256+3208
1Sa 20:42 we have sworn f with each other in the NDT
Ezr 9:12 seek a **treaty of** f *with* them H8934+2256+3208
Job 29: 4 when God's **intimate** f blessed my house, H6051
Ps 109: 4 In return for my f they accuse me, but I am H173
Ps 109: 5 repay me evil for good, and hatred for my f. H173
Lk 11: 8 up and give you the bread because of f, G5813
Jas 4: 4 don't you know that f with the world G5802

FRIGHT (1) [FEAR]
Lk 24: 5 *In* their f the women bowed down G1873+1181

FRIGHTEN (7) [FEAR]
Dt 28:26 there will be no *one to* f them **away**. H3006
Ne 6: 9 They *were* all *trying to* f us, thinking H3707
Job 7:14 even then *you* f me with dreams and H3169
Job 9:34 so that his terror *would* f me no more. H1286
Jer 7:33 there will be no *one to* f them **away**. H3006
Eze 30: 9 me in ships to f Cush *out of* her H3006
2Co 10: 9 seem to be trying to f you with my letters. G1768

FRIGHTENED (10) [FEAR]
Ge 42:35 saw the money pouches, *they were* f. H3707
Ge 43:18 Now the men *were* f when they were taken H3707
Isa 31: 4 *it is* not f by their shouts or disturbed by H3169
Da 5: 6 turned pale and he *was so* f that his legs A10097
Mk 9: 6 did not know what to say, they were **so** f.) G1769
Lk 21: 9 hear of wars and uprisings, *do* not *be* f. G4765
Lk 24:37 They were startled and f, thinking they G1873
Jn 6:19 walking on the water; and *they were* f. G5828
Php 1:28 without *being* f in any way by those who G4769
1Pe 3:14 "Do not fear their threats; *do* not *be* f." G5429

FRIGHTENING (2) [FEAR]
Job 13:21 from me, and stop f me *with* your terrors. H1286
Da 7: 7 terrifying and f and very powerful. A10028

FRINGE (1)
Job 26:14 And these are but the **outer** f *of* his works H7896

FRO (1)
Ps 104:26 There the ships **go to and** f, and H2143

FROGS (14)
Ex 8: 2 send a plague of f on your whole country H7630
Ex 8: 3 The Nile will teem with f. H7630
Ex 8: 4 The f will come up on you and your H7630
Ex 8: 5 make f come up on the land of Egypt. H7630
Ex 8: 6 the f came up and covered the land. H7630
Ex 8: 7 they also made f come up on the land of H7630
Ex 8: 8 LORD to take the f away from me and my H7630
Ex 8: 9 you and your houses may be rid of the f, H7630
Ex 8:11 The f will leave you and your houses, your H7630
Ex 8:12 to the LORD about the f he had brought on H7630
Ex 8:13 The f died in the houses, in the courtyards H7630
Ps 78:45 and f that devastated them. H7630
Ps 105:30 Their land teemed with f, which went up H7630
Rev 16:13 saw three impure spirits that looked like f; G1005

FROLIC (3)
Ps 104:26 Leviathan, which you formed to f there. H8471
Jer 50:11 because *you* f like a heifer threshing grain H7055
Mal 4: 2 you will go out and f like well-fed calves. H7055

FROM (5029) See Index of Articles Etc.

FRONT (160) [FRONTAL]
Ge 30:38 would be **directly in** f **of** the flocks H4200+5790
Ge 30:39 they mated **in** f **of** the branches. H448
Ge 30:41 in the troughs **in** f **of** the animals H4200+6524
Ge 31:37 Put it here **in** f **of** your relatives and mine H5584
Ge 32:17 owns all these animals **in** f **of** you? H4200+7156
Ge 33: 2 female servants and their children *in* f, H8037
Ge 40: 9 my dream I saw a vine **in** f **of** me, H4200+7156
Ex 7:10 his staff down **in** f **of** Pharaoh and H4200+7156
Ex 13:22 left its place **in** f **of** the people. H4200+7156
Ex 14:19 been traveling **in** f **of** Israel's army, H4200+7156
Ex 14:19 also moved from **in** f and stood behind H7156
Ex 17: 5 Moses, "Go out **in** f **of** the people. H4200+7156
Ex 19: 2 there in the desert **in** f **of** the mountain. H5584
Ex 25:37 on it so that they light the space **in** f **of** it. H7156
Ex 26: 9 sixth curtain double at the f *of* the tent. H7156
Ex 28:25 the shoulder pieces of the ephod at the f. H7156
Ex 28:27 the shoulder pieces on the f *of* the ephod, H7156
Ex 28:37 it is to be on the f *of* the turban. H7156
Ex 29:10 the bull to the f *of* the tent of meeting, H7156
Ex 30: 6 Put the altar **in** f **of** the curtain that H4200+7156
Ex 30:36 and place it **in** f **of** the ark of the H4200+7156
Ex 32: 5 he built an altar **in** f **of** the calf and H4200+7156
Ex 32:15 were inscribed on both sides, f and back. H2296S
Ex 33:19 all my goodness to pass **in** f **of** you, H6584+7156
Ex 34: 3 may graze **in** f **of** the mountain." H448+4578
Ex 34: 6 And he passed **in** f **of** Moses H6584+7156
Ex 39:18 the shoulder pieces of the ephod at the f. H7156
Ex 39:20 the shoulder pieces on the f *of* the ephod, H7156
Ex 40: 5 of incense **in** f **of** the ark of the H4200+7156
Ex 40: 6 burnt offering **in** f **of** the entrance H4200+7156
Ex 40:26 tent of meeting **in** f **of** the curtain H4200+7156
Lev 3: 8 and slaughter it **in** f **of** the tent of H4200+7156

Lev 3:13 and slaughter it **in f of** the tent of H4200+7156
Lev 4:6 **in f of** the curtain of the sanctuary. H907+7156
Lev 4:17 LORD seven times **in f of** the curtain. H907+7156
Lev 6:14 it before the LORD, **in f of** the altar. H448+7156
Lev 8:9 sacred emblem, on the **f** *of* it, as the LORD H7156
Lev 9:5 commanded to the **f** *of* the tent of H7156
Lev 10:4 away from the **f** *of* the sanctuary. H7156
Lev 13:41 his hair from the **f** *of* his scalp and has a H6991
Lev 16:2 the curtain **in f of** the atonement H448+7156
Lev 16:14 sprinkle it on the **f** *of* the atonement cover H7156
Lev 16:15 the atonement cover and **in f of** it. H4200+7156
Lev 17:4 to the LORD **in f of** the tabernacle of H4200+7156
Lev 19:14 a stumbling block **in f of** the blind, H4200+7156
Nu 3:38 sunrise, **in f of** the tent of meeting. H4200+7156
Nu 8:2 up the area **in f of** the H448+4578+7156
Nu 8:9 the Levites to the **f** *of* the tent of meeting H7156
Nu 8:13 Levites stand **in f of** Aaron and his H4200+7156
Nu 14:5 fell facedown **in f of** the whole H4200+7156
Nu 16:43 Aaron went to the **f** *of* the tent of meeting H7156
Nu 17:4 of meeting **in f of** the ark of the H4200+7156
Nu 17:10 Aaron's staff **in f of** the ark of the H4200+7156
Nu 19:4 times toward the **f** *of* the tent of meeting. H7156
Nu 20:10 together **in f of** the rock and H448+7156
Dt 14:1 shave the **f of** your **heads** for the H1068+6524
Dt 26:4 and set it down **in f of** the altar of H4200+7156
Jos 4:12 battle, **in f of** the Israelites H4200+7156
Jos 5:13 a man standing **in f of** him with a H4200+5584
Jos 6:4 of rams' horns **in f of** the ark. H4200+7156
Jos 6:6 priests carry trumpets **in f of** it." H4200+7156
Jos 8:11 approached the city and arrived **in f of** it. H5584
Jos 8:33 people stood **in f of** Mount Gerizim H448+4578
Jos 8:33 and half of them **in f of** Mount Ebal, H448+4578
Jdg 18:21 and their possessions **in f of** them, H4200+7156
1Sa 8:11 and they will run **in f of** his chariots. H4200+7156
1Sa 9:24 was on it and set it **in f of** Saul. H4200+7156
1Sa 16:8 and had him pass **in f of** Samuel. H4200+7156
1Sa 17:41 with his shield bearer **in f of** him H4200+7156
1Sa 21:15 fellow here to carry on like this **in f of** me? H6584
2Sa 2:14 and fight hand to hand **in f of** us." H4200+7156
2Sa 3:31 walk in mourning **in f of** Abner." H4200+7156
2Sa 5:23 and attack them **in f of** the poplar H4946+4578
2Sa 5:24 has gone out **in f of** you to strike H4200+7156
2Sa 6:4 and Ahio was walking **in f of** it. H4200+7156
2Sa 10:9 battle lines **in f of** him and behind H4946+7156
2Sa 11:15 "Put Uriah **out in f** where the H448+4578+7156
1Ki 6:3 The portico at the **f** *of* the main hall of the H7156
1Ki 6:3 ten cubits from the **f** *of* the temple. H7156
1Ki 6:17 The main hall **in f of** this room was H4200+7156
1Ki 6:21 chains across the **f** *of* the inner sanctuary, H7156
1Ki 7:5 they were **in the f part** in sets of three H4578
1Ki 7:6 **In f of** it was a portico, and in front H6584+7156
1Ki 7:6 and **in f of** that were pillars and an H6584+7156
1Ki 7:49 the left, **in f of** the inner sanctuary); H4200+7156
1Ki 8:8 the Holy Place **in f of** the inner H6584+7156
1Ki 8:22 altar of the LORD **in f of** the whole H5584
1Ki 8:64 the courtyard **in f of** the temple of H4200+7156
2Ki 11:18 the priest of Baal **in f of** the altars. H4200+7156
2Ki 15:10 He attacked him **in f of** the people H7692
2Ki 16:14 he brought it from the **f** *of* the temple H7156
1Ch 14:14 and attack them **in f of** the poplar H4946+4578
1Ch 14:15 has gone out **in f of** you to strike H4200+7156
1Ch 19:10 were battle lines **in f of** him and behind H7156
2Ch 1:5 was in Gibeon **in f of** the H4200+7156
2Ch 3:4 The portico at the **f** *of* the temple was H7156
2Ch 3:15 **For** the **f of** the temple he made H4200+7156
2Ch 3:17 erected the pillars in the **f** *of* the temple, H7156
2Ch 4:20 to burn **in f of** the inner sanctuary H4200+7156
2Ch 5:9 could be seen from **in f of** the inner H6584+7156
2Ch 6:12 altar of the LORD **in f of** the whole H5584
2Ch 7:7 the courtyard **in f of** the temple of H4200+7156
2Ch 8:12 that he had built **in f of** the portico, H4200+7156
2Ch 13:13 while he was **in f of** Judah the H4200+7156
2Ch 13:14 were being attacked at both **f** and rear. H7156
2Ch 15:8 LORD that was **in f of** the portico of H4200+7156
2Ch 20:5 of the LORD **in** the **f of** the new H4200+7156
2Ch 23:17 the priest of Baal **in f of** the altars. H4200+7156
2Ch 29:19 They are now **in f of** the LORD's altar H4200+7156
Ne 3:23 Hasshub made repairs **in f of** their house; H5584
Ne 3:28 repairs, each **in f of** his own house. H4200+5584
Est 4:6 of the city **in f of** the king's gate. H4200+7156
Est 5:1 court of the palace, **in f of** the king's hall. H5790
Ps 68:25 **In f** *are* the singers, after them the H7709
Pr 21:29 The wicked **put up a bold f** H6451+928+7156
Jer 24:1 of figs placed **in f of** the temple of H4200+7156
Jer 36:22 burning in the firepot **in f of** him. H4200+7156
Eze 4:1 put it **in f of** you and draw the city H4200+7156
Eze 6:4 slay your people **in f of** your idols. H4200+7156
Eze 6:5 of the Israelites **in f of** their idols, H4200+7156
Eze 8:11 **In f of** them stood seventy elders of H4200+7156
Eze 9:6 men who were **in f of** the temple. H4200+7156
Eze 14:1 to me and sat down **in f of** me. H4200+7156
Eze 16:37 all around and will strip you **in f of** them, H448
Eze 20:1 and they sat down **in f of** me. H4200+7156
Eze 40:12 **In f of** each alcove was a wall one H4200+7156
Eze 40:47 the altar was **in f of** the temple. H4200+7156
Eze 40:49 and twelve cubits **from f to back.** H8145
Eze 41:14 including the **f** *of* the temple, was a H7156
Eze 41:21 the one at the **f** *of* the Most Holy H7156
Eze 41:25 wooden overhang on the **f** *of* the portico. H7156
Eze 42:4 **In f of** the rooms was an inner H4200+7156
Eze 42:7 it extended **in f of** the rooms for fifty H448+7156
Eze 42:11 with a passageway **in f of** them H4200+7156
Eze 44:4 of the north gate to the **f** *of* the temple. H7156
Zec 3:9 the stone I have set **in f of** Joshua! H4200+7156
Zec 14:20 the sacred bowls **in f of** the altar. H4200+7156
Mt 5:24 leave your gift there **in f of** the altar. G1869
Mt 6:1 righteousness **in f of** others to be seen G1869
Mt 27:24 washed his hands **in f of** the crowd. G595
Mt 27:29 Then they knelt **in f of** him and mocked G1869
Mt 27:60 *He* **rolled** a big stone **in f of** the entrance G4685
Mk 3:3 "Stand up **in f of everyone.**" G1650+3836+3545
Mk 5:6 he ran and **fell on** *his* **knees in f of** him. G4686
Mk 15:39 who stood there **in f of** Jesus, saw G1666+1885
Lk 5:19 middle of the crowd, **right in f of** Jesus. G1869
Lk 5:25 Immediately he stood up **in f of** them, took G1967
Lk 6:8 and stand **in f of everyone.**" G1650+3836+3545
Lk 14:2 There **in f of** him was a man suffering from G1869
Lk 19:27 bring them here and kill them **in f of** me. G1869
Ac 18:17 leader and beat him **in f of** the proconsul; G1869
Ac 19:33 in the crowd **pushed** Alexander **to the f,** G4582
Ac 27:35 gave thanks to God **in f of** them all. G1967
1Co 6:6 to court—and this **in f of** unbelievers! G2093
Gal 2:14 I said to Cephas **in f of** them all, "You are G1869
Rev 4:5 **In f of** the throne, seven lamps were G1967
Rev 4:6 Also **in f of** the throne there was what G1967
Rev 4:6 were covered with eyes, **in f** and in back. G1869
Rev 8:3 on the golden altar **in f of** the throne. G1967
Rev 12:4 The dragon stood **in f of** the woman who G1967

FRONTAL (1) [FRONT]

Jdg 20:34 men made a **f** attack on Gibeah H4946+5584

FRONTIER (2) [FRONTIERS]

Eze 25:9 beginning at its **f** towns—Beth Jeshimoth, H7895
Eze 48:1 At the northern **f**, Dan will have one H7895

FRONTIERS (1) [FRONTIER]

Ne 9:22 allotting to them even the **remotest f.** H6992

FROST (4) [FROSTY]

Ex 16:14 thin flakes like **f** on the ground appeared H4095
Job 38:29 Who gives birth to the **f** *from* the heavens H4095
Ps 147:16 like wool and scatters the **f** like ashes. H4095
Jer 36:30 to the heat by day and the **f** by night. H7943

FROSTY (1) [FROST]

Zec 14:6 be neither sunlight nor cold, **f darkness.** H7885

FROWARD, FROWARDNESS (KJV) CORRUPT, CROOKED, DEVIOUS, HARSH, PERVERSE, PERVERSENESS, PERVERSITY, SHREWD, WICKED

FROWN (1)

Jer 3:12 the LORD, '*I will* **f** on you no longer H5877+7156

FROZE (1) [FROZEN]

2Sa 23:10 till his hand grew tired and **f** to the sword. H1815

FROZEN (2) [FROZE]

Job 37:10 and the broad waters become **f.** H3668
Job 38:30 when the surface of the deep *is* **f?** H4334

FRUIT (175) [FIRSTFRUITS, FRUITFUL, FRUITFULNESS, FRUITION, FRUITLESS, FRUITS]

Ge 1:11 on the land that bear **f** with seed in it, H7262
Ge 1:12 kinds and trees bearing **f** with seed in it H7262
Ge 1:29 every tree that has **f** with seed in it. H7262
Ge 3:2 "We may eat **f** from the trees in the H7262
Ge 3:3 'You must not eat **f** from the tree that is in H7262
Ge 3:6 woman saw that the **f** of the tree was H7262
Ge 3:12 she gave me some **f** from the tree, and NDT
Ge 3:17 to your wife and ate **f** from the tree about NDT
Ex 10:15 in the fields and the **f** *on* the trees. H7262
Lev 19:23 the land and plant any kind of **f** tree, H4407
Lev 19:23 kind of fruit tree, regard its **f** as forbidden. H7262
Lev 19:24 In the fourth year all its **f** will be holy, an H7262
Lev 19:25 But in the fifth year you may eat its **f.** H7262
Lev 25:19 Then the land will yield its **f**, and you will H7262
Lev 26:4 will yield its crops and the trees their **f.** H7262
Lev 26:20 will the trees of your land yield their **f.** H7262
Lev 27:30 grain from the soil or **f** *from* the trees, H7262
Nu 13:20 to bring back some of the **f** *of* the land." H7262
Nu 13:26 showed them the **f** *of* the land. H7262
Nu 13:27 flow with milk and honey! Here is its **f.** H7262
Dt 1:25 with them some of the **f** *of* the land, H7262
Dt 7:13 He will bless the **f** *of* your womb, the H7262
Dt 20:19 an ax to them, because you can eat their **f.** NDT
Dt 20:20 you know are not **f** trees and use them to H4407
Dt 22:9 plant but also the **f** *of* the vineyard will be H9311
Dt 28:4 The **f** *of* your womb will be blessed, and H7262
Dt 28:11 prosperity—in the **f** *of* your womb, the H7262
Dt 28:18 The **f** *of* your womb will be cursed, and H7262
Dt 28:30 you will not even begin to enjoy its **f.** NDT
Dt 28:53 you will eat the **f** *of* the womb, the flesh H7262
Dt 30:9 of your hands and in the **f** *of* your womb, H7262
Dt 32:13 land and fed him with the **f** *of* the fields. H9482
Jdg 9:11 'Should I give up my **f**, so good and sweet H9482
2Sa 16:2 the bread and **f** are for the men to eat H7811
2Ki 18:31 each of you *will* **eat** *f* **from** your own vine AIT
2Ki 19:29 reap, plant vineyards and eat their **f.** H7262
2Ki 19:30 will take root below and bear **f** above. H7262
Ne 9:25 olive groves and **f** trees in abundance. H4407
Ne 9:36 so they could eat its **f** and the other good H7262
Ne 10:35 firstfruits of our crops and of every **f** tree. H7262
Ne 10:37 of the **f** *of* all our trees and of our new H7262
Ps 1:3 which yields its **f** in season and whose H7262
Ps 72:3 the people, the hills the **f** of righteousness. NDT
Ps 92:14 *They will* still **bear f** in old age, they will H5649
Ps 104:13 the land is satisfied by the **f** *of* his work. H7262
Ps 128:2 You will eat the **f of** your **labor** H3330+4090
Ps 148:9 all hills, **f** trees and all cedars, H7262
Pr 1:31 they will eat the **f** *of* their ways and be H7262
Pr 1:31 be filled with the **f** of their schemes. NDT
Pr 8:19 My **f** is better than fine gold; what I yield H7262
Pr 10:31 *From* the mouth of the righteous **comes the f** *of* H5649
Pr 11:30 The **f** *of* the righteous is a tree of life, and H7262
Pr 12:14 From the **f** *of* their lips people are filled H7262
Pr 13:2 From the **f** *of* their lips people enjoy good H7262
Pr 18:20 From the **f** *of* their mouth a person's H7262
Pr 18:21 and those who love it will eat its **f.** H7262
Pr 27:18 one who guards a fig tree will eat its **f,** H7262
Ecc 2:5 planted all kinds of **f** trees in them. H7262
Ecc 2:19 over all the **f of** my **toil** into which I have H6662
SS 2:3 his shade, and his **f** is sweet to my taste. H7262
SS 2:13 The fig tree forms its **early f**; the H7001
SS 7:7 the palm, and your breasts like **clusters of f.** H864
SS 7:8 the palm tree; I will take hold of its **f.**" H6180
SS 8:11 was to bring for its **f** a thousand shekels of H7262
SS 8:12 two hundred are for those who tend its **f.** H7262
Isa 3:10 they will enjoy the **f** *of* their deeds. H7262
Isa 4:2 the **f** *of* the land will be the pride and H7262
Isa 5:2 of good grapes, but it yielded only **bad f.** H946
Isa 11:1 from his roots a Branch *will* **bear f.** H7238
Isa 14:29 spring up a viper, its **f** will be a darting H7262
Isa 16:9 of joy over your **ripened f** and over your H7811
Isa 27:6 blossom and fill all the world with **f.** H9482
Isa 27:9 this will be the full **f** *of* the removal of his H7262
Isa 32:10 will fail, and the **harvest of f** will not come. H668
Isa 32:17 The **f** *of* that righteousness will be peace H5126
Isa 36:16 each of you *will* **eat** *f* **from** your own vine AIT
Isa 37:30 reap, plant vineyards and eat their **f.** H7262
Isa 37:31 will take root below and bear **f** above. H7262
Isa 65:21 they will plant vineyards and eat their **f.** H7262
Jer 2:7 a fertile land to eat its **f** and rich produce. H7262
Jer 6:19 on this people, the **f** *of* their schemes H7262
Jer 11:16 thriving olive tree with **f** beautiful in form. H7262
Jer 11:19 "Let us destroy the tree and its **f**; let us cut H4312
Jer 12:2 have taken root; they grow and bear **f.** H7262
Jer 17:8 a year of drought and never fails to bear **f.**" H7262
Jer 31:5 the farmers will plant them and enjoy their **f.** NDT
Jer 40:10 harvest the wine, **summer f** and olive oil H7811
Jer 40:12 an abundance of wine and **summer f.** H7811
Jer 48:32 has fallen on your **ripened f** and grapes. H7811
Eze 17:8 bear **f** and become a splendid vine. H7262
Eze 17:9 stripped of its **f** so that it withers? H7262
Eze 17:23 branches and bear **f** and become a H7262
Eze 19:12 it was stripped of its **f**; its strong branches H7262
Eze 19:14 of its main branches and consumed its **f.** H7262
Eze 25:4 they will eat your **f** and drink your milk. H7262
Eze 34:27 trees will yield their **f** and the ground will H7262
Eze 36:8 branches and **f** for my people Israel H7262
Eze 36:30 I will increase the **f** *of* the trees and the H7262
Eze 47:12 **F** trees of all kinds will grow on both banks H4407
Eze 47:12 leaves will not wither, nor will their **f** fail. H7262
Eze 47:12 Every month *they will* **bear f**, because the H1144
Eze 47:12 Their **f** will serve for food and their leaves H7262
Da 4:12 were beautiful, its **f** abundant, and on it A10004
Da 4:14 strip off its leaves and scatter its **f.** A10004
Da 4:21 with beautiful leaves and abundant **f** A10004
Hos 9:10 was like seeing the **early f** on the fig tree. H1136
Hos 9:16 their root is withered, they yield no **f.** H7262
Hos 10:1 he brought forth **f** for himself. H7262
Hos 10:1 As his **f** increased, he built more altars; as H7262
Hos 10:12 reap the **f** *of* unfailing love, and H7023
Hos 10:13 you have eaten the **f** *of* deception. H7262
Hos 14:2 that we may offer the **f** *of* our lips. H7262
Joel 2:22 The trees are bearing their **f**; the fig tree H7262
Am 2:9 I destroyed their **f** above and their roots H7262
Am 6:12 poison and the **f** *of* righteousness into H7262
Am 8:1 LORD showed me: a basket of **ripe f.** H7811
Am 8:2 "A basket of **ripe f,**" I answered. H7811
Am 9:14 they will make gardens and eat their **f.** H7262
Mic 6:7 the **f** *of* my body for the sin of my soul? H7262
Mic 7:1 one who gathers **summer f** at the H7811
Na 3:12 are like fig trees with their **first ripe f**; H1137
Hag 2:19 the olive tree *have* not **borne f.** H5951
Zec 8:12 the vine will yield its **f**, the ground will H7262
Mal 3:11 fields *will* not **drop** *their* **f before it is ripe,** H8897
Mt 3:8 Produce **f** in keeping with repentance. G2843
Mt 3:10 not produce good **f** will be cut down and G2843
Mt 7:16 By their **f** you will recognize them. G2843
Mt 7:17 every good tree bears good **f**, but a bad G2843
Mt 7:17 good fruit, but a bad tree bears bad **f.** G2843
Mt 7:18 A good tree cannot bear bad **f**, and a bad G2843
Mt 7:18 and a bad tree cannot bear good **f.** G2843
Mt 7:19 does not bear good **f** is cut down and G2843
Mt 7:20 by their **f** you will recognize them. G2843
Mt 12:33 "Make a tree good and its **f** will be good G2843
Mt 12:33 make a tree bad and its **f** will be bad G2843
Mt 12:33 be bad, for a tree is recognized by its **f.** G2843
Mt 21:19 he said to it, "May you never bear **f** again!" G2843
Mt 21:34 his servants to the tenants to collect his **f.** G2843
Mt 21:43 given to a people who will produce its **f.** G2843
Mt 26:29 not drink from this **f** of the vine from now G1163
Mk 11:13 he went to find out if it had **any** *f.* AIT
Mk 11:14 "May no one ever eat **f** from you again." G2843

Mk 12: 2 from them some *of* the f of the vineyard. *G2843*
Mk 14:25 drink again from the f of the vine until *G1163*
Lk 3: 8 Produce f in keeping with repentance. *G2843*
Lk 3: 9 not produce good f will be cut down and *G2843*
Lk 6:43 "No good tree bears bad f, nor does a *G2843*
Lk 6:43 bad fruit, nor does a bad tree bear good f. *G2843*
Lk 6:44 Each tree is recognized by its own f *G2843*
Lk 13: 6 he went to look for f on it but did not find *G2843*
Lk 13: 7 coming to look for f on this fig tree and *G2843*
Lk 13: 9 If it bears f next year, fine! If not, then cut *G2843*
Lk 20:10 give him some of the f of the vineyard. *G2843*
Lk 22:18 drink again from the f of the vine until the *G1163*
Jn 15: 2 off every branch in me that bears no f, *G2843*
Jn 15: 2 that does bear f he prunes so that it *G2843*
Jn 15: 4 No branch can bear f by itself; it must *G2843*
Jn 15: 4 Neither *can* you **bear** f unless you *G4048S*
Jn 15: 5 you will bear much f; apart from me you *G2843*
Jn 15: 8 that you bear much f, showing yourselves *G2843*
Jn 15:16 you so that you might go and bear f— *G2843*
Jn 15:16 go and bear fruit—f that will last—and so *G2843*
Ro 7: 4 in order that *we might* **bear** f for God. *G2844*
Ro 7: 5 at work in us, so that *we* **bore** f for death. *G2844*
Gal 5:22 But the f of the Spirit is love, joy, peace *G2843*
Eph 5: 9 the f of the light consists in all *G2843*
Php 1:11 filled with the f of righteousness that *G2843*
Col 1: 6 the gospel is **bearing** f and growing *G2844*
Col 1:10 **bearing** f in every good work, growing in *G2844*
Heb 13:15 the f of lips that openly profess his name. *G2843*
Jas 3:17 full of mercy and good f, impartial and *G2843*
Jude 12 autumn trees, **without** f and uprooted *G182*
Rev 18:14 'The f you longed for is gone from you. *G3967*
Rev 22: 2 bearing twelve **crops of** f, yielding its fruit *G2843*
Rev 22: 2 crops of fruit, yielding its f every month. *G2843*

FRUITFUL (30) [FRUIT]

Ge 1:22 "*Be* f and increase in number and fill the H7238
Ge 1:28 to them, "*Be* f and increase in number H7238
Ge 8:17 on the earth and *be* f and increase in H7238
Ge 9: 1 "*Be* f and increase in number and fill the H7238
Ge 9: 7 As for you, *be* f and increase in number H7238
Ge 17: 6 *I will* **make** you very f; I will make nations H7238
Ge 17:20 *I will* **make** him f and will greatly increase H7238
Ge 28: 3 bless you and **make** you f and increase H7238
Ge 35:11 Almighty; *be* f and increase in number. H7238
Ge 41:52 because God *has* **made** me f in the land H7238
Ge 47:27 property there and *were* f and increased H7238
Ge 48: 4 'I *am going to* **make** you f and increase H7238
Ge 49:22 "Joseph is a **f vine**, a fruitful vine H1201+7238
Ge 49:22 fruitful vine, a f **vine** near a spring H1201+7238
Ex 1: 7 the Israelites *were* **exceedingly** f; they H7238
Lev 26: 9 with favor and **make** you f and increase H7238
Ps 105:24 The LORD **made** his people very f; he H7238
Ps 107:34 f land into a salt waste, because of H7262
Ps 107:37 planted vineyards that yielded a f harvest; H7262
Ps 128: 3 Your wife *will be* like a f vine within your H7238
Isa 17: 6 four or five on the f boughs," declares the H7238
Isa 27: 2 In that day—"Sing about a f vineyard: H2774
Isa 32:12 the pleasant fields, for the f vines H7238
Jer 4:26 I looked, and the f **land** was a desert; all H4149
Jer 23: 3 where *they will be* f and increase in H7238
Jer 49: 4 of your valleys, boast of your valleys *so* f? H2307
Eze 19:10 it was f and full of branches because of H7238
Eze 36:11 and *they will be* f and become numerous. H7238
Jn 15: 2 so that *it will be* even more f. *G2843+5770*
Php 1:22 in the body, this will mean f labor for me. *G2843*

FRUITFULNESS (2) [FRUITFUL]

Dt 33:15 mountains and the f *of* the everlasting H4458
Hos 14: 8 flourishing juniper; your f comes from me." H7262

FRUITION (2) [FRUIT]

2Sa 23: 5 surely he *would* not **bring to** f my H7541
2Th 1:11 by his power *he may* **bring to** f your every *G4444*

FRUITLESS (1) [FRUIT]

Eph 5:11 nothing to do with the f deeds of darkness, *G182*

FRUITS (5) [FRUIT]

Ge 4: 3 brought some of the f *of* the soil as an H7262
Ps 109:11 may strangers plunder the f **of** his **labor**. H3330
SS 4:13 an orchard of pomegranates with choice f, H7262
SS 4:16 into his garden and taste its choice f. H7262
Jer 3:24 consumed the f **of** our ancestors' **labor**— H3330

FRUSTRATE (4) [FRUSTRATED, FRUSTRATES, FRUSTRATING, FRUSTRATION]

2Sa 17:14 had determined to f the good advice of H7296
Ezr 4: 5 against them and f their plans during H7296
Ps 14: 6 *You* evildoers f the plans of the poor, but H1017
1Co 1:19 the intelligence of the intelligent *I will* f." *G119*

FRUSTRATED (2) [FRUSTRATE]

Ne 4:15 aware of their plot and that God *had* f it, H7296
Eze 24:12 *It has* f all efforts; its heavy deposit has H4206

FRUSTRATES (2) [FRUSTRATE]

Ps 146: 9 but *he* f the ways of the wicked. H6430
Pr 22:12 but *he* f the words of the unfaithful. H6156

FRUSTRATING (1) [FRUSTRATE]

2Sa 15:34 then *you can* help me *by* f Ahithophel's H7296

FRUSTRATION (3) [FRUSTRATE]

Ecc 5:17 darkness, with great f, affliction and anger H4087
Ecc 7: 3 **F** is better than laughter, because a sad H4088
Ro 8:20 For the creation was subjected *to* f, not by *G3470*

FUEL (13)

Isa 9: 5 destined for burning, will be **f** *for* the fire. H4409
Isa 9:19 the people will be **f** *for* the fire; H4409
Isa 44:15 It is used as *f* for **burning**; some of it he takes AIT
Isa 44:19 "Half of it *I* **used for** f; I even H8596+1198+836
Jer 51:58 labor is only **f for the flames**." H928+1896+836
Eze 4:12 of the people, using human excrement for f." NDT
Eze 15: 4 thrown on the fire as f and the fire burns H433
Eze 15: 6 the trees of the forest as f for the fire, H433
Eze 21:32 You will be f for the fire, your blood will be H433
Eze 39: 9 out and **use** the weapons **for f** and burn H1277
Eze 39: 9 seven years *they will* **use** them **for f**. H1277+836
Eze 39:10 *they will* **use** the weapons **for f**. H1277+836
Hab 2:13 labor is only **f for the fire**, H928+1896+836

FUGITIVE (4) [FUGITIVES]

Jos 20: 4 are to admit **the f** into their city and H2257S
Jos 20: 5 the elders must not surrender the f H8357S
Jos 20: 5 because the f killed their neighbor NDT
Eze 24:26 on that day a f will come to tell you the H7127

FUGITIVES (15) [FUGITIVE]

Nu 21:29 up his sons as f and his daughters as H7128
Jos 8:22 leaving them neither survivors nor f. H7127
Isa 15: 5 out over Moab; her f flee as far as Zoar H1371
Isa 15: 9 a lion upon the f *of* Moab and upon those H7129
Isa 16: 3 Hide the f, do not betray the H5615
Isa 16: 4 Let the Moabite f stay with you; be their H5615
Isa 21:14 you who live in Tema, bring food for the f. H5610
Isa 43:14 bring down as f all the Babylonians, H1371
Isa 45:20 assemble, you f *from* the nations. H7127
Jer 44:14 live; none will return except a *few* f." H7128
Jer 48:45 shadow of Heshbon the f stand helpless, H5674
Jer 49: 5 driven away, and no one will gather the f. H5610
Jer 50:28 Listen to the f and refugees from Babylon H5674
Eze 7:16 The f who escape will flee to the H7127
Ob 14 wait at the crossroads to cut down their f, H7127

FULFILL (54) [FULFILLED, FULFILLING, FULFILLMENT, FULFILLS]

Ge 38: 8 **f** *your* **duty** to her **as a brother-in-law** to H3302
Lev 22:18 either **to f** a vow or as a freewill offering, H4200
Lev 22:21 the LORD to **f a special vow** or as a H7098+5624
Nu 6:21 *They must* f the vows H6913+7023+3869+4027
Nu 23:19 Does he promise and not f? H7756
Dt 25: 5 and **f the duty of a brother-in-law** *to* her. H3302
Dt 25: 7 not **f the duty of a brother-in-law** *to* me." H3302
1Sa 1:21 annual sacrifice to the LORD and to f his vow, NDT
2Sa 15: 7 go to Hebron and f a vow I made to the H8966
1Ki 6:12 *I will* f through you the promise I gave to H7756
1Ki 12:15 to f the word the LORD had spoken to H7756
2Ki 23:24 This he did to f the requirements of the H7756
2Ch 10:15 to f the word the LORD had spoken to H7756
2Ch 36:22 in order to f the word of the LORD spoken H3983
Ezr 1: 1 in order to f the word of the LORD spoken H3983
Est 5: 8 to grant my petition and f my request, H6913
Job 22:27 he will hear you, and *you will* f your vows. H8966
Ps 22:25 before those who fear you *I will* f my vows. H8966
Ps 50:14 f your vows to the Most High, H8966
Ps 61: 8 of your name and f my vows day after day. H8966
Ps 66:13 burnt offerings and f my vows to you— H8966
Ps 76:11 vows to the LORD your God and f them; H8966
Ps 116:14 *I will* f my vows to the LORD in the H8966
Ps 116:18 *I will* f my vows to the LORD in the H8966
Ps 119:38 **F** your promise to your servant, so that you H7756
Ecc 5: 4 make a vow to God, do not delay to f it. H8966
Ecc 5: 4 He has no pleasure in fools; f your vow. H8966
Ecc 5: 5 a vow than to make one and not f it. H8966
Isa 46:11 from a far-off land, a **man** *to f* my purpose. AIT
Jer 11: 5 Then *I will* f the oath I swore to your H7756
Jer 28: 6 *May* the LORD f the words you have H7756
Jer 29:10 come to you and f my good promise to H7756
Jer 33:14 'when *I will* f the good promise I made to H7756
Jer 39:16 I *am about to* f my words against this city H995
Eze 12:25 rebellious people, *I will* f whatever I say H6913
Eze 13: 6 declares," and expect him to f their words. H7756
Na 1:15 your festivals, Judah, and f your vows. H8966
Mt 1:22 this took place to f what the Lord had said *G4444*
Mt 3:15 us to do this *to* f all righteousness. *G4444*
Mt 4:14 to f what was said through the prophet *G4444*
Mt 5:17 not come to abolish them but *to* f them. *G4444*
Mt 5:33 f to the Lord the vows you have made. *G625*
Mt 8:17 This *was to* f what was spoken through the *G4444*
Mt 12:17 This was to f what was spoken through the *G4444*
Mt 21: 4 This took place to f what was spoken *G4444*
Lk 1:45 that the Lord *would* f his promises *G1639+5459*
Jn 12:38 This was to f the word of Isaiah the *G4444*
Jn 13:18 But this is to f this passage of Scripture *G4444*
Jn 15:25 But *this is* to f what is written in their Law *G4444*
Jn 18:32 This took place to f what Jesus had said *G4444*
Ac 7:17 God *to* f his **promise** to *G2039+4005+3933*
1Co 7: 3 The husband *should* f his marital duty to his *G625*
Gal 6: 2 in this way *you will* f the law of Christ. *G405*
Php 2:13 will and to act **in order to** f his good *G5642*

FULFILLED (61) [FULFILL]

Jos 21:45 promises to Israel failed; every one *was* f. H995
Jos 23:14 Every promise *has been* f; not one has H995
Jdg 13:12 "When your words *are* f, what is to be the H995
1Sa 10: 7 Once these signs *are* f, do whatever your H995
1Sa 10: 9 and all these signs *were* f that day. H995
1Sa 25:30 When the LORD *has* f for my lord every H6913
1Ki 8:15 *who* with his own hand *has* f what he H4848
1Ki 8:24 with your hand *you have* f it— H4848
1Ki 9:25 and so f the temple **obligations**. H8966
2Ki 15:12 of the LORD spoken to Jehu *was* f: H2118+4027
2Ch 6: 4 *who* with his hands *has* f what he H4848
2Ch 6:15 with your hand *you have* f it— H4848
Ps 65: 1 our God, in Zion; to you our vows *will* **be f**. H8966
Pr 7:14 "Today *I* f my vows, and I have food from H8966
Pr 13:12 heart sick, but a longing f is a tree of life. H995
Pr 13:19 A longing **f** is sweet to the soul, but fools H2118
Jer 1:12 I am watching to *see that* my word *is* f." H6913
Jer 17:15 is the word of the LORD? *Let it* now *be* f!" H995
Jer 25:12 "But when the seventy years *are* f, I will H4848
Jer 34:18 my covenant and *have* not f the terms of H7756
Jer 39:16 At that time *they will* **be f** before your H2118
La 2:17 he planned; *he has* f his word, which H1298
Eze 12:23 days are near when every vision will be f. H1821
Eze 12:25 what I will, and *it shall* **be f** without delay. H6913
Eze 12:28 whatever I say *will* **be f**, declares the H6913
Da 4:33 been said about Nebuchadnezzar *was* f. A10508
Da 8:13 "How long will it take for the vision to be f NDT
Da 9:12 *You have* f the words spoken against us H7756
Da 12: 6 be before these astonishing things are f?" H7891
Mt 2:15 And so *was* f what the Lord had said *G4444*
Mt 2:17 said through the prophet Jeremiah *was* f: *G4444*
Mt 2:23 So *was* f what was said through the *G4444*
Mt 13:14 In them *is* f the prophecy of Isaiah: " 'You *G405*
Mt 13:35 So *was* f what was spoken through the *G4444*
Mt 26:54 how then *would* the Scriptures *be* f that *G4444*
Mt 26:56 the writings of the prophets *might be* f." *G4444*
Mt 27: 9 spoken by Jeremiah the prophet *was* f: *G4444*
Mk 13: 4 be the sign that they are all about to *be* f?" *G5334*
Mk 14:49 But the Scriptures must *be* f." *G4444*
Lk 1: 1 of the things *that have been* f among us, *G4442*
Lk 1:38 "*May* your word to me *be* f." Then the *G1181*
Lk 4:21 "Today this scripture *is* f in your hearing." *G4444*
Lk 18:31 prophets about the Son of Man *will be* f. *G5464*
Lk 21:24 until the times of the Gentiles *are* f. *G4444*
Lk 22:37 I tell you that this must *be* f in me. *G5464*
Lk 24:44 Everything must *be* f that is written about *G4444*
Jn 17:12 to destruction so that Scripture *would be* f. *G4444*
Jn 18: 9 that the words he had spoken *would be* f: *G4444*
Jn 19:24 that the scripture *might be* f that said, *G4444*
Jn 19:28 so that Scripture *would be* f, Jesus *G5457*
Jn 19:36 so that the scripture *would be* f: *G4444*
Ac 1:16 the Scripture had to *be* f in which the Holy *G4444*
Ac 3:18 But this is how God f what he had foretold *G4444*
Ac 13:27 condemning him *they* f the words of the *G4444*
Ac 13:33 he *has* f for us, their children, by raising up *G1740*
Ac 23: 1 I *have* f *my* **duty** to God in all good *G4488*
Ac 26: 7 tribes are hoping *to* **see** f as they *G2918*
Ro 13: 8 whoever loves others *has* f the law. *G4444*
Gal 5:14 For the entire law *is* f in keeping this one *G4444*
Jas 2:23 And the scripture *was* f that says *G4444*
Rev 17:17 royal authority, until God's words *are* f. *G5464*

FULFILLING (2) [FULFILL]

Nu 3: 8 f the obligations of the Israelites **by doing** H6268
1Ki 2:27 f the word the LORD had spoken at Shiloh H4848

FULFILLMENT (9) [FULFILL]

Lev 22:23 it will not be accepted **in** f **of** a vow. H4200
2Ch 36:21 were completed *in* f *of* the word of the H4848
Da 11:14 own people will rebel in f *of* the vision, H6641
Lk 9:31 he was about to **bring to** f at Jerusalem. *G4444*
Lk 21:22 of punishment *in* f *of* all that has been *G4398*
Lk 22:16 it again until *it* **finds** f in the kingdom of *G4444*
Lk 22:37 what is written about me is reaching its f." *G5465*
Ro 13:10 Therefore love is the f of the law. *G4445*
Eph 1:10 into effect when the times reach their f— *G4445*

FULFILLS (2) [FULFILL]

Ps 145:19 *He* f the desires of those who fear him; he H6913
Isa 44:26 of his servants and f the predictions of his H8966

FULL (203) [FILL]

Ge 6:11 in God's sight and *was* f *of* violence. H4848
Ge 14:10 the Valley of Siddim was **f** of tar **pits**, H931+931
Ge 15:16 has not yet reached its **f measure**. H8969
Ge 23: 9 sell it to me for the f price as a burial site H4849
Ge 25: 8 an old man and f of years; and he H8428
Ge 35:29 gathered to his people, old and f *of* years. H8428
Ge 41: 1 When *two* **f years** had passed H9102+3427
Ge 41: 7 swallowed up the seven healthy, f heads. H4849
Ge 41:22 heads of grain, f and good, growing on H4849
Ge 50: 3 **taking** a f forty days, for that was the time H4848
Ex 5:18 you must produce your **f quota** *of* bricks." H9420
Ex 8:21 houses of the Egyptians *will be* f *of* flies; H4848
Ex 9:14 I will send the **f force** *of* my plagues H3972
Ex 16:20 but *it was* f *of* maggots and began to H8249
Ex 23:26 *I will* **give** you a f life span. H4848
Lev 6: 5 They must make restitution in f, add a H8031
Lev 16:12 is to take a censer f *of* burning coals from H4850
Lev 23:15 wave offering, count off seven f weeks. H9459
Lev 25:29 right of redemption a f year after its sale. H9462
Lev 25:30 not redeemed before a f year has passed, H9459
Nu 5: 7 *They must* **make f restitution** *for* the wrong H8740+928+8031

F

Nu 33: 3 out defiantly in f view of all the Egyptians, H6524
Dt 21:13 her father and mother for a f month, H3427
Dt 33:23 favor of the LORD and is f of his blessing; H4849
Jos 10:13 delayed going down about a f day. H9459
Jdg 8: 2 better than the f grape harvest of Abiezer? H1292
Ru 1:21 I went away f, but the LORD has brought me H4849
1Sa 2: 5 Those who were f hire themselves out H8428
1Sa 18:27 They counted out the f number to the king H4848
1Sa 28:20 Saul fell f length on the ground, H4850
2Sa 5:17 they went up in f force to search for him H3972
2Sa 6:20 half-naked in f view of the slave H4200+6524
2Sa 11:18 Joab sent David a f account of the battle. H3972
2Sa 23:11 place where there was a field f of lentils, H4849
2Ki 4: 6 When all the jars were f, she said to her H4848
2Ki 6:17 saw the hills f of horses and chariots H4848
2Ki 10:21 of Baal until it was f from one end to the H4848
1Ch 11:13 place where there was a field f of barley, H4849
1Ch 14: 8 they went up in f force to search for him H3972
1Ch 21:22 Sell it to me at the f price." H4849
1Ch 21:24 I insist on paying the f price. H4849
1Ch 23: 1 When David was old and f of years, he H8425
2Ch 24:10 dropping them into the chest until it was f. H3983
2Ch 24:15 Now Jehoiada was old and f of years, and H8425
Ne 9:25 They ate to the f and were well-nourished H8425
Est 1: 4 For a f 180 days he displayed the vast H8041
Est 9:29 wrote with f authority to confirm this H3972
Est 10: 2 together with a f account of the greatness H7308
Job 5:26 You will come to the grave in f vigor, like H3995
Job 10:15 I am f of shame and drowned in my H8428
Job 14: 1 woman, are of few days and f of trouble. H8428
Job 20:22 the f force of misery will come upon him. H3972
Job 21:23 One person dies in f vigor, completely H9448
Job 21:27 "I know f well what you are thinking, the H2176
Job 26: 9 He covers the face of the f moon H4057
Job 32:12 I gave you my f attention. But not one of H1067
Job 32:18 For I am f of words, and the spirit within H4848
Job 33:26 he will restore them to f well-being. H7407
Job 42:17 so Job died, an old man and f of years. H8428
Ps 10: 7 His mouth is f of lies and threats; trouble H4848
Ps 26:10 whose right hands are f of bribes. H4848
Ps 31:23 but the proud he pays back in f. H3856
Ps 33: 5 the earth is f of his unfailing love. H4848
Ps 75: 8 the LORD is a cup f of foaming wine mixed H4849
Ps 78:38 his anger and did not stir up his f wrath. H3972
Ps 81: 3 when the moon is f, on the day of H4057
Ps 94: 4 all the evildoers are f of boasting. H607
Ps 104:24 them all; the earth is f of your creatures. H4848
Ps 116: 5 righteous; our God is f of compassion. H8163
Ps 127: 5 is the man whose quiver is f of them. H4848
Ps 130: 7 love and with him is f redemption. H2221
Ps 139:14 works are wonderful, I know that f well. H4394
Ps 144: 8 whose mouths are f of lies, whose right H1819
Ps 144:11 of foreigners whose mouths are f of lies, H1819
Pr 4:18 shining ever brighter till the f light of day. H3922
Pr 5:21 your ways are in f view of the LORD, H5790+6524
Pr 7:20 and will not be home till f moon." H3427+4057
Pr 8:21 love me and making their treasuries f. H4848
Pr 17: 1 quiet than a house f of feasting, H4849
Pr 20:17 one ends up with a mouth f of gravel. H4848
Pr 27: 7 One who is f loathes honey from the H8428
Pr 29:11 Fools give f vent to their rage, but the H3972
Pr 31:11 husband has f confidence in her H1053+4213
Ecc 1: 7 flow into the sea, yet the sea is never f. H4849
Ecc 9: 3 are f of evil and there is madness in their H4848
Ecc 11: 3 If clouds are f of water, they pour rain on H4848
Isa 1:15 Your hands are f of blood! H4848
Isa 1:21 She once was f of justice; righteousness H4849
Isa 2: 6 They are f of superstitions from the East H4848
Isa 2: 7 Their land is f of silver and gold; there is H4848
Isa 2: 7 Their land is f of horses; there is no end H4848
Isa 2: 8 Their land is f of idols; they bow down to H4848
Isa 6: 3 Almighty; the whole earth is f of his glory." H4850
Isa 15: 9 The waters of Dimon are f of blood, but I H4848
Isa 22: 2 you town so f of commotion, you city of H4849
Isa 22: 7 Your choicest valleys are f of chariots, and H4848
Isa 27: 9 this will be the f fruit of the removal H3972
Isa 30:26 like the light of seven f days, when the LORD AIT
Isa 30:27 of smoke; his lips are f of wrath, and his H4848
Isa 47: 9 They will come upon you in f measure, in H9448
Isa 65: 6 I will not keep silent but will pay back in f H8966
Isa 65: 7 I will measure into their laps the f payment for H4499
Jer 5:27 Like cages f of birds, their houses are full H4849
Jer 5:27 their houses are f of deceit; they have H4849
Jer 6:11 But I am f of the wrath of the LORD, and I H4848
Jer 23:10 The land is f of adulterers; because of the H4848
Jer 35: 5 Then I set bowls f of wine and some cups H4849
Jer 51: 5 though their land is f of guilt before the H4848
Jer 51:56 of retribution; he will repay in f. H8966+8966
La 1: 1 deserted lies the city, once so f of people! H8041
La 4:11 The LORD has given f vent to his wrath; he H3983
Eze 1:18 all four rims were f of eyes all around. H4849
Eze 1:27 metal, as if f of fire, and that from H1074+6017
Eze 7:23 For the land is f of bloodshed, and the city H4848
Eze 7:23 of bloodshed, and the city is f of violence. H4848
Eze 9: 9 the land is f of bloodshed and the city is H4848
Eze 9: 9 of bloodshed and the city is f of injustice. H4848
Eze 10: 4 the court was f of the radiance of the H4848
Eze 10:12 were completely f of eyes, as were their H4849
Eze 17: 3 long feathers and f plumage of varied H4849
Eze 17: 7 with powerful wings and f plumage. H8041
Eze 19:10 was fruitful and f of branches because of H6734
Eze 22: 5 mock you, you infamous city, f of turmoil. H8041
Eze 23:12 warriors in f dress, mounted horsemen H4814
Eze 28:12 f of wisdom and perfect in beauty. H4849
Eze 37: 1 the middle of a valley; it was f of bones. H4849
Joel 2:26 plenty to eat, until you are f, and you will H8425
Joel 3:13 the winepress is f and the vats H4848
Na 3: 1 the city of blood, f of lies, full of plunder H3972
Na 3: 1 full of lies, f of plunder, never without H4849
Zec 9:15 they will be f like a bowl used for H4848
Mt 6: 2 they have received their reward in f. G600
Mt 6: 5 they have received their reward in f. G600
Mt 6:16 they have received their reward in f. G600
Mt 6:22 healthy, your whole body will be f of light. G5893
Mt 6:23 your whole body will be f of darkness. G5027
Mt 12:34 the mouth speaks what the heart is f of. G4354
Mt 13:48 When it was f, the fishermen pulled it up G4444
Mt 23:25 inside they are f of greed and G1154
Mt 23:27 on the inside are f of the bones of the G1154
Mt 23:28 on the inside you are f of hypocrisy and G3550
Mk 2:12 mat and walked out in f view of them all. G1869
Mk 4:28 the head, then the f kernel in the head. G4441
Lk 4: 1 f of the Holy Spirit, left the Jordan G4441
Lk 5: 7 came and filled both boats so f that they G4398
Lk 6:34 sinners, expecting to be repaid in f. G3836+2698
Lk 6:45 the mouth speaks what the heart is f of. G4354
Lk 10:21 time Jesus, f of joy through the Holy Spirit G22
Lk 11:34 healthy, your whole body also is f of light. G5893
Lk 11:34 unhealthy, your body also is f of darkness. G5027
Lk 11:36 if your whole body is f of light, and no G5893
Lk 11:36 it will be just as f of light as when a lamp G3910
Lk 11:39 inside you are f of greed and G1154
Lk 14:23 to come in, so that my house will be f. G1153
Jn 1:14 came from the Father, f of grace and truth. G4441
Jn 3:29 and is f of joy when he hears the G5915+5897
Jn 6:63 to you—they are f of the Spirit and life. AIT
Jn 10:10 they may have life, and have it to the f. G4356
Jn 17:13 may have the f measure of my joy within G4444
Jn 21: 8 towing the net f of fish, for they were not AIT
Jn 21:11 It was f of large fish, 153, but even with G3550
Ac 5: 2 With his wife's f knowledge he kept back G5323
Ac 5:21 the f assembly of the elders of Israel G4246
Ac 6: 3 who are known to be f of the Spirit and G4441
Ac 6: 5 a man f of faith and of the Holy Spirit G4441
Ac 6: 8 a man f of God's grace and power G4441
Ac 7:55 But Stephen, f of the Holy Spirit, looked up G4441
Ac 8:23 see that you are f of bitterness and G1650+5958
Ac 11:24 a good man, f of the Holy Spirit and faith G4441
Ac 13:10 You are f of all kinds of deceit and trickery. G4441
Ac 17:16 to see that the city was f of idols. G2977
Ro 1:29 They are f of envy, murder, strife, deceit G3550
Ro 3:14 "Their mouths are f of cursing and G1154
Ro 11:12 greater riches will their f inclusion bring! G4445
Ro 11:25 in part until the f number of the Gentiles G4445
Ro 13: 6 who give their f time to governing. G4674
Ro 15:14 that you yourselves are f of goodness G3550
Ro 15:29 I will come in the f measure of the G4445
1Co 9:18 so not make f use of my rights as a G2974
2Co 13:11 Strive for f restoration, encourage one G2936
Eph 4:19 kind of impurity, and they are f of greed. G1877
Eph 6:11 Put on the f armor of God, so that you can G4110
Eph 6:13 Therefore put on the f armor of God, so G4110
Php 4:18 I have received f payment and have more G4246
Col 2: 2 they may have the f riches of complete G4246
Col 4: 6 Let your conversation be always f of grace G1877
1Ti 1:15 saying that deserves f acceptance: G4246
1Ti 2:11 learn in quietness and f submission. G4246
1Ti 3: 4 do so in a manner worthy of f respect. G4246
1Ti 4: 9 saying that deserves f acceptance. G4246
1Ti 6: 1 consider their masters worthy of f respect, G4246
Titus 1:10 f of meaningless talk and deception G3468
Heb 10:22 with the f assurance that faith brings G4443
Heb 10:32 you endured in a great conflict f of suffering. AIT
Jas 3: 8 It is a restless evil, f of deadly poison. G3550
Jas 3:17 submissive, f of mercy and good fruit G3550
Jas 5:11 The Lord is f of compassion and mercy. G4499
2Pe 2:14 With eyes f of adultery, they never stop G3550
Rev 5: 8 were holding golden bowls f of incense, G1154
Rev 6:11 until the f number of their fellow servants G4444
Rev 13:13 to the earth in f view of the people. G1967
Rev 14:10 has been poured f strength into the cup of G204
Rev 21: 9 had the seven bowls f of the seven last G1154

FULL-GROWN (1) [GROW]

Jas 1:15 and sin, when it is f, gives birth to G699

FULLER'S, FULLERS' (KJV) LAUNDERER'S, WASHERMAN'S

FULLNESS (9) [FILL]

Dt 33:16 of the earth and its f and the favor of him H4850
Jn 1:16 Out of his f we have all received grace in G4445
Eph 1:23 the f of him who fills everything in every G4445
Eph 3:19 filled to the measure of all the f of God. G4445
Eph 4:13 to the whole measure of the f of Christ. G4445
Col 1:19 pleased to have all his f dwell in him, G4445
Col 1:25 to present to you the word of God in its f G4444
Col 2: 9 For in Christ all the f of the Deity lives in G4445
Col 2:10 in Christ you have been brought to f G4444

FULLY (50) [FILL]

Ex 6: 3 LORD I did not make myself f known to H3359
Ex 19: 5 if you obey me f and H9048+928+7754+9048
Dt 15: 5 if only you f obey the H9048+928+7754+9048
Dt 28: 1 If you f obey the LORD H9048+928+7754+9048
Jos 1:17 Just as we f obeyed Moses, so we will H3972
1Ki 8:61 your hearts be f committed to the LORD our H8969
1Ki 11: 4 his heart was not f devoted to the LORD his H8969
1Ki 15: 3 his heart was not f devoted to the LORD his H8969
1Ki 15:14 Asa's heart was f committed to the LORD H8969
1Ch 12:38 Hebron f determined to make H928+4222+8969
2Ch 15:17 Asa's heart was f committed to the LORD H8969
2Ch 16: 9 whose hearts are f committed to him. H8969
Ezr 6: 8 expenses are to be f paid out of the A10056
Ps 63: 5 I will be f satisfied as with the richest of AIT
Ps 106: 2 acts of the LORD or f declare his praise? H3972
Ps 119: 4 down precepts that are to be f obeyed. H4394
Ps 119:138 down are righteous; they are f trustworthy. H4394
Pr 13: 4 the desires of the diligent are f satisfied. H2014
Pr 14:14 The faithless will be f repaid for their H8425
Pr 28: 5 those who seek the LORD understand it f. H3972
Isa 21: 7 riders on camels, let him be alert, f alert." H8041
Jer 23:20 until he f accomplishes the H6913+2256+7756
Jer 30:24 until he f accomplishes the H6913+2256+7756
Jer 35:10 tents and have f obeyed H9048+2256+6913
Eze 38: 4 your horsemen f armed, and a great H4814
Da 11:13 advance with a huge army f equipped. H8041
Joel 2:19 olive oil, enough to satisfy you f; never H8425
Lk 6:40 everyone who is f trained will be like G2936
Lk 9:32 but when they became f awake, they saw G1340
Lk 11:21 a strong man, f armed, guards his own G2774
Jn 7: 8 because my time has not yet f come." G4444
Ro 4:21 being f persuaded that God had power to G4442
Ro 8: 4 of the law might be f met in us, G4444
Ro 14: 5 of them should be f convinced in their G4442
Ro 14:14 being f persuaded in the Lord Jesus G4275
Ro 15:19 I have f proclaimed the gospel of Christ. G4444
1Co 13:12 then I shall know f, even as I am G2105
1Co 13:12 I shall know fully, even as I am f known. G2105
1Co 15:58 Always give yourselves f to the work of the G4355
2Co 1:14 to understand f that you can boast G2401+5465
2Co 13: 9 our prayer is that you may be f restored. G2937
Gal 4: 4 But when the set time had f come, God G4445
Col 1:28 may present everyone f mature in Christ. G5455
Col 4:12 all the will of God, mature and f assured. G4442
2Ti 4:17 message might be f proclaimed and all G4442
Titus 2:10 to show that they can be f trusted G4246+19
Heb 2:17 be made like them, f human in every way, in G81
Heb 6:11 that what you hope for may be f realized. G4443
1Pe 1:13 with minds that are alert and f sober, set G5458
2Jn 8 but that you may be rewarded f. G4441

FUN (1)

Ac 2:13 however, made f of them and said, "They G1430

FUNCTION (2) [FUNCTIONING]

Ex 27:19 whatever their f, including all the tent NDT
Ro 12: 4 members do not all have the same f, G4552

FUNCTIONING (1) [FUNCTION]

Heb 9: 8 as the first tabernacle was still f. G2400+5087

FUNERAL (5)

2Ch 21:19 His people made no f fire in his honor, as AIT
Jer 16: 5 not enter a house where there is a f meal; H5301
Jer 34: 5 As people made a f fire in honor of your H5386
Eze 43: 7 the f offerings for their kings at H7007
Eze 43: 9 the f offerings for their kings, H7007

FURBISHED (KJV) POLISHED

FURIOUS (21) [FURY]

Ge 34: 7 They were shocked and f, because H3013+4394
Dt 29:28 In f anger and in great wrath the LORD H2779
2Sa 13:21 King David heard all this, he was f. H3013+4394
2Ch 25:10 They were f with Judah and H3013+678+4394
Est 1:12 the king became f and burned H7911+4394
Ps 78:21 LORD heard them, he was f; his fire broke H6297
Ps 78:59 God heard them, he was f; he rejected H6297
Ps 78:62 the sword; he was f with his inheritance. H6297
Jer 21: 5 a mighty arm in f anger and in great H2779
Jer 32:37 I banish them in my f anger and great H2779
Da 2:12 king so angry and f that he ordered the A10633
Da 3:13 F with rage, Nebuchadnezzar summoned A10270
Da 3:19 was f with Shadrach, A10416+10270
Mt 2:16 by the Magi, he was f, and he gave G2597+3336
Mt 8:24 Suddenly a f storm came up on the lake G3489
Mk 4:37 A f squall came up, and the waves broke G3489
Lk 4:28 the people in the synagogue were f G4398+2596
Lk 6:11 of the law were f and began to G4398+486
Ac 5:33 they were f and wanted to put them to G1391
Ac 7:54 they were f and gnashed G1391+3836+2840
Ac 19:28 they were f and began shouting: G4441+2596

FURIOUSLY (2) [FURY]

Jer 46: 9 Drive f, you charioteers! March H2147
Da 8: 7 I saw it attack the ram f, striking the ram H5352

FURLONGS (KJV) MILES, STADIA

FURNACE (30)

Ge 19:28 rising from the land, like smoke from a f. H3901
Ex 9: 8 of soot from a f and have Moses toss it H3901
Ex 9:10 they took soot from a f and stood before H3901
Ex 19:18 billowed up from it like smoke from a f, H3901
Dt 4:20 brought you out of the iron-smelting f, H3929
1Ki 8:51 out of Egypt, out of that iron-smelting f, H3929
Ps 21: 9 you will burn them up as in a blazing f. H9486

Pr 17: 3 The crucible for silver and the f for gold H3929
Pr 27:21 The crucible for silver and the f for gold H3929
Isa 31: 9 fire is in Zion, whose f is in Jerusalem. H9486
Isa 48:10 I have tested you in the f *of* affliction. H3929
Jer 11: 4 out of Egypt, out of the iron-smelting f. H3929
Eze 22:18 tin, iron and lead left inside a f. H3929
Eze 22:20 are gathered into a f to be melted with a H3929
Eze 22:22 As silver is melted in a f, so you will be H3929
Da 3: 6 immediately be thrown into a blazing f." A10086
Da 3:11 worship will be thrown into a blazing f. A10086
Da 3:15 be thrown immediately into a blazing f. A10086
Da 3:17 If we are thrown into the blazing f, the A10086
Da 3:19 He ordered the f heated seven times A10086
Da 3:20 throw them into the blazing f. A10086
Da 3:21 bound and thrown into the blazing f. A10086
Da 3:22 was so urgent and the f so hot that the A10086
Da 3:23 firmly tied, fell into the blazing f. A10086
Da 3:26 opening of the blazing f and shouted, A10086
Mal 4: 1 the day is coming; it will burn like a f. H9486
Mt 13:42 They will throw them into the blazing f G2825
Mt 13:50 throw them into the blazing f, where G2825
Rev 1:15 His feet were like bronze glowing in a f G2825
Rev 9: 2 from it like the smoke *from* a gigantic f. G2825

FURNISHED (4) [FURNISHINGS]

Eze 16:52 for *you have* f *some* **justification** for your H7136
Mk 14:15 you a large room upstairs, f and ready. G5143
Lk 22:12 will show you a large room upstairs, **all** f. G5143
Ac 28:10 *they* f us with the supplies we needed. G2202

FURNISHINGS (21) [FURNISHED]

Ex 25: 9 tabernacle and all its f exactly like the H3998
Ex 31: 7 and all the other f *of* the tent— H3998
Ex 39:33 the tent and all its f, its clasps, frames H3998
Ex 39:40 courtyard; all the f *for* the tabernacle, the H3998
Ex 40: 9 consecrate it and all its f, and it will be H3998
Nu 1:50 over all its f and everything belonging to it. H3998
Nu 1:50 are to carry the tabernacle and all its f; H3998
Nu 3: 8 care of all the f *of* the tent of meeting H3998
Nu 4:15 covering the **holy** f and all the holy H7731
Nu 4:16 including its **holy** f and articles. H7731
Nu 7: 1 anointed and consecrated it and all its f. H3998
Nu 18: 3 must not go near the f *of* the sanctuary H3998
Nu 19:18 the tent and all the f and the people who H3998
1Ki 7:48 also made all the f that were in the LORD's H3998
1Ki 7:51 the silver and gold and the f—and he H3998
1Ki 8: 4 tent of meeting and all the sacred f in it. H3998
1Ch 9:29 to take care of the f and all the other H3998
2Ch 4:19 also made all the f that were in God's H3998
2Ch 5: 1 the silver and gold and all the f—and he H3998
2Ch 5: 5 tent of meeting and all the sacred f in it. H3998
2Ch 28:24 together the f *from* the temple of God H3998

FURNITURE (KJV) ACCESSORIES, ARTICLES, FURNISHINGS, SADDLES, TREASURES, UTENSILS

FURROW (1) [FURROWS]

Job 39:10 Can you hold it to the f with a harness H9439

FURROWS (3) [FURROW]

Job 31:38 against me and all its f are wet with tears, H9439
Ps 65:10 You drench its f and level its ridges; you H9439
Ps 129: 3 plowed my back and made their f long. H5103

FURTHER (18) [FURTHERMORE]

1Sa 10:22 So they inquired f of the LORD, "Has the H6388
2Ch 32:16 officers spoke f against the LORD God and H6388
Job 34:23 God has no need to examine people f H6388
Job 35:15 f, that his anger never punishes and H6964
Ecc 9: 5 nothing; they have no f reward, and even H6388
Eze 23:14 "But *she* **carried** her prostitution **still** f. H3578
Zec 1:17 "Proclaim f: This is what the LORD H6388
Ac 4:17 from spreading **any** f among the G2093+4498
Ac 4:21 *After* f **threats** they let them go. G4653
Ac 8:25 *After* they *had* f **proclaimed** the word of the AIT
Ac 11:18 *they* **had no** f **objections** and praised God G2483
Ac 13:42 invited them *to* **speak** f about these things AIT
Ac 19:39 If there is anything f you want to bring up G4304
Ac 24: 4 But in order not to weary you f, G2093+4498
1Co 11:34 And when I come I will give f directions. G3370
Php 3: 1 F, my brothers and sisters, rejoice G3836+3370
Titus 1: 1 of Jesus Christ **to** f the faith of God's G2848
Heb 12:19 it begged *that* no f word *be* **spoken to** them, AIT

FURTHERMORE (12) [FURTHER]

2Sa 16:19 F, whom should I serve H2256+2021+9108
2Ki 18:25 F, have I come to attack and destroy this H6964
2Ki 23:24 F, Josiah got rid of the mediums H2256+1685
2Ch 17: 6 ways of the LORD; f, he removed the H2256+6388
2Ch 36:14 F, all the leaders of the priests and the H1685
Ezr 4:13 F, the king should know that if this city is A10363
Ezr 6:11 F, I decree that if anyone defies this A10221
Ne 5:17 F, a hundred and fifty Jews and officials H2256
Isa 36:10 F, have I come to attack and H2256+6964
Jer 21: 8 "F, tell the people, 'This is what the LORD H2256
Jer 26:24 F, Ahikam son of Shaphan supported H421
Ro 1:28 F, just as they did not think it worthwhile G2779

FURY (26) [FURIOUS, FURIOUSLY]

Ge 27:44 a while until your brother's f subsides. H2779
Ge 49: 7 their anger, so fierce, and their f, so cruel! H6301
2Ki 3:27 The f against Israel was great; they H7912
Est 2: 1 Later when King Xerxes' f had subsided H2779
Est 7:10 Mordecai. Then the king's f subsided. H2779
Job 40:11 Unleash the f *of* your wrath, look at all H6301
Pr 6:34 For jealousy arouses a husband's f, and H2779
Pr 14:35 a shameful servant arouses his f. H6301
Pr 21:24 is his name—behaves with insolent f. H6301
Pr 22: 8 the rod they wield in f will be broken. H6301
Pr 27: 4 Anger is cruel and f overwhelming, but H678
Isa 14: 4 come to an end! How his f has ended! H5290
Isa 14: 6 in f subdued nations with relentless H678
Isa 66:14 but *his* f *will be* **shown** *to* his foes. H2404
Isa 66:15 he will bring down his anger with f, and H2779
Eze 13:13 torrents of rain will fall with destructive f. H2779
Eze 16:30 " '*I am* **filled with** f **against** you H582+4226
Eze 19:12 But it was uprooted in f and thrown to the H2779
Eze 23:25 and they will deal with you in f. H2779
Da 11:30 turn back and **vent** *his* f against the holy H2404
Am 1:11 continually and his f flamed unchecked, H6301
Heb 11:34 quenched the f of the flames, and G1539
Rev 12:12 He is filled with f, because he G2596+3489
Rev 14:10 will drink the wine of God's f, which has G2596
Rev 16:19 filled with the wine *of* the f of his wrath. G2596
Rev 19:15 the winepress *of* the f of the wrath of God G2596

FUTILE (6) [FUTILITY]

Ps 94:11 all human plans; he knows that they are f. H2039
Jer 48:30 I know her insolence but it is f," H4202+4027
Mal 3:14 have said, 'It is f to serve God. What do H8736
Ro 1:21 their thinking *became* f and their foolish G3471
1Co 3:20 knows that the thoughts of the wise are f." G3469
1Co 15:17 your faith is f; you are still in your G3469

FUTILITY (4) [FUTILE]

Job 7: 3 so I have been allotted months of f, and H8736
Ps 78:33 he ended their days in f and their years in H2039
Ps 89:47 For what f you have created all humanity H8736
Eph 4:17 the Gentiles do, in the f of their thinking. G3470

FUTURE (31)

Ge 30:33 honesty will testify for me in the f, H3427+4737
Dt 6:20 **In the** f, when your son asks you, "What is H4737
Jos 4: 6 **In the** f, when your children ask you H4737
Jos 4:21 "**In the** f when your descendants ask their H4737
Jos 22:27 Then **in the** f your descendants will not be H4737
2Sa 7:19 spoken about the f of the house of H4946+8158
1Ch 17:17 spoken about the f of the house of H4946+8158
Job 8: 7 seem humble, so prosperous will your f be. H344
Ps 22:30 f generations will be told about the Lord. H995
Ps 37:37 a f awaits those who seek peace. H344
Ps 37:38 destroyed; there will be no f *for* the wicked. H344
Ps 102:18 Let this be written for a f generation, that a H340
Pr 23:18 There is surely a f **hope** for you, and your H344
Pr 24:14 there is a f **hope** for you, and your H344
Pr 24:20 the evildoer has no f **hope**, and the H344
Ecc 7:14 no one can discover anything about their f. H339
Ecc 8: 7 Since no one knows the f H4537+8611+2118
Isa 9: 1 but *in the* f he will honor Galilee of the H340
Isa 41:23 tell us what the f holds, so we may know H294
Jer 29:11 harm you, plans to give you hope and a f. H344
La 1: 9 to her skirts; she did not consider her f. H344
Eze 12:27 he prophesies about the distant f. H6961
Eze 38: 8 In f years you will invade a land that has H344
Da 2:45 what will take place **in the** f. A10021+10180
Da 8:26 vision, for it concerns the **distant** f." H3427+8041
Da 10:14 will happen to your people in the f, H344+3427
Ac 16:16 had a spirit by **which** she **predicted the** f. G4780
Ro 8:38 neither the present nor the f, nor any G3516
1Co 3:22 life or death or the present or the f— G3516
Heb 3: 5 to what *would be* **spoken** by God *in the* f. AIT
Heb 11:20 Jacob and Esau in regard to their f. G3516

G

GAAL (10)

Jdg 9:26 Now G son of Ebed moved with his clan H1720
Jdg 9:28 Then G son of Ebed said, "Who is H1720
Jdg 9:30 of the city heard what G son of Ebed said, H1720
Jdg 9:31 "G son of Ebed and his clan have come to H1720
Jdg 9:33 When G and his men come out against H2085S
Jdg 9:35 Now G son of Ebed had gone out and was H1720
Jdg 9:36 When G saw them, he said to Zebul H1720
Jdg 9:37 But G spoke up again: "Look, people are H1720
Jdg 9:39 So G led out the citizens of Shechem and H1720
Jdg 9:41 Zebul drove G and his clan out of H1720

GAASH (4)

Jos 24:30 hill country of Ephraim, north of Mount G. H1724
Jdg 2: 9 hill country of Ephraim, north of Mount G. H1724
2Sa 23:30 Pirathonite, Hiddai from the ravines of G, H1724
1Ch 11:32 Hurai from the ravines of G, Abiel the H1724

GABBAI (1)

Ne 11: 8 his followers, G and Sallai—928 men H1480

GABBATHA (1)

Jn 19:13 Stone Pavement (which in Aramaic is G). G1119

GABRIEL (4)

Da 8:16 from the Ulai calling, "G, tell this man the H1508
Da 9:21 was still in prayer, G, the man I had seen H1508
Lk 1:19 said to him, "I am G. I stand in the G1120
Lk 1:26 God sent the angel G to Nazareth, a town G1120

GAD (55) [BAAL GAD, DIBON GAD, GAD'S, GADITES, MIGDAL GAD]

Ge 30:11 good fortune!" So she named him G. H1514
Ge 35:26 servant Zilpah: G and Asher. These were H1514
Ge 46:16 The sons of G: Zephon, Haggi, Shuni H1514
Ge 49:19 "G will be attacked by a band of raiders H1514
Ex 1: 4 Dan and Naphtali; G and Asher. H1514
Nu 1:14 from G, Eliasaph son of Deuel; H1514
Nu 1:24 From the descendants of G: All the men H1514
Nu 1:25 number from the tribe of G was 45,650. H1514
Nu 2:14 The tribe of G will be next. The leader of H1514
Nu 2:14 of the people of G is Eliasaph son of H1514
Nu 7:42 the leader of the people of G, brought his H1514
Nu 10:20 over the division of the tribe of G. H1201+1514
Nu 13:15 from the tribe of G, Geuel son of Maki. H1514
Nu 26:15 The descendants of G by their clans were H1514
Nu 26:18 These were the clans of G; those H1201+1514
Nu 34:14 the tribe of G and the half-tribe of H1201+1532
Dt 27:13 Reuben, G, Asher, Zebulun, Dan and H1514
Dt 33:20 About G he said: "Blessed is he who H1514
Dt 33:20 G lives there like a lion, tearing at arm or NDT
Jos 4:12 G and the half-tribe of Manasseh crossed H1514
Jos 13:24 is what Moses had given to the tribe of G, H1514
Jos 18: 7 And G, Reuben and the half-tribe of H1514
Jos 20: 8 Ramoth in Gilead in the tribe of G, and H1514
Jos 21: 7 the tribes of Reuben, G and Zebulun. H1514
Jos 21:38 from the tribe of G, Ramoth in Gilead (a H1514
Jos 22:13 G and the half-tribe of Manasseh. H1201+1514
Jos 22:15 G and the half-tribe of Manasseh— H1201+1514
Jos 22:21 G and the half-tribe of Manasseh H1201+1514
Jos 22:30 G and Manasseh had to say H1201+1514
Jos 22:31 said to Reuben, G and Manasseh H1201+1514
1Sa 13: 7 the Jordan to the land of G and Gilead. H1514
1Sa 22: 5 But the prophet G said to David, "Do not H1514
2Sa 24: 5 then went through G and on to Jazer. H1514
2Sa 24:11 of the LORD had come to G the prophet, H1514
2Sa 24:13 So G went to David and said to him H1514
2Sa 24:14 David said to G, "I am in deep distress H1514
2Sa 24:18 On that day G went to David and said to H1514
2Sa 24:19 as the LORD had commanded through G. H1514
2Ki 10:33 Gilead (the region **of** G, Reuben and H1532
1Ch 2: 2 Joseph, Benjamin, Naphtali, G and Asher. H1514
1Ch 6:63 the tribes of Reuben, G and Zebulun. H1514
1Ch 6:80 from the tribe of G they received Ramoth H1514
1Ch 12:37 G and the half-tribe of Manasseh H1532
1Ch 21: 9 The LORD said to G, David's seer, H1514
1Ch 21:11 So G went to David and said to him, "This H1514
1Ch 21:13 David said to G, "I am in deep distress H1514
1Ch 21:18 of the LORD ordered G to tell David to go H1514
1Ch 21:19 to the word that G had spoken in the H1514
1Ch 29:29 the prophet and the records of G the seer, H1514
2Ch 29:25 by David and G the king's seer and H1514
Jer 49: 1 then has Molek taken possession of G? H1514
Eze 48:27 "G will have one portion; it will border the H1514
Eze 48:28 boundary of G will run south from H1514
Eze 48:34 the gate of G, the gate of Asher and the H1514
Rev 7: 5 12,000, from the tribe *of* G 12,000, G1122

GAD'S (1) [GAD]

Dt 33:20 "Blessed is he who enlarges G domain H1514

GADARENES (1)

Mt 8:28 at the other side in the region *of* the G, G1123

GADDAH See HAZAR GADDAH

GADDI (1)

Nu 13:11 a tribe of Joseph), G son of Susi; H1534

GADDIEL (1)

Nu 13:10 from the tribe of Zebulun, G son of Sodi; H1535

GADER See BETH GADER

GADFLY (1)

Jer 46:20 a g is coming against her from the H7976

GADI (2)

2Ki 15:14 Then Menahem son of G went from Tirzah H1533
2Ki 15:17 Menahem son of G became king of Israel H1533

GADITES (29) [GAD]

Nu 32: 1 The Reubenites and G, who had H1201+1514
Nu 32: 6 said to the G and Reubenites, H1201+1514
Nu 32:25 The G and Reubenites said to H1201+1514
Nu 32:29 to them, "If the G and Reubenites H1201+1514
Nu 32:31 The G and Reubenites answered H1201+1514
Nu 32:33 Then Moses gave to the G, the H1201+1514
Nu 32:34 The G built up Dibon, Ataroth H1201+1514
Dt 3:12 Reubenites and the G the territory north of H1532
Dt 3:16 Reubenites and the G I gave the territory H1532
Dt 4:43 in Gilead, for the G; and Golan in Bashan H1532
Dt 29: 8 the G and the half-tribe of Manasseh. H1532
Jos 1:12 the G and the half-tribe of Manasseh H1532
Jos 12: 6 the G and the half-tribe of Manasseh to H1532
Jos 13: 8 Reubenites and the G had received the H1532
Jos 13:28 were the inheritance of the G, H1201+1514
Jos 22: 1 the G and the half-tribe of Manasseh H1532
Jos 22: 9 the G and the half-tribe of H1201+1514
Jos 22:10 the G and the half-tribe of H1201+1514
Jos 22:25 and you—you Reubenites and G! H1201+1514
Jos 22:32 Reubenites and G in Gilead and H1201+1514

Jos 22:33 the Reubenites and the **G** lived. H1201+1514
Jos 22:34 and the **G** gave the altar H1201+1514
1Ch 5:11 The **G** lived next to them in Bashan H1201+1514
1Ch 5:16 The **G** lived in Gilead, in Bashan and its NDT
1Ch 5:18 the **G** and the half-tribe of Manasseh had H1532
1Ch 5:26 the **G** and the half-tribe of Manasseh into H1532
1Ch 12: 8 Some **G** defected to David at his H1532
1Ch 12:14 These **G** were army commanders H1201+1514
1Ch 26:32 the **G** and the half-tribe of Manasseh H1532

GAHAM (1)
Ge 22:24 Tebah, **G**, Tahash and Maakah H1626

GAHAR (2)
Ezr 2:47 Giddel, **G**, Reaiah, H1627
Ne 7:49 Hanan, Giddel, **G**, H1627

GAIN (69) [GAINED, GAINING, GAINS, REGAIN, REGAINED]
Ge 15: 8 can I know that *I will* **g possession** *of* it?" H3769
Ge 37:26 "What will we **g** if we kill our brother and H1299
Ex 14: 4 But *I will* **g glory for myself** through H3877
Ex 14:17 And *I will* **g glory** through Pharaoh and all H3877
Ex 14:18 the LORD when I **g glory** through Pharaoh, H3877
Ex 18:21 trustworthy men who hate **dishonest g** H1299
1Sa 8: 3 aside after **dishonest g** and accepted H1299
2Ki 15:19 of silver to **g** his **support** and H2118+3338+907
Job 21:15 What *would* **we g** by praying to him H3603
Job 22: 3 What would he **g** if your ways were H1299
Job 35: 3 it to me, and what *do I* **g** by not sinning? H3603
Ps 60:12 With God *we will* **g** the victory, and he H6913
Ps 90:12 our days, that *we may* **g** a heart of wisdom. H995
Ps 108:13 With God *we will* **g** the victory, and he H6913
Ps 119:36 your statutes and not toward **selfish g**. H1299
Ps 119:104 *I* **g understanding** from your precepts H1067
Pr 1:19 of all *who* **go after ill-gotten g**; H1298+1299
Pr 3:13 find wisdom, those *who* **g** understanding, H7049
Pr 4: 1 pay attention and **g** understanding. H3359
Pr 8: 5 You who are simple, **g** prudence; you who H1067
Pr 11:16 but ruthless men **g** only wealth. H9461
Pr 16: 8 righteousness than much **g** with injustice. H9311
Pr 19:25 discerning, and *they will* **g** knowledge. H1067
Pr 21:11 punished, the simple **g wisdom**; by paying AIT
Pr 28:16 one who hates **ill-gotten g** will enjoy a H1299
Pr 28:23 a person *will* in the end **g** favor rather H5162
Pr 29:23 person low, but the lowly in spirit **g** honor. H9461
Ecc 1: 3 What do people **g** from all their labors at H3862
Ecc 2:15 What then do I **g** by being wise?" I H3463
Ecc 3: 9 What do workers **g** from their toil? H3862
Ecc 5:16 what do they **g**, since they toil for the H3862
Ecc 6: 8 What do the poor **g** by knowing how to H4200
Isa 29:24 wayward in spirit *will* **g** understanding; H3359
Isa 33:15 who reject **g** *from* extortion and keep their H1299
Isa 56:11 to their own way, they seek their own **g**. H1299
Isa 63:12 to **g** for himself everlasting renown, H6913
Jer 6:13 all are greedy for **g**; prophets and priests H1299
Jer 8:10 all are greedy for **g**; prophets and priests H1299
Jer 12:13 will wear themselves out but **g** nothing. H3603
Jer 17:11 did not lay are *those who* **g** riches by H6913
Jer 22:17 your heart are set only on **dishonest g**, H1299
Eze 22:12 *You* extort **unjust g** *from* your neighbors H1298
Eze 22:13 together at the **unjust g** you have made H1299
Eze 22:27 and kill people to **make unjust g**. H1298+1299
Eze 33:31 their hearts are greedy for **unjust g**. H1299
Da 2: 8 am certain that you *are trying to* **g** time, A10223
Da 10:12 your mind to **g understanding** and to H1067
Da 11:43 *He will* **g control** of the treasures of gold H5440
Hab 2: 9 to him who builds his house by unjust **g**, H1299
Mal 3:14 What do we **g** by carrying out his H1299
Mt 16:26 it be for someone *to* **g** the whole world, *G3045*
Mk 8:36 is it for someone *to* **g** the whole world, *G3045*
Lk 9:25 is it for someone *to* **g** the whole world, *G3045*
Lk 16: 9 use worldly wealth *to* **g** friends for *G4472*
Jn 7:18 on their own do so *to* **g** personal glory, *G2426*
Ac 7:10 enabled him to **g** the goodwill of NDT
1Co 7:21 although if you can **g** your freedom, do so. *G1181*
1Co 13: 3 but do not have love, *I* **g** nothing. *G6067*
Php 1:21 For to me, to live is Christ and to die is **g**. *G3046*
Php 3: 8 them garbage, that *I may* **g** Christ *G3045*
1Ti 3: 8 much wine, and not **pursuing dishonest g**. *G153*
1Ti 3:13 who have served well **g** an excellent *G4347*
1Ti 6: 5 that godliness is a **means to financial g**. *G4516*
1Ti 6: 6 But godliness with contentment is great **g**. *G4516*
2Ti 3: 6 into homes and **g control over** gullible *G170*
Titus 1: 7 not violent, not **pursuing dishonest g**. *G153*
Titus 1:11 that for the sake of dishonest **g**. *G3046*
Heb 11:35 so that *they might* **g** an even better *G5593*
1Pe 5: 2 not **pursuing dishonest g**, but eager *G154*

GAINED (23) [GAIN]
Ge 31: 1 father owned and *has* **g** all this wealth H6913
2Sa 15:12 And so the conspiracy **g** strength, and H2118
2Ch 32: 8 And the people **g confidence** from what H6164
Job 31:25 great wealth, the fortune my hands *had* **g**, H5162
Ps 30: 9 "What is **g** if I am silenced, if I go down H1299
Ps 129: 2 but *they have* not **g the victory** over me. H3523
Pr 20:17 **Food g** *by* fraud tastes sweet, but one ends AIT
Ecc 2:11 the wind; nothing was **g** under the sun. H3862
Isa 26:15 *You have* **g glory for yourself**; you have H3877
Jer 32:20 and *have* **g** the renown that is still yours. H6913
Eze 28: 4 understanding *you have* **g** wealth for H6913
Da 11: 2 When he has **g power** by his wealth, he H2621
Mt 25:16 his money to work and **g** five bags more. *G3045*
Mt 25:17 the one with two bags of gold **g** two more. *G3045*
Mt 25:20 See, *I have* **g** five more.' *G3045*
Mt 25:22 two bags of gold; see, *I have* **g** two more. *G3045*
Lk 19:15 order to find out what *they had* **g** with it. *G1390*
Ro 5: 2 through whom *we have* **g** access by faith *G2400*
1Co 15:32 more than human hopes, what have I **g**? *G4055*
2Co 12: 1 *Although there is* nothing to *be* **g**, I will *G5237*
Gal 2:21 if righteousness could be **g** through the law, NDT
Heb 11:33 and **g** what was promised; who *G2209*
Rev 18:15 things and **g** *their* **wealth** from her will *G4456*

GAINING (4) [GAIN]
Ge 3: 6 also desirable for **g wisdom**, she took H8505
Ps 44:12 a pittance, **g** nothing from their sale. H8049
Pr 1: 2 **g** wisdom and instruction; for H3359
Jn 4: 1 had heard that he *was* **g** and baptizing *G4472*

GAINS (5) [GAIN]
Pr 11:16 A kindhearted woman **g** honor, but H9461
Pr 11:24 gives freely, yet **g** even more; another H3578
Pr 15:32 who heeds correction **g** understanding. H7864
Mic 4:13 will devote their **ill-gotten g** to the LORD, H1299
Php 3: 7 But whatever were **g** to me I now consider *G3046*

GAINSAY, GAINSAYERS, GAINSAYING (KJV) CONTRADICT, OBSTINATE, OPPOSE, RAISING OBJECTION, REBELLION

GAIUS (5)
Ac 19:29 The people seized **G** and Aristarchus *G1127*
Ac 20: 4 from Thessalonica, **G** from Derbe *G1127*
Ro 16:23 **G**, whose hospitality I and the whole *G1127*
1Co 1:14 baptize any of you except Crispus and **G**, *G1127*
3Jn 1 The elder, *To* my dear friend **G**, whom I *G1127*

GALAL (3)
1Ch 9:15 Heresh, **G** and Mattaniah son of Mika, the H1674
1Ch 9:16 the son of **G**, the son of Jeduthun H1674
Ne 11:17 Shammua, the son of **G**, the son of H1674

GALATIA (5) [GALATIAN, GALATIANS]
Ac 16: 6 throughout the region **of** Phrygia and **G**, *G1131*
Ac 18:23 throughout the region *of* **G** and Phrygia, *G1131*
Gal 1: 2 sisters with me, To the churches *in* **G**: *G1130*
2Ti 4:10 Crescens has gone to **G**, and Titus to *G1130*
1Pe 1: 1 the provinces of Pontus, **G**, Cappadocia, *G1130*

GALATIAN (1) [GALATIA]
1Co 16: 1 Do what I told the **G** churches to do. *G1130*

GALATIANS (1) [GALATIA]
Gal 3: 1 You foolish **G**! Who has bewitched you *G1129*

GALBANUM (1)
Ex 30:34 gum resin, onycha and **g**—and pure H2697

GALE (3)
Job 21:18 the wind, like chaff swept away by a **g**? H6070
Isa 17:13 on the hills, like tumbleweed before a **g**. H6070
Isa 41:16 them up, and a **g** will blow them away. H6194

GALEED (2)
Ge 31:47 it Jegar Sahadutha, and Jacob called it **G**. H1681
Ge 31:48 That is why it was called **G**. H1681

GALILEAN (4) [GALILEE]
Mk 14:70 you are one of them, for you are a **G**." *G1134*
Lk 22:59 this fellow was with him, for he is a **G**." *G1134*
Lk 23: 6 Pilate asked if the man was a **G**. *G1134*
Ac 5:37 Judas the **G** appeared in the days of the *G1134*

GALILEANS (5) [GALILEE]
Lk 13: 1 Jesus about the **G** whose blood Pilate *G1134*
Lk 13: 2 you think that these **G** were worse sinners *G1134*
Lk 13: 2 than all the other **G** because they suffered *G1134*
Jn 4:45 arrived in Galilee, the **G** welcomed him. *G1134*
Ac 2: 7 "Aren't all these who are speaking **G**? *G1134*

GALILEE (75) [GALILEAN, GALILEANS, TIBERIAS]
Nu 34:11 along the slopes east of the Sea of **G**. H4055
Jos 12: 3 from the Sea of **G** to the Sea of the H4054
Jos 13:27 the territory up to the end of the Sea of **G**). H4055
Jos 20: 7 set apart Kedesh in **G** in the hill country of H1665
Jos 21:32 Naphtali, Kedesh in **G** (a city of refuge H1665
1Ki 9:11 twenty towns in **G** to Hiram king of H824+1665
2Ki 15:29 He took Gilead and **G**, including all the H1665
1Ch 6:76 of Naphtali they received Kedesh in **G**, H1665
Isa 9: 1 the future he will honor **G** *of* the nations, H1665
Mt 2:22 a dream, he withdrew to the district *of* **G**, *G1133*
Mt 3:13 Jesus came from **G** to the Jordan to be *G1133*
Mt 4:12 had been put in prison, he withdrew to **G**. *G1133*
Mt 4:15 beyond the Jordan, **G** of the Gentiles— *G1133*
Mt 4:18 Jesus was walking beside the Sea *of* **G**, *G1133*
Mt 4:23 Jesus went throughout **G**, teaching in *G1133*
Mt 4:25 Large crowds from **G**, the Decapolis *G1133*
Mt 11: 1 to teach and preach in the towns *of* **G**. *G899S*
Mt 15:29 left there and went along the Sea *of* **G**. *G1133*
Mt 17:22 When they came together in **G**, he said to *G1133*
Mt 19: 1 he left **G** and went into the region of *G1133*
Mt 21:11 is Jesus, the prophet from Nazareth *in* **G**." *G1133*
Mt 26:32 I have risen, I will go ahead of you into **G**." *G1133*
Mt 26:69 "You also were with Jesus **of G**," she said *G1134*
Mt 27:55 followed Jesus from **G** to care for his *G1133*
Mt 28: 7 dead and is going ahead of you into **G**. *G1133*
Mt 28:10 Go and tell my brothers to go to **G**; there *G1133*
Mt 28:16 Then the eleven disciples went to **G**, to *G1133*
Mk 1: 9 from Nazareth in **G** and was baptized *G1133*
Mk 1:14 Jesus went into **G**, proclaiming the good *G1133*
Mk 1:16 As Jesus walked beside the Sea *of* **G**, he *G1133*
Mk 1:28 spread quickly over the whole region *of* **G**. *G1133*
Mk 1:39 So he traveled throughout **G**, preaching in *G1133*
Mk 3: 7 and a large crowd from **G** followed. *G1133*
Mk 6:21 commanders and the leading men *of* **G**. *G1133*
Mk 7:31 down to the Sea *of* **G** and into the region *G1133*
Mk 9:30 left that place and passed through **G**. *G1133*
Mk 14:28 I have risen, I will go ahead of you into **G**." *G1133*
Mk 15:41 In **G** these women had followed him and *G1133*
Mk 16: 7 'He is going ahead of you into **G**. *G1133*
Lk 1:26 angel Gabriel to Nazareth, a town *in* **G**, *G1133*
Lk 2: 4 from the town of Nazareth in **G** to Judea, *G1133*
Lk 2:39 they returned to **G** to their own town of *G1133*
Lk 3: 1 Herod tetrarch *of* **G**, his brother Philip *G1133*
Lk 4:14 Jesus returned to **G** in the power of the *G1133*
Lk 4:31 Capernaum, a town *in* **G**, and on the *G1133*
Lk 5:17 every village *of* **G** and from Judea and *G1133*
Lk 8:26 which is across the lake from **G**. *G1133*
Lk 17:11 the border between Samaria and **G**. *G1133*
Lk 23: 5 He started in **G** and has come all the way *G1133*
Lk 23:49 women who had followed him from **G**, *G1133*
Lk 23:55 with Jesus from **G** followed Joseph and *G1133*
Lk 24: 6 told you, while he was still with you in **G**: *G1133*
Jn 1:43 The next day Jesus decided to leave for **G**. *G1133*
Jn 2: 1 day a wedding took place at Cana *in* **G**. *G1133*
Jn 2:11 did here in Cana *of* **G** was the first of the *G1133*
Jn 4: 3 left Judea and went back once more to **G**. *G1133*
Jn 4:43 After the two days he left for **G**. *G1133*
Jn 4:45 When he arrived in **G**, the Galileans *G1133*
Jn 4:46 Once more he visited Cana *in* **G**, where *G1133*
Jn 4:47 that Jesus had arrived in **G** from Judea, *G1133*
Jn 4:54 performed after coming from Judea to **G**. *G1133*
Jn 6: 1 crossed to the far shore of the Sea *of* **G** *G1133*
Jn 7: 1 Jesus went around in **G**. He did not want *G1133*
Jn 7: 3 "Leave **G** and go to Judea, so *G1949S*
Jn 7: 9 After he had said this, he stayed in **G**. *G1133*
Jn 7:41 "How can the Messiah come from **G**? *G1133*
Jn 7:52 replied, "Are you from **G**, too? Look into it, *G1133*
Jn 7:52 that a prophet does not come out of **G**." *G1133*
Jn 12:21 who was from Bethsaida *in* **G**, with a *G1133*
Jn 21: 1 again to his disciples, by the Sea *of* **G**. *G5500*
Jn 21: 2 Nathanael from Cana *in* **G**, the sons of *G1133*
Ac 1:11 "Men **of G**," they said, "why do you stand *G1134*
Ac 9:31 **G** and Samaria enjoyed a time of peace *G1133*
Ac 10:37 beginning in **G** after the baptism that *G1133*
Ac 13:31 traveled with him from **G** to Jerusalem. *G1133*

GALL (6)
Job 16:13 my kidneys and spills my **g** on the ground. H5354
Ps 69:21 They put **g** in my food and gave me H8032
Pr 5: 4 in the end she is bitter as **g**, sharp as H4360
La 3:15 with bitter herbs and given me **g** to drink. H4360
La 3:19 my wandering, the bitterness and the **g**. H4360
Mt 27:34 to drink, mixed with **g**; but after tasting it, *G5958*

GALLERIES (3) [GALLERY]
Eze 41:15 including its **g** on each side; it was H916
Eze 41:16 narrow windows and **g** around the three of H916
Eze 42: 5 the **g** took more space from them than H916

GALLERY (2) [GALLERIES]
Eze 42: 3 **g** faced gallery at the three levels. H916
Eze 42: 3 gallery faced **g** at the three levels. H916

GALLEY (1)
Isa 33:21 No **g** *with* oars will ride them, no mighty H639

GALLIM (2)
1Sa 25:44 to Paltiel son of Laish, who was from **G**. H1668
Isa 10:30 Daughter **G**! Listen, Laishah! Poor H1668

GALLIO (3)
Ac 18:12 While **G** was proconsul of Achaia, the *G1136*
Ac 18:14 was about to speak, **G** said to them, "If *G1136*
Ac 18:17 **G** showed no concern whatever. *G1136*

GALLONS (2)
Lk 16: 6 " '**Nine hundred g** of olive oil,' he *G1669+1004*
Jn 2: 6 holding from **twenty** to thirty **g**. *G3583+1545*
[Jn 2: 6 holding from twenty to **thirty g**. *G3583+5552*]

GALLOP (1) [GALLOPING, GALLOPS]
Joel 2: 4 of horses; *they* **g along** like cavalry. H8132

GALLOPING (4) [GALLOP]
Jdg 5:22 the horses' hooves—**g**, galloping go his H1852
Jdg 5:22 galloping, **g** go his mighty steeds. H1852
Jer 47: 3 at the sound of the hooves of **g** steeds, at H9121
Na 3: 2 of wheels, **g** horses and jolting chariots! H1851

GALLOPS (1) [GALLOP]
Hab 1: 8 Their cavalry **g headlong**; their horsemen H7055

GALLOWS (NIV84) POLE

GAMALIEL (7)
Nu 1:10 from Manasseh, **G** son of Pedahzur; H1697
Nu 2:20 of Manasseh is **G** son of Pedahzur. H1697
Nu 7:54 On the eighth day **G** son of Pedahzur, the H1697

Nu 7:59 was the offering of G son of Pedahzur. H1697
Nu 10:23 G son of Pedahzur was over the division of H1697
Ac 5:34 But a Pharisee named G, a teacher of the G1137
Ac 22: 3 I studied under G and was thoroughly G1137

GAME (10) [GAMES]
Ge 25:28 who had a taste for wild g, loved Esau, H7473
Ge 27: 3 open country to hunt some wild g for me. H7473
Ge 27: 5 open country to hunt g and bring it back, H7473
Ge 27: 7 'Bring me some g and prepare me some H7473
Ge 27:19 Please sit up and eat some of my g, so H7473
Ge 27:25 bring me some of your g to eat, so that I H7473
Ge 27:31 please sit up and eat some of my g, so H7473
Ge 27:33 that hunted g and brought it to me? H7473
Ps 76: 4 more majestic than mountains rich with g. H3272
Pr 12:27 The lazy do not roast any g, but the H7473

GAMES (1) [GAME]
1Co 9:25 Everyone who competes in the g goes into G76

GAMMAD (1)
Eze 27:11 every side; men of G were in your towers. H1689

GAMUL (1) [BETH GAMUL]
1Ch 24:17 to Jakin, the twenty-second to G, H1690

GANG (1)
Jdg 11: 3 where a g of scoundrels gathered around H408

GANGRENE (1)
2Ti 2:17 Their teaching will spread like g. G1121

GANNIM See EN GANNIM

GAP (4) [GAPS]
Jdg 21:15 the LORD had made a g in the tribes of H7288
1Ki 11:27 had filled in the g in the wall of the city of H7288
Ne 6: 1 the wall and not a g was left in it— H7288
Eze 22:30 before me in the g on behalf of the land H7288

GAPING (1)
Job 30:14 They advance as through a g breach H8146

GAPS (1) [GAP]
Ne 4: 7 ahead and that the g were being closed, H7287

GARBAGE (2)
1Co 4:13 of the earth, the g of the world—right up G4370
Php 3: 8 I consider them g, that I may gain Christ G5032

GARDEN (55) [GARDENER, GARDENS]
Ge 2: 8 the LORD God had planted a g in the east, H1703
Ge 2: 9 In the middle of the g were the tree of life H1703
Ge 2:10 A river watering the g flowed from Eden H1703
Ge 2:15 put him in the G of Eden to work it H1703
Ge 2:16 "You are free to eat from any tree in the g; H1703
Ge 3: 1 'You must not eat from any tree in the g'?" H1703
Ge 3: 2 "We may eat fruit from the trees in the g, H1703
Ge 3: 3 the tree that is in the middle of the g, H1703
Ge 3: 8 he was walking in the g in the cool of the H1703
Ge 3: 8 the LORD God among the trees of the g. H1703
Ge 3:10 "I heard you in the g, and I was afraid H1703
Ge 3:23 him from the G of Eden to work the H1703
Ge 3:24 east side of the G of Eden cherubim and H1703
Ge 13:10 watered, like the g of the LORD, like the H1703
Dt 11:10 irrigated it by foot as in a vegetable g. H1703
1Ki 21: 2 your vineyard to use for a vegetable g, H1703
2Ki 21:18 ancestors and was buried in his palace g, H1703
2Ki 21:18 in his palace garden, the g of Uzza. H1703
2Ki 21:26 was buried in his tomb in the g of Uzza. H1703
2Ki 25: 4 between the two walls near the king's g, H1703
Ne 3:15 by the King's G, as far as the steps H1703
Est 1: 5 in the enclosed g of the king's palace H1708
Est 1: 6 The g had hangings of white and blue linen NDT
Est 7: 7 his wine and went out into the palace g. H1708
Est 7: 8 from the palace g to the banquet hall, H1708
Job 8:16 sunshine, spreading its shoots over the g; H1708
SS 4:12 You are a g locked up, my sister, my bride; H1703
SS 4:15 You are a g fountain, a well of flowing H1703
SS 4:16 Blow on my g, that its fragrance may H1703
SS 4:16 come into his g and taste its choice H1703
SS 5: 1 I have come into my g, my sister, my bride H1703
SS 6: 2 My beloved has gone down to his g, to H1703
Isa 1:30 with fading leaves, like a g without water. H1708
Isa 51: 3 her wastelands like the g of the LORD. H1703
Isa 58:11 You will be like a well-watered g, like a H1703
Isa 61:11 come up and a g causes seeds to grow H1708
Jer 31:12 They will be like a well-watered g, and H1703
Jer 39: 4 left the city at night by way of the king's g, H1703
Jer 52: 7 between the two walls near the king's g, H1703
La 2: 6 He has laid waste his dwelling like a g H1703
Eze 28:13 were in Eden, the g of God; every H1703
Eze 31: 8 The cedars in the g of God could not rival H1703
Eze 31: 8 no tree in the g of God could match its H1703
Eze 31: 9 of all the trees of Eden in the g of God. H1703
Eze 36:35 laid waste has become like the g of Eden; H1703
Joel 2: 3 Before them the land is like the g of Eden, H1703
Mt 13:32 it is the largest of g plants and becomes a G3303
Mk 4:32 becomes the largest of all g plants, G3303
Lk 11:42 rue and all other kinds of g herbs, but you G3303
Lk 13:19 which a man took and planted in his g. G3057
Jn 18: 1 On the other side there was a g, and he G3057
Jn 18: 3 So Judas came to the g, guiding a G1695S
Jn 18:26 "Didn't I see you with him in the g?" G3057
Jn 19:41 there was a g, and in the garden a G3057
Jn 19:41 garden, and in the g a new tomb, in G3057

GARDENER (2) [GARDEN]
Jn 15: 1 am the true vine, and my Father is the g. G1177
Jn 20:15 Thinking he was the g, she said, "Sir, if G3058

GARDENS (11) [GARDEN]
Nu 24: 6 they spread out, like g beside a river, like H1708
Ecc 2: 5 I made g and parks and planted all kinds H1708
SS 6: 2 to browse in the g and to gather lilies. H1703
SS 8:13 You who dwell in the g with friends in H1703
Isa 1:29 because of the g that you have chosen. H1708
Isa 65: 3 sacrifices in g and burning incense on H1708
Isa 66:17 purify themselves to go into the g, H1708
Jer 29: 5 plant g and eat what they produce. H1708
Jer 29:28 plant g and eat what they produce.' H1708
Am 4: 9 "Many times I struck your g and vineyards H1708
Am 9:14 they will make g and eat their fruit. H1708

GAREB (3)
2Sa 23:38 Ira the Ithrite, G the Ithrite H1735
1Ch 11:40 Ira the Ithrite, G the Ithrite, H1735
Jer 31:39 to the hill of G and then turn to Goah. H1736

GARLAND (2)
Pr 1: 9 They are a g to grace your head and a H4292
Pr 4: 9 She will give you a g to grace your head H4292

GARLIC (1)
Nu 11: 5 cucumbers, melons, leeks, onions and g. H8770

GARMENT (49) [GARMENTS, UNDERGARMENT, UNDERGARMENTS]
Ge 9:23 Japheth took a g and laid it across H8529
Ge 25:25 his whole body was like a hairy g; so H168
Ex 22: 9 a sheep, a g, or any other lost property H8515
Lev 6:27 if any of the blood is spattered on a g H955
Nu 31:20 Purify every g as well as everything made of H955
Jdg 8:25 So they spread out a g, and each of them H8529
Ru 3: 9 "Spread the corner of your g over me H4053
1Sa 19:13 covering it with a g and putting some H955
2Sa 13:18 this was the kind of g the virgin daughters H5077
2Sa 20:12 road into a field and threw a g over him. H955
2Ki 1: 8 "He had a g of hair and had a leather H8552
2Ki 2:12 he took hold of his g and tore it in two. H955
2Ki 4:39 as many of its gourds as his g could hold. H955
Job 13:28 something rotten, like a g eaten by moths. H955
Job 30:18 he binds me like the neck of my g. H4189
Job 38: 9 I made the clouds its g and wrapped it in H4230
Job 38:14 its features stand out like those of a g. H4230
Ps 22:18 among them and cast lots for my g. H4230
Ps 74:11 from the folds of your g and destroy them! H2668
Ps 102:26 you remain; they will all wear out like a g. H955
Ps 104: 2 LORD wraps himself in light as with a g; H8515
Ps 104: 6 it with the watery depths as with a g; H4230
Ps 109:18 He wore cursing as his g; it entered into H4496
Pr 20:16 Take the g of one who puts up security H955
Pr 25:20 Like one who takes away a g on a cold day H955
Pr 27:13 Take the g of one who puts up security H955
Isa 9: 5 in battle and every g rolled in blood will H8529
Isa 50: 9 They will all wear out like a g; the moths H955
Isa 51: 6 will wear out like a g and its inhabitants H955
Isa 51: 8 For the moth will eat them up like a g; the H955
Isa 61: 3 a g of praise instead of a spirit of H5073
Jer 43:12 As a shepherd picks his g clean of lice, so H955
Eze 5: 3 tuck them away in the folds of your g. H4053
Eze 16: 8 I spread the corner of my g over you and H4053
Eze 44:17 must not wear any woolen g while H7547
Hag 2:12 consecrated meat in the fold of their g, H955
Zec 13: 4 not put on a prophet's g of hair in order to H168
Mt 9:16 a patch of unshrunk cloth on an old g, G2668
Mt 9:16 the patch will pull away from the g G2668
Mk 2:21 a patch of unshrunk cloth on an old g. G2668
Mk 14:51 wearing nothing but a linen g, was G4984
Mk 14:52 he fled naked, leaving his g behind. G4984
Lk 5:36 piece out of a new g to patch an old one. G2668
Lk 5:36 they will have torn the new g, and the patch AIT
Jn 19:23 This g was seamless, woven in one piece G5945
Jn 19:24 among them and cast lots for my g." G2669
Jn 21: 7 he wrapped his outer g around him (for G2087
Heb 1:11 you remain; they will all wear out like a g. G2668
Heb 1:12 like a robe; like a g they will be changed. G2668

GARMENTS (73) [GARMENT]
Ge 3:21 The LORD God made g of skin for Adam H4189
Ge 49:11 he will wash his g in wine, his robes in H4230
Ex 28: 2 Make sacred g for your brother Aaron to H955
Ex 28: 3 matters that they are to make g for Aaron, H955
Ex 28: 4 These are the g they are to make: H955
Ex 28: 4 to make these sacred g for your brother H955
Ex 29: 5 Take the g and dress Aaron with the tunic H955
Ex 29:21 it on Aaron and his g and on his sons and H955
Ex 29:21 his garments and on his sons and their g. H955
Ex 29:21 his sons and their g will be consecrated. H955
Ex 29:29 "Aaron's sacred g will belong to his H955
Ex 31:10 also the woven g, both the sacred H955
Ex 31:10 both the sacred g for Aaron the priest and H955
Ex 31:10 the priest and the g for his sons when they H955
Ex 35:19 the woven g worn for ministering in the H955
Ex 35:19 both the sacred g for Aaron the priest and H955
Ex 35:19 the priest and the g for his sons when they H955
Ex 35:21 all its service, and for the sacred g. H955
Ex 39: 1 yarn they made woven g for ministering in H955
Ex 39: 1 They also made sacred g for Aaron, as the H955
Ex 39:41 the woven g worn for ministering in the H955
Ex 39:41 both the sacred g for Aaron the priest and H955
Ex 39:41 the priest and the g for his sons when H955
Ex 40:13 Then dress Aaron in the sacred g, anoint H955
Lev 8: 2 his sons, their g, the anointing oil, H955
Lev 8:30 on Aaron and his g and on his sons and H955
Lev 8:30 his garments and on his sons and their g. H955
Lev 8:30 Aaron and his g and his sons and their H955
Lev 8:30 his garments and his sons and their g. H955
Lev 16: 4 These are sacred g; so he must bathe H955
Lev 16:23 take off the linen g he put on before he H955
Lev 16:24 sanctuary area and put on his regular g. H955
Lev 16:32 He is to put on the sacred linen g H955
Lev 21:10 has been ordained to wear the priestly g, H955
Nu 15:38 to make tassels on the corners of your g, H955
Nu 20:26 Remove Aaron's g and put them on his son H955
Nu 20:28 removed Aaron's g and put them on his H955
Jdg 5:30 each man, colorful g as plunder for Sisera H7389
Jdg 5:30 Sisera, colorful g embroidered, highly H7389
Jdg 5:30 highly embroidered g for my neck—all H7389
Jdg 8:26 the purple g worn by the kings of H955
Jdg 14:12 give you thirty linen g and thirty sets of H6041
Jdg 14:13 give me thirty linen g and thirty sets of H6041
1Sa 19:24 He stripped off his g, and he too H955
2Sa 1:24 who adorned your g with ornaments of H4230
2Sa 10: 4 cut off their g at the buttocks, and H4503
1Ch 19: 4 cut off their g at the buttocks, and H4503
Ezr 2:69 5,000 minas of silver and 100 priestly g. H4189
Ne 7:70 of gold, 50 bowls and 530 g for priests. H4189
Ne 7:72 2,000 minas of silver and 67 g for priests. H4189
Est 8:15 he was wearing royal g of blue and white H4230
Job 31:19 lack of clothing, or the needy without g, H4064
Ps 45:14 In embroidered g she is led to the king H8391
Pr 31:24 She makes linen g and sells them, and H6041
SS 4:11 fragrance of your g is like the fragrance H8515
Isa 3:23 the linen g and tiaras and shawls. H6041
Isa 52: 1 Put on your g of splendor, Jerusalem, the H955
Isa 59:17 he put on the g of vengeance and wrapped H955
Isa 61:10 has clothed me with g of salvation and H955
Isa 63: 1 from Bozrah, with his g stained crimson? H955
Isa 63: 2 Why are your g red, like those of one H4230
Isa 63: 3 their blood spattered my g, and I stained H955
La 4:14 blood that no one dares to touch their g. H4230
Eze 16:10 fine linen and covered you with costly g. H5429
Eze 16:16 took some of your g to make gaudy high H955
Eze 26:16 robes and take off their embroidered g. H955
Eze 27:24 they traded with you beautiful g, H4815
Eze 42:14 they leave behind the g in which they H955
Eze 44:19 consecrated through contact with their g. H955
Joel 2:13 Rend your heart and not your g. Return to H955
Am 2: 8 beside every altar on g taken in pledge. H955
Zec 3: 4 your sin, and I will put fine g on you." H4711
Mt 23: 5 wide and the tassels on their g long; G3192

GARMITE (1)
1Ch 4:19 the father of Keilah the G, and Eshtemoa H1753

GARNER, GARNERS (KJV) BARN, BARNS, STOREHOUSES

GARRISON (2) [GARRISONS]
2Sa 23:14 the Philistine g was at Bethlehem. H5163
1Ch 11:16 the Philistine g was at Bethlehem. H5907

GARRISONS (5) [GARRISON]
2Sa 8: 6 He put g in the Aramean kingdom of H5907
2Sa 8:14 He put g throughout Edom, and all the H5907
1Ch 18: 6 He put g in the Aramean kingdom of NDT
1Ch 18:13 He put g in Edom, and all the Edomites H5907
2Ch 17: 2 of Judah and put g in Judah and in the H5907

GASP (2) [GASPING]
Job 11:20 their hope will become a dying g. H5134
Isa 42:14 in childbirth, I cry out, I g and pant. H5971

GASPING (1) [GASP]
Jer 4:31 the cry of Daughter Zion g for breath H3640

GATAM (3)
Ge 36:11 Teman, Omar, Zepho, G and Kenaz. H1725
Ge 36:16 G and Amalek. These were the H1725
1Ch 1:36 Zepho, G and Kenaz; by Timna H1725

GATE (223) [GATEKEEPERS, GATEPOST, GATEPOSTS, GATES, GATEWAY, GATEWAYS]
Ge 23:10 Hittites who had come to the g of his city. H9133
Ge 23:18 Hittites who had come to the g of the city. H9133
Ge 28:17 the house of God; this is the g of heaven." H9133
Ge 34:20 Shechem went to the g of their city to H9133
Ge 34:24 went out of the city g agreed with Hamor H9133
Dt 17: 5 evil deed to your city g and stone that H9133
Dt 21:19 him to the elders at the g of his town. H9133
Dt 22:15 town elders at the g proof that she was a H9133
Dt 22:24 both of them to the g of that town and H9133
Dt 25: 7 go to the elders at the town g and say, H9133
Jos 2: 5 when it was time to close the city g, they H9133
Jos 2: 7 pursuers had gone out, the g was shut. H9133
Jos 7: 5 Israelites from the city g as far as the H9133
Jos 8:29 throw it down at the entrance of the city g. H9133
Jos 20: 4 entrance of the city g and state their case H9133
Jdg 9:35 of the city g just as Abimelek and H9133

G

Jdg 9:40 him all the way to the entrance of the g, H9133
Jdg 9:44 to a position at the entrance of the city g. H9133
Jdg 16: 2 lay in wait for him all night at the city g. H9133
Jdg 16: 3 took hold of the doors of the city g, H9133
Jdg 18:16 battle, stood at the entrance of the g. H9133
Jdg 18:17 men stood at the entrance of the g. H9133
Ru 4: 1 went up to the **town** g and sat down there H9133
Ru 4:11 elders and all the people at the g said, H9133
1Sa 4:18 backward off his chair by the side of the g. H9133
1Sa 21:13 on the doors of the g and letting saliva H9133
2Sa 10: 8 formation at the entrance of their **city** g, H9133
2Sa 11:23 them back to the entrance of the **city** g. H9133
2Sa 15: 2 the side of the road leading to the **city** g. H9133
2Sa 18: 4 king stood beside the g while all his men H9133
2Sa 23:15 from the well near the g of Bethlehem!" H9133
2Sa 23:16 the well near the g of Bethlehem and H9133
1Ki 4:13 large walled cities with bronze g **bars**); H1378
1Ki 17:10 When he came to the town g, a widow H7339
1Ki 22:10 floor by the entrance of the g *of* Samaria, H9133
2Ki 7: 1 of barley for a shekel at the g *of* Samaria." H9133
2Ki 7: 3 with leprosy at the entrance of the **city** g. H9133
2Ki 7:17 whose arm he leaned in charge of the g, H9133
2Ki 7:18 of barley for a shekel at the g *of* Samaria." H9133
2Ki 9:31 As Jehu entered the g, she asked, "Have H9133
2Ki 10: 8 at the entrance of the **city** g until morning." H9133
2Ki 11: 6 a third at the Sur G, and a third at the gate H9133
2Ki 11: 6 a third at the g behind the guard H9133
2Ki 11:19 entering by way of the g *of* the guards. H9133
2Ki 14:13 from the Ephraim G to the Corner Gate— H9133
2Ki 14:13 from the Ephraim Gate to the Corner G— H9133
2Ki 15:35 rebuilt the Upper G *of* the temple of the H9133
2Ki 23: 8 at the entrance of the G *of* Joshua, H9133
2Ki 23: 8 which was on the left of the city g. H9133
2Ki 25: 4 at night through the g between the two H9133
1Ch 9:18 stationed at the King's G on the east, H9133
1Ch 11:17 from the well near the g of Bethlehem!" H9133
1Ch 11:18 the well near the g of Bethlehem and H9133
1Ch 16:42 sons of Jeduthun were stationed at the g. H9133
1Ch 26:13 Lots were cast for **each g** H9133+2256+9133
1Ch 26:14 The lot for the East G fell to Shelemiah NDT
1Ch 26:14 the lot for the North G fell to him. NDT
1Ch 26:15 The lot for the South G fell to Obed-Edom NDT
1Ch 26:16 The lots for the West G and the Shalleketh NDT
1Ch 26:16 the Shalleketh G on the upper road H9133
2Ch 18: 9 floor by the entrance of the g *of* Samaria, H9133
2Ch 23: 5 palace and a third at the Foundation G, H9133
2Ch 23:15 of the Horse G on the palace grounds H9133
2Ch 23:20 through the Upper G and seated the king H9133
2Ch 24: 8 at the g *of* the temple of the LORD. H9133
2Ch 25:23 from the Ephraim G to the Corner Gate— H9133
2Ch 25:23 from the Ephraim Gate to the Corner G— H9133
2Ch 26: 9 built towers in Jerusalem at the Corner G, H9133
2Ch 26: 9 at the Valley G and at the angle of the H9133
2Ch 27: 3 rebuilt the Upper G *of* the temple of the H9133
2Ch 31:14 the Levite, **keeper of** the East G, was in H8788
2Ch 32: 6 square at the city g and encouraged them H9133
2Ch 33:14 entrance of the Fish G and encircling the H9133
2Ch 35:15 at **each g** did not need H9133+2256+9133
Ne 2:13 through the Valley G toward the Jackal H9133
Ne 2:13 toward the Jackal Well and the Dung G, H9133
Ne 2:14 the Fountain G and the King's Pool H9133
Ne 2:15 back and reentered through the Valley G. H9133
Ne 3: 1 went to work and rebuilt the Sheep G. H9133
Ne 3: 3 The Fish G was rebuilt by the sons of H9133
Ne 3: 6 The Jeshanah G was repaired by Joiada H9133
Ne 3:13 The Valley G was repaired by Hanun and H9133
Ne 3:13 cubits of the wall as far as the Dung G. H9133
Ne 3:14 The Dung G was repaired by Malkijah son H9133
Ne 3:15 The Fountain G was repaired by Shallun H9133
Ne 3:26 opposite the Water G toward the east H9133
Ne 3:28 Above the Horse G, the priests made H9133
Ne 3:29 the guard at the East G, made repairs. H9133
Ne 3:31 opposite the Inspection G, and as far as H9133
Ne 3:32 the Sheep G the goldsmiths and H9133
Ne 8: 1 as one in the square before the Water G. H9133
Ne 8: 3 before the Water G in the presence of the H9133
Ne 8:16 square by the Water G and the one by the H9133
Ne 8:16 Gate and the one by the G *of* Ephraim. H9133
Ne 12:31 the wall to the right, toward the Dung G. H9133
Ne 12:37 At the Fountain G they continued directly H9133
Ne 12:37 palace to the Water G on the east. H9133
Ne 12:39 over the G *of* Ephraim, the Jeshanah Gate H9133
Ne 12:39 Ephraim, the Jeshanah G, the Fish Gate, H9133
Ne 12:39 the Fish G, the Tower of Hananel H9133
Ne 12:39 of the Hundred, as far as the Sheep G. H9133
Ne 12:39 At the G *of* the Guard they stopped H9133
Est 2:19 Mordecai was sitting at the king's g. H9133
Est 2:21 time Mordecai was sitting at the king's g, H9133
Est 3: 2 at the king's g knelt down and paid H9133
Est 3: 3 officials at the king's g asked Mordecai, H9133
Est 4: 2 But he went only as far as the king's g H9133
Est 4: 6 square of the city in front of the king's g. H9133
Est 5: 9 at the king's g and observed that he H9133
Est 5:13 that Jew Mordecai sitting at the king's g." H9133
Est 6:10 the Jew, who sits at the king's g. H9133
Est 6:12 Mordecai returned to the king's g. H9133
Job 29: 7 "When I went to the g of the city and took H9133
Ps 69:12 Those who sit at the g mock me, and I am H9133
Ps 118:20 This is the g of the LORD through which the H9133
Pr 1:21 at the city g she makes her speech: H7339+9133
Pr 8: 3 beside the g leading into the city, at the H9133
Pr 17:19 builds a high g invites destruction. H7339
Pr 24: 7 in the **assembly at the g** they must not H9133
Pr 31:23 Her husband is respected at the **city g** H9133
Pr 31:31 let her works bring her praise at the **city** g. H9133
SS 7: 4 of Heshbon by the g *of* Bath Rabbim. H9133
Isa 14:31 you g! Howl, you city! Melt away, all H9133
Isa 24:12 is left in ruins, its g is battered to pieces. H9133
Isa 28: 6 to those who turn back the battle at the g. H9133
Jer 7: 2 "Stand at the g *of* the LORD's house and H9133
Jer 17:19 "Go and stand at the G *of* the People H9133
Jer 19: 2 near the entrance of the Potsherd G. H9133
Jer 20: 2 stocks at the Upper G *of* Benjamin at the H9133
Jer 26:10 of the New G *of* the LORD's house. H9133
Jer 31:38 the Tower of Hananel to the Corner G. H9133
Jer 31:40 east as far as the corner of the Horse G, H9133
Jer 36:10 the entrance of the New G *of* the temple, H9133
Jer 37:13 But when he reached the Benjamin G, the H9133
Jer 38: 7 the king was sitting in the Benjamin G, H9133
Jer 39: 3 came and took seats in the Middle G: H9133
Jer 39: 4 through the g between the two walls H9133
Jer 52: 7 at night through the g between the two H9133
La 5:14 The elders are gone from the **city** g; the H9133
Eze 8: 3 entrance of the north g *of* the inner court, H9133
Eze 8: 5 north of the g *of* the altar I saw this H9133
Eze 8:14 of the north g *of* the house of the H9133
Eze 9: 2 coming from the direction of the upper g, H9133
Eze 10:19 entrance of the east g *of* the LORD's house, H9133
Eze 11: 1 brought me to the g *of* the house of the H9133
Eze 11: 1 the entrance of the g were twenty-five H9133
Eze 26: 2 The g *to* the nations is broken, and its H1946
Eze 40: 6 Then he went to the east g. He climbed H9133
Eze 40: 6 measured the threshold of the g; H9133
Eze 40: 7 the threshold of the g next to the portico H9133
Eze 40:10 Inside the east g were three alcoves on H9133
Eze 40:20 the length and width of the north g, H9133
Eze 40:22 as those of the g facing east. H9133
Eze 40:23 There was a g to the inner court facing the H9133
Eze 40:23 gate to the inner court facing the north g, H9133
Eze 40:23 measured from one g to the opposite one H9133
Eze 40:24 to the south side and I saw the south g. H9133
Eze 40:27 The inner court also had a g facing south H9133
Eze 40:27 measured from this g to the outer gate on H9133
Eze 40:27 this gate to the outer g *on* the south side; H9133
Eze 40:28 into the inner court through the south g, H9133
Eze 40:28 he measured the south g; it had the H9133
Eze 40:35 me to the north g and measured it. H9133
Eze 40:44 Outside the inner g, within the inner court, H9133
Eze 40:44 the side of the north g and facing south, H9133
Eze 40:44 the side of the south g and facing north. H9133
Eze 42:15 me out by the east g and measured the H9133
Eze 43: 1 the man brought me to the g facing east, H9133
Eze 43: 4 the temple through the g facing east. H9133
Eze 44: 1 me back to the outer g *of* the sanctuary, H9133
Eze 44: 2 LORD said to me, "This g is to remain shut. H9133
Eze 44: 4 by way of the north g to the front of the H9133
Eze 46: 1 The g *of* the inner court facing east is to H9133
Eze 46: 2 the g will not be shut until evening. H9133
Eze 46: 9 enters by the north g to worship is to go H9133
Eze 46: 9 gate to worship is to go out the south g; H9133
Eze 46: 9 enters by the south g is to go out the H9133
Eze 46: 9 by the south gate is to go out the north g. H9133
Eze 46: 9 return through the g by which they H9133
Eze 46: 9 each is to go out the opposite g. NDT
Eze 46:12 the g facing east is to be opened for him. H9133
Eze 46:12 after he has gone out, the g will be shut. H9133
Eze 46:19 at the side of the g to the sacred rooms H9133
Eze 47: 2 through the north g and led me around H9133
Eze 47: 2 the outside to the outer g facing east, H9133
Eze 48:31 on the north side will be the g *of* Reuben, H9133
Eze 48:31 the g *of* Judah and the gate of Levi. H9133
Eze 48:31 the gate of Judah and the g *of* Levi. H9133
Eze 48:32 the g *of* Joseph, the gate of Benjamin H9133
Eze 48:32 the g *of* Benjamin and the gate of Dan. H9133
Eze 48:32 the gate of Benjamin and the g *of* Dan. H9133
Eze 48:33 the g *of* Simeon, the gate of Issachar and H9133
Eze 48:33 the g *of* Issachar and the gate of Zebulun. H9133
Eze 48:33 the gate of Issachar and the g *of* Zebulun. H9133
Eze 48:34 the g *of* Gad, the gate of Asher and the H9133
Eze 48:34 the g *of* Asher and the gate of Naphtali. H9133
Eze 48:34 the gate of Asher and the g *of* Naphtali. H9133
Am 1: 5 I will break down the g *of* Damascus; H1378
Mic 1: 9 It has reached the very g *of* my people H9133
Mic 1:12 from the LORD, even to the g *of* Jerusalem. H9133
Mic 2:13 they will break through the g and go out. H9133
Zep 1:10 "a cry will go up from the Fish G, wailing H9133
Zec 14:10 from the Benjamin G to the site of the H9133
Zec 14:10 Benjamin Gate to the site of the First G, H9133
Zec 14:10 to the Corner G, and from the Tower H9133
Mt 7:13 "Enter through the narrow g. For wide is *G4783*
Mt 7:13 For wide is the g and broad is the road *G4783*
Mt 7:14 But small is the g and narrow the road that *G4783*
Lk 7:12 As he approached the town g, a dead *G4783*
Lk 16:20 At his g was laid a beggar named Lazarus *G4784*
Jn 5: 2 is in Jerusalem near the **Sheep G** a pool, *G4583*
Jn 10: 1 does not enter the sheep pen by the g, *G2598*
Jn 10: 2 who enters by the g is the shepherd of *G2598*
Jn 10: 3 The gatekeeper opens the g for him, and the NDT
Jn 10: 7 truly I tell you, I am the g for the sheep. *G2598*
Jn 10: 9 I am the g; whoever enters through me *G2598*
Ac 3: 2 carried to the temple g called Beautiful, *G2598*
Ac 3:10 begging at the temple g called Beautiful, *G4783*
Ac 10:17 Simon's house was and stopped at the g. *G4784*
Ac 12:10 came to the iron g leading to the city. *G4783*
Ac 16:13 we went outside the **city** g to the river, *G4783*
Heb 13:12 outside the **city** g to make the people *G4783*
Rev 21:21 each g made of a single pearl. *G4784*

GATEKEEPER (3) [GATE, KEEP]

2Sa 18:26 he called down to the g, "Look, H8788
1Ch 9:21 was the g *at* the entrance to H8788
Jn 10: 3 The g opens the gate for him, and the *G2601*

GATEKEEPERS (37) [GATE,KEEP]

2Ki 7:10 called out to the city g and told them, H8788
2Ki 7:11 The g shouted the news, and it was H8788
1Ch 9:17 The g: Shallum, Akkub, Talmon, Ahiman H8788
1Ch 9:18 These were the g belonging to the camp H8788
1Ch 9:19 and his fellow g from his family (the NDT
1Ch 9:20 was the official in charge of **the g**, H2157S
1Ch 9:22 those chosen to be g at the thresholds H8788
1Ch 9:22 **The** g had been assigned to their H2156S
1Ch 9:24 The g were on the four sides: east, west H8788
1Ch 9:26 But the four principal g, who were Levites H8788
1Ch 15:18 Mikneiah, Obed-Edom and Jeiel, the g. H8788
1Ch 16:38 son of Jeduthun, and also Hosah, were g. H8788
1Ch 23: 5 thousand are to be g and four thousand H8788
1Ch 26: 1 The divisions of the g: From the Korahites H8788
1Ch 26:12 These divisions of the g, through their H8788
1Ch 26:19 divisions of the g who were descendants H8788
2Ch 8:14 also appointed the g by divisions for the H8788
2Ch 23:19 He also stationed g at the gates of the H8788
2Ch 34: 9 the Levites *who were* the g had H6197+9068
2Ch 34:13 Levites were secretaries, scribes and g. H8788
2Ch 35:15 The g at each gate did not need to leave H8788
Ezr 2:42 The g of the temple: the descendants of H8788
Ezr 2:70 the g and the temple servants settled in H8788
Ezr 7: 7 musicians, g and temple servants, also H8788
Ezr 7:24 musicians, g, temple servants or other A10777
Ezr 10:24 From the g: Shallum, Telem and H8788
Ne 7: 1 doors in place, the g, the musicians and H8788
Ne 7: 3 While **the g** are still on duty, have them H2156S
Ne 7:45 The g: the descendants of Shallum, Ater H8788
Ne 7:73 the Levites, the g, the musicians and the H8788
Ne 10:28 Levites, g, musicians, temple H8788
Ne 10:39 the g and the musicians are also kept. H8788
Ne 11:19 The g: Akkub, Talmon and their H8788
Ne 12:25 Akkub were g who guarded the H8788
Ne 12:45 as did also the musicians and g H8788
Ne 12:47 daily portions for the musicians and the g. H8788
Ne 13: 5 musicians and g, as well as the H8788

GATEPOST (1) [GATE, POST]

Eze 46: 2 of the gateway and stand by the g. H4647+9133

GATEPOSTS (1) [GATE, POST]

Eze 45:19 and on the g *of* the inner court H4647+9133

GATES (107) [GATE]

Dt 3: 5 with high walls and with g and bars, H1946
Dt 6: 9 doorframes of your houses and on your g. H9133
Dt 11:20 doorframes of your houses and on your g, H9133
Dt 20:11 If they accept and open their g, all the NDT
Dt 33:25 The **bolts of** your g will be iron and H4981
Jos 6: 1 Now the *g of* **Jericho** were securely barred AIT
Jos 6:26 cost of his youngest he will set up its g." H1946
Jdg 5: 8 new leaders when war came to the **city g**, H9133
Jdg 5:11 of the LORD went down to the **city** g. H9133
1Sa 17:52 entrance of Gath and to the g *of* Ekron. H9133
1Sa 23: 7 by entering a town with g and bars." H1946
2Sa 18:24 sitting between the inner and outer g, H9133
1Ki 16:34 he set up its g at the cost of his H1946
2Ki 15:16 because they refused to open their g. NDT
1Ch 9:23 of guarding the g of the house of the H9133
2Ch 8: 5 with walls and with g and bars, H1946
2Ch 8:14 divisions for the **various** g, H9133+2256+9133
2Ch 14: 7 around them, with towers, g and bars. H1946
2Ch 23:19 gatekeepers at the g *of* the LORD's temple H9133
2Ch 31: 2 sing praises at the g *of* the LORD's H9133
Ne 1: 3 its g have been burned with fire. H9133
Ne 2: 3 its g have been destroyed by fire? H9133
Ne 2: 8 make beams for the g *of* the citadel by H9133
Ne 2:13 broken down, and its g, which had been H9133
Ne 2:17 its g have been burned with fire. H9133
Ne 6: 1 time I had not set the doors in the g— H9133
Ne 7: 3 "The g *of* Jerusalem are not to be opened H9133
Ne 11:19 who kept watch at the g—172 men. H9133
Ne 12:25 who guarded the storerooms at the g. H9133
Ne 12:30 purified the people, the g and the wall. H9133
Ne 13:19 shadows fell on the g *of* Jerusalem before H9133
Ne 13:19 of my own men at the g so that no load H9133
Ne 13:22 go and guard the g in order to keep the H9133
Job 17:16 Will it go down to the g *of* death? Will we H964
Job 38:17 Have the g *of* death been shown to you H9133
Job 38:17 Have you seen the g *of* the deepest H9133
Ps 9:13 mercy and lift me up from the g *of* death, H9133
Ps 9:14 your praises in the g *of* Daughter Zion, H9133
Ps 24: 7 Lift up your heads, you g; be lifted up, you H9133
Ps 24: 9 Lift up your heads, you g; lift them up, you H9133
Ps 87: 2 The LORD loves the g *of* Zion more than all H9133
Ps 100: 4 Enter his g with thanksgiving and his H9133
Ps 107:16 he breaks down g *of* bronze and cuts H1946
Ps 107:18 all food and drew near the g *of* death. H9133
Ps 118:19 Open for me the g *of* the righteous; I will H9133
Ps 122: 2 Our feet are standing in your g, Jerusalem H9133
Ps 147:13 the bars of your g and blesses your H9133
Pr 14:19 the wicked at the g *of* the righteous. H9133

Pr 18:19 disputes are like the **barred** g *of* a citadel. H1378
Isa 3:26 The g *of* Zion will lament and mourn H7339
Isa 13: 2 to them to enter the g *of* the nobles. H7339
Isa 22: 7 horsemen are posted at the **city** g. H9133
Isa 26: 2 Open the g that the righteous nation may H9133
Isa 38:10 I go through the g *of* death and be H9133
Isa 45: 1 before him so that g will not be shut: H9133
Isa 45: 2 I will break down g *of* bronze and cut H1946
Isa 54:12 of rubies, your g of sparkling jewels, and H9133
Isa 60:11 Your g will always stand open, they will H9133
Isa 60:18 your walls Salvation and your g Praise. H9133
Isa 62:10 pass through the g! Prepare the way for H9133
Jer 1:15 in the entrance of the g *of* Jerusalem; H9133
Jer 7: 2 come through these g to worship the LORD. H9133
Jer 15: 7 a winnowing fork at the **city** g *of* the land. H9133
Jer 17:19 stand also at all the other g *of* Jerusalem. H9133
Jer 17:20 in Jerusalem who come through these g. H9133
Jer 17:21 day or bring it through the g *of* Jerusalem. H9133
Jer 17:24 no load through the g *of* this city on the H9133
Jer 17:25 come through the g *of* this city with their H9133
Jer 17:27 come through the g *of* Jerusalem on the H9133
Jer 17:27 fire in the g *of* Jerusalem that will H9133
Jer 22: 2 your people who come through these g. H9133
Jer 22: 4 will come through the g *of* this palace, H9133
Jer 22:19 thrown outside the g *of* Jerusalem." H9133
Jer 49:31 "a nation that has neither g nor bars; its H1946
Jer 51:30 set on fire; the **bars of** her g are broken. H1378
Jer 51:58 will be leveled and her high g set on fire; H9133
La 2: 9 Her g have sunk into the ground; their H9133
La 4:12 foes could enter the g *of* Jerusalem. H9133
Eze 21:15 the sword for slaughter at all their g. H9133
Eze 21:22 to set battering rams against the g, to H9133
Eze 26:10 when he enters your g as men enter a city H9133
Eze 38:11 without walls and without g and bars. H1946
Eze 44:11 having charge of the g *of* the temple and H9133
Eze 44:17 'When they enter the g *of* the inner court, H9133
Eze 44:17 ministering at the g *of* the inner court H9133
Eze 48:31 the g *of* the city will be named after the H9133
Eze 48:31 The three g on the north side will be the H9133
Eze 48:32 which is 4,500 cubits long, will be three g: H9133
Eze 48:33 measures 4,500 cubits, will be three g: H9133
Eze 48:34 which is 4,500 cubits long, will be three g: H9133
Ob 11 foreigners entered his g and cast lots for H9133
Ob 13 march through the g *of* my people in the H9133
Na 2: 6 The river g are thrown open and the H9133
Na 3:13 The g *of* your land are wide open to your H9133
Na 3:13 fire has consumed the bars of your g. NDT
Mt 16:18 the g of Hades will not overcome it. *G4783*
Ac 9:24 close watch *on* the **city** g in order to kill *G4783*
Ac 14:13 wreaths to the **city** g because he and *G4784*
Ac 21:30 temple, and immediately the g were shut. *G2598*
Rev 21:12 high wall with twelve g, and with twelve *G4784*
Rev 21:12 and with twelve angels at the g. *G4784*
Rev 21:12 On the g were written the names of the NDT
Rev 21:13 There were three g on the east, three on *G4784*
Rev 21:15 to measure the city, its g and its walls. *G4784*
Rev 21:21 The twelve g were twelve pearls, each *G4784*
Rev 21:25 On no day will its g ever be shut, for there *G4784*
Rev 22:14 may go *through* the g into the city. *G4784*

GATEWAY (35) [GATE, WAY]

Ge 19: 1 Lot was sitting in the g *of* the city. H9133
1Sa 9:18 approached Samuel in the g and asked, H9133
2Sa 18:24 went up to the roof of the g by the wall. H9133
2Sa 18:33 went up to the room over the g and wept. H9133
2Sa 19: 8 the king got up and took his seat in the g. H9133
2Sa 19: 8 "The king is sitting in the g," they all H9133
2Ki 7:17 the people trampled him in the g H9133
2Ki 7:20 the people trampled him in the g, and H9133
2Ki 23: 8 broke down the g at the entrance H1195+9133
Eze 27: 3 situated at the g *to* the sea, merchant of H4427
Eze 40: 3 was standing in the g with a linen cord H9133
Eze 40: 8 Then he measured the portico of the g; H9133
Eze 40: 9 The portico of the g faced the temple. H9133
Eze 40:11 the width of the entrance of the g; H9133
Eze 40:13 he measured the g from the top of the H9133
Eze 40:14 walls all around the inside of the g— H9133
Eze 40:15 the entrance of the g to the far end of its H9133
Eze 40:16 walls inside the g were surmounted by H9133
Eze 40:19 inside of the lower g to the outside of the H9133
Eze 40:21 measurements as those of the first g. H9133
Eze 40:25 **The** g and its portico had narrow H2257S
Eze 40:29 **The** g and its portico had openings all H2257S
Eze 40:32 he measured the g; it had the same H9133
Eze 40:33 **The** g and its portico had openings all H2257S
Eze 40:39 In the portico of the g were two tables on H9133
Eze 40:40 By the outside wall of the portico of the g H9133
Eze 40:40 entrance of the north g were two tables, H9133
Eze 40:41 on one side of the g and four on the other H9133
Eze 44: 3 who may sit inside **the** g to eat in the H2257S
Eze 44: 3 the portico of the g and go out the same H9133
Eze 46: 2 the portico of the g and stand by the H9133
Eze 46: 2 at the threshold of the g and then go out, H9133
Eze 46: 3 of the LORD at the entrance of that g. H9133
Eze 46: 8 he is to go in through the portico of the g H9133
Mt 26:71 Then he went out to the g, where another *G4784*

GATEWAYS (5) [GATE, WAY]

1Ch 22: 3 the doors of the g and for the fittings, H9133
La 1: 4 All her g are desolate, her priests groan H9133
Eze 40:18 the sides of the g and was as wide as H9133
Eze 40:30 The porticoes of the g around the inner court NDT
Eze 40:38 was by the portico in each of the inner g, H9133

GATH (36) [GATH HEPHER, GATH RIMMON, MORESHETH GATH]

Jos 11:22 in Gaza, G and Ashdod did any survive. H1781
Jos 13: 3 Ashkelon, G and Ekron; the territory of the H1785
1Sa 5: 8 the ark of the god of Israel moved to G." H1781
1Sa 6:17 Ashdod, Gaza, Ashkelon, G and Ekron. H1781
1Sa 7:14 towns from Ekron to G that the Philistines H1781
1Sa 17: 4 Goliath, who was from G, came out of the H1781
1Sa 17:23 the Philistine champion from G, stepped H1781
1Sa 17:52 to the entrance of G and to the gates of H1781
1Sa 17:52 along the Shaaraim road to G and Ekron. H1781
1Sa 21:10 from Saul and went to Achish king of G. H1781
1Sa 21:12 was very much afraid of Achish king of G. H1781
1Sa 22: 1 David left G and escaped to the cave of H9004S
1Sa 27: 2 over to Achish son of Maok king of G. H1781
1Sa 27: 3 his men settled in G with Achish. H1781
1Sa 27: 4 Saul was told that David had fled to G, H1781
1Sa 27:11 a man or woman alive to be brought to G, H1781
2Sa 1:20 "Tell it not in G, proclaim it not in the H1781
2Sa 15:18 him from G marched before the H1781
2Sa 21:20 which took place at G, there was a huge H1781
2Sa 21:22 four were descendants of Rapha in G, H1781
1Ki 2:39 of Maakah, king of G, and Shimei was H1781
1Ki 2:39 Shimei was told, "Your slaves are in G." H1781
1Ki 2:40 went to Achish at G in search of his H1781
1Ki 2:40 away and brought the slaves back from G. H1781
1Ki 2:41 from Jerusalem to G and had returned, H1781
2Ki 12:17 went up and attacked G and captured it. H1781
1Ch 7:21 were killed by the native-born men of G, H1781
1Ch 8:13 who drove out the inhabitants of G. H1781
1Ch 18: 1 he took G and its surrounding H1781
1Ch 20: 6 which took place at G, there was a huge H1781
1Ch 20: 8 These were descendants of Rapha in G H1781
2Ch 11: 8 G, Mareshah, Ziph, H1781
2Ch 26: 6 Philistines and broke down the walls of G, H1781
Ps 56: T When the Philistines had seized him in G. H1781
Am 6: 2 then go down to G *in* Philistia. H1781
Mic 1:10 Tell it not in G; weep not at all. H1781

GATH HEPHER (2) [GATH, HEPHER]

Jos 19:13 eastward to G and Eth Kazin; H1783
2Ki 14:25 of Amittai, the prophet from G. H1783

GATH RIMMON (4) [GATH, RIMMON]

Jos 19:45 Bene Berak, G, H1784
Jos 21:24 Aijalon and G, together with H1784
Jos 21:25 they received Taanach and G, H1784
1Ch 6:69 Aijalon and G, together with H1784

GATHER (116) [GATHERED, GATHERING, GATHERS, INGATHERING]

Ge 31:46 to his relatives, "G some stones." So they H4377
Ge 49: 1 "G **around** so I can tell you what will H665
Ex 5: 7 let them go and g their own straw. H8006
Ex 5:12 all over Egypt to g stubble to use for straw H8006
Ex 16: 4 out each day and g enough for that day H4377
Ex 16: 5 twice as much as *they* g on the other days H4377
Ex 16:16 'Everyone *is to* g as much as they need H4377
Ex 16:26 Six days *you are to* g it, but on the seventh H4377
Ex 16:27 went out on the seventh day to g it, H4377
Ex 23:16 when you g **in** your crops from the field. H665
Lev 8: 3 g the entire assembly at the entrance H7735
Lev 19: 9 of your field or g the gleanings of your H4377
Lev 23:22 of your field or g the gleanings of your H4377
Lev 25: 3 prune your vineyards and g their crops. H665
Nu 10: 7 *To* g the assembly, blow the trumpets, but H7735
Nu 19: 9 man who is clean *shall* g **up** the ashes of H665
Nu 20: 8 brother Aaron g the assembly **together**. H7735
Nu 21:16 "G the people **together** and I will give H665
Dt 11:14 so that *you may* g **in** your grain, new H665
Dt 13:16 *You are to* g all the plunder of the town H7695
Dt 28:39 you will not drink the wine or g *the* **grapes**, H112
Dt 30: 3 on you and g you again from all H7695
Dt 30: 4 the LORD your God *will* g you and bring H7695
Ru 2: 7 let me glean and g among the sheaves H665
Ru 2:15 "*Let her* g among the sheaves and don't H4377
2Ki 4:39 into the fields to g herbs and found a wild H4377
2Ki 22:20 Therefore I *will* g you to your ancestors, and H665
1Ch 16:35 g us and deliver us from the nations H7695
2Ch 34:28 Now I *will* g you to your ancestors, and you H665
Ne 1: 9 *I will* g them from there and bring them to H7695
Est 4:16 **g together** all the Jews who are in Susa H4043
Job 24: 6 *They* g fodder in the fields and glean in H7917
Ps 7: 7 *Let* the assembled peoples g **around** you H6015
Ps 50: 5 "G to me this consecrated people, who H665
Ps 104:28 it to them, *they* g it **up**; when you open H4377
Ps 106:47 LORD our God, and g us from the nations H7695
Ps 142: 7 the righteous *will* g **about** me because of H4193
Ecc 3: 5 to scatter stones and a time *to* g them, H4043
SS 6: 2 to browse in the gardens and to g lilies. H4377
Isa 10:14 the nations; as *people* g abandoned eggs H665
Isa 11:12 the nations and g the exiles of Israel; H665
Isa 34:15 there also the falcons *will* g, each with its H7695
Isa 34:16 and his Spirit *will* g them **together**. H7695
Isa 43: 5 from the east and g you from the west. H7695
Isa 43: 9 All the nations g together and the H7695
Isa 45:20 "**G together** and come; assemble, you H7695
Isa 49: 5 Jacob back to him and g Israel to himself, H665
Isa 49:18 all your children g and come to you. H7695
Isa 56: 8 "*I will* g still others to them besides those H7695
Isa 62: 9 and *those who* g the grapes will drink it in H7695
Isa 66:18 am about to come and g the people of all H7695
Jer 3:17 all nations *will* g in Jerusalem to H7748
Jer 4: 5 aloud and say: '**G together**! Let us flee to H665
Jer 7:18 The children g wood, the fathers light the H4377
Jer 8:14 we sitting here? **G together**! Let us flee to H665
Jer 9:22 behind the reaper, with no *one to* g them. H665
Jer 10:17 **G up** your belongings to leave the land H665
Jer 12: 9 Go and g all the wild beasts; bring them to H665
Jer 21: 4 And *I will* g them inside this city H665
Jer 23: 3 "*I myself will* g the remnant of my flock out H7695
Jer 29:14 *I will* g you from all the nations and H7695
Jer 31: 8 of the north and g them from the ends of H7695
Jer 31:10 scattered Israel *will* g them and will watch H7695
Jer 32:37 I *will* surely g them from all the lands H7695
Jer 49: 5 and no *one will* g the fugitives. H7695
Eze 11:17 *I will* g you from the nations and bring H7695
Eze 16:37 therefore I *am going to* g all your lovers H7695
Eze 16:37 *I will* g them against you from all around H7695
Eze 20:34 from the nations and g you from the H7695
Eze 20:41 from the nations and g you from the H7695
Eze 22:19 become dross, I *will* g you into Jerusalem. H7695
Eze 22:20 so *will I* g you in my anger and my wrath H7695
Eze 22:21 *I will* g you and I will blow on you with my H4043
Eze 28:25 When I g the people of Israel from the H7695
Eze 29:13 end of forty years *I will* g the Egyptians H7695
Eze 34:13 from the nations and g them from the H7695
Eze 36:24 *I will* g you from all the countries and H7695
Eze 37:21 *I will* g them from all around and bring H7695
Eze 39:10 *They will* not *need to* g wood from the H5951
Eze 39:28 nations, *I will* g them to their own land H4043
Hos 8:10 the nations, *I will* now g them **together**. H7695
Hos 9: 6 Egypt *will* g them, and Memphis H7695
Joel 2:16 G the people, consecrate the assembly H665
Joel 2:16 together the elders, g the children, those H665
Joel 3: 2 *I will* g all nations and bring them down H7695
Mic 2:12 "*I will* **surely** g all of you, Jacob; I will H665+665
Mic 4: 6 declares the LORD, "*I will* g the lame; I will H665
Na 3:18 on the mountains with no *one to* g them. H7695
Hab 1: 9 a desert wind and g prisoners like sand. H665
Zep 2: 1 **G together**, gather yourselves together H8006
Zep 2: 1 together, g *yourselves* **together**, you H8006
Zep 3: 8 to g the kingdoms and to pour out my H7695
Zep 3:19 rescue the lame; *I will* g the exiles. I will H7695
Zep 3:20 At that time I *will* g you; at that time I will H7695
Zec 10: 8 I will signal for them and g them **in** H7695
Zec 10:10 back from Egypt and g them from Assyria. H7695
Zec 14: 2 *I will* g all the nations to Jerusalem to fight H665
Mt 12:30 whoever *does* not g with me scatters. *G5251*
Mt 13:30 then g the wheat and bring it into my *G5251*
Mt 18:20 where two or three g in my name, *G1639+5251*
Mt 23:37 I have longed *to* g your children **together**, *G2190*
Mt 24:28 is a carcass, there the vultures *will* g. *G5251*
Mt 24:31 and *they will* g his elect from the four *G2190*
Mt 25:26 I have not sown and g where I have not *G5251*
Mk 13:27 send his angels and g his elect from the *G2190*
Lk 3:17 threshing floor and *to* g the wheat into his *G5251*
Lk 11:23 whoever *does* not g with me scatters. *G5251*
Lk 13:34 I have longed *to* g your children **together**, *G2190*
Lk 17:37 is a dead body, there the vultures *will* g." *G2190*
Jn 6:12 disciples, "G the pieces that are left over. *G5251*
1Co 11:33 sisters, *when you* g to eat, you should *G5302*
2Ti 4: 3 *they will* g **around** them **a great number** *G2197*
Rev 14:18 your sharp sickle and g the clusters of *G5582*
Rev 16:14 *to* g them for the battle on the great day *G5251*
Rev 19:17 **g together** for the great supper of God, *G5251*
Rev 20: 8 Gog and Magog—and *to* g them for battle. *G5251*

GATHERED (140) [GATHER]

Ge 1: 9 "*Let* the water under the sky **be** g to one H7748
Ge 1:10 and the g waters he called "seas. H5224
Ge 25: 8 full of years; and *he* **was** g to his people. H665
Ge 25:17 last and died, and *he* **was** g to his people. H665
Ge 29: 3 When all the flocks **were** g there, the H665
Ge 29: 7 it is not time for the flocks *to* **be** g. H665
Ge 29: 8 "until all the flocks **are** g and the stone has H665
Ge 35:29 his last and died and **was** g to his people, H665
Ge 37: 7 your sheaves g **around** mine and bowed H6015
Ge 49:29 "I *am about to* **be** g to my people H665
Ge 49:33 breathed his last and **was** g to his people. H665
Ex 16:17 they were told; *some* g much, some little. H4377
Ex 16:18 the *one who* g **much** did not have too H8049
Ex 16:18 the *one who* g **little** did not have too H5070
Ex 16:18 Everyone *had* g just as much as they H4377
Ex 16:21 Each morning everyone g as much as they H4377
Ex 16:22 On the sixth day, *they* g twice as much H4377
Ex 32: 1 mountain, they g around Aaron and said H7735
Lev 8: 4 the assembly g at the entrance to the H7735
Lev 23:39 after you *have* g the crops of the land H665
Nu 11:32 next day the people went out and g quail. H665
Nu 11:32 No one g less than ten homers H665
Nu 14: 5 of the whole Israelite assembly g there. H7736
Nu 16:19 When Korah *had* g all his followers in H7735
Nu 16:42 But when the assembly g in opposition to H7735
Nu 20: 2 the people g in opposition to Moses H7735
Nu 20:10 Aaron g the assembly **together** in front H7735
Nu 20:24 "Aaron *will* **be** g to his people. He will not H665
Nu 20:26 Aaron *will* **be** g to his people; he H665
Nu 27:13 you too *will* **be** g to your people, as H665
Nu 31: 2 After that, *you will* **be** g to your people." H665
Dt 16:13 days after you *have* g the produce of your H665
Dt 32:50 you will die and **be** g to your people, H665

G

Dt 32:50 on Mount Hor and **was** g to his people. H665
Jos 18: 1 of the Israelites g *at* Shiloh and set up the H7735
Jos 22:12 assembly of Israel g at Shiloh to go to war H7735
Jdg 2:10 whole generation *had* **been** g to their H665
Jdg 9: 6 Beth Millo g beside the great tree H665
Jdg 9:27 into the fields and g the grapes and H1305
Jdg 11: 3 a gang of scoundrels g around him and H4377
Ru 2:17 Then she threshed the barley *she had* g H4377
Ru 2:18 mother-in-law saw how much *she had* g. H4377
1Sa 8: 4 elders of Israel g **together** and came to H7695
1Sa 17: 1 Now the Philistines g their forces for war H665
1Sa 17:47 All those g here will know that it is not by H7736
1Sa 22: 2 in debt or discontented g around him, H7695
1Sa 28: 1 days the Philistines g their forces to fight H7695
1Sa 28: 4 while Saul g all Israel and set up camp at H7695
1Sa 29: 1 The Philistines g all their forces at Aphek H7695
2Sa 10:17 was told of this, *he* g all Israel, crossed the H665
2Sa 17:11 *Let* all Israel, ... **be** g H665+665
2Sa 20:14 *who* g **together** and followed him. H7735
2Sa 21:13 had been killed and exposed *were* **g up**. H665
2Sa 23: 6 like thorns, *which* **are** not g with the hand. H4374
2Sa 23: 9 the Philistines g at Pas Dammim for H665
1Ki 8: 5 of Israel that *had* g about him were H3585
1Ki 11:24 Rezon g a band of men around him and H7695
1Ch 11:13 when the Philistines g there for battle. H665
1Ch 19:17 *he* g all Israel and crossed the Jordan H665
1Ch 23: 2 *He* also g **together** all the leaders of Israel H665
2Ch 5: 6 of Israel that *had* g about him were H3585
2Ch 13: 7 worthless scoundrels g around him and H7695
2Ch 23: 2 Judah and g the Levites and the H7695
2Ch 28:24 Ahaz g **together** the furnishings from the H665
2Ch 29:20 g the city officials **together** and went H665
2Ch 32: 4 *They* g a large group of people who H7695
Ezr 7:28 I took courage and g leaders from Israel H7695
Ezr 9: 4 the God of Israel g around me because of H665
Ezr 10: 1 women and children—g around him. H7695
Ezr 10: 9 Judah and Benjamin *had* g *in* Jerusalem. H7695
Ne 8:13 g around Ezra the teacher to give attention H665
Ne 9: 1 the Israelites g **together**, fasting and H665
Job 5:26 in full vigor, like sheaves g in season. H6590
Job 24:24 are brought low and g **up** like all others; H7890
Job 30: 4 In the brush *they* g salt herbs, and their H7786
Ps 35:15 when I stumbled, *they* g in glee; assailants H665
Ps 35:15 assailants g against me without my H665
Ps 107: 3 those *he* g from the lands, from east and H7695
Pr 27:25 appears and the grass from the hills **is g in**, H665
Pr 30: 4 Whose hands *have* **g up** the wind? Who H665
SS 5: 1 my bride; *I have* g my myrrh with my spice. H768
Isa 10:14 abandoned eggs, so I g all the countries H665
Isa 27:12 Israel, *will* **be g up** one by one. H4377
Isa 56: 8 others to them besides *those already* g." H7695
Isa 60: 7 All Kedar's flocks *will* **be** g to you, the H7695
Jer 6:11 street and on the young men g together; H6051
Jer 8: 2 *They will* not **be g up** or buried, but will be H665
Jer 25:33 They will not be mourned or **g up** or buried, H665
Jer 40:15 all the Jews who *are* g around you to be H7695
Eze 22:20 lead and tin are g into a furnace to be H7697
Eze 29: 5 the open field and not **be g** or picked up. H665
Eze 38: 7 you and all the hordes g about you, and H7735
Eze 38: 8 whose *people* **were** g from many nations H7695
Eze 38:12 ruins and the people g from the nations, H665
Eze 38:13 *Have you* g your hordes to loot, to carry off H7735
Eze 39:27 the nations and *have* g them from the H7695
Hos 10:10 nations *will* **be** g against them to put them H665
Mic 1: 7 Since *she* g her gifts from the wages of H7695
Mic 4:11 But now many nations *are* g against you H665
Mic 4:12 that *he has* g them like sheaves to the H7695
Zec 12: 3 the nations of the earth *are* g against her, H665
Mt 13: 2 large crowds g **around** him that he got *G5251*
Mt 16: 9 how many basketfuls *you* g? *G3284*
Mt 16:10 how many basketfuls *you* g? *G3284*
Mt 22:10 into the streets and g all the people they *G5251*
Mt 22:41 *While* the Pharisees *were* **g together** *G5251*
Mt 25:32 All the nations *will be* g before him, and *G5251*
Mt 27:17 So *when* the crowd *had* g, Pilate asked *G5251*
Mt 27:27 the Praetorium and g the whole company *G5251*
Mk 1:33 The whole town g at the door, *G1639+2190*
Mk 2: 2 *They* g in such large numbers that there *G5251*
Mk 3:20 again a crowd g, so that he and his *G5302*
Mk 4: 1 The crowd *that* g around him was so large *G5251*
Mk 5:21 a large crowd g around him while he was *G5251*
Mk 6:30 The apostles g around Jesus and reported *G5251*
Mk 7: 1 had come from Jerusalem g around Jesus *G5251*
Mk 8: 1 During those days another large crowd g *G1639*
Lk 12: 1 *when* a crowd of many thousands *had* g *G2190*
Lk 23:48 all the people *who had* g to witness this *G5219*
Jn 6:13 So *they* g them and filled twelve baskets *G5251*
Jn 8: 2 where all the people g around him, and *G2262*
Jn 10:24 The Jews who were there g **around** him *G3240*
Jn 18:38 out again to the Jews g there and said, NDT
Jn 19: 4 came out and said to the Jews g there, NDT
Ac 1: 6 Then they g **around** him and asked him *G5302*
Ac 5:16 Crowds g also from the towns around *G5302*
Ac 6: 2 Twelve g all the disciples **together** and *G4673*
Ac 12:12 many people *had* g and were *G1639+5255*
Ac 13:44 the whole city g to hear the word of *G5251*
Ac 14:20 But *after* the disciples *had* **g around** him *G3240*
Ac 14:27 *they* g the church **together** and reported *G5251*
Ac 15:30 where *they* g the church **together** and *G5251*
Ac 16:13 to speak to the women *who had* g there. *G5302*
Ac 28: 3 Paul g a pile of brushwood and, as he put *G5370*
2Co 8:15 "The one who g much did not have too NDT
2Co 8:15 the one who g little did not have too NDT
2Th 2: 1 Lord Jesus Christ and our being **g to** him, *G2191*
Rev 14:19 g its grapes and threw them into the great *G5582*
Rev 16:16 Then *they* g the kings **together** to the *G5251*
Rev 19:19 their armies g **together** to wage war *G5251*

GATHERING (13) [GATHER]

Nu 11: 8 The people went around g it, and then H4377
Nu 15:32 a man was found g wood on the Sabbath H8006
Nu 15:33 Those who found him g wood brought him H8006
1Ki 17:10 the town gate, a widow was there g sticks. H8006
1Ki 17:12 I *am* g a few sticks to take home and H8006
Ecc 2:26 he gives the task of g and storing up H665
Isa 17: 5 g the grain *in* their arms—as H7917
Jer 6: 9 the branches again, like *one* **g grapes**." H1305
Mt 3:12 g his wheat into the barn and burning up *G5251*
Mt 25:24 have not sown and g where you have not *G5251*
Lk 8: 4 *While* a large crowd *was* g and people *G5290*
Lk 15: 1 sinners were all **g around** to hear Jesus. *G1581*
Ac 10:27 inside and found a large g *of people*. *G5302*

GATHERS (15) [GATHER]

Nu 19:10 The *man who* **g up** the ashes of the heifer H665
Ps 33: 7 *He* g the waters of the sea into jars; he H4043
Ps 41: 6 falsely, *while* his heart g slander; then H7695
Ps 129: 7 hands with it, nor *one who* g fill his arms. H6682
Ps 147: 2 up Jerusalem; *he* g the exiles of Israel. H4043
Pr 6: 8 in summer and g its food at harvest. H112
Pr 10: 5 *He who* g **crops** in summer is a prudent son H112
Pr 13:11 but *whoever* g money little by little makes H7695
Isa 40:11 *He* g the lambs in his arms and carries H7695
Isa 56: 8 declares—*he who* g the exiles of Israel: H7695
Mic 7: 1 I am like *one who* g summer fruit at the H668
Hab 1:15 in his net, *he* g them **up** in his dragnet H665
Hab 2: 5 *he* g to himself all the nations and takes H665
Mt 23:37 as a hen g her chicks under her wings *G2190*
Lk 13:34 as a hen g her chicks under her wings NDT

GAUDY (1)

Eze 16:16 of your garments to make g high places, H3229

GAUNT (3) [GAUNTNESS]

Ge 41: 3 ugly and g, came up out of H1987+1414
Ge 41: 4 were ugly and g ate up the seven H1987+1414
Ps 109:24 from fasting; my body is thin and g. H4946+9043

GAUNTNESS (1) [GAUNT]

Job 16: 8 my g rises up and testifies against me. H3951

GAVE (660) [GIVE]

Ge 2:20 So the man g names to all the livestock H7924
Ge 3: 6 *She* also g some to her husband, who H5989
Ge 3:12 she g me some fruit from the tree H5989
Ge 4: 1 she became pregnant and **g birth** *to* Cain. H3528
Ge 4: 2 Later *she* **g birth** *to* his brother Abel. H3528
Ge 4:17 became pregnant and **g birth** *to* Enoch. H3528
Ge 4:20 Adah **g birth** *to* Jabal; he was the father of H3528
Ge 4:25 and *she* **g birth** *to* a son and named him H3528
Ge 9: 3 Just as *I* g you the green plants, I now H5989
Ge 12:20 Pharaoh g **orders** about Abram *to* his men H7422
Ge 14:20 Then Abram g him a tenth of everything. H5989
Ge 16: 3 slave Hagar and g her to her husband to H5989
Ge 16:13 *She* g this name *to* the LORD who spoke to H7924
Ge 16:15 Abram g the name Ishmael to the H7924
Ge 18: 7 tender calf and g it to a servant, who H5989
Ge 20:14 female slaves and g them to Abraham, H5989
Ge 21: 3 Abraham g the name Isaac *to* the son H7924
Ge 21:14 a skin of water and g them to Hagar. H5989
Ge 21:19 the skin with water and g the boy **a drink**. H9197
Ge 21:27 cattle and g them to Abimelek, H5989
Ge 24:18 the jar to her hands and g him **a drink**. H9197
Ge 24:53 of clothing and g them to Rebekah; H5989
Ge 24:53 *he* also g costly gifts to her brother and to H5989
Ge 25: 6 he g gifts to the sons of his concubines H5989
Ge 25:26 years old when Rebekah **g birth** *to* them. H3528
Ge 25:34 Then Jacob g Esau some bread and some H5989
Ge 26:11 So Abimelek g **orders** *to* all the people H7422
Ge 26:18 and *he* g them the same names his father H7924
Ge 27:20 "The LORD your God g me **success**," he H7936
Ge 28: 4 a foreigner, the land God g to Abraham." H5989
Ge 29:22 all the people of the place and g a feast. H6913
Ge 29:24 g his servant Zilpah to his daughter *as* her H5989
Ge 29:28 then Laban g him his daughter H5989
Ge 29:29 Laban g his servant Bilhah to his daughter H5989
Ge 29:32 became pregnant and **g birth** *to* a son. H3528
Ge 29:33 when *she* **g birth** *to* a son she said H3528
Ge 29:33 that I am not loved, *he* g me this one too." H5989
Ge 29:34 when *she* **g birth** *to* a son she said H3528
Ge 29:35 when *she* **g birth** *to* a son she said H3528
Ge 30: 4 So *she* g him her servant Bilhah as a wife H5989
Ge 30: 9 servant Zilpah and g her to Jacob as a H5989
Ge 30:21 time later *she* **g birth** *to* a daughter and H3528
Ge 30:23 pregnant and **g birth** *to* a son and said, H3528
Ge 30:25 After Rachel **g birth** *to* Joseph, Jacob said H3528
Ge 31: 8 all the flocks **g birth** *to* speckled young; H3528
Ge 35: 4 So *they* g Jacob all the foreign gods they H5989
Ge 35:12 The land *I* g to Abraham and Isaac I also H5989
Ge 38: 3 she became pregnant and **g birth** *to* a son H3528
Ge 38: 4 again and **g birth** *to* a son and named H3528
Ge 38: 5 *She* **g birth** *to* still another son and named H3528
Ge 38: 5 It was at Kezib that she **g birth** *to* him. H3528
Ge 38:18 So *he* g them to her and slept with her H5989
Ge 39: 3 that the LORD g him **success** *in* everything H7503
Ge 39:23 Joseph and g him **success** *in* whatever he H7503
Ge 40:20 and *he* g a feast for all his officials. H6913
Ge 41:45 Pharaoh g Joseph the name H7924
Ge 41:45 g him Asenath daughter H5989
Ge 42:25 Joseph g **orders** to fill their bags with H7422
Ge 43:24 g them water to wash their feet and H5989
Ge 44: 1 Now Joseph g *these* **instructions** *to* the H7422
Ge 45:21 Joseph g them carts, as Pharaoh had H5989
Ge 45:21 and *he* also g them provisions for their H5989
Ge 45:22 To each of them *he* g new clothing, but to H5989
Ge 45:22 to Benjamin *he* g three hundred H5989
Ge 47:11 in Egypt and g them property in the H5989
Ge 47:17 he g them food in exchange for their H5989
Ge 47:22 from the allotment Pharaoh g them. H5989
Ge 49:29 Then *he* g them *these* **instructions**: "I am H7422
Ex 1:21 *he* g them families of their own. H6913
Ex 1:22 Then Pharaoh g *this* **order** to all his H7422
Ex 2: 2 became pregnant and **g birth** *to* a son. H3528
Ex 2:21 *who* g his daughter Zipporah to Moses **in marriage** H5989
Ex 2:22 Zipporah **g birth** *to* a son, and Moses H3528
Ex 4:11 "Who g human beings their mouths? H8492
Ex 5: 6 day Pharaoh g *this* **order** *to* the slave H7422
Ex 12:36 and *they* g them **what** they **asked for**; so H8626
Ex 16:32 see the bread *I* g you **to eat** in the H430
Ex 31:18 *he* g him the two tablets of the covenant H5989
Ex 32:24 Then *they* g me the gold, and I threw it H5989
Ex 34:32 and *he* g them all *the* **commands** the LORD H7422
Ex 36: 6 Then Moses g **an order** and they sent this H7422
Lev 7:38 which the LORD g Moses at Mount Sinai in H7422
Lev 27:34 commands the LORD g Moses at Mount H7422
Nu 3:51 Moses g the redemption money to Aaron H5989
Nu 7: 6 carts and oxen and g them to the Levites. H5989
Nu 7: 7 *He* g two carts and four oxen to the H5989
Nu 7: 8 and *he* g four carts and eight oxen to the H5989
Nu 13:16 Moses g Hoshea son of Nun *the* **name** H7924
Nu 13:27 *They* g Moses *this* **account**: "We went into H6218
Nu 15:22 of these commands the LORD g Moses— H1819
Nu 15:23 the day the LORD g them and continuing H7422
Nu 17: 6 their leaders g him twelve staffs, one H5989
Nu 21: 3 plea and g the Canaanites **over** to them. H5989
Nu 22:18 "Even if Balak g me all the silver and gold H5989
Nu 22:40 g some to Balaam and the officials H8938
Nu 24:13 'Even if Balak g me all the silver and gold H5989
Nu 30:16 regulations the LORD g Moses concerning H7422
Nu 31:21 required by the law that the LORD g Moses: H7422
Nu 31:41 Moses g the tribute to Eleazar the priest H5989
Nu 31:47 and g them to the Levites H5989
Nu 32:28 Moses g **orders** about them *to* Eleazar H7422
Nu 32:33 Then Moses g to the Gadites, the H5989
Nu 32:38 *They* g names *to* the cities they rebuilt H7924
Nu 32:40 So Moses g Gilead to the Makirites, the H5989
Nu 36: 5 command Moses g *this* **order** *to* the H7422
Nu 36:13 the LORD g through Moses to the H7422
Dt 2:12 in the land the LORD g them as their H5989
Dt 2:36 The LORD our God g us all of them. H5989
Dt 3: 3 the LORD our God also g into our hands Og H5989
Dt 3:12 *I* g the Reubenites and the Gadites the H5989
Dt 3:13 *I* g to the half-tribe of Manasseh. H5989
Dt 3:15 And *I* g Gilead to Makir. H5989
Dt 3:16 the Gadites *I* g the territory extending H5989
Dt 4:45 laws Moses g them when they came H1819
Dt 5:22 on two stone tablets and g them to me. H5989
Dt 8:16 He g you manna **to eat** in the wilderness H430
Dt 9:10 The LORD g me two stone tablets inscribed H5989
Dt 9:11 the LORD g me the two stone tablets H5989
Dt 10: 4 And the LORD g them to me. H5989
Dt 22:16 "*I* g my daughter **in marriage** H5989+4200+851
Dt 26: 9 us to this place and g us this land, H5989
Dt 28:45 the commands and decrees *he* g you. H7422
Dt 29: 8 took their land and g it as an inheritance H5989
Dt 31: 9 down this law and g it to the Levitical H5989
Dt 31:23 The LORD g *this* **command** to Joshua son H7422
Dt 31:25 he g *this* **command** *to* the Levites who H7422
Dt 32: 8 Most High g the nations their **inheritance**, H5706
Dt 32:18 you forgot the God *who* g you **birth**. H2655
Dt 33: 4 the law that Moses g us, the possession H7422
Jos 1: 7 obey all the law my servant Moses g you; H7422
Jos 1:13 the servant of the LORD g you after he said, H7422
Jos 1:14 the land that Moses g you east of the H5989
Jos 1:15 servant of the LORD g you east of the H5989
Jos 6:20 when the men g a loud **shout**, the H8131+9558
Jos 8:33 commanded when he g instructions to bless NDT
Jos 10:12 day the LORD g the Amorites **over** to Israel, H5989
Jos 10:27 sunset Joshua g *the* **order** and they took H7422
Jos 10:30 The LORD also g that city and its king into H5989
Jos 10:32 The LORD g Lachish into Israel's hands, and H5989
Jos 11: 8 the LORD g them into the hand of H5989
Jos 11:23 he g it as an inheritance to Israel H5989
Jos 12: 6 the servant of the LORD g their land to the H5989
Jos 12: 7 Joshua g their lands as an inheritance to H5989
Jos 13:14 to the tribe of Levi *he* g no inheritance, H5989
Jos 14:13 of Jephunneh and g him Hebron as his H5989
Jos 15:13 Joshua g to Caleb son of Jephunneh a H5989
Jos 15:17 g his daughter Aksah to him **in marriage** H5989+4200+851
Jos 15:19 So Caleb g her the upper and lower H5989
Jos 17: 4 So Joshua g them an inheritance along H5989
Jos 18: 7 Moses the servant of the LORD g it to them. H5989
Jos 19:49 the Israelites g Joshua son of Nun an H5989
Jos 19:50 *They* g him the town he asked for H5989
Jos 21: 3 the Israelites g the Levites the following H5989

Jos 21:11 *They* g them Kiriath Arba (that is, Hebron), H5989
Jos 21:13 of Aaron the priest *they* g Hebron H5989
Jos 21:17 the tribe of Benjamin they g them Gibeon, NDT
Jos 21:43 So the LORD g Israel all the land he had H5989
Jos 21:44 The LORD g them **rest** on every side, just as H5663
Jos 21:44 the LORD g all their enemies into their H5989
Jos 22: 3 out the mission the LORD your God g you. H5184
Jos 22: 4 servant of the LORD g you on the other side H5989
Jos 22: 5 that Moses the servant of the LORD g you: H7422
Jos 22: 7 of the tribe Joshua g land on the west H5989
Jos 22:34 the Gadites g the altar *this* **name**: H7924
Jos 23:14 the LORD your God g you has failed. H1819
Jos 24: 3 Canaan and g him **many** descendants. H8049
Jos 24: 3 him many descendants. *I* g him Isaac, H5989
Jos 24: 4 to Isaac *I* g Jacob and Esau. H5989
Jos 24: 8 against you, but *I* g them into your hands. H5989
Jos 24:11 Jebusites, but *I* g them into your hands. H5989
Jos 24:13 So *I* g you a land on which you did not toil H5989
Jdg 1: 4 the LORD g the Canaanites and Perizzites H5989
Jdg 1:13 g his daughter Aksah to him **in marriage** H5989+4200+851
Jdg 1:15 So Caleb g her the upper and lower H5989
Jdg 2:14 Israel the LORD g them into the hands of H5989
Jdg 3: 6 in marriage and g their own daughters to H5989
Jdg 3:10 The LORD g Cushan-Rishathaim king of H5989
Jdg 3:12 the LORD g Eglon king of Moab **power** over H2616
Jdg 3:15 to the LORD, and he g them a deliverer H7756
Jdg 4:19 a skin of milk, g him **a drink**, and covered H9197
Jdg 5:25 water, and *she* g him milk; in a bowl H5989
Jdg 6: 1 seven years he g them into the hands H5989
Jdg 6: 9 them out before you and g you their land. H5989
Jdg 6:32 *they* g him **the name** Jerub-Baal that day H7924
Jdg 8: 3 God g Oreb and Zeeb, the Midianite H5989
Jdg 9: 4 *They* g him seventy shekels of silver from H5989
Jdg 11:21 g Sihon and his whole army into Israel's H5989
Jdg 11:32 the LORD g them into his hands. H5989
Jdg 12: 3 LORD g me the **victory** *over* H5989+928+3338
Jdg 12: 9 *He* g his daughters **away in marriage** to H8938
Jdg 13:24 The woman g **birth** *to* a boy and named H3528
Jdg 14: 9 his parents, *he* g them some, and they H5989
Jdg 14:19 of everything and g their clothes to those H5989
Jdg 15: 2 he said, "that *I* g her to your companion. H5989
Jdg 17: 4 of silver and g them to a silversmith H5989
Ru 1:12 tonight and then g **birth** *to* sons— H3528
Ru 2:15 to glean, Boaz g **orders** *to* his men, "Let H7422
Ru 2:18 also brought out and g her what she had H5989
Ru 3:17 "*He* g me these six measures of barley H5989
Ru 4: 7 took off his sandal and g it to the other. H5989
Ru 4:13 her to conceive, and *she* g **birth** *to* a son. H3528
1Sa 1: 5 But to Hannah *he* g a double portion H5989
1Sa 1:20 became pregnant and g **birth** *to* a son. H3528
1Sa 2:20 the one she prayed for and g to the LORD." H8626
1Sa 2:21 *she* g **birth** *to* three sons and two H3528
1Sa 2:28 *I* also g your ancestor's family all the food H5989
1Sa 4:19 she went into labor and g **birth**, but was H3528
1Sa 9:23 "Bring the piece of meat *I* g you, the one I H5989
1Sa 13:13 the command the LORD your God g you; H7422
1Sa 15:24 men and so *I* g **in** *to* them. H9048+928+7754
1Sa 18: 4 robe he was wearing and g it to David, H5989
1Sa 18: 5 Saul g him **a high rank in** the army H8492+6584
1Sa 18:13 away from him and g him command over H8492
1Sa 18:27 g him his daughter Michal **in marriage** H5989+4200+851
1Sa 20:40 Then Jonathan g his weapons to the boy H5989
1Sa 21: 6 So the priest g him the consecrated bread H5989
1Sa 22:10 *he* also g him provisions and the sword of H5989
1Sa 24:22 So David g *his* **oath** to Saul. Then Saul H8678
1Sa 25: 9 *they* g Nabal this message in David's H1819
1Sa 27: 6 So on that day Achish g him Ziklag, and it H5989
1Sa 30:11 *They* g him water to drink and food to eat H5989
2Sa 3:15 So Ish-Bosheth g **orders** and had her H8938
2Sa 4:10 That was the reward I g him for his news! H5989
2Sa 4:12 So David g *an* **order** *to* his men, and they H7422
2Sa 6:19 Then *he* g a loaf of bread, a cake of dates H2745
2Sa 8: 6 The LORD g David **victory** wherever he H3828
2Sa 8:14 The LORD g David **victory** wherever he H3828
2Sa 12: 8 *I* g your master's house to you, and your H5989
2Sa 12: 8 *I* g you all Israel and Judah H5989
2Sa 12:24 *She* g **birth** *to* a son, and they named him H3528
2Sa 13:25 still refused to go but g him *his* **blessing**. H1385
2Sa 16:23 days the **advice** Ahithophel g was H3619+6783
2Sa 19:28 but *you* g your servant a **place** among H8883
1Ki 1: 7 and *they* g him *their* **support**. H6468+339
1Ki 2: 1 *he* g **a charge** *to* Solomon his son. H7422
1Ki 2:25 So King Solomon g **orders** to Benaiah son H8938
1Ki 2:43 the LORD and obey the command *I* g you?" H7422
1Ki 2:46 Then the king g **the order** *to* Benaiah son H7422
1Ki 3:15 Then *he* g a feast for all his court H6913
1Ki 3:25 He then g **an order**: "Cut the living child in H606
1Ki 3:27 Then the king g *his* **ruling**: "Give the H6699
1Ki 4:29 God g Solomon wisdom and very great H5989
1Ki 5:11 Solomon g Hiram twenty thousand H5989
1Ki 5:12 The LORD g Solomon wisdom, just as he H5989
1Ki 6:12 you the promise *I* g to David your father. H1819
1Ki 8:34 back to the land *you* g to their ancestors. H5989
1Ki 8:36 rain on the land *you* g your people for an H5989
1Ki 8:40 they live in the land *you* g our ancestors. H5989
1Ki 8:48 you toward the land *you* g their ancestors, H5989
1Ki 8:56 the good promises *he* g through his H1819
1Ki 8:58 decrees and laws *he* g our ancestors. H7422
1Ki 9:11 King Solomon g twenty towns in Galilee to H5989
1Ki 9:16 then g it as a wedding gift H5989
1Ki 10:10 And *she* g the king 120 talents of gold H5989
1Ki 10:10 the queen of Sheba g to King Solomon. H5989
1Ki 10:13 King Solomon g the queen of Sheba all H5989
1Ki 11:18 *who* g Hadad a house and land and H5989
1Ki 11:19 *he* g him a sister of his own wife, Queen Tahpenes, **in marriage** H5989+851
1Ki 12: 8 the **advice** the elders g him and H6783+3619
1Ki 13: 3 That same day the man of God g a sign H5989
1Ki 13:21 the command the LORD your God g you. H7422
1Ki 14: 8 from the house of David and g it to you, H5989
1Ki 14:15 this good land that *he* g to their ancestors H5989
1Ki 15: 4 sake the LORD his God g him a lamp in H5989
1Ki 17:23 *He* g him to his mother and said, "Look H5989
1Ki 19:21 to cook the meat and g it to the people, H5989
2Ki 4:17 about that same time *she* g **birth** *to* a son, H3528
2Ki 5:23 *He* g them to two of his servants, and they H5989
2Ki 11:10 Then he g the commanders the spears H5989
2Ki 12:11 *they* g the money to the men appointed H5989
2Ki 12:15 those to whom *they* g the money to pay H5989
2Ki 15:19 Menahem g him a thousand talents H5989
2Ki 16:15 Ahaz then g *these* **orders** *to* Uriah the H7422
2Ki 17:20 afflicted them and g them into the hands H5989
2Ki 17:27 Then the king of Assyria g *this* **order** H7422
2Ki 17:34 that the LORD g the descendants of H7422
2Ki 18:15 So Hezekiah g him all the silver that was H5989
2Ki 18:16 of the LORD, and g it to the king of Assyria. H5989
2Ki 21: 8 wander from the land *I* g their ancestors, H5989
2Ki 21: 8 whole Law that my servant Moses g them." H7422
2Ki 22: 8 He g it to Shaphan, who H5989
2Ki 22:12 He g *these* **orders** *to* Hilkiah the priest H7422
2Ki 23:21 The king g *this* **order** *to* all the people H7422
2Ki 25:28 kindly to him and g him a seat of honor H5989
2Ki 25:30 Day by day the king g Jehoiachin a regular H5989
1Ch 2:35 g his daughter **in marriage** to H5989+4200+851
1Ch 2:49 *She* also g **birth** *to* Shaaph the father of Madmannah and *to* H3528
1Ch 4: 9 saying, "*I* g **birth** to him in pain. H3528
1Ch 4:17 One of Mered's wives g **birth** *to* Miriam H2225
1Ch 4:18 tribe of Judah g **birth** *to* Jered the father H3528
1Ch 6:64 So the Israelites g the Levites these towns H5989
1Ch 6:70 Manasseh the Israelites g Aner and Bileam, NDT
1Ch 7:14 *She* g **birth** *to* Makir the father of Gilead. H3528
1Ch 7:16 wife Maakah g **birth** *to* a son and named H3528
1Ch 7:18 His sister Hammoleketh g **birth** *to* Ishhod H3528
1Ch 7:23 became pregnant and g **birth** *to* a son. H3528
1Ch 11:10 g his kingship **strong support** to H2616+6640
1Ch 14:12 David g **orders** to burn them in the fire. H606
1Ch 16: 3 Then *he* g a loaf of bread, a cake of dates H2745
1Ch 18: 6 The LORD g David **victory** wherever he H3828
1Ch 18:13 The LORD g David **victory** wherever he H3828
1Ch 22: 2 So David g **orders** to assemble the H606
1Ch 22:13 laws that the LORD g Moses for Israel. H7422
1Ch 25: 5 God g Heman fourteen sons and three H5989
1Ch 28:11 Then David g his son Solomon the plans H5989
1Ch 28:12 He g him the plans of all that the Spirit had NDT
1Ch 28:13 He g him instructions for the divisions of the NDT
1Ch 28:18 He also g him the plan for the chariot, that NDT
1Ch 29: 6 in charge of the king's work g **willingly**. H5605
1Ch 29: 7 *They* g toward the work on the temple of H5989
1Ch 29: 8 had precious stones g them to the H5989
2Ch 2: 1 Solomon g **orders** to build a temple for the H606
2Ch 6:25 back to the land *you* g to them and their H5989
2Ch 6:27 rain on the land *you* g your people for an H5989
2Ch 6:31 they live in the land *you* g our ancestors. H5989
2Ch 6:38 toward the land *you* g their ancestors, H5989
2Ch 7: 3 they worshiped and g **thanks** to the LORD, H3344
2Ch 7: 6 which were used when he g **thanks**, H2146
2Ch 9: 9 Then *she* g the king 120 talents of gold H5989
2Ch 9: 9 the queen of Sheba g to King Solomon. H5989
2Ch 9:12 King Solomon g the queen of Sheba all H5989
2Ch 9:12 he g her more than she had brought to him. NDT
2Ch 10: 8 the **advice** the elders g him and H3619+6783
2Ch 11:23 *He* g them abundant provisions and took H5989
2Ch 14: 6 during those years, for the LORD g him **rest**. H5663
2Ch 15:15 So the LORD g them **rest** on every side. H5663
2Ch 19: 9 *He* g them *these* **orders**: "You must serve H7422
2Ch 20:11 possession *you* g us **as an inheritance**. H3769
2Ch 23: 9 Then he g the commanders of units of a H5989
2Ch 24:12 The king and Jehoiada g it to those who H5989
2Ch 26: 5 as he sought the LORD, God g him **success**. H7503
2Ch 28: 9 with Judah, *he* g them into your hand. H5989
2Ch 28:14 So the soldiers g **up** the prisoners and H6440
2Ch 28:20 but *he* g him **trouble** instead of help. H7674
2Ch 29:27 Hezekiah g **the order** to sacrifice the burnt H606
2Ch 31: 5 the Israelites **generously** g the firstfruits of H8049
2Ch 31:11 Hezekiah g **orders** to prepare storerooms in H606
2Ch 32:24 answered him and g him a miraculous H5989
2Ch 34: 9 the high priest and g him the money that H5989
2Ch 34:11 *They* also g money to the carpenters and H5989
2Ch 34:15 temple of the LORD." He g it to Shaphan. H5989
2Ch 34:20 He g *these* **orders** *to* Hilkiah, Ahikam son H7422
2Ch 35: 8 g the priests twenty-six hundred Passover H5989
2Ch 36:17 God g them all into the hands of H5989
Ezr 2:68 families g **freewill offerings** toward the H5605
Ezr 2:69 to their ability *they* g to the treasury for H5989
Ezr 3: 7 Then *they* g money to the masons and H5989
Ezr 3: 7 g food and drink and olive oil to the NDT
Ezr 3:11 people g **a** great **shout** of praise H8131+9558
Ezr 5:11 This is the answer *they* g us: "We are A10754
Ezr 5:12 *he* g them into the hands of A10314
Ezr 5:14 King Cyrus g *them* to a man named A10314
Ezr 8:36 *who* then g **assistance** *to* the people and *to* H5951
Ezr 9:11 *you* g through your servants the prophets H7422
Ezr 10:19 *They all* g their hands **in pledge** to put H5989
Ne 1: 7 decrees and laws *you* g your servant H7422
Ne 1: 8 the instruction *you* g your servant Moses, H7422
Ne 2: 1 I took the wine and g it to the king. H5989
Ne 2: 9 of Trans-Euphrates and g them the king's H5989
Ne 6: 4 each time *I* g them the same answer. H8740
Ne 7:70 The governor g to the treasury 1,000 H5989
Ne 7:71 heads of the families g to the treasury H5989
Ne 9:13 *You* g them regulations and laws that are H5989
Ne 9:14 holy Sabbath and g them commands, H7422
Ne 9:15 In their hunger *you* g them bread from H5989
Ne 9:20 *You* g your good Spirit to instruct them H5989
Ne 9:20 and *you* g them water for their thirst. H5989
Ne 9:22 "*You* g them kingdoms and nations H5989
Ne 9:24 *you* g the Canaanites into their hands H5989
Ne 9:27 great compassion *you* g them deliverers, H5989
Ne 9:30 so *you* g them into the hands of the H5989
Ne 9:35 the spacious and fertile land *you* g them, H5989
Ne 9:36 slaves in the land *you* g our ancestors so H5989
Ne 12:40 The two **choirs that** g **thanks** then took H9343
Ne 13: 9 *I* g **orders** to purify the rooms, and then I put H606
Est 1: 3 year of his reign *he* g a banquet for all his H6913
Est 1: 5 were over, the king g a banquet, lasting H6913
Est 1: 9 Queen Vashti also g a banquet for the H6913
Est 2:18 And the king g a great banquet, Esther's H6913
Est 3:10 from his finger and g it to Haman son of H5989
Est 4: 8 *He* also g him a copy of the text of the H5989
Est 5:12 accompany the king to the banquet *she* g. H6913
Est 8: 1 same day King Xerxes g Queen Esther the H5989
Job 1:21 The LORD g and the LORD has taken away H5989
Job 8: 4 *he* g them **over** to the penalty of their sin. H8938
Job 10:12 You g me life and showed me kindness NDT
Job 22: 7 *You* g no water *to* the weary and you H9197
Job 32:12 *I* g you *my* **full attention**. But not one of H1067
Job 39: 6 *I* g it the wasteland as its home, the salt H8492
Job 42:10 his fortunes and g him twice as much as H3578
Job 42:11 each one g him a piece of silver and H5989
Ps 21: 4 you for life, and *you* g it to him—length H5989
Ps 21: 5 Through the victories you g, his glory is NDT
Ps 40: 2 on a rock and g me **a firm** place to stand. H3922
Ps 44:11 *You* g us **up** to be devoured like sheep H5989
Ps 68: 9 *You* g abundant showers, O God; you H5678
Ps 69:21 gall in my food and g me vinegar for my H9197
Ps 74:14 heads of Leviathan and g it as food to the H5989
Ps 78:15 wilderness and g them **water** as abundant H9197
Ps 78:23 Yet *he* g *a* **command** *to* the skies above H7422
Ps 78:24 *he* g them the grain of heaven. H5989
Ps 78:46 *He* g their crops to the grasshopper, their H5989
Ps 78:48 *He* g **over** their cattle to the hail, their H6037
Ps 78:50 from death but g them **over** to the plague. H6037
Ps 78:62 *He* g his people **over** to the sword; he was H6037
Ps 81:12 So *I* g them **over** to their stubborn hearts H8938
Ps 99: 7 his statutes and the decrees *he* g them. H5989
Ps 105:44 *he* g them the lands of the nations, and H5989
Ps 106: 7 *they* g no **thought** *to* your miracles H8505
Ps 106:14 the desert *they* g **in** *to their* **craving**; H203+9294
Ps 106:15 So *he* g them what they asked for, but H5989
Ps 106:41 *He* g them into the hands of the nations H5989
Ps 119:26 *I* g **an account** *of* my ways and you H6218
Ps 135:12 and *he* g their land as an inheritance, an H5989
Ps 136:21 g their land as an inheritance, His H5989
Pr 8:29 when he g the sea its boundary so the H8492
Pr 23:22 to your father, who g you **life**, and do not H3528
Pr 23:25 may *she who* g you **birth** be joyful! H3528
Ecc 12: 7 the spirit returns to God who g it. H5989
SS 8: 5 there she who was in labor g you **birth**. H3528
Isa 8: 3 she conceived and g **birth** *to* a son. H3528
Isa 22:16 here and who g you **permission** to cut out H4200
Isa 26:18 writhed in labor, but *we* g **birth** *to* wind. H3528
Isa 41:27 *I* g to Jerusalem a messenger of good H5989
Isa 47: 6 my inheritance; *I* g them into your hand H5989
Isa 51: 2 your father, and to Sarah, *who* g you **birth**. H2655
Isa 63: 5 I was appalled that no *one* g **support**; so H6164
Jer 2:27 my father,' and to stone, 'You g me **birth**. H3528
Jer 3: 8 *I* g faithless Israel her certificate of divorce H5989
Jer 3:18 land *I* g your ancestors *as an* **inheritance**. H5706
Jer 7: 7 in the land *I* g your ancestors for ever and H5989
Jer 7:14 the place *I* g to you and your ancestors. H5989
Jer 7:23 but *I* g them this **command**: Obey me, and H7422
Jer 12:14 seize the inheritance *I* g my people Israel, H5706
Jer 15:10 mother, that *you* g me **birth**, a man with H3528
Jer 16:15 them to the land *I* g their ancestors. H5989
Jer 17: 4 fault you will lose the inheritance *I* g you. H5989
Jer 22:26 the mother who g you **birth** into another H3528
Jer 23:39 along with the city *I* g to you and your H5989
Jer 24:10 from the land *I* g to them and their H5989
Jer 25: 5 in the land the LORD g to you and your H5989
Jer 27:12 *I* g **the** same **message** to Zedekiah H1819+3972+2021+2021+465+1821
Jer 30: 3 them to the land *I* g their ancestors to H5989
Jer 32:12 and *I* g this deed to Baruch son of Neriah H5989
Jer 32:13 presence *I* g Baruch *these* **instructions**: H7422
Jer 32:22 *You* g them this land you had sworn to H5989
Jer 35: 6 son of Rekab g us *this* **command**: H7422
Jer 35:16 out the command their forefather g them, H7422
Jer 36:32 another scroll and g it to the scribe Baruch H5989
Jer 37:21 Zedekiah then g **orders** *for* Jeremiah to be H7422
Jer 39:10 at that time *he* g them vineyards and H5989
Jer 40: 5 the commander g him provisions and H5989
Jer 44:30 just as *I* g Zedekiah king of Judah into the H5989
Jer 50:12 *she who* g you **birth** will be disgraced. H3528

Jer 51:59 Jeremiah the prophet **g** *to* the staff officer H7422
Jer 52:32 kindly to him and **g** him a seat of honor H5989
Jer 52:34 the king of Babylon **g** Jehoiachin a H5989
La 2:14 The prophecies *they* **g** you were false H2600
Eze 3: 2 my mouth, and *he* **g** me the scroll **to eat**. H430
Eze 16: 8 *I* **g** you *my* **solemn oath** and entered into H8678
Eze 16:17 You also took the fine jewelry *I* **g** you, the H5989
Eze 16:19 olive oil and honey *I* **g** you **to eat**—you H430
Eze 16:27 *I* **g** you **over** to the greed of your enemies H5989
Eze 16:36 because *you* **g** them your children's H5989
Eze 20:11 *I* **g** them my decrees and made known to H5989
Eze 20:12 Also *I* **g** them my Sabbaths as a sign H5989
Eze 20:25 So I **g** them other statutes that were not H5989
Eze 23: 4 They were mine and **g birth** *to* sons and H3528
Eze 23: 7 *She* **g** herself as a prostitute to all the elite H5989
Eze 28:25 own land, which *I* **g** to my servant Jacob. H5989
Eze 31: 6 of the wild **g birth** under its branches; H3528
Eze 31:11 *I* **g** it into the hands of the ruler of the H5989
Eze 36:28 you will live in the land *I* **g** your ancestors; H5989
Eze 37:25 live in the land *I* **g** to my servant Jacob, H5989
Da 1: 7 The chief official **g** them new names: to H8492
Da 1:16 they were to drink and **g** them vegetables H5989
Da 1:17 four young men God **g** knowledge and H5989
Da 5: 1 King Belshazzar **g** a great banquet for a A10522
Da 5: 2 *he* **g orders** to bring in the gold and A10042
Da 5:18 the Most High God **g** your father A10314
Da 5:19 Because of the high position *he* **g** him A10314
Da 6:16 So the king **g the order**, and they A10042
Da 6:23 was overjoyed and **g orders** to lift Daniel A10042
Da 7:16 "So he told me and **g** me the A10313
Da 7:23 "*He* **g** me this **explanation**: 'The fourth A10042
Da 9:10 God or kept the laws *he* **g** us through his H5989
Da 10:18 a man touched me and **g** me **strength**. H2616
Hos 1: 6 again and **g birth** *to* a daughter. H3528
Hos 2: 8 that I was the *one who* **g** her the grain, H5989
Hos 12:10 **g** them **many** visions and told parables H8049
Hos 13:11 So in my anger *I* **g** you a king, and in my H5989
Am 4: 6 "I **g** you empty stomachs in every city and H5989
Hag 1:13 **g** this message of the LORD to the people: H606
Zec 3: 6 angel of the LORD **g** *this* **charge** to Joshua: H6386
Mal 2: 5 life and peace, and *I* **g** them to him; this H5989
Mal 4: 4 decrees and laws *I* **g** him at Horeb for all H7422
Mt 1:25 their marriage until *she* **g birth to** a son. *G5503*
Mt 1:25 And *he* **g** him the name Jesus. *G2813*
Mt 2:16 and *he* **g orders** to kill all the boys in *G690*
Mt 8:18 *he* **g orders** to cross to the other side of *G3027*
Mt 10: 1 disciples to him and **g** them authority to *G1443*
Mt 14:19 *he* **g thanks** and broke the loaves. *G2328*
Mt 14:19 Then *he* **g** them to the disciples, and the *G1443*
Mt 14:19 the disciples **g** them to the people. NDT
Mt 15:36 he broke them and **g** them to the *G1443*
Mt 20:14 one who was hired last the same as I **g** you. NDT
Mt 21:23 "And who **g** you this authority? *G1443*
Mt 25:15 To one *he* **g** five bags of gold, to another *G1443*
Mt 25:35 hungry and *you* **g** me *something* to eat, *G1443*
Mt 25:35 thirsty and *you* **g** me **something to drink**, *G4540*
Mt 25:42 I was hungry and *you* **g** me nothing to eat *G1443*
Mt 25:42 was thirsty and *you* **g** me nothing **to drink**, *G4540*
Mt 26:26 he broke it and **g** it to his disciples *G1443*
Mt 26:27 had given thanks, *he* **g** it to them, saying, *G1443*
Mt 27:12 priests and the elders, *he* **g** no **answer**. *G646*
Mt 27:50 again in a loud voice, *he* **g up** his spirit. *G918*
Mt 28:12 *they* **g** the soldiers a large sum of money *G1443*
Mk 2:26 And *he* also **g** some to his companions." *G1443*
Mk 3:12 But *he* **g** them strict **orders** not to tell *G2203*
Mk 3:16 Simon (to whom *he* **g** the name Peter), *G2202*
Mk 3:17 to them *he* **g** the name Boanerges *G2202*
Mk 5:13 *He* **g** them **permission**, and the impure *G2205*
Mk 5:43 *He* **g** strict **orders** not to let anyone know *G1403*
Mk 6: 7 out two by two and **g** them authority over *G1443*
Mk 6:21 On his birthday Herod **g** a banquet for his *G4472*
Mk 6:28 it to the girl, and she **g** it to her mother. *G1443*
Mk 6:41 *he* **g thanks** and broke the loaves. *G2328*
Mk 6:41 Then *he* **g** them to his disciples to *G1443*
Mk 8: 6 he broke them and **g** them to his disciples *G1443*
Mk 8: 7 *he* **g thanks** for them also and told the *G2328*
Mk 9: 9 Jesus **g** them **orders** not to tell anyone *G1403*
Mk 11:28 "And who **g** you authority to do this?" *G1443*
Mk 12:44 They all **g** out of their wealth; but she, out *G965*
Mk 14:22 he broke it and **g** it to his disciples *G1443*
Mk 14:23 had given thanks, *he* **g** it to them, and *G1443*
Mk 14:57 up and **g** *this* **false testimony** against him *G6018*
Mk 14:61 But Jesus remained silent and **g** no **answer** *G646*
Mk 15:45 that it was so, *he* **g** the body to Joseph. *G1563*
Lk 1:57 to have her baby, *she* **g birth to** a son. *G1164*
Lk 2: 7 and *she* **g birth to** her firstborn, a son. *G5503*
Lk 2:38 *she* **g thanks** to God and spoke about the *G469*
Lk 4:20 **g** it **back** to the attendant and sat down. *G625*
Lk 5:26 was amazed and **g praise** to God. *G1519*
Lk 6: 4 And *he* also **g** some to his companions." *G1443*
Lk 7:15 and Jesus **g** him **back** to his mother. *G1443*
Lk 7:21 **g** sight to many who were blind. *G5919*
Lk 8:32 into the pigs, and *he* **g** them **permission**. *G2205*
Lk 9: 1 *he* **g** them power and authority to drive *G1443*
Lk 9:16 to heaven, *he* **g thanks** and broke them. *G2328*
Lk 9:16 Then *he* **g** them to the disciples to *G1443*
Lk 9:42 healed the boy and **g** him **back** to his father. AIT
Lk 10:35 out two denarii and **g** them to the *G1443*
Lk 11:27 the mother who **g** you **birth** and nursed *G1002*
Lk 15:16 were eating, but no one **g** him anything. *G1443*
Lk 15:29 Yet *you* never **g** me even a young goat so *G1443*
Lk 19:13 ten of his servants and **g** them ten minas. *G1443*
Lk 20: 2 "Who **g** you this authority?" *G1443*
Lk 21: 4 All these people **g** their gifts out of their *G965*
Lk 22:17 the cup, *he* **g thanks** and said, "Take *G2373*
Lk 22:19 he took bread, **g thanks** and broke it, and *G2373*
Lk 22:19 broke it, and **g** it to them, saying, *G1443*
Lk 23: 9 questions, but Jesus **g** him no **answer**. *G646*
Lk 24:30 he took bread, **g thanks**, broke it and *G2328*
Lk 24:42 They **g** him a piece of broiled fish, *G2113*
Jn 1:12 *he* **g** the right to become children of God *G1443*
Jn 1:32 Then John **g this testimony**: "I saw the *G3455*
Jn 3:16 the world that *he* **g** his one and only *G1443*
Jn 4:12 who **g** us the well and drank from it *G1443*
Jn 5:19 Jesus **g** them *this* **answer**: "Very truly I tell *G646*
Jn 5:35 John was a lamp that burned and **g light** *G5743*
Jn 6:11 took the loaves, **g thanks**, and distributed *G2373*
Jn 6:31 '*He* **g** them bread from heaven to eat *G1443*
Jn 7:22 because Moses **g** you circumcision *G1443*
Jn 13:26 the piece of bread, *he* **g** it to Judas, the *G1443*
Jn 17: 4 by finishing the work *you* **g** me to do. *G1443*
Jn 17: 6 you to those whom *you* **g** me out of the *G1443*
Jn 17: 6 *you* **g** them to me and they have obeyed *G1443*
Jn 17: 8 For *I* **g** them the words you gave me and *G1443*
Jn 17: 8 gave them the words *you* **g** me and they *G1443*
Jn 17:11 the name *you* **g** me, so that they *G1443*
Jn 17:12 kept them safe by that name *you* **g** me. *G1443*
Jn 17:22 I have given them the glory that *you* **g** me, *G1443*
Jn 18: 9 "I have not lost one of those *you* **g** me." *G1443*
Jn 19: 9 asked Jesus, but Jesus **g** him no answer. *G1443*
Jn 19:30 he bowed his head and **g up** his spirit. *G4140*
Jn 21:13 took the bread and **g** it to them, and did *G1443*
Ac 1: 3 himself to them and **g** many convincing *G1877*
Ac 1: 4 with them, *he* **g** them *this* **command**: *G4133*
Ac 3: 5 So the man **g** them *his* **attention** *G2091*
Ac 5:28 "*We* **g** you **strict orders** not to teach *G4132+4133*
Ac 6:10 the wisdom the Spirit **g** him as he spoke. NDT
Ac 7: 5 *He* **g** him no inheritance here, not even *G1443*
Ac 7: 8 Then *he* **g** Abraham the covenant of *G1443*
Ac 7:10 *He* **g** Joseph wisdom and enabled him to *G1443*
Ac 7:42 from them and **g** them **over** to the worship *G4140*
Ac 8:10 **g** him *their* **attention** and exclaimed *G4668*
Ac 8:38 And *he* **g orders** to stop the chariot. *G3027*
Ac 10: 2 *he* **g** generously **to** those **in need** *G4472+1797*
Ac 11:17 So if God **g** them the same gift he gave us *G1443*
Ac 11:17 them the same gift he **g** us who believed in NDT
Ac 13:20 God **g** them judges until the time of *G1443*
Ac 13:21 a king, and he **g** them Saul son of Kish *G1443*
Ac 19:16 *He* **g** them such a **beating** that they ran *G2710*
Ac 21:14 not be dissuaded, *we* **g up** and said, "The *G2483*
Ac 27:15 so *we* **g way** to it and were driven along. *G2113*
Ac 27:20 we finally **g up** all hope of being saved. *G4311*
Ac 27:35 some bread and **g thanks** to God in front *G2373*
Ro 1:21 glorified him as God nor **g thanks** to him, *G2373*
Ro 1:24 Therefore God **g** them **over** in the sinful *G4140*
Ro 1:26 God **g** them **over** to shameful lusts. *G4140*
Ro 1:28 so God **g** them **over** to a depraved mind *G4140*
Ro 4:20 in his faith and **g** glory to God, *G1443*
Ro 8:32 his own Son, but **g** him **up** for us all—how *G4140*
Ro 11: 8 "God **g** them a spirit of stupor, eyes that *G1443*
Ro 15:15 because of the grace God **g** me *G1443*
Ro 15:16 He **g** me the priestly duty of proclaiming the NDT
1Co 3: 2 *I* **g** you milk, not solid food, for you were *G4540*
2Co 5:18 through Christ and **g** us the ministry of *G1443*
2Co 8: 3 For I testify that they **g** as much as they were NDT
2Co 8: 5 *They* **g** themselves first of all to the Lord *G1443*
2Co 10: 8 authority the Lord **g** us for building you up *G1443*
2Co 13: 2 *I* **already g** you **a warning** when I was with *G4625*
2Co 13:10 authority the Lord **g** me for building you *G1443*
Gal 1: 4 who **g** himself for our sins to rescue us *G1443*
Gal 2: 9 **g** me and Barnabas the right hand of *G1443*
Gal 2:20 who loved me and **g** himself for me. *G4140*
Gal 3:18 God **in** *his* **grace g** it to Abraham *G5919*
Eph 4: 8 many captives and **g** gifts to his people." *G1443*
Eph 4:11 So Christ himself **g** the apostles, the *G1443*
Eph 5: 2 loved us and **g** himself **up** for us as a *G4140*
Eph 5:25 loved the church and **g** himself **up** for her *G4140*
Php 2: 9 highest place and **g** him the name that is *G5919*
Col 1:25 the commission God **g** me to present to *G1443*
1Th 1: 9 report what kind of reception you **g** *us*. *G2400S*
1Th 4: 2 what instructions *we* **g** you by the *G1443*
2Th 2:16 us and by his grace **g** us eternal *G1443*
2Th 3:10 we were with you, *we* **g** you this **rule**: *G4133*
1Ti 2: 6 who **g** himself as a ransom for all people *G1443*
2Ti 1: 7 For the Spirit God **g** us does not make us *G1443*
2Ti 4:17 Lord stood at my side and **g** me **strength**, *G1904*
Titus 2:14 who **g** himself for us to redeem us from all *G1443*
Heb 7: 2 Abraham **g** him a tenth of everything *G3532*
Heb 7: 4 patriarch Abraham **g** him a tenth of the *G1443*
Heb 11:22 from Egypt and **g instructions** concerning *G1948*
Jas 2:25 what she did *when she* **g lodging** to the *G5685*
Jas 5:18 the heavens **g** rain, and the earth *G1443*
2Pe 3:15 you with the wisdom that God **g** him. *G1443*
1Jn 3:24 We know it by the Spirit *he* **g** us. *G1443*
3Jn 3 It **g** *me* great **joy** when some believers *G5897*
Jude 7 **g** *themselves* **up to sexual immorality** *G1745*
Rev 1: 1 which God **g** him to show his servants *G1443*
Rev 10: 3 and *he* **g** a loud **shout** like the roar *G3189+5889*
Rev 11:13 were terrified and **g** glory to the God of *G1443*
Rev 12: 5 *She* **g birth** to a son, a male child, who *G5503*
Rev 13: 2 The dragon **g** the beast his power and his *G1443*
Rev 15: 7 four living creatures **g** to the seven angels *G1443*
Rev 16:19 Babylon the Great and **g** her the cup filled *G1443*
Rev 18: 7 grief as the **glory** and luxury *she* **g** herself. *G1519*
Rev 20:13 The sea **g up** the dead that were in it, and *G1443*
Rev 20:13 death and Hades **g up** the dead that were *G1443*

GAY (KJV) FINE

GAZA (23)

Ge 10:19 from Sidon toward Gerar as far as **G**, H6445
Dt 2:23 Avvites who lived in villages as far as **G**, H6445
Jos 10:41 Kadesh Barnea to **G** and from the whole H6445
Jos 11:22 territory; only in **G**, Gath and Ashdod did H6445
Jos 13: 3 held by the five Philistine rulers in **G**, H6484
Jos 15:47 villages; and **G**, its settlements and H6445
Jdg 1:18 Judah also took **G**, Ashkelon and Ekron H6445
Jdg 6: 4 crops all the way to **G** and did not spare a H6445
Jdg 16: 1 One day Samson went to **G**, where he H6445
Jdg 16: 2 The **people of G** were told, "Samson is H6484
Jdg 16:21 out his eyes and took him down to **G**. H6445
1Sa 6:17 each for Ashdod, **G**, Ashkelon, Gath and H6445
1Ki 4:24 from Tiphsah to **G**, and had peace on all H6445
2Ki 18: 8 the Philistines, as far as **G** and its territory. H6445
Jer 25:20 those of Ashkelon, **G**, Ekron, and the H6445
Jer 47: 1 the Philistines before Pharaoh attacked **G**: H6445
Jer 47: 5 **G** will shave her head in mourning H6445
Am 1: 6 "For three sins of **G**, even for four, I will H6445
Am 1: 7 fire on the walls of **G** that will consume H6445
Zep 2: 4 **G** will be abandoned and Ashkelon left in H6445
Zec 9: 5 will see it and fear; **G** will writhe in agony H6445
Zec 9: 5 **G** will lose her king and Ashkelon will be H6445
Ac 8:26 that goes down from Jerusalem to **G**." *G1124*

GAZE (11) [GAZING]

2Ki 8:11 He **stared** *at* him **with a fixed g** H6641+906+7156+2256+8492
Job 35: 5 **g** *at* the clouds so high above you. H8800
Job 36:25 has seen it; mortals **g** *on* it from afar. H5564
Ps 27: 4 to **g** on the beauty of the LORD and to seek H2600
Ps 68:16 why **g in envy**, *you* rugged mountain, at H8353
Pr 4:25 fix your **g** directly before you. H6757
Pr 23:31 *Do* not **g** *at* wine when it is red, when it H8011
SS 6:13 come back, that *we may* **g** on you! H2600
SS 6:13 Why *would you* **g** on the Shulammite as H2600
Hab 2:15 so that *he can* **g** on their naked bodies! H5564
Rev 11: 9 nation *will* **g** on their bodies *G1063*

GAZELLE (13) [GAZELLES]

Dt 12:15 as if it were **g** or deer, according to H7383
Dt 12:22 Eat them as you would **g** or deer. Both the H7383
Dt 14: 5 the deer, the **g**, the roe deer, the wild goat H7383
Dt 15:22 clean may eat it, as if it were **g** or deer. H7383
2Sa 1:19 "A **g** lies slain on your heights, Israel H7383
2Sa 2:18 Asahel was as fleet-footed as a wild **g**. H7383
Pr 6: 5 like a **g** from the hand of the hunter H7383
SS 2: 9 My beloved is like a **g** or a young stag H7383
SS 2:17 be like a **g** or like a young stag on H7383
SS 4: 5 like twin fawns of a **g** that browse among H7386
SS 7: 3 are like two fawns, like twin fawns of a **g**. H7386
SS 8:14 be like a **g** or like a young stag on H7383
Isa 13:14 Like a hunted **g**, like sheep without a H7383

GAZELLES (4) [GAZELLE]

1Ki 4:23 as well as deer, **g**, roebucks and choice H7383
1Ch 12: 8 they were as swift as **g** in the mountains. H7373
SS 2: 7 I charge you by the **g** and by the does of H7374
SS 3: 5 I charge you by the **g** and by the does of H7374

GAZEZ (2)

1Ch 2:46 was the mother of Haran, Moza and **G**. H1606
1Ch 2:46 Haran was the father of **G**. H1606

GAZING (2) [GAZE]

SS 2: 9 behind our wall, **g** through the windows H8708
Da 10: 8 So I was left alone, **g** *at* this great vision; H8011

GAZINGSTOCK (KJV) PUBLICLY EXPOSED, SPECTACLE

GAZZAM (2)

Ezr 2:48 Rezin, Nekoda, **G**, H1613
Ne 7:51 **G**, Uzza, Paseah, H1613

GE HARASHIM (2)

1Ch 4:14 father of Joab, the father of **G**. H1629
Ne 11:35 in Lod and Ono, and in **G**. H1629

GEBA (15)

Jos 18:24 Ophni and **G**—twelve towns and H1494
Jos 21:17 of Benjamin they gave them Gibeon, **G**, H1494
1Sa 13: 3 attacked the Philistine outpost at **G**, H1494
1Sa 14: 5 Mikmash, the other to the south toward **G**. H1494
1Ki 15:22 them King Asa built up **G** *in* Benjamin, H1494
2Ki 23: 8 high places, from **G** to Beersheba, where H1494
1Ch 6:60 were given Gibeon, **G**, Alemeth and H1494
1Ch 8: 6 of those living in **G** and were deported to H1494
2Ch 16: 6 With them he built up **G** and Mizpah. H1494
Ezr 2:26 of Ramah and **G** 621 H1494
Ne 7:30 of Ramah and **G** 621 H1494
Ne 11:31 the Benjamites from **G** lived in Mikmash, H1494
Ne 12:29 from the area of **G** and Azmaveth, for H1494
Isa 10:29 say, "We will camp overnight at **G**." H1494
Zec 14:10 whole land, from **G** to Rimmon, south of H1494

GEBAL (NIV84) BYBLOS

GEBER (1) [BEN-GEBER, EZION GEBER]
1Ki 4:19 **G** son of Uri—in Gilead (the country of H1506

GEBIM (1)
Isa 10:31 is in flight; the people of **G** take cover. H1481

GECKO (1)
Lev 11:30 the **g**, the monitor lizard, the wall lizard, the H652

GEDALIAH (31) [GEDALIAH'S]
2Ki 25:22 of Babylon appointed **G** son of Ahikam, H1546
2Ki 25:23 of Babylon had appointed **G** as governor, H1546
2Ki 25:23 they came to **G** at Mizpah—Ishmael son H1546
2Ki 25:24 **G** took an oath to reassure them and their H1546
2Ki 25:25 assassinated **G** and also the men of H1546
1Ch 25: 3 **G**, Zeri, Jeshaiah, Shimei, Hashabiah H1546
1Ch 25: 9 his sons and relatives 12 the second to **G** H1546
Ezr 10:18 Maaseiah, Eliezer, Jarib and **G**. H1545
Jer 38: 1 son of Mattan, **G** son of Pashhur, Jehukal H1546
Jer 39:14 They turned him over to **G** son of Ahikam H1546
Jer 40: 5 "Go back to **G** son of Ahikam, the H1545
Jer 40: 6 So Jeremiah went to **G** son of Ahikam at H1545
Jer 40: 7 had appointed **G** son of Ahikam as H1546
Jer 40: 8 they came to **G** at Mizpah—Ishmael son of H1545
Jer 40: 9 **G** son of Ahikam, the son of Shaphan H1546
Jer 40:11 had appointed **G** son of Ahikam, H1546
Jer 40:12 land of Judah, to **G** at Mizpah, from all H1546
Jer 40:13 in the open country came to **G** at Mizpah H1546
Jer 40:14 But **G** son of Ahikam did not believe them H1546
Jer 40:15 of Kareah said privately to **G** in Mizpah, H1546
Jer 40:16 But **G** son of Ahikam said to Johanan son H1546
Jer 41: 1 came with ten men to **G** son of Ahikam at H1546
Jer 41: 2 got up and struck down **G** son of Ahikam, H1546
Jer 41: 3 of Judah who were with **G** at Mizpah, H1546
Jer 41: 6 he said, "Come to **G** son of Ahikam." H1546
Jer 41: 9 killed along with **G** was the one King Asa H1546
Jer 41:10 guard had appointed **G** son of Ahikam. H1546
Jer 41:16 had assassinated **G** son of Ahikam— H1545
Jer 41:18 of Nethaniah had killed **G** son of Ahikam, H1546
Jer 43: 6 guard had left with **G** son of Ahikam, H1546
Zep 1: 1 the son of **G**, the son of Amariah, H1545

GEDALIAH'S (1) [GEDALIAH]
Jer 41: 4 The day after **G** assassination, before H1546

GEDER (1) [GEDERITE]
Jos 12:13 the king of Debir one the king of **G** one H1554

GEDERAH (2) [GEDERATHITE]
Jos 15:36 Adithaim and **G** (or Gederothaim) H1557
1Ch 4:23 the potters who lived at Netaim and **G**; H1557

GEDERATHITE (1) [GEDERAH]
1Ch 12: 4 Jahaziel, Johanan, Jozabad the **G**, H1561

GEDERITE (1) [GEDER]
1Ch 27:28 Baal-Hanan the **G** was in charge of the H1559

GEDEROTH (2)
Jos 15:41 **G**, Beth Dagon, Naamah and Makkedah— H1558
2Ch 28:18 Shemesh, Aijalon and **G**, as well as Soko, H1558

GEDEROTHAIM (1)
Jos 15:36 Gederah (or **G**)—fourteen towns and H1562

GEDI See EN GEDI

GEDOR (7)
Jos 15:58 Beth Zur, **G**, H1530
1Ch 4: 4 Penuel was the father of **G**, and Ezer the H1529
1Ch 4:18 Judah gave birth to Jered the father of **G**, H1529
1Ch 4:39 to the outskirts of **G** to the east of the H1530
1Ch 8:31 **G**, Ahio, Zeker H1529
1Ch 9:37 **G**, Ahio, Zechariah and Mikloth. H1529
1Ch 12: 7 Zebadiah the sons of Jeroham from **G**. H1530

GEHAZI (20)
2Ki 4:12 He said to his servant **G**, "Call the H1634
2Ki 4:14 **G** said, "She has no son, and her H1634
2Ki 4:25 the man of God said to his servant **G** H1634
2Ki 4:27 **G** came over to push her away, but the H1634
2Ki 4:29 Elisha said to **G**, "Tuck your cloak into H1634
2Ki 4:31 **G** went on ahead and laid the staff on the H1634
2Ki 4:31 So **G** went back to meet Elisha and told him, NDT
2Ki 4:36 Elisha summoned **G** and said, "Call the H1634
2Ki 5:20 **G**, the servant of Elisha the man of God H1634
2Ki 5:21 So **G** hurried after Naaman. H1634
2Ki 5:22 is all right," **G** answered. "My master sent NDT
2Ki 5:23 He urged **G** to accept them, and then H2257S
2Ki 5:23 they carried them ahead of **G**. H2257S
2Ki 5:24 When **G** came to the hill, he took the things NDT
2Ki 5:25 asked him, "Where have you been, **G**?" H1634
2Ki 5:25 servant didn't go anywhere," **G** answered. NDT
2Ki 5:27 Then **G** went from Elisha's presence and his NDT
2Ki 8: 4 The king was talking to **G**, the servant of H1634
2Ki 8: 5 Just as **G** was telling the king how Elisha H2085S
2Ki 8: 5 **G** said, "This is the woman, my lord the H1634

GELILOTH (3)
Jos 18:17 continued to **G**, which faces the Pass H1667
Jos 22:10 When they came to **G** *near* the Jordan in H1667
Jos 22:11 of Canaan at **G** *near* the Jordan on the H1667

GEM (1) [GEMS]
Ex 28:11 two stones the way a **g** cutter engraves a H74

GEMALLI (1)
Nu 13:12 from the tribe of Dan, Ammiel son of **G**; H1696

GEMARIAH (5)
Jer 29: 3 son of Shaphan and to **G** son of Hilkiah, H1701
Jer 36:10 From the room of **G** son of Shaphan the H1702
Jer 36:11 When Micaiah son of **G**, the son of H1702
Jer 36:12 Elnathan son of Akbor, **G** son of Shaphan H1702
Jer 36:25 Delaiah and **G** urged the king not to burn H1702

GEMS (4) [GEM]
Ex 25: 7 onyx stones and *other* **g** to be mounted on H74
Ex 35: 9 stones and other **g** to be mounted on the H74
Ex 35:27 stones and other **g** to be mounted on the H74
La 4: 1 The sacred **g** are scattered at every street H74

GENDER, GENDERED, GENDERETH (KJV) BIRTH, BREED, CORRESPONDS, MATE, PRODUCE

GENEALOGICAL (11) [GENEALOGY]
1Ch 4:33 And they **kept a g record**. H3509
1Ch 5: 1 he *could* **not be listed in the g record** in H3509
1Ch 5: 7 listed according to their **g records**: H9352
1Ch 5:17 these **were entered in the g records** H3509
1Ch 7: 7 Their **g record listed** 22,034 fighting men H3509
1Ch 7: 9 Their **g record** listed the heads of families H9352
1Ch 26:31 according to the **g records** of their families H9352
2Ch 31:16 whose **names** *were* **in the g records**— H3509
2Ch 31:17 **enrolled** by their families **in the g records** H3509
2Ch 31:18 community **listed in** *these* **g records**. H3509
Ne 7: 5 I found the **g** record of those who had H3510

GENEALOGIES (5) [GENEALOGY]
1Ch 9: 1 All Israel **was listed in the g** recorded in H3509
2Ch 12:15 of Iddo the seer *that* **deal with g**? H3509
2Ch 31:19 to all *who* **were recorded in the g** of the H3509
1Ti 1: 4 themselves to myths and endless **g**. *G1157*
Titus 3: 9 controversies and **g** and arguments and *G1157*

GENEALOGY (10) [GENEALOGICAL, GENEALOGIES]
1Ch 7: 2 fighting men in their **g** numbered 22,600. H9352
1Ch 7: 4 According to their family **g**, they had H9352
1Ch 7: 5 Issachar, *as* **listed in** their **g**, were 87,000 H3509
1Ch 7:40 battle, *as* **listed in** their **g**, was 26,000. H3509
1Ch 8:28 chiefs as **listed** in their **g**, and they lived H9352
1Ch 9: 9 Benjamin, as **listed** in their **g**, numbered H9352
1Ch 9:22 They **were registered by g** in their villages. H3509
1Ch 9:34 chiefs as **listed** in their **g**, and they lived H9352
Mt 1: 1 This is the **g** of Jesus the Messiah *G1047+1161*
Heb 7: 3 father or mother, **without g**, without *G37*

GENERALS (2)
Rev 6:15 the princes, the **g**, the rich, the mighty, *G5941*
Rev 19:18 eat the flesh of kings, **g**, and the mighty, *G5941*

GENERATION (85) [GENERATIONS]
Ge 7: 1 I have found you righteous in this **g**. H1887
Ge 15:16 In the fourth **g** your descendants will come H1887
Ge 50:23 saw the **third g** of Ephraim's children H9000
Ex 1: 6 all his brothers and all that **g** died, H1887
Ex 3:15 you shall call me *from* **g** to generation. H1887
Ex 3:15 you shall call me from generation to **g**. H1887
Ex 17:16 the Amalekites from **g** *to* generation." H1887
Ex 17:16 the Amalekites from generation to **g**." H1887
Ex 20: 5 to the third and **fourth g** of those who H8067
Ex 34: 7 of the parents to the third and **fourth g**." H8067
Nu 14:18 of the parents to the third and **fourth g**. H8067
Nu 32:13 until the whole **g** *of* those who had done H1887
Dt 1:35 one from this evil **g** shall see the good H1887
Dt 2:14 that entire **g** *of* fighting men had perished H1887
Dt 5: 9 to the third and **fourth g** of those who H8067
Dt 23: 2 of the LORD, not even in the tenth **g**. H1887
Dt 23: 3 of the LORD, not even in the tenth **g**. H1887
Dt 23: 8 The third **g** of children born to them may H1887
Dt 32: 5 shame they are a warped and crooked **g**. H1887
Dt 32:20 they are a perverse **g**, children who are H1887
Jdg 2:10 After that whole **g** had been gathered to H1887
Jdg 2:10 another **g** grew up who knew neither the H1887
2Ki 10:30 sit on the throne of Israel to the **fourth g**." H8055
2Ki 15:12 sit on the throne of Israel to the **fourth g**." H8055
Est 9:28 observed in every **g** by every family, H1887
Job 8: 8 "Ask the former **g** and find out what their H1887
Job 42:16 children and their children to the fourth **g**. H1887
Ps 24: 6 Such is the **g** *of* those who seek him, who H1887
Ps 48:13 that you may tell of them to the next **g**. H1887
Ps 71:18 till I declare your power to the next **g**, your H1887
Ps 78: 4 we will tell the next **g** the praiseworthy H1887
Ps 78: 6 so the next **g** would know them, even the H1887
Ps 78: 8 a stubborn and rebellious **g**, whose hearts H1887
Ps 79:13 from **g** to generation we will proclaim H1887
Ps 79:13 from generation to **g** we will proclaim H1887
Ps 95:10 For forty years I was angry with that **g**; H1887
Ps 102:18 Let this be written for a future **g**, that a H1887
Ps 109:13 their names blotted out from the next **g**. H1887
Ps 112: 2 the **g** *of* the upright will be blessed. H1887
Ps 145: 4 *One* **g** commends your works to another H1887
Isa 34:10 From **g** to generation it will lie desolate H1887
Isa 34:10 From generation to **g** it will lie desolate H1887
Isa 34:17 dwell there from **g** to generation. H1887
Isa 34:17 dwell there from generation to **g**. H1887
Isa 53: 8 Yet who of his **g** protested? For he H1887
Jer 2:31 "You of this **g**, consider the word of the H1887
Jer 7:29 abandoned this **g** *that is under* his wrath. H1887
Jer 50:39 inhabited or lived in from **g** to generation. H1887
Jer 50:39 inhabited or lived in from generation to **g**. H1887
La 5:19 your throne endures from **g** to generation. H1887
La 5:19 your throne endures from generation to **g**. H1887
Da 4: 3 dominion endures from **g** to generation. A10183
Da 4: 3 dominion endures from generation to **g**. A10183
Da 4:34 kingdom endures from **g** to generation. A10183
Da 4:34 kingdom endures from generation to **g**. A10183
Joel 1: 3 children, and their children to the next **g**. H1887
Mt 11:16 "To what can I compare this **g**? They are *G1155*
Mt 12:39 wicked and adulterous **g** asks for a sign! *G1155*
Mt 12:41 the judgment with this **g** and condemn it; *G1155*
Mt 12:42 the judgment with this **g** and condemn it; *G1155*
Mt 12:45 That is how it will be *with* this wicked **g**." *G1155*
Mt 16: 4 A wicked and adulterous **g** looks for a sign, *G1155*
Mt 17:17 "You unbelieving and perverse **g**," Jesus *G1155*
Mt 23:36 Truly I tell you, all this will come on this **g**. *G1155*
Mt 24:34 this **g** will certainly not pass away until all *G1155*
Mk 8:12 said, "Why does this **g** ask for a sign? *G1155*
Mk 8:38 my words in this adulterous and sinful **g**, *G1155*
Mk 9:19 "You unbelieving **g**," Jesus replied, "how *G1155*
Mk 13:30 this **g** will certainly not pass away until all *G1155*
Lk 1:50 those who fear him, from **g** to generation. *G1155*
Lk 1:50 those who fear him, from generation *to* **g**. *G1155*
Lk 7:31 can I compare the people *of* this **g**? *G1155*
Lk 9:41 "You unbelieving and perverse **g**," Jesus *G1155*
Lk 11:29 increased, Jesus said, "This is a wicked **g**. *G1155*
Lk 11:30 so also will the Son of Man be *to* this **g**. *G1155*
Lk 11:31 with the people *of* this **g** and condemn *G1155*
Lk 11:32 the judgment with this **g** and condemn it, *G1155*
Lk 11:50 Therefore this **g** will be held responsible *G1155*
Lk 11:51 this **g** will be held responsible for it all. *G1155*
Lk 17:25 many things and be rejected by this **g**. *G1155*
Lk 21:32 this **g** will certainly not pass away until all *G1155*
Ac 2:40 "Save yourselves from this corrupt **g**." *G1155*
Ac 13:36 had served God's purpose *in* his own **g**, *G1155*
Php 2:15 without fault in a warped and crooked **g**." *G1155*
Heb 3:10 That is why I was angry *with* that **g**; I said *G1155*

GENERATIONS (81) [GENERATION]
Ge 9:12 with you, a covenant for all **g** to come: H1887
Ge 17: 7 descendants after you for the **g to come**, H1887
Ge 17: 9 descendants after you for the **g to come**. H1887
Ge 17:12 For the **g to come** every male among you H1887
Ex 12:14 the **g to come** you shall celebrate it as H1887
Ex 12:17 as a lasting ordinance for the **g to come**. H1887
Ex 12:42 vigil to honor the LORD for the **g to come**. H1887
Ex 16:32 of manna and keep it for the **g to come**, H1887
Ex 16:33 the LORD to be kept for the **g to come**." H1887
Ex 20: 6 showing love to a **thousand g** of those who H547
Ex 27:21 among the Israelites for the **g to come**. H1887
Ex 29:42 "For the **g to come** this burnt offering is to H1887
Ex 30: 8 before the LORD for the **g to come**. H1887
Ex 30:10 the atoning sin offering for the **g to come**. H1887
Ex 30:21 his descendants for the **g to come**. H1887
Ex 30:31 my sacred anointing oil for the **g to come**. H1887
Ex 31:13 between me and you for the **g to come**, H1887
Ex 31:16 it for the **g to come** as a lasting covenant H1887
Ex 40:15 that will continue throughout their **g**." H1887
Lev 3:17 is a lasting ordinance for the **g to come**, H1887
Lev 6:18 For *all* **g to come** it is his perpetual share H1887
Lev 7:36 as their perpetual share for the **g to come**. H1887
Lev 10: 9 is a lasting ordinance for the **g to come**, H1887
Lev 17: 7 ordinance for them and for the **g to come**. H1887
Lev 21:17 'For the **g to come** none of your H1887
Lev 22: 3 'For the **g to come**, if any of your H1887
Lev 23:14 be a lasting ordinance for the **g to come**, H1887
Lev 23:21 be a lasting ordinance for the **g to come**, H1887
Lev 23:31 be a lasting ordinance for the **g to come**, H1887
Lev 23:41 be a lasting ordinance for the **g to come**; H1887
Lev 24: 3 be a lasting ordinance for the **g to come**. H1887
Nu 10: 8 ordinance for you and the **g to come**. H1887
Nu 15:14 For the **g to come**, whenever a foreigner H1887
Nu 15:15 is a lasting ordinance for the **g to come**. H1887
Nu 15:21 Throughout the **g to come** you are to give H1887
Nu 15:23 continuing through the **g to come**— H1887
Nu 15:38 'Throughout the **g to come** you are to H1887
Nu 18:23 is a lasting ordinance for the **g to come**. H1887
Nu 35:29 of law for you throughout the **g to come**, H1887
Dt 5:10 showing love to a **thousand g** of those who H547
Dt 7: 9 love to a thousand **g** of those who love H1887
Dt 29:22 follow you in later **g** and foreigners who H1887
Dt 32: 7 consider the **g long past**. H9102+1887+2256+1887
Jos 22:27 us and you and the **g** that follow, H1887
1Ch 16:15 the promise he made, for a thousand **g**, H1887
Ps 22:30 future **g** will be told about the Lord. H1887
Ps 33:11 of his heart through **all g**. H1887+2256+1887
Ps 45:17 your memory through all **g**; H1887+2256+1887
Ps 49:11 their dwellings for **endless g**, H1887+2256+1887
Ps 61: 6 his years for **many g**. H1887+2256+1887
Ps 72: 5 as long as the moon, **through all g**. H1887+1887
Ps 79: 8 Do not hold against us the sins of **past g** H8037
Ps 85: 5 your anger through **all g**? H1887+2256+1887
Ps 89: 1 known through **all g**. H1887+2256+1887
Ps 89: 4 throne firm through **all g**. H1887+2256+1887
Ps 90: 1 place throughout **all g**. H1887+2256+1887
Ps 100: 5 continues through **all g**. H1887+2256+1887
Ps 102:12 endures through **all g**. H1887+2256+1887
Ps 102:24 your years go on through **all g**. H1887+1887

G

Ps 105: 8 the promise he made, for a thousand g, H1887
Ps 106:31 endless g to come. H1887+2256+1887
Ps 119:90 continues through all g; H1887+2256+1887
Ps 135:13 renown, LORD, through all g. H1887+2256+1887
Ps 145:13 endures through all g. H1887+2256+1887
Ps 146:10 your God, O Zion, for all g. H1887+2256+1887
Pr 27:24 crown is not secure for all g. H1887+2256+1887
Ecc 1: 4 G come and generations go, but the earth H1887
Ecc 1: 4 Generations come and g go, but the earth H1887
Ecc 1:11 No one remembers the former g, and even AIT
Isa 13:20 lived in through all g; H1887+2256+1887
Isa 41: 4 calling forth the g from the beginning? H1887
Isa 51: 8 forever, my salvation through all g." H1887+1887
Isa 51: 9 days gone by, as in g of old. Was it not H1887
Isa 60:15 pride and the joy of all g. H1887+2256+1887
Isa 61: 4 have been devastated for g. H1887+2256+1887
Joel 3:20 Jerusalem through all g. H1887+2256+1887
Mt 1:17 were fourteen g in all from Abraham G1155
Lk 1:48 From now on all g will call me blessed, G1155
Eph 3: 5 known to people *in* other g as it has now G1155
Eph 3:21 in Christ Jesus throughout all g, G1155
Col 1:26 that has been kept hidden for ages and g, G1155

GENEROSITY (3) [GENEROUS]
2Co 8: 2 their extreme poverty welled up in rich g. G605
2Co 9:11 through us your g will result in G4015S
2Co 9:13 and *for* your g in sharing with them and G605

GENEROUS (11) [GENEROSITY, GENEROUSLY]
Ps 37:26 *They are* always g and lend freely; their H2858
Ps 112: 5 come to those *who are* g and lend freely, H2858
Pr 11:25 A g person will prosper; whoever H1388
Pr 22: 9 The g will themselves be blessed H3202+6524
Mt 20:15 Or are you envious because I am g?' G19
Lk 11:41 inside you—be g to the poor, and G1443+1797
Ac 28: 7 home and showed us g hospitality for G5819
2Co 9: 5 the arrangements *for* the g gift you had G2330
2Co 9: 5 Then it will be ready as a g gift, not as G2330
2Co 9:11 so that you can be g on every occasion, G605
1Ti 6:18 and to be g and willing to share. G2331

GENEROUSLY (10) [GENEROUS]
Dt 15:10 Give g to them and do so without a H5989+5989
1Ch 29:14 we should be able to give as g as this? H5605
2Ch 31: 5 the Israelites g gave the firstfruits of their H8049
Ps 37:21 do not repay, but the righteous give g; H2858
Ac 10: 2 he gave g to those in need and prayed to G4498
Ro 12: 8 is giving, then give g; if it is to lead, G1877+605
2Co 9: 6 and whoever sows g will also reap G2093+2330
2Co 9: 6 sows generously will also reap g. G2093+2330
Titus 3: 6 he poured out on us g through Jesus G4455
Jas 1: 5 who gives g to all without finding fault G607

GENITALS (2)
Eze 16:26 your neighbors *with* large g, and aroused H1414
Eze 23:20 whose g were like those of donkeys and H1414

GENNESARET (3)
Mt 14:34 they had crossed over, they landed at G. G1166
Mk 6:53 they landed at G and anchored there. G1166
Lk 5: 1 as Jesus was standing by the Lake *of* G, G1166

GENTILE (13) [GENTILES]
Ezr 6:21 practices of their G neighbors in order to H1580
Ne 5: 9 to avoid the reproach of our G enemies? H1580
Ac 10:28 law for a Jew to associate with or visit a G. G260
Ac 15:23 brothers, To the G believers in Antioch G1620
Ac 21:25 As for the G believers, we have written to G1620
Ro 1:16 first to the Jew, then *to* the G. G1818
Ro 2: 9 first for the Jew, then *for* the G; G1818
Ro 2:10 first for the Jew, then *for* the G. G1818
Ro 3:22 There is no difference between Jew and G, NDT
Ro 10:12 is no difference between Jew and G— G1818
Gal 2:14 you live like a G and not like a Jew. G1619
Gal 3:28 There is neither Jew nor G, neither slave G1818
Col 3:11 Here there is no G or Jew, circumcised G1818

GENTILES (94) [GENTILE]
Ne 5: 8 our fellow Jews who were sold to the G. H1580
Isa 42: 6 the people and a light for the G, H1580
Isa 49: 6 I will also make you a light for the G, that H1580
Mt 4:15 beyond the Jordan, Galilee *of* the G— G1620
Mt 10: 5 not go among the G or enter any town of G1620
Mt 10:18 kings as witnesses to them and *to* the G. G1620
Mt 20:19 hand him over to the G to be mocked G1620
Mt 20:25 that the rulers *of* the G lord it over them, G1620
Mk 10:33 to death and will hand him over *to* the G, G1620
Mk 10:42 as rulers *of* the G lord it over them G1620
Lk 2:32 a light for revelation *to* the G, and the G1620
Lk 18:32 He will be delivered over *to* the G. G1620
Lk 21:24 be trampled on by the G until the times of G1620
Lk 21:24 until the times *of* the G are fulfilled. G1620
Lk 22:25 "The kings *of* the G lord it over them G1620
Ac 4:27 together with the G and the people of G1620
Ac 9:15 my name to the G and their kings and to G1620
Ac 10:45 Spirit had been poured out even on G. G1620
Ac 11: 1 Judea heard that the G also had received G1620
Ac 11:18 even *to* G God has granted repentance G1620
Ac 13:16 Israelites and you *G who* worship God, AIT
Ac 13:26 and you God-fearing G, G5828+3836+2536
Ac 13:46 of eternal life, we now turn to the G. G1620
Ac 13:47 " 'I have made you a light *for* the G, that G1620
Ac 13:48 When the G heard this, they were glad G1620
Ac 14: 2 stirred up the *other* G and poisoned their G1620
Ac 14: 5 was a plot afoot *among* both G and Jews, G1620
Ac 14:27 he had opened a door of faith *to* the G. G1620
Ac 15: 3 they told how the G had been converted. G1620
Ac 15: 5 "The G must be circumcised and required G899S
Ac 15: 7 among you that the G might hear from my G1620
Ac 15:10 on the necks *of* G a yoke that neither G3412S
Ac 15:12 had done among the G through them. G1620
Ac 15:14 choose a people for his name from the G. G1620
Ac 15:17 even all the G who bear my name G1620
Ac 15:19 it difficult for the G who are turning to G1620
Ac 18: 6 From now on I will go to the G." G1620
Ac 21:11 this belt and will hand him over to the G." G1620
Ac 21:19 had done among the G through his G1620
Ac 21:21 who live among the G to turn away from G1620
Ac 22:21 'Go; I will send you far away to the G.' G1620
Ac 26:17 from your own people and from the G. G1620
Ac 26:20 and then *to* the G, I preached that G1620
Ac 26:23 of light to his own people and *to* the G." G1620
Ac 28:28 God's salvation has been sent *to* the G, G1620
Ro 1: 5 to call all the G to the obedience that G1620
Ro 1: 6 also are among those G who are called G4005S
Ro 1:13 just as I have had among the other G. G1620
Ro 2:14 when G, who do not have the law G1620
Ro 2:24 among the G because of you. G1620
Ro 3: 9 that Jews and G alike are all under G1818
Ro 3:29 Is he not the God *of* G too? Yes, G1620
Ro 3:29 the God of Gentiles too? Yes, *of* G too, G1620
Ro 9:24 only from the Jews but also from the G? G1620
Ro 9:30 That the G, who did not pursue G1620
Ro 11:11 has come *to* the G to make Israel G1620
Ro 11:12 their loss means riches *for* the G, how G1620
Ro 11:13 I am talking to you G. Inasmuch as I am G1620
Ro 11:13 Inasmuch as I am the apostle *to* the G, G1620
Ro 11:25 the full number *of* the G has come in, G1620
Ro 15: 9 that the G might glorify God for his mercy. G1620
Ro 15: 9 "Therefore I will praise you among the G G1620
Ro 15:10 "Rejoice, you G, with his people." G1620
Ro 15:11 the Lord, all you G; let all the peoples G1620
Ro 15:12 over the nations; in him the G will hope." G1620
Ro 15:16 to be a minister of Christ Jesus to the G G1620
Ro 15:16 so that the G might become an offering G1620
Ro 15:18 me in leading the G to obey God by what G1620
Ro 15:27 For if the G have shared in the Jews' G1620
Ro 16: 4 all the churches *of* the G are grateful to G1620
Ro 16:26 so that all the G might come to the G1620
1Co 1:23 block to Jews and foolishness *to* G, G1620
1Co 12:13 whether Jews or G, slave or free— G1818
2Co 11:26 in danger from G; in danger in the G1620
Gal 1:16 so that I might preach him among the G, G1620
Gal 2: 2 the gospel that I preach among the G. G1620
Gal 2: 8 also at work in me as an apostle to the G. G1620
Gal 2: 9 They agreed that we should go to the G G1620
Gal 2:12 from James, he used to eat with the G. G1620
Gal 2:12 himself from the G because he was afraid of NDT
Gal 2:14 that you force G to follow Jewish customs? G1620
Gal 2:15 who are Jews by birth and not sinful G G1620
Gal 3: 8 that God would justify the G by faith, G1620
Gal 3:14 might come to the G through Christ Jesus, G1620
Eph 2:11 you who are G by birth and called G1620
Eph 3: 1 of Christ Jesus for the sake of you G— G1620
Eph 3: 6 the gospel the G are heirs together G1620
Eph 3: 8 to preach *to* the G the boundless riches of G1620
Eph 4:17 that you must no longer live as the G do G1620
Col 1:27 known among the G the glorious riches G1620
1Th 2:16 us from speaking *to* the G so that they G1620
1Ti 2: 7 a true and faithful teacher *of* the G. G1620
2Ti 4:17 proclaimed and all the G might hear it. G1620
Rev 11: 2 because it has been given *to* the G. G1620

GENTLE (17) [GENTLENESS, GENTLY]
Dt 28:54 Even the most g and sensitive man among H8205
Dt 28:56 The most g and sensitive woman among H8205
Dt 28:56 so sensitive and g that she would not H8204
2Sa 18: 5 "Be g with the young man Absalom for my H351
1Ki 19:12 And after the fire came a g whisper. H1987
Job 41: 3 Will it speak to you with g words? H8205
Pr 15: 1 A g answer turns away wrath, but a harsh H8205
Pr 25:15 a g tongue can break a bone. H8205
Jer 11:19 I had been like a g lamb led to the H476
Mt 11:29 from me, for I am g and humble in heart G4558
Mt 21: 5 comes to you, g and riding on a donkey G4558
Ac 27:13 *When* a g south wind *began to* blow, they G5710
1Co 4:21 shall I come in love and with a g spirit? G4559
Eph 4: 2 Be completely humble and g; be patient G4559
1Ti 3: 3 not violent but g, not quarrelsome, G2117
Titus 3: 2 always to be g toward everyone. G4559
1Pe 3: 4 unfading beauty of a g and quiet spirit, G4558

GENTLENESS (6) [GENTLE]
2Co 10: 1 By the humility and g of Christ, I appeal to G2116
Gal 5:23 g and self-control. Against such things G4559
Php 4: 5 Let your g be evident to all. The Lord is G2117
Col 3:12 kindness, humility, g and patience. G4559
1Ti 6:11 godliness, faith, love, endurance and g. G4557
1Pe 3:15 But do this with g and respect, G4559

GENTLY (8) [GENTLE]
Job 15:11 you, words spoken g to you? H4200+351
Job 29:22 no more; my words fell g on their ears. H5752
SS 7: 9 my beloved, flowing g *over* lips and teeth. H1803
Isa 8: 6 has rejected the g flowing waters of H4200+351
Isa 40:11 *he* g leads those that have young. H5633
Gal 6: 1 should restore that person g. G1877+4460+4559
2Ti 2:25 Opponents must be g instructed, in G1877+4559
Heb 5: 2 He is able *to* deal g with those who are G3584

GENUBATH (2)
1Ki 11:20 of Tahpenes bore him a son named G, H1707
1Ki 11:20 There G lived with Pharaoh's own H1707

GENUINE (2) [GENUINENESS]
2Co 6: 8 report and good report; g, yet regarded as G239
Php 2:20 who will show g concern for your welfare. G1189

GENUINENESS (1) [GENUINE]
1Pe 1: 7 come so that the proven g of your faith— G1510

GERA (9)
Ge 46:21 Ashbel, G, Naaman, Ehi, Rosh, H1733
Jdg 3:15 the son of G the Benjamite. H1733
2Sa 16: 5 His name was Shimei son of G, and he H1733
2Sa 19:16 Shimei son of G, the Benjamite from H1733
2Sa 19:18 When Shimei son of G crossed the Jordan H1733
1Ki 2: 8 you have with you Shimei son of G, the H1733
1Ch 8: 3 The sons of Bela were: Addar, G, Abihud, H1733
1Ch 8: 5 G, Shephuphan and Huram. H1733
1Ch 8: 7 and G, who deported them and H1733

GERAHS (5)
Ex 30:13 sanctuary shekel, which weighs twenty g. H1743
Lev 27:25 sanctuary shekel, twenty g to the shekel. H1743
Nu 3:47 sanctuary shekel, which weighs twenty g. H1743
Nu 18:16 sanctuary shekel, which weighs twenty g. H1743
Eze 45:12 The shekel is to consist of twenty g H1743

GERAR (10)
Ge 10:19 from Sidon toward G as far as Gaza, H1761
Ge 20: 1 For a while he stayed in G, H1761
Ge 20: 2 Abimelek king of G sent for Sarah and H1761
Ge 26: 1 to Abimelek king of the Philistines in G. H1761
Ge 26: 6 So Isaac stayed in G. H1761
Ge 26:17 there and encamped in the Valley of G, H1761
Ge 26:20 But the herders of G quarreled with those H1761
Ge 26:26 Abimelek had come to him from G, with H1761
2Ch 14:13 his army pursued them as far as G. H1761
2Ch 14:14 They destroyed all the villages around G H1761

GERASENES (3)
Mk 5: 1 across the lake to the region *of* the G. G1170
Lk 8:26 They sailed to the region *of* the G, which G1170
Lk 8:37 of the region *of* the G asked Jesus to G1170

GERIZIM (4)
Dt 11:29 are to proclaim on Mount G the blessings, H1748
Dt 27:12 stand on Mount G to bless the people: H1748
Jos 8:33 in front of Mount G and half of them in H1748
Jdg 9: 7 the top of Mount G and shouted to them H1748

GERSHOM (7)
Ex 2:22 and Moses named him G, saying, H1768
Ex 18: 3 One son was named G, for Moses said, "I H1768
Jdg 18:30 Jonathan son of G, the son of Moses, H1768
1Ch 23:15 The sons of Moses: G and Eliezer. H1768
1Ch 23:16 The descendants of G: Shubael was the H1768
1Ch 26:24 a descendant of G son of Moses, was the H1768
Ezr 8: 2 of Phinehas, G; of the descendants of H1768

GERSHON (15) [GERSHONITE, GERSHONITES]
Ge 46:11 The sons of Levi: G, Kohath and Merari. H1767
Ex 6:16 to their records: G, Kohath and Merari H1767
Ex 6:17 The sons of G, by clans, were Libni and H1767
Nu 3:17 of the sons of Levi: G, Kohath and Merari. H1767
Nu 3:21 To G belonged the clans of the Libnites H1767
Nu 26:57 through G, the Gershonite clan; through H1767
Jos 21: 6 The descendants of G were allotted H1767
1Ch 6: 1 The sons of Levi: G, Kohath and Merari. H1767
1Ch 6:16 The sons of Levi: G, Kohath and Merari. H1768
1Ch 6:17 These are the names of the sons of G H1768
1Ch 6:20 Of G: Libni his son, Jahath his son H1768
1Ch 6:43 of Jahath, the son of G, the son of Levi; H1768
1Ch 6:62 The descendants of G, clan by clan, were H1768
1Ch 15: 7 from the descendants of G, Joel the H1768
1Ch 23: 6 to the sons of Levi: G, Kohath and Merari. H1767

GERSHONITE (10) [GERSHON]
Nu 3:18 were the names of the G clans: H1201+1767
Nu 3:21 Shimeites; these were the G clans. H1769
Nu 3:23 The G clans were to camp on the west H1769
Nu 4:24 is the service of the G clans in their H1769
Nu 4:28 service of the G clans at the tent H1201+1769
Nu 4:41 of those in the G clans who served H1201+1767
Nu 26:57 Gershon, the G clan; through Kohath H1769
Jos 21:33 of towns of the G clans came to thirteen H1769
1Ch 26:21 of families belonging to Ladan the G, H1769
1Ch 29: 8 of the LORD in the custody of Jehiel the G. H1769

GERSHONITES (12) [GERSHON]
Nu 3:24 the families of the G was Eliasaph son of H1769
Nu 3:25 of meeting the G were responsible H1201+1767
Nu 4:22 also of the G by their families H1201+1767
Nu 4:26 The G are to do all that needs to be done NDT
Nu 4:38 The G were counted by their clans H1201+1767
Nu 7: 7 two carts and four oxen to the G, H1201+1767
Nu 10:17 and the G and Merarites H1201+1767
Jos 21:27 Levite clans of the G were given: H1201+1767

1Ch 6:71 The **G** received the following: From H1201+1768
1Ch 23: 7 Belonging to the **G**: Ladan and Shimei. H1769
1Ch 26:21 who were **G** through Ladan and H1201+1769
2Ch 29:12 from the **G**, Joah son of Zimmah H1769

GERUTH KIMHAM (1) [KIMHAM]

Jer 41:17 stopping at **G** near Bethlehem H1745

GESHAN (1)

1Ch 2:47 Regem, Jotham, **G**, Pelet, Ephah and H1642

GESHEM (4)

Ne 2:19 official and **G** the Arab heard about H1774
Ne 6: 1 **G** the Arab and the rest of our enemies H1774
Ne 6: 2 Sanballat and **G** sent me this message H1774
Ne 6: 6 the nations—and **G** says it is true—that H1776

GESHUR (11) [GESHURITES]

Jos 12: 5 border of the **people of G** and Maakah, H1771
Jos 13:11 territory of the **people of G** and Maakah, H1771
Jos 13:13 drive out the **people of G** and Maakah, H1771
2Sa 3: 3 of Maakah daughter of Talmai king of **G**; H1770
2Sa 13:37 to Talmai son of Ammihud, the king of **G**. H1770
2Sa 13:38 After Absalom fled and went to **G**, he H1770
2Sa 14:23 Then Joab went to **G** and brought H1770
2Sa 14:32 king to ask, "Why have I come from **G**? H1770
2Sa 15: 8 your servant was living at **G** in Aram, H1770
1Ch 2:23 But **G** and Aram captured Havvoth Jair H1770
1Ch 3: 2 of Maakah daughter of Talmai king of **G**; H1770

GESHURITES (3) [GESHUR]

Dt 3:14 the border of the **G** and the Maakathites; H1771
Jos 13: 2 all the regions of the Philistines and **G**, H1771
1Sa 27: 8 his men went up and raided the **G**, H1771

GET (319) [GETS, GETTING, GOT, ILL-GOTTEN]

Ge 18: 5 *Let me* **g** you something to eat, so you can H4374
Ge 18: 6 "**g** three seahs of the finest flour and knead NDT
Ge 19: 9 "**G out** *of* our way," they replied. H5602
Ge 19:12 who belongs to you? **G** them **out** of here, H3655
Ge 19:14 He said, "Hurry and **g out** of this place H3655
Ge 19:32 *Let's* **g** our father **to drink** wine and then H9197
Ge 19:34 *Let's* **g** him **to drink** wine again tonight H9197
Ge 21:10 "**G rid of** that slave woman and her son H1763
Ge 24: 3 that *you will* not **g** a wife for my son from H4374
Ge 24: 4 my own relatives and **g** a wife for my son H4374
Ge 24: 7 you so that *you can* **g** a wife for my son H4374
Ge 24:37 '*You must* not **g** a wife for my son from H4374
Ge 24:38 to my own clan, and **g** a wife for my son. H4374
Ge 24:40 so that *you can* **g** a wife for my son from H4374
Ge 24:48 the right road to **g** the granddaughter of H4374
Ge 27: 3 Now then, **g** your equipment—your quiver H5951
Ge 27:13 do what I say; go and **g** them for me." H4374
Ge 29:20 So Jacob served seven years to **g** Rachel H928
Ge 34: 4 father Hamor, "**G** me this girl as my wife." H4374
Ge 35: 2 "**G rid of** the foreign gods you have with H6073
Ge 38:20 in order to **g** his pledge **back** from the H4374
Ge 40:14 to Pharaoh and **g** me **out** of this prison. H3655
Ge 42:16 Send one of your number *to* **g** your brother; H4374
Ge 42:27 opened his sack to **g** feed for his donkey, H5989
Ge 45:19 your wives, and **g** your father and come. H5951
Ge 46:28 him to Joseph to **g directions** to Goshen. H3723
Ex 2: 5 reeds and sent her female slave *to* **g** it. H4374
Ex 2: 7 "Shall I go and **g** one of the Hebrew H7924
Ex 5: 4 from their labor? **G back** to your work!" H2143
Ex 5:11 Go and **g** your own straw wherever you can H4374
Ex 5:18 Now **g** to work. You will not be given any H2143
Ex 7:24 dug along the Nile to *g* **drinking** water, AIT
Ex 8:20 "**G up early** in the morning and confront H8899
Ex 9:13 said to Moses, "**G up early** in the morning H8899
Ex 10:26 until we **g** there we will not know what H995
Ex 10:28 said to Moses, "**G** out of my sight! Make H2143
Ex 14:25 "*Let's* **g away** from the Israelites! H5674
Ex 16:24 it did not stink or **g** maggots in it. H2118
Ex 21:19 if the other *can* **g up** and walk around H7756
Ex 23:11 among your people *may* **g food** from it, H430
Ex 32:25 Aaron *had let* them **g out of control** and H7277
Nu 11:13 Where *can* I **g** meat for all these people H5989
Nu 16:10 now *you are* **trying to g** the priesthood H1335
Nu 16:45 "**G away** from this assembly so I can put H8250
Nu 17: 2 to the Israelites and **g** twelve staffs from H4374
Nu 20:25 **G** Aaron and his son Eleazar and take H4374
Nu 22:23 Balaam beat it to **g** it **back on** the road. H5742
Dt 2:13 "Now **g up** and cross the Zered Valley." H7756
Dt 6: 7 when you lie down and when you **g up**. H7756
Dt 11:19 when you lie down and when you **g up**. H7756
Dt 17:16 people return to Egypt to **g more** *of* them, H8049
Dt 22: 4 Help the owner **g it to its feet**. H7756+7756
Dt 24:10 into their house to **g** what is offered to H6292
Dt 24:19 overlook a sheaf, do not go back to **g** it. H4374
Dt 30:12 ascend into heaven *to* **g** it and proclaim it H4374
Dt 30:13 will cross the sea *to* **g** it and proclaim it to H4374
Jos 1: 2 **g ready** to cross the Jordan River into the H7756
Jos 1:11 tell the people, '**G** your provisions **ready**. H3922
Jos 18: 7 however, do not **g** a portion among you H4200
Jos 22:26 we said, '*Let us* **g ready** and build an altar H6913
Jdg 1:24 "Show us **how to g into** the city and we H4427
Jdg 7: 9 said to Gideon, "**G up**, go down against H7756
Jdg 7:15 the camp of Israel and called out, "**G up**! H7756
Jdg 7:17 When I **g** to the edge of the camp, do H995
Jdg 9:29 Then *I would* **g rid of** him. I would H6073
Jdg 11: 2 "*You are* not *going to* **g** *any* **inheritance** in H5706
Jdg 11: 5 of Gilead went to **g** Jephthah from the H4374
Jdg 14: 2 in Timnah; now **g** her for me as my wife." H4374
Jdg 14: 3 the uncircumcised Philistines to **g** a wife?" H4374
Jdg 14: 3 Samson said to his father, "**G** her for me. H4374
Jdg 15: 3 time *I* **have a right to g even** with the H5927
Jdg 15: 7 I won't stop until *I* **g** *my* **revenge** on you." H5933
Jdg 16:28 *let me with* one blow **g revenge** on H5934+5933
Jdg 16:31 father's whole family went down *to* **g** him. H5951
Jdg 18:10 When you **g there**, you will find an H995
Jdg 18:25 some of the men may **g** angry and attack NDT
Jdg 19: 9 **Early** tomorrow **morning** *you can* **g up** H8899
Jdg 19:28 He said to her, "**G up**; let's go." But there H7756
Jdg 20:10 ten thousand, to **g** provisions for the army. H4374
Jdg 21:22 because *we did* not **g** wives for them H4374
Ru 2: 9 go and **g a drink** from the water jars the H9272
Ru 3: 3 and **g dressed** in your best clothes. H8492
1Sa 6: 7 "Now then, **g** a new cart ready, with two H4374
1Sa 9:26 Saul on the roof, "**G ready**, and I will send H7756
1Sa 18: 8 What more can he **g** but the kingdom?" H4200
1Sa 19:17 told him, "He said to me, '**Let** me **g away**. H8938
1Sa 20:29 **let** *me* **g away** to see my brothers. H4880
1Sa 23:22 Go and **g** more **information**. Find out H3922
1Sa 23:26 other side, hurrying to **g away** from Saul. H2143
1Sa 24:19 *does he* **let** him **g away** H8938+928+2006
1Sa 26:11 Now **g** the spear and water jug that are H4374
1Sa 26:22 of your young men come over and **g** it. H4374
1Sa 29:10 Now **g up early**, along with your master's H8899
2Sa 2:14 "*Let's have* some of the young men **g up** H7756
2Sa 4: 6 part of the house as if *to* **g** some wheat, H4374
2Sa 5: 6 to David, "*You will* not **g in** here; even the H995
2Sa 5: 6 They thought, "David cannot **g in** here." H995
2Sa 11: 4 Then David sent messengers *to* **g** her. H4374
2Sa 11:20 'Why *did you* **g so close** to the city to fight H5602
2Sa 11:21 Why *did you* **g so close** to the wall H5602
2Sa 12:17 beside him to **g** him **up** from the ground, H7756
2Sa 12:21 that the child is dead, *you* **g up** and eat!" H7756
2Sa 13:13 Where *could I* **g rid** of my disgrace H2143
2Sa 13:15 Amnon said to her, "**G up** and get out!" H7756
2Sa 13:15 Amnon said to her, "Get up and **g out**!" H2143
2Sa 13:17 "**G** this woman **out** of my sight H8938+2021+2575+2025
2Sa 14: 7 then *we will* **g rid of** the heir as well. H9012
2Sa 15: 2 He *would* **g up early** and stand by the side H8899
2Sa 16: 7 Shimei said, "**G out**, get out, you H3655
2Sa 16: 7 "Get out, **g out**, *you* murderer, you H3655
2Sa 20:18 to say, '**G** *your* **answer** at Abel,' H8626+8626
2Sa 23:15 someone *would* **g** me **a drink** *of* water H9197
1Ki 12:18 managed to **g** into his chariot and escape H6590
1Ki 17:11 As she was going to **g** it, he called, "And H4374
1Ki 18:23 **G** two bulls for us. Let Baal's prophets H5989
1Ki 18:40 Don't **let** anyone **g away**!" They H4880
1Ki 19: 5 touched him and said, "**G up** and eat." H7756
1Ki 19: 7 him and said, "**G up** and eat, for the H7756
1Ki 19:15 When *you* **g there**, anoint Hazael king over H995
1Ki 20:33 "Go and **g** him," the king said H4374
1Ki 21: 7 king over Israel? **G up** and eat! Cheer up. H7756
1Ki 21: 7 I'll **g** you the vineyard of Naboth the H5989
1Ki 21:15 "**G up** and take possession of the vineyard H7756
1Ki 22:34 around and **g** me **out** of the fighting. H3655
2Ki 2:23 jeered at him. "**G out of here**, baldy!" H6590
2Ki 2:23 they said. "**G out of here**, baldy!" H6590
2Ki 4:41 Elisha said, "**G** some flour." He put it into H4374
2Ki 5:20 run after him and **g** something from him." H4374
2Ki 6: 2 where each of *us can* **g** a pole; and let us H4374
2Ki 6:27 not help you, where *can I* **g help for** you? H3828
2Ki 7:12 we will take them alive and **g** into the city. H995
2Ki 9: 2 When *you* **g** there, look for Jehu son of H995
2Ki 9: 2 **g** him **away** from his companions and H7756
2Ki 9:17 troops coming." "**G** a horseman," Joram H4374
2Ki 13:15 Elisha said, "**G** a bow and some arrows," H4374
2Ki 22: 4 priest and **have** *him* **g ready** the money H9462
1Ch 11: 5 said to David, "*You will* not **g in** here." H995
1Ch 11:17 someone *would* **g** me **a drink** *of* water H9197
2Ch 10:18 managed to **g** into his chariot and escape H6590
2Ch 18:33 around and **g** me **out** of the fighting. H3655
Ne 2: 6 journey take, and when *will you* **g back**?" H8740
Ne 2:14 enough room for my mount to **g through**; H6296
Ne 5: 2 us to eat and stay alive, *we must* **g** grain." H5989
Ne 5: 3 our homes *to* **g** grain during the H4374
Ne 6: 7 Now this report *will* **g back to** the king; so H9048
Ne 6: 9 "Their hands *will* **g** too **weak** for the work AIT
Est 6:10 "**G** the robe and the horse and do just as H4374
Est 9:16 themselves and **g relief** from their H5663
Job 7: 4 lie down I think, 'How long before *I* **g up**? H7756
Job 15:31 worthless, for he *will* **g** nothing in return. H2118
Job 19: 7 *I* **g** no **response**; though I call for help H6699
Job 19:22 *Will you* never **g enough** of my flesh? H8425
Job 33:27 but I *did* not **g what** I **deserved**. H8750
Job 36: 3 *I* **g** my knowledge from afar; I will ascribe H5951
Ps 41: 8 *he will* never **g up** *from* the place where H7756
Ps 89:22 enemy *will* not **g the better of** him; H5957+928
Pr 1: 5 and *let* the discerning **g** guidance— H7864
Pr 1:13 *we will* **g** all sorts of valuable things and H5162
Pr 1:19 it takes away the life of **those who g** it. H1251
Pr 3:35 inherit honor, but fools **g** only shame. H8123
Pr 4: 5 **G** wisdom, get understanding; do not H7864
Pr 4: 5 Get wisdom, **g** understanding; do not H7864
Pr 4: 7 of wisdom is this: **G** wisdom. Though it H7864
Pr 4: 7 it cost all you have, **g** understanding. H7864
Pr 6: 9 When *will you* **g up** from your sleep H7756
Pr 16:16 How much better *to* **g** wisdom than gold H7864
Pr 16:16 *to* **g** insight rather than silver! H7864+1047
Pr 21:10 their neighbors **g** no **mercy** from them. H2858
Pr 21:11 attention to the wise *they* **g** knowledge. H4374
Pr 22:25 learn their ways and **g** yourself ensnared. H4374
Pr 23: 4 Do not wear yourself out to *g* **rich**; do not AIT
Pr 24:27 work in order and **g** your fields **ready**; H6963
Pr 28:20 one eager to **g rich** will not go H6947
Pr 28:22 stingy are eager to **g** rich and are unaware NDT
Ecc 2:22 What *do* people **g** for all the toil and H2093
Ecc 8:14 the righteous who **g** what the wicked H5595
Ecc 8:14 the wicked who **g** what the righteous H5595
SS 3: 2 *I will* **g up** now and go about the city H7756
Isa 21: 5 **G up**, *you* officers, oil the H7756
Isa 30:11 Leave this way, **g off** this path, and stop H5742
Isa 56:12 each one cries, "*let me* **g** wine! Let us H4374
Jer 1:17 "**G** yourself **ready**! Stand up and say H273+5516
Jer 8: 4 people fall down, *do they* not **g up**? H7756
Jer 13: 6 now to Perath and **g** the belt I told you H4374
Jer 25:27 **g drunk** and vomit, and fall to rise H8910
Jer 28:13 in its place *you will* **g** a yoke of iron. H6913
Jer 35: 3 So *I went to* **g** Jaazaniah son of Jeremiah H4374
Jer 36:21 The king sent Jehudi to **g** the scroll, and H4374
Jer 37:12 to **g** *his* **share of** *the* **property** among the H2745
Jer 46:11 "Go up to Gilead and **g** balm, Virgin H4374
Jer 46:14 'Take your positions and **g ready**, for the H3922
Jer 46:16 They will say, '**G up**, let us go back to our H7756
Jer 51: 8 **G** balm for her pain; perhaps she can be H4374
Jer 51:61 Seraiah, "When you **g** *to* Babylon, see that H995
La 3:44 a cloud so that no prayer *can* **g through**. H6296
La 5: 6 to Egypt and Assyria to **g enough** bread. H8425
La 5: 9 *We* **g** our bread at the risk of our lives H995
Eze 3:22 said to me, "**G up** and go out to the plain H7756
Eze 17:15 envoys to Egypt to **g** horses and a large H5989
Eze 18:31 **g** a new heart and a new spirit. H6913
Eze 20: 7 **g rid of** the vile images you have set your H8959
Eze 20: 8 they *did* not **g rid of** the vile images they H8959
Eze 38: 7 " '**G ready**; be prepared, you and all the H3922
Da 7: 5 was told, '**G up** and eat your fill of flesh! A10624
Hos 12:12 Israel served to **g** a wife, and to pay H928
Am 2:15 the fleet-footed soldier *will* not **g away** H4880
Am 4: 8 water but *did* not **g enough** to drink, H8425
Am 7:12 Amaziah said to Amos, "**G out**, you seer! H2143
Am 9: 1 Not one *will* **g away**, none will H5674+5674
Jnh 1: 6 can you sleep? **G up** and call on your god H7756
Mic 2:10 **G up**, go away! For this is not your resting H7756
Zep 2:10 This is what they will **g** in return for their H4200
Mal 3:15 put God to the test, *they* **g away with** it. H4880
Mt 2:13 "**G up**," he said, "take the child and his *G1586*
Mt 2:20 said, "**G up**, take the child and his *G1586*
Mt 5:26 *you will* not **g out** until you have paid the *G2002*
Mt 5:46 who love you, what reward *will you* **g**? *G2400*
Mt 9: 5 are forgiven,' or to say, '**G up** and walk'? *G1586*
Mt 9: 6 paralyzed man, "**G up**, take your mat and *G1586*
Mt 10: 9 "*Do* not **g** any gold or silver or copper to *G3227*
Mt 13:54 "Where did this man **g** this wisdom and NDT
Mt 13:56 Where then did this man **g** all these things?" NDT
Mt 14:22 made the disciples **g into** the boat and go *G1832*
Mt 15:33 "Where could we **g** enough bread in this NDT
Mt 16:23 said to Peter, "**G** behind me, Satan! *G5632*
Mt 17: 7 touched them. "**G up**," he said. *G1586*
Mt 19:16 good thing must I do to **g** eternal life?" *G2400*
Mt 22:12 'How *did you* **g in** here without wedding *G1656*
Mt 24:18 no one in the field go back to **g** their cloak. *G149*
Mt 24:32 As soon as its twigs **g** tender and its *G1181*
Mk 2: 4 they could not **g** him **to** Jesus because of *G4712*
Mk 2: 9 to say, '**G up**, take your mat and *G1586*
Mk 2:11 "I tell you, **g up**, take your mat and go *G1586*
Mk 5:41 means "Little girl, I say to you, **g up**!" *G1586*
Mk 6: 2 "Where did this man **g** these things?" NDT
Mk 6:31 to a quiet place and **g** some **rest**. *G399*
Mk 6:45 made his disciples **g into** the boat and go *G1832*
Mk 8: 4 can anyone *g enough* bread *to* **feed** them?" AIT
Mk 8:33 he rebuked Peter. "**G** behind me, Satan!" *G5632*
Mk 13:16 no one in the field go back to **g** their cloak. *G149*
Mk 13:28 As soon as its twigs **g** tender and its *G1181*
Mk 15:24 they cast lots to see what each *would* **g**. *G149*
Mk 16:18 on sick people, and *they will* **g** well." *G2400*
Lk 5:23 are forgiven,' or to say, '**G up** and walk'? *G1586*
Lk 5:24 "I tell you, **g up**, take your mat and go *G1586*
Lk 6: 8 "**G up** and stand in front of everyone." *G1586*
Lk 6:35 them without **expecting to g** anything **back**. *G594*
Lk 7:14 "Young man, I say to you, **g up**!" *G1586*
Lk 8:19 were not able *to* **g near** him because of *G5344*
Lk 8:54 her by the hand and said, "My child, **g up**!" *G1586*
Lk 9:52 village to **g** *things* **ready** for him; *G2286*
Lk 11: 7 I can't **g up** and give you anything *G482*
Lk 11: 8 even though *he will* not **g up** and give you *G482*
Lk 11: 8 audacity *he will surely* **g up** and give you *G1586*
Lk 12:20 Then who *will* **g** what you have prepared *G1639*
Lk 12:45 and to eat and drink and *g* **drunk**. AIT
Lk 12:47 will and *does* not **g ready** or does not do *G2286*
Lk 12:59 *you will* not **g out** until you have paid the *G2002*
Lk 14:24 were invited *will* **g a taste** of my banquet. *G1174*
Lk 17: 8 **g** *yourself* **ready** and wait on me while I *G4322*
Lk 17:31 should go down *to* **g** them. *G149*
Lk 18: 8 I tell you, *he will see that* they **g** justice *G4472*
Lk 18:12 twice a week and give a tenth of all *I* **g**. *G3227*
Lk 21:21 *let* those in the city **g out**, and let *G1774*
Lk 22: 2 looking for some way *to* **g rid** of Jesus, *G359*
Lk 22:46 "**G up** and pray so that you will not fall into *G482*
Jn 2:16 sold doves he said, "**G** these out of here! *G149*
Jn 4:11 Where *can you* **g** this living water *G2400*
Jn 4:15 water so that *I* won't *g* **thirsty** and have to AIT
Jn 5: 6 he asked him, "Do you want *to* **g** well?" *G1181*

Jn 5: 7 While I *am trying to* **g in**, someone else *G2262*
Jn 5: 8 Jesus said to him, "**G up**! Pick up your mat *G1586*
Jn 6:25 asked him, "Rabbi, when *did you* **g** here?" *G1181*
Jn 7:15 "How *did* this man **g** *such* **learning** *G1207+3857*
Jn 11:12 if he sleeps, *he will* **g better**. *G5392*
Jn 19:24 "Let's decide by lot who *will* **g** it." This *G1639*
Jn 20:15 where you have put him, and I *will* **g** him." *G149*
Ac 3: 5 expecting *to* **g** something from them. *G3284*
Ac 7:31 As he went over *to* **g a closer look**, he *G2917*
Ac 9: 6 "Now **g up** and go into the city, and you will *G482*
Ac 9:34 Christ heals you. **G up** and roll up your mat." *G482*
Ac 9:40 the dead woman, he said, "Tabitha, **g up**." *G482*
Ac 10:13 a voice told him, "**G up**, Peter. Kill and eat." *G482*
Ac 10:20 So **g up** and go downstairs. Do not hesitate *G482*
Ac 10:26 But Peter *made* him **g up**. "Stand up," *G1586*
Ac 11: 7 I heard a voice telling me, '**G up**, Peter. *G482*
Ac 12: 7 woke him up. "Quick, **g up**!" he said, *G482*
Ac 16:37 And now *do they want to* **g rid of** us *G1675*
Ac 21:34 could not **g at the truth** because of *G1182+855*
Ac 21:36 that followed kept shouting, "**G rid of** him!" *G149*
Ac 22:10 " '**G up**,' the Lord said, 'and go into *G482*
Ac 22:16 **G up**, be baptized and wash your sins away *G482*
Ac 23:23 "**G ready** a detachment of two hundred *G2286*
Ac 23:35 hear your case when your accusers **g here**." *G4134*
Ac 26:16 'Now **g up** and stand on your feet. I have *G482*
Ac 27:43 to jump overboard first and **g to** land. *G1996*
Ac 27:44 The rest were to **g** there on planks or on NDT
1Co 5: 7 **G rid of** the old yeast, so that you may be *G1705*
1Co 7:36 He is not sinning. *They should* **g married**. AIT
1Co 9:13 in the temple **g** *their* **food** from the *G2266*
1Co 9:24 Run in such a way as to **g** the prize. *G2898*
1Co 9:25 They do it to **g** a crown that will not last *G3284*
1Co 9:25 we do it to **g** a crown that will last NDT
1Co 14: 8 a clear call, who *will* **g ready** for battle? AIT
2Co 10:14 for *we did* **g** as far as you with the gospel *G5777*
Gal 1:18 Jerusalem *to* **g acquainted with** Cephas *G2707*
Gal 4:30 "**G rid of** the slave woman and her son *G1675*
Eph 4:31 **G rid of** all bitterness, rage and anger *G149+608*
Eph 5:18 *Do* not **g drunk** on wine, which leads to AIT
1Th 5: 7 at night, and those *who* **g drunk**, get drunk at AIT
1Th 5: 7 those who get drunk, **g drunk** at night. AIT
1Ti 5:13 *they* **g into the habit** of being idle and *G3443*
1Ti 6: 9 Those who want *to* **g rich** fall into temptation AIT
2Ti 3: 9 But *they will* not **g** very **far** because, as in *G4621*
2Ti 4:11 **G** Mark and bring him with you, because *G377*
2Ti 4:21 Do your best *to* **g here** before winter *G2262*
Jas 1:21 **g rid of** all moral filth and the evil that is so *G700*
Jas 4: 2 covet but you cannot **g** what you want, *G2209*
Jas 4: 3 may spend what you **g** on your pleasures. NDT

GETHER (2)

Ge 10:23 sons of Aram: Uz, Hul, **G** and Meshek. H1788
1Ch 1:17 sons of Aram: Uz, Hul, **G** and Meshek. H1788

GETHSEMANE (2)

Mt 26:36 with his disciples to a place called **G**, *G1149*
Mk 14:32 They went to a place called **G**, and Jesus *G1149*

GETS (14) [GET]

Pr 19: 8 The *one who* **g** wisdom loves life; the one H7864
Pr 29:26 it is from the LORD that one **g** justice. NDT
Pr 30:22 a godless fool *who* **g plenty** to eat, H8425
Pr 30:23 a contemptible woman *who* **g married**, and a AIT
Pr 31:15 *She* **g up** while it is still night; she H7756
Isa 44:12 *He* **g hungry** and loses his strength; he drinks AIT
Mt 28:14 If this report **g to** the governor, we will satisfy AIT
Mk 4:27 whether he sleeps or **g up**, the seed *G1586*
Lk 13:25 owner of the house **g up** and closes the *G1586*
Lk 18: 5 *I will see that* she **g justice**, so that *G1688*
Ac 23:15 We are ready to kill him before he **g here**." *G1581*
1Co 9:24 the runners run, but only one **g** the prize? *G3284*
1Co 11:21 person remains hungry and another **g drunk**. AIT
2Ti 2: 4 as a soldier **g entangled in** civilian affairs, *G1861*

GETTING (12) [GET]

Jdg 3:13 *G* the Ammonites and Amalekites *to* **join** him, AIT
1Ki 16: 9 **g drunk** in the home of Arza H9272+8893
1Ki 20:16 him were in their tents **g drunk**. H9272+8893
Ecc 8:16 people **g** no sleep day or night H8011ˢ
Jnh 1:11 The sea *was* **g rougher and rougher**. So they AIT
Mt 14:15 and *it's* already **g late**. *G3836+6052+4216*
Mt 27:24 When Pilate saw that *he was* **g** nowhere *G6067*
Mk 5:18 *As* Jesus *was* **g into** the boat, the man *G1832*
Mk 5:26 instead of **g better** she grew worse. *G6067*
Lk 23:41 for *we are* **g** what our deeds deserve. *G655*
Jn 12:19 "See, *this is* **g** us **nowhere**. *G4024+6067+4029*
3Jn 2 even as your soul *is* **g along well**. *G2338*

GEUEL (1)

Nu 13:15 from the tribe of Gad, **G** son of Maki. H1451

GEZER (14)

Jos 10:33 Horam king of **G** had come up to help H1618
Jos 12:12 the king of Eglon one the king of **G** one H1618
Jos 16: 3 region of Lower Beth Horon and on to **G**, H1618
Jos 16:10 not dislodge the Canaanites living in **G**; H1618
Jos 21:21 refuge for one accused of murder) and **G**, H1618
Jdg 1:29 drive out the Canaanites living in **G**, H1618
2Sa 5:25 Philistines all the way from Gibeon to **G**. H1618
1Ki 9:15 of Jerusalem, and Hazor, Megiddo and **G**. H1618
1Ki 9:16 of Egypt had attacked and captured **G**. H1618
1Ki 9:17 And Solomon rebuilt **G**.) He built up Lower H1618
1Ch 6:67 given Shechem (a city of refuge), and **G**, H1618
1Ch 7:28 to the east, **G** and its villages to the west H1618
1Ch 14:16 all the way from Gibeon to **G**. H1618
1Ch 20: 4 war broke out with the Philistines, at **G**. H1618

(GAVE/GIVE UP THE) GHOST (KJV) BREATHED HIS LAST, DIE, DIED, DYING, GAVE UP HIS SPIRIT, PERISH, PERISHED

(HOLY) GHOST (KJV) (HOLY) SPIRIT

GHOST (4) [GHOSTLIKE, GHOSTLY]

Mt 14:26 "It's a **g**," they said, and cried *G5753*
Mk 6:49 on the lake, they thought he was a **g**. *G5753*
Lk 24:37 frightened, thinking they saw a **g**. *G4460*
Lk 24:39 a **g** does not have flesh and bones *G4460*

GHOSTLIKE (1) [GHOST]

Isa 29: 4 voice will come **g** from the earth; H3869+200

GHOSTLY (1) [GHOST]

1Sa 28:13 "I see a **g figure** coming up out of the earth H466

GIAH (1)

2Sa 2:24 near **G** on the way to the wasteland of H1632

GIANT, GIANTS (KJV) NEPHILIM, RAPHA, REPHAIM, REPHAITES, WARRIOR

GIBBAR (1)

Ezr 2:20 of **G** 95 H1507

GIBBETHON (5)

Jos 19:44 Eltekeh, **G**, Baalath, H1510
Jos 21:23 the tribe of Dan they received Eltekeh, **G**, H1510
1Ki 15:27 he struck him down at **G**, a Philistine H1510
1Ki 16:15 The army was encamped near **G**, H1510
1Ki 16:17 him withdrew from **G** and laid siege to H1510

GIBEA (1) [GIBEATHITE]

1Ch 2:49 to Sheva the father of Makbenah and **G**. H1495

GIBEAH (48)

Jos 15:57 **G** and Timnah—ten towns and their H1497
Jos 18:28 **G** and Kiriath—fourteen towns and their H1497
Jos 24:33 son of Aaron died and was buried at **G**, H1497
Jdg 19:12 are not Israelites. We will go on to **G**." H1497
Jdg 19:13 let's try to reach **G** or Ramah and spend H1497
Jdg 19:14 the sun set as they neared **G** in Benjamin. H1497
Jdg 19:16 who was living in **G** (the inhabitants of H1497
Jdg 20: 4 concubine came to **G** in Benjamin to H1497
Jdg 20: 5 night the men of **G** came after me and H1497
Jdg 20: 9 But now this is what we'll do to **G**: We'll H1497
Jdg 20:10 when the army arrives at **G** *in* Benjamin, it H1497
Jdg 20:13 those wicked men of **G** over to us so that H1497
Jdg 20:14 came together at **G** to fight against the H1497
Jdg 20:15 able young men from those living in **G**. H1497
Jdg 20:19 got up and pitched camp near **G**. H1497
Jdg 20:20 up battle positions against them at **G**. H1497
Jdg 20:21 Benjamites came out of **G** and cut down H1497
Jdg 20:25 came out from **G** to oppose them, H1497
Jdg 20:29 Then Israel set an ambush around **G**. H1497
Jdg 20:30 up positions against **G** as they had done H1497
Jdg 20:31 one leading to Bethel and the other to **G**. H1497
Jdg 20:33 charged out of its place on the west of **G**. H1497
Jdg 20:34 young men made a frontal attack on **G**. H1497
Jdg 20:36 on the ambush they had set near **G**. H1497
Jdg 20:37 in ambush made a sudden dash into **G**, H1497
Jdg 20:43 them in the vicinity of **G** on the east. H1497
1Sa 10: 5 "After that you will go to **G** *of* God, where H1497
1Sa 10:10 When he and his servant arrived at **G**, H1497
1Sa 10:26 Saul also went to his home in **G** H1497
1Sa 11: 4 came to **G** *of* Saul and reported H1497
1Sa 13: 2 were with Jonathan at **G** *in* Benjamin. H1497
1Sa 13:15 left Gilgal and went up to **G** *in* Benjamin, H1497
1Sa 13:16 with them were staying in **G** *in* Benjamin, H1497
1Sa 14: 2 the outskirts of **G** under a pomegranate H1497
1Sa 14:16 Saul's lookouts at **G** *in* Benjamin saw the H1497
1Sa 15:34 Saul went up to his home in **G** *of* Saul. H1497
1Sa 22: 6 under the tamarisk tree on the hill at **G** H1497
1Sa 23:19 Ziphites went up to Saul at **G** and said, H1497
1Sa 26: 1 The Ziphites went to Saul at **G** and said H1497
2Sa 21: 6 exposed before the LORD at **G** *of* Saul— H1497
2Sa 23:29 Ithai son of Ribai from **G** *in* Benjamin, H1497
1Ch 11:31 Ithai son of Ribai from **G** in Benjamin H1497
2Ch 13: 2 was Maakah, a daughter of Uriel of **G**. H1497
Isa 10:29 Ramah trembles; **G** *of* Saul flees. H1497
Hos 5: 8 "Sound the trumpet in **G**, the horn in H1497
Hos 9: 9 deep into corruption, as in the days of **G**. H1497
Hos 10: 9 "Since the days of **G**, you have sinned H1497
Hos 10: 9 not war again overtake the evildoers in **G**? H1497

GIBEATH HAARALOTH (1)

Jos 5: 3 circumcised the Israelites at **G**. H1502

GIBEATHITE (1) [GIBEA]

1Ch 12: 3 Joash the sons of Shemaah the **G**; H1503

GIBEON (40) [GIBEONITE, GIBEONITES]

Jos 9: 3 when the people of **G** heard what Joshua H1500
Jos 9:17 came to their cities: **G**, Kephirah, Beeroth H1500
Jos 10: 1 that the people of **G** had made a treaty of H1500
Jos 10: 2 because **G** was an important city H1500
Jos 10: 4 "Come up and help me attack **G**," he said H1500
Jos 10: 5 up positions against **G** and attacked it. H1500
Jos 10:10 Israelites defeated them completely at **G**. H1500
Jos 10:12 stand still over **G**, and you, moon, over H1500
Jos 10:41 from the whole region of Goshen to **G**. H1500
Jos 11:19 Except for the Hivites living in **G**, not one H1500
Jos 18:25 **G**, Ramah, Beeroth, H1500
Jos 21:17 the tribe of Benjamin they gave them **G**, H1500
2Sa 2:12 of Saul, left Mahanaim and went to **G**. H1500
2Sa 2:13 went out and met them at the pool of **G**. H1500
2Sa 2:16 So that place in **G** was called Helkath H1500
2Sa 2:24 Giah on the way to the wasteland of **G**. H1500
2Sa 3:30 their brother Asahel in the battle at **G**.) H1500
2Sa 5:25 Philistines all the way from **G** to Gezer. H1500
2Sa 20: 8 While they were at the great rock in **G** H1500
1Ki 3: 4 The king went to **G** to offer sacrifices, for H1500
1Ki 3: 5 At **G** the LORD appeared to Solomon during H1500
1Ki 9: 2 as he had appeared to him at **G**. H1500
1Ch 6:60 the tribe of Benjamin they were given **G**, H1500
1Ch 8:29 Jeiel the father of **G** lived in Gibeon. H1500
1Ch 8:29 Jeiel the father of Gibeon lived in **G**. H1500
1Ch 9:35 Jeiel the father of **G** lived in Gibeon. H1500
1Ch 9:35 Jeiel the father of Gibeon lived in **G**. H1500
1Ch 14:16 all the way from **G** to Gezer. H1500
1Ch 16:39 of the LORD at the high place in **G** H1500
1Ch 21:29 were at that time on the high place at **G**. H1500
2Ch 1: 3 assembly went to the high place at **G**, H1500
2Ch 1: 5 had made was in **G** in front of the NDT
2Ch 1:13 to Jerusalem from the high place at **G**, H1500
Ne 3: 7 were made by men from **G** and Mizpah— H1500
Ne 3: 7 Melatiah **of G** and Jadon of Meronoth H1498
Ne 7:25 of **G** 95 H1500
Isa 28:21 will rouse himself as in the Valley of **G**— H1500
Jer 28: 1 who was from **G**, said to me in the H1500
Jer 41:12 up with him near the great pool in **G**. H1500
Jer 41:16 court officials he had recovered from **G**. H1500

GIBEONITE (1) [GIBEON]

1Ch 12: 4 Ishmaiah the **G**, a mighty warrior H1498

GIBEONITES (10) [GIBEON]

Jos 9:16 after they made the treaty with **the G**, H2157ˢ
Jos 9:22 Then Joshua summoned **the G** and said H2157ˢ
Jos 9:27 That day he made **the G** woodcutters H4392ˢ
Jos 10: 6 The **G** then sent word to Joshua in H408+1500
2Sa 21: 1 it is because he put the **G** to death." H1498
2Sa 21: 2 king summoned the **G** and spoke to them. H1498
2Sa 21: 2 Now the **G** were not a part of Israel but H1498
2Sa 21: 3 David asked the **G**, "What shall I do for H1498
2Sa 21: 4 The **G** answered him, "We have no right H1498
2Sa 21: 9 He handed them over to the **G**, who killed H1498

GIDDALTI (2)

1Ch 25: 4 Eliathah, **G** and Romamti-Ezer H1547
1Ch 25:29 the twenty-second to **G**, his sons and H1547

GIDDEL (4)

Ezr 2:47 **G**, Gahar, Reaiah, H1543
Ezr 2:56 Jaala, Darkon, **G**, H1543
Ne 7:49 Hanan, **G**, Gahar, H1543
Ne 7:58 Jaala, Darkon, **G**, H1543

GIDEON (47) [GIDEON'S, JERUB-BAAL]

Jdg 6:11 where his son **G** was threshing wheat in a H1549
Jdg 6:12 the angel of the LORD appeared to **G**, H2257ˢ
Jdg 6:13 **G** replied, "but if the LORD is with H1549
Jdg 6:15 **G** replied, "but how can I save NDT
Jdg 6:17 **G** replied, "If now I have found favor in your NDT
Jdg 6:19 **G** went inside, prepared a young goat H1549
Jdg 6:20 and pour out the broth." And **G** did so. NDT
Jdg 6:22 When **G** realized that it was the angel of H1549
Jdg 6:24 So **G** built an altar to the LORD there and H1549
Jdg 6:27 So **G** took ten of his servants and did as H1549
Jdg 6:29 they were told, "**G** son of Joash did it." H1549
Jdg 6:32 So because **G** broke down Baal's altar, they NDT
Jdg 6:34 Then the Spirit of the LORD came on **G**, H1549
Jdg 6:36 **G** said to God, "If you will save Israel by H1549
Jdg 6:38 **G** rose early the next day; he squeezed the NDT
Jdg 6:39 Then **G** said to God, "Do not be angry H1549
Jdg 7: 1 **G**) and all his men camped at the H1549
Jdg 7: 2 The LORD said to **G**, "You have too many H1549
Jdg 7: 4 But the LORD said to **G**, "There are still too H1549
Jdg 7: 5 So **G** took the men down to the water H1549
Jdg 7: 7 The LORD said to **G**, "With the three H1549
Jdg 7: 8 So **G** sent the rest of the Israelites home NDT
Jdg 7: 9 During that night the LORD said to **G**, "Get H2257ˢ
Jdg 7:13 **G** arrived just as a man was telling a H1549
Jdg 7:14 other than the sword of **G** son of Joash, H1549
Jdg 7:15 When **G** heard the dream and its H1549
Jdg 7:18 yours and shout, 'For the LORD and for **G**. H1549
Jdg 7:19 **G** and the hundred men with him reached H1549
Jdg 7:20 shouted, "A sword for the LORD and for **G**!" H1549
Jdg 7:24 **G** sent messengers throughout the hill H1549
Jdg 7:25 brought the heads of Oreb and Zeeb to **G**, H1549
Jdg 8: 1 Now the Ephraimites asked **G**, "Why H2257ˢ
Jdg 8: 4 **G** and his three hundred men, exhausted H1549
Jdg 8: 7 Then **G** replied, "Just for that, when the H1549
Jdg 8:11 **G** went up by the route of the nomads east H1549
Jdg 8:13 **G** son of Joash then returned from the H1549
Jdg 8:15 Then **G** came and said to the men of NDT
Jdg 8:19 **G** replied, "Those were my brothers, the NDT
Jdg 8:21 So **G** stepped forward and killed them H1549
Jdg 8:22 The Israelites said to **G**, "Rule over us H1549
Jdg 8:23 But **G** told them, "I will not rule over you H1549
Jdg 8:27 **G** made the gold into an ephod, which he H1549

Jdg 8:27 it became a snare to **G** and his family. H1549
Jdg 8:32 **G** son of Joash died at a good old age H1549
Jdg 8:33 No sooner had **G** died than the Israelites H1549
Jdg 8:35 **G**) in spite of all the good things H1549
Heb 11:32 I do not have time to tell about **G**, Barak *G1146*

GIDEON'S (1) [GIDEON]
Jdg 8:28 During **G** lifetime, the land had peace H1549

GIDEONI (5)
Nu 1:11 from Benjamin, Abidan son of **G**; H1551
Nu 2:22 people of Benjamin is Abidan son of **G**. H1551
Nu 7:60 On the ninth day Abidan son of **G**, the H1551
Nu 7:65 This was the offering of Abidan son of **G**. H1551
Nu 10:24 Abidan son of **G** was over the division H1551

GIDOM (1)
Jdg 20:45 as far as **G** and struck down two H1550

GIER (KJV) OSPREY

GIFT (80) [GIFTED, GIFTS]
Ge 30:20 "God has presented me with a precious **g**. H2273
Ge 32:13 him he selected a **g** for his brother Esau: H4966
Ge 32:18 They are a **g** sent to my lord Esau, and he H4966
Ge 33:10 favor in your eyes, accept this **g** from me. H4966
Ge 34:12 the bride and the **g** I am to bring as H5508
Ge 43:11 take them down to the man as a **g**— H4966
Lev 22:18 presents a **g** for a burnt offering to the LORD H7933
Nu 18: 6 from among the Israelites as a **g** to you, H5510
Nu 18: 7 you the service of the priesthood as a **g**. H5510
Nu 31:52 presented as a **g** to the LORD weighed H9556
Dt 16:17 of you must bring a **g** in proportion to the H5510
1Sa 6: 3 do not send it back to him **without a g**; by H8200
1Sa 9: 7 We have no **g** to take to the man of God H9593
1Sa 25:27 And let this **g**, which your servant has H1388
1Sa 30:26 "Here is a **g** for you from the plunder of H1388
2Sa 11: 8 a **g** *from* the king was sent after him. H5368
1Ki 9:16 gave it as a **wedding g** to his daughter, H8933
1Ki 10:25 everyone who came brought a **g**—articles H4966
1Ki 13: 7 me for a meal, and I will give you a **g**." H5522
1Ki 15:19 I am sending you a **g** *of* silver and gold. H8816
2Ki 5:15 So please accept a **g** from your servant." H1388
2Ki 8: 8 "Take a **g** with you and go to meet the H4966
2Ki 8: 9 with him as a **g** forty camel-loads of H4966
2Ki 16: 8 sent it as a **g** to the king of Assyria. H8816
2Ki 20:12 of Babylon sent Hezekiah letters and a **g**, H4966
2Ch 9:24 everyone who came brought a **g**—articles H4966
Ps 45:12 The city of Tyre will come with a **g** H4966
Pr 18:16 A **g** opens the way and ushers the giver H5508
Pr 21:14 A **g** given in secret soothes anger, and a H5508
Ecc 3:13 in all their toil—this is the **g** *of* God. H5522
Ecc 5:19 be happy in their toil—this is a **g** *of* God. H5522
Isa 39: 1 of Babylon sent Hezekiah letters and a **g**, H4966
Eze 45:13 " 'This is the **special g** you are to offer: H9556
Eze 46:16 the prince makes a **g** from his inheritance H5510
Eze 46:17 he makes a **g** from his inheritance to one H5510
Eze 48: 8 **portion** you are to present **as a special g**. H9556
Eze 48:12 It will be a **special g** to them from the H9557
Eze 48:20 **As a special g** *you will* **set aside** the H8123
Mt 5:23 you are offering your **g** at the altar and *G1565*
Mt 5:24 leave your **g** there in front of the altar. *G1565*
Mt 5:24 to them; then come and offer your **g**. *G1565*
Mt 8: 4 priest and offer the **g** Moses commanded, *G1565*
Mt 23:18 who swears by the **g** on the altar is bound *G1565*
Mt 23:19 the **g**, or the altar that makes the gift *G1565*
Mt 23:19 or the altar that makes the **g** sacred? *G1565*
Jn 4:10 "If you knew the **g** of God and who it is *G1561*
Ac 1: 4 wait for the *g* my Father **promised**, which AIT
Ac 2:38 you will receive the **g** of the Holy Spirit. *G1561*
Ac 8:20 you could buy the **g** of God with money! *G1561*
Ac 10:45 astonished that the **g** of the Holy Spirit *G1561*
Ac 11:17 gave them the same **g** he gave us who *G1561*
Ac 11:30 sending their **g** to the elders by Barnabas NDT
Ro 1:11 you some spiritual **g** to make you strong— *G5922*
Ro 4: 4 not credited as a **g** but as an obligation. *G5921*
Ro 5:15 But the **g** is not like the trespass. For if the *G5922*
Ro 5:15 God's grace and the **g** that came by the *G1561*
Ro 5:16 Nor can the **g** of God be compared with *G1564*
Ro 5:16 the **g** followed many trespasses and *G5922*
Ro 5:17 of grace and *of* the **g** of righteousness *G1561*
Ro 6:23 the **g** of God is eternal life in Christ *G5922*
Ro 12: 6 If your **g** is prophesying, then prophesy in NDT
1Co 1: 7 do not lack any **spiritual g** as you eagerly *G5922*
1Co 7: 7 But each of you has your own **g** from God *G5922*
1Co 7: 7 from God; one has **this** *g*, another has that. AIT
1Co 13: 2 If I have the **g of prophecy** and can fathom *G4735*
1Co 16: 3 send them with your **g** to Jerusalem. *G5921*
2Co 8:12 the **g** is acceptable according to what one NDT
2Co 8:20 of the way we administer this **liberal g**. *G103*
2Co 9: 5 arrangements *for* the **generous g** you had *G2330*
2Co 9: 5 Then it will be ready as a **generous g**, not *G2330*
2Co 9:15 Thanks be to God for his indescribable **g**! *G1561*
Eph 2: 8 not from yourselves, it is the **g** of God— *G1565*
Eph 3: 7 this gospel by the **g** of God's grace given *G1561*
1Ti 4:14 Do not neglect your **g**, which was given *G5922*
2Ti 1: 6 you to fan into flame the **g** of God, *G5922*
Heb 6: 4 who have tasted the heavenly **g**, who *G1561*
Jas 1:17 Every good and perfect **g** is from above *G1521*
1Pe 3: 7 as heirs with you *of* the **gracious g** of life, *G5921*
1Pe 4:10 should use whatever **g** you have received *G5922*
Rev 22:17 who wishes take the **free g** of the water of *G1562*

GIFTED (1) [GIFT]
1Co 14:37 are a prophet or otherwise **g by the Spirit**, *G4461*

GIFTS (87) [GIFT]
Ge 24:53 he also gave **costly g** to her brother and to H4458
Ge 25: 6 he gave **g** to the sons of his concubines H5510
Ge 32:20 him with these **g** I am sending on ahead H4966
Ge 32:21 So Jacob's **g** went on ahead of him, but H4966
Ge 43:15 So the men took the **g** and double the H4966
Ge 43:25 They prepared their **g** for Joseph's arrival H4966
Ge 43:26 presented to him the **g** they had brought H4966
Ex 28:38 involved in the **sacred g** the Israelites H7731
Ex 28:38 consecrate, whatever their **g** may be. H5510
Lev 23:38 in addition to your **g** and whatever you H5510
Nu 7: 3 They brought as their **g** before the LORD six H7933
Nu 8:19 given the Levites as **g** to Aaron and his H5989
Nu 18: 9 From all the **g** they bring me as most holy H7933
Nu 18:11 is set aside from the **g** of all the wave H5508
Dt 12: 6 your tithes and **special g**, what you H9556+3338
Dt 12:11 your tithes and **special g**, and all H9556+3338
Dt 12:17 your freewill offerings or **special g**. H9556+3338
Dt 33:15 with the **choicest g** *of* the ancient H8031
Dt 33:16 with the best **g** of the earth and its fullness NDT
1Sa 10:27 They despised him and brought him no **g**. H4966
2Ki 12:18 the **g** he himself had **dedicated** and H7731
2Ch 17: 5 all Judah brought **g** to Jehoshaphat H4966
2Ch 17:11 brought Jehoshaphat **g** and silver as H4966
2Ch 21: 3 had given them many **g** of silver and gold H5510
2Ch 31:12 the contributions, tithes and **dedicated g**. H7731
2Ch 31:14 LORD and also the **consecrated g**. H7731+7731
2Ch 32:23 the LORD and **valuable g** for Hezekiah H4458
Ezr 1: 6 with **valuable g**, in addition to all H4458
Est 2:18 distributed **g** with royal liberality. H5368
Est 9:22 of food to one another and **g** to the poor. H5510
Ps 68:18 you received **g** from people, even from H5510
Ps 68:29 at Jerusalem kings will bring you **g**. H8856
Ps 72:10 kings of Sheba and Seba present him **g**. H868
Ps 76:11 lands bring **g** to the One to be feared H8856
Ps 112: 9 have freely scattered *their* **g** to the poor, H5989
Pr 19: 6 everyone is the friend of one who gives **g**. H5508
Pr 22:16 wealth and *one who* **gives g** to the rich— H5989
Pr 25:14 is one who boasts of **g never given**. H5522+9214
Isa 1:23 they all love bribes and chase after **g**. H8988
Isa 18: 7 At that time **g** will be brought to the LORD H8856
Isa 18: 7 the **g** will be brought to Mount Zion NDT
Eze 16:33 All prostitutes receive **g**, but you give gifts H5613
Eze 16:33 but you give **g** to all your lovers H5621
Eze 20:26 I defiled them through their **g**—the H5510
Eze 20:31 When you offer your **g**—the sacrifice of H5510
Eze 20:39 my holy name with your **g** and idols. H5510
Eze 20:40 require your offerings and your choice **g**, H5368
Eze 44:30 of all your **special g** will belong to H9556
Da 2: 6 will receive from me **g** and rewards and A10448
Da 2:48 position and lavished many **g** on him. A10448
Da 5:17 "You may keep your **g** for yourself and A10448
Da 11:38 with precious stones and **costly g**. H2776
Hos 8:13 Though they offer sacrifices as **g** *to* me H2037
Mic 1: 7 all her **temple g** will be burned with fire H924
Mic 1: 7 Since she gathered her **g** from the wages of NDT
Mic 1:14 you will give **parting g** to Moresheth Gath. H8933
Mic 7: 3 the ruler demands **g**, the judge accepts NDT
Mt 2:11 presented him with **g** of gold, *G1565*
Mt 7:11 know how to give good **g** to your children *G1517*
Mt 7:11 in heaven give good **g** to those who ask him NDT
Lk 11:13 know how to give good **g** to your children *G1517*
Lk 21: 1 the rich putting their **g** into the temple *G1565*
Lk 21: 4 people gave their **g** out of their wealth; *G1565*
Lk 21: 5 stones and *with* **g dedicated to God**. *G356*
Ac 10: 4 prayers and **g to the poor** have come up *G1797*
Ac 10:31 remembered your **g to the poor**. *G1797*
Ac 24:17 my people **g for the poor** and to present *G1797*
Ro 11:29 God's **g** and his call are irrevocable. *G5922*
Ro 12: 6 We have different **g**, according to the *G5922*
1Co 12: 1 Now about the **g of the Spirit**, brothers *G4461*
1Co 12: 4 There are different kinds *of* **g**, but the *G5922*
1Co 12: 9 to another **g** of healing by that one Spirit *G5922*
1Co 12:28 then miracles, then **g** of healing, of *G5922*
1Co 12:30 Do all have **g** of healing? Do all speak in *G5922*
1Co 12:31 Now eagerly desire the greater **g**. *G5922*
1Co 14: 1 of love and eagerly desire **g of the Spirit**, *G4461*
1Co 14:12 Since you are eager *for g of* the **Spirit**, try to AIT
2Co 9: 9 have freely scattered *their* **g** to the poor; *G1443*
Eph 4: 8 many captives and gave **g** to his people." *G1517*
Php 4:17 Not that I desire your **g**; what I desire is *G1517*
Php 4:18 received from Epaphroditus **the** *g* you sent. AIT
Heb 2: 4 and *by g* of the Holy Spirit **distributed** AIT
Heb 5: 1 to offer **g** and sacrifices for sins. *G1565*
Heb 8: 3 is appointed to offer both **g** and sacrifices, *G1565*
Heb 8: 4 who offer the **g** prescribed by the law *G1565*
Heb 9: 9 indicating that the **g** and sacrifices being *G1565*
Rev 11:10 will celebrate by sending each other **g**, *G1565*

GIGANTIC (1)
Rev 9: 2 from it like the smoke from a **g** furnace. *G3489*

GIHON (6)
Ge 2:13 The name of the second river is the **G**; it H1633
1Ki 1:33 my own mule and take him down to **G**. H1633
1Ki 1:38 David's mule, and they escorted him to **G**. H1633
1Ki 1:45 the prophet have anointed him king at **G**. H1633
2Ch 32:30 upper outlet of the **G** spring and H1633
2Ch 33:14 west of the **G** spring in the valley H1633

GILALAI (1)
Ne 12:36 Milalai, **G**, Maai, Nethanel, Judah H1675

GILBOA (8)
1Sa 28: 4 gathered all Israel and set up camp at **G**. H1648
1Sa 31: 1 and many fell dead on Mount **G**. H1648
1Sa 31: 8 his three sons fallen on Mount **G**. H1648
2Sa 1: 6 "I happened to be on Mount **G**," the H1648
2Sa 1:21 "Mountains of **G**, may you have neither H1648
2Sa 21:12 them after they struck Saul down on **G**.) H1648
1Ch 10: 1 and many fell dead on Mount **G**. H1648
1Ch 10: 8 Saul and his sons fallen on Mount **G**. H1648

GILEAD (97) [GILEAD'S, GILEADITE, GILEADITES, JABESH GILEAD, RAMOTH GILEAD]
Ge 31:21 headed for the hill country of **G**. H1680
Ge 31:23 up with him in the hill country of **G**. H1680
Ge 31:25 the hill country of **G** when Laban overtook H1680
Ge 37:25 a caravan of Ishmaelites coming from **G**. H1680
Nu 26:29 Makir was the father of **G**); through Gilead, H1680
Nu 26:29 of Gilead); through **G**, the Gileadite clan. H1680
Nu 26:30 These were the descendants of **G** H1680
Nu 27: 1 of Hepher, the son of **G**, the son of Makir, H1680
Nu 32: 1 the lands of Jazer and **G** were suitable H1680
Nu 32:26 herds will remain here in the cities of **G**. H1680
Nu 32:29 them the land of **G** as their possession. H1680
Nu 32:39 of Makir son of Manasseh went to **G**, H1680
Nu 32:40 So Moses gave **G** to the Makirites, the H1680
Nu 36: 1 of the clan of **G** son of Makir, H1201+1680
Dt 2:36 even as far as **G**, not one town was too H1680
Dt 3:10 the plateau, and all **G**, and all Bashan as H1680
Dt 3:12 including half the hill country of **G** H1680
Dt 3:13 The rest of **G** and also all of Bashan, the H1680
Dt 3:15 And I gave **G** to Makir. H1680
Dt 3:16 extending from **G** down to the Arnon H1680
Dt 4:43 Reubenites; Ramoth in **G**, for the Gadites; H1680
Dt 34: 1 him the whole land—from **G** to Dan, H1680
Jos 12: 2 the Ammonites. This included half of **G**. H1680
Jos 12: 5 half of **G** to the border of Sihon king H1680
Jos 13:11 It also included **G**, the territory of the H1680
Jos 13:25 all the towns of **G** and half the Ammonite H1680
Jos 13:31 half of **G**, and Ashtaroth and Edrei (the H1680
Jos 17: 1 who had received **G** and Bashan because H1680
Jos 17: 3 of Hepher, the son of **G**, the son of Makir, H1680
Jos 17: 5 of land besides **G** and Bashan east of the H1680
Jos 17: 6 The land of **G** belonged to the rest of the H1680
Jos 20: 8 Reuben, Ramoth in **G** in the tribe of Gad H1680
Jos 21:38 Ramoth in **G** (a city of refuge for H1680
Jos 22: 9 at Shiloh in Canaan to return to **G**, H824+1680
Jos 22:13 to the land of **G**—to Reuben, Gad and the H1680
Jos 22:15 When they went to **G**—to Reuben H824+1680
Jos 22:32 and Gadites in **G** and reported to H824+1680
Jdg 5:17 **G** stayed beyond the Jordan. And Dan H1680
Jdg 7: 3 fear may turn back and leave Mount **G**. H1680
Jdg 10: 3 He was followed by Jair **of G**, who led H1682
Jdg 10: 4 They controlled thirty towns in **G** H824+1680
Jdg 10: 8 on the east side of the Jordan in **G**, H1680
Jdg 10:17 were called to arms and camped in **G**, H1680
Jdg 10:18 of the people of **G** said to each other, H1680
Jdg 10:18 will be head over all who live in **G**." H1680
Jdg 11: 1 His father was **G**; his mother was a H1680
Jdg 11: 5 the elders of **G** went to get Jephthah from H1680
Jdg 11: 8 The elders of **G** said to him H1680
Jdg 11: 8 will be head over all of us who live in **G**." H1680
Jdg 11:10 The elders of **G** replied, "The LORD is our H1680
Jdg 11:11 So Jephthah went with the elders of **G** H1680
Jdg 11:29 He crossed **G** and Manasseh, passed H1680
Jdg 11:29 passed through Mizpah of **G**, and from H1680
Jdg 12: 4 together the men of **G** and fought against H1680
Jdg 12: 5 the men of **G** asked him, "Are you an H1680
Jdg 12: 7 died and was buried in a town in **G**. H1680
Jdg 20: 1 from the land of **G** came together as one H1680
1Sa 13: 7 the Jordan to the land of Gad and **G**. H1680
2Sa 2: 9 He made him king over **G**, Ashuri and H1680
2Sa 17:26 Absalom camped in the land of **G**. H1680
2Sa 24: 6 They went to **G** and the region of Tahtim H1680
1Ki 2: 7 sons of Barzillai **of G** and let them be H1682
1Ki 4:13 of Jair son of Manasseh in **G** were his, H1680
1Ki 4:19 son of Uri—in **G** (the country of H824+1680
1Ki 17: 1 Tishbite, from Tishbe in **G**, said to Ahab, H1680
2Ki 10:33 east of the Jordan in all the land of **G** (the H1680
2Ki 10:33 by the Arnon Gorge through **G** to Bashan. H1680
2Ki 15:25 Taking fifty men **of G** with him, he H1201+1682
2Ki 15:29 He took **G** and Galilee, including all the H1680
1Ch 2:21 the daughter of Makir the father of **G**. H1680
1Ch 2:22 controlled twenty-three towns in **G**. H824+1680
1Ch 2:23 descendants of Makir the father of **G**. H1680
1Ch 5: 9 their livestock had increased in **G**. H824+1680
1Ch 5:10 throughout the entire region east of **G**. H1680
1Ch 5:14 the son of **G**, the son of Michael, H1680
1Ch 5:16 The Gadites lived in **G**, in Bashan and its H1680
1Ch 6:80 tribe of Gad they received Ramoth in **G**, H1680
1Ch 7:14 She gave birth to Makir the father of **G**. H1680
1Ch 7:17 These were the sons of **G** son of Makir H1680
1Ch 26:31 the Hebronites were found at Jazer in **G**. H1680
1Ch 27:21 over the half-tribe of Manasseh in **G**: Iddo H1680
Ps 60: 7 **G** is mine, and Manasseh is mine H1680
Ps 108: 8 **G** is mine, Manasseh is mine; Ephraim is H1680
SS 4: 1 of goats descending from the hills of **G**. H1680
SS 6: 5 is like a flock of goats descending from **G**. H1680
Jer 8:22 Is there no balm in **G**? Is there no H1680
Jer 22: 6 "Though you are like **G** to me, like the H1680

Jer 46:11 "Go up to G and get balm, Virgin H1680
Jer 50:19 satisfied on the hills of Ephraim and G. H1680
Eze 47:18 the Jordan between G and the land of H1680
Hos 6: 8 G is a city of evildoers, stained with H1680
Hos 12:11 Is G wicked? Its people are worthless! Do H1680
Am 1: 3 she threshed G with sledges having H1680
Am 1:13 pregnant women of G in order to extend H1680
Ob 19 Samaria, and Benjamin will possess G. H1680
Mic 7:14 feed in Bashan and G as in days long ago H1680
Zec 10:10 I will bring them to G and Lebanon H824+1680

GILEAD'S (1) [GILEAD]
Jdg 11: 2 G wife also bore him sons, and when they H1680

GILEADITE (8) [GILEAD]
Nu 26:29 of Gilead); through Gilead, the G clan. H1682
Jdg 11: 1 Jephthah the G was a mighty warrior. H1682
Jdg 11:40 the daughter of Jephthah the G. H1682
Jdg 12: 7 Then Jephthah the G died and was H1682
2Sa 17:27 and Barzillai the G from Rogelim H1682
2Sa 19:31 Barzillai the G also came down from H1682
Ezr 2:61 of Barzillai the G and was called by that H1682
Ne 7:63 of Barzillai the G and was called by that H1682

GILEADITES (4) [GILEAD]
Jos 17: 1 Makir was the ancestor of the G, who had H1680
Jdg 12: 4 The G struck them down because H408+1680
Jdg 12: 4 "You G are renegades from Ephraim and H1680
Jdg 12: 5 The G captured the fords of the Jordan H1680

GILGAL (39) [BETH GILGAL]
Dt 11:30 living in the Arabah in the vicinity of G. H1652
Jos 4:19 Jordan and camped at G on the eastern H1652
Jos 4:20 And Joshua set up at G the twelve stones H1652
Jos 5: 9 the place has been called G to this day. H1652
Jos 5:10 while camped at G on the plains of H1652
Jos 9: 6 in the camp at G and said to him and H1652
Jos 10: 6 sent word to Joshua in the camp at G: H1652
Jos 10: 7 marched up from G with his entire army, H1652
Jos 10: 9 After an all-night march from G, Joshua H1652
Jos 10:15 returned with all Israel to the camp at G. H1652
Jos 10:43 returned with all Israel to the camp at G. H1652
Jos 12:23 one the king of Goyim in G one H1652
Jos 14: 6 people of Judah approached Joshua at G, H1652
Jos 15: 7 the Valley of Achor and turned north to G, H1652
Jdg 2: 1 LORD went up from G to Bokim and said, H1652
Jdg 3:19 stone images near G he himself went H1652
1Sa 7:16 on a circuit from Bethel to G to Mizpah, H1652
1Sa 10: 8 "Go down ahead of me to G. I will surely H1652
1Sa 11:14 let us go to G and there renew the H1652
1Sa 11:15 the people went to G and made Saul king H1652
1Sa 13: 4 people were summoned to join Saul at G. H1652
1Sa 13: 7 Saul remained at G, and all the troops H1652
1Sa 13: 8 Samuel did not come to G, and Saul's H1652
1Sa 13:12 will come down against me at G, H1652
1Sa 13:15 Then Samuel left G and went up to H1652
1Sa 15:12 has turned and gone on down to G." H1652
1Sa 15:21 sacrifice them to the LORD your God at G." H1652
1Sa 15:33 put Agag to death before the LORD at G. H1652
2Sa 19:15 Judah had come to G to go out and meet H1652
2Sa 19:40 When the king crossed over to G, Kimham H1652
2Ki 2: 1 Elisha were on their way from G. H1652
2Ki 4:38 Elisha returned to G and there was a H1652
Hos 4:15 "Do not go to G; do not go up to Beth H1652
Hos 9:15 "Because of all their wickedness in G, H1652
Hos 12:11 Do they sacrifice bulls in G? Their altars H1652
Am 4: 4 Bethel and sin; go to G and sin yet more. H1652
Am 5: 5 do not go to G, do not journey to H1652
Am 5: 5 For G will surely go into exile, and Bethel H1652
Mic 6: 5 Remember your journey from Shittim to G H1652

GILOH (2)
Jos 15:51 Goshen, Holon and G—eleven towns H1656
2Sa 15:12 to come from G, his hometown. H1656

GILONITE (2)
2Sa 15:12 he also sent for Ahithophel the G, David's H1639
2Sa 23:34 Eliam son of Ahithophel the G, H1639

GIMZO (1)
2Ch 28:18 as Soko, Timnah and G, with their H1693

GIN, GINS (KJV) TRAP, TRAPS

GINATH (2)
1Ki 16:21 half supported Tibni son of G for king H1640
1Ki 16:22 stronger than those of Tibni son of G. H1640

GINNETHON (2) [GINNETHON'S]
Ne 10: 6 G, Baruch, H1715
Ne 12: 4 G, Abijah, H1715

GINNETHON'S (1) [GINNETHON]
Ne 12:16 of Iddo's, Zechariah; of G, Meshullam; H1715

GIRD, GIRDED, GIRDETH (KJV) ARMED, ARMS, BRACE, CLOTHED, DRESSED, FASTEN, FASTENED, PREPARE, PUT ON, READY, STRAP, STRAPPED, TIE, TIED, TUCKED, WEAR, WEARING, WRAP, WRAPPED

GIRD (1)
Ps 45: 3 G your sword on your side, you mighty H2520

GIRGASHITES (7)
Ge 10:16 Jebusites, Amorites, G, H1739
Ge 15:21 Amorites, Canaanites, G and Jebusites." H1739
Dt 7: 1 the Hittites, G, Amorites, Canaanites H1739
Jos 3:10 Perizzites, G, Amorites and H1739
Jos 24:11 Canaanites, Hittites, G, Hivites and H1739
1Ch 1:14 Jebusites, Amorites, G, H1739
Ne 9: 8 Amorites, Perizzites, Jebusites and G. H1739

GIRL (24) [GIRLS]
Ge 34: 4 father Hamor, "Get me this g as my wife." H3530
Ex 1:16 kill him; but if it is a g, let her live. H1426
Ex 1:22 throw into the Nile, but let every g live." H1426
Ex 2: 8 So the g went and got the baby's mother H6625
Lev 12: 7 woman who gives birth to a boy or a g. H5922
Nu 31:18 yourselves every g who has never H3251+851
1Sa 30:19 boy or g, plunder or anything H1426
2Ki 5: 2 had taken captive a young g from Israel, H5855
2Ki 5: 4 told him what the g from Israel had said. H5855
Am 2: 7 son use the same g and so profane my H5855
Mt 9:24 The g is not dead but asleep. *G3166*
Mt 9:25 he went in and took the g by the hand *G3166*
Mt 14:11 brought in on a platter and given *to* the g, *G3166*
Mt 26:69 courtyard, and a **servant** g came to him. *G4087*
Mt 26:71 where **another** servant g saw him and said to AIT
Mk 5:41 which means "**Little** g, I say to you, get *G3166*
Mk 5:42 Immediately the g stood up and began to *G3166*
Mk 6:22 The king said *to* the g, "Ask me for *G3166*
Mk 6:25 At once the g hurried in to the king with the NDT
Mk 6:28 He presented it *to* the g, and she gave it *G3166*
Mk 14:69 When the **servant** g saw him there, she *G4087*
Lk 8:42 only daughter, a g of about twelve, was *G899S*
Lk 22:56 A **servant** g saw him seated there in the *G4087*
Jn 18:16 spoke *to* the **servant** g **on duty** there and *G2601*

GIRLS (6) [GIRL]
Ex 2:18 When *the* g **returned** to Reuel their father, he AIT
2Sa 6:20 in full view of the **slave** g *of* his servants as H563
2Sa 6:22 But by these **slave** g you spoke of, I will be H563
Joel 3: 3 prostitutes; they sold g for wine to drink. H3530
Zec 8: 5 be filled with boys and g playing there." H3530
Mk 14:66 one *of* the **servant** g of the high priest *G4087*

GIRZITES (1)
1Sa 27: 8 the Geshurites, the G and the Amalekites. H1747

GISHPA (1)
Ne 11:21 Ziha and G were in charge of them. H1778

GITTAIM (2)
2Sa 4: 3 of Beeroth fled to G and have resided H1786
Ne 11:33 in Hazor, Ramah and G, H1786

GITTITE (8) [GITTITES]
2Sa 6:10 took it to the house of Obed-Edom the G. H1785
2Sa 6:11 of Obed-Edom the G for three months, H1785
2Sa 15:19 The king said to Ittai the G, "Why should H1785
2Sa 15:22 So Ittai the G marched on with all his H1785
2Sa 18: 2 of Zeruiah, and a third under Ittai the G. H1785
2Sa 21:19 killed the brother of Goliath the G, H1785
1Ch 13:13 took it to the house of Obed-Edom the G. H1785
1Ch 20: 5 killed Lahmi the brother of Goliath the G, H1785

GITTITES (1) [GITTITE]
2Sa 15:18 the six hundred G who had accompanied H1785

GITTITH (3)
Ps 8: T According to g. A psalm of David. H1787
Ps 81: T According to g. Of Asaph. H1787
Ps 84: T According to g. Of the Sons of H1787

GIVE (912) [GAVE, GIVEN, GIVER, GIVES, GIVING, LIFE-GIVING]
Ge 1:15 the vault of the sky to g **light** on the earth." H239
Ge 1:17 the vault of the sky to g **light** on the earth, H239
Ge 1:29 "*I* g you every seed-bearing plant on the H5989
Ge 1:30 of life in it—I g every green plant for food." NDT
Ge 3:16 painful labor *you will* g **birth** *to* children. H3528
Ge 9: 3 the green plants, I now g you everything. NDT
Ge 12: 7 "To your offspring *I will* g this land." H5989
Ge 13:15 land that you see *I will* g to you and your H5989
Ge 14:21 "G me the people and keep the goods H5989
Ge 15: 2 what *can you* g me since I remain H5989
Ge 15: 7 of the Chaldeans to g you this land to H5989
Ge 15:18 "To your descendants *I* g this land, from H5989
Ge 16:11 pregnant and *you will* g **birth** *to* a son. H3528
Ge 17: 8 *I will* g as an everlasting possession to H5989
Ge 17:16 bless her and *will* surely g you a son by H5989
Ge 19:31 man around here to g us **children**— H995+6584
Ge 23:11 "Listen to me; *I* g you the field, and I give H5989
Ge 23:11 the field, and *I* g you the cave that is in it. H5989
Ge 23:11 *I* g it to you in the presence of my people H5989
Ge 24: 7 'To your offspring *I will* g this land'—he H5989
Ge 24:17 "Please g me a little water from your jar." H1686
Ge 24:41 go to my clan, *they* refuse *to* g her to you H5989
Ge 24:45 I said to her, 'Please g me **a drink**. H9197
Ge 25:24 When the time came for her to g **birth** H3528
Ge 26: 3 your descendants *I will* g all these lands H5989
Ge 26: 4 stars in the sky and *will* g them all these H5989
Ge 27: 4 so that I *may* g you my **blessing** before I H1385
Ge 27: 7 so that *I may* g you my **blessing** in the H1385
Ge 27:10 so that *he may* g you his **blessing** before H1385
Ge 27:19 so that you *may* g me your **blessing**." H1385
Ge 27:25 so that I *may* g you my **blessing**. H1385
Ge 27:28 *May* God g you heaven's dew and earth's H5989
Ge 27:31 so that you *may* g me your **blessing**." H1385
Ge 28: 4 *May he* g you and your descendants the H5989
Ge 28:13 *I will* g you and your descendants the H5989
Ge 28:20 I am taking and *will* g me food to eat H5989
Ge 28:22 of all that *you* g me I will give you a H5989
Ge 28:22 *of* all that you give me *I will* g you **a tenth** H6923+6923
Ge 29:19 "It's better *that* I g her to you than to H5989
Ge 29:21 Then Jacob said to Laban, "G me my wife. H2035
Ge 29:26 to g the younger daughter **in marriage** H5989
Ge 29:27 then *we will* g you the younger one also H5989
Ge 30: 1 she said to Jacob, "G me children, or I'll H2035
Ge 30:14 "Please g me some of your son's H5989
Ge 30:26 G me my wives and children, for whom I H5989
Ge 30:31 "What *shall I* g you?" he asked. H5989
Ge 30:31 "Don't g me anything," Jacob H5989
Ge 34: 8 Please g her to him as his wife. H5989
Ge 34: 9 g us your daughters and take our H5989
Ge 34:11 and *I will* g you whatever you ask. H5989
Ge 34:12 Only g me the young woman as my wife." H5989
Ge 34:14 we can't g our sister to a man who is not H5989
Ge 34:16 Then *we will* g you our daughters and take H5989
Ge 35:12 to Abraham and Isaac *I* also g to you, H5989
Ge 35:12 and *I will* g this land to your descendants H5989
Ge 35:16 Rachel *began to* g **birth** and had great H3528
Ge 38:16 "And what *will you* g me to sleep with H5989
Ge 38:17 "*Will you* g me something *as* a pledge H5989
Ge 38:18 "What pledge *should I* g you?" "Your seal H5989
Ge 38:26 since *I* wouldn't g her to my son Shelah." H5989
Ge 38:27 When the time came for her *to* g **birth** H3528
Ge 41:16 "but God *will* g Pharaoh *the* **answer** he H6699
Ge 42:22 Now *we must* g **an accounting** *for* his H2011
Ge 42:25 to g them provisions for their journey. H5989
Ge 42:34 Then *I will* g your brother **back** to you, and H5989
Ge 45:18 *I will* g you the best of the land of Egypt H5989
Ge 47:15 came to Joseph and said, "G us food. H2035
Ge 47:19 G us seed so that we may live and not die H5989
Ge 47:24 crop comes in, g a fifth of it to Pharaoh. H5989
Ge 48: 4 and *I will* g this land as an everlasting H5989
Ge 48:22 I g one more ridge of land than *to* your H5989
Ex 1:19 are vigorous and g **birth** before the H3528
Ex 5:10 'I *will* not g you any more straw H5989
Ex 6: 4 covenant with them to g them the land of H5989
Ex 6: 8 with uplifted hand to g to Abraham, H5989
Ex 6: 8 *I will* g it to you as a possession H5989
Ex 9:19 G **an order** now to bring your livestock H8938
Ex 12:25 land that the LORD *will* g you as he H5989
Ex 13: 5 land he swore to your ancestors to g you, H5989
Ex 13:12 *you are to* g **over** to the LORD the first H6296
Ex 13:21 by night in a pillar of fire to g them **light**, H239
Ex 17: 2 with Moses and said, "G us water to drink." H5989
Ex 18:19 now to me and *I will* g you *some* **advice**, H3619
Ex 20:16 "*You shall* not g false testimony against H6699
Ex 22:17 father absolutely refuses to g her to him, H5989
Ex 22:29 "*You must* g me the firstborn of your sons. H5989
Ex 22:30 but g them to me on the eighth day. H5989
Ex 23: 2 When *you* g **testimony** in a lawsuit, do H6699
Ex 23:26 *I will* g you *a* **full** life span. H4848
Ex 23:31 *I will* g into your hands the people who H5989
Ex 24:12 and *I will* g you the tablets of stone with H5989
Ex 25: 2 everyone whose heart **prompts** them **to** g. H5605
Ex 25:16 of the covenant law, which *I will* g you. H5989
Ex 25:21 of the covenant law that *I will* g you. H5989
Ex 25:22 meet with you and g you all my H1819
Ex 28: 2 brother Aaron to g him dignity and honor NDT
Ex 28:40 Aaron's sons to g them dignity and NDT
Ex 30:13 already counted *is to* g a half shekel, H5989
Ex 30:14 more, *are to* g an offering to the LORD. H5989
Ex 30:15 The rich *are* not *to* g **more** than a half H8049
Ex 30:15 the poor *are* not *to* g **less** when you H5070
Ex 32:13 in the sky and *I will* g your descendants H5989
Ex 33: 1 '*I will* g it to your descendants.' H5989
Ex 33:14 will go with you, and *I will* g you **rest**." H5663
Lev 5:16 a fifth of its value and g it all to the priest. H5989
Lev 6: 5 the value to it and g it all to the owner on H5989
Lev 6: 9 "G Aaron and his sons *this* **command** H7422
Lev 7:32 *You are to* g the right thigh of your H5989
Lev 7:36 that the Israelites g this to them as their H5989
Lev 15:14 tent of meeting and g them to the priest. H5989
Lev 18:21 " '*Do* not g any of your children to be H5989
Lev 20:24 I *will* g it to you as an inheritance H5989
Lev 23:10 the land I *am going to* g you and you H5989
Lev 23:38 all the freewill offerings *you* g to the LORD.) H5989
Lev 25: 2 you enter the land I *am going to* g you, H5989
Lev 25:38 you out of Egypt to g you the land of H5989
Nu 3: 9 G the Levites to Aaron and his sons; they H5989
Nu 3:48 G the money for the redemption of the H5989
Nu 5: 7 of the value to it and g it all to the person H5989
Nu 5:10 what they g to the priest will belong H5989
Nu 6:26 turn his face toward you and g you peace." H8492
Nu 7: 5 G them to the Levites as each man's work H5989
Nu 7: 9 But Moses *did* not g any to the Kohathites H5989
Nu 10:29 which the LORD said, '*I will* g it to you. H5989
Nu 11:12 *Did* I g them **birth**? Why do you H3528
Nu 11:13 keep wailing to me, 'G us meat to eat! H5989
Nu 11:18 Now the LORD *will* g you meat, and you H5989
Nu 11:21 '*I will* g them meat to eat for a whole H5989
Nu 14: 8 with milk and honey, and *will* g it to us. H5989
Nu 15:21 to come *you are to* g this offering to H5989
Nu 18: 8 the Israelites g me I give to you and NDT

Nu 18: 8 Israelites give me *I* **g** to you and your sons H5989
Nu 18:11 *I* **g** this to you and your sons and H5989
Nu 18:12 "*I* **g** you all the finest olive oil and all the H5989
Nu 18:12 new wine and grain *they* **g** the LORD as the H5989
Nu 18:19 present to the LORD *I* **g** to you and your H5989
Nu 18:21 "*I* **g** to the Levites all the tithes in Israel as H5989
Nu 18:24 *I* **g** to the Levites as their inheritance the H5989
Nu 18:26 Israelites the tithe *I* **g** you as your H5989
Nu 18:28 From these tithes *you must* **g** the LORD's H5989
Nu 19: 3 **G** it to Eleazar the priest; it is to be taken H5989
Nu 20:12 this community into the land *I* **g** them." H5989
Nu 20:24 will not enter the land *I* **g** the Israelites, H5989
Nu 21:16 people together and *I will* **g** them water." H5989
Nu 23: 5 "Go back to Balak and **g** him this **word**." H1819
Nu 23:16 "Go back to Balak and **g** him this **word**." H1819
Nu 26:54 To a larger group **g** a **larger** inheritance H8049
Nu 27: 4 **G** us property among our father's relatives."H5989
Nu 27: 7 *You* **must certainly g** them property H5989+5989
Nu 27: 7 father's relatives and **g** their father's H6296
Nu 27: 8 **g** his inheritance to his daughter. H6296
Nu 27: 9 **g** his inheritance to his brothers. H5989
Nu 27:10 **g** his inheritance to his father's brothers. H5989
Nu 27:11 **g** his inheritance to the nearest relative in H5989
Nu 27:20 **G** him some of your authority so the whole H5989
Nu 28: 2 "**G** *this* **command** *to* the Israelites and say H7422
Nu 31:29 their half share and **g** it to Eleazar the H5989
Nu 31:30 **G** them to the Levites, who are H5989
Nu 32:29 *you must* **g** them the land of Gilead as H5989
Nu 33:54 To a larger group **g** a **larger** inheritance H8049
Nu 33:55 *They will* **g** you **trouble** in the land where H7675
Nu 35: 2 the Israelites *to* **g** the Levites towns to H5989
Nu 35: 2 And **g** them pasturelands around the H5989
Nu 35: 4 the towns that *you* **g** the Levites will H5989
Nu 35: 6 "Six of the towns *you* **g** the Levites will be H5989
Nu 35: 6 In addition, **g** them forty-two other towns H5989
Nu 35: 7 In all *you must* **g** the Levites forty-eight H5989
Nu 35: 8 The towns *you* **g** the Levites from the land H5989
Nu 35:13 These six towns *you* **g** will be your cities of H5989
Nu 35:14 **G** three on this side of the Jordan and H5989
Nu 36: 2 commanded my lord to **g** the land as an H5989
Nu 36: 2 he ordered you to **g** the inheritance of our H5989
Dt 1: 8 the LORD swore *he would* **g** to your fathers H5989
Dt 1:35 the good land I swore to **g** your ancestors, H5989
Dt 1:36 and *I will* **g** him and his descendants the H5989
Dt 1:39 *I will* **g** it to them and they will take H5989
Dt 2: 4 **G** the people *these* **orders**: 'You are about H7422
Dt 2: 5 for *I will* not **g** you any of their land H5989
Dt 2: 9 for *I will* not **g** you any part of their land. H5989
Dt 2:19 for *I will* not **g** you possession *of* any land H5989
Dt 2:30 in order to **g** him into your hands, H5989
Dt 4: 2 of the LORD your God that I **g** you. H7422
Dt 4:38 you into their land to **g** it to you for your H5989
Dt 5:20 "*You shall* not **g** false testimony against H6699
Dt 5:31 here with me so that *I may* **g** you all the H1819
Dt 6: 2 his decrees and commands that I **g** you, H7422
Dt 6: 6 that I **g** you today are to be H7422
Dt 6:10 Isaac and Jacob, to **g** you—a land with H5989
Dt 6:23 to bring us in and **g** us the land he H5989
Dt 7: 3 *Do* not **g** your daughters to their sons or H5989
Dt 7:11 decrees and laws I **g** you today. H7422
Dt 7:13 land he swore to your ancestors to **g** you. H5989
Dt 7:24 *He will* **g** their kings into your hand, and H5989
Dt 10:11 land I swore to their ancestors to **g** them." H5989
Dt 11: 9 to your ancestors to **g** to them and their H5989
Dt 11:21 land the LORD swore to **g** your ancestors, H5989
Dt 12: 6 what you have vowed to **g** and your freewill NDT
Dt 12:10 and *he will* **g** you **rest** from all your H5663
Dt 12:17 whatever you have vowed to **g**, or your NDT
Dt 12:26 things and whatever you have vowed to **g**, NDT
Dt 14:21 *You may* **g** it to the foreigner residing in H5989
Dt 15: 9 your fellow Israelites and **g** them nothing. H5989
Dt 15:10 **G generously** to them and do so H5989+5989
Dt 15:14 **G** to them as the LORD your God has H5989
Dt 15:15 That is why I **g** you this command today H7422
Dt 17: 9 of them and *they will* **g** you the verdict. H5583
Dt 17:10 to the decisions *they* **g** you at the place H5583
Dt 17:11 teach you and the decisions *they* **g** you. H606
Dt 18: 4 *You are to* **g** them the firstfruits of your H5989
Dt 20: 4 you against your enemies to **g** you **victory**."H3828
Dt 21:16 not **g the rights of the firstborn** *to* the son H1144
Dt 22: 2 they come looking for it. Then **g** it **back**. H8740
Dt 22:19 shekels of silver and **g** them to the young H5989
Dt 26: 3 the LORD swore to our ancestors to **g** us." H5989
Dt 26:12 of the tithe, *you shall* **g** it to the Levite H5989
Dt 27: 1 all these commands that I **g** you today. H7422
Dt 27:10 decrees that I **g** you today. H7422
Dt 28: 1 follow all his commands I **g** you today, H7422
Dt 28:11 land he swore to your ancestors to **g** you. H5989
Dt 28:13 LORD your God that I **g** you this day and H7422
Dt 28:14 from any of the commands I **g** you today, H7422
Dt 28:55 he *will* not **g** to one of them any of H5989
Dt 28:65 There the LORD *will* **g** you an anxious mind H5989
Dt 30:20 he *will* **g** you many years in the land H3782
Dt 30:20 in the land he swore to **g** to your fathers, H5989
Dt 31: 7 LORD swore to their ancestors to **g** them, H5989
Dt 32:38 *Let them* **g** you **shelter**! H2118+6261
Dt 34: 4 '*I will* **g** it to your descendants. H5989
Jos 1: 2 into the land I *am about to* **g** to them— H5989
Jos 1: 3 *I will* **g** you every place where you set your H5989
Jos 1: 6 land I swore to their ancestors to **g** them. H5989
Jos 1:13 LORD your God *will* **g** you **rest** by giving H5663
Jos 2:12 shown kindness to you. **G** me a sure sign H5989
Jos 5: 6 solemnly promised their ancestors to **g** us, H5989
Jos 6: 5 *have* the whole army **g** a loud **shout** H8131+9558
Jos 6:10 the army, "*Do* not **g a war cry**, do not raise H8131
Jos 7:19 "My son, **g** glory to the LORD, the God of H8492
Jos 8: 7 The LORD your God *will* **g** it into your hand.H5989
Jos 9:24 his servant Moses to **g** you the whole land H5989
Jos 14:12 Now **g** me this hill country that the LORD H5989
Jos 15:16 *I will* **g** my daughter Aksah **in marriage** H5989+4200+851
Jos 15:19 in the Negev, **g** me also springs of water." H5989
Jos 17: 4 commanded Moses to **g** us an inheritance H5989
Jos 21: 2 Moses that you **g** us towns to live in, H5989
Jos 21:43 land he had sworn to **g** their ancestors, H5989
Jdg 1:12 *I will* **g** my daughter Aksah **in marriage** H5989+4200+851
Jdg 1:15 in the Negev, **g** me also springs of water." H5989
Jdg 2: 1 into the land I swore to **g** to your ancestors. NDT
Jdg 2:19 *They* refused *to* **g up** their evil practices H5877
Jdg 4: 7 Kishon River and **g** him into your hands. H5989
Jdg 4:19 "Please **g** me some water." She H9197
Jdg 6:17 **g** me a sign that it is really you talking to H6913
Jdg 7: 7 I will save you and **g** the Midianites into H5989
Jdg 7: 9 because *I am going to* **g** it into your H5989
Jdg 8: 5 men of Sukkoth, "**G** my troops some bread H5989
Jdg 8: 6 Why *should we* **g** bread to your troops?" H5989
Jdg 8:15 Why *should we* **g** bread to your exhausted H5989
Jdg 8:24 that each of you **g** me an earring from H5989
Jdg 8:25 "*We'll* be **glad to g** them. H5989+5989
Jdg 9: 9 tree answered, '*Should I* **g up** my oil, by H2532
Jdg 9:11 tree replied, '*Should I* **g up** my fruit, so H2532
Jdg 9:13 answered, '*Should I* **g up** my wine, which H2532
Jdg 11:13 to the Jordan. Now **g** it **back** peaceably." H8740
Jdg 11:17 '*G us permission to* **go** through your country AIT
Jdg 11:30 "If *you* **g** the Ammonites into my H5989+5989
Jdg 11:37 "**G** me two months to roam the hills and H8332
Jdg 13: 2 wife who was childless, unable *to* **g birth**. H3528
Jdg 13: 3 to become pregnant and **g birth** *to* a son. H3528
Jdg 14:12 "If *you can* **g** me *the* **answer** within H5583+5583
Jdg 14:12 *I will* **g** you thirty linen garments and thirty H5989
Jdg 14:13 you *must* **g** me thirty linen garments and H5989
Jdg 14:14 three days they could not **g** the answer. H5583
Jdg 16: 5 Each one of us *will* **g** you eleven hundred H5989
Jdg 17: 3 *I will* **g** it **back** to you." H8740
Jdg 17:10 I'll **g** you ten shekels of silver a year H5989
Jdg 20:10 it *can* **g** them what they deserve for this H6913
Jdg 20:28 tomorrow *I will* **g** them into your hands." H5989
Jdg 21: 1 *will* **g** his daughter **in marriage** H5989+4200+851
Jdg 21: 7 the LORD not *to* **g** them any of H5989+4200+851
Jdg 21:18 We can't **g** them our daughters as wives H5989
Jdg 21:22 because you *did* not **g** your daughters H5989
1Sa 1: 4 *he would* **g** portions of the meat to his H5989
1Sa 1:11 not forget your servant but **g** her a son, H5989
1Sa 1:11 then *I will* **g** him to the LORD for all the H5989
1Sa 1:28 So now I **g** him to the LORD. For his whole H8626
1Sa 2:10 "*He will* **g** strength to his king and exalt H5989
1Sa 2:15 "**G** the priest some meat to roast H5989
1Sa 2:20 "*May* the LORD **g** you children by this H8492
1Sa 6: 5 the country, and **g** glory to Israel's god. H5989
1Sa 8: 6 when they said, "**G** us a king to lead us," H5989
1Sa 8:14 olive groves and **g** them to his H5989
1Sa 8:15 of your vintage and **g** it to his officials H5989
1Sa 8:22 "Listen to them and **g** them a **king**." H4887+4889
1Sa 9: 7 "If we go, what *can we* **g** the man? H995
1Sa 9: 8 *I will* **g** it to the man of God so that he H5989
1Sa 9:27 so that *I may* **g** you a message from God." H9048
1Sa 11: 3 "**G** us seven days so we can send H8332
1Sa 14:37 *Will you* **g** them into Israel's hand?" H5989
1Sa 17:10 **G** me a man and let us fight each other." H5989
1Sa 17:25 king *will* **g** great **wealth** *to* the man H6947+6948
1Sa 17:25 *He will* also **g** him his daughter **in marriage**H5989
1Sa 17:44 "and *I'll* **g** your flesh to the birds and the H5989
1Sa 17:46 This very day *I will* **g** the carcasses of the H5989
1Sa 17:47 and *he will* **g** all of you into our hands." H5989
1Sa 18:17 *I will* **g** her to you **in marriage**; H5989+4200+851
1Sa 18:21 "*I will* **g** her to him," he thought, "so that H5989
1Sa 21: 3 **G** me five loaves of bread, or H5989+928+3338
1Sa 21: 9 "There is none like it; **g** it to me. H5989
1Sa 22: 7 *Will* the son of Jesse **g** all of you fields H5989
1Sa 23: 4 *I am going to* **g** the Philistines into H5989
1Sa 23:14 God *did* not **g** David into his hands. H5989
1Sa 24: 4 '*I will* **g** your enemy into your hands for H5989
1Sa 25: 8 Please **g** your servants and your son David H5989
1Sa 25:11 **g** it to men coming from who knows H5989
1Sa 25:14 wilderness to **g** our master his **greetings**, H1385
1Sa 27: 1 Then Saul *will* **g up** searching for me H3286
1Sa 28:19 The LORD *will* also **g** the army of Israel into H5989
1Sa 28:22 your servant and *let me* **g** you some food H8492
2Sa 2:23 But Asahel refused to **g up the pursuit**; so H6073
2Sa 3:14 demanding, "**G** me my wife Michal H5989
2Sa 7:11 *I will* also **g** you **rest** from all your H5663
2Sa 12:11 take your wives and **g** them to one who is H5989
2Sa 13: 5 to come and **g** me something **to eat**. H1356
2Sa 16:20 said to Ahithophel, "**G** us your advice. H2035
2Sa 17: 6 what he says? If not, **g** us your **opinion**." H1819
2Sa 18: 3 now for you to **g** us **support** from the city." H6468
2Sa 18:11 I would have had to **g** you ten shekels of H5989
2Sa 21: 6 So the king said, "I *will* **g** them to you." H5989
2Sa 22:37 my feet, so that my ankles *do* not **g way**. H5048
1Ki 2:17 *to* **g** me Abishag the Shunammite as my H5989
1Ki 3: 5 "Ask for whatever you want *me to* **g** you." H5989
1Ki 3: 9 So **g** your servant a discerning heart to H5989
1Ki 3:12 *I will* **g** you a wise and discerning heart H5989
1Ki 3:13 *I will* **g** you what you have not asked for H5989
1Ki 3:14 your father did, *I will* **g** you a **long** life." H799
1Ki 3:25 child in two and **g** half to one and half to H5989
1Ki 3:26 "Please, my lord, **g** her the living baby! H5989
1Ki 3:27 "**G** the living baby to the first woman H5989
1Ki 5: 6 "So **g orders** that cedars of Lebanon be H7422
1Ki 8:28 Yet **g attention** to your servant's prayer H7155
1Ki 8:33 back to you and **g praise** *to* your name, H3344
1Ki 8:35 this place and **g praise** *to* your name and H3344
1Ki 8:46 with them and **g** them **over** to their H5989
1Ki 11:11 away from you and **g** it to one of your H5989
1Ki 11:13 but *will* **g** him one tribe for the sake of H5989
1Ki 11:31 of Solomon's hand and **g** you ten tribes. H5989
1Ki 11:35 from his son's hands and **g** you ten tribes. H5989
1Ki 11:36 *I will* **g** one tribe to his son so that David H5989
1Ki 11:38 I built for David and *will* **g** Israel to you. H5989
1Ki 12: 7 and **g** them a favorable **answer**, H1819+1821
1Ki 12:27 *will* **again g** their **allegiance** to H8740+4213
1Ki 13: 7 with me for a meal, and *I will* **g** you a gift." H5989
1Ki 13: 8 "Even if *you were to* **g** me half your H5989
1Ki 14: 5 *you are to* **g** her such and such **an answer**. H1819
1Ki 14:16 And *he will* **g** Israel **up** because of the sins H5989
1Ki 17:19 "**G** me your son," Elijah replied. He took H5989
1Ki 20:10 remains in Samaria to **g** each of my men a NDT
1Ki 20:13 I *will* **g** it into your hand today, and then H5989
1Ki 21: 2 In exchange *I will* **g** you a better vineyard H5989
1Ki 21: 3 LORD forbid that I *should* **g** you the H5989
1Ki 21: 4 "*I will* not **g** you the inheritance of my H5989
1Ki 21: 6 *I will* **g** you another vineyard in its place. H5989
1Ki 21: 6 But he said, '*I will* not **g** you my vineyard H5989
1Ki 22: 6 "for the Lord *will* **g** it into the king's hand." H5989
1Ki 22:12 "for the LORD *will* **g** it into the king's hand."H5989
1Ki 22:15 "for the LORD *will* **g** it into the king's hand."H5989
1Ki 22:27 fellow in prison and **g** him nothing but H430S
2Ki 4:42 "**G** it to the people to eat, H5989
2Ki 4:43 answered, "**G** it to the people to eat. H5989
2Ki 5:22 Please **g** them a talent of silver and two H5989
2Ki 6:28 '**G up** your son so we may eat him today H5989
2Ki 6:29 '**G up** your son so we may eat him H5989
2Ki 8: 6 "**G back** everything that belonged to her H8740
2Ki 10:15 said Jehu, "**g** me your hand." So he H5989
2Ki 14: 9 **G** your daughter to my son **in marriage** H5989+4200+851
2Ki 18:23 *I will* **g** you two thousand horses—if you H5989
2Ki 19:16 **G ear**, LORD, and hear; open your H5742+265
2Ki 21:14 my inheritance and **g** them into the hands H5989
1Ch 16: 7 his associates to **g praise** to the LORD in H3344
1Ch 16: 8 **G praise** to the LORD, proclaim his name H3344
1Ch 16:18 "To you *I will* **g** the land of Canaan as the H5989
1Ch 16:34 **G thanks** to the LORD, for he is good; his H3344
1Ch 16:35 that we *may* **g thanks** to your holy name H3344
1Ch 16:41 by name to **g thanks** to the LORD, H3344
1Ch 21:23 *I will* **g** the oxen for the burnt offerings H5989
1Ch 21:23 the grain offering. *I will* **g** all this." H5989
1Ch 22: 9 and *I will* **g** him **rest** from all his enemies H5663
1Ch 22:12 *May* the LORD **g** you discretion and H5989
1Ch 29: 3 temple of my God *I now* **g** my personal H5989
1Ch 29:12 power to exalt and **g strength** to all. H2616
1Ch 29:13 our God, we **g** you **thanks**, and praise your H3344
1Ch 29:14 should be able to **g** as **generously** as this? H5605
1Ch 29:19 And **g** my son Solomon the wholehearted H5989
2Ch 1: 7 "Ask for whatever you want *me to* **g** you." H5989
2Ch 1:10 **G** me wisdom and knowledge, that I may H5989
2Ch 1:12 And *I will* also **g** you wealth, possessions H5989
2Ch 2:10 *I will* **g** your servants, the woodsmen who H5989
2Ch 5:13 in unison to **g praise** and thanks to the H2146
2Ch 6:19 **g attention** to your servant's prayer and H7155
2Ch 6:24 they turn back and **g praise to** your name, H3344
2Ch 6:26 this place and **g praise to** your name and H3344
2Ch 6:36 with them and **g** them **over** to the enemy, H5989
2Ch 10: 7 and **g** them a favorable **answer**, H1819+1821
2Ch 12: 7 destroy them but *will* soon **g** them H5989
2Ch 15: 7 be strong and *do* not **g up**, for your H8332+3338
2Ch 18: 5 "for God *will* **g** it into the king's hand." H5989
2Ch 18:11 "for the LORD *will* **g** it into the king's hand."H5989
2Ch 18:26 fellow in prison and **g** him nothing but H430S
2Ch 19: 6 who is with you whenever you **g** a verdict. NDT
2Ch 20: 7 your people Israel and **g** it forever to the H5989
2Ch 20:17 see the deliverance the LORD will **g** you, H6640
2Ch 20:21 **G thanks** to the LORD, for his love endures H3344
2Ch 25: 9 "The LORD *can* **g** you much more than that. H5989
2Ch 25:18 **G** your daughter to my son **in marriage** H5989+4200+851
2Ch 30:12 on the people to **g** them unity of mind H5989
2Ch 31: 2 to **g thanks** and to sing praises at the H3344
2Ch 31: 4 in Jerusalem to **g** the portion due the H5989
2Ch 35:12 the burnt offerings to **g** them to the H5989
Ezr 9:12 *do* not **g** your daughters **in marriage** to H5989
Ne 1:11 **G** your servant **success** today by granting H7503
Ne 2: 8 so *he will* **g** me timber to make beams H5989
Ne 2:20 "The God of heaven *will* **g** us **success**. H7503
Ne 4: 4 **G** them **over** as plunder in a land of H5989
Ne 5:11 **G back** to them immediately their fields H8740
Ne 5:12 "*We will* **g** it **back**," they said. "And we H8740
Ne 6:13 and then they *would* **g** me a bad H2118+4200
Ne 8:13 the teacher to **g attention** to the words of H8505
Ne 9: 6 You **g life** *to* everything, and the H2649
Ne 9: 8 covenant with him to **g** to his descendants H5989
Ne 9:12 pillar of fire to **g** them **light** *on* the way they H239
Ne 9:15 had sworn with uplifted hand to **g** them. H5989
Ne 10:30 not *to* **g** our daughters **in marriage** to the H5989
Ne 10:32 out the commands to **g** a third of a shekel H5989

Ne 12:24 opposite them to g **praise** and H2146
Ne 12:31 assigned two large **choirs** to **g thanks**. H9343
Ne 13:25 *You are* not *to* g your daughters **in marriage** H5989
Est 1:19 Also *let* the king g her royal position to H5989
Est 3: 9 and *I will* g ten thousand H9202+4200+995
Est 9:13 "g the Jews in Susa **permission** to carry H5989
Job 2: 4 "A man *will* g all he has for his own life H5989
Job 6:22 I ever said, 'G something on my behalf H2035
Job 7:17 that *you* g them so much attention, H8883
Job 9:16 believe *he would* g me **a hearing**. H263+7754
Job 10: 1 therefore *I will* g **free rein** to my complaint H6440
Job 15:35 They conceive trouble and **g birth** *to* evil H3528
Job 17: 3 "G me, O God, the pledge you demand H8492
Job 20:10 his own hands *must* **g back** his wealth. H8740
Job 20:18 he toiled for *he must* **g back** uneaten; H8740
Job 21: 2 let this be the consolation you g me. NDT
Job 22: 3 pleasure would it g the Almighty if you H4200
Job 31:37 *I would* g him an account of my every step H5583
Job 35: 7 righteous, what *do you* g to him, or what H5989
Job 39: 1 know when the mountain goats **g birth**? H3528
Job 39: 2 Do you know the time they **g birth**? H3528
Job 39:17 wisdom or g her **a share** of good sense H2745
Job 39:19 "*Do you* g the horse its strength or clothe H5989
Ps 4: 1 G me **relief** from my distress; have mercy H8143
Ps 7:17 *I will* **g thanks** *to* the LORD because of his H3344
Ps 9: 1 *I will* **g thanks** *to* you, LORD, with all my H3344
Ps 13: 3 **G light** *to* my eyes, or I will H239
Ps 18:36 my feet, so that my ankles *do* not **g way**. H5048
Ps 20: 4 *May he* g you the desire of your heart H5989
Ps 20: 9 **g victory** *to* the king! Answer us H3828
Ps 21: 1 How great is his joy in the victories you **g**! NDT
Ps 35:18 *I will* g you **thanks** in the great assembly H3344
Ps 36: 8 *you* g them **drink** *from* your river of H9197
Ps 37: 4 and *he will* g you the desires of your heart H5989
Ps 37:21 not repay, but the righteous g generously; H5989
Ps 41: 2 *he does* not g them over to the desire of H5989
Ps 44: 7 but *you* g us **victory** over our enemies, H3828
Ps 46: 2 though the earth **g way** and the H4614
Ps 49: 3 of my heart will g you understanding. NDT
Ps 49: 7 life of another or g to God a ransom for H5989
Ps 60:11 **G** us aid against the enemy, for human H2035
Ps 71: 3 always go; g *the* **command** to save me H7422
Ps 78:20 abundantly, but can he also g us bread? H5989
Ps 85:12 The LORD *will* indeed g what is good, and H5989
Ps 86:11 g me an **undivided** heart, that I H3479
Ps 86:17 G me a sign of your goodness, that my H6913
Ps 100: 4 **g thanks** to him and praise his name. H3344
Ps 104:11 *They* g **water** *to* all the beasts of the field H9197
Ps 104:27 look to you to g them their food at the H5989
Ps 104:28 *When you* g it to them, they gather it up H5989
Ps 105: 1 **G praise** *to* the LORD, proclaim his name H3344
Ps 105:11 "To you *I will* g the land of Canaan as the H5989
Ps 105:39 as a covering, and a fire to **g light** at night. H239
Ps 106: 1 **G thanks** *to* the LORD, for he is good; his H3344
Ps 106:47 that we *may* **g thanks** to your holy name H3344
Ps 107: 1 **G thanks** *to* the LORD, for he is good; his H3344
Ps 107: 8 *Let them* **g thanks** *to* the LORD *for* his H3344
Ps 107:15 *Let them* **g thanks** *to* the LORD *for* his H3344
Ps 107:21 *Let them* **g thanks** *to* the LORD *for* his H3344
Ps 107:31 *Let them* **g thanks** *to* the LORD *for* his H3344
Ps 108:12 **G** us aid against the enemy, for human H2035
Ps 109:24 My knees **g way** from fasting; my body is H4173
Ps 118: 1 **G thanks** *to* the LORD, for he is good; his H3344
Ps 118:19 I will enter and g **thanks** *to* the LORD. H3344
Ps 118:21 *I will* g you **thanks**, for you answered me H3344
Ps 118:29 **G thanks** *to* the LORD, for he is good; his H3344
Ps 119:34 **G** me **understanding**, so that I may keep H1067
Ps 119:62 midnight I rise to g you **thanks** for your H3344
Ps 119:73 **g** me **understanding** to learn your H1067
Ps 119:125 **g** me **discernment** that I may understand H1067
Ps 119:143 upon me, but your commands g me delight. NDT
Ps 119:144 **g** me **understanding** that I may live. H1067
Ps 119:169 **g** me **understanding** according to your H1067
Ps 136: 1 **G thanks** *to* the LORD, for he is good. H3344
Ps 136: 2 **G thanks** *to* the God of gods. His love H3344
Ps 136: 3 **G thanks** *to* the Lord of lords: His love H3344
Ps 136:26 **G thanks** *to* the God of heaven. His love H3344
Ps 141: 8 I take refuge—*do* not g me **over to death**. H6867
Ps 145:15 you g them their food at the proper H5989
Pr 1:10 sinful men entice you, *do* not **g in** *to* them. H995
Pr 3:28 "Come back tomorrow and *I'll* g it to you" H5989
Pr 4: 2 *I* g you sound learning, so do not forsake H5989
Pr 4: 9 *She will* g you a garland to grace your H5989
Pr 4:26 **G careful thought** *to* the paths for your H7143
Pr 6: 3 exhaustion—and g your neighbor **no rest**! H8104
Pr 14: 8 the prudent is *to* **g thought** *to* their ways, H1067
Pr 14:15 the prudent **g thought** to their steps. H1067
Pr 21:26 but the righteous g without sparing. H5989
Pr 21:29 the upright **g thought** *to* their ways. H1067
Pr 23:26 **g** me your heart and let your eyes delight H5989
Pr 25:21 enemy is hungry, g him food **to eat**; if he is H430
Pr 25:21 if he is thirsty, g him water **to drink**. H9197
Pr 25:26 the righteous *who* **g way** to the wicked. H4572
Pr 27:23 g careful attention to your herds H8883
Pr 28:27 *Those who* g to the poor will lack nothing H5989
Pr 29:11 Fools g full **vent to** their rage, but the wise H3655
Pr 29:17 and *they will* g you **peace**; they will H5663
Pr 30: 8 from me; g me neither poverty nor riches H5989
Pr 30: 8 riches, but g me only my daily bread. H3271
Pr 30:15 has two daughters. '**G**! Give!' they cry. H2035
Pr 30:15 two daughters. 'Give! **G**!' they cry. H2035
Ecc 3: 6 a time to search and a time to **g up**, a time to H6
Ecc 10: 1 dead flies g perfume **a bad smell**, H944+5580
Ecc 11: 9 and *let* your heart g you **joy** in the days of H3512
SS 7:12 are in bloom—there *I will* g you my love. H5989
SS 8: 2 *I would* g you spiced wine **to drink**, the H9197
SS 8: 7 If one *were to* g all the wealth of one's H5989
SS 8:12 But my own vineyard is mine to g H4200+7156
Isa 7:14 the Lord himself *will* g you a sign: H5989
Isa 7:14 virgin *will* conceive and **g birth** *to* a son, H3528
Isa 7:22 of the abundance of the milk *they* g, H6913
Isa 11: 4 with justice *he will* g **decisions** for the H3519
Isa 12: 4 "**G praise** to the LORD, proclaim his name H3344
Isa 13:10 the moon *will* not g its light. H5585
Isa 19:11 counselors of Pharaoh g **senseless** advice. H1279
Isa 22:25 peg driven into the firm place *will* **g way**; H4631
Isa 24:15 Therefore in the east **g glory** *to* the LORD H3877
Isa 26:17 woman about to **g birth** writhes and cries H3528
Isa 26:19 the earth *will* **g birth** *to* her dead. H5877
Isa 29:11 And if *you* g the scroll to someone who H5989
Isa 29:12 Or if you g the scroll to someone who H5989
Isa 30:10 "G us no *more* **visions** *of* what is right! H2600
Isa 33:11 conceive chaff, *you* **g birth** *to* straw; your H3528
Isa 34: 2 *he will* g them **over** to slaughter. H5989
Isa 35: 3 steady the knees *that* **g way**; H4173
Isa 36: 8 *I will* g you two thousand horses—if you H5989
Isa 37:17 **G ear**, LORD, and hear; open your H5742+265
Isa 41:28 no *one* among the gods *to* **g counsel**, no H3446
Isa 41:28 no *one to* g answer when I ask them. H8740
Isa 42:12 *Let them* g glory to the LORD and proclaim H8492
Isa 43: 3 your Savior; *I* g Egypt for your ransom H5989
Isa 43: 4 *I will* g people in exchange for you H5989
Isa 43: 6 to the north, '**G** them **up**!' and to the H5989
Isa 43:20 wasteland, to **g drink** *to* my people, my H9197
Isa 45: 3 *I will* g you hidden treasures, riches stored H5989
Isa 45:11 or g me **orders** about the work of my H7422
Isa 49:20 small for us; g us **more space** to live in. H5602
Isa 53:12 Therefore *I will* g him **a portion** among H2745
Isa 55: 3 **G ear** and come to me; listen, that H5742+265
Isa 56: 5 to them *I will* g within my temple and its H5989
Isa 56: 5 *I will* g them an everlasting name that H5989
Isa 56: 7 mountain and g them **joy** in my house of H8523
Isa 59: 4 they conceive trouble and **g birth** *to* evil. H3528
Isa 62: 6 who call on the LORD, g yourselves no rest, H4200
Isa 62: 7 g him no rest till he establishes H5989
Isa 62: 8 "Never again *will I* g your grain as food H5989
Isa 65:15 to his servants *he will* g another name. H7924
Isa 66: 9 to the moment of birth and not g **delivery**?" H3528
Jer 3:15 Then *I will* g you shepherds after my own H5989
Jer 3:19 my children and g you a pleasant land, H5989
Jer 6:10 To whom can I speak and **g warning** H6386
Jer 7:22 *I did* not *just* g them **commands** about H7422
Jer 8:10 Therefore *I will* g their wives to other men H5989
Jer 11: 5 to g them a land flowing with milk and H5989
Jer 12: 7 *I will* g the one I love into the hands of H5989
Jer 13:16 **G** glory to the LORD your God before he H5989
Jer 14:13 *I will* g you lasting peace in this place. H5989
Jer 15:13 your treasures *I will* g as plunder, H5989
Jer 16: 7 nor *will anyone* g them **a drink** to H9197+3926
Jer 17: 3 all your treasures *I will* **g away** as plunder, H5989
Jer 18: 2 there *I will* g you my message. H9048
Jer 18:21 So g their children **over** to famine; hand H5989
Jer 19: 7 and *I will* g their carcasses as food to the H5989
Jer 20: 4 *I will* g all Judah into the hands of the H5989
Jer 20:13 Sing to the LORD! **G praise** *to* the LORD! H2146
Jer 21: 7 the LORD, *I will* g Zedekiah king of Judah H5989
Jer 24: 7 *I will* g them a heart to know me, that I am H5989
Jer 27: 4 **G** them **a message** for their masters and H7422
Jer 27: 5 are on it, and *I* g it to anyone I please. H5989
Jer 27: 6 Now I *will* g all your countries into the H5989
Jer 28:14 *I will* even g him control over the wild H5989
Jer 29: 6 g your daughters **in marriage**, H5989+4200+408
Jer 29:11 plans to g you hope and a future. H5989
Jer 31: 2 wilderness; I will come to **g rest** *to* Israel." H8089
Jer 31:13 *I will* g them **comfort** and joy instead of H5714
Jer 32: 3 I *am about to* g this city into the hands of H5989
Jer 32:22 land you had sworn to g their ancestors, H5989
Jer 32:28 I *am about to* g this city into the hands of H5989
Jer 32:39 *I will* g them singleness of heart and H5989
Jer 32:42 so I *will* g them all the prosperity I have H995
Jer 33:11 "**G thanks** *to* the LORD Almighty, for H3344
Jer 34: 2 I *am about to* g this city into the hands of H5989
Jer 34:22 I *am going to* **g the order**, declares the H7422
Jer 35: 2 of the LORD and g them wine **to drink**." H9197
Jer 38:15 Zedekiah, "If *I* g you **an answer**, will you H5583
Jer 38:15 Even if *I did* g you **counsel**, you would not H3619
Jer 46:26 *I will* g them into the hands of those who H5989
La 2:18 a river day and night; g yourself no relief H5989
Eze 2: 8 open your mouth and eat what I g you." H5989
Eze 3:17 I speak and g them **warning** from me. H2302
Eze 7:21 *I will* g their wealth as plunder to H5989
Eze 11:17 and *I will* g you **back** the land of Israel H5989
Eze 11:19 *I will* g them an undivided heart and put a H5989
Eze 11:19 heart of stone and g them a heart of flesh H5989
Eze 16:33 but you g gifts to all your lovers H5989
Eze 16:34 you g payment and none is given to H5989
Eze 16:61 *I will* g them to you as daughters, but not H5989
Eze 20:28 land I had sworn to g them and they saw H5989
Eze 20:42 with uplifted hand to g to your ancestors. H5989
Eze 21:22 to g *the* **command** to slaughter H7337+7023
Eze 21:27 belongs shall come; to him *I will* g it. H5989
Eze 23: 8 *She did* not **g up** the prostitution she H6440
Eze 23:46 them and g them **over** to terror and H5989
Eze 25: 4 therefore I *am going to* g you to the H5989
Eze 25: 7 hand against you and g you as plunder to H5989
Eze 25:10 *I will* g Moab along with the Ammonites H5989
Eze 29: 5 *I will* g you as food to the beasts of the H5989
Eze 29:19 I *am going to* g Egypt to Nebuchadnezzar H5989
Eze 32: 7 the moon *will* not g its **light**. H239+240
Eze 33: 7 I speak and g them **warning** from me. H2302
Eze 33:15 if they **g back** what they took in pledge H8740
Eze 33:15 follow the **decrees** *that* g life, and do no AIT
Eze 33:27 out in the country *I will* g to the wild H5989
Eze 35: 6 *I will* g you **over** to bloodshed and it will H6913
Eze 36:26 *I will* g you a new heart and put a new H5989
Eze 36:26 heart of stone and g you a heart of flesh. H5989
Eze 39: 4 *I will* g you as food to all kinds of carrion H5989
Eze 39:11 " 'On that day *I will* g Gog a burial place H5989
Eze 43:19 *You are to* g a young bull as a sin offering H5989
Eze 44: 5 closely and g attention *to* everything I tell H8492
Eze 44: 5 **G** attention to the entrance to the temple H8492
Eze 44:28 *You are to* g them no possession in Israel H5989
Eze 44:30 *You are to* g them the first portion of your H5989
Eze 45: 6 " '*You are to* g the city as its property an H5989
Eze 45: 9 **G up** your violence and oppression and H6073
Eze 45:16 of the land *will be* **required to g** this H2118+448
Eze 46: 7 lambs as much as he **wants to g**, H5952+3338
Eze 46:18 *He is to* g his sons their **inheritance** out of H5706
Eze 47:14 uplifted hand to g it to your ancestors, H5989
Eze 47:23 there *you are to* g them their inheritance," H5989
Da 1:12 **G** us nothing but vegetables to eat and H5989
Da 3:28 command and *were willing to* **g up** their A10314
Da 5:16 able to g **interpretations** and to A10599+10600
Da 5:17 gifts for yourself and g your rewards to A10314
Da 9:18 **G ear**, our God, and hear; open your H5742+265
Da 9:22 have now come to g you **insight** and H8505
Da 11:17 *he will* g him a daughter **in marriage** H5989+2021+851
Hos 2: 5 *who* g me my food and my water H5989
Hos 2:15 There *I will* g her **back** her vineyards, and H5989
Hos 4:10 have deserted the LORD to g *themselves* H9068
Hos 5: 7 *they* **g birth** *to* illegitimate children. H3528
Hos 9:14 **G** them, LORD—what will you give them H5989
Hos 9:14 what *will you* g them? Give them H5989
Hos 9:14 **G** them wombs that miscarry and breasts H5989
Hos 11: 8 "How *can I* g you **up**, Ephraim? How can I H5989
Hos 13:10 you said, '**G** me a king and princes'? H5989
Am 2:10 in the wilderness to g you the land of the H3769
Am 9: 9 "For I *will* g *the* **command**, and I will H7422
Jnh 3: 2 proclaim to it the message I g you." H1819
Jnh 3: 8 *Let* them **g up** their evil ways and H8740+4946
Jnh 4: 6 up over Jonah to g shade for his head to H2118
Mic 1:14 Therefore *you will* g parting gifts to H5989
Mic 4:13 for *I will* g you horns of iron H8492
Mic 4:13 *I will* g you hooves of bronze H8492
Mic 6:14 what you save *I will* g to the sword. H5989
Mic 6:16 Therefore I *will* g you **over** to ruin and H5989
Na 2:10 Hearts melt, knees **g way**, bodies tremble H7211
Hab 2: 1 what **answer** *I am to* g to this H8740
Hab 2:19 *Can* it g **guidance**? It is H3723
Zep 3:19 *I will* g them praise and honor in every H8492
Zep 3:20 *I will* g you honor and praise among all H5989
Hag 1: 5 "**G careful thought** to your ways H8492+4222
Hag 1: 7 "**G careful thought** to your ways H8492+4222
Hag 2:15 " 'Now **g careful thought** to this H8492+4222
Hag 2:18 **g careful thought** to the day when H8492+4222
Hag 2:18 temple was laid. **G careful thought**: H8492+4222
Zec 3: 7 and *I will* g you a place among these H5989
Zec 8:12 *I will* g all these things **as an inheritance** *to* H5706
Zec 10: 2 that are false, *they* g **comfort** in vain. H5714
Zec 11: 6 "I *will* g everyone into the hands of their H5162
Zec 11:12 you think it best, g me my pay; but if not, H2035
Mal 1:14 male in his flock and **vows to g** it, H5623
Mt 1:21 *She will* **g birth to** a son, and you are to *G5503*
Mt 1:21 and *you are to* g him the name Jesus *G2813*
Mt 1:23 virgin will conceive and **g birth to** a son, *G5503*
Mt 4: 9 "All this *I will* g you," he said, "if you will *G1443*
Mt 5:31 divorces his wife *must* g her a certificate *G1443*
Mt 5:42 **G** to the one who asks you, and do not *G1443*
Mt 6: 2 "So when *you* **g to the needy**, do *G4472+1797*
Mt 6: 3 But *when* you **g to the needy**, do *G4472+1797*
Mt 6:11 **G** us today our daily bread. *G1443*
Mt 7: 6 "*Do* not g dogs what is sacred; do not *G1443*
Mt 7: 9 son asks for bread, *will* g him a stone? *G2113*
Mt 7:10 Or if he asks for a fish, *will* g him a snake? *G2113*
Mt 7:11 know how *to* g good gifts to your children *G1443*
Mt 7:11 more *will* your Father in heaven g good *G1443*
Mt 10: 8 Freely you have received; freely **g**. *G1443*
Mt 10:12 As you enter the home, g it *your* **greeting**. *G832*
Mt 11:28 weary and burdened, and I *will* g you **rest**. *G399*
Mt 12:36 that everyone *will have to* g account on the *G625*
Mt 14: 7 with an oath *to* g her whatever she *G1443*
Mt 14: 8 "**G** me here on a platter the head of John *G1443*
Mt 14:16 You g them something to eat. *G1443*
Mt 16:19 *I will* g you the keys of the kingdom of *G1443*
Mt 16:26 Or what *can* anyone g in exchange for *G1443*
Mt 17:27 Take it and g it to them for my tax and *G1443*
Mt 19: 7 Moses command *that* a man g his wife a *G1443*
Mt 19:18 not steal, *you shall* not **g false testimony**, *G6018*
Mt 19:21 sell your possessions and g to the poor *G1443*
Mt 20:14 I want *to* g the one who was hired last the *G1443*
Mt 20:28 and *to* g his life as a ransom for many." *G1443*
Mt 21:41 who *will* g him his **share** of the crop at *G625*
Mt 22:21 "So **g back** to Caesar what is Caesar's *G625*
Mt 23:23 *You* **g a tenth** of your spices—mint, dill *G620*

Mt 24:29 the moon *will* not g its light; the stars *G1443*
Mt 24:45 in his household *to* g them their food at *G1443*
Mt 25: 8 said to the wise, '**G** us some of your oil *G1443*
Mt 25:28 of gold from him and g it to the one who *G1443*
Mt 25:37 thirsty and g you **something to drink**? *G4540*
Mt 26:15 are you willing *to* g me if I deliver him *G1443*
Mt 27:64 So g **the order** *for* the tomb to be made *G3027*
Mk 5:43 told them *to* g her something to eat. *G1443*
Mk 6:22 anything you want, and *I'll* g it to you." *G1443*
Mk 6:23 "Whatever you ask *I will* g you, up to half *G1443*
Mk 6:25 "I want *you* to g me right now the head of *G1443*
Mk 6:37 answered, "You g them something to eat." *G1443*
Mk 6:37 much on bread and g it to them to eat?" *G1443*
Mk 7: 3 *they* g their hands **a ceremonial washing**, *G3782*
Mk 8:37 Or what *can* anyone g in exchange for *G1443*
Mk 10:19 *you shall* not g **false testimony**, you *G6018*
Mk 10:21 everything you have and g to the poor, *G1443*
Mk 10:45 and *to* g his life as a ransom for many." *G1443*
Mk 12: 9 those tenants and g the vineyard to others *G1443*
Mk 12:17 "**G back** to Caesar what is Caesar's and to *G625*
Mk 13:24 the moon *will* not g its light; *G1443*
Mk 14:11 hear this and promised *to* g him money. *G1443*
Lk 1:31 You will conceive and g **birth to** a son, and *G5503*
Lk 1:32 The Lord God *will* g him the throne of his *G1443*
Lk 1:77 *to* g his people the knowledge of *G1443*
Lk 4: 6 "*I will* g you all their authority and *G1443*
Lk 4: 6 and *I can* g it to anyone I want to. *G1443*
Lk 6:30 **G** to everyone who asks you, and if anyone *G1443*
Lk 6:38 **G**, and it will be given to you. A good *G1443*
Lk 7:44 *You did* not g me any water for my feet *G1443*
Lk 7:45 *You did* not g me a kiss, but this woman *G1443*
Lk 8:55 Jesus told them *to* g her something to *G1443*
Lk 9:13 replied, "You g them something to eat." *G1443*
Lk 10: 7 eating and drinking whatever they g you *G4123*
Lk 11: 3 **G** us each day our daily bread. *G1443*
Lk 11: 7 I can't get up and g you anything.' *G1443*
Lk 11: 8 will not get up and g you the bread *G1443*
Lk 11: 8 surely get up and g you as much as you *G1443*
Lk 11:11 asks for a fish, *will* g him a snake instead? *G2113*
Lk 11:12 he asks for an egg, *will* g him a scorpion? *G2113*
Lk 11:13 know how *to* g good gifts to your children *G1443*
Lk 11:13 more *will* your Father in heaven g the *G1443*
Lk 11:42 because *you* g God **a tenth** of your mint *G620*
Lk 12:32 has been pleased *to* g you the kingdom. *G1443*
Lk 12:33 your possessions and g **to the poor**. *G1443+1797*
Lk 12:42 charge of his servants *to* g them their food *G1443*
Lk 13:15 from the stall and lead it out *to* g it **water**? *G4540*
Lk 14: 9 say to you, '**G** this person your seat. *G1443*
Lk 14:12 "When *you* g a luncheon or dinner *G4472*
Lk 14:13 But when *you* g a banquet, invite the poor *G4472*
Lk 14:33 of you who *do* not g **up** everything you *G698*
Lk 15:12 g me my share of the estate.' *G1443*
Lk 16: 2 **G** an account of your management *G625*
Lk 16:12 who *will* g you property of your own? *G1443*
Lk 17:18 Has no one returned *to* g praise to God *G1443*
Lk 18: 1 they should always pray and not g **up**. *G1591*
Lk 18:12 I fast twice a week and g **a tenth** of all I get *G620*
Lk 18:20 *you shall* not g **false testimony**, honor *G6018*
Lk 18:22 everything you have and g to the poor, *G1344*
Lk 19: 8 *Here and now I* g half of my possessions *G1443*
Lk 19:24 away from him and g it to the one who *G1443*
Lk 20:10 the tenants so *they would* g him some of *G1443*
Lk 20:16 those tenants and g the vineyard to others *G1443*
Lk 20:25 "Then g **back** to Caesar what is Caesar's *G625*
Lk 21:15 For I *will* g you words and wisdom that *G1443*
Lk 22: 5 delighted and agreed *to* g him money. *G1443*
Lk 24:30 broke it and *began to* g it to them. *G2113*
Jn 1:22 **G** us an answer to take back to those who NDT
Jn 4: 7 Jesus said to her, "*Will you* g me a drink?" *G1443*
Jn 4:14 drinks the water I g them will never thirst. *G1443*
Jn 4:14 the water *I* g them will become in them a *G1443*
Jn 4:15 g me this water so that I won't get thirsty *G1443*
Jn 5:21 Son gives life to whom he is pleased to g it. NDT
Jn 6:27 which the Son of Man *will* g you. *G1443*
Jn 6:30 "What sign then *will* you g that we may *G4472*
Jn 6:34 they said, "always g us this bread. *G1443*
Jn 6:51 which I *will* g for the life of the world." *G1443*
Jn 6:52 "How can this man g us his flesh to eat?" *G1443*
Jn 9:24 "**G** glory to God by telling the truth," *G1443*
Jn 10:28 I g them eternal life, and they shall never *G1443*
Jn 11:22 even now God *will* g you whatever you *G1443*
Jn 13:26 the one to whom I *will* g this piece of *G1443*
Jn 13:29 the festival, or to g something to the poor. *G1443*
Jn 13:34 "A new command *I* g you: Love one *G1443*
Jn 14:16 and *he will* g you another advocate to *G1443*
Jn 14:27 with you; my peace *I* g you. I do not give *G1443*
Jn 14:27 I *do* not g to you as the world gives *G1443*
Jn 15:16 you ask in my name the Father *will* g you. *G1443*
Jn 16:23 my Father *will* g you whatever you ask in *G1443*
Jn 17: 2 all people that *he might* g eternal life to *G1443*
Jn 18:40 **G** us Barabbas!" Now Barabbas NDT
Ac 2:45 possessions *to* g to anyone who had *G1374*
Ac 3: 6 I do not have, but what I do have *I* g you. *G1443*
Ac 6: 4 *will* g *our* **attention** to prayer and the *G4674*
Ac 8:19 "**G** me also this ability so that everyone *G1443*
Ac 12:23 because Herod *did* not g praise to God *G1443*
Ac 13:34 " '*I will* g you the holy and sure blessings *G1443*
Ac 20:32 build you up and g you an inheritance *G1443*
Ac 20:35 'It is more blessed *to* g than to receive.' " *G1443*
Ac 21:26 to the temple *to* g **notice** of the date *G1334*
Ac 23:21 Don't g **in to** them, because more than *G4275*
Ac 24:23 under guard but *to* g him some freedom *G2400*

Ro 2: 7 honor and immortality, he will g eternal life. NDT
Ro 8:11 from the dead *will* also g **life** to your *G2443*
Ro 8:32 along with him, **graciously** g us all things? *G5919*
Ro 12: 8 is to encourage, then g encouragement; if it NDT
Ro 12: 8 if it is giving, then g generously; if it is to NDT
Ro 12:20 if he is thirsty, g him **something to drink**. *G4540*
Ro 13: 6 *who* g *their* **full time** to governing. *G4674*
Ro 13: 7 **G** to everyone what you owe them: If you *G625*
Ro 14: 6 to the Lord, for *they* g **thanks** to God; and *G2373*
Ro 14:12 each of us *will* g an account of ourselves *G1443*
Ro 15: 5 *May* the God who gives endurance and encouragement g *G1443*
Ro 16: 2 of his people and *to* g her any help she *G4225*
1Co 7:10 To the married *I* g *this* **command** (not I *G4133*
1Co 7:25 but *I* g a judgment as one who by the *G1443*
1Co 10:16 which *we* g **thanks** a participation in *G2328*
1Co 11:34 when I come *I will* g further **directions**. *G1411*
1Co 13: 3 If *I* g all I possess **to the poor** and give *G6039*
1Co 13: 3 g **over** my body *to hardship* that I *G4140*
1Co 15:58 Always g *yourselves* **fully** to the work of *G4355*
1Co 16: 3 I will g letters of introduction to the men *G1328*
2Co 1:11 Then many *will* g **thanks** on our behalf *G2373*
2Co 4: 6 in our hearts to g us the **light** of the *G5895*
2Co 8:10 the first not only *to* g but also to have the *G4472*
2Co 9: 2 last year you in Achaia were ready to g; NDT
2Co 9: 7 Each of you should g what you have decided NDT
2Co 9: 7 what you have decided in your heart to g, NDT
Gal 2: 5 *We did* not g **in** to them for a *G1634+3836+5717*
Gal 3: 5 *does* God g you his Spirit and work *G2220*
Gal 6: 9 we will reap a harvest *if we do* not g **up**. *G1725*
Eph 1:17 *may* g you the Spirit of wisdom and *G1443*
Eph 4:27 and *do* not g the devil a foothold. *G1443*
Php 2:30 the help you yourselves **could not** g me. *G5729*
Col 4:15 **G** my **greetings** to the brothers and sisters at *G832*
1Th 5:18 g **thanks** in all circumstances; for this is *G2373*
2Th 1: 7 g relief to you who are troubled, and to NDT
2Th 3:16 Now *may* the Lord of peace himself g you *G1443*
1Ti 4:15 matters; g **yourself wholly** to them, so *G3509*
1Ti 5: 3 **G proper recognition** to those widows *G5506*
1Ti 5: 7 **G** the people these **instructions**, so that no *G4133*
1Ti 5:14 their homes and *to* g the enemy no *G1443*
2Ti 2: 7 the Lord *will* g you insight into all this. *G1443*
2Ti 4: 1 his kingdom, *I* g you *this* **charge**: *G1371*
Heb 4:13 eyes of him to whom we must g account. NDT
Heb 6:14 you and g you **many descendants**." *G4437+4437*
Heb 13:17 over you as *those who must* g an account. *G625*
Jas 1:18 He chose *to* g us **birth** through the word of *G652*
1Pe 3: 6 do what is right and *do* not g **way to** fear. *G5828*
1Pe 3:15 Always be prepared to g an answer to AIT
1Pe 3:15 to everyone who **asks** you *to* g the reason AIT
1Pe 4: 5 But they *will have to* g account to him who *G625*
1Jn 5:16 you should pray and God *will* g them life. *G1443*
Rev 2: 7 *I will* g *the right* to eat from the tree of life *G1443*
Rev 2:10 and *I will* g you life as your victor's crown. *G1443*
Rev 2:17 *I will* g some of the hidden manna. *G1443*
Rev 2:17 *I will* also g that person a white stone *G1443*
Rev 2:26 end, *I will* g authority over the nations— *G1443*
Rev 2:28 *I will* also g that one the morning star. *G1443*
Rev 3:21 *I will* g *the right* to sit with me on my *G1443*
Rev 4: 9 Whenever the living creatures g glory *G1443*
Rev 10: 9 angel and asked him *to* g me the little *G1443*
Rev 11:17 "*We* g **thanks** to you, Lord God Almighty *G2373*
Rev 12: 2 out in pain *as she was about to* g **birth**. *G5503*
Rev 12: 4 of the woman who was about to g **birth**, *G5503*
Rev 13:15 was given power *to* g breath to the image *G1443*
Rev 14: 7 "Fear God and g him glory, because *G1443*
Rev 17:13 one purpose and *will* g their power and *G1443*
Rev 18: 6 **G back** to her as she has given; pay her *G625*
Rev 18: 7 **G** her as much torment and grief as the *G1443*
Rev 19: 7 us rejoice and be glad and g him glory! *G1443*
Rev 21: 6 To the thirsty I *will* g water without cost *G1443*
Rev 22: 5 for the Lord God *will* g them **light**. *G5894*
Rev 22:12 and *I will* g to each person according to *G625*
Rev 22:16 my angel *to* g you this **testimony** for the *G3455*

GIVEN (483) [GIVE]

Ge 9: 2 fish in the sea; *they* **are** g into your hands. H5989
Ge 15: 3 Abram said, "*You have* g me no children H5989
Ge 24:19 After *she had* g him **a drink**, she said, "I'll H9197
Ge 24:35 *He has* g him sheep and cattle, silver H5989
Ge 24:36 and *he has* g him everything he owns. H5989
Ge 26:18 the same names his father *had* g them. H7924
Ge 26:22 "Now the LORD *has* g us **room** and we will H8143
Ge 27:41 of the blessing his father *had* g him. H1385
Ge 28: 4 your descendants the **blessing** g *to* Abraham, AIT
Ge 30: 6 has listened to my plea and g me a son." H5989
Ge 31: 9 father's livestock and *has* g them to me. H5989
Ge 33: 5 children God *has* **graciously** g your servant H2858
Ge 38:14 she *had* not **been** g to him as his wife. H5989
Ge 40:16 Joseph *had* g a favorable **interpretation**, H7354
Ge 41:32 reason the dream **was** g to Pharaoh in H9101
Ge 43:23 father, *has* g you treasure in your sacks H5989
Ge 46:18 whom Laban *had* g to his daughter Leah H5989
Ge 46:25 whom Laban *had* g to his daughter H5989
Ge 48: 9 "They are the sons God *has* g me here," H5989
Ex 4:21 all the wonders *I have* g you the power to H8492
Ex 5:16 Your servants **are** g no straw, yet we are H5989
Ex 5:18 You *will* not **be** g any straw, yet you must H5989
Ex 16:15 "It is the bread the LORD *has* g you to eat. H5989
Ex 16:29 mind that the LORD *has* g you the Sabbath; H5989
Ex 28: 3 workers *to* whom *I have* g wisdom in such H4848
Ex 31: 6 Also *I have* g ability to all the skilled H5989

Ex 34:32 commands the LORD *had* g him on Mount H1819
Ex 35:34 And *he has* g both him and Oholiab son H5989
Ex 36: 1 to whom the LORD *has* g skill and ability to H5989
Ex 36: 2 person *to* whom the LORD *had* g ability H5989
Lev 6:17 *I have* g it as their share of the food H5989
Lev 7:34 is presented and *have* g them to Aaron H5989
Lev 10:11 decrees the LORD *has* g them through H1819
Lev 10:14 *they have* **been** g *to* you and your children H5989
Lev 10:17 it *was* g to you to take away the guilt of H5989
Lev 17:11 I *have* g it to you to make atonement H5989
Lev 19:20 has not been ransomed or g her freedom, H5989
Lev 26:25 and *you will* **be** g into enemy hands. H5989
Lev 27: 9 such an animal g to the LORD becomes H5989
Nu 3: 9 *who are to* **be** g **wholly** to him. H5989+5989
Nu 5: 8 to the LORD and must be g to the priest, NDT
Nu 8:16 *who are to* **be** g **wholly** to me. H5989+5989
Nu 8:19 *I have* g the Levites as gifts to Aaron and H5989
Nu 16:14 milk and honey or g us an inheritance of H5989
Nu 18:29 holiest part of everything g *to* you. H5510
Nu 21:29 *He has* g **up** his sons as fugitives and his H5989
Nu 27:12 the land *I have* g the Israelites. H5989
Nu 32: 5 "*let* this land **be** g to your servants as our H5989
Nu 32: 7 over into the land the LORD *has* g them? H5989
Nu 32: 9 entering the land the LORD *had* g them. H5989
Nu 33:53 for *I have* g you the land to possess. H5989
Nu 34:13 has ordered that it *be* g to the nine and a H5989
Nu 35: 8 possess *are to be* g in proportion to H5989
Dt 1: 8 *I have* g you this land. Go in and take H5989
Dt 1:21 the LORD your God *has* g you the land. H5989
Dt 2: 5 *I have* g Esau the hill country of Seir as H5989
Dt 2: 9 *I have* g Ar to the descendants of Lot as a H5989
Dt 2:19 *I have* g it as a possession to the H5989
Dt 2:24 *I have* g into your hand Sihon the Amorite H5989
Dt 3:18 "The LORD your God *has* g you this land to H5989
Dt 3:19 may stay in the towns *I have* g you, H5989
Dt 3:20 go back to the possession *I have* g you." H5989
Dt 6:17 stipulations and decrees *he has* g you. H7422
Dt 8:10 your God for the good land *he has* g you. H5989
Dt 9:23 take possession of the land *I have* g you." H5989
Dt 12: 1 your ancestors, *has* g you to possess—as H5989
Dt 12:21 the herds and flocks the LORD *has* g you, H5989
Dt 16:10 the **blessings** the LORD your God *has* g you H1385
Dt 22:19 because this man *has* g an Israelite virgin H3655
Dt 26:10 of the soil that *you*, LORD, *have* g me." H5989
Dt 26:11 the LORD your God *has* g to you and your H5989
Dt 26:13 sacred portion and *have* g it to the Levite, H5989
Dt 26:15 the land *you have* g us as you H5989
Dt 28:31 Your sheep *will* **be** g to your enemies H5989
Dt 28:32 daughters *will* **be** g to another nation H5989
Dt 28:53 daughters the LORD your God *has* g you. H5989
Dt 29: 4 day the LORD *has* not g you a mind that H5989
Dt 29:26 did not know, gods *he had* not g them. H2745
Dt 32:30 unless the LORD *had* g them **up**? H6037
Jos 2: 9 that the LORD *has* g you this land and H5989
Jos 2:24 "The LORD *has* surely g the whole land H5989
Jos 6:16 For the LORD *has* g you the city! H5989
Jos 9:19 "We *have* g them *our* **oath** by the LORD H8678
Jos 10: 8 of them; *I have* g them into your hand. H5989
Jos 10:19 the LORD your God *has* g them into your H5989
Jos 13: 8 that Moses *had* g them east of the H5989
Jos 13:15 This is what Moses *had* g to the tribe of H5989
Jos 13:24 This is what Moses *had* g to the tribe of H5989
Jos 13:29 This is what Moses *had* g to the half-tribe H5989
Jos 13:32 is *the* **inheritance** Moses *had* g when he H5706
Jos 13:33 Moses *had* g no inheritance; the H5989
Jos 15:19 Since *you have* g me land in the Negev H5989
Jos 17:14 "Why *have you* g us only one allotment H5989
Jos 18: 3 the God of your ancestors, *has* g you? H5989
Jos 21:12 around the city *they had* g to Caleb son of H5989
Jos 21:21 country of Ephraim they *were* g Shechem H5989
Jos 21:26 their pasturelands were g to the rest of the NDT
Jos 21:27 Levite clans of the Gershonites were g: H4200
Jos 21:34 the Merarite clans ... were g: H4200
Jos 22: 4 LORD your God *has* g them **rest** as he H5663
Jos 22: 7 Manasseh Moses *had* g land in Bashan, H5989
Jos 23: 1 the LORD *had* g Israel **rest** from all H5663
Jos 23:13 which the LORD your God *has* g you. H5989
Jos 23:15 you from this good land *he has* g you. H5989
Jos 23:16 perish from the good land *he has* g you." H5989
Jdg 1: 2 *I have* g the land into their hands. H5989
Jdg 1:15 Since *you have* g me land *in* the Negev H5989
Jdg 1:20 promised, Hebron *was* g to Caleb, who H5989
Jdg 3: 4 which *he had* g their ancestors through H7422
Jdg 3:28 "for the LORD *has* g Moab, your enemy, H5989
Jdg 4:14 is the day the LORD *has* g Sisera into your H5989
Jdg 6:13 abandoned us and g us into the hand of H5989
Jdg 7:14 God *has* g the Midianites and the whole H5989
Jdg 7:15 The LORD *has* g the Midianite camp into H5989
Jdg 8: 7 when the LORD *has* g Zebah and H5989
Jdg 11:24 whatever the LORD our God *has* g us, we H3769
Jdg 11:36 "*you have* g your **word** to the H7198+906+7023
Jdg 14:16 *You've* g my people a riddle, but you H2554
Jdg 14:20 And Samson's wife *was* g to one of his H2118
Jdg 15: 6 because his wife *was* g to his companion." H5989
Jdg 15:18 "You *have* g your servant this great victory. H5989
Jdg 20:36 the men of Israel *had* g way before H5989
Jdg 21:14 at that time and *were* g the women of H5989
Ru 4:15 to you than seven sons, *has* g him **birth**." H3528
1Sa 1:28 whole life he *will* **be** g **over** to the LORD." H8626
1Sa 4:20 "Don't despair; *you have* g **birth** to a son." H3528
1Sa 14:10 sign that the LORD *has* g them into our H5989
1Sa 14:12 the LORD *has* g them into the hand of H5989

1Sa 15:28 from you today and *has* g it to one of your H5989
1Sa 18:19 Saul's daughter, *to be* g to David, she H5989
1Sa 18:19 she **was** g **in marriage** to H5989+4200+851
1Sa 25:27 *let* this gift, which your servant has brought to my lord, **be** g H5989
1Sa 25:44 But Saul *had* g his daughter Michal H5989
1Sa 28:17 out of your hands and g it to one of your H5989
1Sa 30:23 not do that with what the LORD *has* g us. H5989
2Sa 7: 1 the LORD *had* g him **rest** from all his H5663
2Sa 9: 9 "*I have* g your master's grandson H5989
2Sa 12: 8 *I would have* g you **even more** H3578+3869+2179+2256+3869+2179
2Sa 13:28 Haven't I g you *this* **order**? Be strong and H7422
2Sa 16: 8 The LORD *has* g the kingdom into the H5989
2Sa 17: 6 "Ahithophel *has* g this advice. H1819
2Sa 17: 7 "The **advice** Ahithophel *has* g is H3619+6783
2Sa 21: 6 *let* seven of his male descendants **be** g to H5989
1Ki 2:21 *Let* Abishag the Shunammite **be** g **in marriage** H5989+4200+851
1Ki 3: 3 to the **instructions** *g* him *by* his father AIT
1Ki 3: 6 to him and *have* g him a son to sit H5989
1Ki 3:28 Israel heard the verdict the king *had* g, H9149S
1Ki 5: 4 LORD my God *has* g me **rest** on every side, H5663
1Ki 5: 7 for *he has* g David a wise son to rule over H5989
1Ki 8:56 who *has* g rest to his people Israel just as H5989
1Ki 9: 6 decrees *I have* g you and go off to H5989
1Ki 9: 7 from the land *I have* g them and will H5989
1Ki 9:12 to see the towns that Solomon *had* g him, H5989
1Ki 9:13 kind of towns are these *you have* g me, H5989
1Ki 10:13 besides what *he had* g her out of his royal H5989
1Ki 12:13 Rejecting the **advice** g him by the H3619+6783
1Ki 13: 5 to the sign g *by* the man of God by the H5989
1Ki 13:26 The LORD *has* g him **over** to the lion, which H5989
1Ki 15:29 the word of the LORD g through his servant H1819
1Ki 18:26 they took the bull g them and prepared it H5989
1Ki 20:27 were also mustered and g **provisions**, H3920
2Ki 5: 1 him the LORD *had* g victory to Aram. H5989
2Ki 5:17 "please *let me*, your servant, **be** g as H5989
2Ki 15:20 shekels of silver to *be* g to the king of H5989
2Ki 18: 6 the commands the LORD *had* g Moses. H7422
2Ki 18:30 this city *will* not **be** g into the hand of the H5989
2Ki 19:10 'Jerusalem *will* not **be** g into the hands of H5989
2Ki 22:10 "Hilkiah the priest *has* g me a book." H5989
1Ch 5: 1 rights as firstborn **were** g to the sons of H5989
1Ch 6:55 They *were* g Hebron in Judah with its H5989
1Ch 6:56 around the city *were* g to Caleb son of H5989
1Ch 6:57 descendants of Aaron *were* g Hebron H5989
1Ch 6:60 the tribe of Benjamin they were g Gibeon, NDT
1Ch 6:66 Kohathite clans *were* g as their territory H2118
1Ch 6:67 country of Ephraim they *were* g Shechem H5989
1Ch 16:40 Law of the LORD, which *he had* g Israel. H7422
1Ch 22:18 For *he has* g the inhabitants of the land H5989
1Ch 25: 5 They were g him through the promises of NDT
1Ch 28: 5 the LORD *has* g me many—he has H5989
1Ch 29: 9 for *they had* g **freely** and wholeheartedly H5605
1Ch 29:14 and *we have* g you only what comes from H5989
1Ch 29:17 these things *I have* g **willingly** and with H5605
1Ch 29:17 **willingly** your people who are here *have* g H5605
2Ch 1:12 wisdom and knowledge *will* **be** g you. H5989
2Ch 2:12 *He has* g King David a wise son H5989
2Ch 2:14 can execute any design g to him. H5989
2Ch 7:19 commands *I have* g you and go off to H5989
2Ch 7:20 my land, which *I have* g them, and will H5989
2Ch 8: 2 rebuilt the villages that Hiram *had* g him, H5989
2Ch 13: 5 *has* g the kingship of Israel to David and H5989
2Ch 14: 7 him and *he has* g us **rest** on every side H5663
2Ch 18:14 "for *they will* **be** g into your hand. H5989
2Ch 20:27 the LORD *had* g them **cause to rejoice** over H8523
2Ch 20:30 his God *had* g him **rest** on every side. H5663
2Ch 21: 3 Their father *had* g them many gifts of H5989
2Ch 21: 3 but *he had* g the kingdom to Jehoram H5989
2Ch 28: 5 *He* **was** also g into the hands of the king H5989
2Ch 31:14 in charge of the **freewill offerings** *g to* God, AIT
2Ch 32:29 God *had* g him very great riches. H5989
2Ch 33: 8 decrees and regulations g through Moses." NDT
2Ch 34:14 of the LORD that had been g through Moses. NDT
2Ch 34:18 "Hilkiah the priest *has* g me a book." H5989
2Ch 36:23 *has* g me all the kingdoms of the earth H5989
Ezr 1: 2 *has* g me all the kingdoms of the earth H5989
Ezr 6: 9 must be g them daily without fail A10314
Ezr 7: 6 which the LORD, the God of Israel, *had* g. H5989
Ezr 7:11 King Artaxerxes *had* g to Ezra the priest, H5989
Ezr 7:15 his advisers *have* **freely** g to the God of A10461
Ezr 9: 9 he *has* g us a wall of protection in H5989
Ezr 9:13 sins deserved and *have* g us a remnant H5989
Ne 7:72 The total g *by* the rest of the people was H5989
Ne 10:29 the Law of God g through Moses the H5989
Ne 12:43 because God *had* g them great **joy**. H8523+8525
Ne 13:10 to the Levites *had* not **been** g to them, H5989
Est 2: 3 and *let* beauty treatments **be** g *to* them. H5989
Est 2:13 she wanted **was** g her to take with H5989
Est 5: 3 up to half the kingdom, *it will* **be** g you." H5989
Est 5: 6 your petition? *It will* **be** g you. And what is H5989
Est 7: 2 your petition? *It will* **be** g you. What is H5989
Est 8: 7 the Jews, *I have* g his estate to Esther H5989
Est 9:12 your petition? *It will* **be** g you. What is H5989
Job 3:20 "Why *is* light g to those in misery, and life H5989
Job 3:23 Why is life g to a man whose way is hidden NDT
Job 15:19 alone the land **was** g when no foreigners H5989
Job 38:12 "*Have you* ever g **orders** *to* the morning H7422
Ps 31: 8 *You have* not g me into the hands of the H6037
Ps 60: 3 *you have* g us wine that makes us stagger. H9197
Ps 61: 5 *you have* g me the heritage of those who H5989
Ps 63:10 They *will be* g **over** *to* the H5599+6584+3338
Ps 72:15 *May* gold from Sheba *be* g him. H5989
Ps 74: 9 *We* **are** g no signs from God; no prophets H8011
Ps 78:29 gorged—*he had* g them what they craved. H995
Ps 94:17 Unless the LORD had g me help, I would NDT
Ps 105:42 his holy promise g to his servant Abraham. H907
Ps 115:16 but the earth *he has* g to mankind. H5989
Ps 118:18 but *he has* not g me **over** to death. H5989
Ps 119:49 to your servant, for *you have* g me **hope**. H3498
Ps 122: 4 LORD according to the statute **g to** Israel. H4200
Pr 8:24 watery depths, *I* **was** g **birth**, when there H2655
Pr 8:25 in place, before the hills, *I* **was** g **birth**, H2655
Pr 21:14 A gift g in secret soothes anger, and a bribe NDT
Pr 23: 2 your throat if you are g **to gluttony**. H1251+5883
Pr 25:11 in settings of silver is a ruling rightly g. H1819
Pr 25:14 is one who boasts of **gifts never** g. H5522+9214
Ecc 5:18 the few days of life God *has* g them— H5989
Ecc 8:15 of the life God *has* g them under the sun. H5989
Ecc 9: 9 life that God *has* g you under the sun— H5989
Ecc 12:11 embedded nails—g by one shepherd. H5989
Isa 1: 4 of evildoers, children **g to corruption**! H8845
Isa 8:18 and the children the LORD *has* g me. H5989
Isa 9: 6 to us a son **is** g, and the H5989
Isa 14:32 What **answer** *shall* **be** g *to* the envoys of H6699
Isa 23: 4 "I have neither been in labor nor g **birth**; H3528
Isa 23:11 *He has* **g an order** concerning Phoenicia H7422
Isa 34:16 For it is his mouth *that has* g *the* **order** H7422
Isa 35: 2 The glory of Lebanon *will* **be** g to it, the H5989
Isa 36:15 this city *will* not **be** g into the hand of the H5989
Isa 37:10 'Jerusalem *will* not **be** g into the hands of H5989
Isa 50: 4 The Sovereign LORD *has* g me a H5989
Isa 63:14 they *were* g **rest** *by* the Spirit of the LORD. H5663
Isa 64: 7 from us and *have* g us **over** to our sins. H4481
Jer 4:31 fainting; my life is **g over to** murderers." H4200
Jer 8:13 What *I have* g them will be taken from H5989
Jer 8:14 perish and g us poisoned water **to drink**, H9197
Jer 21:10 *It will* **be** g into the hands of the king of H5989
Jer 32: 4 but *will* **certainly be** g into the H5989+5989
Jer 32:16 "After I *had* g the deed of purchase to H5989
Jer 32:24 the city *will* **be** g into the hands of the H5989
Jer 32:25 though the city *will* **be** g into the hands of H5989
Jer 32:36 plague *it will* **be** g into the hands H5989
Jer 32:43 for *it has* **been** g into the hands of the H5989
Jer 34: 3 surely be captured and g into his hands. H5989
Jer 35:15 live in the land *I have* g to you and your H5989
Jer 37:21 of the guard and g a loaf of bread from H5989
Jer 38: 3 'This city *will* **certainly be** g into the H5989+5989
Jer 38:16 the LORD lives, who *has* g us breath, I will H6913
Jer 38:18 this city *will* **be** g into the hands of the H5989
Jer 39:11 of Babylon *had* g *these* **orders** about H7422
Jer 39:17 *you will* not **be** g into the hands of those H5989
Jer 46:24 g into the hands of the people of the H5989
La 1:14 *He has* g me into the hands of those I H5989
La 2: 7 *He has* g the walls of her palaces into the H6037
La 3:15 with bitter herbs and g me gall **to drink**. H8115
La 4:11 The LORD *has* g **full vent** *to* his wrath; he H3983
Eze 11:15 this land **was** g to us as our possession. H5989
Eze 11:24 in the vision g **by** the Spirit of God. H928
Eze 15: 6 As *I have* g the wood of the vine among H5989
Eze 16:14 the splendor *I had* g you made your H8492
Eze 16:34 you give payment and none **is** g to you. H5989
Eze 17:18 *he had* g his hand **in pledge** and yet H5989
Eze 20:15 bring them into the land *I had* g them— H5989
Eze 29:20 *I have* g him Egypt as a reward for his H5989
Eze 33:24 surely the land *has* **been** g to us as our H5989
Eze 35:12 laid waste and *have been* g **over** to us to H5989
Eze 46: 5 The grain offering g with the ram is to be an NDT
Da 2:23 *You have* g me wisdom and power, you A10314
Da 2:37 God of heaven *has* g you dominion and A10314
Da 4:16 of a man and *let* him **be** g the mind of A10314
Da 5:21 away from people and g the mind of an A10702
Da 5:28 is divided and g to the Medes and A10314
Da 7: 4 the mind of a human **was** g to it. A10314
Da 7: 6 and it **was** g authority to rule. A10314
Da 7:14 He **was** g authority, glory and sovereign A10314
Da 8:12 the daily sacrifice **were** g **over** to it. H5989
Da 8:26 mornings that *has* **been** g you is true, H606
Da 9: 2 the word of the LORD g to Jeremiah the H2118
Da 10: 1 a revelation **was** g to Daniel (who was H1655
Da 10:19 my lord, since *you have* g me **strength**." H2616
Da 11: 4 empire will be uprooted and g to others. H4200
Da 11:21 person who *has* not *been* g the honor of H5989
Hos 6:10 There Ephraim is **g to** prostitution, Israel H4200
Joel 2:23 *for he has* g you the autumn rains H5989
Am 6:11 For the LORD *has* **g the command**, and he H7422
Am 9:15 be uprooted from the land *I have* g them," H5989
Na 1:14 The LORD *has* **g a command** concerning H7422
Zec 6: 8 country *have* g my Spirit **rest** in the land H5663
Zec 6:14 The crown will be g to Heldai, Tobijah H4200
Zec 13: 6 'The **wounds** *I* **was** g at the house of my H5782
Mt 6:33 all these things *will be* g to you **as well**. *G4707*
Mt 7: 7 "Ask and *it will be* g to you; seek and you *G1443*
Mt 9: 8 who *had* g such authority to man. *G1443*
Mt 10:19 At that time you *will be* g what to say, *G1443*
Mt 12:39 But none *will be* g it except the sign of *G1443*
Mt 13:11 kingdom of heaven *has been* g to you, *G1443*
Mt 13:12 Whoever has *will be* g *more*, and they will *G1443*
Mt 14:11 brought in on a platter and g to the girl, *G1443*
Mt 15:36 and *when he had* g **thanks**, he broke *G2373*
Mt 16: 4 none *will be* g it except the sign of *G1443*
Mt 19:11 only those to whom *it has been* g. *G1443*
Mt 21:43 away from you and g to a people who will *G1443*
Mt 22:30 will neither marry nor *be* g **in marriage**; *G1139*
Mt 25:29 For whoever has *will be* g *more*, and they *G1443*
Mt 26: 9 a high price and the money g to the poor." *G1443*
Mt 26:26 and *when he had* g **thanks**, he broke *G2328*
Mt 26:27 and *when he had* g **thanks**, he gave *G2373*
Mt 27:58 Pilate ordered *that it be* g to him. *G625*
Mt 28:18 heaven and on earth *has been* g to me. *G1443*
Mk 4:11 of the kingdom of God *has been* g to you. *G1443*
Mk 4:25 Whoever has *will be* g more; whoever *G1443*
Mk 6: 2 "What's this wisdom that *has been* g him? *G1443*
Mk 6:17 Herod himself *had* g **orders** to have John *G690*
Mk 8: 6 had taken the seven loaves and g **thanks**, *G2373*
Mk 8:12 Truly I tell you, no sign *will be* g to it." *G1443*
Mk 12:25 will neither marry nor *be* g **in marriage**; *G1139*
Mk 12:28 that Jesus *had* g them **a** good **answer**, *G646*
Mk 13:11 Just say whatever *is* g you at the time, for *G1443*
Mk 14: 5 wages and the money g to the poor." *G1443*
Mk 14:22 and *when he had* g **thanks**, he broke *G2328*
Mk 14:23 and *when he had* g **thanks**, he gave *G2373*
Lk 2:21 the **name** the angel *had* g him before he *G2813*
Lk 4: 6 splendor; *it has been* g to me, and I *G4140*
Lk 6:38 and *it will be* g to you. A good *G1443*
Lk 8:10 of the kingdom of God *has been* g to you, *G1443*
Lk 8:18 Whoever has *will be* g *more*; whoever *G1443*
Lk 10:19 *I have* g you authority to trample on *G1443*
Lk 11: 9 Ask and *it will be* g to you; seek and you *G1443*
Lk 11:29 none *will be* g it except the sign of *G1443*
Lk 12:31 these things *will be* g to you **as well**. *G4707*
Lk 12:48 From everyone who *has been* g much *G1443*
Lk 17:27 and *being* g **in marriage** up to the *G1139*
Lk 19:15 servants to whom *he had* g the money, *G1443*
Lk 19:26 who has, *more will be* g, but as for the *G1443*
Lk 20:34 of this age marry and *are* g **in marriage**. *G1140*
Lk 20:35 will neither marry nor *be* g **in marriage**, *G1139*
Lk 22:19 "This is my body g for you; do this in *G1443*
Jn 1:16 received grace **in place of** grace **already** g. *G505*
Jn 1:17 For the law *was* g through Moses; grace *G1443*
Jn 3:27 can receive only *what* is g them from *G1443*
Jn 4: 5 of ground Jacob *had* g to his son Joseph. *G1443*
Jn 4:10 him and *he* would have g you living *G1443*
Jn 5:27 And *he has* g him authority to judge *G1443*
Jn 5:36 works that the Father *has* g me to finish— *G1443*
Jn 6:23 the bread *after* the Lord *had* g **thanks**. *G2373*
Jn 6:32 it is not Moses *who has* g you the bread *G1443*
Jn 6:39 shall lose none of all those *he has* g me, *G1443*
Jn 7:19 *Has* not Moses g you the law? Yet not one *G1443*
Jn 7:39 Up to that time the Spirit *had* not *been* g *G1639*
Jn 10:29 My Father, who *has* g them to me, is *G1443*
Jn 11:57 the Pharisees *had* g orders that *G1443*
Jn 12: 2 Here a dinner *was* g in Jesus' honor *G4472*
Jn 12: 5 sold and the money g to the poor? *G1443*
Jn 17: 2 eternal life to all those *you have* g him. *G1443*
Jn 17: 7 everything *you have* g me comes from *G1443*
Jn 17: 9 for those *you have* g me, for they are *G1443*
Jn 17:14 I *have* g them your word and the world *G1443*
Jn 17:22 I *have* g them the glory that you gave me *G1443*
Jn 17:24 I want those *you have* g me to be with me *G1443*
Jn 17:24 the glory *you have* g me because you *G1443*
Jn 18:11 I not drink the cup the Father *has* g me?" *G1443*
Jn 19:11 me if it were not g to you from above. *G1443*
Jn 19:35 The man who saw it *has* g **testimony**, and *G3455*
Ac 4:12 name under heaven g to mankind by *G1443*
Ac 5:32 whom God *has* g to those who obey him." *G1443*
Ac 7:53 the law that was g through angels but *G1408*
Ac 8:18 saw that the Spirit *was* g at the laying on *G1443*
Ac 17:31 *He has* g proof of this to everyone by *G4218*
Ac 20:24 the task the Lord Jesus *has* g *me*— *G3284+4123*
Ac 27:24 God *has* **graciously** g you the lives of *G5919*
Ro 3:22 This righteousness is *g* **through** faith in Jesus AIT
Ro 5: 5 the Holy Spirit, who *has been* g to us. *G1443*
Ro 5:13 sin was in the world before the law was g NDT
Ro 11:35 "Who *has ever* g to God, that God should *G4594*
Ro 12: 3 For by the grace g me I say to every one of *G1443*
Ro 12: 6 according to the grace g to each of us. *G1443*
1Co 1: 4 because of his grace g you in Christ Jesus. *G1443*
1Co 2:12 may understand what God *has* **freely** g us. *G5919*
1Co 3:10 By the grace God *has* g me, I laid a *G1443*
1Co 4: 2 those who have been **g a trust** must prove *G3874*
1Co 11:15 For long hair *is* g to her as a covering *G1443*
1Co 11:24 and *when he had* g **thanks**, he broke it *G2373*
1Co 12: 7 of the Spirit *is* g for the common good. *G1443*
1Co 12: 8 To one *there is* g through the Spirit a *G1443*
1Co 12:13 and *we were* all g the one Spirit **to drink**. *G4540*
2Co 4:11 are alive are always *being* g **over** to death *G4140*
2Co 5: 5 who *has* g us the Spirit as a deposit *G1443*
2Co 7: 7 also by the comfort you *had* g *him*. *G4151S*
2Co 8: 1 the grace that God *has* g the Macedonian *G1443*
2Co 9: 5 a generous gift, not as **one grudgingly** g. *G4432*
2Co 9:14 of the surpassing grace God *has* g you. *G2093*
2Co 12: 7 conceited, I *was* g a thorn in my flesh *G1443*
Gal 2: 9 when they recognized the grace g to me. *G1443*
Gal 3:14 the blessing *g to* **Abraham** might come to AIT
Gal 3:19 was the law g at all? It was added NDT
Gal 3:19 The law *was* g through angels and *G1411*
Gal 3:21 For if a law *had been* g that could impart *G1443*
Gal 3:22 being **g through** faith in Jesus Christ *G1666*
Gal 3:22 *might be* g to those who believe. *G1443*
Gal 4:15 torn out your eyes and g them to me. *G1443*
Eph 1: 6 which *he has* **freely** g us in the One he *G5923*
Eph 3: 2 of God's grace that *was* g to me for you, *G1443*
Eph 3: 7 gift of God's grace g me through the *G1443*

Eph 3: 8 the Lord's people, this grace *was* g me: *G1443*
Eph 4: 7 each one of us grace *has been* g as Christ *G1443*
Eph 4:19 they *have* g themselves **over** to sensuality *G4140*
Eph 6:19 words *may be* g me so that I will *G1443*
1Th 1: 6 suffering with the joy *g by* the Holy **Spirit**. AIT
1Ti 1:12 our Lord, who *has* g me **strength**, that he *G1904*
1Ti 3: 3 not **g to drunkenness**, not violent but *G4232*
1Ti 4:14 which *was* g you through prophecy when *G1443*
2Ti 1: 9 This grace *was* g us in Christ Jesus before *G1443*
Titus 1: 7 not **g to drunkenness**, not violent, *G4232*
Phm 7 Your love *has* g *me* great joy and *G2400*
Heb 2:13 and the children God *has* g me. *G1443*
Heb 4: 8 For if Joshua *had* g them **rest**, God would *G2924*
Heb 7:11 indeed *the* **law** g *to* the people *G3793*
Jas 1: 5 finding fault, and *it will be* g to you. *G1443*
1Pe 1: 3 great mercy *he has* g us **new birth** into a *G335*
2Pe 1: 3 His divine power *has* g us everything we *G1563*
2Pe 1: 4 Through these *he has* g us his very great *G1563*
2Pe 3: 2 the command *g by* our **Lord** and Savior AIT
1Jn 4:13 *He has* g us of his Spirit. *G1443*
1Jn 4:21 And he *has* g *us* this command *G2400+608*
1Jn 5: 9 which *he has* g about his Son. *G3455S*
1Jn 5:10 the testimony God *has* g about his Son. *G3455S*
1Jn 5:11 God *has* g us eternal life, and this life is *G1443*
1Jn 5:20 God has come and *has* g us *G1443*
2Jn 4 *It has* g *me* great **joy** to find some of your *G5897*
Rev 2:21 *I have* g her time to repent of her *G1443*
Rev 6: 2 and he *was* g a crown, and he *G1443*
Rev 6: 4 Its rider *was* g power to take peace from *G1443*
Rev 6: 4 To him *was* g a large sword. *G1443*
Rev 6: 8 They *were* g power over a fourth of the *G1443*
Rev 6:11 Then each of them *was* g a white robe *G1443*
Rev 7: 2 angels who *had been* g *power* to harm *G1443*
Rev 8: 2 and seven trumpets *were* g to them. *G1443*
Rev 8: 3 He *was* g much incense to offer, with the *G1443*
Rev 9: 1 The star *was* g the key to the shaft of the *G1443*
Rev 9: 3 on the earth and *were* g power like that of *G1443*
Rev 11: 1 I *was* g a reed like a measuring rod and *G1443*
Rev 11: 2 because *it has been* g to the Gentiles. *G1443*
Rev 12:13 the woman who *had* **g birth** to the male *G5503*
Rev 12:14 The woman *was* g the two wings of a *G1443*
Rev 13: 4 dragon because *he had* g authority to the *G1443*
Rev 13: 5 The beast *was* g a mouth to utter proud *G1443*
Rev 13: 7 It *was* g power to wage war against God's *G1443*
Rev 13: 7 And it *was* g authority over every tribe *G1443*
Rev 13:14 of the signs it *was* g power to perform on *G1443*
Rev 13:15 The second beast *was* g power to give *G1443*
Rev 15: 2 They held harps g them *by* **God** AIT
Rev 16: 6 and *you have* g them blood to drink as *G1443*
Rev 18: 6 Give back to her as she *has* g; pay her back *G625*
Rev 19: 8 bright and clean, *was* g her to wear." *G1443*
Rev 20: 4 seated those *who had been* g authority to *G1443*

GIVER (2) [GIVE]

Pr 18:16 way and ushers the g into the presence of H132S
2Co 9: 7 compulsion, for God loves a cheerful **g**. *G1522*

GIVES (130) [GIVE]

Ex 4:11 Who g them sight or makes them blind NDT
Ex 13:11 land of the Canaanites and g it to you, H5989
Ex 16: 8 was the LORD when *he* g you meat to eat H5989
Ex 16:29 on the sixth day he g you bread for two H5989
Ex 21: 4 If his master g him a wife and she bears H5989
Ex 21:22 and she **g birth prematurely** but H3655+3529
Ex 22: 7 "If anyone g a neighbor silver or goods H5989
Ex 22:10 "If anyone g a donkey, an ox, a sheep H5989
Lev 12: 2 pregnant and **g birth** *to* a son will be H3528
Lev 12: 5 If *she* **g birth** *to* a daughter, for two weeks H3528
Lev 12: 7 the *woman who* **g birth** to a boy or a H3528
Nu 10:32 you whatever good things the LORD g us." H3512
Nu 16:22 the **God** *who* g breath to all living things AIT
Nu 22: 8 to you with the answer the LORD g me." H1819
Nu 27:16 the **God** *who* g breath to all living things AIT
Dt 3:20 the LORD **g rest** to your fellow H5663
Dt 4:40 land the LORD your God g you for all time. H5989
Dt 7:16 peoples the LORD your God **g over** to you. H5989
Dt 8:18 it is he who g you the ability to H5989
Dt 12:15 to the blessing the LORD your God g you. H5989
Dt 16: 5 in any town the LORD your God g you H5989
Dt 17: 2 of the towns the LORD g you is found doing H5989
Dt 19: 8 g you the whole land he promised H5989
Dt 20:14 the LORD your God g you from your H5989
Dt 22:14 slanders her and g her a bad name H3655
Dt 24: 1 g it to her and sends her from his house H5989
Dt 24: 3 g it to her and sends her from his house H5989
Dt 25:19 the LORD your God g you **rest** from all the H5663
Jos 1:15 the LORD g them **rest**, as he has done H5663
Jos 2:14 faithfully when the LORD g us the land." H5989
Jdg 11: 9 Ammonites and the LORD g them to me— H5989
Jdg 11:24 not take what your god Chemosh g you? H3769
Jdg 21:18 'Cursed be *anyone who* g a wife to a' H5989
Ru 4:12 the offspring the LORD g you by this young H5989
2Sa 22:51 "*He* g his king **great** victories; he shows H1540
2Sa 24:23 Majesty, Araunah g all this to the king." H5989
Ezr 9: 8 so our God **g light** *to* our eyes and a H239
Est 5:13 But all this g me no **satisfaction** as long as H8750
Job 8:15 the web, but *it* **g way**; they cling to H4202+6641
Job 32: 8 the Almighty, *that* g them **understanding**. H1067
Job 33: 4 the breath of the Almighty g me **life**. H2649
Job 35:10 God my Maker, *who* g songs in the night, H5989
Job 36: 6 the wicked alive but g the afflicted their H5989
Job 38:29 Who **g birth** *to* the frost from the heavens H3528
Job 38:36 Who g the ibis wisdom or gives the H8883
Job 38:36 gives the ibis wisdom or g the rooster H5989
Ps 7:14 trouble and **g birth** *to* disillusionment. H3528
Ps 18:50 *He* g his king **great** victories; he shows H1540
Ps 20: 6 The LORD **g victory** *to* his anointed H3828
Ps 29:11 The LORD g strength to his people; the H5989
Ps 68:35 the God of Israel g power and strength to H5989
Ps 119:130 The unfolding of your words **g light**; H239
Ps 119:130 *it* **g understanding** *to* the simple. H1067
Ps 119:174 salvation, LORD, and your law g me delight. NDT
Ps 136:25 *He* g food to every creature. His love H5989
Ps 144:10 to the *One who* g victory to kings, who H5989
Ps 146: 7 the oppressed and g food to the hungry. H5989
Ps 146: 8 the LORD **g sight** *to* the blind, the LORD lifts H7219
Pr 2: 6 For the LORD g wisdom; from his mouth H5989
Pr 5: 6 *She* g no **thought** *to* the way of life; her H7143
Pr 11:24 *One person* g **freely**, yet gains even more H7061
Pr 14:30 A heart at peace g life to the body, but envy NDT
Pr 15:30 good news g **health** *to* the bones. H2014
Pr 16:20 *Whoever* g **heed** to instruction prospers H8505
Pr 17: 8 is seen as a charm by the **one who** g it; H1251
Pr 19: 6 everyone is the friend of **one** *who* g gifts. AIT
Pr 22:16 wealth and *one who* g **gifts** to the rich— H5989
Pr 25:18 sharp arrow is one *who* g false testimony H6699
Pr 29: 4 By justice a king g a country **stability**, but H6641
Pr 29:13 The LORD g **sight** *to* the eyes of both H239
Ecc 2:26 pleases him, God g wisdom, knowledge H5989
Ecc 2:26 to the sinner *he* g the task of H5989
Ecc 5:19 when God g someone wealth and H5989
Ecc 6: 2 God g some people wealth, possessions H5989
Isa 14: 3 On the day the LORD g you **relief** from your H5663
Isa 21: 9 And *he* g **back** *the* **answer**: 'Babylon H6699
Isa 30:20 Although the Lord g you the bread of H5989
Isa 40:29 *He* g strength to the weary and increases H5989
Isa 42: 5 springs from it, *who* g breath to its people H5989
Isa 66: 7 goes into labor, *she* **g birth**; before the H3528
Isa 66: 8 in labor than *she* g **birth** *to* her children. H3528
Jer 5:24 who g autumn and spring rains in season H5989
La 4: 4 beg for bread, but no *one* g it to them. H7298
Eze 18: 7 commit robbery but g his food to the H5989
Eze 18:16 commit robbery but g his food to the H5989
Da 2:21 *He* g wisdom to the wise and knowledge A10314
Da 4:17 on earth and g them to anyone he A10498
Da 4:25 on earth and g them to anyone he A10498
Da 4:32 on earth and g them to anyone he A10498
Hab 2:15 "Woe to *him who* g **drink** *to* his neighbors, H9197
Zec 10: 1 *He* g showers of rain to all people, and H5989
Mt 5:15 and *it* **g light** to everyone in the house. *G3290*
Mt 10:42 anyone g even a cup of cold **water to** one *G4540*
Mt 26:73 of them; your accent g you **away**." *G1316+4472*
Mk 1:27 *He* even g **orders** to impure spirits and *G2199*
Mk 9:41 anyone *who* g you **a cup** of water *G4540+4539*
Lk 4:36 power *he* g **orders** to impure spirits *G2199*
Jn 1: 9 The true light that g **light to** everyone was *G5894*
Jn 3: 6 Flesh g **birth to** flesh, but the Spirit gives *G1164*
Jn 3: 6 to flesh, but the Spirit g **birth** *to* spirit. *G1164*
Jn 3:34 for God g the Spirit without limit. *G1443*
Jn 5:21 Father raises the dead and g them **life**, *G2443*
Jn 5:21 even so the Son g **life** to whom he is *G2443*
Jn 6:32 it is my Father *who* g you the true bread *G1443*
Jn 6:33 down from heaven and g life to the world." *G1443*
Jn 6:37 All those the Father g me will come to me *G1443*
Jn 6:63 The Spirit g **life**; the flesh counts for *G2443*
Jn 14:27 I do not give to you as the world g. Do not *G1443*
Ac 17:25 *he* himself g everyone life and breath *G1443*
Ro 4:17 the God who g **life** to the dead and calls *G2443*
Ro 8: 2 law of the Spirit who *g* **life** has set you free AIT
Ro 8:10 the Spirit g life because of righteousness. NDT
Ro 14: 6 does so to the Lord and **g thanks** to God. *G2373*
Ro 15: 5 May the God who g endurance and NDT
1Co 15:38 But God g it a body as he has determined *G1443*
1Co 15:38 to each kind of seed he g its own body. NDT
1Co 15:57 He g us the victory through our Lord Jesus *G1443*
2Co 3: 6 the letter kills, but the Spirit g **life**. *G2443*
Php 4:13 all this through him *who* g me **strength**. *G1904*
Col 1: 9 understanding **that the Spirit g**, *G4461*
1Th 4: 8 the very God *who* g you his Holy Spirit. *G1443*
1Ti 6:13 sight of God, who g **life** to everything, and *G2441*
2Ti 1: 7 not make us timid, but g us power, love NDT
Jas 1: 5 who g generously to all without finding *G1443*
Jas 1:15 has conceived, *it* **g birth** to sin; and sin, *G5503*
Jas 1:15 when it is full-grown, g **birth** to death. *G652*
Jas 1:25 intently into the perfect law that g **freedom**, AIT
Jas 2:12 to be judged by the law *that g* **freedom**, AIT
Jas 4: 6 But *he* g us more grace. That is why *G1443*
Rev 21:23 the glory of God g it **light**, and the *G5894*

GIVING (121) [GIVE]

Ge 13:17 breadth of the land, for *I am* g it to you." H5989
Ge 20:16 "*I am* g your brother a thousand shekels H5989
Ge 30:18 has rewarded me for g my servant to my H5989
Ge 38:28 As she *was* **g birth**, one of them put out H3528
Ge 41:12 g each man *the* **interpretation** *of* his H7354
Ge 49:28 g each the **blessing** appropriate to H1385+1388
Ge 49:33 had finished g **instructions** *to* his sons, H7422
Ex 20:12 in the land the LORD your God *is* g you. H5989
Lev 14:34 which I *am* g you as your possession H5989
Lev 27: 2 to the LORD by g the equivalent value, NDT
Nu 13: 2 of Canaan, which I *am* g to the Israelites. H5989
Nu 15: 2 you enter the land I *am* g you as a home H5989
Nu 18: 7 *I am* g you the service of the priesthood H5989
Dt 1:20 Amorites, which the LORD our God *is* g us. H5989
Dt 1:25 a good land that the LORD our God *is* g us." H5989
Dt 2:29 into the land the LORD our God *is* g us." H5989
Dt 3:20 the LORD your God *is* g them across the H5989
Dt 4: 1 the God of your ancestors, *is* g you. H5989
Dt 4:21 land the LORD your God *is* g you as your H5989
Dt 4:40 commands, which I *am* g you today, so H7422
Dt 5:16 in the land the LORD your God *is* g you. H5989
Dt 5:31 follow in the land I *am* g them to possess." H5989
Dt 8: 1 follow every command I *am* g you today, H7422
Dt 8:11 his decrees that I *am* g you this day. H7422
Dt 9: 6 the LORD your God *is* g you this good land H5989
Dt 10:13 decrees that I *am* g you today for your H7422
Dt 10:18 among you, g them food and clothing. H5989
Dt 11: 8 all the commands I *am* g you today, H7422
Dt 11:13 obey the commands I *am* g you today— H7422
Dt 11:17 from the good land the LORD *is* g you. H5989
Dt 11:22 these commands I *am* g you to follow— H7422
Dt 11:27 the LORD your God that I *am* g you today; H7422
Dt 11:31 of the land the LORD your God *is* g you. H5989
Dt 12: 9 inheritance the LORD your God *is* g you. H5989
Dt 12:10 LORD your God *is* g you **as an inheritance**, H5706
Dt 12:28 to obey all these regulations I *am* g you, H7422
Dt 13:12 towns the LORD your God *is* g you to live in H5989
Dt 13:18 his commands that I *am* g you today and H7422
Dt 15: 4 the LORD your God *is* g you to possess as H5989
Dt 15: 5 all these commands I *am* g you today. H7422
Dt 15: 7 of the land the LORD your God *is* g you, H5989
Dt 16:10 the LORD your God *by* g a freewill offering H5989
Dt 16:18 in every town the LORD your God *is* g you, H5989
Dt 16:20 the land the LORD your God *is* g you. H5989
Dt 17:14 the LORD your God *is* g you and have taken H5989
Dt 18: 9 enter the land the LORD your God *is* g you, H5989
Dt 19: 1 the nations whose land he *is* g you, H5989
Dt 19: 2 the LORD your God *is* g you to possess. H5989
Dt 19: 3 LORD your God *is* g you **as an inheritance**, H5706
Dt 19:10 which the LORD your God *is* g you as your H5989
Dt 19:14 the LORD your God *is* g you to possess. H5989
Dt 19:18 g false **testimony** against a fellow H6699
Dt 20:16 the LORD your God *is* g you as an H5989
Dt 21: 1 the LORD your God *is* g you to possess, H5989
Dt 21:17 as the firstborn by g him a double share H5989
Dt 21:23 the LORD your God *is* g you as an H5989
Dt 24: 4 the LORD your God *is* g you as an H5989
Dt 25:15 in the land the LORD your God *is* g you. H5989
Dt 25:19 you in the land he *is* g you to possess as H5989
Dt 26: 1 the LORD your God *is* g you as an H5989
Dt 26: 2 the LORD your God *is* g you and put them H5989
Dt 27: 2 into the land the LORD your God *is* g you, H5989
Dt 27: 3 enter the land the LORD your God *is* g you, H5989
Dt 28: 8 God will bless you in the land *he is* g you. H5989
Dt 28:15 commands and decrees I *am* g you today, H7422
Dt 28:52 the land the LORD your God *is* g you. H5989
Dt 30: 8 all his commands I *am* g you today. H7422
Dt 32:49 the land I *am* g the Israelites as their own H5989
Dt 32:52 not enter the land I *am* g to the people of H5989
Jos 1:11 the LORD your God *is* g you for your own. H5989
Jos 1:13 God will give you rest *by* g you this land. H5989
Jos 1:15 of the land the LORD your God *is* g them. H5989
Jos 3: 3 g **orders** *to* the people: "When you see the H7422
Jdg 2:23 them out at once *by* g them into the H5989
1Sa 22:13 g him bread and a sword and inquiring of H5989
1Sa 23:20 be responsible for g him into your hands." H6037
2Sa 11:19 you have finished g the king this account H1819
2Sa 18: 5 king g **orders** concerning Absalom *to* each H7422
2Sa 24:12 the LORD says: I am g you three options H5747
1Ch 21:10 the LORD says: I *am* g you three options H5742
Ezr 9: 8 us a remnant and g us a firm place in his H5989
Ne 4:10 "The strength of the laborers *is* **g out**, and H4173
Ne 8: 8 making it clear and g the meaning so that H8492
Est 2:22 it to the king, g **credit** to Mordecai. H928+9005
Est 3: 1 elevating him and g him a seat of honor H8492
Est 9:19 a day for g presents to each other. H5447
Est 9:22 feasting and joy and g presents of food to H5447
Ps 19: 8 of the LORD are right, g **joy** *to* the heart. H8523
Ps 19: 8 of the LORD are radiant, g **light** *to* the eyes. H239
Ps 100: T For g **grateful praise**. H9343
Ps 106: 5 join your inheritance in g **praise**. H2146
Ps 111: 6 g them the lands of other nations. H5989
Pr 1: 4 g prudence to those who are simple H5989
Pr 15:23 person finds joy in **g an apt reply**— H5101+7023
Pr 26: 8 stone in a sling is the g *of* honor to a fool. H5989
Eze 3: 3 eat this scroll I *am* g you and fill your H5989
Eze 11: 2 evil and g wicked **advice** in this city H3619+6783
Eze 16:54 of all you have done in g them **comfort**. H5714
Da 4:21 food for all, *g* **shelter** to the wild animals AIT
Da 6:10 prayed, g **thanks** to his God, just A10312
Da 9:13 from our sins and g **attention** to your truth. H8505
Mt 6: 4 so that your g may be in secret. Then your *G1797*
Mt 24:38 marrying and **g in marriage**, up to the day *G1139*
Jn 16:21 A woman **g birth to a child** has pain *G5503*
Ac 1: 2 *after* g **instructions** through the Holy Spirit *G1948*
Ac 13:19 g their land to his people **as their inheritance** *G2883*
Ac 14:17 has shown kindness *by* g you rain from *G1443*
Ac 15: 8 he accepted them *by* g the Holy Spirit to *G1443*
Ac 22:20 I stood there g *my* **approval** and guarding *G5306*
Ro 12: 8 if it is g, then give generously; *G3556*
1Co 12:24 g greater honor to the parts that lacked it *G1443*
1Co 14:17 You *are* g **thanks** well enough, but no one *G2373*
2Co 5:12 but *are* g you an opportunity to take pride *G1443*
2Co 8: 7 see that you also excel in this **grace of g**. *G5921*
Eph 1:16 I have not stopped **g thanks** for you *G2373*

Eph 5:20 always g thanks to God the Father for G2373
Php 4:15 with me in the matter of g and receiving, G1521
Col 1:12 and g joyful thanks to the Father, who has G2373
Col 3:17 g thanks to God the Father through him. G2373
1Ti 1:18 I am g you this command in keeping with G4192
Heb 10:25 not g up meeting together, as some are in G1593

GIZONITE (1)

1Ch 11:34 the sons of Hashem the G, Jonathan son H1604

GLAD (75) [GLADDENS, GLADLY, GLADNESS]

Ex 4:14 to meet you, and he will be g to see you. H8523
Jos 22:33 They were g to hear the report H3512+928+6524
Jdg 8:25 "We'll be g to give them. H5989+5989
1Sa 19: 5 all Israel, and you saw it and were g. H8523
2Sa 1:20 lest the daughters of the Philistines be g H8523
1Ki 8:66 joyful and g in heart for all the good H3202
1Ch 16:31 let the earth be g; let them say H1635
2Ch 7:10 joyful and g in heart for the good things H3202
Ps 5:11 But let all who take refuge in you be g; let H8523
Ps 9: 2 I will be g and rejoice in you; I will sing H8523
Ps 14: 7 people, let Jacob rejoice and Israel be g! H8523
Ps 16: 9 Therefore my heart is g and my tongue H8523
Ps 21: 6 blessings and made him g with the joy of H2525
Ps 31: 7 I will be g and rejoice in your love, for you H1635
Ps 32:11 in the LORD and be g, you righteous; H1635
Ps 40:16 all who seek you rejoice and be g in you; H8523
Ps 45: 8 ivory the music of the strings makes you g. H8523
Ps 46: 4 whose streams make g the city of God, H8523
Ps 48:11 villages of Judah are g because of your H1635
Ps 53: 6 people, let Jacob rejoice and Israel be g! H8523
Ps 58:10 The righteous will be g when they are H8523
Ps 67: 4 May the nations be g and sing for joy, for H8523
Ps 68: 3 But may the righteous be g and rejoice H8523
Ps 69:32 The poor will see and be g—you who H8523
Ps 70: 4 all who seek you rejoice and be g in you; H8523
Ps 90:14 we may sing for joy and be g all our days. H8523
Ps 90:15 Make us g for as many days as you have H8523
Ps 92: 4 For you make me g by your deeds, LORD; H8523
Ps 96:11 let the earth be g; let the sea H1635
Ps 97: 1 The LORD reigns, let the earth be g; let the H8523
Ps 97: 8 villages of Judah are g because of your H1635
Ps 105:38 Egypt was g when they left, because H8523
Ps 107:30 They were g when it grew calm, and he H8523
Ps 118:24 very day; let us rejoice today and be g. H8523
Ps 149: 2 let the people of Zion be g in their King. H1635
Pr 23:15 then my heart will be g indeed; H8523
Pr 29: 6 the righteous shout for joy and are g. H8523
Ecc 8:15 the sun than to eat and drink and be g. H8523
Isa 25: 9 let us rejoice and be g in his salvation." H8523
Isa 35: 1 desert and the parched land will be g; H8464
Isa 65:18 But be g and rejoice forever in what I will H8464
Isa 66:10 and be g for her, all you who love her H1635
Jer 20:15 who made him very g H8523+8523
Jer 31:13 Then young women will dance and be g H8523
Jer 41:13 officers who were with him, they were g. H8523
Jer 50:11 "Because you rejoice and are g, you who H6600
La 4:21 Rejoice and be g, Daughter Edom, you H8523
Joel 2:21 land of Judah; be g and rejoice. H1635
Joel 2:23 Be g, people of Zion, rejoice in the LORD H1635
Hab 1:15 his dragnet; and so he rejoices and is g. H1635
Zep 3:14 Be g and rejoice with all your heart H8523
Zec 2:10 "Shout and be g, Daughter Zion. For I am H8523
Zec 8:19 become joyful and g occasions and happy H8525
Zec 10: 7 their hearts will be g as with wine. H8523
Mt 5:12 Rejoice and be g, because great is your G22
Lk 15:32 But we had to celebrate and be g G5897
Jn 4:36 sower and the reaper may be g together. G5897
Jn 8:56 of seeing my day; he saw it and was g." G5897
Jn 11:15 for your sake I am g I was not there G5897
Jn 14:28 you would be g that I am going to the G5897
Ac 2:26 Therefore my heart is g and my tongue G2370
Ac 2:46 ate together with g and sincere hearts, G21
Ac 11:23 he was g and encouraged them all to G5897
Ac 13:48 they were g and honored the word of the G5897
Ac 15: 3 This news made all the believers very g. G5915
Ac 15:31 people read it and were g for its G5897
1Co 16:17 I was g when Stephanas, Fortunatus and G5897
2Co 2: 2 who is left to make me g but you whom I G2370
2Co 7:16 I am g I can have complete confidence in G5897
2Co 13: 9 We are g whenever we are weak but you G5897
Gal 4:27 "Be g, barren woman, you who never bore G2370
Php 2:17 I am g and rejoice with all of you. G5897
Php 2:18 So you too should be g and rejoice with G5897
Php 2:28 see him again you may be g and I may G5897
Rev 19: 7 Let us rejoice and be g and give him glory G22

GLADDENS (1) [GLAD]

Ps 104:15 wine that g human hearts, oil to make H8523

GLADLY (11) [GLAD]

Dt 28:47 joyfully and g in the time of H928+3206+4222
Jdg 19: 3 her father saw him, he g welcomed him. H8523
2Ch 24:10 the people brought their contributions g, H8523
Isa 39: 2 Hezekiah received the envoys g and H8523+6584
Isa 64: 5 come to the help of those who g do right, H8464
Jer 3:19 " 'How g would I treat you like my children H375
Lk 19: 6 came down at once and welcomed him g. G5897
Ac 24:10 over this nation; so I g make my defense. G2315
2Co 11:19 You g put up with fools since you are so G2452
2Co 12: 9 boast all the more g about my G2452
2Co 12:15 So I will very g spend for you everything I G2452

GLADNESS (22) [GLAD]

2Ch 29:30 sang praises with g and bowed down H8525
Est 8:16 a time of happiness and joy, g and honor. H8607
Est 8:17 there was joy and g among the Jews, with H8607
Job 3:22 who are filled with g and H8524+448+1637
Ps 35:27 in my vindication shout for joy and g; H8523
Ps 45:15 Led in with joy and g, they enter the H1637
Ps 51: 8 Let me hear joy and g; let the bones you H8525
Ps 65:12 overflow; the hills are clothed with g. H1637
Ps 100: 2 Worship the LORD with g; come before him H8525
Ecc 5:20 God keeps them occupied with g of heart. H8525
Ecc 9: 7 eat your food with g, and drink your wine H8525
Isa 16:10 Joy and g are taken away from the H1637
Isa 35:10 G and joy will overtake them, and sorrow H8607
Isa 51: 3 Joy and g will be found in her H8525
Isa 51:11 G and joy will overtake them, and sorrow H8607
Jer 7:34 sounds of joy and g and to the voices of H8525
Jer 16: 9 sounds of joy and g and to the voices of H8525
Jer 25:10 from them the sounds of joy and g, H8525
Jer 31:13 I will turn their mourning into g; I will give H8607
Jer 33:11 the sounds of joy and g, the voices of H8525
Jer 48:33 Joy and g are gone from the orchards H1637
Joel 1:16 joy and g from the house of our God? H1637

GLANCE (2) [GLANCES]

Pr 23: 5 Cast but a g at riches, and they are gone H6524
SS 4: 9 stolen my heart with one g of your eyes, NDT

GLANCES (1) [GLANCE]

Pr 30:13 so haughty, whose g are so disdainful; H6757

GLASS (4)

GLASS, GLASSES (KJV) MIRROR, MIRRORS

Rev 4: 6 there was what looked like a sea of g, G5612
Rev 15: 2 looked like a sea of g glowing with fire G5612
Rev 21:18 the city of pure gold, as pure as g. G5613
Rev 21:21 city was of gold, as pure as transparent g. G5613

GLAZE (NIV84) DROSS

GLEAM (1) [GLEAMED, GLEAMING]

Da 10: 6 legs like the g of burnished bronze, H6524

GLEAMED (2) [GLEAM]

Eze 1: 7 those of a calf and g like burnished H5913
Lk 24: 4 in clothes that g like lightning stood beside G848

GLEAMING (1) [GLEAM]

Job 20:25 out of his back, the g point out of his liver. H1398

GLEAN (8) [GLEANED, GLEANING, GLEANINGS, GLEANS]

Ru 2: 3 a field and began to g behind the H4377
Ru 2: 7 'Please let me g and gather among the H4377
Ru 2: 8 Don't go and g in another field and don't H4377
Ru 2:15 As she got up to g, Boaz gave orders to his H4377
Ru 2:19 asked her, "Where did you g today? H4377
Ru 2:23 women of Boaz to g until the barley and H4377
Job 24: 6 in the fields and g in the vineyards of the H4380
Jer 6: 9 Let them g the remnant of Israel as thoroughly H6618+6618

GLEANED (1) [GLEAN]

Ru 2:17 So Ruth g in the field until evening. H4377

GLEANING (1) [GLEAN]

Mic 7: 1 summer fruit at the g of the vineyard; H6622

GLEANINGS (5) [GLEAN]

Lev 19: 9 your field or gather the g of your harvest. H4378
Lev 23:22 your field or gather the g of your harvest. H4378
Jdg 8: 2 Aren't the g of Ephraim's grapes better H6622
Isa 17: 6 Yet some g will remain, as when an olive H6622
Isa 24:13 as when g are left after the grape H6622

GLEANS (1) [GLEAN]

Isa 17: 5 as when someone g heads of grain in the H4377

GLEE (2)

Ps 35:15 they gathered in g; assailants gathered H8523
Eze 36: 5 with g and with malice in their hearts H8525

GLIDE (1) [GLIDED, GLIDING]

Dt 32:24 the venom of vipers that g in the dust. H2323

GLIDED (1) [GLIDE]

Job 4:15 A spirit g past my face, and the hair on H2736

GLIDING (2) [GLIDE]

Job 26:13 his hand pierced the g serpent. H1371
Isa 27: 1 Leviathan the g serpent, Leviathan H1371

GLIMPSE (2)

Job 9:25 a runner; they fly away without a g of joy. H8011
Job 23: 9 he turns to the south, I catch no g of him. H8011

GLINT (1)

Hab 3:11 the heavens at the g of your flying arrows, H240

GLISTENING (1)

Job 41:32 It leaves a g wake behind it; one would H239

GLITTERING (3)

Na 3: 3 flashing swords and g spears! H1398

Rev 17: 4 scarlet, and was g with gold, precious G5998
Rev 18:16 scarlet, and g with gold, precious G5998

GLOAT (15) [GLOATED, GLOATING, GLOATS]

Ps 22:17 on display; people stare and g over me. H8011
Ps 30: 1 and did not let my enemies g over me. H8523
Ps 35:19 Do not let those g over me who are my H8523
Ps 35:24 LORD my God; do not let them g over me. H8523
Ps 35:26 May all who g over my distress be put to H8524
Ps 38:16 "Do not let them g or exalt themselves H8523
Ps 59:10 before me and will let me g over those H8011
Pr 24:17 Do not g when your enemy falls; when H8523
Isa 14: 8 the cedars of Lebanon g over you and say, H8523
La 2:17 he has let the enemy g over you, he H8523
Ob 12 You should not g over your brother in the H8011
Ob 13 nor g over them in their calamity in the H8011
Mic 4:11 her be defiled, let our eyes g over Zion!" H2600
Mic 7: 8 Do not g over me, my enemy! Though I H8523
Rev 11:10 of the earth will g over them and will G5897

GLOATED (1) [GLOAT]

Job 31:29 misfortune or g over the trouble that H6424

GLOATING (1) [GLOAT]

Hab 3:14 g as though about to devour the wretched H6617

GLOATS (1) [GLOAT]

Pr 17: 5 whoever g over disaster will not go H8524

GLOOM (12)

Job 3: 5 May g and utter darkness claim it once H3125
Job 10:21 to the land of g and utter darkness, H3125
Isa 8:22 only distress and darkness and fearful g, H5066
Isa 9: 1 will be no more g for those who were in H4599
Isa 24:11 wine; all joy turns to g, all joyful H6845
Isa 29:18 out of g and darkness the eyes of the H694
Jer 13:16 to utter darkness and change it to deep g. H6906
Eze 31:15 Because of it I clothed Lebanon with g H7722
Joel 2: 2 a day of darkness and g, a day of clouds H696
Zep 1:15 a day of darkness and g, a day of clouds H696
Heb 12:18 with fire; to darkness, g and storm; G2432
Jas 4: 9 laughter to mourning and your joy to g. G2993

GLORIES (1) [GLORY]

1Pe 1:11 the Messiah and the g that would follow. G1518

GLORIFIED (17) [GLORY]

Isa 66: 5 have said, 'Let the LORD be g, that we may H3877
Da 4:34 I honored and g him who lives forever. A10198
Jn 7:39 since Jesus had not yet been g. G1519
Jn 11: 4 so that God's Son may be g through it." G1519
Jn 12:16 Only after Jesus was g did they realize G1519
Jn 12:23 has come for the Son of Man to be g. G1519
Jn 12:28 came from heaven, "I have g it, and will G1519
Jn 13:31 "Now the Son of Man is g and God is G1519
Jn 13:31 of Man is glorified and God is g in him. G1519
Jn 13:32 If God is g in him, God will glorify the Son G1519
Jn 14:13 so that the Father may be g in the Son. G1519
Ac 3:13 of our fathers, has g his servant Jesus. G1519
Ro 1:21 they neither g him as God nor gave G1519
Ro 8:30 justified; those he justified, he also g. G1519
2Th 1:10 on the day he comes to be g in his holy G1901
2Th 1:12 name of our Lord Jesus may be g in you, G1901
1Pe 1:21 him from the dead and g him, G1518+1443

GLORIFIES (2) [GLORY]

Lk 1:46 And Mary said: "My soul g the Lord G3486
Jn 8:54 claim as your God, is the one who g me. G1519

GLORIFY (21) [GLORY]

Ps 34: 3 G the LORD with me; let us exalt his name H1540
Ps 63: 3 love is better than life, my lips will g you. H8655
Ps 69:30 name in song and g him with H1540
Ps 86:12 all my heart; I will g your name forever. H3877
Isa 60:13 and I will g the place for my feet. H3877
Da 4:37 exalt and g the King of heaven, A10198
Mt 5:16 your good deeds and g your Father in G1519
Jn 8:54 Jesus replied, "If I g myself, my glory G1519
Jn 12:28 g your name!" Then a voice came G1519
Jn 12:28 "I have glorified it, and will g it again." G1519
Jn 13:32 God will g the Son in himself G1519
Jn 13:32 Son in himself, and will g him at once. G1519
Jn 16:14 He will g me because it is from me that he G1519
Jn 17: 1 the hour has come. G your Son, that your G1519
Jn 17: 1 Glorify your Son, that your Son may g you. G1519
Jn 17: 5 g me in your presence with the glory I had G1519
Jn 21:19 of death by which Peter would g God. G1519
Ro 15: 6 one voice you may g the God and G1519
Ro 15: 9 that the Gentiles might g God for his G1519
1Pe 2:12 good deeds and g God on the day he G1519
Rev 16: 9 they refused to repent and g him. G1443+1518

GLORIFYING (1) [GLORY]

Lk 2:20 g and praising God for all the things they G1519

GLORIOUS (51) [GLORY]

Dt 28:58 not revere this g and awesome name— H3877
Dt 33:29 your shield and helper and your g sword. H1452
1Ch 29:13 give you thanks, and praise your g name. H9514
Ne 9: 5 "Blessed be your g name, and may it be H3883
Ps 45:13 All g is the princess within her chamber H3884
Ps 66: 2 the glory of his name; make his praise g. H3883
Ps 72:19 Praise be to his g name forever; may the H3883
Ps 87: 3 G things are said of you, city of God: H3877

Ps 106:20 exchanged their g God for an image of a H3883
Ps 111: 3 G and majestic are his deeds, and his H2086
Ps 145: 5 They speak of the g splendor of your H3883
Ps 145:12 mighty acts and the g splendor of your H3883
Pr 4: 9 head and present you with a g crown." H9514
Isa 3: 8 against the LORD, defying his g presence. H3883
Isa 4: 2 Branch of the LORD will be beautiful and g, H3883
Isa 11:10 and his resting place will be g. H3883
Isa 12: 5 he has done g things; let this be H1455
Isa 28: 1 the fading flower, his g beauty, set on the H9514
Isa 28: 4 fading flower, his g beauty, set on the H9514
Isa 28: 5 day the LORD Almighty will be a g crown, H9514
Isa 42:21 righteousness to make his law great and g. H158
Isa 60: 7 on my altar, and I will adorn my g temple. H9514
Isa 63:12 who sent his g arm of power to be at H9514
Isa 63:14 people to make for yourself a g name. H9514
Isa 63:15 from your lofty throne, holy and g. H9514
Isa 64:11 Our holy and g temple, where our H9514
Jer 2:11 exchanged their g God for worthless idols H3883
Jer 13:18 your g crowns will fall from your heads." H9514
Jer 14:21 despise us; do not dishonor your g throne. H3883
Jer 17:12 A g throne, exalted from the beginning, is H3883
Jer 48:17 mighty scepter, how broken the g staff! H9514
Hos 4: 7 they exchanged their g God for something H3883
Zec 2: 8 "After the G One has sent me against the H3883
Mt 19:28 when the Son of Man sits on his g throne G1518
Mt 25:31 with him, he will sit on his g throne. G1518
Lk 9:30 appeared in g splendor, talking with G1518
Ac 2:20 coming of the great and g day of the Lord. G2212
2Co 3: 8 the Spirit be even more g? G1877+1518+1506
2Co 3: 9 that brought condemnation was g, G1518
2Co 3: 9 how much more g is the ministry that G1518
2Co 3:10 For what *was* g has no glory now in G1519
Eph 1: 6 to the praise *of* his g grace, which he has G1518
Eph 1:17 Jesus Christ, the g Father, may give you G1518
Eph 1:18 the riches of his g inheritance in his holy G1518
Eph 3:16 I pray that out of his g riches he may G1518
Php 3:21 bodies so that they will be like his g body. G1518
Col 1:11 according to his g might so that you may G1518
Col 1:27 the Gentiles the g riches of this mystery G1518
Jas 2: 1 believers in our g Lord Jesus Christ must G1518
1Pe 1: 8 are filled with an inexpressible and g joy, G1519
Jude 24 you before his g *presence* without fault G1518

GLORY (300) [GLORIES, GLORIFIED, GLORIFIES, GLORIFY, GLORIFYING, GLORIOUS]

Ex 14: 4 But *I will* gain g for myself through H3877
Ex 14:17 And *I will* gain g through Pharaoh and all H3877
Ex 14:18 the LORD when I gain g through Pharaoh, H3877
Ex 15:11 awesome in g, working wonders? H9335
Ex 16: 7 morning you will see the g *of* the LORD, H3883
Ex 16:10 there was the g *of* the LORD appearing H3883
Ex 24:16 the g *of* the LORD settled on Mount H3883
Ex 24:17 To the Israelites the g *of* the LORD looked H3883
Ex 29:43 the place will be consecrated by my g. H3883
Ex 33:18 Then Moses said, "Now show me your g." H3883
Ex 33:22 When my g passes by, I will put you in a H3883
Ex 40:34 the g *of* the LORD filled the tabernacle. H3883
Ex 40:35 the g *of* the LORD filled the tabernacle. H3883
Lev 9: 6 so that the g *of* the LORD may appear to H3883
Lev 9:23 the g *of* the LORD appeared to all the H3883
Nu 14:10 Then the g *of* the LORD appeared at the H3883
Nu 14:21 as surely as the g *of* the LORD fills the H3883
Nu 14:22 of those who saw my g and the signs I H3883
Nu 16:19 the g *of* the LORD appeared to the entire H3883
Nu 16:42 covered it and the g *of* the LORD appeared. H3883
Nu 20: 6 the g *of* the LORD appeared to them. H3883
Dt 5:24 God has shown us his g and his majesty, H3883
Jos 7:19 "My son, give g to the LORD, the God of H3883
1Sa 4:21 "The G has departed from Israel" H3883
1Sa 4:22 She said, "The G has departed from Israel H3883
1Sa 6: 5 the country, and give g to Israel's god. H3883
1Sa 15:29 He who is the G *of* Israel does not lie or H5905
1Ki 8:11 the g *of* the LORD filled his temple. H3883
2Ki 14:10 you are arrogant. G in your victory, but H3877
1Ch 16:10 G in his holy name; let the hearts of those H2146
1Ch 16:24 Declare his g among the nations, his H3883
1Ch 16:28 ascribe to the LORD g and strength. H3883
1Ch 16:29 Ascribe to the LORD the g *due* his name H3883
1Ch 16:35 to your holy name, and g in your praise." H8655
1Ch 29:11 the power and the g and the majesty and H9514
2Ch 5:14 the g *of* the LORD filled the temple of H3883
2Ch 7: 1 the g *of* the LORD filled the temple. H3883
2Ch 7: 2 LORD because the g *of* the LORD filled it. H3883
2Ch 7: 3 down and the g *of* the LORD above the H3883
Est 1: 4 the splendor and g *of* his majesty. H9514
Job 29:20 My g will not fade; the bow will be ever H3883
Job 40:10 Then adorn yourself with g and splendor H1454
Ps 3: 3 shield around me, my g, the One who lifts H3883
Ps 4: 2 will you people turn my g into shame? H3883
Ps 8: 1 You have set your g in the heavens. H2086
Ps 8: 5 crowned them with g and honor. H3883
Ps 19: 1 The heavens declare the g *of* God; the H3883
Ps 21: 5 victories you gave, his g is great; you have H3883
Ps 24: 7 that the King of g may come in. H3883
Ps 24: 8 Who is this King of g? The LORD strong H3883
Ps 24: 9 that the King of g may come in. H3883
Ps 24:10 this King of g? The LORD Almighty— H3883
Ps 24:10 The LORD Almighty—he is the King of g. H3883
Ps 26: 8 you live, the place where your g dwells. H3883
Ps 29: 1 ascribe to the LORD g and strength. H3883
Ps 29: 2 Ascribe to the LORD the g *due* his name H3883
Ps 29: 3 the God of g thunders, the LORD H3883
Ps 29: 9 And in his temple all cry, "G!" H3883
Ps 34: 2 I *will* g in the LORD; let the afflicted hear H2146
Ps 57: 5 heavens; let your g be over all the earth. H3883
Ps 57:11 heavens; let your g be over all the earth. H3883
Ps 63: 2 beheld your power and your g. H3883
Ps 63:11 all who swear by God *will* g in him, while H2146
Ps 64:10 all the upright in heart *will* g in him! H2146
Ps 66: 2 Sing the g *of* his name; make his praise H3883
Ps 72:19 may the whole earth be filled with his g. H3883
Ps 73:24 afterward you will take me into g. H3883
Ps 79: 9 our Savior, for the g *of* your name; deliver H3883
Ps 85: 9 fear him, that his g may dwell in our land. H3883
Ps 86: 9 Lord; *they will* bring g to your name. H3877
Ps 89:17 For you are their g and strength, and by H9514
Ps 96: 3 Declare his g among the nations, his H3883
Ps 96: 6 strength and g are in his sanctuary. H9514
Ps 96: 7 ascribe to the LORD g and strength. H3883
Ps 96: 8 Ascribe to the LORD the g *due* his name H3883
Ps 97: 6 righteousness, and all peoples see his g. H3883
Ps 102:15 the kings of the earth will revere your g. H3883
Ps 102:16 LORD will rebuild Zion and appear in his g. H3883
Ps 104:31 May the g *of* the LORD endure forever; may H3883
Ps 105: 3 G in his holy name; let the hearts of those H2146
Ps 106:47 to your holy name and g in your praise. H8655
Ps 108: 5 heavens; let your g be over all the earth. H3883
Ps 113: 4 all the nations, his g above the heavens. H3883
Ps 115: 1 not to us but to your name be the g H3883
Ps 138: 5 of the LORD, for the g *of* the LORD is great. H3883
Ps 145:11 They tell of the g *of* your kingdom and H3883
Ps 149: 9 this is the g of all his faithful people. H2077
Pr 14:28 A large population is a king's g, but H2079
Pr 19:11 it is to one's g to overlook an offense. H9514
Pr 20:29 The g *of* young men is their strength, gray H9514
Pr 25: 2 It is the g *of* God to conceal a matter; to H3883
Pr 25: 2 to search out a matter is the g *of* kings. H3883
Isa 4: 2 will be the pride and g of the survivors in H9514
Isa 4: 5 over everything the g will be a canopy. H3883
Isa 6: 3 Almighty; the whole earth is full of his g." H3883
Isa 13:19 the pride and g *of* the Babylonians, will H9514
Isa 17: 3 of Aram will be like the g *of* the Israelites," H3883
Isa 17: 4 "In that day the g *of* Jacob will fade; the H3883
Isa 22:24 All the g *of* his family will hang on him: its H3883
Isa 24:15 Therefore in the east give g *to* the LORD H3877
Isa 24:16 "G to the Righteous One." H7382
Isa 24:23 before its elders—*with great* g. H3883
Isa 26:15 *You have* gained g for yourself; you have H3877
Isa 35: 2 The g *of* Lebanon will be given to it, the H3883
Isa 35: 2 they will see the g *of* the LORD, the H3883
Isa 40: 5 And the g *of* the LORD will be revealed H3883
Isa 41:16 in the LORD and g in the Holy One of H2146
Isa 42: 8 I will not yield my g to another or my H3883
Isa 42:12 Let them give g to the LORD and proclaim H3883
Isa 43: 7 whom I created for my g, whom I formed H3883
Isa 44:13 human form in *all* its g, that it may dwell H9514
Isa 44:23 *he* displays *his* g in Israel. H6995
Isa 48:11 I will not yield my g to another. H3883
Isa 58: 8 the g *of* the LORD will be your rear H3883
Isa 59:19 rising of the sun, they will revere his g. H3883
Isa 60: 1 the g *of* the LORD rises upon you. H3883
Isa 60: 2 upon you and his g appears over you. H3883
Isa 60:13 "The g *of* Lebanon will come to you, the H3883
Isa 60:19 and your God will be your g. H9514
Isa 62: 2 all kings your g; you will be called by H3883
Isa 66:18 they will come and see my g. H3883
Isa 66:19 have not heard of my fame or seen my g. H3883
Isa 66:19 will proclaim my g among the nations. H3883
Jer 13:16 Give g to the LORD your God before he H3883
Jer 48:18 "Come down from your g and sit on the H3883
Eze 1:28 of the likeness of the g *of* the LORD. H3883
Eze 3:12 sound as the g *of* the LORD rose from H3883
Eze 3:23 And the g *of* the LORD was standing there H3883
Eze 3:23 like the g I had seen by the Kebar River H3883
Eze 8: 4 before me was the g *of* the God of Israel, H3883
Eze 9: 3 Now the g *of* the God of Israel went up H3883
Eze 10: 4 Then the g *of* the LORD rose from above the H3883
Eze 10: 4 full of the radiance of the g *of* the LORD. H3883
Eze 10:18 Then the g *of* the LORD departed from over H3883
Eze 10:19 the g *of* the God of Israel was above H3883
Eze 11:22 the g *of* the God of Israel was above H3883
Eze 11:23 The g *of* the LORD went up from within the H3883
Eze 24:25 their joy and g, the delight of their H9514
Eze 25: 9 Meon and Kiriathaim—the g *of* that land. H7382
Eze 28:22 and among you *I will* display *my* g. H3877
Eze 39:13 the day I display *my* g will be a H3877
Eze 39:21 "I will display my g among the nations H3883
Eze 43: 2 I saw the g *of* the God of Israel H3883
Eze 43: 2 the land was radiant with his g. H3883
Eze 43: 4 The g *of* the LORD entered the temple H3883
Eze 43: 5 the g *of* the LORD filled the temple. H3883
Eze 44: 4 I looked and saw the g *of* the LORD filling H3883
Da 2:37 dominion and power and might and g; A10331
Da 4:30 power and for the g *of* my majesty?" A10331
Da 4:36 returned to me for the g *of* my kingdom. A10331
Da 5:18 greatness and g and splendor. A10331
Da 5:20 his royal throne and stripped of his g. A10331
Da 7:14 given authority, g and sovereign power A10331
Hos 9:11 Ephraim's g will fly away like a bird—no H3883
Hab 2:14 the knowledge of the g *of* the LORD as the H3883
Hab 2:16 You will be filled with shame instead of g. H3883
Hab 2:16 and disgrace will cover your g. H3883
Hab 3: 3 His g covered the heavens and his praise H2086
Hag 2: 3 is left who saw this house in its former g? H3883
Hag 2: 7 I will fill this house with g,' says the H3883
Hag 2: 9 'The g *of* this present house will be H3883
Hag 2: 9 be greater than the g of the former house, NDT
Zec 2: 5 the LORD, 'and I will be its g within. H3883
Mt 16:27 to come in his Father's g with his angels, G1518
Mt 24:30 clouds of heaven, with power and great g. G1518
Mt 25:31 "When the Son of Man comes in his g G1518
Mk 8:38 in his Father's g with the holy angels." G1518
Mk 10:37 right and the other at your left in your g." G1518
Mk 13:26 coming in clouds with great power and g. G1518
Lk 2: 9 the g of the Lord shone around them G1518
Lk 2:14 "G to God in the highest heaven, and on G1518
Lk 2:32 Gentiles, and the g of your people Israel." G1518
Lk 9:26 he comes in his g and in the glory of G1518
Lk 9:26 in his glory and in the g of the Father and of NDT
Lk 9:32 they saw his g and the two men standing G1518
Lk 19:38 "Peace in heaven and g in the highest!" G1518
Lk 21:27 in a cloud with power and great g. G1518
Lk 24:26 suffer these things and then enter his g?" G1518
Jn 1:14 We have seen his g, the glory of the one G1518
Jn 1:14 his glory, the g of the one and only Son G1518
Jn 2:11 signs through which he revealed his g; G1518
Jn 5:41 "I do not accept g from human beings, G1518
Jn 5:44 since you accept g from one another but G1518
Jn 5:44 do not seek the g that comes from the G1518
Jn 7:18 on their own does so to gain personal g, G1518
Jn 7:18 he who seeks the g of the one who sent G1518
Jn 8:50 I am not seeking g for myself; but there is G1518
Jn 8:54 "If I glorify myself, my g means nothing. G1518
Jn 9:24 "Give g to God by telling the truth," they G1518
Jn 11: 4 it is for God's g so that God's Son may be G1518
Jn 11:40 if you believe, you will see the g of God?" G1518
Jn 12:41 he saw Jesus' g and spoke about him. G1518
Jn 15: 8 This is to my Father's g, that you bear G1519
Jn 17: 4 I *have* brought you g on earth by finishing G1519
Jn 17: 5 in your presence *with* the g I had with you G1518
Jn 17:10 And g *has* come *to me* through them. G1519
Jn 17:22 I have given them the g that you gave me, G1518
Jn 17:24 and to see my g, the glory you have G1518
Jn 17:24 the g you have given me because you G4005S
Ac 7: 2 The God *of* g appeared to our father G1518
Ac 7:55 up to heaven and saw the g of God, G1518
Ro 1:23 exchanged the g of the immortal God G1518
Ro 2: 7 who by persistence in doing good seek g, G1518
Ro 2:10 g, honor and peace for everyone who G1518
Ro 3: 7 God's truthfulness and so increases his g, G1518
Ro 3:23 sinned and fall short *of* the g of God, G1518
Ro 4:20 in his faith and gave g to God, G1518
Ro 5: 2 And we boast in the hope *of* the g of God. G1518
Ro 5: 3 Not only so, but *we* also g in our sufferings G3016
Ro 6: 4 from the dead through the g of the Father, G1518
Ro 8:17 in order that *we may* also share in his g. G5280
Ro 8:18 comparing with the g that will be G1518
Ro 8:21 into the freedom and g of the children of G1518
Ro 9: 4 theirs the divine g, the covenants, G1518
Ro 9:23 to make the riches *of* his g known to the G1518
Ro 9:23 whom he prepared in advance for g— G1518
Ro 11:36 To him be the g forever! Amen. G1518
Ro 15:17 Therefore *I* g in Christ Jesus in my G2400+3018
Ro 16:27 the only wise God be g forever through G1518
1Co 2: 7 destined for our g before time began. G1518
1Co 2: 8 would not have crucified the Lord *of* g. G1518
1Co 10:31 do it all for the g of God. G1518
1Co 11: 7 since he is the image and g of God; but G1518
1Co 11: 7 glory of God; but woman is the g of man. G1518
1Co 11:15 that if a woman has long hair, it is her g? G1518
1Co 15:43 it is raised in g; it is sown in weakness, G1518
2Co 1:20 "Amen" is spoken by us to the g of God. G1518
2Co 3: 7 on stone, came with g, so that the G1518
2Co 3: 7 at the face of Moses because of its g, G1518
2Co 3:10 was glorious has no g *now* in comparison G1519
2Co 3:10 now in comparison with the surpassing g. G1518
2Co 3:11 And if what was transitory came with g G1518
2Co 3:11 much greater is the g of that which lasts! G1518
2Co 3:18 unveiled faces contemplate the Lord's g, G1518
2Co 3:18 with ever-increasing g, G608+1518+1650+1518
2Co 4: 4 of the gospel *that displays* the g of Christ, G1518
2Co 4: 6 the knowledge *of* God's g displayed in G1518
2Co 4:15 thanksgiving to overflow to the g of God. G1518
2Co 4:17 us an eternal g that far outweighs G1518
2Co 6: 8 through g and dishonor, bad report and G1518
Gal 1: 5 to whom be g for ever and ever. Amen. G1518
Eph 1:12 in Christ, might be for the praise *of* his g. G1518
Eph 1:14 God's possession—to the praise *of* his g. G1518
Eph 3:13 of my sufferings for you, which are your g. G1518
Eph 3:21 to him be g in the church and in Christ G1518
Php 1:11 Jesus Christ—to the g and praise of God. G1518
Php 2:11 Christ is Lord, to the g of God the Father. G1518
Php 3:19 stomach, and their g is in their shame. G1518
Php 4:19 to the riches of his g in Christ Jesus. G1518
Php 4:20 God and Father be g for ever and ever. G1518
Col 1:27 which is Christ in you, the hope *of* g. G1518
Col 3: 4 then you also will appear with him in g. G1518
1Th 2:12 who calls you into his kingdom and g. G1518
1Th 2:19 the crown *in* which we will g in the G3018
1Th 2:20 you are our g and joy. G1518
2Th 1: 9 of the Lord and from the g of his might G1518
2Th 2:14 you might share in the g of our Lord Jesus G1518
1Ti 1:11 to the gospel *concerning* the g of the G1518
1Ti 1:17 be honor and g for ever and ever. G1518
1Ti 3:16 on in the world, was taken up in g. G1518

2Ti 2:10 that is in Christ Jesus, with eternal g. G1518
2Ti 4:18 To him be g for ever and ever G1518
Titus 2:13 the appearing *of* the g of our great God G1518
Heb 1: 3 is the radiance *of* God's g and the exact G1518
Heb 2: 7 you crowned them *with* g and honor G1518
Heb 2: 9 now crowned *with* g and honor because G1518
Heb 2:10 In bringing many sons and daughters to g, G1518
Heb 3: 6 confidence and the hope *in* which we g. G3017
Heb 5: 5 Christ *did* not take on himself *the* g of G1519
Heb 9: 5 Above the ark were the cherubim *of* the G G1518
Heb 13:21 to whom be g for ever and ever. G1518
1Pe 1: 7 g and honor when Jesus Christ is revealed G1518
1Pe 1:24 all their g is like the flowers of the G1518
1Pe 4:11 To him be the g and the power for ever G1518
1Pe 4:13 may be overjoyed when his g is revealed. G1518
1Pe 4:14 the Spirit *of* g and of God rests on you. G1518
1Pe 5: 1 also will share *in* the g to be revealed: G1518
1Pe 5: 4 receive the crown *of* g that will never fade G1518
1Pe 5:10 who called you to his eternal g in Christ G1518
2Pe 1: 3 who called us *by* his own g and goodness G1518
2Pe 1:17 received honor and g from God the Father G1518
2Pe 1:17 voice came to him from the Majestic G, G1518
2Pe 3:18 To him be g both now and forever G1518
Jude 25 to the only God our Savior be g, majesty G1518
Rev 1: 6 to him be g and power for ever and ever! G1518
Rev 4: 9 Whenever the living creatures give g G1518
Rev 4:11 to receive g and honor and power G1518
Rev 5:12 strength and honor and g and praise!" G1518
Rev 5:13 be praise and honor and g and power, G1518
Rev 7:12 Praise and g and wisdom and thanks and G1518
Rev 11:13 terrified and gave g to the God of heaven. G1518
Rev 14: 7 "Fear God and give him g, because the G1518
Rev 15: 4 fear you, Lord, and **bring** g to your name? G1519
Rev 15: 8 smoke from the g of God and from his G1518
Rev 18: 7 grief as the g and luxury *she* **gave** herself. G1519
Rev 19: 1 Salvation and g and power belong to our G1518
Rev 19: 7 Let us rejoice and be glad and give him g! G1518
Rev 21:11 It shone with the g of God, and its G1518
Rev 21:23 shine on it, for the g of God gives it light G1518
Rev 21:26 The g and honor of the nations will be G1518

GLOW (1) [GLOWING, GLOWS]
Isa 4: 5 of smoke by day and a g *of* flaming fire by H5586

GLOWING (8) [GLOW]
1Sa 16:12 He was g **with health** and had a fine H145
1Sa 17:42 than a boy, g **with health** and handsome H145
Ps 102: 3 like smoke; my bones burn like g **embers**. H4611
Eze 1: 4 The center of the fire looked like g **metal**, H3133
Eze 1:27 to be his waist up he looked like g **metal**, H3133
Eze 8: 2 his appearance was as bright as g **metal**. H3133
Rev 1:15 His feet were like bronze g in a furnace G4792
Rev 15: 2 looked like a sea of glass g with fire and, G3502

GLOWS (1) [GLOW]
Eze 24:11 coals till it becomes hot and its copper g, H3081

GLUTTED (1) [GLUTTON]
Eze 39:19 eat fat till you are g and drink blood till H8429

GLUTTON (3) [GLUTTED, GLUTTONS, GLUTTONY]
Dt 21:20 *He is a* g and a drunkard." H2361
Mt 11:19 'Here is a g and a drunkard, G476+5741
Lk 7:34 'Here is a g and a drunkard, G476+5741

GLUTTONS (3) [GLUTTON]
Pr 23:21 drunkards and g become poor, and H2361
Pr 28: 7 a companion of g disgraces his father. H2361
Titus 1:12 are always liars, evil brutes, lazy g." G1143

GLUTTONY (1) [GLUTTON]
Pr 23: 2 to your throat if you are **given to** g. H1251+5883

GNASH (3) [GNASHED, GNASHES, GNASHING]
Ps 37:12 the righteous and g their teeth at them; H3080
Ps 112:10 *they will* g their teeth and waste away H3080
La 2:16 they scoff and g their teeth and say H3080

GNASHED (2) [GNASH]
Ps 35:16 mocked; *they* g their teeth at me. H3080
Ac 7:54 they were furious and g their teeth at him. G1107

GNASHES (2) [GNASH]
Job 16: 9 me in his anger and g his teeth at me; H3080
Mk 9:18 the mouth, g his teeth and becomes rigid. G5563

GNASHING (7) [GNASH]
Mt 8:12 there will be weeping and g of teeth." G1106
Mt 13:42 there will be weeping and g of teeth. G1106
Mt 13:50 there will be weeping and g of teeth. G1106
Mt 22:13 there will be weeping and g of teeth. G1106
Mt 24:51 there will be weeping and g of teeth. G1106
Mt 25:30 there will be weeping and g of teeth. G1106
Lk 13:28 weeping there, and g of teeth, when you G1106

GNAT (1) [GNATS]
Mt 23:24 You strain out a g but swallow a camel. G3270

GNATS (6) [GNAT]
Ex 8:16 the land of Egypt the dust will become g." H4031
Ex 8:17 ground, g came on people and animals. H4038
Ex 8:17 throughout the land of Egypt became g. H4031
Ex 8:18 tried to produce g by their secret arts, H4031
Ex 8:18 Since the g were on people and animals H4038
Ps 105:31 and g throughout their country. H4031

GNAWED (1) [GNAWING]
Rev 16:10 *People* g their tongues in agony G3460

GNAWING (1) [GNAWED]
Job 30:17 pierces my bones; my g **pains** never rest. H6908

GO (1427) [GOES, GOING, GONE, WENT]
Ge 4: 8 his brother Abel, "*Let's* g **out** *to* the field." H2143
Ge 7: 1 then said to Noah, "G into the ark, you H995
Ge 11: 7 *let us* g **down** and confuse their language H3718
Ge 11:31 from Ur of the Chaldeans to g to Canaan. H2143
Ge 12: 1 had said to Abram, "G from your country H2143
Ge 12:19 here is your wife. Take her and g!" H2143
Ge 13: 9 If you g to the left, I'll go to the right; if you NDT
Ge 13: 9 to the left, *I'll* g **to the right**; if you go to H3554
Ge 13: 9 go to the right; if you g to the right, I'll go to NDT
Ge 13: 9 if you go to the right, *I'll* g **to the left**." H8521
Ge 13:17 G, walk through the length and breadth of H7756
Ge 15:15 *will* g to your ancestors in peace and be H995
Ge 16: 2 G, **sleep with** my slave; perhaps I can H995+448
Ge 16: 9 "G **back** to your mistress and submit to her H8740
Ge 18: 5 be refreshed and then g **on** *your* **way**— H6296
Ge 18:21 that *I will* g **down** and see if what they H3718
Ge 19: 2 the night and then g on your way early in H2143
Ge 19: 3 so strongly that *they did* g with him and H6073
Ge 19:34 and *you* g **in** and sleep with him so we can H995
Ge 20:13 Everywhere *we* g, say of me, "He is my H995
Ge 22: 2 and g to the region of Moriah. H2143
Ge 22: 5 donkey while I and the boy g over there. H2143
Ge 24: 4 but *will* g to my country and my own H2143
Ge 24:11 the time the women g **out** to draw water. H3655
Ge 24:38 g to my father's family and to my own H2143
Ge 24:41 my oath if, when *you* g to my clan, they H995
Ge 24:51 take her and g, and let her become H2143
Ge 24:55 with us ten days or so; then *you may* g." H2143
Ge 24:56 me on my way so *I may* g to my master." H2143
Ge 24:58 asked her, "*Will you* g with this man?" H2143
Ge 24:58 go with this man?" "*I will* g," she said. H2143
Ge 25:18 border of Egypt, *as* you g toward Ashur. H995
Ge 26: 2 said, "*Do* not g **down** to Egypt; live H3718
Ge 27: 3 and g **out** *to* the open country to hunt H3655
Ge 27: 9 G **out** to the flock and bring me two choice H2143
Ge 27:13 Just do what I say; g and get them for me." H2143
Ge 28: 2 G at once to Paddan Aram, to the house H2143
Ge 28:15 will watch over you wherever *you* g, H2143
Ge 30:25 me on my way so *I can* g **back** to my own H2143
Ge 30:31 *I will* g **on** tending your flocks and H8740
Ge 30:32 *Let me* g through all your flocks today and H6296
Ge 31: 3 "G **back** to the land of your fathers and to H8740
Ge 31:13 land at once and g **back** to your native H8740
Ge 31:18 to g to his father Isaac in the land of H995
Ge 31:52 that I *will* not g **past** this heap to your side H6296
Ge 31:52 that you *will* not g **past** this heap and H6296
Ge 32: 9 'G **back** to your country and your relatives H8740
Ge 32:16 to his servants, "G ahead of me, and keep H6296
Ge 32:26 Then the man said, "**Let** me g, for it is H8938
Ge 32:26 "*I will* not **let** you g unless you bless me." H8938
Ge 33:14 So *let* my lord g **on** ahead of his servant H6296
Ge 34:17 circumcised, we'll take our sister and g." H2143
Ge 35: 1 to Jacob, "G up to Bethel and settle there H7756
Ge 35: 3 Then come, *let us* g **up** *to* Bethel, where I H6590
Ge 37:14 "G and see if all is well with your brothers H2143
Ge 37:17 "I heard them say, '*Let's* g to Dothan.'" H2143
Ge 39:10 refused to g **to bed with** her or even H8886+725
Ge 41:55 "G to Joseph and do what he tells you." H2143
Ge 42: 2 G **down** there and buy some for us, so H3718
Ge 42:19 the rest of you g and take grain back H2143
Ge 42:33 food for your starving households and g. H2143
Ge 42:38 "My son *will* not g **down** there with you H3718
Ge 43: 2 "G **back** and buy us a little more food." H8740
Ge 43: 4 *we will* g **down** and buy food for you. H3718
Ge 43: 5 send him, *we will* not g **down**, because H3718
Ge 43: 8 boy along with me and *we will* g at once, H2143
Ge 43:13 brother also and g **back** to the man at H8740
Ge 44: 4 to his steward, "G after those men at once H8103
Ge 44:17 rest of you, g **back** to your father in peace." H6590
Ge 44:25 'G **back** and buy a little more food. H8740
Ge 44:26 we said, 'We cannot g **down**. Only if our H3718
Ge 44:26 our youngest brother is with us *will we* g. H3718
Ge 44:30 not with us when I g **back** to your servant H995
Ge 44:34 How *can I* g **back** to my father if the boy is H6590
Ge 45:28 *I will* g and see him before I die. H2143
Ge 46: 3 "Do not be afraid *to* g **down** to Egypt, for I H3718
Ge 46: 4 I *will* g **down** to Egypt with you, and I will H3718
Ge 46:31 "*I will* g **up** and speak to Pharaoh and will H6590
Ge 50: 5 Now *let me* g **up** and bury my father H6590
Ge 50: 6 Pharaoh said, "G **up** and bury your father H6590
Ex 2: 7 "*Shall I* g and get one of the Hebrew H2143
Ex 2: 8 g," she answered. So the girl went H2143
Ex 3: 3 "*I will* g **over** and see this strange sight H6073
Ex 3:10 g. I am sending you to Pharaoh to H2143
Ex 3:11 "Who am I that *I should* g to Pharaoh H2143
Ex 3:13 "Suppose I g to the Israelites and say to H995
Ex 3:16 "G, assemble the elders of Israel and say H2143
Ex 3:18 you and the elders *are to* g to the king of H995
Ex 3:19 will not let you g unless a mighty hand H2143
Ex 3:20 among them. After that, *he will* **let** you g. H8938
Ex 3:21 you leave *you will* not g empty-handed. H2143
Ex 4:12 Now g; I will help you speak and will H2143
Ex 4:18 Jethro said, "G, and I wish you well." H2143
Ex 4:19 to Moses in Midian, "G back to Egypt, for H2143
Ex 4:21 heart so that *he will* not **let** the people g. H8938
Ex 4:23 I told you, "**Let** my son g, so he may H8938
Ex 4:23 But you refused to **let** him g; so I will kill H8938
Ex 4:27 "G into the wilderness to meet Moses." H2143
Ex 5: 1 '**Let** my people g, so that they may hold a H8938
Ex 5: 2 that I should obey him and **let** Israel g? H8938
Ex 5: 2 know the LORD and *I will* not **let** Israel g." H8938
Ex 5: 7 *let* them g and gather their own straw. H2143
Ex 5: 8 '*Let us* g and sacrifice to our God. H2143
Ex 5:11 G and get your own straw wherever you H2143
Ex 5:17 '*Let us* g and sacrifice to the LORD. H2143
Ex 6: 1 of my mighty hand *he will* **let** them g; H8938
Ex 6:11 "G, tell Pharaoh king of Egypt to let the H995
Ex 6:11 of Egypt *to* **let** the Israelites g out of his H8938
Ex 7: 2 Pharaoh *to* **let** the Israelites g out of his H8938
Ex 7:14 unyielding; he refuses to **let** the people g. H8938
Ex 7:15 G to Pharaoh in the morning as he goes H2143
Ex 7:16 **Let** my people g, so that they may worship H8938
Ex 8: 1 to Moses, "G to Pharaoh and say to him H995
Ex 8: 1 **Let** my people g, so that they may worship H8938
Ex 8: 2 If you refuse to **let** them g, I will send a H8938
Ex 8: 8 and *I will* **let** your people g to offer H8938
Ex 8:20 **Let** my people g, so that they may worship H8938
Ex 8:21 If you *do* not **let** my people g, I will send H8938
Ex 8:25 Aaron and said, "G, sacrifice to your H2143
Ex 8:28 "I *will* **let** you g to offer sacrifices to the H8938
Ex 8:28 wilderness, but you must not g very far. H2143
Ex 8:29 again by not **letting** the people g to offer H8938
Ex 8:32 his heart and *would* not **let** the people g. H8938
Ex 9: 1 to Moses, "G to Pharaoh and say to him H995
Ex 9: 1 "**Let** my people g, so that they may H8938
Ex 9: 2 If you refuse to **let** them g and continue to H8938
Ex 9: 7 and *he would* not **let** the people g. H8938
Ex 9:13 **Let** my people g, so that they may worship H8938
Ex 9:17 my people and *will* not **let** them g. H8938
Ex 9:28 *I will* **let** you g; you don't have to stay any H8938
Ex 9:35 hard and *he would* not **let** the Israelites g, H8938
Ex 10: 1 LORD said to Moses, "G to Pharaoh, for I H995
Ex 10: 3 **Let** my people g, so that they may worship H8938
Ex 10: 4 If you refuse to **let** them g, I will bring H8938
Ex 10: 7 **Let** the people g, so that they may H8938
Ex 10: 8 back to Pharaoh. "G, worship the LORD H2143
Ex 10: 9 "*We will* g with our young and our old H2143
Ex 10:10 be with you—if *I* **let** you g, along with H8938
Ex 10:11 *Have* only the men g and worship the H2143
Ex 10:20 and *he would* not **let** the Israelites g. H8938
Ex 10:24 Moses and said, "G, worship the LORD. H2143
Ex 10:24 your women and children *may* g with you; H2143
Ex 10:26 Our livestock too *must* g with us; not a H2143
Ex 10:27 he was not willing to **let** them g. H8938
Ex 11: 1 After that, *he will* **let** you g from here, and H8938
Ex 11: 4 'About midnight I *will* g throughout Egypt. H3655
Ex 11: 8 before me and saying, 'G, you and all the H3655
Ex 11:10 and *he would* not **let** the Israelites g out H8938
Ex 12:21 "G **at once** and select the animals for your H5432
Ex 12:22 None of you *shall* g **out** of the door of H3655
Ex 12:31 G, worship the LORD as you have H2143
Ex 12:32 flocks and herds, as you have said, and g. H2143
Ex 13:15 Pharaoh stubbornly refused to **let** us g, H8938
Ex 13:17 When Pharaoh **let** the people g, God did H8938
Ex 14: 5 *We have* **let** the Israelites g and have lost H8938
Ex 14:16 that the Israelites *can* g through the sea on H995
Ex 14:17 Egyptians so that *they will* g **in** after them. H995
Ex 16: 4 The people *are to* g **out** each day and H3655
Ex 16:29 on the seventh day; no one *is to* g **out**." H3655
Ex 17: 5 "G **out** in front of the people. H6296
Ex 17: 5 staff with which you struck the Nile, and g. H2143
Ex 17: 9 some of our men and g **out** to fight the H3655
Ex 18:23 all these people *will* g home satisfied." H995
Ex 19:10 "G to the people and consecrate them H2143
Ex 19:21 "G **down** and warn the people so they do H3718
Ex 19:24 "G down and bring Aaron up with you. H2143
Ex 20:26 And *do* not g **up** to my altar on steps, or H6590
Ex 21: 2 the seventh year, *he shall* g free, without H3655
Ex 21: 3 comes alone, *he is to* g **free** alone; but if H3655
Ex 21: 3 wife when he comes, she *is to* g with him. H3655
Ex 21: 4 her master, and only the man *shall* g **free**. H3655
Ex 21: 5 children and *do* not *want to* g free, H3655
Ex 21: 7 *she is* not *to* g **free** as male servants do. H3655
Ex 21:11 three things, *she is to* g **free**, without any H3655
Ex 21:26 destroys it *must* **let** the slave g free to H8938
Ex 21:27 female slave *must* **let** the slave g free to H8938
Ex 23:23 My angel *will* g ahead of you and bring H2143
Ex 24:14 involved in a dispute *can* g to them." H5602
Ex 26:19 make forty silver bases to g under them— NDT
Ex 32: 1 make us gods who *will* g before us. H2143
Ex 32: 7 said to Moses, "G down, because your H2143
Ex 32:23 'Make us gods who *will* g before us. H2143
Ex 32:27 G **back** and forth through the camp from H8740
Ex 32:30 But now *I will* g **up** to the LORD; perhaps I H6590
Ex 32:34 Now g, lead the people to the place I H2143
Ex 32:34 spoke of, and my angel *will* g before you. H2143
Ex 33: 1 and g **up** to the land I promised on oath H6590
Ex 33: 3 G up to the land flowing with milk and NDT
Ex 33: 3 But *I will* not g with you, because you are H6590
Ex 33: 5 *If I were to* g with you even for a moment H6590
Ex 33: 7 of the LORD *would* g to the tent of H3655
Ex 33:14 "My Presence *will* g with you, and I will H2143
Ex 33:15 "If your Presence *does* not g with us, do H2143
Ex 33:16 with your people unless you g with us? H2143
Ex 34: 9 in your eyes, then *let* the Lord g with us. H2143

Ex 34:24 your land when you **g up** three times each H6590
Ex 36:24 made forty silver bases to g under them— NDT
Lev 6:12 must be kept burning; *it must* not **g out**. H3882
Lev 6:13 the altar continuously; *it must* not **g out**. H3882
Lev 10: 9 drink whenever you **g into** the tent of H995
Lev 12: 4 anything sacred or g to the sanctuary until H995
Lev 13:16 turns white, *they must* g to the priest. H995
Lev 14: 3 The priest *is to* g outside the camp and H3655
Lev 14:35 owner of the house *must* g and tell the H995
Lev 14:36 this the priest *is to* **g in** and inspect the H995
Lev 14:38 the priest *shall* **g out** the doorway of the H3655
Lev 14:44 the priest *is to* g and examine it and, if the H995
Lev 16:23 "Then Aaron *is to* g into the tent of H995
Lev 19:10 *Do* not **g over** your vineyard **a second time** H6618
Lev 19:16 " '*Do* not **g about** spreading slander H2143
Lev 21:23 *he must* not **g near** the curtain or approach H995
Lev 25:27 *they can* then **g back** to their own property. H8740
Lev 25:28 and *they can* then **g back** to their property. H8740
Lev 25:41 and *they will* **g back** to their own clans H8740
Nu 4: 5 his sons *are to* **g in** and take down the H995
Nu 4:19 his sons *are to* **g into** the sanctuary H995
Nu 4:20 the Kohathites *must* not **g in** to look at the H995
Nu 6: 6 the Nazirite *must* not **g near** a dead body. H995
Nu 8:19 Israelites when they **g near** the sanctuary." H5602
Nu 10: 9 When *you* **g into** battle in your own land H995
Nu 10:30 *I will* not g; I am going back to my H2143
Nu 11:15 please *g ahead and* **kill** me—if I have AIT
Nu 11:26 the elders, but *did* not **g out** to the tent. H3655
Nu 13:17 "**G up** through the Negev and on into the H6590
Nu 13:30 "*We* **should g up** and take H6590+6590
Nu 14: 3 it be better for us *to* **g back** to Egypt?" H8740
Nu 14: 4 choose a leader and **g back** to Egypt." H8740
Nu 14:14 that you g before them in a pillar of H2143
Nu 14:40 "Now we *are ready to* **g up** to the land the H6590
Nu 14:42 *Do* not **g up**, because the LORD is not with H6590
Nu 16:30 and *they* **g down** alive into the realm of H3718
Nu 18: 3 but *they must* not **g near** the furnishings H7928
Nu 18:22 the Israelites *must* not **g near** the tent of H7928
Nu 20:17 *We will* not g through any field or H6296
Nu 20:19 "*We will* g along the main road, and if H6590
Nu 20:21 refused to let them g through their H6296
Nu 21: 4 route to the Red Sea, to **g around** Edom. H6015
Nu 22:12 God said to Balaam, "*Do* not g with them. H2143
Nu 22:13 officials, "**G back** to your own country H2143
Nu 22:13 the LORD has refused to let me g with you." H2143
Nu 22:18 small to **g beyond** the command of H6296
Nu 22:20 to summon you, g with them, but do H2143
Nu 22:34 Now if you are displeased, *I will* **g back**." H8740
Nu 22:35 LORD said to Balaam, "**G** with the men, but H2143
Nu 23: 3 here beside your offering while *I* **g aside**. H2143
Nu 23: 5 "**G back** to Balak and give him this word." H8740
Nu 23:16 "**G back** to Balak and give him this word." H8740
Nu 24:11 Now leave at once and g home! I said I NDT
Nu 24:13 *to* **g beyond** the command of the LORD H6296
Nu 27:12 "**G up** this mountain in the Abarim Range H6590
Nu 27:17 *to* **g out** and come in before them, one H3655
Nu 27:21 community of the Israelites *will* **g out**, H3655
Nu 31: 3 some of your men *to* g to war against the H2118
Nu 32: 6 "*Should* your fellow Israelites g to war H995
Nu 32:17 battle and g ahead of the Israelites NDT
Nu 34: 4 on to Zin and g south of Kadesh Barnea H2118
Nu 34: 4 Then *it will* g *to* Hazar Addar and over to H3655
Nu 34: 8 Then the boundary *will* g to Zedad, H2118
Nu 34:11 *will* **g down** from Shepham *to* Riblah H3718
Nu 34:12 Then the boundary *will* **g down** along the H3718
Nu 35:32 so *allow* them *to* **g back** and live on H8740
Dt 1: 2 eleven days to g from Horeb to Kadesh NDT
Dt 1: 7 g to all the neighboring peoples in the H995
Dt 1: 8 **G in** and take possession of the land the H995
Dt 1:21 **G up** and take possession of it as the LORD, H6590
Dt 1:26 But you were unwilling to **g up**; you H6590
Dt 1:28 Where *can* we g? Our brothers have made H6590
Dt 1:33 to show you the way *you should* g. H2143
Dt 1:41 We *will* **g up** and fight, as the LORD our H6590
Dt 1:41 thinking it easy to **g up** into the hill H6590
Dt 1:42 "Tell them, '*Do* not **g up** and fight H6590
Dt 3:20 each of you *may* **g back** to the possession H8740
Dt 3:25 *Let me* **g over** and see the good land H6296
Dt 3:27 **G up** *to* the top of Pisgah and look west H6590
Dt 4: 1 you may live and *may* **g in** and take H995
Dt 4:40 so that *it may* **g well** with you and your H3512
Dt 5: 5 of the fire and *did* not **g up** the mountain.) H6590
Dt 5:16 long and that *it may* **g well** with you in H3512
Dt 5:27 **G near** and listen to all that the LORD our H7928
Dt 5:29 so that *it might* **g well** with them and their H3512
Dt 5:30 "**G**, tell them to return to their tents. H2143
Dt 6: 3 to obey so that *it may* **g well** with you H3512
Dt 6:18 so that *it may* **g well** with you and you H3512
Dt 6:18 with you and *you may* **g in** and take over H995
Dt 8:16 that in the end *it might* **g well** *with* you. H3512
Dt 9: 1 to cross the Jordan to **g in** and dispossess H995
Dt 9:12 LORD told me, "**G down** from here at once H3718
Dt 9:23 "**G up** and take possession of the land I H6590
Dt 10:11 "**G**," the LORD said to me, "and lead the H7756
Dt 11: 8 have the strength to **g in** and take over the H995
Dt 11:25 of you on the whole land, wherever *you* **g**. H2005
Dt 12: 5 his dwelling. To that place *you must* g; H995
Dt 12:25 so that *it may* **g well** with you and your H3512
Dt 12:26 g to the place the LORD will choose. H995
Dt 12:28 so that *it may* always **g well** with you and H3512
Dt 13: 6 "*Let us* g and worship other gods" H2143
Dt 13:13 "*Let us* g and worship other gods" H2143
Dt 14:25 silver with you and g to the place the LORD H2143
Dt 15:12 the seventh year *you must* **let** them g free. H8938
Dt 17: 9 **G** to the Levitical priests and to the judge H995
Dt 17:16 "*You are* not *to* **g back** that way again." H8740
Dt 19: 5 a man *may* g into the forest with his H995
Dt 19:13 so that *it may* **g well** with you. H3201
Dt 20: 1 When *you* g to war against your enemies H3655
Dt 20: 2 When you *are about to* g into battle, the H7928
Dt 20: 5 *Let him* **g** home, or he may H2143+2256+8740
Dt 20: 6 *Let him* **g** home, or he may H2143+2256+8740
Dt 20: 7 *Let him* **g** home, or he may H2143+2256+8740
Dt 20: 8 *Let him* **g** home so that his H2143+2256+8740
Dt 21: 2 judges *shall* **g out** and measure the H3655
Dt 21:10 When *you* g to war against your enemies H3655
Dt 21:13 then *you may* g to her and be her husband H995
Dt 21:14 with her, **let** her g wherever she wishes. H8938
Dt 22: 7 but **be sure to let** the mother g, so H8938+8938
Dt 22: 7 so that *it may* **g well** with you and you H3512
Dt 23:10 *he is to* g outside the camp and stay there H3655
Dt 23:12 the camp where *you can* g to relieve H3655
Dt 24:10 *do* not g into their house to get what is H995
Dt 24:12 *do* not **g to sleep** with their pledge in your H8886
Dt 24:19 overlook a sheaf, *do* not **g back** to get it. H8740
Dt 24:20 *do* not **g over the branches a second time** H6994+339
Dt 24:21 vineyard, *do* not **g over the vines again**. H6618
Dt 25: 7 she *shall* g to the elders at the town gate H6590
Dt 25: 9 brother's widow *shall* **g up** to him in the H5602
Dt 26: 2 Then g to the place the LORD your God will H2143
Dt 28: 6 you come in and blessed when you **g out**. H3655
Dt 28:19 you come in and cursed when you **g out**. H3655
Dt 28:41 because *they will* g into captivity. H2143
Dt 29:18 the LORD our God to g and worship the H2143
Dt 31: 7 you *must* g with this people into the H995
Dt 32:49 "**G up** into the Abarim Range to Mount H6590
Jos 1: 7 you may be successful wherever *you* g. H2143
Jos 1: 9 your God will be with you wherever *you* g." H2143
Jos 1:11 "**G** through the camp and tell the people H6296
Jos 1:11 the Jordan here to **g in** and take H995
Jos 1:15 *you may* **g back** and occupy your own land H8740
Jos 1:16 and wherever you send us *we will* g. H2143
Jos 2: 1 "**G**, look over the land," he said H2143
Jos 2: 5 which way they went. **G** after them quickly H8103
Jos 2:16 "**G** to the hills so the pursuers will not find H2143
Jos 2:16 until they return, and then g on your way." H2143
Jos 2:19 If any of *them* g outside your house into H3655
Jos 3: 4 Then you will know which way *to* g, since H2143
Jos 3: 4 between you and the ark; *do* not **g near** it." H7928
Jos 3: 8 the Jordan's waters, g and stand in the river. NDT
Jos 3:11 Lord of all the earth *will* g into the Jordan H6296
Jos 4: 5 "**G over** before the ark of the LORD your H6296
Jos 6: 5 city will collapse and the army *will* **g up**, H6590
Jos 6:19 to the LORD and *must* **g into** his treasury." H995
Jos 6:22 "**G into** the prostitute's house and bring her H995
Jos 7: 2 told them, "**G up** and spy out the region." H6590
Jos 7: 3 all the army *will have to* **g up** *against* Ai. H6590
Jos 7:13 "**G**, consecrate the people. Tell them H7756
Jos 8: 1 army with you, and **g up** and attack Ai. H7756
Jos 8: 4 Don't g very **far** from it. All of you H8178
Jos 8:17 in Ai or Bethel who *did* not g after Israel. H3655
Jos 9:11 g and meet them and say to them H2143
Jos 14:11 just as vigorous to **g out** to battle now as I H3655
Jos 17:15 **g up** into the forest and clear land for H6590
Jos 18: 8 "**G** and make a survey of the land and H2143
Jos 20: 6 Then they may g back to their own home in H995
Jos 22:12 at Shiloh to g to war against them. H6590
Jos 23:14 "Now I *am about to* g the way of all the H2143
Jos 23:16 g and serve other gods and bow H2143
Jdg 1: 1 "Who of us *is to* **g up** first to fight against H6590
Jdg 1: 2 answered, "Judah *shall* **g up**; I have given H6590
Jdg 1: 3 We in turn *will* g with you into yours." H2143
Jdg 4: 6 commands *you*: '**G**, take with you H2143
Jdg 4: 8 said to her, "If *you* g with me, I will go; H2143
Jdg 4: 8 you go with me, *I will* g; but if you don't H2143
Jdg 4: 8 but if *you* don't g with me, I won't H2143
Jdg 4: 8 but if you don't go with me, *I* won't g." H2143
Jdg 4: 9 "**Certainly** *I will* g with you," said H2143+2143
Jdg 4:14 said to Barak, "**G**! This is the day the H7756
Jdg 5:22 galloping, galloping g his mighty steeds. NDT
Jdg 6:14 "**G** in the strength you have and save H2143
Jdg 6:18 Please *do* not **g away** until I come back H4631
Jdg 7: 4 'This one *shall* g with you,' he H2143
Jdg 7: 4 shall go with you,' he *shall* g; but if I say, H2143
Jdg 7: 4 'This one *shall* not g with you,' he H2143
Jdg 7: 4 one shall not go with you,' he *shall* not g." H2143
Jdg 7: 7 *Let* all the others g home." H2143
Jdg 7: 9 "Get up, **g down** against the camp H3718
Jdg 7:10 **g down** to the camp with your servant H3718
Jdg 9:38 you ridiculed? **G out** and fight them!" H3655
Jdg 10:14 **G** and cry out to the gods you have chosen. H2143
Jdg 11:17 '*Give us permission to* g through your H6296
Jdg 11:38 "*You may* g," he said. And he let her go H2143
Jdg 11:38 And *he* **let** her g for two months H8938
Jdg 11:40 women of Israel *g out* for four days to H2143
Jdg 12: 1 "Why *did you* g to fight the Ammonites H6296
Jdg 12: 1 without calling us to g with you? H2143
Jdg 14: 3 *Must* you g to the uncircumcised H2143
Jdg 15: 1 But her father would not let him **g in**. H995
Jdg 16:20 "*I'll* **g out** as before and shake myself free." H3655
Jdg 18: 2 They told them, "**G**, explore the land." H2143
Jdg 18: 6 answered them, "**G** in peace. H2143
Jdg 18: 9 Don't hesitate to g there and take it over. H2143
Jdg 19: 5 with something to eat; then *you can* g." H2143
Jdg 19: 7 And when the man got up to g, his H2143
Jdg 19: 8 when he rose to g, the woman's father H2143
Jdg 19:12 *We* won't g into any city whose people H6073
Jdg 19:12 not Israelites. *We will* **g on** to Gibeah." H6296
Jdg 19:25 the night, and at dawn *they* **let** her g. H8938
Jdg 19:28 "Get up; *let's* g." But there was no H2143
Jdg 20: 8 saying, "None of *us will* g home. H2143
Jdg 20: 9 We'll g up against it in the order decided by NDT
Jdg 20:18 "Who of us *is to* **g up** first to fight against H6590
Jdg 20:18 The LORD replied, "Judah shall g first." NDT
Jdg 20:23 "Shall we **g up** again to fight against the H5602
Jdg 20:23 The LORD answered, "**G up** against them." H6590
Jdg 20:28 "Shall we **g up** again to fight against the H3655
Jdg 20:28 LORD responded, "**G**, for tomorrow I will H6590
Jdg 21:10 instructions *to* g to Jabesh Gilead and H2143
Jdg 21:20 "**G** and hide in the vineyards H2143
Ru 1: 8 "**G** back, each of *you*, to your mother's H2143
Ru 1:10 "*We will* **g back** with you to your people." H8740
Ru 1:15 people and her gods. **G back** with her." H8740
Ru 1:16 Where *you* g I will go, and where you stay H2143
Ru 1:16 Where you go *I will* g, and where you stay H2143
Ru 1:18 that Ruth was determined to g with her, H2143
Ru 2: 2 "*Let me* g *to* the fields and pick up the H2143
Ru 2: 2 said to her, "**G ahead**, my daughter." H2143
Ru 2: 8 Don't g and glean in another field and H2143
Ru 2: 8 another field and don't **g away** from here. H6296
Ru 2: 9 g and get a drink from the water jars the H2143
Ru 2:22 *to* g with the women who work for him H3655
Ru 3: 3 Then **g down** *to* the threshing floor, but H3718
Ru 3: 4 Then g and uncover his feet and lie down H995
Ru 3:16 "**How did it** g, my daughter? H4769+905
Ru 3:17 'Don't **g back** to your mother-in-law H995
1Sa 1:17 Eli answered, "**G** in peace, and may the H2143
1Sa 1:22 Hannah *did* not g. She said to her H6590
1Sa 2:20 Then *they would* g home. H2143
1Sa 2:28 to be my priest, to **g up** to my altar, to H6590
1Sa 3: 5 "I did not call; **g back** and lie down." H8740
1Sa 3: 6 "I did not call; **g back** and lie down." H8740
1Sa 3: 9 So Eli told Samuel, "**G** and lie down, and H2143
1Sa 4: 3 so that *he may* g with us and save us from H995
1Sa 5:11 Israel away; *let* it **g back** to its own place H8740
1Sa 6: 6 out so *they could* **g on** *their* **way**? H2143
1Sa 6:20 To whom *will* the ark **g up** from here?" H6590
1Sa 8:20 king to lead us and *to* **g out** before us H3655
1Sa 8:22 "Everyone **g back** to your own town." H2143
1Sa 9: 3 servants with you and g and look for the H2143
1Sa 9: 5 *let's* **g back**, or my father will stop H8740
1Sa 9: 6 says comes true. *Let's* g there now H2143
1Sa 9: 7 to his servant, "If *we* g, what can we give H2143
1Sa 9: 9 *let us* g to the seer," because the H2143
1Sa 9:10 "Come, *let's* g." So they set out H2143
1Sa 9:13 **G up** now; you should find him about this H6590
1Sa 9:19 "**G up** ahead of me *to* the high place, for H6590
1Sa 9:27 "Tell the servant *to* **g on** ahead of us"— H6296
1Sa 10: 3 "Then *you will* g on from there until you H2736
1Sa 10: 5 "After that *you will* g *to* Gibeah of God H995
1Sa 10: 8 "**G down** ahead of me *to* Gilgal. I will H3718
1Sa 10:25 the people to g to their own homes. NDT
1Sa 11:14 *let us* g *to* Gilgal and there renew the H2143
1Sa 14: 1 *let's* **g over** to the Philistine outpost on H6296
1Sa 14: 6 *let's* **g over** to the outpost of those H6296
1Sa 14: 7 "**G ahead**; I am with you H5742
1Sa 14: 9 stay where we are and not **g up** to them. H6590
1Sa 14:34 "**G out** among the men and tell them H7046
1Sa 14:36 "*Let us* **g down** and pursue the Philistines H3718
1Sa 14:37 "*Shall I* **g down** and pursue the Philistines H3718
1Sa 15: 3 Now **g**, attack the Amalekites and totally H2143
1Sa 15: 6 he said to the Kenites, "**G** away, leave the H2143
1Sa 15:18 '**G** and completely destroy those wicked H2143
1Sa 15:26 said to him, "*I will* not **g back** with you. H8740
1Sa 15:35 he did not g to see Saul again NDT
1Sa 16: 2 Samuel said, "How *can I* g? If Saul hears H2143
1Sa 17:32 your servant *will* g and fight him. H2143
1Sa 17:33 "You are not able to **g out** against this H2143
1Sa 17:37 Saul said to David, "**G**, and the LORD be H2143
1Sa 17:39 "I cannot g in these," he said to Saul H2143
1Sa 18:30 commanders *continued to* **g out** to battle, H3655
1Sa 19: 2 morning; g into hiding and stay there. H3782
1Sa 19: 3 I *will* **g out** and stand with my father in the H3655
1Sa 20: 5 but **let** me g and hide in the field until H8938
1Sa 20:11 Jonathan said, "*let's* **g out** *into* the field." H3655
1Sa 20:19 g to the place where you hid when this H995
1Sa 20:21 send a boy and say, '**G**, find the arrows. H2143
1Sa 20:22 then *you must* g, because the H2143
1Sa 20:28 asked me for permission to g to Bethlehem. NDT
1Sa 20:29 He said, '**Let** me g, because our family is H8938
1Sa 20:38 shouted, "Hurry! **G quickly**! Don't stop!" H2590
1Sa 20:40 the boy and said, "**G**, carry them back to H2143
1Sa 20:42 said to David, "**G** in peace, for we have H2143
1Sa 22: 5 the stronghold. **G** into the land of Judah." H2143
1Sa 23: 2 "*Shall I* g and attack these Philistines?" H2143
1Sa 23: 2 LORD answered him, "**G**, attack the H2143
1Sa 23: 3 if *we* g *to* Keilah against the Philistine H3718
1Sa 23: 4 answered him, "**G down** *to* Keilah, for I H3718
1Sa 23: 8 to **g down** *to* Keilah to besiege David H3718
1Sa 23:13 escaped from Keilah, *he did* not g there. H3655
1Sa 23:22 **G** and get more information. Find out H2143
1Sa 23:23 Then *I will* g with you; if he is in the area H2143
1Sa 25: 5 "**G** up to Nabal at Carmel and greet him in H995
1Sa 25:19 told her servants, "**G on** ahead; I'll follow H6296
1Sa 25:35 brought him and said, "**G** home in peace. H6590

1Sa 26: 6 "Who *will* **g down** into the camp with me H3718
1Sa 26: 6 "I'll **g** with you," said H3718
1Sa 26:10 or *he will* **g** into battle and perish. H3718
1Sa 26:11 jug that are near his head, and *let's* **g**." H2143
1Sa 26:19 have said, '**G**, serve other gods. H2143
1Sa 27:10 "Where *did you* **g raiding** today? H7320
1Sa 28: 7 a medium, so *I may* **g** and inquire of her." H2143
1Sa 28:22 have the strength *to* **g** on your way." H2143
1Sa 29: 4 *He must* not **g** with us into battle, or he H3718
1Sa 29: 7 Now turn back and **g** in peace; do nothing H2143
1Sa 29: 8 Why can't *I* **g** and fight against the H995
1Sa 29: 9 '*He must* not **g up** with us into battle. H6590
1Sa 29:11 in the morning to **g** back to the land of H2143
1Sa 30:22 "Because *they did* not **g out** with us, we H2143
1Sa 30:22 may take his wife and children and **g**." H2143
2Sa 1:15 of his men and said, "**G**, strike him down!" H5602
2Sa 2: 1 "*Shall I* **g up** to one of the towns of Judah H6590
2Sa 2: 1 The LORD said, "**G up**." David asked, H6590
2Sa 2: 1 "Where *shall I* **g**?" "To Hebron, H6590
2Sa 3:16 Abner said to him, "**G** back home!" So he H2143
2Sa 3:21 "*Let me* **g** at once and assemble all Israel H2143
2Sa 3:24 Why *did you* **let** him **g**? Now he is H8938
2Sa 5:19 "*Shall I* **g** and attack the Philistines? H6590
2Sa 5:19 LORD answered him, "**G**, for I will surely H6590
2Sa 5:23 answered, "*Do* not **g straight up**, but circle H6590
2Sa 7: 3 you have in mind, **g ahead** and do it, for H2143
2Sa 7: 5 "**G** and tell my servant David, 'This is H2143
2Sa 11: 1 at the time when kings **g off to war**, David H3655
2Sa 11: 8 "**G down** to your house and wash your H3718
2Sa 11: 9 servants and *did* not **g down** to his house. H3718
2Sa 11:10 was told, "Uriah *did* not **g** home." So he H3718
2Sa 11:10 Why didn't *you* **g** home?" H3718
2Sa 11:11 *How could* I **g** to my house to eat and drink H995
2Sa 11:13 his master's servants; *he did* not **g** home. H3718
2Sa 12:23 that he is dead, why *should* I **g** *on* **fasting**? AIT
2Sa 12:23 I *will* **g** to him, but he will not return to H2143
2Sa 13: 5 "**G** to bed and pretend to be ill," Jonadab H8886
2Sa 13: 7 "**G** *to* the house of your brother Amnon H2143
2Sa 13:25 "All of us *should* not **g**; we would only be H2143
2Sa 13:25 he still refused to **g** but gave him his H2143
2Sa 13:26 asked him, "Why *should he* **g** with you?" H2143
2Sa 13:39 And King David longed to **g** to Absalom H3655
2Sa 14: 3 Then **g** to the king and speak these words H995
2Sa 14: 8 said to the woman, "**G** home, and I will H2143
2Sa 14:21 **G**, bring back the young man H2143
2Sa 14:24 king said, "*He must* **g** to his own house H6015
2Sa 14:30 he has barley there. **G** and set it on fire." H2143
2Sa 14:31 Then Joab *did* **g** to Absalom's house, and H995
2Sa 15: 7 "*Let me* **g** to Hebron and fulfill a vow I H2143
2Sa 15: 9 king said to him, "**G** in peace." So he H2143
2Sa 15:19 **G back** and stay with King Absalom H8740
2Sa 15:20 where I am going? **G back**, and take your H8740
2Sa 15:22 said to Ittai, "**G ahead**, march on." So Ittai H2143
2Sa 15:27 **G back** *to* the city with my blessing H8740
2Sa 15:33 said to him, "If *you* **g** with me, you will be H6296
2Sa 16: 9 *Let me* **g over** and cut off his head." H6296
2Sa 16:17 your friend, why didn't *you* **g** with him?" H2143
2Sa 17:17 female servant *was to* **g** and inform them H2143
2Sa 17:17 they *were to* **g** and tell King David H2143
2Sa 18: 3 men said, "*You must* not **g out**; if we are H3655
2Sa 18:21 said to a Cushite, "**G**, tell the king what H2143
2Sa 18:22 replied, "My son, why *do you want to* **g**? H8132
2Sa 19: 7 Now **g** out and encourage your men. H7756
2Sa 19: 7 I swear by the LORD that if you don't **g out** H3655
2Sa 19:15 come to Gilgal to **g out** and meet the king H2143
2Sa 19:25 "Why didn't *you* **g** with me H2143
2Sa 19:26 will ride on it, so *I can* **g** with the king. H2143
2Sa 19:34 that *I should* **g up** *to* Jerusalem with the H6590
2Sa 21:17 "Never again *will you* **g out** with us to H3655
2Sa 24: 1 "**G** and take a census of Israel and Judah." H2143
2Sa 24: 2 "**G** throughout the tribes of Israel from H8763
2Sa 24:12 "**G** and tell David, 'This is what the LORD H2143
2Sa 24:18 "**G up** and build an altar to the LORD on H6590
1Ki 1:13 **G in** to King David and say to H2143+2256+995
1Ki 1:35 Then *you are to* **g up** with him, and he is H6590
1Ki 1:53 Solomon said, "**G** to your home. H2143
1Ki 2: 2 "*I am about to* **g** the way of all the earth," H2143
1Ki 2: 3 prosper in all you do and wherever *you* **g** H7155
1Ki 2: 6 but *do* not **let** his gray head **g down** *to* the H3718
1Ki 2:26 "**G back** to your fields in Anathoth. H2143
1Ki 2:29 son of Jehoiada, "**G**, strike him down!" H2143
1Ki 2:36 live there, but *do* not **g** anywhere else. H3655
1Ki 2:42 'On the day you leave *to* **g** anywhere else H2143
1Ki 7:38 one basin to **g** on each of the ten stands. NDT
1Ki 8:44 "When your people **g** to war against their H3655
1Ki 9: 6 have given you and **g off** to serve other H2143
1Ki 11:21 said to Pharaoh, "**Let** me **g**, that I may H8938
1Ki 11:22 that you want to **g back** to your own H2143
1Ki 11:22 Hadad replied, "but **do let me g**!" H8938+8938
1Ki 12: 5 "**G away** for three days and then come H2143
1Ki 12:21 to **g to war** against Israel and to regain the H4309
1Ki 12:24 *Do* not **g up** to fight against your brothers H6590
1Ki 12:24 **G** home, every one of you, for this is my H8740
1Ki 12:27 If these people **g up** to offer sacrifices at H6590
1Ki 12:28 is too much for you *to* **g up** *to* Jerusalem. H6590
1Ki 13: 8 possessions, *I would* not **g** with you, nor H995
1Ki 13:12 father asked them, "Which way *did he* **g**?" H2143
1Ki 13:16 "I cannot turn back and **g** with you, nor can H995
1Ki 14: 2 said to his wife, "**G**, disguise yourself, H7756
1Ki 14: 2 Then **g** *to* Shiloh. Ahijah H2143
1Ki 14: 3 cakes and a jar of honey, and **g** to him. H995
1Ki 14: 7 **G**, tell Jeroboam that this is what the LORD H2143
1Ki 14:12 "As for you, **g back** home. When you set H2143
1Ki 17: 9 "**G** at once to Zarephath in the region of H2143
1Ki 17:13 **G home** and do as you have said H995
1Ki 18: 1 "**G** and present yourself to Ahab, and I H2143
1Ki 18: 5 "**G** through the land to all the springs H2143
1Ki 18: 8 "**G** tell your master, 'Elijah is H2143
1Ki 18:11 But now you tell me *to* **g** to my master H2143
1Ki 18:12 If *I* **g** and tell Ahab and he doesn't find you H995
1Ki 18:14 now you tell me *to* **g** to my master and H2143
1Ki 18:41 Elijah said to Ahab, "**G**, eat and drink, H6590
1Ki 18:43 "**G** and look toward the sea," he told his H6590
1Ki 18:43 Seven times Elijah said, "**G back**." H8740
1Ki 18:44 So Elijah said, "**G** and tell Ahab, 'Hitch H6590
1Ki 18:44 your chariot and **g down** before the rain H3718
1Ki 19:11 "**G out** and stand on the mountain in the H3655
1Ki 19:15 said to him, "**G** back the way you came H2143
1Ki 19:15 you came, and **g** to the Desert of Damascus. NDT
1Ki 19:20 come with you." "**G** back," Elijah replied H2143
1Ki 20:31 *Let us* **g** to the king of Israel with sackcloth H3655
1Ki 20:33 "**G** and get him," the king said H995
1Ki 20:34 he made a treaty with him, and **let** him **g**. H8938
1Ki 21:18 "**G** down to meet Ahab king of Israel, who H7756
1Ki 22: 4 "*Will you* **g** with me to fight against H2143
1Ki 22: 6 "*Shall I* **g** to war against Ramoth Gilead H2143
1Ki 22: 6 "**G**," they answered, "for the Lord will H6590
1Ki 22:15 *shall we* **g** to war against Ramoth Gilead H2143
1Ki 22:17 *Let* each one **g** home in peace H8740
1Ki 22:22 " '*I will* **g out** and be a deceiving spirit in H3655
1Ki 22:22 said the LORD. '**G** and do it.' H3655
1Ki 22:24 way *did* the spirit from the LORD **g** when he H6296
1Ki 22:25 out on the day *you* **g** to hide in an inner H995
1Ki 22:48 of trading ships to **g** to Ophir for gold, H2143
2Ki 1: 2 to them, "**G** and consult Baal-Zebub H2143
2Ki 1: 3 "**G up** and meet the messengers of the H6590
2Ki 1: 6 '**G** back to the king who sent you and tell H2143
2Ki 1:15 said to Elijah, "**G down** with him; do not H3718
2Ki 2:16 *Let them* **g** and look for your master H2143
2Ki 2:18 said to them, "Didn't I tell you not *to* **g**?" H2143
2Ki 3: 7 *Will you* **g** with me to fight against Moab?" H2143
2Ki 3: 7 against Moab?" "*I will* **g** with you," he H6590
2Ki 3:13 **G** to the prophets of your father and the H2143
2Ki 4: 3 "**G** around and ask all your neighbors H2143
2Ki 4: 4 Then **g** *inside* and shut the door behind you H995
2Ki 4: 7 he said, "**G**, sell the oil and pay your H2143
2Ki 4:22 so *I can* **g** to the man of God **quickly** and H8132
2Ki 4:23 "Why **g** to him today?" he asked. "It's not H2143
2Ki 5: 5 "**By all means, g**," the king of Aram H2143+995
2Ki 5:10 to say to him, "**G**, wash yourself seven H2143
2Ki 5:19 "**G** in peace," Elisha said. After Naaman H2143
2Ki 5:25 "Your servant didn't **g** anywhere," Gehazi H2143
2Ki 6: 2 *Let us* **g** to the Jordan, where each of us H2143
2Ki 6: 2 there for us to meet." And he said, "**G**." H2143
2Ki 6:13 "**G**, find out where he is," the king H2143
2Ki 6:22 drink and then **g back** to their master." H2143
2Ki 7: 4 If we say, '*We'll* **g into** the city'—the famine H995
2Ki 7: 4 So *let's* **g over** to the camp of the H2143
2Ki 7: 9 *Let's* **g at once** and report this H2143+2256+995
2Ki 7:14 "**G** and find out what has happened." H2143
2Ki 8: 1 "**G away** with your family and stay for a H2143
2Ki 8: 8 a gift with you and **g** to meet the man of H2143
2Ki 8:10 Elisha answered, "**G** and say to him, 'You H2143
2Ki 9: 1 oil with you and **g** *to* Ramoth Gilead. H2143
2Ki 9: 2 **G** *to* him, get him away from his H995
2Ki 9:15 out of the city to **g** and tell the news in H2143
2Ki 10:25 "**G in** and kill them; let no H995
2Ki 11: 7 *that* normally **g off** Sabbath **duty** are all H3655
2Ki 17:27 **Have** one of the priests you took captive
from Samaria **g** H2143
2Ki 19:27 when you come and **g** and how you rage H3655
2Ki 20: 5 "**G back** and tell Hezekiah, the ruler of my H8740
2Ki 20: 5 day from now *you will* **g up** *to* the temple H6590
2Ki 20: 8 me and that *I will* **g up** *to* the temple of H6590
2Ki 20: 9 *Shall* the shadow **g forward** ten steps, or H2143
2Ki 20: 9 ten steps, or *shall it* **g back** ten steps?" H8740
2Ki 20:10 the shadow to **g forward** ten steps, H5742
2Ki 20:10 "Rather, *have* it **g back** ten steps." H8740+345
2Ki 20:11 the LORD **made** the shadow **g back** the ten H8740
2Ki 22: 4 "**G up** to Hilkiah the high priest and have H6590
2Ki 22:13 "**G** and inquire of the LORD for me and for H2143
2Ki 25:24 of Babylon, and *it will* **g well** with you." H3512
1Ch 7:11 fighting men **ready to g out** to war. H3655+7372
1Ch 14:10 "*Shall I* **g** and attack the Philistines H6590
1Ch 14:10 LORD answered him, "**G**, I will deliver them H6590
1Ch 14:14 "*Do* not **g directly** after them H6590
1Ch 17: 4 "**G** and tell my servant David, 'This is H2143
1Ch 17:11 days are over and you **g** to be with your H2143
1Ch 20: 1 at the time when kings **g off** to war, Joab H3655
1Ch 21: 2 "**G** and count the Israelites from H2143
1Ch 21:10 "**G** and tell David, 'This is what the LORD H2143
1Ch 21:18 Gad to tell David *to* **g up** and build an H6590
1Ch 21:30 But David could not **g** before it to inquire H2143
2Ch 6:34 "When your people **g** to war against their H3655
2Ch 7:19 have given you and **g off** to serve other H2143
2Ch 11: 1 to **g to war** against Israel and to regain the H4309
2Ch 11: 4 *Do* not **g up** to fight against your fellow H6590
2Ch 11: 4 **G** home, every one of you, for this is my H8740
2Ch 17:10 so that *they did* not **g to war** against H4309
2Ch 18: 3 "*Will you* **g** with me *against* Ramoth H2143
2Ch 18: 5 "*Shall we* **g** to war against Ramoth Gilead H2143
2Ch 18: 5 "**G**," they answered, "for God will give it H6590
2Ch 18:14 *shall we* **g** to war against Ramoth Gilead H2143
2Ch 18:16 *Let* each one **g** home in peace H8740
2Ch 18:21 " '*I will* **g** and be a deceiving spirit in the H3655
2Ch 18:21 said the LORD. '**G** and do it.' H3655
2Ch 18:23 way *did* the spirit from the LORD **g** when he H6296
2Ch 18:24 out on the day *you* **g** to hide in an inner H995
2Ch 20:17 **G out** to face them tomorrow, and the H3655
2Ch 24: 5 "**G** to the towns of Judah and collect the H3655
2Ch 25: 8 Even if you **g** and fight courageously in H995
2Ch 26:11 **ready to g out** by divisions H3655+7372
2Ch 34:21 "**G** and inquire of the LORD for me and for H2143
2Ch 36:23 Any of his people among you *may* **g up** H6590
Ezr 1: 3 among you *may* **g up** to Jerusalem in H6590
Ezr 1: 5 prepared to **g up** and build the house of H6590
Ezr 4: 4 make them afraid to **g** *on* **building**. AIT
Ezr 5: 5 until a report *could* **g** to Darius and his A10207
Ezr 5:15 these articles and **g** and deposit them in A10016
Ezr 7:13 who volunteer to **g** to Jerusalem with A10207
Ezr 7:13 to go to Jerusalem with you, *may* **g**. A10207
Ezr 7:28 leaders from Israel to **g up** with me. H6590
Ezr 8:17 I ordered them *to* **g** *to* Iddo, the leader in AIT
Ezr 8:31 from the Ahava Canal to **g** *to* Jerusalem. H2143
Ne 6: 3 on a great project and cannot **g down**. H3718
Ne 6: 3 stop while I leave it and **g down** to you?" H3718
Ne 6:11 Or *should* someone like me **g** into the H995
Ne 6:11 the temple to save his life? *I will* not **g**!" H995
Ne 8:10 "**G** and enjoy choice food and sweet H2143
Ne 8:15 "**G out** *into* the hill country and bring back H3655
Ne 9:15 you told them to **g in** and take possession H995
Ne 12:31 *I* **had** the leaders of Judah **g up** on top of H6590
Ne 13:22 themselves and **g** and guard the gates H995
Est 2:12 woman's turn came to **g in** to King Xerxes, H995
Est 2:13 And this is how she *would* **g** to the king H995
Est 2:14 In the evening she *would* **g** there and in the H995
Est 2:15 his uncle Abihail) to **g** to the king, she H995
Est 4: 8 him to instruct her to **g** into the king's H995
Est 4:11 passed since I was called to **g** to the king." H995
Est 4:16 "**G**, gather together all the Jews who are H2143
Est 4:16 this is done, *I will* **g** to the king, even H995
Est 5:14 Then **g** with the king to the banquet and H995
Est 6:10 "**G at once**," the king commanded Haman H4554
Job 2:11 by agreement to **g** and sympathize with H995
Job 6:18 *they* **g off** into the wasteland and perish. H6590
Job 10:14 *would* not **let** my offense **g unpunished**. H5927
Job 10:21 before *I* **g** to the place of no return, to the H2143
Job 11: 2 *Are* all these words *to* **g unanswered** H4202+6699
Job 16: 6 if I refrain, *it does* not **g** away. H2143
Job 17:16 *Will it* **g down** *to* the gates of death? Will H3718
Job 20:13 he cannot bear *to let* it **g** and lets it linger H6440
Job 21:13 in prosperity and **g down** *to* the grave in H5737
Job 23: 3 find him; if only *I could* **g** to his dwelling! H995
Job 23: 8 "But if *I* **g** *to* the east, he is not there; if I H2143
Job 23: 8 he is not there; if I **g** to the west, I do not NDT
Job 24: 5 the poor **g about** their labor of foraging H3655
Job 24:10 Lacking clothes, *they* **g about** naked; they H2143
Job 24:10 they carry the sheaves, but still **g** hungry. NDT
Job 27: 6 my innocence and never **let g** *of it*; H8332
Job 30:28 *I* **g about** blackened, but not by the sun; H2143
Job 31:34 I kept silent and *would* not **g** outside— H3655
Job 33:27 And *they will* **g** to others and say, 'I have H8801
Job 39: 5 "Who **let** the wild donkey **g** free? Who H8938
Job 42: 8 seven rams and **g** to my servant Job H2143
Ps 9:17 The wicked **g down** to the realm of the H8740
Ps 22:29 all *who* **g down** *to* the dust will kneel H3718
Ps 26: 6 in innocence, and **g about** your altar, LORD H6015
Ps 28: 1 I will be like *those who* **g down** *to* the pit. H3718
Ps 30: 9 if I am silenced, if I **g down** to the pit? H3718
Ps 32: 8 teach you in the way *you should* **g**; H2143
Ps 37:20 be consumed, *they will* **g up** in smoke. H3983
Ps 38: 6 very low; all day long *I* **g about** mourning. H2143
Ps 42: 2 When *can I* **g** and meet with God H995
Ps 42: 4 how *I used to* **g** to the house of God H6296
Ps 42: 9 Why *must I* **g about** mourning, oppressed H2143
Ps 43: 2 Why *must I* **g about** mourning, oppressed H2143
Ps 43: 4 Then *I will* **g** to the altar of God, to God H995
Ps 44: 9 *you* no *longer* **g out** with our armies. H3655
Ps 48:12 Walk about Zion, **g around** her, count her H5938
Ps 55:15 *let them* **g down** alive *to* the realm of the H3718
Ps 58: 3 Even from birth the wicked **g astray**; from H2319
Ps 59:10 God *will* **g before** me and will let me H7709
Ps 60:10 us and no longer **g out** with our armies? H3655
Ps 63: 9 *they will* **g down** to the depths of the earth. H995
Ps 68:21 crowns of *those who* **g on** in their sins. H2143
Ps 71: 3 to which I *can* always **g**; give the command H995
Ps 73:12 free of care, *they* **g on amassing** wealth. H8436
Ps 84: 7 *They* **g** from strength to strength, till each H2143
Ps 88: 4 among *those who* **g down** *to* the pit; H3718
Ps 89:14 love and faithfulness **g** before you. H7709
Ps 95:10 'They are a people whose hearts **g astray** H9494
Ps 102:24 your years **g** on through all generations. NDT
Ps 104:19 the sun knows when to **g down**. H4427
Ps 104:23 Then people **g out** to their work, to their H3655
Ps 104:26 There the ships **g to and fro**, and H2143
Ps 108:11 us and no longer **g out** with our armies? H3655
Ps 115:17 those *who* **g down** *to* the place of silence H3718
Ps 122: 1 "*Let us* **g** *to* the house of the LORD. H2143
Ps 122: 4 That is where the tribes **g up**—the tribes H6590
Ps 126: 6 *Those who* **g out** weeping, carrying H2143+2143
Ps 132: 3 "I will not enter my house or **g** to my bed, H6590
Ps 132: 7 "*Let us* **g** to his dwelling place, let us H995
Ps 139: 7 Where *can I* **g** from your Spirit? Where H2143
Ps 139: 8 If *I* **g up** *to* the heavens, you are there; if I H6158
Ps 143: 7 I will be like *those who* **g down** *to* the pit. H3718
Ps 143: 8 Show me the way *I should* **g**, for to you I H2143

Book	Ref	Context	Number
Pr	1:12	like *those who* **g down** *to* the pit;	H3718
Pr	1:15	*do* not g along with them	H2143+928+2006
Pr	1:19	of all *who* **g after ill-gotten gain**;	H1298+1299
Pr	2:19	None *who* g *to* her return or attain the	H995
Pr	3:23	Then *you will* g *on* your way in safety, and	H2143
Pr	4:13	to instruction, *do* not **let** it g; guard it well,	H8332
Pr	4:15	turn from it and **g on** *your* **way**.	H6296
Pr	5:5	Her feet **g down** *to* death; her steps lead	H3718
Pr	5:8	*do* not **g near** the door of her house	H7928
Pr	6:3	**G**—to the point of exhaustion—and give	H2143
Pr	6:6	**G** to the ant, *you* sluggard; consider its	H2143
Pr	6:29	one who touches her *will* **g unpunished**.	H5927
Pr	9:15	who pass by, who **g straight** *on* their way,	H3837
Pr	10:3	LORD *does* not **let** the righteous **g hungry**,	H8279
Pr	11:21	The wicked *will* not **g unpunished**, but	H5927
Pr	11:21	those who are righteous *will* **g free**.	H4880
Pr	14:22	*Do* not those who plot evil **g astray**? But	H9494
Pr	16:5	*They will* not **g unpunished**.	H5927
Pr	17:5	over disaster *will* not **g unpunished**.	H5927
Pr	18:8	morsels; they **g down** *to* the inmost parts.	H3718
Pr	19:5	A false witness *will* not **g unpunished**	H5927
Pr	19:5	whoever pours out lies *will* not **g free**.	H4880
Pr	19:9	A false witness *will* not **g unpunished**	H5927
Pr	19:15	on deep sleep, and the shiftless **g hungry**.	H8279
Pr	21:22	who is wise *can* **g up** *against* the city of	H6590
Pr	22:6	Start children off on the **way** they *should* g	AIT
Pr	23:30	who g to sample bowls of mixed wine.	H995
Pr	24:25	But *it will* **g well** with those who convict	H5838
Pr	26:22	morsels; they **g down** *to* the inmost parts.	H3718
Pr	27:10	and *do* not g *to* your relative's house when	H995
Pr	28:12	rise to power, people **g into hiding**.	H2924
Pr	28:20	eager to get rich *will* not **g unpunished**.	H5927
Pr	28:28	people **g into hiding**; but when	H6259
Pr	31:18	her lamp *does* not **g out** at night.	H3882
Ecc	1:4	Generations come and generations g, but	H995
Ecc	3:20	All g to the same place; all come from	H2143
Ecc	5:1	your steps when *you* g to the house of	H2143
Ecc	5:1	**G near** to listen rather than to offer the	H7928
Ecc	6:6	*Do* not all g to the same place?	H2143
Ecc	7:2	It is better to g to a house of mourning	H2143
Ecc	7:2	of mourning than *to* g to a house of	H2143
Ecc	7:18	one and not **let** g of the other	H5663+906+3338
Ecc	8:10	used to come and g from the holy place	H2143
Ecc	8:12	I know that *it will* g better with those who	H2118
Ecc	8:13	not fear God, *it will* not g well with them	H2118
Ecc	9:7	**G**, eat your food with gladness, and drink	H2143
Ecc	10:7	while princes g on foot like slaves.	H2143
Ecc	12:5	Then people g to their eternal home and	H2143
Ecc	12:5	home and mourners **g about** the streets.	H6015
SS	3:2	I will get up now and **g about** the city	H6015
SS	3:4	him and *would* not **let** him g till I had	H8332
SS	4:6	*I will* g to the mountain of myrrh and to	H2143
SS	7:9	*May* the wine g straight to my beloved	H2143
SS	7:11	my beloved, *let us* g to the countryside	H3655
SS	7:12	*Let us* **g early** to the vineyards to see if the	H8899
Isa	2:3	*let us* **g up** to the mountain of the LORD	H6590
Isa	2:3	The law *will* **g out** from Zion, the word of	H3655
Isa	2:10	**G** into the rocks, hide in the ground from	H995
Isa	5:13	my people *will* **g into exile** for lack of	H1655
Isa	6:8	And who *will* g for us?" And I said	H2143
Isa	6:9	He said, "**G** and tell this people: " 'Be	H2143
Isa	7:3	said to Isaiah, "**G out**, you and your son	H3655
Isa	7:24	*Hunters will* g there with bow and arrow, for	H995
Isa	7:25	*you will* no longer g there for fear of the	H995
Isa	10:29	*They* **g over** the pass, and say, "We will	H6296
Isa	13:7	all hands *will* **g limp**, every heart will	H8332
Isa	14:17	and *would* not *let* his captives g home?"	H7337
Isa	15:5	*They* **g up** the hill to Luhith, weeping as	H6590
Isa	15:5	weeping as they g; on the road to	NDT
Isa	18:2	**G**, swift messengers, to a people tall and	H2143
Isa	19:23	The Assyrians *will* g to Egypt and the	H995
Isa	21:6	"**G**, post a lookout and have him report	H2143
Isa	22:15	"**G**, say to this steward, to Shebna	H2143+995
Isa	23:18	Her profits *will* g to those who live before	H2118
Isa	26:10	uprightness *they* **g on doing evil** and do not	AIT
Isa	26:20	**G**, my people, enter your rooms and shut	H2143
Isa	28:13	so that *as they* g they will fall backward	H2143
Isa	28:28	so *one does* not **g on threshing** it	H1889+1889
Isa	29:1	to year and *let* your **cycle** of festivals **g on**.	H5938
Isa	29:15	to those *who* **g to great depths** to hide	H6676
Isa	30:2	who g down to Egypt without consulting	H3718
Isa	30:8	**G** now, write it on a tablet for them	H995
Isa	30:29	playing pipes g up to the mountain	H2143
Isa	31:1	Woe to those *who* **g down** *to* Egypt for	H3718
Isa	35:8	wicked fools *will* not **g about** on it.	H9494
Isa	37:28	when you come and g and how you rage	H3655
Isa	38:5	"**G** and tell Hezekiah, 'This is what the	H2143
Isa	38:8	I *will* **make** the shadow cast by the sun **g**	H8740
Isa	38:10	prime of my life *must I* g through the	H2143
Isa	38:18	*those who* **g down** *to* the pit cannot hope	H3718
Isa	38:22	the sign that *I will* **g up** to the temple of	H6590
Isa	40:9	news to Zion, **g up** on a high mountain.	H6590
Isa	42:10	you *who* **g down** *to* the sea, and	H3718
Isa	45:2	I *will* g before you and will level the	H2143
Isa	45:16	*they will* **g off** into disgrace together.	H2143
Isa	46:2	*they* themselves **g off** into captivity.	H2143
Isa	47:1	"**G down**, sit in the dust, Virgin Daughter	H3718
Isa	47:5	"Sit in silence, g into darkness, queen city	H995
Isa	47:15	All of them **g on** in their error; there is not	H6298
Isa	48:17	who directs you in the way *you should* **g**.	H2143
Isa	50:11	*g*, **walk** in the light of your fires and of the	AIT
Isa	51:4	Instruction *will* **g out** from me; my justice	H3655
Isa	52:11	depart, **g out** from there! Touch	H3655
Isa	52:12	you will not leave in haste or g in flight;	H2143
Isa	52:12	the LORD *will* g before you, the God	H2143
Isa	55:12	*You will* **g out** in joy and be led forth in	H3655
Isa	58:8	then your righteousness *will* g before you	H2143
Isa	63:14	like cattle *that* **g down** to the plain, they	H3718
Isa	65:13	but you *will* g **hungry**; my servants	AIT
Isa	65:13	but you *will* g **thirsty**; my servants will	AIT
Isa	66:17	purify themselves to g into the gardens,	NDT
Isa	66:24	"And *they will* **g out** and look on the dead	H3655
Jer	1:7	*You must* g to everyone I send you to	H2143
Jer	2:2	"**G** and proclaim in the hearing of	H2143
Jer	2:18	Now why **g to** Egypt to drink water from	H2006
Jer	2:18	And why **g to** Assyria to drink water from	H2006
Jer	2:25	foreign gods, and *I must* g after them.	H2143
Jer	2:36	Why *do you* **g about** so much, changing	H261
Jer	3:12	**G**, proclaim this message toward the north:	H2143
Jer	4:1	out of my sight and no longer **g astray**,	H5653
Jer	4:6	Raise the signal to g to Zion! Flee for safety	NDT
Jer	4:29	*Some* g into the thickets; some climb up	H995
Jer	5:1	"**G up and down** the streets of Jerusalem	H8763
Jer	5:5	So *I will* g to the leaders and speak to	H2143
Jer	5:10	"**G** through her vineyards and ravage	H6590
Jer	6:25	*Do* not **g out** *to* the fields or walk on the	H3655
Jer	7:12	" '**G** now to the place in Shiloh where I	H2143
Jer	7:21	*G ahead*, **add** your burnt offerings to your	AIT
Jer	7:23	that *it may* **g well** with you.	H3512
Jer	9:2	leave my people and g away from them;	H2143
Jer	9:3	*They* g from one sin to another; they do	H3655
Jer	11:12	of Jerusalem *will* g and cry out to the	H2143
Jer	12:9	**G** and gather all the wild beasts; bring	H2143
Jer	13:1	"**G** and buy a linen belt and put it around	H2143
Jer	13:4	g now to Perath and hide it there in a	H2143
Jer	13:6	"**G** now to Perath and get the belt I told	H2143
Jer	13:10	of their hearts and g after other gods to	H2143
Jer	14:3	*they* g to the cisterns but find no water.	H995
Jer	14:18	If *I* **g into** the country, I see those slain by	H3655
Jer	14:18	by the sword; if *I* **g into** the city, I see the	H995
Jer	15:1	my heart would not g out to this people.	NDT
Jer	15:1	away from my presence! *Let them* **g**!	H3655
Jer	15:2	ask you, 'Where *shall we* g?' tell them,	H3655
Jer	16:5	*do* not g to mourn or show sympathy	H2143
Jer	17:19	"**G** and stand at the Gate of the People	H2143
Jer	17:19	which the kings of Judah **g in** and out;	H995
Jer	18:2	"**G down** *to* the potter's house, and there I	H3718
Jer	19:1	"**G** and buy a clay jar from a potter	H2143
Jer	19:2	and **g out** to the Valley of Ben Hinnom	H3655
Jer	19:10	jar while those who g with you are	H2143
Jer	20:6	live in your house *will* g into exile to	H2143
Jer	22:1	"**G down** *to* the palace of the king of	H3718
Jer	22:20	"**G up** *to* Lebanon and cry out, let your	H6590
Jer	22:22	and your allies *will* g into exile.	H2143
Jer	25:16	will stagger and **g mad** because of the	H2147
Jer	25:29	and *will* you **indeed g unpunished**?	H5927+5927
Jer	25:29	*You will* not **g unpunished**, for I am	H5927
Jer	28:13	"**G** and tell Hananiah, 'This is what the	H2143
Jer	29:16	fellow citizens who *did* not **g** with you into	H3655
Jer	30:11	*I will* not **let** you **g entirely unpunished**	H5927+5927
Jer	30:16	all your enemies *will* g into exile.	H2143
Jer	31:4	your timbrels and **g out** to dance with the	H3655
Jer	31:6	*let us* **g up** *to* Zion, to the LORD our	H6590
Jer	32:39	that all will then g well for them and for	NDT
Jer	34:2	**G** to Zedekiah king of Judah and tell him	H2143
Jer	34:3	And *you will* g to Babylon.	H995
Jer	34:14	you six years, *you must* **let** them g free.	H8938
Jer	34:16	you had set free to g where they wished.	NDT
Jer	35:2	"**G** to the Rekabite family and invite them	H2143
Jer	35:11	*we must* g to Jerusalem to escape the	H995
Jer	35:13	**G** and tell the people of Judah and those	H2143
Jer	36:5	I am not allowed to g *to* the LORD's temple.	H995
Jer	36:6	So you g *to* the house of the LORD on a day	H995
Jer	36:19	"You and Jeremiah, g and hide.	H2143
Jer	37:4	free to come and g among the people,	H3655
Jer	37:7	to support you, *will* **g back** to its own land	H8740
Jer	37:12	to leave the city to g *to* the territory of	H2143
Jer	38:20	Then *it will* **g well** with you, and your life	H3512
Jer	39:16	"**G** and tell Ebed-Melek the Cushite, 'This	H2143
Jer	40:4	lies before you; g wherever you please."	H2143
Jer	40:5	before Jeremiah **turned to g**	H8740
Jer	40:5	"**G back** to Gedaliah son of Ahikam	H8740
Jer	40:5	people, or g anywhere else you please."	H2143
Jer	40:5	provisions and a present and **let** him **g**.	H8938
Jer	40:9	of Babylon, and *it will* **g well** with you.	H3512
Jer	40:15	"*Let me* g and kill Ishmael son of	H2143
Jer	42:3	tell us where *we should* g and what we	H2143
Jer	42:6	so that *it will* **g well** with us, for we	H3512
Jer	42:14	*we will* g and live in Egypt, where we	H995
Jer	42:15	are determined to g *to* Egypt and you do	H995
Jer	42:15	to go to Egypt and *you do* g to settle there,	H995
Jer	42:17	who are determined to g *to* Egypt to settle	H995
Jer	42:18	be poured out on you when you g *to* Egypt.	H995
Jer	42:19	the LORD has told you, '*Do* not g *to* Egypt.	H995
Jer	42:22	in the place where you want to g to settle."	H995
Jer	43:2	'*You must* not g to Egypt to settle there.	H995
Jer	44:12	were determined to g *to* Egypt to settle	H995
Jer	44:25	"*G ahead* then, **do** what you promised	AIT
Jer	45:5	wherever *you* g I will let you escape	H2143
Jer	46:11	"**G up** to Gilead and get balm, Virgin	H6590
Jer	46:16	*let us* **g back** to our own people and our	H8740
Jer	46:28	*I will* not **let** you **g entirely unpunished**	H5927+5927
Jer	48:5	*They* **g up** the hill to Luhith, weeping	H6590
Jer	48:5	weeping bitterly as they g; on the road	NDT
Jer	48:7	captive, and Chemosh *will* g into exile	H3655
Jer	48:15	finest young men *will* **g down** in the	H3718
Jer	49:3	the walls, for Molek *will* g into exile	H2143
Jer	49:12	why *should* you **g unpunished**?	H5927+5927
Jer	49:12	*You will* not **g unpunished**, but must drink	H5927
Jer	49:36	be a nation where Elam's exiles *do* not **g**.	H995
Jer	50:4	of Judah together *will* g in tears to seek the	H995
Jer	50:27	*let them* **g down** to the slaughter!	H3718
Jer	50:33	hold them fast, refusing *to* **let** them **g**.	H8938
Jer	50:38	of idols, idols *that will* **g mad** with terror.	H2147
Jer	51:9	us leave her and each g to our own land,	H2143
La	4:15	"**G away**! You are unclean!" people cry to	H6073
Eze	1:12	Wherever the spirit *would* g, they would	H2143
Eze	1:12	would go, *they would* **g**, without turning	H2143
Eze	1:17	*they would* **g** in any one of the four	H2143
Eze	1:20	Wherever the spirit *would* g, they would	H2143
Eze	1:20	would go, *they would* **g**, and the wheels	H2143
Eze	3:1	then g and speak to the people of Israel."	H2143
Eze	3:4	**g now** to the people of Israel and	H2143+995
Eze	3:11	**G now** to your people in exile and	H2143+995
Eze	3:22	"Get up and **g out** to the plain, and	H3655
Eze	3:24	to me and said: "**G**, shut yourself inside	H995
Eze	3:25	so that *you* cannot **g out** among the	H3655
Eze	7:14	but no *one will* g into battle, for my	H2143
Eze	7:17	Every hand *will* **g limp**; every leg will be	H8332
Eze	7:26	*They will* **g searching for** a vision from the	H1335
Eze	8:9	"**G in** and see the wicked and detestable	H995
Eze	9:4	"**G** throughout the city of Jerusalem and	H6296
Eze	9:7	with the slain. **G**!" So they went out and	H3655
Eze	10:2	"**G** in among the wheels beneath the	H995
Eze	10:11	*they would* g in any one of the four	H2143
Eze	12:3	set out and g from where you are to	H1655
Eze	12:4	**g out** like those who go into exile.	H3655
Eze	12:4	go out like *those who* g *into* exile.	H4604
Eze	12:11	*They will* g into exile as captives.	H2143
Eze	12:12	be dug in the wall for him to g through.	H3655
Eze	12:16	in the nations where *they* g they may	H995
Eze	12:22	'The days **g by** and every vision comes to	H799
Eze	14:4	before their faces and then g to a prophet,	H995
Eze	14:7	their faces and then g to a prophet to	H995
Eze	20:29	What is this high place you g *to*?' "	H995
Eze	20:39	**G** and serve your idols	H2143
Eze	21:7	will melt with fear and every hand **g limp**;	H8332
Eze	24:6	encrusted, whose deposit *will* not g away!	H3655
Eze	26:20	down with *those who* **g down** *to* the pit,	H3718
Eze	26:20	with *those who* **g down** *to* the pit	H3718
Eze	30:9	day messengers *will* **g out** from me in	H3655
Eze	30:17	the cities themselves *will* g into captivity.	H2143
Eze	30:18	her villages *will* g into captivity.	H2143
Eze	31:14	mortals *who* **g down** *to* the realm of	H3718
Eze	31:16	to be with *those who* **g down** *to* the pit.	H3718
Eze	32:18	along with *those who* **g down** *to* the pit.	H3718
Eze	32:19	**G down** and be laid among the	H3718
Eze	32:24	shame with *those who* **g down** *to* the pit.	H3718
Eze	32:25	shame with *those who* **g down** *to* the pit;	H3718
Eze	32:29	with *those who* **g down** *to* the pit.	H3718
Eze	32:30	shame with *those who* **g down** *to* the pit.	H3718
Eze	35:7	cut off from it all who come and g.	H8740
Eze	38:9	the many nations with you *will* **g up**,	H6590
Eze	39:9	the towns of Israel *will* **g out** and use the	H3655
Eze	39:15	As they g through the land, anyone who	H6296
Eze	42:14	*they are* not *to* g into the outer court until	H3655
Eze	42:14	clothes before *they* **g near** the places that	H7928
Eze	44:3	of the gateway and **g out** the same way."	H3655
Eze	44:19	When they **g out** into the outer court	H3655
Eze	46:2	threshold of the gateway and then **g out**,	H3655
Eze	46:8	*he is to* **g in** through the portico of the	H995
Eze	46:9	gate to worship *is to* **g out** the south gate;	H3655
Eze	46:9	the south gate *is to* **g out** the north gate.	H3655
Eze	46:9	but *each is to* **g out** the opposite gate.	H3655
Eze	46:10	going in when they **g in** and going out	H995
Eze	46:10	they go in and going out when they **g out**.	H3655
Eze	46:12	Then *he shall* **g out**, and after he has	H3655
Eze	48:11	me and *did* not **g astray** as the Levites	H9494
Da	10:20	and when I g, the prince of Greece	H3655
Da	11:4	It will not g to his descendants, nor will it	NDT
Da	11:6	king of the South *will* g to the king of the	H995
Da	12:4	Many *will* **g here and there** to increase	H8763
Da	12:9	He replied, "**G** *your* **way**, Daniel, because	H2143
Da	12:13	"As for you, g *your* **way** till the end.	H2143
Hos	1:2	LORD said to him, "**G**, marry a promiscuous	H2143
Hos	2:5	She said, '*I will* g after my lovers, who	H2143
Hos	2:7	'*I will* g back to my husband as at first	H2143
Hos	3:1	LORD said to me, "**G**, show your love to	H2143
Hos	4:15	"*Do* not g *to* Gilgal; do not go up to Beth	H995
Hos	4:15	go to Gilgal; *do* not **g up** to Beth Aven.	H6590
Hos	5:6	*When they* g with their flocks and herds to	H2143
Hos	5:14	I will tear them to pieces and **g away**;	H2143
Hos	6:5	then my judgments **g forth** like the sun.	H3655
Hos	7:12	When *they* **g**, I will throw my net over	H2143
Joel	2:20	And its stench *will* **g up**; its smell will	H6590
Am	1:5	people of Aram *will* **g into exile** to Kir,"	H1655
Am	1:15	Her king *will* g into exile, he and his	H2143
Am	2:2	Moab *will* **g down** in great tumult amid	H4637
Am	4:3	*You will* each g straight **out** through	H3655
Am	4:4	"**G** *to* Bethel and sin; go to Gilgal and sin	H995
Am	4:4	Bethel and sin; g to Gilgal and sin yet more.	NDT
Am	5:5	not seek Bethel, *do* not g *to* Gilgal, do not	H995
Am	5:5	For Gilgal *will* **surely g into exile**	H1655+1655
Am	6:2	**G** *to* Kalneh and look at it; go from there	H6296

Am 6: 2 look at it; g from there to great Hamath H2143
Am 6: 2 then g down to Gath in Philistia. H3718
Am 6: 7 you will be among the first to g into exile H1655+1655
Am 6:10 "No," then he will g on to say, "Hush! AIT
Am 7:11 and Israel will surely g into exile H1655+1655
Am 7:12 you seer! G back to the land of Judah H1368
Am 7:15 said to me, 'G, prophesy to my H2143
Am 7:17 And Israel will surely g into exile H1655+1655
Am 8: 9 "I will make the sun g down at noon and H995
Ob 1 "Rise, let us g against her for battle"— H7756
Ob 21 Deliverers will g up on Mount Zion to H6590
Jnh 1: 2 "G to the great city of Nineveh and preach H2143
Jnh 3: 2 "G to the great city of Nineveh and H2143
Jnh 3: 3 it took three days to g through it. H4544
Mic 1: 8 I will g about barefoot and naked. H2143
Mic 1:16 for they will g from you into exile. H1655
Mic 2:10 g away! For this is not your resting H2143
Mic 2:13 open the way will g up before them; H6590
Mic 2:13 will break through the gate and g out. H3655
Mic 3: 6 the day will g dark for them. H7722
Mic 4: 2 let us g up to the mountain of the LORD H6590
Mic 4: 2 The law will g out from Zion, the word of H3655
Mic 4:10 You will g to Babylon; there you will be H995
Na 3:11 you will g into hiding and seek refuge H2118
Hab 1:11 they sweep past like the wind and g on— H6296
Hab 2: 6 How long must this g on?' NDT
Zep 1:10 the LORD, "a cry will g up from the Fish Gate NDT
Hag 1: 8 G up into the mountains and bring down H6590
Zec 1:10 LORD has sent to g throughout the earth H2143
Zec 6: 7 were straining to g throughout the H2143+2143
Zec 6: 7 he said, "G throughout the earth!" H2143+2143
Zec 6:10 G the same day to the house of Josiah son H995
Zec 8:10 could g about their business H3655+2256+995
Zec 8:21 of one city will g to another and say, H2143
Zec 8:21 'Let us g at once to entreat the LORD H2143+2143
Zec 8:23 robe and say, 'Let us g with you, because H2143
Zec 11: 5 buyers slaughter them and g unpunished. AIT
Zec 14: 2 Half of the city will g into exile, but the H3655
Zec 14: 3 Then the LORD will g out and fight against H3655
Zec 14:16 Jerusalem will g up year after year to H6590
Zec 14:17 of the earth do not g up to Jerusalem to H6590
Zec 14:18 people do not g up and take part, H6590
Zec 14:18 the nations that do not g up to celebrate H6590
Zec 14:19 the nations that do not g up to celebrate H6590
Mal 4: 2 And you will g out and frolic like well-fed H3655
Mt 2: 8 "G and search carefully for the child. G4513
Mt 2: 8 so that I too may g and worship him." G2262
Mt 2:12 warned in a dream not to g back to Herod, G366
Mt 2:20 his mother and g to the land of Israel G4513
Mt 2:22 his father Herod, he was afraid to g there. G599
Mt 5:24 First g and be reconciled to them; then G5632
Mt 5:30 than for your whole body to g into hell. G599
Mt 5:41 If anyone forces you to g one mile, go with G30
Mt 5:41 to go one mile, g with them two miles. G5632
Mt 6: 6 But when you pray, g into your room, close G1656
Mt 8: 4 But g, show yourself to the priest and offer G5632
Mt 8: 9 I tell this one, 'G,' and he goes; and that G4513
Mt 8:13 to the centurion, "G! Let it be done just as G5632
Mt 8:19 "Teacher, I will follow you wherever you g." G599
Mt 8:21 first let me g and bury my father. G599
Mt 8:32 He said to them, "G!" So they came out G5632
Mt 9: 6 "Get up, take your mat and g home." G5632
Mt 9:13 But g and learn what this means: 'I desire G4513
Mt 9:24 "G away. The girl is not dead but G432
Mt 10: 5 "Do not g among the Gentiles or enter any G599
Mt 10: 6 G rather to the lost sheep of Israel. G4513
Mt 10: 7 As you g, proclaim this message: 'The G4513
Mt 11: 4 "G back and report to John what you hear G4513
Mt 11: 7 "What did you g out into the wilderness G2002
Mt 11: 8 what did you g out to see? A man G2002
Mt 11: 9 Then what did you g out to see? A prophet G2002
Mt 11:23 No, you will g down to Hades G2849
Mt 12:45 than itself, and they g in and live there. G1656
Mt 13:28 'Do you want us to g and pull them up? G599
Mt 14:15 so they can g to the villages and buy G599
Mt 14:16 "They do not need to g away. G599
Mt 14:22 the boat and g on ahead of him to the G4575
Mt 16:21 disciples that he must g to Jerusalem and G599
Mt 17:27 g to the lake and throw out your line. G4513
Mt 18:12 on the hills and g to look for the one that G4513
Mt 18:15 sister sins, g and point out their fault G5632
Mt 18:27 canceled the debt and let him g. G918
Mt 19:21 want to be perfect, g, sell your G5632
Mt 19:24 a camel to g through the eye of a G1451
Mt 20: 4 'You also g and work in my vineyard G5632
Mt 20: 7 'You also g and work in my vineyard.' G5632
Mt 20:14 Take your pay and g. I want to give the G5632
Mt 21: 2 to them, "G to the village ahead of you G4513
Mt 21:21 say to this mountain, 'G, throw yourself into G149
Mt 21:28 g and work today in the vineyard.' G5632
Mt 21:30 He answered, 'I will, sir,' but he did not g. G599
Mt 22: 9 So g to the street corners and invite to the G4513
Mt 23:32 G ahead, then, and complete what your AIT
Mt 24:17 Let no one on the housetop g down to G2849
Mt 24:18 Let no one in the field g back to get their G2188
Mt 24:26 wilderness,' do not g out; or, 'Here he is G2002
Mt 25: 9 g to those who sell oil and buy some for G4513
Mt 25:39 you sick or in prison and g to visit you?' G2262
Mt 25:46 "Then they will g away to eternal G599
Mt 26:18 "G into the city to a certain man and tell G5632
Mt 26:24 The Son of Man will g just as it is written G5632
Mt 26:32 I will g ahead of you into Galilee. G4575
Mt 26:36 "Sit here while I g over there and pray." G599
Mt 26:46 Let us g! Here comes my betrayer! G72
Mt 27:65 "G, make the tomb as secure as you know G5632
Mt 28: 7 Then g quickly and tell his disciples: 'He G4513
Mt 28:10 G and tell my brothers to go to Galilee G5632
Mt 28:10 Go and tell my brothers to g to Galilee G599
Mt 28:16 mountain where Jesus had told them to g. NDT
Mt 28:19 Therefore g and make disciples of all G4513
Mk 1:38 Jesus replied, "Let us g somewhere else—to G72
Mk 1:44 But g, show yourself to the priest and offer G5632
Mk 2:11 get up, take your mat and g home." G5632
Mk 4:35 disciples, "Let us g over to the other side." G1451
Mk 5:12 among the pigs; allow us to g into them." G1656
Mk 5:18 demon-possessed begged to g with him. G1639
Mk 5:19 "G home to your own people and tell G5632
Mk 5:34 G in peace and be freed from your G5632
Mk 6:36 away so that they can g to the surrounding G599
Mk 6:37 Are we to g and spend that much on bread G599
Mk 6:38 "G and see." When they found G5632
Mk 6:45 into the boat and g on ahead of him to G4575
Mk 7: 8 You have let g of the commands of God G918
Mk 7:19 For it doesn't g into their heart but into G1660
Mk 7:29 such a reply, you may g; the demon has G5632
Mk 8:26 "Don't even g into the village. G1656
Mk 9:43 maimed than with two hands to g into hell, G599
Mk 10:21 "G, sell everything you have and give to G5632
Mk 10:25 a camel to g through the eye of a G1451
Mk 10:52 "G," said Jesus, "your faith has healed G5632
Mk 11: 2 to them, "G to the village ahead of you G5632
Mk 11: 6 told them to, and the people let them g. G918
Mk 11:23 to this mountain, 'G, throw yourself into G149
Mk 13:15 Let no one on the housetop g down or G2849
Mk 13:16 Let no one in the field g back to get their G2188
Mk 14:12 asked him, "Where do you want us to g G599
Mk 14:13 telling them, "G into the city, and a man G5632
Mk 14:21 The Son of Man will g just as it is written G5632
Mk 14:28 I will g ahead of you into Galilee. G4575
Mk 14:42 Let us g! Here comes my betrayer! G72
Mk 16: 1 spices so that they might g to anoint G2262
Mk 16: 7 But g, tell his disciples and Peter, 'He is G5632
Mk 16:15 "G into all the world and preach the G4513
Lk 1: 9 to g into the temple of the Lord and burn G1656
Lk 1:17 And he will g on before the Lord, in the G4601
Lk 1:76 for you will g on before the Lord to G4638
Lk 2:15 "Let's g to Bethlehem and see this thing G1451
Lk 4:34 "G away! What do you want with us, Jesus G1568
Lk 5: 8 knees and said, "G away from me, Lord; G2002
Lk 5:14 tell anyone, but g, show yourself to the G599
Lk 5:24 get up, take your mat and g home." G4513
Lk 5:33 yours g on eating and drinking. AIT
Lk 6:25 are well fed now, for you will g hungry. G4277
Lk 7: 8 I tell this one, 'G,' and he goes; and that G4513
Lk 7:22 "G back and report to John what you have G4513
Lk 7:24 "What did you g out into the wilderness G2002
Lk 7:25 what did you g out to see? A man G2002
Lk 7:26 But what did you g out to see? A prophet G2002
Lk 7:50 "Your faith has saved you; g in peace." G4513
Lk 8:14 but as they g on their way they are choked G4513
Lk 8:22 "Let us g over to the other side of the lake." G1451
Lk 8:31 not to order them to g into the Abyss. G599
Lk 8:32 begged Jesus to let them g into the pigs, G1656
Lk 8:38 had gone out begged to g with him, G1639
Lk 8:47 seeing that she could not g unnoticed G3291
Lk 8:48 your faith has healed you. G in peace." G4513
Lk 8:51 did not let anyone g in with him except G1656
Lk 9:12 the crowd away so they can g to the G4513
Lk 9:13 unless we g and buy food for all this crowd G4513
Lk 9:57 "I will follow you wherever you g." G599
Lk 9:59 first let me g and bury my father." G599
Lk 9:60 you g and proclaim the kingdom of G599
Lk 9:61 first let me g back and say goodbye to NDT
Lk 10: 1 town and place where he was about to g. G2262
Lk 10: 3 G! I am sending you out like lambs among G5632
Lk 10:10 not welcomed, g into its streets and say, G2002
Lk 10:15 No, you will g down to Hades. G2849
Lk 10:37 Jesus told him, "G and do likewise." G4513
Lk 11: 5 and you g to him at midnight and say G4513
Lk 11:26 than itself, and they g in and live there. G1656
Lk 13:31 "Leave this place and g somewhere else. G4513
Lk 13:32 He replied, "G tell that fox, 'I will keep on G4513
Lk 14:18 bought a field, and I must g and see it. G2002
Lk 14:21 'G out quickly into the streets and alleys G2002
Lk 14:23 'G out to the roads and country lanes and G2002
Lk 14:31 a king is about to g to war against G5202
Lk 15: 4 open country and g after the lost sheep G4513
Lk 15:18 I will set out and g back to my father and G4513
Lk 15:28 brother became angry and refused to g in. G1656
Lk 16:26 that those who want to g from here to you G1329
Lk 17:14 he said, "G, show yourselves to the priests G4513
Lk 17:19 "Rise and g; your faith has made G4513
Lk 17:23 Do not g running off after them. G599
Lk 17:31 should g down to get them. G2849
Lk 17:31 should g back for anything G2188+1650+3836+3958
Lk 18:25 easier for a camel to g through the eye of G1656
Lk 19:30 "G to the village ahead of you, and as you G5632
Lk 22: 8 "G and make preparations for us to eat G4513
Lk 22:22 The Son of Man will g as it has been G4513
Lk 22:33 I am ready to g with you to prison and to G4513
Jn 4: 4 Now he had to g through Samaria. G1451
Jn 4:16 He told her, "G, call your husband and G5632
Jn 4:50 "G," Jesus replied, "your son will live." G4513
Jn 6: 9 how far will they g among so many?" G1639
Jn 6:35 comes to me will never g hungry, G4277
Jn 6:68 answered him, "Lord, to whom shall we g? G599
Jn 7: 1 He did not want to g about in Judea G4344
Jn 7: 3 "Leave Galilee and g to Judea, so that G5632
Jn 7: 8 You g to the festival. I am not going up to G326
Jn 7:14 the festival did Jesus g up to the temple G326
Jn 7:35 this man intend to g that we cannot find G4513
Jn 7:35 Will he g where our people live scattered G4513
Jn 8: 9 who heard began to g away one at a time G2002
Jn 8:11 "G now and leave your life of sin. G4513
Jn 8:21 Where I g, you cannot come." G5632
Jn 8:22 he says, 'Where I g, you cannot come'?" G5632
Jn 9: 7 "G," he told him, "wash in the Pool of G5632
Jn 9:11 He told me to g to Siloam and wash G5632
Jn 10: 9 They will come in and g out, and find G2002
Jn 11: 7 said to his disciples, "Let us g back to Judea." G72
Jn 11:15 that you may believe. But let us g to him." G72
Jn 11:16 the disciples, "Let us also g, that we may die G72
Jn 11:44 "Take off the grave clothes and let him g." G5632
Jn 11:48 If we let him g on like this, everyone will G918
Jn 13: 1 him to leave this world and g to the Father. AIT
Jn 14: 3 And if I g and prepare a place for you, G4513
Jn 15:16 you so that you might g and bear fruit— G5632
Jn 16: 7 Unless I g away, the Advocate will not G599
Jn 16: 7 come to you; but if I g, I will send him to G4513
Jn 18: 8 are looking for me, then let these men g." G5632
Jn 19:12 shouting, "If you let this man g, you are no G668
Jn 20: 5 strips of linen lying there but did not g in. G1656
Jn 20:17 G instead to my brothers and tell them, 'I G4513
Jn 21: 3 and they said, "We'll g with you. G2262
Jn 21:18 lead you where you do not want to g." NDT
Ac 1:11 way you have seen him g into heaven." G4513
Ac 1:25 which Judas left to g where he belongs." G4513
Ac 3:13 though he had decided to let him g. G668
Ac 4:21 After further threats they let them g. G668
Ac 5:20 "G, stand in the temple courts," he said G4513
Ac 5:38 these men alone! Let them g! For if their G918
Ac 5:40 in the name of Jesus, and let them g. G668
Ac 7: 3 'and g to the land I will show you.' G1306
Ac 7:40 'Make us gods who will g before us. G4638
Ac 8:26 said to Philip, "G south to the road—the G4513
Ac 8:29 "G to that chariot and stay near it. G4665
Ac 9: 6 "Now get up and g into the city, and you G1656
Ac 9:11 "G to the house of Judas on Straight G4513
Ac 9:15 said to Ananias, "G! This man is my G4513
Ac 10:20 So get up and g downstairs. Do not G2849
Ac 10:20 Do not hesitate to g with them, for I have G4513
Ac 14:16 he let all nations g their own way. G4513
Ac 14:22 "We must g through many hardships to enter AIT
Ac 15: 2 to g up to Jerusalem to see the apostles G326
Ac 15:36 "Let us g back and visit the believers in all G2188
Ac 16:36 Now you can leave. G in peace." G4513
Ac 17: 9 the others post bond and let them g. G668
Ac 18: 6 From now on I will g to the Gentiles." G4513
Ac 18:27 When Apollos wanted to g to Achaia, the G1451
Ac 19:21 Paul decided to g to Jerusalem, passing G4513
Ac 20: 3 he decided to g back through Macedonia. G5715
Ac 21: 4 they urged Paul not to g on to Jerusalem. G2094
Ac 21:12 with Paul not to g up to Jerusalem. G326
Ac 22:10 the Lord said, 'and g into Damascus. G4513
Ac 22:21 the Lord said to me, 'G; I will send you far G4513
Ac 23:10 the troops to g down and take him away G2849
Ac 23:23 spearmen to g to Caesarea at nine G4513
Ac 23:32 next day they let the cavalry g on with him, G599
Ac 25: 9 "Are you willing to g up to Jerusalem and G326
Ac 25:12 To Caesar you will g!" G4513
Ac 25:20 would be willing to g to Jerusalem and G4513
Ac 27: 3 allowed him to g to his friends so they G4513
Ac 28:26 " 'G to this people and say, "You will be G4513
Ro 6: 1 Shall we g on sinning so that grace may G2152
Ro 15:24 I plan to do so when I g to Spain. I hope G4513
Ro 15:28 I will g to Spain and visit you on the way. G599
1Co 4: 6 "Do not g beyond what is written." G5642
1Co 4:11 To this very hour we g hungry and thirsty G4277
1Co 10:27 invites you to a meal and you want to g, G4513
1Co 11:21 some of you g ahead with your own G4624
1Co 16: 4 If it seems advisable for me to g also, they G4513
1Co 16: 5 After I g through Macedonia, I will come G1451
1Co 16: 6 can help me on my journey, wherever I g. G4513
1Co 16:12 I strongly urged him to g to you with the G2262
1Co 16:12 He was quite unwilling to g now, but he G2262
1Co 16:12 but he will g when he has the opportunity. G2262
2Co 9:14 you their hearts will g out to you, G2160
2Co 10:15 Neither do we g beyond our limits by AIT
2Co 12: 1 I must g on boasting. Although there is AIT
2Co 12: 1 I will g on to visions and revelations from G2262
2Co 12:18 I urged Titus to g to you and I sent our NDT
Gal 1:17 I did not g up to Jerusalem to see those G456
Gal 2: 9 agreed that we should g to the Gentiles, AIT
Gal 5:12 they would g the whole way and emasculate themselves AIT
Eph 4:26 Do not let the sun g down while you are G2115
Eph 6: 3 "so that it may g well with you and that G1181
Php 1:22 If I am to g on living in the body, this will AIT
Php 2:23 him as soon as I see how things g with me. AIT
2Ti 3:13 while evildoers and impostors will g from G4621
Heb 4: 6 to them did not g in because of their G1656
Heb 11: 8 when called to g to a place he would G2002
Heb 13:13 Let us, then, g to him outside the camp G2002
Jas 1:11 even while they g about their business. G4512

Jas 2:16 you says to them, "**G** in peace; keep warm G5632
Jas 3: 4 rudder wherever the pilot wants *to* **g**. G2316
Jas 4:13 tomorrow *we will* **g** to this or that G4513
1Jn 3: 9 they cannot *g on* **sinning**, because they AIT
3Jn 2 health and *that* all **may g well** with you, G2338
Rev 10: 8 "**G**, take the scroll that lies open in the G5632
Rev 11: 1 "**G** and measure the temple of God and G1586
Rev 13:10 "If anyone is to **g** into captivity, into captivity NDT
Rev 13:10 **g** into captivity, into captivity *they will* **g**. G5632
Rev 16: 1 the seven angels, "**G**, pour out the seven G5632
Rev 16:14 they **g out** to the kings of the whole G1744
Rev 16:15 so as not to **g** naked and be shamefully G4344
Rev 17: 8 out of the Abyss and **g** to its destruction. G5632
Rev 20: 8 and *will* **g out** to deceive the nations in G2002
Rev 22:14 life and *may* **g** through the gates **into** the G1656

GOADS (3)

1Sa 13:21 forks and axes and for repointing **g**. H1995
Ecc 12:11 The words of the wise are like **g**, their H1996
Ac 26:14 It is hard for you to kick against the **g**.' G3034

GOAH (1)

Jer 31:39 to the hill of Gareb and then turn to **G**. H1717

GOAL (8)

Lk 13:32 on the third day *I will* **reach** *my* **g**. G5457
Ro 9:31 righteousness, have not attained their **g**. G3795S
2Co 5: 9 So *we* **make it** *our* **g** to please him G5818
2Co 8:14 supply what you need. **The g** is equality, G3968
Php 3:12 or *have* already **arrived at** *my* **g**, but I G5457
Php 3:14 I press on toward the **g** to win the prize G5024
Col 2: 2 My **g** is **that** they may be encouraged in G2671
1Ti 1: 5 The **g** of this command is love, which G5465

GOAT (86) [GOAT'S, GOATS, GOATS', GOATSKINS, HE-GOAT, SCAPEGOAT]

Ge 15: 9 me a heifer, a **g** and a ram, each three H6436
Ge 30:32 lamb and every spotted or speckled **g**. H6436
Ge 30:33 Any **g** in my possession that is not H6436
Ge 37:31 slaughtered a **g** and dipped the H8538+6436
Ge 38:17 send you a **young g** from my flock," H1531+6436
Ge 38:20 sent the **young g** by his friend H1531+6436
Ge 38:23 I did send her this **young g**, but you didn't H1531
Ex 23:19 "Do not cook a **young g** in its mother's H1531
Ex 25: 4 scarlet yarn and fine linen; **g hair**; H6436
Ex 26: 7 "Make curtains of **g hair** for the tent over H6436
Ex 34:26 "Do not cook a **young g** in its mother's H1531
Ex 35: 6 scarlet yarn and fine linen; **g hair**; H6436
Ex 35:23 fine linen, or **g hair**, ram skins dyed red H6436
Ex 35:26 willing and had the skill spun the **g hair**. H6436
Ex 36:14 made curtains of **g hair** for the tent over H6436
Lev 3:12 " 'If your offering is a **g**, you are to present H6436
Lev 4:23 offering a male **g** without defect. H8538+6436
Lev 4:28 a female **g** without defect. H8544+6436
Lev 5: 6 a female lamb or **g** from the flock H8544+6436
Lev 9: 3 'Take a **male g** for a sin offering, H8538+6436
Lev 9:15 He took the **g** for the people's sin offering H8538
Lev 10:16 inquired about the **g** *of* the sin offering H8538
Lev 10:18 should have eaten **the g** in the sanctuary H2023S
Lev 16: 9 Aaron shall bring the **g** whose lot falls to H8538
Lev 16:10 But the **g** chosen by lot as the scapegoat H8538
Lev 16:15 then slaughter the **g** *for* the sin offering H8538
Lev 16:20 the altar, he shall bring forward the live **g**. H8538
Lev 16:21 the head of the live **g** and confess over it H8538
Lev 16:21 He shall send the **g** away into the NDT
Lev 16:22 The **g** will carry on itself all their sins to a H8538
Lev 16:26 who releases the **g** as a scapegoat must H8538
Lev 16:27 The bull and the **g** *for* the sin offerings H8538
Lev 17: 3 a lamb or a **g** in the camp or outside of it H6436
Lev 17: 7 their sacrifices to the **g idols** to whom they H8539
Lev 22:27 a lamb or a **g** is born, it is to H6436
Lev 23:19 Then sacrifice one **male g** for a sin H8538+6436
Nu 7:16 one **male g** for a sin offering; H8538+6436
Nu 7:22 one **male g** for a sin offering; H8538+6436
Nu 7:28 one **male g** for a sin offering; H8538+6436
Nu 7:34 one **male g** for a sin offering; H8538+6436
Nu 7:40 one **male g** for a sin offering; H8538+6436
Nu 7:46 one **male g** for a sin offering; H8538+6436
Nu 7:52 one **male g** for a sin offering; H8538+6436
Nu 7:58 one **male g** for a sin offering; H8538+6436
Nu 7:64 one **male g** for a sin offering; H8538+6436
Nu 7:70 one **male g** for a sin offering; H8538+6436
Nu 7:76 one **male g** for a sin offering; H8538+6436
Nu 7:82 one **male g** for a sin offering; H8538+6436
Nu 15:11 each lamb or **young g**, is to be H6436
Nu 15:24 and a **male g** for a sin offering. H8538+6436
Nu 15:27 a year-old female **g** for a sin offering. H6436
Nu 18:17 of a cow, a sheep or a **g**; they are holy. H6436
Nu 28:15 one **male g** is to be presented to H8538+6436
Nu 28:22 Include one **male g** as a sin offering to H8538
Nu 28:30 Include one **male g** to make H8538+6436
Nu 29: 5 Include one **male g** as a sin H8538+6436
Nu 29:11 Include one **male g** as a sin H8538+6436
Nu 29:16 Include one **male g** as a sin H8538+6436
Nu 29:19 Include one **male g** as a sin H8538+6436
Nu 29:22 Include one **male g** as a sin offering, in H8538
Nu 29:25 Include one **male g** as a sin H8538+6436
Nu 29:28 Include one **male g** as a sin offering, in H8538
Nu 29:31 Include one **male g** as a sin offering, in H8538
Nu 29:34 Include one **male g** as a sin offering, in H8538
Nu 29:38 Include one **male g** as a sin offering, in H8538
Nu 31:20 made of leather, **g hair** or wood. H6436
Dt 14: 4 the ox, the sheep, the **g**, H8445+6436
Dt 14: 5 the roe deer, the **wild g**, the ibex, the H735
Dt 14:21 Do not cook a **young g** in its mother's milk H1531
Jdg 6:19 prepared a **young g**, and from an H1531+6436
Jdg 13:15 until we prepare a **young g** for you." H1531+6436
Jdg 13:19 Then Manoah took a **young g** H1531+6436
Jdg 14: 6 hands as he might have torn a **young g**. H1531
Jdg 15: 1 took a **young g** and went to H1531+6436
1Sa 16:20 of wine and a **young g** and sent H1531+6436
2Ch 11:15 for the **g** and calf **idols** he had made. H8539
Isa 11: 6 the leopard will lie down with the **g**, the H1531
Eze 43:22 are to offer a **male g** without defect H8538+6436
Eze 43:25 you are to provide a **male g** daily for a sin H8538
Eze 45:23 and a **male g** for a sin offering. H6436+8538
Da 8: 5 suddenly a **g** with a prominent H7618+6436
Da 8: 7 the **g** knocked it to the ground and trampled NDT
Da 8: 8 The **g** became very great, but at the H7618+6436
Da 8:21 The shaggy **g** is the king of Greece, and H7618
Lk 15:29 never gave me even a **young g** so I could G2253
Rev 6:12 turned black like sackcloth **made of g hair**, G5570

GOAT'S (3) [GOAT]

Lev 4:24 lay his hand on the **g** head and slaughter H8538
Lev 16:18 some of the **g** blood and put it on H8538
Lev 16:21 their sins—and put them on the **g** head. H8538

GOATS (77) [GOAT]

Ge 27: 9 and bring me two choice **young g**, H6436+1531
Ge 30:35 he removed all the **male g** that were H9411
Ge 30:35 all the speckled or spotted *female* **g** H6436
Ge 31:10 saw that the **male g** mating with the H6966
Ge 31:12 see that all the **male g** mating with the H6966
Ge 31:38 Your sheep and **g** have not miscarried H6436
Ge 32: 5 donkeys, **sheep and g**, male and H7366
Ge 32:14 two hundred *female* **g** and twenty male H6436
Ge 32:14 hundred female goats and twenty **male g**, H9411
Ge 47:17 horses, their **sheep and g**, their H5238+7366
Ex 9: 3 camels and on your cattle, **sheep and g**. H7366
Ex 12: 5 may take them from the sheep or the **g**. H6436
Ex 20:24 your **sheep and g** and your cattle. H7366
Lev 1:10 from either the sheep or the **g**, you are to H6436
Lev 7:23 not eat any of the fat of cattle, sheep or **g**. H6436
Lev 16: 5 he is to take two **male g** for a sin H8538+6436
Lev 16: 7 he is to take the two **g** and present them H8538
Lev 16: 8 He is to cast lots for the two **g**—one lot H8538
Lev 22:19 sheep or **g** in order that it may be H6436
Nu 7:17 five **male g** and five male lambs a year H6966
Nu 7:23 five **male g** and five male lambs a year H6966
Nu 7:29 five **male g** and five male lambs a year H6966
Nu 7:35 five **male g** and five male lambs a year H6966
Nu 7:41 five **male g** and five male lambs a year H6966
Nu 7:47 five **male g** and five male lambs a year H6966
Nu 7:53 five **male g** and five male lambs a year H6966
Nu 7:59 five **male g** and five male lambs a year H6966
Nu 7:65 five **male g** and five male lambs a year H6966
Nu 7:71 five **male g** and five male lambs a year H6966
Nu 7:77 five **male g** and five male lambs a year H6966
Nu 7:83 five **male g** and five male lambs a year H6966
Nu 7:87 Twelve **male g** were used for the H8538+6436
Nu 7:88 sixty **male g** and sixty male lambs a year H6966
Dt 32:14 flock and with fattened lambs and **g**, H6966
1Sa 10: 3 One will be carrying three **young g** H1531
1Sa 24: 2 his men near the Crags of the **Wild G**. H3604
1Sa 25: 2 He had a thousand **g** and three thousand H6436
1Ki 4:23 cattle and a hundred **sheep and g**, H7366
1Ki 8:63 twenty thousand **sheep and g**. H7366
1Ki 20:27 opposite them like two small flocks of **g**, H6436
2Ch 7: 5 twenty thousand **sheep and g**. H7366
2Ch 14:15 off droves of **sheep and g** and camels. H7366
2Ch 15:11 seven thousand **sheep and g** from the H7366
2Ch 17:11 seven thousand seven hundred **g**. H9411
2Ch 29:21 lambs and seven **male g** as a sin H7618+6436
2Ch 29:23 The **g** *for* the sin offering were brought H8538
2Ch 29:24 then slaughtered **the g** and presented H4392S
2Ch 29:33 bulls and three thousand **sheep and g**. H7366
2Ch 30:24 seven thousand **sheep and g** for the H7366
2Ch 30:24 bulls and ten thousand **sheep and g**. H7366
2Ch 35: 7 lambs and **g** for the Passover H1201+6436
Ezr 6:17 twelve **male g**, one for each A10615+10535
Ezr 8:35 as a sin offering, twelve **male g**. H7618
Job 39: 1 know when the mountain **g** give birth? H3604
Ps 50: 9 bull from your stall or of **g** from your pens, H6966
Ps 50:13 the flesh of bulls or drink the blood of **g**? H6966
Ps 66:15 offering of rams; I will offer bulls and **g**. H6966
Ps 104:18 The high mountains belong to the **wild g** H3604
Pr 27:26 the **g** with the price of a field. H6966
SS 1: 8 graze your **young g** by the tents of the H1537
SS 4: 1 is like a flock of **g** descending from the H6436
SS 6: 5 is like a flock of **g** descending from Gilead H6436
Isa 1:11 in the blood of bulls and lambs and **g**. H6966
Isa 7:21 will keep alive a young cow and two **g**. H7366
Isa 13:21 there the **wild g** will leap about. H8538
Isa 34: 6 the blood of lambs and **g**, fat from the H6966
Isa 34:14 and **wild g** will bleat to each other H8538
Jer 50: 8 be like the **g** that lead the flock. H6966
Jer 51:40 lambs to the slaughter, like rams and **g**. H6966
Eze 27:21 business with you in lambs, rams and **g**. H6966
Eze 34:17 another, and between rams and **g**. H6966
Eze 39:18 were rams and lambs, **g** and bulls—all of H6966
Mt 25:32 shepherd separates the sheep from the **g**. G2253
Mt 25:33 sheep on his right and the **g** on his left. G2252
Heb 9:12 by means of the blood *of* **g** and calves; G5543
Heb 9:13 The blood *of* **g** and bulls and the ashes of G5543
Heb 10: 4 blood of bulls and **g** to take away sins. G5543

GOATS' (3) [GOAT]

1Sa 19:13 putting some **g hair** at the head. H3889+6436
1Sa 19:16 and at the head was some **g hair**. H3889+6436
Pr 27:27 will have plenty of **g** milk to feed your H6436

GOATSKINS (2) [GOAT, SKIN]

Ge 27:16 part of his neck with the **g**. H6425+1531+6436
Heb 11:37 went about in sheepskins and **g**, G128+1293

GOB (2)

2Sa 21:18 another battle with the Philistines, at **G**. H1570
2Sa 21:19 In another battle with the Philistines at **G** H1570

GOBLET (3) [GOBLETS]

SS 7: 2 Your navel is a rounded **g** that never lacks H110
Isa 51:17 to its dregs the **g** that makes H7694+3926
Isa 51:22 that cup, the **g** *of* my wrath, you H7694+3926

GOBLETS (6) [GOBLET]

1Ki 10:21 All King Solomon's **g** were gold H3998+5482
2Ch 9:20 All King Solomon's **g** were gold H3998+5482
Est 1: 7 Wine was served in **g** *of* gold, each one H3998
Da 5: 2 gold and silver **g** that Nebuchadnezzar A10398
Da 5: 3 in the gold **g** that had been taken A10398
Da 5:23 You had the **g** from his temple brought A10398

GOD (3991) [GOD'S, GOD-BREATHED, GOD-FEARING, GOD-HATERS, GODDESS, GODLESS, GODLESSNESS, GODLINESS, GODLY, GODS]

Ge 1: 1 In the beginning **G** created the heavens H466
Ge 1: 2 the Spirit of **G** was hovering over the H466
Ge 1: 3 And **G** said, "Let there be light," and there H466
Ge 1: 4 **G** saw that the light was good, and he H466
Ge 1: 5 **G** called the light "day," and the darkness H466
Ge 1: 6 And **G** said, "Let there be a vault between H466
Ge 1: 7 So **G** made the vault and separated the H466
Ge 1: 8 **G** called the vault "sky." And there was H466
Ge 1: 9 And **G** said, "Let the water under the sky be H466
Ge 1:10 **G** called the dry ground "land," and the H466
Ge 1:10 And **G** saw that it was good. H466
Ge 1:11 Then **G** said, "Let the land produce H466
Ge 1:12 And **G** saw that it was good. H466
Ge 1:14 And **G** said, "Let there be lights in the vault H466
Ge 1:16 **G** made two great lights—the greater light H466
Ge 1:17 **G** set them in the vault of the sky to give H466
Ge 1:18 from darkness. And **G** saw that it was good. H466
Ge 1:20 And **G** said, "Let the water teem with living H466
Ge 1:21 So **G** created the great creatures of the sea H466
Ge 1:21 And **G** saw that it was good. H466
Ge 1:22 **G** blessed them and said, "Be fruitful and H466
Ge 1:24 And **G** said, "Let the land produce living H466
Ge 1:25 **G** made the wild animals according to their H466
Ge 1:25 And **G** saw that it was good. H466
Ge 1:26 Then **G** said, "Let us make mankind in our H466
Ge 1:27 So **G** created mankind in his own image, in H466
Ge 1:27 in the image of **G** he created them; male H466
Ge 1:28 **G** blessed them and said to them, "Be H466
Ge 1:29 Then **G** said, "I give you every H466
Ge 1:31 **G** saw all that he had made, and it was H466
Ge 2: 2 By the seventh day **G** had finished the work H466
Ge 2: 3 Then **G** blessed the seventh day and made H466
Ge 2: 4 when the LORD **G** made the earth and the H466
Ge 2: 5 the LORD **G** had not sent rain on the H466
Ge 2: 7 Then the LORD **G** formed a man from the H466
Ge 2: 8 Now the LORD **G** had planted a garden in H466
Ge 2: 9 The LORD **G** made all kinds of trees grow out H466
Ge 2:15 The LORD **G** took the man and put him in H466
Ge 2:16 And the LORD **G** commanded the man, "You H466
Ge 2:18 The LORD **G** said, "It is not good for the man H466
Ge 2:19 Now the LORD **G** had formed out of the H466
Ge 2:21 So the LORD **G** caused the man to fall into a H466
Ge 2:22 Then the LORD **G** made a woman from the H466
Ge 3: 1 of the wild animals the LORD **G** had made. H466
Ge 3: 1 to the woman, "Did **G** really say, 'You must H466
Ge 3: 3 **G** did say, 'You must not eat fruit from H466
Ge 3: 5 "For **G** knows that when you eat from it your H466
Ge 3: 5 you will be like **G**, knowing good and H466
Ge 3: 8 sound of the LORD **G** as he was walking in H466
Ge 3: 8 hid from the LORD **G** among the trees of the H466
Ge 3: 9 But the LORD **G** called to the man, "Where H466
Ge 3:13 Then the LORD **G** said to the woman, "What H466
Ge 3:14 So the LORD **G** said to the serpent, "Because H466
Ge 3:21 The LORD **G** made garments of skin for H466
Ge 3:22 And the LORD **G** said, "The man has now H466
Ge 3:23 So the LORD **G** banished him from the H466
Ge 4:25 "**G** has granted me another child in place H466
Ge 5: 1 When **G** created mankind, he made them H466
Ge 5: 1 he made them in the likeness of **G**. H466
Ge 5:22 walked faithfully with **G** 300 years and had H466
Ge 5:24 Enoch walked faithfully with **G**; then he was H466
Ge 5:24 was no more, because **G** took him away. H466
Ge 6: 2 the sons of **G** saw that the daughters of H466
Ge 6: 4 when the sons of **G** went to the daughters H466
Ge 6: 9 his time, and he walked faithfully with **G**. H466
Ge 6:12 **G** saw how corrupt the earth had become H466
Ge 6:13 So **G** said to Noah, "I am going to put an H466
Ge 6:22 did everything just as **G** commanded him. H466
Ge 7: 9 as **G** had commanded Noah. H466
Ge 7:16 living thing, as **G** had commanded Noah. H466
Ge 8: 1 But **G** remembered Noah and all the wild H466

Ge 8:15 Then **G** said to Noah, H466
Ge 9:1 Then **G** blessed Noah and his sons, saying H466
Ge 9:6 in the image of **G** has God made H466
Ge 9:6 in the image of God has **G** made mankind. NDT
Ge 9:8 Then **G** said to Noah and to his sons with H466
Ge 9:12 And **G** said, "This is the sign of the H466
Ge 9:16 covenant between **G** and all living H466
Ge 9:17 So **G** said to Noah, "This is the sign of the H466
Ge 9:26 "Praise be to the LORD, the **G** *of* Shem! H466
Ge 9:27 May **G** extend Japheth's territory; may H466
Ge 14:18 He was priest of **G** Most High, H446
Ge 14:19 "Blessed be Abram by **G** Most High H446
Ge 14:20 And praise be to **G** Most High, who H446
Ge 14:22 an oath to the LORD, **G** Most High, Creator H446
Ge 16:13 "You are the **G** who sees me," for she said H446
Ge 17:1 him and said, "I am **G** Almighty; walk H446
Ge 17:3 Abram fell facedown, and **G** said to him, H466
Ge 17:7 to be your **G** and the God of your H466
Ge 17:7 be your God and the **G** of your descendants NDT
Ge 17:8 after you; and I will be their **G**. H466
Ge 17:9 Then **G** said to Abraham, "As for you, you H466
Ge 17:15 **G** also said to Abraham, "As for Sarai your H466
Ge 17:18 And Abraham said to **G**, "If only Ishmael H466
Ge 17:19 Then **G** said, "Yes, but your wife Sarah will H466
Ge 17:22 with Abraham, **G** went up from him. H466
Ge 17:23 circumcised them, as **G** told him. H466
Ge 19:29 So when **G** destroyed the cities of the plain, H466
Ge 20:3 But **G** came to Abimelek in a dream one H466
Ge 20:6 Then **G** said to him in the dream, "Yes, H466
Ge 20:11 'There is surely no fear of **G** in this place H466
Ge 20:13 And when **G** had me wander from my H466
Ge 20:17 Then Abraham prayed to **G**, and God H466
Ge 20:17 prayed to God, and **G** healed Abimelek H466
Ge 21:2 at the very time **G** had promised him. H466
Ge 21:4 circumcised him, as **G** commanded him. H466
Ge 21:6 Sarah said, "**G** has brought me laughter H466
Ge 21:12 But **G** said to him, "Do not be so distressed H466
Ge 21:17 **G** heard the boy crying, and the angel of H466
Ge 21:17 the angel of **G** called to Hagar from H466
Ge 21:17 **G** has heard the boy crying as he lies there. H466
Ge 21:19 Then **G** opened her eyes and she saw a H466
Ge 21:20 **G** was with the boy as he grew up. He lived H466
Ge 21:22 "**G** is with you in everything you do. H466
Ge 21:23 to me here before **G** that you will not deal H466
Ge 21:33 on the name of the LORD, the Eternal **G**. H446
Ge 22:1 Some time later **G** tested Abraham. H466
Ge 22:2 Then **G** said, "Take your son, your only son NDT
Ge 22:3 set out for the place **G** had told him about. H466
Ge 22:8 "**G** himself will provide the lamb for the H466
Ge 22:9 reached the place **G** had told him about, H466
Ge 22:12 Now I know that you fear **G**, because you H466
Ge 24:3 the **G** *of* heaven and the God of earth H466
Ge 24:3 the God of heaven and the **G** *of* earth, that H466
Ge 24:7 "The LORD, the **G** *of* heaven, who brought H466
Ge 24:12 **G** *of* my master Abraham, make me H466
Ge 24:27 to the LORD, the **G** *of* my master Abraham H466
Ge 24:42 'LORD, **G** *of* my master Abraham, if H466
Ge 24:48 the LORD, the **G** *of* my master Abraham H466
Ge 25:11 Abraham's death, **G** blessed his son Isaac H466
Ge 26:24 "I am the **G** *of* your father Abraham. H466
Ge 27:20 "The LORD your **G** gave me success," he H466
Ge 27:28 May **G** give you heaven's dew and earth's H466
Ge 28:3 May **G** Almighty bless you and make you H446
Ge 28:4 a foreigner, the land **G** gave to Abraham." H466
Ge 28:12 the angels of **G** were ascending and H466
Ge 28:13 the **G** *of* your father Abraham and the God H466
Ge 28:13 of your father Abraham and the **G** *of* Isaac. H466
Ge 28:17 This is none other than the house of **G**; this H466
Ge 28:20 "If **G** will be with me and will watch over H466
Ge 28:21 household, then the LORD will be my **G** H466
Ge 30:2 "Am I in the place of **G**, who has kept you H466
Ge 30:6 Then Rachel said, "**G** has vindicated me; he H466
Ge 30:17 **G** listened to Leah, and she became H466
Ge 30:18 "**G** has rewarded me for giving my servant H466
Ge 30:20 "**G** has presented me with a precious gift. H466
Ge 30:22 Then **G** remembered Rachel; he listened to H466
Ge 30:23 said, "**G** has taken away my disgrace." H466
Ge 31:5 the **G** *of* my father has been with me. H466
Ge 31:7 **G** has not allowed him to harm me. H466
Ge 31:9 So **G** has taken away your father's livestock H466
Ge 31:11 The angel of **G** said to me in the dream H466
Ge 31:13 I am the **G** *of* Bethel, where you anointed a H446
Ge 31:16 all the wealth that **G** took away from our H466
Ge 31:16 So do whatever **G** has told you." H466
Ge 31:24 Then **G** came to Laban the Aramean in a H466
Ge 31:29 last night the **G** *of* your father said to H466
Ge 31:42 If the **G** of my father, the God of Abraham H466
Ge 31:42 the **G** *of* Abraham and the Fear of Isaac H466
Ge 31:42 But **G** has seen my hardship and the toil of H466
Ge 31:50 remember that **G** is a witness between you H466
Ge 31:53 May the **G** *of* Abraham and the God of H466
Ge 31:53 the God of Abraham and the **G** *of* Nahor, H466
Ge 31:53 God of Nahor, the **G** *of* their father, judge H466
Ge 32:1 on his way, and the angels of **G** met him. H466
Ge 32:2 saw them, he said, "This is the camp of **G**!" H466
Ge 32:9 Jacob prayed, "O **G** *of* my father Abraham H466
Ge 32:9 my father Abraham, **G** *of* my father Isaac H466
Ge 32:28 struggled with **G** and with humans and H466
Ge 32:30 "It is because I saw **G** face to face, and H466
Ge 33:5 are the children **G** has graciously given H466
Ge 33:10 see your face is like seeing the face of **G**, H466
Ge 33:11 **G** has been gracious to me and I have H466
Ge 35:1 Then **G** said to Jacob, "Go up to Bethel H466
Ge 35:1 build an altar there to **G**, who H446
Ge 35:3 where I will build an altar to **G**, who H446
Ge 35:5 the terror of **G** fell on the towns all H466
Ge 35:7 it was there that **G** revealed himself to him H466
Ge 35:9 **G** appeared to him again and blessed him. H466
Ge 35:10 **G** said to him, "Your name is Jacob, but you H466
Ge 35:11 And **G** said to him, "I am God Almighty; be H466
Ge 35:11 said to him, "I am **G** Almighty; be fruitful H446
Ge 35:13 Then **G** went up from him at the place H466
Ge 35:14 at the place where **G** had talked with him, NDT
Ge 35:15 the place where **G** had talked with him H466
Ge 39:9 I do such a wicked thing and sin against **G**?" H466
Ge 40:8 "Do not interpretations belong to **G**? H466
Ge 41:16 "but **G** will give Pharaoh the answer he H466
Ge 41:25 **G** has revealed to Pharaoh what he is H466
Ge 41:28 **G** has shown Pharaoh what he is about to H466
Ge 41:32 the matter has been firmly decided by **G**, H466
Ge 41:32 decided by God, and **G** will do it soon. H466
Ge 41:38 this man, one in whom is the spirit of **G**?" H466
Ge 41:39 "Since **G** has made all this known to you H466
Ge 41:51 "It is because **G** has made me forget all my H466
Ge 41:52 "It is because **G** has made me fruitful in H466
Ge 42:18 "Do this and you will live, for I fear **G**: H466
Ge 42:28 "What is this that **G** has done to us?" H466
Ge 43:14 And may **G** Almighty grant you mercy H446
Ge 43:23 Your **G**, the God of your father, has given H466
Ge 43:23 Your God, the **G** *of* your father, has given H466
Ge 43:29 And he said, "**G** be gracious to you, my son H466
Ge 44:16 **G** has uncovered your servants' guilt H466
Ge 45:5 to save lives that **G** sent me ahead of you. H466
Ge 45:7 But **G** sent me ahead of you to preserve H466
Ge 45:8 it was not you who sent me here, but **G**. H466
Ge 45:9 **G** has made me lord of all Egypt H466
Ge 46:1 sacrifices to the **G** *of* his father Isaac. H466
Ge 46:2 And **G** spoke to Israel in a vision at night H466
Ge 46:3 "I am **G**, the God of your father," he said H446
Ge 46:3 "I am God, the **G** *of* your father," he said H466
Ge 48:3 "**G** Almighty appeared to me at Luz in the H446
Ge 48:9 "They are the sons **G** has given me here," H466
Ge 48:11 now **G** has allowed me to see your H466
Ge 48:15 "May the **G** before whom my fathers H466
Ge 48:15 the **G** who has been my shepherd all my H466
Ge 48:20 'May **G** make you like Ephraim and H466
Ge 48:21 **G** will be with you and take you back to H466
Ge 49:25 because of your father's **G**, who helps you H446
Ge 50:17 sins of the servants of the **G** *of* your father." H466
Ge 50:19 "Don't be afraid. Am I in the place of **G**? H466
Ge 50:20 **G** intended it for good to accomplish H466
Ge 50:24 But **G** will surely come to your aid and take H466
Ge 50:25 said, "**G** will surely come to your aid H466
Ex 1:17 feared **G** and did not do what the king of H466
Ex 1:20 So **G** was kind to the midwives and the H466
Ex 1:21 And because the midwives feared **G**, he H466
Ex 2:23 help because of their slavery went up to **G**. H466
Ex 2:24 **G** heard their groaning and he remembered H466
Ex 2:25 So **G** looked on the Israelites and was H466
Ex 3:1 came to Horeb, the mountain of **G**. H466
Ex 3:4 **G** called to him from within the bush H466
Ex 3:5 not come any closer," **G** said. "Take off your NDT
Ex 3:6 he said, "I am the **G** *of* your father, the God H466
Ex 3:6 of your father, the **G** *of* Abraham, the God H466
Ex 3:6 the **G** *of* Isaac and the God of Jacob." H466
Ex 3:6 the God of Isaac and the **G** *of* Jacob." H466
Ex 3:6 because he was afraid to look at **G**. H466
Ex 3:11 But Moses said to **G**, "Who am I that I H466
Ex 3:12 And **G** said, "I will be with you. And this will NDT
Ex 3:12 you will worship **G** on this mountain." H466
Ex 3:13 Moses said to **G**, "Suppose I go to the H466
Ex 3:13 'The **G** *of* your fathers has sent me to you H466
Ex 3:14 **G** said to Moses, "I AM WHO I AM. H466
Ex 3:15 **G** also said to Moses, "Say to the Israelites H466
Ex 3:15 'The LORD, the **G** *of* your fathers—the God H466
Ex 3:15 your fathers—the **G** *of* Abraham, the God H466
Ex 3:15 the **G** *of* Isaac and the God of Jacob H466
Ex 3:15 the God of Isaac and the **G** *of* Jacob—has H466
Ex 3:16 'The LORD, the **G** *of* your fathers—the God H466
Ex 3:16 your fathers—the **G** *of* Abraham, Isaac H466
Ex 3:18 'The LORD, the **G** *of* the Hebrews, has met H466
Ex 3:18 to offer sacrifices to the LORD our **G**. H466
Ex 4:5 that the LORD, the **G** *of* their fathers—the H466
Ex 4:5 their fathers—the **G** *of* Abraham, the God H466
Ex 4:5 the **G** *of* Isaac and the God of Jacob H466
Ex 4:5 the God of Isaac and the **G** *of* Jacob—has H466
Ex 4:16 your mouth and as if you were **G** to him. H466
Ex 4:20 And he took the staff of **G** in his hand. H466
Ex 4:27 at the mountain of **G** and kissed him. H466
Ex 5:1 "This is what the LORD, the **G** *of* Israel, says: H466
Ex 5:3 "The **G** *of* the Hebrews has met with us. H466
Ex 5:3 to offer sacrifices to the LORD our **G**, H466
Ex 5:8 crying out, 'Let us go and sacrifice to our **G**. H466
Ex 6:2 **G** also said to Moses, "I am the LORD. H466
Ex 6:3 to Isaac and to Jacob as **G** Almighty, but by H446
Ex 6:7 as my own people, and I will be your **G**. H466
Ex 6:7 you will know that I am the LORD your **G**, H466
Ex 7:1 I have made you like **G** to Pharaoh, and H466
Ex 7:16 'The LORD, the **G** *of* the Hebrews, has sent H466
Ex 8:10 know there is no one like the LORD our **G**. H466
Ex 8:19 said to Pharaoh, "This is the finger of **G**." H466
Ex 8:25 sacrifice to your **G** here in the land. H466
Ex 8:26 offer the LORD our **G** would be detestable H466
Ex 8:27 to offer sacrifices to the LORD our **G**, H466
Ex 8:28 to the LORD your **G** in the wilderness, H466
Ex 9:1 what the LORD, the **G** *of* the Hebrews, says: H466
Ex 9:13 what the LORD, the **G** *of* the Hebrews, says: H466
Ex 9:30 your officials still do not fear the LORD **G**." H466
Ex 10:3 what the LORD, the **G** *of* the Hebrews, says: H466
Ex 10:7 so that they may worship the LORD their **G**. H466
Ex 10:8 worship the LORD your **G**," he said. "But tell H466
Ex 10:16 against the LORD your **G** and against you. H466
Ex 10:17 pray to the LORD your **G** to take this deadly H466
Ex 10:25 burnt offerings to present to the LORD our **G**. H466
Ex 10:26 some of them in worshiping the LORD our **G**, H466
Ex 13:17 **G** did not lead them on the road through H466
Ex 13:17 For **G** said, "If they face war, they might H466
Ex 13:18 So **G** led the people around by the desert H466
Ex 13:19 had said, "**G** will surely come to your aid H466
Ex 14:19 Then the angel of **G**, who had been H466
Ex 15:2 He is my **G**, and I will praise him, my H446
Ex 15:2 my father's **G**, and I will exalt him. H466
Ex 15:26 to the LORD your **G** and do what is right in H466
Ex 16:12 you will know that I am the LORD your **G**. H466
Ex 17:9 of the hill with the staff of **G** in my hands." H466
Ex 18:1 heard of everything **G** had done for Moses H466
Ex 18:4 he said, "My father's **G** was my helper; he H466
Ex 18:5 he was camped near the mountain of **G**. H466
Ex 18:12 a burnt offering and other sacrifices to **G**, H466
Ex 18:12 Moses' father-in-law in the presence of **G**. H466
Ex 18:19 you some advice, and may **G** be with you. H466
Ex 18:19 representative before **G** and bring their H466
Ex 18:21 people—men who fear **G**, trustworthy men H466
Ex 18:23 If you do this and **G** so commands, you will H466
Ex 19:3 Then Moses went up to **G**, and the LORD H466
Ex 19:17 the people out of the camp to meet with **G**, H466
Ex 19:19 spoke and the voice of **G** answered him. H466
Ex 20:1 And **G** spoke all these words: H466
Ex 20:2 "I am the LORD your **G**, who brought you out H466
Ex 20:5 the LORD your **G**, am a jealous God H466
Ex 20:5 your God, am a jealous **G**, punishing the H446
Ex 20:7 not misuse the name of the LORD your **G**, H466
Ex 20:10 day is a sabbath to the LORD your **G**. H466
Ex 20:12 in the land the LORD your **G** is giving you. H466
Ex 20:19 But do not have **G** speak to us or we will H466
Ex 20:20 **G** has come to test you, so that the fear of H466
Ex 20:20 so that the fear of **G** will be with you to H2257S
Ex 20:21 the thick darkness where **G** was. H466
Ex 21:13 intentionally, but **G** lets it happen, they H466
Ex 22:20 sacrifices to any **g** other than the LORD must H466
Ex 22:28 "Do not blaspheme **G** or curse the ruler of H466
Ex 23:19 of your soil to the house of the LORD your **G**. H466
Ex 23:25 Worship the LORD your **G**, and his blessing H466
Ex 24:10 saw the **G** *of* Israel. Under his feet was H466
Ex 24:11 But **G** did not raise his hand against these NDT
Ex 24:11 Israelites; they saw **G**, and they ate and H466
Ex 24:13 Moses went up on the mountain of **G**. H466
Ex 29:45 dwell among the Israelites and be their **G**. H466
Ex 29:46 They will know that I am the LORD their **G** H466
Ex 29:46 dwell among them. I am the LORD their **G**. H466
Ex 31:3 I have filled him with the Spirit of **G** H466
Ex 31:18 of stone inscribed by the finger of **G**. H466
Ex 32:11 Moses sought the favor of the LORD his **G**. H466
Ex 32:16 The tablets were the work of **G**; the writing H466
Ex 32:16 the writing was the writing of **G**, engraved H466
Ex 32:27 "This is what the LORD, the **G** *of* Israel, says: H466
Ex 34:6 the compassionate and gracious **G**, slow to H446
Ex 34:14 Do not worship any other **g**, for the LORD H446
Ex 34:14 whose name is Jealous, is a jealous **G**. H446
Ex 34:23 before the Sovereign LORD, the **G** *of* Israel. H466
Ex 34:24 each year to appear before the LORD your **G**. H466
Ex 34:26 of your soil to the house of the LORD your **G**. H466
Ex 35:31 he has filled him with the Spirit of **G** H466
Lev 2:13 of the covenant of your **G** out of your grain H466
Lev 4:22 in any of the commands of the LORD his **G**, H466
Lev 11:44 I am the LORD your **G**; consecrate yourselves H466
Lev 11:45 brought you up out of Egypt to be your **G**; H466
Lev 18:2 say to them: 'I am the LORD your **G**. H466
Lev 18:4 to follow my decrees. I am the LORD your **G**. H466
Lev 18:21 you must not profane the name of your **G**. H466
Lev 18:30 I am the LORD your **G**.'" H466
Lev 19:2 holy because I, the LORD your **G**, am holy. H466
Lev 19:3 observe my Sabbaths. I am the LORD your **G**. H466
Lev 19:4 gods for yourselves. I am the LORD your **G**. H466
Lev 19:10 the foreigner. I am the LORD your **G**. H466
Lev 19:12 name and so profane the name of your **G**. H466
Lev 19:14 block in front of the blind, but fear your **G**. H466
Lev 19:25 will be increased. I am the LORD your **G**. H466
Lev 19:31 be defiled by them. I am the LORD your **G**. H466
Lev 19:32 respect for the elderly and revere your **G**. H466
Lev 19:34 foreigners in Egypt. I am the LORD your **G**. H466
Lev 19:36 I am the LORD your **G**, who brought you out H466
Lev 20:7 be holy, because I am the LORD your **G**. H466
Lev 20:24 I am the LORD your **G**, who has set you H466
Lev 21:6 be holy to their **G** and must not profane H466
Lev 21:6 must not profane the name of their **G**. H466
Lev 21:6 the food of their **G**, they are to be holy. H466
Lev 21:7 because priests are holy to their **G**. H466
Lev 21:8 because they offer up the food of your **G**. H466
Lev 21:12 leave the sanctuary of his **G** or desecrate it, H466
Lev 21:12 dedicated by the anointing oil of his **G**. H466
Lev 21:17 may come near to offer the food of his **G**. H466
Lev 21:21 not come near to offer the food of his **G**. H466
Lev 21:22 He may eat the most holy food of his **G**, as H466
Lev 22:25 offer them as the food of your **G**. H466
Lev 22:33 who brought you out of Egypt to be your **G**. H466

Book	Ref	Context	Number
Lev	23:14	very day you bring this offering to your G.	H466
Lev	23:22	I am the LORD your G.' "	H466
Lev	23:28	is made for you before the LORD your G.	H466
Lev	23:40	before the LORD your G for seven days.	H466
Lev	23:43	them out of Egypt. I am the LORD your G.' "	H466
Lev	24:15	who curses their G will be held responsible	H466
Lev	24:22	the native-born. I am the LORD your G.' "	H466
Lev	25:17	advantage of each other, but fear your G.	H466
Lev	25:17	fear your God. I am the LORD your G.	H466
Lev	25:36	but fear your G, so that they may	H466
Lev	25:38	I am the LORD your G, who brought you out	H466
Lev	25:38	you the land of Canaan and to be your G.	H466
Lev	25:43	rule over them ruthlessly, but fear your G.	H466
Lev	25:55	brought out of Egypt. I am the LORD your G.	H466
Lev	26: 1	bow down before it. I am the LORD your G.	H466
Lev	26:12	I will walk among you and be your G, and	H466
Lev	26:13	I am the LORD your G, who brought you out	H466
Lev	26:44	covenant with them. I am the LORD their G.	H466
Lev	26:45	in the sight of the nations to be their G.	H466
Nu	6: 7	of their dedication to G is on their head.	H466
Nu	10: 9	by the LORD your G and rescued from your	H466
Nu	10:10	will be a memorial for you before your G.	H466
Nu	10:10	before your God. I am the LORD your G."	H466
Nu	12:13	cried out to the LORD, "Please, G, heal her!"	H446
Nu	15:40	will be consecrated to your G.	H466
Nu	15:41	I am the LORD your G, who brought you out	H466
Nu	15:41	who brought you out of Egypt to be your G.	H466
Nu	15:41	to be your God. I am the LORD your G.' "	H466
Nu	16: 9	you that the G *of* Israel has separated	H466
Nu	16:22	cried out, "O G, the God who gives	H446
Nu	16:22	the G *who gives* breath to all living things	H466
Nu	21: 5	they spoke against G and against Moses	H466
Nu	22: 9	G came to Balaam and asked, "Who are	H466
Nu	22:10	Balaam said to G, "Balak son of Zippor	H466
Nu	22:12	But G said to Balaam, "Do not go with	H466
Nu	22:18	go beyond the command of the LORD my G.	H466
Nu	22:20	That night G came to Balaam and said	H466
Nu	22:22	But G was very angry when he went, and	H466
Nu	22:38	I must speak only what G puts in my mouth."	H466
Nu	23: 4	G met with him, and Balaam said, "I have	H466
Nu	23: 8	can I curse those whom G has not cursed?	H446
Nu	23:19	G is not human, that he should lie, not a	H446
Nu	23:21	The LORD their G is with them; the shout of	H466
Nu	23:22	G brought them out of Egypt; they have the	H446
Nu	23:23	Jacob and of Israel, 'See what G has done!	H446
Nu	23:27	it will please G to let you curse them	H466
Nu	24: 2	tribe by tribe, the Spirit of G came on him	H466
Nu	24: 4	prophecy of one who hears the words of G,	H446
Nu	24: 8	"G brought them out of Egypt; they have	H446
Nu	24:16	prophecy of one who hears the words of G,	H446
Nu	24:23	Who can live when G does this?	H446
Nu	25:13	the honor of his G and made atonement	H466
Nu	27:16	the G *who gives* breath to all living things	H466
Dt	1: 6	The LORD our G said to us at Horeb, "You	H466
Dt	1:10	The LORD your G has increased your	H466
Dt	1:11	May the LORD, the G *of* your ancestors	H466
Dt	1:17	of anyone, for judgment belongs to G.	H466
Dt	1:19	as the LORD our G commanded us, we set	H466
Dt	1:20	which the LORD our G is giving us.	H466
Dt	1:21	the LORD your G has given you the land.	H466
Dt	1:21	it as the LORD, the G *of* your ancestors, told	H466
Dt	1:25	good land that the LORD our G is giving us."	H466
Dt	1:26	against the command of the LORD your G.	H466
Dt	1:30	The LORD your G, who is going before you	H466
Dt	1:31	you saw how the LORD your G carried you,	H466
Dt	1:32	you did not trust in the LORD your G,	H466
Dt	1:41	as the LORD our G commanded us.	H466
Dt	2: 7	The LORD your G has blessed you in all the	H466
Dt	2: 7	years the LORD your G has been with you,	H466
Dt	2:29	into the land the LORD our G is giving us."	H466
Dt	2:30	For the LORD your G had made his spirit	H466
Dt	2:33	the LORD our G delivered him over to us	H466
Dt	2:36	The LORD our G gave us all of them.	H466
Dt	2:37	with the command of the LORD our G,	H466
Dt	3: 3	So the LORD our G also gave into our hands	H466
Dt	3:18	"The LORD your G has given you this land to	H466
Dt	3:20	that the LORD your G is giving them across	H466
Dt	3:21	that the LORD your G has done to these two	H466
Dt	3:22	the LORD your G himself will fight for you."	H466
Dt	3:24	For what g is there in heaven or on earth	H446
Dt	4: 1	land the LORD, the G *of* your ancestors, is	H466
Dt	4: 2	of the LORD your G that I give you.	H466
Dt	4: 3	The LORD your G destroyed from among you	H466
Dt	4: 4	fast to the LORD your G are still alive today.	H466
Dt	4: 5	laws as the LORD my G commanded me,	H466
Dt	4: 7	the way the LORD our G is near us whenever	H466
Dt	4:10	you stood before the LORD your G at Horeb,	H466
Dt	4:19	things the LORD your G has apportioned to	H466
Dt	4:21	land the LORD your G is giving you as your	H466
Dt	4:23	of the LORD your G that he made with you;	H466
Dt	4:23	of anything the LORD your G has forbidden.	H466
Dt	4:24	For the LORD your G is a consuming fire,	H466
Dt	4:24	your God is a consuming fire, a jealous G.	H446
Dt	4:25	eyes of the LORD your G and arousing his	H466
Dt	4:29	But if from there you seek the LORD your G	H466
Dt	4:30	will return to the LORD your G and obey him.	H466
Dt	4:31	For the LORD your G is a merciful God; he	H466
Dt	4:31	For the LORD your God is a merciful G; he	H446
Dt	4:32	from the day G created human beings on	H466
Dt	4:33	heard the voice of G speaking out of fire,	H466
Dt	4:34	Has any g ever tried to take for himself one	H466
Dt	4:34	things the LORD your G did for you in Egypt	H466
Dt	4:35	so that you might know that the LORD is G;	H466
Dt	4:39	day that the LORD is G in heaven above	H466
Dt	4:40	land the LORD your G gives you for all time	H466
Dt	5: 2	The LORD our G made a covenant with us at	H466
Dt	5: 6	"I am the LORD your G, who brought you out	H466
Dt	5: 9	the LORD your G, am a jealous God	H466
Dt	5: 9	your God, am a jealous G, punishing the	H446
Dt	5:11	not misuse the name of the LORD your G,	H466
Dt	5:12	as the LORD your G has commanded you.	H466
Dt	5:14	day is a sabbath to the LORD your G.	H466
Dt	5:15	that the LORD your G brought you out of	H466
Dt	5:15	the LORD your G has commanded you to	H466
Dt	5:16	as the LORD your G has commanded you, so	H466
Dt	5:16	in the land the LORD your G is giving you.	H466
Dt	5:24	"The LORD our G has shown us his glory	H466
Dt	5:24	person can live even if G speaks with them.	H466
Dt	5:25	hear the voice of the LORD our G any longer.	H466
Dt	5:26	voice of the living G speaking out of fire,	H466
Dt	5:27	listen to all that the LORD our G says.	H466
Dt	5:27	tell us whatever the LORD our G tells you.	H466
Dt	5:32	what the LORD your G has commanded you;	H466
Dt	5:33	that the LORD your G has commanded you,	H466
Dt	6: 1	laws the LORD your G directed me to teach	H466
Dt	6: 2	fear the LORD your G as long as you live by	H466
Dt	6: 3	just as the LORD, the G *of* your ancestors	H466
Dt	6: 4	The LORD our G, the LORD is one.	H466
Dt	6: 5	Love the LORD your G with all your heart	H466
Dt	6:10	When the LORD your G brings you into the	H466
Dt	6:13	Fear the LORD your G, serve him only and	H466
Dt	6:15	the LORD your G, who is among you, is a	H466
Dt	6:15	is a jealous G and his anger will burn	H446
Dt	6:16	not put the LORD your G to the test as you	H466
Dt	6:17	of the LORD your G and the stipulations	H466
Dt	6:20	laws the LORD our G has commanded you?"	H466
Dt	6:24	these decrees and to fear the LORD our G,	H466
Dt	6:25	to obey all this law before the LORD our G,	H466
Dt	7: 1	When the LORD your G brings you into the	H466
Dt	7: 2	when the LORD your G has delivered them	H466
Dt	7: 6	you are a people holy to the LORD your G.	H466
Dt	7: 6	The LORD your G has chosen you out of all	H466
Dt	7: 9	Know therefore that the LORD your G is God	H466
Dt	7: 9	Know therefore that the LORD your God is G	H466
Dt	7: 9	he is the faithful G, keeping his covenant	H446
Dt	7:12	then the LORD your G will keep his covenant	H466
Dt	7:16	peoples the LORD your G gives over to you.	H466
Dt	7:18	what the LORD your G did to Pharaoh and to	H466
Dt	7:19	which the LORD your G brought you out.	H466
Dt	7:19	The LORD your G will do the same to all the	H466
Dt	7:20	the LORD your G will send the hornet among	H466
Dt	7:21	the LORD your G, who is among you,	H466
Dt	7:21	is among you, is a great and awesome G.	H446
Dt	7:22	LORD your G will drive out those nations	H466
Dt	7:23	But the LORD your G will deliver them over	H466
Dt	7:25	for it is detestable to the LORD your G.	H466
Dt	8: 2	how the LORD your G led you all the way in	H466
Dt	8: 5	so the LORD your G disciplines you.	H466
Dt	8: 6	Observe the commands of the LORD your G	H466
Dt	8: 7	For the LORD your G is bringing you into a	H466
Dt	8:10	praise the LORD your G for the good land he	H466
Dt	8:11	that you do not forget the LORD your G,	H466
Dt	8:14	proud and you will forget the LORD your G,	H466
Dt	8:18	But remember the LORD your G, for it is he	H466
Dt	8:19	forget the LORD your G and follow other	H466
Dt	8:20	destroyed for not obeying the LORD your G.	H466
Dt	9: 3	that the LORD your G is the one who goes	H466
Dt	9: 4	After the LORD your G has driven them out	H466
Dt	9: 5	the LORD your G will drive them out before	H466
Dt	9: 6	that the LORD your G is giving you this good	H466
Dt	9: 7	anger of the LORD your G in the wilderness.	H466
Dt	9:10	stone tablets inscribed by the finger of G.	H466
Dt	9:16	you had sinned against the LORD your G;	H466
Dt	9:23	against the command of the LORD your G.	H466
Dt	10: 9	inheritance, as the LORD your G told them.)	H466
Dt	10:12	does the LORD your G ask of you but to fear	H466
Dt	10:12	God ask of you but to fear the LORD your G,	H466
Dt	10:12	to serve the LORD your G with all your heart	H466
Dt	10:14	To the LORD your G belong the heavens	H466
Dt	10:17	the LORD your G is God of gods and Lord	H466
Dt	10:17	the LORD your God is G *of* gods and Lord of	H466
Dt	10:17	of lords, the great G, mighty and awesome,	H446
Dt	10:20	Fear the LORD your G and serve him.	H466
Dt	10:21	he is your G, who performed for you	H466
Dt	10:22	now the LORD your G has made you as	H466
Dt	11: 1	Love the LORD your G and keep his	H466
Dt	11: 2	the discipline of the LORD your G:	H466
Dt	11:12	It is a land the LORD your G cares for; the	H466
Dt	11:12	eyes of the LORD your G are continually on	H466
Dt	11:13	to love the LORD your G and to serve him	H466
Dt	11:22	to love the LORD your G, to walk in	H466
Dt	11:25	The LORD your G, as he promised you, will	H466
Dt	11:27	of the LORD your G that I am giving you	H466
Dt	11:28	of the LORD your G and turn from the way	H466
Dt	11:29	When the LORD your G has brought you into	H466
Dt	11:31	of the land the LORD your G is giving you.	H466
Dt	12: 1	that the LORD, the G *of* your ancestors, has	H466
Dt	12: 4	not worship the LORD your G in their way.	H466
Dt	12: 5	place the LORD your G will choose from	H466
Dt	12: 7	in the presence of the LORD your G, you	H466
Dt	12: 7	because the LORD your G has blessed you.	H466
Dt	12: 9	inheritance the LORD your G is giving you.	H466
Dt	12:10	the land the LORD your G is giving you as	H466
Dt	12:11	the place the LORD your G will choose as a	H466
Dt	12:12	And there rejoice before the LORD your G	H466
Dt	12:15	to the blessing the LORD your G gives you.	H466
Dt	12:18	of the LORD your G at the place the LORD	H466
Dt	12:18	at the place the LORD your G will choose—	H466
Dt	12:18	before the LORD your G in everything you	H466
Dt	12:20	When the LORD your G has enlarged your	H466
Dt	12:21	where the LORD your G chooses to put his	H466
Dt	12:27	offerings on the altar of the LORD your G,	H466
Dt	12:27	poured beside the altar of the LORD your G,	H466
Dt	12:28	right in the eyes of the LORD your G.	H466
Dt	12:29	The LORD your G will cut off before you the	H466
Dt	12:31	not worship the LORD your G in their way,	H466
Dt	13: 3	The LORD your G is testing you to find out	H466
Dt	13: 4	It is the LORD your G you must follow, and	H466
Dt	13: 5	inciting rebellion against the LORD your G,	H466
Dt	13: 5	the way the LORD your G commanded you to	H466
Dt	13:10	to turn you away from the LORD your G,	H466
Dt	13:12	towns the LORD your G is giving you to live	H466
Dt	13:16	a whole burnt offering to the LORD your G.	H466
Dt	13:18	you obey the LORD your G by keeping all	H466
Dt	14: 1	You are the children of the LORD your G.	H466
Dt	14: 2	you are a people holy to the LORD your G	H466
Dt	14:21	you are a people holy to the LORD your G.	H466
Dt	14:23	of the LORD your G at the place he will	H466
Dt	14:23	may learn to revere the LORD your G always.	H466
Dt	14:24	by the LORD your G and cannot carry your	H466
Dt	14:25	go to the place the LORD your G will choose.	H466
Dt	14:26	presence of the LORD your G and rejoice.	H466
Dt	14:29	so that the LORD your G may bless you in all	H466
Dt	15: 4	the land the LORD your G is giving you to	H466
Dt	15: 5	obey the LORD your G and are careful to	H466
Dt	15: 6	For the LORD your G will bless you as he	H466
Dt	15: 7	of the land the LORD your G is giving you,	H466
Dt	15:10	of this the LORD your G will bless you in all	H466
Dt	15:14	them as the LORD your G has blessed you.	H466
Dt	15:15	Egypt and the LORD your G redeemed you.	H466
Dt	15:18	And the LORD your G will bless you in	H466
Dt	15:19	the LORD your G every firstborn male of	H466
Dt	15:20	of the LORD your G at the place he will	H466
Dt	15:21	you must not sacrifice it to the LORD your G.	H466
Dt	16: 1	celebrate the Passover of the LORD your G,	H466
Dt	16: 2	to the LORD your G an animal from your	H466
Dt	16: 5	in any town the LORD your G gives you	H466
Dt	16: 7	it at the place the LORD your G will choose.	H466
Dt	16: 8	to the LORD your G and do no work.	H466
Dt	16:10	to the LORD your G by giving a freewill	H466
Dt	16:10	blessings the LORD your G has given you.	H466
Dt	16:11	before the LORD your G at the place he will	H466
Dt	16:15	to the LORD your G at the place the LORD	H466
Dt	16:15	For the LORD your G will bless you in all	H466
Dt	16:16	before the LORD your G at the place he will	H466
Dt	16:17	to the way the LORD your G has blessed you.	H466
Dt	16:18	every town the LORD your G is giving you,	H466
Dt	16:20	the land the LORD your G is giving you.	H466
Dt	16:21	the altar you build to the LORD your G,	H466
Dt	16:22	for these the LORD your G hates.	H466
Dt	17: 1	to the LORD your G an ox or a sheep that	H466
Dt	17: 2	eyes of the LORD your G in violation of his	H466
Dt	17: 8	to the place the LORD your G will choose.	H466
Dt	17:12	to the LORD your G is to be put to death.	H466
Dt	17:14	land the LORD your G is giving you and	H466
Dt	17:15	over you a king the LORD your G chooses.	H466
Dt	17:19	revere the LORD his G and follow carefully	H466
Dt	18: 5	the LORD your G has chosen them and	H466
Dt	18: 7	name of the LORD his G like all his fellow	H466
Dt	18: 9	the land the LORD your G is giving you,	H466
Dt	18:12	the LORD your G will drive out those	H466
Dt	18:13	must be blameless before the LORD your G.	H466
Dt	18:14	the LORD your G has not permitted you to do	H466
Dt	18:15	The LORD your G will raise up for you a	H466
Dt	18:16	of the LORD your G at Horeb on the day of	H466
Dt	18:16	voice of the LORD our G nor see this great	H466
Dt	19: 1	When the LORD your G has destroyed the	H466
Dt	19: 2	the land the LORD your G is giving you to	H466
Dt	19: 3	the land the LORD your G is giving you as	H466
Dt	19: 8	If the LORD your G enlarges your territory,	H466
Dt	19: 9	to love the LORD your G and to walk always	H466
Dt	19:10	which the LORD your G is giving you as	H466
Dt	19:14	the land the LORD your G is giving you to	H466
Dt	20: 1	because the LORD your G, who brought you	H466
Dt	20: 4	For the LORD your G is the one who goes	H466
Dt	20:13	When the LORD your G delivers it into your	H466
Dt	20:14	plunder the LORD your G gives you from	H466
Dt	20:16	nations the LORD your G is giving you as an	H466
Dt	20:17	as the LORD your G has commanded you.	H466
Dt	20:18	you will sin against the LORD your G.	H466
Dt	21: 1	the land the LORD your G is giving you to	H466
Dt	21: 5	the LORD your G has chosen them to	H466
Dt	21:10	the LORD your G delivers them into your	H466
Dt	21:23	the land the LORD your G is giving you as	H466
Dt	22: 5	the LORD your G detests anyone who	H466
Dt	23: 5	the LORD your G would not listen to Balaam	H466
Dt	23: 5	you, because the LORD your G loves you.	H466
Dt	23:14	For the LORD your G moves about in your	H466
Dt	23:18	house of the LORD your G to pay any vow,	H466
Dt	23:18	because the LORD your G detests them both.	H466
Dt	23:20	so that the LORD your G may bless you in	H466
Dt	23:21	If you make a vow to the LORD your G, do	H466
Dt	23:21	the LORD your G will certainly demand it	H466
Dt	23:23	to the LORD your G with your own mouth.	H466
Dt	24: 4	the land the LORD your G is giving you as an	H466
Dt	24: 9	what the LORD your G did to Miriam along	H466

Dt 24:13 act in the sight of the LORD your G. H466
Dt 24:18 the LORD your G redeemed you from H466
Dt 24:19 so that the LORD your G may bless you in all H466
Dt 25:15 in the land the LORD your G is giving you. H466
Dt 25:16 For the LORD your G detests anyone who H466
Dt 25:18 lagging behind; they had no fear of G. H466
Dt 25:19 When the LORD your G gives you rest from H466
Dt 26: 1 the land the LORD your G is giving you as an H466
Dt 26: 2 land the LORD your G is giving you and put H466
Dt 26: 2 the place the LORD your G will choose as a H466
Dt 26: 3 to the LORD your G that I have come to H466
Dt 26: 4 in front of the altar of the LORD your G. H466
Dt 26: 5 you shall declare before the LORD your G: H466
Dt 26: 7 out to the LORD, the G of our ancestors, and H466
Dt 26:10 the LORD your G and bow down before H466
Dt 26:11 things the LORD your G has given to you H466
Dt 26:13 Then say to the LORD your G: "I have H466
Dt 26:14 I have obeyed the LORD my G; I have done H466
Dt 26:16 The LORD your G commands you this day to H466
Dt 26:17 that the LORD is your G and that you will H466
Dt 26:19 will be a people holy to the LORD your G, H466
Dt 27: 2 into the land the LORD your G is giving you, H466
Dt 27: 3 the land the LORD your G is giving you, H466
Dt 27: 3 just as the LORD, the G of your ancestors H466
Dt 27: 5 Build there an altar to the LORD your G, an H466
Dt 27: 6 of the LORD your G with fieldstones and H466
Dt 27: 6 burnt offerings on it to the LORD your G. H466
Dt 27: 7 in the presence of the LORD your G. H466
Dt 27: 9 now become the people of the LORD your G. H466
Dt 27:10 Obey the LORD your G and follow his H466
Dt 28: 1 obey the LORD your G and carefully follow H466
Dt 28: 1 the LORD your G will set you high above all H466
Dt 28: 2 you if you obey the LORD your G: H466
Dt 28: 8 The LORD your G will bless you in the land H466
Dt 28: 9 of the LORD your G and walk in obedience H466
Dt 28:13 of the LORD your G that I give you this day H466
Dt 28:15 obey the LORD your G and do not carefully H466
Dt 28:45 not obey the LORD your G and observe the H466
Dt 28:47 serve the LORD your G joyfully and gladly in H466
Dt 28:52 the land the LORD your G is giving you. H466
Dt 28:53 daughters the LORD your G has given you. H466
Dt 28:58 awesome name—the LORD your G— H466
Dt 28:62 because you did not obey the LORD your G. H466
Dt 29: 6 you might know that I am the LORD your G." H466
Dt 29:10 today in the presence of the LORD your G— H466
Dt 29:12 enter into a covenant with the LORD your G, H466
Dt 29:13 that he may be your G as he promised you H466
Dt 29:15 of the LORD our G but also with those who H466
Dt 29:18 from the LORD our G to go and worship the H466
Dt 29:25 of the LORD, the G of their ancestors, the H466
Dt 29:29 The secret things belong to the LORD our G H466
Dt 30: 1 the LORD your G disperses you among H466
Dt 30: 2 to the LORD your G and obey him with all H466
Dt 30: 3 then the LORD your G will restore your H466
Dt 30: 4 there the LORD your G will gather you and H466
Dt 30: 6 The LORD your G will circumcise your hearts H466
Dt 30: 7 The LORD your G will put all these curses on H466
Dt 30: 9 Then the LORD your G will make you most H466
Dt 30:10 obey the LORD your G and keep his H466
Dt 30:10 turn to the LORD your G with all your heart H466
Dt 30:16 you today to love the LORD your G, H466
Dt 30:16 the LORD your G will bless you in the H466
Dt 30:20 that you may love the LORD your G H466
Dt 31: 3 The LORD your G himself will cross over H466
Dt 31: 6 the LORD your G goes with you; he will H466
Dt 31:11 before the LORD your G at the place he will H466
Dt 31:12 to fear the LORD your G and follow carefully H466
Dt 31:13 to fear the LORD your G as long as you live H466
Dt 31:17 come on us because our G is not with us? H466
Dt 31:26 the ark of the covenant of the LORD your G. H466
Dt 32: 3 Oh, praise the greatness of our G! H466
Dt 32: 4 A faithful G who does no wrong, upright H446
Dt 32:12 alone led him; no foreign g was with him. H446
Dt 32:15 abandoned the G who made them and H468
Dt 32:17 which are not G—gods they had not H468
Dt 32:18 you forgot the G who gave you birth. H446
Dt 32:21 by what is no g and angered me with H446
Dt 32:39 There is no g besides me. I put to H466
Dt 33: 1 Moses the man of G pronounced on the H466
Dt 33:26 "There is no one like the G of Jeshurun H446
Dt 33:27 The eternal G is your refuge, and H466
Jos 1: 9 the LORD your G will be with you H466
Jos 1:11 land the LORD your G is giving you for your H466
Jos 1:13 LORD your G will give you rest by giving H466
Jos 1:15 of the land the LORD your G is giving them. H466
Jos 1:17 may the LORD your G be with you as he was H466
Jos 2:11 the LORD your G is God in heaven above H466
Jos 2:11 LORD your God is G in heaven above and H466
Jos 3: 3 the ark of the covenant of the LORD your G, H466
Jos 3: 9 listen to the words of the LORD your G. H466
Jos 3:10 know that the living G is among you and H446
Jos 4: 5 ark of the LORD your G into the middle of H466
Jos 4:23 For the LORD your G dried up the Jordan H466
Jos 4:23 The LORD your G did to the Jordan what he H466
Jos 4:24 you might always fear the LORD your G." H466
Jos 7:13 this is what the LORD, the G of Israel, says: H466
Jos 7:19 to the LORD, the G of Israel, and honor him H466
Jos 7:20 sinned against the LORD, the G of Israel. H466
Jos 8: 7 The LORD your G will give it into your hand. H466
Jos 8:30 Ebal an altar to the LORD, the G of Israel, H466
Jos 9: 9 because of the fame of the LORD your G. H466
Jos 9:18 oath to them by the LORD, the G of Israel. H466
Jos 9:19 oath by the LORD, the G of Israel, and we H466
Jos 9:23 water carriers for the house of my G." H466
Jos 9:24 how the LORD your G had commanded his H466
Jos 10:19 the LORD your G has given them into H466
Jos 10:40 just as the LORD, the G of Israel, had H466
Jos 10:42 because the LORD, the G of Israel, fought H466
Jos 13:14 to the LORD, the G of Israel, are their H466
Jos 13:33 the LORD, the G of Israel, is their inheritance H466
Jos 14: 6 to Moses the man of G at Kadesh Barnea H466
Jos 14: 8 followed the LORD my G wholeheartedly. H466
Jos 14: 9 followed the LORD my G wholeheartedly. H466
Jos 14:14 followed the LORD, the G of Israel H466
Jos 18: 3 that the LORD, the G of your ancestors, has H466
Jos 18: 6 you in the presence of the LORD our G. H466
Jos 22: 3 out the mission the LORD your G gave you. H466
Jos 22: 4 that the LORD your G has given them rest H466
Jos 22: 5 to love the LORD your G, to walk in H466
Jos 22:16 break faith with the G of Israel like this? H466
Jos 22:19 other than the altar of the LORD our G. H466
Jos 22:22 "The Mighty One, G, the LORD! The Mighty H446
Jos 22:22 The Mighty One, G, the LORD! He knows! H466
Jos 22:24 have to do with the LORD, the G of Israel? H466
Jos 22:29 altar of the LORD our G that stands before H466
Jos 22:33 were glad to hear the report and praised G. H466
Jos 22:34 A Witness Between Us—that the LORD is G. H466
Jos 23: 3 the LORD your G has done to all these H466
Jos 23: 3 it was the LORD your G who fought for you. H466
Jos 23: 5 The LORD your G himself will push them out H466
Jos 23: 5 as the LORD your G promised you. H466
Jos 23: 8 But you are to hold fast to the LORD your G H466
Jos 23:10 because the LORD your G fights for you, just H466
Jos 23:11 So be very careful to love the LORD your G. H466
Jos 23:13 that the LORD your G will no longer drive H466
Jos 23:13 which the LORD your G has given you. H466
Jos 23:14 the LORD your G gave you has failed. H466
Jos 23:15 things the LORD your G has promised you H466
Jos 23:15 the LORD your G has destroyed you H466
Jos 23:16 you violate the covenant of the LORD your G, H466
Jos 24: 1 they presented themselves before G. H466
Jos 24: 2 "This is what the LORD, the G of Israel, says: H466
Jos 24:17 It was the LORD our G himself who brought H466
Jos 24:18 will serve the LORD, because he is our G." H466
Jos 24:19 He is a holy G; he is a jealous God H466
Jos 24:19 he is a jealous G. He will not forgive H446
Jos 24:23 your hearts to the LORD, the G of Israel." H466
Jos 24:24 will serve the LORD our G and obey him." H466
Jos 24:26 these things in the Book of the Law of G. H466
Jos 24:27 against you if you are untrue to your G." H466
Jdg 1: 7 Now G has paid me back for what I did to H466
Jdg 2:12 the LORD, the G of their ancestors, who H466
Jdg 3: 7 forgot the LORD their G and served the Baals H466
Jdg 3:20 "I have a message from G for you. H466
Jdg 4: 6 "The LORD, the G of Israel, commands H466
Jdg 4:23 On that day G subdued Jabin king of H466
Jdg 5: 3 praise the LORD, the G of Israel, in song. H466
Jdg 5: 5 of Sinai, before the LORD, the G of Israel. H466
Jdg 5: 8 G chose new leaders when war came to H466
Jdg 6: 8 "This is what the LORD, the G of Israel, says: H466
Jdg 6:10 'I am the LORD your G; do not worship the H466
Jdg 6:20 The angel of G said to him, "Take the H466
Jdg 6:26 altar to the LORD your G on the top of this H466
Jdg 6:31 If Baal really is a g, he can defend himself H466
Jdg 6:36 Gideon said to G, "If you will save Israel by H466
Jdg 6:39 Then Gideon said to G, "Do not be angry H466
Jdg 6:40 That night G did so. Only the fleece was dry; H466
Jdg 7:14 G has given the Midianites and the whole H466
Jdg 8: 3 G gave Oreb and Zeeb, the Midianite H466
Jdg 8:33 They set up Baal-Berith as their g H466
Jdg 8:34 did not remember the LORD their G, who H466
Jdg 9: 7 of Shechem, so that G may listen to you. H466
Jdg 9:23 G stirred up animosity between Abimelek H466
Jdg 9:24 G did this in order that the crime against NDT
Jdg 9:27 they held a festival in the temple of their g. H466
Jdg 9:56 Thus G repaid the wickedness that H466
Jdg 9:57 G also made the people of Shechem pay H466
Jdg 10:10 forsaking our G and serving the Baals." H466
Jdg 11:21 "Then the LORD, the G of Israel, gave Sihon H466
Jdg 11:23 since the LORD, the G of Israel, has driven H466
Jdg 11:24 not take what your g Chemosh gives you? H466
Jdg 11:24 whatever the LORD our G has given us, we H466
Jdg 13: 5 a Nazirite, dedicated to G from the womb. H466
Jdg 13: 6 told him, "A man of G came to me. H466
Jdg 13: 6 He looked like an angel of G, very H466
Jdg 13: 7 will be a Nazirite of G from the womb until H466
Jdg 13: 8 to let the man of G you sent to us come H466
Jdg 13: 9 G heard Manoah, and the angel of God H466
Jdg 13: 9 the angel of G came again to the H466
Jdg 13:22 he said to his wife. "We have seen G!" H466
Jdg 15:19 Then G opened up the hollow place in Lehi, H466
Jdg 16:17 dedicated to G from my mother's womb H466
Jdg 16:23 sacrifice to Dagon their g and to celebrate, H466
Jdg 16:23 "Our g has delivered Samson, our H466
Jdg 16:24 saw him, they praised their g, saying, H466
Jdg 16:24 "Our g has delivered our enemy into our H466
Jdg 16:28 G, strengthen me just once more H466
Jdg 18: 5 "Please inquire of G to learn whether our H466
Jdg 18:10 a spacious land that G has put into your H466
Jdg 18:31 all the time the house of G was in Shiloh. H466
Jdg 20:18 went up to Bethel and inquired of G. H466
Jdg 20:27 the ark of the covenant of G was there, H466
Jdg 21: 2 where they sat before G until evening H466
Jdg 21: 3 G of Israel," they cried, "why has this H466
Ru 1:16 will be my people and your G my God. H466
Ru 1:16 will be my people and your God my G. H466
Ru 2:12 by the LORD, the G of Israel, under whose H466
1Sa 1:17 may the G of Israel grant you what you H466
1Sa 2: 2 besides you; there is no Rock like our G. H466
1Sa 2: 3 the LORD is a G who knows, and by him H446
1Sa 2:25 another, G may mediate for the offender H466
1Sa 2:27 Now a man of G came to Eli and said to H466
1Sa 2:30 the LORD, the G of Israel, declares: H466
1Sa 3: 3 The lamp of G had not yet gone out, and H466
1Sa 3: 3 house of the LORD, where the ark of G was. H466
1Sa 3:13 his sons blasphemed G, and he failed to H466
1Sa 3:17 May G deal with you, be it ever so severely H466
1Sa 4: 4 there with the ark of the covenant of G. H466
1Sa 4: 7 "A g has come into the camp," H466
1Sa 4:11 The ark of G was captured, and Eli's two H466
1Sa 4:13 because his heart feared for the ark of G. H466
1Sa 4:17 and the ark of G has been captured." H466
1Sa 4:18 When he mentioned the ark of G, Eli fell H466
1Sa 4:19 news that the ark of G had been captured H466
1Sa 4:21 of the ark of G and the deaths of her H466
1Sa 4:22 for the ark of G has been captured. H466
1Sa 5: 1 the Philistines had captured the ark of G, H466
1Sa 5: 7 "The ark of the g of Israel must not stay H466
1Sa 5: 7 hand is heavy on us and on Dagon our g." H466
1Sa 5: 8 shall we do with the ark of the g of Israel?" H466
1Sa 5: 8 "Have the ark of the g of Israel moved to H466
1Sa 5: 8 So they moved the ark of the G of Israel. H466
1Sa 5:10 So they sent the ark of G to Ekron. H466
1Sa 5:10 As the ark of G was entering Ekron, the H466
1Sa 5:10 the ark of the g of Israel around to us H466
1Sa 5:11 "Send the ark of the g of Israel away; let it H466
1Sa 6: 3 "If you return the ark of the g of Israel, do H466
1Sa 6: 5 the country, and give glory to Israel's g. H466
1Sa 6: 6 When Israel's g dealt harshly with them, did NDT
1Sa 6:19 But G struck down some of the inhabitants NDT
1Sa 6:20 in the presence of the LORD, this holy G? H466
1Sa 7: 8 not stop crying out to the LORD our G for us, H466
1Sa 9: 6 in this town there is a man of G; he is H466
1Sa 9: 7 We have no gift to take to the man of G H466
1Sa 9: 8 give it to the man of G so that he will tell H466
1Sa 9: 9 if someone went to inquire of G, they H466
1Sa 9:10 out for the town where the man of G was. H466
1Sa 9:27 so that I may give you a message from G." H466
1Sa 10: 3 going up to worship G at Bethel will meet H466
1Sa 10: 5 "After that you will go to Gibeah of G H466
1Sa 10: 7 your hand finds to do, for G is with you. H466
1Sa 10: 9 to leave Samuel, G changed Saul's heart H466
1Sa 10:10 the Spirit of G came powerfully upon him H466
1Sa 10:18 "This is what the LORD, the G of Israel, says: H466
1Sa 10:19 But you have now rejected your G, who H466
1Sa 10:26 valiant men whose hearts G had touched. H466
1Sa 11: 6 the Spirit of G came powerfully upon him H466
1Sa 12: 9 "But they forgot the LORD their G; so he sold H466
1Sa 12:12 even though the LORD your G was your king. H466
1Sa 12:14 reigns over you follow the LORD your G— H466
1Sa 12:19 "Pray to the LORD your G for your servants H466
1Sa 13:13 the command the LORD your G gave you; H466
1Sa 14:15 the ground shook. It was a panic sent by G. H466
1Sa 14:18 "Bring the ark of G." (At that time it was H466
1Sa 14:36 the priest said, "Let us inquire of G here." H466
1Sa 14:37 So Saul asked G, "Shall I go down and H466
1Sa 14:37 But G did not answer him that day NDT
1Sa 14:41 to the LORD, the G of Israel, "Why have you H466
1Sa 14:44 Saul said, "May G deal with me, be it ever H466
1Sa 15:15 cattle to sacrifice to the LORD your G, H466
1Sa 15:21 the best of what was devoted to G, in H3051
1Sa 15:21 sacrifice them to the LORD your G at Gilgal." H466
1Sa 15:30 so that I may worship the LORD your G." H466
1Sa 16:15 an evil spirit from G is tormenting you. H466
1Sa 16:16 when the evil spirit from G comes on you, H466
1Sa 16:23 Whenever the spirit from G came on Saul H466
1Sa 17:26 he should defy the armies of the living G?" H466
1Sa 17:36 he has defied the armies of the living G. H466
1Sa 17:45 LORD Almighty, the G of the armies of Israel H466
1Sa 17:46 world will know that there is a G in Israel. H466
1Sa 18:10 an evil spirit from G came forcefully on H466
1Sa 19:20 the Spirit of G came on Saul's men H466
1Sa 19:23 But the Spirit of G came even on him, and H466
1Sa 20:12 swear by the LORD, the G of Israel, that I will H466
1Sa 22: 3 you until I learn what G will do for me?" H466
1Sa 22:13 a sword and inquiring of G for him, H466
1Sa 22:15 day the first time I inquired of G for him? H466
1Sa 23: 7 "G has delivered him into my hands H466
1Sa 23:10 G of Israel, your servant has heard H466
1Sa 23:11 LORD, G of Israel, tell your H466
1Sa 23:14 G did not give David into his hands. H466
1Sa 23:16 Horesh and helped him find strength in G. H466
1Sa 25:22 May G deal with David, be it ever so H466
1Sa 25:26 as the LORD your G lives and as you live, NDT
1Sa 25:28 The LORD your G will certainly make a NDT
1Sa 25:29 the bundle of the living by the LORD your G, H466
1Sa 25:31 when the LORD your G has brought my lord NDT
1Sa 25:32 be to the LORD, the G of Israel, who has H466
1Sa 25:34 as the LORD, the G of Israel, lives, who has H466
1Sa 26: 8 "Today G has delivered your enemy into H466
1Sa 28:15 against me, and G has departed from me. H466
1Sa 29: 9 as pleasing in my eyes as an angel of G; H466
1Sa 30: 6 But David found strength in the LORD his G. H466
1Sa 30:15 "Swear to me before G that you will not kill H466
2Sa 2:27 "As surely as G lives, if you had not H466
2Sa 3: 9 May G deal with Abner, be it ever so H466

Book	Ref	Context	Number
2Sa	3:35	"May G deal with me, be it ever so	H466
2Sa	5:10	because the LORD G Almighty was with him.	H466
2Sa	6: 2	Judah to bring up from there the ark of G,	H466
2Sa	6: 3	They set the ark of G on a new cart and	H466
2Sa	6: 4	with the ark of G on it, and Ahio was	H466
2Sa	6: 6	reached out and took hold of the ark of G,	H466
2Sa	6: 7	therefore G struck him down, and he	H466
2Sa	6: 7	he died there beside the ark of G.	H466
2Sa	6:12	everything he has, because of the ark of G."	H466
2Sa	6:12	to bring up the ark of G from the house of	H466
2Sa	7: 2	while the ark of G remains in a tent."	H466
2Sa	7:22	and there is no G but you, as we have	H466
2Sa	7:23	nation on earth that G went out to redeem	H466
2Sa	7:24	LORD, have become their G.	H466
2Sa	7:25	"And now, LORD G, keep forever the	H466
2Sa	7:26	'The LORD Almighty is G over Israel!	H466
2Sa	7:27	"LORD Almighty, G *of* Israel, you have	H466
2Sa	7:28	Sovereign LORD, you are G! Your covenant	H466
2Sa	10:12	our people and the cities of our G.	H466
2Sa	12: 7	is what the LORD, the G *of* Israel, says: 'I	H466
2Sa	12:16	David pleaded with G for the child.	H466
2Sa	14:11	invoke the LORD his G to prevent the	H466
2Sa	14:13	a thing like this against the people of G?	H466
2Sa	14:14	But that is not what G desires; rather, he	H466
2Sa	14:17	is like an angel of G in discerning good	H466
2Sa	14:17	May the LORD your G be with you.'"	H466
2Sa	14:20	has wisdom like that of an angel of G—	H466
2Sa	15:24	were carrying the ark of the covenant of G.	H466
2Sa	15:24	They set down the ark of G, and Abiathar	H466
2Sa	15:25	"Take the ark of G back into the city.	H466
2Sa	15:29	took the ark of G back to Jerusalem and	H466
2Sa	15:32	where people used to worship G, Hushai	H466
2Sa	16:23	was like that of one who inquires of G.	H466
2Sa	18:28	said, "Praise be to the LORD your G!	H466
2Sa	19:13	May G deal with me, be it ever so severely	H466
2Sa	19:27	My lord the king is like an angel of G; so	H466
2Sa	21:14	G answered prayer in behalf of the land.	H466
2Sa	22: 3	my G is my rock, in whom I take refuge, my	H466
2Sa	22: 7	I called to the LORD; I called out to my G.	H466
2Sa	22:22	I am not guilty of turning from my G.	H466
2Sa	22:30	with my G I can scale a wall.	H466
2Sa	22:31	"As for G, his way is perfect: The LORD's	H446
2Sa	22:32	For who is G besides the LORD? And who is	H446
2Sa	22:32	And who is the Rock except our G?	H466
2Sa	22:33	It is G who arms me with strength and	H446
2Sa	22:47	Exalted be my G, the Rock, my Savior!	H466
2Sa	22:48	He is the G who avenges me, who puts the	H446
2Sa	23: 1	the man anointed by the G *of* Jacob, the	H466
2Sa	23: 3	The G *of* Israel spoke, the Rock of Israel	H466
2Sa	23: 3	when he rules in the fear of G,	H466
2Sa	23: 5	"If my house were not right with G, surely	H446
2Sa	24: 3	"May the LORD your G multiply the troops a	H466
2Sa	24:23	"May the LORD your G accept you.	H466
2Sa	24:24	to the LORD my G burnt offerings that	H466
1Ki	1:17	to me your servant by the LORD your G:	H466
1Ki	1:30	I swore to you by the LORD, the G *of* Israel:	H466
1Ki	1:36	May the LORD, the G *of* my lord the king, so	H466
1Ki	1:47	'May your G make Solomon's name more	H466
1Ki	1:48	be to the LORD, the G *of* Israel, who has	H466
1Ki	2: 3	observe what the LORD your G requires	H466
1Ki	2:23	"May G deal with me, be it ever so severely	H466
1Ki	3: 5	night in a dream, and G said, "Ask for	H466
1Ki	3: 7	LORD my G, you have made your	H466
1Ki	3:11	So G said to him, "Since you have asked	H466
1Ki	3:28	he had wisdom from G to administer	H466
1Ki	4:29	G gave Solomon wisdom and very great	H466
1Ki	5: 3	Name of the LORD his G until the LORD put	H466
1Ki	5: 4	But now the LORD my G has given me rest	H466
1Ki	5: 5	a temple for the Name of the LORD my G,	H466
1Ki	8:15	be to the LORD, the G *of* Israel, who with his	H466
1Ki	8:17	the Name of the LORD, the G *of* Israel.	H466
1Ki	8:20	the Name of the LORD, the G *of* Israel.	H466
1Ki	8:23	the G *of* Israel, there is no God like	H466
1Ki	8:23	there is no G like you in heaven above	H466
1Ki	8:25	"Now LORD, the G *of* Israel, keep for your	H466
1Ki	8:26	And now, G *of* Israel, let your word that you	H466
1Ki	8:27	"But will G really dwell on earth? The	H466
1Ki	8:28	prayer and his plea for mercy, LORD my G.	H466
1Ki	8:57	May the LORD our G be with us as he was	H466
1Ki	8:59	be near to the LORD our G day and night	H466
1Ki	8:60	know that the LORD is G and that there is no	H466
1Ki	8:61	hearts be fully committed to the LORD our G,	H466
1Ki	8:65	it before the LORD our G for seven days and	H466
1Ki	9: 9	they have forsaken the LORD their G,	H466
1Ki	10: 9	Praise be to the LORD your G, who has	H466
1Ki	10:24	to hear the wisdom G had put in his heart.	H466
1Ki	11: 4	was not fully devoted to the LORD his G,	H466
1Ki	11: 5	Molek the **detestable** g *of* the	H9199
1Ki	11: 7	Chemosh the **detestable** g *of* Moab,	H9199
1Ki	11: 7	Molek the **detestable** g *of* the	H9199
1Ki	11: 9	from the LORD, the G *of* Israel, who had	H466
1Ki	11:23	And G raised up against Solomon another	H466
1Ki	11:31	this is what the LORD, the G *of* Israel, says:	H466
1Ki	11:33	Chemosh the g *of* the Moabites, and	H466
1Ki	11:33	Molek the g *of* the Ammonites, and	H466
1Ki	12:22	But this word of G came to Shemaiah the	H466
1Ki	12:22	of God came to Shemaiah the man of G:	H466
1Ki	13: 1	of the LORD a man of G came from Judah to	H466
1Ki	13: 3	That same day the man of G gave a sign	NDT
1Ki	13: 4	what the man of G cried out against the	H466
1Ki	13: 5	given by the man of G by the word of the	H466
1Ki	13: 6	Then the king said to the man of G	H466
1Ki	13: 6	with the LORD your G and pray for me that	H466
1Ki	13: 6	So the man of G interceded with the LORD	H466
1Ki	13: 7	The king said to the man of G, "Come	H466
1Ki	13: 8	But the man of G answered the king, "Even	H466
1Ki	13:11	all that the man of G had done there that	H466
1Ki	13:12	road the man of G from Judah had taken.	H466
1Ki	13:14	rode after the man of G. He found him	H466
1Ki	13:14	you the man of G who came from Judah	H466
1Ki	13:16	The man of G said, "I cannot turn back and	NDT
1Ki	13:19	So the man of G returned with him and ate	NDT
1Ki	13:21	out to the man of G who had come from	H466
1Ki	13:21	the command the LORD your G gave you.	H466
1Ki	13:23	When the man of G had finished eating	NDT
1Ki	13:26	"It is the man of G who defied the word of	H466
1Ki	13:29	picked up the body of the man of G,	H466
1Ki	13:31	in the grave where the man of G is buried;	H466
1Ki	14: 7	this is what the LORD, the G *of* Israel, says:	H466
1Ki	14:13	whom the LORD, the G *of* Israel, has found	H466
1Ki	15: 3	was not fully devoted to the LORD his G,	H466
1Ki	15: 4	sake the LORD his G gave him a lamp in	H466
1Ki	15:30	the anger of the LORD, the G *of* Israel.	H466
1Ki	16:13	anger of the LORD, the G *of* Israel, by their	H466
1Ki	16:26	anger of the LORD, the G *of* Israel, by their	H466
1Ki	16:33	of the LORD, the G *of* Israel, than did all	H466
1Ki	17: 1	"As the LORD, the G *of* Israel, lives, whom I	H466
1Ki	17:12	"As surely as the LORD your G lives," she	H466
1Ki	17:14	this is what the LORD, the G *of* Israel, says:	H466
1Ki	17:18	"What do you have against me, man of G?	H466
1Ki	17:20	to the LORD, "LORD my G, have you brought	H466
1Ki	17:21	to the LORD, "LORD my G, let this boy's life	H466
1Ki	17:24	you are a man of G and that the word of	H466
1Ki	18:10	As surely as the LORD your G lives, there is	H466
1Ki	18:21	If the LORD is G, follow him; but if Baal is	H466
1Ki	18:21	follow him; but if Baal is G, follow him."	NDT
1Ki	18:24	Then you call on the name of your g, and I	H466
1Ki	18:24	The g who answers by fire	H466
1Ki	18:24	by fire—he is G." Then all the people	H466
1Ki	18:25	Call on the name of your g, but do not light	H466
1Ki	18:27	"Surely he is a g! Perhaps he is deep	H466
1Ki	18:36	the G *of* Abraham, Isaac and Israel	H466
1Ki	18:36	today that you are G in Israel and that I am	H466
1Ki	18:37	are G, and that you are turning their	H466
1Ki	18:39	prostrate and cried, "The LORD—he is G!	H466
1Ki	18:39	LORD—he is God! The LORD—he is G!"	H466
1Ki	19: 8	he reached Horeb, the mountain of G.	H466
1Ki	19:10	been very zealous for the LORD G Almighty.	H466
1Ki	19:14	been very zealous for the LORD G Almighty.	H466
1Ki	20:28	The man of G came up and told the king of	H466
1Ki	20:28	think the LORD is a g *of* the hills and not a	H466
1Ki	20:28	god of the hills and not a g *of* the valleys,	H466
1Ki	21:10	that he has cursed both G and the king.	H466
1Ki	21:13	"Naboth has cursed both G and the king."	H466
1Ki	22:53	of the LORD, the G *of* Israel, just as his	H466
2Ki	1: 2	Baal-Zebub, the g *of* Ekron, to see if I	H466
2Ki	1: 3	because there is no G in Israel that you are	H466
2Ki	1: 3	off to consult Baal-Zebub, the g *of* Ekron?	H466
2Ki	1: 6	because there is no G in Israel that you are	H466
2Ki	1: 6	to consult Baal-Zebub, the g *of* Ekron?	H466
2Ki	1: 9	said to him, "Man of G, the king says	H466
2Ki	1:10	"If I am a man of G, may fire come down	H466
2Ki	1:11	said to him, "Man of G, this is what the	H466
2Ki	1:12	"If I am a man of G," Elijah replied, "may	H466
2Ki	1:12	Then the fire of G fell from heaven and	H466
2Ki	1:13	"Man of G," he begged, "please have	H466
2Ki	1:16	it because there is no G in Israel for you to	H466
2Ki	1:16	to consult Baal-Zebub, the g *of* Ekron?	H466
2Ki	2:14	now is the LORD, the G *of* Elijah?" he asked.	H466
2Ki	4: 7	She went and told the man of G, and he	H466
2Ki	4: 9	often comes our way is a holy man of G.	H466
2Ki	4:16	"Please, man of G, don't mislead your	H466
2Ki	4:21	laid him on the bed of the man of G,	H466
2Ki	4:22	I can go to the man of G quickly and return."	H466
2Ki	4:25	came to the man of G at Mount Carmel.	H466
2Ki	4:25	the man of G said to his servant Gehazi	H466
2Ki	4:27	she reached the man of G at the mountain,	H466
2Ki	4:27	but the man of G said, "Leave her	H466
2Ki	4:40	cried out, "Man of G, there is death in the	H466
2Ki	4:42	bringing the man of G twenty loaves of	H466
2Ki	5: 7	he tore his robes and said, "Am I G?	H466
2Ki	5: 8	Elisha the man of G heard that the king of	H466
2Ki	5:11	call on the name of the LORD his G,	H466
2Ki	5:14	as the man of G had told him, and	H466
2Ki	5:15	his attendants went back to the man of G.	H466
2Ki	5:15	know that there is no G in all the world	H466
2Ki	5:17	sacrifices to any other g but the LORD.	H466
2Ki	5:20	the servant of Elisha the man of G, said to	H466
2Ki	6: 6	The man of G asked, "Where did it fall?"	H466
2Ki	6: 9	The man of G sent word to the king of	H466
2Ki	6:10	on the place indicated by the man of G.	H466
2Ki	6:15	of the man of G got up and went out	H466
2Ki	6:31	"May G deal with me, be it ever so	H466
2Ki	7: 2	the king was leaning said to the man of G,	H466
2Ki	7:17	just as the man of G had foretold when the	H466
2Ki	7:18	as the man of G had said to the king:	H466
2Ki	7:19	The officer had said to the man of G, "Look,	H466
2Ki	7:19	The man of G had replied, "You will see it	NDT
2Ki	8: 2	proceeded to do as the man of G said.	H466
2Ki	8: 4	the servant of the man of G, and had said,	H466
2Ki	8: 7	"The man of G has come all the way up	H466
2Ki	8: 8	gift with you and go to meet the man of G.	H466
2Ki	8:11	Then the man of G began to weep.	H466
2Ki	9: 6	"This is what the LORD, the G *of* Israel, says:	H466
2Ki	10:31	law of the LORD, the G *of* Israel, with all his	H466
2Ki	13:19	The man of G was angry with him and said	H466
2Ki	14:25	word of the LORD, the G *of* Israel, spoken	H466
2Ki	16: 2	was right in the eyes of the LORD his G.	H466
2Ki	17: 7	had sinned against the LORD their G,	H466
2Ki	17: 9	against the LORD their G that were not right.	H466
2Ki	17:14	who did not trust in the LORD their G.	H466
2Ki	17:16	of the LORD their G and made for	H466
2Ki	17:19	not keep the commands of the LORD their G.	H466
2Ki	17:26	do not know what the g *of* that country	H466
2Ki	17:27	the people what the g *of* the land requires."	H466
2Ki	17:39	worship the LORD your G; it is he who will	H466
2Ki	18: 5	trusted in the LORD, the G *of* Israel.	H466
2Ki	18:12	they had not obeyed the LORD their G,	H466
2Ki	18:22	"We are depending on the LORD our G"—	H466
2Ki	18:33	Has the g *of* any nation ever delivered his	H466
2Ki	19: 4	be that the LORD your G will hear all the	H466
2Ki	19: 4	has sent to ridicule the living G, and that	H466
2Ki	19: 4	the words the LORD your G has heard.	H466
2Ki	19:10	Do not let the g you depend on deceive	H466
2Ki	19:15	the G *of* Israel, enthroned between	H466
2Ki	19:15	you alone are G over all the kingdoms of	H466
2Ki	19:16	has sent to ridicule the living G.	H466
2Ki	19:19	LORD our G, deliver us from his hand	H466
2Ki	19:19	may know that you alone, LORD, are G."	H466
2Ki	19:20	what the LORD, the G *of* Israel, says: I have	H466
2Ki	19:37	worshiping in the temple of his g Nisrok,	H466
2Ki	20: 5	is what the LORD, the G *of* your father David	H466
2Ki	21:12	this is what the LORD, the G *of* Israel, says:	H466
2Ki	21:22	the LORD, the G *of* his ancestors, and	H466
2Ki	22:15	"This is what the LORD, the G *of* Israel, says:	H466
2Ki	22:18	is what the LORD, the G *of* Israel, says	H466
2Ki	23:13	Chemosh the **vile** g *of* Moab, and for	H9199
2Ki	23:13	Molek the **detestable** g *of* the people	H9359
2Ki	23:16	by the man of G who foretold these	H466
2Ki	23:17	tomb of the man of G who came from	H466
2Ki	23:21	"Celebrate the Passover to the LORD your G	H466
1Ch	4:10	Jabez cried out to the G *of* Israel, "Oh, that	H466
1Ch	4:10	free from pain." And G granted his request	H466
1Ch	5:20	G delivered the Hagrites and all their	H466
1Ch	5:25	unfaithful to the G *of* their ancestors and	H466
1Ch	5:25	whom G had destroyed before them.	H466
1Ch	5:26	So the G *of* Israel stirred up the spirit of Pul	H466
1Ch	6:48	duties of the tabernacle, the house of G.	H466
1Ch	6:49	Moses the servant of G had commanded.	H466
1Ch	9:11	the official in charge of the house of G;	H466
1Ch	9:13	ministering in the house of G.	H466
1Ch	9:26	the rooms and treasuries in the house of G.	H466
1Ch	9:27	the night stationed around the house of G,	H466
1Ch	11: 2	And the LORD your G said to you, 'You will	H466
1Ch	11:19	"G forbid that I should do this!" he said	H466
1Ch	12:17	may the G *of* our ancestors see it and	H466
1Ch	12:18	who help you, for your G will help you."	H466
1Ch	12:22	he had a great army, like the army of G.	H466
1Ch	13: 2	to you and if it is the will of the LORD our G,	H466
1Ch	13: 3	Let us bring the ark of our G back to us, for	H466
1Ch	13: 5	to bring the ark of G from Kiriath Jearim.	H466
1Ch	13: 6	to bring up from there the ark of G the LORD	H466
1Ch	13: 7	moved the ark of G from Abinadab's house	H466
1Ch	13: 8	celebrating with all their might before G,	H466
1Ch	13:10	So he died there before G.	H466
1Ch	13:12	David was afraid of G that day and asked	H466
1Ch	13:12	"How can I ever bring the ark of G to me?"	H466
1Ch	13:14	The ark of G remained with the family of	H466
1Ch	14:10	so David inquired of G: "Shall I go and	H466
1Ch	14:11	G has broken out against my enemies by	H466
1Ch	14:14	so David inquired of G again, and God	H466
1Ch	14:14	of God again, and G answered him, "Do	H466
1Ch	14:15	that will mean G has gone out in front	H466
1Ch	14:16	So David did as G commanded him, and	H466
1Ch	15: 1	place for the ark of G and pitched a tent	H466
1Ch	15: 2	one but the Levites may carry the ark of G,	H466
1Ch	15:12	ark of the LORD, the G *of* Israel, to the place	H466
1Ch	15:13	time that the LORD our G broke out in anger	H466
1Ch	15:14	bring up the ark of the LORD, the G *of* Israel.	H466
1Ch	15:15	carried the ark of G with the poles on their	H466
1Ch	15:24	were to blow trumpets before the ark of G.	H466
1Ch	15:26	Because G had helped the Levites who	H466
1Ch	16: 1	brought the ark of G and set it inside the	H466
1Ch	16: 1	offerings and fellowship offerings before G.	H466
1Ch	16: 4	and praise the LORD, the G *of* Israel:	H466
1Ch	16: 6	before the ark of the covenant of G.	H466
1Ch	16:14	He is the LORD our G; his judgments are in	H466
1Ch	16:35	"Save us, G our Savior; gather us and	H466
1Ch	16:36	be to the LORD, the G *of* Israel, from	H466
1Ch	17: 2	you have in mind, do it, for G is with you."	H466
1Ch	17: 3	that night the word of G came to Nathan,	H466
1Ch	17:16	"Who am I, LORD G, and what is my family	H466
1Ch	17:17	in your sight, my G, you have spoken about	H466
1Ch	17:17	LORD G, have looked on me as though	H466
1Ch	17:20	and there is no G but you, as we have	H466
1Ch	17:21	on earth whose G went out to redeem a	H466
1Ch	17:22	LORD, have become their G.	H466
1Ch	17:24	LORD Almighty, the G *over* Israel, is Israel's	H466
1Ch	17:24	Almighty, the God over Israel, is Israel's G!	H466
1Ch	17:25	my G, have revealed to your servant	H466
1Ch	17:26	LORD, are G! You have promised these	H466
1Ch	19:13	our people and the cities of our G.	H466
1Ch	21: 7	command was also evil in the sight of G;	H466
1Ch	21: 8	Then David said to G, "I have sinned	H466
1Ch	21:15	And G sent an angel to destroy Jerusalem	H466
1Ch	21:17	David said to G, "Was it not I who ordered	H466

1Ch 21:17 LORD my **G**, let your hand fall on me and my H466
1Ch 21:30 could not go before it to inquire of **G**, H466
1Ch 22: 1 "The house of the LORD **G** is to be here, and H466
1Ch 22: 2 dressed stone for building the house of **G**. H466
1Ch 22: 6 build a house for the LORD, the **G** *of* Israel. H466
1Ch 22: 7 a house for the Name of the LORD my **G**. H466
1Ch 22:11 build the house of the LORD your **G**, H466
1Ch 22:12 you may keep the law of the LORD your **G**. H466
1Ch 22:18 to them, "Is not the LORD your **G** with you? H466
1Ch 22:19 heart and soul to seeking the LORD your **G**. H466
1Ch 22:19 Begin to build the sanctuary of the LORD **G** H466
1Ch 22:19 articles belonging to **G** into the temple that H466
1Ch 23:14 of Moses the man of **G** were counted as H466
1Ch 23:25 the LORD, the **G** *of* Israel, has granted H466
1Ch 23:28 of other duties at the house of **G**. H466
1Ch 24: 5 officials of **G** among the descendants H466
1Ch 24:19 as the LORD, the **G** *of* Israel, had H466
1Ch 25: 5 through the promises of **G** to exalt him. H466
1Ch 25: 5 **G** gave Heman fourteen sons and three H466
1Ch 25: 6 for the ministry at the house of **G**. H466
1Ch 26: 5 (For **G** had blessed Obed-Edom. H466
1Ch 26:20 of the house of **G** and the treasuries for the H466
1Ch 26:32 matter pertaining to **G** and for the affairs of H466
1Ch 28: 2 the footstool of our **G**, and I made plans H466
1Ch 28: 3 But **G** said to me, 'You are not to build a H466
1Ch 28: 4 "Yet the LORD, the **G** *of* Israel, chose me H466
1Ch 28: 8 of the LORD, and in the hearing of our **G**: H466
1Ch 28: 8 all the commands of the LORD your **G**, H466
1Ch 28: 9 acknowledge the **G** *of* your father, and H466
1Ch 28:12 of the temple of **G** and for the treasuries H466
1Ch 28:20 discouraged, for the LORD **G**, my God, H466
1Ch 28:20 the LORD God, my **G**, is with you. H466
1Ch 28:21 ready for all the work on the temple of **G**, H466
1Ch 29: 1 the one whom **G** has chosen, is young H466
1Ch 29: 1 structure is not for man but for the LORD **G**. H466
1Ch 29: 2 I have provided for the temple of my **G**— H466
1Ch 29: 3 to the temple of my **G** I now give my H466
1Ch 29: 3 of gold and silver for the temple of my **G**, H466
1Ch 29: 7 on the temple of **G** five thousand talents H466
1Ch 29:10 the **G** *of* our father Israel, from H466
1Ch 29:13 our **G**, we give you thanks, and praise H466
1Ch 29:16 LORD our **G**, all this abundance that we have H466
1Ch 29:17 my **G**, that you test the heart and H466
1Ch 29:18 the **G** *of* our fathers Abraham, Isaac H466
1Ch 29:20 whole assembly, "Praise the LORD your **G**." H466
1Ch 29:20 praised the LORD, the **G** *of* their fathers; they H466
2Ch 1: 1 the LORD his **G** was with him and made H466
2Ch 1: 4 brought up the ark of **G** from Kiriath Jearim H466
2Ch 1: 7 That night **G** appeared to Solomon and H466
2Ch 1: 8 Solomon answered **G**, "You have shown H466
2Ch 1: 9 LORD **G**, let your promise to my father H466
2Ch 1:11 **G** said to Solomon, "Since this is your H466
2Ch 2: 4 Name of the LORD my **G** and to dedicate it H466
2Ch 2: 4 at the appointed festivals of the LORD our **G**. H466
2Ch 2: 5 because our **G** is greater than all other H466
2Ch 2:12 be to the LORD, the **G** *of* Israel, who made H466
2Ch 3: 3 the temple of **G** was sixty cubits long H466
2Ch 4:11 King Solomon in the temple of **G**: H466
2Ch 5:14 the glory of the LORD filled the temple of **G**. H466
2Ch 6: 4 be to the LORD, the **G** *of* Israel, who with his H466
2Ch 6: 7 the Name of the LORD, the **G** *of* Israel. H466
2Ch 6:10 the Name of the LORD, the **G** *of* Israel. H466
2Ch 6:14 the **G** *of* Israel, there is no God like H466
2Ch 6:14 there is no **G** like you in heaven or on earth H466
2Ch 6:16 the **G** *of* Israel, keep for your servant H466
2Ch 6:17 the **G** *of* Israel, let your word that you H466
2Ch 6:18 "But will **G** really dwell on earth with H466
2Ch 6:19 LORD my **G**, give attention to your H466
2Ch 6:40 my **G**, may your eyes be open and H466
2Ch 6:41 "Now arise, LORD **G**, and come to your H466
2Ch 6:41 May your priests, LORD **G**, be clothed with H466
2Ch 6:42 LORD **G**, do not reject your anointed one H466
2Ch 7: 5 all the people dedicated the temple of **G**. H466
2Ch 7:22 the LORD, the **G** *of* their ancestors, who H466
2Ch 8:14 was what David the man of **G** had ordered. H466
2Ch 9: 8 Praise be to the LORD your **G**, who has H466
2Ch 9: 8 throne as king to rule for the LORD your **G**. H466
2Ch 9: 8 of the love of your **G** for Israel and his H466
2Ch 9:23 to hear the wisdom **G** had put in his heart. H466
2Ch 10:15 this turn of events was from **G**, to fulfill H466
2Ch 11: 2 the LORD came to Shemaiah the man of **G**: H466
2Ch 11:16 the LORD, the **G** *of* Israel, followed the H466
2Ch 11:16 to the LORD, the **G** *of* their ancestors. H466
2Ch 13: 5 that the LORD, the **G** *of* Israel, has given the H466
2Ch 13:10 the LORD is our **G**, and we have not H466
2Ch 13:11 the requirements of the LORD our **G**. H466
2Ch 13:12 **G** is with us; he is our leader. His priests H466
2Ch 13:12 the LORD, the **G** *of* your ancestors, for H466
2Ch 13:15 **G** routed Jeroboam and all Israel before H466
2Ch 13:16 **G** delivered them into their hands. H466
2Ch 13:18 relied on the LORD, the **G** *of* their ancestors. H466
2Ch 14: 2 right in the eyes of the LORD his **G**. H466
2Ch 14: 4 seek the LORD, the **G** *of* their ancestors, and H466
2Ch 14: 7 because we have sought the LORD our **G** H466
2Ch 14:11 Then Asa called to the LORD his **G** and said H466
2Ch 14:11 Help us, LORD our **G**, for we rely on you, andH466
2Ch 14:11 you are our **G**; do not let mere H466
2Ch 15: 1 The Spirit of **G** came on Azariah son of H466
2Ch 15: 3 a long time Israel was without the true **G**, H466
2Ch 15: 4 to the LORD, the **G** *of* Israel, and sought him H466
2Ch 15: 6 because **G** was troubling them with every H466
2Ch 15: 9 they saw that the LORD his **G** was with him. H466
2Ch 15:12 to seek the LORD, the **G** *of* their ancestors H466
2Ch 15:13 seek the LORD, the **G** *of* Israel, were to be H466
2Ch 15:15 They sought **G** eagerly, and he was H2084S
2Ch 15:18 into the temple of **G** the silver and gold H466
2Ch 16: 7 king of Aram and not on the LORD your **G**, H466
2Ch 17: 4 sought the **G** *of* his father and followed H466
2Ch 18: 5 "for **G** will give it into the king's hand." H466
2Ch 18:13 I can tell him only what my **G** says. H466
2Ch 18:31 **G** drew them away from him H466
2Ch 19: 3 have set your heart on seeking **G**. H466
2Ch 19: 4 back to the LORD, the **G** *of* their ancestors. H466
2Ch 19: 7 with the LORD our **G** there is no injustice H466
2Ch 20: 6 the **G** *of* our ancestors, are you not H466
2Ch 20: 6 are you not the **G** who is in heaven? H466
2Ch 20: 7 Our **G**, did you not drive out the inhabitants H466
2Ch 20:12 Our **G**, will you not judge them? For we H466
2Ch 20:19 praised the LORD, the **G** *of* Israel, with a very H466
2Ch 20:20 in the LORD your **G** and you will be upheld H466
2Ch 20:29 The fear of **G** came on all the surrounding H466
2Ch 20:30 his **G** had given him rest on every side. H466
2Ch 20:33 set their hearts on the **G** *of* their ancestors. H466
2Ch 21:10 forsaken the LORD, the **G** *of* his ancestors. H466
2Ch 21:12 is what the LORD, the **G** *of* your father David H466
2Ch 22: 7 **G** brought about Ahaziah's downfall. H466
2Ch 22:12 them at the temple of **G** for six years while H466
2Ch 23: 3 covenant with the king at the temple of **G**. H466
2Ch 23: 9 David and that were in the temple of **G**. H466
2Ch 24: 5 all Israel, to repair the temple of your **G**. H466
2Ch 24: 7 into the temple of **G** and had used even its H466
2Ch 24: 9 Moses the servant of **G** had required of H466
2Ch 24:13 rebuilt the temple of **G** according to its H466
2Ch 24:16 he had done in Israel for **G** and his temple. H466
2Ch 24:18 of the LORD, the **G** *of* their ancestors, and H466
2Ch 24:20 Then the Spirit of **G** came on Zechariah H466
2Ch 24:20 the people and said, "This is what **G** says: H466
2Ch 24:24 forsaken the LORD, the **G** *of* their ancestors H466
2Ch 24:27 of the temple of **G** are written in the H466
2Ch 25: 7 But a man of **G** came to him and said H466
2Ch 25: 8 **G** will overthrow you before the enemy H466
2Ch 25: 8 **G** has the power to help or to overthrow." H466
2Ch 25: 9 Amaziah asked the man of **G**, "But what H466
2Ch 25: 9 The man of **G** replied, "The LORD can give H466
2Ch 25:16 "I know that **G** has determined to destroy H466
2Ch 25:20 **G** so worked that he might deliver them H466
2Ch 25:24 in the temple of **G** that had been in the H466
2Ch 26: 5 He sought **G** during the days of Zechariah H466
2Ch 26: 5 who instructed him in the fear of **G**. H466
2Ch 26: 5 as he sought the LORD, **G** gave him success. H466
2Ch 26: 7 **G** helped him against the Philistines and H466
2Ch 26:16 He was unfaithful to the LORD his **G**, and H466
2Ch 26:18 you will not be honored by the LORD **G**." H466
2Ch 27: 6 walked steadfastly before the LORD his **G**. H466
2Ch 28: 5 the LORD his **G** delivered him into the H466
2Ch 28: 6 forsaken the LORD, the **G** *of* their ancestors. H466
2Ch 28: 9 the LORD, the **G** *of* your ancestors, was H466
2Ch 28:10 also guilty of sins against the LORD your **G**? H466
2Ch 28:24 from the temple of **G** and cut them in H466
2Ch 28:25 anger of the LORD, the **G** *of* his ancestors. H466
2Ch 29: 5 temple of the LORD, the **G** *of* your ancestors. H466
2Ch 29: 6 the eyes of the LORD our **G** and forsook him. H466
2Ch 29: 7 offerings at the sanctuary to the **G** *of* Israel. H466
2Ch 29:10 with the LORD, the **G** *of* Israel, so that his H466
2Ch 29:36 rejoiced at what **G** had brought about for H466
2Ch 30: 1 the Passover to the LORD, the **G** *of* Israel. H466
2Ch 30: 5 the Passover to the LORD, the **G** *of* Israel. H466
2Ch 30: 6 to the LORD, the **G** *of* Abraham, Isaac and H466
2Ch 30: 7 to the LORD, the **G** *of* their ancestors, so that H466
2Ch 30: 8 Serve the LORD your **G**, so that his fierce H466
2Ch 30: 9 the LORD your **G** is gracious and H466
2Ch 30:12 Judah the hand of **G** was on the people to H466
2Ch 30:16 in the Law of Moses the man of **G**. H466
2Ch 30:19 sets their heart on seeking **G**—the LORD, H466
2Ch 30:19 the LORD, the **G** *of* their ancestors—even if H466
2Ch 30:22 praised the LORD, the **G** *of* their ancestors. H466
2Ch 30:27 the people, and **G** heard them, for their NDT
2Ch 31: 6 holy things dedicated to the LORD their **G**, H466
2Ch 31:13 the official in charge of the temple of **G**. H466
2Ch 31:14 charge of the freewill offerings given to **G**, H466
2Ch 31:20 right and faithful before the LORD his **G**. H466
2Ch 31:21 he sought his **G** and worked H466
2Ch 32: 8 us is the LORD our **G** to help us and to fight H466
2Ch 32:11 'The LORD our **G** will save us from the hand H466
2Ch 32:14 How then can your **g** deliver you from my H466
2Ch 32:15 no **g** *of* any nation or kingdom has been H468
2Ch 32:15 much less will your **g** deliver you from my H466
2Ch 32:16 against the LORD **G** and against his servant H466
2Ch 32:17 the LORD, the **G** *of* Israel, and saying this H466
2Ch 32:17 so the **g** *of* Hezekiah will not rescue his H466
2Ch 32:19 spoke about the **G** *of* Jerusalem as they H466
2Ch 32:21 And when he went into the temple of his **g**, H466
2Ch 32:29 **G** had given him very great riches. H466
2Ch 32:31 **G** left him to test him and to know H466
2Ch 33: 7 of which **G** had said to David and to his H466
2Ch 33:12 of the LORD his **G** and humbled himself H466
2Ch 33:12 greatly before the **G** *of* his ancestors. H466
2Ch 33:13 Then Manasseh knew that the LORD is **G**. H466
2Ch 33:16 Judah to serve the LORD, the **G** *of* Israel. H466
2Ch 33:17 high places, but only to the LORD their **G**. H466
2Ch 33:18 his prayer to his **G** and the words the seers H466
2Ch 33:18 of the LORD, the **G** *of* Israel, are written H466
2Ch 33:19 His prayer and how **G** was moved by his NDT
2Ch 34: 3 he began to seek the **G** *of* his father David. H466
2Ch 34: 8 to repair the temple of the LORD his **G**. H466
2Ch 34: 9 had been brought into the temple of **G**, H466
2Ch 34:23 "This is what the LORD, the **G** *of* Israel, says: H466
2Ch 34:26 is what the LORD, the **G** *of* Israel, says H466
2Ch 34:27 yourself before **G** when you heard what he H466
2Ch 34:32 this in accordance with the covenant of **G**, H466
2Ch 34:32 covenant of God, the **G** *of* their ancestors. H466
2Ch 34:33 present in Israel serve the LORD their **G**. H466
2Ch 34:33 to follow the LORD, the **G** *of* their ancestors. H466
2Ch 35: 3 serve the LORD your **G** and his people Israel. H466
2Ch 35:21 **G** has told me to hurry; so stop opposing H466
2Ch 35:21 so stop opposing **G**, who is with me, H466
2Ch 36: 5 He did evil in the eyes of the LORD his **G**. H466
2Ch 36:12 eyes of the LORD his **G** and did not humble H466
2Ch 36:13 would not turn to the LORD, the **G** *of* Israel. H466
2Ch 36:15 The LORD, the **G** *of* their ancestors, sent H466
2Ch 36:17 **G** gave them all into the hands of NDT
2Ch 36:18 all the articles from the temple of **G**, H466
2Ch 36:23 " 'The LORD, the **G** *of* heaven, has given me H466
2Ch 36:23 and may the LORD their **G** be with them. H466
Ezr 1: 2 " 'The LORD, the **G** *of* heaven, has given me H466
Ezr 1: 3 of the LORD, the **G** *of* Israel, the God who is H466
Ezr 1: 3 God of Israel, the **G** who is in Jerusalem H466
Ezr 1: 3 Jerusalem, and may their **G** be with them. H466
Ezr 1: 4 offerings for the temple of **G** in Jerusalem. H466
Ezr 1: 5 everyone whose heart **G** had moved H466
Ezr 1: 7 had placed in the temple of his **g**. H466
Ezr 2:68 the rebuilding of the house of **G** on its site. H466
Ezr 3: 2 build the altar of the **G** *of* Israel to sacrifice H466
Ezr 3: 2 written in the Law of Moses the man of **G**. H466
Ezr 3: 8 their arrival at the house of **G** in Jerusalem, H466
Ezr 3: 9 those working on the house of **G**. H466
Ezr 4: 1 a temple for the LORD, the **G** *of* Israel, H466
Ezr 4: 2 we seek your **G** and have been sacrificing H466
Ezr 4: 3 part with us in building a temple to our **G**. H466
Ezr 4: 3 the LORD, the **G** *of* Israel, as King Cyrus H466
Ezr 4:24 on the house of **G** in Jerusalem came to A10033
Ezr 5: 1 in the name of the **G** *of* Israel, A10033
Ezr 5: 2 to rebuild the house of **G** in Jerusalem. A10033
Ezr 5: 2 And the prophets of **G** were with them A10033
Ezr 5: 5 But the eye of their **G** was watching over A10033
Ezr 5: 8 of Judah, to the temple of the great **G**. A10033
Ezr 5:11 servants of the **G** *of* heaven and earth, A10033
Ezr 5:12 our ancestors angered the **G** *of* heaven, A10033
Ezr 5:13 a decree to rebuild this house of **G**. A10033
Ezr 5:14 silver articles of the house of **G**, A10033
Ezr 5:15 And rebuild the house of **G** on its site.' A10033
Ezr 5:16 of the house of **G** in Jerusalem. A10033
Ezr 5:17 to rebuild this house of **G** in Jerusalem. A10033
Ezr 6: 3 the temple of **G** in Jerusalem: A10033
Ezr 6: 5 silver articles of the house of **G**, A10033
Ezr 6: 5 are to be deposited in the house of **G**. A10033
Ezr 6: 7 with the work on this temple of **G**. A10033
Ezr 6: 7 elders rebuild this house of **G** on its site. A10033
Ezr 6: 8 in the construction of this house of **G**: A10033
Ezr 6: 9 burnt offerings to the **G** *of* heaven, A10033
Ezr 6:10 pleasing to the **G** *of* heaven and pray A10033
Ezr 6:12 May **G**, who has caused his Name to A10033
Ezr 6:14 the command of the **G** *of* Israel and the A10033
Ezr 6:16 dedication of the house of **G** with joy. A10033
Ezr 6:17 of this house of **G** they offered a A10033
Ezr 6:18 groups for the service of **G** at Jerusalem, A10033
Ezr 6:21 in order to seek the LORD, the **G** *of* Israel. H466
Ezr 6:22 them in the work on the house of **G**, H466
Ezr 6:22 work on the house of God, the **G** *of* Israel. H466
Ezr 7: 6 which the LORD, the **G** *of* Israel, had given. H466
Ezr 7: 6 the hand of the LORD his **G** was on him. H466
Ezr 7: 9 the gracious hand of his **G** was on him. H466
Ezr 7:12 teacher of the Law of the **G** *of* heaven: A10033
Ezr 7:14 with regard to the Law of your **G**, A10033
Ezr 7:15 have freely given to the **G** *of* Israel, A10033
Ezr 7:16 the temple of their **G** in Jerusalem. A10033
Ezr 7:17 of the temple of your **G** in Jerusalem. A10033
Ezr 7:18 in accordance with the will of your **G**. A10033
Ezr 7:19 Deliver to the **G** *of* Jerusalem all the A10033
Ezr 7:19 you for worship in the temple of your **G**. A10033
Ezr 7:20 the temple of your **G** that you are A10033
Ezr 7:21 teacher of the Law of the **G** *of* heaven, A10033
Ezr 7:23 Whatever the **G** *of* heaven has A10033
Ezr 7:23 the temple of the **G** *of* heaven. A10033
Ezr 7:24 other workers at this house of **G**. A10033
Ezr 7:25 in accordance with the wisdom of your **G**, A10033
Ezr 7:25 all who know the laws of your **G**. A10033
Ezr 7:26 the law of your **G** and the law of the A10033
Ezr 7:27 be to the LORD, the **G** *of* our ancestors, who H466
Ezr 7:28 the hand of the LORD my **G** was on me, H466
Ezr 8:17 attendants to us for the house of our **G**. H466
Ezr 8:18 the gracious hand of our **G** was on us, H466
Ezr 8:21 ourselves before our **G** and ask him for a H466
Ezr 8:22 gracious hand of our **G** is on everyone who H466
Ezr 8:23 we fasted and petitioned our **G** about this, H466
Ezr 8:25 there had donated for the house of our **G**. H466
Ezr 8:28 to the LORD, the **G** *of* your ancestors. H466
Ezr 8:30 taken to the house of our **G** in Jerusalem. H466
Ezr 8:31 The hand of our **G** was on us, and he H466
Ezr 8:33 in the house of our **G**, we weighed out the H466
Ezr 8:35 sacrificed burnt offerings to the **G** *of* Israel: H466
Ezr 8:36 to the people and to the house of **G**. H466
Ezr 9: 4 at the words of the **G** *of* Israel gathered H466
Ezr 9: 5 with my hands spread out to the LORD my **G** H466
Ezr 9: 6 disgraced, my **G**, to lift up my face to H466
Ezr 9: 8 the LORD our **G** has been gracious in H466

Ezr 9: 8 so our **G** gives light to our eyes and a H466
Ezr 9: 9 our **G** has not forsaken us in our bondage. H466
Ezr 9: 9 the house of our **G** and repair its ruins, H466
Ezr 9:10 "But now, our **G**, what can we say after this? H466
Ezr 9:13 our **G**, you have punished us less H466
Ezr 9:15 the **G** *of* Israel, you are righteous! We H466
Ezr 10: 1 himself down before the house of **G**, H466
Ezr 10: 2 unfaithful to our **G** by marrying foreign H466
Ezr 10: 3 a covenant before our **G** to send away all H466
Ezr 10: 3 of those who fear the commands of our **G**. H466
Ezr 10: 6 before the house of **G** and went to the H466
Ezr 10: 9 sitting in the square before the house of **G**, H466
Ezr 10:11 honor the LORD, the **G** *of* your ancestors H466
Ezr 10:14 the fierce anger of our **G** in this matter is H466
Ne 1: 4 fasted and prayed before the **G** *of* heaven. H466
Ne 1: 5 the **G** *of* heaven, the great and H466
Ne 1: 5 the great and awesome **G**, who keeps his H446
Ne 2: 4 Then I prayed to the **G** *of* heaven, H466
Ne 2: 8 the gracious hand of my **G** was on me, H466
Ne 2:12 told anyone what my **G** had put in my heart H466
Ne 2:18 gracious hand of my **G** on me and what the H466
Ne 2:20 "The **G** *of* heaven will give us success. H466
Ne 4: 4 Hear us, our **G**, for we are despised. H466
Ne 4: 9 But we prayed to our **G** and posted a guard H466
Ne 4:15 of their plot and that **G** had frustrated it, H466
Ne 4:20 Our **G** will fight for us!" H466
Ne 5: 9 in the fear of our **G** to avoid the reproach H466
Ne 5:13 "In this way may **G** shake out of their house H466
Ne 5:15 out of reverence for **G** I did not act like that. H466
Ne 5:19 me with favor, my **G**, for all I have done H466
Ne 6:10 "Let us meet in the house of **G**, inside the H466
Ne 6:12 I realized that **G** had not sent him, but that H466
Ne 6:14 Sanballat, my **G**, because of what they H466
Ne 6:16 had been done with the help of our **G**. H466
Ne 7: 2 integrity and feared **G** more than most H466
Ne 7: 5 So my **G** put it into my heart to assemble H466
Ne 8: 6 the LORD, the great **G**; and all the people H466
Ne 8: 8 They read from the Book of the Law of **G** H466
Ne 8: 9 "This day is holy to the LORD your **G**. H466
Ne 8:16 of the house of **G** and in the square by H466
Ne 8:18 Ezra read from the Book of the Law of **G**. H466
Ne 9: 3 Law of the LORD their **G** for a quarter of the H466
Ne 9: 3 in worshiping the LORD their **G**. H466
Ne 9: 4 out with loud voices to the LORD their **G**. H466
Ne 9: 5 "Stand up and praise the LORD your **G**, who H466
Ne 9: 7 "You are the LORD **G**, who chose Abram H466
Ne 9:17 But you are a forgiving **G**, gracious and H468
Ne 9:18 'This is your **g**, who brought you up H466
Ne 9:31 you are a gracious and merciful **G**. H446
Ne 9:32 "Now therefore, our **G**, the great God H466
Ne 9:32 our God, the great **G**, mighty and awesome H446
Ne 10:28 peoples for the sake of the Law of **G**, H466
Ne 10:29 to follow the Law of **G** given through Moses H466
Ne 10:29 Moses the servant of **G** and to obey H466
Ne 10:32 year for the service of the house of our **G**: H466
Ne 10:33 for all the duties of the house of our **G**. H466
Ne 10:34 to the house of our **G** at set times each H466
Ne 10:34 wood to burn on the altar of the LORD our **G**, H466
Ne 10:36 of our flocks to the house of our **G**, H466
Ne 10:37 to the storerooms of the house of our **G**, H466
Ne 10:38 tenth of the tithes up to the house of our **G**, H466
Ne 10:39 "We will not neglect the house of our **G**." H466
Ne 11:11 the official in charge of the house of **G**, H466
Ne 11:16 of the outside work of the house of **G**; H466
Ne 11:22 the service of the house of **G**. H466
Ne 12:24 as prescribed by David the man of **G**. H466
Ne 12:36 prescribed by David the man of **G**. H466
Ne 12:40 then took their places in the house of **G**; H466
Ne 12:43 rejoicing because **G** had given them great H466
Ne 12:45 the service of their **G** and the service of H466
Ne 12:46 the songs of praise and thanksgiving to **G**. H466
Ne 13: 1 ever be admitted into the assembly of **G**, H466
Ne 13: 2 Our **G**, however, turned the curse into a H466
Ne 13: 4 of the storerooms of the house of our **G**. H466
Ne 13: 7 a room in the courts of the house of **G**. H466
Ne 13: 9 them the equipment of the house of **G**, H466
Ne 13:11 "Why is the house of **G** neglected? H466
Ne 13:14 me for this, my **G**, and do not blot out H466
Ne 13:14 the house of my **G** and its services. H466
Ne 13:18 so that our **G** brought all this calamity on H466
Ne 13:22 me for this also, my **G**, and show mercy to H466
Ne 13:26 He was loved by his **G**, and God made him H466
Ne 13:26 and **G** made him king over all Israel H466
Ne 13:27 unfaithful to our **G** by marrying foreign H466
Ne 13:29 Remember them, my **G**, because they H466
Ne 13:31 Remember me with favor, my **G**. H466
Job 1: 1 upright; he feared **G** and shunned evil. H466
Job 1: 5 have sinned and cursed **G** in their hearts." H466
Job 1: 8 a man who fears **G** and shuns evil. H466
Job 1: 9 "Does Job fear **G** for nothing?" Satan H466
Job 1:16 "The fire of **G** fell from the heavens and H466
Job 1:22 did not sin by charging **G** with wrongdoing. H466
Job 2: 3 a man who fears **G** and shuns evil. H466
Job 2: 9 Curse **G** and die!" H466
Job 2:10 Shall we accept good from **G**, and not H466
Job 3: 4 to darkness; may **G** above not care about it H468
Job 3:23 way is hidden, whom **G** has hedged in? H468
Job 4: 9 At the breath of **G** they perish; at the blast H468
Job 4:17 'Can a mortal be more righteous than **G** H468
Job 4:18 If **G** places no trust in his servants, if he NDT
Job 5: 8 I would appeal to **G**; I would lay my cause H446
Job 5:17 "Blessed is the one whom **G** corrects; so do H468
Job 6: 8 that **G** would grant what I hope for, H468
Job 6: 9 that **G** would be willing to crush me, to let H468
Job 7: 7 Remember, O **G**, that my life is but a breath NDT
Job 8: 3 Does **G** pervert justice? Does the Almighty H446
Job 8: 5 But if you will seek **G** earnestly and plead H446
Job 8:13 Such is the destiny of all who forget **G**; so H446
Job 8:20 "Surely **G** does not reject one who is H446
Job 9: 2 mortals prove their innocence before **G**? H446
Job 9:13 **G** does not restrain his anger; even the H468
Job 10: 2 I say to **G**: Do not declare me guilty, but H468
Job 11: 4 You say to **G**, 'My beliefs are flawless and I NDT
Job 11: 5 how I wish that **G** would speak, that he H468
Job 11: 6 **G** has even forgotten some of your sin. H468
Job 11: 7 "Can you fathom the mysteries of **G**? Can H468
Job 12: 4 though I called on **G** and he answered—a H468
Job 12: 6 those who provoke **G** are secure H446
Job 12: 6 God are secure—those **G** has in his hand. H468
Job 12:13 "To **G** belong wisdom and power H2257S
Job 13: 3 the Almighty and to argue my case with **G**. H446
Job 13: 8 Will you argue the case for **G**? H446
Job 13:20 me these two things, **G**, and then I will not H446
Job 15: 4 undermine piety and hinder devotion to **G**. H446
Job 15:13 vent your rage against **G** and pour out such H446
Job 15:15 If **G** places no trust in his holy ones, if even NDT
Job 15:25 he shakes his fist at **G** and vaunts himself H446
Job 16: 7 **G**, you have worn me out; you have NDT
Job 16: 9 **G** assails me and tears me in his anger NDT
Job 16:11 **G** has turned me over to the ungodly and H446
Job 16:20 is my friend as my eyes pour out tears to **G**; H468
Job 16:21 man he pleads with **G** as one pleads for a H468
Job 17: 3 "Give me, O **G**, the pledge you demand NDT
Job 17: 6 "**G** has made me a byword to everyone, NDT
Job 18:21 is the place of one who does not know **G**." H446
Job 19: 6 then know that **G** has wronged me and H468
Job 19:21 have pity, for the hand of **G** has struck me. H468
Job 19:22 Why do you pursue me as **G** does? Will H446
Job 19:26 destroyed, yet in my flesh I will see **G**; H468
Job 20:15 **G** will make his stomach vomit them up. H446
Job 20:23 **G** will vent his burning anger against him NDT
Job 20:29 Such is the fate **G** allots the wicked, the H466
Job 20:29 the heritage appointed for them by **G**." H446
Job 21: 9 free from fear; the rod of **G** is not on them. H468
Job 21:14 Yet they say to **G**, 'Leave us alone! We H446
Job 21:17 upon them, the fate **G** allots in his anger? NDT
Job 21:19 '**G** stores up the punishment of the wicked H468
Job 21:22 "Can anyone teach knowledge to **G**, since H446
Job 22: 2 "Can a man be of benefit to **G**? Can even a H446
Job 22:12 "Is not **G** in the heights of heaven? And H468
Job 22:13 'What does **G** know? Does he judge H446
Job 22:17 They said to **G**, 'Leave us alone! What can H446
Job 22:21 "Submit to **G** and be at peace with him H2257S
Job 22:26 the Almighty and will lift up your face to **G**. H468
Job 23:16 **G** has made my heart faint; the Almighty H446
Job 24:12 But **G** charges no one with wrongdoing. H468
Job 24:22 But **G** drags away the mighty by his power NDT
Job 25: 2 "Dominion and awe belong to **G**; he H2257S
Job 25: 4 then can a mortal be righteous before **G**? H446
Job 26: 6 realm of the dead is naked before **G**; H2257S
Job 27: 2 "As surely as **G** lives, who has denied me H446
Job 27: 3 within me, the breath of **G** in my nostrils, H468
Job 27: 8 are cut off, when **G** takes away their life? H468
Job 27: 9 Does **G** listen to their cry when distress H446
Job 27:10 Will they call on **G** at all times? H468
Job 27:11 "I will teach you about the power of **G**; the H446
Job 27:13 "Here is the fate **G** allots to the wicked, the H446
Job 28:23 **G** understands the way to it and he alone H466
Job 29: 2 for the days when **G** watched over me, H468
Job 30:11 Now that **G** has unstrung my bow and NDT
Job 30:18 In his great power **G** becomes like clothing NDT
Job 30:20 "I cry out to you, **G**, but you do not answer; NDT
Job 31: 2 For what is our lot from **G** above, our H468
Job 31: 6 let **G** weigh me in honest scales and he H468
Job 31:14 what will I do when **G** confronts me? What H446
Job 31:23 For I dreaded destruction from **G**, and for H446
Job 31:28 I would have been unfaithful to **G** on high. H446
Job 32: 2 Job for justifying himself rather than **G**. H466
Job 32:13 found wisdom; let **G**, not a man, refute him H446
Job 33: 4 The Spirit of **G** has made me; the breath of H446
Job 33:10 Yet **G** has found fault with me; he considers NDT
Job 33:12 not right, for **G** is greater than any mortal. H468
Job 33:14 For **G** does speak—now one way, now H446
Job 33:24 he is gracious to that person and says to **G**, NDT
Job 33:26 person can pray to **G** and find favor with H468
Job 33:28 **G** has delivered me from going down to the NDT
Job 33:29 "**G** does all these things to a person H446
Job 34: 5 'I am innocent, but **G** denies me justice. H446
Job 34: 9 'There is no profit in trying to please **G**. H466
Job 34:10 Far be it from **G** to do evil, from the H446
Job 34:12 It is unthinkable that **G** would do wrong H446
Job 34:23 **G** has no need to examine people further H446
Job 34:31 "Suppose someone says to **G**, 'I am guilty H446
Job 34:33 Should **G** then reward you on your terms NDT
Job 34:37 us and multiplies his words against **G**." H446
Job 35: 2 You say, 'I am in the right, not **G**.' H446
Job 35:10 one says, 'Where is **G** my Maker, who gives H468
Job 35:13 **G** does not listen to their empty plea H446
Job 36: 5 "**G** is mighty, but despises no one; he is H446
Job 36:22 "**G** is exalted in his power. Who is a H446
Job 36:26 How great is **G**—beyond our understanding H446
Job 37:10 The breath of **G** produces ice, and the H446
Job 37:15 Do you know how **G** controls the clouds H468
Job 37:22 splendor; **G** comes in awesome majesty. H468
Job 38:41 its young cry out to **G** and wander about H446
Job 39:17 **G** did not endow her with wisdom or H468
Job 40: 2 Let him who accuses **G** answer him!" H468
Job 40:19 It ranks first among the works of **G**, yet its H446
Ps 3: 2 are saying of me, "**G** will not deliver him." H466
Ps 3: 7 Deliver me, my **G**! Strike all my H466
Ps 4: 1 me when I call to you, my righteous **G**. H466
Ps 5: 2 my King and my **G**, for to you I pray. H466
Ps 5: 4 For you are not a **G** who is pleased with H446
Ps 5:10 Declare them guilty, O **G**! Let their intrigues H466
Ps 7: 1 LORD my **G**, I take refuge in you; save and H466
Ps 7: 3 LORD my **G**, if I have done this and there is H466
Ps 7: 6 Awake, my **G**; decree justice. H446
Ps 7: 9 the righteous **G** who probes minds and H466
Ps 7:10 My shield is **G** Most High, who saves the H466
Ps 7:11 **G** is a righteous judge, a God who displays H466
Ps 7:11 a **G** who displays his wrath every day. H446
Ps 9:17 of the dead, all the nations that forget **G**. H466
Ps 9:18 But **G** will never forget the needy; the hope NDT
Ps 10: 4 in all his thoughts there is no room for **G**. H466
Ps 10:11 He says to himself, "**G** will never notice; he H446
Ps 10:12 Lift up your hand, O **G**. Do not forget the H446
Ps 10:13 Why does the wicked man revile **G**? Why H466
Ps 10:14 **G**, see the trouble of the afflicted NDT
Ps 13: 3 answer, LORD my **G**. Give light to my H466
Ps 14: 1 his heart, "There is no **G**." They are corrupt, H466
Ps 14: 2 are any who understand, any who seek **G**. H466
Ps 14: 5 **G** is present in the company of the H466
Ps 16: 1 Keep me safe, my **G**, for in you I take H446
Ps 17: 6 I call on you, my **G**, for you will answer me H446
Ps 18: 2 my deliverer; my **G** is my rock, in whom H446
Ps 18: 6 called to the LORD; I cried to my **G** for help. H466
Ps 18:21 I am not guilty of turning from my **G**. H466
Ps 18:28 burning; my **G** turns my darkness into light. H466
Ps 18:29 with my **G** I can scale a wall. H466
Ps 18:30 As for **G**, his way is perfect: The LORD's H446
Ps 18:31 For who is **G** besides the LORD? And who is H468
Ps 18:31 And who is the Rock except our **G**? H466
Ps 18:32 It is **G** who arms me with strength and H446
Ps 18:46 be to my Rock! Exalted be **G** my Savior! H466
Ps 18:47 He is the **G** who avenges me, who subdues H446
Ps 19: 1 The heavens declare the glory of **G**; the H446
Ps 19: 4 In the heavens **G** has pitched a tent for the NDT
Ps 20: 1 the name of the **G** *of* Jacob protect you. H466
Ps 20: 5 lift up our banners in the name of our **G**. H466
Ps 20: 7 we trust in the name of the LORD our **G**. H466
Ps 22: 1 My **G**, my God, why have you forsaken me H446
Ps 22: 1 My God, my **G**, why have you forsaken me H446
Ps 22: 2 My **G**, I cry out by day, but you do not H466
Ps 22:10 my mother's womb you have been my **G**. H446
Ps 24: 4 not trust in an idol or swear by a **false** *g*. AIT
Ps 24: 5 LORD and vindication from **G** their Savior. H466
Ps 24: 6 seek him, who seek your face, **G** *of* Jacob. H466
Ps 25: 1 LORD my **G**, I put my trust. H466
Ps 25: 5 teach me, for you are **G** my Savior, and my H466
Ps 25:22 Deliver Israel, O **G**, from all their troubles! H466
Ps 27: 9 not reject me or forsake me, **G** my Savior. H466
Ps 29: 3 the waters; the **G** *of* glory thunders, the H446
Ps 30: 2 LORD my **G**, I called to you for help, and H466
Ps 30:12 LORD my **G**, I will praise you H466
Ps 31: 5 my spirit; deliver me, LORD, my faithful **G**. H446
Ps 31:14 I trust in you, LORD; I say, "You are my **G**." H466
Ps 33:12 Blessed is the nation whose **G** is the LORD H466
Ps 35:23 Contend for me, my **G** and Lord. H466
Ps 35:24 LORD my **G**; do not let them gloat H466
Ps 36: 1 a **message from G** in my heart *concerning* H5536
Ps 36: 1 There is no fear of **G** before their eyes. H466
Ps 36: 7 unfailing love, O **G**! People take refuge in H466
Ps 37:31 The law of their **G** is in their hearts; their H466
Ps 38:15 I wait for you; you will answer, Lord my **G**. H466
Ps 38:21 forsake me; do not be far from me, my **G**. H466
Ps 40: 3 in my mouth, a hymn of praise to our **G**. H466
Ps 40: 5 LORD my **G**, are the wonders you H466
Ps 40: 8 do your will, my **G**; your law is within my H466
Ps 40:17 my deliverer; you are my **G**, do not delay. H466
Ps 41:13 be to the LORD, the **G** *of* Israel, from H466
Ps 42: 1 of water, so my soul pants for you, my **G**. H466
Ps 42: 2 My soul thirsts for **G**, for the living God H466
Ps 42: 2 for the living **G**. When can I go and H446
Ps 42: 2 When can I go and meet with **G**? H466
Ps 42: 3 say to me all day long, "Where is your **G**?" H466
Ps 42: 4 go to the house of **G** under the protection H466
Ps 42: 5 Put your hope in **G**, for I will yet praise him H466
Ps 42: 5 I will yet praise him, my Savior and my **G**. H466
Ps 42: 8 is with me—a prayer to the **G** *of* my life. H446
Ps 42: 9 I say to **G** my Rock, "Why have you H446
Ps 42:10 to me all day long, "Where is your **G**?" H466
Ps 42:11 Put your hope in **G**, for I will yet praise him H466
Ps 42:11 I will yet praise him, my Savior and my **G**. H466
Ps 43: 1 Vindicate me, my **G**, and plead my cause H466
Ps 43: 2 You are **G** my stronghold. Why have you H466
Ps 43: 4 Then I will go to the altar of **G**, to God, my H466
Ps 43: 4 the altar of God, to **G**, my joy and my H446
Ps 43: 4 will praise you with the lyre, O **G**, my God. H466
Ps 43: 4 will praise you with the lyre, O God, my **G**. H466
Ps 43: 5 Put your hope in **G**, for I will yet praise him H466
Ps 43: 5 I will yet praise him, my Savior and my **G**. H466
Ps 44: 1 it with our ears, O **G**; our ancestors have H466
Ps 44: 4 You are my King and my **G**, who decrees H466
Ps 44: 8 In **G** we make our boast all day long, and H466
Ps 44:20 the name of our **G** or spread out our hands H466
Ps 44:20 God or spread out our hands to a foreign **g**, H446

Ps 44:21 would not G have discovered it, since he H466
Ps 45: 2 since G has blessed you forever. H466
Ps 45: 6 Your throne, O G, will last for ever and ever; H466
Ps 45: 7 hate wickedness; therefore G, your God, H466
Ps 45: 7 therefore God, your G, has set you above H466
Ps 46: 1 G is our refuge and strength, an H466
Ps 46: 4 whose streams make glad the city of G, H466
Ps 46: 5 G is within her, she will not fall; God will H466
Ps 46: 5 will not fall; G will help her at break of day. H466
Ps 46: 7 is with us; the G *of* Jacob is our fortress. H466
Ps 46:10 know that I am G; I will be exalted H466
Ps 46:11 is with us; the G *of* Jacob is our fortress. H466
Ps 47: 1 all you nations; shout to G with cries of joy. H466
Ps 47: 5 G has ascended amid shouts of joy, the H466
Ps 47: 6 Sing praises to G, sing praises; sing praises H466
Ps 47: 7 For G is the King of all the earth; sing to H466
Ps 47: 8 G reigns over the nations; God is seated on H466
Ps 47: 8 the nations; G is seated on his holy throne. H466
Ps 47: 9 as the people of the G *of* Abraham, H466
Ps 47: 9 the kings of the earth belong to G; he is H466
Ps 48: 1 in the city of our G, his holy mountain. H466
Ps 48: 3 G is in her citadels; he has shown himself H466
Ps 48: 8 of the LORD Almighty, in the city of our G: H466
Ps 48: 8 city of our God: G makes her secure forever. H466
Ps 48: 9 your temple, O G, we meditate on your H466
Ps 48:10 Like your name, O G, your praise reaches to H466
Ps 48:14 For this G is our God for ever and ever; he H466
Ps 48:14 For this God is our G for ever and ever; he H466
Ps 49: 7 another or give to G a ransom for them— H466
Ps 49:15 But G will redeem me from the realm of H466
Ps 50: 1 The Mighty One, G, the LORD, speaks and H410
Ps 50: 2 From Zion, perfect in beauty, G shines forth. H466
Ps 50: 3 Our G comes and will not be silent; a fire H466
Ps 50: 6 his righteousness, for he is a G of justice. H466
Ps 50: 7 against you, Israel: I am G, your God. H466
Ps 50: 7 against you, Israel: I am God, your G. H466
Ps 50:14 "Sacrifice thank offerings to G, fulfill your H466
Ps 50:16 to the wicked person, G says: "What right H466
Ps 50:22 you who forget G, or I will tear you to H468
Ps 51: 1 Have mercy on me, O G, according to your H466
Ps 51:10 in me a pure heart, O G, and renew a H466
Ps 51:14 of bloodshed, O G, you who are God my H466
Ps 51:14 you who are G my Savior, and my H466
Ps 51:17 My sacrifice, O G, is a broken spirit; H466
Ps 51:17 contrite heart you, G, will not despise. H466
Ps 52: 1 you who are a disgrace in the eyes of G? H446
Ps 52: 5 Surely G will bring you down to everlasting H446
Ps 52: 7 who did not make G his stronghold but H466
Ps 52: 8 an olive tree flourishing in the house of G; H466
Ps 53: 1 his heart, "There is no G." They are corrupt, H466
Ps 53: 2 G looks down from heaven on all mankind H466
Ps 53: 2 are any who understand, any who seek G. H466
Ps 53: 4 though eating bread; they never call on G. H466
Ps 53: 5 G scattered the bones of those who H466
Ps 53: 5 put them to shame, for G despised them. H466
Ps 53: 6 When G restores his people, let Jacob H466
Ps 54: 1 Save me, O G, by your name; vindicate me H466
Ps 54: 2 Hear my prayer, O G; listen to the words of H466
Ps 54: 3 to kill me—people without regard for G. H466
Ps 54: 4 Surely G is my help; the Lord is the one H466
Ps 55: 1 to my prayer, O G, do not ignore my plea H466
Ps 55:14 sweet fellowship at the house of G, H466
Ps 55:16 As for me, I call to G, and the LORD saves H466
Ps 55:19 G, who is enthroned from of old, who does H446
Ps 55:19 because they have no fear of G. H466
Ps 55:23 But you, G, will bring down the wicked into H466
Ps 56: 1 merciful to me, my G, for my enemies are H466
Ps 56: 4 In G, whose word I praise—in God I trust H466
Ps 56: 4 I praise—in G I trust and am not afraid. H466
Ps 56: 7 in your anger, G, bring the nations H466
Ps 56: 9 By this I will know that G is for me. H466
Ps 56:10 In G, whose word I praise, in the LORD H466
Ps 56:11 in G I trust and am not afraid. What can H466
Ps 56:12 under vows to you, my G; I will present my H466
Ps 56:13 that I may walk before G in the light of life. H466
Ps 57: 1 mercy on me, my G, have mercy on me, H466
Ps 57: 2 I cry out to G Most High, to God, who H466
Ps 57: 2 God Most High, to G, who vindicates me. H446
Ps 57: 3 G sends forth his love and his faithfulness. H466
Ps 57: 5 Be exalted, O G, above the heavens; let H466
Ps 57: 7 My heart, O G, is steadfast, my heart is H466
Ps 57:11 Be exalted, O G, above the heavens; let H466
Ps 58: 6 in their mouths, O G; LORD, tear out the H466
Ps 58:11 surely there is a G who judges the earth." H466
Ps 59: 1 me from my enemies, O G; be my fortress H466
Ps 59: 5 LORD G Almighty, you who are the God H466
Ps 59: 5 you who are the G *of* Israel, rouse yourself H466
Ps 59: 9 I watch for you; you, G, are my fortress, H466
Ps 59:10 my G *on whom* I can rely. God will go H466
Ps 59:10 G will go before me and will let me gloat H466
Ps 59:13 ends of the earth that G rules over Jacob. H466
Ps 59:17 praise to you; you, G, are my fortress, my H466
Ps 59:17 are my fortress, my G *on whom* I can rely. H466
Ps 60: 1 You have rejected us, G, and burst upon us; H466
Ps 60: 6 G has spoken from his sanctuary: "In H466
Ps 60:10 Is it not you, G, you who have now rejected H466
Ps 60:12 With G we will gain the victory, and he will H466
Ps 61: 1 Hear my cry, O G; listen to my prayer. H466
Ps 61: 5 G, have heard my vows; you have H466
Ps 62: 1 Truly my soul finds rest in G; my salvation H466
Ps 62: 5 find rest in G; my hope comes from H466
Ps 62: 7 My salvation and my honor depend on G H466
Ps 62: 8 out your hearts to him, for G is our refuge. H466
Ps 62:11 One thing G has spoken, two things I have H466
Ps 62:11 "Power belongs to you, G, H466
Ps 63: 1 G, are my God, earnestly I seek you; H466
Ps 63: 1 God, are my G, earnestly I seek you; H446
Ps 63:11 But the king will rejoice in G; all who swear H466
Ps 63:11 all who swear by G will glory in him H2257S
Ps 64: 1 Hear me, my G, as I voice my complaint H466
Ps 64: 7 But G will shoot them with his arrows; they H466
Ps 64: 9 the works of G and ponder what he H466
Ps 65: 1 awaits you, our G, in Zion; to you our H466
Ps 65: 5 righteous deeds, G our Savior, the hope H466
Ps 65: 9 The streams of G are filled with water to H466
Ps 66: 1 Shout for joy to G, all the earth! H466
Ps 66: 3 Say to G, "How awesome are your deeds H466
Ps 66: 5 Come and see what G has done, his H466
Ps 66: 8 Praise our G, all peoples, let the sound of H466
Ps 66:10 G, tested us; you refined us like H466
Ps 66:16 all you who fear G; let me tell you what H466
Ps 66:19 G has surely listened and has heard my H466
Ps 66:20 Praise be to G, who has not rejected my H466
Ps 67: 1 May G be gracious to us and bless us and H466
Ps 67: 3 peoples praise you, G; may all the peoples H466
Ps 67: 5 peoples praise you, G; may all the peoples H466
Ps 67: 6 yields its harvest; G, our God, blesses us. H466
Ps 67: 6 yields its harvest; God, our G, blesses us. H466
Ps 67: 7 May G bless us still, so that all the ends of H466
Ps 68: 1 May G arise, may his enemies be scattered; H466
Ps 68: 2 may the wicked perish before G. H466
Ps 68: 3 the righteous be glad and rejoice before G; H466
Ps 68: 4 Sing to G, sing in praise of his name, extol H466
Ps 68: 5 of widows, is G in his holy dwelling. H466
Ps 68: 6 G sets the lonely in families, he leads out H466
Ps 68: 7 When you, G, went out before your people H466
Ps 68: 8 down rain, before G, the One of Sinai, H466
Ps 68: 8 One of Sinai, before G, the God of Israel. H466
Ps 68: 8 One of Sinai, before God, the G *of* Israel. H466
Ps 68: 9 abundant showers, O G; you refreshed your H466
Ps 68:10 from your bounty, G, you provided for the H466
Ps 68:16 at the mountain where G chooses to reign H466
Ps 68:17 The chariots of G are tens of thousands H466
Ps 68:18 that you, LORD G, might dwell there. H466
Ps 68:19 be to the Lord, to G our Savior, who daily H446
Ps 68:20 Our G is a God who saves; from the H446
Ps 68:20 Our God is a G who saves; from the H446
Ps 68:21 Surely G will crush the heads of his H466
Ps 68:24 Your procession, G, has come into view H466
Ps 68:24 the procession of my G and King into the H446
Ps 68:26 Praise G in the great congregation; praise H466
Ps 68:28 Summon your power, G; show us your H466
Ps 68:28 us your strength, our G, as you have done H466
Ps 68:31 from Egypt; Cush will submit herself to G. H466
Ps 68:32 Sing to G, you kingdoms of the earth, sing H466
Ps 68:34 Proclaim the power of G, whose majesty is H466
Ps 68:35 G, are awesome in your sanctuary; the H466
Ps 68:35 the G *of* Israel gives power and strength to H446
Ps 68:35 strength to his people. Praise be to G! H466
Ps 69: 1 Save me, O G, for the waters have come up H466
Ps 69: 3 My eyes fail, looking for my G. H466
Ps 69: 5 G, know my folly; my guilt is not H466
Ps 69: 6 because of me; G *of* Israel, may those who H466
Ps 69:13 your great love, O G, answer me with your H466
Ps 69:29 may your salvation, G, protect me. H466
Ps 69:32 you who seek G, may your hearts H466
Ps 69:35 G will save Zion and rebuild the cities H466
Ps 70: 1 O G, to save me; come quickly H466
Ps 70: 5 poor and needy; come quickly to me, O G. H466
Ps 71: 4 Deliver me, my G, from the hand of the H466
Ps 71:11 They say, "G has forsaken him; pursue him H466
Ps 71:12 be far from me, my G; come quickly, God, H466
Ps 71:12 my God; come quickly, G, to help me. H466
Ps 71:17 Since my youth, G, you have taught me H466
Ps 71:18 do not forsake me, my G, till I declare your H466
Ps 71:19 Your righteousness, G, reaches to the H466
Ps 71:19 done great things. Who is like you, G? H466
Ps 71:22 your faithfulness, my G; I will sing praise to H466
Ps 72: 1 with your justice, O G, the royal son with H466
Ps 72:18 Praise be to the LORD G, the God of Israel H466
Ps 72:18 to the LORD God, the G *of* Israel, who alone H466
Ps 73: 1 Surely G is good to Israel, to those who are H466
Ps 73:11 "How would G know? Does the Most H446
Ps 73:17 till I entered the sanctuary of G; then I H446
Ps 73:26 G is the strength of my heart and my H466
Ps 73:28 it is good to be near G. I have made the H466
Ps 74: 1 O G, why have you rejected us forever H466
Ps 74: 8 every place where G was worshiped in the H446
Ps 74: 9 We are given no **signs** *from* G; no prophets AIT
Ps 74:10 the enemy mock you, G? Will the foe revile H466
Ps 74:12 But G is my King from long ago; he brings H466
Ps 74:22 Rise up, O G, and defend your cause H466
Ps 75: 1 We praise you, G, we praise you, for your H466
Ps 75: 7 It is G who judges: He brings one down, he H466
Ps 75: 9 I will sing praise to the G *of* Jacob, H466
Ps 76: 1 G is renowned in Judah; in Israel his name H466
Ps 76: 6 At your rebuke, G *of* Jacob, both horse H466
Ps 76: 9 when you, G, rose up to judge, to save all H466
Ps 76:11 vows to the LORD your G and fulfill them; H466
Ps 77: 1 I cried out to G for help; I cried out to God H466
Ps 77: 1 to God for help; I cried out to G to hear me. H466
Ps 77: 3 I remembered you, G, and I groaned; H466
Ps 77: 9 Has G forgotten to be merciful? Has he in H446
Ps 77:13 Your ways, G, are holy. What god is as H466
Ps 77:13 What g is as great as our God? H446
Ps 77:13 What god is as great as our G? H466
Ps 77:14 You are the G who performs miracles; you H446
Ps 77:16 The waters saw you, G, the waters saw you H466
Ps 78: 7 put their trust in G and would not forget his H466
Ps 78: 8 whose hearts were not loyal to G, whose H446
Ps 78:18 They willfully put G to the test by H446
Ps 78:19 They spoke against G; they said, "Can God H466
Ps 78:19 "Can G really spread a table in the H446
Ps 78:22 they did not believe in G or trust in his H466
Ps 78:34 Whenever G slew them, they would seek H446
Ps 78:35 They remembered that G was their Rock H466
Ps 78:35 that G Most High was their Redeemer. H446
Ps 78:41 Again and again they put G to the test H446
Ps 78:56 But they put G to the test and rebelled H466
Ps 78:59 When G heard them, he was furious; he H466
Ps 79: 1 O G, the nations have invaded your H466
Ps 79: 9 Help us, G our Savior, for the glory of your H466
Ps 79:10 should the nations say, "Where is their G?" H466
Ps 80: 3 Restore us, O G; make your face shine on H466
Ps 80: 4 How long, LORD G Almighty, will your H466
Ps 80: 7 Restore us, G Almighty; make your face H466
Ps 80:14 Return to us, G Almighty! Look down from H466
Ps 80:19 Restore us, LORD G Almighty; make your H466
Ps 81: 1 Sing for joy to G our strength; shout aloud H466
Ps 81: 1 our strength; shout aloud to the G of Jacob! H466
Ps 81: 4 Israel, an ordinance of the G *of* Jacob. H466
Ps 81: 5 When G went out against Egypt, he H2257S
Ps 81: 9 You shall have no foreign g among you H446
Ps 81: 9 you shall not worship any g other than me. H446
Ps 81:10 I am the LORD your G, who brought you up H466
Ps 82: 1 G presides in the great assembly; he H466
Ps 82: 8 Rise up, O G, judge the earth, for all the H466
Ps 83: 1 O G, do not remain silent; do not turn a H466
Ps 83: 1 turn a deaf ear, do not stand aloof, O G. H446
Ps 83:12 take possession of the pasturelands of G." H466
Ps 83:13 like tumbleweed, my G, like chaff before H466
Ps 84: 2 heart and my flesh cry out for the living G. H446
Ps 84: 3 LORD Almighty, my King and my G. H466
Ps 84: 7 till each appears before G in Zion. H466
Ps 84: 8 Hear my prayer, LORD G Almighty; listen to H466
Ps 84: 8 God Almighty; listen to me, G *of* Jacob. H466
Ps 84: 9 Look on our shield, O G; look with favor on H466
Ps 84:10 in the house of my G than dwell in the H466
Ps 84:11 For the LORD G is a sun and shield; the LORD H466
Ps 85: 4 Restore us again, G our Savior, and put H466
Ps 85: 8 I will listen to what G the LORD says; he H446
Ps 86: 2 servant who trusts in you. You are my G; H466
Ps 86:10 do marvelous deeds; you alone are G. H466
Ps 86:12 praise you, Lord my G, with all my heart; H466
Ps 86:14 are attacking me, O G; ruthless people are H466
Ps 86:15 are a compassionate and gracious G, slow H446
Ps 87: 3 Glorious things are said of you, city of G: H466
Ps 88: 1 you are the G who saves me; day and H466
Ps 89: 7 council of the holy ones G is greatly feared; H446
Ps 89: 8 is like you, LORD G Almighty? You, LORD, H466
Ps 89:26 are my Father, my G, the Rock my Savior. H446
Ps 90: T A prayer of Moses the man of G. H466
Ps 90: 2 from everlasting to everlasting you are G. H446
Ps 90:17 May the favor of the Lord our G rest on us H466
Ps 91: 2 my fortress, my G, in whom I trust. H466
Ps 92:13 they will flourish in the courts of our G. H466
Ps 94: 1 The LORD is a G *who* avenges. O God who H446
Ps 94: 1 O G *who* avenges, shine H446
Ps 94: 7 not see; the G *of* Jacob takes no notice." H466
Ps 94:22 my G the rock in whom I take refuge. H466
Ps 94:23 the LORD our G will destroy them. H466
Ps 95: 3 For the LORD is the great G, the great King H446
Ps 95: 7 he is our G and we are the people of H466
Ps 98: 3 the earth have seen the salvation of our G. H466
Ps 99: 5 Exalt the LORD our G and worship at his H466
Ps 99: 8 LORD our G, you answered them; you were H466
Ps 99: 8 you were to Israel a forgiving G, though H446
Ps 99: 9 Exalt the LORD our G and worship at his holy H466
Ps 99: 9 holy mountain, for the LORD our G is holy. H466
Ps 100: 3 Know that the LORD is G. It is he who made H466
Ps 102:24 not take me away, my G, in the midst of my H446
Ps 104: 1 LORD my G, you are very great; you are H466
Ps 104:21 their prey and seek their food from G. H446
Ps 104:33 I will sing praise to my G as long as I live. H466
Ps 105: 7 He is the LORD our G; his judgments are in H466
Ps 106:14 in the wilderness they put G to the test. H446
Ps 106:20 exchanged their **glorious** G for an image H3883
Ps 106:21 They forgot the G who saved them, who H446
Ps 106:33 they rebelled against the Spirit of G H2257S
Ps 106:47 Save us, LORD our G, and gather us from the H466
Ps 106:48 be to the LORD, the G *of* Israel, from H466
Ps 108: 1 My heart, O G, is steadfast; I will sing and H466
Ps 108: 5 Be exalted, O G, above the heavens; let H466
Ps 108: 7 G has spoken from his sanctuary: "In H466
Ps 108:11 Is it not you, G, you who have rejected us H466
Ps 108:13 With G we will gain the victory, and he will H466
Ps 109: 1 My G, whom I praise, do not remain silent, H466
Ps 109:26 Help me, LORD my G; save me according to H466
Ps 113: 5 Who is like the LORD our G, the One who H466
Ps 114: 7 at the presence of the G *of* Jacob, H468
Ps 115: 2 Why do the nations say, "Where is their G?" H466
Ps 115: 3 Our G is in heaven; he does whatever H466
Ps 116: 5 righteous; our G is full of compassion. H466
Ps 118:27 The LORD is G, and he has made his light H446
Ps 118:28 You are my G, and I will praise you; you H446
Ps 118:28 you are my G, and I will exalt you. H466

Ps 119:115 that I may keep the commands of my **G**! H466
Ps 119:116 Sustain me, my **G**, according to your NDT
Ps 122: 9 For the sake of the house of the Lord our **G** H466
Ps 123: 2 so our eyes look to the Lord our **G**, till he H466
Ps 135: 2 in the courts of the house of our **G**. H466
Ps 136: 2 Give thanks to the **G** *of* gods. His love H466
Ps 136:26 Give thanks to the **G** *of* heaven. His love H446
Ps 139:17 are your thoughts, **G**! How vast is the sum H446
Ps 139:19 If only you, **G**, would slay the wicked! Away H468
Ps 139:23 Search me, **G**, and know my heart; test me H446
Ps 140: 6 say to the Lord, "You are my **G**." Hear, H446
Ps 143:10 for you are my **G**; may your good Spirit H466
Ps 144: 2 He is my loving **G** and my fortress, my NDT
Ps 144: 9 new song to you, my **G**; on the ten-stringed H466
Ps 144:15 blessed is the people whose **G** is the Lord. H466
Ps 145: 1 I will exalt you, my **G** the King; I will praise H466
Ps 146: 2 I will sing praise to my **G** as long as I live. H466
Ps 146: 5 are those whose help is the **G** *of* Jacob, H446
Ps 146: 5 of Jacob, whose hope is in the Lord their **G**. H466
Ps 146:10 Lord reigns forever, your **G**, O Zion, for all H466
Ps 147: 1 How good it is to sing praises to our **G** H466
Ps 147: 7 make music to our **G** on the harp. H466
Ps 147:12 the Lord, Jerusalem; praise your **G**, Zion. H466
Ps 149: 6 May the praise of **G** be in their mouths H446
Ps 150: 1 Praise **G** in his sanctuary; praise him in his H446
Pr 2: 5 of the Lord and find the knowledge of **G**. H466
Pr 2:17 ignored the covenant she made before **G**. H466
Pr 3: 4 a good name in the sight of **G** and man. H466
Pr 14:31 whoever is kind to the needy honors **G**. H2257S
Pr 14:32 in death the righteous seek refuge in **G**. NDT
Pr 17:11 Evildoers foster **rebellion** *against* **G**; the AIT
Pr 25: 2 It is the glory of **G** to conceal a matter; to H466
Pr 28:14 is the one who always trembles before **G**, NDT
Pr 30: 1 "I am weary, **G**, but I can prevail. H445
Pr 30: 5 "Every word of **G** is flawless; he is a shield H468
Pr 30: 9 and so dishonor the name of my **G**. H466
Ecc 1:13 a heavy burden **G** has laid on mankind H466
Ecc 2:24 This too, I see, is from the hand of **G**, H466
Ecc 2:26 who pleases him, **G** gives wisdom NDT
Ecc 2:26 to hand it over to the one who pleases **G**. H466
Ecc 3:10 have seen the burden **G** has laid on the H466
Ecc 3:11 no one can fathom what **G** has done from H466
Ecc 3:13 in all their toil—this is the gift of **G**. H466
Ecc 3:14 I know that everything **G** does will endure H466
Ecc 3:14 **G** does it so that people will fear him. H466
Ecc 3:15 and **G** will call the past to account. H466
Ecc 3:17 "**G** will bring into judgment both the H466
Ecc 3:18 **G** tests them so that they may see that they H466
Ecc 5: 1 your steps when you go to the house of **G**. H466
Ecc 5: 2 in your heart to utter anything before **G**. H466
Ecc 5: 2 **G** is in heaven and you are on earth, so let H466
Ecc 5: 4 When you make a vow to **G**, do not delay H466
Ecc 5: 6 Why should **G** be angry at what you say H466
Ecc 5: 7 words are meaningless. Therefore fear **G**. H466
Ecc 5:18 the few days of life **G** has given them— H466
Ecc 5:19 when **G** gives someone wealth and H466
Ecc 5:19 be happy in their toil—this is a gift of **G**. H466
Ecc 5:20 because **G** keeps them occupied with H466
Ecc 6: 2 **G** gives some people wealth, possessions H466
Ecc 6: 2 **G** does not grant them the ability to H466
Ecc 7:13 Consider what **G** has done: Who can H466
Ecc 7:14 **G** has made the one as well as the other H466
Ecc 7:18 Whoever fears **G** will avoid all extremes. H466
Ecc 7:26 The man who pleases **G** will escape her H466
Ecc 7:29 **G** created mankind upright, but they have H466
Ecc 8: 2 because you took an oath before **G**. H466
Ecc 8:12 that it will go better with those who fear **G**, H466
Ecc 8:13 Yet because the wicked do not fear **G**, it will H466
Ecc 8:15 the days of the life **G** has given them under H466
Ecc 8:17 then I saw all that **G** has done. No one can H466
Ecc 9: 7 **G** has already approved what you do. H466
Ecc 9: 9 meaningless life that **G** has given you under NDT
Ecc 11: 5 so you cannot understand the work of **G** H466
Ecc 11: 9 all these things **G** will bring you into H466
Ecc 12: 7 the spirit returns to **G** who gave it. H466
Ecc 12:13 Fear **G** and keep his commandments, for H466
Ecc 12:14 For **G** will bring every deed into judgment H466
Isa 1:10 listen to the instruction of our **G**, you H466
Isa 2: 3 the Lord, to the temple of the **G** *of* Jacob. H466
Isa 5:16 the holy **G** will be proved holy by his H446
Isa 5:19 those who say, "Let **G** hurry; let him hasten NDT
Isa 7:11 "Ask the Lord your **G** for a sign, whether in H466
Isa 7:13 Will you try the patience of my **G** also? H466
Isa 8:10 but it will not stand, for **G** is with us. H446
Isa 8:19 should not a people inquire of their **G**? H466
Isa 8:21 upward, will curse their king and their **G**. H466
Isa 9: 6 Counselor, Mighty **G**, Everlasting Father, H446
Isa 10:21 of Jacob will return to the Mighty **G**. H446
Isa 12: 2 Surely **G** is my salvation; I will trust and not H446
Isa 13:19 will be overthrown by **G** like Sodom and H466
Isa 14:13 I will raise my throne above the stars of **G**; H446
Isa 17: 6 boughs," declares the Lord, the **G** *of* Israel. H466
Isa 17:10 You have forgotten **G** your Savior; you have H466
Isa 21:10 the Lord Almighty, from the **G** *of* Israel. H466
Isa 21:17 The Lord, the **G** *of* Israel, has spoken. H466
Isa 24:15 name of the Lord, the **G** *of* Israel, in the H466
Isa 25: 1 you are my **G**; I will exalt you and H466
Isa 25: 9 "Surely this is our **G**; we trusted in him, H466
Isa 25:11 **G** will bring down their pride despite the NDT
Isa 26: 1 **G** makes salvation its walls and ramparts. NDT
Isa 26:13 Lord our **G**, other lords besides you have H466
Isa 28:11 lips and strange tongues **G** will speak to this NDT
Isa 28:26 His **G** instructs him and teaches him the H466
Isa 29:23 will stand in awe of the **G** *of* Israel. H466
Isa 30:18 For the Lord is a **G** *of* justice. Blessed are H466
Isa 31: 3 the Egyptians are mere mortals and not **G**; H446
Isa 34:11 **G** will stretch out over Edom the measuring NDT
Isa 35: 2 the glory of the Lord, the splendor of our **G**. H466
Isa 35: 4 do not fear; your **G** will come, he will come H466
Isa 36: 7 "We are depending on the Lord our **G**"— H466
Isa 37: 4 be that the Lord your **G** will hear the words H466
Isa 37: 4 has sent to ridicule the living **G**, and that H466
Isa 37: 4 the words the Lord your **G** has heard. H466
Isa 37:10 Do not let the **g** you depend on deceive H466
Isa 37:16 "Lord Almighty, the **G** *of* Israel, enthroned H466
Isa 37:16 you alone are **G** over all the kingdoms of H466
Isa 37:17 has sent to ridicule the living **G**. H466
Isa 37:20 Lord our **G**, deliver us from his hand H466
Isa 37:20 may know that you, Lord, are the only **G**." H466
Isa 37:21 what the Lord, the **G** *of* Israel, says H466
Isa 37:38 worshiping in the temple of his **g** Nisrok, H466
Isa 38: 5 is what the Lord, the **G** *of* your father David H466
Isa 40: 1 Comfort, comfort my people, says your **G**. H466
Isa 40: 3 straight in the desert a highway for our **G**. H466
Isa 40: 8 but the word of our **G** endures forever." H466
Isa 40: 9 say to the towns of Judah, "Here is your **G**!" H466
Isa 40:18 will you compare **G**? To what image will H446
Isa 40:27 my cause is disregarded by my **G**"? H466
Isa 40:28 The Lord is the everlasting **G**, the Creator H466
Isa 41:10 do not be dismayed, for I am your **G**. H466
Isa 41:13 I am the Lord your **G** who takes hold of H466
Isa 41:17 will answer them; I, the **G** *of* Israel, will not H466
Isa 42: 5 This is what **G** the Lord says—the Creator H446
Isa 43: 3 For I am the Lord your **G**, the Holy One of H466
Isa 43:10 Before me no **g** was formed, nor will there H446
Isa 43:12 and not some foreign **g** among you. NDT
Isa 43:12 witnesses," declares the Lord, "that I am **G**. H446
Isa 44: 6 I am the last; apart from me there is no **G**. H466
Isa 44: 8 Is there any **G** besides me? No, H468
Isa 44:10 Who shapes a **g** and casts an idol, which H446
Isa 44:15 But he also fashions a **g** and worships it H446
Isa 44:17 From the rest he makes a **g**, his idol; he H446
Isa 44:17 to it and says, "Save me! You are my **g**!" H446
Isa 45: 3 I am the Lord, the **G** *of* Israel, who H466
Isa 45: 5 is no other; apart from me there is no **G**. H466
Isa 45:14 'Surely **G** is with you, and there is H446
Isa 45:14 there is no other; there is no other **g**. H466
Isa 45:15 Truly you are a **G** who has been hiding H446
Isa 45:15 hiding himself, the **G** and Savior *of* Israel. H466
Isa 45:18 the heavens, he is **G**; he who fashioned H466
Isa 45:21 And there is no **G** apart from me, H466
Isa 45:21 from me, a righteous **G** and a Savior; there H446
Isa 45:22 the earth; for I am **G**, and there is no other H446
Isa 46: 6 they hire a goldsmith to make it into a **g** H446
Isa 46: 9 of long ago; I am **G**, and there is no other; H446
Isa 46: 9 is no other; I am **G**, and there is none like H466
Isa 48: 1 of the Lord and invoke the **G** *of* Israel— H466
Isa 48: 2 city and claim to rely on the **G** *of* Israel— H466
Isa 48: 5 image and **metal g** ordained them. H5822
Isa 48:17 "I am the Lord your **G**, who teaches you H466
Isa 49: 4 Lord's hand, and my reward is with my **G**." H466
Isa 49: 5 of the Lord and my **G** has been my strength H466
Isa 50:10 in the name of the Lord and rely on their **G**. H466
Isa 51:15 For I am the Lord your **G**, who stirs up the H466
Isa 51:20 of the Lord, with the rebuke of your **G**. H466
Isa 51:22 Lord says, your **G**, who defends his people: H466
Isa 52: 7 salvation, who say to Zion, "Your **G** reigns!" H466
Isa 52:10 of the earth will see the salvation of our **G**. H466
Isa 52:12 the **G** *of* Israel will be your rear guard. H466
Isa 53: 4 we considered him punished by **G** H466
Isa 54: 5 he is called the **G** *of* all the earth. H466
Isa 54: 6 only to be rejected," says your **G**. H466
Isa 55: 5 because of the Lord your **G**, the Holy One H466
Isa 55: 7 on them, and to our **G**, for he will freely H466
Isa 57:21 is no peace," says my **G**, "for the wicked." H466
Isa 58: 2 has not forsaken the commands of its **G**. H466
Isa 58: 2 seem eager for **G** to come near them. H466
Isa 59: 2 iniquities have separated you from your **G**; H466
Isa 59:13 turning our backs on our **G**, inciting revolt H466
Isa 60: 9 to the honor of the Lord your **G**, the Holy H466
Isa 60:19 and your **G** will be your glory. H466
Isa 61: 2 favor and the day of vengeance of our **G**, H466
Isa 61: 6 you will be named ministers of our **G**. H466
Isa 61:10 in the Lord; my soul rejoices in my **G**. H466
Isa 62: 3 a royal diadem in the hand of your **G**. H466
Isa 62: 5 his bride, so will your **G** rejoice over you. H466
Isa 64: 4 no eye has seen any **G** besides you, who H466
Isa 65:16 in the land will do so by the one true **G**; H466
Isa 65:16 in the land will swear by the one true **G**. H466
Isa 66: 9 when I bring to delivery?" says your **G**. H466
Jer 2:11 exchanged their **glorious G** for worthless H3883
Jer 2:17 the Lord your **G** when he led you in the H466
Jer 2:19 the Lord your **G** and have no awe of me H466
Jer 3:13 you have rebelled against the Lord your **G** H466
Jer 3:21 ways and have forgotten the Lord their **G**. H466
Jer 3:22 come to you, for you are the Lord our **G**. H466
Jer 3:23 surely in the Lord our **G** is the salvation of H466
Jer 3:25 We have sinned against the Lord our **G** H466
Jer 3:25 day we have not obeyed the Lord our **G**." H466
Jer 5: 4 of the Lord, the requirements of their **G**. H466
Jer 5: 5 of the Lord, the requirements of their **G**." H466
Jer 5:14 this is what the Lord **G** Almighty says: H466
Jer 5:19 Why has the Lord our **G** done all this to us? H466
Jer 5:24 'Let us fear the Lord our **G**, who gives H466
Jer 7: 3 the Lord Almighty, the **G** *of* Israel, says: H466
Jer 7:21 the Lord Almighty, the **G** *of* Israel, says: H466
Jer 7:23 I will be your **G** and you will be my H466
Jer 7:28 not obeyed the Lord its **G** or responded to H466
Jer 8:14 For the Lord our **G** has doomed us to perish H466
Jer 9:15 the Lord Almighty, the **G** *of* Israel, says: H466
Jer 10:10 But the Lord is the true **G**; he is the living H466
Jer 10:10 he is the living **G**, the eternal King. H466
Jer 10:12 But **G** made the earth by his power; he NDT
Jer 11: 3 this is what the Lord, the **G** *of* Israel, says: H466
Jer 11: 4 will be my people, and I will be your **G**. H466
Jer 11:13 incense to that **shameful g** Baal are as H1425
Jer 13:12 is what the Lord, the **G** *of* Israel, says: Every H466
Jer 13:16 to the Lord your **G** before he brings the H466
Jer 14:22 it is you, Lord our **G**. Therefore our hope is H466
Jer 15:16 I bear your name, Lord **G** Almighty. H466
Jer 16: 9 the Lord Almighty, the **G** *of* Israel, says: H466
Jer 16:10 have we committed against the Lord our **G**? H466
Jer 19: 3 the Lord Almighty, the **G** *of* Israel, says: H466
Jer 19:15 the Lord Almighty, the **G** *of* Israel, says: H466
Jer 21: 4 is what the Lord, the **G** *of* Israel, says: I am H466
Jer 22: 9 of the Lord their **G** and have worshiped H466
Jer 23: 2 is what the Lord, the **G** *of* Israel, says to the H466
Jer 23:23 "Am I only a **G** nearby," declares the Lord H466
Jer 23:23 declares the Lord, "and not a **G** far away? H466
Jer 23:36 So you distort the words of the living **G**, H466
Jer 23:36 the living God, the Lord Almighty, our **G**. H466
Jer 24: 5 is what the Lord, the **G** *of* Israel, says: H466
Jer 24: 7 I will be their **G**, for they will return to H466
Jer 25:15 what the Lord, the **G** *of* Israel, said to me: H466
Jer 25:27 the Lord Almighty, the **G** *of* Israel, says: H466
Jer 26:13 your actions and obey the Lord your **G**. H466
Jer 26:16 to us in the name of the Lord our **G**." H466
Jer 27: 4 the Lord Almighty, the **G** *of* Israel, says: H466
Jer 27:21 Lord Almighty, the **G** *of* Israel, says about H466
Jer 28: 2 the Lord Almighty, the **G** *of* Israel, says: H466
Jer 28:14 the Lord Almighty, the **G** *of* Israel, says: H466
Jer 29: 4 Lord Almighty, the **G** *of* Israel, says to all H466
Jer 29: 8 the Lord Almighty, the **G** *of* Israel, says: H466
Jer 29:21 Lord Almighty, the **G** *of* Israel, says about H466
Jer 29:25 the Lord Almighty, the **G** *of* Israel, says: H466
Jer 30: 2 what the Lord, the **G** *of* Israel, says: 'Write H466
Jer 30: 9 serve the Lord their **G** and David their king, H466
Jer 30:22 will be my people, and I will be your **G**. H466
Jer 31: 1 "I will be the **G** of all the families of Israel H466
Jer 31: 6 let us go up to Zion, to the Lord our **G**. H466
Jer 31:18 will return, because you are the Lord my **G**. H466
Jer 31:23 the Lord Almighty, the **G** *of* Israel, says: H466
Jer 31:33 I will be their **G**, and they will be my H466
Jer 32:14 the Lord Almighty, the **G** *of* Israel, says: H466
Jer 32:15 the Lord Almighty, the **G** *of* Israel, says: H466
Jer 32:18 Great and mighty **G**, whose name is the H446
Jer 32:27 "I am the Lord, the **G** *of* all mankind. H466
Jer 32:36 this is what the Lord, the **G** *of* Israel, says: H466
Jer 32:38 will be my people, and I will be their **G**. H466
Jer 33: 4 is what the Lord, the **G** *of* Israel, says about H466
Jer 34: 2 is what the Lord, the **G** *of* Israel, says: Go H466
Jer 34:13 what the Lord, the **G** *of* Israel, says: I made H466
Jer 35: 4 of Hanan son of Igdaliah the man of **G**. H466
Jer 35:13 the Lord Almighty, the **G** *of* Israel, says: H466
Jer 35:17 this is what the Lord **G** Almighty, H466
Jer 35:17 Lord God Almighty, the **G** *of* Israel, says: H466
Jer 35:18 the Lord Almighty, the **G** *of* Israel, says: H466
Jer 35:19 the Lord Almighty, the **G** *of* Israel, says: H466
Jer 37: 3 "Please pray to the Lord our **G** for us." H466
Jer 37: 7 is what the Lord, the **G** *of* Israel, says: Tell H466
Jer 38:17 "This is what the Lord **G** Almighty, H466
Jer 38:17 Lord God Almighty, the **G** *of* Israel, says: H466
Jer 39:16 the Lord Almighty, the **G** *of* Israel, says: H466
Jer 40: 2 "The Lord your **G** decreed this disaster for H466
Jer 42: 2 pray to the Lord your **G** for this entire H466
Jer 42: 3 that the Lord your **G** will tell us where we H466
Jer 42: 4 to the Lord your **G** as you have requested H466
Jer 42: 5 the Lord your **G** sends you to tell us. H466
Jer 42: 6 we will obey the Lord our **G**, to whom we H466
Jer 42: 6 for we will obey the Lord our **G**. H466
Jer 42: 9 what the Lord, the **G** *of* Israel, to whom you H466
Jer 42:13 this land,' and so disobey the Lord your **G**, H466
Jer 42:15 the Lord Almighty, the **G** *of* Israel, says: H466
Jer 42:18 the Lord Almighty, the **G** *of* Israel, says: H466
Jer 42:20 you sent me to the Lord your **G** and said, H466
Jer 42:20 'Pray to the Lord our **G** for us; tell us H466
Jer 42:21 obeyed the Lord your **G** in all he sent me to H466
Jer 43: 1 people all the words of the Lord their **G**— H466
Jer 43: 2 The Lord our **G** has not sent you to say H466
Jer 43:10 the Lord Almighty, the **G** *of* Israel, says: H466
Jer 44: 2 the Lord Almighty, the **G** *of* Israel, says: H466
Jer 44: 7 "Now this is what the Lord **G** Almighty, H466
Jer 44: 7 Lord God Almighty, the **G** *of* Israel, says: H466
Jer 44:11 the Lord Almighty, the **G** *of* Israel, says: H466
Jer 44:25 the Lord Almighty, the **G** *of* Israel, says: H466
Jer 45: 2 what the Lord, the **G** *of* Israel, says to you, H466
Jer 46:25 Lord Almighty, the **G** *of* Israel, says: "I am H466
Jer 46:25 to bring punishment on Amon **g** of Thebes, NDT
Jer 48: 1 the Lord Almighty, the **G** *of* Israel, says: H466
Jer 50: 4 will go in tears to seek the Lord their **G**. H466
Jer 50:18 the Lord Almighty, the **G** *of* Israel, says: H466
Jer 50:28 how the Lord our **G** has taken vengeance, H466
Jer 51: 5 Judah have not been forsaken by their **G**, H466
Jer 51:10 tell in Zion what the Lord our **G** has done. H466
Jer 51:33 the Lord Almighty, the **G** *of* Israel, says: H466
Jer 51:56 For the Lord is a **G** *of* retribution; he will H446

G

La 3:41 our hearts and our hands to G in heaven, H466
Eze 1: 1 were opened and I saw visions of G. H466
Eze 8: 3 in visions of G he took me to H466
Eze 8: 4 before me was the glory of the G *of* Israel, H466
Eze 8:14 sitting there, mourning the g **Tammuz**. H9452
Eze 9: 3 the glory of the G of Israel went up from H466
Eze 10: 5 like the voice of G Almighty when he H446
Eze 10:19 the glory of the G *of* Israel was above H466
Eze 10:20 seen beneath the G *of* Israel by the Kebar H466
Eze 11:20 will be my people, and I will be their G. H466
Eze 11:22 the glory of the G *of* Israel was above H466
Eze 11:24 in the vision given by the Spirit of G. H466
Eze 14:11 I will be their G, declares the H466
Eze 20: 5 hand I said to them, "I am the LORD your G." H466
Eze 20: 7 the idols of Egypt. I am the LORD your G." H466
Eze 20:19 I am the LORD your G; follow my decrees H466
Eze 20:20 you will know that I am the LORD your G." H466
Eze 28: 2 heart you say, "I am a g; I sit on the throne H446
Eze 28: 2 sit on the throne of a g in the heart of the H466
Eze 28: 2 But you are a mere mortal and not a g H446
Eze 28: 2 though you think you are as wise as a g. H466
Eze 28: 6 you think you are wise, as wise as a g, H466
Eze 28: 9 you then say, "I am a g," in the presence of H466
Eze 28: 9 a mortal, not a g, in the hands of those H446
Eze 28:13 the garden of G; every precious H466
Eze 28:14 You were on the holy mount of G; you H466
Eze 28:16 drove you in disgrace from the mount of G, H466
Eze 28:26 they will know that I am the LORD their G. H466
Eze 31: 8 cedars in the garden of G could not rival it, H466
Eze 31: 8 tree in the garden of G could match its H466
Eze 31: 9 of all the trees of Eden in the garden of G. H466
Eze 34:24 I the LORD will be their G, and my servant H466
Eze 34:30 the LORD their G, am with them and that H466
Eze 34:31 pasture, and I am your G, declares the H466
Eze 36:28 you will be my people, and I will be your G. H466
Eze 37:23 will be my people, and I will be their G. H466
Eze 37:27 I will be their G, and they will be my H466
Eze 39:22 Israel will know that I am the LORD their G. H466
Eze 39:28 they will know that I am the LORD their G, H466
Eze 40: 2 In visions of G he took me to the land of H466
Eze 43: 2 the glory of the G *of* Israel coming from H466
Eze 44: 2 the LORD, the G *of* Israel, has entered H466
Da 1: 2 some of the articles from the temple of G. H466
Da 1: 2 to the temple of his g in Babylonia and put H466
Da 1: 2 put in the treasure house of his g. H466
Da 1: 9 Now G had caused the official to show favor H466
Da 1:17 four young men G gave knowledge and H466
Da 2:18 mercy from the G *of* heaven concerning A10033
Da 2:19 Then Daniel praised the G *of* heaven A10033
Da 2:20 be to the name of G for ever and ever; A10033
Da 2:23 thank and praise you, G *of* my ancestors: A10033
Da 2:28 there is a G in heaven who reveals A10033
Da 2:37 The G *of* heaven has given you A10033
Da 2:44 the G *of* heaven will set up a kingdom A10033
Da 2:45 "The great G has shown the king what A10033
Da 2:47 "Surely your G is the God of gods and A10033
Da 2:47 your God is the G *of* gods and the Lord A10033
Da 3:15 Then what g will be able to rescue you A10033
Da 3:17 the G we serve is able to deliver us from A10033
Da 3:26 servants of the Most High G, come out! A10033
Da 3:28 "Praise be to the G of Shadrach A10033
Da 3:28 worship any g except their own God A10033
Da 3:28 worship any god except their own G. A10033
Da 3:29 say anything against the G of Shadrach, A10033
Da 3:29 no other g can save in this way. A10033
Da 4: 2 that the Most High G has performed A10033
Da 4: 8 after the name of my g, and the spirit of A10033
Da 5: 3 from the temple of G in Jerusalem, A10033
Da 5:18 the Most High G gave your father A10033
Da 5:21 that the Most High G is sovereign over A10033
Da 5:23 did not honor the G who holds in his A10033
Da 5:26 G has numbered the days of your reign A10033
Da 6: 5 something to do with the law of his G." A10033
Da 6: 7 who prays to any g or human being A10033
Da 6:10 giving thanks to his G, just as he had A10033
Da 6:11 Daniel praying and asking G for help. A10033
Da 6:12 who prays to any g or human being A10033
Da 6:16 to Daniel, "May your G, whom you serve A10033
Da 6:20 servant of the living G, has your God, A10033
Da 6:20 living God, has your G, whom you serve A10033
Da 6:22 My G sent his angel, and he shut the A10033
Da 6:23 on him, because he had trusted in his G. A10033
Da 6:26 must fear and reverence the G of Daniel. A10033
Da 6:26 "For he is the living G and he endures A10033
Da 9: 3 turned to the Lord G and pleaded with him H466
Da 9: 4 I prayed to the LORD my G and confessed H466
Da 9: 4 the great and awesome G, who keeps his H446
Da 9: 9 The Lord our G is merciful and forgiving H466
Da 9:10 obeyed the LORD our G or kept the laws he H466
Da 9:11 the servant of G, have been poured out H466
Da 9:13 favor of the LORD our G by turning from our H466
Da 9:14 the LORD our G is righteous in everything H466
Da 9:15 Lord our G, who brought your people H466
Da 9:17 our G, hear the prayers and petitions H466
Da 9:18 Give ear, our G, and hear; open your eyes H466
Da 9:19 For your sake, my G, do not delay, because H466
Da 9:20 request to the LORD my G for his holy hill— H466
Da 10:12 to humble yourself before your G, H466
Da 11:32 people who know their G will firmly resist H466
Da 11:36 himself above every g and will say H446
Da 11:36 unheard-of things against the G *of* gods. H446
Da 11:37 will he regard any g, but will exalt H468
Da 11:38 he will honor a g *of* fortresses; a god H468
Da 11:38 a g unknown to his ancestors he will honor H468
Da 11:39 the help of a foreign g and will greatly H468
Hos 1: 7 the LORD their G, will save them. H466
Hos 1: 9 you are not my people, and I am not your G. NDT
Hos 1:10 they will be called 'children of the living G. H446
Hos 2:23 people'; and they will say, 'You are my G. H466
Hos 3: 5 seek the LORD their G and David their king. H466
Hos 4: 1 no acknowledgment of G in the land. H466
Hos 4: 6 you have ignored the law of your G, H466
Hos 4: 7 exchanged their **glorious** G for something H3883
Hos 4:12 them astray; they are unfaithful to their G. H466
Hos 5: 4 do not permit them to return to their G. H466
Hos 6: 6 acknowledgment of G rather than burnt H466
Hos 7:10 return to the LORD his G or search for him. H466
Hos 8: 2 out to me, 'Our G, we acknowledge you! H466
Hos 8: 6 a metalworker has made it; it is not G. H466
Hos 9: 1 For you have been unfaithful to your G; you H466
Hos 9: 8 along with my G, is the watchman over H466
Hos 9: 8 and hostility in the house of his G. H466
Hos 9: 9 G will remember their wickedness and NDT
Hos 9:17 My G will reject them because they have H466
Hos 11: 7 Even though they call me G Most High, H446
Hos 11: 9 For I am G, and not a man—the Holy One H446
Hos 11:12 And Judah is unruly against G, even H446
Hos 12: 3 as a man he struggled with G. H466
Hos 12: 5 the LORD G Almighty, the LORD is his name! H466
Hos 12: 6 But you must return to your G; maintain H466
Hos 12: 6 justice, and wait for your G always. H466
Hos 12: 9 been the LORD your G ever since you came H466
Hos 13: 4 been the LORD your G ever since you came H466
Hos 13: 4 You shall acknowledge no G but me, no H466
Hos 13:16 because they have rebelled against their G. H466
Hos 14: 1 to the LORD your G. Your sins have been H466
Joel 1:13 you who minister before my G; for the grain H466
Joel 1:13 are withheld from the house of your G. H466
Joel 1:14 in the land to the house of the LORD your G, H466
Joel 1:16 joy and gladness from the house of our G? H466
Joel 2:13 Return to the LORD your G, for he is gracious H466
Joel 2:14 drink offerings for the LORD your G. H466
Joel 2:17 say among the peoples, 'Where is their G? H466
Joel 2:23 rejoice in the LORD your G, for he has given H466
Joel 2:26 will praise the name of the LORD your G, H466
Joel 2:27 that I am the LORD your G, and that there is H466
Joel 3:17 know that I, the LORD your G, dwell in Zion, H466
Am 2: 8 the house of their g they drink wine taken H466
Am 3:13 declares the Lord, the LORD G Almighty. H466
Am 4:12 this to you, Israel, prepare to meet your G." H466
Am 4:13 the LORD G Almighty is his name. H466
Am 5:14 Then the LORD G Almighty will be with you H466
Am 5:15 Perhaps the LORD G Almighty will have H466
Am 5:16 is what the Lord, the LORD G Almighty, says: H466
Am 5:26 the star of your g—which you made for H466
Am 5:27 says the LORD, whose name is G Almighty. H466
Am 6: 8 by himself—the LORD G Almighty declares: H466
Am 6:14 the LORD G Almighty declares, "I will stir H466
Am 8:14 'As surely as your g lives, Dan,' or, H466
Am 8:14 'As surely as the g *of* Beersheba lives' H2006
Am 9:15 I have given them," says the LORD your G. H466
Jnh 1: 5 afraid and each cried out to his own g. H466
Jnh 1: 6 Get up and call on your g! Maybe he will H466
Jnh 1: 9 the LORD, the G *of* heaven, who made the H466
Jnh 2: 1 the fish Jonah prayed to the LORD his G. H466
Jnh 2: 6 But you, LORD my G, brought my life up H466
Jnh 3: 5 The Ninevites believed G. A fast was H466
Jnh 3: 8 Let everyone call urgently on G. Let them H466
Jnh 3: 9 G may yet relent and with compassion turn H466
Jnh 3:10 When G saw what they did and how they H466
Jnh 4: 2 you are a gracious and compassionate G, H446
Jnh 4: 2 a G who relents from sending calamity. NDT
Jnh 4: 6 Then the LORD G provided a leafy plant and H466
Jnh 4: 7 at dawn the next day G provided a worm, H466
Jnh 4: 8 sun rose, G provided a scorching east wind H466
Jnh 4: 9 But G said to Jonah, "Is it right for you to H466
Mic 3: 7 faces because there is no answer from G." H466
Mic 4: 2 the LORD, to the temple of the G *of* Jacob. H466
Mic 4: 5 name of the LORD our G for ever and ever. H466
Mic 5: 4 the majesty of the name of the LORD his G. H466
Mic 6: 6 LORD and bow down before the exalted G? H466
Mic 6: 8 love mercy and to walk humbly with your G. H466
Mic 7: 4 The day G visits you has come, the day your NDT
Mic 7: 7 the LORD, I wait for G my Savior; my God H466
Mic 7: 7 wait for God my Savior; my G will hear me. H466
Mic 7:10 said to me, "Where is the LORD your G?" H466
Mic 7:17 fear to the LORD our G and will be afraid of H466
Mic 7:18 Who is a G like you, who pardons sin and H446
Na 1: 2 The LORD is a jealous and avenging G; the H446
Hab 1:11 whose own strength is their g. H468
Hab 1:12 from everlasting? My G, my Holy One, you H466
Hab 3: 3 G came from Teman, the Holy One from H468
Hab 3:18 in the LORD, I will be joyful in G my Savior. H466
Zep 2: 7 The LORD their G will care for them; he will H466
Zep 2: 9 LORD Almighty, the G *of* Israel, "surely H466
Zep 3: 2 the LORD, she does not draw near to her G. H466
Zep 3:17 The LORD your G is with you, the Mighty H466
Hag 1:12 of the LORD their G and the message of the H466
Hag 1:12 because the LORD their G had sent him. H466
Hag 1:14 on the house of the LORD Almighty, their G, H466
Zec 4: 7 out the capstone to shouts of 'G bless it! NDT
Zec 4: 7 to shouts of 'God bless it! G bless it!'" NDT
Zec 6:15 if you diligently obey the LORD your G." H466
Zec 8: 8 faithful and righteous to them as their G." H466
Zec 8:23 because we have heard that G is with you. H466
Zec 9: 7 will belong to our G and become a clan in H466
Zec 9:16 The LORD their G will save his people on H466
Zec 10: 6 I am the LORD their G and I will answer H466
Zec 11: 4 This is what the LORD my G says: H466
Zec 12: 5 because the LORD Almighty is their G. H466
Zec 12: 8 the house of David will be like G, like H466
Zec 13: 9 they will say, 'The LORD is our G. H466
Zec 14: 5 Then the LORD my G will come, and all the H466
Mal 1: 9 "Now plead with G to be gracious to us H446
Mal 2:10 Did not one G create us? Why do H446
Mal 2:11 marrying women who worship a foreign g. H446
Mal 2:15 Has not the one G made you? You belong NDT
Mal 2:15 And what does the one G seek? Godly NDT
Mal 2:16 says the LORD, the G *of* Israel, "does H466
Mal 2:17 with them" or "Where is the G *of* justice?" H466
Mal 3: 8 "Will a mere mortal rob G? Yet you rob me H466
Mal 3:14 'It is futile to serve G. What do we gain by H466
Mal 3:15 even when they put G to the test, they H466
Mal 3:18 those who serve G and those who do not. H466
Mt 1:23 Immanuel" (which means "G with us") *G2536*
Mt 3: 9 out of these stones G can raise up *G2536*
Mt 3:16 he saw the Spirit *of* G descending like a *G2536*
Mt 4: 3 "If you are the Son *of* G, tell these stones *G2536*
Mt 4: 4 word that comes from the mouth *of* G. *G2536*
Mt 4: 6 "If you are the Son *of* G," he said, "throw *G2536*
Mt 4: 7 'Do not put the Lord your G to the test.'" *G2536*
Mt 4:10 'Worship the Lord your G, and serve him *G2536*
Mt 5: 8 are the pure in heart, for they will see G. *G2536*
Mt 5: 9 they will be called children *of* G. *G2536*
Mt 6:24 You cannot serve both G and money. *G2536*
Mt 6:30 If that is how G clothes the grass of the *G2536*
Mt 8:29 want with us, Son *of* G?" they shouted. *G2536*
Mt 9: 8 they praised G, who had given such *G2536*
Mt 12: 4 He entered the house *of* G, and he and *G2536*
Mt 12:28 if it is by the Spirit *of* G that I drive out *G2536*
Mt 12:28 then the kingdom *of* G has come upon *G2536*
Mt 14:33 saying, "Truly you are the Son *of* G." *G2536*
Mt 15: 3 break the command *of* G for the sake of *G2536*
Mt 15: 4 For G said, 'Honor your father and mother' *G2536*
Mt 15: 5 their father or mother is '**devoted to G**, *G1565*
Mt 15: 6 nullify the word *of* G for the sake of your *G2536*
Mt 15:31 And they praised the G of Israel. *G2536*
Mt 16:16 are the Messiah, the Son *of* the living G." *G2536*
Mt 16:23 do not have in mind the concerns *of* G, *G2536*
Mt 19: 6 Therefore what G has joined together, let *G2536*
Mt 19:24 who is rich to enter the kingdom *of* G." *G2536*
Mt 19:26 with G all things are possible. *G2536*
Mt 21:31 entering the kingdom *of* G ahead of you. *G2536*
Mt 21:43 that the kingdom *of* G will be taken away *G2536*
Mt 22:16 you teach the way *of* G in accordance with *G2536*
Mt 22:21 what is Caesar's, and *to* G what is God's." *G2536*
Mt 22:29 not know the Scriptures or the power *of* G. *G2536*
Mt 22:31 have you not read what G said to you, *G2536*
Mt 22:32 'I am the G of Abraham, the God of Isaac *G2536*
Mt 22:32 God of Abraham, the G of Isaac, and the *G2536*
Mt 22:32 the God of Isaac, and the G of Jacob'? *G2536*
Mt 22:32 He is not the G of the dead but of the *G2536*
Mt 22:37 " 'Love the Lord your G with all your heart *G2536*
Mt 26:61 destroy the temple *of* G and rebuild it in *G2536*
Mt 26:63 "I charge you under oath by the living G: *G2536*
Mt 26:63 us if you are the Messiah, the Son *of* G." *G2536*
Mt 27:40 from the cross, if you are the Son *of* G!" *G2536*
Mt 27:43 He trusts in G. Let God rescue him now if *G2536*
Mt 27:43 Let G rescue him now if he wants him, for NDT
Mt 27:43 for he said, 'I am the Son *of* G. *G2536*
Mt 27:46 which means "My G, my God, why have *G2536*
Mt 27:46 means "My God, my G, why have you *G2536*
Mt 27:54 exclaimed, "Surely he was the Son *of* G!" *G2536*
Mk 1: 1 about Jesus the Messiah, the Son *of* G, *G2536*
Mk 1:14 Galilee, proclaiming the good news *of* G. *G2536*
Mk 1:15 "The kingdom *of* G has come near *G2536*
Mk 1:24 I know who you are—the Holy One *of* G!" *G2536*
Mk 2: 7 Who can forgive sins but G alone?" *G2536*
Mk 2:12 amazed everyone and they praised G, *G2536*
Mk 2:26 he entered the house *of* G and ate the *G2536*
Mk 3:11 him and cried out, "You are the Son *of* G." *G2536*
Mk 4:11 of the kingdom *of* G has been given to *G2536*
Mk 4:26 "This is what the kingdom *of* G is like. *G2536*
Mk 4:30 shall we say the kingdom *of* G is like, *G2536*
Mk 5: 7 with me, Jesus, Son *of* the Most High G? *G2536*
Mk 7: 8 of the commands *of* G and are holding on *G2536*
Mk 7: 9 aside the commands *of* G in order to *G2536*
Mk 7:11 is Corban (that is, **devoted to G**)— *G1565*
Mk 7:13 you nullify the word *of* G by your tradition *G2536*
Mk 8:33 do not have in mind the concerns *of* G, *G2536*
Mk 9: 1 that the kingdom *of* G has come with *G2536*
Mk 9:47 enter the kingdom *of* G with one eye than *G2536*
Mk 10: 6 of creation G 'made them male and NDT
Mk 10: 9 Therefore what G has joined together, let *G2536*
Mk 10:14 the kingdom *of* G belongs to such as *G2536*
Mk 10:15 receive the kingdom *of* G like a little child *G2536*
Mk 10:18 "No one is good—except G alone. *G2536*
Mk 10:23 it is for the rich to enter the kingdom *of* G!" *G2536*
Mk 10:24 how hard it is to enter the kingdom *of* G! *G2536*
Mk 10:25 who is rich to enter the kingdom *of* G." *G2536*
Mk 10:27 not with G; all things are possible *G2536*
Mk 10:27 with God; all things are possible with G." *G2536*
Mk 11:22 "Have faith *in* G," Jesus answered. *G2536*
Mk 12:14 you teach the way *of* G in accordance with *G2536*
Mk 12:17 what is Caesar's and *to* G what is God's." *G2536*
Mk 12:24 not know the Scriptures or the power *of* G? *G2536*

Mk 12:26 burning bush, how G said to him, 'I am G2536
Mk 12:26 'I am the G of Abraham, the God G2536
Mk 12:26 God of Abraham, the G of Isaac, and the G2536
Mk 12:26 the God of Isaac, and the G of Jacob'? G2536
Mk 12:27 He is not the G of the dead, but of the G2536
Mk 12:29 The Lord our G, the Lord is one. G2536
Mk 12:30 Love the Lord your G with all your heart G2536
Mk 12:32 right in saying that G is one and there is no NDT
Mk 12:34 "You are not far from the kingdom of G." G2536
Mk 13:19 the beginning, when G created the world G2536
Mk 14:25 when I drink it new in the kingdom of G." G2536
Mk 15:34 which means "My G, my God, why have G2536
Mk 15:34 means "My God, my G, why have you G2536
Mk 15:39 "Surely this man was the Son of G!" G2536
Mk 15:43 was himself waiting for the kingdom of G, G2536
Mk 16:19 heaven and he sat at the right hand of G. G2536
Lk 1: 6 of them were righteous in the sight of G, G2536
Lk 1: 8 he was serving as priest before G, G2536
Lk 1:16 of the people of Israel to the Lord their G. G2536
Lk 1:19 I stand in the presence of G, and I have G2536
Lk 1:26 G sent the angel Gabriel to Nazareth G2536
Lk 1:30 Mary; you have found favor with G. G2536
Lk 1:32 The Lord G will give him the throne of his G2536
Lk 1:35 to be born will be called the Son of G. G2536
Lk 1:37 For no word from G will ever fail. G2536
Lk 1:47 my spirit rejoices in G my Savior, G2536
Lk 1:64 and he began to speak, praising G. G2536
Lk 1:68 be to the Lord, the G of Israel, because he G2536
Lk 1:78 because of the tender mercy of our G, by G2536
Lk 2:13 with the angel, praising G and saying, G2536
Lk 2:14 "Glory to G in the highest heaven, and on G2536
Lk 2:20 praising G for all the things they G2536
Lk 2:28 took him in his arms and praised G, G2536
Lk 2:38 she gave thanks to G and spoke about the G2536
Lk 2:40 wisdom, and the grace of G was on him. G2536
Lk 2:52 stature, and in favor with G and man. G2536
Lk 3: 2 the word of G came to John son of G2536
Lk 3: 8 out of these stones G can raise up G2536
Lk 3:38 of Seth, the son of Adam, the son of G. G2536
Lk 4: 3 "If you are the Son of G, tell this stone to G2536
Lk 4: 8 the Lord your G and serve him only. G2536
Lk 4: 9 "If you are the Son of G," he said, "throw G2536
Lk 4:12 'Do not put the Lord your G to the test.'" G2536
Lk 4:34 I know who you are—the Holy One of G!" G2536
Lk 4:41 people, shouting, "You are the Son of G!" G2536
Lk 4:43 of the kingdom of G to the other towns G2536
Lk 5: 1 him and listening to the word of G. G2536
Lk 5:21 Who can forgive sins but G alone?" G2536
Lk 5:25 been lying on and went home praising G. G2536
Lk 5:26 was amazed and gave praise to G. G2536
Lk 6: 4 He entered the house of G, and taking the G2536
Lk 6:12 and spent the night praying to G. G2536
Lk 6:20 are poor, for yours is the kingdom of G. G2536
Lk 7:16 were all filled with awe and praised G. G2536
Lk 7:16 "G has come to help his people. G2536
Lk 7:28 in the kingdom of G is greater than he." G2536
Lk 8: 1 the good news of the kingdom of G. G2536
Lk 8:10 of the kingdom of G has been given to G2536
Lk 8:11 of the parable: The seed is the word of G. G2536
Lk 8:28 with me, Jesus, Son of the Most High G? G2536
Lk 8:39 tell how much G has done for you. G2536
Lk 9: 2 the kingdom of G and to heal the sick G2536
Lk 9:11 spoke to them about the kingdom of G, G2536
Lk 9:27 death before they see the kingdom of G." G2536
Lk 9:43 were all amazed at the greatness of G. G2536
Lk 9:60 you go and proclaim the kingdom of G." G2536
Lk 9:62 back is fit for service in the kingdom of G." G2536
Lk 10: 9 'The kingdom of G has come near to you. G2536
Lk 10:11 The kingdom of G has come near.' G2536
Lk 10:27 " 'Love the Lord your G with all your heart G2536
Lk 11:20 But if I drive out demons by the finger of G, G2536
Lk 11:20 then the kingdom of G has come upon G2536
Lk 11:28 those who hear the word of G and obey it." G2536
Lk 11:42 because you give G a tenth of your mint, rue NDT
Lk 11:42 you neglect justice and the love of G. G2536
Lk 11:49 Because of this, G in his wisdom said, 'I G2536
Lk 12: 6 Yet not one of them is forgotten by G. G2536
Lk 12: 8 also acknowledge before the angels of G. G2536
Lk 12: 9 will be disowned before the angels of G. G2536
Lk 12:20 "But G said to him, 'You fool! This very G2536
Lk 12:21 themselves but is not rich toward G." G2536
Lk 12:24 no storeroom or barn; yet G feeds them. G2536
Lk 12:28 If that is how G clothes the grass of the G2536
Lk 13:13 she straightened up and praised G. G2536
Lk 13:18 "What is the kingdom of G like? G2536
Lk 13:20 shall I compare the kingdom of G to? G2536
Lk 13:28 all the prophets in the kingdom of G, G2536
Lk 13:29 places at the feast in the kingdom of G. G2536
Lk 14:15 will eat at the feast in the kingdom of G." G2536
Lk 15:10 of the angels of G over one sinner who G2536
Lk 16:13 You cannot serve both G and money." G2536
Lk 16:15 eyes of others, but G knows your hearts. G2536
Lk 16:16 of the kingdom of G is being preached, G2536
Lk 17:15 came back, praising G in a loud voice. G2536
Lk 17:18 to give praise to G except this foreigner?" G2536
Lk 17:20 when the kingdom of G would come, G2536
Lk 17:20 of the kingdom of G is not something that G2536
Lk 17:21 the kingdom of G is in your midst. G2536
Lk 18: 2 who neither feared G nor cared what G2536
Lk 18: 4 though I don't fear G or care what people G2536
Lk 18: 7 And will not G bring about justice for his G2536
Lk 18:11 'G, I thank you that I am not like other G2536
Lk 18:13 breast and said, 'G, have mercy on me, G2536
Lk 18:14 the other, went home justified before G. G1467
Lk 18:16 the kingdom of G belongs to such as G2536
Lk 18:17 receive the kingdom of G like a little child G2536
Lk 18:19 "No one is good—except G alone. G2536
Lk 18:24 it is for the rich to enter the kingdom of G! G2536
Lk 18:25 who is rich to enter the kingdom of G." G2536
Lk 18:27 is impossible with man is possible with G." G2536
Lk 18:29 children for the sake of the kingdom of G G2536
Lk 18:43 his sight and followed Jesus, praising G. G2536
Lk 18:43 all the people saw it, they also praised G. G2536
Lk 19:11 that the kingdom of G was going to G2536
Lk 19:37 joyfully to praise G in loud voices for all G2536
Lk 20:16 heard this, they said, "G forbid!" G3590+1181S
Lk 20:21 teach the way of G in accordance with G2536
Lk 20:25 what is Caesar's, and to G what is God's." G2536
Lk 20:37 he calls the Lord 'the G of Abraham G2536
Lk 20:37 of Abraham, and the G of Isaac, and the G2536
Lk 20:37 the God of Isaac, and the G of Jacob. G2536
Lk 20:38 He is not the G of the dead, but of the G2536
Lk 21: 5 stones and with gifts dedicated to G. G356
Lk 21:31 you know that the kingdom of G is near. G2536
Lk 22:16 it finds fulfillment in the kingdom of G." G2536
Lk 22:18 of the vine until the kingdom of G comes." G2536
Lk 22:69 seated at the right hand of the mighty G." G2536
Lk 22:70 all asked, "Are you then the Son of G?" G2536
Lk 23:40 "Don't you fear G," he said, "since you G2536
Lk 23:47 happened, praised G and said, "Surely G2536
Lk 23:51 himself was waiting for the kingdom of G. G2536
Lk 24:19 deed before G and all the people. G2536
Lk 24:53 continually at the temple, praising G. G2536
Jn 1: 1 the Word was with G, and the Word G2536
Jn 1: 1 Word was with God, and the Word was G. G2536
Jn 1: 2 He was with G in the beginning. G2536
Jn 1: 6 a man sent from G whose name was John G2536
Jn 1:12 gave the right to become children of G— G2536
Jn 1:13 a husband's will, but born of G. G2536
Jn 1:18 No one has ever seen G, but the one and G2536
Jn 1:18 who is himself G and is in closest G2536
Jn 1:29 the Lamb of G, who takes away the G2536
Jn 1:36 passing by, he said, "Look, the Lamb of G!" G2536
Jn 1:49 you are the Son of G; you are the king of G2536
Jn 1:51 the angels of G ascending and G2536
Jn 3: 2 you are a teacher who has come from G. G2536
Jn 3: 2 you are doing if G were not with him." G2536
Jn 3: 3 can see the kingdom of G unless they are G2536
Jn 3: 5 enter the kingdom of G unless they are G2536
Jn 3:16 For G so loved the world that he gave his G2536
Jn 3:17 For G did not send his Son into the world G2536
Jn 3:21 done has been done in the sight of G. G2536
Jn 3:33 accepted it has certified that G is truthful. G2536
Jn 3:34 For the one whom G has sent speaks the G2536
Jn 3:34 God has sent speaks the words of G, G2536
Jn 3:34 for G gives the Spirit without limit. NDT
Jn 4:10 you knew the gift of G and who it is that G2536
Jn 4:24 G is spirit, and his worshipers must G2536
Jn 5:18 he was even calling G his own Father G2536
Jn 5:18 own Father, making himself equal with G. G2536
Jn 5:25 voice of the Son of G and those who hear G2536
Jn 5:42 do not have the love of G in your hearts. G2536
Jn 5:44 the glory that comes from the only G? G2536
Jn 6:27 For on him G the Father has placed his G2536
Jn 6:28 must we do to do the works G requires?" G2536
Jn 6:29 "The work of G is this: to believe G2536
Jn 6:33 For the bread of G is the bread that comes G2536
Jn 6:45 'They will all be taught by G.' Everyone G2536
Jn 6:46 the Father except the one who is from G; G2536
Jn 6:69 to know that you are the Holy One of G." G2536
Jn 7:17 to do the will of G will find out whether G899S
Jn 7:17 teaching comes from G or whether I speak G2536
Jn 8:40 has told you the truth that I heard from G. G2536
Jn 8:41 "The only Father we have is G himself." G2536
Jn 8:42 said to them, "If G were your Father, you G2536
Jn 8:42 love me, for I have come here from G. G2536
Jn 8:42 I have not come on my own; G sent me. G1697S
Jn 8:47 Whoever belongs to G hears what God G2536
Jn 8:47 belongs to God hears what G says. G2536
Jn 8:47 not hear is that you do not belong to G." G2536
Jn 8:54 whom you claim as your G, is the one G2536
Jn 9: 3 so that the works of G might be displayed G2536
Jn 9:16 "This man is not from G, for he does not G2536
Jn 9:24 "Give glory to G by telling the truth," G2536
Jn 9:29 We know that G spoke to Moses, but as G2536
Jn 9:31 We know that G does not listen to sinners G2536
Jn 9:33 If this man were not from G, he could do G2536
Jn 10:33 because you, a mere man, claim to be G." G2536
Jn 10:35 to whom the word of G came—and G2536
Jn 11:22 I know that even now G will give you G2536
Jn 11:27 Messiah, the Son of G, who is to come G2536
Jn 11:40 if you believe, you will see the glory of G?" G2536
Jn 11:52 also for the scattered children of G, G2536
Jn 12:43 human praise more than praise from G. G2536
Jn 13: 3 he had come from G and was returning to G2536
Jn 13: 3 come from God and was returning to G; G2536
Jn 13:31 Man is glorified and G is glorified in him. G2536
Jn 13:32 If G is glorified in him, God will glorify G2536
Jn 13:32 G will glorify the Son in himself G2536
Jn 14: 1 You believe in G; believe also in me. G2536
Jn 16: 2 will think they are offering a service to G. G2536
Jn 16:27 have believed that I came from G. G2536
Jn 16:30 makes us believe that you came from G." G2536
Jn 17: 3 the only true G, and Jesus Christ, G2536
Jn 19: 7 because he claimed to be the Son of G." G2536
Jn 20:17 your Father, to my G and your God. G2536
Jn 20:17 your Father, to my God and your G. G2536
Jn 20:28 Thomas said to him, "My Lord and my G!" G2536
Jn 20:31 the Messiah, the Son of G, and that by G2536
Jn 21:19 of death by which Peter would glorify G. G2536
Ac 1: 3 days and spoke about the kingdom of G. G2536
Ac 2:11 the wonders of G in our own tongues!" G2536
Ac 2:17 " 'In the last days, G says, I will pour out G2536
Ac 2:22 a man accredited by G to you by miracles, G2536
Ac 2:22 which G did among you through him G2536
Ac 2:24 But G raised him from the dead, freeing G2536
Ac 2:30 knew that G had promised him on G2536
Ac 2:32 G has raised this Jesus to life, and we are G2536
Ac 2:33 Exalted to the right hand of G, he has G2536
Ac 2:36 G has made this Jesus, whom you G2536
Ac 2:39 for all whom the Lord our G will call." G2536
Ac 2:47 praising G and enjoying the favor of all G2536
Ac 3: 8 walking and jumping, and praising G. G2536
Ac 3: 9 people saw him walking and praising G, G2536
Ac 3:13 The G of Abraham, Isaac and Jacob, the G2536
Ac 3:13 Isaac and Jacob, the G of our fathers, has G2536
Ac 3:15 but G raised him from the dead. G2536
Ac 3:18 But this is how G fulfilled what he had G2536
Ac 3:19 and turn to G, so that your sins may be AIT
Ac 3:21 the time comes for G to restore everything G2536
Ac 3:22 'The Lord your G will raise up for you a G2536
Ac 3:25 of the covenant G made with your G2536
Ac 3:26 When G raised up his servant, he sent him G2536
Ac 4:10 crucified but whom G raised from the G2536
Ac 4:21 people were praising G for what had G2536
Ac 4:24 raised their voices together in prayer to G. G2536
Ac 4:31 Spirit and spoke the word of G boldly. G2536
Ac 5: 4 not lied just to human beings but to G." G2536
Ac 5:29 "We must obey G rather than human G2536
Ac 5:30 The G of our ancestors raised Jesus from G2536
Ac 5:31 G exalted him to his own right hand as G2536
Ac 5:32 whom G has given to those who obey him G2536
Ac 5:39 But if it is from G, you will not be able to G2536
Ac 5:39 only find yourselves fighting against G." G2534
Ac 6: 2 of the word of G in order to wait on G2536
Ac 6: 7 So the word of G spread. The number of G2536
Ac 6:11 words against Moses and against G." G2536
Ac 7: 2 The G of glory appeared to our father G2536
Ac 7: 3 your people,' G said, 'and go to the NDT
Ac 7: 4 G sent him to this land where you are now NDT
Ac 7: 5 But G promised him that he and his NDT
Ac 7: 6 G spoke to him in this way: 'For four G2536
Ac 7: 7 serve as slaves,' G said, 'and afterward G2536
Ac 7: 9 as a slave into Egypt. But G was with him G2536
Ac 7:17 time drew near for G to fulfill his promise G2536
Ac 7:25 would realize that G was using him to G2536
Ac 7:32 'I am the G of your fathers, the God of G2536
Ac 7:32 of your fathers, the G of Abraham, Isaac G2536
Ac 7:35 be their ruler and deliverer by G himself, G2536
Ac 7:37 'G will raise up for you a prophet like me G2536
Ac 7:42 But G turned away from them and gave G2536
Ac 7:43 of Molek and the star of your g Rephan, G2536
Ac 7:44 been made as G directed Moses, G3836+3281S
Ac 7:45 from the nations G drove out before them G2536
Ac 7:46 a dwelling place for the G of Jacob. G2536
Ac 7:55 up to heaven and saw the glory of G, G2536
Ac 7:55 Jesus standing at the right hand of G. G2536
Ac 7:56 of Man standing at the right hand of G." G2536
Ac 8:10 is rightly called the Great Power of G." G2536
Ac 8:12 of the kingdom of G and the name of G2536
Ac 8:14 that Samaria had accepted the word of G, G2536
Ac 8:20 you could buy the gift of G with money! G2536
Ac 8:21 because your heart is not right before G. G2536
Ac 9:20 synagogues that Jesus is the Son of G. G2536
Ac 10: 2 those in need and prayed to G regularly. G2536
Ac 10: 3 He distinctly saw an angel of G, who G2536
Ac 10: 4 come up as a memorial offering before G. G2536
Ac 10:15 anything impure that G has made clean." G2536
Ac 10:28 But G has shown me that I should not call G2536
Ac 10:31 G has heard your prayer and remembered G2536
Ac 10:33 in the presence of G to listen to G2536
Ac 10:34 how true it is that G does not show G2536
Ac 10:36 You know the message G sent to the people NDT
Ac 10:38 how G anointed Jesus of Nazareth with G2536
Ac 10:38 of the devil, because G was with him. G2536
Ac 10:40 G raised him from the dead on the G2536
Ac 10:41 by witnesses whom G had already chosen G2536
Ac 10:42 is the one whom G appointed as judge G2536
Ac 10:46 them speaking in tongues and praising G. G2536
Ac 11: 1 Gentiles also had received the word of G. G2536
Ac 11: 9 anything impure that G has made clean. G2536
Ac 11:17 So if G gave them the same gift he gave G2536
Ac 11:18 had no further objections and praised G, G2536
Ac 11:18 even to Gentiles G has granted G2536
Ac 11:23 saw what the grace of G had done, G2536
Ac 12: 5 church was earnestly praying to G for him. G2536
Ac 12:22 "This is the voice of a g, not of a man." G2536
Ac 12:23 because Herod did not give praise to G G2536
Ac 12:24 But the word of G continued to spread G2536
Ac 13: 5 proclaimed the word of G in the Jewish G2536
Ac 13: 7 because he wanted to hear the word of G. G2536
Ac 13:16 you Gentiles who worship G, G2536
Ac 13:17 The G of the people of Israel chose our G2536
Ac 13:20 G gave them judges until the time of NDT
Ac 13:22 David their king. G testified concerning him NDT
Ac 13:23 man's descendants G has brought to G2536

Ac 13:30 But G raised him from the dead, G2536
Ac 13:32 What G promised our ancestors NDT
Ac 13:34 G raised him from the dead so that he will NDT
Ac 13:34 As G has said, " 'I will give you the holy NDT
Ac 13:37 But the one whom G raised from the dead G2536
Ac 13:43 urged them to continue in the grace *of* G. G2536
Ac 13:46 had to speak the word *of* G to you first. G2536
Ac 14:15 these worthless things to the living G, G2536
Ac 14:22 hardships to enter the kingdom *of* G," G2536
Ac 14:26 to the grace *of* G for the work they had G2536
Ac 14:27 reported all that G had done through G2536
Ac 15: 4 reported everything G had done through G2536
Ac 15: 7 that some time ago G made a choice G2536
Ac 15: 8 G, who knows the heart, showed that he G2536
Ac 15:10 why do you try to test G by putting on the G2536
Ac 15:12 signs and wonders G had done among G2536
Ac 15:14 described to us how G first intervened to G2536
Ac 15:19 the Gentiles who are turning to G. G2536
Ac 16:10 concluding that G had called us to preach G2536
Ac 16:14 She was a worshiper *of* G. The Lord G2536
Ac 16:17 men are servants *of* the Most High G, G2536
Ac 16:25 were praying and singing hymns *to* G, G2536
Ac 16:34 because he had come to believe *in* G— G2536
Ac 17:13 was preaching the word *of* G at Berea, G2536
Ac 17:23 TO AN UNKNOWN G. So you are G2536
Ac 17:24 "The G who made the world and G2536
Ac 17:27 G did this so that they would seek him G2536
Ac 17:30 In the past G overlooked such ignorance G2536
Ac 18: 7 house of Titius Justus, a worshiper *of* G. G2536
Ac 18:11 a half, teaching them the word *of* G. G2536
Ac 18:13 people to worship G in ways contrary to G2536
Ac 18:26 to him the way *of* G more adequately. G2536
Ac 19: 8 persuasively about the kingdom *of* G. G2536
Ac 19:11 G did extraordinary miracles through Paul, G2536
Ac 20:21 they must turn to G in repentance and G2536
Ac 20:27 to proclaim to you the whole will *of* G. G2536
Ac 20:28 Be shepherds of the church *of* G, which he G2536
Ac 20:32 "Now I commit you *to* G and to the word G2536
Ac 21:19 in detail what G had done among the G2536
Ac 21:20 they praised G. Then they said to G2536
Ac 22: 3 just as zealous *for* G as any of you are G2536
Ac 22:14 'The G of our ancestors has chosen you to G2536
Ac 23: 1 fulfilled my duty *to* G in all good G2536
Ac 23: 3 Paul said to him, "G will strike you, you G2536
Ac 24:14 that I worship the G of our ancestors as a G2536
Ac 24:15 have the same hope in G as these men G2536
Ac 24:16 my conscience clear before G and man. G2536
Ac 26: 6 of my hope in what G has promised our G2536
Ac 26: 7 as they earnestly serve G day and night. NDT
Ac 26: 8 it incredible that G raises the dead? G2536
Ac 26:18 from the power of Satan to G, so that G2536
Ac 26:20 repent and turn to G and demonstrate G2536
Ac 26:22 But G has helped me to this very day; so I G2536
Ac 26:29 I pray *to* G that not only you but all who G2536
Ac 27:23 night an angel *of* the G to whom I belong G2536
Ac 27:24 G has graciously given you the lives G2536
Ac 27:25 I have faith *in* G that it will happen G2536
Ac 27:35 gave thanks *to* G in front of them all. G2536
Ac 28: 6 changed their minds and said he was a g. G2536
Ac 28:15 Paul thanked G and was encouraged. G2536
Ac 28:23 explaining about the kingdom *of* G, and G2536
Ac 28:31 the kingdom *of* G and taught about the G2536
Ro 1: 1 set apart for the gospel *of* G— G2536
Ro 1: 4 appointed the Son *of* G in power by his G2536
Ro 1: 7 who are loved *by* G and called to be G2536
Ro 1: 7 peace to you from G our Father and from G2536
Ro 1: 8 I thank my G through Jesus Christ for all of G2536
Ro 1: 9 G, whom I serve in my spirit in preaching G2536
Ro 1:16 it is the power *of* G that brings salvation G2536
Ro 1:17 the righteousness *of* G is revealed— G2536
Ro 1:18 The wrath *of* G is being revealed from G2536
Ro 1:19 may be known *about* G is plain to them, G2536
Ro 1:19 because G has made it plain to them. G2536
Ro 1:21 For although they knew G, they neither G2536
Ro 1:21 glorified him as G nor gave thanks to him, G2536
Ro 1:23 the glory *of* the immortal G for images G2536
Ro 1:24 Therefore G gave them over in the sinful G2536
Ro 1:25 They exchanged the truth *about* G for a lie, G2536
Ro 1:26 G gave them over to shameful lusts. G2536
Ro 1:28 worthwhile to retain the knowledge *of* G, G2536
Ro 1:28 so G gave them over to a depraved mind G2536
Ro 2: 6 G "will repay each person according to G4005S
Ro 2:11 For G does not show favoritism. G2536
Ro 2:16 place on the day when G judges people's G2536
Ro 2:17 if you rely on the law and boast in G; G2536
Ro 2:23 do you dishonor G by breaking the law? G2536
Ro 2:29 is not from other people, but from G. G2536
Ro 3: 2 been entrusted with the very words *of* G. G2536
Ro 3: 4 Let G be true, and every human being a G2536
Ro 3: 5 That G is unjust in bringing his wrath on G2536
Ro 3: 6 were so, how could G judge the world? G2536
Ro 3:11 there is no one who seeks G. G2536
Ro 3:18 "There is no fear *of* G before their eyes." G2536
Ro 3:19 the whole world held accountable *to* G. G2536
Ro 3:21 the righteousness *of* G has been made G2536
Ro 3:23 sinned and fall short of the glory *of* G, G2536
Ro 3:25 G presented Christ as a sacrifice of G2536
Ro 3:29 Or is G the God of Jews only? Is he not the NDT
Ro 3:29 Or is God the G of Jews only? Is he not the G2536
Ro 3:29 Is he not the G of Gentiles too? Yes, NDT
Ro 3:30 since there is only one G, who will justify G2536
Ro 4: 2 to boast about—but not before G. G2536
Ro 4: 3 "Abraham believed G, and it was credited G2536
Ro 4: 5 not work but trusts G who justifies the G3836S
Ro 4: 6 of the one to whom G credits G2536
Ro 4:17 He is our father in the sight of G, in whom G2536
Ro 4:17 the G who gives life to the dead and calls NDT
Ro 4:20 unbelief regarding the promise *of* G, G2536
Ro 4:20 in his faith and gave glory *to* G, G2536
Ro 4:21 persuaded that G had power to do what NDT
Ro 4:24 to whom G will credit righteousness NDT
Ro 5: 1 we have peace with G through our Lord G2536
Ro 5: 2 we boast in the hope of the glory *of* G. G2536
Ro 5: 8 But G demonstrates his own love for us in G2536
Ro 5:11 we also boast in G through our Lord G2536
Ro 5:16 Nor can the gift of G be compared with the NDT
Ro 6:10 but the life he lives, he lives *to* G. G2536
Ro 6:11 dead to sin but alive *to* G in Christ Jesus. G2536
Ro 6:13 offer yourselves *to* G as those who have G2536
Ro 6:17 But thanks be *to* G that, though you used G2536
Ro 6:22 from sin and have become slaves *of* G, G2536
Ro 6:23 the gift *of* G is eternal life in Christ G2536
Ro 7: 4 in order that we might bear fruit *for* G. G2536
Ro 7:25 Thanks be *to* G, who delivers me through G2536
Ro 8: 3 G did by sending his own Son in the G2536
Ro 8: 7 governed by the flesh is hostile to G; G2536
Ro 8: 8 in the realm of the flesh cannot please G. G2536
Ro 8: 9 if indeed the Spirit *of* G lives in you. G2536
Ro 8:14 led by the Spirit *of* G are the children of G2536
Ro 8:14 by the Spirit of God are the children *of* G. G2536
Ro 8:17 heirs *of* G and co-heirs with Christ G2536
Ro 8:19 the children *of* G to be revealed. G2536
Ro 8:21 freedom and glory of the children *of* G. G2536
Ro 8:27 people in accordance with the will of G. G2536
Ro 8:28 that in all things G works for the good of G2536
Ro 8:29 For those G foreknew he also predestined to NDT
Ro 8:31 to these things? If G is for us, who can be G2536
Ro 8:33 against those whom G has chosen? G2536
Ro 8:33 God has chosen? It is G who justifies. G2536
Ro 8:34 is at the right hand *of* G and is also G2536
Ro 8:39 us from the love *of* G that is in Christ G2536
Ro 9: 5 of the Messiah, who is G over all, forever G2536
Ro 9:14 then shall we say? Is G unjust? Not at all! G2536
Ro 9:18 "Therefore G has mercy on whom he wants to NDT
Ro 9:19 "Then why does G still blame us? For NDT
Ro 9:20 a human being, to talk back *to* G? G2536
Ro 9:22 What if G, although choosing to show his G2536
Ro 9:26 will be called 'children *of* the living G.' G2536
Ro 10: 1 desire and prayer to G for the Israelites is G2536
Ro 10: 2 about them that they are zealous *for* G, G2536
Ro 10: 3 the righteousness *of* G and sought to G2536
Ro 10: 9 in your heart that G raised him from the G2536
Ro 11: 1 Did G reject his people? By no G2536
Ro 11: 2 G did not reject his people, whom he G2536
Ro 11: 2 how he appealed *to* G against Israel: G2536
Ro 11: 8 "G gave them a spirit of stupor, eyes that G2536
Ro 11:21 For if G did not spare the natural branches G2536
Ro 11:22 therefore the kindness and sternness *of* G: G2536
Ro 11:23 for G is able to graft them in again. G2536
Ro 11:30 time disobedient *to* G have now received G2536
Ro 11:32 For G has bound everyone over to G2536
Ro 11:33 riches of the wisdom and knowledge *of* G! G2536
Ro 11:35 "Who has ever given *to* G, that God G899S
Ro 11:35 given to God, that G should repay them?" NDT
Ro 12: 1 holy and pleasing *to* G—this is your true G2536
Ro 12: 3 with the faith G has distributed to each G2536
Ro 13: 1 except that which G has established. G2536
Ro 13: 1 that exist have been established by G. G2536
Ro 13: 2 is rebelling against what G has instituted, G2536
Ro 14: 3 one who does, for G has accepted them. G2536
Ro 14: 6 they give thanks *to* G; and whoever G2536
Ro 14: 6 does so to the Lord and gives thanks *to* G. G2536
Ro 14:11 every tongue will acknowledge G. G2536
Ro 14:12 us will give an account of ourselves *to* G. G2536
Ro 14:17 For the kingdom *of* G is not a matter of G2536
Ro 14:18 way is pleasing *to* G and receives human G2536
Ro 14:20 destroy the work *of* G for the sake of food G2536
Ro 14:22 things keep between yourself and G. G2536
Ro 15: 5 May the G who gives endurance and G2536
Ro 15: 6 you may glorify the G and Father of our G2536
Ro 15: 7 in order to bring praise *to* G. G2536
Ro 15: 9 the Gentiles might glorify G for his mercy. G2536
Ro 15:13 May the G of hope fill you with all joy G2536
Ro 15:15 because of the grace G gave me G2536
Ro 15:16 duty of proclaiming the gospel *of* G, G2536
Ro 15:16 might become an offering acceptable to G, NDT
Ro 15:17 I glory in Christ Jesus in my service to G. G2536
Ro 15:18 the Gentiles to obey G by what I have said NDT
Ro 15:19 through the power of the Spirit *of* G. G2536
Ro 15:30 me in my struggle by praying to G for me. G2536
Ro 15:33 The G of peace be with you all. Amen. G2536
Ro 16:20 The G of peace will soon crush Satan G2536
Ro 16:26 writings by the command of the eternal G, G2536
Ro 16:27 *to* the only wise G be glory forever through G2536
1Co 1: 1 an apostle of Christ Jesus by the will *of* G, G2536
1Co 1: 2 To the church *of* G in Corinth, to those G2536
1Co 1: 3 peace to you from G our Father and the G2536
1Co 1: 4 I always thank my G for you because of G2536
1Co 1: 6 G thus confirming our testimony about Christ NDT
1Co 1: 9 G is faithful, who has called you into G2536
1Co 1:14 I thank G that I did not baptize any of you G2536
1Co 1:18 who are being saved it is the power *of* G. G2536
1Co 1:20 Has not G made foolish the wisdom of G2536
1Co 1:21 in the wisdom *of* G the world through G2536
1Co 1:21 G was pleased through the foolishness of G2536
1Co 1:24 to those whom G has called, both Jews NDT
1Co 1:24 Christ the power *of* G and the wisdom of G2536
1Co 1:24 the power of God and the wisdom *of* G. G2536
1Co 1:25 For the foolishness *of* G is wiser than G2536
1Co 1:25 the weakness *of* G is stronger than G2536
1Co 1:27 But G chose the foolish things of the world G2536
1Co 1:27 G chose the weak things of the world to G2536
1Co 1:28 G chose the lowly things of this world and G2536
1Co 1:30 who has become for us wisdom from G G2536
1Co 2: 1 proclaimed to you the testimony *about* G. G2536
1Co 2: 7 been hidden and that G destined for our G2536
1Co 2: 9 the things G has prepared for those who G2536
1Co 2:10 these are the things G has revealed to us G2536
1Co 2:10 all things, even the deep things *of* G. G2536
1Co 2:11 knows the thoughts *of* G except the Spirit G2536
1Co 2:11 the thoughts of God except the Spirit *of* G. G2536
1Co 2:12 the Spirit who is from G, so that we G2536
1Co 2:12 understand what G has freely given us G2536
1Co 2:14 from the Spirit *of* G but considers them G2536
1Co 3: 6 but G has been making it grow. G2536
1Co 3: 7 is anything, but only G, who makes things G2536
1Co 3:10 By the grace G has given me, I laid a G2536
1Co 3:17 God's temple, G will destroy that person G2536
1Co 3:23 you are of Christ, and Christ is *of* G. G2536
1Co 4: 1 with the mysteries G *has revealed.* G2536
1Co 4: 5 time each will receive their praise from G. G2536
1Co 4: 9 it seems to me that G has put us apostles G2536
1Co 4:20 For the kingdom *of* G is not a matter of talk G2536
1Co 5:13 G will judge those outside. "Expel the G2536
1Co 6: 9 will not inherit the kingdom *of* G? G2536
1Co 6:10 swindlers will inherit the kingdom *of* G. G2536
1Co 6:11 Jesus Christ and by the Spirit *of* our G. G2536
1Co 6:13 food, and G will destroy them both." G2536
1Co 6:14 By his power G raised the Lord from the G2536
1Co 6:19 whom you have received from G? G2536
1Co 6:20 Therefore honor G with your bodies. G2536
1Co 7: 7 But each of you has your own gift from G G2536
1Co 7:15 G has called us to live in peace. G2536
1Co 7:17 to them, just as G has called them. G2536
1Co 7:20 situation they were in when G called them. NDT
1Co 7:24 as responsible to G, should remain in the G2536
1Co 7:24 situation they were in when G called them. NDT
1Co 7:40 I think that I too have the Spirit *of* G. G2536
1Co 8: 3 But whoever loves G is known by God. G2536
1Co 8: 3 But whoever loves God is known by G. G899S
1Co 8: 4 and that "There is no G but one. G2536
1Co 8: 6 for us there is but one G, the Father G2536
1Co 8: 7 of it as having been **sacrificed to a g**, G1628
1Co 8: 8 But food does not bring us near *to* G; we G2536
1Co 9: 9 Is it about oxen that G is concerned? G2536
1Co 10: 5 G was not pleased with most of them G2536
1Co 10:13 And G is faithful; he will not let you be G2536
1Co 10:20 to demons, not *to* G, and I do not want G2536
1Co 10:30 because of something I thank G for? NDT
1Co 10:31 do it all for the glory *of* G. G2536
1Co 10:32 Greeks or the church *of* G— G2536
1Co 11: 3 and the head of Christ is G. G2536
1Co 11: 7 since he is the image and glory *of* G; but G2536
1Co 11:12 But everything comes from G. G2536
1Co 11:13 a woman to pray *to* G with her head G2536
1Co 11:16 other practice—nor do the churches *of* G. G2536
1Co 11:22 despise the church *of* G by humiliating G2536
1Co 12: 3 who is speaking by the Spirit *of* G says, G2536
1Co 12: 6 in everyone it is the same G at work. G2536
1Co 12:18 But in fact G has placed the parts in the G2536
1Co 12:24 But G has put the body together, giving G2536
1Co 12:28 And G has placed in the church first of all G2536
1Co 14: 2 does not speak to people but *to* G. G2536
1Co 14:16 when you are praising G in the Spirit, NDT
1Co 14:18 I thank G that I speak in tongues more G2536
1Co 14:25 So they will fall down and worship G G2536
1Co 14:25 exclaiming, "G is really among you!" G2536
1Co 14:28 the church and speak to himself and *to* G. G2536
1Co 14:33 For G is not a God of disorder but of peace G2536
1Co 14:33 For God is not a G of disorder but of peace NDT
1Co 14:36 Or did the word *of* G originate with you G2536
1Co 15: 9 because I persecuted the church *of* G. G2536
1Co 15:10 But by the grace *of* G I am what I am, and G2536
1Co 15:10 but the grace *of* G that was with me. G2536
1Co 15:15 then found to be false witnesses *about* G, G2536
1Co 15:15 have testified about G that he raised G2536
1Co 15:24 over the kingdom *to* G the Father after he G2536
1Co 15:27 is clear that this does not include G himself, NDT
1Co 15:28 under him, so that G may be all in all. G2536
1Co 15:34 there are some who are ignorant *of* G— G2536
1Co 15:38 But G gives it a body as he has G2536
1Co 15:50 blood cannot inherit the kingdom *of* G, G2536
1Co 15:57 But thanks be *to* G! He gives us the victory G2536
2Co 1: 1 an apostle of Christ Jesus by the will *of* G G2536
2Co 1: 1 To the church *of* G in Corinth, together G2536
2Co 1: 2 peace to you from G our Father and the G2536
2Co 1: 3 Praise be to the G and Father of our Lord G2536
2Co 1: 3 of compassion and the G of all comfort, G2536
2Co 1: 4 the comfort we ourselves receive from G. G2536
2Co 1: 9 we might not rely on ourselves but on G, G2536
2Co 1:18 But as surely as G is faithful, our message G2536
2Co 1:19 For the Son *of* G, Jesus Christ, who was G2536
2Co 1:20 matter how many promises G has made, G2536
2Co 1:20 "Amen" is spoken by us to the glory *of* G. G2536
2Co 1:21 Now it is G who makes both us and you G2536
2Co 1:23 I call G as my witness—and I stake my life G2536

Book	Ref	Context	Number
2Co	2:14	But thanks be *to* **G**, who always leads us	G2536
2Co	2:15	For we are *to* **G** the pleasing aroma of	G2536
2Co	2:17	we do not peddle the word *of* **G** for profit.	G2536
2Co	2:17	in Christ we speak before **G** with sincerity	G2536
2Co	2:17	God with sincerity, as those sent from **G**.	G2536
2Co	3: 3	with ink but with the Spirit *of* the living **G**,	G2536
2Co	3: 4	we have through Christ before **G**.	G2536
2Co	3: 5	our competence comes from **G**.	G2536
2Co	4: 2	do we distort the word *of* **G**.	G2536
2Co	4: 2	to everyone's conscience in the sight of **G**.	G2536
2Co	4: 4	The **g** of this age has blinded the minds of	G2536
2Co	4: 4	the glory of Christ, who is the image *of* **G**.	G2536
2Co	4: 6	For **G**, who said, "Let light shine out of	G2536
2Co	4: 7	power is *from* **G** and not from us.	G2536
2Co	4:15	thanksgiving to overflow to the glory *of* **G**.	G2536
2Co	5: 1	we have a building from **G**, an eternal	G2536
2Co	5: 5	fashioned us for this very purpose is **G**,	G2536
2Co	5:11	What we are is plain *to* **G**, and I hope it is	G2536
2Co	5:13	as some say, it is *for* **G**; if we are in our	G2536
2Co	5:18	All this is from **G**, who reconciled us to	G2536
2Co	5:19	that **G** was reconciling the world to himself	G2536
2Co	5:20	as though **G** were making his appeal	G2536
2Co	5:20	you on Christ's behalf: Be reconciled *to* **G**.	G2536
2Co	5:21	**G** made him who had no sin to be sin for us	NDT
2Co	5:21	we might become the righteousness *of* **G**.	G2536
2Co	6: 4	as servants *of* **G** we commend ourselves	G2536
2Co	6: 7	in truthful speech and in the power *of* **G**	G2536
2Co	6:16	there between the temple *of* **G** and idols?	G2536
2Co	6:16	For we are the temple *of* the living **G**.	G2536
2Co	6:16	of the living God. As **G** has said: "I will	G2536
2Co	6:16	I will be their **G**, and they will be my	G2536
2Co	7: 1	perfecting holiness out of reverence *for* **G**.	G2536
2Co	7: 6	But **G**, who comforts the downcast	G2536
2Co	7: 9	became sorrowful as **G** intended and so	G2536
2Co	7:12	rather that before **G** you could see for	G2536
2Co	8: 1	about the grace that **G** has given the	G2536
2Co	8: 5	and then by the will *of* **G** also to us.	G2536
2Co	8:16	Thanks be *to* **G**, who put into the heart of	G2536
2Co	9: 7	compulsion, for **G** loves a cheerful giver.	G2536
2Co	9: 8	And **G** is able to bless you abundantly, so	G2536
2Co	9:11	generosity will result in thanksgiving *to* **G**.	G2536
2Co	9:12	in many expressions of thanks *to* **G**.	G2536
2Co	9:13	others will praise **G** for the obedience that	G2536
2Co	9:14	of the surpassing grace **G** has given you.	G2536
2Co	9:15	Thanks be *to* **G** for his indescribable gift!	G2536
2Co	10: 5	sets itself up against the knowledge *of* **G**,	G2536
2Co	10:13	sphere of service **G** himself has assigned	G2536
2Co	11: 7	preaching the gospel *of* **G** to you free of	G2536
2Co	11:11	Because I do not love you? **G** knows I do!	G2536
2Co	11:31	The **G** and Father of the Lord Jesus, who is	G2536
2Co	12: 2	out of the body I do not know—**G** knows.	G2536
2Co	12: 3	the body I do not know, but **G** knows—	G2536
2Co	12:19	in the sight of **G** as those in Christ;	G2536
2Co	12:21	when I come again my **G** will humble me	G2536
2Co	13: 7	Now we pray to **G** that you will not do	G2536
2Co	13:11	And the **G** of love and peace will be with	G2536
2Co	13:14	the love *of* **G**, and the fellowship	G2536
Gal	1: 1	by Jesus Christ and **G** the Father, who	G2536
Gal	1: 3	peace to you from **G** our Father and the	G2536
Gal	1: 4	according to the will *of* our **G** and Father,	G2536
Gal	1:10	the approval of human beings, or *of* **G**?	G2536
Gal	1:13	the church *of* **G** and tried to destroy	G2536
Gal	1:15	But when **G**, who set me apart from my	G2536
Gal	1:20	I assure you before **G** that what I am	G2536
Gal	1:24	And they praised **G** because of me.	G2536
Gal	2: 6	**G** does not show favoritism	G2536
Gal	2: 8	For **G**, who was at work in Peter as an	NDT
Gal	2:19	I died to the law so that I might live *for* **G**.	G2536
Gal	2:20	I live by faith in the Son *of* **G**, who loved	G2536
Gal	2:21	I do not set aside the grace *of* **G**, for if	G2536
Gal	3: 5	does **G** give you his Spirit and work	G3836S
Gal	3: 6	So also Abraham "believed **G**, and it was	G2536
Gal	3: 8	Scripture foresaw that **G** would justify the	G2536
Gal	3:11	relies on the law is justified before **G**,	G2536
Gal	3:17	established by **G** and thus do away with	G2536
Gal	3:18	**G** in his grace gave it to Abraham	G2536
Gal	3:20	implies more than one party; but **G** is one.	G2536
Gal	3:21	therefore, opposed to the promises *of* **G**?	G2536
Gal	3:26	you are all children *of* **G** through faith,	G2536
Gal	4: 4	time had fully come, **G** sent his Son, born	G2536
Gal	4: 6	**G** sent the Spirit of his Son into our hearts,	G2536
Gal	4: 7	his child, **G** has made you also an heir.	G2536
Gal	4: 8	when you did not know **G**, you were	G2536
Gal	4: 9	But now that you know **G**—or rather are	G2536
Gal	4: 9	rather are known by **G**—how is it that	G2536
Gal	4:14	welcomed me as if I were an angel *of* **G**,	G2536
Gal	5:21	like this will not inherit the kingdom *of* **G**.	G2536
Gal	6: 7	not be deceived: **G** cannot be mocked.	G2536
Gal	6:16	who follow this rule—to the Israel *of* **G**.	G2536
Eph	1: 1	an apostle of Christ Jesus by the will *of* **G**	G2536
Eph	1: 2	peace to you from **G** our Father and the	G2536
Eph	1: 3	Praise be to the **G** and Father of our Lord	G2536
Eph	1:17	I keep asking that the **G** of our Lord Jesus	G2536
Eph	1:22	And **G** placed all things under his feet and	NDT
Eph	2: 4	great love for us, **G**, who is rich in mercy,	G2536
Eph	2: 6	And **G** raised us up with Christ and seated us	NDT
Eph	2: 8	is not from yourselves, it is the gift *of* **G**—	G2536
Eph	2:10	which **G** prepared in advance for us to do.	G2536
Eph	2:12	without hope and **without G** in the world.	G117
Eph	2:16	both of them *to* **G** through the cross,	G2536
Eph	2:22	a dwelling in which **G** lives by his Spirit.	G2536
Eph	3: 9	which for ages past was kept hidden in **G**	G2536
Eph	3:10	manifold wisdom *of* **G** should be made	G2536
Eph	3:12	him we may approach **G** with freedom and	NDT
Eph	3:19	to the measure of all the fullness *of* **G**.	G2536
Eph	4: 6	one **G** and Father of all, who is over all	G2536
Eph	4:13	of the Son *of* **G** and become mature,	G2536
Eph	4:18	from the life *of* **G** because of the	G2536
Eph	4:24	created to be like **G** in true righteousness	G2536
Eph	4:30	And do not grieve the Holy Spirit *of* **G**	G2536
Eph	4:32	each other, just as in Christ **G** forgave you.	G2536
Eph	5: 2	as a fragrant offering and sacrifice *to* **G**.	G2536
Eph	5: 5	in the kingdom of Christ and *of* **G**.	G2536
Eph	5:20	always giving thanks *to* **G** the Father for	G2536
Eph	6: 6	doing the will *of* **G** from your heart.	G2536
Eph	6:11	Put on the full armor *of* **G**, so that you can	G2536
Eph	6:13	Therefore put on the full armor *of* **G**, so	G2536
Eph	6:17	sword of the Spirit, which is the word *of* **G**.	G2536
Eph	6:23	love with faith from **G** the Father and the	G2536
Php	1: 2	peace to you from **G** our Father and the	G2536
Php	1: 3	I thank my **G** every time I remember you.	G2536
Php	1: 8	**G** can testify how I long for all of you with	G2536
Php	1:11	Jesus Christ—to the glory and praise *of* **G**.	G2536
Php	1:28	that you will be saved—and that by **G**.	G2536
Php	2: 6	being in very nature **G**, did not consider	G2536
Php	2: 6	consider equality *with* **G** something to be	G2536
Php	2: 9	Therefore **G** exalted him to the highest	G2536
Php	2:11	Christ is Lord, to the glory *of* **G** the Father.	G2536
Php	2:13	it is **G** who works in you to will and to	G2536
Php	2:15	"children *of* **G** without fault in a warped	G2536
Php	2:27	But **G** had mercy on him, and not on him	G2536
Php	3: 3	we who serve **G** by his Spirit, who boast	G2536
Php	3: 9	that comes from **G** on the basis of faith.	G2536
Php	3:14	win the prize for which **G** has called me	G2536
Php	3:15	that too **G** will make clear to you.	G2536
Php	3:19	destruction, their **g** is their stomach, and	G2536
Php	4: 6	thanksgiving, present your requests to **G**.	G2536
Php	4: 7	And the peace *of* **G**, which transcends all	G2536
Php	4: 9	And the **G** of peace will be with you	G2536
Php	4:18	an acceptable sacrifice, pleasing *to* **G**.	G2536
Php	4:19	And my **G** will meet all your needs	G2536
Php	4:20	*To* our **G** and Father be glory for ever and	G2536
Col	1: 1	an apostle of Christ Jesus by the will *of* **G**	G2536
Col	1: 2	Grace and peace to you from **G** our Father.	G2536
Col	1: 3	We always thank **G**, the Father of our Lord	G2536
Col	1: 9	We continually ask **G** to fill you with the	NDT
Col	1:10	growing in the knowledge *of* **G**,	G2536
Col	1:15	The Son is the image *of* the invisible **G**	G2536
Col	1:19	For **G** was pleased to have all his fullness	NDT
Col	1:21	were alienated from **G** and were enemies in	NDT
Col	1:25	by the commission **G** gave me to present	G2536
Col	1:25	to you the word *of* **G** in its fullness—	G2536
Col	1:27	To them **G** has chosen to make known	G2536
Col	2: 2	that they may know the mystery *of* **G**,	G2536
Col	2:12	through your faith in the working *of* **G**,	G2536
Col	2:13	of your flesh, **G** made you alive with Christ.	NDT
Col	2:19	sinews, grows as **G** causes it to grow.	G2536
Col	3: 1	Christ is, seated at the right hand *of* **G**.	G2536
Col	3: 3	your life is now hidden with Christ in **G**.	G2536
Col	3: 6	of these, the wrath *of* **G** is coming.	G2536
Col	3:16	singing *to* **G** with gratitude in your hearts.	G2536
Col	3:17	giving thanks *to* **G** the Father through him.	G2536
Col	4: 3	that **G** may open a door for our message	G2536
Col	4:11	my co-workers for the kingdom *of* **G**,	G2536
Col	4:12	you may stand firm in all the will *of* **G**,	G2536
1Th	1: 1	the Thessalonians in **G** the Father and the	G2536
1Th	1: 2	We always thank **G** for all of you and	G2536
1Th	1: 3	remember before our **G** and Father your	G2536
1Th	1: 4	brothers and sisters loved by **G**, that he	G2536
1Th	1: 8	your faith in **G** has become known	G2536
1Th	1: 9	how you turned to **G** from idols to serve	G2536
1Th	1: 9	from idols to serve the living and true **G**,	G2536
1Th	2: 2	the help of our **G** we dared to tell you	G2536
1Th	2: 4	those approved by **G** to be entrusted with	G2536
1Th	2: 4	We are not trying to please people but **G**	G2536
1Th	2: 5	mask to cover up greed—**G** is our witness.	G2536
1Th	2: 8	not only the gospel *of* **G** but our lives as	G2536
1Th	2: 9	we preached the gospel *of* **G** to you.	G2536
1Th	2:10	are witnesses, and so is **G**, of how holy,	G2536
1Th	2:12	urging you to live lives worthy *of* **G**,	G2536
1Th	2:13	And we also thank **G** continually because	G2536
1Th	2:13	when you received the word *of* **G**, which	G2536
1Th	2:13	the word *of* **G**, which is indeed at	G2536
1Th	2:15	They displease **G** and are hostile to	G2536
1Th	2:16	The wrath of **G** has come upon them at last.	NDT
1Th	3: 9	How can we thank **G** enough for you in	G2536
1Th	3: 9	in the presence of our **G** because of you?	G2536
1Th	3:11	Now may our **G** and Father himself and	G2536
1Th	3:13	presence of our **G** and Father when our	G2536
1Th	4: 1	you how to live in order to please **G**,	G2536
1Th	4: 5	lust like the pagans, who do not know **G**;	G2536
1Th	4: 7	For **G** did not call us to be impure, but to	G2536
1Th	4: 8	does not reject a human being but **G**,	G2536
1Th	4: 8	the very **G** who gives you his Holy Spirit.	NDT
1Th	4: 9	have been **taught by G** to love each other.	G2531
1Th	4:14	so we believe that **G** will bring with Jesus	G2536
1Th	4:16	archangel and with the trumpet call *of* **G**,	G2536
1Th	5: 9	For **G** did not appoint us to suffer wrath	G2536
1Th	5:23	May **G** himself, the God of peace, sanctify	G2536
1Th	5:23	May God himself, the **G** of peace, sanctify	NDT
2Th	1: 1	the Thessalonians in **G** our Father and the	G2536
2Th	1: 2	peace to you from **G** the Father and the	G2536
2Th	1: 3	We ought always to thank **G** for you	G2536
2Th	1: 5	be counted worthy of the kingdom *of* **G**,	G2536
2Th	1: 6	**G** is just: He will pay back trouble to those	G2536
2Th	1: 8	who do not know **G** and do not obey the	G2536
2Th	1:11	that our **G** may make you worthy of his	G2536
2Th	1:12	to the grace *of* our **G** and the Lord Jesus	G2536
2Th	2: 4	that is called **G** or is worshiped,	G2536
2Th	2: 4	temple, proclaiming himself to be **G**.	G2536
2Th	2:11	For this reason **G** sends them a powerful	G2536
2Th	2:13	But we ought always to thank **G** for you	G2536
2Th	2:13	because **G** chose you as firstfruits to be	G2536
2Th	2:16	Jesus Christ himself and **G** our Father,	G2536
1Ti	1: 1	by the command *of* **G** our Savior and of	G2536
1Ti	1: 2	mercy and peace from **G** the Father and	G2536
1Ti	1:11	concerning the glory *of* the blessed **G**,	G2536
1Ti	1:17	invisible, the only **G**, be honor and glory	G2536
1Ti	2: 3	This is good, and pleases **G** our Savior,	G2536
1Ti	2: 5	For there is one **G** and one mediator	G2536
1Ti	2: 5	one mediator *between* **G** and mankind,	G2536
1Ti	2:10	women who profess *to* **worship G**.	G2537
1Ti	3:15	which is the church *of* the living **G**, the	G2536
1Ti	4: 3	which **G** created to be received with	G2536
1Ti	4: 4	For everything **G** created is good, and	G2536
1Ti	4: 5	consecrated by the word *of* **G** and prayer.	G2536
1Ti	4:10	we have put our hope in the living **G**,	G2536
1Ti	5: 4	grandparents, for this is pleasing to **G**.	G2536
1Ti	5: 5	puts her hope in **G** and continues night	G2536
1Ti	5: 5	night and day to pray and to ask **G** for help.	NDT
1Ti	5:21	in the sight of **G** and Christ Jesus and the	G2536
1Ti	6:11	But you, man *of* **G**, flee from all this, and	G2536
1Ti	6:13	In the sight of **G**, who gives life to	G2536
1Ti	6:15	which **G** will bring about in his own time	NDT
1Ti	6:15	in his own time—**G**, the blessed and only	NDT
1Ti	6:17	to put their hope in **G**, who richly	G2536
2Ti	1: 1	an apostle of Christ Jesus by the will *of* **G**	G2536
2Ti	1: 2	mercy and peace from **G** the Father and	G2536
2Ti	1: 3	I thank **G**, whom I serve, as my ancestors	G2536
2Ti	1: 6	remind you to fan into flame the gift *of* **G**,	G2536
2Ti	1: 7	For the Spirit **G** gave us does not make us	G2536
2Ti	1: 8	the gospel, by the power *of* **G**.	G2536
2Ti	2:14	Warn them before **G** against quarreling	G2536
2Ti	2:15	to present yourself *to* **G** as one approved,	G2536
2Ti	2:25	in the hope that **G** will grant them	G2536
2Ti	3: 4	of pleasure rather than **lovers of G**—	G5806
2Ti	3:17	so that the servant *of* **G** may be thoroughly	G2536
2Ti	4: 1	In the presence of **G** and of Christ Jesus	G2536
Titus	1: 1	a servant *of* **G** and an apostle of Jesus	G2536
Titus	1: 2	of eternal life, which **G**, who does not lie,	G2536
Titus	1: 3	to me by the command *of* **G** our Savior,	G2536
Titus	1: 4	Grace and peace from **G** the Father and	G2536
Titus	1:16	They claim to know **G**, but by their actions	G2536
Titus	2: 5	so that no one will malign the word *of* **G**.	G2536
Titus	2:10	make the teaching *about* **G** our Savior	G2536
Titus	2:11	For the grace *of* **G** has appeared that	G2536
Titus	2:13	of the glory *of* our great **G** and Savior,	G2536
Titus	3: 4	kindness and love *of* **G** our Savior	G2536
Titus	3: 8	who have trusted *in* **G** may be careful to	G2536
Phm	3	peace to you from **G** our Father and the	G2536
Phm	4	I always thank my **G** as I remember you in	G2536
Heb	1: 1	In the past **G** spoke to our ancestors	G2536
Heb	1: 5	For to which of the angels did **G** ever say	NDT
Heb	1: 6	when **G** brings his firstborn into the world	NDT
Heb	1: 8	"Your throne, *O* **G**, will last for ever and	G2536
Heb	1: 9	hated wickedness; therefore **G**, your God,	G2536
Heb	1: 9	therefore God, your **G**, has set you above	G2536
Heb	1:13	To which of the angels did **G** ever say, "Sit	NDT
Heb	2: 4	**G** also testified to it by signs, wonders	G2536
Heb	2: 8	**G** left nothing that is not subject to them.	NDT
Heb	2: 9	so that by the grace *of* **G** he might taste	G2536
Heb	2:10	it was fitting that **G**, for whom and	G899S
Heb	2:13	and the children **G** has given me.	G2536
Heb	2:17	faithful high priest in service to **G**,	G2536
Heb	3: 4	**G** is the builder of everything.	G2536
Heb	3: 5	to what would be spoken by **G** in the future.	NDT
Heb	3:12	heart that turns away from the living **G**.	G2536
Heb	3:18	And to whom did **G** swear that they would	NDT
Heb	4: 3	that rest, just as **G** has said, "So I declared	NDT
Heb	4: 4	"On the seventh day **G** rested from all his	G2536
Heb	4: 7	**G** again set a certain day, calling it "Today."	NDT
Heb	4: 8	**G** would not have spoken later about	NDT
Heb	4: 9	a Sabbath-rest for the people *of* **G**;	G2536
Heb	4:10	from their works, just as **G** did from his.	G2536
Heb	4:12	For the word *of* **G** is alive and active	G2536
Heb	4:14	Jesus the Son *of* **G**, let us hold firmly	G2536
Heb	5: 1	the people in matters related to **G**,	G2536
Heb	5: 4	he receives it when called by **G**, just	G2536
Heb	5: 5	But **G** said to him, "You are my Son; today I	NDT
Heb	5:10	was designated by **G** to be high priest in	G2536
Heb	6: 1	acts that lead to death, and of faith in **G**,	G2536
Heb	6: 3	And **G** permitting, we will do so.	G2536
Heb	6: 5	of the word *of* **G** and the powers of	G2536
Heb	6: 6	crucifying the Son *of* **G** all over again and	G2536
Heb	6: 7	it is farmed receives the blessing of **G**.	G2536
Heb	6:10	**G** is not unjust; he will not forget your work	G2536
Heb	6:13	When **G** made his promise to Abraham	G2536
Heb	6:17	Because **G** wanted to make the	G2536
Heb	6:18	**G** did this so that, by two unchangeable	NDT
Heb	6:18	in which it is impossible *for* **G** to lie,	G2536
Heb	7: 1	king of Salem and priest *of* **G** Most High.	G2536
Heb	7: 3	resembling the Son *of* **G**, he remains a	G2536
Heb	7:19	introduced, by which we draw near *to* **G**.	G2536
Heb	7:21	priest with an oath when **G** said to him:	G3836S
Heb	7:25	those who come to **G** through him,	G2536
Heb	8: 8	But **G** found fault with the people and said	NDT

Heb 8:10 I will be their G, and they will be my G2536
Heb 9:14 Spirit offered himself unblemished *to* G, G2536
Heb 9:14 so that we may serve the living G! G2536
Heb 9:20 which G has commanded you to keep." G2536
Heb 10: 7 I have come to do your will, my G. G2536
Heb 10:12 he sat down at the right hand *of* G, G2536
Heb 10:21 have a great priest over the house *of* G, G2536
Heb 10:22 let us draw near to G with a sincere heart NDT
Heb 10:27 fire that will consume the enemies of G. NDT
Heb 10:29 who has trampled the Son *of* G underfoot, G2536
Heb 10:31 thing to fall into the hands *of* the living G. G2536
Heb 10:36 so that when you have done the will *of* G, G2536
Heb 11: 4 By faith Abel brought G a better offering G2536
Heb 11: 4 when G spoke well of his offerings. G2536
Heb 11: 5 because G had taken him away. G2536
Heb 11: 5 was commended as one who pleased G. G2536
Heb 11: 6 without faith it is impossible to please G, G2536
Heb 11:10 whose architect and builder is G. G2536
Heb 11:16 Therefore G is not ashamed to be called G2536
Heb 11:16 God is not ashamed to be called their G, G2536
Heb 11:17 faith Abraham, when G tested him, offered NDT
Heb 11:18 even though G had said to him, "It is NDT
Heb 11:19 reasoned that G could even raise the G2536
Heb 11:25 with the people *of* G rather than to enjoy G2536
Heb 11:40 since G had planned something better G2536
Heb 12: 2 down at the right hand of the throne *of* G. G2536
Heb 12: 7 G is treating you as his children. G2536
Heb 12:10 but G disciplines us for our good G3836[S]
Heb 12:15 short of the grace *of* G and that no bitter G2536
Heb 12:22 to the city *of* the living G, the heavenly G2536
Heb 12:23 You have come *to* G, the Judge of all, to G2536
Heb 12:28 so worship G acceptably with G2536
Heb 12:29 our "G is a consuming fire. G2536
Heb 13: 4 G will judge the adulterer and all the G2536
Heb 13: 5 you have, because G has said, "Never will G899[S]
Heb 13: 7 leaders, who spoke the word *of* G to you. G2536
Heb 13:15 us continually offer *to* G a sacrifice of G2536
Heb 13:16 with such sacrifices G is pleased. G2536
Heb 13:20 Now may the G of peace, who through G2536
Jas 1: 1 a servant *of* G and of the Lord Jesus Christ, G2536
Jas 1: 5 you should ask G, who gives generously G2536
Jas 1:13 no one should say, "G is tempting me." G2536
Jas 1:13 For G cannot be tempted by evil, nor G2536
Jas 1:20 produce the righteousness *that* G *desires*. G2536
Jas 1:27 Religion that G our Father accepts as pure G2536
Jas 2: 5 Has not G chosen those who are poor in G2536
Jas 2:19 You believe that there is one G. Good G2536
Jas 2:23 "Abraham believed G, and it was credited G2536
Jas 4: 2 You do not have because you do not ask G. NDT
Jas 4: 4 with the world means enmity *against* G? G2536
Jas 4: 4 of the world becomes an enemy *of* G. G2536
Jas 4: 6 "G opposes the proud but shows favor to G2536
Jas 4: 7 yourselves, then, *to* G. Resist the devil, G2536
Jas 4: 8 Come near *to* G and he will come near to G2536
1Pe 1: 2 to the foreknowledge *of* G the Father, G2536
1Pe 1: 3 Praise be to the G and Father of our Lord G2536
1Pe 1:21 Through him you believe in G, who raised G2536
1Pe 1:21 and so your faith and hope are in G. G2536
1Pe 1:23 the living and enduring word *of* G. G2536
1Pe 2: 4 chosen by G and precious to him— G2536
1Pe 2: 5 acceptable *to* G through Jesus Christ G2536
1Pe 2:10 now you are the people *of* G; once G2536
1Pe 2:12 deeds and glorify G on the day he visits G2536
1Pe 2:17 of believers, fear G, honor the emperor. G2536
1Pe 2:18 in reverent fear of G submit yourselves to NDT
1Pe 2:19 suffering because they are conscious *of* G. G2536
1Pe 2:20 endure it, this is commendable before G. G2536
1Pe 3: 5 who put their hope in G used to adorn G2536
1Pe 3:18 the unrighteous, to bring you to G. G2536
1Pe 3:20 long ago when G waited patiently in the G2536
1Pe 3:21 pledge of a clear conscience toward G. G2536
1Pe 4: 2 desires, but rather for the will *of* G. G2536
1Pe 4: 6 live according to G in regard to the G2536
1Pe 4:11 so as one who speaks the very words *of* G. G2536
1Pe 4:11 should do so with the strength G provides, G2536
1Pe 4:11 so that in all things G may be praised G2536
1Pe 4:14 the Spirit of glory and *of* G rests on you. G2536
1Pe 4:16 praise G that you bear that name. G2536
1Pe 4:17 those who do not obey the gospel *of* G? G2536
1Pe 5: 2 you are willing, as G wants you to be; not G2536
1Pe 5: 5 "G opposes the proud but shows favor to G2536
1Pe 5:10 And the G of all grace, who called you to G2536
1Pe 5:12 testifying that this is the true grace *of* G. G2536
2Pe 1: 1 righteousness *of* our G and Savior Jesus G2536
2Pe 1: 2 the knowledge *of* G and of Jesus our Lord G2536
2Pe 1:17 glory from G the Father when the G2536
2Pe 1:21 spoke from G as they were carried along G2536
2Pe 2: 4 For if G did not spare angels when they G2536
2Pe 3:12 forward to the day *of* G and speed its G2536
2Pe 3:15 wrote you with the wisdom that G gave him. NDT
1Jn 1: 5 G is light; in him there is no darkness at G2536
1Jn 2: 5 love *for* G is truly made complete in them. G2536
1Jn 2:14 the word *of* G lives in you, and G2536
1Jn 2:17 whoever does the will *of* G lives forever. G2536
1Jn 3: 1 that we should be called children *of* G! G2536
1Jn 3: 2 now we are children *of* G, and what we G2536
1Jn 3: 8 The reason the Son *of* G appeared was to G2536
1Jn 3: 9 one who is born of G will continue to sin G2536
1Jn 3: 9 because they have been born of G. G2536
1Jn 3:10 who the children *of* G are and who the G2536
1Jn 3:17 how can the love *of* G be in that person? G2536
1Jn 3:20 we know that G is greater than our hearts G2536
1Jn 3:21 we have confidence before G G2536
1Jn 4: 1 the spirits to see whether they are from G, G2536
1Jn 4: 2 is how you can recognize the Spirit *of* G: G2536
1Jn 4: 2 Christ has come in the flesh is from G, G2536
1Jn 4: 3 not acknowledge Jesus is not from G. G2536
1Jn 4: 4 are from G and have overcome them G2536
1Jn 4: 6 We are from G, and whoever knows God G2536
1Jn 4: 6 whoever knows G listens to us; but G2536
1Jn 4: 6 whoever is not from G does not listen to G2536
1Jn 4: 7 love one another, for love comes from G. G2536
1Jn 4: 7 loves has been born of G and knows God. G2536
1Jn 4: 7 loves has been born of God and knows G. G2536
1Jn 4: 8 Whoever does not love does not know G G2536
1Jn 4: 8 does not know God, because G is love. G2536
1Jn 4: 9 This is how G showed his love among us G2536
1Jn 4:10 not that we loved G, but that he loved us G2536
1Jn 4:11 Dear friends, since G so loved us, we also G2536
1Jn 4:12 No one has ever seen G; but if we love G2536
1Jn 4:12 G lives in us and his love is made G2536
1Jn 4:15 acknowledges that Jesus is the Son *of* G, G2536
1Jn 4:15 G lives in them and they in God. G2536
1Jn 4:15 God lives in them and they in G. G2536
1Jn 4:16 know and rely on the love G has for us. G2536
1Jn 4:16 love God has for us. G is love. Whoever G2536
1Jn 4:16 Whoever lives in love lives in G, and God G2536
1Jn 4:16 lives in love lives in God, and G in them. G2536
1Jn 4:20 claims to love G yet hates a brother G2536
1Jn 4:20 cannot love G, whom they have not G2536
1Jn 4:21 Anyone who loves G must also love their G2536
1Jn 5: 1 that Jesus is the Christ is born of G, G2536
1Jn 5: 2 we know that we love the children *of* G: G2536
1Jn 5: 2 by loving G and carrying out his G2536
1Jn 5: 3 this is love *for* G: to keep his G2536
1Jn 5: 4 everyone born of G overcomes the world G2536
1Jn 5: 5 who believes that Jesus is the Son *of* G. G2536
1Jn 5: 9 is greater because it is the testimony *of* G, G2536
1Jn 5:10 believes in the Son *of* G accepts this G2536
1Jn 5:10 does not believe G has made him out to G2536
1Jn 5:10 the testimony G has given about his G2536
1Jn 5:11 G has given us eternal life, and this life is G2536
1Jn 5:12 not have the Son *of* G does not have life. G2536
1Jn 5:13 the name of the Son *of* G so that you may G2536
1Jn 5:14 confidence we have in approaching G: G899[S]
1Jn 5:16 you should pray and G will give them life. NDT
1Jn 5:18 that anyone born of G does not continue G2536
1Jn 5:18 One who was born of G keeps them safe, G2536
1Jn 5:19 We know that we are children of G, and G2536
1Jn 5:20 also that the Son *of* G has come and has G2536
1Jn 5:20 He is the true G and eternal life. G2536
2Jn 1 To the lady **chosen** *by G* and to her children AIT
2Jn 3 peace from G the Father and from G2536
2Jn 9 in the teaching of Christ does not have G; G2536
2Jn 13 your sister, who is **chosen** *by G*, send their AIT
3Jn 6 on their way in a manner that honors G. G2536
3Jn 11 Anyone who does what is good is from G G2536
3Jn 11 who does what is evil has not seen G. G2536
Jude 1 who are loved in G the Father and kept G2536
Jude 4 pervert the grace *of* our G into a license G2536
Jude 25 *to* the only G our Savior be glory, majesty G2536
Rev 1: 1 which G gave him to show his servants G2536
Rev 1: 2 the word *of* G and the testimony of Jesus G2536
Rev 1: 6 priests *to serve* his G and Father— G2536
Rev 1: 8 says the Lord G, "who is, and who was G2536
Rev 1: 9 of the word *of* G and the testimony G2536
Rev 2: 7 tree of life, which is in the paradise *of* G. G2536
Rev 2:18 These are the words of the Son *of* G G2536
Rev 3: 1 the seven spirits *of* G and the seven stars. G2536
Rev 3: 2 deeds unfinished in the sight of my G. G2536
Rev 3:12 I will make a pillar in the temple *of* my G. G2536
Rev 3:12 them the name *of* my G and the name of G2536
Rev 3:12 my God and the name of the city *of* my G, G2536
Rev 3:12 is coming down out of heaven from my G; G2536
Rev 4: 5 These are the seven spirits *of* G. G2536
Rev 4: 8 holy is the Lord G Almighty,' who was, G2536
Rev 4:11 our Lord and G, to receive glory G2536
Rev 5: 6 the seven spirits *of* G sent out into all the G2536
Rev 5: 9 you purchased *for* G persons from every G2536
Rev 5:10 be a kingdom and priests *to serve* our G, G2536
Rev 6: 9 of the word *of* G and the testimony G2536
Rev 7: 2 the east, having the seal *of* the living G. G2536
Rev 7: 3 on the foreheads of the servants *of* our G." G2536
Rev 7:10 "Salvation *belongs to* our G, who sits on G2536
Rev 7:11 faces before the throne and worshiped G, G2536
Rev 7:12 strength be *to* our G for ever and ever G2536
Rev 7:15 before the throne *of* G and serve him day G2536
Rev 7:17 'And G will wipe away every tear from G2536
Rev 8: 2 the seven angels who stand before G, G2536
Rev 8: 4 went up before G from the angel's hand. G2536
Rev 9: 4 not have the seal *of* G on their foreheads. G2536
Rev 9:13 horns of the golden altar that is before G. G2536
Rev 10: 7 the mystery *of* G will be accomplished G2536
Rev 11: 1 measure the temple *of* G and the altar, G2536
Rev 11:11 the breath of life from G entered them, G2536
Rev 11:13 gave glory *to* the G of heaven. G2536
Rev 11:16 were seated on their thrones before G, G2536
Rev 11:16 fell on their faces and worshiped G, G2536
Rev 11:17 thanks to you, Lord G Almighty, the One G2536
Rev 12: 5 was snatched up to G and to his throne. G2536
Rev 12: 6 to a place prepared for her by G, G2536
Rev 12:10 the power and the kingdom *of* our G, G2536
Rev 12:10 accuses them before our G day and night, G2536
Rev 13: 6 It opened its mouth to blaspheme G, and G2536
Rev 14: 4 offered as firstfruits *to* G and the Lamb. G2536
Rev 14: 7 a loud voice, "Fear G and give him glory G2536
Rev 14:12 *on the part of* the **people of** G who keep G41
Rev 15: 2 They held harps *given* them *by* G G2536
Rev 15: 3 are your deeds, Lord G Almighty. G2536
Rev 15: 7 golden bowls filled with the wrath *of* G, G2536
Rev 15: 8 from the glory *of* G and from his power, G2536
Rev 16: 7 Lord G Almighty, true and just are G2536
Rev 16: 9 heat and they cursed the name *of* G, G2536
Rev 16:11 cursed the G of heaven because of G2536
Rev 16:14 the battle on the great day *of* G Almighty. G2536
Rev 16:19 G remembered Babylon the Great and G2536
Rev 16:21 And they cursed G on account of the G2536
Rev 17:17 For G has put it into their hearts to G2536
Rev 18: 5 G has remembered her crimes. G2536
Rev 18: 8 mighty is the Lord G who judges her. G2536
Rev 18:20 Rejoice, you **people of** G! Rejoice, G41
Rev 18:20 For G has judged her with the judgment G2536
Rev 19: 1 glory and power *belong to* our G, G2536
Rev 19: 4 creatures fell down and worshiped G, G2536
Rev 19: 5 "Praise our G, all you his servants, you G2536
Rev 19: 6 For our Lord G Almighty reigns. G2536
Rev 19: 9 he added, "These are the true words *of* G." G2536
Rev 19:10 Worship G! For it is the Spirit of G2536
Rev 19:13 in blood, and his name is the Word *of* G. G2536
Rev 19:15 of the fury of the wrath *of* G Almighty. G2536
Rev 19:17 gather together for the great supper *of* G, G2536
Rev 20: 4 Jesus and because of the word *of* G. G2536
Rev 20: 6 they will be priests *of* G and of Christ and G2536
Rev 21: 2 coming down out of heaven from G G2536
Rev 21: 3 G himself will be with them and be G2536
Rev 21: 3 himself will be with them and be their G. G2536
Rev 21: 7 I will be their G and they will be my G2536
Rev 21:10 coming down out of heaven from G. G2536
Rev 21:11 It shone with the glory *of* G, and its G2536
Rev 21:22 because the Lord G Almighty and the G2536
Rev 21:23 for the glory *of* G gives it light, and G2536
Rev 22: 1 from the throne *of* G and of the Lamb G2536
Rev 22: 3 The throne *of* G and of the Lamb will be G2536
Rev 22: 5 for the Lord G will give them light. G2536
Rev 22: 6 The Lord, the G who inspires the prophets G2536
Rev 22: 9 keep the words of this scroll. Worship G!" G2536
Rev 22:18 G will add to that person the plagues G2536
Rev 22:19 G will take away from that person any G2536

GOD'S (248) [GOD]

Ge 6:11 earth was corrupt in G sight and was full of H466
Ge 28:22 I have set up as a pillar will be G house, H466
Ex 18:15 the people come to me to seek G will. H466
Ex 18:16 inform them of G decrees and H466
Dt 21:23 who is hung on a pole is under G curse. H466
Jos 9:20 so that G wrath will not fall on us for NDT
Jdg 20: 2 their places in the assembly of G people, H466
1Sa 5:11 with panic; G hand was very heavy on it. H466
1Sa 14:45 for he did this today with G help. H466
2Sa 9: 3 of Saul to whom I can show G kindness?" H466
2Sa 14:16 both me and my son from G inheritance. H466
1Ch 5:22 fell slain, because the battle was G. H4946+466
1Ch 27:24 G wrath came on Israel on account of this NDT
2Ch 1: 3 at Gibeon, for G tent of meeting was there H466
2Ch 4:19 all the furnishings that were in G temple: H466
2Ch 5: 1 placed them in the treasuries of G temple. H466
2Ch 20:15 For the battle is not yours, but G. H4200+466
2Ch 24:18 G anger came on Judah and Jerusalem. NDT
2Ch 31:21 in the service of G temple and in H466
2Ch 32:12 himself remove **this g** high places and H2257[S]
2Ch 33: 7 he had made and put it in G temple, H466
2Ch 35: 8 the officials in charge of G temple, gave H466
2Ch 35:22 Necho had said at G command but went to H466
2Ch 36:13 had made him take an oath in G name. H466
2Ch 36:16 But they mocked G messengers, despised H466
2Ch 36:19 They set fire to G temple and broke down H466
Ne 13:25 them take an oath in G name and said: H466
Job 6: 4 G terrors are marshaled against me. H468
Job 9:34 someone to remove G rod from me, so H2257[S]
Job 13: 7 Will you speak wickedly on G behalf? Will H446
Job 15: 8 Do you listen in on G council? Do you have H468
Job 15:11 Are G consolations not enough for you H446
Job 15:30 the breath of G mouth will carry him H2257[S]
Job 20:28 rushing waters on the day of G wrath. H2257[S]
Job 29: 4 when G intimate friendship blessed my H468
Job 33: 6 I am the same as you in G sight; I too am a H446
Job 33:26 they will see G face and shout for joy H2257[S]
Job 36: 2 that there is more to be said in G behalf. H468
Job 37: 5 G voice thunders in marvelous ways; he H446
Job 37:14 Job; stop and consider G wonders. H446
Job 38:33 Can you set up G dominion over the H2257[S]
Job 40: 9 Do you have an arm like G, and can your H446
Ps 52: 8 I trust in G unfailing love for ever and ever. H466
Ps 61: 7 he be enthroned in G presence forever; H466
Ps 69:30 I will praise G name in song and glorify H466
Ps 78:10 they did not keep G covenant and refused H466
Ps 78:31 G anger rose against them; he put to death H466
Ps 107:11 rebelled against G commands and H446
Ps 114: 2 Judah became G sanctuary, Israel his H2257[S]
Ps 133: 1 it is when G **people** live together in H278
Pr 5:14 trouble in the assembly of G **people**." H6337
Pr 11:26 they pray *G* **blessing** on the one who is AIT
Ecc 9: 1 the wise and what they do are in G hands, H466
Isa 8:16 seal up G **instruction** among my H9368
Isa 8:20 Consult G **instruction** and the testimony of H9368
Jnh 2: 8 idols turn away from G **love** *for* them. H2876

Mt 5:34 either by heaven, for it is **G** throne; *G2536*
Mt 22:21 what is Caesar's, and to God what is **G**." *G2536*
Mt 23:22 by heaven swears by **G** throne and by the *G2536*
Mk 3:35 Whoever does **G** will is my brother and *G2536*
Mk 5: 7 **In G name** don't torture me!" *G3991+3836+2536*
Mk 12:17 what is Caesar's and to God what is **G**." *G2536*
Lk 3: 6 And all people will see **G** salvation.'" *G2536*
Lk 7:29 acknowledged that **G** way was right *G2536*
Lk 7:30 in the law rejected **G** purpose for *G2536*
Lk 8:21 are those who hear **G** word and put it into *G2536*
Lk 9:20 Peter answered, "**G** Messiah." *G2536*
Lk 16:15 value highly is detestable in **G** sight. *G2536*
Lk 19:44 recognize the time *of* **G coming** to you." *G2175*
Lk 20:25 what is Caesar's, and to God what is **G**." *G2536*
Lk 20:36 They are **G** children, since they are *G2536*
Lk 23:35 let him save himself if he is **G** Messiah *G2536*
Jn 1:34 I testify that this is **G** Chosen One. *G2536*
Jn 3:18 in the name of **G** one and only Son. *G2536*
Jn 3:36 not see life, for **G** wrath remains on them. *G2536*
Jn 10:36 blasphemy because I said, 'I am **G** Son'? *G2536*
Jn 11: 4 it is for **G** glory so that God's Son may be *G2536*
Jn 11: 4 God's glory so that **G** Son may be *G2536*
Ac 2:23 over to you by **G** deliberate plan and *G2536*
Ac 4:19 John replied, "Which is right in **G** eyes: *G2536*
Ac 4:33 And **G** grace was so powerfully at work in NDT
Ac 6: 8 Stephen, a man full of **G** grace and power NDT
Ac 7:46 who enjoyed **G** favor and asked that he *G2536*
Ac 11:17 was I to think that I could stand in **G** way?" *G2536*
Ac 13:36 David had served **G** purpose in his own *G2536*
Ac 17:29 "Therefore since we are **G** offspring, we *G2536*
Ac 18:21 promised, "I will come back if it is **G** will." *G2536*
Ac 20:24 of testifying to the good news of **G** grace. *G2536*
Ac 23: 4 "How dare you insult **G** high priest!" *G2536*
Ac 28:28 you to know that **G** salvation has been *G2536*
Ro 1:10 that now at last by **G** will the way may be *G2536*
Ro 1:20 of the world **G** invisible qualities— *G899S*
Ro 1:32 Although they know **G** righteous decree *G2536*
Ro 2: 2 Now we know that **G** judgment against *G2536*
Ro 2: 3 do you think you will escape **G** judgment? *G2536*
Ro 2: 4 not realizing that **G** kindness is intended *G2536*
Ro 2: 5 against yourself for the day of **G** wrath, *G2536*
Ro 2:13 hear the law who are righteous in **G** sight, *G2536*
Ro 2:24 "**G** name is blasphemed among the *G2536*
Ro 3: 3 their unfaithfulness nullify **G** faithfulness? *G2536*
Ro 3: 5 brings out **G** righteousness more clearly *G2536*
Ro 3: 7 falsehood enhances **G** truthfulness and so *G2536*
Ro 3:20 righteous in **G** sight by the works of *G899S*
Ro 5: 5 because **G** love has been poured out into *G2536*
Ro 5: 9 we be saved from **G** wrath through him! *G3836S*
Ro 5:10 while we were **G** enemies, we were *G2536*
Ro 5:15 how much more did **G** grace and the gift *G2536*
Ro 5:17 those who receive **G** abundant provision of NDT
Ro 7:22 For in my inner being I delight in **G** law; *G2536*
Ro 7:25 I myself in my mind am a slave to **G** law *G2536*
Ro 8: 7 it does not submit to **G** law, nor can it do *G2536*
Ro 8:16 with our spirit that we are **G** children. *G2536*
Ro 8:27 intercedes for **G people** in accordance with *G41*
Ro 9: 6 It is not as though **G** word had failed. *G2536*
Ro 9: 8 by physical descent who are **G** children, *G2536*
Ro 9:11 in order that **G** purpose in election might *G2536*
Ro 9:16 human desire or effort, but on **G** mercy. *G2536*
Ro 10: 3 they did not submit to **G** righteousness. *G2536*
Ro 11: 4 And what was **G answer** to him? "I have *G5977*
Ro 11:29 **G** gifts and his call are irrevocable. *G2536*
Ro 11:31 receive mercy as a result of **G** mercy to you. NDT
Ro 12: 1 in view of **G** mercy, to offer your *G2536*
Ro 12: 2 able to test and approve what **G** will is— *G2536*
Ro 12:19 leave room for **G** wrath, for it is *G3836S*
Ro 13: 4 one in authority is **G** servant for your good *G2536*
Ro 13: 4 They are **G** servants, agents of wrath to *G2536*
Ro 13: 6 the authorities are **G** servants, who *G2536*
Ro 14:10 we will all stand before **G** judgment seat. *G2536*
Ro 15: 8 a servant of the Jews on behalf of **G** truth, *G2536*
Ro 15:32 to you with joy, by **G** will, and in your *G2536*
1Co 2: 5 rest on human wisdom, but on **G** power. *G2536*
1Co 2: 7 we declare **G** wisdom, a mystery that *G2536*
1Co 3: 9 For we are co-workers in **G** service; you are *G2536*
1Co 3: 9 you are **G** field, God's building. *G2536*
1Co 3: 9 you are God's field, **G** building. *G2536*
1Co 3:16 you yourselves are **G** temple and that *G2536*
1Co 3:16 temple and that **G** Spirit dwells in your *G2536*
1Co 3:17 If anyone destroys **G** temple, God will *G2536*
1Co 3:17 that person; for **G** temple is sacred, and *G2536*
1Co 3:19 of this world is foolishness in **G** sight. *G2536*
1Co 7:19 Keeping **G** commands is what counts *G2536*
1Co 9:21 I am not free from **G** law but am under *G2536*
1Co 11:19 you to show which of you have **G** approval. NDT
2Co 1:12 not on worldly wisdom but on **G** grace. *G2536*
2Co 4: 1 since through **G** mercy we have this ministry NDT
2Co 4: 6 of the knowledge of **G** glory displayed in *G2536*
2Co 6: 1 As **G** co-workers we urge you not to receive NDT
2Co 6: 1 urge you not to receive **G** grace in vain. *G2536*
2Co 6: 2 now is the time of **G** favor, now is the day NDT
2Co 13: 4 in weakness, yet he lives by **G** power. *G2536*
2Co 13: 4 by **G** power we will live with him in *G2536*
2Co 13:13 All **G people** here send their greetings. *G41*
Gal 1: 8 let them be **under G curse**! *G353*
Gal 1: 9 you accepted, let them be **under G curse**! *G353*
Gal 4: 7 longer a slave, but **G** child; and since you NDT
Eph 1: 1 will of God, *To* **G holy people** in Ephesus *G41*
Eph 1: 7 in accordance with the riches *of* **G** grace *G899S*
Eph 1:14 of those who are **G** possession— NDT
Eph 1:15 Lord Jesus and your love for all **G people**, *G41*
Eph 2:10 For we are **G** handiwork, created in Christ *G899S*
Eph 2:19 fellow citizens *with* **G people** and also *G41*
Eph 3: 2 the administration *of* **G** grace that was *G2536*
Eph 3: 5 by the Spirit to **G** holy apostles and *G899S*
Eph 3: 7 gospel by the gift *of* **G** grace given me *G2536*
Eph 5: 1 Follow **G** example, therefore, as dearly *G2536*
Eph 5: 3 these are improper *for* **G holy people**. *G41*
Eph 5: 6 of such things **G** wrath comes on those *G2536*
Php 1: 1 To all **G holy people** in Christ Jesus at *G41*
Php 1: 7 all of you share in **G** grace with me. *G3836S*
Php 1:19 your prayers and **G** provision of the Spirit NDT
Php 4:21 Greet all **G people** in Christ Jesus. *G41*
Php 4:22 All **G people** here send you greetings *G41*
Col 1: 2 *To* **G holy people** in Colossae, the faithful *G41*
Col 1: 4 of the love you have for all **G people**— *G41*
Col 1: 6 you heard it and truly understood **G** grace. *G2536*
Col 3:12 Therefore, as **G** chosen people, holy and *G2536*
1Th 2:14 became imitators of **G** churches in Judea *G2536*
1Th 3: 2 co-worker in **G** service in spreading *G2536*
1Th 4: 3 It is **G** will that you should be sanctified *G2536*
1Th 4:10 you do love all *of* **G family** throughout *G3836+81*
1Th 5:18 this is **G** will for you in Christ Jesus. *G2536*
1Th 5:26 Greet all **G people** with a holy kiss. *G81*
2Th 1: 4 among **G** churches we boast about your *G2536*
2Th 1: 5 this is evidence that **G** judgment is right, *G2536*
2Th 2: 4 so that he sets himself up in **G** temple *G2536*
2Th 3: 5 direct your hearts into **G** love and Christ's *G2536*
1Ti 1: 4 rather than advancing **G** work— *G2536*
1Ti 3: 5 how can he take care of **G** church? *G2536*
1Ti 3:15 to conduct themselves in **G** household, *G2536*
1Ti 6: 1 so that **G** name and our teaching may not *G2536*
2Ti 2: 9 like a criminal. But **G** word is not chained *G2536*
2Ti 2:14 Keep reminding **G** people of these things NDT
2Ti 2:19 **G** solid foundation stands firm *G2536*
Titus 1: 1 to further the faith of **G** elect and their *G2536*
Titus 1: 7 Since an overseer manages **G** household *G2536*
Heb 1: 3 Son is the radiance of **G** glory and the exact NDT
Heb 1: 6 he says, "Let all **G** angels worship him." *G2536*
Heb 3: 2 just as Moses was faithful in all **G** house. *G899S*
Heb 3: 5 was faithful as a servant in all **G** house," *G899S*
Heb 3: 6 Christ is faithful as the Son over **G** house. *G899S*
Heb 4:10 anyone who enters **G** rest also rests from *G899S*
Heb 4:13 in all creation is hidden from **G** sight. *G899S*
Heb 4:16 Let us then approach **G** throne of grace with NDT
Heb 5:12 elementary truths *of* **G** word all over again *G2536*
Heb 9:24 now to appear for us in **G** presence. *G2536*
Heb 11: 3 the universe was formed at **G** command, *G2536*
Jas 2:23 and he was called **G** friend. *G2536*
Jas 3: 9 who have been made in **G** likeness. *G2536*
1Pe 1: 1 of Jesus Christ, *To* **G elect**, exiles scattered AIT
1Pe 1: 5 faith are shielded by **G** power until the *G2536*
1Pe 2: 9 a holy nation, **G** special possession, that NDT
1Pe 2:15 For it is **G** will that by doing good you *G2536*
1Pe 2:16 as a cover-up for evil; live as **G** slaves. *G2536*
1Pe 3: 4 which is of great worth in **G** sight. *G2536*
1Pe 3:17 it is better, if it is **G** will, to suffer for doing *G2536*
1Pe 3:22 into heaven and is at **G** right hand— *G2536*
1Pe 4:10 faithful stewards of **G** grace in its various *G2536*
1Pe 4:17 judgment to begin with **G** household; *G2536*
1Pe 4:19 suffer according to **G** will should commit *G2536*
1Pe 5: 2 Be shepherds of **G** flock that is under your *G2536*
1Pe 5: 6 therefore, under **G** mighty hand, that he *G2536*
2Pe 3: 5 that long ago by **G** word the heavens *G2536*
1Jn 3: 9 because **G** seed remains in them *G899S*
1Jn 3:10 does not do what is right is not **G** child, *G2536*
1Jn 3:24 The one who keeps **G** commands lives in *G899S*
1Jn 5: 9 **G** testimony is greater because it is *G2536*
Jude 3 was once for all entrusted *to* **G holy people**. *G41*
Jude 21 keep yourselves in **G** love as you wait for *G2536*
Rev 3:14 true witness, the ruler *of* **G** creation. *G2536*
Rev 5: 8 incense, which are the prayers *of* **G people**. *G41*
Rev 8: 3 with the prayers *of* all **G people**, on the *G41*
Rev 8: 4 together with the prayers *of* **G people**, went *G41*
Rev 11:19 Then **G** temple in heaven was opened *G2536*
Rev 12:17 those who keep **G** commands and hold *G2536*
Rev 13: 7 war against **G holy people** and to conquer *G41*
Rev 13:10 faithfulness *on the part of* **G people**. *G41*
Rev 14:10 will drink the wine *of* **G** fury, which has *G2536*
Rev 14:19 them into the great winepress of **G** wrath. *G2536*
Rev 15: 1 because with them **G** wrath is completed. *G2536*
Rev 15: 3 sang the song of **G** servant Moses and *G2536*
Rev 16: 1 the seven bowls of **G** wrath on the earth." *G2536*
Rev 17: 6 was drunk with the blood *of* **G holy people**, *G41*
Rev 17:17 royal authority, until **G** words are fulfilled. *G2536*
Rev 18:24 the blood of prophets and *of* **G holy people**, *G41*
Rev 19: 8 the righteous acts *of* **G holy people**. *G41*
Rev 20: 9 earth and surrounded the camp *of* **G people**, *G41*
Rev 21: 3 **G** dwelling place is now among the *G2536*
Rev 22:21 grace of the Lord Jesus be with **G people**. *G41*

GOD-BREATHED (1) [GOD, BREATH]

2Ti 3:16 All Scripture is **G** and is useful for teaching *G2535*

GOD-FEARING (7) [GOD, FEAR]

Ac 2: 5 staying in Jerusalem **G** Jews from every *G2327*
Ac 10: 2 family were devout and **G**; *G5828+3836+2536*
Ac 10:22 is a righteous and **G** man, *G5828+3836+2536*
Ac 13:26 and you **G Gentiles**, *G5828+3836+2536*
Ac 13:50 leaders incited the **G** women of high *G4936*
Ac 17: 4 did a large number *of* **G** Greeks and quite *G4936*
Ac 17:17 synagogue with both Jews and **G Greeks**, *G4936*

GOD-HATERS (1) [GOD, HATE]

Ro 1:30 slanderers, **G**, insolent, arrogant and *G2539*

GODDESS (7) [GOD]

1Ki 11: 5 followed Ashtoreth the **g** *of* the Sidonians, H466
1Ki 11:33 Ashtoreth the **g** *of* the Sidonians, H466
2Ki 23:13 Ashtoreth the **vile g** *of* the Sidonians, H9199
Ac 19:27 that the temple *of* the great **g** Artemis will *G2516*
Ac 19:27 be discredited; and the **g** herself, who is NDT
Ac 19:37 robbed temples nor blasphemed our **g**. *G2536*
Ac 28: 4 the **g Justice** has not allowed him to live." *G1472*

GODHEAD (KJV) DEITY, DIVINE BEING, DIVINE NATURE

GODLESS (19) [GOD]

Job 8:13 forget God; so perishes the hope of the **g**. H2868
Job 13:16 no **g** *person* would dare come before H2868
Job 15:34 For the company of the **g** will be barren H2868
Job 20: 5 the joy of the **g** lasts but a moment. H2868
Job 20: 6 the pride of the **g** *person* reaches to the H2257S
Job 27: 8 what hope have the **g** when they are cut H2868
Job 34:30 to keep the **g** from ruling, from H2868+132
Job 36:13 "The **g** *in* heart harbor resentment; even H2868
Pr 11: 9 With their mouths the **g** destroy their H2868
Pr 17: 7 Eloquent lips are unsuited to a **g fool** H5572
Pr 17:21 there is no joy for the parent of a **g fool**. H5572
Pr 30:22 a **g fool** who gets plenty to eat H5572
Isa 10: 6 I send him against a **g** nation, I dispatch H2868
Isa 33:14 in Zion are terrified; trembling grips the **g**: H2868
Jer 23:11 "Both prophet and priest *are* **g**; even in H2866
1Ti 4: 7 nothing to do with **g** myths and old wives' *G1013*
1Ti 6:20 Turn away from **g** chatter and the *G1013*
2Ti 2:16 Avoid **g** chatter, because those who *G1013*
Heb 12:16 immoral, or is **g** like Esau, who for a *G1013*

GODLESSNESS (2) [GOD]

Ro 1:18 heaven against all the **g** and wickedness of *G813*
Ro 11:26 from Zion; he will turn **g** away from Jacob. *G813*

GODLINESS (11) [GOD]

Ac 3:12 by our own power or **g** we had made this *G2354*
1Ti 2: 2 quiet lives in all **g** and holiness. *G2354*
1Ti 3:16 mystery *from which* **true g** *springs* is great: *G2354*
1Ti 4: 8 some value, but **g** has value for all things *G2354*
1Ti 6: 5 who think that **g** is a means to *G2354*
1Ti 6: 6 But **g** with contentment is great gain. *G2354*
1Ti 6:11 pursue righteousness, **g**, faith, love, *G2354*
2Ti 3: 5 having a form *of* **g** but denying its power *G2354*
Titus 1: 1 knowledge of the truth that leads to **g**— *G2354*
2Pe 1: 6 perseverance; and to perseverance, **g**; *G2354*
2Pe 1: 7 to **g**, mutual affection; and to mutual *G2354*

GODLY (14) [GOD]

Mal 2:15 the one God seek? **G** offspring. So be on H466
Jn 9:31 He listens *to* the **g** *person* who does his *G2538*
Ac 8: 2 **G** men buried Stephen and mourned *G2327*
2Co 1:12 with you, with integrity and **g** sincerity. *G2536*
2Co 7:10 **G** sorrow brings repentance that *G2848+2536*
2Co 7:11 See what this **g** sorrow has *G2848+2536*
2Co 11: 2 I am jealous for you with a **g** jealousy. *G2536*
1Ti 4: 7 wives' tales; rather, train yourself to be **g**. *G2354*
1Ti 6: 3 of our Lord Jesus Christ and to **g** teaching, *G2354*
2Ti 3:12 who wants to live a **g** life in Christ Jesus *G2357*
Titus 2:12 upright and **g** lives in this present age, *G2357*
2Pe 1: 3 we need for a **g** life through our *G2354*
2Pe 2: 9 how to rescue the **g** from trials and to *G2356*
2Pe 3:11 You ought to live holy and **g** *lives* *G2354*

GODS (280) [GOD]

Ge 31:19 Rachel stole her father's **household g**. H9572
Ge 31:30 But why did you steal my **g**?" H466
Ge 31:32 But if you find anyone who has your **g**, that H466
Ge 31:32 not know that Rachel had stolen **the g**. H4392S
Ge 31:34 had taken the **household g** and put them H9572
Ge 31:35 could not find the **household g**. H9572
Ge 35: 2 "Get rid of the foreign **g** you have with you H466
Ge 35: 4 Jacob all the foreign **g** they had and the H466
Ex 12:12 I will bring judgment on all the **g** *of* Egypt. H466
Ex 15:11 Who among the **g** is like you, LORD? Who is H446
Ex 18:11 that the LORD is greater than all other **g**, H466
Ex 20: 3 "You shall have no other **g** before me. H466
Ex 20:23 Do not make any **g** to be alongside me; do NDT
Ex 20:23 make for yourselves **g** *of* silver or gods of H466
Ex 20:23 yourselves gods of silver or **g** *of* gold. H466
Ex 23:13 Do not invoke the names of other **g**; do not H466
Ex 23:24 down before their **g** or worship them or H466
Ex 23:32 make a covenant with them or with their **g**. H466
Ex 23:33 the worship of their **g** will certainly be a H466
Ex 32: 1 make us **g** who will go before us. H466
Ex 32: 4 "These are your **g**, Israel, who brought H466
Ex 32: 8 it and have said, 'These are your **g**, Israel, H466
Ex 32:23 'Make us **g** who will go before us. H466
Ex 32:31 They have made themselves **g** *of* gold. H466
Ex 34:15 themselves to their **g** and sacrifice to them, H466
Ex 34:16 daughters prostitute themselves to their **g**, H466
Lev 19: 4 to idols or make metal **g** for yourselves. H466
Nu 25: 2 who invited them to the sacrifices to their **g** H466
Nu 25: 2 meal and bowed down before these **g**. H466
Nu 33: 4 the LORD had brought judgment on their **g**. H466
Dt 4: 7 as to have their **g** near them the way the H466
Dt 4:28 worship man-made **g** of wood and stone, H466
Dt 5: 7 "You shall have no other **g** before me. H466

Dt 6:14 Do not follow other g, the gods of the H466
Dt 6:14 the g of the peoples around you H466
Dt 7: 4 away from following me to serve other g, H466
Dt 7:16 on them with pity and do not serve their g, H466
Dt 7:25 The images of their g you are to burn in the H466
Dt 8:19 follow other g and worship and bow H466
Dt 10:17 your God is God of g and Lord of lords, H466
Dt 11:16 worship other g and bow down to H466
Dt 11:28 I command you today by following other g, H466
Dt 12: 2 you are dispossessing worship their g. H466
Dt 12: 3 down the idols of their g and wipe out their H466
Dt 12:30 to be ensnared by inquiring about their g, H466
Dt 12:30 "How do these nations serve their g? H466
Dt 12:31 because in worshiping their g, they do all H466
Dt 12:31 daughters in the fire as sacrifices to their g. H466
Dt 13: 2 the prophet says, "Let us follow other g" H466
Dt 13: 2 (g you have not known) "and let us H4392S
Dt 13: 6 "Let us go and worship other g" (gods that H466
Dt 13: 6 g that neither you nor your ancestors have NDT
Dt 13: 7 g of the peoples around you, whether near H466
Dt 13:13 "Let us go and worship other g" (gods you H466
Dt 13:13 other gods" (g you have not known), H889S
Dt 17: 3 to my command has worshiped other g, H466
Dt 18:20 who speaks in the name of other g, H466
Dt 20:18 things they do in worshiping their g, H466
Dt 28:14 following other g and serving them. H466
Dt 28:36 There you will worship other g, gods of H466
Dt 28:36 worship other gods, g of wood and stone. NDT
Dt 28:64 There you will worship other g—gods of H466
Dt 28:64 worship other gods—g of wood and stone NDT
Dt 29:18 to go and worship the g of those nations; H466
Dt 29:26 worshiped other g and bowed down to H466
Dt 29:26 bowed down to them, g they did not know H466
Dt 29:26 they did not know, g he had not given them. NDT
Dt 30:17 to bow down to other g and worship them, H466
Dt 31:16 to the foreign g of the land they are H466
Dt 31:18 of all their wickedness in turning to other g. H466
Dt 31:20 they will turn to other g and worship them H466
Dt 32:16 with their foreign g and angered him with NDT
Dt 32:17 They sacrificed to false g, which are not H8717
Dt 32:17 which are not God—g they had not known H466
Dt 32:17 had not known, g that recently appeared NDT
Dt 32:17 appeared, g your ancestors did not fear. H4392S
Dt 32:37 "Now where are their g, the rock they took H466
Dt 32:38 the g who ate the fat of their sacrifices and NDT
Jos 23: 7 the names of their g or swear by them. H466
Jos 23:16 go and serve other g and bow down to H466
Jos 24: 2 the Euphrates River and worshiped other g. H466
Jos 24:14 Throw away the g your ancestors worshiped H466
Jos 24:15 whether the g your ancestors served H466
Jos 24:15 the Euphrates, or the g of the Amorites, in H466
Jos 24:16 from us to forsake the LORD to serve other g! H466
Jos 24:20 If you forsake the LORD and serve foreign g H466
Jos 24:23 away the foreign g that are among you H466
Jdg 2: 3 and their g will become snares to you. H466
Jdg 2:12 worshiped various g of the peoples around H466
Jdg 2:17 themselves to other g and worshiped them. H466
Jdg 2:19 following other g and serving and H466
Jdg 3: 6 daughters to their sons, and served their g. H466
Jdg 6:10 do not worship the g of the Amorites, in H466
Jdg 9: 9 by which both g and humans are honored H466
Jdg 9:13 which cheers both g and humans, to hold H466
Jdg 10: 6 Ashtoreths, and the g of Aram, the gods of H466
Jdg 10: 6 gods of Aram, the g of Sidon, the gods of H466
Jdg 10: 6 gods of Sidon, the g of Moab, the gods of H466
Jdg 10: 6 the g of the Ammonites and the gods of H466
Jdg 10: 6 Ammonites and the g of the Philistines. H466
Jdg 10:13 you have forsaken me and served other g, H466
Jdg 10:14 Go and cry out to the g you have chosen H466
Jdg 10:16 rid of the foreign g among them and H466
Jdg 17: 5 an ephod and some household g and H9572
Jdg 18:14 some household g and an image overlaid H9572
Jdg 18:17 ephod and the household g while the H9572
Jdg 18:18 the ephod and the household g, the H9572
Jdg 18:20 the household g and the idol and went H9572
Jdg 18:24 "You took the g I made, and my priest, H466
Ru 1:15 is going back to her people and her g. H466
1Sa 4: 8 deliver us from the hand of these mighty g? H466
1Sa 4: 8 They are the g who struck the Egyptians H466
1Sa 6: 5 hand from you and your g and your land. H466
1Sa 7: 3 of the foreign g and the Ashtoreths and H466
1Sa 8: 8 forsaking me and serving other g, so they H466
1Sa 17:43 And the Philistine cursed David by his g. H466
1Sa 26:19 have said, 'Go, serve other g.' H466
2Sa 7:23 out nations and their g from before your H466
1Ki 9: 6 go off to serve other g and worship them, H466
1Ki 9: 9 have embraced other g, worshiping H466
1Ki 11: 2 will surely turn your hearts after their g." H466
1Ki 11: 4 his wives turned his heart after other g, and H466
1Ki 11: 8 incense and offered sacrifices to their g. H466
1Ki 11:10 had forbidden Solomon to follow other g, H466
1Ki 12:28 Here are your g, Israel, who brought you up H466
1Ki 14: 9 You have made for yourself other g, idols H466
1Ki 19: 2 "May the g deal with me, be it H466
1Ki 20:10 "May the g deal with me, be it ever so H466
1Ki 20:23 advised him, "Their g are gods of the hills. H466
1Ki 20:23 advised him, "Their gods are g of the hills. H466
2Ki 17: 7 They worshiped other g H466
2Ki 17:29 group made its own g in the several towns H466
2Ki 17:31 Anammelek, the g of Sepharvaim. H466
2Ki 17:33 also served their own g in accordance with H466
2Ki 17:35 worship any other g or bow down to them, H466
2Ki 17:37 he wrote for you. Do not worship other g. H466
2Ki 17:38 with you, and do not worship other g. H466
2Ki 18:34 Where are the g of Hamath and Arpad H466
2Ki 18:34 Where are the g of Sepharvaim, Hena H466
2Ki 18:35 Who of all the g of these countries has H466
2Ki 19:12 Did the g of the nations that were destroyed H466
2Ki 19:12 deliver them—the g of Gozan, Harran, NDT
2Ki 19:18 They have thrown their g into the fire and H466
2Ki 19:18 they were not g but only wood and H466
2Ki 22:17 incense to other g and aroused my anger H466
2Ki 23:24 spiritists, the household g, the idols and H9572
1Ch 5:25 themselves to the g of the peoples of the H466
1Ch 10:10 the temple of their g and hung up his head H466
1Ch 14:12 Philistines had abandoned their g there, H466
1Ch 16:25 of praise; he is to be feared above all g. H466
1Ch 16:26 For all the g of the nations are idols, but H466
2Ch 2: 5 because our God is greater than all other g. H466
2Ch 7:19 go off to serve other g and worship them, H466
2Ch 7:22 have embraced other g, worshiping H466
2Ch 13: 8 calves that Jeroboam made to be your g. H466
2Ch 13: 9 may become a priest of what are not g. H466
2Ch 25:14 he brought back the g of the people of Seir. H466
2Ch 25:14 He set them up as his own g, bowed down H466
2Ch 25:15 "Why do you consult this people's g, which H466
2Ch 25:20 because they sought the g of Edom. H466
2Ch 28:23 He offered sacrifices to the g of Damascus H466
2Ch 28:23 "Since the g of the kings of Aram have H466
2Ch 28:25 sacrifices to other g and aroused the anger H466
2Ch 32:13 Were the g of those nations ever able to H466
2Ch 32:14 Who of all the g of these nations that my H466
2Ch 32:17 "Just as the g of the peoples of the other H466
2Ch 32:19 they did about the g of the other peoples H466
2Ch 33:15 rid of the foreign g and removed the image H466
2Ch 34:25 incense to other g and aroused my anger H466
Ps 4: 2 will you love delusions and seek false g? H3942
Ps 16: 4 Those who run after other g will suffer more AIT
Ps 16: 4 of blood to such g or take up their H2157S
Ps 40: 4 to those who turn aside to false g. H3942
Ps 82: 1 he renders judgment among the "g": H466
Ps 82: 5 "The 'g' know nothing, they understand NDT
Ps 82: 6 'You are "g"; you are all sons of the H466
Ps 86: 8 Among the g there is none like you, Lord H466
Ps 95: 3 the great God, the great King above all g. H466
Ps 96: 4 of praise; he is to be feared above all g. H466
Ps 96: 5 For all the g of the nations are idols, but H466
Ps 97: 7 boast in idols—worship him, all you g! H466
Ps 97: 9 the earth; you are exalted far above all g. H466
Ps 106:28 Peor and ate sacrifices offered to lifeless g; NDT
Ps 106:37 their sons and their daughters to false g. H8717
Ps 135: 5 is great, that our Lord is greater than all g. H466
Ps 136: 2 Give thanks to the God of g. His love H466
Ps 138: 1 my heart; before the "g" I will sing your H466
Isa 21: 9 All the images of its g lie shattered on the H466
Isa 36:18 Have the g of any nations ever delivered H466
Isa 36:19 Where are the g of Hamath and Arpad H466
Isa 36:19 Where are the g of Sepharvaim? Have H466
Isa 36:20 Who of all the g of these countries have H466
Isa 37:12 Did the g of the nations that were destroyed H466
Isa 37:12 deliver them—the g of Gozan, Harran, NDT
Isa 37:19 They have thrown their g into the fire and H466
Isa 37:19 they were not g but only wood and H466
Isa 41:23 so we may know that you are g. H466
Isa 41:28 no one among the g to give counsel H465S
Isa 42:17 images, 'You are our g,' will be turned H466
Isa 43: 9 Which of their g foretold this and H2157S
Isa 45:20 of wood, who pray to g that cannot save. H446
Jer 1:16 incense to other g and in worshiping what H466
Jer 2:11 Has a nation ever changed its g? (Yet they H466
Jer 2:11 Yet they are not g at all.) But my people H466
Jer 2:25 I love foreign g, and I must go after NDT
Jer 2:28 Where then are the g you made for H466
Jer 2:28 have as many g as you have towns. H466
Jer 3:13 favors to foreign g under every spreading NDT
Jer 3:24 our youth shameful g have consumed H1425
Jer 5: 7 me and sworn by g that are not gods. NDT
Jer 5: 7 me and sworn by gods that are not g. H466
Jer 5:19 me and served foreign g in your own land, H466
Jer 7: 6 do not follow other g to your own harm, H466
Jer 7: 9 follow other g you have not known, H466
Jer 7:18 offerings to other g to arouse my anger. H466
Jer 10:11 'These g, who did not make the heavens A10033
Jer 11:10 They have followed other g to serve them H466
Jer 11:12 go and cry out to the g to whom they burn H466
Jer 11:13 have as many g as you have towns H466
Jer 13:10 go after other g to serve and worship H466
Jer 13:25 have forgotten me and trusted in false g. H9214
Jer 16:11 'and followed other g and served and H466
Jer 16:13 there you will serve other g day and night, H466
Jer 16:19 ancestors possessed nothing but false g, H9214
Jer 16:20 Do people make their own g? Yes, but they H466
Jer 16:20 their own gods? Yes, but they are not g!" H466
Jer 19: 4 me and made this a place of foreign g; NDT
Jer 19: 4 incense in it to g that neither they nor H466
Jer 19:13 poured out drink offerings to other g. H466
Jer 22: 9 have worshiped and served other g. H466
Jer 25: 6 Do not follow other g to serve and worship H466
Jer 32:29 by pouring out drink offerings to other g. H466
Jer 35:15 do not follow other g to serve them. H466
Jer 43:12 set fire to the temples of the g of Egypt; H466
Jer 43:12 their temples and take their g captive. H4392S
Jer 43:13 burn down the temples of the g of Egypt. H466
Jer 44: 3 worshiping other g that neither they H466
Jer 44: 5 stop burning incense to other g. H466
Jer 44: 8 burning incense to other g in Egypt, where H466
Jer 44:15 wives were burning incense to other g, H466
Jer 46:25 on Egypt and her g and her kings, and on H466
Jer 48:35 high places and burn incense to their g," H466
Da 2:11 can reveal it to the king except the g, A10033
Da 2:47 God is the God of g and the Lord of A10033
Da 3:12 neither serve your g nor worship the A10033
Da 3:14 you do not serve my g or worship the A10033
Da 3:18 will not serve your g or worship the A10033
Da 3:25 the fourth looks like a son of the g." A10033
Da 4: 8 the spirit of the holy g is in him. A10033
Da 4: 9 that the spirit of the holy g is in you, A10033
Da 4:18 because the spirit of the holy g is in you." A10033
Da 5: 4 they praised the g of gold and silver, of A10033
Da 5:11 who has the spirit of the holy g in him. A10033
Da 5:11 wisdom like that of the g. A10033
Da 5:14 the spirit of the g is in you and that you A10033
Da 5:23 You praised the g of silver and gold, of A10033
Da 11: 8 He will also seize their g, their metal H466
Da 11:36 unheard-of things against the God of g. H446
Da 11:37 no regard for the g of his ancestors or for H466
Hos 3: 1 they turn to other g and love the sacred H466
Hos 3: 4 without ephod or household g. H9572
Hos 7:14 They slash themselves, appealing to their g H1517
Hos 14: 3 never again say 'Our g' to what our own H466
Am 2: 4 they have been led astray by false g, H3942
Am 2: 4 false gods, the g their ancestors followed, H889S
Mic 4: 5 nations may walk in the name of their g, H466
Na 1:14 idols that are in the temple of your g. H466
Zep 1: 9 the temple of their g with violence and H123
Zep 2:11 when he destroys all the g of the earth. H466
Jn 10:34 in your Law, 'I have said you are "g" '? G2536
Jn 10:35 If he called them 'g,' to whom the word of G2536
Ac 7:40 'Make us g who will go before us. G2536
Ac 14:11 "The g have come down to us in human G2536
Ac 17:18 "He seems to be advocating foreign g." G1228
Ac 19:26 He says that g made by human hands are NDT
Ac 19:26 made by human hands are no g at all. G2536
Ac 28:11 of the twin g Castor and Pollux. G1483
1Co 8: 5 For even if there are so-called g, whether G2536
1Co 8: 5 as indeed there are many "g" and many G2536
Gal 4: 8 slaves to those who by nature are not g. G2536

GOES (84) [GO]

Ge 40:14 But when all g well with you, remember H3512
Ex 7:15 in the morning as he g out to the river. H3655
Ex 8:20 confront Pharaoh as he g to the river and H3655
Ex 12:23 When the LORD g through the land to strike H6296
Lev 14:36 emptied before he g in to examine the H995
Lev 14:46 "Anyone who g into the house while it is H995
Lev 16:17 the time Aaron g in to make atonement H995
Lev 22: 7 When the sun g down, he will be clean H995
Nu 5:12 'If a man's wife g astray and is unfaithful H8474
Nu 5:29 when a woman g astray and makes H8474
Nu 35:26 accused ever g outside the limits H3655+3655
Dt 9: 3 God is the one who g across ahead of you H6296
Dt 16: 6 when the sun g down, on the anniversary H995
Dt 20: 4 your God is the one who g with you to H2143
Dt 31: 6 the LORD your God g with you; he will H2143
Dt 31: 8 The LORD himself g before you and will be H2143
Jdg 21:19 east of the road that g from Bethel to H6590
1Sa 6: 9 If it g up to its own territory, toward Beth H6590
1Sa 9:13 find him before he g up to the high place H6590
1Sa 23:22 David usually g and who has H2118+8079
1Sa 24:13 As the old saying g, 'From evildoers come H606
1Sa 25:25 his name means Fool, and folly g with him. NDT
2Ki 11: 8 close to the king wherever he g." H928+3655+2256+928+995
2Ch 23: 7 close to the king wherever he g." H928+995+2256+928+3655
Ne 9:37 its abundant harvest g to the kings you have NDT
Job 7: 9 so one who g down to the grave does not H3718
Job 9:11 see him; when he g by, I cannot perceive H2736
Job 18: 6 the lamp beside him g out. H1980
Job 21:33 a countless throng g before them. NDT
Job 22:14 not see us as he g about in the vaulted H2143
Job 24:18 so that no one g to the vineyards. H7155
Job 41:22 resides in its neck; dismay g before it. H1881
Ps 19: 4 Yet their voice g out into all the earth H3655
Ps 39: 6 "Surely everyone g around like a mere H2143
Ps 41: 6 then he g out and spreads it around. H3655
Ps 85:13 Righteousness g before him and prepares H2143
Ps 97: 3 Fire g before him and consumes his foes H2143
Pr 6:12 who g about with a corrupt mouth H2143
Pr 13:25 the stomach of the wicked g hungry. H2893
Pr 16:18 Pride g before destruction, a haughty spirit NDT
Pr 20:14 then g off and boasts about the purchase. H261
Pr 22:10 out the mocker, and out g strife; quarrels H3655
Pr 23:31 in the cup, when it g down smoothly! H2143
Pr 26:20 Without wood a fire g out; without a H3882
Pr 29: 9 If a wise person g to court with a fool, the H9149
Ecc 1: 6 round and round it g, ever returning on H2143
Ecc 3:21 the animal g down into the H3718+4200+4752
Ecc 8:17 comprehend what g on under the sun. H6913
Isa 15: 2 Dibon g up to its temple, to its high H6590
Isa 16:12 when she g to her shrine to pray H995
Isa 55:11 so is my word that g out from my mouth: It H3655
Isa 66: 7 "Before she g into labor, she gives birth H2655
Jer 6:29 but the refining g on in vain H7671+7671
Jer 14: 2 the land, and a cry g up from Jerusalem. H6590

Jer 21: 9 But whoever **g out** and surrenders to the H3655
Jer 38: 2 whoever **g over** to the Babylonians H3655
Eze 43:14 to the lower **ledge that g around** the altar H6478
Eze 43:14 to the upper **ledge that g around** the altar H6478
Eze 44:27 On the day he **g** into the inner court of the H995
Eze 47: 8 region and **g down** into the Arabah, H3718
Da 9:25 the time the word **g out** to restore and H4604
Mic 5: 8 which mauls and mangles as *it* **g**, and no H6296
Mt 8: 9 this one, 'Go,' and *he* **g**; and that one G4513
Mt 12:43 *it* **g through** arid places seeking rest and G1451
Mt 12:45 Then *it* **g** and takes with it seven other G4513
Mt 15:11 What **g into** someone's mouth does not G1656
Mt 15:17 enters the mouth **g** into the stomach and G6003
Mk 9:43 to go into hell, where the fire **never g out**. G812
Lk 7: 8 this one, 'Go,' and *he* **g**; and that one G4513
Lk 11:24 *it* **g through** arid places seeking rest and G1451
Lk 11:26 Then *it* **g** and takes seven other spirits G4513
Lk 15: 6 **g** home. Then he calls his friends and G2262
Lk 16:30 'but if someone from the dead **g** to them G4513
Lk 19:37 near the **place where the road g down** the G2853
Jn 5: 7 someone else **g down** ahead of me." G2849
Jn 10: 4 out all his own, *he* **g on** ahead of them G4513
Jn 15:26 Spirit of truth who **g out** from the Father— G1744
Ac 8:26 that **g down** from Jerusalem to Gaza." G2849
1Co 9:25 in the games **g into** strict **training**. G1603
Col 2:18 *Such a person* also **g into great detail** G1836
Jas 1:24 **g away** and immediately forgets what he G599
2Pe 3: 4 everything **g on** as it has since the G1373
Rev 14: 4 They follow the Lamb wherever *he* **g** G5632
Rev 19: 3 The smoke from her **g up** for ever and ever." G326

GOG (12) [HAMON GOG]

1Ch 5: 4 Shemaiah his son, **G** his son, Shimei his H1573
Eze 38: 2 your face against **G**, *of* the land of Magog H1573
Eze 38: 3 I am against you, **G**, chief prince of H1573
Eze 38:14 son of man, prophesy and say to **G**: H1573
Eze 38:16 In days to come, **G**, I will bring you H1573
Eze 38:18 When **G** attacks the land of Israel, my hot H1573
Eze 38:21 a sword against **G** on all my mountains, H2257S
Eze 39: 1 prophesy against **G** and say: 'This is H1573
Eze 39: 1 I am against you, **G**, chief prince of H1573
Eze 39:11 that day I will give **G** a burial place in H1573
Eze 39:11 because **G** and all his hordes will be H1573
Rev 20: 8 of the earth—**G** and Magog—and to G1223

GOIIM (NIV84) GOYIM

GOING (307) [GO]

Ge 6:13 to Noah, "I *am* **g** *to* **put** an end to all people AIT
Ge 6:13 I *am* surely **g** *to* **destroy** both them and the AIT
Ge 6:17 I *am* **g** *to* **bring** floodwaters on the earth to AIT
Ge 7:16 The *animals* **g in** were male and female of H995
Ge 16: 8 you come from, and where *are you* **g**?" H2143
Ge 19:13 because we *are* **g** *to* **destroy** this place. AIT
Ge 32:17 and where *are you* **g**, and who owns H2143
Ge 37:13 Come, *I am* **g** *to* **send** you to them. AIT
Ge 48: 4 'I *am* **g** *to* **make** *you* **fruitful** and increase AIT
Ex 10: 8 "But tell me who *will be* **g**." H2143
Ex 19: 9 "I *am* **g** *to* **come** to you in a dense cloud AIT
Ex 34:12 those who live in the land where you *are* **g**, H995
Lev 18:24 nations that I *am* **g** *to* **drive out** before you AIT
Lev 20:23 of the nations I *am* **g** *to* **drive out** before you. AIT
Lev 23:10 enter the land I *am* **g** *to* **give** you and you AIT
Lev 25: 2 'When you enter the land I *am* **g** *to* **give** you AIT
Nu 10:30 *I am* **g back** to my own land and my own H2143
Nu 11:15 If this is how you *are* **g** *to* **treat** me, please go AIT
Nu 16:34 shouting, "The earth *is* **g** *to* **swallow** us too!" AIT
Nu 17:13 of the LORD will die. Are we all **g** *to* **die**?" AIT
Nu 22: 4 "This horde is **g** to lick up everything H6964
Nu 24:14 Now I *am* **g back** to my people, but come H2143
Dt 1:30 LORD your God, who *is* **g** before you, will H2143
Dt 3:21 the kingdoms **over** there where you *are* **g**. H6296
Dt 3:27 since *you are* not **g** *to* **cross** this Jordan. AIT
Dt 9: 4 the LORD *is* **g** *to* **drive** them **out** before you. AIT
Dt 9: 5 integrity that you *are* **g in** to take H995
Dt 20: 3 Today you are **g** into battle against your H7929
Dt 29:19 even though *I* persist in **g** my own way," H2143
Dt 31:16 "You *are* **g** *to* **rest** with your ancestors, and AIT
Dt 33:18 Zebulun, in your **g out**, and you, Issachar, H3655
Jos 6: 7 an armed guard **g** ahead of the ark of H6296
Jos 8:21 the city and that smoke *was* **g up** *from* it, H6590
Jos 10:10 along the road **g up** *to* Beth Horon and H5090
Jos 10:13 sky and delayed **g down** about a full day. H995
Jos 10:25 will do to all the enemies you *are* **g** *to* **fight**." AIT
Jos 19:11 **G** west it ran to Maralah, touched H4200
Jos 22:33 no more about **g** to war against them H6590
Jdg 6:23 Do not be afraid. *You are* not **g** *to* **die**." AIT
Jdg 6:31 "*Are* you **g** *to* **plead** Baal's **cause**? AIT
Jdg 7: 9 because *I am* **g** *to* **give** it into your hands. AIT
Jdg 11: 2 "*You are* not **g** *to* **get** *any* **inheritance** in our AIT
Jdg 12: 1 *We're* **g** *to* **burn down** your house over your AIT
Jdg 13: 3 but *you are* **g** *to* **become pregnant** and give AIT
Jdg 15: 1 He said, "*I'm* **g** to my wife's room. H995
Jdg 18: 9 **Aren't** you **g** *to* **do something**? Don't AIT
Jdg 19:17 the old man asked, "Where *are you* **g**? H2143
Jdg 19:18 Judah and now I *am* **g** *to* the house of the H2143
Jdg 20:40 city **g up** in smoke. H6590+2021+9028+2025
Ru 1:11 Am I **g** to have any more sons, who could NDT
Ru 1:15 sister-in-law *is* **g back** to her people and H8740
1Sa 1:14 "How long *are you* **g** *to* **stay drunk**? AIT
1Sa 9:11 As they *were* **g up** the hill to the town H6590
1Sa 9:27 *As* they *were* **g down** to the edge of the H3718
1Sa 10: 3 Three men **g up** to worship God at Bethel H6590
1Sa 12: 7 *I am* **g** *to* **confront** you **with evidence** before AIT
1Sa 17:20 camp as the army *was* **g out** to its battle H3655
1Sa 17:55 As Saul watched David **g out** to meet the H3655
1Sa 20: 2 Jonathan replied. "*You are* not **g** *to* **die**! Look, AIT
1Sa 23: 4 I *am* **g** *to* **give** the Philistines into your AIT
1Sa 23:26 Saul *was* **g** along one side of the H2143
1Sa 26:14 "Aren't *you* **g** *to* **answer** me, Abner? AIT
2Sa 6:20 **g around half-naked** in full view of the H1655
2Sa 11: 7 were and **how** the war **was g**. H4200+8934
2Sa 12:11 own household I *am* **g** *to* **bring** calamity on AIT
2Sa 12:13 taken away your sin. *You are* not **g** *to* **die**. AIT
2Sa 14:18 me the answer to what I *am* **g** *to* **ask** you." AIT
2Sa 15:20 **I do not know where I am g** H2143+6584+889+2143
2Sa 16:13 road while Shimei *was* **g** along the H2143
2Sa 18: 9 while the mule he was riding **kept on g**. H6296
2Sa 18:14 Joab said, "*I'm* not **g** *to* **wait** like this for you." AIT
1Ki 11:29 time Jeroboam *was* **g out** of Jerusalem, H3655
1Ki 11:31 I *am* **g** *to* **tear** the kingdom out of Solomon's AIT
1Ki 14:10 I *am* **g** *to* **bring** disaster on the house of AIT
1Ki 17:11 As *she was* **g** to get it, he called, "And H2143
1Ki 18: 6 Ahab **g** in one direction and Obadiah in H2143
1Ki 20: 6 time tomorrow *I am* **g** *to* **send** my officials to AIT
1Ki 21:21 'I *am* **g** *to* **bring** disaster on you. AIT
1Ki 21:26 in the vilest manner by **g** after idols, H2143
1Ki 22:20 Ramoth Gilead and **g** *to his* **death** there? H5877
2Ki 1: 3 in Israel that you *are* **g off** to consult H2143
2Ki 2: 3 that the LORD *is* **g** *to* **take** your master from AIT
2Ki 2: 5 that the LORD *is* **g** *to* **take** your master from AIT
2Ki 6: 9 because the Arameans are **g down** there." H5741
2Ki 10:19 because I am **g** to hold a great sacrifice NDT
2Ki 11: 5 companies *that are* **g on duty** *on* the H995
2Ki 11: 9 *those who were* **g on duty** *on* the Sabbath H995
2Ki 11: 9 Sabbath and *those who were* **g off duty**— H3655
2Ki 20: 1 because you *are* **g** *to* **die**; you will not AIT
2Ki 21:12 I *am* **g** *to* **bring** such disaster on Jerusalem AIT
2Ki 22:16 I *am* **g** *to* **bring** disaster on this place and its AIT
2Ki 22:20 all the disaster I *am* **g** *to* **bring** on this place. AIT
2Ch 2: 5 "The temple I *am* **g** *to* **build** will be great AIT
2Ch 18:19 Ramoth Gilead and **g** *to his* **death** there? H5877
2Ch 23: 4 Levites *who are* **g on duty** *on* the H995
2Ch 23: 8 *those who were* **g on duty** *on* the Sabbath H995
2Ch 23: 8 Sabbath and *those who were* **g off duty**— H3655
2Ch 34:24 I *am* **g** *to* **bring** disaster on this place and its AIT
2Ch 34:28 the disaster I *am* **g** *to* **bring** on this place AIT
Ne 3:15 as far as the steps **g down** from the City of H3718
Ne 13: 6 But while all this was **g** on, I was not in NDT
Job 1: 7 the earth, **g back and forth** on it. H2143
Job 2: 2 the earth, **g back and forth** on it. H2143
Job 33:24 'Spare them from **g down** *to* the pit; H3718
Job 33:28 has delivered me from **g down** to the pit, H6296
Ps 30: 3 you spared me from **g down** *to* the pit. H3718
Ps 121: 8 over your coming and **g** both now and H3655
Ps 139: 3 You discern my **g out** and my lying down H782
Ps 144:14 of walls, no **g into captivity**, no cry of H3448
Pr 7: 8 *He was* **g down** the street near her corner H6296
Pr 7:22 followed her like an ox **g** to the slaughter, H995
Pr 15:24 keep them from **g down** *to* the realm of H4752
Pr 22: 3 the simple *keep* **g** and pay the H6296
Pr 27:12 the simple *keep* **g** and pay the H6296
Ecc 9:10 where you *are* **g**, there is neither H2143
Isa 5: 5 tell you what I *am* **g** *to* **do** to my vineyard: AIT
Isa 20: 2 **g around** stripped and barefoot. H2143
Isa 24: 1 the LORD *is* **g** *to* **lay waste** the earth and AIT
Isa 38: 1 because you *are* **g** *to* **die**; you will not AIT
Isa 41:22 you idols, what *is* **g** *to* **happen**. Tell us what AIT
Isa 57:10 You wearied yourself by such **g about**, but H2006
Isa 58:13 you honor it by not **g** your own way and H6913
Jer 6:28 all hardened rebels, **g about** to slander. H2143
Jer 13:13 I *am* **g** *to* **fill** *with* drunkenness all who live in AIT
Jer 19: 3 I *am* **g** *to* **bring** a disaster on this place that AIT
Jer 19:15 I *am* **g** *to* **bring** on this city and all the AIT
Jer 28:16 This very year you *are* **g** *to* **die**, because you AIT
Jer 32: 7 your uncle *is* **g** *to* **come** to you and say, AIT
Jer 34:22 I *am* **g** *to* **give the order**, declares the LORD AIT
Jer 35:17 I *am* **g** *to* **bring** on Judah and on everyone AIT
Jer 38:14 "I *am* **g** *to* **ask** you something," the king said AIT
Jer 44:30 'I *am* **g** *to* **deliver** Pharaoh Hophra king of AIT
Eze 9: 8 *Are* you **g** *to* **destroy** the entire remnant of AIT
Eze 11: 5 I know **what is g through** your mind. H5091
Eze 12:23 *I am* **g** *to* **put an end** *to* this proverb, and they AIT
Eze 13:11 cover it with whitewash that *it is* **g** *to* **fall**. AIT
Eze 16:37 therefore I *am* **g** *to* **gather** all your lovers, AIT
Eze 21: 4 Because *I am* **g** *to* **cut off** the righteous and AIT
Eze 25: 4 therefore I *am* **g** *to* **give** you to the people of AIT
Eze 26: 7 From the north I *am* **g** *to* **bring** against Tyre AIT
Eze 28: 7 I *am* **g** *to* **bring** foreigners against you, the AIT
Eze 29:19 I *am* **g** *to* **give** Egypt to Nebuchadnezzar king AIT
Eze 36:22 of Israel, that I *am* **g** *to* **do** these things, but AIT
Eze 37:12 I *am* **g** *to* **open** your graves and bring you up AIT
Eze 37:19 I *am* **g** *to* **take** the stick of Joseph—which is AIT
Eze 40: 4 attention to everything I *am* **g** *to* **show** you, AIT
Eze 44:25 not defile himself by **g** near a dead person; H995
Eze 46:10 **g in** when they go in and going out when H995
Eze 46:10 they go in and **g out** when they go out. H3655
Da 2:29 mysteries showed you what *is* **g** *to* **happen**. AIT
Da 8:19 "I *am* **g** *to* **tell** you what will happen later in AIT
Hos 2:14 "Therefore I *am* now **g** *to* **allure** her; I will AIT
Joel 3: 7 I *am* **g** *to* **rouse** them out of the places to AIT
Jnh 3: 4 Jonah began by **g** a day's journey into the H995
Hab 1: 5 For *I am* **g** *to* **do** something in your days that AIT
Hag 2:21 of Judah that I *am* **g** *to* **shake** the heavens AIT
Zec 2: 2 "Where *are* you **g**?" He answered H2143
Zec 3: 8 I *am* **g** *to* **bring** my servant, the AIT
Zec 5: 3 is the curse that *is* **g out** over the whole H3655
Zec 6: 5 **g out** from standing in the presence of the H3655
Zec 6: 6 with the black horses *is* **g** toward the north H3655
Zec 6: 8 those **g** toward the north country have H3655
Zec 8:21 seek the LORD Almighty. *I* myself *am* **g**. H2143
Zec 11:16 For I *am* **g** *to* **raise up** a shepherd over the AIT
Zec 12: 2 "I *am* **g** *to* **make** Jerusalem a cup that sends AIT
Zec 12: 8 like the angel of the LORD **g** before them. NDT
Mal 3:14 requirements and **g about** like mourners H2143
Mt 2:13 Herod *is* **g to** search for the child to kill G3516
Mt 4:21 **G on** from there, he saw two other G4581
Mt 8:25 "Lord, save us! *We're* **g** *to* **drown**!" AIT
Mt 9:32 *While* they *were* **g out**, a man who was G2002
Mt 10:23 *you will* not **finish g** *through* the towns of AIT
Mt 12: 9 **G on** from that place, he went into their G3553
Mt 16:27 For the Son of Man *is* **g to** come in his G3516
Mt 17:12 way the Son of Man *is* **g to** suffer at their G3516
Mt 17:22 "The Son of Man *is* **g to** be delivered G3516S
Mt 20: 8 the last ones hired and **g on to** the first. G2401
Mt 20:17 Now Jesus *was* **g up** to Jerusalem. On the G326
Mt 20:18 "*We are* **g up** to Jerusalem, and the Son of G326
Mt 20:22 "Can you drink the cup I *am* **g to** drink?" G3516
Mt 20:30 when they heard that Jesus *was* **g by** G4135
Mt 25: 8 us some of your oil; our lamps *are* **g out**. G4931
Mt 25:14 it will be like a man **g on a journey**, who G623
Mt 26:18 *I am* **g** *to* **celebrate** the Passover with my AIT
Mt 26:39 **G** a little **farther**, he fell with his face to G4601
Mt 26:49 **G** at once to Jesus, Judas said, "Greetings G4665
Mt 26:62 said to Jesus, "*Are you* not **g** *to* **answer**? AIT
Mt 27:32 *As they were* **g out**, they met a man from G2002
Mt 27:40 "You *who are* **g** *to* **destroy** the temple and AIT
Mt 27:58 **G** to Pilate, he asked for Jesus' body, and G4665
Mt 28: 2 from heaven and, **g** to the tomb, rolled G4665
Mt 28: 7 from the dead and *is* **g ahead** of you into G4575
Mk 2:23 One Sabbath Jesus *was* **g** through the G4182
Mk 6:31 were coming and **g** that they did not even G5632
Mk 7:15 a person can defile them *by* **g into** them. G1660
Mk 9:31 Son of Man is *g to be* **delivered** into the AIT
Mk 10:32 told them what *was* **g to** happen to him. G3516
Mk 10:33 "*We are* **g up** to Jerusalem," he said, "and G326
Mk 13:34 It's like a man **g away**: He leaves his house G624
Mk 14:35 **G** a little **farther**, he fell to the ground G4601
Mk 14:45 **G** at once to Jesus, Judas said, "Rabbi!" G2262
Mk 14:60 asked Jesus, "*Are you* not **g** *to* **answer**? AIT
Mk 15: 4 Pilate asked him, "Aren't *you* **g** *to* **answer**? AIT
Mk 15:29 You *who are* **g** *to* **destroy** the temple and AIT
Mk 16: 7 '*He is* **g ahead** of you into Galilee. G4575
Lk 1:36 your relative *is* **g** *to* **have** a child in her old AIT
Lk 1:59 and *they were* **g** *to* **name** him after his father AIT
Lk 1:66 asking, "What then *is* this child **g** *to* **be**?" AIT
Lk 6: 1 Sabbath Jesus *was* **g through** the G1388
Lk 8:24 "Master, Master, *we're* **g** *to* **drown**! AIT
Lk 9: 7 the tetrarch heard about all that *was* **g on**. G1181
Lk 9:44 The Son of Man *is* **g to** be delivered into G3516
Lk 10:30 "A man *was* **g down** from Jerusalem to G2849
Lk 10:31 happened *to be* **g down** the same road, G2849
Lk 12:54 you say, '*It's* **g to** rain,' and it does. G2262
Lk 12:55 you say, '*It's* **g** *to* **be** hot,' and it is. AIT
Lk 12:58 As *you are* **g** with your adversary to the G5632
Lk 13:23 *are* only a few people **g** *to* **be saved**? AIT
Lk 15:26 servants and asked him what *was* **g on**. G1639
Lk 17:12 *As* he *was* **g into** a village, ten men who G1656
Lk 18:31 told them, "*We are* **g up** to Jerusalem G326
Lk 18:36 When he heard the crowd **g by**, he asked G1388
Lk 19:11 kingdom of God *was* **g to** appear at once. G3516
Lk 19:28 he went on ahead, **g up** to Jerusalem. G326
Lk 22:21 the hand of him *who is* **g** *to* **betray** me is with AIT
Lk 22:49 Jesus' followers saw what *was* **g** *to* **happen**, AIT
Lk 23:52 **G** to Pilate, he asked for Jesus' body. G4665
Lk 24:13 day two of them were **g** to a village called G4513
Lk 24:21 he was the *one who was* **g to** redeem G3516
Lk 24:28 the village to which *they were* **g**, G4513
Lk 24:28 Jesus continued on as if *he were* **g** farther. G4513
Lk 24:49 I *am* **g** *to* **send** you what my Father has AIT
Jn 2:20 you *are* **g** *to* **raise** it in three days? AIT
Jn 3: 8 tell where it comes from or where *it is* **g**. G5632
Jn 3:26 he is baptizing, and everyone *is* **g** to him." G2262
Jn 5:47 how *are you* **g** *to* **believe** what I say? AIT
Jn 6: 6 already had in mind what *he was* **g to** do. G3516
Jn 7: 8 *I am* not **g up** to this festival, because my G326
Jn 7:33 then *I am* **g** to the one who sent me. G5632
Jn 8:14 where I came from and where *I am* **g**. G5632
Jn 8:14 idea where I come from or where *I am* **g**. G5632
Jn 8:21 said to them, "*I am* **g away**, and you will G5632
Jn 11: 8 tried to stone you, and yet *you are* **g** back?" G5632
Jn 11:11 but *I am* **g** there to wake him up. G4513
Jn 11:31 supposing *she was* **g** to the tomb to G5632
Jn 12:11 of the Jews *were* **g over** to Jesus and G5632
Jn 12:33 to show the kind of death *he was* **g to** die. G3516
Jn 12:35 "You *are* **g** *to* **have** the light just a little while AIT
Jn 12:35 the dark does not know where *they are* **g**. G5632
Jn 13: 6 "Lord, *are* you **g** *to* **wash** my feet? AIT
Jn 13:11 For he knew who *was* **g** *to* **betray** him, and AIT
Jn 13:21 truly I tell you, one of you *is* **g** *to* **betray** me." AIT
Jn 13:33 Where *I am* **g**, you cannot come G5632
Jn 13:36 Peter asked him, "Lord, where *are you* **g**?" G5632
Jn 13:36 replied, "Where *I am* **g**, you cannot follow G5632
Jn 14: 2 have told you that *I am* **g** there to prepare G4513
Jn 14: 4 know the way to the place where *I am* **g**." G5632
Jn 14: 5 we don't know where *you are* **g**, so how G5632

Jn 14:12 than these, because I *am* g to the Father. G4513
Jn 14:28 '*I am* g **away** and I am coming back to G5632
Jn 14:28 would be glad that *I am* g to the Father, G4513
Jn 16: 5 now *I am* g to him who sent me. G5632
Jn 16: 5 None of you asks me, 'Where *are you* g?' G5632
Jn 16: 7 it is for your good that I *am* g **away**. G599
Jn 16:10 because *I am* g to the Father, where G5632
Jn 16:17 and 'Because *I am* g to the Father'?" G5632
Jn 16:28 the world and g back to the Father." G4513
Jn 18: 4 knowing all that *was* g *to* **happen** to him AIT
Jn 18:32 about the kind of death *he was* g **to** die. G3516
Jn 21: 3 "*I'm* g **out** to fish," Simon Peter told them G5632
Jn 21:20 had said, "Lord, who is *g to* **betray** you?" AIT
Ac 1: 6 *are you* at this time *g to* **restore** the kingdom AIT
Ac 1:10 intently up into the sky *as* he *was* g, G4513
Ac 3: 1 Peter and John *were* g **up** to the temple at G326
Ac 3: 2 to beg from those g **into** the temple courts G1660
Ac 4:16 "What *are we g to* **do** with these men?" AIT
Ac 8: 3 G from house to house, he dragged off G1660
Ac 11:12 to have no hesitation *about* g **with** them. G5302
Ac 13:11 *You are g to* **be** blind for a time, not even AIT
Ac 13:41 I *am g to* **do** something in your days that AIT
Ac 14:24 *After* g **through** Pisidia, they came into G1451
Ac 16:16 Once *when* we *were* g to the place of G4513
Ac 17:23 this is what I *am g to* **proclaim** to you. AIT
Ac 18:10 and no one *is g to* **attack** and harm you AIT
Ac 20:13 where *we were* g **to** take Paul aboard. G3516
Ac 20:13 because he was g there **on foot**. G4269
Ac 20:22 by the Spirit, I *am* g to Jerusalem, not G4513
Ac 22:26 "What *are you* g **to** do?" he asked. G3516
Ac 25: 4 Caesarea, and I myself am g there soon. G1744
Ac 26:12 these journeys *I was* g to Damascus with G4513
Ac 27:10 that our voyage *is* g **to** be disastrous and G3516
Ac 27:30 pretending *they were* g **to** lower some G3516
1Co 16: 5 for *I will be* g **through** Macedonia. G1451
2Co 10:14 *We are* not g **too far** in our boasting, as G2391
Php 1:30 *since* you *are* g **through** the same struggle G2400
1Ti 5:13 of being idle and g **about** from house to G4320
Heb 3:10 'Their hearts *are* always g **astray**, and they G4414
Heb 5: 2 those who are ignorant and *are* g **astray**, G4414
Heb 11: 8 though he did not know where *he was* g. G2262
Jas 2:12 act as *those who are* g **to** be judged G3516
1Pe 2:25 For "you were like sheep g **astray**," but G4414
1Pe 3:13 Who *is g to* **harm** you if you are eager to do AIT
2Pe 2: 6 an example *of what is* g **to happen** to the G3516
1Jn 2:11 They do not know where *they are* g G5632
1Jn 2:19 their g showed that none of them NDT
Rev 3:10 of trial that *is* g **to** come on the whole G3516
Rev 17:11 to the seven and *is* g to his destruction. G5632

GOLAN (4)

Dt 4:43 the Gadites; and G in Bashan, for the H1584
Jos 20: 8 G in Bashan in the tribe of Manasseh. H1584
Jos 21:27 of Manasseh, G in Bashan (a city of H1584
1Ch 6:71 they received G in Bashan and also H1584

GOLD (467) [GOLD-COVERED, GOLDEN, GOLDSMITH, GOLDSMITHS]

Ge 2:11 entire land of Havilah, where there is g. H2298
Ge 2:12 The g *of* that land is good; aromatic resin H2298
Ge 13: 2 wealthy in livestock and in silver and g. H2298
Ge 24:22 the man took out a g nose ring weighing H2298
Ge 24:22 a beka and two g bracelets weighing ten H2298
Ge 24:35 cattle, silver and g, male and female H2298
Ge 24:53 servant brought out g and silver jewelry H2298
Ge 41:42 fine linen and put a g chain around his H2298
Ge 44: 8 we steal silver or g from your master's H2298
Ex 3:22 articles of silver and g and for clothing, H2298
Ex 11: 2 their neighbors for articles of silver and g." H2298
Ex 12:35 articles of silver and g and for clothing. H2298
Ex 20:23 yourselves gods of silver or gods of g. H2298
Ex 25: 3 receive from them: g, silver and bronze; H2298
Ex 25:11 Overlay it with pure g, both inside and out H2298
Ex 25:11 out, and make a g molding around it. H2298
Ex 25:12 Cast four g rings for it and fasten them to H2298
Ex 25:13 of acacia wood and overlay them with g. H2298
Ex 25:17 "Make an atonement cover of pure g H2298
Ex 25:18 out of hammered g at the ends of the H2298
Ex 25:24 Overlay it with pure g and make a gold H2298
Ex 25:24 gold and make a g molding around it. H2298
Ex 25:25 wide and put a g molding on the rim. H2298
Ex 25:26 Make four g rings for the table and fasten H2298
Ex 25:28 overlay them with g and carry the table H2298
Ex 25:29 And make its plates and dishes of pure g H2298
Ex 25:31 "Make a lampstand of pure g. Hammer H2298
Ex 25:36 the lampstand, hammered out of pure g. H2298
Ex 25:38 trimmers and trays are to be of pure g. H2298
Ex 25:39 A talent of pure g is to be used for the H2298
Ex 26: 6 Then make fifty g clasps and use them to H2298
Ex 26:29 the frames with g and make gold rings to H2298
Ex 26:29 with gold and make g rings to hold the H2298
Ex 26:29 Also overlay the crossbars with g. H2298
Ex 26:32 Hang it with g hooks on four posts of H2298
Ex 26:32 wood overlaid with g and standing on H2298
Ex 26:37 Make g hooks for this curtain and five H2298
Ex 26:37 five posts of acacia wood overlaid with g. H2298
Ex 28: 5 Have them use g, and blue, purple and H2298
Ex 28: 6 "Make the ephod of g, and of blue H2298
Ex 28: 8 piece with the ephod and made with g, H2298
Ex 28:11 mount the stones in g filigree settings H2298
Ex 28:13 Make g filigree settings H2298
Ex 28:14 two braided chains of pure g, like a H2298
Ex 28:15 of g, and of blue, purple and scarlet yarn H2298
Ex 28:20 Mount them in g filigree settings. H2298
Ex 28:22 make braided chains of pure g, H2298
Ex 28:23 Make two g rings for it and fasten them to H2298
Ex 28:24 Fasten the two g chains to the rings at the H2298
Ex 28:26 Make two g rings and attach them to the H2298
Ex 28:27 Make two more g rings and attach them to H2298
Ex 28:33 of the robe, with g bells between them. H2298
Ex 28:34 The g bells and the pomegranates are to H2298
Ex 28:36 a plate of pure g and engrave on it as H2298
Ex 30: 3 all the sides and the horns with pure g, H2298
Ex 30: 3 and make a g molding around it. H2298
Ex 30: 4 Make two g rings for the altar below the H2298
Ex 30: 5 of acacia wood and overlay them with g. H2298
Ex 31: 4 to make artistic designs for work in g, silver H2298
Ex 31: 8 the pure g lampstand and all its accessories, NDT
Ex 32: 2 "Take off the g earrings that your wives H2298
Ex 32:24 'Whoever has any g jewelry, take it off. H2298
Ex 32:24 Then they gave me the g, and I threw it NDT
Ex 32:31 They have made themselves gods of g. H2298
Ex 35: 5 is to bring to the LORD an offering of g, H2298
Ex 35:22 came and brought g jewelry of all kinds: H2298
Ex 35:22 all presented their g as a wave offering to H2298
Ex 35:32 to make artistic designs for work in g, silver H2298
Ex 36:13 Then they made fifty g clasps and used H2298
Ex 36:34 the frames with g and made gold rings to H2298
Ex 36:34 with gold and made g rings to hold the H2298
Ex 36:34 They also overlaid the crossbars with g. H2298
Ex 36:36 wood for it and overlaid them with g. H2298
Ex 36:36 They made g hooks for them and cast H2298
Ex 36:38 their bands with g and made their five H2298
Ex 37: 2 He overlaid it with pure g, both inside H2298
Ex 37: 2 and made a g molding around it. H2298
Ex 37: 3 He cast four g rings for it and fastened H2298
Ex 37: 4 of acacia wood and overlaid them with g. H2298
Ex 37: 6 He made the atonement cover of pure g— H2298
Ex 37: 7 out of hammered g at the ends of the H2298
Ex 37:11 overlaid it with pure g and made a gold H2298
Ex 37:11 gold and made a g molding around it. H2298
Ex 37:12 wide and put a g molding on the rim. H2298
Ex 37:13 They cast four g rings for the table and H2298
Ex 37:15 of acacia wood and were overlaid with g. H2298
Ex 37:16 they made from pure g the articles for the H2298
Ex 37:17 They made the lampstand of pure g. H2298
Ex 37:22 the lampstand, hammered out of pure g. H2298
Ex 37:23 as its wick trimmers and trays, of pure g. H2298
Ex 37:24 its accessories from one talent of pure g. H2298
Ex 37:26 all the sides and the horns with pure g, H2298
Ex 37:26 and made a g molding around it. H2298
Ex 37:27 They made two g rings below the molding H2298
Ex 37:28 of acacia wood and overlaid them with g. H2298
Ex 38:24 amount of the g *from* the wave offering H2298
Ex 39: 2 They made the ephod of g, and of blue H2298
Ex 39: 3 out thin sheets of g and cut strands to be H2298
Ex 39: 5 piece with the ephod and made with g, H2298
Ex 39: 6 the onyx stones in g filigree settings and H2298
Ex 39: 8 of g, and of blue, purple and scarlet yarn H2298
Ex 39:13 They were mounted in g filigree settings. H2298
Ex 39:15 they made braided chains of pure g, H2298
Ex 39:16 They made two g filigree settings and two H2298
Ex 39:16 two gold filigree settings and two g rings, H2298
Ex 39:17 fastened the two g chains to the rings H2298
Ex 39:19 They made two g rings and attached them H2298
Ex 39:20 they made two more g rings and attached H2298
Ex 39:25 made bells of pure g and attached them H2298
Ex 39:30 emblem, out of pure g and engraved on it H2298
Ex 39:37 the pure g lampstand with its row of lamps NDT
Ex 39:38 the g altar, the anointing oil, the fragrant H2298
Ex 40: 5 Place the g altar of incense in front of the H2298
Ex 40:26 Moses placed the g altar in the tent of H2298
Lev 8: 9 on Aaron's head and set the g plate, H2298
Lev 24: 4 lamps on the pure g lampstand before the NDT
Lev 24: 6 on the table of pure g before the LORD. NDT
Nu 4:11 "Over the g altar they are to spread a blue H2298
Nu 7:14 one g dish weighing ten shekels, filled H2298
Nu 7:20 one g dish weighing ten shekels, filled H2298
Nu 7:26 one g dish weighing ten shekels, filled H2298
Nu 7:32 one g dish weighing ten shekels, filled H2298
Nu 7:38 one g dish weighing ten shekels, filled H2298
Nu 7:44 one g dish weighing ten shekels, filled H2298
Nu 7:50 one g dish weighing ten shekels, filled H2298
Nu 7:56 one g dish weighing ten shekels, filled H2298
Nu 7:62 one g dish weighing ten shekels, filled H2298
Nu 7:68 one g dish weighing ten shekels, filled H2298
Nu 7:74 one g dish weighing ten shekels, filled H2298
Nu 7:80 one g dish weighing ten shekels, filled H2298
Nu 7:84 sprinkling bowls and twelve g dishes. H2298
Nu 7:86 The twelve g dishes filled with incense H2298
Nu 7:86 the g dishes weighed a hundred and H2298
Nu 8: 4 It was made of hammered g—from its H2298
Nu 22:18 gave me all the silver and g in his palace, H2298
Nu 24:13 gave me all the silver and g in his palace, H2298
Nu 31:22 G, silver, bronze, iron, tin, lead H2298
Nu 31:50 to the LORD the g articles each of us H2298
Nu 31:51 the priest accepted from them the g— H2298
Nu 31:52 All the g from the commanders of H2298
Nu 31:54 accepted the g from the commanders H2298
Dt 7:25 Do not covet the silver and g on them H2298
Dt 8:13 your silver and g increase and all you H2298
Dt 17:17 accumulate large amounts of silver and g. H2298
Dt 29:17 idols of wood and stone, of silver and g. H2298
Jos 6:19 All the silver and g and the articles of H2298
Jos 6:24 put the silver and g and the articles of H2298
Jos 7:21 silver and a bar of g weighing fifty shekels H2298
Jos 7:24 the robe, the g bar, his sons and H2298
Jos 22: 8 with silver, g, bronze and iron, and a H2298
Jdg 8:24 of the Ishmaelites to wear g earrings.) H2298
Jdg 8:26 The weight of the g rings he asked for H2298
Jdg 8:27 Gideon made **the** g into an ephod, which H2257S
1Sa 6: 4 replied, "Five g tumors and five gold rats H2298
1Sa 6: 4 "Five gold tumors and five g rats H2298
1Sa 6: 8 beside it put the g objects you are H2298
1Sa 6:11 containing the g rats and the models H2298
1Sa 6:15 with the chest containing the g objects, H2298
1Sa 6:17 These are the g tumors the Philistines H2298
1Sa 6:18 the number of the g rats was according H2298
2Sa 1:24 your garments with ornaments of g. H2298
2Sa 8: 7 David took the g shields that belonged to H2298
2Sa 8:10 him articles of silver, of g and of bronze. H2298
2Sa 8:11 with the silver and g from all the nations H2298
2Sa 12:30 It weighed a talent of g, and it was set H2298
2Sa 21: 4 to demand silver or g from Saul or his H2298
1Ki 6:20 He overlaid the inside with pure g, and H2298
1Ki 6:21 the inside of the temple with pure g, H2298
1Ki 6:21 he extended g chains across the front H2298
1Ki 6:21 sanctuary, which was overlaid with g. H2298
1Ki 6:22 So he overlaid the whole interior with g H2298
1Ki 6:22 He also overlaid with g the altar that H2298
1Ki 6:28 He overlaid the cherubim with g. H2298
1Ki 6:30 outer rooms of the temple with g. H2298
1Ki 6:32 palm trees with hammered g. H2298
1Ki 6:35 overlaid them with g hammered evenly H2298
1Ki 7:49 the lampstands of pure g (five on the right H2298
1Ki 7:49 the g floral work and lamps and tongs H2298
1Ki 7:50 the pure g basins, wick trimmers H2298
1Ki 7:50 the g sockets for the doors of the H2298
1Ki 7:51 the silver and g and the furnishings—and H2298
1Ki 9:11 the cedar and juniper and g he wanted. H2298
1Ki 9:14 had sent to the king 120 talents of g. H2298
1Ki 9:28 Ophir and brought back 420 talents of g, H2298
1Ki 10: 2 large quantities of g, and precious stones H2298
1Ki 10:10 And she gave the king 120 talents of g H2298
1Ki 10:11 Hiram's ships brought g from Ophir; and H2298
1Ki 10:14 The weight of the g that Solomon H2298
1Ki 10:16 hundred large shields of hammered g; H2298
1Ki 10:16 hundred shekels of g went into each H2298
1Ki 10:17 hundred small shields of hammered g, H2298
1Ki 10:17 with three minas of g in each shield. H2298
1Ki 10:18 with ivory and overlaid with fine g. H2298
1Ki 10:21 All King Solomon's goblets were g, and H2298
1Ki 10:21 of the Forest of Lebanon were pure g. H2298
1Ki 10:22 it returned, carrying g, silver and ivory, H2298
1Ki 10:25 articles of silver and g, robes, H2298
1Ki 14:26 including all the g shields Solomon had H2298
1Ki 15:15 LORD the silver and g and the articles that H2298
1Ki 15:18 all the silver and g that was left in the H2298
1Ki 15:19 I am sending you a gift of silver and g. H2298
1Ki 20: 3 'Your silver and g are mine, and the best H2298
1Ki 20: 5 'I sent to demand your silver and g, your H2298
1Ki 20: 7 my silver and my g, I did not refuse him." H2298
1Ki 22:48 fleet of trading ships to go to Ophir for g, H2298
2Ki 5: 5 six thousand shekels of g and ten sets of H2298
2Ki 7: 8 they took silver, g and clothes, and went H2298
2Ki 12:13 any other articles of g or silver for the H2298
2Ki 12:18 dedicated and all the g found in the H2298
2Ki 14:14 He took all the g and silver and all the H2298
2Ki 16: 8 took the silver and g found in the temple H2298
2Ki 18:14 talents of silver and thirty talents of g. H2298
2Ki 18:16 Judah stripped off the g with which he had NDT
2Ki 20:13 the silver, the g, the spices and the fine H2298
2Ki 23:33 hundred talents of silver and a talent of g. H2298
2Ki 23:35 Necho the silver and g he demanded. H2298
2Ki 23:35 the silver and g from the people of the H2298
2Ki 24:13 cut up the g articles that Solomon H2298
2Ki 25:15 that were made of **pure** g or silver. H2298+2298
1Ch 18: 7 David took the g shields carried by the H2298
1Ch 18:10 Hadoram brought all kinds of articles of g H2298
1Ch 18:11 with the silver and g he had taken from H2298
1Ch 20: 2 its weight was found to be a talent of g H2298
1Ch 21:25 six hundred shekels of g for the site. H2298
1Ch 22:14 the LORD a hundred thousand talents of g, H2298
1Ch 22:16 in g and silver, bronze and iron H2298
1Ch 28:14 the weight of g for all the gold H2298
1Ch 28:14 of gold for all the g articles to be used in H2298
1Ch 28:15 the weight of g for the gold lampstands H2298
1Ch 28:15 of gold for the g lampstands and their H2298
1Ch 28:16 the weight of g for each table for H2298
1Ch 28:17 the weight of pure g for the forks H2298
1Ch 28:17 the weight of g for each gold dish; the H2298
1Ch 28:17 the weight of gold for each g dish; the NDT
1Ch 28:18 weight of the refined g for the altar of H2298
1Ch 28:18 the cherubim of g that spread their wings H2298
1Ch 29: 2 temple of my God—g for the gold work H2298
1Ch 29: 2 my God—gold for the g *work*, silver for the H2298
1Ch 29: 3 personal treasures of g and silver for the H2298
1Ch 29: 4 three thousand talents of g (gold of Ophir H2298
1Ch 29: 4 talents of gold (g *of* Ophir) and seven H2298
1Ch 29: 5 the g *work* and the silver work, and for H2298
1Ch 29: 7 talents and ten thousand darics of g, H2298
2Ch 1:15 king made silver and g as common in H2298
2Ch 2: 7 a man skilled to work in g and silver H2298
2Ch 2:14 He is trained to work in g and silver H2298
2Ch 3: 4 He overlaid the inside with pure g. H2298
2Ch 3: 5 covered it with fine g and decorated it H2298

2Ch 3: 6 And the g he used was gold of Parvaim H2298
2Ch 3: 6 And the gold he used was g of Parvaim. H2298
2Ch 3: 7 walls and doors of the temple with g, and H2298
2Ch 3: 8 inside with six hundred talents of fine g. H2298
2Ch 3: 9 The g nails weighed fifty shekels. He also H2298
2Ch 3: 9 He also overlaid the upper parts with g. H2298
2Ch 3:10 cherubim and overlaid them with g. H2298
2Ch 4: 7 He made ten g lampstands according to H2298
2Ch 4: 8 also made a hundred g sprinkling bowls. H2298
2Ch 4:20 the lampstands of pure g with their lamps, H2298
2Ch 4:21 the g floral work and lamps and tongs H2298
2Ch 4:21 lamps and tongs (they were solid g); H2298
2Ch 4:22 the pure g wick trimmers, sprinkling bowls, H2298
2Ch 4:22 censers; and the g doors of the temple: H2298
2Ch 5: 1 the silver and g and all the furnishings H2298
2Ch 8:18 back four hundred and fifty talents of g, H2298
2Ch 9: 1 large quantities of g, and precious stones H2298
2Ch 9: 9 Then she gave the king 120 talents of g H2298
2Ch 9:10 of Solomon brought g from Ophir; H2298
2Ch 9:13 The weight of the g that Solomon H2298
2Ch 9:14 territories brought g and silver to Solomon H2298
2Ch 9:15 hundred large shields of hammered g; H2298
2Ch 9:15 shekels of hammered g went into each H2298
2Ch 9:16 hundred small shields of hammered g, H2298
2Ch 9:16 three hundred shekels of g in each shield. H2298
2Ch 9:17 with ivory and overlaid with pure g. H2298
2Ch 9:18 a footstool of g was attached to it. H2298
2Ch 9:20 All King Solomon's goblets were g, and H2298
2Ch 9:20 of the Forest of Lebanon were pure g. H2298
2Ch 9:21 it returned, carrying g, silver and ivory, H2298
2Ch 9:24 articles of silver and g, and robes, H2298
2Ch 12: 9 including the g shields Solomon had H2298
2Ch 13:11 light the lamps on the g lampstand every H2298
2Ch 15:18 God the silver and g and the articles that H2298
2Ch 16: 2 took the silver and g out of the treasuries H2298
2Ch 16: 3 I am sending you silver and g. Now break H2298
2Ch 21: 3 gifts of silver and g and articles of value, H2298
2Ch 24:14 dishes and other objects of g and silver. H2298
2Ch 25:24 He took all the g and silver and all the H2298
2Ch 32:27 his silver and g and for his precious H2298
2Ch 36: 3 hundred talents of silver and a talent of g. H2298
Ezr 1: 4 are to provide them with silver and g, H2298
Ezr 1: 6 assisted them with articles of silver and g, H2298
Ezr 1: 9 g dishes 30 silver dishes 1,000 silver pans H2298
Ezr 1:10 g bowls 30 matching silver bowls 410 H2298
Ezr 1:11 were 5,400 articles of g and of silver. H2298
Ezr 2:69 treasury for this work 61,000 darics of g, H2298
Ezr 5:14 of Babylon the g and silver articles A10160
Ezr 6: 5 the g and silver articles of the house of A10160
Ezr 7:15 you the silver and g that the king and his A10160
Ezr 7:16 all the silver and g you may obtain from A10160
Ezr 7:18 best with the rest of the silver and g, A10160
Ezr 8:25 of silver and g and the articles that H2298
Ezr 8:26 weighing 100 talents, 100 talents of g, H2298
Ezr 8:27 20 bowls of g valued at 1,000 darics, and H2298
Ezr 8:27 of polished bronze, as precious as g. H2298
Ezr 8:28 The silver and g are a freewill offering to H2298
Ezr 8:30 the silver and g and sacred articles H2298
Ezr 8:33 out the silver and g and the sacred H2298
Ne 7:70 gave to the treasury 1,000 darics of g, H2298
Ne 7:71 20,000 darics of g and 2,200 minas of H2298
Ne 7:72 rest of the people was 20,000 darics of g, H2298
Est 1: 6 There were couches of g and silver on a H2298
Est 1: 7 Wine was served in goblets of g, each one H2298
Est 4:11 king extends the g scepter to them and H2298
Est 5: 2 held out to her the g scepter that was in H2298
Est 8: 4 king extended the g scepter to Esther and H2298
Est 8:15 a large crown of g and a purple robe of H2298
Job 3:15 with princes who had g, who filled their H2298
Job 22:24 your g of Ophir to the rocks in the ravines, H234
Job 22:25 then the Almighty will be your g, the H1309
Job 23:10 he has tested me, I will come forth as g. H2298
Job 28: 1 silver and a place where g is refined. H2298
Job 28: 6 and its dust contains nuggets of g. H2298
Job 28:15 It cannot be bought with the finest g, nor H6034
Job 28:16 It cannot be bought with the g of Ophir H4188
Job 28:17 Neither g nor crystal can compare with it H2298
Job 28:17 nor can it be had for jewels of g. H7058
Job 28:19 it cannot be bought with pure g. H4188
Job 31:24 If I have put my trust in g or said to pure gold H2298
Job 31:24 put my trust in gold or said to pure g, H4188
Job 42:11 gave him a piece of silver and a g ring. H2298
Ps 12: 6 in a crucible, like g refined seven times. H3021
Ps 19:10 They are more precious than g, than H2298
Ps 19:10 than much pure g; they are sweeter H7058
Ps 21: 3 placed a crown of pure g on his head. H7058
Ps 45: 9 right hand is the royal bride in g of Ophir. H4188
Ps 45:13 chamber; her gown is interwoven with g. H2298
Ps 68:13 with silver, its feathers with shining g." H3021
Ps 72:15 May g from Sheba be given him H2298
Ps 105:37 laden with silver and g, and from among H2298
Ps 115: 4 But their idols are silver and g, made by H2298
Ps 119:72 than thousands of pieces of silver and g. H2298
Ps 119:127 I love your commands more than g, H2298
Ps 119:127 more than gold, more than pure g, H7058
Ps 135:15 The idols of the nations are silver and g H2298
Pr 3:14 silver and yields better returns than g. H3021
Pr 8:10 of silver, knowledge rather than choice g, H3021
Pr 8:19 My fruit is better than fine g; what I yield H7058
Pr 11:22 Like a g ring in a pig's snout is a beautiful H2298
Pr 16:16 How much better to get wisdom than g, to H3021
Pr 17: 3 crucible for silver and the furnace for g, H2298
Pr 20:15 G there is, and rubies in abundance, but H2298
Pr 22: 1 to be esteemed is better than silver or g. H2298
Pr 25:11 Like apples of g in settings of silver is a H2298
Pr 25:12 Like an earring of g or an ornament of H2298
Pr 25:12 an ornament of fine g is the rebuke of H4188
Pr 27:21 crucible for silver and the furnace for g, H2298
Ecc 2: 8 I amassed silver and g for myself, and the H2298
SS 1:11 We will make you earrings of g, studded H2298
SS 3:10 of silver, its base of g. Its seat was H2298
SS 5:11 His head is purest g; his hair is H4188+7058
SS 5:14 His arms are rods of g set with topaz. H2298
SS 5:15 pillars of marble set on bases of pure g. H7058
Isa 2: 7 Their land is full of silver and g; there is H2298
Isa 2:20 bats their idols of silver and idols of g, H2298
Isa 13:12 I will make people scarcer than pure g H7058
Isa 13:12 pure gold, more rare than the g of Ophir. H4188
Isa 13:17 care for silver and have no delight in g. H2298
Isa 30:22 silver and your images covered with g; H2298
Isa 31: 7 idols of silver and g your sinful hands H2298
Isa 39: 2 the silver, the g, the spices, the fine olive H2298
Isa 40:19 overlays it with g and fashions silver H2298
Isa 46: 6 Some pour out g from their bags and H2298
Isa 60: 6 bearing g and incense and proclaiming H2298
Isa 60: 9 with their silver and g, to the honor of the H2298
Isa 60:17 Instead of bronze I will bring you g, and H2298
Jer 4:30 yourself in scarlet and put on jewels of g? H2298
Jer 10: 4 They adorn it with silver and g; they H2298
Jer 10: 9 brought from Tarshish and g from Uphaz. H2298
Jer 51: 7 Babylon was a g cup in the LORD's hand H2298
Jer 52:19 that were made of pure g or silver. H2298+2298
La 4: 1 How the g has lost its luster, the fine gold H2298
La 4: 1 has lost its luster, the fine g become dull! H4188
La 4: 2 once worth their weight in g, are now H7058
Eze 7:19 their g will be treated as a thing H2298
Eze 7:19 Their silver and g will not be able to H2298
Eze 16:13 So you were adorned with g and silver H2298
Eze 16:17 the jewelry made of my g and silver, and H2298
Eze 27:22 of spices and precious stones, and g. H2298
Eze 28: 4 yourself and amassed g and silver in your H2298
Eze 28:13 settings and mountings were made of g; H2298
Eze 38:13 to carry off silver and g, to take away H2298
Da 2:32 head of the statue was made of pure g, A10160
Da 2:35 the silver and the g were all broken to A10160
Da 2:38 over them all. You are that head of g. A10160
Da 2:45 the clay, the silver and the g to pieces. A10160
Da 3: 1 Nebuchadnezzar made an image of g, A10160
Da 3: 5 worship the image of g that King A10160
Da 3: 7 worshiped the image of g that King A10160
Da 3:10 fall down and worship the image of g, A10160
Da 3:12 worship the image of g you have set up." A10160
Da 3:14 worship the image of g I have set up? A10160
Da 3:18 worship the image of g you have set up." A10160
Da 5: 2 to bring in the g and silver goblets A10160
Da 5: 3 they brought in the g goblets that had A10160
Da 5: 4 they praised the gods of g and silver, of A10160
Da 5: 7 purple and have a g chain placed A10160
Da 5:16 purple and have a g chain placed A10160
Da 5:23 You praised the gods of silver and g, of A10160
Da 5:29 a g chain was placed around his neck A10160
Da 10: 5 with a belt of fine g from Uphaz around H4188
Da 11: 8 of silver and g and carry them off to H2298
Da 11:38 ancestors he will honor with g and silver, H2298
Da 11:43 of the treasures of g and silver and all the H2298
Hos 2: 8 who lavished on her the silver and g H2298
Hos 8: 4 With their silver and g they make idols H2298
Joel 3: 5 took my silver and my g and carried off my H2298
Na 2: 9 Plunder the g! The supply is H2298
Hab 2:19 It is covered with g and silver; there is no H2298
Zep 1:18 their silver nor their g will be able to save H2298
Hag 2: 8 'The silver is mine and the g is mine,' H2298
Zec 4: 2 "I see a solid g lampstand with a bowl at H2298
Zec 4:12 beside the two g pipes that pour out H2298
Zec 6:10 "Take silver and g from the exiles Heldai NDT
Zec 6:11 Take the silver and g and make a crown H2298
Zec 9: 3 like dust, and g like the dirt of the streets. H3021
Zec 13: 9 them like silver and test them like g. H2298
Zec 14:14 great quantities of g and silver and H2298
Mal 3: 3 Levites and refine them like g and silver. H2298
Mt 2:11 presented him with gifts of g, G5996
Mt 10: 9 "Do not get any g or silver or copper to G5996
Mt 18:24 ten thousand bags of g was brought to G5419
Mt 23:16 who swears by the g of the temple is G5996
Mt 23:17 the g, or the temple that makes the gold G5996
Mt 23:17 the temple that makes the g sacred? G5996
Mt 25:15 To one he gave five bags of g, to another G5419
Mt 25:16 received five bags of g went at once and G5419
Mt 25:17 one with two bags of g gained two more. NDT
Mt 25:20 had received five bags of g brought the G5419
Mt 25:20 'you entrusted me with five bags of g. G5419
Mt 25:22 "The man with two bags of g also came G5419
Mt 25:22 'you entrusted me with two bags of g; see G5419
Mt 25:24 who had received one bag of g came. G5419
Mt 25:25 went out and hid your g in the ground. G5419
Mt 25:28 " 'So take the bag of g from him and give G5419
Ac 3: 6 Peter said, "Silver or g I do not have, but G5992
Ac 17:29 divine being is like g or silver or stone— G5996
Ac 20:33 coveted anyone's silver or g or clothing. G5992
1Co 3:12 anyone builds on this foundation using g, G5996
1Ti 2: 9 hairstyles or g or pearls or expensive G5992
2Ti 2:20 there are articles not only of g and silver, G5997
Heb 9: 4 This ark contained the g jar of manna G5997
Jas 2: 2 your meeting wearing a g ring and fine G5993
Jas 5: 3 Your g and silver are corroded. Their G5996
1Pe 1: 7 of greater worth than g, which perishes G5992
1Pe 1:18 such as silver or g that you were G5992
1Pe 3: 3 the wearing of g jewelry or fine G5992
Rev 3:18 you to buy from me g refined in the fire, G5992
Rev 4: 4 white and had crowns of g on their heads. G5997
Rev 9: 7 they wore something like crowns of g, G5996
Rev 9:20 worshiping demons, and idols of g, silver, G5997
Rev 14:14 man with a crown of g on his head and a G5997
Rev 17: 4 was glittering with g, precious stones G5992
Rev 18:12 cargoes of g, silver, precious stones and G5996
Rev 18:16 glittering with g, precious stones and G5992
Rev 21:15 had a measuring rod of g to measure the G5997
Rev 21:18 the city of pure g, as pure as glass. G5992
Rev 21:21 The great street of the city was of g, as G5992

GOLD-COVERED (1) [GOLD, COVER]

Heb 9: 4 incense and the g ark of the G4328+4119+5992

GOLDEN (21) [GOLD]

1Ki 7:48 the g altar; the golden table on which H2298
1Ki 7:48 the g table on which was the bread of the H2298
1Ki 12:28 the king made two g calves. H2298
2Ki 10:29 the worship of the g calves at Bethel and H2298
2Ch 4:19 the g altar; the tables on which was the H2298
2Ch 13: 8 have with you the g calves that Jeroboam H2298
Job 37:22 Out of the north he comes in g splendor H2298
Ecc 12: 6 is severed, and the g bowl is broken H2298
Zec 4:12 the two gold pipes that pour out g oil?" H2298
Heb 9: 4 which had the g altar of incense and the G5997
Rev 1:12 when I turned I saw seven g lampstands, G5997
Rev 1:13 his feet and with a g sash around his G5997
Rev 1:20 of the seven g lampstands is this: G5997
Rev 2: 1 walks among the seven g lampstands. G5997
Rev 5: 8 they were holding g bowls full of incense G5997
Rev 8: 3 who had a g censer, came and G5997
Rev 8: 3 on the g altar in front of the throne. G5997
Rev 9:13 the four horns of the g altar that is before G5997
Rev 15: 6 linen and wore g sashes around their G5997
Rev 15: 7 seven angels seven g bowls filled with G5997
Rev 17: 4 She held a g cup in her hand, filled with G5997

GOLDSMITH (6) [GOLD]

Isa 40:19 a g overlays it with gold and fashions H7671
Isa 41: 7 The metalworker encourages the g, and H7671
Isa 46: 6 they hire a g to make it into a god H7671
Jer 10: 9 the craftsman and g have made is then H7671
Jer 10:14 every g is shamed by his idols. H7671
Jer 51:17 every g is shamed by his idols. H7671

GOLDSMITHS (3) [GOLD]

Ne 3: 8 Harhaiah, one of the g, repaired the next H7671
Ne 3:31 one of the g, made repairs as far H7672
Ne 3:32 Sheep Gate the g and merchants made H7671

GOLGOTHA (3)

Mt 27:33 They came to a place called G (which G1201
Mk 15:22 They brought Jesus to the place called G G1201
Jn 19:17 the Skull (which in Aramaic is called G). G1201

GOLIATH (7)

1Sa 17: 4 A champion named G, who was from H1669
1Sa 17: 8 G stood and shouted to the ranks of Israel NDT
1Sa 17:23 was talking with them, G, the Philistine H1669
1Sa 21: 9 "The sword of G the Philistine, whom H1669
1Sa 22:10 the sword of G the Philistine. H1669
2Sa 21:19 killed the brother of G the Gittite, H1669
1Ch 20: 5 killed Lahmi the brother of G the Gittite, H1669

GOMER (8)

Ge 10: 2 G, Magog, Madai, Javan, Tubal, Meshek H1699
Ge 10: 3 The sons of G: Ashkenaz, Riphath and H1699
1Ch 1: 5 G, Magog, Madai, Javan, Tubal, Meshek H1699
1Ch 1: 6 The sons of G: Ashkenaz, Riphath and H1699
Eze 38: 6 also G with all its troops, and Beth H1699
Hos 1: 3 So he married G daughter of Diblaim, and H1700
Hos 1: 6 G conceived again and gave birth to a NDT
Hos 1: 8 weaned Lo-Ruhamah, G had another son. NDT

GOMORRAH (23)

Ge 10:19 toward Sodom, G, Admah and Zeboyim H6686
Ge 13:10 before the LORD destroyed Sodom and G.) H6686
Ge 14: 2 Birsha king of G, Shinab king of Admah H6686
Ge 14: 8 Sodom, the king of G, the king of Admah, H6686
Ge 14:10 when the kings of Sodom and G fled H6686
Ge 14:11 goods of Sodom and G and all their food; H6686
Ge 18:20 against Sodom and G is so great and H6686
Ge 19:24 down burning sulfur on Sodom and G— H6686
Ge 19:28 He looked down toward Sodom and G H6686
Dt 29:23 be like the destruction of Sodom and G, H6686
Dt 32:32 vine of Sodom and from the fields of G. H6686
Isa 1: 9 like Sodom, we would have been like G. H6686
Isa 1:10 instruction of our God, you people of G! H6686
Isa 13:19 be overthrown by God like Sodom and G. H6686
Jer 23:14 the people of Jerusalem are like G." H6686
Jer 49:18 As Sodom and G were overthrown, along H6686
Jer 50:40 I overthrew Sodom and G along with their H6686
Am 4:11 some of you as I overthrew Sodom and G. H6686
Zep 2: 9 the Ammonites like G—a place of weeds H6686
Mt 10:15 Sodom and G on the day of judgment G1202
Ro 9:29 like Sodom, we would have been like G." G1202
2Pe 2: 6 cities of Sodom and G by burning them to G1202
Jude 7 Sodom and G and the surrounding towns G1202

G

GONE (208) [GO]

Ge 8: 3 fifty days the water *had* **g down,** H2893
Ge 19: 4 Before *they had* **g to bed,** all the men from H8886
Ge 20: 4 Now Abimelek *had* not **g near** her, so he H7928
Ge 21:15 When the water in the skin *was* g, she put H3983
Ge 28: 7 mother and *had* g to Paddan Aram. H2143
Ge 31:19 When Laban *had* **g to** shear his sheep H2143
Ge 31:30 Now *you have* **g off** because you H2143+2143
Ge 35: 3 who has been with me wherever *I have* g." H2143
Ge 37:12 Now his brothers *had* g to graze their H2143
Ge 43:10 we could have g and returned twice." NDT
Ge 44: 4 They *had* not g far **from** the city when H3655
Ge 47:15 of the people of Egypt and Canaan *was* g, H9462
Ge 47:15 die before your eyes? Our money *is* **all g."** H699
Ge 47:16 your livestock, since your money *is* g." H699
Ge 47:18 since our money *is* g and our livestock H9462
Ge 50:14 all the *others who had* g with him to H6590
Ex 3: 4 the LORD saw that *he had* **g over** to look, H6073
Ex 9:29 replied, "When I *have* **g out** *of* the city, H3655
Ex 16:14 When the dew *was* g, thin flakes like frost H6590
Ex 19:14 After Moses *had* **g down** the mountain to H3718
Lev 14:48 because the defiling mold *is* g. H8324
Nu 5:19 you and *you have* not **g astray** and H8474
Nu 5:20 But if you *have* **g astray** while married to H8474
Nu 13:31 But the men who *had* **g up** with him said H6590
Nu 14: 9 Their protection *is* g, but the LORD is with H6073
Nu 16: 3 said to them, "You have **g too far!** H8041
Nu 16: 7 You Levites have **g too far!"** H8041
Nu 16:33 and were **g from** the community. H4946+9348
Nu 31:21 said to the soldiers who *had* g into battle, H995
Nu 32:13 who had done evil in his sight *was* g. H9462
Dt 32:36 sees their strength *is* g and no one is left, H261
Dt 34: 7 his eyes were not weak nor his strength **g.** H5674
Jos 2: 7 as soon as the pursuers *had* **g out** H3655
Jdg 3:24 After he *had* g, the servants came and H3655
Jdg 4:12 of Abinoam *had* **g up** *to* Mount Tabor, H6590
Jdg 4:14 *Has* not the LORD **g** ahead of you? H3655
Jdg 9:27 After *they had* **g out** *into* the fields and H3655
Jdg 9:35 Gaal son of Ebed *had* **g out** and was H3655
Jdg 18:22 When they *had* **g some distance** from H8178
Jdg 19:11 near Jebus and the day *was* almost g, H3718
Jdg 20: 3 that the Israelites *had* **g up** *to* Mizpah.) H6590
1Sa 3: 3 The lamp of God *had* not yet **g out,** and H3882
1Sa 9: 7 The food in our sacks *is* g. We have no gift H261
1Sa 13:23 of Philistines *had* **g out** to the pass at H3655
1Sa 14:21 Philistines and *had* **g up** with them to H6590
1Sa 15:12 he was told, "Saul *has* g to Carmel. H995
1Sa 15:12 has turned and **g on** down to Gilgal." H6296
1Sa 20:41 After the boy *had* g, David got up from the H995
1Sa 23: 7 Saul was told that David *had* g *to* Keilah H995
1Sa 28:20 His strength *was* g, for he had H4202+2118+928
2Sa 3:22 sent him away, and *he had* g in peace. H2143
2Sa 3:23 him away and that *he had* g in peace. H2143
2Sa 3:24 did you let him go? Now *he is* g! H2143+2143
2Sa 4: 7 *They had* **g into** the house while he was H995
2Sa 5:24 mean the LORD *has* **g out** in front of you H3655
2Sa 7: 9 have been with you wherever *you have* g, H2143
2Sa 12:15 After Nathan *had* g home, the LORD struck H2143
2Sa 16: 1 When David *had* g a short distance H6296
2Sa 17:21 After they *had* g, the two climbed out of H2143
2Sa 24: 8 After *they had* g through the entire land H8763
1Ki 1:25 Today *he has* **g down** and sacrificed great H3718
1Ki 1:45 From there *they have* **g up** cheering, and H6590
1Ki 2:15 the kingdom *has* g to my brother; for H2118
1Ki 2:41 Shimei *had* g from Jerusalem *to* Gath H2143
1Ki 11:15 the army, *who had* **g up** to bury the dead H6590
1Ki 12: 1 all Israel *had* g there to make him king. H995
1Ki 14: 4 his sight *was* g because of his age. H7756
1Ki 14:10 as one burns dung, until it *is* **all g.** H9462
1Ki 21:18 where *he has* g to take possession of it. H3718
1Ki 22:13 The messenger who *had* g to summon H2143
2Ki 3:26 saw that the battle *had* g against him, H2616S
2Ki 4:13 '*You have* **g** to all this **trouble** for H3006+3010
2Ki 5: 2 of raiders **from** Aram *had* **g out** and had H3655
2Ki 9:16 king of Judah *had* **g down** to see him. H3718
2Ki 20:11 the ten steps *it had* **g down** on the H3718+345
2Ki 22:13 us because **those who have g before** us have H3
1Ch 14:15 will mean God *has* **g out** in front of you H3655
1Ch 17: 8 have been with you wherever *you have* g, H2143
2Ch 10: 1 all Israel *had* g there to make him king. H995
2Ch 18:12 The messenger who *had* g to summon H2143
2Ch 34:21 us because **those who have g before** us have H3
Ezr 4:12 to us from you *have* g to Jerusalem and A10085
Ne 2:16 did not know where *I had* g or what I was H2143
Ne 4: 7 walls *had* **g ahead** and that the H6590
Ne 13:10 the service *had* **g back** to their own H1368
Job 7: 9 As a cloud vanishes and *is* g, so one who H2143
Job 11:16 trouble, recalling it only as waters **g by.** H6296
Job 14:20 once for all, and *they are* g; you change H2143
Job 19: 4 If it is true that *I have* **g astray,** my error H8706
Job 19:10 tears me down on every side till *I am* g; H2143
Job 19:14 My relatives *have* **g away;** my closest H2532
Job 24:14 When daylight is g, the murderer rises up NDT
Job 24:24 then they are g; they are brought low H401
Job 27:19 no more; when he opens his eyes, all is **g.** H401
Job 27:21 him off, and *he is* g; it sweeps him out H2143
Job 29: 2 "How I long for the months **g by,** for the H7710
Job 30: 2 since their vigor *had* g from them? H6
Ps 38:10 even the light has **g from** my eyes. H401+907
Ps 49:19 join *those* **who have g before** them, H1887+3
Ps 52: T Doeg the Edomite *had* g to Saul and told H995
Ps 52: T "David *has* g to the house of Ahimelek." H995
Ps 54: T When the Ziphites *had* g to Saul and said H995
Ps 71: 9 do not forsake me when my strength *is* **g.** H3983
Ps 90: 4 your sight are like a day that *has just* **g by,** H6296
Ps 103:16 the wind blows over it and it is g, and its H401
Pr 7:19 not at home; *he has* g on a long journey. H2143
Pr 10:25 the wicked are g, but the righteous H401
Pr 23: 5 at riches, and they are g, for they will surely H401
Pr 30: 4 Who *has* **g up** *to* heaven and come down? H6590
Ecc 6:12 will happen under the sun after they are g? NDT
Ecc 7:29 they *have* **g in search of** many H1335
SS 2:11 winter is past; the rains are over and **g.** H2143
SS 5: 6 my beloved had left; *he was* **g.** H6296
SS 6: 1 Where *has* your beloved g, most beautiful H2143
SS 6: 2 My beloved *has* **g down** to his garden, to H3718
Isa 15: 6 the vegetation *is* g and nothing green is H3983
Isa 17:14 the morning, they are g! This is the portion H401
Isa 18: 5 when the blossom *is* g and the flower H9462
Isa 20: 3 as my servant Isaiah *has* g stripped and H2143
Isa 22: 1 that you *have* all **g up** on the roofs, H6590
Isa 38: 8 the ten steps *it has* **g down** on the H3718
Isa 38: 8 went back the ten steps *it had* **g down.** H3718
Isa 51: 9 as in days **g by,** as in generations H7710
Isa 53: 6 like sheep, *have* **g astray,** each of us has H9494
Jer 3: 6 She *has* **g up** on every high hill and under H2143
Jer 4:23 at the heavens, and their light was g. H401
Jer 5:23 they have turned aside and **g away.** H2143
Jer 9:10 birds have all fled and the animals *are* g. H2143
Jer 10:20 My children *are* **g from** me and are no H3655
Jer 14:18 prophet and priest *have* g to a land they H6086
Jer 17:11 When their lives are **half** *g*, their riches will AIT
Jer 22:11 king of Judah but *has* g from this place: H3655
Jer 29: 2 the artisans *had* g into exile from H3655
Jer 37:21 day until all the bread in the city *was* **g.** H9462
Jer 38:19 of the Jews who *have* **g over** to the H5877
Jer 39: 9 along with those who *had* **g over** to him H5877
Jer 44:14 of Judah who *have* g to live in Egypt H995
Jer 48:11 jar to another—*she has* not g into exile. H2143
Jer 48:33 Joy and gladness *are* g from the orchards H665
Jer 48:36 The wealth they acquired *is* **g.** H6
Jer 48:45 a fire *has* **g out** from Heshbon, H3655
Jer 51: 7 her wine; therefore they *have now* **g mad.** H2147
La 1: 3 harsh labor, Judah *has* **g into exile.** H1655
La 1: 5 Her children *have* **g** *into* exile, captive H2143
La 1:18 men and young women *have* g into exile. H2143
La 3:18 "My splendor *is* g and all that I had hoped H6
La 5:14 The elders *are* g from the city gate; the H8697
La 5:15 Joy *is* **g** *from* our hearts; our dancing has H8697
Eze 11:16 them in the countries where *they have* g. H995
Eze 13: 5 *You have* not **g up** to the breaches in the H6590
Eze 13:15 "The wall is g and so are those who H401
Eze 19: 5 her expectation **g,** she took another of her H6
Eze 23:31 *You have* g the way of your sister; so I will H2143
Eze 27:34 all your company *have* **g down** with you. H5877
Eze 31:17 *had* **g down** to the realm of the dead H3718
Eze 36:21 among the nations where *they had* g. H995
Eze 36:22 among the nations where *you have* g. H995
Eze 37:11 'Our bones are dried up and our hope *is* **g** H6
Eze 37:21 out of the nations where *they have* g. H2143
Eze 45: 9 You have **g far enough,** princes of H8041
Eze 46:12 and after he *has* **g out,** the gate will H3655
Da 2:14 *had* **g out** to put to death the wise men A10485
Da 10:17 My strength *is* g and I can H4202+6641+928
Hos 4:18 Even when their drinks *are* g, they H6073
Hos 8: 9 For they *have* **g up** *to* Assyria like a wild H6590
Jnh 1: 5 But Jonah *had* g below deck, where he H3718
Jnh 4: 5 Jonah *had* **g out** and sat down at a place H3655
Zec 1:11 "*We have* g throughout the earth and H2143
Mal 3: 4 as in days **g by,** as in former years H6409
Mt 2:13 *When* they *had* g, an angel of the Lord *G432*
Mt 9:28 *When he had* g indoors, the blind men *G2262*
Mk 1:19 *When he had* g a little **farther,** he saw *G4581*
Mk 5:30 realized that power *had* **g out** from him. *G2002*
Mk 7:30 child lying on the bed, and the demon **g.** *G2002*
Mk 9:28 *After* Jesus *had* g indoors, his disciples *G1656*
Lk 2:15 the angels had left them and *g* **into** heaven, AIT
Lk 8:30 because many demons *had* **g into** him. *G1656*
Lk 8:35 man from whom the demons *had* **g out,** *G2002*
Lk 8:38 the demons *had* **g out** begged to go *G2002*
Lk 8:46 I know that power *has* **g out** from me." *G2002*
Lk 16: 9 so that when it *is* g, you will be welcomed *G1722*
Lk 19: 7 "*He has* g to be the guest of a sinner." *G1656*
Jn 2: 3 *When* the wine *was* g, Jesus' mother said *G5728*
Jn 3:13 No one *has ever* g into heaven except the *G326*
Jn 4: 8 His disciples *had* g into the town to buy *G599*
Jn 6:22 disciples, but that they *had* **g away** alone. *G599*
Jn 7:50 who *had* g to Jesus earlier and who was *G2262*
Jn 12:19 Look how the whole world *has* g after him!" *G599*
Jn 13:31 When *he was* g, Jesus said, "Now the *G2002*
Ac 8:27 This man *had* g to Jerusalem to worship, *G2262*
Ac 9:23 After many days *had* **g by,** there was a *G4444*
Ac 10: 7 When the angel who spoke to him *had* **g** *G599*
Ac 16:19 that their hope of making money *was* g, *G2002*
Ac 20:25 among whom *I have* **g about** preaching *G1451*
Ac 27:21 *After they had* g a long time without food *G5639*
Ac 27:33 suspense and *have* g without food— *G1412*
Ro 10:18 "Their voice *has* **g out** into all the earth *G2002*
1Co 5: 2 *you* rather *have* **g into mourning** and have *G4291*
2Co 5:17 The old *has* g, the new is here! *G4216*
2Co 11:27 toiled and have often **g without sleep;** *G71*
2Co 11:27 thirst and have often **g without food;** *G3763*
2Ti 4:10 deserted me and *has* g to Thessalonica. *G4513*
2Ti 4:10 Crescens has g to Galatia, and Titus to NDT
1Pe 3:22 who *has* g into heaven and is at God's *G4513*
1Jn 4: 1 false prophets *have* **g out** into the world. *G2002*
2Jn 7 in the flesh, *have* **g out** into the world. *G2002*
Rev 12:12 because the devil *has* **g down** to you! *G2849*
Rev 18:14 'The fruit you longed for *is* g from you. *G599*

GONG (1)

1Co 13: 1 only a resounding **g** or a clanging cymbal *G5910*

GOOD (594) [BETTER, BEST, GOODNESS, WELL]

Ge 1: 4 God saw that the light was g, and he H3202
Ge 1:10 And God saw that it was **g.** H3202
Ge 1:12 to their kinds. And God saw that it was **g.** H3202
Ge 1:18 from darkness. And God saw that it was **g.** H3202
Ge 1:21 And God saw that it was **g.** H3202
Ge 1:25 to their kinds. And God saw that it was **g.** H3202
Ge 1:31 all that he had made, and it was very **g.** H3202
Ge 2: 9 were pleasing to the eye and g for food. H3202
Ge 2: 9 the tree of the knowledge of g and evil. H3202
Ge 2:12 The gold of that land is g; aromatic resin H3202
Ge 2:17 the tree of the knowledge of g and evil, H3202
Ge 2:18 "It is not g for the man to be alone. H3202
Ge 3: 5 you will be like God, knowing g and evil." H3202
Ge 3: 6 of the tree was g for food and pleasing H3202
Ge 3:22 like one of us, knowing g and evil. H3202
Ge 15:15 in peace and be buried at a g old age. H3202
Ge 20: 3 "You *are* **as g as dead** because of the H4637
Ge 24:10 with all kinds of **g things** *from* his master. H3206
Ge 25: 8 breathed his last and died at a g old age, H3202
Ge 25:32 "**What** *g* is the birthright to me? AIT
Ge 30:11 "What **g fortune!"** So she named H1513
Ge 31:24 to say anything to Jacob, either g or bad." H3202
Ge 31:29 to say anything to Jacob, either g or bad. H3202
Ge 34:18 proposal seemed **g** *to* Hamor and his son H3512
Ge 41: 5 healthy and g, were growing on a H3202
Ge 41:22 of grain, full and g, growing on a single H3202
Ge 41:24 of grain swallowed up the seven g heads. H3202
Ge 41:26 The seven g cows are seven years, and the H3202
Ge 41:26 the seven g heads of grain are seven H3202
Ge 41:35 the food of these g years that are coming H3202
Ge 41:37 The plan seemed g to Pharaoh and to all H3512
Ge 44: 4 'Why have you repaid g with evil? H3208
Ge 49:15 When he sees how g is his resting place H3202
Ge 50:20 God intended it for g to accomplish what H3208
Ex 3: 8 of that land into a g and spacious land, H3202
Ex 18: 9 about all the **g things** the LORD had done H3208
Ex 18:17 replied, "What you are doing is not g. H3202
Lev 5: 4 an oath to **do** anything, whether g or evil H3512
Lev 27:10 substitute a g one for a bad one, H3202
Lev 27:10 a bad one for a g *one;* if they should H3202
Lev 27:12 who will judge its quality as g or bad H3202
Lev 27:14 priest will judge its quality as g or bad. H3202
Lev 27:33 may pick out the g from the bad or make H3202
Nu 10:29 the LORD has promised g *things* to Israel." H3202
Nu 10:32 with you whatever g things the LORD gives H3202
Nu 13:19 Is it g or bad? What kind of H3202
Nu 14: 7 through and explored is exceedingly **g.** H3202
Nu 24:13 not do *anything* of my own accord, g or H3208
Dt 1:14 "What you propose to do is **g.** H3202
Dt 1:23 The idea seemed **g** to me; so I selected H3512
Dt 1:25 "It is a **g** land that the LORD our God is H3202
Dt 1:35 shall see the g land I swore to give H3202
Dt 1:39 who do not yet know g from bad— H3202
Dt 3:25 go over and see the **g** land beyond the H3202
Dt 4:21 Jordan and enter the g land the LORD your H3202
Dt 4:22 over and take possession of that g land. H3202
Dt 5:28 Everything they said *was* **g.** H3512
Dt 6:11 with all kinds of **g things** you did not H3206
Dt 6:18 Do what is right and g in the LORD's sight H3202
Dt 6:18 in and take over the g land the LORD H3202
Dt 8: 7 your God is bringing you into a g land— H3202
Dt 8:10 your God for the **g** land he has given you H3202
Dt 9: 6 God is giving you this g land to possess, H3202
Dt 10:13 that I am giving you today for your own g? H3202
Dt 11:17 soon perish from the g land the LORD is H3202
Dt 12:28 be doing what is g and right in the eyes H3202
Dt 18:17 The LORD said to me: "What they say *is* **g.** H3512
Dt 26:11 in all the g *things* the LORD your God H3202
Jos 9:25 to us whatever seems **g** and right to you." H3202
Jos 10: 2 than Ai, and all its men were **g fighters.** H1475
Jos 21:45 one of all the LORD's g promises to Israel H3202
Jos 23:13 until you perish from this g land, which H3202
Jos 23:14 not one of all the g promises the LORD H3202
Jos 23:15 But just as all the g things the LORD your H3202
Jos 23:15 you from this g land he has given you. H3202
Jos 23:16 perish from the g land he has given you." H3202
Jos 24:20 an end of you, after *he has been* g to you." H3512
Jdg 8:32 of Joash died at a g old age and was H3202
Jdg 8:35 spite of all the **g things** he had done for H3208
Jdg 9:11 I give up my fruit, so g and sweet, to hold H3202
Jdg 9:16 honorably and in **g faith** by making H9459
Jdg 9:19 honorably and in **g faith** toward H9459
Jdg 17:13 "Now I know that the LORD *will be* g to me H3512
Jdg 18: 9 and it is very **g.** Aren't you going to H3202
Ru 2:22 "It will be **g** for you, my daughter, H3202
Ru 3: 7 and drinking and *was* **in g spirits,** H3512+4213
Ru 3:13 guardian-redeemer, g; let him redeem H3202
1Sa 1:23 only *may* the LORD **make g** his word." H7756
1Sa 2:24 among the LORD's people is not g. H3202
1Sa 2:32 Although g *will be* **done** *to* Israel, no one H3512
1Sa 3:18 the LORD; let him do what is g in his eyes." H3202
1Sa 9:10 "**G,"** Saul said to his servant. "Come, let's H3202

1Sa 12:14 over you follow the LORD your God—g! NDT
1Sa 12:21 *They can* **do** you no g, nor can they rescue H3603
1Sa 12:23 will teach you the way that is g and right. H3202
1Sa 15: 9 calves and lambs—everything that was g. H3202
1Sa 19:10 David **made g** *his* **escape**. H5674+2256+4880
1Sa 24:18 now told me about the g you did to me; H3208
1Sa 25: 6 **G health** to you and your household H8934
1Sa 25: 6 And g **health** to all that is yours! H8934
1Sa 25:15 Yet these men were very g to us. They did H3202
1Sa 25:21 He has paid me back evil for g. H3208
1Sa 25:30 my lord every g **thing** he promised H3208
1Sa 25:33 your g **judgment** and for keeping H3248
1Sa 26:16 What you have done is not g. As surely as H3202
2Sa 3:13 "G," said David. "I will make an H3202
2Sa 4:10 and thought he was **bringing g news**, H1413
2Sa 7:28 promised these g **things** to your servant. H3208
2Sa 10:12 The LORD will do what is g in his sight." H3202
2Sa 13:22 word to Amnon, either g or bad; he hated H3202
2Sa 14:17 an angel of God in discerning g and evil. H3202
2Sa 15:26 him do to me whatever seems g to him." H3202
2Sa 17: 4 This plan seemed g to Absalom and to all H3837
2Sa 17: 7 Ahithophel has given is not g this time. H3202
2Sa 17:14 to frustrate the g advice of Ahithophel in H3202
2Sa 18:25 "If he is alone, he must have g **news**." H1415
2Sa 18:26 "He *must be* **bringing g news**, too. H1413
2Sa 18:27 "He's a g man," the king said H3202
2Sa 18:27 the king said. "He comes with g news." H3202
2Sa 18:31 "My lord the king, **hear** *the* **g news**! H1413
1Ki 1:42 man like you must be bringing g news." H3202
1Ki 2:38 answered the king, "What you say is g. H3202
1Ki 2:42 time you said to me, 'What you say is g. H3202
1Ki 7:10 were laid with large stones of g **quality**, H3701
1Ki 8:56 has failed of all the g promises he gave H3202
1Ki 8:66 heart for all the g **things** the LORD had H3208
1Ki 14:13 the God of Israel, has found anything g. H3202
1Ki 14:15 Israel from this g land that he gave to H3202
1Ki 18:24 all the people said, "What you say is g." H3202
1Ki 20:33 The men **took** *this* **as a g sign** and were H5727
1Ki 22: 8 never prophesies *anything* g about me, H3202
1Ki 22:18 never prophesies *anything* g about me, H3202
2Ki 3:19 You will cut down every g tree, stop up all H3202
2Ki 3:19 springs, and ruin every g field with stones." H3202
2Ki 3:25 threw a stone on every g field until it was H3202
2Ki 3:25 all the springs and cut down every g tree. H3202
2Ki 7: 9 This is a day of g **news** and we are H1415
2Ki 20: 3 have done what is g in your eyes. H3202
2Ki 20:19 word of the LORD you have spoken is g," H3202
1Ch 4:40 They found rich, g pasture, and the land H3202
1Ch 13: 2 "If it seems g to you and if it is the will of H3202
1Ch 16:34 to the LORD, for he is g; his love endures H3202
1Ch 17:26 promised these g **things** to your servant. H3208
1Ch 19:13 The LORD will do what is g in his sight." H3202
1Ch 28: 8 may possess this g land and pass it on H3202
1Ch 29:28 He died at a g old age, having enjoyed H3202
2Ch 5:13 LORD and sang: "He is g; his love endures H3202
2Ch 7: 3 saying, "He is g; his love endures H3202
2Ch 7:10 in heart for the g **things** the LORD had H3208
2Ch 12:12 Indeed, there was some g in Judah. H3202
2Ch 14: 2 Asa did what was g and right in the eyes H3202
2Ch 18: 7 never prophesies *anything* g about me, H3208
2Ch 18:17 never prophesies *anything* g about me, H3202
2Ch 19: 3 however, some g in you, for you have rid H3202
2Ch 24:16 because of the g he had done in Israel H3208
2Ch 30:18 "May the LORD, who is g, pardon everyone H3202
2Ch 30:22 who showed g understanding of the H3202
2Ch 31:20 doing what was g and right and faithful H3202
Ezr 3:11 "He is g; his love toward Israel endures H3202
Ezr 7:28 has extended his g **favor** to me before the H2876
Ezr 9:12 eat the g **things** *of* the land and H3206
Ne 2:18 So they began this g **work**. H3208
Ne 5: 5 though our children are **as g as** theirs, H3869
Ne 6:19 to me his g **deeds** and then telling H3208
Ne 9:13 decrees and commands that are g. H3202
Ne 9:20 You gave your g Spirit to instruct them H3202
Ne 9:25 of houses filled with all kinds of g **things**, H3206
Ne 9:36 its fruit and the other g **things** it *produces*. H3206
Est 10: 3 he worked for the g of his people and H3202
Job 2:10 Shall we accept g from God, and not H3202
Job 21:25 never having enjoyed anything g. H3208
Job 22:18 he who filled their houses with g *things*, H3202
Job 30:26 Yet when I hoped for g, evil came; when I H3202
Job 34: 4 let us learn together what is g. H3202
Job 39:17 wisdom or give her a share of g **sense**. H1069
Ps 13: 6 LORD's praise, for *he has* **been** g to me. H1694
Ps 14: 1 are vile; there is no one who does g. H3202
Ps 14: 3 there is no one who does g, not even one H3202
Ps 16: 2 Lord; apart from you I have no g **thing**." H3208
Ps 25: 7 love remember me, for you, LORD, are g. H3206
Ps 25: 8 **G** and upright is the LORD; therefore he H3202
Ps 31:19 abundant are the g *things* that you have H3206
Ps 34: 8 Taste and see that the LORD is g; blessed H3202
Ps 34:10 those who seek the LORD lack no g *thing*. H3202
Ps 34:12 loves life and desires to see many g days, H3202
Ps 34:14 Turn from evil and do g; seek peace and H3202
Ps 35:12 repay me evil for g and leave me like one H3208
Ps 36: 3 deceitful; they fail to act wisely or **do** g. H3512
Ps 37: 3 Trust in the LORD and do g; dwell in the H3202
Ps 37:27 Turn from evil and do g; then you will H3202
Ps 38:20 Those who repay my g with evil lodge H3208
Ps 38:20 though I seek only to do *what* is g. H3202
Ps 39: 2 utterly silent, not even saying *anything* g. H3202
Ps 52: 3 You love evil rather than g, falsehood H3202

Ps 52: 9 hope in your name, for your name is g. H3202
Ps 53: 1 ways are vile; there is no one who does g. H3202
Ps 53: 3 there is no one who does g, not even one H3202
Ps 54: 6 I will praise your name, LORD, for it is g. H3202
Ps 65: 4 with the g **things** *of* your house, *of* your H3206
Ps 73: 1 Surely God is g to Israel, to those who are H3202
Ps 73:28 But as for me, it is g to be near God. H3202
Ps 84:11 no g *thing* does he withhold from those H3202
Ps 85:12 The LORD will indeed give what is g, and H3202
Ps 86: 5 are forgiving and g, abounding in love to H3202
Ps 92: 1 It is g to praise the LORD and make music H3202
Ps 100: 5 For the LORD is g and his love endures H3202
Ps 103: 5 your desires with g *things* so that your H3202
Ps 104:28 they are satisfied with g *things*. H3202
Ps 106: 1 to the LORD, for he is g; his love endures H3202
Ps 107: 1 to the LORD, for he is g; his love endures H3202
Ps 107: 9 thirsty and fills the hungry with g *things*. H3202
Ps 109: 5 They repay me evil for g, and hatred for H3208
Ps 111:10 follow his precepts have g understanding. H3202
Ps 112: 5 **G** will come to those who are generous H3202
Ps 116: 7 my soul, for the LORD *has been* g to you. H1694
Ps 118: 1 to the LORD, for he is g; his love endures H3202
Ps 118:29 to the LORD, for he is g; his love endures H3202
Ps 119:17 *Be* g to your servant while I live, that I H1694
Ps 119:39 the disgrace I dread, for your laws are g. H3202
Ps 119:65 Do g to your servant according to your H3202
Ps 119:66 Teach me knowledge and g judgment, for H3206
Ps 119:68 You are g, and what you do is good H3202
Ps 119:68 are good, and *what you* **do** *is* g; teach me H3512
Ps 119:71 It was g for me to be afflicted so that I H3202
Ps 125: 4 **do** g to those who are good, to H3512
Ps 125: 4 do good to those *who* are g, to those who H3202
Ps 133: 1 How g and pleasant it is when God's H3202
Ps 135: 3 for the LORD is g; sing praise to his H3202
Ps 136: 1 to the LORD, for he is g. His love endures H3202
Ps 143:10 may your g Spirit lead me on level ground H3202
Ps 145: 9 The LORD is g to all; he has compassion H3202
Ps 147: 1 How g it is to sing praises to our God H3202
Pr 2: 9 is right and just and fair—every g path. H3202
Pr 2:20 in the ways of the g and keep to the paths H3202
Pr 3: 4 win favor and a g name in the sight of H3202
Pr 3:27 Do not withhold g from those to whom it H3202
Pr 11:23 The desire of the righteous ends only in g, H3202
Pr 11:27 Whoever seeks g finds favor, but evil H3202
Pr 12: 2 **G** *people* obtain favor from the LORD, but H3202
Pr 12:14 their lips people are filled with g *things*, H3202
Pr 13: 2 fruit of their lips people enjoy g *things*, H3202
Pr 13:15 **G** judgment wins favor, but the way of the H3202
Pr 13:21 the righteous are rewarded with g *things*. H3202
Pr 13:22 A g *person* leaves an inheritance for their H3202
Pr 14:14 and the g rewarded for theirs. H3202+408
Pr 14:19 will bow down in the presence of the g, H3202
Pr 14:22 those who plan *what* is g find love and H3202
Pr 15: 3 keeping watch on the wicked and the g. H3202
Pr 15:23 apt reply—and how g is a timely word! H3202
Pr 15:30 g news gives health to the bones. H3202
Pr 16:29 leads them down a path that is not g. H3202
Pr 17:13 the house of one who pays back evil for g. H3208
Pr 17:22 A cheerful heart *is* g medicine, but a H3512
Pr 17:26 imposing a fine on the innocent is not g, H3202
Pr 18: 5 It is not g to be partial to the wicked and H3202
Pr 18:22 finds a wife finds *what* is g and receives H3202
Pr 19: 2 Desire without knowledge is not g—how H3202
Pr 20:14 "It's **no** g, it's no good!" says the buyer H8273
Pr 20:14 "It's no good, it's **no** g!" says the buyer H8273
Pr 22: 1 A g name is more desirable than great NDT
Pr 24:13 my son, for it is g; honey from the comb is H3202
Pr 24:23 To show partiality in judging is not g: H3202
Pr 25:25 to a weary soul is g news from a distant H3202
Pr 25:27 It is not g to eat too much honey, nor is it H3202
Pr 28:10 blameless will receive a g inheritance. H3202
Pr 28:21 To show partiality is not g—yet a person H3202
Pr 31:12 She brings him g, not harm, all the days H3202
Ecc 2: 1 you with pleasure to find out *what* is g." H3202
Ecc 2: 3 to see what was g for people to do under H3202
Ecc 3:12 to be happy and to do g while they live. H3202
Ecc 4: 9 because they have a g return for their H3202
Ecc 5:18 This is what I have observed to be g: that H3202
Ecc 6:12 who knows what is g for a person in life, H3202
Ecc 7: 1 A g name is better than fine perfume H3202
Ecc 7: 3 because a sad face is g *for* the heart. H3512
Ecc 7:11 is a g *thing* and benefits those who see H3202
Ecc 7:14 When times are g, be happy; but when H3208
Ecc 7:18 It is g to grasp the one and not let go of H3202
Ecc 9: 2 the wicked, the g and the bad, the H3202
Ecc 9: 2 As it is with the g, so with the sinful; as it H3202
Ecc 9:18 but one sinner destroys much g. H3208
Ecc 12:14 every hidden thing, whether it is g or evil. H3202
Isa 1:19 you will eat the g *things of* the land; H3206
Isa 5: 2 Then he looked for a crop of g **grapes**, but H6694
Isa 5: 4 When I looked for g **grapes**, why did it H6694
Isa 5:20 to those who call evil g and good evil, H3202
Isa 5:20 to those who call evil good and g evil, H3202
Isa 38: 3 have done what is g in your eyes. H3202
Isa 39: 8 word of the LORD you have spoken is g," H3202
Isa 40: 9 You *who* **bring g news** *to* Zion, go up on a H1413
Isa 40: 9 You *who* **bring g news** *to* Jerusalem, lift H1413
Isa 41: 7 the welding, "It is g." The other nails H3202
Isa 41:23 **Do** *something*, whether g or bad, so that H3512
Isa 41:27 to Jerusalem a **messenger of g news**. H1413
Isa 52: 7 are the feet of *those who* **bring g news**, H1413
Isa 52: 7 who bring g tidings, who proclaim H3202

Isa 55: 2 and eat *what* is g, and you will H3202
Isa 61: 1 me to **proclaim g news** *to* the poor. H1413
Isa 63: 7 the many g **things** he has done for Israel H3206
Isa 65: 2 who walk in ways not g, pursuing their H3202
Jer 4:22 in doing evil; they know not how to **do** g." H3512
Jer 5:25 your sins have deprived you of g. H3202
Jer 6:16 ask where the g way is, and walk in H3202
Jer 8:15 We hoped for peace but no g has come H3202
Jer 10: 5 can do no harm nor *can* they **do** *any* g." H3512
Jer 13:23 Neither can you **do** g who are accustomed H3512
Jer 14:19 We hoped for peace but no g has come H3202
Jer 15:11 "Surely I will deliver you for a g *purpose* H3202
Jer 16:19 worthless idols *that* **did** them no g. H3603
Jer 18:10 the g I had intended to **do** *for* it. H3208+3512
Jer 18:20 Should g be repaid with evil? Yet they H3208
Jer 21:10 determined to do this city harm and not g, H3208
Jer 24: 2 One basket had very g figs, like those that H3202
Jer 24: 3 "The g ones are very good, but the bad H3202
Jer 24: 3 "The good ones are very g, but the bad H3202
Jer 24: 5 'Like these g figs, I regard as good the H3202
Jer 24: 5 I regard as g the exiles from Judah H3208
Jer 24: 6 My eyes will watch over them for their g H3208
Jer 26:14 with me whatever you think is g and right. H3202
Jer 29:10 you and fulfill my g promise to bring you H3202
Jer 29:32 will he see the g *things* I will do for my H3202
Jer 32:40 I will never stop **doing** g *to* them, and I H3512
Jer 32:41 I will rejoice in **doing** them g and will H3201
Jer 33: 9 that hear of all the g **things** I do for it; H3208
Jer 33:11 the LORD is g; his love endures forever H3202
Jer 33:14 I will fulfill the g promise I made to the H3202
Jer 38: 4 is not seeking the g of these people but H8934
Jer 44:27 harm, not for g; the Jews in Egypt H3208
La 3:25 The LORD is g to those whose hope is in H3202
La 3:26 it is g to wait quietly for the salvation of H3202
La 3:27 It is g for a man to bear the yoke while he H3202
La 3:38 that both calamities and g *things* come? H3202
Eze 17: 8 It had been planted in g soil by abundant H3202
Eze 20:25 that were not g and laws through which H3202
Eze 30:22 the g arm as well as the broken one H2617
Eze 34:14 I will tend them in a g pasture, and the H3202
Eze 34:14 There they will lie down in g grazing land, H3202
Eze 34:18 enough for you to feed on the g pasture? H3202
Da 3:15 worship the image I made, very g. NDT
Hos 8: 3 But Israel has rejected what is g; an H3202
Am 5:14 Seek g, not evil, that you may live. H3202
Am 5:15 Hate evil, love g; maintain justice in the H3202
Am 9: 4 my eye on them for harm and not for g." H3208
Jnh 2: 9 What I have vowed *I will* **make** g. I will H8966
Mic 2: 7 "*Do* not my words **do** g to the one whose H3512
Mic 3: 2 you who hate g and love evil; who tear H3202
Mic 6: 8 O mortal, what is g. And what does the H3202
Na 1: 7 The LORD is g, a refuge in times of trouble H3202
Na 1:15 the feet of *one who* **brings g news**, who H1413
Zep 1:12 'The LORD *will do* nothing, either g or bad. H3512
Zec 8:15 have determined to **do** g again to H3512
Mal 2:17 "All who do evil are g in the eyes of the H3202
Mt 3:10 that does not produce g fruit will be cut *G2819*
Mt 4:23 proclaiming the g **news** of the kingdom *G2295*
Mt 5:13 *It is* no longer g for anything, except to be *G2710*
Mt 5:16 they may see your g deeds and glorify *G2819*
Mt 5:45 causes his sun to rise on the evil and the g, *G19*
Mt 7:11 know how to give g gifts to your children *G19*
Mt 7:11 Father in heaven give g gifts to those who *G19*
Mt 7:17 Likewise, every g tree bears good fruit, but a *G19*
Mt 7:17 every good tree bears g fruit, but a bad *G2819*
Mt 7:18 A g tree cannot bear bad fruit, and a bad *G19*
Mt 7:18 and a bad tree cannot bear g fruit. *G2819*
Mt 7:19 that does not bear g fruit is cut down and *G2819*
Mt 9:35 proclaiming the g **news** of the kingdom *G2295*
Mt 11: 5 and **the g news is proclaimed** to the poor. *G2294*
Mt 12:12 it is lawful to do g on the Sabbath." *G2822*
Mt 12:33 "Make a tree g and its fruit will be good *G2819*
Mt 12:33 "Make a tree good and its fruit will be g *G2819*
Mt 12:34 how can you who are evil say *anything* g? *G19*
Mt 12:35 A g man brings good things out of the good *G19*
Mt 12:35 A good man brings g *things* out of the good *G19*
Mt 12:35 good things out of the g stored up in him, *G19*
Mt 13: 8 Still other seed fell on g soil, where it *G2819*
Mt 13:23 the seed falling on g soil refers to *G2819*
Mt 13:24 like a man who sowed g seed in his field. *G2819*
Mt 13:27 didn't you sow g seed in your field? *G2819*
Mt 13:37 one who sowed the g seed is the Son of *G2819*
Mt 13:38 the g seed stands for the people of *G2819*
Mt 13:48 down and collected the g *fish* in baskets, *G2819*
Mt 16:26 What g *will it be* **for** someone to gain the *G6067*
Mt 17: 4 to Jesus, "Lord, it is g for us to be here. *G2819*
Mt 19:16 what g *thing* must I do to get eternal life?" *G19*
Mt 19:17 "Why do you ask me about what is g?" *G19*
Mt 19:17 "There is only One who is g. If you want to *G19*
Mt 22:10 the bad as well as the g, and the wedding *G19*
Mt 24:46 It will be g *for* that servant whose master *G3421*
Mt 25:21 'Well done, g and faithful servant! *G19*
Mt 25:23 'Well done, g and faithful servant! *G19*
Mk 1: 1 The beginning *of* the g **news** about Jesus *G2295*
Mk 1:14 Galilee, proclaiming the g **news** of God. *G2295*
Mk 1:15 Repent and believe the g **news**!" *G2295*
Mk 3: 4 on the Sabbath: to do g or to do evil, to save *G19*
Mk 4: 8 Still other seed fell on g soil. It came up *G2819*
Mk 4:20 like seed sown on g soil, hear the word, *G2819*
Mk 8:36 What g *is it for* someone to gain the *G6067*
Mk 9: 5 to Jesus, "Rabbi, it is g for us to be here. *G2819*
Mk 9:50 "Salt is g, but if it loses its saltiness, how *G2819*

Mk 10:17 "G teacher," he asked, "what must I do to G19
Mk 10:18 "Why do you call me g?" Jesus answered G19
Mk 10:18 "No one is g—except God alone. G19
Mk 12:28 that Jesus had given them a g answer, G2822
Lk 1:19 speak to you and to tell you this g news. G2294
Lk 1:53 the hungry with g things but has sent the G19
Lk 2:10 I bring you g news that will cause great G2294
Lk 3: 9 that does not produce g fruit will be cut G2819
Lk 3:18 and proclaimed the g news to them. G2294
Lk 4:18 anointed me to proclaim g news to the G2294
Lk 4:43 "I must proclaim the g news of the G2294
Lk 6: 9 to do g or to do evil, to save life or to destroy G16
Lk 6:27 enemies, do g to those who hate you, G2822
Lk 6:33 And if you do g to those who are good to you G16
Lk 6:33 if you do good to those who are g to you, G16
Lk 6:35 love your enemies, do g to them, and lend G16
Lk 6:38 A g measure, pressed down, shaken G2819
Lk 6:43 "No g tree bears bad fruit, nor does a bad G2819
Lk 6:43 bad fruit, nor does a bad tree bear g fruit. G2819
Lk 6:45 A g man brings good things out of the good G19
Lk 6:45 A good man brings g things out of the good G19
Lk 6:45 things out of the g stored up in his heart G19
Lk 7:22 and the g news is proclaimed to the poor. G2294
Lk 8: 1 proclaiming the g news of the kingdom of G2294
Lk 8: 8 Still other seed fell on g soil. It came up G19
Lk 8:15 But the seed on g soil stands for those G2819
Lk 8:15 stands for those with a noble and g heart, G19
Lk 9: 6 proclaiming the g news and healing G2294
Lk 9:25 What g is it for someone to gain the G6067
Lk 9:33 "Master, it is g for us to be here. G2819
Lk 11:13 know how to give g gifts to your children G19
Lk 12:37 It will be g for those servants whose G3421
Lk 12:38 It will be g for those servants whose G3421
Lk 12:43 It will be g for that servant whom the G3421
Lk 14:34 "Salt is g, but if it loses its saltiness, how G2819
Lk 16:16 the g news of the kingdom of God is being preached G2294
Lk 16:25 in your lifetime you received your g things, G19
Lk 18:18 ruler asked him, "G teacher, what must I do G19
Lk 18:19 "Why do you call me g?" Jesus answered G19
Lk 18:19 "No one is g—except God alone. G19
Lk 19:17 " 'Well done, my g servant!' his master G19
Lk 20: 1 courts and proclaiming the g news, G2294
Lk 23:50 of the Council, a g and upright man, G19
Jn 1:46 Can anything g come from there? G19
Jn 5:29 who have done what is g will rise to live, G19
Jn 7:12 Some said, "He is a g man." Others replied, G19
Jn 10:11 "I am the g shepherd. The good shepherd G2819
Jn 10:11 The g shepherd lays down his life for the G2819
Jn 10:14 "I am the g shepherd; I know my sheep G2819
Jn 10:32 have shown you many g works from the G2819
Jn 10:33 "We are not stoning you for any g work," G2240
Jn 16: 7 it is for your g that I am going away. G5237
Jn 18:14 leaders that it would be g if one man G5237
Ac 5:42 and proclaiming the g news that Jesus is G2294
Ac 8:12 Philip as he proclaimed the g news of the G2294
Ac 8:35 and told him the g news about Jesus. G2294
Ac 9:36 was always doing g and helping the poor G19
Ac 10:33 immediately, and it was g of you to come. G2822
Ac 10:36 announcing the g news of peace through G2294
Ac 10:38 he went around doing g and healing all G2308
Ac 11:20 telling them the g news about the Lord G2294
Ac 11:24 He was a g man, full of the Holy Spirit and G19
Ac 13:32 "We tell you the g news: What God G2294
Ac 14:15 We are bringing you g news, telling you G2294
Ac 15:28 It seemed g to the Holy Spirit and to us G1506
Ac 17:18 Paul was preaching the g news about G2294
Ac 19:25 that we receive a g income from this G2345
Ac 19:27 that our trade will lose its g name G1650+591+2262
Ac 20:24 of testifying to the g news of God's grace. G2295
Ac 23: 1 my duty to God in all g conscience to this G19
Ro 2: 7 who by persistence in doing g seek glory, G19
Ro 2:10 honor and peace for everyone who does g: G19
Ro 3: 8 "Let us do evil that g may result"? G19
Ro 3:12 there is no one who does g, not even one G5983
Ro 4:19 the fact that his body was as g as dead— G3739
Ro 5: 7 though for a g person someone might G19
Ro 7:12 the commandment is holy, righteous and g. G19
Ro 7:13 Did that which is g, then, become death to G19
Ro 7:13 it used what is g to bring about my death G19
Ro 7:16 not want to do, I agree that the law is g. G2819
Ro 7:18 For I know that g itself does not dwell in me G19
Ro 7:18 For I have the desire to do what is g, but I G2819
Ro 7:19 For I do not do the g I want to do, but the evil G19
Ro 7:21 Although I want to do g, evil is right there G2819
Ro 8:28 God works for the g of those who love him, G19
Ro 9:11 were born or had done anything g or bad— G19
Ro 10:15 are the feet of those who bring g news!" G19
Ro 10:16 not all the Israelites accepted the g news. G2295
Ro 12: 2 God's will is—his g, pleasing and perfect G19
Ro 12: 9 Hate what is evil; cling to what is g. G19
Ro 12:21 overcome by evil, but overcome evil with g. G19
Ro 13: 4 one in authority is God's servant for your g. G19
Ro 14:16 let what you know is g be spoken of as evil. G19
Ro 15: 2 us should please our neighbors for their g, G19
Ro 16:19 I want you to be wise about what is g G19
1Co 5: 6 Your boasting is not g. Don't you know G2819
1Co 7: 1 "It is g for a man not to have sexual G2819
1Co 7: 8 It is g for them to stay unmarried G2819
1Co 7:26 I think that it is g for a man to remain as G2819
1Co 7:35 I am saying this for your own g, not to G5239
1Co 10:24 No one should seek their own g, but the good AIT
1Co 10:24 seek their own good, but the g of others. AIT
1Co 10:33 not seeking my own g but the good of G5239
1Co 10:33 seeking my own good but the g of many, NDT
1Co 11:17 your meetings do more harm than g. G3202
1Co 12: 7 of the Spirit is given for the common g. G5237
1Co 14: 6 in tongues, what g will I be to you, unless G6067
1Co 15:33 "Bad company corrupts g character." G5982
2Co 5:10 done while in the body, whether g or bad. G19
2Co 6: 8 bad report and g report; genuine, G2367
2Co 9: 8 you need, you will abound in every g work. G19
Gal 4:17 are zealous to win you over, but for no g. G2822
Gal 4:18 provided the purpose is g, and to be so G2819
Gal 5: 7 You were running a g race. Who cut in on G2822
Gal 6: 6 word should share all g things with their G19
Gal 6: 9 Let us not become weary in doing g, for at G2819
Gal 6:10 opportunity, let us do g to all people G19
Eph 1: 9 of his will according to his g pleasure, G2306
Eph 2:10 created in Christ Jesus to do g works, which G19
Eph 6: 8 will reward each one for whatever g they do, G19
Php 1: 6 that he who began a g work in you will carry G19
Php 2:13 to act in order to fulfill his g purpose. G2306
Php 4:14 Yet it was g of you to share in my troubles. G2822
Col 1:10 bearing fruit in every g work, growing in the G19
1Th 3: 6 you and has brought g news about your G2294
1Th 5:15 strive to do what is g for each other and G19
1Th 5:21 test them all; hold on to what is g, G2819
2Th 2:16 gave us eternal encouragement and g hope, G19
2Th 2:17 strengthen you in every g deed and word. G19
2Th 3:13 sisters, never tire of doing what is g. G2818
1Ti 1: 5 from a pure heart and a g conscience and a G19
1Ti 1: 8 know that the law is g if one uses it G2819
1Ti 1:19 holding on to faith and a g conscience G19
1Ti 2: 3 This is g, and pleases God our Savior, G2819
1Ti 2:10 with g deeds, appropriate for women G19
1Ti 3: 7 He must also have a g reputation with G2819
1Ti 4: 4 For everything God created is g, and G2819
1Ti 4: 6 you will be a g minister of Christ Jesus G2819
1Ti 4: 6 the faith and of the g teaching that you G2819
1Ti 5:10 is well known for her g deeds, such as G2819
1Ti 5:10 devoting herself to all kinds of g deeds. G19
1Ti 5:25 In the same way, g deeds are obvious G2819
1Ti 6:12 Fight the g fight of the faith. Take hold of G2819
1Ti 6:12 when you made your g confession in the G2819
1Ti 6:13 Pontius Pilate made the g confession, G2819
1Ti 6:18 Command them to do g, to be rich in good G14
1Ti 6:18 do good, to be rich in g deeds, and to be G2819
2Ti 1:14 Guard the g deposit that was entrusted to G2819
2Ti 2: 3 suffering, like a g soldier of Christ Jesus. G2819
2Ti 2:21 the Master and prepared to do any g work. G19
2Ti 3: 3 self-control, brutal, not lovers of the g, G920
2Ti 3:17 be thoroughly equipped for every g work. G19
2Ti 4: 7 I have fought the g fight, I have finished G2819
Titus 1: 8 one who loves what is g, who is G5787
Titus 1:16 disobedient and unfit for doing anything g. G19
Titus 2: 3 to much wine, but to teach what is g. G2815
Titus 2: 7 set them an example by doing what is g. G2819
Titus 2:14 are his very own, eager to do what is g. G2819
Titus 3: 1 obedient, to be ready to do whatever is g, G19
Titus 3: 8 to devote themselves to doing what is g. G2819
Titus 3:14 to devote themselves to doing what is g, G2819
Phm 6 understanding of every g thing we share G19
Heb 4: 2 have had the g news proclaimed to us, G2294
Heb 4: 6 who formerly had the g news proclaimed to them G2294
Heb 5:14 themselves to distinguish g from evil. G2819
Heb 9:11 as high priest of the g things that are now G19
Heb 10: 1 only a shadow of the g things that are G19
Heb 10:24 one another on toward love and g deeds, G2819
Heb 11:12 one man, and he as g as dead, came AIT
Heb 12:10 God disciplines us for our g, in order G5237
Heb 13: 9 It is g for our hearts to be strengthened by G2819
Heb 13:16 do not forget to do g and to share with G2343
Heb 13:21 equip you with everything g for doing his will, G19
Jas 1:17 Every g and perfect gift is from above G19
Jas 2: 3 say, "Here's a g seat for you," but say G2822
Jas 2:14 What g is it, my brothers and sisters, if G4055
Jas 2:16 about their physical needs, what g is it? G4055
Jas 2:19 is one God. G! Even the demons G2822+4472
Jas 3:13 Let them show it by their g life, by deeds G2819
Jas 3:17 full of mercy and g fruit, impartial and G19
Jas 4:17 knows the g they ought to do and doesn't G2819
1Pe 2: 3 now that you have tasted that the Lord is g. G5982
1Pe 2:12 Live such g lives among the pagans that G2819
1Pe 2:12 they may see your g deeds and glorify G2819
1Pe 2:15 it is God's will that by doing g you should G16
1Pe 2:18 not only to those who are g and considerate G19
1Pe 2:20 But if you suffer for doing g and you endure G16
1Pe 3:10 love life and see g days must keep their G19
1Pe 3:11 They must turn from evil and do g; they must G19
1Pe 3:13 going to harm you if you are eager to do g? G19
1Pe 3:16 against your g behavior in Christ may G19
1Pe 3:17 to suffer for doing g than for doing evil. G16
1Pe 4:19 to their faithful Creator and continue to do g. G17
3Jn 2 I pray that you may enjoy g health and G5617
3Jn 11 do not imitate what is evil but what is g. G19
3Jn 11 Anyone who does what is g is from God G16

GOODBYE (8)

Ge 31:28 kiss my grandchildren and my daughters g H5975
Ru 1: 9 Then she kissed them g and they wept H5975
Ru 1:14 Then Orpah kissed her mother-in-law g H5975
1Ki 19:20 "Let me kiss my father and mother g," H5975
Lk 9:61 first let me go back and say g to my family." G698
Ac 20: 1 said g and set out for Macedonia. G832
Ac 21: 6 After saying g to each other, we went G571
2Co 2:13 So I said g to them and went on to G698

GOODMAN (KJV) HUSBAND, LANDOWNER, OWNER

GOODNESS (20) [GOOD]

Ex 33:19 "I will cause all my g to pass in front of H3206
2Ch 6:41 may your faithful people rejoice in your g. H3202
Ne 9:25 they reveled in your great g. H3206
Ne 9:35 enjoying your great g to them in the H3206
Ps 23: 6 Surely your g and love will follow me all H3202
Ps 27:13 I will see the g of the LORD in the land of H3206
Ps 69:16 out of the g of your love; in your H3202
Ps 86:17 Give me a sign of your g, that my H3208
Ps 109:21 out of the g of your love, deliver me. H3202
Ps 116:12 I return to the LORD for all his g to me? H9326
Ps 142: 7 gather about me because of your g to me. H1694
Ps 145: 7 your abundant g and joyfully sing of H3206
Ro 15:14 that you yourselves are full of g, filled with G20
Gal 5:22 forbearance, kindness, g, faithfulness, G20
Eph 5: 9 the fruit of the light consists in all g G20
2Th 1:11 your every desire for g and your every deed G20
Heb 6: 5 who have tasted the g of the word of God G2819
2Pe 1: 3 him who called us by his own glory and g. G746
2Pe 1: 5 make every effort to add to your faith g G746
2Pe 1: 5 your faith goodness; and to g, knowledge; G746

GOODS (23)

Ge 14:11 seized all the g of Sodom and Gomorrah H8214
Ge 14:16 He recovered all the g and brought back H8214
Ge 14:21 the people and keep the g for yourself." H8214
Ge 31:18 along with all the g he had accumulated H8214
Ge 31:37 that you have searched through all my g, H3998
Ge 36: 6 animals and all the g he had acquired in H7871
Ge 40:17 kinds of baked g for Pharaoh, H4407+5126+685
Ex 22: 7 a neighbor silver or g for safekeeping H3998
Nu 31: 9 Midianite herds, flocks and g as plunder. H2657
2Ch 21:17 carried off all the g found in the king's H8214
Ezr 1: 4 silver and gold, with g and livestock, and H8214
Ezr 1: 6 silver and gold, with g and livestock, and H8214
Ne 13: 8 all Tobiah's household g out of the room. H3998
Ne 13:20 of all kinds of g spent the night outside H4928
Est 3:13 the month of Adar, and to plunder their g. H8965
Ps 62:10 in extortion or put vain hope in stolen g; H1610
Ecc 5:11 As g increase, so do those who consume H3208
Jer 49:29 be carried off with all their g and camels. H3998
Eze 27:12 you because of your great wealth of g; H2104
Eze 27:18 your many products and great wealth of g. H2104
Eze 38:12 rich in livestock and g, living at the center H7871
Eze 38:13 away livestock and g and to seize much H7871
Hab 2: 6 piles up stolen g and makes H4202+4200+2257

GOODWILL (4)

Est 9:30 kingdom—words of g and assurance— H8934
Pr 14: 9 but g is found among the upright. H8356
Ac 7:10 him to gain the g of Pharaoh king of G5921
Php 1:15 out of envy and rivalry, but others out of g. G2306

GOPHER (KJV) CYPRESS

GORE (3) [GORES, GORING]

Dt 33:17 With them he will g the nations, even H5590
1Ki 22:11 'With these you will g the Arameans until H5590
2Ch 18:10 'With these you will g the Arameans until H5590

GORES (3) [GORE]

Ex 21:28 "If a bull g a man or woman to death, the H5590
Ex 21:31 applies if the bull g a son or daughter. H5590
Ex 21:32 If the bull g a male or female slave, the H5590

GORGE (23) [GORGED]

Ex 15: 9 divide the spoils; I will g myself on them. H4848
Dt 2:24 "Set out now and cross the Arnon G. H5707
Dt 2:36 From Aroer on the rim of the Arnon G, and H5707
Dt 2:36 from the town in the g, even as far as H5707
Dt 3: 8 from the Arnon G as far as Mount Hermon H5707
Dt 3:12 the territory north of Aroer by the Arnon G, H5707
Dt 3:16 from Gilead down to the Arnon G H5707
Dt 3:16 the middle of the g being the border H5707
Dt 4:48 the rim of the Arnon G to Mount Sirion H5707
Jos 12: 1 from the Arnon G to Mount Hermon H5707
Jos 12: 2 from Aroer on the rim of the Arnon G— H5707
Jos 12: 2 from the middle of the g—to the Jabbok H5707
Jos 13: 9 from Aroer on the rim of the Arnon G, H5707
Jos 13: 9 from the town in the middle of the g H5707
Jos 13:16 from Aroer on the rim of the Arnon G, H5707
Jos 13:16 from the town in the middle of the g H5707
Jos 15: 7 the Pass of Adummim south of the g. H5707
2Sa 24: 5 south of the town in the g, and then went H5707
2Ki 10:33 Aroer by the Arnon G through Gilead to H5707
2Ch 20:16 them at the end of the g in the Desert of H5707
Ps 17:14 may their children g themselves on it H8425
Pr 23:20 too much wine or g themselves on meat, H2361
Eze 32: 4 animals of the wild g themselves on you. H8425

GORGED (2) [GORGE]

Ps 78:29 They ate till they were g—he had H8425+4394
Rev 19:21 all the birds g themselves on their flesh. G5963

GORING (2) [GORE]

Ex 21:29 has had the habit of g and the owner has H5591

Ex 21:36 known that the bull had the habit of g, H5591

GOSHEN (15)

Ge 45:10 live in the region of G and be near me— H1777
Ge 46:28 of him to Joseph to get directions to G. H1777
Ge 46:28 When they arrived in the region of G, H1777
Ge 46:29 ready and went to G to meet his father H1777
Ge 46:34 be allowed to settle in the region of G." H1777
Ge 47: 1 land of Canaan and are now in G." H824+1777
Ge 47: 4 please let your servants settle in G." H824+1777
Ge 47: 6 Let them live in G. And if you know H824+1777
Ge 47:27 settled in Egypt in the region of G. H1777
Ge 50: 8 their flocks and herds were left in G. H824+1777
Ex 8:22 I will deal differently with the land of G, H1777
Ex 9:26 place it did not hail was the land of G, H1777
Jos 10:41 from the whole region of G to Gibeon. H1777
Jos 11:16 the whole region of G, the western H1777
Jos 15:51 G, Holon and Giloh—eleven towns and H1777

GOSPEL (95)

Mt 24:14 And this g of the kingdom will be G2295
Mt 26:13 wherever this g is preached throughout G2295
Mk 8:35 their life for me and for the g will save it. G2295
Mk 10:29 children or fields for me and the g G2295
Mk 13:10 And the g must first be preached to all G2295
Mk 14: 9 wherever the g is preached throughout G2295
Mk 16:15 the world and preach the g to all creation. G2295
Ac 8:25 **preaching the g** in many Samaritan G2294
Ac 8:40 **preaching the g** in all the towns until he G2294
Ac 14: 7 where they continued *to* **preach the g**. G2294
Ac 14:21 *They* **preached the g** in that city and won G2294
Ac 15: 7 my lips the message *of* the g and believe. G2295
Ac 16:10 had called us *to* **preach the g** to them. G2294
Ro 1: 1 apostle and set apart for the g of God— G2295
Ro 1: 2 **the g** he promised beforehand through G4005S
Ro 1: 9 in my spirit in **preaching the g** of his Son, G2295
Ro 1:15 I am so eager *to* **preach the g** also to you G2294
Ro 1:16 For I am not ashamed *of* the g, because it G2295
Ro 1:17 For in **the g** the righteousness of God is G899S
Ro 2:16 through Jesus Christ, as my g declares. G2295
Ro 11:28 As far as the g is concerned, they are G2295
Ro 15:16 priestly duty *of* **proclaiming the g** of God, G2295
Ro 15:19 I have fully **proclaimed the g** of Christ. G2295
Ro 15:20 my ambition *to* **preach the g** where Christ G2294
Ro 16:25 to establish you in accordance with my g, G2295
1Co 1:17 to baptize, but *to* **preach the g**—not with G2294
1Co 4:15 Jesus I became your father through the g. G2295
1Co 9:12 rather than hinder the g of Christ. G2295
1Co 9:14 who preach the g should receive their G2295
1Co 9:14 should receive their living from the g. G2295
1Co 9:16 For when *I* **preach the g**, I cannot boast G2294
1Co 9:16 Woe to me if *I do* not **preach the g**! G2294
1Co 9:18 that *in* **preaching the g** I may offer it free G2294
1Co 9:18 use of my rights as a **preacher of the g**. G2295
1Co 9:23 I do all this for the sake of the g, that I G2295
1Co 15: 1 to remind you *of* the g I preached to you G2295
1Co 15: 2 By **this g** you are saved, if you hold firmly G4005S
2Co 2:12 to Troas to **preach the g** of Christ and G2295
2Co 4: 3 And even if our g is veiled, it is veiled to G2295
2Co 4: 4 see the light *of* the g that displays the G2295
2Co 8:18 by all the churches for his service to the g. G2295
2Co 9:13 your confession of the g of Christ, G2295
2Co 10:14 did get as far as you with the g of Christ. G2295
2Co 10:16 *so that we can* **preach the g** in the regions G2294
2Co 11: 4 a different g from the one you accepted G2295
2Co 11: 7 you by preaching the g of God to you free G2295
Gal 1: 6 of Christ and are turning to a different g— G2295
Gal 1: 7 which is really no g at all. Evidently some G257S
Gal 1: 7 are trying to pervert the g of Christ. G2295
Gal 1: 8 from heaven *should* **preach a g** other than G2294
Gal 1: 9 If anybody *is* **preaching** to you a g other G2294
Gal 1:11 that the g I preached is not of human G2295
Gal 2: 2 to them the g that I preach among G2295
Gal 2: 5 so that the truth *of* the g might be G2295
Gal 2: 7 with the task *of* **preaching the g** to the G2295
Gal 2:14 not acting in line with the truth *of* the g, G2295
Gal 3: 8 and **announced the g in advance** to G4603
Gal 4:13 illness *that I* first **preached the g** to you, G2294
Eph 1:13 message of truth, the g of your salvation. G2295
Eph 3: 6 is that through the g the Gentiles are G2295
Eph 3: 7 I became a servant *of* **this g** by the gift of G4005S
Eph 6:15 readiness that *comes from* the g of peace. G2295
Eph 6:19 make known the mystery *of* the g, G2295
Php 1: 5 your partnership in the g from the first day G2295
Php 1: 7 chains or defending and confirming the g, G2295
Php 1:12 me has actually served to advance the g. G2295
Php 1:14 the more to proclaim the g without fear. G3364
Php 1:16 I am put here for the defense *of* the g. G2295
Php 1:27 in a manner worthy *of* the g of Christ. G2295
Php 1:27 together as one for the faith *of* the g G2295
Php 2:22 has served with me in the **work of** the g. G2295
Php 4: 3 at my side in the cause of the g, G2295
Php 4:15 days *of* your *acquaintance with* the g, G2295
Col 1: 5 heard in the true message *of* the g G2295
Col 1: 6 the g is bearing fruit and growing NDT
Col 1:23 not move from the hope *held out in* the g. G2295
Col 1:23 This is the g that you heard and that has NDT
1Th 1: 5 because our g came to you not simply with G2295
1Th 2: 2 to tell you his g in the face of strong G2295
1Th 2: 4 by God to be entrusted *with* the g. G2295
1Th 2: 8 you not only the g of God but our lives G2295
1Th 2: 9 while we preached the g of God to you. G2295
1Th 3: 2 God's service in spreading the g of Christ, G2295
2Th 1: 8 do not obey the g of our Lord Jesus. G2295
2Th 2:14 He called you to this through our g, that G2295
1Ti 1:11 that conforms to the g concerning the glory G2295
2Ti 1: 8 join with me in suffering *for* the g, by the G2295
2Ti 1:10 life and immortality to light through the g. G2295
2Ti 1:11 And of **this g** I was appointed a herald G4005S
2Ti 2: 8 descended from David. This is my g, G2295
Phm 13 helping me while I am in chains *for* the g. G2295
1Pe 1:12 by those *who have* **preached the g** to you G2294
1Pe 4: 6 is the reason **the g** *was* **preached** even to G2294
1Pe 4:17 those who do not obey the g of God? G2295
Rev 14: 6 he had the eternal g to proclaim to those G2295

GOSSIP (7) [GOSSIPS]

Pr 11:13 A g betrays a confidence, but a H2143+8215
Pr 16:28 conflict, and a g separates close friends. H8087
Pr 18: 8 The words of a g are like choice morsels H8087
Pr 20:19 A g betrays a confidence; so avoid H2143+8215
Pr 26:20 without a g a quarrel dies down. H8087
Pr 26:22 The words of a g are like choice morsels H8087
2Co 12:20 ambition, slander, g, arrogance and G6030

GOSSIPS (1) [GOSSIP]

Ro 1:29 deceit and malice. They are g, G6031

GOT (158) [GET]

Ge 18:16 When the men g **up** to leave, they looked H7756
Ge 19: 1 *he* g **up** to meet them and bowed down H7756
Ge 19:27 **Early** the next morning Abraham g **up** H8899
Ge 19:33 night *they* g their father **to drink** wine, H9197
Ge 19:33 it when she lay down or when she g **up**. H7756
Ge 19:35 So *they* g their father **to drink** wine that H9197
Ge 19:35 it when she lay down or when she g **up**. H7756
Ge 21:21 his mother g a wife for him from Egypt. H4374
Ge 22: 3 **Early** the next morning Abraham g **up** H8899
Ge 24:54 When *they* g **up** the next morning, he H7756
Ge 24:61 her attendants g **ready** and mounted the H7756
Ge 24:64 *She* g **down** from her camel H5877
Ge 25:34 and then g **up** and left. So Esau H7756
Ge 27:14 So he went and g them and brought them H4374
Ge 32:22 That night Jacob g **up** and took his two H7756
Ge 37:31 Then *they* g Joseph's robe, slaughtered a H4374
Ge 38: 6 Judah g a wife for Er, his firstborn, and H4374
Ex 2: 3 *she* g a papyrus basket for him and H4374
Ex 2: 8 So the girl went and g the baby's mother. H7924
Ex 2:17 Moses g **up** and came to their rescue H7756
Ex 12:30 all the Egyptians g **up** during the night, H7756
Ex 24: 4 *He* g **up early** the next morning and built H8899
Ex 32: 6 to eat and drink and g **up** to indulge in H7756
Nu 16:25 Moses g **up** and went to Dathan and H7756
Nu 22:13 next morning Balaam g **up** and said to H7756
Nu 22:21 Balaam g **up** in the morning, saddled his H7756
Nu 24:25 Then Balaam g **up** and returned home H7756
Jos 6:12 Joshua g **up early** the next morning and H8899
Jos 6:15 *they* g **up** at daybreak and marched H8899
Jos 15:18 When *she* g **off** her donkey H7563+4946+6584
Jdg 1:14 When *she* g **off** her donkey H7563+4946+6584
Jdg 3:26 they waited, Ehud g **away**. He passed by H4880
Jdg 4:15 Sisera g **down** from his chariot and H3718
Jdg 6:28 when the people of the town g **up**, H8899
Jdg 7: 6 All the rest g **down** on their knees to drink. H4156
Jdg 10:16 Then *they* g **rid of** the foreign gods among H6073
Jdg 13:11 Manoah g **up** and followed his wife H7756
Jdg 16: 3 Then *he* g **up** and took hold of the doors H7756
Jdg 19: 5 the fourth day *they* g **up early** and he H8899
Jdg 19: 7 And when the man g **up** to go, his H7756
Jdg 19: 9 his servant, g **up** to leave, his H7756
Jdg 19:27 When her master g **up** in the morning H7756
Jdg 20:11 the Israelites g **together** and united as one H665
Jdg 20:19 the Israelites g **up** and pitched camp near H7756
Ru 2:15 As *she* g **up** to glean, Boaz gave orders to H7756
Ru 3:14 but g **up** before anyone could be H7756
1Sa 3: 6 And Samuel g **up** and went to Eli and H7756
1Sa 3: 8 And Samuel g **up** and went to Eli and H7756
1Sa 9:26 When Saul g **ready**, he and Samuel H7756
1Sa 15:12 **Early** in the morning Samuel g **up** and H8899
1Sa 20:34 Jonathan g **up** from the table in fierce H7756
1Sa 20:41 David g **up** from the south side of the H7756
1Sa 25:23 she quickly g **off** her donkey H3718+4946+6584
1Sa 25:42 Abigail quickly g **on** a donkey and H8206
1Sa 28:23 *He* g **up** from the ground and sat on the H7756
1Sa 28:25 That same night *they* g **up** and left. H7756
1Sa 29:11 his men g **up early** in the morning H8899
1Sa 30:17 none of them g **away**, except four H4880
2Sa 11: 2 One evening David g **up** from his bed H7756
2Sa 12:20 Then David g **up** from the ground. After H7756
2Sa 13:29 Then all the king's sons g **up**, mounted H7756
2Sa 14: 6 *They* g **into a fight** *with* each other in the H5897
2Sa 18: 9 Absalom's hair *g* **caught** in the tree. AIT
2Sa 19: 8 So the king g **up** and took his seat in the H7756
2Sa 24:11 Before David g **up** the next morning, the H7756
1Ki 1: 5 So *he* g chariots and horses **ready**, with H6913
1Ki 3:20 So *she* g **up** in the middle of the night H7756
1Ki 3:21 The next morning, *I* g **up** to nurse my son H7756
1Ki 14:17 Jeroboam's wife g **up** and left and went H7756
1Ki 15:12 from the land and g **rid of** all the idols his H6073
1Ki 19: 8 So *he* g **up** and ate and drank H7756
1Ki 21:16 he g **up** and went down to take H7756
2Ki 1:15 So Elijah g **up** and went down with him to H7756
2Ki 3: 2 *He* g **rid of** the sacred stone of Baal that H6073
2Ki 3:22 When *they* g **up early** in the morning, the H8899
2Ki 4:30 So *he* g **up** and followed her H7756
2Ki 4:34 Then *he* g **on** the bed and lay on the boy H6590
2Ki 4:35 in the room and then g **on** the bed and H6590
2Ki 5:21 *he* g **down** from the chariot to meet him. H5877
2Ki 5:26 you when the man g **down** from his H2200
2Ki 6:15 of the man of God g **up** and went out H7756
2Ki 7: 5 At dusk *they* g **up** and went to the camp H7756
2Ki 7: 7 So *they* g **up** and fled in the dusk and H7756
2Ki 7:12 The king g **up** in the night and said to his H7756
2Ki 9: 6 Jehu g **up** and went into the house. H7756
2Ki 9:16 Then he g **into** *his* **chariot** and rode to H8206
2Ki 19:35 When *the people* g **up** the next morning H8899
2Ki 23:24 Josiah g **rid of** the mediums and spiritists H1278
2Ch 33:15 *He* g **rid of** the foreign gods and removed H6073
Est 6:11 So Haman g the robe and the horse. H4374
Est 7: 7 The king g **up** in a rage, left his wine and H7756
Est 9: 1 the Jews g **the upper hand** over those H8948
Est 9:22 time when the Jews g **relief** from their H5663
Job 1:20 Job g **up** and tore his robe and shaved his H7756
Isa 37:36 When *the people* g **up** the next morning H8899
Jer 41: 2 who were with him g **up** and struck down H7756
Eze 3:23 So *I* g **up** and went out to the plain. H7756
Eze 29:18 he and his army g no reward from H2118+4200
Da 6:10 times a day he g **down** on his knees A10121
Da 6:19 the king g **up** and hurried to the lions' A10624
Da 8:27 Then *I* g **up** and went about the king's H7756
Zec 11: 8 In one month *I* g **rid of** the three H3948
Mt 2:14 So he g **up**, took the child and his mother G1586
Mt 2:21 So he g **up**, took the child and his mother G1586
Mt 8:15 and *she* g **up** and began to wait on him. G1586
Mt 8:23 Then he g **into** the boat and his disciples G1832
Mt 8:26 Then *he* g **up** and rebuked the winds and G1586
Mt 9: 7 Then the man g **up** and went home. G1586
Mt 9: 9 and Matthew g **up** and followed him. G482
Mt 9:19 Jesus g **up** and went with him, and so did G1586
Mt 9:25 took the girl by the hand, and *she* g **up**. G1586
Mt 13: 2 him that he g **into** a boat and sat in G1832
Mt 14:29 Then Peter g **down** out of the boat G2849
Mt 15:39 *he* g **into** the boat and went to the vicinity G1832
Mt 22:34 the Pharisees g **together**. G5251+2093+3836+899
Mt 27:48 one of them ran and g a sponge. G3284
Mk 1:35 still dark, Jesus g **up**, left the house and G482
Mk 2:12 *He* g **up**, took his mat and walked out in G1586
Mk 2:14 told him, and Levi g **up** and followed him. G482
Mk 4: 1 so large that he g **into** a boat and sat in G1832
Mk 4:39 *He* g **up**, rebuked the wind and said to G1444
Mk 5: 2 *When* Jesus g **out** of the boat, a man with G2002
Mk 6:33 all the towns and g there **ahead of** them. G4601
Mk 6:54 As soon as they g **out** of the boat, people G2002
Mk 8:10 *he* g **into** the boat with his disciples and G1832
Mk 8:13 g back **into** the boat and crossed to the G1832
Lk 1:39 At that time Mary g **ready** and hurried to a G482
Lk 4:29 *They* g **up**, drove him out of the town, and G482
Lk 4:39 *She* g **up** at once and began to wait on G482
Lk 5: 3 *He* g **into** one of the boats, the one G1832
Lk 5:28 Levi g **up**, left everything and followed G482
Lk 6: 8 So *he* g **up** and stood there. G482
Lk 8:22 So *they* g **into** a boat and set out G1832
Lk 8:24 He g **up** and rebuked the wind and the G1444
Lk 8:37 So he g **into** the boat and left. G1832
Lk 14:20 '*I just* g **married**, so I can't G1222+1138
Lk 15:13 the younger son g **together** all he had, set G5251
Lk 15:20 So *he* g **up** and went to his father. "But G482
Lk 24:12 however, g **up** and ran to the tomb G482
Lk 24:33 *They* g **up** and returned at once to G482
Jn 4:52 as to the time when his son g better, G2400
Jn 6:17 where *they* g **into** a boat and set off across G1832
Jn 6:24 they g **into** the boats and went to G1832
Jn 11:29 *she* g **up** quickly and went to him. G1586
Jn 11:31 noticed how quickly she g **up** and went out G482
Jn 13: 4 so *he* g **up** from the meal, took off his G1586
Jn 21: 3 So they went out and g **into** the boat, but G1832
Ac 5: 8 the price *you* and Ananias g for the land?" G625
Ac 9: 8 Saul g **up** from the ground, but when he G1586
Ac 9:18 *He* g **up** and was baptized, G482
Ac 9:34 Immediately Aeneas g **up**. G482
Ac 9:40 then *he* g **down on** his knees and prayed. G5502
Ac 14:20 *he* g **up** and went back into the city. G482
Ac 15: 7 Peter g **up** and addressed them: G482
Ac 16:10 *we* g **ready** at once to leave for G2426
Ac 25:18 *When* his accusers g **up** to speak, they did G2705
Ac 28:16 When *we* g to Rome, Paul was allowed to G1656
1Co 10: 7 to eat and drink and g **up** to indulge in G482

GOUGE (3) [GOUGED]

1Sa 11: 2 the condition that I g **out** the right eye of H5941
Mt 5:29 you to stumble, g it **out** and throw it away. G1975
Mt 18: 9 you to stumble, g it **out** and throw it away. G1975

GOUGED (1) [GOUGE]

Jdg 16:21 g **out** his eyes and took him down to Gaza H5941

GOURD (KJV) (LEAFY) PLANT

GOURDS (4)

1Ki 6:18 carved with g and open flowers. H7225
1Ki 7:24 Below the rim, g encircled it—ten to a H7225
1Ki 7:24 The g were cast in two rows in one piece H7225
2Ki 4:39 as many of its g as his garment H7226+8441

GOVERN (14) [GOVERNED, GOVERNING, GOVERNMENT, GOVERNOR, GOVERNOR'S, GOVERNORS, GOVERNS]

Ge 1:16 the greater light to g the day and the H4939
Ge 1:16 the day and the lesser light to g the night. H4939
Ge 1:18 to g the day and the night, and to H5440
1Sa 9:17 I spoke to you about; he *will* g my people." H6806
1Ki 3: 9 a discerning heart to g your people and to H9149
1Ki 3: 9 For who is able to g this great people of H9149
2Ch 1:10 who *is able to* g this great people of H9149
2Ch 1:11 knowledge *to* g my people over H9149
Job 34:17 Can someone who hates justice g? Will H2502
Ps 136: 8 the sun to g the day, His love endures H4939
Ps 136: 9 the moon and stars to g the night; His H4939
Pr 8:16 by me princes g, and nobles—all who H8606
Ob 21 up on Mount Zion to g the mountains of H9149
Zec 3: 7 then you *will* g my house and have H1906

GOVERNED (6) [GOVERN]

Jdg 9:22 After Abimelek *had* g Israel three years, H8606
2Ki 15: 5 of the palace and g the people of the H9149
2Ch 26:21 of the palace and g the people of the H9149
Ro 8: 6 The mind g *by* the **flesh** is death, but the AIT
Ro 8: 6 the mind g *by* the **Spirit** is life and peace. AIT
Ro 8: 7 The mind g *by* the **flesh** is hostile to God; it AIT

GOVERNING (2) [GOVERN]

Ro 13: 1 everyone be subject to the g authorities, *G5660*
Ro 13: 6 who give their full time to g. *G899+4047S*

GOVERNMENT (4) [GOVERN]

1Ki 9:22 fighting men, his g **officials**, his officers, H6269
Isa 9: 6 and the g will be on his shoulders. H5385
Isa 9: 7 greatness of his g and peace there will H5385
Da 6: 4 Daniel in his conduct of g **affairs**, A10424

GOVERNMENTS (KJV) GUIDANCE

GOVERNOR (51) [GOVERN]

Ge 42: 6 Now Joseph was the g of the land, the H8954
Jdg 9:30 When Zebul the g *of* the city heard what H8569
1Ki 4:19 He was the only g over the district. H5907
1Ki 22:47 no king in Edom; a **provincial** g ruled. H5893
2Ki 10: 5 the city g, the elders and the H889+6584S
2Ki 23: 8 of Joshua, the city g, which was on the H8569
2Ki 25:23 of Babylon *had* **appointed** Gedaliah **as** g, H7212
Ezr 2:63 The g ordered them not to eat any of the H9579
Ezr 5: 3 that time Tattenai, g *of* Trans-Euphrates A10580
Ezr 5: 6 that Tattenai, g *of* Trans-Euphrates, and A10580
Ezr 5:14 whom he had appointed g, A10580
Ezr 6: 6 Tattenai, g *of* Trans-Euphrates, and A10580
Ezr 6: 7 Let the g *of* the Jews and the Jewish A10580
Ezr 6:13 Tattenai, g *of* Trans-Euphrates, and A10580
Ne 3: 7 the authority of the g *of* Trans-Euphrates. H7068
Ne 5:14 to be their g in the land of Judah, H7068
Ne 5:14 my brothers ate the food allotted to the g. H7068
Ne 5:18 demanded the food allotted to the g, H7068
Ne 7:65 The g, therefore, ordered them not to eat H9579
Ne 7:70 The g gave to the treasury 1,000 darics of H9579
Ne 8: 9 Then Nehemiah the g, Ezra the priest H9579
Ne 10: 1 Nehemiah the g, the son of H9579
Ne 12:26 days of Nehemiah the g and of Ezra the H7068
Isa 60:17 make peace your g and well-being your H7213
Jer 40: 7 *had* **appointed** Gedaliah son of Ahikam **as** g H7212
Jer 40:11 *had* **appointed** Gedaliah son of Ahikam, the son of Shaphan, **as** g H7212
Jer 41: 2 of Babylon *had* **appointed as** g over the H7212
Jer 41:18 of Babylon *had* **appointed as** g over the H7212
Hag 1: 1 son of Shealtiel, g *of* Judah, and to H7068
Hag 1:14 son of Shealtiel, g *of* Judah, and the spirit H7068
Hag 2: 2 son of Shealtiel, g *of* Judah, to Joshua H7068
Hag 2:21 "Tell Zerubbabel g *of* Judah that I am H7068
Mal 1: 8 Try offering them to your g! Would he be H7068
Mt 27: 2 handed him over to Pilate the g. *G2450*
Mt 27:11 Meanwhile Jesus stood before the g, and *G2450*
Mt 27:11 governor, and the g asked him, "Are you *G2450*
Mt 27:14 charge—to the great amazement *of* the g. *G2450*
Mt 27:21 release to you?" asked the g. "Barabbas," *G2450*
Mt 28:14 If this report gets to the g, we will satisfy *G2450*
Lk 2: 2 took place *while* Quirinius *was* g of Syria.) *G2448*
Lk 3: 1 *when* Pontius Pilate *was* g of Judea *G2448*
Lk 20:20 over to the power and authority *of* the g. *G2450*
Jn 18:28 Caiaphas to the **palace of the Roman** g. *G4550*
Ac 23:24 so that he may be taken safely to G Felix." *G2450*
Ac 23:26 Lysias, To His Excellency, G Felix: *G2450*
Ac 23:33 the letter *to* the g and handed Paul *G2450*
Ac 23:34 The g read the letter and asked what NDT
Ac 24: 1 their charges against Paul *before* the g. *G2450*
Ac 24:10 When the g motioned for him to speak *G2450*
Ac 26:30 with him the g and Bernice and those *G2450*
2Co 11:32 In Damascus the g under King Aretas had *G1617*

GOVERNOR'S (2) [GOVERN]

Mt 27:15 Now it was the g custom at the festival to *G2450*
Mt 27:27 Then the g soldiers took Jesus into the *G2450*

GOVERNORS (26) [GOVERN]

1Ki 4: 5 in charge of the **district** g; Zabud son of H5893
1Ki 4: 7 had twelve **district** g over all Israel, H5893
1Ki 4:27 The **district** g, each in his month, supplied H5893
1Ki 10:15 Arabian kings and the g *of* the territories. H7068
2Ch 9:14 kings of Arabia and the g *of* the territories H7068
Ezr 8:36 satraps and to the g *of* Trans-Euphrates, H7068
Ne 2: 7 I have letters to the g *of* Trans-Euphrates, H7068
Ne 2: 9 So I went to the g *of* Trans-Euphrates and H7068
Ne 5:15 But the earlier g—those preceding me H7068
Est 3:12 the g of the various provinces and the H7068
Est 8: 9 g and nobles of the 127 provinces H7068
Est 9: 3 the g and the king's administrators H7068
Jer 51:23 with you I shatter g and officials. H7068
Jer 51:28 of the Medes, their g and all their officials H7068
Jer 51:57 wise men drunk, her g, officers and H7068
Eze 23: 6 clothed in blue, g and commanders, all of H7068
Eze 23:12 after the Assyrians—g and commanders H7068
Eze 23:23 all of them g and commanders H7068
Da 3: 2 satraps, prefects, g, advisers, treasurers, A10580
Da 3: 3 satraps, prefects, g, advisers, treasurers, A10580
Da 3:27 g and royal advisers crowded around A10580
Da 6: 7 advisers and g have all agreed that the A10580
Mt 10:18 be brought before g and kings as *G2450*
Mk 13: 9 you will stand before g and kings as *G2450*
Lk 21:12 you will be brought before kings and g, *G2450*
1Pe 2:14 or *to* g, who are sent by him to punish *G2450*

GOVERNS (2) [GOVERN]

Jdg 13:12 what is to be the **rule that** g the boy's life H5477
Job 36:31 This is the way *he* g the nations and H1906

GOWN (1)

Ps 45:13 chamber; her g is interwoven with gold. H4230

GOYIM (3)

Ge 14: 1 king of Elam and Tidal king of G, H1582
Ge 14: 9 Tidal king of G, Amraphel king of H1582
Jos 12:23 one the king of G in Gilgal one H1582

GOZAN (5)

2Ki 17: 6 in G on the Habor River and in the towns H1579
2Ki 18:11 in G on the Habor River and in towns of H1579
2Ki 19:12 deliver them—the gods of G, Harran, H1579
1Ch 5:26 Hara and the river of G, where they are to H1579
Isa 37:12 deliver them—the gods of G, Harran, H1579

GRABBED (4) [GRABS]

Jdg 15:15 *he* g it and struck down a thousand men. H4374
2Sa 2:16 Then each man g his opponent by the H2616
2Sa 13:11 it to him to eat, *he* g her and said, "Come H2616
Mt 18:28 *He* g him and began to choke him *G3195*

GRABS (1) [GRABBED]

Pr 26:17 Like *one who* g a stray dog by the ears is H2616

GRACE (128) [GRACIOUS, GRACIOUSLY]

Ps 45: 2 your lips have been anointed with g, H2834
Pr 1: 9 are a garland to g your head and a chain H2834
Pr 3:22 life for you, an **ornament to** g your neck. H2834
Pr 4: 9 you a garland to g your head and present H2834
Pr 22:11 who speaks *with* g will have the king H2834
Isa 26:10 But *when* g **is shown** *to* the wicked, they H2858
Zec 12:10 Jerusalem a spirit of g and supplication. H2834
Lk 2:40 wisdom, and the g of God was on him. *G5921*
Jn 1:14 came from the Father, full *of* g and truth. *G5921*
Jn 1:16 we have all received g in place of grace *G5921*
Jn 1:16 grace in place of g already given. *G5921*
Jn 1:17 g and truth came through Jesus Christ. *G5921*
Ac 4:33 And God's g was so powerfully at work in *G5921*
Ac 6: 8 Stephen, a man full *of* God's g and power *G5921*
Ac 11:23 saw what the g of God had done, *G5921*
Ac 13:43 urged them to continue *in* the g of God. *G5921*
Ac 14: 3 the message *of* his g by enabling them to *G5921*
Ac 14:26 been committed *to* the g of God for the *G5921*
Ac 15:11 it is through the g of our Lord Jesus that *G5921*
Ac 15:40 by the believers *to* the g of the Lord. *G5921*
Ac 18:27 help to those who by g had believed. *G5921*
Ac 20:24 of testifying to the good news *of* God's g. *G5921*
Ac 20:32 you to God and to the word *of* his g, *G5921*
Ro 1: 5 him we received g and apostleship to *G5921*
Ro 1: 7 G and peace to you from God our Father *G5921*
Ro 3:24 are justified freely *by* his g through the *G5921*
Ro 4:16 so that it may be by g and may be *G5921*
Ro 5: 2 by faith into this g in which we now stand. *G5921*
Ro 5:15 much more did God's g and the gift that *G5921*
Ro 5:15 gift that came by the g of the one man, *G5921*
Ro 5:17 abundant provision *of* g and of the gift of *G5921*
Ro 5:20 sin increased, g increased all the more, *G5921*
Ro 5:21 so also g might reign through *G5921*
Ro 6: 1 we go on sinning so that g may increase? *G5921*
Ro 6:14 you are not under the law, but under g. *G5921*
Ro 6:15 are not under the law but under g? *G5921+5920*
Ro 11: 5 time there is a remnant chosen by g. *G5921*
Ro 11: 6 And if *by* g, then it cannot be based on *G5921*
Ro 11: 6 if it were, g would no longer be grace. *G5921*
Ro 11: 6 if it were, grace would no longer be g. *G5921*
Ro 12: 3 For by the g given me I say to every one of *G5921*
Ro 12: 6 according to the g given to each of us. *G5921*
Ro 15:15 because of the g God gave me *G5921*
Ro 16:20 The g of our Lord Jesus be with you. *G5921*
1Co 1: 3 G and peace to you from God our Father *G5921*
1Co 1: 4 you because of his g given you in Christ *G5921*
1Co 3:10 By the g God has given me, I laid a *G5921*
1Co 15:10 But *by* the g of God I am what I am, and *G5921*
1Co 15:10 his g to me was not without effect. *G5921*
1Co 15:10 but the g of God that was with me. *G5921*
1Co 16:23 The g of the Lord Jesus be with you. *G5921*
2Co 1: 2 G and peace to you from God our Father *G5921*
2Co 1:12 not on worldly wisdom but on God's g. *G5921*
2Co 4:15 so that the g that is reaching more and *G5921*
2Co 6: 1 urge you not to receive God's g in vain. *G5921*
2Co 8: 1 you to know *about* the g that God has *G5921*
2Co 8: 6 to completion this **act of** g on your part. *G5921*
2Co 8: 7 see that you also excel in this g **of giving**. *G5921*
2Co 8: 9 For you know the g of our Lord Jesus Christ *G5921*
2Co 9:14 of the surpassing g God has given you. *G5921*
2Co 12: 9 he said to me, "My g is sufficient for you *G5921*
2Co 13:14 May the g of the Lord Jesus Christ, and *G5921*
Gal 1: 3 G and peace to you from God our Father *G5921*
Gal 1: 6 you to live in the g of Christ and are *G5921*
Gal 1:15 mother's womb and called me by his g, *G5921*
Gal 2: 9 when they recognized the g given to me. *G5921*
Gal 2:21 I do not set aside the g of God, for if *G5921*
Gal 3:18 God **in** *his* g **gave** it to Abraham *G5919*
Gal 5: 4 from Christ; you have fallen away from g. *G5921*
Gal 6:18 The g of our Lord Jesus Christ be with your *G5921*
Eph 1: 2 G and peace to you from God our Father *G5921*
Eph 1: 6 to the praise of his glorious g, which he *G5921*
Eph 1: 7 in accordance with the riches of God's g *G5921*
Eph 2: 5 it is *by* g you have been saved. *G5921*
Eph 2: 7 show the incomparable riches *of* his g, *G5921*
Eph 2: 8 For it is *by* g you have been saved, through *G5921*
Eph 3: 2 of God's g that was given to me *G5921*
Eph 3: 7 the gift of God's g given me through the *G5921*
Eph 3: 8 the Lord's people, this g was given me: *G5921*
Eph 4: 7 But to each one of us g has been given as *G5921*
Eph 6:24 G to all who love our Lord Jesus Christ *G5921*
Php 1: 2 G and peace to you from God our Father *G5921*
Php 1: 7 all of you share in God's g with me. *G5921*
Php 4:23 The g of the Lord Jesus Christ be with your *G5921*
Col 1: 2 G and peace to you from God our Father. *G5921*
Col 1: 6 you heard it and truly understood God's g. *G5921*
Col 4: 6 Let your conversation be always full of g *G5921*
Col 4:18 Remember my chains. G be with you. *G5921*
1Th 1: 1 the Lord Jesus Christ: G and peace to you. *G5921*
1Th 5:28 The g of our Lord Jesus Christ be with you. *G5921*
2Th 1: 2 G and peace to you from God the Father *G5921*
2Th 1:12 according to the g of our God and the *G5921*
2Th 2:16 who loved us and by his g gave us eternal *G5921*
2Th 3:18 The g of our Lord Jesus Christ be with you *G5921*
1Ti 1: 2 G, mercy and peace from God the Father *G5921*
1Ti 1:14 The g of our Lord was poured out on me *G5921*
1Ti 6:21 departed from the faith. G be with you all. *G5921*
2Ti 1: 2 G, mercy and peace from God the Father *G5921*
2Ti 1: 9 because of his own purpose and g. *G5921*
2Ti 1: 9 This g was given us in Christ Jesus before NDT
2Ti 2: 1 be strong in the g that is in Christ Jesus. *G5921*
2Ti 4:22 Lord be with your spirit. G be with you all. *G5921*
Titus 1: 4 G and peace from God the Father and *G5921*
Titus 2:11 For the g of God has appeared that offers *G5921*
Titus 3: 7 having been justified *by* his g, we might *G5921*
Titus 3:15 love us in the faith. G be with you all. *G5921*
Phm 3 G and peace to you from God our Father *G5921*
Phm 25 The g of the Lord Jesus Christ be with your *G5921*
Heb 2: 9 so that *by* the g of God he might taste *G5921*
Heb 4:16 God's throne *of* g with confidence, *G5921*
Heb 4:16 mercy and find g to help us in our time *G5921*
Heb 10:29 who has insulted the Spirit *of* g? *G5921*
Heb 12:15 one falls short of the g of God and that no *G5921*
Heb 13: 9 our hearts to be strengthened *by* g, *G5921*
Heb 13:25 G be with you all. *G5921*
Jas 4: 6 But he gives us more g. That is why *G5921*
1Pe 1: 2 G and peace be yours in abundance. *G5921*
1Pe 1:10 who spoke of the g that was to come to *G5921*
1Pe 1:13 your hope on the g to be brought to you *G5921*
1Pe 4:10 faithful stewards *of* God's g in its various *G5921*
1Pe 5:10 And the God *of* all g, who called you to *G5921*
1Pe 5:12 testifying that this is the true g of God. *G5921*
2Pe 1: 2 G and peace be yours in abundance *G5921*
2Pe 3:18 But grow in the g and knowledge of our *G5921*
2Jn 3 G, mercy and peace from God the Father *G5921*
Jude 4 who pervert the g of our God into a *G5921*
Rev 1: 4 G and peace to you from him who is, and *G5921*
Rev 22:21 The g of the Lord Jesus be with God's *G5921*

GRACEFUL (3)

Job 41:12 its strength and its g form. H2665
Pr 5:19 A loving doe, a g deer—may her breasts H2834
SS 7: 1 Your g legs are like jewels, the work of an H2788

GRACIOUS (41) [GRACE]

Ge 21: 1 Now the LORD *was* g *to* Sarah as he had H7212
Ge 33:11 God *has been* g *to* me and I have all I H2858
Ge 43:29 And he said, "God *be* g *to* you, my son." H2858
Ex 34: 6 the compassionate and g God, slow to H2843
Nu 6:25 his face shine on you and *be* g *to* you; H2858
1Sa 2:21 And the LORD *was* g *to* Hannah; she gave H7212
2Sa 12:22 The LORD *may be* g *to* me and let the child H2858
2Ki 13:23 But the LORD *was* g *to* them and had H2858
2Ch 30: 9 LORD your God is g and compassionate. H2843
Ezr 7: 9 the g hand of his God was on him. H3202
Ezr 8:18 Because the g hand of our God was on us H3202
Ezr 8:22 "The g hand of our God is on everyone H3208
Ezr 9: 8 LORD our God has been g in leaving us a H9382
Ne 2: 8 And because the g hand of my God was H3202
Ne 2:18 told them about the g hand of my God on H3202
Ne 9:17 are a forgiving God, g and compassionate H2843
Ne 9:31 for you are a g and merciful God. H2843
Job 33:24 and *he is* g *to* that person and says to H2858

Ps 25:16 Turn to me and be g to me, for I am H2858
Ps 67: 1 May God be g to us and bless us and H2858
Ps 86:15 are a compassionate and g God, slow to H2843
Ps 103: 8 The LORD is compassionate and g, slow to H2843
Ps 111: 4 the LORD is g and compassionate. H2843
Ps 112: 4 for those who are g and compassionate H2843
Ps 116: 5 The LORD is g and righteous; our God is H2843
Ps 119:29 be g to me and teach me your law. H2858
Ps 119:58 be g to me according to your promise. H2858
Ps 145: 8 The LORD is g and compassionate, slow to H2843
Pr 15:26 but g words are pure in his sight. H5840
Pr 16:21 g words promote instruction. H5518
Pr 16:24 G words are a honeycomb, sweet to the H5840
Ecc 10:12 Words from the mouth of the wise are g H2834
Isa 30:18 Yet the LORD longs to be g to you H2858
Isa 30:19 How g he will be when you cry for H2858+2858
Isa 33: 2 be g to us; we long for you. Be our H2858
Joel 2:13 your God, for he is g and compassionate H2843
Jnh 4: 2 knew that you are a g and compassionate H2843
Mal 1: 9 "Now plead with God to be g to us. H2858
Lk 4:22 were amazed at the g words that came G5921
2Co 1:11 on our behalf for the g favor granted us in G5922
1Pe 3: 7 as heirs with you of the g gift of life, G5921

GRACIOUSLY (4) [GRACE]

Ge 33: 5 the children God has g given your servant." H2858
Hos 14: 2 "Forgive all our sins and receive us g, that H3202
Ac 27:24 God has g given you the lives of all G5919
Ro 8:32 along with him, g give us all things? G5919

GRAFF, GRAFFED (KJV) GRAFT, GRAFTED

GRAFT (1) [GRAFTED]

Ro 11:23 for God is able to g them in again. G1596

GRAFTED (5) [GRAFT]

Ro 11:17 have been g in among the others and G1596
Ro 11:19 were broken off so that I could be g in." G1596
Ro 11:23 in unbelief, they will be g in, for God is G1596
Ro 11:24 contrary to nature were g into a cultivated G1596
Ro 11:24 branches, be g into their own olive tree! G1596

GRAIN (268) [GRAINS, GRANARIES]

Ge 27:28 an abundance of g and new wine. H1841
Ge 27:37 have sustained him with g and new wine. H1841
Ge 37: 7 We were binding sheaves of g out in the H524
Ge 41: 5 Seven heads of g, healthy and good H8672
Ge 41: 6 seven other heads of g sprouted—thin H8672
Ge 41: 7 The thin heads of g swallowed up the H8672
Ge 41:22 "In my dream I saw seven heads of g, full H8672
Ge 41:24 The thin heads of g swallowed up the H8672
Ge 41:26 the seven good heads of g are seven H8672
Ge 41:27 seven worthless heads of g scorched by H8672
Ge 41:35 store up the g under the authority of H1339
Ge 41:49 Joseph stored up huge quantities of g, like H1339
Ge 41:56 storehouses and sold g to the Egyptians, H8690
Ge 41:57 came to Egypt to buy g from Joseph, H8690
Ge 42: 1 Jacob learned that there was g in Egypt, H8692
Ge 42: 2 "I have heard that there is g in Egypt. H8692
Ge 42: 3 brothers went down to buy g from Egypt. H1339
Ge 42: 5 were among those who went to buy g, H8690
Ge 42: 6 the person who sold g to all its people. H8690
Ge 42:19 of you go and take g back for your starving H8692
Ge 42:25 gave orders to fill their bags with g, H1339
Ge 42:26 they loaded their g on their donkeys and H8692
Ge 43: 2 had eaten all the g they had brought from H8692
Ge 44: 2 one's sack, along with the silver for his g." H8692
Ge 45:23 loaded with g and bread and other H1339
Ge 47:14 in payment for the g they were buying, H8692
Ex 22: 6 so that it burns shocks of g or standing H1538
Ex 22: 6 of grain or standing g or the whole field H7850
Ex 29:41 with the same g offering and its drink H4966
Ex 30: 9 incense or any burnt offering or g offering, H4966
Ex 40:29 on it burnt offerings and g offerings, H4966
Lev 2: 1 anyone brings a g offering to the LORD, H4966
Lev 2: 3 The rest of the g offering belongs to Aaron H4966
Lev 2: 4 'If you bring a g offering baked in an oven H4966
Lev 2: 5 If your g offering is prepared on a griddle H4966
Lev 2: 6 it and pour oil on it; it is a g offering. H4966
Lev 2: 7 If your g offering is cooked in a pan, it is to H4966
Lev 2: 8 Bring the g offering made of these things H4966
Lev 2: 9 portion from the g offering and burn it on H4966
Lev 2:10 The rest of the g offering belongs to Aaron H4966
Lev 2:11 " 'Every g offering you bring to the LORD H4966
Lev 2:13 Season all your g offerings with salt. H4966
Lev 2:13 of your God out of your g offerings; H4966
Lev 2:14 " 'If you bring a g offering of firstfruits to H4966
Lev 2:14 crushed heads of new g roasted in the fire H4152
Lev 2:15 Put oil and incense on it; it is a g offering. H4966
Lev 2:16 portion of the crushed g and the oil, H1762
Lev 5:13 the priest, as in the case of the g offering. H4966
Lev 6:14 are the regulations for the g offering: H4966
Lev 6:15 with all the incense on the g offering, H4966
Lev 6:20 of the finest flour as a regular g offering, H4966
Lev 6:21 present the g offering broken in H4966
Lev 6:23 Every g offering of a priest shall be burned H4966
Lev 7: 9 Every g offering baked in an oven or H4966
Lev 7:10 every g offering, whether mixed with H4966
Lev 7:37 offering, the g offering, the sin offering, H4966
Lev 9: 4 together with a g offering mixed with H4966
Lev 9:17 He also brought the g offering, took a H4966
Lev 10:12 "Take the g offering left over from the H4966
Lev 14:10 flour mixed with olive oil for a g offering, H4966
Lev 14:20 together with the g offering, and make H4966
Lev 14:21 flour mixed with olive oil for a g offering, H4966
Lev 14:31 offering, together with the g offering. H4966
Lev 23:10 priest a sheaf of the first g you harvest. H6684
Lev 23:13 together with its g offering of two-tenths of H4966
Lev 23:14 roasted or new g, until the very day H4152
Lev 23:16 present an offering of new g to the LORD. H4966
Lev 23:18 together with their g offerings and drink H4966
Lev 23:37 the burnt offerings and g offerings H4966
Lev 27:30 whether g from the soil or fruit from the H2446
Nu 4:16 the regular g offering and the anointing H4966
Nu 5:15 because it is a g offering for jealousy, H4966
Nu 5:18 the g offering for jealousy, while he H4966
Nu 5:25 from her hands the g offering for jealousy, H4966
Nu 5:26 a handful of the g offering as a memorial H4966
Nu 6:15 together with their g offerings and drink H4966
Nu 6:17 together with its g offering and drink H4966
Nu 7:13 flour mixed with olive oil as a g offering; H4966
Nu 7:19 flour mixed with olive oil as a g offering; H4966
Nu 7:25 flour mixed with olive oil as a g offering; H4966
Nu 7:31 flour mixed with olive oil as a g offering; H4966
Nu 7:37 flour mixed with olive oil as a g offering; H4966
Nu 7:43 flour mixed with olive oil as a g offering; H4966
Nu 7:49 flour mixed with olive oil as a g offering; H4966
Nu 7:55 flour mixed with olive oil as a g offering; H4966
Nu 7:61 flour mixed with olive oil as a g offering; H4966
Nu 7:67 flour mixed with olive oil as a g offering; H4966
Nu 7:73 flour mixed with olive oil as a g offering; H4966
Nu 7:79 flour mixed with olive oil as a g offering; H4966
Nu 7:87 a year old, together with their g offering. H4966
Nu 8: 8 bull with its g offering of the finest flour H4966
Nu 15: 4 to the LORD a g offering of a tenth of an H4966
Nu 15: 6 ram prepare a g offering of two-tenths of H4966
Nu 15: 9 with the bull a g offering of three-tenths H4966
Nu 15:24 its prescribed g offering and drink offering H4966
Nu 18: 9 whether g or sin or guilt offerings H4966
Nu 18:12 finest new wine and g they give the LORD H1841
Nu 18:27 reckoned to you as g from the threshing H1841
Nu 20: 5 It has no g or figs, grapevines or H2446
Nu 28: 5 together with a g offering of a tenth of an H4966
Nu 28: 8 the same kind of g offering and drink H4966
Nu 28: 9 offering and a g offering of two-tenths of H4966
Nu 28:12 there is to be a g offering of three-tenths H4966
Nu 28:12 a g offering of two-tenths of an ephah of H4966
Nu 28:13 a g offering of a tenth of an ephah of the H4966
Nu 28:20 each bull offer a g offering of three-tenths H4966
Nu 28:26 the LORD an offering of new g during the H4966
Nu 28:28 there is to be a g offering of three-tenths H4966
Nu 28:31 regular burnt offering and its g offering. H4966
Nu 29: 3 the bull offer a g offering of three-tenths H4966
Nu 29: 6 with their g offerings and drink offerings H4966
Nu 29: 9 the bull offer a g offering of three-tenths H4966
Nu 29:11 regular burnt offering with its g offering, H4966
Nu 29:14 bulls offer a g offering of three-tenths of H4966
Nu 29:16 offering with its g offering and drink H4966
Nu 29:18 offer their g offerings and drink offerings H4966
Nu 29:19 regular burnt offering with its g offering, H4966
Nu 29:21 offer their g offerings and drink offerings H4966
Nu 29:22 offering with its g offering and drink H4966
Nu 29:24 offer their g offerings and drink offerings H4966
Nu 29:25 offering with its g offering and drink H4966
Nu 29:27 offer their g offerings and drink offerings H4966
Nu 29:28 offering with its g offering and drink H4966
Nu 29:30 offer their g offerings and drink offerings H4966
Nu 29:31 offering with its g offering and drink H4966
Nu 29:33 offer their g offerings and drink offerings H4966
Nu 29:34 offering with its g offering and drink H4966
Nu 29:37 offer their g offerings and drink offerings H4966
Nu 29:38 offering with its g offering and drink H4966
Nu 29:39 burnt offerings, g offerings, drink offerings H4966
Dt 7:13 of your land—your g, new wine and olive H1841
Dt 11:14 so that you may gather in your g, new H1841
Dt 12:17 the tithe of your g and new wine and H1841
Dt 14:23 Eat the tithe of your g, new wine and olive H1841
Dt 16: 9 begin to put the sickle to the standing g. H7850
Dt 18: 4 are to give them the firstfruits of your g, H1841
Dt 23:25 must not put a sickle to their standing g. H7850
Dt 25: 4 an ox while it is treading out the g. H1889
Dt 28:51 They will leave you no g, new wine or H1841
Dt 33:28 dwell secure in a land of g and new wine, H1841
Jos 5:11 unleavened bread and roasted g. H7828
Jos 22:23 to offer burnt offerings and g offerings, H4966
Jos 22:29 burnt offerings, g offerings and sacrifices H4966
Jdg 13:19 together with the g offering, and H4966
Jdg 13:23 offering and g offering from our hands, H4966
Jdg 15: 5 loose in the standing g of the Philistines. H7850
Jdg 15: 5 He burned up the shocks and standing g H7850
Jdg 16:21 they set him to grinding g in the prison. H3221
Ru 2: 2 pick up the leftover g behind anyone H8672
Ru 2:14 harvesters, he offered her some roasted g. H7833
Ru 2:21 until they finish harvesting all my g. H7907
Ru 3: 7 to lie down at the far end of the g pile. H6894
1Sa 8:15 take a tenth of your g and of your vintage H2446
1Sa 17:17 this ephah of roasted g and these ten H7833
1Sa 25:18 five seahs of roasted g, a hundred cakes H7833
2Sa 17:19 of the well and scattered g over it. H8195
2Sa 17:28 flour and roasted g, beans and H7833
1Ki 8:64 g offerings and the fat of the fellowship H4966
1Ki 8:64 the g offerings and the fat of the H4966
2Ki 4:42 of barley bread baked from the first ripe g, H1137
2Ki 4:42 along with some heads of new g. H4152
2Ki 16:13 up his burnt offering and g offering, H4966
2Ki 16:15 burnt offering and the evening g offering, H4966
2Ki 16:15 king's burnt offering and his g offering, H4966
2Ki 16:15 their g offering and their drink H4966
2Ki 18:32 your own—a land of g and new wine, H1841
1Ch 21:23 and the wheat for the g offering. H4966
1Ch 23:29 the special flour for the g offerings, the H4966
2Ch 7: 7 the g offerings and the fat portions. H4966
2Ch 31: 5 generously gave the firstfruits of their g, H1841
2Ch 32:28 made buildings to store the harvest of g, H1841
Ezr 7:17 together with their g offerings and drink A10432
Ne 5: 2 us to eat and stay alive, we must get g." H1841
Ne 5: 3 our homes to get g during the famine." H1841
Ne 5:10 also lending the people money and g. H1841
Ne 5:11 of the money, g, new wine and olive H1841
Ne 10:31 bring merchandise or g to sell on the H8692
Ne 10:33 the regular g offerings and burnt H4966
Ne 10:37 ground meal, of our g offerings, of the fruit AIT
Ne 10:39 are to bring their contributions of g, new H1841
Ne 13: 5 to store the g offerings and incense and H4966
Ne 13: 5 also the tithes of g, new wine and H1841
Ne 13: 9 with the g offerings and the incense. H4966
Ne 13:12 All Judah brought the tithes of g, new H1841
Ne 13:15 bringing in g and loading it on H6894
Job 24:24 all others; they are cut off like heads of g. H8672
Job 31:10 then may my wife grind another man's g H3221
Job 39:12 it to haul in your g and bring it to your H2446
Ps 4: 7 joy when their g and new wine abound H1841
Ps 65: 9 with water to provide the people with g, H1841
Ps 65:13 flocks and the valleys are mantled with g; H1339
Ps 72:16 May g abound throughout the land; on H1339
Ps 78:24 he gave them the g of heaven. H1841
Pr 11:26 People curse the one who hoards g, but H1339
Pr 27:22 grinding them like g with a pestle, you H8195
Ecc 11: 1 Ship your g across the sea; after many H4312
Isa 5:10 homer of seed will yield only an ephah of g." NDT
Isa 17: 5 as when reapers harvest the standing g, H7850
Isa 17: 5 gathering the g in their arms—as H8672
Isa 17: 5 someone gleans heads of g in the Valley H8672
Isa 19:21 worship with sacrifices and g offerings; H4966
Isa 23: 3 the great waters came the g of the Shihor; H2446
Isa 28:28 G must be ground to make bread; so one NDT
Isa 28:28 one does not use horses to grind g. H5647S
Isa 36:17 your own—a land of g and new wine, H1841
Isa 43:23 you with g offerings nor wearied you H4966
Isa 57: 6 out drink offerings and offered g offerings. H4966
Isa 62: 8 again will I give your g as food for your H1841
Isa 66: 3 whoever makes a g offering is like one H4966
Isa 66:20 as the Israelites bring their g offerings, to H4966
Jer 9:22 open field, like cut g behind the reaper H6658
Jer 14:12 they offer burnt offerings and g offerings, H4966
Jer 17:26 sacrifices, g offerings and incense H4966
Jer 23:28 For what has straw to do with g?" declares H1339
Jer 31:12 of the LORD—the g, the new wine and the H1841
Jer 33:18 to burn g offerings and to present H4966
Jer 41: 5 bringing g offerings and incense with H4966
Jer 50:11 like a heifer threshing g and neigh like H1889
Jer 50:26 her granaries; pile her up like heaps of g. H6894
Eze 36:29 I will call for the g and make it plentiful H1841
Eze 42:13 holy offerings—the g offerings, the sin H4966
Eze 44:29 They will eat the g offerings, the sin H4966
Eze 45:15 These will be used for the g offerings H4966
Eze 45:17 g offerings and drink offerings at the H4966
Eze 45:17 sin offerings, g offerings, burnt offerings H4966
Eze 45:24 to provide as a g offering an ephah for H4966
Eze 45:25 burnt offerings, g offerings and oil. H4966
Eze 46: 5 The g offering given with the ram is to be H4966
Eze 46: 5 the g offering with the lambs is to be H4966
Eze 46: 7 to provide as a g offering one ephah with H4966
Eze 46:11 the g offering is to be an ephah with a H4966
Eze 46:14 with it morning by morning a g offering, H4966
Eze 46:14 of this g offering to the LORD is a H4966
Eze 46:15 the lamb and the g offering and the oil H4966
Eze 46:20 the sin offering and bake the g offering, H4966
Hos 2: 8 that I was the one who gave her the g, H1841
Hos 2: 9 I will take away my g when it ripens, H1841
Hos 2:22 the earth will respond to the g, the H1841
Hos 7:14 to their gods for g and new wine, H1841
Hos 8: 7 Were it to yield g, foreigners would swallow NDT
Hos 14: 7 they will flourish like the g, they will H1841
Joel 1: 9 G offerings and drink offerings are cut off H4966
Joel 1:10 is dried up; the g is destroyed, the new H1841
Joel 1:13 the g offerings and drink offerings are H4966
Joel 1:17 been broken down, for the g has dried up. H1841
Joel 2:14 g offerings and drink offerings for the H4966
Joel 2:19 "I am sending you g, new wine and olive H1841
Joel 2:24 The threshing floors will be filled with g H1339
Am 2:13 you as a cart crushes when loaded with g. H6658
Am 5:11 on the poor and impose a tax on their g. H1339
Am 5:22 bring me burnt offerings and g offerings, H4966
Am 8: 5 New Moon be over that we may sell g, H8692
Am 9: 9 all the nations as g is shaken in a sieve, NDT
Hag 1:11 the mountains, on the g, the new wine, H1841
Zec 9:17 G will make the young men thrive, and H1841
Mt 12: 1 to pick some heads of g and eat them G5092
Mk 2:23 they began to pick some heads of g. G5092
Mk 4: 7 the plants, so that they did not bear g. G2843
Mk 4:28 All by itself the soil produces g—first the G2844
Mk 4:29 As soon as the g is ripe, he puts the sickle G2843
Lk 6: 1 disciples began to pick some heads of g, G5092
Lk 12:18 and there I will store my surplus g. G4992
Lk 12:19 "You have plenty of g laid up for many G19S
Lk 17:35 Two women will be grinding g together G241

Ac 7:12 Jacob heard that there was g in Egypt, *G4989*
Ac 27:38 the ship by throwing the g into the sea. *G4992*
1Co 9: 9 muzzle an ox *while it is* **treading out the g.**" *G262*
1Ti 5:18 muzzle an ox *while it is* **treading out the g,**" *G262*

GRAINFIELD (1) [FIELD]
Dt 23:25 If you enter your neighbor's g, you may H7850

GRAINFIELDS (3) [FIELD]
Mt 12: 1 Jesus went through the g on the Sabbath. *G5077*
Mk 2:23 Sabbath Jesus was going through the g, *G5077*
Lk 6: 1 Sabbath Jesus was going through the g, *G5077*

GRAINS (3) [GRAIN]
Job 29:18 my days as numerous as the **g of sand.** H2567
Ps 139:18 they would outnumber the **g of sand** H2567
Isa 48:19 your children like its **numberless** g; their H5054

GRANARIES (3) [GRAIN]
Ex 22:29 back offerings from your g or your vats. H4852
Jer 50:26 Break open her g; pile her up like heaps H4393
Joel 1:17 in ruins, the g have been broken down H4923

GRANDCHILDREN (7) [CHILD]
Ge 31:28 even let me kiss my g and my daughters H1201
Ge 31:55 Laban kissed his g and his daughters and H1201
Ge 45:10 your children and g, your flocks and H1201+1201
Ex 10: 2 your children and g how I dealt H1201+1201
Dt 4:25 had children and g and have lived H1201+1201
2Ki 17:41 children and g continue to do as H1201+1201
1Ti 5: 4 But if a widow has children or g, these *G1681*

GRANDDAUGHTER (5) [DAUGHTER]
Ge 24:48 road to get the g *of* my master's brother H1426
Ge 36: 2 of Anah and g *of* Zibeon the Hivite— H1426
Ge 36:14 daughter of Anah and g *of* Zibeon, H1426
2Ki 8:26 was Athaliah, a g *of* Omri king of Israel. H1426
2Ch 22: 2 mother's name was Athaliah, a g *of* Omri. H1426

GRANDDAUGHTERS (1) [DAUGHTER]
Ge 46: 7 and his daughters and g— H1426+1201

GRANDFATHER (1) [FATHER]
2Sa 9: 7 you all the land that belonged to your g Saul, H3

GRANDFATHER'S (2) [FATHER]
2Sa 16: 3 Israelites will restore to me my g kingdom. H3
2Sa 19:28 All my g descendants deserved nothing but H3

GRANDMOTHER (3) [MOTHER]
1Ki 15:13 He even deposed his g Maakah from her H562
2Ch 15:16 Asa also deposed his g Maakah from her H562
2Ti 1: 5 first lived in your g Lois and in your *G3439*

GRANDMOTHER'S (1) [MOTHER]
1Ki 15:10 His g name was Maakah daughter of H562

GRANDPARENTS (1) [PARENT]
1Ti 5: 4 so repaying their **parents and g,** *G4591*

GRANDSON (9) [SON]
Ge 11:31 son Abram, his g Lot son of Haran H1201+1201
Ge 29: 5 to them, "Do you know Laban, Nahor's g?" H1201
Jdg 8:22 your son and your g—because you H1201+1201
2Sa 9: 9 given your master's g everything that H1201
2Sa 9:10 that your master's g may be provided for. H1201
2Sa 9:10 And Mephibosheth, g *of* your master, will H1201
2Sa 16: 3 then asked, "Where is your master's g?" H1201
2Sa 19:24 Saul's g, also went down to H1201
Jer 27: 7 his son and his g until the time H1201+1201

GRANDSONS (7) [SON]
Ge 36:12 These were g *of* Esau's wife Adah. H1201
Ge 36:13 These were g *of* Esau's wife Basemath. H1201
Ge 36:16 Eliphaz in Edom; they were g *of* Adah. H1201
Ge 36:17 they were g *of* Esau's wife Basemath. H1201
Ge 46: 7 his sons and g and his daughters H1201+1201
Jdg 12:14 He had forty sons and thirty g, who H1201+1201
1Ch 8:40 They had many sons and g—150 H1201+1201

GRANT (36) [GRANTED, GRANTING, GRANTS]
Ge 19:21 "Very well, *I will* g this request too H5951+7156
Ge 24:42 please g **success** *to* the journey on which I H7503
Ge 43:14 And *may* God Almighty g you mercy H5989
Ex 21: 9 *he must* g her the rights of a daughter. H6913
Lev 26: 6 " '*I will* g peace in the land, and you will H5989
Dt 28: 7 The LORD *will* g that the enemies who rise H5989
Dt 28:11 The LORD *will* g you **abundant** prosperity H3855
Jdg 11:37 But g me this one request," she said H6913
Ru 1: 9 *May* the LORD g that each of you will find H5989
1Sa 1:17 and *may* the God of Israel g you what you H5989
2Sa 14:15 perhaps he *will* g his servant's request. H6913
2Sa 23: 5 my salvation and g me my every desire. NDT
1Ki 5: 9 And you *are to* g my wish by providing H6913
1Ch 22: 9 and *I will* g Israel peace and quiet during H5989
Est 5: 8 it pleases the king to g my petition and H5989
Est 7: 3 if it pleases you, g me my life—this is my H5989
Job 6: 8 that God *would* g what I hope for, H5989
Job 13:20 "Only g me these two things, God, and H6913
Ps 20: 2 sanctuary and g you **support** from Zion. H6184
Ps 20: 5 *May* the LORD g all your requests. H4848
Ps 51:12 of your salvation and g me a willing spirit, NDT
Ps 85: 7 LORD, and g us your salvation. H5989
Ps 94:13 you g them **relief** from days of trouble, till H9200
Ps 118:25 save us! LORD, g us **success!** H7503
Ps 140: 8 *Do* not g the wicked their desires, LORD; do H5989
Ecc 6: 2 God *does* not g them **the ability** to H8948
Isa 46:13 *I will* g salvation to Zion, my splendor to H5989
Hag 2: 9 'And in this place *I will* g peace,' declares H5989
Mt 20:21 "G that one of these two sons of mine *G3306*
Mt 20:23 to sit at my right or left is not for me *to* g. *G1443*
Mk 10:40 to sit at my right or left is not for me *to* g. *G1443*
Lk 18: 3 'G me **justice** against my adversary.' *G1688*
Lk 23:24 So Pilate decided *to* g their demand. *G1181*
Ac 24:27 Felix wanted *to* g a favor to the Jews *G2960*
2Ti 1:18 *May* the Lord g that he will find mercy *G1443*
2Ti 2:25 the hope that God *will* g them repentance *G1443*

GRANTED (30) [GRANT]
Ge 4:25 "God *has* g me another child in place of H8883
Ge 24:56 that the LORD *has* g **success** *to* my journey. H7503
Ge 39:21 him kindness and g him favor in the eyes H5989
Jos 14: 3 Moses *had* g the two and a half tribes H5989
Jos 14: 3 of the Jordan but *had* not g the Levites an H5989
1Sa 1:27 the LORD *has* g me what I asked of H5989
1Sa 25:35 your words and g your **request.**" H5951+7156
2Sa 14:22 because the king *has* g his servant's H6913
1Ch 4:10 be free from pain." And God g his request. H995
1Ch 22:18 And *has he* not g you **rest** on every side H5663
1Ch 23:25 *has* g **rest** to his people and has come to H5663
Ezr 7: 6 The king *had* g him everything he asked H5989
Ezr 9: 9 He *has* g us new life to rebuild the house H5989
Ne 2: 8 God was on me, the king g my **requests.** H5989
Est 5: 6 up to half the kingdom, *it will* **be g.**" H6913
Est 7: 2 up to half the kingdom, *it will* **be g.**" H6913
Est 8:11 The king's edict g the Jews in every city H5989
Est 9:12 What is your request? *It will* also **be g.**" H6913
Job 42:15 their father g them an inheritance H5989
Ps 21: 2 *You have* g him his heart's desire and H5989
Ps 21: 6 Surely *you have* g him unending H8883
Pr 10:24 what the righteous desire *will be* g. H5989
Mt 14: 9 he ordered that her request *be* g *G1443*
Mt 15:28 Your request *is* g." And her daughter *G1181*
Jn 5:26 so *he has* g the Son also to have life in *G1443*
Jn 17: 2 For *you* g him authority over all people *G1443*
Ac 11:18 to Gentiles God *has* g repentance that *G1443*
Ro 11:20 **G.** But they were broken off because of *G2822*
2Co 1:11 the gracious favor g us in answer to the *G1650*
Php 1:29 For *it has been* g to you on behalf of Christ *G5919*

GRANTING (1) [GRANT]
Ne 1:11 success today *by* g him favor in the H5989

GRANTS (2) [GRANT]
Ps 127: 2 to eat—for *he* g sleep to those he loves. H5989
Ps 147:14 He g peace *to* your borders and satisfies H8492

GRAPE (10) [GRAPES, GRAPEVINE, GRAPEVINES]
Lev 26: 5 continue until **g harvest** and the grape H1292
Lev 26: 5 harvest and the g **harvest** will continue H1292
Nu 6: 3 They must not drink g juice or eat grapes H6694
Dt 32:14 You drank the foaming blood of the g. H6694
Jdg 8: 2 better than the **full g harvest** *of* Abiezer? H1292
Isa 18: 5 the flower becomes a ripening g, H1235
Isa 24:13 gleanings are left after the **g harvest.** H1292
Isa 32:10 will tremble; the **g harvest** will fail, and H1292
Jer 49: 9 If **g pickers** came to you, would they not H1305
Ob 5 If **g pickers** came to you, would they not H1305

GRAPES (44) [GRAPE]
Ge 40:10 its clusters ripened into g. H6694
Ge 40:11 I took the g, squeezed them into H6694
Ge 49:11 in wine, his robes in the blood of g. H6694
Lev 19:10 time or pick up the **g that have fallen.** H7261
Lev 25: 5 harvest the g *of* your untended vines. H6694
Nu 6: 3 juice or eat **g or raisins.** H6694+4300+2256+3313
Nu 13:20 It was the season for the first ripe g.) H6694
Nu 13:23 off a branch bearing a single cluster of g. H6694
Nu 13:24 because of the **cluster of g** the Israelites cut H864
Dt 23:24 you may eat all the g you want, but do H6694
Dt 24:21 When *you* **harvest** *the* g *in* your vineyard H1305
Dt 28:39 you will not drink the wine or **gather** *the* g, H112
Dt 32:32 Their g are *filled with* poison, and their H6694
Jdg 8: 2 Aren't the **gleanings of** Ephraim's g better H6622
Jdg 9:27 gathered the g and trodden them, H4142
Ne 13:15 together with wine, g, figs and all other H6694
Job 15:33 will be like a vine stripped of its **unripe** g, H1235
Ps 80:12 its walls so that all who pass by pick its g? NDT
SS 7: 8 breasts be like **clusters of** g *on* the vine, H864
Isa 5: 2 Then he looked for a crop of **good** g, but H6694
Isa 5: 4 When I looked for **good** g, why did it yield H6694
Isa 62: 9 those who gather **the** g will drink it in H2257S
Isa 65: 8 still found in a **cluster of** g and people say, H864
Jer 6: 9 the branches again, like *one* **gathering** g." H1305
Jer 8:13 There will be no g on the vine. There H6694
Jer 25:30 He will shout like those who tread the g NDT
Jer 31:29 'The parents have eaten **sour** g, and the H1235
Jer 31:30 whoever eats **sour** g—their own teeth H1235
Jer 48:32 has fallen on your ripened fruit and g. H1292
Jer 49: 9 would they not leave a **few** g? H6622
Eze 18: 2 " 'The parents eat **sour** g, and the H1235
Hos 9:10 it was like finding g in the desert; when I H6694
Joel 3:13 **trample the** g, for the winepress is H8097
Am 9:13 the planter by the one treading g. H6694
Ob 5 would they not leave a **few** g? H6622
Mic 6:15 you will crush g but not drink the wine. H9408
Mic 7: 1 there is no **cluster of** g to eat, none of the H864
Hab 3:17 not bud and there are no g on the vines, H3292
Mt 7:16 Do people pick g from thornbushes, or *G5091*
Lk 6:44 figs from thornbushes, or g from briers. *G5091*
1Co 9: 7 plants a vineyard and does not eat its g? *G2843*
Rev 14:18 gather the **clusters of** g from the *G1084*
Rev 14:18 the earth's vine, because its g are ripe." *G5091*
Rev 14:19 gathered its g and threw them into the *G306*

GRAPEVINE (3) [GRAPE, VINE]
Nu 6: 4 anything that comes from the g, H1728+3516
Jdg 13:14 anything that comes from the g, H1728+3516
Jas 3:12 can a fig tree bear olives, or a g bear figs? *G306*

GRAPEVINES (1) [GRAPE, VINE]
Nu 20: 5 no grain or figs, g or pomegranates. H1728

GRASP (9) [GRASPED, GRASPING, GRASPS]
2Ki 14: 5 After the kingdom was firmly in his g, he H3338
Ps 71: 4 from the g *of* those who are evil and cruel. H4090
Ecc 7:18 It is good *to* g the one and not let go of the H296
Jer 15:21 deliver you from the g *of* the cruel. H4090
Jer 34: 3 not escape from his g but will surely be H3338
Lk 9:45 so that *they did* not g it, and they *G150*
Jn 10:39 tried to seize him, but he escaped their g. *G5931*
1Co 14:11 If then *I do* not g the meaning of what *G3857*
Eph 3:18 *to* g how wide and long and high and *G2898*

GRASPED (5) [GRASP]
Ge 19:16 the men g his hand and the hands of his H2616
Eze 21:11 to be polished, to *be* g with the hand; it is H9530
Eze 21:15 to strike like lightning, *it is* g for slaughter. H6487
Eze 29: 7 When they g you with their hands, you H9530
Hos 12: 3 In the womb *he* g his brother's **heel**; as a H6810

GRASPING (3) [GRASP]
Ge 25:26 with his hand g Esau's heel; so he was H296
Jdg 7:20 **G** the torches in their left hands and H2616
Pr 27:16 the wind or g oil *with* the hand. H7924

GRASPS (2) [GRASP]
Dt 32:41 sword and my hand g it in judgment, H296
Pr 31:19 distaff and g the spindle *with* her fingers. H9461

GRASS (53)
Nu 22: 4 as an ox licks up the g *of* the field. H3764
Dt 11:15 I will provide g in the fields for your cattle H6912
Dt 32: 2 like showers on **new** g, like abundant rain H2013
2Sa 23: 4 after rain that brings g from the earth. H2013
1Ki 18: 5 Maybe we can find *some* g to keep the H2945
2Ki 19:26 green shoots, like g *sprouting on* the roof H2945
Job 5:25 your descendants like the g *of* the earth. H6912
Job 6: 5 Does a wild donkey bray when it has g, or H2013
Job 8:12 they wither more quickly than g. H2945
Job 38:27 and make it sprout with g? H4604+2013
Job 40:15 with you and which feeds on g like an ox. H2945
Ps 37: 2 like the g they will soon wither, like H2945
Ps 72:16 Lebanon and thrive like the g *of* the field. H6912
Ps 90: 5 they are like the new g of the morning: H2945
Ps 92: 7 wicked spring up like g and all evildoers H6912
Ps 102: 4 My heart is blighted and withered like g; H6912
Ps 102:11 the evening shadow; I wither away like g. H6912
Ps 103:15 The life of mortals is like g, they flourish H2945
Ps 104:14 He makes g grow for the cattle, and H2945
Ps 106:20 God for an image of a bull, which eats g. H6912
Ps 129: 6 May they be like g *on* the roof, which H2945
Ps 147: 8 with rain and makes g grow on the hills. H2945
Pr 19:12 but his favor is like dew on the g. H6912
Pr 27:25 appears and the g *from* the hills is H6912
Isa 5:24 up straw and as **dry** g sinks down in the H3143
Isa 15: 6 are dried up and the g is withered; H2945
Isa 35: 7 g and reeds and papyrus will grow. H2945
Isa 37:27 green shoots, like g *sprouting on* the roof H2945
Isa 40: 6 "All people are like g, and all their H2945
Isa 40: 7 The g withers and the flowers fall H2945
Isa 40: 7 blows on them. Surely the people are g. H2945
Isa 40: 8 The g withers and the flowers fall, but the H2945
Isa 44: 4 They will spring up like g in a meadow H2945
Isa 51:12 mortals, human beings who are but g, H2945
Isa 66:14 will rejoice and you will flourish like g; H2013
Jer 12: 4 lie parched and the g *in* every field be H6912
Jer 14: 5 her newborn fawn because there is no g. H2013
Da 4:15 in the ground, in the g of the field. A10187
Da 4:23 bronze, in the g of the field, while A10187
Da 4:25 you will eat g like the ox and be A10572
Da 4:32 wild animals; you will eat g like the ox. A10572
Da 4:33 away from people and ate g like the ox. A10572
Da 5:21 the wild donkeys and ate g like the ox; A10572
Mic 5: 7 like showers on the g, which do not wait H6912
Mt 6:30 that is how God clothes the g of the field, *G5965*
Mt 14:19 directed the people to sit down on the g. *G5965*
Mk 6:39 people sit down in groups on the green g. *G5965*
Lk 12:28 that is how God clothes the g of the field, *G5965*
Jn 6:10 There was plenty *of* g in that place, and *G5965*
1Pe 1:24 "All people are like g, and all their glory *G5965*
1Pe 1:24 the g withers and the flowers fall *G5965*
Rev 8: 7 and all the green g was burned up. *G5965*
Rev 9: 4 told not to harm the g of the earth or any *G5965*

GRASSHOPPER (3) [GRASSHOPPERS]
Lev 11:22 eat any kind of locust, katydid, cricket or g. H2506
Ps 78:46 He gave their crops to the g, their produce H2885
Ecc 12: 5 tree blossoms and the g drags itself along H2506

GRASSHOPPERS (6) [GRASSHOPPER]
Nu 13:33 We seemed like g in our own eyes, and H2506
1Ki 8:37 mildew, locusts or g, or when an enemy H2885
2Ch 6:28 mildew, locusts or g, or when enemies H2885
Ps 105:34 the locusts came, g without number; H3540
Isa 40:22 of the earth, and its people are like g. H2506
Na 3:15 Multiply like g, multiply like locusts H3540

GRASSLANDS (2) [LAND]
Ps 65:12 The g *of* the wilderness overflow; the hills H5661
Jer 9:10 up a lament concerning the wilderness g. H5661

GRATEFUL (4) [GRATIFY, GRATIFYING, GRATITUDE]
Ps 100: T For **giving g praise**. H9343
Ps 147: 7 Sing to the LORD with **g praise**; make H9343
Jnh 2: 9 with shouts of **g praise**, will sacrifice to H9343
Ro 16: 4 churches of the Gentiles *are* g to them. *G2373*

GRATIFY (2) [GRATEFUL]
Ro 13:14 do not think about **how to g** the desires of *G1650*
Gal 5:16 and *you will* not g the desires of the flesh. *G5464*

GRATIFYING (1) [GRATEFUL]
Eph 2: 3 g the cravings of our flesh and following *G1877S*

GRATING (6)
Ex 27: 4 Make a g for it, a bronze network, and H4803
Ex 35:16 the altar of burnt offering with its bronze g H4803
Ex 38: 4 They made a g for the altar, a bronze H4803
Ex 38: 5 poles for the four corners of the bronze g. H4803
Ex 38:30 altar with its bronze g and all its utensils, H4803
Ex 39:39 the bronze altar with its bronze g, its poles H4803

GRATITUDE (2) [GRATEFUL]
Ac 24: 3 we acknowledge this with profound g. *G2374*
Col 3:16 singing to God with g in your hearts. *G5921*

GRAVE (54) [GRAVES]

GRAVE, GRAVED, GRAVEN (KJV) CARVED, ENGRAVE, ENGRAVED, IDOL, IDOLS, IMAGES, INSCRIBED
Ge 37:35 to mourn until I join my son in the g." H8619
Ge 42:38 my gray head down to the g in sorrow." H8619
Ge 44:29 my gray head down to the g in misery. H8619
Ge 44:31 of our father down to the g in sorrow. H8619
Nu 19:16 who touches a human bone or a g, H7700
Nu 19:18 a human bone or a g or anyone who has H7700
Dt 34: 6 to this day no one knows where his g is. H7690
1Sa 2: 6 he brings down to the g and raises up. H8619
2Sa 22: 6 The cords of the g coiled around me; the H8619
1Ki 2: 6 his gray head go down to the g in peace. H8619
1Ki 2: 9 his gray head down to the g in blood." H8619
1Ki 13:31 bury me in the g where the man of God is H7700
Job 3:22 rejoice when they reach the g? H7700
Job 5:26 You will come to the g in full vigor, like H7700
Job 7: 9 who goes down to the g does not return. H8619
Job 10:19 carried straight from the womb to the g! H7700
Job 14:13 hide me in the g and conceal me till H8619
Job 17: 1 my days are cut short, the g awaits me. H7700
Job 17:13 If the only home I hope for is the g, if I H8619
Job 21:13 prosperity and go down to the g in peace. H8619
Job 21:32 They are carried to the g, and watch is H7700
Job 24:19 so the g snatches away those who have H8619
Job 40:13 dust together; shroud their faces in the g. H3243
Ps 5: 9 Their throat is an open g; with their H7700
Ps 6: 5 Who praises you from the g? H8619
Ps 18: 5 The cords of the g coiled around me; the H8619
Ps 49:14 Their forms will decay in the g, far from H8619
Ps 88: 5 like the slain who lie in the g, whom you H7700
Ps 88:11 Is your love declared in the g, your H7700
Ps 89:48 who can escape the power of the g? H8619
Ps 107:20 he rescued them from the g. H8827
Ps 116: 3 the anguish of the g came over me; I was H8619
Ps 141: 7 been scattered at the mouth of the g." H8619
Pr 1:12 them alive, like the g, and whole, H8619
Pr 5: 5 to death; her steps lead straight to the g. H8619
Pr 7:27 Her house is a highway to the g, leading H8619
Pr 28:17 guilt of murder will seek refuge in the g; H1014
Pr 30:16 the g, the barren womb, land, which is H8619
SS 8: 6 as death, its jealousy unyielding as the g. H8619
Isa 14:11 pomp has been brought down to the g, H8619
Isa 22:16 permission to cut out a g for yourself here, H7700
Isa 22:16 hewing your g on the height and H7700
Isa 38:18 For the g cannot praise you, death cannot H8619
Isa 53: 9 He was assigned a g with the wicked, and H7700
Jer 5:16 Their quivers are like an open g; all of H7700
Jer 20:17 with my mother as my g, her womb H7700
Eze 32:23 of the pit and her army lies around her g. H7690
Eze 32:24 is there, with all her hordes around her g. H7690
Eze 32:25 with all her hordes around her g. H7700
Hos 13:14 this people from the power of the g; H8619
Hos 13:14 Where, O g, is your destruction H8619
Na 1:14 I will prepare your g, for you are vile." H7700
Hab 2: 5 he is as greedy as the g and like death is H8619
Jn 11:44 "Take off the g clothes and let him go." NDT

GRAVEDIGGERS (1) [DIG]
Eze 39:15 beside it until the g bury it in the Valley of H7699

GRAVEL (2)
Pr 20:17 one ends up with a mouth full of g. H2953
La 3:16 He has broken my teeth with g; he has H2953

GRAVES (14) [GRAVE]
Ex 14:11 because there were no g in Egypt that you H7700
2Ki 23: 6 the dust over the g *of* the common people H7700
2Ch 34: 4 scattered over the g of those who had H7700
Isa 65: 4 who sit among the g and spend their H7700
Jer 8: 1 Jerusalem will be removed from their g. H7700
Eze 32:22 she is surrounded by the g *of* all her slain H7700
Eze 32:23 Their g are in the depths of the pit and her H7700
Eze 32:26 with all their hordes around their g. H7700
Eze 37:12 going to open your g and bring you up H7700
Eze 37:13 when I open your g and bring you up from H7700
Mt 23:29 decorate the g of the righteous. *G3646*
Lk 11:44 because you are like unmarked g, which *G3646*
Jn 5:28 all who are in their g will hear his voice *G3646*
Ro 3:13 "Their throats are open g; their tongues *G5439*

GRAVITY (KJV) RESPECT, SERIOUSNESS

GRAY (12)
Ge 42:38 you will bring my **g head** down to the H8484
Ge 44:29 you will bring my **g head** down to the H8484
Ge 44:31 will bring the **g head** *of* our father down H8484
Dt 32:25 the infants and those with **g hair**. H8484
1Sa 12: 2 I am old and g, and my sons are H8482
1Ki 2: 6 do not let his **g head** go down to the H8484
1Ki 2: 9 Bring his **g head** down to the grave in H8484
Ps 71:18 Even when I am old and g, do not forsake H8484
Pr 16:31 **G hair** is a crown of splendor; it is H8484
Pr 20:29 strength, **g hair** the splendor of the old. H8484
Isa 46: 4 Even to your old age and **g hairs** I am he H8484
Hos 7: 9 His **hair** is sprinkled with g, but he does H8484

GRAY-HAIRED (1) [HAIR]
Job 15:10 The g and the aged are on our side, men H8482

GRAZE (9) [GRAZED, GRAZES, GRAZING]
Ge 37:12 brothers had gone to g their father's flocks H8286
Ex 22: 5 them stray and *they* g in someone else's H1278
Ex 34: 3 the flocks and herds *may* g in front of the H8286
SS 1: 7 where *you* g *your* **flock** and where you rest H8286
SS 1: 8 of the sheep and g your young goats by H8286
Isa 5:17 Then sheep *will* g as in their own pasture H8286
Isa 27:10 there the calves g, there they lie down; H8286
Isa 30:23 day your cattle *will* g *in* broad meadows. H8286
Jer 50:19 and *they will* g *on* Carmel and Bashan H8286

GRAZED (2) [GRAZE]
Ge 41: 2 fat, and *they* g among the reeds. H8286
Ge 41:18 sleek, and *they* g among the reeds. H8286

GRAZES (1) [GRAZE]
Ex 22: 5 "If anyone g their livestock *in* a field or H1278

GRAZING (7) [GRAZE]
Ge 36:24 desert while he *was* g the donkeys of his H8286
Ge 37:13 brothers *are* **g the flocks** near Shechem H8286
Ge 37:16 you tell me where they *are* **g** *their* **flocks**?" H8286
1Ch 27:29 was in charge of the herds g in Sharon. H8286
Job 1:14 plowing and the donkeys *were* g nearby, H8286
Eze 34:14 heights of Israel will be their **g land**. H5659
Eze 34:14 There they will lie down in good **g land** H5659

GREAT (685) [GREATER, GREATEST, GREATLY, GREATNESS]
Ge 1:16 God made two g lights—the greater light H1524
Ge 1:21 So God created the g creatures of the sea H1524
Ge 6: 5 The LORD saw how g the wickedness of the H8041
Ge 7:11 all the springs of the g deep burst forth, H8041
Ge 10:12 Nineveh and Calah—which is the g city. H1524
Ge 12: 2 "I will make you into a g nation, and I will H1524
Ge 12: 2 *I will* **make** your name g, and you H1540
Ge 12: 6 the site of the **g tree** *of* Moreh at Shechem. H471
Ge 13: 6 possessions were **so g** that they were not H8041
Ge 13:18 to live near the **g trees** *of* Mamre at Hebron H471
Ge 14:13 living near the **g trees** *of* Mamre the H471
Ge 15: 1 I am your shield, your very g reward." H2221
Ge 15:14 they will come out with g possessions. H1524
Ge 15:18 from the Wadi of Egypt to the g river, the H1524
Ge 17:20 I will make him into a g nation. H1524
Ge 18: 1 near the **g trees** *of* Mamre while he H471
Ge 18:18 surely become a g and powerful nation, H1524
Ge 18:20 Gomorrah *is* so g and their sin so H8045
Ge 19:13 against its people *is* so g that he has sent H1540
Ge 19:19 you *have* shown g kindness to me in H1540
Ge 20: 9 you have brought *such* g guilt upon me H1524
Ge 21: 8 was weaned Abraham held a g feast. H1524
Ge 21:18 for I will make him into a g nation." H1524
Ge 30: 8 "I have had a g struggle with my sister H466
Ge 32: 7 In g fear and distress Jacob divided the H4394
Ge 34:12 **Make** the price ... **as g as you like** H8049+4394
Ge 35:16 began to give birth and *had* **g difficulty**. H7996
Ge 35:17 And as she *was* **having g difficulty** in H7996
Ge 36: 7 were too g for them to remain H8041
Ge 41:29 Seven years of g abundance are coming H1524
Ge 45: 7 to save your lives by a g deliverance. H1524
Ge 46: 3 I will make you into a g nation there. H1524
Ge 48:19 a people, and he too *will become* g. H1540
Ex 10:14 area of the country *in* **g numbers**. H3878+4394
Ex 32:10 Then I will make you into a g nation." H1524
Ex 32:11 out of Egypt with g power and a mighty H1524
Ex 32:21 that you led them into *such* g sin? H1524
Ex 32:30 the people, "You have committed a g sin. H1524
Ex 32:31 what a g sin these people have H1524
Lev 11:17 the little owl, the cormorant, the **g owl**, H3568
Lev 11:29 the weasel, the rat, any kind of **g lizard**, H7370
Lev 19:15 partiality to the poor or favoritism to the g, H1524
Nu 13:32 All the people we saw there are of **g size**. H4500
Nu 14:19 In accordance with your g love, forgive the H1542
Nu 22:18 I could not do *anything* g or small to go H1524
Dt 1: 7 as far as the g river, the Euphrates. H1524
Dt 1:17 in judging; hear both small and g alike. H1524
Dt 3: 5 there were also a g many unwalled H4394
Dt 4: 6 "Surely this g nation is a wise and H1524
Dt 4: 7 other nation is so g as to have their gods H1524
Dt 4: 8 what other nation is so g as to have such H1524
Dt 4:32 Has anything so g as this ever happened H1524
Dt 4:34 or by g and awesome deeds, like H1524
Dt 4:36 On earth he showed you his g fire, and H1524
Dt 4:37 Egypt by his Presence and his g strength, H1524
Dt 5:25 This g fire will consume us, and we will H1524
Dt 6:22 signs and wonders—g and terrible—on H1524
Dt 7:19 You saw with your own eyes the g trials H1524
Dt 7:21 is among you, is a g and awesome God. H1524
Dt 7:23 throwing them into g confusion until they H1524
Dt 9:26 by your **g power** and brought out H1542
Dt 9:29 you brought out by your g power and your H1524
Dt 10:17 Lord of lords, the g God, mighty and H1524
Dt 10:21 you those g and awesome wonders H1524
Dt 11: 7 that saw all these g things the LORD has H1524
Dt 11:30 near the **g trees** *of* Moreh, in the H471
Dt 14:16 the little owl, the **g owl**, the white owl, H3568
Dt 17:16 *must* not **acquire g numbers** *of* horses H8049
Dt 18:16 LORD our God nor see this g fire anymore, H1524
Dt 19: 6 overtake him if the distance *is too* g, and H8049
Dt 26: 5 lived there and became a g nation, H1524
Dt 26: 8 with g terror and with signs and wonders. H1524
Dt 29: 3 With your own eyes you saw those g trials H1524
Dt 29: 3 great trials, those signs and g wonders. H1524
Dt 29:28 In furious anger and in g wrath the LORD H1524
Jos 1: 4 from the g river, the Euphrates— H1524
Jos 2: 9 land and that a **g fear** *of* you has fallen on H399
Jos 3:16 It piled up in a heap a g distance away H4394
Jos 7: 9 then will you do for your own g name?" H1524
Jos 17: 1 the Makirites were **g soldiers**. H408+4878
Jos 22: 8 to your homes with your g wealth— H8041
Jos 22: 8 and a **g quantity** *of* clothing H2221+4394
Jos 23: 9 out before you g and powerful nations; H1524
Jos 24:17 performed those g signs before our H1524
Jdg 2: 7 had seen all the g things the LORD had H1524
Jdg 2:15 sworn to them. They were in g distress. H4394
Jdg 4:11 his tent by the **g tree** in Zaanannim near H471
Jdg 9: 6 gathered beside the **g tree** *at* the pillar in H471
Jdg 10: 9 Ephraim; Israel was in g distress. H4394
Jdg 12: 2 were engaged in a g struggle with the H4394
Jdg 15:18 "You have given your servant this g victory. H1524
Jdg 16: 5 the secret of his g strength and how we H1524
Jdg 16: 6 the secret of your g strength and how you H1524
Jdg 16:15 told me the secret of your g strength." H1524
Jdg 16:23 assembled to offer a g sacrifice to Dagon H1524
Jdg 20:38 should send up a g cloud of smoke from H8049
1Sa 1:16 here out of my g anguish and grief." H8044
1Sa 2:17 young men was very g in the LORD's sight, H1524
1Sa 4: 5 Israel raised such a g shout that the H1524
1Sa 4:10 The slaughter was very g; Israel lost thirty H1524
1Sa 5: 9 that city, throwing it into a g panic. H1524+4394
1Sa 6: 9 the LORD has brought this g disaster on us. H1524
1Sa 10: 3 there until you reach the **g tree** *of* Tabor. H471
1Sa 11:15 all the Israelites held a g celebration. H4394
1Sa 12:16 still and see this g thing the LORD is about H1524
1Sa 12:22 For the sake of his g name the LORD will H1524
1Sa 12:24 what **g things** *he has* **done** for you. H1540
1Sa 14:45 brought about this g deliverance in Israel? H1524
1Sa 17:24 the man, they all fled from him in g fear. H4394
1Sa 17:25 The king will give g wealth to the man H1524
1Sa 18:14 In everything he did he **had g success** H8505
1Sa 19: 1 Jonathan had taken a g liking to David H4394
1Sa 19: 5 The LORD won a g victory for all Israel, and H1524
1Sa 19:22 Ramah and went to the g cistern at Seku. H1524
1Sa 20: 2 doesn't do anything, g or small, without H1524
1Sa 26:25 *you will* **do g things** and surely H6913+6913
1Sa 28:15 "I am in g distress," Saul said H4394
1Sa 30:16 because of the g **amount** of plunder they H1524
2Sa 3:22 brought with them a **g deal** of plunder. H8041
2Sa 3:38 a commander and a g *man* has fallen in H1524
2Sa 7: 9 Now I will make your name g, like the H1524
2Sa 7:21 have done this **g thing** and made it H1525
2Sa 7:22 "How **g** *you are*, Sovereign LORD! There is H1540
2Sa 7:23 to perform g and awesome wonders H1525
2Sa 7:26 so that your name *will be* g forever. H1540
2Sa 8: 8 David took a **g quantity** of bronze. H2221+4394
2Sa 12:30 David took a **g quantity** *of* plunder H2221+4394
2Sa 18: 7 the casualties that day were g H1524
2Sa 18:29 "I saw g confusion just as Joab was about H1524
2Sa 20: 8 While they were at the g rock in Gibeon H1524
2Sa 22:15 *with* **g bolts of lightning** he routed them. H1398
2Sa 22:36 my shield; your help *has* **made** me g. H8049
2Sa 22:51 "*He* **gives** his king g victories; he shows H1540
2Sa 23:10 LORD brought about a g victory that day. H1524
2Sa 23:12 the LORD brought about a g victory. H1524
2Sa 23:20 from Kabzeel, performed g exploits. H8041
2Sa 24:14 for his mercy is g; but do not let me H8041
1Ki 1:19 He has sacrificed **g numbers** of cattle H8044
1Ki 1:25 down and sacrificed **g numbers** of cattle, H8044
1Ki 3: 6 "You have shown g kindness to your H1524
1Ki 3: 6 continued this g kindness to him and H1524

1Ki 3: 8 you have chosen, a g people, too H8041
1Ki 3: 9 is able to govern this g people of yours?" H3878
1Ki 4:29 gave Solomon wisdom and very g insight, H2221
1Ki 5: 7 a wise son to rule over this g nation." H8041
1Ki 7: 9 the outside to the g courtyard and from H1524
1Ki 7:12 The g courtyard was surrounded by a wall H1524
1Ki 8:42 will hear of your g name and your mighty H1524
1Ki 10: 2 at Jerusalem with a very g caravan— H3878
1Ki 10:11 brought g *cargoes of* almugwood H2221+4394
1Ki 10:18 the king made a g throne covered with H1524
1Ki 19:11 Then a g and powerful wind tore the H1524
1Ki 22:31 anyone, small or g, except the king of H1524
2Ki 3:27 The fury against Israel was g; they H1524
2Ki 5: 1 He was a g man in the sight of his master H1524
2Ki 5:13 prophet had told you to do some g thing, H1524
2Ki 6:23 So he prepared a g feast for them, and H1524
2Ki 6:25 There was a g famine in the city; the siege H1524
2Ki 7: 6 of chariots and horses and a g army, H1524
2Ki 8: 4 me about all the g *things* Elisha has done H1524
2Ki 10:19 I am going to hold a g sacrifice for Baal. H1524
2Ki 17:21 LORD and caused them to commit a g sin. H1524
2Ki 18:19 " 'This is what the g king, the king of H1524
2Ki 18:28 "Hear the word of the g king, the king of H1524
2Ki 22:13 G is the LORD's anger that burns against us H1524
1Ch 10:12 their bones under the g **tree** in Jabesh, H461
1Ch 11:14 the LORD brought about a g victory. H1524
1Ch 11:22 from Kabzeel, performed g exploits. H8041
1Ch 12:22 until he had a g army, like the army H1524
1Ch 16:25 For g is the LORD and most worthy of praise H1524
1Ch 17:19 have done this g **thing** and made known H1525
1Ch 17:19 made known all these g *promises*. H1525
1Ch 17:21 to perform g and awesome wonders H1525
1Ch 17:24 that your name *will be* g forever. H1540
1Ch 18: 8 David took a g quantity of bronze H4394
1Ch 20: 2 He took a g **quantity** *of* plunder H2221+4394
1Ch 21:13 his mercy is very g; but do not let me H8041
1Ch 22: 5 the LORD *should be* of g magnificence H1540
1Ch 22:14 "I have **taken** g **pains** to provide for H928+6715
1Ch 22:14 and iron too g to be weighed, H4200+8044
1Ch 29: 1 The task is g, because this palatial H1524
1Ch 29:22 ate and drank with g joy in the presence H1524
2Ch 1: 1 with him and **made** him exceedingly g. H1540
2Ch 1: 8 "You have shown g kindness to David my H1524
2Ch 1:10 is able to govern this g people of yours?" H1524
2Ch 2: 5 "The temple I am going to build will be g, H1524
2Ch 2:13 a man of g **skill**, H2682+3359+1069
2Ch 6:32 because of your g name and your mighty H1524
2Ch 6:42 the g **love** *promised to* David your H2876
2Ch 9: 1 Arriving with a very g caravan—with H3878
2Ch 9:17 the king made a g throne covered with H1524
2Ch 14:13 Such a g number of Cushites fell that they NDT
2Ch 15: 5 inhabitants of the lands were in g turmoil. H8041
2Ch 15:13 whether small or g, man or woman. H1524
2Ch 16: 8 army with g **numbers** of chariots H2221+4394
2Ch 17: 5 so that he had g wealth and honor. H4200+8044
2Ch 18: 1 Jehoshaphat had g wealth and H4200+8044
2Ch 18:30 anyone, small or g, except the king of H1524
2Ch 20:25 among them a g **amount** of H4200+8044
2Ch 21:19 of the disease, and he died in g pain. H8273
2Ch 24:11 collected a g **amount** of money. H4200+8044
2Ch 25:10 Judah and left for home in a g **rage**. H3034+678
2Ch 25:13 carried off g **quantities** of plunder. H8041
2Ch 28: 8 They also took a g **deal** of plunder, which H8041
2Ch 28:13 For our guilt is already g, and his fierce H8041
2Ch 30:21 Bread for seven days with g rejoicing, H1524
2Ch 30:24 A g **number** of priests consecrated H4200+8044
2Ch 30:26 There was g joy in Jerusalem, for since the H1524
2Ch 31: 5 They brought a g **amount**, a tithe H4200+8044
2Ch 31:10 his people, and this g **amount** is left over." H2162
2Ch 32:27 Hezekiah had very g wealth and honor H2221
2Ch 32:29 and acquired g **numbers** of flocks H4200+8044
2Ch 32:29 God had given him very g riches. H8041
2Ch 34:21 G is the LORD's anger that is poured out on H1524
Ezr 3:11 all the people gave a g shout of praise to H1524
Ezr 4:10 other people whom the g and honorable A10647
Ezr 5: 8 of Judah, to the temple of the g God. A10647
Ezr 5:11 one that a g king of Israel built and A10647
Ezr 8:22 his g anger is against all who forsake H6437
Ezr 9: 7 ancestors until now, our guilt has been g. H1524
Ezr 9:13 a result of our evil deeds and our g guilt, H1524
Ne 1: 3 the province are in g trouble and disgrace H1524
Ne 1: 5 God of heaven, the g and awesome God H1524
Ne 1:10 you redeemed by your g strength and your H1524
Ne 3:27 from the g projecting tower to the wall of H1524
Ne 4:14 the Lord, who is g and awesome, and H1524
Ne 5: 1 their wives raised a g outcry against their H1524
Ne 6: 3 "I am carrying on a g project and cannot H1524
Ne 8: 6 praised the LORD, the g God; and all the H1524
Ne 8:12 of food and to celebrate with g joy, H1524
Ne 8:17 And their joy was very g. H1524
Ne 9:19 "Because of your g compassion you did H8041
Ne 9:25 they reveled in your g goodness. H1524
Ne 9:27 in your g compassion you gave them H8041
Ne 9:31 But in your g mercy you did not put an H8041
Ne 9:32 our God, the g God, mighty and awesome H1524
Ne 9:35 enjoying your g goodness to them in the H8041
Ne 9:37 as they please. We are in g distress. H1524
Ne 12:43 And on that day they offered g sacrifices H1524
Ne 12:43 because God had given them g joy. H1524
Ne 13:22 mercy to me according to your g love. H8044
Est 2:18 And the king gave a g banquet, Esther's H1524
Est 4: 3 there was g mourning among the Jews H1524
Est 4: 4 her about Mordecai, she was in g distress. H4394
Job 2:13 they saw how g his suffering *was*. H1540+4394
Job 3:19 The small and the g are there, and the H1524
Job 4:10 the teeth of the g **lions** are broken. H4097
Job 12:23 *He* **makes** nations g, and destroys them H8434
Job 21:28 'Where now is the house of the g, the H5618
Job 22: 5 Is not your wickedness g? Are not your H8041
Job 26: 3 And what g insight you have H4200+8044
Job 30:18 In his g power God becomes like clothing H8044
Job 31:25 if I have rejoiced over my g wealth, the H8041
Job 36:26 *How* g is God—beyond our understanding H8438
Job 37: 5 he does g *things* beyond our H1524
Job 37:23 in his justice and g righteousness, he H8044
Job 39:11 Will you rely on it for its g strength? Will H8041
Ps 5: 7 by your g love, can come into your H8044
Ps 17: 7 Show me the wonders of your g **love**, you H2876
Ps 18:14 with g bolts of lightning he routed them. H8041
Ps 18:35 sustains me; your help *has* **made** me g. H8049
Ps 18:50 *He* **gives** his king g victories; he shows H1540
Ps 19:11 in keeping them there is g reward. H8041
Ps 19:13 blameless, innocent of g transgression. H8041
Ps 21: 1 How g is his joy in the victories you give! H4394
Ps 21: 5 his glory is g; you have bestowed H1524
Ps 22:25 the theme of my praise in the g assembly; H8041
Ps 25: 6 your g **mercy** and love, for they are H8171
Ps 25:11 forgive my iniquity, though it is g. H8041
Ps 26:12 in the g **congregation** I will praise the H5220
Ps 33:16 no warrior escapes by his g strength. H8044
Ps 33:17 despite *all* its g strength it cannot save. H8044
Ps 35:18 I will give you thanks in the g assembly H8041
Ps 36: 6 mountains, your justice like the g deep. H8041
Ps 40: 9 your saving acts in the g assembly; H8041
Ps 40:10 your faithfulness from the g assembly. H8041
Ps 40:16 saving help always say, "The LORD *is* g!" H1540
Ps 47: 2 is awesome, the g King over all the earth. H1524
Ps 48: 1 G is the LORD, and most worthy of praise H1524
Ps 48: 2 is Mount Zion, the city of the G King. H8041
Ps 49: 6 in their wealth and boast of their g riches? H8044
Ps 51: 1 according to your g compassion blot out H8044
Ps 52: 7 trusted in his g wealth and grew H8044
Ps 57:10 For g is your love, reaching to the heavens H1524
Ps 66: 3 *So* g is your power that your enemies H8044
Ps 68:26 Praise God in the g **congregation**; praise H5220
Ps 68:27 there the g **throng** *of* Judah's princes H8086
Ps 69:13 time of your favor; in your g love, O God, H8041
Ps 69:16 of your love; in your g mercy turn to me. H8044
Ps 70: 4 saving help always say, "The LORD *is* g!" H1540
Ps 71:19 heavens, you who have done g *things*. H1524
Ps 76: 1 in Judah; in Israel his name is g. H1524
Ps 77:13 What god is *as* g as our God? H1524
Ps 82: 1 God presides in the g assembly; he renders H446
Ps 86:10 For you are g and do marvelous deeds H1524
Ps 86:13 For g is your love toward me; you have H1524
Ps 89: 1 I will sing of the LORD's g **love** forever; H2876
Ps 89:49 where is your former g **love**, which in your H2876
Ps 90:11 Your wrath is as g as the fear that is your NDT
Ps 91:13 will trample the g **lion** and the serpent. H4097
Ps 92: 5 How g *are* your works, LORD, how H1540
Ps 93: 4 Mightier than the thunder of the g waters H8041
Ps 94:19 When anxiety was g within me, your H8044
Ps 95: 3 For the LORD is the g God, the great King H1524
Ps 95: 3 the great God, the g King above all gods. H1524
Ps 96: 4 For g is the LORD and most worthy of praise H1524
Ps 99: 2 G is the LORD in Zion; he is exalted over H1524
Ps 99: 3 them praise your g and awesome name— H1524
Ps 102:10 because of your g **wrath**, for H2405+2256+7912
Ps 103:11 *so* g *is* his love for those who fear him; H1504
Ps 104: 1 LORD my God, *you are* very g; you are H1540
Ps 106:21 who had done g *things* in Egypt, H1524
Ps 106:45 out of his g love he relented. H8044
Ps 108: 4 For g is your love, higher than the H1524
Ps 109:30 in the g *throng of worshipers* I will praise H8041
Ps 111: 2 G are the works of the LORD; they are H1524
Ps 112: 1 who find g delight in his commands. H4394
Ps 115:13 who fear the LORD—small and g alike. H1524
Ps 117: 2 For g *is* his love toward us, and the H1504
Ps 119:14 your statutes as one rejoices in g riches. H3972
Ps 119:156 is g; preserve my life according to H8041
Ps 119:162 your promise like one who finds g spoil. H8041
Ps 119:165 G peace have those who love your law H8041
Ps 126: 2 "The LORD has done g *things* for them." H1540
Ps 126: 3 The LORD has done g *things* for us, and we H1540
Ps 131: 1 myself with g *matters* or things too H1524
Ps 135: 5 I know that the LORD is g, that our Lord is H1524
Ps 136: 4 to him who alone does g wonders, His H1524
Ps 136: 7 who made the g lights—His love endures H1524
Ps 136:17 to him who struck down g kings, His love H1524
Ps 138: 5 of the LORD, for the glory of the LORD is g. H1524
Ps 145: 3 G is the LORD and most worthy of praise H1524
Ps 145: 6 works—and I will proclaim your g **deeds**. H1525
Ps 147: 5 G is our Lord and mighty in power; his H1524
Ps 148: 7 you g **sea creatures** and all ocean depths, H9490
Pr 5:23 will die, led astray by their own g folly. H8044
Pr 6:35 he will refuse a bribe, however g it is. H8049
Pr 13: 7 pretends to be poor, yet has g wealth. H8041
Pr 14:29 Whoever is patient has g understanding H8041
Pr 15: 6 of the righteous contains g treasure, H8041
Pr 15:16 of the LORD than g wealth with turmoil. H8041
Pr 18:16 the giver into the presence of the g. H1524
Pr 21:14 concealed in the cloak pacifies g wrath. H6434
Pr 22: 1 name is more desirable than g riches; H8041
Pr 23:24 of a righteous child *has* g **joy**; H1635+1635
Pr 24: 5 The wise prevail through g **power**, and H6437
Pr 25: 6 do not claim a place among his g *men*; H1524
Pr 28:12 triumph, there is g elation; but when the H8041
Ecc 2: 4 *I* **undertook** g projects: I built houses for H1540
Ecc 2:21 too is meaningless and a g misfortune. H8041
Ecc 5:17 eat in darkness, with g frustration H2221
Ecc 10: 4 calmness can lay g offenses to rest. H1524
Isa 1: 4 a people whose guilt is g, a brood of H3878
Isa 5: 9 "Surely the g houses will become H8041
Isa 9: 2 walking in darkness have seen a g light; H1524
Isa 10:33 will lop off the boughs with g **power**. H5124
Isa 12: 6 g is the Holy One of Israel among you." H1524
Isa 13: 4 the mountains, like that of a g multitude! H8041
Isa 16: 6 Moab's pride—**how** g is her arrogance!— H4394
Isa 17:12 they roar like the roaring of g waters! H3888
Isa 23: 3 On the g waters came the grain of the H8041
Isa 24:23 before its elders—*with* g **glory**. AIT
Isa 27: 1 his fierce, g and powerful sword H1524
Isa 27:13 And in that day a g trumpet will sound H1524
Isa 29: 6 with thunder and earthquake and g noise, H1524
Isa 29:15 Woe to those *who* **go to** g **depths** to hide H6676
Isa 30:25 In the day of g slaughter, when the towers H8041
Isa 31: 1 their chariots and in the g strength of their H4394
Isa 31: 4 a lion growls, a g **lion** over its prey—and H4097
Isa 32: 2 the shadow of a g rock in a thirsty H3878
Isa 34: 6 in Bozrah and a g slaughter in the land of H1524
Isa 34: 7 with them, the bull calves and the g bulls. H52
Isa 34:11 the g **owl** and the raven will nest there. H3568
Isa 36: 4 " 'This is what the g king, the king of H1524
Isa 36:13 "Hear the words of the g king, the king of H1524
Isa 40:26 Because of his g power and mighty H8044
Isa 42:21 *to* **make** *his* law g and glorious. H1540
Isa 51:10 the waters of the g deep, who made a H8041
Isa 53:12 I will give him a portion among the g, H8041
Isa 54:13 by the LORD, and g will be their peace. H8041
Jer 2:12 shudder with g horror," declares the H4394
Jer 2:31 a desert to Israel or a land of g **darkness**? H4420
Jer 5: 6 their rebellion *is* g and their H8045
Jer 6:22 a g nation is being stirred up from the H1524
Jer 9:19 ruined we are! How g is our shame! We H4394
Jer 10: 6 you are g, and your name is mighty H1524
Jer 10:22 a g commotion from the land of the north! H1524
Jer 13: 9 of Judah and the g pride of Jerusalem. H8041
Jer 16:10 LORD decreed such a g disaster against us? H1524
Jer 21: 5 arm in furious anger and in g wrath. H1524
Jer 22: 8 the LORD done such a thing to this g city? H1524
Jer 22:14 will build myself a g palace with spacious H4500
Jer 25:14 be enslaved by many nations and g kings; H1524
Jer 27: 5 With my g power and outstretched arm I H1524
Jer 27: 7 many nations and g kings will subjugate H1524
Jer 28: 8 against many countries and g kingdoms. H1524
Jer 30:14 because your guilt is *so* g and your sins so H8044
Jer 30:15 Because of your g guilt and many sins I H8044
Jer 31: 8 women in labor; a g throng will return. H1524
Jer 31:15 Ramah, mourning and g weeping, Rachel H9476
Jer 31:20 *I* **have** g **compassion** *for* him, H8163+8163
Jer 32:17 the earth by your g power and H1524
Jer 32:18 G and mighty God, whose name is the H1524
Jer 32:19 g are your purposes and mighty are your H1524
Jer 32:21 an outstretched arm and with g terror. H1524
Jer 32:37 them in my furious anger and g wrath; H1524
Jer 32:42 have brought all this g calamity on this H1524
Jer 33: 3 you and tell you g and unsearchable H1524
Jer 36: 7 against this people by the LORD are g." H1524
Jer 41:12 up with him near the g pool in Gibeon. H8041
Jer 44: 2 You saw the g disaster I brought on H3972
Jer 44: 7 Why bring *such* g disaster on yourselves H1524
Jer 44:26 'I swear by my g name,' says the LORD H1524
Jer 45: 5 Should you then seek g *things* for yourself H1524
Jer 48: 3 cries of g havoc and destruction. H1524
Jer 48:29 of Moab's pride—*how* g is her arrogance!—H4394
Jer 50: 9 an alliance of g nations from the land H1524
Jer 50:22 is in the land, the noise of g destruction! H1524
Jer 50:41 a g nation and many kings are being H1524
Jer 51:54 the sound of g destruction from the land H1524
Jer 51:55 Waves of enemies will rage like g waters H8041
La 1: 1 who once was g among the nations! H8041
La 3:22 of the LORD's g **love** we are not consumed, H2876
La 3:23 new every morning; g is your faithfulness. H8041
La 3:32 compassion, so g is his unfailing love. H8044
Eze 9: 9 of Israel and Judah is exceedingly g; H1524
Eze 14: 4 myself in keeping with their g idolatry. H8044
Eze 17: 3 A g eagle with powerful wings, long H1524
Eze 17: 7 there was another g eagle with powerful H1524
Eze 17:17 his mighty army and g horde will be of no H8041
Eze 21:14 a sword for g slaughter, closing in H1524
Eze 25:17 I will carry out g vengeance on them and H1524
Eze 26: 7 chariots, with horsemen and a g army. H8041
Eze 27:12 because of your g wealth of goods; H8044+3972
Eze 27:18 products and g wealth of goods. H8044+3972
Eze 27:33 with your g wealth and your wares you H8044
Eze 28: 5 By your g skill in trading you have H8044
Eze 29: 3 you g monster lying among your streams. H1524
Eze 31: 6 all the g nations lived in its shade. H8041
Eze 31:10 Because the g cedar towered over the thick NDT
Eze 31:17 They too, like **the** g **cedar**, had gone H2257S
Eze 32: 3 " 'With a g throng of people I will cast my H8041
Eze 36:23 I will show the holiness of my g name H1524
Eze 37: 2 I saw a g many bones on the floor of H4394
Eze 38: 4 a g horde with large and small H8041
Eze 38:15 riding on horses, a g horde, a mighty H1524
Eze 38:19 time there shall be a g earthquake in the H1524

Eze 39:17 the g sacrifice on the mountains of Israel. H1524
Eze 47: 7 I saw a g number of trees on each side of H4394
Da 2: 6 from me gifts and rewards and g honor. A10678
Da 2:10 No king, however g and mighty, has ever A10647
Da 2:45 "The g God has shown the king what A10647
Da 4: 3 How g are his signs, how mighty his A10647
Da 4:22 *You have become* g and strong; your A10648
Da 4:30 "Is not this the g Babylon I have built as A10647
Da 5: 1 Belshazzar gave a g banquet for a A10647
Da 7: 2 winds of heaven churning up the g sea. A10647
Da 7: 3 Four g beasts, each different from the A10647
Da 7:17 'The four g beasts are four kings that will A10647
Da 8: 4 It did as it pleased and *became* g. H1540
Da 8: 6 the canal and charged at it in g rage. H3946
Da 8: 8 The goat *became* very g, but at the height H1540
Da 8:11 *It* **set** *itself* **up to be** as g as the H1540
Da 9: 4 the g and awesome God, who H1524
Da 9:12 our rulers by bringing on us g disaster. H1524
Da 9:18 righteous, but because of your g mercy. H8041
Da 10: 1 was true and it concerned a g war. H1524
Da 10: 4 I was standing on the bank of the g river, H1524
Da 10: 8 gazing at this g vision; I had no H1524
Da 11: 3 who will rule with g power and do as he H8041
Da 11: 5 will rule his own kingdom with g power. H8041
Da 11:10 prepare for war and assemble a g army, H8041
Da 11:28 return to his own country with g wealth, H1524
Da 11:40 chariots and cavalry and a g fleet of ships. H8041
Da 11:44 he will set out in a g rage to destroy and H1524
Da 12: 1 the g prince who protects your people H1524
Hos 1:11 the land, for g will be the day of Jezreel. H1524
Hos 5:13 to Assyria, and sent to the g king for help. H3714
Hos 5:14 a lion to Ephraim, like a g **lion** to Judah. H4097
Hos 9: 7 sins are so many and your hostility **so** g, H8041
Hos 10: 6 carried to Assyria as tribute for the g king. H3714
Hos 10:15 because your **wickedness is** g. H8288+8288
Joel 1: 4 swarm has left the g **locusts** have eaten; H746
Joel 1: 4 what the g **locusts** have left the young H746
Joel 2:11 The day of the LORD is g; it is dreadful H1524
Joel 2:20 Surely he has done g *things*! H1540
Joel 2:21 Surely the LORD has done g *things*! H1540
Joel 2:25 eaten—the g **locust** and the young locust H746
Joel 2:25 my g army that I sent among you. H1524
Joel 2:31 the coming of the g and dreadful day of H1524
Joel 3:13 vats overflow—so g is their wickedness!" H8041
Am 2: 2 will go down in g **tumult** amid war cries H8623
Am 3: 9 see the g unrest within her and the H8041
Am 5:12 are your offenses and how g your sins. H6786
Am 6: 2 go from there to g Hamath, and then go H8041
Am 6:11 he will smash the g house into pieces H1524
Am 7: 4 it dried up the g deep and devoured the H8041
Jnh 1: 2 "Go to the g city of Nineveh and preach H1524
Jnh 1: 4 Then the LORD sent a g wind on the sea H1524
Jnh 1:12 my fault that this g storm has come upon H1524
Jnh 3: 2 "Go to the g city of Nineveh and proclaim H1524
Jnh 4:11 not have concern for the g city of Nineveh, H1524
Na 1: 3 The LORD is slow to anger but g *in* power H1524
Na 3:10 all her g *men* were put in chains. H1524
Hab 3:15 with your horses, churning the g waters. H8041
Zep 1:14 The g day of the LORD is near—near and H1524
Zep 3:17 *He will* **take** g **delight** in you H8464+928+8525
Zec 2: 4 because of the g **number** *of* people and H8044
Zec 12:11 in Jerusalem *will be* as g as the weeping H1540
Zec 14: 4 forming a g valley, with half H1524+4394
Zec 14:13 will be *stricken* by the LORD *with* g panic. H8041
Zec 14:14 g **quantities** *of* gold and H4200+8044+4394
Mal 1: 5 own eyes and say, 'G *is* the LORD—even H1540
Mal 1:11 My name will be g among the nations H1524
Mal 1:11 my name will be g among the nations," H1524
Mal 1:14 For I am a g king," says the LORD Almighty H1524
Mal 4: 5 to you before that g and dreadful day of H1524
Mt 2:18 Ramah, weeping and g mourning, Rachel G4498
Mt 4:16 living in darkness have seen a g light; G3489
Mt 5:12 because g is your reward in heaven G4498
Mt 5:19 will be called g in the kingdom of G3489
Mt 5:35 Jerusalem, for it is the city of the G King. G3489
Mt 6:23 you is darkness, **how** g is that darkness! G4531
Mt 7:27 that house, and it fell with a g crash." G3489
Mt 8:10 found anyone in Israel with **such** g faith. G5537
Mt 13:46 When he found one **of** g **value**, he went G4501
Mt 15:28 said to her, "Woman, you have g faith! G3489
Mt 15:30 G crowds came to him, bringing the lame G4498
Mt 19:22 went away sad, because he had g wealth. G4498
Mt 20:26 wants to become g among you must be G3489
Mt 24:21 For then there will be g distress G3489
Mt 24:24 appear and perform g signs and wonders G3489
Mt 24:30 clouds of heaven, with power and g glory. G4498
Mt 27:14 to the g amazement of the governor. G3336
Mt 27:19 I have suffered **a** g **deal** today in a dream G4498
Mk 5:26 She had suffered a g **deal** under the care G4498
Mk 10:22 went away sad, because he had g wealth. G4498
Mk 10:43 wants to become g among you must be G3489
Mk 13: 2 "Do you see all these g buildings? G3489
Mk 13:26 coming in clouds with g power and glory. G4498
Lk 1:15 he will be g in the sight of the Lord. G3489
Lk 1:32 He will be g and will be called the Son of G3489
Lk 1:49 Mighty One has done g *things* for me— G3489
Lk 1:58 that the Lord *had* **shown** her g mercy, G3486
Lk 2:10 news that will cause g joy for all the G3489
Lk 2:13 Suddenly a g **company** of the heavenly G4436
Lk 5:29 Then Levi held a g banquet for Jesus at G3489
Lk 6:17 was there and a g number of people from G4498
Lk 6:23 because g is your reward in heaven. G4498
Lk 6:35 Then your reward will be g, and you will G4498
Lk 7: 9 I have not found **such** g faith even in G5537
Lk 7:16 "A g prophet has appeared among us," G3489
Lk 7:47 been forgiven—as her g love has shown. G4498
Lk 8:23 swamped, and *they were* **in** g **danger**. G3073
Lk 14:16 was preparing a g banquet and invited G3489
Lk 16:26 us and you a g chasm has been set G3489
Lk 21:11 There will be g earthquakes, famines and G3489
Lk 21:11 fearful events and g signs from heaven. G3489
Lk 21:23 There will be g distress in the land and G3489
Lk 21:27 coming in a cloud with power and g glory. G4498
Lk 24:52 him and returned to Jerusalem with g joy. G3489
Jn 5: 3 Here a g **number** of disabled people used G4436
Jn 6: 2 a g crowd of people followed him G4498
Jn 6: 5 up and saw a g crowd coming toward G4498
Jn 12:12 The next day the g crowd that had come G4498
Ac 2:20 the coming of the g and glorious day of G3489
Ac 4:29 to speak your word with g boldness. G4246
Ac 4:33 With g power the apostles continued to G3489
Ac 5: 5 And g fear seized all who heard what had G3489
Ac 5:11 G fear seized the whole church and all G3489
Ac 6: 8 performed g wonders and signs among G3489
Ac 7:11 Canaan, bringing g suffering, and our G3489
Ac 8: 1 On that day a g persecution broke out G3489
Ac 8: 8 So there was g joy in that city. G4498
Ac 8: 9 He boasted that he was someone g, G3489
Ac 8:10 man is rightly called the G Power of God." G3489
Ac 8:13 astonished by the g signs and miracles he G3489
Ac 11:21 a g number of people believed and G4498
Ac 11:24 a g number of people were brought G2653
Ac 11:26 church and taught g numbers of people. G2653
Ac 14: 1 so effectively that a g number of Jews G4498
Ac 16:16 She earned a g **deal** of money for her G4498
Ac 17:11 the message with g eagerness and G4246
Ac 18:25 he spoke **with** g **fervor** and G2417+3836+4460
Ac 18:27 he was a g help to those who by grace G4498
Ac 19:23 there arose a g disturbance about G4024+3900
Ac 19:27 the temple of the g goddess Artemis will G3489
Ac 19:28 "G is Artemis of the Ephesians! G3489
Ac 19:34 "G is Artemis of the Ephesians! G3489
Ac 19:35 of the temple *of* the g Artemis and of her G3489
Ac 20:19 I served the Lord with g humility and with G4246
Ac 21:35 of the mob was **so** g he had to be carried G1328
Ac 23: 9 There was a g uproar, and some of the G3489
Ac 25:23 Bernice came with g pomp and entered G4498
Ac 26:22 here and testify to small and g alike. G3489
Ac 26:24 "Your g learning is driving you insane." G4498
Ac 27:10 disastrous and bring g loss to ship and G4498
Ro 9: 2 I have g sorrow and unceasing anguish in G3489
Ro 9:22 bore with g patience the objects of his G4498
1Co 2: 3 in weakness with g fear and trembling. G4498
1Co 16: 9 because a g door for effective work has G3489
2Co 1: 8 We were under g pressure, far G2848+5651
2Co 2: 4 I wrote you out of g distress and anguish G4498
2Co 6: 4 in g endurance; in troubles, hardships G4498
2Co 7: 4 I have spoken to you with g frankness; G4498
2Co 7: 4 with great frankness; I take g pride in you. G4498
2Co 8:22 so because of his g confidence in you. G4498
2Co 12: 7 of these **surpassingly** g revelations. G5651
Eph 1:19 his incomparably g power for us who G3490
Eph 2: 4 But because of his g love for us, God, who G4498
Php 2:29 welcome him in the Lord with g joy, and G4246
Col 1:11 so that you may have g endurance and G4246
Col 2:18 *Such a person* also **goes into** g **detail** G1836
1Ti 3:13 standing and g assurance in their G4498
1Ti 3:16 from which true godliness springs is g: G3489
1Ti 6: 6 But godliness with contentment is g gain. G3489
2Ti 4: 2 with g patience and careful instruction. G4246
2Ti 4: 3 *they will* **gather around** them **a** g **number** G2197
2Ti 4:14 the metalworker did me a g **deal** *of* harm. G4498
Titus 2:13 of the glory of our g God and Savior, G3489
Phm 7 love has given me g joy and G4498
Heb 2: 3 we escape if we ignore **so** g a salvation? G5496
Heb 4:14 since we have a g high priest who has G3489
Heb 7: 4 Just think **how** g he was: Even the G4383
Heb 10:21 since we have a g priest over the G3489
Heb 10:32 when you endured in a g conflict full of G4498
Heb 12: 1 are surrounded by **such a** g cloud of G5537
Heb 13:20 Lord Jesus, that g Shepherd of the sheep, G3489
Jas 3: 5 part of the body, but it makes g boasts. G3489
Jas 3: 5 Consider **what a** g forest is set on fire by a G2462
1Pe 1: 3 In his g mercy he has given us new birth G4498
1Pe 3: 4 which is *of* g **worth** in God's sight. G4500
2Pe 1: 4 he has given us his **very** g and precious G3492
1Jn 3: 1 See **what** g love the Father has lavished G4534
2Jn 4 It has given me g joy to find some of your G3336
3Jn 3 It gave me g joy when some believers G3336
Jude 6 chains for judgment on the g Day. G3489
Jude 24 presence without fault and with g **joy**— G21
Rev 6:12 There was a g earthquake. The sun G3489
Rev 6:17 For the g day of their wrath has come, and G3489
Rev 7: 9 before me was a g multitude that no one G4498
Rev 7:14 who have come out of the g tribulation; G3489
Rev 8:10 his trumpet, and a g star, blazing like a G3489
Rev 9:14 who are bound at the g river Euphrates." G3489
Rev 11: 8 will lie in the public square of the g city— G3489
Rev 11:17 you have taken your g power and have G3489
Rev 11:18 your name, both g and small—and for G3489
Rev 12: 1 A g sign appeared in heaven: a woman G3489
Rev 12: 9 The g dragon was hurled down—that G3489
Rev 12:14 was given the two wings of a g eagle, G3489
Rev 13: 2 his power and his throne and g authority. G3489
Rev 13:13 And it performed g signs, even causing G3489
Rev 13:16 forced all people, g and small, rich and G3489
Rev 14: 8 Fallen is Babylon the G,' which made all G3489
Rev 14:19 threw them into the g winepress of God's G3489
Rev 15: 1 in heaven another g and marvelous sign: G3489
Rev 15: 3 "G and marvelous are your deeds, Lord G3489
Rev 16:12 out his bowl on the g river Euphrates, G3489
Rev 16:14 the battle on the g day of God Almighty. G3489
Rev 16:19 The g city split into three parts, and the G3489
Rev 16:19 Babylon the G and gave her the cup G3489
Rev 17: 1 you the punishment of the g prostitute, G3489
Rev 17: 5 BABYLON THE G THE MOTHER OF G3489
Rev 17:18 you saw is the g city that rules over G3489
Rev 18: 1 He had g authority, and the earth was G3489
Rev 18: 2 Fallen is Babylon the G!' She has become G3489
Rev 18:10 Woe to you, g city, you mighty city of G3489
Rev 18:16 Woe to you, g city, dressed in fine linen G3489
Rev 18:17 In one hour **such** g wealth has been G5537
Rev 18:18 'Was there ever a city like this g city? G3489
Rev 18:19 Woe to you, g city, where all who had G3489
Rev 18:21 such violence the g city of Babylon will be G3489
Rev 19: 1 like the roar of a g multitude in heaven G4498
Rev 19: 2 He has condemned the g prostitute who G3489
Rev 19: 5 you who fear him, both g and small!" G3489
Rev 19: 6 I heard what sounded like a g multitude, G4498
Rev 19:17 gather together for the g supper of God, G3489
Rev 19:18 of all people, free and slave, g and small." G3489
Rev 20: 1 Abyss and holding in his hand a g chain. G3489
Rev 20:11 Then I saw a g white throne and him who G3489
Rev 20:12 And I saw the dead, g and small, standing G3489
Rev 21:10 in the Spirit to a mountain g and high, G3489
Rev 21:12 It had a g, high wall with twelve gates G3489
Rev 21:21 The g **street** of the city was of gold, as G4423
Rev 22: 2 down the middle *of* the g **street** of the city G4423

GREATER (80) [GREAT]

Ge 1:16 the g light to govern the day and the H1524
Ge 29:30 Rachel was g **than** his love for Leah. H4946
Ge 39: 9 No one is g in this house than I am. H1524
Ge 41:40 respect to the throne *will I be* g than you." H1540
Ge 48:19 his younger brother *will be* g than he, and H1540
Ge 49:26 father's blessings *are* g than the blessings H1504
Ex 18:11 that the LORD is g than all other gods, H1524
Nu 14:12 you into a nation g and stronger than they H1524
Nu 24: 7 "Their king *will be* g than Agag; their H8123
Dt 4:38 before you nations g and stronger than H1524
Dt 9: 1 dispossess nations g and stronger than H1524
Dt 20: 1 chariots and an army g than yours, H8041
Ru 3:10 "This kindness *is* g than that which you H3512
1Sa 14:30 *Would* not the slaughter of the Philistines *have been* even g H8049
2Sa 13:16 me away would be a g wrong than what H1524
2Sa 19:43 have a g claim on David **than** you have H4946
2Sa 23:19 Was he not held in g honor than the H3954
2Sa 23:23 He was held in g honor **than** any of the H4946
1Ki 1:37 Solomon *to* **make** his throne *even* g than H1540
1Ki 1:47 than yours and his throne g than yours! H1540
1Ki 4:30 Solomon's wisdom *was* g than the wisdom H8049
1Ki 4:30 and g than all the wisdom of Egypt. NDT
1Ki 10:23 King Solomon *was* g in riches and H1540
1Ch 11:25 He was held in g honor than any of the H4946
2Ch 2: 5 because our God is g than all other gods. H1524
2Ch 9:22 King Solomon *was* g in riches and H1540
2Ch 32: 7 there is a g **power** with us than with H8041
Job 33:12 are not right, for God *is* g than any mortal. H8049
Ps 135: 5 is great, that our Lord is g **than** all gods. H4946
Ecc 2: 9 *I became* g by far than anyone in H1540
La 4: 6 of my people *is* g than that of Sodom, H1540
Da 2:30 I have g wisdom **than** anyone else A10427
Da 4:36 and **became even** g A10650+10339+10323
Hag 2: 9 house will be g than the glory of the H1524
Zec 12: 7 inhabitants *may* not *be* g than that of H1540
Mt 11:11 has not risen anyone g than John the G3505
Mt 11:11 in the kingdom of heaven is g than he. G3505
Mt 12: 6 I tell you that *something* g than the G3505
Mt 12:41 now *something* g than Jonah is here. G4498
Mt 12:42 now *something* g than Solomon is G4498
Mt 23:17 Which is g: the gold, or the G3505
Mt 23:19 You blind men! Which is g: the gift, or the G3505
Mk 12:31 There is no commandment g than these." G3505
Lk 7:28 of women there is no one g than John; G3505
Lk 7:28 least in the kingdom of God is g than he." G3505
Lk 11:31 now *something* g than Solomon is G4498
Lk 11:32 now *something* g than Jonah is here. G4498
Lk 22:27 For who is g, the one who is at the table G3505
Jn 1:50 You will see g *things* than that." G3505
Jn 3:30 He must *become* g; I must become less." G889
Jn 4:12 Are you g than our father Jacob, who gave G3505
Jn 5:20 he will show him *even* g works than these G3505
Jn 8:53 Are you g than our father Abraham? He G3505
Jn 10:29 them to me, is g than all; no one can G3505
Jn 13:16 no servant is g than his master, nor is G3505
Jn 13:16 is a messenger g than the one who G3505
Jn 14:12 they will do *even* g *things* than these G3505
Jn 14:28 to the Father, for the Father is g than I. G3505
Jn 15:13 G love has no one than this: to lay down G3505
Jn 15:20 'A servant is not g than his master.' If G3505
Jn 19:11 handed me over to you is guilty of a g sin." G3505
Ro 11:12 how much g riches will their full inclusion G3437
1Co 12:24 giving g honor to the parts that lacked it G4358
1Co 12:31 Now eagerly desire the g gifts. And yet I G3505
1Co 14: 5 who prophesies is g than the one who G3505

2Co 3:11 how much **g** is the glory of that which G3437
2Co 7: 7 so that my joy was **g than ever**. G3437
2Co 7:15 you is **all the g** when he remembers G4359
Heb 3: 3 found worthy of **g** honor than Moses, G4498
Heb 3: 3 of a house has **g** honor than the house G4498
Heb 6:13 there was no one **g** for him to swear by, G3505
Heb 6:16 swear by someone **g** than themselves, G3505
Heb 7: 7 doubt the lesser is blessed by the **g**. G3202
Heb 9:11 he went through the **g** and more perfect G3505
Heb 11:26 sake of Christ as of **g** value than the G3505
1Pe 1: 7 of your faith—*of* **g worth** than gold, which G4501
1Jn 3:20 we know that God is **g** than our hearts G3505
1Jn 4: 4 who is in you is **g** than the one who is G3505
1Jn 5: 9 God's testimony is **g** because it is the G3505
3Jn 4 I have no **g** joy *than* to hear that my G3505

GREATER SIDON (2) [SIDON]

Jos 11: 8 pursued them all the way to **G**, H7478
Jos 19:28 Hammon and Kanah, as far as **G**. H7478

GREATEST (31) [GREAT]

Jos 14:15 who was the **g** man among the Anakites.) H1524
2Sa 7: 9 like the names of the **g** *men* on earth. H1524
2Ki 23: 2 all the people from the least to the **g**. H1524
2Ki 25:26 all the people from the least to the **g** H1524
1Ch 12:14 a hundred, and the **g** for a thousand. H1524
1Ch 17: 8 like the names of the **g** *men* on earth. H1524
2Ch 34:30 all the people from the least to the **g**. H1524
Est 1: 5 from the least to the **g** who were in the H1524
Est 1:20 their husbands, from the least to the **g**." H1524
Job 1: 3 He was the **g** man among all the people H1524
Jer 6:13 "From the least to the **g**, all are greedy H1524
Jer 8:10 From the least to the **g**, all are greedy H1524
Jer 31:34 from the least of them to the **g**," declares H1524
Jer 42: 1 from the least to the **g** approached H1524
Jer 42: 8 all the people from the least to the **g**. H1524
Jer 44:12 From the least to the **g**, they will die by H1524
Jnh 3: 5 all of them, from the **g** to the least, put on H1524
Mt 18: 1 is the **g** in the kingdom of heaven? G3505
Mt 18: 4 of this child is the **g** in the kingdom of G3505
Mt 22:36 which is the **g** commandment in the Law?" G3489
Mt 22:38 This is the first and **g** commandment. G3489
Mt 23:11 The **g** among you will be your servant. G3505
Mk 9:34 they had argued about who was the **g**. G3505
Lk 9:46 as to which of them would be the **g**. G3505
Lk 9:48 who is least among you all who is the **g**." G3489
Lk 22:24 to which of them was considered to be **g**. G3505
Lk 22:26 the **g** among you should be like the G3505
Jn 7:37 On the last and **g** day of the festival G3489
1Co 13:13 hope and love. But the **g** of these is love. G3505
Heb 8:11 know me, from the least of them to the **g**. G3489
1Pe 1:10 searched intently and **with the g care**, G2001

GREATLY (71) [GREAT]

Ge 7:18 waters rose and increased **g** on the earth, H4394
Ge 7:19 They rose **g** on the earth, and all H4394+4394
Ge 13:13 were sinning **g** against the LORD. H4394
Ge 17: 2 you and will **g** increase your H928+4394+4394
Ge 17:20 fruitful and will **g** increase his H4394+928+4394
Ge 21:11 distressed Abraham **g** because it H4394
Ge 30:30 had before I came has increased **g**, H4200+8044
Ge 47:27 were fruitful and increased **g** in number. H4394
Ge 48:16 may they increase **g** on the earth." H4200+8044
Ex 1: 7 *they* **multiplied g**, increased in H9237
Dt 6: 3 that you may increase **g** in a land flowing H4394
1Sa 18: 8 this refrain **displeased** him **g**. H8317+928+6524
1Sa 19: 4 what he has done has benefited you **g**. H4394
1Sa 28:21 to Saul and saw that he was **g** shaken, H4394
1Sa 30: 6 David was **g** distressed because the men H4394
2Sa 10: 5 the men, for they were **g** humiliated. H4394
2Sa 24:10 "I have sinned **g** in what I have done. H4394
1Ki 1:40 playing pipes and rejoicing **g**, so that the H1524
1Ki 5: 7 message, he was **g** pleased and said H4394
1Ch 4:38 Their families increased **g**, H4200+8044
1Ch 19: 5 to meet them, for they were **g** humiliated. H4394
1Ch 21: 8 "I have sinned **g** by doing this. H4394
1Ch 29: 9 David the king also rejoiced **g**. H1524
2Ch 26:15 he was **g** helped until he became H7098
2Ch 33:12 humbled himself **g** before the God of H4394
Ezr 10: 9 **g distressed** by the occasion and because H8283
Ezr 10:13 because *we have* sinned **g** in this thing. H8049
Ne 4: 1 he became angry and was **g** incensed. H2221
Ne 13: 8 I was **g** displeased and threw all Tobiah's H4394
Job 20: 2 me to answer because I am **g disturbed**. H2591
Ps 47: 9 the earth belong to God; he is **g** exalted. H4394
Ps 89: 7 council of the holy ones God is **g** feared; H8041
Ps 107:38 their numbers **g** increased, and he H4394
Ps 109:30 With my mouth I will **g** extol the LORD; in H4394
Ps 116:10 the LORD when I said, "I am **g** afflicted"; H4394
Ps 119:167 I obey your statutes, for I love them **g**. H4394
Ps 129: 1 "They have **g** oppressed me from my H8041
Ps 129: 2 "they have **g** oppressed me from my youth H8041
Ps 138: 3 *you* **g emboldened** me. H8104+6437
Ecc 9:13 example of wisdom that **g** impressed me: H1524
Isa 31: 6 to the One *you have so* **g** revolted against. H6676
Isa 35: 2 *it will* **rejoice g** and shout for H1635+677+1638
Isa 61:10 *I* **delight g** in the LORD; my soul H8464+8464
Isa 66:10 who love her; **rejoice g** with her, all H8464+5375
Jer 3:16 *your* **numbers** *have* **increased g** H8049+2256+7238
Jer 14:10 "They **g** love to wander; they do not H4027
Jer 50:12 your mother will be **g** ashamed; she who H4394
La 1: 8 Jerusalem *has* **sinned g** and so has H2627+2628
Da 4: 1 live in all the earth: *May* you prosper **g**! A10677
Da 4:19 Belteshazzar) *was* **g perplexed** for a time A10724
Da 6:14 heard this, he was **g** distressed; he was A10678
Da 6:25 in all the earth: "*May* you prosper **g**! A10677
Da 11:39 a foreign god and *will* **g** honor those who H8049
Jnh 1:16 At this the men **g** feared the LORD, and H1524
Zec 9: 9 Rejoice **g**, Daughter Zion! Shout H4394
Mt 17:15 "He has seizures and is suffering **g**. G2809
Mt 19:25 they were **g** astonished and asked G5379
Mk 6:20 heard John, he was **g** puzzled; yet he G4498
Mk 6:26 The king was **g distressed**, but because of G4337
Lk 1:29 Mary *was* **g troubled** at his words and G1410
Lk 23: 8 saw Jesus, he was **g** pleased, because G3336
Ac 4: 2 *They were* **g disturbed** because the G1387
Ac 7:17 *the* **number** of our people in Egypt *had* **g increased** G889+2779+4437
Ac 17:16 he *was* **g distressed** to see that the city G4236
Ac 20:12 home alive and were **g** comforted. G4024+3585
2Co 7: 4 *I am* **g** encouraged; in all our troubles my G4444
2Co 10:15 activity among you will **g** expand, G1650+4353
Php 4:10 I rejoiced **g** in the Lord that at last you G3487
Heb 6:18 hope set before us may be **g** encouraged. G2708
1Pe 1: 6 In all this *you* **g rejoice**, though now for a G22
Rev 17: 6 saw her, *I was* **g astonished**. G2513+2512+3489

GREATNESS (16) [GREAT]

Ex 15: 7 "In the **g** *of* your majesty you threw down H8044
Dt 3:24 your servant your **g** and your strong hand H1542
Dt 32: 3 Oh, praise the **g** of our God! H1542
1Ch 29:11 is the **g** and the power and the glory and H1525
2Ch 9: 6 not even half the **g** *of* your wisdom was H5270
Est 10: 2 with a full account of the **g** *of* Mordecai, H1525
Ps 145: 3 worthy of praise; his **g** no one can fathom. H1525
Ps 150: 2 of power; praise him for his surpassing **g**. H1542
Isa 9: 7 Of the **g** *of* his government and peace H5269
Isa 63: 1 striding forward in the **g** *of* his strength? H8044
Eze 38:23 And so *I will* **show** *my* **g** and my holiness H1540
Da 4:22 your **g** has grown until it reaches the sky A10650
Da 5:18 sovereignty and **g** and glory and A10650
Da 7:27 power and **g** of all the kingdoms under A10650
Mic 5: 4 then *his* **g** will reach to the ends of the H1540
Lk 9:43 And they were all amazed at the **g** of God G3484

GREAVES (1)

1Sa 17: 6 on his legs he wore bronze **g**, and a H5196

GRECIA, GRECIANS (KJV) GREECE, GREEKS, HELLENISTIC

GREECE (7) [GREEK, GREEKS]

Isa 66:19 to Tubal and **G**, and to the distant H3430
Eze 27:13 " '**G**, Tubal and Meshek did business with H3430
Da 8:21 The shaggy goat is the king of **G**, and the H3430
Da 10:20 when I go, the prince of **G** will come; H3430
Da 11: 2 up everyone against the kingdom of **G**. H3430
Zec 9:13 against your sons, **G**, and make you like a H3430
Ac 20: 2 to the people, and finally arrived in **G**, G1817

GREED (13) [GREEDY]

Isa 57:17 I was enraged by their sinful **g**; I punished H1299
Eze 16:27 I gave you over to the **g** *of* your enemies H5883
Mt 23:25 they are full of **g** and self-indulgence. G771
Mk 7:22 adultery, **g**, malice, deceit, lewdness, envy, G4432
Lk 11:39 inside you are full *of* **g** and wickedness. G771
Lk 12:15 Be on your guard against all kinds of **g** G4432
Ro 1:29 kind of wickedness, evil, **g** and depravity. G4432
Eph 4:19 kind of impurity, and they are full of **g**. G4432
Eph 5: 3 of impurity, or of **g**, because these are G4432
Col 3: 5 evil desires and **g**, which is idolatry. G4432
1Th 2: 5 did we put on a mask to cover up **g** G4432
2Pe 2: 3 In their **g** these teachers will exploit you G4432
2Pe 2:14 they are experts *in* **g**—an accursed brood! G4432

GREEDY (12) [GREED]

Ps 10: 3 he blesses the **g** and reviles the LORD. H1298
Pr 15:27 The **g** bring ruin to their H1298+1299
Pr 28:25 The **g** stir up conflict, but those H8146+5883
Pr 29: 4 but **those** *who are* **g** *for* bribes tear it down. AIT
Jer 6:13 the greatest, all *are* **g** *for* gain; prophets H1298
Jer 8:10 the greatest, all *are* **g** *for* gain; prophets H1298
Eze 33:31 their hearts *are* **g** *for* unjust gain. H2143+339
Hab 2: 5 Because he *is* as **g** as the grave and like H8143
1Co 5:10 are immoral, or the **g** and swindlers, or G4431
1Co 5:11 sister but is sexually immoral or **g**, G4431
1Co 6:10 thieves nor the **g** nor drunkards nor G4431
Eph 5: 5 impure or **g** *person*—such a person is G4431

GREEK (10) [GREECE]

Mk 7:26 The woman was a **G**, born in Syrian G1820
Jn 19:20 sign was written in Aramaic, Latin and **G**. G1822
Ac 9:36 Tabitha (**in G** her name *is* Dorcas); G1450+3306
Ac 16: 1 a believer but whose father was a **G**. G1818
Ac 16: 3 they all knew that his father was a **G**. G1818
Ac 17:12 number of prominent **G** women and many G1820
Ac 17:12 prominent Greek women and many **G** men. NDT
Ac 21:37 "Do you speak **G**?" he replied. G1822
Gal 2: 3 be circumcised, even though he was a **G**. G1818
Rev 9:11 is Abaddon and in **G** is Apollyon G1819

GREEKS (17) [GREECE]

Joel 3: 6 of Judah and Jerusalem to the **G**, H1201+3436
Jn 7:35 our people live scattered *among* the **G**, G1818
Jn 7:35 among the Greeks, and teach the **G**? G1818
Jn 12:20 there were some **G** among those who G1818
Ac 11:20 to Antioch and began to speak to **G** also, G1821
Ac 14: 1 a great number of Jews and **G** believed. G1818
Ac 17: 4 number of God-fearing **G** and quite a few G1818
Ac 17:17 with both Jews and **God-fearing G**, G4936
Ac 18: 4 trying to persuade Jews and **G**. G1818
Ac 19:10 that all the Jews and **G** who lived in the G1818
Ac 19:17 to the Jews and **G** living in Ephesus, G1818
Ac 20:21 to both Jews and **G** that they must turn to G1818
Ac 21:28 he has brought **G** into the temple and G1818
Ro 1:14 I am obligated both *to* **G** and Non-Greeks, G1818
1Co 1:22 demand signs and **G** look for wisdom, G1818
1Co 1:24 both Jews and **G**, Christ the power of G1818
1Co 10:32 whether Jews, **G** or the church of God— G1818

GREEN (20) [GREENISH]

Ge 1:30 of life in it—I give every **g** plant for food." H3764
Ge 9: 3 Just as I gave you the **g** plants, I now give H3764
Ex 10:15 Nothing **g** remained on tree or plant in all H3764
2Ki 19:26 the field, like tender **g** shoots, like grass H2013
Job 39: 8 its pasture and searches for any **g thing**. H3728
Ps 23: 2 He makes me lie down in **g** pastures, he H2013
Ps 37: 2 like **g** plants they will soon die away. H2013
Ps 58: 9 whether they be **g** or dry—the wicked will H2645
Ps 92:14 fruit in old age, they will stay fresh and **g**, H8316
Ps 105:35 they ate up every **g thing** in their land, ate H6912
Pr 11:28 the righteous will thrive like a **g leaf**. H6591
Isa 15: 6 vegetation is gone and nothing **g** is left. H3764
Isa 37:27 the field, like tender **g** shoots, like grass H2013
Jer 17: 8 when heat comes; its leaves are always **g**. H8316
Eze 17:24 I dry up the **g** tree and make the dry tree H4300
Eze 20:47 consume all your trees, both **g** and dry. H4300
Joel 2:22 in the wilderness *are becoming* **g**. H2012
Mk 6:39 people sit down in groups on the **g** grass. G5952
Lk 23:31 do these things when the tree is **g**, G5619
Rev 8: 7 and all the **g** grass was burned up. G5952

GREENISH (2) [GREEN]

Lev 13:49 any leather article, is **g** or reddish, it is a H3768
Lev 14:37 if it has **g** or reddish depressions that H3768

GREET (40) [GREETED, GREETING, GREETINGS, GREETS]

1Sa 10: 4 *They will* **g** you and offer you H8626+4200+8934
1Sa 13:10 and Saul went out to **g** him. H7925+1385
1Sa 25: 5 at Carmel and **g** him in my H8626+4200+8934
2Sa 8:10 to King David to **g** him and H8626+4200+8934
2Ki 4:29 Don't **g** anyone you meet, and if anyone H1385
2Ki 10:13 have come down to **g** the families of the H8934
1Ch 18:10 to King David to **g** him and H8626+4200+8934
Ps 21: 3 *You* **came to g** him *with* rich blessings H7709
Isa 14: 9 rouses the spirits of the departed to **g** you— NDT
Mt 5:47 And if *you* **g** only your own people, what G832
Mk 9:15 with wonder and ran *to* **g** him. G832
Lk 10: 4 sandals; and *do* not **g** anyone on the road. G832
Ro 16: 3 **G** Priscilla and Aquila, my co-workers in G832
Ro 16: 5 **G** also the church that meets at their house NDT
Ro 16: 5 **G** my dear friend Epenetus, who was the G832
Ro 16: 6 **G** Mary, who worked very hard for you. G832
Ro 16: 7 **G** Andronicus and Junia, my fellow Jews G832
Ro 16: 8 **G** Ampliatus, my dear friend in the Lord. G832
Ro 16: 9 **G** Urbanus, our co-worker in Christ, and my G832
Ro 16:10 **G** Apelles, whose fidelity to Christ has G832
Ro 16:10 **G** those who belong to the household of G832
Ro 16:11 **G** Herodion, my fellow Jew. Greet those in G832
Ro 16:11 **G** those in the household of Narcissus who G832
Ro 16:12 **G** Tryphena and Tryphosa, those women G832
Ro 16:12 **G** my dear friend Persis, another woman G832
Ro 16:13 **G** Rufus, chosen in the Lord, and his G832
Ro 16:14 **G** Asyncritus, Phlegon, Hermes, Patrobas G832
Ro 16:15 **G** Philologus, Julia, Nereus and his sister G832
Ro 16:16 **G** one another with a holy kiss. All the G832
Ro 16:22 wrote down this letter, **g** you in the Lord. G832
1Co 16:19 Aquila and Priscilla **g** you warmly in the G832
1Co 16:20 **G** one another with a holy kiss. G832
2Co 13:12 **G** one another with a holy kiss. G832
Php 4:21 **G** all God's people in Christ Jesus. G832
1Th 5:26 **G** all God's people with a holy kiss. G832
2Ti 4:19 **G** Priscilla and Aquila and the household G832
Titus 3:15 **G** those who love us in the faith G832
Heb 13:24 **G** all your leaders and all the Lord's people G832
1Pe 5:14 **G** one another with a kiss of love. Peace to G832
3Jn 14 **G** the friends there by name. G832

GREETED (11) [GREET]

Ex 18: 7 *They* **g** each other and then H8626+4200+8934
Jdg 18:15 at Micah's place and **g** him. H8626+4200+8934
Ru 2: 4 from Bethlehem and **g** the harvesters, H606
2Ki 10:15 Jehu **g** him and said, "Are you in accord H1385
Mt 23: 7 they love to be **g with respect** in the G833
Mk 12:38 robes and be **g with respect** in the G833
Lk 1:40 entered Zechariah's home and **g** Elizabeth. G832
Lk 20:46 love to be **g with respect** in the G833
Ac 18:22 up to Jerusalem and **g** the church and then G832
Ac 21: 7 where *we* **g** the brothers and sisters and G832
Ac 21:19 Paul **g** them and reported in detail what G832

GREETING (7) [GREET]

Mt 10:12 As you enter the home, **give** it *your* **g**. G832
Lk 1:29 wondered what kind of **g** this might be. G833
Lk 1:41 When Elizabeth heard Mary's **g**, the baby G833
Lk 1:44 as the sound *of* your **g** reached my ears, G833

1Co 16:21 Paul, write this **g** in my own hand. *G833*
Col 4:18 Paul, write this **g** in my own hand *G833*
2Th 3:17 write this **g** in my own hand, which is *G833*

GREETINGS (31) [GREET]
1Sa 25:14 the wilderness to **give** our master his **g**, H1385
Ezr 4:17 elsewhere in Trans-Euphrates: **G**. A10720
Ezr 5: 7 King Darius: **Cordial g**. A10720+10353+10002+10002
Ezr 7:12 of the Law of the God of heaven: **G**. A10147
Mt 26:49 at once to Jesus, Judas said, "**G**, Rabbi!" *G5897*
Mt 28: 9 Jesus met them. "**G**," he said. They came *G5897*
Lk 1:28 to her and said, "**G**, you who are highly *G5897*
Lk 11:43 the synagogues and **respectful g** in the *G833*
Ac 15:23 believers in Antioch, Syria and Cilicia: **G**. *G5897*
Ac 23:26 To His Excellency, Governor Felix: **G**. *G5897*
Ro 16:16 All the churches of Christ **send g**. *G832*
Ro 16:21 my co-worker, **sends** *his* **g** to you, as do *G832*
Ro 16:23 whole church here enjoy, **sends** you *his* **g**. *G832*
Ro 16:23 our brother Quartus **send** you *their* **g**. *G832*
1Co 16:19 in the province of Asia **send** you **g**. *G832*
1Co 16:20 All the brothers and sisters here **send** you **g** *G832*
2Co 13:13 All God's people here **send** *their* **g**. *G832*
Php 4:21 sisters who are with me **send g**. *G832*
Php 4:22 All God's people here **send** you **g** *G832*
Col 4:10 fellow prisoner Aristarchus **sends** you *his* **g**, *G832*
Col 4:11 also sends **g**. These are the only NDT
Col 4:12 you and a servant of Christ Jesus, **sends g**. *G832*
Col 4:14 friend Luke, the doctor, and Demas **send g**. *G832*
Col 4:15 **Give** my **g** to the brothers and sisters at *G832*
Titus 3:15 Everyone with me **sends** you **g**. Greet those *G832*
Phm 23 fellow prisoner in Christ Jesus, **sends** you **g**. *G832*
Heb 13:24 Those from Italy **send** you *their* **g**. *G832*
Jas 1: 1 tribes scattered among the nations: **G**. *G5897*
1Pe 5:13 with you, **sends** you *her* **g**, and so does my *G832*
2Jn 13 who is chosen by God, **send** *their* **g**. *G832*
3Jn 14 The friends here **send** *their* **g**. Greet the *G832*

GREETS (2) [GREET]
2Ki 4:29 if anyone **g** you, do not answer. H1385
2Ti 4:21 Eubulus **g** you, and so do Pudens, Linus *G832*

GREW (67) [GROW]
Ge 21: 8 The child **g** and was weaned, and on the H1540
Ge 21:20 God was with the boy as *he* **g up**. H1540
Ge 25:27 The boys **g up**, and Esau became a H1540
Ge 30:43 the man *g* exceedingly **prosperous** and came AIT
Ex 2:10 When the child **g older**, she took him to H1540
Ex 16:21 when the sun *g* **hot**, it melted away. AIT
Ex 17:12 When Moses' hands **g** tired, they took a NDT
Ex 19:19 *As* the sound of the trumpet **g louder and louder** H2143+2256+2618+4394
Nu 21: 4 But the people *g* **impatient** on the way; AIT
Dt 32:15 Jeshurun **g fat** and kicked; filled with food, H9042
Jos 17:13 when the Israelites *g* **stronger**, they subjected AIT
Jdg 2:10 generation **g up** who knew neither H7756
Jdg 13:24 He **g** and the LORD blessed him, H1540
Ru 1:13 would you wait until *they* **g up**? Would you H1540
1Sa 2:21 the boy Samuel **g up** in the presence of H1540
1Sa 3:19 The LORD was with Samuel as he **g up** H1540
1Sa 8: 1 When Samuel **g old**, he appointed his H2416
1Sa 31: 3 The fighting *g* **fierce** around Saul, and when AIT
2Sa 3: 1 **g stronger and stronger**, H2143+2256+2618
2Sa 3: 1 Saul **g weaker and weaker**. H2143+2256+1924
2Sa 12: 3 and *it* **g up** with him and his children. H1540
2Sa 23:10 till his hand *g* **tired** and froze to the sword. AIT
1Ki 11: 4 As Solomon **g old**, his wives turned his H2420
1Ki 17:17 He **g worse and worse** H2118+2716+2617+4394
1Ki 18:45 the sky *g* **black** *with* clouds, the wind AIT
2Ki 4:18 The child **g**, and one day he went out to H1540
2Ki 4:34 himself out on him, the boy's body *g* **warm**. AIT
1Ch 10: 3 The fighting **g fierce** around Saul, and H3877
2Ch 13:21 But Abijah **g in strength**. He married H2616
2Ch 27: 6 Jotham *g* **powerful** because he walked AIT
Ps 39: 3 my heart *g* **hot** within me. While I meditated AIT
Ps 52: 7 his great wealth and *g* **strong** by destroying AIT
Ps 77: 3 I groaned; I meditated, and my spirit *g* **faint**. AIT
Ps 106:16 In the camp *they g* **envious** of Moses and of AIT
Ps 107:30 They were glad when *it g* **calm**, and he AIT
Isa 38:14 My eyes **g weak** as I looked to the heavens AIT
Isa 53: 2 *He* **g up** before him like a tender shoot H6590
Eze 16: 7 *You* **g** and developed and entered H8049
Eze 17:10 wither away in the plot where it **g**? H7542
Eze 31: 5 its boughs increased and its branches *g* **long** AIT
Da 4:11 The tree **g large** and strong and its top A10648
Da 4:20 you saw, which **g large** and strong, with A10648
Da 4:33 until his hair **g** like the feathers of A10648
Da 5: 9 more terrified and his face **g** more pale. A10731
Da 8: 3 was longer than the other but **g up** later. H6590
Da 8: 8 four prominent horns **g up** toward the four H6590
Da 8: 9 started small but **g** *in* power to the south H1540
Da 8:10 *It* **g** until it reached the host of the H1540
Jnh 1:13 the sea **g even wilder** than H6192+2143+2256
Jnh 1:15 him overboard, and the raging sea **g calm**. AIT
Jnh 4: 8 blazed on Jonah's head so that *he g* **faint**. AIT
Zec 11: 8 flock detested me, and I **g weary** of them H7918
Mt 13: 7 which **g up** and choked the plants. *G326*
Mk 4: 7 which **g up** and choked the plants *G326*
Mk 4: 8 It came up, **g** and produced a crop, some *G889*
Mk 5:26 of getting better *she* **g** worse. *G1650+2262*
Lk 1:80 And the child **g** and became strong in spirit *G889*
Lk 2:40 And the child **g** and became strong; he was *G889*
Lk 2:52 And Jesus **g** in wisdom and stature, and in *G4621*
Lk 8: 7 which **g up with** it and choked the plants. *G5243*
Lk 13:19 *It* **g** and became a tree, and the birds *G889*
Jn 6:18 wind was blowing and the waters *g* **rough**. AIT
Ac 4: 4 of men who believed **g** *to* about five *G1181*
Ac 9:22 Yet Saul *g* more and more **powerful** and AIT
Ac 16: 5 in the faith and **g** daily in numbers. *G4355*
Ac 19:20 of the Lord spread widely and **g** in power. *G2710*
Rev 18: 3 of the earth *g* **rich** from her excessive AIT

GREYHOUND (KJV) ROOSTER

GRIDDLE (3)
Lev 2: 5 If your grain offering is prepared on a **g**, it H4679
Lev 6:21 It must be prepared with oil on a **g**; bring H4679
Lev 7: 9 in a pan or on a **g** belongs to the priest H4679

GRIEF (30) [GRIEFS, GRIEVANCE, GRIEVE, GRIEVED, GRIEVES, GRIEVING, GRIEVOUS]
Ge 26:35 They were a **source of g** to Isaac H5289+8120
Ge 38:12 When Judah *had* **recovered from** *his* **g**, he H5714
1Sa 1:16 here out of my great anguish and **g**." H4088
Est 6:12 rushed home, with his head covered in **g**, H63
Job 17: 7 My eyes have grown dim with **g**; my H4089
Ps 10:14 you consider their **g** and take it in hand. H4088
Ps 31: 9 weak with sorrow, my soul and body with **g**. NDT
Ps 35:14 I bowed my head *in* **g** as though weeping H7722
Ps 88: 9 my eyes are dim with **g**. I call to you, LORD H6715
Pr 10: 1 a foolish son brings **g** *to* his mother. H9342
Pr 10:10 Whoever winks maliciously causes **g**, and H6780
Pr 14:13 may ache, and rejoicing may end in **g**. H9342
Pr 17:21 To have a fool for a child brings **g**; there H9342
Pr 17:25 A foolish son brings **g** to his father and H4088
Ecc 1:18 the more knowledge, the more **g**. H4799
Ecc 2:23 All their days their work is **g** and pain H4088
La 1: 5 The LORD *has* **brought** her **g** because of H3324
La 3:32 Though *he* **brings g**, he will show H3324
La 3:33 willingly bring affliction or **g** *to* anyone. H3324
La 3:51 What I see **brings g** to my soul because of H6618
Eze 13:22 when I *had* **brought** them no **g**, and H3872
Eze 21: 6 them with broken heart and **bitter g**. H5320
Mic 4: 6 the exiles and those *I have* **brought to g**. H8317
Mt 17:23 And the disciples *were* filled with **g**. *G3382*
Jn 16: 6 you are filled with **g** because I have said *G3383*
Jn 16:20 You will grieve, but your **g** will turn to joy. *G3383*
Jn 16:22 Now is your **time of g**, but I will see you *G3383*
2Co 2: 5 If anyone *has* **caused g**, he has not so *G3382*
1Pe 1: 6 may have had to **suffer g** in all kinds of *G3382*
Rev 18: 7 as much torment and **g** as the glory and *G4292*

GRIEFS (1) [GRIEF]
1Ti 6:10 pierced themselves *with* many **g**. *G3850*

GRIEVANCE (3) [GRIEF]
Job 31:13 female, when they had a **g** against me, H8190
Ac 19:38 craftsmen have a **g** against anybody, *G3364*
Col 3:13 if any of you has a **g** against someone. *G3664*

GRIEVE (17) [GRIEF]
2Sa 1:26 I **g** for you, Jonathan my brother; you were H7639
Ne 8:10 *Do* not **g**, for the joy of the LORD is your H6772
Ne 8:11 "Be still, for this is a holy day. *Do* not **g**." H6772
Isa 16: 7 Lament and **g** for the raisin cakes of Kir H5778
Isa 61: 3 provide for *those who* **g** *in* Zion—to H63
La 1: 4 her young women **g**, and she is in bitter H3324
Eze 7:12 Let not the buyer rejoice nor the seller **g**, for H61
Eze 9: 4 of those who **g** and lament over all H634
Joel 1:11 vine growers; **g** for the wheat and the barley NDT
Am 6: 6 but *you do* not **g** over the ruin of Joseph. H2703
Zec 12:10 and **g bitterly** for him as one grieves for a H5352
Jn 16:20 world rejoices. You *will* **g**, but your grief *G3382*
2Co 2: 2 For if I **g** you, who is left to make me glad *G3382*
2Co 2: 4 not to **g** *you* but to let you know the depth *G3382*
Eph 4:30 And *do* not **g** the Holy Spirit of God, with *G3382*
1Th 4:13 so that *you do* not **g** like the rest of *G3382*
Jas 4: 9 **G**, mourn and wail. Change your laughter *G5415*

GRIEVED (15) [GRIEF]
Dt 34: 8 The Israelites **g** *for* Moses in the plains of H1134
Jdg 21: 6 Now the Israelites **g** for the tribe of H5714
Jdg 21:15 The people **g** for Benjamin, because the H5714
1Sa 20: 3 must not know this or *he will* **be g**. H6772
1Sa 20:34 because *he* **was g** at his father's shameful H6772
Job 30:25 *Has* not my soul **g** for the poor? H6327
Ps 73:21 When my heart **was g** and my spirit H2806
Ps 78:40 the wilderness and **g** him in the H6772
Isa 63:10 Yet they rebelled and **g** his Holy Spirit. H6772
Eze 6: 9 how *I have* **been g** *by* their adulterous H8689
Ac 20:38 What **g** *them* most was his statement that *G3849*
2Co 2: 2 to make me glad but you *whom I have* **g**? *G3382*
2Co 2: 5 *he has* not so much **g** me as he has *G3382*
2Co 2: 5 grieved me as he has **g** all of you to some NDT
2Co 12:21 and *I will be* **g** over many who have *G4291*

GRIEVES (1) [GRIEF]
Zec 12:10 bitterly for him as *one* **g** for a firstborn son H5352

GRIEVING (3) [GRIEF]
2Sa 14: 2 a woman *who has spent* many days **g** for the H61
2Sa 19: 2 heard it said, "The king *is* **g** for his son." H6772
Joel 1: 8 a virgin in sackcloth **g** for the betrothed of NDT

GRIEVOUS (7) [GRIEF]
Ge 18:20 Gomorrah is so great and their sin so **g** H3877
Ecc 2:17 that is done under the sun was **g** to me. H8273
Ecc 5:13 I have seen a **g** evil under the sun: wealth H2703
Ecc 5:16 This too *is* a **g** evil: As everyone comes H2703
Ecc 6: 2 This is meaningless, a **g** evil. H8273
Jer 14:17 has suffered a **g** wound, a crushing blow H1524
Jer 15:18 unending and my wound **g** and incurable? H631

GRIND (5) [GRINDERS, GRINDING]
Ex 30:36 **G** some of it to powder and place it in H8835
Job 31:10 then *may* my wife **g** another man's **grain** H3221
Pr 27:22 Though *you* **g** a fool in a mortar, grinding H4197
Isa 28:28 but one *does* not **use** horses **to g** grain. H1990
Isa 47: 2 Take millstones and **g** flour; take off your H3221

GRINDERS (1) [GRIND]
Ecc 12: 3 when the **g** cease because they are few H3223

GRINDING (6) [GRIND]
Jdg 16:21 they set him to **g grain** in the prison. H3221
Pr 27:22 in a mortar, **g** them like grain with a pestle NDT
Ecc 12: 4 are closed and the sound of **g** fades; H3222
Isa 3:15 my people and **g** the faces of the poor?" H3221
Mt 24:41 Two women *will be* **g** with a hand mill; one *G241*
Lk 17:35 Two women will be **g grain** together; one *G241*

GRIP (4) [GRIPPED, GRIPS]
Ex 15:14 anguish *will* **g** the people of Philistia. H296
Job 30:16 my life ebbs away; days of suffering **g** me. H296
Isa 13: 8 pain and anguish *will* **g** them; they will H296
Jer 13:21 *Will* not pain **g** you like that of a woman in H296

GRIPPED (4) [GRIP]
Jer 6:24 Anguish *has* **g** us, pain like that of a H2616
Jer 49:24 has turned to flee and panic *has* **g** her; H2616
Jer 50:43 Anguish *has* **g** him, pain like that of a H2616
Lk 1:12 he was startled and *was* **g with** fear. *G2158*

GRIPS (3) [GRIP]
Ps 119:53 Indignation **g** me because of the wicked H296
Isa 33:14 Zion are terrified; trembling **g** the godless: H296
Jer 8:21 I am crushed; I mourn, and horror **g** me. H2616

GRISLED (KJV) DAPPLED, SPOTTED

GROAN (21) [GROANED, GROANING, GROANS]
Ps 12: 5 the poor are plundered and the needy **g**, H651
Ps 38: 8 utterly crushed; *I* **g** in anguish of heart. H8613
Ps 102: 5 In my distress I **g** aloud and am reduced to H635
Pr 5:11 At the end of your life *you will* **g**, when H5637
Pr 29: 2 when the wicked rule, the people **g**. H634
Isa 19: 8 The fishermen *will* **g** and lament, all who H627
Isa 24: 7 the vine withers; all the merrymakers **g**. H634
Jer 4:31 a **g** as of one bearing her first child H7650
Jer 22:23 how *you will* **g** when pangs come upon you H634
Jer 51:52 throughout her land the wounded *will* **g**. H650
La 1: 4 desolate, her priests **g**, her young women H634
La 1:11 All her people **g** as they search for bread H634
Eze 21: 6 "Therefore **g**, son of man! Groan before H634
Eze 21: 6 **G** before them with broken heart and bitter H634
Eze 24:17 **G** quietly; do not mourn for the dead. H650
Eze 24:23 of your sins and **g** among yourselves. H5637
Eze 26:15 when the wounded **g** and the slaughter H650
Eze 30:24 and *he will* **g** before him like a H5543+5544
Ro 8:23 **g** inwardly as we wait eagerly for our *G5100*
2Co 5: 2 Meanwhile *we* **g**, longing to be clothed *G5100*
2Co 5: 4 are in this tent, *we* **g** and are burdened *G5100*

GROANED (2) [GROAN]
Ex 2:23 The Israelites **g** in their slavery and cried H634
Ps 77: 3 God, and *I* **g**; I meditated, and my H2159

GROANING (13) [GROAN]
Ex 2:24 God heard their **g** and he remembered his H5544
Ex 6: 5 I have heard the **g** *of* the Israelites, whom H5544
Jdg 2:18 because of their **g** under those who H5544
Job 23: 2 is bitter; his hand is heavy in spite of my **g**. H635
Ps 6: 6 I am worn out from my **g**. All night long I H635
Ps 31:10 is consumed by anguish and my years by **g**; H635
Ps 32: 3 wasted away through my **g** all day long. H8614
Isa 21: 2 I will bring to an end all the **g** she caused. H635
Jer 45: 3 I am worn out with **g** and find no rest. H635
La 1:21 "People have heard my **g**, but there is no H634
Eze 21: 7 ask you, 'Why *are* you **g**?' you shall say, H634
Ac 7:34 I have heard their **g** and have come down *G5099*
Ro 8:22 whole creation *has been* **g** as in the pains *G5367*

GROANS (7) [GROAN]
Job 3:24 my daily food; my **g** pour out like water. H8614
Job 24:12 *The* **g** of the dying *rise* from the city, and H5543
Ps 79:11 May the **g** *of* the prisoners come before you H651
Ps 102:20 to hear the **g** *of* the prisoners and release H651
La 1: 8 her naked; *she* herself **g** and turns away. H634
La 1:22 My **g** are many and my heart is faint." H635
Ro 8:26 intercedes for us *through* wordless **g**. *G5099*

GROPE (6) [GROPED]
Dt 28:29 At midday *you will* **g about** like a blind H5491
Job 5:14 daytime; at noon *they* **g** as in the night. H5491
Job 12:25 *They* **g** *in* darkness with no light; he H5491
Isa 59:10 Like the blind *we* **g along** the wall H1779
La 4:14 Now *they* **g** through the streets as if they H5675

Zep 1:17 people that *they will* **g about** like those H2143

GROPED (1) [GROPE]

Ac 13:11 over him, and *he* **g about**, seeking *G4310*

GROSS (KJV) CALLOUSED, DEEP, THICK

GROUND (309) [AGROUND, GROUNDS]

Ge 1: 9 to one place, and let **dry g** appear." H3317
Ge 1:10 God called the **dry g** "land," and the H3317
Ge 1:24 the creatures that move along the **g**, and NDT
Ge 1:25 that move along the **g** according to their H141
Ge 1:26 all the creatures that move along the **g**." H824
Ge 1:28 every living creature that moves on the **g**." H824
Ge 1:30 all the creatures that move along the **g**— H824
Ge 2: 5 earth and there was no one to work the **g**, H141
Ge 2: 6 watered the whole surface of the **g**. H141
Ge 2: 7 from the dust of the **g** and breathed into H141
Ge 2: 9 made all kinds of trees grow out of the **g**— H141
Ge 2:19 formed out of the **g** all the wild animals H141
Ge 3:17 "Cursed is the **g** because of you H141
Ge 3:19 will eat your food until you return to the **g**, H141
Ge 3:23 of Eden to work the **g** from which he had H141
Ge 4:10 brother's blood cries out to me from the **g**. H141
Ge 4:11 are under a curse and driven from the **g**, H141
Ge 4:12 When you work the **g**, it will no longer yield H141
Ge 5:29 hands caused by the **g** the LORD has cursed." H141
Ge 6: 7 the **creatures that move along the g**— H8254
Ge 6:20 that moves along the **g** will come to you to H141
Ge 7: 8 of all creatures that move along the **g**, H141
Ge 7:14 that moves along the **g** according to its H824
Ge 7:23 that move along the **g** and the birds were NDT
Ge 8: 8 had receded from the surface of the **g**. H141
Ge 8:13 saw that the surface of the **g** was dry. H141
Ge 8:17 all the creatures that move along the **g**— H824
Ge 8:19 that move along the **g** and all the birds— NDT
Ge 8:21 will I curse the **g** because of humans, H141
Ge 9: 2 on every creature that moves along the **g** H141
Ge 18: 2 tent to meet them and bowed low to the **g**. H824
Ge 19: 1 bowed down with his face to the **g**. H824
Ge 24:52 he bowed down to the **g** before the LORD. H824
Ge 33: 3 bowed down to the **g** seven times as he H824
Ge 33:19 the plot of **g** where he pitched his tent. H8441
Ge 37:10 come and bow down to the **g** before you?" H824
Ge 38: 9 his semen on the **g** to keep from providing H824
Ge 42: 6 down to him with their faces to the **g**. H824
Ge 43:26 they bowed down before him to the **g**. H824
Ge 44:11 lowered his sack to the **g** and opened it. H824
Ge 44:14 they threw themselves to the **g** before him. H824
Ge 47:23 is seed for you so you can plant the **g**. H141
Ge 48:12 bowed down with his face to the **g**. H824
Ex 3: 5 the place where you are standing is holy **g**." H141
Ex 4: 3 "Throw it on the **g**." Moses threw it on H824
Ex 4: 3 threw it on the **g** and it became a snake H824
Ex 4: 9 from the Nile and pour it on the **dry g**. H3317
Ex 4: 9 from the river will become blood on the **g**." H3318
Ex 8:16 out your staff and strike the dust of the **g**, H824
Ex 8:17 with the staff and struck the dust of the **g**, H824
Ex 8:21 even the **g** will be covered with them. H141
Ex 9:23 and lightning flashed down to the **g**. H824
Ex 10: 5 cover the face of the **g** so that it cannot be H824
Ex 10:15 They covered all the **g** until it was black H824
Ex 14:16 Israelites can go through the sea on **dry g**. H3317
Ex 14:22 Israelites went through the sea on **dry g**, H3317
Ex 14:29 Israelites went through the sea on **dry g**, H3317
Ex 15:19 walked through the sea on **dry g**. H3317
Ex 16:14 like frost on the **g** appeared on the desert H824
Ex 16:25 You will not find any of it on the **g** today. H8441
Ex 32:20 it in the fire; then *he* **g** it to powder H3221
Ex 34: 8 Moses bowed to the **g** at once and H824
Lev 5: 2 unclean **creature that moves along the g**) H9238
Lev 7:21 **creature that moves along the g**— H9238
Lev 11:21 have jointed legs for hopping on the **g**. H824
Lev 11:29 " 'Of the animals that move along the **g** H824
Lev 11:31 Of all those that move along the **g**, these are NDT
Lev 11:41 moves along the **g** is to be regarded as H824
Lev 11:42 to eat any creature that moves along the **g**, H824
Lev 11:44 by any creature that moves along the **g**. H824
Lev 11:46 every creature that moves along the **g**. H824
Lev 16:12 two handfuls of **finely g** fragrant incense H1987
Lev 20:25 bird or anything that moves along the **g**— H141
Lev 26: 4 the **g** will yield its crops and the trees H824
Lev 26:19 iron and the **g** *beneath* you like bronze. H824
Nu 11: 8 then **g** it in a hand mill or crushed it H3221
Nu 15:20 the first of your **g meal** and present it as H6881
Nu 15:21 to the LORD from the first of your **g meal**. H6881
Nu 16:31 saying all this, the **g** under them split apart H141
Dt 4:18 that moves along the **g** or any fish in the H141
Dt 9:21 it and **g** it **to powder** as fine as H3221+3512
Dt 11:17 not rain and the **g** will yield no produce H141
Dt 12:16 the blood; pour it out on the **g** like water. H824
Dt 12:24 the blood; pour it out on the **g** like water. H824
Dt 15:23 the blood; pour it out on the **g** like water. H824
Dt 22: 6 either in a tree or on the **g**, and the mother H824
Dt 28:11 of your livestock and the crops of your **g**— H141
Dt 28:23 will be bronze, the **g** beneath you iron. H824
Dt 28:56 venture to touch the **g** with the sole of her H824
Jos 3:17 middle of the Jordan and stood on **dry g**, H3000
Jos 3:17 had completed the crossing on **dry g**. H3000
Jos 4:18 their feet on the **dry g** than the waters of H3000
Jos 4:22 'Israel crossed the Jordan on **dry g**.' H3317
Jos 5:14 Joshua fell facedown to the **g** in reverence, H824
Jos 7: 6 fell facedown to the **g** before the ark of the H824
Jos 7:21 They are hidden in the **g** inside my tent H824
Jdg 4:21 the peg through his temple into the **g**, H824
Jdg 6:37 dew only on the fleece and all the **g** is dry, H824
Jdg 6:39 dry and let the **g** be covered with dew." H824
Jdg 6:40 was dry; all the **g** was covered with dew. H824
Jdg 13:20 his wife fell with their faces to the **g**. H824
Ru 2:10 she bowed down with her face to the **g**. H824
1Sa 3:19 he let none of Samuel's words fall to the **g**. H824
1Sa 4: 5 raised such a great shout that the **g** shook. H824
1Sa 5: 3 on his face on the **g** before the ark of the H824
1Sa 5: 4 on his face on the **g** before the ark of the H824
1Sa 8:12 others to plow his **g** and reap his harvest, H3045
1Sa 14:15 raiding parties—and the **g** shook. H824
1Sa 14:25 the woods, and there was honey on the **g**. H8441
1Sa 14:32 butchered them on the **g** and ate them, H824
1Sa 14:45 not a hair of his head will fall to the **g**, for H824
1Sa 17:49 forehead, and he fell facedown on the **g**. H824
1Sa 20:41 three times, with his face to the **g**. H824
1Sa 24: 8 prostrated himself with his face to the **g**. H824
1Sa 25:23 down before David with her face to the **g**. H824
1Sa 25:41 down with her face to the **g** and said, H824
1Sa 26: 7 with his spear stuck in the **g** near his head. H824
1Sa 26: 8 let me pin him to the **g** with one thrust of H824
1Sa 26:20 my blood fall to the **g** far from the presence H824
1Sa 28:14 prostrated himself with his face to the **g**. H824
1Sa 28:20 Immediately Saul fell full length on the **g** H824
1Sa 28:23 He got up from the **g** and sat on the couch H824
2Sa 1: 2 to David, he fell to the **g** to pay him honor. H824
2Sa 8: 2 lie down on the **g** and measured them H824
2Sa 12:16 spent the nights lying in sackcloth on the **g**. H824
2Sa 12:17 stood beside him to get him up from the **g**, H824
2Sa 12:20 Then David got up from the **g**. After he had H824
2Sa 13:31 tore his clothes and lay down on the **g**; and H824
2Sa 14: 4 fell with her face to the **g** to pay him honor, H824
2Sa 14:11 hair of your son's head will fall to the **g**." H824
2Sa 14:14 Like water spilled on the **g**, which cannot be H824
2Sa 14:22 fell with his face to the **g** to pay him honor, H824
2Sa 14:33 down with his face to the **g** before the king. H824
2Sa 17:12 we will fall on him as dew settles on the **g**. H141
2Sa 18:11 didn't you strike him to the **g** right there? H824
2Sa 18:28 the king with his face to the **g** and said, H824
2Sa 20:10 his intestines spilled out on the **g**. H824
2Sa 23:10 Eleazar **stood** *his* **g** and struck down H7756
2Sa 24:20 down before the king with his face to the **g**. H824
1Ki 1:23 the king and bowed with his face to the **g**. H824
1Ki 1:31 bowed down with her face to the **g**, H824
1Ki 1:40 so that the **g** shook with the sound. H824
1Ki 1:52 not a hair of his head will fall to the **g**; but H824
1Ki 18: 7 **bowed down to the g**, and H5877+6584+7156
1Ki 18:42 bent down to the **g** and put his face H824
2Ki 2: 8 the two of them crossed over on **dry g**. H3000
2Ki 2:15 meet him and bowed to the **g** before him. H824
2Ki 4:37 fell at his feet and bowed to the **g**. H824
2Ki 8:12 **dash** their little children **to the g**, and H8187
2Ki 9:10 will devour her on the **plot of g** *at* Jezreel, H2750
2Ki 9:21 at the **plot of g** *that had belonged to* H2754
2Ki 9:26 make you pay for it on this **plot of g**, H2754
2Ki 9:36 On the **plot of g** *at* Jezreel dogs will H2750
2Ki 9:37 be like dung on the **g** in the plot at H8441
2Ki 13:18 told him, "Strike the **g**." He struck it three H824
2Ki 13:19 should have struck the **g** five or six times; NDT
2Ki 23: 6 *He* **g** it to powder and scattered the dust H1990
2Ki 23:15 burned the high place and **g** it to powder, H1990
1Ch 21:21 down before David with his face to the **g**. H824
2Ch 2:10 twenty thousand cors of **g** wheat, twenty H4804
2Ch 7: 3 on the pavement with their faces to the **g**, H824
2Ch 20:18 bowed down with his face to the **g**, H824
2Ch 20:24 they saw only dead bodies lying on the **g** H824
Ne 8: 6 the LORD with their faces to the **g**. H824
Ne 9:11 so that they passed through it on **dry g** H3317
Ne 10:37 the first of our **g meal**, of our grain H6881
Job 1:20 Then he fell to the **g** in worship H824
Job 2:13 Then they sat on the **g** with him for seven H824
Job 3:16 hidden away in the **g** like a stillborn child NDT
Job 5: 6 the soil, nor does trouble sprout from the **g**. H141
Job 14: 8 may grow old in the **g** and its stump die in H824
Job 16:13 my kidneys and spills my gall on the **g**. H824
Job 18:10 A noose is hidden for him on the **g**; a trap H824
Job 30: 6 among the rocks and in holes in the **g**. H6760
Job 39:14 lays her eggs on the **g** and lets them warm H824
Job 39:24 In frenzied excitement it eats up the **g**; it H824
Ps 7: 5 my life to the **g** and make me sleep in H824
Ps 17:11 with eyes alert, to throw me to the **g**. H824
Ps 26:12 My feet stand on **level g**; in the great H4793
Ps 44:25 down to the dust; our bodies cling to the **g**. H824
Ps 73:18 Surely you place them on **slippery** *g*; you cast AIT
Ps 74: 7 They burned your sanctuary to the **g**; they H824
Ps 80: 9 *You* **cleared** *the* **g** for it, and it took root H7155
Ps 83:10 at Endor and became like dung on the **g**. H141
Ps 89:44 to his splendor and cast his throne to the **g**. H824
Ps 104:30 created, and you renew the face of the **g**. H141
Ps 107:33 a desert, flowing springs into **thirsty g**, H7536
Ps 107:35 the parched **g** into flowing springs; H824
Ps 143: 3 he crushes me to the **g**; he makes me H824
Ps 143:10 may your good Spirit lead me on level **g**. H824
Ps 146: 4 they return to the **g**; on that very day their H141
Ps 147: 6 the humble but casts the wicked to the **g**. H824
Pr 24:31 the **g** was covered with weeds H7156
Ecc 12: 7 the dust returns to the **g** it came from H824
Isa 2:10 hide in the **g** from the fearful presence of H6760
Isa 2:19 to holes in the **g** from the fearful H6760
Isa 3:26 mourn; destitute, she will sit on the **g**. H824
Isa 21: 9 images of its gods lie shattered on the **g**!' H824
Isa 25:12 he will bring them down to the **g**, to the H824
Isa 26: 5 he levels it to the **g** and casts it down to H824
Isa 28: 2 he will throw it forcefully to the **g**. H824
Isa 28:28 Grain *must* **be g** to make bread; so one H1990
Isa 29: 4 you will speak from the **g**; your speech will H824
Isa 30:23 you rain for the seed you sow in the **g**, H141
Isa 35: 7 the **thirsty g** bubbling springs. H7536
Isa 40: 4 the **rough g** shall become level H6815
Isa 40:24 no sooner do they take root in the **g**, than H824
Isa 41:18 of water, and the parched **g** into springs. H824
Isa 44: 3 streams on the **dry g**; I will pour out H3317
Isa 45: 9 potsherds among the potsherds on the **g**. H141
Isa 47: 1 Babylon; sit on the **g** without a throne H824
Isa 49:23 down before you with their faces to the **g**; H824
Isa 51:23 And you made your back like the **g**, like a H824
Isa 53: 2 a tender shoot, and like a root out of dry **g**. H824
Isa 63: 6 drunk and poured their blood on the **g**." H824
Jer 4: 3 "Break up your **unplowed g** and do not H5776
Jer 8: 2 but will be like dung lying on the **g**. H141
Jer 14: 4 The **g** is cracked because there is no rain in H141
Jer 16: 4 buried but will be like dung lying on the **g**. H141
Jer 25:33 but will be like dung lying on the **g**. H141
Jer 46:21 *they will* not **stand** *their* **g**, for the H6641
Jer 48:18 from your glory and sit on the **parched g**, H7533
La 2: 2 its princes down to the **g** in dishonor. H824
La 2: 9 Her gates have sunk into the **g**; their bars H824
La 2:10 of Daughter Zion sit on the **g** in silence; H824
La 2:10 have bowed their heads to the **g**. H824
La 2:11 is poured out on the **g** because my people H824
Eze 1:15 saw a wheel on the **g** beside each creature H824
Eze 1:19 when the living creatures rose from the **g**, H824
Eze 1:21 when the creatures rose from the **g** H824
Eze 10:16 spread their wings to rise from the **g**, H824
Eze 10:19 spread their wings and rose from the **g**, H824
Eze 13:14 will level it to the **g** so that its foundation H824
Eze 19:12 it was uprooted in fury and thrown to the **g**. H824
Eze 24: 7 she did not pour it on the **g**, where the dust H824
Eze 26:11 your strong pillars will fall to the **g**. H824
Eze 26:16 they will sit on the **g**, trembling every H824
Eze 28:18 you to ashes on the **g** in the sight of all H824
Eze 34:27 their fruit and the **g** will yield its crops; H824
Eze 38:20 every creature that moves along the **g**, and H141
Eze 38:20 crumble and every wall will fall to the **g**. H824
Eze 39:14 will bury any bodies that are lying on the **g**. H824
Eze 43:14 the gutter on the **g** up to the lower ledge H824
Eze 44:30 portion of your **g meal** so that a blessing H6881
Da 4:15 remain in the **g**, in the grass of the A10075
Da 4:23 the field, while its roots remain in the **g**. A10075
Da 7: 4 was lifted from the **g** so that it stood on A10075
Da 8: 5 the whole earth without touching the **g**. H824
Da 8: 7 goat knocked it to the **g** and trampled on it, H824
Da 8:12 and truth was thrown to the **g**. H824
Da 8:18 was in a deep sleep, with my face to the **g**. H824
Da 10: 9 I fell into a deep sleep, my face to the **g**. H824
Da 10:15 my face toward the **g** and was speechless. H824
Hos 2:18 the creatures that move along the **g**. H141
Hos 10:11 and Jacob *must* **break up the g**. H8440
Hos 10:12 break up your **unplowed g**; for it is H5776
Hos 10:14 mothers **were dashed to the g** with their H8187
Hos 13:16 their little ones *will* **be dashed to the g** H8187
Joel 1:10 are ruined, the **g** is dried up; the grain H141
Am 2: 7 as on the dust of the **g** and deny justice to H824
Am 2:15 The archer *will* not **stand** *his* **g**, the H6641
Am 3: 5 to a trap on the **g** when no bait is there H824
Am 3: 5 spring up from the **g** if it has not caught H141
Am 3:14 of the altar will be cut off and fall to the **g**. H824
Am 5: 7 bitterness and cast righteousness to the **g**. H824
Am 9: 9 and not a pebble will reach the **g**. H824
Ob 3 'Who can bring me down to the **g**?' H824
Mic 7:17 a snake, like creatures that crawl on the **g**. H824
Hag 1:11 oil and everything else the **g** produces, H141
Zec 4: 7 Zerubbabel you will become **level g**. H4793
Zec 8:12 yield its fruit, the **g** will produce its crops H824
Mt 10:29 will fall to the **g** outside your Father's *G1178*
Mt 13:20 seed falling on **rocky g** refers to someone *G4378*
Mt 15:35 He told the crowd to sit down on the **g**. *G1178*
Mt 17: 6 they fell **facedown to the g** *G2093+4725*
Mt 25:18 dug a hole *in* the **g** and hid his master's *G1178*
Mt 25:25 went out and hid your gold in the **g**. *G1178*
Mt 26:39 he fell **with** his **face to the g** and *G2093+4725*
Mk 4:26 A man scatters seed on the **g**. *G1178*
Mk 8: 6 He told the crowd to sit down on the **g**. *G1178*
Mk 9:18 it seizes him, *it* **throws** him **to the g**. *G4838*
Mk 9:20 He fell to the **g** and rolled around *G1178*
Mk 14:35 he fell to the **g** and prayed that if possible *G1178*
Lk 5:12 he fell **with** his **face to the g** and *G2093+4725*
Lk 6:49 a house on the **g** without a foundation *G1178*
Lk 8: 6 Some fell on **rocky g**, and when it came up *G4376*
Lk 8:13 Those on the **rocky g** are the ones who *G4376*
Lk 9:42 the demon **threw** him **to the g** in a *G4838*
Lk 12:16 "The **g** of a certain rich man yielded an *G6001*
Lk 19:44 *They will* **dash** you **to the g**, you and the *G1610*
Lk 22:44 was like drops of blood falling to the **g**. *G1178*
Lk 24: 5 bowed down with their faces to the **g**, *G1178*
Jn 4: 5 near the **plot of g** Jacob had given to his *G6005*
Jn 8: 6 started to write on the **g** with his finger. *G1178*
Jn 8: 8 he stooped down and wrote on the **g**. *G1178*
Jn 9: 6 he spit **on the g**, made some mud *G5912*
Jn 12:24 a kernel of wheat falls to the **g** and dies, *G1178*
Jn 18: 6 they drew back and fell *to* the **g**. *G5912*
Ac 7: 5 not even enough **g** to set his foot on. NDT

Ac 7:33 place where you are standing is holy g. *G1178*
Ac 9: 4 He fell to the g and heard a voice say to *G1178*
Ac 9: 8 Saul got up from the g, but when he *G1178*
Ac 13:28 Though they found no **proper g** for a death *G162*
Ac 20: 9 he fell **to the g** from the third story and *G3004*
Ac 22: 7 I fell to the g and heard a voice say to me *G1611*
Ac 26:14 We all fell to the g, and I heard a voice *G1178*
2Co 11:12 in order to cut the g from under those who *G929*
Eph 6:13 you may be able *to* **stand** your g, and after *G468*
Heb 11:38 living in caves and in holes *in* the g. *G1178*

GROUNDS (5) [GROUND]
2Ki 11:16 the horses enter the **palace g**. H1074+4889
2Ch 23:15 of the Horse Gate on the **palace g**, H1074+4889
Da 6: 4 tried to find **g for charges** against Daniel A10544
Lk 23:22 in him no **g for the death penalty**. *G165+2505*
Jn 8:59 himself, slipping away from the **temple g**. *G2639*

GROUP (25) [GROUPS, REGROUPED]
Ge 32: 8 "If Esau comes and attacks one g, the H4722
Ge 32: 8 one group, the g that is left may escape." H4722
Ge 48:19 descendants will become a g *of* nations." H4850
Nu 16: 3 *They* **came as a g** to oppose Moses and H7735
Nu 26:54 To a **larger** *g* give a larger inheritance, and to AIT
Nu 26:54 to a **smaller** *g* a smaller one; each AIT
Nu 26:55 What each **g** inherits will be according to NDT
Nu 33:54 To a **larger** *g* give a larger inheritance, and AIT
Nu 33:54 to a **smaller** *g* a smaller one. AIT
1Sa 19:20 But when they saw a **g** *of* prophets H4272
2Sa 2:13 **One g** sat down on one side of the pool H465S
2Sa 2:13 of the pool and **one g** on the other side. H465S
2Sa 2:25 themselves into a **g** and took their stand on H99
2Ki 17:29 **each national g** made its own gods H1580+1580
2Ch 32: 4 a large **g of people** who blocked all H6639
2Ch 35: 5 holy place with a **g** of Levites H2755+1074+3
Da 6: 6 satraps **went as a g** to the king and A10656
Da 6:11 Then these men **went as a g** and found A10656
Da 6:15 Then the men **went as a g** to King A10656
Jn 8: 3 They made her stand before the g *G1877+3545*
Ac 1:15 a g numbering about a hundred *G4063+3950*
Ac 6: 5 This proposal pleased the whole g. *G4436*
Ac 17:18 *A* g of Epicurean and Stoic philosophers *G5516*
Gal 2:12 who belonged to the **circumcision** g. *G4364*
Titus 1:10 especially those of the **circumcision** g. *G4364*

GROUPS (7) [GROUP]
Ge 32: 7 the people who were with him into two **g**, H4722
Nu 26:56 by lot among the larger and smaller g." NDT
Ezr 6:18 the Levites in their g for the service of A10412
Mk 6:39 people sit down **in g** on the green *G5235+5235*
Mk 6:40 So they sat down **in g** of hundreds *G4555+4555*
Lk 9:14 them sit down *in g of* about fifty each." *G3112*
Eph 2:14 who has made the **two** g one and has AIT

GROVE (2) [GROVES]
Ex 23:11 same with your vineyard and your **olive** g. H2339
SS 6:11 I went down to the g *of* nut trees to look H1708

GROVES (8) [GROVE]
Dt 6:11 vineyards and **olive** g you did not H2339
Jos 24:13 vineyards and **olive** g that you did not H2339
Jdg 15: 5 together with the vineyards and **olive** g. H2339
1Sa 8:14 vineyards and **olive** g and give them to H2339
2Ki 5:26 accept clothes—or **olive** g and vineyards H2339
Ne 5:11 vineyards, **olive** g and houses, and also H2339
Ne 9:25 **olive** g and fruit trees in abundance. H2339
Ecc 2: 6 reservoirs to water g *of* flourishing trees. H3623

GROW (71) [FULL-GROWN, GREW, GROWERS, GROWING, GROWN, GROWS, GROWTH, OVERGROWN]
Ge 2: 9 LORD God **made** all kinds of trees g out of H7541
Ge 26:13 wealth continued *to* g until he became H2143
Ge 27:40 But when *you* g **restless**, you will throw his AIT
Nu 6: 5 *they must let* their hair **g long**. H1540
Nu 24:18 will be conquered, but Israel *will* g strong. H6913
Dt 8:13 herds and flocks **g large** and your silver H8049
Jdg 16:22 on his head began to **g** again after it had H7541
1Sa 2:26 the boy Samuel **continued to g** in stature H2143
Ezr 4:22 Why *let* this threat **g**, to the detriment of A10677
Job 8:11 *Can* papyrus **g tall** where there is no H1448
Job 8:19 and from the soil other plants **g**. H7541
Job 14: 8 Its roots *may* **g old** in the ground and its H2416
Job 17: 9 *those with* clean hands *will* **g stronger** H601+3578
Job 31:16 poor or *let* the eyes of the widow **g weary**, H3983
Job 39: 4 young thrive and **g strong** in the wilds; H2730
Ps 6: 7 My eyes *g* **weak** with sorrow; they fail AIT
Ps 31: 9 in distress; my eyes *g* **weak** with sorrow, my AIT
Ps 31:10 of my affliction, and my bones *g* **weak**. AIT
Ps 34:10 The lions *may g* **weak** and hungry, but those AIT
Ps 49:16 Do not be overawed when others *g* **rich** AIT
Ps 92:12 *they will* g like a cedar of Lebanon; H8436
Ps 104:14 *He* **makes** grass g for the cattle, and H7541
Ps 129: 6 on the roof, which withers before *it can* g; H8990
Ps 132:17 "Here *I will* **make** a horn g for David and H7541
Ps 147: 8 with rain and **makes** grass g *on* the hills. H7541
Pr 13:11 gathers money little by little **makes** it g. H8049
Pr 20:13 Do not love sleep or *you will* **g poor**; stay H3769
Ecc 12: 2 the light and the moon and the stars **g dark**, AIT
Ecc 12: 3 those looking through the windows **g dim**; AIT
Ecc 12: 4 the sound of birds, but all their songs *g* **faint**; AIT
Isa 5: 6 briers and thorns *will* g there. H6590
Isa 17:11 them out, *you* **make** them g, and on the H8451
Isa 29:22 no longer *will* their faces **g pale**. H2578
Isa 35: 7 grass and reeds and papyrus will g. NDT
Isa 40:28 *He will* not *g* **tired** or weary, and his AIT
Isa 40:30 Even youths *g* **tired** and weary, and young AIT
Isa 40:31 they will run and not *g* **weary**, they will walk AIT
Isa 44:14 *He* **let** it g among the trees of the forest, or H599
Isa 44:14 planted a pine, and the rain **made** it g. H1540
Isa 55:13 of the thornbush *will* g the juniper, H6590
Isa 55:13 instead of briers the myrtle *will* g. H6590
Isa 61:11 come up and a garden **causes** seeds to g, H7541
Jer 4:28 will mourn and the heavens above *g* **dark**, AIT
Jer 6: 4 the shadows of evening **g long**. H5742
Jer 12: 2 have taken root; *they* g and bear fruit. H2143
Jer 15: 9 mother of seven *will* **g faint** and breathe her AIT
La 3: 4 *He has* **made** my skin and my flesh **g old** H1162
La 5:17 because of these things our eyes **g dim** AIT
Eze 16: 7 I made you g like a plant of the field. H8047
Eze 17:24 the tall tree and **make** the low tree **g tall**. H1467
Eze 29:21 "On that day *I will* **make** a horn g for the H7541
Eze 31: 4 deep springs **made** it **g tall**; their streams H8123
Eze 44:20 shave their heads or **let** their hair g long, H8938
Eze 47:12 trees of all kinds *will* g on both banks of H6590
Hos 10: 8 thistles *will* **g up** and cover their H6590
Hos 14: 6 his young shoots *will* g. His splendor will H2143
Jnh 4: 6 plant and **made** it **g up** over Jonah to H6590
Jnh 4:10 though you did not tend it or **make** it g. H1540
Zec 8:12 "The seed will **g well**, the vine will yield H8934
Mt 6:28 See how the flowers of the field **g**. They do *G889*
Mt 13:30 Let both **g together** until the harvest. *G5277*
Mt 24:12 wickedness, the love of most *will* **g cold**, *G6038*
Lk 12:27 "Consider how the wild flowers **g**. They do *G889*
1Co 3: 6 watered it, but God *has been* **making** it g. *G889*
1Co 3: 7 only God, who **makes** things g. *G889*
2Co 10:15 hope is *that, as* your faith *continues to* g, *G889*
Eph 4:15 *we will* **g to become** in every respect the **mature** *G889*
Col 2:19 sinews, grows as God **causes** it **to g**. *G890*
Heb 12: 3 so that *you will* not *g* **weary** and lose heart. AIT
1Pe 2: 2 so that by it *you may* **g up** in your salvation *G889*
2Pe 3:18 But g in the grace and knowledge of our *G889*

GROWERS (1) [GROW]
Joel 1:11 you **vine** g; grieve for the wheat and H4144

GROWING (14) [GROW]
Ge 41: 5 good, *were* g on a single stalk. H6590
Ge 41:22 full and good, g on a single stalk. H6590
Ex 9:22 on everything **g** in the fields of Egypt." H6912
Ex 9:25 beat down everything **g** *in* the fields and H6912
Ex 10: 5 including every tree that *is* **g** in your fields. H7541
Ex 10:12 devour everything **g** *in* the fields, H6912
Ex 10:15 everything **g** *in* the fields and the fruit on H6912
Dt 29:23 nothing sprouting, no vegetation **g** on it. H6590
Job 8:12 While still g and uncut, they wither more H4
Job 21: 7 **g old** and increasing in power? H6980
Lk 13: 6 "A man had a fig tree **g** in his vineyard *G5885*
Col 1: 6 is bearing fruit and **g** throughout the whole *G889*
Col 1:10 good work, **g** in the knowledge of God, *G889*
2Th 1: 3 because your faith *is* **g more and more** *G5647*

GROWL (6) [GROWLED, GROWLS]
Job 4:10 The lions may roar and g, yet the teeth of H7754
Ps 83: 2 See how your enemies g, how your foes H2159
Isa 5:29 *they* g as they seize their prey and carry it H5637
Isa 59:11 We all g like bears; we moan mournfully H2159
Jer 51:38 roar like young lions, *they* g like lion cubs. H5849
Am 3: 4 *Does* it **g** in its den when it has H5989+7754

GROWLED (1) [GROWL]
Jer 2:15 have roared; *they have* g at him. H5989+7754

GROWLS (1) [GROWL]
Isa 31: 4 "As a lion g, a great lion over its prey H2047

GROWN (22) [GROW]
Ge 38:14 *though* Shelah *had* now **g up**, she H1540
Ge 41:48 each city he put the **food** *g in* the fields AIT
Ex 2:11 after Moses *had* **g up**, he went out to H1540
Lev 13:37 if black hair *has* g in it, the affected H7541
Jos 13: 1 When Joshua *had* **g old** H2416+995+928+2021+3427
Jdg 11: 2 when they *were* **g up**, they drove H1540
2Sa 10: 5 "Stay at Jericho till your beards *have* **g** H7541
1Ki 12: 8 young men who *had* **g up** with him and H1540
1Ki 12:10 young men who *had* **g up** with him H1540
1Ch 19: 5 "Stay at Jericho till your beards *have* **g** H7541
2Ch 10: 8 young men who *had* **g up** with him and H1540
2Ch 10:10 young men who *had* **g up** with him H1540
Job 17: 7 My eyes *have* **g dim** with grief; my whole H3908
Ps 102: T person *who has* **g weak** and pours out a AIT
SS 8: 8 a little sister, and her breasts are not yet g. NDT
Isa 10:27 will be broken because you have g so fat. NDT
Jer 5:28 and *have* **g fat** and sleek. Their evil deeds AIT
Eze 16: 7 breasts had formed and your hair *had* **g**, H7541
Eze 28: 5 of your wealth your heart *has* **g proud**. AIT
Da 4:22 your greatness *has* g until it reaches the A10648
Heb 11:24 Moses, *when he had* **g up**, refused *G3489+1181*
Rev 2: 3 my name, and *have* not **g weary**. AIT

GROWS (21) [GROW]
Ge 38:11 household until my son Shelah **g up**." H1540
Lev 25: 5 Do not reap **what g of itself** or harvest the H6206
Lev 25:11 do not reap **what g of itself** or harvest the H6206
1Ki 4:33 Lebanon to the hyssop that **g out** of walls. H3655
2Ki 19:26 on the roof, scorched before *it* **g up**. H7850
2Ki 19:29 "This year you will eat **what g by itself** H6206
Job 30:30 My skin **g black** and peels; my body burns H8837
Ps 61: 2 I call as my heart *g* **faint**; lead me to the rock AIT
Ps 142: 3 When my spirit *g* **faint** within me, it is you AIT
Ps 143: 4 So my spirit *g* **faint** within me; my heart AIT
Isa 5:27 Not one of them g tired or stumbles, not NDT
Isa 37:27 on the roof, scorched before *it* **g up**. H7850
Isa 37:30 "This year you will eat **what g by itself** H6206
Isa 44:12 his strength; he drinks no water and *g* **faint**. AIT
Na 2:10 bodies tremble, every face **g pale**. H6999+7695
Mt 13:32 all seeds, yet when *it* g, it is the largest of *G889*
Mk 4:27 the seed sprouts and g, though he does *G3602*
Mk 4:32 *it* g and becomes the largest of all garden *G326*
Eph 4:16 **g** and builds itself up in love *G890+4472*
Col 2:19 sinews, **g** as God causes it to grow. *G889*
Heb 12:15 that no bitter root **g** up to cause trouble *G5886*

GROWTH (3) [GROW, UNDERGROWTH]
Pr 27:25 is removed and **new g** appears and the H2013
SS 6:11 of nut trees to look at the **new g** *in* the valley, H4
Eze 17: 9 All its new **g** will wither. It will H7542

GRUDGE (4) [GRUDGING, GRUDGINGLY]
Ge 27:41 Esau **held a g against** Jacob because of H8475
Ge 50:15 if Joseph **holds a g against** us and pays H8475
Lev 19:18 revenge or **bear a g against** anyone H5757
Mk 6:19 So Herodias **nursed a g against** John and *G1923*

GRUDGING (1) [GRUDGE]
Dt 15:10 to them and do so without a g heart; H8317

GRUDGINGLY (1) [GRUDGE]
2Co 9: 5 as a generous gift, not as **one g given**. *G4432*

GRUMBLE (8) [GRUMBLED, GRUMBLERS, GRUMBLING]
Ex 16: 7 that *you should* g against us? H4296
Nu 14:27 long *will* this wicked community **g** against H4296
Nu 14:36 and **made** the whole community **g** H4296
Nu 16:11 is Aaron that *you should* g against him?" H4296
Mt 20:11 *they began to* g against the landowner. *G1197*
Jn 6:41 the Jews there *began to* g about him *G1197*
1Co 10:10 And *do* not g, as some of them did—and *G1197*
Jas 5: 9 Don't g against one another, brothers and *G5100*

GRUMBLED (9) [GRUMBLE]
Ex 15:24 So the people g against Moses, saying H4296
Ex 16: 2 whole community g against Moses and H4296
Ex 17: 3 water there, and they g against Moses. H4296
Nu 14: 2 All the Israelites g against Moses and H4296
Nu 14:29 in the census and who *has* g against me. H4296
Nu 16:41 Israelite community g against Moses and H4296
Dt 1:27 *You* g in your tents and said, "The LORD H8087
Jos 9:18 The whole assembly g against the H4296
Ps 106:25 *They* g in their tents and did not obey the H8087

GRUMBLERS (1) [GRUMBLE]
Jude 16 These people are g and faultfinders; they *G1199*

GRUMBLING (12) [GRUMBLE]
Ex 16: 7 because he has heard your **g** against him. H9442
Ex 16: 8 he has heard your **g** against him. H9442+4296
Ex 16: 8 You are not **g** against us, but against the H9442
Ex 16: 9 before the LORD, for he has heard your **g**. H9442
Ex 16:12 "I have heard the g *of* the Israelites. H9442
Nu 14:27 heard the complaints of these **g** Israelites. H4296
Nu 17: 5 this **constant g** against you *by* the H9442+4296
Nu 17:10 This will put an end to their **g** against me H9442
Jn 6:43 "Stop **g** among yourselves," Jesus *G1197*
Jn 6:61 Aware that his disciples *were* **g** about this, *G1197*
Php 2:14 Do everything without **g** or arguing, *G1198*
1Pe 4: 9 Offer hospitality to one another without **g**. *G1198*

GUARANTEE (1) [GUARANTEED, GUARANTEEING, GUARANTOR]
Ge 43: 9 *I* myself *will* **g** his **safety**; you can hold me H6842

GUARANTEED (2) [GUARANTEE]
Ge 44:32 Your servant **g** the boy's **safety** to my father H6842
Ro 4:16 by grace and may be **g** to all Abraham's *G1010*

GUARANTEEING (3) [GUARANTEE]
2Co 1:22 our hearts *as* a **deposit**, **g what is to come**. *G775*
2Co 5: 5 the Spirit *as* a **deposit**, **g what is to come**. *G775*
Eph 1:14 who is a **deposit g** our inheritance until the *G775*

GUARANTOR (1) [GUARANTEE]
Heb 7:22 has become the **g** of a better covenant *G1583*

GUARD (132) [BODYGUARD, GUARDED, GUARDIAN, GUARDIAN-REDEEMER, GUARDIAN-REDEEMERS, GUARDIANS, GUARDING, GUARDROOM, GUARDS, SAFEGUARD]
Ge 3:24 back and forth to **g** the way to the tree of H9068
Ge 37:36 Pharaoh's officials, the captain of the **g**. H3184
Ge 39: 1 the captain of the **g**, bought him from the H3184
Ge 40: 3 in the house of the captain of the **g**, H3184
Ge 40: 4 The captain of the **g** assigned them to H3184
Ge 41:10 baker in the house of the captain of the **g**. H3184
Ge 41:12 with us, a servant of the captain of the **g**. H3184
Ex 23:20 ahead of you to **g** you along the way and H9068

Nu 10:25 as the **rear** g for all the units, the H665
Jos 6: 7 with an **armed** g going ahead of the ark H2741
Jos 6: 9 The **armed** g marched ahead of the priests H2741
Jos 6: 9 trumpets, and the **rear** g followed the ark. H665
Jos 6:13 of them and the **rear** g followed the ark of H665
Jos 10:18 and post some men there to g it. H9068
Jdg 7:19 just after they had changed the g. H9068
1Sa 2: 9 *He will* g the feet of his faithful servants H9068
1Sa 7: 1 Eleazar his son to g the ark of the LORD. H9068
1Sa 19: 2 *Be* **on** *your* g tomorrow morning; go into H9068
1Sa 26:15 Why didn't *you* g your lord the king H9068
1Sa 26:16 because *you did* not g your master H9068
2Sa 16: 6 troops and the **special** g were on David's H1475
2Sa 20: 3 palace and put them in a house **under** g. H5466
2Sa 20:10 Amasa *was* not **on** *his* g against the H9068
1Ki 1: 8 Rei and David's **special** g did not join H1475
1Ki 1:10 Benaiah or the **special** g or his brother H1475
1Ki 14:27 the commanders of the g on duty at the H8132
1Ki 20:39 me with a captive and said, 'G this man. H9068
2Ki 6:10 so that *he was* **on** *his* g in such places. H9068
2Ki 11: 6 a third at the gate behind the g, who H8132
2Ki 11: 7 duty *are* all *to* g the temple H9068+5466
2Ki 25: 8 commander of the **imperial** g, H3184
2Ki 25:10 of the **imperial** g broke down the H3184
2Ki 25:11 the commander of the g carried into exile H3184
2Ki 25:15 of the **imperial** g took away the H3184
2Ki 25:18 The commander of the g took as prisoners H3184
1Ch 9:27 because they had to g it; and they had H5466
1Ch 26:16 **G** was alongside of guard H5464
1Ch 26:16 Guard was alongside of g: H5464
2Ch 12:10 the commanders of the g on duty at the H8132
Ezr 8:29 **G** them carefully until you weigh them out H9193
Ne 3:25 the upper palace near the court of the g. H4766
Ne 3:29 of Shekaniah, the g *at* the East Gate H9068
Ne 4: 9 our God and posted a g day and night to H5464
Ne 12:39 At the Gate of the **G** they stopped. H4766
Ne 13:22 go and g the gates in order to H9068
Job 7:12 the deep, that you put me **under** g? H5464+6584
Ps 25:20 **G** my life and rescue me; do not let me H9068
Ps 86: 2 **G** my life, for I am faithful to you; save H9068
Ps 91:11 concerning you to g you in all your ways; H9068
Ps 141: 3 Set a g over my mouth, LORD; keep watch H9072
Pr 2:11 protect you, and understanding *will* g you. H5915
Pr 4:13 do not let it go; g it **well**, for it is your life. H5915
Pr 4:23 Above all else, g your heart, for H5915
Pr 7: 2 g my teachings as the apple of your eye. NDT
Pr 13: 3 *Those who* g their lips preserve their lives H5915
Pr 16:17 *those who* g their ways preserve their lives H5915
Pr 21:23 *Those who* g their mouths and their H9068
Ecc 5: 1 G your steps when you go to the house of H9068
Isa 27: 3 *I* g it day and night so that no one may H5915
Isa 52:12 the God of Israel will be your **rear** g. H665
Isa 58: 8 the glory of the LORD *will be* your **rear** g. H665
Jer 32: 2 the courtyard of the g in the royal palace H4766
Jer 32: 8 to me in the courtyard of the g and said, H4766
Jer 32:12 the Jews sitting in the courtyard of the g. H4766
Jer 33: 1 still confined in the courtyard of the g, H4766
Jer 37:13 the captain of the g, whose name was H7215
Jer 37:21 the courtyard of the g and given a loaf of H4766
Jer 37:21 remained in the courtyard of the g. H4766
Jer 38: 6 which was in the courtyard of the g. H4766
Jer 38:13 remained in the courtyard of the g. H4766
Jer 38:28 the courtyard of the g until the day H4766
Jer 39: 9 commander of the **imperial** g carried into H3184
Jer 39:10 the commander of the g left behind in the H3184
Jer 39:11 commander of the **imperial** g: H3184
Jer 39:13 So Nebuzaradan the commander of the g H3184
Jer 39:14 taken out of the courtyard of the g. H4766
Jer 39:15 been confined in the courtyard of the g, H4766
Jer 40: 1 of the **imperial** g had released H3184
Jer 40: 2 the commander of the g found Jeremiah, H3184
Jer 41:10 of the **imperial** g had appointed H3184
Jer 43: 6 of the **imperial** g had left with H3184
Jer 51:12 Reinforce the g, station the watchmen H5464
Jer 52:12 commander of the **imperial** g, H3184
Jer 52:14 under the commander of the **imperial** g H3184
Jer 52:15 the commander of the g carried into exile H3184
Jer 52:19 of the **imperial** g took away the H3184
Jer 52:24 The commander of the g took as prisoners H3184
Jer 52:30 the commander of the **imperial** g. H3184
Eze 40:45 is for the priests *who* g the temple, H9068+5466
Eze 40:46 is for the priests *who* g the altar. H9068+5466
Eze 44:14 appoint them **to** g the temple for H9068+5466
Da 1:11 then said to the g whom the chief official H4915
Da 1:16 So the g took away their choice food and H4915
Da 2:14 the commander of the king's g, had A10295
Mic 7: 5 lies in your embrace g the words of your H9068
Na 2: 1 **G** the fortress, watch the road, brace H5915
Zec 9: 8 at my temple to g it against marauding H5166
Mal 2:15 So *be* **on** your g, and do not H9068+928+8120
Mal 2:16 So *be* **on** *your* g, and do not H9068+928+8120
Mt 10:17 *Be* **on** *your* g; you will be handed over to *G4668*
Mt 16: 6 "*Be* **on** *your* g against the yeast of the *G4668*
Mt 16:11 But *be* **on** *your* g against the yeast of the *G4668*
Mt 16:12 not telling them **to** g against the yeast *G4668*
Mt 27:65 "Take a g," Pilate answered. "Go, make *G3184*
Mt 27:66 a seal on the stone and posting the g. *G3184*
Mk 13: 9 "You *must be* **on** your g. You will be *G1063*
Mk 13:23 So *be* **on** your g; I have told you everything *G1063*
Mk 13:33 *Be* **on** g! Be alert! You do not know when *G1063*
Mk 14:44 arrest him and lead him away **under** g." *G857*
Lk 4:10 angels concerning you *to* g you **carefully**; *G1428*
Lk 8:29 chained hand and foot and **kept under** g, *G5875*
Lk 12: 1 "*Be* **on** *your* g against the yeast of the *G4668*
Lk 12:15 *Be on your* g against all kinds of greed *G5875*
Lk 22: 4 the **officers of the temple** g and *G5130*
Lk 22:52 the **officers of** the temple g, and the *G5130*
Ac 4: 1 the **captain of** the temple g and the *G5130*
Ac 5:24 the **captain of** the temple g and the chief *G5130*
Ac 12: 6 sentries stood g at the entrance. *G5871*
Ac 16:23 was commanded *to* g them carefully. *G5498*
Ac 20:31 So *be* **on** *your* g! Remember that for three *G1213*
Ac 23:35 he ordered *that* Paul *be* **kept under** g in *G5875*
Ac 24:23 centurion *to* **keep** Paul **under** g but to give *G5498*
Ac 28:16 to live by himself, with a soldier *to* g him. *G5875*
1Co 16:13 *Be* **on** *your* g; stand firm in the faith; be *G1213*
Php 1:13 the whole **palace** g and to everyone *G4550*
Php 4: 7 *will* g your hearts and your minds in Christ *G5864*
1Ti 6:20 **g** what has been entrusted to your care. *G5875*
2Ti 1:12 that he is able *to* g what I have entrusted *G5875*
2Ti 1:14 **G** the good deposit that was entrusted to *G5875*
2Ti 1:14 g it with the help of the Holy Spirit who lives NDT
2Ti 4:15 You too *should be* **on** *your* g against him *G5875*
2Pe 3:17 *be* **on** *your* g so that you may not be *G5875*

GUARDED (10) [GUARD]

Dt 32:10 him; *he* g him as the apple of his eye, H5915
Dt 33: 9 over your word and g your covenant. H5915
2Ki 12: 9 The priests *who* g the entrance put into H9068
Ne 12:25 gatekeepers *who* g the storerooms H9068+5464
Est 2:21 of the king's officers *who* g the doorway, H9068
Est 6: 2 of the king's officers *who* g the doorway, H9068
Eze 27:11 of Arvad and Helek g your walls on every H6584
Eze 44:15 of Zadok and who g my sanctuary H9068+5466
Ac 12: 4 handing him over *to be* g by four squads *G5875*
2Co 11:32 *had* the city of the Damascenes g in *G5864*

GUARDIAN (5) [GUARD]

Eze 28:14 You were anointed as a g cherub, for so I H6114
Eze 28:16 I expelled you, g cherub, from among H6114
Ac 19:35 is the **g of the temple** of the great *G3753*
Gal 3:24 So the law was our g until Christ came that *G4080*
Gal 3:25 has come, we are no longer under a g. *G4080*

GUARDIAN-REDEEMER (8) [GUARD, REDEEM]

Ru 3: 9 over me, since you *are a* **g of** our **family**." H1457
Ru 3:12 it is true that *I am a* **g of** our **family**, H1457
Ru 3:13 if *he wants to* **do his duty as** your g, H1457
Ru 4: 1 there just as the g he had mentioned H1457
Ru 4: 3 Then he said to the g, "Naomi, who has H1457
Ru 4: 6 the g said, "Then I cannot redeem H1457
Ru 4: 8 So the g said to Boaz, "Buy it yourself." H1457
Ru 4:14 who this day has not left you without a g. H1457

GUARDIAN-REDEEMERS (1) [GUARD, REDEEM]

Ru 2:20 is our close relative; he is one of our g." H1457

GUARDIANS (4) [GUARD]

2Ki 10: 1 the elders and to the **g of** Ahab's **children**. H587
2Ki 10: 5 the elders and the g sent this message to H587
1Co 4:15 Even if you had ten thousand g in Christ *G4080*
Gal 4: 2 The heir is subject to g and trustees until *G2208*

GUARDING (9) [GUARD]

2Ki 11: 5 a third of you g the royal palace, H9068+5466
2Ki 11: 6 guard, *who* take turns g the temple H9068+5466
1Ch 9:19 were responsible for g the thresholds of H9068
1Ch 9:19 been responsible for g the entrance to the H9068
1Ch 9:23 were in charge of g the gates of the H5466
Jer 4:17 They surround her like *men* g a field H9068
Mt 27:54 those with him *who were* g Jesus saw the *G5498*
Lk 22:63 The men who *were* g Jesus began *G5309*
Ac 22:20 my approval and g the clothes of those *G5875*

GUARDROOM (2) [GUARD]

1Ki 14:28 they returned them to the g. H9288+8132
2Ch 12:11 they returned them to the g. H9288+8132

GUARDS (35) [GUARD]

1Sa 22:17 Then the king ordered the g at his side H8132
1Ki 14:28 LORD's temple, the g bore the shields, and H8132
2Ki 10:25 offering, he ordered the g and officers: H8132
2Ki 10:25 The g and officers threw the bodies out H8132
2Ki 11: 4 the Carites and the g and had them H8132
2Ki 11:11 The g, each with weapon in hand H8132
2Ki 11:13 the noise made by the g and the people, H8132
2Ki 11:18 the priest posted g at the temple of the H7213
2Ki 11:19 the g and all the people of the land H8132
2Ki 11:19 entering by way of the gate of the g. H8132
2Ch 12:11 LORD's temple, the g went with him H8132
Ne 4:22 they can serve us as g by night and as H5464
Ne 4:23 my men nor the g with me took off H408+5464
Ne 7: 3 Also appoint residents of Jerusalem as g H5466
Ps 97:10 for *he* g the lives of his faithful ones and H9068
Ps 127: 1 over the city, the g stand watch in vain. H9068
Pr 2: 8 he g the course of the just and protects H5915
Pr 13: 6 Righteousness g the person of integrity H5915
Pr 24:12 Does not he *who* g your life know it H5915
Pr 27:18 The *one who* g a fig tree will eat its fruit H5915
Eze 40: 7 The **alcoves for the** g were one rod long H9288
Eze 44:16 to minister before me and serve me as g. H5466
Na 3:17 Your g are like locusts, your officials like H4964
Mt 26:58 sat down with the g to see the outcome. *G5677*
Mt 28: 4 The g were so afraid of him that they *G5498*
Mt 28:11 some *of* the g went into the city and *G3184*
Mk 14:54 he sat with the g and warmed himself at *G5677*
Mk 14:65 And the g took him and beat him. *G5677*
Lk 11:21 fully armed, g his own house, his *G5875*
Jn 7:32 the Pharisees sent **temple** g to arrest him. *G5677*
Jn 7:45 Finally the **temple** g went back to the *G5677*
Jn 7:46 the way this man does," the g replied. *G5677*
Ac 5:23 with the g standing at the doors *G5874*
Ac 12:10 first and second g and came to the iron *G5871*
Ac 12:19 cross-examined the g and ordered that *G5874*

GUDGODAH (1)

Dt 10: 7 they traveled to **G** and on to Jotbathah, H1516

GUEST (9) [GUESTS]

Lev 22:10 may the g *of* a priest or his hired H9369
Jdg 19:23 Since this man *is* my g, don't H995+448+1074
Est 1: 8 king's command each g was allowed to NDT
Mk 14:14 Where is my g **room**, where I may eat the *G2906*
Lk 2: 7 was no g **room** available for them. *G5536+1877+3836+2906*
Lk 19: 7 "He has gone *to* **be the** g of a sinner." *G2907*
Lk 22:11 Where is the g **room**, where I may eat the *G2906*
Ac 10:32 He *is a* g in the home of Simon the *G3826*
Phm 22 Prepare a g **room** for me, because I hope *G3825*

GUESTS (20) [GUEST]

1Sa 9:24 from the time I said, 'I have invited g. H6639
2Sa 15:11 *They had* **been invited as** g and went H7924
1Ki 1:41 all the g who were with him H7924
1Ki 1:49 all Adonijah's g rose in alarm and H7924
Job 19:15 My g and my female servants count H1591+1074
Pr 9:18 that her g are deep in the realm of the H7924
Mt 9:15 "How can the **g of the bridegroom** mourn *G5626*
Mt 14: 6 danced for the g and pleased Herod so *G3345S*
Mt 14: 9 because of his oaths and his **dinner** g *G5263*
Mt 22:10 the wedding hall was filled with g. *G367*
Mt 22:11 "But when the king came in to see the g *G367*
Mk 2:19 "How can the **g of the bridegroom** fast *G5626*
Mk 6:22 she pleased Herod and his **dinner** g. *G5263*
Mk 6:26 because of his oaths and his **dinner** g *G367*
Lk 7:49 The **other** g began to say among *G5263*
Lk 14: 7 he noticed how the g picked the places of *G2813*
Lk 14:10 in the presence of all the **other** g. *G5263*
Lk 14:16 a great banquet and invited **many** g. AIT
Jn 2:10 wine after the g have had too much to NDT
Ac 10:23 the men into the house *to be* his g. *G3826*

GUIDANCE (8) [GUIDE]

2Ki 16:15 I will use the bronze altar for **seeking** g." H1329
1Ch 10:13 LORD and even consulted a medium for g, H2011
Pr 1: 5 learning, and let the discerning get g— H9374
Pr 11:14 For lack of g a nation falls, but victory is H9374
Pr 20:18 so if you wage war, obtain g. H9374
Pr 24: 6 Surely you need g to wage war, and H9374
Hab 2:19 *Can* it **give** g? It is covered H3723
1Co 12:28 of helping, *of* g, and of different kinds of *G3236*

GUIDE (20) [GUIDANCE, GUIDED, GUIDEPOSTS, GUIDES, GUIDING]

Ex 13:21 of cloud to g them *on* their way and by H5697
Ex 15:13 In your strength *you will* g them to your H5633
Ne 9:19 cloud did not fail to g them on their path, H5697
Ps 25: 5 **G** me in your truth and teach me, for you H2005
Ps 31: 3 the sake of your name lead and g me. H5633
Ps 48:14 he *will be* our g even to the end. H5627
Ps 67: 4 with equity and g the nations of the H5697
Ps 73:24 *You* g me with your counsel, and H5697
Ps 139:10 even there your hand *will* g me, your right H5697
Pr 6:22 When you walk, *they will* g you; when you H5697
Isa 9:16 *Those who* g this people mislead them H886
Isa 42:16 along unfamiliar paths *I will* g them; I will H2005
Isa 49:10 on them *will* g them and lead H5627
Isa 51:18 she bore there was none *to* g her; H5633
Isa 57:18 *I will* g them and restore comfort to H5697
Isa 58:11 The LORD *will* g you always; he will satisfy H5697
Lk 1:79 *to* g our feet into the path of peace." *G2985*
Jn 16:13 *he will* g you into all the truth. *G3842*
Ac 1:16 who served as g for those who arrested *G3843*
Ro 2:19 convinced that you are a g for the blind, *G3843*

GUIDED (6) [GUIDE]

Job 31:18 and from my birth *I* g the widow— H5697
Ps 78:14 *He* g them with the cloud by day and with H5697
Ps 78:53 *He* g them safely, so they were unafraid H5697
Ps 107:30 and *he* g them to their desired haven. H5697
Isa 9:16 and *those who* **are** g are led astray. H886
Isa 63:14 This is how *you* g your people to make H5627

GUIDEPOSTS (1) [GUIDE]

Jer 31:21 up road signs; put up g. Take note of the H9477

GUIDES (7) [GUIDE]

Ps 23: 3 *He* g me along the right paths for his H5697
Ps 25: 9 *He* g the humble in what is right and H2005
Pr 11: 3 The integrity of the upright g them, but H5697
Isa 3:12 My people, your g lead you astray; they H886
Mt 15:14 they are blind g. If the blind lead *G3843*
Mt 23:16 "Woe to you, blind g! You say, 'If anyone *G3843*
Mt 23:24 *You* blind g! You strain out a gnat but *G3843*

GUIDING (4) [GUIDE]

2Sa 6: 3 sons of Abinadab, *were* g the new cart H5627
1Ch 13: 7 on a new cart, with Uzzah and Ahio g it. H5627

Ecc 2: 3 my mind *still* **g** me with wisdom. H5627
Jn 18: 3 **g** a detachment of soldiers and some G3284

GUILE (KJV) DECEIT, LIE, LIES, TRICK, TRICKERY

GUILT (109) [GUILTLESS, GUILTY]
Ge 20: 9 brought such great **g** upon me and my H2631
Ge 26:10 you would have brought **g** upon us. H871
Ge 44:16 God has uncovered your servants' **g**. H6411
Ex 28:38 he will bear the **g** *involved in* the sacred H6411
Ex 28:43 so that they will not incur **g** and die. H6411
Lev 4: 3 bringing **g** *on* the people, he must H873
Lev 4:13 of the matter, when *they* **realize** *their* **g** H870
Lev 4:22 of the LORD his God, *when he* **realizes** *his* **g** H870
Lev 4:27 LORD's commands, when *they* **realize** *their* **g** H870
Lev 5: 2 then *they come to* **realize** *their* **g**; H870
Lev 5: 3 then they learn of it and **realize** *their* **g** H870
Lev 5: 4 then they learn of it and **realize** *their* **g**— H870
Lev 5:15 to the sanctuary shekel. It is a **g offering**. H871
Lev 5:16 them with the ram as a **g offering**, H871
Lev 5:18 to the priest as a **g offering** a ram from the H871
Lev 5:19 It is a **g offering**; they have been guilty of H871
Lev 6: 4 sin in any of these ways and **realize** *their* **g**, H870
Lev 6: 5 on the day they present their **g offering**. H873
Lev 6: 6 to the LORD, their **g offering**, a ram from the H871
Lev 6:17 Like the sin offering and the **g offering**, it is H871
Lev 7: 1 are the regulations for the **g offering**, H871
Lev 7: 2 The **g offering** is to be slaughtered in the H871
Lev 7: 5 presented to the LORD. It is a **g offering**. H871
Lev 7: 7 to both the sin offering and the **g offering**: H871
Lev 7:37 sin offering, the **g offering**, the ordination H871
Lev 10:17 to take away the **g** *of* the community by H6411
Lev 14:12 the male lambs and offer it as a **g offering**, H871
Lev 14:13 the **g offering** belongs to the priest H871
Lev 14:14 the blood of the **g offering** and put it on H871
Lev 14:17 on top of the blood of the **g offering**. H871
Lev 14:21 male lamb as a **g offering** to be waved to H871
Lev 14:24 priest is to take the lamb for the **g offering**, H871
Lev 14:25 the lamb for the **g offering** and take some H871
Lev 14:28 places he put the blood of the **g offering**— H871
Lev 19:17 frankly so you will not share in their **g**. H2628
Lev 19:21 tent of meeting for a **g offering** to the LORD. H871
Lev 19:22 the ram of the **g offering** the priest is to H871
Lev 22:16 so bring upon them **g** requiring payment. H6411
Nu 5:28 she *will* **be cleared of g** and will be able H5927
Nu 6:12 bring a year-old male lamb as a **g offering**. H871
Nu 15:31 surely be cut off; their **g** remains on them. H6411
Nu 18: 9 whether grain or sin or **g offerings**, that part H871
Dt 19:13 Israel the **g of shedding** innocent **blood**, H1947
Dt 21: 9 the **g of shedding** innocent **blood**, H1947
Dt 22: 8 not bring the **g of bloodshed** on your H1947
1Sa 3:14 'The **g** *of* Eli's house will never be atoned H6411
1Sa 6: 3 by all means send a **g offering** to him. H871
1Sa 6: 4 "What **g offering** should we send to him?" H871
1Sa 6: 8 are sending back to him as a **g offering**. H871
1Sa 6:17 sent as a **g offering** to the LORD— H871
1Sa 14:39 even if **the g** lies with my son Jonathan H5647S
2Sa 14: 9 let the king and his throne be **without g**." H5929
2Sa 24:10 I beg you, take away the **g** *of* your servant. H6411
1Ki 2:31 of the **g of** the innocent **blood** that Joab H1947
1Ki 2:33 May the **g of** their **blood** rest on the head H1947
2Ki 12:16 The money from the **g offerings** and sin H871
1Ch 21: 3 Why should he bring **g** on Israel?" H873
1Ch 21: 8 I beg you, take away the **g** *of* your servant. H6411
2Ch 24:18 Because of their **g**, God's anger came on H873
2Ch 28:13 Do you intend to add to our sin and **g**? For H873
2Ch 28:13 For our **g** is already great, and his fierce H873
2Ch 33:23 before the LORD; Amon increased his **g**. H873
Ezr 9: 6 our heads and our **g** has reached to the H873
Ezr 9: 7 ancestors until now, our **g** has been great. H873
Ezr 9:13 a result of our evil deeds and our great **g**, H873
Ezr 9:15 Here we are before you in our **g**, though H873
Ezr 10:10 foreign women, adding to Israel's **g**. H873
Ezr 10:19 for their **g** they each presented a ram H873
Ezr 10:19 a ram from the flock as a **g offering**.) H871
Ne 4: 5 Do not cover up their **g** or blot out their H6411
Job 20:27 The heavens will expose his **g**; the earth H6411
Job 31:33 as people do, by hiding my **g** in my heart H6411
Ps 7: 3 done this and there is **g** on my hands— H6404
Ps 32: 5 And you forgave the **g** *of* my sin. H6411
Ps 38: 4 My **g** has overwhelmed me like a burden H6411
Ps 51:14 Deliver me from the **g of bloodshed**, H1947
Ps 69: 5 know my folly; my **g** is not hidden from you. H873
Pr 28:17 by the **g of murder** will seek H1947+5883
Isa 1: 4 a people whose **g** is great, a brood of H6411
Isa 6: 7 your **g** is taken away and your sin atoned H6411
Isa 24: 6 the earth; its people *must* **bear** *their* **g**. H870
Isa 24:20 upon it is the **g of** its **rebellion** that it falls H7322
Isa 27: 9 will Jacob's **g** be atoned for, and H6411
Isa 59: 3 stained with blood, your fingers with **g**. H6411
Jer 2:22 the stain of your **g** is still before me," H6411
Jer 3:13 Only acknowledge your **g**—you have H6411
Jer 14:20 and the **g** *of* our ancestors; we have H6411
Jer 25:12 their **g**," declares the LORD, H6411
Jer 26:15 bring the **g of** innocent **blood** on H1947
Jer 30:14 because your **g** is so great and your sins H6411
Jer 30:15 of your great **g** and many sins I have H6411
Jer 50:20 "search will be made for Israel's **g**, but H6411
Jer 51: 5 their land is full of **g** before the Holy One H871
Eze 14:10 They will bear their **g**—the prophet will be H6411
Eze 18:19 does the son not share the **g** *of* his father? H6411
Eze 18:20 child will not share the **g** *of* the parent, H6411
Eze 18:20 will the parent share the **g** *of* the child. H6411
Eze 21:23 remind them of their **g** and take them H6411
Eze 21:24 brought to mind your **g** by your open H6411
Eze 40:39 offerings and **g offerings** were slaughtered. H871
Eze 42:13 the sin offerings and the **g offerings**—for H871
Eze 44:29 the sin offerings and the **g offerings**; and H871
Eze 46:20 are to cook the **g offering** and the sin H871
Hos 5:15 lair until *they have* **borne** *their* **g** and seek H870
Hos 10: 2 deceitful, and now *they must* **bear** *their* **g**. H870
Hos 12:14 on him the **g of** his **bloodshed** and will H1947
Hos 13:12 The **g** *of* Ephraim is stored up, his sins are H6411
Hos 13:16 The people of Samaria *must* **bear** *their* **g** H870
Jn 9:41 that you claim you can see, your **g** remains. G281

GUILTLESS (4) [GUILT]
Ex 20: 7 the LORD *will* not **hold** anyone **g** who H5927
Dt 5:11 the LORD *will* not **hold** anyone **g** who H5927
1Sa 26: 9 a hand on the LORD's anointed and *be* **g**? H5927
Job 34: 6 although I am **g**, his arrow inflicts H1172+7322

GUILTY (81) [GUILT]
Ge 38:24 Tamar *is* **g of prostitution**, H2388
Ex 21:19 the **g** party must pay the injured person NDT
Ex 22: 2 the defender is not **g of bloodshed**; H1947
Ex 22: 3 sunrise, the defender is **g of bloodshed**. H1947
Ex 22: 9 whom the judges **declare g** must pay back H8399
Ex 23: 1 Do not help a **g** *person* by being a H8401
Ex 23: 7 person to death, for I will not acquit the **g**. H8401
Ex 34: 7 *he does* not **leave the g unpunished** H5927+5927
Lev 5: 2 'If anyone becomes aware that they are **g**— NDT
Lev 5: 5 *anyone becomes* **aware that** *they are* **g** in H870
Lev 5:17 *they are* **g** and will be held responsible. H870
Lev 5:19 *they have been* **g of wrongdoing** H870+870
Lev 6: 7 of the things they did that made them **g**." H873
Lev 17: 4 shall be considered **g of bloodshed**; H1947
Lev 22: 9 they *do* not **become g** and H2628+5951+6584
Nu 5: 6 any way and so is unfaithful to the LORD *is* **g** H870
Nu 14:18 *he does* not **leave the g unpunished** H5927+5927
Nu 18:32 part of it *you will* not *be* **g** in this H5951+2628
Nu 35:27 the accused without being **g of murder**. H1947
Dt 15: 9 and you will be found **g of sin**. H2628
Dt 19:10 so that you will not be **g of bloodshed**. H1947
Dt 21: 8 your people **g of** *the* **blood** *of* an innocent H1947
Dt 21:22 If someone **g** *of* a capital offense is put to H2628
Dt 23:21 demand it of you and you will be **g of sin**. H2628
Dt 23:22 from making a vow, you will not be **g**. H2628
Dt 24:15 LORD against you, and you will be **g of sin**. H2628
Dt 25: 1 the innocent and condemning the **g**. H8401
Dt 25: 2 If the **g** *person* deserves to be beaten, the H8401
Dt 25: 3 If **the g party** is flogged more than that H2257S
Jdg 21:22 *You will* **not be g** of breaking your oath H870
1Sa 20: 8 If I am **g**, then kill me yourself H6411
1Sa 24:11 that I am **g of wrongdoing** or rebellion. H8288
1Sa 26:18 I done, and what wrong am I **g** *of*? H928+3338
2Sa 14:32 and if I am **g** of anything, let him H6411
2Sa 19:19 said to him, "May my lord not hold me **g**. H6411
2Sa 22:22 *I am* not **g** *of* turning from my God. H8399
1Ki 8:32 condemning the **g** by bringing down on H8401
2Ch 6:23 condemning the **g** and bringing down on H8401
2Ch 28:10 aren't you also **g of sins** against the LORD H873
2Ch 28:13 they said, "or we will be **g** *before* the LORD. H873
Job 9:20 blameless, *it would* **pronounce** me **g**. H6835
Job 9:29 Since I *am already found* **g**, why should I H8399
Job 10: 2 *Do* not **declare** me **g**, but tell me what H8399
Job 10: 7 you know that *I am* not **g** and that no one H8399
Job 10:15 If *I am* **g**—woe to me! Even if I am H8399
Job 34:31 '*I am* **g** but will offend no more. H5951
Ps 5:10 **Declare** them **g**, O God! Let their intrigues H870
Ps 18:21 *I am* not **g** *of* turning from my God. H8399
Ps 109: 7 let him be found **g**, and may his prayers H8401
Pr 17:15 Acquitting the **g** and condemning the H8401
Pr 21: 8 The way of the **g** is devious, but the H2261
Pr 24:24 Whoever says to the **g**, "You are innocent," H8401
Pr 24:25 it will go well with those who convict the **g**, NDT
Isa 5:23 who acquit the **g** for a bribe, but deny H8401
Isa 29:21 *those who* with a word **make** someone **out to be g** H2627
Jer 2: 3 all who devoured her *were* **held g**, and H870
Jer 50: 7 enemies said, '*We are* not **g**, for they H870
Eze 14:10 the prophet will be as **g** as the one who H6411
Eze 18:24 the **unfaithfulness** *they are* **g of** H5086+5085
Eze 22: 4 *you have become* **g** because of the blood H870
Eze 25:12 Judah and *became* **very g** by doing so H870+870
Hos 1: 2 land *is* **g of unfaithfulness** to the LORD." H2388
Hos 4:15 adultery, *do not let* Judah *become* **g**. H870
Hos 13: 1 But *he became* **g** of Baal worship and died H870
Na 1: 3 *will* not **leave the g unpunished**. H5927+5927
Hab 1:11 wind and go on—**g** *people*, whose own H870
Mk 3:29 be forgiven; they are **g** of an eternal sin." G1944
Lk 13: 4 think they were more **g** than all the others G4050
Jn 8:46 *Can* any of you **prove** me **g** of sin? If I am G1794
Jn 9:41 you would not be **g of sin**; but now that you G281
Jn 15:22 *they would* not *be* **g of sin**; but G281+2400
Jn 15:24 else did, *they would* not *be* **g of sin**. G281+2400
Jn 19:11 me over to you *is* **g** of a greater **sin**." G281+2400
Ac 5:28 determined *to* **make** us **g** of this man's G2042
Ac 22:25 citizen who **hasn't** even **been found g**?" G185
Ac 25:11 *I am* **g** of doing anything deserving death G92
Ac 28:18 because I was not **g** of any crime G1877
1Co 11:27 manner will be **g of sinning** against the G1944
Heb 10: 2 would no longer have felt **g** for their sins. G5287
Heb 10:22 to cleanse us from a **g** conscience and G4505
Jas 2:10 at just one point is **g** of breaking all of it. G1944

GULF (1)
Isa 11:15 LORD will dry up the **g** *of* the Egyptian sea; H4383

GULL (2)
Lev 11:16 the screech owl, the **g**, any kind of hawk, H8830
Dt 14:15 the screech owl, the **g**, any kind of hawk, H8830

GULLIBLE (1)
2Ti 3: 6 homes and gain control over **g women**, G1220

GULP (1) [GULPS]
Pr 21:20 olive oil, but fools **g** theirs down. H1180

GULPS (1) [GULP]
Pr 19:28 the mouth of the wicked **g down** evil. H1180

GUM (1)
Ex 30:34 fragrant spices—**g resin**, onycha and H5753

GUNI (4) [GUNITE]
Ge 46:24 Jahziel, **G**, Jezer and Shillem. H1586
Nu 26:48 through **G**, the Gunite clan; H1586
1Ch 5:15 of Abdiel, the son of **G**, was head of their H1586
1Ch 7:13 Jahziel, **G**, Jezer and Shillem—the H1586

GUNITE (1) [GUNI]
Nu 26:48 through Guni, the **G** clan; H1587

GUR (1) [GUR BAAL]
2Ki 9:27 chariot on the way up to **G** near Ibleam, H1595

GUR BAAL (1) [BAAL, GUR]
2Ch 26: 7 who lived in **G** and against the H1597

GUSH (1) [GUSHED, GUSHES, GUSHING]
Isa 35: 6 Water *will* **g forth** in the wilderness and H1324

GUSHED (4) [GUSH]
Nu 20:11 Water **g out**, and the community H8041+3655
Ps 78:20 the rock, and water **g out**, streams flowed H2307
Ps 105:41 the rock, and water **g out**; it flowed like a H2307
Isa 48:21 the rock; he split the rock and water **g out**. H2307

GUSHES (2) [GUSH]
Pr 15: 2 the mouth of the fool **g** folly. H5580
Pr 15:28 the mouth of the wicked **g** evil. H5580

GUSHING (1) [GUSH]
Dt 8: 7 deep springs **g out** into the valleys H3655

GUTTER (3)
Eze 43:13 Its **g** is a cubit deep and a cubit wide H2668
Eze 43:14 From the **g** *on* the ground up to the lower H2668
Eze 43:17 around the altar is a **g** of one cubit with a H2668

H

HAAHASHTARI (1)
1Ch 4: 6 him Ahuzzam, Hepher, Temeni and **H**. H2028

HAARALOTH See GIBEATH HAARALOTH

HABAKKUK (2)
Hab 1: 1 The prophecy that **H** the prophet received. H2487
Hab 3: 1 A prayer of **H** the prophet. On shigionoth. H2487

HABAZZINIAH (1)
Jer 35: 3 Jeremiah, the son of **H**, and his brothers H2484

HABERGEON, HABERGEONS (KJV) ARMOR, COLLAR, JAVELIN

HABIT (5)
Ex 21:29 bull has **had the h** of goring H4946+9453+8997
Ex 21:36 the bull **had the h** of goring, H4946+9453+8997
Nu 22:30 *Have I* **been in the h of** doing this H6122+6122
1Ti 5:13 *they* **get into the h** of being idle and G3443
Heb 10:25 as some are **in the h of** doing, but G1621

HABITAT (1) [INHABIT]
Job 39: 6 as its home, the salt flats as its **h**. H5438

HABITATION, HABITATIONS (KJV) ABODE, DWELL, DWELLING, DWELLINGS, FOUNDATION, HAUNT, HOME, HOMELAND, HOUSE, LIVE, PLACE, PLACES, PROPERTY, SETTLE, SETTLEMENT, SETTLEMENTS, TENTS

HABOR (3)
2Ki 17: 6 in Gozan on the **H** River and in the towns H2466
2Ki 18:11 in Gozan on the **H** River and in towns of H2466
1Ch 5:26 took them to Halah, **H**, Hara and the river H2466

HACALIAH (NIV84) HAKALIAH

HACK (1)
Eze 16:40 stone you and **h** you **to pieces** with their H1438

HACMONI (NIV84) HAKMONI

HACMONITE (NIV84) HAKMONITE

HAD (597 of 2808) [HAVE] See Index of Articles Etc. for an Exhaustive Index

Ge 4:22 Zillah also **h a son,** Tubal-Cain, who H3528
Ge 4:26 Seth also **h** a son, and he named him H3528
Ge 5: 3 130 years, *he* **h a son** in his own likeness H3528
Ge 5: 4 lived 800 years and **h** other sons and H3528
Ge 5: 7 lived 807 years and **h** other sons and H3528
Ge 5:10 lived 815 years and **h** other sons and H3528
Ge 5:13 lived 840 years and **h** other sons and H3528
Ge 5:16 lived 830 years and **h** other sons and H3528
Ge 5:19 lived 800 years and **h** other sons and H3528
Ge 5:22 with God 300 years and **h** other sons and H3528
Ge 5:26 lived 782 years and **h** other sons and H3528
Ge 5:28 Lamech had lived 182 years, *he* **h** a son. H3528
Ge 5:30 lived 595 years and **h** other sons and H3528
Ge 6: 4 of humans and **h children** by them. H3528
Ge 6:10 Noah **h** three sons: Shem, Ham and H3528
Ge 7:14 They **h** with them every wild animal NDT
Ge 7:22 on dry land that **h** the breath of life in its NDT
Ge 10: 1 who themselves **h** sons after the flood. H3528
Ge 11: 1 the whole world **h** one language and a H2118
Ge 11:11 lived 500 years and **h** other sons and H3528
Ge 11:13 lived 403 years and **h** other sons and H3528
Ge 11:15 lived 403 years and **h** other sons and H3528
Ge 11:17 lived 430 years and **h** other sons and H3528
Ge 11:19 lived 209 years and **h** other sons and H3528
Ge 11:21 Reu lived 207 years and **h** other sons and H3528
Ge 11:23 lived 200 years and **h** other sons and H3528
Ge 11:25 lived 119 years and **h** other sons and H3528
Ge 12:20 with his wife and everything he **h.** H4200
Ge 13: 1 with his wife and everything he **h,** and Lot H4200
Ge 13: 5 also **h** flocks and herds and tents. H2118+4200
Ge 16: 1 But she **h** an Egyptian slave named Hagar H4200
Ge 19:37 The older daughter **h** a son, and she H3528
Ge 19:38 The younger daughter also **h** a son, and H3528
Ge 20:13 And when God **h** me **wander** from my H9494
Ge 22:24 whose name was Reumah, also **h sons:** H3528
Ge 24: 2 the one in charge of all that he **h,** "Put H4200
Ge 24:11 *He* **h** the camels **kneel down** near the well H1384
Ge 24:19 until *they have* **h enough** to drink. H3983
Ge 24:29 Now Rebekah **h** a brother named Laban H4200
Ge 25:28 who **h** a taste for wild game, loved H928
Ge 26:14 He **h** so many flocks and herds and H4200
Ge 27:15 older son, which she **h** in the house, and H907
Ge 28:12 *He* **h a dream** in which he saw a stairway H2731
Ge 29:16 Now Laban **h** two daughters; the name of H4200
Ge 29:17 Rachel **h** a lovely figure and was H2118
Ge 30: 8 "*I have* **h** a great **struggle** with my H7349+5887
Ge 30:30 The little you **h** before I came has H2118+4200
Ge 30:35 all that **h** white on them) and all NDT
Ge 31: 2 toward him was not what *it* **h been.** H9453+8997
Ge 31:10 breeding season *I once* **h** a dream in H8011S
Ge 31:21 So he fled with all he **h,** crossed the H4200
Ge 32:10 I **h** only my staff when I crossed this Jordan H928
Ge 32:13 from what he **h** *with* him he selected H928+3338
Ge 35: 4 foreign gods they **h** and the rings in H928+3338
Ge 35:22 Israel heard of it. Jacob **h** twelve sons: H2118
Ge 36:12 son Eliphaz also **h** a concubine H2118+4200
Ge 37: 5 Joseph **h a dream,** and when he H2731+2706
Ge 37: 6 to them, "Listen to this **dream** *I* **h:** H2706+2731
Ge 37: 9 Then *he* **h** another **dream,** and he H2731+2706
Ge 37: 9 "*I* **h** another **dream,** and this H2731+2706
Ge 37:10 "What is this **dream** *you* **h?** H2706+2731
Ge 38:30 who **h** the scarlet thread on his wrist NDT
Ge 39: 5 LORD was on everything Potiphar **h,** H4200+3780
Ge 39: 6 left everything he **h** in Joseph's care; H4200
Ge 40: 5 prison—**h a dream** the same night H2731+2706
Ge 40: 5 each dream **h** a meaning of its own. H3869
Ge 40: 8 "*We both* **h dreams,**" they H2731+2706
Ge 40:16 he said to Joseph, "I too **h** a dream: NDT
Ge 41: 1 years had passed, Pharaoh **h a dream:** H2731
Ge 41: 5 fell asleep again and **h** a second **dream:** H2731
Ge 41:11 Each of us **h a dream** the same H2731+2706
Ge 41:11 each dream **h** a meaning of its own. H3869
Ge 41:15 Joseph, "*I* **h a dream,** and no one H2731+2706
Ge 41:43 *He* **h** him **ride** in a chariot as his H8206
Ge 43: 6 by telling the man you **h** another brother?" H4200
Ge 47:22 Pharaoh and **h food enough** *from* the H430
Ex 2:16 Now a priest of Midian **h** seven daughters H4200
Ex 5:13 each day, just as when you **h** straw." H2118
Ex 9:28 we *have* **h** enough thunder and hail. H2118
Ex 10:23 all the Israelites **h** light in the H2118+4200
Ex 14: 6 So *he* **h** his chariot **made ready** and took his H673
Ex 14:25 chariots so that they **h** difficulty driving. H928
Ex 21:29 bull has **h the habit** of H4946+9453+8997
Ex 21:36 the bull **h the habit** of H4946+9453+8997
Ex 35:23 Everyone who **h** blue, purple or H5162+907
Ex 35:24 and everyone who **h** acacia wood H5162+907
Ex 35:26 who were willing and **h** the skill spun the H928
Ex 36: 7 because what *they already* **h** was more H2118
Ex 37: 9 The cherubim **h** their wings spread upward H2118
Ex 38: 9 cubits long and **h** curtains of finely H4200
Ex 38:11 cubits long and **h** twenty posts and twenty H4200
Ex 38:12 end was fifty cubits wide and **h** curtains, H4200
Ex 38:17 all the posts of the courtyard **h** silver bands. NDT
Lev 23:43 know that *I* **h** the Israelites **live** in H3782
Nu 3: 4 They **h** no sons, so Eleazar and H2118+4200
Nu 5:18 the priest *has* **h** the woman **stand** before H6641
Nu 5:19 other man *has* **h sexual relations** with you H8886
Nu 11: 4 wailing and said, "If only we **h** meat **to eat!** H430
Nu 11:18 you wailed, "If only we **h** meat **to eat!** H430
Nu 11:24 elders and **h** them **stand** around the tent H6641
Nu 12:10 saw that *she* **h a defiling skin disease,** H7665
Nu 22:29 If only I **h** a sword in my hand, I would kill H3780
Nu 26:33 son of Hepher **h** no sons; H2118+4200
Nu 26:33 had no sons; he **h** only daughters, whose NDT
Nu 26:46 Asher **h** a daughter named Serah.) NDT
Nu 27: 4 from his clan because he **h** no son? H4200
Nu 27:11 If his father **h** no brothers, give his H4200
Nu 27:22 Joshua and **h** him **stand** before Eleazar H6641
Nu 32: 1 who **h** very large herds and flocks H2118+4200
Dt 4:25 After *you have* **h** children and H3528
Jos 5: 1 and they no longer **h** the courage to H2118+928
Jos 5: 5 during the journey from Egypt **h** not. H4576S
Jos 7:16 Joshua **h** Israel **come forward** by tribes, H7928
Jos 7:17 *He* **h** the clan of the Zerahites **come forward** H7928
Jos 7:18 Joshua **h** his family **come forward** man by H7928
Jos 7:24 his tent and all that he **h,** to the Valley of H4200
Jos 8:20 but they **h** no **chance** to H2118+928+3338
Jos 11:10 Hazor **h been** the head of all these H4200+7156
Jos 11:23 Then the land **h rest** from war. H9200
Jos 14:15 Then the land **h rest** from war. H9200
Jos 17: 3 **h** no sons but only daughters H2118+4200
Jos 17: 8 Manasseh **h** the land of Tappuah H2118+4200
Jos 17:11 Manasseh also **h** Beth Shan H2118+4200
Jos 18:21 to its clans, **h** the following towns: H2118+4200
Jos 21:42 Each of these towns **h** pasturelands H2118
Jdg 1:19 because they **h** chariots fitted with iron. H4200
Jdg 3: 2 who *had* not **h** previous battle **experience**): H3359
Jdg 3:11 So the land **h peace** for forty years, until H9200
Jdg 3:30 the land **h peace** for eighty years. H9200
Jdg 4: 3 Because he **h** nine hundred chariots fitted H4200
Jdg 5:31 Then the land **h peace** forty years. H9200
Jdg 7:13 "*I* **h a dream,**" he was H2731+2706
Jdg 8: 8 they answered as the men of Sukkoth **h.** H6699S
Jdg 8:28 lifetime, the land **h peace** forty years. H9200
Jdg 8:30 He **h** seventy sons of his own, for he H2118+4200
Jdg 8:30 of his own, for he **h** many wives. H2118+4200
Jdg 10: 4 He **h** thirty sons, who rode thirty H2118+4200
Jdg 11:34 Except for her he **h** neither son nor H4200
Jdg 12: 9 He **h** thirty sons and thirty daughters H2118+4200
Jdg 12:14 He **h** forty sons and thirty grandsons, H2118+4200
Jdg 13: 2 of the Danites, **h** a wife who was childless H2118
Jdg 17: 5 Now this man Micah **h** a shrine, and he H4200
Jdg 17: 6 In those days Israel **h** no king; everyone did H928
Jdg 18: 1 In those days Israel **h** no king. And in those H928
Jdg 18: 7 the Sidonians and **h** no relationship with H4200
Jdg 18:28 way from Sidon and **h** no relationship H4200
Jdg 19: 1 In those days Israel **h** no king. Now a Levite H928
Jdg 19: 3 He **h** with him his servant and two donkeys NDT
Jdg 21:25 In those days Israel **h** no king; everyone did H928
Ru 1:12 even if *I* **h** a husband tonight and H2118+4200
Ru 2: 1 Now Naomi **h** a relative on her husband's H4200
Ru 2:14 ate all she wanted and **h some left over.** H3855
Ru 2:18 gave her what *she* **h left over** after she H3855
1Sa 1: 2 He **h** two wives; one was called Hannah H4200
1Sa 1: 2 Peninnah **h** children, but Hannah H2118+4200
1Sa 1: 2 had children, but Hannah **h** none. H4200
1Sa 2:12 scoundrels; *they* **h** no **regard for** the LORD. H3359
1Sa 9: 2 Kish **h** a son named Saul, as H2118+4200
1Sa 10:20 Samuel **h** all Israel **come forward** by tribes H7928
1Sa 13: 3 Then Saul **h** the trumpet **blown** H9546
1Sa 13:13 your God gave you; if you **h,** he would have NDT
1Sa 13:22 Saul and Jonathan **h** a sword or spear in H5162
1Sa 13:22 Saul and his son Jonathan **h** them. H4200+5162
1Sa 16: 8 Abinadab and **h** him **pass** in front of H6296
1Sa 16: 9 Jesse then **h** Shammah **pass by,** but H6296
1Sa 16:10 Jesse **h** seven of his sons **pass** before H6296
1Sa 16:12 So he sent for him and **h** him **brought in** H995
1Sa 16:12 with health and **h** a fine appearance and H6640
1Sa 17: 5 He **h** a bronze helmet on his head and wore NDT
1Sa 17:12 Jesse **h** eight sons, and in Saul's time he H4200
1Sa 18:10 as he usually did. Saul **h** a spear in his hand NDT
1Sa 18:14 In everything he did he **h great success** H8505
1Sa 20: 9 "If *I* **h the least inkling** that my H3359+3359
1Sa 20:17 And Jonathan **h** David **reaffirm** his oath H3578
1Sa 20:35 He **h** a small boy with him, NDT
1Sa 25: 2 in Maon, who **h** property there at Carmel NDT
1Sa 25: 2 He **h** a thousand goats and three H4200
1Sa 27: 3 Each man **h** his family with him, and David NDT
1Sa 27: 3 family with him, and David **h** his two wives: NDT
1Sa 28:24 The woman **h** a fattened calf at the house H4200
1Sa 30: 4 wept aloud until they **h** no strength left to H928
2Sa 3: 7 Now Saul had **h** a concubine named H4200
2Sa 3:20 When Abner, who **h** twenty men with him NDT
2Sa 3:37 the king **h** no **part in** the murder H2118+4946
2Sa 4: 2 Now Saul's son **h** two men who were H2118
2Sa 4: 4 son of Saul **h** a son who was lame H4200
2Sa 6:23 daughter of Saul **h** no children to H2118+4200
2Sa 9: 5 David **h** him **brought** from Lo H8938+2256+4374
2Sa 9:10 Now Ziba **h** fifteen sons and twenty H4200
2Sa 9:12 Mephibosheth **h** a young son named H4200
2Sa 10:16 Hadadezer **h** Arameans **brought** from H3655
2Sa 11:27 was over, David **h** her **brought** to his house H665
2Sa 12: 2 The rich man **h** a very large number H2118+4200
2Sa 12: 3 the poor man **h** nothing except one H4200
2Sa 12: 6 he did such a thing and **h** no **pity.** H2798
2Sa 13: 3 Now Amnon **h** an adviser named H4200
2Sa 14: 2 Tekoa and **h** a wise woman **brought** from H4374
2Sa 14: 6 I your servant **h** two sons. They got into a H4200
2Sa 16: 1 He **h** a string of donkeys saddled and NDT
2Sa 17:18 He **h** a well in his courtyard, and they H4200
2Sa 18:11 Then I would have **h to** give you ten H6584
2Sa 20: 3 but **h** no **sexual relations with** them. H995+448
2Sa 21:19 who **h** a spear with a shaft like a weaver's NDT
2Sa 23:21 the Egyptian **h** a spear in his hand, NDT
1Ki 1: 4 the king **h** no **sexual relations with** her. H3359
1Ki 1:38 down and **h** Solomon **mount** King H8206+6584
1Ki 2:19 *He* **h** a throne **brought** for the king's H8492
1Ki 3:17 and *I* **h a baby** while she was there with H3528
1Ki 3:18 child was born, this woman also **h a baby.** H3528
1Ki 3:28 they saw that he **h** wisdom from God H928+7931
1Ki 4: 7 Solomon **h** twelve district governors over H4200
1Ki 4: 7 Each one **h to** provide supplies for H2118+6584
1Ki 4:24 to Gaza, and **h** peace on all sides. H2118+4200
1Ki 4:26 Solomon **h** four thousand stalls H2118+4200
1Ki 5:15 Solomon **h** seventy thousand H2118+4200
1Ki 7: 5 All the doorways **h** rectangular frames; they NDT
1Ki 7:28 They **h** side panels attached to uprights H4200
1Ki 7:30 Each stand **h** four bronze wheels with H4200
1Ki 7:30 each **h** a basin resting on four H4200
1Ki 7:31 was an opening that **h** a circular frame one NDT
1Ki 7:34 Each stand **h** four handles, one on each NDT
1Ki 8:17 "My father David **h** *it* in his heart to build H2118
1Ki 10: 2 him about all that *she* **h** on her mind. H2118
1Ki 10:19 The throne **h** six steps, and its back had a H4200
1Ki 10:19 had six steps, and its back **h** a rounded top. NDT
1Ki 10:22 The king **h** a fleet of trading ships at sea H4200
1Ki 10:26 he **h** fourteen hundred chariots and H2118+4200
1Ki 11: 3 He **h** seven hundred wives of royal H2118+4200
1Ki 19: 4 "I have **h** enough, LORD," NDT
1Ki 20:33 Ahab **h** him **come up** into his chariot. H6590
2Ki 1: 8 "He **h** a garment of hair and had a H1251
2Ki 1: 8 garment of hair and **h** a leather belt around NDT
2Ki 1:17 Because Ahaziah **h** no son, Joram H2118+4200
2Ki 3: 9 the army **h** no more water for H2118+4200
2Ki 4:44 they ate and **h** *some* **left over** H3855
2Ki 5: 1 He was a valiant soldier, but *he* **h leprosy.** H7665
2Ki 6:30 under his robes, he **h** sackcloth on his body. NDT
2Ki 7: 8 The *men who* **h leprosy** reached the edge H7665
2Ki 10:16 Then *he* **h** him **ride along** in his chariot H8206
2Ki 10:30 to the house of Ahab all I **h** in mind to do, NDT
2Ki 11: 4 guards and **h** them **brought** to him at the H995
2Ki 13: 5 lived in their own homes as they **h** before. NDT
2Ki 13:23 to them and **h compassion** and showed H8163
2Ki 15: 5 the king's son **h charge of** the palace and H6584
2Ki 15:20 Every wealthy person **h** to contribute fifty NDT
2Ki 23:16 *he* **h** the bones **removed** H8938+2256+4374
1Ch 2: 4 Zerah to Judah. He **h** five sons in all. NDT
1Ch 2:18 son of Hezron **h children** by his wife H3528
1Ch 2:26 Jerahmeel **h** another wife, whose H2118+4200
1Ch 2:34 Sheshan **h** no sons—only H2118+4200
1Ch 2:34 He **h** an Egyptian servant named Jarha H4200
1Ch 4: 5 the father of Tekoa **h** two wives, H2118+4200
1Ch 4:27 Shimei **h** sixteen sons and six daughters H4200
1Ch 5:18 of Manasseh **h** 44,760 men ready for NDT
1Ch 7: 4 they **h** 36,000 men ready for battle H6584
1Ch 7: 4 for *they* **h many** wives and children. H8049
1Ch 7:15 who **h** only daughters. H2118+4200
1Ch 8: 9 By his wife Hodesh *he* **h** Jobab, Zibia H3528
1Ch 8:11 By Hushim *he* **h** Abitub and Elpaal. H3528
1Ch 8:38 Azel **h** six sons, and these were their H4200
1Ch 8:40 *They* **h many** sons and grandsons—150 in H8049
1Ch 9:27 because they **h to** guard it; and they H6584
1Ch 9:27 they **h charge of** the key for opening H6584
1Ch 9:44 Azel **h** six sons, and these were their H4200
1Ch 11:23 Although the Egyptian **h** a spear like a NDT
1Ch 12:22 help David, until he **h** a great army, like the NDT
1Ch 13:14 his household and everything he **h.** H4200
1Ch 19:16 and **h** Arameans **brought** from beyond H3655
1Ch 20: 5 who **h** a spear with a shaft like a weaver's NDT
1Ch 22: 7 I **h** *it* in my heart to build a house for the H2118
1Ch 23:17 Eliezer **h** no other sons, but the H2118+4200
1Ch 23:22 he **h** only daughters. NDT
1Ch 24: 2 and they **h** no sons; so Eleazar H2118+4200
1Ch 24:28 Eleazar, who **h** no sons. H2118+4200
1Ch 26: 2 Meshelemiah **h** sons: Zechariah the H4200
1Ch 26: 4 Obed-Edom also **h** sons: Shemaiah the H4200
1Ch 26: 6 Obed-Edom's son Shemaiah also **h** sons H3528
1Ch 26: 9 Meshelemiah **h** sons and relatives, who H4200
1Ch 26:10 Hosah the Merarite **h** sons: Shimri the first H4200
1Ch 26:12 **h** duties for ministering in the temple of H4200
1Ch 26:12 temple of the LORD, just as their relatives **h.** NDT
1Ch 26:32 Jeriah **h** twenty-seven hundred relatives NDT
1Ch 28: 2 I **h** it in my heart to build a house as a place NDT
1Ch 29: 8 Anyone who **h** precious stones gave H5162+907
1Ch 29:25 no king over Israel ever **h** before. H2118+6584
2Ch 1:12 who was before you *ever* **h** and none after H2118
2Ch 1:14 he **h** fourteen hundred chariots and H2118+4200
2Ch 6: 7 "My father David **h** *it* in his heart to build H2118
2Ch 7:11 in carrying out all he **h** in mind to do in the H995
2Ch 9: 1 with him about all *she* **h** on her mind. H2118
2Ch 9:18 The throne **h** six steps, and a footstool of H4200
2Ch 9:21 The king **h** a fleet of trading ships manned H4200
2Ch 9:25 Solomon **h** four thousand stalls H2118+4200
2Ch 11:21 *he* **h** eighteen wives and sixty concubines H5951
2Ch 13:21 fourteen wives and **h** twenty-two sons H3528
2Ch 14: 8 Asa **h** an army of three hundred H2118+4200
2Ch 17: 5 so that he **h** great wealth and H2118+4200
2Ch 17:13 and **h** large supplies in the towns H2118+4200
2Ch 18: 1 Now Jehoshaphat **h** great wealth H2118+4200
2Ch 21:19 in his honor, as they **h** for his predecessors. NDT
2Ch 24: 3 him, and *he* **h** sons and daughters. H3528
2Ch 26:10 because he **h** much livestock in the H2118+4200

2Ch 26:10 He **h** people working his fields and NDT
2Ch 26:11 Uzziah **h** a well-trained army H2118+4200
2Ch 26:19 who **h** a censer in his hand ready to burn NDT
2Ch 26:20 saw that he **h** **leprosy** on his forehead H7665
2Ch 26:21 King Uzziah **h** **leprosy** until the day he H7665
2Ch 26:21 Jotham his son **h** **charge of** the palace H6584
2Ch 26:23 the kings, for people said, "He **h** **leprosy**." H7665
2Ch 30:17 the Levites **h** **to** kill the Passover lambs H6584
2Ch 31:10 we *have* **h** **enough** to eat and plenty to H8425
2Ch 32:27 Hezekiah **h** very great wealth and H2118+4200
2Ch 34:13 **h** **charge of** the laborers and supervised all H6584
2Ch 34:32 *he* **h** everyone in Jerusalem and Benjamin **pledge** *themselves to* H6641
2Ch 34:33 *he* **h** all who were present in Israel **serve** H6641
2Ch 36:15 because *he* **h** **pity** on his people and on H2798
Ezr 1: 8 of Persia **h** them **brought** by Mithredath H3655
Ezr 2:65 they also **h** 200 male and female H4200
Ezr 2:66 They **h** 736 horses, 245 mules, NDT
Ezr 4:20 Jerusalem *has* **h** powerful kings A10201+10542
Ezr 10:44 some of them **h** children by these H8492
Ne 4:23 our clothes; each **h** his weapon, even when NDT
Ne 7:67 they also **h** 245 male and female H4200
Ne 11:16 who **h** **charge of** the outside work of the H6584
Ne 12:31 *I* **h** the leaders of Judah **go up** on top of H6590
Est 1: 6 The garden **h** hangings of white and blue NDT
Est 1:14 Media *who* **h** **special access to** the H8011+7156
Est 2: 7 Mordecai **h** a cousin named Hadassah NDT
Est 2: 7 up because she **h** neither father nor H4200
Est 2: 7 **h** a lovely figure and was beautiful. NDT
Est 2: 8 to Hegai, *who* **h** **charge of** the harem. H9068
Job 1: 2 He **h** seven sons and three daughters, H3528
Job 1: 3 donkeys, and **h** a large number of servants. NDT
Job 3:15 with princes who **h** gold, who filled their H4200
Job 28:17 nor can it be **h** **for** jewels of gold. H9455
Job 29:12 the fatherless who **h** none to assist them. NDT
Job 31:13 when they **h** a grievance against me, NDT
Job 31:35 that I **h** someone to hear me! I sign H4200
Job 32: 5 the three men **h** nothing more to H928+7023
Job 34:27 him and **h** no **regard for** any of his ways. H8505
Job 41:32 one would think the deep **h** white hair. NDT
Job 42:10 gave him twice as much as he **h** before. H4200
Job 42:12 He **h** fourteen thousand sheep, six H2118+4200
Job 42:13 And he also **h** seven sons and three H2118+4200
Ps 55: 6 "Oh, that I **h** the wings of a dove! H4200
Ps 78:63 their young women **h** no **wedding songs**; H2146
Pr 6:26 a prostitute can be **h** **for** a loaf of bread, H6330
Pr 7: 7 the young men, a youth who **h** **no** sense. H2894
Ecc 2: 7 slaves and **h** other slaves who H2118+4200
Ecc 4: 8 all alone; he **h** neither son nor brother. H4200
SS 8:11 Solomon **h** a vineyard in Baal H2118+4200
Isa 5: 1 My loved one **h** a vineyard on a H2118+4200
Isa 53: 2 He **h** no beauty or majesty to attract us to H4200
Jer 9: 2 that I **h** in the desert a lodging place for NDT
Jer 20: 2 he **h** Jeremiah the prophet **beaten** and put H5782
Jer 23:25 They say, '*I* **h** **a dream**! I had a dream! H2731
Jer 23:25 They say, 'I had a dream! *I* **h** **a dream**!' H2731
Jer 24: 2 One basket **h** very good figs, like those that NDT
Jer 24: 2 the other basket **h** very bad figs, so bad NDT
Jer 26:23 *who* **h** him **struck down** with a sword and H5782
Jer 32:10 the deed, **h** it **witnessed**, and H6386+6332
Jer 35: 9 houses to live in or **h** vineyards, H2118+4200
Jer 37:15 Jeremiah and **h** him **beaten** and H5782
Jer 38: 6 into the cistern; it **h** no water in it, only mud, NDT
Jer 41:13 the people Ishmael **h** with him saw NDT
Jer 44:17 At that time *we* **h** **plenty** *of* food and were H8425
Jer 44:18 *we have* **h** **nothing** and have been H2893+3972
Jer 52:27 the king **h** them **executed**. H5782+2256+4637
La 5: 4 our wood *can be* **h** only at a price. H995[S]
Eze 1: 6 each of them **h** four faces and four H4200
Eze 1: 8 on their four sides they **h** human hands. NDT
Eze 1: 8 All four of them **h** faces and wings, H4200
Eze 1:10 Each of the four **h** the face of a human H4200
Eze 1:10 on the right side each **h** the face of a lion, H4200
Eze 1:10 each also **h** the face of an eagle. H4200
Eze 1:11 They each **h** two wings spreading out H4200
Eze 1:11 each **h** two other wings covering its NDT
Eze 1:23 each **h** two wings covering its body. H4200
Eze 8:11 Each **h** a censer in his hand, and a fragrant NDT
Eze 9: 2 clothed in linen who **h** a writing kit at his NDT
Eze 9: 3 clothed in linen who **h** the writing kit at his NDT
Eze 10:14 Each of the cherubim **h** four faces: One H4200
Eze 10:21 Each **h** four faces and four wings, and H4200
Eze 10:22 Their faces **h** the same appearance as those NDT
Eze 16: 5 pity or **h** **compassion** *enough* to do any of H2798
Eze 36:21 *I* **h** **concern** for my holy name, which the H2798
Eze 40:10 the three **h** the same measurements H4200
Eze 40:10 walls on each side **h** the same H4200
Eze 40:21 its portico **h** the same measurements H2118
Eze 40:22 tree decorations **h** the same measurements NDT
Eze 40:24 they **h** the same measurements as the NDT
Eze 40:25 its portico **h** narrow openings all H4200
Eze 40:26 it **h** palm tree decorations on the faces of H4200
Eze 40:27 The inner court also **h** a gate facing south H4200
Eze 40:28 it **h** the same measurements as the others. NDT
Eze 40:29 its portico **h** the same measurements NDT
Eze 40:29 its portico **h** openings all around. H4200
Eze 40:32 it **h** the same measurements as the others. NDT
Eze 40:33 its portico **h** the same measurements NDT
Eze 40:33 its portico **h** openings all around. H4200
Eze 40:35 It **h** the same measurements as the others NDT
Eze 40:36 its portico, and it **h** openings all around. H4200
Eze 41: 8 I saw that the temple **h** a raised base all H4200
Eze 41:18 with cherubim. Each cherub **h** two faces: H4200
Eze 41:21 The main hall **h** a rectangular doorframe NDT
Eze 41:23 the Most Holy Place **h** double doors. H4200
Eze 41:24 Each door **h** two leaves—two hinged H4200
Eze 41:26 side rooms of the temple also **h** overhangs. NDT
Eze 42: 6 The rooms on the top floor **h** no pillars, as H4200
Eze 42: 6 as the courts **h**; so they were smaller NDT
Eze 42: 9 The lower rooms **h** an entrance on the east NDT
Eze 42:11 the north; they **h** the same length and width NDT
Eze 42:20 It **h** a wall around it, five hundred cubits H4200
Da 2: 1 Nebuchadnezzar **h** **dreams**; his H2731+2706
Da 2: 3 "*I have* **h** **a dream** that troubles me H2731+2706
Da 4: 5 *I* **h** a dream that made me afraid. A10255[S]
Da 4:18 dream that I, King Nebuchadnezzar, **h**. A10255[S]
Da 5:23 You **h** the goblets from his temple brought NDT
Da 7: 1 of Babylon, Daniel **h** a dream, and A10255[S]
Da 7: 4 and it **h** the wings of an eagle. A10378
Da 7: 5 it **h** three ribs in its mouth between its NDT
Da 7: 6 And on its back it **h** four wings like those A10378
Da 7: 6 This beast **h** four heads, and it was A10378
Da 7: 7 It **h** large iron teeth; it crushed and A10378
Da 7: 7 all the former beasts, and it **h** ten horns. A10378
Da 7: 8 This horn **h** eyes like the eyes of a A10089
Da 7:20 the others and that **h** eyes and a mouth A10378
Da 8: 1 **h** a vision, after the one that had H8011[S]
Da 10: 8 at this great vision; I **h** no strength left, my H928
Hos 1: 8 Lo-Ruhamah, Gomer **h** another son. H3528
Hos 10: 3 But even if we **h** a king, what could he do NDT
Am 4: 7 One field **h** **rain**; another had none and H4763
Am 4: 7 had rain; another **h** none and dried up. H4763[S]
Zec 1: 8 During the night *I* **h** **a vision**, and there H8011
Zec 5: 9 They **h** wings like those of a stork, and H4200
Zec 6: 2 The first chariot **h** red horses, the second H928
Mt 1:19 *he* **h** **in mind** to divorce her quietly. *G1089*
Mt 3: 4 he **h** a leather belt around his waist. NDT
Mt 4: 5 holy city and **h** him **stand** on the highest *G2705*
Mt 7:29 because he taught as *one who* **h** authority *G2400*
Mt 8:33 including **what h happened** to the *G3836*
Mt 9:36 the crowds, *he* **h** **compassion** on them *G5072*
Mt 13: 6 they withered because *they* **h** no root. *G2400*
Mt 13:44 went and sold all *he* **h** and bought that *G2400*
Mt 13:46 sold everything *he* **h** and bought it. *G2400*
Mt 14:10 **h** John beheaded in the prison. *G4287*
Mt 14:14 *he* **h** **compassion** on them and healed *G5072*
Mt 18:25 all that *he* **h** be sold to repay the *G2400*
Mt 18:33 Shouldn't you *have* **h** **mercy** on your fellow *G1796*
Mt 18:33 on your fellow servant just as I **h** on you? *G1796[S]*
Mt 19:22 because *he* **h** great wealth. *G1639+2400*
Mt 20:34 Jesus **h** **compassion** on them and touched *G5072*
Mt 21:28 *There was* a man *who* **h** two sons *G2400*
Mt 22:25 died, and *since he* **h** no children, he *G2400*
Mt 27:16 At that time *they* **h** a well-known prisoner *G2400*
Mt 27:26 But *he* **h** Jesus **flogged**, and handed him *G5849*
Mk 1:22 he taught them as *one who* **h** authority, *G2400*
Mk 1:34 healed many *who* **h** various diseases *G2400*
Mk 4: 6 they withered because *they* **h** no root. *G2400*
Mk 5:19 you, and how *he has* **h** **mercy** on you." *G1796*
Mk 5:26 of many doctors and had spent all she **h**, *G4123*
Mk 6:17 and *he* **h** him **bound** and put in prison. *G1313*
Mk 6:34 a large crowd, *he* **h** **compassion** on them *G5072*
Mk 8: 1 *Since they* **h** nothing to eat, Jesus called *G2400*
Mk 8: 7 *They* **h** a few small fish as well; he gave *G2400*
Mk 8:14 one loaf *they* **h** with them in the *G2400*
Mk 10:22 because *he* **h** great wealth. *G1639+2400*
Mk 11:13 he went to find out if it **h** any fruit. *G1877*
Mk 12: 6 "*He* **h** one left to send, a son, whom he *G2400*
Mk 12:44 put in everything—all she **h** to live on." *G2400*
Lk 2:49 "Didn't you know I **h** **to** be in my Father's *G1256*
Lk 4: 9 Jerusalem and **h** him **stand** on the *G2705*
Lk 4:32 because his words **h** authority. *G1877+1639*
Lk 4:40 to Jesus all who **h** various kinds of *G2400*
Lk 7:21 very time Jesus cured many who **h** diseases, NDT
Lk 7:42 Neither of them **h** the money to pay him *G2400*
Lk 8: 6 withered because *they* **h** no moisture. *G2400*
Lk 10:37 replied, "The *one who* **h** mercy on him." *G4472*
Lk 10:39 She **h** a sister called Mary, who sat at the *G1639*
Lk 13: 6 "A man **h** a fig tree growing in his *G2400*
Lk 14: 6 And *they* **h** nothing to say. *G2710*
Lk 15:11 "There was a man *who* **h** two sons. *G2400*
Lk 15:13 the younger son got together all he **h**, set NDT
Lk 15:32 But *we* **h** **to** celebrate and be glad *G1256*
Lk 17:12 ten men *who* **h** **leprosy** met him. *G3320*
Lk 18:28 "We have left **all** *we* **h** to follow *G3836+2625*
Lk 21: 4 of her poverty put in all *she* **h** to live on." *G2400*
Lk 22: 7 the Passover lamb **h** **to** be sacrificed. *G1256*
Lk 24:35 two told **what h happened** on the way, *G3836*
Jn 2:10 after the guests *have* **h** **too much to drink**; *G3499*
Jn 4: 4 Now he **h** **to** go through Samaria. *G1256*
Jn 4:18 The fact is, *you have* **h** five husbands, and *G2400*
Jn 5: 6 learned that he **h** **been** in this condition *G2453*
Jn 5:13 who was healed **h** no **idea** who it was, *G3857*
Jn 6: 6 he *already* **h** **in mind** what he was *G3857*
Jn 6:12 When *they had all* **h** **enough to eat**, he *G1855*
Jn 6:26 you ate the loaves and **h** *your* **fill**. *G5963*
Jn 9:13 the Pharisees the man who **h** **been** blind. *G4537*
Jn 13:10 "Those *who have* **h** **a bath** need only to *G3374*
Jn 13:29 Since Judas **h** **charge of** the money, some *G2400*
Jn 17: 5 with the glory *I* **h** with you before the *G2400*
Jn 18:10 Then Simon Peter, *who* **h** a sword, drew it *G2400*
Jn 20: 9 that Jesus **h** **to** rise from the dead. *G1256*
Jn 21: 7 around him (for *he* **h** taken it off) and *G1639*
Ac 1:16 the Scripture **h** **to** be fulfilled in which the *G1256*
Ac 2:13 said, "They have **h** **too much** wine." *G3551*
Ac 2:44 were together and **h** everything in *G2400*
Ac 2:45 to give to anyone who **h** need. *G2400*
Ac 4: 7 *They* **h** Peter and John **brought** before *G2705*
Ac 4:32 but they shared everything they **h**. *G1639*
Ac 4:35 it was distributed to anyone who **h** need. *G2400*
Ac 7: 5 *even though at that time* Abraham **h** no *G1639*
Ac 7:29 he settled as a foreigner and **h** two sons. *G1164*
Ac 7:44 "Our ancestors **h** the tabernacle of the *G1639*
Ac 8:16 the Holy Spirit **h** not yet come on any of *G1639*
Ac 10: 3 three in the afternoon he **h** a vision. *G1877*
Ac 11:18 *they* **h** **no further objections** and praised *G2483*
Ac 12: 9 but *he* **h** no **idea** that what the angel was *G3857*
Ac 13:46 "We **h** **to** speak the word of God to *G1639+338*
Ac 14: 9 saw that *he* **h** faith to be healed *G2400*
Ac 15:39 *They* **h** such a sharp disagreement that *G1181*
Ac 16: 9 the night Paul **h** a vision of a man of *G3972[S]*
Ac 16:16 by a female slave *who* **h** a spirit by which *G2400*
Ac 17: 3 that the Messiah **h** **to** suffer and rise from *G1256*
Ac 19: 9 with him and **h** **discussions** daily in the *G1363*
Ac 19:16 Then the man who **h** the evil spirit *G1877+1639*
Ac 21: 9 He **h** four unmarried daughters who *G1639*
Ac 21:29 *They* **h** previously seen Trophimus the *G1639*
Ac 21:35 was so great he **h** **to** be carried by the *G5201*
Ac 23:29 the accusation **h** **to do with** questions *G4309*
Ac 25:16 accusers and *have* **h** an opportunity to *G3284*
Ac 25:19 *they* **h** some points of dispute with him *G2400*
Ro 1:13 just as I have **h** among the other Gentiles. NDT
Ro 4: 2 by works, *he* **h** something to boast about *G2400*
Ro 4:11 that he **h** by faith while he was NDT
Ro 4:12 that our father Abraham **h** before he was NDT
Ro 4:21 persuaded that God **h** power to do what *G1639*
Ro 7: 7 what sin was **h** **it** not **been** for the law. *G1623*
Ro 15: 5 toward each other that Christ Jesus **h**, *G2848*
1Co 2: 8 for if *they* **h**, they would not have *G1182[S]*
1Co 4:15 Even if *you* **h** ten thousand guardians in *G2400*
2Co 2: 3 *I* **h** **confidence** in all of you, that you *G4275*
2Co 2:13 *I still* **h** no peace of mind, because I did *G2400*
2Co 5:21 God made him *who* **h** no sin to be sin *G1182*
2Co 7: 5 into Macedonia, we **h** no rest, but we *G2400*
Gal 4:22 For it is written that Abraham **h** two sons *G2400*
Php 1:30 through the same struggle you saw I **h**, *G1877*
Php 2:27 But God **h** **mercy** on him, and not on him *G1796*
Php 4:10 but *you* **h** **no opportunity** *to show it*. *G177*
Heb 2:17 For this reason *he* **h** **to** be made like them *G4053*
Heb 4: 2 For *we* also *have* **h** the good news *G1639*
Heb 7: 6 blessed him *who* **h** the promises. *G2400*
Heb 9: 1 Now the first covenant **h** regulations for *G2400*
Heb 9: 4 *which* **h** the golden altar of incense and *G2400*
Heb 9:26 Christ *would have* **h** **to** suffer many *G1256*
Heb 10:34 you knew *that you* yourselves **h** better *G2400*
Heb 11:15 *they* would have **h** opportunity to return. *G2400*
Heb 12: 9 we *have all* **h** human fathers who *G2400*
1Pe 1: 6 little while *you may have* **h** **to** suffer grief *G1256*
1Pe 1:14 to the evil desires you **h** when you lived in NDT
2Pe 1:21 prophecy never **h** *its* **origin** in the human *G5770*
1Jn 2: 7 which *you have* **h** since the beginning. *G2400*
1Jn 2:19 For if *they* **h** belonged to us, they would *G1639*
2Jn 5 command but one *we have* **h** from the *G2400*
Rev 4: 3 the one who sat there **h** the appearance of NDT
Rev 4: 4 dressed in white and **h** crowns of gold on NDT
Rev 4: 7 like an ox, the third **h** a face like a man *G2400*
Rev 4: 8 four living creatures **h** six wings and was *G2400*
Rev 5: 6 The Lamb **h** seven horns and seven eyes *G2400*
Rev 5: 8 Each one **h** a harp and they were holding *G2400*
Rev 8: 3 Another angel, *who* **h** a golden censer *G2400*
Rev 8: 6 seven angels who **h** the seven trumpets *G2400*
Rev 9: 9 *They* **h** breastplates like breastplates of *G2400*
Rev 9:10 *They* **h** tails with stingers, like scorpions *G2400*
Rev 9:10 in their tails they **h** power to torment people NDT
Rev 9:11 *They* **h** as king over them the angel of the *G2400*
Rev 9:14 said to the sixth angel who **h** the trumpet, *G2400*
Rev 13: 1 *It* **h** ten horns and seven heads, with ten *G2400*
Rev 13: 2 **h** feet like those of a bear and a mouth NDT
Rev 13: 3 beast seemed *to have* **h** a fatal **wound**, *G5377*
Rev 13:11 *It* **h** two horns like a lamb, but it spoke *G2400*
Rev 13:17 not buy or sell unless they **h** the mark, *G2400*
Rev 14: 1 with him 144,000 *who* **h** his name and *G2400*
Rev 14: 6 and *he* **h** the eternal gospel to proclaim *G2400*
Rev 14:17 in heaven, and he too **h** a sharp sickle. *G2400*
Rev 14:18 another angel, who **h** charge of the fire *G2400*
Rev 14:18 in a loud voice *to* him *who* **h** the sharp *G2400*
Rev 16: 2 on the people who **h** the mark of the *G2400*
Rev 16: 9 who **h** control over these plagues *G2400*
Rev 17: 1 seven angels who **h** the seven bowls *G2400*
Rev 17: 3 names and **h** seven heads and ten *G2400*
Rev 18: 1 *He* **h** great authority, and the earth was *G2400*
Rev 18:19 where all who **h** ships on the sea became *G2400*
Rev 21: 9 seven angels who **h** the seven bowls full *G2400*
Rev 21:12 *It* **h** a great, high wall with twelve gates *G2400*
Rev 21:14 The wall of the city **h** twelve foundations *G2400*
Rev 21:15 who talked with me **h** a measuring rod of *G2400*

HADAD (17) [BEN-HADAD, HADAD RIMMON]

Ge 25:15 **H**, Tema, Jetur, Naphish and Kedemah. H2524
Ge 36:35 Husham died, **H** son of Bedad, who H2060
Ge 36:36 When **H** died, Samlah from Masrekah H2060
Ge 36:39 of Akbor died, **H** succeeded him as king. H2060
1Ki 11:14 an adversary, **H** the Edomite, from the H2060
1Ki 11:17 But **H**, still only a boy, fled to Egypt with H119
1Ki 11:18 who gave **H** a house and land and H2257[S]
1Ki 11:19 was so pleased with **H** that he gave him a H2060

1Ki 11:21 **H** heard that David rested with his H2060
1Ki 11:21 Then **H** said to Pharaoh, "Let me go, that H2060
1Ki 11:22 "Nothing," **H** replied, "but do let me NDT
1Ki 11:25 adding to the trouble caused by **H**. H2060
1Ch 1:30 Mishma, Dumah, Massa, **H**, Tema, H2524
1Ch 1:46 Husham died, **H** son of Bedad, who H2060
1Ch 1:47 When **H** died, Samlah from Masrekah H2060
1Ch 1:50 **H** succeeded him as king. H2060
1Ch 1:51 **H** also died. The chiefs of Edom were H2060

HADAD RIMMON (1) [HADAD, RIMMON]
Zec 12:11 the weeping of **H** in the plain of H2062

HADADEZER (17) [HADADEZER'S]
2Sa 8: 3 David defeated **H** son of Rehob, king of H2061
2Sa 8: 5 Damascus came to help **H** king of Zobah, H2061
2Sa 8: 7 to the officers of **H** and brought them to H2061
2Sa 8: 8 towns that belonged to **H**, King David H2061
2Sa 8: 9 David had defeated the entire army of **H**, H2061
2Sa 8:10 him on his victory in battle over **H**, H2061
2Sa 8:12 the plunder taken from **H** son of Rehob, H2061
2Sa 10:16 **H** had Arameans brought from beyond the H2061
2Sa 10:19 who were vassals of **H** saw that they had H2061
1Ki 11:23 fled from his master, **H** king of Zobah. H2061
1Ch 18: 3 David defeated **H** king of Zobah, in the H2061
1Ch 18: 5 Damascus came to help **H** king of Zobah, H2061
1Ch 18: 7 by the officers of **H** and brought them to H2061
1Ch 18: 8 towns that belonged to **H**, David took a H2061
1Ch 18: 9 the entire army of **H** king of Zobah, H2061
1Ch 18:10 him on his victory in battle over **H**, H2061
1Ch 19:19 When the vassals of **H** saw that they had H2061

HADADEZER'S (2) [HADADEZER]
2Sa 10:16 the commander of **H** army leading them. H2061
1Ch 19:16 the commander of **H** army leading them. H2061

HADASHAH (1)
Jos 15:37 **H**, Migdal Gad, H2546

HADASSAH (1)
Est 2: 7 Mordecai had a cousin named **H**, whom H2073

HADATTAH See HAZOR HADATTAH

HADDAH See EN HADDAH

HADES (8)
Mt 11:23 you will go down to **H**. For if the miracles *G87*
Mt 16:18 the gates *of* **H** will not overcome it. *G87*
Lk 10:15 to the heavens? No, you will go down to **H**. *G87*
Lk 16:23 In **H**, where he was in torment, he looked up *G87*
Rev 1:18 And I hold the keys of death and **H**. *G87*
Rev 6: 8 **H** was following close behind him. *G87*
Rev 20:13 death and **H** gave up the dead that *G87*
Rev 20:14 Then death and **H** were thrown into the lake *G87*

HADID (3)
Ezr 2:33 **H** and Ono 725 H2531
Ne 7:37 **H** and Ono 721 H2531
Ne 11:34 in **H**, Zeboim and Neballat, H2531

HADLAI (1)
2Ch 28:12 Amasa son of **H**—confronted those H2536

HADORAM (4)
Ge 10:27 **H**, Uzal, Diklah, H2066
1Ch 1:21 **H**, Uzal, Diklah, H2066
1Ch 18:10 he sent his son **H** to King David to greet H2067
1Ch 18:10 **H** brought all kinds of articles of gold, of NDT

HADRAK (1)
Zec 9: 1 against the land of **H** and will come to H2541

HAELEPH (1)
Jos 18:28 **H**, the Jebusite city (that is H2030

HAGAB (1)
Ezr 2:46 **H**, Shalmai, Hanan, H2507

HAGABA (1)
Ne 7:48 Lebana, **H**, Shalmai, H2509

HAGABAH (1)
Ezr 2:45 Lebanah, **H**, Akkub, H2509

HAGAR (15)
Ge 16: 1 But she had an Egyptian slave named **H**; H2057
Ge 16: 3 her Egyptian slave **H** and gave her to her H2057
Ge 16: 4 He slept with **H**, and she conceived. H2057
Ge 16: 6 Then Sarai mistreated **H**; so she fled H2023S
Ge 16: 7 of the LORD found **H** near a spring in the H2023S
Ge 16: 8 And he said, "**H**, slave of Sarai, where H2057
Ge 16:15 So **H** bore Abram a son, and Abram gave H2057
Ge 16:16 years old when **H** bore him Ishmael. H2057
Ge 21: 9 that the son whom **H** the Egyptian had H2057
Ge 21:14 a skin of water and gave them to **H**. H2057
Ge 21:17 of God called to **H** from heaven and said H2057
Ge 21:17 said to her, "What is the matter, **H**? H2057
Ge 25:12 whom Sarah's slave, **H** the Egyptian, bore H2057
Gal 4:24 children who are to be slaves: This is **H**. *G29*
Gal 4:25 Now **H** stands for Mount Sinai in Arabia and *G29*

HAGGAI (11)
Ezr 5: 1 Now **H** the prophet and Zechariah the A10247
Ezr 6:14 the preaching of **H** the prophet and A10247
Hag 1: 1 through the prophet **H** to Zerubbabel son H2516
Hag 1: 3 of the LORD came through the prophet **H**: H2516
Hag 1:12 God and the message of the prophet **H**, H2516
Hag 1:13 Then **H**, the LORD's messenger, gave this H2516
Hag 2: 1 of the LORD came through the prophet **H**: H2516
Hag 2:10 word of the LORD came to the prophet **H**: H2516
Hag 2:13 Then **H** said, "If a person defiled by H2516
Hag 2:14 Then **H** said, " 'So it is with this people H2516
Hag 2:20 of the LORD came to **H** a second time on H2516

HAGGAN See BETH HAGGAN

HAGGARD (2)
2Sa 13: 4 look so **h** morning after morning? H1924
Job 30: 3 **H** from want and hunger, they roamed the H1678

HAGGEDOLIM (1)
Ne 11:14 Their chief officer was Zabdiel son of **H**. H2045

HAGGI (2) [HAGGITE]
Ge 46:16 Zephon, **H**, Shuni, Ezbon, Eri, Arodi and H2515
Nu 26:15 through **H**, the Haggite clan; H2515

HAGGIAH (1)
1Ch 6:30 his son, **H** his son and Asaiah his son. H2517

HAGGIDGAD See HOR HAGGIDGAD

HAGGITE (1) [HAGGI]
Nu 26:15 through Haggi, the **H** clan; through Shuni H2515

HAGGITH (5)
2Sa 3: 4 Adonijah the son of **H**; the fifth, H2518
1Ki 1: 5 whose mother was **H**, put himself forward H2518
1Ki 1:11 Adonijah, the son of **H**, has become king, H2518
1Ki 2:13 the son of **H**, went to Bathsheba, H2518
1Ch 3: 2 the fourth, Adonijah the son of **H**; H2518

HAGGOYIM See HAROSHETH HAGGOYIM

HAGRI (2) [HAGRITE, HAGRITES]
2Sa 23:36 son of Nathan from Zobah, the son of **H**, H2058
1Ch 11:38 the brother of Nathan, Mibhar son of **H**, H2058

HAGRITE (1) [HAGRI]
1Ch 27:31 Jaziz the **H** was in charge of the flocks. H2058

HAGRITES (6) [HAGRI]
1Ch 5:10 reign they waged war against the **H**, H2058
1Ch 5:10 the dwellings of **the H** throughout the H2157S
1Ch 5:19 They waged war against the **H**, Jetur H2058
1Ch 5:20 God delivered the **H** and all their allies H2058
1Ch 5:21 They seized the livestock of **the H**—fifty H2157S
Ps 83: 6 the Ishmaelites, of Moab and the **H**, H2058

HAHIROTH See PI HAHIROTH

HAI (KJV) AI

HAIL (30) [HAILSTONES, HAILSTORM]
Ex 9:19 because the **h** will fall on every person H1352
Ex 9:22 toward the sky so that **h** will fall all over H1352
Ex 9:23 the LORD sent thunder and **h**, and H1352
Ex 9:23 So the LORD rained **h** on the land of Egypt; H1352
Ex 9:24 **h** fell and lightning flashed back and forth H1352
Ex 9:25 Throughout Egypt **h** struck everything in H1352
Ex 9:26 only place it did not **h** was the land of H1352
Ex 9:28 we have had enough thunder and **h**. H1352
Ex 9:29 will stop and there will be no more **h**, H1352
Ex 9:33 the thunder and **h** stopped, and the rain H1352
Ex 9:34 saw that the rain and **h** and thunder had H1352
Ex 10: 5 what little you have left after the **h**, H1352
Ex 10:12 in the fields, everything left by the **h**." H1352
Ex 10:15 devoured all that was left after the **h**— H1352
Jos 10:11 them died from the **h** than were killed H74+1352
Job 38:22 snow or seen the storehouses of the **h**, H1352
Ps 78:47 their vines with **h** and their sycamore-figs H1352
Ps 78:48 He gave over their cattle to the **h**, their H1352
Ps 105:32 He turned their rain into **h**, with lightning H1352
Ps 147:17 He hurls down his **h** like pebbles. H7943
Ps 148: 8 lightning and **h**, snow and clouds, stormy H1352
Isa 28:17 **h** will sweep away your refuge H1352
Isa 30:30 with cloudburst, thunderstorm and **h**. H74+1352
Isa 32:19 Though **h** flattens the forest and the city is H1351
Hag 2:17 mildew and **h**, yet you did not H1352
Mt 27:29 mocked him. "**H**, king of the Jews! *G5897*
Mk 15:18 to call out to him, "**H**, king of the Jews!" *G5897*
Jn 19: 3 again, saying, "**H**, king of the Jews!" *G5897*
Rev 8: 7 there came **h** and fire mixed with *G5898*
Rev 16:21 cursed God on account of the plague *of* **h**, *G5898*

HAILSTONES (6) [HAIL]
Jos 10:11 the LORD hurled large **h** down on them, and H74
Ps 18:12 advanced, with **h** and bolts of lightning. H1352
Eze 13:11 I will send **h** hurtling down, and H74+453
Eze 13:13 in my anger **h** and torrents of rain H74+453
Eze 38:22 **h** and burning sulfur on him and on his H74+453
Rev 16:21 From the sky huge **h**, each weighing about *G5898*

HAILSTORM (3) [HAIL]
Ex 9:18 I will send the worst **h** that has ever fallen H1352
Isa 28: 2 Like a **h** and a destructive wind H2443+1352
Rev 11:19 of thunder, an earthquake and a severe **h**. *G5898*

HAIR (93) [GRAY-HAIRED, HAIRS, HAIRSTYLES, HAIRY]
Ex 25: 4 scarlet yarn and fine linen; **goat h**; H6436
Ex 26: 7 "Make curtains of **goat h** for the tent over H6436
Ex 35: 6 scarlet yarn and fine linen; **goat h**; H6436
Ex 35:23 fine linen, or **goat h**, ram skins dyed H6436
Ex 35:26 willing and had the skill spun the **goat h**. H6436
Ex 36:14 made curtains of **goat h** for the tent over H6436
Lev 10: 6 "Do not let your **h** become unkempt and H8031
Lev 13: 3 if the **h** in the sore has turned white H8552
Lev 13: 4 skin deep and the **h** *in* it has not turned H8552
Lev 13:10 that has turned the **h** white and if there is H8552
Lev 13:20 skin deep and the **h** *in* it has turned white H8552
Lev 13:21 there is no white **h** in it and it is not more H8552
Lev 13:25 and if the **h** in it has turned white H8552
Lev 13:26 there is no white **h** in the spot and if it H8552
Lev 13:30 skin deep and the **h** in it is yellow and H8552
Lev 13:31 skin deep and there is no black **h** in it, H8552
Lev 13:32 there is no yellow **h** in it and it does not H8552
Lev 13:36 he does not need to look for yellow **h** H8552
Lev 13:37 and if black **h** has grown in it, the H8552
Lev 13:40 "A man *who has* **lost** his **h** and is H5307+8031
Lev 13:41 If *he has* **lost** his **h** from the front of H5307+8031
Lev 13:45 clothes, let their **h** be unkempt, cover the H8031
Lev 14: 8 shave off all their **h** and bathe with water H8552
Lev 14: 9 day they must shave off all their **h**; H8552
Lev 14: 9 their eyebrows and the rest of their **h**. H8552
Lev 19:27 " '*Do* not **cut** the **h** at the sides of your H5938
Lev 21:10 must not let his **h** become unkempt or H8031
Nu 5:18 he shall loosen her **h** and place in her H8031
Nu 6: 5 must let their **h** grow long. H7279+8552+8031
Nu 6: 9 defiling the **h** *that symbolizes* their H8031
Nu 6:18 shave off the **h** *that symbolizes* their H8031
Nu 6:18 They are to take the **h** and put it in the H8552
Nu 6:19 has shaved off the **h** that symbolizes their NDT
Nu 31:20 made of leather, **goat h** or wood. H6436
Dt 32:25 the infants and those with **gray h**. H8484
Jdg 16:19 to shave off the seven braids of his **h**, H8031
Jdg 16:22 But the **h** *on* his head began to grow H8552
Jdg 20:16 could sling a stone at a **h** and not miss. H8553
1Sa 14:45 not a **h** of his head will fall to the ground H8553
1Sa 17:35 I seized it by its **h**, struck it and killed H2417
1Sa 19:13 putting some **goats' h** at the head. H3889+6436
1Sa 19:16 at the head was some **goats' h**. H3889+6436
2Sa 14:11 "not one **h** of your son's **head** will fall to H8553
2Sa 14:26 Whenever he **cut** *the* **h** *of* his head—he H1662
2Sa 14:26 he used to **cut** *his* **h** once a year because it H1662
2Sa 18: 9 Absalom's **h** got caught in the tree. H8031
1Ki 1:52 not a **h of** his **head** will fall to the ground H8553
2Ki 1: 8 "He had a **garment of h** and had a H8552
2Ki 9:30 arranged her **h** and looked out of a H8031
Ezr 9: 3 pulled **h** from my head and beard and sat H8552
Ne 13:25 some of the men and **pulled out** their **h**. H5307
Job 4:15 and the **h** *on* my body stood on end. H8553
Job 41:32 one would think the deep had **white h**. H8484
Pr 16:31 **Gray h** is a crown of splendor; it is H8484
Pr 20:29 strength, **gray h** the splendor of the old. H8484
SS 4: 1 Your **h** is like a flock of goats descending H8552
SS 5: 2 my **h** with the dampness of the night." H7767
SS 5:11 his **h** is wavy and black as a raven. H7767
SS 6: 5 Your **h** is like a flock of goats descending H8552
SS 7: 5 Your **h** is like royal tapestry; the H1929+8031
Isa 3:24 instead of **well-dressed h** H5126+5250
Isa 22:12 to **tear out** your **h** and put on sackcloth. H7947
Jer 7:29 " 'Cut off your **h** and throw it away; take H5694
Eze 5: 1 take a set of scales and divide up the **h**. H4392S
Eze 5: 2 burn a third of the **h** inside the city. NDT
Eze 8: 3 a hand and took me by the **h** *of* my head. H7492
Eze 16: 7 had formed and your **h** had grown, H8552
Eze 44:20 shave their heads or let their **h** grow **long**, H7279
Eze 44:20 *they are to* **keep** *the* **h** of their heads **trimmed** H4080+4080
Da 3:27 was a **h** *of* their heads singed A10687
Da 4:33 of heaven until his **h** grew like the A10687
Da 7: 9 the **h** *of* his head was white like wool. A10687
Hos 7: 9 His **h** is sprinkled with **gray**, but he does H8484
Zec 13: 4 garment of **h** in order to deceive. H8552
Mt 3: 4 John's clothes were made of camel's **h** *G2582*
Mt 5:36 cannot make even one **h** white or black. *G2582*
Mk 1: 6 John wore clothing *made of* camel's **h** *G2582*
Lk 7:38 she wiped them *with* her **h**, *G2582+3836+3051*
Lk 7:44 with her tears and wiped them *with* her **h**. *G2582*
Lk 21:18 But not a **h** of your head will perish. *G2582*
Jn 11: 2 on the Lord and wiped his feet *with* her **h**.) *G2582*
Jn 12: 3 Jesus' feet and wiped his feet *with* her **h**. *G2582*
Ac 18:18 he had his **h** cut off at Cenchreae because *G3051*
Ac 27:34 of you will lose *a single* **h** from his head." *G2582*
1Co 11: 6 *she might as well* **have** *her* **h cut off**; but *G3025*
1Co 11: 6 a woman to **have** her **h cut off** or her head *G3025*
1Co 11:14 things teach you that if a man **has long h**, *G3150*
1Co 11:15 that if a woman **has long h**, it is her *G3150*
1Co 11:15 For **long h** is given to her as a covering *G3151*
Rev 1:14 The **h** on his head was white like wool, as *G2582*
Rev 6:12 black like sackcloth **made of goat h**, *G5570*
Rev 9: 8 Their **h** was like women's hair, and their *G2582*
Rev 9: 8 Their hair was like women's **h**, and their *G2582*

HAIRS (6) [HAIR]
Ps 40:12 They are more than the **h** *of* my head H8553
Ps 69: 4 reason outnumber the **h** *of* my head; H8553
Isa 46: 4 Even to your old age and **gray h** I am he, H8484
Eze 5: 3 But take a few **h** and tuck them away in the NDT
Mt 10:30 And even the very **h** of your head are all *G2582*

Lk 12: 7 the very **h** of your head are all numbered. *G2582*

HAIRSTYLES (2) [HAIR]
1Ti 2: 9 not with **elaborate h** or gold or pearls *G4427*
1Pe 3: 3 such as **elaborate h** and the *G1862+2582*

HAIRY (4) [HAIR]
Ge 25:25 his whole body was like a **h** garment H8552
Ge 27:11 my brother Esau is a **h** man while I have H8537
Ge 27:23 his hands were **h** like those of his H8537
Ps 68:21 the **h** crowns of those who go on in their H8552

HAKALIAH (2)
Ne 1: 1 The words of Nehemiah son of **H**: In the H2678
Ne 10: 1 the governor, the son of **H**. Zedekiah, H2678

HAKILAH (3)
1Sa 23:19 on the hill of **H**, south of Jeshimon? H2677
1Sa 26: 1 "Is not David hiding on the hill of **H** H2677
1Sa 26: 3 the road on the hill of **H** facing Jeshimon, H2677

HAKKATAN (1)
Ezr 8:12 Johanan son of **H**, and with him 110 men H2214

HAKKEREM See BETH HAKKEREM

HAKKORE See EN HAKKORE

HAKKOZ (5)
1Ch 24:10 the seventh to **H**, the eighth to Abijah, H2212
Ezr 2:61 of Hobaiah, **H** and Barzillai (a man H2212
Ne 3: 4 of Uriah, the son of **H**, repaired the next H2212
Ne 3:21 of Uriah, the son of **H**, repaired another H2212
Ne 7:63 of Hobaiah, **H** and Barzillai (a man H2212

HAKMONI (1) [HAKMONITE]
1Ch 27:32 Jehiel son of **H** took care of the king's H2685

HAKMONITE (1) [HAKMONI]
1Ch 11:11 Jashobeam, a **H**, was chief of the H1201+2685

HAKUPHA (2)
Ezr 2:51 Bakbuk, **H**, Harhur, H2979
Ne 7:53 Bakbuk, **H**, Harhur, H2979

HALAH (3)
2Ki 17: 6 He settled them in **H**, in Gozan on the H2712
2Ki 18:11 Israel to Assyria and settled them in **H**, H2712
1Ch 5:26 He took them to **H**, Habor, Hara and the H2712

HALAK (2)
Jos 11:17 from Mount **H**, which rises toward Seir, to H2748
Jos 12: 7 Gad in the Valley of Lebanon to Mount **H**, H2748

HALF (113) [HALF-DISTRICT, HALF-NAKED, HALF-TRIBE, HALFWAY, HALVES]
Ge 15:10 the birds, however, *he did* not **cut in h**. H1439
Ex 24: 6 Moses took **h** *of* the blood and put it in H2942
Ex 24: 6 the other **h** he splashed against the H2942
Ex 25:10 wood—two and a **h** cubits long, a cubit H2942
Ex 25:10 a cubit and a **h** wide, and a cubit H2942
Ex 25:10 a half wide, and a cubit and a **h** high. H2942
Ex 25:17 two and a **h** cubits long and a cubit and a H2942
Ex 25:17 half cubits long and a cubit and a **h** wide. H2942
Ex 25:23 a cubit wide and a cubit and a **h** high. H2942
Ex 26:12 the **h** curtain that is left over is to hang H2942
Ex 26:16 ten cubits long and a cubit and a **h** wide, H2942
Ex 30:13 already counted is to give a **h** shekel, H4734
Ex 30:13 This **h** shekel is an offering to the LORD H4734
Ex 30:15 to give more than a **h** shekel and the poor H4734
Ex 30:23 shekels of liquid myrrh, **h as much** (that is, H4734
Ex 36:21 ten cubits long and a cubit and a **h** wide, H2942
Ex 37: 1 wood—two and a **h** cubits long, a cubit H2942
Ex 37: 1 a cubit and a **h** wide, and a cubit H2942
Ex 37: 1 a half wide, and a cubit and a **h** high. H2942
Ex 37: 6 two and a **h** cubits long and a cubit and a H2942
Ex 37: 6 half cubits long and a cubit and a **h** wide. H2942
Ex 37:10 a cubit wide and a cubit and a **h** high. H2942
Ex 38:26 **h** a shekel, according to the H4734
Lev 6:20 **h** *of* it in the morning and half in the H4734
Lev 6:20 of it in the morning and **h** in the evening. H4734
Nu 12:12 womb with its flesh **h** eaten away. H2942
Nu 15: 9 finest flour mixed with **h** a hin of olive oil, H2942
Nu 15:10 also bring **h** a hin of wine as a drink H2942
Nu 28:14 is to be a drink offering of **h** a hin of wine; H2942
Nu 31:29 tribute from their **h share** and give it to H4734
Nu 31:30 From the Israelites' **h**, select one out of H4734
Nu 31:36 The **h** share of those who fought in the H4733
Nu 31:42 The **h** *belonging to* the Israelites, which H4734
Nu 31:43 the community's **h**—was 337,500 sheep, H4733
Nu 31:47 From the Israelites' **h**, Moses selected one H4734
Nu 34:13 that it be given to the nine and a **h** tribes, H2942
Nu 34:15 These two and a **h** tribes have received H2942
Dt 3:12 including **h** the hill country of Gilead H2942
Jos 8:33 **H** *of* the people stood in front of Mount H2942
Jos 8:33 Mount Gerizim and **h** *of* them in front of H2942
Jos 12: 2 This included **h** *of* Gilead. H2942
Jos 12: 5 and **h** *of* Gilead to the border of Sihon H2942
Jos 13: 7 the nine tribes and **h** *of* the tribe of H2942
Jos 13: 8 **The other h of Manasseh**, the H2257S
Jos 13:25 towns of Gilead and **h** the Ammonite H2942
Jos 13:29 to **h** the family of the descendants of H2942
Jos 13:31 **h** *of* Gilead, and Ashtaroth and Edrei (the H2942
Jos 13:31 of Manasseh—for **h** *of* the sons of Makir H2942
Jos 14: 2 assigned by lot to the nine and *a* **h** tribes, H2942
Jos 14: 3 had granted the two and *a* **h** tribes their H2942
Jos 21: 5 of Ephraim, Dan and **h** *of* Manasseh. H2942
Jos 21:25 From **h** the tribe of Manasseh they H4734
Jos 22: 7 to the other **h** *of* the tribe Joshua H2942
1Sa 14:14 twenty men in an area of about **h** an acre. H2942
2Sa 10: 4 shaved off **h** *of* each man's beard H2942
2Sa 18: 3 Even if **h** *of* us die, they won't care; but H2942
2Sa 19:40 troops of Judah and **h** the troops of Israel H2942
1Ki 3:25 child in two and give **h** to one and half to H2942
1Ki 3:25 give half to one and **h** to the other." H2942
1Ki 7:31 its basework it measured a cubit and a **h**. H2942
1Ki 7:32 of each wheel was a cubit and a **h**. H2942
1Ki 7:35 there was a circular band **h** a cubit deep. H2942
1Ki 10: 7 Indeed, not even **h** was told me; in H2942
1Ki 13: 8 if you were to give me **h** your possessions, H2942
1Ki 16: 9 who had command of **h** his chariots H4734
1Ki 16:21 **h** supported Tibni son of Ginath for king H2942
1Ki 16:21 king, and the other **h** supported Omri. H2942
1Ch 2:52 Haroeh, **h** the Manahathites, H2942
1Ch 2:54 Atroth Beth Joab, **h** the Manahathites, the H2942
1Ch 6:61 from the clans of **h** the tribe of Manasseh. H4734
1Ch 6:70 And from **h** the tribe of Manasseh the H4734
1Ch 12:31 from **h** the tribe of Manasseh, designated H2942
1Ch 27:20 of Azaziah; over **h** the tribe of Manasseh: H2942
2Ch 9: 6 not even **h** the greatness of your wisdom H2942
Ne 3:17 Hashabiah, ruler of **h** the district of Keilah H2942
Ne 4: 6 the wall till all of it reached **h** its height, H2942
Ne 4:16 that day on, **h** *of* my men did the work H2942
Ne 4:16 while the other **h** were equipped with H2942
Ne 4:21 the work with **h** the men holding spears, H2942
Ne 12:32 Hoshaiah and **h** the leaders of Judah H2942
Ne 12:38 together with **h** the people—past the H2942
Ne 12:40 so did I, together with **h** the officials, H2942
Ne 13:24 **H** *of* their children spoke the language of H2942
Est 5: 3 Even up to **h** the kingdom, it will be given H2942
Est 5: 6 Even up to **h** the kingdom, it will be H2942
Est 7: 2 Even up to **h** the kingdom, it will be H2942
Ps 55:23 deceitful *will* not **live out h** their days. H2936
Isa 44:16 **H** *of* the wood he burns in the fire; over it H2942
Isa 44:19 "**H** *of* it I used for fuel; H2942
Jer 17:11 When their lives are **h** *gone*, their riches H2942
Eze 16:51 Samaria did not commit **h** the sins you did. H2942
Eze 40:42 each a cubit and a **h** long, a cubit and a H2942
Eze 40:42 a cubit and a **h** wide and a cubit high. H2942
Eze 43:17 gutter of one cubit with a rim of **h** a cubit. H2942
Da 7:25 his hands for a time, times and **h** a time. A10584
Da 12: 7 "It will be for a time, times and **h** a time. H2942
Zec 14: 2 **H** *of* the city will go into exile, but the rest H2942
Zec 14: 4 with **h** *of* the mountain moving north and H2942
Zec 14: 4 moving north and **h** moving south. H2942
Zec 14: 8 **h** *of* it east to the Dead Sea and half of it H2942
Zec 14: 8 to the Dead Sea and **h** *of* it west to the H2942
Mk 6:23 ask I will give you, up to **h** my kingdom." *G2468*
Mk 6:37 take **more than h a year's wages**! *G1324+1357*
Lk 4:25 sky was shut for **three and a h years** *G2291+5552+2779+3604+1971*
Lk 10:30 him and went away, leaving him **h dead**. *G2467*
Lk 19: 8 Here and now I give **h** of my possessions *G2468*
Jn 6: 7 take **more than h a year's wages** to *G1357+1324*
Ac 18:11 in Corinth for a **year** and a **h**, *G3604+1971*
Jas 5:17 on the land for three and a **h years**. *G3604+1971*
Rev 8: 1 silence in heaven *for* about **h an hour**. *G2469*
Rev 11: 9 For three and a **h** days some from every *G2468*
Rev 11:11 after the three and a **h** days the breath of *G2468*
Rev 12:14 a time, times and **h** a time, out of the *G2468*

HALF-DISTRICT (4) [HALF, DISTRICT]
Ne 3: 9 of Hur, ruler of a **h** *of* Jerusalem H2942+7135
Ne 3:12 ruler of a **h** *of* Jerusalem, repaired H2942+7135
Ne 3:16 ruler of a **h** *of* Beth Zur, made H2942+7135
Ne 3:18 ruler of the other **h** *of* Keilah. H2942+7135

HALF-NAKED (1) [HALF, NAKED]
2Sa 6:20 **going around h** in full view of the slave H1655

HALF-TRIBE (25) [HALF, TRIBE]
Nu 32:33 and the **h** *of* Manasseh son of H2942+8657
Nu 34:14 Gad and the **h** *of* Manasseh have H2942+4751
Dt 3:13 I gave to the **h** *of* Manasseh. H2942+8657
Dt 29: 8 Gadites and the **h** *of* Manasseh. H2942+8657
Jos 1:12 Gadites and the **h** *of* Manasseh, H2942+8657
Jos 4:12 Gad and the **h** *of* Manasseh H2942+8657
Jos 12: 6 and the **h** *of* Manasseh to be H2942+8657
Jos 13:29 had given to the **h** *of* Manasseh, H2942+8657
Jos 18: 7 and the **h** *of* Manasseh have H2942+8657
Jos 21: 6 Naphtali and the **h** *of* Manasseh in H2942+4751
Jos 21:27 from the **h** *of* Manasseh, Golan in H2942+4751
Jos 22: 1 the Gadites and the **h** *of* Manasseh H2942+4751
Jos 22: 7 To the **h** *of* Manasseh Moses had H2942+8657
Jos 22: 9 Gadites and the **h** *of* Manasseh left H2942+8657
Jos 22:10 and the **h** *of* Manasseh built H2942+8657
Jos 22:13 Gad and the **h** *of* Manasseh. H2942+8657
Jos 22:15 Gad and the **h** *of* Manasseh—they H2942+8657
Jos 22:21 Gad and the **h** *of* Manasseh H2942+8657
1Ch 5:18 and the **h** *of* Manasseh had H2942+8657
1Ch 5:23 people of the **h** *of* Manasseh were H2942+8657
1Ch 5:26 and the **h** *of* Manasseh into H2942+8657
1Ch 6:71 the clan of the **h** *of* Manasseh they H2942+4751
1Ch 12:37 Gad and the **h** *of* Manasseh H2942+8657
1Ch 26:32 Gadites and the **h** *of* Manasseh H2942+8657
1Ch 27:21 over the **h** *of* Manasseh in Gilead: Iddo H2942

HALFWAY (3) [HALF]
Ex 27: 5 of the altar so that it is **h** up the altar. H2942
Ex 38: 4 to be under its ledge, **h** up the altar. H2942
Jn 7:14 Not until **h through** the festival did Jesus *G3548*

HALHUL (1)
Jos 15:58 **H**, Beth Zur, Gedor, H2713

HALI (1)
Jos 19:25 Helkath, **H**, Beten, Akshaph, H2718

HALL (28)
1Sa 9:22 his servant into the **h** and seated them at H4384
1Ki 6: 3 at the front of the **main h** *of* the temple H2121
1Ki 6: 5 the walls of the **main h** and inner H2121
1Ki 6:17 The **main h** in front of this room was forty H2121
1Ki 6:33 entrance to the **main h** he made H2121
1Ki 6:33 that were one fourth of the width of the **h**. NDT
1Ki 7: 7 He built the throne **h**, the Hall of Justice H395
1Ki 7: 7 the throne hall, the **H** *of* Justice, where he H395
1Ki 7: 8 a palace like this **h** for Pharaoh's daughter, H395
1Ki 7:50 the doors of the **main h** of the temple. H2121
2Ch 3: 5 He paneled the main **h** with juniper and H1074
2Ch 3:13 stood on their feet, facing the **main h**. H1074
2Ch 4:22 Holy Place and the doors of the **main h**. H2121
Est 5: 1 of the palace, in front of the king's **h**. H1074
Est 5: 1 was sitting on his royal throne in the **h**, H1074
Est 7: 8 from the palace garden to the banquet **h**, H1074
SS 2: 4 Let him lead me to the **banquet h** H1074+3516
Eze 41: 1 me to the **main h** and measured the H2121
Eze 41: 2 He also measured the main **h**; it was forty NDT
Eze 41: 4 cubits across the end of the **main h**. H2121
Eze 41:15 The **main h**, the inner sanctuary and the H2121
Eze 41:20 were carved on the wall of the **main h**. H2121
Eze 41:21 The **main h** had a rectangular doorframe H2121
Eze 41:23 Both the **main h** and the Most Holy Place H2121
Eze 41:25 on the doors of the **main h** were carved H2121
Da 5:10 his nobles, came into the banquet **h**. A10103
Mt 22:10 the **wedding h** was filled with guests. *G1141*
Ac 19: 9 daily in the **lecture h** of Tyrannus. *G5391*

HALLELUJAH (4)
Rev 19: 1 heaven shouting: "**H**! Salvation and glory *G252*
Rev 19: 3 "**H**! The smoke from her *G252*
Rev 19: 4 on the throne. And they cried: "Amen, **H**!" *G252*
Rev 19: 6 "**H**! For our Lord God Almighty *G252*

HALLOHESH (2)
Ne 3:12 Shallum son of **H**, ruler of a half-district of H2135
Ne 10:24 **H**, Pilha, Shobek, H2135

HALLOW, HALLOWED (KJV) CONSECRATE, CONSECRATED, HOLY, SACRED, SET APART

HALLOWED (2) [HOLY]
Mt 6: 9 " 'Our Father in heaven, **h** *be* your name, *G39*
Lk 11: 2 " 'Father, **h** *be* your name, your kingdom *G39*

HALT (4) [HALTED]
2Sa 2:28 all the troops **came to a h**; they no H6641
2Sa 20:12 saw that all the troops **came to a h** there. H6641
Job 38:11 here is where your proud waves **h**'? H8883
Isa 10:32 This day they *will* **h** at Nob; they will H6641

HALTED (2) [HALT]
2Sa 15:17 and *they* **h** *at* the edge of the city. H6641
2Sa 18:16 stopped pursuing Israel, for Joab **h** them. H3104

HALVES (3) [HALF]
Ge 15:10 arranged the **h** opposite each other; H1440
SS 4: 3 your veil are like the **h** *of* a pomegranate. H7115
SS 6: 7 your veil are like the **h** *of* a pomegranate. H7115

HAM (16) [HAMITES]
Ge 5:32 the father of Shem, **H** and Japheth. H2769
Ge 6:10 had three sons: Shem, **H** and Japheth. H2769
Ge 7:13 **H** and Japheth, together with his H2769
Ge 9:18 out of the ark were Shem, **H** and Japheth. H2769
Ge 9:18 (**H** was the father of Canaan. H2769
Ge 9:22 **H**, the father of Canaan, saw his father H2769
Ge 10: 1 account of Shem, **H** and Japheth, Noah's H2769
Ge 10: 6 The sons of **H**: Cush, Egypt, Put and H2769
Ge 10:20 These are the sons of **H** by their clans H2769
Ge 14: 5 the Zuzites in **H**, the Emites in Shaveh H2154
1Ch 1: 4 The sons of Noah: Shem, **H** and Japheth. H2769
1Ch 1: 8 The sons of **H**: Cush, Egypt, Put and H2769
Ps 78:51 the firstfruits of manhood in the tents of **H**. H2769
Ps 105:23 resided as a foreigner in the land of **H**. H2769
Ps 105:27 his wonders in the land of **H**. H2769
Ps 106:22 in the land of **H** and awesome deeds by H2769

HAMAN (44) [HAMAN'S]
Est 3: 1 Xerxes honored **H** son of Hammedatha, H2172
Est 3: 2 gate knelt down and paid honor to **H**, H2172
Est 3: 4 Therefore they told **H** about it to see H2172
Est 3: 5 When **H** saw that Mordecai would not H2172
Est 3: 6 Instead **H** looked for a way to destroy all H2172
Est 3: 7 in the presence of **H** to select a day and H2172
Est 3: 8 Then **H** said to King Xerxes, "There is a H2172
Est 3:10 gave it to **H** son of Hammedatha, H2172
Est 3:11 the king said to **H**, "and do with the H2172
Est 3:15 The king and **H** sat down to drink, but the H2172
Est 4: 7 amount of money **H** had promised to pay H2172

H

Est 5: 4 the king, together with **H**, come today to a H2172
Est 5: 5 "Bring **H** at once," the king said, "so that H2172
Est 5: 5 So the king and **H** went to the banquet H2172
Est 5: 8 let the king and **H** come tomorrow to the H2172
Est 5: 9 **H** went out that day happy and in high H2172
Est 5:10 **H** restrained himself and went home. H2172
Est 5:11 **H** boasted to them about his vast wealth H2172
Est 5:12 that's not all," **H** added. "I'm the only H2172
Est 5:14 This suggestion delighted **H**, and he had H2172
Est 6: 4 Now **H** had just entered the outer court of H2172
Est 6: 5 answered, "**H** is standing in the court." H2172
Est 6: 6 When **H** entered, the king asked him H2172
Est 6: 6 Now **H** thought to himself, "Who is there H2172
Est 6:10 the king commanded **H**. "Get the robe H2172
Est 6:11 So **H** got the robe and the horse. H2172
Est 6:12 But **H** rushed home, with his head H2172
Est 6:14 hurried **H** away to the banquet H2172
Est 7: 1 So the king and **H** went to Queen Esther's H2172
Est 7: 6 This vile **H**!" Then Haman was H2172
Est 7: 6 Then **H** was terrified before the king and H2172
Est 7: 7 But **H**, realizing that the king had already H2172
Est 7: 8 **H** was falling on the couch where Esther H2172
Est 7:10 So they impaled **H** on the pole he had set H2172
Est 8: 1 Xerxes gave Queen Esther the estate of **H**, H2172
Est 8: 2 which he had reclaimed from **H**, and H2172
Est 8: 3 an end to the evil plan of **H** the Agagite, H2172
Est 8: 5 dispatches that **H** son of Hammedatha, H2172
Est 8: 7 the Jew, "Because **H** attacked the Jews, H2172
Est 9:10 the ten sons of **H** son of Hammedatha, the H2172
Est 9:12 the ten sons of **H** in the citadel of H2172
Est 9:14 and they impaled the ten sons of **H**. H2172
Est 9:24 For **H** son of Hammedatha, the Agagite H2172
Est 9:25 the evil scheme **H** had devised against H2257S

HAMAN'S (5) [HAMAN]
Est 3:12 of each people all **H** orders to the king's H2172
Est 7: 8 left the king's mouth, they covered **H** face. H2172
Est 7: 9 a height of fifty cubits stands by **H** house. H2172
Est 8: 2 And Esther appointed him over **H** estate. H2172
Est 9:13 let **H** ten sons be impaled on poles." H2172

HAMATH (24) [HAMATH ZOBAH, HAMATHITES, LEBO HAMATH]
2Sa 8: 9 When Tou king of **H** heard that David had H2828
2Ki 14:28 Israel both Damascus and **H**, H2828
2Ki 17:24 **H** and Sepharvaim and settled them in H2828
2Ki 17:30 and those from **H** made Ashima; H2828
2Ki 18:34 Where are the gods of **H** and Arpad H2828
2Ki 19:13 Where is the king of **H** or the king of H2828
2Ki 23:33 in the land of **H** so that he might not H2828
2Ki 25:21 in the land of **H**, the king had them H2828
1Ch 18: 3 in the vicinity of **H**, when he went to set H2828
1Ch 18: 9 When Tou king of **H** heard that David had H2828
2Ch 8: 4 all the store cities he had built in **H**. H2828
Isa 10: 9 Is not **H** like Arpad, and Samaria like H2828
Isa 11:11 from **H** and from the islands of the H2828
Isa 36:19 Where are the gods of **H** and Arpad H2828
Isa 37:13 Where is the king of **H** or the king of H2828
Jer 39: 5 king of Babylon at Riblah in the land of **H**, H2828
Jer 49:23 "**H** and Arpad are dismayed, for they have H2828
Jer 52: 9 king of Babylon at Riblah in the land of **H**, H2828
Jer 52:27 in the land of **H**, the king had them H2828
Eze 47:16 on the border between Damascus and **H**), H2828
Eze 47:17 with the border of **H** to the north. H2828
Eze 48: 1 of Damascus next to **H** will be part of its H2828
Am 6: 2 go from there to great **H**, and then go H2828
Zec 9: 2 on **H** too, which borders on it, and on H2828

HAMATH ZOBAH (1) [HAMATH, ZOBAH]
2Ch 8: 3 then went to **H** and captured it. H2832

HAMATHITES (2) [HAMATH]
Ge 10:18 Zemarites and **H**. Later the Canaanite H2833
1Ch 1:16 Arvadites, Zemarites and **H**. H2833

HAMITES (2) [HAM]
1Ch 4:40 Some **H** had lived there formerly H2769
1Ch 4:41 They attacked the **H** in their dwellings and NDT

HAMMAHLEKOTH See SELA HAMMAHLEKOTH

HAMMATH (2)
Jos 19:35 were Ziddim, Zer, **H**, Rakkath, Kinnereth, H2829
1Ch 2:55 These are the Kenites who came from **H** H2830

HAMMEDATHA (5)
Est 3: 1 King Xerxes honored Haman son of **H**, the H2158
Est 3:10 his finger and gave it to Haman son of **H**, H2158
Est 8: 5 the dispatches that Haman son of **H**, H2158
Est 9:10 the ten sons of Haman son of **H**, the H2158
Est 9:24 For Haman son of **H**, the Agagite, the H2158

HAMMER (9) [HAMMERED, HAMMERS]
Ex 25:31 **H out** its base and shaft, and make H5251+6913
Nu 16:38 **H** the censers *into* sheets to overlay H6913+8393
Jdg 4:21 up a tent peg and a **h** and went quietly to H5216
Jdg 5:26 *her right hand* for the workman's **h**. H2153
1Ki 6: 7 were used, and no **h**, chisel or any other H5216
Isa 41: 7 smooths with the **h** spurs on the one who H7079
Jer 10: 4 they fasten it with **h** and nails so it will H5216
Jer 23:29 "and like a **h** that breaks a rock in pieces? H7079
Jer 50:23 shattered is the **h** *of* the whole earth! H7079

HAMMERED (18) [HAMMER]
Ex 25:18 two cherubim out of **h** gold at the ends of H5251
Ex 25:36 with the lampstand, **h** out of pure gold. H5251
Ex 37: 7 two cherubim out of **h** gold at the ends of H5251
Ex 37:17 They **h out** its base and shaft, and made H5251
Ex 37:22 with the lampstand, **h out** *of* pure gold. H5251
Ex 39: 3 *They* **h out** thin sheets of gold and cut H8392
Nu 8: 4 It was made of **h** gold—from its base to H5251
Nu 10: 2 "Make two trumpets of **h** silver, and use H5251
Nu 16:39 and *he had* them **h out** to overlay the H8392
1Ki 6:32 the cherubim and palm trees with **h** gold. H8096
1Ki 6:35 them with gold **h evenly** over the carvings. H3837
1Ki 7:29 lions and bulls were wreaths of **h** work. H4618
1Ki 10:16 two hundred large shields of **h** gold; H8822
1Ki 10:17 three hundred small shields of **h** gold, H8822
2Ch 9:15 two hundred large shields of **h** gold; H8822
2Ch 9:15 hundred shekels of **h** gold went into each H8822
2Ch 9:16 three hundred small shields of **h** gold, H8822
Jer 10: 9 **H** silver is brought from Tarshish and gold H8392

HAMMERS (1) [HAMMER]
Isa 44:12 he shapes an idol with **h**, he forges it with H5216

HAMMOLEKETH (1)
1Ch 7:18 His sister **H** gave birth to Ishhod, Abiezer H2168

HAMMON (2)
Jos 19:28 **H** and Kanah, as far as Greater H2785
1Ch 6:76 Kedesh in Galilee, **H** and Kiriathaim H2785

HAMMOTH DOR (1) [DOR]
Jos 21:32 **H** and Kartan, together with their H2831

HAMMUEL (1)
1Ch 4:26 **H** his son, Zakkur his son and Shimei his H2781

HAMON See BAAL HAMON, HAMON GOG

HAMON GOG (2) [BAAL HAMON]
Eze 39:11 So it will be called the Valley of **H**. H2163
Eze 39:15 bury it in the Valley of **H**, H2163

HAMONAH (1)
Eze 39:16 near a town called **H**. And so they will H2164

HAMOR (13)
Ge 33:19 he bought from the sons of **H**, the father H2791
Ge 34: 2 When Shechem son of **H** the Hivite, the H2791
Ge 34: 4 And Shechem said to his father **H**, "Get H2791
Ge 34: 6 Shechem's father **H** went out to talk with H2791
Ge 34: 8 But **H** said to them, "My son Shechem has H2791
Ge 34:13 they spoke to Shechem and his father **H**. H2791
Ge 34:18 seemed good to **H** and his son Shechem. H2791
Ge 34:20 So **H** and his son Shechem went to the H2791
Ge 34:24 gate agreed with **H** and his son Shechem, H2791
Ge 34:26 They put **H** and his son Shechem to the H2791
Jos 24:32 pieces of silver from the sons of **H**, H2791
Jdg 9:28 Serve the family of **H**, Shechem's father H2791
Ac 7:16 from the sons *of* **H** at Shechem for a *G1846*

HAMPERED (1)
Pr 4:12 your steps *will* not *be* **h**; when you run, H7674

HAMSTRING (1) [HAMSTRUNG]
Jos 11: 6 *You are to* **h** their horses and burn their H6828

HAMSTRUNG (4) [HAMSTRING]
Ge 49: 6 in their anger and **h** oxen as they pleased H6828
Jos 11: 9 *He* **h** their horses and burned their H6828
2Sa 8: 4 He **h** all but a hundred of the chariot H6828
1Ch 18: 4 He **h** all but a hundred of the chariot H6828

HAMUL (3) [HAMULITE]
Ge 46:12 The sons of Perez: Hezron and **H**. H2783
Nu 26:21 through **H**, the Hamulite clan. H2783
1Ch 2: 5 The sons of Perez: Hezron and **H**. H2783

HAMULITE (1) [HAMUL]
Nu 26:21 through Hamul, the **H** clan. H2784

HAMUTAL (3)
2Ki 23:31 mother's name was **H** daughter of H2782
2Ki 24:18 mother's name was **H** daughter of H2782
Jer 52: 1 mother's name was **H** daughter of H2782

HANAMEL (4)
Jer 32: 7 **H** son of Shallum your uncle is going to H2856
Jer 32: 8 my cousin **H** came to me in the courtyard H2856
Jer 32: 9 from my cousin **H** and weighed out for H2856
Jer 32:12 of my cousin **H** and of the witnesses H2856

HANAN (12) [BAAL-HANAN, BEN-HANAN]
1Ch 8:23 Zikri, **H**, H2860
1Ch 8:38 Ishmael, Sheariah, Obadiah and **H**. H2860
1Ch 9:44 Ishmael, Sheariah, Obadiah and **H**. H2860
1Ch 11:43 **H** son of Maakah, Joshaphat the Mithnite, H2860
Ezr 2:46 Hagab, Shalmai, **H**, H2860
Ne 7:49 **H**, Giddel, Gahar, H2860
Ne 8: 7 Jozabad, **H** and Pelaiah—instructed the H2860
Ne 10:10 Shebaniah, Hodiah, Kelita, Pelaiah, **H**, H2860
Ne 10:22 Pelatiah, **H**, Anaiah, H2860
Ne 10:26 Ahiah, **H**, Anan, H2860
Ne 13:13 storerooms and made **H** son of Zakkur, H2860
Jer 35: 4 room of the sons of **H** son of Igdaliah the H2860

HANANEL (4)
Ne 3: 1 dedicated, and as far as the Tower of **H**. H2861
Ne 12:39 the Tower of **H** and the Tower of the H2861
Jer 31:38 from the Tower of **H** to the Corner Gate. H2861
Zec 14:10 from the Tower of **H** to the royal H2861

HANANI (11)
1Ki 16: 1 to Jehu son of **H** concerning Baasha: H2862
1Ki 16: 7 prophet Jehu son of **H** to Baasha and his H2862
1Ch 25: 4 Jerimoth; Hananiah, **H**, Eliathah, Giddalti H2862
1Ch 25:25 the eighteenth to **H**, his sons and H2862
2Ch 16: 7 At that time **H** the seer came to Asa king H2862
2Ch 19: 2 the seer, the son of **H**, went out to meet H2862
2Ch 20:34 are written in the annals of Jehu son of **H** H2862
Ezr 10:20 descendants of Immer: **H** and Zebadiah. H2862
Ne 1: 2 **H**, one of my brothers, came from Judah H2862
Ne 7: 2 I put in charge of Jerusalem my brother **H** H2862
Ne 12:36 Nethanel, Judah and **H**—with musical H2862

HANANIAH (28)
1Ch 3:19 Meshullam and **H**. Shelomith was their H2863
1Ch 3:21 The descendants of **H**: Pelatiah and H2863
1Ch 8:24 **H**, Elam, Anthothijah, H2863
1Ch 25: 4 Jerimoth; **H**, Hanani, Eliathah, H2863
1Ch 25:23 the sixteenth to **H**, his sons and relatives H2864
2Ch 26:11 the officer under the direction of **H**, H2864
Ezr 10:28 Jehohanan, **H**, Zabbai and Athlai. H2863
Ne 3: 8 the next section; and **H**, one of the H2863
Ne 3:30 Next to him, **H** son of Shelemiah, and H2863
Ne 7: 2 along with **H** the commander of the H2863
Ne 10:23 Hoshea, **H**, Hasshub, H2863
Ne 12:12 Meraiah; of Jeremiah's, **H**; H2863
Ne 12:41 Zechariah and **H** with their trumpets— H2863
Jer 28: 1 the prophet **H** son of Azzur, who H2863
Jer 28: 5 to the prophet **H** before the priests and H2863
Jer 28:10 Then the prophet **H** took the yoke off the H2863
Jer 28:12 After the prophet **H** had broken the yoke H2863
Jer 28:13 "Go and tell **H**, 'This is what the LORD says H2863
Jer 28:15 prophet Jeremiah said to **H** the prophet, H2863
Jer 28:15 said to Hananiah the prophet, "Listen, **H**! H2863
Jer 28:17 of that same year, **H** the prophet died. H2863
Jer 36:12 Zedekiah son of **H**, and all the other H2864
Jer 37:13 the son of **H**, arrested him and H2863
Da 1: 6 Daniel, **H**, Mishael and H2863
Da 1: 7 Belteshazzar; to **H**, Shadrach; to Mishael H2863
Da 1:11 over Daniel, **H**, Mishael and Azariah, H2863
Da 1:19 equal to Daniel, **H**, Mishael and Azariah; H2863
Da 2:17 explained the matter to his friends **H**, A10275

HAND (813) [HANDBREADTH, HANDED, HANDFUL, HANDFULS, HANDING, HANDS, LEFT-HANDED, OPENHANDED, RIGHT-HANDED]
Ge 3:22 to reach out his **h** and take also from the H3338
Ge 4:11 receive your brother's blood from your **h**. H3338
Ge 8: 9 He reached out his **h** and took the dove H3338
Ge 14:20 who delivered your enemies into your **h**." H3338
Ge 14:22 "With raised **h** I have sworn an oath to H3338
Ge 16:12 his **h** will be against everyone and H3338
Ge 16:12 everyone and everyone's **h** against him, H3338
Ge 19:16 the men grasped his **h** and the hands of H3338
Ge 21:18 Lift the boy up and take him by the **h**, for I H3338
Ge 21:30 seven lambs from my **h** as a witness that I H3338
Ge 22:10 he reached out his **h** and took the knife to H3338
Ge 22:12 "Do not lay a **h** on the boy," he said. "Do H3338
Ge 24: 2 that he had, "Put your **h** under my thigh. H3338
Ge 24: 9 So the servant put his **h** under the thigh of H3338
Ge 25:26 came out, with his **h** grasping Esau's heel H3338
Ge 32:11 from the **h** *of* my brother Esau, for I H3338
Ge 37:22 the wilderness, but don't lay a **h** on him." H3338
Ge 38:18 the staff in your **h**," she answered. H3338
Ge 38:28 one of them put out his **h**; so the midwife H3338
Ge 38:29 But when he drew back his **h**, his brother H3338
Ge 39:12 left his cloak in her **h** and ran out of the H3338
Ge 39:13 left his cloak in her **h** and had run out of H3338
Ge 40:11 Pharaoh's cup was in my **h**, and I took the H3338
Ge 40:11 Pharaoh's cup and put the cup in his **h**." H4090
Ge 40:13 you will put Pharaoh's cup in his **h** H3338
Ge 40:21 again put the cup into Pharaoh's **h**— H4090
Ge 41:44 word no one will lift **h** or foot in all Egypt." H3338
Ge 46: 4 And Joseph's own **h** will close your eyes." H3338
Ge 47:29 put your **h** under my thigh and promise H3338
Ge 48:13 toward Israel's left **h** and Manasseh on his NDT
Ge 48:13 Manasseh on his left toward Israel's **right** *h*. AIT
Ge 48:14 Israel reached out his **right** *h* and put it on AIT
Ge 48:14 he put his left **h** on Manasseh's head NDT
Ge 48:17 placing his right **h** on Ephraim's head he H3338
Ge 48:17 hold of his father's **h** to move it from H3338
Ge 48:18 is the firstborn; put your **right** *h* on his head." AIT
Ge 49: 8 your **h** will be on the neck of your H3338
Ge 49:24 because of the **h** *of* the Mighty One of H3338
Ex 3: 8 them from the **h** *of* the Egyptians and H3338
Ex 3:19 you go unless a mighty **h** compels him. H3338
Ex 3:20 So I will stretch out my **h** and strike the H3338
Ex 4: 2 LORD said to him, "What is that in your **h**?" H3338
Ex 4: 4 "Reach out your **h** and take it by the tail." H3338
Ex 4: 4 it turned back into a staff in his **h**. H4090
Ex 4: 6 LORD said, "Put your **h** inside your cloak." H3338
Ex 4: 6 So Moses put his **h** into his cloak, and H3338
Ex 4: 7 So Moses put his **h** back into his cloak H3338
Ex 4:17 this staff in your **h** so you can perform the H3338
Ex 4:20 And he took the staff of God in his **h**. H3338
Ex 5:21 have put a sword in their **h** to kill us." H3338

Ex 6: 1 of my mighty **h** he will let them go; H3338
Ex 6: 1 of my mighty **h** he will drive them H3338
Ex 6: 8 swore with uplifted **h** to give to Abraham, H3338
Ex 7: 4 Then I will lay my **h** on Egypt and with H3338
Ex 7: 5 when I stretch out my **h** against Egypt H3338
Ex 7:15 take in your **h** the staff that was H3338
Ex 7:17 staff that is in my **h** I will strike the water H3338
Ex 7:19 stretch out your **h** over the waters of H3338
Ex 8: 5 'Stretch out your **h** with your staff over the H3338
Ex 8: 6 stretched out his **h** over the waters of H3338
Ex 8:17 stretched out his **h** with the staff and H3338
Ex 9: 3 the **h** *of* the LORD will bring a terrible H3338
Ex 9:15 stretched out my **h** and struck you and H3338
Ex 9:22 "Stretch out your **h** toward the sky so that H3338
Ex 10:12 "Stretch out your **h** over Egypt so that H3338
Ex 10:21 "Stretch out your **h** toward the sky so that H3338
Ex 10:22 Moses stretched out his **h** toward the sky, H3338
Ex 11: 5 who is at her **h mill**, and all the H8160
Ex 12:11 on your feet and your staff in your **h**. H3338
Ex 13: 3 LORD brought you out of it with a mighty **h**. H3338
Ex 13: 9 like a sign on your **h** and a reminder on H3338
Ex 13: 9 you out of Egypt with his mighty **h**. H3338
Ex 13:14 'With a mighty **h** the LORD brought us out H3338
Ex 13:16 like a sign on your **h** and a symbol on H3338
Ex 13:16 brought us out of Egypt with his mighty **h**." H3338
Ex 14:16 stretch out your **h** over the sea to H3338
Ex 14:21 Moses stretched out his **h** over the sea, H3338
Ex 14:26 "Stretch out your **h** over the sea so that H3338
Ex 14:27 Moses stretched out his **h** over the sea H3338
Ex 14:31 saw the mighty **h** *of* the LORD displayed H3338
Ex 15: 6 Your **right** *h*, LORD, was majestic in power AIT
Ex 15: 6 Your **right** *h*, LORD, shattered the AIT
Ex 15: 9 my sword and my **h** will destroy them. H3338
Ex 15:12 "You stretch out your **right** *h*, and the earth AIT
Ex 15:20 took a timbrel in her **h**, and all the H3338
Ex 16: 3 only we had died by the LORD's **h** in Egypt! H3338
Ex 17: 5 take in your **h** the staff with which H3338
Ex 18: 9 them from the **h** *of* the Egyptians. H3338
Ex 18:10 you from the **h** *of* the Egyptians and H3338
Ex 18:10 the people from the **h** *of* the Egyptians. H3338
Ex 19:13 with arrows; not a **h** is to be laid on them. H3338
Ex 21:24 tooth for tooth, **h** for hand, foot for H3338
Ex 21:24 tooth for tooth, hand for **h**, foot for foot, H3338
Ex 24:11 did not raise his **h** against these leaders H3338
Ex 32:11 of Egypt with great power and a mighty **h**? H3338
Ex 33:22 cover you with my **h** until I have passed H4090
Ex 33:23 I will remove my **h** and you will see my H4090
Lev 1: 4 You are to lay your **h** on the head of the H3338
Lev 3: 2 You are to lay your **h** on the head of your H3338
Lev 3: 8 lay your **h** on its head and slaughter it in H3338
Lev 3:13 lay your **h** on its head and slaughter it in H3338
Lev 4: 4 He is to lay his **h** on its head and H3338
Lev 4:24 He is to lay his **h** on the goat's head and H3338
Lev 4:29 They are to lay their **h** on the head of the H3338
Lev 4:33 They are to lay their **h** on its head and H3338
Lev 8:23 thumb of his right **h** and on the big toe of H3338
Lev 14:14 thumb of their right **h** and on the big toe H3338
Lev 14:15 pour it in the **palm of** his own left **h**, H4090
Lev 14:17 thumb of their right **h** and on the big toe H3338
Lev 14:25 thumb of their right **h** and on the big toe H3338
Lev 14:26 of the oil into the **palm of** his own left **h**, H4090
Lev 14:28 thumb of their right **h** and on the big toe H3338
Lev 21:19 no man with a crippled foot or **h**, H3338
Lev 22:25 animals from the **h** *of* a foreigner and H3338
Nu 11: 8 ground it in a **h mill** or crushed it in a H8160
Nu 14:30 swore with uplifted **h** to make your home, H3338
Nu 22:23 in the road with a drawn sword in his **h**, H3338
Nu 22:29 If only I had a sword in my **h**, I would kill H3338
Nu 25: 7 he left the assembly, took a spear in his **h** H3338
Nu 27:18 of leadership, and lay your **h** on him. H3338
Dt 2:15 The LORD's **h** was against them until he H3338
Dt 2:24 have given into your **h** Sihon the Amorite, H3338
Dt 3:24 servant your greatness and your strong **h**. H3338
Dt 4:34 by a mighty **h** and an outstretched arm H3338
Dt 5:15 there with a mighty **h** and an outstretched H3338
Dt 6:21 brought us out of Egypt with a mighty **h**. H3338
Dt 7: 8 out with a mighty **h** and redeemed you H3338
Dt 7:19 the mighty **h** and outstretched arm H3338
Dt 7:24 He will give their kings into your **h**, and H3338
Dt 9:26 brought out of Egypt with a mighty **h**. H3338
Dt 11: 2 majesty, his mighty **h**, his outstretched H3338
Dt 12: 7 in everything you have put your **h** to, H3338
Dt 12:18 your God in everything you put your **h** to. H3338
Dt 13: 9 Your **h** must be the first in putting them to H3338
Dt 15:10 work and in everything you put your **h** to. H3338
Dt 15:18 worth twice as much as that of a **hired h**. H8502
Dt 19:21 tooth for tooth, **h** for hand, foot for H3338
Dt 19:21 tooth for tooth, hand for **h**, foot for foot. H3338
Dt 20:13 the LORD your God delivers it into your **h**, H3338
Dt 23:15 *do* not **h** them **over** to their master. H6037
Dt 23:20 you put your **h** to in the land you are H3338
Dt 25:12 you shall cut off her **h**. Show her no pity. H4090
Dt 26: 8 Egypt with a mighty **h** and an outstretched H3338
Dt 28: 8 barns and on everything you put your **h** to. H3338
Dt 28:20 rebuke in everything you put your **h** to, H3338
Dt 28:32 them day after day, powerless to lift a **h**. H3338
Dt 32:27 say, 'Our **h** has triumphed; the LORD H3338
Dt 32:39 and no one can deliver out of my **h**. H3338
Dt 32:40 I lift my **h** to heaven and solemnly swear H3338
Dt 32:41 sword and my **h** grasps it in judgment H3338
Dt 33: 3 people; all the holy ones are in your **h**. H3338
Jos 2:19 will be on our head if a **h** is laid on them. H3338
Jos 4:24 might know that the **h** *of* the LORD is H3338
Jos 5:13 front of him with a drawn sword in his **h**. H3338
Jos 8: 7 The LORD your God will give it into your **h**. H3338
Jos 8:18 out toward Ai the javelin that is in your **h**, H3338
Jos 8:18 for into your **h** I will deliver the city." H3338
Jos 8:18 the city the javelin that was in his **h**. H3338
Jos 8:26 did not draw back the **h** that held out his H3338
Jos 10: 8 of them; I have given them into your **h**. H3338
Jos 10:19 your God has given them into your **h**." H3338
Jos 10:30 gave that city and its king into Israel's **h**. H3338
Jos 11: 6 I *will* **h** all of them, slain, **over** to Israel H5989
Jos 11: 8 the LORD gave them into the **h** *of* Israel. H3338
Jos 22:31 rescued the Israelites from the LORD's **h**." H3338
Jos 24:10 and I delivered you out of his **h**. H3338
Jdg 2:15 the **h** *of* the LORD was against them to H3338
Jdg 3:21 Ehud reached with his left **h**, drew the H3338
Jdg 4:24 And the **h** *of* the Israelites pressed harder H3338
Jdg 5:26 Her **h** reached for the tent peg, her right H3338
Jdg 5:26 her **right** *h* for the workman's hammer. AIT
Jdg 6: 9 I rescued you from the **h** *of* the Egyptians H3338
Jdg 6: 9 you from the **h** *of* all your oppressors; H3338
Jdg 6:13 us and given us into the **h** *of* Midian." H4090
Jdg 6:14 have and save Israel out of Midian's **h**. H4090
Jdg 6:21 with the tip of the staff that was in his **h**. H3338
Jdg 6:36 save Israel by my **h** as you have promised H3338
Jdg 6:37 know that you will save Israel by my **h**, H3338
Jdg 8: 7 given Zebah and Zalmunna into my **h**, H3338
Jdg 8:22 you have saved us from the **h** *of* Midian." H3338
Jdg 9:17 life to rescue you from the **h** *of* Midian. H3338
Jdg 15:12 you up and **h** you **over** *to* the H928+5989+3338
Jdg 15:13 up and **h** you **over** *to* them. H5989+3338+928
Jdg 16:26 Samson said to the servant who held his **h**, H3338
Jdg 16:29 his **right** *h* on the one and his left hand on AIT
Jdg 16:29 hand on the one and his left **h** on the other, NDT
Ru 1:13 because the LORD's **h** has turned against H3338
Ru 2: 9 I have told the men not *to* **lay a h on** you H5595
1Sa 2:13 fork in his **h** while the meat was being H3338
1Sa 2:16 answer, "No, **h** it **over** now; if you don't H5989
1Sa 4: 3 us and save us from the **h** *of* our enemies." H4090
1Sa 4: 8 us from the **h** *of* these mighty gods? H3338
1Sa 5: 6 The LORD's **h** was heavy on the people of H3338
1Sa 5: 7 because his **h** is heavy on us and on H3338
1Sa 5: 9 the LORD's **h** was against that city H3338
1Sa 5:11 with panic; God's **h** was very heavy on it. H3338
1Sa 6: 3 will know why his **h** has not been lifted H3338
1Sa 6: 5 he will lift his **h** from you and your gods H3338
1Sa 6: 9 that it was not his **h** that struck us but that H3338
1Sa 7: 3 deliver you out of the **h** *of* the Philistines." H3338
1Sa 7: 8 rescue us from the **h** *of* the Philistines." H3338
1Sa 7:13 the **h** *of* the LORD was against the H3338
1Sa 9:16 deliver them from the **h** *of* the Philistines. H3338
1Sa 10: 7 do whatever your **h** finds to do, for God is H3338
1Sa 12: 3 From whose **h** have I accepted a bribe to H3338
1Sa 12: 4 have not taken anything from anyone's **h**." H3338
1Sa 12: 5 that you have not found anything in my **h**." H3338
1Sa 12: 9 so he sold them into the **h** *of* Sisera, the H3338
1Sa 12:15 his commands, his **h** will be against you H3338
1Sa 13:22 Jonathan had a sword or spear in his **h**; H3338
1Sa 14:12 LORD has given them into the **h** *of* Israel." H3338
1Sa 14:19 Saul said to the priest, "Withdraw your **h**." H3338
1Sa 14:26 no one put his **h** to his mouth H3338
1Sa 14:27 staff that was in his **h** and dipped it into H3338
1Sa 14:27 He raised his **h** to his mouth, and his eyes H3338
1Sa 14:37 Will you give them into Israel's **h**?" But H3338
1Sa 17:37 rescue me from the **h** *of* this Philistine." H3338
1Sa 17:40 Then he took his staff in his **h**, chose five H3338
1Sa 17:40 with his sling in his **h**, approached the H3338
1Sa 17:50 a sword in his **h** he struck down the H3338
1Sa 18:10 he usually did. Saul had a spear in his **h** H3338
1Sa 18:17 himself, "I will not raise a **h** against him. H3338
1Sa 18:21 him and so that the **h** *of* the Philistines H3338
1Sa 19: 9 sitting in his house with his spear in his **h**. H3338
1Sa 20: 8 Why **h** me **over** to your father? H995
1Sa 21: 3 what *do* you **have on h**? H3780+9393+3338
1Sa 21: 4 **have** any ordinary bread **on h**; H448+9393+3338
1Sa 22: 6 spear in **h**, under the tamarisk H3338
1Sa 22:17 unwilling to raise a **h** to strike the priests H3338
1Sa 23: 4 going to give the Philistines into your **h**." H3338
1Sa 23:17 "My father Saul will not lay a **h** on you H3338
1Sa 24: 6 anointed, or lay my **h** on him; for he is the H3338
1Sa 24:10 'I will not lay my **h** on my lord, because H3338
1Sa 24:11 look at this piece of your robe in my **h**! H3338
1Sa 24:11 is nothing in my **h** to indicate that I am H3338
1Sa 24:12 done to me, but my **h** will not touch you. H3338
1Sa 24:13 evil deeds,' so my **h** will not touch you. H3338
1Sa 24:15 me by delivering me from your **h**." H3338
1Sa 25:35 accepted from her **h** what she had H3338
1Sa 26: 9 Who can lay a **h** on the LORD's anointed H3338
1Sa 26:11 that I should lay a **h** on the LORD's H3338
1Sa 26:23 I would not lay a **h** on the LORD's H3338
1Sa 27: 1 days I will be destroyed by the **h** *of* Saul. H3338
1Sa 27: 1 in Israel, and I will slip out of his **h**." H3338
1Sa 30:15 me or **h** me **over** *to* my master H6037+928+3338
2Sa 1:14 afraid to lift your **h** to destroy the LORD's H3338
2Sa 2:14 men get up and **fight h to hand** in front of H8471
2Sa 2:14 men get up and **fight hand to h** in front of H8471
2Sa 3:18 Israel from the **h** *of* the Philistines and H3338
2Sa 3:18 from the **h** *of* all their enemies. H3338
2Sa 4:11 his blood from your **h** and rid the earth of H3338
2Sa 12: 7 I delivered you from the **h** *of* Saul. H3338
2Sa 13: 5 may watch her and then eat it from her **h**. H3338
2Sa 13: 6 in my sight, so I may eat from her **h**." H3338
2Sa 13:10 my bedroom so I may eat from your **h**." H3338
2Sa 14: 7 '**H over** the one who struck his brother H5989
2Sa 14:16 his servant from the **h** *of* the man who is H4090
2Sa 14:19 "Isn't the **h** *of* Joab with you in all this?" H3338
2Sa 15: 5 Absalom would reach out his **h**, take hold H3338
2Sa 18:12 I would not lay a **h** on the king's son." H3338
2Sa 18:14 javelins in his **h** and plunged them into H4090
2Sa 18:19 delivering him from the **h** *of* his enemies." H3338
2Sa 18:31 you from the **h** *of* all who rose up H3338
2Sa 19: 9 delivered us from the **h** *of* our enemies; H4090
2Sa 19: 9 rescued us from the **h** *of* the Philistines. H4090
2Sa 20: 9 by the beard with his right **h** to kiss him. H3338
2Sa 20:10 his guard against the dagger in Joab's **h**, H3338
2Sa 20:21 has lifted up his **h** against the king H3338
2Sa 20:21 **H over** this one man, and I'll withdraw H5989
2Sa 21:20 six fingers on each **h** and six toes on each H3338
2Sa 22: 1 him from the **h** *of* all his enemies and H4090
2Sa 22: 1 of all his enemies and from the **h** *of* Saul. H4090
2Sa 23: 6 which are not gathered with the **h**. H3338
2Sa 23:10 Philistines till his **h** grew tired and froze to H3338
2Sa 23:21 the Egyptian had a spear in his **h**, H3338
2Sa 23:21 from the Egyptian's **h** and killed him with H3338
2Sa 24:16 stretched out his **h** to destroy Jerusalem, H3338
2Sa 24:16 Withdraw your **h**." The angel of the H3338
2Sa 24:17 Let your **h** fall on me and my family." H3338
1Ki 2:19 and she sat down at his **right** *h*. AIT
1Ki 8:15 who with his own **h** has fulfilled what he H3338
1Ki 8:24 with your **h** you have fulfilled it— H3338
1Ki 8:42 name and your mighty **h** and your H3338
1Ki 11:12 I will tear it out of the **h** *of* your son. H3338
1Ki 11:31 out of Solomon's **h** and give you ten H3338
1Ki 11:34 the whole kingdom out of Solomon's **h**; H3338
1Ki 13: 4 he stretched out his **h** from the altar and H3338
1Ki 13: 4 But the **h** he stretched out toward the man H3338
1Ki 13: 6 pray for me that my **h** may be restored." H3338
1Ki 13: 6 the king's **h** was restored and H3338
1Ki 18:44 as small as a man's **h** is rising from the H4090
1Ki 20:13 I will give it into your **h** today, and then H3338
1Ki 22: 6 "for the Lord will give it into the king's **h**." H3338
1Ki 22:12 "for the LORD will give it into the king's **h**." H3338
1Ki 22:15 "for the LORD will give it into the king's **h**." H3338
2Ki 3:15 playing, the **h** *of* the LORD came on Elisha H3338
2Ki 4:29 your belt, take my staff in your **h** and run. H3338
2Ki 5:11 wave his **h** over the spot and cure me of H3338
2Ki 6: 7 the man reached out his **h** and took it. H3338
2Ki 10:15 said Jehu, "give me your **h**." So he did, H3338
2Ki 11: 8 the king, each of you with weapon in **h**. H3338
2Ki 11:11 each with weapon in **h**, stationed H3338
2Ki 12: 7 but **h** it **over** for repairing the temple." H5989
2Ki 14:27 saved them by the **h** *of* Jeroboam son of H3338
2Ki 16: 7 save me out of the **h** *of* the king of Aram H4090
2Ki 17:39 you from the **h** *of* all your enemies." H3338
2Ki 18:21 which pierces the **h** *of* anyone who leans H4090
2Ki 18:29 He cannot deliver you from my **h**. H3338
2Ki 18:30 be given into the **h** *of* the king of Assyria. H3338
2Ki 18:33 his land from the **h** *of* the king of Assyria? H3338
2Ki 18:34 Have they rescued Samaria from my **h**? H3338
2Ki 18:35 the LORD deliver Jerusalem from my **h**?" H3338
2Ki 19:19 deliver us from his **h**, so that all the H3338
2Ki 20: 6 this city from the **h** *of* the king of Assyria. H4090
1Ch 4:10 Let your **h** be with me, and keep me from H3338
1Ch 6:15 into exile by the **h** *of* Nebuchadnezzar. H3338
1Ch 6:39 associate Asaph, who served at his **right** *h*: AIT
1Ch 6:44 their associates, the Merarites, at his left **h**: NDT
1Ch 11:23 had a spear like a weaver's rod in his **h**, H3338
1Ch 11:23 from the Egyptian's **h** and killed him with H3338
1Ch 13: 9 Uzzah reached out his **h** to steady the ark H3338
1Ch 13:10 because he had put his **h** on the ark. H3338
1Ch 14:11 broken out against my enemies by my **h**." H3338
1Ch 20: 6 six fingers on each **h** and six toes on each NDT
1Ch 21:15 Withdraw your **h**." The angel of the H3338
1Ch 21:16 a drawn sword in his **h** extended over H3338
1Ch 21:17 let your **h** fall on me and my family H3338
1Ch 28:19 writing as a result of the LORD's **h** on me, H3338
1Ch 29:14 given you only what comes from your **h**. H3338
1Ch 29:16 your Holy Name comes from your **h**, H3338
2Ch 6:15 with your **h** you have fulfilled it— H3338
2Ch 6:32 name and your mighty **h** and your H3338
2Ch 16: 7 king of Aram has escaped from your **h**. H3338
2Ch 16: 8 the LORD, he delivered them into your **h**. H3338
2Ch 18: 5 "for God will give it into the king's **h**." H3338
2Ch 18:11 "for the LORD will give it into the king's **h**." H3338
2Ch 18:14 "for they will be given into your **h**." H3338
2Ch 20: 6 Power and might are in your **h**, and no H3338
2Ch 23: 7 around the king, each with weapon in **h**. H3338
2Ch 23:10 each with his weapon in his **h**, around the H3338
2Ch 25:15 not save their own people from your **h**?" H3338
2Ch 26:19 had a censer in his **h** ready to burn H3338
2Ch 28: 9 with Judah, he gave them into your **h**. H3338
2Ch 30: 6 escaped from the **h** *of* the kings of Assyria H4090
2Ch 30:12 Also in Judah the **h** *of* God was on the H3338
2Ch 32:11 save us from the **h** *of* the king of Assyria, H4090
2Ch 32:13 ever able to deliver their land from my **h**? H3338
2Ch 32:14 then can your god deliver you from my **h**? H3338
2Ch 32:15 his people from my **h** or the hand of my H3338
2Ch 32:15 my hand or the **h** *of* my predecessors. H3338
2Ch 32:15 less will your god deliver you from my **h**!" H3338
2Ch 32:17 did not rescue their people from my **h**, H3338
2Ch 32:17 will not rescue his people from my **h**." H3338
2Ch 32:22 Jerusalem from the **h** *of* Sennacherib king H3338
2Ch 32:22 of Assyria and from the **h** *of* all others. H3338
Ezr 6:12 people who lifts a **h** to change this A10311

Ezr 7: 6 the **h** *of* the LORD his God was on him. H3338
Ezr 7: 9 the gracious **h** *of* his God was on him. H3338
Ezr 7:14 the Law of your God, which is in your **h**. A10311
Ezr 7:28 Because the **h** *of* the LORD my God was on H3338
Ezr 8:18 the gracious **h** *of* our God was on us, H3338
Ezr 8:22 "The gracious **h** *of* our God is on everyone H3338
Ezr 8:31 The **h** *of* our God was on us, and he H3338
Ezr 9: 7 humiliation at the **h** *of* foreign kings, H3338
Ne 1:10 by your great strength and your mighty **h**. H3338
Ne 2: 8 the gracious **h** *of* my God was on me, H3338
Ne 2:18 the gracious **h** *of* my God on me and H3338
Ne 4:17 their work with one **h** and held a weapon H3338
Ne 6: 5 in his **h** was an unsealed letter H3338
Ne 9:15 had sworn with uplifted **h** to give them. H3338
Ne 9:27 rescued them from the **h** *of* their enemies. H3338
Ne 9:28 them to the **h** *of* their enemies so H3338
Est 5: 2 to her the gold scepter that was in his **h**. H3338
Est 9: 1 the Jews **got the upper h** over those H8948
Job 1:11 now stretch out your **h** and strike H3338
Job 2: 5 now stretch out your **h** and strike his flesh H3338
Job 6: 9 to let loose his **h** and cut off my life! H3338
Job 6:23 deliver me from the **h** *of* the enemy H3338
Job 10: 7 that no one can rescue me from your **h**? H3338
Job 11:14 sin that is in your **h** and allow no evil to H3338
Job 12: 6 God are secure—those God has in his **h**. H3338
Job 12: 9 not know that the **h** *of* the LORD has done H3338
Job 12:10 In his **h** is the life of every creature and H3338
Job 13:21 Withdraw your **h** far from me, and stop H4090
Job 15:23 he knows the day of darkness is at **h**. H3338
Job 19:21 have pity, for the **h** *of* God has struck me. H3338
Job 21: 5 be appalled; clap your **h** over your mouth. H3338
Job 23: 2 his **h** is heavy in spite of my groaning. H3338
Job 26:13 his **h** pierced the gliding serpent. H3338
Job 29:20 the bow will be ever new in my **h**. H3338
Job 30:21 with the might of your **h** you attack me. H3338
Job 30:24 no one lays a **h** on a broken man when H3338
Job 31:21 if I have raised my **h** against the H3338
Job 31:27 enticed and my **h** offered them a kiss of H3338
Job 33: 7 nor should my **h** be heavy on you. H437
Job 34:20 the mighty are removed without human **h**. H3338
Job 35: 7 or what does he receive from your **h**? H3338
Job 40: 4 I reply to you? I put my **h** over my mouth. H3338
Job 40:14 to you that your own **right** *h* can save you. AIT
Job 41: 8 If you lay a **h** on it, you will remember the H4090
Ps 10:12 Lift up your **h**, O God. Do not forget H3338
Ps 10:14 you consider their grief and take it in **h**. H3338
Ps 16: 8 With him at my **right** *h*, I will not be AIT
Ps 16:11 with eternal pleasures at your **right** *h*. AIT
Ps 17: 7 you who save by your **right** *h* those who take AIT
Ps 17:14 By your **h** save me from such people, LORD H3338
Ps 18: T him from the **h** *of* all his enemies and H4090
Ps 18: T of all his enemies and from the **h** *of* Saul. H3338
Ps 18:35 my shield, and your **right** *h* sustains me; your AIT
Ps 20: 6 with the victorious power of his **right** *h*. AIT
Ps 21: 8 Your **h** will lay hold on all your enemies H3338
Ps 21: 8 enemies; your **right** *h* will seize your foes. AIT
Ps 32: 4 day and night your **h** was heavy on me; H3338
Ps 36:11 the **h** *of* the wicked drive me away. H3338
Ps 37:24 for the LORD upholds him with his **h**. H3338
Ps 38: 2 and your **h** has come down on me. H3338
Ps 39:10 I am overcome by the blow of your **h**. H3338
Ps 44: 2 With your **h** you drove out the nations H3338
Ps 44: 3 them victory; it was your **right** *h*, your arm, AIT
Ps 45: 4 let your **right** *h* achieve awesome deeds. AIT
Ps 45: 9 at your **right** *h* is the royal bride in gold of AIT
Ps 48:10 your **right** *h* is filled with righteousness. AIT
Ps 60: 5 Save us and help us with your **right** *h*, that AIT
Ps 63: 8 I cling to you; your **right** *h* upholds me. AIT
Ps 71: 4 my God, from the **h** *of* the wicked, from H3338
Ps 73:23 with you; you hold me by my right **h**. H3338
Ps 74:11 Why do you hold back your **h**, your right H3338
Ps 74:11 do you hold back your hand, your **right** *h*? AIT
Ps 74:19 *Do* not **h over** the life of your dove to wild H5989
Ps 75: 8 In the **h** *of* the LORD is a cup full of H3338
Ps 77:10 when the Most High stretched out his **right** *h*. AIT
Ps 77:20 like a flock by the **h** *of* Moses and Aaron. H3338
Ps 78:54 to the hill country his **right** *h* had taken. AIT
Ps 80:15 the root your **right** *h* has planted, the son you AIT
Ps 80:17 Let your **h** rest on the man at your right H3338
Ps 80:17 Let your hand rest on the man at your **right** *h* AIT
Ps 81:14 enemies and turn my **h** against their foes! H3338
Ps 82: 4 deliver them from the **h** *of* the wicked. H3338
Ps 89:13 with power; your **h** is strong, your right H3338
Ps 89:13 your hand is strong, your **right** *h* exalted. AIT
Ps 89:21 My **h** will sustain him; surely my arm will H3338
Ps 89:25 I will set his **h** over the sea, his right hand H3338
Ps 89:25 hand over the sea, his **right** *h* over the rivers. AIT
Ps 89:42 You have exalted the **right** *h of* his foes; you AIT
Ps 91: 7 ten thousand at your **right** *h*, but it will not AIT
Ps 95: 4 In his **h** are the depths of the earth, and H3338
Ps 97:10 delivers them from the **h** *of* the wicked. H3338
Ps 98: 1 his **right** *h* and his holy arm have worked AIT
Ps 104:28 when you open your **h**, they are satisfied H3338
Ps 106:10 He saved them from the **h** *of* the foe; from H3338
Ps 106:10 from the **h** *of* the enemy he redeemed H3338
Ps 106:26 them with uplifted **h** that he would make H3338
Ps 107: 2 those he redeemed from the **h** *of* the foe, H3338
Ps 108: 6 Save us and help us with your **right** *h*, that AIT
Ps 109: 6 my enemy; let an accuser stand at his **right** *h*. AIT
Ps 109:27 Let them know that it is your **h**, that you H3338
Ps 109:31 For he stands at the **right** *h of* the needy, to AIT
Ps 110: 1 "Sit at my **right** *h* until I make your enemies a AIT
Ps 110: 5 The Lord is at your **right** *h*; he will crush AIT
Ps 118:15 "The LORD's **right** *h* has done mighty things! AIT
Ps 118:16 The LORD's **right** *h* is lifted high; the LORD's AIT
Ps 118:16 the LORD's **right** *h* has done mighty things!" AIT
Ps 118:27 **With** boughs **in h**, join in the festal H928
Ps 119:173 May your **h** be ready to help me, for I H3338
Ps 121: 5 the LORD is your shade at your right **h**; H3338
Ps 123: 2 of slaves look to the **h** *of* their master, H3338
Ps 123: 2 female slave look to the **h** *of* her mistress, H3338
Ps 136:12 with a mighty **h** and outstretched arm; His H3338
Ps 137: 5 Jerusalem, may my **right** *h* forget its skill. AIT
Ps 138: 7 stretch out your **h** against the anger of H3338
Ps 138: 7 of my foes; with your **right** *h* you save me. AIT
Ps 139: 5 before, and you lay your **h** upon me. H4090
Ps 139:10 even there your **h** will guide me, your H3338
Ps 139:10 will guide me, your **right** *h* will hold me fast. AIT
Ps 142: 4 there is no one *at* my **right** *h*; no one is AIT
Ps 144: 7 Reach down your **h** from on high; deliver H3338
Ps 145:16 You open your **h** and satisfy the desires of H3338
Pr 1:24 pays attention when I stretch out my **h**, H3338
Pr 3:16 Long life is in her **right** *h*; in her left hand are AIT
Pr 3:16 in her left **h** are riches and honor. NDT
Pr 6: 5 like a gazelle from the **h** of the hunter H3338
Pr 17:16 fools have money in **h** to buy wisdom, H3338
Pr 19:24 A sluggard buries his **h** in the dish; he H3338
Pr 21: 1 In the LORD's **h** the king's heart is a stream H3338
Pr 26: 9 in a drunkard's **h** is a proverb in the H3338
Pr 26:15 A sluggard buries his **h** in the dish; he is H3338
Pr 27:16 the wind or grasping oil with the **h**. H3545
Pr 30:28 a lizard can be caught with the **h**, yet it is H3338
Pr 30:32 plan evil, clap your **h** over your mouth! H3338
Pr 31:19 In her **h** she holds the distaff and grasps H3338
Ecc 2:24 This too, I see, is from the **h** *of* God, H3338
Ecc 2:26 up wealth to **h** it **over** to the one who H5989
Ecc 9:10 Whatever your **h** finds to do, do it with all H3338
SS 5: 4 My beloved thrust his **h** through the H3338
Isa 1:25 I will turn my **h** against you; I will H3338
Isa 5:25 his **h** is raised and he strikes them down. H3338
Isa 5:25 is not turned away, his **h** is still upraised. H3338
Isa 6: 6 flew to me with a live coal in his **h**, H3338
Isa 8:11 says to me with his strong **h** upon me, H3338
Isa 9:12 is not turned away, his **h** is still upraised. H3338
Isa 9:17 is not turned away, his **h** is still upraised. H3338
Isa 9:21 is not turned away, his **h** is still upraised. H3338
Isa 10: 4 is not turned away, his **h** is still upraised. H3338
Isa 10: 5 in whose **h** is the club of my wrath! H3338
Isa 10:10 As my **h** seized the kingdoms of the idols H3338
Isa 10:13 " 'By the strength of my **h** I have done this, H3338
Isa 10:14 so my **h** reached for the wealth of the H3338
Isa 11: 8 child will put its **h** into the viper's nest. H3338
Isa 11:11 Lord will reach out his **h** a second time to H3338
Isa 11:15 he will sweep his **h** over the Euphrates H3338
Isa 13:22 Her time *is* **at h**, and her days H7940+4200+995
Isa 14:26 this is the **h** stretched out over all nations. H3338
Isa 14:27 His **h** is stretched out, and who can turn it H3338
Isa 19: 4 *I will* **h** the Egyptians **over** to the power of H6127
Isa 19:16 fear at the uplifted **h** that the LORD H3338
Isa 22:21 and **h** your authority **over** *to* H5989+928+3338
Isa 23:11 stretched out his **h** over the sea and made H3338
Isa 25:10 The **h** *of* the LORD will rest on this H3338
Isa 26:11 your **h** is lifted high, but they do not H3338
Isa 28: 4 as people see them and take them in **h**, H4090
Isa 31: 3 When the LORD stretches out his **h**, those H3338
Isa 34:17 his **h** distributes them by measure. H3338
Isa 36: 6 which pierces the **h** *of* anyone who leans H4090
Isa 36:15 be given into the **h** *of* the king of Assyria. H3338
Isa 36:18 lands from the **h** *of* the king of Assyria H3338
Isa 36:19 Have they rescued Samaria from my **h**? H3338
Isa 36:20 the LORD deliver Jerusalem from my **h**?" H3338
Isa 37:20 deliver us from his **h**, so that all the H3338
Isa 38: 6 this city from the **h** *of* the king of Assyria. H4090
Isa 40: 2 from the LORD's **h** double for all her sins. H3338
Isa 40:12 the waters in the **hollow of** his **h**, H9123
Isa 40:12 with the **breadth of** his **h** marked off the H2455
Isa 41:10 I will uphold you with my righteous **right** *h*. AIT
Isa 41:13 takes hold of your **right** *h* and says to you, AIT
Isa 41:20 that the **h** *of* the LORD has done this H3338
Isa 42: 6 righteousness; I will take hold of your **h**. H3338
Isa 43:13 No one can deliver out of my **h**. When I H3338
Isa 44: 5 still others will write on their **h**, 'The H3338
Isa 44:20 "Is not this thing in my **right** *h* a lie? AIT
Isa 45: 1 whose **right** *h* I take hold of to subdue AIT
Isa 47: 6 I gave them into your **h**, and you showed H3338
Isa 48:13 My own **h** laid the foundations of the H3338
Isa 48:13 and my **right** *h* spread out the heavens AIT
Isa 49: 2 in the shadow of his **h** he hid me; he H3338
Isa 49: 4 Yet what is due me is **in** the LORD's **h**, and H907
Isa 50:11 This is what you shall receive from my **h** H3338
Isa 51:16 covered you with the shadow of my **h**— H3338
Isa 51:17 have drunk from the **h** *of* the LORD the cup H3338
Isa 51:18 there was none to take her by the **h**. H3338
Isa 51:22 taken out of your **h** the cup that made you H3338
Isa 53:10 the will of the LORD will prosper in his **h**. H3338
Isa 56: 1 salvation is close **at h** and my H995
Isa 62: 3 be a crown of splendor in the LORD's **h**, H3338
Isa 62: 3 a royal diadem in the **h** *of* your God. H4090
Isa 62: 8 has sworn by his **right** *h* and by his mighty AIT
Isa 63:12 arm of power to be at Moses' **right** *h*, AIT
Isa 64: 8 the potter; we are all the work of your **h**. H3338
Isa 66: 2 Has not my **h** made all these things, and H3338
Isa 66:14 the **h** *of* the LORD will be made known to H3338
Jer 1: 9 reached out his **h** and touched my mouth H3338
Jer 6: 9 pass your **h** over the branches again H3338
Jer 6:12 when I stretch out my **h** against those who H3338
Jer 15:17 alone because your **h** was on me and you H3338
Jer 18: 6 "Like clay in the **h** *of* the potter, so are you H3338
Jer 18: 6 of the potter, so are you in my **h**, Israel. H3338
Jer 18:21 **h** them **over** to the power of the sword. H5599
Jer 21: 5 an outstretched **h** and a mighty arm in H3338
Jer 21:12 rescue from the **h** *of* the oppressor the H3338
Jer 22: 3 Rescue from the **h** *of* the oppressor the H3338
Jer 22:24 were a signet ring on my right **h**, I would H3338
Jer 25:15 "Take from my **h** this cup filled with the H3338
Jer 25:17 cup from the LORD's **h** and made all the H3338
Jer 25:28 to take the cup from your **h** and drink, H3338
Jer 27: 8 the LORD, until I destroy it by his **h**. H3338
Jer 31:11 them from the **h** *of* those stronger than H3338
Jer 31:32 I took them by the **h** to lead them out of H3338
Jer 32:21 by a mighty **h** and an outstretched arm H3338
Jer 33:13 pass under the **h** *of* the one who counts H3338
Jer 36:14 went to them with the scroll in his **h**. H3338
Jer 38:16 you nor **h** you **over** *to* those H5989+928+3338
Jer 38:19 *may* **h** me **over** *to* them and H5989+928+3338
Jer 38:20 "*They will* not **h** you **over**," Jeremiah H5989
Jer 43: 3 against us to **h** us **over** *to* the H5989+928+3338
Jer 48:16 "The fall of Moab *is* **at h**; her H7940+995
Jer 48:37 every **h** is slashed and every waist is H3338
Jer 51: 7 Babylon was a gold cup in the LORD's **h** H3338
Jer 51:25 "I will stretch out my **h** against you, roll H3338
La 2: 3 has withdrawn his **right** *h* at the approach of AIT
La 2: 4 he has strung his bow; his **right** *h* is ready. AIT
La 2: 8 did not withhold his **h** from destroying. H3338
La 3: 3 he has turned his **h** against me again H3338
La 4: 6 a moment without a **h** turned to help her. H3338
Eze 1: 3 There the **h** *of* the LORD was on him. H3338
Eze 2: 9 and I saw a **h** stretched out to me. H3338
Eze 3:14 with the strong **h** *of* the LORD on me. H3338
Eze 3:22 The **h** *of* the LORD was on me there, and H3338
Eze 6:14 will stretch out my **h** against them and H3338
Eze 7:17 Every **h** will go limp; every leg will be wet H3338
Eze 8: 1 the **h** *of* the Sovereign LORD came on me H3338
Eze 8: 3 what looked like a **h** and took me by the H3338
Eze 8:11 Each had a censer in his **h**, and a fragrant H3338
Eze 9: 1 on the city, each with a weapon in his **h**." H3338
Eze 9: 2 each with a deadly weapon in his **h**. H3338
Eze 10: 7 reached out his **h** to the fire that was H3338
Eze 13: 9 My **h** will be against the prophets who see H3338
Eze 14: 9 I will stretch out my **h** against him and H3338
Eze 14:13 I stretch out my **h** against it to cut off H3338
Eze 16:27 So I stretched out my **h** against you and H3338
Eze 17:18 he had given his **h** in pledge and yet did H3338
Eze 18: 8 He withholds his **h** from doing wrong and H3338
Eze 18:17 He withholds his **h** from mistreating the H3338
Eze 20: 5 swore with uplifted **h** to the descendants H3338
Eze 20: 5 With uplifted **h** I said to them, "I am the H3338
Eze 20:15 Also with uplifted **h** I swore to them in the H3338
Eze 20:22 But I withheld my **h**, and for the sake of my H3338
Eze 20:23 Also with uplifted **h** I swore to them in the H3338
Eze 20:33 you with a mighty **h** and an outstretched H3338
Eze 20:34 with a mighty **h** and an outstretched arm H3338
Eze 20:42 had sworn with uplifted **h** to give to your H3338
Eze 21: 7 will melt with fear and every **h** go limp; H3338
Eze 21:11 to be grasped with the **h**; it is sharpened H4090
Eze 21:11 made ready for the **h** *of* the slayer. H3338
Eze 21:22 Into his **right** *h* will come the lot for Jerusalem AIT
Eze 23:31 so I will put her cup into your **h**. H3338
Eze 25: 7 will stretch out my **h** against you and give H3338
Eze 25:13 will stretch out my **h** against Edom and H3338
Eze 25:14 on Edom by the **h** *of* my people Israel, H3338
Eze 25:16 to stretch out my **h** against the Philistines H3338
Eze 30:10 of Egypt by the **h** *of* Nebuchadnezzar king H3338
Eze 30:12 by the **h** *of* foreigners I will lay waste the H3338
Eze 30:22 and make the sword fall from his **h**. H3338
Eze 30:24 of Babylon and put my sword in his **h**, H3338
Eze 30:25 my sword into the **h** *of* the king of Babylon H3338
Eze 33:22 man arrived, the **h** *of* the LORD was on me H3338
Eze 35: 3 will stretch out my **h** against you and H3338
Eze 36: 7 I swear with uplifted **h** that the nations H3338
Eze 37: 1 The **h** *of* the LORD was on me, and he H3338
Eze 37:17 so that they will become one in your **h**. H3338
Eze 37:19 which is in Ephraim's **h**—and of the H3338
Eze 37:19 and they will become one in my **h**. H3338
Eze 38:12 loot and turn my **h** against the H3338
Eze 39: 3 bow from your left **h** and make your H3338
Eze 39: 3 make your arrows drop from your right **h**. H3338
Eze 39:21 I inflict and the **h** I lay on them. H3338
Eze 40: 1 that very day the **h** *of* the LORD was on me H3338
Eze 40: 3 a linen cord and a measuring rod in his **h**. H3338
Eze 40: 5 rod in the man's **h** was six long cubits, H3338
Eze 44:12 sworn with uplifted **h** that they must bear H3338
Eze 47: 3 eastward with a measuring line in his **h**, H3338
Eze 47:14 I swore with uplifted **h** to give it to your H3338
Da 1: 2 Jehoiakim king of Judah into his **h**, H3338
Da 3:15 will be able to rescue you from my **h**?" A10311
Da 3:17 he will deliver us from Your Majesty's **h**. A10311
Da 4:35 one can hold back his **h** or say to him: A10311
Da 5: 5 of a human **h** appeared and wrote A10311
Da 5: 5 king watched the **h** as it wrote. A10589+10311
Da 5:23 God who holds in his **h** your life and all A10311
Da 5:24 he sent the **h** that wrote the A10589+10311
Da 9:15 Egypt with a mighty **h** and who made H3338
Da 10:10 A **h** touched me and set me trembling on H3338
Da 11:41 of Ammon will be delivered from his **h**. H3338
Da 12: 7 lifted his **right** *h* and his left hand toward AIT

Da 12: 7 his right hand and his left h toward heaven, NDT
Hos 9: 7 are coming, the days of reckoning *are* at h. H995
Hos 11: 8 How *can I* h you over, Israel H4481
Joel 2: 1 of the LORD is coming. It is close at h— H7940
Am 1: 8 I will turn my h against Ekron, till the last H3338
Am 5:19 house and rested his h on the wall only to H3338
Am 7: 7 true to plumb, with a plumb line in his h. H3338
Am 9: 2 from there my h will take them. H3338
Ob 14 nor h over their survivors in the day of H6037
Jnh 4:11 who cannot tell their right *h* from their left— AIT
Mic 4:10 redeem you out of the h *of* your enemies. H4090
Mic 5: 9 Your h will be lifted up in triumph over H3338
Hab 2:16 cup from the LORD's right *h* is coming around AIT
Hab 3: 4 rays flashed from his h, where his power H3338
Zep 1: 4 "I will stretch out my h against Judah and H3338
Zep 2:13 will stretch out his h against the north H3338
Zec 2: 1 was a man with a measuring line in his h. H3338
Zec 2: 9 will surely raise my h against them so that H3338
Zec 4:10 chosen capstone in the h *of* Zerubbabel?" H3338
Zec 8: 4 them with cane in h because of their age H3338
Zec 13: 7 I will turn my h against the little ones. H3338
Zec 14:13 seize each other *by* the h and attack one H3338
Mt 3:12 His winnowing fork is in his h, and he will G5931
Mt 5:25 adversary *may* h you over to the judge, G4140
Mt 5:25 the judge may h you over to the officer NDT
Mt 5:30 And if your right h causes you to stumble G5931
Mt 5:40 take your shirt, h over your coat as well. G918
Mt 6: 3 do not let your left h know what your right G754
Mt 6: 3 left hand know what your right h is doing, G1288
Mt 8: 3 reached out his h and touched the man. G5931
Mt 8:15 He touched her h and the fever left her G5931
Mt 9:18 But come and put your h on her, and she G5931
Mt 9:25 he went in and took the girl *by* the h, and G5931
Mt 12:10 a man with a shriveled h was there G5931
Mt 12:13 he said to the man, "Stretch out your h." G5931
Mt 14:31 Jesus reached out his h and caught him. G5931
Mt 18: 8 If your h or your foot causes you to stumble G5931
Mt 20:19 and *will* h him over to the Gentiles to be G4140
Mt 22:13 'Tie him h and foot, and throw G4546
Mt 22:44 "Sit at my right h until I put your enemies G1288
Mt 24:41 Two women will be grinding with a h mill G3685
Mt 26:16 watched for an opportunity to h him over. G4140
Mt 26:23 who has dipped his h into the bowl with G5931
Mt 26:64 sitting at the right h of the Mighty One G1288
Mt 27:29 They put a staff in his right h. Then they G1288
Mk 1:31 took her h and helped her up. G5931
Mk 1:41 He reached out his h and touched the G5931
Mk 3: 1 a man with a shriveled h was there. G5931
Mk 3: 3 Jesus said to the man with the shriveled h G5931
Mk 3: 5 said to the man, "Stretch out your h." G5931
Mk 3: 5 and his h was completely restored. G5931
Mk 5: 4 For he *had* often *been* chained h and G268+1313
Mk 5:41 He took her *by* the h and said to her G5931
Mk 7:32 they begged Jesus to place his h on him. G5931
Mk 8:23 took the blind man *by* the h and led him G5931
Mk 9:27 But Jesus took him *by* the h and lifted him G5931
Mk 9:43 If your h causes you to stumble, cut it off. G5931
Mk 10:33 to death and *will* h him over to the G4140
Mk 12:36 "Sit at my right h until I put your enemies G1288
Mk 14:11 watched for an opportunity *to* h him over. G4140
Mk 14:62 sitting at the right h of the Mighty One G1288
Mk 16:19 heaven and he sat at the right h of God. G1288
Lk 1:66 For the Lord's h was with him. G5931
Lk 1:71 from the h of all who hate us— G5931
Lk 1:74 to rescue us from the h of our enemies G5931
Lk 3:17 fork is in his h to clear his threshing G5931
Lk 5:13 reached out his h and touched the man. G5931
Lk 6: 6 was there whose right h was shriveled. G5931
Lk 6: 8 said to the man with the shriveled h, G5931
Lk 6:10 then said to the man, "Stretch out your h." G5931
Lk 6:10 and his h was completely restored. G5931
Lk 8:29 and *though he was* chained h and G1297+268
Lk 8:54 But he took her *by* the h and said, "My G5931
Lk 9:62 "No one who puts a h to the plow and G5931
Lk 20:20 so that *they might* h him over to the G4140
Lk 20:42 Lord said to my Lord: "Sit at my right h G1288
Lk 21:12 *They will* h you over to synagogues and G4140
Lk 22: 6 opportunity *to* h Jesus over to them when G4140
Lk 22:21 But the h of him who is going to betray me G5931
Lk 22:53 and you did not lay a h on me. G5931
Lk 22:69 be seated at the right h of the mighty God G1288
Jn 7:30 no one laid a h on him, because his G5931
Jn 7:44 to seize him, but no one laid a h on him. G5931
Jn 10:12 The hired h is not the shepherd and does G3638
Jn 10:13 because he is a hired h and cares nothing G3638
Jn 10:28 no one will snatch them out of my h. G5931
Jn 10:29 one can snatch them out of my Father's h. G5931
Jn 20:25 and put my h into his side, I will G5931
Jn 20:27 Reach out your h and put it into my side G5931
Ac 2:25 Because he is at my right h, I will not be G1288
Ac 2:33 Exalted *to* the right h of God, he has G1288
Ac 2:34 Lord said to my Lord: "Sit at my right h G1288
Ac 3: 7 Taking him *by* the right h, he helped him G5931
Ac 4:30 Stretch out your h to heal and perform G5931
Ac 5:31 exalted him *to* his own right h as Prince G1288
Ac 7:50 Has not my h made all these things? G5931
Ac 7:55 Jesus standing at the right h of God. G1288
Ac 7:56 of Man standing at the right h of God." G1288
Ac 9: 8 So they led him by the h into Damascus. G5932
Ac 9:41 He took her *by* the h and helped her to her G5931
Ac 11:21 The Lord's h was with them, and a great G5931
Ac 12:17 Peter motioned *with* his h for them to be G5931
Ac 13:11 Now the h of the Lord is against you. G5931
Ac 13:11 seeking someone to lead him by the h. G5933
Ac 13:16 Paul motioned *with* his h and said: G5931
Ac 21:11 and *will* h him over to the G4140+1650+5931
Ac 22:11 My companions led me by the h into G5932
Ac 23:19 commander took the young man *by* the h, G5931
Ac 25:11 no one has the right *to* h me over to them. G5919
Ac 25:16 Roman custom *to* h over anyone before G5919
Ac 26: 1 Paul motioned *with* his h and began his G5931
Ac 28: 3 out by the heat, fastened itself on his h. G5931
Ac 28: 4 saw the snake hanging from his h, G5931
Ro 8:34 is at the right h of God and is also G1288
1Co 5: 5 h this man over to Satan for the G4140
1Co 12:15 "Because I am not a h, I do not belong to G5931
1Co 12:21 The eye cannot say *to* the h, "I don't need G5931
1Co 16:21 Paul, write this greeting *in* my own h. G5931
2Co 6: 7 righteousness *in* the right h and in the left G1288
Gal 2: 9 Barnabas the right h of fellowship G1288
Gal 6:11 I use as I write to you *with* my own h! G5931
Eph 1:20 seated him at his right h in the heavenly G1288
Col 3: 1 Christ is, seated at the right h of God. G1288
Col 4:18 write this greeting *in* my own h G5931
2Th 3:17 write this greeting *in* my own h, which is G5931
Phm 19 am writing this *with* my own h. I will pay it G5931
Heb 1: 3 sat down at the right h of the Majesty in G1288
Heb 1:13 "Sit at my right h until I make your G1288
Heb 8: 1 sat down at the right h of the throne of G1288
Heb 8: 9 I took them by the h to lead them out of G5931
Heb 10:12 sins, he sat down at the right h of God, G1288
Heb 12: 2 sat down at the right h of the throne of G1288
1Pe 3:22 into heaven and is at God's right h— G1288
1Pe 5: 6 under God's mighty h, that he may lift you G5931
Rev 1:16 In his right h he held seven stars, and G5931
Rev 1:17 he placed his right h on me and said: G1288
Rev 1:20 you saw in my right h and of the seven G1288
Rev 2: 1 stars in his right h and walks among G1288
Rev 5: 1 Then I saw in the right h of him who sat G1288
Rev 5: 7 scroll from the right h of him who sat on G1288
Rev 6: 5 rider was holding a pair of scales in his h. G5931
Rev 8: 4 went up before God from the angel's h. G5931
Rev 10: 2 a little scroll, which lay open in his h. G5931
Rev 10: 5 on the land raised his right h to heaven. G5931
Rev 10: 8 that lies open in the h of the angel who is G5931
Rev 10:10 little scroll from the angel's h and ate it. G5931
Rev 14: 9 its mark on their forehead or on their h, G5931
Rev 14:14 on his head and a sharp sickle in his h. G5931
Rev 17: 4 She held a golden cup in her h, filled G5931
Rev 17:17 by agreeing *to* h over to the beast their G1443
Rev 20: 1 Abyss and holding in his h a great chain. G5931

HANDBREADTH (8) [HAND]

Ex 25:25 around it a rim a h *wide* and put a gold H3256
Ex 37:12 around it a rim a h wide and put a gold H3256
1Ki 7:26 It was a h in thickness, and its rim was like H3255
2Ch 4: 5 It was a h in thickness, and its rim was like H3255
Ps 39: 5 You have made my days a mere h; the H3257
Eze 40: 5 each of which was a cubit and a h. H3256
Eze 40:43 each a h long, were attached to H3256
Eze 43:13 that cubit being a cubit and a h: H3256

HANDED (41) [HAND]

Ge 27:17 Then *she* h *to* her son Jacob H5989+928+3338
Ex 32: 4 He took what they h him and made it into H3338
Lev 9:12 His sons h him the blood, and he H5162
Lev 9:13 *They* h him the burnt offering piece by H5162
Lev 9:18 His sons h him the blood, and he H5162
Dt 19:12 and *be* h over *to* the avenger H5989+928+3338
2Sa 3: 8 *I haven't* h you over *to* David H5162+928+3338
2Sa 21: 9 *He* h them over *to* the H5989+928+3338
2Ch 30:16 the altar the blood h to them by the H3338
2Ch 35:11 the altar the blood h *to* them, H4946+3338
Isa 42:24 Who h Jacob over to become loot, and H5989
Jer 26:24 so he *was* not h over *to* the H5989+928+3338
Eze 39:23 them and h them over *to* their H5989+928+3338
Da 7:27 under heaven *will* be h over to the holy A10314
Mt 10:17 you *will be* h over to the local councils G4140
Mt 18:34 anger his master h him over to the jailers G4140
Mt 24: 9 "Then you *will be* h over to be persecuted G4140
Mt 26: 2 the Son of Man *will be* h over to be G4140
Mt 27: 2 led him away and h him over to Pilate the G4140
Mt 27:18 *that they had* h Jesus over to him. G4140
Mt 27:26 flogged, and h him over to be crucified. G4140
Mk 7:13 by your tradition that *you have* h down. G4140
Mk 13: 9 You *will be* h over to the local councils G4140
Mk 15: 1 led him away and h him over to Pilate. G4140
Mk 15:10 the chief priests *had* h Jesus over to him. G4140
Mk 15:15 flogged, and h him over to be crucified. G4140
Lk 1: 2 just as *they were* h down to us *by* those G4140
Lk 4:17 scroll of the prophet Isaiah *was* h to him. G2113
Lk 24:20 our rulers h him over to be sentenced G4140
Jn 18:30 "*we* would not have h him over to you." G4140
Jn 18:35 people and chief priests h you over to me. G4140
Jn 19:11 the *one who* h me over to you is G4140
Jn 19:16 Finally Pilate h him over to them to be G4140
Ac 2:23 This man was h over to you by God's G1692
Ac 3:13 You h him over *to be killed*, and you G4140
Ac 6:14 change the customs Moses h down to us." G4140
Ac 23:33 to the governor and h Paul over to him. G4225
Ac 27: 1 other prisoners *were* h over to a centurion G4140
Ac 28:17 *I was* arrested in Jerusalem and h over G4140+3836+5931
1Ti 1:20 whom *I have* h over to Satan to be taught G4140
1Pe 1:18 of life h down to you from your ancestors, G4261

HANDFUL (8) [HAND]

Lev 2: 2 priest *shall* take a h of the H7858+4850+7859
Lev 5:12 who *shall* take a h of it as a H7858+4850+7859
Lev 6:15 The priest is to take a h of the finest flour H7859
Lev 9:17 took a h of it and burned it on the H4848+4090
Nu 5:26 The priest *is* then *to* take a h of the grain H7858
1Ki 17:12 only a h *of* flour in a jar and a little H4850+4090
1Ki 20:10 in Samaria to give each of my men a h." H9123
Ecc 4: 6 Better *one* h with tranquillity than H4850+4090

HANDFULS (4) [HAND]

Ex 9: 8 "Take h *of* soot from a furnace and H4850+2908
Lev 16:12 the LORD and two h *of* finely ground H2908+4850
Ecc 4: 6 tranquillity than *two* h with toil and H4850+2908
Eze 13:19 my people for a *few* h *of* barley and H9123

HANDING (2) [HAND]

1Ki 18: 9 you *are* h your servant over *to* H5989+928+3338
Ac 12: 4 h him over to be guarded by four squads G4140

HANDIWORK (2)

Isa 19:25 Assyria my h, and Israel my H5126+3338
Eph 2:10 For we are God's h, created in Christ Jesus G4473

HANDKERCHIEFS (1)

Ac 19:12 so that even h and aprons that had G5051

HANDLE (10) [HANDLED, HANDLES, HANDLING]

Ex 18:18 too heavy for you; you cannot h it alone. H6913
Jdg 3:22 Even the h sank in after the blade, and his H5896
2Sa 24: 9 able-bodied men *who could* h a sword, H8990
1Ch 5:18 able-bodied men *who could* h shield and H5951
1Ch 8:40 were brave warriors *who could* h the bow. H2005
1Ch 12: 8 battle and *able to* h the shield and H6885
1Ch 21: 5 thousand men *who could* h a sword, H8990
2Ch 25: 5 service, *able to* h the spear and shield. H296
Eze 27:29 All *who* h the oars will abandon their H9530
Col 2:21 "*Do* not h! Do not taste! Do not touch!" G721

HANDLED (1) [HANDLE]

Jer 8: 8 lying pen of the scribes *has* h it falsely? H6913

HANDLES (3) [HANDLE]

1Ki 7:34 Each stand had four h, one on each H4190
SS 5: 5 with flowing myrrh, on the h *of* the bolt. H4090
2Ti 2:15 ashamed and *who* correctly h the word of G3982

HANDLING (1) [HANDLE]

Lk 16:11 not been trustworthy in h worldly wealth, G1877

HANDMAID, HANDMAIDS (KJV) SERVANT, SERVANT'S, (FEMALE) SERVANTS, SLAVE

HANDS (610) [HAND]

Ge 5:29 painful toil of our h caused by the ground H3338
Ge 9: 2 fish in the sea; they are given into your h. H3338
Ge 16: 6 "Your slave is in your h," Abram said. "Do H3338
Ge 19:16 his hand and the h *of* his wife and of his H3338
Ge 20: 5 this with a clear conscience and clean h." H4090
Ge 24:18 the jar to her h and gave him a drink. H3338
Ge 27:16 also covered his h and the smooth part H3338
Ge 27:22 of Jacob, but the h are the hands of Esau." H3338
Ge 27:22 of Jacob, but the hands are the h *of* Esau." H3338
Ge 27:23 his h were hairy like those of his H3338
Ge 31:42 seen my hardship and the toil of my h, H4090
Ge 37:21 he tried to rescue him from their h. H3338
Ge 37:27 the Ishmaelites and not lay our h on him; H3338
Ex 9:29 I will spread out my h in prayer to the LORD H4090
Ex 9:33 He spread out his h toward the LORD; the H4090
Ex 14:30 saved Israel from the h *of* the Egyptians, H3338
Ex 15:17 the sanctuary, Lord, your h established. H3338
Ex 17: 9 of the hill with the staff of God in my h." H3338
Ex 17:11 As long as Moses held up his h, the H3338
Ex 17:11 whenever he lowered his h, the H3338
Ex 17:12 When Moses' h grew tired, they took a H3338
Ex 17:12 Aaron and Hur held his h up—one on H3338
Ex 17:12 so that his h remained steady till sunset. H3338
Ex 17:16 "Because h were lifted up against the H3338
Ex 22: 8 the house has laid h on the other H3338
Ex 22:11 neighbor did not lay h on the other H3338
Ex 23:31 I will give into your h the people who live H3338
Ex 28: 6 finely twisted linen—the work of skilled h. H3110
Ex 28:15 making decisions—the work of skilled h. H3110
Ex 29:10 his sons shall lay their h on its head. H3338
Ex 29:15 his sons shall lay their h on its head. H3338
Ex 29:19 his sons shall lay their h on its head. H3338
Ex 29:20 on the thumbs of their right h, and on the H3338
Ex 29:24 all these in the h *of* Aaron and his sons H4090
Ex 29:25 them from their h and burn them on the H3338
Ex 30:19 are to wash their h and feet with water H3338
Ex 30:21 they shall wash their h and feet so that H3338
Ex 32:15 two tablets of the covenant law in his h. H3338
Ex 32:19 he threw the tablets out of his h, H3338
Ex 34: 4 he carried the two stone tablets in his h. H3338
Ex 34:29 two tablets of the covenant law in his h, H3338
Ex 35:25 woman spun with her h and brought what H3338
Ex 36: 8 cherubim woven into them by expert h. H3110
Ex 39: 3 yarn and fine linen—the work of skilled h. H3110
Ex 40:31 his sons used it to wash their h and feet. H3338
Lev 4:15 are to lay their h on the bull's head H3338
Lev 7:30 With their own h they are to present the H3338
Lev 8:14 his sons laid their h on its head. H3338

H

Lev 8:18 his sons laid their **h** on its head. H3338
Lev 8:22 his sons laid their **h** on its head. H3338
Lev 8:24 of their right **h** and on the big toes H3338
Lev 8:27 all these in the **h** *of* Aaron and his sons, H4090
Lev 8:28 them from their **h** and burned them on H4090
Lev 9:22 Aaron lifted his **h** toward the people and H3338
Lev 15:11 without rinsing his **h** with water must H3338
Lev 16:21 He is to lay both **h** on the head of the live H3338
Lev 24:14 heard him are to lay their **h** on his head, H3338
Lev 26:25 and you will be given into enemy **h**. H3338
Nu 5:18 place in her **h** the reminder-offering H4090
Nu 5:25 is to take from her **h** the grain offering H3338
Nu 6:19 is to place in their **h** a boiled shoulder of H4090
Nu 8:10 the Israelites are to lay their **h** on them. H3338
Nu 8:12 are to lay their **h** on the heads of the H3338
Nu 21: 2 you will deliver these people into our **h**, H3338
Nu 21:34 I have delivered him into your **h**, along H3338
Nu 24:10 He struck his **h** together and said to him H4090
Nu 27:23 Then he laid his **h** on him and H3338
Dt 1:27 to deliver us into the **h** *of* the Amorites to H3338
Dt 2: 7 has blessed you in all the work of your **h**. H3338
Dt 2:30 obstinate in order to give him into your **h**, H3338
Dt 3: 2 I have delivered him into your **h**, along H3338
Dt 3: 3 also gave into our **h** Og king of Bashan H3338
Dt 6: 8 as symbols on your **h** and bind them on H3338
Dt 8:17 the strength of my **h** have produced this H3338
Dt 9:15 two tablets of the covenant were in my **h**. H3338
Dt 9:17 two tablets and threw them out of my **h**, H3338
Dt 10: 3 mountain with the two tablets in my **h**. H3338
Dt 11:18 as symbols on your **h** and bind them on H3338
Dt 13: 9 and then the **h** *of* all the people. H3338
Dt 13:17 things are to be found in your **h**. H3338
Dt 14:29 may bless you in all the work of your **h**. H3338
Dt 16:15 your harvest and in all the work of your **h**, H3338
Dt 17: 7 The **h** *of* the witnesses must be the first in H3338
Dt 17: 7 and then the **h** *of* all the people. H3338
Dt 21: 6 shall wash their **h** over the heifer whose H3338
Dt 21: 7 "Our **h** did not shed this blood, nor did H3338
Dt 21:10 them into your **h** and you take captives, H3338
Dt 23:25 you may pick kernels with your **h**, but you H3338
Dt 24:19 may bless you in all the work of your **h**. H3338
Dt 26: 4 the basket from your **h** and set it down in H3338
Dt 27:15 the work of skilled **h**—and sets it up in H3338
Dt 28:12 season and to bless all the work of your **h**. H3338
Dt 30: 9 in all the work of your **h** and in the fruit of H3338
Dt 31:29 his anger by what your **h** have made." H3338
Dt 33: 7 With his own **h** he defends his cause H3338
Dt 33:11 be pleased with the work of his **h**. H3338
Dt 34: 9 because Moses had laid his **h** on him. H3338
Jos 2:24 surely given the whole land into our **h**; H3338
Jos 6: 2 I have delivered Jericho into your **h**, along H3338
Jos 7: 7 to deliver us into the **h** *of* the Amorites to H3338
Jos 8: 1 I have delivered into your **h** the king of Ai, H3338
Jos 9:25 We are now in your **h**. Do to us whatever H3338
Jos 10:32 The LORD gave Lachish into Israel's **h**, and H3338
Jos 21:44 LORD gave all their enemies into their **h**. H3338
Jos 24: 8 against you, but I gave them into your **h**. H3338
Jos 24:11 Jebusites, but I gave them into your **h**. H3338
Jdg 1: 2 I have given the land into their **h**. H3338
Jdg 1: 4 the Canaanites and Perizzites into their **h**, H3338
Jdg 2:14 gave them into the **h** *of* raiders who H3338
Jdg 2:14 sold them into the **h** *of* their enemies all H3338
Jdg 2:16 saved them out of the **h** *of* these raiders. H3338
Jdg 2:18 them out of the **h** *of* their enemies as H3338
Jdg 2:23 once by giving them into the **h** *of* Joshua. H3338
Jdg 3: 8 them into the **h** *of* Cushan-Rishathaim H3338
Jdg 3:10 king of Aram into the **h** *of* Othniel, H3338
Jdg 3:28 has given Moab, your enemy, into your **h**." H3338
Jdg 4: 2 sold them into the **h** *of* Jabin king of H3338
Jdg 4: 7 the Kishon River and give him into your **h**. H3338
Jdg 4: 9 will deliver Sisera into the **h** *of* a woman." H3338
Jdg 4:14 day the LORD has given Sisera into your **h**. H3338
Jdg 6: 1 gave them into the **h** *of* the Midianites. H3338
Jdg 7: 2 I cannot deliver Midian into their **h**, or H3338
Jdg 7: 6 hundred of them drank from cupped **h**, H3338
Jdg 7: 7 you and give the Midianites into your **h**. H3338
Jdg 7: 9 because I am going to give it into your **h**. H3338
Jdg 7:14 the whole camp into his **h**. H3338
Jdg 7:15 has given the Midianite camp into your **h**." H3338
Jdg 7:16 empty jars in the **h** *of* all of them, H3338
Jdg 7:19 broke the jars that were in their **h**. H3338
Jdg 7:20 torches in their left **h** and holding in their H3338
Jdg 7:20 in their right **h** the trumpets they were H3338
Jdg 8: 3 the Midianite leaders, into your **h**. H3338
Jdg 8: 6 already have the **h** *of* Zebah and H4090
Jdg 8:15 already have the **h** *of* Zebah and H4090
Jdg 8:34 them from the **h** *of* all their enemies on H3338
Jdg 10: 7 sold them into the **h** *of* the Philistines H3338
Jdg 10:12 help, did I not save you from their **h**? H3338
Jdg 11:21 Sihon and his whole army into Israel's **h**, H3338
Jdg 11:30 "If you give the Ammonites into my **h**, H3338
Jdg 11:32 the LORD gave them into his **h**. H3338
Jdg 12: 2 I called, you didn't save me out of their **h**. H3338
Jdg 12: 3 I took my life in my **h** and crossed over to H4090
Jdg 13: 1 them into the **h** *of* the Philistines for H3338
Jdg 13: 5 Israel from the **h** *of* the Philistines. H3338
Jdg 13:23 offering and grain offering from our **h**, H3338
Jdg 14: 6 apart with his bare **h** as he might have H3338
Jdg 14: 9 the honey with his **h** and ate as he went H4090
Jdg 15:14 and the bindings dropped from his **h**. H3338
Jdg 15:18 fall into the **h** *of* the uncircumcised?" H3338
Jdg 16:18 returned with the silver in their **h**. H3338
Jdg 16:23 delivered Samson, our enemy, into our **h**." H3338
Jdg 16:24 god has delivered our enemy into our **h**, H3338
Jdg 18:10 land that God has put into your **h**, H3338
Jdg 19:27 of the house, with her **h** on the threshold. H3338
Jdg 20:28 tomorrow I will give them into your **h**." H3338
1Sa 5: 4 His head and **h** had been broken H4090+3338
1Sa 7:14 territory from the **h** *of* the Philistines. H3338
1Sa 12: 9 into the **h** *of* the Philistines and the H3338
1Sa 12:10 now deliver us from the **h** *of* our enemies, H3338
1Sa 12:11 you from the **h** *of* your enemies all H3338
1Sa 14:10 that the LORD has given them into our **h**." H3338
1Sa 14:13 climbed up, using his **h** and feet, with his H3338
1Sa 14:48 Israel from the **h** *of* those who had H3338
1Sa 17:46 day the LORD will deliver you into my **h**, H3338
1Sa 17:47 he will give all of you into our **h**. H3338
1Sa 18:25 have David fall by the **h** *of* the Philistines. H3338
1Sa 19: 5 He took his life in his **h** when he killed the H4090
1Sa 21:13 while he was in their **h** he acted like a H3338
1Sa 23: 7 "God has delivered him into my **h**, for H3338
1Sa 23:14 God did not give David into his **h**. H3338
1Sa 23:20 be responsible for giving him into your **h**." H3338
1Sa 24: 4 enemy into your **h** for you to deal with H3338
1Sa 24:10 LORD delivered you into my **h** in the cave. H3338
1Sa 24:18 the LORD delivered me into your **h**, but you H3338
1Sa 24:20 of Israel will be established in your **h**. H3338
1Sa 25:26 from avenging yourself with your own **h**, H3338
1Sa 25:33 from avenging myself with my own **h**. H3338
1Sa 26: 8 has delivered your enemy into your **h**. H3338
1Sa 26:23 The LORD delivered you into my **h** today H3338
1Sa 28:17 kingdom out of your **h** and given it to one H3338
1Sa 28:19 you into the **h** *of* the Philistines, H3338
1Sa 28:19 army of Israel into the **h** *of* the Philistines." H3338
1Sa 28:21 I took my life in my **h** and did what you H4090
1Sa 30:23 delivered into our **h** the raiding party that H3338
2Sa 3:34 Your **h** were not bound, your feet were not H3338
2Sa 4:12 They cut off their **h** and feet and hung the H3338
2Sa 5:19 Will you deliver them into my **h**?" The H3338
2Sa 5:19 surely deliver the Philistines into your **h**." H3338
2Sa 7:14 with floggings inflicted by **human h**. H1201+132
2Sa 13:19 She put her **h** on her head and went away H3338
2Sa 16: 8 kingdom into the **h** *of* your son Absalom. H3338
2Sa 16:21 the **h** *of* everyone with you will be H3338
2Sa 18:12 shekels were weighed out into my **h**, H4090
2Sa 18:28 who lifted their **h** against my lord the H3338
2Sa 21:22 they fell at the **h** *of* David and his men. H3338
2Sa 22:21 cleanness of my **h** he has rewarded me. H3338
2Sa 22:35 He trains my **h** for battle; my arms can H3338
2Sa 24:14 Let us fall into the **h** *of* the LORD, for his H3338
2Sa 24:14 do not let me fall into human **h**. H3338
1Ki 2:46 was now established in Solomon's **h**. H3338
1Ki 8:22 of Israel, spread out his **h** toward heaven H4090
1Ki 8:38 out their **h** toward this temple— H4090
1Ki 8:54 kneeling with his **h** spread out toward H4090
1Ki 11:35 from his son's **h** and give you ten H3338
1Ki 20:28 I will deliver this vast army into your **h** H3338
2Ki 3:10 only to deliver us into the **h** *of* Moab?" H3338
2Ki 3:11 He used to pour water on the **h** *of* Elijah." H3338
2Ki 3:13 together to deliver us into the **h** *of* Moab." H3338
2Ki 3:18 he will also deliver Moab into your **h**. H3338
2Ki 4:34 mouth to mouth, eyes to eyes, **h** to hands. H4090
2Ki 4:34 mouth to mouth, eyes to eyes, hands to **h**. H4090
2Ki 9:35 except her skull, her feet and her **h**. H4090+3338
2Ki 10:24 of the men I am placing in your **h** escape, H3338
2Ki 11:12 the people clapped their **h** and shouted, H4090
2Ki 13:16 "Take the bow in your **h**," he said to the H3338
2Ki 13:16 Elisha put his **h** on the king's hands. H3338
2Ki 13:16 Elisha put his hands on the king's **h**. H3338
2Ki 17:20 gave them into the **h** *of* plunderers, H3338
2Ki 19:10 be given into the **h** *of* the king of Assyria. H3338
2Ki 19:18 wood and stone, fashioned by human **h**. H3338
2Ki 21:14 give them into the **h** *of* enemies. H3338
2Ki 22:17 anger by all the idols their **h** have made, H3338
1Ch 5:10 who were defeated at their **h**; they H3338
1Ch 5:20 Hagrites and all their allies into their **h**, H3338
1Ch 12:17 to my enemies when my **h** are free from H4090
1Ch 14:10 Will you deliver them into my **h**?" The H3338
1Ch 14:10 "Go, I will deliver them into your **h**." H3338
1Ch 20: 8 they fell at the **h** *of* David and his men. H3338
1Ch 21:13 Let me fall into the **h** *of* the LORD, for his H3338
1Ch 21:13 do not let me fall into human **h**. H3338
1Ch 22:18 the inhabitants of the land into my **h**, H3338
1Ch 29:12 In your **h** are strength and power to exalt H3338
2Ch 6: 4 who with his **h** has fulfilled what he H3338
2Ch 6:12 assembly of Israel and spread out his **h**. H4090
2Ch 6:13 spread out his **h** toward heaven. H4090
2Ch 6:29 out their **h** toward this temple— H4090
2Ch 13: 8 which is in the **h** *of* David's descendants. H3338
2Ch 13:16 God delivered them into their **h**. H3338
2Ch 23:18 of the LORD in the **h** *of* the Levitical priests, H3338
2Ch 24:24 delivered into their **h** a much larger army. H3338
2Ch 25:20 might deliver them into the **h** *of* Jehoash, H3338
2Ch 28: 5 him into the **h** *of* the king of Aram. H3338
2Ch 28: 5 also given into the **h** *of* the king of Israel, H3338
2Ch 29:23 assembly, and they laid their **h** on them. H3338
2Ch 32:19 of the world—the work of human **h**. H3338
2Ch 34:25 my anger by all that their **h** have made, H3338
2Ch 36:17 them all into the **h** *of* Nebuchadnezzar. H3338
Ezr 5:12 gave them into the **h** *of* Nebuchadnezzar A10311
Ezr 8:33 articles into the **h** *of* Meremoth son of H3338
Ezr 9: 5 on my knees with my **h** spread out to the H4090
Ezr 10: 4 this matter is **in** your **h**. We will support H6584
Ezr 10:19 They all gave their **h** in pledge to put H3338
Ne 6: 9 "Their **h** will get too weak for the work H3338
Ne 6: 9 But I prayed, "Now strengthen my **h**." H3338
Ne 8: 6 the people lifted their **h** and responded, H3338
Ne 9:24 you gave the Canaanites into their **h** H3338
Ne 9:27 them into the **h** *of* their enemies, H3338
Ne 9:30 gave them into the **h** *of* the neighboring H3338
Est 9:10 But they did not lay their **h** on the plunder. H3338
Est 9:15 they did not lay their **h** on the plunder. H3338
Est 9:16 did not lay their **h** on the plunder. H3338
Job 1:10 You have blessed the work of his **h**, so H3338
Job 2: 6 he is in your **h**; but you must spare H3338
Job 4: 3 how you have strengthened feeble **h**. H3338
Job 5:12 so that their **h** achieve no success. H3338
Job 5:18 binds up; he injures, but his **h** also heal. H3338
Job 8:20 strengthen the **h** *of* evildoers. H3338
Job 9:24 a land falls into the **h** *of* the wicked, H3338
Job 9:30 with soap and my **h** with cleansing H4090
Job 10: 3 to spurn the work of your **h**, while you H4090
Job 10: 8 "Your **h** shaped me and made me. H3338
Job 11:13 heart to him and stretch out your **h** to him, H4090
Job 13:14 in jeopardy and take my life in my **h**? H4090
Job 14:15 long for the creature your **h** have made. H3338
Job 16:17 my **h** have been free of violence and H4090
Job 17: 9 those with clean **h** will grow stronger. H3338
Job 20:10 his own **h** must give back his wealth. H3338
Job 21:16 But their prosperity is not in their own **h** H3338
Job 22:30 delivered through the cleanness of your **h**." H4090
Job 27:23 It claps its **h** in derision and hisses him H4090
Job 28: 9 rock with their **h** and lay bare the roots H3338
Job 29: 9 covered their mouths with their **h**; H4090
Job 30: 2 use was the strength of their **h** to me, H3338
Job 31: 7 by my eyes, or if my **h** have been defiled, H4090
Job 31:25 the fortune my **h** had gained, H3338
Job 34:19 the poor, for they are all the work of his **h**? H3338
Job 34:37 **scornfully** *he* **claps** his **h** among us and H6215
Job 36:32 He fills his **h** with lightning and H4090
Ps 7: 3 done this and there is guilt on my **h**— H4090
Ps 8: 6 them rulers over the works of your **h**; H3338
Ps 9:16 are ensnared by the work of their **h**. H4090
Ps 18:20 cleanness of my **h** he has rewarded me. H3338
Ps 18:24 to the cleanness of my **h** in his sight. H3338
Ps 18:34 He trains my **h** for battle; my arms can H3338
Ps 19: 1 the skies proclaim the work of his **h**. H3338
Ps 22:16 they pierce my **h** and my feet. H3338
Ps 24: 4 one who has clean **h** and a pure heart, H4090
Ps 26: 6 I wash my **h** in innocence, and go about H4090
Ps 26:10 in whose **h** are wicked schemes, whose H3338
Ps 26:10 schemes, whose **right** *h* are full of bribes. AIT
Ps 28: 2 as I lift up my **h** toward your Most Holy H3338
Ps 28: 4 what their **h** have done and bring H3338
Ps 28: 5 of the LORD and what his **h** have done, H3338
Ps 31: 5 Into your **h** I commit my spirit; deliver me H3338
Ps 31: 8 given me into the **h** *of* the enemy but H3338
Ps 31:15 My times are in your **h**; deliver me from H3338
Ps 31:15 deliver me from the **h** *of* my enemies H3338
Ps 44:20 God or spread out our **h** to a foreign god, H4090
Ps 47: 1 Clap your **h**, all you nations; shout to God H4090
Ps 58: 2 your **h** mete out violence on the earth H3338
Ps 63: 4 and in your name I will lift up my **h**. H4090
Ps 73:13 have washed my **h** in innocence. H4090
Ps 76: 5 not one of the warriors can lift his **h**. H3338
Ps 77: 2 at night I stretched out untiring **h**, and I H3338
Ps 78:61 his splendor into the **h** *of* the enemy. H3338
Ps 78:72 of heart; with skillful **h** he led them. H4090
Ps 81: 6 their **h** were set free from the basket. H4090
Ps 88: 9 every day; I spread out my **h** to you. H4090
Ps 90:17 establish the work of our **h** for us—yes, H3338
Ps 90:17 us—yes, establish the work of our **h**. H3338
Ps 91:12 they will lift you up in their **h**, so that you H4090
Ps 92: 4 I sing for joy at what your **h** have done. H3338
Ps 95: 5 made it, and his **h** formed the dry land. H3338
Ps 98: 8 Let the rivers clap their **h**, let the H4090
Ps 102:25 the heavens are the work of your **h**. H3338
Ps 106:41 He gave them into the **h** of the nations H3338
Ps 111: 7 The works of his **h** are faithful and just; all H3338
Ps 115: 4 are silver and gold, made by human **h**. H3338
Ps 115: 7 They have **h**, but cannot feel, feet, but H3338
Ps 119:73 Your **h** made me and formed me; give me H3338
Ps 119:109 Though I constantly take my life in my **h**, H4090
Ps 125: 3 the righteous might use their **h** to do evil. H3338
Ps 127: 4 Like arrows in the **h** *of* a warrior are H3338
Ps 129: 7 a reaper cannot fill his **h** with it, nor one H4090
Ps 134: 2 Lift up your **h** in the sanctuary and praise H3338
Ps 135:15 are silver and gold, made by human **h**. H3338
Ps 138: 8 do not abandon the works of your **h**. H3338
Ps 140: 4 from the **h** *of* the wicked; protect me H3338
Ps 141: 2 the lifting up of my **h** be like the evening H4090
Ps 143: 5 consider what your **h** have done. H3338
Ps 143: 6 I spread out my **h** to you; I thirst for you H3338
Ps 144: 1 who trains my **h** for war, my fingers H3338
Ps 144: 7 mighty waters, from the **h** *of* foreigners H3338
Ps 144: 8 are full of lies, whose **right** *h* are deceitful. AIT
Ps 144:11 rescue me from the **h** *of* foreigners whose H3338
Ps 144:11 are full of lies, whose **right** *h* are deceitful. AIT
Ps 149: 6 a double-edged sword in their **h**, H3338
Pr 6: 1 if you have shaken **h** in pledge for a H4090
Pr 6: 3 you have fallen into your neighbor's **h**: H4090
Pr 6:10 slumber, a little folding of the **h** to rest— H3338
Pr 6:17 lying tongue, **h** that shed innocent blood, H3338
Pr 10: 4 Lazy **h** make for poverty, but diligent H4090
Pr 10: 4 poverty, but diligent **h** bring wealth. H3338
Pr 11:15 refuses to **shake h in pledge** is safe. H9364

Pr 12:14 the work of their **h** brings them reward. H3338
Pr 12:24 Diligent **h** will rule, but laziness ends in H3338
Pr 14: 1 with her own **h** the foolish one tears H3338
Pr 17:18 has no sense shakes **h** in pledge and puts H4090
Pr 21:25 because his **h** refuse to work. H3338
Pr 22:26 be one who shakes **h** in pledge or puts up H4090
Pr 24:33 slumber, a little folding of the **h** to rest— H3338
Pr 26: 6 a message by the **h** *of* a fool is like H3338
Pr 30: 4 Whose **h** have gathered up the wind H2908
Pr 31:13 wool and flax and works with eager **h**. H4090
Pr 31:20 the poor and extends her **h** to the needy. H3338
Pr 31:31 Honor her for all that her **h** have done H3338
Ecc 2:11 all that my **h** had done and what I H3338
Ecc 4: 5 Fools fold their **h** and ruin themselves. H3338
Ecc 5: 6 you say and destroy the work of your **h**? H3338
Ecc 5:15 their toil that they can carry in their **h**. H3338
Ecc 7:26 heart is a trap and whose **h** are chains. H3338
Ecc 9: 1 the wise and what they do are in God's **h**, H3338
Ecc 10:18 because of idle **h**, the house leaks. H3338
Ecc 11: 6 at evening let your **h** not be idle, for H3338
SS 5: 5 my beloved, and my **h** dripped with myrrh H3338
SS 7: 1 are like jewels, the work of an artist's **h**. H3338
Isa 1:15 When you spread out your **h** in prayer, H4090
Isa 1:15 am not listening. Your **h** are full of blood! H3338
Isa 2: 8 they bow down to the work of their **h**, to H3338
Isa 3:11 be paid back for what their **h** have done. H3338
Isa 5:12 the LORD, no respect for the work of his **h**. H3338
Isa 13: 7 Because of this, all **h** will go limp, every H3338
Isa 17: 8 the work of their **h**, and they will have no H3338
Isa 25:11 They will stretch out their **h** in it, as H3338
Isa 25:11 as swimmers stretch out their **h** to swim. NDT
Isa 25:11 pride despite the cleverness of their **h**. H3338
Isa 29:23 the work of my **h**, they will keep my name H3338
Isa 31: 7 silver and gold your sinful **h** have made. H3338
Isa 33:15 keep their **h** from accepting bribes, H4090
Isa 35: 3 Strengthen the feeble **h**, steady the knees H3338
Isa 37:10 be given into the **h** *of* the king of Assyria. H3338
Isa 37:19 wood and stone, fashioned by human **h**. H3338
Isa 41: 2 *He* **h** nations **over** *to* him and subdues H5989
Isa 45: 9 Does your work say, 'The potter has no **h**'? H3338
Isa 45:11 give me orders about the work of my **h**? H3338
Isa 45:12 My own **h** stretched out the heavens; H3338
Isa 49:16 have engraved you on the **palms** of my **h**; H4090
Isa 51:23 I will put it into the **h** *of* your tormentors H3338
Isa 55:12 all the trees of the field will clap their **h**. H4090
Isa 56: 2 and keeps their **h** from doing any evil." H3338
Isa 59: 3 For your **h** are stained with blood, your H4090
Isa 59: 6 and acts of violence are in their **h**. H4090
Isa 60:21 the work of my **h**, for the display of my H3338
Isa 65: 2 I have held out my **h** to an obstinate H3338
Isa 65:22 ones will long enjoy the work of their **h**. H3338
Jer 1:16 in worshiping what their **h** have made. H3338
Jer 2:37 leave that place with your **h** on your head, H3338
Jer 4:31 stretching out her **h** and saying, "Alas! H4090
Jer 6:24 reports about them, and our **h** hang limp. H3338
Jer 11:21 of the LORD or you will die by our **h**"— H3338
Jer 12: 7 the one I love into the **h** *of* her enemies. H4090
Jer 15:21 will save you from the **h** *of* the wicked H3338
Jer 18: 4 from the clay was marred in his **h**; H3338
Jer 19: 7 at the **h** *of* those who want to kill them H3338
Jer 20: 4 all Judah into the **h** *of* the king of Babylon H3338
Jer 20: 5 of this city into the **h** *of* their enemies— H3338
Jer 20:13 life of the needy from the **h** *of* the wicked. H3338
Jer 21: 4 you the weapons of war that are in your **h**, H3338
Jer 21: 7 into the **h** *of* Nebuchadnezzar king of H3338
Jer 21:10 be given into the **h** *of* the king of Babylon, H3338
Jer 22:25 you into the **h** *of* those who want to H3338
Jer 23:14 They strengthen the **h** *of* evildoers, so that H3338
Jer 25: 6 my anger with what your **h** have made. H3338
Jer 25: 7 my anger with what your **h** have made, H3338
Jer 25:14 to their deeds and the work of their **h**." H3338
Jer 26:14 I am in your **h**; do with me whatever H3338
Jer 27: 6 your countries into the **h** *of* my servant H3338
Jer 29:21 them into the **h** *of* Nebuchadnezzar king H3338
Jer 30: 6 strong man with his **h** on his stomach like H3338
Jer 32: 3 this city into the **h** *of* the king of Babylon, H3338
Jer 32: 4 be given into the **h** *of* the king of Babylon, H3338
Jer 32:24 be given into the **h** *of* the Babylonians H3338
Jer 32:25 be given into the **h** *of* the Babylonians, H3338
Jer 32:28 this city into the **h** *of* the Babylonians and H3338
Jer 32:30 my anger with what their **h** have made, H3338
Jer 32:36 be given into the **h** *of* the king of Babylon' H3338
Jer 32:43 been given into the **h** *of* the Babylonians. H3338
Jer 34: 2 this city into the **h** *of* the king of Babylon, H3338
Jer 34: 3 surely be captured and given into his **h**. H3338
Jer 34:20 deliver into the **h** *of* their enemies who H3338
Jer 34:21 officials into the **h** *of* their enemies who H3338
Jer 37:17 delivered into the **h** *of* the king of Babylon H3338
Jer 38: 3 be given into the **h** *of* the army of the king H3338
Jer 38: 5 "He is in your **h**," King Zedekiah H3338
Jer 38:18 be given into the **h** *of* the Babylonians H3338
Jer 38:23 escape from their **h** but will be captured H3338
Jer 39:17 not be given into the **h** *of* those you fear. H3338
Jer 42:11 will save you and deliver you from his **h**. H3338
Jer 44: 8 my anger with what your **h** have made, H3338
Jer 44:30 of Egypt into the **h** *of* his enemies who H3338
Jer 44:30 of Judah into the **h** *of* Nebuchadnezzar H3338
Jer 46:24 given into the **h** *of* the people of the north H3338
Jer 46:26 give them into the **h** *of* those who want to H3338
Jer 47: 3 help their children; their **h** will hang limp. H3338
Jer 50:43 reports about them, and his **h** hang limp. H3338
La 1: 7 When her people fell into enemy **h**, there H3338
La 1:10 The enemy laid **h** on all her treasures H3338
La 1:14 by his **h** they were woven together. H3338
La 1:14 has given me into the **h** *of* those I cannot H3338
La 1:17 Zion stretches out her **h**, but there is no H3338
La 2: 7 of her palaces into the **h** *of* the enemy; H3338
La 2:15 All who pass your way clap their **h** at you H4090
La 2:19 Lift up your **h** to him for the lives of your H4090
La 3:41 up our hearts and our **h** to God in heaven, H4090
La 3:64 deserve, LORD, for what their **h** have done. H3338
La 4: 2 as pots of clay, the work of a potter's **h**! H3338
La 4:10 With their own **h** compassionate women H3338
La 5: 8 there is no one to free us from their **h**. H3338
La 5:12 Princes have been hung up by their **h** H3338
Eze 1: 8 on their four sides they had human **h**. H3338
Eze 6:11 Strike your **h** together and stamp your feet H4090
Eze 7:27 the **h** *of* the people of the land will H3338
Eze 10: 2 Fill your **h** with burning coals from among H2908
Eze 10: 7 put it into the **h** *of* the man in linen, H2908
Eze 10: 8 could be seen what looked like human **h**.) H3338
Eze 10:12 their backs, their **h** and their wings, were H3338
Eze 10:21 wings was what looked like human **h**. H3338
Eze 11: 9 deliver you into the **h** *of* foreigners and H3338
Eze 12: 7 evening I dug through the wall with my **h**. H3338
Eze 13:21 veils and save my people from your **h**, H3338
Eze 13:23 I will save my people from your **h**. H3338
Eze 16:39 I will deliver you into the **h** of your lovers, H3338
Eze 21:14 and strike your **h together**. H4090+448+4090
Eze 21:17 I too will strike my **h together** H4090+448+4090
Eze 21:31 I will deliver you into the **h** *of* brutal men H3338
Eze 22:13 will surely strike my **h** together at the H4090
Eze 22:14 endure or your **h** be strong in the day I H3338
Eze 23: 9 I delivered her into the **h** *of* her lovers, H3338
Eze 23:28 deliver you into the **h** *of* those you hate, H3338
Eze 23:37 adultery and blood is on their **h**. H3338
Eze 23:45 are adulterous and blood is on their **h**. H3338
Eze 25: 6 have clapped your **h** and stamped your H3338
Eze 28: 9 not a god, in the **h** *of* those who slay you. H3338
Eze 28:10 the uncircumcised at the **h** *of* foreigners. H3338
Eze 29: 7 When they grasped you with their **h**, you H4090
Eze 31:11 I gave it into the **h** *of* the ruler of the H3338
Eze 34:27 them from the **h** *of* those who enslaved H3338
Eze 48:14 the land and *must* not **pass into other h**, H6296
Da 2:34 a rock was cut out, but not by human **h**. A10311
Da 2:38 in your **h** he has placed all mankind and A10311
Da 2:45 not by human **h**—a rock that broke A10311
Da 7:25 will be delivered into his **h** for a time, A10311
Da 10:10 me trembling on my **h** and knees. H4090+3338
Hos 2:10 no one will take her out of my **h**. H3338
Hos 7: 5 and he joins **h** with the mockers. H3338
Hos 14: 3 'Our gods' to what our own **h** have made, H3338
Mic 5:13 no longer bow down to the work of your **h**. H3338
Mic 7: 3 *Both* **h** are skilled in doing evil; the ruler H4090
Mic 7:16 They will put their **h** over their mouths H3338
Na 3:19 news about you clap their **h** at your fall, H4090
Zep 3:16 Zion; do not let your **h** hang limp. H3338
Hag 1:11 livestock, and on all the labor of your **h**." H4090
Hag 2:17 I struck all the work of your **h** with blight H3338
Zec 4: 9 "The **h** *of* Zerubbabel have laid the H3338
Zec 4: 9 of this temple; his **h** will also complete it. H3338
Zec 8: 9 'Let your **h** be strong so that the temple H3338
Zec 8:13 not be afraid, but let your **h** be strong." H3338
Zec 11: 6 everyone into the **h** *of* their neighbors H3338
Zec 11: 6 I will not rescue anyone from their **h**." H3338
Mal 1: 9 With such offerings from your **h**, will he H3338
Mal 1:10 "and I will accept no offering from your **h**. H3338
Mal 1:13 should I accept them from your **h**? H3338
Mal 2:13 accepts them with pleasure from your **h**. H3338
Mt 4: 6 they will lift you up in their **h**, so that *G5931*
Mt 15: 2 They don't wash their **h** before they eat!" *G5931*
Mt 15:20 eating *with* unwashed **h** does not *G5931*
Mt 16:21 suffer many things **at the h of** the elders, *G608*
Mt 17:12 Son of Man is going to suffer **at** their **h**." *G5679*
Mt 17:22 going to be delivered into the **h** of men. *G5931*
Mt 18: 8 than to have two **h** or two feet and be *G5931*
Mt 19:13 him to place his **h** on them and pray for *G5931*
Mt 19:15 When he had placed his **h** on them, he *G5931*
Mt 26:45 of Man is delivered into the **h** of sinners. *G5931*
Mt 27:24 water and washed his **h** in front of the *G5931*
Mk 5:23 come and put your **h** on her so that she *G5931*
Mk 6: 5 except lay his **h** on a few sick people and *G5931*
Mk 7: 2 eating food *with* **h** that were defiled, *G5931*
Mk 7: 3 they give their **h** a ceremonial washing, *G5931*
Mk 7: 5 of eating their food *with* defiled **h**? *G5931*
Mk 8:23 on the man's eyes and put his **h** on him, *G5931*
Mk 8:25 more Jesus put his **h** on the man's eyes. *G5931*
Mk 9:31 going to be delivered into the **h** of men. *G5931*
Mk 9:43 maimed than with two **h** to go into hell, *G5931*
Mk 10:13 to Jesus for him *to* **place** *his* **h on** them, *G721*
Mk 10:16 placed his **h** on them and blessed them. *G5931*
Mk 14:41 of Man is delivered into the **h** of sinners. *G5931*
Mk 14:58 this temple **made with human h** and in *G5935*
Mk 14:58 days will build another, **not made with h**. *G942*
Mk 16:18 they will pick up snakes with their **h**; and *G5931*
Mk 16:18 they will place their **h** on sick people, and *G5931*
Lk 4:11 they will lift you up in their **h**, so that you *G5931*
Lk 4:40 laying his **h** on each one, he healed *G5931*
Lk 6: 1 rub them *in* their **h** and eat the kernels. *G5931*
Lk 9:44 going to be delivered into the **h** of men." *G5931*
Lk 10:36 to the *man who* **fell into the h of** robbers?" *G1860*
Lk 13:13 Then he put his **h** on her, and *G5931*
Lk 18:15 to Jesus for *him to* **place** *his* **h on** them. *G721*
Lk 23:46 "Father, into your **h** I commit my spirit." *G5931*
Lk 24: 7 must be delivered over to the **h** of sinners, *G5931*
Lk 24:39 Look at my **h** and my feet. It is I myself *G5931*
Lk 24:40 said this, he showed them his **h** and feet. *G5931*
Lk 24:50 he lifted up his **h** and blessed them. *G5931*
Jn 3:35 Son and has placed everything in his **h**. *G5931*
Jn 11:44 his **h** and feet wrapped with strips of linen *G5931*
Jn 13: 9 my feet but my **h** and my head as well *G5931*
Jn 20:20 said this, he showed them his **h** and side. *G5931*
Jn 20:25 the nail marks in his **h** and put my finger *G5931*
Jn 20:27 Thomas, "Put your finger here; see my **h**. *G5931*
Jn 21:18 you are old you will stretch out your **h**, *G5931*
Ac 6: 6 who prayed and laid their **h** on them. *G5931*
Ac 7:41 reveled in what their own **h** had made. *G5931*
Ac 7:48 not live in houses **made by human h**. *G5935*
Ac 8:17 Peter and John placed their **h** on them, *G5931*
Ac 8:18 given at the laying on of the apostles' **h**, *G5931*
Ac 8:19 on whom I lay my **h** may receive the Holy *G5931*
Ac 9:12 come and place his **h** on him to restore *G5931*
Ac 9:17 Placing his **h** on Saul, he said, "Brother *G5931*
Ac 13: 3 they placed their **h** on them and sent *G5931*
Ac 17:24 not live in temples **built by human h**. *G5935*
Ac 17:25 And he is not served by human **h**, as if he *G5931*
Ac 19: 6 When Paul placed his **h** on them, the Holy *G5931*
Ac 19:26 gods made by *human* **h** are no gods at *G5931*
Ac 20:34 know that these **h** of mine have supplied *G5931*
Ac 21:11 tied his own **h** and feet with it and said *G5931*
Ac 27:19 ship's tackle overboard **with their own h**. *G901*
Ac 28: 8 placed his **h** on him and healed him. *G5931*
Ro 10:21 I have held out my **h** to a disobedient *G5931*
1Co 4:12 We work hard *with* our own **h**. When we *G5931*
1Co 15:24 when *he* **h over** the kingdom to God the *G4140*
2Co 5: 1 house in heaven, **not built by human h**. *G942*
2Co 11:33 in the wall and slipped through his **h**. *G5931*
Eph 2:11 which is **done** in the body **by human h**)— *G5935*
Eph 4:28 doing something useful *with* their own **h** *G5931*
Col 2:11 a circumcision **not performed by human h**. *G942*
1Th 4:11 your own business and work *with* your **h**, *G5931*
1Ti 2: 8 lifting up holy **h** without anger or *G5931*
1Ti 4:14 the body of elders laid their **h** on you. *G5931*
1Ti 5:22 Do not be hasty in the laying on *of* **h**, and *G5931*
2Ti 1: 6 is in you through the laying on *of* my **h**. *G5931*
Heb 1:10 the heavens are the work *of* your **h**. *G5931*
Heb 6: 2 the laying on *of* **h**, the resurrection of *G5931*
Heb 9:11 that is not **made with human h**, *G5935*
Heb 9:24 a sanctuary **made with human h** that was *G5935*
Heb 10:31 thing to fall into the **h** of the living God. *G5931*
Jas 4: 8 Wash your **h**, you sinners, and purify your *G5931*
1Jn 1: 1 have looked at and our **h** have touched— *G5931*
Rev 7: 9 were holding palm branches in their **h**. *G5931*
Rev 9:20 still did not repent of the work *of* their **h**; *G5931*
Rev 13:16 mark on their right **h** or on their foreheads *G5931*
Rev 20: 4 its mark on their foreheads or their **h**. *G5931*

HANDSOME (12) [HANDSOMELY]

Ge 39: 6 Now Joseph was well-built and **h**, H3637+5260
1Sa 9: 2 *as* **h** a young man as could be found H3202
1Sa 16:12 had a fine appearance and **h** features. H3202
1Sa 17:42 glowing with health and **h**, and he H3637+5260
2Sa 14:25 praised for his **h appearance** as Absalom. H3637
1Ki 1: 6 He was also very **h** and was born H3202+9307
SS 1:16 How **h** you are, my beloved! Oh, how H3637
Eze 23: 6 all of them **h** young men, and mounted H2774
Eze 23:12 mounted horsemen, all **h** young men. H2774
Eze 23:23 Assyrians with them, **h** young men, all of H2774
Da 1: 4 physical defect, **h**, showing H3202+5260
Zec 11:13 the **h** price at which they valued me! H159

HANDSOMELY (2) [HANDSOME]

Nu 22:17 *I will* **reward** you **h** and do H3877+4394+3877
Nu 24:11 I said *I would* **reward** you **h**, but the H3877+3877

HANES (1)

Isa 30: 4 Zoan and their envoys have arrived in **H**, H2865

HANG (13) [HANGED, HANGING, HANGINGS, HANGS, HUNG, OVERHANG, OVERHANGING, OVERHANGS]

Ex 26:12 that is left over *is to* **h down** at the rear of H6243
Ex 26:13 what is left *will* **h** over the sides of the H6243
Ex 26:32 **H** it *with* gold hooks on four posts of H5989
Ex 26:33 **H** the curtain from the clasps and place H5989
Job 37:16 Do you know how the clouds **h poised** H5146
SS 4: 4 of stone; on it **h** a thousand shields, all H9434
Isa 22:24 All the glory of his family *will* **h** on him: its H9434
Jer 6:24 about them, and our hands **h limp**. H8332
Jer 47: 3 their children; their hands will **h limp**. H8342
Jer 50:43 reports about them, and his hands **h limp**. H8332
Eze 15: 3 Do they make pegs from it to **h** things on? H9434
Zep 3:16 Zion; *do* not *let* your hands **h limp**. H8332
Mt 22:40 the Law and the Prophets **h** on these two *G3203*

HANGED (2) [HANG]

2Sa 17:23 put his house in order and then **h himself**. H2871
Mt 27: 5 Then he went away and **h** *himself*. *G551*

HANGING (10) [HANG]

Dt 21:23 not leave the body **h** on the pole overnight. NDT
Jos 10:26 they were *left* **h** on the poles until H9434
1Sa 25:17 because disaster *is* **h** over our master and H3983
2Sa 18: 9 *He* **was left h** in midair, while the mule H5989
2Sa 18:10 "I just saw Absalom **h** in an oak tree." H9434
Isa 22:25 and the load **h on** it will be cut down." H6584
Ac 5:30 whom you killed *by* **h** him on a cross. *G3203*

Ac 10:39 They killed him *by* **h** him on a cross, G3203
Ac 28: 4 islanders saw the snake **h** from his hand, G3203
2Pe 2: 3 *has* long *been* **h over** them, G4024+733

HANGINGS (1) [HANG]
Est 1: 6 The garden had **h of** white and blue **linen** H4158

HANGS (1) [HANG]
Isa 33:23 Your rigging **h loose**: The mast is not held H5759

HANNAH (14) [HANNAH'S]
1Sa 1: 2 one was called **H** and the other Peninnah. H2839
1Sa 1: 2 Peninnah had children, but **H** had none. H2839
1Sa 1: 5 But to **H** he gave a double portion H2839
1Sa 1: 7 Whenever **H** went up to the house of the H2023S
1Sa 1: 8 would say to her, "**H**, why are you H2839
1Sa 1: 9 eating and drinking in Shiloh, **H** stood up. H2839
1Sa 1:10 In her deep anguish **H** prayed to the LORD, H2085S
1Sa 1:13 **H** was praying in her heart, and her lips H2839
1Sa 1:15 **H** replied, "I am a woman who is deeply H2839
1Sa 1:19 Elkanah made love to his wife **H**, and the H2839
1Sa 1:20 the course of time **H** became pregnant H2839
1Sa 1:22 **H** did not go. She said to her husband H2839
1Sa 2: 1 Then **H** prayed and said: "My heart H2839
1Sa 2:21 And the LORD was gracious to **H**; she gave H2839

HANNAH'S (1) [HANNAH]
1Sa 1: 6 Because the LORD had closed **H** womb H2023S

HANNATHON (1)
Jos 19:14 on the north to **H** and ended at the H2872

HANNIEL (2)
Nu 34:23 **H** son of Ephod, the leader from the tribe H2848
1Ch 7:39 The sons of Ulla: Arah, **H** and Rizia. H2848

HANOK (6) [HANOKITE]
Ge 25: 4 were Ephah, Epher, **H**, Abida and Eldaah. H2840
Ge 46: 9 The sons of Reuben: **H**, Pallu, Hezron H2840
Ex 6:14 firstborn son of Israel were **H** and Pallu, H2840
Nu 26: 5 through **H**, the Hanokite clan; through H2840
1Ch 1:33 Epher, **H**, Abida and Eldaah H2840
1Ch 5: 3 firstborn of Israel: **H**, Pallu, Hezron and H2840

HANOKITE (1) [HANOK]
Nu 26: 5 through Hanok, the **H** clan; through Pallu H2854

HANUN (13)
2Sa 10: 1 his son **H** succeeded him as king. H2842
2Sa 10: 2 "I will show kindness to **H** son of Nahash H2842
2Sa 10: 2 his sympathy to **H** concerning his father. NDT
2Sa 10: 3 commanders said to **H** their lord, H2842
2Sa 10: 4 So **H** seized David's envoys, shaved off H2842
1Ch 19: 2 "I will show kindness to **H** son of Nahash H2842
1Ch 19: 2 his sympathy to **H** concerning his father. H2257S
1Ch 19: 2 envoys came to **H** in the land of the H2842
1Ch 19: 3 the Ammonite commanders said to **H**, "Do H2842
1Ch 19: 4 So **H** seized David's envoys, shaved them H2842
1Ch 19: 6 **H** and the Ammonites sent a thousand H2842
Ne 3:13 was repaired by **H** and the residents of H2842
Ne 3:30 son of Shelemiah, and **H**, the sixth son of H2842

HAPHARAIM (1)
Jos 19:19 **H**, Shion, Anaharath, H2921

HAPPEN (58) [HAPPENED, HAPPENING, HAPPENS]
Ge 49: 1 I can tell you what *will* **h** *to* you in days to H7925
Ex 2: 4 at a distance to see what *would* **h** to him. H6913
Ex 21:13 But God **lets** *it* **h**, they are to H628+4200+3338
1Ki 14: 3 He will tell you what *will* **h** to the boy." H2118
1Ki 14:14 Even now this is beginning to **h**. NDT
2Ki 7: 2 floodgates of the heavens, *could* this **h**?" H2118
2Ki 7:19 floodgates of the heavens, *could* this **h**?" H2118
Ecc 3:22 bring them to see what *will* **h** after them? H2118
Ecc 6:12 can tell them what *will* **h** under the sun H2118
Ecc 9:11 time and chance **h** *to* them all. H7936
Ecc 10:14 tell someone else what *will* **h** after them? H2118
Isa 7: 7 " 'It will not take place, *it will* not **h**, H2118
Isa 14:24 and as I have purposed, so it *will* **h**. H7756
Isa 23:15 *it will* **h** to Tyre as in the song of the H2118
Isa 41:22 you idols, what *is going to* **h**. Tell us what H7936
Isa 47: 7 these things or reflect on **what might h**. H344
Jer 6:18 are witnesses, observe what will **h** to them. NDT
La 3:37 can speak and *have it* **h** if the Lord has H2118
Eze 20:32 But what you have in mind *will* never **h**. H2118
Eze 38:18 *This is what will* **h** in that day: When Gog H2118
Da 2:28 what *will* **h** in days to come. A10201
Da 2:29 showed you what *is going to* **h**. A10201
Da 8:19 to tell you what *will* **h** later in the time of H2118
Da 10:14 to you what *will* **h** to your people in H7936
Hos 10:15 So *will it* **h** to you, Bethel, because your H6913
Am 7: 3 "*This will* not **h**," the LORD said H2118
Am 7: 6 "This *will* not **h** either," the Sovereign H2118
Jnh 4: 5 waited to see what *would* **h** to the city. H2118
Zec 6:15 *This will* **h** if you diligently obey the LORD H2118
Mt 16:22 "This *shall* never **h** to you!" G1639
Mt 24: 3 they said, "when *will* this **h**, and what will G1639
Mt 24: 6 *Such things* must **h**, but the end is still to G1181
Mt 24:39 about what would **h** until the flood came NDT
Mt 26:54 be fulfilled that say *it* must **h** in this way?" G1181
Mk 10:32 told them what was going to **h** to him. G5201
Mk 11:23 believes that what they say *will* **h**, G1181
Mk 13: 4 when *will* these things **h**? And what G1639
Mk 13: 7 Such things must **h**, but the end is still to G1181
Lk 21: 7 they asked, "when *will* these things **h**? G1639
Lk 21: 9 These things must **h** first, but the end will G1181
Lk 21:36 be able to escape all that is about to **h**, G1181
Lk 22:49 Jesus' followers saw what *was going to* **h**, G1639
Lk 23:31 tree is green, what *will* **h** when it is dry?" G1181
Jn 5:14 sinning or something worse *may* **h** to you." G1181
Jn 13:19 so that when *it does* **h** you will believe G1181
Jn 14:29 so that when *it does* **h** you will believe. G1181
Jn 18: 4 knowing all that *was going to* **h** to him G2262
Ac 4:28 will had decided beforehand *should* **h**. G1181
Ac 8:24 that nothing you have said *may* **h** to me." G2088
Ac 12:11 the Jewish people were **hoping would h**." G4660
Ac 13:40 the prophets have said *does* not **h** to you: G2088
Ac 20:22 not knowing what *will* **h** to me there. G5267
Ac 26:22 the prophets and Moses said would **h**— G1181
Ac 27:25 faith in God that *it will* **h** just as he told G1639
Ac 28: 6 seeing nothing unusual **h** to him, G1181
2Th 1: 7 This will **h** when the Lord Jesus is revealed NDT
Jas 4:14 you do not even know what will **h** tomorrow. NDT
2Pe 2: 6 an example *of what is* **going to h** to the G3516

HAPPENED (107) [HAPPEN]
Ge 20: 8 told them all **that** had **h**, H1821+2021+465+2021
Ge 34: 7 the fields as soon as they heard what had **h**. NDT
Ge 42:29 they told him all that *had* **h** *to* them. H7936
Ex 32: 1 we don't know what *has* **h** to him. H2118
Ex 32:23 we don't know what *has* **h** to him. H2118
Lev 10:19 but such things as this *have* **h** to me. H7925
Dt 4:30 all these things *have* **h** to you, H5162
Dt 4:32 *Has* anything so great as this *ever* **h**, or H2118
Jos 2:23 told him everything that *had* **h** *to* them. H5162
Jdg 6:13 LORD is with us, why *has* all this **h to** us? H5162
Jdg 6:38 And that *is what* **h**. Gideon rose early the H2118
Jdg 20: 3 "Tell us how this awful thing **h**. H2118
Jdg 21: 3 they cried, "why *has* this **h** to Israel? H2118
1Sa 4: 7 Nothing like this *has* **h** before. H2118
1Sa 4:13 man entered the town and told what had **h**, NDT
1Sa 4:16 Eli asked, "What **h**, my son?" H2118
1Sa 6: 9 that struck us but that it **h** to us by chance." H2118
1Sa 10:11 "What is this *that has* **h** to the son of Kish? H2118
1Sa 20:26 "**Something** must have **h** to David to H5247
2Sa 1: 4 "What **h**?" David asked. "Tell me." "The H2118
2Sa 1: 6 "*I* **h to be** on Mount Gilboa," the H7936+7925
2Sa 13:35 *it has* **h** just as your servant said. H2118
2Sa 18: 9 Now Absalom **h** to meet David's men. H7925
2Sa 18:10 When one of the men saw what had **h**, he NDT
2Sa 20: 1 son of Bikri, a Benjamite, **h** *to be* there. H7925
1Ki 15:30 This **h** because of the sins Jeroboam had NDT
2Ki 7:13 So let us send them to find out what **h**." NDT
2Ki 7:14 the drivers, "Go and find out what has **h**." NDT
2Ki 7:18 *It* **h** as the man of God had said to the H2118
2Ki 7:20 And that is exactly *what* **h** to him, for the H2118
2Ki 9:27 Ahaziah king of Judah saw what had **h**, NDT
2Ki 18:12 This **h** because they had not obeyed the LORD NDT
2Ki 24: 3 Surely *these things* **h** to Judah according H2118
2Ki 24:20 anger that *all this* **h** to Jerusalem and H2118
Ezr 9:13 "What *has* **h** to us is a result of our evil H995
Ne 9:33 In all that *has* **h** to us, you have remained H995
Est 1: 1 *This is what* **h** during the time of Xerxes H2118
Est 4: 7 told him everything that *had* **h** *to* him, H7936
Est 6:13 his friends everything that *had* **h** *to* him. H7936
Est 9:17 This **h** on the thirteenth day of the month of NDT
Est 9:26 they had seen and what *had* **h** to them, H5595
Job 3:25 upon me; what I dreaded *has* **h** to me. H995
Isa 20: 6 'See **what** has **h** *to* those we relied on H3907
Isa 44: 7 lay out before me **what has h** since I H2023S
Isa 48: 5 before *they* **h** I announced them to you so H995
Jer 5:30 shocking thing *has* **h** in the land: H2118
Jer 13:22 you ask yourself, "Why *has* this **h** to me?" H7925
Jer 32:24 What you said *has* **h**, as you now see. H2118
Jer 40: 3 All this **h** because you people sinned H2118
Jer 48:19 woman escaping, ask them, 'What *has* **h**? H2118
Jer 52: 3 anger that *all this* **h** to Jerusalem and H2118
La 4:13 But it **h** because of the sins of her prophets NDT
La 5: 1 what *has* **h** to us; look, and H2118
Eze 16:19 *That is what* **h**, declares the Sovereign H2118
Da 4:28 All this **h** to King Nebuchadnezzar. A10413
Da 12: 1 distress such as *has* not **h** from the H2118
Joel 1: 2 *Has* anything like this *ever* **h** in your days H2118
Mt 8:33 including **what had h** to the G3836
Mt 14:13 When Jesus heard what had **h**, he withdrew NDT
Mt 18:31 When the other servants saw what *had* **h** G1181
Mt 18:31 told their master everything that *had* **h**. G1181
Mt 22:26 The same thing **h** to the second and third NDT
Mt 24:34 pass away until all these things *have* **h**. G1181
Mt 27:54 saw the earthquake and all *that had* **h**, G1181
Mt 28:11 to the chief priests everything that *had* **h**. G1181
Mk 5:14 went out to see what *had* **h**. G1639+1181
Mk 5:16 told the people what *had* **h** to the G1181
Mk 5:33 knowing what *had* **h** to her, came and G1181
Mk 13:30 pass away until all these things *have* **h**. G1181
Lk 2:15 Bethlehem and see this thing that *has* **h**, G1181
Lk 8:34 those tending the pigs saw what *had* **h**, G1181
Lk 8:35 the people went out to see what *had* **h**. G1181
Lk 8:56 them not to tell anyone what *had* **h**. G1181
Lk 10:31 A priest **h** to be going down the G2848+5175
Lk 21:32 pass away until all these things *have* **h**. G1181
Lk 23:47 seeing what *had* **h**, praised God and said G1181
Lk 24:12 wondering to himself what *had* **h**. G1181
Lk 24:14 each other about everything that *had* **h**. G5201
Lk 24:18 not know the *things that have* **h** there in G1181
Lk 24:35 Then the two told **what had h** on the way G3836
Jn 1:28 This all **h** at Bethany on the other side of G1181
Jn 9: 3 "but this **h** so that the works of God might NDT
Jn 18: 9 This **h** so that the words he had spoken NDT
Jn 19:24 This **h** that the scripture might be fulfilled NDT
Jn 19:36 These things **h** so that the scripture would G1181
Jn 21: 1 by the Sea of Galilee. *It* **h** this way: G5746
Ac 3:10 amazement at what *had* **h** to him. G5201
Ac 4:21 people were praising God for what *had* **h**. G1181
Ac 5: 5 great fear seized all who heard what had **h**. NDT
Ac 5: 7 wife came in, not knowing what *had* **h**. G1181
Ac 7:40 Egypt—we don't know what *has* **h** to him! G1181
Ac 10: 8 everything that had **h** and sent them to NDT
Ac 10:16 This **h** three times, and immediately the G1181
Ac 10:37 You know what *has* **h** throughout the G1181
Ac 11:10 This **h** three times, and then it was all G1181
Ac 11:28 This **h** during the reign of Claudius.) G1181
Ac 12: 3 *This* **h** during the Festival of Unleavened G1639
Ac 13:12 When the proconsul saw what *had* **h**, he G1181
Ac 17:17 day by day with those *who* **h to be there**. G4193
Ac 19:21 After all this *had* **h**, Paul decided to go to G4444
Ac 19:40 with rioting because of **what h** today. G3836S
Ac 28: 9 *When* this *had* **h**, the rest of the sick on G1181
1Co 10:11 These things **h** to them as examples and G5201
2Co 1: 9 But this **h** that we might not rely on NDT
Php 1:12 that **what has h to** me has actually G3836+2848
Php 1:19 of Jesus Christ **what** has **h** to me will turn G4047
2Ti 3:11 what kinds of things **h** to me in Antioch G1181

HAPPENING (10) [HAPPEN]
Ge 25:22 and she said, "Why is this **h** to me? NDT
1Sa 5: 7 the people of Ashdod saw what was **h**, H4027S
Ne 6: 8 "Nothing like what you are saying *is* **h** H2118
Est 2:11 how Esther was and what **was h** to her. H6913
Mk 13:29 when you see these things **h**, you know G1181
Lk 18:36 crowd going by, he asked what was **h**. G4047S
Lk 21:31 when you see these things **h**, you know G1181
Ac 12: 9 what the angel was doing was really **h**; G1181
Col 4: 9 They will tell you everything that is **h** here. NDT
1Pe 4:12 though something strange *were* **h** to you. G5201

HAPPENS (16) [HAPPEN]
Ex 22: 3 if it **h** after sunrise, the defender is guilty NDT
Dt 22:23 If a man *h to* **meet** in a town a virgin AIT
Dt 22:25 the country a man *h to* **meet** a young woman AIT
Dt 22:28 If a man *h to* **meet** a virgin who is not AIT
Ru 3:18 my daughter, until you find out what **h**. H5877
1Sa 2:34 " 'And what **h** to your two sons, Hophni H995
2Sa 14:20 he knows everything that **h** in the land." NDT
Ecc 9: 3 evil in everything that **h** under the sun: H6913
Ecc 9: 6 a part in anything that **h** under the sun. H6913
Isa 48:16 in secret; at the time it **h**, I am there." H2118
Jer 12: 4 are saying, "He will not see **what h** *to* us." H344
Eze 24:24 When this **h**, you will know that I am the H995
Lk 1:20 not able to speak until the day this **h**, G1181
Jn 13:19 "I am telling you now before *it* **h**, so that G1181
Jn 14:29 I have told you now before *it* **h**, so that G1181
Php 1:27 **Whatever h**, conduct yourselves in a G3667

HAPPIER (3) [HAPPY]
Ecc 4: 2 had already died, are **h** than the living, who NDT
Mt 18:13 *he is* **h** about that one sheep than G5897+3437
1Co 7:40 judgment, she is **h** if she stays as she is G3421

HAPPINESS (6) [HAPPY]
Dt 24: 5 at home and **bring h** *to* the wife he has H8523
Est 8:16 For the Jews it was a **time of h** and joy H245
Job 7: 7 a breath; my eyes will never see **h** again. H3202
Ecc 2:26 knowledge and **h**, but to the sinner he H8525
Mt 25:21 Come and share your master's **h**!' G5915
Mt 25:23 Come and share your master's **h**!' G5915

HAPPIZZEZ (1)
1Ch 24:15 to Hezir, the eighteenth to **H**, H2204

HAPPY (23) [HAPPIER, HAPPINESS]
Ge 30:13 Then Leah said, "How **h** I am! The women H891
Ge 30:13 The women *will* **call** me **h**." So she H887
1Ki 4:20 they ate, they drank and they were **h**. H8524
1Ki 10: 8 **How h** your people must be! How happy H897
1Ki 10: 8 **How h** your officials, who continually stand H897
2Ch 9: 7 **How h** your people must be! How happy H897
2Ch 9: 7 **How h** your officials, who continually stand H897
Est 5: 9 went out that day **h** and in high spirits. H8524
Ps 68: 3 before God; *may they be* **h** and joyful. H8464
Ps 113: 9 in her home as a **h** mother of children. H8524
Ps 137: 8 **h** is the one who repays you according to H897
Ps 137: 9 **H** is the one who seizes your infants and H897
Pr 15:13 A **h** heart makes the face cheerful, but H8524
Ecc 3:12 people than to *be* **h** and to do good H8523
Ecc 5:19 to accept their lot and *be* **h** in their toil H8523
Ecc 7:14 times are good, be **h**; but when times are H3202
Ecc 11: 9 *You* who are young, *be* **h** while you are H8523
Jnh 4: 6 and Jonah *was* very **h** about the H8523+8525
Zec 8:19 glad occasions and **h** festivals for Judah. H3202
1Co 7:30 did not; those *who are* **h**, as if they were G5897
2Co 7: 9 now *I am* **h**, not because you were G5897
2Co 7:13 delighted to see *how* **h** Titus was, G5915
Jas 5:13 Let them pray. *Is* anyone **h**? Let them sing G2313

HARA (1)
1Ch 5:26 **H** and the river of Gozan, where H2217

HARADAH (2)
Nu 33:24 left Mount Shepher and camped at H. H3011
Nu 33:25 They left H and camped at Makheloth. H3011

HARAM See BETH HARAM

HARAN (9) [BETH HARAN]
Ge 11:26 the father of Abram, Nahor and H. H2237
Ge 11:27 the father of Abram, Nahor and H. H2237
Ge 11:27 And H became the father of Lot. H2237
Ge 11:28 still alive, H died in Ur of the Chaldeans H2237
Ge 11:29 she was the daughter of H, the father of H2237
Ge 11:31 his grandson Lot son of H, and his H2237
1Ch 2:46 concubine Ephah was the mother of H, H3060
1Ch 2:46 H was the father of Gazez H3060
1Ch 23: 9 Haziel and H—three in all. H2237

HARARITE (5)
2Sa 23:11 to him was Shammah son of Agee the H. H2240
2Sa 23:33 son of Shammah the H, Ahiam son of H2240
2Sa 23:33 the Hararite, Ahiam son of Sharar the H, H2240
1Ch 11:34 Gizonite, Jonathan son of Shagee the H, H2240
1Ch 11:35 Ahiam son of Sakar the H, Eliphal son of H2240

HARASHIM See GE HARASHIM

HARASS (2) [HARASSED]
Dt 2: 9 "Do not h the Moabites or provoke them H7444
Dt 2:19 do not h them or provoke them to war H7444

HARASSED (2) [HARASS]
Mt 9:36 because they were h and helpless, like G5035
2Co 7: 5 had no rest, but we were h at every turn G2567

HARBONA (2)
Est 1:10 Mehuman, Biztha, H, Bigtha, Abagtha H3002
Est 7: 9 Then H, one of the eunuchs attending the H3003

HARBOR (12) [HARBORED]
Dt 15: 9 careful not to h this wicked H2118+6640+4222
Job 36:13 "The godless in heart h resentment; even H8492
Ps 12: 2 their lips but h deception in their hearts. H1819
Ps 28: 3 their neighbors but h malice in their hearts. H928
Ps 103: 9 nor will he h his anger forever; H5757
Pr 26:24 their lips, but in their hearts they h deceit. H8883
Isa 23: 1 is destroyed and left without house or h. H4427
Isa 23:10 Tarshish, for you no longer have a h. H4651
Jer 4:14 How long will you h wicked H4328+928+7931
Ac 27:12 Since the h was unsuitable to winter in G3348
Ac 27:12 This was a h in Crete, facing both G3348
Jas 3:14 But if you h bitter envy and selfish G2400

HARBORED (1) [HARBOR]
Eze 35: 5 " 'Because you h an ancient H2118+4200

HARD (62) [HARDEN, HARDENED, HARDENING, HARDENS, HARDER, HARDEST, HARDSHIP, HARDSHIPS]
Ge 18:14 Is anything too h for the LORD? I will return H7098
Ge 33:13 If they are driven h just one day, all the H1985
Ex 2:11 were and watched them at their h labor. H6026
Ex 7:13 Pharaoh's heart became h and he would H2616
Ex 7:22 Pharaoh's heart became h; he would H2616
Ex 8:19 Pharaoh's heart was h and he would not H2616
Ex 9:35 Pharaoh's heart was h and he would not H2616
Dt 1:17 Bring me any case too h for you, and I will H7996
Dt 8:15 He brought you water out of h rock. H2734
1Sa 13: 6 critical and that their army was h pressed, H5601
1Ki 10: 1 came to test Solomon with h questions. H2648
1Ki 10: 3 nothing was too h for the king to explain H6623
2Ch 9: 1 to Jerusalem to test him with h questions. H2648
2Ch 9: 2 nothing was too h for him to explain to H6623
2Ch 32: 5 Then he worked h repairing all the broken H2616
Job 7: 1 "Do not mortals have h service on earth H7372
Job 14:14 All the days of my h service I will wait H7372
Job 37:18 out the skies, h as a mirror of cast bronze? H2617
Job 38:30 when the waters become h as stone H2461
Job 38:38 dust becomes h and the H3668+4200+2021+4607
Job 41:24 Its chest is h as rock, hard as a lower H3668
Job 41:24 is hard as rock, h as a lower millstone. H3668
Ps 114: 8 the h rock into springs of water. H2734
Ps 118: 5 When h pressed, I cried to the LORD; he H5210
Pr 14:23 All h work brings a profit, but mere talk H6776
Ecc 8: 1 their face and changes its h appearance. H6437
Isa 40: 2 to her that her h service has been H7372
Jer 19: 9 press the siege so h against them to H928+5186
Jer 32:17 Nothing is too h for you. H7098
Jer 32:27 of all mankind. Is anything too h for me? H7098
Eze 29:18 drove his army in a h campaign against H1524
Zec 7:12 their hearts as h as flint and would not H9032
Mt 19: 8 your wives because your hearts were h. G5016
Mt 19:23 it is h for someone who is rich to enter the G1552
Mt 25:24 'I knew that you are a h man, harvesting G5017
Mk 10: 5 because your hearts were h that Moses G5016
Mk 10:23 "How h it is for the rich to enter the G1552
Mk 10:24 how h it is to enter the kingdom of God! G1551
Lk 5: 5 we've worked h all night and haven't G3159
Lk 12:58 try h to be reconciled on the way G1443+2238
Lk 18:24 "How h it is for the rich to enter the G1552
Lk 19:21 afraid of you, because you are a h man. G893
Lk 19:22 did you, that I am a h man, taking out what G893
Jn 4:38 Others have done the h work, and you G3159
Jn 6:60 of his disciples said, "This is a h teaching. G5017
Ac 20:35 by this kind of h work we must help the G3159
Ac 26:14 It is h for you to kick against the goads G5017
Ro 16: 6 Greet Mary, who worked very h for you. G3159
Ro 16:12 those women who work h in the Lord. G3159
Ro 16:12 woman who has worked very h in the Lord G3159
1Co 4:12 We work h with our own hands G3159+2237
2Co 4: 8 We are h pressed on every side, but not G2567
2Co 6: 5 riots; in h work, sleepless nights and G3160
2Co 8:13 be relieved while you are h pressed, G2568
Col 2: 1 want you to know how h I am contending G2462
Col 4:13 that he is working h for you and for those G4498
1Th 5:12 those who work h among you, G3159
2Ti 1:17 he searched h for me until he found me. G5081
Heb 5:11 but it is h to make it clear to you G1549+3306
1Pe 4:18 "If it is h for the righteous to be saved G3660
2Pe 3:16 some things that are h to understand, G1554
Rev 2: 2 your h work and your perseverance. G3160

HARDEN (11) [HARD]
Ex 4:21 But I will h his heart so that he will not let H2616
Ex 7: 3 But I will h Pharaoh's heart, and though I H7996
Ex 14: 4 And I will h Pharaoh's heart, and he will H2616
Ex 14:17 I will h the hearts of the Egyptians so that H2616
1Sa 6: 6 Why do you h your hearts as the Egyptians H3877
Ps 95: 8 "Do not h your hearts as you did at H7996
Isa 63:17 from your ways and h our hearts so we do H7998
Ro 9:18 and he hardens whom he wants to h. NDT
Heb 3: 8 do not h your hearts as you did in the G5020
Heb 3:15 do not h your hearts as you did in the G5020
Heb 4: 7 if you hear his voice, do not h your hearts." G5020

HARDENED (20) [HARD]
Ex 8:15 he h his heart and would not listen to H3877
Ex 8:32 time also Pharaoh h his heart and would H3877
Ex 9:12 But the LORD h Pharaoh's heart and he H2616
Ex 9:34 He and his officials h their hearts. H3877
Ex 10: 1 I have h his heart and the hearts of his H3877
Ex 10:20 But the LORD h Pharaoh's heart, and he H2616
Ex 10:27 But the LORD h Pharaoh's heart, and he H2616
Ex 11:10 the LORD h Pharaoh's heart, and H2616
Ex 14: 8 The LORD h the heart of Pharaoh king of H2616
Jos 11:20 the LORD himself who h their hearts to H2616
2Ch 36:13 stiff-necked and h his heart and would not H599
Jer 6:28 They are all h rebels, going about H6253+6073
Eze 3: 7 the Israelites are h and obstinate. H2617+5195
Eze 3: 8 as unyielding and h as they are. H2617+5195
Da 5:20 heart became arrogant and h with pride, A10772
Mk 6:52 about the loaves; their hearts were h. G4800
Mk 8:17 understand? Are your hearts h? G4800+2400
Jn 12:40 has blinded their eyes and h their hearts, G4800
Ro 11: 7 among them did, but the others were h, G4800
Heb 3:13 so that none of you may be h by sin's G5020

HARDENING (2) [HARD]
Ro 11:25 has experienced a h in part until the full G4801
Eph 4:18 is in them due to the h of their hearts. G4801

HARDENS (2) [HARD]
Pr 28:14 but whoever h their heart falls into trouble H7996
Ro 9:18 and he h whom he wants to harden. G5020

HARDER (7) [HARD]
Ex 5: 9 Make the work h for the people so that H3877
Jdg 4:24 pressed h and harder H2143+2256+7997
Jdg 4:24 pressed harder and h H2143+2256+7997
Jer 5: 3 They made their faces h than stone and H2616
Eze 3: 9 like the hardest stone, h than flint. H2617
1Co 15:10 I worked h than all of them—yet not I G4358
2Co 11:23 I have worked much h, been in prison G4359

HARDEST (1) [HARD]
Eze 3: 9 I will make your forehead like the h stone H9032

HARDHEARTED (1) [HEART]
Dt 15: 7 do not be h or tightfisted H599+906+4222

HARDLY (8)
Ge 48:10 because of old age, and he could h see. H4202
Job 2:12 distance, they could h recognize him; they H4202
Da 10:17 is gone and I can h breathe." H5972+4202+8636
Mt 13:15 calloused; they h hear with their ears G977
Mk 7:32 a man who was deaf and could h talk, G3652
Lk 11:46 down with burdens they can h carry, G1546
Ac 27:16 we were h able to make the lifeboat G3660
Ac 28:27 calloused; they h hear with their ears G977

HARDSHIP (12) [HARD]
Ge 31:42 But God has seen my h and the toil of my H6715
Dt 15:18 Do not consider it a h to set your servant H7996
Ne 9:32 do not let all this h seem trifling in your H9430
Ne 9:32 in your eyes—the h that has come on us, on NDT
Job 5: 6 For h does not spring from the soil, nor H224
Isa 30: 6 Through a land of h and distress, of lions H7650
La 3: 5 surrounded me with bitterness and h. H9430
Ro 8:35 Shall trouble or h or persecution or G5103
1Co 13: 3 poor and give over my body to h that I may AIT
1Th 2: 9 our toil and h; we worked night and G3677
2Ti 4: 5 all situations, endure h, do the work of an G2802
Heb 12: 7 Endure h as discipline; God is treating G5702

HARDSHIPS (9) [HARD]
Ex 18: 8 about all the h they had met along H9430
Nu 11: 1 about their h in the hearing of the H8273
Nu 20:14 know about all the h that have come on H9430
1Ki 2:26 shared all my father's h." H6700+928+889+6700
Ac 14:22 go through many h to enter the kingdom G2568
Ac 20:23 me that prison and h are facing me. G2568
2Co 6: 4 endurance; in troubles, h and distresses; G340
2Co 12:10 in insults, in h, in persecutions, in G340
Rev 2: 3 and have endured h for my name, G1002

HARDWORKING (1) [WORK]
2Ti 2: 6 The h farmer should be the first to receive G3159

HARE (KJV) RABBIT

HAREM (8)
Est 2: 3 women into the h at the citadel of H1074+851
Est 2: 8 to Hegai, who had charge of the h. H851
Est 2: 9 into the best place in the h. H1074+851
Est 2:11 courtyard of the h to find out how H1074+851
Est 2:13 with her from the h to the king's H1074+851
Est 2:14 another part of the h to the care of H1074+851
Est 2:15 king's eunuch who was in charge of the h, H851
Ecc 2: 8 and a h as well—the delights H8721+2256+8721

HAREPH (1)
1Ch 2:51 H the father of Beth Gader. H3073

HARESETH See KIR HARESETH

HARHAIAH (1)
Ne 3: 8 Uzziel son of H, one of the goldsmiths H3015

H

HARHAS (1)
2Ki 22:14 of Tikvah, the son of H, keeper of the H3030

HARHUR (2)
Ezr 2:51 Bakbuk, Hakupha, H, H3028
Ne 7:53 Bakbuk, Hakupha, H, H3028

HARIM (10) [HARIM'S]
1Ch 24: 8 the third to H, the fourth to Seorim, H3053
Ezr 2:32 of H 320 H3053
Ezr 2:39 of H 1,017 H3053
Ezr 10:21 From the descendants of H: Maaseiah H3053
Ezr 10:31 From the descendants of H: Eliezer H3053
Ne 3:11 Malkijah son of H and Hasshub son of H3053
Ne 7:35 of H 320 H3053
Ne 7:42 of H 1,017 H3053
Ne 10: 5 H, Meremoth, Obadiah, H3053
Ne 10:27 H and Baanah. H3053

HARIM'S (1) [HARIM]
Ne 12:15 of H, Adna; of Meremoth's, Helkai; H3053

HARIPH (2)
Ne 7:24 of H 112 H3040
Ne 10:19 H, Anathoth, Nebai, H3040

HARLOT, HARLOT'S, HARLOTS (KJV) ADULTERY, PROSTITUTE, PROSTITUTE'S, PROSTITUTES, PROSTITUTION

HARLOTS (1)
Hos 4:14 consort with h and sacrifice with H2390

HARM (75) [HARMED, HARMFUL, HARMING, HARMLESS, HARMS]
Ge 26:29 that you will do us no h, just as we did not H8288
Ge 26:29 just as we did not h you but always H5595
Ge 31: 7 God has not allowed him to h me. H8317
Ge 31:29 I have the power to h you; but last H6913+8273
Ge 31:52 heap to your side to h you and that you will NDT
Ge 31:52 this heap and pillar to my side to h me. H8288
Ge 42: 4 he was afraid that h might come to him. H656
Ge 42:38 If h comes to him on the journey you are H656
Ge 44:29 this one from me too and h comes to him, H656
Ge 48:16 Angel who has delivered me from all h— H8273
Ge 50:20 You intended to h me, but God intended it H8288
Nu 5:19 may this bitter water that brings a curse not h you H5927+4946
Nu 35:23 not an enemy and no h was intended, H8288
Jdg 15: 3 the Philistines; I will really h them." H6913+8288
1Sa 20: 7 be sure that he is determined to h me. H8288
1Sa 20: 9 that my father was determined to h you, H8288
1Sa 20:13 But if my father intends to h you, may the H8288
1Sa 26:21 I will not try to h you again. H8317
2Sa 18:32 all who rise up to h you be like that young H8288
2Sa 20: 6 son of Bikri will do us more h than H8317
2Ki 8:12 "Because I know the h you will do to the H8288
1Ch 4:10 keep me from h so that I will be free H8288
1Ch 16:22 my anointed ones; do my prophets no h." H8317
Ne 6: 2 But they were scheming to h me; H6913+8288
Job 5:19 rescue you; in seven no h will touch you. H8273
Ps 10: 6 He swears, "No one will ever do me h." H8273
Ps 38:12 those who would h me talk of my ruin H8288
Ps 71:13 those who want to h me be covered with H8288
Ps 71:24 who wanted to h me have been put to H8288
Ps 91:10 no h will overtake you, no disaster will H8288
Ps 105:15 my anointed ones; do my prophets no h." H8317
Ps 121: 6 the sun will not h you by day, nor the H5782
Ps 121: 7 The LORD will keep you from all h—he H8273
Pr 1:33 safety and be at ease, without fear of h." H8288
Pr 3:29 Do not plot h against your neighbor, who H8288
Pr 3:30 reason—when they have done you no h. H8288
Pr 8:36 those who fail to find me h themselves; H2803

Pr 12:21 No **h** overtakes the righteous, but the H224
Pr 13:20 for a companion of fools **suffers h**. H8317
Pr 31:12 brings him good, not **h**, all the days of her H8273
Ecc 5:13 wealth hoarded to the **h** *of* its owners, H8288
Ecc 8: 5 his command will come to no **h**, H1821+8273
Isa 11: 9 *They will* neither **h** nor destroy on all my H8317
Isa 27: 3 it day and night so that no *one may* **h** it. H7212
Isa 65:25 *They will* neither **h** nor destroy on all my H8317
Jer 5:12 No **h** will come to us; we will never see H8288
Jer 7: 6 do not follow other gods to your own **h**, H8273
Jer 10: 5 *they can* **do** no **h** nor can they do any H8317
Jer 21:10 determined to do this city **h** and not good, H8288
Jer 23:17 hearts they say, 'No **h** will come to you. H8288
Jer 25: 6 hands have made. Then *I will* not **h** you." H8317
Jer 25: 7 you have brought **h** to yourselves. H8273
Jer 29:11 "plans to prosper you and not to **h** you H8288
Jer 39:12 don't **h** him but do for him H6913+8273
Jer 44:17 food and were well off and suffered no **h**. H8288
Jer 44:27 For I am watching over them for **h**, not H8288
Jer 44:29 that my threats of **h** against you will surely H8288
Am 9: 4 my eye on them for **h** and not for good." H8288
Zep 3:15 with you; never again will you fear any **h**. H8273
Lk 10:19 the power of the enemy; nothing *will* **h** you. G92
Ac 9:13 man and all the **h** he has done to your G2805
Ac 16:28 shouted, "Don't **h** yourself! We are G4556+2805
Ac 18:10 no one is going to attack and **h** you G2808
Ro 13:10 Love does no **h** to a neighbor. Therefore G2805
1Co 11:17 your meetings do more **h** than good. G2482
2Ti 4:14 the metalworker did me a great deal of **h**. G2805
1Pe 3:13 Who *is going to* **h** you if you are eager to G2808
2Pe 2:13 will be paid back *with* **h** for the harm they G94
2Pe 2:13 back with harm *for the* **h** *they have* **done**. G92
1Jn 5:18 them safe, and the evil one cannot **h** them. G721
Rev 7: 2 been given power *to* **h** the land and the sea G92
Rev 7: 3 "*Do* not **h** the land or the sea or the trees G92
Rev 9: 4 They were told not to **h** the grass of the earth G92
Rev 11: 5 If anyone tries *to* **h** them, fire comes from G92
Rev 11: 5 how anyone who wants *to* **h** them must die. G92

HARMED (3) [HARM]

Ru 2:22 in someone else's field you *might be* **h**." H7003
Da 3:27 saw that the fire *had* not **h** their bodies, A10715
2Co 7: 9 intended and so *were* not **h** in any way by G2423

HARMFUL (3) [HARM]

2Ki 4:41 And there was nothing **h** in the pot. H8273
Ps 52: 4 You love every **h** word, you deceitful H1184
1Ti 6: 9 many foolish and **h** desires that plunge G1054

HARMING (4) [HARM]

1Sa 24: 9 when men say, 'David is bent on **h** you'? H8288
1Sa 25:26 who are intent on **h** my lord be like Nabal H8288
1Sa 25:34 who has kept me from **h** you, if you had H8317
Jer 7:19 Are they not rather **h** themselves, to their NDT

HARMLESS (2) [HARM]

Lev 13:39 it is a **h rash** that has broken out on the H993
Pr 1:11 blood, let's ambush some **h soul**; H5929+2855

HARMON (1)

Am 4: 3 you will be cast out toward **H**, H2236

HARMONY (3)

Zec 6:13 there will be **h** between the two. H6783+8934
Ro 12:16 **Live in h** with one another. G3836+899+5858
2Co 6:15 What **h** is there between Christ and Belial G5245

HARMS (1) [HARM]

Ge 26:11 "Anyone *who* **h** this man or his wife shall H5595

HARNEPHER (1)

1Ch 7:36 Suah, **H**, Shual, Beri, Imrah, H3062

HARNESS (4)

Job 39:10 Can you hold it to the furrow with a **h** H6310
Ps 50:19 evil and **h** your tongue *to* deceit. H7537
Jer 46: 4 **H** the horses, mount the steeds! Take your H673
Mic 1:13 in Lachish, **h** fast horses to the chariot. H8412

HAROD (1) [HARODITE]

Jdg 7: 1 all his men camped at the spring of **H**. H3008

HARODITE (2) [HAROD]

2Sa 23:25 Shammah the **H**, Elika the Harodite, H3012
2Sa 23:25 Shammah the Harodite, Elika the **H**, H3012

HAROEH (1)

1Ch 2:52 Kiriath Jearim were: **H**, half the H2218

HARORITE (1)

1Ch 11:27 Shammoth the **H**, Helez the Pelonite, H2229

HAROSHETH HAGGOYIM (3)

Jdg 4: 2 of his army, was based in **H**. H3099
Jdg 4:13 summoned from **H** to the H3099
Jdg 4:16 chariots and army as far as **H**, H3099

HARP (23) [HARPIST, HARPISTS, HARPS]

1Ch 25: 3 using the **h** in thanking and praising the H4036
Ps 33: 2 Praise the LORD with the **h**; make music to H4036
Ps 49: 4 with the **h** I will expound my riddle: H4036
Ps 57: 8 Awake, **h** and lyre! I will awaken H4036
Ps 71:22 praise you with the **h** for your faithfulness, H5575
Ps 81: 2 timbrel, play the melodious **h** and lyre. H4036
Ps 92: 3 ten-stringed lyre and the melody of the **h**. H4036
Ps 98: 5 make music to the LORD with the **h**, with H4036
Ps 98: 5 with the **h** and the sound of singing, H4036
Ps 108: 2 **h** and lyre! I will awaken the H4036
Ps 147: 7 make music to our God on the **h**. H4036
Ps 149: 3 make music to him with timbrel and **h**. H4036
Ps 150: 3 trumpet, praise him with the **h** and lyre, H4036
Isa 16:11 My heart laments for Moab like a **h**, my H4036
Isa 23:16 "Take up a **h**, walk through the city, you H4036
Isa 23:16 prostitute; **play the h** well, sing many a H5594
Isa 24: 8 revelers has stopped, the joyful **h** is silent. H4036
Da 3: 5 lyre, **h**, pipe and all kinds of A10590
Da 3: 7 **h** and all kinds of music, all the A10590
Da 3:10 **h**, pipe and all kinds of music must A10590
Da 3:15 lyre, **h**, pipe and all kinds of A10590
1Co 14: 7 such as the pipe or **h**, how will anyone G3067
Rev 5: 8 Each one had a **h** and they were holding G3067

HARPIST (2) [HARP]

2Ki 3:15 But now bring me a **h**." While the harpist H5594
2Ki 3:15 While the **h** was playing, the hand of the H5594

HARPISTS (2) [HARP]

Rev 14: 2 heard was like that *of* **h** playing their G3069
Rev 18:22 The music *of* **h** and musicians, pipers G3069

HARPOONS (1)

Job 41: 7 you fill its hide with **h** or its head with H8496

HARPS (25) [HARP]

Ge 31:27 singing to the music of timbrels and **h**? H4036
1Sa 10: 5 pipes and **h** being played before them H4036
2Sa 6: 5 the LORD, with castanets, **h**, lyres, timbrels, H4036
1Ki 10:12 to make **h** and lyres for the musicians. H4036
1Ch 13: 8 before God, with songs and with **h**, lyres, H4036
1Ch 15:16 musical instruments: lyres, **h** and cymbals. H4036
1Ch 15:21 Jeiel and Azaziah were to play the **h** H4036
1Ch 15:28 cymbals, and the playing of lyres and **h**. H4036
1Ch 16: 5 They were to play the lyres and **h**, Asaph H4036
1Ch 25: 1 accompanied by **h**, lyres and cymbals. H4036
1Ch 25: 6 cymbals, lyres and **h**, for the ministry at H4036
2Ch 5:12 linen and playing cymbals, **h** and lyres. H4036
2Ch 9:11 to make **h** and lyres for the musicians. H4036
2Ch 20:28 of the LORD with **h** and lyres and trumpets. H5575
2Ch 29:25 **h** and lyres in the way prescribed by David H4036
Ne 12:27 with the music of cymbals, **h** and lyres. H4036
Ps 137: 2 There on the poplars we hung our **h**, H4036
Isa 5:12 They have **h** and lyres at their banquets H4036
Isa 14:11 along with the noise of your **h**; maggots H5575
Isa 30:32 will be to the music of timbrels and **h**, H4036
Eze 26:13 the music of your **h** will be heard no more H4036
Am 5:23 I will not listen to the music of your **h**. H5575
Am 6: 5 You strum away on your **h** like David and H5575
Rev 14: 2 was like that of harpists playing their **h**. G3067
Rev 15: 2 They held **h** given them by God G3067

HARRAN (12)

Ge 11:31 But when they came to **H**, they settled H3059
Ge 11:32 Terah lived 205 years, and he died in **H**. H3059
Ge 12: 4 years old when he set out from **H**. H3059
Ge 12: 5 the people they had acquired in **H**, H3059
Ge 27:43 Flee at once to my brother Laban in **H**. H3059
Ge 28:10 Jacob left Beersheba and set out for **H**. H3059
Ge 29: 4 "We're from **H**," they replied. H3059
2Ki 19:12 the gods of Gozan, **H**, Rezeph and the H3059
Isa 37:12 the gods of Gozan, **H**, Rezeph and the H3059
Eze 27:23 " '**H**, Kanneh and Eden and merchants of H3059
Ac 7: 2 in Mesopotamia, before he lived in **H**. G5924
Ac 7: 4 land of the Chaldeans and settled in **H**. G5924

HARROW, HARROWS (KJV) PICKS, TILL

HARSH (16) [HARSHLY]

Ex 1:14 their lives bitter with **h** labor in brick and H7997
Ex 1:14 in all their **h** labor the Egyptians worked NDT
Ex 6: 9 of their discouragement and **h** labor. H7997
Dt 26: 6 made us suffer, subjecting us to **h** labor. H7997
Dt 28:59 descendants, **h** and prolonged disasters H1524
1Ki 12: 4 now lighten the **h** labor and the heavy H7997
2Ch 10: 4 now lighten the **h** labor and the heavy H7997
Pr 15: 1 away wrath, but a **h** word stirs up anger. H6776
Isa 14: 3 from the **h** labor forced on you, H7997
Isa 66: 4 will choose **h treatment** *for* them and will H9500
La 1: 3 After affliction and **h** labor, Judah has H8044
Da 2:15 "Why did the king issue *such* a **h** decree?" A10280
2Co 13:10 I may not have to be **h** in my use of G705
Col 2:23 humility and their **h treatment** of the body, G910
Col 3:19 your wives and *do* not *be* **h** with them. G4393
1Pe 2:18 considerate, but also to those *who* are **h**. G5021

HARSHA (2) [TEL HARSHA]

Ezr 2:52 Bazluth, Mehida, **H**, H3095
Ne 7:54 Bazluth, Mehida, **H**, H3095

HARSHLY (12) [HARSH]

Ge 42: 7 to be a stranger and spoke **h** to them. H7997
Ge 42:30 over the land spoke **h** to us and treated us H7997
Ex 10: 2 grandchildren how *I* **dealt h** with the H6618
1Sa 6: 6 When Israel's god **dealt h** with them, did H6618
1Sa 20:10 will tell me if your father answers you **h**?" H7997
1Ki 12:13 The king answered the people **h** H7997
2Ch 10:13 The king answered them **h**. Rejecting the H7997
Job 39:16 *She* **treats** her young **h**, as if they were not H7998
Pr 18:23 plead for mercy, but the rich answer **h**. H6434
Eze 34: 4 You have ruled them **h** and brutally. H928+2622
Mk 14: 5 And *they* **rebuked** her **h**. G1839
1Ti 5: 1 *Do* not **rebuke** an older man **h**, but exhort G2159

HART, HARTS (KJV) DEER, STAG

HARUM (1)

1Ch 4: 8 of the clans of Aharhel son of **H**. H2227

HARUMAPH (1)

Ne 3:10 Jedaiah son of **H** made repairs opposite H3018

HARUPHITE (1)

1Ch 12: 5 Shemariah and Shephatiah the **H**; H3020

HARUZ (1)

2Ki 21:19 name was Meshullemeth daughter of **H**; H3027

HARVEST (97) [HARVESTED, HARVESTERS, HARVESTING, HARVESTS]

Ge 8:22 endures, seedtime and **h**, cold and heat, H7907
Ge 30:14 During wheat **h**, Reuben went out into the H7907
Ge 41:34 to take a fifth of the **h** of Egypt during the NDT
Ex 23:10 you are to sow your fields and **h** the crops, H665
Ex 23:16 the Festival of **H** with the firstfruits of H7907
Ex 34:21 the plowing season and **h** you must rest. H7907
Ex 34:22 Weeks with the firstfruits of the wheat **h**, H7907
Lev 19: 9 " 'When you reap the **h** *of* your land, do H7907
Lev 19: 9 field or gather the gleanings of your **h**. H7907
Lev 19:25 In this way your **h** will be increased. H9311
Lev 23:10 I am going to give you and you reap its **h**, H7907
Lev 23:10 the priest a sheaf of the first grain you **h**. H7907
Lev 23:22 " 'When you reap the **h** *of* your land, do H7907
Lev 23:22 field or gather the gleanings of your **h**. H7907
Lev 25: 5 grows of itself or **h** the grapes of your H1305
Lev 25:11 grows of itself or **h** the untended vines. H1305
Lev 25:20 year if we do not plant or **h** our crops?" H665
Lev 25:22 eat from it until the **h** of the ninth year H9311
Lev 26: 5 will continue until **grape h** and the grape H1292
Lev 26: 5 harvest and the **grape h** will continue H1292
Lev 26:10 be eating **last year's h** when you H3824+3823
Nu 18:12 give the LORD as the **firstfruits of** their **h**. H8040
Dt 16:15 bless you in all your **h** and in all the work H9311
Dt 24:21 When *you* **h** *the* **grapes** *in* your vineyard H1305
Dt 28:38 much seed in the field but *you will* **h** little, H665
Jos 3:15 the Jordan is at flood stage all during **h**. H7907
Jdg 8: 2 better than the **full grape h** *of* Abiezer? H1292
Jdg 15: 1 at the time of wheat **h**, Samson took a H7907
Ru 1:22 as the barley **h** was beginning. H7907
1Sa 8:12 others to plow his ground and reap his **h**, H7907
1Sa 12:17 Is it not wheat **h** now? I will call on the H7907
2Sa 21: 9 put to death during the first days of the **h**, H7907
2Sa 21: 9 just as the barley **h** was beginning. H7907
2Sa 21:10 the beginning of the **h** till the rain poured H7907
2Sa 23:13 During **h time**, three of the thirty chief H7907
2Ch 32:28 made buildings to store the **h** *of* grain, H9311
Ne 9:37 its abundant **h** goes to the kings you have H9311
Job 5: 5 The hungry consume his **h**, taking it even H7907
Job 31:12 Destruction; it would have uprooted my **h**. H9311
Ps 67: 6 The land yields its **h**; God, our God H3292
Ps 85:12 what is good, and our land will yield its **h**. H3292
Ps 107:37 planted vineyards that yielded a fruitful **h**; H9311
Pr 6: 8 in summer and gathers its food at **h**. H7907
Pr 10: 5 who sleeps during **h** is a disgraceful son H7907
Pr 18:20 with the **h** *of* their lips they are satisfied. H9311
Pr 20: 4 so at **h time** they look but find nothing. H7907
Pr 25:13 snow-cooled drink at **h** time is a H7907
Pr 26: 1 Like snow in summer or rain in **h**, honor is H7907
Isa 9: 3 before you as people rejoice at the **h**, H7907
Isa 17: 5 It will be as *when* reapers **h** the standing H665
Isa 17:11 the **h** will be as nothing in the day of H7907
Isa 18: 4 like a cloud of dew in the heat of **h**." H7907
Isa 18: 5 before the **h**, when the blossom is H7907
Isa 23: 3 the **h** *of* the Nile was the revenue of Tyre H7907
Isa 24:13 when gleanings are left after the **grape h**. H1292
Isa 28: 4 will be like figs ripe before **h**—as soon as H7811
Isa 32:10 will tremble; the **grape h** will fail, and the H1292
Isa 32:10 will fail, and the **h of fruit** will not come. H668
Isa 62: 9 but *those who* **h** it will eat it and praise the H665
Jer 2: 3 the firstfruits of his **h**; all who devoured H9311
Jer 5:24 who assures us of the regular weeks of **h**. H7907
Jer 8:13 'I will take away their **h**, declares the LORD. H658
Jer 8:20 "The **h** is past, the summer has ended H7907
Jer 12:13 the shame of their **h** because of the LORD's H9311
Jer 40:10 but you *are to* **h** the wine, summer H665
Jer 50:16 and the reaper with his sickle at **h**. H7907
Jer 51:33 the time to **h** her will soon come. H7907
Hos 6:11 you, Judah, a **h** is appointed H7907
Joel 1:11 because the **h** *of* the field is destroyed. H7907
Joel 3:13 the sickle, for the **h** is ripe. Come, trample H7907
Am 4: 7 from you when the **h** was still three H7907
Mic 6:15 You will plant but not **h**; you will press H7917
Mt 9:37 "The **h** is plentiful but the workers are few. G2546
Mt 9:38 Ask the Lord *of* the **h**, therefore, to send G2546
Mt 9:38 to send out workers into his **h field**." G2546
Mt 13:30 Let both grow together until the **h**. At that G2546
Mt 13:39 The **h** is the end of the age, and the G2546
Mt 21:34 When the **h** time approached, he sent his G2843
Mt 21:41 give him his share of the crop at **h** time." G899S
Mt 25:26 So you knew that *I* **h** where I have not G2545
Mk 4:29 the sickle to it, because the **h** has come." G2546
Mk 12: 2 *At* **h time** he sent a servant to the tenants G2789

Lk 10: 2 He told them, "The **h** is plentiful, but the *G2546*
Lk 10: 2 Ask the Lord *of* the **h**, therefore, to send *G2546*
Lk 10: 2 to send out workers into his **h field**. *G2546*
Lk 12:16 a certain rich man **yielded an abundant h**. *G2369*
Lk 20:10 *At* **h time** he sent a servant to the tenants *G2789*
Jn 4:35 a saying, 'It's still four months until **h**'? *G2546*
Jn 4:35 look at the fields! They are ripe for **h**. *G2546*
Ro 1:13 in order that I might have a **h** among you *G2843*
1Co 9:10 to do so in the hope of sharing in the **h**. NDT
1Co 9:11 much if we **reap a** material **h** from you? *G2545*
2Co 9:10 will enlarge the **h** of your *G1163*
Gal 6: 9 proper time *we will* **reap a h** if we do not *G2545*
Heb 12:11 it produces a **h** of righteousness and *G2843*
Jas 3:18 sow in peace reap a **h** of righteousness. *G2843*
Rev 14:15 has come, for the **h** of the earth is ripe." *G2546*

HARVESTED (5) [HARVEST]

Isa 33: 4 O nations, **is h** as by young locusts; like a H665
Jer 40:12 And *they* **h** an abundance of wine and H665
Am 7: 1 king's share *had been* **h** and just as the H1600
Hag 1: 6 have planted much, but **h** little. You eat, H995
Rev 14:16 sickle over the earth, and the earth *was* **h**. *G2545*

HARVESTERS (8) [HARVEST]

Ru 2: 3 a field and began to glean behind the **h**. H7917
Ru 2: 4 from Bethlehem and greeted the **h**, H7917
Ru 2: 5 Boaz asked the overseer of his **h**, "Who H7917
Ru 2: 7 gather among the sheaves behind the **h**. H7917
Ru 2:14 When she sat down with the **h**, he offered H7917
Mt 13:30 At that time I will tell the **h**: First collect *G2547*
Mt 13:39 the end of the age, and the **h** are angels. *G2547*
Jas 5: 4 The cries *of* the **h** have reached the ears *G2545*

HARVESTING (6) [HARVEST]

Lev 25:15 of the number of years left for **h crops**. H9311
Dt 24:19 When you *are* **h** in your field and H7917+7907
Ru 2: 9 Watch the field where *the men are* **h**, and H7917
Ru 2:21 my workers until they finish **h** all my **grain**. H7907
1Sa 6:13 Beth Shemesh *were* **h** their wheat H7917+7907
Mt 25:24 **h** where you have not sown and gathering *G2545*

HARVESTS (6) [HARVEST]

Dt 32:22 the earth and its **h** and set afire the H3292
Ru 2:23 the barley and wheat **h** were finished. H7907
Pr 14: 4 the strength of an ox come abundant **h**. H9311
Isa 16: 9 fruit and over your **h** have been stilled. H7907
Jer 5:17 They will devour your **h** and food, devour H7907
Jn 4:36 draws a wage and **h** a crop for eternal *G5251*

HAS (303 of 2328) [HAVE] See Index of Articles Etc. for an Exhaustive Index

Ge 1:29 every tree that **h** fruit with seed in it. NDT
Ge 1:30 everything that **h** the breath of life in it NDT
Ge 6:17 every creature that **h** the breath of life in it. NDT
Ge 9: 4 must not eat meat that **h** its lifeblood still in NDT
Ge 31:32 But if you find anyone who **h** your gods H6640
Ge 34:21 the land **h** plenty of room for them. NDT
Ge 38:23 "Let her keep what she **h**, or we will H4200
Ex 21: 3 but if he **h** a wife when he comes H1251
Ex 21: 8 *He* **h** no **right** to sell her to foreigners H5440
Ex 22:19 *who* **h sexual relations with** an H8886+6640
Ex 22:27 cloak is the only covering your neighbor **h**. H4200
Ex 32:24 I told them, 'Whoever **h** any gold jewelry H4200
Lev 13: 2 "When anyone **h** a swelling or a rash or a H2118
Lev 13: 9 "When anyone **h** a defiling skin H2118+928
Lev 13:18 "When someone **h** a boil on their H2118+928
Lev 13:24 "When someone **h** a burn on their skin H2118
Lev 13:29 a man or woman **h** a sore on their H2118+928
Lev 13:38 a man or woman **h** white spots on the H2118
Lev 13:41 the front of his scalp and **h** a bald forehead, NDT
Lev 13:42 But if *he* **h** a reddish-white sore on his H2118
Lev 13:57 whatever **h** the mold must be burned. H928
Lev 14:32 anyone who **h** a defiling skin disease H928
Lev 14:37 if it **h** greenish or reddish depressions NDT
Lev 15: 2 'When any man **h** an unusual bodily H2118
Lev 15:16 " 'When a man **h** an emission of semen H3655
Lev 15:17 leather that **h** semen on it must be H2118
Lev 15:18 When a man **h sexual relations** with a H8886
Lev 15:19 " 'When a woman **h** her regular flow of H2118
Lev 15:24 a man **h sexual relations** with her H8886+8886
Lev 15:25 a woman **h a discharge** *of* blood H2307+2308
Lev 15:25 be unclean as long as she **h** the discharge, NDT
Lev 15:33 a man who **h sexual relations** with a H8886
Lev 20:11 " 'If a man **h sexual relations** with his H8886
Lev 20:12 " 'If a man **h sexual relations** with his H8886
Lev 20:13 " 'If a man **h sexual relations** with a man H8886
Lev 20:15 'If a man **h sexual relations** with an H5989+8888
Lev 20:18 man **h sexual relations with** a H1655+906+6872
Lev 20:20 " 'If a man **h sexual relations** with his H8886
Lev 21: 3 on him since *she* **h** no husband— H2118+4200
Lev 21:17 descendants who **h** a defect may H2118+928
Lev 21:18 No man who **h** any defect may come near H928
Lev 21:20 a dwarf, or who **h** any eye defect, or who H928
Lev 21:20 who **h** festering or running sores or NDT
Lev 21:21 Aaron the priest who **h** any defect is to H928
Lev 21:21 He **h** a defect; he must not come near to H928
Lev 22: 4 by anyone who **h** an emission of H3655
Lev 22:13 is divorced, yet **h** no children, and she H4200
Nu 5: 2 anyone *who* **h a defiling skin disease** H7665
Nu 5: 8 But if that person **h** no close relative to H4200
Nu 5:13 man **h sexual relations** with H8886+8887+2446
Nu 14:24 my servant Caleb **h** a different spirit H2118+6640
Nu 20: 5 It **h** no grain or figs, grapevines or NDT
Nu 24:16 *who* **h knowledge** *from* the Most H3359+1981
Nu 27: 9 If he **h** no daughter, give his inheritance to H4200
Nu 27:10 If he **h** no brothers, give his inheritance to H4200
Nu 35: 8 Take many towns from a tribe that **h** many NDT
Nu 35: 8 that has many, but few from one that **h** few." NDT
Dt 3:20 rest to your fellow Israelites as he **h** to you, NDT
Dt 14: 9 you may eat any that **h** fins and scales. H4200
Dt 15:21 If an animal **h** a defect, is lame or H2118+928
Dt 15:21 is lame or blind, or **h** any serious flaw, you NDT
Dt 17: 1 ox or a sheep that **h** any defect or flaw in H2118
Dt 21:15 If a man **h** two wives, and he loves H2118+4200
Dt 21:17 him a double share of all he **h**. H5162+4200
Dt 21:18 If someone **h** a stubborn and H2118+4200
Dt 27:21 *anyone who* **h sexual relations with** H8886+6640
Dt 28:55 It will be all he **h** left because of the H4200
Dt 32:21 angry by a nation that **h** no understanding. NDT
Jdg 18: 6 Your journey **h** the LORD's approval." NDT
Jdg 18:14 one of these houses **h** an ephod, H3780+928
Ru 4: 4 For no *one* **h the right to do it** except you, H1457S
Ru 4:17 women living there said, "Naomi **h** a son!" H3528
1Sa 2: 8 princes and **h** them **inherit** a throne of H5706
1Sa 14:33 the LORD by eating meat that **h** blood in it." NDT
1Sa 25:24 hear what your servant **h** to say. NDT
2Sa 6:12 of Obed-Edom and everything he **h**, H4200
2Sa 14:20 My lord **h** wisdom like that of an angel of NDT
2Sa 14:30 is next to mine, and he **h** barley there. H4200
2Sa 15: 4 everyone who **h** a complaint or H2118+4200
2Sa 17: 5 so we can hear what he **h** to say as well." H928
1Ki 18:22 Baal **h** four hundred and fifty prophets. NDT
2Ki 4: 2 "Your servant **h** nothing there at all," H4200
2Ki 4:14 Gehazi said, "She **h** no son, and her H4200
2Ki 14: 7 calling it Joktheel, the name it **h** to this day. NDT
2Ch 25: 8 God **h** the power to help or to H3780+928
Ezr 4:19 found that this city **h** a long history of revolt NDT
Est 4:11 being summoned the king **h** but one law: NDT
Job 1:10 his household and everything he **h**? H4200
Job 1:11 out your hand and strike everything he **h**, H4200
Job 1:12 everything he **h** is in your power, but H4200
Job 2: 4 "A man will give all he **h** for his own life. H4200
Job 6: 5 Does a wild donkey bray when it **h** grass, or NDT
Job 6: 5 has grass, or an ox bellow when it **h** fodder? NDT
Job 11: 6 of wisdom, for true wisdom **h** two sides. H4200
Job 12: 6 God are secure—those God **h** in his hand. H995
Job 18:17 from the earth; he **h** no name in the land. H4200
Job 18:19 He **h** no offspring or descendants among H4200
Job 20:23 When *he* **h** filled his belly, God will vent H2118
Job 23:14 and many such plans he still **h** in store. NDT
Job 37:16 wonders of him who **h** perfect knowledge? NDT
Job 38:37 Who **h** the wisdom to count the clouds H928
Job 40:16 What strength it **h** in its loins, what power in NDT
Job 41:11 Who **h a claim against** me that I must pay H7709
Job 41:15 Its back **h** rows of shields tightly sealed NDT
Job 41:26 The sword that reaches it **h** no **effect**, nor H7756
Job 42: 7 the truth about me, as my servant Job **h**. NDT
Job 42: 8 the truth about me, as my servant Job **h**." NDT
Ps 24: 4 The one who **h** clean hands and a pure NDT
Ps 73:25 And earth **h** nothing I desire besides you. H928
Ps 101: 5 whoever **h** haughty eyes and a proud heart NDT
Ps 103:13 As a father **h compassion** on his children H8163
Ps 103:13 so the LORD **h compassion** on those who H8163
Ps 104:17 the stork **h** its home in the junipers. NDT
Ps 109:11 May a creditor seize all he **h**; may H4200
Ps 145: 9 he **h** compassion on all he has made. NDT
Ps 147: 5 in power; his understanding **h** no limit. H4200
Ps 150: 6 Let everything that **h** breath praise the LORD NDT
Pr 6: 7 It **h** no commander, no overseer or ruler, H4200
Pr 6:32 a man who commits adultery **h no** sense; H2894
Pr 10:13 rod is for the back of one who **h no** sense. H2894
Pr 11:12 derides their neighbor **h no** sense, H2894
Pr 13: 7 pretends to be poor, yet **h** great wealth. NDT
Pr 14:26 Whoever fears the LORD **h** a secure fortress H928
Pr 14:29 Whoever is patient **h** great understanding NDT
Pr 15:15 the cheerful heart **h** a continual feast. NDT
Pr 15:21 Folly brings joy to *one who* **h no** sense H2894
Pr 17:18 One who **h no** sense shakes hands in H2894
Pr 17:27 The *one who* **h knowledge** uses H3359+1981
Pr 18:21 The tongue **h** the power of life and death H928
Pr 23:29 Who **h** woe? Who has sorrow? Who has H4200
Pr 23:29 Who has woe? Who **h** sorrow? Who has H4200
Pr 23:29 Who has sorrow? Who **h** strife? Who has H4200
Pr 23:29 Who **h** complaints? Who has H4200
Pr 23:29 has complaints? Who **h** needless bruises H4200
Pr 23:29 Who **h** bloodshot eyes? H4200
Pr 24:20 the evildoer **h** no future hope H2118+4200
Pr 24:30 the vineyard of someone who **h no** sense; H2894
Pr 28: 2 is rebellious, it **h** many rulers, but a ruler NDT
Pr 30:15 "The leech **h** two daughters. 'Give! Give!' H4200
Pr 31:11 husband **h full confidence** in her H1053+4213
Ecc 1: 8 The eye never **h enough** *of* seeing, nor H8425
Ecc 1:16 than anyone who **h** ruled over Jerusalem H2118
Ecc 5: 4 delay to fulfill it. He **h** no pleasure in fools NDT
Ecc 5:10 Whoever loves money never **h enough** H8425
Ecc 6: 5 it **h** more rest than does that man H4200
Ecc 8: 8 As no one **h** power over the wind to contain NDT
Ecc 8: 8 so no one **h** power over the time of their NDT
Ecc 9: 4 Anyone who is among the living **h** hope— H3780
SS 4: 2 Each **h** *its* **twin**; not one of them H9298
SS 6: 6 Each **h** its **twin**, not one of them is H9298
Isa 2:12 The LORD Almighty **h** a day in store for all H4200
Isa 10: 7 this is not what he **h in mind**; his H3108+4222
Isa 22: 5 **h** a day of tumult and trampling and terror H4200
Isa 28: 2 the Lord **h** one who is powerful and strong H4200
Isa 34: 6 For the LORD **h** a sacrifice in Bozrah and a H4200
Isa 34: 8 For the LORD **h** a day of vengeance, a year H4200
Isa 44:19 no one **h** the knowledge or understanding NDT
Isa 45: 9 your work say, 'The potter **h** no hands'? H4200
Isa 49:10 *He who* **h compassion** *on* them will guide H8163
Isa 50:10 in the dark, who **h** no light, trust in the H4200
Isa 54: 1 woman than of *her who* **h a husband**," H1249
Isa 54:10 says the LORD, *who* **h compassion** *on* you. H8163
Jer 6:25 for the enemy **h** a sword, and there H4200
Jer 17: 8 *It* **h** no **worries** in a year of drought and H1793
Jer 23:28 Let the prophet who **h** a dream recount the H907
Jer 23:28 let the one who **h** my word speak it H907
Jer 23:28 For what **h** straw **to do with** grain? H4200
Jer 30:15 over your wound, your pain that **h** no cure? NDT
Jer 49: 1 what the LORD says: "**H** Israel no sons? H4200
Jer 49: 1 Israel no sons? **H** Israel no heir? Why H4200
Jer 49:31 "a nation that **h** neither gates nor bars H4200
Jer 50:25 LORD Almighty **h** work to do in the land H4200
Eze 9: 6 do not touch anyone who **h** the mark. H6584
Eze 18:10 "Suppose *he* **h** a violent son, who sheds H3528
Eze 18:14 suppose this son **h** a son who sees all H3528
Da 5:11 in your kingdom who **h** the spirit of the holy NDT
Da 6: 5 Daniel unless it **h** something to do with NDT
Hos 4: 1 because the LORD **h** a charge to bring H4200
Hos 8: 7 The stalk **h** no head; it will produce no H4200
Hos 12: 2 The LORD **h** a charge to bring against H4200
Joel 1: 6 without number; it **h** the teeth of a lion H4200
Am 3: 4 lion roar in the thicket when it **h** no prey? H4200
Mic 6: 2 For the LORD **h** a case against his people H4200
Mal 1:14 is the cheat who **h** an acceptable male in H3780
Mal 3:17 a father **h compassion and spares** his son H2798
Mt 5:23 brother or sister **h** something against you, *G2400*
Mt 6:34 Each day **h** enough trouble of its own. NDT
Mt 8:20 the Son of Man **h** no place to lay his *G2400*
Mt 9: 6 that the Son of Man **h** authority on earth *G2400*
Mt 11:15 Whoever **h** ears, let them hear. *G2400*
Mt 11:18 drinking, and they say, '*He* **h** a demon.' *G2400*
Mt 12:11 "If any of you **h** a sheep and it falls into a *G2400*
Mt 13: 9 Whoever **h** ears, let them hear. *G2400*
Mt 13:12 Whoever **h** will be given more, and they *G2400*
Mt 13:43 Whoever **h** ears, let them hear. *G2400*
Mt 17:15 "*He* **h seizures** and is suffering greatly *G4944*
Mt 25:28 give it *to* the *one who* **h** ten bags. *G2400*
Mt 25:29 For whoever **h** will be given more, and *G2400*
Mk 2:10 that the Son of Man **h** authority on earth *G2400*
Mk 3:30 they were saying, "*He* **h** an impure spirit." *G2400*
Mk 4: 9 Jesus said, "Whoever **h** ears to hear, let *G2400*
Mk 4:23 If anyone **h** ears to hear, let them hear." *G2400*
Mk 4:25 Whoever **h** will be given more; whoever *G2400*
Lk 1:61 among your relatives who **h** that name." *G2813S*
Lk 3:11 "Anyone *who* **h** two shirts should share *G2400*
Lk 3:11 should share with the *one who* **h** none, *G2400*
Lk 3:11 anyone *who* **h** food should do the *G2400*
Lk 5:24 that the Son of Man **h** authority on earth *G2400*
Lk 7:33 and you say, '*He* **h** a demon.' *G2400*
Lk 8: 8 called out, "Whoever **h** ears to hear, let *G2400*
Lk 8:18 Whoever **h** will be given more; whoever *G2400*
Lk 9:58 the Son of Man **h** no place to lay his *G2400*
Lk 12: 5 *who*, after your body has been killed, **h** *G2400*
Lk 14: 5 "If one of you **h** a child or an ox that falls NDT
Lk 14:35 "Whoever **h** ears to hear, let *G2400*
Lk 15: 4 "*Suppose* one of you **h** a hundred sheep *G2400*
Lk 15: 8 "Or suppose a woman **h** ten silver coins *G2400*
Lk 15:27 calf because *he* **h** him **back** safe and sound *G655*
Lk 17: 7 "*Suppose* one of you **h** a servant plowing *G2400*
Lk 19:24 give it *to* the *one who* **h** ten minas. *G2400*
Lk 19:25 they said, '*he already* **h** ten! *G2400*
Lk 19:26 'I tell you that to everyone who **h**, more *G2400*
Lk 19:26 as for the *one who* **h** nothing, even *G2400*
Lk 23:15 Neither **h** Herod, for he sent him back to us NDT
Jn 3:36 Whoever believes in the Son **h** eternal life, *G2400*
Jn 4:44 out that a prophet **h** no honor in his own *G2400*
Jn 5:24 him who sent me **h** eternal life and will *G2400*
Jn 5:26 For as the Father **h** life in himself, so he *G2400*
Jn 6:47 the one who believes **h** eternal life. *G2400*
Jn 6:54 flesh and drinks my blood **h** eternal life, *G2400*
Jn 8:35 Now a slave **h** no permanent **place** in the *G3531*
Jn 14: 2 My Father's house **h** many rooms; if *G1877+1639*
Jn 14:21 Whoever **h** my commands and keeps them *G2400*
Jn 14:30 world is coming. *He* **h** no hold over me, *G2400*
Jn 15:13 Greater love **h** no one than this: to lay *G2400*
Jn 16:21 birth to a child **h** pain because her time *G2400*
Ac 23:17 commander; *he* **h** something to tell him." *G2400*
Ac 23:18 man to you *because he* **h** something to *G2400*
Ac 25:11 no one **h the right** to hand me over to *G1538*
Ro 2:25 Circumcision **h value** if you observe the *G6067*
Ro 6: 9 death no longer **h mastery over** him. *G3259*
Ro 7: 1 that the law **h authority over** someone only *G3259*
Ro 7: 3 if *she* **h sexual relations with** another man *G1181*
Ro 9:18 Therefore God **h mercy** on whom he wants *G1796*
Ro 10:19 angry by a nation that **h** no understanding." NDT
Ro 12: 4 For just as *each of us* **h** one body with *G2400*
Ro 14:23 But whoever **h doubts** is condemned if *G1359*
1Co 6: 1 *If* any of you **h** a dispute with another, do *G2400*
1Co 7: 7 But each of you **h** your own gift from God *G2400*
1Co 7: 7 gift from God; one **h** this gift, another has NDT
1Co 7: 7 from God; one has this gift, another **h** that. NDT
1Co 7:12 If any brother **h** a wife who is not a *G2400*
1Co 7:13 And if a woman **h** a husband who is not a *G2400*
1Co 7:37 no compulsion but **h** control over his own *G2400*
1Co 11:14 things teach you that if a man **h long hair**, *G3150*
1Co 11:15 that if a woman **h long hair**, it is her *G3150*

H

1Co 12:12 though one, **h** many parts, but all its G2400
1Co 14:26 together, each *of you* **h** a hymn, or a word G2400
1Co 15:41 The sun **h** one kind of splendor, the moon NDT
1Co 16:10 see to it that he **h** nothing to fear while he NDT
1Co 16:12 he will go when *he* **h the opportunity**. G2320
2Co 3:10 was glorious **h** no **glory** *now* in G1519
2Co 8:12 is acceptable according to what *one* **h**, G2400
Gal 4:27 woman than *of* her *who* **h** a husband." G2400
Gal 5: 6 uncircumcision **h** any **value**. G2710
Eph 5: 5 **h** any inheritance in the kingdom of Christ G2400
Php 1:12 that **what h happened to** me has G3836+2848
Col 3:13 if any of you **h** a grievance against G2400
2Th 3: 2 evil people, for not everyone **h** faith. NDT
1Ti 4: 8 but godliness **h** value for all things G1639
1Ti 5: 4 But if a widow **h** children or grandchildren G2400
1Ti 5:16 who is a believer **h** widows *in her care*, G2400
Heb 3: 3 builder of a house **h** greater honor than G2400
Heb 3:12 sisters, *that* none of you **h** a sinful G1639+1877
Heb 5: 3 This is why *he* **h to** offer sacrifices for his G4053
Heb 7:24 he **h** a permanent priesthood. G2400
Jas 2:14 claims to have faith but **h** no deeds? G2400
2Pe 3: 4 everything goes on **as it h** since the G4048
1Jn 2:23 No one who denies the Son **h** the Father G2400
1Jn 2:23 acknowledges the Son **h** the Father also. G2400
1Jn 3:15 that no murderer **h** eternal life residing G2400
1Jn 3:17 If anyone **h** material possessions and sees G2400
1Jn 3:17 need but **h no pity** on them, G3091+3836+5073
1Jn 4:16 know and rely on the love God **h** for us. G2400
1Jn 4:18 because fear **h to do with** punishment. G2400
1Jn 5:12 Whoever **h** the Son has life; whoever does G2400
1Jn 5:12 Whoever has the Son **h** life; whoever does G2400
2Jn 9 in the teaching **h** both the Father and the G2400
Rev 2: 7 Whoever **h** ears, let them hear what the G2400
Rev 2:11 Whoever **h** ears, let them hear what the G2400
Rev 2:12 are the words of him who **h** the sharp, G2400
Rev 2:13 where you live—where Satan **h** his throne. NDT
Rev 2:17 Whoever **h** ears, let them hear what the G2400
Rev 2:29 Whoever **h** ears, let them hear what the G2400
Rev 3: 6 Whoever **h** ears, let them hear what the G2400
Rev 3:13 Whoever **h** ears, let them hear what the G2400
Rev 3:22 Whoever **h** ears, let them hear what the G2400
Rev 13: 9 Whoever **h** ears, let them hear. G2400
Rev 13:18 Let the *person who* **h** insight calculate the G2400
Rev 17: 7 which **h** the seven heads and ten horns. G2400
Rev 19:12 *He* **h** a name written on him that no one G2400
Rev 19:16 on his thigh *he* **h** this name written: G2400
Rev 20: 6 The second death **h** no power over them G2400

HASADIAH (1)
1Ch 3:20 Berekiah, **H** and Jushab-Hesed. H2878

HASHABIAH (15)
1Ch 6:45 the son of **H**, the son of Amaziah, the son H3116
1Ch 9:14 son of Azrikam, the son of **H**, a Merarite; H3116
1Ch 25: 3 Jeshaiah, Shimei, **H** and Mattithiah, six in H3117
1Ch 25:19 the twelfth to **H**, his sons and relatives 12 H3116
1Ch 26:30 **H** and his relatives—seventeen hundred H3117
1Ch 27:17 **H** son of Kemuel; over Aaron H3116
2Ch 35: 9 his brothers, and **H**, Jeiel and Jozabad H3117
Ezr 8:19 **H**, together with Jeshaiah from the H3116
Ezr 8:24 Sherebiah, **H** and ten of their brothers H3116
Ne 3:17 Beside him, **H**, ruler of half the district of H3116
Ne 10:11 Rehob, **H**, H3116
Ne 11:15 Azrikam, the son of **H**, the son of Bunni; H3116
Ne 11:22 of Bani, the son of **H**, the son of H3116
Ne 12:21 of Hilkiah's, **H**; of Jedaiah's, Nethanel. H3116
Ne 12:24 And the leaders of the Levites were **H** H3116

HASHABNAH (1)
Ne 10:25 Rehum, **H**, Maaseiah, H3118

HASHABNEIAH (2)
Ne 3:10 Hattush son of **H** made repairs next H3119
Ne 9: 5 Kadmiel, Bani, **H**, Sherebiah, Hodiah H3119

HASHBADDANAH (1)
Ne 8: 4 Malkijah, Hashum, **H**, Zechariah and H3111

HASHEM (1)
1Ch 11:34 the sons of **H** the Gizonite, Jonathan son H2244

HASHMONAH (2)
Nu 33:29 They left Mithkah and camped at **H**. H3135
Nu 33:30 They left **H** and camped at Moseroth. H3135

HASHUBAH (1)
1Ch 3:20 **H**, Ohel, Berekiah, Hasadiah and H3112

HASHUM (5)
Ezr 2:19 of **H** 223 H3130
Ezr 10:33 From the descendants of **H**: Mattenai H3130
Ne 7:22 of **H** 328 H3130
Ne 8: 4 Mishael, Malkijah, **H**, Hashbaddanah H3130
Ne 10:18 Hodiah, **H**, Bezai, H3130

HASN'T (7) [HAVE, NOT]
Ge 38:21 "There **h** been any shrine prostitute here," H4202
Ge 38:22 'There **h** been any shrine prostitute here. H4202
Nu 12: 2 "**H** he also spoken through us? H4202
1Sa 20:27 "Why **h** the son of Jesse come to the H4202
2Sa 10: 3 **H** David sent them to you only to explore H4202
Ac 9:21 And **h** he come here to take them as NDT
Ac 22:25 citizen who **h** even **been found guilty**?" G185

HASRAH (1)
2Ch 34:22 of Tokhath, the son of **H**, keeper of the H2897

HASSENAAH (1)
Ne 3: 3 Fish Gate was rebuilt by the sons of **H**. H2189

HASSENUAH (2)
1Ch 9: 7 the son of Hodaviah, the son of **H**; H2190
Ne 11: 9 Judah son of **H** was over the New H2190

HASSHUB (5)
1Ch 9:14 Shemaiah son of **H**, the son of Azrikam H3121
Ne 3:11 son of Harim and **H** son of Pahath-Moab H3121
Ne 3:23 Benjamin and **H** made repairs in front of H3121
Ne 10:23 Hoshea, Hananiah, **H**, H3121
Ne 11:15 Shemaiah son of **H**, the son of Azrikam H3121

HASSOPHERETH (1)
Ezr 2:55 the descendants of Sotai, **H**, Peruda, H2191

HASTE (7) [HASTEN, HASTILY, HASTY]
Ex 12:11 Eat it in **h**; it is the LORD's H2906
Dt 16: 3 because you left Egypt in **h**—so that all H2906
Ps 68:12 "Kings and armies **flee in h**; the H5610+5610
Pr 21: 5 to profit as surely as **h** leads to poverty. H237
Pr 29:20 Do you see someone *who* speaks **in h** H237
Isa 52:12 But you will not leave in **h** or go in flight H2906
Jer 46: 5 *They* **flee in h** without looking back, H5674+4960

HASTEN (4) [HASTE]
Ps 70: 1 **H**, O God, to save me; come quickly, LORD, NDT
Ps 119:60 *I will* **h** and not delay to obey your H2590
Isa 5:19 *let him* **h** his work so we may see it. H2590
Isa 49:17 Your children **h** back, and those who laid H4554

HASTILY (1) [HASTE]
Pr 25: 8 do not bring **h** to court, for what will you H4554

HASTY (3) [HASTE]
Pr 19: 2 how much more will **h** feet miss the way! H237
Ecc 5: 2 *do not be* **h** in your heart to utter anything H4554
1Ti 5:22 Do not be **h** in the laying on of hands G5441

HASUPHA (2)
Ezr 2:43 the descendants of Ziha, **H**, Tabbaoth, H3102
Ne 7:46 the descendants of Ziha, **H**, Tabbaoth, H3102

HATCH (2) [HATCHED, HATCHES]
Isa 34:15 lay eggs, *she will* **h** them, and care H1324
Isa 59: 5 *They* **h** the eggs of vipers and spin a H1324

HATCHED (1) [HATCH]
Isa 59: 5 when one is broken, an adder **is h**. H1324

HATCHES (1) [HATCH]
Jer 17:11 Like a partridge *that* **h eggs** it did not lay H1842

HATCHETS (1) [HATCHET]
Ps 74: 6 the carved paneling with their axes and **h**. H3965

HATE (79) [GOD-HATERS, HATED, HATES, HATING, HATRED]
Ex 18:21 trustworthy men *who* **h** dishonest gain H8533
Ex 20: 5 fourth generation of *those who* **h** me, H8533
Lev 19:17 " '*Do* not **h** a fellow Israelite in your heart H8533
Lev 26:17 *those who* **h** you will rule over you H8533
Dt 5: 9 fourth generation of *those who* **h** me, H8533
Dt 7:10 But *those who* **h** him he will repay to their H8533
Dt 7:10 to repay to their face *those who* **h** him. H8533
Dt 7:15 he will inflict them on all *who* **h** you. H8533
Dt 19:11 But if *out of* someone lies in wait H8533
Dt 30: 7 your enemies who **h** and persecute you. H8533
Dt 32:41 adversaries and repay *those who* **h** me. H8533
Jdg 11: 7 "Didn't you **h** me and drive me from my H8533
Jdg 14:16 herself on him, sobbing, "*You* **h** me! H8533
2Sa 19: 6 You love *those who* **h** you and hate those H8533
2Sa 19: 6 who hate you and **h** those who love you. H8533
1Ki 22: 8 I **h** him because he never prophesies H8533
2Ch 18: 7 I **h** him because he never prophesies H8533
2Ch 19: 2 wicked and love *those who* **h** the LORD? H8533
Ps 5: 5 in your presence. *You* **h** all who do wrong H8533
Ps 25:19 and how fiercely *they* **h** me! H8533+8534
Ps 31: 6 *I* **h** those who cling to worthless idols; as H8533
Ps 35:19 do not let *those who* **h** me without reason H8533
Ps 36: 2 too much to detect or **h** their sin. H8533
Ps 38:19 *those who* **h** me without reason are H8533
Ps 45: 7 You love righteousness and **h** wickedness H8533
Ps 50:17 You **h** my instruction and cast my words H8533
Ps 69: 4 *Those who* **h** me without reason H8533
Ps 69:14 deliver me from *those who* **h** me, from the H8533
Ps 81:15 *Those who* **h** the LORD would cringe before H8533
Ps 97:10 Let those who love the LORD **h** evil, for he H8533
Ps 101: 3 *I* **h** what faithless people do; I will have H8533
Ps 105:25 whose hearts he turned to **h** his people H8533
Ps 119:104 precepts; therefore *I* **h** every wrong path. H8533
Ps 119:113 *I* **h** double-minded people, but I love your H8533
Ps 119:128 your precepts right, *I* **h** every wrong path. H8533
Ps 119:163 *I* **h** and detest falsehood but I love your H8533
Ps 120: 6 have I lived among *those who* **h** peace. H8533
Ps 129: 5 May all *who* **h** Zion be turned back in H8533
Ps 139:21 *Do I* not **h** those who hate you, LORD, and H8533
Ps 139:21 Do I not hate *those who* **h** you, LORD, and H8533
Pr 1:22 in mockery and fools **h** knowledge? H8533
Pr 8:13 To fear the LORD is *to* **h** evil; I hate pride H8533
Pr 8:13 is to hate evil; *I* **h** pride and arrogance H8533
Pr 8:36 themselves; all *who* **h** me love death." H8533
Pr 9: 8 Do not rebuke mockers or *they will* **h** you H8533
Pr 13: 5 The righteous **h** what is false, but the H8533
Pr 25:17 too much of you, and *they will* **h** you. H8533
Pr 29:10 The bloodthirsty **h** a person of integrity H8533
Ecc 3: 8 a time to love and a time to **h**, a time H8533
Ecc 9: 1 one knows whether love or **h** awaits them. H8534
Ecc 9: 6 their **h** and their jealousy have long since H8534
Isa 1:14 appointed festivals I **h** with all my being. H8533
Isa 61: 8 love justice; I **h** robbery and wrongdoing. H8533
Isa 66: 5 "Your own people *who* **h** you, and H8533
Jer 12: 8 She roars at me; therefore *I* **h** her. H8533
Jer 44: 4 'Do not do this detestable thing that *I* **h**! H8533
Eze 23:28 deliver you into the hands of those *you* **h**, H8533
Eze 35: 6 Since *you did* not **h** bloodshed H8533
Am 5:10 There are *those who* **h** the one who H8533
Am 5:15 **H** evil, love good; maintain justice in the H8533
Am 5:21 "*I* **h**, I despise your religious festivals; your H8533
Mic 3: 2 *you who* **h** good and love evil; who tear H8533
Zec 8:17 love to swear falsely. *I* **h** all this," declares H8533
Mt 5:43 'Love your neighbor and **h** your enemy.' G3631
Mt 6:24 Either *you will* **h** the one and love the G3631
Mt 24:10 the faith and will betray and **h** each other, G3631
Mk 13:13 Everyone will **h** *you* because of me, but G3631
Lk 1:71 from the hand of all who **h** us— G3631
Lk 6:22 Blessed are you when people **h** you G3631
Lk 6:27 enemies, do good to those *who* **h** you, G3631
Lk 14:26 comes to me and *does* not **h** father and G3631
Lk 16:13 Either *you will* **h** the one and love the G3631
Lk 21:17 Everyone *will* **h** *you* because of me. G1639+3631
Jn 7: 7 The world cannot **h** you, but it hates me G3631
Ro 7:15 I want to do I do not do, but what *I* **h** I do. G3631
Ro 12: 9 Love must be sincere. **H** what is evil; cling G696
Rev 2: 6 *You* **h** the practices of the Nicolaitans G3631
Rev 2: 6 of the Nicolaitans, which I also **h**. G3631
Rev 17:16 ten horns you saw *will* **h** the prostitute. G3631

HATED (30) [HATE]
Ge 37: 4 *they* **h** him and could not speak a kind H8533
Ge 37: 5 it to his brothers, *they* **h** him all the more. H8533
Ge 37: 8 And *they* **h** him all the more because of H8533
Dt 9:28 because he **h** them, he brought H8534
Jdg 15: 2 "I was so sure *you* **h** her," he said H8533+8533
2Sa 13:15 Then Amnon **h** her *with* intense hatred. H8533
2Sa 13:15 *he* **h** her more than he had loved her. H8533
2Sa 13:22 he **h** Amnon because he had disgraced H8533
Est 9: 1 the upper hand over *those who* **h** them. H8533
Est 9: 5 what they pleased to *those who* **h** them. H8533
Pr 1:29 since *they* **h** knowledge and did not H8533
Pr 5:12 You will say, "How *I* **h** discipline! How my H8533
Pr 14:17 the one who devises evil schemes **is h**. H8533
Ecc 2:17 So *I* **h** life, because the work that is done H8533
Ecc 2:18 I **h** all the things I had toiled for under the H8533
Isa 60:15 "Although you have been forsaken and **h** H8533
Eze 16:37 those you loved as well as those *you* **h**. H8533
Hos 9:15 their wickedness in Gilgal, *I* **h** them there. H8533
Mal 1: 3 Esau *I have* **h**, and I have turned his H8533
Mt 10:22 You will be **h** by everyone because of me G3631
Mt 24: 9 you will be **h** by all nations because G3631
Lk 19:14 "But his subjects **h** him and sent a G3631
Jn 15:18 hates you, keep in mind that *it* **h** me first. G3631
Jn 15:24 yet *they have* **h** both me and my G3631
Jn 15:25 '*They* **h** me without reason.' G3631
Jn 17:14 your word and the world *has* **h** them, G3631
Ro 9:13 "Jacob I loved, but Esau *I* **h**." G3631
Eph 5:29 no one ever **h** their own body, but G3631
Titus 3: 3 being **h** and hating one another. G5144
Heb 1: 9 loved righteousness and **h** wickedness; G3631

HATES (26) [HATE]
Ex 23: 5 the donkey of *someone who* **h** you fallen H8533
Dt 1:27 said, "The LORD **h** us; so he brought H8534
Dt 12:31 all kinds of detestable things the LORD **h**. H8533
Dt 16:22 for these the LORD your God **h**. H8533
Job 34:17 *Can someone who* **h** justice govern? Will H8533
Ps 11: 5 who love violence, *he* **h** with a passion. H8533
Pr 6:16 There are six things the LORD **h**, seven that H8533
Pr 12: 1 but *whoever* **h** correction is stupid. H8533
Pr 13:24 Whoever spares the rod **h** their children H8533
Pr 15:10 the *one who* **h** correction will die. H8533
Pr 15:27 the *one who* **h** bribes will live. H8533
Pr 26:28 A lying tongue **h** those it hurts, and a H8533
Pr 28:16 but *one who* **h** ill-gotten gain will enjoy a H8533
Mal 2:16 "The *man who* **h** and divorces his wife," H8533
Jn 3:20 Everyone who does evil **h** the light, and G3631
Jn 7: 7 but *it* **h** me because I testify that its works G3631
Jn 12:25 while anyone *who* **h** their life in this world G3631
Jn 15:18 "If the world **h** you, keep in mind that it G3631
Jn 15:19 That is why the world **h** you. G3631
Jn 15:23 Whoever **h** me hates my Father as well. G3631
Jn 15:23 Whoever hates me **h** my Father as well. G3631
1Jn 2: 9 be in the light but **h** a brother or sister is G3631
1Jn 2:11 But anyone *who* **h** a brother or sister is in G3631
1Jn 3:13 my brothers and sisters, if the world **h** you. G3631
1Jn 3:15 Anyone who **h** a brother or sister is a G3631
1Jn 4:20 to love God yet **h** a brother or sister is G3631

HATHAK (3)
Est 4: 5 Then Esther summoned **H**, one of the H2251
Est 4: 6 So **H** went out to Mordecai in the open H2251

Est 4: 9 H went back and reported to Esther what H2251

HATHATH (1)
1Ch 4:13 The sons of Othniel: H and Meonothai. H3171

HATING (2) [HATE]
Titus 3: 3 being hated and h one another. G3631
Jude 23 h even the clothing stained by corrupted G3631

HATIPHA (2)
Ezr 2:54 Neziah and H H2640
Ne 7:56 Neziah and H H2640

HATITA (2)
Ezr 2:42 Talmon, Akkub, H and Shobai 139 H2638
Ne 7:45 Talmon, Akkub, H and Shobai 138 H2638

HATRED (10) [HATE]
2Sa 13:15 Then Amnon hated her with intense h. H8534
Ps 109: 3 With words of h they surround me; they H8534
Ps 109: 5 me evil for good, and h for my friendship. H8534
Ps 139:22 I have nothing but h for them; H8533+8534
Pr 10:12 H stirs up conflict, but love covers over all H8534
Pr 10:18 Whoever conceals h with lying lips and H8534
Pr 15:17 with love than a fattened calf with h. H8534
Eze 23:29 will deal with you in h and take away H8534
Eze 35:11 you showed in your h of them and I will H8534
Gal 5:20 idolatry and witchcraft; h, discord, jealousy, G2397

HATTAAVAH See KIBROTH HATTAAVAH

HATTIKON See HAZER HATTIKON

HATTIL (2)
Ezr 2:57 Shephatiah, H, Pokereth-Hazzebaim and H2639
Ne 7:59 Shephatiah, H, Pokereth-Hazzebaim and H2639

HATTUSH (5)
1Ch 3:22 H, Igal, Bariah, Neariah and Shaphat—six H2637
Ezr 8: 2 of the descendants of David, H H2637
Ne 3:10 H son of Hashabneiah made repairs H2637
Ne 10: 4 H, Shebaniah, Malluk, H2637
Ne 12: 2 Amariah, Malluk, H, H2637

HAUGHTINESS (1) [HAUGHTY]
Jer 48:29 her conceit and the h of her heart. H8124

HAUGHTY (15) [HAUGHTINESS]
2Sa 22:28 your eyes are on the h to bring them low. H8123
Job 41:34 It looks down on all that are h; it is king H1469
Ps 18:27 bring low those whose eyes are h. H8123
Ps 101: 5 whoever has h eyes and a proud heart H1468
Ps 131: 1 my eyes are not h; I do not concern H8123
Pr 6:17 h eyes, a lying tongue, hands that shed H8123
Pr 16:18 before destruction, a h spirit before a fall. H1470
Pr 18:12 Before a downfall the heart is h, but H1467
Pr 21: 4 H eyes and a proud heart—the unplowed H8124
Pr 30:13 those whose eyes are ever so h, whose H8123
Isa 3:16 "The women of Zion are h, walking along H1467
Isa 10:12 of his heart and the h look in his eyes. H8124
Isa 13:11 arrogance of the h and will humble the H2294
Eze 16:50 They were h and did detestable things H1467
Zep 3:11 Never again will you be h on my holy hill. H1467

HAUL (4)
1Ki 5: 9 My men will h them down from Lebanon H3718
Job 39:12 Can you trust it to h in your grain and H8740
Eze 32: 3 and they will h you up in my net. H6590
Jn 21: 6 were unable to h the net in because of G1816

HAUNT (9) [HAUNTS]
Ps 44:19 crushed us and made us a h for jackals; H5226
Isa 34:13 She will become a h for jackals, a home H5659
Jer 9:11 a heap of ruins, a h of jackals; and I will H5061
Jer 10:22 towns of Judah desolate, a h of jackals. H5061
Jer 49:33 "Hazor will become a h of jackals, H5061
Jer 51:37 a heap of ruins, a h of jackals, an object H5061
Rev 18: 2 demons and a h for every impure spirit G5871
Rev 18: 2 impure spirit, a h for every unclean bird G5871
Rev 18: 2 a h for every unclean and detestable G5871

HAUNTS (3) [HAUNT]
Ps 74:20 because h of violence fill the dark places H5661
SS 4: 8 dens and the mountain h of leopards. H2215
Isa 35: 7 In the h where jackals once lay, grass H5659

HAURAN (2)
Eze 47:16 Hattikon, which is on the border of H. H2588
Eze 47:18 will run between H and Damascus, H2588

HAVE (1002 of 4448) [HAD, HASN'T, HAVE, HAVEN'T, HAVING] See Index of Articles Etc. for an Exhaustive Index
Ge 7:15 of all creatures that h the breath of life in NDT
Ge 13: 8 "Let's not h any quarreling between you H2118
Ge 14:24 Mamre. Let them h their share." H4374
Ge 18:10 and Sarah your wife will h a son. H4200
Ge 18:12 will I now h this pleasure? H2118+4200
Ge 18:13 say, 'Will I really h a child, now that I H3528
Ge 18:14 time next year, and Sarah will h a son." H4200
Ge 19: 5 out to us so that we can h sex with them." H3359
Ge 19: 8 I h two daughters who have never slept H4200
Ge 19:12 said to Lot, "Do you h anyone else here H4200
Ge 20:17 slaves so they could h children again, H3528
Ge 24:14 let down your jar that I may h a drink, H9272
Ge 24:25 "We h plenty of straw and fodder H6640
Ge 24:33 eat until I have told you what I h to say." H1821
Ge 25:30 let me h some of that red stew! H4358
Ge 26:10 of the men might well h slept with H3869+5071
Ge 27:11 Esau is a hairy man while I h smooth skin. H408S
Ge 27:38 his father, "Do you h only one blessing H4200
Ge 31:14 "Do we still h any share in the inheritance H4200
Ge 31:29 I h the power to harm you; but last H3780+4200
Ge 32: 5 I h cattle and donkeys, sheep and H2118+4200
Ge 33: 9 Esau said, "I already h plenty, my H3780+4200
Ge 33: 9 Keep what you h for yourself." H4200
Ge 33:11 gracious to me and I h all I need." H3780+4200
Ge 35: 2 "Get rid of the foreign gods you h with you NDT
Ge 35:17 "Don't despair, for you h another son." H4200
Ge 43: 7 'Do you h another brother H3780+4200
Ge 44: 9 If any of your servants is found to h it, he H907
Ge 44:10 Whoever is found to h it will become my H907
Ge 44:16 the one who was found to h the cup." H928+3338
Ge 44:17 who was found to h the cup will H928+3338
Ge 44:19 'Do you h a father or a brother? H3780+4200
Ge 44:20 answered, 'We h an aged father H3780+4200
Ge 45: 1 cried out, "H everyone leave my presence!" H3655
Ge 45:10 your flocks and herds, and all you h. H4200
Ge 47: 4 your servants' flocks h no pasture. H4200
Ex 9:19 everything you h in the field to a H4200
Ex 10: 5 devour what little you h left after the hail, H4200
Ex 10:25 must allow us to h sacrifices and H928+3338
Ex 12:39 Egypt and did not h time to H4538+3523
Ex 16:16 each person you h in your tent. H4200+889
Ex 16:18 who gathered much did not h too much, H6369
Ex 16:18 who gathered little did not h too little. H2893
Ex 18:16 Whenever they h a dispute, it is H2118+4200
Ex 20: 3 "You shall h no other gods before H2118+4200
Ex 22: 3 if they h nothing, they must be H4200
Ex 23: 7 H nothing to do with a false charge and H8178
Ex 25:20 The cherubim are to h their wings spread H2118
Ex 27: 9 cubits long and is to h curtains of finely H4200
Ex 27:11 a hundred cubits long and is to h curtains, NDT
Ex 27:12 shall be fifty cubits wide and h curtains, NDT
Ex 27:17 the courtyard are to h silver bands and NDT
Ex 28: 1 "H Aaron your brother brought to you H7928
Ex 28: 7 It is to h two shoulder pieces H2118+4200
Ex 33:19 I will h mercy on whom I will have mercy H2858
Ex 33:19 I will have mercy on whom I will h mercy H2858
Ex 33:19 and I will h compassion on whom I will H8163
Ex 33:19 on whom I will h compassion. H8163
Ex 35: 5 From what you h, take an offering for the H907
Lev 7:33 offering shall h the right thigh as H2118+4200
Lev 11: 9 you may eat any that h fins and scales. H4200
Lev 11:10 streams that do not h fins and scales— H4200
Lev 11:12 water that does not h fins and scales is to H4200
Lev 11:21 those that h jointed legs for hopping on H4200
Lev 11:23 flying insects that h four legs you are to H4200
Lev 13:15 flesh is unclean; they h a defiling disease. NDT
Lev 13:46 As long as they h the disease they remain H928
Lev 14:41 He must h all the inside walls of the house scraped H7909
Lev 18: 6 close relative to h sexual relations. H1655+6872
Lev 18: 7 mother; do not h relations with her. H1655+6872
Lev 18: 8 " 'Do not h sexual relations with H1655+6872
Lev 18: 9 " 'Do not h sexual relations with H1655+6872
Lev 18:10 " 'Do not h sexual relations with H1655+6872
Lev 18:11 " 'Do not h sexual relations with H1655+6872
Lev 18:12 " 'Do not h sexual relations with H1655+6872
Lev 18:13 " 'Do not h sexual relations with H1655+6872
Lev 18:14 Do not dishonor your father's brother by approaching his wife to h sexual relations H1655+6872
Lev 18:15 " 'Do not h sexual relations with H1655+6872
Lev 18:15 do not h relations with her. H1655+6872
Lev 18:16 " 'Do not h sexual relations with H1655+6872
Lev 18:17 " 'Do not h sexual relations with H1655+6872
Lev 18:17 Do not h sexual relations with H1655+6872
Lev 18:18 and h sexual relations with her H1655+6872
Lev 18:19 woman to h sexual relations during H1655+6872
Lev 18:20 Do not h sexual relations H5989+8888+4200+2446
Lev 18:22 " 'Do not h sexual relations with a man as H8886
Lev 18:23 " 'Do not h sexual relations with an H5989+8888
Lev 18:23 to an animal to h sexual relations with it; H8061
Lev 19:10 time or pick up the grapes that h fallen. H7261
Lev 19:30 Sabbaths and h reverence for my H3707
Lev 20:16 an animal to h sexual relations with it, H8061
Lev 20:17 and they h sexual relations, it H8011+906+6872
Lev 20:19 " 'Do not h sexual relations with H1655+6872
Lev 22:25 because they are deformed and h defects. H928
Lev 23:24 month you are to h a day of H2118+4200
Lev 24:22 You are to h the same law for the H2118+4200
Lev 25: 4 year the land is to h a year of H2118+4200
Lev 25: 5 The land is to h a year of rest H2118+4200
Lev 25: 9 Then h the trumpet sounded everywhere H6296
Lev 25:32 Levites always h the right to H2118+4200
Lev 26: 2 Sabbaths and h reverence for my H3707
Lev 26:35 the land will h the rest it did not have H8697
Lev 26:35 will have the rest it did not h during the H8697S
Nu 5:16 bring her and h her stand before the LORD. H6641
Nu 5:26 he is to h the woman drink the water. H9197
Nu 5:28 guilt and will be able to h children. H2445+2446
Nu 5:30 The priest is to h her stand before the H6641
Nu 8: 7 then h them shave their whole H6296+9509
Nu 8:13 H the Levites stand in front of Aaron and H6641
Nu 9:14 You must h the same regulations H2118+4200
Nu 11:16 H them come to the tent of meeting, that H4374
Nu 11:22 Would they h enough if flocks and herds H5162
Nu 11:22 Would they h enough if all the fish in the H5162
Nu 14:34 know what it is like to h me against you. NDT
Nu 15:15 The community is to h the same rules for you NDT
Nu 15:39 You will h these tassels to look at H2118+4200
Nu 16: 5 and he will h that person come near him. H7928
Nu 18: 9 You are to h the part of the most H2118+4200
Nu 18:20 "You will h no inheritance in their land H5706
Nu 18:20 nor will you h any share among H2118+4200
Nu 18:24 'They will h no inheritance among H5706+5709
Nu 23:22 of Egypt; they h the strength of a wild ox. H4200
Nu 24: 7 buckets; their seed will h abundant water. H928
Nu 24: 8 of Egypt; they h the strength of a wild ox. H4200
Nu 25:13 descendants will h a covenant of a H2118+4200
Nu 27:11 This is to h the force of law for the H2118+4200
Nu 27:19 H him stand before Eleazar the priest and H6641
Nu 32: 4 livestock, and your servants h livestock. H4200
Nu 34: 2 as an inheritance is to h these boundaries: NDT
Nu 35: 3 Then they will h towns to live in H2118+4200
Nu 35: 5 They will h this area as H2118+4200
Nu 35:29 " 'This is to h the force of law for H2118+4200
Dt 3:19 I know you h much livestock) may H4200
Dt 4: 7 is so great as to h their gods near them H4200
Dt 4: 8 is so great as to h such righteous decrees H4200
Dt 4:33 speaking out of fire, as you h, and lived? H9048S
Dt 5: 7 "You shall h no other gods before H2118+4200
Dt 5:26 speaking out of fire, as we h, and survived? NDT
Dt 8:13 gold increase and all you h is multiplied, H4200
Dt 9: 1 with large cities that h walls up to the sky. NDT
Dt 10: 9 is why the Levites h no share or H2118+4200
Dt 11: 8 so that you may h the strength to go in H2616
Dt 12:12 from your towns who h no allotment or H4200
Dt 12:26 and whatever you h vowed to give, H2118+4200
Dt 13:17 you mercy, and will h compassion on you. H8163
Dt 14:10 that does not h fins and scales you H4200
Dt 14:27 they h no allotment or inheritance of H4200
Dt 14:29 who h no allotment or inheritance of their H4200
Dt 18: 1 are to h no allotment or inheritance H2118+4200
Dt 18: 2 They shall h no inheritance among H2118+4200
Dt 22: 7 go well with you and you may h a long life. H799
Dt 23:13 your equipment h something to dig H2118+4200
Dt 25: 1 When people h a dispute, they are H2118+1068
Dt 25: 2 lie down and h them flogged in his H5782
Dt 25:13 Do not h two differing weights in H2118+4200
Dt 25:14 Do not h two differing measures in H2118+4200
Dt 25:15 You must h accurate and honest H2118+4200
Dt 28:33 and you will h nothing but cruel H2118
Dt 28:40 You will h olive trees throughout H2118+4200
Dt 28:41 You will h sons and daughters but you will H3528
Dt 28:54 you will h no compassion on his H8317+6524
Dt 30: 3 fortunes and h compassion on you and H8163
Dt 33: 9 mother, 'I h no regard for them. H8011
Jos 17:16 who live in the plain h chariots fitted with H928
Jos 17:17 You will h not only one allotment H2118+4200
Jos 17:18 the Canaanites h chariots fitted with H4200
Jos 22:24 'What do you h to do with the LORD, the H4200
Jos 22:25 You h no share in the LORD.' H4200
Jos 22:27 to say to ours, 'You h no share in the LORD. H4200
Jos 23: 8 to the LORD your God, as you h until now. H6913S
Jdg 3:19 Majesty, I h a secret message for you." H4200
Jdg 3:20 "I h a message from God for you. H4200
Jdg 6:14 in the strength you h and save Israel out of NDT
Jdg 7: 2 LORD said to Gideon, "You h too many men. H907
Jdg 8: 6 "Do you already h the hands of Zebah and NDT
Jdg 8:15 'Do you already h the hands of Zebah and NDT
Jdg 8:24 he said, "I do h one request, that H8626+8629
Jdg 9:19 If you h, may Abimelek be your joy, and NDT
Jdg 9:20 But if you h not, let fire come out from NDT
Jdg 11:12 "What do you h against me that you have H4200
Jdg 13: 5 pregnant and h a son whose head is H3528
Jdg 13: 7 'You will become pregnant and h a son. H3528
Jdg 15: 3 "This time I h a right to get even with the H5927
Jdg 17: 2 you utter a curse—I h that silver with me; NDT
Jdg 18:24 What else do I h? How can you ask, H4200
Jdg 19:19 We h both straw and fodder for our H3780
Jdg 19:22 to your house so we can h sex with him." H3359
Jdg 21:17 The Benjamite survivors must h heirs," H4200
Ru 1:11 Am I going to h any more sons, who H928+5055
Ru 1:12 I am too old to h another husband. H2118+4200
Ru 2:13 though I do not h the standing of one of H2118
Ru 2:14 H some bread and dip it in the wine H430S
Ru 4:11 May you h standing in Ephrathah and be H6913
1Sa 8: 5 to lead us, such as all the other nations h." NDT
1Sa 9: 7 We h no gift to take to the man of God NDT
1Sa 9: 7 take to the man of God. What do we h?" H907
1Sa 9: 8 "I h a quarter of a shekel of H5162+928+3338
1Sa 9:12 the people h a sacrifice at the high H4200
1Sa 12: 2 Now you h a king as your leader. As for me, NDT
1Sa 14: 7 "Do all that you h in mind," his NDT
1Sa 16:11 asked Jesse, "Are these all the sons you h?" NDT
1Sa 18:25 plan was to h David fall by the hands of H5877
1Sa 21: 3 what do you h on hand? H3780+9393+3338
1Sa 21: 4 h any ordinary bread on hand H448+9393+3338
1Sa 21: 8 "Don't you h a spear or a H3780+9393+3338
1Sa 25:31 my lord will not h on his conscience H2118+4200
1Sa 28:22 you may eat and h the strength to H2118+928
2Sa 1:21 of Gilboa, may you h neither dew nor rain H6584
2Sa 7: 3 "Whatever you h in mind, go ahead NDT
2Sa 7:10 so that they can h a home of their H8905+9393
2Sa 16:10 "What does this h to do with you, you H4200

2Sa 18:18 "I h no son to carry on the memory of my H4200
2Sa 18:22 You don't h any news that will bring you a H4200
2Sa 18:25 he is alone, he must h good news." H928+7023
2Sa 19:22 "What does this h to do with you, you H4200
2Sa 19:22 What right do you h to interfere? Should NDT
2Sa 19:26 'I will h my donkey saddled and will ride H2502
2Sa 19:28 what right do I h to make any more H3780+4200
2Sa 19:43 of Judah, "We h ten shares in the king H4200
2Sa 19:43 so we h a greater claim on David than you H928
2Sa 19:43 have a greater claim on David than you h. NDT
2Sa 20: 1 shouted, "We h no share in David H4200
2Sa 21: 4 "We h no right to demand silver or gold H4200
2Sa 21: 4 do we h the right to put anyone in H4200
1Ki 1:33 and h Solomon my son mount my H8206+6584
1Ki 2: 4 you will never fail to h a successor H4162+4200
1Ki 2: 8 you h with you Shimei son of Gera NDT
1Ki 2:14 he added, "I h something to say to you." H4200
1Ki 2:16 Now I h one request to make of you.H8626+8629
1Ki 2:20 "I h one small request to make of H8626+8629
1Ki 3:13 your lifetime you will h no equal among H2118
1Ki 3:26 "Neither I nor you shall h him. H2118+4200
1Ki 5: 6 You know that we h no one so skilled in H928
1Ki 8:18 'You did well to h it in your heart to build H2118
1Ki 8:25 'You shall never fail to h a H4162+4200
1Ki 9: 5 'You shall never fail to h a H4162+4200
1Ki 9:13 Land of Kabul, a name they h to this day. NDT
1Ki 11:32 tribes of Israel, he will h one tribe. H2118+4200
1Ki 11:36 my servant may always h a lamp H2118+4200
1Ki 12:16 "What share do we h in David, what part H4200
1Ki 17:12 "I don't h any bread—only a H3780+4200
1Ki 17:13 me from what you h and bring it to me, NDT
1Ki 17:18 "What do you h against me, man of H4200
1Ki 18:18 "But you and your father's family h. NDT
1Ki 20: 4 my lord the king. I and all I h are yours." H4200
1Ki 21: 2 "Let me h your vineyard to use for a H5989
1Ki 21:10 him and h them bring charges that he has H6386
1Ki 22:17 the Lord said, 'These people h no master. H4200
2Ki 1:13 "please h respect for my life H3700+928+6524
2Ki 1:14 But now h respect for my life!" H3700+928+6524
2Ki 2:16 "we your servants h fifty able men. H3780+907
2Ki 3:14 if I did not h respect for the presence of H5951
2Ki 3:23 "Those kings must h fought and H2991+2991
2Ki 4: 2 what do you h in your house? H3780+4200
2Ki 4:13 "I h a home among my own people." H3782
2Ki 4:43 'They will eat and h some left over.'" H3855
2Ki 9: 5 "I h a message for you, commander," H4200
2Ki 9:18 "What do you h to do with peace?" Jehu H4200
2Ki 9:19 "What do you h to do with peace? H4200
2Ki 10: 2 "You h your master's sons with you and you H907
2Ki 10: 2 with you and you h chariots and horses, H907
2Ki 17:27 H one of the priests you took captive from Samaria go H2143
2Ki 18:20 You say you h the counsel and the might NDT
2Ki 19: 7 there I will h him cut down with the H5877
2Ki 21:15 evil in my eyes and h aroused my anger H2118
2Ki 22: 4 priest and h him get ready the money that H9462
2Ki 22:13 us because those who h gone before us have H3
1Ch 4:27 his brothers did not h many children H4200
1Ch 17: 2 to David, "Whatever you h in mind, do it, NDT
1Ch 17: 9 they can h a home of their own H8905+9393
1Ch 21:22 "Let me h the site of your threshing floor H5989
1Ch 22: 9 But you will h a son who will be a man of H3528
1Ch 22:11 and may you h success and build the H7503
1Ch 22:13 Then you will h success if you are careful H7503
1Ch 22:15 You h many workers: stonecutters, masons H6640
1Ch 23:11 Jeush and Beriah did not h many sons; H8049
1Ch 28:19 "I h in writing as a result of the Lord's hand NDT
2Ch 1:12 you ever had and none after you will h." H2118
2Ch 6: 8 'You did well to h it in your heart to build H2118
2Ch 6:16 'You shall never fail to h a H4162+4200
2Ch 7:18 'You shall never fail to h a H4162+4200
2Ch 10:16 "What share do we h in David, what part H4200
2Ch 13: 8 a vast army and h with you the golden NDT
2Ch 18:16 the Lord said, 'These people h no master. H4200
2Ch 20:12 For we h no power to face this vast army H928
2Ch 20:20 H faith in the Lord your God and you will H586
2Ch 20:20 h faith in his prophets and you will be H586
2Ch 34:21 us because those who h gone before us have H3
Ezr 4: 3 "You h no part with us in building a H4200
Ezr 7:24 also to know that you h no authority to NDT
Ne 2: 7 may I h letters to the governors of H5989+4200
Ne 2: 8 And may I h a letter to Asaph, keeper of the NDT
Ne 2:20 you h no share in Jerusalem or any claim NDT
Est 9:21 to h them celebrate annually the H7756
Job 3:26 I h no peace, no quietness; I have no rest H8922
Job 3:26 no quietness; I h no rest, but only turmoil." H5663
Job 5:16 So the poor h hope, and injustice H2118+4200
Job 5:23 For you will h a covenant with the stones of NDT
Job 6: 8 that I might h my request, that God H995
Job 6:10 Then I would still h this consolation—my H2118
Job 6:11 "What strength do I h, that I should still NDT
Job 6:12 Do I h the strength of stone? Is my flesh NDT
Job 6:13 Do I h any power to help myself, now that H928
Job 7: 1 "Do not mortals h hard service on earth H4200
Job 7:16 Let me alone; my days h no meaning. NDT
Job 9:21 am blameless, I h no concern for myself; H3359
Job 10: 4 Do you h eyes of flesh? Do you see as a H4200
Job 10:20 away from me so I can h a moment's joy H1158
Job 12: 3 But I h a mind as well as you; I am not H4200
Job 12: 5 Those who are at ease h contempt for H6953
Job 15: 3 with speeches that h no value? H3603
Job 15: 8 Do you h a monopoly on wisdom? H1757
Job 15: 9 What insights do you h that we do not H1067
Job 15: 9 insights do you have that we do not h? H6640
Job 19:21 "H pity on me, my friends, have pity, for H2858
Job 19:21 my friends, h pity, for the hand of God has H2858
Job 20:20 "Surely he will h no respite from his H3359
Job 21:14 We h no desire to know your ways. H2911
Job 24: 7 they h nothing to cover themselves in the NDT
Job 24:22 established, they h no assurance of life. H586
Job 27: 3 as long as I h life within me, the breath of NDT
Job 27: 8 For what hope h the godless when they are NDT
Job 27:14 his offspring will never h enough to eat. H8425
Job 32:17 I too will h my say; I too will tell H6699+2750
Job 33:32 If you h anything to say, answer me H3780
Job 34:16 "If you h understanding, hear this; listen to NDT
Job 37:24 for does he not h regard for all the wise in H8011
Job 38:28 Does the rain h a father? Who H3780+4200
Job 40: 5 but I h no answer—twice, but I H6699
Job 40: 9 Do you h an arm like God's, and can your H4200
Ps 4: 1 h mercy on me and hear my prayer. H2858
Ps 6: 2 H mercy on me, Lord, for I am faint; heal H2858
Ps 9:13 H mercy and lift me up from the gates of H2858
Ps 13: 2 day after day h sorrow in my heart? NDT
Ps 16: 2 my Lord; apart from you I h no good thing." NDT
Ps 16: 6 surely I h a delightful inheritance. H6584
Ps 19: 3 They h no speech, they use no words; no H401
Ps 28: 5 Because they h no regard for the deeds of H1067
Ps 32: 9 which h no understanding but must be H1067
Ps 34:19 The righteous person may h many troubles NDT
Ps 36: 1 I h a message from God in my heart NDT
Ps 37:16 that the righteous h than the wealth of H4200
Ps 41: 1 are those who h regard for the weak; H8505
Ps 41: 4 "H mercy on me, Lord; heal me, for H2858
Ps 41:10 But may you h mercy on me, Lord; raise H2858
Ps 49:19 join those who h gone before them, H1887+3
Ps 49:20 People who h wealth but lack H928
Ps 50:16 "What right h you to recite H4537+4200+3870
Ps 51: 1 H mercy on me, O God, according to your H2858
Ps 57: 1 H mercy on me, my God, have mercy on H2858
Ps 57: 1 my God, h mercy on me, for in you I take H2858
Ps 68:23 while the tongues of your dogs h their share." NDT
Ps 72:12 the afflicted who h no one to help. NDT
Ps 73: 4 They h no struggles; their bodies are H4200
Ps 73: 7 their evil imaginations h no limits. H6296
Ps 73:25 Whom h I in heaven but you? And earth H4200
Ps 74:20 H regard for your covenant H5564+4200
Ps 81: 9 You shall h no foreign god among you H2118
Ps 84: 3 where she may h her young—a H8883
Ps 86: 3 h mercy on me, Lord, for I call to you all H2858
Ps 86:14 they h no regard for you. H8492+4200+5584
Ps 86:16 Turn to me and h mercy on me; show your H2858
Ps 90:13 H compassion on your servants. H5714
Ps 101: 3 faithless people do; I will h no part in it. H1815
Ps 101: 4 I will h nothing to do with what is evil. H3359
Ps 102:13 You will arise and h compassion on Zion H8163
Ps 111:10 follow his precepts h good understanding. H4200
Ps 112: 7 They will h no fear of bad news; their H3707
Ps 112: 8 are secure, they will h no fear; in the end H3707
Ps 115: 5 They h mouths, but cannot speak, eyes H4200
Ps 115: 6 They h ears, but cannot hear, noses, but H4200
Ps 115: 7 They h hands, but cannot feel, feet, but NDT
Ps 119:99 I h more insight than all my teachers, for I H8505
Ps 119:100 I h more understanding than the elders H1067
Ps 119:117 I will always h regard for your decrees. H9120
Ps 119:132 Turn to me and h mercy on me, as you H2858
Ps 119:165 Great peace h those who love your law H4200
Ps 123: 3 H mercy on us, Lord, have mercy on us, H2858
Ps 123: 3 h mercy on us, for we have endured H2858
Ps 135:14 his people and h compassion on his H5714
Ps 135:16 They h mouths, but cannot speak, eyes H4200
Ps 135:17 They h ears, but cannot hear, nor is there H4200
Ps 139:22 I h nothing but hatred for them; H8533+8534
Ps 142: 4 I h no refuge; no one H6+4946
Pr 3:28 when you already h it with you. H3780
Pr 4: 7 Though it cost all you h, get H7871
Pr 7:14 h food from my fellowship offering at home H6584
Pr 8:14 judgment are mine; I h insight, I have NDT
Pr 8:14 are mine; I have insight, I h power. H4200
Pr 9: 4 To those who h no sense she says, H2894
Pr 9:16 To those who h no sense she says, H4213
Pr 10: 2 Ill-gotten treasures h no lasting value, but H3603
Pr 12: 9 be a nobody and yet h a servant than H4200
Pr 12: 9 pretend to be somebody and h no food. H2894
Pr 12:11 who work their land will h abundant food, H8425
Pr 12:11 those who chase fantasies h no sense. H2894
Pr 12:20 but those who promote peace h joy. H4200
Pr 12:21 the wicked h their fill of trouble. H4848
Pr 13: 2 the unfaithful h an appetite for violence. NDT
Pr 14:20 their neighbors, but the rich h many friends. NDT
Pr 17:16 Why should fools h money in hand to buy H928
Pr 17:21 To h a fool for a child brings grief; there is H3528
Pr 20: 6 Many claim to h unfailing love, but a NDT
Pr 20:13 stay awake and you will h food to spare. H8425
Pr 22: 2 Rich and poor h this in common: The Lord H7008
Pr 22:11 with grace will h the king for a friend. NDT
Pr 22:18 heart and h all of them ready on your lips. H3922
Pr 27:27 You will h plenty of goats' milk to feed your NDT
Pr 28:19 who work their land will h abundant food, H8425
Pr 28:19 chase fantasies will h their fill of poverty. H8425
Pr 29: 7 the wicked h no such concern. H1067+1981
Pr 29:13 poor and the oppressor h this in common: H7008
Pr 30: 2 I do not h human understanding. H4200
Pr 30: 9 I may h too much and disown you and say H8425
Pr 30:27 locusts h no king, yet they advance H4200
Ecc 2:14 The wise h eyes in their heads, while the NDT
Ecc 2:19 Yet they will h control over all the fruit of H8948
Ecc 3:19 All h the same breath; humans have no H4200
Ecc 3:19 humans h no advantage over animals. NDT
Ecc 4: 1 they h no comforter; power H4200
Ecc 4: 1 oppressors—and they h no comforter. H4200
Ecc 4: 9 because they h a good return for H3780+4200
Ecc 5:14 so that when they h children there is H3528
Ecc 6: 3 A man may h a hundred children and live H3528
Ecc 6: 8 What advantage h the wise over fools H4200
Ecc 7:12 Wisdom preserves those who h it. H1251
Ecc 9: 5 know nothing; they h no further reward H4200
Ecc 9: 6 never again will they h a part in anything H4200
SS 8: 8 We h a little sister, and her breasts are H4200
Isa 1:11 "I h more than enough of burnt offerings H8425
Isa 1:11 I h no pleasure in the blood of bulls and H2911
Isa 2:22 humans, who h but a breath in their nostrils. NDT
Isa 3: 6 say, "You h a cloak, you be our H4200
Isa 3: 7 in that day he will cry out, "I h no remedy. H2118
Isa 3: 7 I h no food or clothing in my house; do not NDT
Isa 5:12 They h harps and lyres at their banquets H2118
Isa 5:12 but they h no regard for the deeds of the H5564
Isa 8:20 to this word, they h no light of dawn. H4200
Isa 10:13 my wisdom, because I h understanding. H1067
Isa 13:17 care for silver and h no delight in gold. H2911
Isa 13:18 they will h no mercy on infants H8163
Isa 14: 1 The Lord will h compassion on Jacob H8163
Isa 17: 8 and they will h no regard for the Asherah H8011
Isa 22:11 h regard for the One who planned it H8011
Isa 23:10 Tarshish, for you no longer h a harbor. NDT
Isa 26: 1 We h a strong city; God makes salvation H4200
Isa 29:20 all who h an eye for evil will be cut H9193
Isa 30: 4 Though they h officials in Zoan and their H2118
Isa 30:15 is your strength, but you would h none of it. H14
Isa 32: 9 who feel secure, hear what I h to say! H614
Isa 34:12 Her nobles will h nothing there to be called NDT
Isa 36: 5 You say you h counsel and might for war NDT
Isa 37: 7 there I will h him cut down with the H5877
Isa 40:11 he gently leads those that h young. H6402
Isa 43: 8 Lead out those who h eyes but are blind H3780
Isa 43: 8 are blind, who h ears but are deaf. H4200
Isa 49:15 breast and h no compassion on the child H8163
Isa 52: 5 "And now what do I h here?" declares the H4200
Isa 54: 8 kindness I will h compassion on you," H8163
Isa 55: 1 and you who h no money, come, H4200
Isa 55: 7 and he will h mercy on them, and to H8163
Isa 56:11 mighty appetites; they never h enough. H3359
Jer 2:19 the Lord your God and h no awe of me," H448
Jer 2:28 h as many gods as you have towns. H2118
Jer 2:28 have as many gods as you h towns. NDT
Jer 3: 3 Yet you h the brazen look of a H2118+4200
Jer 4:10 by saying, 'You will h peace,' when H2118+4200
Jer 4:22 children; they h no understanding. H1067
Jer 5:21 people, who h eyes but do not see H4200
Jer 5:21 do not see, who h ears but do not hear: H4200
Jer 5:23 But these people h stubborn and H2118+4200
Jer 5:28 Their evil deeds h no limit; they do not H6296
Jer 6:15 they h no shame at all; they do H1017+1017
Jer 8: 8 "We are wise, for we h the law of the Lord," H907
Jer 8: 9 the Lord, what kind of wisdom do they h? H4200
Jer 8:12 they h no shame at all; they do H1017+1017
Jer 9:24 that they h the understanding to know me, H8505
Jer 10:14 are a fraud; they h no breath in them. NDT
Jer 11:13 h as many gods as you have towns H2118
Jer 11:13 have as many gods as you h towns; and the NDT
Jer 12:15 I will again h compassion and will bring H8163
Jer 15: 5 "Who will h pity on you, Jerusalem? Who H2798
Jer 16: 2 not marry and h sons or daughters H2118+4200
Jer 22:15 you a king to h more and more cedar? H3013
Jer 22:15 Did not your father h food and drink H430
Jer 22:19 He will h the burial of a donkey H7699+7690
Jer 23:17 You will h peace.' And H2118+4200
Jer 25:35 The shepherds will h nowhere to flee H6+4946
Jer 27:18 are prophets and h the word of the H3780+907
Jer 29: 6 Marry and h sons and daughters; find H3528
Jer 29: 6 so that they too may h sons and H3528
Jer 29: 8 dreams you encourage them to h. H2731+2706
Jer 29:11 For I know the plans I h for you," H3108+4742
Jer 29:32 He will h no one left among this H2118+4200
Jer 30:10 Jacob will again h peace and security H9200
Jer 30:18 tents and h compassion on his dwellings; H8163
Jer 31:20 I h great compassion for him," H8163+8163
Jer 32:25 and h the transaction witnessed. H6386+6332
Jer 33:17 'David will never fail to h a man to H4162+4200
Jer 33:18 will the Levitical priests ever fail to h H4162+4200
Jer 33:21 and David will no longer h a H2118+4200
Jer 33:26 their fortunes and h compassion on them. H8163
Jer 35: 7 you must never h any of these H2118+4200
Jer 35:19 son of Rekab will never fail to h a H4162+4200
Jer 36:30 He will h no one to sit on the H2118+4200
Jer 41: 8 We h wheat and barley, olive oil H3780+4200
Jer 42:12 so that he will h compassion on you and H8163
Jer 46:27 Jacob will again h peace and security H9200
Jer 51:17 are a fraud; they h no breath in them. NDT
Eze 12: 2 They h eyes to see but do not see and H4200
Eze 12:22 is this proverb you h in the land of Israel: H4200
Eze 18: 6 h sexual relations with a woman H7928+448
Eze 20:32 But what you h in mind will never happen. H6590
Eze 24:14 not hold back; I will not h pity, nor will I H2571
Eze 24:19 tell us what these things h to do with us? H4200
Eze 28:24 longer will the people of Israel h H2118+4200

Eze 34:15 will tend my sheep and **h** them **lie down**, H8069
Eze 37:24 and they *will* all **h** one shepherd. H2118+4200
Eze 39:25 of Jacob and *will* **h compassion** *on* all the H8163
Eze 44:28 am to be the only inheritance the priests **h**. NDT
Eze 45: 7 " 'The prince will **h** the land bordering H4200
Eze 47:22 residing among you and who **h** children. H3528
Eze 48: 1 Dan will **h** one portion; it will follow NDT
Eze 48: 2 "Asher will **h** one portion; it will border the NDT
Eze 48: 3 "Naphtali will **h** one portion; it will border NDT
Eze 48: 4 "Manasseh will **h** one portion; it will border NDT
Eze 48: 5 "Ephraim will **h** one portion; it will border NDT
Eze 48: 6 "Reuben will **h** one portion; it will border NDT
Eze 48: 7 "Judah will **h** one portion; it will border the NDT
Eze 48:13 the Levites will **h** an allotment 25,000 cubits NDT
Eze 48:16 will **h** these measurements: the north NDT
Eze 48:23 Benjamin will **h** one portion; it will extend NDT
Eze 48:24 "Simeon will **h** one portion; it will border NDT
Eze 48:25 "Issachar will **h** one portion; it will border NDT
Eze 48:26 "Zebulun will **h** one portion; it will border NDT
Eze 48:27 "Gad will **h** one portion; it will border the NDT
Da 1:10 king would then **h** my head because of H4200
Da 2:30 not because I **h** greater wisdom A10029+10089
Da 2:41 yet *it will* **h** some of the strength of iron A10201
Da 5:11 father he was found to **h** insight and A10089
Da 5:12 was found to **h** a keen mind and A10089
Da 5:14 the gods is in you and that you **h** insight, A10089
Da 8:22 his nation but will not **h** the same power. H928
Da 9:26 will be put to death and will **h** nothing. H4200
Da 11: 4 will it **h** the power he exercised NDT
Da 11:15 best troops will not **h** the strength to stand. NDT
Da 11:16 Land and will **h** the power to destroy H928+3338
Hos 1: 2 woman and **h** children with her, NDT
Hos 4:10 "They will eat but not **h enough**; they will H8425
Hos 10: 3 "We **h** no king because we did not revere H4200
Hos 13:13 he doesn't **h** the sense to come out of the NDT
Hos 13:14 "I *will* **h no** compassion, H6259+4946+6524
Hos 14: 8 what more **h** I **to do with** idols? I will H4200
Joel 1:18 mill about because they **h** no pasture; H4200
Joel 2: 4 They **h** the appearance of horses; they NDT
Joel 2:26 *You will* **h plenty to eat**, until you are H430+430
Joel 3: 4 "Now what **h** you against me, Tyre and NDT
Am 5: 3 strong *will* **h** only a hundred **left**; H8636
Am 5: 3 out a hundred strong *will* **h** only ten **left**." H8636
Am 5: 6 Bethel *will* **h** no one to quench it. H4200
Am 5:15 Almighty *will* **h mercy** *on* the remnant H2858
Am 5:22 offerings, *I will* **h** no **regard for** them. H5564
Jnh 4:11 And *should* I not **h concern** for the great H2571
Mic 2: 5 Therefore you *will* **h** no one in the H2118+4200
Mic 3: 5 if they **h something to eat**, H5966+928+9094
Mic 4: 9 Why do you now cry aloud—**h** you no king? H928
Mic 6: 1 let the hills hear **what** you **h to say**. H7754
Mic 7:19 You will again **h compassion** *on* us; you H8163
Na 1:14 "*You will* **h** no **descendants** to bear your H2445
Hab 1:14 like the sea creatures that **h** no ruler. H928
Hag 1: 6 You eat, but never **h enough**. You drink, H8425
Hag 1: 6 but never **h** *your* **fill**. You put on H8910
Zec 3: 7 my house and **h charge of** my courts, H9068
Zec 10: 6 them because *I* **h compassion** *on* them. H8163
Zec 11: 6 For *I will* no longer **h pity** on the people of H2798
Zec 14:17 LORD Almighty, they *will* **h** no rain. H2118+6584
Zec 14:18 go up and take part, they *will* **h** no rain. H6584
Mal 2:10 Do we not all **h** one Father? Did not one H4200
Mal 3: 3 Then the LORD *will* **h** men who will H2118+4200
Mt 3: 9 yourselves, '*We* **h** Abraham as our father. G2400
Mt 6: 1 *you will* **h** no reward from your Father in G2400
Mt 7:12 others what you would **h** them to do to you, G2671
Mt 8:20 "Foxes **h** dens and birds have nests G2400
Mt 8:20 "Foxes have dens and birds **h** nests, but the NDT
Mt 9:27 calling out, "**H mercy** on us, Son of G1796
Mt 10: 8 cleanse **those who h leprosy**, drive out G3320
Mt 10:21 their parents and **h** them **put to death**. G2506
Mt 11: 5 **those who h leprosy** are cleansed G3320
Mt 11:21 they **would h** repented long ago in G323
Mt 11:23 in Sodom, it **would h** remained to this day. G323
Mt 12: 7 you **would** not **h** condemned the innocent. G323
Mt 13: 5 rocky places, where *it did* not **h** much soil. G2400
Mt 13:12 and *they will* **h an abundance**. G4355
Mt 13:12 Whoever *does* not **h**, even what they have G2400
Mt 13:12 even what *they* **h** will be taken from them. G2400
Mt 13:21 But *since they* **h** no root, they last only a G2400
Mt 14: 4 "It is not lawful for you *to* **h** her." G2400
Mt 14:17 "*We* **h** here only five loaves of bread and G2400
Mt 15: 5 that what **might h been** used to help G1569
Mt 15:22 "Lord, Son of David, **h mercy** on me! G1796
Mt 15:28 said to her, "Woman, you **h** great faith! NDT
Mt 15:32 "*I* **h compassion** for these people G5072
Mt 15:32 with me three days and **h** nothing to eat. G2400
Mt 15:34 "How many loaves *do you* **h**?" Jesus G2400
Mt 16:23 *you do* not **h in mind** the concerns of God G5858
Mt 17:15 **h mercy** on my son," he said. "He G1796
Mt 17:20 if *you* **h** faith as small as a mustard seed G2400
Mt 18: 6 them to **h** a large millstone **hung** around G3203
Mt 18: 8 crippled than *to* **h** two hands or two G2400
Mt 18: 9 with one eye than *to* **h** two eyes and be G2400
Mt 19:21 and *you will* **h** treasure in heaven. G2400
Mt 20:15 Don't I **h the right** to do what I want with G2003
Mt 20:30 Son of David, **h mercy** on us! G1796
Mt 20:31 Son of David, **h mercy** on us! G1796
Mt 21:21 I tell you, if *you* **h** faith and do not doubt G2400
Mt 23: 8 for you **h** one Teacher, and you G1639
Mt 23: 9 for you **h** one Father, and he is G1639
Mt 23:10 instructors, for you **h** one Instructor, the G1639
Mt 23:23 *You* **should h** practiced the latter, without G1256
Mt 23:30 we **would** not **h** taken part with them in G323
Mt 24:43 he **would h** kept watch and would not have G323
Mt 24:43 kept watch and **would** not **h** let his house G323
Mt 25:27 you **should h** put my money on deposit G1256
Mt 25:27 when I returned I **would h** received it back G323
Mt 25:29 and *they will* **h an abundance**. G4355
Mt 25:29 Whoever *does* not **h**, even what they have G2400
Mt 25:29 even what *they* **h** will be taken from them. G2400
Mt 26: 9 "This perfume **could h** *been* sold at a high G1538
Mt 26:11 The poor *you will* always **h** with you, but G2400
Mt 26:11 with you, but *you will* not always **h** me. G2400
Mt 26:35 declared, "Even if I **h to** die with you, G1256
Mt 27: 1 their plans how to **h** Jesus **executed**. G2506
Mt 27:20 ask for Barabbas and *to* **h** Jesus **executed**. G660
Mk 2:19 so long as *they* **h** him with them. G2400
Mk 3:15 and *to* **h** authority to drive out demons. G2400
Mk 4: 5 rocky places, where *it did* not **h** much soil. G2400
Mk 4:17 But *since they* **h** no root, they last only a G2400
Mk 4:25 whoever *does* not **h**, even what G2400
Mk 4:25 even what *they* **h** will be taken from them." G2400
Mk 4:40 you so afraid? *Do you* still **h** no faith?" G2400
Mk 6:17 had given orders *to* **h** John **arrested**, G3195
Mk 6:18 not lawful for you *to* **h** your brother's wife." G2400
Mk 6:31 that *they did* not even **h a chance** to eat, G2320
Mk 6:38 "How many loaves *do you* **h**?" he asked G2400
Mk 6:39 them *to* **h** all the people **sit down** in groups G369
Mk 8: 2 "*I* **h compassion** for these people; they G5072
Mk 8: 2 with me three days and **h** nothing to eat. G2400
Mk 8: 5 "How many loaves *do you* **h**?" Jesus G2400
Mk 8:16 said, "It is because *we* **h** no bread." G2400
Mk 8:18 *Do you* **h** eyes but fail to see, and ears G2400
Mk 8:33 "*You do* not **h in mind** the concerns of G5858
Mk 9:45 life crippled than *to* **h** two feet and be G2400
Mk 9:47 with one eye than *to* **h** two eyes and be G2400
Mk 9:50 **H** salt among yourselves, and be at peace G2400
Mk 10:21 sell everything *you* **h** and give to the poor G2400
Mk 10:21 and *you will* **h** treasure in heaven. G2400
Mk 10:47 Son of David, **h mercy** on me! G1796
Mk 10:48 the more, "Son of David, **h mercy** on me!" G1796
Mk 11:22 "**H** faith in God," Jesus answered. G2400
Mk 12:39 **h** the most important seats in the NDT
Mk 14: 5 It **could h** been sold for more than a year's G1538
Mk 14: 7 The poor *you will* always **h** with you, and G2400
Mk 14: 7 But *you will* not always **h** me. G2400
Mk 14:31 "Even if I **h to** die with you, I will G1256
Lk 1:36 your relative *is going to* **h** a child in her G5197
Lk 1:57 it was time for Elizabeth *to* **h** her **baby**, G5503
Lk 3: 8 yourselves, '*We* **h** Abraham as our father. G2400
Lk 6:31 to others as you would **h** them do to you. G2671
Lk 7:22 *those who* **h leprosy** are cleansed G3320
Lk 7:36 invited Jesus to **h dinner** with him, G2266
Lk 7:40 "Simon, *I* **h** something to tell you. G2400
Lk 8:13 joy when they hear it, but they **h** no root. G2400
Lk 8:18 whoever *does* not **h**, even what G2400
Lk 8:18 what they think *they* **h** will be taken from G2400
Lk 9:13 "We **h** only five loaves of bread and two G1639
Lk 9:58 "Foxes **h** dens and birds have nests G2400
Lk 9:58 "Foxes have dens and birds **h** nests, but the NDT
Lk 10:13 they **would h** repented long ago G323
Lk 10:35 you for any **extra expense** *you may* **h**. G4655
Lk 11: 5 to them, "*Suppose* you **h** a friend, and G2400
Lk 11: 6 come to me, and *I* **h** no food to offer him. G2400
Lk 11:42 *You* **should h** practiced the latter without G1256
Lk 12:17 *I* **h** no place to store my crops G2400
Lk 12:19 "You **h** plenty of grain laid up for many G2400
Lk 12:24 sow or reap, they **h** no storeroom or barn G1639
Lk 12:37 *will* **h** them **recline at the table** and will G369
Lk 12:39 he **would** not **h** let his house be broken G323
Lk 12:50 But *I* **h** a baptism to undergo, and what G2400
Lk 14:28 the cost to see if *you* **h** enough money to G2400
Lk 14:33 up everything you **h** cannot be my G5639
Lk 15:17 my father's hired servants **h** food **to spare**, G4355
Lk 15:23 *Let's* **h a feast** and celebrate. G2266
Lk 15:31 and everything **I h** is yours. G3836+1847
Lk 16:24 **h pity** on me and send Lazarus to dip the G1796
Lk 16:28 for *I* **h** five brothers. Let him warn them, so G2400
Lk 16:29 replied, '*They* **h** Moses and the Prophets G2400
Lk 17: 6 "If *you* **h** faith as small as a mustard seed G2400
Lk 17:13 a loud voice, "Jesus, Master, **h pity** on us!" G1796
Lk 18:13 said, 'God, **h mercy** on me, a sinner.' G2661
Lk 18:22 Sell everything *you* **h** and give to the poor, G2400
Lk 18:22 and *you will* **h** treasure in heaven. G2400
Lk 18:38 "Jesus, Son of David, **h mercy** on me!" G1796
Lk 18:39 the more, "Son of David, **h mercy** on me!" G1796
Lk 19:23 I **could h** collected it with interest? G323
Lk 19:26 even what *they* **h** will be taken away. G2400
Lk 20:46 the marketplaces and **h** the most important NDT
Lk 22:36 to them, "But now *if* you **h** a purse, take it, G2400
Lk 22:36 and *if* you don't **h** a sword, sell G2400
Lk 24:26 *Did* not the Messiah **h to** suffer these G1256
Lk 24:39 a ghost *does* not **h** flesh and bones G2400
Lk 24:39 not have flesh and bones, as you see I **h**." G2400
Lk 24:41 "*Do you* **h** anything here to eat? G2400
Jn 2: 3 said to him, "*They* **h** no more wine." G2400
Jn 3:15 who believes *may* **h** eternal life in him." G2400
Jn 3:16 in him shall not perish but **h** eternal life. G2400
Jn 4:10 you **would h** asked him and he would have G323
Jn 4:10 asked him and he **would h** given you living G323
Jn 4:11 "*you* **h** nothing to draw with and the well G2400
Jn 4:17 "*I* **h** no husband," she replied. Jesus said G2400
Jn 4:17 are right when you say *you* **h** no husband. G2400
Jn 4:18 the man *you* now **h** is not your G2400
Jn 4:32 "I **h** food to eat that you know nothing G2400
Jn 4:35 Don't you **h a saying**, 'It's still four months G3306
Jn 5: 7 "*I* **h** no one to help me into the pool G2400
Jn 5:26 granted the Son also *to* **h** life in himself. G2400
Jn 5:36 "I **h** testimony weightier than that of John G2400
Jn 5:39 you think that in them *you* **h** eternal life. G2400
Jn 5:40 you refuse to come to me to **h** life. G2400
Jn 5:42 I know that *you do* not **h** the love of God G2400
Jn 6: 7 enough bread for each one *to* **h** a bite!" G3284
Jn 6:10 Jesus said, "**H** the people sit down." G4472
Jn 6:40 believes in him *shall* **h** eternal life, G2400
Jn 6:53 drink his blood, *you* **h** no life in you. G2400
Jn 6:68 *You* **h** the words of eternal life. G2400
Jn 8: 6 in order to **h** a basis for accusing him. G2400
Jn 8:12 in darkness, but *will* **h** the light of life." G2400
Jn 8:14 But you **h** no **idea** where I come from or G3857
Jn 8:26 "*I* **h** much to say in judgment of you. G2400
Jn 8:37 because you **h** no **room** *for* my word. G6003
Jn 8:41 "The only Father *we* **h** is God himself." G2400
Jn 10:10 I have come that *they may* **h** life, and G2400
Jn 10:10 they may have life, and **h** it to the full. G2400
Jn 10:16 *I* **h** other sheep that are not of this sheep G2400
Jn 10:18 *I* **h** authority to lay it down and authority G2400
Jn 11:10 they stumble, for they **h** no light." G1639+1877
Jn 11:21 been here, my brother **would** not **h** died. G323
Jn 11:32 been here, my brother **would** not **h** died." G323
Jn 12: 8 *You will* always **h** the poor among you, but G2400
Jn 12: 8 among you, but *you will* not always **h** me." G2400
Jn 12:35 "You *are going to* **h** the light just a G1877+1639
Jn 12:35 Walk while *you* **h** the light, before G2400
Jn 12:36 Believe in the light while *you* **h** the light G2400
Jn 13: 8 I wash you, *you* **h** no part with me. G2400
Jn 15:22 but now *they* **h** no excuse for their sin. G2400
Jn 16:12 "*I* **h** much more to say to you, more than G2400
Jn 16:33 so that in me *you may* **h** peace. G2400
Jn 16:33 In this world *you will* **h** trouble. But take G2400
Jn 17:10 All **I h** is yours, and all you have is G3836+1847
Jn 17:10 is yours, and all **you h** is mine. G3836+5050
Jn 17:13 so that *they may* **h** the full measure of my G2400
Jn 17:26 order that the love *you* **h** for me may be in G26S
Jn 18:30 "we **would** not **h** handed him over to you." G323
Jn 18:31 "But we **h** no **right** to execute anyone," G2003
Jn 19: 7 insisted, "We **h** a law, and according G2400
Jn 19:10 "Don't you realize *I* **h** power either to free G2400
Jn 19:11 "*You would* **h** no power over me if it were G2400
Jn 19:15 "*We* **h** no king but Caesar," the chief G2400
Jn 20:31 by believing *you may* **h** life in his name G2400
Jn 21:12 "Come and **h breakfast**." None of the G753
Jn 21:25 whole world *would* not **h room** for the G6003
Ac 2:13 said, "*They* **h** had too much wine." G1639
Ac 3: 6 "Silver or gold I *do* not **h**, but what I do G5639
Ac 3: 6 I do not have, but what *I do* **h** I give you. G2400
Ac 8:21 You **h** no part or share in this ministry G1639
Ac 10:22 so that he could hear what you **h** to say." G4123
Ac 10:47 have received the Holy Spirit just as we **h**." NDT
Ac 11:12 told me *to* **h** no **hesitation** about going G1359
Ac 13:15 if you **h** a word of exhortation for G1639+1877
Ac 17:28 in him we live and move and **h** *our* **being**. G1639
Ac 18:10 because I **h** many people in this city." G1639
Ac 19:38 his fellow craftsmen **h** a grievance against G2400
Ac 20:21 God in repentance and **h** faith in our Lord NDT
Ac 21:20 how many thousands of Jews **h** believed G1639
Ac 24:15 and *I* **h** the same hope in God as these G2400
Ac 24:15 hope in God as these men themselves **h**, NDT
Ac 24:19 bring charges if *they* **h** anything against G2400
Ac 25:26 But *I* **h** nothing definite to write to His G2400
Ac 25:26 this investigation *I may* **h** something to G2400
Ac 26: 1 "You **h permission** to speak for yourself." G2205
Ac 26:32 "This man **could h** been set free if he had G1538
Ac 27:21 *you* **should h** taken my advice not to sail G1256
Ac 27:25 for *I* **h faith** in God that it will happen just G4409
Ro 1:13 in order that *I might* **h** a harvest among G2400
Ro 1:31 they **h** no understanding, no fidelity, no love NDT
Ro 2: 1 therefore, **h** no excuse, you who pass G1639
Ro 2:14 Gentiles, who *do* not **h** the law, do by G2400
Ro 2:14 *even though they do* not **h** the law. G2400
Ro 2:20 *because you* **h** in the law the G2400
Ro 2:27 even though you **h** the written code and G1328
Ro 3:26 who justifies those who **h** faith in Jesus. G1666
Ro 4:16 also to those who **h** the faith of Abraham. G1666
Ro 5: 1 *we* **h** peace with God through our Lord G2400
Ro 7:18 For I **h** the desire to do what is good, but I G4154
Ro 8: 5 to the flesh **h** *their* **minds set on** what the G5858
Ro 8: 5 with the Spirit **h** their minds set on what NDT
Ro 8: 9 And if anyone *does* not **h** the Spirit of G2400
Ro 8:12 sisters, *we* **h** an obligation—but it G1639
Ro 8:23 ourselves, *who* **h** the firstfruits of the Spirit G2400
Ro 8:24 Who hopes for what *they* **already h**? G1063
Ro 8:25 But if we hope for what *we* **do** not **yet h** G1063
Ro 9: 2 I **h** great sorrow and unceasing anguish in G1639
Ro 9: 9 time I will return, and Sarah *will* **h** a son." G1639
Ro 9:15 "*I will* **h mercy** on whom I have mercy G1796
Ro 9:15 "I will have mercy on whom *I* **h mercy** G1796
Ro 9:15 and *I will* **h compassion** on whom I have G3882
Ro 9:15 compassion on whom *I* **h compassion**." G3882
Ro 9:18 has mercy on whom he wants to **h** mercy, NDT
Ro 9:21 *Does* not the potter **h** the right to make out G2400
Ro 9:29 we **would h** become like Sodom G323
Ro 9:29 we **would h** been like Gomorrah. G323
Ro 11:32 so that *he may* **h mercy** on them all. G1796
Ro 12: 4 these members *do* not all **h** the same G2400

Ro 12: 6 *We* **h** different gifts, according to the grace G2400
Ro 15: 4 they provide *we might* **h** hope. G2400
1Co 2: 8 they **would** not **h** crucified the Lord of glory. G323
1Co 2:16 But we **h** the mind of Christ. G2400
1Co 3: 8 the one who waters **h** one purpose, G1639
1Co 4: 7 What *do you* **h** that you did not receive G2400
1Co 4: 8 Already *you* **h all** *you* **want** G3170+1639
1Co 4:15 in Christ, you do not **h** many fathers, for in NDT
1Co 4:19 people are talking, but what power they **h**. NDT
1Co 5:10 In that case *you would* **h to** leave this G4053
1Co 6: 4 if *you* **h** disputes about such matters G2400
1Co 6: 7 The very fact that *you* **h** lawsuits among G2400
1Co 6: 9 **men who h sex with men** G3434+780
1Co 6:12 "I **h the right** *to do* anything," you say G2003
1Co 6:12 "I **h the right** *to do* anything"—but I will G2003
1Co 7: 1 a man not *to* **h sexual relations** with a G721
1Co 7: 2 man *should* **h sexual relations with** his G2400
1Co 7: 4 The wife *does* not **h authority** over her own G2027
1Co 7: 4 the husband *does* not **h authority** over his G2027
1Co 7:25 *I* **h** no command from the Lord, but I give G2400
1Co 7:29 From now on those *who* **h** wives should G2400
1Co 7:40 I think *that* I too **h** the Spirit of God. G2400
1Co 9: 4 Don't *we* **h** the right to food and drink? G2400
1Co 9: 5 Don't *we* **h** the right to take a believing G2400
1Co 9:12 If others **h** this right of **support** from you G3576
1Co 9:12 from you, shouldn't we **h** it all the more? NDT
1Co 9:17 If I preach voluntarily, *I* **h** a reward; if not G2400
1Co 10:21 you cannot **h a part** in both the Lord's G3576
1Co 10:23 "*I* **h the right** *to do* anything," you say G2003
1Co 10:23 "*I* **h the right** *to do* anything"—but not G2003
1Co 11: 6 *she might as well* **h** *her* **hair cut off**; but G3025
1Co 11: 6 a woman to **h** her **hair cut off** or her head G3025
1Co 11:10 a woman ought to **h** authority over her G2400
1Co 11:16 about this, we **h** no other practice—nor do G2400
1Co 11:17 following directives *I* **h** no **praise** for you, G2046
1Co 11:19 No doubt *there* **h to** be differences among G1256
1Co 11:19 you to show which of you **h** God's approval. NDT
1Co 11:22 Don't *you* **h** homes to eat and drink in? Or G2400
1Co 11:22 God by humiliating those *who* **h** nothing? G2400
1Co 12:25 but *that* its parts *should* **h** equal **concern** G3534
1Co 12:30 *Do* all **h** gifts of healing? Do all speak in G2400
1Co 13: 1 of angels, but *do* not **h** love, I am only G2400
1Co 13: 2 If *I* **h** the gift of prophecy and can fathom G2400
1Co 13: 2 if *I* **h** a faith that can move mountains G2400
1Co 13: 2 mountains, but *do* not **h** love, I am G2400
1Co 13: 3 I may boast, but *do* not **h** love, I gain G2400
1Co 15:19 this life *we* **h hope** in Christ, G1827+1639
1Co 15:39 People **h** one kind of flesh, animals have NDT
1Co 15:39 animals **h** another, birds another NDT
2Co 2: 3 by those who **should h** made me rejoice. G1256
2Co 3: 4 Such confidence *we* **h** through Christ G2400
2Co 3:12 Therefore, *since we* **h** such a hope, we G2400
2Co 4: 1 through God's mercy *we* **h** this ministry, G2400
2Co 4: 7 But *we* **h** this treasure in jars of clay to G2400
2Co 4:13 " *Since we* **h** that same spirit of faith, we G2400
2Co 5: 1 in is destroyed, *we* **h** a building from God G2400
2Co 6:14 wickedness **h** in common? NDT
2Co 6:14 what fellowship can light **h** with darkness? NDT
2Co 6:15 what does a believer **h** in common with an NDT
2Co 7: 1 Therefore, *since we* **h** these promises G2400
2Co 7: 3 before that *you* **h** such a **place** in our G1639
2Co 8:10 to give but also *to* **h the desire** to do so. G2527
2Co 8:12 not according to what *one does* not **h**. G2400
2Co 8:15 who gathered much *did* not **h too much**, G4429
2Co 8:15 who gathered little *did* not **h too little**." G1782
2Co 10: 4 they **h** divine power to demolish strongholds NDT
2Co 12:14 children **should** not **h** to save up for their G4053
2Co 12:15 *will* very gladly **spend** for you **everything** *I* **h** G1251
Gal 2: 4 on the freedom we **h** in Christ Jesus and G2400
Gal 3: 7 that those who **h** faith are children of G1666
Gal 3:21 **would** certainly **h** come by the G323
Gal 4:17 from us, so that *you may* **h zeal** for them. G2420
Gal 6:10 Therefore, as *we* **h** opportunity, let us do G2400
Eph 1: 7 In him *we* **h** redemption through his blood, G2400
Eph 2:18 For through him *we* both **h** access to the G2400
Eph 4:28 that *they may* **h** something to share with G2400
Eph 5:11 **H** nothing **to do with** the fruitless deeds of G5170
Php 1: 7 all of you, since I **h** you in my heart and G2400
Php 1:20 will **h** sufficient courage so that now G1877
Php 1:30 you saw I had, and now hear that I still **h**. G1877
Php 2: 1 Therefore if you **h** any encouragement from NDT
Php 2: 5 **h** the same **mindset** as Christ Jesus: G5858
Php 2:20 *I* **h** no one else like him, who will show G2400
Php 2:28 you may be glad and I *may* **h** less anxiety. G1639
Php 3: 4 though *I* myself **h** *reasons for* such G2400
Php 3: 4 to put confidence in the flesh, I **h** more: NDT
Php 3:17 just as *you* **h** us as a model, keep G2400
Php 4:12 in need, and I know what it is *to* **h plenty**. G4355
Php 4:18 full payment and **h more than enough**. G4355
Col 1: 4 of the love *you* **h** for all God's people G2400
Col 1:11 so that you may **h** great endurance and NDT
Col 1:14 in whom *we* **h** redemption, the forgiveness G2400
Col 1:18 in everything he *might* **h** the supremacy. G1181
Col 2: 2 so that they may **h** the full riches of NDT
Col 2:23 regulations indeed **h** an appearance of G2400
Col 4: 1 know that you also **h** a Master in heaven. G2400
1Th 3: 6 has told us that *you* always **h** pleasant G2400
1Th 3: 9 all the joy *we* **h** in the presence of G5897S
1Th 4:13 like the rest of mankind, who **h** no hope. G2400
1Th 5:27 the Lord *to* **h** this letter **read** to all the G336
2Th 1: 3 the love all of you **h** for one another is NDT
2Th 3: 4 *We* **h confidence** in the Lord that you are G4275
2Th 3: 9 not because *we do* not **h** the right to such G2400
1Ti 3: 7 He must also **h** a good reputation with G2400
1Ti 4: 7 **H nothing to do with** godless myths and G4148
1Ti 5:14 widows to marry, *to* **h children**, to manage G5449
1Ti 6: 2 Those *who* **h** believing masters should not G2400
1Ti 6: 4 *They* **h an unhealthy interest** in G3796
1Ti 6: 8 But *if we* **h** food and clothing, we will be G2400
2Ti 2:23 **Don't h anything to do with** foolish and G4148
2Ti 3: 5 **H nothing to do with** such people. G706
Titus 2: 8 be ashamed *because they* **h** nothing bad G2400
Titus 3:10 After that, **h nothing to do with** them. G4148
Titus 3:13 that they **h everything** they **need**. G3594+3309
Phm 15 was that *you might* **h** him **back** forever— G600
Phm 20 *that I may* **h** *some* **benefit** from you in the G3949
Heb 2:14 Since the children **h** flesh and blood, he G3125
Heb 4: 8 God **would** not **h** spoken later about G323
Heb 4:14 *since we* **h** a great high priest who has G2400
Heb 4:15 For *we do* not **h** a high priest who is G2400
Heb 4:15 we **h** one who has been tempted in NDT
Heb 6: 9 the things *that* **h to do with** salvation. G2400
Heb 6:19 *We* **h** this hope as an anchor for the soul G2400
Heb 8: 1 *We do* **h** such a high priest, who sat down G2400
Heb 8: 3 this one also *to* **h** something to offer. G2400
Heb 10: 2 **would** they not **h** stopped being offered? G323
Heb 10:19 *since we* **h** confidence to enter the Most G2400
Heb 10:21 since we **h** a great priest over the house NDT
Heb 11:15 they **would h** had opportunity to return. G323
Heb 11:32 I *do* **not h** time to tell about Gideon G2142
Heb 13: 5 of money and be content *with* what *you* **h**, G4205
Heb 13:10 *We* **h** an altar from which those who G2400
Heb 13:10 at the tabernacle **h** no right to eat. G2400
Heb 13:14 For here *we do* not **h** an enduring city, but G2400
Heb 13:17 **H confidence** in your leaders and submit G4275
Heb 13:18 We are sure that *we* **h** a clear conscience G2400
Jas 2:14 if someone claims *to* **h** faith but has no G2400
Jas 2:18 will say, "You **h** faith; I have deeds." G2400
Jas 2:18 will say, "You have faith; I **h** deeds." G2400
Jas 3:16 For where you **h** envy and selfish ambition NDT
Jas 4: 2 You desire but *do* not **h**, so you kill. G2400
Jas 4: 2 *You do* not **h** because you do not ask God. G2400
1Pe 1:22 the truth so that you **h** sincere love for each NDT
1Pe 3:15 to give the reason for the hope that you **h**. G1877
2Pe 1: 9 But whoever *does* not **h** them is G4205
2Pe 1:12 firmly established in the truth *you* **now h**. G4205
2Pe 1:19 *We* also **h** the prophetic message as G2400
1Jn 1: 3 so that you also *may* **h** fellowship with us. G2400
1Jn 1: 6 If we claim *to* **h** fellowship with him and G2400
1Jn 1: 7 *we* **h** fellowship with one another G2400
1Jn 2: 1 *we* **h** an advocate with the Father G2400
1Jn 2:19 they **would h** remained with us G323
1Jn 2:20 But you **h** an anointing from the Holy One, G2400
1Jn 3: 3 All who **h** this hope in him purify G2400
1Jn 3:21 condemn us, *we* **h** confidence before God G2400
1Jn 4:17 among us so that *we will* **h** confidence on G2400
1Jn 5:12 whoever *does* not **h** the Son of God does G2400
1Jn 5:12 not have the Son of God *does* not **h** life. G2400
1Jn 5:13 that you may know that *you* **h** eternal life. G2400
1Jn 5:14 is the confidence *we* **h** in approaching G2400
1Jn 5:15 we know that *we* **h** what we asked of him. G2400
2Jn 9 in the teaching of Christ *does* not **h** God; G2400
2Jn 12 *I* **h** much to write to you, but I do not want G2400
3Jn 4 *I* **h** no greater joy than to hear that my G2400
3Jn 13 *I* **h** much to write you, but I do not want to G2400
Jude 19 natural instincts and *do* not **h** the Spirit. G2400
Rev 2: 6 But *you* **h** this *in your favor*: You hate the G2400
Rev 2:14 Nevertheless, *I* **h** a few things against you: G2400
Rev 2:15 you also **h** those who hold to the teaching G2400
Rev 2:25 to hold on to what *you* **h** until I come. G2400
Rev 3: 1 *you* **h** a reputation of being alive G2400
Rev 3: 4 Yet *you* **h** a few people in Sardis who G2400
Rev 3: 8 I know that *you* **h** little strength, yet you G2400
Rev 3:11 Hold on to what *you* **h**, so that no one will G2400
Rev 4:11 will they were created and **h** *their* **being**." G1639
Rev 9: 4 people who *did* not **h** the seal of God G2400
Rev 11: 6 They **h** power to shut up the heavens so G2400
Rev 11: 6 and *they* **h** power to turn the waters into G2026
Rev 17:13 They **h** one purpose and will give their G2400
Rev 22:14 that they *may* **h** the right to the tree of life G1639

HAVEN (2) [FAIR HAVENS]

Ge 49:13 the seashore and become a **h** *for* ships; H2572
Ps 107:30 he guided them to their desired **h**. H4685

HAVEN'T (22) [HAVE, NOT]

Ge 27:36 "**H** you reserved any blessing for me?" H4202
Ex 5:14 "Why **h** you met your quota of bricks H4202
Nu 16:14 you **h** brought us into a land flowing with H4202
Jdg 14:16 a riddle, but you **h** told me the answer." H4202
Jdg 14:16 "I **h** even explained it to my father or H4202
Jdg 16:15 a fool of me and **h** told me the secret of H4202
1Sa 21: 8 I **h** brought my sword or any other weapon H4202
2Sa 3: 8 I **h** handed you over to David H4202
2Sa 11:10 "**H** you just come from a military H4202
2Sa 13:28 Don't be afraid. **H** I given you this order H4202
1Ki 18:13 **H** you heard, my lord, what I did while H4202
1Ch 19: 3 **H** his envoys come to you only to explore H4202
2Ch 24: 6 "Why **h** you required the Levites to bring H4202
Eze 11: 3 '**H** our houses been recently rebuilt? H4202
Mt 12: 3 "**H** you read what David did when he and G4024
Mt 12: 5 Or **h** you read in the Law that the priests G4024
Mt 19: 4 "**H** you read," he replied, "that at the G4024
Mk 12:10 **H** you read this passage of Scripture: G4028
Lk 5: 5 hard all night and **h** caught **anything**. G4029
Lk 13: 7 fruit on this fig tree and **h** found any. G4024
Jn 21: 5 to them, "Friends, **h** *you* any fish?" G3590+2400
Ac 27:33 without food—you **h** eaten **anything**. G3594

HAVENS See FAIR HAVENS

HAVILAH (7)

Ge 2:11 it winds through the entire land *of* **H** H2564
Ge 10: 7 Seba, **H**, Sabtah, Raamah and H2564
Ge 10:29 **H** and Jobab. All these were sons H2564
Ge 25:18 settled in the area from **H** to Shur, H2564
1Sa 15: 7 Amalekites all the way from **H** to Shur, H2564
1Ch 1: 9 Seba, **H**, Sabta, Raamah and H2564
1Ch 1:23 **H** and Jobab. All these were sons H2564

HAVING (63) [HAVE]

Ge 16: 2 "The LORD has kept me from **h children**. H3528
Ge 29:35 Then she stopped **h children**. H3528
Ge 30: 2 who has kept you from *h* **children**? AIT
Ge 30: 9 saw that she had stopped **h children**, H3528
Ge 31:35 up in your presence; I'm **h** my period." H4200
Ge 35:17 And as she *was* **h great difficulty** in H7996
Ex 12: 4 **h** taken into account the number of people NDT
Lev 9:22 And *h* **sacrificed** the sin offering, the burnt AIT
Lev 16:17 he comes out, *h* **made atonement** for himself AIT
Lev 18: 7 *Do* not **dishonor** your father **by h sexual relations with** H1655+6872
Nu 5:20 *by* **h sexual relations with** a H5989+928+8888
Nu 10: 2 together and for **h** the camps **set out**. H5023
1Sa 24: 5 *h* **cut off** a corner of his robe. AIT
1Sa 25:31 needless bloodshed or of *h* **avenged** himself. AIT
1Ki 6:34 each **h** two leaves that turned in sockets. NDT
1Ch 23:22 Eleazar died without **h** sons: he H2118+4200
1Ch 29:28 died at a good old age, **h** enjoyed long life NDT
Est 3: 6 Yet *h* **learned** who Mordecai's people were AIT
Job 21:25 never *h* **enjoyed** anything good. AIT
Ps 65: 6 your power, *h* **armed yourself** with strength, AIT
Isa 22: 3 *h* **fled** while the enemy was still far away. AIT
Eze 44:11 **h charge** of the gates of the temple and H7213
Da 4:21 and *h* **nesting places** in its branches for the AIT
Am 1: 3 threshed Gilead with **sledges** *h* iron teeth, AIT
Zep 2: 6 will become pastures **h** wells for shepherds NDT
Mt 2:12 And *h* **been warned** in a dream not to go AIT
Mt 2:22 *H* **been warned** in a dream, he withdrew to AIT
Mt 4:24 *those* **h seizures**, and the G4944
Mt 9:10 *While* Jesus *was* **h dinner** at Matthew's G367
Mt 16: 8 among yourselves about **h** no bread? G2400
Mt 22:24 us that if a man dies without **h** children, G2400
Mk 2:15 *While* Jesus was **h dinner** at Levi's house G2879
Mk 8:17 "Why are you talking about **h** no bread G2400
Jn 7:15 get such learning without *h* **been taught**?" AIT
Jn 13: 1 *H* **loved** his own who were in the world, he AIT
Ac 8:22 may forgive you for **h** such a thought in your NDT
Ac 16: 6 *h* **been kept** by the Holy Spirit **from** preaching AIT
Ro 5:10 much more, *h* **been reconciled**, shall we be AIT
1Co 8: 7 they think of it as **h** been sacrificed to a god NDT
1Co 9:21 To those **not h the law** I became like one G491
1Co 9:21 the law I became like *one* **not h the law** G491
1Co 9:21 so as to win those **not h the law**. G491
1Co 11: 5 it is the same as *h* her head **shaved**. AIT
2Co 6:10 making many rich; **h** nothing, and yet G2400
2Co 9: 4 would be ashamed of **h** been so confident. NDT
2Co 9: 8 things at all times, **h** all that you need G2400
Eph 1:11 *h* **been predestined** according to the plan of AIT
Eph 4:19 *H* **lost all sensitivity**, they have given AIT
Php 2: 2 being like-minded, **h** the same love G2400
Php 3: 9 not **h** a righteousness of my own that G2400
Col 2:12 *h* **been buried with** him in baptism, in which AIT
Col 2:14 *h* **canceled** the charge of our legal AIT
Col 2:15 And *h* **disarmed** the powers and authorities AIT
2Ti 3: 5 **h** a form of godliness but denying its G2400
Titus 3: 7 *h* **been justified** by his grace, we AIT
Titus 3: 7 might become heirs **h** the hope of eternal G2848
Heb 10:22 *h* our hearts **sprinkled to cleanse** us from a AIT
Heb 10:22 and *h* our bodies **washed** with pure AIT
Jas 1:12 under trial because, *h* **stood** the test, that AIT
2Pe 1: 4 *h* **escaped** the corruption in the world caused AIT
Rev 7: 2 the east, **h** the seal of the living God. G2400
Rev 9:19 **h** heads with which they inflict injury. G2400
Rev 20: 1 **h** the key to the Abyss and holding in his G2400

HAVOC (3)

Isa 54:16 have created the destroyer to **wreak h**; H2472
Jer 48: 3 cries of great **h** and destruction. H8719
Ac 9:21 he the *man who* **raised h** in Jerusalem G4514

HAVVOTH JAIR (4) [JAIR]

Nu 32:41 their settlements and called them **H**. H2596
Dt 3:14 so that to this day Bashan is called **H**. H2596
Jdg 10: 4 which to this day are called **H**. H2596
1Ch 2:23 But Geshur and Aram captured **H**, as H2596

HAWK (3)

Lev 11:16 the screech owl, the gull, any kind of **h**, H5891
Dt 14:15 the screech owl, the gull, any kind of **h**, H5891
Job 39:26 "Does the **h** take flight by your wisdom H5891

HAY (2)

Pr 27:25 When the **h** is removed and new growth H2945
1Co 3:12 costly stones, wood, **h** or straw, G5965

HAZAEL (24)
1Ki 19:15 you get there, anoint H king over Aram. H2599
1Ki 19:17 to death any who escape the sword of H, H2599
2Ki 8: 8 he said to H, "Take a gift with you and go H2599
2Ki 8: 9 H went to meet Elisha, taking with him as H2599
2Ki 8:11 with a fixed gaze until H was embarrassed. NDT
2Ki 8:12 asked H. "Because I know the H2599
2Ki 8:13 H said, "How could your servant, a mere H2599
2Ki 8:14 Then H left Elisha and returned to his NDT
2Ki 8:14 H replied, "He told me that you would NDT
2Ki 8:15 Then H succeeded him as king H2599
2Ki 8:28 Ahab to war against H king of Aram at H2599
2Ki 8:29 Ramoth in his battle with H king of Aram. H2599
2Ki 9:14 Ramoth Gilead against H king of Aram, H2599
2Ki 9:15 on him in the battle with H king of Aram.) H2599
2Ki 10:32 H overpowered the Israelites throughout H2599
2Ki 12:17 About this time H king of Aram went up H2599
2Ki 12:18 he sent them to H king of Aram, who H2599
2Ki 13: 3 under the power of H king of Aram and H2599
2Ki 13:22 H king of Aram oppressed Israel H2599
2Ki 13:24 H king of Aram died, and Ben-Hadad his H2599
2Ki 13:25 Ben-Hadad son of H the towns he had H2599
2Ch 22: 5 to wage war against H king of Aram at H2599
2Ch 22: 6 Ramoth in his battle with H king of Aram. H2599
Am 1: 4 fire on the house of H that will consume H2599

HAZAIAH (1)
Ne 11: 5 the son of H, the son of Adaiah, H2610

HAZAR ADDAR (1) [ADDAR]
Nu 34: 4 it will go to H and over to Azmon H2960

HAZAR ENAN (4) [ENAN]
Nu 34: 9 continue to Ziphron and end at H H2966
Nu 34:10 run a line from H to Shepham. H2966
Eze 47:17 will extend from the sea to H, H2965
Eze 48: 1 H and the northern border of H2966

HAZAR GADDAH (1)
Jos 15:27 H, Heshmon, Beth Pelet, H2961

HAZAR SHUAL (4) [SHUAL]
Jos 15:28 H, Beersheba, Biziothiah, H2967
Jos 19: 3 H, Balah, Ezem, H2967
1Ch 4:28 lived in Beersheba, Moladah, H, H2967
Ne 11:27 in H, in Beersheba and its H2967

HAZAR SUSAH (1)
Jos 19: 5 Beth Markaboth, H, H2963

HAZAR SUSIM (1)
1Ch 4:31 Beth Markaboth, H, Beth Biri and H2964

HAZARMAVETH (2)
Ge 10:26 father of Almodad, Sheleph, H, Jerah, H2975
1Ch 1:20 father of Almodad, Sheleph, H, Jerah, H2975

HAZEL (KJV) ALMOND

HAZER HATTIKON (1)
Eze 47:16 as far as H, which is on the H2962

HAZEROTH (5)
Nu 11:35 people traveled to H and stayed there. H2972
Nu 12:16 the people left H and encamped in the H2972
Nu 33:17 left Kibroth Hattaavah and camped at H. H2972
Nu 33:18 They left H and camped at Rithmah. H2972
Dt 1: 1 Tophel, Laban, H and Dizahab. H2972

HAZEZON TAMAR (2) [EN GEDI, TAMAR]
Ge 14: 7 the Amorites who were living in H. H2954
2Ch 20: 2 It is already in H" (that is, En Gedi). H2954

HAZIEL (1)
1Ch 23: 9 Shelomoth, H and Haran—three in H2609

HAZO (1)
Ge 22:22 H, Pildash, Jidlaph and Bethuel." H2605

HAZOR (18) [BAAL HAZOR, EN HAZOR, HAZOR HADATTAH, KERIOTH HEZRON]
Jos 11: 1 When Jabin king of H heard of this, he H2937
Jos 11:10 back and captured H and put its king to H2937
Jos 11:10 H had been the head of all these H2937
Jos 11:11 that breathed, and he burned H *itself*. H2937
Jos 11:13 their mounds—except H, which Joshua H2937
Jos 12:19 the king of Madon one the king of H one H2937
Jos 15:23 Kedesh, H, Ithnan, H2937
Jos 15:25 Hadattah, Kerioth Hezron (that is, H), H2937
Jos 19:36 Adamah, Ramah, H, H2937
Jdg 4: 2 Jabin king of Canaan, who reigned in H. H2937
Jdg 4:17 between Jabin king of H and the family of H2937
1Sa 12: 9 the commander of the army of H, and into H2937
1Ki 9:15 of Jerusalem, and H, Megiddo and Gezer. H2937
2Ki 15:29 Beth Maakah, Janoah, Kedesh and H. H2937
Ne 11:33 in H, Ramah and Gittaim, H2937
Jer 49:28 Concerning Kedar and the kingdoms of H H2938
Jer 49:30 you who live in H," declares the LORD. H2938
Jer 49:33 "H will become a haunt of jackals, H2938

HAZOR HADATTAH (1) [HAZOR]
Jos 15:25 H, Kerioth Hezron (that is, Hazor H2939

HAZZELELPONI (1)
1Ch 4: 3 Their sister was named H. H2209

HAZZOBEBAH (1)
1Ch 4: 8 father of Anub and H and of the clans of H2206

HAZZURIM See HELKATH HAZZURIM

HE (8526) [HE'S, HIM, HIS] See Index of Articles Etc.

HE'S (13) [BE, HE]
Ge 27:36 my birthright, and now *h* **taken** my blessing!" AIT
Jdg 13:10 woman hurried to tell her husband, "H here! NDT
1Sa 9:12 they answered. "H ahead of you. Hurry now NDT
2Sa 16:17 show your friend? If h your friend, why didn't NDT
2Sa 18:27 son of Zadok." "H a good man," the king H2296
Mt 27:42 he can't save himself! H the king of Israel *G1639*
Mt 27:47 heard this, they said, "H calling Elijah." *G4047*
Mk 2: 7 *H* **blaspheming**! Who can AIT
Mk 9:26 much like a corpse that many said, "*H* **dead**." AIT
Mk 10:49 On your feet! *H* **calling** you." AIT
Mk 15:35 heard this, they said, "Listen, *h* **calling** Elijah." AIT
Ac 20:10 "Don't be alarmed," he said. "H alive!" *G899*
Ac 22:22 "Rid the earth of him! H not fit to live!" *G899*

HE-GOAT (1) [GOAT]
Pr 30:31 a strutting rooster, a h, and a king secure H9411

HEAD (322) [AHEAD, FIGUREHEAD, HEADED, HEADING, HEADS, HOTHEADED]
Ge 3:15 he will crush your h, and you will strike his H8031
Ge 28:11 he put it **under** his h and lay down to H5265
Ge 28:18 he had placed **under** his h and set it up H5265
Ge 40:13 will lift up your h and restore you to your H8031
Ge 40:16 On my h were three baskets of bread. H8031
Ge 40:17 eating them out of the basket on my h." H8031
Ge 40:19 will lift off your h and impale your body H8031
Ge 42:38 you will bring my **gray** h down to the H8484
Ge 44:29 you will bring my **gray** h down to the H8484
Ge 44:31 will bring the **gray** h *of* our father down to H8484
Ge 48:14 his right hand and put it on Ephraim's h, H8031
Ge 48:14 he put his left hand on Manasseh's h H8031
Ge 48:17 hand on Ephraim's h he was displeased; H8031
Ge 48:17 it from Ephraim's h to Manasseh's head. H8031
Ge 48:17 it from Ephraim's head to Manasseh's h. H8031
Ge 48:18 the firstborn; put your right hand on his h." H8031
Ge 49:26 Let all these rest on the h *of* Joseph, on H8031
Ex 12: 9 over a fire—with the h, legs and internal H8031
Ex 22: 1 must pay back five *h of* **cattle** for the ox and AIT
Ex 28:32 with an opening for the h in its center H8031
Ex 29: 6 Put the turban on his h and attach the H8031
Ex 29: 7 oil and anoint him by pouring it on his h. H8031
Ex 29:10 his sons shall lay their hands on its h. H8031
Ex 29:15 his sons shall lay their hands on its h. H8031
Ex 29:17 them with the h and the other pieces. H8031
Ex 29:19 his sons shall lay their hands on its h. H8031
Lev 1: 4 your hand on the h *of* the burnt offering, H8031
Lev 1: 8 including the h and the fat, on the H8031
Lev 1:12 including the h and the fat, on the H8031
Lev 1:15 wring off the h and burn it on the altar H8031
Lev 3: 2 your hand on the h *of* your offering and H8031
Lev 3: 8 lay your hand on its h and slaughter it in H8031
Lev 3:13 lay your hand on its h and slaughter it in H8031
Lev 4: 4 lay his hand on its h and slaughter it H8031
Lev 4:11 as well as the h and legs, the H8031
Lev 4:15 hands on the bull's h before the LORD, H8031
Lev 4:24 hand on the goat's h and slaughter it at H8031
Lev 4:29 their hand on the h *of* the sin offering H8031
Lev 4:33 lay their hand on its h and slaughter it H8031
Lev 5: 8 He is to wring its h from its neck, not H8031
Lev 8: 9 the turban on Aaron's h and set the gold H8031
Lev 8:12 oil on Aaron's h and anointed him to H8031
Lev 8:14 his sons laid their hands on its h. H8031
Lev 8:18 his sons laid their hands on its h. H8031
Lev 8:20 cut the ram into pieces and burned the h, H8031
Lev 8:22 his sons laid their hands on its h. H8031
Lev 9:13 including the h, and he burned them H8031
Lev 13:12 skin of the affected person from h to foot, H8031
Lev 13:29 woman has a sore on their h or chin, H8031
Lev 13:30 is a defiling skin disease on the h or chin. H8031
Lev 13:42 sore on his **bald** h or forehead, H7949
Lev 13:42 breaking out on his h or forehead. H7949
Lev 13:43 if the swollen sore on his h or forehead is H7949
Lev 13:44 him unclean because of the sore on his h. H8031
Lev 14: 9 they must shave their h, their beard, H8031
Lev 14:18 shall put on the h *of* the one to be H8031
Lev 14:29 shall put on the h *of* the one to be H8031
Lev 16:21 both hands on the h *of* the live goat and H8031
Lev 16:21 their sins—and put them on the goat's h. H8031
Lev 19:27 at the sides of your h or clip off the edges H8031
Lev 20: 9 their blood will be on their own h. NDT
Lev 21:10 oil poured on his h and who has been H8031
Lev 24:14 heard him are to lay their hands on his h, H8031
Nu 1: 4 each of them the h of his family, is to H8031
Nu 6: 5 no razor may be used on their h. H8031
Nu 6: 7 of their dedication to God is on their h. H8031
Nu 6: 9 must shave their h on the seventh day— H8031
Nu 6:11 day they are to consecrate their h again. H8031
Nu 17: 3 be one staff for the h *of* each ancestral H8031
Dt 18: 3 internal organs and the **meat from the** h. H4305
Dt 19: 5 the h may fly off and hit his neighbor and H1366
Dt 21:12 into your home and have her shave her h, H8031
Dt 28:13 The LORD will make you the h, not the tail H8031
Dt 28:23 The sky over your h will be bronze, the H8031
Dt 28:35 the soles of your feet to the **top of** your h. H7721
Dt 28:44 They will be the h, but you will be the tail. H8031
Dt 33:16 Let all these rest on the h *of* Joseph, on H8031
Dt 33:20 lives there like a lion, tearing at arm or h. H7721
Jos 2:19 blood will be on our h if a hand is laid on H8031
Jos 11:10 Hazor had been the h *of* all these H8031
Jos 22:14 each the h *of* a family division among the H8031
Jdg 5:26 she crushed his h, she shattered and H8031
Jdg 8:28 Israelites and did not raise its h again. H8031
Jdg 9:53 millstone on his h and cracked his skull. H8031
Jdg 10:18 Ammonites will be h over all who live in H8031
Jdg 11: 8 you will be h over all of us who live H8031
Jdg 11: 9 gives them to me—will I really be your h?" H8031
Jdg 11:11 people made him h and commander over H8031
Jdg 12: 1 going to burn down your house over your h." NDT
Jdg 13: 5 have a son whose h is never to be H8031
Jdg 16:13 seven braids of my h into the fabric on the H8031
Jdg 16:13 Delilah took the seven braids of his h H8031
Jdg 16:17 "No razor has ever been used on my h," H8031
Jdg 16:17 If my h were shaved, my strength would NDT
Jdg 16:22 But the hair on his h began to grow again H8031
1Sa 1:11 no razor will ever be used on his h." H8031
1Sa 4:12 with his clothes torn and dust on his h. H8031
1Sa 5: 4 His h and hands had been broken off H8031
1Sa 9: 2 he was a h taller than anyone H4946+8900+2256+5087+2025
1Sa 9:22 seated them at the h *of* those who were H8031
1Sa 10: 1 poured it on Saul's h and kissed him, H8031
1Sa 10:23 he was a h taller than any of H4946+8900+2256+5087+2025
1Sa 14:45 not a hair of his h will fall to the ground H8031
1Sa 15:17 you not become the h *of* the tribes of H8031
1Sa 17: 5 helmet on his h and wore a coat of H8031
1Sa 17:38 on him and a bronze helmet on his h. H8031
1Sa 17:46 I'll strike you down and cut off your h. H8031
1Sa 17:51 killed him, he cut off his h with the sword. H8031
1Sa 17:54 took the Philistine's h and brought it to H8031
1Sa 17:57 with David still holding the Philistine's h. H8031
1Sa 19:13 putting some goats' hair at the h. H5265
1Sa 19:16 and at the h was some goats' hair. H5265
1Sa 25:39 Nabal's wrongdoing down on his own h." H8031
1Sa 26: 7 his spear stuck in the ground **near** his h. H5265
1Sa 26:11 spear and water jug that are **near** his h, H5265
1Sa 26:12 the spear and water jug **near** Saul's h, H5265
1Sa 26:16 spear and water jug that were **near** his h?" H5265
1Sa 31: 9 They cut off his h and stripped off his H8031
2Sa 1: 2 with his clothes torn and dust on his h. H8031
2Sa 1:10 that was on his h and the band on his H8031
2Sa 1:16 "Your blood be on your own h. H8031
2Sa 2:16 his opponent by the h and thrust his H8031
2Sa 3: 8 "Am I a dog's h—on Judah's side? H8031
2Sa 3:29 his blood fall on the h *of* Joab and on his H8031
2Sa 4: 7 stabbed and killed him, they cut off his h. H8031
2Sa 4: 8 They brought the h *of* Ish-Bosheth to H8031
2Sa 4: 8 "Here is the h *of* Ish-Bosheth son of Saul H8031
2Sa 4:12 But they took the h *of* Ish-Bosheth and H8031
2Sa 12:30 David took the crown from their king's h H8031
2Sa 12:30 and it was placed on his own h. H8031
2Sa 13:19 put ashes on her h and tore the ornate H8031
2Sa 13:19 put her hands on her h and went away, H8031
2Sa 14:11 "not one **hair of** your son's h will fall to H8553
2Sa 14:25 From the **top of** his h to the sole of his H7721
2Sa 14:26 Whenever he cut the hair of his h—he H8031
2Sa 15:30 his h was covered and he was barefoot. H8031
2Sa 15:32 meet him, his robe torn and dust on his h. H8031
2Sa 16: 9 Let me go over and cut off his h." H8031
2Sa 20:21 "His h will be thrown to you from the wall. H8031
2Sa 20:22 they cut off the h *of* Sheba son of Bikri H8031
2Sa 22:44 have preserved me as the h *of* nations. H8031
1Ki 1:52 not a **hair of** his h will fall to the ground H8553
1Ki 2: 6 do not let his **gray** h go down to the H8484
1Ki 2: 9 Bring his **gray** h down to the grave in H8484
1Ki 2:33 their blood rest on the h *of* Joab and his H8031
1Ki 2:37 will die; your blood will be on your own h." H8031
1Ki 4:23 ten *h of* stall-fed **cattle**, twenty of pasture-fed AIT
1Ki 19: 6 there **by** his h was some bread baked H5265
2Ki 4:19 to his father, "My h! My head!" His father H8031
2Ki 4:19 My h!" His father told a servant, H8031
2Ki 6:25 long that a donkey's h sold for eighty H8031
2Ki 6:31 if the h *of* Elisha son of Shaphat remains H8031
2Ki 6:32 is sending someone to cut off my h? H8031
2Ki 9: 3 pour the oil on his h and declare, H8031
2Ki 9: 6 poured the oil on Jehu's h and declared, H8031
2Ki 19:21 Jerusalem tosses her h as you flee. H8031
1Ch 5:15 the son of Guni, was h of their family. H8031
1Ch 10: 9 him and took his h and his armor, H8031
1Ch 10:10 gods and hung up his h in the temple of H1653
1Ch 15:22 Kenaniah the h Levite was in charge of the H8569
1Ch 20: 2 took the crown from the h *of* their king— H8031
1Ch 20: 2 stones—and it was placed on David's h. H8031
1Ch 29:11 kingdom; you are exalted as h over all. H8031
2Ch 7: 5 thousand *h of* **cattle** and a hundred and AIT
2Ch 15:11 LORD seven hundred *h of* **cattle** and seven AIT
2Ch 20:21 they went out **at the h of** the army, H4200+7156
2Ch 35: 9 five hundred *h of* **cattle** for the Levites. AIT
Ezr 9: 3 pulled hair from my h and beard and sat H8031
Ne 6: 8 you are just making it up out of your h." H4213
Est 2:17 royal crown on her h and made her queen H8031
Est 6: 8 one with a royal crest placed on its h. H8031
Est 6:12 rushed home, with his h covered in grief, H8031

Est 9:25 Jews should come back onto his own **h**, H8031
Job 1:20 up and tore his robe and shaved his **h**. H8031
Job 2: 7 the soles of his feet to the **crown of** his **h**. H7721
Job 10:15 I cannot lift my **h**, for I am full of shame H8031
Job 10:16 If I **hold** my **h high**, you stalk me like a H1448
Job 16: 4 against you and shake my **h** at you. H8031
Job 19: 9 honor and removed the crown from my **h**. H8031
Job 20: 6 the heavens and his **h** touches the clouds, H8031
Job 29: 3 his lamp shone on my **h** and by his light I H8031
Job 41: 7 with harpoons or its **h** with fishing spears? H8031
Ps 3: 3 my glory, the One who lifts my **h** high. H8031
Ps 18:43 you have made me the **h** *of* nations. H8031
Ps 21: 3 placed a crown of pure gold on his **h**. H8031
Ps 23: 5 You anoint my **h** with oil; my cup H8031
Ps 27: 6 Then my **h** will be exalted above the H8031
Ps 35:14 ***I* bowed *my* h** in grief as though weeping H8820
Ps 40:12 They are more than the hairs of my **h**, and H8031
Ps 69: 4 reason outnumber the hairs of my **h**; H8031
Ps 110: 7 the way, and so he will lift his **h** high. H8031
Ps 132:18 but **his *h*** will be adorned with a radiant AIT
Ps 133: 2 It is like precious oil poured on the **h** H8031
Ps 140: 7 you shield my **h** in the day of battle. H8031
Ps 141: 5 let him rebuke me—that is oil on my **h**. H8031
Ps 141: 5 My **h** will not refuse it, for my prayer will H8031
Pr 1: 9 to grace your **h** and a chain to adorn H8031
Pr 4: 9 to grace your **h** and present you with H8031
Pr 10: 6 Blessings crown the **h** *of* the righteous H8031
Pr 25:22 you will heap burning coals on his **h**, and H8031
Ecc 9: 8 and always anoint your **h** with oil. H8031
SS 2: 6 His left arm is under my **h**, and his right H8031
SS 5: 2 My **h** is drenched with dew, my hair with H8031
SS 5:11 His **h** is purest gold; his hair is wavy and H8031
SS 7: 5 Your **h** crowns you like Mount Carmel H8031
SS 8: 3 left arm is under my **h** and his right arm H8031
Isa 1: 5 Your whole **h** is injured, your whole heart H8031
Isa 1: 6 of your foot to the *top of* your **h** there is no H8031
Isa 7: 8 the **h** *of* Aram is Damascus, and the H8031
Isa 7: 8 the **h** *of* Damascus is only Rezin. H8031
Isa 7: 9 The **h** *of* Ephraim is Samaria, and the H8031
Isa 7: 9 the **h** *of* Samaria is only Remaliah's H8031
Isa 7:20 Assyria—to shave your **h** and private parts H8031
Isa 9:14 will cut off from Israel both **h** and tail, H8031
Isa 9:15 the elders and dignitaries are the **h**, the H8031
Isa 15: 2 Every **h** is shaved and every beard cut off. H8031
Isa 19:15 Egypt can do—**h** or tail, palm branch H8031
Isa 28: 1 set on the **h** *of* a fertile valley—to H8031
Isa 28: 4 set on the **h** *of* a fertile valley, will H8031
Isa 37:22 Jerusalem tosses her **h** as you flee. H8031
Isa 58: 5 bowing one's **h** like a reed and for H8031
Isa 59:17 the helmet of salvation on his **h**; he H8031
Isa 61:10 as a bridegroom **adorns** his **h** like a priest H6996
Jer 2:37 that place with your hands on your **h**, H8031
Jer 9: 1 that my **h** were a spring of water and my H8031
Jer 16: 6 themselves or **shave** *their* **h** for the dead. H7942
Jer 47: 5 Gaza *will* **shave** *her* **h in mourning** H995+7947
Jer 48:27 that *you* **shake** *your* **h in scorn** whenever H5653
Jer 48:37 Every **h** is shaved and every beard cut off H8031
La 3:54 the waters closed over my **h**, and I H8031
La 5:16 The crown has fallen from our **h**. Woe to H8031
Eze 5: 1 razor to shave your **h** and your beard. H8031
Eze 7:18 with shame, and every **h** will be shaved. H8031
Eze 8: 3 a hand and took me by the hair of my **h**. H8031
Eze 10:11 went in whatever direction the **h** faced, H8031
Eze 16:12 your ears and a beautiful crown on your **h**. H8031
Eze 16:43 bring down on your **h** what you have done H8031
Eze 18:13 put to death; his blood will be on his own **h**. NDT
Eze 29:18 every **h** was rubbed bare and every H8031
Eze 33: 4 their blood will be on their own **h**. H8031
Eze 33: 5 warning, their blood will be on their own **h**. NDT
Da 1:10 would then have my **h** because of you." H8031
Da 2:32 The **h** *of* the statue was made of pure A10646
Da 2:38 over them all. You are that **h** of gold. A10646
Da 7: 9 the hair of his **h** was white like wool. A10646
Da 7:20 ten horns on its **h** and about the other A10646
Hos 8: 7 The stalk has no **h**; it will produce no flour H7542
Joel 2:11 The LORD thunders at the **h** *of* his army; his H7156
Am 3:12 with only the **h** *of* a bed and a piece of H6991
Ob 15 your deeds will return upon your own **h**. H8031
Jnh 2: 5 seaweed was wrapped around my **h**. H8031
Jnh 4: 6 to give shade for his **h** to ease his H8031
Jnh 4: 8 blazed on Jonah's **h** so that he grew faint H8031
Mic 1:16 **Shave** *your* **h** in mourning for the H7942+1605
Mic 2:13 through before them, the LORD at their **h**." H8031
Hab 3:13 you stripped him from **h** to foot. H7418
Hab 3:14 spear you pierced his **h** when his warriors H8031
Zec 1:21 Judah so that no one could raise their **h**, H8031
Zec 3: 5 "Put a clean turban on his **h**." So they put H8031
Zec 3: 5 a clean turban on his **h** and clothed him, H8031
Zec 6:11 set it on the **h** *of* the high priest H8031
Mt 5:36 And do not swear by your **h**, for you cannot *G3051*
Mt 6:17 put oil on your **h** and wash your face, *G3051*
Mt 8:20 the Son of Man has no place to lay his **h**." *G3051*
Mt 10:25 If the **h of the house** has been called *G3867*
Mt 10:30 the very hairs *of* your **h** are all numbered. *G3051*
Mt 14: 8 on a platter the **h** of John the Baptist." *G3051*
Mt 14:11 His **h** was brought in on a platter and *G3051*
Mt 26: 7 she poured on his **h** as he was reclining *G3051*
Mt 27:29 a crown of thorns and set it on his **h**. *G3051*
Mt 27:30 struck him on the **h** again and again. *G3051*
Mt 27:37 Above his **h** they placed the written charge *G3051*
Mk 4:28 the stalk, then the **h**, then the full kernel *G5092*
Mk 4:28 the head, then the full kernel in the **h**. *G5092*

Mk 6:24 "The **h** of John the Baptist," she *G3051*
Mk 6:25 me right now the **h** of John the Baptist *G3051*
Mk 6:27 executioner with orders to bring John's **h**. *G3051*
Mk 6:28 brought back his **h** on a platter. *G3051*
Mk 12: 4 *they* **struck** this man **on the h** and treated *G3052*
Mk 14: 3 the jar and poured the perfume *on* his **h**. *G3051*
Mk 15:19 they struck him *on* the **h** with a staff and *G3051*
Lk 7:46 You did not put oil on my **h**, but she has *G3051*
Lk 9:58 the Son of Man has no place to lay his **h**." *G3051*
Lk 12: 7 the very hairs *of* your **h** are all numbered. *G3051*
Lk 21:18 But not a hair of your **h** will perish. *G3051*
Jn 13: 9 my feet but my hands and my **h** as well!" *G3051*
Jn 19: 2 a crown of thorns and put it on his **h**. *G3051*
Jn 19:30 he bowed his **h** and gave up his spirit. *G3051*
Jn 20: 7 that had been wrapped around Jesus' **h**. *G3051*
Jn 20:12 one at the **h** and the other at the foot. *G3051*
Ac 27:15 by the storm and could not **h into** the wind; *G535*
Ac 27:34 of you will lose a single hair from his **h**." *G3051*
Ro 12:20 you will heap burning coals on his **h**." *G3051*
1Co 11: 3 to realize that the **h** of every man is Christ, *G3051*
1Co 11: 3 is Christ, and the **h** of the woman is man *G3051*
1Co 11: 3 woman is man, and the **h** of Christ is God. *G3051*
1Co 11: 4 prophesies with his **h** covered dishonors *G3051*
1Co 11: 4 with his head covered dishonors his **h**. *G3051*
1Co 11: 5 with her **h** uncovered dishonors *G3051*
1Co 11: 5 her head uncovered dishonors her **h**— *G3051*
1Co 11: 5 it is the same as having her **h** shaved. NDT
1Co 11: 6 For if a woman does not cover her **h**, she NDT
1Co 11: 6 to have her hair cut off or her **h** shaved, NDT
1Co 11: 6 head shaved, then she should cover her **h**. NDT
1Co 11: 7 A man ought not to cover his **h**, since he *G3051*
1Co 11:10 ought to have authority over her own **h**, *G3051*
1Co 11:13 to pray to God with her **h** uncovered? NDT
1Co 12:21 And the **h** cannot say to the feet, "I don't *G3051*
Eph 1:22 appointed him to be **h** over everything *G3051*
Eph 4:15 the mature body of him who is the **h**, *G3051*
Eph 5:23 the husband is the **h** of the wife as Christ *G3051*
Eph 5:23 of the wife as Christ is the **h** of the church, *G3051*
Col 1:18 And he is the **h** of the body, the church; he *G3051*
Col 2:10 He is the **h** over every power and authority *G3051*
Col 2:19 They have lost connection *with* the **h**, from *G3051*
2Ti 4: 5 **keep** *your* **h** in all situations *G3768*
Rev 1:14 The hair *on* his **h** was white like wool, as *G3051*
Rev 10: 1 with a rainbow above his **h**; his face was *G3051*
Rev 12: 1 feet and a crown of twelve stars on her **h**. *G3051*
Rev 13: 1 on each **h** a blasphemous name. *G3051*
Rev 14:14 crown of gold on his **h** and a sharp sickle *G3051*
Rev 19:12 and on his **h** are many crowns. *G3051*

HEADBAND (2) [HEADBANDS]

1Ki 20:38 himself with his **h** down over his eyes. H710
1Ki 20:41 quickly removed the **h** from his eyes, H710

HEADBANDS (1) [HEADBAND]

Isa 3:18 the bangles and **h** and crescent necklaces, H8667

HEADDRESSES (1)

Isa 3:20 the **h** and anklets and sashes, the perfume H6996

HEADED (6) [HEAD]

Ge 31:21 and **h for** the hill country of Gilead. H8492
Ex 9:31 since the barley had **h** and the flax was in H26
Jos 15: 9 the boundary **h** toward the spring of H9305
Jos 18:12 slope of Jericho and **h** west into the hill H6590
Jer 39: 4 the two walls, and **h** toward the Arabah. H3655
Jnh 1: 3 ran away from the LORD and **h** for Tarshish. NDT

HEADING (2) [HEAD]

Lk 9:53 because he was **h** for Jerusalem. *G4513*
Jn 6:21 reached the shore where *they were* **h**. *G5632*

HEADLONG (4)

2Ki 7:15 had thrown away in their **h flight**. H2905
Job 27:22 without mercy *as he* **flees h** from its H1368+1368
Hab 1: 8 Their cavalry **gallops h**; their horsemen H7055
Ac 1:18 a field; there *he* **fell h**, his body *G4568+1181*

HEADS (179) [HEAD]

Ge 40:20 He lifted up the **h** *of* the chief cupbearer H8031
Ge 41: 5 Seven **h of grain**, healthy and good, were H8672
Ge 41: 6 seven other **h of grain** sprouted—thin H8672
Ge 41: 7 The thin **h of grain** swallowed up the H8672
Ge 41: 7 swallowed up the seven healthy, full **h**. H8672
Ge 41:22 "In my dream I saw seven **h of grain**, full H8672
Ge 41:23 seven other **h** sprouted—withered H8672
Ge 41:24 The thin **h of grain** swallowed up the H8672
Ge 41:24 of grain swallowed up the seven good **h**. H8672
Ge 41:26 the seven good **h of grain** are seven years H8672
Ge 41:27 seven worthless **h of grain** scorched by the H8672
Ex 6:14 These were the **h** *of* their families: The H8031
Ex 6:25 These were the **h** *of* the Levite families H8031
Lev 2:14 offer crushed **h** *of* new grain roasted in the H26
Lev 20:11 to death; their blood will be on their own **h**. NDT
Lev 20:12 their blood will be on their own **h**. NDT
Lev 20:13 to death; their blood will be on their own **h**. NDT
Lev 20:16 to death; their blood will be on their own **h**. NDT
Lev 20:27 their blood will be on their own **h**. NDT
Lev 21: 5 must not shave their **h** or shave off the H8031
Lev 26:13 enabled you to walk **with h held high**. H7758
Nu 1:16 They were the **h** *of* the clans of Israel. H8031
Nu 7: 2 the **h** *of* families who were the tribal H8031
Nu 8:12 to lay their hands on the **h** *of* the bulls, H8031
Nu 10: 4 the leaders—the **h** *of* the clans of Israel H8031

Nu 30: 1 Moses said to the **h** *of* the tribes of Israel H8031
Nu 31:26 the family **h** *of* the community are to H8031
Nu 32:28 Nun and to the family **h** of the Israelite H8031
Nu 36: 1 The family **h** of the clan of Gilead son of H8031
Nu 36: 1 the leaders, the **h** of the Israelite families. H8031
Dt 14: 1 shave the **front of** your **h** for the H1068+6524
Dt 32:42 the captives, the **h** *of* the enemy leaders." H8031
Dt 33:21 When the **h** *of* the people assembled, he H8031
Jos 2:19 their blood will be on their own **h**; we will H8031
Jos 7: 6 the same, and sprinkled dust on their **h**. H8031
Jos 14: 1 son of Nun and the **h** *of* the tribal clans of H8031
Jos 19:51 son of Nun and the **h** *of* the tribal clans of H8031
Jos 21: 1 Now the family **h** *of* the Levites H8031
Jos 21: 1 the **h** *of* the other tribal families of H8031
Jos 22:21 replied to the **h** *of* the clans of Israel: H8031
Jos 22:30 the **h** *of* the clans of the Israelites H8031
Jdg 7:25 brought the **h** *of* Oreb and Zeeb to H8031
1Sa 29: 4 than by taking the **h** *of* our own men? H8031
2Sa 15:30 him covered their **h** too and were H8031
1Ki 8: 1 all the **h** *of* the tribes and the chiefs of the H8031
1Ki 8:32 down on their **h** what they have done, H8031
1Ki 20:31 our waists and ropes around our **h**. H8031
1Ki 20:32 their waists and ropes around their **h**, H8031
2Ki 4:42 along with *some* **h of new grain**. H4152
2Ki 10: 6 take the **h** *of* your master's sons and come H8031
2Ki 10: 7 They put their **h** in baskets and sent them H8031
2Ki 10: 8 "They have brought the **h** *of* the princes." H8031
1Ch 5:24 These were the **h** *of* their families: Epher H8031
1Ch 5:24 famous men, and **h** of their families. H8031
1Ch 7: 2 Ibsam and Samuel—**h** of their families. H8031
1Ch 7: 7 Jerimoth and Iri, **h** *of* families—five in all. H8031
1Ch 7: 9 record listed the **h** of families and 20,200 H8031
1Ch 7:11 these sons of Jediael were **h** *of* families. H8031
1Ch 7:40 of Asher—**h** *of* families, choice men H8031
1Ch 8: 6 who were **h** *of* families of those living in H8031
1Ch 8:10 These were his sons, **h** *of* families. H8031
1Ch 8:13 who were **h** *of* families of those living in H8031
1Ch 8:28 All these were **h** *of* families, chiefs as H8031
1Ch 9: 9 All these men were **h** of their families. H8031
1Ch 9:13 who were **h** of families, numbered H8031
1Ch 9:33 who were musicians, **h** of Levite families H8031
1Ch 9:34 All these were **h** of Levite families, chiefs H8031
1Ch 12:19 "It will cost us our **h** if he deserts to his H8031
1Ch 15:12 "You are the **h** of the Levitical families H8031
1Ch 23: 9 These were the **h** *of* the families of Ladan. H8031
1Ch 23:24 the **h** *of* families as they were registered H8031
1Ch 24: 4 sixteen **h** of families from Eleazar's H8031
1Ch 24: 4 descendants and eight **h** of families from NDT
1Ch 24: 6 of Abiathar and the **h** *of* families of the H8031
1Ch 24:31 the **h** *of* families of the priests and of H8031
1Ch 26:21 Ladan and who were **h** *of* families H8031
1Ch 26:26 by the **h** *of* families who were the H8031
1Ch 26:32 who were able men and **h** *of* families H8031
1Ch 27: 1 of the Israelites—**h** *of* families H8031
2Ch 1: 2 the leaders in Israel, the **h** *of* families— H8031
2Ch 5: 2 all the **h** *of* the tribes and the chiefs of the H8031
2Ch 6:23 down on their **h** what they have done, H8031
2Ch 19: 8 priests and **h** of Israelite families to H8031
2Ch 23: 2 the Levites and the **h** of Israelite families H8031
Ezr 1: 5 Then the family **h** of Judah and Benjamin, H8031
Ezr 2:68 some of the **h** *of* the families gave H8031
Ezr 3:12 the older priests and Levites and family **h**, H8031
Ezr 4: 2 to the **h** *of* the families and H8031
Ezr 4: 3 the rest of the **h** *of* the families of H8031
Ezr 8: 1 are the family **h** and those registered H8031
Ezr 8:29 the Levites and the family **h** of Israel." H8569
Ezr 9: 6 are higher than our **h** and our guilt has H8031
Ezr 10:16 priest selected men who were family **h**, H8031
Ne 4: 4 Turn their insults back on their own **h** H8031
Ne 7:70 Some of the **h** *of* the families contributed H8031
Ne 7:71 Some of the **h** *of* the families gave to the H8031
Ne 8:13 day of the month, the **h** of all the families H8031
Ne 9: 1 sackcloth and putting dust on their **h**. NDT
Ne 11:13 who were **h** of families—242 men; H8031
Ne 11:16 Jozabad, two of the **h** *of* the Levites, who H8031
Ne 12:12 these were the **h** *of* the priestly families: H8031
Ne 12:22 The family **h** of the Levites in the days of H8031
Ne 12:23 The family **h** among the descendants of H8031
Job 2:12 their robes and sprinkled dust on their **h**. H8031
Job 24:24 all others; they are cut off like **h** *of* grain. H8672
Ps 7:16 their violence comes down on their own **h**. H7721
Ps 22: 7 they hurl insults, shaking their **h**. H8031
Ps 24: 7 Lift up your **h**, you gates; be lifted up, you H8031
Ps 24: 9 Lift up your **h**, you gates; lift them up, you H8031
Ps 44:14 nations; the peoples shake their **h** at us. H8031
Ps 64: 8 who see them *will* **shake** *their* **h in scorn**. H5653
Ps 66:12 You let people ride over our **h**; we went H8031
Ps 68:21 God will crush the **h** *of* his enemies, H8031
Ps 74:13 you broke the **h** *of* the monster in the H8031
Ps 74:14 who crushed the **h** *of* Leviathan and gave H8031
Ps 83: 2 enemies growl, how your foes rear their **h**. H8031
Ps 109:25 when they see me, they shake their **h**. H8031
Ps 140: 9 who surround me proudly rear their **h**; H8031
Ecc 2:14 The wise have eyes in their **h**, while the H8031
Isa 3:17 bring sores on the **h** of the women of Zion H7721
Isa 17: 5 someone gleans **h of grain** in the Valley H8672
Isa 29:10 he has covered your **h** (the seers). H8031
Isa 35:10 singing; everlasting joy will crown their **h**. H8031
Isa 51:11 singing; everlasting joy will crown their **h**. H8031
Jer 13:18 your glorious crowns will fall from your **h**." H5265
Jer 14: 3 despairing, they cover their **h**. H8031
Jer 14: 4 farmers are dismayed and cover their **h**. H8031

Jer 18:16 by will be appalled and will shake their **h**. H8031
Jer 23:19 swirling down on the **h** *of* the wicked. H8031
Jer 30:23 swirling down on the **h** *of* the wicked. H8031
La 2:10 dust on their **h** and put on sackcloth. H8031
La 2:10 have bowed their **h** to the ground. H8031
La 2:15 shake their **h** at Daughter Jerusalem H8031
Eze 1:22 Spread out above the **h** *of* the living H8031
Eze 1:25 the vault over their **h** as they stood with H8031
Eze 1:26 the vault over their **h** was what looked like H8031
Eze 9:10 down on their own **h** what they have done H8031
Eze 10: 1 vault that was over the **h** *of* the cherubim. H8031
Eze 11:21 down on their own **h** what they have done H8031
Eze 13:18 lengths for their **h** in order to ensnare H8031
Eze 22:31 down on their own **h** all they have done, H8031
Eze 23:15 waists and flowing turbans on their **h**; H8031
Eze 23:42 her sister and beautiful crowns on their **h**. H8031
Eze 24:23 turbans on your **h** and your sandals on H8031
Eze 27:30 sprinkle dust on their **h** and roll in ashes. H8031
Eze 27:31 *They will* **shave** *their* **h** because of H7942+7947
Eze 32:27 placed under their **h** and their shields H8031
Eze 44:18 linen turbans on their **h** and linen H8031
Eze 44:20 must not shave their **h** or let their hair H8031
Eze 44:20 are to keep the hair of their **h** trimmed. H8031
Da 3:27 was a hair of their **h** singed; their A10646
Da 7: 6 This beast had four **h**, and it was given A10646
Joel 3: 4 return on your own **h** what you have done. H8031
Joel 3: 7 return on your own **h** what you have done. H8031
Am 2: 7 trample on the **h** *of* the poor as on the H8031
Am 8:10 of you wear sackcloth and shave your **h**. H8031
Am 9: 1 them down on the **h** *of* all the people; H8031
Mt 12: 1 to pick *some* **h of grain** and eat them G5092
Mt 13:26 When the wheat sprouted and formed **h** G2843
Mt 27:39 by hurled insults at him, shaking their **h** G3051
Mk 2:23 they began to pick some **h of grain**. G5092
Mk 15:29 shaking their **h** and saying, "So! G3051
Lk 6: 1 disciples began to pick some **h of grain**, G5092
Lk 21:28 stand up and lift up your **h**, because your G3051
Ac 18: 6 to them, "Your blood be on your own **h**! G3051
Ac 21:24 so that they can have their **h** shaved. G3051
Rev 4: 4 white and had crowns of gold on their **h**. G3051
Rev 9: 7 On their **h** they wore something like G3051
Rev 9:17 The **h** of the horses resembled the heads G3051
Rev 9:17 of the horses resembled the **h** of lions, G3051
Rev 9:19 having **h** with which they inflict injury. G3051
Rev 12: 3 dragon with seven **h** and ten horns and G3051
Rev 12: 3 ten horns and seven crowns on its **h**. G3051
Rev 13: 1 It had ten horns and seven **h**, with ten G3051
Rev 13: 3 One of the **h** of the beast seemed to have G3051
Rev 17: 3 names and had seven **h** and ten horns. G3051
Rev 17: 7 which has the seven **h** and ten horns. G3051
Rev 17: 9 The seven **h** are seven hills on which the G3051
Rev 18:19 They will throw dust on their **h**, and with G3051

HEADWATERS (1) [WATER]

Ge 2:10 from there it was separated into four **h**. H8031

HEADWAY (1)

Ac 27: 7 *We* **made slow h** for many days and had G1095

HEAL (43) [HEALED, HEALING, HEALS]

Nu 12:13 cried out to the LORD, "Please, God, **h** her!" H8324
Dt 32:39 I have wounded and I *will* **h**, and no one H8324
2Ki 20: 5 prayer and seen your tears; I *will* **h** you. H8324
2Ki 20: 8 sign that the LORD *will* **h** me and that I will H8324
2Ch 7:14 will forgive their sin and *will* **h** their land. H8324
Job 5:18 binds up; he injures, but his hands also **h**. H8324
Ps 6: 2 for I am faint; **h** me, LORD, for my H8324
Ps 41: 4 mercy on me, LORD; **h** me, for I have H8324
Ecc 3: 3 a time to kill and a time to **h**, a time to H8324
Isa 19:22 a plague; he will strike them and **h** them. H8324
Isa 19:22 he will respond to their pleas and **h** them. H8324
Isa 57:18 their ways, but *I will* **h** them; I will guide H8324
Isa 57:19 says the LORD. "And *I will* **h** them." H8324
Jer 17:14 **H** me, LORD, and I will be healed; save me H8324
Jer 30:17 restore you to health and **h** your wounds, H8324
Jer 33: 6 *I will* **h** my people and will let them enjoy H8324
La 2:13 is as deep as the sea. Who *can* **h** you? H8324
Hos 5:13 able to cure you, not able *to* **h** your sores. H1564
Hos 6: 1 He has torn us to pieces but *he will* **h** us H8324
Hos 7: 1 whenever I *would* **h** Israel, the sins of H8324
Hos 14: 4 "*I will* **h** their waywardness and love them H8324
Na 3:19 Nothing can **h** you; your H3911+4200+8691
Zec 11:16 seek the young, or **h** the injured, or feed H8324
Mt 8: 7 said to him, "Shall I come and **h** him?" G2543
Mt 10: 1 impure spirits and *to* **h** every disease and G2543
Mt 10: 8 **H** the sick, raise the dead, cleanse those G2543
Mt 12:10 "Is it lawful *to* **h** on the Sabbath?" G2543
Mt 13:15 their hearts and turn, and *I would* **h** them. G2615
Mt 17:16 your disciples, but *they* could not **h** him." G2543
Mk 3: 2 closely to see if *he would* **h** him on the G2543
Mk 6: 5 hands on a few sick people and **h** them. G2543
Lk 4:23 'Physician, **h** yourself!' And you G2543
Lk 5:17 of the Lord was with Jesus to **h the sick**. G2615
Lk 6: 7 to see if *he would* **h** on the Sabbath. G2543
Lk 7: 3 asking him to come and **h** his servant. G1407
Lk 8:43 twelve years, but no one could **h** her. G2543
Lk 9: 2 the kingdom of God and *to* **h** the sick. G2615
Lk 10: 9 **H** the sick who are there and tell them G2543
Lk 14: 3 "Is it lawful *to* **h** on the Sabbath or not?" G2543
Jn 4:47 begged him to come and **h** his son, G2615
Jn 12:40 nor turn—and *I would* **h** them. G2615
Ac 4:30 out your hand to **h** and perform signs and G2617
Ac 28:27 their hearts and turn, and *I would* **h** them. G2615

HEALED (75) [HEAL]

Ge 20:17 and God **h** Abimelek, his wife H8324
Ex 21:19 **see that** the victim **is completely h**. H8324+8324
Lev 13:37 has grown in it, the affected person *is* **h**. H8324
Lev 14: 3 If they *have* **been h** of their defiling skin H8324
Jos 5: 8 they were in camp until they *were* **h**. H2649
1Sa 6: 3 Then *you will* **be h**, and you will know H8324
2Ki 2:21 the LORD says: '*I have* **h** this water. H8324
2Ch 30:20 LORD heard Hezekiah and **h** the people. H8324
Ps 30: 2 I called to you for help, and *you* **h** me. H8324
Ps 107:20 He sent out his word and **h** them; he H8324
Isa 6:10 with their hearts, and turn and *be* **h**." H8324
Isa 53: 5 was on him, and by his wounds we **are h**. H8324
Jer 14:19 you afflicted us so that we cannot be **h**? H5340
Jer 17:14 and *I will* **be h**; save me and I will H8324
Jer 51: 8 balm for her pain; perhaps *she can* **be h**. H8324
Jer 51: 9 " '*We would have* **h** Babylon, but she H8324
Jer 51: 9 Babylon, but *she* cannot **be h**; let us leave H8324
Eze 30:21 been bound up to be **h** or put in a splint H8337
Eze 34: 4 the weak or **h** the sick or bound up the H8324
Hos 11: 3 they did not realize *it was I who* **h** them. H8324
Mt 4:24 the paralyzed; and *he* **h** them. G2543
Mt 8: 8 say the word, and my servant *will be* **h**. G2615
Mt 8:13 And his servant *was* **h** at that moment. G2615
Mt 8:16 the spirits with a word and **h** all the sick. G2543
Mt 9:21 "If I only touch his cloak, *I will be* **h**." G5392
Mt 9:22 daughter," he said, "your faith *has* **h** you." G5392
Mt 9:22 And the woman *was* **h** at that moment. G5392
Mt 12:15 followed him, and *he* **h** all who were **ill**. G2543
Mt 12:22 mute, and Jesus **h** him, so that he G2543
Mt 14:14 had compassion on them and **h** their sick. G2543
Mt 14:36 his cloak, and all who touched it *were* **h**. G1407
Mt 15:28 And her daughter *was* **h** at that moment. G2615
Mt 15:30 laid them at his feet; and *he* **h** them. G2543
Mt 17:18 of the boy, and he *was* **h** at that moment. G2543
Mt 19: 2 followed him, and *he* **h** them there. G2543
Mt 21:14 to him at the temple, and *he* **h** them. G2543
Mk 1:34 Jesus **h** many who had various G2543
Mk 3:10 For *he had* **h** many, so that those with G2543
Mk 5:23 on her so that *she will be* **h** and live." G5392
Mk 5:28 "If I just touch his clothes, *I will be* **h**." G5392
Mk 5:34 "Daughter, your faith *has* **h** you. G5392
Mk 6:13 many sick people with oil and **h** them. G2543
Mk 6:56 his cloak, and all who touched it *were* **h**. G5392
Mk 10:52 "your faith *has* **h** you." Immediately G5392
Lk 4:40 laying his hands on each one, *he* **h** them. G2543
Lk 5:15 to hear him and *to be* **h** of their G2543
Lk 6:18 to hear him and *to be* **h** of their diseases. G2615
Lk 7: 7 say the word, and my servant *will be* **h**. G2615
Lk 8:47 him and how *she had been* instantly **h**. G2615
Lk 8:48 "Daughter, your faith *has* **h** you. G5392
Lk 8:50 be afraid; just believe, and *she will be* **h**." G5392
Lk 9:11 and **h** those who needed healing. G2615
Lk 9:42 **h** the boy and gave him back to his father. G2615
Lk 13:14 because Jesus *had* **h** on the Sabbath, G2543
Lk 13:14 So come and *be* **h** on those days, not on G2543
Lk 14: 4 *he* **h** him and sent him on his way. G2615
Lk 17:15 when he saw *he was* **h**, came back, G2615
Lk 18:42 "Receive your sight; your faith *has* **h** you." G5392
Lk 22:51 And he touched the man's ear and **h** him. G2615
Jn 5:10 leaders said *to the man who had been* **h**, G2543
Jn 5:13 The *man who was* **h** had no idea who it G2615
Ac 3:16 *that has* **completely h** G1443+3836+3907+4047
Ac 4: 9 lame and are being asked how he *was* **h**, G5392
Ac 4:10 that this man stands before you **h**. G5618
Ac 4:14 the man who *had been* **h** standing there G2543
Ac 4:22 was miraculously **h** was over forty years G2617
Ac 5:16 by impure spirits, and all of them *were* **h**. G2543
Ac 8: 7 who were paralyzed or lame *were* **h**. G2543
Ac 14: 9 saw that he had faith *to be* **h** G5392
Ac 28: 8 placed his hands on him and **h** him. G2615
Heb 12:13 lame may not be disabled, but rather **h**. G2615
Jas 5:16 pray for each other so that *you may be* **h**. G2615
1Pe 2:24 "by his wounds *you have been* **h**." G2615
Rev 13: 3 but the fatal wound *had been* **h**. G2543
Rev 13:12 whose fatal wound *had been* **h**. G2543

HEALING (27) [HEAL]

2Ch 28:15 sandals, food and drink, and **h balm**. H6057
Pr 12:18 the tongue of the wise brings **h**. H5340
Pr 13:17 trouble, but a trustworthy envoy brings **h**. H5340
Pr 16:24 sweet to the soul and **h** to the bones. H5340
Isa 58: 8 the dawn, and your **h** will quickly appear H776
Jer 8:15 a time of **h** but there is only terror. H5340
Jer 8:22 is there no **h for the wound** *of* my people? H776
Jer 14:19 a time of **h** but there is only terror. H5340
Jer 30:12 wound is incurable, your injury **beyond h**. H2703
Jer 30:13 no remedy for your sore, no **h** for you. H9499
Jer 33: 6 I will bring health and **h** to it; I will heal H5340
Jer 46:11 medicines in vain; there is no **h** for you. H9499
Eze 47:12 will serve for food and their leaves for **h**." H9559
Mal 4: 2 of righteousness will rise with **h** in its rays. H5340
Mt 4:23 **h** every disease and sickness among G2543
Mt 9:35 of the kingdom and **h** every disease and G2543
Lk 6:19 was coming from him and **h** them all. G2615
Lk 9: 6 the good news and **h** people everywhere. G2543
Lk 9:11 and healed those who needed **h**. G2542
Lk 13:32 out demons and **h** *people* today and G2617+699
Jn 6: 2 signs he had performed **by h** the sick. G2093S
Jn 7:23 angry with me for **h** a man's whole G5618+4472
Ac 10:38 doing good and **h** all who were under G2615
1Co 12: 9 to another gifts *of* **h** by that one Spirit, G2611
1Co 12:28 miracles, then gifts *of* **h**, of helping, of G2611
1Co 12:30 Do all have gifts *of* **h**? Do all speak in G2611
Rev 22: 2 of the tree are for the **h** of the nations. G2542

HEALS (6) [HEAL]

Ex 15:26 Egyptians, for I am the LORD, *who* **h** you." H8324
Lev 13:18 someone has a boil on their skin and *it* **h**, H8324
Ps 103: 3 all your sins and **h** all your diseases, H8324
Ps 147: 3 He **h** the brokenhearted and binds up H8324
Isa 30:26 of his people and **h** the wounds he H8324
Ac 9:34 Peter said to him, "Jesus Christ **h** you. G2615

HEALTH (13) [HEALTHIER, HEALTHY]

1Sa 16:12 He was **glowing with h** and had a fine H145
1Sa 17:42 than a boy, **glowing with h** and handsome H145
1Sa 25: 6 **Good h** to you and your household H8934
1Sa 25: 6 And **good h** to all that is yours! H8934
Ps 38: 3 of your wrath there is no **h** in my body; H5507
Ps 38: 7 searing pain; there is no **h** in my body. H5507
Pr 3: 8 This will bring **h** to your body and H8326
Pr 4:22 who find them and **h** to one's whole body H5340
Pr 15:30 good news **gives h** *to* the bones. H2014
Isa 38:16 *You* **restored** me **to h** and let me live. H2730
Jer 30:17 will restore you to **h** and heal your wounds, H776
Jer 33: 6 I will bring **h** and healing to it; I will H776
3Jn 2 I pray *that* you *may* **enjoy good h** and that G5617

HEALTHIER (1) [HEALTH]

Da 1:15 days they looked **h** and better nourished H3202

HEALTHY (9) [HEALTH]

Ge 41: 5 Seven heads of grain, **h** and good, were H1374
Ge 41: 7 heads of grain swallowed up the seven **h**, H1374
Ps 73: 4 struggles; their bodies are **h** and strong. H1374
Zec 11:16 injured, or feed the **h**, but will eat the H5893
Mt 6:22 If your eyes are **h**, your whole body will be G606
Mt 9:12 "It is not the **h** who need a doctor G2710
Mk 2:17 "It is not the **h** who need a doctor G2710
Lk 5:31 "It is not the **h** who need a doctor G5617
Lk 11:34 When your eyes are **h**, your whole body G606

HEAP (34) [HEAPED, HEAPING, HEAPS]

Ge 31:46 So they took stones and piled them in a **h**, H1643
Ge 31:46 in a heap, and they ate there by the **h**. H1643
Ge 31:48 "This **h** is a witness between you and me H1643
Ge 31:51 to Jacob, "Here is this **h**, and here is this H1643
Ge 31:52 This **h** is a witness, and this pillar is a H1643
Ge 31:52 will not go past this **h** to your side to harm H1643
Ge 31:52 not go past this **h** and pillar to my side H1643
Lev 4:12 burn it there in a wood fire on the ash **h**. H9162
Dt 32:23 "*I will* **h** calamities on them and spend H3578
Jos 3:13 will be cut off and stand up in a **h**. H5603
Jos 3:16 It piled up in a **h** a great distance away H5603
Jos 8:28 Ai and made it a permanent **h of ruins**, H9424
1Sa 2: 8 the dust and lifts the needy from the **ash h**; H883
2Sa 18:17 piled up a large **h** *of* rocks over him. H1643
1Ki 9: 8 This temple will become a **h of rubble** H6505
2Ch 7:21 This temple will become a **h of rubble** H6505
Ps 113: 7 the dust and lifts the needy from the **ash h**; H883
Pr 25:22 you *will* **h** burning coals on his head H3149
Isa 3: 6 our leader; take charge of this **h of ruins**!" H4843
Isa 17: 1 be a city but will become a **h** *of* ruins. H5075
Isa 25: 2 You have made the city a **h of rubble**, the H1643
Jer 9:11 "I will make Jerusalem a **h of ruins**, H1643
Jer 26:18 Jerusalem will become a **h of rubble**, the H6505
Jer 51:37 Babylon will be a **h of ruins**, a haunt of H1643
Eze 24:10 So **h** *on* the wood and kindle the fire H8049
Mic 1: 6 I will make Samaria a **h of rubble**, H6505
Mic 3:12 Jerusalem will become a **h of rubble**, the H6505
Hag 2:16 anyone came to a **h** *of* twenty measures, H6894
Ro 12:20 *you will* **h** burning coals on his head." G5397
1Th 2:16 way they always **h up** their sins **to the limit**. G405
1Pe 4: 4 wild living, and *they* **h abuse** on you. G1059
2Pe 2:10 they are not afraid *to* **h abuse** on celestial G1059
2Pe 2:11 do not **h** abuse on such beings when NDT
Jude 8 authority and **h abuse on** celestial beings. G1059

HEAPED (5) [HEAP]

Jos 7:26 Over Achan *they* **h up** a large pile of rocks H7756
Zec 9: 3 a stronghold; *she has* **h up** silver like dust H7392
Mt 27:44 crucified with him also **h insults** on him. G3943
Mk 15:32 crucified with him also **h insults on** him. G3943
Ac 13:45 Paul was saying and **h abuse** on him. G1059

HEAPING (3) [HEAP]

Ps 39: 6 **h up wealth** without knowing whose it will H7392
Ps 110: 6 **h up** the dead and crushing the rulers of H4848
Isa 30: 1 not by my Spirit, **h** sin upon sin; H3578

HEAPS (8) [HEAP]

Ex 8:14 They were piled into **h**, and the H2818+2818
2Ch 31: 6 and they piled them **in h**. H6894+6894
2Ch 31: 8 his officials came and saw the **h**, H6894
2Ch 31: 9 asked the priests and Levites about the **h**; H6894
Ne 4: 2 back to life from those **h** *of* rubble— H6894
Job 27:16 Though *he* **h up** silver like dust and H7392
Jer 50:26 her granaries; pile her up like **h of grain**. H6894
La 4: 5 up in royal purple now lie on **ash h**. H883

HEAR (377) [HEARD, HEARERS, HEARING, HEARS, OVERHEARD, OVERHEARING]

Ge 4:23 listen to me; wives of Lamech, **h** my words. H263
Ge 41:15 of you that *when you* **h** a dream you can H9048
Ex 15:14 The nations *will* **h** and tremble; anguish H9048
Ex 18: 9 was delighted to **h** about all the good NDT
Ex 19: 9 that the people *will* **h** me speaking with H9048
Ex 22:23 to me, *I will* **certainly h** their cry. H9048+9048
Ex 22:27 they cry out to me, *I will* **h**, for I am H9048
Ex 32:18 it is the sound of singing that I **h**. H9048
Lev 5: 1 speak up when *they* **h** a public H9048+7754
Nu 14:13 "Then the Egyptians *will* **h** *about* it! H9048
Nu 23:18 and listen; **h** me, son of Zippor. H263
Dt 1:16 "**H** the disputes between your people H9048
Dt 1:17 in judging; **h** both small and great alike. H9048
Dt 1:17 any case too hard for you, and *I will* **h** it." H9048
Dt 2:25 *They will* **h** reports of you and will tremble H9048
Dt 4: 1 **h** the decrees and laws I am about to H9048
Dt 4: 6 who *will* **h** *about* all these decrees and H9048
Dt 4:10 people before me *to* **h** my words so that H9048
Dt 4:28 which cannot see or **h** or eat or smell. H9048
Dt 4:36 From heaven *he* **made** you **h** his voice to H9048
Dt 5: 1 **H**, Israel, the decrees and laws I declare H9048
Dt 5:25 we will die if we **h** the voice of the LORD H9048
Dt 6: 3 **H**, Israel, and be careful to obey so that it H9048
Dt 6: 4 **H**, O Israel: The LORD our God, the LORD is H9048
Dt 9: 1 **H**, Israel: You are now about to cross the H9048
Dt 13:11 Then all Israel *will* **h** and be afraid, and H9048
Dt 13:12 If *you* **h** it said about one of the towns the H9048
Dt 17:13 All the people *will* **h** and be afraid, and H9048
Dt 18:16 "*Let us* not **h** the voice of the LORD our God H9048
Dt 19:20 The rest of the people *will* **h** of this and be H9048
Dt 20: 3 "**H**, Israel: Today you are H9048
Dt 21:21 All Israel *will* **h** of it and be afraid. H9048
Dt 29: 4 eyes that see or ears that **h**. H9048
Dt 31:13 *must* **h** it and learn to fear the LORD your H9048
Dt 32: 1 I will speak; **h**, you earth, the words H9048
Dt 33: 7 "**H**, LORD, the cry of Judah; bring him to his H9048
Jos 6: 5 When you **h** them sound a long blast on H9048
Jos 7: 9 of the country *will* **h** *about* this and they H9048
Jos 22:33 They were glad to **h** the report and praised NDT
Jdg 5: 3 "**H** this, *you* kings! Listen, you rulers! H9048
Jdg 5:16 the sheep pens to **h** the whistling for the H9048
Jdg 14:13 us your riddle," they said. "*Let's* **h** it." H9048
1Sa 2:23 I **h** from all the people *about* these H9048
1Sa 2:24 the report I **h** spreading among the LORD's H9048
1Sa 13: 3 the land and said, "*Let* the Hebrews **h**!" H9048
1Sa 15:14 What is this lowing of cattle that I **h**?" H9048
1Sa 25: 7 " 'Now *I* **h** that it is sheep-shearing time H9048
1Sa 25:24 **h** what your servant has to say. H9048
2Sa 5:24 As soon as you **h** the sound of marching in H9048
2Sa 15: 3 is no representative of the king *to* **h** you." H9048
2Sa 15:10 "As soon as you **h** the sound of the H9048
2Sa 15:35 Tell them anything *you* **h** in the king's H9048
2Sa 15:36 Send them to me with anything *you* **h**." H9048
2Sa 16:21 Then all Israel *will* **h** that you have made H9048
2Sa 17: 5 so *we can* **h** what he has to say as well." H9048
2Sa 18:31 "My lord the king, **h** *the* **good news**! H1413
2Sa 19:35 *Can I* still **h** the voices of male and H9048
2Sa 22:45 as soon as they **h** *of* me, they obey me. H9048
1Ki 1:45 resounds with it. That's the noise *you* **h**. H9048
1Ki 8:28 **H** the cry and the prayer that your servant H9048
1Ki 8:29 so that you *will* **h** the prayer your servant H9048
1Ki 8:30 **H** the supplication of your servant and of H9048
1Ki 8:30 **H** from heaven, your dwelling place, and H9048
1Ki 8:30 dwelling place, and when *you* **h**, forgive. H9048
1Ki 8:32 then **h** from heaven and act. H9048
1Ki 8:34 then **h** from heaven and forgive the sin of H9048
1Ki 8:36 then **h** from heaven and forgive the sin of H9048
1Ki 8:39 then **h** from heaven, your dwelling place H9048
1Ki 8:42 for *they* will **h** *of* your great name and H9048
1Ki 8:43 then **h** from heaven, your dwelling place H9048
1Ki 8:45 then **h** from heaven their prayer and their H9048
1Ki 8:49 **h** their prayer and their plea H9048
1Ki 10: 8 stand before you and **h** your wisdom! H9048
1Ki 10:24 with Solomon to **h** the wisdom God had H9048
1Ki 22:19 "Therefore **h** the word of the LORD: H9048
2Ki 7: 1 Elisha replied, "**H** the word of the LORD H9048
2Ki 7: 6 Lord *had* **caused** the Arameans **to h** the H9048
2Ki 18:28 in Hebrew, "**H** the word of the great king H9048
2Ki 19: 4 the LORD your God *will* **h** all the words of H9048
2Ki 19:16 Give ear, LORD, and **h**; open your eyes, H9048
2Ki 20:16 said to Hezekiah, "**H** the word of the LORD: H9048
1Ch 14:15 As soon as you **h** the sound of marching in H9048
2Ch 6:19 **H** the cry and the prayer that your servant H9048
2Ch 6:20 *May* you **h** the prayer your servant prays H9048
2Ch 6:21 **H** the supplications of your servant and of H9048
2Ch 6:21 **H** from heaven, your dwelling place; and H9048
2Ch 6:21 dwelling place; and when *you* **h**, forgive. H9048
2Ch 6:23 then **h** from heaven and act. H9048
2Ch 6:25 then **h** from heaven and forgive the sin of H9048
2Ch 6:27 then **h** from heaven and forgive the sin of H9048
2Ch 6:30 then **h** from heaven, your dwelling place H9048
2Ch 6:33 then **h** from heaven, your dwelling place H9048
2Ch 6:35 then **h** from heaven their prayer and their H9048
2Ch 6:39 **h** their prayer and their pleas H9048
2Ch 7:14 then I *will* **h** from heaven, and I H9048
2Ch 9: 7 stand before you and **h** your wisdom! H9048
2Ch 9:23 with Solomon to **h** the wisdom God had H9048
2Ch 18:18 "Therefore **h** the word of the LORD: H9048
2Ch 20: 9 distress, and *you will* **h** us and save us. H9048
Ne 1: 6 your eyes open to **h** the prayer your H9048
Ne 4: 4 **H** us, our God, for we are despised. H9048
Ne 4:20 Wherever *you* **h** the sound of the trumpet H9048
Ne 13:27 *Must we* **h** now that you too are doing all H9048
Job 3:18 *they* no longer **h** the slave driver's shout. H9048
Job 5:27 So **h** it and apply it to yourself. H9048
Job 13: 6 **H** now my argument; listen to the pleas of H9048
Job 20: 3 *I* **h** a rebuke that dishonors me, and my H9048
Job 22:27 pray to him, and *he will* **h** you, and you H9048
Job 26:14 how faint the whisper *we* **h** of him! H9048
Job 31:35 that I had *someone to* **h** me! I sign H9048
Job 34: 2 "**H** my words, you wise men; listen to me H9048
Job 34:16 have understanding, **h** this; listen to what H9048
Job 34:34 declare, wise men *who* **h** me say to me, H9048
Job 39: 7 in the town; *it does* not **h** a driver's shout. H9048
Ps 4: 1 have mercy on me and **h** my prayer. H9048
Ps 5: 2 **H** my cry for help, my King and my God H7992
Ps 5: 3 *you* **h** my voice; in the morning I lay H9048
Ps 10:17 **h** the desire of the afflicted; you H9048
Ps 17: 1 **H** me, LORD, my plea is just; listen to my H9048
Ps 17: 1 **H** my prayer—it does not rise from H263
Ps 17: 6 turn your ear to me and **h** my prayer. H9048
Ps 18:44 as soon as they **h** *of* me, they obey me. H9051
Ps 27: 7 **H** my voice when I call, LORD; be merciful H9048
Ps 28: 2 **H** my cry for mercy as I call to you for help H9048
Ps 30:10 **H**, LORD, and be merciful to me; LORD, be H9048
Ps 31:13 For *I* **h** many whispering, "Terror on every H9048
Ps 34: 2 in the LORD; *let* the afflicted **h** and rejoice. H9048
Ps 38:13 like the deaf, *who* cannot **h**, like the mute H9048
Ps 38:14 I have become like one who *does* not **h** H9048
Ps 39:12 "**H** my prayer, LORD, listen to my cry for H9048
Ps 49: 1 **H** this, all you peoples; listen, all who live H9048
Ps 51: 8 **Let** me **h** joy and gladness; let the bones H9048
Ps 54: 2 **H** my prayer, O God; listen to the words of H9048
Ps 55: 2 **h** me and answer me. My thoughts H7992
Ps 55:19 *he will* **h** them and humble them H9048
Ps 59: 7 as swords, and they think, "Who *can* **h** us?" H9048
Ps 61: 1 **H** my cry, O God; listen to my prayer. H9048
Ps 64: 1 **H** me, my God, as I voice my complaint H9048
Ps 66:16 Come and **h**, all *you* who fear God; let me H9048
Ps 77: 1 to God for help; I cried out to God *to* **h** me. H263
Ps 78: 1 My people, **h** my teaching; listen to the H263
Ps 80: 1 **H** us, Shepherd of Israel, you who lead H263
Ps 81: 8 **H** me, my people, and I will warn you—if H9048
Ps 84: 8 **H** my prayer, LORD God Almighty; listen to H9048
Ps 86: 1 **H** me, LORD, and answer me, for I H5742+265
Ps 86: 6 **H** my prayer, LORD; listen to my cry for H263
Ps 94: 9 *Does he* who fashioned the ear not **h** H9048
Ps 95: 7 if only *you would* **h** his voice, H9048
Ps 102: 1 **H** my prayer, LORD; let my cry for help H9048
Ps 102:20 to **h** the groans of the prisoners and H9048
Ps 115: 6 but cannot **h**, noses, but cannot H9048
Ps 119:149 **H** my voice in accordance with your love H9048
Ps 130: 2 **h** my voice. Let your ears be H9048
Ps 135:17 have ears, but cannot **h**, nor is there breath H263
Ps 138: 4 when *they* **h** what you have decreed. H9048
Ps 140: 6 are my God." **H**, LORD, my cry for mercy H263
Ps 141: 1 **h** me when I call to you. H263+7754
Ps 143: 1 **h** my prayer, listen to my cry for H9048
Pr 20:12 Ears *that* **h** and eyes that see—the LORD H9048
Ecc 7:21 or *you may* **h** your servant cursing you H9048
SS 2:14 me your face, **let** me **h** your voice; for H9048
SS 8:13 friends in attendance, **let** me **h** your voice! H9048
Isa 1: 2 **H** me, *you* heavens! Listen, earth! For the H9048
Isa 1:10 **H** the word of the LORD, *you* rulers of H9048
Isa 6:10 see with their eyes, **h** with their ears H9048
Isa 7:13 Then Isaiah said, "**H** now, you house of H9048
Isa 18: 3 when a trumpet sounds, *you will* **h** it. H9048
Isa 21: 3 I am staggered by *what* I **h**, I am H9048
Isa 24:16 From the ends of the earth *we* **h** singing H9048
Isa 28:14 **h** the word of the LORD, *you* scoffers H9048
Isa 28:23 Listen and **h** my voice; pay attention and H9048
Isa 28:23 my voice; pay attention and **h** what I say. H9048
Isa 29:18 that day the deaf *will* **h** the words of the H9048
Isa 30:21 your ears *will* **h** a voice behind you H9048
Isa 30:30 The LORD *will* **cause** people **to h** his H9048
Isa 32: 3 the ears of *those who* **h** will listen. H9048
Isa 32: 9 who feel secure, **h** what I have to say! H263
Isa 33:13 who are far away, **h** what I have done H9048
Isa 34: 1 *Let* the earth **h**, and all that is in it, the H9048
Isa 36:13 in Hebrew, "**H** the words of the great king H9048
Isa 37: 4 the LORD your God *will* **h** the words of the H9048
Isa 37:17 Give ear, LORD, and **h**; open your eyes, H9048
Isa 39: 5 "**H** the word of the LORD Almighty: H9048
Isa 42:18 "**H**, *you* deaf; look, you blind, and see! H9048
Isa 43: 9 so that *others may* **h** and say, "It is H9048
Isa 49: 1 you islands; **h** this, *you* distant nations: H7992
Isa 51: 4 "Listen to me, my people; **h** me, my nation H263
Isa 51: 7 "**H** me, you who know what is right, you H9048
Isa 51:21 Therefore **h** this, *you* afflicted one, made H9048
Isa 59: 1 too short to save, nor his ear too dull *to* **h**. H9048
Isa 59: 2 his face from you, so that *he will* not **h**. H9048
Isa 65:24 while they are still speaking I *will* **h**. H9048
Isa 66: 5 **H** the word of the LORD, you who tremble H9048
Isa 66: 6 **H** that uproar from the city, hear that H7754
Isa 66: 6 from the city, **h** that noise from the temple! NDT
Jer 2: 4 **H** the word of the LORD, *you* descendants H9048
Jer 4:21 battle standard and **h** the sound of the H9048
Jer 4:31 *I* **h** a cry as of a woman in labor, a groan H9048
Jer 5:21 **H** this, *you* foolish and senseless people H9048
Jer 5:21 do not see, who have ears but *do* not **h**: H9048
Jer 6:10 Their ears are closed so they cannot **h** H7992
Jer 6:18 Therefore **h**, you nations; you who are H9048
Jer 6:19 **H**, you earth: I am bringing disaster on H9048
Jer 7: 2 " '**H** the word of the LORD, all you people H9048
Jer 9:20 *you* women, **h** the word of the LORD H9048
Jer 10: 1 **H** what the LORD says to you, people of H9048
Jer 13:15 **H** and pay attention, do not be arrogant H9048
Jer 17:20 '**H** the word of the LORD, *you* kings of H9048
Jer 18:19 LORD; **h** what my accusers are saying! H9048
Jer 19: 3 '**H** the word of the LORD, *you* kings of H9048
Jer 20:10 *I* **h** many whispering, "Terror on every side H9048
Jer 20:16 *May he* **h** wailing in the morning, a battle H9048
Jer 21:11 house of Judah, '**H** the word of the LORD. H9048
Jer 22: 2 '**H** the word of the LORD to you, king of H9048
Jer 22:29 land, land, **h** the word of the LORD! H9048
Jer 23:18 council of the LORD to see or *to* **h** his word? H9048
Jer 25:36 **H** the cry of the shepherds, the wailing of H7754
Jer 29:20 Therefore, **h** the word of the LORD, all you H9048
Jer 31:10 "**H** the word of the LORD, *you* nations H9048
Jer 33: 9 on earth that **h** *of* all the good things H9048
Jer 34: 4 " 'Yet **h** the LORD's promise to you H9048
Jer 36: 3 *when* the people of Judah **h** *about* every H9048
Jer 38:25 If the officials **h** that I talked with you, and H9048
Jer 42: 2 "Please **h** our petition and H5877+4200+7156
Jer 42:14 we will not see war or **h** the trumpet or be H9048
Jer 42:15 then **h** the word of the LORD, *you* remnant H9048
Jer 44:24 "**H** the word of the LORD, all *you people* of H9048
Jer 44:26 But **h** the word of the LORD, all *you* Jews H9048
Jer 46:12 The nations *will* **h** *of* your shame; your H9048
Jer 49:20 **h** what the LORD has planned against H9048
Jer 50:45 **h** what the LORD has planned against H9048
Eze 3:17 so **h** the word I speak and give them H9048
Eze 6: 3 '*You* mountains of Israel, **h** the word of H9048
Eze 12: 2 do not see and ears to **h** but do not hear, H9048
Eze 12: 2 do not see and ears to hear but *do* not **h**, H9048
Eze 13: 2 own imagination: '**H** the word of the LORD! H9048
Eze 16:35 you prostitute, **h** the word of the LORD! H9048
Eze 18:25 Lord is not just.' **H**, *you* Israelites: Is my H9048
Eze 20:47 southern forest: '**H** the word of the LORD H9048
Eze 25: 3 '**H** the word of the Sovereign LORD. H9048
Eze 33: 7 so **h** the word I speak and give them H9048
Eze 33:30 'Come and **h** the message that has come H9048
Eze 33:31 sit before you *to* **h** your words, but H9048
Eze 33:32 for *they* **h** your words but do not put them H9048
Eze 34: 7 you shepherds, **h** the word of the LORD: H9048
Eze 34: 9 you shepherds, **h** the word of the LORD: H9048
Eze 36: 1 of Israel, **h** the word of the LORD. H9048
Eze 36: 4 **h** the word of the Sovereign LORD: H9048
Eze 36:15 No longer *will I* **make** you **h** the taunts of H9048
Eze 37: 4 'Dry bones, **h** the word of the LORD! H9048
Da 3: 5 As soon as *you* **h** the sound of the horn A10725
Da 3:15 Now when *you* **h** the sound of the horn A10725
Da 5:23 which cannot see or **h** or understand. A10725
Da 9:17 **h** the prayers and petitions of your servant. H9048
Da 9:18 our God, and **h**; open your eyes and see H9048
Da 9:19 Lord, **h** and act! For your H7992
Hos 4: 1 **H** the word of the LORD, you Israelites H9048
Hos 5: 1 "**H** this, *you* priests! Pay attention, you H9048
Hos 7:12 When I **h** them flocking together, I will H9051
Joel 1: 2 **H** this, you elders; listen, all who live in H9048
Am 3: 1 **H** this word, people of Israel, the word the H9048
Am 3:13 "**H** this and testify against the H9048
Am 4: 1 **H** this word, you cows of Bashan on H9048
Am 5: 1 **H** this word, Israel, this lament I take up H9048
Am 7:16 Now then, **h** the word of the LORD. You say H9048
Am 8: 4 **H** this, you who trample the needy and do H9048
Mic 1: 2 **H**, *you* peoples, all of you, listen, earth H9048
Mic 3: 9 **H** this, you leaders of Jacob, you rulers of H9048
Mic 6: 1 *let* the hills **h** what you have to say. H9048
Mic 6: 2 "**H**, *you* mountains, the LORD's accusation H9048
Mic 7: 7 wait for God my Savior; my God *will* **h** me. H9048
Na 3:19 All *who* **h** the news about you clap their H9048
Zec 8: 9 "Now **h** these words, 'Let your hands be H9048
Mt 11: 4 report to John what *you* **h** and see: *G201*
Mt 11: 5 cleansed, the deaf **h**, the dead are raised, *G201*
Mt 11:15 Whoever has ears, *let them* **h**. *G201*
Mt 12:19 no one *will* **h** his voice in the streets. *G201*
Mt 13: 9 Whoever has ears, *let them* **h**. *G201*
Mt 13:13 hearing, *they do* not **h** or understand. *G201*
Mt 13:15 calloused; *they* hardly **h** with their ears *G201*
Mt 13:15 might see with their eyes, **h** with their ears *G201*
Mt 13:16 they see, and your ears because *they* **h**. *G201*
Mt 13:17 and *to* **h** what you hear but did not hear it. *G201*
Mt 13:17 to hear what *you* **h** but did not hear it. *G201*
Mt 13:17 to hear what you hear but *did* not **h** it. *G201*
Mt 13:43 Whoever has ears, *let them* **h**. *G201*
Mt 21:16 "*Do you* **h** what these children are saying?" *G201*
Mt 24: 6 You will **h** of wars and rumors of wars, but *G201*
Mt 27:13 "Don't *you* **h** the testimony they are *G201*
Mk 4: 9 "Whoever has ears *to* **h**, let them hear." *G201*
Mk 4: 9 "Whoever has ears to hear, *let them* **h**." *G201*
Mk 4:15 As soon as *they* **h** it, Satan comes and *G201*
Mk 4:16 **h** the word and at once receive it with joy. *G201*
Mk 4:18 like seed sown among thorns, **h** the word; *G201*
Mk 4:20 sown on good soil, **h** the word, accept it, *G201*
Mk 4:23 If anyone has ears *to* **h**, let them hear." *G201*
Mk 4:23 If anyone has ears to hear, *let them* **h**." *G201*
Mk 4:24 "Consider carefully what *you* **h**," he *G201*
Mk 7:37 makes the deaf **h** and the mute speak." *G201*
Mk 8:18 eyes but fail to see, and ears but fail *to* **h**? *G201*
Mk 12:29 '**H**, O Israel: The Lord our *G201*
Mk 13: 7 When *you* **h** of wars and rumors of wars, do *G201*
Mk 14:11 They were delighted *to* **h** this and promised *G201*

Mk 15:44 Pilate was surprised to **h** that he was already NDT
Lk 5:15 of people came *to* **h** him and to be healed *G201*
Lk 6:18 who had come *to* **h** him and to be healed *G201*
Lk 7:22 cleansed, the deaf **h**, the dead are raised, *G201*
Lk 8: 8 "Whoever has ears *to* **h**, let them hear." *G201*
Lk 8: 8 "Whoever has ears to hear, *let them* **h**." *G201*
Lk 8:12 Those along the path are the *ones who* **h** *G201*
Lk 8:13 receive the word with joy when *they* **h** it, *G201*
Lk 8:14 fell among thorns stands for those *who* **h**, *G201*
Lk 8:15 good heart, *who* **h** the word, retain it, *G201*
Lk 8:21 are those who **h** God's word and put it *G201*
Lk 9: 9 then, is this *I* **h** such things about? *G201*
Lk 10:24 and *to* **h** what you hear but did not hear it." *G201*
Lk 10:24 to hear what *you* **h** but did not hear it." *G201*
Lk 10:24 to hear what you hear but *did* not **h** it." *G201*
Lk 11:28 rather are those *who* **h** the word of God *G201*
Lk 14:35 "Whoever has ears *to* **h**, let them hear." *G201*
Lk 14:35 "Whoever has ears to hear, *let them* **h**." *G201*
Lk 15: 1 were all gathering around *to* **h** Jesus. *G201*
Lk 16: 2 asked him, 'What is this *I* **h** about you? *G201*
Lk 21: 9 When *you* **h** of wars and uprisings, do not *G201*
Lk 21:38 in the morning *to* **h** him at the temple. *G201*
Jn 3: 8 *You* **h** its sound, but you cannot tell where *G201*
Jn 5:25 come when the dead *will* **h** the voice of the *G201*
Jn 5:25 the Son of God and those *who* **h** will live. *G201*
Jn 5:28 all who are in their graves *will* **h** his voice *G201*
Jn 5:30 I judge only as *I* **h**, and my judgment is *G201*
Jn 8:43 Because you are unable *to* **h** what I say. *G201*
Jn 8:47 The reason you *do* not **h** is that you do not *G201*
Jn 9:27 Why do you want *to* **h** it again? Do you *G201*
Jn 11:42 I knew that *you* always **h** me, but I said this *G201*
Jn 14:24 These words *you* **h** are not my own; they *G201*
Ac 2:11 *we* **h** them declaring the wonders of God in *G201*
Ac 2:33 has poured out what you now see and **h**. *G201*
Ac 10:22 house so that *he could* **h** what you have to *G201*
Ac 13: 7 because he wanted to **h** the word of God. *G201*
Ac 13:44 whole city gathered *to* **h** the word of the *G201*
Ac 15: 7 you *that* the Gentiles *might* **h** from my *G201*
Ac 17:32 "*We want to* **h** you again on this subject." *G201*
Ac 19:26 And you see and **h** how this fellow Paul has *G201*
Ac 21:22 *They will* certainly **h** that you have come *G201*
Ac 22:14 Righteous One and *to* **h** words from his *G201*
Ac 23:35 "*I will* **h** your **case** when your accusers get *G1358*
Ac 24: 4 that you be kind enough *to* **h** us briefly. *G201*
Ac 25:22 "I would like *to* **h** this man myself. *G201*
Ac 25:22 He replied, "Tomorrow *you will* **h** him." *G201*
Ac 28:22 But we want *to* **h** what your views are, for *G201*
Ac 28:27 calloused; *they* hardly **h** with their ears *G201*
Ac 28:27 might see with their eyes, **h** with their ears *G201*
Ro 2:13 For it is not those *who* **h** the law who are *G212*
Ro 10:14 And how *can they* **h** without someone *G201*
Ro 10:18 *Did they* not **h**? Of course they did *G201*
Ro 11: 8 could not see and ears that *could* not **h**, *G201*
1Co 11:18 *I* **h** that when you come together as a *G201*
Php 1:27 see you or *only* **h** about you in my *G201*
Php 1:30 you saw I had, and now **h** that I still have. *G201*
2Th 3:11 *We* **h** that some among you are idle and *G201*
2Ti 4: 3 *to* **say what** their **itching ears want to h** *G3117+198*
2Ti 4:17 proclaimed and all the Gentiles *might* **h** it. *G201*
Phm 5 *because I* **h** about your love for all his holy *G201*
Heb 3: 7 Holy Spirit says: "Today, if *you* **h** his voice, *G201*
Heb 3:15 if *you* **h** his voice, do not harden *G201*
Heb 4: 7 if *you* **h** his voice, do not harden *G201*
3Jn 4 greater joy than to **h** that my children are *G201*
Rev 1: 3 blessed are those *who* **h** it and take to *G201*
Rev 2: 7 *let them* **h** what the Spirit says to the *G201*
Rev 2:11 *let them* **h** what the Spirit says to the *G201*
Rev 2:17 *let them* **h** what the Spirit says to the *G201*
Rev 2:29 *let them* **h** what the Spirit says to the *G201*
Rev 3: 6 *let them* **h** what the Spirit says to the *G201*
Rev 3:13 *let them* **h** what the Spirit says to the *G201*
Rev 3:22 *let them* **h** what the Spirit says to the *G201*
Rev 9:20 idols that cannot see or **h** or walk. *G201*
Rev 13: 9 Whoever has ears, *let them* **h**. *G201*

HEARD (577) [HEAR]

Ge 3: 8 the man and his wife **h** the sound of the H9048
Ge 3:10 He answered, "*I* **h** you in the garden, and H9048
Ge 14:14 When Abram **h** that his relative had been H9048
Ge 16:11 Ishmael, for the LORD *has* **h** of your misery. H9048
Ge 17:20 as for Ishmael, *I have* **h** you: I will surely H9048
Ge 21:17 God **h** the boy crying, and the angel of H9048
Ge 21:17 God *has* **h** the boy crying as he lies there. H9048
Ge 21:26 not tell me, and I **h** *about* it only today." H9048
Ge 24:30 *had* **h** Rebekah tell what the man H9048
Ge 24:52 Abraham's servant **h** what they said, H9048
Ge 27:34 When Esau **h** his father's words, he burst H9048
Ge 29:13 As soon as Laban **h** the news about Jacob H9048
Ge 29:33 "Because the LORD **h** that I am not loved H9048
Ge 31: 1 Jacob **h** that Laban's sons were saying H9048
Ge 34: 5 When Jacob **h** that his daughter Dinah H9048
Ge 34: 7 as soon as they **h** what had happened. H9048
Ge 35:22 concubine Bilhah, and Israel **h** *of* it. H9048
Ge 37:17 the man answered. "*I* **h** them say, 'Let's H9048
Ge 37:21 When Reuben **h** this, he tried to rescue H9048
Ge 39:15 When he **h** me scream for help, he left his H9048
Ge 39:19 When his master **h** the story his wife told H9048
Ge 41:15 But I *have* **h** it said of you *that* when you H9048
Ge 42: 2 "*I have* **h** that there is grain in Egypt. H9048
Ge 43:25 because *they had* **h** that they were to eat H9048
Ge 45: 2 wept so loudly that the Egyptians **h** him, H9048
Ge 45: 2 and Pharaoh's household **h** *about* it. H9048
Ex 2:15 When Pharaoh **h** *of* this, he tried to kill H9048
Ex 2:24 God **h** their groaning and he remembered H9048
Ex 3: 7 *I have* **h** them crying out because of their H9048
Ex 4:31 And when *they* **h** that the LORD was H9048
Ex 6: 5 I *have* **h** the groaning of the Israelites H9048
Ex 16: 7 because he *has* **h** your grumbling against H9048
Ex 16: 8 because he *has* **h** your grumbling against H9048
Ex 16: 9 the LORD, for *he has* **h** your grumbling. H9048
Ex 16:12 "*I have* **h** the grumbling of the Israelites H9048
Ex 18: 1 **h** *of* everything God had done for Moses H9048
Ex 20:18 lightning and **h** the trumpet and saw H7754
Ex 23:13 gods; *do* not *let them* **be h** on your lips. H9048
Ex 28:35 of the bells *will* **be h** when he enters H9048
Ex 32:17 When Joshua **h** the noise of the people H9048
Ex 33: 4 When the people **h** these distressing H9048
Lev 10:20 When Moses **h** this, he was satisfied. H9048
Lev 24:14 All those *who* **h** him are to lay their hands H9048
Nu 7:89 *he* **h** the voice speaking to him from H9048
Nu 11: 1 when he **h** them his anger was H9048
Nu 11:10 Moses **h** the people of every family H9048
Nu 11:18 The LORD **h** you when you wailed, "If only H265
Nu 12: 2 spoken through us?" And the LORD **h** this. H9048
Nu 14:14 *They have already* **h** that you, LORD, are H9048
Nu 14:15 the nations who *have* **h** this report about H9048
Nu 14:27 *I have* **h** the complaints of these H9048
Nu 14:28 do to you the very thing I **h** you say: H928+265
Nu 16: 4 When Moses **h** this, he fell facedown. H9048
Nu 20:16 *he* **h** our cry and sent an angel and H9048
Nu 21: 1 **h** that Israel was coming along the road H9048
Nu 22:36 When Balak **h** that Balaam was coming H9048
Nu 33:40 **h** that the Israelites were coming. H9048
Dt 1:34 When the LORD **h** what you said, he was H9048
Dt 4:12 You **h** the sound of words but saw no form H9048
Dt 4:32 *has* anything like it *ever* **been h** *of*? H9048
Dt 4:33 *Has* any other people **h** the voice of God H9048
Dt 4:36 and *you* **h** his words from out of the fire. H9048
Dt 5:23 When you **h** the voice out of the darkness H9048
Dt 5:24 and *we have* **h** his voice from the fire. H9048
Dt 5:26 For what mortal *has* ever **h** the voice of the H9048
Dt 5:28 The LORD **h** you when you spoke to me H9048
Dt 5:28 "*I have* **h** what this people said to you. H9048
Dt 9: 2 You know about them and *have* **h** it said H9048
Dt 26: 7 the LORD **h** our voice and saw our H9048
Jos 2:10 *We have* **h** how the LORD dried up the H9048
Jos 2:11 When *we* **h** of it, our hearts melted in fear H9048
Jos 5: 1 kings along the coast **h** how the LORD had H9048
Jos 9: 1 west of the Jordan **h** *about* these things— H9048
Jos 9: 3 people of Gibeon **h** what Joshua had H9048
Jos 9: 9 For *we have* **h** reports of him H9048
Jos 9:16 the Israelites **h** that they were neighbors H9048
Jos 10: 1 king of Jerusalem **h** that Joshua had H9048
Jos 11: 1 When Jabin king of Hazor **h** of this, he H9048
Jos 14:12 *You* yourself **h** then that the Anakites H9048
Jos 22:11 And *when* the Israelites **h** that they had H9048
Jos 22:30 of the Israelites—**h** what Reuben, Gad H9048
Jos 24:27 It *has* **h** all the words the LORD has said to H9048
Jdg 7:15 When Gideon **h** the dream and its H9048
Jdg 9:30 governor of the city **h** what Gaal son of H9048
Jdg 9:47 When Abimelek **h** that they had H5583
Jdg 13: 9 God **h** Manoah, and the angel of H9048+7754
Jdg 17: 2 about which I **h** you utter a curse H606+928+265
Jdg 20: 3 The Benjamites **h** that the Israelites had H9048
Ru 1: 6 When Naomi **h** in Moab that the LORD had H9048
1Sa 1:13 lips were moving but her voice **was** not **h**. H9048
1Sa 2:22 **h** *about* everything his sons were doing to H9048
1Sa 4:14 Eli **h** the outcry and asked, "What is the H9048
1Sa 4:19 When *she* **h** the news that the ark of God H9048
1Sa 7: 7 When the Philistines **h** that Israel had H9048
1Sa 7: 7 When the Israelites **h** *of* it, they were H9048
1Sa 8:21 When Samuel **h** all that the people said H9048
1Sa 11: 6 When Saul **h** their words, the Spirit of H9048
1Sa 13: 3 at Geba, and the Philistines **h** *about* it. H9048
1Sa 13: 4 So all Israel **h** the news: "Saul has H9048
1Sa 14:22 country of Ephraim **h** that the Philistines H9048
1Sa 14:27 But Jonathan *had* not **h** that his father had H9048
1Sa 17:23 his usual defiance, and David **h** it. H9048
1Sa 17:28 brother, **h** him speaking with the men H9048
1Sa 22: 1 his father's household **h** *about* it, H9048
1Sa 22: 6 Now Saul **h** that David and his men had H9048
1Sa 23:10 servant *has* **h definitely** that Saul H9048+9048
1Sa 23:11 Saul come down, as your servant *has* **h**? H9048
1Sa 23:25 When Saul **h** this, he went into the Desert H9048
1Sa 25: 4 *he* **h** that Nabal was shearing sheep. H9048
1Sa 25:35 *I have* **h** your words and granted your H9048
1Sa 25:39 When David **h** that Nabal was dead, he H9048
1Sa 31:11 of Jabesh Gilead **h** what the Philistines H9048
2Sa 3:28 when David **h** *about* this, he said, "I H9048
2Sa 4: 1 son of Saul **h** that Abner had died in H9048
2Sa 5:17 the Philistines **h** that David had been H9048
2Sa 5:17 David **h** *about* it and went down to H9048
2Sa 7:22 you, as *we have* **h** with our own ears. H9048
2Sa 8: 9 Tou king of Hamath **h** that David had H9048
2Sa 11:26 When Uriah's wife **h** that her husband H9048
2Sa 13:21 When King David **h** all this, he was H9048
2Sa 18: 5 And all the troops **h** the king giving orders H9048
2Sa 19: 2 because on that day the troops **h** it said H9048
2Sa 22: 7 From his temple *he* **h** my voice; my cry H9048
1Ki 1:11 mother, "*Have you* not **h** that Adonijah H9048
1Ki 1:41 who were with him **h** it as they were H9048
1Ki 3:28 When all Israel **h** the verdict the king had H9048
1Ki 4:34 of the world, who *had* **h** *of* his wisdom. H9048
1Ki 5: 1 Hiram king of Tyre **h** that Solomon had H9048
1Ki 5: 7 When Hiram **h** Solomon's message, he H9048
1Ki 6: 7 other iron tool **was h** at the temple site H9048
1Ki 9: 3 "*I have* **h** the prayer and plea you have H9048
1Ki 10: 1 the queen of Sheba **h** *about* the fame of H9048
1Ki 10: 6 "The report *I* **h** in my own country about H9048
1Ki 10: 7 you have far exceeded the report *I* **h**. H9048
1Ki 11:21 Hadad **h** that David rested with his H9048
1Ki 12: 2 When Jeroboam son of Nebat **h** this (he H9048
1Ki 12:20 all the Israelites **h** that Jeroboam had H9048
1Ki 13: 4 When King Jeroboam **h** what the man of H9048
1Ki 13:26 brought him back from his journey **h** *of* it, H9048
1Ki 14: 6 So when Ahijah **h** the sound of her H9048
1Ki 15:21 When Baasha **h** this, he stopped building H9048
1Ki 16:16 in the camp **h** that Zimri had plotted H9048
1Ki 17:22 The LORD **h** Elijah's cry, and the boy's life H9048
1Ki 18:13 Haven't you **h**, my lord, what I did while H5583
1Ki 19:13 When Elijah **h** it, he pulled his cloak over H9048
1Ki 20:12 Ben-Hadad **h** this message while he and H9048
1Ki 20:31 *we have* **h** that the kings of Israel are H9048
1Ki 21:15 As soon as Jezebel **h** that Naboth had H9048
1Ki 21:16 When Ahab **h** that Naboth was dead, he H9048
1Ki 21:27 When Ahab **h** these words, he tore his H9048
2Ki 3:21 all the Moabites *had* **h** that the kings had H9048
2Ki 5: 8 Elisha the man of God **h** that the king of H9048
2Ki 6:30 When the king **h** the woman's words, he H9048
2Ki 9:30 When Jezebel **h** *about* it, she put on eye H9048
2Ki 11:13 When Athaliah **h** the noise made by the H9048
2Ki 19: 1 When King Hezekiah **h** this, he tore his H9048
2Ki 19: 4 the words the LORD your God *has* **h**. H9048
2Ki 19: 6 Do not be afraid of what *you have* **h** H9048
2Ki 19: 8 the field commander **h** that the king of H9048
2Ki 19:11 Surely you *have* **h** what the kings of H9048
2Ki 19:20 *I have* **h** your prayer concerning H9048
2Ki 19:25 " '*Have you* not **h**? Long ago I ordained it H9048
2Ki 20: 5 *I have* **h** your prayer and seen your tears; H9048
2Ki 20:12 because *he had* **h** *of* Hezekiah's illness. H9048
2Ki 22:11 When the king **h** the words of the Book of H9048
2Ki 22:18 of Israel, says concerning the words *you* **h**: H9048
2Ki 22:19 the LORD when you **h** what I have spoken H9048
2Ki 22:19 presence, I also *have* **h** you, declares the H9048
2Ki 25:23 officers and their men **h** that the king of H9048
1Ch 10:11 of Jabesh Gilead **h** what the Philistines H9048
1Ch 14: 8 the Philistines **h** that David had been H9048
1Ch 14: 8 David **h** *about* it and went out to meet H9048
1Ch 17:20 you, as *we have* **h** with our own ears. H9048
1Ch 18: 9 Tou king of Hamath **h** that David had H9048
2Ch 7:12 "*I have* **h** your prayer and have chosen H9048
2Ch 9: 1 the queen of Sheba **h** *of* Solomon's fame, H9048
2Ch 9: 5 "The report *I* **h** in my own country about H9048
2Ch 9: 6 you have far exceeded the report *I* **h**. H9048
2Ch 10: 2 When Jeroboam son of Nebat **h** this (he H9048
2Ch 15: 8 When Asa **h** these words and the H9048
2Ch 16: 5 When Baasha **h** this, he stopped building H9048
2Ch 20:29 kingdoms when they **h** how the LORD had H9048
2Ch 23:12 When Athaliah **h** the noise of the people H9048
2Ch 30:20 And the LORD **h** Hezekiah and healed the H9048
2Ch 30:27 people, and God **h** them, for their H9048+7754
2Ch 34:19 When the king **h** the words of the Law, he H9048
2Ch 34:26 of Israel, says concerning the words *you* **h**: H9048
2Ch 34:27 before God when you **h** what he spoke H9048
2Ch 34:27 in my presence, I *have* **h** you, declares the H9048
Ezr 3:13 And the sound **was h** far away. H9048
Ezr 4: 1 Judah and Benjamin **h** that the exiles H9048
Ezr 9: 3 When I **h** this, I tore my tunic and cloak H9048
Ne 1: 4 When I **h** these things, I sat down and H9048
Ne 2:10 the Ammonite official **h** *about* this, H9048
Ne 2:19 official and Geshem the Arab **h** *about* it, H9048
Ne 4: 1 When Sanballat **h** that we were H9048
Ne 4: 7 the people of Ashdod **h** that the repairs to H9048
Ne 4:15 When our enemies **h** that we were aware H9048
Ne 5: 6 When *I* **h** their outcry and these charges, H9048
Ne 6:16 When all our enemies **h** *about* this, all H9048
Ne 9: 9 in Egypt; *you* **h** their cry at the Red Sea. H9048
Ne 9:27 From heaven you **h** them, and in your H9048
Ne 9:28 to you again, you **h** from heaven, and in H9048
Ne 12:43 *The* **sound** of rejoicing in Jerusalem *could* **be h** H9048
Ne 13: 3 When the people **h** this law, they H9048
Est 1:18 nobility who *have* **h** *about* the queen's H9048
Job 2:11 **h** *about* all the troubles that had come H9048
Job 3: 7 be barren; *may* no shout of joy **be h** in it. H995
Job 4:16 before my eyes, and *I* **h** a hushed voice: H9048
Job 13: 1 my ears *have* **h** and understood it. H9048
Job 16: 2 "*I have* **h** many things like these; you are H9048
Job 29:11 Whoever **h** me spoke well of me, and H9048
Job 33: 8 said in my hearing—*I* **h** the very words— H9048
Job 34:28 so that *he* **h** the cry of the needy. H9048
Job 42: 5 My ears *had* **h** *of* you but now my H9048+9051
Ps 6: 8 for the LORD *has* **h** my weeping. H9048
Ps 6: 9 The LORD *has* **h** my cry for mercy; H9048
Ps 18: 6 From his temple *he* **h** my voice; my cry H9048
Ps 19: 3 use no words; no sound **is h** from them. H9048
Ps 28: 6 to the LORD, for *he has* **h** my cry for mercy. H9048
Ps 31:22 Yet *you* **h** my cry for mercy when I called H9048
Ps 34: 6 and the LORD **h** him; he saved him H9048
Ps 40: 1 the LORD; he turned to me and **h** my cry. H9048
Ps 44: 1 *We have* **h** it with our ears, O God; our H9048
Ps 48: 8 As *we have* **h**, so we have seen in the city H9048
Ps 61: 5 *have* **h** my vows; you have given me H9048
Ps 62:11 God has spoken, two things *I have* **h**: H9048
Ps 66: 8 peoples, **let** the sound of his praise **be h**; H9048

Ps 66:19 listened and *has* **h** my prayer. H7992+928+7754
Ps 77:18 Your thunder was **h** in the whirlwind, your H7754
Ps 78: 3 things *we have* **h** and known, things our H9048
Ps 78:21 *When* the LORD **h** them, he was furious H9048
Ps 78:59 *When* God **h** them, he was furious; he H9048
Ps 81: 5 *I* **h** an unknown voice say: H9048
Ps 92:11 my ears *have* **h** the rout of my wicked foes. H9048
Ps 106:44 note of their distress when he **h** their cry; H9048
Ps 116: 1 love the LORD, for *he* **h** my voice; he heard H9048
Ps 116: 1 he heard my voice; he **h** my cry for mercy. NDT
Ps 132: 6 *We* **h** it in Ephrathah, we came upon it in H9048
Ecc 12:13 Now all *has* **been h**; here is the H9048
SS 2:12 the cooing of doves **is h** in our land. H9048
Isa 5: 7 righteousness, but **h** cries of distress. H2180
Isa 6: 8 Then *I* **h** the voice of the Lord saying H9048
Isa 15: 4 their voices **are h** all the way to Jahaz. H9048
Isa 16: 6 *We have* **h** *of* Moab's pride—how great H9048
Isa 21:10 I tell you what *I have* **h** from the LORD H9048
Isa 37: 1 When King Hezekiah **h** this, he tore his H9048
Isa 37: 4 the words the LORD your God *has* **h**. H9048
Isa 37: 6 Do not be afraid of what *you have* **h** H9048
Isa 37: 8 the field commander **h** that the king of H9048
Isa 37: 9 When *he* **h** it, he sent messengers to H9048
Isa 37:11 Surely you *have* **h** what the kings of H9048
Isa 37:26 "*Have you* not **h**? Long ago I ordained it H9048
Isa 38: 5 *I have* **h** your prayer and seen your tears; H9048
Isa 39: 1 because *he had* **h** *of* his illness and H9048
Isa 40:21 you not know? *Have you* not **h**? Has it not H9048
Isa 40:28 *Have you* not **h**? The LORD is H9048
Isa 41:26 foretold it, no *one* **h** any words from you. H9048
Isa 48: 6 *You have* **h** these things; look at them all H9048
Isa 48: 7 *you have* not **h** *of* them before today. H9048
Isa 48: 8 *You have* neither **h** nor understood; from H9048
Isa 52:15 and what *they have* not **h**, they will H9048
Isa 58: 4 **expect** your voice **to be h** on high. H9048
Isa 60:18 No longer *will* violence **be h** in your land H9048
Isa 64: 4 Since ancient times no *one has* **h**, no ear H9048
Isa 65:19 of crying *will* **be h** in it no more. H9048
Isa 66: 8 Who *has ever* **h** *of* such things? Who has H9048
Isa 66:19 islands that *have* not **h** of my fame or H9048
Jer 3:21 A cry **is h** on the barren heights, the H9048
Jer 4:19 For I *have* **h** the sound of the trumpet; H9048
Jer 4:19 sound of the trumpet; I have **h** the battle cry. NDT
Jer 6:24 *We have* **h** reports about them, and our H9048
Jer 8:16 of the enemy's horses **is h** from Dan; H9048
Jer 9:10 the lowing of cattle *is* not **h**. H9048
Jer 9:19 The sound of wailing **is h** from Zion: 'How H9048
Jer 18:13 Who *has ever* **h** anything like this H9048
Jer 18:22 *Let* a cry **be h** from their houses when you H9048
Jer 20: 1 **h** Jeremiah prophesying these things H9048
Jer 22:20 cry out, **let** your voice **be h** in Bashan H5989
Jer 23:18 Who has listened and **h** his word? H9048
Jer 23:25 "*I have* **h** what the prophets say who H9048
Jer 26: 7 all the people **h** Jeremiah speak H9048
Jer 26:10 officials of Judah **h** *about* these things, H9048
Jer 26:11 *You have* **h** it with your own ears! H9048
Jer 26:12 this city all the things *you have* **h**. H9048
Jer 26:21 all his officers and officials **h** his words, H9048
Jer 26:21 But Uriah **h** of it and fled in fear to Egypt H9048
Jer 30: 5 " 'Cries of fear *are* **h**—terror, not peace. H9048
Jer 31: 7 **Make** your praises **h**, and say, 'LORD, save H9048
Jer 31:15 "A voice **is h** in Ramah, mourning and H9048
Jer 31:18 "*I have* **surely h** Ephraim's H9048+9048
Jer 33:10 animals, *there will* **be h** once more H9048
Jer 36:11 **h** all the words of the LORD from the scroll H9048
Jer 36:13 them everything *he had* **h** Baruch read to H9048
Jer 36:16 When they **h** all these words, they looked H9048
Jer 36:24 his attendants who **h** all these words H9048
Jer 37: 5 *when* the Babylonians who were besieging
Jerusalem **h** H9048
Jer 38: 1 son of Malkijah **h** what Jeremiah was H9048
Jer 38: 7 **h** that they had put Jeremiah into the H9048
Jer 38:27 no *one had* **h** his conversation with the H9048
Jer 40: 7 in the open country **h** that the king of H9048
Jer 40:11 all the other countries **h** that the king of H9048
Jer 41:11 who were with him **h** *about* all the crimes H9048
Jer 42: 4 "*I have* **h** you," replied Jeremiah the H9048
Jer 48: 5 cries over the destruction *are* **h**. H9048
Jer 48:29 "*We have* **h** *of* Moab's pride—how great H9048
Jer 49:14 *I have* **h** a message from the LORD; an H9048
Jer 49:23 are dismayed, for *they have* **h** bad news. H9048
Jer 50:43 king of Babylon *has* **h** reports about them H9048
Jer 51:46 be afraid when rumors **are h** in the land; H9048
La 1:21 "*People have* **h** my groaning, but there is H9048
La 1:21 All my enemies *have* **h** *of* my distress H9048
La 3:56 *You* **h** my plea: "Do not close your ears to H9048
La 3:61 *you have* **h** their insults, all their H9048
Eze 1:24 *I* **h** the sound of their wings H9048
Eze 1:28 and *I* **h** the voice of one speaking. H9048
Eze 2: 2 to my feet, and *I* **h** him speaking to me. H9048
Eze 3:12 and *I* **h** behind me a loud rumbling sound H9048
Eze 9: 1 Then I **h** him call out in a loud voice H928+265
Eze 10: 5 of the cherubim *could* **be h** as far away as H9048
Eze 10:13 I **h** the wheels being called "the H928+265
Eze 19: 4 The nations **h** about him, and he was H9048
Eze 19: 9 so his roar **was h** no longer on the H9048
Eze 26:13 the music of your harps *will* **be h** no more. H9048
Eze 33: 5 Since *they* **h** the sound of the trumpet but H9048
Eze 35:12 know that I the LORD *have* **h** all the H9048
Eze 35:13 against me without restraint, and I **h** it. H9048
Eze 43: 6 *I* **h** someone speaking to me from inside H9048
Da 3: 7 as soon as they **h** the sound of the horn A10725
Da 5:14 *I have* **h** that the spirit of the gods is in A10725
Da 5:16 Now I *have* **h** that you are able to give A10725
Da 6:14 When the king **h** this, he was greatly A10725
Da 8:13 Then *I* **h** a holy one speaking, and H9048
Da 8:16 And *I* **h** a man's voice from the Ulai H9048
Da 10: 9 Then *I* **h** him speaking, and as I listened H9048
Da 10:12 your words **were h**, and I have come H9048
Da 12: 7 and *I* **h** him swear by him who lives H9048
Da 12: 8 I **h**, but I did not understand. So I asked H9048
Ob 1 *We have* **h** a message from the LORD: H9048
Na 2:13 of your messengers *will* no longer **be h**." H9048
Hab 3: 2 *I have* **h** *of* your fame; I stand in awe H9048
Hab 3:16 *I* **h** and my heart pounded, my lips H9048
Zep 2: 8 "*I have* **h** the insults of Moab and the H9048
Zec 8:23 because *we have* **h** that God is with you. H9048
Mal 3:16 each other, and the LORD listened and **h**. H9048
Mt 2: 3 *When* King Herod **h** this he was disturbed G201
Mt 2: 9 *After* they *had* **h** the king, they went on G201
Mt 2:18 "A voice *is* **h** in Ramah, weeping and great G201
Mt 2:22 But *when he* **h** that Archelaus was reigning G201
Mt 4:12 *When* Jesus **h** that John had been put in G201
Mt 5:21 "*You have* **h** that it was said to the people G201
Mt 5:27 "*You have* **h** that it was said, 'You shall not G201
Mt 5:33 *you have* **h** that it was said to the people G201
Mt 5:38 "*You have* **h** that it was said, 'Eye for eye G201
Mt 5:43 "*You have* **h** that it was said, 'Love your G201
Mt 6: 7 they think *they will be* **h** because of G1653
Mt 8:10 *When* Jesus **h** this, he was amazed and G201
Mt 11: 2 *When* John, who was in prison, **h** *about* G201
Mt 12:24 But *when* the Pharisees **h** this, they said, "It G201
Mt 14: 1 Herod the tetrarch **h** the reports about G201
Mt 14:13 *When* Jesus **h** what had happened, he G201
Mt 15:12 Pharisees were offended *when they* **h** this?" G201
Mt 17: 6 *When* the disciples **h** this, they fell G201
Mt 19:22 *When* the young man **h** this, he went away G201
Mt 19:25 *When* the disciples **h** this, they were G201
Mt 20:24 *When* the ten **h about** this, they were G201
Mt 20:30 and *when they* **h** that Jesus was going by G201
Mt 21:45 *When* the chief priests and the Pharisees **h** G201
Mt 22:22 *When they* **h** this, they were amazed. G201
Mt 22:33 *When* the crowds **h** this, they were G201
Mt 26:65 now *you have* **h** the blasphemy. G201
Mt 27:47 When some of those standing there **h** this G201
Mk 2: 1 *the people* **h** that he had come home. G201
Mk 3: 8 *When they* **h** about all he was doing, many G201
Mk 3:21 *When* his family **h about** this, they went to G201
Mk 5:27 *When she* **h** about Jesus, she came up G201
Mk 6: 2 many *who* **h** him were amazed. G201
Mk 6:14 King Herod **h about** this, for Jesus' name G201
Mk 6:16 But *when* Herod **h** this, he said, "John G201
Mk 6:20 *When* Herod **h** John, he was greatly G201
Mk 6:55 the sick on mats to wherever *they* **h** he was. G201
Mk 7:25 as soon as *she* **h** about him, G201
Mk 10:41 *When* the ten **h about** this, they became G201
Mk 10:47 *When he* **h** that it was Jesus of Nazareth G201
Mk 11:14 And his disciples **h** him say it. G201
Mk 11:18 teachers of the law **h** this and began G201
Mk 12:28 of the law came and **h** them debating. G201
Mk 14:58 "We **h** him say, 'I will destroy this temple G201
Mk 14:64 "*You have* **h** the blasphemy. What do you G201
Mk 15:35 *When* some of those standing near **h** this G201
Mk 16:11 *When* they **h** that Jesus was alive and that G201
Lk 1:13 Zechariah; your prayer *has been* **h**. G1653
Lk 1:41 When Elizabeth **h** Mary's greeting, the baby G201
Lk 1:58 relatives **h** that the Lord had shown G201
Lk 1:66 Everyone who **h** this wondered about it G201
Lk 2:18 all who **h** it were amazed at what the G201
Lk 2:20 God for all the things *they had* **h** and seen, G201
Lk 2:47 Everyone who **h** him was amazed at his G201
Lk 4:23 hometown what *we have* **h** that you did in G201
Lk 4:28 synagogue were furious *when they* **h** this. G201
Lk 7: 3 The centurion **h** of Jesus and sent some G201
Lk 7: 9 *When* Jesus **h** this, he was amazed at him G201
Lk 7:22 report to John what you have seen and **h**: G201
Lk 7:29 collectors, *when they* **h** Jesus' *words* G201
Lk 9: 7 Herod the tetrarch **h about** all that was G201
Lk 12: 3 said in the dark *will be* **h** in the daylight, G201
Lk 14:15 *When* one of those at the table with him **h** G201
Lk 15:25 near the house, *he* **h** music and dancing. G201
Lk 16:14 **h** all this and were sneering at Jesus. G201
Lk 18:22 *When* Jesus **h** this, he said to him, "You G201
Lk 18:23 *When* he **h** this, he became very sad G201
Lk 18:26 Those *who* **h** this asked, "Who then can be G201
Lk 18:36 *When he* **h** the crowd going by, he asked G201
Lk 20:16 *When* the people **h** this, they said, "God G201
Lk 22:71 We *have* **h** it from his own lips. G201
Lk 23: 8 From what *he had* **h** about him, he hoped G201
Jn 1:37 *When* the two disciples **h** him say this, they G201
Jn 1:40 one of the two who **h** what John had said G201
Jn 3:32 He testifies to what he has seen and **h**, but G201
Jn 4: 1 that the Pharisees *had* **h** that he was G201
Jn 4:42 what you said; now *we have* **h** for ourselves G201
Jn 4:47 *When* this man **h** that Jesus had arrived in G201
Jn 5:37 *You have* never **h** his voice nor seen his G201
Jn 6:45 Everyone who *has* **h** the Father and G201
Jn 7:32 The Pharisees **h** the crowd whispering such G201
Jn 8: 9 those *who* **h** began to go away one at a G201
Jn 8:26 what I *have* **h** from him I tell the world." G201
Jn 8:38 are doing what *you have* **h** from your father G201
Jn 8:40 has told you the truth that *I* **h** from God. G201
Jn 9:32 Nobody *has* ever **h of** opening the eyes of a G201
Jn 9:35 Jesus **h** that they had thrown him out, and G201
Jn 9:40 who were with him **h** him say this and G201
Jn 10:19 The Jews who **h** these words were again NDT
Jn 11: 4 *When he* **h** this, Jesus said, "This sickness G201
Jn 11: 6 So when *he* **h** that Lazarus was sick, he G201
Jn 11:20 When Martha **h** that Jesus was coming, she G201
Jn 11:29 When Mary **h** this, she got up quickly and G201
Jn 11:41 I thank you that *you have* **h** me. G201
Jn 12:12 the festival **h** that Jesus was on his G201
Jn 12:18 because *they had* **h** that he had performed G201
Jn 12:29 that was there and **h** it said it had G201
Jn 12:34 "We *have* **h** from the Law that the Messiah G201
Jn 14:28 "*You* **h** me say, 'I am going away and I am G201
Jn 18:21 Ask those *who* **h** me. Surely they know G201
Jn 19: 8 When Pilate **h** this, he was even more G201
Jn 19:13 *When* Pilate **h** this, he brought Jesus out G201
Jn 21: 7 As soon as Simon Peter **h** him say, "It is G201
Ac 1: 4 which *you have* **h** me *speak about*. G201
Ac 1:19 Everyone in Jerusalem **h about** this G1196+1181
Ac 2: 6 *When they* **h** this sound, a crowd came G1181S
Ac 2: 6 because each one **h** their own language G201
Ac 2:37 *When the people* **h** this, they were cut to G201
Ac 4: 4 But many who **h** the message believed; so G201
Ac 4:20 speaking about what we have seen and **h**." G201
Ac 4:24 *When* they **h** this, they raised their voices G201
Ac 5: 5 *When* Ananias **h** this, he fell down and G201
Ac 5: 5 fear seized all who **h** what had happened. G201
Ac 5:11 church and all who **h** about these events. G201
Ac 5:33 *When* they **h** this, they were furious and G201
Ac 6:11 "*We have* **h** Stephen speak blasphemous G201
Ac 6:14 For *we have* **h** him say that this Jesus of G201
Ac 7:12 *When* Jacob **h** that there was grain in Egypt, G201
Ac 7:29 When Moses **h** this, he fled to Midian G3364
Ac 7:31 to get a closer look, *he* **h** the Lord say: G1181S
Ac 7:34 *I have* **h** their groaning and have come G201
Ac 7:54 *When* the members of the Sanhedrin **h** this G201
Ac 8: 6 When the crowds **h** Philip and saw the G201
Ac 8:14 *When* the apostles in Jerusalem **h** that G201
Ac 8:30 up to the chariot and **h** the man reading G201
Ac 9: 4 fell to the ground and **h** a voice say to him, G201
Ac 9: 7 *they* **h** the sound but did not see anyone. G201
Ac 9:13 "*I have* **h** many reports about this man G201
Ac 9:21 All those *who* **h** him were astonished and G201
Ac 9:38 *so when* the disciples **h** that Peter was in G201
Ac 10:31 God *has* **h** your prayer and remembered G1653
Ac 10:44 Spirit came on all who **h** the message. G201
Ac 10:46 For *they* **h** them speaking in tongues and G201
Ac 11: 1 throughout Judea **h** that the Gentiles also G201
Ac 11: 7 Then *I* **h** a voice telling me, 'Get up, Peter G201
Ac 11:18 *When they* **h** this, they had no further G201
Ac 13:48 *When* the Gentiles **h** this, they were glad G201
Ac 14:14 *when* the apostles Barnabas and Paul **h** of G201
Ac 15:24 *We have* **h** that some went out from us G201
Ac 16:38 and *when they* **h** that Paul and Silas were G201
Ac 17: 8 *When* they **h** this, the crowd and the city G201
Ac 17:32 *When they* **h** about the resurrection of the G201
Ac 18: 8 of the Corinthians *who* **h** Paul believed G201
Ac 18:26 *When* Priscilla and Aquila **h** him, they G201
Ac 19: 2 *we have* not even **h** that there is a Holy G201
Ac 19:10 the province of Asia **h** the word of the Lord. G201
Ac 19:28 *When they* **h** this, they were furious and G201
Ac 21:12 When *we* **h** this, we and the people there G201
Ac 21:20 *When* they **h** this, they praised God. G201
Ac 22: 2 *When they* **h** him speak to them in G201
Ac 22: 7 I fell to the ground and **h** a voice say to me G201
Ac 22:15 to all people of what you have seen and **h**. G201
Ac 22:26 *When* the centurion **h** this, he went to the G201
Ac 23:16 But *when* the son of Paul's sister **h** of this G201
Ac 26:14 and *I* **h** a voice saying to me in Aramaic G201
Ac 28:15 sisters there *had* **h** that we were G201
Ro 10:14 in the one of whom *they have* not **h**? G201
Ro 10:17 the **message** is **h** through the word G198
Ro 15:21 those *who have* not **h** will understand." G201
Ro 16:19 Everyone *has* **h about** your G1650+919
1Co 2: 9 what no ear *has* **h**, and what no G201
2Co 6: 2 "In the time of my favor *I* **h** you, and in G2052
2Co 12: 4 up to paradise and **h** inexpressible things, G201
Gal 1:13 For *you have* **h** of my previous way of life in G201
Gal 1:23 *They* only **h** *the report*: "The man G201+1639
Gal 3: 2 of the law, or by believing **what** you **h**? G198
Gal 3: 5 of the law, or by your believing **what** you **h**? G198
Eph 1:13 in Christ *when you* **h** the message of G201
Eph 1:15 *ever since* I **h** about your faith in the Lord G201
Eph 3: 2 Surely *you have* **h** about the administration G201
Eph 4:21 when *you* **h about** Christ and were taught in G201
Php 2:26 is distressed because *you* **h** he was ill. G201
Php 4: 9 you have learned or received or **h** from me, G201
Col 1: 4 *because we have* **h** of your faith in Christ G201
Col 1: 5 about which *you have* **already h** in the G4578
Col 1: 6 among you since the day *you* **h** it and truly G201
Col 1: 9 since the day *we* **h** about you, we have G201
Col 1:23 is the gospel that *you* **h** and that has been G201
1Th 2:13 which you **h** from us, you accepted G198
2Ti 1:13 What *you* **h** from me, keep as the pattern G201
2Ti 2: 2 And the things *you have* **h** me say in the G201
Heb 2: 1 therefore, to what *we have* **h**, so that we do G201
Heb 2: 3 was confirmed to us by those *who* **h** him. G201
Heb 3:16 Who *were they who* **h** and rebelled? Were G201
Heb 4: 2 the message they **h** was of no value to G198
Heb 5: 7 and *he was* **h** because of his reverent G1653
Heb 12:19 words that those *who* **h** it begged that no G201
Jas 1:25 not forgetting what *they have* **h**, but G212+1181
Jas 5:11 *You have* **h** of Job's perseverance and have G201

2Pe 1:18 *We* ourselves **h** this voice that came from G201
2Pe 2: 8 soul by the lawless deeds he saw and **h**)— G198
1Jn 1: 1 which *we have* **h**, which we have G201
1Jn 1: 3 proclaim to you what we have seen and **h**, G201
1Jn 1: 5 is the message *we have* **h** from him and G201
1Jn 2: 7 old command is the message *you have* **h**. G201
1Jn 2:18 as *you have* **h** that the antichrist is G201
1Jn 2:24 see that what *you have* **h** from the G201
1Jn 3:11 is the message *you* **h** from the beginning: G201
1Jn 4: 3 which *you have* **h** is coming and even now G201
2Jn 6 As *you have* **h** from the beginning, his G201
Rev 1:10 and *I* **h** behind me a loud voice like a G201
Rev 3: 3 what you have received and **h**; hold it fast, G201
Rev 4: 1 And the voice *I had* first **h** speaking to me G201
Rev 5:11 Then I looked and **h** the voice of many G201
Rev 5:13 Then *I* **h** every creature in heaven and on G201
Rev 6: 1 Then *I* **h** one of the four living creatures say G201
Rev 6: 3 *I* **h** the second living creature say G201
Rev 6: 5 third seal, *I* **h** the third living creature say G201
Rev 6: 6 Then *I* **h** what sounded like a voice among G201
Rev 6: 7 *I* **h** the voice of the fourth living creature G201
Rev 7: 4 Then *I* **h** the number of those who were G201
Rev 8:13 *I* **h** an eagle that was flying in midair call G201
Rev 9:13 and *I* **h** a voice coming from the four horns G201
Rev 9:16 times ten thousand. *I* **h** their number. G201
Rev 10: 4 to write; but *I* **h** a voice from heaven say G201
Rev 10: 8 the voice that *I had* **h** from heaven spoke G201
Rev 11:12 Then *they* **h** a loud voice from heaven G201
Rev 12:10 Then *I* **h** a loud voice in heaven say: "Now G201
Rev 14: 2 And *I* **h** a sound from heaven like the roar G201
Rev 14: 2 The sound *I* **h** was like that of harpists G201
Rev 14:13 Then *I* **h** a voice from heaven say, "Write G201
Rev 16: 1 Then *I* **h** a loud voice from the temple G201
Rev 16: 5 Then *I* **h** the angel in charge of the waters G201
Rev 16: 7 And *I* **h** the altar respond: "Yes, Lord God G201
Rev 18: 4 Then *I* **h** another voice from heaven say: G201
Rev 18:22 trumpeters, *will* never *be* **h** in you again. G201
Rev 18:22 of a millstone *will* never *be* **h** in you again. G201
Rev 18:23 bride *will* never *be* **h** in you again. G201
Rev 19: 1 After this *I* **h** what sounded like the roar of G201
Rev 19: 6 Then *I* **h** what sounded like a great G201
Rev 21: 3 And *I* **h** a loud voice from the throne saying G201
Rev 22: 8 am the *one who* **h** and saw these things. G201
Rev 22: 8 And when *I had* **h** and seen them, I fell G201

HEARERS (1) [HEAR]

1Ti 4:16 you will save both yourself and your **h**. G201

HEARING (55) [HEAR]

Ge 23:10 to Abraham in the **h** of all the Hittites who H265
Ge 23:13 he said to Ephron in their **h**, "Listen to H265
Ge 23:16 price he had named in the **h** *of* the Hittites: H265
Nu 11: 1 about their hardships in the **h** *of* the LORD, H265
Dt 5: 1 decrees and laws I declare in your **h** today. H265
Dt 31:11 shall read this law before them in their **h**. H265
Dt 31:28 these words in their **h** and call the heavens H265
Dt 31:30 to end in the **h** *of* the whole assembly of H265
Dt 32:44 words of this song in the **h** *of* the people. H265
Jdg 9:46 On **h** this, the citizens in the tower of H9048
1Sa 4: 6 **H** the uproar, the Philistines asked H9048
1Sa 17:11 On **h** the Philistine's words, Saul and all H9048
2Sa 10: 7 On **h** this, David sent Joab out with the H9048
2Sa 18:12 In our **h** the king commanded you and H265
1Ki 1:41 *On* **h** the sound of the trumpet, Joab H9048
2Ki 18:26 us in Hebrew in the **h** *of* the people on the H265
2Ki 23: 2 He read in their **h** all the words of the Book H265
1Ch 19: 8 On **h** this, David sent Joab out with the H9048
1Ch 28: 8 of the LORD, and in the **h** *of* our God: H265
2Ch 34:30 He read in their **h** all the words of the Book H265
Ne 13: 1 read aloud in the **h** *of* the people and H265
Job 9:16 not believe *he would* **give** me a **h**. H263+7754
Job 33: 8 "But you have said in my **h**—I heard the H265
Ecc 1: 8 enough of seeing, nor the ear its fill of **h**. H9048
Isa 5: 9 The LORD Almighty has declared in my **h** H265
Isa 6: 9 " '*Be* **ever h**, but never H9048+9048
Isa 22:14 LORD Almighty has revealed this in my **h**: H265
Isa 36:11 us in Hebrew in the **h** *of* the people on the H265
Isa 49:20 your bereavement will yet say in your **h**, H265
Jer 2: 2 "Go and proclaim in the **h** *of* Jerusalem H265
Jer 26:15 to you to speak all these words in your **h**." H265
Jer 28: 7 have to say in your **h** and in the hearing of H265
Jer 28: 7 your hearing and in the **h** *of* all the people: H265
Da 5:10 **h** the voices of the king and his nobles NDT
Am 8:11 a famine of **h** the words of the LORD. H9048
Mt 9:12 *On* **h** this, Jesus said, "It is not the healthy G201
Mt 13:13 they do not see; *though* **h**, they do not hear G201
Mt 13:14 " '*You will be* **ever h** but never G198+201
Mt 14:13 **H** of this, the crowds followed him on foot G201
Mt 22:34 **H** that Jesus had silenced the Sadducees G201
Mk 2:17 *On* **h** this, Jesus said to them, "It is not the G201
Mk 4:12 and **ever h** but never understanding G201+201
Mk 6:29 *On* **h** *of* this, John's disciples came and took G201
Lk 4:21 "Today this scripture is fulfilled in your **h**." G4044
Lk 8:10 they may not see; *though* **h**, they may not G201
Lk 8:50 **H** this, Jesus said to Jairus, "Don't be G201
Lk 23: 6 *On* **h** this, Pilate asked if the man was a G201
Jn 6:60 *On* **h** it, many of his disciples said, "This is G201
Jn 7:40 *On* **h** his words, some of the people said G201
Jn 7:51 a man without first **h** him to find out what G201
Ac 5:24 On **h** this report, the captain of the temple G201
Ac 19: 5 *On* **h** this, they were baptized in the name G201
Ac 28:26 "*You will be* **ever h** but never G198+201
Ro 10:17 faith comes from **h** the **message**, and the G198
1Co 12:17 where would the **sense of h** be? G198

HEARKEN, HEARKENED, HEARKENETH, HEARKENING (KJV) AGREE, AGREED, ATTENTION, HEAR, HEARD, LISTENED, LISTENED, OBEY, OBEYED, OBEYING

HEARS (51) [HEAR]

Ge 21: 6 everyone who **h** *about* this will laugh H9048
Ex 17:14 and **make sure** *that* Joshua **h** it H8492+928+265
Nu 24: 4 the prophecy of *one who* **h** the words of H9048
Nu 24:16 the prophecy of *one who* **h** the words of H9048
Nu 30: 4 her father **h** *about* her vow or pledge H9048
Nu 30: 5 her father forbids her when he **h** *about* it, H9048
Nu 30: 7 her husband **h** *about* it but says H9048
Nu 30: 8 husband forbids her when he **h** *about* it, H9048
Nu 30:11 her husband **h** *about* it but says H9048
Nu 30:12 nullifies them when he **h** *about* them, H9048
Nu 30:14 nothing to her when he **h** *about* them. H9048
Nu 30:15 them some time after he **h** *about* them, H9048
Dt 29:19 When such a person **h** the words of this H9048
1Sa 3:11 ears of everyone who **h** *about* it tingle. H9048
1Sa 16: 2 If Saul **h** *about* it, he will kill me H9048
2Sa 17: 9 whoever **h** *about* it will say H9048+9048
2Ki 19: 7 When *he* **h** a certain report, I will make H9048
2Ki 21:12 ears of everyone *who* **h** *of* it will tingle. H9048
Ps 4: 3 himself; the LORD **h** when I call to him. H9048
Ps 34:17 and the LORD **h** them; he delivers H9048
Ps 55:17 I cry out in distress, and *he* **h** my voice. H9048
Ps 69:33 The LORD **h** the needy and does not H9048
Ps 97: 8 Zion **h** and rejoices and the villages of H9048
Ps 145:19 fear him; *he* **h** their cry and saves them. H9048
Pr 15:29 but *he* **h** the prayer of the righteous. H9048
Pr 25:10 the *one who* **h** it may shame you and H9048
Isa 11: 3 decide by **what** he **h** *with* his ears; H5461
Isa 30:19 As soon as he **h**, he will answer you H9048
Isa 37: 7 When *he* **h** a certain report, I will make H9048
Jer 19: 3 the ears of everyone *who* **h** *of* it tingle. H9048
Eze 33: 4 then if *anyone* **h** the trumpet H9048+7754+9048
Da 3:10 that everyone who **h** the sound of the A10725
Mt 7:24 everyone who **h** these words of mine and G201
Mt 7:26 But everyone who **h** these words of mine G201
Mt 13:19 *When* anyone **h** the message about the G201
Mt 13:20 refers to someone *who* **h** the word and at G201
Mt 13:22 thorns refers to someone *who* **h** the word, G201
Mt 13:23 soil refers to someone *who* **h** the word G201
Lk 6:47 who comes to me and **h** my words and puts G201
Lk 6:49 But the *one who* **h** my words and does not G201
Jn 3:29 is full of joy **when** *he* **h** the bridegroom's G1328S
Jn 5:24 whoever **h** my word and believes him who G201
Jn 8:47 Whoever belongs to God **h** what God says G201
Jn 12:47 "If anyone **h** my words but does not keep G201
Jn 16:13 he will speak only what *he* **h**, and he will G201
Ac 2: 8 is it that each of us **h** them in our native G201
1Jn 5:14 ask anything according to his will, *he* **h** us. G201
1Jn 5:15 And if we know that *he* **h** us—whatever we G201
Rev 3:20 If anyone **h** my voice and opens the door, G201
Rev 22:17 And let the *one who* **h** say, "Come!" Let G201
Rev 22:18 I warn everyone who **h** the words of the G201

HEART (532) [BROKENHEARTED, DISHEARTENED, DOWNHEARTED, FAINTHEARTED, HARDHEARTED, HEART'S, HEARTACHE, HEARTFELT, HEARTLESS, HEARTS, HEARTS', KINDHEARTED, STUBBORN-HEARTED, WHOLEHEARTED, WHOLEHEARTEDLY]

Ge 6: 5 of the human **h** was only evil all the H4213
Ge 6: 6 the earth, and his **h** was deeply troubled. H4213
Ge 8:21 the pleasing aroma and said in his **h**: H4213
Ge 8:21 of the human **h** is evil from childhood. H4213
Ge 24:45 "Before I finished praying in my **h** H4213
Ge 34: 3 His **h** was drawn to Dinah daughter of H5883
Ge 34: 8 son Shechem has his **h** set on your H5883
Ex 4:21 But I will harden his **h** so that he will not H4213
Ex 7: 3 But I will harden Pharaoh's **h**, and though H4213
Ex 7:13 Yet Pharaoh's **h** became hard and he H4213
Ex 7:14 to Moses, "Pharaoh's **h** is unyielding; he H4213
Ex 7:22 and Pharaoh's **h** became hard; he H4213
Ex 7:23 and did not take even this to **h**. H4213
Ex 8:15 he hardened his **h** and would not listen to H4213
Ex 8:19 But Pharaoh's **h** was hard and he would H4213
Ex 8:32 hardened his **h** and would not let H4213
Ex 9: 7 Yet his **h** was unyielding and he would H4213
Ex 9:12 hardened Pharaoh's **h** and he would not H4213
Ex 9:35 So Pharaoh's **h** was hard and he would H4213
Ex 10: 1 I have hardened his **h** and the hearts of H4213
Ex 10:20 But the LORD hardened Pharaoh's **h**, and H4213
Ex 10:27 But the LORD hardened Pharaoh's **h**, and H4213
Ex 11:10 the LORD hardened Pharaoh's **h**, and H4213
Ex 14: 4 And I will harden Pharaoh's **h**, and he will H4213
Ex 14: 8 LORD hardened the **h** *of* Pharaoh king of H4213
Ex 15: 8 waters congealed in the **h** *of* the sea. H4213
Ex 25: 2 from everyone whose **h** prompts them to H4213
Ex 28:29 of Israel over his **h** on the breastpiece of H4213
Ex 28:30 be over Aaron's **h** whenever he enters H4213
Ex 28:30 the Israelites over his **h** before the LORD. H4213
Ex 35:21 willing and whose **h** moved them came H4213
Lev 19:17 " 'Do not hate a fellow Israelite in your **h** H4222
Dt 2:30 stubborn and his **h** obstinate in order to H4222
Dt 4: 9 them fade from your **h** as long as you live. H4222
Dt 4:29 him with all your **h** and with all your soul H4222
Dt 4:39 take to **h** this day that the LORD H4222
Dt 6: 5 God with all your **h** and with all your soul H4222
Dt 8: 2 you in order to know what was in your **h**, H4222
Dt 8: 5 Know then in your **h** that as a man H4222
Dt 8:14 then your **h** will become proud and you H4222
Dt 10:12 God with all your **h** and with all your soul H4222
Dt 11: 3 the things he did in the **h** *of* Egypt, H9348
Dt 11:13 him with all your **h** and with all your soul H4222
Dt 13: 3 him with all your **h** and with all your soul H4222
Dt 15:10 to them and do so without a grudging **h**; H4222
Dt 17:17 many wives, or his **h** will be led astray. H4222
Dt 26:16 them with all your **h** and with all your soul H4222
Dt 28:65 weary with longing, and a despairing **h**. H5883
Dt 29:18 you today whose **h** turns away from the H4222
Dt 30: 1 you take them to **h** wherever the LORD H4222
Dt 30: 2 him with all your **h** and with all your soul H4222
Dt 30: 6 him with all your **h** and with all your soul H4222
Dt 30:10 God with all your **h** and with all your soul H4222
Dt 30:14 mouth and in your **h** so you may obey it. H4222
Dt 30:17 But if your **h** turns away and you are not H4222
Dt 32:46 "Take to **h** all the words I have solemnly H4222
Jos 22: 5 him with all your **h** and with all your soul." H4222
Jos 23:14 know with all your **h** and soul that not one H4222
Jdg 5: 9 My **h** is with Israel's princes, with the H4213
Jdg 5:15 of Reuben there was much searching of **h**. H4213
Jdg 5:16 of Reuben there was much searching of **h**. H4213
1Sa 1:13 Hannah was praying in her **h**, and her lips H4213
1Sa 2: 1 "My **h** rejoices in the LORD; in the LORD H4213
1Sa 2:35 do according to what is in my **h** and mind. H4222
1Sa 4:13 because his **h** feared for the ark of God. H4213
1Sa 9:19 way and will tell you all that is in your **h**. H4222
1Sa 10: 9 God changed Saul's **h**, and all these H4213
1Sa 12:20 but serve the LORD with all your **h**. H4222
1Sa 12:24 serve him faithfully with all your **h**; H4222
1Sa 13:14 a man after his own **h** and appointed him H4222
1Sa 14: 7 ahead; I am with you **h and soul**." H3869+4222
1Sa 16: 7 appearance, but the LORD looks at the **h**." H4222
1Sa 17:28 you are and how wicked your **h** is; H4222
1Sa 17:32 "Let no one lose **h** on account of this H4213
1Sa 21:12 took these words to **h** and was very much H4222
1Sa 25:37 his **h** failed him and he became like H4213
1Sa 28: 5 he was afraid; terror filled his **h**. H4213
2Sa 3:21 you may rule over all that your **h** desires." H5883
2Sa 6:16 the LORD, she despised him in her **h**. H4213
2Sa 13:20 Don't take this thing to **h**." And Tamar H4213
2Sa 14: 1 that the king's **h** longed for Absalom. H4213
2Sa 17:10 whose **h** is like the heart of a lion H4213
2Sa 17:10 whose heart is like the **h** *of* a lion, will H4213
2Sa 18:14 into Absalom's **h** while Absalom was H4213
2Sa 22:46 They all **lose h**; they come trembling from H5570
1Ki 2: 4 before me with all their **h** and soul, H4222
1Ki 2:44 You know in your **h** all the wrong you did H4222
1Ki 3: 6 to you and righteous and upright in **h**. H4222
1Ki 3: 9 servant a discerning **h** to govern your H4213
1Ki 3:12 I will give you a wise and discerning **h**, so H4213
1Ki 8:17 David had it in his **h** to build a temple H4222
1Ki 8:18 to have it in your **h** to build a temple for H4222
1Ki 8:39 you alone know every human **h**), H4222
1Ki 8:47 have a change of **h** in the land where H4213
1Ki 8:48 to you with all their **h** and soul in the land H4222
1Ki 8:66 joyful and glad in **h** for all the good H4213
1Ki 9: 3 My eyes and my **h** will always be there. H4213
1Ki 9: 4 with integrity of **h** and uprightness, H4222
1Ki 10:24 to hear the wisdom God had put in his **h**. H4213
1Ki 11: 4 his wives turned his **h** after other gods H4222
1Ki 11: 4 his **h** was not fully devoted to the H4222
1Ki 11: 4 as the **h** *of* David his father had been. H4222
1Ki 11: 9 Solomon because his **h** had turned away H4222
1Ki 11:37 you will rule over all that your **h** desires; H5883
1Ki 14: 8 followed me with all his **h**, H4222
1Ki 15: 3 his **h** was not fully devoted to the LORD his H4222
1Ki 15: 3 as the **h** *of* David his forefather had been. H4222
1Ki 15:14 Asa's **h** was fully committed to the LORD H4222
2Ki 9:24 arrow pierced his **h** and he slumped down H4213
2Ki 10:31 the LORD, the God of Israel, with all his **h**. H4222
2Ki 22:19 Because your **h** was responsive and you H4222
2Ki 23: 3 decrees with all his **h** and all his soul, H4213
2Ki 23:25 with all his **h** and with all his soul and H4222
1Ch 15:29 celebrating, she despised him in her **h**. H4213
1Ch 22: 7 I had it in my **h** to build a house for the H4222
1Ch 22:19 Now devote your **h** and soul to seeking the H4222
1Ch 28: 2 I had it in my **h** to build a house as a H4222
1Ch 28: 9 LORD searches every **h** and understands H4222
1Ch 29:17 that you test the **h** and are pleased with H4222
2Ch 6: 7 David had it in his **h** to build a temple H4222
2Ch 6: 8 to have it in your **h** to build a temple for H4222
2Ch 6:30 for you alone know the human **h**), H4222
2Ch 6:37 have a change of **h** in the land where H4213
2Ch 6:38 to you with all their **h** and soul in the land H4213
2Ch 7:10 joyful and glad in **h** for the good things H4213
2Ch 7:16 My eyes and my **h** will always be there. H4213
2Ch 9:23 to hear the wisdom God had put in his **h**. H4213
2Ch 12:14 he had not set his **h** on seeking the LORD. H4213
2Ch 15:12 their ancestors, with all their **h** and soul. H4222
2Ch 15:17 Asa's **h** was fully committed to the LORD H4222
2Ch 17: 6 His **h** was devoted to the ways of the LORD H4213
2Ch 19: 3 have set your **h** on seeking God. H4222
2Ch 22: 9 who sought the LORD with all his **h**. H4222
2Ch 30:19 sets their **h** on seeking God—the LORD, H4222
2Ch 32:25 But Hezekiah's **h** was proud and he did H4213
2Ch 32:26 Hezekiah repented of the pride of his **h**, H4213
2Ch 32:31 to know everything that was in his **h**. H4222
2Ch 34:27 Because your **h** was responsive and you H4222

2Ch 34:31 decrees with all his **h** and all his soul, H4222
2Ch 36:13 hardened his **h** and would not turn to H4222
2Ch 36:22 the LORD moved the **h** *of* Cyrus king of H8120
Ezr 1: 1 the LORD moved the **h** *of* Cyrus king of H8120
Ezr 1: 5 everyone whose **h** God had moved H8120
Ezr 7:27 it into the king's **h** to bring honor to the H4213
Ne 2: 2 This can be nothing but sadness of **h**." H4213
Ne 2:12 God had put in my **h** to do for Jerusalem. H4213
Ne 4: 6 the people worked *with all* their **h**. H4213
Ne 7: 5 my God put it into my **h** to assemble the H4213
Ne 9: 8 You found his **h** faithful to you, and you H4222
Job 10:13 "But this is what you concealed in your **h** H4222
Job 11:13 if you devote your **h** to him and stretch out H4213
Job 15:12 Why has your **h** carried you away, and H4213
Job 17:11 are shattered. Yet the desires of my **h** H4222
Job 19:27 How my **h** yearns within me! H4000
Job 22:22 his mouth and lay up his words in your **h**. H4222
Job 23:16 God has made my **h** faint; the Almighty H4213
Job 29:13 blessed me; I made the widow's **h** sing. H4213
Job 31: 7 the path, if my **h** has been led by my eyes H4213
Job 31: 9 "If my **h** has been enticed by a woman, or H4213
Job 31:27 so that my **h** was secretly enticed and my H4213
Job 31:33 as people do, by hiding my guilt in my **h** H2460
Job 33: 3 My words come from an upright **h**; my lips H4213
Job 36:13 "The godless in **h** harbor resentment H4213
Job 37: 1 "At this my **h** pounds and leaps from its H4213
Job 37:24 he not have regard for all the wise in **h**?" H4213
Ps 4: 7 Fill my **h** with joy when their grain and H4213
Ps 5: 9 be trusted; their **h** is filled with malice. H7931
Ps 7:10 Most High, who saves the upright in **h**. H4213
Ps 9: 1 with all my **h**; I will tell of all your H4213
Ps 10: 3 He boasts about the cravings of his **h**; he H5883
Ps 11: 2 from the shadows at the upright in **h**. H4213
Ps 13: 2 day after day have sorrow in my **h**? H4222
Ps 13: 5 my **h** rejoices in your salvation. H4213
Ps 14: 1 The fool says in his **h**, "There is no God." H4213
Ps 15: 2 who speaks the truth from their **h**; H4222
Ps 16: 7 even at night my **h** instructs me. H4000
Ps 16: 9 Therefore my **h** is glad and my tongue H4213
Ps 17: 3 Though you probe my **h**, though you H4213
Ps 18:45 They all **lose h**; they come trembling from H5570
Ps 19: 8 of the LORD are right, giving joy to the **h**. H4213
Ps 19:14 meditation of my **h** be pleasing in your H4213
Ps 20: 4 you the desire of your **h** and make all your H4222
Ps 22:14 My **h** has turned to wax; it has melted H4213
Ps 24: 4 one who has clean hands and a pure **h**, H4222
Ps 25:17 the troubles of my **h** and free me from my H4222
Ps 26: 2 try me, examine my **h** and my mind; H4000
Ps 27: 3 army besiege me, my **h** will not fear H4213
Ps 27: 8 My **h** says of you, "Seek his face!" Your H4213
Ps 27:14 be strong and **take h** and wait for H599+4213
Ps 28: 7 my shield; my **h** trusts in him, and he H4213
Ps 28: 7 My **h** leaps for joy, and with my song I H4213
Ps 30:12 that my **h** may sing your praises and not H3883
Ps 31:24 Be strong and **take h**, all you who H599+4222
Ps 32:11 all you who are upright in **h**! H4213
Ps 33:11 the purposes of his **h** through all H4213
Ps 36: 1 from God in my **h** concerning the H4213
Ps 36:10 your righteousness to the upright in **h**. H4213
Ps 37: 4 he will give you the desires of your **h**. H4213
Ps 38: 8 utterly crushed; I groan in anguish of **h**. H4213
Ps 38:10 My **h** pounds, my strength fails me; even H4213
Ps 39: 3 my **h** grew hot within me. While I H4213
Ps 40: 8 will, my God; your law is within my **h**." H5055
Ps 40:10 I do not hide your righteousness in my **h**; H4213
Ps 40:12 of my head, and my **h** fails within me. H4213
Ps 41: 6 while his **h** gathers slander; then H4213
Ps 44:21 since he knows the secrets of the **h**? H4213
Ps 45: 1 My **h** is stirred by a noble theme as I H4213
Ps 46: 2 the mountains fall into the **h** *of* the sea, H4213
Ps 49: 3 the meditation of my **h** will give you H4213
Ps 51:10 Create in me a pure **h**, O God, and renew H4213
Ps 51:17 a broken and contrite **h** you, God, H4213
Ps 53: 1 The fool says in his **h**, "There is no God." H4213
Ps 55: 4 My **h** is in anguish within me; the terrors H4213
Ps 55:21 war is in his **h**; his words are more H4213
Ps 57: 7 My **h**, O God, is steadfast, my heart is H4213
Ps 57: 7 is steadfast, my **h** is steadfast; I will sing H4213
Ps 58: 2 in your **h** you devise injustice, and H4213
Ps 61: 2 I call as my **h** grows faint; lead me H4213
Ps 62:10 increase, do not set your **h** on them. H4213
Ps 64: 6 the human mind and **h** are cunning. H4213
Ps 64:10 all the upright in **h** will glory in him! H4213
Ps 66:18 If I had cherished sin in my **h**, the Lord H4213
Ps 69:20 Scorn has broken my **h** and has left me H4213
Ps 73: 1 good to Israel, to those who are pure in **h**. H4222
Ps 73:13 vain I have kept my **h** pure and have H4222
Ps 73:21 When my **h** was grieved and my spirit H4222
Ps 73:26 My flesh and my **h** may fail, but God is H4222
Ps 73:26 is the strength of my **h** and my portion H4222
Ps 77: 6 My **h** meditated and my spirit asked H4222
Ps 78:72 shepherded them with integrity of **h**; H4222
Ps 84: 2 my **h** and my flesh cry out for the living H4213
Ps 86:11 give me an undivided **h**, that I may fear H4222
Ps 86:12 my God, with all my **h**; I will glorify your H4222
Ps 89:50 how I bear in my **h** the taunts of all the H2668
Ps 90:12 that we may gain a **h** *of* wisdom. H4222
Ps 94:15 all the upright in **h** will follow it. H4213
Ps 97:11 the righteous and joy on the upright in **h**. H4213
Ps 101: 2 affairs of my house with a blameless **h**. H4222
Ps 101: 4 The perverse of **h** shall be far from me; H4222
Ps 101: 5 whoever has haughty eyes and a proud **h** H4222
Ps 102: 4 My **h** is blighted and withered like grass; H4213
Ps 108: 1 My **h**, O God, is steadfast; I will sing and H4213
Ps 109:22 and my **h** is wounded within me. H4213
Ps 111: 1 the LORD with all my **h** in the council of H4222
Ps 119: 2 statutes and seek him with all their **h**— H4213
Ps 119: 7 you with an upright **h** as I learn your H4222
Ps 119:10 I seek you with all my **h**; do not let me H4213
Ps 119:11 your word in my **h** that I might not sin H4213
Ps 119:30 faithfulness; *I have* **set** *my* **h** *on* your laws. H8751
Ps 119:34 keep your law and obey it with all my **h**. H4213
Ps 119:36 Turn my **h** toward your statutes and not H4213
Ps 119:58 I have sought your face with all my **h**; be H4213
Ps 119:69 I keep your precepts with all my **h**. H4213
Ps 119:111 heritage forever; they are the joy of my **h**. H4213
Ps 119:112 My **h** is set on keeping your decrees to H4213
Ps 119:145 I call with all my **h**; answer me, LORD, H4213
Ps 119:161 but my **h** trembles at your word. H4213
Ps 125: 4 are good, to those who are upright in **h**. H4213
Ps 131: 1 My **h** is not proud, LORD, my eyes are not H4213
Ps 138: 1 with all my **h**; before the "gods" I H4213
Ps 139:23 and know my **h**; test me and know H4222
Ps 141: 4 Do not let my **h** be drawn to what is evil H4213
Ps 143: 4 within me; my **h** within me is dismayed. H4213
Ps 148:14 of Israel, the people **close to** his **h**. H7940
Pr 2: 2 applying your **h** to understanding— H4213
Pr 2:10 For wisdom will enter your **h**, and H4213
Pr 3: 1 keep my commands in your **h**, H4213
Pr 3: 3 write them on the tablet of your **h**. H4213
Pr 3: 5 LORD with all your **h** and lean not on your H4213
Pr 4: 4 "Take hold of my words with all your **h** H4213
Pr 4:21 of your sight, keep them within your **h**; H4222
Pr 4:23 all else, guard your **h**, for everything you H4213
Pr 5:12 How my **h** spurned correction! H4213
Pr 6:14 who plots evil with deceit in his **h**—he H4213
Pr 6:18 a **h** that devises wicked schemes, feet that H4213
Pr 6:21 Bind them always on your **h**; fasten them H4213
Pr 6:25 Do not lust in your **h** after her beauty or H4222
Pr 7: 3 write them on the tablet of your **h**. H4213
Pr 7:25 Do not let your **h** turn to her ways or stray H4213
Pr 10: 8 The wise in **h** accept commands, but a H4213
Pr 10:20 the **h** *of* the wicked is of little value. H4213
Pr 12:23 themselves, but a fool's **h** blurts out folly. H4213
Pr 12:25 Anxiety weighs down the **h**, but a kind H4213
Pr 13:12 Hope deferred makes the **h** sick, but a H4213
Pr 14:10 *Each* **h** knows its own bitterness, and no H4213
Pr 14:13 Even in laughter the **h** may ache, and H4213
Pr 14:30 A **h** at peace gives life to the body, but H4213
Pr 14:33 reposes in the **h** *of* the discerning and H4213
Pr 15:13 A happy **h** makes the face cheerful, but H4213
Pr 15:14 The discerning **h** seeks knowledge, but H4213
Pr 15:15 the cheerful **h** has a continual feast. H4213
Pr 15:28 The **h** *of* the righteous weighs its answers H4213
Pr 15:30 in a messenger's eyes brings joy to the **h**, H4213
Pr 16: 1 To humans belong the plans of the **h**, but H4213
Pr 16: 5 The LORD detests all the proud of **h**. H4213
Pr 16:21 The wise in **h** are called discerning, and H4213
Pr 17: 3 furnace for gold, but the LORD tests the **h**. H4213
Pr 17:20 One whose **h** is corrupt does not prosper H4213
Pr 17:22 A cheerful **h** is good medicine, but a H4213
Pr 18:12 Before a downfall the **h** is haughty, but H4213
Pr 18:15 The **h** *of* the discerning acquires H4213
Pr 19: 3 yet their **h** rages against the LORD. H4213
Pr 19:21 Many are the plans in a person's **h**, but it H4213
Pr 20: 5 purposes of a person's **h** are deep waters, H4213
Pr 20: 9 "I have kept my **h** pure; I am clean and H4213
Pr 21: 1 hand the king's **h** is a stream of water H4213
Pr 21: 2 ways are right, but the LORD weighs the **h**. H4213
Pr 21: 4 Haughty eyes and a proud **h**—the H4213
Pr 22:11 who loves a pure **h** and who speaks with H4213
Pr 22:15 Folly is bound up in the **h** *of* a child, but H4213
Pr 22:17 of the wise; apply your **h** to what I teach, H4213
Pr 22:18 keep them in your **h** and have all of them H1061
Pr 23: 7 he says to you, but his **h** is not with you. H4213
Pr 23:12 Apply your **h** to instruction and your ears H4213
Pr 23:15 My son, if your **h** is wise, then my heart H4213
Pr 23:15 then my **h** will be glad indeed; H4213
Pr 23:17 Do not let your **h** envy sinners, but always H4213
Pr 23:19 be wise, and set your **h** on the right path: H4213
Pr 23:26 give me your **h** and let your eyes delight H4213
Pr 24:12 does not he who weighs the **h** perceive it? H4213
Pr 24:17 they stumble, do not let your **h** rejoice, H4213
Pr 24:32 I applied my **h** to what I observed and H4213
Pr 25:20 is one who sings songs to a heavy **h**. H4213
Pr 26:23 are fervent lips with an evil **h**. H4213
Pr 27: 9 Perfume and incense bring joy to the **h** H4213
Pr 27:11 bring joy to my **h**; then I can answer H4213
Pr 27:19 the face, so one's life reflects the **h**. H4213
Pr 28:14 whoever hardens their **h** falls into trouble. H4213
Ecc 2: 8 harem as well—the **delights of a** man's **h**. H9503
Ecc 2:10 eyes desired; I refused my **h** no pleasure. H4213
Ecc 2:10 My **h** took delight in all my labor, and this H4213
Ecc 2:20 So my **h** began to despair over all my H4213
Ecc 3:11 He has also set eternity in the human **h** H4213
Ecc 5: 2 do not be hasty in your **h** to utter anything H4213
Ecc 5:20 keeps them occupied with gladness of **h**. H4213
Ecc 7: 2 everyone; the living should take this to **h**. H4213
Ecc 7: 3 because a sad face is good for the **h**. H4213
Ecc 7: 4 The **h** *of* the wise is in the house of H4213
Ecc 7: 4 the **h** *of* fools is in the house of H4213
Ecc 7: 7 into a fool, and a bribe corrupts the **h**. H4213
Ecc 7:22 you know in your **h** that many times you H4213
Ecc 7:26 whose **h** is a trap and whose hands are H4213
Ecc 8: 5 the wise **h** will know the proper time H4213
Ecc 9: 7 drink your wine with a joyful **h**, for H4213
Ecc 10: 2 The **h** *of* the wise inclines to the right, but H4213
Ecc 10: 2 the right, but the **h** *of* the fool to the left. H4213
Ecc 11: 9 let your **h** give you joy in the days of H4213
Ecc 11: 9 the ways of your **h** and whatever your eyes H4213
Ecc 11:10 anxiety from your **h** and cast off the H4213
SS 3: 1 my bed I looked for the one my **h** loves; H5883
SS 3: 2 I will search for the one my **h** loves. H5883
SS 3: 3 "Have you seen the one my **h** loves?" H5883
SS 3: 4 them when I found the one my **h** loves. H5883
SS 3:11 of his wedding, the day his **h** rejoiced. H4213
SS 4: 9 *You have* **stolen** my **h**, my sister, my bride H4220
SS 4: 9 *you have* **stolen** my **h** with one glance of H4220
SS 5: 2 I slept but my **h** was awake. Listen! My H4213
SS 5: 4 my **h** began to pound for him. H5055
SS 5: 6 he was gone. My **h** sank at his departure H5883
SS 8: 6 Place me like a seal over your **h**, like a H4213
Isa 1: 5 head is injured, your whole **h** afflicted. H4222
Isa 6:10 Make the **h** *of* this people calloused H4213
Isa 7: 4 Do not lose **h** because of these two H4222
Isa 9: 9 who say with pride and arrogance of **h**, H4222
Isa 10:12 willful pride of his **h** and the haughty look H4222
Isa 13: 7 will go limp, every **h** will melt with fear. H4222
Isa 14:13 You said in your **h**, "I will ascend to the H4222
Isa 15: 5 My **h** cries out over Moab; her fugitives H4213
Isa 16:11 My **h** laments for Moab like a harp, my H5055
Isa 19: 3 Egyptians *will* **lose h**, H1327+8120+928+7931
Isa 19:10 all the wage earners will be sick at **h**. H5883
Isa 19:19 be an altar to the LORD in the **h** *of* Egypt, H9348
Isa 21: 4 My **h** falters, fear makes me tremble; the H4222
Isa 32: 4 The fearful **h** will know and understand H4222
Isa 40:11 his arms and carries them close to his **h**; H2668
Isa 42:25 but they did not take it to **h**. H4213
Isa 44:20 on ashes; a deluded **h** misleads him; he H4213
Isa 46: 8 keep it in mind, take it to **h**, you rebels. H4213
Isa 49:21 Then you will say in your **h**, 'Who bore H4222
Isa 51: 7 who have taken my instruction to **h**: H4213
Isa 57: 1 no one takes it to **h**; the devout are H4213
Isa 57:11 remembered me nor taken this to **h**? H4213
Isa 57:15 lowly and to revive the **h** *of* the contrite. H4213
Isa 60: 5 your **h** will throb and swell with joy H4222
Isa 65:14 out from anguish of **h** and wail in H4213
Isa 66:14 your **h** will rejoice and you will flourish H4213
Jer 3:10 Judah did not return to me with all her **h**, H4213
Jer 3:15 I will give you shepherds after my own **h**, H4213
Jer 4: 9 "the king and the officials will lose **h**, the H4213
Jer 4:14 wash the evil from your **h** and be saved. H4213
Jer 4:18 How bitter it is! How it pierces to the **h**!" H4213
Jer 4:19 the agony of my **h**! My heart pounds H4213
Jer 4:19 My **h** pounds within me, I cannot keep H4213
Jer 8:18 in sorrow, my **h** is faint within me. H4213
Jer 9:26 house of Israel is uncircumcised in **h**." H4213
Jer 11:20 righteously and test the **h** and mind, H4213
Jer 15: 1 my **h** would not go out to this people. H5883
Jer 17: 5 flesh and whose **h** turns away from the H4213
Jer 17: 9 The **h** is deceitful above all things and H4213
Jer 17:10 the LORD search the **h** and examine the H4213
Jer 20: 9 his word is in my **h** like a fire, a fire shut H4213
Jer 20:12 the righteous and probe the **h** and mind, H4213
Jer 22:17 "But your eyes and your **h** are set only on H4213
Jer 23: 9 My **h** is broken within me; all my bones H4213
Jer 23:20 fully accomplishes the purposes of his **h**. H4213
Jer 24: 7 I will give them a **h** to know me, that I am H4213
Jer 24: 7 they will return to me with all their **h**. H4213
Jer 29:13 me when you seek me with all your **h**. H4222
Jer 30:24 fully accomplishes the purposes of his **h**. H4213
Jer 31:20 Therefore my **h** yearns for him; I have H5055
Jer 32:39 I will give them singleness of **h** and action, H4213
Jer 32:41 them in this land with all my **h** and soul. H4213
Jer 48:29 her conceit and the haughtiness of her **h**. H4213
Jer 48:36 "So my **h** laments for Moab like the music H4213
Jer 48:41 will be like the **h** *of* a woman in labor. H4213
Jer 49:16 the pride of your **h** have deceived you, H4213
Jer 49:22 will be like the **h** *of* a woman in labor. H4213
Jer 51:46 Do not lose **h** or be afraid when rumors H4222
La 1:20 and in my **h** I am disturbed, for I H4213
La 1:22 My groans are many and my **h** is faint." H4213
La 2:11 my **h** is poured out on the ground H3879
La 2:19 pour out your **h** like water in the presence H4213
La 3:13 He pierced my **h** with arrows from his H4000
Eze 3:10 take to **h** all the words I speak H4222
Eze 11:19 them an undivided **h** and put a new spirit H4213
Eze 11:19 from them their **h** *of* stone and give them H4213
Eze 11:19 heart of stone and give them a **h** *of* flesh. H4213
Eze 18:31 get a new **h** and a new spirit. H4213
Eze 21: 6 them with broken **h** and bitter grief. H5516
Eze 21: 7 Every **h** will melt with fear and every hand H4213
Eze 25: 6 the malice of your **h** against the land of H5883
Eze 27:27 will sink into the **h** *of* the sea on the day H4213
Eze 28: 2 " 'In the pride of your **h** you say, "I am a H4213
Eze 28: 2 the throne of a god in the **h** *of* the seas." H4213
Eze 28: 5 of your wealth your **h** has grown proud. H4222
Eze 28: 8 die a violent death in the **h** *of* the seas. H4213
Eze 28:17 Your **h** became proud on account of your H4213
Eze 36:26 will give you a new **h** and put a new spirit H4213
Eze 36:26 from you your **h** *of* stone and give you H4213
Eze 36:26 heart of stone and give you a **h** *of* flesh. H4213
Eze 44: 7 uncircumcised in **h** and flesh into my H4213
Eze 44: 9 uncircumcised in **h** and flesh is to enter H4213
Da 5:20 But when his **h** became arrogant and A10381
Da 11:28 his **h** will be set against the holy H4222

Da 11:30 will oppose him, and *he will* **lose h**. H3874
Hos 5: 4 A spirit of prostitution is in their **h**; they do H7931
Hos 10: 2 Their **h** is deceitful, and now they must H4213
Hos 11: 8 My **h** is changed within me; all my H4213
Joel 2:12 "return to me with all your **h**, with fasting H4222
Joel 2:13 Rend your **h** and not your garments H4222
Am 7:10 against you in the very **h** *of* Israel. H7931
Ob 3 The pride of your **h** has deceived you, you H4213
Jnh 2: 3 into the *very* **h** *of* the seas, and H4222
Hab 3:16 I heard and my **h** pounded, my lips H1061
Zep 3:14 Be glad and rejoice with all your **h** H4213
Mt 5: 8 Blessed are the pure *in* **h**, for they will see *G2840*
Mt 5:28 committed adultery with her in his **h**. *G2840*
Mt 6:21 your treasure is, there your **h** will be also. *G2840*
Mt 9: 2 said to the man, "**Take h**, son; your sins *G2510*
Mt 9:22 "**Take h**, daughter," he said, "your faith *G2510*
Mt 11:29 I am gentle and humble *in* **h**, and you *G2840*
Mt 12:34 For the mouth speaks what the **h** is full of. *G2840*
Mt 12:40 three nights in the **h** of the earth. *G2840*
Mt 13:15 For this people's **h** has become calloused *G2840*
Mt 13:19 snatches away what was sown in their **h**. *G2840*
Mt 15:18 out of a person's mouth come from the **h**, *G2840*
Mt 15:19 For out of the **h** come evil thoughts *G2840*
Mt 18:35 forgive your brother or sister from your **h**." *G2840*
Mt 22:37 God with all your **h** and with all your soul *G2840*
Mk 7:19 doesn't go into their **h** but into their *G2840*
Mk 7:21 out of a person's **h**, that evil thoughts *G2840*
Mk 11:23 not doubt in their **h** but believes that what *G2840*
Mk 12:30 God with all your **h** and with all your soul *G2840*
Mk 12:33 To love him with all your **h**, with all your *G2840*
Lk 2:19 these things and pondered them in her **h**. *G2840*
Lk 2:51 mother treasured all these things in her **h**. *G2840*
Lk 6:45 things out of the good stored up *in* his **h**, *G2840*
Lk 6:45 things out of the evil stored up *in* his **h**. *G2840*
Lk 6:45 For the mouth speaks what the **h** is full of. *G2840*
Lk 7:13 saw her, *his* **h went out** to her and he said *G5072*
Lk 8:15 stands for those with a noble and good **h**, *G2840*
Lk 10:27 God with all your **h** and with all your soul *G2840*
Lk 12:29 And *do* not **set** *your* **h on** what you will eat *G2426*
Lk 12:34 your treasure is, there your **h** will be also. *G2840*
Jn 16:33 But **take h**! I have overcome *G2510*
Ac 1:24 "Lord, you **know** everyone's **h**. *G2841*
Ac 2:26 Therefore my **h** is glad and my tongue *G2840*
Ac 2:37 they were cut *to* the **h** and said to Peter *G2840*
Ac 4:32 All the believers were one *in* **h** and mind *G2840*
Ac 5: 3 has so filled your **h** that you have lied to *G2840*
Ac 8:21 because your **h** is not right before God. *G2840*
Ac 8:22 you for having such a thought *in* your **h**. *G2840*
Ac 13:22 a man after my own **h**; he will do *G2840*
Ac 15: 8 *who* **knows the h**, showed that he *G2841*
Ac 16:14 The Lord opened her **h** to respond to *G2840*
Ac 21:13 are you weeping and breaking my **h**? *G2840*
Ac 28:27 For this people's **h** has become calloused *G2840*
Ro 2: 5 stubbornness and your unrepentant **h**, *G2840*
Ro 2:29 circumcision is circumcision *of* the **h** *G2840*
Ro 6:17 come to obey from your **h** the pattern of *G2840*
Ro 9: 2 sorrow and unceasing anguish *in* my **h**. *G2840*
Ro 10: 6 "Do not say in your **h**, 'Who will ascend *G2840*
Ro 10: 8 it is in your mouth and in your **h**," that is, *G2840*
Ro 10: 9 believe in your **h** that God raised him *G2840*
Ro 10:10 For it is *with* your **h** that you believe and *G2840*
1Co 4: 5 will expose the motives *of* the **h**. *G2840*
2Co 2: 4 anguish *of* **h** and with many tears *G2840*
2Co 4: 1 we have this ministry, *we do* not **lose h**. *G1591*
2Co 4:16 Therefore *we do* not **lose h**. Though *G1591*
2Co 5:12 is seen rather than in what is *in* the **h**. *G2840*
2Co 8:16 who put into the **h** of Titus the same *G2840*
2Co 9: 7 what you have decided *in* your **h** to give, *G2840*
Eph 1:18 that the eyes *of* your **h** may be *G2840*
Eph 5:19 make music *from* your **h** to the Lord, *G2840*
Eph 6: 5 with sincerity *of* **h**, just as you would *G2840*
Eph 6: 6 doing the will of God from your **h**. *G6034*
Php 1: 7 since I have you in my **h** and, whether I *G2840*
Col 2: 2 may be encouraged *in* **h** and united in *G2840*
Col 3:22 with sincerity *of* **h** and reverence for *G2840*
Col 3:23 work at it with *all* your **h**, as working for *G6034*
1Ti 1: 5 comes from a pure **h** and a good *G2840*
2Ti 2:22 who call on the Lord out of a pure **h**. *G2840*
Phm 12 who is my very **h**—back to you. *G5073*
Phm 20 you in the Lord; refresh my **h** in Christ. *G5073*
Heb 3:12 unbelieving **h** that turns away from the *G2840*
Heb 4:12 the thoughts and attitudes *of* the **h**. *G2840*
Heb 10:22 to God with a sincere **h** and with the full *G2840*
Heb 12: 3 that you will not grow weary and lose **h**. *G6034*
Heb 12: 5 and *do* not **lose h** when he rebukes you *G1725*
1Pe 1:22 love one another deeply, from the **h**. *G2840*
Rev 1: 3 who hear it and **take to h** what is written *G5498*
Rev 18: 7 In her **h** she boasts, 'I sit enthroned as *G2840*

HEART'S (5) [HEART]

2Ch 1:11 "Since this is your **h** desire and you have H4222
Ps 21: 2 granted him his **h** desire and have not H4213
Jer 15:16 they were my joy and my **h** delight, for I H4222
Eze 24:25 of their eyes, their **h** desire, and their sons H5883
Ro 10: 1 my **h** desire and prayer to God for the *G2840*

HEARTACHE (1) [HEART]

Pr 15:13 cheerful, but **h** crushes the spirit. H6780+4213

HEARTFELT (1) [FEEL, HEART]

Pr 27: 9 of a friend springs from their **h** advice. H5883

HEARTH (6)

Lev 6: 9 remain on the altar **h** throughout the H4612
Isa 29: 2 she will be to me like an **altar h**. H789
Isa 30:14 taking coals from a **h** or scooping water H3683
Eze 43:15 Above that, the **altar h** is four cubits high H2219
Eze 43:15 four horns project upward from the **h**. H789
Eze 43:16 The **altar h** is square, twelve cubits long H789

HEARTLESS (1) [HEART]

La 4: 3 people have become **h** like ostriches in the H425

HEARTS (223) [HEART]

Ge 42:28 Their **h** sank and they turned to each H4213
Ex 9:34 He and his officials hardened their **h**. H4213
Ex 10: 1 his heart and the **h** *of* his officials so that I H4213
Ex 14:17 I will harden the **h** *of* the Egyptians so that H4213
Lev 26:36 I will make their **h** so fearful in the lands H4222
Lev 26:41 their uncircumcised **h** are humbled and H4222
Nu 15:39 after the lusts of your own **h** and eyes. H4222
Dt 1:28 Our brothers *have* **made** our **h** melt in fear H4222
Dt 5:29 that their **h** would be inclined to fear me H4222
Dt 6: 6 that I give you today are to be on your **h**. H4222
Dt 10:16 Circumcise your **h**, therefore, and do not H4222
Dt 11:18 these words of mine in your **h** and minds; H4222
Dt 28:67 that will fill your **h** and the sights that your H4222
Dt 30: 6 will circumcise your **h** and the hearts of H4222
Dt 30: 6 hearts and the **h** *of* your descendants, H4222
Jos 2:11 our **h** melted in fear and everyone's H4222
Jos 5: 1 their **h** melted in fear and they no longer H4222
Jos 7: 5 At this the **h** *of* the people melted in fear H4222
Jos 11:20 who hardened their **h** to wage war H4213
Jos 14: 8 with me made the **h** *of* the people melt in H4213
Jos 24:23 among you and yield your **h** to the LORD, H4222
1Sa 6: 6 do you harden your **h** as the Egyptians H4222
1Sa 7: 3 are returning to the LORD with all your **h**, H4222
1Sa 10:26 valiant men whose **h** God had touched. H4213
2Sa 15: 6 so he stole the **h** *of* the people of H4213
2Sa 15:13 "The **h** *of* the people of Israel are with H4213
2Sa 19:14 He won over the **h** *of* the men of Judah so H4222
1Ki 8:38 aware of the afflictions of their own **h**, H4222
1Ki 8:39 since you know their **h** (for you alone H4222
1Ki 8:58 May he turn our **h** to him, to walk in H4222
1Ki 8:61 And may your **h** be fully committed to the H4222
1Ki 11: 2 will surely turn your **h** after their gods." H4222
1Ki 18:37 that you are turning their **h** back again." H4213
1Ch 16:10 let the **h** *of* those who seek the LORD H4213
1Ch 29:18 thoughts in the **h** *of* your people H4222
1Ch 29:18 and keep their **h** loyal to you. H4222
2Ch 6:30 since you know their **h** (for you alone H4222
2Ch 11:16 Israel who set their **h** on seeking the LORD, H4222
2Ch 16: 9 those whose **h** are fully committed to H4222
2Ch 20:33 still had not set their **h** on the God of their H4222
2Ch 29:31 all whose **h** were willing brought H4213
Job 1: 5 have sinned and cursed God in their **h**." H4222
Job 31:20 their **h** did not bless me for warming H2743
Ps 4: 4 on your beds, search your **h** and be silent. H4222
Ps 7: 9 righteous God who probes minds and **h**. H4213
Ps 12: 2 harbor deception in their **h**. H4213+2256+4213
Ps 17:10 They close up their **callous h**, and their H2693
Ps 22:26 will praise him—may your **h** live forever! H4222
Ps 28: 3 neighbors but harbor malice in their **h**. H4222
Ps 33:15 he who forms the **h** *of* all, who considers H4213
Ps 33:21 In him our **h** rejoice, for we trust in his H4213
Ps 37:15 But their swords will pierce their own **h** H4213
Ps 37:31 The law of their God is in their **h**; their H4213
Ps 44:18 Our **h** had not turned back; our feet had H4213
Ps 45: 5 arrows pierce the **h** *of* the king's enemies; H4213
Ps 62: 4 they bless, but in their **h** they curse. H7931
Ps 62: 8 people; pour out your **h** to him, for God is H4222
Ps 69:32 you who seek God, may your **h** live! H4222
Ps 73: 7 From their **callous h** comes iniquity; their H2693
Ps 74: 8 They said in their **h**, "We will crush them H4213
Ps 78: 8 whose **h** were not loyal to God H4213
Ps 78:37 their **h** were not loyal to him, they were H4213
Ps 81:12 to their stubborn **h** to follow their own H4213
Ps 84: 5 is in you, whose **h** are set on pilgrimage. H4222
Ps 95: 8 "Do not harden your **h** as you did at H4222
Ps 95:10 'They are a people whose **h** go astray H4222
Ps 104:15 wine that gladdens human **h**, oil to make H4222
Ps 104:15 and bread that sustains their **h**. H4222
Ps 105: 3 let the **h** *of* those who seek the LORD H4213
Ps 105:25 whose **h** he turned to hate his people, to H4213
Ps 112: 7 of bad news; their **h** are steadfast, trusting H4213
Ps 112: 8 Their **h** are secure, they will have no fear H4213
Ps 119:70 Their **h** are callous and unfeeling, but I H4213
Ps 140: 2 evil plans in their **h** and stir up war every H4213
Pr 8: 5 you who are foolish, set your **h** on it. H4213
Pr 11:20 LORD detests those whose **h** are perverse, H4213
Pr 12:20 Deceit is in the **h** *of* those who plot evil H4213
Pr 15: 7 the **h** *of* fools are not upright. H4213
Pr 15:11 the LORD—how much more do human **h**! H4213
Pr 16: 9 In their **h** humans plan their course, but H4213
Pr 16:23 The **h** *of* the wise make their mouths H4213
Pr 24: 2 their **h** plot violence, and their lips talk H4213
Pr 25: 3 so the **h** *of* kings are unsearchable. H4213
Pr 26:24 their lips, but in their **h** they harbor deceit. H7931
Pr 26:25 for seven abominations fill their **h**. H4213
Ecc 6: 2 so that they lack nothing their **h** desire H5883
Ecc 8:11 people's **h** are filled with schemes to do H4213
Ecc 9: 3 The **h** *of* people, moreover, are full of evil H4213
Ecc 9: 3 is madness in their **h** while they live, H4222
Isa 6:10 understand with their **h**, and turn and be H4222
Isa 7: 2 so the **h** *of* Ahaz and his people were H4222
Isa 15: 4 of Moab cry out, and their **h** are faint. H5883
Isa 19: 1 the **h** *of* the Egyptians melt with fear. H4222
Isa 26: 8 name and renown are the desire of our **h**. H5883
Isa 29:13 with their lips, but their **h** are far from me. H4213
Isa 30:29 your **h** will rejoice as when people H4222
Isa 32: 6 fools speak folly, their **h** are bent on evil: H4213
Isa 35: 4 say to those with fearful **h**, "Be strong, do H4213
Isa 59:13 uttering lies our **h** have conceived. H4213
Isa 63:17 harden our **h** so we do not revere H4213
Isa 65:14 servants will sing out of the joy of their **h**, H4213
Jer 3:17 follow the stubbornness of their evil **h**. H4213
Jer 4: 4 circumcise your **h**, you people of Judah H4222
Jer 5:23 people have stubborn and rebellious **h**; H4213
Jer 7:24 the stubborn inclinations of their evil **h**. H4213
Jer 9: 8 in their **h** they set traps for them. H7931
Jer 9:14 have followed the stubbornness of their **h**; H4213
Jer 11: 8 followed the stubbornness of their evil **h**. H4213
Jer 12: 2 always on their lips but far from their **h**. H4000
Jer 13:10 stubbornness of their **h** and go after other H4213
Jer 16:12 of your evil **h** instead of obeying me. H4213
Jer 17: 1 the tablets of their **h** and on the horns of H4213
Jer 18:12 all follow the stubbornness of our evil **h**. H4213
Jer 23:17 the stubbornness of their **h** they say, H4213
Jer 23:26 this continue in the **h** *of* these lying H4213
Jer 31:33 law in their minds and write it on their **h**. H4213
Jer 48:41 In that day the **h** *of* Moab's warriors will H4213
Jer 49:22 In that day the **h** *of* Edom's warriors will H4213
La 2:18 The **h** *of* the people cry out to the Lord H4213
La 3:41 Let us lift up our **h** and our hands to God H4222
La 3:65 Put a veil over their **h**, and may your curse H4213
La 5:15 Joy is gone from our **h**; our dancing has H4213
La 5:17 Because of this our **h** are faint, because of H4213
Eze 6: 9 I have been grieved by their adulterous **h**, H4213
Eze 11:21 as for those whose **h** are devoted to their H4213
Eze 14: 3 set up idols in their **h** and put wicked H4213
Eze 14: 4 set up idols in their **h** and put a wicked H4213
Eze 14: 5 to recapture the **h** *of* the people of Israel H4213
Eze 14: 7 set up idols in their **h** and put a wicked H4213
Eze 20:16 For their **h** were devoted to their idols. H4213
Eze 21:15 So that **h** may melt with fear and the H4213
Eze 25:15 took revenge with malice in their **h**, H5883
Eze 32: 9 I will trouble the **h** *of* many peoples when H4213
Eze 33:31 their **h** are greedy for unjust gain. H4213
Eze 36: 5 with malice in their **h** they made my land H4222
Da 11:27 two kings, with their **h** bent on evil, will sit H4222
Hos 7: 6 Their **h** are like an oven; they approach H4213
Hos 7:14 out to me from their **h** but wail on their H4213
Na 2:10 **H** melt, knees give way, bodies tremble H4213
Zec 7:12 They made their **h** as hard as flint and H4213
Zec 10: 7 their **h** will be glad as with wine. H4213
Zec 10: 7 be joyful; their **h** will rejoice in the LORD. H4213
Zec 12: 5 Then the clans of Judah will say in their **h** H4213
Mal 4: 6 He will turn the **h** *of* the parents to their H4213
Mal 4: 6 the **h** *of* the children to their parents H4213
Mt 9: 4 do you entertain evil thoughts in your **h**? *G2840*
Mt 13:15 understand with their **h** and turn, and I *G2840*
Mt 15: 8 with their lips, but their **h** are far from me. *G2840*
Mt 19: 8 your wives because your **h** were **hard**. *G5016*
Mk 2: 8 was what they were thinking in *their* **h**, *G1571*
Mk 3: 5 deeply distressed at their stubborn **h**, said *G2840*
Mk 6:52 about the loaves; their **h** were hardened. *G2840*
Mk 7: 6 with their lips, but their **h** are far from me. *G2840*
Mk 8:17 see or understand? Are your **h** hardened? *G2840*
Mk 10: 5 was because your **h** were **hard** that Moses *G5016*
Lk 1:17 to turn the **h** of the parents to their *G2840*
Lk 2:35 the thoughts of many **h** will be revealed. *G2840*
Lk 3:15 wondering in their **h** if John might *G2840*
Lk 5:22 are you thinking these things in your **h**? *G2840*
Lk 8:12 takes away the word from their **h**, *G2840*
Lk 16:15 the eyes of others, but God knows your **h**. *G2840*
Lk 21:34 your **h** will be weighed down with *G2840*
Lk 24:32 "Were not our **h** burning within us while *G2840*
Jn 5:42 you do not have the love of God in **your h**. *G1571*
Jn 12:40 blinded their eyes and hardened their **h**, *G2840*
Jn 12:40 understand *with* their **h**, nor turn— *G2840*
Jn 14: 1 "Do not let your **h** be troubled. *G2840*
Jn 14:27 Do not let your **h** be troubled and do not *G2840*
Ac 2:46 ate together with glad and sincere **h**, *G2840*
Ac 7:39 him and in their **h** turned back to Egypt. *G2840*
Ac 7:51 Your **h** and ears are still uncircumcised *G2840*
Ac 11:23 to remain true to the Lord *with all* their **h**. *G2840*
Ac 14:17 plenty of food and fills your **h** with joy." *G2840*
Ac 15: 9 them, for he purified their **h** by faith. *G2840*
Ac 28:27 understand *with* their **h** and turn, and I *G2840*
Ro 1:21 futile and their foolish **h** were darkened. *G2840*
Ro 1:24 sinful desires *of* their **h** to sexual impurity *G2840*
Ro 2:15 of the law are written on their **h**, *G2840*
Ro 5: 5 poured out into our **h** through the Holy *G2840*
Ro 8:27 he who searches our **h** knows the mind of *G2840*
1Co 10: 6 keep us from **setting** *our* **h on** evil things *G2122*
1Co 14:25 as the secrets *of* their **h** are laid bare. *G2840*
2Co 1:22 put his Spirit in our **h** as a deposit *G2840*
2Co 3: 2 written on our **h**, known and read by *G2840*
2Co 3: 3 of stone but on tablets *of* human **h**. *G2840*
2Co 3:15 when Moses is read, a veil covers their **h**. *G2840*
2Co 4: 6 his light shine in our **h** to give us the light *G2840*
2Co 6:11 opened wide our **h** to you. *G2840*
2Co 6:13 as to my children—open wide your **h** also. NDT
2Co 7: 2 Make room for us in your **h**. We have NDT
2Co 7: 3 such a place in our **h** that we would live *G2840*
2Co 9:14 prayers for you *their* **h** *will* **go out to** you, *G2160*

Gal 4: 6 God sent the Spirit of his Son into our **h** G2840
Eph 3:17 Christ may dwell in your **h** through faith. G2840
Eph 4:18 is in them due to the hardening *of* their **h**. G2840
Php 4: 7 will guard your **h** and your minds in Christ G2840
Col 3: 1 with Christ, **set** *your* **h on** things above G2426
Col 3:15 Let the peace of Christ rule in your **h** G2840
Col 3:16 singing to God with gratitude in your **h**. G2840
Col 4: 8 that he may encourage your **h**. G2840
1Th 2: 4 please people but God, who tests our **h**. G2840
1Th 3:13 he strengthen your **h** so that you will be G2840
2Th 2:17 encourage your **h** and strengthen you in G2840
2Th 3: 5 the Lord direct your **h** into God's love and G2840
Phm 7 have refreshed the **h** of the Lord's people. G5073
Heb 3: 8 do not harden your **h** as you did in the G2840
Heb 3:10 'Their **h** are always going astray G2840
Heb 3:15 do not harden your **h** as you did in the G2840
Heb 4: 7 you hear his voice, do not harden your **h**." G2840
Heb 8:10 in their minds and write them on their **h**. G2840
Heb 10:16 I will put my laws in their **h**, and I will G2840
Heb 10:22 having our **h** sprinkled to cleanse us from G2840
Heb 13: 9 It is good *for* our **h** to be strengthened by G2840
Jas 3:14 bitter envy and selfish ambition in your **h**, G2840
Jas 4: 8 purify your **h**, you double-minded. G2840
1Pe 3:15 But in your **h** revere Christ as Lord. G2840
2Pe 1:19 the morning star rises in your **h**. G2840
1Jn 3:19 how we set our **h** at rest in his G2840
1Jn 3:20 If our **h** condemn us, we know that God is G2840
1Jn 3:20 we know that God is greater *than* our **h** G2840
1Jn 3:21 Dear friends, if our **h** do not condemn us G2840
Rev 2:23 that I am he who searches **h** and minds, G2840
Rev 17:17 has put it into their **h** to accomplish his G2840

HEARTS' (1) [HEART]

Pr 13:25 The righteous eat to their **h** content, but H5883

HEAT (31) [HEATED]

Ge 8:22 harvest, cold and **h**, summer and winter, H2770
Ge 18: 1 entrance to his tent in the **h** *of* the day. H2770
Ge 30:38 When the flocks *were* **in h** and came to H3501
Ge 30:41 Whenever the stronger females *were* **in h** H3501
Ge 31:40 The **h** consumed me in the daytime and H2996
Dt 28:22 with **scorching h** and drought, with H3031
1Sa 11:11 slaughtered them until the **h** *of* the day. H2770
2Sa 4: 5 arrived there in the **h** *of* the day while he H2770
2Ki 23:26 turn away from the **h** *of* his fierce anger, H3019
Job 6:17 in the **h** vanish from their channels. H2801
Job 24:19 As **h** and drought snatch away the melted H2770
Ps 32: 4 was sapped as in the **h** *of* summer. H3001
Ps 58: 9 your pots can feel the **h** of the thorns— NDT
Isa 4: 6 a shelter and shade from the **h** of the day, H2996
Isa 18: 4 like shimmering **h** in the sunshine, like H2770
Isa 18: 4 like a cloud of dew in the **h** *of* harvest." H2770
Isa 21:15 the bent bow and from the **h** *of* battle. H3880
Isa 25: 4 from the storm and a shade from the **h**. H2996
Isa 25: 5 like the **h** of the desert. You silence H2996
Isa 25: 5 as **h** is reduced by the shadow of a cloud H2996
Isa 49:10 will the **desert h** or the sun beat down H9220
Jer 2:24 craving—**in** her **h** who can restrain her? H9299
Jer 17: 8 It does not fear when **h** comes; its leaves H2770
Jer 36:30 exposed to the **h** by day and the frost H2996
Hos 13: 5 the wilderness, in the land of **burning h**. H9429
Mt 20:12 burden of the work and the **h** of the day. G3014
Ac 28: 3 driven out by the **h**, fastened itself on his G2549
Jas 1:11 sun rises with **scorching h** and withers the G3014
2Pe 3:12 and the elements will melt *in the* **h**. G3012
Rev 7:16 beat down on them,' nor any **scorching h**. G3008
Rev 16: 9 were seared *by* the intense **h** and they G3008

HEATED (1) [HEAT]

Da 3:19 ordered the furnace **h** seven times hotter A10015

HEATH (KJV) BUSH

HEATHEN (NIV84) PAGANS

HEAVE OFFERING (KJV) CONTRIBUTION

HEAVEN (415) [HEAVEN'S, HEAVENLY, HEAVENS, HEAVENWARD]

Ge 14:19 by God Most High, Creator of **h** and earth. H9028
Ge 14:22 God Most High, Creator of **h** and earth, H9028
Ge 21:17 called to Hagar from **h** and said to her, H9028
Ge 22:11 of the LORD called out to him from **h**, H9028
Ge 22:15 called to Abraham from **h** a second time H9028
Ge 24: 3 the God of **h** and the God of earth H9028
Ge 24: 7 the God of **h**, who brought me out H9028
Ge 27:39 richness, away from the dew of **h** above. H9028
Ge 28:12 with its top reaching to **h**, and the angels H9028
Ge 28:17 the house of God; this is the gate of **h**." H9028
Ex 16: 4 "I will rain down bread from **h** for you. H9028
Ex 17:14 out the name of Amalek from under **h**." H9028
Ex 20: 4 form of anything in **h** above or on the H9028
Ex 20:22 that I have spoken to you from **h**: H9028
Dt 2:25 fear of you on all the nations under **h**. H9028
Dt 3:24 god is there in **h** or on earth who can H9028
Dt 4:19 apportioned to all the nations under **h**. H9028
Dt 4:36 From **h** he made you hear his voice to H9028
Dt 4:39 the LORD is God in **h** above and on the H9028
Dt 5: 8 form of anything in **h** above or on the H9028
Dt 7:24 will wipe out their names from under **h**. H9028
Dt 9:14 blot out their name from under **h**. H9028
Dt 11:11 valleys that drinks rain from **h**. H9028
Dt 25:19 out the name of Amalek from under **h**. H9028
Dt 26:15 Look down from **h**, your holy dwelling H9028
Dt 29:20 will blot out their names from under **h**. H9028
Dt 30:12 It is not up in **h**, so that you have to ask H9028
Dt 30:12 "Who will ascend into **h** to get it and H9028
Dt 32:40 I lift my hand to **h** and solemnly swear: As H9028
Dt 33:13 precious dew from **h** above and with the H9028
Jos 2:11 your God is God in **h** above and on the H9028
Jdg 13:20 flame blazed up from the altar toward **h**, H9028
1Sa 2:10 The Most High will thunder from **h**; the H9028
1Sa 5:12 the outcry of the city went up to **h**. H9028
2Sa 22:14 The LORD thundered from **h**; the voice of H9028
1Ki 8:22 of Israel, spread out his hands toward **h** H9028
1Ki 8:23 is no God like you in **h** above or on earth H9028
1Ki 8:27 even the **highest h**, cannot contain H9028+9028
1Ki 8:30 Hear from **h**, your dwelling place, and H9028
1Ki 8:32 then hear from **h** and act. Judge between H9028
1Ki 8:34 then hear from **h** and forgive the sin of H9028
1Ki 8:36 then hear from **h** and forgive the sin of H9028
1Ki 8:39 then hear from **h**, your dwelling place H9028
1Ki 8:43 then hear from **h**, your dwelling place. H9028
1Ki 8:45 then hear from **h** their prayer and their H9028
1Ki 8:49 then from **h**, your dwelling place, hear H9028
1Ki 8:54 with his hands spread out toward **h**. H9028
1Ki 22:19 the multitudes of **h** standing around him H9028
2Ki 1:10 come down from **h** and consume you and H9028
2Ki 1:10 Then fire fell from **h** and consumed the H9028
2Ki 1:12 come down from **h** and consume you and H9028
2Ki 1:12 of God fell from **h** and consumed him H9028
2Ki 1:14 fire has fallen from **h** and consumed the H9028
2Ki 2: 1 to take Elijah up to **h** in a whirlwind, H9028
2Ki 2:11 Elijah went up to **h** in a whirlwind. H9028
2Ki 14:27 blot out the name of Israel from under **h**, H9028
2Ki 19:15 You have made **h** and earth. H9028
1Ch 21:16 of the LORD standing between **h** and earth, H9028
1Ch 21:26 him with fire from **h** on the altar of burnt H9028
1Ch 29:11 everything in **h** and earth is yours. H9028
2Ch 2:12 the God of Israel, who made **h** and earth! H9028
2Ch 6:13 Israel and spread out his hands toward **h**. H9028
2Ch 6:14 there is no God like you in **h** or on earth H9028
2Ch 6:21 Hear from **h**, your dwelling place; and H9028
2Ch 6:23 then hear from **h** and act. Judge between H9028
2Ch 6:25 then hear from **h** and forgive the sin of H9028
2Ch 6:27 then hear from **h** and forgive the sin of H9028
2Ch 6:30 then hear from **h**, your dwelling place H9028
2Ch 6:33 then hear from **h**, your dwelling place. H9028
2Ch 6:35 then hear from **h** their prayer and their H9028
2Ch 6:39 then from **h**, your dwelling place, hear H9028
2Ch 7: 1 fire came down from **h** and consumed the H9028
2Ch 7:14 then I will hear from **h**, and I will forgive H9028
2Ch 18:18 the multitudes of **h** standing on his right H9028
2Ch 20: 6 are you not the God who is in **h**? H9028
2Ch 28: 9 them in a rage that reaches to **h**. H9028
2Ch 30:27 their prayer reached **h**, his holy H9028
2Ch 32:20 Amoz cried out in prayer to **h** about this. H9028
2Ch 36:23 the God of **h**, has given me all the H9028
Ezr 1: 2 the God of **h**, has given me all the H9028
Ezr 5:11 the servants of the God of **h** and earth, A10723
Ezr 5:12 our ancestors angered the God of **h**, A10723
Ezr 6: 9 lambs for burnt offerings to the God of **h**, A10723
Ezr 6:10 pleasing to the God of **h** and pray for the A10723
Ezr 7:12 teacher of the Law of the God of **h**: A10723
Ezr 7:21 the teacher of the Law of the God of **h** A10723
Ezr 7:23 Whatever the God of **h** has prescribed A10723
Ezr 7:23 diligence for the temple of the God of **h**. A10723
Ne 1: 4 fasted and prayed before the God of **h**. H9028
Ne 1: 5 the God of **h**, the great and H9028
Ne 2: 4 Then I prayed to the God of **h**, H9028
Ne 2:20 "The God of **h** will give us success. H9028
Ne 9: 6 the multitudes of **h** worship you. H9028
Ne 9:13 Mount Sinai; you spoke to them from **h**. H9028
Ne 9:15 gave them bread from **h** and in their thirst H9028
Ne 9:27 From **h** you heard them, and in your great H9028
Ne 9:28 you heard from **h**, and in your H9028
Job 16:19 Even now my witness is in **h**; my advocate H9028
Job 22:12 "Is not God in the heights of **h**? And see H9028
Job 25: 2 he establishes order in the **heights of h**. H5294
Job 37: 3 beneath the whole **h** and sends it to the H9028
Job 41:11 Everything under **h** belongs to me. H9028
Ps 2: 4 The One enthroned in **h** laughs; the Lord H9028
Ps 14: 2 LORD looks down from **h** on all mankind to H9028
Ps 18:13 The LORD thundered from **h**; the voice of H9028
Ps 33:13 From **h** the LORD looks down and sees all H9028
Ps 53: 2 God looks down from **h** on all mankind to H9028
Ps 57: 3 He sends from **h** and saves me, rebuking H9028
Ps 69:34 Let **h** and earth praise him, the seas and H9028
Ps 73: 9 Their mouths lay claim to **h**, and their H9028
Ps 73:25 Whom have I in **h** but you? And earth has H9028
Ps 75: 5 Do not lift your horns against **h**; do not H5294
Ps 76: 8 From **h** you pronounced judgment, and H9028
Ps 78:24 he gave them the grain of **h**. H9028
Ps 80:14 Look down from **h** and see! Watch over H9028
Ps 85:11 righteousness looks down from **h**. H9028
Ps 89: 2 established your faithfulness in **h** itself. H9028
Ps 102:19 on high, from **h** he viewed the earth, H9028
Ps 103:19 The LORD has established his throne in **h** H9028
Ps 105:40 he fed them well with the bread of **h**. H9028
Ps 115: 3 Our God is in **h**; he does whatever H9028
Ps 115:15 by the LORD, the Maker of **h** and earth. H9028
Ps 121: 2 from the LORD, the Maker of **h** and earth. H9028
Ps 123: 1 to you who sit enthroned in **h**. H9028
Ps 124: 8 of the LORD, the Maker of **h** and earth. H9028
Ps 134: 3 he who is the Maker of **h** and earth. H9028
Ps 136:26 Give thanks to the God of **h**. His love H9028
Ps 146: 6 He is the Maker of **h** and earth, the sea H9028
Pr 30: 4 Who has gone up to **h** and come down H9028
Ecc 5: 2 God is in **h** and you are on earth, so let H9028
Isa 13:10 The stars of **h** and their constellations will H9028
Isa 14:12 How you have fallen from **h**, morning star H9028
Isa 37:16 You have made **h** and earth. H9028
Isa 55:10 the rain and the snow come down from **h**, H9028
Isa 63:15 Look down from **h** and see, from your lofty H9028
Isa 66: 1 "**H** is my throne, and the earth is my H9028
Jer 7:18 make cakes to offer to the Queen of **H**. H9028
Jer 23:24 "Do not I fill **h** and earth?" declares H9028
Jer 33:25 established the laws of **h** and earth, H9028
Jer 44:17 to the Queen of **H** and will pour out drink H9028
Jer 44:18 to the Queen of **H** and pouring out drink H9028
Jer 44:19 to the Queen of **H** and poured out drink H9028
Jer 44:25 out drink offerings to the Queen of **H**. H9028
Jer 49:36 the four winds from the four quarters of **h**; H9028
Jer 51:48 Then **h** and earth and all that is in them H9028
La 2: 1 the splendor of Israel from **h** to earth; H9028
La 3:41 up our hearts and our hands to God in **h**, H9028
La 3:50 until the LORD looks down from **h** and sees. H9028
Eze 8: 3 up between earth and **h** and in visions of H9028
Da 2:18 mercy from the God of **h** concerning this A10723
Da 2:19 Then Daniel praised the God of **h** A10723
Da 2:28 there is a God in **h** who reveals A10723
Da 2:37 The God of **h** has given you dominion A10723
Da 2:44 the God of **h** will set up a kingdom that A10723
Da 4:13 a messenger, coming down from **h**. A10723
Da 4:15 'Let him be drenched with the dew of **h**, A10723
Da 4:23 coming down from **h** and saying, 'Cut A10723
Da 4:23 Let him be drenched with the dew of **h** A10723
Da 4:25 ox and be drenched with the dew of **h**. A10723
Da 4:26 you when you acknowledge that **H** rules. A10723
Da 4:31 a voice came from **h**, "This is what is A10723
Da 4:33 with the dew of **h** until his hair grew like A10723
Da 4:34 raised my eyes toward **h**, and my sanity A10723
Da 4:35 with the powers of **h** and the peoples of A10723
Da 4:37 exalt and glorify the King of **h**, A10723
Da 5:21 body was drenched with the dew of **h**, A10723
Da 5:23 set yourself up against the Lord of **h**. A10723
Da 7: 2 the four winds of **h** churning up the great A10723
Da 7:13 son of man, coming with the clouds of **h**. A10723
Da 7:27 the kingdoms under **h** will be handed A10723
Da 8: 8 horns grew up toward the four winds of **h**. H9028
Da 9:12 Under the whole **h** nothing has ever been H9028
Da 11: 4 parceled out toward the four winds of **h**. H9028
Da 12: 7 his right hand and his left hand toward **h**, H9028
Jnh 1: 9 the LORD, the God of **h**, who made the sea H9028
Zec 2: 6 have scattered you to the four winds of **h**," H9028
Zec 5: 9 lifted up the basket between **h** and earth. H9028
Zec 6: 5 "These are the four spirits of **h**, going out H9028
Mal 3:10 the floodgates of **h** and pour out so much H9028
Mt 3: 2 the kingdom *of* **h** has come near. G4041
Mt 3:16 At that moment **h** was opened, and he G4041
Mt 3:17 And a voice from **h** said, "This is my Son G4041
Mt 4:17 the kingdom *of* **h** has come near. G4041
Mt 5: 3 in spirit, for theirs is the kingdom *of* **h**. G4041
Mt 5:10 theirs is the kingdom *of* **h**. G4041
Mt 5:12 because great is your reward in **h**, for in G4041
Mt 5:16 good deeds and glorify your Father in **h**. G4041
Mt 5:18 truly I tell you, until **h** and earth disappear G4041
Mt 5:19 will be called least in the kingdom *of* **h**, G4041
Mt 5:19 will be called great in the kingdom *of* **h**. G4041
Mt 5:20 will certainly not enter the kingdom *of* **h**. G4041
Mt 5:34 either by **h**, for it is God's G4041
Mt 5:45 you may be children of your Father in **h**. G4041
Mt 6: 1 will have no reward from your Father in **h**. G4041
Mt 6: 9 " 'Our Father in **h**, hallowed be your name G4041
Mt 6:10 your will be done, on earth as it is in **h**. G4041
Mt 6:20 But store up for yourselves treasures in **h** G4041
Mt 7:11 will your Father in **h** give good gifts to G4041
Mt 7:21 will enter the kingdom *of* **h**, but only the G4041
Mt 7:21 does the will of my Father who is in **h**. G4041
Mt 8:11 Isaac and Jacob in the kingdom *of* **h**. G4041
Mt 10: 7 'The kingdom *of* **h** has come near.' G4041
Mt 10:32 also acknowledge before my Father in **h**. G4041
Mt 10:33 I will disown before my Father in **h**. G4041
Mt 11:11 in the kingdom *of* **h** is greater than he. G4041
Mt 11:12 the kingdom *of* **h** has been subjected to G4041
Mt 11:25 Lord *of* **h** and earth, because you G4041
Mt 12:50 will of my Father in **h** is my brother and G4041
Mt 13:11 of the kingdom *of* **h** has been given to G4041
Mt 13:24 "The kingdom *of* **h** is like a man who G4041
Mt 13:31 "The kingdom *of* **h** is like a mustard seed G4041
Mt 13:33 "The kingdom *of* **h** is like yeast that a G4041
Mt 13:44 "The kingdom *of* **h** is like treasure hidden G4041
Mt 13:45 the kingdom *of* **h** is like a merchant G4041
Mt 13:47 the kingdom *of* **h** is like a net that was let G4041
Mt 13:52 in the kingdom *of* **h** is like the owner of a G4041
Mt 14:19 the two fish and looking up to **h**, G4041
Mt 16: 1 asking him to show them a sign from **h**. G4041
Mt 16:17 by flesh and blood, but by my Father in **h**. G4041
Mt 16:19 will give you the keys of the kingdom *of* **h**; G4041
Mt 16:19 you bind on earth will be bound in **h**, G4041
Mt 16:19 you loose on earth will be loosed in **h**." G4041
Mt 18: 1 is the greatest in the kingdom *of* **h**?" G4041
Mt 18: 3 you will never enter the kingdom *of* **h**. G4041
Mt 18: 4 child is the greatest in the kingdom *of* **h**. G4041
Mt 18:10 that their angels in **h** always see the face G4041
Mt 18:10 always see the face of my Father in **h**. G4041
Mt 18:14 way your Father in **h** is not willing that any G4041

Mt 18:18 you bind on earth will be bound in **h**, G4041
Mt 18:18 you loose on earth will be loosed in **h**. G4041
Mt 18:19 it will be done for them by my Father in **h**. G4041
Mt 18:23 the kingdom *of* **h** is like a king who G4041
Mt 19:12 eunuchs for the sake of the kingdom *of* **h**. G4041
Mt 19:14 the kingdom *of* **h** belongs to such as G4041
Mt 19:21 the poor, and you will have treasure in **h**. G4041
Mt 19:23 who is rich to enter the kingdom *of* **h**. G4041
Mt 20: 1 "For the kingdom *of* **h** is like a landowner G4041
Mt 21: 9 "Hosanna in the **highest h**!" G5736
Mt 21:25 Was it from **h**, or of human origin? G4041
Mt 21:25 "If we say, 'From **h**,' he will ask, 'Then G4041
Mt 22: 2 "The kingdom *of* **h** is like a king who G4041
Mt 22:30 they will be like the angels in **h**. G4041
Mt 23: 9 you have one Father, and he is **in h**. G4039
Mt 23:13 of the kingdom *of* **h** in people's faces. G4041
Mt 23:22 anyone who swears by **h** swears by God's G4041
Mt 24:30 appear the sign of the Son of Man in **h**. G4041
Mt 24:30 Son of Man coming on the clouds *of* **h**, G4041
Mt 24:35 **H** and earth will pass away, but my words G4041
Mt 24:36 not even the angels *in* **h**, nor the Son, G4041
Mt 25: 1 that time the kingdom *of* **h** will be like ten G4041
Mt 26:64 One and coming on the clouds *of* **h**." G4041
Mt 28: 2 angel of the Lord came down from **h** and, G4041
Mt 28:18 "All authority in **h** and on earth has been G4041
Mk 1:10 he saw **h** being torn open and the Spirit G4041
Mk 1:11 And a voice came from **h**: "You are my G4041
Mk 6:41 the two fish and looking up to **h**, G4041
Mk 7:34 He looked up to **h** and with a deep sigh G4041
Mk 8:11 test him, they asked him for a sign from **h**. G4041
Mk 10:21 the poor, and you will have treasure in **h**. G4041
Mk 11:10 "Hosanna in the **highest h**!" G5736
Mk 11:25 that your Father in **h** may forgive you your G4041
Mk 11:30 was it from **h**, or of human origin G4041
Mk 11:31 "If we say, 'From **h**,' he will ask, 'Then G4041
Mk 12:25 they will be like the angels in **h**. G4041
Mk 13:31 **H** and earth will pass away, but my words G4041
Mk 13:32 not even the angels in **h**, nor the Son, G4041
Mk 14:62 One and coming on the clouds *of* **h**." G4041
Mk 16:19 he was taken up into **h** and he sat at the G4041
Lk 1:78 the rising sun will come to us from **h** G5737
Lk 2:14 "Glory to God in the **highest h**, and on G5736
Lk 2:15 the angels had left them and gone into **h**, G4041
Lk 3:21 And as he was praying, **h** was opened G4041
Lk 3:22 And a voice came from **h**: "You are my G4041
Lk 6:23 joy, because great is your reward in **h**. G4041
Lk 9:16 the two fish and looking up to **h**, G4041
Lk 9:51 approached for him *to be* **taken up to h**, G378
Lk 9:54 to call fire down from **h** to destroy them?" G4041
Lk 10:18 "I saw Satan fall like lightning from **h**. G4041
Lk 10:20 rejoice that your names are written in **h**." G4041
Lk 10:21 Lord *of* **h** and earth, because you G4041
Lk 11:13 will your Father in **h** give the Holy Spirit to G4041
Lk 11:16 tested him by asking for a sign from **h**. G4041
Lk 12:33 a treasure in **h** that will never fail G4041
Lk 15: 7 more rejoicing in **h** over one sinner who G4041
Lk 15:18 I have sinned against **h** and against you. G4041
Lk 15:21 I have sinned against **h** and against you. G4041
Lk 16:17 It is easier *for* **h** and earth to disappear G4041
Lk 17:29 rained down from **h** and destroyed them G4041
Lk 18:13 He would not even look up to **h**, but beat G4041
Lk 18:22 the poor, and you will have treasure in **h**. G4041
Lk 19:38 "Peace in **h** and glory in the highest!" G4041
Lk 20: 4 was it from **h**, or of human origin G4041
Lk 20: 5 "If we say, 'From **h**,' he will ask, 'Why G4041
Lk 21:11 fearful events and great signs from **h**. G4041
Lk 21:33 **H** and earth will pass away, but my words G4041
Lk 22:43 An angel from **h** appeared to him and G4041
Lk 24:51 he left them and was taken up into **h**. G4041
Jn 1:32 come down from **h** as a dove and remain G4041
Jn 1:51 you will see '**h** open, and the angels G4041
Jn 3:13 has ever gone into **h** except the one who G4041
Jn 3:13 except the one who came from **h**— G4041
Jn 3:27 receive only what is given them from **h**. G4041
Jn 3:31 The one who comes from **h** is above all. G4041
Jn 6:31 'He gave them bread from **h** to eat.'" G4041
Jn 6:32 who has given you the bread from **h**, G4041
Jn 6:32 who gives you the true bread from **h**. G4041
Jn 6:33 that comes down from **h** and gives life to G4041
Jn 6:38 have come down from **h** not to do my will G4041
Jn 6:41 "I am the bread that came down from **h**." G4041
Jn 6:42 can he now say, 'I came down from **h**'?" G4041
Jn 6:50 is the bread that comes down from **h**, G4041
Jn 6:51 the living bread that came down from **h**. G4041
Jn 6:58 This is the bread that came down from **h** G4041
Jn 12:28 Then a voice came from **h**, "I have G4041
Jn 17: 1 said this, he looked toward **h** and prayed: G4041
Ac 1: 2 the day *he was* **taken up** *to h*, after AIT
Ac 1:11 who has been taken from you into **h**, will G4041
Ac 1:11 same way you have seen him go into **h**." G4041
Ac 2: 2 wind came from **h** and filled the whole G4041
Ac 2: 5 Jews from every nation under **h**. G4041
Ac 2:34 For David did not ascend to **h**, and yet he G4041
Ac 3:21 **H** must receive him until the time comes G4041
Ac 4:12 other name under **h** given to mankind by G4041
Ac 7:49 "'**H** is my throne, and the earth is my G4041
Ac 7:55 looked up to **h** and saw the glory of God G4041
Ac 7:56 "I see **h** open and the Son of Man G4041
Ac 9: 3 a light from **h** flashed around him. G4041
Ac 10:11 He saw **h** opened and something like a G4041
Ac 10:16 the sheet was taken back to **h**. G4041
Ac 11: 5 being let down from **h** by its four corners, G4041
Ac 11: 9 "The voice spoke from **h** a second time G4041
Ac 11:10 then it was all pulled up to **h** again. G4041
Ac 14:17 by giving you rain **from h** and crops in G4040
Ac 17:24 in it is the Lord *of* **h** and earth and does G4041
Ac 19:35 and *of* her **image, which fell from h**? G1479
Ac 22: 6 a bright light from **h** flashed around me. G4041
Ac 26:13 I saw a light **from h**, brighter than the G4040
Ac 26:19 I was not disobedient to the vision **from h**. G4039
Ro 1:18 is being revealed from **h** against all the G4041
Ro 10: 6 in your heart, 'Who will ascend into **h**? G4041
1Co 8: 5 whether in **h** or on earth (as indeed G4041
1Co 15:47 dust of the earth; the second man is of **h**. G4041
1Co 15:48 so also are those who are **of h**. G2230
2Co 5: 1 an eternal house in **h**, not built by human G4041
2Co 12: 2 years ago was caught up to the third **h**. G4041
Gal 1: 8 we or an angel from **h** should preach a G4041
Eph 1:10 unity to all things in **h** and on earth under G4041
Eph 3:15 every family in **h** and on earth derives G4041
Eph 6: 9 who is both their Master and yours is in **h**, G4041
Php 2:10 **in h** and on earth and under the earth, G2230
Php 3:20 But our citizenship is **in h**. And we eagerly G4041
Col 1: 5 up for you in **h** and about which you G4041
Col 1:16 things in **h** and on earth, visible and G4041
Col 1:20 whether things on earth or things in **h**, by G4041
Col 1:23 proclaimed to every creature under **h**, G4041
Col 4: 1 know that you also have a Master in **h**. G4041
1Th 1:10 to wait for his Son from **h**, whom he G4041
1Th 4:16 the Lord himself will come down from **h**, G4041
2Th 1: 7 is revealed from **h** in blazing fire with G4041
Heb 1: 3 at the right hand of the Majesty in **h**. G5734
Heb 4:14 high priest who has ascended into **h**, G4041
Heb 8: 1 hand of the throne of the Majesty in **h**, G4041
Heb 8: 5 that is a copy and shadow *of* what is **in h**. G2230
Heb 9:24 true one; he entered **h** itself, now to G4041
Heb 9:25 Nor did he enter **h** to offer himself again NDT
Heb 12:23 firstborn, whose names are written in **h**. G4041
Heb 12:25 turn away from him who warns us from **h**? G4041
Jas 3:15 does not come down **from h** but is earthly G540
Jas 3:17 wisdom that comes **from h** is first of all G540
Jas 5:12 not *by* **h** or by earth or by anything else. G4041
1Pe 1: 4 This inheritance is kept in **h** for you, G4041
1Pe 1:12 to you by the Holy Spirit sent from **h**. G4041
1Pe 3:22 who has gone into **h** and is at God's right G4041
2Pe 1:18 that came from **h** when we were with G4041
2Pe 3:13 forward to a new **h** and a new earth, G4041
Rev 3:12 is coming down out of **h** from my God; G4041
Rev 4: 1 before me was a door standing open in **h**. G4041
Rev 4: 2 me was a throne in **h** with someone G4041
Rev 5: 3 But no one in **h** or on earth or under the G4041
Rev 5:13 every creature in **h** and on earth and G4041
Rev 8: 1 there was silence in **h** for about half an G4041
Rev 10: 1 mighty angel coming down from **h**. G4041
Rev 10: 4 I heard a voice from **h** say, "Seal up G4041
Rev 10: 5 on the land raised his right hand to **h**. G4041
Rev 10: 8 I had heard from **h** spoke to me once G4041
Rev 11:12 heard a loud voice from **h** saying to them, G4041
Rev 11:12 And they went up to **h** in a cloud, while G4041
Rev 11:13 terrified and gave glory to the God *of* **h**. G4041
Rev 11:15 there were loud voices in **h**, which G4041
Rev 11:19 Then God's temple in **h** was opened, and G4041
Rev 12: 1 A great sign appeared in **h**: a woman G4041
Rev 12: 3 Then another sign appeared in **h**: an G4041
Rev 12: 7 Then war broke out in **h**. Michael and his G4041
Rev 12: 8 enough, and they lost their place in **h**. G4041
Rev 12:10 Then I heard a loud voice in **h** say: "Now G4041
Rev 13: 6 dwelling place and those who live in **h**. G4041
Rev 13:13 to come down from **h** to the earth in full G4041
Rev 14: 2 And I heard a sound from **h** like the roar of G4041
Rev 14:13 Then I heard a voice from **h** say, "Write G4041
Rev 14:17 angel came out of the temple in **h**, G4041
Rev 15: 1 I saw in **h** another great and marvelous G4041
Rev 15: 5 I saw in **h** the temple—that is, G4041
Rev 16:11 cursed the God *of* **h** because of their G4041
Rev 18: 1 I saw another angel coming down from **h**. G4041
Rev 18: 4 Then I heard another voice from **h** say: G4041
Rev 18: 5 her sins are piled up to **h**, and God G4041
Rev 19: 1 roar of a great multitude in **h** shouting: G4041
Rev 19:11 I saw **h** standing open and there before G4041
Rev 19:14 The armies of **h** were following him, riding G4041
Rev 20: 1 I saw an angel coming down out of **h**, G4041
Rev 20: 9 came down from **h** and devoured them. G4041
Rev 21: 1 Then I saw "a new **h** and a new earth," G4041
Rev 21: 1 the first **h** and the first earth had G4041
Rev 21: 2 coming down out of **h** from God, prepared G4041
Rev 21:10 coming down out of **h** from God. G4041

HEAVEN'S (1) [HEAVEN]

Ge 27:28 May God give you **h** dew and earth's H9028

HEAVENLY (37) [HEAVEN]

Dt 4:19 the stars—all the **h** array—do not be H9028
Ps 11: 4 holy temple; the LORD is on his **h** throne. H9028
Ps 20: 6 answers him from his **h** sanctuary with the H9028
Ps 29: 1 the LORD, you **h** *beings*, ascribe to H1201+446
Ps 89: 6 is like the LORD among the **h beings**? H1201+446
Ps 103:21 the LORD, all his **h hosts**, you his servants H7372
Ps 148: 2 all his angels; praise him, all his **h hosts**. H7372
Mt 5:48 therefore, as your **h** Father is perfect. G4039
Mt 6:14 your **h** Father will also forgive you. G4039
Mt 6:26 and yet your **h** Father feeds them. G4039
Mt 6:32 your **h** Father knows that you need G4039
Mt 15:13 "Every plant that my **h** Father has not G4039
Mt 18:35 "This is how my **h** Father will treat each of G4039
Mt 24:29 and the **h** bodies will be shaken. G4041
Mk 13:25 and the **h** bodies will be G1877+3836+4041
Lk 2:13 a great company *of* the **h** host appeared G4039
Lk 21:26 the world, for the **h** bodies will be shaken. G4041
Jn 3:12 will you believe if I speak *of* **h things**? G2230
1Co 15:40 There are also **h** bodies and there are G2230
1Co 15:40 the splendor *of* the **h** bodies is one G2230
1Co 15:48 as is the **h** *man*, so also are those G2230
1Co 15:49 so shall we bear the image *of* the **h** *man*. G2230
2Co 5: 2 instead with our **h** dwelling, G1666+4041
2Co 5: 4 to be clothed instead with our **h** dwelling, NDT
Eph 1: 3 blessed us in the **h realms** with every G2230
Eph 1:20 him at his right hand in the **h realms**, G2230
Eph 2: 6 with him in the **h realms** in Christ Jesus, G2230
Eph 3:10 the rulers and authorities in the **h realms**, G2230
Eph 6:12 the spiritual forces of evil in the **h realms**. G2230
2Ti 4:18 will bring me safely to his **h** kingdom. G2230
Heb 3: 1 who share in the **h** calling, fix your G2230
Heb 6: 4 who have tasted the **h** gift, who have G2230
Heb 9:23 copies of the **h** things to be G1877+3836+4041
Heb 9:23 the **h** *things* themselves with better G2230
Heb 11:16 longing for a better country—a **h** *one*. G2230
Heb 12:22 city of the living God, the **h** Jerusalem. G2230
Jas 1:17 coming down from the Father *of* the *h* **lights** AIT

HEAVENS (198) [HEAVEN]

Ge 1: 1 God created the **h** and the earth. H9028
Ge 2: 1 Thus the **h** and the earth were completed H9028
Ge 2: 4 the account of the **h** and the earth when H9028
Ge 2: 4 the LORD God made the earth and the **h**. H9028
Ge 6:17 the earth to destroy all life under the **h**, H9028
Ge 7:11 the floodgates of the **h** were opened. H9028
Ge 7:19 under the entire **h** were covered. H9028
Ge 8: 2 the floodgates of the **h** had been closed, H9028
Ge 11: 4 with a tower that reaches to the **h**, so that H9028
Ge 19:24 Gomorrah—from the LORD out of the **h**. H9028
Ex 20:11 days the LORD made the **h** and the earth, H9028
Ex 31:17 days the LORD made the **h** and the earth, H9028
Dt 4:11 while it blazed with fire to the very **h**, H9028
Dt 4:26 I call the **h** and the earth as witnesses H9028
Dt 4:32 ask from one end of the **h** to the other. H9028
Dt 10:14 To the LORD your God belong the **h**, even H9028
Dt 10:14 even the **highest h**, the earth and H9028+9028
Dt 11:17 he will shut up the **h** so that it will not H9028
Dt 11:21 the days that the **h** are above the earth. H9028
Dt 28:12 The LORD will open the **h**, the storehouse H9028
Dt 30: 4 to the most distant land under the **h**, H9028
Dt 30:19 This day I call the **h** and the earth as H9028
Dt 31:28 hearing and call the **h** and the earth to H9028
Dt 32: 1 you **h**, and I will speak; hear, you H9028
Dt 33:26 who rides across the **h** to help you and on H9028
Dt 33:28 new wine, where the **h** drop dew. H9028
Jdg 5: 4 the earth shook, the **h** poured, the clouds H9028
Jdg 5:20 From the **h** the stars fought, from their H9028
2Sa 21:10 poured down from the **h** on the bodies, H9028
2Sa 22: 8 the foundations of the **h** shook; they H9028
2Sa 22:10 He parted the **h** and came down; dark H9028
1Ki 8:27 The **h**, even the highest heaven, cannot H9028
1Ki 8:35 "When the **h** are shut up and there is no H9028
2Ki 7: 2 LORD should open the floodgates of the **h**, H9028
2Ki 7:19 LORD should open the floodgates of the **h**, H9028
1Ch 16:26 are idols, but the LORD made the **h**. H9028
1Ch 16:31 Let the **h** rejoice, let the earth be glad; let H9028
2Ch 2: 6 him, since the **h**, even the highest H9028
2Ch 2: 6 even the **highest h**, cannot contain H9028+9028
2Ch 6:18 The **h**, even the highest heavens, cannot H9028
2Ch 6:18 even the **highest h**, cannot contain H9028+9028
2Ch 6:26 "When the **h** are shut up and there is no H9028
2Ch 7:13 "When I shut up the **h** so that there is no H9028
Ezr 9: 6 heads and our guilt has reached to the **h**. H9028
Ne 9: 6 You made the **h**, even the highest H9028
Ne 9: 6 even the **highest h**, and all their H9028+9028
Job 1:16 of God fell from the **h** and burned up the H9028
Job 9: 8 stretches out the **h** and treads on the H9028
Job 11: 8 They are higher than the **h above**—what H9028
Job 14:12 not rise; till the **h** are no more, people H9028
Job 15:15 if even the **h** are not pure in his eyes, H9028
Job 20: 6 reaches to the **h** and his head touches H9028
Job 20:27 The **h** will expose his guilt; the earth will H9028
Job 22:14 see us as he goes about in the vaulted **h**. H9028
Job 26:11 The pillars of the **h** quake, aghast at his H9028
Job 28:24 earth and sees everything under the **h**. H9028
Job 35: 5 Look up at the **h** and see; gaze at the H9028
Job 38:29 Who gives birth to the frost from the **h** H9028
Job 38:33 Do you know the laws of the **h**? Can you H9028
Job 38:37 Who can tip over the water jars of the **h** H9028
Ps 8: 1 You have set your glory in the **h**. H9028
Ps 8: 3 When I consider your **h**, the work of your H9028
Ps 18: 9 He parted the **h** and came down; dark H9028
Ps 19: 1 The **h** declare the glory of God; the skies H9028
Ps 19: 4 In **the h** God has pitched a tent for the H2157S
Ps 19: 6 at one end of the **h** and makes its circuit H9028
Ps 33: 6 By the word of the LORD the **h** were made H9028
Ps 36: 5 reaches to the **h**, your faithfulness to H9028
Ps 50: 4 He summons the **h** above, and the earth H9028
Ps 50: 6 And the **h** proclaim his righteousness, for H9028
Ps 57: 5 above the **h**; let your glory be over H9028
Ps 57:10 reaching to the **h**; your faithfulness H9028
Ps 57:11 above the **h**; let your glory be over H9028
Ps 68: 8 the earth shook, the **h** poured down rain H9028
Ps 68:33 him who rides across the **highest h**, H9028+9028

Ps 68:33 heavens, the ancient **h**, who thunders with NDT
Ps 68:34 is over Israel, whose power is in the **h**. H8836
Ps 71:19 reaches to the **h**, you who have done H5294
Ps 77:17 the **h** resounded with thunder H8836
Ps 78:23 above and opened the doors of the **h**; H9028
Ps 78:26 east wind from the **h** and by his power H9028
Ps 89: 5 The **h** praise your wonders, LORD, your H9028
Ps 89:11 The **h** are yours, and yours also the earth H9028
Ps 89:29 his throne as long as the **h** endure. H9028
Ps 96: 5 are idols, but the LORD made the **h**. H9028
Ps 96:11 Let the **h** rejoice, let the earth be glad; let H9028
Ps 97: 6 The **h** proclaim his righteousness, and all H9028
Ps 102:25 the **h** are the work of your hands. H9028
Ps 103:11 For as high as the **h** are above the earth H9028
Ps 104: 2 garment; he stretches out the **h** like a tent H9028
Ps 107:26 mounted up to the **h** and went down to H9028
Ps 108: 4 higher than the **h**; your faithfulness H9028
Ps 108: 5 above the **h**; let your glory be over H9028
Ps 113: 4 over all the nations, his glory above the **h**. H9028
Ps 113: 6 down to look on the **h** and the earth? H9028
Ps 115:16 The **highest h** belong to the LORD H9028+9028
Ps 119:89 is eternal; it stands firm in the **h**. H9028
Ps 135: 6 pleases him, in the **h** and on the earth, in H9028
Ps 136: 5 who by his understanding made the **h** H9028
Ps 139: 8 If I go up to the **h**, you are there; if I make H9028
Ps 144: 5 Part your **h**, LORD, and come down; touch H9028
Ps 148: 1 Praise the LORD from the **h**; praise him in H9028
Ps 148: 4 you **highest h** and you waters H9028+9028
Ps 148:13 his splendor is above the earth and the **h**. H9028
Ps 150: 1 his sanctuary; praise him in his mighty **h**. H8385
Pr 3:19 by understanding he set the **h** in place; H9028
Pr 8:27 I was there when he set the **h** in place H9028
Pr 25: 3 As the **h** are high and the earth is deep H9028
Ecc 1:13 by wisdom all that is done under the **h**. H9028
Ecc 2: 3 to do under the **h** during the few days of H9028
Ecc 3: 1 a season for every activity under the **h**: H9028
Isa 1: 2 Hear me, you **h**! Listen, earth! For the LORD H9028
Isa 13: 5 from the ends of the **h**—the LORD and the H9028
Isa 13:13 Therefore I will make the **h** tremble; and H9028
Isa 14:13 "I will ascend to the **h**; I will raise my H9028
Isa 24: 4 withers, the **h** languish with the earth. H5294
Isa 24:18 The floodgates of the **h** are opened, the H5294
Isa 24:21 the powers in the **h** above and the kings H5294
Isa 34: 4 be dissolved and the **h** rolled up like a H9028
Isa 34: 5 My sword has drunk its fill in the **h**; see, it H9028
Isa 38:14 My eyes grew weak as I looked to the **h**. H5294
Isa 40:12 the breadth of his hand marked off the **h**? H9028
Isa 40:22 He stretches out the **h** like a canopy, and H9028
Isa 40:26 Lift up your eyes and look to the **h**: Who H5294
Isa 42: 5 the Creator of the **h**, who stretches them H9028
Isa 44:23 Sing for joy, you **h**, for the LORD has done H9028
Isa 44:24 who stretches out the **h**, who spreads out H9028
Isa 45: 8 "You **h** above, rain down my H9028
Isa 45:12 My own hands stretched out the **h**; H9028
Isa 45:18 he who created the **h**, he is God; H9028
Isa 48:13 my right hand spread out the **h**; when H9028
Isa 49:13 Shout for joy, you **h**; rejoice, you earth H9028
Isa 50: 3 I clothe the **h** with darkness and make H9028
Isa 51: 6 Lift up your eyes to the **h**, look at the earth H9028
Isa 51: 6 beneath; the **h** will vanish like smoke H9028
Isa 51:13 who stretches out the **h** and who lays the H9028
Isa 51:16 I who set the **h** in place, who laid H9028
Isa 55: 9 "As the **h** are higher than the earth, so H9028
Isa 64: 1 you would rend the **h** and come down, H9028
Isa 65:17 I will create new **h** and a new earth. H9028
Isa 66:22 "As the new **h** and the new earth that I H9028
Jer 2:12 appalled at this, you **h**, and shudder with H9028
Jer 4:23 and at the **h**, and their light was H9028
Jer 4:28 will mourn and the **h** above grow dark, H9028
Jer 8: 2 the moon and all the stars of the **h**, H9028
Jer 10: 2 nations or be terrified by signs in the **h**, H9028
Jer 10:11 who did not make the **h** and the earth A10723
Jer 10:11 from the earth and from under the **h**. A10723
Jer 10:12 stretched out the **h** by his understanding. H9028
Jer 10:13 the waters in the **h** roar; he makes clouds H9028
Jer 31:37 "Only if the **h** above can be measured H9028
Jer 32:17 you have made the **h** and the earth by H9028
Jer 51: 9 to the skies, it rises as high as the **h**. H8836
Jer 51:15 stretched out the **h** by his understanding. H9028
Jer 51:16 the waters in the **h** roar; he makes clouds H9028
Jer 51:53 Babylon ascends to the **h** and fortifies her H9028
La 3:66 destroy them from under the **h** *of* the LORD. H9028
Eze 1: 1 the **h** were opened and I saw visions of H9028
Eze 32: 7 I will cover the **h** and darken their stars H9028
Eze 32: 8 shining lights in the **h** I will darken over H9028
Da 6:27 wonders in the **h** and on the earth. A10723
Da 8:10 It grew until it reached the host of the **h** H9028
Da 12: 3 will shine like the brightness of the **h**, H8385
Joel 2:10 earth shakes, the **h** tremble, the sun and H9028
Joel 2:30 show wonders in the **h** and on the earth, H9028
Joel 3:16 the earth and the **h** will tremble. H9028
Am 9: 2 Though they climb up to the **h** *above* H9028
Am 9: 6 lofty palace in the **h** and sets its H9028
Hab 3: 3 glory covered the **h** and his praise filled H9028
Hab 3:11 stood still in the **h** at the glint of your H2292
Hag 1:10 because of you the **h** have withheld their H9028
Hag 2: 6 will once more shake the **h** and the earth, H9028
Hag 2:21 I am going to shake the **h** and the earth. H9028
Zec 8:12 its crops, and the **h** will drop their dew. H9028
Zec 12: 1 who stretches out the **h**, who lays the H9028
Mt 11:23 Capernaum, will you be lifted to the **h**? *G4041*
Mt 24:31 from one end *of* the **h** to the other. *G4041*
Mk 13:27 the ends of the earth to the ends *of* the **h**. *G4041*
Lk 10:15 Capernaum, will you be lifted to the **h**? *G4041*
Ac 2:19 wonders in the **h** above and signs on *G4041*
Ac 4:24 "you made the **h** and the earth and the *G4041*
Ac 14:15 who made the **h** and the earth and the *G4041*
Eph 4:10 one who ascended higher than all the **h**, *G4041*
Heb 1:10 the **h** are the work of your hands. *G4041*
Heb 7:26 apart from sinners, exalted above the **h**. *G4041*
Heb 12:26 shake not only the earth but also the **h**." *G4041*
Jas 5:18 he prayed, and the **h** gave rain, and the *G4041*
2Pe 3: 5 by God's word the **h** came into being and *G4041*
2Pe 3: 7 same word the present **h** and earth are *G4041*
2Pe 3:10 The **h** will disappear with a roar; the *G4041*
2Pe 3:12 about the destruction of the **h** by fire, *G4041*
Rev 6:14 The **h** receded like a scroll being rolled up, *G4041*
Rev 10: 6 who created the **h** and all that is in them *G4041*
Rev 11: 6 power to shut up the **h** so that it will not rain NDT
Rev 12:12 *you* **h** and you who dwell in them! *G4041*
Rev 14: 7 Worship him who made the **h**, the earth *G4041*
Rev 18:20 "Rejoice over her, *you* **h**! Rejoice, you *G4041*
Rev 20:11 The earth and the **h** fled from his *G4041*

HEAVENWARD (1) [HEAVEN]

Php 3:14 which God has called me **h** in Christ Jesus. *G539*

HEAVIER (6) [HEAVY]

1Ki 12:11 you a heavy yoke; I *will* **make** it **even h**. H3578
1Ki 12:14 your yoke heavy; I *will* **make** it **even h**. H3578
2Ch 10:11 you a heavy yoke; I *will* **make** it **even h**. H3578
2Ch 10:14 your yoke heavy; I *will* **make** it **even h**. H3578
Pr 27: 3 a fool's provocation is **h** than both. H3878
Isa 28:22 your chains *will become* **h**; the Lord, H2616

HEAVILY (2) [HEAVY]

Ps 88: 7 Your wrath **lies h** on me; you have H6164
Ecc 6: 1 the sun, and it **weighs h** on mankind: H8041

HEAVY (49) [HEAVIER, HEAVILY]

Ex 18:18 The work is too **h** for you; you cannot H3878
Nu 11:14 by myself; the burden is too **h** for me. H3878
Nu 35:23 on them a stone **h enough** to kill them, H889S
Dt 1: 9 *are* **too h a burden** for me **to carry** H4202+3523+5951
Dt 25:13 weights in your bag—one **h**, one light. H1524
Dt 32:15 filled with food, *they became* **h** and sleek. H6286
Jdg 20:34 The fighting *was so* **h** that the Benjamites H3877
1Sa 4:17 the army has suffered **h** losses. H1524
1Sa 4:18 he was an old man, and he was **h**. H3878
1Sa 5: 6 The LORD's hand *was* **h** on the people of H3877
1Sa 5: 7 because his hand *is* **h** on us and on H7996
1Sa 5:11 with panic; God's hand *was* very **h** *on* it. H3877
1Sa 6:19 because of the **h** blow the LORD had H1524
1Sa 23: 5 He inflicted **h** losses on the Philistines H1524
2Sa 14:26 a year because it became too **h** for him— H3878
1Ki 12: 4 "Your father **put** *a* **h** yoke on us, but now H7996
1Ki 12: 4 harsh labor and the **h** yoke he put on us, H3878
1Ki 12:10 'Your father **put** *a* **h** yoke on us, but H3877
1Ki 12:11 My father laid on you a **h** yoke; I will make H3878
1Ki 12:14 "My father **made** your yoke **h**; I will make H3877
1Ki 18:41 for there is the sound of a **h** rain." H2162
1Ki 18:45 a **h** rain started falling and Ahab rode off H1524
1Ki 20:21 inflicted **h** losses on the Arameans H1524
2Ch 10: 4 "Your father **put** *a* **h** yoke on us, but now H7996
2Ch 10: 4 harsh labor and the **h** yoke he put on us, H3878
2Ch 10:10 'Your father **put** *a* **h** yoke on us, but H3877
2Ch 10:11 My father laid on you a **h** yoke; I will make H3878
2Ch 10:14 "My father **made** your yoke **h**; I will make H3877
2Ch 13:17 his troops inflicted **h** losses on them, H8041
2Ch 21:14 everything that is yours, with a **h** blow. H1524
2Ch 28: 5 who inflicted **h** casualties on him. H1524
Ne 5:15 **placed a h burden** on the people and took H3877
Ne 5:18 the demands *were* **h** on these people. H3877
Job 23: 2 his hand *is* **h** in spite of my groaning. H3877
Job 33: 7 nor *should* my hand *be* **h** on you. H3877
Job 39:11 Will you leave your **h work** to it? H3330
Ps 32: 4 For day and night your hand *was* **h** on me H3877
Ps 38: 4 me like a burden too **h** to bear. H3878+3877
Ps 144:14 our oxen *will* **draw h loads**. There will be H6022
Pr 25:20 is one who sings songs to a **h** heart. H8273
Pr 27: 3 Stone is **h** and sand a burden, but a fool's H3880
Ecc 1:13 What a **h** burden God has laid on H8273
Isa 24:20 *so* **h** upon it is the guilt of its rebellion H3877
Isa 47: 6 Even on the aged *you* **laid** a very **h** yoke. H3877
Eze 24:12 its **h** deposit has not been removed H8041
Eze 27:25 filled with **h** *cargo* as you sail the H3877+4394
Mt 23: 4 They tie up **h**, cumbersome loads and put *G987*
Mt 26:43 them sleeping, because their eyes were **h**. *G976*
Mk 14:40 sleeping, because their eyes were **h**. *G2852*

HEBER (10) [HEBER'S, HEBERITE]

Ge 46:17 The sons of Beriah: **H** and Malkiel. H2491
Nu 26:45 through **H**, the Heberite clan; through H2491
Jdg 4:11 Now **H** the Kenite had left the other H2491
Jdg 4:17 the wife of **H** the Kenite, because H2491
Jdg 4:17 of Hazor and the family of **H** the Kenite. H2491
Jdg 5:24 be Jael, the wife of **H** the Kenite, most H2491
1Ch 4:18 the father of Gedor, **H** the father of Soko H2491
1Ch 7:31 **H** and Malkiel, who was the father of H2491
1Ch 7:32 **H** was the father of Japhlet, Shomer and H2491
1Ch 8:17 Zebadiah, Meshullam, Hizki, **H**, H2491

HEBER'S (1) [HEBER]

Jdg 4:21 But Jael, **H** wife, picked up a tent peg H2491

HEBERITE (1) [HEBER]

Nu 26:45 through Heber, the **H** clan; through H2499

HEBRAIC (1) [HEBREW]

Ac 6: 1 against the **H Jews** because their widows *G1578*

HEBREW (26) [HEBRAIC, HEBREWS]

Ge 14:13 came and reported this to Abram the **H**. H6303
Ge 39:14 "this **H** has been brought to us to make H6303
Ge 39:17 "That **H** slave you brought us came to me H6303
Ge 41:12 Now a young **H** was there with us, H6303
Ex 1:15 The king of Egypt said to the **H** midwives H6303
Ex 1:16 are helping the **H** *women* during H6303
Ex 1:19 "**H** *women* are not like Egyptian women H6303
Ex 1:22 "Every **H** boy that is born you must throw NDT
Ex 2: 6 "This is one of the **H** babies," she said. H6303
Ex 2: 7 get one of the **H** women to nurse the H6303
Ex 2:11 He saw an Egyptian beating a **H** H6303+408
Ex 2:13 "Why are you hitting your fellow **H**? NDT
Ex 21: 2 "If you buy a **H** servant, he is to serve you H6303
Dt 15:12 of your people—**H** *men* or women—sell H6303
[Dt 15:12 of your people—**H** men or *women*—sell H6303]
1Sa 4: 6 "What's all this shouting in the **H** camp?" H6303
2Ki 18:26 Don't speak to us **in H** in the hearing of H3376
2Ki 18:28 commander stood and called out **in H**, H3376
2Ch 32:18 Then they called out **in H** to the people of H3376
Isa 36:11 Don't speak to us **in H** in the hearing of H3376
Isa 36:13 commander stood and called out **in H**, H3376
Jer 34: 9 Everyone was to free their **H** slaves, both H6303
Jer 34: 9 one was to hold a fellow **H** in bondage. H3374
Jnh 1: 9 "I am a **H** and I worship the LORD H6303
Php 3: 5 tribe of Benjamin, a **H** of Hebrews; in *G1578*
Rev 9:11 whose name *in* **H** is Abaddon and in *G1580*
Rev 16:16 to the place that **in H** is called *G1580*

HEBREWS (19) [HEBREW]

Ge 40:15 forcibly carried off from the land of the **H**, H6303
Ge 43:32 because Egyptians could not eat with **H** H6303
Ex 2:13 he went out and saw two **H** fighting. H408+6303
Ex 3:18 the God of the **H**, has met with us. H6303
Ex 5: 3 "The God of the **H** has met with us. H6303
Ex 7:16 the God of the **H**, has sent me to say H6303
Ex 9: 1 is what the LORD, the God of the **H**, says: H6303
Ex 9:13 is what the LORD, the God of the **H**, says: H6303
Ex 10: 3 is what the LORD, the God of the **H**, says: H6303
1Sa 4: 9 you will be subject to the **H**, as they H6303
1Sa 13: 3 the land and said, "Let the **H** hear!" H6303
1Sa 13: 7 *Some* **H** even crossed the Jordan to the H6303
1Sa 13:19 "Otherwise the **H** will make swords or H6303
1Sa 14:11 "The **H** are crawling out of the holes they H6303
1Sa 14:21 Those **H** who had previously been with the H6303
1Sa 29: 3 Philistines asked, "What about these **H**?" H6303
Jer 34:14 must free any fellow **H** who have sold H6303
2Co 11:22 Are they **H**? So am I. Are they Israelites *G1578*
Php 3: 5 a Hebrew of **H**; in regard to the law *G1578*

HEBRON (74) [HEBRONITE, HEBRONITES, KIRIATH ARBA]

Ge 13:18 to live near the great trees of Mamre at **H**, H2496
Ge 23: 2 that is, **H**) in the land of Canaan H2496
Ge 23:19 Mamre (which is at **H**) in the land of H2496
Ge 35:27 **H**), where Abraham and Isaac had H2496
Ge 37:14 Then he sent him off from the Valley of **H**. H2496
Ex 6:18 Kohath were Amram, Izhar, **H** and Uzziel. H2497
Nu 3:19 Amram, Izhar, **H** and Uzziel. H2497
Nu 13:22 up through the Negev and came to **H**, H2496
Nu 13:22 **H** had been built seven years before Zoan H2496
Jos 10: 3 Jerusalem appealed to Hoham king of **H**, H2496
Jos 10: 5 kings of Jerusalem, **H**, Jarmuth, Lachish H2496
Jos 10:23 kings of Jerusalem, **H**, Jarmuth, Lachish H2496
Jos 10:36 went up from Eglon to **H** and attacked it. H2496
Jos 10:39 had done to Libnah and its king and to **H**. H2496
Jos 11:21 from **H**, Debir and Anab, from all the hill H2496
Jos 12:10 king of Jerusalem one the king of **H** one H2496
Jos 14:13 gave him **H** as his inheritance. H2496
Jos 14:14 So **H** has belonged to Caleb son of H2496
Jos 14:15 **H** used to be called Kiriath Arba after Arba H2496
Jos 15:13 portion in Judah—Kiriath Arba, that is, **H**. H2496
Jos 15:14 From **H** Caleb drove out the three H9004S
Jos 15:54 that is, **H**) and Zior—nine towns H2496
Jos 20: 7 Kiriath Arba (that is, **H**) in the hill country H2496
Jos 21:11 **H**), with its surrounding H2496
Jos 21:13 of Aaron the priest they gave **H** H2496
Jdg 1:10 against the Canaanites living in **H** H2496
Jdg 1:20 had promised, **H** was given to Caleb H2496
Jdg 16: 3 them to the top of the hill that faces **H**. H2496
1Sa 30:31 and **H**; and to those in all the other places H2496
2Sa 2: 1 "To **H**," the LORD answered. H2496
2Sa 2: 3 they settled in **H** and its towns. H2496
2Sa 2: 4 Then the men of Judah came to **H**, and NDT
2Sa 2:11 David was king in **H** over Judah was H2496
2Sa 2:32 all night and arrived at **H** by daybreak. H2496
2Sa 3: 2 Sons were born to David in **H**: His H2496
2Sa 3: 5 These were born to David in **H**. H2496
2Sa 3:19 Then he went to **H** to tell David H2496
2Sa 3:20 came to David at **H**, David prepared a H2496
2Sa 3:22 But Abner was no longer with David in **H** H2496
2Sa 3:27 Now when Abner returned to **H**, Joab took H2496
2Sa 3:32 They buried Abner in **H**, and the king wept H2496
2Sa 4: 1 of Saul heard that Abner had died in **H**, H2496
2Sa 4: 8 to David at **H** and said to the king, H2496
2Sa 4:12 hung the bodies by the pool in **H**. H2496

2Sa 4:12 buried it in Abner's tomb at **H**. H2496
2Sa 5: 1 of Israel came to David at **H** and said, H2496
2Sa 5: 3 of Israel had come to King David at **H**, H2496
2Sa 5: 3 covenant with them at **H** before the LORD, H2496
2Sa 5: 5 In **H** he reigned over Judah seven years H2496
2Sa 5:13 After he left **H**, David took more H2496
2Sa 15: 7 "Let me go to **H** and fulfill a vow I made H2496
2Sa 15: 8 to Jerusalem, I will worship the LORD in **H**. H2496
2Sa 15: 9 "Go in peace." So he went to **H**. H2496
2Sa 15:10 trumpets, then say, 'Absalom is king in **H**. H2496
1Ki 2:11 seven years in **H** and thirty-three in H2496
1Ch 2:42 son Mareshah, who was the father of **H**. H2497
1Ch 2:43 The sons of **H**: Korah, Tappuah, Rekem H2497
1Ch 3: 1 were the sons of David born to him in **H**: H2496
1Ch 3: 4 These six were born to David in **H**, where H2496
1Ch 6: 2 Amram, Izhar, **H** and Uzziel. H2497
1Ch 6:18 Amram, Izhar, **H** and Uzziel. H2497
1Ch 6:55 They were given **H** in Judah with its H2496
1Ch 6:57 the descendants of Aaron were given **H** H2496
1Ch 11: 1 came together to David at **H** and said, H2496
1Ch 11: 3 of Israel had come to King David at **H**, H2496
1Ch 11: 3 covenant with them at **H** before the LORD, H2496
1Ch 12:23 who came to David at **H** to turn Saul's H2496
1Ch 12:38 They came to **H** fully determined to make H2496
1Ch 15: 9 from the descendants of **H**, Eliel the H2497
1Ch 23:12 Amram, Izhar, **H** and Uzziel—four in H2497
1Ch 23:19 The sons of **H**: Jeriah the first, Amariah H2497
1Ch 24:23 The sons of **H**: Jeriah the first, Amariah H2497
1Ch 29:27 seven in **H** and thirty-three in Jerusalem. H2496
2Ch 11:10 Aijalon and **H**. These were fortified H2496

HEBRONITE (1) [HEBRON]
Nu 26:58 the Libnite clan, the **H** clan, the Mahlite H2498

HEBRONITES (5) [HEBRON]
Nu 3:27 Izharites, **H** and Uzzielites; these were the H2498
1Ch 26:23 the Izharites, the **H** and the Uzzielites: H2498
1Ch 26:30 From the **H**: Hashabiah and his relatives— H2498
1Ch 26:31 As for the **H**, Jeriah was their chief H2498
1Ch 26:31 men among **the H** were found at H2157S

HEDGE (3) [HEDGED]
Job 1:10 "*Have* you not **put a h** around him and his H8455
Isa 5: 5 I will take away its **h**, and it will be H5372
Mic 7: 4 the most upright worse than a **thorn h**. H5004

HEDGED (1) [HEDGE]
Job 3:23 way is hidden, whom God *has* **h in**? H6114

HEED (10) [HEEDED, HEEDS]
1Sa 15:22 to **h** is better than the fat of rams. H7992
Ps 58: 5 that *will* not **h** the tune of the charmer H9048
Ps 107:43 *Let* the one who is wise **h** these things H9068
Pr 16:20 *Whoever* **gives h** to instruction prospers H8505
Pr 28: 4 the wicked, but *those who* **h** it resist them. H9068
Ecc 4:13 who no longer knows how to **h a warning**. H2302
Ecc 7: 5 It is better to **h** the rebuke of a wise H9048
Eze 33: 4 but *does* not **h the warning** and the H2302
Eze 33: 5 of the trumpet but *did* not **h the warning**, H2302
Mic 6: 9 "**H** the rod and the One who appointed it. H9048

HEEDED (3) [HEED]
Ecc 9:16 despised, and his words **are** no longer **h**. H9048
Ecc 9:17 of the wise *are* more *to* **be h** than the H9048
Eze 33: 5 If they *had* **h the warning**, they would H2302

HEEDS (8) [HEED]
Pr 10:17 *Whoever* **h** discipline shows the way to H9068
Pr 13: 1 A wise son **h** his father's instruction, but a NDT
Pr 13:18 but *whoever* **h** correction is honored. H9068
Pr 15: 5 but *whoever* **h** correction shows prudence. H9068
Pr 15:31 *Whoever* **h** life-giving correction will H9048+265
Pr 15:32 the *one who* **h** correction gains H9048
Pr 28: 7 A discerning son **h** instruction, but a H5915
Pr 29:18 blessed is the one *who* **h** wisdom's H9068

HEEL (4) [HEELS]
Ge 3:15 crush your head, and you will strike his **h**." H6811
Ge 25:26 with his hand grasping Esau's **h**; so he H6811
Job 18: 9 A trap seizes him by the **h**; a snare holds H6811
Hos 12: 3 In the womb *he* **grasped** his brother's **h** H6810

HEELS (3) [HEEL]
Ge 49:17 that bites the horse's **h** so that its rider H6811
Ge 49:19 but he will attack them at their **h**. H6811
La 5: 5 Those who pursue us are **at our h** H6584+7418

HEGAI (4)
Est 2: 3 Let them be placed under the care of **H** H2043
Est 2: 8 of Susa and put under the care of **H**. H2051
Est 2: 8 to the king's palace and entrusted to **H**, H2051
Est 2:15 she asked for nothing other than what **H** H2051

HEIFER (15) [HEIFER'S]
Ge 15: 9 "Bring me a **h**, a goat and a ram, H6320
Nu 19: 2 to bring you a red **h** without defect or H7239
Nu 19: 5 he watches, the **h** is to be burned—its H7239
Nu 19: 6 wool and throw them onto the burning **h**. H7239
Nu 19: 9 up the ashes of the **h** and put them in a H7239
Nu 19:10 up the ashes of the **h** must also wash his H7239
Dt 21: 3 body shall take a **h** that has never H6320+1330
Dt 21: 6 their hands over the **h** whose neck was H6320
Jdg 14:18 "If you had not plowed with my **h**, you H6320
1Sa 16: 2 "Take a **h** with you and say H6320+1330
Jer 46:20 "Egypt is a beautiful **h**, but a gadfly is H6320
Jer 50:11 you frolic like a **h** threshing grain and H6320
Hos 4:16 Israelites are stubborn, like a stubborn **h**. H7239
Hos 10:11 Ephraim is a trained **h** that loves to thresh; H6320
Heb 9:13 the ashes *of* a **h** sprinkled on those *G1239*

HEIFER'S (1) [HEIFER]
Dt 21: 4 in the valley they are to break the **h** neck. H6320

HEIGHT (17) [HEIGHTS]
Nu 23: 3 Then he went off to a **barren h**. H9155
Jdg 6:26 to the LORD your God on the top of this **h**. H5057
1Sa 16: 7 consider his appearance or his **h**, H1469+7757
1Sa 17: 4 His **h** was six cubits and a span. H1470
1Ki 6:10 The **h** *of* each was five cubits, and they H7757
1Ki 6:26 The **h** *of* each cherub was ten cubits. H7757
Ne 4: 6 wall till all of it **reached** half its **h**, H8003+6330
Est 5:14 pole set up, *reaching to a* **h** *of* fifty cubits H1469
Est 7: 9 "A pole *reaching to a* **h** *of* fifty cubits H1469
Isa 22:16 hewing your grave *on* the **h** and chiseling H5294
Eze 19:11 conspicuous for its **h** and for its many H1470
Eze 31:10 because it was proud of its **h**, H1470
Eze 31:14 well-watered are ever to reach *such a* **h**; H1470
Eze 43:13 And this is the **h** *of* the altar: H1470
Da 4:10 middle of the land. Its **h** was enormous. A10660
Da 8: 8 at the **h of its power** the large horn H6793
Ro 8:39 neither **h** nor depth, nor anything else in *G5739*

HEIGHTS (41) [HEIGHT]
Nu 21:28 Ar of Moab, the citizens of Arnon's **h**. H1195
Nu 23: 9 peaks I see them, from the **h** I view them. H1496
Dt 32:13 him ride on the **h** *of* the land and fed H1195
Dt 33:29 before you, and you will tread on their **h**." H1195
2Sa 1:19 "A gazelle lies slain on your **h**, Israel H1195
2Sa 1:25 Jonathan lies slain on your **h**. H1195
2Sa 22:34 he causes me to stand on the **h**. H1195
2Ki 19:23 I have ascended the **h** *of* the mountains, H5294
2Ki 19:23 the mountains, the **utmost h** *of* Lebanon. H3752
Job 22:12 "Is not God in the **h** *of* heaven? And see H1470
Job 25: 2 he establishes order in the **h of heaven**. H5294
Ps 18:33 he causes me to stand on the **h**. H1195
Ps 42: 6 the Jordan, the **h of Hermon**—from Mount H3056
Ps 48: 2 like the **h** *of* Zaphon is Mount Zion H3752
Ps 78:69 He built his sanctuary like the **h**, like the H8123
Ps 148: 1 the heavens; praise him in the **h above**. H5294
Ecc 12: 5 people are afraid of **h** and of dangers in H1469
Isa 7:11 depths or *in* the highest **h**." H4200+5087+2025
Isa 14:13 on the **utmost h** *of* Mount Zaphon. H3752
Isa 31: 4 to do battle on Mount Zion and on its **h**. H1496
Isa 33:16 they are the ones who will dwell **on** the **h** H5294
Isa 37:24 I have ascended the **h** *of* the mountains, H5294
Isa 37:24 the mountains, the **utmost h** *of* Lebanon. H3752
Isa 37:24 I have reached its remotest **h**, the finest of H5294
Isa 41:18 I will make rivers flow on **barren h**, and H9155
Isa 58:14 in triumph on the **h** *of* the land and to H1195
Jer 3: 2 "Look up to the **barren h** and see. Is there H9155
Jer 3:21 A cry is heard on the **barren h**, the H9155
Jer 4:11 wind from the **barren h** in the desert H9155
Jer 7:29 take up a lament on the **barren h**, for the H9155
Jer 12:12 Over all the **barren h** in the desert H9155
Jer 14: 6 stand on the **barren h** and pant like H9155
Jer 31:12 come and shout for joy on the **h** *of* Zion; H5294
Jer 49:16 of the rocks, who occupy the **h** *of* the hill. H5294
Eze 17:23 On the mountain **h** *of* Israel I will plant it H5294
Eze 34:14 the mountain **h** *of* Israel will be their H5294
Eze 36: 2 The ancient **h** have become our H1195
Am 4:13 treads on the **h** *of* the earth—the H1195
Ob 3 the rocks and make your home on the **h**, H5294
Mic 1: 3 down and treads on the **h** *of* the earth. H1195
Hab 3:19 he enables me to tread on the **h**. H1195

HEIR (15) [INHERIT]
Ge 15: 3 a servant in my household *will be* my **h**." H3769
Ge 15: 4 "This man *will* not *be* your **h**, but a son H3769
Ge 15: 4 your own flesh and blood *will be* your **h**." H3769
2Sa 14: 7 then we will get rid of the **h** as well. H3769
Ps 105:44 and *they* **fell h** to what others had toiled H3769
Jer 49: 1 Has Israel no **h**? Why then has Molek H3769
Mt 21:38 they said to each other, 'This is the **h**. *G3101*
Mk 12: 7 said to one another, 'This is the **h**. *G3101*
Lk 20:14 'This is the **h**,' they said. 'Let's kill *G3101*
Ro 4:13 promise that he would be **h** of the world, *G3101*
Gal 4: 1 is that as long as an **h** is underage, *G3101*
Gal 4: 2 The **h** is subject to guardians and trustees NDT
Gal 4: 7 his child, God has made you also an **h**. *G3101*
Heb 1: 2 whom he appointed **h** of all things, and *G3101*
Heb 11: 7 world and became **h** of the righteousness *G3101*

HEIRS (11) [INHERIT]
Jdg 21:17 The Benjamite survivors must have **h**," H3772
Ac 3:25 And you are **h** of the prophets and of the *G5626*
Ro 4:14 For if those who depend on the law are **h** *G3101*
Ro 8:17 children, then we are **h**—heirs of God *G3101*
Ro 8:17 heirs—**h** of God and co-heirs with Christ *G3101*
Gal 3:29 and **h** according to the promise. *G3101*
Eph 3: 6 the Gentiles are **h together** with Israel, *G5169*
Titus 3: 7 we might become **h** having the hope of *G3101*
Heb 6:17 purpose very clear *to* the **h** of what was *G3101*
Heb 11: 9 who were **h with** him of the same promise *G5169*
1Pe 3: 7 partner and as **h with** you of the gracious *G5169*

HELAH (2)
1Ch 4: 5 of Tekoa had two wives, **H** and Naarah. H2690
1Ch 4: 7 The sons of **H**: Zereth, Zohar, Ethnan, H2690

HELAM (2)
2Sa 10:16 they went to **H**, with Shobak the H2663
2Sa 10:17 crossed the Jordan and went to **H**. H2663

HELBAH (1)
Jdg 1:31 Ahlab or Akzib or **H** or Aphek or Rehob. H2695

HELBON (1)
Eze 27:18 They offered wine from **H**, wool from H2696

HELD (88) [HOLD]
Ge 21: 8 was weaned Abraham **h** a great feast. H6913
Ge 27:41 Esau **h a grudge against** Jacob because H8475
Ge 39:22 in charge of all those **h** in the prison, H659
Ge 40: 5 of Egypt, who **were** *being* **h** in prison—had H673
Ge 41:36 food should be **h in reserve** for the country H7214
Ex 17:11 As long as Moses **h up** his hands, the H8123
Ex 17:12 Aaron and Hur **h** his hands **up**—one on H9461
Ex 21:19 the blow *will* **not be h liable** if the other H5927
Ex 21:28 of the bull will **not** be **h responsible**. H5929
Lev 5: 1 about, they *will be* **h responsible**. H5951+6411
Lev 5:17 guilty and *will be* **h responsible**. H5951+6411
Lev 7:18 eats any of it *will be* **h responsible**. H5951+6411
Lev 17:16 they *will be* **h responsible**. H5951+6411
Lev 19: 8 eats it *will be* **h responsible** H5951+6411
Lev 20:17 his sister and *will be* **h responsible**. H5951+6411
Lev 20:19 of you *would be* **h responsible**. H5951+6411
Lev 20:20 They *will be* **h responsible**; they H5951+2628
Lev 24:15 their God *will be* **h responsible**; H5951+2628
Lev 26:13 enabled you to walk **with heads h high**. H7758
Nu 28:16 first month the LORD's Passover is to be **h**. NDT
Dt 4: 4 all of you who **h fast** to the LORD your H1816
Jos 8:18 So Joshua **h out** toward the city the H5742
Jos 8:26 back the hand that **h out** his javelin until H5742
Jos 13: 3 as Canaanite though **h** by the five Philistine NDT
Jos 21:41 the Levites in the **territory** *h by* the Israelites AIT
Jdg 4: 5 She **h court** under the Palm of Deborah H3782
Jdg 5: 7 not fight; *they* **h back** until I, Deborah H2532
Jdg 7:21 While each man **h** his position around the H6641
Jdg 9:27 *they* **h** a festival in the temple of their god H6913
Jdg 14:10 And there Samson **h** a feast, as was H6913
Jdg 16:26 said to the servant who **h** his hand, H2616
1Sa 7:17 and there *he* also **h court** *for* Israel. H9149
1Sa 11:15 all the Israelites **h a great celebration**. H8523
2Sa 6:22 girls you spoke of, *I will* **be h in honor**." H3877
2Sa 23:19 *Was he* not **h in** greater **honor** than the H3877
2Sa 23:23 *He* **was h in** greater **honor** than any of the H3877
1Ki 3:28 *they* **h** the king **in awe**, because H3707
1Ki 7:26 a lily blossom. *It* **h** two thousand baths. H3920
1Ki 8:47 in the land where *they* **are h captive**, H8647
1Ki 11: 2 Solomon **h fast** to them in love. H1815
1Ki 12:32 like the festival **h** in Judah, and offered NDT
2Ki 18: 6 *He* **h fast** to the LORD and did not stop H1815
1Ch 11:25 He **was h in** greater **honor** than any of the H3877
2Ch 4: 5 a lily blossom. *It* **h** three thousand baths. H3920
2Ch 6:37 in the land where *they* **are h captive**, H8647
2Ch 7: 9 On the eighth day *they* **h** an assembly, for H6913
Ne 4:17 with one hand and **h** a weapon in the H2616
Est 5: 2 with her and **h out** to her the gold H3804
Est 8:15 the city of Susa **h** a joyous **celebration**. H7412
Est 10: 3 and **h in high esteem** by his many fellow H8354
Job 36: 8 in chains, **h fast** by cords of affliction, H4334
Ps 17: 5 My steps *have* **h** to your paths; my feet H9461
Ps 106:46 caused all *who* **h** them **captive** to show H8647
SS 3: 4 *I* **h** him and would not let him go till I had H296
SS 7: 5 tapestry; the king **is h captive** by its tresses. H673
Isa 33:23 The mast *is* not **h secure**, the sail is not H2616
Isa 40:12 *Who has* **h** the dust of the earth in a H3920
Isa 42:14 I have been quiet and **h myself back**. H706
Isa 53: 3 despised, and *we* **h** him **in low esteem**. H3108
Isa 65: 2 All day long *I have* **h out** my hands to an H7298
Jer 2: 3 all who devoured her *were* **h guilty**, and H870
Eze 31:15 mourning for it; *I* **h back** its streams, and H4979
Mt 21:46 the people **h** *that* he was a prophet *G1650+2400*
Mk 11:32 everyone **h** that John really was a *G2400*
Lk 5:29 Then Levi **h** a great banquet for Jesus at *G4472*
Lk 11:50 *will be* **h responsible for** the blood *G1699*
Lk 11:51 generation *will be* **h responsible for** it all. *G1699*
Ac 3:11 *While* the man **h on** to Peter and John *G3195*
Ac 19:17 of the Lord Jesus *was* **h in high honor**. *G3486*
Ac 25: 4 answered, "Paul *is being* **h** at Caesarea *G5498*
Ac 25:21 made his appeal *to be* **h over** for the *G5498*
Ac 25:21 I ordered him **h** until I could send him to *G5498*
Ac 27:32 the ropes that *h* the **lifeboat** and let it drift AIT
Ac 27:40 time untied the ropes that *h* the **rudders**. AIT
Ro 3:19 the whole world **h** accountable to God. *G1181*
Ro 10:21 "All day long *I have* **h out** my hands to a *G1736*
Gal 2: 6 As for those who **h in high esteem** *G1506*
Gal 3:23 faith, *we were* **h in custody** under the law *G5864*
Eph 4:16 joined and **h together** by every supporting *G5204*
Col 1:23 not moved from the hope *h out in* the **gospel**. AIT
Col 2:19 supported and **h together** by its ligaments *G5204*
2Ti 4:16 *May it* not *be* **h** against them. *G3357*
Heb 2:15 all their lives were **h in** slavery by their *G1944*
2Pe 2: 4 chains of darkness *to be* **h** for judgment; *G5498*
Rev 1:16 In his right hand *he* **h** seven stars, and *G2400*
Rev 6: 2 Its rider **h** a bow, and he was given a *G2400*
Rev 15: 2 name. *They* **h** harps given them by God *G2400*
Rev 17: 4 *She* **h** a golden cup in her hand, filled *G2400*

HELDAI (3)
1Ch 27:15 twelfth month, was **H** the Netophathite H2702
Zec 6:10 "Take silver and gold from the exiles **H** H2702
Zec 6:14 The crown will be given to **H**, Tobijah H2702

HELECH (NIV84) HELEK

HELED (2)
2Sa 23:29 **H** son of Baanah the Netophathite, Ithai H2699
1Ch 11:30 **H** son of Baanah the Netophathite H2699

HELEK (3) [HELEKITE]
Nu 26:30 through **H**, the Helekite clan; H2751
Jos 17: 2 the clans of Abiezer, **H**, Asriel, Shechem, H2751
Eze 27:11 Men of Arvad and **H** guarded your walls H2662

HELEKITE (1) [HELEK]
Nu 26:30 Iezerite clan; through Helek, the **H** clan; H2757

HELEM (1)
1Ch 7:35 The sons of his brother **H**: Zophah, Imna H2152

HELEPH (1)
Jos 19:33 boundary went from **H** and the large tree H2738

HELEZ (5)
2Sa 23:26 **H** the Paltite, Ira son of Ikkesh from Tekoa, H2742
1Ch 2:39 Azariah the father of **H**, Helez the father H2742
1Ch 2:39 father of Helez, **H** the father of Eleasah H2742
1Ch 11:27 Shammoth the Harorite, **H** the Pelonite, H2742
1Ch 27:10 seventh month, was **H** the Pelonite, an H2742

HELI (1)
Lk 3:23 it was thought, of Joseph, the son *of* **H**, *G2459*

HELIOPOLIS (1)
Eze 30:17 The young men of **H** and Bubastis will fall H225

HELKAI (1)
Ne 12:15 of Harim's, Adna; of Meremoth's, **H**; H2758

HELKATH (2) [HELKATH HAZZURIM]
Jos 19:25 territory included: **H**, Hali, Beten, Akshaph H2762
Jos 21:31 **H** and Rehob, together with their H2762

HELKATH HAZZURIM (1) [HELKATH]
2Sa 2:16 place in Gibeon was called **H**. H2763

HELL (13)
Mt 5:22 will be in danger of the fire *of* **h**. *G1147*
Mt 5:29 your whole body to be thrown into **h**. *G1147*
Mt 5:30 than for your whole body to go into **h**. *G1147*
Mt 10:28 who can destroy both soul and body in **h**. *G1147*
Mt 18: 9 two eyes and be thrown into the fire *of* **h**. *G1147*
Mt 23:15 twice as much a child *of* **h** as you are. *G1147*
Mt 23:33 will you escape being condemned *to* **h**? *G1147*
Mk 9:43 maimed than with two hands to go into **h**, *G1147*
Mk 9:45 to have two feet and be thrown into **h**. *G1147*
Mk 9:47 to have two eyes and be thrown into **h**, *G1147*
Lk 12: 5 has authority to throw you into **h**. *G1147*
Jas 3: 6 life on fire, and is itself set on fire by **h**. *G1147*
2Pe 2: 4 but **sent** them **to h**, putting them *G5434*

HELLENISTIC (2)
Ac 6: 1 the **H Jews** among them complained *G1821*
Ac 9:29 He talked and debated with the **H Jews** *G1821*

HELM (KJV) RUDDER

HELMET (7) [HELMETS]
1Sa 17: 5 He had a bronze **h** on his head and wore H3916
1Sa 17:38 on him and a bronze **h** on his head. H7746
Ps 60: 7 Ephraim is my **h**, Judah is my H5057+8031
Ps 108: 8 Ephraim is my **h**, Judah is my H5057+8031
Isa 59:17 the **h** *of* salvation on his head H3916
Eph 6:17 Take the **h** of salvation and the sword of *G4330*
1Th 5: 8 the hope of salvation *as* a **h**. *G4330*

HELMETS (5) [HELMET]
2Ch 26:14 shields, spears, **h**, coats of armor, bows H3916
Jer 46: 4 Take your positions with **h** on! Polish your H3916
Eze 23:24 with large and small shields and with **h**. H7746
Eze 27:10 hung their shields and **h** on your walls, H3916
Eze 38: 5 will be with them, all with shields and **h**, H3916

HELON (5)
Nu 1: 9 from Zebulun, Eliab son of **H**; H2735
Nu 2: 7 the people of Zebulun is Eliab son of **H**. H2735
Nu 7:24 third day, Eliab son of **H**, the leader of the H2735
Nu 7:29 This was the offering of Eliab son of **H**. H2735
Nu 10:16 Eliab son of **H** was over the division of H2735

HELP (225) [HELPED, HELPER, HELPERS, HELPFUL, HELPING, HELPLESS, HELPS]
Ge 4: 1 "**With the h of** the LORD I have brought H907
Ge 39:15 heard me **scream for h**, H8123+7754+2256+7924
Ge 39:18 as I **screamed for h**, H8123+7754+2256+7924
Ex 2:23 their **cry for h** because of their slavery H8784
Ex 4:12 I *will* **h** you speak and will teach H2118+6640
Ex 4:15 I *will* **h** both of you speak and will H2118+6640
Ex 23: 1 Do not **h** a guilty person by H8883+3338+6640
Ex 23: 5 it there; **be sure** *you* **h** them with it. H6441+6441
Ex 31: 6 of Ahisamak, of the tribe of Dan, to **h** him. H907
Lev 25:35 **h** them as you would a foreigner and H2616
Nu 1: 4 the head of his family, *is to* **h** you. H2118+907
Nu 34:18 from each tribe to **h assign** the land. H5706
Dt 22: 4 **H** the owner get it to its feet. H6640
Dt 22:24 was in a town and *did* not **scream for h**, H7590
Dt 32:38 Let them rise up *to* **h** you! Let them give H6468
Dt 33: 7 Oh, be his **h** against his foes!" H6469
Dt 33:26 the heavens to **h** you and on the clouds H6469
Jos 1:14 your fellow Israelites. *You are to* **h** them H6468
Jos 10: 4 "Come up and **h** me attack Gibeon," H6468
Jos 10: 6 **H** us, because all the Amorite kings from H6468
Jos 10:33 king of Gezer had come up to **h** Lachish, H6468
Jos 24: 7 But *they* **cried** to the LORD **for h**, and he put H7590
Jdg 4: 3 twenty years, they **cried** to the LORD **for h**. H7590
Jdg 5:23 because they did not come to **h** the LORD H6476
Jdg 5:23 the LORD, to **h** the LORD against the mighty. H6476
Jdg 6: 6 that they **cried out** to the LORD **for h**. H2410
Jdg 10:12 oppressed you and *you* **cried** to me **for h**, H7590
Jdg 12: 3 When I saw that you wouldn't **h**, I took my H3828
1Sa 12: 8 they **cried** to the LORD **for h**, and the H2410
1Sa 14:45 ground, for he did this today **with** God's **h**." H6640
2Sa 3:12 and I will **h** you bring all Israel over H3338+6640
2Sa 8: 5 Damascus came to **h** Hadadezer king of H6468
2Sa 10:19 were afraid to **h** the Ammonites anymore. H3828
2Sa 14: 4 she said, "**H** me, Your Majesty!" H3828
2Sa 15:34 then you can **h** me by frustrating H4200
2Sa 22:30 **With** your **h** I can advance against a troop H928
2Sa 22:36 You make your **saving h** my shield; your H3829
2Sa 22:36 my shield; your **h** has made me great. H6476
2Sa 22:42 *They* **cried for h**, but there was no one to H8775
2Ki 4: 2 replied to her, "How *can I* **h** you? H6913+4200
2Ki 6:26 cried to him, "**H** me, my lord the king H3828
2Ki 6:27 "If the LORD *does* not **h** you, where can I H3828
2Ki 6:27 not help you, where *can I* **get h for** you? H3828
2Ki 14:26 suffering; there was no *one to* **h** them. H6468
2Ki 23:29 Euphrates River to **h** the king of Assyria. H6584
1Ch 12:17 you have come to me in peace to **h** me, H6468
1Ch 12:18 success to *those who* **h** you, for your H6468
1Ch 12:18 who help you, for your God *will* **h** you." H6468
1Ch 12:19 *He and his men did* not **h** the Philistines H6468
1Ch 12:22 Day after day men came to **h** David, until H6468
1Ch 12:33 weapon, to **h** David with undivided loyalty H6370
1Ch 18: 5 Damascus came to **h** Hadadezer king of H6468
1Ch 19:19 were not willing to **h** the Ammonites H3828
1Ch 22:17 leaders of Israel to **h** his son Solomon. H6468
1Ch 23:28 the Levites was to **h** Aaron's H4200+3338
1Ch 24: 3 **With the h of** Zadok a descendant of H2256
1Ch 28:21 in any craft will **h** you in all the work. H6640
2Ch 14:11 no one like you to **h** the powerless H6468
2Ch 14:11 **H** us, LORD our God, for we rely on you H6468
2Ch 16:12 illness *he did* not **seek h** *from* the LORD, H2011
2Ch 19: 2 "*Should you* **h** the wicked and love those H6468
2Ch 20: 4 came together to **seek h** from the LORD; H1335
2Ch 25: 8 God has the power to **h** or to overthrow." H6468
2Ch 28:16 Ahaz sent to the kings of Assyria for **h**. H6468
2Ch 28:20 he gave him trouble instead of **h**. H2616
2Ch 28:21 the king of Assyria, but that did not **h** him. H6476
2Ch 28:23 I will sacrifice to them so *they will* **h** me." H6468
2Ch 32: 8 the LORD our God to **h** us and to fight our H6468
Ezr 4: 2 said, "Let us **h** you build because H6640
Ne 3:12 next section **with the h of** his daughters. H2256
Ne 6:16 been done **with the h of** our God. H4946+907
Est 7: 9 Mordecai, who spoke up to **h** the king." H3202
Job 6:13 Do I have any power to **h** myself, now that H6476
Job 6:21 Now you too have proved to be of no **h**; you NDT
Job 19: 7 response; though *I* **call for h**, there is no H8775
Job 24:12 the souls of the wounded **cry out for h**. H8775
Job 29:12 I rescued the poor *who* **cried for h**, H8775
Job 30:13 'No *one can* **h** him,' they say. H6468
Job 30:24 broken man when *he* **cries for h** in his H8780
Job 30:28 I stand up in the assembly and **cry for h**. H8775
Job 36:13 he fetters them, *they do* not **cry for h**. H8775
Ps 5: 2 Hear my **cry for h**, my King and my H7754+8776
Ps 12: 1 **H**, LORD, for no one is faithful anymore H3828
Ps 18: 6 called to the LORD; *I* **cried** to my God **for h**. H8775
Ps 18:29 **With** your **h** I can advance against a troop H928
Ps 18:35 You make your **saving h** my shield, and H3829
Ps 18:35 sustains me; your **h** has made me great. H6476
Ps 18:41 *They* **cried for h**, but there was no one to H8775
Ps 20: 2 May he send you **h** from the sanctuary H6469
Ps 22:11 trouble is near and there is no *one to* **h**. H6468
Ps 22:19 are my strength; come quickly to **h** me. H6476
Ps 22:24 from him but has listened to his **cry for h**. H8775
Ps 28: 2 Hear my cry for mercy as I **call** to you **for h** H8775
Ps 30: 2 my God, *I* **called** to you **for h**, and you H8775
Ps 30:10 be merciful to me; LORD, be my **h**. H6468
Ps 31:22 cry for mercy when I **called** to you **for h**. H8775
Ps 33:20 the LORD; he is our **h** and our shield. H6469
Ps 38:22 Come quickly to **h** me, my Lord and my H6476
Ps 39:12 listen to my **cry for h**; do not be deaf H8784
Ps 40:10 of your faithfulness and your **saving h**. H9591
Ps 40:13 LORD; come quickly, LORD, to **h** me. H6476
Ps 40:16 who long for your **saving h** always say, H9591
Ps 40:17 You are my **h** and my deliverer; you are H6476
Ps 44:26 Rise up and **h** us; rescue us because of H6476
Ps 46: 1 strength, an ever-present **h** in trouble. H6476
Ps 46: 5 not fall; God *will* **h** her at break of day. H6468
Ps 54: 4 Surely God *is* my **h**; the Lord is the one H6468
Ps 56: 9 enemies will turn back when *I* **call for h**. H7924
Ps 59: 4 Arise to **h** me; look on my H7925
Ps 60: 5 Save us and **h** us with your right hand H6699
Ps 60:11 the enemy, for human **h** is worthless. H9591
Ps 63: 7 Because you are my **h**, I sing in the H6476
Ps 69: 3 I am worn out **calling for h**; my throat is H7924
Ps 70: 1 to save me; come quickly, LORD, to **h** me. H6476
Ps 70: 4 who long for your **saving h** always say, H3802
Ps 70: 5 You are my **h** and my deliverer; LORD, do H6469
Ps 71:12 my God; come quickly, God, to **h** me. H6476
Ps 72:12 the afflicted who have no *one to* **h**. H6468
Ps 77: 1 *I* **cried out** to God **for h**; I cried out H7590+7754
Ps 79: 9 **H** us, God our Savior, for the glory of your H6468
Ps 88:13 I **cry** to you **for h**, LORD; in the morning H8775
Ps 94:17 Unless the LORD had given me **h**, I would H6476
Ps 102: 1 LORD; let my **cry for h** come to you. H8784
Ps 107:12 they stumbled, and there was no *one to* **h**. H6468
Ps 108: 6 Save us and **h** us with your right hand H6699
Ps 108:12 the enemy, for human **h** is worthless. H9591
Ps 109:21 **h** me for your name's sake H6913+907
Ps 109:26 **H** me, LORD my God; save me according H6468
Ps 115: 9 trust in the LORD—he is their **h** and shield. H6469
Ps 115:10 trust in the LORD—he is their **h** and shield. H6469
Ps 115:11 trust in the LORD—he is their **h** and shield. H6469
Ps 119:86 are trustworthy; **h** me, for I am being H6468
Ps 119:147 I rise before dawn and **cry for h**; I have H8775
Ps 119:173 May your hand be ready to **h** me, for I H6468
Ps 121: 1 where does my **h** come from? H6469
Ps 121: 2 My **h** comes from the LORD, the Maker of H6469
Ps 124: 8 Our **h** is in the name of the LORD, the H6469
Ps 146: 5 are those whose **h** is the God of Jacob, H6469
Ecc 4:10 them falls down, one *can* **h** the other **up**. H7756
Ecc 4:10 who falls and has no one to **h** them **up**. H7756
Isa 10: 3 To whom will you run for **h**? Where will H6476
Isa 20: 6 we fled to for **h** and deliverance from H6476
Isa 30: 2 *who* **look for h** to Pharaoh's protection H6395
Isa 30: 5 who bring neither **h** nor advantage, but H6469
Isa 30: 7 to Egypt, *whose* **h** is utterly useless H6468
Isa 30:19 he will be when you **cry for h**! H7754+2410
Isa 31: 1 Woe to those who go down to Egypt for **h** H6476
Isa 31: 1 One of Israel, or **seek h** *from* the LORD. H2011
Isa 31: 2 against *those who* **h** evildoers. H6476
Isa 31: 3 out his hand, *those who* **h** will stumble H6468
Isa 41: 6 *they* **h** each other and say to their H6468
Isa 41:10 I will strengthen you and **h** you; I will H6468
Isa 41:13 says to you, Do not fear; I *will* **h** you. H6468
Isa 41:14 not fear, for *I* myself *will* **h** you," declares H6468
Isa 44: 2 you in the womb, and *who will* **h** you: H6468
Isa 49: 8 in the day of salvation *I will* **h** you; H6468
Isa 57:13 When you **cry out for h**, let your collection H2410
Isa 58: 9 will answer; *you will* **cry for h**, and he will H8775
Isa 63: 5 there was no *one to* **h**, I was appalled H6468
Isa 64: 5 *You* **come to the h of** those who gladly do H7003
Jer 11:12 but *they will* not **h** them **at all** H3828+3828
Jer 47: 3 Parents *will* not **turn to h** their children H7155
Jer 47: 4 all survivors *who could* **h** Tyre and Sidon. H6468
Jer 50:32 fall and no *one will* **h** her **up**; H7756
La 1: 7 enemy hands, there was no *one to* **h** her. H6468
La 3: 8 Even when I call out or **cry for h**, he shuts H8775
La 3:11 mangled me and left me **without h**. H9037
La 4: 6 a moment without a hand turned to **h** her. NDT
La 4:17 looking in vain for **h**; from our towers we H6476
Eze 16:49 *they did* not **h** the poor and needy. H2616+3338
Eze 17:17 great horde *will be of* no **h** *to* him in war, H6913
Eze 29:16 reminder of their sin in turning to her for **h**. NDT
Da 6:11 Daniel praying and **asking** God **for h**. A10274
Da 10:13 princes, came to **h** me, because I was H6468
Da 11:17 his plans will not succeed or **h** him. H2118+4200
Da 11:34 *they will* **receive** a little **h**, and H6468+6469
Da 11:39 fortresses **with the h of** a foreign god and H6640
Da 11:45 come to his end, and no *one will* **h** him. H6468
Hos 5:13 Assyria, and **sent** to the great king **for h**. H8938
Jnh 2: 2 in the realm of the dead *I* **called for h**, H8775
Hab 1: 2 *must I* **call for h**, but you do not H8775
Zec 6:15 will come and *h to* **build** the temple of the AIT
Mt 8: 5 a centurion came to him, **asking for h**. *G4151*
Mt 15: 5 might have been *used to* **h** their father *G6067*
Mt 15:25 knelt before him. "Lord, **h** me!" she said. *G1070*
Mt 25:44 sick or in prison, and *did* not **h** you? *G1354*
Mk 7:11 that what *might have been used to* **h** their *G6067*
Mk 9:22 can do anything, take pity on us and **h** us." *G1070*
Mk 9:24 do believe; **h** me *overcome* my unbelief!" *G1070*
Mk 14: 7 and you can **h** them any time you *G2292+4472*
Lk 4:38 high fever, and they asked Jesus **to h** her. *G4309*
Lk 5: 7 in the other boat to come and **h** them, *G5197*
Lk 7:16 "God *has* **come to h** his people." *G2170*
Lk 10:40 do the work by myself? Tell her to **h** me!" *G5269*
Lk 11:46 *you* yourselves *will* not **lift** one finger **to h** *G4718+3836+5845*
Jn 5: 7 "I have no one to **h** me into the pool when *G965*
Jn 12: 6 *he used to* **h himself to** what was put into *G1002*
Jn 14:16 you another **advocate** to **h** you and be *G4156*
Ac 2:23 you, with the **h** of wicked men, put *G5931*
Ac 4:20 we cannot **h** speaking about what we *G3590S*
Ac 11:29 decided to provide **h** for the brothers and *G1355*
Ac 16: 9 "Come over to Macedonia and **h** us." *G1070*
Ac 18:27 *he was a* great **h** to those who by grace *G5202*
Ac 20:35 this kind of hard work we must **h** the weak, *G514*
Ac 21:28 "Fellow Israelites, **h** us! This is the man *G1070*
Ro 16: 2 to give her any **h** she may need from *G4547*
1Co 16: 6 so that you *can* **h** me **on my journey** *G4636*
2Co 1:11 *as* you **h** us by your prayers. Then many *G5348*
2Co 8:19 Lord himself and to show our **eagerness** *to* **h**. AIT
2Co 9: 2 For I know your **eagerness** *to* **h**, and I have AIT
Php 2:30 to make up for the **h** you yourselves could *G3311*
Php 4: 3 **h** these women since they have *G5197*
1Th 2: 2 but **with the h of** our God we dared to tell *G1877*

1Th 5:14 the disheartened, h the weak, be patient G504
2Th 3: 9 because we do not have the right to such h, NDT
1Ti 5: 5 day to pray and to ask God for h. G1255
1Ti 5:16 she should continue to h them and not let G2064
1Ti 5:16 that the church can h those widows who G2064
2Ti 1:14 guard it with the h of the Holy Spirit who G1328
Titus 3:13 to h Zenas the lawyer and Apollos on their way G4636
Heb 2:18 he is able to h those who are being G1070
Heb 4:16 find grace to h us in our time of need G1069
Heb 6:10 his people and continue to h them. G1354
1Pe 5:12 With the h of Silas, whom I regard as a G1328
3Jn 7 went out, receiving no h from the pagans. AIT

HELPED (31) [HELP]
Jdg 9:24 who had h him murder his H2616+906+3338
1Sa 7:12 "Thus far the LORD has h us." H6468
1Sa 23:16 and h him find strength in H2616+906+3338
2Ki 10:15 and Jehu h him up into the chariot. H6590
1Ch 5:20 They were h in fighting them, and God H6468
1Ch 12: 1 among the warriors who h him in battle; H6468
1Ch 12:21 They h David against raiding bands, for all H6468
1Ch 15:26 Because God had h the Levites who were H6468
2Ch 18:31 cried out, and the LORD h him. H6468
2Ch 20:23 from Seir, they h to destroy one another. H6468
2Ch 26: 7 God h him against the Philistines and H6468
2Ch 26:15 he was greatly h until he became H6468
2Ch 28:23 gods of the kings of Aram have h them, H6468
2Ch 29:34 relatives the Levites h them until the task H2616
2Ch 32: 3 springs outside the city, and they h him. H6468
Est 9: 3 the king's administrators h the Jews, H5951
Job 26: 2 "How you have h the powerless! How you H6468
Job 26: 4 Who has h you utter these words? And H907
Ps 86:17 LORD, have h me and comforted me. H6468
Ps 118:13 back and about to fall, but the LORD h me. H6468
Isa 31: 3 will stumble, those who are h will fall; all H6468
Jer 2:37 those you trust; you will not be h by them. H7503
Mk 1:31 went to her, took her hand and h her up. G1586
Lk 1:54 He has h his servant Israel, remembering G514
Ac 3: 7 the right hand, he h him up, and instantly G1586
Ac 9:41 took her by the hand and h her to her feet. G482
Ac 26:22 But God has h me to this very day G2135+5593
2Co 6: 2 and in the day of salvation I h you." G1070
2Ti 1:18 in how many ways he h me in Ephesus. G1354
Heb 6:10 have shown him as you have h his people G1354
Rev 12:16 But the earth h the woman by opening its G1070

HELPER (11) [HELP]
Ge 2:18 I will make a h suitable for him." H6469
Ge 2:20 But for Adam no suitable h was found. H6469
Ex 18: 4 "My father's God was my h; he saved me H6469
Dt 33:29 He is your shield and h and your glorious H6469
Ne 4:22 every man and his h stay inside H5853
Ps 10:14 you are the h of the fatherless. H6468
Ps 27: 9 away in anger; you have been my h. H6476
Ps 118: 7 LORD is with me; he is my h. I look in H6468
Hos 13: 9 you are against me, against your h. H6469
Ac 13: 5 John was with them as their h. G5677
Heb 13: 6 "The Lord is my h; I will not be afraid. G1071

HELPERS (2) [HELP]
Eze 30: 8 set fire to Egypt and all her h are crushed. H6468
Ac 19:22 He sent two of his h, Timothy and Erastus G1354

HELPFUL (3) [HELP]
Ac 20:20 anything that would be h to you but have G5237
Eph 4:29 only what is h for building others up G19
2Ti 4:11 because he is h to me in my ministry. G2378

HELPING (8) [HELP]
Ex 1:16 are h the Hebrew women during childbirth H3528
Jos 14:12 the LORD h me, I will drive them out H907
Jdg 21:22 'Do us the favor of h them, because we did NDT
Lk 8: 3 These women were h to support them out G1354
Ac 9:36 always doing good and h the poor. G1797+4472
1Co 12:28 gifts of healing, of h, of guidance, and of G516
1Ti 5:10 h those in trouble and devoting herself to G2064
Phm 13 so that he could take your place in h me G1354

HELPLESS (8) [HELP]
Ps 10: 9 He lies in wait to catch the h; he catches H6714
Ps 10: 9 he catches the h and drags them off in his H6714
Ps 10:12 your hand, O God. Do not forget the h. H6705
Ps 69:20 has broken my heart and has left me h; H5683
Pr 28:15 bear is a wicked ruler over a h people. H1924
Jer 48:45 of Heshbon the fugitives stand h, H4946+3946
Da 10: 8 deathly pale and I was h. H4202+6806+3946
Mt 9:36 because they were harassed and h, like G4849

HELPS (7) [HELP]
Ge 49:25 your father's God, who h you, because of H6468
Ps 28: 7 my heart trusts in him, and he h me. H6468
Ps 37:40 The LORD h them and delivers them; he H6468
Isa 50: 7 Because the Sovereign LORD h me, I will H6468
Isa 50: 9 It is the Sovereign LORD who h me. H6468
Ro 8:26 the Spirit h us in our weakness. G5269
Heb 2:16 For surely it is not angels he h, but G2138

HEM (10) [HEMMED]
Ex 28:33 scarlet yarn around the h of the robe, H8767
Ex 28:34 are to alternate around the h of the robe. H8767
Ex 39:24 twisted linen around the h of the robe. H8767
Ex 39:25 them around the h between the H8767
Ex 39:26 around the h of the robe to be worn H8767
1Sa 15:27 Saul caught hold of the h of his robe, and H4053
Ps 139: 5 You h me in behind and before, and you H7443
Hab 1: 4 The wicked h in the righteous, so that H4193
Zec 8:23 of one Jew by the h of his robe and say, H4053
Lk 19:43 encircle you and h you in on every side. G5309

HEMAN (16) [HEMAN'S]
1Ki 4:31 Ezrahite—wiser than H, Kalkol and Darda, H2124
1Ch 2: 6 Ethan, H, Kalkol and Darda—five H2124
1Ch 6:33 H, the musician, the son of Joel, the son H2124
1Ch 15:17 So the Levites appointed H son of Joel H2124
1Ch 15:19 The musicians H, Asaph and Ethan were H2124
1Ch 16:41 With them were H and Jeduthun and the H2124
1Ch 16:42 H and Jeduthun were responsible for the H2124
1Ch 25: 1 H and Jeduthun for the ministry of H2124
1Ch 25: 4 As for H, from his sons: Bukkiah H2124
1Ch 25: 5 All these were sons of H the king's seer H2124
1Ch 25: 5 God gave H fourteen sons and three H2124
1Ch 25: 6 Jeduthun and H were under the H2124
2Ch 5:12 H, Jeduthun and their sons and H2124
2Ch 29:14 from the descendants of H, Jehiel and H2124
2Ch 35:15 H and Jeduthun the king's seer. H2124
Ps 88: T A maskil of H the Ezrahite. H2124

HEMAN'S (1) [HEMAN]
1Ch 6:39 H associate Asaph, who served at H2257S

HEMDAN (2)
Ge 36:26 sons of Dishon: H, Eshban, Ithran and H2777
1Ch 1:41 sons of Dishon: H, Eshban, Ithran and H2777

HEMLOCK (KJV) BITTERNESS, POISONOUS WEEDS

HEMMED (1) [HEM]
Ex 14: 3 the land in confusion, h in by the desert. H6037

HEN (3)
Zec 6:14 Jedaiah and H son of Zephaniah as a H2835
Mt 23:37 as a h gathers her chicks under her wings G3998
Lk 13:34 as a h gathers her chicks under her wings G3998

HENA (3)
2Ki 18:34 are the gods of Sepharvaim, H and Ivvah? H2184
2Ki 19:13 kings of Lair, Sepharvaim, H and Ivvah?" H2184
Isa 37:13 kings of Lair, Sepharvaim, H and Ivvah?" H2184

HENADAD (4)
Ezr 3: 9 the sons of H and their sons and H2836
Ne 3:18 their fellow Levites under Binnui son of H, H2836
Ne 3:24 Binnui son of H repaired another section H2836
Ne 10: 9 Binnui of the sons of H, Kadmiel, H2836

HENCE (KJV) AWAY, FROM HERE, LEAVE, PLACE, SOMEWHERE ELSE

HENNA (2)
SS 1:14 me a cluster of h blossoms from the H4110
SS 4:13 with choice fruits, with h and nard, H4110

HENOCH (KJV) ENOCH, HANOK

HEPHER (9) [GATH HEPHER, HEPHERITE]
Nu 26:32 through H, the Hepherite clan. H2918
Nu 26:33 Zelophehad son of H had no sons; he H2918
Nu 27: 1 The daughters of Zelophehad son of H H2918
Jos 12:17 king of Tappuah one the king of H one H2919
Jos 17: 2 Asriel, Shechem, H and Shemida. H2918
Jos 17: 3 Now Zelophehad son of H, the son of H2918
1Ki 4:10 Sokoh and all the land of H were his); H2919
1Ch 4: 6 bore him Ahuzzam, H, Temeni and H2918
1Ch 11:36 H the Mekerathite, Ahijah the Pelonite, H2918

HEPHERITE (1) [HEPHER]
Nu 26:32 through Hepher, the H clan. H2920

HEPHZIBAH (2)
2Ki 21: 1 fifty-five years. His mother's name was H. H2915
Isa 62: 4 But you will be called H, and your land H2915

HER (1667) [SHE] See Index of Articles Etc.

HERALD (4)
Da 3: 4 Then the h loudly proclaimed, "Nations A10370
Hab 2: 2 on tablets so that a h may run with it. H7924
1Ti 2: 7 I was appointed a h and an apostle— G3061
2Ti 1:11 I was appointed a h and an apostle and a G3061

HERBS (6)
Ex 12: 8 along with bitter h, and bread made H5353
Nu 9:11 with unleavened bread and bitter h. H5353
2Ki 4:39 the fields to gather h and found a wild vine H246
Job 30: 4 In the brush they gathered salt h, and H4865
La 3:15 filled me with bitter h and given me gall H5353
Lk 11:42 rue and all other kinds of garden h, but G3303

HERD (20) [HERDED, HERDERS, HERDING, HERDS]
Ge 18: 7 Then he ran to the h and selected a H1330
Ge 32:16 his servants, each h by itself, and H6373+6373
Ex 34:19 of your livestock, whether from h or flock. H8802
Lev 1: 2 an animal from either the h or the flock. H1330
Lev 1: 3 the offering is a burnt offering from the h, H1330
Lev 3: 1 you offer an animal from the h H1330
Lev 22:21 brings from the h or flock a fellowship H1330
Lev 27:32 Every tithe of the h and flock—every tenth H1330
Nu 15: 3 LORD food offerings from the h or the flock, H1330
Dt 16: 2 from your flock or h at the place the LORD H1330
Dt 32:14 curds and milk from h and flock and with H1330
Jdg 6:25 "Take the second bull from your father's h, H8802
Ps 68:30 the h of bulls among the calves of the H6337
Mt 8:30 from them a large h of pigs was feeding. G36
Mt 8:31 you drive us out, send us into the h of pigs." G36
Mt 8:32 the whole h rushed down the steep G36
Mk 5:11 A large h of pigs was feeding on the nearby G36
Mk 5:13 The h, about two thousand in number G36
Lk 8:32 A large h of pigs was feeding there on the G36
Lk 8:33 the h rushed down the steep bank into G36

HERDED (1) [HERD]
Isa 24:22 They will be h together like prisoners H665+669

HERDERS (4) [HERD]
Ge 13: 7 between Abram's h and Lot's. H8286+5238
Ge 13: 8 or between your h and mine, for we H8286
Ge 26:20 But the h of Gerar quarreled with those of H8286
2Ch 14:15 the camps of the h and carried off droves H5238

HERDING (1) [HERD]
1Sa 25:16 whole time we were h our sheep near H8286

HERDS (55) [HERD]
Ge 13: 5 also had flocks and h and tents. H1330
Ge 26:14 many flocks and h and servants H5238+1330
Ge 32: 7 the flocks and h and camels as well. H1330
Ge 32:16 and keep some space between the h." H6373
Ge 32:19 all the others who followed the h: H6373
Ge 33: 8 meaning of all these flocks and h I met?" H4722
Ge 33:14 pace of the flocks and h before me and H4856
Ge 34:28 seized their flocks and h and donkeys H1330
Ge 45:10 your flocks and h, and all you have. H1330
Ge 46:32 their flocks and h and everything they H1330
Ge 47: 1 with their flocks and h and everything they H1330
Ge 50: 8 their flocks and h were left in Goshen. H1330
Ex 10: 9 with our flocks and h, because we are H1330
Ex 10:24 only leave your flocks and h behind." H1330
Ex 12:32 Take your flocks and h, as you have said H1330
Ex 12:38 droves of livestock, both flocks and h. H1330
Ex 34: 3 even the flocks and h may graze in front H1330
Nu 11:22 if flocks and h were slaughtered for H1330
Nu 31: 9 children and took all the Midianite h, H989
Nu 32: 1 who had very large h and flocks, saw that H5238
Nu 32:26 our flocks and h will remain here in the H989
Dt 7:13 the calves of your h and the lambs of your H546
Dt 8:13 when your h and flocks grow large H1330
Dt 12: 6 the firstborn of your h and flocks. H1330
Dt 12:17 the firstborn of your h and flocks, or H1330
Dt 12:21 animals from the h and flocks the LORD H1330
Dt 14:23 the firstborn of your h and flocks in the H1330
Dt 15:19 every firstborn male of your h and flocks. H1330
Dt 28: 4 the calves of your h and the lambs of your H546
Dt 28:18 the calves of your h and the lambs of your H546
Dt 28:51 any calves of your h or lambs of your H546
Jos 14: 4 with pasturelands for their flocks and h. H7871
Jos 22: 8 with large h of livestock, with silver, H5238
1Sa 30:20 He took all the flocks and h, and his men H1330
2Ki 5:26 flocks and h, or male and female H1330
1Ch 27:29 was in charge of the h grazing in Sharon. H1330
1Ch 27:29 was in charge of the h in the valleys. H1330
2Ch 31: 6 a tithe of their h and flocks and a tithe H1330
2Ch 32:29 acquired great numbers of flocks and h, H1330
Ne 10:36 of our h and of our flocks to the house of H1330
Job 1:10 so that his flocks and h are spread H5238
Ps 8: 7 all flocks and h, and the animals of the H546
Ps 107:38 he did not let their h diminish. H989
Pr 27:23 give careful attention to your h; H6373
Ecc 2: 7 I also owned more h and flocks than H1330
Isa 60: 6 H of camels will cover your land, young H9180
Isa 65:10 the Valley of Achor a resting place for h, H1330
Jer 3:24 their flocks and h, their sons and H1330
Jer 5:17 they will devour your flocks and h, devour H1330
Jer 31:12 olive oil, the young of the flocks and h. H1330
Jer 49:32 their large h will be spoils of war. H5238
Hos 5: 6 go with their flocks and h to seek the LORD, H1330
Joel 1:18 The h mill about because they H6373+1330
Jnh 3: 7 let people or animals, h or flocks, taste H1330
Zep 2:14 Flocks and h will lie down there, creatures H6373

HERE (397) [HERE'S, HEREBY]
Ge 3:12 "The woman you put h with me—she gave AIT
Ge 12:19 Now then, h is your wife. H2180
Ge 15:16 your descendants will come back h, H2178+2025
Ge 19: 9 "This fellow came h as a foreigner, and now NDT
Ge 19:12 "Do you have anyone else h H7024
Ge 19:12 Get them out of h, H2021+5226S
Ge 19:15 wife and your two daughters who are h, H5162
Ge 19:20 h is a town near enough to run to H2296
Ge 19:31 is no man around h to give us H2021+824S
Ge 21:23 Now swear to me h before God that you H2178
Ge 22: 1 "Abraham!" "H I am," he replied. H2180
Ge 22: 5 "Stay h with the donkey while I and the H7024
Ge 22: 7 "The fire and wood are h," Isaac said H2180
Ge 22:11 "H I am," he replied. H2180
Ge 23: 4 a burial site h so I can bury my dead." H6640
Ge 24:31 "Why are you standing out h H928+2021+2575
Ge 24:51 H is Rebekah; take her and go, and let her H2180
Ge 27: 1 "My son." "H I am," he answered. H2180
Ge 27:26 Isaac said to him, "Come h, my son, H5602

H

Ge 29: 6 "and **h** comes his daughter Rachel with H2180
Ge 29:19 than to some other man. **Stay** *h* with me." AIT
Ge 29:26 is not our custom **h** to give the H928+5226S
Ge 30: 3 Then she said, "**H** is Bilhah, my servant H2180
Ge 31:11 the dream, 'Jacob.' I answered, '**H** I am.' H2180
Ge 31:32 whether there is anything of yours *h* **with** me; AIT
Ge 31:37 Put it **h** in front of your relatives and mine H3907
Ge 31:51 also said to Jacob, "**H** is this heap, and H2180
Ge 31:51 **h** is this pillar I have set up between H2180
Ge 37:17 "They have moved on from **h**," the man H2296
Ge 37:19 "**H** comes that dreamer!" they said to H2180
Ge 37:22 him into this cistern **h** in the wilderness, H889
Ge 38:21 hasn't been any shrine prostitute **h**," H928+2296
Ge 38:22 hasn't been any shrine prostitute **h**. H928+2296
Ge 39:14 He came in **h** to sleep with me, but I NDT
Ge 40:15 even **h** I have done nothing to H7024
Ge 42:15 unless your youngest brother comes **h**. H2178
Ge 42:19 let one of your brothers stay *h* **in** prison AIT
Ge 42:28 said to his brothers. "**H** it is in my sack." H2180
Ge 42:33 Leave one of your brothers **h with** me, and AIT
Ge 43: 7 he would say, 'Bring your brother down **h**'?" NDT
Ge 43: 9 him back to you and set him **h** before you, NDT
Ge 43:18 "We were brought **h** because of the silver NDT
Ge 43:20 "we came down **h** the first time to buy food. NDT
Ge 44:33 your servant remain **h** as my lord's slave in NDT
Ge 45: 5 be angry with yourselves for selling me **h**, H2178
Ge 45: 8 it was not you who sent me **h**, but God. H2178
Ge 45:13 And bring my father down **h** quickly." H2178
Ge 46: 2 Jacob!" "**H** I am," he replied. H2180
Ge 47: 4 come to live **h** for a while, H928+2021+824S
Ge 47:23 **h** is seed for you so you can plant the H2026
Ge 48: 5 I came to you **h** will be reckoned H5213+2025S
Ge 48: 9 are the sons God has given me **h**," H928+2296
Ex 3: 4 And Moses said, "**H** I am." H2180
Ex 8:25 sacrifice to your God **h** in the land. NDT
Ex 11: 1 he will let you go from **h**, and when he H2296
Ex 24:12 up to me on the mountain and stay **h**, H9004
Ex 24:14 "Wait **h** for us until we come back to H928+2296
Ex 33:15 not go with us, do not send us up from **h**. H2296
Lev 10: 4 said to them, "**Come h**; carry your H7928
Nu 5:21 **h** the priest is to put the woman under this H2256
Nu 11:21 "**H** I am among six hundred thousand men H889
Nu 13:27 flow with milk and honey! **H** is its fruit. H2296
Nu 14:33 be shepherds **h** for forty H928+2021+4497S
Nu 14:35 end in this wilderness; **h** they will die." H9004
Nu 20: 4 that we and our livestock should die **h**? H9004
Nu 20:16 "Now we are **h** at Kadesh, a town on the NDT
Nu 20:18 "You may not pass through **h**; if you try H3276S
Nu 22: 8 "Spend the night **h**," Balaam said to them H7024
Nu 22:19 spend the night **h** so that I can find H928+2296
Nu 22:32 I have come **h** to oppose you because H2180
Nu 23: 1 "Build me seven altars **h**, and H928+2296
Nu 23: 3 "Stay **h** beside your offering while I go aside NDT
Nu 23:15 "Stay **h** beside your offering while I meet H3907
Nu 23:29 "Build me seven altars **h**, and H928+2296
Nu 32: 6 fellow Israelites go to war while you sit **h**? H7024
Nu 32:14 "And **h** you are, a brood of sinners H2180
Nu 32:16 like to build pens **h** for our livestock and H7024
Nu 32:26 herds will remain **h** in the cities of H9004
Nu 33: 1 **H** are the stages in the journey of the H465
Dt 5: 3 with all of us who are alive **h** today. H7024
Dt 5:31 But you stay **h** with me so that I may give H7024
Dt 9: 4 LORD has brought me **h** to take possession of NDT
Dt 9: 7 left Egypt until you arrived **h**, H2021+5226+2021+2296S
Dt 9:12 "Go down from **h** at once, because H2296
Dt 12: 8 You are not to do as we do **h** today H7024
Dt 22:17 But **h** is the proof of my daughter's virginity H465
Dt 29:12 You are standing **h** in order to enter into a NDT
Dt 29:15 who are standing **h** with us today in the H7024
Dt 29:15 also with those who are not **h** today. H7024
Dt 29:16 passed through the countries on the way **h**. NDT
Jos 1:11 will cross the Jordan **h** to go in and take H2296
Jos 2: 2 Israelites have come **h** tonight to spy out H2178
Jos 3: 9 "Come **h** and listen to the words of the H2178
Jos 10:24 "**Come h** and put your feet on the necks of H7928
Jos 12: 7 **H is a list of** the kings of the land that H465S
Jos 14:10 in the wilderness. So **h** I am today H2180
Jos 18: 6 bring them **h** to me and I will cast lots H2178
Jos 18: 8 I will cast lots for you **h** at Shiloh in the H7024
Jdg 8:15 of Sukkoth, "**H** are Zebah and Zalmunna H2180
Jdg 13:10 hurried to tell her husband, "He's **h**! H2180
Jdg 14:15 Did you invite us **h** to steal our property?" NDT
Jdg 16: 2 people of Gaza were told, "Samson is **h**!" H2178
Jdg 18: 3 asked him, "Who brought you **h**? H2151
Jdg 18: 3 you doing in this place? Why are you **h**?" H7024
Jdg 19: 9 Spend the night **h**; the day is nearly over H7024
Jdg 19:24 **h** is my virgin daughter, and his NDT
Ru 2: 7 has remained **h** from morning till now, NDT
Ru 2: 8 another field and don't go away from **h**. H2296
Ru 2: 8 Stay **h** with the women who work for me H3907
Ru 2:14 mealtime Boaz said to her, "Come **over h**. H2151
Ru 3:13 Stay **h** for the night, and in the morning if he NDT
Ru 3:13 LORD lives I will do it. Lie **h** until morning." NDT
Ru 4: 1 "Come over **h**, my friend, and sit H7024
Ru 4: 2 town and said, "Sit **h**," and they did so. H7024
Ru 4: 4 of these seated **h** and in the presence of NDT
1Sa 1:16 been praying **h** out of my great H6330+2178
1Sa 1:23 "Stay **h** until you have weaned him; only NDT
1Sa 1:26 woman who stood **h** beside you H928+2296
1Sa 3: 4 Samuel answered, "**H** I am." H2180
1Sa 3: 5 to Eli and said, "**H** I am; you called me." H2180
1Sa 3: 6 to Eli and said, "**H** I am; you called me." H2180
1Sa 3: 8 to Eli and said, "**H** I am; you called me." H2180
1Sa 3:16 Samuel answered, "**H** I am." H2180
1Sa 5: 7 of the god of Israel must not stay **h** with us, NDT
1Sa 6:20 To whom will the ark go up from **h**?" H5646S
1Sa 9:11 and they asked them, "Is the seer **h**?" H928+2296
1Sa 9:24 "**H** is what has been kept for you. H2180
1Sa 9:27 did so—"but you stay **h** for a while, so that I NDT
1Sa 10:22 of the LORD, "Has the man come **h** yet?" H2151
1Sa 12: 2 old and gray, and my sons are **h** with you. H2180
1Sa 12: 3 **H** I stand. Testify against me in the H2180
1Sa 12: 7 Now then, stand **h**, because I am going to NDT
1Sa 12:13 Now **h** is the king you have chosen, the H2180
1Sa 14:33 "Roll a large stone over **h** at once." H3276S
1Sa 14:34 and slaughter them **h** and eat them. H928+2296
1Sa 14:36 the priest said, "Let us inquire of God **h**." H2151
1Sa 14:38 therefore said, "Come **h**, all you who are H2151
1Sa 14:40 my son will stand **over h**." H4200+6298+285
1Sa 16: 6 LORD's anointed stands **h** before the LORD." NDT
1Sa 16:16 his servants **h** to search for H4200+7156
1Sa 17:28 asked, "Why have you come down **h**? H2296
1Sa 17:44 "Come **h**," he said, "and I'll give your flesh H448
1Sa 17:47 All those gathered **h** will know that it is not NDT
1Sa 18:17 to David, "**H** is my older daughter Merab. H2180
1Sa 20:21 this side of you; bring them **h**,' then come, NDT
1Sa 21: 4 there is some consecrated bread **h** NDT
1Sa 21: 8 "Don't you have a spear or a sword **h**? H7024
1Sa 21: 9 the Valley of Elah, is **h**; it is wrapped in a H2180
1Sa 21: 9 there is no sword **h** but that one." H928+2296
1Sa 21:15 to bring this fellow **h** to carry on like this in NDT
1Sa 23: 3 said to him, "**H** in Judah we are afraid. H7024
1Sa 26:22 "**H** is the king's spear," David answered H2180
1Sa 30:26 "**H** is a gift for you from the plunder of the H2180
2Sa 1: 9 said to me, 'Stand **h by** me and kill me! H6584
2Sa 1:10 arm and have brought them **h** to my lord." H2178
2Sa 4: 8 "**H** is the head of Ish-Bosheth son of Saul H2180
2Sa 5: 6 "You will not get in **h**; even the blind and H2178
2Sa 5: 6 They thought, "David cannot get in **h**." H2178
2Sa 7: 2 Nathan the prophet, "**H** I am, living in a H8011
2Sa 11:12 to him, "Stay **h** one more day, and H928+2296
2Sa 13: 9 "Send everyone out of **h**," Amnon H6584+3276S
2Sa 13:10 "Bring the food **h** into my bedroom so I may NDT
2Sa 14:32 'Come **h** so I can send you to the king to H2178
2Sa 18:30 "Stand aside and wait **h**." So he stepped H3907
2Sa 19:20 today I have come **h** as the first from the H2180
2Sa 19:37 But **h** is your servant Kimham H2180
2Sa 20: 4 me within three days, and be **h** yourself." H7024
2Sa 20:16 Tell Joab to come **h** so I can speak to him." H2178
2Sa 24:22 **H** are oxen for the burnt offering, and H8011
2Sa 24:22 **h** are threshing sledges and ox yokes NDT
1Ki 1:23 king was told, "Nathan the prophet is **h**." H2180
1Ki 2:30 I will die **h**." Benaiah reported to the H7024
1Ki 3: 8 Your servant is **h** among the people you NDT
1Ki 9:15 **H** is the account of the forced labor King H2296
1Ki 11:22 have you lacked **h** that you want H6640+3276S
1Ki 11:27 **H** is the account of how he rebelled H2296
1Ki 12:28 **H** are your gods, Israel, who brought you H2180
1Ki 13: 2 places who make offerings **h**, H6584+3870S
1Ki 13: 8 bread or drink water **h**. H928+2021+5226+2021+2296S
1Ki 17: 3 "Leave **h**, turn eastward and hide in the H2296
1Ki 18: 8 "Go tell your master, 'Elijah is **h**.'" H2180
1Ki 18:11 to go to my master and say, 'Elijah is **h**. H2180
1Ki 18:14 to go to my master and say, 'Elijah is **h**. H2180
1Ki 18:30 said to all the people, "**Come h** to me." H5602
1Ki 19: 9 "What are you doing **h**, Elijah?" H7024
1Ki 19:13 "What are you doing **h**, Elijah? H7024
1Ki 20:40 While your servant was busy **h** and there H2178
1Ki 22: 7 of the LORD **h** whom we can inquire H7024
2Ki 2: 2 to Elisha, "Stay **h**; the LORD has sent me H7024
2Ki 2: 4 said to him, "Stay **h**, Elisha; the LORD has H7024
2Ki 2: 6 said to him, "Stay **h**; the LORD has sent me H7024
2Ki 2:23 jeered at him. "**Get out of h**, baldy!" H6590
2Ki 2:23 they said. "**Get out of h**, baldy!" H6590
2Ki 3:11 "Is there no prophet of the LORD **h**, through H7024
2Ki 3:11 answered, "Elisha son of Shaphat is **h**. H7024
2Ki 7: 3 to each other, "Why stay **h** until we die? H7024
2Ki 7: 4 And if we stay **h**, we will die. So let's H7024
2Ki 7:13 like that of all the Israelites left **h**— H928+2023S
2Ki 8: 7 man of God has come all the way up **h**," H2178
2Ki 9:12 "**H is what** he told me: H3869+2296+2256+3869+2296
2Ki 10:23 one who serves the LORD is **h** with you— H7024
2Ki 19:32 will not enter this city or shoot an arrow **h**. H9004
1Ch 6:33 **H** are the men who served, together with H465
1Ch 11: 5 "You will not get in **h**." Nevertheless, H2178
1Ch 17: 1 Nathan the prophet, "**H** I am, living in a H2180
1Ch 22: 1 "The house of the LORD God is to be **h** H2296
1Ch 25: 1 *H* **is** the list of the men who performed this AIT
1Ch 29:17 your people who are **h** have given to you. H7024
2Ch 18: 6 of the LORD **h** whom we can inquire H7024
2Ch 20:10 "But now **h** are men from Ammon, Moab H2180
2Ch 28:13 "You must not bring those prisoners **h**," H2178
2Ch 34:28 on this place and on those who live **h**. H2257S
Ezr 4: 2 king of Assyria, who brought us **h**. H7024
Ezr 9:15 **H** we are before you in our guilt, though H2180
Ezr 10:13 there are many people **h** and it is the rainy NDT
Ne 13: 7 **H** I learned about the evil thing Eliashib H2256
Job 27:13 "**H** is the fate God allots to the wicked H2296
Job 38:11 **h** is where your proud waves halt'? H7024
Job 38:35 Do they report to you, '**H** we are'? H2180
Ps 40: 7 Then I said, "**H** I am, I have come—it is H2180
Ps 52: 7 "**H now** is the man who did not make God H2180
Ps 132:14 ever and ever; **h** I will sit enthroned H7024
Ps 132:17 "**H** I will make a horn grow for David and H9004
Pr 25: 7 say to you, "Come up **h**," than for him to H2178
Ecc 1:10 It was **h** already, long ago; it was here NDT
Ecc 1:10 long ago; it was **h** before our time. NDT
Ecc 12:13 **h** is the conclusion of the matter: NDT
SS 2: 8 **H** he comes, leaping across the H2296
Isa 5:26 ends of the earth. **H** they come, swiftly H2180
Isa 6: 8 go for us?" And I said, "**H** am I. Send me!" H2180
Isa 8:18 **H** am I, and the children the LORD has H2180
Isa 21: 9 **h** comes a man in a chariot with a team H2296
Isa 22:16 What are you doing **h** and who gave you H7024
Isa 22:16 to cut out a grave for yourself **h**, H7024
Isa 28:10 a rule for that; a little **h**, a little there." H9004
Isa 28:13 rule for that; a little **h**, a little there—so H9004
Isa 37:33 will not enter this city or shoot an arrow **h**. H9004
Isa 40: 9 say to the towns of Judah, "**H** is your God!" H2180
Isa 41:27 was the first to tell Zion, 'Look, **h** they are! H2180
Isa 42: 1 "**H** is my servant, whom I uphold, my H2176
Isa 52: 5 "And now what do I have **h**?" declares the H7024
Isa 57: 3 "But you—come **h**, you children of a H2178
Isa 58: 9 he will say: **H** am I. "If you do away H2180
Isa 65: 1 on my name, I said, '**H** am I, here am I. H2180
Isa 65: 1 on my name, I said, 'Here am I, **h** am I. H2180
Jer 2:23 she-camel **running h and there**, H8592+2006
Jer 8:14 Why are we sitting **h**? Gather together! Let NDT
Jer 19:12 do to this place and to those who live **h**, H2257S
Jer 28: 3 from **h** and took to H2021+5226+2021+2296S
Jer 38:10 "Take thirty men from **h** with you and lift H2296
Jer 43:10 his throne over these stones I have buried **h**; NDT
Jer 48:47 **H** ends the judgment on Moab H2178
Jer 49: 3 **rush h and there** inside the walls H8763
Jer 51:64 The words of Jeremiah end **h**. H2178
La 4:15 the nations say, "They can stay **h** no longer." NDT
Eze 8: 6 things the Israelites are doing **h**, H7024
Eze 8: 9 detestable things they are doing **h**." H7024
Eze 8:17 the detestable things they are doing **h**? H7024
Eze 40: 4 that is why you have been brought **h**. H2178
Da 3:26 come out! Come **h**!" So Shadrach NDT
Da 4: 9 too difficult for you. **H** is my dream; interpret NDT
Da 5:26 "**H** is what these words mean: Mene A10180
Da 12: 4 Many *will* **go h and there** to increase H8763
Zec 3: 7 give you a place among these standing **h**. NDT
Zec 6:12 '**H** is the man whose name is the Branch H2180
Mt 6:30 *which* **is** *h* today and tomorrow is thrown into AIT
Mt 8:29 "Have you come **h** to torture us before the *G6045*
Mt 11:19 they say, '**H** is a glutton and a drunkard *G2627*
Mt 12: 6 something greater than the temple is **h**. *G6045*
Mt 12:18 "**H** is my servant whom I have chosen, the *G2627*
Mt 12:41 now something greater than Jonah is **h**. *G6045*
Mt 12:42 something greater than Solomon is **h**. *G6045*
Mt 12:49 "**H** are my mother and my brothers. *G2627*
Mt 14: 8 "Give me **h** on a platter the head of John *G6045*
Mt 14:17 "We have **h** only five loaves of bread and *G6045*
Mt 14:18 "Bring them **h** to me," he said. *G6045*
Mt 16:28 who are standing **h** will not taste death *G6045*
Mt 17: 4 to Jesus, "Lord, it is good for us to be **h**. *G6045*
Mt 17:17 put up with you? Bring the boy **h** to me." *G6045*
Mt 17:20 mountain, 'Move **from h** to there,' and it *G1925*
Mt 20: 6 you been standing **h** all day long doing *G6045*
Mt 22:12 'How did you get in **h** without wedding *G6045*
Mt 24: 2 not one stone **h** will be left on another *G6045*
Mt 24:23 says to you, 'Look, **h** is the Messiah! *G6045*
Mt 24:26 do not go out; or, '**H** he is, in the inner *G2627*
Mt 25:25 See, **h** is what belongs to you NDT
Mt 26:36 "Sit **h** while I go over there and pray." *G899*
Mt 26:38 Stay **h** and keep watch with me. *G6045*
Mt 26:46 Let us go! **H** comes my betrayer!" *G2627*
Mt 28: 6 He is not **h**; he has risen, just as he said *G6045*
Mk 3:34 "**H** are my mother and my brothers! *G2623*
Mk 6: 3 Aren't his sisters **h** with us?" And they *G6045*
Mk 9: 1 who are standing **h** will not taste death *G6045*
Mk 9: 5 to Jesus, "Rabbi, it is good for us to be **h**. *G6045*
Mk 11: 2 one has ever ridden. Untie it and bring it **h**. NDT
Mk 11: 3 needs it and will send it back **h** shortly. *G6045*
Mk 13: 2 "Not one stone **h** will be left on another *G6045*
Mk 13:21 says to you, 'Look, **h** is the Messiah! *G6045*
Mk 14:32 said to his disciples, "Sit **h** while I pray." *G6045*
Mk 14:34 "Stay **h** and keep watch." *G6045*
Mk 14:42 Let us go! **H** comes my betrayer!" *G2627*
Mk 16: 6 He is not **h**. See the place where *G6045*
Lk 4: 9 he said, "throw yourself down **from h**. *G1949*
Lk 4:23 'Do **h** in your hometown what we have *G6045*
Lk 7:34 you say, '**H** is a glutton and a drunkard *G2627*
Lk 9:12 because we are in a remote place **h**." *G6045*
Lk 9:27 who are standing **h** will not taste death *G899*
Lk 9:33 "Master, it is good for us to be **h**. *G6045*
Lk 9:41 put up with you? Bring your son **h**." *G6045*
Lk 11:31 something greater than Solomon is **h**. *G6045*
Lk 11:32 now something greater than Jonah is **h**. *G6045*
Lk 12:28 of the field, *which* **is** *h* today, and tomorrow AIT
Lk 15:17 to spare, and **h** I am starving to death! *G6045*
Lk 16: 4 when I lose my job **h**, people will welcome NDT
Lk 16:25 now he is comforted **h** and you are in *G6045*
Lk 16:26 who want to go **from h** to you cannot, *G1925*
Lk 17:21 people say, '**H it is**,' or 'There it is *G2627+6045*
Lk 17:23 or '**H he is**!' Do not go *G2627+6045*
Lk 19: 8 *H and now I* **give** half of my possessions to AIT
Lk 19:20 **h** is your mina; I have kept it laid *G2627*
Lk 19:27 bring them **h** and kill them in front of me. *G6045*
Lk 19:30 one has ever ridden. Untie it and bring it **h**. NDT

Lk 21: 6 "As for what you see **h**, the time will come NDT
Lk 22:38 "See, Lord, **h** are two swords. *G6045*
Lk 23: 5 in Galilee and has come all the way **h**." *G6045*
Lk 24: 6 He is not **h**; he has risen! Remember how *G6045*
Lk 24:41 "Do you have anything **h** to eat? *G1924*
Jn 1:47 "**H** truly is an Israelite in whom there is no *G2623*
Jn 2:11 What Jesus did **h** in Cana of Galilee was NDT
Jn 2:16 sold doves he said, "Get these **out of h**! *G1949*
Jn 4:15 have to keep coming **h** to draw water." *G1924*
Jn 5: 3 **H** a great number of disabled *G1877+4047*
Jn 6: 9 "**H** is a boy with five small barley loaves *G6045*
Jn 6:25 asked him, "Rabbi, when did you get **h**?" *G6045*
Jn 6:50 But *h* **is** the bread that comes down from AIT
Jn 7: 6 "My time *is* not yet **h**; for you any *G4205*
Jn 7:26 **H** he is, speaking publicly, and they are *G2623*
Jn 7:28 *I am* not **h** on my own authority, but he *G2262*
Jn 8:13 challenged him, "**H** you are, appearing as NDT
Jn 8:42 love me, for I have come **h** from God. *G2457*
Jn 11:21 "if you had been **h**, my brother would not *G6045*
Jn 11:28 "The Teacher *is* **h**," she said, "and is *G4205*
Jn 11:32 if you had been **h**, my brother would not *G6045*
Jn 11:42 the benefit of the people **standing h**, *G4325*
Jn 11:47 "**H** is this man performing many signs. *G4022*
Jn 12: 2 **H** a dinner was given in Jesus' honor *G1695*
Jn 19: 5 Pilate said to them, "**H is** the man!" *G2627*
Jn 19:14 it was about noon. "**H is** your king," Pilate *G2623*
Jn 19:26 he said to her, "Woman, **h is** your son," *G2623*
Jn 19:27 to the disciple, "**H is** your mother." From *G2623*
Jn 20:27 "Put your finger **h**; see my hands. *G6045*
Ac 1:11 "why do you stand **h** looking into the sky? NDT
Ac 2:29 and his tomb is **h** to this day. *G1877+1609*
Ac 7: 5 He gave him no inheritance **h**, not *G1877+899*
Ac 8:36 the eunuch said, "Look, **h** is water. NDT
Ac 9:14 And he has come **h** with authority from the *G6045*
Ac 9:17 to you on the road as you were coming **h**— NDT
Ac 9:21 And hasn't he come **h** to take them as *G6045*
Ac 10:33 Now we **are** all *h* in the presence of God to AIT
Ac 16:28 "Don't harm yourself! We are all **h**!" *G1924*
Ac 17: 6 all over the world have now come **h**, *G1924*
Ac 19:26 numbers of people **h** in Ephesus and in NDT
Ac 19:37 You have brought these men **h**, though they NDT
Ac 22:18 because the people **h** will not accept your NDT
Ac 23:15 We are ready to kill him before he **gets h**." *G1581*
Ac 23:35 hear your case when your accusers **get h**." *G4134*
Ac 24:19 who ought to **be h** before you and bring *G4205*
Ac 24:20 Or these who are **h** should state what crime NDT
Ac 25:14 "There is a man **h** whom Felix left as a NDT
Ac 25:17 When they came **h** with me, I did not *G1924*
Ac 25:24 him in Jerusalem and **h** in Caesarea, *G1924*
Ac 26:22 so I stand **h** and testify to small and great NDT
Ro 13:12 night is nearly over; the day *is* **almost h**. *G1581*
Ro 16:23 hospitality I and the whole church **h** enjoy, NDT
1Co 16:20 brothers and sisters **h** send you greetings. NDT
2Co 5:17 The old has gone, the new *is* **h**! *G1181*
2Co 8:10 And **h is** *my* judgment about what is *G1443S*
2Co 13:13 All God's people **h** send their greetings. NDT
Eph 4:14 and **blown h and there** by every wind of *G4367*
Php 1:16 knowing that *I am* **put h** for the defense of *G3023*
Php 4:22 All God's people **h** send you greetings NDT
Col 3:11 **H** there is no Gentile or Jew, circumcised *G3963*
Col 4: 9 tell you everything that is happening **h**. *G6045*
1Ti 1:15 **H** is a trustworthy saying that deserves full NDT
1Ti 3: 1 **H** is a trustworthy saying: Whoever aspires NDT
2Ti 2:11 **H** is a trustworthy saying: If we died with NDT
2Ti 4:21 Do your best *to* **get h** before winter *G2262*
Heb 2:13 And again he says, "**H** am I, and the *G2627*
Heb 9:11 of the good things that **are** *now already h*, AIT
Heb 10: 7 Then I said, '**H** I am—it is written about *G2627*
Heb 10: 9 Then he said, "**H** I am, I have come to do *G2627*
Heb 13:14 For **h** we do not have an enduring city, but *G6045*
1Pe 1:17 your time as foreigners **h** in reverent fear. NDT
3Jn 14 The friends **h** send their greetings NDT
Rev 3:20 **H I am**! I stand at the door and knock. *G2627*
Rev 4: 1 "Come up **h**, and I will show you *G6045*
Rev 11:12 from heaven saying to them, "Come up **h**." *G6045*

HERE'S (2) [BE, HERE]

Mt 25: 6 the cry rang out: '**H** the bridegroom! Come *G2627*
Jas 2: 3 clothes and say, "**H** a good seat for you," *G6045*

HEREAFTER (KJV) AFTER, AFTERWARD, FROM NOW ON, FUTURE, LATER, LONGER, TO COME

HEREBY (2) [HERE]

Ge 41:41 "*I h* **put** you in charge of the whole land of AIT
Ezr 6: 8 I **h** decree what you are to do for these NDT

HEREIN (KJV) HERE, ON CONDITION, THIS, THIS WAY, THUS

HERES (2) [TIMNATH HERES]

Jdg 1:35 determined also to hold out in Mount **H**, H3065
Jdg 8:13 returned from the battle by the Pass of **H**. H3065

HERESH (1)

1Ch 9:15 Bakbakkar, **H**, Galal and Mattaniah son of H3090

HERESIES (1)

2Pe 2: 1 They will secretly introduce destructive **h** *G146*

HERETH (1)

1Sa 22: 5 So David left and went to the forest of **H**. H3101

HERETICK (KJV) DIVISIVE PERSON

HERETOFORE (KJV) BEFORE, EARLIER, IN THE PAST

HERITAGE (7) [INHERIT]

Job 20:29 the **h** appointed for them by God. H5709
Job 27:13 the **h** a ruthless man receives from the H5709
Job 31: 2 our **h** *from* the Almighty on high? H5709
Ps 61: 5 have given me the **h** *of* those who fear H3772
Ps 119:111 Your statutes *are my* **h** forever; they are H5706
Ps 127: 3 Children are a **h** *from* the LORD, offspring a H5709
Isa 54:17 This is the **h** *of* the servants of the LORD H5709

HERMAS (1)

Ro 16:14 **H** and the other brothers and sisters with *G2254*

HERMES (2)

Ac 14:12 Paul they called **H** because he was the *G2258*
Ro 16:14 Asyncritus, Phlegon, **H**, Patrobas, Hermas *G2258*

HERMOGENES (1)

2Ti 1:15 deserted me, including Phygelus and **H**. *G2259*

HERMON (14) [BAAL HERMON, SENIR, SIRION, SIYON]

Dt 3: 8 from the Arnon Gorge as far as Mount **H**. H3056
Dt 3: 9 **H** is called Sirion by the Sidonians; the H3056
Dt 4:48 Arnon Gorge to Mount Sirion (that is, **H**), H3056
Jos 11: 3 to the Hivites below **H** in the region of H3056
Jos 11:17 in the Valley of Lebanon below Mount **H**. H3056
Jos 12: 1 from the Arnon Gorge to Mount **H** H3056
Jos 12: 5 He ruled over Mount **H**, Salekah, all of H3056
Jos 13: 5 Gad below Mount **H** to Lebo Hamath. H3056
Jos 13:11 all of Mount **H** and all Bashan as far as H3056
1Ch 5:23 Baal Hermon, that is, to Senir (Mount **H**). H3056
Ps 42: 6 the Jordan, the **heights of H**—from Mount H3056
Ps 89:12 Tabor and **H** sing for joy at your name. H3056
Ps 133: 3 is as if the dew of **H** were falling on H3056
SS 4: 8 the summit of **H**, from the lions' H3056

HERO (4) [HEROES]

1Sa 17:51 the Philistines saw that their **h** was dead, H1475
2Sa 23: 1 the God of Jacob, the **h** *of* Israel's songs: H5834
Ps 52: 1 you **mighty h**? Why do you boast H1475
Isa 3: 2 the **h** and the warrior, the judge and the H1475

HEROD (43) [HEROD'S, HERODIANS]

Mt 2: 1 during the time of King **H**, Magi from the *G2476*
Mt 2: 3 When King **H** heard this he was disturbed, *G2476*
Mt 2: 7 Then **H** called the Magi secretly and *G2476*
Mt 2:12 warned in a dream not to go back to **H**, *G2476*
Mt 2:13 **H** is going to search for the child to kill *G2476*
Mt 2:15 where he stayed until the death *of* **H**. *G2476*
Mt 2:16 When **H** realized that he had been *G2476*
Mt 2:19 After **H** died, an angel of the Lord *G2476*
Mt 2:22 reigning in Judea in place of his father **H**, *G2476*
Mt 14: 1 At that time **H** the tetrarch heard the *G2476*
Mt 14: 3 Now **H** had arrested John and bound him *G2476*
Mt 14: 5 **H** wanted to kill John, but he was afraid of NDT
Mt 14: 6 the guests and pleased **H** so much *G2476*
Mk 6:14 King **H** heard about this, for Jesus' name *G2476*
Mk 6:16 But when **H** heard this, he said, "John *G2476*
Mk 6:17 For **H** himself had given orders to have *G2476*
Mk 6:18 For John had been saying *to* **H**, "It is not *G2476*
Mk 6:20 because **H** feared John and protected him *G2476*
Mk 6:20 When **H** heard John, he was greatly puzzled NDT
Mk 6:21 On his birthday **H** gave a banquet for his *G2476*
Mk 6:22 she pleased **H** and his dinner guests. *G2476*
Mk 8:15 the yeast of the Pharisees and that *of* **H**." *G2476*
Lk 1: 5 In the time *of* **H** king of Judea there was a *G2476*
Lk 3: 1 governor of Judea, **H** tetrarch of Galilee *G2476*
Lk 3:19 when John rebuked **H** the tetrarch *G2476*
Lk 3:20 **H** added this to them all: He locked John up NDT
Lk 9: 7 Now **H** the tetrarch heard about all that *G2476*
Lk 9: 9 But **H** said, "I beheaded John. Who, then *G2476*
Lk 13:31 go somewhere else. **H** wants to kill you." *G2476*
Lk 23: 7 he sent him to **H**, who was also in *G2476*
Lk 23: 8 When **H** saw Jesus, he was greatly *G2476*
Lk 23:11 Then **H** and his soldiers ridiculed and *G2476*
Lk 23:12 That day **H** and Pilate became friends *G2476*
Lk 23:15 Neither has **H**, for he sent him back to us *G2476*
Ac 4:27 Indeed **H** and Pontius Pilate met together *G2476*
Ac 12: 1 this time that King **H** arrested some who *G2476*
Ac 12: 4 **H** intended to bring him out for public trial NDT
Ac 12: 6 The night before **H** was to bring him to *G2476*
Ac 12:19 After **H** had a thorough search made for *G2476*
Ac 12:19 Then **H** went from Judea to Caesarea and NDT
Ac 12:21 On the appointed day **H**, wearing his *G2476*
Ac 12:23 because **H** did not give praise to God NDT
Ac 13: 1 had been brought up with **H** the tetrarch) *G2476*

HEROD'S (5) [HEROD]

Mt 14: 6 On **H** birthday the daughter of Herodias *G2476*
Lk 8: 3 the manager of **H** household; Susanna; *G2476*
Lk 23: 7 that Jesus was under **H** jurisdiction, *G2476*
Ac 12:11 rescued me from **H** clutches and from *G2476*
Ac 23:35 Paul be kept under guard in **H** palace. *G2476*

HERODIANS (3) [HEROD]

Mt 22:16 their disciples to him along with the **H**. *G2477*
Mk 3: 6 to plot with the **H** how they might kill *G2477*
Mk 12:13 of the Pharisees and **H** to Jesus to catch *G2477*

HERODIAS (6)

Mt 14: 3 him and put him in prison because of **H**, *G2478*
Mt 14: 6 the daughter *of* **H** danced for the guests *G2478*
Mk 6:17 He did this because of **H**, his brother *G2478*
Mk 6:19 So **H** nursed a grudge against John and *G2478*
Mk 6:22 When the daughter *of* **H** came in and *G2478*
Lk 3:19 the tetrarch because of his marriage to **H**, *G2478*

HERODION (1)

Ro 16:11 Greet **H**, my fellow Jew. Greet those in *G2479*

HEROES (3) [HERO]

Ge 6: 4 They were the **h** of old, men of H1475
Ne 3:16 the artificial pool and the House of the **H**. H1475
Isa 5:22 Woe to *those who* are **h** at drinking wine H1475

HERON (2)

Lev 11:19 the stork, any kind of **h**, the hoopoe and the H649
Dt 14:18 the stork, any kind of **h**, the hoopoe and the H649

HERS (4) [SHE]

Ge 3:15 between your offspring and **h**; he will H2023
Job 39:16 as if they were not **h**; she cares not H4200+2023
Pr 14: 1 own hands the foolish one tears **h** down. H5647
La 1: 7 the treasures that were **h** in days of old. H2023

HERSELF (45) [SELF, SHE] See Index of Articles Etc.

HESHBON (37) [HESHBON'S]

Nu 21:25 including **H** and all its surrounding H3114
Nu 21:26 **H** was the city of Sihon king of the H3114
Nu 21:27 "Come to **H** and let it be rebuilt; let H3114
Nu 21:28 "Fire went out from **H**, a blaze from the H3114
Nu 21:34 king of the Amorites, who reigned in **H**." H3114
Nu 32: 3 Nimrah, **H**, Elealeh, Sebam, Nebo H3114
Nu 32:37 And the Reubenites rebuilt **H**, Elealeh H3114
Dt 1: 4 who reigned in **H**, and at Edrei had H3114
Dt 2:24 the Amorite, king of **H**, and his country. H3114
Dt 2:26 to Sihon king of **H** offering peace and H3114
Dt 2:30 But Sihon king of **H** refused to let us pass H3114
Dt 3: 2 king of the Amorites, who reigned in **H**." H3114
Dt 3: 6 as we had done with Sihon king of **H** H3114
Dt 4:46 who reigned in **H** and was defeated by H3114
Dt 29: 7 Sihon king of **H** and Og king of Bashan H3114
Jos 9:10 Jordan—Sihon king of **H**, and Og king of H3114
Jos 12: 2 king of the Amorites, who reigned in **H**. H3114
Jos 12: 5 of Gilead to the border of Sihon king of **H**. H3114
Jos 13:10 who ruled in **H**, out to the border of H3114
Jos 13:17 to **H** and all its towns on the plateau H3114
Jos 13:21 king of the Amorites, who ruled at **H**. H3114
Jos 13:26 from **H** to Ramath Mizpah and H3114
Jos 13:27 the rest of the realm of Sihon king of **H** H3114
Jos 21:39 **H** and Jazer, together with their H3114
Jdg 11:19 who ruled in **H**, and said to him, H3114
Jdg 11:26 For three hundred years Israel occupied **H** H3114
1Ch 6:81 **H** and Jazer, together with their H3114
Ne 9:22 of Sihon king of **H** and the country of Og H3114
SS 7: 4 are the pools of **H** by the gate of Bath H3114
Isa 15: 4 **H** and Elealeh cry out, their voices are H3114
Isa 16: 8 The fields of **H** wither, the vines of H3114
Isa 16: 9 the vines of Sibmah. **H** and Elealeh, H3114
Jer 48: 2 in **H** people will plot her downfall: H3114
Jer 48:34 their cry rises from **H** to Elealeh and Jahaz H3114
Jer 48:45 "In the shadow of **H** the fugitives stand H3114
Jer 48:45 a fire has gone out from **H**, a blaze H3114
Jer 49: 3 **H**, for Ai is destroyed! Cry out, you H3114

HESHBON'S (1) [HESHBON]

Nu 21:30 **H dominion** has been destroyed all the H3114

HESHMON (1)

Jos 15:27 Hazar Gaddah, **H**, Beth Pelet, H3132

HESITATE (4) [HESITATED, HESITATION]

Jdg 18: 9 Don't **h** to go there and take it over. H6788
Job 30:10 distance; *they do* not **h** to spit in my face. H3104
Da 9:14 The LORD **did not h** to bring the disaster on H9193
Ac 10:20 *Do* not **h** to go with them, for I have sent *G1359*

HESITATED (3) [HESITATE]

Ge 19:16 When *he* **h**, the men grasped his hand H4538
Ac 20:20 You know that *I have* not **h** to preach *G5713*
Ac 20:27 For *I have* not **h** to proclaim to you the *G5713*

HESITATION (1) [HESITATE]

Ac 11:12 Spirit told me *to* **have** no **h** about going *G1359*

HETHLON (2)

Eze 47:15 Sea by the **H** road past Lebo Hamath to H3158
Eze 48: 1 it will follow the **H** road to Lebo Hamath H3158

HEW, HEWED (KJV) CHISELED, CUT, DRESSED, PREPARE

HEWING (1) [HEWN]

Isa 22:16 **h** your grave on the height and chiseling H2933

HEWN (1) [HEWING]

Isa 51: 1 to the quarry from which *you* **were h**; H5941

HEZEKIAH (123) [HEZEKIAH'S]

2Ki 16:20 And **H** his son succeeded him as king H2625
2Ki 18: 1 **H** son of Ahaz king of Judah began to H2624
2Ki 18: 5 **H** trusted in the LORD, the God of Israel NDT

2Ki 18:14 So **H** king of Judah sent this message to H2624
2Ki 18:14 exacted from **H** king of Judah three H2624
2Ki 18:15 So **H** gave him all the silver that was H2624
2Ki 18:16 At this time **H** king of Judah stripped off H2624
2Ki 18:17 from Lachish to King **H** at Jerusalem. H2625
2Ki 18:19 field commander said to them, "Tell **H**: H2625
2Ki 18:22 whose high places and altars **H** removed, H2625
2Ki 18:29 Do not let **H** deceive you. H2625
2Ki 18:30 Do not let **H** persuade you to trust in the H2625
2Ki 18:31 "Do not listen to **H**. This is what the king H2625
2Ki 18:32 "Do not listen to **H**, for he is misleading H2625
2Ki 18:37 Joah son of Asaph the recorder went to **H**, H2625
2Ki 19: 1 When King **H** heard this, he tore his H2625
2Ki 19: 3 "This is what **H** says: This day is a H2625
2Ki 19: 9 sent messengers to **H** with this word: H2625
2Ki 19:10 "Say to **H** king of Judah: Do not let the H2625
2Ki 19:14 **H** received the letter from the messengers H2625
2Ki 19:15 And **H** prayed to the LORD: "LORD, the God H2625
2Ki 19:20 Isaiah son of Amoz sent a message to **H**: H2625
2Ki 19:29 be the sign for you, **H**: "This year you will NDT
2Ki 20: 1 In those days **H** became ill and was at the H2625
2Ki 20: 2 **H** turned his face to the wall and prayed to NDT
2Ki 20: 3 good in your eyes." And **H** wept bitterly. H2625
2Ki 20: 5 "Go back and tell **H**, the ruler of my H2625
2Ki 20: 8 **H** had asked Isaiah, "What will be the H2625
2Ki 20:10 shadow to go forward ten steps," said **H**. H3491
2Ki 20:12 king of Babylon sent **H** letters and a gift, H2625
2Ki 20:13 **H** received the envoys and showed them H2625
2Ki 20:13 all his kingdom that **H** did not show them. H2625
2Ki 20:14 the prophet went to King **H** and asked, H2625
2Ki 20:14 a distant land," **H** replied. "They came H2625
2Ki 20:15 saw everything in my palace," **H** said. H2625
2Ki 20:16 Then Isaiah said to **H**, "Hear the word of H2625
2Ki 20:19 LORD you have spoken is good," **H** replied. H2625
2Ki 20:21 **H** rested with his ancestors. H2625
2Ki 21: 3 high places his father **H** had destroyed; H2625
1Ch 3:13 Ahaz his son, **H** his son, Manasseh his H2625
1Ch 4:41 came in the days of **H** king of Judah. H3491
2Ch 28:27 And **H** his son succeeded him as king H3491
2Ch 29: 1 **H** was twenty-five years old when he H3491
2Ch 29:18 Then they went in to King **H** and reported H2625
2Ch 29:20 the next morning King **H** gathered the city H3491
2Ch 29:27 **H** gave the order to sacrifice the burnt H2625
2Ch 29:30 King **H** and his officials ordered the Levites H3491
2Ch 29:31 Then **H** said, "You have now dedicated H3491
2Ch 29:36 **H** and all the people rejoiced at what God H3491
2Ch 30: 1 **H** sent word to all Israel and Judah and H3491
2Ch 30:18 But **H** prayed for them, saying, "May the H3491
2Ch 30:20 And the LORD heard **H** and healed the H3491
2Ch 30:22 **H** spoke encouragingly to all the Levites H3491
2Ch 30:24 **H** king of Judah provided a thousand bulls H2625
2Ch 31: 2 **H** assigned the priests and Levites to H3491
2Ch 31: 8 When **H** and his officials came and saw H3491
2Ch 31: 9 **H** asked the priests and Levites about the H3491
2Ch 31:11 **H** gave orders to prepare storerooms in H3491
2Ch 31:13 appointment of King **H** and Azariah the H3491
2Ch 31:20 This is what **H** did throughout Judah H3491
2Ch 32: 1 After all that **H** had so faithfully done NDT
2Ch 32: 2 When **H** saw that Sennacherib had come H3491
2Ch 32: 8 confidence from what **H** the king of Judah H3491
2Ch 32: 9 this message for **H** king of Judah and H3491
2Ch 32:11 When **H** says, 'The LORD our God will save H3491
2Ch 32:12 Did not **H** himself remove this god's high H3491
2Ch 32:15 Now do not let **H** deceive you and H2625
2Ch 32:16 the LORD God and against his servant **H**. H3491
2Ch 32:17 so the god of **H** will not rescue his people H3491
2Ch 32:20 King **H** and the prophet Isaiah son of H3491
2Ch 32:22 So the LORD saved **H** and the people of H3491
2Ch 32:23 valuable gifts for **H** king of Judah. H3491
2Ch 32:24 In those days **H** became ill and was at the H3491
2Ch 32:26 Then **H** repented of the pride of his heart H3491
2Ch 32:26 not come on them during the days of **H**. H3491
2Ch 32:27 **H** had very great wealth and honor, and H3491
2Ch 32:30 It was **H** who blocked the upper outlet of H3491
2Ch 32:33 **H** rested with his ancestors and was buried H3491
2Ch 33: 3 high places his father **H** had demolished; H3491
Ezr 2:16 of Ater (through **H**) 98 H3490
Ne 7:21 of Ater (through **H**) 98 H2624
Ne 10:17 Ater, **H**, Azzur, H2624
Pr 25: 1 compiled by the men of **H** king of Judah: H2624
Isa 1: 1 Jotham, Ahaz and **H**, kings of Judah. H3491
Isa 36: 2 army from Lachish to King **H** at Jerusalem. H2625
Isa 36: 4 field commander said to them, "Tell **H**: H2625
Isa 36: 7 whose high places and altars **H** removed, H2625
Isa 36:14 Do not let **H** deceive you. H2625
Isa 36:15 Do not let **H** persuade you to trust in the H2625
Isa 36:16 "Do not listen to **H**. This is what the king H2625
Isa 36:18 "Do not let **H** mislead you when he says H2625
Isa 36:22 Joah son of Asaph the recorder went to **H**, H2625
Isa 37: 1 When King **H** heard this, he tore his H2625
Isa 37: 3 "This is what **H** says: This day is a H2625
Isa 37: 9 he sent messengers to **H** with this word: H2625
Isa 37:10 "Say to **H** king of Judah: Do not let the H2625
Isa 37:14 **H** received the letter from the messengers H2625
Isa 37:15 And **H** prayed to the LORD: H2625
Isa 37:21 Isaiah son of Amoz sent a message to **H**: H2625
Isa 37:30 be the sign for you, **H**: "This year you will NDT
Isa 38: 1 In those days **H** became ill and was at the H2625
Isa 38: 2 **H** turned his face to the wall and prayed H2625
Isa 38: 3 good in your eyes." And **H** wept bitterly. H2625
Isa 38: 5 "Go and tell **H**, 'This is what the LORD, the H2625
Isa 38: 9 A writing of **H** king of Judah after his H2625
Isa 38:22 **H** had asked, "What will be the sign that I H2625
Isa 39: 1 king of Babylon sent **H** letters and a gift, H2625
Isa 39: 2 **H** received the envoys gladly and showed H2625
Isa 39: 2 all his kingdom that **H** did not show them. H2625
Isa 39: 3 the prophet went to King **H** and asked, H2625
Isa 39: 3 a distant land," **H** replied. "They came to H2625
Isa 39: 4 saw everything in my palace," **H** said. H2625
Isa 39: 5 Then Isaiah said to **H**, "Hear the word of H2625
Isa 39: 8 LORD you have spoken is good," **H** replied. H2625
Jer 15: 4 Manasseh son of **H** king of Judah did in H3491
Jer 26:18 in the days of **H** king of Judah. H2625
Jer 26:19 "Did **H** king of Judah or anyone else in H2625
Jer 26:19 Did not **H** fear the LORD and seek his favor NDT
Hos 1: 1 Jotham, Ahaz and **H**, kings of Judah, and H3490
Mic 1: 1 of Jotham, Ahaz and **H**, kings of Judah— H3490
Zep 1: 1 Amariah, the son of **H**, during the reign of H2624
Mt 1: 9 the father of Ahaz, Ahaz the father of **H**, *G1614*
Mt 1:10 **H** the father of Manasseh, Manasseh the *G1614*

HEZEKIAH'S (10) [HEZEKIAH]

2Ki 18: 9 In King **H** fourth year, which was H4200+2625
2Ki 18:10 was captured in **H** sixth year, H4200+2624
2Ki 18:13 In the fourteenth year of King **H** reign H2624
2Ki 19: 5 When King **H** officials came to Isaiah, H2625
2Ki 20:12 because he had heard of **H** illness. H2625
2Ki 20:20 As for the other events of **H** reign, all his H2625
2Ch 32:25 But **H** heart was proud and he did not H3491
2Ch 32:32 The other events of **H** reign and his acts H3491
Isa 36: 1 In the fourteenth year of King **H** reign H2625
Isa 37: 5 When King **H** officials came to Isaiah, H2625

HEZION (1)

1Ki 15:18 the son of **H**, the king of Aram, H2611

HEZIR (2)

1Ch 24:15 the seventeenth to **H**, the eighteenth to H2615
Ne 10:20 Magpiash, Meshullam, **H**, H2615

HEZRO (2)

2Sa 23:35 **H** the Carmelite, Paarai the Arbite, H2968
1Ch 11:37 **H** the Carmelite, Naarai son of Ezbai, H2968

HEZRON (20) [HEZRONITE, KERIOTH HEZRON]

Ge 46: 9 Hanok, Pallu, **H** and Karmi. H2969
Ge 46:12 The sons of Perez: **H** and Hamul. H2969
Ex 6:14 were Hanok and Pallu, **H** and Karmi. H2969
Nu 26: 6 through **H**, the Hezronite clan; through H2969
Nu 26:21 through **H**, the Hezronite clan; through H2969
Jos 15: 3 Then it ran past **H** up to Addar and curved H2970
Ru 4:18 Perez was the father of **H**, H2969
Ru 4:19 **H** the father of Ram, Ram the father of H2969
1Ch 2: 5 The sons of Perez: **H** and Hamul. H2969
1Ch 2: 9 The sons born to **H** were: Jerahmeel, Ram H2969
1Ch 2:18 Caleb son of **H** had children by his wife H2969
1Ch 2:21 **H**, when he was sixty years old H2969
1Ch 2:24 After **H** died in Caleb Ephrathah, Abijah H2969
1Ch 2:24 Abijah the wife of **H** bore him Ashhur the H2969
1Ch 2:25 The sons of Jerahmeel the firstborn of **H** H2969
1Ch 4: 1 Perez, **H**, Karmi, Hur and Shobal. H2969
1Ch 5: 3 Hanok, Pallu, **H** and Karmi. H2969
Mt 1: 3 Perez the father of **H**, Hezron the father of *G2272*
Mt 1: 3 the father of Hezron, **H** the father of Ram, *G2272*
Lk 3:33 of Ram, the son of **H**, the son of Perez, *G2272*

HEZRONITE (2) [HEZRON]

Nu 26: 6 Hezron, the **H** clan; through Karmi H2971
Nu 26:21 Hezron, the **H** clan; through Hamul H2971

HID (34) [HIDE]

Ge 3: 8 and *they* **h** from the LORD God among the H2461
Ge 3:10 I was afraid because I was naked; so *I* **h**." H2461
Ex 2: 2 a fine child, *she* **h** him for three months. H7621
Ex 2:12 killed the Egyptian and **h** him in the sand. H3243
Ex 3: 6 Moses **h** his face, because he was H6259
Jos 6:17 because *she* **h** the spies we sent. H2461
Jos 6:25 because *she* **h** the men Joshua had sent H2461
1Sa 13: 6 hard pressed, they **h** in caves and thickets H2461
1Sa 20:19 the place where *you* **h** when this trouble H6259
1Sa 20:24 So David **h** in the field, and when the H6259
1Ki 18:13 *I* **h** a hundred of the LORD's prophets in H2461
1Ki 20:30 fled to the city and **h in** an inner room. H995
2Ki 7: 8 clothes, and went off and **h** them. H3243
2Ki 7: 8 took some things from it and **h** them also. H3243
1Ch 21:20 sons who were with him **h themselves**. H2461
2Ch 22:11 *she* **h** the child from Athaliah so she H6259
Ps 30: 7 stand firm; but *when you* **h** your face, H6259
Ps 35: 7 Since *they* **h** their net for me without H3243
Ps 35: 8 may the net *they* **h** entangle them, may H3243
Isa 49: 2 in the shadow of his hand *he* **h** me; he H2461
Isa 54: 8 In a surge of anger *I* **h** my face from you H6259
Isa 57:17 I punished them, and **h** my face in anger H6259
Jer 13: 5 So I went and **h** it at Perath, as the LORD H3243
Eze 39:23 So *I* **h** my face from them and handed H6259
Eze 39:24 their offenses, and *I* **h** my face from them. H6259
Da 10: 7 them that they fled and **h themselves**. H2461
Mt 13:44 a man found it, *he* **h** it again, and then *G3221*
Mt 25:18 in the ground and **h** his master's money. *G3221*
Mt 25:25 went out and **h** your gold in the *G3221*
Jn 8:59 but Jesus **h** *himself*, slipping away *G3221*
Jn 12:36 Jesus left and **h** *himself* from them. *G3221*
Ac 1: 9 and a cloud **h** him from their sight. *G5696*
Heb 11:23 Moses' parents **h** him for three months *G3221*
Rev 6:15 **h** in caves and among the rocks of the *G3221*

HIDDAI (1)

2Sa 23:30 Pirathonite, **H** from the ravines of Gaash, H2068

HIDDEKEL (KJV) TIGRIS

HIDDEN (82) [HIDE]

Ge 4:14 and *I will be* **h** from your presence H6259
Nu 5:13 and *this is* **h** from her husband and her H6623
Dt 33:19 on the **treasures h** *in the sand*." H3243+8561
Jos 2: 4 had taken the two men and **h** them. H7621
Jos 2: 6 up to the roof and **h** them under the stalks H3243
Jos 7:21 They *are* **h** in the ground inside my tent H3243
Jos 7:22 there it was, **h** in his tent, with the H3243
Jos 10:16 kings had fled and **h** in the cave at H2461
Jdg 16: 9 With men **h** in the room, she called to him H741
Jdg 16:12 with men **h** in the room, she called H741
1Sa 10:22 he *has* **h himself** among the supplies." H2461
1Sa 14:22 the Israelites who *had* **h** in the hill country H2461
2Sa 17: 9 he *is* **h** in a cave or some other place. H2461
2Sa 18:13 and nothing *is* **h** from the king—you H3948
1Ki 18: 4 prophets and **h** them in two caves, H2461
2Ki 4:27 the LORD *has* **h** it from me and has not H6623
2Ki 6:29 so we may eat him,' but *she had* **h** him." H2461
2Ki 11: 3 He remained **h** with his nurse at the H2461
2Ch 22:12 He remained **h** with them at the temple of H2461
Job 3:16 Or why was I not **h away** in the ground H3243
Job 3:21 who search for it more than for **h treasure**, H4759
Job 3:23 is life given to a man whose way *is* **h**, H6259
Job 18:10 A noose *is* **h** for him on the ground; a trap H3243
Job 28: 7 No bird of prey knows that **h path**, no H5985
Job 28:11 of the rivers and bring **h things** to light. H9502
Job 28:21 *It is* **h** from the eyes of every living thing H6623
Job 33:21 their bones, *once* **h**, now stick out. H4202+8011
Job 40:21 **h** *among* the reeds in the marsh. H6260
Ps 9:15 feet are caught in the net *they have* **h**. H3243
Ps 19:12 their own errors? Forgive my **h** *faults*. H6259
Ps 22:24 *he has* not **h** his face from him but has H6259
Ps 38: 9 Lord; my sighing **is** not **h** from you. H6259
Ps 69: 5 know my folly; my guilt *is* not **h** from you. H3948
Ps 78: 2 I will utter **h things**, things from of old— H2648
Ps 119:11 *I have* **h** your word in my heart that I H7621
Ps 139:15 My frame **was** not **h** from you when I was H3948
Ps 140: 5 The arrogant *have* **h** a snare for me; they H3243
Ps 142: 3 where I walk *people have* **h** a snare for H3243
Pr 2: 4 silver and search for it as for **h treasure**, H4759
Pr 27: 5 Better is open rebuke than **h** love. H6259
Ecc 12:14 including every **h** *thing*, whether it is good H6623
Isa 30:20 your teachers *will be* **h** no more; with your H4052
Isa 40:27 "My way *is* **h** from the LORD; my H6259
Isa 42:22 them trapped in pits or **h away** in prisons. H2461
Isa 45: 3 I will give you **h** treasures, riches stored in H3125
Isa 48: 6 new things, of **h** *things* unknown to you. H5915
Isa 59: 2 your sins *have* **h** his face from you H6259
Isa 64: 7 for *you have* **h** your face from us and have H6259
Isa 65:16 will be forgotten and **h** from my eyes. H6259
Jer 13: 7 took it from the place where *I had* **h** it, H3243
Jer 16:17 their ways; *they* **are** not **h** from me, nor is H6259
Jer 18:22 to capture me and *have* **h** snares for my H3243
Jer 36:26 But the LORD *had* **h** them. H6259
Jer 41: 8 olive oil and honey, **h** in a field. H4759
Eze 28: 3 *Is* no secret **h** *from* you? H6670
Da 2:22 He reveals deep and **h** *things*; he knows A10519
Hos 5: 3 about Ephraim; Israel *is* not **h** from me. H3948
Ob 6 be ransacked, his **h treasures** pillaged! H5208
Hab 3: 4 from his hand, where his power was **h**. H2470
Mt 5:14 A town built on a hill cannot *be* **h**. *G3221*
Mt 10:26 **h** that will not be made known. *G3220*
Mt 11:25 because *you have* **h** these things from the *G3221*
Mt 13:35 I will utter *things* **h** since the creation of *G3221*
Mt 13:44 of heaven is like treasure **h** in a field. *G3221*
Mk 4:22 For whatever is **h** is meant to be disclosed *G3220*
Lk 8:17 For there is nothing **h** that will not be *G3220*
Lk 9:45 It was **h** from them, so that they did not *G4152*
Lk 10:21 because *you have* **h** these things from the *G648*
Lk 11:33 puts it in a **place** *where it will be* **h**, *G3219*
Lk 12: 2 **h** that will not be made known. *G3220*
Lk 18:34 Its meaning was **h** from them, and they *G3221*
Lk 19:42 peace—but now *it is* **h** from your eyes. *G3221*
Ro 16:25 of the mystery **h** for long ages past, *G4967*
1Co 2: 7 a mystery that *has been* **h** and that God *G648*
1Co 4: 5 to light what is **h** in darkness and will *G3220*
Eph 3: 9 which for ages past *was kept* **h** in God, who *G648*
Col 1:26 mystery that *has been kept* **h** for ages and *G648*
Col 2: 3 in whom are **h** all the treasures of wisdom *G649*
Col 3: 3 your life *is now* **h** with Christ in God. *G3221*
1Ti 5:25 are not obvious cannot *remain* **h** *forever*. *G3221*
Heb 4:13 Nothing in all creation is **h from** God's sight. *G905*
Rev 2:17 I will give some of the **h** manna. *G3221*

HIDE (74) [HID, HIDDEN, HIDES, HIDING]

Ge 18:17 "*Shall* I **h** from Abraham what I am about H4059
Ge 47:18 "*We* cannot **h** from our lord the fact that H3948
Ex 2: 3 But when she could **h** him no longer, she H7621
Ex 29:14 the bull's flesh and its **h** and its intestines H6425
Lev 4:11 But the **h** *of* the bull and all its flesh, as H6425
Lev 7: 8 anyone may keep its **h** for himself. H6425
Lev 8:17 But the bull with its **h** and its flesh and its H6425
Lev 9:11 the flesh and the **h** he burned up outside H6425
Lev 11:32 it is made of wood, cloth, **h** or sackcloth. H6425
Nu 19: 5 is to be burned—its **h**, flesh, blood and H6425
Dt 7:20 the survivors who **h** from you have H6259
Dt 31:17 forsake them; *I will* **h** my face from them H6259

Dt 31:18 And I *will* **certainly h** my face in that H6259+6259
Dt 32:20 "*I will* **h** my face from them," he said H6259
Jos 2:16 **H yourselves** there three days until they H2461
Jos 7:19 what you have done; *do* not **h** it from me." H3948
Jdg 21:20 "Go and **h** in the vineyards H741
1Sa 3:17 "Do not **h** it from me. May God H3948
1Sa 3:17 if *you* **h** from me anything he told you." H3948
1Sa 20: 2 Why *would* he **h** this from me H6259
1Sa 20: 5 let me go and **h** in the field until the H6259
1Ki 17: 3 turn eastward and **h** in the Kerith Ravine H6259
1Ki 22:25 on the day you go to **h** *in* an inner room." H2464
2Ki 7:12 have left the camp to **h** in the countryside, H2464
2Ki 11: 2 in a bedroom *to* **h** him from Athaliah; H6259
2Ch 18:24 on the day you go to **h** *in* an inner room." H2461
Job 3:10 of the womb on me *to* **h** trouble from my H6259
Job 13:20 and then *I will* not **h** from you: H6259
Job 13:24 Why *do you* **h** your face and consider me H6259
Job 14:13 "If only *you would* **h** me in the grave and H7621
Job 34:22 no utter darkness, where evildoers *can* **h**. H6259
Job 41: 7 Can you fill its **h** with harpoons or its head H6425
Ps 10: 1 *Why do you* **h** *yourself* in times of trouble H6623
Ps 13: 1 How long *will you* **h** your face from me H6259
Ps 17: 8 **h** me in the shadow of your wings H6259
Ps 27: 5 *he will* **h** me in the shelter of his sacred H6259
Ps 27: 9 *Do* not **h** your face from me, do not turn H6259
Ps 31:20 of your presence *you* **h** them from all H6259
Ps 40:10 *I do* not **h** your righteousness in my heart H4059
Ps 44:24 Why *do you* **h** your face and forget our H6259
Ps 51: 9 **H** your face from my sins and blot out all H6259
Ps 55:12 if a foe were rising against me, *I could* **h**. H6259
Ps 64: 2 **H** me from the conspiracy of the wicked H6259
Ps 69:17 *Do* not **h** your face from your servant H6259
Ps 78: 4 *We will* not **h** them from their H3948
Ps 88:14 you reject me and **h** your face from me? H6259
Ps 89:46 *Will you* **h yourself** forever? How H6259
Ps 102: 2 *Do* not **h** your face from me when I am in H6259
Ps 104:29 *When you* **h** your face, they are terrified H6259
Ps 119:19 *do* not **h** your commands from me. H6259
Ps 139:11 the darkness *will* **h** me and the light H8789
Ps 143: 7 *Do* not **h** your face from me or I will be H6259
Ps 143: 9 my enemies, LORD, for *I* **h** *myself* in you. H4059
Isa 1:15 your hands in prayer, *I* **h** my eyes from you H6623
Isa 2:10 **h** in the ground from the fearful presence H3243
Isa 3: 9 their sin like Sodom; *they do* not **h** it. H3948
Isa 16: 3 **H** the fugitives, do not betray the refugees H6259
Isa 26:20 **h** *yourselves* for a little while until his H2464
Isa 29:15 to great depths to **h** their plans from the H6259
Isa 50: 6 *I did* not **h** my face from mocking and H6259
Isa 53: 3 Like *one* from whom people **h** their faces H5040
Jer 13: 4 go now to Perath and **h** it there in a H3243
Jer 13: 6 get the belt I told you to **h** there. H3243
Jer 23:24 Who *can* **h** in secret places so that I H6259
Jer 33: 5 *I will* **h** my face from this city because of H6259
Jer 36:19 to Baruch, "You and Jeremiah, go and **h**. H6259
Jer 38:14 "*Do* not **h** anything from me. H3948
Jer 38:25 *do* not **h** it from us or we will kill you H3948
Jer 49: 8 Turn and flee, **h** in deep caves, you who H3782
Eze 39:29 *I will* no longer **h** my face from them, for I H6259
Am 9: 3 Though *they* **h themselves** on the top of H2461
Am 9: 3 Though *they* **h** from my eyes at the H6259
Mic 3: 4 At that time *he will* **h** his face from them H6259
Rev 6:16 "Fall on us and **h** us from the face of him *G3221*

HIDES (4) [HIDE]

Lev 16:27 the camp; their **h**, flesh and intestines H6425
Job 20:12 in his mouth and *he* **h** it under his tongue H3948
Job 34:29 condemn him? If *he* **h** his face, who can H6259
Lk 8:16 one lights a lamp and **h** it in a clay jar *G2821*

HIDING (30) [HIDE]

Jos 10:17 kings had been found **h** in the cave at H2461
Jos 10:27 into the cave where *they had been* **h**. H2461
Jdg 9: 5 son of Jerub-Baal, escaped by **h**. H2461
Jdg 9:35 his troops came out from their **h place**. H4422
1Sa 3:18 told him everything, **h** nothing from him. H3948
1Sa 14:11 crawling out of the holes *they were* **h** in." H2461
1Sa 19: 2 morning; go into **h** and stay there. H6260
1Sa 23:19 "*Is* not David **h** among us in the H6259
1Sa 23:23 about all the **h places** he uses and come H4676
1Sa 26: 1 "*Is* not David **h** on the hill of Hakilah H6259
2Ch 22: 9 captured him while he *was* **h** in Samaria. H2461
Job 15:18 **h** nothing received from their ancestors H3948
Job 24: 4 and **force** all the poor of the land **into h**. H2461
Job 31:33 as people do, by **h** my guilt in my heart H3243
Ps 32: 7 You are my **h place**; you will protect me H6260
Ps 54: T Saul and said, "*Is* not David **h** among us?" H6259
Ps 64: 5 they talk about **h** their snares; they say H3243
Pr 28:12 wicked rise to power, people **go into h**. H2924
Pr 28:28 to power, people **go into h**; but when the H6259
SS 2:14 in the **h places** *on* the mountainside H6260
Isa 4: 6 a refuge and **h place** from the storm H5039
Isa 8:17 who *is* **h** his face from the descendants of H6259
Isa 28:15 lie our refuge and falsehood *our* **h place**." H6259
Isa 28:17 and water will overflow your **h place**. H6260
Isa 45:15 you are a God *who has been* **h himself**, H6259
Jer 49:10 I will uncover his **h places**, so that he H5041
La 3:10 Like a bear lying in wait, like a lion in **h**, H5041
Am 6:10 them asks anyone who might be **h** there, NDT
Na 3:11 you will go into **h** and seek refuge from H6623
Hab 3:14 to devour the wretched who were in **h**. H5041

HIEL (1)

1Ki 16:34 Ahab's time, **H** of Bethel rebuilt Jericho. H2647

HIERAPOLIS (1)

Col 4:13 you and for those at Laodicea and **H**. *G2631*

HIGGAION (NIV84) Not translated in 2011 NIV; see footnote to Psalm 9:16.

HIGH (377) [HIGH-GRADE, HIGH-PRIESTHOOD, HIGH-RANKING, HIGHBORN, HIGHER, HIGHEST, HIGHLY]

Ge 6:15 fifty cubits wide and thirty cubits **h**. H7757
Ge 6:16 the roof an opening one cubit **h** all around. H448
Ge 7:17 they lifted the ark **h** above the earth. H8123
Ge 7:19 all the **h** mountains under the entire H1469
Ge 14:18 He was priest of God **Most H**, H6610
Ge 14:19 "Blessed be Abram by God **Most H** H6610
Ge 14:20 And praise be to God **Most H**, who H6610
Ge 14:22 to the LORD, God **Most H**, Creator of H6610
Ge 29: 7 "the sun is still **h**; it is not time for the H1524
Ex 25:10 a half wide, and a cubit and a half **h**. H7757
Ex 25:23 a cubit wide and a cubit and a half **h**. H7757
Ex 27: 1 three cubits **h**; it is to be square, H7757
Ex 27:18 of finely twisted linen five cubits **h**, H7757
Ex 30: 2 and two cubits **h**—its horns of one H7757
Ex 37: 1 a half wide, and a cubit and a half **h**. H7757
Ex 37:10 a cubit wide and a cubit and a half **h**. H7757
Ex 37:25 long and a cubit wide and two cubits **h**— H7757
Ex 38: 1 three cubits **h**; it was square, H7757
Ex 38:18 the curtains of the courtyard, five cubits **h**, H7757
Lev 16:32 his father as **h priest** is to make H3912
Lev 21:10 " 'The **h** priest, the one among his H1524
Lev 26:13 enabled you to walk **with heads held h**. H7758
Lev 26:30 I will destroy your **h places**, cut down your H1195
Nu 24:16 who has knowledge from the **Most H**, who H6610
Nu 33:52 and demolish all their **h places**. H1195
Nu 35:25 stay there until the death of the **h** priest, H1524
Nu 35:28 of refuge until the death of the **h** priest; H1524
Nu 35:28 the death of the **h** priest may they return H1524
Nu 35:32 own land before the death of the **h** priest. NDT
Dt 3: 5 were fortified with **h** walls and with gates H1469
Dt 12: 2 all the places on the **h** mountains, H8123
Dt 26:19 fame and honor **h** above all the nations H6609
Dt 28: 1 God will set you **h** above all the nations H6609
Dt 28:52 your land until the **h** fortified walls in H1469
Dt 32: 8 When the **Most H** gave the nations their H6610
Jos 20: 6 the death of the **h** priest who is serving H1524
Jdg 16:25 While they *were* **in h spirits**, they H3201+4213
1Sa 2: 1 the LORD; in the LORD my horn *is* **lifted h**. H8123
1Sa 2:10 The **Most H** will thunder from heaven; the H6583
1Sa 9:12 the people have a sacrifice at the **h place**. H1195
1Sa 9:13 before he goes up to the **h place** to eat. H1195
1Sa 9:14 toward them on his way up to the **h place**. H1195
1Sa 9:19 "Go up ahead of me to the **h place**, for H1195
1Sa 9:25 came down from the **h place** to the town, H1195
1Sa 10: 5 coming down from the **h place** with lyres, H1195
1Sa 10:13 prophesying, he went to the **h place**. H1195
1Sa 18: 5 Saul **gave** him **a h rank in** the army H8492+6584
1Sa 25:36 He *was* **in h spirits** and very drunk H3201+4213
2Sa 13:28 When Amnon *is* **in h spirits** from H3201+4213
2Sa 22:14 the voice of the **Most H** resounded. H6610
2Sa 22:17 reached down from **on h** and took hold of H5294
2Sa 23: 1 of the man exalted by the **Most H**, H6583
1Ki 3: 2 were still sacrificing at the **h places** H1195
1Ki 3: 3 burned incense on the **h places**. H1195
1Ki 3: 4 that was the most important **h place** H1195
1Ki 6: 2 sixty cubits long, twenty wide and thirty **h**. H7757
1Ki 6: 4 made narrow windows **h up** in the temple H9209
1Ki 6:20 cubits long, twenty wide and twenty **h**. H7757
1Ki 6:23 out of olive wood, each ten cubits **h**. H7757
1Ki 7: 2 fifty wide and thirty **h**, with four rows of H7757
1Ki 7: 4 Its **windows** were **placed h** in sets of three H9209
1Ki 7:15 eighteen cubits **h** and twelve cubits in H7757
1Ki 7:16 the pillars; each capital was five cubits **h**. H7757
1Ki 7:19 were in the shape of lilies, four cubits **h**. NDT
1Ki 7:23 cubits from rim to rim and five cubits **h**. H7757
1Ki 7:27 four cubits long, four wide and three **h**. H7757
1Ki 11: 7 Solomon built a **h place** for Chemosh the H1195
1Ki 12:31 built shrines on **h places** and appointed H1195
1Ki 12:32 priests at the **h places** he had made. H1195
1Ki 13: 2 the priests of the **h places** who make H1195
1Ki 13:32 shrines on the **h places** in the towns of H1195
1Ki 13:33 priests for the **h places** from all sorts of H1195
1Ki 13:33 a priest he consecrated for the **h places**. H1195
1Ki 14:23 They also set up for themselves **h places** H1195
1Ki 14:23 poles on every **h** hill and under every H1469
1Ki 15:14 Although he did not remove the **h places** H1195
1Ki 22:43 The **h places**, however, were not removed, H1195
2Ki 12: 3 The **h places**, however, were not removed H1195
2Ki 12:10 the royal secretary and the **h** priest came H1524
2Ki 14: 4 The **h places**, however, were not removed H1195
2Ki 15: 4 The **h places**, however, were not removed H1195
2Ki 15:35 The **h places**, however, were not removed H1195
2Ki 16: 4 burned incense at the **h places**, H1195
2Ki 17: 9 built themselves **h places** in all their H1195
2Ki 17:10 poles on every **h** hill and under every H1469
2Ki 17:11 At every **h place** they burned incense, as H1195
2Ki 17:29 of Samaria had made at the **h places**. H1195
2Ki 17:32 as priests in the shrines at the **h places**. H1195
2Ki 18: 4 He removed the **h places**, smashed the H1195
2Ki 18:22 he the one whose **h places** and altars H1195
2Ki 21: 3 He rebuilt the **h places** his father Hezekiah H1195
2Ki 22: 4 up to Hilkiah the **h** priest and have him H1524
2Ki 22: 8 Hilkiah the **h** priest said to Shaphan the H1524
2Ki 23: 4 The king ordered Hilkiah the **h** priest, the H1524
2Ki 23: 5 incense on the **h places** of the towns of H1195
2Ki 23: 8 of Judah and desecrated the **h places**, H1195
2Ki 23: 9 the priests of the **h places** did not serve at H1195
2Ki 23:13 desecrated the **h places** that were east of H1195
2Ki 23:15 the **h place** made by Jeroboam son of H1195
2Ki 23:15 that altar and **h place** he demolished. H1195
2Ki 23:15 He burned the **h place** and ground it to H1195
2Ki 23:19 shrines at the **h places** that the kings of H1195
2Ki 23:20 priests of those **h places** on the altars H1195
2Ki 25:17 Each pillar was eighteen cubits **h**. H7757
2Ki 25:17 was three cubits **h** and was decorated H7757
1Ch 16:39 of the LORD at the **h place** in Gibeon H1195
1Ch 21:29 at that time on the **h place** at Gibeon. H1195
2Ch 1: 3 assembly went to the **h place** at Gibeon, H1195
2Ch 1:13 to Jerusalem from the **h place** at Gibeon, H1195
2Ch 3: 4 width of the building and twenty cubits **h**. H1470
2Ch 3:15 each with a capital five cubits **h**. H6584+8031
2Ch 4: 1 twenty cubits wide and ten cubits **h**. H7757
2Ch 4: 2 cubits from rim to rim and five cubits **h**. H7757
2Ch 6:13 five cubits wide and three cubits **h**, and H7757
2Ch 11:15 priests for the **h places** and for the goat H1195
2Ch 14: 3 the foreign altars and the **h places**, H1195
2Ch 14: 5 He removed the **h places** and incense H1195
2Ch 15:17 did not remove the **h places** from Israel, H1195
2Ch 17: 6 he removed the **h places** and the Asherah H1195
2Ch 20:33 The **h places**, however, were not removed H1195
2Ch 21:11 He had also built **h places** on the hills of H1195
2Ch 28: 4 burned incense at the **h places**, H1195
2Ch 28:25 in Judah he built **h places** to burn H1195
2Ch 31: 1 destroyed the **h places** and the altars H1195
2Ch 32:12 remove this god's **h places** and altars, H1195
2Ch 33: 3 He rebuilt the **h places** his father Hezekiah H1195
2Ch 33:17 continued to sacrifice at the **h places**, but H1195
2Ch 33:19 where he built **h places** and set up H1195
2Ch 34: 3 purge Judah and Jerusalem of **h places**, H1195
2Ch 34: 9 went to Hilkiah the **h** priest and gave him H1524
Ezr 6: 3 to be sixty cubits **h** and sixty cubits wide A10660
Ne 3: 1 Eliashib the **h** priest and his fellow priests H1524
Ne 3:20 of the house of Eliashib the **h** priest. H1524
Ne 8: 4 stood on a **h** wooden **platform** built for H4463
Ne 13:28 son of Eliashib the **h** priest was H1524
Est 1:10 Xerxes *was* **in h spirits** from wine, H3201+4213
Est 5: 9 out that day happy and **in h spirits**. H3201+4213
Est 10: 3 and **held in h esteem** by his many fellow H8354
Job 5:11 The lowly he sets **on h**, and those who H5294
Job 10:16 If I **hold** my **head h**, you stalk me like a H1448
Job 16:19 heaven; my advocate is **on h**. H928+2021+5294
Job 31: 2 heritage from the Almighty **on h**? H4946+5294
Job 31:28 have been unfaithful to God **on h**. H4946+5087
Job 35: 5 gaze at the clouds *so* **h** above you. H1467
Job 39:27 at your command and **build** its nest **on h**? H8123
Ps 3: 3 my glory, the *One who* **lifts** my head **h**. H8123
Ps 7: 7 enthroned over them **on h**. H4200+2021+5294
Ps 7: 8 according to my integrity, O **Most H**. H6604
Ps 7:10 My shield is God **Most H**, who saves the H6583
Ps 7:17 praises of the name of the LORD **Most H**. H6610
Ps 9: 2 sing the praises of your name, O **Most H**. H6610
Ps 18:13 the voice of the **Most H** resounded. H6610
Ps 18:16 reached down from **on h** and took hold of H5294
Ps 21: 7 love of the **Most H** he will not be H6610
Ps 27: 5 his sacred tent and **set** me **h** upon a rock. H8123
Ps 46: 4 the holy place where the **Most H** dwells. H6610
Ps 47: 2 For the LORD **Most H** is awesome, the great H6610
Ps 49: 2 both low and **h**, rich and poor alike: H1201+408
Ps 50:14 fulfill your vows to the **Most H**, H6610
Ps 57: 2 I cry out to God **Most H**, to God, who H6610
Ps 68:18 When you ascended **on h** H4200+2021+5294
Ps 73:11 Does the **Most H** know anything?" H6610
Ps 77:10 years when the **Most H** stretched out his H6610
Ps 78:17 in the wilderness against the **Most H**. H6610
Ps 78:35 that God **Most H** was their Redeemer. H6610
Ps 78:56 the test and rebelled against the **Most H**; H6610
Ps 78:58 They angered him with their **h places** H1195
Ps 82: 6 you are all sons of the **Most H**. H6610
Ps 83:18 you alone are the **Most H** over all the H6610
Ps 87: 5 the **Most H** himself will establish her." H6610
Ps 91: 1 in the shelter of the **Most H** will rest in the H6610
Ps 91: 9 and you make the **Most H** your dwelling, H6610
Ps 92: 1 make music to your name, O **Most H**, H6610
Ps 93: 4 sea—the LORD **on h** is mighty. H928+2021+5294
Ps 97: 9 are the **Most H** over all the earth H6610
Ps 102:19 LORD looked down from his sanctuary **on h**, H5294
Ps 103:11 For as **h** as the heavens are above the H1469
Ps 104:18 The **h** mountains belong to the wild goats H1469
Ps 107:11 despised the plans of the **Most H**. H6610
Ps 107:25 up a tempest *that* **lifted h** the waves. H8123
Ps 110: 7 the way, and so *he will* **lift** his head **h**. H8123
Ps 112: 9 their horn *will be* **lifted h** in honor. H8123
Ps 113: 5 the *One who* sits enthroned **on h**, H1467
Ps 118:16 The LORD's right hand *is* **lifted h**; H8123
Ps 144: 7 Reach down your hand from **on h**; deliver H5294
Pr 17:19 *whoever* **builds** a **h** gate invites H1467
Pr 18:11 they imagine it a wall **too h to scale**. H8435
Pr 23:34 be like one sleeping on the **h seas**, H4213+3542
Pr 24: 7 Wisdom *is too* **h** for fools; in the assembly H8123
Pr 25: 3 As the heavens are **h** and the earth is H8124
Pr 30:19 the way of a ship on the **h seas** H4213+3542
Ecc 10: 6 Fools are put in many **h positions**, while H5294
Isa 2:14 towering mountains and all the **h hills**, H5951

Isa 5:13 *those* **of h rank** will die of hunger and the H3883
Isa 6: 1 I saw the Lord, **h** and exalted, seated on a H8123
Isa 14:14 I will make myself like the **Most H.** H6610
Isa 15: 2 its temple, to its **h places** to weep; Moab H1195
Isa 16: 3 like night—**at h noon.** Hide the fugitives, H7416
Isa 16:12 When Moab appears at her **h place,** she H1195
Isa 25:12 will bring down your **h** fortified walls and H5369
Isa 26: 5 He humbles those who dwell **on h,** he H5294
Isa 26:11 your hand *is* **lifted h,** but they do not H8123
Isa 30:13 this sin will become for you like a **h** wall H8435
Isa 30:25 will flow on every **h** mountain and every H1469
Isa 32:15 till the Spirit is poured on us from **on h** H5294
Isa 33: 5 he dwells **on h;** he will fill Zion H5294
Isa 36: 7 he the one whose **h places** and altars H1195
Isa 40: 9 news to Zion, go up on a **h** mountain. H1469
Isa 57: 7 have made your bed on a **h** and lofty hill; H1469
Isa 57:15 this is what the **h** and exalted One says H8123
Isa 57:15 "I live in a **h** and holy place, but also with H5294
Isa 58: 4 your voice to be heard **on h.** H928+2021+5294
Jer 2:20 on every **h** hill and under every spreading H1469
Jer 3: 6 gone up on every **h** hill and under every H1469
Jer 7:31 have built the **h places** *of* Topheth in the H1195
Jer 16: 6 "Both **h** and low will die in this land. H1524
Jer 17: 2 the spreading trees and on the **h** hills. H1469
Jer 17: 3 together with your **h places,** because of H1195
Jer 19: 5 have built the **h places** *of* Baal to burn H1195
Jer 25:30 " 'The LORD will roar from **on h;** he will H5294
Jer 32:35 They built **h places** *for* Baal in the Valley H1195
Jer 39: 3 Nergal-Sharezer a **h** official and all the H8042
Jer 39:13 Nergal-Sharezer a **h** official and all the H8042
Jer 48:35 offerings on the **h places** and burn H1195
Jer 49:16 Though *you* **build** your nest as **h** as the H1467
Jer 51: 9 to the skies, *it* **rises** as **h** as the heavens. H5951
Jer 51:58 be leveled and her **h** gates set on fire; H1469
Jer 52:21 was eighteen cubits **h** and twelve cubits H7757
Jer 52:22 was five cubits **h** and was decorated with H7757
La 1:13 "From **on h** he sent fire, sent it down into H5294
La 3:35 people their rights before the **Most H,** H6610
La 3:38 the mouth of the **Most H** that both H6610
Eze 1:18 Their rims were **h** and awesome, and all H1470
Eze 1:26 and **h above** on the H4946+4200+5087+2025
Eze 6: 3 and I will destroy your **h places.** H1195
Eze 6: 6 laid waste and the **h places** demolished, H1195
Eze 6:13 on every **h** hill and on all the H8123
Eze 16:16 of your garments to make gaudy **h places,** H1195
Eze 17:22 plant it on a **h** and lofty mountain. H1469
Eze 19:11 It towered **h** above the thick foliage H7757
Eze 20:28 them and they saw any **h** hill or any leafy H8123
Eze 20:29 What is this **h place** you go to?' " H1195
Eze 20:40 holy mountain, the **h** mountain of Israel H5294
Eze 23:23 chariot officers and **men of h rank,** all H7924
Eze 24: 9 of bloodshed! I, too, *will* **pile** the wood **h.** H1540
Eze 27: 4 Your domain was on the **h seas** H4213+3542
Eze 27:26 Your oarsmen take you out to the **h** seas H8041
Eze 31: 3 it towered **on h,** its top above the H7757
Eze 31:14 are ever to tower proudly **on h,** H928+7757
Eze 34: 6 all the mountains and on every **h** hill. H8123
Eze 40: 2 Israel and set me on a very **h** mountain, H1469
Eze 40: 5 one measuring rod thick and one rod **h.** H7757
Eze 40:12 front of each alcove was a wall one cubit **h,** NDT
Eze 40:42 a cubit and a half wide and a cubit **h.** H1470
Eze 41:22 altar three cubits **h** and two cubits square; H1469
Eze 43:14 that goes around the altar it is two cubits **h,** NDT
Eze 43:14 that goes around the altar it is four cubits **h,** NDT
Eze 43:15 the altar hearth is four cubits **h,** and four NDT
Da 2:48 king **placed** Daniel **in a h position** and A10648
Da 3: 1 of gold, sixty cubits **h** and six cubits wide A10660
Da 3:26 servants of the **Most H** God, come out! A10546
Da 4: 2 wonders that the **Most H** God has A10546
Da 4:17 may know that the **Most H** is sovereign A10546
Da 4:24 is the decree the **Most H** has issued A10546
Da 4:25 that the **Most H** is sovereign over A10546
Da 4:32 that the **Most H** is sovereign over A10546
Da 4:34 Then I praised the **Most H;** I honored A10546
Da 5:18 the **Most H** God gave your father A10546
Da 5:19 Because of the **h position** he gave him A10650
Da 5:21 that the **Most H** God is sovereign A10546
Da 7:18 people of the **Most H** will receive the A10548
Da 7:22 favor of the holy people of the **Most H,** A10548
Da 7:25 against the **Most H** and oppress his A10546
Da 7:27 over to the holy people of the **Most H.** A10548
Hos 7:16 They do not turn to the **Most H;** they are H6583
Hos 10: 8 The **h places** *of* wickedness will be H1195
Hos 11: 7 Even though they call me God **Most H,** H6583
Am 7: 9 "The **h places** *of* Isaac will be destroyed H1195
Mic 1: 5 What is Judah's **h place?** Is it not H1195
Hab 2: 9 setting his nest **on h** to escape the H5294
Hab 3:10 the deep roared and lifted its waves *on* **h.** H8125
Hag 1: 1 to Joshua son of Jozadak, the **h** priest: H1524
Hag 1:12 son of Jozadak, the **h** priest, and the H1524
Hag 1:14 son of Jozadak, the **h** priest, and the spirit H1524
Hag 2: 2 son of Jozadak, the **h** priest, and to the H1524
Hag 2: 4 Joshua son of Jozadak, the **h** priest. H1524
Zec 3: 1 showed me Joshua the **h** priest standing H1524
Zec 3: 8 " 'Listen, **H** Priest Joshua, you and your H1524
Zec 6:11 set it on the head of the **h** priest H1524
Zec 14:10 Jerusalem *will be* **raised up h** from the H8027
Mt 4: 8 took him to a very **h** mountain and *G5734*
Mt 17: 1 led them up a **h** mountain by *G5734*
Mt 20:25 their **h officials** exercise authority over *G3489*
Mt 26: 3 assembled in the palace *of* the **h priest,** *G797*
Mt 26: 9 been sold at a **h** price and the money *G4498*
Mt 26:51 it out and struck the servant *of* the **h priest,** *G797*
Mt 26:57 Jesus took him to Caiaphas the **h priest,** *G797*
Mt 26:58 right up to the courtyard *of* the **h priest.** *G797*
Mt 26:62 Then the **h priest** stood up and said to *G797*
Mt 26:63 The **h priest** said to him, "I charge you *G797*
Mt 26:65 Then the **h priest** tore his clothes and said *G797*
Mk 2:26 In the days of Abiathar the **h priest,** he *G797*
Mk 5: 7 with me, Jesus, Son of the **Most H** God? *G5736*
Mk 6:21 a banquet *for* his **h officials** and military *G3491*
Mk 9: 2 with him and led them up a **h** mountain, *G5734*
Mk 10:42 their **h officials** exercise authority over *G3489*
Mk 14:47 sword and struck the servant *of* the **h priest,** *G797*
Mk 14:53 They took Jesus to the **h priest,** and all the *G797*
Mk 14:54 right into the courtyard *of* the **h priest.** *G797*
Mk 14:60 Then the **h priest** stood up before them *G797*
Mk 14:61 Again the **h priest** asked him, "Are you the *G797*
Mk 14:63 The **h priest** tore his clothes. "Why do we *G797*
Mk 14:66 of the servant girls *of* the **h priest** came by. *G797*
Lk 1:32 will be called the Son *of* the **Most H.** *G5736*
Lk 1:35 the power *of* the **Most H** will *G5736*
Lk 1:76 will be called a prophet *of* the **Most H;** for *G5736*
Lk 4: 5 led him up to a **h** place and showed him *G5734*
Lk 4:38 was suffering from a **h** fever, *G3489*
Lk 6:35 you will be children *of* the **Most H** *G5736*
Lk 8:28 with me, Jesus, Son of the **Most H** God? *G5736*
Lk 22:50 of them struck the servant *of* the **h priest,** *G797*
Lk 22:54 took him into the house *of* the **h priest.** *G797*
Lk 24:49 have been clothed with power from **on h.**" *G5737*
Jn 11:49 who was **h priest** that year, spoke *G797*
Jn 11:51 as **h priest** that year he prophesied that *G797*
Jn 18:10 drew it and struck the **h priest's** servant *G797*
Jn 18:13 of Caiaphas, the **h priest** that year. *G797*
Jn 18:15 this disciple was known *to* the **h priest,** *G797*
Jn 18:15 with Jesus into the **h priest's** courtyard, *G797*
Jn 18:16 who was known *to* the **h priest,** came back, *G797*
Jn 18:19 the **h priest** questioned Jesus about his *G797*
Jn 18:22 "Is this the way you answer the **h priest?**" *G797*
Jn 18:24 sent him bound to Caiaphas the **h priest.** *G797*
Jn 18:26 One of the **h priest's** servants, a relative of *G797*
Ac 4: 6 Annas the **h priest** was there, and so were *G797*
Ac 4: 6 others of the **h priest's** family. *G796*
Ac 5:17 Then the **h priest** and all his associates *G797*
Ac 5:21 When the **h priest** and his associates *G797*
Ac 5:27 Sanhedrin to be questioned by the **h priest.** *G797*
Ac 7: 1 Then the **h priest** asked Stephen, "Are *G797*
Ac 7:48 the **Most H** does not live in houses made *G5736*
Ac 8:10 all the people, both **h** and low, gave him *G3489*
Ac 9: 1 the Lord's disciples. He went to the **h priest** *G797*
Ac 13:50 women *of* **h standing** and the leading *G2363*
Ac 16:17 men are servants of the **Most H** God, *G5736*
Ac 19:17 of the Lord Jesus *was* **held in h honor.** *G3486*
Ac 22: 5 as the **h priest** and all the Council can *G797*
Ac 23: 2 At this the **h priest** Ananias ordered those *G797*
Ac 23: 4 "How dare you insult God's **h priest!**" *G797*
Ac 23: 5 I did not realize that he was the **h priest** *G797*
Ac 24: 1 days later the **h priest** Ananias went down *G797*
Gal 2: 6 As for those who were **held in h esteem** *G1506*
Eph 3:18 wide and long and **h** and deep is the love *G5737*
Eph 4: 8 "When he ascended on **h,** he took many *G5737*
Heb 2:17 faithful **h priest** in service to God, *G797*
Heb 3: 1 acknowledge as our apostle and **h priest.** *G797*
Heb 4:14 we have a great **h priest** who has ascended *G797*
Heb 4:15 we do not have a **h priest** who is unable to *G797*
Heb 5: 1 Every **h priest** is selected from among the *G797*
Heb 5: 5 himself the glory of becoming a **h priest.** *G797*
Heb 5:10 by God to be **h priest** in the order of *G797*
Heb 6:20 He has become a **h priest** forever, in the *G797*
Heb 7: 1 king of Salem and priest of God **Most H.** *G5736*
Heb 7:26 Such a **h priest** truly meets our need—one *G797*
Heb 7:27 Unlike the other **h priests,** he does not need *G797*
Heb 7:28 the law appoints *as* **h priests** men in all *G797*
Heb 8: 1 We do have such a **h priest,** who sat down *G797*
Heb 8: 3 Every **h priest** is appointed to offer both *G797*
Heb 9: 7 But only the **h priest** entered the inner room, *G797*
Heb 9:11 when Christ came *as* **h priest** of the good *G797*
Heb 9:25 the way the **h priest** enters the Most Holy *G797*
Heb 13:11 The **h priest** carries the blood of animals *G797*
Jas 1: 9 ought to take pride in their **h position.** *G5737*
Rev 14:20 rising **as h as** the horses' bridles for a *G948*
Rev 21:10 in the Spirit to a mountain great and **h,** *G5734*
Rev 21:12 It had a great, **h** wall with twelve gates *G5734*
Rev 21:16 in length, and as wide and **h** as it is long. *G5737*

HIGH-GRADE (3) [HIGH]

1Ki 5:17 quarry large blocks of **h** stone to provide a H3701
1Ki 7: 9 made of blocks of **h** stone cut to size and H3701
1Ki 7:11 Above were **h** stones, cut to size, and H3701

HIGH-PRIESTHOOD (1) [HIGH, PRIEST]

Lk 3: 2 during the **h** of Annas and Caiaphas, the *G797*

HIGH-RANKING (1) [HIGH, RANK]

Ac 25:23 room with the **h military officers** and the *G5941*

HIGHBORN (1) [BEAR, HIGH]

Ps 62: 9 are but a breath, the **h** are but a lie. H1201+408

HIGHER (16) [HIGH]

Dt 28:43 will rise above you **h** and higher, H5087+2025
Dt 28:43 will rise above you higher and **h,** H5087+2025
2Ki 25:28 a seat of honor **h than** those of the H4946+6584
2Ch 33:14 the hill of Ophel; *he* also **made** it much **h.** H1467
Ezr 9: 6 our sins *are* **h than** our H8049+4200+5087+2025
Est 3: 1 a seat of honor **h than** that of all H6584+4946
Job 11: 8 They are **h** *than* the heavens above H1470
Ps 61: 2 lead me to the rock *that is* **h** than I. H8123
Ps 108: 4 is your love, **h than** the heavens H4946+6584
Ecc 5: 8 one official is eyed by a **h** one H4946+6584
Ecc 5: 8 and **over** them both are others **h** still. H6584
Isa 55: 9 "As the heavens *are* **h** than the earth, so H1467
Isa 55: 9 so *are* my ways **h** than your ways and my H1467
Jer 52:32 a seat of honor **h** than those of the H4946+5087
Eze 31: 5 So it towered **h** than all the trees of the H7757
Eph 4:10 one who ascended **h** than all the heavens *G5645*

HIGHEST (32) [HIGH]

Nu 14:40 set out for the **h point** *in* the hill country, H8031
Nu 14:44 up toward the **h point** *in* the hill country, H8031
Dt 10:14 even the **h heavens,** the earth and H9028+9028
1Ki 8:27 even the **h heaven,** cannot contain H9028+9028
2Ch 2: 6 even the **h heavens,** cannot H9028+9028
2Ch 6:18 even the **h heavens,** cannot H9028+9028
Ne 9: 6 even the **h heavens,** and all their H9028+9028
Est 1:14 to the king and were **h** in the kingdom. H8037
Job 21:22 since he judges even the **h?** H8123
Job 22:12 And see how lofty are the **h** stars! H8031
Ps 36: 6 Your righteousness is like the **h** mountains H446
Ps 68:33 who rides across the **h heavens,** H9028+9028
Ps 115:16 The **h heavens** belong to the LORD H9028+9028
Ps 137: 6 not consider Jerusalem my **h** joy. H6584+8031
Ps 148: 4 you **h heavens** and you waters H9028+9028
Pr 8: 2 At the **h point** along the way H8031+5294
Pr 9: 3 calls from the **h point** *of* the city, H1726+5294
Pr 9:14 on a seat at the **h point** *of* the city, H5294
Isa 2: 2 be established as the **h** *of* the mountains; H8031
Isa 7:11 in the deepest depths or in the **h** heights." H1467
Da 5: 7 he will be made the **third h** ruler in the A10761
Da 5:16 you will be made the **third h** ruler in the A10761
Da 5:29 was proclaimed the **third h** ruler in the A10761
Mic 4: 1 be established as the **h** *of* the mountains; H8031
Mt 4: 5 him stand on the **h point** of the temple. *G4762*
Mt 21: 9 "Hosanna in the **h heaven!**" *G5736*
Mk 11:10 "Hosanna in the **h heaven!**" *G5736*
Lk 2:14 "Glory to God in the **h heaven,** and on *G5736*
Lk 4: 9 him stand on the **h point** of the temple. *G4762*
Lk 19:38 "Peace in heaven and glory in the **h!**" *G5736*
Php 2: 9 God **exalted** him **to the h place** and gave *G5671*
1Th 5:13 Hold them in the **h** regard in love because *G5655*

HIGHLIGHT (1)

Jer 4:30 Why **h** your eyes with makeup H7973

HIGHLY (22) [HIGH]

Ex 11: 3 himself was **h regarded** in Egypt by H1524+4394
Ex 15: 1 sing to the LORD, for *he is* **h exalted.** H1448+1448
Ex 15:21 to the LORD, for *he is* **h exalted.** H1448+1448
Jdg 5:30 **h embroidered** garments for my neck H8391
1Sa 9: 6 man of God; he is **h respected,** and H3877
1Sa 22:14 bodyguard and **h respected** in your H3877
2Sa 14:25 there was not a man **so h** praised for his H4394
2Ki 5: 1 sight of his master and **h regarded,** H5951+7156
1Ch 14: 2 had been **h** exalted for the H4200+5087+2025
1Ch 29:25 The LORD **h** exalted Solomon H4200+5087+2025
2Ch 32:23 then on *he* **was h regarded** by all the H5951
Isa 32: 5 noble nor the scoundrel be **h respected.** H8777
Isa 52:13 will be raised and lifted up and **h** exalted. H4394
Da 9:23 come to tell you, for you are **h esteemed.** H2776
Da 10:11 you who are **h esteemed,** consider H2776
Da 10:19 you who are **h esteemed,**" he said. H2776
Lk 1:28 "Greetings, *you who are* **h favored!** *G5923*
Lk 7: 2 whom his master **valued h,** was *G1639+1952*
Lk 16:15 What people **value h** is detestable in *G5734*
Ac 5:13 they *were* **h regarded** *by* the people *G3486*
Ac 22:12 of the law and **h respected** by all the Jews *G3455*
Ro 12: 3 *Do* not **think of yourself more h** than you *G5672*

HIGHMINDED (KJV) ARROGANT, CONCEITED

HIGHWAY (11) [HIGHWAYS]

Nu 20:17 along the King's **H** and not turn to the H2006
Nu 21:22 along the King's **H** until we have passed H2006
Pr 7:27 Her house is a **h** *to* the grave, leading H2006
Pr 15:19 but the path of the upright **is a h.** H6148
Pr 16:17 The **h** *of* the upright avoids evil; those H5019
Isa 11:16 There will be a **h** for the remnant of his H5019
Isa 19:23 day there will be a **h** from Egypt to Assyria H5019
Isa 35: 8 And a **h** will be there; it will be called the H5020
Isa 40: 3 straight in the desert a **h** for our God. H5019
Isa 62:10 build up the **h!** Remove the stones. H5019
Jer 31:21 Take note of the **h,** the road that you take H5019

HIGHWAYS (3) [HIGHWAY]

Jdg 5: 6 in the days of Jael, the **h** were abandoned H784
Isa 33: 8 The **h** are deserted, no travelers are on H5019
Isa 49:11 into roads, and my **h** will be raised up. H5019

HILEN (1)

1Ch 6:58 **H,** Debir, H2664

HILKIAH (31) [HILKIAH'S]

2Ki 18:18 Eliakim son of **H** the palace H2760
2Ki 18:26 Then Eliakim son of **H,** and Shebna and H2760
2Ki 18:37 Then Eliakim son of **H** the palace H2759
2Ki 22: 4 "Go up to **H** the high priest and have him H2760
2Ki 22: 8 **H** the high priest said to Shaphan the H2760
2Ki 22:10 "**H** the priest has given me a book." H2759

2Ki 22:12 He gave these orders to **H** the priest H2759
2Ki 22:14 **H** the priest, Ahikam, Akbor, Shaphan H2760
2Ki 23: 4 The king ordered **H** the high priest, the H2760
2Ki 23:24 written in the book that **H** the priest had H2760
1Ch 6:13 Shallum the father of **H**, Hilkiah the father H2759
1Ch 6:13 father of Hilkiah, **H** the father of Azariah H2759
1Ch 6:45 the son of Amaziah, the son of **H**, H2759
1Ch 9:11 Azariah son of **H**, the son of Meshullam H2759
1Ch 26:11 **H** the second, Tabaliah the third and H2760
2Ch 34: 9 They went to **H** the high priest and gave H2760
2Ch 34:14 **H** the priest found the Book of the Law of H2760
2Ch 34:15 **H** said to Shaphan the secretary, "I have H2760
2Ch 34:18 "**H** the priest has given me a book." H2760
2Ch 34:20 He gave these orders to **H**, Ahikam son of H2760
2Ch 34:22 **H** and those the king had sent with him H2760
2Ch 35: 8 **H**, Zechariah and Jehiel, the officials in H2759
Ezr 7: 1 Seraiah, the son of Azariah, the son of **H**, H2759
Ne 8: 4 **H** and Maaseiah; and on his left H2759
Ne 11:11 Seraiah son of **H**, the son of Meshullam H2759
Ne 12: 7 Amok, **H** and Jedaiah. These were H2759
Isa 22:20 summon my servant, Eliakim son of **H**. H2760
Isa 36: 3 Eliakim son of **H** the palace administrator H2760
Isa 36:22 Then Eliakim son of **H** the palace H2760
Jer 1: 1 The words of Jeremiah son of **H**, one of H2760
Jer 29: 3 of Shaphan and to Gemariah son of **H**, H2759

HILKIAH'S (1) [HILKIAH]

Ne 12:21 of **H**, Hashabiah; of Jedaiah's, Nethanel. H2759

HILL (158) [FOOTHILLS, HILLS, HILLSIDE, HILLTOP, HILLTOPS]

Ge 10:30 toward Sephar, in the eastern **h country**. H2215
Ge 14: 6 the Horites in the **h country** *of* Seir, as H2215
Ge 31:21 headed for the **h country** *of* Gilead. H2215
Ge 31:23 up with him in the **h country** *of* Gilead. H2215
Ge 31:25 his tent in the **h country** *of* Gilead when H2215
Ge 31:54 there in the **h country** and invited his H2215
Ge 36: 8 Edom) settled in the **h country** *of* Seir. H2215
Ge 36: 9 of the Edomites in the **h country** *of* Seir. H2215
Ex 17: 9 stand on top of the **h** with the staff of God H1496
Ex 17:10 Aaron and Hur went to the top of the **h**. H1496
Nu 13:17 the Negev and on into the **h country**. H2215
Nu 13:29 Amorites live in the **h country**; H2215
Nu 14:40 out for the highest point in the **h country**, H2215
Nu 14:44 toward the highest point in the **h country**, H2215
Nu 14:45 lived in that **h country** came down and H2215
Dt 1: 7 into the **h country** *of* the Amorites; H2215
Dt 1:19 went toward the **h country** *of* the Amorites H2215
Dt 1:20 reached the **h country** *of* the Amorites, H2215
Dt 1:24 They left and went up into the **h country** H2215
Dt 1:41 it easy to go up into the **h country**. H2215
Dt 1:43 you marched up into the **h country**. H2215
Dt 2: 1 our way around the **h country** *of* Seir. H2215
Dt 2: 3 way around this **h country** long enough; H2215
Dt 2: 5 given Esau the **h country** *of* Seir as his H2215
Dt 3:12 including half the **h country** *of* Gilead H2215
Dt 3:25 Jordan—that fine **h country** and Lebanon." H2215
Jos 9: 1 the kings in the **h country**, in the western H2215
Jos 10: 6 kings from the **h country** have joined H2215
Jos 10:40 including the **h country**, the Negev, H2215
Jos 11: 3 Perizzites and Jebusites in the **h country** H2215
Jos 11:16 the **h country**, all the Negev, the whole H2215
Jos 11:21 destroyed the Anakites from the **h country**: H2215
Jos 11:21 from all the **h country** *of* Judah, and from H2215
Jos 11:21 from all the **h country** *of* Israel. H2215
Jos 12: 8 The lands included the **h country**, the H2215
Jos 13:19 Zereth Shahar on the **h** *in* the valley, H2215
Jos 14:12 Now give me this **h country** that the LORD H2215
Jos 15: 8 to the top of the **h** west of the Hinnom H2215
Jos 15:48 In the **h country**: Shamir, Jattir, Sokoh, H2215
Jos 16: 1 the desert into the **h country** *of* Bethel. H2215
Jos 17:15 "and if the **h country** *of* Ephraim is too H2215
Jos 17:16 "The **h country** is not enough for us H2215
Jos 17:18 the forested **h country** as well. Clear it H2215
Jos 18:12 headed west into the **h country**, H2215
Jos 18:13 Addar on the **h** south of Lower Beth H2215
Jos 18:14 From the **h** facing Beth Horon on the H2215
Jos 18:16 to the foot of the **h** facing the Valley of H2215
Jos 19:50 Timnath Serah in the **h country** *of* Ephraim. H2215
Jos 20: 7 in Galilee in the **h country** *of* Naphtali, H2215
Jos 20: 7 Shechem in the **h country** *of* Ephraim, and H2215
Jos 20: 7 that is, Hebron) in the **h country** *of* Judah. H2215
Jos 21:11 pastureland, in the **h country** *of* Judah. H2215
Jos 21:21 In the **h country** *of* Ephraim they were H2215
Jos 24: 4 I assigned the **h country** *of* Seir to Esau H2215
Jos 24:30 Serah in the **h country** *of* Ephraim, H2215
Jos 24:33 son Phinehas in the **h country** *of* Ephraim. H2215
Jdg 1: 9 the Canaanites living in the **h country**, H2215
Jdg 1:19 They took possession of the **h country**, but H2215
Jdg 1:34 confined the Danites to the **h country**, H2215
Jdg 2: 9 Heres in the **h country** *of* Ephraim, H2215
Jdg 3:27 a trumpet in the **h country** *of* Ephraim, H2215
Jdg 4: 5 Bethel in the **h country** *of* Ephraim, H2215
Jdg 7: 1 of them in the valley near the **h** *of* Moreh. H1496
Jdg 7:24 throughout the **h country** *of* Ephraim, H2215
Jdg 9:37 are coming down from the **central h**, H3179+824
Jdg 10: 1 in Shamir, in the **h country** *of* Ephraim. H2215
Jdg 12:15 in the **h country** *of* the Amalekites. H2215
Jdg 16: 3 to the top of the **h** that faces Hebron. H2215
Jdg 17: 1 Micah from the **h country** *of* Ephraim H2215
Jdg 17: 8 house in the **h country** *of* Ephraim. H2215
Jdg 18: 2 they entered the **h country** *of* Ephraim H2215
Jdg 18:13 went on to the **h country** *of* Ephraim and H2215
Jdg 19: 1 area in the **h country** *of* Ephraim took a H2215
Jdg 19:16 old man from the **h country** *of* Ephraim, H2215
Jdg 19:18 area in the **h country** *of* Ephraim where I H2215
1Sa 1: 1 a Zuphite from the **h country** *of* Ephraim H2215
1Sa 7: 1 house on the **h** and consecrated Eleazar H1496
1Sa 9: 4 through the **h country** *of* Ephraim and H2215
1Sa 9:11 As they were going up the **h** *to* the town H5090
1Sa 13: 2 Mikmash and in the **h country** *of* Bethel, H2215
1Sa 14:22 hidden in the **h country** *of* Ephraim heard H2215
1Sa 17: 3 occupied one **h** and the Israelites H2215
1Sa 22: 6 the tamarisk tree on the **h** at Gibeah, H8229
1Sa 23:19 at Horesh, on the **h** *of* Hakilah, south of H1496
1Sa 26: 1 "Is not David hiding on the **h** *of* Hakilah H1496
1Sa 26: 3 the road on the **h** *of* Hakilah facing H1496
1Sa 26:13 on top of the **h** some distance away; H2215
2Sa 2:24 they came to the **h** *of* Ammah, near Giah H1496
2Sa 2:25 group and took their stand on top of a **h**. H1496
2Sa 6: 3 house of Abinadab, which was on the **h**. H1496
2Sa 13:34 coming down the side of the **h**. H2215
2Sa 13:34 of Horonaim, on the side of the **h**. H2215
2Sa 20:21 from the **h country** *of* Ephraim, has H2215
2Sa 21: 9 their bodies on a **h** before the LORD. H2215
1Ki 4: 8 Ben-Hur—in the **h country** *of* Ephraim; H2215
1Ki 11: 7 On a **h** east of Jerusalem, Solomon built H2215
1Ki 12:25 Shechem in the **h country** *of* Ephraim and H2215
1Ki 14:23 poles on every high **h** and under every H1496
1Ki 16:24 He bought the **h** *of* Samaria from Shemer H2215
1Ki 16:24 talents of silver and built a city on the **h**, H2215
1Ki 16:24 the name of the former owner of the **h**. H2215
2Ki 1: 9 who was sitting on the top of a **h**, and H2215
2Ki 5:22 to me from the **h country** *of* Ephraim. H2215
2Ki 5:24 When Gehazi came to the **h**, he took the H6755
2Ki 17:10 poles on every high **h** and under every H1496
2Ki 23:13 on the south of the **H** *of* Corruption— H2215
1Ch 4:42 sons of Ishi, invaded the **h country** *of* Seir. H2215
1Ch 6:67 In the **h country** *of* Ephraim they were H2215
2Ch 13: 4 in the **h country** *of* Ephraim, and H2215
2Ch 19: 4 to the **h country** *of* Ephraim and H2215
2Ch 27: 3 work on the wall at the **h of Ophel**. H6755
2Ch 27: 4 towns in the **h country** *of* Judah and forts H2215
2Ch 32:33 was buried on the **h** *where* the tombs of H5090
2Ch 33:14 Fish Gate and encircling the **h of Ophel**; H6755
2Ch 33:15 built on the temple **h** and in Jerusalem; H2215
Ne 3:26 living on the **h of Ophel** made repairs up H6755
Ne 8:15 "Go out into the **h country** and bring back H2215
Ne 11:21 temple servants lived on the **h of Ophel**, H6755
Ps 78:54 to the **h country** his right hand had taken. H2215
SS 4: 6 of myrrh and to the **h** *of* incense. H1496
Isa 10:32 of Daughter Zion, at the **h** *of* Jerusalem. H1496
Isa 15: 5 They go up the **h** *to* Luhith, weeping as H5090
Isa 30:17 on a mountaintop, like a banner on a **h**." H1496
Isa 30:25 on every high mountain and every lofty **h**. H1496
Isa 40: 4 every mountain and **h** made low; the H1496
Isa 49: 9 roads and find pasture on every **barren h**. H9155
Isa 57: 7 made your bed on a high and lofty **h**; H2215
Jer 2:20 on every high **h** and under every H1496
Jer 3: 6 gone up on every high **h** and under every H2215
Jer 16:16 every mountain and **h** and from the H1496
Jer 17:26 from the **h country** and the Negev H2215
Jer 26:18 the temple **h** a mound overgrown with H2215
Jer 31:39 straight to the **h** *of* Gareb and then turn H1496
Jer 32:44 Judah and in the towns of the **h country**, H2215
Jer 33:13 In the towns of the **h country**, of the H2215
Jer 48: 5 They go up the **h** *to* Luhith, weeping H5090
Jer 49:16 who occupy the heights of the **h**. H1496
Jer 50: 6 over mountain and **h** and forgot their own H1496
Eze 6:13 on every high **h** and on all the H1496
Eze 20:28 they saw any high **h** or any leafy tree, H1496
Eze 34: 6 all the mountains and on every high **h**. H1496
Eze 34:26 the places surrounding my **h** a blessing. H1496
Da 9:16 from Jerusalem, your city, your holy **h**. H2215
Da 9:20 to the LORD my God for his holy **h**— H2215
Joel 2: 1 in Zion; sound the alarm on my holy **h**. H2215
Joel 3:17 LORD your God, dwell in Zion, my holy **h**. H2215
Ob 16 Just as you drank on my holy **h**, so all the H2215
Mic 3:12 the temple **h** a mound overgrown with H2215
Zep 3:11 again will you be haughty on my holy **h**. H2215
Mal 1: 3 have turned his **h country** into a H2215
Mt 5:14 A town built on a **h** cannot be hidden. *G4001*
Lk 1:39 to a town in the **h country** of Judea, *G3978*
Lk 1:65 throughout the **h country** of Judea people *G3978*
Lk 3: 5 filled in, every mountain and **h** made low. *G1090*
Lk 4:29 him to the brow *of* the **h** on which the *G4001*
Lk 19:29 Bethany at the **h** called the Mount of *G4001*
Lk 21:37 the night on the **h** called the Mount of *G4001*
Ac 1:12 Jerusalem from the **h** called the Mount of *G4001*

HILLEL (2)

Jdg 12:13 Abdon son of **H**, from Pirathon, led H2148
Jdg 12:15 Then Abdon son of **H** died and was buried H2148

HILLS (79) [HILL]

Ge 12: 8 went on toward the **h** east of Bethel and H2215
Ge 14:10 fell into them and the rest fled to the **h**. H2215
Ge 49:26 than the bounty of the age-old **h**. H1496
Dt 1:44 who lived in those **h** came out against H2215
Dt 2:37 that around the towns in the **h**. H2215
Dt 8: 7 gushing out into the valleys and **h**; H2215
Dt 8: 9 iron and you can dig copper out of the **h**. H2215
Dt 12: 2 on the **h** and under every spreading tree H1496
Dt 33:15 the fruitfulness of the everlasting **h**; H1496
Jos 2:16 "Go to the **h** so the pursuers will not find H2215
Jos 2:22 they went into the **h** and stayed there H2215
Jos 2:23 They went down out of the **h**, forded the H2215
Jdg 3:27 Israelites went down with him from the **h**, H2215
Jdg 11:37 months to roam the **h** and weep with my H2215
Jdg 11:38 went into the **h** and wept because she H2215
1Sa 23:14 in the **h** of the Desert of Ziph. H2215
1Ki 5:15 eighty thousand stonecutters in the **h**, H2215
1Ki 20:23 "Their gods are gods of the **h**. H2215
1Ki 20:28 is a god of the **h** and not a god of the H2215
1Ki 22:17 scattered on the **h** like sheep without a H2215
2Ki 6:17 looked and saw the **h** full of horses and H2215
2Ch 2: 2 stonecutters in the **h** and 3,600 as H2215
2Ch 2:18 80,000 to be stonecutters in the **h**, H2215
2Ch 15: 8 he had captured in the **h** *of* Ephraim. H2215
2Ch 18:16 scattered on the **h** like sheep without a H2215
2Ch 21:11 high places on the **h** *of* Judah and had H2215
2Ch 26:10 vineyards in the **h** and in the fertile H2215
Job 15: 7 Were you brought forth before the **h**? H1496
Job 39: 8 It ranges the **h** for its pasture and H2215
Job 40:20 The **h** bring it their produce, and all the H2215
Ps 50:10 is mine, and the cattle on a thousand **h**. H2215
Ps 65:12 overflow; the **h** are clothed with gladness. H1496
Ps 72: 3 people, the **h** the fruit of righteousness. H1496
Ps 72:16 the land; on the tops of the **h** may it sway. H2215
Ps 114: 4 leaped like rams, the **h** like lambs. H1496
Ps 114: 6 did you leap like rams, you **h**, like lambs? H1496
Ps 147: 8 with rain and makes grass grow on the **h**. H2215
Ps 148: 9 you mountains and all **h**, fruit trees and H1496
Pr 8:25 in place, before the **h**, I was given birth, H1496
Pr 27:25 the grass from the **h** is gathered in, H2215
SS 2: 8 the mountains, bounding over the **h**. H1496
SS 2:17 like a young stag on the rugged **h**. H2215
SS 4: 1 of goats descending from the **h** *of* Gilead. H2215
Isa 2: 2 it will be exalted above the **h**, and all H1496
Isa 2:14 towering mountains and all the high **h**, H1496
Isa 7:25 As for all the **h** once cultivated by the hoe H2215
Isa 17:13 driven before the wind like chaff on the **h** H2215
Isa 40:12 on the scales and the **h** in a balance? H1496
Isa 41:15 crush them, and reduce the **h** to chaff. H1496
Isa 42:15 the mountains and **h** and dry up all their H1496
Isa 54:10 be shaken and the **h** be removed, H1496
Isa 55:12 the mountains and **h** will burst into song H1496
Isa 65: 7 the mountains and defied me on the **h**, H1496
Jer 3:23 commotion on the **h** and mountains is a H1496
Jer 4:15 disaster from the **h** *of* Ephraim. H2215
Jer 4:24 were quaking; all the **h** were swaying. H1496
Jer 13:16 your feet stumble on the darkening **h**. H2215
Jer 13:27 detestable acts on the **h** and in the fields. H1496
Jer 17: 2 the spreading trees and on the high **h**. H1496
Jer 31: 5 will plant vineyards on the **h** *of* Samaria; H2215
Jer 31: 6 watchmen cry out on the **h** *of* Ephraim, H2215
Jer 50:19 satisfied on the **h** *of* Ephraim and Gilead H2215
Eze 6: 3 LORD says to the mountains and **h**, H1496
Eze 35: 8 will fall on your **h** and in your valleys and H1496
Eze 36: 4 LORD says to the mountains and **h**, H1496
Eze 36: 6 of Israel and say to the mountains and **h**, H1496
Hos 4:13 burn offerings on the **h**, H1496
Hos 10: 8 and to the **h**, "Fall on us!" H1496
Joel 3:18 new wine, and the **h** will flow with milk H1496
Am 9:13 the mountains and flow from all the **h**, H1496
Mic 4: 1 it will be exalted above the **h**, and H1496
Mic 6: 1 let the **h** hear what you have to say. H1496
Na 1: 5 quake before him and the **h** melt away. H1496
Hab 3: 6 crumbled and the age-old **h** collapsed— H1496
Zep 1:10 New Quarter, and a loud crash from the **h**. H1496
Mt 18:12 ninety-nine on the **h** and go to look for *G4001*
Mk 5: 5 tombs and in the **h** he would cry out and *G4001*
Lk 23:30 and to the **h**, "Cover us!" ' *G1090*
Rev 17: 9 heads are seven **h** on which the woman *G4001*

HILLSIDE (5) [HILL]

2Sa 16:13 going along the **h** opposite him, H7521+2215
2Ki 23:16 saw the tombs that were there on the **h**, H2215
Isa 5: 1 loved one had a vineyard on a fertile **h**. H7967
Mk 5:11 herd of pigs was feeding on the nearby **h**. *G4001*
Lk 8:32 herd of pigs was feeding there on the **h**. *G4001*

HILLTOP (2) [HILL]

Jos 15: 9 From the **h** the boundary headed H2215+8031
Isa 13: 2 Raise a banner on a bare **h**, shout to H2215

HILLTOPS (3) [HILL]

Jdg 9:25 set men on the **h** to ambush and H8031+2215
2Ki 16: 4 on the **h** and under every spreading tree. H1496
2Ch 28: 4 on the **h** and under every spreading tree. H1496

HIM (4822) [HE] See Index of Articles Etc.

HIMSELF (346) [HE, SELF] See Index of Articles Etc.

HIN (22)

Ex 29:40 with a quarter of a **h** *of* oil from pressed H2125
Ex 29:40 a quarter of a **h** *of* wine as a drink H2125
Ex 30:24 the sanctuary shekel—and a **h** *of* olive oil. H2125
Lev 19:36 an honest ephah and an honest **h**. H2125
Lev 23:13 drink offering of a quarter of a **h** of wine. H2125
Nu 15: 4 mixed with a quarter of a **h** *of* olive oil. H2125
Nu 15: 5 prepare a quarter of a **h** *of* wine as a drink H2125
Nu 15: 6 flour mixed with a third of a **h** *of* olive oil, H2125
Nu 15: 7 a third of a **h** *of* wine as a drink H2125
Nu 15: 9 flour mixed with half a **h** *of* olive oil, H2125
Nu 15:10 also bring half a **h** *of* wine as a drink H2125

Nu 28: 5 with a quarter of a **h** *of* oil from pressed H2125
Nu 28: 7 to be a quarter of a **h** of fermented drink H2125
Nu 28:14 to be a drink offering of half a **h** of wine; H2125
Nu 28:14 a third of a **h**; and with each lamb, H2125
Nu 28:14 and with each lamb, a quarter of a **h**. H2125
Eze 4:11 out a sixth of a **h** of water and drink it at H2125
Eze 45:24 along with a **h** *of* olive oil for each ephah. H2125
Eze 46: 5 along with a **h** *of* olive oil for each ephah. H2125
Eze 46: 7 along with a **h** of oil for each ephah. H2125
Eze 46:11 along with a **h** of oil for each ephah. H2125
Eze 46:14 with a third of a **h** of oil to moisten the H2125

HIND, HINDS, HINDS' (KJV) DEER, DOE, DOES

HINDER (7) [HINDERED, HINDERS, HINDRANCE]
1Sa 14: 6 Nothing can **h** the LORD *from* saving H5109
Job 15: 4 undermine piety and **h** devotion to God. H1757
Mt 19:14 come to me, and *do* not **h** them, for the G3266
Mk 10:14 come to me, and *do* not **h** them, for the G3266
Lk 18:16 come to me, and *do* not **h** them, for the G3266
1Co 9:12 rather than **h** the gospel of Christ G1600+1443
1Pe 3: 7 so that nothing *will* **h** your prayers. G1601

HINDERED (2) [HINDER]
Lk 11:52 and *you have* **h** those who were entering." G3266
Ro 15:22 is why *I have* often *been* **h** from coming G1601

HINDERMOST, HINDMOST (KJV) LAST, LAGGING, LEAST, REAR

H

HINDERS (1) [HINDER]
Heb 12: 1 off everything that **h** and the sin that so G3839

HINDQUARTERS (2)
1Ki 7:25 and their **h** were toward the center. H294
2Ch 4: 4 and their **h** were toward the center. H294

HINDRANCE (1) [HINDER]
Ac 28:31 with all boldness and **without h**! G219

HINGED (1) [HINGES]
Eze 41:24 two leaves—two **h** leaves for each door. H6015

HINGES (1) [HINGED]
Pr 26:14 As a door turns on its **h**, so a sluggard H7494

HINNOM (3) [BEN HINNOM]
Jos 15: 8 the hill west of the **H** Valley at the H2183
Jos 18:16 It continued down the **H** Valley along the H2183
Ne 11:30 way from Beersheba to the Valley of **H**. H2183

HINT (1)
Eph 5: 3 you *there must* not *be* even a **h of** sexual G3951

HIP (6) [HIPS]
Ge 32:25 the socket of Jacob's **h** so that his hip was H3751
Ge 32:25 hip so that his **h** was wrenched as he H3751
Ge 32:31 he was limping because of his **h**. H3751
Ge 32:32 tendon attached to the socket of the **h**, H3751
Ge 32:32 socket of Jacob's **h** was touched near the H3751
Isa 60: 4 your daughters are carried on the **h**. H7396

HIPS (2) [HIP]
Isa 3:16 **strutting along with swaying h** H2143+2256+3262
Isa 49:22 arms and carry your daughters on their **h**. H4190

HIRAH (2)
Ge 38: 1 to stay with a man of Adullam named **H**. H2669
Ge 38:12 his friend **H** the Adullamite went with H2669

HIRAM (23) [HIRAM'S]
2Sa 5:11 Now **H** king of Tyre sent envoys to David H2671
1Ki 5: 1 When **H** king of Tyre heard that Solomon H2671
1Ki 5: 2 Solomon sent back this message to **H**: H2671
1Ki 5: 7 When **H** heard Solomon's message, he H2671
1Ki 5: 8 So **H** sent word to Solomon: "I have H2671
1Ki 5:10 In this way **H** kept Solomon supplied with H2670
1Ki 5:11 Solomon gave **H** twenty thousand cors H2671
1Ki 5:11 continued to do this for **H** year after year. H2671
1Ki 5:12 relations between **H** and Solomon, H2671
1Ki 5:18 of Solomon and **H** and workers from H2670
1Ki 9:11 twenty towns in Galilee to **H** king of Tyre, H2671
1Ki 9:11 because **H** had supplied him with all the H2671
1Ki 9:12 But when **H** went from Tyre to see the H2671
1Ki 9:14 Now **H** had sent to the king 120 talents of H2671
1Ki 9:27 And **H** sent his men—sailors who knew H2671
1Ki 10:22 ships at sea along with the ships of **H**. H2671
1Ch 14: 1 Now **H** king of Tyre sent messengers to H2671
2Ch 2: 3 sent this message to **H** king of Tyre: H2586
2Ch 2:11 **H** king of Tyre replied by letter to H2586
2Ch 2:12 And **H** added: "Praise be to the LORD, the H2586
2Ch 8: 2 rebuilt the villages that **H** had given him, H2586
2Ch 8:18 And **H** sent him ships commanded by his H2586
2Ch 9:10 The servants of **H** and the servants of H2586

HIRAM'S (2) [HIRAM]
1Ki 10:11 (**H** ships brought gold from Ophir; and H2671
2Ch 9:21 of trading ships manned by **H** servants. H2586

HIRE (7) [HIRED, HIRES]
Ex 22:15 the **money paid for** *the* **h** covers the loss. H8510
Jdg 9: 4 Abimelek used it *to* **h** reckless scoundrels H8509
1Sa 2: 5 who were full **h themselves out** for food, H8509
1Ch 19: 6 talents of silver to **h** chariots and H8509
Isa 46: 6 *they* **h** a goldsmith to make it into a god H8509
Zec 8:10 no wages for people or **h** *for* animals. H8510
Mt 20: 1 early in the morning *to* **h** workers for his G3636

HIRED (37) [HIRE]
Ge 30:16 "*I have* **h** you with my son's H8509+8509
Ex 12:45 resident or a **h worker** may not eat it. H8502
Ex 22:15 If the animal was **h**, the money paid for H8502
Lev 19:13 back the wages of a **h worker** overnight. H8502
Lev 22:10 the guest of a priest or his **h worker** eat it. H8502
Lev 25: 6 the **h worker** and temporary resident H8502
Lev 25:40 to be treated as **h workers** or temporary H8502
Lev 25:50 rate paid to a **h worker** for that number H8502
Lev 25:53 be treated as **workers h** *from* year to year; H8502
Dt 15:18 worth twice as much as that of a **h hand**. H8502
Dt 23: 4 *they* **h** Balaam son of Beor from H8509
Dt 24:14 advantage of a **h worker** who is poor and H8502
Jdg 18: 4 "*He has* **h** me and I am his priest. H8509
2Sa 10: 6 they **h** twenty thousand Aramean foot H8509
2Ki 7: 6 the king of Israel *has* **h** the Hittite and H8509
1Ch 19: 7 *They* **h** thirty-two thousand chariots and H8509
2Ch 24:12 *They* **h** masons and carpenters to restore H8509
2Ch 25: 6 *He* also **h** a hundred thousand fighting H8509
Ne 6:12 Tobiah and Sanballat *had* **h** him. H8509
Ne 6:13 He *had* **been h** to intimidate me so that I H8509
Ne 13: 2 water but *had* **h** Balaam to call a H8509
Job 7: 1 Are not their days like those of **h laborers**? H8502
Job 7: 2 a **h laborer** waiting to be paid, H8502
Job 14: 6 till he has put in his time like a **h laborer**. H8502
Isa 7:20 Lord will use a razor **h** from beyond the H8502
Mt 20: 7 " 'Because no one *has* **h** us,' they G3636
Mt 20: 8 with the last ones **h** and going on to the first NDT
Mt 20: 9 "**The workers who were h** about five in G3836S
Mt 20:10 So when those came **who were h** first G3836S
Mt 20:12 'These **who were h** last worked only one G3836S
Mt 20:14 to give the one **who was h** last the same G3836S
Mk 1:20 boat with the **h men** and followed him G3638
Lk 15:15 So he went and **h** *himself* **out** to a citizen G3140
Lk 15:17 of my father's **h servants** have food to G3634
Lk 15:19 make me like one *of* your **h servants**. G3634
Jn 10:12 The **h hand** is not the shepherd and does G3638
Jn 10:13 because he is a **h hand** and cares nothing G3638

HIRELING (KJV) HIRED, LABORERS, SERVANT

HIRES (1) [HIRE]
Pr 26:10 at random is *one who* **h** a fool or any H8509

HIS (6189) [HE] See Index of Articles Etc.

HISS (1) [HISSES]
Jer 46:22 Egypt will **h** like a fleeing serpent as the H7754

HISSES (1) [HISS]
Job 27:23 in derision and **h** him out of his place." H9239

HISTORIC (1) [HISTORY]
Ne 2:20 in Jerusalem or any claim or **h right** to it." H2355

HISTORY (3) [HISTORIC]
Ezr 4:15 a place with a long **h** of sedition. A10317
Ezr 4:19 has a **long h** of revolt A10427+10317+10550
Ac 17:26 their appointed **times in h** and the G2789

HIT (7) [HITS, HITTING]
Ex 21:22 are fighting and **h** a pregnant woman H5597
Dt 19: 5 head may fly off and **h** his neighbor and H5162
1Ki 22:34 bow at random and **h** the king of Israel H5782
2Ch 18:33 bow at random and **h** the king of Israel H5782
Pr 23:35 "*They* **h** me," you will say, "but I'm not H5782
Mt 26:68 "Prophesy to us, Messiah. Who **h** you?" G4091
Lk 22:64 demanded, "Prophesy! Who **h** you?" G4091

HITCH (3) [HITCHED]
1Sa 6: 7 **H** the cows to the cart, but take their calves H673
1Ki 18:44 '**H up** your chariot and go down before the H673
2Ki 9:21 "**H up** my chariot," Joram ordered. H673

HITCHED (2) [HITCH]
1Sa 6:10 two such cows and **h** them to the cart and H673
2Ki 9:21 And when *it was* **h up**, Joram king of Israel H673

HITHER (KJV) BACK, HERE, RIGHT

HITHERTO (KJV) ABUNDANTLY, IN THE PAST, THIS FAR, THUS FAR, TO THIS DAY, UNTIL NOW, UP TO

HITS (3) [HIT]
Ex 21:18 one person **h** another with a stone H5782
Ex 21:26 "An owner *who* **h** a male or female slave H5782
Nu 35:21 if out of enmity *one person* **h** another with H5782

HITTING (1) [HIT]
Ex 2:13 "Why *are you* **h** your fellow Hebrew?" H5782

HITTITE (25) [HITTITES]
Ge 23:10 Ephron the **H** was sitting among his H3153
Ge 25: 9 in the field of Ephron son of Zohar the **H**, H3153
Ge 26:34 he married Judith daughter of Beeri the **H**, H3153
Ge 26:34 also Basemath daughter of Elon the **H**. H3153
Ge 27:46 with living because of these **H** women. H3147
Ge 27:46 of this land, from **H** women like these, my H3147
Ge 36: 2 Adah daughter of Elon the **H**, and H3153
Ge 49:29 in the cave in the field of Ephron the **H**, H3153
Ge 49:30 field as a burial place from Ephron the **H**. H3153
Ge 50:13 field as a burial place from Ephron the **H**. H3153
Jos 1: 4 the Euphrates—all the **H** country—to the H3153
1Sa 26: 6 asked Ahimelek the **H** and Abishai son of H3153
2Sa 11: 3 of Eliam and the wife of Uriah the **H**." H3153
2Sa 11: 6 "Send me Uriah the **H**." And Joab sent H3153
2Sa 11:17 army fell; moreover, Uriah the **H** died. H3153
2Sa 11:21 your servant Uriah the **H** is dead. H3153
2Sa 11:24 your servant Uriah the **H** is dead. H3153
2Sa 12: 9 down Uriah the **H** with the sword and H3153
2Sa 12:10 the wife of Uriah the **H** to be your own. H3153
2Sa 23:39 Uriah the **H**. There were thirty-seven H3153
1Ki 15: 5 except in the case of Uriah the **H**. H3153
2Ki 7: 6 Israel has hired the **H** and Egyptian kings H3153
1Ch 11:41 Uriah the **H**, Zabad son of Ahlai, H3153
Eze 16: 3 was an Amorite and your mother a **H**. H3153
Eze 16:45 Your mother was a **H** and your father an H3153

HITTITES (36) [HITTITE]
Ge 10:15 father of Sidon his firstborn, and of the **H**, H3147
Ge 15:20 **H**, Perizzites, Rephaites, H3153
Ge 23: 3 his dead wife and spoke to the **H**. H1201+3147
Ge 23: 5 The **H** replied to Abraham, H1201+3147
Ge 23: 7 the people of the land, the **H**. H1201+3147
Ge 23:10 of all the **H** who had come to H1201+3147
Ge 23:16 named in the hearing of the **H**: H1201+3147
Ge 23:18 of all the **H** who had come to the H1201+3147
Ge 23:20 Abraham by the **H** as a burial site. H1201+3147
Ge 25:10 Abraham had bought from the **H**. H1201+3147
Ge 49:32 cave in it were bought from the **H**." H1201+3147
Ex 3: 8 of the Canaanites, **H**, Amorites, Perizzites, H3153
Ex 3:17 the land of the Canaanites, **H**, Amorites, H3153
Ex 13: 5 the land of the Canaanites, **H**, Amorites, H3153
Ex 23:23 the land of the Amorites, **H**, Perizzites, H3153
Ex 23:28 Canaanites and **H** out of your way. H3153
Ex 33: 2 Amorites, **H**, Perizzites, Hivites H3153
Ex 34:11 Canaanites, **H**, Perizzites, Hivites H3153
Nu 13:29 live in the Negev; the **H**, Jebusites and H3153
Dt 7: 1 you many nations—the **H**, Girgashites, H3153
Dt 20:17 destroy them—the **H**, Amorites, H3153
Jos 3:10 out before you the Canaanites, **H**, Hivites, H3153
Jos 9: 1 as Lebanon (the kings of the **H**, Amorites, H3153
Jos 11: 3 to the Amorites, **H**, Perizzites and H3153
Jos 12: 8 These were the lands of the **H**, Amorites H3153
Jos 24:11 Canaanites, **H**, Girgashites, Hivites H3153
Jdg 1:26 He then went to the land of the **H**, where H3153
Jdg 3: 5 lived among the Canaanites, **H**, Amorites, H3153
1Ki 9:20 left from the Amorites, **H**, Perizzites, H3153
1Ki 10:29 the kings of the **H** and of the Arameans. H3153
1Ki 11: 1 Ammonites, Edomites, Sidonians and **H**. H3153
1Ch 1:13 father of Sidon his firstborn, and of the **H**, H3147
2Ch 1:17 the kings of the **H** and of the Arameans. H3153
2Ch 8: 7 There were still people left from the **H** H3153
Ezr 9: 1 of the Canaanites, **H**, Perizzites, Jebusites H3153
Ne 9: 8 the land of the Canaanites, **H**, Amorites, H3153

HIVITE (2) [HIVITES]
Ge 34: 2 When Shechem son of Hamor the **H**, the H2563
Ge 36: 2 granddaughter of Zibeon the **H**— H2563

HIVITES (23) [HIVITE]
Ge 10:17 **H**, Arkites, Sinites, H2563
Ex 3: 8 Amorites, Perizzites, **H** and Jebusites. H2563
Ex 3:17 Perizzites, **H** and Jebusites—a land H2563
Ex 13: 5 Amorites, **H** and Jebusites—the land he H2563
Ex 23:23 Canaanites, **H** and Jebusites, and I will H2563
Ex 23:28 the hornet ahead of you to drive the **H**, H2563
Ex 33: 2 Hittites, Perizzites, **H** and Jebusites. H2563
Ex 34:11 Hittites, Perizzites, **H** and Jebusites. H2563
Dt 7: 1 Perizzites, **H** and Jebusites, seven nations H2563
Dt 20:17 Perizzites, **H** and Jebusites—as the LORD H2563
Jos 3:10 Canaanites, Hittites, **H**, Perizzites H2563
Jos 9: 1 Perizzites, **H** and Jebusites)— H2563
Jos 9: 7 The Israelites said to the **H**, "But perhaps H2563
Jos 11: 3 to the **H** below Hermon in the region H2563
Jos 11:19 Except for the **H** living in Gibeon, not one H2563
Jos 12: 8 Canaanites, Perizzites, **H** and Jebusites. H2563
Jos 24:11 Girgashites, **H** and Jebusites, but I gave H2563
Jdg 3: 3 the **H** living in the Lebanon H2563
Jdg 3: 5 Amorites, Perizzites, **H** and Jebusites. H2563
2Sa 24: 7 all the towns of the **H** and Canaanites. H2563
1Ki 9:20 Perizzites, **H** and Jebusites (these peoples H2563
1Ch 1:15 **H**, Arkites, Sinites, H2563
2Ch 8: 7 Perizzites, **H** and Jebusites (these people H2563

HIZKI (1)
1Ch 8:17 Zebadiah, Meshullam, **H**, Heber, H2623

HIZKIAH (1)
1Ch 3:23 Elioenai, **H** and Azrikam—three H2624

HO (KJV) COME

HOAR, HOARY (KJV) AGED, GRAY, THIN FLAKES, WHITE HAIR

HOARDED (3) [HOARDS]
Ecc 5:13 wealth **h** to the harm of its owners H9068
Isa 23:18 the LORD; they will not be stored up or **h**. H2889
Jas 5: 3 *You have* **h wealth** in the last days. G2564

HOARDS (1) [HOARDED]
Pr 11:26 People curse the *one who* **h** grain, but H4979

HOBAB (2)
Nu 10:29 Now Moses said to H son of Reuel the H2463
Jdg 4:11 the descendants of H, Moses' H2463

HOBAH (1)
Ge 14:15 pursuing them as far as H, north of H2551

HOBAIAH (2)
Ezr 2:61 The descendants of H, Hakkoz and H2469
Ne 7:63 the descendants of H, Hakkoz and H2469

HOD (1)
1Ch 7:37 H, Shamma, Shilshah, Ithran and H2087

HODAVIAH (6)
1Ch 3:24 H, Eliashib, Pelaiah, Akkub, Johanan H2090
1Ch 5:24 Azriel, Jeremiah, H and Jahdiel. H2089
1Ch 9: 7 the son of H, the son of Hassenuah H2089
Ezr 2:40 Jeshua and Kadmiel (of the line of H) 74 H2089
Ezr 3: 9 descendants of H) and the sons of H3373
Ne 7:43 through Kadmiel through the line of H) 74 H2088

HODESH (1)
1Ch 8: 9 By his wife H he had Jobab, Zibia, Mesha, H2545

HODIAH (5) [HODIAH'S]
Ne 8: 7 Shabbethai, H, Maaseiah, Kelita H2091
Ne 9: 5 Sherebiah, H, Shebaniah and Pethahiah H2091
Ne 10:10 Shebaniah, H, Kelita, Pelaiah H2091
Ne 10:13 H, Bani and Beninu. H2091
Ne 10:18 H, Hashum, Bezai, H2091

HODIAH'S (1) [HODIAH]
1Ch 4:19 The sons of H wife, the sister of Naham H2091

HODSHI See TAHTIM HODSHI

HOE (1)
Isa 7:25 As for all the hills once cultivated by the h H5053

HOGLAH (4) [BETH HOGLAH]
Nu 26:33 were Mahlah, Noah, H, Milkah and Tirzah H2519
Nu 27: 1 were Mahlah, Noah, H, Milkah and Tirzah H2519
Nu 36:11 Mahlah, Tirzah, H, Milkah and Noah H2519
Jos 17: 3 were Mahlah, Noah, H, Milkah and Tirzah H2519

HOHAM (1)
Jos 10: 3 Jerusalem appealed to H king of Hebron, H2097

HOISTED (2)
Ac 27:17 so the men h it aboard. Then they passed G149
Ac 27:40 Then they h the foresail to the wind and G2048

HOLD (170) [HELD, HOLDING, HOLDS]
Ge 43: 9 you can h me personally responsible for H1335+4946+3338
Ge 48:17 so he took h of his father's hand to move H9461
Ex 4: 4 reached out and took h of the snake and H2616
Ex 5: 1 so that they may h a festival to me in the H2510
Ex 9: 2 let them go and continue to h them back, H2616
Ex 12:16 On the first day h a sacred assembly, and H2118
Ex 13: 6 on the seventh day h a festival to the LORD NDT
Ex 20: 7 the LORD will not h anyone guiltless who H5927
Ex 22:29 "Do not h back offerings from your H336
Ex 25:27 be close to the rim to h the poles used in H1074
Ex 26:29 make gold rings to h the crossbars. H1074
Ex 30: 4 to h the poles used to carry it. H1074
Ex 36:34 made gold rings to h the crossbars. H1074
Ex 37:14 put close to the rim to h the poles used in H1074
Ex 37:27 to h the poles used to carry it. H1074
Ex 38: 5 cast bronze rings to h the poles for the H1074
Lev 19:13 Do not h back the wages of a hired worker overnight H4328+6330+1332
Lev 23: 7 On the first day h a sacred assembly and H2118
Lev 23: 8 on the seventh day h a sacred assembly NDT
Lev 23:27 H a sacred assembly and deny yourselves H2118
Lev 23:36 on the eighth day h a sacred assembly H2118
Lev 25:24 the land that you h as a possession, H299
Lev 25:33 a house sold in any town they h—and is to H299
Nu 12:11 I ask you not to h against us the sin we H8883
Nu 28:18 On the first day h a sacred assembly and do NDT
Nu 28:25 On the seventh day h a sacred assembly H2118
Nu 28:26 h a sacred assembly and do no regular H2118
Nu 29: 1 of the seventh month h a sacred assembly H2118
Nu 29: 7 this seventh month h a sacred assembly. H2118
Nu 29:12 h a sacred assembly and do no regular H2118
Nu 29:35 " 'On the eighth day h a closing special H2118
Dt 5:11 the LORD will not h anyone guiltless who H5927
Dt 10:20 H fast to him and take your oaths in his H1815
Dt 11:22 obedience to him and to h fast to him— H1815
Dt 13: 4 obey him; serve him and h fast to him. H1815
Dt 16: 8 on the seventh day h an assembly to the NDT
Dt 21: 8 and do not h your people guilty of the H5989
Dt 21:19 mother shall take h of him and bring H9530
Dt 30:20 listen to his voice, and h fast to him. H1815
Jos 8:18 "H out toward Ai the javelin that is in your H5742
Jos 22: 5 to h fast to him and to serve him with all H1815
Jos 23: 8 But you are to h fast to the LORD your God H1815
Jdg 1:35 determined also to h out in Mount Heres, H3782
Jdg 9: 9 are honored, to h sway over the trees? H5675
Jdg 9:11 good and sweet, to h sway over the trees? H5675
Jdg 9:13 humans, to h sway over the trees? H5675
Jdg 16: 3 Then he got up and took h of the doors of H296
Ru 3:15 me the shawl you are wearing and h it out." H296
1Sa 15:27 Saul caught h of the hem of his robe H2616
1Sa 17:51 He took h of the Philistine's sword and H4374
2Sa 1:11 the men with him took h of their clothes H2616
2Sa 6: 6 reached out and took h of the ark of God, H296
2Sa 15: 5 out his hand, take h of him and kiss him. H2616
2Sa 19:19 said to him, "May my lord not h me guilty. H3108
2Sa 22:17 down from on high and took h of me; H4374
1Ki 1:50 went and took h of the horns of the altar. H2616
1Ki 2:28 of the LORD and took h of the horns of the H2616
1Ki 8:64 LORD was too small to h the burnt offerings H3920
1Ki 11:30 Ahijah took h of the new cloak he was H9530
1Ki 18:32 it large enough to h two seahs of seed. H1074
2Ki 2:12 Then he took h of his garment and tore it H2616
2Ki 4:16 said, "you will h a son in your arms." H2485
2Ki 4:27 at the mountain, she took h of his feet. H2616
2Ki 4:39 as many of its gourds as his garment could h H4850
2Ki 6:32 shut the door and h it shut against him. H4315
2Ki 10:19 I am going to h a great sacrifice for H4200
2Ki 15:19 strengthen his own h on the kingdom. H3338
2Ch 7: 7 had made could not h the burnt offerings, H3920
Job 1: 4 His sons used to h feasts in their homes H6913
Job 8:15 they cling to it, but it does not h. H7756
Job 9:28 I know you will not h me innocent. H5927
Job 10:16 If I h my head high, you stalk me like a H1448
Job 17: 9 the righteous will h to their ways, and H296
Job 36:17 judgment and justice have taken h of you. H9461
Job 39:10 Can you h it to the furrow with a harness H8003
Ps 18:16 down from on high and took h of me; H4374
Ps 21: 8 Your hand will lay h on all your enemies H5162
Ps 73:23 with you; you h me by my right hand. H296
Ps 74:11 Why do you h back your hand, your right H8740
Ps 75: 3 people quake, it is I who h its pillars firm. H9419
Ps 79: 8 Do not h against us the sins of past H2349
Ps 119:31 I h fast to your statutes, LORD; do not let H1815
Ps 139:10 guide me, your right hand will h me fast. H296
Pr 3:18 is a tree of life to those who take h of her; H2616
Pr 3:18 those who h her fast will be blessed. H9461
Pr 4: 4 "Take h of my words with all your heart H9461
Pr 4:13 H on to instruction, do not let it go; guard H2616
Pr 5:22 the cords of their sins h them fast. H9461
Pr 7:13 She took h of him and kissed him and H2616
Pr 10:19 but the prudent h their tongues. H3104
Pr 17:28 discerning if they h their tongues. H357
Pr 20:16 h it in pledge if it is done for an outsider. H2471
Pr 24:11 h back those staggering toward slaughter. H3104
Pr 27:13 h it in pledge if it is done for an outsider. H2471
Pr 28:17 in the grave; let no one h them back. H9461
SS 7: 8 climb the palm tree; I will take h of its fruit." H296
Isa 2:22 in their nostrils. Why h them in esteem? H3108
Isa 4: 1 seven women will take h of one man and H2616
Isa 22:17 LORD is about to take firm h of you H6487+6487
Isa 41:13 LORD your God who takes h of your right H2616
Isa 42: 6 righteousness; I will take h of your hand. H2616
Isa 43: 6 the south, 'Do not h them back.' Bring my H3973
Isa 45: 1 whose right hand I take h of to subdue H2616
Isa 48: 9 the sake of my praise I h it back from you, H2641
Isa 54: 2 do not h back; lengthen your H3104
Isa 56: 4 pleases me and h fast to my covenant— H2616
Isa 56: 6 it and who h fast to my covenant— H2616
Isa 58: 1 "Shout it aloud, do not h back. Raise your H3104
Isa 64: 7 on your name or strives to lay h of you; H2616
Isa 64:12 LORD, will you h yourself back? Will you H706
Isa 65: 4 whose pots h broth of impure meat NDT
Jer 2:13 broken cisterns that cannot h water. H3920
Jer 6:11 the wrath of the LORD, and I cannot h it in. H3920
Jer 34: 9 was to h a fellow Hebrew in bondage. H6268
Jer 34:10 slaves and no longer h them in bondage. H6268
Jer 50:33 All their captors h them fast, refusing to H2616
Eze 3:18 I will h you accountable for H1335+4946+3338
Eze 3:20 I will h you accountable for H1335+4946+3338
Eze 17: 3 Taking h of the top of a cedar H4374
Eze 24:14 I will not h back; I will not have pity, nor H7277
Eze 30: 9 Anguish will take h of them on the H2118+928
Eze 30:21 may become strong enough to h a sword. H9530
Eze 33: 6 I will h the watchman accountable for H2011+4946+3338
Eze 33: 8 I will h you accountable for H1335+4946+3338
Eze 34:10 will h them accountable for H2011+4946+3338
Eze 37:20 H before their eyes the sticks H2118+928+3338
Da 4:35 No one can h back his hand or say to A10411
Jnh 1:14 Do not h us accountable for killing H5989+6584
Zec 8:23 nations will take firm h of one Jew by H2616
Mt 12:11 will you not take h of it and lift it out? G3195
Mt 21:26 for they all h that John was a G6055+2400
Mk 11:25 praying, if you h anything against anyone G2400
Lk 14: 4 So taking h of the man, he healed him G2138
Jn 8:31 Jesus said, "If you h to my teaching, you G3531
Jn 14:30 He has no h over me, G4024+4029
Jn 20:17 Jesus said, "Do not h on to me, for I have G721
Ac 2:24 impossible for death to keep its h on him. G3195
Ac 7:60 "Lord, do not h this sin against them." G2705
Ac 27: 7 When the wind did not allow us to h our course G4661
Ac 27:17 ropes under the ship itself to h it together. G5690
Ro 13: 3 rulers h no terror for those who do right, G1639
1Co 15: 2 if you h firmly to the word I preached to G2988
Php 2:16 as you h firmly to the word of life. G2091
Php 3:12 I press on to take h of that for which G2898
Php 3:12 of that for which Christ Jesus took h of me. G2898
Php 3:13 consider myself yet to have taken h of it. G2898
Col 1:17 and in him all things h together. G5319
1Th 5:13 H them in the highest regard in love G2451
1Th 5:21 test them all; h on to what is good, G2988
2Th 2:15 stand firm and h fast to the teachings we G3195
1Ti 3: 9 They must keep h of the deep truths of the G2400
1Ti 6:12 Take h of the eternal life to which you G2138
1Ti 6:19 so that they may take h of the life that is G2138
Titus 1: 9 He must h firmly to the trustworthy message G504
Heb 3: 6 if indeed we h firmly to our confidence G2988
Heb 3:14 if indeed we h our original conviction G2988
Heb 4:14 let us h firmly to the faith we profess. G3195
Heb 6:18 who have fled to take h of the hope set G3195
Heb 10:23 Let us h unswervingly to the hope we G2988
2Pe 2: 9 from trials and to h the unrighteous for G5498
Rev 1:18 And I h the keys of death and Hades. G2400
Rev 2: 4 Yet I h this against you: You have G2400
Rev 2:14 There are some among you who h to the G3195
Rev 2:15 also have those who h to the teaching G3195
Rev 2:24 to you who do not h to her teaching and G2400
Rev 2:25 except to h on to what you have until I G3195
Rev 3: 3 received and heard; h it fast, and repent. G5498
Rev 3:11 H on to what you have, so that no one G3195
Rev 12:17 commands and h fast their testimony G2400
Rev 19:10 sisters who h to the testimony of G2400

HOLDING (26) [HOLD]
Ge 50:11 "The Egyptians are h a solemn ceremony H4200
Nu 2: 2 their standard and h the banners of their H928
Nu 35:17 Or if anyone is h a stone and strikes H928+3338
Nu 35:18 Or if anyone is h a wooden object H928+3338
Jdg 7:20 in their left hands and h in their right hands NDT
1Sa 17:57 with David still h the Philistine's H928+3338
1Sa 25:36 he was in the house h a banquet like that H4200
1Ki 7:38 each h forty baths and measuring four H3920
Ne 4:21 the work with half the men h spears, H2616
Jer 15: 6 out and destroy you; I am tired of h back. H5714
Jer 20: 9 I am weary of h it in; indeed, I cannot. H3920
Jer 34: 7 cities of Judah that were still h out— H3855
Mk 7: 3 washing, h to the tradition of the elders. G3195
Mk 7: 8 of God and are h on to human traditions." G3195
Jn 2: 6 each h from twenty to thirty gallons. G6003
Jn 8:44 the beginning, not h to the truth, for there G2705
1Co 11: 2 in everything and for h to the traditions G2988
2Th 2: 6 And now you know what is h him back, so G2988
1Ti 1:19 h on to faith and a good conscience G2400
1Ti 4: 8 h promise for both the present life and G2400
Rev 5: 8 a harp and they were h golden bowls full of NDT
Rev 6: 5 Its rider was h a pair of scales in his hand G2400
Rev 7: 1 h back the four winds of the earth to G3195
Rev 7: 9 were h palm branches in their hands. AIT
Rev 10: 2 He was h a little scroll, which lay open in G2400
Rev 20: 1 key to the Abyss and h in his hand a great AIT

HOLDS (19) [HOLD]
Ge 50:15 if Joseph h a grudge against us and pays H8475
Nu 5:18 he himself h the bitter water H2118+928+3338
Job 12:15 If he h back the waters, there is drought; if H6806
Job 18: 9 him by the heel; a snare h him fast. H2616
Job 37: 4 his voice resounds, he h nothing back. H6810
Pr 2: 7 He h success in store for the upright, he is H7621
Pr 11:12 who has understanding h their tongue. H3087
Pr 31:19 In her hand she h the distaff and grasps H8938
Isa 41:23 tell us what the future h, so we may know H910
Isa 56: 2 the person who h it fast, who keeps the H2616
Eze 23:32 bring scorn and derision, for it h so much. H3920
Da 5:23 honor the God who h in his hand your life NDT
Am 1: 5 of Aven and the one who h the scepter in H9461
Am 1: 8 Ashdod and the one who h the scepter in H9461
2Th 2: 7 the one who now h it back will G2988
Heb 2:14 the power of him who h the power of G2400
Rev 2: 1 the words of him who h the seven stars in G3195
Rev 3: 1 words of him who h the seven spirits of G2400
Rev 3: 7 is holy and true, who h the key of David. G2400

HOLE (6) [HOLES]
Dt 23:13 dig a h and cover up your excrement. H2916
2Ki 12: 9 priest took a chest and bored a h in its lid. H2986
Ps 7:15 Whoever digs a h and scoops it out falls H1014
Eze 8: 7 I looked, and I saw a h in the wall. H2986
Eze 12:12 a h will be dug in the wall for him to go NDT
Mt 25:18 dug a h in the ground and hid his G4002

HOLES (6) [HOLE]
1Sa 14:11 crawling out of the h they were hiding in." H2986
Job 30: 6 among the rocks and in h in the ground. H2986
Isa 2:19 in the rocks and to h in the ground from H4704
Isa 7:19 all the thornbushes and at all the water h. H5635
Hag 1: 6 only to put them in a purse with h in it." H5918
Heb 11:38 living in caves and in h in the ground. G3956

HOLIDAY (1)
Est 2:18 He proclaimed a h throughout the H2182

HOLIEST (1) [HOLY]
Nu 18:29 portion the best and h part of everything H5219

HOLINESS (24) [HOLY]
Ex 15:11 majestic in h, awesome in glory, H7731
Dt 32:51 because you did not uphold my h among H7727
1Ch 16:29 Worship the LORD in the splendor of his h. H7731
2Ch 20:21 the splendor of his h as they went out at H7731
Ps 29: 2 worship the LORD in the splendor of his h. H7731
Ps 89:35 I have sworn by my h—and I will not lie H7731
Ps 93: 5 h adorns your house for endless days. H7731

Ps 96: 9 Worship the LORD in the splendor of his **h** H7731
Isa 29:23 *they will* **acknowledge** *the* **h** *of* the Holy H7727
Isa 35: 8 it will be called the Way of **H**; it will be H7731
Eze 36:23 *I will* **show** *the* **h** *of* my great name, which H7727
Eze 38:23 And so I will show my greatness and *my* **h** H7727
Am 4: 2 The Sovereign LORD has sworn by his **h** H7731
Lk 1:75 in **h** and righteousness before him all our G4009
Ro 1: 4 through the Spirit *of* **h** was appointed the G43
Ro 6:19 as slaves to righteousness leading to **h**. G40
Ro 6:22 the benefit you reap leads to **h**, and the G40
1Co 1:30 our righteousness, **h** and redemption. G40
2Co 7: 1 perfecting **h** out of reverence for God. G43
Eph 4:24 be like God in true righteousness and **h**. G4009
1Ti 2: 2 quiet lives in all godliness and **h**. G4949
1Ti 2:15 continue in faith, love and **h** with propriety. G40
Heb 12:10 in order that we may share in his **h**. G42
Heb 12:14 without **h** no one will see the Lord. G4005S

HOLLOW (7)

Ex 27: 8 Make the altar **h**, out of boards. It is to be H5554
Ex 38: 7 They made it **h**, *out of* boards. H5554
Jdg 15:19 Then God opened up the **h place** in Lehi H4847
Isa 40:12 measured the waters in the **h of** his **hand**, H9123
Jer 52:21 each was four fingers thick, and **h**. H5554
2Co 9: 3 you in this matter *should* not **prove h**, G3033
Col 2: 8 you captive through **h** and deceptive G3031

HOLON (3)

Jos 15:51 Goshen, **H** and Giloh—eleven towns and H2708
Jos 21:15 **H**, Debir, H2708
Jer 48:21 to the plateau—to **H**, Jahzah and H2708

HOLPEN (KJV) HELP, HELPED, REINFORCE

HOLY (601) [HALLOWED, HOLIEST, HOLINESS]

Ge 2: 3 blessed the seventh day and **made** it **h**, H7727
Ex 3: 5 place where you are standing is **h** ground." H7731
Ex 15:13 you will guide them to your **h** dwelling. H7731
Ex 16:23 of sabbath rest, a **h** sabbath to the LORD. H7731
Ex 19: 6 me a kingdom of priests and a **h** nation. H7705
Ex 19:23 the mountain and **set** it **apart as h**. H7727
Ex 20: 8 the Sabbath day by **keeping** it **h**. H7727
Ex 20:11 blessed the Sabbath day and **made** it **h**. H7727
Ex 22:31 "You are to be my **h** people. So do not H7731
Ex 26:33 will separate the **H Place** from the Most H7731
Ex 26:33 Holy Place from the **Most H Place**. H7731+7731
Ex 26:34 covenant law in the **Most H Place**. H7731+7731
Ex 28:29 "Whenever Aaron enters the **H Place**, he H7731
Ex 28:35 he enters the **H Place** before the LORD H7731
Ex 28:36 engrave on it as on a seal: **H** TO THE LORD. H7731
Ex 28:43 the altar to minister in the **H Place**, H7731
Ex 29:30 to minister in the **H Place** is to wear them H7731
Ex 29:37 Then the altar will be **most h**, and H7731+7731
Ex 29:37 and whatever touches it *will be* **h**. H7727
Ex 30:10 It is **most h** to the LORD." H7731+7731
Ex 30:29 them so they will be **most h**, H7731+7731
Ex 30:29 whatever touches them *will be* **h**. H7727
Ex 30:36 It shall be **most h** to you. H7731+7731
Ex 30:37 yourselves; consider it **h** to the LORD. H7731
Ex 31:11 oil and fragrant incense for the **H Place**. H7731
Ex 31:13 that I am the LORD, *who* **makes** you **h**. H7727
Ex 31:14 the Sabbath, because it is **h** to you. H7731
Ex 31:15 day is a day of sabbath rest, **h** to the LORD. H7731
Ex 35: 2 the seventh day shall be your **h** day, H7731
Ex 39:30 an inscription on a seal: **H** TO THE LORD. H7731
Ex 40: 9 it and all its furnishings, and it will be **h**. H7731
Ex 40:10 the altar, and it will be **most h**. H7731+7731
Lev 2: 3 it is a **most h** *part* of the food H7731+7731
Lev 2:10 it is a **most h** *part* of the food H7731+7731
Lev 5:15 in regard to any of the LORD's **h things**, H7731
Lev 5:16 failed to do in regard to the **h things**, H7731
Lev 6:17 and the guilt offering, it is **most h**. H7731+7731
Lev 6:18 Whatever touches them *will become* **h**.'" H7727
Lev 6:25 offering is slaughtered; it is **most h**. H7731+7731
Lev 6:27 touches any of the flesh *will become* **h**, H7727
Lev 6:29 family may eat it; it is **most h**. H7731+7731
Lev 6:30 atonement in the **H Place** must not be H7731
Lev 7: 1 the guilt offering, which is **most h**: H7731+7731
Lev 7: 6 in the sanctuary area; it is **most h**. H7731+7731
Lev 10: 3 who approach me *I will* **be proved h**; H7727
Lev 10:10 between the **h** and the common, H7731
Lev 10:12 it beside the altar, for it is **most h**. H7731+7731
Lev 10:17 It is **most h**; it was given to you to H7731+7731
Lev 10:18 its blood was not taken into the **H Place**, H7731
Lev 11:44 consecrate yourselves and be **h**, because I H7705
Lev 11:44 yourselves and be holy, because I am **h**. H7705
Lev 11:45 therefore be **h**, because I am holy. H7705
Lev 11:45 therefore be holy, because I am **h**. H7705
Lev 14:13 belongs to the priest; it is **most h**. H7731+7731
Lev 16: 2 chooses into the **Most H Place** behind the H7731
Lev 16: 3 is how Aaron is to enter the **Most H Place**: H7731
Lev 16:16 the **Most H Place** because of the H7731
Lev 16:17 in the **Most H Place** until he comes H7731
Lev 16:20 making atonement for the **Most H Place**, H7731
Lev 16:23 on before he entered the **Most H Place**, H7731
Lev 16:27 brought into the **Most H Place** to make H7731
Lev 16:33 atonement for the **Most H Place**, H7731+5219
Lev 19: 2 'Be **h** because I, the LORD your God, am H7705
Lev 19: 2 holy because I, the LORD your God, am **h**. H7705
Lev 19: 8 have desecrated **what** is **h** *to* the LORD; H7731
Lev 19:24 In the fourth year all its fruit will be **h**, an H7731
Lev 20: 3 my sanctuary and profaned my **h** name. H7731
Lev 20: 7 "'Consecrate yourselves and be **h** H7705
Lev 20: 8 I am the LORD, *who* **makes** you **h**. H7727
Lev 20:26 You are to be **h** to me because I, the LORD H7705
Lev 20:26 the LORD, am **h**, and I have set you apart H7705
Lev 21: 6 They must be **h** to their God and must not H7705
Lev 21: 6 the food of their God, they are to be **h**. H7731
Lev 21: 7 because priests are **h** to their God. H7705
Lev 21: 8 **Regard** them **as h**, because they offer up H7727
Lev 21: 8 Consider them **h**, because I the LORD am H7705
Lev 21: 8 because I the LORD am **h**—I who make you H7705
Lev 21: 8 I the LORD am holy—I *who* **make** you **h**. H7727
Lev 21:15 I am the LORD, *who* **makes** him **h**.'" H7727
Lev 21:22 He may eat the **most h** food of his H7731+7731
Lev 21:22 food of his God, as well as the **h** food; H7731
Lev 21:23 I am the LORD, *who* **makes** them **h**.'" H7727
Lev 22: 2 so they will not profane my **h** name. H7731
Lev 22: 9 I am the LORD, *who* **makes** them **h**. H7727
Lev 22:16 I am the LORD, *who* **makes** them **h**.'" H7727
Lev 22:32 Do not profane my **h** name, for I must be H7731
Lev 22:32 for *I must* **be acknowledged as h** by the H7727
Lev 22:32 I am the LORD, *who* **made** you **h** H7727
Lev 24: 9 because it is a **most h** part of their H7731+7731
Lev 25:12 For it is a jubilee and is to be **h** for you H7731
Lev 27: 9 an animal given to the LORD becomes **h**. H7731
Lev 27:10 both it and the substitute become **h**. H7731
Lev 27:14 their house as **something h** to the LORD, H7731
Lev 27:21 it will become **h**, like a field devoted H7731
Lev 27:23 on that day as **something h** to the LORD. H7731
Lev 27:28 so devoted is **most h** to the LORD. H7731+7731
Lev 27:30 belongs to the LORD; it is **h** to the LORD. H7731
Lev 27:32 the shepherd's rod—will be **h** to the LORD. H7731
Lev 27:33 its substitute become **h** and cannot be H7731
Nu 4: 4 the care of the **most h things**. H7731+7731
Nu 4:15 covering the **h furnishings** and all the holy H7731
Nu 4:15 the holy furnishings and all the **h** articles, H7731
Nu 4:15 not touch the **h things** or they will die. H7731
Nu 4:16 including its **h furnishings** and articles." H7731
Nu 4:19 they come near the **most h things**, H7731+7731
Nu 4:20 must not go in to look at the **h things**, H7731
Nu 5:17 he shall take some **h** water in a clay jar H7705
Nu 6: 5 They must be **h** until the period of their H7705
Nu 6:20 they are **h** and belong to the priest H7731
Nu 7: 9 to carry on their shoulders the **h things**, H7731
Nu 10:21 Kohathites set out, carrying the **h things**. H5219
Nu 16: 3 The whole community is **h**, every one of H7705
Nu 16: 5 show who belongs to him and who is **h**, H7705
Nu 16: 7 the LORD chooses will be the one who is **h**. H7705
Nu 16:37 distance away, for the censers *are* **h**— H7727
Nu 16:38 before the LORD and *have become* **h**. H7727
Nu 18: 8 all the **h offerings** the Israelites give me I H7731
Nu 18: 9 part of the **most h offerings** that is H7731+7731
Nu 18: 9 they bring me as **most h offerings**, H7731+7731
Nu 18:10 Eat it as something **most h**; every H7731+7731
Nu 18:10 male shall eat it. You must regard it as **h**. H7731
Nu 18:17 of a cow, a sheep or a goat; they are **h**. H7731
Nu 18:19 aside from the **h offerings** the Israelites H7731
Nu 18:32 not defile the **h offerings** *of* the Israelites, H7731
Nu 20:12 me enough to **honor** me **as h** in the sight H7727
Nu 20:13 where *he was* **proved h** among them. H7727
Nu 27:14 command to **honor** me **as h** before their H7727
Nu 35:25 who was anointed with the **h** oil. H7731
Dt 5:12 "Observe the Sabbath day by **keeping** it **h** H7727
Dt 7: 6 For you are a people **h** to the LORD your H7705
Dt 14: 2 you are a people **h** to the LORD your H7705
Dt 14:21 you are a people **h** to the LORD your God H7705
Dt 23:14 Your camp must be **h**, so that he will not H7705
Dt 26:15 from heaven, your **h** dwelling place, and H7731
Dt 26:19 will be a people **h** to the LORD your God H7705
Dt 28: 9 LORD will establish you as his **h** people, H7705
Dt 33: 2 with myriads of **h ones** from the south, H7731
Dt 33: 3 people; all the **h** *ones* are in your hand. H7705
Jos 5:15 the place where you are standing is **h**." H7731
Jos 24:19 He is a **h** God; he is a jealous H7705
Jos 24:26 the oak near the **h place** *of* the LORD. H5219
1Sa 2: 2 "There is no *one* **h** like the LORD; there is H7705
1Sa 6:20 in the presence of the LORD, this **h** God? H7705
1Sa 21: 5 The men's bodies are **h** even on missions H7731
1Sa 21: 5 are holy even on missions that are **not h**. H2687
1Ki 6:16 inner sanctuary, the **Most H Place**. H7731+7731
1Ki 7:50 the **Most H Place**, and also H7731+7731
1Ki 8: 6 the **Most H Place**, and put it H7731+7731
1Ki 8: 8 be seen from the **H Place** in front of the H7731
1Ki 8: 8 not from outside the H Place; and they NDT
1Ki 8:10 the priests withdrew from the **H Place**, H7731
2Ki 4: 9 often comes our way is a **h** man of God. H7705
2Ki 19:22 Against the **H** *One of* Israel! H7705
1Ch 6:49 that was done in the **Most H Place**, H7731+7731
1Ch 16:10 Glory in his **h** name; let the hearts of H7731
1Ch 16:35 that we may give thanks to your **h** name H7731
1Ch 23:13 to consecrate the **most h things**, to H7731+7731
1Ch 23:32 meeting, for the **H Place** and, under their H7731
1Ch 29: 3 I have provided for this **h** temple: H7731
1Ch 29:16 a temple for your **H** Name comes from H7731
2Ch 3: 8 He built the **Most H Place**, its H7731+7731
2Ch 3:10 For the **Most H** Place he made a H7731+7731
2Ch 4:22 doors to the **Most H Place** and the H7731+7731
2Ch 5: 7 temple, the **Most H Place**, and put H7731+7731
2Ch 5: 9 not from outside the H Place; and they NDT
2Ch 5:11 priests then withdrew from the **H Place**. H7731
2Ch 8:11 the ark of the LORD has entered are **h**." H7731
2Ch 30:27 reached heaven, his **h** dwelling place. H7731
2Ch 31: 6 a tithe of the **h things** dedicated to the H7731
2Ch 35: 5 "Stand in the **h place** with a group of H7731
2Ch 35:13 boiled the **h offerings** in pots H7731
Ezr 9: 2 have mingled the **h** race with the H7731
Ne 8: 9 "This day is **h** to the LORD your God. H7705
Ne 8:10 This day is **h** to our Lord. Do not H7705
Ne 8:11 "Be still, for this is a **h** day. H7705
Ne 9:14 known to them your **h** Sabbath and gave H7731
Ne 10:31 them on the Sabbath or on any **h** day. H7731
Ne 10:33 festivals; for the **h offerings**; for sin H7731
Ne 11: 1 live in Jerusalem, the **h** city, while the H7731
Ne 11:18 The Levites in the **h** city totaled 284. H7731
Ne 13:22 gates in order to **keep** the Sabbath day **h**. H7727
Job 5: 1 To which of the **h** *ones* will you turn? H7705
Job 6:10 I had not denied the words of the **H One**. H7705
Job 15:15 If God places no trust in his **h** *ones*, if H7705
Ps 2: 6 my king on Zion, my **h** mountain. H7731
Ps 3: 4 he answers me from his **h** mountain. H7731
Ps 5: 7 I bow down toward your **h** temple. H7731
Ps 11: 4 The LORD is in his **h** temple; the LORD is on H7731
Ps 15: 1 Who may live on your **h** mountain? H7731
Ps 16: 3 I say of the **h people** who are in the land H7705
Ps 22: 3 Yet you are enthroned as the **H One**; you H7705
Ps 24: 3 Who may stand in his **h** place? H7731
Ps 28: 2 hands toward your **Most H Place**. H7731+1808
Ps 30: 4 you his faithful people; praise his **h** name. H7731
Ps 33:21 hearts rejoice, for we trust in his **h** name. H7731
Ps 34: 9 the LORD, you his **h people**, for those who H7705
Ps 43: 3 let them bring me to your **h** mountain, to H7731
Ps 46: 4 the **h** *place* where the Most High dwells. H7705
Ps 47: 8 nations; God is seated on his **h** throne. H7731
Ps 48: 1 in the city of our God, his **h** mountain. H7731
Ps 51:11 presence or take your **H** Spirit from me. H7731
Ps 65: 4 things of your house, of your **h** temple. H7705
Ps 68: 5 of widows, is God in his **h** dwelling. H7731
Ps 71:22 to you with the lyre, **H One** *of* Israel. H7705
Ps 77:13 Your ways, God, are **h**. What god is as H7731
Ps 78:41 to the test; they vexed the **H One** *of* Israel. H7705
Ps 78:54 brought them to the border of his **h** land, H7731
Ps 79: 1 they have defiled your **h** temple, they H7731
Ps 87: 1 has founded his city on the **h** mountain. H7731
Ps 89: 5 in the assembly of the **h** *ones*. H7705
Ps 89: 7 In the council of the **h** *ones* God is greatly H7705
Ps 89:18 the LORD, our king to the **H One** *of* Israel. H7705
Ps 97:12 are righteous, and praise his **h** name. H7731
Ps 98: 1 his right hand and his **h** arm have worked H7731
Ps 99: 3 your great and awesome name—he is **h**. H7705
Ps 99: 5 God and worship at his footstool; he is **h**. H7705
Ps 99: 9 our God and worship at his **h** mountain, H7731
Ps 99: 9 holy mountain, for the LORD our God is **h**. H7705
Ps 103: 1 all my inmost being, praise his **h** name. H7731
Ps 105: 3 Glory in his **h** name; let the hearts of H7731
Ps 105:42 he remembered his **h** promise given to H7731
Ps 106:47 give thanks to your **h** name and glory in H7731
Ps 110: 3 Arrayed in **h** splendor, your young men H7731
Ps 111: 9 forever—**h** and awesome is his name. H7705
Ps 138: 2 bow down toward your **h** temple and will H7731
Ps 145:21 creature praise his **h** name for ever and H7731
Pr 9:10 knowledge of the **H One** is understanding H7705
Pr 30: 3 I attained to the knowledge of the **H One**. H7705
Ecc 8:10 go from the **h** place and receive H7705
Isa 1: 4 have spurned the **H One** *of* Israel and H7705
Isa 4: 3 will be called **h**, all who are recorded H7705
Isa 5:16 the **h** God will be proved holy by his H7705
Isa 5:16 the holy God *will* **be proved h** by his H7727
Isa 5:19 The plan of the **H One** *of* Israel—let it H7705
Isa 5:24 spurned the word of the **H One** *of* Israel. H7705
Isa 6: 3 "**H**, holy, holy is the LORD Almighty; the H7705
Isa 6: 3 **h**, holy is the LORD Almighty; the H7705
Isa 6: 3 **h** is the LORD Almighty; the whole H7705
Isa 6:13 so the **h** seed will be the stump in the H7731
Isa 8:13 is the one *you are to* **regard as h**, H7727
Isa 8:14 He will be a **h place**; for both Israel and H5219
Isa 10:17 become a fire, their **H One** a flame; in a H7705
Isa 10:20 truly rely on the LORD, the **H One** *of* Israel. H7705
Isa 11: 9 harm nor destroy on all my **h** mountain, H7731
Isa 12: 6 great is the **H One** *of* Israel among you H7705
Isa 17: 7 turn their eyes to the **H One** *of* Israel. H7705
Isa 27:13 the LORD on the **h** mountain in Jerusalem. H7731
Isa 29:19 needy will rejoice in the **H One** *of* Israel. H7705
Isa 29:23 my hands, *they will* **keep** my name **h**; they H7727
Isa 29:23 the holiness of the **H One** *of* Jacob, H7705
Isa 30:11 confronting us with the **H One** *of* Israel!" H7705
Isa 30:12 this is what the **H One** *of* Israel says: H7705
Isa 30:15 Sovereign LORD, the **H One** *of* Israel, says: H7705
Isa 30:29 as on the night you **celebrate** a **h** festival; H7727
Isa 31: 1 do not look to the **H One** *of* Israel, or H7705
Isa 37:23 Against the **H One** *of* Israel! H7705
Isa 40:25 Or who is my equal?" says the **H One**. H7705
Isa 41:14 your Redeemer, the **H One** *of* Israel. H7705
Isa 41:16 the LORD and glory in the **H One** *of* Israel. H7705
Isa 41:20 that the **H One** *of* Israel has created it. H7705
Isa 43: 3 LORD your God, the **H One** *of* Israel, your H7705
Isa 43:14 your Redeemer, the **H One** *of* Israel: H7705
Isa 43:15 I am the LORD, your **H One**, Israel's H7705
Isa 45:11 LORD says—the **H One** *of* Israel, and its H7705
Isa 47: 4 is his name—is the **H One** *of* Israel. H7705
Isa 48: 2 citizens of the **h** city and claim to rely on H7731
Isa 48:17 your Redeemer, the **H One** *of* Israel: H7705
Isa 49: 7 the Redeemer and **H One** *of* Israel—to H7705
Isa 49: 7 is faithful, the **H One** *of* Israel, who has H7731
Isa 52: 1 of splendor, Jerusalem, the **h** city. H7731
Isa 52:10 LORD will lay bare his **h** arm in the sight of H7731
Isa 54: 5 the **H One** *of* Israel is your Redeemer H7705

Isa 55: 5 LORD your God, the **H One** *of* Israel, for he H7705
Isa 56: 7 I will bring to my **h** mountain and give H7731
Isa 57:13 the land and possess my **h** mountain." H7731
Isa 57:15 he who lives forever, whose name is **h**: H7705
Isa 57:15 "I live in a high and **h** *place*, but also with H7705
Isa 58:13 from doing as you please on my **h** day, H7731
Isa 58:13 a delight and the LORD's **h** day honorable, H7705
Isa 60: 9 LORD your God, the **H One** *of* Israel, for he H7705
Isa 60:14 of the LORD, Zion of the **H One** *of* Israel. H7705
Isa 62:12 They will be called the **H** People, the H7731
Isa 63:10 Yet they rebelled and grieved his **H** Spirit H7731
Isa 63:11 is he who set his **H** Spirit among them, H7731
Isa 63:15 from your lofty throne, **h** and glorious. H7731
Isa 63:18 your people possessed your **h place**, H7731
Isa 64:11 Our **h** and glorious temple, where our H7731
Isa 65:11 the LORD and forget my **h** mountain, H7731
Isa 65:25 harm nor destroy on all my **h** mountain," H7731
Isa 66:20 to my **h** mountain in Jerusalem as an H7731
Jer 2: 3 Israel was **h** to the LORD, the firstfruits of H7731
Jer 17:22 Sabbath, but **keep** the Sabbath day **h**, as I H7727
Jer 17:24 **keep** the Sabbath day **h** by not doing H7727
Jer 17:27 me to **keep** the Sabbath day **h** by not H7727
Jer 23: 9 because of the LORD and his **h** words. H7731
Jer 25:30 will thunder from his **h** dwelling and roar H7731
Jer 31:40 of the Horse Gate, will be **h** to the LORD. H7731
Jer 50:29 has defied the LORD, the **H One** *of* Israel. H7705
Jer 51: 5 is full of guilt before the **H One** *of* Israel. H7705
Jer 51:51 have entered the **h places** *of* the LORD's H5219
Eze 20:12 would know that I the LORD **made** them **h**. H7727
Eze 20:20 **Keep** my Sabbaths **h**, that they may be a H7727
Eze 20:39 longer profane my **h** name with your gifts H7731
Eze 20:40 For on my **h** mountain, the high mountain H7731
Eze 20:40 along with all your **h** sacrifices. H7731
Eze 20:41 and *I will* **be proved h** through you in the H7727
Eze 22: 8 despised my **h things** and desecrated H7731
Eze 22:26 to my law and profane my **h things**; H7731
Eze 22:26 between the **h** and the common; H7731
Eze 28:14 You were on the **h** mount of God; you H7731
Eze 28:22 on you and within you *am* **proved to be h**. H7727
Eze 28:25 *I will* **be proved h** through them in the H7727
Eze 36:20 the nations they profaned my **h** name, H7731
Eze 36:21 I had concern for my **h** name, which the H7731
Eze 36:22 for the sake of my **h** name, which you H7731
Eze 36:23 when I *am* **proved h** through you before H7727
Eze 37:28 will know that I the LORD **make** Israel **h**, H7727
Eze 38:16 know me when I *am* **proved h** through you H7727
Eze 39: 7 will make known my **h** name among my H7731
Eze 39: 7 no longer let my **h** name be profaned, H7731
Eze 39: 7 that I the LORD am the **H One** in Israel. H7705
Eze 39:25 I will be zealous for my **h** name. H7731
Eze 39:27 *I will* **be proved h** through them in the H7727
Eze 41: 4 to me, "This is the **Most H Place**." H7731+7731
Eze 41:21 the front of the **Most H Place** was similar. H7731
Eze 41:23 hall and the **Most H Place** had double H7731
Eze 42:13 LORD will eat the **most h offerings**. H7731+7731
Eze 42:13 they will put the **most h offerings**— H7731+7731
Eze 42:13 the guilt offerings—for the place is **h**. H7705
Eze 42:14 Once the priests enter the **h precincts**, they H7731
Eze 42:14 in which they minister, for these are **h**. H7731
Eze 42:20 to separate the **h** from the common. H7731
Eze 43: 7 will never again defile my **h** name— H7731
Eze 43: 8 they defiled my **h** name by their H7731
Eze 43:12 top of the mountain will be **most h**. H7731+7731
Eze 44: 8 out your duty in regard to my **h things**, H7731
Eze 44:13 near any of my **h things** or my most holy H7731
Eze 44:13 holy things or my **most h offerings**; H7731+7731
Eze 44:23 between the **h** and the common and H7731
Eze 44:24 and *they are to* **keep** my Sabbaths **h**. H7727
Eze 45: 1 cubits wide; the entire area will be **h**. H7731
Eze 45: 3 be the sanctuary, the **Most H Place**. H7731+7731
Eze 45: 4 as well as a **h place** for the sanctuary. H5219
Eze 48:12 of the land, a **most h** portion H7731+7731
Eze 48:14 other hands, because it is **h** to the LORD. H7731
Da 4: 8 the spirit of the **h** gods is in him. A10620
Da 4: 9 that the spirit of the **h** gods is in you, A10620
Da 4:13 there before me was a **h** *one*, A10620
Da 4:17 the **h** *ones* declare the verdict A10620
Da 4:18 because the spirit of the **h** gods is in you." A10620
Da 4:23 "Your Majesty saw a **h** *one*, a messenger A10620
Da 5:11 who has the spirit of the **h** gods in him. A10620
Da 7:18 But the **h people** *of* the Most High will A10620
Da 7:21 war against the **h people** and defeating A10620
Da 7:22 favor of the **h people** *of* the Most High, A10620
Da 7:25 oppress his **h people** and try to A10620
Da 7:25 The **h** people will be delivered into his NDT
Da 7:27 handed over to the **h** people of the Most A10620
Da 8:13 Then I heard a **h** *one* speaking, and H7705
Da 8:13 another **h** *one* said to him, "How H7705
Da 8:24 those who are mighty, the **h** people. H7705
Da 9:16 from Jerusalem, your city, your **h** hill. H7731
Da 9:20 request to the LORD my God for his **h** hill—H7731
Da 9:24 your people and your **h** city to finish H7731
Da 9:24 and to anoint the **Most H Place**. H7731+7731
Da 11:28 heart will be set against the **h** covenant. H7731
Da 11:30 vent his fury against the **h** covenant. H7731
Da 11:30 favor to those who forsake the **h** covenant. H7731
Da 11:45 the seas at the beautiful **h** mountain. H7731
Da 12: 7 the power of the **h** people has been H7731
Hos 11: 9 not a man—the **H One** among you. H7705
Hos 11:12 even against the faithful **H One**. H7705
Joel 1:14 **Declare** *a* **h** fast; call a sacred assembly H7727
Joel 2: 1 in Zion; sound the alarm on my **h** hill. H7731
Joel 2:15 trumpet in Zion, **declare** a **h** fast, call a H7727
Joel 3:17 LORD your God, dwell in Zion, my **h** hill. H7731
Joel 3:17 Jerusalem will be **h**; never again will H7731
Am 2: 7 the same girl and so profane my **h** name. H7731
Ob 16 Just as you drank on my **h** hill, so all the H7731
Ob 17 it will be **h**, and Jacob will possess H7731
Jnh 2: 4 I will look again toward your **h** temple. H7731
Jnh 2: 7 my prayer rose to you, to your **h** temple. H7731
Mic 1: 2 against you, the Lord from his **h** temple. H7731
Hab 1:12 My God, my **H One**, you will never die H7705
Hab 2:20 The LORD is in his **h** temple; let all the H7731
Hab 3: 3 Teman, the **H One** from Mount Paran. H7705
Zep 3:11 again will you be haughty on my **h** hill. H7731
Zec 2:12 as his portion in the **h** land and will again H7731
Zec 2:13 has roused himself from his **h** dwelling." H7731
Zec 8: 3 Almighty will be called the **H** Mountain." H7731
Zec 14: 5 will come, and all the **h** *ones* with him. H7705
Zec 14:20 that day **H** TO THE LORD will be inscribed H7731
Zec 14:21 Judah will be **h** to the LORD Almighty, H7731
Mt 1:18 found to be pregnant through the **H** Spirit. *G41*
Mt 1:20 what is conceived in her is from the **H** Spirit. *G41*
Mt 3:11 He will baptize you with the **H** Spirit and fire. *G41*
Mt 4: 5 devil took him to the **h** city and had him *G41*
Mt 12:32 who speaks against the **H** Spirit will not be *G41*
Mt 24:15 see standing in the **h** place 'the *G41*
Mt 27:52 The bodies *of* many **h** *people* who had died *G41*
Mt 27:53 went into the **h** city and appeared to *G41*
Mt 28:19 Father and of the Son and *of* the **H** Spirit, *G41*
Mk 1: 8 he will baptize you with the **H** Spirit. *G41*
Mk 1:24 I know who you are—the **H** *One* of God!" *G41*
Mk 3:29 against the **H** Spirit will never be *G41*
Mk 6:20 knowing him to be a righteous and **h** man. *G41*
Mk 8:38 in his Father's glory with the **h** angels." *G41*
Mk 12:36 speaking by the **H** Spirit, declared: *G41*
Mk 13:11 it is not you speaking, but the **H** Spirit. *G41*
Lk 1:15 be filled with the **H** Spirit even before he *G41*
Lk 1:35 answered, "The **H** Spirit will come on you *G41*
Lk 1:35 So the **h** *one* to be born will be called the *G41*
Lk 1:41 Elizabeth was filled with the **H** Spirit. *G41*
Lk 1:49 done great things for me—**h** is his name. *G41*
Lk 1:67 was filled with the **H** Spirit and prophesied: *G41*
Lk 1:70 he said through his **h** prophets of long ago), *G41*
Lk 1:72 ancestors and to remember his **h** covenant, *G41*
Lk 2:25 of Israel, and the **H** Spirit was on him. *G41*
Lk 2:26 to him by the **H** Spirit that he would *G41*
Lk 3:16 He will baptize you with the **H** Spirit and fire. *G41*
Lk 3:22 the **H** Spirit descended on him in bodily *G41*
Lk 4: 1 full of the **H** Spirit, left the Jordan and *G41*
Lk 4:34 I know who you are—the **H** *One* of God!" *G41*
Lk 9:26 the glory of the Father and *of* the **h** angels. *G41*
Lk 10:21 full of joy through the **H** Spirit, said, *G41*
Lk 11:13 in heaven give the **H** Spirit to those who ask *G41*
Lk 12:10 blasphemes against the **H** Spirit will not be *G41*
Lk 12:12 the **H** Spirit will teach you at that time *G41*
Jn 1:33 is the one who will baptize with the **H** Spirit. *G41*
Jn 6:69 to know that you are the **H** *One* of God." *G41*
Jn 14:26 But the Advocate, the **H** Spirit, whom the *G41*
Jn 17:11 **H** Father, protect them by the power of your *G41*
Jn 20:22 on them and said, "Receive the **H** Spirit. *G41*
Ac 1: 2 through the **H** Spirit to the apostles *G41*
Ac 1: 5 days you will be baptized with the **H** Spirit." *G41*
Ac 1: 8 power when the **H** Spirit comes on you; *G41*
Ac 1:16 fulfilled in which the **H** Spirit spoke long ago *G41*
Ac 2: 4 were filled with the **H** Spirit and began to *G41*
Ac 2:27 you will not let your **h** *one* see decay. *G4008*
Ac 2:33 Father the promised **H** Spirit and has poured *G41*
Ac 2:38 And you will receive the gift *of* the **H** Spirit. *G41*
Ac 3:14 You disowned the **H** and Righteous One *G41*
Ac 3:21 promised long ago through his **h** prophets. *G41*
Ac 4: 8 filled with the **H** Spirit, said to them: *G41*
Ac 4:25 You spoke by the **H** Spirit through the mouth *G41*
Ac 4:27 city to conspire against your **h** servant Jesus, *G41*
Ac 4:30 through the name of your **h** servant Jesus." *G41*
Ac 4:31 all filled with the **H** Spirit and spoke the *G41*
Ac 5: 3 you have lied to the **H** Spirit and have kept *G41*
Ac 5:32 and so is the **H** Spirit, whom God has *G41*
Ac 6: 5 a man full of faith and of the **H** Spirit; also *G41*
Ac 6:13 against this **h** place and against the *G41*
Ac 7:33 place where you are standing is **h** ground. *G41*
Ac 7:51 You always resist the **H** Spirit! *G41*
Ac 7:55 But Stephen, full of the **H** Spirit, looked up to *G41*
Ac 8:15 there that they might receive the **H** Spirit, *G41*
Ac 8:16 because the **H** Spirit had not yet come on NDT
Ac 8:17 on them, and they received the **H** Spirit. *G41*
Ac 8:19 I lay my hands may receive the **H** Spirit." *G41*
Ac 9:13 he has done *to* your **h people** in Jerusalem. *G41*
Ac 9:17 see again and be filled with the **H** Spirit." *G41*
Ac 9:31 of the Lord and encouraged by the **H** Spirit, *G41*
Ac 10:22 A **h** angel told him to ask you to come to his *G41*
Ac 10:38 of Nazareth with the **H** Spirit and power, *G41*
Ac 10:44 the **H** Spirit came on all who heard the *G41*
Ac 10:45 that the gift of the **H** Spirit had been poured *G41*
Ac 10:47 have received the **H** Spirit just as we have *G41*
Ac 11:15 the **H** Spirit came on them as he had come *G41*
Ac 11:16 you will be baptized with the **H** Spirit. *G41*
Ac 11:24 good man, full of the **H** Spirit and faith, and *G41*
Ac 13: 2 Lord and fasting, the **H** Spirit said, "Set apart *G41*
Ac 13: 4 sent on their way by the **H** Spirit, went down *G41*
Ac 13: 9 filled with the **H** Spirit, looked straight *G41*
Ac 13:34 you the **h** and sure **blessings promised** to *G4008*
Ac 13:35 " 'You will not let your **h** *one* see decay.' *G4008*
Ac 13:52 were filled with joy and with the **H** Spirit. *G41*
Ac 15: 8 them by giving the **H** Spirit to them, *G41*
Ac 15:28 It seemed good to the **H** Spirit and to us not *G41*
Ac 16: 6 been kept by the **H** Spirit from preaching *G41*
Ac 19: 2 "Did you receive the **H** Spirit when you *G41*
Ac 19: 2 have not even heard that there is a **H** Spirit." *G41*
Ac 19: 6 hands on them, the **H** Spirit came on them *G41*
Ac 20:23 that in every city the **H** Spirit warns me that *G41*
Ac 20:28 the flock of which the **H** Spirit has made you *G41*
Ac 21:11 with it and said, "The **H** Spirit says, 'In this *G41*
Ac 21:28 into the temple and defiled this **h** place." *G41*
Ac 28:25 "The **H** Spirit spoke the truth to your *G41*
Ro 1: 2 through his prophets in the **H** Scriptures *G41*
Ro 1: 7 loved by God and called to be his **h** *people*: *G41*
Ro 5: 5 out into our hearts through the **H** Spirit, *G41*
Ro 7:12 the law is **h**, and the commandment *G41*
Ro 7:12 the commandment is **h**, righteous and *G41*
Ro 9: 1 conscience confirms it through the **H** Spirit— *G41*
Ro 11:16 part of the dough offered as firstfruits is **h**, *G41*
Ro 11:16 then the whole batch is **h**; if the root is holy, NDT
Ro 11:16 if the root is **h**, so are the branches. *G41*
Ro 12: 1 as a living sacrifice, **h** and pleasing to God *G41*
Ro 14:17 righteousness, peace and joy in the **H** Spirit, *G41*
Ro 15:13 with hope by the power of the **H** Spirit. *G41*
Ro 15:16 acceptable to God, sanctified by the **H** Spirit. *G41*
Ro 16:16 Greet one another with a **h** kiss. All the *G41*
1Co 1: 2 Christ Jesus and called to be **his h people**, *G41*
1Co 6:19 that your bodies are temples *of* the **H** Spirit, *G41*
1Co 7:14 would be unclean, but as it is, they are **h**. *G41*
1Co 12: 3 "Jesus is Lord," except by the **H** Spirit. *G41*
1Co 16:20 Greet one another with a **h** kiss. *G41*
2Co 1: 1 with all his **h people** throughout Achaia: *G41*
2Co 6: 6 kindness; in the **H** Spirit and in sincere love; *G41*
2Co 13:12 Greet one another with a **h** kiss. *G41*
2Co 13:14 the fellowship *of* the **H** Spirit be with *G41*
Eph 1: 1 will of God, *To* **God's h people** in Ephesus *G41*
Eph 1: 4 of the world to be **h** and blameless in his *G41*
Eph 1:13 in him with a seal, the promised **H** Spirit, *G41*
Eph 1:18 of his glorious inheritance in his **h people**, *G41*
Eph 2:21 rises to become a **h** temple in the Lord. *G41*
Eph 3: 5 the Spirit to God's **h** apostles and prophets. *G41*
Eph 3:18 together with all **the Lord's h people**, to *G41*
Eph 4:30 And do not grieve the **H** Spirit of God, with *G41*
Eph 5: 3 these are improper *for* **God's h people**. *G41*
Eph 5:26 to **make** her **h**, cleansing her by the washing *G39*
Eph 5:27 any other blemish, but **h** and blameless. *G41*
Php 1: 1 To all **God's h people** in Christ Jesus at *G41*
Col 1: 2 *To* **God's h people** in Colossae, the faithful *G41*
Col 1:12 inheritance *of* **his h people** in the kingdom *G41*
Col 1:22 through death to present you **h** in his sight, *G41*
Col 3:12 as God's chosen people, **h** and dearly loved *G41*
1Th 1: 5 with the **H** Spirit and deep conviction. *G41*
1Th 1: 6 suffering with the joy given by the **H** Spirit. *G41*
1Th 2:10 so is God, of how **h**, righteous and *G4010*
1Th 3:13 will be blameless and **h** in the presence of *G43*
1Th 3:13 our Lord Jesus comes with all his **h** *ones*. *G41*
1Th 4: 4 own body in a way that is **h** and honorable, *G40*
1Th 4: 7 not call us to be impure, but to live a **h** *life*. *G40*
1Th 4: 8 the very God who gives you his **H** Spirit. *G41*
1Th 5:26 Greet all God's people with a **h** kiss. *G41*
2Th 1:10 glorified in his **h** *people* and to be marveled *G41*
1Ti 2: 8 lifting up **h** hands without anger or *G4008*
2Ti 1: 9 He has saved us and called us to a **h** life *G41*
2Ti 1:14 with the help of the **H** Spirit who lives in us. *G41*
2Ti 2:21 special purposes, **made h**, useful to the *G39*
2Ti 3:15 infancy you have known the **H** Scriptures, *G2641*
Titus 1: 8 self-controlled, upright, **h** and disciplined. *G4008*
Titus 3: 5 of rebirth and renewal by the **H** Spirit, *G41*
Phm 5 love for all **his h people** and your faith in *G41*
Heb 2: 4 by gifts *of* the **H** Spirit distributed *G4460*
Heb 2:11 Both the *one who* **makes** people **h** and those *G39*
Heb 2:11 those who *are* **made h** are of the same *G39*
Heb 3: 1 Therefore, **h** brothers and sisters, who share *G41*
Heb 3: 7 as the **H** Spirit says: "Today, if you hear *G41*
Heb 6: 4 who have shared in the **H** Spirit, *G41*
Heb 7:26 our need—one who is **h**, blameless, *G4008*
Heb 9: 2 this was called the **H Place**. *G41*
Heb 9: 3 was a room called the **Most H Place**, *G41+41*
Heb 9: 8 The **H** Spirit was showing by this that the way *G41*
Heb 9: 8 the way *into* the **Most H Place** had not yet *G41*
Heb 9:12 he entered the **Most H Place** once for all by *G41*
Heb 9:25 enters the **Most H Place** every year with *G41*
Heb 10:10 we have been **made h** through the sacrifice *G39*
Heb 10:14 perfect forever those *who are being* **made h**. *G39*
Heb 10:15 The **H** Spirit also testifies to us about this *G41*
Heb 10:19 to enter the **Most H Place** by the blood of *G41*
Heb 11: 7 *in* **h fear** built an ark to save his family. *G2326*
Heb 12:14 to live in peace with everyone and to be **h**; *G40*
Heb 13:11 animals into the **Most H Place** as a sin *G41*
Heb 13:12 city gate to **make** the people **h** through his *G39*
1Pe 1:12 gospel to you by the **H** Spirit sent from *G41*
1Pe 1:15 But just as he who called you is **h**, so be holy *G41*
1Pe 1:15 who called you is holy, so be **h** in all you do; *G41*
1Pe 1:16 it is written: "Be **h**, because I am holy." *G41*
1Pe 1:16 it is written: "Be holy, because I am **h**." *G41*
1Pe 2: 5 into a spiritual house to be a **h** priesthood, *G41*
1Pe 2: 9 a royal priesthood, a **h** nation, God's special *G41*
1Pe 3: 5 this is the way the **h** women of the past who *G41*
2Pe 1:21 as they were carried along by the **H** Spirit. *G41*
2Pe 3: 2 in the past by the **h** prophets and the *G41*
2Pe 3:11 You ought to live **h** and godly lives *G41*
1Jn 2:20 But you have an anointing from the **H** *One* *G41*
Jude 3 once for all entrusted *to* **God's h people**. *G41*

Jude 14 thousands upon thousands *of* his **h** *ones* G41
Jude 20 up in your *most* **h** faith and praying in G41
Jude 20 most holy faith and praying in the **H** Spirit, G41
Rev 3: 7 are the words of him who is **h** and true, G41
Rev 4: 8 " '**H**, holy, holy is the Lord God Almighty,' G41
Rev 4: 8 **h**, holy is the Lord God Almighty,' G41
Rev 4: 8 holy, **h** is the Lord God Almighty,' G41
Rev 6:10 Sovereign Lord, **h** and true, until you judge G41
Rev 11: 2 will trample on the **h** city for 42 months. G41
Rev 13: 7 war against **God's h people** and to conquer G41
Rev 14:10 the presence of the **h** angels and of the G41
Rev 15: 4 For you alone are **h**. All nations will come G4008
Rev 16: 5 judgments, O **H** *One*, you who are and G4008
Rev 16: 6 shed the blood *of* **your h people** and your G41
Rev 17: 6 was drunk with the blood *of* **God's h people**, G41
Rev 18:24 blood of prophets and *of* **God's h people**, G41
Rev 19: 8 the righteous acts *of* **God's h people**.) G41
Rev 20: 6 Blessed and **h** are those who share in the G41
Rev 21: 2 I saw the **H** City, the new Jerusalem, coming G41
Rev 21:10 and showed me the **H** City, Jerusalem, G41
Rev 22:11 let the **h** *person* continue to be holy. G41
Rev 22:11 and *let* the holy person continue *to be* **h**." G39
Rev 22:19 share in the tree of life and in the **H** City, G41

HOLYDAY (KJV) FESTIVE, RELIGIOUS FESTIVAL

HOMAGE (3)

2Ch 24:17 of Judah came and **paid h** to the king, H2556
Job 31:27 **offered** them **a kiss of h**, H5975+4200+7023
Mk 15:19 on their knees, *they* **paid h** to him. G4686

HOMAM (2)

Ge 36:22 Hori and **H**. Timna was Lotan's H2123
1Ch 1:39 Hori and **H**. Timna was Lotan's H2102

HOME (191) [HOMELAND, HOMELESS, HOMES]

Ge 18:33 and Abraham returned **h**. H5226
Ge 25:27 was content *to* **stay at h** *among* the tents. H3782
Ge 29:13 kissed him and brought him to his **h**, H1074
Ge 31:55 Then he left and returned **h**. H5226
Ge 34: 5 he did nothing about it until they **came h**. H995
Ge 35:27 Jacob **came h** to his father Isaac in Mamre H995
Ge 39:16 cloak beside her until his master came **h**. H1074
Ge 43:26 When Joseph came **h**, they presented to H1074
Ex 3: 8 milk and honey—the **h** *of* the Canaanites H5226
Ex 18:23 all these people will go **h** satisfied." H5226
Lev 18: 9 she was **born in the same h** or H4580+1074
Nu 14:30 I swore with uplifted hand to **make** your **h**, H8905
Nu 15: 2 you enter the land I am giving you as a **h** H4632
Nu 24:11 Now leave at once and go **h**! I said I H5226
Nu 24:25 Then Balaam got up and returned **h**, and H5226
Nu 30:16 his young daughter still living at **h**. H1074
Dt 6: 7 when you sit at **h** and when you walk H1074
Dt 11:19 when you sit at **h** and when you walk H1074
Dt 20: 5 Let him go **h**, or he may die in battle and H1074
Dt 20: 6 Let him go **h**, or he may die in battle and H1074
Dt 20: 7 Let him go **h**, or he may die in battle and H1074
Dt 20: 8 Let him go **h** so that his fellow soldiers H1074
Dt 21:12 Bring her into your **h** and have her shave H1074
Dt 22: 2 take it **h** with you and keep it until they H1074
Dt 24: 5 be free to stay at **h** and bring happiness H1074
Jos 9:12 when we packed it at **h** on the day we left H1074
Jos 20: 6 go back to their own **h** in the town from H1074
Jos 22: 7 When Joshua sent them **h**, he blessed H185
Jdg 7: 7 Let all the others go **h**." H5226+2257
Jdg 7: 8 of the Israelites **h** but kept the three H185+2257
Jdg 8:29 son of Joash went back **h** to live. H1074
Jdg 9: 5 to his father's **h** in Ophrah and on one H1074
Jdg 9:55 that Abimelek was dead, they went **h**. H5226
Jdg 11:34 Jephthah returned to his **h** in Mizpah, H1074
Jdg 14:19 with anger, he returned to his father's **h**. H1074
Jdg 18:26 him, turned around and went back **h**. H1074
Jdg 19: 2 went back to her parents' **h** in Bethlehem, H1074
Jdg 19: 3 She took him into her parents' **h**, and H1074
Jdg 19: 9 you can get up and be on your way **h**." H185
Jdg 19:28 put her on his donkey and set out for **h**. H5226
Jdg 19:29 When he reached **h**, he took a knife and H1074
Jdg 20: 8 saying, "None of us will go **h**. H185
Jdg 21:24 left that place and went **h** to their tribes NDT
Ru 1: 6 prepared to return **h** from there. NDT
Ru 1: 8 "Go back, each of you, to your mother's **h**. H1074
Ru 1: 9 will find rest in the **h** *of* another husband." H1074
Ru 1:11 Naomi said, "Return **h**, my daughters. NDT
Ru 1:12 Return **h**, my daughters; I am too old to have NDT
Ru 3: 1 I must find a **h** for you, where you will H4955
Ru 4:11 is coming into your **h** like Rachel and H1074
1Sa 1:19 then went back to their **h** at Ramah. H1074
1Sa 1:23 So the woman **stayed at h** and nursed her H3782
1Sa 2:11 Then Elkanah went **h** to Ramah, but the H1074
1Sa 2:20 gave to the LORD." Then they would go **h**. H5226
1Sa 7:17 to Ramah, where his **h** was, and there he H1074
1Sa 10:26 Saul also went to his **h** in Gibeah, H1074
1Sa 15:34 Saul went up to his **h** *in* Gibeah of Saul. H1074
1Sa 18: 2 did not let him return **h** to his family. H1074
1Sa 18: 6 men were returning **h** after David had killed NDT
1Sa 23:18 Then Jonathan went **h**, but David H1074
1Sa 24:22 Then Saul returned **h**, but David and his H1074
1Sa 25: 1 they buried him at his **h** in Ramah. H1074
1Sa 25:35 brought him and said, "Go **h** in peace. H1074
1Sa 26:25 went on his way, and Saul returned **h**. H5226
2Sa 3:16 said to him, "Go back **h**!" So he went back. NDT
2Sa 6:20 When David returned **h** to bless his NDT
2Sa 7:10 so that *they can* **have a h** *of* their H8905+9393
2Sa 11: 4 Then she went back **h**. H1074
2Sa 11:10 "Uriah did not go **h**." So he asked Uriah, H1074
2Sa 11:10 Why didn't you go **h**?" H1074
2Sa 11:13 his master's servants; he did not go **h**. H1074
2Sa 12:15 After Nathan had gone **h**, the LORD struck H1074
2Sa 14: 8 to the woman, "Go **h**, and I will issue an H1074
2Sa 19:30 my lord the king has returned **h** safely." H1074
2Sa 19:39 farewell, and Barzillai returned to his **h**. H5226
2Sa 20:22 from the city, each returning to his **h**. H185
1Ki 1:53 Solomon said, "Go to your **h**. H1074
1Ki 2:34 he was buried at his **h** out in the country. H1074
1Ki 5:14 month in Lebanon and two months at **h**. H1074
1Ki 8:66 They blessed the king and then went **h** H185
1Ki 12:16 So the Israelites went **h**. H185
1Ki 12:24 Go **h**, every one of you, for this is my H1074
1Ki 12:24 the word of the LORD and **went h** again, H2143
1Ki 13: 7 man of God, "Come **h** with me for a meal H1074
1Ki 13:15 said to him, "Come **h** with me and eat." H1074
1Ki 14:12 "As for you, go back **h**. When you set foot H1074
1Ki 16: 9 getting drunk in the **h** *of* Arza, the palace H1074
1Ki 17:12 a few sticks *to* **take h** and make a meal H995
1Ki 17:13 **Go h** and do as you have said H995
1Ki 21: 4 So Ahab went **h**, sullen and angry H1074
1Ki 22:17 Let each one go **h** in peace.' " H1074
2Ki 4:13 "**I have a h** among my own people." H3782
2Ki 8:21 by night; his army, however, fled back **h**. H185
2Ki 14:10 but stay at **h**! Why ask for trouble H1074
2Ki 14:12 by Israel, and every man fled to his **h**. H185
1Ch 16:43 each for their own **h**, and David returned H1074
1Ch 16:43 David **returned h** to bless his family. H6015
1Ch 17: 9 *they can* **have a h** *of their own* and H8905+9393
2Ch 10:16 So all the Israelites went **h**. H185
2Ch 11: 4 Go **h**, every one of you, for this is my H1074
2Ch 18:16 Let each one go **h** in peace.' " H1074
2Ch 25:10 to him from Ephraim and sent them **h**. H5226
2Ch 25:10 with Judah and left for **h** in a great rage. H5226
2Ch 25:19 But stay at **h**! Why ask for trouble H1074
2Ch 25:22 by Israel, and every man fled to his **h**. H185
Ne 6:10 son of Mehetabel, who was shut in at his **h**. NDT
Est 5:10 Haman restrained himself and went **h**. H1074
Est 6:12 But Haman rushed **h**, with his head H1074
Job 17:13 If the only **h** I hope for is the grave, if I H1074
Job 39: 6 I gave it the wasteland as its **h**, the salt H1074
Ps 68:12 the women **at h** divide the plunder. H5661+1074
Ps 84: 3 Even the sparrow has found a **h**, and the H1074
Ps 104:17 the stork has its **h** in the junipers. H1074
Ps 113: 9 woman in her **h** as a happy mother of H1074
Pr 3:33 he blesses the **h** *of* the righteous. H5659
Pr 7:11 defiant, her feet never stay at **h**; H1074
Pr 7:14 I **have** food from my fellowship offering *at h*. AIT
Pr 7:19 My husband is not at **h**; he has gone on a H1074
Pr 7:20 money and will not be **h** till full moon." H1074
Pr 15:31 correction *will be* **at h** among the wise. H4328
Pr 27: 8 flees its nest is anyone who flees from **h**. H5226
Pr 30:26 yet they make their **h** in the crags; H1074
Ecc 12: 5 go to their eternal **h** and mourners go H1074
Isa 14:17 cities and would not let his captives go **h**?" H1074
Isa 34:13 become a haunt for jackals, a **h** for owls. H2948
Jer 39:14 son of Shaphan, to take him back to his **h**. H1074
Eze 36: 8 people Israel, for *they will* soon **come h**. H995
Da 4: 4 Nebuchadnezzar, was at **h** in my palace A10103
Da 6:10 he went **h** to his upstairs room where the A10103
Ob 3 the rocks and make your **h** on the heights, H8699
Jnh 4: 2 this what I said, LORD, when I was still at **h**? H141
Zep 3:20 gather you; at that time *I will* **bring** you **h**. H995
Hag 1: 9 What you brought **h**, I blew away. Why?" H1074
Mt 1:20 not be afraid *to* **take** Mary **h** as your wife, G4161
Mt 1:24 him and **took** Mary **h** as his wife. G4161
Mt 8: 6 "my servant lies at **h** paralyzed, suffering G3864
Mt 9: 6 "Get up, take your mat and go **h**." G3875+5148
Mt 9: 7 Then the man got up and went **h**. G3875+899
Mt 10:12 As you enter the **h**, give it your greeting. G3864
Mt 10:13 If the **h** is deserving, let your peace rest on G3864
Mt 10:14 leave that **h** or town and shake the dust G3864
Mt 13:57 except in his own town and in his own **h**." G3864
Mt 26: 6 in Bethany in the **h** of Simon the Leper, G3864
Mk 1:29 John to the **h** of Simon and Andrew. G3864
Mk 2: 1 the people heard that he had come **h**. G3875
Mk 2:11 get up, take your mat and go **h**." G3875+5148
Mk 5:19 "Go **h** to your own people and tell G3875+5148
Mk 5:38 they came to the **h** of the synagogue G3875
Mk 6: 4 among his relatives and in his own **h**." G3864
Mk 7:30 She went **h** and found her child G3875+899
Mk 8: 3 If I send them **h** hungry, they will G3875+899
Mk 8:26 Jesus sent him **h**, saying, "Don't G3875+899
Mk 10:29 "no one who has left **h** or brothers or G3864
Mk 14: 3 at the table in the **h** of Simon the Leper, G3864
Lk 1:23 was completed, he returned **h**. G3875+899
Lk 1:40 entered Zechariah's **h** and greeted G3875
Lk 1:56 three months and then returned **h**. G3875+899
Lk 2:43 while his parents *were* **returning h**, the G5715
Lk 4:38 synagogue and went to the **h** of Simon. G3864
Lk 5:24 get up, take your mat and go **h**." G3875+5148
Lk 5:25 lying on and went **h** praising God. G3875+899
Lk 8:39 "Return **h** and tell how much God G3875+5148
Lk 10:38 named Martha **opened** *her* **h** to him. G5685
Lk 15: 6 goes **h**. Then he calls his friends and G3875
Lk 15:30 your property with prostitutes comes **h**, NDT
Lk 18:14 went **h** justified before God. G3875+899
Lk 18:29 "no one who has left **h** or wife or brothers G3864
Lk 19:15 was made king, however, and **returned h**. G2059
Lk 23:56 Then *they* **went h** and prepared spices G5715
Jn 7:53 Then they all went **h**, G3875+899
Jn 9: 7 man went and washed, and **came** *h* seeing. AIT
Jn 11:20 out to meet him, but Mary stayed at **h**. G3875
Jn 14:23 come to them and make our **h** with them. G3665
Jn 16:32 be scattered, each to **your own h**. G3836+2625
Jn 19:27 this disciple took her into **his h**. G3836+2625
Ac 8:28 and **on** *his* **way h** was sitting in his chariot G5715
Ac 10:32 is a guest in the **h** of Simon the tanner, G3864
Ac 16:15 were baptized, she invited us to her **h**. NDT
Ac 18:26 *they* **invited** him to *their* **h** and explained G4689
Ac 20:12 *The people* **took** the young man **h** alive and G72
Ac 21: 6 the ship, and they returned **h**. G3836+2625
Ac 21:16 us and brought us to the **h** of Mnason, NDT
Ac 28: 7 He **welcomed** us to *his* **h** and showed us G346
1Co 11:34 who is hungry should eat something at **h**, G3875
1Co 14:35 they should ask their own husbands at **h** G3875
2Co 5: 6 know that *as long as we are* **at h** in the G1897
2Co 5: 8 from the body and **at h** with the Lord. G1897
2Co 5: 9 whether *we are* **at h** in the body or away G1897
Titus 2: 5 pure, to be **busy at h**, to be kind, G3877
Phm 2 to the church that meets in your **h**: G3875
Heb 11: 9 By faith *he* **made** *his* **h** in the promised G4228

HOMELAND (7) [HOME]

Ge 30:25 way so I can go back to my own **h**. H5226+824
Ru 2:11 mother and your **h** and came to live H824+4580
2Sa 15:19 You are a foreigner, an exile from your **h**. H5226
2Ki 17:23 were taken from their **h** into exile in Assyria H141
Ps 79: 7 devoured Jacob and devastated his **h**. H5659
Jer 10:25 him completely and destroyed his **h**. H5659
Joel 3: 6 that you might send them far from their **h**. H1473

HOMELESS (1) [HOME]

1Co 4:11 we are brutally treated, *we are* **h**. G841

HOMER (10) [HOMERS]

Lev 27:16 fifty shekels of silver to a **h** *of* barley seed. H2818
Isa 5:10 a **h** of seed will yield only an ephah of H2818
Eze 45:11 a tenth of a **h** and the ephah a tenth H2818
Eze 45:11 of a homer and the ephah a tenth of a **h**; H2818
Eze 45:11 the **h** is to be the standard measure for H2818
Eze 45:13 ephah from each **h** *of* wheat and a sixth H2818
Eze 45:13 a sixth of an ephah from each **h** *of* barley. H2818
Eze 45:14 which consists of ten baths or one **h**, for H2818
Eze 45:14 ten baths are equivalent to a **h**). H2818
Hos 3: 2 of silver and about a **h** and a lethek of H2818

HOMERS (1) [HOMER]

Nu 11:32 No one gathered less than ten **h**. H2818

HOMES (31) [HOME]

Ex 12:27 spared our **h** when he struck down H1074
Nu 32:18 will not return to our **h** until each of the H1074
Dt 32:25 them childless; in their **h** terror will reign. H2540
Jos 22: 4 return to your **h** in the land that Moses the H185
Jos 22: 6 sent them away, and they went to their **h**. H185
Jos 22: 8 "Return to your **h** with your great wealth H185
1Sa 10:25 the people to go to their own **h**. H1074
1Sa 13: 2 The rest of the men he sent back to their **h** H185
2Sa 6:19 And all the people went to their **h**. H1074
2Sa 18:17 all the Israelites fled to their **h**. H185
2Sa 19: 8 the Israelites had fled to their **h**. H185
2Ki 13: 5 lived in their own **h** as they had before. H185
2Ch 7:10 month he sent the people to their **h**, H185
Ne 4:14 your daughters, your wives and your **h**." H1074
Ne 5: 3 vineyards and our **h** to get grain during H1074
Job 1: 4 to hold feasts in their **h** on their birthdays, H1074
Job 2:11 set out from their **h** and met together by H5226
Job 21: 9 Their **h** are safe and free from fear; the H1074
Job 36:20 to drag people away from their **h**. H9393
Ps 78:55 he settled the tribes of Israel in their **h**. H185
Ps 109:10 may they be driven from their **ruined h**. H2999
Isa 32:18 in secure **h**, in undisturbed places H5438
La 5: 2 over to strangers, our **h** to foreigners. H1074
Hos 11:11 I will settle them in their **h**," declares the H1074
Mic 2: 2 They defraud people of their **h**, they rob H1074
Mic 2: 9 of my people from their pleasant **h**. H1074
Mk 10:30 **h**, brothers, sisters, mothers, children and G3864
Ac 2:46 broke bread in their **h** and ate together G3875
1Co 11:22 Don't you have **h** to eat and drink in? Or G3864
1Ti 5:14 *to* **manage** *their* **h** and to give the enemy G3866
2Ti 3: 6 worm their way into **h** and gain control G3864

HOMETOWN (8) [TOWN]

Ru 4:10 among his family or from his **h**. H9133+5226
1Sa 20: 6 to Bethlehem, his **h**, because an annual H6551
2Sa 15:12 counselor, to come from Giloh, his **h**. H6551
2Sa 17:23 donkey and set out for his house in his **h**. H6551
Mt 13:54 Coming to his **h**, he began teaching the G4258
Mk 6: 1 Jesus left there and went to his **h** G4258
Lk 4:23 'Do here in your **h** what we have heard G4258
Lk 4:24 "no prophet is accepted in his **h**. G4258

HOMOSEXUALITY (1)

1Ti 1:10 immoral, *for those* **practicing h**, for slave G780

HONEST (22) [HONESTLY, HONESTY]

Ge 42:11 Your servants are **h** *men*, not spies." H4026
Ge 42:19 If you are **h** *men*, let one of your brothers H4026
Ge 42:31 'We are **h** *men*; we are not spies. H4026
Ge 42:33 is how I will know whether you are **h** *men*: H4026
Ge 42:34 know that you are not spies but **h** *men*. H4026
Ex 23: 7 not put an innocent or **h** *person* to death, H7404

Lev 19:36 Use h scales and honest weights, an H7406
Lev 19:36 Use honest scales and h weights, an H7406
Lev 19:36 weights, an honest ephah and an honest hin. H7406
Lev 19:36 weights, an honest ephah and an h hin. H7406
Dt 25:15 have accurate and h weights and H7406
2Ki 22: 7 because they are h in their dealings." H575
1Ch 29:17 I have given willingly and with h intent. H3841
Job 6:25 How painful are h words! But what do H3841
Job 31: 6 let God weigh me in h scales and he will H7406
Pr 12:17 An h witness tells the truth, but a false H575
Pr 14: 5 An h witness does not deceive, but a false H574
Pr 16:11 H scales and balances belong to the LORD H5477
Pr 16:13 Kings take pleasure in h lips; they value H7406
Pr 17:26 surely to flog h officials is not right. H5618
Pr 22:21 teaching you to be h and to speak the H7999
Pr 24:26 An h answer is like a kiss on the lips. H5791

HONESTLY (1) [HONEST]

Jer 5: 1 person who deals h and seeks the truth, H5477

HONESTY (3) [HONEST]

Ge 30:33 And my h will testify for me in the future H7407
2Ki 12:15 because they acted with complete h. H575
Isa 59:14 stumbled in the streets, h cannot enter. H5791

HONEY (62) [HONEYCOMB]

Ge 43:11 a little balm and a little h, some spices H1831
Ex 3: 8 a land flowing with milk and h—the H1831
Ex 3:17 a land flowing with milk and h. H1831
Ex 13: 5 a land flowing with milk and h—you are H1831
Ex 16:31 seed and tasted like wafers made with h. H1831
Ex 33: 3 Go up to the land flowing with milk and h H1831
Lev 2:11 to burn any yeast or h in a food offering H1831
Lev 20:24 a land flowing with milk and h. H1831
Nu 13:27 sent us, and it does flow with milk and h! H1831
Nu 14: 8 a land flowing with milk and h, and will H1831
Nu 16:13 flowing with milk and h to kill us in the H1831
Nu 16:14 flowing with milk and h or given us an H1831
Dt 6: 3 greatly in a land flowing with milk and h, H1831
Dt 8: 8 fig trees, pomegranates, olive oil and h; H1831
Dt 11: 9 a land flowing with milk and h. H1831
Dt 26: 9 this land, a land flowing with milk and h; H1831
Dt 26:15 ancestors, a land flowing with milk and h." H1831
Dt 27: 3 a land flowing with milk and h, just as the H1831
Dt 31:20 into the land flowing with milk and h, H1831
Dt 32:13 He nourished him with h from the rock H1831
Jos 5: 6 to give us, a land flowing with milk and h. H1831
Jdg 14: 8 in it he saw a swarm of bees and *some* h. H1831
Jdg 14: 9 He scooped out the h with his hands H2084S
Jdg 14: 9 that he had taken the h from the lion's H1831
Jdg 14:18 said to him, "What is sweeter than h? H1831
1Sa 14:25 and there was h on the ground. H1831
1Sa 14:26 they saw the h oozing out; yet no H1831
1Sa 14:29 brightened when I tasted a little of this h. H1831
1Sa 14:43 "I tasted a little h with the end of my staff. H1831
2Sa 17:29 h and curds, sheep, and cheese from H1831
1Ki 14: 3 some cakes and a jar of h, and go to him. H1831
2Ki 18:32 vineyards, a land of olive trees and h. H1831
2Ch 31: 5 olive oil and h and all that the fields H1831
Job 20:17 the rivers flowing with h and cream. H1831
Ps 19:10 they are sweeter than h, than honey from H1831
Ps 19:10 than honey, than h *from* the honeycomb. H5885
Ps 81:16 with h from the rock I would satisfy you." H1831
Ps 119:103 to my taste, sweeter than h to my mouth! H1831
Pr 5: 3 the lips of the adulterous woman drip h, H5885
Pr 24:13 Eat h, my son, for it is good; honey from H1831
Pr 24:13 h from the comb is sweet to your taste. H5885
Pr 24:14 Know also that wisdom is like *h* for you: If AIT
Pr 25:16 If you find h, eat just enough—too much H1831
Pr 25:27 It is not good to eat too much h, nor is it H1831
Pr 27: 7 One who is full loathes h from the comb H5885
SS 4:11 milk and h are under your tongue. H1831
SS 5: 1 I have eaten my honeycomb and my h; H1831
Isa 7:15 be eating curds and h when he knows H1831
Isa 7:22 remain in the land will eat curds and h. H1831
Jer 11: 5 them a land flowing with milk and h'— H1831
Jer 32:22 ancestors, a land flowing with milk and h. H1831
Jer 41: 8 olive oil and h, hidden in a field. H1831
Eze 3: 3 it tasted as sweet as h in my mouth. H1831
Eze 16:13 Your food was h, olive oil and the finest H1831
Eze 16:19 olive oil and h I gave you to eat H1831
Eze 20: 6 a land flowing with milk and h, the most H1831
Eze 20:15 a land flowing with milk and h, the most H1831
Eze 27:17 confections, h, olive oil and balm for H1831
Mt 3: 4 His food was locusts and wild h. *G3510*
Mk 1: 6 his waist, and he ate locusts and wild h. *G3510*
Rev 10: 9 'in your mouth it will be as sweet as h. *G3510*
Rev 10:10 It tasted as sweet as h in my mouth, but *G3510*

HONEYCOMB (5) [HONEY]

1Sa 14:27 his hand and dipped it into the h. H3626+1831
Ps 19:10 than honey, than honey from the h. H7430
Pr 16:24 Gracious words are a h, sweet to H7430+1831
SS 4:11 Your lips drop sweetness as the h, my H5885
SS 5: 1 I have eaten my h and my honey; I have H3624

HONOR (174) [HONORABLE, HONORABLY, HONORED, HONORING, HONORS]

Ge 30:20 time my husband *will* treat me with h, H2290
Ge 45:13 about all the h *accorded* me in Egypt and H3883
Ge 49: 3 excelling in h, excelling in power. H8420
Ex 8: 9 "I leave *to you* the h *of* setting the time H6995
Ex 12:42 are to keep vigil to h the LORD for the H4200
Ex 20:12 "H your father and your mother, so that H3877
Ex 28: 2 brother Aaron to give him dignity and h. H9514
Ex 28:40 Aaron's sons to give them dignity and h. H9514
Nu 20:12 in me enough to h me as holy in the sight H7727
Nu 25:11 Since he *was* as zealous *for* my *h* among AIT
Nu 25:13 was zealous for the h of his God and made NDT
Nu 27:14 my command to h me as holy before their H7727
Dt 5:16 "H your father and your mother, as the H3877
Dt 26:19 fame and h high above all the nations he H9514
Jos 7:19 the God of Israel, and h him. H5989+9343
Jdg 4: 9 you are taking, the h will not be yours, for H9514
Jdg 13:17 so that *we may* h you when your word H3877
1Sa 2: 8 has them inherit a throne of h. H3883
1Sa 2:29 Why *do you* h your sons more than me by H3877
1Sa 2:30 *Those who* h me I will honor, but those H3877
1Sa 2:30 Those who honor me *I will* h, but those H3877
1Sa 15:12 up a monument in his own h and has H4200
1Sa 15:30 But please h me before the elders of my H3877
2Sa 1: 2 he fell to the ground *to* pay him h. H2556
2Sa 6:22 girls you spoke of, *I will* be held in h." H3877
2Sa 9: 6 to David, he bowed down *to* pay him h. H2556
2Sa 14: 4 with her face to the ground *to* pay him h, H2556
2Sa 14:22 with his face to the ground *to* pay him h, H2556
2Sa 23:19 *Was he* not held in greater h than the H3877
2Sa 23:23 *He* was held in greater h than any of the H3877
1Ki 3:13 both wealth and h—so that in your H3883
2Ki 10:20 "Call an assembly in h of Baal." H7727+4200
2Ki 25:28 gave him a seat of h higher than H4058
1Ch 11:25 He was held in greater h than any of the H3877
1Ch 29:12 Wealth and h come from you; you are the H3883
1Ch 29:28 having enjoyed long life, wealth and h. H3883
2Ch 1:11 possessions or h, nor for the death of H3883
2Ch 1:12 possessions and h, such as no king who H3883
2Ch 16:14 they made a huge fire in his h. H4200
2Ch 17: 5 so that he had great wealth and h. H3883
2Ch 18: 1 Jehoshaphat had great wealth and h, H3883
2Ch 21:19 His people made no funeral fire in his h H4200
2Ch 32:27 Hezekiah had very great wealth and h H3883
Ezr 7:27 king's heart to bring h *to* the house of the H6995
Ezr 10:11 Now h the LORD, the God of your H5989+9343
Est 3: 1 giving him a seat of h higher than H4058
Est 3: 2 gate knelt down and paid h to Haman, H2556
Est 3: 2 would not kneel down or pay him h. H2556
Est 3: 5 would not kneel down or pay him h, H2556
Est 6: 3 "What h and recognition has Mordecai H3702
Est 6: 6 done for the man the king delights to h?" H3702
Est 6: 6 the king would rather h than me?" H6913+3702
Est 6: 7 "For the man the king delights to h, H3702
Est 6: 9 them robe the man the king delights to h, H3702
Est 6: 9 is done for the man the king delights to h! H3702
Est 6:11 is done for the man the king delights to h!" H3702
Est 8:16 of happiness and joy, gladness and h. H3702
Job 19: 9 stripped me of my h and removed the H3883
Job 40:10 clothe yourself in h and majesty. H2086
Ps 8: 5 crowned them with glory and h. H2077
Ps 22:23 All *you* descendants of Jacob, h him H3877
Ps 45:11 by your beauty; h him, for he is your lord. H2556
Ps 50:15 I will deliver you, and *you will* h me." H3877
Ps 50:23 Those who sacrifice thank offerings h me H3877
Ps 62: 7 My salvation and my h depend on God H3883
Ps 71:21 will increase my h and comfort me once H1525
Ps 84:11 the LORD bestows favor and h; no good H3883
Ps 91:15 in trouble, I will deliver him and h him. H3877
Ps 112: 9 their horn will be lifted high in h. H3883
Ps 149: 5 rejoice in this h and sing for joy on H3883
Pr 3: 9 H the LORD with your wealth, with the H3877
Pr 3:16 in her left hand are riches and h. H3883
Pr 3:35 The wise inherit h, but fools get only H3883
Pr 4: 8 embrace her, and *she will* h you. H3877
Pr 5: 9 lest you lose your h to others and your H2086
Pr 8:18 With me are riches and h, enduring H3883
Pr 11:16 A kindhearted woman gains h, but H3883
Pr 15:33 the LORD, and humility comes before h. H3883
Pr 18:12 is haughty, but humility comes before h. H3883
Pr 20: 3 It is to one's h to avoid strife, but every H3883
Pr 21:21 love finds life, prosperity and h. H3883
Pr 22: 4 its wages are riches and h and life. H3883
Pr 26: 1 rain in harvest, h is not fitting for a fool. H3883
Pr 26: 8 in a sling is the giving of h to a fool. H3883
Pr 29:23 person low, but the lowly in spirit gain h. H3883
Pr 31:31 H her for all that her hands have done H5989
Ecc 6: 2 possessions and h, so that they lack H3883
Ecc 10: 1 so a little folly outweighs wisdom and h. H3883
Isa 9: 1 in the future *he will* h Galilee of the H3877
Isa 22:23 become a seat of h for the house of his H3883
Isa 25: 3 Therefore strong peoples *will* h you; cities H3877
Isa 26:13 over us, but your name alone *do we* h. H2349
Isa 29:13 with their mouth and h me with their lips, H3877
Isa 43:20 The wild animals h me, the jackals and H3877
Isa 45: 4 by name and bestow *on* you a title of h, H4033
Isa 58:13 if *you* h it by not going your own way H3877
Isa 60: 9 gold, to the h *of* the LORD your God H9005
Jer 3:17 in Jerusalem to h the name of the LORD. NDT
Jer 13:11 people for my renown and praise and h. H9514
Jer 30:19 decreased; *I will* bring them h, and they H3877
Jer 33: 9 praise and h before all nations on earth H9514
Jer 34: 5 As people made a funeral fire *in h of* your AIT
Jer 34: 5 will make a fire in your h and lament, H4200
Jer 52:32 gave him a seat of h higher than H4058
La 4:16 The priests *are* shown no h, the H5951+7156
Da 2: 6 from me gifts and rewards and great h. A10331
Da 2:46 Daniel and paid him h and ordered that A10504
Da 4:36 my h and splendor were returned to me A10199
Da 5:23 But *you did* not h the God who holds in A10198
Da 11:21 who has not been given the h *of* royalty. H2086
Da 11:38 of them, *he will* h a god of fortresses H3877
Da 11:38 to his ancestors *he will* h with gold and H3877
Da 11:39 god and will greatly h those who H3883
Hab 1: 7 to themselves and promote their own h. H8420
Zep 3:19 them praise and h in every land where H9005
Zep 3:20 I will give you h and praise among all the H9005
Zec 12: 7 so that the h *of* the house of David and of H9514
Mal 1: 6 where is the h *due* me? If I am a H3883
Mal 2: 2 if you do not resolve to h my name," H5989+3883
Mal 2: 2 because you have not resolved to h me. NDT
Mt 13:57 "A prophet is not without h except in his *G872*
Mt 15: 4 'H your father and mother' and 'Anyone *G5506*
Mt 15: 6 *they are* not *to* 'h their father or mother' *G5506*
Mt 15: 8 " 'These people h me with their lips, but *G5506*
Mt 19:19 h your father and mother,' and 'love your *G5506*
Mt 23: 6 they love the place of h at banquets and *G4752*
Mk 6: 4 "A prophet is not without h except in his *G872*
Mk 7: 6 " 'These people h me with their lips, but *G5506*
Mk 7:10 For Moses said, 'H your father and mother *G5506*
Mk 10:19 not defraud, h your father and mother. *G5506*
Mk 12:39 the places of h at banquets. *G4752*
Lk 14: 7 guests picked the places of h at the table, *G4752*
Lk 14: 8 do not take the place of h, for a person *G4752*
Lk 18:20 false testimony, h your father and mother. *G5506*
Lk 20:46 the places of h at banquets. *G4752*
Jn 4:44 a prophet has no h in his own country.) *G5507*
Jn 5:23 that all *may* h the Son just as they honor *G5506*
Jn 5:23 honor the Son just as *they* h the Father. *G5506*
Jn 5:23 Whoever *does* not h the Son does not *G5506*
Jn 5:23 not honor the Son *does* not h the Father, *G5506*
Jn 8:49 "but *I* h my Father and you dishonor me. *G5506*
Jn 12: 2 Here a dinner was given *in* Jesus' *h*. Martha AIT
Jn 12:26 My Father *will* h the one who serves me *G5506*
Ac 19:17 of the Lord Jesus *was* held in high h. *G3486*
Ro 2: 7 good seek glory, h and immortality, he *G5507*
Ro 2:10 h and peace for everyone who does good: *G5507*
Ro 12:10 H one another above yourselves. *G5507*
Ro 13: 7 if respect, then respect; if h, then honor. *G5507*
Ro 13: 7 if respect, then respect; if honor, then h. *G5507*
1Co 6:20 Therefore h God with your bodies. *G1519*
1Co 12:23 less honorable we treat with special h. *G5507*
1Co 12:24 giving greater h to the parts that lacked it *G5507*
2Co 8:19 in order to h the Lord himself and *G1518*
2Co 8:23 of the churches and an h to Christ. *G1518*
Eph 6: 2 "H your father and mother"—which is the *G5506*
Php 2:29 great joy, and h people like him, *G1952+2400*
1Ti 1:17 be h and glory for ever and ever. *G5507*
1Ti 5:17 of the church well are worthy *of* double h, *G5507*
1Ti 6:16 To him be h and might forever *G5507*
Heb 2: 7 you crowned them with glory and h *G5507*
Heb 2: 9 with glory and h because he suffered *G5507*
Heb 3: 3 found worthy *of* greater h than Moses, *G1518*
Heb 3: 3 a house has greater h than the house *G5507*
Heb 5: 4 And no one takes this h on himself, but he *G5507*
1Pe 1: 7 glory and h when Jesus Christ is revealed. *G5507*
1Pe 2:17 of believers, fear God, h the emperor. *G5506*
2Pe 1:17 He received h and glory from God the *G5507*
Rev 4: 9 h and thanks to him who sits on the *G5507*
Rev 4:11 to receive glory and h and power, for you *G5507*
Rev 5:12 strength and h and glory and praise!" *G5507*
Rev 5:13 Lamb be praise and h and glory and *G5507*
Rev 7:12 wisdom and thanks and h and power and *G5507*
Rev 13:14 set up an image *in h of* the beast who was AIT
Rev 21:26 The glory and h of the nations will be *G5507*

HONORABLE (6) [HONOR]

1Ch 4: 9 Jabez was more h than his brothers. H3877
Ezr 4:10 whom the great and h Ashurbanipal A10330
Pr 25:27 is it h to search out matters that are H3883
Isa 58:13 a delight and the LORD's holy day h, H3877
1Co 12:23 that we think are less h we treat with *G872*
1Th 4: 4 your own body in a way that is holy and h, *G5507*

HONORABLY (4) [HONOR]

Jdg 9:16 "Have you acted h and in good faith H928+622
Jdg 9:19 So have you acted h and in good faith H928+622
1Co 7:36 *that he might* not be acting h toward *G858*
Heb 13:18 desire to live h in every way. *G2822*

HONORED (32) [HONOR]

Ge 34:19 who *was* the most h of all his father's H3877
Ex 20:24 Wherever *I* cause my name to be h, I will H2349
Lev 10: 3 in the sight of all the people *I will* be h. H3877
Jdg 9: 9 by which both gods and humans *are* h, to H3877
1Ch 11:21 *He* was doubly h above the Three and H3877
2Ch 26:18 you will not be h by the LORD God. H3883
2Ch 32:33 of Jerusalem h him when he died. H6913+3883
Est 3: 1 King Xerxes h Haman son of H1540
Est 5:11 the ways the king *had* h him and how he H1540
Job 14:21 If their children *are* h, they do not know it H3877
Job 22: 8 land—an h *man*, living on it. H5951+7156
Ps 12: 8 when what is vile *is* h by the human race. H8123
Ps 45: 9 of kings are among your h *women*; H3701
Pr 13:18 but whoever heeds correction is h. H3877
Pr 27:18 whoever protects their master *will* be h. H3877
Isa 3: 5 against the old, the nobody against the h. H3877
Isa 43: 4 Since you are precious and h in my sight H3877
Isa 43:23 offerings, nor h me *with* your sacrifices. H3877
Isa 49: 5 for *I* am h in the eyes of the LORD and my H3877

La 1: 8 All *who* **h** her despise her, for they have H3877
Da 4:34 *I* **h** and glorified him who lives forever. A10693
Hag 1: 8 so that I may take pleasure in it and **be h**," H3877
Mal 3:16 who feared the LORD and **h** his name. H3108
Mt 6: 2 on the streets, to *be* **h** by others. *G1519*
Lk 14:10 Then you will be **h** in the presence of all *G1518*
Ac 5:34 of the law, who was **h** by all the people *G5508*
Ac 13:48 they were glad and **h** the word of the Lord; *G1519*
Ac 28:10 They **h** us in many ways; and when *G5507+5506*
1Co 4:10 You are **h**, we are dishonored! *G1902*
1Co 12:26 if one part *is* **h**, every part rejoices *G1519*
2Th 3: 1 of the Lord may spread rapidly and *be* **h**, *G1519*
Heb 13: 4 Marriage should be **h** by all, and the *G5508*

HONORING (3) [HONOR]

2Sa 10: 3 "Do you think David *is* **h** your father by H3877
1Ch 17:18 can David say to you for **h** your servant? H3883
1Ch 19: 3 "Do you think David *is* **h** your father by H3877

HONORS (4) [HONOR]

Ps 15: 4 a vile person but **h** those who fear the H3877
Pr 14:31 whoever is kind to the needy **h** God. H3877
Mal 1: 6 "A son **h** his father, and a slave his H3877
3Jn 6 them on their way **in a manner that h** God. *G547*

HOOF (12) [HOOVES]

Ex 10:26 go with us; not a **h** is to be left behind. H7274
Lev 11: 3 that has a divided **h** and that chews the H7274
Lev 11: 4 chew the cud or only have a divided **h**, H7274
Lev 11: 4 does not have a divided **h**; it is H7274
Lev 11: 5 does not have a divided **h**; it is unclean H7274
Lev 11: 6 does not have a divided **h**; it is unclean H7274
Lev 11: 7 though it has a divided **h**, does not chew H7274
Lev 11:26 not have a divided **h** or that does not H7274
Dt 14: 6 that has a divided **h** and that chews the H7274
Dt 14: 7 that have a divided **h** you may not eat the H7274
Dt 14: 7 they do not have a divided **h**; they are H7274
Dt 14: 8 although it has a divided **h**, it does not H7274

HOOK (4) [FISHHOOK, FISHHOOKS, HOOKS]

2Ki 19:28 I will put my **h** in your nose and my bit in H2626
2Ch 33:11 prisoner, put a **h** in his nose, bound him H2560
Job 41: 2 through its nose or pierce its jaw with a **h**? H2560
Isa 37:29 I will put my **h** in your nose and my bit in H2626

HOOKS (24) [HOOK]

Ex 26:32 Hang it with gold **h** on four posts of acacia H2260
Ex 26:37 Make gold **h** for this curtain and five posts H2260
Ex 27:10 with silver **h** and bands *on* the posts. H2260
Ex 27:11 with silver **h** and bands *on* the posts. H2260
Ex 27:17 courtyard are to have silver bands and **h**, H2260
Ex 36:36 They made gold **h** for them and cast their H2260
Ex 36:38 they made five posts with **h** *for* them H2260
Ex 38:10 with silver **h** and bands *on* the posts. H2260
Ex 38:11 with silver **h** and bands *on* the posts. H2260
Ex 38:12 with silver **h** and bands *on* the posts. H2260
Ex 38:17 The **h** and bands *on* the posts were silver H2260
Ex 38:19 Their **h** and bands were silver, and their H2260
Ex 38:28 1,775 shekels to make the **h** for the posts, H2260
Isa 2: 4 their spears into **pruning h**. H4661
Isa 19: 8 lament, all who cast **h** into the Nile; those H2676
Eze 19: 4 They led him with **h** to the land of Egypt. H2626
Eze 19: 9 With **h** they pulled him into a cage and H2626
Eze 29: 4 But I will put **h** in your jaws and make the H2626
Eze 38: 4 put **h** in your jaws and bring you out with H2626
Eze 40:43 And **double-pronged h**, each a H9191
Joel 3:10 swords and your **pruning h** into spears. H4661
Am 4: 2 when you will be taken away with **h**, H7553
Mic 4: 3 their spears into **pruning h**. H4661
Hab 1:15 wicked foe pulls all of them up with **h**, H2676

HOOPOE (2)

Lev 11:19 any kind of heron, the **h** and the bat. H1871
Dt 14:18 any kind of heron, the **h** and the bat. H1871

HOOTING (1)

Zep 2:14 Their **h** will echo through the windows H7754

HOOVES (8) [HOOF]

Jdg 5:22 Then thundered the horses' **h**—galloping H6811
Ps 69:31 more than a bull with its horns and **h**. H7271
Isa 5:28 their horses' **h** seem like flint, their H7274
Jer 47: 3 at the sound of the **h** *of* galloping steeds H7274
Eze 26:11 The **h** *of* his horses will trample all your H7274
Eze 32:13 foot of man or muddied by the **h** *of* cattle. H7274
Mic 4:13 I will give you **h** *of* bronze, and you will H7274
Zec 11:16 of the choice sheep, tearing off their **h**. H7274

HOPE (167) [HOPED, HOPELESS, HOPES, HOPING]

Ru 1:12 Even if I thought there was still **h** for me H9536
1Ch 29:15 on earth are like a shadow, without **h**. H5223
Ezr 10: 2 in spite of this, there is still **h** for Israel. H5223
Job 4: 6 your blameless ways your **h**? H9536
Job 5:16 So the poor have **h**, and injustice shuts its H9536
Job 6: 8 that God would grant *what* I **h** *for*, H9536
Job 6:11 strength do I have, that *I should still* **h**? H3498
Job 6:19 traveling merchants of Sheba **look in h**. H7747
Job 7: 6 they come to an end without **h**. H9536
Job 8:13 so perishes the **h** *of* the godless. H9536
Job 11:18 because there is **h**; you will look about H9536
Job 11:20 their **h** will become a dying gasp. H9536
Job 13:15 he slay me, yet *will I* **h** in him; I will surely H3498
Job 14: 7 "At least there is **h** for a tree: If it is cut H9536
Job 14:19 away the soil, so you destroy a person's **h**. H9536
Job 17:13 If the only home *I* **h for** is the grave, if I H7747
Job 17:15 where then is my **h**—who can see any H9536
Job 17:15 is my hope—who can see any **h** *for* me? H9536
Job 19:10 till I am gone; he uproots my **h** like a tree. H9536
Job 27: 8 For what **h** have the godless when they H9536
Job 41: 9 Any **h** *of* subduing it is false; the mere H9347
Ps 9:18 the **h** *of* the afflicted will never perish. H9536
Ps 25: 5 and *my* **h** *is* **in** you all day long. H7747
Ps 25:21 protect me, because *my* **h**, LORD, *is* in you. H7747
Ps 31:24 take heart, all you who **h** in the LORD. H3498
Ps 33:17 A horse is a **vain h** for deliverance H9214
Ps 33:18 on those *whose* **h** *is* in his unfailing love, H3498
Ps 33:20 We **wait in h** for the LORD; he is our help H2675
Ps 33:22 with us, LORD, even as *we* **put** *our* **h** in you. H3498
Ps 37: 9 but *those who* **h in** the LORD will inherit H7747
Ps 37:34 **H** in the LORD and keep his way. He will H7747
Ps 39: 7 what do I look for? *My* **h** *is* in you. H3498
Ps 42: 5 **Put** *your* **h** in God, for I will yet praise him H3498
Ps 42:11 **Put** *your* **h** in God, for I will yet praise him H3498
Ps 43: 5 **Put** *your* **h** in God, for I will yet praise him H3498
Ps 52: 9 And *I will* **h in** your name, for your name H7747
Ps 62: 5 find rest in God; my **h** comes from him. H9536
Ps 62:10 in extortion or **put vain h** in stolen goods; H2038
Ps 65: 5 the **h** *of* all the ends of the earth and of H4440
Ps 69: 6 may *those who* **h in** you not be disgraced H7747
Ps 71: 5 For you have been my **h**, Sovereign LORD H9536
Ps 71:14 As for me, *I will* always *have* **h**; I will H3498
Ps 119:43 for *I have* **put** *my* **h** in your laws. H3498
Ps 119:49 to your servant, for *you have* **given** me **h**. H3498
Ps 119:74 see me, for *I have* **put** *my* **h** in your word. H3498
Ps 119:81 but *I have* **put** *my* **h** in your word. H3498
Ps 119:114 my shield; *I have* **put** *my* **h** in your word. H3498
Ps 119:147 for help; *I have* **put** *my* **h** in your word. H3498
Ps 130: 5 being waits, and in his word *I* **put** *my* **h**. H3498
Ps 130: 7 **put** *your* **h** in the LORD, for with the H3498
Ps 131: 3 **put** *your* **h** in the LORD both now and H3498
Ps 146: 5 Jacob, whose **h** is in the LORD their God. H8433
Ps 147:11 who **put** *their* **h** in his unfailing love. H3498
Pr 11:23 the **h** *of* the wicked only in wrath. H9536
Pr 13:12 **H** deferred makes the heart sick, but a H9347
Pr 19:18 in that there is **h**; do not be a willing H9536
Pr 23:18 There is surely a **future h** for you, and your H344
Pr 23:18 you, and your **h** will not be cut off. H9536
Pr 24:14 there is a **future h** for you, and your H344
Pr 24:14 you, and your **h** will not be cut off. H9536
Pr 24:20 the evildoer has no **future h**, and the H344
Pr 26:12 There is more **h** for a fool than for them. H9536
Pr 29:20 There is more **h** for a fool than for them. H9536
Ecc 9: 4 Anyone who is among the living has **h** H1059
Isa 19: 9 the weavers of fine linen will lose **h**. NDT
Isa 38:18 to the pit cannot **h** for your faithfulness. H8432
Isa 40:31 but *those who* **h in** the LORD will renew H7747
Isa 42: 4 In his teaching the islands *will* **put** *their* **h**." H3498
Isa 49:23 those *who* **h in** me will not be H7747
Isa 51: 5 will look to me and **wait in h** for my arm. H3498
Jer 13:16 *You* **h** for light, but he will turn it to utter H7747
Jer 14: 8 You who are the **h** *of* Israel, its Savior in H5223
Jer 14:22 Therefore *our* **h** *is* in you, for you are the H7747
Jer 17:13 you are the **h** *of* Israel; all who H5223
Jer 29:11 plans to give you **h** and a future. H9536
Jer 31:17 So there is **h** for your descendants, H9536
Jer 50: 7 pasture, the LORD, the **h** *of* their ancestors. H5223
La 3:21 this I call to mind and therefore *I have* **h**: H3498
La 3:25 LORD is good to *those whose* **h** *is in* him, H7747
La 3:29 his face in the dust—there may yet be **h**. H9536
Eze 19: 5 " 'When she saw *her* **h unfulfilled**, her H3498
Eze 37:11 bones are dried up and our **h** is gone; H9536
Hos 2:15 will make the Valley of Achor a door of **h**. H9536
Mic 7: 7 But as for me, *I* **watch in h** for the LORD, H7595
Zec 9: 5 Ekron too, for her **h** will wither. H4438
Zec 9:12 you prisoners of **h**; even now I announce H9536
Mt 12:21 In his name the nations *will* **put** *their* **h**." *G1827*
Ac 2:26 rejoices; my body also will rest in **h**, *G1828*
Ac 8:22 to the Lord **in the h that** he may *G1623+726*
Ac 16:19 realized that their **h** of making money was *G1828*
Ac 23: 6 trial because of the **h** of the resurrection *G1828*
Ac 24:15 I have the same **h** in God as these *G1828*
Ac 26: 6 it is because of my **h** in what God has *G1828*
Ac 26: 7 it is because of this **h** that these Jews are *G1828*
Ac 27:20 we finally gave up all **h** of being saved. *G1828*
Ac 28:20 It is because of the **h** of Israel that I am *G1828*
Ro 4:18 Against all **h**, Abraham in hope believed *G1828*
Ro 4:18 Abraham in **h** believed and so became *G1828*
Ro 5: 2 And we boast in the **h** of the glory of God *G1828*
Ro 5: 4 perseverance, character; and character, **h**. *G1828*
Ro 5: 5 And **h** does not put us to shame, because *G1828*
Ro 8:20 the will of the one who subjected it, in **h** *G1828*
Ro 8:24 For *in* this **h** we were saved. But hope that *G1828*
Ro 8:24 But **h** that is seen is no hope at all *G1828*
Ro 8:24 But hope that is seen is no **h** at all. *G1828*
Ro 8:25 But if *we* **h for** what we do not yet have *G1827*
Ro 11:14 **in the h that** I may somehow arouse my *G1623*
Ro 12:12 Be joyful *in* **h**, patient in affliction, faithful *G1828*
Ro 15: 4 they provide we might have **h**. *G1828*
Ro 15:12 the nations; in him the Gentiles *will* **h**." *G1827*
Ro 15:13 May the God *of* **h** fill you with all joy and *G1828*
Ro 15:13 may overflow with **h** by the power of the *G1828*
Ro 15:24 *I* **h** to see you while passing through and *G1827*
1Co 9:10 be able to do so in the **h** of sharing in the *G1828*
1Co 9:15 not writing this **in the h that** you will do *G2671*
1Co 13:13 three remain: faith, **h** and love. But the *G1828*
1Co 15:19 this life *we* **have h** in Christ, *G1827+1639*
1Co 16: 7 *I* **h** to spend some time with you *G1827*
2Co 1: 7 And our **h** for you is firm, because we *G1828*
2Co 1:10 On him *we have* **set** *our* **h** that he will *G1827*
2Co 1:13 cannot read or understand. And *I* **h** that, *G1827*
2Co 3:12 since we have such a **h**, we are very bold. *G1828*
2Co 5:11 and *I* **h** it is also plain to your conscience. *G1827*
2Co 10:15 Our **h** is that, as your faith continues to *G1828*
2Co 11: 1 *I* **h** you will put up with me in a little *G4054*
Gal 5: 5 by faith the righteousness for which we **h**. *G1828*
Eph 1:12 who *were* **the first to put** our **h** in Christ *G4598*
Eph 1:18 that you may know the **h** to which he has *G1828*
Eph 2:12 without **h** and without God in the world. *G1828*
Eph 4: 4 were called to one **h** when you were *G1828*
Php 1:20 I eagerly expect and **h** that I will in no way *G1828*
Php 2:19 *I* **h** in the Lord Jesus to send Timothy to *G1827*
Php 2:23 *I* **h**, therefore, to send him as soon as I see *G1827*
Col 1: 5 that spring from the **h** stored up for you in *G1828*
Col 1:23 do not move from the **h** held out in the *G1828*
Col 1:27 which is Christ in you, the **h** of glory. *G1828*
1Th 1: 3 your endurance *inspired by* **h** in our Lord *G1828*
1Th 2:19 For what is our **h**, our joy, or the crown in *G1828*
1Th 4:13 like the rest of mankind, who have no **h**. *G1828*
1Th 5: 8 the **h** of salvation as a helmet. *G1828*
2Th 2:16 us eternal encouragement and good **h**, *G1828*
1Ti 1: 1 God our Savior and of Christ Jesus our **h**, *G1828*
1Ti 3:14 *Although I* **h** to come to you soon, I am *G1827*
1Ti 4:10 because *we have* **put** *our* **h** in the living *G1827*
1Ti 5: 5 left all alone **puts** *her* **h** in God and *G1827*
1Ti 6:17 to be arrogant nor *to* **put** *their* **h** in wealth, *G1827*
1Ti 6:17 to put their **h** in God, who richly provides NDT
2Ti 2:25 **in the h that** God will grant them *G3607*
Titus 1: 2 in the **h** of eternal life, which God, who *G1828*
Titus 2:13 while we wait for the blessed **h**—the *G1828*
Titus 3: 7 become heirs having the **h** of eternal life. *G1828*
Phm 22 because *I* **h** to be restored to you in *G1827*
Heb 3: 6 confidence and the **h** in which we glory. *G1828*
Heb 6:11 so that what you **h** *for* may be fully *G1828*
Heb 6:18 to take hold of the **h** set before us may be *G1828*
Heb 6:19 We have **this h** as an anchor for the soul *G4005S*
Heb 7:19 and a better **h** is introduced, by which we *G1828*
Heb 10:23 us hold unswervingly *to* the **h** we profess, *G1828*
Heb 11: 1 is confidence *in what we* **h for** and *G1827*
1Pe 1: 3 new birth into a living **h** through the *G1828*
1Pe 1:13 **set** *your* **h** on the grace to be brought to *G1827*
1Pe 1:21 and so your faith and **h** are in God. *G1828*
1Pe 3: 5 of the past who **put** *their* **h** in God used to *G1827*
1Pe 3:15 to give the reason for the **h** that you have. *G1828*
1Jn 3: 3 All who have this **h** in him purify *G1828*
2Jn 12 *I* **h** to visit you and talk with you face to *G1827*
3Jn 14 *I* **h** to see you soon, and we will talk face *G1827*

HOPED (8) [HOPE]

Est 9: 1 of the Jews *had* **h** to overpower them, H8432
Job 30:26 Yet *when I* **h for** good, evil came; when I H7747
Jer 8:15 We **h** for peace but no good has come H7747
Jer 14:19 We **h** for peace but no good has come H7747
La 3:18 is gone and *all that* I had **h** from the LORD." H9347
Lk 20:20 They **h** to catch Jesus in something he *G2671*
Lk 23: 8 *he* **h** to see him perform a sign of some *G1827*
Lk 24:21 we *had* **h** that he was the one who *G1827*

HOPELESS (1) [HOPE]

Isa 57:10 but you would not say, '*It is* **h**. H3286

HOPES (10) [HOPE]

2Ki 4:28 "Didn't I tell you, 'Don't **raise** my **h**'?" H8922
Ps 25: 3 No one *who* **h** in you will ever be put to H7747
Ps 119:116 I will live; do not let my **h** be dashed. H8433
Pr 10:28 the **h** *of* the wicked come to nothing. H9536
Pr 11: 7 **H** placed in mortals die with them; all the H9536
Jer 23:16 they **fill** you **with false h**. H2038
Jn 5:45 accuser is Moses, on whom your **h** *are* **set**. *G1827*
Ro 8:24 Who **h for** what they already have *G1827*
1Co 13: 7 always trusts, always **h**, always perseveres. *G1827*
1Co 15:32 in Ephesus **with** no more than human **h**, *G2848*

HOPHNI (5)

1Sa 1: 3 at Shiloh, where **H** and Phinehas, the two H2909
1Sa 2:34 to your two sons, **H** and Phinehas, will be H2909
1Sa 4: 4 And Eli's two sons, **H** and Phinehas, were H2909
1Sa 4:11 Eli's two sons, **H** and Phinehas, died. H2909
1Sa 4:17 Also your two sons, **H** and Phinehas, are H2909

HOPHRA (1)

Jer 44:30 to deliver Pharaoh **H** king of Egypt into H2922

HOPING (6) [HOPE]

Ps 56: 6 they watch my steps, **h** *to take* my life. H7747
Da 2: 9 **h** the situation will change. A10527+10168
Ac 12:11 the Jewish people were **h would happen**." *G4660*
Ac 24:26 the same time *he was* **h** that Paul would *G1827*
Ac 26: 7 our twelve tribes *are* **h** to see fulfilled as *G1827*
Ac 27:12 **h** to reach Phoenix and *G1623+4803+1538*

HOPPING (1)

Lev 11:21 have jointed legs for **h** on the ground. H6001

HOR (12) [HOR HAGGIDGAD]

Nu 20:22 out from Kadesh and came to Mount **H**. H2216
Nu 20:23 At Mount **H**, near the border of Edom, the H2216
Nu 20:25 son Eleazar and take them up Mount **H**. H2216
Nu 20:27 They went up Mount **H** in the sight of the H2216

Nu 21: 4 traveled from Mount **H** along the route to H2216
Nu 33:37 They left Kadesh and camped at Mount **H**, H2216
Nu 33:38 Aaron the priest went up Mount **H**, H2216
Nu 33:39 years old when he died on Mount **H**. H2216
Nu 33:41 They left Mount **H** and camped at H2216
Nu 34: 7 from the Mediterranean Sea to Mount **H** H2216
Nu 34: 8 from Mount **H** to Lebo Hamath. H2216
Dt 32:50 died on Mount **H** and was gathered to H2216

HOR HAGGIDGAD (2) [HOR]

Nu 33:32 Jaakan and camped at **H**. H2988
Nu 33:33 They left **H** and camped at H2988

HORAM (1)

Jos 10:33 **H** king of Gezer had come up to help H2235

HORDE (5) [HORDES]

Nu 22: 4 "This **h** is going to lick up everything H7736
Eze 17:17 army and great **h** will be of no help to H7736
Eze 38: 4 a great **h** with large and small H7736
Eze 38:15 on horses, a great **h**, a mighty army. H7736
Joel 2:20 "I will drive the **northern** *h* far from you AIT

HORDES (21) [HORDE]

Isa 29: 5 fine dust, the ruthless **h** like blown chaff. H2162
Isa 29: 7 Then the **h** *of* all the nations that fight H2162
Isa 29: 8 will it be with the **h** *of* all the nations that H2162
Eze 30:10 put an end to the **h** *of* Egypt by the hand H2162
Eze 30:15 of Egypt, and wipe out the **h** *of* Thebes. H2162
Eze 31: 2 say to Pharaoh king of Egypt and to his **h**: H2162
Eze 31:18 " 'This is Pharaoh and all his **h**, declares H2162
Eze 32:12 I will cause your **h** to fall by the swords of H2162
Eze 32:12 of Egypt, and all her **h** will be overthrown. H2162
Eze 32:16 for Egypt and all her **h** they will chant it H2162
Eze 32:18 wail for the **h** *of* Egypt and consign to the H2162
Eze 32:20 let her be dragged off with all her **h**. H2162
Eze 32:24 is there, with all her **h** around her grave. H2162
Eze 32:25 the slain, with all her **h** around her grave. H2162
Eze 32:26 with all their **h** around their graves. H2162
Eze 32:31 consoled for all his **h** that were killed by H2162
Eze 32:32 Pharaoh and all his **h** will be laid among H2162
Eze 38: 7 you and all the **h** gathered about you H7736
Eze 38:13 Have you gathered your **h** to loot, to carry H7736
Eze 39:11 Gog and all his **h** will be buried there. H2162
Hab 1: 9 Their **h** advance like a desert wind and H4480

HOREB (17)

Ex 3: 1 far side of the wilderness and came to **H**, H2998
Ex 17: 6 stand there before you by the rock at **H**. H2998
Ex 33: 6 stripped off their ornaments at Mount **H**. H2998
Dt 1: 2 days to go from **H** to Kadesh Barnea by H2998
Dt 1: 6 The LORD our God said to us at **H**, "You H2998
Dt 1:19 we set out from **H** and went toward the H2998
Dt 4:10 you stood before the LORD your God at **H**, H2998
Dt 4:15 the LORD spoke to you at **H** out of the fire. H2998
Dt 5: 2 our God made a covenant with us at **H**. H2998
Dt 9: 8 At **H** you aroused the LORD's wrath so that H2998
Dt 18:16 the LORD your God at **H** on the day of the H2998
Dt 29: 1 covenant he had made with them at **H**. H2998
1Ki 8: 9 tablets that Moses had placed in it at **H**, H2998
1Ki 19: 8 days and forty nights until he reached **H**, H2998
2Ch 5:10 tablets that Moses had placed in it at **H**, H2998
Ps 106:19 At **H** they made a calf and worshiped an H2998
Mal 4: 4 laws I gave him at **H** for all Israel. H2998

HOREM (1)

Jos 19:38 Migdal El, **H**, Beth Anath and Beth H3054

HORESH (4)

1Sa 23:15 While David was at **H** in the Desert of H3092
1Sa 23:16 went to David at **H** and helped him find H3092
1Sa 23:18 went home, but David remained at **H**. H3092
1Sa 23:19 hiding among us in the strongholds at **H**, H3092

HORI (3) [HORITE, HORITES]

Ge 36:22 The sons of Lotan: **H** and Homam. H3036
Nu 13: 5 the tribe of Simeon, Shaphat son of **H**; H3036
1Ch 1:39 The sons of Lotan: **H** and Homam. H3036

HORITE (4) [HORI]

Ge 36:20 These were the sons of Seir the **H**, who H3037
Ge 36:21 These sons of Seir in Edom were **H** chiefs. H3037
Ge 36:29 These were the **H** chiefs: Lotan, Shobal H3037
Ge 36:30 These were the **H** chiefs, according to H3037

HORITES (4) [HORI]

Ge 14: 6 the **H** in the hill country of Seir, as far H3037
Dt 2:12 **H** used to live in Seir, but the descendants H3037
Dt 2:12 They destroyed **the H** from before them H4392S
Dt 2:22 he destroyed the **H** from before them. H3037

HORIZON (3)

Ne 1: 9 if your exiled people are at the farthest **h**, H9028
Job 26:10 He marks out the **h** on the face of the H2976
Pr 8:27 he marked out the **h** on the face of the H2553

HORMAH (9)

Nu 14:45 beat them down all the way to **H**. H3055
Nu 21: 3 their towns; so the place was named **H**. H3055
Dt 1:44 beat you down from Seir all the way to **H**. H3055
Jos 12:14 the king of **H** one the king of Arad one H3055
Jos 15:30 Eltolad, Kesil, **H**, H3055
Jos 19: 4 Eltolad, Bethul, **H**, H3055
Jdg 1:17 Therefore it was called **H**. H3055
1Sa 30:30 to those in **H**, Bor Ashan, Athak H3055
1Ch 4:30 Bethuel, **H**, Ziklag, H3055

HORN (38) [HORNED, HORNS, TWO-HORNED]

Ex 19:13 Only when the **ram's h** sounds a long H3413
Ex 27: 2 Make a **h** at each of the four corners, so H7967
Ex 38: 2 They made a **h** at each of the four corners H7967
1Sa 2: 1 the LORD; in the LORD my **h** is lifted high. H7967
1Sa 2:10 his king and exalt the **h** *of* his anointed." H7967
1Sa 16: 1 Fill your **h** with oil and be on your way; H7967
1Sa 16:13 So Samuel took the **h** *of* oil and anointed H7967
2Sa 22: 3 my shield and the **h** *of* my salvation. H7967
1Ki 1:39 the priest took the **h** *of* oil from the sacred H7967
Ps 18: 2 my shield and the **h** *of* my salvation, my H7967
Ps 81: 3 Sound the **ram's h** at the New Moon, and H8795
Ps 89:17 by your favor you exalt our **h**. H7967
Ps 89:24 through my name his **h** will be exalted. H7967
Ps 92:10 You have exalted my **h** like that of a wild H7967
Ps 98: 6 trumpets and the blast of the **ram's h**— H8795
Ps 112: 9 their **h** will be lifted high in honor. H7967
Ps 132:17 "Here I will make a **h** grow for David and H7967
Ps 148:14 And he has raised up for his people a **h** H7967
Jer 48:25 Moab's **h** is cut off; her arm is broken," H7967
La 2: 3 anger he has cut off every **h** *of* Israel. H7967
La 2:17 he has exalted the **h** *of* your foes. H7967
Eze 29:21 that day I will make a **h** grow for the H7967
Da 3: 5 As soon as you hear the sound of the **h** A10641
Da 3: 7 soon as they heard the sound of the **h**, A10641
Da 3:10 everyone who hears the sound of the **h**, A10641
Da 3:15 Now when you hear the sound of the **h** A10641
Da 7: 8 there before me was another **h**, a little A10641
Da 7: 8 This **h** had eyes like the eyes of a A10641
Da 7:11 the boastful words the **h** was speaking. A10641
Da 7:20 head and about the other **h** that came up, NDT
Da 7:20 the **h** that looked more imposing than A10641
Da 7:21 this **h** was waging war against the holy A10641
Da 8: 5 with a prominent **h** between its eyes H7967
Da 8: 8 of its power the large **h** was broken off, H7967
Da 8: 9 Out of one of them came another **h** H7967
Da 8:21 the large **h** between its eyes is the H7967
Hos 5: 8 the trumpet in Gibeah, the **h** in Ramah. H2956
Lk 1:69 He has raised up a **h** of salvation for us in *G3043*

HORNED (2) [HORN]

Lev 11:16 the **h owl**, the screech owl, the gull H1426+3613
Dt 14:15 the **h owl**, the screech owl, the gull H1426+3613

HORNET (3)

Ex 23:28 I will send the **h** ahead of you to drive the H7667
Dt 7:20 God will send the **h** among them until H7667
Jos 24:12 I sent the **h** ahead of you, which drove H7667

HORNS (66) [HORN]

Ge 22:13 in a thicket he saw a ram caught by its **h**. H7967
Ex 27: 2 so that the **h** and the altar are of one H7967
Ex 29:12 put it on the **h** *of* the altar with your H7967
Ex 30: 2 cubits high—its **h** of one piece with it. H7967
Ex 30: 3 all the sides and the **h** with pure gold, H7967
Ex 30:10 Aaron shall make atonement on its **h**. H7967
Ex 37:25 cubits high—its **h** of one piece with it. H7967
Ex 37:26 all the sides and the **h** with pure gold, H7967
Ex 38: 2 so that the **h** and the altar were of one H7967
Lev 4: 7 of the blood on the **h** *of* the altar of H7967
Lev 4:18 of the blood on the **h** *of* the altar that is H7967
Lev 4:25 put it on the **h** *of* the altar of burnt H7967
Lev 4:30 put it on the **h** *of* the altar of burnt H7967
Lev 4:34 put it on the **h** *of* the altar of burnt H7967
Lev 8:15 he put it on all the **h** *of* the altar to purify H7967
Lev 9: 9 the blood and put it on the **h** *of* the altar; H7967
Lev 16:18 blood and put it on all the **h** *of* the altar. H7967
Dt 33:17 his **h** are the horns of a wild ox. H7967
Dt 33:17 his horns are the **h** *of* a wild ox. H7967
Jos 6: 4 carry trumpets of **rams' h** in front of the ark H3413
1Ki 1:50 went and took hold of the **h** *of* the altar. H7967
1Ki 1:51 is clinging to the **h** *of* the altar. H7967
1Ki 2:28 LORD and took hold of the **h** *of* the altar. H7967
1Ki 22:11 had made iron **h** and he declared, H7967
1Ch 15:28 the sounding of **rams' h** and trumpets, H8795
2Ch 15:14 with shouting and with trumpets and **h**. H8795
2Ch 18:10 son of Kenaanah had made iron **h**, H7967
Ps 22:21 save me from the **h** *of* the wild oxen. H7967
Ps 69:31 more than a bull *with its* **h** and hooves. H7966
Ps 75: 4 and to the wicked, 'Do not lift up your **h**. H7967
Ps 75: 5 Do not lift your **h** against heaven; do not H7967
Ps 75:10 "I will cut off the **h** *of* all the wicked, but H7967
Ps 75:10 the **h** *of* the righteous will be lifted up." H7967
Ps 118:27 festal procession up to the **h** *of* the altar. H7967
Jer 17: 1 of their hearts and on the **h** *of* their altars. H7967
Eze 34:21 weak sheep with your **h** until you have H7967
Eze 43:15 four **h** project upward from the hearth. H7967
Eze 43:20 put it on the four **h** *of* the altar and on the H7967
Da 7: 7 all the former beasts, and it had ten **h**. A10641
Da 7: 8 "While I was thinking about the **h**, there A10641
Da 7: 8 three of the first **h** were uprooted before A10641
Da 7:20 know about the ten **h** on its head and A10641
Da 7:24 The ten **h** are ten kings who will come A10641
Da 8: 3 there before me was a ram with *two* **h**, H7967
Da 8: 3 beside the canal, and the **h** were long. H7967
Da 8: 3 One of the **h** was longer than the other but NDT
Da 8: 7 striking the ram and shattering its two **h**. H7967
Da 8: 8 place four prominent **h** grew up toward the NDT
Da 8:22 The four **h** that replaced the one that was NDT
Am 3:14 the **h** *of* the altar will be cut off and fall to H7967
Mic 4:13 I will give you **h** *of* iron; I will give you H7967
Zec 1:18 and there before me were four **h**. H7967
Zec 1:19 "These are the **h** that scattered Judah H7967
Zec 1:21 "These are the **h** that scattered Judah so H7967
Zec 1:21 throw down these **h** *of* the nations who H7967
Zec 1:21 who lifted up their **h** against the land of H7967
Rev 5: 6 The Lamb had seven **h** and seven eyes *G3043*
Rev 9:13 coming from the four **h** of the golden altar *G3043*
Rev 12: 3 heads and ten **h** and seven crowns on *G3043*
Rev 13: 1 It had ten **h** and seven heads, with ten *G3043*
Rev 13: 1 with ten crowns on its **h**, and on each *G3043*
Rev 13:11 It had two **h** like a lamb, but it spoke like *G3043*
Rev 17: 3 names and had seven heads and ten **h**. *G3043*
Rev 17: 7 which has the seven heads and ten **h**. *G3043*
Rev 17:12 "The ten **h** you saw are ten kings who *G3043*
Rev 17:16 The beast and the ten **h** you saw will hate *G3043*

HORON See BETH HORON

HORONAIM (5)

2Sa 13:34 "I see men in the direction of **H**, on the H2589
Isa 15: 5 on the road to **H** they lament their H2589
Jer 48: 3 Cries of anguish arise from **H**, cries of H2589
Jer 48: 5 on the road down to **H** anguished cries H2589
Jer 48:34 from Zoar as far as **H** and Eglath H2589

HORONITE (3) [BETH HORON]

Ne 2:10 When Sanballat the **H** and Tobiah the H3061
Ne 2:19 But when Sanballat the **H**, Tobiah the H3061
Ne 13:28 priest was son-in-law to Sanballat the **H**. H3061

HORRIBLE (8) [HORROR]

Dt 7:15 inflict on you the **h** diseases you knew in H8273
Jer 5:30 "A **h** and shocking thing has happened in H9014
Jer 18:13 A most **h thing** has been done by Virgin H9137
Jer 23:14 of Jerusalem I have seen **something h**: H9136
Eze 26:21 bring you to a **h end** and you will be no H1166
Eze 27:36 you have come to a **h end** and will be no H1166
Eze 28:19 you have come to a **h end** and will be no H1166
Hos 6:10 I have seen a **h thing** in Israel: There H9137

HORRIFIED (2) [HORROR]

Pr 25:23 is a sly tongue—which provokes a **h** look. H2404
Jer 4: 9 the priests *will be* **h**, and the prophets H9037

HORROR (24) [HORRIBLE, HORRIFIED]

Dt 28:25 you will become a **thing of h** to all the H2400
Dt 28:37 You will become a **thing of h**, a byword H9014
2Ch 29: 8 them an object of dread and **h** and scorn, H9014
2Ch 30: 7 so that he made them an **object of h**, as H9014
Job 18:20 those of the east are seized with **h**. H8550
Ps 55: 5 have beset me; **h** has overwhelmed me. H7146
Isa 21: 4 I longed for has become a **h** to me. H3010
Jer 2:12 shudder with great **h**," declares the H2990
Jer 8:21 I am crushed; I mourn, and **h** grips me. H9014
Jer 18:16 land will be an **object of h** and of lasting H9014
Jer 19: 8 city and make it an **object of h** and scorn; H9014
Jer 25: 9 make them an **object of h** and scorn, H9014
Jer 25:18 them a ruin and an **object of h** and scorn, H9014
Jer 29:18 a curse and an **object of h**, of scorn and H9014
Jer 42:18 You will be a curse and an **object of h**, H9014
Jer 44:12 will become a curse and an **object of h**, H9014
Jer 48:39 an **object of h** to all those around her." H4745
Jer 49:13 a curse, an **object of h** and reproach H2997
Jer 49:17 "Edom will become an **object of h**; all H9014
Jer 51:37 of jackals, an **object of h** and scorn, H9014
Eze 5:15 warning and an **object of h** to the nations H5457
Eze 20:26 that *I might* **fill** them **with h** so they would H9037
Eze 27:35 kings shudder with **h** and their faces are H8550
Eze 32:10 will shudder with **h** because of you when I H8550

HORSE (37) [HORSE'S, HORSEBACK, HORSEMAN, HORSEMEN, HORSES, HORSES', WARHORSES]

Ex 15: 1 Both **h** and driver he has hurled into the H6061
Ex 15:21 Both **h** and driver he has hurled into the H6061
1Ki 10:29 of silver, and a **h** for a hundred and fifty. H6061
1Ki 20:25 horse—**h** for horse and chariot for chariot H6061
1Ki 20:25 horse for **h** and chariot for chariot H6061
2Ki 14:20 was brought back by **h** and was buried in H6061
2Ch 1:17 of silver, and a **h** for a hundred and fifty. H6061
2Ch 23:15 the entrance of the **H** Gate on the palace H6061
2Ch 25:28 brought back by **h** and was buried with H6061
Ne 3:28 Above the **H** Gate, the priests made H6061
Est 6: 8 king has worn and a **h** the king has ridden H6061
Est 6: 9 let the robe and **h** be entrusted to one H6061
Est 6: 9 lead him on the **h** through the city H6061
Est 6:10 the robe and the **h** and do just as you H6061
Est 6:11 So Haman got the robe and the **h**. H6061
Job 39:18 feathers to run, she laughs at **h** and rider. H6061
Job 39:19 "Do you give the **h** its strength or clothe H6061
Ps 32: 9 Do not be like the **h** or the mule, which H6061
Ps 33:17 A **h** is a vain hope for deliverance H6061
Ps 76: 6 God of Jacob, both **h** and chariot lie still. H6061
Ps 147:10 pleasure is not in the strength of the **h**, H6061
Pr 21:31 The **h** is made ready for the day of battle H6061
Pr 26: 3 A whip for the **h**, a bridle for the donkey H6061
Isa 63:13 Like a **h** in open country, they did not H6061
Jer 8: 6 own course like a **h** charging into battle. H6061
Jer 31:40 east as far as the corner of the **H** Gate, H6061
Jer 51:21 with you I shatter **h** and rider, with you I H6061
Zec 1: 8 me was a man mounted on a red **h**. H6061
Zec 10: 3 make them like a proud **h** in battle. H6061
Zec 12: 4 day I will strike every **h** with panic and its H6061

Rev 6: 2 there before me was a white **h**! *G2691*
Rev 6: 4 Then another **h** came out, a fiery red one *G2691*
Rev 6: 5 there before me was a black **h**! *G2691*
Rev 6: 8 there before me was a pale **h**! *G2691*
Rev 19:11 open and there before me was a white **h**, *G2691*
Rev 19:19 against the rider on the **h** and his army. *G2691*
Rev 19:21 out of the mouth of the rider on the **h**, *G2691*

HORSE'S (1) [HORSE]

Ge 49:17 that bites the **h** heels so that its rider H6061

HORSEBACK (3) [HORSE]

1Ki 20:20 of Aram escaped on **h** with some of his H6061
Est 6:11 and **led** him **on h** through the city streets H8206
Ecc 10: 7 I have seen slaves on **h**, while princes go H6061

HORSEMAN (4) [HORSE, MAN]

2Ki 9:17 "Get a **h**," Joram ordered. "Send H8208
2Ki 9:18 The **h** rode off to meet Jehu and H8206+6061
2Ki 9:19 So the king sent out a second **h** H8206+6061
Am 2:15 and the **h** will not save his life. H8206+6061

HORSEMEN (29) [HORSE, MAN]

Ge 50: 9 Chariots and **h** also went up with him. H7305
Ex 14: 9 chariots, **h** and troops—pursued H7305
Ex 14:17 his army, through his chariots and his **h**. H7305
Ex 14:18 through Pharaoh, his chariots and his **h**." H7305
Ex 14:23 chariots and **h** followed them into the H7305
Ex 14:26 the Egyptians and their chariots and **h**." H7305
Ex 14:28 back and covered the chariots and **h**— H7305
Ex 15:19 chariots and **h** went into the sea H7305
Jos 24: 6 with chariots and **h** as far as the Red Sea. H7305
1Ki 20:20 escaped on horseback with *some* of his **h**. H7305
2Ki 2:12 The chariots and **h** *of* Israel!" And Elisha H7305
2Ki 13: 7 left of the army of Jehoahaz except fifty **h**, H7305
2Ki 13:14 "The chariots and **h** *of* Israel!" H7305
2Ki 18:24 depending on Egypt for chariots and **h**? H7305
2Ch 12: 3 sixty thousand **h** and the H7305
2Ch 16: 8 with great numbers of chariots and **h**? H7305
Ezr 8:22 king for soldiers and **h** to protect us from H7305
Isa 22: 7 **h** are posted at the city gates. H7305
Isa 31: 1 in the great strength of their **h**, H7305
Isa 36: 9 depending on Egypt for chariots and **h**? H7305
Jer 4:29 At the sound of **h** and archers every town H7305
Eze 23: 6 handsome young men, and mounted **h**. H7305
Eze 23:12 mounted **h**, all handsome young H7305
Eze 26: 7 chariots, with **h** and a great army. H7305
Eze 38: 4 your horses, your **h** fully armed, and a H7305
Hos 1: 7 by horses and **h**, but I, the LORD their H7305
Hab 1: 8 gallops headlong; their **h** come from afar. H7305
Zec 10: 5 will put the enemy **h** to shame. H8206+6061
Ac 23:23 seventy **h** and two hundred spearmen to *G2689*

HORSES (125) [HORSE]

Ge 47:17 gave them food in exchange for their **h**, H6061
Ex 9: 3 the field—on your **h**, donkeys and camels H6061
Ex 14: 9 all Pharaoh's **h** and chariots, horsemen H6061
Ex 14:23 all Pharaoh's **h** and chariots and H6061
Ex 15:19 When Pharaoh's **h**, chariots and H6061
Dt 11: 4 to its **h** and chariots, how he H6061
Dt 17:16 great numbers of **h** for himself or make H6061
Dt 20: 1 enemies and see **h** and chariots and an H6061
Jos 11: 4 a large number of **h** and chariots— H6061
Jos 11: 6 are to hamstring their **h** and burn their H6061
Jos 11: 9 He hamstrung their **h** and burned their H6061
1Sa 8:11 make them serve with his chariots and **h**, H7304
2Sa 8: 4 all but a hundred of the **chariot h**. H8207
2Sa 15: 1 with a chariot and **h** and with fifty men to H6061
1Ki 1: 5 So he got chariots and **h** ready, with fifty H7304
1Ki 4:26 had four thousand stalls for chariot **h**, H6061
1Ki 4:26 chariot horses, and twelve thousand **h**. H7304
1Ki 4:28 straw for the **chariot h** and the other H8224
1Ki 4:28 the chariot horses and the other **h**. H6061
1Ki 9:19 the towns for his chariots and for his **h**— H7304
1Ki 10:25 weapons and spices, and **h** and mules. H6061
1Ki 10:26 Solomon accumulated chariots and **h**; he H7304
1Ki 10:26 hundred chariots and twelve thousand **h**, H7304
1Ki 10:28 Solomon's **h** were imported from Egypt H6061
1Ki 18: 5 grass to keep the **h** and mules alive so we H6061
1Ki 20: 1 thirty-two kings with their **h** and chariots, H6061
1Ki 20:21 overpowered the **h** and chariots and H6061
1Ki 22: 4 as your people, my **h** as your horses." H6061
1Ki 22: 4 as your people, my horses as your **h**." H6061
2Ki 2:11 chariot of fire and **h** *of* fire appeared and H6061
2Ki 3: 7 as your people, my **h** as your horses." H6061
2Ki 3: 7 as your people, my horses as your **h**." H6061
2Ki 5: 9 Naaman went with his **h** and chariots H6061
2Ki 6:14 Then he sent **h** and chariots and a strong H6061
2Ki 6:15 an army with **h** and chariots had H6061
2Ki 6:17 saw the hills full of **h** and chariots of fire H6061
2Ki 7: 6 sound of chariots and **h** and a great army, H6061
2Ki 7: 7 their tents and their **h** and donkeys. H6061
2Ki 7:10 only tethered **h** and donkeys, and the H6061
2Ki 7:13 men take five of the **h** that are left in the H6061
2Ki 7:14 So they selected two chariots with their **h** H6061
2Ki 9:33 the wall and the **h** as they trampled her H6061
2Ki 10: 2 with you and you have chariots and **h**, H6061
2Ki 11:16 the place where the **h** enter the palace H6061
2Ki 18:23 I will give you two thousand **h**—if you can H6061
2Ki 23:11 temple of the LORD the **h** that the kings of H6061
1Ch 18: 4 all but a hundred of the **chariot h**. H8207
2Ch 1:14 Solomon accumulated chariots and **h**; he H7304
2Ch 1:14 hundred chariots and twelve thousand **h**, H7304
2Ch 1:16 Solomon's **h** were imported from Egypt H6061
2Ch 8: 6 the cities for his chariots and for his **h**— H7304
2Ch 9:24 weapons and spices, and **h** and mules. H6061
2Ch 9:25 four thousand stalls for **h** and chariots, H6061
2Ch 9:25 twelve thousand **h**, which he kept in H7304
2Ch 9:28 Solomon's **h** were imported from Egypt H6061
Ezr 2:66 They had 736 **h**, 245 mules, H6061
Ne 7:68 There were 736 **h**, 245 mules, H6061
Est 8:10 who rode **fast h** especially bred for the H8224
Est 8:14 riding the royal **h**, went out, spurred on by H8224
Ps 20: 7 Some trust in chariots and some in **h**, but H6061
SS 1: 9 to a mare among Pharaoh's **chariot h**. H8207
Isa 2: 7 Their land is full of **h**; there is no end to H6061
Isa 21: 7 When he sees chariots with teams of **h** H7304
Isa 21: 9 a man in a chariot with a team of **h**. H7304
Isa 22: 6 with her charioteers and **h**; Kir uncovers H7304
Isa 28:28 but one does not use **h** to grind grain. H7304
Isa 30:16 we will flee on **h**.' Therefore you will H6061
Isa 30:16 'We will ride off on swift **h**.' Therefore your NDT
Isa 31: 1 help, who rely on **h**, who trust in the H6061
Isa 31: 3 not God; their **h** are flesh and not spirit. H6061
Isa 36: 8 I will give you two thousand **h**—if you can H6061
Isa 43:17 who drew out the chariots and **h**, the army H6061
Isa 66:20 to the LORD—on **h**, in chariots and wagons H6061
Jer 4:13 a whirlwind, his **h** are swifter than eagles. H6061
Jer 6:23 the roaring sea as they ride on their **h**; H6061
Jer 8:16 of the enemy's **h** is heard from Dan; H6061
Jer 12: 5 you out, how can you compete with **h**? H6061
Jer 17:25 will come riding in chariots and on **h**, H6061
Jer 22: 4 riding in chariots and on **h**, accompanied H6061
Jer 46: 4 Harness the **h**, mount the steeds! Take H6061
Jer 46: 9 Charge, you **h**! Drive furiously, you H6061
Jer 50:37 A sword against her **h** and chariots and H6061
Jer 50:42 the roaring sea as they ride on their **h**; H6061
Jer 51:27 send up **h** like a swarm of locusts. H6061
Eze 17:15 envoys to Egypt to get **h** and a large army. H6061
Eze 23:20 whose emission was like that of **h**. H6061
Eze 23:23 men of high rank, all mounted on **h**. H6061
Eze 26: 7 king of kings, with **h** and chariots, with H6061
Eze 26:10 His **h** will be so many that they will cover H6061
Eze 26:11 The hooves of his **h** will trample all your H6061
Eze 27:14 of Beth Togarmah exchanged **chariot h**, H6061
Eze 27:14 **cavalry h** and mules for your merchandise. H7304
Eze 38: 4 whole army—your **h**, your horsemen fully H6061
Eze 38:15 all of them riding on **h**, a great horde, H6061
Eze 39:20 table you will eat your fill of **h** and riders, H6061
Hos 1: 7 battle, or by **h** and horsemen, but I, H6061
Joel 2: 4 They have the appearance of **h**; they H6061
Am 4:10 the sword, along with your captured **h**. H6061
Am 6:12 Do **h** run on the rocky crags? Does one H6061
Mic 1:13 in Lachish, harness **fast h** to the chariot. H8224
Mic 5:10 "I will destroy your **h** from among you H6061
Na 3: 2 wheels, galloping **h** and jolting chariots! H6061
Hab 1: 8 Their **h** are swifter than leopards, fiercer H6061
Hab 3: 8 when you rode your **h** and your chariots to H6061
Hab 3:15 You trampled the sea with your **h** H6061
Hag 2:22 their drivers; **h** and their riders will fall H6061
Zec 1: 8 Behind him were red, brown and white **h**. H6061
Zec 6: 2 The first chariot had red **h**, the second H6061
Zec 6: 6 one with the black **h** is going toward the H6061
Zec 6: 6 the one with the white **h** toward the west NDT
Zec 6: 6 one with the dappled **h** toward the south." NDT
Zec 6: 7 When the powerful **h** went out, they were NDT
Zec 12: 4 I will blind all the **h** *of* the nations. H6061
Zec 14:15 similar plague will strike the **h** and mules, H6061
Zec 14:20 will be inscribed on the bells of the **h**, H6061
Ac 23:24 Provide **h** for Paul so that he may be taken *G3229*
Jas 3: 3 into the mouths *of* **h** to make them obey *G2691*
Rev 9: 7 locusts looked like **h** prepared for battle. *G2691*
Rev 9: 9 the thundering *of* many **h** and chariots *G2691*
Rev 9:17 The **h** and riders I saw in my vision looked *G2691*
Rev 9:17 The heads *of* the **h** resembled the heads *G2691*
Rev 9:19 The power *of* the **h** was in their mouths *G2691*
Rev 18:13 cattle and sheep; **h** and carriages; and *G2691*
Rev 19:14 riding on white **h** and dressed in fine *G2691*
Rev 19:18 the mighty, *of* **h** and their riders, and *G2691*

HORSES' (3) [HORSE]

Jdg 5:22 Then thundered the **h** hooves H6061
Isa 5:28 are strung; their **h** hooves seem like flint H6061
Rev 14:20 rising as high as the **h** bridles for a distance *G2691*

HOSAH (5)

Jos 19:29 turned toward **H** and came out at the H2881
1Ch 16:38 Jeduthun, and also **H**, were gatekeepers. H2880
1Ch 26:10 **H** the Merarite had sons: Shimri the first H2880
1Ch 26:11 The sons and relatives of **H** were 13 in all. H2880
1Ch 26:16 on the upper road fell to Shuppim and **H**. H2880

HOSANNA (6)

Mt 21: 9 followed shouted, "**H** to the Son of David!" *G6057*
Mt 21: 9 "**H** in the highest heaven! *G6057*
Mt 21:15 the temple courts, "**H** to the Son of David," *G6057*
Mk 11: 9 those who followed shouted, "**H**! *G6057*
Mk 11:10 "**H** in the highest heaven! *G6057*
Jn 12:13 went out to meet him, shouting, "**H**!" *G6057*

HOSEA (5)

Hos 1: 1 LORD that came to **H** son of Beeri during H2107
Hos 1: 2 When the LORD began to speak through **H** H2107
Hos 1: 4 Then the LORD said to **H**, "Call him H2257S
Hos 1: 6 Then the LORD said to **H**, "Call her H2257S
Ro 9:25 As he says in **H**: "I will call them 'my *G6060*

HOSHAIAH (3)

Ne 12:32 **H** and half the leaders of Judah followed H2108
Jer 42: 1 son of Kareah and Jezaniah son of **H**, H2108
Jer 43: 2 Azariah son of **H** and Johanan son of H2108

HOSHAMA (1)

1Ch 3:18 Shenazzar, Jekamiah, **H** and Nedabiah. H2106

HOSHEA (12) [JOSHUA]

Nu 13: 8 from the tribe of Ephraim, **H** son of Nun; H2107
Nu 13:16 Moses gave **H** son of Nun the name H2107
2Ki 15:30 Then **H** son of Elah conspired against H2107
2Ki 17: 1 **H** son of Elah became king of Israel in H2107
2Ki 17: 3 king of Assyria came up to attack **H**, H2107
2Ki 17: 4 of Assyria discovered that **H** was a traitor, H2107
2Ki 17: 6 In the ninth year of **H**, the king of Assyria H2107
2Ki 18: 1 In the third year of **H** son of Elah king of H2107
2Ki 18: 9 the seventh year of **H** son of Elah king of H2107
2Ki 18:10 was the ninth year of **H** king of Israel. H2107
1Ch 27:20 **H** son of Azaziah; over half the tribe of H2107
Ne 10:23 **H**, Hananiah, Hasshub, H2107

HOSPITABLE (2) [HOSPITALITY]

1Ti 3: 2 respectable, **h**, able to teach, *G5811*
Titus 1: 8 he must be **h**, one who loves what *G5811*

HOSPITALITY (8) [HOSPITABLE]

Ac 28: 7 home and **showed** us generous **h** for *G3826*
Ro 12:13 Lord's people who are in need. Practice **h**. *G5810*
Ro 16:23 **h** I and the whole church here **enjoy**, *G3828*
1Ti 5:10 up children, **showing h**, washing the feet *G3827*
Heb 13: 2 Do not forget to **show h to strangers**, for *G5810*
Heb 13: 2 some people *have* **shown h** to angels *G3826*
1Pe 4: 9 **Offer h** to one another without grumbling. *G5811*
3Jn 8 ought therefore *to* **show h** to such people *G5696*

HOST (12) [HOSTS]

Ne 9: 6 all their **starry h**, the earth and all H7372
Ps 33: 6 their **starry h** by the breath of his mouth. H7372
Pr 23: 6 not eat the food of a **begrudging h**, H8273+6524
Isa 34: 4 all the **starry h** will fall like withered H7372
Isa 40:26 brings out the **starry h** one by one and H7372
Da 8:10 until it reached the **h** *of* the heavens, H7372
Da 8:10 some of the starry **h** down to the earth H7372
Zep 1: 5 down on the roofs to worship the starry **h**, H7372
Lk 2:13 of the heavenly **h** appeared with the *G5131*
Lk 14: 9 the **h** *who* **invited** both of you will come *G2813*
Lk 14:10 so that when your **h** comes, he will say to *G2813*
Lk 14:12 Then Jesus said *to* his **h**, "When you give *G2813*

HOSTAGES (2)

2Ki 14:14 He also took **h** and returned to H1201+9510
2Ch 25:24 the palace treasures and the **h**, H1201+9510

HOSTILE (13) [HOSTILITY]

Ge 26:27 since you *were* **h** *to* me and sent me away H8533
Lev 26:21 " 'If you remain **h** toward me and refuse H7950
Lev 26:23 continue to be **h** toward me, H7950
Lev 26:24 I myself will be **h** toward you and will H7950
Lev 26:27 to me but continue to be **h** toward me, H7950
Lev 26:28 then in my anger I will be **h** toward you H7950
Lev 26:41 which made me **h** toward them so that I H7950
Nu 24: 8 They devour **h** nations and break their H7640
Jdg 6:31 Joash replied to the **h** crowd around him, NDT
1Ki 11:25 ruled in Aram and *was* **h** toward Israel. H7762
Isa 11:13 of Judah, nor Judah **h** *toward* Ephraim. H7675
Ro 8: 7 mind governed by the flesh is **h** to God; *G2397*
1Th 2:15 They displease God and are **h** to everyone *G1885*

HOSTILITY (13) [HOSTILE]

Ge 16:12 and he will live in **h toward** all his H6584+7156
Ge 25:18 And *they* **lived in h toward** H5877+6584+7156
Ge 49:23 attacked him; they shot at him *with* **h**. H8475
Lev 26:40 their unfaithfulness and their **h** toward me H7950
2Ch 21:16 against Jehoram the **h** *of* the Philistines H8120
Job 17: 2 my eyes must dwell on their **h**. H5286
Ps 78:49 indignation and **h**—a band of destroying H7650
Eze 25:15 with ancient **h** sought to destroy Judah, H368
Eze 35: 5 harbored an ancient **h** and delivered the H368
Hos 9: 7 your sins are so many and your **h** so great, H5378
Hos 9: 8 his paths, and **h** in the house of his God. H5378
Eph 2:14 the barrier, the dividing wall *of* **h**, *G2397*
Eph 2:16 by which he put to death their **h**. *G2397*

HOSTS (11) [HOST]

2Ki 17:16 They bowed down to all the starry **h**, and H7372
2Ki 21: 3 to all the starry **h** and worshiped them. H7372
2Ki 21: 5 the LORD, he built altars to all the starry **h**. H7372
2Ki 23: 4 Baal and Asherah and all the starry **h**. H7372
2Ki 23: 5 the constellations and to all the starry **h**. H7372
2Ch 33: 3 to all the starry **h** and worshiped them. H7372
2Ch 33: 5 the LORD, he built altars to all the starry **h**. H7372
Ps 103:21 the LORD, all his **heavenly h**, you his H7372
Ps 148: 2 his angels; praise him, all his **heavenly h**. H7372
Isa 45:12 the heavens; I marshaled their **starry h**. H7372
Jer 19:13 to all the starry **h** and poured out drink H7372

HOT (25) [HOTLY, HOTTER]

Ge 36:24 who discovered the **h springs** in the desert H3553
Ex 11: 8 Then Moses, **h** with anger, left H3034
Ex 16:21 when the sun *grew* **h**, it melted away. H2801
1Sa 11: 9 'By the time the sun *is* **h** tomorrow, you H2801
1Sa 14:22 they joined the battle **in h pursuit**. H339

1Sa 21: 6 replaced by **h** bread on the day it H2770
1Sa 31: 2 Philistines *were* **in h pursuit** *of* Saul and H1815
2Sa 1: 6 the chariots and their drivers **in h pursuit.** H1815
1Ki 19: 6 head was some bread **baked over h coals,** H8363
1Ch 10: 2 Philistines *were* **in h pursuit** of Saul and H1815
Ne 7: 3 are not to be opened until the sun *is* **h**. H2801
Job 15: 2 fill their belly with the **h east wind**? H7708
Ps 39: 3 my heart *grew* **h** within me. While I H2801
Ps 56: 1 my enemies *are* **in h pursuit**; all day H8634
Ps 78:49 He unleashed against them his **h** anger H3019
Pr 6:28 a man walk on **h coals** without his feet H1624
La 5:10 Our skin *is* **h** as an oven, feverish from H4023
Eze 24:11 the coals till *it becomes* **h** and its copper H2801
Eze 38:18 land of Israel, my **h** anger will be aroused H2779
Da 3:22 the furnace so **h** that the flames of A10015
Hos 7: 7 All of them *are* **h** as an oven; they devour H2801
Lk 12:55 you say, 'It's going to be **h**,' and it is. *G3014*
1Ti 4: 2 *have been* **seared as with a h iron**. *G3013*
Rev 3:15 that you are neither cold nor **h**. *G2412*
Rev 3:16 lukewarm—neither **h** nor cold—I am *G2412*

HOT-TEMPERED (4) [TEMPER]

Pr 15:18 A **h** person stirs up conflict, but the one H2779
Pr 19:19 A **h** *person* must pay the penalty H1524+2779
Pr 22:24 Do not make friends with a **h** person, do H678
Pr 29:22 and a **h** *person* commits many sins. H1251+2779

HOTHAM (2)

1Ch 7:32 Shomer and **H** and of their sister Shua. H2598
1Ch 11:44 Jeiel the sons of **H** the Aroerite, H2598

HOTHEADED (1) [HEAD]

Pr 14:16 but a fool *is* **h** and yet feels secure. H6297

HOTHIR (2)

1Ch 25: 4 Mallothi, **H** and Mahazioth. H2110
1Ch 25:28 the twenty-first to **H**, his sons and H2110

HOTLY (1) [HOT]

Ps 57: 3 rebuking *those who* **h pursue** me—God H8634

HOTTER (1) [HOT]

Da 3:19 furnace heated seven times **h** than usual A10015

HOUGHED (KJV) HAMSTRUNG

HOUND (1) [HOUNDED]

Job 19:28 "If you say, 'How *we will* **h** him, since the H8103

HOUNDED (1) [HOUND]

Ps 109:16 **h** to death the poor and the needy H8103

HOUR (45) [HOURS]

Ecc 9:12 no one knows when their **h** will come: H6961
Mt 6:27 by worrying add a single **h** to your life? *G4388*
Mt 20:12 who were hired last worked only one **h**, *G6052*
Mt 24:36 "But about that day or **h** no one knows *G6052*
Mt 24:44 Man will come *at* an **h** when you do not *G6052*
Mt 24:50 him and at an **h** he is not aware of. *G6052*
Mt 25:13 because you do not know the day or the **h**. *G6052*
Mt 26:40 you men keep watch with me *for* one **h**?" *G6052*
Mt 26:45 the **h** has come, and the Son of *G6052*
Mt 26:55 In that **h** Jesus said to the crowd, "Am I *G6052*
Mk 13:32 "But about that day or **h** no one knows *G6052*
Mk 14:35 if possible the **h** might pass from him. *G6052*
Mk 14:37 Couldn't you keep watch *for* one **h**? *G6052*
Mk 14:41 The **h** has come. Look, the Son *G6052*
Lk 12:25 worrying can add a *single* **h** to your life? *G4388*
Lk 12:39 had known at what **h** the thief was *G6052*
Lk 12:40 Man will come *at* an **h** when you do not *G6052*
Lk 12:46 him and at an **h** he is not aware of. *G6052*
Lk 22:14 When the **h** came, Jesus and his apostles *G6052*
Lk 22:53 But this is your **h**—when darkness reigns *G6052*
Lk 22:59 About an **h** later another asserted *G6052*
Jn 2: 4 Jesus replied. "My **h** has not yet come." *G6052*
Jn 7:30 on him, because his **h** had not yet come. *G6052*
Jn 8:20 because his **h** had not yet come. *G6052*
Jn 12:23 "The **h** has come for the Son of Man to be *G6052*
Jn 12:27 'Father, save me from this **h**'? No, *G6052*
Jn 12:27 it was for this very reason I came to this **h**. *G6052*
Jn 13: 1 knew that the **h** had come for him to *G6052*
Jn 17: 1 "Father, the **h** has come. Glorify *G6052*
Ac 10:30 ago I was in my house praying at this **h**, *G6052*
Ac 16:33 At that **h** of the night the jailer took them *G6052*
Ro 13:11 The **h** has already come for you to wake *G6052*
1Co 4:11 To this very **h** we go hungry and thirsty, we *G6052*
1Co 15:30 why do we endanger ourselves every **h**? *G6052*
1Jn 2:18 this is the last **h**; and as you have heard *G6052*
1Jn 2:18 This is how we know it is the last **h**. *G6052*
Rev 3:10 keep you from the **h** of trial that is going *G6052*
Rev 8: 1 was silence in heaven *for* about **half an h**. *G2469*
Rev 9:15 ready for this very **h** and day and month *G6052*
Rev 11:13 At that very **h** there was a severe *G6052*
Rev 14: 7 because the **h** of his judgment has come. *G6052*
Rev 17:12 who *for* one **h** will receive authority as *G6052*
Rev 18:10 *In* one **h** your doom has come *G6052*
Rev 18:17 *In* one **h** such great wealth has been *G6052*
Rev 18:19 *In* one **h** she has been brought to ruin *G6052*

HOURS (4) [HOUR]

2Sa 2:29 through the **morning h** and came to H1443
Jn 11: 9 "Are there not twelve **h** of daylight? *G6052*
Ac 5: 7 About three **h** later his wife came in, not *G6052*
Ac 19:34 they all shouted in unison for about two **h**: *G6052*

HOUSE (744) [HOUSEHOLD, HOUSEHOLDS, HOUSES, HOUSETOP, STOREHOUSE, STOREHOUSES]

Ge 19: 2 "please turn aside to your servant's **h**. H1074
Ge 19: 3 they did go with him and entered his **h**. H1074
Ge 19: 4 both young and old—surrounded the **h**. H1074
Ge 19:10 Lot back into the **h** and shut the door. H1074
Ge 19:11 the men who were at the door of the **h**, H1074
Ge 24:23 room in your father's **h** for us to spend the H1074
Ge 24:27 on the journey to the **h** *of* my master's H1074
Ge 24:31 I have prepared the **h** and a place for the H1074
Ge 24:32 So the man went to the **h**, and the camels H1074
Ge 27:15 which she had in the **h**, and put them on H1074
Ge 28: 2 to the **h** *of* your mother's father Bethuel. H1074
Ge 28:17 This is none other than the **h** *of* God; this H1074
Ge 28:22 I have set up as a pillar will be God's **h**, H1074
Ge 34:26 took Dinah from Shechem's **h** and left. H1074
Ge 39: 2 he lived in the **h** *of* his Egyptian H1074
Ge 39: 5 both in the **h** and in the field. H1074
Ge 39: 8 concern himself with anything in the **h**; H1074
Ge 39: 9 No one is greater in this **h** than I am. H1074
Ge 39:11 day he went into the **h** to attend to his H1074
Ge 39:12 his cloak in her hand and ran out of the **h**. NDT
Ge 39:13 cloak in her hand and had run out of the **h**, NDT
Ge 39:15 his cloak beside me and ran out of the **h**." NDT
Ge 39:18 his cloak beside me and ran out of the **h**." NDT
Ge 40: 3 in custody in the **h** *of* the captain of the H1074
Ge 40: 7 in custody with him in his master's **h**, H1074
Ge 41:10 chief baker in the **h** *of* the captain of the H1074
Ge 43:16 he said to the steward of his **h**, "Take H1074
Ge 43:16 "Take these men to my **h**, slaughter an H1074
Ge 43:17 told him and took the men to Joseph's **h**. H1074
Ge 43:18 frightened when they were taken to his **h**. H1074
Ge 43:19 spoke to him at the entrance to the **h**. H1074
Ge 43:24 The steward took the men into Joseph's **h**, H1074
Ge 43:26 him the gifts they had brought into the **h**, H1074
Ge 44: 1 these instructions to the steward of his **h**: H1074
Ge 44: 8 steal silver or gold from your master's **h**? H1074
Ge 44:14 was still in the **h** when Judah and his H1074
Ex 3:22 woman living in her **h** for articles of silver H1074
Ex 12:22 go out of the door of your **h** until morning. H1074
Ex 12:30 there was not a **h** without someone H1074
Ex 12:46 "It must be eaten inside the **h**; take none H1074
Ex 12:46 take none of the meat outside the **h**. H1074
Ex 20:17 "You shall not covet your neighbor's **h** H1074
Ex 22: 7 they are stolen from the neighbor's **h**, H1074
Ex 22: 8 the owner of the **h** must appear before H1074
Ex 22: 8 the owner of the **h** has laid hands on the NDT
Ex 23:19 of your soil to the **h** *of* the LORD your God. H1074
Ex 34:26 of your soil to the **h** *of* the LORD your God. H1074
Lev 14:34 I put a spreading mold in a **h** *in* that land, H1074
Lev 14:35 the owner of the **h** must go and tell the H1074
Lev 14:35 that looks like a defiling mold in my **h**. H1074
Lev 14:36 is to order the **h** to be emptied before H1074
Lev 14:36 that nothing in the **h** will be pronounced H1074
Lev 14:36 the priest is to go in and inspect the **h**. H1074
Lev 14:38 the doorway of the **h** and close it up for H1074
Lev 14:39 day the priest shall return to inspect the **h**. NDT
Lev 14:41 the inside walls of the **h** scraped and the H1074
Lev 14:42 take new clay and plaster the **h**. H1074
Lev 14:43 reappears in the **h** after the stones have H1074
Lev 14:43 torn out and the **h** scraped and plastered H1074
Lev 14:44 if the mold has spread in the **h**, it is a H1074
Lev 14:44 persistent defiling mold; the **h** is unclean. H1074
Lev 14:46 who goes into the **h** while it is closed up H1074
Lev 14:47 sleeps or eats in the **h** must wash their H1074
Lev 14:48 not spread after the **h** has been plastered, H1074
Lev 14:48 he shall pronounce the **h** clean, because H1074
Lev 14:49 To purify the **h** he is to take two birds and H1074
Lev 14:51 and sprinkle the **h** seven times. H1074
Lev 14:52 He shall purify the **h** with the bird's blood H1074
Lev 14:53 way he will make atonement for the **h**, H1074
Lev 14:55 defiling molds in fabric or in a **h**, H1074
Lev 25:29 who sells a **h** *in* a walled city H1074+4632
Lev 25:30 the **h** in the walled city shall belong H1074
Lev 25:33 a **h** sold in any town they hold H1074
Lev 27:14 dedicates their **h** as something holy to H1074
Lev 27:15 who dedicates their **h** wishes to redeem it H1074
Lev 27:15 and the **h** will again become theirs. NDT
Nu 12: 7 servant Moses; he is faithful in all my **h**. H1074
Dt 5:21 your desire on your neighbor's **h** or land, H1074
Dt 7:26 a detestable thing into your **h** or you, H1074
Dt 20: 5 anyone built a new **h** and not yet begun H1074
Dt 21:13 she has lived in your **h** and mourned her H1074
Dt 22: 8 When you build a new **h**, make a parapet H1074
Dt 22: 8 of bloodshed on your **h** if someone falls H1074
Dt 22:21 of her father's **h** and there the men of H1074
Dt 22:21 promiscuous while still in her father's **h**. H1074
Dt 23:18 prostitute into the **h** *of* the LORD your God H1074
Dt 24: 1 gives it to her and sends her from his **h**, H1074
Dt 24: 2 she leaves his **h** she becomes the wife H1074
Dt 24: 3 gives it to her and sends her from his **h**, or H1074
Dt 24:10 do not go into their **h** to get what is H1074
Dt 25:14 have two differing measures in your **h**— H1074
Dt 26:13 removed from my **h** the sacred portion H1074
Dt 28:30 You will build a **h**, but you will not live in H1074
Jos 2: 1 entered the **h** *of* a prostitute named H1074
Jos 2: 3 who came to you and entered your **h**, H1074
Jos 2:15 the **h** she lived in was part of the city H1074
Jos 2:18 brothers and all your family into your **h**. H1074
Jos 2:19 of them go outside your **h** into the street, H1074
Jos 2:19 As for those who are in the **h** with you H1074
Jos 6:17 who are with her in her **h** shall be spared, H1074
Jos 6:22 the prostitute's **h** and bring her out and H1074
Jos 6:24 iron into the treasury of the LORD's **h**. H1074
Jos 9:23 water carriers for the **h** *of* my God. H1074
Jdg 11: 7 hate me and drive me from my father's **h**? H1074
Jdg 11:31 of the door of my **h** to meet me when I H1074
Jdg 12: 1 to burn down your **h** over your head." H1074
Jdg 17: 4 And it was put in Micah's **h**. H1074
Jdg 17: 8 he came to Micah's **h** in the hill country of H1074
Jdg 17:12 man became his priest and lived in his **h**. H1074
Jdg 18: 2 of Ephraim and came to the **h** *of* Micah, H1074
Jdg 18: 3 When they were near Micah's **h**, they H1074
Jdg 18:13 of Ephraim and came to Micah's **h**. H1074
Jdg 18:15 went to the **h** *of* the young Levite at H1074
Jdg 18:18 went into Micah's **h** and took the idol, H1074
Jdg 18:22 had gone some distance from Micah's **h**, H1074
Jdg 18:31 all the time the **h** *of* God was in Shiloh. H1074
Jdg 19:18 now I am going to the **h** *of* the LORD. H1074
Jdg 19:20 "You are welcome at my **h**," the old man NDT
Jdg 19:21 took him into his **h** and fed his donkeys. H1074
Jdg 19:22 wicked men of the city surrounded the **h**. H1074
Jdg 19:22 shouted to the old man who owned the **h**, H1074
Jdg 19:22 who came to your **h** so we can have sex H1074
Jdg 19:23 The owner of the **h** went outside and said H1074
Jdg 19:26 went back to the **h** where her master was H1074
Jdg 19:27 the door of the **h** and stepped out to H1074
Jdg 19:27 fallen in the doorway of the **h**, with her H1074
Jdg 20: 5 came after me and surrounded the **h**, H1074
Jdg 20: 8 not one of us will return to his **h**. H1074
1Sa 1: 7 Hannah went up to the **h** *of* the LORD, H1074
1Sa 1: 9 his chair by the doorpost of the LORD's **h**. H2121
1Sa 1:24 brought him to the **h** *of* the LORD at Shiloh. H1074
1Sa 2:31 the strength of your priestly **h**, H1074
1Sa 2:35 I will firmly establish his priestly **h**, and H1074
1Sa 3: 3 was lying down in the **h** *of* the LORD, H2121
1Sa 3:14 Therefore I swore to the **h** *of* Eli, 'The guilt H1074
1Sa 3:14 'The guilt of Eli's **h** will never be atoned H1074
1Sa 3:15 opened the doors of the **h** *of* the LORD. H1074
1Sa 7: 1 brought it to Abinadab's **h** on the hill H1074
1Sa 9:18 you please tell me where the seer's **h** is?" H1074
1Sa 9:25 talked with Saul on the **roof of** his **h**. H1511
1Sa 18:10 He was prophesying in his **h**, while David H1074
1Sa 19: 9 was sitting in his **h** with his spear in his H1074
1Sa 19:11 sent men to David's **h** to watch it and to H1074
1Sa 20:16 made a covenant with the **h** *of* David, H1074
1Sa 21:15 Must this man come into my **h**?" H1074
1Sa 25:36 he was in the **h** holding a banquet like H1074
1Sa 28:24 The woman had a fattened calf at the **h** H1074
2Sa 3: 1 war between the **h** *of* Saul and the house H1074
2Sa 3: 1 of Saul and the **h** *of* David lasted a long H1074
2Sa 3: 1 while the **h** *of* Saul grew weaker and H1074
2Sa 3: 6 war between the **h** *of* Saul and the house H1074
2Sa 3: 6 the house of Saul and the **h** *of* David, H1074
2Sa 3: 6 his own position in the **h** *of* Saul. H1074
2Sa 3: 8 I am loyal to the **h** *of* your father Saul H1074
2Sa 3:10 kingdom from the **h** *of* Saul and establish H1074
2Sa 4: 5 set out for the **h** *of* Ish-Bosheth, and they H1074
2Sa 4: 6 the inner part of the **h** as if to get some H1074
2Sa 4: 7 had gone into the **h** while he was lying H1074
2Sa 4:11 man in his own **h** and on his own bed— H1074
2Sa 6: 3 brought it from the **h** *of* Abinadab, H1074
2Sa 6:10 he took it to the **h** *of* Obed-Edom the H1074
2Sa 6:11 LORD remained in the **h** *of* Obed-Edom the H1074
2Sa 6:12 of God from the **h** *of* Obed-Edom to the H1074
2Sa 6:21 anyone from his **h** when he appointed H1074
2Sa 7: 2 living in a **h** *of* cedar, while the ark H1074
2Sa 7: 5 you the one to build me a **h** to dwell in? H1074
2Sa 7: 6 I have not dwelt in a **h** from the day I H1074
2Sa 7: 7 "Why have you not built me a **h** *of* cedar?" H1074
2Sa 7:11 the LORD himself will establish a **h** for you: H1074
2Sa 7:13 the one who will build a **h** for my Name, H1074
2Sa 7:16 Your **h** and your kingdom will endure H1074
2Sa 7:19 about the future of the **h** *of* your servant— H1074
2Sa 7:25 made concerning your servant and his **h**. H1074
2Sa 7:26 And the **h** *of* your servant David will be H1074
2Sa 7:27 servant, saying, 'I will build a **h** for you. H1074
2Sa 7:29 be pleased to bless the **h** *of* your servant, H1074
2Sa 7:29 your blessing the **h** *of* your servant will be H1074
2Sa 9: 1 still left of the **h** *of* Saul to whom I can H1074
2Sa 9: 3 alive from the **h** *of* Saul to whom I can H1074
2Sa 9: 4 "He is at the **h** *of* Makir son of Ammiel in H1074
2Sa 9: 5 from the **h** *of* Makir son of Ammiel. H1074
2Sa 11: 8 "Go down to your **h** and wash your feet." H1074
2Sa 11: 9 servants and did not go down to his **h**. H1074
2Sa 11:11 could I go to my **h** to eat and drink and H1074
2Sa 11:27 David had her brought to his **h**, and she H1074
2Sa 12: 8 I gave your master's **h** to you, and your H1074
2Sa 12:10 the sword will never depart from your **h** H1074
2Sa 12:20 he went into the **h** *of* the LORD and H1074
2Sa 12:20 Then he went to his own **h**, and at his H1074
2Sa 13: 7 "Go to the **h** *of* your brother Amnon and H1074
2Sa 13: 8 Tamar went to the **h** *of* her brother H1074
2Sa 13:20 Tamar lived in her brother Absalom's **h**, H1074
2Sa 14:24 "He must go to his own **h**; he must not H1074
2Sa 14:24 went to his own **h** and did not see the H1074
2Sa 14:31 Then Joab did go to Absalom's **h**, and he H1074
2Sa 17:18 went to the **h** *of* a man in Bahurim. H1074
2Sa 17:20 men came to the woman at the **h**, H1074
2Sa 17:23 set out for his **h** in his hometown. H1074
2Sa 17:23 He put his **h** in order and then hanged H1074
2Sa 19: 5 Joab went into the **h** to the king and said, H1074
2Sa 20: 3 palace and put them in a **h** under guard. H1074

2Sa 21: 1 account of Saul and his blood-stained **h**; H1074
2Sa 23: 5 "If my **h** were not right with God, surely he H1074
1Ki 2:27 had spoken at Shiloh about the **h** *of* Eli. H1074
1Ki 2:33 descendants, his **h** and his throne, may H1074
1Ki 2:36 "Build yourself a **h** in Jerusalem and live H1074
1Ki 3:17 This woman and I live in the same **h**, and H1074
1Ki 3:18 was no one in the **h** but the two of us. H1074
1Ki 8:43 may know that this **h** I have built bears H1074
1Ki 11:18 who gave Hadad a **h** and land and H1074
1Ki 12:16 Look after your own **h**, David!" So the H1074
1Ki 12:19 against the **h** *of* David to this day. H1074
1Ki 12:20 Judah remained loyal to the **h** *of* David. H1074
1Ki 12:26 will now likely revert to the **h** *of* David. H1074
1Ki 13: 2 Josiah will be born to the **h** *of* David. H1074
1Ki 13:18 back with you to your **h** so that he may eat H1074
1Ki 13:19 with him and ate and drank in his **h**. H1074
1Ki 13:34 was the sin of the **h** *of* Jeroboam that led H1074
1Ki 14: 4 he said and went to Ahijah's **h** in Shiloh. H1074
1Ki 14: 8 away from the **h** *of* David and gave it to H1074
1Ki 14:10 to bring disaster on the **h** *of* Jeroboam. H1074
1Ki 14:10 I will burn up the **h** *of* Jeroboam as one H1074
1Ki 14:13 only one in the **h** *of* Jeroboam in whom H1074
1Ki 14:17 she stepped over the threshold of the **h**, H1074
1Ki 16: 3 I am about to wipe out Baasha and his **h**, H1074
1Ki 16: 3 I will make your **h** like that of H1074
1Ki 16: 7 Jehu son of Hanani to Baasha and his **h**, H1074
1Ki 16: 7 becoming like the **h** *of* Jeroboam—and H1074
1Ki 17:17 the woman who owned the **h** became ill. H1074
1Ki 17:23 him down from the room into the **h**. H1074
1Ki 21:22 I will make your **h** like that of Jeroboam H1074
1Ki 21:29 will bring it on his **h** in the days of his son H1074
2Ki 4: 2 what do you have in your **h**?" "Your H1074
2Ki 4:32 When Elisha reached the **h**, there was the H1074
2Ki 5: 9 stopped at the door of Elisha's **h**. H1074
2Ki 5:24 the servants and put them away in the **h**. H1074
2Ki 6:32 Now Elisha was sitting in his **h**, and the H1074
2Ki 7:17 foretold when the king came down to his **h**. NDT
2Ki 8: 3 to appeal to the king for her **h** and land. H1074
2Ki 8: 5 to appeal to the king for her **h** and land. H1074
2Ki 8:18 of Israel, as the **h** *of* Ahab had done, for H1074
2Ki 8:27 the ways of the **h** *of* Ahab and did evil in H1074
2Ki 8:27 the LORD, as the **h** *of* Ahab had done, for H1074
2Ki 9: 6 Jehu got up and went into the **h**. H1074
2Ki 9: 7 are to destroy the **h** *of* Ahab your master, H1074
2Ki 9: 8 The whole **h** *of* Ahab will perish. I will cut H1074
2Ki 9: 9 I will make the **h** *of* Ahab like the house of H1074
2Ki 9: 9 of Ahab like the **h** *of* Jeroboam son of H1074
2Ki 9: 9 Nebat and like the **h** *of* Baasha son of H1074
2Ki 10: 1 in Samaria seventy sons of the **h** of Ahab. NDT
2Ki 10: 3 Then fight for your master's **h**." H1074
2Ki 10:10 spoken against the **h** *of* Ahab will fail. H1074
2Ki 10:11 Jezreel who remained of the **h** *of* Ahab, H1074
2Ki 10:30 have done to the **h** *of* Ahab all I had in H1074
2Ki 13: 6 away from the sins of the **h** *of* Jeroboam, H1074
2Ki 15: 5 day he died, and he lived in a separate **h**. H1074
2Ki 17:21 he tore Israel away from the **h** *of* David, H1074
2Ki 20: 1 Put your **h** in order, because you are H1074
2Ki 21:13 plumb line used against the **h** *of* Ahab. H1074
1Ch 6:31 of the music in the **h** *of* the LORD after the H1074
1Ch 6:48 duties of the tabernacle, the **h** *of* God. H1074
1Ch 9:11 the official in charge of the **h** *of* God; H1074
1Ch 9:13 ministering in the **h** *of* God. H1074
1Ch 9:23 guarding the gates of the **h** *of* the LORD— H1074
1Ch 9:23 the **h** called the tent of meeting. H1074
1Ch 9:26 the rooms and treasuries in the **h** *of* God. H1074
1Ch 9:27 the night stationed around the **h** *of* God, H1074
1Ch 10: 6 sons died, and all his **h** died together. H1074
1Ch 12:29 had remained loyal to Saul's **h** until then; H1074
1Ch 13: 7 of God from Abinadab's **h** on a new cart, H1074
1Ch 13:13 he took it to the **h** *of* Obed-Edom the H1074
1Ch 13:14 of Obed-Edom in his **h** for three months, H1074
1Ch 15:25 of the LORD from the **h** *of* Obed-Edom, H1074
1Ch 17: 1 living in a **h** *of* cedar, while the ark H1074
1Ch 17: 4 not the one to build me a **h** to dwell in. H1074
1Ch 17: 5 I have not dwelt in a **h** from the day I H1074
1Ch 17: 6 "Why have you not built me a **h** *of* cedar?" H1074
1Ch 17:10 to you that the LORD will build a **h** for you: H1074
1Ch 17:12 He is the one who will build a **h** for me H1074
1Ch 17:14 will set him over my **h** and my kingdom H1074
1Ch 17:17 about the future of the **h** *of* your servant. H1074
1Ch 17:23 your servant and his **h** be established H1074
1Ch 17:24 And the **h** *of* your servant David will be H1074
1Ch 17:25 servant that you will build a **h** for him. H1074
1Ch 17:27 pleased to bless the **h** *of* your servant, H1074
1Ch 22: 1 "The **h** *of* the LORD God is to be here H1074
1Ch 22: 2 dressed stone for building the **h** *of* God. H1074
1Ch 22: 5 the **h** to be built for the LORD should H1074
1Ch 22: 6 charged him to build a **h** for the LORD, H1074
1Ch 22: 7 my heart to build a **h** for the Name of the H1074
1Ch 22: 8 You are not to build a **h** for my Name H1074
1Ch 22:10 the one who will build a **h** for my Name. H1074
1Ch 22:11 build the **h** *of* the LORD your God, H1074
1Ch 23:28 of other duties at the **h** *of* God. H1074
1Ch 25: 6 for the ministry at the **h** *of* God. H1074
1Ch 26:20 the treasuries of the **h** *of* God and the H1074
1Ch 28: 2 my heart to build a **h** as a place of rest H1074
1Ch 28: 3 'You are not to build a **h** for my Name H1074
1Ch 28: 6 one who will build my **h** and my courts, H1074
1Ch 28:10 chosen you to build a **h** as the sanctuary. H1074
2Ch 6:33 may know that this **h** I have built bears H1074
2Ch 10:16 Look after your own **h**, David!" So all the H1074
2Ch 10:19 against the **h** *of* David to this day. H1074
2Ch 21: 6 of Israel, as the **h** *of* Ahab had done, for H1074
2Ch 21: 7 was not willing to destroy the **h** *of* David. H1074
2Ch 21:13 themselves, just as the **h** *of* Ahab did. H1074
2Ch 22: 3 too followed the ways of the **h** *of* Ahab, H1074
2Ch 22: 4 the LORD, as the **h** *of* Ahab had done, for H1074
2Ch 22: 7 had anointed to destroy the **h** *of* Ahab. H1074
2Ch 22: 8 executing judgment on the **h** *of* Ahab, H1074
2Ch 22: 9 was no one in the **h** *of* Ahaziah powerful H1074
2Ch 22:10 the whole royal family of the **h** *of* Judah. H1074
2Ch 26:21 He lived in a separate **h**—leprous, and H1074
2Ch 35:21 but the **h** *with which* I am at war. H1074
Ezr 1: 5 go up and build the **h** *of* the LORD in H1074
Ezr 2:68 they arrived at the **h** *of* the LORD in H1074
Ezr 2:68 the rebuilding of the **h** *of* God on its site. H1074
Ezr 3: 8 their arrival at the **h** *of* God in Jerusalem, H1074
Ezr 3: 8 the building of the **h** *of* the LORD. H1074
Ezr 3: 9 those working on the **h** *of* God. H1074
Ezr 3:11 foundation of the **h** *of* the LORD was laid. H1074
Ezr 4:24 the work on the **h** *of* God in Jerusalem A10103
Ezr 5: 2 to rebuild the **h** *of* God in Jerusalem. A10103
Ezr 5:13 issued a decree to rebuild this **h** *of* God. A10103
Ezr 5:14 gold and silver articles of the **h** *of* God, A10103
Ezr 5:15 And rebuild the **h** *of* God on its site.' A10103
Ezr 5:16 of the **h** *of* God in Jerusalem. A10103
Ezr 5:17 to rebuild this **h** *of* God in Jerusalem. A10103
Ezr 6: 5 gold and silver articles of the **h** *of* God, A10103
Ezr 6: 5 they are to be deposited in the **h** *of* God. A10103
Ezr 6: 7 elders rebuild this **h** *of* God on its site. A10103
Ezr 6: 8 Jews in the construction of this **h** *of* God: A10103
Ezr 6:11 be pulled from their **h** and they are to be A10103
Ezr 6:11 this crime their **h** is to be made a pile A10103
Ezr 6:16 the dedication of the **h** *of* God with joy. A10103
Ezr 6:17 dedication of this **h** *of* God they offered A10103
Ezr 6:22 them in the work on the **h** *of* God, H1074
Ezr 7:24 other workers at this **h** *of* God. A10103
Ezr 7:27 to bring honor to the **h** *of* the LORD in H1074
Ezr 8:17 attendants to us for the **h** *of* our God. H1074
Ezr 8:25 there had donated for the **h** *of* our God. H1074
Ezr 8:29 the chambers of the **h** *of* the LORD in H1074
Ezr 8:30 to be taken to the **h** *of* our God in H1074
Ezr 8:33 fourth day, in the **h** *of* our God, we H1074
Ezr 8:36 to the people and to the **h** *of* God. H1074
Ezr 9: 9 life to rebuild the **h** *of* our God and repair H1074
Ezr 10: 1 himself down before the **h** *of* God, H1074
Ezr 10: 6 from before the **h** *of* God and went to the H1074
Ezr 10: 9 sitting in the square before the **h** *of* God, H1074
Ne 3:10 Harumaph made repairs opposite his **h**, H1074
Ne 3:16 artificial pool and the **H** *of* the Heroes. H1074
Ne 3:20 the entrance of the **h** *of* Eliashib the high H1074
Ne 3:21 entrance of Eliashib's **h** to the end of it. H1074
Ne 3:23 Hasshub made repairs in front of their **h**; H1074
Ne 3:23 of Ananiah, made repairs beside his **h**. H1074
Ne 3:24 from Azariah's **h** to the angle and the H1074
Ne 3:28 made repairs, each in front of his own **h**. H1074
Ne 3:29 of Immer made repairs opposite his **h**. H1074
Ne 3:31 as far as the **h** *of* the temple servants H1074
Ne 5:13 shake out of their **h** and possessions H1074
Ne 6:10 day I went to the **h** *of* Shemaiah son of H1074
Ne 6:10 "Let us meet in the **h** *of* God, inside the H1074
Ne 8:16 in the courts of the **h** *of* God and in the H1074
Ne 10:32 year for the service of the **h** *of* our God: H1074
Ne 10:33 for all the duties of the **h** *of* our God. H1074
Ne 10:34 is to bring to the **h** *of* our God at set times H1074
Ne 10:35 bringing to the **h** *of* the LORD each year H1074
Ne 10:36 of our flocks to the **h** *of* our God, H1074
Ne 10:37 to the storerooms of the **h** *of* our God, H1074
Ne 10:38 tenth of the tithes up to the **h** *of* our God, H1074
Ne 10:39 "We will not neglect the **h** *of* our God." H1074
Ne 11:11 the official in charge of the **h** *of* God, H1074
Ne 11:16 of the outside work of the **h** *of* God; H1074
Ne 11:22 the service of the **h** *of* God. H1074
Ne 12:40 then took their places in the **h** *of* God; H1074
Ne 13: 4 of the storerooms of the **h** *of* our God. H1074
Ne 13: 7 a room in the courts of the **h** *of* God. H1074
Ne 13: 9 into them the equipment of the **h** *of* God, H1074
Ne 13:11 "Why is the **h** *of* God neglected? H1074
Ne 13:14 faithfully done for the **h** *of* my God and its H1074
Est 4:13 are in the king's **h** you alone of all the H1074
Est 7: 8 the queen while she is with me in the **h**?" H1074
Est 7: 9 height of fifty cubits stands by Haman's **h**. H1074
Job 1:13 drinking wine at the oldest brother's **h**, H1074
Job 1:18 drinking wine at the oldest brother's **h**, H1074
Job 1:19 desert and struck the four corners of the **h**. H1074
Job 5: 3 but suddenly his **h** was cursed. H5659
Job 7:10 He will never come to his **h** again; his H1074
Job 20:28 A flood will carry off his **h**, rushing waters H1074
Job 21:28 'Where now is the **h** *of* the great, the H1074
Job 27:18 The **h** he builds is like a moth's cocoon H1074
Job 29: 4 God's intimate friendship blessed my **h**, H185
Job 29:18 'I will die in my own **h**, my days as H7860
Job 41: 5 it on a leash for the young women *in* **your** *h*? AIT
Job 42:11 before came and ate with him in his **h**. H1074
Ps 5: 7 can come into your **h**; in reverence I bow H1074
Ps 23: 6 I will dwell in the **h** *of* the LORD forever. H1074
Ps 26: 8 I love the **h** where you live, the H1074
Ps 27: 4 I may dwell in the **h** *of* the LORD all the H1074
Ps 36: 8 They feast on the abundance of your **h** H1074
Ps 42: 4 I used to go to the **h** *of* God under the H1074
Ps 45:10 Forget your people and your father's **h**. H1074
Ps 52: T "David has gone to the **h** *of* Ahimelek." H1074
Ps 52: 8 an olive tree flourishing in the **h** *of* God; H1074
Ps 55:14 enjoyed sweet fellowship at the **h** *of* God, H1074
Ps 59: T to watch David's **h** in order to kill him H1074
Ps 65: 4 are filled with the good things of your **h**, H1074
Ps 69: 9 zeal for your **h** consumes me, and the H1074
Ps 84: 4 Blessed are those who dwell in your **h** H1074
Ps 84:10 doorkeeper in the **h** *of* my God than dwell H1074
Ps 92:13 planted in the **h** *of* the LORD, they will H1074
Ps 93: 5 holiness adorns your **h** for endless days. H1074
Ps 101: 2 the affairs of my **h** with a blameless heart. H1074
Ps 101: 7 who practices deceit will dwell in my **h**; H1074
Ps 115:10 **H** *of* Aaron, trust in the LORD—he is their H1074
Ps 115:12 he will bless the **h** *of* Aaron, H1074
Ps 116:19 in the courts of the **h** *of* the LORD—in your H1074
Ps 118: 3 Let the **h** *of* Aaron say: "His love endures H1074
Ps 118:26 From the **h** *of* the LORD we bless you. H1074
Ps 122: 1 said to me, "Let us go to the **h** *of* the LORD."H1074
Ps 122: 5 judgment, the thrones of the **h** *of* David. H1074
Ps 122: 9 For the sake of the **h** *of* the LORD our God, H1074
Ps 127: 1 Unless the LORD builds the **h**, the builders H1074
Ps 128: 3 will be like a fruitful vine within your **h**; H1074
Ps 132: 3 will not enter my **h** or go to my bed, H185+1074
Ps 134: 1 who minister by night in the **h** *of* the LORD. H1074
Ps 135: 2 you who minister in the **h** *of* the LORD, in H1074
Ps 135: 2 the LORD, in the courts of the **h** *of* our God. H1074
Ps 135:19 praise the LORD; **h** *of* Aaron, praise the H1074
Ps 135:20 **h** *of* Levi, praise the LORD; you who fear H1074
Pr 2:18 Surely her **h** leads down to death and her H1074
Pr 3:33 The LORD's curse is on the **h** *of* the wicked H1074
Pr 5: 8 do not go near the door of her **h**, H1074
Pr 5:10 your toil enrich the **h** *of* another. H1074
Pr 6:31 though it costs him all the wealth of his **h**. H1074
Pr 7: 6 At the window of my **h** I looked down H1074
Pr 7: 8 walking along in the direction of her **h** H1074
Pr 7:27 Her **h** is a highway to the grave, leading H1074
Pr 9: 1 Wisdom has built her **h**; she has set up its H1074
Pr 9: 4 "Let all who are simple come to my **h**!" H2178
Pr 9:14 She sits at the door of her **h**, on a seat at H1074
Pr 9:16 "Let all who are simple come **to** my **h**!" H2178S
Pr 12: 7 the **h** *of* the righteous stands firm. H1074
Pr 14: 1 The wise woman builds her **h**, but with H1074
Pr 14:11 The **h** *of* the wicked will be destroyed, but H1074
Pr 15: 6 The **h** *of* the righteous contains great H1074
Pr 15:25 The LORD tears down the **h** *of* the proud H1074
Pr 17: 1 peace and quiet than a **h** full of feasting, H1074
Pr 17:13 never leave the **h** *of* one who pays back H1074
Pr 21: 9 roof than share a **h** with a quarrelsome H1074
Pr 21:12 One takes note of the **h** *of* the wicked H1074
Pr 24: 3 By wisdom a **h** is built, and through H1074
Pr 24:15 like a thief near the **h** *of* the righteous, H5659
Pr 24:27 your fields ready; after that, build your **h**. H1074
Pr 25:17 Seldom set foot in your neighbor's **h** H1074
Pr 25:24 roof than share a **h** with a quarrelsome H1074
Pr 27:10 to your relative's **h** when disaster strikes H1074
Ecc 2: 7 had other slaves who were born in my **h**. H1074
Ecc 5: 1 your steps when you go to the **h** *of* God. H1074
Ecc 7: 2 better to go to a **h** *of* mourning than to go H1074
Ecc 7: 2 of mourning than to go to a **h** *of* feasting, H1074
Ecc 7: 4 heart of the wise is in the **h** *of* mourning, H1074
Ecc 7: 4 the heart of fools is in the **h** *of* pleasure. H1074
Ecc 10:18 because of idle hands, the **h** leaks. H1074
Ecc 12: 3 when the keepers of the **h** tremble, and H1074
SS 1:17 The beams of our **h** are cedars; our rafters H1074
SS 3: 4 till I had brought him to my mother's **h**, H1074
SS 8: 2 you and bring you to my mother's **h**— H1074
SS 8: 7 to give all the wealth of one's **h** for love, H1074
Isa 3: 6 seize one of his brothers in his father's **h**, H1074
Isa 3: 7 I have no food or clothing in my **h**; do not H1074
Isa 5: 8 Woe to you who add **h** to house and join H1074
Isa 5: 8 you who add house to **h** and join field to H1074
Isa 7: 2 Now the **h** *of* David was told, "Aram has H1074
Isa 7:13 Isaiah said, "Hear now, you **h** *of* David! H1074
Isa 7:17 people and on the **h** *of* your father a time H1074
Isa 16: 5 one from the **h** *of* David—one who in H185
Isa 22:18 will become a disgrace to your master's **h**. H1074
Isa 22:22 on his shoulder the key to the **h** *of* David; H1074
Isa 22:23 a seat of honor for the **h** *of* his father. H1074
Isa 23: 1 is destroyed and left without **h** or harbor. H1074
Isa 24:10 the entrance to every **h** is barred. H1074
Isa 38: 1 Put your **h** in order, because you are H1074
Isa 38:12 shepherd's tent my **h** has been pulled H1886
Isa 52:11 you who carry the **articles** *of* the LORD's *h*. AIT
Isa 56: 7 give them joy in my **h** *of* prayer. H1074
Isa 56: 7 my **h** will be called a house of prayer H1074
Isa 56: 7 house will be called a **h** *of* prayer for all H1074
Isa 66: 1 Where is the **h** you will build for me H1074
Jer 7: 2 gate of the LORD's **h** and there proclaim H1074
Jer 7:10 then come and stand before me in this **h**, H1074
Jer 7:11 Has this **h**, which bears my Name, become H1074
Jer 7:14 will now do to the **h** that bears my Name, H1074
Jer 7:30 idols in the **h** that bears my Name and H1074
Jer 9:26 even the whole **h** *of* Israel is H1074
Jer 12: 7 "I will forsake my **h**, abandon my H1074
Jer 16: 5 "Do not enter a **h** *where there* is a funeral H1074
Jer 16: 8 do not enter a **h** *where there* is feasting H1074
Jer 17:26 thank offerings to the **h** *of* the LORD. H1074
Jer 18: 2 "Go down to the potter's **h**, and there I will H1074
Jer 18: 3 So I went down to the potter's **h**, and I saw H1074
Jer 20: 6 all who live in your **h** will go into exile to H1074
Jer 21:11 say to the royal **h** *of* Judah, 'Hear the H1074
Jer 21:12 is what the LORD says to you, **h** *of* David: H1074
Jer 26: 2 of the LORD's **h** and speak to all the H1074
Jer 26: 2 who come to worship in the **h** *of* the LORD. H1074
Jer 26: 6 then I will make this **h** like Shiloh and this H1074

Jer 26: 7 speak these words in the **h** *of* the LORD. H1074
Jer 26: 9 LORD's name that this **h** will be like Shiloh H1074
Jer 26: 9 around Jeremiah in the **h** *of* the LORD. H1074
Jer 26:10 royal palace to the **h** *of* the LORD and took H1074
Jer 26:10 entrance of the New Gate of the LORD's **h**. NDT
Jer 26:12 against this **h** and this city all the H1074
Jer 27:16 from the LORD's **h** will be brought back H1074
Jer 27:18 remaining in the **h** *of* the LORD and in the H1074
Jer 27:21 that are left in the **h** *of* the LORD and in the H1074
Jer 28: 1 said to me in the **h** *of* the LORD in the H1074
Jer 28: 3 of the LORD's **h** that Nebuchadnezzar H1074
Jer 28: 5 who were standing in the **h** *of* the LORD. H1074
Jer 28: 6 articles of the LORD's **h** and all the exiles H1074
Jer 29:26 to be in charge of the **h** *of* the LORD; H1074
Jer 32:34 vile images in the **h** that bears my Name H1074
Jer 33:11 bring thank offerings to the **h** *of* the LORD, H1074
Jer 34:15 before me in the **h** that bears my Name. H1074
Jer 35: 2 side rooms of the **h** *of* the LORD and give H1074
Jer 35: 4 I brought them into the **h** *of* the LORD, into H1074
Jer 36: 6 So you go to the **h** *of* the LORD on a day of H1074
Jer 37:15 imprisoned in the **h** *of* Jonathan the H1074
Jer 37:20 send me back to the **h** *of* Jonathan the H1074
Jer 38:26 me back to Jonathan's **h** to die there. H1074
Jer 41: 5 incense with them to the **h** *of* the LORD. H1074
Jer 51:51 entered the holy places of the LORD's **h**." H1074
La 2: 7 a shout in the **h** *of* the LORD as on the H1074
Eze 3:24 "Go, shut yourself inside your **h**. H1074
Eze 8: 1 I was sitting in my **h** and the elders of H1074
Eze 8:14 of the north gate of the **h** *of* the LORD, H1074
Eze 8:16 into the inner court of the **h** *of* the LORD, H1074
Eze 10:19 entrance of the east gate of the LORD's **h**, H1074
Eze 11: 1 to the gate of the **h** *of* the LORD that faces H1074
Eze 23:39 That is what they did in my **h**. H1074
Da 1: 2 put in the treasure **h** *of* his god. H1074
Da 2:17 returned to his **h** and explained the A10103
Hos 1: 4 will soon punish the **h** *of* Jehu for the H1074
Hos 5: 1 royal **h**! This judgment is against H1074
Hos 8: 1 eagle is over the **h** *of* the LORD because H1074
Hos 9: 8 and hostility in the **h** *of* his God. H1074
Hos 9:15 sinful deeds, I will drive them out of my **h**. H1074
Joel 1: 9 offerings are cut off from the **h** *of* the LORD. H1074
Joel 1:13 are withheld from the **h** *of* your God. H1074
Joel 1:14 in the land to the **h** *of* the LORD your God, H1074
Joel 1:16 joy and gladness from the **h** *of* our God? H1074
Joel 3:18 flow out of the LORD's **h** and will water the H1074
Am 1: 4 I will send fire on the **h** *of* Hazael that will H1074
Am 2: 8 In the **h** *of* their god they drink wine taken H1074
Am 3:15 tear down the winter **h** along with the H1074
Am 3:15 winter house along with the summer **h**; H1074
Am 5:19 he entered his **h** and rested his hand H1074
Am 6: 9 If ten people are left in one **h**, they too H1074
Am 6:10 the bodies out of the **h** to burn them asks H1074
Am 6:11 will smash the great **h** into pieces and the H1074
Am 6:11 into pieces and the small **h** into bits. H1074
Am 7: 9 I will rise against the **h** *of* Jeroboam." H1074
Mic 6:10 you wicked **h**, and the short ephah, H1074
Mic 6:16 of Omri and all the practices of Ahab's **h**; H1074
Hab 2: 9 to him who builds his **h** by unjust gain, H1074
Hab 2:10 shaming your own **h** and forfeiting your H1074
Hag 1: 2 has not yet come to rebuild the LORD's **h**. H1074
Hag 1: 4 houses, while this **h** remains a ruin?" H1074
Hag 1: 8 bring down timber and build my **h**, H1074
Hag 1: 9 "Because of my **h**, which remains a ruin H1074
Hag 1: 9 while each of you is busy with your own **h**. H1074
Hag 1:14 to work on the **h** *of* the LORD Almighty, H1074
Hag 2: 3 is left who saw this **h** in its former glory? H1074
Hag 2: 7 I will fill this **h** with glory,' says the H1074
Hag 2: 9 glory of this present **h** will be greater than H1074
Hag 2: 9 be greater than the glory of the former **h**, NDT
Zec 1:16 with mercy, and there my **h** will be rebuilt. H1074
Zec 3: 7 you will govern my **h** and have charge of H1074
Zec 5: 4 it will enter the **h** *of* the thief and the H1074
Zec 5: 4 the thief and the **h** *of* anyone who swears H1074
Zec 5: 4 It will remain in that **h** and destroy it H1074
Zec 5:11 the country of Babylonia to build a **h** for it. H1074
Zec 5:11 When the **h** is ready, the basket will be set NDT
Zec 6:10 Go the same day to the **h** *of* Josiah son of H1074
Zec 7: 3 the priests of the **h** *of* the LORD Almighty H1074
Zec 8: 9 was laid for the **h** *of* the LORD Almighty. H1074
Zec 11:13 them to the potter at the **h** *of* the LORD. H1074
Zec 12: 7 so that the honor of the **h** *of* David and of H1074
Zec 12: 8 and the **h** *of* David will be like God H1074
Zec 12:10 I will pour out on the **h** *of* David and the H1074
Zec 12:12 the clan of the **h** *of* David and their wives H1074
Zec 12:12 the clan of the **h** *of* Nathan and their H1074
Zec 12:13 the clan of the **h** *of* Levi and their wives H1074
Zec 13: 1 will be opened to the **h** *of* David and the H1074
Zec 13: 6 wounds I was given at the **h** *of* my friends. H1074
Zec 14:20 pots in the LORD's **h** will be like the sacred H1074
Zec 14:21 a Canaanite in the **h** *of* the LORD Almighty. H1074
Mal 3:10 that there may be food in my **h**. H1074
Mt 2:11 On coming to the **h**, they saw the child G3864
Mt 5:15 it gives light to everyone in the **h**. G3864
Mt 7:24 a wise man who built his **h** on the rock. G3864
Mt 7:25 the winds blew and beat against that **h**; G3864
Mt 7:26 a foolish man who built his **h** on sand. G3864
Mt 7:27 the winds blew and beat against that **h**, G3864
Mt 8:14 When Jesus came into Peter's **h**, he saw G3864
Mt 9:10 Jesus was having dinner at Matthew's **h**, G3864
Mt 9:23 synagogue leader's **h** and saw the noisy G3864
Mt 10:11 worthy person **and** stay **at** their **h** until you G2795
Mt 10:25 If the **head of the h** has been called G3867
Mt 12: 4 He entered the **h** of God, and he and his G3875
Mt 12:29 enter a strong man's **h** and carry off his G3864
Mt 12:29 Then he can plunder his **h**. G3864
Mt 12:44 'I will return to the **h** I left.' When it G3875
Mt 12:44 it finds the **h** unoccupied, swept NDT
Mt 13: 1 went out of the **h** and sat by the lake. G3864
Mt 13:36 he left the crowd and went into the **h**. G3864
Mt 13:52 is like the **owner of a h** who brings G476+3867
Mt 17:25 When Peter came into the **h**, Jesus was G3864
Mt 21:13 " 'My **h** will be called a house of prayer G3875
Mt 21:13 " 'My house will be called a **h** of prayer,' G3875
Mt 23:38 your **h** is left to you desolate. G3875
Mt 24:17 go down to take anything out of the **h**. G3864
Mt 24:43 If the **owner of the h** had known at what G3867
Mt 24:43 would not have let his **h** be broken into. G3864
Mt 26:18 the Passover with my disciples at your **h**. NDT
Mk 1:35 left the **h** and went off to a solitary place NDT
Mk 2:15 While Jesus was having dinner at Levi's **h**, G3864
Mk 2:26 he entered the **h** of God and ate the G3875
Mk 3:20 Then Jesus entered a **h**, and again a G3875
Mk 3:25 If a **h** is divided against itself, that house G3864
Mk 3:25 divided against itself, that **h** cannot stand. G3864
Mk 3:27 enter a strong man's **h** without first tying G3864
Mk 3:27 Then he can plunder the strong man's **h**. G3864
Mk 5:35 some people came from the **h** of Jairus, the NDT
Mk 6:10 Whenever you enter a **h**, stay there until G3864
Mk 7:17 he had left the crowd and entered the **h**, G3875
Mk 7:24 He entered a **h** and did not want anyone G3864
Mk 9:33 When he was in the **h**, he asked them G3864
Mk 10:10 When they were in the **h** again, the G3864
Mk 11:17 'My **h** will be called a house of prayer G3875
Mk 11:17 house will be called a **h** of prayer for all G3875
Mk 13:15 down or enter the **h** to take anything out G3864
Mk 13:34 He leaves his **h** and puts his servants in G3864
Mk 13:35 when the owner *of* the **h** will come back— G3864
Mk 14:14 Say *to* the **owner of the h** he enters, 'The G3867
Lk 1:69 us in the **h** of his servant David G3875
Lk 2: 4 he belonged to the **h** and line of David. G3875
Lk 2:49 you know I had to be in my Father's **h**?" G3836S
Lk 5:18 tried *to* **take** him **into** *the h* to lay him AIT
Lk 5:29 held a great banquet for Jesus at his **h**, G3864
Lk 6: 4 He entered the **h** of God, and taking the G3875
Lk 6:48 They are like a man building a **h**, who dug G3864
Lk 6:48 torrent struck that **h** but could not shake it, G3864
Lk 6:49 a man who built a **h** on the ground G3864
Lk 6:49 The moment the torrent struck that **h**, it G3864
Lk 7: 6 was not far from the **h** when the centurion G3864
Lk 7:10 sent returned to the **h** and found the G3875
Lk 7:36 to the Pharisee's **h** and reclined at the G3875
Lk 7:37 that Jesus was eating at the Pharisee's **h**, G3864
Lk 7:44 I came into your **h**. You did not give me G3864
Lk 8:27 man had not worn clothes or lived in a **h**, G3864
Lk 8:41 pleading with him to come to his **h** G3875
Lk 8:49 someone came from the **h** of Jairus, NDT
Lk 8:51 When he arrived at the **h** of Jairus, he did G3864
Lk 9: 4 Whatever **h** you enter, stay there until you G3864
Lk 10: 5 "When you enter a **h**, first say, 'Peace to G3864
Lk 10: 5 enter a house, first say, 'Peace *to* this **h**. G3875
Lk 10: 7 Do not move around from **h** to house. G3864
Lk 10: 7 Do not move around from house to **h**. G3864
Lk 11:17 a **h** divided against itself will fall. G3875
Lk 11:21 guards his own **h**, his possessions are G885
Lk 11:24 Then it says, 'I will return to the **h** I left.' G3875
Lk 11:25 it finds the **h** swept clean and put in order. NDT
Lk 12:39 If the **owner of the h** had known at what G3867
Lk 12:39 would not have let his **h** be broken into. G3875
Lk 13:25 Once the **owner of the h** gets up and G3867
Lk 13:35 your **h** is left to you desolate. I tell G3875
Lk 14: 1 went to eat in the **h** of a prominent G3875
Lk 14:21 Then the **owner of the h** became angry G3867
Lk 14:23 them to come in, so that my **h** will be full. G3875
Lk 15: 8 sweep the **h** and search carefully until she G3864
Lk 15:25 When he came near the **h**, he heard G3864
Lk 19: 5 I must stay at your **h** today." G3875
Lk 19: 9 "Today salvation has come *to* this **h** G3875
Lk 19:46 to them, " 'My **h** will be a house of prayer' G3875
Lk 19:46 " 'My house will be a **h** of prayer'; but you G3875
Lk 22:10 Follow him to the **h** that he enters, G3864
Lk 22:11 say to the owner *of* the **h**, 'The G3864
Lk 22:54 took him into the **h** of the high priest. G3864
Jn 2:16 Stop turning my Father's **h** into a market!" G3875
Jn 2:17 "Zeal *for* your **h** will consume me. G3875
Jn 11:31 Jews who had been with Mary in the **h**, G3864
Jn 12: 3 And the **h** was filled with the fragrance of G3864
Jn 14: 2 My Father's **h** has many rooms; if that were G3864
Jn 20:26 week later his disciples were in the **h** again, NDT
Ac 2: 2 filled the whole **h** where they were G3875
Ac 5:42 temple courts and **from h to house**, G2848+3875
Ac 5:42 temple courts and **from house to h**, G2848+3875
Ac 7:47 But it was Solomon who built a **h** for him. G3875
Ac 7:49 What kind of **h** will you build for me G3875
Ac 8: 3 Going **from h to house**, he G2848+3836+3875
Ac 8: 3 Going **from house to h**, he G2848+3836+3875
Ac 9:11 "Go to the **h** of Judas on Straight Street G3864
Ac 9:17 Ananias went to the **h** and entered it. G3864
Ac 10: 6 Simon the tanner, whose **h** is by the sea." G3864
Ac 10:17 out where Simon's **h** was and stopped at G3864
Ac 10:22 you to come to his **h** so that he could hear G3875
Ac 10:23 invited the men into the **h** to be his guests. NDT
Ac 10:25 As Peter entered the **h**, Cornelius met him NDT
Ac 10:30 ago I was in my **h** praying at this hour G3875
Ac 11: 3 "You went into the **h** of uncircumcised men NDT
Ac 11:11 stopped at the **h** where I was staying. G3864
Ac 11:12 with me, and we entered the man's **h**. G3875
Ac 11:13 seen an angel appear in his **h** and say, G3875
Ac 12:12 he went to the **h** of Mary the mother of G3864
Ac 16:15 she said, "come and stay at my **h**. G3875
Ac 16:32 Lord to him and to all the others in his **h**. G3864
Ac 16:34 them into his **h** and set a meal before G3875
Ac 16:40 they went to Lydia's **h**, where they met with NDT
Ac 17: 5 They rushed *to* Jason's **h** in search of Paul G3864
Ac 17: 7 Jason *has* **welcomed** them **into** his **h** G5685
Ac 18: 7 went next door to the **h** of Titius Justus, G3864
Ac 19:16 they ran out of the **h** naked and bleeding. G3875
Ac 20:20 you publicly and **from h to house**. G2848+3875
Ac 20:20 you publicly and **from house to h**. G2848+3875
Ac 21: 8 stayed at the **h** of Philip the G3875
Ac 28:30 there in his own **rented h** and welcomed G3637
Ro 16: 5 also the church that meets at their **h**. G3875
1Co 16:19 so does the church that meets at their **h**. G3875
2Co 5: 1 an eternal **h** in heaven, not built G3864
Col 4:15 to Nympha and the church in her **h**. G3875
1Ti 5:13 and going about **from h to house**. G3836+3864
1Ti 5:13 and going about **from house to h**. G3836+3864
2Ti 2:20 In a large **h** there are articles not only of G3864
Heb 3: 2 just as Moses was faithful in all God's **h**. G3875
Heb 3: 3 as the builder of a **h** has greater honor than NDT
Heb 3: 3 house has greater honor *than* the **h** itself. G3875
Heb 3: 4 For every **h** is built by someone, but God is G3875
Heb 3: 5 was faithful as a servant in all God's **h**," G3875
Heb 3: 6 Christ is faithful as the Son over God's **h**. G3875
Heb 3: 6 And we are his **h**, if indeed we hold firmly G3875
Heb 10:21 we have a great priest over the **h** of God, G3875
1Pe 2: 5 being built *into* a spiritual **h** to be a holy G3875
2Jn 10 take them into your **h** or welcome them. G3864

HOUSEHOLD (128) [HOUSE]

Ge 12: 1 your father's **h** to the land I will show H1074
Ge 12:17 on Pharaoh and his **h** because of Abram's H1074
Ge 14:14 men born in his **h** and went in pursuit as H1074
Ge 15: 3 so a servant in my **h** will be my heir." H1074
Ge 17:12 those born in your **h** or bought with H1074
Ge 17:13 born in your **h** or bought with your H1074
Ge 17:23 all those born in his **h** or bought with his H1074
Ge 17:23 every male in his **h**, and circumcised them H1074
Ge 17:27 And every male in Abraham's **h**, including H1074
Ge 17:27 those born in his **h** or bought from a H1074
Ge 18:19 his children and his **h** after him to keep H1074
Ge 20:13 God had me wander from my father's **h**, H1074
Ge 20:18 women in Abimelek's **h** from conceiving H1074
Ge 24: 2 He said to the senior servant in his **h**, the H1074
Ge 24: 7 out of my father's **h** and my native land H1074
Ge 24:28 told her mother's **h** about these things. H1074
Ge 28:21 so that I return safely to my father's **h**, then H1074
Ge 30:30 when may I do something for my own **h**?" H1074
Ge 31:19 Rachel stole her father's **h gods**. H9572
Ge 31:30 you longed to return to your father's **h**. H1074
Ge 31:34 had taken the **h gods** and put them inside H9572
Ge 31:35 searched but could not find the **h gods**. H9572
Ge 31:37 have you found that belongs to your **h**? H1074
Ge 31:41 this for the twenty years I was in your **h**. H1074
Ge 34:30 attack me, I and my **h** will be destroyed." H1074
Ge 35: 2 Jacob said to his **h** and to all who were H1074
Ge 36: 6 daughters and all the members of his **h**, H1074
Ge 38:11 in your father's **h** until my son Shelah H1074
Ge 38:11 So Tamar went to live in her father's **h**. H1074
Ge 39: 4 Potiphar put him in charge of his **h**, and H1074
Ge 39: 5 him in charge of his **h** and of all that he H1074
Ge 39: 5 the LORD blessed the **h** *of* the Egyptian H1074
Ge 39:11 none of the **h** servants was inside. H1074
Ge 39:14 she called her **h** servants. "Look," she said H1074
Ge 41:51 forget all my trouble and all my father's **h**." H1074
Ge 45: 2 and Pharaoh's **h** heard about it. H1074
Ge 45: 8 lord of his entire **h** and ruler of all Egypt. H1074
Ge 45:11 you and your **h** and all who belong to H1074
Ge 46:31 said to his brothers and to his father's **h**, H1074
Ge 46:31 'My brothers and my father's **h**, who were H1074
Ge 47:12 brothers and all his father's **h** with food, H1074
Ge 50: 8 members of Joseph's **h** and his brothers H1074
Ge 50: 8 and *those belonging to* his father's **h**. H1074
Ex 12: 3 take a lamb for his family, one for each **h**. H1074
Ex 12: 4 If any **h** is too small for a whole lamb, they H1074
Ex 12:48 have all the males in his **h** circumcised; NDT
Ex 23:12 that the **slave born in** your **h** and the H1201+563
Lev 16: 6 to make atonement for himself and his **h**. H1074
Lev 16:11 to make atonement for himself and his **h**, H1074
Lev 16:17 his **h** and the whole community of Israel. H1074
Lev 22:11 if slaves are born in his **h**, they may eat H1074
Lev 22:13 to live in her father's **h** as in her youth, H1074
Nu 18:11 Everyone in your **h** who is ceremonially H1074
Nu 18:13 Everyone in your **h** who is ceremonially H1074
Nu 30: 3 living in her father's **h** makes a vow to the H1074
Dt 6:22 on Egypt and Pharaoh and his whole **h**. H1074
Dt 14:26 Then you and your **h** shall eat there in the H1074
Dt 26:11 your God has given to you and your **h**. H1074
Jos 24:15 But as for me and my **h**, we will serve the H1074
Jdg 14:15 will burn you and your father's **h** to death. H1074
Jdg 17: 5 an ephod and *some* **h gods** and installed H9572
Jdg 18:14 *some* **h gods** and an image overlaid with H9572
Jdg 18:17 the ephod and the **h gods** while the priest H9572
Jdg 18:18 the ephod and the **h gods**, the priest said H9572
Jdg 18:19 as priest rather than just one man's **h**?" H1074
Jdg 18:20 the **h gods** and the idol and went along H9572
1Sa 22: 1 brothers and his father's **h** heard about it, H1074

H

1Sa 22:14 highly respected in your **h**? H1074
1Sa 25: 6 Good health to you and your **h**! And good H1074
1Sa 25:17 hanging over our master and his whole **h**. H1074
2Sa 6:11 the LORD blessed him and his entire **h**. H1074
2Sa 6:12 has blessed the **h** *of* Obed-Edom and H1074
2Sa 6:20 When David returned home to bless his **h**, H1074
2Sa 9: 2 was a servant of Saul's **h** named Ziba. H1074
2Sa 9:12 the members of Ziba's **h** were servants of H1074
2Sa 12:11 'Out of your own **h** I am going to bring H1074
2Sa 12:17 The elders of his **h** stood beside him to H1074
2Sa 15:16 with his entire **h** following him; but H1074
2Sa 16: 2 donkeys are for the king's **h** to ride on, H1074
2Sa 16: 8 all the blood you shed in the **h** *of* Saul, H1074
2Sa 19:17 the steward of Saul's **h**, and his fifteen H1074
2Sa 19:18 to take the king's **h** over and to do H1074
2Sa 19:41 bring him and his **h** across the Jordan, H1074
1Ki 4: 7 provisions for the king and the royal **h**. H1074
1Ki 5: 9 my wish by providing food for my royal **h**." H1074
1Ki 5:11 thousand cors of wheat as food for his **h**, H1074
1Ki 10:21 all the **h articles** *in* the Palace of the H3998
2Ki 23:24 spiritists, the **h gods**, the idols and all H9572
1Ch 13:14 the LORD blessed his **h** and everything he H1074
2Ch 9:20 all the **h articles** *in* the Palace of the H3998
Ne 13: 8 threw all Tobiah's **h** goods out of the H1074
Est 1:22 every man should be ruler over his own **h**, H1074
Job 1:10 around him and his **h** and everything he H1074
Job 16: 7 me out; you have devastated my entire **h**. H6337
Job 31:31 if those of my **h** have never said, 'Who has H185
Ps 105:21 He made him master of his **h**, ruler over H1074
Pr 31:21 she has no fear for her **h**; for all of them H1074
Pr 31:27 the affairs of her **h** and does not eat the H1074
Jer 23:34 the LORD,' I will punish them and their **h**. H1074
Eze 44:30 so that a blessing may rest on your **h**. H1074
Hos 3: 4 sacred stones, without ephod or **h gods**. H9572
Mic 7: 6 enemies are the members of his own **h**. H1074
Mt 10:25 how much more the **members of** his **h**! *G3865*
Mt 10:36 will be the **members of** his own **h**. *G3865*
Mt 12:25 every city or **h** divided against itself *G3864*
Mt 24:45 of the **servants in** his **h** to give them *G3859*
Lk 8: 3 the **manager of** Herod's **h**; Susanna; *G2208*
Jn 4:53 So he and his whole **h** believed. *G3864*
Ac 11:14 which you and all your **h** will be saved. *G3875*
Ac 16:15 she and the **members of** her **h** were *G3875*
Ac 16:31 you will be saved—you and your **h**." *G3875*
Ac 16:33 he and all his **h** were baptized. *G3836S*
Ac 16:34 to believe in God—he and his **whole h**. *G4109*
Ac 18: 8 his entire **h** believed in the Lord *G3875*
Ro 16:10 those who **belong to** the **h** of Aristobulus *G1666*
Ro 16:11 Greet those **in** the **h of** Narcissus who are *G1666*
1Co 1:11 some from Chloe's **h** have informed me *G3836*
1Co 1:16 I also baptized the **h** of Stephanas *G3875*
1Co 16:15 You know that the **h** of Stephanas were *G3864*
Eph 2:19 God's people and also **members of** his **h**, *G3858*
Php 4:22 those who belong to Caesar's **h**. *G3864*
1Ti 3:12 must manage his children and his **h** well. *G3875*
1Ti 3:15 ought to conduct themselves in God's **h**, *G3875*
1Ti 5: 8 especially for their own **h**, has denied *G3858*
2Ti 1:16 Lord show mercy *to* the **h** of Onesiphorus, *G3875*
2Ti 4:19 Aquila and the **h** of Onesiphorus. *G3875*
Titus 1: 7 Since an overseer **manages** God's **h**, he *G3874*
1Pe 4:17 time for judgment to begin with God's **h**; *G3875*

HOUSEHOLDS (8) [HOUSE]

Ge 42:19 go and take grain back for your starving **h**. H1074
Ge 42:33 take food for your starving **h** and go. H1074
Ge 47:24 yourselves and your **h** and your children." H1074
Nu 16:32 mouth and swallowed them and their **h**, H1074
Nu 18:31 You and your **h** may eat the rest of it H1074
Dt 11: 6 swallowed them up with their **h**, H1074
Pr 15:27 The greedy bring ruin to their **h**, but the H1074
Titus 1:11 are disrupting whole **h** by teaching things *G3875*

HOUSES (95) [HOUSE]

Ge 34:29 taking as plunder everything in the **h**. H1074
Ex 8: 3 into the **h** *of* your officials and on your H1074
Ex 8: 9 that you and your **h** may be rid of the H1074
Ex 8:11 The frogs will leave you and your **h**, your H1074
Ex 8:13 The frogs died in the **h**, in the courtyards H1074
Ex 8:21 officials, on your people and into your **h**. H1074
Ex 8:21 The **h** *of* the Egyptians will be full of flies H1074
Ex 8:24 palace and into the **h** *of* his officials; H1074
Ex 10: 6 They will fill your **h** and those of all your H1074
Ex 12: 7 doorframes of the **h** where they eat the H1074
Ex 12:13 be a sign for you on the **h** where you are, H1074
Ex 12:15 the first day remove the yeast from your **h**, H1074
Ex 12:19 days no yeast is to be found in your **h**. H1074
Ex 12:23 to enter your **h** and strike you down. H1074
Ex 12:27 who passed over the **h** *of* the Israelites in H1074
Lev 25:31 But **h** *in* villages without walls around H1074
Lev 25:32 to redeem their **h** *in* the Levitical towns, H1074
Lev 25:33 because the **h** *in* the towns of the Levites H1074
Dt 6: 9 doorframes of your **h** and on your gates. H1074
Dt 6:11 **h** filled with all kinds of good things you H1074
Dt 8:12 when you build fine **h** and settle down, H1074
Dt 11:20 doorframes of your **h** and on your gates, H1074
Dt 19: 1 them out and settled in their towns and **h**, H1074
Jdg 18:14 know that one of these **h** has an ephod, H1074
1Ki 20: 6 your palace and the **h** *of* your officials. H1074
2Ki 25: 9 royal palace and all the **h** *of* Jerusalem. H1074
Ne 5:11 olive groves and **h**, and also the interest H1074
Ne 7: 3 at their posts and some near their own **h**." H1074
Ne 7: 4 and the **h** had not yet been rebuilt. H1074
Ne 9:25 took possession of **h** filled with all kinds H1074
Job 3:15 had gold, who filled their **h** with silver. H1074
Job 4:19 much more those who live in **h** *of* clay, H1074
Job 15:28 ruined towns and **h** where no one lives, H1074
Job 15:28 no one lives, **h** crumbling to rubble. H889S
Job 20:19 he has seized **h** he did not build. H1074
Job 22:18 he who filled their **h** with good things, H1074
Job 24:16 thieves break into **h**, but by day they shut H1074
Ps 49:11 Their tombs will remain their **h** forever H1074
Ps 49:16 when the splendor of their **h** increases; H1074
Ps 112: 3 Wealth and riches are in their **h**, and their H1074
Pr 1:13 things and fill our **h** with plunder; H1074
Pr 19:14 **H** and wealth are inherited from parents H1074
Ecc 2: 4 I built **h** for myself and planted vineyards. H1074
Isa 3:14 the plunder from the poor is in your **h**. H1074
Isa 5: 9 "Surely the great **h** will become desolate H1074
Isa 6:11 until the **h** are left deserted and the fields H1074
Isa 13:16 their **h** will be looted and their wives H1074
Isa 13:21 jackals will fill her **h**; there the owls will H1074
Isa 22:10 tore down **h** to strengthen the wall. H1074
Isa 32:13 mourn for all **h** *of* merriment and for this H1074
Isa 65:21 They will build **h** and dwell in them; they H1074
Isa 65:22 longer will they build **h** and others live in NDT
Jer 5: 7 thronged to the **h** *of* prostitutes. H1074
Jer 5:27 full of birds, their **h** are full of deceit; they H1074
Jer 6:12 Their **h** will be turned over to others H1074
Jer 9:19 leave our land because our **h** are in ruins. H5438
Jer 17:22 a load out of your **h** or do any work on the H1074
Jer 18:22 be heard from their **h** when you suddenly H1074
Jer 19:13 The **h** *in* Jerusalem and those of the kings H1074
Jer 19:13 all the **h** where they burned incense on H1074
Jer 29: 5 "Build **h** and settle down; plant gardens H1074
Jer 29:28 Therefore build **h** and settle down; plant H1074
Jer 32:15 **H**, fields and vineyards will again be H1074
Jer 32:29 along with the **h** where the people H1074
Jer 33: 4 says about the **h** *in* this city and the royal H1074
Jer 35: 7 Also you must never build **h**, sow seed H1074
Jer 35: 9 built **h** to live in or had vineyards, fields H1074
Jer 39: 8 royal palace and the **h** *of* the people and H1074
Jer 52:13 royal palace and all the **h** *of* Jerusalem. H1074
Eze 7:24 of nations to take possession of their **h**. H1074
Eze 11: 3 'Haven't our **h** been recently rebuilt? H1074
Eze 16:41 will burn down your **h** and inflict H1074
Eze 23:47 daughters and burn down their **h**. H1074
Eze 26:12 demolish your fine **h** and throw your H1074
Eze 28:26 will build **h** and plant vineyards; H1074
Eze 33:30 you by the walls and at the doors of the **h**, H1074
Eze 45: 4 be a place for their **h** as well as a holy H1074
Eze 48:15 use of the city, for **h** and for pastureland. H4632
Da 2: 5 pieces and your **h** turned into piles of A10103
Da 3:29 pieces and their **h** be turned into piles A10103
Hos 7: 1 thieves break into **h**, bandits rob in the NDT
Joel 2: 9 They climb into the **h**; like thieves they H1074
Am 3:15 the **h** *adorned with* ivory will be destroyed H1074
Mic 2: 2 seize them, and **h**, and take them. H1074
Zep 1:13 will be plundered, their **h** demolished. H1074
Zep 1:13 Though they build **h**, they will not live in H1074
Zep 2: 7 they will lie down in the **h** *of* Ashkelon. H1074
Hag 1: 4 yourselves to be living in your paneled **h**, H1074
Zec 14: 2 will be captured, the **h** ransacked, and the H1074
Mt 19:29 everyone who has left **h** or brothers or *G3864*
Mk 12:40 They devour widows' **h** and for a show *G3864*
Lk 16: 4 people will welcome me into their **h**. *G3875*
Lk 20:47 They devour widows' **h** and for a show *G3864*
Ac 4:34 those who owned land or **h** sold them, *G3864*
Ac 7:48 does not live in **h** made by human hands. NDT

HOUSETOP (3) [HOUSE, TOP]

Mt 24:17 Let no one on the **h** go down to take *G1560*
Mk 13:15 Let no one on the **h** go down or enter the *G1560*
Lk 17:31 On that day no one who is on the **h**, with *G1560*

HOVERING (2) [HOVERS]

Ge 1: 2 the Spirit of God *was* **h** over the waters. H8173
Isa 31: 5 Like birds **h overhead**, the LORD Almighty H6414

HOVERS (1) [HOVERING]

Dt 32:11 that stirs up its nest and **h** over its young, H8173

HOW (735) [HOWEVER, SOMEHOW]

Ge 6: 5 The LORD saw **h** great the wickedness of H3954
Ge 6:12 God saw *h* **corrupt** the earth *had become*, for AIT
Ge 6:15 This is **h** you are to build it: The ark is to be H889
Ge 15: 8 **h** can I know that I will gain H928+4537
Ge 20: 9 **H** have I wronged you that you have H4537
Ge 20:13 'This is **h** you can show your love to me: H889
Ge 27:20 "**H** did you find it so quickly H4537+2296
Ge 28: 8 Esau then realized **h** displeasing the H3954
Ge 28:17 said, "**H** awesome is this place! H4537
Ge 30:13 Then Leah said, "**H** happy I am! The H928
Ge 30:26 You know **h much** work I've done for you." H889
Ge 30:29 "You know **h** I have worked for you and H889
Ge 30:29 worked for you and **h** your livestock has H889
Ge 31:36 "**H** *have* I wronged you that you hunt me H4537
Ge 38:29 "*So* **this is h** you have broken out! H4537
Ge 39: 9 **H** then could I do such a wicked thing and H375
Ge 39:19 "**This is h** your slave treated H3869+2021+1821+2021+465
Ge 42:15 And **this is h** you will be tested: As H928+2296
Ge 42:21 We saw *h* **distressed** he was when he AIT
Ge 42:33 '**This is h** I will know whether you H928+2296
Ge 43: 7 *H were we to* **know** he would say, 'Bring your AIT
Ge 43:27 *He* **asked** them **h they were** H4200+8934+8626
Ge 43:27 "**H is** your aged father you told me about? H8934
Ge 44:16 **H** can we prove our innocence H4537
Ge 44:34 **H** can I go back to my father if the boy is not H375
Ge 47: 8 asked him, "**H** old are you?" H3869+4537
Ge 49:15 When he sees **h** good is his resting place H3954
Ge 49:15 resting place and **h** pleasant is his land, H3954
Ex 10: 2 grandchildren **h** I dealt harshly with H889
Ex 10: 2 the Egyptians and **h** I performed my signs H889
Ex 10: 3 '**H long** will you refuse to humble H6330+5503
Ex 10: 7 "**H long** will this man be a snare to H6330+5503
Ex 12:11 **This is h** you are to eat it: with your cloak H3970
Ex 16:28 "**H long** will you refuse to H6330+625+2025
Ex 18: 1 **h** the LORD had brought Israel out of H3954
Ex 18: 8 along the way and **h** the LORD had saved NDT
Ex 18:20 are to live and **h** they are to behave. H5126S
Ex 19: 4 **h** I carried you on eagles' wings and NDT
Ex 23: 9 yourselves know **h it feels** to be foreigners H5883
Ex 32:22 "You know **h** prone these people are to H3954
Ex 33:16 **H** will anyone know that H928+2021+4537+686
Ex 34:10 among will see **h** awesome is the work H3954
Ex 36: 1 skill and ability to **know h** to carry out all H3359
Lev 15: 3 **This is h** his discharge will bring about H2296
Lev 16: 3 "**This is h** Aaron is to enter the Most H928+2296
Lev 18:24 because **this is h** the nations H928+3972+465
Nu 6:23 '**This is h** you are to bless the Israelites. H3907
Nu 8: 4 **This is h** the lampstand was made: It was H2296
Nu 8:26 **This**, then, **is h** you are to assign the H3970
Nu 9:16 **That is h** it continued to be; the cloud H4027
Nu 11:15 If **this is h** you are going to treat me H3970
Nu 13:20 **H** is the soil? Is it fertile or poor? Are there H4537
Nu 14:11 "**H long** will these people H6330+625+2025
Nu 14:11 **H long** will they refuse to H6330+625+2025
Nu 14:27 "**H long** will this wicked community H6330+5503
Nu 16:28 "**This is h** you will know that the LORD H928+2296
Nu 23: 8 **H** can I curse those whom God has not H4537
Nu 23: 8 **H** can I denounce those whom the LORD H4537
Nu 24: 5 "**H** beautiful are your tents, Jacob, your H4537
Dt 1:12 **But h** can I bear your problems and your H377
Dt 1:31 There you saw **h** the LORD your God carried H889
Dt 7:17 **H** can we drive them out? H377
Dt 8: 2 Remember **h** the LORD your God led you all H889
Dt 9: 7 never forget **h** you aroused the anger H889
Dt 11: 4 **h** he overwhelmed them with the waters of H889
Dt 11: 4 **h** the LORD brought lasting ruin on them. NDT
Dt 12:30 "**H** do these nations serve their gods? H377
Dt 15: 2 This is **h** it is to be done: Every creditor H1821
Dt 18:21 "**H** can we know when a message has not H377
Dt 20:15 **This is h** you are to treat all the cities that H4027
Dt 29:16 You yourselves know **h** we lived in Egypt H889
Dt 29:16 lived in Egypt and **h** we passed through the H889
Dt 31:27 For I know **h** rebellious and stiff-necked you NDT
Dt 31:27 **h much more** will you rebel H2256+677+3954
Dt 32:30 **H** could one man chase a thousand, or two H377
Jos 2:10 We have heard **h** the LORD dried up the H889
Jos 3:10 **This is h** you will know that the living H2296+928
Jos 5: 1 the coast heard **h** the LORD had dried up H889
Jos 9: 7 so **h** can we make a treaty with you?" H375
Jos 9:12 But now see **h** dry and moldy it is. NDT
Jos 9:13 filled were new, but see **h** cracked they are. NDT
Jos 9:24 were clearly told **h** the LORD your God had H889
Jos 18: 3 "**H long** will you wait before H6330+625+2025
Jos 22:16 '**H** could you break faith with the God of H4537
Jos 22:16 **H** could you turn away from the LORD and NDT
Jos 23: 4 Remember **h** I have allotted as an NDT
Jdg 1:24 "Show us **h to get into** the city and we will H4427
Jdg 6:15 replied, "but **h** can I save Israel? H928+4537
Jdg 13: 8 again to teach us **h** to bring up the boy H4537
Jdg 16: 5 strength and **h** we can overpower H928+4537
Jdg 16: 6 strength and **h** you can be tied up H928+4537
Jdg 16:10 tell me **h** you can be tied. H928+4537
Jdg 16:13 Tell me **h** you can be tied. H928+4537
Jdg 16:15 she said to him, "**H** can you say, 'I love H375
Jdg 18: 8 asked them, "**H** did you **find things**?" H4537
Jdg 18:24 **H** can you ask, 'What's the matter with H4537
Jdg 20: 3 "Tell us **h** this awful thing happened." H377
Jdg 20:34 did not realize **h** near disaster was. H3954
Jdg 21: 7 "**H** can we provide wives for those who are H4537
Jdg 21:16 **h** shall we provide wives for the men who H4537
Ru 2:11 **h** you left your father and mother and your H2256
Ru 2:18 saw **h much** she had gathered. H889
Ru 3:16 "**H did it go**, my daughter? H4769+905
1Sa 1:14 "**H long** are you going to stay drunk H6330+5503
1Sa 2:14 **This is h** they treated all the Israelites H3970
1Sa 2:22 doing to all Israel and **h** they slept with the H889
1Sa 6: 2 Tell us **h** we should send it back to H928+4537
1Sa 10:27 "**H** can this fellow save us? H4537
1Sa 14:29 See **h** my eyes brightened when I tasted a H3954
1Sa 14:30 **H much better** it would have been if H677+3954
1Sa 16: 1 "**H long** will you mourn for Saul H6330+5503
1Sa 16: 2 But Samuel said, "**H** can I go? If Saul hears H375
1Sa 16:18 of Bethlehem *who* **knows h** to play the H3359
1Sa 17:18 See **h** your brothers **are** and bring back H8934
1Sa 17:22 **asked** his brothers **h** they **were** H8626+4200+8934
1Sa 17:25 "Do you see **h** this man keeps coming out H3954
1Sa 17:28 I know **h** conceited you are and how wicked NDT
1Sa 17:28 you are and **h** wicked your heart is; NDT
1Sa 18:15 When Saul saw **h** successful he was, he H4394
1Sa 20: 1 **H** have I wronged your father, that he is H4537
1Sa 21: 5 **H much more so** today!" H677+3954
1Sa 23: 3 **H much more**, then, if we go to Keilah H677
1Sa 24:10 with your own eyes **h** the LORD delivered H889

1Sa 29: 4 **H** better could he regain his H928+4537
1Sa 30:21 he asked them **h** they **were**. H4200+8934
2Sa 1: 5 "**H** do you know that Saul and his son H375
2Sa 1:19 heights, Israel. **H** the mighty have fallen! H375
2Sa 1:25 "**H** the mighty have fallen in battle H375
2Sa 1:27 "**H** the mighty have fallen! The weapons of H375
2Sa 2:22 **H** could I look your brother Joab in the face H375
2Sa 2:26 **H long** before you order your men H6330+5503
2Sa 4:11 **H much more**—when wicked men have H677
2Sa 6: 9 **H** can the ark of the LORD ever come to me? H375
2Sa 6:20 "**H** the king of Israel has distinguished H4537
2Sa 7:22 "**H** great you are, Sovereign LORD H6584+4027
2Sa 11: 7 David asked him **h** Joab **was**, how H4200+8934
2Sa 11: 7 **h** the soldiers **were** and how the H4200+8934
2Sa 11: 7 were and **h** the war **was going**. H4200+8934
2Sa 11:11 *H could* I **go** to my house to eat and drink AIT
2Sa 12:18 **H** can we now tell him the child is dead H375
2Sa 16:11 **H much more**, then, this H677+3954
2Sa 16:23 **That was h** both David and Absalom H4027
2Sa 19:19 Do not remember **h** your servant did wrong H889
2Sa 19:34 "**H many more** years will I live H3869+4537
2Sa 20: 9 said to Amasa, "**H are** you, my brother?" H8934
2Sa 21: 3 **H** shall I make atonement so that H928+4537
2Sa 24: 2 so that I may know **h many** there are." H5031
2Sa 24:13 it over and decide **h** I should answer the H4537
1Ki 1:12 let me advise you **h** you can save your H2256
1Ki 2: 4 'If your descendants watch **h** they **live** H2006
1Ki 2:30 to the king, "**This is h** Joab answered me." H3907
1Ki 3: 7 child and *do* not **know h** to carry out my H3359
1Ki 7:28 This is **h** the stands were **made**: They had H5126
1Ki 8:27 **H much less** this temple I have built H677+3954
1Ki 10: 8 **H happy** your people must be! How happy H897
1Ki 10: 8 **H happy** your officials, who continually H897
1Ki 11:27 is the account of **h** he rebelled against H889
1Ki 11:28 when Solomon saw **h well** the young man H3954
1Ki 12: 6 "**H** would you advise me to answer these H375
1Ki 12: 9 **H** should we answer these people who say NDT
1Ki 14:19 his wars and **h** he ruled, are written H889
1Ki 18:21 "**H long** will you waver between H6330+5503
1Ki 19: 1 Elijah had done and **h** he had killed all the H889
1Ki 20: 7 "See **h** this man is looking for trouble! H3954
1Ki 21: 7 "Is this **h** you act as king over Israel? NDT
1Ki 21:29 "Have you noticed **h** Ahab has humbled H3954
1Ki 22:16 "**H many** times must I make H6330+3869+4537
2Ki 4: 2 replied to her, "**H** can I help you? Tell me H4537
2Ki 4:43 "**H** can I set this before a hundred men?" H4537
2Ki 5: 7 See **h** he is trying to pick a quarrel with H3954
2Ki 5:13 **H much more**, then, when he tells you H677
2Ki 6:32 "Don't you see **h** this murderer is sending H3954
2Ki 8: 5 was telling the king **h** Elisha had restored H889
2Ki 8:13 Hazael said, "**H** could your servant, H4537
2Ki 9:22 "**H** can there be peace," Jehu replied H4537
2Ki 9:25 Remember **h** you and I were riding H3954
2Ki 10: 4 two kings could not resist him, **h** can we?" H375
2Ki 13: 4 he saw **h** severely the king of Aram H3954
2Ki 14:26 The LORD had seen **h** bitterly everyone in H4394
2Ki 14:28 including **h** he recovered for Israel both H889
2Ki 17:28 taught them **h** to worship the LORD. H375
2Ki 18:24 **H** can you repulse one officer of the least H375
2Ki 18:35 **H** then can the LORD deliver Jerusalem H3954
2Ki 19:27 come and go and *h* you **rage** against me. AIT
2Ki 20: 3 **h** I have walked before you faithfully and H889
2Ki 20:20 achievements and **h** he made the pool H889
1Ch 13:12 "**H** can I ever bring the ark of God to me?" H2120
1Ch 15:13 not inquire of him about **h** to do it in the NDT
1Ch 21: 2 me so that I may know **h many** there are." H5031
1Ch 21:12 decide **h** I should answer the one who H4537
1Ch 29:17 I have seen with joy **h** willingly your people NDT
2Ch 6:18 **H much less** this temple I have built H677+3954
2Ch 9: 7 **H happy** your people must be! How happy H897
2Ch 9: 7 **H happy** your officials, who continually H897
2Ch 10: 6 "**H** would you advise me to answer these H375
2Ch 10: 9 **H** should we answer these people who say NDT
2Ch 18:15 "**H many** times must I make H6330+3869+4537
2Ch 20:11 See *h* they *are* **repaying** us by coming to AIT
2Ch 20:29 when they heard **h** the LORD had fought H3954
2Ch 32:14 **H** then can your god deliver you from my H3954
2Ch 32:15 **H much less** will your god H677+3954+4202
2Ch 33:19 His prayer and **h** God was moved by his NDT
Ne 2: 6 "**H long** will your journey take H6330+5503
Ne 6:14 prophet Noadiah and **h** she and the rest of NDT
Ne 9:10 you knew **h** arrogantly the Egyptians H3954
Ne 13:24 and *did* not **know h** to speak the H5795
Est 2:11 to find out **h** Esther **was** and what was H8934
Est 2:13 And this is **h** she would go to the H928+2296
Est 5:11 honored him and **h** he had elevated him H889
Est 8: 1 Esther had told **h** he was related to her H4537
Est 8: 6 For **h** can I bear to see disaster fall on my H379
Est 8: 6 **H** can I bear to see the destruction of my H379
Job 2:13 because they saw **h** great his suffering H3954
Job 4: 3 Think **h** you have instructed many, how you NDT
Job 4: 3 **h** you have strengthened feeble hands. NDT
Job 4:19 **h much more** those who live in houses of H677
Job 6:25 **H** painful are honest words! But what do H4537
Job 7: 4 I lie down I think, '**H long** *before* I get up? H5503
Job 8: 2 "**H long** will you say such things H6330+625
Job 9: 2 But **h** can mere mortals prove their H4537
Job 9:14 "**H** then can I dispute with him? How can I H3954
Job 9:14 *H can I* **find** words to argue with him? AIT
Job 11: 5 **Oh, h I wish** that God would speak H4769+5989
Job 13:23 **H many** wrongs and sins have I H3869+4537
Job 15:16 **h much less** mortals, who are vile H677+3954
Job 19: 2 "**H long** will you torment me H6330+625+2025
Job 19:27 **H** my heart yearns within me NDT
Job 19:28 "If you say, '**H** we will hound him, since H4537
Job 20: 4 "Surely you know **h** it has been from of H2296
Job 21:17 "Yet **h often** is the lamp of the H3869+4537
Job 21:17 **H** often does calamity come upon them, the NDT
Job 21:18 **H** often are they like straw before the wind NDT
Job 21:34 "So **h** can you console me with your H375
Job 22:12 And see **h** lofty are the highest stars H3954
Job 25: 4 **H** then can a mortal be righteous before H4537
Job 25: 4 **H** can one born of woman be pure? H4537
Job 25: 6 **h much less** a mortal, who is but a H677+3954
Job 26: 2 "**H** you have helped the powerless! How H4537
Job 26: 2 **H** you have saved the arm that is feeble! NDT
Job 26:14 **h** faint the whisper we hear of him! H4537
Job 29: 2 "**H I long for** the months H4769+5989+5761
Job 33:23 thousand, sent to tell them **h** to be upright, NDT
Job 35: 6 If you sin, **h** does that affect him? If your H4537
Job 35:14 **H much less**, then, will he listen H677+3954
Job 36:26 *H* **great** is God—beyond our understanding AIT
Job 36:29 Who can understand **h** he spreads out the NDT
Job 36:29 the clouds, **h** he thunders from his pavilion? NDT
Job 36:30 See **h** he scatters his lightning about him NDT
Job 37:15 Do you know **h** God controls the clouds and NDT
Job 37:16 Do you know **h** the clouds hang poised H6584
Job 40: 4 "I am unworthy—**h** can I reply to you? H4537
Ps 3: 1 **h** many are my foes! How many rise H4537
Ps 3: 1 **H** many rise up against me NDT
Ps 4: 2 **H long** will you people turn my H6330+4537
Ps 4: 2 **H** long will you love delusions and seek NDT
Ps 6: 3 deep anguish. **H long**, LORD, how H6330+5503
Ps 6: 3 is in deep anguish. How long, LORD, **h** long? NDT
Ps 8: 1 **h** majestic is your name in all the earth! H4537
Ps 8: 9 **h** majestic is your name in all the earth! H4537
Ps 9:13 see **h** my enemies persecute me! Have NDT
Ps 11: 1 **H** *then* can you say to me H375
Ps 13: 1 **H long**, LORD? Will you forget H6330+625+2025
Ps 13: 1 **H long** will you hide your face H6330+625+2025
Ps 13: 2 **H long** must I wrestle with my H6330+625+2025
Ps 13: 2 **H long** will my enemy H6330+625+2025
Ps 21: 1 **H** great is his joy in the victories you give! H4537
Ps 25:19 See **h** numerous are my enemies and H3954
Ps 25:19 are my enemies and **h** fiercely they hate me NDT
Ps 31:19 **H** abundant are the good things that you H4537
Ps 35:17 **H long**, Lord, will you look on H3869+4537
Ps 36: 7 **H** priceless is your unfailing love, O God H4537
Ps 36:12 See **h** the evildoers lie fallen—thrown NDT
Ps 39: 4 my days; let me know **h** fleeting my life is. H4537
Ps 42: 4 **h** I used to go to the house of God under H3954
Ps 59: 3 See **h** they lie in wait for me! Fierce men H3954
Ps 62: 3 **H long** will you assault me H6330+625+2025
Ps 66: 3 Say to God, "**H** awesome are your deeds H4537
Ps 69:19 You know **h** I am scorned, disgraced and NDT
Ps 71:15 though I know not *h to* **relate** them all. AIT
Ps 73:11 They say, "**H** would God know? Does the H377
Ps 73:19 **H** suddenly are they destroyed, completely H375
Ps 74: 9 of us knows **h long** this will be. H6330+4537
Ps 74:10 **H long** will the enemy mock you H6330+5503
Ps 74:18 Remember **h** the enemy has mocked you H2296
Ps 74:18 **h** foolish people have reviled your name. NDT
Ps 74:22 remember **h** fools mock you all day long. NDT
Ps 78:40 **H often** they rebelled against him H3869+4537
Ps 79: 5 **H long**, LORD? Will you be angry H6330+4537
Ps 79: 5 **H** long will your jealousy burn like fire? NDT
Ps 80: 4 **H long**, LORD God Almighty, will H6330+5503
Ps 81:14 **h quickly** I would subdue their H3869+5071
Ps 82: 2 "**H long** will you defend the unjust H6330+5503
Ps 83: 2 See **h** your enemies growl, how your foes NDT
Ps 83: 2 enemies growl, **h** your foes rear their heads. NDT
Ps 84: 1 **H** lovely is your dwelling place, LORD H4537
Ps 89:46 **H long**, LORD? Will you hide H6330+4537
Ps 89:46 **H** long will your wrath burn like fire? NDT
Ps 89:47 Remember **h** fleeting is my life. For what H4537
Ps 89:50 **h** your servant has been mocked, how I NDT
Ps 89:50 **h** I bear in my heart the taunts of all the NDT
Ps 90:13 **H long** will it be? Have H6330+5503
Ps 92: 5 **H** great are your works, LORD, how H4537
Ps 92: 5 LORD, **h** profound your thoughts! H4394
Ps 94: 3 **H long**, LORD, will the wicked, how H6330+5503
Ps 94: 3 **h long** will the wicked be jubilant? H6330+5503
Ps 103:14 he **knows h** we are formed, he H3359
Ps 104:24 **H** many are your works, LORD! In wisdom H4537
Ps 119: 9 **H** can a young person stay on the H928+4537
Ps 119:40 **H** I long for your precepts! In your H2180
Ps 119:84 **H long must** your servant **wait** H3869+4537+3427
Ps 119:97 **h** I love your law! I meditate on it all H4537
Ps 119:103 **H** sweet are your words to my taste H4537
Ps 119:159 See **h** I love your precepts; preserve my H3954
Ps 133: 1 **H** good and pleasant it is when God's H4537
Ps 137: 4 **H** can we sing the songs of the LORD while H375
Ps 139:17 **H** precious to me are your thoughts, God H4537
Ps 139:17 thoughts, God! **H** vast is the sum of them H4537
Ps 147: 1 **H** good it is to sing praises to our God H3954
Ps 147: 1 **h** pleasant and fitting to praise him! H3954
Pr 1:17 **H** useless to spread a net where every H3954
Pr 1:22 "**H long** will you who are simple H6330+5503
Pr 1:22 **H** long will mockers delight in mockery and NDT
Pr 5:12 You will say, "**H** I hated discipline! How my H375
Pr 5:12 **H** my heart spurned correction! NDT
Pr 6: 9 **H long** will you lie there, you H6330+5503
Pr 11:31 **h much more** the ungodly and the H677+3954
Pr 15:11 **h much more** do human hearts! H677+3954
Pr 15:23 apt reply—and **h** good is a timely word! H4537
Pr 16:16 **H much** better to get wisdom than gold H4537
Pr 17: 7 **h much worse** lying lips to a ruler! H677+3954
Pr 19: 2 **h much more** will hasty feet miss the way! H2256
Pr 19: 7 **h much more** do their friends avoid H677+3954
Pr 19:10 **h much worse** for a slave to rule over H677+3954
Pr 20:24 **H** then can anyone understand their own H4537
Pr 21:27 **h much more so** when brought with H677+3954
Pr 24:10 in a time of trouble, **h** small is your strength! NDT
Pr 28:11 discerning sees **h** deluded they are. NDT
Ecc 4:11 But **h** can one keep warm alone H375
Ecc 4:13 who no longer **knows h** to heed a warning H3359
Ecc 6: 3 yet no matter **h** long he lives, if he H8611
Ecc 6: 8 do the poor gain *by* **knowing h** to conduct H3359
Ecc 6:11 meaning, and **h** does that profit anyone? H4537
Ecc 10: 3 sense and show everyone *h* **stupid** they are. AIT
Ecc 11: 5 **h** the body is formed in a mother's H3869
SS 1: 4 *H* **right** they are to adore you AIT
SS 1:15 **H** beautiful you are, my darling! Oh, how H2180
SS 1:15 Oh, **h** beautiful! Your eyes are H2180
SS 1:16 **H** handsome you are, my beloved! Oh H2180
SS 1:16 Oh, **h** charming! And our bed H677
SS 4: 1 **H** beautiful you are, my darling! Oh, how H2180
SS 4: 1 Oh, **h** beautiful! Your eyes H2180
SS 4:10 **H** delightful is your love, my sister, my H4537
SS 4:10 **H** much more pleasing is your love than H4537
SS 5: 9 **H** is your beloved better than others, most H4537
SS 5: 9 **H** is your beloved better than others, that H4537
SS 7: 1 **H** beautiful your sandaled feet, O prince's H4537
SS 7: 6 **H** beautiful you are and how pleasing, my H4537
SS 7: 6 How beautiful you are and **h** pleasing, my H4537
Isa 1:21 **See h** the faithful city has become a H377
Isa 6:11 "**For h long**, Lord?" And H6330+5503
Isa 8: 4 For before the boy **knows h** to say 'My H3359
Isa 14: 4 **H** the oppressor has come to an end H375
Isa 14: 4 has come to an end! **H** his fury has ended! NDT
Isa 14:12 **H** you have fallen from heaven, morning H375
Isa 16: 6 Moab's pride—**h great** is her arrogance!— H4394
Isa 19:11 **H** can you say to Pharaoh, "I am one of the H375
Isa 20: 6 the king of Assyria! **H** then can we escape?' H375
Isa 29:12 answer, "*I* don't **know h to read**." H3359+6219
Isa 30:19 *H* **gracious** *he will be* when you cry for help AIT
Isa 32:20 *h* **blessed** you will be, sowing your seed by AIT
Isa 36: 9 **H** then can you repulse one officer of the H375
Isa 36:20 **H** then can the LORD deliver Jerusalem H3954
Isa 37:28 come and go and *h* you **rage** against me. AIT
Isa 38: 3 **h** I have walked before you faithfully and H889
Isa 47:11 and *you will* not **know h** to conjure it away H3359
Isa 48: 4 For I knew **h** stubborn you were; your neck H3954
Isa 48: 8 Well do I know **h treacherous** *you are* H953+953
Isa 48:11 **H** can I let myself be defamed? H375
Isa 52: 7 **H** beautiful on the mountains are the feet H4537
Isa 63:14 **This is h** you guided your people to make H4027
Isa 64: 5 you were angry. **H** then can we be saved NDT
Jer 1: 6 "*I do* not **know h** to speak; I am too H3359
Jer 2: 2 **h** as a bride you loved me and followed me NDT
Jer 2:19 then and realize **h** evil and bitter it is for H3954
Jer 2:21 **H** then did you turn against me into a H375
Jer 2:23 "**H** can you say, 'I am not defiled; I have H375
Jer 2:23 See **h** you **behaved** in the valley; consider H2006
Jer 2:33 **H** skilled you are at pursuing love! Even H4537
Jer 3: 5 **This is h** you talk, but you do all the evil H2180
Jer 3:19 " '**H gladly** would I treat you like my H375
Jer 4:10 **H** completely you have deceived this H434
Jer 4:14 **H long** will you harbor wicked H6330+5503
Jer 4:18 is your punishment. **H** bitter it is! How it H3954
Jer 4:18 How bitter it is! **H** it pierces to the heart!" H3954
Jer 4:21 **H long** must I see the battle H6330+5503
Jer 4:22 in doing evil; *they* **know** not **h** to do good." H3359
Jer 6:15 *they do* not even **know h** to blush. H3359
Jer 8: 8 " '**H** can you say, "We are wise, for we H377
Jer 8:12 *they do* not even **know h** to blush. H3359
Jer 9:19 is heard from Zion: '**H** ruined we are! How H375
Jer 9:19 'How ruined we are! **H** great is our shame NDT
Jer 9:20 Teach your daughters **h** to wail; teach one NDT
Jer 12: 4 **H long** will the land lie parched H6330+5503
Jer 12: 5 you out, **h** can you compete with horses? H375
Jer 12: 5 **h** will you manage in the thickets by the H375
Jer 13:27 **H long** will you be unclean?" H339+5503+6388
Jer 15: 5 Who will stop to ask **h** you **are**? H8934
Jer 15:15 think of *h* I **suffer** reproach for your sake. AIT
Jer 16:12 See **h** all of you are following the NDT
Jer 22:23 **h** you will groan when pangs come upon H4537
Jer 23:26 **H long** will this continue in the H6330+5503
Jer 30: 7 **H** awful that day will be! No other will be H3954
Jer 31:22 **H long** will you wander, unfaithful H6330+5503
Jer 32:24 "See **h** the siege ramps are built up to take NDT
Jer 36:17 "Tell us, **h** did you come to write all this? H375
Jer 38:28 **This is h** Jerusalem was taken H3869+889
Jer 47: 2 "See **h** the waters are rising in the north NDT
Jer 47: 5 **h long** will you cut yourselves? H6330+5503
Jer 47: 6 the LORD, **h long** till you rest? H6330+625+2025
Jer 47: 7 But **h** can it rest when the LORD has H375
Jer 48:14 "**H** can you say, 'We are warriors, men H375
Jer 48:17 '**H** broken is the mighty scepter, how H377
Jer 48:17 mighty scepter, **h** broken the glorious staff! NDT
Jer 48:29 of Moab's pride—*h* **great** is her arrogance!— AIT
Jer 48:39 "**H** shattered she is! How they wail! How H375
Jer 48:39 shattered she is! **H** they wail! How Moab H375
Jer 48:39 **H** Moab turns her back in shame NDT
Jer 50:23 **H** broken and shattered is the hammer of H375
Jer 50:23 **H** desolate is Babylon among the nations H375

Jer 50:28 declaring in Zion **h** the LORD our God has NDT
Jer 51:41 "**H** Sheshak will be captured, the boast of H375
Jer 51:41 **H** desolate Babylon will be among the H375
La 1: 1 **H** deserted lies the city, once so full of H377
La 1: 1 **H** like a widow is she, who once was great NDT
La 1:20 LORD, **h** distressed I am! I am in H3954
La 2: 1 **H** the Lord has covered Daughter Zion with H377
La 4: 1 **H** the gold has lost its luster, the fine gold H377
La 4: 2 **H** the precious children of Zion, once worth H377
Eze 6: 9 **h** I have been grieved by their adulterous H889
Eze 14:21 **H much worse** will it be when I send H677+3954
Eze 15: 2 **h** is the wood of a vine different from that H4537
Eze 15: 5 **h much less** can it be made into H677+3954
Eze 22: 6 " 'See **h** each of the princes of Israel who NDT
Eze 26:17 " '**H** you are destroyed, city of renown H375
Eze 33:10 because of them. **H** then can we live?" H375
Eze 35:15 became desolate, **that is h** I will treat you. H4027
Eze 44:23 and **show** them **h to distinguish** between H3359
Da 4: 3 **H** great are his signs, how A10341+10408
Da 4: 3 his signs, **h** mighty his wonders! A10341+10408
Da 8:13 "**H long** will it take *for* the vision to H6330+5503
Da 10:17 **H** can I, your servant, talk with you, H2120
Da 12: 6 "**H long** will it be before these H6330+5503
Hos 4:16 **H** then can the LORD pasture them like lambs NDT
Hos 8: 5 **H long** will they be incapable of purity? H5503
Hos 11: 8 "**H** can I give you up, Ephraim? How can I H375
Hos 11: 8 **H** can I hand you over, Israel NDT
Hos 11: 8 **H** can I treat you like Admah? How H375
Hos 11: 8 **H** can I make you like Zeboyim NDT
Joel 1:18 **H** the cattle moan! The herds mill about H4537
Am 3:10 "*They do* not **know h** to do right," declares H3359
Am 5:12 For I know **h** many are your offenses and NDT
Am 5:12 are your offenses and **h** great your sins. NDT
Am 7: 2 **H** can Jacob survive? He is so H4769
Am 7: 5 I beg you, stop! **H** can Jacob survive? He H4769
Ob 6 But **h** Esau will be ransacked, his hidden H375
Jnh 1: 6 went to him and said, "**H** can you sleep? H4537
Jnh 3:10 saw what they did and **h** they turned from H3954
Mic 6: 3 I done to you? **H** have I burdened you H4537
Hab 1: 2 **H long**, LORD, must I call for H6330+625+2025
Hab 2: 6 **H long** must this go on H5503+6330
Hag 2: 3 its former glory? **H** does it look to you now H4537
Hag 2:15 consider **h** things were before one stone was NDT
Zec 1:12 **h long** will you withhold mercy H6330+5503
Zec 2: 2 to find out **h** wide and how long it H3869+4537
Zec 2: 2 find out how wide and **h** long it is." H3869+4537
Zec 7:14 **This is h** they made the pleasant land H2256
Zec 9:17 **H** attractive and beautiful they will be H4537
Mal 1: 2 "But you ask, '**H** have you loved us?' H928+4537
Mal 1: 6 '**H** have we shown contempt for your H928+4537
Mal 1: 7 you ask, '**H** have we defiled you? H928+4537
Mal 2:17 "**H** have we wearied him? H928+4537
Mal 3: 7 "But you ask, '**H** are we to return?' H928+4537
Mal 3: 8 "But you ask, '**H** are we robbing you H928+4537
Mt 1:18 **This is h** the birth of Jesus the Messiah *G4048*
Mt 5:13 **h** can it be made salty again? *G1877+5515*
Mt 6: 9 "**This**, then, **is h** you should pray: " 'Our *G4048*
Mt 6:23 you is darkness, **h great** is that darkness! *G4531*
Mt 6:28 See **h** the flowers of the field grow *G4802*
Mt 6:30 If **that is h** God clothes the grass of the *G4048*
Mt 7: 4 **H** can you say to your brother, 'Let me take *G4802*
Mt 7:11 **know h** to give good gifts to your children *G3857*
Mt 7:11 **h much** more will your Father in heaven *G4531*
Mt 9:14 "**H is it that** we and the Pharisees *G1328+5515*
Mt 9:15 "**H** can the guests of the bridegroom *G3590*
Mt 10:19 not worry about what to say or **h** to say it. *G4802*
Mt 10:25 **h much** more the members of his *G4531*
Mt 12:12 **H much** more valuable is a person than a *G4531*
Mt 12:14 went out and plotted **h** they might kill *G3968*
Mt 12:26 **H** then can his kingdom stand? *G4802*
Mt 12:29 **h** can anyone enter a strong man's house *G4802*
Mt 12:34 **h** can you who are evil say anything good? *G4802*
Mt 12:45 **That is h** it will be with this wicked *G4048*
Mt 13:49 **This is h** it will be at the end of the age *G4048*
Mt 15:34 "**H many** loaves do you have?" Jesus *G4531*
Mt 16: 3 *You* **know h** to interpret the appearance *G1182*
Mt 16: 9 and **h many** basketfuls you gathered? *G4531*
Mt 16:10 and **h many** basketfuls you gathered? *G4531*
Mt 16:11 **H is it** you don't understand that I was not *G4802*
Mt 17:17 "**h long** shall I stay with you? *G2401+4536*
Mt 17:17 **H long** shall I put up with you *G2401+4536*
Mt 18:21 **h many times** shall I forgive my brother *G4529*
Mt 18:35 "**This is h** my heavenly Father will treat *G4048*
Mt 21:20 "**H** did the fig tree wither so quickly?" *G4802*
Mt 22:12 '**H** did you get in here without wedding *G4802*
Mt 22:43 He said to them, "**H is it** then that David *G4802*
Mt 22:45 calls him 'Lord,' **h** can he be his son?" *G4802*
Mt 23:33 **H** will you escape being condemned to *G4802*
Mt 23:37 **h often** I have longed to gather your *G4529*
Mt 24:19 **H dreadful** it will be in those days for *G4026*
Mt 24:39 **That is h** it will be at the coming of the *G4048*
Mt 26:54 But **h** then would the Scriptures be fulfilled *G4802*
Mt 27: 1 made their plans **h** to have Jesus *G6063*
Mt 27:65 make the tomb as secure as *you* **know h**." *G3857*
Mk 2:18 "**H is it that** John's disciples and *G1328+5515*
Mk 2:19 "**H** can the guests of the bridegroom fast *G3590*
Mk 3: 6 with the Herodians **h** they might kill Jesus *G3968*
Mk 3:23 "**H** can Satan drive out Satan? *G4802*
Mk 4:13 **H** then will you understand any parable? *G4802*
Mk 4:27 grows, though he *does* not **know h**. *G3857*
Mk 5:19 tell them **h much** the Lord has done *G4012*
Mk 5:19 you, and **h** he has had mercy on you." NDT

Mk 5:20 in the Decapolis **h much** Jesus had done *G4012*
Mk 6:38 "**H many** loaves do you have?" he asked *G4531*
Mk 8: 5 "**H many** loaves do you have?" Jesus *G4531*
Mk 8:19 **h many** basketfuls of pieces did you pick *G4531*
Mk 8:20 **h many** basketfuls of pieces did you pick *G4531*
Mk 9:19 "**h long** shall I stay with you? *G2401+4536*
Mk 9:19 **H long** shall I put up with you *G2401+4536*
Mk 9:21 "**H** long has he been like this? *G4531*
Mk 9:50 **h** can you make it salty again? *G1877+5515*
Mk 10:23 "**H** hard it is for the rich to enter the *G4802*
Mk 10:24 **h** hard it is to enter the kingdom of God! *G4802*
Mk 12:26 of the burning bush, **h** God said to him, 'I *G4802*
Mk 12:37 **H** then can he be his son? *G4470*
Mk 13:17 **H dreadful** it will be in those days for *G4026*
Mk 15: 4 See **h many** *things* they are accusing you *G4531*
Mk 15:39 in front of Jesus, saw **h** he died, he said, *G4048*
Lk 1:18 the angel, "**H** can I be sure of this? *G2848+5515*
Lk 1:34 "**H** will this be," Mary asked the angel *G4802*
Lk 6:23 For **that is h** their ancestors *G2848+3836+899*
Lk 6:26 for **that is h** their ancestors *G2848+3836+899*
Lk 6:42 **H** can you say to your brother, 'Brother, let *G4802*
Lk 8:18 Therefore consider carefully **h** you listen *G4802*
Lk 8:36 it told the people **h** the demon-possessed *G4802*
Lk 8:39 home and tell **h much** God has done for *G4012*
Lk 8:39 told all over town **h much** Jesus had done *G4012*
Lk 8:47 had touched him and **h** she had been *G6055*
Lk 9:41 "**h long** shall I stay with you and *G2401+4536*
Lk 10:26 he replied. "**H** do you read it?" *G4802*
Lk 11:13 **know h** to give good gifts to your children *G3857*
Lk 11:13 **h much** more will your Father in heaven *G4531*
Lk 11:18 against himself, **h** can his kingdom stand? *G4802*
Lk 12:11 do not worry about **h** you will defend *G4802*
Lk 12:21 "**This is h** it will be with whoever stores up *G4048*
Lk 12:24 And **h much** more valuable you are than *G4531*
Lk 12:27 "Consider **h** the wild flowers grow. *G4802*
Lk 12:28 If **that is h** God clothes the grass of the *G4048*
Lk 12:28 the fire, **h much** more will he clothe you *G4531*
Lk 12:49 **h** I wish it were already kindled! *G5515*
Lk 12:56 *You* **know h** to interpret the appearance of *G3857*
Lk 12:56 **H is it** that you don't know how to *G4802*
Lk 12:56 is it that *you* don't **know h** to interpret *G3857*
Lk 13:34 **h often** I have longed to gather your *G4529*
Lk 14: 7 When he noticed **h** the guests picked the *G4802*
Lk 14:34 **h** can it be made salty again? *G1877+5515*
Lk 15:17 '**H many** of my father's hired servants *G4531*
Lk 16: 5 the first, '**H much** do you owe my master? *G4531*
Lk 16: 7 the second, 'And **h much** do you owe? *G4531*
Lk 18:24 "**H** hard it is for the rich to enter the *G4802*
Lk 20:44 **H** then can he be his son? *G4802*
Lk 21: 5 were remarking about **h** the temple was *G4022*
Lk 21:14 beforehand *h you will* **defend** *yourselves*. AIT
Lk 21:23 **H dreadful** it will be in those days for *G4026*
Lk 22: 4 discussed with them **h** he might betray *G4802*
Lk 23:55 saw the tomb and **h** his body was laid in *G6055*
Lk 24: 6 Remember **h** he told you, while he was *G6055*
Lk 24:25 them, "**H foolish** you are *G6043+1639+6042+485*
Lk 24:25 and **h slow** to believe all *G1096+3836+2840*
Lk 24:35 **h** Jesus was recognized by them *G6055*
Jn 1:48 "**H** do you know me?" Nathanael asked *G4470*
Jn 3: 4 "**H** can someone be born when they are *G4802*
Jn 3: 9 "**H** can this be?" Nicodemus asked. *G4802*
Jn 3:12 **h** then will you believe if I speak of *G4802*
Jn 4: 9 **H** can you ask me for a drink? *G4802*
Jn 5:44 **H** can you believe since you accept glory *G4802*
Jn 5:47 **h** are you going to believe what I say?" *G4802*
Jn 6: 9 but **h far** will they go among so many?" *G5515*
Jn 6:42 **H** can he now say, 'I came down from *G4802*
Jn 6:52 "**H** can this man give us his flesh to eat?" *G4802*
Jn 7:15 "**H** did this man get such learning without *G4802*
Jn 7:41 "**H** can the Messiah come from *G3590+1142*
Jn 8:33 **H** can you say that we shall be set free?" *G4802*
Jn 9:10 "**H** then were your eyes opened?" they *G4802*
Jn 9:15 also asked him **h** he had received his *G4802*
Jn 9:16 "**H** can a sinner perform such signs?" *G4802*
Jn 9:19 **H** is it that now he can see? *G4802*
Jn 9:21 But **h** he can see now, or who opened his *G4802*
Jn 9:26 he do to you? **H** did he open your eyes?" *G4802*
Jn 9:34 steeped in sin at birth; *h dare* you **lecture** us!" AIT
Jn 10:24 "**H long** will you keep us in *G2401+4536*
Jn 11:31 noticed **h** quickly she got up and went out, *G4022*
Jn 11:36 Then the Jews said, "See **h** he loved him!" *G4802*
Jn 12:19 **Look h** the whole world has gone after *G2623*
Jn 12:34 remain forever, so **h** can you say, 'The *G4802*
Jn 14: 5 you are going, *so* **h** can we know the way?" *G4802*
Jn 14: 9 has seen the Father. **H** can you say, 'Show *G4802*
Ac 2: 8 Then **h** is it that each of us hears them in *G4802*
Ac 3:18 But **this is h** God fulfilled what he had *G4048*
Ac 4: 9 are being asked **h** he was healed, *G1877+5515*
Ac 4:21 They could not decide **h** to punish them *G4802*
Ac 5: 3 **h is it that** Satan has so filled your *G1328+5515*
Ac 5: 9 "**H could** you conspire to test *G5515+5516+4022*
Ac 8:31 "**H** can I," he said, "unless someone *G4802+323*
Ac 9:16 I will show him **h much** he must suffer *G4012*
Ac 9:27 He told them **h** Saul on his journey had *G4802*
Ac 9:27 **h** in Damascus he had preached *G4802*
Ac 10:34 "I now realize **h true** it is that God *G2093+237*
Ac 10:38 **h** God anointed Jesus of Nazareth with the *G6055*
Ac 10:38 **h** he went around doing good and NDT
Ac 11:13 He told us **h** he had seen an angel appear *G4802*
Ac 12:17 quiet and described **h** the Lord had *G4802*
Ac 14:27 through them and **h** he had opened a *G4022*
Ac 15: 3 *they* **told** *h* the Gentiles had been converted. AIT

Ac 15:14 has described to us **h** God first intervened *G2777*
Ac 15:36 of the Lord and see **h** they are doing." *G4802*
Ac 19:26 And you see and hear **h** this fellow Paul *G4022*
Ac 20:18 "You know **h** I lived the whole time I was *G4802*
Ac 21:20 **h** many thousands of Jews have believed *G4531*
Ac 23: 4 "*H dare you* **insult** God's high priest! AIT
Ac 25:20 I was at a loss **h** to investigate such matters NDT
Ro 1: 9 is my witness **h** constantly I remember you *G6055*
Ro 3: 6 were so, **h** could God judge the world? *G4802*
Ro 5: 9 **h much** more shall we be saved from *G4498*
Ro 5:10 of his Son, **h much** more, having been *G4498*
Ro 5:15 **h much** more did God's grace and the gift *G4498*
Ro 5:17 **h much** more will those who receive *G4498*
Ro 6: 2 died to sin; **h** can we live in it any longer? *G4802*
Ro 8:32 gave him up for us all—**h** will he not also *G4802*
Ro 9: 9 For this was **h** the promise was stated: "At NDT
Ro 10:14 **H**, then, can they call on the one they *G4802*
Ro 10:14 And **h** can they believe in the one of *G4802*
Ro 10:14 And **h** can they hear without someone *G4802*
Ro 10:15 And **h** can anyone preach unless they are *G4802*
Ro 10:15 "**H** beautiful are the feet of those who *G6055*
Ro 11: 2 **h** he appealed to God against Israel: *G6055*
Ro 11:12 **h much** greater riches will their full *G4531*
Ro 11:24 olive tree, **h much** more readily will these *G4531*
Ro 11:33 **H** unsearchable his judgments, and his *G6055*
Ro 13:14 not think about **h to gratify** the desires of *G1650*
1Co 4: 1 **This**, then, **is h** you ought to regard us: as *G4048*
1Co 4: 8 **H I wish that** you really had begun to *G4054*
1Co 4:19 find out not only **h** these arrogant people *G3836*
1Co 6: 3 **H much more** the things of this life *G3615+3615*
1Co 7:16 **H** do you know, wife, whether you will *G5515*
1Co 7:16 **h** do you know, husband, whether you *G5515*
1Co 7:32 Lord's affairs—**h** he can please the Lord. *G4802*
1Co 7:33 of this world—**h** he can please his wife *G4802*
1Co 7:34 world—**h** she can please her husband. *G4802*
1Co 14: 7 **h** will anyone know what tune is being *G4802*
1Co 14: 9 **h** will anyone know what you are saying? *G4802*
1Co 14:16 God in the Spirit, **h** can someone else *G4802*
1Co 15:12 **h** can some of you say that there is no *G4802*
1Co 15:35 will ask, "**H** are the dead raised? *G4802*
1Co 15:36 *H* **foolish**! What you sow does not come to AIT
2Co 1:20 For **no matter h many** promises God has *G4012*
2Co 3: 9 **h much** more glorious is the ministry that *G4498*
2Co 3:11 **h much** greater is the glory of that which *G4498*
2Co 7:12 see for yourselves *h* **devoted** to us you are. AIT
2Co 7:13 delighted to see *h* **happy** Titus was, AIT
2Co 12:13 **H** were you inferior to the other churches *G5515*
Gal 1:13 **h** intensely I persecuted the church of God *G4022*
Gal 2:14 **H is it**, then, that you force Gentiles to *G4802*
Gal 4: 9 **h is it** that you are turning back to those *G4802*
Gal 4:20 *h I* **wish** I could be with you now and change AIT
Eph 3:18 to grasp **h** wide and long and high and *G5515*
Eph 5:15 **h** you live—not as unwise but as *G4802*
Eph 6:21 also may know **h** I am and what I *G3836+2848*
Eph 6:22 that you may know **h** we are, and *G3836+4309*
Php 1: 8 God can testify **h** I long for all of you with *G6055*
Php 2:23 him as soon as I see *h* things *go* **with** me. AIT
Col 2: 1 want you to know **h hard** I am contending *G2462*
Col 2: 5 delight to see *h* **disciplined** you are and how AIT
Col 2: 5 you are and *h* **firm** your faith in Christ is AIT
Col 4: 6 that you may know **h** to answer everyone. *G4802*
1Th 1: 5 You know **h** we lived among you for your *G3888*
1Th 1: 9 They tell **h** you turned to God from idols *G4802*
1Th 2:10 so is God, of **h** holy, righteous and *G6055*
1Th 3: 9 **H** can we thank God enough for you in *G5515*
1Th 4: 1 we instructed you **h** to live in order to *G4802*
2Th 2: 9 will be in accordance with *h* Satan **works**. AIT
2Th 3: 7 you yourselves know **h** you ought to follow *G4802*
2Th 3:17 mark in all my letters. **This is h** I write. *G4048*
1Ti 3: 5 If anyone *does* not **know h** to manage his *G3857*
1Ti 3: 5 **h** can he take care of God's church?) *G4802*
1Ti 3:15 you will know **h** people ought to conduct *G4802*
2Ti 1:18 very well *in* **h many** *ways* he helped me *G4012*
2Ti 3:15 **h** from infancy you have known the *G4022*
Heb 2: 3 **h** shall we escape if we ignore so great a *G4802*
Heb 7: 4 Just think **h great** he was: Even the *G4383*
Heb 9:14 **H much** more, then, will the blood of *G4531*
Heb 10:24 And let us consider **h** we may spur one NDT
Heb 10:29 **H much** more severely do you think *G4531*
Heb 12: 9 **H much** more should we submit to the *G4498*
Heb 12:25 them on earth, **h much** less will we, if we *G4498*
Jas 5: 7 See *h* the farmer **waits for** the land to yield AIT
1Pe 2:20 But **h** is it to your credit if you receive a *G4481*
2Pe 2: 9 then the Lord **knows h** to rescue the godly *G3857*
1Jn 2: 5 **This is h** we know we are in him *G1877+4047*
1Jn 2:18 come. **This is h** we know it is the last hour *G3854*
1Jn 3:10 **This is h** we know who the children *G1877+4047*
1Jn 3:16 **This is h** we know what love is *G1877+4047*
1Jn 3:17 **h** can the love of God be in that person? *G4802*
1Jn 3:19 **This is h** we know that we belong *G1877+4047*
1Jn 3:19 to the truth and **h** we set our hearts at NDT
1Jn 3:24 And **this is h** we know that he lives *G1877+4047*
1Jn 4: 2 **This is h** you can recognize the *G1877+4047*
1Jn 4: 6 **This is h** we recognize the Spirit of *G1666+4047*
1Jn 4: 9 **This is h** God showed his love *G1877+4047*
1Jn 4:13 **This is h** we know that we live in *G1877+4047*
1Jn 4:17 **This is h** love is made complete *G1877+4047*
1Jn 5: 2 **This is h** we know that we love the *G1877+4047*
3Jn 3 telling **h** you continue to walk in it. *G2777*
Rev 2: 5 Consider **h far** you have fallen! Repent *G4470*
Rev 6:10 a loud voice, "**H long**, Sovereign *G2401+4536*
Rev 11: 5 **This is h** anyone who wants to harm them *G4048*

HOWBEIT (KJV) ALTHOUGH, BUT, HOWEVER, NEVERTHELESS, THOUGH, YET

HOWEVER (144) [HOW]

Ge 15:10 each other; the birds, **h**, he did not cut in H2256
Ge 15:15 **h**, will go to your ancestors in peace H2256
Ge 30:37 **h**, took fresh-cut branches from H2256
Ge 31: 7 my wages ten times. **H**, God has not H2256
Ge 33:17 **h**, went to Sukkoth, where he built H2256
Ge 40:23 The chief cupbearer, **h**, did not remember H2256
Ge 47:13 There was no food, **h**, in the whole region H2256
Ge 47:22 **H**, he did not buy the land of the priests H8370
Ex 1:17 The midwives, **h**, feared God and did not H2256
Ex 9:32 wheat and spelt, **h**, were not destroyed H2256
Ex 16:20 **H**, some of them paid no attention to H2256
Ex 21:13 **H**, if it is not done intentionally, but God H2256
Ex 21:19 outside with a staff; **h**, the guilty party H8370
Ex 21:29 **h**, the bull has had the habit of goring H2256
Ex 21:30 **H**, if payment is demanded, the owner may NDT
Ex 21:36 **H**, if it was known that the bull had the habit NDT
Ex 32:34 **H**, when the time comes for me to punish H2256
Lev 5:11 **h**, they cannot afford two doves or H2256
Lev 7:16 **h**, their offering is the result of a vow H2256
Lev 11:21 There are, **h**, some flying insects that walk H421
Lev 11:36 A spring, **h**, or a cistern for collecting water H421
Lev 13:28 **h**, the spot is unchanged and has not H2256
Lev 13:37 **h**, the sore is unchanged so far as the H2256
Lev 14:21 **h**, they are poor and cannot afford H2256
Lev 19:21 The man, **h**, must bring a ram to the H2256
Lev 22:13 No unauthorized person, **h**, may eat it. H2256
Lev 22:23 You may, **h**, present as a freewill offering H2256
Lev 25:26 **h**, there is no one to redeem it for them H2256
Lev 27:20 **h**, they do not redeem the field, or if H2256
Lev 27:26 " 'No one, **h**, may dedicate the firstborn of H421
Nu 1:47 tribe of the Levites, **h**, was not counted H2256
Nu 1:53 The Levites, **h**, are to set up their tents H2256
Nu 2:33 The Levites, **h**, were not counted along H2256
Nu 3: 4 Nadab and Abihu, **h**, died before the LORD H2256
Nu 5:28 **h**, the woman has not made herself H2256
Nu 11:26 **H**, two men, whose names were Eldad H2256
Nu 21:24 **h**, put him to the sword and took H2256
Nu 26:11 The line of Korah, **h**, did not die out. H2256
Nu 30:15 **h**, he nullifies them some time after he H2256
Dt 3:19 **H**, your wives, your children and your H8370
Dt 14: 7 **H**, of those that chew the cud or that have a H421
Dt 15: 4 **H**, there need be no poor people H700+3954
Dt 20:16 **H**, in the cities of the nations the LORD H8370
Dt 20:20 **H**, you may cut down trees that you know H8370
Dt 22:20 **h**, the charge is true and no proof of H2256
Dt 23: 5 **H**, the LORD your God would not listen to H2256
Dt 25: 7 **H**, if a man does not want to marry his H2256
Dt 28:15 **H**, if you do not obey the LORD your God H2256
Jos 9: 3 **H**, when the people of Gibeon heard H2256
Jos 14: 8 **h**, followed the LORD my God H2256
Jos 17:13 **H**, when the Israelites grew stronger, they H2256
Jos 18: 7 The Levites, **h**, do not get a portion among H3954
Jdg 1:21 The Benjamites, **h**, did not drive out the H2256
Jdg 9:51 Inside the city, **h**, was a strong tower, to H2256
Jdg 11:20 **h**, did not trust Israel to pass H2256
Jdg 11:28 The king of Ammon, **h**, paid no attention H2256
1Sa 2:25 His sons, **h**, did not listen to their father's H2256
1Sa 21: 4 bread on hand; **h**, there is some H3954+561
1Sa 26:19 **h**, people have done it, may they be H2256
1Sa 30:22 **H**, each man may take his wife and H3954+561
2Sa 2:10 The tribe of Judah, **h**, remained loyal to H421
2Sa 3:16 Her husband, **h**, went with her, weeping H2256
2Sa 24: 4 The king's word, **h**, overruled Joab and H2256
1Ki 3: 2 The people, **h**, were still sacrificing at the H8370
1Ki 7: 1 thirteen years, **h**, to complete the H2256
1Ki 11: 1 King Solomon, **h**, loved many foreign H2256
1Ki 11:37 **H**, as for you, I will take you, and you will H2256
1Ki 12:18 King Rehoboam, **h**, managed to get into H2256
1Ki 15:23 In his old age, **h**, his feet became H8370
1Ki 22:43 The high places, **h**, were not removed, and H421
2Ki 8:21 by night; his army, **h**, fled back home. H2256
2Ki 10:29 **H**, he did not turn away from the sins of H8370
2Ki 12: 3 The high places, **h**, were not removed; the H8370
2Ki 14: 4 The high places, **h**, were not removed; the H8370
2Ki 14:11 Amaziah, **h**, would not listen, so Jehoash H2256
2Ki 15: 4 The high places, **h**, were not removed; the H8370
2Ki 15:35 The high places, **h**, were not removed; the H8370
2Ki 17:40 They would not listen, **h**, but persisted in H2256
2Ki 25:25 In the seventh month, **h**, Ishmael son of H2256
1Ch 21: 4 The king's word, **h**, overruled Joab; so H2256
2Ch 10:18 King Rehoboam, **h**, managed to get into H2256
2Ch 12: 8 They will, **h**, become subject to him, so H3954
2Ch 19: 3 **h**, some good in you, for you have H66
2Ch 20:33 The high places, **h**, were not removed, and H421
2Ch 25:20 Amaziah, **h**, would not listen, for God so H2256
2Ch 27: 2 The people, **h**, continued their corrupt H2256
2Ch 29:34 The priests, **h**, were too few to skin all the H8370
2Ch 33:17 The people, **h**, continued to sacrifice at the H66
2Ch 35:22 **h**, would not turn away from him H2256
Ezr 5:13 "**H**, in the first year of Cyrus king of A10124
Ne 13: 2 Our God, **h**, turned the curse into a H2256
Est 9:18 The Jews in Susa, **h**, had assembled on H2256
Job 13: 4 **h**, smear me with lies; you are H2256+219
Job 27:14 **H** many his children, their fate is the sword H561
Ps 58: 5 charmer, **h** skillful the enchanter may be. NDT
Pr 6:35 he will refuse a bribe, **h** great it is. H3954
Ecc 11: 8 **H** many years anyone may live, let H3954+561
Jer 16:14 "**H**, the days are coming," declares H4200+4027
Jer 26:15 Be assured, **h**, that if you put me to death H421
Jer 26:22 King Jehoiakim, **h**, sent Elnathan son of H2256
Jer 27: 8 **h**, any nation or kingdom will not H2256
Jer 29:29 Zephaniah the priest, **h**, read the letter to H2256
Jer 34:14 Your ancestors, **h**, did not listen to me H2256
Jer 37: 3 King Zedekiah, **h**, sent Jehukal son of H2256
Jer 40: 5 **H**, before Jeremiah turned to go H2256
Jer 42:13 "**H**, if you say, 'We will not stay in this H2256
Jer 46:26 **h**, Egypt will be inhabited as in H2256
Eze 16:53 " '**H**, I will restore the fortunes of Sodom H2256
Eze 44:25 near a dead person; **h**, if the dead person H3954
Eze 46:17 **h**, he makes a gift from his inheritance H2256
Da 2:10 No king, **h** great and mighty, has ever asked NDT
Da 11:20 In a few years, **h**, he will be destroyed, yet NDT
Mt 25: 4 The wise ones, **h**, took oil in jars along *G1254*
Lk 10:20 **H**, do not rejoice that the spirits submit to *G4440*
Lk 18: 8 **H**, when the Son of Man comes, will he *G4440*
Lk 19:15 "He was made king, **h**, and returned home NDT
Lk 24:12 **h**, got up and ran to the tomb *G1254*
Jn 7:10 **H**, after his brothers had left for the *G1254*
Ac 2:13 **h**, made fun of them and said *G1254*
Ac 6: 9 Opposition arose, **h**, from members of the *G1254*
Ac 7:48 "**H**, the Most High does not live in houses *G247*
Ac 8:40 **h**, appeared at Azotus and traveled *G1254*
Ac 11:20 Some of them, **h**, men from Cyprus and *G1254*
Ac 20:24 **H**, I consider my life worth nothing to me *G247*
Ac 24:14 **H**, I admit that I worship the God of our *G1254*
Ac 25:11 **h**, I am guilty of doing anything *G4036*
Ro 4: 5 **H**, to the one who does not work but trusts *G1254*
Ro 8: 9 **h**, are not in the realm of the flesh *G1254*
Ro 15:25 **h**, I am on my way to Jerusalem in *G1254*
1Co 2: 6 **h**, speak a message of wisdom *G1254*
1Co 2: 9 **H**, as it is written: "What no eye has seen *G247*
1Co 6:13 The body, **h**, is not meant for sexual *G1254*
1Co 8: 9 Be careful, **h**, that the exercise of your *G1254*
1Co 14:22 prophecy, **h**, is not for unbelievers but *G1254*
2Co 10:13 **h**, will not boast beyond proper limits *G1254*
Gal 3:20 A mediator, **h**, implies more than one *G1254*
Eph 4:20 **h**, is not the way of life you learned *G1254*
Eph 5:33 **H**, each one of you also must love his wife *G4440*
Col 2:17 to come; the reality, **h**, is found in Christ. *G1254*
2Ti 3:10 **h**, know all about my teaching, my *G1254*
Titus 2: 1 **h**, must teach what is appropriate to *G1254*
Heb 7: 6 This man, **h**, did not trace his descent from *G1254*
Heb 12:11 Later on, **h**, it produces a harvest of *G1254*
1Pe 4:16 **H**, if you suffer as a Christian, do not be *G1254*

HOWL (3) [HOWLING]

Ps 59:15 about for food and **h** if not satisfied. H4296
Isa 14:31 you gate! **H**, *you* city! Melt away, all H2410
Mic 1: 8 *I will* **h** like a jackal and moan like H5027+6913

HOWLING (1) [HOWL]

Dt 32:10 he found him, in a barren and **h** waste. H3537

HUBBAH (1)

1Ch 7:34 Ahi, Rohgah, **H** and Aram. H2465

HUBS (1)

1Ki 7:33 spokes and **h** were all of cast metal. H3141

HUDDLED (1)

Job 30: 7 the bushes and **h** in the undergrowth. H6202

HUG (1)

Job 24: 8 mountain rains and **h** the rocks for lack of H2485

HUGE (13)

Ge 41:49 Joseph stored up **h** quantities of grain, like H4394
Jos 11: 4 chariots—a **h** army, as numerous as H8041
2Sa 21:20 there was a **h** man with six fingers on H4500
2Sa 23:21 And he struck down a **h** Egyptian H5260
1Ch 20: 6 there was a **h** man with six fingers on H4500
2Ch 16:14 they made a **h** fire in his H1524+6330+4200+4394
Ecc 9:14 it and built **h** siege works against it. H1524
Da 2:35 statue became a **h** mountain and filled A10647
Da 11:13 will advance with a **h** army fully equipped H1524
Jnh 1:17 the LORD provided a **h** fish to swallow H1524
Mt 12:40 three nights in the belly *of* a **h fish**, *G3063*
Rev 8: 8 something like a **h** mountain, all *G3489*
Rev 16:21 From the sky **h** hailstones, each weighing *G3489*

HUKKOK (1)

Jos 19:34 through Aznoth Tabor and came out at **H**. H2982

HUKOK (1)

1Ch 6:75 **H** and Rehob, together with their H2577

HUL (2)

Ge 10:23 sons of Aram: Uz, **H**, Gether and Meshek. H2566
1Ch 1:17 sons of Aram: Uz, **H**, Gether and Meshek. H2566

HULDAH (2)

2Ki 22:14 Asaiah went to speak to the prophet **H**, H2701
2Ch 34:22 with him went to speak to the prophet **H**, H2701

HUMAN (196) [HUMANITY, HUMANS]

Ge 6: 1 When **h beings** began to increase in H132
Ge 6: 5 wickedness of the **h race** had become on H132
Ge 6: 5 the thoughts of the **h** heart was only evil H2257S
Ge 6: 6 that he had made **h beings** on the earth, H132
Ge 6: 7 of the earth the **h race** I have created— H132
Ge 8:21 every inclination of the **h** heart is evil from H132
Ge 9: 5 And from each **h being**, too, I will demand H132
Ge 9: 5 accounting for the life of another **h being**. H132
Ge 9: 6 "Whoever sheds **h** blood, by humans shall H132
Ex 4:11 "Who gave **h beings** their mouths? H132
Ex 13: 2 belongs to me, whether **h** or animal." H132
Lev 5: 3 if they touch **h** uncleanness (anything H132
Lev 7:21 whether **h** uncleanness or an unclean H132
Lev 24:17 takes the life of a **h being** is to be put to H132
Lev 24:21 whoever kills a **h being** is to be put to H132
Lev 27:28 whether a **h being** or an animal or family H132
Nu 3:13 firstborn in Israel, whether **h** or animal. H132
Nu 8:17 in Israel, whether **h** or animal, is mine. H132
Nu 18:15 of every womb, both **h** and animal, that is H132
Nu 19:11 "Whoever touches a **h** corpse will be H5883+132
Nu 19:13 after touching a **h** corpse, H5883+132
Nu 19:16 anyone who touches a **h** bone or a grave, H132
Nu 19:18 who has touched a **h** bone or a grave or NDT
Nu 23:19 God is not **h**, that he should lie, not a H408
Nu 23:19 not a **h being**, that he should H1201+132
Dt 4:32 the day God created **h beings** on the earth; H132
Dt 32:26 erase their name from **h** memory, H632
Jos 10:14 a day when the LORD listened to a **h being**. H408
1Sa 15:29 he is not a **h being**, that he should H132
2Sa 7:14 with floggings inflicted by **h hands**. H1201+132
2Sa 7:19 this decree, Sovereign LORD, is for a *mere* **h**! H132
2Sa 24:14 but do not let me fall into **h** hands. H132
1Ki 8:39 you alone know every **h** heart), H1201+2021+132
1Ki 13: 2 and **h** bones will be burned on you. H132
2Ki 19:18 wood and stone, fashioned by **h** hands. H132
2Ki 23:14 poles and covered the sites with **h** bones. H132
2Ki 23:20 on the altars and burned **h** bones on them. H132
1Ch 21:13 but do not let me fall into **h** hands. H132
2Ch 6:30 you alone know the **h** heart), H1201+132
2Ch 32:19 peoples of the world—the work of **h** hands. H132
Job 11:12 than a wild donkey's colt can be born **h**. H132
Job 21: 4 "Is my complaint directed to a **h being** H132
Job 25: 6 a maggot—a **h being**, who is only a H1201+132
Job 28: 4 Far from *h* **dwellings** they cut a shaft, in AIT
Job 28: 4 in places untouched by **h** feet; far from other NDT
Job 28:28 And he said to the **h race**, "The fear of the H132
Job 30: 5 They were banished from **h society** H1569
Job 34:20 the mighty are removed without **h** hand. NDT
Ps 8: 4 **h beings** that you care for them? H1201+132
Ps 12: 1 loyal have vanished from the **h race**. H1201+132
Ps 12: 8 what is vile is honored by the **h race**. H1201+132
Ps 31:20 you hide them from all **h** intrigues; H408
Ps 60:11 against the enemy, for **h** help is worthless. H132
Ps 64: 6 Surely the **h** mind and heart are cunning H408
Ps 73: 5 They are free from *common* **h** burdens H632
Ps 73: 5 burdens; they are not plagued by **h** ills. H132
Ps 78:25 **H beings** ate the bread of angels; he sent H408
Ps 94:11 The LORD knows all **h** plans; he knows that H132
Ps 104:15 wine that gladdens **h** hearts, oil to make H632
Ps 108:12 against the enemy, for **h** help is worthless. H132
Ps 115: 4 idols are silver and gold, made by **h** hands. H132
Ps 119:134 Redeem me from **h** oppression, that I may H132
Ps 135:15 are silver and gold, made by **h** hands. H132
Ps 144: 3 what are **h beings** that you care for them H132
Ps 146: 3 in princes, in **h beings**, who cannot H1201+132
Pr 15:11 how much more do **h** hearts! H1201+132
Pr 18:14 The **h** spirit can endure in sickness, but a H408
Pr 20:27 The **h** spirit is the lamp of the LORD that H132
Pr 27:20 are never satisfied, and neither are **h** eyes. H132
Pr 30: 2 not a man; I do not have **h** understanding. H132
Ecc 3:10 burden God has laid on the **h race**. H1201+132
Ecc 3:11 He has also set eternity in the **h** heart H4392S
Ecc 3:19 the fate of **h beings** is like H1201+2021+132
Ecc 3:21 Who knows if the **h** spirit rises H1201+2021+132
Isa 2:11 will be humbled and **h** pride brought low; H408
Isa 2:17 will be brought low and **h** pride humbled; H408
Isa 29:13 of me is based on *merely* **h** rules they have H408
Isa 31: 8 "Assyria will fall by no **h** sword; a sword H408
Isa 37:19 wood and stone, fashioned by **h** hands. H132
Isa 44:11 such craftsmen are *only* **h beings**. H132
Isa 44:13 He shapes it in **h** form, human form in all H408
Isa 44:13 it in human form, **h** form in all its glory H132
Isa 51:12 mortals, **h beings** who are but grass, H1201+132
Isa 52:14 beyond that of *any* **h being** and his form H408
Isa 52:14 his form marred beyond **h** likeness— H1201+132
Eze 1: 5 In appearance their form was **h**, H132
Eze 1: 8 wings on their four sides they had **h** hands. H132
Eze 1:10 Each of the four had the face of a **h being** H132
Eze 4:12 of the people, using **h** excrement for fuel." H132
Eze 4:15 over cow dung instead of **h** excrement." H132
Eze 10: 8 could be seen what looked like **h** hands.) H132
Eze 10:14 the second the face of a **h being**, the third H132
Eze 10:21 their wings was what looked like **h** hands. H132
Eze 27:13 they traded **h beings** and articles of H5883+132
Eze 39:15 anyone who sees a **h** bone will leave a H132
Eze 41:19 the face of a **h being** toward the palm tree H132
Da 2:34 a rock was cut out, but not by **h** hands. NDT
Da 2:45 a mountain, but not by **h** hands—a rock that NDT
Da 5: 5 the fingers of a **h** hand appeared and A10050
Da 6: 7 to any god or **h being** during the next A10050
Da 6:12 to any god or **h being** except to you, A10050
Da 7: 4 that it stood on two feet like a **h being**, A10050
Da 7: 4 the mind of a **h** was given to it. A10050
Da 7: 8 the eyes of a **h being** and a mouth that A10050
Da 8:25 Yet he will be destroyed, but not by **h** power. NDT
Hos 11: 4 I led them with cords of **h** kindness, with H132
Hos 13: 2 of these people, "They offer **h** sacrifices! H132
Hab 2: 8 For you have shed **h** blood; you have H132
Hab 2:17 For you have shed **h** blood; you have H132

Zec 12: 1 who forms the **h** spirit within a person H132
Mt 15: 9 their teachings are *merely* **h** rules. G476
Mt 16:23 concerns of God, but *merely* **h** concerns." G476
Mt 21:25 it from heaven, or of **h** origin?" They G476
Mt 21:26 But if we say, 'Of **h** origin'—we are afraid of G476
Mk 7: 7 their teachings are *merely* **h** rules. G476
Mk 7: 8 of God and are holding on to **h** traditions." G476
Mk 8:33 concerns of God, but *merely* **h** concerns." G476
Mk 11:30 was it from heaven, or of **h** origin? G476
Mk 11:32 But if we say, 'Of **h** origin' . . ." (They feared G476
Mk 14:58 this temple **made with h hands** and in G5935
Lk 20: 4 was it from heaven, or of **h** origin? G476
Lk 20: 6 But if we say, 'Of **h** origin,' all the people G476
Jn 1:13 of **h** decision or a husband's will G4922
Jn 5:34 Not that I accept **h** testimony; but I mention G476
Jn 5:41 "I do not accept glory from **h beings**, G476
Jn 8:15 You judge by **h standards**; I pass judgment G4922
Jn 12:43 they loved **h** praise more than praise G476
Ac 5: 4 have not lied *just to* **h beings** but to God." G476
Ac 5:29 "We must obey God rather than **h beings**! G476
Ac 5:38 For if their purpose or activity is of **h** origin G476
Ac 7:48 does not live in houses **made by h hands**. G5935
Ac 14:11 "The gods have come down to us in **h** form!" G476
Ac 14:15 We too are *only* **h**, like you. We are G476
Ac 17:24 does not live in temples **built by h hands**. G5935
Ac 17:25 And he is not served by **h** hands, as if he G474
Ac 17:29 an image *made by* **h** design and skill. G476
Ac 19:26 that gods made by *h* **hands** are no gods at AIT
Ro 1:23 to look like a mortal **h being** and birds G476
Ro 2: 3 So when you, a *mere* **h being**, pass G476
Ro 2: 9 every **h being** who does evil: G6034+476
Ro 3: 4 and every **h being** a liar. As it is G476
Ro 3: 5 (I am using a **h argument**.) G2848+476
Ro 6:19 life because of your **h** limitations. G4922
Ro 9: 5 is traced the **h ancestry** of the G2848+4922
Ro 9:16 therefore, depend on **h** desire or effort, but NDT
Ro 9:20 But who are you, a **h being**, to talk back to G476
Ro 14:18 is pleasing to God and receives **h** approval. G476
1Co 1:25 foolishness of God is wiser *than* **h** wisdom, G476
1Co 1:25 of God is stronger *than* **h** strength. G476
1Co 1:26 many of you were wise by **h standards**; G4922
1Co 2: 1 with eloquence or *h* **wisdom** as I proclaimed AIT
1Co 2: 5 that your faith might not rest on **h** wisdom, G476
1Co 2: 9 and what no **h** mind has conceived G476
1Co 2:13 words taught us by **h** wisdom but in words G474
1Co 2:15 person *is* not **subject to** *merely h* **judgments**, AIT
1Co 3: 4 Apollos," are you not *mere* **h beings**? G476
1Co 3:21 no more boasting about **h** *leaders*! All G476
1Co 4: 3 if I am judged by you or by any **h** court; G474
1Co 4: 9 universe, to angels as well as *to* **h beings**. G476
1Co 7:23 do not become slaves *of* **h beings**. G476
1Co 9: 8 Do I say this *merely* on **h** authority? Doesn't G476
1Co 15:32 in Ephesus with *no more than* **h** hopes, G476
2Co 3: 3 tablets of stone but on tablets of **h** hearts. G4921
2Co 5: 1 house in heaven, **not built by h hands**. G942
Gal 1:10 now trying to win the approval *of* **h beings**, G476
Gal 1:11 the gospel I preached is not of **h** origin. G476
Gal 1:16 not to consult any **h being**. G4922+2779+135
Gal 3:15 set aside or add to a **h** covenant that has G476
Eph 2:11 which is **done** in the body **by h hands**)— G5935
Php 2: 7 of a servant, being made in **h** likeness. G476
Col 2: 8 which depends on **h** tradition and the G476
Col 2:11 a circumcision **not performed by h hands**. G942
Col 2:22 are based on *merely* **h** commands and G476
Col 3:23 as working for the Lord, not *for* **h** masters, G476
1Th 2:13 you accepted it not as a **h** word, but as it G476
1Th 4: 8 does not reject a **h being** but God, G476
Titus 1:14 myths or to the *merely* **h** commands of G476
Heb 2:17 be made like them, **fully h** in every way, in G81
Heb 8: 2 set up by the Lord, not by a *mere* **h being**. G476
Heb 9:11 tabernacle that is not **made with h hands**, G5935
Heb 9:24 a sanctuary **made with h hands** that was G5935
Heb 12: 9 we have all had **h** fathers who disciplined G4922
Jas 1:20 because **h** anger does not produce the G467
Jas 3: 8 no **h being** can tame the tongue. It is a G476
Jas 3: 9 with it we curse **h beings**, who have G476
Jas 5:17 Elijah was a **h being**, even as we are. G476
1Pe 2:13 the Lord's sake to every **h** authority: G474
1Pe 4: 2 rest of their earthly lives for evil **h** desires, G476
1Pe 4: 6 according to **h standards** in regard to the G476
2Pe 1:21 prophecy never had its origin in the **h** will, G476
2Pe 1:21 prophets, *though* **h**, spoke from God as G476
2Pe 2:16 who spoke with a **h** voice and restrained the G476
1Jn 5: 9 We accept **h** testimony, but God's testimony G476
Rev 9: 7 and their faces resembled **h** faces. G476
Rev 18:13 carriages; and **h beings** sold as slaves. G476
Rev 21:17 measured the wall using **h** measurement, G476

HUMANITY (6) [HUMAN]
Job 34:15 all **h** would perish together and mankind H1414
Job 36:25 All **h** has seen it; mortals gaze on it from H132
Ps 89:47 what futility you have created all **h**! H1201+132
Ecc 6:10 and what **h** is has been known H132
Eph 2:15 create in himself one new **h** out of the two, G476
Heb 2:14 he too shared in **their** *h* so that by his death AIT

HUMANS (21) [HUMAN]
Ge 6: 2 saw that the daughters of **h** were beautiful, H132
Ge 6: 3 "My Spirit will not contend with **h** forever H132
Ge 6: 4 to the daughters of **h** and had children by H132
Ge 8:21 again will I curse the ground because of **h**, H132
Ge 9: 6 by **h** shall their blood be shed H132
Ge 32:28 with God and with **h** and have overcome." H408
Jdg 9: 9 by which both gods and **h** are honored, to H408
Jdg 9:13 which cheers both gods and **h**, to hold H408
2Ch 6:18 "But will God really dwell on earth with **h** H132
Job 35: 8 Your wickedness *only* affects **h** like yourself H408
Ps 78:60 of Shiloh, the tent he had set up among **h**. H132
Ps 118: 8 to take refuge in the LORD than to trust in **h**. H132
Pr 16: 1 To **h** belong the plans of the heart, but H132
Pr 16: 9 In their hearts **h** plan their course, but the H132
Ecc 3:18 "As for **h**, God tests them H1201+2021+132
Ecc 3:19 **h** have no advantage over animals. H132
Isa 2:22 Stop trusting in *mere* **h**, who have but a H132
Isa 7:13 Is it not enough to try the patience of **h** H408
Da 2:11 the gods, and they do not live among **h**." A10125
1Co 3: 3 Are you not acting like *mere* **h**? G476
1Pe 2: 4 rejected by **h** but chosen by God and G476

HUMBLE (43) [HUMBLED, HUMBLES, HUMBLY, HUMILIATE, HUMILIATED, HUMILIATING, HUMILIATION, HUMILITY]
Ex 10: 3 will you refuse to **h yourself** before me? H6700
Nu 12: 3 Now Moses was a very **h** man, more H6705
Nu 12: 3 more **h** than anyone else on the face of the NDT
Dt 8: 2 to **h** and test you in order to know what H6700
Dt 8:16 to **h** and test you so that in the end it H6700
2Sa 22:28 You save the **h**, but your eyes are H6639+6714
1Ki 11:39 *I will* **h** David's descendants because of H6700
2Ch 7:14 *will* **h themselves** and pray and seek my H4044
2Ch 33:23 *he did* not **h himself** before the LORD H4044
2Ch 36:12 his God and *did* not **h himself** before H4044
Ezr 8:21 so that we *might* **h ourselves** before our H6700
Job 8: 7 Your beginnings will seem **h**, so H5203
Job 40:12 look at all who are proud and **h** them H4044
Ps 18:27 You save the **h** but bring low those H6639+6714
Ps 25: 9 He guides the **h** in what is right and H6705
Ps 55:19 he will hear them and **h** them, because H6700
Ps 147: 6 LORD sustains the **h** but casts the wicked H6705
Ps 149: 4 his people; he crowns the **h** with victory. H6705
Pr 3:34 shows favor to the **h and oppressed**. H6705
Isa 13:11 of the haughty and *will* **h** the pride of the H9164
Isa 23: 9 her splendor and to **h** all who are H7837
Isa 29:19 Once more the **h** will rejoice in the LORD H6705
Isa 58: 5 only a day for people *to* **h** themselves? H6700
Isa 66: 2 *those who* are **h** and contrite in spirit, and H6714
Da 4:37 those who walk in pride he is able to **h**. A10737
Da 5:19 those he wanted to **h**, he humbled. NDT
Da 10:12 to **h yourself** before your God, H6700
Zep 2: 3 the LORD, all you **h** *of* the land, you who H6705
Zep 3:12 I will leave within you the meek and **h**. H1924
Mt 11:29 I am gentle and **h** in heart, and you G5424
Mt 23:12 those who **h** themselves will be G5427
Lk 1:48 been mindful of the **h state** of his servant. G5428
Lk 1:52 from their thrones but has lifted up the **h**. G5424
Lk 14:11 those *who* **h** themselves will be G5427
Lk 18:14 those *who* **h** themselves will be G5427
2Co 12:21 come again my God *will* **h** me before you, G5427
Eph 4: 2 Be completely **h** and gentle; be patient G5425
Jas 1: 9 Believers **in h circumstances** ought to take G5424
Jas 4: 6 the proud but shows favor *to* the **h**." G5424
Jas 4:10 **H** *yourselves* before the Lord, and he will G5427
1Pe 3: 8 one another, be compassionate and **h**. G5426
1Pe 5: 5 the proud but shows favor *to* the **h**." G5424
1Pe 5: 6 **H** *yourselves*, therefore, under God's G5427

HUMBLED (36) [HUMBLE]
Lev 26:41 hearts **are h** and they pay for H4044
Dt 8: 3 *He* **h** you, causing you to hunger and then H6700
2Sa 22:40 *you* **h** my adversaries before me. H4156
1Ki 21:29 how Ahab *has* **h himself** before me? H4044
1Ki 21:29 Because *he has* **h himself**, I will not bring H4044
2Ki 22:19 responsive and *you* **h yourself** before the H4044
2Ch 12: 6 the king **h themselves** and said, H4044
2Ch 12: 7 the LORD saw that *they* **h themselves**, H4044
2Ch 12: 7 "Since *they have* **h themselves**, I will not H4044
2Ch 12:12 Because Rehoboam **h himself**, the LORD's H4044
2Ch 28:19 The LORD *had* **h** Judah because of Ahaz H4044
2Ch 30:11 Zebulun **h themselves** and went to H4044
2Ch 33:12 LORD his God and **h himself** greatly before H4044
2Ch 33:19 poles and idols before he **h himself**— H4044
2Ch 34:27 responsive and *you* **h yourself** before God H4044
2Ch 34:27 because *you* **h yourself** before me H4044
Ps 18:39 *you* **h** my adversaries before me. H4156
Ps 35:13 on sackcloth and **h** myself with fasting. H6700
Ps 44: 9 But now you have rejected and **h** us; you H4007
Ps 68:30 of the nations. **H**, may the beast bring H8346
Ps 107:39 decreased, and *they were* **h** by oppression H8820
Isa 2: 9 will be brought low and everyone **h**— H9164
Isa 2:11 of the arrogant *will be* **h** and human pride H9164
Isa 2:12 all that is exalted (and *they will be* **h**), H9164
Isa 2:17 will be brought low and human pride **h**; H9164
Isa 5:15 will be brought low and everyone **h**, H9164
Isa 5:15 humbled, the eyes of the arrogant **h**. H9164
Isa 9: 1 In the past *he* **h** the land of Zebulun and H7837
Isa 58: 3 Why *have we* **h** ourselves, and you have H6700
Jer 44:10 this day *they have* not **h themselves** or H1917
Da 5:19 those he wanted to humble, *he* **h**. A10737
Da 5:22 his son, *have* not **h** yourself, though you A10737
Mt 23:12 For those who exalt themselves *will be* **h** G5427
Lk 14:11 all those who exalt themselves *will be* **h**, G5427
Lk 18:14 all those who exalt themselves *will be* **h**, G5427
Php 2: 8 *he* **h** himself by becoming obedient to G5427

HUMBLES (2) [HUMBLE]
1Sa 2: 7 poverty and wealth; *he* **h** and he exalts. H9164
Isa 26: 5 *He* **h** those who dwell on high, he lays H8820

HUMBLY (5) [HUMBLE]
2Sa 16: 4 "*I* **h bow**," Ziba said. "May I H2556
Isa 38:15 *I will* **walk h** all my years because of this H1844
Mic 6: 8 love mercy and to walk **h** with your God. H7570
Gal 5:13 rather, **serve** one another **h** in love. G1526
Jas 1:21 so prevalent and **h** accept the word G1877+4559

HUMILIATE (1) [HUMBLE]
Pr 25: 7 than for him *to* **h** you before his nobles. H9164

HUMILIATED (10) [HUMBLE]
2Sa 6:22 than this, and I will be **h** in my own eyes. H9166
2Sa 10: 5 to meet the men, for they were greatly **h**. H4007
2Sa 19: 5 said, "Today *you have* **h** all your men H1017
1Ch 19: 5 to meet them, for they were greatly **h**. H4007
Isa 54: 4 fear disgrace; *you will* not *be* **h**. You will H2917
Jer 15: 9 it is still day; she will be disgraced and **h**. H2917
Jer 31:19 I was ashamed and **h** because I bore the H4007
Mal 2: 9 to be despised and **h** before all the H9166
Lk 13:17 all his opponents *were* **h**, but the people G2875
Lk 14: 9 **h**, you will have to take the G3552+158

HUMILIATING (1) [HUMBLE]
1Co 11:22 the church of God *by* **h** those who have G2875

HUMILIATION (5) [HUMBLE]
Ezr 9: 7 to pillage and **h** at the hand of H1425+7156
Job 19: 5 above me and use my **h** against me, H3075
Eze 16:63 open your mouth because of your **h**, H4009
Ac 8:33 In his **h** he was deprived of justice. G5428
Jas 1:10 But the rich should take pride in their **h** G5428

HUMILITY (14) [HUMBLE]
Ps 45: 4 the cause of truth, **h** and justice; let your H6708
Pr 11: 2 disgrace, but with **h** comes wisdom. H7560
Pr 15:33 fear the LORD, and **h** comes before honor. H6708
Pr 18:12 is haughty, but **h** comes before honor. H6708
Pr 22: 4 **H** is the fear of the LORD; its wages are H6708
Zep 2: 3 righteousness, seek **h**; perhaps you will H6708
Ac 20:19 the Lord with great **h** and with tears and G5425
2Co 10: 1 By the **h** and gentleness of Christ, G4559
Php 2: 3 *in* **h** value others above yourselves, G5425
Col 2:18 who delights in *false* **h** and the worship of G5425
Col 2:23 their *false* **h** and their harsh treatment of G5425
Col 3:12 compassion, kindness, **h**, gentleness and G5425
Jas 3:13 by deeds done in the **h** that comes from G4559
1Pe 5: 5 yourselves with **h** toward one another, G5425

HUMPS (1)
Isa 30: 6 their treasures on the **h** *of* camels, to that H1832

HUMTAH (1)
Jos 15:54 **H**, Kiriath Arba (that is, Hebron) and Zior H2794

HUNCHBACK (1)
Lev 21:20 who is a **h** or a dwarf, or who has any H1492

HUNDRED (288) [HUNDREDFOLD, HUNDREDS, HUNDREDTH, 100]
Ge 6: 3 their days will be a **h** and twenty years." H4395
Ge 6:15 The ark is to be three **h** cubits long, fifty H4395
Ge 7: 6 Noah was six **h** years old when the H4395
Ge 7:24 flooded the earth for a **h** and fifty days. H4395
Ge 8: 3 At the end of the **h** and fifty days the H4395
Ge 8:13 first month of Noah's six **h** and first year, H4395
Ge 15:13 certain that for four **h** years your H4395
Ge 17:17 a son be born to a man a **h** years old? H4395
Ge 21: 5 Abraham was a **h** years old when his son H4395
Ge 23: 1 Sarah lived to be a **h** and twenty-seven H4395
Ge 23:15 the land is worth four **h** shekels of silver H4395
Ge 23:16 four **h** shekels of silver, according to the H4395
Ge 25: 7 Abraham lived a **h** and seventy-five years. H4395
Ge 25:17 Ishmael lived a **h** and thirty-seven years H4395
Ge 32: 6 meet you, and four **h** men are with him." H4395
Ge 32:14 *two* **h** female goats and twenty male goats H4395
Ge 32:14 male goats, *two* **h** ewes and twenty rams, H4395
Ge 33: 1 coming with his four **h** men; so he divided H4395
Ge 33:19 For a **h** pieces of silver, he bought from the H4395
Ge 35:28 Isaac lived a **h** and eighty years. H4395
Ge 45:22 he gave three **h** shekels of silver and H4395
Ge 47: 9 years of my pilgrimage are a **h** and thirty. H4395
Ge 47:28 years of his life were a **h** and forty-seven. H4395
Ge 50:22 father's family. He lived a **h** and ten years H4395
Ge 50:26 So Joseph died at the age of a **h** and ten H4395
Ex 12:37 were about six **h** thousand men on foot H4395
Ex 14: 7 He took six **h** *of* the best chariots, along H4395
Ex 27: 9 side shall be a **h** cubits long and is to H4395
Ex 27:11 side shall also be a **h** cubits long and is H4395
Ex 27:18 courtyard shall be a **h** cubits long and fifty H4395
Ex 38: 9 south side was a **h** cubits long and had H4395
Ex 38:11 side was also a **h** cubits long and had H4395
Lev 26: 8 Five of you will chase a **h**, and a hundred H4395
Lev 26: 8 a **h** of you will chase ten thousand H4395
Nu 7:13 plate weighing a **h** and thirty shekels and H4395
Nu 7:19 plate weighing a **h** and thirty shekels and H4395
Nu 7:25 plate weighing a **h** and thirty shekels and H4395
Nu 7:31 plate weighing a **h** and thirty shekels and H4395
Nu 7:37 plate weighing a **h** and thirty shekels and H4395
Nu 7:43 plate weighing a **h** and thirty shekels and H4395

Nu 7:49 plate weighing a **h** and thirty shekels and H4395
Nu 7:55 plate weighing a **h** and thirty shekels and H4395
Nu 7:61 plate weighing a **h** and thirty shekels and H4395
Nu 7:67 plate weighing a **h** and thirty shekels and H4395
Nu 7:73 plate weighing a **h** and thirty shekels and H4395
Nu 7:79 plate weighing a **h** and thirty shekels and H4395
Nu 7:85 plate weighed a **h** and thirty shekels, H4395
Nu 7:85 weighed two thousand four **h** shekels, H4395
Nu 7:86 dishes weighed a **h** and twenty shekels. H4395
Nu 11:21 I am among six **h** thousand men on foot H4395
Nu 31:28 tribute for the LORD one out of every five **h**, H4395
Nu 33:39 Aaron was a **h** and twenty-three years old H4395
Dt 22:19 They shall fine him a **h** shekels of silver H4395
Dt 31: 2 "I am now a **h** and twenty years old and I H4395
Dt 34: 7 Moses was a **h** and twenty years old when H4395
Jos 7:21 *two* **h** shekels of silver and a bar of gold H4395
Jos 24:29 the LORD, died at the age of a **h** and ten. H4395
Jos 24:32 Jacob bought for a **h** pieces of silver from H4395
Jdg 2: 8 the LORD, died at the age of a **h** and ten. H4395
Jdg 3:31 who struck down six **h** Philistines with an H4395
Jdg 4: 3 Because he had nine **h** chariots fitted with H4395
Jdg 4:13 his men and his nine **h** chariots fitted with H4395
Jdg 7: 6 Three **h** of them drank from cupped hands H4395
Jdg 7: 7 "With the three **h** men that lapped I will H4395
Jdg 7: 8 the Israelites home but kept the three **h**, H4395
Jdg 7:16 Dividing the three **h** men into three H4395
Jdg 7:19 Gideon and the **h** men with him reached H4395
Jdg 7:22 When the three **h** trumpets sounded, the H4395
Jdg 8: 4 Gideon and his three **h** men, exhausted H4395
Jdg 8:10 a **h** and twenty thousand swordsmen had H4395
Jdg 8:26 came to **seventeen h** H8679+4395+2256+547
Jdg 11:26 For three **h** years Israel occupied Heshbon, H4395
Jdg 15: 4 caught three **h** foxes and tied them H4395
Jdg 16: 5 give you **eleven h** shekels of H547+2256+4395
Jdg 17: 2 "The **eleven h** shekels of H547+2256+4395
Jdg 17: 3 the **eleven h** shekels of H547+2256+4395
Jdg 17: 4 she took *two* **h** shekels of silver and gave H4395
Jdg 18:11 Then six **h** men of the Danites, armed H4395
Jdg 18:16 The six **h** Danites, armed for battle, stood H4395
Jdg 18:17 priest and the six **h** armed men stood at H4395
Jdg 20: 2 four **h** thousand men armed with swords. H4395
Jdg 20:10 ten men out of every **h** from all the tribes H4395
Jdg 20:10 of Israel, and a **h** from a thousand, and a H4395
Jdg 20:15 addition to seven **h** able young men from H4395
Jdg 20:16 there were seven **h** select troops who H4395
Jdg 20:17 mustered four **h** thousand swordsmen, all H4395
Jdg 20:47 But six **h** of them turned and fled into the H4395
Jdg 21:12 Jabesh Gilead four **h** young women who H4395
1Sa 11: 8 numbered three **h** thousand and those of H4395
1Sa 13:15 They numbered about six **h**. H4395
1Sa 14: 2 With him were about six **h** men, H4395
1Sa 15: 4 *two* **h** thousand foot soldiers and ten H4395
1Sa 17: 7 its iron point weighed six **h** shekels. H4395
1Sa 18:25 the bride than a **h** Philistine foreskins, H4395
1Sa 18:27 went out and killed *two* **h** Philistines and H4395
1Sa 22: 2 About four **h** men were with him. H4395
1Sa 23:13 his men, about six **h** in number, left H4395
1Sa 25:13 About four **h** men went up with David H4395
1Sa 25:13 while *two* **h** stayed with the supplies. H4395
1Sa 25:18 She took *two* **h** loaves of bread, two skins H4395
1Sa 25:18 a **h** cakes of raisins and two hundred H4395
1Sa 25:18 of raisins and *two* **h** cakes of pressed H4395
1Sa 27: 2 So David and the six **h** men with him left H4395
1Sa 30: 9 David and the six **h** men with him came H4395
1Sa 30:10 *Two* **h** of them were too exhausted to cross H4395
1Sa 30:10 the other four **h** continued the pursuit H4395
1Sa 30:17 except four **h** young men who rode off on H4395
1Sa 30:21 came to the *two* **h** men who had been H4395
2Sa 2:31 had killed three **h** and sixty Benjamites H4395
2Sa 3:14 the price of a **h** Philistine foreskins." H4395
2Sa 8: 4 hamstrung all but a **h** of the chariot H4395
2Sa 10:18 David killed seven **h** of their charioteers H4395
2Sa 14:26 its weight was *two* **h** shekels by the H4395
2Sa 15:11 *Two* **h** men from Jerusalem had H4395
2Sa 15:18 all the six **h** Gittites who had H4395
2Sa 16: 1 loaded with *two* **h** loaves of bread, H4395
2Sa 16: 1 loaves of bread, a **h** cakes of raisins, H4395
2Sa 16: 1 a **h** cakes of figs and a skin of wine. H4395
2Sa 21:16 weighed three **h** shekels and who was H4395
2Sa 23: 8 he raised his spear against eight **h** men H4395
2Sa 23:18 He raised his spear against three **h** men H4395
2Sa 24: 3 God multiply the troops a **h** times over, H4395
2Sa 24: 9 there were eight **h** thousand able-bodied H4395
2Sa 24: 9 a sword, and in Judah five **h** thousand. H4395
1Ki 4:23 cattle and a **h** sheep and goats, H4395
1Ki 5:16 well as **thirty-three h** foremen H8993+547+2256+8993+4395
1Ki 6: 1 In the four **h** and eightieth year after the H4395
1Ki 7: 2 of the Forest of Lebanon a **h** cubits long, H4395
1Ki 7:20 were the *two* **h** pomegranates in rows all H4395
1Ki 7:42 the four **h** pomegranates for the two sets H4395
1Ki 8:63 cattle and a **h** and twenty thousand H4395
1Ki 10:16 Solomon made *two* **h** large shields of H4395
1Ki 10:16 six **h** shekels of gold went into each H4395
1Ki 10:17 He also made three **h** small shields of H4395
1Ki 10:26 he had **fourteen h** chariots H547+2256+752+4395
1Ki 10:29 from Egypt for six **h** shekels of silver, H4395
1Ki 10:29 of silver, and a horse for a **h** and fifty. H4395
1Ki 11: 3 He had seven **h** wives of royal birth and H4395
1Ki 11: 3 of royal birth and three **h** concubines, H4395
1Ki 12:21 a **h** and eighty thousand able young men H4395
1Ki 18: 4 had taken a **h** prophets and hidden H4395
1Ki 18:13 I hid a **h** of the LORD's prophets in two H4395
1Ki 18:19 And bring the four **h** and fifty prophets of H4395
1Ki 18:19 Baal and the four **h** prophets of Asherah, H4395
1Ki 18:22 but Baal has four **h** and fifty prophets. H4395
1Ki 20:29 inflicted a **h** thousand casualties on H4395
1Ki 22: 6 about four **h** men—and asked them, H4395
2Ki 3: 4 Israel a tribute of a **h** thousand lambs H4395
2Ki 3: 4 the wool of a **h** thousand rams. H4395
2Ki 3:26 with him seven **h** swordsmen to break H4395
2Ki 4:43 "How can I set this before a **h** men?" H4395
2Ki 11: 4 sent for the commanders of **units of a h**, H4395
2Ki 11: 9 commanders of **units of a h** did just as H4395
2Ki 11:15 ordered the commanders of **units of a h**, H4395
2Ki 14:13 a section about four **h** cubits long. H4395
2Ki 18:14 king of Judah three **h** talents of silver and H4395
2Ki 19:35 out and put to death a **h** and eighty-five H4395
2Ki 23:33 on Judah a levy of a **h** talents of silver H4395
1Ch 4:42 And five **h** of these Simeonites, led by H4395
1Ch 5:21 *two* **h** fifty thousand sheep and two H4395
1Ch 5:21 They also took *one* **h** thousand people H4395
1Ch 11:11 he raised his spear against three **h** men H4395
1Ch 11:20 He raised his spear against three **h** men H4395
1Ch 12:14 the least was a match for a **h**, and the H4395
1Ch 18: 4 hamstrung all but a **h** of the chariot H4395
1Ch 21: 3 LORD multiply his troops a **h** times over. H4395
1Ch 21: 5 one million *one* **h** thousand men who H4395
1Ch 21: 5 including four **h** and seventy thousand in H4395
1Ch 21:25 paid Araunah six **h** shekels of gold for H4395
1Ch 22:14 temple of the LORD a **h** thousand talents of H4395
1Ch 26:30 **seventeen h** able men H547+2256+8679+4395
1Ch 26:32 had **twenty-seven h** H547+2256+8679+4395
1Ch 29: 7 of bronze and a **h** thousand talents of H4395
2Ch 1:14 he had **fourteen h** chariots H547+2256+752+4395
2Ch 1:17 from Egypt for six **h** shekels of silver, H4395
2Ch 1:17 of silver, and a horse for a **h** and fifty. H4395
2Ch 3: 8 the inside with six **h** talents of fine gold. H4395
2Ch 3:16 He also made a **h** pomegranates and H4395
2Ch 4: 8 He also made a **h** gold sprinkling bowls. H4395
2Ch 4:13 the four **h** pomegranates for the two sets H4395
2Ch 7: 5 of cattle and a **h** and twenty thousand H4395
2Ch 8:10 **two h** and fifty officials supervising the H4395
2Ch 8:18 brought back four **h** and fifty talents of H4395
2Ch 9:15 Solomon made *two* **h** large shields of H4395
2Ch 9:15 six **h** shekels of hammered gold went into H4395
2Ch 9:16 He also made three **h** small shields of H4395
2Ch 9:16 with three **h** shekels of gold in each H4395
2Ch 11: 1 a **h** and eighty thousand able young men H4395
2Ch 12: 3 With **twelve h** chariots and H547+2256+4395
2Ch 13: 3 with an army of four **h** thousand able H4395
2Ch 13: 3 him with eight **h** thousand able troops. H4395
2Ch 13:17 that there were five **h** thousand casualties H4395
2Ch 14: 8 an army of three **h** thousand men from H4395
2Ch 14: 8 and *two* **h** and eighty thousand from H4395
2Ch 14: 9 upon thousands and three **h** chariots, H4395
2Ch 15:11 to the LORD seven **h** head of cattle and H4395
2Ch 17:11 seven thousand seven **h** rams and seven H4395
2Ch 17:11 rams and seven thousand seven **h** goats. H4395
2Ch 18: 5 the prophets—four **h** men—and asked H4395
2Ch 23: 1 with the commanders of **units of a h**: H4395
2Ch 23: 9 commanders of **units of a h** the spears H4395
2Ch 23:14 sent out the commanders of **units of a h**, H4395
2Ch 24:15 he died at the age of a **h** and thirty. H4395
2Ch 25: 5 there were three **h** thousand men fit for H4395
2Ch 25: 6 He also hired a **h** thousand fighting men H4395
2Ch 25: 6 men from Israel for a **h** talents of silver. H4395
2Ch 25: 9 "But what about the **h** talents I paid for H4395
2Ch 25:23 a section about four **h** cubits long. H4395
2Ch 27: 5 Ammonites paid him a **h** talents of silver, H4395
2Ch 28: 6 Remaliah killed a **h** and twenty thousand H4395
2Ch 28: 8 were from Judah *two* **h** thousand wives, H4395
2Ch 29:32 a **h** rams and two hundred male lambs H4395
2Ch 29:32 a hundred rams and *two* **h** male lambs H4395
2Ch 29:33 amounted to six **h** bulls and three H4395
2Ch 35: 8 priests **twenty-six h** H547+2256+9252+4395
2Ch 35: 8 Passover offerings and three **h** cattle. H4395
2Ch 35: 9 offerings and five **h** head of cattle for the H4395
2Ch 36: 3 on Judah a levy of a **h** talents of silver H4395
Ezr 6:17 this house of God they offered a **h** bulls, A10395
Ezr 6:17 a hundred bulls, *two* **h** rams, four A10395
Ezr 6:17 four **h** male lambs and, as A10395
Ezr 7:22 up to a **h** talents of silver, a hundred cors A10395
Ezr 7:22 talents of silver, a **h** cors of wheat, A10395
Ezr 7:22 cors of wheat, a **h** baths of wine, A10395
Ezr 7:22 baths of wine, a **h** baths of olive oil, and A10395
Ne 3: 1 building as far as the Tower of the **H** H4396
Ne 5:17 a **h** and fifty Jews and officials ate at my H4395
Ne 12:39 of Hananel and the Tower of the **H**, H4396
Est 9: 6 the Jews killed and destroyed five **h** men. H4395
Est 9:12 destroyed five **h** men and the ten H4395
Est 9:15 they put to death in Susa three **h** men, H4395
Job 1: 3 five **h** yoke of oxen and five hundred H4395
Job 1: 3 hundred yoke of oxen and five **h** donkeys, H4395
Job 42:16 Job lived a **h** and forty years; he saw H4395
Pr 17:10 person more than a **h** lashes a fool. H4395
Ecc 6: 3 A man may have a **h** children and live H4395
Ecc 8:12 who commits a **h** crimes may live a H4395
SS 8:12 and *two* **h** are for those who tend its fruit. H4395
Isa 37:36 out and put to death a **h** and eighty-five H4395
Isa 65:20 the one who dies at a **h** will be thought a H4395
Isa 65:20 who fails to reach a **h** will be considered H4395
Jer 52:23 above the surrounding network was a **h**. H4395
Eze 40:19 it was a **h** cubits on the east side as well H4395
Eze 40:23 to the opposite one; it was a **h** cubits. H4395
Eze 40:27 gate on the south side; it was a **h** cubits. H4395
Eze 40:47 a **h** cubits long and a hundred cubits wide. H4395
Eze 40:47 a hundred cubits long and a **h** cubits wide. H4395
Eze 41:13 temple; it was a **h** cubits long, and the H4395
Eze 41:13 with its walls were also a **h** cubits long. H4395
Eze 41:14 the front of the temple, was a **h** cubits. H4395
Eze 41:15 galleries on each side; it was a **h** cubits. H4395
Eze 42: 2 faced north was a **h** cubits long and fifty H4395
Eze 42: 4 ten cubits wide and a **h** cubits long. H4395
Eze 42: 8 nearest the sanctuary was a **h** cubits long. H4395
Eze 42:16 the measuring rod; it was five **h** cubits. H4395
Eze 42:17 it was five **h** cubits by the measuring rod. H4395
Eze 42:18 it was five **h** cubits by the measuring rod. H4395
Eze 42:19 it was five **h** cubits by the measuring rod. H4395
Eze 42:20 five **h** cubits long and five hundred cubits H4395
Eze 42:20 cubits long and five **h** cubits wide, H4395
Eze 45:15 from every flock of *two* **h** from the H4395
Am 5: 3 a thousand strong will have only a **h** left; H4395
Am 5: 3 that marches out a **h** strong will have only H4395
Jnh 4:11 a **h and twenty thousand** H8052+9109+6926
Mt 13: 8 it produced a crop—a **h**, sixty or thirty *G1669*
Mt 13:23 yielding a **h**, sixty or thirty times *G1669*
Mt 18:12 If a man owns a **h** sheep, and one of *G1669*
Mt 18:28 servants who owed him a **h** silver coins. *G1669*
Mt 19:29 will receive a **h times** *as much* and will *G1671*
Mk 4: 8 some sixty, some a **h** *times.* *G1669*
Mk 4:20 some a **h** *times* what was sown. *G1669*
Mk 10:30 to receive a **h times** *as much* in this *G1671*
Lk 7:41 One owed him **five h** denarii, and the *G4296*
Lk 8: 8 a **h times** *more* than was sown. *G1671*
Lk 15: 4 one of you has a **h** sheep and loses one *G1669*
Lk 16: 6 " '**Nine h gallons** of olive oil,' he *G1669+1004*
Lk 16: 6 down quickly, and make it **four h and fifty**. *G4299*
Lk 16: 7 'Take your bill and make it **eight h**. *G3837*
Jn 21: 8 not far from shore, about **a h yards**. *G4388+1357*
Ac 1:15 a group numbering about a **h** and twenty) *G1669*
Ac 5:36 about **four h** men rallied to him. *G5484*
Ac 7: 6 'For **four h** years your descendants will be *G5484*
Ac 23:23 ready a detachment of **two h** soldiers, *G1357*
Ac 23:23 horsemen and **two h** spearmen to go to *G1357*
Ac 27:28 was **a h and twenty feet deep**. *G3976+1633*
Ro 4:19 since he was about **a h years old**—and *G1670*
1Co 15: 6 he appeared *to* more than **five h** of the *G4296*
Rev 16:21 each **weighing** about **a h pounds**, fell on *G5418*

HUNDREDFOLD (1) [HUNDRED]

Ge 26:12 and the same year reaped a **h**, H4395+9134

HUNDREDS (21) [HUNDRED]

Ex 18:21 over thousands, **h**, fifties and tens. H4395
Ex 18:25 over thousands, **h**, fifties and tens. H4395
Nu 31:14 of thousands and commanders of **h**— H4395
Nu 31:48 of thousands and commanders of **h**— H4395
Nu 31:52 commanders of **h** that Moses and H4395
Nu 31:54 commanders of **h** and brought it into H4395
Dt 1:15 of thousands, of **h**, of fifties and of tens H4395
1Sa 22: 7 of thousands and commanders of **h**? H4395
1Sa 29: 2 with their **units of h** and thousands, H4395
2Sa 18: 1 of thousands and commanders of **h**. H4395
2Sa 18: 4 marched out in **units of h** and of H4395
2Ki 11:19 He took with him the commanders of **h** H4395
1Ch 13: 1 of thousands and commanders of **h**. H4395
1Ch 26:26 of thousands and commanders of **h**, H4395
1Ch 27: 1 of thousands and commanders of **h**, H4395
1Ch 28: 1 of thousands and commanders of **h**, H4395
1Ch 29: 6 of thousands and commanders of **h**, H4395
2Ch 1: 2 of thousands and commanders of **h**, H4395
2Ch 23:20 He took with him the commanders of **h** H4395
2Ch 25: 5 commanders of **h** for all Judah and H4395
Mk 6:40 So they sat down in groups of **h** and fifties. *G1669*

HUNDREDTH (1) [HUNDRED]

Ge 7:11 In the six **h** year of Noah's life, on the H4395

HUNG (15) [HANG]

Ex 40:21 the tabernacle and **h** the shielding curtain H8492
Dt 21:23 because *anyone who* is **h** on a pole is H9434
2Sa 4:12 hands and feet and **h** the bodies by the H9434
2Sa 21:12 the Philistines *had* **h** them after they H9428
1Ch 10:10 gods and **h up** his head *in* the temple of H9546
Ps 137: 2 There on the poplars *we* **h** our harps, H9434
La 1:14 *They have been* **h** on my neck, and the H6590
La 5:12 Princes *have* **been h up** by their hands H9434
Eze 27:10 *They* **h** their shields and helmets on your H9434
Eze 27:11 *They* **h** their shields around your walls H9434
Mt 18: 6 them to **have** a large millstone **h** around *G3203*
Mk 9:42 a large millstone *were* **h** around their *G4329*
Lk 19:48 because all the people **h on** his words. *G1717*
Lk 23:39 One of the criminals *who* **h** there hurled *G3203*
Gal 3:13 "Cursed is everyone who *is* **h** on a pole." *G3203*

HUNGER (19) [HUNGRY]

Dt 8: 3 **causing** you **to h** and then feeding you H8279
Dt 28:48 therefore in **h** and thirst, in nakedness H8280
2Ch 32:11 to let you die of **h** and thirst. H8280
Ne 9:15 In their **h** you gave them bread from H8280
Job 30: 3 Haggard from want and **h**, they roamed H4103
Job 38:39 the lioness and satisfy the **h** *of* the lions H2652
Pr 6:30 steals to satisfy his **h** when he is starving. H5883
Pr 16:26 works for them; their **h** drives them on. H7023
Isa 5:13 rank will die of **h** and the common people H8280
Isa 49:10 *They will* neither **h** nor thirst, nor will the H8279

La 2:19 who faint from **h** at every street corner. H8280
La 4: 9 die of famine; **racked with h**, they waste H1991
La 5:10 Our skin is hot as an oven, feverish from **h**. H8280
Eze 7:19 will not satisfy their **h** or fill their stomachs H5883
Mt 5: 6 Blessed are those *who* **h** and thirst for *G4277*
Lk 6:21 Blessed are you who **h** now, for you will *G4277*
2Co 6: 5 in hard work, sleepless nights and **h**; *G3763*
2Co 11:27 I have known **h** and thirst and have often *G3350*
Rev 7:16 'Never again *will they* **h**; never again will *G4277*

HUNGRY (54) [HUNGER]

1Sa 2: 5 but *those who were* **h** are hungry no more. H8281
1Sa 2: 5 those who were hungry are **h** no more. NDT
2Sa 17:29 exhausted and **h** and thirsty in the H8281
Job 5: 5 The **h** consume his harvest, taking it even H8281
Job 18:12 Calamity is **h** *for* him; disaster is ready H8281
Job 22: 7 weary and you withheld food from the **h**, H8281
Job 24:10 they carry the sheaves, but still go **h**. H8281
Ps 17:12 They are like a lion **h** for prey, like a fierce H4083
Ps 34:10 The lions may grow weak and **h**, but H8279
Ps 50:12 If *I were* **h** I would not tell you, for the H8279
Ps 107: 5 *They* were **h** and thirsty, and their lives H8281
Ps 107: 9 and fills the **h** with good things. H5883+8281
Ps 107:36 there he brought the **h** to live, and they H8281
Ps 146: 7 of the oppressed and gives food to the **h**. H8281
Pr 10: 3 The LORD *does* not **let** the righteous **go h** H8279
Pr 13:25 the stomach of the wicked **goes h**. H2893
Pr 19:15 on deep sleep, and the shiftless **go h**. H8279
Pr 25:21 If your enemy is **h**, give him food to eat; if H8281
Pr 27: 7 to the **h** even what is bitter tastes H8281
Isa 8:21 Distressed and **h**, they will roam through H8281
Isa 9:20 will devour, but *still be* **h**; on the left they H8279
Isa 29: 8 as when a **h** *person* dreams of eating, but H8281
Isa 29: 8 awakens **h** *still*; as when a H8199+5883
Isa 32: 6 the **h** they leave empty and from H5883+8281
Isa 44:12 *He gets* **h** and loses his strength; he H8279
Isa 58: 7 your food with the **h** and to provide the H8281
Isa 58:10 in behalf of the **h** and satisfy the needs of H8281
Isa 65:13 will eat, but you *will* **go h**; my servants H8279
Jer 42:14 war or hear the trumpet or *be* **h** for bread, H8279
Eze 18: 7 his food to the **h** and provides clothing H8281
Eze 18:16 his food to the **h** and provides clothing H8281
Mt 4: 2 forty days and forty nights, *he was* **h**. *G4277*
Mt 12: 1 His disciples *were* **h** and began to pick *G4277*
Mt 12: 3 did when *he* and his companions *were* **h**? *G4277*
Mt 15:32 I do not want to send them away **h**, or *G3765*
Mt 21:18 was on his way back to the city, *he was* **h**. *G4277*
Mt 25:35 For *I was* **h** and you gave me something to *G4277*
Mt 25:37 when did we see you **h** and feed you, or *G4277*
Mt 25:42 For *I was* **h** and you gave me nothing to *G4277*
Mt 25:44 when did we see you **h** or thirsty or a *G4277*
Mk 2:25 his companions *were* **h** and in need? *G4277*
Mk 8: 3 If I send them home **h**, they will collapse *G3765*
Mk 11:12 they were leaving Bethany, Jesus *was* **h**. *G4277*
Lk 1:53 He has filled the **h** with good things but *G4277*
Lk 4: 2 and at the end of them *he was* **h**. *G4277*
Lk 6: 3 did when he and his companions *were* **h**? *G4277*
Lk 6:25 who are well fed now, for *you will* **go h**. *G4277*
Jn 6:35 Whoever comes to me *will* never **go h** *G4277*
Ac 10:10 He became **h** and wanted something to *G4698*
Ro 12:20 "If your enemy *is* **h**, feed him; if he is *G4277*
1Co 4:11 To this very hour *we* **go h** and thirsty, we *G4277*
1Co 11:21 one person *remains* **h** and another gets *G4277*
1Co 11:34 Anyone *who is* **h** should eat something at *G4277*
Php 4:12 whether well fed or **h**, whether living in *G4277*

HUNT (9) [HUNTED, HUNTER, HUNTERS, HUNTING, HUNTS]

Ge 27: 3 the open country *to* **h** some wild game H7421
Ge 27: 5 the open country to **h** game and bring it H7421
Ge 31:36 have I wronged you that *you* **h** me **down**? H1944
Job 38:39 "*Do you* **h** the prey for the lioness and H7421
Ps 140:11 *may* disaster **h down** the H7421+4200+4511
Pr 12:27 the diligent feed on the riches of the **h**. H1353
Jer 16:16 and *they will* **h** them **down** on every H7421
Am 9: 3 there *I will* **h** them **down** and seize them. H2924
Mic 7: 2 shed blood; *they* **h** each other with nets. H7421

HUNTED (4) [HUNT]

Ge 27:33 that **h** game and brought it to me? H7421
Isa 13:14 Like a **h** gazelle, like sheep without a H5615
La 3:52 without cause **h** me like a bird. H7421+7421
Ac 26:11 them that I even **h** them down in foreign NDT

HUNTER (4) [HUNT]

Ge 10: 9 He was a mighty **h** before the LORD; that is H7473
Ge 10: 9 "Like Nimrod, a mighty **h** before the LORD." H7473
Ge 25:27 and Esau became a skillful **h**, a man H408+7473
Pr 6: 5 like a gazelle from the hand of the **h**, like a NDT

HUNTERS (2) [HUNT]

Isa 7:24 *H will* **go** there with bow and arrow, for the AIT
Jer 16:16 After that I will send for many **h**, and they H7475

HUNTING (2) [HUNT]

Ge 27:30 his brother Esau came in from **h**. H7473
1Sa 24:11 you *are* **h** me **down** to take my life. H7399

HUNTS (3) [HUNT]

Lev 17:13 among you who **h** any animal or bird H7421
1Sa 26:20 as *one* **h** a partridge in the mountains." H8103
Ps 10: 2 the wicked man **h down** the weak, H1944

HUPHAM (1) [HUPHAMITE]

Nu 26:39 through **H**, the Huphamite clan. H2573

HUPHAMITE (1) [HUPHAM]

Nu 26:39 through Hupham, the **H** clan. H2574

HUPPAH (1)

1Ch 24:13 the thirteenth to **H**, the fourteenth to H2904

HUPPIM (1)

Ge 46:21 Naaman, Ehi, Rosh, Muppim, **H** and Ard. H2907

HUPPITES (2)

1Ch 7:12 The Shuppites and **H** were the H2907
1Ch 7:15 a wife from among the **H** and Shuppites. H2907

HUR (15) [BEN-HUR]

Ex 17:10 Aaron and **H** went to the top of the hill. H2581
Ex 17:12 Aaron and **H** held his hands up—one on H2581
Ex 24:14 Aaron and **H** are with you, and anyone H2581
Ex 31: 2 the son of **H**, of the tribe of Judah H2581
Ex 35:30 the son of **H**, of the tribe of Judah H2581
Ex 38:22 the son of **H**, of the tribe of Judah H2581
Nu 31: 8 **H** and Reba—the five kings of Midian H2581
Jos 13:21 **H** and Reba—princes allied with H2581
1Ch 2:19 Caleb married Ephrath, who bore him **H**. H2581
1Ch 2:20 **H** was the father of Uri, and Uri the father H2581
1Ch 2:50 The sons of **H** the firstborn of Ephrathah H2581
1Ch 4: 1 Hezron, Karmi, **H** and Shobal. H2581
1Ch 4: 4 These were the descendants of **H**, the H2581
2Ch 1: 5 son of Uri, the son of **H**, had made was in H2581
Ne 3: 9 Rephaiah son of **H**, ruler of a half-district H2581

HURAI (1)

1Ch 11:32 **H** from the ravines of Gaash, Abiel the H2584

HURAM (7)

1Ki 7:13 King Solomon sent to Tyre and brought **H**, H2671
1Ki 7:14 **H** was filled with wisdom, with NDT
1Ki 7:40 So **H** finished all the work he had H2671
1Ki 7:45 these objects that **H** made for King H2671
1Ch 8: 5 Shephuphan and **H**. H2586
2Ch 4:11 And **H** also made the pots and shovels H2586
2Ch 4:11 So **H** finished the work he had undertaken H2586

HURAM-ABI (2)

2Ch 2:13 "I am sending you **H**, a man of great skill, H2587
2Ch 4:16 All the objects that **H** made for King H2587

HURI (1)

1Ch 5:14 These were the sons of Abihail son of **H** H2585

HURL (8) [HURLED, HURLS]

1Sa 25:29 your enemies *he will* **h away** as from the H7843
2Ch 26:15 shoot arrows and **h** large stones from the NDT
Ps 22: 7 *they* **h insults**, shaking H7080+928+8557
Isa 22:17 firm hold of you and **h** you **away**, H3214+3232
Jer 10:18 "At this time I *will* **h out** those who live in H7843
Jer 22:26 *I will* **h** you and the mother who gave you H3214
Eze 32: 4 you on the land and **h** you on the open H3214
Mic 7:19 our sins underfoot and **h** all our iniquities H8959

HURLED (23) [HURL]

Ex 15: 1 horse and driver *he has* **h** into the sea. H8227
Ex 15: 4 his army *he has* **h** into the sea. H3721
Ex 15:21 horse and driver *he has* **h** into the sea." H8227
Jos 10:11 the LORD **h** large hailstones down on them, H8959
1Sa 18:11 he **h** it, saying to himself, "I'll pin H3214
1Sa 20:33 But Saul **h** his spear at him to kill him H3214
1Sa 25:14 his greetings, but *he* **h insults** at them. H6512
Ne 9:11 but *you* **h** their pursuers into the depths H8959
Ps 79:12 times the contempt *they have* **h** *at* you, H3070
Jer 22:28 Why *will* he and his children **be h out** H3214
La 2: 1 *He has* **h down** the splendor of Israel from H8959
Jnh 2: 3 *You* **h** me into the depths, into the very H8959
Mt 27:39 Those who passed by **h insults** at him *G1059*
Mk 15:29 Those who passed by **h insults** at him *G1059*
Lk 23:39 criminals who hung there **h insults at** him: *G1059*
Jn 9:28 Then *they* **h insults** at him and said, "You *G3366*
1Pe 2:23 *When they* **h** *their* **insults** at him, he did *G3366*
Rev 8: 5 from the altar, and **h** it on the earth; and *G965*
Rev 8: 7 and *it was* **h down** on the earth. *G965*
Rev 12: 9 The great dragon *was* **h down**—that ancient *G965*
Rev 12: 9 *He was* **h** to the earth, and his angels with *G965*
Rev 12:10 our God day and night, *has been* **h down**. *G965*
Rev 12:13 saw that *he had been* **h** to the earth, *G965*

HURLS (2) [HURL]

Job 27:22 *It* **h** *itself* against him without mercy as he H8959
Ps 147:17 *He* **h down** his hail like pebbles. Who can H8959

HURRICANE (1)

Ac 27:14 very long, a wind **of h force**, called the *G5607*

HURRIED (24) [HURRY]

Ge 18: 2 *he* **h** from the entrance of his tent to meet H8132
Ge 18: 6 So Abraham **h** into the tent to Sarah H4554
Ge 18: 7 gave it to a servant, *who* **h** to prepare it. H4554
Ge 24:17 The servant **h** to meet her and said H8132
Ge 24:29 he **h** out to the man at the spring. H8132
Ge 29:13 his sister's son, *he* **h** to meet him. H8132
Ge 43:15 *They* **h** down to Egypt and presented H7756
Ge 43:30 Joseph **h** *out* and looked for a place to H4554
Ex 9:20 word of the LORD **h to bring** their slaves H5674
Jos 4:10 had directed Joshua. The people **h** over, H4554
Jos 8:14 all the men of the city **h** out early in the H4554
Jdg 13:10 The woman **h** to tell her husband, "He's H4554
1Sa 4:14 of this uproar?" The man **h** over to Eli, H4554
2Sa 4: 4 fled, but as she **h** to leave, he fell H2905
2Sa 19:16 **h** down with the men of Judah to meet H4554
2Ki 5:21 So Gehazi **h** after Naaman. H8103
2Ch 26:20 leprosy on his forehead, so *they* **h** him out. H987
Est 6:14 eunuchs arrived and **h** Haman away to the H987
Job 31: 5 falsehood or my foot *has* **h** after deceit— H2590
Da 6:19 the king got up and **h** to the lions' den. A10097
Mt 28: 8 So the women **h** away from the tomb *G5444*
Mk 6:25 At once the girl **h** in to the king *G3552+5082*
Lk 1:39 got ready and **h** to a town in *G4513+3552+5082*
Lk 2:16 So *they* **h off** and found Mary and *G2262+5067*

HURRIEDLY (1) [HURRY]

Jdg 9:54 **H** he called to his armor-bearer, "Draw H4559

HURRIES (1) [HURRY]

Ecc 1: 5 the sun sets, and **h back** to where it rises. H8634

HURRY (15) [HURRIED, HURRIES, HURRIEDLY, HURRYING]

Ge 19:14 He said, "**H** and get out of this place H7756
Ge 19:15 of dawn, the angels urged Lot, saying, "**H**! H7756
Ge 45: 9 Now **h** back to my father and say to him H4554
Ex 12:33 urged the people to **h** and leave the H4554
Nu 16:46 and **h** to the assembly to make H2143+4559
1Sa 9:12 **H** now; he has just come to our town H4554
1Sa 17:17 your brothers and **h** to their camp. H8132
1Sa 20: 6 asked my permission to **h** *to* Bethlehem, H8132
1Sa 20:38 Then he shouted, "**H**! Go quickly! Don't H4559
2Ch 35:21 God has told me to **h**; so stop opposing H987
Ps 55: 8 *I would* **h** to my place of shelter, far from H2590
Ecc 8: 3 *Do* not *be* **in a h** to leave the king's H987
SS 1: 4 me away with you—*let us* **h**! Let the king H8132
Isa 5:19 those who say, "*Let* God **h**; let him hasten H4554
Ac 20:16 for *he was* **in a h** to reach Jerusalem *G5067*

HURRYING (1) [HURRY]

1Sa 23:26 the other side, **h** to get away from Saul. H2905

HURT (9) [HURTS]

Ps 69:26 talk about the pain of *those* you **h**. H2728
Pr 23:35 "They hit me," you will say, "but *I'm* not **h**! H2703
Ecc 8: 9 a man lords it over others to his own **h**. H8273
Da 6:22 *They have* not **h** me, because I was A10243
Mk 16:18 deadly poison, *it will* not **h** them at all *G1055*
Jn 21:17 Peter *was* **h** because Jesus asked him the *G3382*
Ac 7:26 brothers; why *do you want to* **h** each other? *G92*
2Co 7: 8 I see that my letter **h** you, but only for a *G3382*
Rev 2:11 who is victorious *will* not *be* **h** at all by the *G92*

HURTLING (1)

Eze 13:11 I will send hailstones **h down**, and H5877

HURTS (2) [HURT]

Ps 15: 4 who keeps an oath even when *it* **h**, and H8317
Pr 26:28 A lying tongue hates *those* it **h**, and a H1916

HUSBAND (114) [HUSBAND'S, HUSBANDS]

Ge 3: 6 She also gave some to her **h**, who was with H408
Ge 3:16 Your desire will be for your **h**, and he will H408
Ge 16: 3 Hagar and gave her to her **h** to be his wife. H408
Ge 29:32 Surely my **h** will love me now." H408
Ge 29:34 "Now at last my **h** will become attached to H408
Ge 30:15 it enough that you took away my **h**? H408
Ge 30:18 rewarded me for giving my servant to my **h**." H408
Ge 30:20 This time my **h** will treat me with honor H408
Ex 21:22 the woman's **h** demands and the H1251
Lev 21: 3 is dependent on him since she has no **h**— H408
Nu 5:13 is hidden from her **h** and her impurity is H408
Nu 5:14 come over her **h** and he suspects H2257S
Nu 5:19 become impure while married to your **h**, H408
Nu 5:20 married to your **h** and you have made H408
Nu 5:20 relations with a man other than your **h**"— H408
Nu 5:27 impure and been unfaithful to her **h**, H408
Nu 5:29 herself impure while married to her **h**, H408
Nu 5:31 The **h** will be innocent of any wrongdoing H408
Nu 30: 7 her **h** hears about it but says nothing to H408
Nu 30: 8 But if her **h** forbids her when he hears about H408
Nu 30:10 a woman living with her **h** makes a vow H408
Nu 30:11 her **h** hears about it but says nothing to H408
Nu 30:12 But if her **h** nullifies them when he hears H408
Nu 30:12 Her **h** has nullified them, and the LORD will H408
Nu 30:13 Her **h** may confirm or nullify any vow she H408
Nu 30:14 But if her **h** says nothing to her about it from H408
Dt 21:13 go to her and *be* her **h** and she shall be H1249
Dt 24: 3 her second **h** dislikes her and writes her H408
Dt 24: 4 then her first **h**, who divorced her, is not H1251
Dt 25:11 comes to rescue her **h** from his assailant, H408
Dt 28:56 will begrudge the **h** she loves and her own H408
Jdg 13: 6 the woman went to her **h** and told him, H408
Jdg 13: 9 but her **h** Manoah was not with her. H408
Jdg 13:10 The woman hurried to tell her **h**, "He's here! H408
Jdg 14:15 "Coax your **h** into explaining the riddle H408
Jdg 19: 3 her **h** went to her to persuade her to return H408
Jdg 20: 4 the Levite, the **h** *of* the murdered woman H408
Ru 1: 3 Elimelek, Naomi's **h**, died, and she was H408
Ru 1: 5 was left without her two sons and her **h**. H408
Ru 1: 9 you will find rest in the home of another **h**." H408
Ru 1:12 daughters; I am too old to have another **h**. H408

Ru 1:12 even if I had a **h** tonight and then gave H408
Ru 2:11 mother-in-law since the death of your **h**— H408
1Sa 1: 8 Her **h** Elkanah would say to her, "Hannah H408
1Sa 1:21 When her **h** Elkanah went up with all his H408
1Sa 1:22 She said to her **h**, "After the boy is weaned, H408
1Sa 1:23 seems best to you," her **h** Elkanah told her. H408
1Sa 2:19 she went up with her **h** to offer the annual H408
1Sa 4:19 her father-in-law and her **h** were dead, H408
1Sa 4:21 the deaths of her father-in-law and her **h**. H408
1Sa 25: 3 her **h** was surly and mean in his H408
1Sa 25:19 But she did not tell her **h** Nabal. H408
2Sa 3:15 taken away from her **h** Paltiel son of Laish. H408
2Sa 3:16 Her **h**, however, went with her, weeping H408
2Sa 11:26 Uriah's wife heard that her **h** was dead, H408
2Sa 14: 5 She said, "I am a widow; my **h** is dead. H408
2Sa 14: 7 leaving my **h** neither name nor descendant H408
2Ki 4: 1 "Your servant my **h** is dead, and you know H408
2Ki 4: 9 She said to her **h**, "I know that this man H408
2Ki 4:14 "She has no son, and her **h** is old. H408
2Ki 4:22 She called her **h** and said, "Please send H408
2Ki 4:26 Is your **h** all right? Is your H408
Pr 7:19 My **h** is not at home; he has gone on a H408
Pr 31:11 Her **h** has full confidence in her and lacks H1251
Pr 31:23 Her **h** is respected at the city gate, where H1251
Pr 31:28 her blessed; her **h** also, and he praises H1251
Isa 54: 1 desolate woman than of *her who* **has a h**," H1249
Isa 54: 5 For your Maker *is* your **h**—the LORD H1249
Jer 3:14 declares the LORD, "for I *am* your **h**. H1249
Jer 3:20 But like a woman unfaithful to her **h**, so H8276
Jer 6:11 both **h** and wife will be caught in it H408
Jer 31:32 covenant, though I *was a* **h** to them," H1249
Eze 16:32 You prefer strangers to your own **h**! H408
Eze 16:45 who despised her **h** and her children; and H408
Hos 2: 2 she is not my wife, and I am not her **h**. H408
Hos 2: 7 'I will go back to my **h** as at first, for then I H408
Hos 2:16 "you will call me 'my **h**'; you will no longer H408
Mt 1:16 of Joseph, the **h** of Mary, and Mary was *G467*
Mt 1:19 Because Joseph her **h** was faithful to the *G467*
Mt 19:10 this is the situation between a **h** and wife, *G476*
Mk 10:12 if she divorces her **h** and marries another *G467*
Lk 2:36 had lived with her **h** seven years after her *G467*
Jn 4:16 told her, "Go, call your **h** and come back." *G467*
Jn 4:17 "I have no **h**," she replied. Jesus said to *G467*
Jn 4:17 "You are right when you say you have no **h**. *G467*
Jn 4:18 the man you now have is not your **h**. *G467*
Ac 5: 9 the men who buried your **h** are at the door, *G467*
Ac 5:10 carried her out and buried her beside her **h**. *G467*
Ro 7: 2 woman is bound *to* her **h** as long as he is *G467*
Ro 7: 2 but if her **h** dies, she is released *G467*
Ro 7: 3 with another man while her **h** is still alive, *G467*
Ro 7: 3 But if her **h** dies, she is released from that *G467*
1Co 7: 2 and each woman *with* her own **h**. *G467*
1Co 7: 3 The **h** should fulfill his marital duty to his *G467*
1Co 7: 3 to his wife, and likewise the wife *to* her **h**. *G467*
1Co 7: 4 over her own body but yields it to her **h**. *G467*
1Co 7: 4 the **h** does not have authority over his own *G467*
1Co 7:10 A wife must not separate from her **h**. *G467*
1Co 7:11 unmarried or else be reconciled *to* her **h**. *G467*
1Co 7:11 And a **h** must not divorce his wife *G467*
1Co 7:13 And if a woman has a **h** who is not a *G467*
1Co 7:14 For the unbelieving **h** has been sanctified *G467*
1Co 7:14 has been sanctified through her believing **h**. *G81*
1Co 7:16 wife, whether you will save your **h**? *G467*
1Co 7:16 how do you know, **h**, whether you will save *G467*
1Co 7:34 of this world—how she can please her **h**. *G467*
1Co 7:39 is bound to her **h** as long as he lives. *G467*
1Co 7:39 But if her **h** dies, she is free to marry *G467*
2Co 11: 2 I promised you to one **h**, to Christ, so that I *G467*
Gal 4:27 desolate woman than of her who has a **h**." *G467*
Eph 5:23 For the **h** is the head of the wife as Christ is *G467*
Eph 5:33 himself, and the wife must respect her **h**. *G467*
1Ti 5: 9 has been **faithful to her h**, *G1651+467+1222*
Rev 21: 2 as a bride beautifully dressed *for* her **h**. *G467*

HUSBAND'S (6) [HUSBAND]

Dt 25: 5 Her **h brother** shall take her and marry her H3303
Dt 25: 7 "My **h brother** refuses to carry on his H3303
Ru 2: 1 Now Naomi had a relative on her **h** side, H408
Pr 6:34 For jealousy arouses a **h** fury, and he will H1505
Pr 12: 4 A wife of noble character is her **h** crown H1251
Jn 1:13 of human decision or a **h** will, but born *G467*

HUSBANDMAN, HUSBANDMEN (KJV) FARMER, FARMERS, GARDENER, MAN OF THE SOIL, TENANTS, WORK THE FIELDS

HUSBANDS (21) [HUSBAND]

Lev 21: 7 by prostitution or divorced from their **h**, H408
Ru 1: 8 shown kindness to your **dead** *h* and to me. AIT
Ru 1:11 any more sons, who could become your **h**? H408
Est 1:17 so they will despise their **h** and say H1251
Est 1:20 all the women will respect their **h**, from H1251
Jer 44:19 did not our **h** know that we were making H408
Eze 16:45 who despised their **h** and their children. H408
Am 4: 1 crush the needy and say to your **h**, H123
Jn 4:18 you have had five **h**, and the man you now *G467*
1Co 14:35 they should ask their own **h** at home; for it *G467*
Eph 5:22 yourselves *to* your own **h** as you do to the *G467*
Eph 5:24 should submit *to* their **h** in everything. *G467*
Eph 5:25 **H**, love your wives, just as Christ loved the *G467*
Eph 5:28 **h** ought to love their wives as their own *G467*
Col 3:18 submit yourselves *to* your **h**, as is fitting in *G467*
Col 3:19 **H**, love your wives and do not be harsh *G467*
Titus 2: 4 women *to* **love** their **h** and children *G5791+1639*
Titus 2: 5 to be subject *to* their **h**, so that no one *G467*
1Pe 3: 1 submit yourselves *to* your own **h** so that, *G467*
1Pe 3: 5 They submitted themselves *to* their own **h**, *G467*
1Pe 3: 7 **H**, in the same way be considerate as you *G467*

HUSH (1) [HUSHED]

Am 6:10 "No," then he will go on to say, "**H**! H2187

HUSHAH (1)

1Ch 4: 4 father of Gedor, and Ezer the father of **H**. H2592

HUSHAI (12)

2Sa 15:32 **H** the Arkite was there to meet him H2593
2Sa 15:37 So **H**, David's confidant, arrived at H2593
2Sa 16:16 Then **H** the Arkite, David's confidant, went H2593
2Sa 16:17 Absalom said to **H**, "So this is the love H2593
2Sa 16:18 **H** said to Absalom, "No, the one chosen H2593
2Sa 17: 5 "Summon also **H** the Arkite, so we H2593
2Sa 17: 6 When **H** came to him, Absalom said H2593
2Sa 17: 7 **H** replied to Absalom, "The advice H2593
2Sa 17:14 "The advice of **H** the Arkite is better than H2593
2Sa 17:15 **H** told Zadok and Abiathar, the priests H2593
1Ki 4:16 Baana son of **H**—in Asher and in Aloth; H2593
1Ch 27:33 **H** the Arkite was the king's confidant H2593

HUSHAM (4)

Ge 36:34 **H** from the land of the Temanites H2595
Ge 36:35 When **H** died, Hadad son of Bedad, who H2595
1Ch 1:45 **H** from the land of the Temanites H2595
1Ch 1:46 When **H** died, Hadad son of Bedad, who H2595

HUSHATHITE (5)

2Sa 21:18 At that time Sibbekai the **H** killed Saph H3144
2Sa 23:27 Abiezer from Anathoth, Sibbekai the **H**, H3144
1Ch 11:29 Sibbekai the **H**, Ilai the Ahohite, H3144
1Ch 20: 4 At that time Sibbekai the **H** killed Sippai H3144
1Ch 27:11 was Sibbekai the **H**, a Zerahite. H3144

HUSHED (4) [HUSH]

Job 4:16 before my eyes, and I heard a **h** voice: H1960
Job 29:10 the voices of the nobles *were* **h**, and their H2461
Job 37:17 when the land **lies h** under the south H9200
Ps 107:29 to a whisper; the waves of the sea *were* **h**. H3120

HUSHIM (3)

Ge 46:23 The son of Dan: **H**. H3123
1Ch 8: 8 he had divorced his wives **H** and Baara. H2594
1Ch 8:11 By **H** he had Abitub and Elpaal. H2594

HUSHITES (1)

1Ch 7:12 and the **H** the descendants of Aher. H3131

HUSK, HUSKS (KJV) PODS, SKINS

HUT (3)

Job 27:18 cocoon, like a **h** made by a watchman. H6109
Isa 1: 8 in a vineyard, like a **h** in a cucumber field H4870
Isa 24:20 it sways like a **h** in the wind; so heavy H4870

HUZOTH See KIRIATH HUZOTH

HYENAS (3)

Isa 13:22 **H** will inhabit her strongholds, jackals her H363
Isa 34:14 Desert creatures will meet with **h**, and wild H363
Jer 50:39 "So desert creatures and **h** will live there H363

HYMENAEUS (2)

1Ti 1:20 Among them are **H** and Alexander, whom *G5628*
2Ti 2:17 Among them are **H** and Philetus, *G5628*

HYMN (4) [HYMNS]

Ps 40: 3 in my mouth, a **h of praise** to our God. H9335
Mt 26:30 *When they had* **sung a h**, they went out to *G5630*
Mk 14:26 *When they had* **sung a h**, they went out to *G5630*
1Co 14:26 each of you has a **h**, or a word of *G6011*

HYMNS (3) [HYMN]

Ac 16:25 Silas were praying and **singing h** to God, *G5630*
Eph 5:19 with psalms, **h**, and songs from the *G5631*
Col 3:16 through psalms, **h**, and songs from the *G5631*

HYPOCRISY (6) [HYPOCRITE, HYPOCRITES, HYPOCRITICAL]

Mt 23:28 inside you are full *of* **h** and wickedness. *G5694*
Mk 12:15 But Jesus knew their **h**. "Why are you *G5694*
Lk 12: 1 the yeast of the Pharisees, which is **h**. *G5694*
Gal 2:13 The other Jews **joined** him **in** his **h**, so that *G5347*
Gal 2:13 so that *by* their **h** even Barnabas was led *G5694*
1Pe 2: 1 of all malice and all deceit, **h**, envy, *G5694*

HYPOCRITE (2) [HYPOCRISY]

Mt 7: 5 *You* **h**, first take the plank out of your own *G5695*
Lk 6:42 *You* **h**, first take the plank out of your eye *G5695*

HYPOCRITES (16) [HYPOCRISY]

Ps 26: 4 the deceitful, nor do I associate with **h**. H6623
Mt 6: 2 as the **h** do in the synagogues and on the *G5695*
Mt 6: 5 do not be like the **h**, for they love to pray *G5695*
Mt 6:16 do not look somber as the **h** do, for they *G5695*
Mt 15: 7 You **h**! Isaiah was right when he *G5695*
Mt 22:18 "*You* **h**, why are you trying to trap *G5695*
Mt 23:13 teachers of the law and Pharisees, *you* **h**! *G5695*
Mt 23:15 teachers of the law and Pharisees, *you* **h**! *G5695*
Mt 23:23 teachers of the law and Pharisees, *you* **h**! *G5695*
Mt 23:25 teachers of the law and Pharisees, *you* **h**! *G5695*
Mt 23:27 teachers of the law and Pharisees, *you* **h**! *G5695*
Mt 23:29 teachers of the law and Pharisees, *you* **h**! *G5695*
Mt 24:51 pieces and assign him a place with the **h**, *G5695*
Mk 7: 6 right when he prophesied about you **h**; *G5695*
Lk 12:56 **H**! You know how to interpret the *G5695*
Lk 13:15 answered him, "You **h**! Doesn't each of *G5695*

HYPOCRITICAL (1) [HYPOCRISY]

1Ti 4: 2 Such teachings come through **h** liars *G5694*

HYRAX (3) [HYRAXES]

Lev 11: 5 The **h**, though it chews the cud, does not H9176
Dt 14: 7 not eat the camel, the rabbit or the **h**. H9176
Ps 104:18 the crags are a refuge for the **h**. H9176

HYRAXES (1) [HYRAX]

Pr 30:26 **h** are creatures of little power, yet they H9176

HYSSOP (12)

Ex 12:22 Take a bunch of **h**, dip it into the blood in H257
Lev 14: 4 scarlet yarn and **h** be brought for the H257
Lev 14: 6 the scarlet yarn and the **h**, into the blood of H257
Lev 14:49 some cedar wood, scarlet yarn and **h**. H257
Lev 14:51 the cedar wood, the **h**, the scarlet yarn H257
Lev 14:52 the cedar wood, the **h** and the scarlet yarn. H257
Nu 19: 6 **h** and scarlet wool and throw them onto H257
Nu 19:18 is ceremonially clean is to take *some* **h**, H257
1Ki 4:33 of Lebanon to the **h** that grows out of walls H257
Ps 51: 7 Cleanse me with **h**, and I will be clean H257
Jn 19:29 put the sponge on a **stalk of the h plant** *G5727*
Heb 9:19 scarlet wool and **branches of h**, and *G5727*

I

I (8795) [I'LL, I'M, I'VE, ME, MINE, MYSELF] See Index of Articles Etc.

I AM (70 of 1038) See Index of Articles Etc. for Exhaustive Indexes to I and AM (See Introduction, pages x-xi)

Ge 15: 1 **I** am your shield, your very great reward. H644
Ge 17: 1 "**I** am God Almighty; walk before me H638
Ex 3:14 God said to Moses, "*I* AM WHO I AM. This is AIT
Ex 3:14 to Moses, "I AM WHO *I* AM. This is what you AIT
Ex 3:14 to the Israelites: '*I* AM has sent me to you.'" AIT
Ps 46:10 "Be still, and know that I am God; H644
Isa 41:10 So do not fear, for **I** am with you; do not be H638
Isa 41:10 do not be dismayed, for **I** am your God. H638
Isa 43: 3 For **I** am the LORD your God, the Holy One H638
Isa 43:11 **I**, even I, am the LORD, and apart from me H644
Isa 43:15 **I** am the LORD, your Holy One, Israel's H638
Isa 44: 6 **I** am the first and I am the last; apart from H638
Isa 44: 6 I am the first and **I** am the last; apart from H638
Isa 48:12 **I** am he; I am the first and I am the last. H638
Isa 48:12 I am he; **I** am the first and I am the last. H638
Isa 48:12 I am he; I am the first and **I** am the last. H638
Jer 3:14 declares the LORD, "for **I** am your husband. H644
Jer 32:27 "**I** am the LORD, the God of all mankind. H638
Hos 11: 9 For **I** am God, and not a man—the Holy H644
Mt 16:15 he asked. "Who do you say **I** am?" *G1609*
Mt 28:20 And surely **I** am with you always, to the *G1609*
Mk 8:29 "Who do you say **I** am?" Peter answered, *G1609*
Mk 14:62 "**I** am," said Jesus. "And you will see the *G1609*
Lk 9:20 "Who do you say **I** am?" Peter answered, *G1609*
Lk 22:70 He replied, "You say that **I** am." *G1609*
Jn 6:35 Jesus declared, "**I** am the bread of life. *G1609*
Jn 6:41 "**I** am the bread that came down from *G1609*
Jn 6:48 **I** am the bread of life. *G1609*
Jn 6:51 **I** am the living bread that came down from *G1609*
Jn 8:12 he said, "**I** am the light of the world. *G1609*
Jn 8:24 if you do not believe that **I** am he, you *G1609*
Jn 8:28 you will know that **I** am he and that I do *G1609*
Jn 8:58 "before Abraham was born, **I** am! *G1609*
Jn 9: 5 While *I* **am** in the world, I am the light of the AIT
Jn 9: 5 I am in the world, *I* **am** the light of the world." AIT
Jn 10: 7 I tell you, **I** am the gate for the sheep. *G1609*
Jn 10: 9 **I** am the gate; whoever enters through me *G1609*
Jn 10:11 "**I** am the good shepherd. The good *G1609*
Jn 10:14 "**I** am the good shepherd; I know my *G1609*
Jn 10:36 blasphemy because I said, '*I* **am** God's Son'? AIT
Jn 11:25 "**I** am the resurrection and the life. *G1609*
Jn 13:19 you will believe that **I** am who I am. *G1609*
Jn 13:19 happen you will believe that I *am who I* **am**. AIT
Jn 14: 6 "**I** am the way and the truth and the life. *G1609*
Jn 14:10 Don't you believe that **I** am in the Father *G1609*
Jn 14:11 when I say that **I** am in the Father *G1609*
Jn 14:20 you will realize that **I** am in my Father, *G1609*
Jn 14:20 you are in me, **and I** am in you. *G2743*
Jn 15: 1 "**I** am the true vine, and my Father is the *G1609*
Jn 15: 5 "**I** am the vine; you are the branches. *G1609*
Jn 17:21 just as you are in me **and I** am in you. *G2743*
Jn 18: 5 "**I** am he," Jesus said. *G1609*
Jn 18: 6 When Jesus said, "**I** am he," they drew *G1609*
Jn 18: 8 "I told you that **I** am he. If you are looking *G1609*
Ac 7:32 '**I** am the God of your fathers, the God of *G1609*
Ac 9: 5 "**I** am Jesus, whom you are persecuting," *G1609*
Ac 18:10 For **I** am with you, and no one is going to *G1609*

Ac 22: 8 " '**I** am Jesus of Nazareth, whom you are *G1609*
Ac 26:15 " '**I** am Jesus, whom you are persecuting *G1609*
Rev 1: 8 "**I** am the Alpha and the Omega," says *G1609*
Rev 1:17 not be afraid. **I** am the First and the Last. *G1609*
Rev 1:18 **I** am the Living One; I was dead, and now NDT
Rev 1:18 now look, *I* **am** alive for ever and ever! AIT
Rev 3:11 *I am* **coming** soon. Hold on to what you have, AIT
Rev 21: 6 **I** am the Alpha and the Omega, the *G1609*
Rev 22: 7 *I am* **coming** soon! Blessed is the one AIT
Rev 22:12 *I am* **coming** soon! My reward is with AIT
Rev 22:13 **I** am the Alpha and the Omega, the First *G1609*
Rev 22:16 **I** am the Root and the Offspring of David *G1609*
Rev 22:20 to these things says, "Yes, *I am* **coming** soon." AIT

I'LL (38) [I, WILL] See Index of Articles Etc.

I'M (25) [BE, I] See Index of Articles Etc.

I'VE (8) [HAVE, I]

Ge 30:26 You know how much work **I** done for you." H3276
Ge 31: 6 You know that *I* **worked for** your father with AIT
Ru 2:11 "**I** been told all about what you have H3276
1Ki 22:34 me out of the fighting. *I* **been wounded**." AIT
2Ch 18:33 me out of the fighting. *I* **been wounded**." AIT
Pr 30:20 her mouth and says, '*I* **done** nothing wrong. AIT
Lk 13: 7 three years now *I been* **coming** to look for AIT
Lk 15:29 All these years *I been* **slaving** for you and AIT

IBEX (1)

Dt 14: 5 the wild goat, the **i**, the antelope and the H1913

IBHAR (3)

2Sa 5:15 **I**, Elishua, Nepheg, Japhia, H3295
1Ch 3: 6 There were also **I**, Elishua, Eliphelet, H3295
1Ch 14: 5 **I**, Elishua, Elpelet, H3295

IBIS (1)

Job 38:36 Who gives the **i** wisdom or gives the H3219

IBLEAM (3)

Jos 17:11 had Beth Shan, **I** and the people of Dor H3300
Jdg 1:27 Taanach or Dor or **I** or Megiddo and their H3300
2Ki 9:27 in his chariot on the way up to Gur near **I**, H3300

IBNEIAH (1)

1Ch 9: 8 **I** son of Jeroham; Elah son of Uzzi, the H3307

IBNIJAH (1)

1Ch 9: 8 the son of Reuel, the son of **I**. H3308

IBRI (1)

1Ch 24:27 Beno, Shoham, Zakkur and **I**. H6304

IBSAM (1)

1Ch 7: 2 Jahmai, **I** and Samuel—heads of their H3311

IBZAN (3)

Jdg 12: 8 After him, **I** of Bethlehem led Israel. H83
Jdg 12: 9 outside his clan. **I** led Israel seven years NDT
Jdg 12:10 Then **I** died and was buried in Bethlehem. H83

ICE (3) [ICY]

Job 6:16 darkened by thawing **i** and swollen with H7943
Job 37:10 The breath of God produces **i**, and the H7943
Job 38:29 From whose womb comes the **i**? Who H7943

ICHABOD (1) [ICHABOD'S]

1Sa 4:21 She named the boy **I**, saying, "The Glory H376

ICHABOD'S (1) [ICHABOD]

1Sa 14: 3 He was a son of **I** brother Ahitub son of H376

ICONIUM (6)

Ac 13:51 feet as a warning to them and went to **I**. *G2658*
Ac 14: 1 At **I** Paul and Barnabas went as usual into *G2658*
Ac 14:19 from Antioch and **I** and won the crowd *G2658*
Ac 14:21 they returned to Lystra, **I** and Antioch, *G2658*
Ac 16: 2 at Lystra and **I** spoke well of him. *G2658*
2Ti 3:11 to me in Antioch, **I** and Lystra, the *G2658*

ICY (1) [ICE]

Ps 147:17 Who can withstand his **i** **blast**? H7938

IDALAH (1)

Jos 19:15 Nahalal, Shimron, **I** and Bethlehem. H3339

IDBASH (1)

1Ch 4: 3 Jezreel, Ishma and **I**. Their sister was H3340

IDDO (13) [IDDO'S]

1Ki 4:14 Ahinadab son of **I**—in Mahanaim; H6333
1Ch 6:21 Joah his son, **I** his son, Zerah his son and H6341
1Ch 27:21 Manasseh in Gilead: **I** son of Zechariah H3346
2Ch 9:29 in the visions of **I** the seer concerning H3587
2Ch 12:15 the prophet and of **I** the seer that deal H6341
2Ch 13:22 in the annotations of the prophet **I**. H6341
Ezr 5: 1 a descendant of **I**, prophesied to the A10529
Ezr 6:14 Zechariah, a descendant of **I**. A10529
Ezr 8:17 I ordered them to go to **I**, the leader in H120
Ezr 8:17 them what to say to **I** and his fellow Levites H120
Ne 12: 4 **I**, Ginnethon, Abijah, H6342
Zec 1: 1 Zechariah son of Berekiah, the son of **I**: H6341
Zec 1: 7 Zechariah son of Berekiah, the son of **I**. H6342

IDDO'S (1) [IDDO]

Ne 12:16 of **I**, Zechariah; of Ginnethon's H6342

IDEA (8) [IDEAS]

Nu 16:28 things and that it was not my **i**: H4946+4213
Dt 1:23 The **i** seemed good to me; so I selected H1821
Est 3: 6 he **scorned the i** of killing H1022+928+6524
Jn 5:13 who was healed **had** no **i** who it was, *G3857*
Jn 8:14 But you **have** no **i** where I come from or *G3857*
Jn 18:34 "*Is* that **your own i**," Jesus *G608+4932+3306*
Ac 12: 9 but *he* **had** no **i** that what the angel was *G3857*
2Pe 2:13 *Their* **i** of pleasure is to carouse in broad *G2451*

IDEAS (3) [IDEA]

Ac 17:20 You are bringing some **strange** *i* to our ears AIT
Ac 17:21 talking about and listening to the **latest** *i*.) AIT
1Ti 6:20 chatter and the **opposing** *i* of what is falsely AIT

IDENTICAL (2)

1Ki 6:25 the two cherubim were **i** in size and shape. H285
1Ki 7:37 same molds and were **i** in size and shape. H285

IDLE (11) [IDLENESS, IDLERS]

Dt 32:47 They are not just **i** words for you—they are H8199
Job 11: 3 Will your **i talk** reduce others to silence H966
Ecc 10:18 because of **i** hands, the house leaks. H9170
Ecc 11: 6 at evening **let** your hands not **be i**, for H5663
Isa 58:13 doing as you please or speaking **i** words, NDT
Col 2:18 they are puffed up *with* **i notions** by their *G1632*
1Th 5:14 warn those who are **i and disruptive** *G864*
2Th 3: 6 who is **i and disruptive** and does not *G865*
2Th 3: 7 *We were* not **i** when we were with you *G863*
2Th 3:11 that some among you are **i and disruptive**. *G865*
1Ti 5:13 into the habit *of* being **i** and going about *G734*

IDLENESS (1) [IDLE]

Pr 31:27 does not eat the bread of **i**. H6791

IDLERS (1) [IDLE]

1Ti 5:13 And not only do they become **i**, but also *G734*

IDOL (36) [CALF-IDOL, CALF-IDOLS, IDOL'S, IDOLATER, IDOLATERS, IDOLATRIES, IDOLATROUS, IDOLATRY, IDOLS]

Ex 32: 4 made it into an **i cast** in the shape of a H5011
Ex 32: 8 themselves an **i cast** in the shape of a H5011
Dt 4:16 corrupt and make for yourselves an **i**, H7181
Dt 4:23 yourselves an **i** *in* the form of anything H7181
Dt 4:25 become corrupt and make any kind of **i**, H7181
Dt 9:12 them and have made an **i** for themselves." H5011
Dt 9:16 yourselves an **i cast** in the shape of a H5011
Dt 27:15 is anyone who makes an **i**— H7181+2256+5011
Jdg 17: 4 used them to make the **i**. H7181+2256+5011
Jdg 18:17 out the land went inside and took the **i**, H7181
Jdg 18:18 house and took the **i**, H7181+2256+5011
Jdg 18:20 gods and the **i** and went along with H7181
Jdg 18:30 the Danites set up for themselves the **i**, H7181
Jdg 18:31 continued to use the **i** Micah had made, H7181
1Sa 19:13 Then Michal took an **i** and laid it on the H9572
1Sa 19:16 there was the **i** in the bed, and at the H9572
Ps 24: 4 does not trust in an **i** or swear by a false H8736
Ps 106:19 a calf and worshiped an **i cast from metal**. H5011
Isa 40:19 As for an **i**, a metalworker casts it, and a H7181
Isa 40:20 worker to set up an **i** that will not topple. H7181
Isa 41: 7 The other nails down **the i** so it will not H2084S
Isa 44:10 Who shapes a god and casts an **i**, which H7181
Isa 44:12 he shapes an **i** with hammers, he H2084S
Isa 44:15 he makes an **i** and bows down to it. H7181
Isa 44:17 he makes a god, his **i**; he bows down to it H7181
Isa 66: 3 incense is like one who worships an **i**. H224
Eze 8: 3 where the **i** that provokes to jealousy H6166
Eze 8: 5 gate of the altar I saw this **i** *of* jealousy. H6166
Eze 8:12 darkness, each at the shrine of his own **i**? H5381
Hos 4:12 My people consult a **wooden i**, and a H6770
Hos 9:10 to that **shameful i** and became as H1425
Hab 2:18 "Of what value is an **i** carved by a H7181
Ac 7:41 time *they* **made an i in the form of a calf**. *G3674*
1Co 8: 4 We know that "An **i** is nothing at all in *G1631*
1Co 10:19 then that **food sacrificed to an i** is *G1628*
1Co 10:19 idol is anything, or that an **i** is anything? *G1631*

IDOL'S (1) [IDOL]

1Co 8:10 eating in an **i temple**, won't that person *G1627*

IDOLATER (2) [IDOL]

1Co 5:11 immoral or greedy, an **i** or slanderer, *G1629*
Eph 5: 5 such a person is an **i**—has any inheritance *G1629*

IDOLATERS (5) [IDOL]

1Co 5:10 the greedy and swindlers, or **i**. *G1629*
1Co 6: 9 sexually immoral nor **i** nor adulterers nor *G1629*
1Co 10: 7 Do not be **i**, as some of them were; as it is *G1629*
Rev 21: 8 magic arts, the **i** and all liars—they will *G1629*
Rev 22:15 the **i** and everyone who loves and *G1629*

IDOLATRIES (1) [IDOL]

Jer 14:14 **i** and the delusions of their own minds. H496

IDOLATROUS (4) [IDOL]

2Ki 23: 5 away with the **i priests** appointed by the H4024
Jer 3:23 Surely the **i** commotion on the hills and NDT
Hos 10: 5 and so will its **i priests**, those who had H4024
Zep 1: 4 very names of the **i priests**— H4024+6640+3913

IDOLATRY (8) [IDOL]

1Sa 15:23 arrogance like the evil of **i**. H9572
2Ki 9:22 "as long as all the **i** and witchcraft of your H2393
Eze 14: 4 them myself in keeping with their great **i**. H1658
Eze 23:49 bear the consequences of your sins of **i**. H1658
1Co 10:14 Therefore, my dear friends, flee from **i**. *G1630*
Gal 5:20 **i** and witchcraft; hatred, discord, jealousy *G1630*
Col 3: 5 evil desires and greed, which is **i**. *G1630*
1Pe 4: 3 carousing and detestable **i**. *G1630*

IDOLS (165) [IDOL]

Ex 34:17 "Do not make any **i**. H5011+466
Lev 17: 7 their sacrifices to the **goat i** to whom they H8539
Lev 19: 4 " 'Do not turn to **i** or make metal gods for H496
Lev 26: 1 " 'Do not make **i** or set up an image or a H496
Lev 26:30 bodies on the lifeless forms of your **i**, H1658
Nu 33:52 all their carved images and their cast **i**, H7512
Dt 7: 5 Asherah poles and burn their **i** in the fire. H7178
Dt 12: 3 cut down the **i** *of* their gods and wipe out H7178
Dt 29:17 images and **i** of wood and stone, H1658
Dt 32:16 angered him with their **detestable i**. H9359
Dt 32:21 angered me with their **worthless i**. H2039
1Sa 12:21 Do not turn away after **useless i**. They can H9332
1Sa 31: 9 the temple of their **i** and among their H6773
2Sa 5:21 The Philistines abandoned their **i** there H6773
1Ki 14: 9 other gods, **i made of metal**; you have H5011
1Ki 15:12 got rid of all the **i** his ancestors had made H1658
1Ki 16:13 the God of Israel, by their **worthless i**. H2039
1Ki 16:26 the God of Israel, by their **worthless i**. H2039
1Ki 21:26 in the vilest manner by going after **i**, H1658
2Ki 11:18 the altars and **i** to pieces and killed H7512
2Ki 17:12 They worshiped **i**, though the LORD had H1658
2Ki 17:15 They followed **worthless i** and themselves H2039
2Ki 17:16 themselves two **i cast** in the shape of H5011
2Ki 17:41 the LORD, they were serving their **i**. H7178
2Ki 21:11 him and has led Judah into sin with his **i**. H1658
2Ki 21:21 worshiping the **i** his father had worshiped H1658
2Ki 22:17 anger by all the **i** their hands have **made**, H5126
2Ki 23:24 the **i** and all the other detestable things H1658
1Ch 10: 9 the news among their **i** and their people. H6773
1Ch 16:26 For all the gods of the nations are **i**, but the H496
2Ch 11:15 for the **goat** and calf **i** he had made. H8539
2Ch 15: 8 He removed the **detestable i** from the H9199
2Ch 23:17 the altars and **i** and killed Mattan the H7512
2Ch 24:18 worshiped Asherah poles and **i**. H6773
2Ch 28: 2 Israel and also made **i** for worshiping the H5011
2Ch 33:19 Asherah poles and **i** before he humbled H7178
2Ch 33:22 to all the **i** Manasseh had made. H7178
2Ch 34: 3 places, Asherah poles and **i**. H7178+2256+5011
2Ch 34: 4 the Asherah poles and the **i**. H7178+2256+5011
2Ch 34: 7 crushed the **i** to powder and cut to H7178
2Ch 34:33 removed all the **detestable i** from all the H9359
Ps 31: 6 hate those who cling to **worthless i**; H2039+8736
Ps 78:58 they aroused his jealousy with their **i**. H7178
Ps 96: 5 For all the gods of the nations are **i**, but the H496
Ps 97: 7 those who boast in **i**—worship him, H496
Ps 106:36 They worshiped their **i**, which became a H6773
Ps 106:38 whom they sacrificed to the **i** *of* Canaan H6773
Ps 115: 4 But their **i** are silver and gold, made by H6773
Ps 135:15 The **i** *of* the nations are silver and gold H6773
Isa 2: 8 Their land is full of **i**; they bow down to the H496
Isa 2:18 the **i** will totally disappear. H496
Isa 2:20 moles and bats their **i** *of* silver and idols of H496
Isa 2:20 bats their idols of silver and **i** *of* gold, H496
Isa 10:10 As my hand seized the kingdoms of the **i** H496
Isa 10:11 images as I dealt with Samaria and her **i**? H496
Isa 19: 1 The **i** *of* Egypt tremble before him, and the H496
Isa 19: 3 they will consult the **i** and the spirits of the H496
Isa 30:22 will desecrate your **i** overlaid with silver H7178
Isa 31: 7 you will reject the **i** *of* silver and gold your H496
Isa 41:22 "Tell us, you **i**, what is going to happen NDT
Isa 42: 8 yield my glory to another or my praise to **i**. H7178
Isa 42:17 But those who trust in **i**, who say to H7181
Isa 44: 9 All who make **i** are nothing, and the H7181
Isa 45:16 All the makers of **i** will be put to shame H7497
Isa 45:20 are those who carry about **i** *of* wood, H7181
Isa 46: 1 their **i** are borne by beasts of burden. H6773
Isa 48:14 Which of **the i** has foretold these things H2157S
Isa 57: 6 The **i** among the smooth stones of the NDT
Isa 57:13 out for help, let your **collection** *of* **i** save you! AIT
Jer 2: 5 They followed **worthless i** and became H2039
Jer 2: 8 by Baal, following **worthless i**. H4202+3603
Jer 2:11 their glorious God for **worthless i**. H4202+3603
Jer 4: 1 you put your **detestable i** out of my sight H9199
Jer 7:30 set up their **detestable i** in the house H9199
Jer 8:19 images, with their **worthless** foreign **i**?" H2039
Jer 10: 5 a cucumber field, **their i** cannot speak H2156S
Jer 10: 8 they are taught by **worthless** wooden **i**. H2039
Jer 10:14 every goldsmith is shamed by his **i**. H7181
Jer 14:22 Do any of the **worthless i** *of* the nations H2039
Jer 16:18 my inheritance with their **detestable i**." H9359
Jer 16:19 **worthless i** that did them no good. H2039
Jer 18:15 they burn incense to **worthless i**, which H8736
Jer 50: 2 put to shame and her **i** filled with terror. H1658
Jer 50:38 For it is a land of **i**, idols that will go mad H7178
Jer 50:38 land of idols, **i** that will go mad with terror. NDT
Jer 51:17 every goldsmith is shamed by his **i**. H7181
Jer 51:47 come when I will punish the **i** *of* Babylon; H7178
Jer 51:52 "when I will punish her **i**, and throughout H7178
Eze 5: 9 Because of all your **detestable i**, I will do H9359
Eze 6: 4 I will slay your people in front of your **i**. H1658
Eze 6: 5 bodies of the Israelites in front of their **i**, H1658

Eze 6: 6 devastated, your **i** smashed and ruined H1658
Eze 6: 9 their eyes, which have lusted after their **i**. H1658
Eze 6:13 lie slain among their **i** around their altars, H1658
Eze 6:13 they offered fragrant incense to all their **i**. H1658
Eze 7:20 used it to make their detestable **i**. H7512
Eze 8:10 unclean animals and all the **i** *of* Israel. H1658
Eze 11:18 all its vile images and **detestable i**. H9359
Eze 11:21 to their vile images and **detestable i**, H9359
Eze 14: 3 men have set up **i** in their hearts and H1658
Eze 14: 4 the Israelites set up **i** in their hearts and H1658
Eze 14: 5 who have all deserted me for their **i**. H1658
Eze 14: 6 Turn from your **i** and renounce all your H1658
Eze 14: 7 from me and set up **i** in their hearts and H1658
Eze 16:17 made for yourself male **i** and engaged in H7512
Eze 16:20 me and sacrificed them as food to **the i**. H2157S
Eze 16:21 my children and sacrificed them to **the i**. H2157S
Eze 16:36 because of all your detestable **i**, and H1658
Eze 18: 6 mountain shrines or look to the **i** *of* Israel. H1658
Eze 18:12 He looks to the **i**. He does detestable H1658
Eze 18:15 mountain shrines or look to the **i** *of* Israel. H1658
Eze 20: 7 not defile yourselves with the **i** *of* Egypt. H1658
Eze 20: 8 nor did they forsake the **i** *of* Egypt. H1658
Eze 20:16 For their hearts were devoted to their **i**. H1658
Eze 20:18 their laws or defile yourselves with their **i**. H1658
Eze 20:24 their eyes lusted after their parents' **i**. H1658
Eze 20:31 yourselves with all your **i** to this day. H1658
Eze 20:39 Go and serve your **i**, every one of you! But H1658
Eze 20:39 my holy name with your gifts and **i**. H1658
Eze 21:21 he will consult his **i**, he will examine the H9572
Eze 22: 3 her midst and defiles herself by making **i**, H1658
Eze 22: 4 become defiled by the **i** you have made. H1658
Eze 23: 7 with all the **i** *of* everyone she lusted H1658
Eze 23:30 nations and defiled yourself with their **i**. H1658
Eze 23:37 They committed adultery with their **i**; they H1658
Eze 23:39 day they sacrificed their children to their **i**, H1658
Eze 30:13 'I will destroy the **i** and put an end to the H1658
Eze 33:25 in it and look to your **i** and shed blood, H1658
Eze 36:18 because they had defiled it with their **i**. H1658
Eze 36:25 all your impurities and from all your **i**. H1658
Eze 37:23 themselves with their **i** and vile images H1658
Eze 44:10 from me after their **i** must bear the H1658
Eze 44:12 presence of their **i** and made the people H1658
Hos 4:17 Ephraim is joined to **i**; leave him alone! H6773
Hos 5:11 in judgment, intent on pursuing **i**. H7417
Hos 8: 4 gold they make **i** for themselves to H6773
Hos 13: 2 they make **i** for themselves from their H5011
Hos 14: 8 what more have I to do with **i**? I will H6773
Am 5:26 the pedestal of your **i**, the star of your god H7512
Jnh 2: 8 cling to worthless **i** turn away from God's H8736
Mic 1: 7 All her **i** will be broken to pieces; all her H7178
Mic 5:13 I will destroy your **i** and your sacred stones H7178
Na 1:14 the images and **i** that are in the temple H5011
Hab 2:18 creation; he makes **i** that cannot speak. H496
Zep 1: 3 the **i that cause** the wicked **to stumble**." H4843
Zec 10: 2 The **i** speak deceitfully, diviners see H9572
Zec 13: 2 banish the names of the **i** from the land, H6773
Ac 7:43 god Rephan, the **i** you made to worship. *G5596*
Ac 15:20 them to abstain from food polluted *by* **i**, *G1631*
Ac 15:29 are to abstain *from* **food sacrificed to i**, *G1628*
Ac 17:16 distressed to see that the city was **full of i**. *G2977*
Ac 21:25 should abstain *from* **food sacrificed to i**, *G1628*
Ro 2:22 You who abhor **i**, do you rob temples? *G1631*
1Co 8: 1 Now about **food sacrificed to i**: We know *G1628*
1Co 8: 4 about eating **food sacrificed to i**: We *G1628*
1Co 8: 7 still so accustomed to **i** that when they eat *G1631*
1Co 8:10 emboldened to eat what is **sacrificed to i**? *G1628*
1Co 12: 2 were influenced and led astray to mute **i**. *G1631*
2Co 6:16 there between the temple of God and **i**? *G1631*
1Th 1: 9 turned to God from **i** to serve the living *G1631*
1Jn 5:21 Dear children, keep yourselves from **i**. *G1631*
Rev 2:14 that they ate **food sacrificed to i** and *G1628*
Rev 2:20 the eating *of* **food sacrificed to i**. *G1628*
Rev 9:20 worshiping demons, and **i** of gold, silver, *G1631*
Rev 9:20 wood—**i** that cannot see or hear or walk. *G4005S*

IDUMEA (1)

Mk 3: 8 Jerusalem, **I**, and the regions across the *G2628*

IEZER (1) [IEZERITE]

Nu 26:30 through **I**, the Iezerite clan; through Helek H404

IEZERITE (1) [IEZER]

Nu 26:30 through Iezer, the **I** clan; through Helek H405

IF (1715)

Ge 4: 7 **I** you do what is right, will you not be H561
Ge 4: 7 But **i** you do not do what is right, sin is H561
Ge 4:24 **I** Cain is avenged seven times, then H3954
Ge 8: 8 out a dove to see **i** the water had receded H2022
Ge 11: 6 "**I** as one people speaking the same H2176
Ge 13: 9 **I** you go to the left, I'll go to the right; if H561
Ge 13: 9 I'll go to the right; **i** you go to the right, I'll H561
Ge 13:16 so that **i** anyone could count the dust H561
Ge 15: 5 the stars—**i indeed** you can count them." H561
Ge 17:18 "**I only** Ishmael might live under your H4273
Ge 18: 3 He said, "**I** I have found favor in your eyes H561
Ge 18:21 go down and see **i** what they have done H2022
Ge 18:21 that has reached me. **I** not, I will know." H561
Ge 18:24 **What i** there are fifty righteous people in H218
Ge 18:26 "**I** I find fifty righteous people in the city of H561
Ge 18:28 **what i** the number of the righteous is five H218
Ge 18:28 "**I** I find forty-five there," he said, "I will H561
Ge 18:29 "**What i** only forty are found there? H218
Ge 18:30 **What i** only thirty can be found there?" H218
Ge 18:30 "I will not do it **i** I find thirty there. H561
Ge 18:31 **what i** only twenty can be found there?" H218
Ge 18:32 more. **What i** only ten can be found there?" H218
Ge 20: 7 But **i** you do not return her, you may be H561
Ge 23: 8 "**I** you are willing to let me bury my dead H561
Ge 23:13 in their hearing, "Listen to me, **i** you will. H561
Ge 24: 5 "**What i** the woman is unwilling to come H218
Ge 24: 8 **I** the woman is unwilling to come back with H561
Ge 24:39 '**What i** the woman will not come back with H218
Ge 24:41 You will be released from my oath **i**, when H561
Ge 24:42 of my master Abraham, **i** you will, please H561
Ge 24:43 *I* a young woman **comes out** to draw water AIT
Ge 24:44 **i** she says to me, "Drink, and I'll draw NDT
Ge 24:49 Now **i** you will show kindness and H561
Ge 24:49 tell me; and **i** not, tell me, so I may H561
Ge 27:12 **What i** my father touches me? I would H218
Ge 27:46 **I** Jacob takes a wife from among the H561
Ge 28:20 "**I** God will be with me and will watch over H561
Ge 30:27 "**I** I have found favor in your eyes H561
Ge 30:31 "**But i** you will do this one thing for me, H561
Ge 30:42 **i** the animals were weak, he would not H928
Ge 31: 8 **I** he said, 'The speckled ones will be H561+3907
Ge 31: 8 speckled young; and **i** he said, 'The H561+3907
Ge 31:32 But **i** you find anyone who has your gods NDT
Ge 31:32 of yours here with me; and **i** so, take it." NDT
Ge 31:42 **I** the God of my father, the God of Abraham
and the Fear of Isaac, had **not** H4295
Ge 31:50 **I** you mistreat my daughters or if you take H561
Ge 31:50 my daughters or **i** you take any wives H561
Ge 32: 8 "**I** Esau comes and attacks one group H561
Ge 33:10 "**I** I have found favor in your eyes, accept H561
Ge 33:13 **I** they are driven hard just one day, all the H2256
Ge 34:17 But **i** you will not agree to be circumcised H561
Ge 34:30 and *i they* **join forces** against me and attack AIT
Ge 37:14 "Go and see **i** all is well with your brothers NDT
Ge 37:26 "What will we gain **i** we kill our brother H3954
Ge 38:25 "*See i you* **recognize** whose seal and cord AIT
Ge 42:16 may be tested to see **i** you are telling the H2022
Ge 42:16 **I** you are not, then as surely as Pharaoh H561
Ge 42:19 **I** you are honest men, let one of your H561
Ge 42:37 of my sons to death **i** I do not bring him H561
Ge 42:38 **I** harm comes to him on the journey you H2256
Ge 43: 4 **I** you will send our brother along with us H561
Ge 43: 5 But **i** you will not send him, we will not go H561
Ge 43: 9 **I** I do not bring him back to you and set H561
Ge 43:10 As it is, **i** we had **not** delayed, we H3954+4295
Ge 43:11 Israel said to them, "**I** it must be, then do H561
Ge 43:14 As for me, **i** I am bereaved, I am H3869+889
Ge 44: 9 **I** any of your servants is found to have it, he NDT
Ge 44:22 leave his father; **i** he leaves him, his H2256
Ge 44:26 **Only i** our youngest brother is with us will H561
Ge 44:29 **I** you take this one from me too and harm H2256
Ge 44:30 **i** the boy is not with us when I go back to H2256
Ge 44:30 my father, and **i** my father, whose life NDT
Ge 44:32 '**I** I do not bring him back to you, H561
Ge 44:34 go back to my father **i** the boy is not with H2256
Ge 47: 6 And **i** you know of any among them with H561
Ge 47:29 "**I** I have found favor in your eyes H561
Ge 50: 4 "**I** I have found favor in your eyes H561
Ge 50:15 "**What i** Joseph holds a grudge against us H4273
Ex 1:10 more numerous and, **i** war breaks out, will H3954
Ex 1:16 **i** you see that the baby is a boy H561
Ex 1:16 is a boy, kill him; but **i** it is a girl, let her H561
Ex 4: 1 "**What i** they do not believe me or listen H2176
Ex 4: 8 "**I** they do not believe you or pay attention H561
Ex 4: 9 But **i** they do not believe these two signs H561
Ex 4:16 it will be **as i** he were your mouth H4200
Ex 4:16 your mouth and **as i** you were God to H4200
Ex 4:18 in Egypt to see **i** any of them are still H2022
Ex 6:12 "**I** the Israelites will not listen to me H2176
Ex 8: 2 **I** you refuse to let them go, I will send a H561
Ex 8:21 **I** you do not let my people go, I will H3954+561
Ex 8:26 And **i** we offer sacrifices that are H2176
Ex 9: 2 **I** you refuse to let them go and H3954+561
Ex 10: 4 **I** you refuse to let them go, I will H3954+561
Ex 10:10 LORD be with you—**i** I let you go H3869+889
Ex 12: 4 **I** any household is too small for a whole H561
Ex 12:10 it till morning; **i** some is left till morning H2256
Ex 13:13 firstborn donkey, but **i** you do not redeem it H561
Ex 13:17 For God said, "**I** they face war, they might H928
Ex 15:26 "**I** you listen carefully to the LORD your God H561
Ex 15:26 **i** you pay attention to his commands and H2256
Ex 16: 3 "**I only** we had died by the LORD's H4769+5989
Ex 18:23 **I** you do this and God so commands, you H561
Ex 19: 5 Now **i** you obey me fully and keep my H561
Ex 20:25 **I** you make an altar of stones for me, do not H561
Ex 20:25 you will defile it **i** you use a tool on it. NDT
Ex 21: 2 "**I** you buy a Hebrew servant, he is to H3954
Ex 21: 3 **I** he comes alone, he is to go free alone H561
Ex 21: 3 **but i** he has a wife when he comes H561
Ex 21: 4 **I** his master gives him a wife and she bears H561
Ex 21: 5 "But **i** the servant declares, 'I love my H561
Ex 21: 7 "**I** a man sells his daughter as a servant H3954
Ex 21: 8 **I** she does not please the master who has H561
Ex 21: 9 **I** he selects her for his son, he must grant H561
Ex 21:10 **I** he marries another woman, he must not H561
Ex 21:11 **I** he does not provide her with these three H561
Ex 21:13 However, **i** it is not done intentionally, but NDT
Ex 21:14 But **i** anyone schemes and kills someone H3954
Ex 21:18 "**I** people quarrel and one person hits H3954
Ex 21:19 not be held liable **i** the other can get up H561
Ex 21:20 must be punished **i** the slave dies as a H3954
Ex 21:21 are not to be punished **i** the slave recovers H561
Ex 21:22 "**I** people are fighting and hit a pregnant H3954
Ex 21:23 But **i** there is serious injury, you are to take H561
Ex 21:28 "**I** a bull gores a man or woman to death H3954
Ex 21:29 **I**, however, the bull has had the habit of H561
Ex 21:30 However, **i** payment is demanded, the H561
Ex 21:31 This law also applies **i** the bull gores a son H196
Ex 21:32 **I** the bull gores a male or female slave, the H561
Ex 21:33 "**I** anyone uncovers a pit or digs one and H3954
Ex 21:35 "**I** anyone's bull injures someone else's H3954
Ex 21:36 **i** it was known that the bull had the habit H196
Ex 22: 2 "**I** a thief is caught breaking in at night H561
Ex 22: 3 **but i** it happens after sunrise, the defender H561
Ex 22: 3 make restitution, **but i** they have nothing H561
Ex 22: 4 **I** the stolen animal is found alive in their H561
Ex 22: 5 "**I** anyone grazes their livestock in a field H3954
Ex 22: 6 "**I** a fire breaks out and spreads into H3954
Ex 22: 7 "**I** anyone gives a neighbor silver or goods H3954
Ex 22: 7 the thief, **i** caught, must pay back H561
Ex 22: 8 **But i** the thief is not found, the owner of the H561
Ex 22:10 "**I** anyone gives a donkey, an ox, a sheep H3954
Ex 22:12 But **i** the animal was stolen from the H561
Ex 22:13 **I** it was torn to pieces by a wild animal, the H561
Ex 22:14 "**I** anyone borrows an animal from their H3954
Ex 22:15 **But i** the owner is with the animal, the H561
Ex 22:15 **I** the animal was hired, the money paid H561
Ex 22:16 "**I** a man seduces a virgin who is not H3954
Ex 22:17 **I** her father absolutely refuses to give her to H561
Ex 22:23 **I** you do and they cry out to me, I will H561
Ex 22:25 "**I** you lend money to one of my people H561
Ex 22:26 **I** you take your neighbor's cloak as a pledge H561
Ex 23: 4 "**I** you come across your enemy's ox or H3954
Ex 23: 5 **I** you see the donkey of someone who H3954
Ex 23:22 **I** you listen carefully to what he says H3954+561
Ex 29:34 And **i** any of the meat of the ordination ram H561
Ex 32:32 their sin—but **i** not, then blot me out H561
Ex 33: 5 *I I were to* **go** with you even for a moment, AIT
Ex 33:13 **I** you are pleased with me, teach me your H561
Ex 33:15 "**I** your Presence does not go with us H561
Ex 34: 9 he said, "**I** I have found favor in your eyes H561
Ex 34:20 with a lamb, but **i** you do not redeem it H561
Ex 40:37 **i** the cloud did not lift, they did not set H561
Lev 1: 3 " '**I** the offering is a burnt offering from the H561
Lev 1:10 " '**I** the offering is a burnt offering from the H561
Lev 1:14 " '**I** the offering to the LORD is a burnt H561
Lev 2: 4 " '**I** you bring a grain offering baked in an H3954
Lev 2: 5 **I** your grain offering is prepared on a H561
Lev 2: 7 **I** your grain offering is cooked in a pan, it is H561
Lev 2:14 " '**I** you bring a grain offering of firstfruits to H561
Lev 3: 1 " '**I** your offering is a fellowship offering H561
Lev 3: 6 " '**I** you offer an animal from the flock as a H561
Lev 3: 7 **I** you offer a lamb, you are to present it H561
Lev 3:12 " '**I** your offering is a goat, you are to H561
Lev 4: 3 " '**I** the anointed priest sins, bringing guilt H561
Lev 4:13 " '**I** the whole Israelite community sins H561
Lev 4:27 " '**I** any member of the community sins H561
Lev 4:32 " '**I** someone brings a lamb as their sin H561
Lev 5: 1 " '**I** anyone sins because they do not H3954
Lev 5: 2 " '**I** anyone becomes aware that they are H889
Lev 5: 2 *i they* unwittingly **touch** anything AIT
Lev 5: 3 **i** they touch human uncleanness H3954
Lev 5: 4 **i** anyone thoughtlessly takes an oath to H3954
Lev 5:11 " 'I, however, they cannot afford two doves H561
Lev 5:17 "**I** anyone sins and does what is forbidden H561
Lev 6: 2 "**I** anyone sins and is unfaithful to the LORD H3954
Lev 6: 2 or **i** they cheat their neighbor NDT
Lev 6: 3 **i** they find lost property and lie about it, or NDT
Lev 6: 3 **i** they swear falsely about any such sin NDT
Lev 6:27 **i** any of the blood is spattered on a H889
Lev 6:28 be broken; but **i** it is cooked in a bronze pot H561
Lev 7:12 " '**I** they offer it as an expression of H561
Lev 7:16 " 'I, however, their offering is the result of a H561
Lev 7:18 **I** any meat of the fellowship offering is H561
Lev 7:20 But **i** anyone who is unclean eats any meat NDT
Lev 10:19 have been pleased **i** I had eaten the sin H2256
Lev 11:33 **I** one of them falls into a clay pot H2256
Lev 11:37 **I** a carcass falls on any seeds that are to H3954
Lev 11:38 But **i** water has been put on the seed and H3954
Lev 11:39 " '**I** an animal that you are allowed to eat H3954
Lev 12: 5 **I** she gives birth to a daughter, for two H561
Lev 12: 8 But **i** she cannot afford a lamb, she is to H561
Lev 13: 3 **i** the hair in the sore has turned white NDT
Lev 13: 4 **I** the shiny spot on the skin is white but H561
Lev 13: 5 **i** he sees that the sore is unchanged H2180
Lev 13: 6 **i** the sore has faded and has not H2180
Lev 13: 7 But **i** the rash does spread in their skin after H561
Lev 13: 8 **i** the rash has spread in the skin H2180
Lev 13:10 **i** there is a white swelling in the skin H2180
Lev 13:10 the hair white and **i** there is raw flesh in the NDT
Lev 13:12 "**I** the disease breaks out all over their skin H561
Lev 13:13 **i** the disease has covered their whole H2180
Lev 13:16 **I** the raw flesh changes and turns white H3954
Lev 13:17 and **i** the sores have turned white H2180
Lev 13:20 **i** it appears to be more than skin H2180
Lev 13:21 But **i**, when the priest examines it, there is H561
Lev 13:22 **I** it is spreading in the skin, the priest shall H561
Lev 13:23 But **i** the spot is unchanged and has not H561
Lev 13:25 and **i** the hair in it has turned white H2180
Lev 13:26 But **i** the priest examines it and there is no H561
Lev 13:26 hair in the spot and **i** it is not more than skin NDT
Lev 13:27 that person, and **i** it is spreading in the skin H561

Lev 13:28 **I**, however, the spot is unchanged and has H561
Lev 13:29 "**I** a man or woman has a sore on their H3954
Lev 13:30 **i** it appears to be more than skin H2180
Lev 13:31 But **i**, when the priest examines the sore, it NDT
Lev 13:32 **i** it has not spread and there is no H2180
Lev 13:34 **i** it has not spread in the skin and H2180
Lev 13:35 But **i** the sore does spread in the skin after H561
Lev 13:36 and **i** *he finds that* the sore has spread in H2180
Lev 13:37 **I**, however, the sore is unchanged so far as H561
Lev 13:37 can see, and **i** black hair has grown in it NDT
Lev 13:39 and **i** the spots are dull white H2180
Lev 13:41 **I** he has lost his hair from the front of his H561
Lev 13:42 But **i** he has a reddish-white sore on his H3954
Lev 13:43 **i** the swollen sore on his head or H2180
Lev 13:49 **i** the affected area in the fabric, the H2256
Lev 13:51 and **i** the mold has spread in the fabric H3954
Lev 13:53 "But **i**, when the priest examines it, the H561
Lev 13:55 **i** the mold has not changed its H2180
Lev 13:56 **I**, when the priest examines it, the mold has H561
Lev 13:57 But **i** it reappears in the fabric, in the woven H561
Lev 14: 3 **I** they have been healed of their defiling H2180
Lev 14:21 "**I**, however, they are poor and cannot H561
Lev 14:37 **i** it has greenish or reddish H2180
Lev 14:39 **I** the mold has spread on the walls, H2180
Lev 14:43 "**I** the defiling mold reappears in the house H561
Lev 14:44 **i** the mold has spread in the house H2180
Lev 14:48 "But **i** the priest comes to examine it and H561
Lev 15: 8 " '**I** the man with the discharge spits on H3954
Lev 15:24 " '**I** a man has sexual relations with her H561
Lev 17:16 But **i** they do not wash their clothes and H561
Lev 18:28 And **i** you defile the land, it will vomit you H928
Lev 19: 7 **I** any of it is eaten on the third day, it is H561
Lev 19:20 " '**I** a man sleeps with a female slave who H3954
Lev 20: 4 **I** the members of the community close their H561
Lev 20: 4 children to Molek and **i** they fail to put him NDT
Lev 20:10 " '**I** a man commits adultery with another H2256
Lev 20:11 " '**I** a man has sexual relations with his H2256
Lev 20:12 " '**I** a man has sexual relations with his H2256
Lev 20:13 " '**I** a man has sexual relations with a H2256
Lev 20:14 " '**I** a man marries both a woman and her H2256
Lev 20:15 " '**I** a man has sexual relations with an H2256
Lev 20:16 " '**I** a woman approaches an animal to H2256
Lev 20:17 " '**I** a man marries his sister, the daughter H2256
Lev 20:18 " '**I** a man has sexual relations with a H2256
Lev 20:20 " '**I** a man has sexual relations with his H2256
Lev 20:21 " '**I** a man marries his brother's wife, it is H2256
Lev 21: 9 " '**I** a priest's daughter defiles herself by H3954
Lev 22: 3 **i** any of your descendants is ceremonially H889
Lev 22: 4 " '**I** a descendant of Aaron has a defiling NDT
Lev 22: 4 will also be unclean **i** he touches something NDT
Lev 22: 5 **i** he touches any crawling thing that NDT
Lev 22:11 But **i** a priest buys a slave with money, or if H3954
Lev 22:11 or **i** slaves are born in his household NDT
Lev 22:12 **I** a priest's daughter marries anyone other H3954
Lev 22:13 But **i** a priest's daughter becomes a widow H3954
Lev 22:18 '**I** any of you—whether an Israelite or a H889
Lev 25:14 " '**I** you sell land to any of your own H3954
Lev 25:20 in the seventh year **i** we do not plant or H2176
Lev 25:25 " '**I** one of your fellow Israelites becomes H3954
Lev 25:26 **I**, however, there is no one to redeem it H3954
Lev 25:28 But **i** they do not acquire the means to H561
Lev 25:30 **I** it is not redeemed before a full year has H561
Lev 25:35 " '**I** any of your fellow Israelites become H3954
Lev 25:39 " '**I** any of your fellow Israelites become H3954
Lev 25:47 " '**I** a foreigner residing among you H3954
Lev 25:49 Or **i** they prosper, they may redeem NDT
Lev 25:51 **I** many years remain, they must pay for their H561
Lev 25:52 **I** only a few years remain until the Year of H561
Lev 25:54 " 'Even **i** someone is not redeemed in any H561
Lev 26: 3 " '**I** you follow my decrees and are careful H561
Lev 26:14 " 'But **i** you will not listen to me and carry H561
Lev 26:15 **i** you reject my decrees and abhor my H561
Lev 26:18 " '**I** after all this you will not listen to me, H561
Lev 26:21 " '**I** you remain hostile toward me and H561
Lev 26:23 " '**I** in spite of these things you do not H561
Lev 26:27 " '**I** in spite of this you still do not listen to H561
Lev 26:40 " 'But **i** they will confess their sins and the NDT
Lev 27: 2 '**I** anyone makes a special vow to H3954
Lev 27: 8 **I** anyone making the vow is too poor to pay H561
Lev 27: 9 " '**I** what they vowed is an animal that is H561
Lev 27:10 **i** they should substitute one animal for H561
Lev 27:11 **I** what they vowed is a ceremonially H561
Lev 27:13 **I** the owner wishes to redeem the animal, H561
Lev 27:14 " '**I** anyone dedicates their house as H3954
Lev 27:15 **I** the one who dedicates their house wishes H561
Lev 27:16 " '**I** anyone dedicates to the LORD part of H561
Lev 27:17 **I** they dedicate a field during the Year of H561
Lev 27:18 But **i** they dedicate a field after the Jubilee H561
Lev 27:19 **I** the one who dedicates the field wishes to H561
Lev 27:20 **I**, however, they do not redeem the field, or H561
Lev 27:20 or **i** they have sold it to someone else H561
Lev 27:22 " '**I** anyone dedicates to the LORD a field H561
Lev 27:27 **I** it is one of the unclean animals, it may be H561
Lev 27:27 **I** it is not redeemed, it is to be sold at its H561
Lev 27:33 **I** anyone does make a substitution, both H561
Nu 5: 8 But **i** that person has no close relative to H561
Nu 5:12 '**I** a man's wife goes astray and is H3954
Nu 5:14 **i** feelings of jealousy come over her H561
Nu 5:14 **i** he is jealous and suspects her even NDT
Nu 5:19 "**I** no other man has had sexual relations H561
Nu 5:20 But **i** you have gone astray while married H3954
Nu 5:27 **I** she has made herself impure and been H561
Nu 5:28 **I**, however, the woman has not made H561
Nu 6: 2 "**I** a man or woman wants to make a H3954
Nu 6: 7 **Even i** their own father or mother or brother H928
Nu 6: 9 " '**I** someone dies suddenly in the H3954
Nu 9:13 But **i** anyone who is ceremonially clean and NDT
Nu 10: 4 **I** only one is sounded, the leaders—the H561
Nu 10:32 **I** you come with us, we will share with you H3954
Nu 11: 4 said, "**I only** we had meat to eat! H4769
Nu 11:15 **I** this is how you are going to treat me H561
Nu 11:15 kill me—**i** I have found favor in your eyes H561
Nu 11:18 you wailed, "**I only** we had meat to eat! H4769
Nu 11:22 they have enough **i** flocks and herds were H2022
Nu 11:22 they have enough **i** all the fish in the H561
Nu 12:14 to Moses, "**I** her father had spit in her face H2256
Nu 14: 2 to them, "**I only** we had died in Egypt! H4273
Nu 14: 8 **I** the LORD is pleased with us, he will lead us H561
Nu 14:15 **I** you put all these people to death H2256
Nu 15:22 " 'Now **i** you as a community H3954
Nu 15:24 **i** this is done unintentionally without H561
Nu 15:27 " 'But **i** just one person sins unintentionally, H561
Nu 16:29 **I** these men die a natural death and suffer H561
Nu 16:30 But **i** the LORD brings about something H561
Nu 19:12 But **i** they do not purify themselves on the H561
Nu 19:13 **I** they fail to purify themselves after H2256
Nu 19:20 But **i** those who are unclean do not purify H2256
Nu 20: 3 "**I only** we had died when our brothers fell H4273
Nu 20:18 pass through here; **i** you try, we will march H7153
Nu 20:19 **i** we or our livestock drink any of your H561
Nu 21: 2 "**I** you will deliver these people into our H561
Nu 22:18 "**Even i** Balak gave me all the silver and H561
Nu 22:29 **I only** I had a sword in my hand, I would H4273
Nu 22:33 **I** it had **not** turned away, I would certainly H218
Nu 22:34 to oppose me. Now **i** you are displeased, H561
Nu 24:13 '**Even i** Balak gave me all the silver and H561
Nu 27: 8 '**I** a man dies and leaves no son H3954
Nu 27: 9 **I** he has no daughter, give his inheritance H561
Nu 27:10 **I** he has no brothers, give his inheritance to H561
Nu 27:11 **I** his father had no brothers, give his H561
Nu 30: 5 But **i** her father forbids her when he hears H561
Nu 30: 6 "**I** she marries after she makes a vow or H561
Nu 30: 8 But **i** her husband forbids her when he H561
Nu 30:10 "**I** a woman living with her husband makes H561
Nu 30:12 But **i** her husband nullifies them when he H561
Nu 30:14 But **i** her husband says nothing to her about H561
Nu 30:15 **I**, however, he nullifies them some time H561
Nu 32: 5 **I** we have found favor in your eyes," they H561
Nu 32:15 **I** you turn away from following him, he will H3954
Nu 32:20 Moses said to them, "**I** you will do this—if H561
Nu 32:20 **i** you will arm yourselves before the LORD H561
Nu 32:21 **i** all of you who are armed cross over the NDT
Nu 32:23 "But **i** you fail to do this, you will be H561
Nu 32:29 to them, "**I** the Gadites and Reubenites H561
Nu 32:30 But **i** they do not cross over with you armed H561
Nu 33:55 " 'But **i** you do not drive out the inhabitants H561
Nu 35:16 " '**I** anyone strikes someone a fatal blow H561
Nu 35:17 Or **i** anyone is holding a stone and strikes H561
Nu 35:18 Or **i** anyone is holding a wooden object and NDT
Nu 35:20 **I** anyone with malice aforethought shoves H561
Nu 35:21 **i** out of enmity one person hits another NDT
Nu 35:22 " 'But **i** without enmity someone suddenly H561
Nu 35:26 " 'But **i** the accused ever goes outside the H561
Dt 4:25 **i** you **then** become corrupt and make any H2256
Dt 4:29 But **i** from there you seek the LORD your God NDT
Dt 4:29 you will find him **i** you seek him with all H3954
Dt 4:42 a person could flee **i** they had NDT
Dt 5:24 can live even **i** God speaks with them NDT
Dt 5:25 we will die **i** we hear the voice of the H561
Dt 6:25 And **i** we are careful to obey all this law H3954
Dt 7:12 **I** you pay attention to these laws and are H6813
Dt 8:19 **I** you ever forget the LORD your God and H561
Dt 11:13 So **i** you faithfully obey the commands I am H561
Dt 11:22 **I** you carefully observe all these commands H561
Dt 11:27 the blessing **i** you obey the commands of H889
Dt 11:28 the curse **i** you disobey the commands of H561
Dt 12:15 as you want, **as i** it were gazelle or deer H3869
Dt 12:21 **I** the place where the LORD your God H3954
Dt 13: 1 **I** a prophet, or one who foretells by H3954
Dt 13: 2 **i** the sign or wonder spoken of takes NDT
Dt 13: 6 **I** your very own brother, or your son or H3954
Dt 13:12 **I** you hear it said about one of the towns H3954
Dt 13:14 And **i** it is true and it has been proved H2180
Dt 14:24 But **i** that place is too distant and you have H3954
Dt 15: 5 **i** only you fully obey the LORD your God H561
Dt 15: 7 **I** anyone is poor among your fellow H3954
Dt 15:12 **I** any of your people—Hebrew men or H3954
Dt 15:16 But **i** your servant says to you, "I do not H3954
Dt 15:21 **I** an animal has a defect, is lame or blind H3954
Dt 15:22 may eat it, **as i** it were gazelle or deer. H3869
Dt 17: 2 **I** a man or woman living among you in H3954
Dt 17: 4 **I** it is true and it has been proved that this H2180
Dt 17: 8 **I** cases come before your courts that are H3954
Dt 18: 6 **I** a Levite moves from one of your towns H3954
Dt 18:22 **I** what a prophet proclaims in the name of H2256
Dt 19: 6 overtake him **i** the distance is too great H3954
Dt 19: 8 **I** the LORD your God enlarges your territory H561
Dt 19:11 But **i** out of hate someone lies in wait H3954
Dt 19:16 **I** a malicious witness takes the stand to H3954
Dt 19:18 **i** the witness proves to be a liar H2180
Dt 20:11 **I** they accept and open their gates, all the H561
Dt 20:12 **I** they refuse to make peace and they H561
Dt 21: 1 **I** someone is found slain, lying in a field H3954
Dt 21:11 **i** you notice among the captives a H2256
Dt 21:14 **I** you are not pleased with her, let her go H561
Dt 21:15 **I** a man has two wives, and he loves one H3954
Dt 21:18 **I** someone has a stubborn and rebellious H3954
Dt 21:22 **I** someone guilty of a capital offense is H3954
Dt 22: 1 **I** you see your fellow Israelite's ox or sheep NDT
Dt 22: 2 **I** they do not live near you or if you do not H561
Dt 22: 2 not live near you or **i** you do not know who NDT
Dt 22: 3 Do the same **i** you find their donkey or cloak NDT
Dt 22: 4 **I** you see your fellow Israelite's donkey or ox NDT
Dt 22: 6 **I** you come across a bird's nest beside the H3954
Dt 22: 8 on your house **i** someone falls from the H3954
Dt 22: 9 in your vineyard; **i** you do, not only the H7153
Dt 22:13 **I** a man takes a wife and, after sleeping H3954
Dt 22:20 **I**, however, the charge is true and no proof H561
Dt 22:22 **I** a man is found sleeping with another H3954
Dt 22:23 **I** a man happens to meet in a town a H3954
Dt 22:25 But **i** out in the country a man happens to H561
Dt 22:28 **I** a man happens to meet a virgin who is H3954
Dt 23:10 **I** one of your men is unclean because of a H3954
Dt 23:15 **I** a slave has taken refuge with you, do not H889
Dt 23:21 **I** you make a vow to the LORD your God, H3954
Dt 23:22 But **i** you refrain from making a vow, you H3954
Dt 23:24 **I** you enter your neighbor's vineyard, you H3954
Dt 23:25 **I** you enter your neighbor's grainfield, you H3954
Dt 24: 1 **I** a man marries a woman who becomes H3954
Dt 24: 2 **i** after she leaves his house she NDT
Dt 24: 3 sends her from his house, or **i** he dies, H3954
Dt 24: 5 **I** a man has recently married, he must not H3954
Dt 24: 7 **I** someone is caught kidnapping a fellow H3954
Dt 24:12 **I** the neighbor is poor, do not go to sleep H561
Dt 25: 2 **I** the guilty person deserves to be beaten H561
Dt 25: 3 **I** the guilty party is flogged more than that H7153
Dt 25: 5 **I** brothers are living together and one of H3954
Dt 25: 7 **i** a man does not want to marry his H561
Dt 25: 8 **I** he persists in saying, "I do not want to H2256
Dt 25:11 **I** two men are fighting and the wife of H3954
Dt 28: 1 **I** you fully obey the LORD your God and H561
Dt 28: 2 accompany you **i** you obey the LORD H3954
Dt 28: 9 **i** you keep the commands of the LORD your H3954
Dt 28:13 **I** you pay attention to the commands of H3954
Dt 28:15 **i** you do not obey the LORD your God and do H561
Dt 28:58 **I** you do not carefully follow all the words H561
Dt 28:67 will say, "**I only** it were evening!" H4769+5989
Dt 28:67 evening, "**I only** it were morning!" H4769+5989
Dt 30: 4 **Even i** you have been banished to the most H561
Dt 30:10 **i** you obey the LORD your God and keep his H3954
Dt 30:17 But **i** your heart turns away and you are not H561
Dt 30:17 **i** you are drawn away to bow down to NDT
Dt 31:27 **I** you have been rebellious against the H2176
Dt 32:29 **I only** they were wise and would H4273
Jos 2:14 "**I** you don't tell what we are doing, we will H561
Jos 2:19 **I** any of them go outside your house into H889
Jos 2:19 will be on our head **i** a hand is laid on H561
Jos 2:20 But **i** you tell what we are doing, we will be H561
Jos 7: 7 **I only** we had been content to stay on the H4273
Jos 17:15 "**I** you are so numerous," Joshua answered H561
Jos 17:15 "and **i** the hill country of Ephraim is too H3954
Jos 20: 5 **I** the avenger of blood comes in pursuit H3954
Jos 22:18 " '**I** you rebel against the LORD today H2256
Jos 22:19 **I** the land you possess is defiled, come over H561
Jos 22:22 **I** this has been in rebellion or H561
Jos 22:23 **I** we have built our own altar to turn away H561
Jos 22:28 "And we said, '**I** they ever say this to us H3954
Jos 23:12 "But **i** you turn away and ally yourselves H561
Jos 23:12 remain among you and **i** you intermarry with NDT
Jos 23:16 **I** you violate the covenant of the LORD your H928
Jos 24:15 But **i** serving the LORD seems undesirable to H561
Jos 24:20 **I** you forsake the LORD and serve foreign H3954
Jos 24:27 a witness against you **i** you are untrue to H7153
Jdg 4: 8 Barak said to her, "**I** you go with me, I will H561
Jdg 4: 8 I will go; but **i** you don't go with me, H561
Jdg 4:20 "**I** someone comes by and asks you, 'Is H561
Jdg 6:13 Gideon replied, "**but i** the LORD is with us H2256
Jdg 6:17 "**I** now I have found favor in your eyes H561
Jdg 6:31 **I** Baal really is a god, he can defend H561
Jdg 6:36 "**I** you will save Israel by my hand as you H561
Jdg 6:37 **I** there is dew only on the fleece and all H561
Jdg 7: 4 **I** I say, 'This one shall go with you,' he H889
Jdg 7: 4 he shall go; but **i** I say, 'This one shall not H889
Jdg 7:10 **I** you are afraid to attack, go down to the H561
Jdg 8:19 the LORD lives, **i** you had spared their lives H4273
Jdg 9:15 '**I** you really want to anoint me king over H561
Jdg 9:15 in my shade; but **i** not, then let fire come H561
Jdg 9:19 **I** you have, may Abimelek be your joy, and H561
Jdg 9:20 But **i** you have not, let fire come out from H561
Jdg 9:29 **I only** this people were under my H4769+5989
Jdg 11:30 "**I** you give the Ammonites into my hands H561
Jdg 12: 5 you an Ephraimite?" **I** he replied, "No," H2256
Jdg 12: 6 **I** he said, "Sibboleth," because he H2256
Jdg 13:16 But **i** you prepare a burnt offering, offer it to H561
Jdg 13:23 answered, "**I** the LORD had meant to kill us H4273
Jdg 14:12 "**I** you can give me the answer within the H561
Jdg 14:13 **I** you can't tell me the answer, you must H561
Jdg 14:18 "**I** you had **not** plowed with my heifer H4295
Jdg 16: 5 "*See i you can* **lure** him *into* showing you the AIT
Jdg 16: 7 "**I** anyone ties me with seven fresh H561
Jdg 16:11 "**I** anyone ties me securely with new ropes H561
Jdg 16:12 ropes off his arms **as i** they were threads. H3869
Jdg 16:13 "**I** you weave the seven braids of my head H561
Jdg 16:17 **I** my head were shaved, my strength would H561
Ru 1:12 **Even i** I thought there was still hope for H3954
Ru 1:12 even **i** I had a husband tonight and then NDT

Ru 1:17 i even death separates you and me." H3954
Ru 3:13 in the morning i he wants to do his H561
Ru 3:13 But i he is not willing, as surely as the LORD H561
Ru 4: 4 elders of my people. I you will redeem it H561
Ru 4: 4 But i you will not, tell me, so I will H561
1Sa 1:11 i you will only look on your servant's misery H561
1Sa 2:16 I the person said to him, "Let the fat be H2256
1Sa 2:16 hand it over now; i you don't, I'll take it by H561
1Sa 2:25 I one person sins against another, God may H561
1Sa 2:25 offender; but i anyone sins against the LORD H561
1Sa 3: 9 "Go and lie down, and i he calls you, say H561
1Sa 3:17 i you hide from me anything he told you." H561
1Sa 6: 3 "I you return the ark of the god of Israel H561
1Sa 6: 9 I it goes up to its own territory, toward Beth H561
1Sa 6: 9 But i it does not, then we will know that it H561
1Sa 7: 3 "I you are returning to the LORD with all H561
1Sa 9: 7 said to his servant, "I we go, what can we H2180
1Sa 9: 9 in Israel, i someone went to inquire of God H928
1Sa 9:20 i not to you and your whole family line?" H2022
1Sa 11: 3 i no one comes to rescue us H561
1Sa 12: 3 I I have done any of these things, I will NDT
1Sa 12:14 I you fear the LORD and serve and obey him H561
1Sa 12:14 i both you and the king who reigns over NDT
1Sa 12:15 But i you do not obey the LORD, and if you H561
1Sa 12:15 and i you rebel against his commands NDT
1Sa 12:25 Yet i you persist in doing evil, both you H561
1Sa 13:13 your God gave you; i you had, he would H3954
1Sa 14: 9 I they say to us, 'Wait there until we come H561
1Sa 14:10 But i they say, 'Come up to us,' we will H561
1Sa 14:30 it would have been i the men had eaten H4273
1Sa 14:39 even i the guilt lies with my son Jonathan H561
1Sa 14:41 I the fault is in me or my son Jonathan H561
1Sa 14:41 but i the men of Israel are at fault H561
1Sa 14:44 so severely, i you do not die, Jonathan." H3954
1Sa 16: 2 "How can I go? I Saul hears about it, he H2256
1Sa 17: 9 I he is able to fight and kill me, we will H561
1Sa 17: 9 subjects; but i I overcome him and kill him H561
1Sa 19:11 "I you don't run for your life tonight H561
1Sa 20: 6 I your father misses me at all, tell him H561
1Sa 20: 7 I he says, 'Very well,' then your servant is H561
1Sa 20: 7 But i he loses his temper, you can be sure H561
1Sa 20: 8 you before the LORD. I I am guilty, then kill H561
1Sa 20: 9 "I I had the least inkling that my H3954+561
1Sa 20:10 "Who will tell me i your father H196+4537
1Sa 20:12 I he is favorably disposed toward you, will H2180
1Sa 20:13 But i my father intends to harm you, may H3954
1Sa 20:13 i I do not let you know and send you away H2256
1Sa 20:21 I I say to him, 'Look, the arrows are on this H561
1Sa 20:22 But i I say to the boy, 'Look, the arrows are H561
1Sa 20:29 I I have found favor in your eyes, let me get H561
1Sa 21: 9 I you want it, take it; there is no sword here H561
1Sa 23: 3 i we go to Keilah against the Philistine H3954
1Sa 23:23 I will go with you; i he is in the area, H561
1Sa 25:22 i by morning I leave alive one male of all H561
1Sa 25:34 i you had not come quickly to meet H3954+4295
1Sa 26:19 I the LORD has incited you against me, then H561
1Sa 26:19 I, however, people have done it, may they H561
1Sa 27: 5 to Achish, "I I have found favor in your eyes H561
2Sa 2:27 God lives, i you had not spoken H3954+4295
2Sa 3: 9 i I do not do for David what the LORD H3954
2Sa 3:27 chamber, as i to speak with him privately. NDT
2Sa 3:35 i I taste bread or anything else H3954+561
2Sa 4: 6 part of the house as i to get some wheat, NDT
2Sa 7:19 And as i this were not enough in your sight NDT
2Sa 10:11 "I the Arameans are too strong for me H561
2Sa 10:11 i the Ammonites are too strong for you H561
2Sa 11:21 I he asks you this, then say to him NDT
2Sa 12: 8 And i all this had been too little, I would H561
2Sa 13:26 Then Absalom said, "I not, please let my H2256
2Sa 14:10 king replied, "I anyone says anything to you NDT
2Sa 14:32 It would be better for me i I were still there!" NDT
2Sa 14:32 king's face, and i I am guilty of anything H561
2Sa 15: 4 "I only I were appointed judge in the land H4769
2Sa 15: 8 'I the LORD takes me back to Jerusalem, H561
2Sa 15:25 I I find favor in the LORD's eyes, he will H561
2Sa 15:26 But i he says, 'I am not pleased with you,' H561
2Sa 15:33 David said to him, "I you go with me, you H561
2Sa 15:34 But i you return to the city and say to H561
2Sa 16:10 I he is cursing because the LORD said to H3954
2Sa 16:17 I he's your friend, why didn't you go with NDT
2Sa 17: 6 we do what he says? I not, give us your H561
2Sa 17: 9 I he should attack your troops first H3869
2Sa 17:13 I he withdraws into a city, then all Israel will H561
2Sa 18: 3 not go out; i we are forced to flee H3954+561
2Sa 18: 3 Even i half of us die, they won't care; but H561
2Sa 18:12 "Even i a thousand shekels were weighed H4273
2Sa 18:13 And i I had put my life in jeopardy—and H196
2Sa 18:25 The king said, "I he is alone, he must have H561
2Sa 18:33 I only I had died instead of you—O H4769+5989
2Sa 19: 6 would be pleased i Absalom were alive H4273
2Sa 19: 7 I swear by the LORD that i you don't go out H3954
2Sa 19:13 i you are not the commander of my army H561
2Sa 23: 5 "I my house were not right with God H3954
1Ki 1:52 "I he shows himself to be worthy H561
1Ki 1:52 fall to the ground; but i evil is found in him H561
1Ki 2: 4 'I your descendants watch how they live H561
1Ki 2: 4 i they walk faithfully before me with all NDT
1Ki 2: 5 their blood in peacetime as i in battle, AIT
1Ki 2:23 i Adonijah does not pay with his life for H3954
1Ki 3:14 And i you walk in obedience to me and H561
1Ki 6:12 you are building, i you follow my decrees H561
1Ki 8:25 i only your descendants are careful in all H561
1Ki 8:47 i they have a change of heart in the NDT
1Ki 8:48 i they turn back to you with all their NDT
1Ki 9: 4 i you walk before me faithfully with H561
1Ki 9: 6 "But i you or your descendants turn away H561
1Ki 11:38 I I you do whatever I command you and walk H561
1Ki 12: 7 "I today you will be a servant to these H561
1Ki 12:27 I these people go up to offer sacrifices at H561
1Ki 13: 8 "Even i you were to give me half your H561
1Ki 18:12 I I go and tell Ahab and he doesn't find H2256
1Ki 18:21 I the LORD is God, follow him; but if Baal is H561
1Ki 18:21 follow him; but i Baal is God, follow H561
1Ki 19: 2 i by this time tomorrow I do not make your H3954
1Ki 20:10 i enough dust remains in Samaria to give H561
1Ki 20:18 He said, "I they have come out for peace H561
1Ki 20:18 them alive; i they have come out for war H561
1Ki 20:23 But i we fight them on the plains, surely we H219
1Ki 20:39 I he is missing, it will be your life for his H561
1Ki 21: 2 a better vineyard or, i you prefer, I will pay H561
1Ki 21: 6 me your vineyard; or i you prefer, I will give H561
1Ki 22:28 Micaiah declared, "I you ever return safely H561
2Ki 1: 2 to see i I will recover from this injury." H561
2Ki 1:10 the captain, "I I am a man of God, may H561
2Ki 1:12 "I I am a man of God," Elijah replied, "may H561
2Ki 2:10 "yet i you see me when I am taken from H561
2Ki 3:14 i I did not have respect for the H3954+4295
2Ki 4:29 you meet, and i anyone greets you H3954
2Ki 5: 3 "I only my master would see the prophet H332
2Ki 5:13 i the prophet had told you to do some H2022
2Ki 5:17 "I you will not," said Naaman, "please let H2256
2Ki 6:27 king replied, "I the LORD does not help you NDT
2Ki 6:31 i the head of Elisha son of Shaphat H561
2Ki 7: 2 *even i* the LORD *should* open the floodgates AIT
2Ki 7: 4 I we say, 'We'll go into the city'—the H561
2Ki 7: 4 we will die. And i we stay here, we H561
2Ki 7: 4 I they spare us, we live; if they kill us, then H561
2Ki 7: 4 spare us, we live; i they kill us, then we H561
2Ki 7: 9 I we wait until daylight, punishment will H2256
2Ki 7:19 *even i* the LORD *should* open the floodgates AIT
2Ki 9:15 Jehu said, "I you desire to make me king H561
2Ki 10: 4 said, "I two kings could not resist him H2180
2Ki 10: 6 "I you are on my side and will obey me H561
2Ki 10:15 Jehonadab answered. "I so," said Jehu H2256
2Ki 10:24 "I one of you lets any of the men I am H561
2Ki 18:22 But i you say to me, "We are depending H3954
2Ki 18:23 horses—i you can put riders on them! H561
2Ki 21: 8 i only they will be careful to do everything I H561
1Ch 12:17 "I you have come to me in peace to help H561
1Ch 12:17 But i you have come to betray me to my H561
1Ch 12:19 cost us our heads *i he* deserts to his master AIT
1Ch 13: 2 "I it seems good to you and if it is the will H561
1Ch 13: 2 seems good to you and i it is the will of the NDT
1Ch 17:17 And as i this were not enough in your sight NDT
1Ch 19:12 "I the Arameans are too strong for me H561
1Ch 19:12 i the Ammonites are too strong for you H561
1Ch 22:13 you will have success i you are careful to H561
1Ch 28: 7 his kingdom forever i he is unswerving in H561
1Ch 28: 9 I you seek him, he will be found by you H561
1Ch 28: 9 be found by you; but i you forsake him, he H561
2Ch 6:16 i only your descendants are careful in all H561
2Ch 6:37 i they have a change of heart in the NDT
2Ch 6:38 i they turn back to you with all their NDT
2Ch 7:14 i my people, who are called by my name H2256
2Ch 7:17 i you walk before me faithfully as David H561
2Ch 7:19 "But i you turn away and forsake the H561
2Ch 10: 7 "I you will be kind to these people and H561
2Ch 15: 2 I you seek him, he will be found by you H561
2Ch 15: 2 be found by you, but i you forsake him, he H561
2Ch 18:27 Micaiah declared, "I you ever return safely H561
2Ch 20: 9 "I calamity comes upon us, whether the H561
2Ch 25: 8 Even i you go and fight courageously in H561
2Ch 30: 9 I you return to the LORD, then your fellow H3954
2Ch 30: 9 turn his face from you i you return to him." H561
2Ch 30:19 even i they are not clean according to the H2256
2Ch 33: 8 i only they will be careful to do everything I H561
Ezr 4:13 king should know that i this city is built A10213
Ezr 4:16 inform the king that i this city is built A10213
Ezr 5:17 Now i it pleases the king, let a search be A10213
Ezr 5:17 of Babylon to see i King Cyrus did in fact A10213
Ezr 6:11 I decree that i anyone defies this edict A10168
Ne 1: 8 'I you are unfaithful, I will scatter NDT
Ne 1: 9 i you return to me and obey my NDT
Ne 1: 9 then even i your exiled people are at the H561
Ne 2: 5 "I it pleases the king and if your servant H561
Ne 2: 5 pleases the king and i your servant has H561
Ne 2: 7 I also said to him, "I it pleases the king H561
Ne 13:21 the night by the wall? I you do this again, H561
Est 1:19 "Therefore, i it pleases the king, let him H561
Est 3: 9 I it pleases the king, let a decree be issued H561
Est 4:14 For i you remain silent at this time, relief H561
Est 4:16 And i I perish, I perish." H3869+889
Est 5: 4 "I it pleases the king," replied Esther, "let H561
Est 5: 8 I the king regards me with favor and if it H561
Est 5: 8 me with favor and i it pleases the king to H561
Est 7: 3 answered, "I I have found favor with you H561
Est 7: 3 Your Majesty, and i it pleases you, grant H561
Est 7: 4 I we had merely been sold as male and H467
Est 8: 5 "I it pleases the king," she said, "and if he H561
Est 8: 5 "and i he regards me with favor and thinks H561
Est 8: 5 thing to do, and i he is pleased with me NDT
Est 9:13 "I it pleases the king," Esther answered H561
Job 4: 2 "I someone ventures a word with you, will H2022
Job 4:18 I God places no trust in his servants, if he H2176
Job 4:18 servants, i he charges his angels with error, NDT
Job 5: 1 "Call i you will, but who will answer you H5528
Job 5: 8 "But i I were you, I would appeal to God; H219
Job 6: 2 "I only my anguish could be weighed H4273
Job 7:20 I I have sinned, what have I done to you NDT
Job 8: 5 But i you will seek God earnestly and plead H561
Job 8: 6 i you are pure and upright, even now he H561
Job 9:12 I he snatches away, who can stop him H2176
Job 9:16 Even i I summoned him and he responded H561
Job 9:19 I it is a matter of strength, he is mighty H561
Job 9:19 And i it is a matter of justice, who can H561
Job 9:20 Even i I were innocent, my mouth would H561
Job 9:20 would condemn me; i I were blameless, it NDT
Job 9:24 I it is not he, then who H561
Job 9:27 I I say, 'I will forget my complaint, I will H561
Job 9:30 Even i I washed myself with soap and my H561
Job 9:33 I only there were someone to mediate H4273
Job 10:14 I I sinned, you would be watching me and H561
Job 10:15 I I am guilty—woe to me! Even if I am H561
Job 10:15 Even i I am innocent, I cannot lift my H2256
Job 10:16 I I hold my head high, you stalk me like a H2256
Job 10:19 I only I had never come into being H3869+889
Job 11:10 "I he comes along and confines you in H561
Job 11:13 "Yet i you devote your heart to him and H561
Job 11:14 i you put away the sin that is in your hand H561
Job 12:15 I he holds back the waters, there is H2176
Job 12:15 there is drought; i he lets them loose H2256
Job 13: 5 I only you would be altogether H4769+5989
Job 13: 9 Would it turn out well i he examined you H3954
Job 13:10 call you to account i you secretly showed H561
Job 13:19 against me? I so, I will be silent H3954+6964
Job 14: 7 I it is cut down, it will sprout again, and its H561
Job 14:13 "I only you would hide me in the H4769+5989
Job 14:13 I only you would set me a time and then NDT
Job 14:14 I someone dies, will they live again? All H561
Job 14:21 I their children are honored, they do not NDT
Job 14:21 know it; i their offspring are brought low H2256
Job 15:15 I God places no trust in his holy ones, if H2176
Job 15:15 i even the heavens are not pure in his eyes, NDT
Job 16: 4 speak like you, i you were in my place H4273
Job 16: 6 "Yet i I speak, my pain is not relieved; and H561
Job 16: 6 is not relieved; and i I refrain, it does not go NDT
Job 17: 5 I anyone denounces their friends for reward NDT
Job 17:13 I the only home I hope for is the grave, if I H561
Job 17:13 i I spread out my bed in the realm of NDT
Job 17:14 i I say to corruption, 'You are my father,' NDT
Job 19: 4 I it is true that I have gone astray, my error H677
Job 19: 5 I indeed you would exalt yourselves above H561
Job 19:28 "I you say, 'How we will hound him, since H3954
Job 22: 3 it give the Almighty i you were righteous? H3954
Job 22: 3 What would he gain i your ways were H3954
Job 22:23 I you return to the Almighty, you will be H561
Job 22:23 I you remove wickedness far from your tent NDT
Job 23: 3 I only I knew where to find him; if H4769+5989
Job 23: 3 to find him; i only I could go to his dwelling! NDT
Job 23: 8 "But i I go to the east, he is not there; if I H2176
Job 23: 8 he is not there; i I go to the west, I do not H2256
Job 24:25 "I this is not so, who can prove me false H561
Job 25: 5 I even the moon is not bright and the H2176
Job 30: 5 shouted at as i they were thieves. H3869
Job 31: 5 "I I have walked with falsehood or my foot H561
Job 31: 7 i my steps have turned from the path, if my H561
Job 31: 7 i my heart has been led by my eyes H2256
Job 31: 7 my eyes, or i my hands have been defiled, NDT
Job 31: 9 "I my heart has been enticed by a woman H561
Job 31: 9 i I have lurked at my neighbor's door NDT
Job 31:13 "I I have denied justice to any of my H561
Job 31:16 "I I have denied the desires of the poor H561
Job 31:17 i I have kept my bread to myself, not H2256
Job 31:19 i I have seen anyone perishing for lack of H561
Job 31:21 i I have raised my hand against the H561
Job 31:24 "I I have put my trust in gold or said to pure H561
Job 31:25 i I have rejoiced over my great wealth, the H561
Job 31:26 i I have regarded the sun in its radiance H561
Job 31:29 "I I have rejoiced at my enemy's misfortune H561
Job 31:31 i those of my household have never said H561
Job 31:33 i I have concealed my sin as people do, by H561
Job 31:38 "i my land cries out against me and all its H561
Job 31:39 i I have devoured its yield without payment H561
Job 32:22 i I were skilled in flattery, my Maker H4202
Job 33: 5 Answer me then, i you can; stand up and H561
Job 33:23 Yet i there is an angel at their side, H561
Job 33:32 I you have anything to say, answer me H561
Job 33:33 But i not, then listen to me; be silent, and I H561
Job 34:14 I it were his intention and he withdrew his H561
Job 34:16 "I you have understanding, hear this; listen H561
Job 34:29 But i he remains silent, who can condemn NDT
Job 34:29 can condemn him? I he hides his face H2256
Job 34:32 what I cannot see; i I have done wrong, H561
Job 35: 6 I you sin, how does that affect him? If your H561
Job 35: 6 I your sins are many, what does that do to H2256
Job 35: 7 I you are righteous, what do you give to H561
Job 36: 8 But i people are bound in chains, held fast H561
Job 36:11 I they obey and serve him, they will spend H561
Job 36:12 But i they do not listen, they will perish by H561
Job 38: 4 Tell me, i you understand. H561
Job 38:18 Tell me, i you know all this. H561
Job 39:16 her young harshly, as i they were not hers H4200
Job 41: 8 I you lay a hand on it, you will remember NDT
Ps 7: 3 i I have done this and there is guilt on my H561
Ps 7: 4 i I have repaid my ally with evil or without H561
Ps 7:12 I he does not relent, he will sharpen his H561

Ps 14: 2 on all mankind to see i there are any who H2022
Ps 28: 1 For i you remain silent, I will be like those H7153
Ps 30: 9 "What is gained i I am silenced, if I go H928
Ps 30: 9 if I am silenced, i I go down to the pit? H928
Ps 44:20 I we had forgotten the name of our God H561
Ps 50:12 I I were hungry I would not tell you, for the H561
Ps 53: 2 on all mankind to see i there are any who H2022
Ps 55:12 I an enemy were insulting me, I could H4273
Ps 55:12 endure it; i a foe were rising against me H4273
Ps 59:15 about for food and howl i not satisfied. H561
Ps 62: 9 I weighed on a balance, they are nothing NDT
Ps 66:18 I I had cherished sin in my heart, the Lord H561
Ps 73:15 I I had spoken out like that, I would have H561
Ps 81: 8 warn you—i you would only listen to me H561
Ps 81:13 "I my people would only listen to me, if H4273
Ps 81:13 i Israel would only follow my ways NDT
Ps 89:30 "I his sons forsake my law and do not H561
Ps 89:31 i they violate my decrees and fail to keep H561
Ps 90:10 eighty, i our strength endures; yet the H561
Ps 90:11 I only we knew the power of your anger H4769
Ps 91: 9 I you say, "The LORD is my refuge," and you NDT
Ps 95: 7 i only you would hear his voice H561
Ps 119:92 I your law had not been my delight, H4295
Ps 124: 1 I the LORD had not been on our side—let H4295
Ps 124: 2 i the LORD had not been on our side when H4295
Ps 130: 3 I you, LORD, kept a record of sins, Lord, who H561
Ps 132:12 I your sons keep my covenant and the H561
Ps 133: 3 It is as i the dew of Hermon were falling H3869
Ps 137: 5 I I forget you, Jerusalem, may my right H561
Ps 137: 6 the roof of my mouth i I do not remember H561
Ps 137: 6 i I do not consider Jerusalem my highest H561
Ps 139: 8 I I go up to the heavens, you are there; if I H561
Ps 139: 8 are there; i I make my bed in the depths H2256
Ps 139: 9 I I rise on the wings of the dawn, if I settle NDT
Ps 139: 9 the dawn, i I settle on the far side of the sea NDT
Ps 139:11 I I say, "Surely the darkness will hide me H2256
Ps 139:19 I only you, God, would slay the wicked H561
Ps 139:24 See i there is any offensive way in me, and H561
Pr 1:10 i sinful men entice you, do not H561
Pr 1:11 I they say, "Come along with us; let's lie in H561
Pr 2: 1 i you accept my words and store up my H561
Pr 2: 3 i you call out for insight and cry aloud for H561
Pr 2: 4 i you look for it as for silver and search H561
Pr 6: 1 i you have put up security for your neighbor, H561
Pr 6: 1 i you have shaken hands in pledge for a NDT
Pr 6:30 do not despise a thief i he steals to satisfy H3954
Pr 6:31 Yet i he is caught, he must pay sevenfold NDT
Pr 9:12 I you are wise, your wisdom will reward you H561
Pr 9:12 will reward you; i you are a mocker, you H2256
Pr 11:31 I the righteous receive their due on earth H2176
Pr 17:26 I imposing a fine on the innocent is not NDT
Pr 17:28 fools are thought wise i they keep silent, NDT
Pr 17:28 discerning i they hold their tongues. NDT
Pr 20:16 hold it in pledge i it is done for an outsider. NDT
Pr 20:18 by seeking advice; so i you wage war H2256
Pr 20:20 I someone curses their father or mother NDT
Pr 22:27 i you lack the means to pay, your very bed H561
Pr 23: 2 a knife to your throat i you are given to H561
Pr 23:13 i you punish them with the rod H3954
Pr 23:15 i your heart is wise, then my heart H561
Pr 24:10 I you falter in a time of trouble, how small is NDT
Pr 24:12 I you say, "But we knew nothing about H3954
Pr 24:14 I you find it, there is a future hope for you H561
Pr 25: 8 you do in the end i your neighbor puts you H928
Pr 25: 9 I you take your neighbor to court, do not NDT
Pr 25:16 I you find honey, eat just enough—too NDT
Pr 25:21 I your enemy is hungry, give him food to H561
Pr 25:21 give him food to eat; i he is thirsty, give H561
Pr 26:27 a pit will fall into it; i someone rolls a stone NDT
Pr 27:13 hold it in pledge i it is done for an H2256
Pr 27:14 I anyone loudly blesses their neighbor early NDT
Pr 28: 9 I anyone turns a deaf ear to my instruction NDT
Pr 29: 9 I a wise person goes to court with a fool, the NDT
Pr 29:12 I a ruler listens to lies, all his officials NDT
Pr 29:14 I a king judges the poor with fairness, his NDT
Pr 30:32 "I you play the fool and exalt yourself, or if H561
Pr 30:32 exalt yourself, or i you plan evil, clap H561
Ecc 3:21 Who knows i the human spirit rises upward NDT
Ecc 3:21 spirit rises upward and i the spirit of the NDT
Ecc 4:10 I either of them falls down, one can H3954+561
Ecc 4:11 i two lie down together, they will H561
Ecc 5: 8 I you see the poor oppressed in a district H561
Ecc 6: 3 i he cannot enjoy his prosperity and does H2256
Ecc 6: 6 even i he lives a thousand years twice over H467
Ecc 8:17 Even i the wise claim they know, they H561
Ecc 10: 4 I a ruler's anger rises against you, do not H561
Ecc 10:10 I the ax is dull and its edge unsharpened H561
Ecc 10:11 I a snake bites before it is charmed, the H561
Ecc 11: 3 I clouds are full of water, they pour rain on H561
SS 1: 8 I you do not know, most beautiful of H561
SS 5: 8 I charge you—i you find my beloved, what H561
SS 6:11 to see i the vines had budded or the H2022
SS 7:12 the vineyards to see i the vines have H561
SS 7:12 have budded, i their blossoms have opened NDT
SS 7:12 i the pomegranates are in bloom NDT
SS 8: 1 I only you were to me like a brother H4769+5989
SS 8: 1 i I found you outside, I would kiss you, NDT
SS 8: 7 I one were to give all the wealth of one's H561
SS 8: 9 I she is a wall, we will build towers of silver H561
SS 8: 9 I she is a door, we will enclose her with H561
Isa 1:19 I you are willing and obedient, you will eat H561
Isa 1:20 i you resist and rebel, you will be H561
Isa 5:30 And i one looks at the land, there is only NDT
Isa 7: 9 I you do not stand firm in your faith, you H561
Isa 8:20 I anyone does not speak according to this H561
Isa 10:15 As i a rod were to wield the person who H3869
Isa 21:12 I you would ask, then ask; and come back H561
Isa 27: 4 I only there were briers and thorns H4769+5989
Isa 29:11 And i you give the scroll to someone who NDT
Isa 29:12 Or i you give the scroll to someone who NDT
Isa 29:16 as i the potter were thought to be like the H561
Isa 36: 7 But i you say to me, "We are depending H3954
Isa 36: 8 horses—i you can put riders on them! H561
Isa 41:25 He treads on rulers as *i* they were mortar, as AIT
Isa 41:25 as *i* he were a potter treading the clay. AIT
Isa 48:18 I only you had paid attention to my H4273
Isa 54: 6 will call you back as i you were a wife H3869
Isa 54:15 I anyone does attack you, it will not be my H2176
Isa 58: 2 as i they were a nation that does what is H3869
Isa 58: 9 "I you do away with the yoke of oppression H561
Isa 58:10 i you spend yourselves in behalf of the NDT
Isa 58:13 "I you keep your feet from breaking the H561
Isa 58:13 i you call the Sabbath a delight and the NDT
Isa 58:13 i you honor it by not going your own NDT
Isa 59:10 midday we stumble as i it were twilight; H3869
Jer 2:10 see i there has ever been anything like H2176
Jer 2:28 Let them come i they can save you when H561
Jer 3: 1 "I a man divorces his wife and she leaves H2176
Jer 4: 1 "I you, Israel, will return, then return to me," H561
Jer 4: 1 I you put your detestable idols out of my H561
Jer 4: 2 i in a truthful, just and righteous way NDT
Jer 5: 1 I you can find but one person who deals H561
Jer 7: 5 I you really change your ways and H3954+561
Jer 7: 6 i you do not oppress the foreigner, the NDT
Jer 7: 6 i you do not follow other gods to your NDT
Jer 12: 5 "I you have raced with men on foot and H3954
Jer 12: 5 I you stumble in safe country, how will H2256
Jer 12:16 And i they learn well the ways of my people H561
Jer 12:17 But i any nation does not listen, I will H561
Jer 13:12 And i they say to you, 'Don't we know that NDT
Jer 13:17 I you do not listen, I will weep in secret H561
Jer 13:22 And i you ask yourself, "Why has this H3954
Jer 14:18 I I go into the country, I see those slain by H561
Jer 14:18 slain by the sword; i I go into the city, I see H561
Jer 15: 1 "Even i Moses and Samuel were to stand H561
Jer 15: 2 And i they ask you, 'Where shall we go?' H3954
Jer 15:19 "I you repent, I will restore you that you H561
Jer 15:19 you may serve me; i you utter worthy, not H561
Jer 17:24 But i you are careful to obey me, declares H561
Jer 17:27 But i you do not obey me to keep the H561
Jer 18: 7 I at any time I announce that a nation or NDT
Jer 18: 8 i that nation I warned repents of its evil NDT
Jer 18: 9 And i at another time I announce that a NDT
Jer 18:10 i it does evil in my sight and does not NDT
Jer 20: 9 But i I say, "I will not mention his word or NDT
Jer 22: 4 For i you are careful to carry out these H561
Jer 22: 5 But i you do not obey these commands H561
Jer 22:24 the LORD, "even i you, Jehoiachin son of H561
Jer 22:30 "Record this man as i childless, a man who NDT
Jer 23:22 But i they had stood in my council, they H561
Jer 23:34 I a prophet or a priest or anyone else claims NDT
Jer 25:28 But i they refuse to take the cup from your H3954
Jer 26: 4 I you do not listen to me and follow my law H561
Jer 26: 5 i you do not listen to the words of my NDT
Jer 26:15 however, that i you put me to death, you H561
Jer 27: 8 " ' "I, however, any nation or kingdom will NDT
Jer 27:11 But i any nation will bow its neck under the NDT
Jer 27:18 I they are prophets and have the word of H561
Jer 28: 9 sent by the LORD only i his prediction comes H928
Jer 29: 7 LORD for it, because i it prospers, you too H928
Jer 31:36 "Only i these decrees vanish from my sight," H561
Jer 31:37 "Only i the heavens above can be H561
Jer 32: 5 I you fight against the Babylonians, you H3954
Jer 33:20 'I you can break my covenant with the day H561
Jer 33:25 'I I have not made my covenant with day H561
Jer 37:10 Even i you were to defeat the entire H561
Jer 38:15 said to Zedekiah, "I I give you an answer H3954
Jer 38:15 Even i I did give you counsel, you would H3954
Jer 38:17 'I you surrender to the officers of the king of H561
Jer 38:18 But i you will not surrender to the officers of H561
Jer 38:21 But i you refuse to surrender, this is what H561
Jer 38:25 I the officials hear that I talked with you H3954
Jer 40: 4 with me to Babylon, i you like, and I will H561
Jer 40: 4 look after you; but i you do not want to H561
Jer 42: 5 witness against us i we do not act in H561
Jer 42:10 'I you stay in this land, I will build you up H561
Jer 42:13 "However, i you say, 'We will not stay in H561
Jer 42:14 i you say, 'No, we will go and live in NDT
Jer 42:15 'I you are determined to go to Egypt and H561
Jer 49: 9 I grape pickers came to you, would they not H561
Jer 49: 9 I thieves came during the night, would they H561
Jer 49:12 "I those who do not deserve to drink the H2180
Jer 51:53 Even i Babylon ascends to the heavens H3954
La 3:37 have it happen i the Lord has not NDT
La 4:14 through the streets as i they were blind. NDT
Eze 1:27 like glowing metal, as i full of fire, and H3869
Eze 3: 6 Surely i I had sent you to them, they would H3954
Eze 3:19 But i you do warn the wicked person and H3954
Eze 3:21 But i you do warn the righteous person not H3954
Eze 14: 9 " 'And i the prophet is enticed to utter a H3954
Eze 14:13 i a country sins against me by being H3954
Eze 14:14 even i these three men—Noah, Daniel H2256
Eze 14:15 "Or i I send wild beasts through that H4273
Eze 14:16 even i these three men were in it NDT
Eze 14:17 "Or i I bring a sword against that country NDT
Eze 14:18 even i these three men were in it H2256
Eze 14:19 "Or i I send a plague into that land and NDT
Eze 14:20 Sovereign LORD, even i Noah, Daniel and H2256
Eze 15: 5 I it was not useful for anything when it was H2180
Eze 18:21 "But i a wicked person turns away from all H3954
Eze 18:24 "But i a righteous person turns from their H928
Eze 18:26 I a righteous person turns from their H928
Eze 18:27 But i a wicked person turns away from the H928
Eze 21:13 And what i even the scepter, which the H561
Eze 33: 4 then i anyone hears the trumpet but does NDT
Eze 33: 5 I they had heeded the warning, they H2256
Eze 33: 6 But i the watchman sees the sword coming H3954
Eze 33: 9 But i you do warn the wicked person to H3954
Eze 33:12 'I someone who is righteous H928+3427
Eze 33:12 And i someone who is wicked H928+3427
Eze 33:13 I I tell a righteous person that they will H928
Eze 33:14 And i I say to a wicked person, 'You will H928
Eze 33:15 i they give back what they took in pledge NDT
Eze 33:18 I a righteous person turns from their H928
Eze 33:19 And i a wicked person turns away from their H928
Eze 39:18 princes of the earth as i they were rams NDT
Eze 43:11 i they are ashamed of all they have H561
Eze 44:25 i the dead person was his father or mother H561
Eze 46:16 I the prince makes a gift from his H3954
Eze 46:17 I, however, he makes a gift from his H3954
Da 2: 5 I you do not tell me what my dream was A10213
Da 2: 6 But i you tell me the dream and explain A10213
Da 2: 9 I you do not tell me the dream, there is A10213
Da 3:15 i you are ready to fall down and worship A10213
Da 3:15 But i you do not worship it, you will be A10213
Da 3:17 I we are thrown into the blazing furnace A10213
Da 3:18 But even i he does not, we want you to A10213
Da 4:19 i only the dream applied to your enemies NDT
Da 5:16 I you can read this writing and tell me A10213
Hos 9: 6 Even i they escape from destruction, Egypt H3954
Hos 9:12 Even i they rear children, I will bereave H561
Hos 9:16 Even i they bear children, I will slay their H3954
Hos 10: 3 But even i we had a king, what could he do NDT
Joel 3: 4 I you are paying me back, I will swiftly and H561
Am 3: 5 up from the ground i it has not caught H2256
Am 6: 9 I ten people are left in one house, they too H561
Am 6:10 And i the relative who comes to carry the NDT
Ob 5 "I thieves came to you, if robbers in the H561
Ob 5 thieves came to you, i robbers in the night H561
Ob 5 I grape pickers came to you, would they not H561
Ob 16 drink and be as i they had never H3869
Mic 2:11 I a liar and deceiver comes and says, 'I H4273
Mic 3: 5 they proclaim 'peace' i they have something NDT
Hab 1: 5 would not believe, even i you were told. H3954
Hag 2:12 I someone carries consecrated meat in the H2176
Hag 2:13 "I a person defiled by contact with a dead H561
Zec 3: 7 'I you will walk in obedience to me and H561
Zec 6:15 This will happen i you diligently obey the H561
Zec 11:12 I told them, "I you think it best, give me my H561
Zec 11:12 give me my pay; but i not, keep it." H561
Zec 13: 3 And i anyone still prophesies, their father H3954
Zec 13: 6 I someone asks, 'What are these wounds H2256
Zec 14:17 I any of the peoples of the earth do not go H889
Zec 14:18 I the Egyptian people do not go up and H561
Mal 1: 6 a slave his master. I I am a father, where is H561
Mal 1: 6 I I am a master, where is the respect due H561
Mal 2: 2 I you do not listen, and if you do not resolve H561
Mal 2: 2 i you do not resolve to honor my name," H561
Mal 3:10 "and see i I will not throw open the H561
Mt 4: 3 him and said, "I you are the Son of God *G1623*
Mt 4: 6 "I you are the Son of God," he said, "throw *G1623*
Mt 4: 9 "i you will bow down and worship me." *G1569*
Mt 5:13 But i the salt loses its saltiness, how can it *G1569*
Mt 5:23 i you are offering your gift at the altar *G1569*
Mt 5:29 I your right eye causes you to stumble *G1623*
Mt 5:30 And i your right hand causes you to *G1623*
Mt 5:39 I anyone slaps you on the right cheek, turn *G247*
Mt 5:40 And i anyone wants to sue you and take your NDT
Mt 5:41 I anyone forces you to go one mile, go with NDT
Mt 5:46 I you love those who love you, what *G1569*
Mt 5:47 And i you greet only your own people *G1569*
Mt 6: 1 I you do, you will have no reward from *G1623*
Mt 6:14 For i you forgive other people when they *G1569*
Mt 6:15 But i you do not forgive others their sins *G1569*
Mt 6:22 I your eyes are healthy, your whole body *G1569*
Mt 6:23 But i your eyes are unhealthy, your whole *G1569*
Mt 6:23 I then the light within you is darkness *G1623*
Mt 6:30 I that is how God clothes the grass of the *G1623*
Mt 7: 6 I you do, they may trample them under *G3607*
Mt 7: 9 "Which of you, i your son asks for bread, NDT
Mt 7:10 Or i he asks for a fish, will give him a *G2779*
Mt 7:11 I you, then, though you are evil, know how *G1623*
Mt 8: 2 i you are willing, you can make me *G1569*
Mt 8:31 demons begged Jesus, "I you drive us out *G1623*
Mt 9:17 I they do, the skins will burst; the wine *G1623*
Mt 9:21 said to herself, "I I only touch his cloak *G1569*
Mt 10:13 I the home is deserving, let your peace *G1569*
Mt 10:13 your peace rest on it; i it is not, let your *G1569*
Mt 10:14 I anyone will not welcome you or listen to *G323*
Mt 10:25 I the head of the house has been called *G1623*
Mt 10:42 And i anyone gives even a cup of cold *G323*
Mt 11: 8 I not, what did you go out to see? A man *G247*
Mt 11:14 And i you are willing to accept it, he is the *G1623*
Mt 11:21 For i the miracles that were performed in *G1623*
Mt 11:23 For i the miracles that were performed in *G1623*
Mt 12: 7 I you had known what these words mean *G1623*

Mt 12:11 "I any of you has a sheep and it falls into G1569
Mt 12:26 I Satan drives out Satan, he is divided G1623
Mt 12:27 And i I drive out demons by Beelzebul, by G1623
Mt 12:28 But i it is by the Spirit of God that I drive G1623
Mt 14:28 i it's you," Peter replied, "tell me to G1623
Mt 15: 5 But you say that i anyone declares that what G323
Mt 15:14 I the blind lead the blind, both will fall G1569
Mt 17: 4 I you wish, I will put up three shelters G1623
Mt 17:20 i you have faith as small as a mustard G1569
Mt 18: 6 *I* anyone **causes** one of these little ones—those who believe in me—**to stumble** AIT
Mt 18: 8 I your hand or your foot causes you to G1623
Mt 18: 9 And i your eye causes you to stumble G1623
Mt 18:12 I a man owns a hundred sheep, and one G1569
Mt 18:13 And i he finds it, truly I tell you, he is G1569
Mt 18:15 "I your brother or sister sins, go and point G1569
Mt 18:15 I they listen to you, you have won them G1569
Mt 18:16 But i they will not listen, take one or two G1569
Mt 18:17 I they still refuse to listen, tell it to the G1569
Mt 18:17 i they refuse to listen even to the G1569
Mt 18:19 truly I tell you that i two of you on earth G1569
Mt 19:10 "I this is the situation between a husband G1623
Mt 19:17 I you want to enter life, keep the G1623
Mt 19:21 Jesus answered, "I you want to be perfect G1623
Mt 21: 3 I anyone says anything to you, say that the G1569
Mt 21:21 tell you, i you have faith and do not doubt G1569
Mt 21:22 *I you* **believe**, you will receive whatever you AIT
Mt 21:24 I you answer me, I will tell you by what G1569
Mt 21:25 said, "I we say, 'From heaven, G1569
Mt 21:26 But i we say, 'Of human origin'—we are G1569
Mt 22:24 "Moses told us that i a man dies without G1569
Mt 22:45 I then David calls him 'Lord,' how can he G1623
Mt 23:16 You say, 'I anyone swears by the temple, it G323
Mt 23:18 You also say, 'I anyone swears by the altar G323
Mt 23:30 'I we had lived in the days of our G1623
Mt 24:22 "I those days had not been cut short, no G1623
Mt 24:23 At that time i anyone says to you, 'Look G1569
Mt 24:24 wonders to deceive, i possible, even the G1623
Mt 24:26 "So i anyone tells you, 'There he is, out in G1569
Mt 24:43 I the owner of the house had known at G1623
Mt 26:15 willing to give me i I deliver him over to G2743
Mt 26:24 be better for him i he had not been born." G1623
Mt 26:33 "**Even** i all fall away on account of you G1623
Mt 26:35 declared, "**Even** i I have to die with you G2829
Mt 26:39 "My Father, i it is possible, may this cup G1623
Mt 26:42 i it is not possible for this cup to be taken G1623
Mt 26:63 Tell us i you are the Messiah, the Son of G1623
Mt 27:40 from the cross, i you are the Son of God!" G1623
Mt 27:43 Let God rescue him now i he wants him G1623
Mt 27:49 Let's see i Elijah comes to save him." G1623
Mt 28:14 I this report gets to the governor, we will G1569
Mk 1:40 him on his knees, "I you are willing, you G1569
Mk 3: 2 him closely to see i he would heal him on G1623
Mk 3:24 I a kingdom is divided against itself, that G1569
Mk 3:25 I a house is divided against itself, that G1569
Mk 3:26 And i Satan opposes himself and is G1623
Mk 4:23 I anyone has ears to hear, let them hear." G1623
Mk 4:38 "Teacher, don't you care i we drown?" G4022
Mk 5:28 she thought, "I I just touch his clothes G1569
Mk 6:11 And i **any** place will not welcome G4005+323
Mk 7:11 But you say that i anyone declares that G1569
Mk 8: 3 I I send them home hungry, they will G1569
Mk 8:38 I anyone is ashamed of me and my words G1569
Mk 9:22 But i you can do anything, take pity on us G1623
Mk 9:23 " 'I you can'?" said Jesus. "Everything is G1623
Mk 9:42 "I anyone causes one of these little ones G323
Mk 9:42 be better for them i a large millstone G1623
Mk 9:43 I your hand causes you to stumble, cut it G1569
Mk 9:45 And i your foot causes you to stumble, cut G1569
Mk 9:47 And i your eye causes you to stumble G1569
Mk 9:50 "Salt is good, but i it loses its saltiness G1569
Mk 10:12 And i she divorces her husband and G1569
Mk 11: 3 I anyone asks you, 'Why are you doing this G1569
Mk 11:13 he went to find out i it had any fruit. G1623+726
Mk 11:23 I tell you, i anyone says to this mountain G323
Mk 11:25 i you hold anything against anyone G1623
Mk 11:31 said, "I we say, 'From heaven, G1569
Mk 11:32 But *i we* **say**, 'Of human origin' . . ." (They AIT
Mk 12:19 wrote for us that i a man's brother dies G1569
Mk 13:20 "I the Lord had not cut short those days G1623
Mk 13:21 At that time i anyone says to you, 'Look G1569
Mk 13:22 wonders to deceive, i possible, even the G1623
Mk 13:36 *I he* **comes** suddenly, do not let him find you AIT
Mk 14:21 be better for him i he had not been born." G1623
Mk 14:29 Peter declared, "Even i all fall away, I will G1623
Mk 14:31 "**Even** i I have to die with you G1569
Mk 14:35 prayed that i possible the hour G1623
Mk 15:36 Let's see i Elijah comes to take him down," G1623
Mk 15:44 he asked him i Jesus had already died. G1623
Lk 3:15 in their hearts i John might possibly be G3607
Lk 4: 3 said to him, "I you are the Son of God G1623
Lk 4: 7 I you worship me, it will all be yours." G1569
Lk 4: 9 "I you are the Son of God," he said G1623
Lk 5:12 i you are willing, you can make me G1569
Lk 6: 7 him closely to see i he would heal on the G1623
Lk 6:29 *I* someone **slaps** you on one cheek, turn to AIT
Lk 6:29 *I* someone **takes** your coat, do not withhold AIT
Lk 6:30 and *i* anyone **takes** what belongs to you AIT
Lk 6:32 "I you love those who love you, what G1623
Lk 6:33 And i you do good to those who are good G1569
Lk 6:34 And i you lend to those from whom you G1569
Lk 7:25 I **not**, what did you go out to see? A man G247

Lk 7:39 to himself, "I this man were a prophet G1623
Lk 9: 5 I people do not welcome you, leave their G323
Lk 10: 6 I someone who promotes peace is there G1569
Lk 10: 6 will rest on them; i not, it will return to G1623
Lk 10:13 For i the miracles that were performed in G1623
Lk 11:11 of you fathers, *i* your son **asks for** a fish, will AIT
Lk 11:12 Or *i he* **asks for** an egg, will give him a AIT
Lk 11:13 I you then, though you are evil, know how G1623
Lk 11:18 I Satan is divided against himself, how G1623
Lk 11:19 Now i I drive out demons by Beelzebul, by G1623
Lk 11:20 But i I drive out demons by the finger of G1623
Lk 11:36 Therefore, i your whole body is full of light G1623
Lk 12:28 I that is how God clothes the grass of the G1623
Lk 12:38 **even** i he comes in the middle of the G2829
Lk 12:39 I the owner of the house had known at G1623
Lk 13: 9 I it bears fruit next year, fine! If not, then G2829
Lk 13: 9 fruit next year, fine! I not, then cut it down G1623
Lk 14: 5 "I one of you has a child or an ox that falls NDT
Lk 14: 9 I **so**, the host who invited both of you will G2779
Lk 14:12 rich neighbors; **i you do**, they may invite G3607
Lk 14:26 "I anyone comes to me and does not hate G1623
Lk 14:28 the cost *to see* i you have enough G1623
Lk 14:29 For i you lay the foundation and are not G3607
Lk 14:32 I he is not able, he will send a delegation G1623
Lk 14:34 "Salt is good, but i it loses its saltiness G1569
Lk 16:11 So i you have not been trustworthy in G1623
Lk 16:12 And i you have not been trustworthy with G1623
Lk 16:30 'but i someone from the dead goes to G1569
Lk 16:31 'I they do not listen to Moses and the G1623
Lk 16:31 be convinced even i someone rises from G1569
Lk 17: 3 "I your brother or sister sins against you G1569
Lk 17: 3 rebuke them; and i they repent, forgive G1569
Lk 17: 4 Even i they sin against you seven times in G1569
Lk 17: 6 "I you have faith as small as a mustard G1623
Lk 19: 8 i I have cheated anybody out of G1623
Lk 19:31 I anyone asks you, 'Why are you untying it?G1569
Lk 19:40 he replied, "i they keep quiet, the stones G1569
Lk 19:42 "I you, even you, had **only** known on this G1623
Lk 20: 5 said, "I we say, 'From heaven, G1569
Lk 20: 6 But i we say, 'Of human origin,' all the G1569
Lk 20:28 wrote for us that i a man's brother dies G1569
Lk 22:36 to them, "But now *i* you **have** a purse, take it, AIT
Lk 22:36 and *i* you don't **have** a sword, sell AIT
Lk 22:42 i you are willing, take this cup G1623
Lk 22:67 "I you are the Messiah," they said, "tell us."G1623
Lk 22:67 Jesus answered, "I I tell you, you will not G1569
Lk 22:68 i I asked you, you would not answer. G1569
Lk 23: 6 Pilate asked i the man was a Galilean. G1623
Lk 23:31 For i people do these things when the G1623
Lk 23:35 him save himself i he is God's Messiah, G1623
Lk 23:37 "I you are the king of the Jews G1623
Lk 24:28 Jesus **continued on as** i he were going G4701
Jn 1:25 then do you baptize i you are not the G1623
Jn 3: 2 signs you are doing i God were not with G1569
Jn 3:12 then will you believe i I speak of heavenly G1569
Jn 4:10 "I you knew the gift of God and who it is G1623
Jn 5:31 "I I testify about myself, my testimony is G1569
Jn 5:43 i someone else comes in his own G1569
Jn 5:46 I you believed Moses, you would believe G1623
Jn 6:62 Then **what** i you see the Son of Man G1569
Jn 7:23 *Now* i a boy can be circumcised on the G1623
Jn 8:14 "**Even** i I testify on my own behalf G2829
Jn 8:16 But i I do judge, my decisions are true G1569
Jn 8:19 "I you knew me, you would know my G1623
Jn 8:24 i you do not believe that I am he G1569
Jn 8:31 Jesus said, "I you hold to my teaching G1569
Jn 8:36 So i the Son sets you free, you will be free G1569
Jn 8:39 "I you were Abraham's children," said G1623
Jn 8:42 said to them, "I God were your Father G1623
Jn 8:46 I I am telling the truth, why don't you G1623
Jn 8:54 Jesus replied, "I I glorify myself, my glory G1569
Jn 8:55 I I said I did not, I would be a liar like you, G2829
Jn 9:33 I this man were not from God, he could do G1623
Jn 9:41 Jesus said, "I you were blind, you would G1623
Jn 10:24 us in suspense? I you are the Messiah G1623
Jn 10:35 I he called them 'gods,' to whom the word G1623
Jn 10:38 But i I do them, even though you do not G1623
Jn 11:12 replied, "Lord, i he sleeps, he will get G1623
Jn 11:21 said to Jesus, "i you had been here, my G1623
Jn 11:32 i you had been here, my brother G1623
Jn 11:40 "Did I not tell you that i you believe, you G1569
Jn 11:48 I we let him go on like this, everyone will G1569
Jn 12:24 a single seed. But i it dies, it produces G1569
Jn 12:47 "I anyone hears my words but does not G1569
Jn 13:17 you will be blessed i you do them. G1569
Jn 13:32 I God is glorified in him, God will glorify G1623
Jn 13:35 are my disciples, i you love one another." G1569
Jn 14: 2 house has many rooms; i that were not so G1623
Jn 14: 3 And i I go and prepare a place for you, G1569
Jn 14: 7 I you really know me, you will know my G1623
Jn 14:15 "I you love me, keep my commands. G1569
Jn 14:28 I you loved me, you would be glad that I G1623
Jn 15: 5 *I* you **remain** in me and I in you, you will AIT
Jn 15: 6 I you do not remain in me, you are like a G1569
Jn 15: 7 I you remain in me and my words remain G1569
Jn 15:10 I you keep my commands, you will remain G1569
Jn 15:14 You are my friends i you do what I G1569
Jn 15:18 "I the world hates you, keep in mind that G1623
Jn 15:19 I you belonged to the world, it would love G1623
Jn 15:20 I they persecuted me, they will persecute G1623
Jn 15:20 I they obeyed my teaching, they will obey G1623
Jn 15:22 I I had not come and spoken to them, they G1623

Jn 15:24 I I had not done among them the works no G1623
Jn 16: 7 not come to you; but i I go, I will send G1569
Jn 18: 8 I you are looking for me, then let these G1623
Jn 18:14 would be good *i* one man **died** for the AIT
Jn 18:23 "I I said something wrong," Jesus replied G1623
Jn 18:23 But i I spoke the truth, why did you strike G1623
Jn 18:30 "I he were not a criminal," they replied G1623
Jn 18:36 I it were, my servants would fight to G1623
Jn 19:11 no power over me i it were not given to G1623
Jn 19:12 kept shouting, "I you let this man go G1569
Jn 20:15 i you have carried him away, tell me G1623
Jn 20:23 I you forgive anyone's sins, their sins are G323
Jn 20:23 sins are forgiven; i you do not forgive them G323
Jn 21:22 "I I want him to remain alive until I return G1569
Jn 21:23 "I I want him to remain alive until I return G1569
Jn 21:25 I every one of them were written down, G1569
Ac 3:12 do you stare at us **as** i by our own power G6055
Ac 4: 9 I we are being called to account today G1623
Ac 5:38 For i their purpose or activity is of human G1569
Ac 5:39 But i it is from God, you will not be able to G1623
Ac 9: 2 so that i he found any there who G1569
Ac 10:18 asking i Simon who was known as Peter G1623
Ac 11:17 So i God gave them the same gift he gave G1623
Ac 13:15 i you have a word of exhortation for the G1623
Ac 13:41 never believe, **even** i someone told you. G1569
Ac 16:15 "I you consider me a believer in the Lord," G1623
Ac 17:11 every day *to see* i what Paul said was G1623
Ac 17:25 by human hands, *as i he* **needed** anything. AIT
Ac 18:14 "I you Jews were making a complaint G1623
Ac 18:21 promised, "I will come back *i it is* God's **will**." AIT
Ac 19:38 I, then, Demetrius and his fellow G1623
Ac 19:39 I there is anything further you want to G1623
Ac 20:16 to reach Jerusalem, i possible, by the day G1623
Ac 23: 9 "**What** i a spirit or an angel has spoken to G1623
Ac 24:19 bring charges i they have anything G1623
Ac 25: 5 i the man has done anything wrong G1623
Ac 25:11 I, however, I am guilty of doing anything G1623
Ac 25:11 But i the charges brought against me by G1623
Ac 25:20 so I asked i he would be willing to go to G1623
Ac 26: 5 time and can testify, i they are willing G1569
Ac 26:32 have been set free i he had not appealed G1623
Ac 27:39 to run the ship aground i they could. G1623
Ro 2:17 Now you, i you call yourself a Jew; if you G1623
Ro 2:17 i you rely on the law and boast in God; NDT
Ro 2:18 i you know his will and approve of what is NDT
Ro 2:19 i you are convinced that you are a guide NDT
Ro 2:25 has value i you observe the law, G1569
Ro 2:25 observe the law, but i you break the law G1569
Ro 2:26 i those who are not circumcised keep the G1569
Ro 3: 3 What i some were unfaithful? Will their G1623
Ro 3: 5 But i our unrighteousness brings out G1623
Ro 3: 6 **I that were so**, how could God judge the G2075
Ro 3: 7 "I my falsehood enhances God's G1623
Ro 4: 2 I, in fact, Abraham was justified by works G1623
Ro 4:14 For i those who depend on the law are G1623
Ro 5:10 For i, while we were God's enemies, we G1623
Ro 5:15 For i the many died by the trespass of the G1623
Ro 5:17 For i, by the trespass of the one man G1623
Ro 6: 5 For i we have been united with him in a G1623
Ro 6: 8 Now i we died with Christ, we believe that G1623
Ro 7: 2 as he is alive, but i her husband dies, she G1569
Ro 7: 3 i she has sexual relations with another G1569
Ro 7: 3 But i her husband dies, she is released G1569
Ro 7: 3 not an adulteress *i she* **marries** another man. AIT
Ro 7: 7 coveting really was i the law had not said, G1623
Ro 7:16 And i I do what I do not want to do, G1623
Ro 7:20 Now i I do what I do not want to do, it is G1623
Ro 8: 9 i **indeed** the Spirit of God lives in you. G1642
Ro 8: 9 And i anyone does not have the Spirit of G1623
Ro 8:10 But i Christ is in you, then even though G1623
Ro 8:11 And i the Spirit of him who raised Jesus G1623
Ro 8:13 For i you live according to the flesh, you G1623
Ro 8:13 i by the Spirit you put to death the G1623
Ro 8:17 Now i we are children, then we are heirs G1623
Ro 8:17 i **indeed** we share in his sufferings in G1642
Ro 8:25 But i we hope for what we do not yet have G1623
Ro 8:31 to these things? I God is for us, who can G1623
Ro 9:22 What i God, although choosing to show G1623
Ro 9:23 **What** i he did this to make the riches of G2779
Ro 9:32 it not by faith but **as** i it were by works. G6055
Ro 10: 9 I you declare with your mouth, "Jesus is G1569
Ro 11: 6 And i by grace, then it cannot be based on G1623
Ro 11: 6 based on works; **i it were**, grace would no G2075
Ro 11:12 But i their transgression means riches for G1623
Ro 11:15 For i their rejection brought reconciliation G1623
Ro 11:16 I the part of the dough offered as firstfruits G1623
Ro 11:16 whole batch is holy; i the root is holy, so G1623
Ro 11:17 I some of the branches have been broken G1623
Ro 11:18 other branches. I you do, consider this G1623
Ro 11:21 For i God did not spare the natural G1623
Ro 11:23 And i they do not persist in unbelief, they G1569
Ro 11:24 i you were cut out of an olive tree that is G1623
Ro 12: 6 I your gift is prophesying, then prophesy G1664
Ro 12: 7 i it is serving, then serve; if it is teaching G1664
Ro 12: 7 is serving, then serve; i it is teaching, then G1664
Ro 12: 8 i it is to encourage, then give G1664
Ro 12: 8 give encouragement; i it is giving, then give NDT
Ro 12: 8 then give generously; i it is to lead, do it NDT
Ro 12: 8 do it diligently; i it is to show mercy, do it NDT
Ro 12:18 I it is possible, as far as it depends on you G1623
Ro 12:20 "I your enemy is hungry, feed him; if he is G1569
Ro 12:20 feed him; i he is thirsty, give him G1569

Ro 13: 4 But i you do wrong, be afraid, for rulers do G1569
Ro 13: 7 I you owe taxes, pay taxes; if revenue, then NDT
Ro 13: 7 pay taxes; i revenue, then revenue NDT
Ro 13: 7 then revenue; i respect, then respect NDT
Ro 13: 7 if respect, then respect; i honor, then honor. NDT
Ro 14: 8 I we live, we live for the Lord; and if we G1569
Ro 14: 8 the Lord; and i we die, we die for the G1569
Ro 14:14 But i anyone regards something as G1623+3590
Ro 14:15 I your brother or sister is distressed G1623
Ro 14:23 has doubts is condemned i they eat, G1569
Ro 15:27 For i the Gentiles have shared in the G1623
1Co 1:16 I don't remember i I baptized anyone else G1623
1Co 2: 8 understood it, for i they had, they would G1623
1Co 3:12 I anyone builds on this foundation using G1623
1Co 3:14 I what has been built survives, the builder G1623
1Co 3:15 I it is burned up, the builder will suffer loss G1623
1Co 3:17 I anyone destroys God's temple, God will G1623
1Co 3:18 I any of you think you are wise by the G1623
1Co 4: 3 I care very little i I am judged by you or by G2671
1Co 4: 7 And i you did receive it, why do you boast G1623
1Co 4:15 Even i you had ten thousand guardians in G1569
1Co 4:18 arrogant, as i I were not coming to you. G6055
1Co 4:19 to you very soon, i the Lord is willing G1569
1Co 6: 1 *I* any of you **has** a dispute with another, do AIT
1Co 6: 2 And i you are to judge the world, are you G1623
1Co 6: 4 i you have disputes about such matters G1569
1Co 7: 9 But i they cannot control themselves, they G1623
1Co 7:11 But i she does, she must remain G1569
1Co 7:12 I any brother has a wife who is not a G1623
1Co 7:13 And i a woman has a husband who is not G1623
1Co 7:15 But i the unbeliever leaves, let it be so G1623
1Co 7:21 although i you can gain your freedom G1623
1Co 7:28 But i you do marry, you have not sinned G1569
1Co 7:28 have not sinned; and i a virgin marries G1569
1Co 7:29 have wives should live as i they do not; G6055
1Co 7:30 those who mourn, as i they did not; those G6055
1Co 7:30 who are happy, as i they were not; those G6055
1Co 7:30 something, as i it were not theirs to keep G6055
1Co 7:31 of the world, as i not engrossed in them. G6055
1Co 7:36 I anyone is worried that he might not be G1623
1Co 7:36 i his passions are too strong and he G1569
1Co 7:39 But i her husband dies, she is free to G1569
1Co 7:40 she is happier i she stays as she is—and G1569
1Co 8: 5 For even i there are so-called gods G1642
1Co 8: 8 we are no worse i we do not eat, and G1569
1Co 8: 8 if we do not eat, and no better i we do. G1569
1Co 8:10 For i someone with a weak conscience G1569
1Co 8:13 i what I eat causes my brother or sister to G1623
1Co 9:11 I we have sown spiritual seed among you G1623
1Co 9:11 is it too much i we reap a material harvest G1623
1Co 9:12 I others have this right of support from you G1623
1Co 9:16 Woe to me i I do not preach the gospel G1569
1Co 9:17 I I preach voluntarily, I have a reward; if G1623
1Co 9:17 I have a reward; i not voluntarily, I am G1623
1Co 10:12 *i* you **think** you are standing firm, be AIT
1Co 10:27 I an unbeliever invites you to a meal and G1623
1Co 10:28 But i someone says to you, "This has been G1569
1Co 10:30 I I take part in the meal with thankfulness G1623
1Co 11: 6 For i a woman does not cover her head G1623
1Co 11: 6 i it is a disgrace for a woman to have G1623
1Co 11:14 teach you that i a man has long hair, G1569
1Co 11:15 that i a woman has long hair, it is her G1569
1Co 11:16 I anyone wants to be contentious about G1623
1Co 11:31 But i we were more discerning with regard G1623
1Co 12:15 Now i the foot should say, "Because I am G1569
1Co 12:16 And i the ear should say, "Because I am G1569
1Co 12:17 I the whole body were an eye, where G1623
1Co 12:17 I the whole body were an ear, where G1623
1Co 12:19 I they were all one part, where would the G1623
1Co 12:26 I one part suffers, every part suffers with it G1664
1Co 12:26 part suffers with it; i one part is honored G1664
1Co 13: 1 I I speak in the tongues of men or of G1569
1Co 13: 2 I I have the gift of prophecy and can G1569
1Co 13: 2 i I have a faith that can move G1569
1Co 13: 3 I I give all I possess to the poor and give G2829
1Co 14: 6 i I come to you and speak in tongues G1569
1Co 14: 8 i the trumpet does not sound a clear call G1569
1Co 14:11 I then I do not grasp the meaning of what G1569
1Co 14:14 For i I pray in a tongue, my spirit prays, but G1569
1Co 14:23 So i the whole church comes together and G1569
1Co 14:24 But i an unbeliever or an inquirer comes in G1569
1Co 14:27 I anyone speaks in a tongue, two—or at G1664
1Co 14:28 I there is no interpreter, the speaker G1569
1Co 14:30 And i a revelation comes to someone who G1569
1Co 14:35 I they want to inquire about something G1623
1Co 14:37 I anyone thinks they are a prophet or G1623
1Co 14:38 But i anyone ignores this, they will G1623
1Co 15: 2 i you hold firmly to the word I preached to G1623
1Co 15:12 But i it is preached that Christ has been G1623
1Co 15:13 I there is no resurrection of the dead, then G1623
1Co 15:14 And i Christ has not been raised, our G1623
1Co 15:15 he did not raise him i in fact the dead are G1642
1Co 15:16 For i the dead are not raised, then Christ G1623
1Co 15:17 And i Christ has not been raised, your faith G1623
1Co 15:19 I only for this life we have hope in Christ G1623
1Co 15:29 Now i there is no resurrection, what will G2075
1Co 15:29 I the dead are not raised at all, why are G1623
1Co 15:32 I I fought wild beasts in Ephesus with no G1623
1Co 15:32 I the dead are not raised, "Let us eat and G1623
1Co 15:44 I there is a natural body, there is also a G1623
1Co 16: 4 I it seems advisable for me to go also G1569
1Co 16: 7 some time with you, i the Lord permits. G1569
1Co 16:22 I anyone does not love the Lord, let that G1623
2Co 1: 6 I we are distressed, it is for your comfort G1664
2Co 1: 6 salvation; i we are comforted, it G1664
2Co 2: 2 For i I grieve you, who is left to make me G1623
2Co 2: 5 I anyone has caused grief, he has not so G1623
2Co 2: 9 you was to see i you would stand the G1623
2Co 2:10 forgiven—i there was anything to forgive G1623
2Co 3: 7 Now i the ministry that brought death G1623
2Co 3: 9 I the ministry that brought condemnation G1623
2Co 3:11 And i what was transitory came with glory G1623
2Co 4: 3 And even i our gospel is veiled, it is veiled G1623
2Co 5: 1 For we know that i the earthly tent we live G1569
2Co 5:13 I we are "out of our mind," as some say, it G1664
2Co 5:13 it is for God; i we are in our right mind, it G1664
2Co 5:17 Therefore, i anyone is in Christ, the new G1623
2Co 7: 8 Even i I caused you sorrow by my letter, G1623
2Co 8:12 For i the willingness is there, the gift is G1623
2Co 9: 4 For i any Macedonians come with me and G1569
2Co 10: 7 I anyone is confident that they belong to G1623
2Co 10: 8 So even i I boast somewhat freely about G1569
2Co 10:14 would be the case *i we had* not **come** to you, AIT
2Co 11: 4 For i someone comes to you and preaches G1623
2Co 11: 4 i you receive a different spirit from the NDT
2Co 11:15 i his servants also masquerade as G1623
2Co 11:16 But i you do, then tolerate me just as you G1623
2Co 11:30 I I must boast, I will boast of the things G1623
2Co 12: 6 Even i I should choose to boast, I would G1569
2Co 12:15 myself as well. I I love you more, will G1623
Gal 1: 8 But even i we or an angel from heaven G1569
Gal 1: 9 I anybody is preaching to you a gospel G1623
Gal 1:10 I I were still trying to please people, G1623
Gal 2:17 "But i, in seeking to be justified in Christ G1623
Gal 2:18 I I rebuild what I destroyed, then I really G1623
Gal 2:21 i righteousness could be gained G1623
Gal 3: 4 so much in vain—i it really was in vain? G1623
Gal 3:18 For i the inheritance depends on the law G1623
Gal 3:21 For i a law had been given that could G1623
Gal 3:29 I you belong to Christ, then you are G1623
Gal 4:14 you welcomed me as i I were an angel of G6055
Gal 4:14 as i I were Christ Jesus himself. G6055
Gal 4:15 I can testify that, i you could have done so G1623
Gal 5: 2 tell you that i you let yourselves be G1569
Gal 5:11 i I am still preaching circumcision G1623
Gal 5:15 I you bite and devour each other, watch G1623
Gal 5:18 But i you are led by the Spirit, you are not G1623
Gal 6: 1 sisters, i someone is caught in a sin G1569
Gal 6: 3 I anyone thinks they are something when G1623
Gal 6: 9 we will reap a harvest *i we do* not **give up**. AIT
Eph 6: 7 as i you were serving the Lord G6055
Php 1:22 I I am to go on living in the body, this will G1623
Php 2: 1 Therefore i you have any encouragement G1623
Php 2: 1 with Christ, i any comfort from his love G1623
Php 2: 1 i any common sharing in the Spirit G1623
Php 2: 1 i any tenderness and compassion, G1623
Php 2:17 But even i I am being poured out like a G1623
Php 3: 4 I someone else thinks they have reasons G1623
Php 3:15 And i on some point you think differently G1623
Php 4: 8 i anything is excellent or praiseworthy G1623
Col 1:23 i you continue in your faith, established G1623
Col 3:13 forgive one another i any of you has a G1569
Col 4:10 instructions about him; i he comes to you G1569
1Ti 1: 8 that the law is good i one uses it properly. G1569
1Ti 2:15 childbearing—i they continue in faith G1569
1Ti 3: 5 I anyone does not know how to manage G1623
1Ti 3:10 then *i there* **is** nothing against them AIT
1Ti 3:15 i I am delayed, you will know how people G1569
1Ti 4: 4 is to be rejected *i it is* **received** with AIT
1Ti 4: 6 *I you* **point** these things **out** to the brothers AIT
1Ti 4:16 in them, because *i you* **do**, you will save both AIT
1Ti 5: 1 exhort him as i he were your father. G6055
1Ti 5: 4 But i a widow has children or G1623
1Ti 5:16 I any woman who is a believer has G1623
1Ti 6: 3 I anyone teaches otherwise and does not G1623
1Ti 6: 8 But *i we* **have** food and clothing, we will be AIT
2Ti 2:11 I we died with him, we will also live with G1623
2Ti 2:12 i we endure, we will also reign with him G1623
2Ti 2:12 also reign with him. I we disown him, he G1623
2Ti 2:13 i we are faithless, he remains faithful, for G1623
Phm 17 So i you consider me a partner, welcome G1623
Phm 18 I he has done you any wrong or owes you G1623
Heb 2: 3 how shall we escape *i we* **ignore** so great a AIT
Heb 3: 6 i indeed we hold firmly to our confidence G1569
Heb 3: 7 "Today, i you hear his voice, G1569
Heb 3:14 i indeed we hold our original conviction G1570
Heb 3:15 "Today, i you hear his voice, do not G1569
Heb 3:18 never enter his rest i not to those who G1623
Heb 4: 7 "Today, i you hear his voice, do not G1569
Heb 4: 8 For i Joshua had given them rest, God G1623
Heb 7:11 I perfection could have been attained G1623
Heb 7:15 is even more clear i another priest like G1623
Heb 8: 4 I he were on earth, he would not be a G1623
Heb 8: 7 For i there had been nothing wrong with G1623
Heb 10:26 *I we* deliberately **keep on sinning** after we AIT
Heb 11:15 I they had been thinking of the country G1623
Heb 12: 8 I you are not disciplined—and everyone G1623
Heb 12:20 "I even an animal touches the mountain G2829
Heb 12:25 I they did not escape when they refused G1623
Heb 12:25 i we turn away from him who warns us from NDT
Heb 13: 3 those in prison as i you were together G6055
Heb 13: 3 who are mistreated as i you yourselves G6055
Heb 13:23 I he arrives soon, I will come with him to G1569
Jas 1: 5 I any of you lacks wisdom, you should ask G1623
Jas 2: 3 *I you* **show special attention** to the man AIT
Jas 2: 8 I you really keep the royal law found in G1623
Jas 2: 9 But i you show favoritism, you sin and are G1623
Jas 2:11 I you do not commit adultery but do G1623
Jas 2:14 i someone claims to have faith but has no G1569
Jas 2:16 *I* one of you **says** to them, "Go in peace; keep AIT
Jas 2:17 by itself, i it is not accompanied by action G1569
Jas 3:14 But i you harbor bitter envy and selfish G1623
Jas 4:15 you ought to say, "I it is the Lord's will, we G1569
Jas 4:17 *I anyone*, then, **knows** the good they ought to AIT
Jas 5:15 will raise them up. I they have sinned G2829
Jas 5:19 i one of you should wander from the truth G1569
1Pe 2:19 For it is commendable i someone bears up G1623
1Pe 2:20 is it to your credit i you receive a beating G1623
1Pe 2:20 But i you suffer for doing good and you G1623
1Pe 3: 1 i any of them do not believe the word G1623
1Pe 3: 6 daughters *i you* **do** *what is* **right** and do not AIT
1Pe 3:13 is going to harm you i you are eager to do G1569
1Pe 3:14 But even i you should suffer for what is G1623
1Pe 3:17 For it is better, i it is God's will, to suffer G1623
1Pe 4:11 I anyone speaks, they should do so as one G1623
1Pe 4:11 I anyone serves, they should do so with G1623
1Pe 4:14 I you are insulted because of the name of G1623
1Pe 4:15 *I you* **suffer**, it should not be as a murderer AIT
1Pe 4:16 However, i you suffer as a Christian, do not G1623
1Pe 4:17 God's household; and i it begins with us G1623
1Pe 4:18 "I it is hard for the righteous to be saved G1623
2Pe 1: 8 For *i you* **possess** these qualities in increasing AIT
2Pe 1:10 For *i you* **do** these things, you will never AIT
2Pe 2: 4 For i God did not spare angels when they G1623
2Pe 2: 5 i he did not spare the ancient world when he NDT
2Pe 2: 6 *i he* **condemned** the cities of Sodom and AIT
2Pe 2: 7 i he rescued Lot, a righteous man, who NDT
2Pe 2: 9 i this is so, then the Lord knows how to NDT
2Pe 2:20 I they have escaped the corruption of the G1623
1Jn 1: 6 I we claim to have fellowship with him G1569
1Jn 1: 7 But i we walk in the light, as he is in the G1569
1Jn 1: 8 I we claim to be without sin, we deceive G1569
1Jn 1: 9 I we confess our sins, he is faithful and G1569
1Jn 1:10 I we claim we have not sinned, we make G1569
1Jn 2: 1 But i anybody does sin, we have an G1569
1Jn 2: 3 come to know him i we keep his G1569
1Jn 2: 5 But i anyone obeys his word, love for God is G323
1Jn 2:15 I anyone loves the world, love for the G1569
1Jn 2:19 For i they had belonged to us, they would G1623
1Jn 2:24 I it does, you also will remain in the Son G1569
1Jn 2:29 I you know that he is righteous, you know G1569
1Jn 3:13 brothers and sisters, i the world hates you. G1623
1Jn 3:17 I anyone has material possessions and sees G323
1Jn 3:20 I our hearts condemn us, we know that G1569
1Jn 3:21 i our hearts do not condemn us G1569
1Jn 4:12 ever seen God; but i we love one another G1569
1Jn 4:15 I anyone acknowledges that Jesus is the G1569
1Jn 5:14 that i we ask anything according to his G1569
1Jn 5:15 And i we know that he hears us—whatever G1569
1Jn 5:16 I you see any brother or sister commit a G1569
2Jn 10 I anyone comes to you and does not bring G1623
Rev 2: 5 I you do not repent, I will come to you G1569
Rev 3: 3 But i you do not wake up, I will come like G1569
Rev 3:20 I anyone hears my voice and opens the G1569
Rev 5: 6 a Lamb, *looking* as i it had been slain G6055
Rev 11: 5 I anyone tries to harm them, fire comes G1623
Rev 13:10 "I anyone is to go into captivity, into G1623
Rev 13:10 I anyone is to be killed with the sword G1623
Rev 14: 9 "I anyone worships the beast and its G1623
Rev 22:18 I anyone adds anything to them, God will G1569
Rev 22:19 And i anyone takes words away from this G1569

IGAL (3)

Nu 13: 7 from the tribe of Issachar, I son of Joseph; H3319
2Sa 23:36 I son of Nathan from Zobah, the son of H3319
1Ch 3:22 Hattush, I, Bariah, Neariah and Shaphat— H3319

IGDALIAH (1)

Jer 35: 4 sons of Hanan son of I the man of God. H3323

IGNORANCE (7) [IGNORE]

Eze 45:20 who sins unintentionally or through i; H7344
Ac 3:17 I know that you acted in i, as did your G53
Ac 17:30 In the past God overlooked such i, but now G53
Eph 4:18 of God because of the i that is in them due G53
1Ti 1:13 mercy because I acted in i and unbelief. G51
Heb 9: 7 *for* the **sins** the people *had* **committed in i**. G52
1Pe 1:14 the evil desires you had when you lived in i. G53

IGNORANT (10) [IGNORE]

Ps 73:22 I was senseless and i; I was a brute H4202+3359
Isa 44: 9 are blind; *they are* i, to their own H1153+3359
Isa 45:20 I *are* those who carry about idols of H4202+3359
Ac 17:23 So *you are* i of the very thing you worship G51
Ro 11:25 I do not want you *to be* i of this mystery G51
1Co 10: 1 For I do not want you *to be* **i of the fact** G51
1Co 15:34 there are some who are i of God—I say G57
Heb 5: 2 gently with those *who are* i and are going G51
1Pe 2:15 should silence the i talk of foolish people G57
2Pe 3:16 which i and unstable people distort G276

IGNORE (9) [IGNORANCE, IGNORANT, IGNORED, IGNORES]

Dt 22: 1 *do* not i it but be sure to take it back to its H6623
Dt 22: 3 anything else they have lost. *Do* not i it. H6623
Dt 22: 4 ox fallen on the road, *do* not i it. H6623
Ps 9:12 *he does* not i the cries of the afflicted. H8894

Ps 55: 1 to my prayer, O God, *do* not i my plea; H6623
Ps 74:23 *Do* not i the clamor of your adversaries H8894
Ps 119:139 me out, for my enemies i your words. H8894
Hos 4: 6 law of your God, I also *will* i your children. H8894
Heb 2: 3 how shall we escape *if we* i so great a *G288*

IGNORED (4) [IGNORE]
Ex 9:21 But those who i the word of H4202+8492+4213
Pr 2:17 of her youth and i the covenant she made H8894
Hos 4: 6 because *you have* i the law of your God H8894
1Co 14:38 ignores this, *they will themselves be* i. *G51*

IGNORES (2) [IGNORE]
Pr 10:17 but *whoever* i correction leads others H6440
1Co 14:38 But if anyone i this, they will themselves be *G51*

IIM (NIV84) IYIM

IJON (3)
1Ki 15:20 He conquered I, Dan, Abel Beth Maakah H6510
2Ki 15:29 king of Assyria came and took I, H6510
2Ch 16: 4 They conquered I, Dan, Abel Maim and H6510

IKKESH (3)
2Sa 23:26 Helez the Paltite, Ira son of I from Tekoa, H6837
1Ch 11:28 Ira son of I from Tekoa, Abiezer from H6837
1Ch 27: 9 was Ira the son of I the Tekoite. H6837

ILAI (1)
1Ch 11:29 Sibbekai the Hushathite, I the Ahohite, H6519

ILL (25) [ILLNESS, ILLNESSES, ILLS]
Ge 48: 1 later Joseph was told, "Your father *is* i." H2703
Dt 15: 9 that you *do* not show i will toward H8317+6524
1Sa 19:14 to capture David, Michal said, "He *is* i." H2703
1Sa 30:13 me when *I became* i three days ago. H2703
2Sa 12:15 wife had borne to David, and *he became* i. H653
2Sa 13: 2 his sister Tamar that *he* made himself i. H2703
2Sa 13: 5 "Go to bed and pretend to be i," Jonadab H2703
2Sa 13: 6 Amnon lay down and pretended to be i. H2703
1Ki 14: 1 time Abijah son of Jeroboam *became* i, H2703
1Ki 14: 5 her son, for he *is* i, and you are to give H2703
1Ki 17:17 woman who owned the house *became* i. H2703
2Ki 8: 7 Ben-Hadad king of Aram *was* i. H2703
2Ki 20: 1 days Hezekiah *became* i and was at the H2703
2Ch 21:15 yourself will be very i with a lingering H2716
2Ch 32:24 days Hezekiah *became* i and was at the H2703
Ne 2: 2 your face look so sad when you *are* not i? H2703
Job 6: 7 I refuse to touch it; such food makes me i. H1867
Ps 35:13 Yet when they *were* i, I put on sackcloth H2703
Isa 33:24 in Zion will say, "*I am* i"; and the sins of H2703
Isa 38: 1 days Hezekiah *became* i and was at the H2703
Mt 4:24 to him all who *were* i with various *G2809+2400*
Mt 12:15 and *he* healed all who were i. *G2543*
Ac 28: 5 off into the fire and suffered no i effects. *G2805*
Php 2:26 is distressed because you heard *he was* i. *G820*
Php 2:27 Indeed *he was* i, and almost died. But God *G820*

ILL-GOTTEN (5) [GET]
Pr 1:19 the paths of all *who* go after i gain; H1298+1299
Pr 10: 2 I treasures have no lasting value, but H8400
Pr 28:16 one who hates i gain will enjoy a H1299
Mic 4:13 You will devote their i gains to the LORD H1299
Mic 6:10 Am I still to forget your i treasures, you H8400

ILLEGAL (1) [LEGAL]
Ex 22: 9 In all cases of i possession of an ox, H7322

ILLEGITIMATE (2)
Hos 5: 7 to the LORD; they give birth to i children. H2424
Jn 8:41 "We are not i children," they *G1666+4518*

ILLICIT (1)
Eze 16:33 to you from everywhere for your i favors. H9373

ILLNESS (10) [ILL]
2Ki 8: 8 ask him, 'Will I recover from this i?' H2716
2Ki 8: 9 sent me to ask, 'Will I recover from this i?' H2716
2Ki 13:14 suffering from the i from which he died. H2716
2Ki 20:12 because he had heard of Hezekiah's i. H2703
2Ch 16:12 even in his i he did not seek help from H2716
Ps 41: 3 restores them from their bed of i. H2716
Isa 38: 9 king of Judah after his i and recovery: H2703
Isa 39: 1 he had heard of *his* i and recovery. H2703
Gal 4:13 was because of an i that I first *G819+3836+4922*
Gal 4:14 though my i was a trial to *G1877+3836+4922*

ILLNESSES (3) [ILL]
Dt 28:59 disasters, and severe and lingering i. H2716
Ac 19:12 their i were cured and the evil spirits *G3798*
1Ti 5:23 of your stomach and your frequent i. *G819*

ILLS (1) [ILL]
Ps 73: 5 burdens; they are not plagued by human i. NDT

ILLUMINATED (2)
Eph 5:13 everything that *is* i becomes a light. *G5746*
Rev 18: 1 the earth *was* i by his splendor. *G5894*

ILLUSIONS (1)
Isa 30:10 Tell us pleasant things, prophesy i. H4562

ILLUSTRATION (1)
Heb 9: 9 This is an i for the present time, indicating *G4130*

ILLYRICUM (1)
Ro 15:19 So from Jerusalem all the way around to I, *G2665*

IMAGE (54) [IMAGES]
Ge 1:26 "Let us make mankind in our i, in our H7512
Ge 1:27 So God created mankind in his own i, in H7512
Ge 1:27 in the i *of* God he created them H7512
Ge 5: 3 likeness, in his own i; and he named him H7512
Ge 9: 6 in the i *of* God has God made H7512
Ex 20: 4 make for yourself an i in the form of H7181
Lev 26: 1 idols or set up an i or a sacred stone for H7181
Dt 4:16 an idol, an i *of* any shape, whether H9454
Dt 5: 8 yourself an i in the form *of* anything in H7181
Jdg 17: 3 my son to make an i overlaid with silver. H7181
Jdg 18:14 gods and an i overlaid with silver? H7181
1Ki 15:13 she had made a repulsive i for the H5145
2Ch 15:16 she had made a repulsive i for the H5145
2Ch 33: 7 He took the i he had made and put H7181+6166
2Ch 33:15 removed the i from the temple of H6166
Ne 9:18 cast for themselves an i of a calf and said, H5011
Ps 106:20 their glorious God for an i *of* a bull, H9322
Isa 40:18 To what i will you liken him? H1952
Isa 48: 5 my wooden i and metal god ordained H7181
Jer 44:19 cakes impressed with her i and pouring H6771
Da 3: 1 King Nebuchadnezzar made an i of gold, A10614
Da 3: 2 to the dedication of the i he had set up. A10614
Da 3: 3 the dedication of the i that King A10614
Da 3: 5 down and worship the i *of* gold that King A10614
Da 3: 7 worshiped the i *of* gold that King A10614
Da 3:10 fall down and worship the i *of* gold, A10614
Da 3:12 worship the i *of* gold you have set A10614
Da 3:14 worship the i *of* gold I have set up A10614
Da 3:15 to fall down and worship the i I made, A10614
Da 3:18 worship the i *of* gold you have set A10614
Hab 2:18 by a craftsman? Or an i that teaches lies H5011
Mt 22:20 asked them, "Whose i is this? And whose *G1635*
Mk 12:16 he asked them, "Whose i is this? *G1635*
Lk 20:24 Whose i and inscription are on it? *G1635*
Ac 17:29 an i made by human design and skill. *G5916*
Ac 19:35 and *of* her i, which fell from heaven? *G1479*
Ro 8:29 to be conformed to the i of his Son, *G1635*
1Co 11: 7 since he is the i and glory of God; but *G1635*
1Co 15:49 we have borne the i of the earthly man, *G1635*
1Co 15:49 shall we bear the i of the heavenly man. *G1635*
2Co 3:18 being transformed *into* his i with *G1635*
2Co 4: 4 the glory of Christ, who is the i of God. *G1635*
Col 1:15 The Son is the i of the invisible God, the *G1635*
Col 3:10 in knowledge in the i of its Creator. *G1635*
Rev 13:14 them to set up an i in honor of the beast *G1635*
Rev 13:15 to give breath *to* the i of the first beast, *G1635*
Rev 13:15 so that the i could speak and cause all *G1635*
Rev 13:15 who refused to worship the i to be killed. *G1635*
Rev 14: 9 the beast and its i and receives its mark *G1635*
Rev 14:11 those who worship the beast and its i, *G1635*
Rev 15: 2 the beast and its i and over the number of *G1635*
Rev 16: 2 the mark of the beast and worshiped its i. *G1635*
Rev 19:20 the mark of the beast and worshiped its i. *G1635*
Rev 20: 4 the beast or its i and had not received its *G1635*

IMAGES (36) [IMAGE]
Nu 33:52 Destroy all their carved i and their cast H5381
Dt 7:25 The i *of* their gods you are to burn in the H7178
Dt 29:17 them their detestable i and idols of H9199
Jdg 3:19 But on reaching the stone i near Gilgal he H7178
Jdg 3:26 He passed by the stone i and escaped to H7178
Ps 97: 7 All who worship i are put to shame, those H7181
Isa 10:10 kingdoms whose i excelled those of H7178
Isa 10:11 with Jerusalem and her i as I dealt with H6773
Isa 21: 9 All the i *of* its gods lie shattered on the H7178
Isa 30:22 with silver and your i covered with gold; H5011
Isa 41:29 their i are but wind and confusion. H5822
Isa 42:17 in idols, who say to i, 'You are our gods, H5011
Isa 46: 1 The i that are carried about are H5953
Isa 48: 5 could not say, 'My i brought them about H6777
Jer 8:19 have they aroused my anger with their i, H7178
Jer 10:14 The i he makes are a fraud; they have no H5822
Jer 16:18 forms of their vile i and have filled my H9199
Jer 32:34 They set up their vile i in the house that H9199
Jer 50: 2 Her i will be put to shame and her idols H6773
Jer 51:17 The i he makes are a fraud; they have no H5822
Eze 5:11 with all your vile i and detestable H9199
Eze 7:20 They made it into vile i; therefore I will H9199
Eze 11:18 remove all its vile i and detestable H9199
Eze 11:21 are devoted to their vile i and detestable H9199
Eze 20: 7 get rid of the vile i you have set your eyes H9199
Eze 20: 8 not get rid of the vile i they had set their H9199
Eze 20:30 ancestors did and lust after their vile i? H9199
Eze 30:13 idols and put an end to the i in Memphis. H496
Eze 37:23 their idols and vile i or with any of their H9199
Da 4: 5 the i and visions that passed through my A10217
Da 11: 8 their metal i and their valuable articles of H5816
Hos 11: 2 to the Baals and they burned incense to i. H7178
Hos 13: 2 cleverly fashioned i, all of them the work H6773
Mic 1: 7 be burned with fire; I will destroy all her i. H6773
Na 1:14 I will destroy the i and idols that are in H7181
Ro 1:23 the immortal God for i made to look like a *G1635*

IMAGINATION (2) [IMAGINE]
Eze 13: 2 to those who prophesy out of their own i: H4213
Eze 13:17 people who prophesy out of their own i. H4213

IMAGINATIONS (2) [IMAGINE]
Ps 73: 7 iniquity; their evil i have no limits. H5381+4222
Isa 65: 2 in ways not good, pursuing their own i— H4742

IMAGINE (5) [IMAGINATION, IMAGINATIONS]
Jdg 19:30 up out of Egypt. Just i! We must do H8492+4200
Ps 41: 7 against me; *they* i the worst for me H3108
Pr 18:11 they i it a wall too high to scale. H928+5381
Pr 23:33 your mind *will* i confusing things. H1819
Eph 3:20 immeasurably more than all we ask or i, *G3783*

IMITATE (7) [IMITATED, IMITATORS]
Dt 18: 9 do not learn to i the detestable H6913+3869
Eze 23:48 may take warning and not i you. H6913+3869
1Co 4:16 Therefore I urge you *to* i me. *G3629+1181*
2Th 3: 9 to offer ourselves as a model for you to i. *G3628*
Heb 6:12 to i those who through faith and *G3629*
Heb 13: 7 of their way of life and i their faith. *G3628*
3Jn 11 *do* not i what is evil but what is good. *G3628*

IMITATED (1) [IMITATE]
2Ki 17:15 They i the nations around them although H339

IMITATORS (2) [IMITATE]
1Th 1: 6 You became i of us and of the Lord, for *G3629*
1Th 2:14 became i of God's churches in Judea *G3629*

IMLAH (4)
1Ki 22: 8 He is Micaiah son of I." "The king should H3551
1Ki 22: 9 said, "Bring Micaiah son of I at once." H3551
2Ch 18: 7 He is Micaiah son of I." "The king should H3550
2Ch 18: 8 said, "Bring Micaiah son of I at once." H3550

IMMANUEL (3)
Isa 7:14 give birth to a son, and will call him I. H6672
Isa 8: 8 will cover the breadth of your land, I!" H6672
Mt 1:23 birth to a son, and they will call him I" *G1842*

IMMEASURABLY (1) [MEASURE]
Eph 3:20 who is able to do i more than all we ask *G5655*

IMMEDIATE (1) [IMMEDIATELY]
Gal 1:16 my i response was not to consult any *G2311*

IMMEDIATELY (54) [IMMEDIATE]
1Sa 28:20 I Saul fell full length on the ground, filled H4554
2Sa 15:14 *We must* leave i, or he will move quickly H4554
Ezr 4:23 they went i to the Jews in A10089+10096
Ne 5:11 back to them i their fields, H3869+2021+3427
Est 2: 9 I *he* provided her with her beauty H987
Da 3: 6 worship will i be thrown into a A10734+10002
Da 3:15 will be thrown i into a blazing A10734+10191
Da 4:33 I what had been said about A10734+10002
Mt 4:22 i they left the boat and their father *G2311*
Mt 8: 3 I he was cleansed of his leprosy *G2311*
Mt 14:22 I Jesus made the disciples get into the *G2311*
Mt 14:27 But Jesus i said to them: "Take courage! It *G2317*
Mt 14:31 I Jesus reached out his hand and caught *G2311*
Mt 20:34 I they received their sight and followed *G2311*
Mt 21:19 bear fruit again!" I the tree withered. *G4202*
Mt 24:29 "I after the distress of those days " 'the *G2311*
Mt 26:74 don't know the man!" I a rooster crowed. *G2311*
Mt 27:48 I one of them ran and got a sponge. *G2311*
Mk 1:30 and they i told Jesus about her. *G2317*
Mk 1:42 I the leprosy left him and he was cleansed. *G2317*
Mk 2: 8 I Jesus knew in his spirit that this was *G2317*
Mk 5:29 I her bleeding stopped and she felt in her *G2317*
Mk 5:42 I the girl stood up and began to walk *G2317*
Mk 6:27 So he i sent an executioner with orders to *G2317*
Mk 6:45 I Jesus made his disciples get into the *G2317*
Mk 6:50 I he spoke to them and said, "Take *G2317*
Mk 9:20 it i threw the boy into a convulsion. *G2317*
Mk 9:24 I the boy's father exclaimed, "I do believe; *G2317*
Mk 10:52 I he received his sight and followed Jesus *G2317*
Mk 14:72 I the rooster crowed the second time *G2317*
Lk 1:64 I his mouth was opened and his tongue *G4202*
Lk 5:13 And i the leprosy left him *G2311*
Lk 5:25 I he stood up in front of them, took what *G4202*
Lk 8:44 of his cloak, and i her bleeding stopped. *G4202*
Lk 12:36 knocks they can i open the door for *G2311*
Lk 12:54 rising in the west, i you say, 'It's going to *G2311*
Lk 13:13 i she straightened up and praised *G4202*
Lk 14: 5 the Sabbath day, will you not i pull it out?" *G2311*
Lk 18:43 I he received his sight and followed Jesus *G4202*
Lk 19: 5 said to him, "Zacchaeus, come down i. *G5067*
Lk 20:19 for a way to arrest him i, *G1877+899+3836+6052*
Jn 6:21 i the boat reached the shore where *G2311*
Ac 9:18 I, something like scales fell from Saul's *G2311*
Ac 9:34 roll up your mat." I Aeneas got up. *G2311*
Ac 10:16 i the sheet was taken back to heaven. *G2317*
Ac 10:33 So I sent for you i, and it was good of you *G1994*
Ac 12:23 I, because Herod did not give praise to *G4202*
Ac 13:11 I mist and darkness came over him, and *G4202*
Ac 16:33 then i he and all his household were *G4202*
Ac 17:14 The believers i sent Paul to the coast, but *G2311*
Ac 21:30 the temple, and i the gates were shut. *G2311*
Ac 22:18 'Leave Jerusalem i, because the *G1877+5443*
Ac 22:29 were about to interrogate him withdrew i. *G2311*
Jas 1:24 goes away and i forgets what he looks *G2311*

IMMENSE (2)
Eze 1: 4 an i cloud with flashing lightning and H1524
1Ti 1:16 might display his i patience as an example *G570*

IMMER (10)
1Ch 9:12 the son of Meshillemith, the son of **I**. H612
1Ch 24:14 the fifteenth to Bilgah, the sixteenth to **I**, H612
Ezr 2:37 of **I** 1,052 H612
Ezr 2:59 Addon and **I**, but they could not H613
Ezr 10:20 From the descendants of **I**: Hanani and H612
Ne 3:29 Zadok son of **I** made repairs opposite his H612
Ne 7:40 of **I** 1,052 H612
Ne 7:61 Addon and **I**, but they could not H613
Ne 11:13 the son of Meshillemoth, the son of **I**, H612
Jer 20:1 When the priest Pashhur son of **I**, the H612

IMMORAL (10) [IMMORALITY]
1Co 5:9 not to associate with **sexually i people**— G4521
1Co 5:10 the **people** of this world who are **i**, G4521
1Co 5:11 brother or sister but is **sexually i** or greedy, G4521
1Co 6:9 Neither the **sexually i** nor idolaters nor G4521
Eph 5:5 No **i**, impure or greedy person—such a G4521
1Ti 1:10 *for* the **sexually i**, for those practicing G4521
Heb 12:16 See that no one is **sexually i**, or is godless G4521
Heb 13:4 judge the adulterer and *all* the **sexually i**. G4521
Rev 21:8 the murderers, the **sexually i**, those who G4521
Rev 22:15 magic arts, the **sexually i**, the murderers, G4521

IMMORALITY (25) [IMMORAL]
Nu 25:1 men began to **indulge in sexual i** with H2388
Jer 3:9 Because Israel's **i** mattered so little to her H2394
Mt 5:32 except for **sexual i**, makes her the G4518
Mt 15:19 adultery, **sexual i**, theft, false G4518
Mt 19:9 his wife, except for **sexual i**, and marries G4518
Mk 7:21 thoughts come—**sexual i**, theft, murder, G4518
Ac 15:20 by idols, *from* **sexual i**, from the meat of G4518
Ac 15:29 of strangled animals and *from* **sexual i**. G4518
Ac 21:25 of strangled animals and *from* **sexual i**." G4518
Ro 13:13 not *in* **sexual i** and debauchery G3130
1Co 5:1 reported that there is **sexual i** among you, G4518
1Co 6:13 is not *meant for* **sexual i** but for the Lord G4518
1Co 6:18 Flee *from* **sexual i**. All other sins a person G4518
1Co 7:2 But since **sexual i** is occurring, each man G4518
1Co 10:8 *We should* not **commit sexual i**, as some G4519
Gal 5:19 flesh are obvious: **sexual i**, impurity and G4518
Eph 5:3 there must not be even a hint of **sexual i**, G4518
Col 3:5 **sexual i**, impurity, lust, evil desires and G4518
1Th 4:3 that you should avoid **sexual i**; G4518
Jude 4 our God into a **license for i** and deny Jesus G816
Jude 7 towns **gave** *themselves* **up to sexual i** G1745
Rev 2:14 sacrificed to idols and **committed sexual i**. G4519
Rev 2:20 my servants *into* **sexual i** and the eating G4519
Rev 2:21 I have given her time to repent of her **i** G4518
Rev 9:21 magic arts, their **sexual i** or their thefts. G4518

IMMORTAL (3) [IMMORTALITY]
Ro 1:23 the glory of the **i** God for images made to G915
1Ti 1:17 to the King eternal, **i**, invisible, the only G915
1Ti 6:16 who alone is **i** and who lives in G114

IMMORTALITY (5) [IMMORTAL]
Pr 12:28 there is life; along that path is **i**. H440+4638
Ro 2:7 seek glory, honor and **i**, he will give eternal G914
1Co 15:53 the imperishable, and the mortal *with* **i**. G114
1Co 15:54 the mortal *with* **i**, then the saying that G114
2Ti 1:10 has brought life and **i** to light through the G914

IMMOVABLE (2)
Job 41:23 tightly joined; they are firm and **i**. H1153+4572
Zec 12:3 will make Jerusalem an **i** rock for all the H5098

IMMUTABILITY, IMMUTABLE (KJV) UNCHANGEABLE, UNCHANGING

IMNA (1)
1Ch 7:35 Zophah, **I**, Shelesh and Amal. H3557

IMNAH (4) [IMNITE]
Ge 46:17 The sons of Asher: **I**, Ishvah, Ishvi and H3555
Nu 26:44 through **I**, the Imnite clan; through Ishvi H3555
1Ch 7:30 The sons of Asher: **I**, Ishvah, Ishvi and H3555
2Ch 31:14 Kore son of **I** the Levite, keeper of the East H3555

IMNITE (1) [IMNAH]
Nu 26:44 through Imnah, the **I** clan; through Ishvi H3555

IMPALE (2) [IMPALED, IMPALING]
Ge 40:19 off your head and **i** your body on a pole. H9434
Est 7:9 The king said, "**I** him on it!" H9434

IMPALED (11) [IMPALE]
Ge 40:22 but *he* **i** the chief baker, just as Joseph H9434
Ge 41:13 to my position, and the other man *was* **i**." H9434
Jos 8:29 *He* **i** the body of the king of Ai on a pole H9434
Ezr 6:11 their house and *they are to* **be i** on it. A10411
Est 2:23 be true, the two officials **were i** on poles. H9434
Est 5:14 in the morning *to have* Mordecai **i** on it. H9434
Est 7:10 So *they* **i** Haman on the pole he had set H9434
Est 8:7 and *they have* **i** him on the pole he set up H9434
Est 9:13 and *let* Haman's ten sons *be* **i** on poles." H9434
Est 9:14 and *they* **i** the ten sons of Haman. H9434
Est 9:25 that he and his sons *should be* **i** on poles. H9434

IMPALING (1) [IMPALE]
Est 6:4 to the king about **i** Mordecai on the pole H9434

IMPART (3) [IMPARTED]
Pr 29:15 A rod and a reprimand **i** wisdom, but a H5989
Ro 1:11 to see you so that *I may* **i** to you some G3556
Gal 3:21 if a law had been given that could **i** life, G2443

IMPARTED (1) [IMPART]
Ecc 12:9 but *he* also **i** knowledge to the people. H4340

IMPARTIAL (1) [IMPARTIALLY]
Jas 3:17 full of mercy and good fruit, **i** and sincere. G88

IMPARTIALLY (2) [IMPARTIAL]
1Ch 24:5 divided them **i** by casting lots, H465+6640+465
1Pe 1:17 a Father who judges each person's work **i**, G719

IMPATIENT (4)
Nu 21:4 But the people *grew* **i** on the way; H7918+5883
Job 4:2 ventures a word with you, *will you be* **i**? H4206
Job 21:4 to a human being? Why *should* I not *be* **i**? H7918
Mic 2:7 be said, "*Does the* LORD *become* **i**? H7918+8120

IMPERIAL (15) [EMPIRE]
2Ki 25:8 Nebuzaradan commander of the **i guard** H3184
2Ki 25:10 commander of the **i guard** broke down the H3184
2Ki 25:15 commander of the **i guard** took away the H3184
Jer 39:9 commander of the **i guard** carried into H3184
Jer 39:11 Nebuzaradan commander of the **i guard**: H3184
Jer 40:1 commander of the **i guard** had released H3184
Jer 41:10 commander of the **i guard** had appointed H3184
Jer 43:6 commander of the **i guard** had left with H3184
Jer 52:12 Nebuzaradan commander of the **i guard** H3184
Jer 52:14 under the commander of the **i guard** H3184
Jer 52:19 commander of the **i guard** took away the H3184
Jer 52:30 the commander of the **i guard**. H3184
Mt 22:17 Is it right to pay the **i tax** to Caesar or not?" G3056
Mk 12:14 Is it right to pay the **i tax** to Caesar or not? G3056
Ac 27:1 who belonged to the **I** Regiment. G4935

IMPERISHABLE (6)
1Co 15:42 is sown is perishable, it is raised **i**; G1877+914
1Co 15:50 nor does the perishable inherit the **i**. G914
1Co 15:52 the dead will be raised **i**, and we will be G915
1Co 15:53 the perishable must clothe itself with the **i**, G914
1Co 15:54 the perishable has been clothed with the **i**, G914
1Pe 1:23 perishable seed, but *of* **i**, through the living G915

IMPETUOUS (2)
Job 6:3 no wonder my words *have been* **i**. H4362
Hab 1:6 that ruthless and **i** people, who sweep H4554

IMPLIES (1)
Gal 3:20 however, **i** more than one party; but God G1639

IMPLORE (1)
2Co 5:20 through us. *We* **i** you on Christ's behalf G1289

IMPORTANCE (1) [IMPORTANT]
1Co 15:3 I passed on to you **as of first i**: G1877+4755

IMPORTANT (16) [IMPORTANCE]
Jos 10:2 because Gibeon was an **i** city, like one of H1524
1Ki 3:4 that was the **most i** high place, and H1524
2Ki 25:9 Every **i** building he burned down. H1524
Jer 52:13 Every **i** building he burned down. H1524
Mt 23:6 banquets and the **most i seats** in the G4751
Mt 23:23 neglected the **more i matters** of the law— G987
Mk 12:28 the commandments, which is the **most i**?" G4755
Mk 12:29 "The **most i** *one*," answered Jesus, "is this G4755
Mk 12:33 as yourself is **more i** than all burnt G4358
Mk 12:39 have the **most i seats** in the G4751
Lk 11:43 you love the **most i seats** in the G4751
Lk 14:9 you will have to take the **least i** place. G2274
Lk 20:46 have the **most i seats** in the G4751
Ac 8:27 an **i official** in charge of all the treasury of G1541
Php 1:18 The **i thing** is that in every way, whether G4440
Rev 18:23 Your merchants were the world's **i people** G3491

IMPORTED (7)
1Ki 10:12 almugwood *has* never *been* **i** or seen since H995
1Ki 10:28 horses were **i** from Egypt and from H4604
1Ki 10:29 *They* **i** a chariot from Egypt H6590+2256+3655
2Ch 1:16 horses were **i** from Egypt and from H4604
2Ch 1:17 *They* **i** a chariot from Egypt H6590+2256+3655
2Ch 9:28 Solomon's horses *were* **i** from Egypt and H3655
Isa 17:10 set out the finest plants and plant **i** vines, H2424

IMPOSE (4) [IMPOSED, IMPOSING, SELF-IMPOSED]
Dt 25:3 judge *must* not **i** more than forty **lashes**. H5782
Ezr 7:24 that you have no authority to **i** taxes, A10667
Am 5:11 tax on the poor and **i** a tax on their grain. H4374
Rev 2:24 '*I will* not **i** any other burden on you, G965

IMPOSED (5) [IMPOSE]
2Ki 23:33 and *he* **i** on Judah a levy of a hundred H5989
2Ch 24:6 Jerusalem the **tax** *i* by Moses the servant AIT
2Ch 36:3 and **i** *on* Judah a **levy** *of* a hundred H6740
Est 10:1 King Xerxes **i** tribute throughout the H8492
Rev 18:20 her with the judgment she **i on** you." G1666

IMPOSING (3) [IMPOSE]
Jos 22:10 built an **i** altar there by H1524+4200+5260
Pr 17:26 If **i a fine** on the innocent is not good H6740
Da 7:20 that looked more **i** than the others and A10647

IMPOSSIBLE (12)
Ge 11:6 nothing they plan to do *will be* **i** for them. H1307
Jdg 6:5 **It was i** to count them or their camels; they H401
2Sa 13:2 it seemed **i** *for* him to do anything to H7098
Mt 17:20 Nothing *will be* **i** for you." G104
Mt 19:26 "With man this is **i**, but with God all G105
Mk 10:27 "With man this is **i**, but not with God; G105
Lk 18:27 "What is **i** with man is possible with God." G105
Ac 2:24 because it was **i** for death to keep G4024+1543
Heb 6:4 It is **i** for those who have once been G105
Heb 6:18 things in which it is **i** for God to lie, G105
Heb 10:4 It is **i** for the blood of bulls and goats to G105
Heb 11:6 And without faith it is **i** to please God G105

IMPOSTORS (2)
2Co 6:8 good report; genuine, yet regarded as **i**; G4418
2Ti 3:13 while evildoers and **i** will go from bad to G1200

IMPOTENT (KJV) DISABLED, INVALID, LAME

IMPOVERISHED (1) [POOR]
Jdg 6:6 Midian so **i** the Israelites that they cried H1937

IMPRESS (2) [IMPRESSED, IMPRESSES]
Dt 6:7 **I** them on your children. Talk about them H9112
Gal 6:12 Those who want *to* **i** people by means of G2349

IMPRESSED (2) [IMPRESS]
Ecc 9:13 this example of wisdom that greatly **i** me: H448
Jer 44:19 cakes **i with** her **image** and pouring H6771

IMPRESSES (1) [IMPRESS]
Pr 17:10 A rebuke **i** a discerning person more than H5737

IMPRISON (1) [PRISON]
Ac 22:19 to another *to* **i** and beat those who G5872

IMPRISONED (5) [PRISON]
Ge 41:10 *he* **i** me and the chief baker *in* H5989+928+5464
1Sa 23:7 David *has* **i himself** by entering a town H6037
Jer 32:3 Zedekiah king of Judah *had* **i** him there, H3973
Jer 37:15 and **i** *in* the house H5989+1074+2021+657
1Pe 3:19 proclamation to the **i** spirits— G1877+5871

IMPRISONMENT (4) [PRISON]
Ezr 7:26 confiscation of property, or **i**. A10054
Ac 23:29 against him that deserved death or **i**. G1301
Ac 26:31 doing anything that deserves death or **i**." G1301
Heb 11:36 flogging, and even chains and **i**. G5871

IMPRISONMENTS (1) [PRISON]
2Co 6:5 in beatings, **i** and riots; in hard work G5871

IMPRISONS (1) [PRISON]
Job 12:14 be rebuilt; those *he* **i** cannot be released. H6037

IMPROPER (1)
Eph 5:3 because these *are* **i** for God's holy G4560S

IMPROVISE (1)
Am 6:5 harps like David and **i** on musical H3108

IMPUDENT (KJV) BRAZEN, HARDENED, OBSTINATE

IMPURE (45) [IMPURITIES, IMPURITY]
Lev 7:18 it has become **i**; the person who eats H7002
Lev 19:7 third day, it is **i** and will not be accepted. H7002
Nu 5:14 he suspects his wife and she *is* **i**— H3237
Nu 5:14 suspects her even though she *is* not **i**— H3237
Nu 5:19 astray and become **i** while married to your H3240
Nu 5:20 *you have* **made yourself i** by having H3237
Nu 5:27 If *she has* **made herself i** and been H3237
Nu 5:28 the woman *has* not **made herself i**, but is H3237
Nu 5:29 astray and **makes herself i** while married H3237
Dt 23:9 enemies, keep away from everything **i**. H8273
Job 14:4 Who can bring what is pure from the **i** H3238
Isa 65:4 whose pots hold broth of **i meat**; H7002
Eze 4:14 No **i** meat has ever entered my mouth." H7002
Mt 10:1 authority to drive out **i** spirits and to heal G176
Mt 12:43 "When an **i** spirit comes out of a person, it G176
Mk 1:23 who was possessed by an **i** spirit cried out, G176
Mk 1:26 The **i** spirit shook the man violently and G176
Mk 1:27 even gives orders to **i** spirits and they obey G176
Mk 3:11 Whenever the **i** spirits saw him, they fell G176
Mk 3:30 they were saying, "He has an **i** spirit." G176
Mk 5:2 a man with an **i** spirit came from the tombs G176
Mk 5:8 "Come out of this man, you **i** spirit! G176
Mk 5:13 the **i** spirits came out and went into G176
Mk 6:7 two and gave them authority over **i** spirits. G176
Mk 7:25 was possessed by an **i** spirit came and fell G176
Mk 9:25 to the scene, he rebuked the **i** spirit. G176
Lk 4:33 a man possessed by a demon, an **i** spirit. G176
Lk 4:36 he gives orders to **i** spirits and they come G176
Lk 6:18 Those troubled by **i** spirits were cured, G176
Lk 8:29 had commanded the **i** spirit to come out of G176
Lk 9:42 But Jesus rebuked the **i** spirit, healed the G176
Lk 11:24 "When an **i** spirit comes out of a person, it G176
Ac 5:16 their sick and those tormented by **i** spirits, G176
Ac 8:7 For with shrieks, **i** spirits came out of many G176
Ac 10:14 "I have never eaten anything **i** or unclean." G3123
Ac 10:15 "*Do* not **call** anything **i** that God has G3124
Ac 10:28 that I should not call anyone **i** or unclean. G3123
Ac 11:8 Nothing **i** or unclean has ever entered my G3123
Ac 11:9 '*Do* not **call** anything **i** that God has made G3124

Eph 5: 5 No immoral, i or greedy person—such a G176
1Th 2: 3 does not spring from error or i *motives*, G174
1Th 4: 7 For God did not call us to be i, but to live a G174
Rev 16:13 Then I saw three i spirits that looked like G176
Rev 18: 2 demons and a haunt for every i spirit, G176
Rev 21:27 Nothing i will ever enter it, nor will anyone G3123

IMPURITIES (3) [IMPURE]
Isa 1:25 away your dross and remove all your i. H975
Eze 24:11 so that its i may be melted and its deposit H3240
Eze 36:25 you from all your i and from all your idols. H3240

IMPURITY (15) [IMPURE]
Lev 15:19 the i of her monthly period will last seven H5614
Lev 20:21 it is an act of i; he has dishonored H5614
Nu 5:13 her husband and *her* i is undetected H3237
Ezr 9:11 filled it with their i from one end to the H3240
Eze 24:13 " 'Now your i is lewdness. Because I tried H3240
Eze 24:13 you would not be cleansed from your i, H3240
Zec 13: 1 to cleanse them from sin and i. H5614
Zec 13: 2 prophets and the spirit of i from the land. H3240
Ro 1:24 of their hearts to sexual i for the degrading G174
Ro 6:19 yourselves as slaves *to* i and to G174
2Co 12:21 earlier and have not repented of the i, G174
Gal 5:19 sexual immorality, i and debauchery; G174
Eph 4:19 so as to indulge in every kind of i, G174
Eph 5: 3 immorality, or of any kind of i, or of greed, G174
Col 3: 5 sexual immorality, i, lust, evil desires and G174

IMPUTE, IMPUTED, IMPUTETH, IMPUTING
(KJV) ACCUSE, CHARGED, COUNT, COUNTING, CREDIT, CREDITED, HOLD GUILTY, RECKONED

IMRAH (1)
1Ch 7:36 Suah, Harnepher, Shual, Beri, I, H3559

IMRI (2)
1Ch 9: 4 son of Omri, the son of I, the son of Bani, H617
Ne 3: 2 Zakkur son of I built next to them. H617

IN (11336) [INASMUCH, INMOST, INNER, INNERMOST, INSIDE, WITHIN] See Index of Articles Etc.

INASMUCH (2) [IN]
Ro 11:13 I as I am the apostle to G2093+4012+3525+4036
1Pe 4:13 But rejoice i as you participate in the G2771

INCAPABLE (1)
Hos 8: 5 How long *will they be* i *of* purity? H3523+4202

INCENSE (151) [FRANKINCENSE, INCENSED]
Ex 25: 6 the anointing oil and for the fragrant i; H7792
Ex 30: 1 an altar of acacia wood for burning i. H7792
Ex 30: 7 must burn fragrant i on the altar every H7792
Ex 30: 8 He must burn i again when he lights the H5626S
Ex 30: 8 lamps at twilight so i will burn regularly H7792
Ex 30: 9 this altar any other i or any burnt offering H7792
Ex 30:27 its accessories, the altar of i, H7792
Ex 30:35 make a fragrant blend of i, the work of H7792
Ex 30:37 Do not make any i with this formula for H7792
Ex 30:38 Whoever makes i like it to enjoy its fragrance NDT
Ex 31: 8 all its accessories, the altar of i, H7792
Ex 31:11 oil and fragrant i for the Holy Place. H7792
Ex 35: 8 the anointing oil and for the fragrant i; H7792
Ex 35:15 the altar of i with its poles, the anointing H7792
Ex 35:15 the anointing oil and the fragrant i; the H7792
Ex 35:28 the anointing oil and for the fragrant i. H7792
Ex 37:25 made the altar of i out of acacia wood. H7792
Ex 37:29 the pure, fragrant i—the work of a H7792
Ex 39:38 the fragrant i, and the curtain for the H7792
Ex 40: 5 the gold altar of i in front of the ark of H7792
Ex 40:27 burned fragrant i on it, as the LORD H7792
Lev 2: 1 They are to pour olive oil on it, put i on it H4247
Lev 2: 2 together with all the i, and burn this as a H4247
Lev 2:15 Put oil and i on it; it is a grain offering. H4247
Lev 2:16 together with all the i, as a food offering H4247
Lev 4: 7 the altar of fragrant i that is before the H7792
Lev 5:11 They must not put olive oil or i on it H4247
Lev 6:15 with all the i on the grain offering H4247
Lev 10: 1 put fire in them and added i; and they H7792
Lev 16:12 ground fragrant i and take them behind H7792
Lev 16:13 He is to put the i on the fire before the H7792
Lev 16:13 the smoke of the i will conceal the H7792
Lev 24: 7 each stack put *some* pure i as a memorial H4247
Lev 26:30 cut down your i altars and pile your dead H2802
Nu 4:16 the light, the fragrant i, the regular grain H7792
Nu 5:15 must not pour olive oil on it or put i on it, H4247
Nu 7:14 dish weighing ten shekels, filled with i; H7792
Nu 7:20 dish weighing ten shekels, filled with i; H7792
Nu 7:26 dish weighing ten shekels, filled with i; H7792
Nu 7:32 dish weighing ten shekels, filled with i; H7792
Nu 7:38 dish weighing ten shekels, filled with i; H7792
Nu 7:44 dish weighing ten shekels, filled with i; H7792
Nu 7:50 dish weighing ten shekels, filled with i; H7792
Nu 7:56 dish weighing ten shekels, filled with i; H7792
Nu 7:62 dish weighing ten shekels, filled with i; H7792
Nu 7:68 dish weighing ten shekels, filled with i; H7792
Nu 7:74 dish weighing ten shekels, filled with i; H7792
Nu 7:80 dish weighing ten shekels, filled with i; H7792
Nu 7:86 dishes filled with i weighed ten shekels H7792
Nu 16: 7 burning coals and i in them before the H7792
Nu 16:17 man is to take his censer and put i in it— H7792
Nu 16:18 put burning coals and i in it, and stood H7792
Nu 16:35 the 250 men who were offering the i. H7792
Nu 16:40 should come to burn i before the LORD, H7792
Nu 16:46 "Take your censer and put i in it, along H7792
Nu 16:47 Aaron offered the i and made atonement H7792
Dt 33:10 He offers i before you and whole burnt H7777
1Sa 2:28 to my altar, to burn i, and to wear an H7787
1Ki 3: 3 sacrifices and burned i on the high places H7787
1Ki 9:25 burning i before the LORD along with them, H7787
1Ki 11: 8 *who* burned i and offered sacrifices to H7787
1Ki 22:43 to offer sacrifices and burn i there. H7787
2Ki 12: 3 to offer sacrifices and burn i there. H7787
2Ki 14: 4 to offer sacrifices and burn i there. H7787
2Ki 15: 4 to offer sacrifices and burn i there. H7787
2Ki 15:35 to offer sacrifices and burn i there. H7787
2Ki 16: 4 sacrifices and burned i at the high places, H7787
2Ki 17:11 At every high place *they* burned i, as the H7787
2Ki 18: 4 the Israelites had been burning i to it. H7787
2Ki 22:17 forsaken me and burned i to other gods H7787
2Ki 23: 5 kings of Judah *to* burn i on the high H7787
2Ki 23: 5 those *who* burned i to Baal, to H7787
2Ki 23: 8 where the priests *had* burned i. H7787
1Ch 6:49 on the altar of i in connection with all H7792
1Ch 9:29 wine, and the olive oil, i and spices. H4247
1Ch 28:18 of the refined gold for the altar of i. H7792
2Ch 2: 4 it to him for burning fragrant i before him, H7792
2Ch 13:11 burnt offerings and fragrant i to the LORD. H7792
2Ch 14: 5 high places and i altars in every town in H2802
2Ch 26:16 temple of the LORD to burn i on the altar of H7787
2Ch 26:16 the LORD to burn incense on the altar of i. H7792
2Ch 26:18 for you, Uzziah, to burn i to the LORD. H7787
2Ch 26:18 who have been consecrated to burn i. H7787
2Ch 26:19 had a censer in his hand *ready* to burn i, H7787
2Ch 26:19 presence before the i altar in the LORD's H7792
2Ch 28: 4 sacrifices and burned i at the high places, H7787
2Ch 29: 7 They did not burn i or present any burnt H7792
2Ch 29:11 to minister before him and *to* burn i." H7787
2Ch 30:14 cleared away the i altars and threw them H5232
2Ch 34: 4 cut to pieces the i altars that were above H2802
2Ch 34: 7 to pieces all the i altars throughout Israel. H2802
2Ch 34:25 forsaken me and burned i to other gods H7787
Ne 13: 5 grain offerings and i and temple articles, H4247
Ne 13: 9 with the grain offerings and the i. H4247
Ps 141: 2 May my prayer be set before you like i H7792
Pr 27: 9 Perfume and i bring joy to the heart, and H7792
SS 3: 6 with myrrh and i made from all the H4247
SS 4: 6 the mountain of myrrh and to the hill of i. H4247
SS 4:14 with every kind of i tree, with myrrh and H4247
Isa 1:13 Your i is detestable to me. H7792
Isa 17: 8 poles and the i altars their fingers have H2802
Isa 27: 9 no Asherah poles or i altars will be left H2802
Isa 43:23 wearied you with demands for i. H4247
Isa 60: 6 bearing gold and i and proclaiming the H4247
Isa 65: 3 in gardens and burning i on altars of brick H7787
Isa 66: 3 whoever burns memorial i is like one who H4247
Jer 1:16 *in* burning i to other gods and in H7787
Jer 6:20 do I care about i from Sheba or sweet H4247
Jer 7: 9 burn i to Baal and follow other gods you H7787
Jer 11:12 cry out to the gods to whom they burn i, H7787
Jer 11:13 you have set up to burn i to that shameful H7787
Jer 11:17 aroused my anger by burning i to Baal. H7787
Jer 17:26 grain offerings and i, and bringing thank H4247
Jer 18:15 *they* burn i to worthless idols H7787
Jer 19: 4 *they have* burned i in it to gods that H7787
Jer 19:13 houses where *they* burned i on the roofs H7787
Jer 32:29 my anger by burning i on the roofs to H7787
Jer 41: 5 grain offerings and i with them to the H4247
Jer 44: 3 my anger by burning i to and worshiping H7787
Jer 44: 5 stop burning i to other gods. H7787
Jer 44: 8 burning i to other gods in Egypt H7787
Jer 44:15 their wives *were* burning i to other gods, H7787
Jer 44:17 We *will* burn i to the Queen of Heaven H7787
Jer 44:18 we stopped burning i to the Queen of H7787
Jer 44:19 "When we burned i to the Queen of H7787
Jer 44:21 call to mind the i burned in the towns H7789
Jer 44:23 Because *you have* burned i and have H7787
Jer 44:25 vows we made to burn i and pour out H7787
Jer 48:35 the high places and burn i to their gods," H7787
Eze 6: 4 your i altars will be smashed; H2802
Eze 6: 6 ruined, your i altars broken down H2802
Eze 6:13 they offered fragrant i to all their H8194+5767
Eze 8:11 and a fragrant cloud of i was rising. H7792
Eze 16:18 you offered my oil and i before them. H7792
Eze 16:19 offered as fragrant i before them. H8194+5767
Eze 20:28 their fragrant i and poured out H8194+5767
Eze 20:41 you as fragrant i when I bring H8194+5767
Eze 23:41 you had placed the i and olive oil that H7792
Da 2:46 an offering and i be presented to him. A10478
Hos 2:13 her for the days she burned i to the Baals; H7787
Hos 11: 2 to the Baals and *they* burned i to images. H7787
Hab 1:16 to his net and burns i to his dragnet, H7787
Mal 1:11 In every place i and pure offerings will be H5231
Lk 1: 9 go into the temple of the Lord and burn i. G2594
Lk 1:10 when the time *for* the burning of i came, G2592
Lk 1:11 standing at the right side of the altar *of* i. G2592
Heb 9: 4 which had the golden altar of i and the G2593
Rev 5: 8 they were holding golden bowls full of i, G2592
Rev 8: 3 He was given much i to offer, with the G2592
Rev 8: 4 The smoke *of* the i, together with the G2592
Rev 18:13 of cinnamon and spice, *of* i, myrrh and G2592

INCENSED (1) [INCENSE]
Ne 4: 1 he became angry and *was* greatly i. H4087

INCIDENT (4)
Nu 25:18 you in the Peor i involving their sister H1821
Nu 25:18 the plague came as a result of that i." H1821S
Nu 31:16 to be unfaithful to the LORD in the Peor i, H1821
1Ki 21: 1 later there was an i involving a vineyard NDT

INCITED (6) [INCITING]
1Sa 22: 8 me that my son *has* i my servant to lie H7756
1Sa 26:19 If the LORD *has* i you against me, then may H6077
2Sa 24: 1 and *he* i David against them H6077
1Ch 21: 1 up against Israel and i David to take a H6077
Job 2: 3 though *you* i me against him to ruin him H6077
Ac 13:50 the Jewish leaders i the God-fearing G4241

INCITING (4) [INCITED]
Dt 13: 5 be put to death for i rebellion against the H1819
Isa 59:13 backs on our God, i revolt and oppression H1819
Jer 43: 3 Baruch son of Neriah *is* i you against us to H6077
Lk 23:14 as *one who was* i the people to rebellion. G695

INCLINATION (2) [INCLINATIONS, INCLINED, INCLINES]
Ge 6: 5 that every i *of* the thoughts of the H3671
Ge 8:21 even though every i *of* the human heart is H3671

INCLINATIONS (1) [INCLINATION]
Jer 7:24 the stubborn i *of* their evil hearts. H4600

INCLINED (2) [INCLINATION]
Dt 5:29 their hearts *would be* i to fear me H2118+2296
Jdg 9: 3 they *were* i to follow Abimelek H5742+4213

INCLINES (1) [INCLINATION]
Ecc 10: 2 The heart of the wise i to the right, but H4200

INCLUDE (18) [INCLUDED, INCLUDES, INCLUDING, INCLUSION]
Nu 1:49 i them in the census of the H5951+906+8031
Nu 28:22 I one male goat as a sin offering to make H2256
Nu 28:30 I one male goat to make atonement for you. NDT
Nu 29: 5 I one male goat as a sin offering to make H2256
Nu 29:11 I one male goat as a sin offering, in addition NDT
Nu 29:16 I one male goat as a sin offering, in H2256
Nu 29:19 I one male goat as a sin offering, in H2256
Nu 29:22 I one male goat as a sin offering, in H2256
Nu 29:25 I one male goat as a sin offering, in H2256
Nu 29:28 I one male goat as a sin offering, in H2256
Nu 29:31 I one male goat as a sin offering, in H2256
Nu 29:34 I one male goat as a sin offering, in H2256
Nu 29:38 I one male goat as a sin offering, in H2256
Nu 34: 3 southern side *will* i some of the Desert H2118
Jos 17: 7 from there to i the people living at En H448
1Ch 21: 6 But Joab did not i Levi and H928+9348
Eze 16:29 increased your promiscuity to i Babylonia, H448
1Co 15:27 it is clear that this does not i God himself G1760

INCLUDED (19) [INCLUDE]
Dt 4:49 and i all the Arabah east of the Jordan, as H2256
Jos 12: 2 of the Ammonites. This i half of Gilead. H2256
Jos 12: 8 The lands i the hill country, the western NDT
Jos 13: 9 and i the whole plateau of Medeba as far H2256
Jos 13:11 It also i Gilead, the territory of the people H2256
Jos 16: 9 It also i all the towns and their villages that NDT
Jos 19: 2 It i: Beersheba (or Sheba), Moladah, H2118
Jos 19:15 I were Kattath, Nahalal, Shimron, Idalah H2256
Jos 19:18 Their territory i: Jezreel, Kesulloth H2118
Jos 19:25 Their territory i: Helkath, Hali, Beten H2118
Jos 19:41 The territory of their inheritance i: Zorah H2118
2Sa 23:19 even though *he was* not i among them. H995
2Sa 23:23 but *he was* not i among the Three. H995
1Ch 7:28 lands and settlements i Bethel and its NDT
1Ch 11:21 even though *he was* not i among them. H995
1Ch 11:25 but *he was* not i among the Three. H995
2Ch 31:18 They i all the little ones, the wives, and the NDT
Job 3: 6 *may it* not be i among the days of the H2526
Eph 1:13 And you also were i in Christ when you G1877

INCLUDES (2) [INCLUDE]
2Co 10:13 a sphere *that* also i you. G2391+948
2Th 1:10 This i you, because you believed our NDT

INCLUDING (67) [INCLUDE]
Ge 17:12 i those born in your household or bought NDT
Ge 17:27 i those born in his household or bought NDT
Ex 10: 5 i every tree that is growing in your fields. H2256
Ex 27:19 i all the tent pegs for it and those for the H2256
Ex 34:19 i all the firstborn males of your livestock H2256
Lev 1: 8 the pieces, i the head and the fat, on the H2256
Lev 1:12 shall arrange them, i the head and the fat H2256
Lev 9:13 piece by piece, i the head, and he burned H2256
Nu 3:39 i every male a month old or more NDT
Nu 4:14 at the altar, i the firepans, meat forks, NDT
Nu 4:16 i its holy furnishings and articles. H928
Nu 21:25 i Heshbon and all its surrounding H928
Nu 31:11 spoils, i the people and animals, H928
Dt 3:12 i half the hill country of Gilead H2256
Jos 8:35 of Israel, i the women and children H2256
Jos 10: 7 entire army, i all the best fighting men. H2256
Jos 10:40 the whole region, i the hill country, the H2256
Jos 12: 1 i all the eastern side of the Arabah: H2256
Jos 13:17 on the plateau, i Dibon, Bamoth Baal, NDT
Jos 13:30 from Mahanaim and i all of Bashan, NDT
Jos 24: 2 i Terah the father of Abraham and Nahor NDT

Jos 24:18 us all the nations, i the Amorites, who H2256
Jdg 20:48 i the animals and everything else they H6330
Jdg 21:10 living there, i the women and children. H2256
1Sa 30:18 the Amalekites had taken, i his two wives. H2256
1Ki 4:31 than anyone else, i Ethan the Ezrahite H4946
1Ki 10:15 not i the revenues from H4200+963+4946
1Ki 14:26 i all the gold shields Solomon had made. H2256
1Ki 22:39 of Ahab's reign, i all he did, the palace H2256
2Ki 8: 6 i all the income from her land from the H2256
2Ki 13:12 i his war against Amaziah king of Judah H889
2Ki 14:15 i his war against Amaziah king of Judah H2256
2Ki 14:28 i how he recovered for Israel both H2256
2Ki 15:29 Galilee, i all the land of Naphtali NDT
2Ki 21:17 all he did, i the sin he committed H2256
2Ki 24: 4 i the shedding of innocent blood H2256+1685
1Ch 12:27 i Jehoiada, leader of the family of Aaron H2256
1Ch 21: 5 i four hundred and seventy thousand in H2256
2Ch 8:15 in any matter, i that of the treasuries. H2256
2Ch 9:14 not i the revenues brought in H4200+963+4946
2Ch 12: 9 i the gold shields Solomon had made. H2256
2Ch 27: 7 i all his wars and the other things he did H2256
2Ch 30:25 i the foreigners who had come from Israel H2256
2Ch 33:18 i his prayer to his God and the words the H2256
Ezr 7: 7 Some of the Israelites, i priests, Levites H2256
Ezr 7:13 in my kingdom, i priests and Levites A10221
Ezr 9: 1 of Israel, i the priests and the Levites H2256
Ne 1: 6 Israelites, i myself and my father's family H2256
Ne 10:39 The people of Israel, i the Levites, are to H2256
Est 4: 7 i the exact amount of money Haman had H2256
Ecc 12:14 deed into judgment, i every hidden thing H6584
Jer 10:16 Maker of all things, i Israel, the people of H2256
Jer 13:13 i the kings who sit on David's throne H2256
Jer 42: 1 i Johanan son of Kareah and Jezaniah H2256
Jer 44:24 to all the people, i the women, "Hear the H2256
Jer 51:19 all things, i the people of his inheritance H2256
Eze 10:12 Their entire bodies, i their backs, their H2256
Eze 41:14 on the east, i the front of the temple H2256
Eze 41:15 of the temple, i its galleries on each side H2256
Eze 41:16 everything beyond and i the threshold was NDT
Mt 8:33 i what had happened to the G2779
Lk 23:27 i women who mourned and wailed for G2779
Lk 23:49 i the women who had followed him from G2779
Ac 21: 5 All of them, i wives and children G5250
Ro 16: 2 the benefactor of many people, i me. G2779
2Co 12:12 of a true apostle, i signs, wonders and G5445
2Ti 1:15 i Phygelus and Hermogenes. G4005+1639

INCLUSION (1) [INCLUDE]

Ro 11:12 much greater riches will their full i bring! G4445

INCOME (5)

2Ki 8: 6 including all the i *from* her land from the H9311
Pr 15: 6 the i *of* the wicked brings ruin. H9311
Ecc 5:10 loves wealth is never satisfied with their i. H9311
Ac 19:25 that we receive a good i from this G2345
1Co 16: 2 a sum of money in keeping with *your* i, G2338

INCOMPARABLE (1) [INCOMPARABLY]

Eph 2: 7 he might show the i riches of his grace, G5650

INCOMPARABLY (1) [INCOMPARABLE]

Eph 1:19 his i great power for us who believe G5650

INCOMPREHENSIBLE (1)

Isa 33:19 whose language is strange and i. H401+1069

INCORRUPTIBLE, INCORRUPTION (KJV)

IMPERISHABLE, LAST FOREVER, NEVER PERISH

INCREASE (47) [EVER-INCREASING, INCREASED, INCREASES, INCREASING]

Ge 1:22 "Be fruitful and i in number and fill the H8049
Ge 1:22 the seas, and *let* the birds i on the earth." H8049
Ge 1:28 "Be fruitful and i in number; fill the earth H8049
Ge 6: 1 beings began to i in number on the earth H8045
Ge 8:17 be fruitful and i in number on it. H8049
Ge 9: 1 "Be fruitful and i in number and fill the H8049
Ge 9: 7 be fruitful and i in number; multiply on H8049
Ge 9: 7 multiply on the earth and i upon it." H8049
Ge 16:10 "*I will* i your descendants so much H8049+8049
Ge 17: 2 you and *will* greatly i your numbers." H8049
Ge 17:20 him fruitful and *will* greatly i his numbers. H8049
Ge 24:60 *may* you i to thousands upon thousands H2118
Ge 26:24 bless you and *will* i the number *of* your H8049
Ge 28: 3 you fruitful and i your numbers until you H8049
Ge 35:11 God Almighty; be fruitful and i in number. H8049
Ge 48: 4 to make you fruitful and i your numbers. H8049
Ge 48:16 and *may they* i greatly on the earth." H1835
Lev 25:16 years are many, *you are to* i the price, and H8049
Lev 26: 9 make you fruitful and i your numbers, H8049
Dt 1:11 *May* the LORD, the God of your ancestors, i H3578+6584
Dt 6: 3 with you and that *you may* i greatly in a H8049
Dt 7:13 you and bless you and i your numbers. H8049
Dt 8: 1 you may live and i and may enter and H8049
Dt 8:13 your silver and gold i and all you have is H8049
Dt 13:17 *He will* i your numbers, as he promised H8049
Dt 28:63 to make you prosper and i in number, H8049
Dt 30:16 then you will live and i, and the LORD your H8049
Job 10:17 against me and i your anger toward me; H8049
Ps 61: 6 I the days of the king's life, his years for H3578
Ps 62:10 though your riches i, do not set your heart H5649
Ps 71:21 *You will* i my honor and comfort me once H8049
Ps 144:13 Our sheep *will* i by thousands, by tens of H545
Pr 22:16 the poor to i his wealth and one H8049
Ecc 5: 9 The i *from* the land is taken by all; the H3862
Ecc 5:11 As goods i, so do those who consume H8049
Jer 23: 3 they will be fruitful and i in number. H8049
Jer 29: 6 I in number there; do not H8049
Eze 36:11 *I will* i the number *of* people and animals H8049
Eze 36:30 *I will* i the fruit of the trees and the crops H8049
Eze 37:26 I will establish them and i their numbers H8049
Da 12: 4 will go here and there *to* i knowledge." H8049
Mt 24:12 Because of the i of wickedness, the love of G4437
Lk 17: 5 apostles said to the Lord, "I our faith!" G4707
Ro 5:20 brought in so that the trespass *might* i. G4429
Ro 6: 1 we go on sinning so that grace *may* i? G4429
2Co 9:10 will also supply and i your store of seed G4437
1Th 3:12 *May* the Lord make your love i and G4429

INCREASED (32) [INCREASE]

Ge 7:17 and *as* the waters i they lifted the ark high H8049
Ge 7:18 The waters rose and i greatly on the earth H8049
Ge 30:30 little you had before I came *has* i greatly, H7287
Ge 47:27 were fruitful and i greatly in number. H8049
Ex 1: 7 i in numbers and became so numerous H8049
Ex 1:20 the people i and became even more H8049
Ex 23:30 until *you have* i *enough* to take H7238
Lev 19:25 In this way your harvest *will be* i. I am the H3578
Dt 1:10 LORD your God *has* i your numbers so that H8049
Jdg 1:35 when the power of the tribes of Joseph i, H3877
1Sa 14:19 camp i more and more. H2143+2256+8041+2143
1Ch 4:38 of their clans. Their families i greatly, H7287
1Ch 5: 9 because their livestock *had* i in Gilead. H8049
2Ch 33:23 himself before the LORD; Amon i his guilt. H8049
Ps 39: 2 saying anything good. But my anguish i; H6579
Ps 107:38 and *their* numbers greatly i, and he H8049
Ps 107:41 of their affliction and i their families like H8492
Ecc 1:16 I *have* i in wisdom more H1540+2256+3578
Isa 9: 3 have enlarged the nation and i their joy; H1540
Isa 57: 9 Molek with olive oil and i your perfumes. H8049
Jer 3:16 *your* numbers *have* i greatly H8049+2256+7238
Eze 16:29 Then *you* i your promiscuity to include H8049
Eze 28: 5 skill in trading *you have* i your wealth, H8049
Eze 31: 5 its boughs i and its branches grew long H8049
Hos 10: 1 As his fruit i, he built more altars; as his H8044
Na 3:16 *You have* i *the* number *of* your merchants H8049
Lk 11:29 *As* the crowds i, Jesus said, "This is a G2044
Ac 6: 7 of disciples in Jerusalem i rapidly, G4437
Ac 7:17 *the* number of our people in Egypt *had* greatly i G889+2779+4437
Ac 9:31 by the Holy Spirit, *it* i in numbers. G4437
Ro 5:20 But where sin i, grace increased all the G4429
Ro 5:20 where sin increased, grace i all the more, G5668

INCREASES (4) [INCREASE]

Ps 49:16 when the splendor of their houses i; H8049
Pr 28: 8 *Whoever* i wealth by taking interest or H8049
Isa 40:29 to the weary and i the power of the weak. H8049
Ro 3: 7 God's truthfulness and so i his glory, G1650

INCREASING (7) [INCREASE]

2Sa 15:12 Absalom's following kept on i. H8041
Job 21: 7 growing old and i *in* power? H1504
Eze 16:25 spreading your legs *with* i promiscuity to H8049
Eze 16:26 aroused my anger with your i promiscuity. H8049
Ac 6: 1 days *when the* number of disciples *was* i, G4437
2Th 1: 3 love all of you have for one another *is* i. G4429
2Pe 1: 8 you possess these qualities *in* i measure, G4429

INCREDIBLE (1)

Ac 26: 8 any of you consider it i that God raises the G603

INCUR (1) [INCURS]

Ex 28:43 so that *they will* not i guilt and die. H5951

INCURABLE (7)

2Ch 21:18 Jehoram with an i disease of the H401+5340
Job 34: 6 I am guiltless, his arrow inflicts an i wound. H631
Isa 17:11 nothing in the day of disease and i pain. H631
Jer 10:19 My wound *is* i! Yet I said to H2703
Jer 15:18 and my wound grievous and i? H4412+8324
Jer 30:12 " 'Your wound is i, your injury beyond H631
Mic 1: 9 For Samaria's plague is i; it has spread to H631

INCURS (1) [INCUR]

Pr 9: 7 whoever rebukes the wicked i abuse. NDT

INDEBTEDNESS (1) [DEBT]

Col 2:14 having canceled the charge of our legal i G5934

INDECENT (2)

Dt 23:14 among you anything i and turn away from H6872
Dt 24: 1 because he finds something i about her, H6872

INDECISIVE (1)

2Ch 13: 7 he was young and i and not strong H8205+4222

INDEED (75)

Ge 15: 5 count the stars—if i you can count them." H561
Ge 27:33 I blessed him—and i he will be blessed!" H1685
Ex 3: 7 "*I have* i seen the misery of my H8011+8011
Nu 22: 3 I, Moab was filled with dread because of H2256
Dt 9:13 they are a stiff-necked people i! H2180
Dt 18: 1 The Levitical priests—i, the whole tribe of NDT
Jdg 5:29 ladies answer her; i, she keeps saying to H677
1Sa 21: 5 "I women have been kept from us H3954+561
2Sa 3:36 were pleased; i, everything the king H3869
1Ki 8:13 *I have* i built a magnificent temple H1215+1215
1Ki 10: 7 I, not even half was told me; in wisdom H2180
2Ki 14:10 *You have* i defeated Edom and now H5782+5782
1Ch 16:19 few in number, few i, and strangers in it, H3869
2Ch 9: 6 I, not even half the greatness of your H2180
2Ch 12:12 totally destroyed. I, there was some H2256+1685
2Ch 13: 8 You are i a vast army and have with you H2256
2Ch 20: 4 help from the LORD; i, they came from H1685
2Ch 26:20 I, he himself was eager to leave H2256+1685
Job 9: 2 "I, I know that this is true. But how can H597
Job 13:16 I, this will turn out for my deliverance, for H1685
Job 19: 5 If i you would exalt yourselves above me H597
Job 35:13 I, God does not listen to their empty plea H421
Ps 58: 1 Do you rulers i speak justly? Do you judge H598
Ps 85:12 The LORD will i give what is good, and our H1685
Ps 87: 5 I, of Zion it will be said, "This one and H2256
Ps 89:18 I, our shield belongs to the LORD, our king H3954
Ps 89:43 I, you have turned back the edge of his H677
Ps 93: 1 armed with strength; i, the world is H677
Ps 105:12 few in number, few i, and strangers in it, NDT
Ps 121: 4 i, he who watches over Israel will neither H2180
Pr 2: 3 i, if you call out for insight and cry aloud H3954
Pr 23:15 heart is wise, then my heart will be glad i; H1685
Ecc 7:20 I, there is no one on earth who is H3954
Isa 57: 6 your portion; i, they are your lot. H2156+2156
Jer 2:20 I, on every high hill and under every H3954
Jer 14:13 I, I will give you lasting peace in this H3954
Jer 14:20 ancestors; we have i sinned against you. H3954
Jer 20: 9 I am weary of holding it in; i, I cannot. H2256
Jer 23:32 I, I am against those who prophesy false H2180
Jer 25:29 and *will* you i go unpunished? H5927+5927
Jer 32:30 from their youth; i, the people of Israel H3954
Jer 42:17 I, all who are determined to go to Egypt to H2256
La 3: 3 i, he has turned his hand against me again H421
Eze 33:32 I, to them you are nothing more than one H2180
Hab 2: 5 i, wine betrays him; he is H2256+677+3954
Mt 20:23 "You will i drink from my cup G3836+3525
Lk 10:42 things are needed—or *i* only one. Mary has AIT
Lk 12: 7 I, the very hairs of your head are all G247+2779
Lk 13:30 I there are those who are last who G2779+2627
Lk 18:25 I, it is easier for a camel to go through the G1142
Jn 4:14 I, the water I give them will become in G247
Jn 8:24 that I am he, *you will i* die in your sins." AIT
Jn 8:36 if the Son sets you free, you will be free i. G3953
Ac 3:24 "I, beginning with Samuel, all the G2779
Ac 4:27 I Herod and Pontius Pilate G1142+2093+237
Ac 7:34 *I have* i seen the oppression of my G3972+3972
Ro 2:14 I, when Gentiles, who do not have the law, G1142
Ro 8: 9 if i the Spirit of God lives in you. G1642
Ro 8:17 if i we share in his sufferings in order that G1642
Ro 15:27 to do it, and i they owe it to them. G2779
1Co 3: 2 not yet ready for it. I, you are still not ready G247
1Co 4: 3 by any human court; i, I do not even judge G247
1Co 8: 5 on earth (as i there are many "gods G6061
1Co 14: 2 I, no one understands them; they utter G1142
1Co 15:20 But Christ has i been raised from the dead G3815
2Co 1: 9 I, we felt we had received the sentence of G247
2Co 11: 6 I may i be untrained as a speaker, but I do G2779
Php 2:27 I he was ill, and almost died. But God had G2779
Php 4:10 I, you were concerned, but you had no G2779
Col 2:23 Such regulations i have an appearance of G3525
1Th 2:13 which is i at work in you who believe. G2779
1Th 2:20 I, you are our glory and joy. G1142
Heb 3: 6 if i we hold firmly to our confidence and G1569
Heb 3:14 if i we hold our original conviction firmly G1570
Heb 7:11 and i the law given to the people G1142

INDEPENDENT (2)

1Co 11:11 in the Lord woman is not i of man, nor is G6006
1Co 11:11 of man, nor is man i of woman. G6006

INDESCRIBABLE (1)

2Co 9:15 Thanks be to God for his i gift! G442

INDESTRUCTIBLE (1)

Heb 7:16 on the basis of the power of an i life. G186

INDIA (2)

Est 1: 1 127 provinces stretching from I to Cush: H2064
Est 8: 9 127 provinces stretching from I to Cush. H2064

INDICATE (4) [INDICATED, INDICATING]

1Sa 16: 3 You are to anoint for me the one *I* i." H606
1Sa 24:11 nothing in my hand *to* i *that* I am guilty of H3359
Jn 21:19 Jesus said this *to* i the kind of death by G4955
Heb 12:27 i the removing of what can be shaken G1317

INDICATED (1) [INDICATE]

2Ki 6:10 checked on the place i *by* the man of God. H606

INDICATING (1) [INDICATE]

Heb 9: 9 i that the gifts and sacrifices being G2848+4005

INDICTMENT (1)

Job 31:35 let my accuser put his i in writing. H6219

INDIGNANT (7) [INDIGNANTLY, INDIGNATION]

Mt 20:24 about this, *they were* i with the two brothers. G24
Mt 21:15 "Hosanna to the Son of David," *they were* i. G24
Mt 26: 8 saw this, *they were* i. "Why this waste?" G24
Mk 1:41 Jesus *was* i. He reached out his hand G3974
Mk 10:14 Jesus saw this, *he was* i. He said to them, G24

Mk 10:41 they became i with James and John. G24
Lk 13:14 I because Jesus had healed on the Sabbath G24

INDIGNANTLY (1) [INDIGNANT]
Mk 14: 4 those present were saying i to one another, G24

INDIGNATION (6) [INDIGNANT]
Ps 78:49 his wrath, i and hostility—a band of H2405
Ps 90: 7 by your anger and terrified by your i. H2779
Ps 119:53 I grips me because of the wicked, who H2363
Jer 15:17 was on me and you had filled me with i. H2405
Na 1: 6 Who can withstand his i? Who can H2405
2Co 7:11 to clear yourselves, what i, what alarm, G25

INDISPENSABLE (1)
1Co 12:22 of the body that seem to be weaker are i, G338

INDIVIDUAL (1) [INDIVIDUALLY, INDIVIDUALS]
Job 34:29 Yet he is over i and nation alike, H132

INDIVIDUALLY (1) [INDIVIDUAL]
1Ch 23:24 under their names and counted i, H4200+1653

INDIVIDUALS (1) [INDIVIDUAL]
Jude 4 For certain i whose condemnation was G476

INDOORS (2)
Mt 9:28 When he had gone i, the G1650+3836+3864
Mk 9:28 After Jesus had gone i, his G1650+3875

INDULGE (7) [INDULGED, INDULGENCE, INDULGING, SELF-INDULGENCE]
Ex 32: 6 to eat and drink and got up to i in revelry. H7464
Nu 25: 1 men began to i in sexual immorality with H2388
Lk 7:25 expensive clothes and i in luxury are in G5639
1Co 10: 7 to eat and drink and got up to i in revelry." G4089
Gal 5:13 But do not use your freedom to i the flesh G929
Eph 4:19 to sensuality so as to i in every kind of G2238
2Ti 2:16 because those who i in it will become more NDT

INDULGED (1) [INDULGE]
2Co 12:21 sin and debauchery in which they have i. G4556

INDULGENCE (1) [INDULGE]
Col 2:23 lack any value in restraining sensual i. G4447

INDULGING (1) [INDULGE]
1Ti 3: 8 sincere, not i in much wine, and not G4668

INEFFECTIVE (1)
2Pe 1: 8 keep you from being i and unproductive in G734

INEXPERIENCED (2)
1Ch 22: 5 "My son Solomon is young and i, and the H8205
1Ch 29: 1 whom God has chosen, is young and i. H8205

INEXPRESSIBLE (2)
2Co 12: 4 caught up to paradise and heard i things, G777
1Pe 1: 8 are filled with an i and glorious joy, G443

INFAMOUS (1)
Eze 22: 5 mock you, you i city, full of H3238+2021+9005

INFANCY (1) [INFANT]
2Ti 3:15 how from i you have known the Holy G1100

INFANT (7) [INFANCY, INFANT'S, INFANTS]
Nu 11:12 as a nurse carries an i, to the land you H3437
Nu 12:12 let her be like a stillborn i coming from its H4637
Job 3:16 like an i who never saw the light of day? H6407
Job 24: 9 the i of the poor is seized for a debt. H6403
Isa 11: 8 The i will play near the cobra's den, and H3437
Isa 65:20 will there be in it an i who lives but a few H6403
Heb 5:13 being still an i, is not acquainted G3758

INFANT'S (1) [INFANT]
La 4: 4 Because of thirst the i tongue sticks to the H3437

INFANTS (14) [INFANT]
Dt 32:25 will perish, the i and those with gray hair. H3437
1Sa 15: 3 women, children and i, cattle and sheep, H3437
1Sa 22:19 women, its children and i, and its cattle, H3437
Ps 8: 2 of children and i you have established a H3437
Ps 137: 9 one who seizes your i and dashes them H6408
Isa 13:16 Their i will be dashed to pieces before H6407
Isa 13:18 they will have no mercy on i, nor H7262+1061
Jer 44: 7 women, the children and i, and so leave H3437
La 2:11 because children and i faint in the streets H3437
Na 3:10 Her i were dashed to pieces at every H6408
Mt 21:16 " 'From the lips of children and i you, Lord G2558
1Co 3: 1 who are still worldly—mere i in Christ. G3758
1Co 14:20 In regard to evil be i, but in your thinking G3757
Eph 4:14 Then we will no longer be i, tossed back G3758

INFERIOR (6)
Job 12: 3 a mind as well as you; I am not i to you. H5877
Job 13: 2 you know, I also know; I am not i to you. H5877
Da 2:39 another kingdom will arise, i to yours. A10075
2Co 11: 5 I do not think I am in the least i to those G5728
2Co 12:11 for I am not in the least i to the G5728
2Co 12:13 How were you i to the other churches G2273

INFIDEL (KJV) UNBELIEVER

INFILTRATED (1)
Gal 2: 4 believers had i our ranks to spy on G4207+4209

INFINITE (KJV) BOUNDLESS, ENDLESS, NO LIMIT

INFIRM (1) [INFIRMITIES, INFIRMITY]
2Ch 36:17 men or young women, the elderly or the i. H3844

INFIRMITIES (1) [INFIRM]
Mt 8:17 "He took up our i and bore our diseases." G819

INFIRMITY (1) [INFIRM]
Lk 13:12 "Woman, you are set free from your i." G819

INFLAMED (3) [INFLAMMATION]
Isa 5:11 up late at night till they are i with wine. H1944
Hos 7: 5 the princes become i with wine, H2703+2779
Ro 1:27 with women and were i with lust for one G1706

INFLAMMATION (1) [INFLAMED]
Dt 28:22 with fever and i, with scorching heat H1945

INFLICT (23) [INFLICTED, INFLICTS]
Dt 7:15 He will not i on you the horrible diseases H8492
Dt 7:15 but he will i them on all who hate you. H5989
Dt 28:53 your enemy will i on you during the H7439
Dt 28:55 your enemy will i on you during the H7439
Dt 28:57 your enemy will i on you during the H7439
Jdg 20:31 They began to i casualties on the H5782
Jdg 20:39 had begun to i casualties on the H5782
Ps 149: 7 to i vengeance on the nations and H6913
Jer 18: 8 I will relent and not i on it the disaster I H6913
Jer 26: 3 I will relent and not i on them the disaster H6913
Jer 36: 3 about every disaster I plan to i on them, H6913
Eze 5: 8 and I will i punishment on you in the H6913
Eze 5:10 I will i punishment on you and will scatter H6913
Eze 5:15 around you when I i punishment on you H6913
Eze 11: 9 of foreigners and i punishment on you. H6913
Eze 16:41 your houses and i punishment on you in H6913
Eze 25:11 and I will i punishment on Moab. H6913
Eze 28:22 when I i punishment on you and within H6913
Eze 28:26 live in safety when I i punishment on all H6913
Eze 30:14 fire to Zoan and i punishment on Thebes H6913
Eze 30:19 So I will i punishment on Egypt, and they H6913
Eze 39:21 see the punishment I i and the hand I lay H6913
Rev 9:19 having heads with which they i injury. G92

INFLICTED (17) [INFLICT]
Ge 12:17 the LORD i serious diseases on Pharaoh H5595
Lev 24:20 The one who has i the injury must suffer H5989
1Sa 14:47 he turned, he i punishment on them. H8399
1Sa 23: 5 He i heavy losses on the Philistines and H5782
2Sa 7:14 with floggings i by human hands. AIT
1Ki 20:21 chariots and i heavy losses on the H5782
1Ki 20:29 i a hundred thousand casualties on the H5782
2Ki 8:29 the Arameans had i on him at Ramoth in H5782
2Ki 9:15 the Arameans had i on him in the battle H5782
2Ch 13:17 his troops i heavy losses on them H5782
2Ch 22: 6 the wounds they had i on him at Ramoth H5782
2Ch 28: 5 of Israel, who i heavy casualties on him. H5782
Isa 30:26 of his people and heals the wounds he i. H4804
Jer 42:10 concerning the disaster I have i on you. H6913
La 1:12 like my suffering that was i on me, H6618
Eze 23:10 women, and punishment was i on her. H6913
2Co 2: 6 The punishment i on him by the majority is AIT

INFLICTS (2) [INFLICT]
Job 34: 6 guiltless, his arrow i an incurable wound. NDT
Zec 14:18 on them the plague he i on the nations H5597

INFLUENCE (1) [INFLUENCED, INFLUENTIAL]
Job 31:21 fatherless, knowing that I had i in court, H6476

INFLUENCED (1) [INFLUENCE]
1Co 12: 2 somehow or other you were i and led astray G72

INFLUENTIAL (1) [INFLUENCE]
1Co 1:26 not many were i; not many were of noble G1543

INFORM (8) [INFORMATION, INFORMED]
Ex 18:16 the parties and i them of God's decrees H3359
1Sa 27:11 he thought, "They might i on us and say H5583
2Sa 15:28 until word comes from you to i me." H5583
2Sa 17:17 A female servant was to go and i them H5583
2Sa 17:21 out of the well and went to i King David. H5583
Ezr 4:14 are sending this message to i the king, A10313
Ezr 4:16 We i the king that if this city is built and A10313
Job 12: 8 teach you, or let the fish in the sea i you. H6218

INFORMATION (5) [INFORM]
1Sa 23:22 Go and get more i. Find out where David H3922
1Sa 23:23 uses and come back to me with definite i. H3922
Ezr 5:10 the names of their leaders for your i. A10313
Ac 23:15 wanting more accurate i about his case. G1336
Ac 23:20 of wanting more accurate i about him. G4785

INFORMED (6) [INFORM]
2Ki 22:10 Then Shaphan the secretary i the king H5583
2Ch 34:18 Then Shaphan the secretary i the king H5583
Da 1: 4 kind of learning, well i, quick to H3359+1981
Ac 21:21 They have been i that you teach all the G2994
Ac 23:30 When I was i of a plot to be carried out G3606
1Co 1:11 some from Chloe's household have i me G1317

INGATHERING (2) [GATHER]
Ex 23:16 the Festival of I at the end of the year, H658
Ex 34:22 the Festival of I at the turn of the year. H658

INHABIT (3) [HABITAT, INHABITANT, INHABITANTS, INHABITED]
Job 15:28 he will i ruined towns and houses where H8905
Isa 13:22 Hyenas will i her strongholds, jackals her H6410
Ac 17:26 that they should i the whole earth G2997

INHABITANT (3) [INHABIT]
Isa 6:11 "Until the cities lie ruined and without i H3782
Jer 4: 7 Your towns will lie in ruins without i. H3782
Jer 46:19 be laid waste and lie in ruins without i. H3782

INHABITANTS (50) [INHABIT]
Lev 18:25 its sin, and the land vomited out its i. H3782
Lev 25:10 liberty throughout the land to all its i. H3782
Nu 14:14 And they will tell the i of this land about it. H3782
Nu 32:17 for protection from the i of the land. H3782
Nu 33:52 drive out all the i of the land before you H3782
Nu 33:55 if you do not drive out the i of the land, H3782
Jos 9:24 to wipe out all its i from before you. H3782
Jos 13: 6 "As for all the i of the mountain regions H3782
Jdg 1:16 to live among the i of the Desert of Judah H6639
Jdg 1:32 the Canaanite i of the land because H3782
Jdg 1:33 lived among the Canaanite i of the land, H3782
Jdg 19:16 the i of the place were Benjamites) H408
1Sa 6:19 down some of the i of Beth Shemesh, H408
1Ki 9:16 killed its Canaanite i and then gave it as H3782
2Ki 16: 9 He deported its i to Kir and put Rezin to H2023S
2Ki 23: 2 people of Judah, the i of Jerusalem, the H3782
1Ch 8:13 Aijalon and who drove out the i of Gath. H3782
1Ch 10:11 When all the i of Jabesh Gilead heard what NDT
1Ch 22:18 For he has given the i of the land into my H3782
2Ch 15: 5 all the i of the lands were in great H3782
2Ch 20: 7 you not drive out the i of this land before H3782
2Ch 34: 9 Benjamin and the i of Jerusalem. H3782
2Ch 34:30 people of Judah, the i of Jerusalem, the H3782
Isa 9: 9 Ephraim and the i of Samaria—who say H3782
Isa 24: 1 he will ruin its face and scatter its i— H3782
Isa 24: 6 Therefore earth's i are burned up, and H3782
Isa 51: 6 out like a garment and its i die like flies. H3782
Jer 4: 4 you people of Judah and i of Jerusalem H3782
Jer 25: 9 this land and its i and against all the H3782
Jer 44:22 a curse and a desolate waste without i, H3782
Jer 48:18 parched ground, you i of Daughter Dibon H3782
Jer 49: 3 you i of Rabbah! Put on H1426
Jer 51:35 flesh be on Babylon," say the i of Zion. H3782
Da 9: 7 of Judah and the i of Jerusalem and all H3782
Mic 6:12 your i are liars and their tongues speak H3782
Mic 7:13 will become desolate because of its i, H3782
Zec 8:20 peoples and the i of many cities will yet H3782
Zec 8:21 the i of one city will go to another and H3782
Zec 12: 7 of Jerusalem's i may not be greater H3782
Zec 12:10 of David and the i of Jerusalem a spirit of H3782
Zec 13: 1 house of David and the i of Jerusalem, H3782
Rev 3:10 the whole world to test the i of the earth. G2997
Rev 6:10 until you judge the i of the earth and G2997
Rev 8:13 Woe to the i of the earth, because of the G2997
Rev 11:10 The i of the earth will gloat over them G2997
Rev 13: 8 All i of the earth will worship the beast G2997
Rev 13:12 made the earth and its i worship the first G2997
Rev 13:14 first beast, it deceived the i of the earth. G2997
Rev 17: 2 the i of the earth were intoxicated G2997
Rev 17: 8 The i of the earth whose names have not G2997

INHABITED (16) [INHABIT]
Isa 13:20 She will never be i or lived in through all H3782
Isa 44:26 of Jerusalem, 'It shall be i,' of the towns H3782
Isa 45:18 be empty, but formed it to be i—he says: H3782
Jer 17:25 Jerusalem, and this city will be i forever. H3782
Jer 22: 6 you like a wasteland, like towns not i. H3782
Jer 33:10 deserted, i by neither people nor animals H3782
Jer 46:26 however, Egypt will be i as in times past," H8905
Jer 50:13 LORD's anger she will not be i but will be H3782
Jer 50:39 It will never again be i or lived in from H3782
Eze 12:20 The i towns will be laid waste and the H3782
Eze 26:19 like cities no longer i, and when I bring H3782
Eze 35: 9 desolate forever; your towns will not be i. H3782
Eze 36:10 The towns will be i and the ruins rebuilt. H3782
Eze 36:35 destroyed, are now fortified and i. H3782
Joel 3:20 Judah will be i forever and Jerusalem H3782
Zec 14:11 It will be i; never again will it be destroyed H3782

INHERIT (45) [CO-HEIRS, HEIR, HEIRS, HERITAGE, INHERITANCE, INHERITANCES, INHERITED, INHERITS]
Ge 15: 2 and the one who will i my estate is H1201+5479
Ge 48: 6 in the territory they i they will be reckoned H5709
Nu 14:24 he went to, and his descendants will i it. H3769
Nu 32:32 the property we i will be on this side H5709
Dt 1:38 because he will lead Israel to i it. H5706
Dt 3:28 across and will cause them to i the land H5706
Dt 33:23 blessing; he will i southward to the lake." H3769
Jos 1: 6 you will lead these people to i the land I H5706
1Sa 2: 8 with princes and has them i a throne of H5706
2Ki 2: 9 "Let me i a double portion of your H2118+448
1Ch 16:18 land of Canaan as the portion you will i." H5709
Ps 25:13 their descendants will i the land. H3769
Ps 37: 9 who hope in the LORD will i the land. H3769
Ps 37:11 But the meek will i the land and enjoy H3769

Ps 37:22 those the LORD blesses will i the land, but H3769
Ps 37:29 The righteous will i the land and dwell in H3769
Ps 37:34 He will exalt you to i the land; when the H3769
Ps 69:36 the children of his servants will i it, and H5706
Ps 105:11 land of Canaan as the portion you will i." H5709
Pr 3:35 The wise i honor, but fools get only H5706
Pr 11:29 brings ruin on their family will i only wind, H5706
Pr 14:18 The simple i folly, but the prudent are H5706
Ecc 5:14 children there is nothing left for them to i. AIT
Isa 14:21 they are not to rise to i the land and cover H3769
Isa 57:13 takes refuge in me will i the land and H5706
Isa 61: 7 And so you will i a double portion in your H3769
Isa 65: 9 my chosen people will i them, and there H3769
Zep 2: 9 the survivors of my nation will i their land." H5706
Zec 2:12 The LORD will i Judah as his portion in the H5706
Mt 5: 5 are the meek, for they will i the earth. G3099
Mt 19:29 times as much and will i eternal life. G3099
Mk 10:17 he asked, "what must I do to i eternal life?" G3099
Lk 10:25 he asked, "what must I do to i eternal life?" G3099
Lk 18:18 teacher, what must I do to i eternal life?" G3099
1Co 6: 9 that wrongdoers will not i the kingdom of G3099
1Co 6:10 swindlers will i the kingdom of God. G3099
1Co 15:50 blood cannot i the kingdom of God, G3099
1Co 15:50 nor does the perishable i the G3099
Gal 5:21 who live like this will not i the kingdom of G3099
Heb 1:14 sent to serve those who will i salvation? G3099
Heb 6:12 who through faith and patience i what G3099
Heb 12:17 when he wanted to i this blessing, he G3099
Jas 2: 5 rich in faith and to i the kingdom he G3101
1Pe 3: 9 were called so that you may i a blessing. G3099
Rev 21: 7 Those who are victorious will i all this, and G3099

INHERITANCE (242) [INHERIT]

Ge 21:10 son will never share in the i with my H3769
Ge 31:14 any share in the i of our father's estate? H5709
Ex 15:17 plant them on the mountain of your i— H5709
Ex 32:13 and it will be their i forever. H5706
Ex 34: 9 our sin, and take us as your i. H5706
Lev 20:24 I will give it to you as an i, a land flowing H3769
Nu 16:14 honey or given us an i of fields and H5709
Nu 18:20 to Aaron, "You will have no i in their land H5706
Nu 18:20 your share and your i among the Israelites H5709
Nu 18:21 in Israel as their i in return for the work H5709
Nu 18:23 They will receive no i among the H5706+5709
Nu 18:24 to the Levites as their i the tithes that the H5709
Nu 18:24 'They will have no i among the H5706+5709
Nu 18:26 the Israelites the tithe I give you as your i, H5709
Nu 26:53 to them as an i based on the number of H5709
Nu 26:54 To a larger group give a larger i, and to a H5709
Nu 26:54 each is to receive its i according to the H5709
Nu 26:56 Each i is to be distributed by lot among H5709
Nu 26:62 because they received no i among them. H5709
Nu 27: 7 them property as an i among their father's H5709
Nu 27: 7 relatives and give their father's i to them. H5709
Nu 27: 8 leaves no son, give his i to his daughter. H5709
Nu 27: 9 has no daughter, give his i to his brothers. H5709
Nu 27:10 brothers, give his i to his father's brothers. H5709
Nu 27:11 give his i to the nearest relative in his H5709
Nu 32:18 each of the Israelites has received their i. H5709
Nu 32:19 We will not receive any i with them on the H5706
Nu 32:19 because our i has come to us on the east H5709
Nu 33:54 To a larger group give a larger i, and to a H5709
Nu 34: 2 be allotted to you as an i is to have these H5709
Nu 34:13 "Assign this land by lot as an i. The LORD H5706
Nu 34:14 of Manasseh have received their i. H5709
Nu 34:15 have received their i east of the Jordan H5709
Nu 34:17 who are to assign the land for you as an i: H5706
Nu 34:29 commanded to assign the i to the H5706
Nu 35: 2 to live in from the i the Israelites will H5709
Nu 35: 8 given in proportion to the i of each tribe: H5709
Nu 36: 2 to give the land as an i to the Israelites by H5709
Nu 36: 2 you to give the i of our brother H5709
Nu 36: 3 then their i will be taken from our H5709
Nu 36: 3 from our ancestral i and added to that of H5709
Nu 36: 3 so part of the i allotted to us will be taken H5709
Nu 36: 4 their i will be added to that of the tribe H5709
Nu 36: 4 be taken from the tribal i of our ancestors." H5709
Nu 36: 7 No i in Israel is to pass from one tribe to H5709
Nu 36: 7 shall keep the tribal i of their ancestors. H5709
Nu 36: 8 will possess the i of their ancestors. H5709
Nu 36: 9 No i may pass from one tribe to another H5709
Nu 36:12 their i remained in their father's tribe H5709
Dt 4:20 to be the people of his i, as you now are. H5709
Dt 4:21 the LORD your God is giving you as your i. H5709
Dt 4:38 into their land to give it to you for your i, H5709
Dt 9:26 your own i that you redeemed by your H5709
Dt 9:29 your i that you brought out by your great H5709
Dt 10: 9 have no share or i among their fellow H5709
Dt 10: 9 the LORD is their i, as the LORD your God H5709
Dt 12: 9 place and the i the LORD your God is H5709
Dt 12:10 the LORD your God is giving you as an i, H5706
Dt 12:12 who have no allotment or i of their own. H5709
Dt 14:27 they have no allotment or i of their own. H5709
Dt 14:29 who have no allotment or i of their own H5709
Dt 15: 4 God is giving you to possess as your i, H5709
Dt 18: 1 are to have no allotment or i with Israel. H5709
Dt 18: 1 presented to the LORD, for that is their i. H5709
Dt 18: 2 They shall have no i among their fellow H5709
Dt 18: 2 the LORD is their i, as he promised them. H5709
Dt 19: 3 the LORD your God is giving you as an i, H5706
Dt 19:10 the LORD your God is giving you as your i, H5709
Dt 19:14 predecessors in the i you receive in the H5709
Dt 20:16 the LORD your God is giving you as an i, H5709
Dt 21:23 the LORD your God is giving you as an i. H5709
Dt 24: 4 the LORD your God is giving you as an i. H5709
Dt 25:19 land he is giving you to possess as an i, H5709
Dt 26: 1 God is giving you as an i and have taken H5709
Dt 29: 8 gave it as an i to the Reubenites, H5709
Dt 31: 7 you must divide it among them as their i. H5706
Dt 32: 8 the Most High gave the nations their i, H5706
Dt 32: 9 portion is his people, Jacob his allotted i. H5709
Jos 11:23 he gave it as an i to Israel according H5709
Jos 12: 7 gave their lands as an i to the tribes of H3772
Jos 13: 6 sure to allocate this land to Israel for an i, H5709
Jos 13: 7 divide it as an i among the nine tribes H5709
Jos 13: 8 had received the i that Moses had given H5709
Jos 13:14 But to the tribe of Levi he gave no i, since H5709
Jos 13:14 of Israel, are their i, as he promised them. H5709
Jos 13:23 villages were the i of the Reubenites, H5709
Jos 13:28 their villages were the i of the Gadites, H5709
Jos 13:32 This is the i Moses had given when he H5706
Jos 13:33 Moses had given no i; the LORD, H5709
Jos 13:33 of Israel, is their i, as he promised them. H5709
Jos 14: 1 the Israelites received as an i in the land H5706
Jos 14: 3 a half tribes their i east of the Jordan but H5709
Jos 14: 3 granted the Levites an i among the rest, H5709
Jos 14: 9 walked will be your i and that of your H5709
Jos 14:13 Jephunneh and gave him Hebron as his i. H5709
Jos 15:20 This is the i of the tribe of Judah H5709
Jos 16: 4 descendants of Joseph, received their i. H5706
Jos 16: 5 The boundary of their i went from Ataroth H5709
Jos 16: 8 This was the i of the tribe of the H5709
Jos 16: 9 within the i of the Manassites. H5709
Jos 17: 4 Moses to give us an i among our relatives H5709
Jos 17: 4 So Joshua gave them an i along with the H5709
Jos 17: 6 Manasseh received an i among the sons. H5709
Jos 17:14 one allotment and one portion for an i? H5709
Jos 18: 2 tribes who had not yet received their i. H5709
Jos 18: 4 according to the i of each. H5709
Jos 18: 7 the priestly service of the LORD is their i. H5709
Jos 18: 7 already received their i on the east side of H5709
Jos 18:20 that marked out the i of the clans of H5709
Jos 18:28 This was the i of Benjamin for its clans. H5709
Jos 19: 1 Their i lay within the territory of Judah. H5709
Jos 19: 8 This was the i of the tribe of the H5709
Jos 19: 9 The i of the Simeonites was taken from H5709
Jos 19: 9 the Simeonites received their i within the H5706
Jos 19:10 boundary of their i went as far as Sarid. H5709
Jos 19:16 their villages were the i of Zebulun, H5709
Jos 19:23 villages were the i of the tribe of Issachar, H5709
Jos 19:31 villages were the i of the tribe of Asher, H5709
Jos 19:39 villages were the i of the tribe of Naphtali H5709
Jos 19:41 The territory of their i included: Zorah H5709
Jos 19:48 villages were the i of the tribe of Dan, H5709
Jos 19:49 Joshua son of Nun an i among them, H5709
Jos 21: 3 towns and pasturelands out of their own i: H5709
Jos 23: 4 I have allotted as an i for your tribes all H5709
Jos 24:28 dismissed the people, each to their own i. H5709
Jos 24:30 And they buried him in the land of his i, at H5709
Jos 24:32 This became the i of Joseph's H5709
Jdg 2: 6 of the land, each to their own i. H5709
Jdg 2: 9 And they buried him in the land of his i, at H5709
Jdg 11: 2 "You are not going to get any i in our H5706
Jdg 18: 1 not yet come into an i among the tribes of H5709
Jdg 20: 6 sent one piece to each region of Israel's i, H5709
Jdg 21:23 returned to their i and rebuilt the towns H5709
Jdg 21:24 their tribes and clans, each to his own i. H5709
1Sa 10: 1 not the LORD anointed you ruler over his i? H5709
1Sa 26:19 my share in the LORD's i and have said, H5709
2Sa 14:16 cut off both me and my son from God's i. H5709
2Sa 14:17 the word of my lord the king secure my i, H4957
2Sa 20:19 do you want to swallow up the LORD's i?" H5709
2Sa 21: 3 so that you will bless the LORD's i? H5709
1Ki 8:36 on the land you gave your people for an i. H5709
1Ki 8:51 they are your people and your i, whom H5709
1Ki 8:53 the nations of the world to be your own i, H5709
1Ki 21: 3 I should give you the i of my ancestors." H5709
1Ki 21: 4 "I will not give you the i of my ancestors." H5709
2Ki 21:14 the remnant of my i and give them into H5709
1Ch 28: 8 good land and pass it on as an i to your H5706
2Ch 6:27 on the land you gave your people for an i. H5709
2Ch 20:11 out of the possession you gave us as an i. H3769
Ezr 9:12 leave it to your children as an everlasting i H3769
Job 42:15 father granted them an i along with their H5709
Ps 2: 8 I will make the nations your i, the H5709
Ps 16: 6 surely I have a delightful i. H5709
Ps 28: 9 Save your people and bless your i; be H5709
Ps 33:12 is the LORD, the people he chose for his i. H5709
Ps 37:18 LORD's care, and their i will endure forever. H5709
Ps 47: 4 He chose our i for us, the pride of Jacob H5709
Ps 68: 9 you refreshed your weary i. H5709
Ps 74: 2 the people of your i, whom you redeemed H5709
Ps 78:55 allotted their lands to them as an i; H5709
Ps 78:62 to the sword; he was furious with his i. H5709
Ps 78:71 of his people Jacob, of Israel his i. H5709
Ps 79: 1 the nations have invaded your i; they H5709
Ps 82: 8 the earth, for all the nations are your i. H5706
Ps 94: 5 your people, LORD; they oppress your i. H5709
Ps 94:14 his people; he will never forsake his i. H5709
Ps 106: 5 nation and join your i in giving praise. H5709
Ps 106:40 angry with his people and abhorred his i. H5709
Ps 135:12 he gave their land as an i, an H5709
Ps 135:12 an inheritance, an i to his people Israel. H5709
Ps 136:21 gave their land as an i, His love H5709
Ps 136:22 an i to his servant Israel. His love endures H5709
Pr 8:21 bestowing a rich i on those who love me H5706
Pr 13:22 A good person leaves an i for their H5706
Pr 17: 2 will share the i as one of the family. H5709
Pr 20:21 An i claimed too soon will not be blessed H5709
Pr 28:10 the blameless will receive a good i. H5706
Ecc 7:11 Wisdom, like an i, is a good thing and H5709
Isa 19:25 Assyria my handiwork, and Israel my i." H5709
Isa 47: 6 with my people and desecrated my i; H5709
Isa 58:14 to feast on the i of your father Jacob." H5709
Isa 61: 7 of disgrace you will rejoice in your i. H2750
Isa 63:17 of your servants, the tribes that are your i. H5709
Jer 2: 7 my land and made my i detestable. H5709
Jer 3:18 to the land I gave your ancestors as an i. H5706
Jer 3:19 the most beautiful i of any nation. H5709
Jer 10:16 the people of his i—the LORD Almighty is H5709
Jer 12: 7 abandon my i; I will give the one H5709
Jer 12: 8 My i has become to me like a lion in the H5709
Jer 12: 9 Has not my i become to me like a H5709
Jer 12:14 who seize the i I gave my people Israel H5709
Jer 12:15 back to their own i and their own country. H5709
Jer 16:18 have filled my i with their detestable H5709
Jer 17: 4 own fault you will lose the i I gave you. H5709
Jer 50:11 you who pillage my i, because you frolic H5709
Jer 51:19 including the people of his i—the LORD H5709
La 5: 2 Our i has been turned over to strangers H5709
Eze 35:15 you rejoiced when the i of Israel became H5709
Eze 36:12 you will be their i; you will never H5709
Eze 44:28 " 'I am to be the only i the priests have H5709
Eze 45: 1 " 'When you allot the land as an i, you H5709
Eze 46:16 makes a gift from his i to one of his sons, H5709
Eze 46:16 descendants; it is to be their property by i. H5709
Eze 46:17 makes a gift from his i to one of his H5709
Eze 46:17 His i belongs to his sons only H5709
Eze 46:18 must not take any of the i of the people, H5709
Eze 46:18 He is to give his sons their i out of his H5706
Eze 47:13 you will divide among the twelve tribes of Israel as their i H5706
Eze 47:14 ancestors, this land will become your i. H5709
Eze 47:22 are to allot it as an i for yourselves and H5709
Eze 47:22 are to be allotted an i among the tribes of H5709
Eze 47:23 there you are to give them their i, H5709
Eze 48:29 you are to allot as an i to the tribes of H5709
Da 12:13 you will rise to receive your allotted i." H1598
Joel 2:17 Do not make your i an object of scorn, H5709
Joel 3: 2 put them on trial for what they did to my i, H5709
Ob 17 will be holy, and Jacob will possess his i. H4625
Mic 2: 2 of their homes, they rob them of their i. H5709
Mic 7:14 the flock of your i, which lives by itself H5709
Mic 7:18 the transgression of the remnant of his i? H5709
Zec 8:12 I will give all these things as an i to the H5706
Mal 1: 3 left his i to the desert jackals. H5709
Mt 21:38 Come, let's kill him and take his i.' G3100
Mt 25:34 by my Father; take your i, the kingdom G3099
Mk 12: 7 let's kill him, and the i will be ours. G3100
Lk 12:13 tell my brother to divide the i with me." G3100
Lk 20:14 'Let's kill him, and the i will be ours.' G3100
Ac 7: 5 He gave him no i here, not even enough G3100
Ac 13:19 giving their land to his people as their i. G2883
Ac 20:32 up and give you an i among all those G3100
Gal 3:18 For if the i depends on the law, then it no G3100
Gal 4:30 son will never share in the i with the G3099
Eph 1:14 guaranteeing our i until the redemption G3100
Eph 1:18 the riches of his glorious i in his holy G3100
Eph 5: 5 has any i in the kingdom of Christ and of G3100
Col 1:12 you to share in the i of his holy people in G3102
Col 3:24 you will receive an i from the Lord as a G3100
Heb 9:15 may receive the promised eternal i— G3100
Heb 11: 8 to a place he would later receive as his i, G3100
Heb 12:16 meal sold his i rights as the oldest son. G4757
1Pe 1: 4 into an i that can never perish, spoil G3100
1Pe 1: 4 This i is kept in heaven for you, NDT

INHERITANCES (2) [INHERIT]

Jos 14: 2 Their i were assigned by lot to the nine H5709
Isa 49: 8 the land and to reassign its desolate i, H5709

INHERITED (3) [INHERIT]

Lev 25:46 to your children as i property and can H3769
Pr 19:14 Houses and wealth are i from parents, but H5709
Heb 1: 4 angels as the name he has i is superior to G3099

INHERITS (3) [INHERIT]

Nu 26:55 What each group i will be according to H5706
Nu 36: 8 Every daughter who i land in any Israelite H3769
Nu 36: 9 each Israelite tribe is to keep the land it i." H5709

INIQUITIES (11) [INIQUITY]

Ps 78:38 he forgave their i and did not destroy H6411
Ps 90: 8 You have set our i before you, our secret H6411
Ps 103:10 deserve or repay us according to our i. H6411
Ps 107:17 suffered affliction because of their i. H6411
Isa 53: 5 he was crushed for our i; the punishment H6411
Isa 53:11 will justify many, and he will bear their i. H6411
Isa 59: 2 But your i have separated you from your H6411
Isa 59:12 ever with us, and we acknowledge our i: H6411
La 4:13 of her prophets and the i of her priests, H6411
Da 9:16 Our sins and the i of our ancestors have H6411
Mic 7:19 hurl all our i into the depths of the H2633

INIQUITY (13) [INIQUITIES]

Ps 25:11 forgive my i, though it is great. H6411
Ps 32: 5 my sin to you and did not cover up my i. H6411

Ps 38:18 I confess my **i**; I am troubled by my sin. H6411
Ps 51: 2 Wash away all my **i** and cleanse me from H6411
Ps 51: 9 face from my sins and blot out all my **i**. H6411
Ps 73: 7 From their callous hearts comes **i**; their H6411
Ps 85: 2 You forgave the **i** *of* your people and H6411
Ps 89:32 their sin with the rod, their **i** with flogging; H6411
Ps 109:14 May the **i** *of* his fathers be remembered H6411
Isa 53: 6 the LORD has laid on him the **i** *of* us all. H6411
Hos 12: 8 they will not find in me any **i** or sin." H6411
Mic 2: 1 Woe to those who plan **i**, to those who plot H224
Zec 5: 6 "This is the **i** *of* the people throughout the H6411

INITIATIVE (1)

2Co 8:17 with much enthusiasm and **on his own i**. *G882*

INJURE (1) [INJURED, INJURES, INJURING, INJURY]

Zec 12: 3 try to move it *will* **i themselves**. H8581+8581

INJURED (15) [INJURE]

Ex 21:19 party must pay **the i person** for any loss H2257S
Ex 22:10 it dies or **is i** or is taken away while H8689
Ex 22:14 their neighbor and *it* **is i** or dies while the H8689
Lev 22:22 the LORD the blind, the **i** or the maimed, or H8653
Lev 24:19 their neighbor *is to* **be i** in the same H6913
2Ki 1: 2 his upper room in Samaria and **i** *himself.* H2703
Ecc 10: 9 quarries stones *may* **be i** by them; H6772
Isa 1: 5 Your whole head is **i**, your whole heart H2716
Isa 28:13 *they will* **be i** and snared and captured. H8689
Eze 34: 4 weak or healed the sick or bound up the **i**. H8689
Eze 34:16 I will bind up the **i** and strengthen the H8689
Hos 6: 1 *he has* **i** us but he will bind up our H5782
Zec 11:16 or heal the **i**, or feed the healthy, H8689
Mal 1:13 "When you bring **i**, lame or diseased H1608
2Co 7:12 did the wrong nor on account of the **i** *party*, *G92*

INJURES (3) [INJURE]

Ex 21:35 "If anyone's bull **i** someone else's bull H5597
Lev 24:19 Anyone *who* **i** their neighbor is to H5989+4583
Job 5:18 he also binds up; *he* **i**, but his hands also H4730

INJURING (2) [INJURE]

Ge 4:23 wounding me, a young man for **i** me. H2467
Lk 4:35 them all and came out without **i** him. *G1055*

INJURY (8) [INJURE]

Ex 21:22 birth prematurely but there is no **serious i**, H656
Ex 21:23 But if there is **serious i**, you are to take life H656
Lev 24:20 has inflicted the **i** must suffer the same H4583
Lev 24:20 inflicted the injury must suffer the same **i**. NDT
2Ki 1: 2 Ekron, to see if I will recover from this **i**." H2716
Jer 10:19 Woe to me because of my **i**! My wound is H8691
Jer 30:12 is incurable, your **i** beyond healing. H4804
Rev 9:19 having heads with which *they* **inflict i**. *G92*

INJUSTICE (12)

2Ch 19: 7 our God there is no **i** or partiality or H6406
Job 5:16 poor have hope, and **i** shuts its mouth. H6637
Ps 58: 2 in your heart you devise **i**, and your hands H6406
Ps 64: 6 They plot **i** and say, "We have devised a H6406
Pr 13:23 the poor, but **i** sweeps it away. H4202+5477
Pr 16: 8 than much gain with **i**. H4202+5477
Pr 22: 8 Whoever sows **i** reaps calamity, and the H6406
Isa 58: 6 loose the chains of **i** and untie the cords H8400
Jer 22:13 his upper rooms by **i**, making his H4202+5477
Eze 9: 9 is full of bloodshed and the city is full of **i**. H4754
Hab 1: 3 Why do you make me look at **i**? Why do H224
Hab 2:12 bloodshed and establishes a town by **i**! H6406

INK (4)

Jer 36:18 and I wrote them in **i** on the scroll. H1902
2Co 3: 3 written not *with* **i** but with the Spirit of the *G3506*
2Jn 12 but I do not want to use paper and **i**. *G3506*
3Jn 13 I do not want to do so with pen and **i**. *G3506*

INKHORN (KJV) WRITING KIT

INKLING (1)

1Sa 20: 9 "If *I* **had the least i** that my father H3359+3359

INLAID (1)

SS 3:10 with purple, its interior **i** *with* love. H8362

INMOST (9) [IN, MOST]

Ps 103: 1 my soul; all my **i being**, praise his holy H7931
Ps 139:13 For you created my **i being**; you knit me H4000
Pr 18: 8 they go down to the **i parts**. H2540+1061
Pr 20:27 sheds light on one's **i being**. H3972+2540+1061
Pr 20:30 and beatings purge the **i being**. H2540+1061
Pr 23:16 my **i being** will rejoice when your lips H4000
Pr 26:22 they go down to the **i parts**. H2540+1061
Isa 16:11 like a harp, my **i being** for Kir Hareseth. H7931
Lk 1:51 those who are proud in their **i** thoughts. *G2840*

INN (1) [INNKEEPER]

Lk 10:34 brought him to an **i** and took care of him. *G4106*

INNER (67) [IN]

Ge 30:37 exposing the white **i** wood of the H6584
Jdg 3:24 himself in the **i room** *of* the palace." H2540
2Sa 3:27 Joab took him aside into an **i chamber**, as H9133
2Sa 4: 6 They went into the **i part** *of* the house as if H9348
2Sa 18:24 sitting between the **i and outer** gates, H9109S
1Ki 6: 5 the main hall and **i sanctuary** he built a H1808
1Ki 6:16 to form within the temple an **i sanctuary**, H1808
1Ki 6:19 He prepared the **i sanctuary** within the H1808
1Ki 6:20 The **i sanctuary** was twenty cubits long H1808
1Ki 6:21 chains across the front of the **i sanctuary**, H1808
1Ki 6:22 the altar that belonged to the **i sanctuary**. H1808
1Ki 6:23 For the **i sanctuary** he made a pair of H1808
1Ki 6:29 in both the **i** and outer rooms, he H4200+7156
1Ki 6:30 of both the **i** and outer rooms of H4200+7163
1Ki 6:31 entrance to the **i sanctuary** he made doors H1808
1Ki 6:36 And he built the **i** courtyard of three H7164
1Ki 7: 9 smoothed on their **i** and outer faces. H1074
1Ki 7:12 as was the **i** courtyard of the temple of the H7164
1Ki 7:49 in front of the **i sanctuary**); the gold floral H1808
1Ki 8: 6 its place in the **i sanctuary** *of* the temple, H1808
1Ki 8: 8 the Holy Place in front of the **i sanctuary**, H1808
1Ki 20:30 the city and hid in an **i room**. H2540+928+2540
1Ki 22:25 you go to hide in an **i room**." H2540+928+2540
2Ki 9: 2 and take him into an **i room**. H2540+928+2540
2Ki 10:25 then entered the **i shrine** *of* the temple of H6551
1Ch 28:11 its **i** rooms and the place of atonement. H7164
2Ch 4:20 in front of the **i sanctuary** as prescribed; H1808
2Ch 4:22 the **i** doors to the Most Holy Place and the H7164
2Ch 5: 7 its place in the **i sanctuary** *of* the temple, H1808
2Ch 5: 9 be seen from in front of the **i sanctuary**, H1808
2Ch 18:24 you go to hide in an **i room**." H2540+928+2540
Est 4:11 the king in the **i** court without being H7164
Est 5: 1 stood in the **i** court of the palace, H7164
Eze 8: 3 entrance of the north gate of the **i** court, H7164
Eze 8:16 brought me into the **i** court of the house H7164
Eze 10: 3 went in, and a cloud filled the **i** court. H7164
Eze 40:19 gateway to the outside of the **i** court; H7164
Eze 40:23 was a gate to the **i** court facing the north H7164
Eze 40:27 The **i** court also had a gate facing south H7164
Eze 40:28 he brought me into the **i** court through the H7164
Eze 40:30 gateways around the **i** court were NDT
Eze 40:32 he brought me to the **i** court on the east H7164
Eze 40:38 was by the portico in each of the **i** gateways, NDT
Eze 40:44 Outside the **i** gate, within the inner court H7164
Eze 40:44 within the **i** court, were two rooms, H6584
Eze 41: 3 went into the **i sanctuary** and measured H7163
Eze 41: 4 measured the length of the **i sanctuary**; H2257S
Eze 41:15 the **i sanctuary** and the portico facing the H7164
Eze 41:17 the entrance to the **i** sanctuary and on the H7164
Eze 41:17 all around the **i** and outer **sanctuary** H7164
Eze 42: 3 twenty cubits from the **i** court and in the H7164
Eze 42: 4 of the rooms was an **i** passageway ten H7164
Eze 43: 5 me up and brought me into the **i** court, H7164
Eze 44:17 'When they enter the gates of the **i** court, H7164
Eze 44:17 at the gates of the **i** court or inside the H7164
Eze 44:21 to drink wine when he enters the **i** court. H7164
Eze 44:27 day he goes into the **i** court of the H7164
Eze 45:19 altar and on the gateposts of the **i** court. H7164
Eze 46: 1 The gate of the **i** court facing east is to be H7164
Mt 24:26 in the **i rooms**,' do not believe *G5421*
Lk 12: 3 in the ear in the **i rooms** will be *G5421*
Ac 16:24 he put them in the **i** cell and fastened *G2278*
Ro 7:22 For in my **i being** I delight in God's law; *G2276*
Eph 3:16 power through his Spirit in your **i** being, *G2276*
Heb 6:19 It enters the **i** *sanctuary* behind the curtain *G2278*
Heb 9: 7 But only the high priest entered the **i** *room*, *G1311*
1Pe 3: 4 it should be that of your **i** self, the *G3220*

INNERMOST (2) [IN, MOST]

1Ki 6:27 cherubim inside the **i** *room* of the temple, H7164
1Ki 7:50 gold sockets for the doors of the **i** room, H7164

INNKEEPER (1) [INN]

Lk 10:35 out two denarii and gave them *to* the **i**. *G4107*

INNOCENCE (9) [INNOCENT]

Ge 44:16 How *can we* **prove** *our* **i**? God has H7405
1Ki 8:32 treating them in accordance with their **i**. H7407
2Ch 6:23 treating them in accordance with their **i**. H7407
Job 9: 2 how *can* mere mortals **prove** *their* **i** before H7405
Job 23: 7 upright *can* **establish** their **i** before him H3519
Job 27: 6 I will maintain my **i** and never let go of it H7407
Ps 26: 6 I wash my hands in **i**, and go about your H5931
Ps 73:13 pure and have washed my hands in **i**. H5931
Isa 43:26 matter together; state the *case for* your **i**. H7405

INNOCENT (75) [INNOCENCE, INNOCENTLY]

Ge 20: 4 "Lord, will you destroy an **i** nation? H7404
Ex 23: 7 do not put an **i** or honest person to H5929
Ex 23: 8 who see and twists the words of the **i**. H7404
Nu 5:31 The husband *will be* **i** of any wrongdoing H5927
Dt 16:19 of the wise and twists the words of the **i**. H7404
Dt 19:10 Do this so that **i** blood will not be shed in H5929
Dt 19:13 from Israel the guilt of shedding **i** blood, H5929
Dt 21: 8 people guilty of the blood of an **i** *person*." H5929
Dt 21: 9 yourselves the guilt of shedding **i** blood, H5929
Dt 25: 1 acquitting the **i** and condemning the H7404
Dt 27:25 who accepts a bribe to kill an **i** person." H5929
1Sa 19: 5 do wrong to an **i man** like David by H5929+1947
2Sa 3:28 my kingdom are forever **i** before the LORD H5929
2Sa 4:11 men have killed an **i** man in his own H7404
1Ki 2: 9 But now, *do* not **consider** him **i**. You are a H5927
1Ki 2:31 of the guilt of the **i** blood that Joab shed. H2855
1Ki 8:32 vindicating the **i** by treating them H7404
2Ki 10: 9 all the people and said, "You are **i**. H7404
2Ki 21:16 also shed so much **i** blood that he filled H5929
2Ki 24: 4 including the shedding of **i** blood. For he H5929
2Ki 24: 4 For he had filled Jerusalem with **i** blood H5929
2Ch 6:23 vindicating the **i** by treating them in H7404
Job 4: 7 Who, being **i**, has ever perished H5929
Job 9:15 Though *I were* **i**, I could not answer him; H7405
Job 9:20 Even if *I were* **i**, my mouth would H7405
Job 9:23 he mocks the despair of the **i**. H5929
Job 9:28 I know *you will* not **hold** me **i**. H5927
Job 10:15 Even if *I am* **i**, I cannot lift my head, for I H7405
Job 17: 8 the **i** are aroused against the ungodly. H5929
Job 22:19 ruin and rejoice; the **i** mock them, saying, H5929
Job 22:30 He will deliver even *one who* is not **i**, who H5929
Job 27:17 will wear, and the **i** will divide his silver. H5929
Job 34: 5 "Job says, '*I am* **i**, but God denies me H7405
Ps 10: 8 villages; from ambush he murders the **i**. H5929
Ps 15: 5 who does not accept a bribe against the **i**. H5929
Ps 19:13 be blameless, **i** of great transgression. H5927
Ps 64: 4 They shoot from ambush at the **i**; they H9447
Ps 94:21 righteous and condemn the **i** to death. H5929
Ps 106:38 They shed **i** blood, the blood of their sons H5929
Pr 1:11 let's lie in wait for *i* **blood**, let's ambush AIT
Pr 6:17 a lying tongue, hands that shed **i** blood, H5929
Pr 12:13 sinful talk, and so the **i** escape trouble. H7404
Pr 17:15 the guilty and condemning the **i**— H7404
Pr 17:26 If imposing a fine on the **i** is not good H7404
Pr 18: 5 the wicked and so deprive the **i** of justice. H7404
Pr 21: 8 the conduct of the **i** is upright. H3838
Pr 24:24 to the guilty, "You are **i**," will be cursed by H7404
Isa 5:23 guilty for a bribe, but deny justice to the **i**. H7404
Isa 29:21 false testimony deprive the **i** of justice. H7404
Isa 59: 7 into sin; they are swift to shed **i** blood. H5929
Jer 2:34 is found the lifeblood of the **i** poor, H5929
Jer 2:35 you say, '*I am* **i**; he is not angry with me.' H5927
Jer 7: 6 do not shed **i** blood in this place, H5929
Jer 19: 4 filled this place with the blood of the **i**. H5929
Jer 22: 3 do not shed **i** blood in this place. H5929
Jer 22:17 on shedding **i** blood and on oppression H5929
Jer 26:15 bring the guilt of **i** blood on yourselves H5929
Da 6:22 because I was found **i** in his sight. A10229
Joel 3:19 in whose land they shed **i** blood. H5929
Joel 3:21 Shall I leave their *i* **blood** unavenged? No, AIT
Am 2: 6 They sell the **i** for silver, and the needy H7404
Am 5:12 who oppress the **i** and take bribes and H7404
Jnh 1:14 hold us accountable for killing an **i** *man*, H5929
Mt 10:16 be as shrewd as snakes and as **i** as doves. *G193*
Mt 12: 5 desecrate the Sabbath and yet are **i**? *G360*
Mt 12: 7 you would not have condemned the **i**. *G360*
Mt 27: 4 he said, "for I have betrayed **i** blood." *G127*
Mt 27:19 *have* anything *to do with* that **i** *man*, *G1465*
Mt 27:24 "I am **i** of this man's blood, *G127*
Ac 18: 6 I am **i** of it. From now on I *G2754*
Ac 20:26 you today that I am **i** of the blood of any *G2754*
Ro 16:19 what is good, and **i** about what is evil. *G193*
1Co 4: 4 is clear, but that *does* not **make** *me* **i**. *G1467*
2Co 7:11 have proved yourselves to be **i** in this matter. *G54*
Jas 5: 6 condemned and murdered the **i** *one*, *G1465*

INNOCENTLY (1) [INNOCENT]

2Sa 15:11 invited as guests and went **quite i**, H4200+9448

INNUMERABLE (1)

2Ch 12: 3 horsemen and the **i** troops of H401+5031

INORDINATE (KJV) LUST

INQUIRE (37) [INQUIRED, INQUIRER, INQUIRERS, INQUIRES, INQUIRING, INQUIRY]

Ge 25:22 So she went to **i** of the LORD. H2011
Dt 13:14 then *you must* **i**, probe and investigate it H2011
Dt 17: 9 **I** of them and they will give you the H2011
Jos 9:14 but *did* not **i** of the LORD. H8626+906+7023
Jdg 18: 5 "Please **i** of God to learn whether H8626+928
1Sa 9: 9 if someone went to **i** of God, they would H2011
1Sa 14:36 the priest said, "*Let us* **i** of God here." H7928+448
1Sa 28: 7 a medium, so I may go and **i** of her." H2011+928
1Ki 22: 7 LORD here whom *we can* **i** of?" H2011+4946+907
1Ki 22: 8 through whom we *can* **i** of the LORD, H2011
2Ki 3:11 through whom *we may* **i** of the LORD?" H2011
2Ki 22:13 "Go and **i** of the LORD for me and for the H2011
2Ki 22:18 who sent you to **i** of the LORD, 'This is H2011
1Ch 10:14 and *did* not **i** of the LORD. So the LORD H2011+928
1Ch 13: 3 for *we did* not **i** of it during the reign of H2011
1Ch 15:13 *We did* not **i** of him *about* how to do it in H2011
1Ch 21:30 David could not go before it to **i** of God, H2011
2Ch 18: 6 of the LORD here whom *we can* **i** of?" H2011
2Ch 18: 7 through whom we *can* **i** of the LORD, H2011
2Ch 20: 3 resolved to **i** of the LORD, H2011+4200
2Ch 34:21 "Go and **i** of the LORD for me and for the H2011
2Ch 34:26 who sent you to **i** of the LORD, 'This is H2011+928
Ezr 7:14 his seven advisers to **i** about Judah and A10118
Isa 8:19 *should* not a people **i** of their God? H2011+448
Jer 10:21 are senseless and *do* not **i** of the LORD; H2011
Jer 18:13 what the LORD says: "**I** among the nations H8626
Jer 21: 2 "**I** now of the LORD for us because H2011
Jer 37: 7 who sent you to **i** of me, 'Pharaoh's army, H2011
Eze 14: 3 *Should I* **let** them **i** of *me* **at all** H2011+4200+2011
Eze 14: 7 and then go to a prophet to **i** of me, H2011+928
Eze 20: 1 the elders of Israel came to **i** of the LORD, H2011
Eze 20: 3 Have you come to **i** of me? As surely as I H2011
Eze 20: 3 *I will* not **let** you **i** of *me*, declares H2011
Eze 20:31 *Am I to* **let** you **i** of *me*, you H2011+4200
Eze 20:31 *I will* not **let** you **i** of *me*. H2011+4200
Zep 1: 6 neither seek the LORD nor **i** of him. H2011
1Co 14:35 If they want *to* **i** about something, they *G3443*

INQUIRED (20) [INQUIRE]

Lev 10:16 When Moses **i** about the goat of H2011+2011

Jdg 13:17 Then Manoah **i of** the angel of the H606+448
Jdg 20:18 went up to Bethel and **i of** God. H8626+928
Jdg 20:23 until evening, and *they* **i of** the LORD. H8626+928
Jdg 20:27 And the Israelites **i of** the LORD. H8626+928
1Sa 10:22 So *they* **i** further **of** the LORD, "Has the H8626+928
1Sa 22:10 Ahimelek **i of** the LORD for him; he H8626+928
1Sa 22:15 day the first time I **i of** God for him? H8626+928
1Sa 23: 2 he **i of** the LORD, saying, "Shall I go H8626+928
1Sa 23: 4 Once again David **i of** the LORD, and H8626+928
1Sa 28: 6 He **i of** the LORD, but the LORD did not H8626+928
1Sa 30: 8 David **i of** the LORD, "Shall I H8626+928
2Sa 2: 1 course of time, David **i of** the LORD. H8626+928
2Sa 5:19 so David **i of** the LORD, "Shall I go H8626+928
2Sa 5:23 so David **i of** the LORD, and he H8626+928
1Ch 14:10 so David **i of** God: "Shall I go and H8626+928
1Ch 14:14 so David **i of** God again, and God H8626+928
2Ch 1: 5 Solomon and the assembly **i of** him there. H2011
Mt 19:18 "Which ones?" *he* **i**. Jesus replied, " 'You G3306
Jn 4:52 *When he* **i** *as to* the time when his son got G4785

INQUIRER (2) [INQUIRE]

1Co 14:16 who is now put in the position *of* an **i**, say G2626
1Co 14:24 if an unbeliever or an **i** comes in while G2626

INQUIRERS (1) [INQUIRE]

1Co 14:23 in tongues, and **i** or unbelievers come in G2626

INQUIRES (1) [INQUIRE]

2Sa 16:23 like that of one *who* **i of** God. H8626+928+1821

INQUIRING (4) [INQUIRE]

Ex 33: 7 Anyone **i of** the LORD would go to the tent H1335
Nu 27:21 him by **i** *of* the Urim before the H5477
Dt 12:30 not to be ensnared *by* **i** about their gods, H2011
1Sa 22:13 and a sword and **i of** God for him, H8626+928

INQUIRY (1) [INQUIRE]

Job 34:24 Without **i** he shatters the mighty and sets H2984

INQUISITION (KJV) AVENGES, INVESTIGATED, INVESTIGATION

INSANE (5)

1Sa 21:13 So *he* **pretended to be i** in their H9101+3248
1Sa 21:14 *He is* **i**! Why bring him to H8713
Ps 34: T When he **pretended to be i** before H9101+3248
Ac 26:24 "Your great learning is driving you **i**." G3444
Ac 26:25 "*I am* not **i**, most excellent Festus," Paul G3419

INSATIABLE (1)

Eze 16:28 because you were **i**; and even after H1194+8429

INSCRIBE (1) [INSCRIBED, INSCRIPTION]

Isa 30: 8 on a tablet for them, **i** it on a scroll, that H2980

INSCRIBED (6) [INSCRIBE]

Ex 31:18 the tablets of stone **i** by the finger of God. H4180
Ex 32:15 They *were* **i** on both sides H4180
Dt 9:10 two stone tablets **i** by the finger of God H4180
Job 19:24 that they were **i** with an iron tool on lead, or NDT
Jer 17: 1 with an iron tool, **i** with a flint point, on H3086
Zec 14:20 to the Lord will be *i* **on** the bells of the horses AIT

INSCRIPTION (9) [INSCRIBE]

Ex 39:30 engraved on it, like an **i** *on* a seal: H4844+7334
Da 5:24 he sent the hand that wrote the **i**. A10375
Da 5:25 "This is the **i** that was written: MENE A10375
Zec 3: 9 I will engrave an **i** *on* it,' says the H7334
Mt 22:20 "Whose image is this? And whose **i**?" G2107
Mk 12:16 image is this? And whose **i**?" "Caesar's," G2107
Lk 20:24 Whose image and **i** are on it?" "Caesar's," G2107
Ac 17:23 worship, I even found an altar with *this* **i**: G2108
2Ti 2:19 foundation stands firm, sealed *with* **this** *i*: AIT

INSECTS (6)

Lev 11:20 " 'All flying **i** that walk on all fours are to H9238
Lev 11:21 some flying **i** that walk on all fours that H9238
Lev 11:23 But all other flying **i** that have four legs H9238
Dt 14:19 All flying **i** are unclean to you; do not eat H9238
Ps 50:11 the **i** *in* the fields are mine. H2328
Ps 80:13 ravage it, and **i** *from* the fields feed on it. H2328

INSERT (1) [INSERTED]

Ex 25:14 **I** the poles into the rings on the sides of the H995

INSERTED (6) [INSERT]

Ex 27: 7 The poles *are to* **be i** into the rings so they H995
Ex 37: 5 And *he* **i** the poles into the rings on the H995
Ex 38: 7 *They* **i** the poles into the rings so they H995
Ex 40:18 **i** the crossbars and set up the posts. H5989
1Ki 6: 6 so that nothing *would be* **i** into the temple H296
Eze 41: 6 the supports were not **i into** the wall of the H928

INSIDE (80) [IN]

Ge 6:14 it and coat it with pitch **i** and out. H4946+1074
Ge 9:21 drunk and lay uncovered **i** his tent. H928+9348
Ge 19:10 But the men **i** reached out and pulled Lot H448
Ge 31:34 gods and put them **i** her camel's saddle H928
Ge 39:11 the household servants was **i**. H928+2021+1074
Ge 44: 8 the silver we found **i** the mouths of our H928
Ex 4: 6 the LORD said, "Put your hand **i** your cloak." H928
Ex 9:20 slaves and their livestock **i**. H448+2021+1074
Ex 12:46 "It must be eaten **i** the house; take none of H928
Ex 25:11 pure gold, both **i** and out, and H4946+1074
Ex 28:26 on the **i** edge next to the H1074+2025
Ex 37: 2 pure gold, both **i** and out, and H4946+1074
Ex 39:19 on the **i** edge next to the H1074+2025
Lev 14:41 must have all the **i** walls of the H4946+1074
Nu 18: 7 at the altar and **i** the curtain. H4200+4946+1074
Jos 7:21 are hidden in the ground **i** my tent, H928+9348
Jdg 6:19 Gideon **went i**, prepared a young goat, and H995
Jdg 7:16 hands of all of them, with torches **i**. H928+9348
Jdg 9:49 set it on fire **with** the people **still i**. H6584
Jdg 9:51 **I** the city, however, was a strong H928+9348
Jdg 18:17 the land went **i** and took the idol H9004+2025S
1Sa 26: 5 Saul was lying **i** the camp, with the army H928
1Sa 26: 7 lying asleep **i** the camp with his spear stuck H928
2Sa 6:17 it in its place **i** the tent that David H928+9348
2Sa 10:14 they fled before Abishai and **went i** the city. H995
1Ki 6:18 The **i** of the temple was cedar, carved with H7163
1Ki 6:20 He overlaid the **i** with pure gold H4200+7156
1Ki 6:21 covered the **i** *of* the temple with H4946+7163
1Ki 6:27 the cherubim **i** the innermost room H928+9348
1Ki 7:31 On the **i** of the stand there was an H1074
2Ki 4: 4 Then **go** *i* and shut the door behind you and AIT
2Ki 6:20 and there they were, **i** Samaria. H928+9348
1Ch 16: 1 of God and set it **i** the tent that H928+9348
1Ch 19:15 his brother Abishai and went **i** the city. H2025
2Ch 3: 4 He overlaid the **i** with pure gold. H7163
2Ch 3: 8 He overlaid **the i** with six hundred H2084S
Ne 4:22 his helper stay **i** Jerusalem at night, H928+9348
Ne 6:10 the house of God, **i** the temple, and H448+9348
Job 30:27 The churning **i** me never stops; days of H5055
Job 32:19 **i** I am like bottled-up wine, like new H1061
Ps 78:28 them come down **i** their camp, H928+7931
Jer 21: 4 And I will gather them **i** this city. H448+9348
Jer 49: 3 rush here and there **i** the walls, for Molek H928
La 1:20 bereaves; **i**, there is only H928+2021+1074
Eze 3:24 "Go, shut yourself **i** your house. H928+9348
Eze 5: 2 burn a third of the hair **i** the city. H928+9348
Eze 5:12 plague or perish by famine **i** you; H928+9348
Eze 7:15 sword; **i** are plague and famine. H4946+1074
Eze 22:18 iron and lead left **i** a furnace. H928+9348
Eze 22:20 my wrath and put you **i** the city and melt you NDT
Eze 22:21 and you will be melted **i** her. H928+9348
Eze 22:22 so you will be melted **i** her, and you H928+9348
Eze 40:10 **I** the east gate were three alcoves on each NDT
Eze 40:14 walls all around the **i** of the gateway— NDT
Eze 40:16 projecting walls **i** the gateway were H4200+7163
Eze 40:19 distance from the **i** *of* the lower H4200+7156
Eze 42:15 measuring what was **i** the temple area, H7164
Eze 43: 6 speaking to me **from i** the temple. H4946
Eze 44: 3 only one who may sit **i** the gateway to eat H928
Eze 44:17 gates of the inner court or **i** the temple. H2025
Eze 46:23 Around the **i** of each of the four courts was H928
Jnh 2: 1 From **i** the fish Jonah prayed to the LORD H5055
Mt 23:25 **i** they are full of greed and G2277
Mt 23:26 First clean the **i** of the cup and dish, and G1955
Mt 23:27 on the outside but **on the i** are full of the G2277
Mt 23:28 as righteous but **on the i** you are full of G2277
Mk 7:23 All these evils come **from i** and defile a G2277
Lk 11: 7 And suppose the one **i** answers, 'Don't G2277
Lk 11:39 **i** you are full of greed and wickedness. G2277
Lk 11:40 who made the outside make the **i** also? G2277
Lk 11:41 But now as for what *is* **i** you—be generous G1913
Lk 17:31 with possessions **i**, should G1877+3836+3864
Jn 18:33 Pilate then **went** back **i** the palace G1656
Jn 19: 9 and *he* **went** back **i** the palace. "Where do G1656
Jn 20: 8 had reached the tomb first, also **went i**. G1656
Ac 5:23 we opened them, we found no one **i**." G2276
Ac 10:27 Peter **went i** and found a large gathering G1656
1Co 5:12 Are you not to judge those **i**? G2276
Rev 5: 3 earth could open the scroll or even look *i* **it**. AIT
Rev 5: 4 who was worthy to open the scroll or look **i**. NDT

INSIGHT (23) [INSIGHTS]

1Ki 4:29 gave Solomon wisdom and very great **i**, H9312
1Ch 27:32 was a counselor, a man of **i** and a scribe. H1067
Job 12:16 To him belong strength and **i**; both H9370
Job 26: 3 And what great **i** you have displayed! H9370
Job 34:35 without knowledge; his words lack **i**. H8505
Ps 119:99 *I have* more **i** than all my teachers, for I H8505
Pr 1: 2 instruction; for understanding words of **i**; H1069
Pr 2: 3 if you call out for **i** and cry aloud for H1069
Pr 5: 1 wisdom, turn your ear to my **words of i**, H9312
Pr 7: 4 my sister," and to **i**, "You are my relative." H1069
Pr 8:14 are mine; I have **i**, I have power. H1069
Pr 9: 6 you will live; walk in the way of **i**. H1069
Pr 16:16 than gold, to get **i** rather than silver! H1069
Pr 20: 5 one who has **i** draws them out. H9312
Pr 21:30 is no wisdom, no **i**, no plan that can H9312
Pr 23:23 sell it—wisdom, instruction and **i** as well. H1069
Da 5:11 was found to have **i** and intelligence A10467
Da 5:14 of the gods is in you and that you have **i**, A10467
Da 9:22 have now come to **give** you **i** and H8505
Eph 3: 4 to understand my **i** into the mystery of G5304
Php 1: 9 more in knowledge and depth *of* **i**, G151
2Ti 2: 7 the Lord will give you **i** into all this. G5304
Rev 13:18 the person who has **i** calculate the G3808

INSIGHTS (1) [INSIGHT]

Job 15: 9 What **i** *do you* **have** that we do not have? H1067

INSIST (4) [INSISTED, INSISTING, INSISTENTLY]

2Sa 24:24 *I* **i on paying** you **for** it. H7864+928+4697+7864
1Ch 21:24 *I* **i on paying** the full price. H7864+7864
Eph 4:17 I tell you this, and **i on** it in the Lord, that G3458
1Ti 6: 2 are the things you are to teach and **i on**. G4151

INSISTED (7) [INSIST]

Ge 19: 3 But *he* **i** so strongly that they did go with H7210
Ge 33:11 And because Jacob **i**, Esau accepted it. H7210
1Ki 3:22 But the first one **i**, "No! The dead one is H606
Mk 14:31 But Peter **i** emphatically, "Even if I have to G3281
Lk 23: 5 But they **i**, "He stirs up the people G2196+3306
Jn 9: 9 But *he himself* **i**, "I am the man G3306
Jn 19: 7 The Jewish leaders **i**, "We have a law, and G646

INSISTENTLY (1) [INSIST]

Lk 23:23 loud shouts they **i** demanded that he be G2130

INSISTING (1) [INSIST]

Ac 12:15 *When she kept* **i** *that* it was so, they said G1462

INSOLENCE (7) [INSOLENT]

2Ki 19:28 because your **i** has reached my ears H8633
Isa 16: 6 her pride and her **i**; but her boasts are H6301
Isa 37:29 because your **i** has reached my ears H8633
Jer 48:29 of her **i**, her pride, her conceit and the H1470
Jer 48:30 I know her **i** but it is futile," declares the H6301
Da 11:18 will put an end to his **i** and will turn his H3075
Da 11:18 insolence and will turn his **i** back on him. H3075

INSOLENT (5) [INSOLENCE]

Nu 16: 1 of Eliab, and On son of Peleth—*became* **i** H3689
Pr 21:24 is his name—behaves with **i** fury. H2295
Pr 29:21 pampered from youth will turn out to be **i**. H4959
Hos 7:16 fall by the sword because of their **i** words. H2405
Ro 1:30 God-haters, **i**, arrogant and boastful G5616

INSPECT (2) [INSPECTED, INSPECTION]

Lev 14:36 this the priest is to go in and **i** the house. H8011
Lev 14:39 day the priest shall return *to* **i** the house. H8011

INSPECTED (1) [INSPECT]

Ex 39:43 Moses **i** the work and saw that they had H8011

INSPECTION (1) [INSPECT]

Ne 3:31 opposite the **I** Gate, and as far as the H5152

INSPIRE (2) [INSPIRED, INSPIRES]

Jer 32:40 and *I will* **i** them to fear me H5989+928+4222
Jer 49:16 The terror you **i** and the pride of your heart NDT

INSPIRED (5) [INSPIRE]

2Sa 23: 1 "The **i utterance** *of* David son of Jesse H5536
Pr 30: 1 of Agur son of Jakeh—an **i utterance**. H5363
Pr 31: 1 an **i utterance** his mother taught him. H5363
Hos 9: 7 considered a fool, the **i** person a maniac. H8120
1Th 1: 3 your endurance *i by* **hope** in our Lord Jesus AIT

INSPIRES (2) [INSPIRE]

Job 20: 3 and my understanding **i** me to reply. H8120
Rev 22: 6 the God who **i** the prophets, sent G4460

INSTALLED (5)

Jdg 17: 5 gods and **i** one of his sons as H4848+906+3338
Jdg 17:12 Then Micah **i** the Levite, and H4848+906+3338
1Ki 12:32 And at Bethel *he* also **i** priests at the high H6641
Ezr 6:18 And *they* **i** the priests in their divisions A10624
Ps 2: 6 "I *have* **i** my king on Zion, my holy H5820

INSTANCE (1)

Dt 19: 5 **For i**, a man may go into the forest with his H2256

INSTANT (9) [INSTANTLY]

Job 7:19 let me alone even **for an i**? H6330+1180+8371
Job 34:20 They die **in an i**, in the middle of the H8092
Pr 6:15 disaster will overtake him **in an i**; H7328
Isa 29: 5 like blown chaff. Suddenly, in an **i**, H7353
Isa 30:13 bulging, that collapses suddenly, in an **i**. H7353
Jer 4:20 **In an i** my tents are destroyed, my shelter H7328
Jer 49:19 I will chase Edom from its land *in an* **i**. H8088
Jer 50:44 I will chase Babylon from its land **in an i**. H8088
Lk 4: 5 him in an **i** all the kingdoms G5117+5989

INSTANTLY (2) [INSTANT]

Lk 8:47 him and how she had been **i** healed. G4202
Ac 3: 7 **i** the man's feet and ankles became G4202

INSTEAD (104) [STEAD]

Ge 11: 3 They used brick **i of** stone, and tar for H4200
Ge 22:13 it as a burnt offering **i of** his son. H9393
Ex 7:23 **I**, he turned and went into his palace, and H2256
Lev 17: 4 **i of** bringing it to the entrance to the tent H4202
Nu 1:50 **I**, appoint the Levites to be in charge of H2256
Nu 18:24 **I**, I give to the Levites as their inheritance H3954
Dt 12:18 **I**, you are to eat them in the H3954+561
Jos 23:13 **I**, they will become snares and traps for H2256
Jdg 15: 2 sister more attractive? Take her **i**." H9393
2Sa 6:10 **I**, he took it to the house of Obed-Edom H2256
2Sa 12: 4 **I**, he took the ewe lamb that belonged to H2256
2Sa 16:12 his covenant blessing **i of** his curse today." H9393
2Sa 18:33 If only I had died **i of** you—O Absalom H9393
2Sa 23:16 he refused to drink it; **i**, he poured it out H2256
1Ch 11:18 refused to drink it; **i**, he poured it out to H2256
1Ch 13:13 **I**, he took it to the house of Obed-Edom H2256
2Ch 28:20 but he gave him trouble **i of** help. H4202
Ne 5:16 **I**, I devoted myself to the work on H2256+1685
Est 2: 4 pleases the king be queen **i of** Vashti." H9393

Est 2:17 her head and made her queen i of Vashti. H9393
Est 3: 6 I Haman looked for a way to destroy all H2256
Est 4: 4 clothes for him to put on i of his sackcloth, H6073
Job 31:40 let briers come up i of wheat and H9393
Job 31:40 of wheat and stinkweed i of barley." H9393
Pr 8:10 Choose my instruction i of silver H440
Pr 11: 8 from trouble, and it falls on the wicked i. H9393
Ecc 6: 2 enjoy them, and strangers enjoy them i. H3954
Isa 3:24 I of fragrance there will be a stench H9393
Isa 3:24 there will be a stench; i of a sash, a rope; H9393
Isa 3:24 of a sash, a rope; i of well-dressed hair H9393
Isa 3:24 baldness; i of fine clothing, sackcloth H9393
Isa 3:24 clothing, sackcloth; i of beauty, branding. H9393
Isa 55:13 I of the thornbush will grow the juniper H9393
Isa 55:13 and i of briers the myrtle will grow. H9393
Isa 60:17 I of bronze I will bring you gold, and silver H9393
Isa 60:17 I of wood I will bring you bronze, and iron H9393
Isa 61: 3 on them a crown of beauty i of ashes, H9393
Isa 61: 3 the oil of joy i of mourning, and a H9393
Isa 61: 3 a garment of praise i of a spirit of despair. H9393
Isa 61: 7 I of your shame you will receive a double H9393
Isa 61: 7 i of disgrace you will rejoice in your NDT
Jer 7:24 pay attention; i, they followed the H2256
Jer 9:14 I, they have followed the stubbornness of H2256
Jer 11: 8 pay attention; i, they followed the H2256
Jer 14:12 I, I will destroy them with the sword H3954
Jer 16:12 of your evil hearts i of obeying me. H4200+1194
Jer 30: 9 I, they will serve the LORD their God and H2256
Jer 31:13 will give them comfort and joy i of sorrow. H4946
Jer 31:30 I, everyone will die for their own sin H3954+561
Jer 36:26 I, the king commanded Jerahmeel, a son H2256
Jer 37:14 not listen to him; i, he arrested Jeremiah H2256
Jer 43: 5 I, Johanan son of Kareah and all the army H2256
Eze 4:15 over cow dung i of human excrement." H9393
Eze 36:34 be cultivated i of lying desolate in H9393+889
Eze 44: 8 I of carrying out your duty in regard to my H4202
Da 1:16 were to drink and gave them vegetables i. NDT
Da 5:23 I, you have set yourself up against the A10221
Da 11:38 I of them, he will honor a god of H6584+4030
Jnh 1:13 I, the men did their best to row back to H2256
Hab 2:16 You will be filled with shame i of glory H4946
Mt 5:15 I they put it on its stand, and it gives light G247
Mt 18:30 I, he went off and had the man thrown into G247
Mt 20:26 I, whoever wants to become great among G247
Mt 25: 9 I, go to those who sell oil and buy some G3437
Mt 27:24 nowhere, but that i an uproar was starting G3437
Mk 1:45 I he went out and began to talk freely G1254
Mk 4:21 a bowl or a bed? I, don't you put it on G2671
Mk 5:26 yet i of getting better she grew worse. G3594
Mk 7: 5 of the elders i of eating their food with G247
Mk 10:43 I, whoever wants to become great among G247
Mk 15:11 crowd to have Pilate release Barabbas i. G3437
Lk 8:16 I, they put it on a stand, so that those who G247
Lk 11:11 son asks for a fish, will give him a snake i? G505
Lk 11:33 I they put it on its stand, so that those who G247
Lk 22:26 I, the greatest among you should be like G247
Jn 3:19 loved darkness i of light because G3437+2445
Jn 7:24 by mere appearances, but i judge correctly." G247
Jn 11:54 I he withdrew to a region near the G247
Jn 15:15 I, I have called you friends, for everything G1254
Jn 19:34 I, one of the soldiers pierced Jesus' side G247
Jn 20:17 Go i to my brothers and tell them, 'I am G1254
Ac 7:39 I, they rejected him and in their hearts G247
Ac 15:20 I we should write to them, telling them to G247
Ac 25:19 I, they had some points of dispute with G1254
Ac 27:11 i of listening to what Paul said G3437+2445
Ro 14:13 I, make up your mind not to G247+4047+3437
1Co 6: 1 judgment i of before the Lord's G2779+4049
1Co 6: 6 But i, one brother takes another to court G247
1Co 6: 8 I, you yourselves cheat and do wrong, and G247
2Co 2: 7 Now i, you ought to forgive and G5539+3437
2Co 5: 2 longing *to be* clothed *i* with our heavenly AIT
2Co 5: 4 to be unclothed but to be clothed i with our G247
Gal 4:14 I, you welcomed me as if I were an angel G247
Eph 4:15 I, speaking the truth in love, we will grow G1254
Eph 5:18 leads to debauchery. I, be filled with the G247
Eph 6: 4 your children; i, bring them up in the G247
1Th 2: 7 I, we were like young children among you G247
1Ti 6: 2 I, they should serve them even better G247
2Ti 4: 3 I, to suit their own desires, they will gather G247
Heb 11:16 I, they were longing for a better G3814+1254
Jas 4:15 I, you ought to say, "If it is the Lord's will G505
1Pe 2:23 I, he entrusted himself to him who judges G1254
2Pe 3: 9 I he is patient with you, not wanting G247
2Jn 12 I, I hope to visit you and talk with you face G247

INSTINCT (2) [INSTINCTS]
2Pe 2:12 animals, creatures of i, born only to be G5879
Jude 10 the very things they do understand by i— G5880

INSTINCTS (1) [INSTINCT]
Jude 19 who follow mere natural i and do not G6035

INSTITUTED (4)
Nu 28: 6 burnt offering i at Mount Sinai as a H6913
1Ki 12:32 He i a festival on the fifteenth day of the H6913
1Ki 12:33 So *he* i the festival for the Israelites and H6913
Ro 13: 2 is rebelling against what God has i, G1408

INSTRUCT (15) [INSTRUCTED, INSTRUCTING, INSTRUCTION, INSTRUCTIONS, INSTRUCTOR, INSTRUCTORS, INSTRUCTS, WELL-INSTRUCTED]
Dt 17:10 careful to do everything *they* i you to do. H3723
Dt 24: 8 to do exactly as the Levitical priests i you. H3723
Ne 9:20 You gave your good Spirit to i them. H8505
Est 4: 8 he told him to i her to go into the H7422
Job 8:10 *Will* they not i you and tell you? Will they H3723
Ps 25:12 *He will* i them in the ways they should H3723
Ps 32: 8 *I will* i you and teach you in the way you H8505
Ps 105:22 to i his princes as he pleased and teach his H673
Pr 4:11 *I* i you in the way of wisdom and lead you H3723
Pr 9: 9 I the wise and they will be wiser still H5989
Isa 40:13 of the LORD, or i the LORD as his counselor? H3359
Da 11:33 "Those who are wise *will* i many, though H1067
Ro 15:14 competent *to* i one another. G3805
1Co 2:16 the mind of the Lord *so as to* i him?" G5204
1Co 14:19 intelligible words to i others than ten G2994

INSTRUCTED (31) [INSTRUCT]
Ge 32: 4 *He* i them: "This is what you are to say to H7422
Ge 32:17 *He* i the one in the lead: "When my H7422
Ge 32:19 *He* also i the second, the third and all the H7422
Ex 12:35 did as Moses i and asked the Egyptians H1821
Nu 5: 4 They did just as the LORD *had* i Moses. H1819
Nu 27:23 as the LORD i through Moses. H1819
Jos 8:27 of this city, as the LORD *had* i Joshua. H7422
Jos 13: 6 Israel for an inheritance, as *I have* i you, H7422
Jos 18: 8 the land, Joshua i them, "Go and make a H7422
Jos 20: 2 cities of refuge, as *I* i you through Moses, H1819
Jdg 21:20 So *they* i the Benjamites, saying, "Go H7422
2Sa 11:19 *He* i the messenger: "When you have H7422
2Sa 14:19 your servant Joab *who* i me to do this H7422
2Ki 12: 2 all the years Jehoiada the priest i him. H3723
2Ch 26: 5 Zechariah, who i him in the fear of God. H1067
2Ch 35: 3 who i all Israel and who had been H1067
Ne 8: 7 i the people in the Law while the people H1067
Est 1: 8 the king i all the wine stewards to H3569
Est 4:10 Then she i him to say to Mordecai, H606
Job 4: 3 Think how *you have* i many, how you H3579
Isa 50: 4 wakens my ear to listen like one being i. H4341
Jer 9:12 Who *has been* i *by* the LORD and H7023+1819
Da 9:22 *He* i me and said to me, "Daniel, I have H1067
Mt 17: 9 the mountain, Jesus i them, "Don't tell G1948
Mt 21: 6 went and did as Jesus *had* i them. G5332
Mt 28:15 took the money and did as *they were* i. G1438
Ac 18:25 He had been i in the way of the Lord, and G2994
Ro 2:18 is superior *because you are* i by the law; G2994
1Co 14:31 that everyone *may be* i and encouraged. G3443
1Th 4: 1 we i *you* how to live in order to please G4161
2Ti 2:25 Opponents *must be* gently i, in the hope G4084

INSTRUCTING (2) [INSTRUCT]
Ne 8: 9 the Levites who *were* i the people said to H1067
Mt 11: 1 Jesus had finished i his twelve disciples, G1411

INSTRUCTION (48) [INSTRUCT]
Ex 15:25 issued a ruling and i for them and put H5477
Ex 24:12 commandments I have written for their i." H3723
Dt 33: 3 all bow down, and from you receive i, H1830
Ne 1: 8 "Remember the i you gave your servant H1821
Job 22:22 Accept i from his mouth and lay up his H9368
Ps 50:17 You hate my i and cast my words behind H4592
Pr 1: 2 gaining wisdom and i; for H4592
Pr 1: 3 receiving i *in* prudent behavior, doing H4592
Pr 1: 7 fools despise wisdom and i. H4592
Pr 1: 8 to your father's i and do not forsake your H4592
Pr 4: 1 my sons, to a father's i; pay attention and H4592
Pr 4:13 Hold on to i, do not let it go; guard it well, H4592
Pr 6:23 correction and i are the way to life, H4592
Pr 8:10 Choose my i instead of silver, knowledge H4592
Pr 8:33 Listen to my i and be wise; do not H4592
Pr 13: 1 A wise son heeds his father's i, but a H4592
Pr 13:13 Whoever scorns i will pay for it, but H1821
Pr 15:33 Wisdom's i is to fear the LORD, and H4592
Pr 16:20 Whoever gives heed to i prospers, and H1821
Pr 16:21 discerning, and gracious words promote i. H4375
Pr 16:23 mouths prudent, and their lips promote i. H4375
Pr 19:27 Stop listening to i, my son, and you will H4592
Pr 23:12 Apply your heart to i and your ears to H4592
Pr 23:23 not sell it—wisdom, i and insight as well. H4592
Pr 28: 4 Those who forsake i praise the wicked H9368
Pr 28: 7 A discerning son heeds i, but a H9368
Pr 28: 9 If anyone turns a deaf ear to my i, even H9368
Pr 29:18 blessed is the one who heeds wisdom's i. H9368
Pr 31:26 wisdom, and faithful i is on her tongue. H9368
Isa 1:10 listen to the i *of* our God, you people H9368
Isa 8:16 seal up God's i among my disciples H9368
Isa 8:20 Consult God's i and the testimony of H9368
Isa 29:24 those who complain will accept i. H4375
Isa 30: 9 children unwilling to listen to the LORD's i. H9368
Isa 51: 4 I will go out from me; my justice will H9368
Isa 51: 7 you people who have taken my i to heart: H9368
Eze 7:26 priestly i in the law will cease, the H9368
Mal 2: 6 True i was in his mouth and nothing false H9368
Mal 2: 7 people seek i from his mouth. H9368
1Co 14: 6 knowledge or prophecy or word of i? G1439
1Co 14:26 has a hymn, or a word of i, a revelation, G1439
Gal 6: 6 the *one who* receives i in the word should G2994
Eph 6: 4 them up in the training and i of the Lord. G3804
1Th 4: 8 who rejects this i does not reject a human NDT
2Th 3:14 who does not obey our i in this letter. G3364
1Ti 6: 3 not agree to the sound i of our Lord Jesus G3364
2Ti 4: 2 with great patience and careful i. G1439
Heb 6: 2 i about cleansing rites, the laying on of G1439

INSTRUCTIONS (35) [INSTRUCT]
Ge 26: 5 my commands, my decrees and my i." H9368
Ge 44: 1 Now Joseph gave *these* i *to* the steward H7422
Ge 49:29 Then *he* gave them *these* i: "I am about H7422
Ge 49:33 Jacob had finished giving i *to* his sons, H7422
Ge 50:16 "Your father left *these* i before he died: H7422
Ex 12:24 "Obey these i as a lasting ordinance for H1821
Ex 16: 4 see whether they will follow my i. H9368
Ex 16:28 refuse to keep my commands and my i? H9368
Ex 18:16 inform them of God's decrees and i." H9368
Ex 18:20 Teach them his decrees and i, and show H9368
Jos 8:33 when he gave i to bless the people of NDT
Jdg 21:10 fighting men with i to go to Jabesh H7422
1Sa 15:11 from me and has not carried out my i." H1821
1Sa 15:13 I have carried out the LORD's i." H1821
1Sa 15:24 I violated the LORD's command and your i H1821
1Ki 3: 3 according to the i *given* him *by* his father H2978
1Ch 23:27 According to the last i *of* David, the Levites H1821
1Ch 28:13 He gave him i for the divisions of the priests NDT
2Ch 35: 4 according to the i written *by* David king of H4181
Est 2:20 follow Mordecai's i as she had done H4411
Est 4:17 away and carried out all of Esther's i. H7422
Jer 32:13 "In their presence *I* gave Baruch *these* i: H7422
Jer 35:18 have followed all his i and have done H5184
Eze 44: 5 regulations and i *regarding* the temple of H9368
Mt 10: 5 twelve Jesus sent out *with* the following i: G4133
Mk 6: 8 *These were his* i: "Take nothing for the G4133
Ac 1: 2 *after* giving i through the Holy Spirit to the G1948
Ac 17:15 then left with i for Silas and Timothy G1953
Ac 19:33 to the front, and *they* shouted i to him. G5204
Col 4:10 You have received i about him; if he G1953
1Th 4: 2 For you know what i we gave you by the G4132
1Ti 3:14 to you soon, I am writing you these *i* so that, AIT
1Ti 5: 7 Give the people these i, so that no one G4133
1Ti 5:21 to keep these *i* without partiality AIT
Heb 11:22 from Egypt and gave i concerning the G1948

INSTRUCTOR (3) [INSTRUCT]
Mt 23:10 you have one I, the Messiah. G2762
Ro 2:20 an i of the foolish, a teacher of little G4083
Gal 6: 6 should share all good things *with* their i. G2994

INSTRUCTORS (2) [INSTRUCT]
Pr 5:13 obey my teachers or turn my ear to my i. H4340
Mt 23:10 Nor are you to be called i, for you have G2762

INSTRUCTS (3) [INSTRUCT]
Ps 16: 7 counsels me; even at night my heart i me. H3579
Ps 25: 8 therefore *he* i sinners in his ways. H3723
Isa 28:26 His God i him and teaches him the right H3579

INSTRUMENT (4) [INSTRUMENTS]
Eze 33:32 with a beautiful voice and plays an i well, H5594
Ac 9:15 man is my chosen i to proclaim my name G5007
Ro 6:13 of yourself to sin *as* an i of wickedness, G3960
Ro 6:13 yourself to him *as* an i of righteousness. G3960

INSTRUMENTS (23) [INSTRUMENT]
Ge 4:21 of all who play stringed i and pipes. H4036
1Ch 15:16 to make a joyful sound with musical i: H3998
1Ch 16:42 the playing of the other i *for* sacred song. H3998
1Ch 23: 5 LORD with the *musical* i I have provided H3998
2Ch 5:13 cymbals and other i, the singers H3998+8877
2Ch 7: 6 did the Levites with the LORD's musical i, H3998
2Ch 23:13 with their i were leading the H8877+3998
2Ch 29:26 So the Levites stood ready with David's i H3998
2Ch 29:27 by trumpets and the i *of* David king of H3998
2Ch 30:21 day with resounding i dedicated to the H3998
2Ch 34:12 all who were skilled in playing musical i— H3998
Ne 12:36 with musical i prescribed by David the H3998
Ps 4: T With stringed i. A psalm of H5593
Ps 6: T With stringed i. According to H5593
Ps 54: T With stringed i. A maskil of H5593
Ps 55: T With stringed i. A maskil of H5593
Ps 61: T With stringed i. Of David. H5593
Ps 67: T With stringed i. A psalm. H5593
Ps 76: T With stringed i. A psalm of H5593
Isa 38:20 we will sing with stringed i all the days of H5593
Am 6: 5 like David and improvise on musical i. H3998
Hab 3:19 the director of music. On my stringed i. H5593
2Ti 2:21 the latter will be i for special purposes, G5007

INSULT (12) [INSULTED, INSULTING, INSULTS]
Ps 69: 9 the insults of *those who* i you fall on me. H3070
Pr 12:16 at once, but the prudent overlook an i. H7830
Jer 20: 8 LORD has brought me i and reproach all H3075
Mt 5:11 "Blessed are you when *people* i you G3943
Lk 6:22 they exclude you and i you and reject your G3943
Lk 11:45 when you say these things, *you* i us also." G5614
Lk 18:32 will mock him, i him and spit on him; G5614
Ac 23: 4 "*How dare you* i God's high priest! G3366
Ro 15: 3 "The insults *of* those who i you have G3943
Heb 10:33 publicly exposed *to* i and persecution; G3944
1Pe 3: 9 Do not repay evil with evil or i with insult G3367
1Pe 3: 9 Do not repay evil with evil or insult with i G3367

INSULTED (4) [INSULT]
Jer 51:51 we have been i and shame covers our H3075
Zep 2: 8 who i my people and made threats H3070

Heb 10:29 and *who has* i the Spirit of grace? *G1964*
1Pe 4:14 If *you are* i because of the name of Christ *G3943*

INSULTING (3) [INSULT]

Ps 55:12 If an enemy *were* i me, I could endure it H3070
Zep 2:10 i and mocking the people of the LORD H3070
Lk 22:65 And they said many other i things to him. *G1059*

INSULTS (20) [INSULT]

1Sa 25:14 his greetings, but *he* **hurled** i at them. H6512
Ne 4: 4 Turn their i back on their own heads H3075
Ne 4: 5 for *they have* **thrown** i in the face of the H4087
Ps 22: 7 mock me; *they* **hurl** i, shaking H7080+928+8557
Ps 69: 9 the i *of* those who insult you fall on H3075
Pr 9: 7 Whoever corrects a mocker invites i H7830
Pr 22:10 out goes strife; quarrels and i are ended. H7830
Isa 51: 7 of mere mortals or be terrified by their i. H1528
La 3:61 you have heard their i, all their plots H3075
Eze 21:28 says about the Ammonites and their i: H3075
Zep 2: 8 "I have heard the i *of* Moab and the H3075
Mt 27:39 Those who passed by **hurled** i at him *G1059*
Mt 27:44 crucified with him also **heaped** i on him. *G3943*
Mk 15:29 Those who passed by **hurled** i at him *G1059*
Mk 15:32 crucified with him also **heaped** i on him. *G3943*
Lk 23:39 criminals who hung there **hurled** i at him: *G1059*
Jn 9:28 Then *they* **hurled** i at him and said, "You *G3366*
Ro 15: 3 "The i of those who insult you have fallen *G3944*
2Co 12:10 in weaknesses, in i, in hardships, in *G5615*
1Pe 2:23 *When they* **hurled** *their* i at him, he did *G3366*

INSURRECTION (2) [INSURRECTIONISTS]

Lk 23:19 thrown into prison for an i in the city, *G5087*
Lk 23:25 been thrown into prison for i and murder, *G5087*

INSURRECTIONISTS (1) [INSURRECTION]

Mk 15: 7 in prison with the i who had committed *G5086*

INTACT (1)

Zec 12: 6 Jerusalem *will* remain i in her place. H3782

INTEGRITY (22)

Dt 9: 5 your i that you are going in H3841+4222
1Ki 9: 4 me faithfully with i *of* heart and H9448
1Ch 29:17 you test the heart and are pleased with i. H4797
Ne 7: 2 he was a man of i and feared God more H622
Job 2: 3 And he still maintains his i, though you H9450
Job 2: 9 "Are you still maintaining your i? H9450
Job 6:29 be unjust; reconsider, for my i is at stake. H7406
Job 27: 5 in the right; till I die, I will not deny my i. H9450
Ps 7: 8 according to my i, O Most High. H9448
Ps 25:21 May i and uprightness protect me H9448
Ps 41:12 Because of my i you uphold me and set H9448
Ps 78:72 David shepherded them with i *of* heart; H9448
Pr 10: 9 Whoever walks in i walks securely, but H9448
Pr 11: 3 The i *of* the upright guides them, but the H9450
Pr 13: 6 guards the **person of** i, H9448+2006
Pr 29:10 hate a *person of* i and seek to kill H9447
Isa 45:23 mouth has uttered *in all* i a word that will H7407
Isa 59: 4 justice; no one pleads a case with i. H575
Mt 22:16 that you are a *man of* i and that you teach *G239*
Mk 12:14 "Teacher, we know that you are a *man of* i. *G239*
2Co 1:12 with you, with i and godly sincerity. *G605*
Titus 2: 7 In your teaching show i, seriousness *G917*

INTELLIGENCE (5) [INTELLIGENT]

2Ch 2:12 endowed with i and discernment H8507
Isa 29:14 the i *of* the intelligent will vanish. H1069
Da 5:11 to have insight and i and wisdom like A10684
Da 5:14 have insight, i and outstanding wisdom. A10684
1Co 1:19 the i of the intelligent I will frustrate." *G5304*

INTELLIGENT (4) [INTELLIGENCE]

1Sa 25: 3 She was an i and beautiful woman, H3202+8507
Isa 29:14 the intelligence of the i will vanish." H1067
Ac 13: 7 The proconsul, an i man, sent for *G5305*
1Co 1:19 the intelligence *of* the i I will frustrate." *G5305*

INTELLIGIBLE (2)

1Co 14: 9 Unless you speak i words with your *G2358*
1Co 14:19 would rather speak five i words to instruct *G3808*

INTEND (10) [INTENDED, INTENDING, INTENDS, INTENT, INTENTION, INTENTIONAL, INTENTIONALLY, INTENTLY]

Ge 37: 8 to him, "*Do you* i **to reign** over us? H4887+4887
1Ki 5: 5 I i, therefore, to build a temple for the H606
2Ch 28:10 And now you i to make the men and H606
2Ch 28:13 *Do* you i to add to our sin and guilt H606
2Ch 29:10 Now I i to make a covenant with the H6640+4222
Ps 62: 4 Surely *they* i to topple me from my lofty H3619
Jn 7:35 "Where *does* this man i to go that we *G3516*
Jn 14:22 why *do you* i to show yourself to us and *G3516*
Ac 5:35 carefully what *you* i to do to these men. *G3516*
Ac 28:19 *I certainly did* not i to bring any charge *G2400*

INTENDED (17) [INTEND]

Ge 50:20 You i *to* harm me, but God intended it H3108
Ge 50:20 God i it for good to accomplish what H3108
Nu 35:23 was not an enemy and no harm *was* i, H1335
Dt 19:19 witness as that witness i to do to the other H2372
1Sa 14: 4 pass that Jonathan i to cross to reach the H1335
1Sa 20:33 knew that his father i to kill David. H3983
2Ch 32: 2 come and that he i to wage war against H7156
Jer 18:10 will reconsider the good *I had* i to do for it. H606
Hos 2: 9 my linen, i to cover her naked body. NDT
Jn 6:15 knowing that *they* i **to** come and make *G3516*
Jn 12: 7 "*It was* i **that** she should save this perfume AIT
Ac 12: 4 Herod i to bring him out for public trial *G1089*
Ac 20: 7 *because he* i to leave the next day *G3516*
Ro 2: 4 God's kindness *is* i *to* **lead** you to repentance AIT
Ro 7:10 commandment that was i to bring life NDT
2Co 1:17 Was I fickle *when I* i *to do* this? Or do I *G1089*
2Co 7: 9 sorrowful **as** God i and so were not *G2848*

INTENDING (2) [INTEND]

Jdg 20: 5 surrounded the house, i to kill me. H1948
Ac 12: 1 belonged to the church, *i to* **persecute** them. AIT

INTENDS (3) [INTEND]

Dt 28:57 For in her dire need *she* i *to* **eat** them secretly AIT
1Sa 20:13 But if my father i to harm you, may the H3512
Isa 10: 7 But this is not what *he* i, this is not what H1948

INTENSE (3) [INTENSELY]

2Sa 13:15 Amnon hated her with i hatred. H1524+4394
1Th 2:17 out of our i longing we made every effort *G4498*
Rev 16: 9 were seared by the i heat and they cursed *G3489*

INTENSELY (2) [INTENSE]

Gal 1:13 how i I persecuted the church of *G2848+5651*
Rev 2:22 who commit adultery with her suffer i, *G3489*

INTENT (11) [INTEND]

Ex 32:12 'It was with **evil** i that he brought them H8288
1Sa 25:26 enemies and *all* who *are* i **on** harming my H1335
1Ch 29:17 I have given willingly and with honest i. H4222
Ps 37:32 the righteous, i **on** putting them to death H1335
Ps 139:20 They speak of you with **evil** i; your H4659
Pr 7:10 dressed like a prostitute and with crafty i. H4213
Pr 21:27 much more so when brought with **evil** i! H2365
Hos 5:11 trampled in judgment, i **on** pursuing idols. H3283
Hab 1: 9 they all come i **on** violence. Their hordes H4200
Mt 22:18 knowing their **evil** *i*, said, "You AIT
Eph 3:10 His i was **that** now, through the church, the *G2671*

INTENTION (2) [INTEND]

2Sa 13:32 Absalom's express i ever since the day H8461
Job 34:14 If *it were* his i and he withdrew his H8492+4213

INTENTIONAL (1) [INTEND]

Nu 15:25 it was **not** i and they have presented to H8705

INTENTIONALLY (2) [INTEND]

Ex 21:13 However, if it *is* not **done** i, but God lets it H7399
Nu 35:20 something at them i so that they die H928+7402

INTENTLY (4) [INTEND]

Ac 1:10 They were **looking** i **up** into the sky as he *G867*
Ac 6:15 in the Sanhedrin **looked** i at Stephen, *G867*
Jas 1:25 But whoever **looks** i into the perfect law *G4160*
1Pe 1:10 **searched** i and with the greatest care, *G1699*

INTERCEDE (5) [INTERCEDED, INTERCEDES, INTERCEDING, INTERCESSION, INTERCESSOR]

Ge 23: 8 then listen to me and i with Ephron son of H7003
1Sa 2:25 sins against the LORD, who *will* i for them?" H7137
1Sa 7: 5 Mizpah, and *I will* i with the LORD for you." H7137
1Ki 13: 6 **"I with** the LORD your God and H2704+906+7156
Heb 7:25 because he always lives to i for them. *G1961*

INTERCEDED (1) [INTERCEDE]

1Ki 13: 6 man of God i **with** the LORD, H2704+906+7156

INTERCEDES (2) [INTERCEDE]

Ro 8:26 the Spirit himself i for us through *G5659*
Ro 8:27 because the Spirit i for God's people in *G1961*

INTERCEDING (1) [INTERCEDE]

Ro 8:34 the right hand of God and *is* also i for us. *G1961*

INTERCESSION (2) [INTERCEDE]

Isa 53:12 of many, and **made** i for the transgressors. H7003
1Ti 2: 1 i and thanksgiving be made for all people *G1950*

INTERCESSOR (1) [INTERCEDE]

Job 16:20 My i is my friend as my eyes pour out H4885

INTEREST (19) [INTERESTS, SELF-INTEREST]

Ex 22:25 treat it like a business deal; charge no i. H5968
Lev 25:36 Do not take i or any profit from them, but H5968
Lev 25:37 lend them money at i or sell them food at H5968
Dt 23:19 *Do* not **charge** a fellow Israelite i H5967+5968
Dt 23:19 food or anything else that *may* **earn** i. H5967
Dt 23:20 *You may* **charge** a foreigner i, but not a H5967
Ne 5: 7 "You are charging your own people i!" H5391
Ne 5:10 But let us stop **charging** i! H5391
Ne 5:11 also *the* i you *are* **charging** them H5957
Est 3: 8 it is not **in** the king's **best** i to tolerate H8750
Ps 15: 5 who lends money to the poor without i H5968
Pr 28: 8 wealth by **taking** i or profit from the H5968
Eze 18: 8 not lend to them at i or take a profit from H5968
Eze 18:13 He lends at i and takes a profit. Will such H5968
Eze 18:17 poor and takes no i or profit from them. H5968
Eze 22:12 you take i and make a profit from the poor H5968
Mt 25:27 I would have received it back with i. *G5527*
Lk 19:23 I could have collected it with i? *G5527*
1Ti 6: 4 *They* **have an unhealthy** i in controversies *G3796*

INTERESTS (5) [INTEREST]

Ezr 4:22 to the detriment of the **royal** i? A10421
1Co 7:34 his i are divided. An unmarried woman NDT
Php 2: 4 looking to your own i but each of you to *G3836*
Php 2: 4 each of you to **the** i of the others. *G3836*
Php 2:21 For everyone looks out for their own i, not *G3836*S

INTERFERE (2)

2Sa 19:22 What right do you have to i H2118+8477
Ezr 6: 7 *Do* **not** i with the work on this temple of A10697

INTERIOR (4)

1Ki 6:15 He lined its i walls with H4946+1074+2025
1Ki 6:22 So he overlaid the whole i with gold. H1074
SS 3:10 with purple, its i inlaid with love. H9348
Ac 19: 1 the road through the i and arrived at *G541+3538*

INTERMARRY (5) [MARRY]

Ge 34: 9 **I** *with* us; give us your daughters and take H3161
Dt 7: 3 *Do* not i with them. Do not give your H3161
Jos 23:12 among you and if *you* i with them and H3161
1Ki 11: 2 the Israelites, "*You must* not i with them H995
Ezr 9:14 commands again and i with the peoples H3161

INTERMITTENT (1)

Job 6:15 are as undependable as **i streams**, H5707

INTERNAL (17)

Ex 12: 9 with the head, legs and **i organs**. H7931
Ex 29:13 Then take all the fat on the **i organs**, the H7931
Ex 29:17 wash the **i organs** and the legs, H7931
Ex 29:22 the fat on the **i organs**, the long lobe of H7931
Lev 1: 9 are to wash the **i organs** and the legs with H7931
Lev 1:13 are to wash the **i organs** and the legs with H7931
Lev 3: 3 the **i organs** and all the fat that is H7931
Lev 3: 9 the **i organs** and all the fat that is H7931
Lev 3:14 the **i organs** and all the fat that is H7931
Lev 4: 8 all the fat that is connected to the **i organs**, H7931
Lev 4:11 legs, the **i organs** and the intestines H7931
Lev 7: 3 tail and the fat that covers the **i organs**, H7931
Lev 8:16 also took all the fat around the **i organs**, H7931
Lev 8:21 He washed the **i organs** and the legs with H7931
Lev 8:25 all the fat around the **i organs**, the long H7931
Lev 9:14 He washed the **i organs** and the legs and H7931
Dt 18: 3 the **i organs** and the meat from the head. H7687

INTERPRET (25) [INTERPRETATION, INTERPRETATIONS, INTERPRETED, INTERPRETER, INTERPRETERS, INTERPRETS]

Ge 40: 8 answered, "but there is no *one to* i them." H7354
Ge 41: 8 dreams, but no *one could* i them for him. H7354
Ge 41:15 "I had a dream, and no *one can* i it. H7354
Ge 41:15 that when you hear a dream *you can* i it." H7354
Da 2: 4 the dream, and *we will* i it." A10252+10600
Da 2: 5 not tell me what my dream was and i it, A10600
Da 2: 6 So tell me the dream and i it for me." A10600
Da 2: 7 the dream, and *we will* i it." A10252+10600
Da 2: 9 know that *you can* i it *for* me." A10252+10600
Da 2:16 so that he *might* i the dream for A10252+10600
Da 2:24 and *I will* i his dream for him." A10252+10600
Da 2:26 tell me what I saw in my dream and i it?" A10600
Da 2:36 and now *we will* i it to the king. A10042+10600
Da 4: 6 before me *to* i the dream *for* me. A10313+10600
Da 4: 7 but *they could* not i it for me. A10313+10600
Da 4: 9 Here is my dream; i it for me. A10042+10600
Da 4:18 in my kingdom can i it *for* me. A10313+10600
Da 5:12 also the *ability to* i dreams, explain A10599
Mt 16: 3 You know how *to* i the appearance of the *G1359*
Mt 16: 3 but you cannot i the signs of the times. NDT
Lk 12:56 You know how *to* i the appearance of the *G1507*
Lk 12:56 you don't know how *to* i this present time? *G1507*
1Co 12:30 Do all speak in tongues? *Do* all i? *G1450*
1Co 14:13 should pray that *they may* i what they say. *G1450*
1Co 14:27 one at a time, and someone *must* i. *G1450*

INTERPRETATION (11) [INTERPRET]

Ge 40:16 saw that Joseph *had* **given** *a* favorable i, H7354
Ge 40:22 just as Joseph *had* **said** to them in *his* i. H7354
Ge 41:12 **giving** each man *the* i *of* his dream. H7354
Jdg 7:15 When Gideon heard the dream and its i H8694
Da 2:30 may know the i and that you may A10600
Da 2:45 The dream is true and its i is trustworthy." A10600
Da 4:24 "This is the i, Your Majesty, and this is A10600
Da 7:16 me and gave me the i *of* these things: A10600
1Co 12:10 to still another the i of tongues. *G2255*
1Co 14:26 instruction, a revelation, a tongue or an i. *G2255*
2Pe 1:20 about *by* the prophet's own i *of things*. *G2146*

INTERPRETATIONS (2) [INTERPRET]

Ge 40: 8 said to them, "Do not i belong to God? H7355
Da 5:16 are able to **give** i and to solve A10599+10600

INTERPRETED (2) [INTERPRET]

Ge 41:12 him our dreams, and *he* i them for us H7354
Ge 41:13 turned out exactly as *he* i them to us: H7354

INTERPRETER (2) [INTERPRET]

Ge 42:23 since he was using an i. H4885
1Co 14:28 If there is no i, the speaker should keep *G1449*

INTERPRETERS (1) [INTERPRET]

Jer 27: 9 diviners, your **i of dreams**, your mediums H2706

INTERPRETS (2) [INTERPRET]
Dt 18:10 divination or sorcery, **i omens**, engages in H5727
1Co 14: 5 in tongues, unless *someone* **i**, so that the *G1450*

INTERROGATE (1) [INTERROGATED]
Ac 22:29 Those who were about to **i** him withdrew *G458*

INTERROGATED (1) [INTERROGATE]
Ac 22:24 directed *that* he *be* flogged and **i** in order *G458*

INTERRUPTED (1)
Ac 26:24 At this point Festus **i** Paul's defense. "You NDT

INTERSECTING (2)
Eze 1:16 to be made like a wheel **i** a wheel. H928+9348
Eze 10:10 each was like a wheel **i** a wheel. H928+9348

INTERVALS (1)
Eze 41:17 on the walls **at regular i** all around the H4500

INTERVENE (1) [INTERVENED]
Isa 59:16 was appalled that there was no *one to* **i**; H7003

INTERVENED (2) [INTERVENE]
Ps 106:30 But Phinehas stood up and **i**, and the H7136
Ac 15:14 to us how God first **i** to choose a people *G2170*

INTERWOVEN (3) [WEAVE]
1Ki 7:17 A network of **i chains** adorned the H5126+9249
2Ch 3:16 He made **i** chains and put them on H3869+8054
Ps 45:13 her chamber; her gown is **i** *with* gold. H5401

INTESTINES (7)
Ex 29:14 its hide and its **i** outside the camp. H7302
Lev 4:11 legs, the internal organs and the **i**— H7302
Lev 8:17 its flesh and its **i** he burned up outside H7302
Lev 16:27 flesh and **i** are to be burned up. H7302
Nu 19: 5 to be burned—its hide, flesh, blood and **i**. H7302
2Sa 20:10 and his **i** spilled out on the ground. H5055
Ac 1:18 body burst open and all his **i** spilled out. *G5073*

INTIMATE (3)
Job 19:19 All my **i** friends detest me; those I love H6051
Job 29: 4 when God's **i friendship** blessed my H6051
Hos 3: 3 not be a prostitute or be **i with** any man, H4200

INTIMIDATE (3)
Ne 6:13 He had been hired to **i** *me* so that I would H3707
Ne 6:14 of the prophets have been *trying to* **i** me. H3707
Ne 6:19 And Tobiah sent letters to **i** me. H3707

INTO (1349)
Ge 2: 7 ground and breathed **i** his nostrils the H928
Ge 2:10 there it was separated **i** four headwaters. H4200
Ge 2:21 the LORD God **caused** the man **to fall** *i* a deep AIT
Ge 6:19 You are to bring **i** the ark two of all living H448
Ge 7: 1 said to Noah, "Go **i** the ark, you and your H448
Ge 9: 2 fish in the sea; they are given **i** your hands. H928
Ge 10: 5 peoples spread out **i** their territories by H928
Ge 12: 2 "I will make you **i** a great nation, and I H4200
Ge 12:15 to Pharaoh, and she **was taken** *i* his palace. AIT
Ge 14:10 some of the men fell **i** them and the rest H2025
Ge 14:20 who delivered your enemies **i** your hand." H928
Ge 15:12 was setting, Abram **fell** *i* a deep sleep, and a AIT
Ge 17:20 I will make him **i** a great nation. H4200
Ge 18: 6 So Abraham hurried **i** the tent to Sarah H2025
Ge 19:10 pulled Lot back **i** the house and shut H2025
Ge 20: 1 moved on from there **i** the region of the H2025
Ge 21:13 make the son of the slave **i** a nation also, H4200
Ge 21:18 for I will make him **i** a great nation." H4200
Ge 24:20 So she quickly emptied her jar **i** the trough H448
Ge 24:67 Isaac brought her **i** the tent of his mother H2025
Ge 30:14 Reuben went out **i** the fields and found H928
Ge 31:33 So Laban went **i** Jacob's tent and into H928
Ge 31:33 into Jacob's tent and **i** Leah's tent and into H928
Ge 31:33 into Leah's tent and **i** the tent of the two H928
Ge 32: 7 people who were with him **i** two groups, H4200
Ge 34:15 *We will* **enter i an agreement** with you on H252
Ge 37:20 him and throw him **i** one of these cisterns H928
Ge 37:22 Throw him **i** this cistern here in the H448
Ge 37:24 they took him and threw him **i** the cistern. H2025
Ge 39:11 One day he went **i** the house to attend to H2025
Ge 40:10 blossomed, and its clusters **ripened** *i* grapes. AIT
Ge 40:11 squeezed them **i** Pharaoh's cup and put H448
Ge 40:21 again put the cup **i** Pharaoh's hand— H6584
Ge 43:12 that was put back **i** the mouths of your H928
Ge 43:18 that was put back **i** our sacks the first time H928
Ge 43:24 steward took the men **i** Joseph's house, H2025
Ge 43:26 the gifts they had brought **i** the house, H2025
Ge 43:30 He went **i** his private room and wept there H2025
Ge 45: 4 brother Joseph, the one you sold **i** Egypt! H2025
Ge 46: 3 I will make you **i** a great nation there. H4200
Ge 49:33 he drew his feet up **i** the bed, breathed his H448
Ex 1:22 boy that is born you must throw **i** the Nile, H2025
Ex 3: 8 up out of that land **i** a good and spacious H448
Ex 3:17 of your misery in Egypt **i** the land of the H448
Ex 3:18 a three-day journey **i** the wilderness to H928
Ex 4: 4 snake and *it* **turned** *back* **i** a staff in H2118+4200
Ex 4: 6 So Moses put his hand **i** his cloak, and H928
Ex 4: 7 "Now put it back **i** your cloak," he said. H448
Ex 4: 7 So Moses put his hand back **i** his cloak H448
Ex 4:27 "Go **i** the wilderness to meet Moses." H2025
Ex 5: 3 a three-day journey **i** the wilderness to H928
Ex 7:15 the staff that was changed **i** a snake. H4200
Ex 7:17 the Nile, and it will be changed **i** blood. H4200
Ex 7:20 all the water was changed **i** blood. H4200
Ex 7:23 he turned and went **i** his palace, and did H448
Ex 8: 3 They will come up **i** your palace and your H928
Ex 8: 3 **i** the houses of your officials and on your H928
Ex 8: 3 **i** your ovens and kneading troughs. H928
Ex 8:14 They *were* **piled** *i* heaps, and the land reeked AIT
Ex 8:21 officials, on your people and **i** your houses. H928
Ex 8:24 of flies poured **i** Pharaoh's palace and H2025
Ex 8:24 Pharaoh's palace and **i** the houses of his NDT
Ex 8:27 a three-day journey **i** the wilderness to H928
Ex 9: 8 have Moses toss it **i** the air in the H2025
Ex 9:10 Moses tossed it **i** the air, and festering H2025
Ex 10: 4 I will bring locusts **i** your country tomorrow. H928
Ex 10:19 locusts and carried them **i** the Red Sea. H2025
Ex 12: 4 having **taken i account** the number of H928
Ex 12:11 with your **cloak tucked i** your **belt** H2520+5516
Ex 12:22 dip it **i** the blood in the basin and put H928
Ex 13: 5 When the LORD brings you **i** the land of the H448
Ex 13:11 the LORD brings you **i** the land of the H448
Ex 14:21 strong east wind and turned it **i** dry land. H4200
Ex 14:23 horsemen followed them **i** the sea. H448+9348
Ex 14:24 Egyptian army and **threw** it **i confusion**. H2169
Ex 14:27 and the LORD swept them **i** the sea. H928+9348
Ex 14:28 that had followed the Israelites **i** the sea. H928
Ex 15: 1 horse and driver he has hurled **i** the sea. H928
Ex 15: 4 his army he has hurled **i** the sea. H928
Ex 15:19 chariots and horsemen went **i** the sea, the H928
Ex 15:21 horse and driver he has hurled **i** the sea." H928
Ex 15:22 Sea and they went **i** the Desert of Shur. H448
Ex 15:25 He threw it **i** the water, and the water H448
Ex 16: 3 have brought us out **i** this desert to starve H448
Ex 18: 7 each other and then went **i** the tent. H2025
Ex 21:33 to cover it and an ox or a donkey falls **i** it, H2025
Ex 22: 6 fire breaks out and **spreads** *i* thornbushes so AIT
Ex 23:23 of you and bring you **i** the land of the H448
Ex 23:27 of you and **throw** *i* **confusion** every nation H2169
Ex 23:31 I will give **i** your hands the people who live H928
Ex 25:14 Insert the poles **i** the rings on the sides of H928
Ex 26: 1 with cherubim **woven** *i* them *by* a skilled AIT
Ex 26: 9 together **i one set** and the other H4200+963
Ex 26: 9 set and the other six **i another set.** H4200+963
Ex 26:24 the way to the top and fitted **i** a single ring; H448
Ex 26:31 with cherubim **woven** *i* it *by* a skilled worker. AIT
Ex 27: 7 are to be inserted **i** the rings so they will H928
Ex 29:17 Cut the ram **i** pieces and wash the internal H4200
Ex 30:25 **Make** these *i* a sacred anointing oil, AIT
Ex 32: 4 handed him and **made** it *i* an idol cast in AIT
Ex 32:10 Then I will make you **i** a great nation." H4200
Ex 32:21 that *you* **led** them **i** such great sin? H995
Ex 32:24 and I threw it **i** the fire, and out came H928
Ex 33: 9 As Moses went **i** the tent, the pillar of H2025
Ex 36: 8 with cherubim **woven** *i* them *by* expert hands. AIT
Ex 36:16 five of the curtains **i** one set and the other H4200
Ex 36:16 one set and the other six **i** another set. H4200
Ex 36:29 the way to the top and fitted **i** a single ring; H448
Ex 36:35 with cherubim **woven** *i* it *by* a skilled worker. AIT
Ex 37: 5 he inserted the poles **i** the rings on the H928
Ex 38: 7 They inserted the poles **i** the rings so they H928
Ex 39: 3 cut strands to be worked **i** the blue, H928+9348
Ex 40:21 he brought the ark **i** the tabernacle and H448
Lev 1: 6 skin the burnt offering and cut it **i** pieces. H4200
Lev 1:12 You are to cut it **i** pieces, and the priest H4200
Lev 4: 5 blood and carry it **i** the tent of meeting. H448
Lev 4: 6 is to dip his finger **i** the blood and sprinkle H928
Lev 4:16 of the bull's blood **i** the tent of meeting. H448
Lev 4:17 shall dip his finger **i** the blood and H4946
Lev 6:30 blood is brought **i** the tent of meeting to H448
Lev 8:20 He cut the ram **i** pieces and burned the H4200
Lev 9: 9 he dipped his finger **i** the blood and put it H928
Lev 9:23 Aaron then went **i** the tent of meeting. H448
Lev 10: 9 whenever you go **i** the tent of meeting, H448
Lev 10:18 was not taken **i** the Holy Place, H448+7163
Lev 11:33 If one of them falls **i** a clay pot H448+9348
Lev 11:34 to eat that *has* **come** *i* contact with water AIT
Lev 14: 6 **i** the blood of the bird that was killed over H928
Lev 14: 8 After this they may come **i** the camp, but H448
Lev 14:16 dip his right forefinger **i** the oil in his palm, H4946
Lev 14:26 pour some of the oil **i** the palm of his own H6584
Lev 14:40 be torn out and thrown **i** an unclean place H448
Lev 14:41 is scraped off dumped **i** an unclean place H448
Lev 14:46 "Anyone who goes **i** the house while it is H448
Lev 14:51 dip them **i** the blood of the dead bird and H928
Lev 16: 2 whenever he chooses **i** the Most Holy Place H448
Lev 16:10 by sending it **i** the wilderness as a H2025
Lev 16:21 send the goat away **i** the wilderness in H2025
Lev 16:23 "Then Aaron is to go **i** the tent of meeting H448
Lev 16:26 afterward he may come **i** the camp. H448
Lev 16:27 blood was brought **i** the Most Holy Place to H928
Lev 16:28 afterward he may come **i** the camp. H448
Lev 26:25 When you withdraw **i** your cities, I will send H448
Lev 26:25 and you will be given **i** enemy hands. H928
Lev 26:31 *I will* **turn** your cities **i** ruins and lay waste H5989
Lev 26:41 them so that I sent them **i** the land of their H928
Nu 4:19 his sons *are to* **go i** the sanctuary and H995
Nu 5:17 dust from the tabernacle floor **i** the water. H448
Nu 5:23 then wash them off **i** the bitter water. H448
Nu 10: 9 When *you* **go i** battle in your own land H995
Nu 11: 8 They cooked it in a pot or **made** it *i* loaves AIT
Nu 13:17 through the Negev and **on** *i* the hill country. AIT
Nu 13:27 "We went **i** the land to which you sent us H448
Nu 14: 8 he will lead us **i** that land, a land H448
Nu 14:12 I will make you **i** a nation greater and H4200
Nu 14:16 bring these people **i** the land he promised H448
Nu 14:24 I will bring him **i** the land he went to, and H448
Nu 16:14 haven't brought us **i** a land flowing with H448
Nu 16:30 they go down alive **i** the realm of the H2025
Nu 16:33 They went down alive **i** the realm of the H2025
Nu 16:38 **Hammer** the censers *i* sheets to overlay the AIT
Nu 16:47 and ran **i** the midst of the assembly. H448
Nu 19: 7 He may then come **i** the camp, but he will H448
Nu 19:17 purification offering **i** a jar and pour fresh H448
Nu 20: 4 the LORD's community **i** this wilderness, H448
Nu 20:12 bring this community **i** the land I give them H448
Nu 20:15 Our ancestors went down **i** Egypt, and we H2025
Nu 21: 2 you will deliver these people **i** our hands, H928
Nu 21:13 wilderness extending **i** Amorite territory. H4946
Nu 21:22 will not turn aside **i** any field or vineyard, H928
Nu 21:23 army and marched out **i** the wilderness H2025
Nu 21:34 I have delivered him **i** your hands H928
Nu 22:23 in his hand, it turned off the road **i** a field. H928
Nu 25: 6 man brought **i** the camp a Midianite H448
Nu 25: 8 followed the Israelite **i** the tent. H448
Nu 25: 8 *He* **drove** the spear **i** both of them, right H1991
Nu 25: 8 Israelite man and **i** the woman's stomach. H448
Nu 31: 4 Send **i** battle a thousand men from each H4200
Nu 31: 6 Moses sent them **i** battle, a thousand from H4200
Nu 31:21 to the soldiers who had gone **i** battle, H4200
Nu 31:24 Then you may come **i** the camp." H448
Nu 31:54 brought it **i** the tent of meeting as H448
Nu 32: 7 from crossing over **i** the land the LORD has H448
Nu 32:32 We *will* **cross over** before the LORD *i* Canaan AIT
Nu 33: 8 passed through the sea **i** the desert, H2025
Nu 33:51 'When you cross the Jordan **i** Canaan, H448
Nu 35:10 'When you cross the Jordan **i** Canaan, H2025
Nu 36: 3 to that of the tribe *they* **marry i.** H2118+4200
Nu 36: 4 that of the tribe **i** which *they* **marry**, H2118+4200
Dt 1: 7 Break camp and **advance** *i* the hill country of AIT
Dt 1:24 They left and went up **i** the hill country H2025
Dt 1:27 of Egypt to deliver us **i** the hands of the H928
Dt 1:41 thinking it easy to go up **i** the hill country. H2025
Dt 1:43 you marched up **i** the hill country. H2025
Dt 2:24 I have given **i** your hand Sihon the Amorite, H928
Dt 2:29 we cross the Jordan **i** the land the LORD our H448
Dt 2:30 obstinate in order to give him **i** your hands, H928
Dt 3: 2 I have delivered him **i** your hands H928
Dt 3: 3 our God also gave **i** our hands Og king of H928
Dt 4:19 *do* not **be enticed** *i* bowing down to them AIT
Dt 4:38 than you and to **bring** you **i** their land to H995
Dt 4:42 They could flee **i** one of these cities and H448
Dt 6:10 your God brings you **i** the land he swore to H448
Dt 7: 1 LORD your God brings you **i** the land you are H448
Dt 7:23 **throwing** them **i** great **confusion** H2169+4539
Dt 7:24 He will give their kings **i** your hand, and you H928
Dt 7:26 a detestable thing **i** your house or you, H448
Dt 8: 7 your God is bringing you **i** a good land— H448
Dt 8: 7 springs gushing out **i** the valleys and hills; H928
Dt 9:14 And I will make you **i** a nation stronger H4200
Dt 9:21 threw the dust **i** a stream that flowed H448
Dt 9:28 not able to take them **i** the land he had H448
Dt 10:22 who went down **i** Egypt were seventy in H2025
Dt 11:29 God has brought you **i** the land you are H448
Dt 13:16 the plunder of the town **i** the middle of the H448
Dt 15:17 push it through his earlobe **i** the door, H928
Dt 19: 3 involved and **divide i three** parts the land H8992
Dt 19: 5 a man may go **i** the forest with his H928
Dt 20: 2 When you are about to go **i** battle, the H448
Dt 20: 3 Today you are going **i** battle against your H4200
Dt 20:13 the LORD your God delivers it **i** your hand, H928
Dt 21:10 God delivers them **i** your hands and you H928
Dt 21:12 Bring her **i** your home and have her H448+9348
Dt 23: 5 turned the curse **i** a blessing for you, H4200
Dt 23:18 of a male prostitute **i** the house of the LORD NDT
Dt 24:10 do not go **i** their house to get what is H448
Dt 26: 5 he went down **i** Egypt with a few H2025
Dt 27: 2 crossed the Jordan **i** the land the LORD your H448
Dt 28:24 LORD *will* **turn** the rain of your country **i** H5989
Dt 28:41 keep them, because they will go **i** captivity. H928
Dt 29:12 here in order to enter **i** a covenant with the H928
Dt 29:28 their land and thrust them **i** another land, H448
Dt 30:12 "Who will ascend **i** heaven to get it and H2025
Dt 31: 7 go with this people **i** the land that the LORD H448
Dt 31:20 I have brought them **i** the land flowing with H448
Dt 31:21 before I bring them **i** the land I promised H448
Dt 31:23 bring the Israelites **i** the land I promised H448
Dt 32:49 "Go up **i** the Abarim Range to Mount Nebo H448
Dt 34: 4 your eyes, but you will not cross over **i** it." H2025
Jos 1: 2 the Jordan River **i** the land I am about to H448
Jos 2:18 brothers and all your family **i** your house. H2025
Jos 2:19 them go outside your house **i** the street, H2025
Jos 2:22 they went **i** the hills and stayed there H2025
Jos 2:24 surely given the whole land **i** our hands; H928
Jos 3:11 all the earth will go **i** the Jordan ahead of H928
Jos 4: 5 of the LORD your God **i** the middle of the H448
Jos 6: 2 I have delivered Jericho **i** your hands H928
Jos 6:19 to the LORD and *must* **go i** his treasury." H995
Jos 6:22 "**Go i** the prostitute's house and bring her H995
Jos 6:24 *they* **put** the silver and gold and the articles of bronze and iron *i* AIT
Jos 7: 7 the Jordan to deliver us **i** the hands of the H928
Jos 8: 1 For I have delivered **i** your hands the king H928
Jos 8: 7 The LORD your God will give it **i** your hand. H928
Jos 8:13 That night Joshua went **i** the valley. H928+9348

Jos 8:18 for **i** your hand I will deliver the city." H928
Jos 8:20 the smoke of the city rising up **i** the sky, H2025
Jos 10: 8 of them; I have given them **i** your hand. H928
Jos 10:10 The LORD **threw** them **i confusion** before H2169
Jos 10:19 LORD your God has given them **i** your hand." H928
Jos 10:27 threw them **i** the cave where they H448
Jos 10:30 gave that city and its king **i** Israel's hand. H928
Jos 10:32 The LORD gave Lachish **i** Israel's hand, and H928
Jos 11: 8 the LORD gave them **i** the hand of Israel H928
Jos 16: 1 there through the desert **i** the hill country of H928
Jos 17:15 go up **i** the forest and clear land for H2025
Jos 18: 5 You are to divide the land **i** seven parts H4200
Jos 18:12 Jericho and headed west **i** the hill country, H928
Jos 18:18 Beth Arabah and on down **i** the Arabah. H2025
Jos 19:49 dividing the land **i** its allotted portions, H4200
Jos 20: 4 to admit the fugitive **i** their city and H2025
Jos 21:44 LORD gave all their enemies **i** their hands. H928
Jos 24: 8 against you, but I gave them **i** your hands. H928
Jos 24:11 Jebusites, but I gave them **i** your hands. H928
Jdg 1: 2 I have given the land **i** their hands. H928
Jdg 1: 3 "Come up with us **i** the territory allotted to H928
Jdg 1: 3 We in turn will go with you **i** yours." So the H928
Jdg 1: 4 the Canaanites and Perizzites **i** their hands, H928
Jdg 1:24 "Show us **how to get i** the city and we will H4427
Jdg 1:28 the Canaanites **i** forced labor but never H4200
Jdg 1:34 allowing them to come down **i** the plain. H4200
Jdg 1:35 they too were pressed **i** forced labor. H4200
Jdg 2: 1 of Egypt and led you **i** the land I swore to H448
Jdg 2:14 the LORD gave them **i** the hands of raiders H928
Jdg 2:14 He sold them **i** the hands of their enemies H928
Jdg 2:23 once by giving them **i** the hands of Joshua. H928
Jdg 3: 8 Israel so that he sold them **i** the hands of H928
Jdg 3:10 king of Aram **i** the hands of Othniel, H928
Jdg 3:21 right thigh and plunged it **i** the king's belly. H928
Jdg 3:28 has given Moab, your enemy, **i** your hands." H928
Jdg 4: 2 So the LORD sold them **i** the hands of Jabin H928
Jdg 4: 7 the Kishon River and give him **i** your hands. H928
Jdg 4: 9 will deliver Sisera **i** the hands of a woman." H928
Jdg 4:14 day the LORD has given Sisera **i** your hands. H928
Jdg 4:21 the peg through his temple **i** the ground, H928
Jdg 5:15 sent under his command **i** the valley. H928
Jdg 6: 1 years he gave them **i** the hands of the H928
Jdg 6:13 us and given us **i** the hand of Midian." H928
Jdg 6:35 to arms, and also **i** Asher, Zebulun and H928
Jdg 7: 2 I cannot deliver Midian **i** their hands, or H928
Jdg 7: 7 you and give the Midianites **i** your hands. H928
Jdg 7: 9 because I am going to give it **i** your hands. H928
Jdg 7:13 came tumbling **i** the Midianite camp. H928
Jdg 7:14 the whole camp **i** his hands. H928
Jdg 7:15 has given the Midianite camp **i** your hands." H928
Jdg 7:16 the three hundred men **i** three companies, NDT
Jdg 8: 3 the Midianite leaders, **i** your hands. H928
Jdg 8: 7 has given Zebah and Zalmunna **i** my hand, H928
Jdg 8:27 Gideon made the gold **i** an ephod, which H4200
Jdg 9:26 of Ebed moved with his clan **i** Shechem, H928
Jdg 9:27 After *they had* **gone out** *i* the fields and AIT
Jdg 9:43 divided them **i** three companies and set H4200
Jdg 9:46 of Shechem went **i** the stronghold of the H448
Jdg 10: 7 He sold them **i** the hands of the Philistines H928
Jdg 11:21 Sihon and his whole army **i** Israel's hands, H928
Jdg 11:30 "If you give the Ammonites **i** my hands, H928
Jdg 11:32 the LORD gave them **i** his hands. H928
Jdg 11:38 her friends went **i** the hills and wept H6584
Jdg 13: 1 the LORD delivered them **i** the hands of the H928
Jdg 14:15 "**Coax** your husband *i* explaining the riddle AIT
Jdg 15:18 now die of thirst and fall **i** the hands of the H928
Jdg 16: 5 "*See if you can* **lure** him *i* showing you the AIT
Jdg 16:13 braids of my head **i** the fabric on the loom H6640
Jdg 16:13 braids of his head, wove them **i** the fabric H6640
Jdg 16:23 delivered Samson, our enemy, **i** our hands." H928
Jdg 16:24 god has delivered our enemy **i** our hands, H928
Jdg 18: 1 because they *had* not yet **come i** an H5877+928
Jdg 18:10 land that God has put **i** your hands, H928
Jdg 18:18 When the five men **went i** Micah's house H995
Jdg 19: 3 *She* **took** him **i** her parents' home, and H995
Jdg 19:12 We won't go **i** any city whose people are H448
Jdg 19:21 So he took him **i** his house and fed his H4200
Jdg 19:29 **i** twelve parts and sent them into all the H4200
Jdg 19:29 parts and sent them **i** all the areas of Israel H928
Jdg 20: 6 **cut** her **i pieces** and sent one piece to H5983
Jdg 20:28 tomorrow I will give them **i** your hands." H928
Jdg 20:37 in ambush made a sudden dash **i** Gibeah, H448
Jdg 20:47 them turned and fled **i** the wilderness to H2025
Ru 2: 7 *She* **came i** the field and has remained H995
Ru 3:15 *he* **poured i** it six **measures** of barley and H4499
Ru 4:11 woman who is coming **i** your home like H448
1Sa 2:14 would plunge the fork **i** the pan or kettle H928
1Sa 4: 5 ark of the LORD's covenant came **i** the camp, H448
1Sa 4: 6 the ark of the LORD had come **i** the camp, H448
1Sa 4: 7 "A god has come **i** the camp," they said H448
1Sa 4:19 *she* **went i labor** and gave birth H4156
1Sa 5: 2 Then they **carried** the ark *i* Dagon's temple AIT
1Sa 5: 9 against that city, throwing it **i** a great panic. NDT
1Sa 6:19 because they looked **i** the ark of the LORD. H928
1Sa 7:10 and **threw** them **i** *such* **a panic** that they H2169
1Sa 9: 4 They went on **i** the district of Shaalim, but H928
1Sa 9:22 Saul and his servant **i** the hall and seated H2025
1Sa 10: 6 you will be changed **i** a different person. H4200
1Sa 11: 7 of oxen, **cut** them **i pieces**, and sent the H5983
1Sa 11:11 next day Saul **separated** his men *i* three AIT
1Sa 11:11 night they broke **i** the camp of the H928+9348
1Sa 12: 9 so he sold them **i** the hand of Sisera H928
1Sa 12: 9 **i** the hands of the Philistines and the H928
1Sa 14:10 that the LORD has given them **i** our hands." H928
1Sa 14:12 LORD has given them **i** the hand of Israel." H928
1Sa 14:26 When they went **i** the woods, they saw the H448
1Sa 14:27 in his hand and dipped it **i** the honeycomb. H928
1Sa 14:37 Will you give them **i** Israel's hand?" But H928
1Sa 14:52 brave man, *he* **took** him **i** his **service**. H665
1Sa 17:46 day the LORD will deliver you **i** my hands, H928
1Sa 17:47 he will give all of you **i** our hands. H928
1Sa 17:49 Reaching **i** his bag and taking out a stone H448
1Sa 17:49 The stone sank **i** his forehead, and he fell H928
1Sa 19: 2 morning; go **i** hiding and stay there. H928
1Sa 19:10 him as Saul drove the spear **i** the wall. H928
1Sa 20: 8 have brought him **i** a covenant with you H928
1Sa 20:11 Jonathan said, "*let's* **go out** *i* the field." AIT
1Sa 21:15 Must this man come **i** my house?" H448
1Sa 22: 5 in the stronghold. Go **i** the land of Judah." H995
1Sa 23: 4 going to give the Philistines **i** your hand." H928
1Sa 23: 7 "God has delivered him **i** my hands, for H928
1Sa 23:14 God did not give David **i** his hands. H928
1Sa 23:20 be responsible for giving him **i** your hands." H928
1Sa 23:25 *he* **went** *i* the Desert of Maon **in pursuit** of AIT
1Sa 24: 4 will give your enemy **i** your hands for you to H928
1Sa 24:10 LORD delivered you **i** my hands in the cave. H928
1Sa 24:18 the LORD delivered me **i** your hands, but you H928
1Sa 25: 1 David moved down **i** the Desert of Paran. H448
1Sa 25:20 riding her donkey **i** a mountain ravine, H928
1Sa 26: 6 "Who will go down **i** the camp with me to H448
1Sa 26: 8 has delivered your enemy **i** your hands. H928
1Sa 26:10 will die, or he will go **i** battle and perish. H928
1Sa 26:12 the LORD *had* **put** them *i* a deep sleep. AIT
1Sa 26:23 The LORD delivered you **i** my hands today H928
1Sa 28:19 both Israel and you **i** the hands of the H928
1Sa 28:19 give the army of Israel **i** the hands of the H928
1Sa 29: 4 He must not go with us **i** battle, or he will H928
1Sa 29: 9 'He must not go up with us **i** battle. H928
1Sa 30:23 us and delivered **i** our hands the raiding H928
2Sa 2:16 thrust his dagger **i** his opponent's side, H928
2Sa 2:23 the butt of his spear **i** Asahel's stomach, H448
2Sa 2:25 formed themselves **i** a group and took H4200
2Sa 3:13 *Do* not **come i** my **presence** H8011+906+7156
2Sa 3:27 took him aside **i** an inner chamber, H448+9348
2Sa 4: 6 They went **i** the inner part of the house as H6330
2Sa 4: 7 *They had* **gone i** the house while he was H995
2Sa 5:19 Will you deliver them **i** my hands?" The H928
2Sa 5:19 surely deliver the Philistines **i** your hands." H928
2Sa 12: 8 and your master's wives **i** your arms. H928
2Sa 12:20 *he* **went i** the house of the LORD and H995
2Sa 13:10 "**Bring** the food here **i** my bedroom so I H995
2Sa 14: 6 *They* **got i a fight** *with* each other in the H5897
2Sa 14:19 who put all these words **i** the mouth of your H928
2Sa 15:25 Zadok, "**Take** the ark of God **back** *i* the city. AIT
2Sa 15:31 **turn** Ahithophel's counsel **i foolishness**." H6118
2Sa 16: 8 given the kingdom **i** the hands of your son H928
2Sa 17:11 with you yourself leading them **i** battle. H928
2Sa 17:13 If he withdraws **i** a city, then all Israel will H448
2Sa 17:18 in his courtyard, and *they* **climbed down** *i* it. AIT
2Sa 18:12 shekels were weighed out **i** my hands, H6584
2Sa 18:14 plunged them **i** Absalom's heart while H928
2Sa 18:17 threw him **i** a big pit in the forest and piled H448
2Sa 19: 2 that day *was* **turned i** mourning, H2118+4200
2Sa 19: 3 The men **stole i** the city that H1704+4200+995
2Sa 19: 5 Then Joab went **i** the house to the king H448
2Sa 20:10 Joab plunged it **i** his belly, and his H448
2Sa 20:12 *he* **dragged** him from the road *i* a field and AIT
2Sa 22:20 He brought me out **i** a spacious place; he H4200
2Sa 22:29 the LORD **turns** my darkness **i light**. H5585
2Sa 23:20 also went down **i** a pit on a snowy H928+9348
2Sa 24:14 Let us fall **i** the hands of the LORD, for his H928
2Sa 24:14 do not let me fall **i** human hands. H928
1Ki 1:28 So she came *i* the king's **presence** and stood AIT
1Ki 6: 6 would be inserted **i** the temple walls. H928
1Ki 8: 1 summoned **i** his **presence** at Jerusalem H448
1Ki 10:16 shekels of gold went **i** each shield. H6584
1Ki 11:30 he was wearing and **tore** it *i* twelve pieces. AIT
1Ki 12:18 managed to get **i** his chariot and escape to H928
1Ki 15:15 *He* **brought i** the temple of the LORD the H995
1Ki 16:18 he went **i** the citadel of the royal palace H448
1Ki 16:21 people of Israel were split **i** two factions; H4200
1Ki 17:23 him down from the room **i** the house. H2025
1Ki 18:23 and *let them* **cut** it **i pieces** and put it on H5983
1Ki 18:33 **cut** the bull **i pieces** and laid it on the H5983
1Ki 18:46 **tucking** his **cloak i** *his* **belt**, he H9113+5516
1Ki 19: 4 went a day's journey **i** the wilderness. H928
1Ki 19: 9 There he went **i** a cave and spent the night H448
1Ki 20: 2 He sent messengers **i** the city to Ahab king H2025
1Ki 20:13 I will give it **i** your hand today, and then H928
1Ki 20:28 I will deliver this vast army **i** your hands H928
1Ki 20:33 Ahab had him come up **i** his chariot. H6584
1Ki 20:39 "Your servant went **i** the thick of the battle H928
1Ki 22: 6 "for the Lord will give it **i** the king's hand." H928
1Ki 22:12 "for the LORD will give it **i** the king's hand." H928
1Ki 22:15 "for the LORD will give it **i** the king's hand." H928
1Ki 22:20 'Who *will* **entice** Ahab *i* attacking Ramoth AIT
1Ki 22:30 Israel disguised himself and went **i** battle. H928
2Ki 2:21 out to the spring and threw the salt **i it**, H9004S
2Ki 3:10 only to deliver us **i** the hands of Moab?" H928
2Ki 3:13 together to deliver us **i** the hands of Moab." H928
2Ki 3:18 he will also deliver Moab **i** your hands. H928
2Ki 4: 4 Pour oil **i** all the jars, and as each is filled, H6584
2Ki 4:29 "**Tuck** your **cloak i** your **belt**, take H2520+5516
2Ki 4:39 One of them went out **i** the fields to gather H448
2Ki 4:39 he cut them up **i** the pot of stew, though H448
2Ki 4:41 He put it **i** the pot and said, "Serve it to H448
2Ki 6: 5 the iron axhead fell **i** the water. H448
2Ki 7: 4 If we say, '*We'll* **go i** the city'—the famine H995
2Ki 7:10 "We went **i** the Aramean camp and no one H448
2Ki 7:12 we will take them alive and get **i** the city. H448
2Ki 9: 1 "**Tuck** *your* **cloak i** your **belt**, take H2520+5516
2Ki 9: 2 companions and **take** him **i** an inner room. H995
2Ki 9: 6 Jehu got up and went **i** the house. H2025
2Ki 9:16 Then he **got i** *his* **chariot** and rode to H8206
2Ki 10:15 and Jehu helped him up **i** the chariot. H448
2Ki 10:21 *They* **crowded** *i* the temple of Baal until it H995
2Ki 10:23 son of Rekab **went i** the temple of Baal. H995
2Ki 11:19 temple of the LORD and **went i** the palace, H995
2Ki 12: 9 the entrance put **i** the chest all the money H2025
2Ki 12:10 money that *had* **been brought** *i* the temple of AIT
2Ki 12:10 the temple of the LORD and **put** it **i bags**. H7443
2Ki 12:13 The money **brought i** the temple was not H995
2Ki 12:16 sin offerings **was** not **brought i** the temple H995
2Ki 13:21 they threw the man's body **i** Elisha's tomb. H928
2Ki 16: 6 Edomites then **moved i** Elath and have H995
2Ki 17:20 them and gave them **i** the hands of H928
2Ki 17:23 *were* **taken** from their homeland **i exile** in H1655
2Ki 18: 4 *He* **broke i pieces** the bronze snake Moses H4198
2Ki 18:30 city will not be given **i** the hand of the king H928
2Ki 19: 1 on sackcloth and **went i** the temple of the H995
2Ki 19:10 will not be given **i** the hands of the king of H928
2Ki 19:18 thrown their gods **i** the fire and destroyed H928
2Ki 19:25 that you *have* **turned** fortified cities **i** piles H8615
2Ki 20:20 by which he brought water **i** the city, H2025
2Ki 21:11 him and *has* **led** Judah **i sin** with his idols H2627
2Ki 21:14 give them **i** the hands of enemies. H928
2Ki 22: 4 money that *has* **been brought i** the temple H995
2Ki 23:12 threw the rubble **i** the Kidron Valley. H448
2Ki 24:14 *He* **carried** all Jerusalem **i exile**: all H1655+1655
2Ki 25:11 of the guard **carried i exile** the people H1655
2Ki 25:21 So Judah **went i captivity**, away from her H1655
1Ch 5: 6 Tiglath-Pileser king of Assyria **took i exile**. H1655
1Ch 5:20 Hagrites and all their allies **i** their hands, H928
1Ch 5:26 *who* **took** the Reubenites, the Gadites and the half-tribe of Manasseh **i exile** H1655
1Ch 6:15 LORD **sent** Judah and Jerusalem **i exile** by H1655
1Ch 11:22 also went down **i** a pit on a snowy H928+9348
1Ch 14:10 Will you deliver them **i** my hands?" The H928
1Ch 14:10 "Go, I will deliver them **i** your hands." H928
1Ch 21:13 Let me fall **i** the hands of the LORD, for his H928
1Ch 21:13 do not let me fall **i** human hands. H928
1Ch 21:27 he put his sword back **i** its sheath. H448
1Ch 22:18 the inhabitants of the land **i** my hands, H928
1Ch 22:19 belonging to God **i** the temple that will H4200
1Ch 23: 6 David **separated** the Levites *i* divisions AIT
1Ch 24: 3 David **separated** them **i divisions** for their H2745
2Ch 3:14 fine linen, with cherubim worked **i** it. H6584
2Ch 9:15 of hammered gold went **i** each shield. H6584
2Ch 10:18 managed to get **i** his chariot and escape to H928
2Ch 13: 3 Abijah **went i** battle with an army of four H673
2Ch 13:16 God delivered them **i** their hands. H928
2Ch 15:12 They entered **i** a covenant to seek the LORD H928
2Ch 15:18 *He* **brought i** the temple of God the silver H995
2Ch 16: 8 on the LORD, he delivered them **i** your hand. H928
2Ch 18: 5 "for God will give it **i** the king's hand." H928
2Ch 18:11 "for the LORD will give it **i** the king's hand." H928
2Ch 18:14 "for they will be given **i** your hand. H928
2Ch 18:19 'Who *will* **entice** Ahab king of Israel *i* AIT
2Ch 18:29 Israel disguised himself and went **i** battle. H928
2Ch 22: 1 who came with the Arabs **i** the camp, had H4200
2Ch 23:20 *They* **went i** the palace through the Upper H995
2Ch 24: 7 Athaliah *had* **broken i** the temple of H7287
2Ch 24:10 dropping them **i** the chest until it was full. H4200
2Ch 24:24 the LORD delivered **i** their hands a much H928
2Ch 25:20 might deliver them **i** the hands of Jehoash, H928
2Ch 28: 5 God delivered him **i** the hands of the king H928
2Ch 28: 5 He was also given **i** the hands of the king H928
2Ch 28: 9 with Judah, he gave them **i** your hand. H928
2Ch 29:16 The priests went **i** the sanctuary of H4200+7163
2Ch 30:14 altars and threw them **i** the Kidron Valley. H4200
2Ch 32:21 And when *he* **went i** the temple of his god H995
2Ch 34: 9 money that *had* **been brought i** the temple H995
2Ch 34:11 kings of Judah *had* **allowed to fall i ruin**. H8845
2Ch 34:14 money that *had* **been taken i** the temple of H995
2Ch 36:17 God gave them all **i** the hands of H928
2Ch 36:20 *He* **carried i exile** to Babylon the remnant H1655
Ezr 5:12 he gave them **i** the hands of A10089
Ezr 7:27 who has put it **i** the king's heart to bring H928
Ezr 8:33 the sacred articles **i** the hands of H6584
Ne 6:11 someone like me go **i** the temple to save H448
Ne 7: 5 So my God put it **i** my heart to assemble the H448
Ne 8:15 "**Go out** *i* the hill country and bring back AIT
Ne 9:11 you hurled their pursuers **i** the depths H928
Ne 9:11 the depths, like a stone **i** mighty waters. H928
Ne 9:23 you brought them **i** the land that you H448
Ne 9:24 you gave the Canaanites **i** their hands H928
Ne 9:27 So you delivered them **i** the hands of their H928
Ne 9:30 so you gave them **i** the hands of the H928
Ne 12:44 they were to bring **i** the storerooms the H928
Ne 13: 1 ever be admitted **i** the assembly of God, H928
Ne 13: 2 however, turned the curse **i** a blessing.) H4200
Ne 13: 9 then *I* **put back** *i* them the equipment of AIT
Ne 13:12 new wine and olive oil **i** the storerooms. H4200
Ne 13:15 And *they were* **bringing** all this **i** Jerusalem H995
Ne 13:26 even he *was* **led i sin** *by* foreign H2627
Est 2: 3 beautiful young women **i** the harem at the H448

Est 2: 6 who *had* **been carried i exile** from H1655
Est 2: 9 her attendants **i** the best place in the H4200
Est 4: 1 and went out **i** the city, wailing H928+9348
Est 4: 7 had promised to pay **i** the royal treasury H6584
Est 4: 8 her to go **i** the king's **presence** to beg for H448
Est 7: 7 his wine and went out **i** the palace garden. H448
Est 8: 1 And Mordecai came **i** the presence of the H4200
Est 9:22 sorrow was turned **i** joy and their H4200
Est 9:22 their mourning **i** a day of celebration. H4200
Job 6:18 they go off **i** the wasteland and perish. H928
Job 9:24 When a land falls **i** the hands of the H928
Job 9:31 you would plunge me **i** a slime pit so that H928
Job 10:19 If only *I had* never **come i being**, or H2118+2118
Job 12:22 brings utter darkness **i** the light. H4200
Job 16:11 thrown me **i** the clutches of the H6584
Job 17:12 turn night **i** day; in the face of the H4200
Job 17:16 Will we descend together **i** the dust?" H6584
Job 18: 8 His feet thrust him **i** a net; he wanders into H928
Job 18: 8 him into a net; he wanders **i** its mesh. H6584
Job 18:18 is driven from light **i** the realm of darkness H448
Job 24: 4 and **force** all the poor of the land **i hiding**. H2461
Job 24:16 In the dark, *thieves* **break i** houses, but by H3168
Job 30:19 He throws me **i** the mud, and I am H4200
Job 39:21 in its strength, and charges **i** the fray. H7925
Ps 4: 2 will you people **turn** my glory **i** shame? H4200
Ps 5: 7 your great love, *can* **come i** your house; in H995
Ps 7:15 scoops it out falls **i** the pit they have made. H928
Ps 9:15 nations have fallen **i** the pit they have dug; H928
Ps 18: 6 my cry came before him, **i** his ears. H928
Ps 18:19 He brought me out **i** a spacious place; he H4200
Ps 18:28 burning; my God **turns** my darkness **i light**. H5585
Ps 19: 4 Yet their voice goes out **i** all the earth, their H928
Ps 30:11 You turned my wailing **i** dancing; you H4200
Ps 31: 5 **I** your hands I commit my spirit; deliver me H928
Ps 31: 8 You have not given me **i** the hands of the H928
Ps 33: 7 He gathers the waters of the sea **i** jars; he H3869
Ps 33: 7 into jars; he puts the deep **i** storehouses. H928
Ps 35: 8 may they fall **i** the pit, to their ruin. H928
Ps 46: 2 the mountains fall **i** the heart of the sea, H928
Ps 55:23 bring down the wicked **i** the pit of decay; H4200
Ps 57: T When he had fled from Saul **i** the cave. H928
Ps 57: 6 they have fallen **i** it themselves. H928+9348
Ps 66: 6 He turned the sea **i** dry land, they passed H4200
Ps 66:11 You brought us **i** prison and laid burdens H928
Ps 68:17 Lord has come from Sinai **i** his sanctuary. H928
Ps 68:24 *has* **come i view**, the procession of H8011
Ps 68:24 of my God and King **i** the sanctuary. H928
Ps 69: 2 I have come **i** the deep waters; the floods H928
Ps 73:24 afterward *you will* **take** me *i* glory. AIT
Ps 78:44 He turned their river **i** blood; they could H4200
Ps 78:61 He sent the ark of his might **i** captivity, his H4200
Ps 78:61 his splendor **i** the hands of the enemy. H928
Ps 79:12 Pay back **i** the laps of our neighbors seven H448
Ps 96: 8 bring an offering and come **i** his courts. H4200
Ps 98: 4 all the earth, **burst** *i* jubilant song with music AIT
Ps 104: 8 the mountains, *they* **went down** *i* the valleys AIT
Ps 104:10 He makes springs pour water **i** the ravines H928
Ps 105:29 He turned their waters **i** blood, causing H4200
Ps 105:30 which went up **i** the bedrooms of their H928
Ps 105:32 *He* **turned** their rain **i** hail, with lightning H5989
Ps 106:41 He gave them **i** the hands *of* the nations H928
Ps 107:33 He turned rivers **i** a desert, flowing springs H4200
Ps 107:33 a desert, flowing springs **i** thirsty ground, H4200
Ps 107:34 fruitful land **i** a salt waste, because of H4200
Ps 107:35 He turned the desert **i** pools of water and H4200
Ps 107:35 the parched ground **i** flowing springs; H4200
Ps 109:18 his garment; it entered **i** his body like water H928
Ps 109:18 into his body like water, **i** his bones like oil. H928
Ps 114: 8 who **turned** the rock **i** a pool, the hard rock H2200
Ps 114: 8 the hard rock **i** springs of water. H4200
Ps 118: 5 the LORD; he brought me **i** a spacious place. H928
Ps 135: 9 He sent his signs and wonders **i** your midst H928
Ps 136:15 swept Pharaoh and his army **i** the Red Sea; H928
Ps 140:10 may they be thrown **i** the fire, into miry pits H928
Ps 140:10 thrown into the fire, **i** miry pits, never to rise H928
Ps 141:10 Let the wicked fall **i** their own nets, while I H928
Ps 143: 2 Do not bring your servant **i** judgment, for H928
Ps 144:14 of walls, no **going i captivity**, no cry of H3448
Pr 1:16 their feet rush **i** evil, they are swift to H4200
Pr 3:32 takes the upright **i** his confidence. H907
Pr 6: 3 you have fallen **i** your neighbor's hands H928
Pr 6:18 schemes, feet that are quick to rush **i** evil, H4200
Pr 6:27 Can a man scoop fire **i** his lap without his H928
Pr 7:22 slaughter, like a deer stepping **i** a noose H448
Pr 7:23 like a bird darting **i** a snare, little knowing H448
Pr 7:25 heart turn to her ways or stray **i** her paths. H928
Pr 8: 3 beside the gate **leading i** the city H4200+7023
Pr 13:17 A wicked messenger falls **i** trouble, but a H928
Pr 16:33 The lot is cast **i** the lap, but its every H928
Pr 17:20 whose tongue is perverse falls **i** trouble. H928
Pr 18:16 ushers the giver **i** the presence of the H4200
Pr 22:14 a man who is under the LORD's wrath **falls** *i* it. AIT
Pr 26:17 someone who rushes **i** a quarrel not their H6584
Pr 26:27 Whoever digs a pit will fall **i** it; if someone H928
Pr 28:10 along an evil path will fall **i** their own trap, H928
Pr 28:12 wicked rise to power, people **go i hiding**. H2924
Pr 28:14 whoever hardens their heart falls **i** trouble. H928
Pr 28:18 whose ways are perverse will fall **i** the pit. H928
Pr 28:28 people **go i hiding**; but when the H6259
Ecc 1: 7 All streams flow **i** the sea, yet the sea is H448
Ecc 2:19 the fruit of my toil *i* **which** I have poured my AIT
Ecc 3:17 "God *will* **bring i judgment** both the H9149
Ecc 3:21 of the animal goes down **i** the earth?" H4200
Ecc 5: 6 Do not let your mouth **lead** you **i sin**. H2627
Ecc 7: 7 Extortion **turns** a wise person **i a fool**, and H2147
Ecc 10: 8 Whoever digs a pit may fall **i** it; whoever H928
Ecc 11: 9 these things God will bring you **i** judgment. H928
Ecc 12:14 For God will bring every deed **i** judgment H928
SS 1: 4 *Let* the king **bring** me **i** his chambers H995
SS 4:16 Let my beloved come **i** his garden and H4200
SS 5: 1 I have come **i** my garden, my sister, my H4200
Isa 2: 4 beat their swords **i** plowshares and their H4200
Isa 2: 4 their spears **i** pruning hooks. H4200
Isa 2:10 Go **i** the rocks, hide in the ground from the H928
Isa 3:14 The LORD enters **i** judgment against the H928
Isa 5:13 my people *will* **go i exile** for lack of H1655
Isa 5:14 **i** it will descend their nobles and masses H928
Isa 5:19 it approach, *let it* **come i view**, so we may H995
Isa 8: 8 sweep on **i** Judah, swirling over it H928
Isa 8:22 and *they will* **be thrust** *i* utter darkness. AIT
Isa 10:14 As one reaches **i** a nest, so my hand H3869
Isa 11: 8 child will put his hand **i** the viper's nest. H6584
Isa 11:15 He will break it up **i** seven streams so that H4200
Isa 14: 7 are at rest and at peace; *they* **break** *i* singing. AIT
Isa 14:23 "I will turn her **i** a place for owls and into H4200
Isa 14:23 her into a place for owls and **i** swampland; NDT
Isa 19: 8 all who cast hooks **i** the Nile; those who H928
Isa 19:14 LORD has poured **i** them a spirit of H928+7931
Isa 22:18 like a ball and throw you **i** a large country. H448
Isa 22:23 I will drive him like a peg **i** a firm place; he H928
Isa 22:25 "the peg driven **i** the firm place will give H928
Isa 23:13 its fortresses bare and turned it **i** a ruin. H4200
Isa 24:18 flees at the sound of terror will fall **i** a pit; H448
Isa 28:15 "*We have* **entered** *i* a covenant with death AIT
Isa 29:17 not Lebanon be turned **i** a fertile field H4200
Isa 34: 9 Edom's streams will be turned **i** pitch, her H4200
Isa 34: 9 into pitch, her dust **i** burning sulfur; her H4200
Isa 35: 2 *it will* **burst i bloom**; it will rejoice H7255+7255
Isa 36:15 city will not be given **i** the hand of the king H928
Isa 37: 1 on sackcloth and **went i** the temple of the H995
Isa 37:10 will not be given **i** the hands of the king of H928
Isa 37:19 thrown their gods **i** the fire and destroyed H928
Isa 37:26 that you *have* **turned** fortified cities **i** piles H8615
Isa 41:15 I will make you **i** a threshing sledge H4200
Isa 41:18 I will turn the desert **i** pools of water, and H4200
Isa 41:18 and the parched ground **i** springs. H4200
Isa 42: 9 before *they* **spring i being** I announce H7541
Isa 42:15 I will turn rivers **i** islands and dry up the H4200
Isa 42:16 turn the darkness **i** light before them and H4200
Isa 44:23 **Burst** *i* song, *you* mountains, you forests and AIT
Isa 44:25 of the wise and **turns** it **i nonsense**, H6118
Isa 45:16 they will go off **i** disgrace together. H928
Isa 46: 2 they themselves go off **i** captivity. H928
Isa 46: 6 they hire a goldsmith *to* **make** it *i* a god, and AIT
Isa 47: 5 "Sit in silence, go **i** darkness, queen city of H928
Isa 47: 6 I gave them **i** your hand, and you H928
Isa 49: 2 he made me **i** a polished arrow and H4200
Isa 49:11 I will turn all my mountains **i** roads, and H4200
Isa 49:13 you earth; **burst** *i* song, *you* mountains! AIT
Isa 50: 2 dry up the sea, *I* **turn** rivers **i** a desert; their H8492
Isa 51:23 I will put it **i** the hands of your tormentors H928
Isa 52: 9 **Burst** *i* songs of joy together, you ruins of AIT
Isa 54: 1 never bore a child; **burst** *i* song, shout for joy, AIT
Isa 54:16 blacksmith *who* **fans** the coals *i* flame and AIT
Isa 55:12 hills *will* **burst** *i* song before you, AIT
Isa 57: 2 Those who walk uprightly **enter** *i* peace; they AIT
Isa 57: 8 *you* **climbed** *i* it and opened it wide AIT
Isa 59: 7 Their feet rush **i** sin; they are swift to shed H4200
Isa 59: 8 *They have* **turned** them *i* **crooked** roads; no AIT
Isa 65: 6 I will pay it back **i** their laps— H6584
Isa 65: 7 I will measure **i** their laps the full payment H448
Isa 66: 2 these things, and so they **came i being**?" H2118
Isa 66: 7 "Before *she* **goes i labor**, she gives birth H2655
Isa 66:17 purify themselves to go **i** the gardens, H448
Jer 1: 3 the people of Jerusalem **went i exile**. H1655
Jer 2: 7 I brought you **i** a fertile land to eat its fruit H448
Jer 2:21 How then *did you* **turn** against me **i** a H2200
Jer 4:29 Some go **i** the thickets; some climb up H928
Jer 8: 6 own course like a horse charging **i** battle. H928
Jer 12: 7 give the one I love **i** the hands of her H928
Jer 12:10 my pleasant field **i** a desolate wasteland. H4200
Jer 13:19 All Judah *will* **be carried i exile**, carried H1655
Jer 14:16 to will be thrown out **i** the streets of H928
Jer 14:18 If *I* **go i** the country, I see those slain by H3655
Jer 14:18 by the sword; if *I* **go i** the city, I see the H995
Jer 16:13 you out of this land **i** a land neither you H6584
Jer 18: 4 so the potter **formed** it *i* another pot, shaping AIT
Jer 20: 4 I will give all Judah **i** the hands of the king H928
Jer 20: 5 the wealth of this city **i** the hands of their H928
Jer 20: 6 in your house will go **i** exile to Babylon. H928
Jer 21: 7 **i** the hands of Nebuchadnezzar king of H928
Jer 21:10 It will be given **i** the hands of the king of H928
Jer 22: 7 cedar beams and throw them **i** the fire. H6584
Jer 22:22 and your allies will go **i** exile. H928
Jer 22:25 I will deliver you **i** the hands of those who H928
Jer 22:26 who gave you birth **i** another country, H6584
Jer 22:28 cast **i** a land they do not know? H6584
Jer 24: 1 of Judah *were* **carried i exile** from H1655
Jer 26:23 his body thrown **i** the burial place of H448
Jer 27: 6 all your countries **i** the hands of my servant H928
Jer 27:20 **carried** Jehoiachin son of Jehoiakim king of Judah **i exile** H1655
Jer 29: 1 Nebuchadnezzar *had* **carried i exile** from H1655
Jer 29: 2 artisans had gone **i** exile from Jerusalem.) NDT
Jer 29: 4 to all those *I* **carried i exile** from H1655
Jer 29: 7 the city to which *I have* **carried** you **i exile**. H1655
Jer 29:14 the place from which *I* **carried** you **i exile**." H1655
Jer 29:16 citizens who did not go with you **i** exile— H928
Jer 29:21 "I will deliver them **i** the hands of H928
Jer 29:26 who acts like a prophet **i** the stocks and H448
Jer 30:16 devoured; all your enemies will go **i** exile. H928
Jer 31:13 I will turn their mourning **i** gladness; I will H4200
Jer 32: 3 to give this city **i** the hands of the king H928
Jer 32: 4 certainly be given **i** the hands of the king H928
Jer 32:18 the parents' sins **i** the laps of their H448
Jer 32:24 the city will be given **i** the hands of the H928
Jer 32:25 the city will be given **i** the hands of the H928
Jer 32:28 am about to give this city **i** the hands of the H928
Jer 32:36 it will be given **i** the hands of the king H928
Jer 32:43 it has been given **i** the hands of the H928
Jer 34: 2 to give this city **i** the hands of the king H928
Jer 34: 3 surely be captured and given **i** his hands. H928
Jer 34:10 people who entered **i** this covenant agreed H928
Jer 34:20 I will deliver **i** the hands of their enemies H928
Jer 34:21 Judah and his officials **i** the hands of their H928
Jer 35: 4 I brought them **i** the house of the LORD, into NDT
Jer 35: 4 **i** the room of the sons of Hanan son of H448
Jer 36:23 scribe's knife and threw them **i** the firepot, H448
Jer 37:15 secretary, which they had made **i** a prison. H4200
Jer 37:16 Jeremiah was put **i** a vaulted cell in a H448
Jer 37:17 will be delivered **i** the hands of the king H928
Jer 38: 3 certainly be given **i** the hands of the army H928
Jer 38: 6 Jeremiah and put him **i** the cistern of H448
Jer 38: 6 lowered Jeremiah by ropes **i** the cistern; H928
Jer 38: 6 and Jeremiah sank down **i** the mud. H928
Jer 38: 7 that they had put Jeremiah **i** the cistern. H448
Jer 38: 9 They have thrown him **i** a cistern, where he H448
Jer 38:18 this city will be given **i** the hands of the H928
Jer 39: 9 guard **carried i exile** *to* Babylon the H1655
Jer 39:17 you will not be given **i** the hands of those H928
Jer 40: 1 Judah who *were* **being carried i exile** to H1655
Jer 40: 7 who *had* not **been carried i exile** to H1655
Jer 41: 7 When they went **i** the city, Ishmael H448+9348
Jer 41: 7 them and threw them **i** a cistern. H448+9348
Jer 42:16 the famine you dread *will* **follow** you *i* Egypt, AIT
Jer 43: 3 may kill us or **carry** us **i exile** *to* Babylon." H1655
Jer 44:30 Hophra king of Egypt **i** the hands of his H928
Jer 44:30 Zedekiah king of Judah **i** the hands of H928
Jer 46:24 given **i** the hands of the people of the H928
Jer 46:26 I will give them **i** the hands of those who H928
Jer 48: 7 Chemosh will go **i** exile, together with H928
Jer 48:11 jar to another—she has not gone **i** exile. H928
Jer 48:44 flees from the terror will fall **i** a pit, H448
Jer 48:46 your sons are taken **i** exile and your H928
Jer 48:46 into exile and your daughters **i** captivity. H928
Jer 49: 3 Molek will go **i** exile, together with his H928
Jer 51:34 *he has* **thrown** us **i confusion**, he has H2169
Jer 51:63 to it and throw it **i** the Euphrates. H448+9348
Jer 52:15 of the guard **carried i exile** some of the H1655
Jer 52:27 So Judah **went i captivity**, away from her H1655
Jer 52:28 people Nebuchadnezzar **carried i exile**: H1655
Jer 52:30 745 Jews **taken i exile** *by* Nebuzaradan H1655
La 1: 3 harsh labor, Judah *has* **gone i exile**. H1655
La 1: 5 Her children *have* **gone** *i* exile, captive AIT
La 1: 7 When her people fell **i** enemy hands, there H928
La 1:13 high he sent fire, sent it down **i** my bones. H928
La 1:14 "My sins *have* **been bound** *i* a yoke; by his AIT
La 1:14 He has given me **i** the hands of those I H928
La 1:18 men and young women have gone **i** exile. H928
La 2: 7 walls of her palaces **i** the hands of the H928
La 2: 9 Her gates have sunk **i** the ground; their H928
Eze 2: 2 the Spirit came **i** me and raised me to my H928
Eze 3:24 the Spirit came **i** me and raised me to H928
Eze 5: 4 and throw them **i** the fire and burn H448+9348
Eze 7:14 no one will go **i** battle, for my wrath is H4200
Eze 7:19 " 'They will throw their silver **i** the streets H928
Eze 7:19 it has caused them to **stumble** *i* sin. AIT
Eze 7:20 They made it **i** vile images; therefore I will NDT
Eze 8: 8 "Son of man, now dig **i** the wall. H928
Eze 8: 8 So I dug **i** the wall and saw a doorway H928
Eze 8:16 He then brought me **i** the inner court of the H448
Eze 10: 7 of it and put it **i** the hands of the man H448
Eze 11: 9 city and deliver you **i** the hands of H928
Eze 12: 4 watching, go out like *those who* **go** *i* exile. AIT
Eze 12:11 They will go **i** exile as captives. H928
Eze 14:19 if I send a plague **i** that land and pour out H448
Eze 15: 5 less can it be made **i** something useful H4200
Eze 16: 5 you were thrown out **i** the open field, for on H448
Eze 16: 8 oath and entered **i** a covenant with you, H928
Eze 16:39 I will deliver you **i** the hands *of* your lovers, H928
Eze 19: 9 they pulled him **i** a cage and brought H928
Eze 20: 6 them out of Egypt **i** a land I had searched H448
Eze 20:10 Egypt and brought them **i** the wilderness. H448
Eze 20:15 not bring them **i** the land I had given H448
Eze 20:28 When I brought them **i** the land I had sworn H448
Eze 20:35 I will bring you **i** the wilderness of the H448
Eze 20:37 I will bring you **i** the bond of the H928
Eze 20:42 when I bring you **i** the land of Israel H448
Eze 21:22 **I** his right hand will come the lot for H928
Eze 21:31 I will deliver you **i** the hands of brutal men H928
Eze 22:19 I will gather you **i** Jerusalem. H448+9348
Eze 22:20 tin are gathered **i** a furnace to be H448+9348
Eze 23: 9 I delivered her **i** the hands of her lovers, H928
Eze 23:28 about to deliver you **i** the hands of those H928
Eze 23:31 your sister; so I will put her cup **i** your hand. H928
Eze 24: 3 cooking pot; put it on and pour water **i** it. H928

Eze 24: 4 Put **i** it the pieces of meat, all the choice H448
Eze 25: 3 people of Judah when they went **i** exile, H928
Eze 25: 5 I will turn Rabbah **i** a pasture for camels H4200
Eze 25: 5 camels and Ammon **i** a resting place for H4200
Eze 26:12 stones, timber and rubble **i** the sea. H928+9348
Eze 27:27 on board will sink **i** the heart of the sea on H928
Eze 30:17 the cities themselves will go **i** captivity. H928
Eze 30:18 and her villages will go **i** captivity. H928
Eze 30:25 when I put my sword **i** the hand of the king H928
Eze 31:11 I gave it **i** the hands of the ruler of the H928
Eze 33:31 but *they do* not **put** them **i practice**. H6913
Eze 33:32 your words but *do* not **put** them **i practice**. H6913
Eze 34:13 I will bring them **i** their own land. H448
Eze 35: 4 *I will* **turn** your towns **i** ruins and you will H8492
Eze 36:24 bring you back **i** your own land. H448
Eze 37: 9 the four winds and breathe **i** these slain, H928
Eze 37:17 Join them together **i** one stick so that they H4200
Eze 37:19 I will make them **i** a single stick of wood H4200
Eze 37:21 bring them back **i** their own land. H448
Eze 37:22 two nations or be divided **i** two kingdoms. H4200
Eze 38:10 thoughts will come **i** your mind and you H6584
Eze 39:23 people of Israel **went i** exile for their sin, H1655
Eze 39:28 though I **sent** them **i exile** among the H1655
Eze 40:17 Then he brought me **i** the outer court H448
Eze 40:20 the north gate, **leading i** the outer court. H4200
Eze 40:28 Then he brought me **i** the inner court H448
Eze 41: 3 Then he went **i** the inner sanctuary and H4200
Eze 41: 6 supports were not **inserted i** the wall of the H928
Eze 42: 1 led me northward **i** the outer court and H448
Eze 42:14 they are not to go **i** the outer court until H448
Eze 43: 5 me up and brought me **i** the inner court, H448
Eze 44: 7 in heart and flesh **i** my sanctuary, H928
Eze 44:12 idols and **made** the people of Israel **fall** *i* sin, AIT
Eze 44:19 When they go out **i** the outer court where H448
Eze 44:27 On the day he goes **i** the inner court of the H448
Eze 46:20 avoid bringing them **i** the outer court and H448
Eze 47: 8 region and goes down **i** the Arabah, H6584
Eze 47: 8 When it empties **i** the sea, the salty water H448
Eze 48:14 the land and *must* not **pass i other hands**, H6296
Da 1: 2 Jehoiakim king of Judah **i** his hand, H928
Da 1: 3 to **bring i** the king's service some of the H995
Da 1:18 set by the king to **bring** them **i** his service, H995
Da 2: 5 I *will have you* **cut i** pieces and your A10522
Da 2: 5 your houses **turned i** piles of rubble. A10682
Da 3: 6 be thrown **i** a blazing furnace." A10378+10135
Da 3:11 will be thrown **i** a blazing A10378+10135
Da 3:15 immediately **i** a blazing furnace. A10378+10135
Da 3:17 If we are thrown **i** the blazing furnace, the NDT
Da 3:20 throw them **i** the blazing furnace. A10378
Da 3:21 bound and thrown **i** the blazing A10378+10135
Da 3:23 fell **i** the blazing furnace. A10378+10135
Da 3:24 we tied up and threw **i** the fire?" A10378+10135
Da 3:29 Abednego **be cut i** pieces and their A10522
Da 3:29 their houses **be turned i** piles of rubble A10702
Da 4: 8 Daniel **came i** my presence and I told A10549
Da 5:10 his nobles, came **i** the banquet hall. A10378
Da 6: 7 Majesty, shall be thrown **i** the lions' den. A10378
Da 6:12 would be thrown **i** the lions' den? A10378
Da 6:16 Daniel and threw him **i** the lions' den. A10378
Da 6:24 brought in and thrown **i** the lions' den, A10378
Da 7:11 destroyed and thrown **i** the blazing fire. A10378
Da 7:13 of Days and was led **i** his **presence**. A10621
Da 7:25 will be delivered **i** his hands for a time, A10089
Da 10: 9 I **fell i a deep sleep**, my face to H8101
Hos 2: 3 a desert, turn her **i** a parched land, and H3869
Hos 2:14 I will lead her **i** the wilderness and speak NDT
Hos 7: 1 thieves **break i** houses, bandits rob H995
Hos 9: 4 *it will* not **come i** the temple of the LORD. H995
Hos 9: 9 *They have* **sunk deep** *i* corruption, as in the AIT
Hos 10: 5 because *it is* **taken** from them **i exile**. H1655
Joel 2: 9 They climb **i** the houses; like thieves they H928
Joel 2:20 pushing it **i** a parched and barren land H448
Joel 3:10 Beat your plowshares **i** swords and your H4200
Joel 3:10 swords and your pruning hooks **i** spears. H4200
Joel 3:12 let them advance **i** the Valley of H448
Am 1: 5 The people of Aram *will* **go i exile** to Kir," H1655
Am 1:15 Her king will go **i** exile, he and his officials H928
Am 5: 5 For Gilgal *will* **surely go i exile**, and H1655+1655
Am 5: 7 who turn justice **i** bitterness and cast H4200
Am 5: 8 who turns midnight **i** dawn and darkens H4200
Am 5: 8 midnight into dawn and **darkens** day *i* night, AIT
Am 5:27 Therefore *I will* **send** you **i** exile beyond H1655
Am 6: 7 *you will* be among the first to **go i exile** H1655+1655
Am 6:11 and *he will* **smash** the great house *i* pieces AIT
Am 6:11 into pieces and the small house **i** bits. NDT
Am 6:12 have turned justice **i** poison and the fruit H4200
Am 6:12 the fruit of righteousness **i** bitterness— H4200
Am 7:11 and Israel *will* **surely go i exile** H1655+1655
Am 7:17 And Israel *will* **surely go i exile** H1655+1655
Am 8:10 religious festivals **i** mourning and all your H4200
Am 8:10 mourning and all your singing **i** weeping. H4200
Am 9: 4 they are driven **i** exile by their enemies H928
Jnh 1: 5 they threw the cargo **i** the sea to lighten H448
Jnh 1: 5 he lay down and **fell i a deep sleep**. H8101
Jnh 1:12 "Pick me up and throw me **i** the sea," H448
Jnh 2: 3 You hurled me **i** the depths, into the very NDT
Jnh 2: 3 into the depths, **i** the very heart of the seas H928
Jnh 3: 4 began by going a day's journey **i** the city, H928
Mic 1: 6 I will pour her stones **i** the valley and lay H4200
Mic 1:16 for *they will* **go** from you **i** exile. H1655
Mic 4: 3 beat their swords **i** plowshares and their H4200
Mic 4: 3 their spears **i** pruning hooks. H4200
Mic 7: 9 He will bring me out **i** the light; I will see H4200
Mic 7:19 all our iniquities **i** the depths of the sea. H928
Na 1: 8 will pursue his foes **i** the realm of darkness. NDT
Na 3:10 Yet she was taken captive and went **i** exile H928
Na 3:11 *you will* **go** *i* hiding and seek refuge from the AIT
Na 3:12 the figs fall **i** the mouth of the eater. H6584
Hab 3:16 decay crept **i** my bones, and my H928
Hag 1: 8 **Go up** *i* the mountains and bring down timber AIT
Zec 5: 8 he pushed her back **i** the basket and H448+9348
Zec 10: 5 trampling their enemy **i** the mud of the H928
Zec 11: 6 "I will give everyone **i** the hands of their H928
Zec 13: 9 This third I will put **i** the fire; I will refine H928
Zec 14: 2 Half of the city will go **i** exile, but the rest H928
Mal 1: 3 and *I have* **turned** his hill country **i** a H8492
Mal 3:10 Bring the whole tithe **i** the storehouse, that H448
Mt 3:10 will be cut down and thrown **i** the fire. G1650
Mt 3:12 gathering his wheat **i** the barn and G1650
Mt 4: 1 led by the Spirit **i** the wilderness to be G1650
Mt 4:18 They were casting a net **i** the lake, for G1650
Mt 5:25 and you may be thrown **i** prison. G1650
Mt 5:29 your whole body to be thrown **i** hell. G1650
Mt 5:30 than for your whole body to go **i** hell. G1650
Mt 6: 6 But when you pray, **go i** your room, close G1656
Mt 6:13 And lead us not **i** temptation, but deliver G1650
Mt 6:30 today and tomorrow is thrown **i** the fire, G1650
Mt 7:19 fruit is cut down and thrown **i** the fire. G1650
Mt 7:24 of mine and **puts** them **i practice** is like a G4472
Mt 7:26 and *does* not **put** them **i practice** is like G4472
Mt 8:12 be thrown outside, **i** the darkness, where G1650
Mt 8:14 When Jesus came **i** Peter's house, he saw G1650
Mt 8:23 Then he **got i** the boat and his disciples G1832
Mt 8:31 drive us out, send us **i** the herd of pigs." G1650
Mt 8:32 So they came out and went **i** the pigs G1650
Mt 8:32 down the steep bank **i** the lake and died G1650
Mt 8:33 went **i** the town and reported all this G1650
Mt 9: 1 Jesus **stepped i** a boat, crossed over and G1832
Mt 9:17 do people pour new wine **i** old wineskins. G1650
Mt 9:17 they pour new wine **i** new wineskins, and G1650
Mt 9:38 to send out workers **i** his harvest field." G1650
Mt 11: 7 "What did you go out **i** the wilderness to G1650
Mt 12: 9 that place, he went **i** their synagogue, G1650
Mt 12:11 a sheep and it falls **i** a pit on the Sabbath G1650
Mt 13: 2 around him that he **got i** a boat and sat in G1832
Mt 13:30 gather the wheat and **bring** it **i** my barn. G1650
Mt 13:33 took and mixed **i** about sixty pounds G1650
Mt 13:36 he left the crowd and went **i** the house. G1650
Mt 13:42 They will throw them **i** the blazing furnace G1650
Mt 13:47 that was let down **i** the lake and caught G1650
Mt 13:50 throw them **i** the blazing furnace G1650
Mt 14:22 made the disciples **get i** the boat and go G1832
Mt 14:32 And when they climbed **i** the boat, the G1650
Mt 15:11 What **goes i** someone's mouth does not G1656
Mt 15:14 blind lead the blind, both will fall **i** a pit." G1650
Mt 15:17 the mouth goes **i** the stomach and then G1650
Mt 15:39 *he* **got i** the boat and went to the vicinity G1832
Mt 17:15 He often falls **i** the fire or into the water G1650
Mt 17:15 He often falls into the fire or **i** the water. G1650
Mt 17:22 going to be delivered **i** the hands of men. G1650
Mt 17:25 When Peter came **i** the house, Jesus was G1650
Mt 18: 8 two feet and be thrown **i** eternal fire. G1650
Mt 18: 9 two eyes and be thrown **i** the fire of hell. G1650
Mt 18:30 had the man thrown **i** prison until he G1650
Mt 19: 1 Galilee and went **i** the region of Judea G1650
Mt 20: 2 the day and sent them **i** his vineyard. G1650
Mt 21:21 throw yourself **i** the sea,' and it will G1650
Mt 22:10 So the servants went out **i** the streets and G1650
Mt 22:13 throw him outside, **i** the darkness, where G1650
Mt 24:43 would not have let his house *be* **broken i**. G1482
Mt 25:30 servant outside, **i** the darkness, where G1650
Mt 25:41 **i** the eternal fire prepared for the devil G1650
Mt 26:18 "Go **i** the city to a certain man and tell G1650
Mt 26:23 has dipped his hand **i** the bowl with me G1877
Mt 26:32 I will go ahead of you **i** Galilee. G1650
Mt 26:41 pray so that *you will* not **fall i** temptation. G1656
Mt 26:45 of Man is delivered **i** the hands of sinners. G1650
Mt 27: 5 threw the money **i** the temple and left. G1650
Mt 27: 6 against the law to put this **i** the treasury, G1650
Mt 27:27 soldiers took Jesus **i** the Praetorium and G1650
Mt 27:53 resurrection and **went i** the holy city and G1656
Mt 28: 7 dead and is going ahead of you **i** Galilee. G1650
Mt 28:11 of the guards went **i** the city and reported G1650
Mk 1:12 the Spirit sent him out **i** the wilderness, G1650
Mk 1:14 Jesus went **i** Galilee, proclaiming G1650
Mk 1:16 brother Andrew casting a net **i** the lake, G1877
Mk 1:21 Jesus **went i** the synagogue and began to G1656
Mk 2:22 no one pours new wine **i** old wineskins. G1650
Mk 2:22 they pour new wine **i** new wineskins." G1650
Mk 3: 1 Another time Jesus **went i** the synagogue G1656
Mk 4: 1 so large that he **got i** a boat and sat in G1832
Mk 4:22 is meant to be brought *out* **i** the open. G1650
Mk 5:12 us among the pigs; allow *us to* **go i** them." G1656
Mk 5:13 spirits came out and **went i** the pigs. G1656
Mk 5:13 down the steep bank **i** the lake and were G1650
Mk 5:18 *As* Jesus *was* **getting i** the boat, the man G1832
Mk 6:45 made his disciples **get i** the boat and go G1832
Mk 6:51 Then he climbed **i** the boat with them G1650
Mk 6:56 wherever he went—**i** villages, towns or G1650
Mk 7:15 a person can defile them *by* **going i** them. G1660
Mk 7:19 For *it* doesn't **go i** their heart but into their G1660
Mk 7:19 go into their heart but **i** their stomach, G1650
Mk 7:31 of Galilee and **i** the region of the G324+3545
Mk 7:33 Jesus put his fingers **i** the man's ears. G1650
Mk 8:10 *he* **got i** the boat with his disciples and G1832
Mk 8:13 **got** back **i** the boat and crossed to the G1832
Mk 8:26 "Don't even **go i** the village. G1656
Mk 9:20 *it* immediately **threw** the boy **i a convulsion** G5360
Mk 9:22 has often thrown him **i** fire or water to kill G1650
Mk 9:31 going to be delivered **i** the hands of men. G1650
Mk 9:42 their neck and they were thrown **i** the sea. G1650
Mk 9:43 maimed than with two hands to go **i** hell, G1650
Mk 9:45 to have two feet and be thrown **i** hell. G1650
Mk 9:47 to have two eyes and be thrown **i** hell, G1650
Mk 10: 1 that place and went **i** the region of Judea G1650
Mk 11:11 Jerusalem and *went* **i** the temple courts. G1650
Mk 11:23 throw yourself **i** the sea,' and does G1650
Mk 12:41 putting their money **i** the temple treasury. G1650
Mk 12:43 widow has put more **i** the treasury than all G1650
Mk 14:13 telling them, "Go **i** the city, and a man G1650
Mk 14:16 went **i** the city and found things just as G1650
Mk 14:20 "one who dips bread **i** the bowl with me. G1650
Mk 14:28 I will go ahead of you **i** Galilee. G1650
Mk 14:38 pray so that you will not fall **i** temptation. G1650
Mk 14:41 of Man is delivered **i** the hands of sinners. G1650
Mk 14:54 **right i** the courtyard of the G2401+2276+1650
Mk 14:68 he said, and went out **i** the entryway. G1650
Mk 15:16 The soldiers led Jesus away **i** the palace G2276
Mk 16: 7 'He is going ahead of you **i** Galilee. G1650
Mk 16:15 "Go **i** all the world and preach the gospel G1650
Mk 16:19 he was taken up **i** heaven and he sat at G1650
Lk 1: 9 *to* **go i** the temple of the Lord and burn G1656
Lk 1:79 to guide our feet **i** the path of peace." G1650
Lk 2:15 angels had left them and *gone* **i** heaven, G1650
Lk 2:27 by the Spirit, he went **i** the temple courts. G1650
Lk 3: 3 He went **i** all the country around the G1650
Lk 3: 9 will be cut down and thrown **i** the fire." G1650
Lk 3:17 floor and to gather the wheat **i** his barn, G1650
Lk 4: 1 was led by the Spirit **i** the wilderness, G1877
Lk 4:16 Sabbath day *he* **went i** the synagogue, G1656
Lk 5: 3 *He* **got i** one of the boats, the one G1832
Lk 5: 4 to Simon, "Put out **i** deep water, and let G1650
Lk 5:18 tried *to* **take** him **i** *the house* to lay G1662
Lk 5:19 mat through the tiles **i** the middle of the G1650
Lk 5:37 no one pours new wine **i** old wineskins. G1650
Lk 5:38 wine must be poured **i** new wineskins. G1650
Lk 6: 6 Sabbath he **went i** the synagogue and G1656
Lk 6:38 running over, will be poured **i** your lap. G1650
Lk 6:39 *Will they* not both **fall i** a pit? G1860
Lk 6:47 hears my words and **puts** them **i practice**, G4472
Lk 6:49 and *does* not **put** them **i practice** is like G4472
Lk 7:24 "What did you go out **i** the wilderness to G1650
Lk 7:44 see this woman? *I* **came i** your house. G1656
Lk 8:17 not be known or brought out **i** the open. G1650
Lk 8:21 who hear God's word and **put** it **i practice**." G4472
Lk 8:22 So *they* **got i** a boat and set out G1832
Lk 8:29 driven by the demon **i** solitary places. G1650
Lk 8:30 because many demons *had* **gone i** him. G1656
Lk 8:31 not to order them to go **i** the Abyss. G1650
Lk 8:32 begged Jesus to let them **go i** the pigs, G1656
Lk 8:33 out of the man, *they* **went i** the pigs, and G1656
Lk 8:33 down the steep bank **i** the lake and was G1650
Lk 8:37 So he **got i** the boat and left. G1832
Lk 9:39 *it* **throws** him **i convulsions** so that he G5057
Lk 9:44 going to be delivered **i** the hands of men." G1650
Lk 9:52 *who* **went i** a Samaritan village to get G1656
Lk 10: 2 to send out workers **i** his harvest field. G1650
Lk 10:10 are not welcomed, go **i** its streets and say, G1650
Lk 10:36 to the *man who* **fell i the hands of** robbers G1860
Lk 11: 4 And **lead** us not **i** temptation.' G1662
Lk 12: 5 has authority *to* **throw** you **i** hell. G1833
Lk 12:28 tomorrow is thrown **i** the fire, how G1650
Lk 12:39 would not have let his house *be* **broken i**. G1482
Lk 12:58 and the officer throw you **i** prison. G1650
Lk 13:21 a woman took and **mixed i** about sixty G1606
Lk 14: 5 an ox that falls **i** a well on the Sabbath G1650
Lk 14:21 'Go out quickly **i** the streets and alleys of G1650
Lk 16: 4 people will welcome me **i** their houses. G1650
Lk 16: 9 you will be welcomed **i** eternal dwellings. G1650
Lk 16:16 everyone is forcing their way **i** it. G1650
Lk 17: 2 them to be thrown **i** the sea with a G1650
Lk 17:12 *As* he *was* **going i** a village, ten men who G1656
Lk 21: 1 putting their gifts **i** the temple treasury. G1650
Lk 22:40 "Pray *that you will* not **fall i** temptation." G1656
Lk 22:46 pray so that *you will* not **fall i** temptation." G1656
Lk 22:54 led him away and **took** him **i** the house of G1652
Lk 23:19 Barabbas had been thrown **i** prison for an G1877
Lk 23:25 who had been thrown **i** prison for G1650
Lk 23:42 me when you come **i** your kingdom." G1650
Lk 23:46 "Father, **i** your hands I commit my spirit." G1650
Lk 24:51 he left them and was taken up **i** heaven. G1650
Jn 1: 9 light to everyone was coming **i** the world. G1650
Jn 2: 9 the water *that had been* **turned i** wine. G1181
Jn 2:16 Stop **turning** my Father's house **i** a market! G4472
Jn 3: 4 a second time **i** their mother's womb G1650
Jn 3:13 No one has ever gone **i** heaven except the G1650
Jn 3:17 not send his Son **i** the world to condemn G1650
Jn 3:19 Light has come **i** the world, but people G1650
Jn 3:20 will not come **i** the light for fear that G4639
Jn 3:21 lives by the truth comes **i** the light, G4639
Jn 3:22 disciples went out **i** the Judean G1650
Jn 4: 8 disciples had gone **i** the town to buy food.) G1650
Jn 4:46 where *he had* **turned** the water **i** wine. G4472
Jn 5: 7 no one to help me **i** the pool when the G1650

Jn 5:13 had slipped away *i* the **crowd** that was there. AIT
Jn 6:14 is the Prophet who is to come **i** the world." *G1650*
Jn 6:17 where *they* **got i** a boat and set off across *G1832*
Jn 6:21 they were willing to take him **i** the boat, *G1650*
Jn 6:24 they **got i** the boats and went to *G1832*
Jn 7:52 **Look i** it, and you will find that a prophet *G2236*
Jn 9:39 "For judgment I have come **i** this world, so *G1650*
Jn 10:36 as his very own and sent **i** the world? *G1650*
Jn 11:27 Son of God, who is to come **i** the world." *G1650*
Jn 12: 6 he used to help himself to what *was* **put** *i* it. AIT
Jn 12:46 I have come **i** the world as a light, so that *G1650*
Jn 13: 5 he poured water **i** a basin and began to *G1650*
Jn 13:27 took the bread, Satan entered **i** him. *G1650*
Jn 15: 6 picked up, thrown **i** the fire and burned. *G1650*
Jn 16:13 he will guide you **i** all the truth. *G1877*
Jn 16:21 of her joy that a child is born **i** the world. *G1650*
Jn 17:18 As you sent me **i** the world, I have sent *G1650*
Jn 17:18 the world, I have sent them **i** the world. *G1650*
Jn 18: 1 garden, and he and his disciples **went i** it. *G1656*
Jn 18:15 **he went with** Jesus **i** the high priest's *G5291*
Jn 18:37 I was born and came **i** the world is to *G1650*
Jn 19:23 his clothes, **dividing** them *i* four shares, one AIT
Jn 19:27 time on, this disciple took her **i** his home. *G1650*
Jn 20: 6 behind him and **went straight i** the tomb. *G1656*
Jn 20:11 she wept, she bent over to look **i** the tomb *G1650*
Jn 20:25 put my hand **i** his side, I will not *G1650*
Jn 20:27 Reach out your hand and put it **i** my side *G1650*
Jn 21: 3 So they went out and **got i** the boat, but *G1832*
Jn 21: 7 had taken it off) and jumped **i** the water. *G1650*
Jn 21:11 So Simon Peter **climbed back i** the boat *G326*
Ac 1:10 looking intently up **i** the sky as he was *G1650*
Ac 1:11 "why do you stand here looking **i** the sky? *G1650*
Ac 1:11 who has been taken from you **i** heaven *G1650*
Ac 1:11 way you have seen him go **i** heaven." *G1650*
Ac 3: 2 to beg from those **going i** the temple *G1660*
Ac 3: 8 Then *he* **went** with them **i** the temple *G1656*
Ac 5:15 brought the sick **i** the streets and laid *G1650*
Ac 7: 9 Joseph, they sold him as a slave **i** Egypt. *G1650*
Ac 7:43 Therefore *I will* **send** you **i exile**' beyond *G3579*
Ac 8:38 eunuch went down **i** the water and Philip *G1650*
Ac 9: 6 "Now get up and **go i** the city, and you will *G1656*
Ac 9: 8 So they led him by the hand **i** Damascus. *G1650*
Ac 10:10 was being prepared, he fell **i** a trance. *G2093*
Ac 10:23 Then Peter **invited** the men **i** the house to *G1657*
Ac 11: 3 "*You* **went i** the house of uncircumcised *G1656*
Ac 11: 6 I looked **i** it and saw four-footed animals *G1650*
Ac 14: 1 Barnabas **went** as usual **i** the Jewish *G1656*
Ac 14:14 their clothes and rushed out **i** the crowd, *G1650*
Ac 14:20 he got up and went back **i** the city. *G1650*
Ac 14:24 through Pisidia, they came **i** Pamphylia, *G1650*
Ac 15: 2 This **brought** Paul and Barnabas *i* sharp AIT
Ac 16:19 dragged them **i** the marketplace to *G1650*
Ac 16:20 and *are* **throwing** our city **i an uproar** *G1752*
Ac 16:23 they were thrown **i** prison, and the jailer *G1650*
Ac 16:34 jailer brought them **i** his house and set a *G1650*
Ac 16:37 are Roman citizens, and threw us **i** prison. *G1650*
Ac 17: 2 his custom, Paul **went i** the synagogue *G1656*
Ac 17: 7 Jason *has* **welcomed** them **i** his **house**. *G5685*
Ac 17: 8 the city officials *were* **thrown i turmoil**. *G5429*
Ac 18:19 *He* himself **went i** the synagogue and *G1656*
Ac 19:29 all of them rushed **i** the theater together. *G1650*
Ac 19:31 begging him not to venture **i** the theater. *G1650*
Ac 20: 9 was sinking *i* a deep **sleep** as Paul talked AIT
Ac 20:18 from the first day *I* **came i** the province of *G2094*
Ac 21:28 *he has* **brought** Greeks **i** the temple and *G1652*
Ac 21:29 that Paul *had* **brought** him **i** the temple.) *G1652*
Ac 21:34 ordered that Paul be taken **i** the barracks. *G1650*
Ac 21:37 were about to **take** Paul **i** the barracks, *G1652*
Ac 21:38 terrorists out **i** the wilderness some *G1650*
Ac 22: 4 women and throwing them **i** prison, *G1650*
Ac 22:10 the Lord said, 'and go **i** Damascus. *G1650*
Ac 22:11 led me by the hand **i** Damascus, *G1650*
Ac 22:17 was praying at the temple, I fell **i** a trance *G1877*
Ac 22:23 off their cloaks and flinging dust **i** the air, *G1650*
Ac 22:24 ordered *that* Paul *be* **taken i** the barracks. *G1652*
Ac 23:10 by force and bring him **i** the barracks. *G1650*
Ac 23:16 *he* **went i** the barracks and told Paul. *G1656*
Ac 27:15 the storm and could not **head i** the wind; *G535*
Ac 27:30 the sailors let the lifeboat down **i** the sea *G1650*
Ac 27:38 the ship by throwing the grain **i** the sea. *G1650*
Ac 28: 5 shook the snake off **i** the fire and suffered *G1650*
Ro 4:17 the dead and calls *i* **being** things that were AIT
Ro 5: 2 access by faith **i** this grace in which we *G1650*
Ro 5: 5 has been poured out **i** our hearts through *G1877*
Ro 6: 3 us who were baptized **i** Christ Jesus were *G1650*
Ro 6: 3 Christ Jesus were baptized **i** his death? *G1650*
Ro 6: 4 him through baptism **i** death in order that, *G1650*
Ro 8:21 to decay and *brought* **i** the freedom and *G1650*
Ro 10: 6 in your heart, 'Who will ascend **i** heaven? *G1650*
Ro 10: 7 "or 'Who will descend **i** the deep?' " (that *G1650*
Ro 10:18 "Their voice has gone out **i** all the earth *G1650*
Ro 11:24 to nature *were* **grafted i** a cultivated *G1596*
Ro 11:24 *be* **grafted i** their own olive tree! *G1596*
1Co 1: 9 who has called you **i** fellowship with his *G1650*
1Co 5: 2 *you* rather *have* **gone i mourning** and *G4291*
1Co 8:13 eat **causes** my brother or sister **to fall i sin**, *G4997*
1Co 9:25 in the games **goes i** strict **training**. *G1603*
1Co 10: 2 were all baptized **i** Moses in the cloud *G1650*
1Co 14: 9 You will just be speaking **i** the air. *G1650*
2Co 3:18 being transformed *i* his **image** with AIT
2Co 7: 5 For when we came **i** Macedonia, we had *G1650*
2Co 8:16 who put **i** the heart of Titus the same *G1877*
2Co 11:29 Who *is* **led i sin**, and I do not inwardly *G4997*
Gal 1: 7 are **throwing** you **i confusion** and are *G5429*
Gal 1:17 apostles before I was, but I went **i** Arabia. *G1650*
Gal 3:27 who were baptized **i** Christ have clothed *G1650*
Gal 4: 6 God sent the Spirit of his Son **i** our hearts *G1650*
Gal 5:10 The *one who is* **throwing** you **i confusion** *G5429*
Eph 1:10 to be **put i effect** when the times reach *G3873*
Eph 3: 4 my insight **i** the mystery of Christ *G1877*
Php 4: 9 from me, or seen in me—**put** it **i practice**. *G4556*
Col 1:13 brought us **i** the kingdom of the Son *G1650*
Col 2:18 *Such a person* also **goes i great detail** *G1836*
1Th 2:12 who calls you **i** his kingdom and glory. *G1650*
2Th 3: 5 direct your hearts **i** God's love and Christ's *G1650*
1Ti 1: 3 As I urged you when I went **i** Macedonia *G1650*
1Ti 1:15 Christ Jesus came **i** the world to save *G1650*
1Ti 3: 7 so that *he will* not **fall i** disgrace and into *G1860*
1Ti 3: 7 not fall into disgrace and **i** the devil's trap. NDT
1Ti 5: 4 *to* **put** *their* **religion i practice by caring for** *G2355*
1Ti 5:13 *they* **get i the habit** of being idle and *G3443*
1Ti 6: 7 For *we* **brought** nothing **i** the world, and *G1662*
1Ti 6: 9 want to get rich **fall i** temptation and a *G1860*
1Ti 6: 9 a trap and **i** many foolish and harmful NDT
1Ti 6: 9 that plunge people **i** ruin and destruction. *G1650*
2Ti 1: 6 I remind you *to* **fan i flame** the gift of God, *G351*
2Ti 2: 7 the Lord will give you insight **i** all this. *G1877*
2Ti 3: 6 the kind who **worm their way i** homes *G1905*
Heb 1: 6 when God **brings** his firstborn **i** the world *G1652*
Heb 4:14 high priest *who has* **ascended i** heaven, *G1451*
Heb 9: 6 entered regularly **i** the outer room to carry *G1650*
Heb 9: 8 the way *i* the **Most Holy Place** had not yet AIT
Heb 9:18 covenant *was* not **put i effect** without *G1590*
Heb 10: 5 Therefore, *when* Christ **came i** the world *G1656*
Heb 10:31 a dreadful thing *to* **fall i** the hands of the *G1860*
Heb 13:11 priest **carries** the blood of animals **i** the *G1662*
Jas 1:25 looks intently **i** the perfect law that *G1650*
Jas 2: 2 Suppose a man **comes i** your meeting *G1656*
Jas 2: 6 the ones who are dragging you **i** court? *G1650*
Jas 3: 3 When we put bits **i** the mouths of horses *G1650*
1Pe 1: 3 given us new birth **i** a living hope through *G1650*
1Pe 1: 4 **i** an inheritance that can never perish *G1650*
1Pe 1:12 Even angels long to look **i** these things. *G1650*
1Pe 2: 5 being built *i* a spiritual **house** to be a holy AIT
1Pe 2: 9 you out of darkness **i** his wonderful light. *G1650*
1Pe 3:22 who has gone **i** heaven and is at God's *G1650*
2Pe 1:11 a rich welcome **i** the eternal kingdom of *G1650*
2Pe 2: 2 *will* **bring** the way of truth **i disrepute**. *G1059*
2Pe 3: 5 the heavens **came i being** and the earth *G1639*
1Jn 4: 1 false prophets have gone out **i** the world. *G1650*
1Jn 4: 9 his one and only Son **i** the world that we *G1650*
2Jn 7 in the flesh, have gone out **i** the world. *G1650*
2Jn 10 do not take them **i** your house or welcome *G1650*
Jude 4 the grace of our God **i** a license for *G1650*
Jude 11 they have rushed for profit *i* Balaam's **error** AIT
Rev 2:20 my servants *i* **sexual immorality** and the AIT
Rev 5: 6 spirits of God sent out **i** all the earth. *G1650*
Rev 8: 8 all ablaze, was thrown **i** the sea. *G1650*
Rev 8: 8 A third of the sea **turned i** blood, *G1181*
Rev 9: 9 many horses and chariots rushing **i** battle. *G1650*
Rev 11: 6 to turn the waters **i** blood and to strike the *G1650*
Rev 12: 6 The woman fled **i** the wilderness to a *G1650*
Rev 13:10 "If anyone is to go **i** captivity, into captivity *G1650*
Rev 13:10 to go into captivity, **i** captivity they will go. *G1650*
Rev 14:10 poured full strength **i** the cup of his wrath. *G1877*
Rev 14:19 threw them **i** the great winepress *G1650*
Rev 16: 3 and *it* **turned i** blood like that of a dead *G1181*
Rev 16:10 its kingdom was **plunged i darkness**. *G5031*
Rev 16:17 angel poured out his bowl **i** the air, *G2093*
Rev 16:19 The great city split **i** three parts, and the *G1650*
Rev 17: 3 me away in the Spirit **i** a wilderness. *G1650*
Rev 17:17 For God has put it **i** their hearts to *G1650*
Rev 18:21 of a large millstone and threw it **i** the sea, *G1650*
Rev 19:20 them were thrown alive **i** the fiery lake of *G1650*
Rev 20: 3 He threw him **i** the Abyss, and locked and *G1650*
Rev 20:10 was thrown **i** the lake of burning sulfur *G1650*
Rev 20:14 Hades were thrown **i** the lake of fire. *G1650*
Rev 20:15 book of life was thrown **i** the lake of fire. *G1650*
Rev 21:24 of the earth will bring their splendor **i** it. *G1650*
Rev 21:26 honor of the nations will be brought **i** it. *G1650*
Rev 22:14 life and *may* **go** through the gates **i** the *G1656*

INTOXICATED (3)

Pr 5:19 *may you* ever *be* **i** with her love. H8706
Pr 5:20 my son, *be* **i** with another man's wife? H8706
Rev 17: 2 of the earth were **i** with the wine of her *G3499*

INTREAT, INTREATED, INTREATIES, INTREATY (KJV) ANSWERED PRAYER, ASK, BEG, BEGGED, CURRY, EXHORT, INTERCEDE, PLEAD, PRAY, PRAYED, SEEK, SOUGHT, URGE

INTRIGUE (3) [INTRIGUES]

Da 8:23 a master of **i**, will arise. H2648
Da 11:21 feel secure, and he will seize it through **i**. H2761
Hos 7: 6 are like an oven; they approach him with **i**. H744

INTRIGUES (2) [INTRIGUE]

Ps 5:10 Let their **i** be their downfall H4600
Ps 31:20 presence you hide them from *all* human **i**; H8222

INTRODUCE (1) [INTRODUCED, INTRODUCTION]

2Pe 2: 1 They *will* **secretly i** destructive heresies *G4206*

INTRODUCED (4) [INTRODUCE]

2Ki 17: 8 the practices that the kings of Israel *had* **i**. H6913
2Ki 17:19 They followed the practices Israel *had* **i**. H6913
Gal 3:17 The law, **i** 430 years later, does not set *G1181*
Heb 7:19 and a better hope is **i**, by which we draw *G2081*

INTRODUCTION (1) [INTRODUCE]

1Co 16: 3 I will give **letters of i** to the men you *G2186*

INVADE (15) [INVADED, INVADER, INVADERS, INVADING]

Dt 12:29 you *are about to* **i** and H995+9004+2025
2Ch 20:10 allow Israel to **i** when they came from H995+928
Isa 7: 6 "*Let us* **i** Judah; let us tear it apart H6590+928
Eze 38: 8 In future years *you will* **i** a land that H995+448
Eze 38:11 "*I will* **i** a land of unwalled villages; H6590+6584
Da 11: 9 of the North *will* **i** the realm of the H995+928
Da 11:21 *He will* **i** the kingdom when its people feel H995
Da 11:24 *he will* **i** them and will achieve what H995
Da 11:29 appointed time *he will* **i** the South H995+928
Da 11:40 *He will* **i** many countries and sweep H995+928
Da 11:41 *He will* also **i** the Beautiful Land H995+928
Joel 3:17 never again *will* foreigners **i** her. H6296+928
Mic 5: 5 the Assyrians **i** our land and march H995+928
Mic 5: 6 Assyrians when *they* **i** our land and H995+928
Na 1:15 No more *will* the wicked **i** you; they will H6296

INVADED (15) [INVADE]

Ex 10:14 they **i** all Egypt and settled down in H6590+6584
Jdg 6: 3 other eastern peoples **i** the country. H6590+6584
Jdg 6: 5 camels; *they* **i** the land to ravage it. H995+928
2Ki 3:24 And the Israelites **i** the land and H995+928
2Ki 15:19 Then Pul king of Assyria **i** the land H995+6584
2Ki 17: 5 The king of Assyria **i** the entire land H6590+928
2Ki 24: 1 king of Babylon **i** the land, H6590
1Ch 4:42 of Ishi, **i** the hill country of Seir. H2143+4200
2Ch 21:17 **i** it and carried off all the goods found in H1324
2Ch 24:23 *it* **i** Judah and Jerusalem and killed H995+448
2Ch 32: 1 king of Assyria came and **i** Judah. H995+928
Ps 79: 1 the nations *have* **i** your inheritance H995+928
Jer 35:11 king of Babylon **i** this land, H6590+448
Jer 48:15 Moab will be destroyed and her towns **i** H6590
Joel 1: 6 A nation *has* **i** my land, a mighty H6590+6584

INVADER (2) [INVADE]

Isa 21: 1 the southland, *an i* **comes** from the desert AIT
Da 11:16 The **i** will do as he pleases; no one H995+448

INVADERS (1) [INVADE]

Jer 18:22 when you suddenly bring **i** against them, H1522

INVADING (3) [INVADE]

1Sa 7:13 they stopped **i** Israel's territory. H995+928
2Ch 20:22 and Mount Seir who *were* **i** Judah, H995+4200
Hab 3:16 of calamity to come on the nation **i** us. H1574

INVALID (2)

Jn 5: 5 there *had been an* **i** for *G2400+1877+3836+819*
Jn 5: 7 the **i** replied, "I have no one to help me *G820*

INVENT (1) [INVENTED]

Ro 1:30 boastful; *they* **i** ways of doing evil *G2388*

INVENTED (1) [INVENT]

2Ch 26:15 he made devices **i** for use on the H4742+3110

INVENTORY (1)

Ezr 1: 9 This was the **i**: gold dishes 30 silver H5031

INVEST (1)

Ecc 11: 2 **I** in seven ventures, yes, in eight H5989+2750

INVESTIGATE (5) [INVESTIGATED, INVESTIGATION]

Dt 13:14 must inquire, probe and **i** it thoroughly. H8626
Dt 17: 4 attention, then *you must* **i** it thoroughly. H2011
Ezr 10:16 tenth month they sat down to **i** the cases, H2011
Ecc 7:25 to **i** and to search out wisdom and the H9365
Ac 25:20 I was at a loss how to **i** such matters; so I *G2428*

INVESTIGATED (4) [INVESTIGATE]

Ex 9: 7 Pharaoh **i** and found that not even one of H8938
Jdg 6:29 When *they* **carefully i**, they H2011+2256+1335
Est 2:23 when the report **was i** and found to be H1335
Lk 1: 3 *since I myself have* carefully **i** everything *G4158*

INVESTIGATION (2) [INVESTIGATE]

Dt 19:18 The judges *must* **make** *a* thorough **i**, and if H2011
Ac 25:26 as a result of this **i** I may have something *G374*

INVISIBLE (5)

Ro 1:20 creation of the world God's **i** *qualities*— *G548*
Col 1:15 The Son is the image of the **i** God, the *G548*
Col 1:16 on earth, visible and **i**, whether thrones *G548*
1Ti 1:17 immortal, **i**, the only God, be *G548*
Heb 11:27 persevered because he saw him who is **i**. *G548*

INVITATION (1) [INVITE]

2Sa 11:13 *At* David's **i**, he ate and drank with him H7924

INVITE (16) [INVITATION, INVITED, INVITES, INVITING]

Ex 2:20 **I** him to have something to eat. H7924
Ex 34:15 *they will* **i** you and you will eat their H7924
Jdg 14:15 *Did you* **i** us here to steal our property?" H7924
1Sa 16: 3 **I** Jesse to the sacrifice, and I will show you H7924

1Ki 1:10 but *he did* not i Nathan the prophet or H7924
1Ki 1:26 your servant Solomon *he did* not i. H7924
Job 1: 4 and *they would* i their three H8938+2256+7924
Pr 18: 6 them strife, and their mouths i a beating. H7924
Jer 35: 2 family and i them to come to one H1819
Zec 3:10 day each of you *will* i your neighbor to H7924
Mt 22: 9 street corners and i to the banquet G2813
Mt 25:38 did we see you a stranger and **i** you **in,** G5251
Mt 25:43 I was a stranger and *you did* not i me **in,** G5251
Lk 14:12 dinner, *do* not i your friends, your G5888
Lk 14:12 they *may* i you **back** and so you will be G511
Lk 14:13 you give a banquet, i the poor, the G2813

INVITED (37) [INVITE]

Ge 31:54 the hill country and i his relatives to a H7924
Nu 25: 2 *who* i them to the sacrifices to their gods H7924
1Sa 9:13 afterward, those *who are* i will eat. H7924
1Sa 9:22 them at the head of those *who* **were i**— H7924
1Sa 9:24 from the time I said, '*I have* i guests. H7924
1Sa 16: 5 his sons and i them to the sacrifice. H7924
2Sa 13:23 he i all the king's sons to come there. H7924
2Sa 15:11 *They had* **been i as guests** and went quite H7924
1Ki 1: 9 *He* i all his brothers, the king's sons, and H7924
1Ki 1:19 sheep, and *has* i all the king's sons H7924
1Ki 1:19 but *he has* not i Solomon your servant. H7924
1Ki 1:25 *He has* i all the king's sons, the H7924
Est 5:12 person Queen Esther i to accompany the H995
Est 5:12 And she *has* i me along with the king H7924
Zep 1: 7 he has consecrated *those* he *has* i. H7924
Mt 22: 3 servants *to* those *who had been* i to the G2813
Mt 22: 4 'Tell those *who have been* i that I have G2813
Mt 22: 8 those *I* i did not deserve to come. G2813
Mt 22:14 "For many are i, but few are chosen." G3105
Mt 25:35 to drink, I was a stranger and *you* i me **in,** G5251
Lk 7:36 *When* one of the Pharisees i Jesus to G2263
Lk 7:39 the Pharisee who *had* i him saw this, G2813
Lk 11:37 a Pharisee i him to eat with him G2263
Lk 14: 8 distinguished than you may have been i. G2813
Lk 14: 9 the **host** *who* i both of you will come and G2813
Lk 14:10 But when *you are* i, take the lowest place G2813
Lk 14:16 a great banquet and i many guests. G2813
Lk 14:17 his servant to tell those *who had been* i, G2813
Lk 14:24 one of those who *were* i will get a taste of G2813
Jn 2: 2 his disciples *had* also *been* i to the G2813
Ac 8:31 So *he* i Philip to come up and sit with him G4151
Ac 10:23 Then Peter i the men **into** the house to be G1657
Ac 13:42 *the people* i them to speak further about G4151
Ac 16:15 were baptized, *she* i us to her home. G4151
Ac 18:26 *they* i him **to** *their* **home** and explained to G4689
Ac 28:14 sisters who i *us* to spend a week with G4151
Rev 19: 9 are those *who are* i to the wedding G2813

INVITES (5) [INVITE]

Pr 9: 7 Whoever corrects a mocker i insults H4374
Pr 10:14 knowledge, but the mouth of a fool i ruin. H7940
Pr 17:19 whoever builds a high gate i destruction. H1335
Lk 14: 8 "When someone i *you* to a wedding feast G2813
1Co 10:27 If an unbeliever i you to a meal and you G2813

INVITING (1) [INVITE]

2Ch 30: 1 i them to come to the temple of the LORD in NDT

INVOKE (8) [INVOKED, INVOKES, INVOKING]

Ex 23:13 *Do* not i the names of other gods; do not H2349
Dt 29:19 oath and *they* i **a blessing on themselves,** H1385
Jos 23: 7 *do* not i the names of their gods or swear H2349
2Sa 14:11 "Then *let* the king i the LORD his God to H2349
Isa 48: 1 of the LORD and i the God of Israel— H2349
Jer 4: 2 the nations *will* i **blessings** by him and in H1385
Jer 44:26 Egypt *will* ever again i my H7924+928+7023
Ac 19:13 evil spirits tried *to* i the name of the Lord G3951

INVOKED (2) [INVOKE]

Hos 2:17 her lips; no longer *will* their names **be i**. H2349
Eph 1:21 every name *that is* i, not only in the G3951

INVOKES (1) [INVOKE]

Isa 65:16 Whoever **i a blessing** in the land will do H1385

INVOKING (1) [INVOKE]

Job 31:30 to sin by i a curse *against* their life— H8626

INVOLVE (2) [INVOLVED, INVOLVES, INVOLVING]

2Ki 3:13 king of Israel, "Why do you want to i me? H4200
Jn 2: 4 "Woman, **why do** you i me?" G5515+5516+2779

INVOLVED (7) [INVOLVE]

Ex 24:14 anyone **i in** a dispute can go to them." H1251
Ex 28:38 he will bear the **guilt** *i in* the sacred gifts AIT
Nu 15:26 all the people were **i in** the unintentional H928
Dt 19: 3 Determine the **distances** *i* and divide into AIT
Dt 19:17 the two people **i in** the dispute must stand H4200
Ac 23:13 More than forty men were **i in** this plot. G4472
Ac 24:18 with me, nor was I **i in** any disturbance. G3552

INVOLVES (1) [INVOLVE]

Ac 18:15 But since *it* i questions about words and G1639

INVOLVING (3) [INVOLVE]

Nu 25:18 in the Peor incident i their sister Kozbi, H6584
2Sa 3: 8 you accuse me of an **offense** *i* this woman! AIT
1Ki 21: 1 was an incident i a vineyard belonging NDT

INWARD (2) [INWARDLY]

2Sa 5: 9 area around it, from the terraces **i**. H1074+2025
Eze 40:16 the openings all around faced **i**. H7163

INWARDLY (5) [INWARD]

Mt 7:15 clothing, but **i** they are ferocious wolves. G2277
Ro 2:29 is a Jew who is one **i**; G1877+3836+3220
Ro 8:23 groan **i** as we wait eagerly for our G1877+1571
2Co 4:16 **i** we are being renewed day by G3836+2276
2Co 11:29 Who is led into sin, and I *do* not *i* **burn**? AIT

INWARDS (KJV) INTERNAL ORGANS

IPHDEIAH (1)

1Ch 8:25 **I** and Penuel were the sons of Shashak. H3635

IPHTAH (1) [IPHTAH EL]

Jos 15:43 **I**, Ashnah, Nezib, H3652

IPHTAH EL (2) [IPHTAH]

Jos 19:14 ended at the Valley of **I**. H3654
Jos 19:27 touched Zebulun and the Valley of **I** H3654

IR (1) [IR NAHASH, IR SHEMESH, REHOBOTH IR]

1Ch 7:12 Huppites were the descendants of **I**, H6553

IR NAHASH (1) [NAHASH]

1Ch 4:12 Tehinnah the father of **I**. H6560

IR SHEMESH (1)

Jos 19:41 Zorah, Eshtaol, **I**, H6561

IRA (6)

2Sa 20:26 **I** the Jairite was David's priest. H6562
2Sa 23:26 the Paltite, **I** son of Ikkesh from Tekoa H6562
2Sa 23:38 **I** the Ithrite, Gareb the Ithrite H6562
1Ch 11:28 **I** son of Ikkesh from Tekoa, Abiezer from H6562
1Ch 11:40 **I** the Ithrite, Gareb the Ithrite, H6562
1Ch 27: 9 was **I** the son of Ikkesh the Tekoite. H6562

IRAD (2)

Ge 4:18 To Enoch was born **I**, and Irad was the H6563
Ge 4:18 and **I** was the father of Mehujael H6563

IRAM (2)

Ge 36:43 Magdiel and **I**. These were the chiefs of H6566
1Ch 1:54 Magdiel and **I**. These were the chiefs of H6566

IRI (1)

1Ch 7: 7 Jerimoth and **I**, heads of families— H6565

IRIJAH (2)

Jer 37:13 whose name was **I** son of Shelemiah, the H3713
Jer 37:14 But **I** would not listen to him; instead, he H3713

IRON (95) [IRON-SMELTING, IRONS, NECK-IRONS]

Ge 4:22 all kinds of tools out of bronze and **i**. H1366
Lev 26:19 sky above you like **i** and the ground H1366
Nu 31:22 silver, bronze, **i**, tin, lead H1366
Nu 35:16 someone a fatal blow with an **i** object, H1366
Dt 3:11 was decorated with **i** and was more than H1366
Dt 8: 9 where the rocks are **i** and you can dig H1366
Dt 27: 5 Do not use any **i tool** on them. H1366
Dt 28:23 will be bronze, the ground beneath you **i**. H1366
Dt 28:48 He will put an **i** yoke on your neck until he H1366
Dt 33:25 bolts of your gates will be **i** and bronze, H1366
Jos 6:19 of bronze and **i** are sacred to the LORD H1366
Jos 6:24 articles of bronze and **i** into the treasury of H1366
Jos 8:31 on which no **i tool** had been used. H1366
Jos 17:16 live in the plain have chariots fitted with **i**, H1366
Jos 17:18 chariots fitted with **i** and though they are H1366
Jos 19:38 **I**, Migdal El, Horem, Beth Anath and Beth H3712
Jos 22: 8 bronze and **i**, and a great quantity H1366
Jdg 1:19 because they had chariots fitted with **i**. H1366
Jdg 4: 3 chariots fitted with **i** and had cruelly H1366
Jdg 4:13 his nine hundred chariots fitted with **i**. H1366
1Sa 17: 7 its **i** point weighed six hundred H1366
2Sa 12:31 labor with saws and with **i** picks and axes, H1366
2Sa 23: 7 thorns uses a **tool of i** or the shaft of a H1366
1Ki 6: 7 chisel or any other **i** tool was heard at the H1366
1Ki 22:11 of Kenaanah had made **i** horns and he H1366
2Ki 6: 5 the **i axhead** fell into the water. H1366
2Ki 6: 6 threw it there, and made the **i** float. H1366
1Ch 20: 3 labor with saws and with **i** picks and axes. H1366
1Ch 22: 3 a large amount of **i** to make nails for the H1366
1Ch 22:14 of bronze and **i** too great to be weighed, H1366
1Ch 22:16 bronze and **i**—craftsmen beyond H1366
1Ch 29: 2 **i** for the iron and wood for the wood H1366
1Ch 29: 2 iron for the **i** and wood for the wood H1366
1Ch 29: 7 a hundred thousand talents of **i**. H1366
2Ch 2: 7 silver, bronze and **i**, and in purple, H1366
2Ch 2:14 silver, bronze and **i**, stone and wood, H1366
2Ch 18:10 son of Kenaanah had made **i** horns, H1366
2Ch 24:12 also workers in **i** and bronze to repair H1366
Job 19:24 they were inscribed with an **i** tool on lead, H1366
Job 20:24 Though he flees from an **i** weapon, H1366
Job 28: 2 **I** is taken from the earth, and copper is H1366
Job 40:18 tubes of bronze, its limbs like rods of **i**. H1366
Job 41:27 **I** it treats like straw and bronze like rotten H1366
Ps 2: 9 You will break them with a rod of **i**; you H1366
Ps 107:10 darkness, prisoners suffering in **i chains**, H1366
Ps 107:16 gates of bronze and cuts through bars of **i**. H1366
Ps 149: 8 their nobles with shackles of **i**, H1366
Pr 27:17 As **i** sharpens iron, so one person H1366
Pr 27:17 As iron sharpens **i**, so one person H1366
Isa 45: 2 gates of bronze and cut through bars of **i**. H1366
Isa 48: 4 your neck muscles were **i**, your forehead H1366
Isa 60:17 bring you gold, and silver in place of **i**. H1366
Isa 60:17 bring you bronze, and **i** in place of stones. H1366
Jer 1:18 an **i** pillar and a bronze wall to stand H1366
Jer 6:28 They are bronze and **i**; they all act H1366
Jer 15:12 "Can a man break **i**—iron from the north H1366
Jer 15:12 a man break iron—**i** from the north—or H1366
Jer 17: 1 "Judah's sin is engraved with an **i** tool H1366
Jer 28:13 in its place you will get a yoke of **i**. H1366
Jer 28:14 I will put an **i** yoke on the necks of all H1366
Eze 4: 3 Then take an **i** pan, place it as an iron H1366
Eze 4: 3 place it as an **i** wall between you and the H1366
Eze 22:18 **i** and lead left inside a furnace. H1366
Eze 22:20 **i**, lead and tin are gathered into a H1366
Eze 27:12 exchanged silver, **i**, tin and lead for your H1366
Eze 27:19 wrought **i**, cassia and calamus H1366
Da 2:33 its legs of **i**, its feet partly of iron and A10591
Da 2:33 its feet partly of **i** and partly of baked A10591
Da 2:34 on its feet of **i** and clay and smashed A10591
Da 2:35 Then the **i**, the clay, the bronze, the silver A10591
Da 2:40 kingdom, strong as **i**—for iron breaks A10591
Da 2:40 **i** breaks and smashes everything A10591
Da 2:40 as **i** breaks things to pieces A10591
Da 2:41 were partly of baked clay and partly of **i**, A10591
Da 2:41 will have some of the strength of **i** in it, A10591
Da 2:41 even as you saw **i** mixed with clay. A10591
Da 2:42 As the toes were partly **i** and partly clay A10591
Da 2:43 just as you saw the **i** mixed with baked A10591
Da 2:43 any more than **i** mixes with clay. A10591
Da 2:45 a rock that broke the **i**, the bronze, A10591
Da 4:15 bound with **i** and bronze, remain A10591
Da 4:23 bound with **i** and bronze, in the A10591
Da 5: 4 silver, of bronze, **i**, wood and stone. A10591
Da 5:23 gold, of bronze, **i**, wood and stone A10591
Da 7: 7 It had large **i** teeth; it crushed and A10591
Da 7:19 with its **i** teeth and bronze claws A10591
Am 1: 3 Gilead with sledges having **i** teeth, H1366
Mic 4:13 I will give you horns of **i**; I will give you H1366
Ac 12:10 came to the **i** gate leading to the G4971
1Ti 4: 2 *have been* **seared as with a hot i**. G3013
Rev 2:27 rule them with an **i** scepter and will dash G4971
Rev 9: 9 had breastplates like breastplates *of* **i**, G4971
Rev 12: 5 "will rule all the nations with an **i** scepter." G4971
Rev 18:12 costly wood, bronze, **i** and marble; G4970
Rev 19:15 "He will rule them with an **i** scepter." G4971

IRON-SMELTING (3) [IRON]

Dt 4:20 you and brought you out of the **i** furnace, H1366
1Ki 8:51 brought out of Egypt, out of that **i** furnace. H1366
Jer 11: 4 them out of Egypt, out of the **i** furnace. H1366

IRONS (2) [IRON]

Ps 105:18 feet with shackles, his neck was put in **i**, H1366
Mk 5: 4 chains apart and broke the **i on** his **feet**. G4267

IRPEEL (1)

Jos 18:27 **I**, Taralah, H3761

IRRATIONAL (1)

Jude 10 by instinct—as **i** animals do—will destroy G263

IRRELIGIOUS (1)

1Ti 1: 9 the unholy and **i**, for those who kill G1013

IRRESISTIBLE (1)

Da 11:10 will sweep on like an **i** flood and carry the H6296

IRREVERENT (1)

2Sa 6: 7 against Uzzah because of his **i act**; H8915

IRREVOCABLE (1)

Ro 11:29 God's gifts and his call are **i**. G294

IRRIGATED (1) [IRRIGATE]

Dt 11:10 planted your seed and **i** it by foot as in a H9197

IRRITATE (1)

1Sa 1: 6 rival kept provoking her in order to **i** her. H8307

IRU (1)

1Ch 4:15 son of Jephunneh: **I**, Elah and Naam. H6564

IS (7121) [BE] See Index of Articles Etc.

ISAAC (133) [ISAAC'S]

Ge 17:19 bear you a son, and you will call him **I**. H3663
Ge 17:21 But my covenant I will establish with **I** H3663
Ge 21: 3 gave the name **I** to the son Sarah H3663
Ge 21: 4 When his son **I** was eight days old H3663
Ge 21: 5 years old when his son **I** was born to him. H3663
Ge 21: 8 on the day **I** was weaned Abraham H3663
Ge 21:10 share in the inheritance with my son **I**." H3663
Ge 21:12 because it is through **I** that your offspring H3663
Ge 22: 2 whom you love—**I**—and go to the region H3663
Ge 22: 3 with him two of his servants and his son **I**. H3663
Ge 22: 6 burnt offering and placed it on his son **I**, H3663
Ge 22: 7 **I** spoke up and said to his father Abraham H3663
Ge 22: 7 **I** said, "but where is the lamb for the burnt NDT
Ge 22: 9 He bound his son **I** and laid him on the H3663
Ge 24: 4 own relatives and get a wife for my son **I**." H3663
Ge 24:14 one you have chosen for your servant **I**. H3663
Ge 24:62 Now **I** had come from Beer Lahai Roi, for H3663

Ge	24:64	Rebekah also looked up and saw **I**.	H3663
Ge	24:66	Then the servant told **I** all he had done.	H3663
Ge	24:67	**I** brought her into the tent of his mother	H3663
Ge	24:67	**I** was comforted after his mother's	H3663
Ge	25: 5	Abraham left everything he owned to **I**.	H3663
Ge	25: 6	away from his son **I** to the land of the	H3663
Ge	25: 9	His sons **I** and Ishmael buried him in the	H3663
Ge	25:11	God blessed his son **I**, who then lived	H3663
Ge	25:19	of the family line of Abraham's son **I**.	H3663
Ge	25:19	Abraham became the father of **I**,	H3663
Ge	25:20	**I** was forty years old when he married	H3663
Ge	25:21	**I** prayed to the LORD on behalf of his wife	H3663
Ge	25:26	**I** was sixty years old when Rebekah gave	H3663
Ge	25:28	**I**, who had a taste for wild game, loved	H3663
Ge	26: 1	**I** went to Abimelek king of the	H3663
Ge	26: 2	The LORD appeared to **I** and said, "Do not	H2257S
Ge	26: 6	So **I** stayed in Gerar.	H3663
Ge	26: 8	When **I** had been there a long time	H2257S
Ge	26: 8	a window and saw **I** caressing his wife	H3663
Ge	26: 9	So Abimelek summoned **I** and said, "She	H3663
Ge	26: 9	**I** answered him, "Because I thought I	H3663
Ge	26:12	**I** planted crops in that land and the same	H3663
Ge	26:16	Then Abimelek said to **I**, "Move away	H3663
Ge	26:17	So **I** moved away from there and	H3663
Ge	26:18	**I** reopened the wells that had been dug in	H3663
Ge	26:20	Gerar quarreled with those of **I** and said,	H3663
Ge	26:25	**I** built an altar there and called on the	NDT
Ge	26:27	**I** asked them, "Why have you come to me	H3663
Ge	26:30	**I** then made a feast for them, and they ate	NDT
Ge	26:31	Then **I** sent them on their way, and they	H3663
Ge	26:35	were a source of grief to **I** and Rebekah.	H3663
Ge	27: 1	When **I** was old and his eyes were so	H3663
Ge	27: 2	**I** said, "I am now an old man and don't	NDT
Ge	27: 5	was listening as **I** spoke to his son Esau.	H3663
Ge	27:20	**I** asked his son, "How did you find it so	H3663
Ge	27:21	Then **I** said to Jacob, "Come near so I can	H3663
Ge	27:22	Jacob went close to his father **I**, who	H3663
Ge	27:26	Then his father **I** said to him, "Come here	H3663
Ge	27:27	When **I** caught the smell of his clothes, he	NDT
Ge	27:30	After **I** finished blessing him, and Jacob	H3663
Ge	27:32	His father **I** asked him, "Who are you?"	H3663
Ge	27:33	**I** trembled violently and said, "Who was it	H3663
Ge	27:37	**I** answered Esau, "I have made him lord	H3663
Ge	27:39	His father **I** answered him, "Your dwelling	H3663
Ge	27:46	Then Rebekah said to **I**, "I'm disgusted	H3663
Ge	28: 1	So **I** called for Jacob and blessed him	H3663
Ge	28: 5	Then **I** sent Jacob on his way, and he went	H3663
Ge	28: 6	Esau learned that **I** had blessed Jacob	H3663
Ge	28: 8	the Canaanite women were to his father **I**;	H3663
Ge	28:13	of your father Abraham and the God of **I**.	H3663
Ge	31:18	to go to his father **I** in the land of Canaan.	H3663
Ge	31:42	the God of Abraham and the Fear of **I**,	H3663
Ge	31:53	in the name of the Fear of his father **I**.	H3663
Ge	32: 9	father Abraham, God of my father **I**, LORD,	H3663
Ge	35:12	gave to Abraham and **I** I also give to you,	H3663
Ge	35:27	came home to his father **I** in Mamre,	H3663
Ge	35:27	where Abraham and **I** had stayed.	H3663
Ge	35:28	**I** lived a hundred and eighty years.	H3663
Ge	46: 1	sacrifices to the God of his father **I**.	H3663
Ge	48:15	fathers Abraham and **I** walked faithfully,	H3663
Ge	48:16	the names of my fathers Abraham and **I**,	H3663
Ge	49:31	there **I** and his wife Rebekah were buried	H3663
Ge	50:24	on oath to Abraham, **I** and Jacob.	H3663
Ex	2:24	with Abraham, with **I** and with Jacob.	H3663
Ex	3: 6	the God of **I** and the God of Jacob."	H3663
Ex	3:15	the God of **I** and the God of Jacob	H3663
Ex	3:16	God of Abraham, **I** and Jacob—appeared	H3663
Ex	4: 5	the God of **I** and the God of Jacob	H3663
Ex	6: 3	to **I** and to Jacob as God Almighty	H3663
Ex	6: 8	to give to Abraham, to **I** and to Jacob.	H3663
Ex	32:13	servants Abraham, **I** and Israel, to whom	H3663
Ex	33: 1	on oath to Abraham, **I** and Jacob, saying,	H3663
Lev	26:42	my covenant with **I** and my covenant with	H3663
Nu	32:11	on oath to Abraham, **I** and Jacob—	H3663
Dt	1: 8	to Abraham, **I** and Jacob—and to their	H3663
Dt	6:10	to Abraham, **I** and Jacob, to give	H3663
Dt	9: 5	to your fathers, to Abraham, **I** and Jacob.	H3663
Dt	9:27	your servants Abraham, **I** and Jacob.	H3663
Dt	29:13	to your fathers, Abraham, **I** and Jacob.	H3663
Dt	30:20	to your fathers, Abraham, **I** and Jacob.	H3663
Dt	34: 4	oath to Abraham, **I** and Jacob when I said	H3663
Jos	24: 3	him many descendants. I gave him **I**,	H3663
Jos	24: 4	to **I** I gave Jacob and Esau. I assigned	H3663
1Ki	18:36	the God of Abraham, **I** and Israel, let it be	H3663
2Ki	13:23	his covenant with Abraham, **I** and Jacob.	H3663
1Ch	1:28	The sons of Abraham: **I** and Ishmael.	H3663
1Ch	1:34	Abraham was the father of **I**. The sons of	H3663
1Ch	1:34	The sons of **I**: Esau and Israel.	H3663
1Ch	16:16	with Abraham, the oath he swore to **I**.	H3663
1Ch	29:18	our fathers Abraham, **I** and Israel, keep	H3663
2Ch	30: 6	the God of Abraham, **I** and Israel, that he	H3663
Ps	105: 9	with Abraham, the oath he swore to **I**.	H3773
Jer	33:26	descendants of Abraham, **I** and Jacob.	H3773
Am	7: 9	"The high places of **I** will be destroyed	H3773
Am	7:16	preaching against the descendants of **I**.	H3773
Mt	1: 2	Abraham was the father of **I**, Isaac the	*G2693*
Mt	1: 2	the father of Isaac, **I** the father of Jacob	*G2693*
Mt	8:11	**I** and Jacob in the kingdom of heaven.	*G2693*
Mt	22:32	of Abraham, the God of **I**, and the God of	*G2693*
Mk	12:26	of Abraham, the God *of* **I**, and the God of	*G2693*
Lk	3:34	of Jacob, the son *of* **I**, the son of Abraham	*G2693*
Lk	13:28	**I** and Jacob and all the prophets in the	*G2693*
Lk	20:37	the God *of* **I**, and the God of	*G2693*
Ac	3:13	God of Abraham, **I** and Jacob, the God	*G2693*
Ac	7: 8	the father of **I** and circumcised him	*G2693*
Ac	7: 8	Later **I** became the father of Jacob, and	*G2693*
Ac	7:32	the God of Abraham, **I** and Jacob.	*G2693*
Ro	9: 7	"It is through **I** that your offspring will be	*G2693*
Ro	9:10	at the same time *by* our father **I**.	*G2693*
Gal	4:28	sisters, like **I**, are children of promise.	*G2693*
Heb	11: 9	in tents, as did **I** and Jacob, who were	*G2693*
Heb	11:17	God tested him, offered **I** as a sacrifice.	*G2693*
Heb	11:18	"It is through **I** that your offspring will be	*G2693*
Heb	11:19	speaking he did receive **I** back from death.	*G899*
Heb	11:20	By faith **I** blessed Jacob and Esau in	*G2693*
Jas	2:21	when he offered his son **I** on the altar?	*G2693*

ISAAC'S (2) [ISAAC]

Ge	26:19	**I** servants dug in the valley and	H3663
Ge	26:32	That day **I** servants came and told him	H3663

ISAIAH (53)

2Ki	19: 2	sackcloth, to the prophet **I** son of Amoz.	H3833
2Ki	19: 5	When King Hezekiah's officials came to **I**,	H3833
2Ki	19: 6	**I** said to them, "Tell your master, 'This is	H3833
2Ki	19:20	Then **I** son of Amoz sent a message to	H3833
2Ki	20: 1	The prophet **I** son of Amoz went to him	H3833
2Ki	20: 4	Before **I** had left the middle court, the	H3833
2Ki	20: 7	Then **I** said, "Prepare a poultice of figs."	H3833
2Ki	20: 8	Hezekiah had asked **I**, "What will be the	H3833
2Ki	20: 9	**I** answered, "This is the LORD's sign to you	H3833
2Ki	20:11	Then the prophet **I** called on the LORD	H3833
2Ki	20:14	Then **I** the prophet went to King Hezekiah	H3833
2Ki	20:16	Then **I** said to Hezekiah, "Hear the word	H3833
2Ch	26:22	recorded by the prophet **I** son of Amoz.	H3833
2Ch	32:20	the prophet **I** son of Amoz cried out	H3833
2Ch	32:32	vision of the prophet **I** son of Amoz in the	H3833
Isa	1: 1	Jerusalem that **I** son of Amoz saw	H3833
Isa	2: 1	This is what **I** son of Amoz saw	H3833
Isa	7: 3	Then the LORD said to **I**, "Go out, you and	H3833
Isa	7:13	Then **I** said, "Hear now, you house of David	NDT
Isa	13: 1	against Babylon that **I** son of Amoz saw:	H3833
Isa	20: 2	the LORD spoke through **I** son of Amoz.	H3833
Isa	20: 3	"Just as my servant **I** has gone stripped	H3833
Isa	37: 2	sackcloth, to the prophet **I** son of Amoz.	H3833
Isa	37: 5	When King Hezekiah's officials came to **I**,	H3833
Isa	37: 6	**I** said to them, "Tell your master, 'This is	H3833
Isa	37:21	Then **I** son of Amoz sent a message to	H3833
Isa	38: 1	The prophet **I** son of Amoz went to him	H3833
Isa	38: 4	Then the word of the LORD came to **I**:	H3833
Isa	38:21	**I** had said, "Prepare a poultice of figs	H3833
Isa	39: 3	Then **I** the prophet went to King Hezekiah	H3833
Isa	39: 5	Then **I** said to Hezekiah, "Hear the word	H3833
Mt	3: 3	who was spoken of through the prophet **I**:	*G2480*
Mt	4:14	what was said through the prophet **I**:	*G2480*
Mt	8:17	what was spoken through the prophet **I**:	*G2480*
Mt	12:17	what was spoken through the prophet **I**:	*G2480*
Mt	13:14	In them is fulfilled the prophecy *of* **I**:	*G2480*
Mt	15: 7	**I** was right when he prophesied about you	*G2480*
Mk	1: 2	as it is written in **I** the prophet: "I will send	*G2480*
Mk	7: 6	"**I** was right when he prophesied about	*G2480*
Lk	3: 4	in the book of the words *of* **I** the prophet:	*G2480*
Lk	4:17	scroll of the prophet **I** was handed to him.	*G2480*
Jn	1:23	John replied in the words of **I** the prophet	*G2480*
Jn	12:38	This was to fulfill the word *of* **I** the prophet:	*G2480*
Jn	12:39	not believe, because, as **I** says elsewhere:	*G2480*
Jn	12:41	**I** said this because he saw Jesus' glory	*G2480*
Ac	8:28	chariot reading the **Book of I** the prophet.	*G2480*
Ac	8:30	heard the man reading **I** the prophet.	*G2480*
Ac	28:25	when he said through **I** the prophet:	*G2480*
Ro	9:27	**I** cries out concerning Israel: "Though the	*G2480*
Ro	9:29	It is just as **I** said previously: "Unless the	*G2480*
Ro	10:16	For **I** says, "Lord, who has believed our	*G2480*
Ro	10:20	And **I** boldly says, "I was found by those	*G2480*
Ro	15:12	And again, **I** says, "The Root of Jesse will	*G2480*

ISCAH (NIV84) ISKAH

ISCARIOT (11)

Mt	10: 4	Simon the Zealot and Judas **I**, who	*G2697*
Mt	26:14	the one called Judas **I**—went to the chief	*G2697*
Mk	3:19	Judas **I**, who betrayed him.	*G2697*
Mk	14:10	Then Judas **I**, one of the Twelve, went to	*G2697*
Lk	6:16	of James, and Judas **I**, who became a	*G2697*
Lk	22: 3	called **I**, one of the Twelve.	*G2697*
Jn	6:71	the son of Simon **I**, who, though one of	*G2697*
Jn	12: 4	of his disciples, Judas **I**, who was later to	*G2697*
Jn	13: 2	the son of Simon **I**, to betray Jesus.	*G2697*
Jn	13:26	he gave it to Judas, the son of Simon **I**.	*G2697*
Jn	14:22	Then Judas (not Judas **I**) said, "But, Lord	*G2697*

ISH-BOSHETH (14)

2Sa	2: 8	had taken **I** son of Saul and brought him	H410
2Sa	2:10	**I** son of Saul was forty years old when he	H410
2Sa	2:12	together with the men of **I** son of Saul, left	H410
2Sa	2:15	twelve men for Benjamin and **I** son of Saul	H410
2Sa	3: 7	And **I** said to Abner, "Why did you sleep	NDT
2Sa	3: 8	was very angry because of what **I** said.	H410
2Sa	3:11	**I** did not dare to say another word to Abner	NDT
2Sa	3:14	David sent messengers to **I** son of Saul,	H410
2Sa	3:15	So **I** gave orders and had her taken away	H410
2Sa	4: 1	When **I** son of Saul heard that Abner had	NDT
2Sa	4: 5	set out for the house of **I**, and they arrived	H410
2Sa	4: 8	brought the head of **I** to David at Hebron	H410
2Sa	4: 8	"Here is the head of **I** son of Saul, your	H410
2Sa	4:12	they took the head of **I** and buried it in	H410

ISHBAH (1)

1Ch	4:17	Shammai and **I** the father of Eshtemoa.	H3786

ISHBAK (2)

Ge	25: 2	Jokshan, Medan, Midian, **I** and Shuah.	H3791
1Ch	1:32	Jokshan, Medan, Midian, **I** and Shuah.	H3791

ISHBI-BENOB (1)

2Sa	21:16	And **I**, one of the descendants of Rapha	H3787

ISHHOD (1)

1Ch	7:18	His sister Hammoleketh gave birth to **I**	H412

ISHI (4)

1Ch	2:31	The son of Appaim: **I**, who was the father	H3831
1Ch	4:20	The descendants of **I**: Zoheth and	H3831
1Ch	4:42	Uzziel, the sons of **I**, invaded the hill	H3831
1Ch	5:24	**I**, Eliel, Azriel, Jeremiah, Hodaviah	H3831

ISHIAH (6)

1Ch	7: 3	Obadiah, Joel and **I**. All five of them were	H3807
1Ch	12: 6	Elkanah, **I**, Azarel, Joezer and Jashobeam	H3808
1Ch	23:20	Micah the first and **I** the second.	H3807
1Ch	24:21	Rehabiah, from his sons: **I** was the first.	H3807
1Ch	24:25	The brother of Micah: **I**; from the sons of	H3807
1Ch	24:25	from the sons of **I**: Zechariah.	H3807

ISHIJAH (1)

Ezr	10:31	Eliezer, **I**, Malkijah, Shemaiah	H3807

ISHMA (1)

1Ch	4: 3	sons of Etam: Jezreel, **I** and Idbash. Their	H3816

ISHMAEL (48) [ISHMAELITE, ISHMAELITES]

Ge	16:11	You shall name him **I**, for the LORD has	H3817
Ge	16:15	gave the name **I** to the son she had	H3817
Ge	16:16	years old when Hagar bore him **I**.	H3817
Ge	17:18	"If only **I** might live under your blessing!"	H3817
Ge	17:20	And as for **I**, I have heard you: I will surely	H3817
Ge	17:23	Abraham took his son **I** and all those born	H3817
Ge	17:25	his son **I** was thirteen;	H3817
Ge	17:26	Abraham and his son **I** were both	H3817
Ge	25: 9	His sons Isaac and **I** buried him in the	H3817
Ge	25:12	of the family line of Abraham's son **I**,	H3817
Ge	25:13	These are the names of the sons of **I**	H3817
Ge	25:13	Nebaioth the firstborn of **I**, Kedar, Adbeel	H3817
Ge	25:16	These were the sons of **I**, and these are	H3817
Ge	25:17	**I** lived a hundred and thirty-seven years	H3817
Ge	28: 9	so he went to **I** and married Mahalath, the	H3817
Ge	28: 9	daughter of **I** son of Abraham,	H3817
Ge	36: 3	Basemath daughter of **I** and sister of	H3817
2Ki	25:23	Gedaliah at Mizpah—**I** son of Nethaniah	H3817
2Ki	25:25	however, **I** son of Nethaniah, the son of	H3817
1Ch	1:28	The sons of Abraham: Isaac and **I**.	H3817
1Ch	1:29	Nebaioth the firstborn of **I**, Kedar, Adbeel	H3817
1Ch	1:31	Kedemah. These were the sons of **I**.	H3817
1Ch	8:38	Azrikam, Bokeru, **I**, Sheariah, Obadiah	H3817
1Ch	9:44	Azrikam, Bokeru, **I**, Sheariah, Obadiah	H3817
2Ch	19:11	Zebadiah son of **I**, the leader of the	H3817
2Ch	23: 1	son of Jeroham, **I** son of Jehohanan	H3817
Ezr	10:22	Elioenai, Maaseiah, **I**, Nethanel, Jozabad	H3817
Jer	40: 8	Gedaliah at Mizpah—**I** son of Nethaniah	H3817
Jer	40:14	Ammonites has sent **I** son of Nethaniah	H3817
Jer	40:15	"Let me go and kill **I** son of Nethaniah	H3817
Jer	40:16	What you are saying about **I** is not true."	H3817
Jer	41: 1	In the seventh month **I** son of Nethaniah	H3817
Jer	41: 2	**I** son of Nethaniah and the ten men who	H3817
Jer	41: 3	**I** also killed all the men of Judah who	H3817
Jer	41: 6	**I** son of Nethaniah went out from Mizpah	H3817
Jer	41: 7	**I** son of Nethaniah and the men who	H3817
Jer	41: 8	But ten of them said to **I**, "Don't kill us	H3817
Jer	41: 9	**I** son of Nethaniah filled it with the dead	H3817
Jer	41:10	**I** made captives of all the rest of the	H3817
Jer	41:10	**I** son of Nethaniah took them captive and	H3817
Jer	41:11	all the crimes **I** son of Nethaniah had	H3817
Jer	41:12	men and went to fight **I** son of Nethaniah.	H3817
Jer	41:13	When all the people **I** had with him saw	H3817
Jer	41:14	All the people **I** had taken captive at	H3817
Jer	41:15	But **I** son of Nethaniah and eight of his	H3817
Jer	41:16	had recovered from **I** son of Nethaniah	H3817
Jer	41:16	son of Nethaniah after **I** had assassinated	NDT
Jer	41:18	of them because **I** son of Nethaniah had	H3817

ISHMAELITE (3) [ISHMAEL]

2Sa	17:25	of Jether, an **I** who had married Abigail	H3818
1Ch	2:17	of Amasa, whose father was Jether the **I**.	H3818
1Ch	27:30	Obil the **I** was in charge of the camels	H3818

ISHMAELITES (6) [ISHMAEL]

Ge	37:25	saw a caravan of **I** coming from Gilead.	H3818
Ge	37:27	sell him to the **I** and not lay our hands	H3818
Ge	37:28	him for twenty shekels of silver to the **I**,	H3818
Ge	39: 1	bought him from the **I** who had taken him	H3818
Jdg	8:24	the custom of the **I** to wear gold earrings	H3818
Ps	83: 6	the tents of Edom and the **I**, of Moab and	H3818

ISHMAIAH (2)

1Ch	12: 4	**I** the Gibeonite, a mighty warrior	H3819
1Ch	27:19	over Zebulun: **I** son of Obadiah; over	H3820

ISHMERAI (1)

1Ch	8:18	**I**, Izliah and Jobab were the sons of	H3821

ISHPAH (1)
1Ch 8:16 **I** and Joha were the sons of Beriah. H3834

ISHPAN (1)
1Ch 8:22 **I**, Eber, Eliel, H3836

ISHVAH (2)
Ge 46:17 sons of Asher: Imnah, **I**, Ishvi and Beriah H3796
1Ch 7:30 sons of Asher: Imnah, **I**, Ishvi and Beriah H3796

ISHVI (4) [ISHVITE]
Ge 46:17 Imnah, Ishvah, **I** and Beriah. Their H3798
Nu 26:44 the Imnite clan; through **I**, the Ishvite clan; H3798
1Sa 14:49 sons were Jonathan, **I** and Malki-Shua. H3798
1Ch 7:30 Imnah, Ishvah, **I** and Beriah. Their H3798

ISHVITE (1) [ISHVI]
Nu 26:44 through Ishvi, the **I** clan; through Beriah H3799

ISKAH (1)
Ge 11:29 of Haran, the father of both Milkah and **I**. H3576

ISLAND (13) [ISLANDERS, ISLANDS]
Isa 23: 2 you people of the **i** and you merchants of H362
Isa 23: 6 over to Tarshish; wail, you people of the **i**. H362
Ac 13: 6 through the whole **i** until they came to G3762
Ac 27:14 the Northeaster, swept down from **the i**. G899S
Ac 27:16 to the lee of a **small i** called Cauda, G3761
Ac 27:26 we must run aground on some **i**. G3762
Ac 28: 1 we found out that the **i** was called Malta. G3762
Ac 28: 7 to Publius, the chief official *of* the **i**. G3762
Ac 28: 9 of the sick on the **i** came and were cured. G3762
Ac 28:11 sea in a ship that had wintered in the **i**— G3762
Rev 1: 9 was on the **i** of Patmos because of the G3762
Rev 6:14 every mountain and **i** was removed from G3762
Rev 16:20 Every **i** fled away and the mountains could G3762

ISLANDERS (2) [ISLAND]
Ac 28: 2 The **i** showed us unusual kindness. G975
Ac 28: 4 When the **i** saw the snake hanging from his G975

ISLANDS (15) [ISLAND]
Isa 11:11 from the **i** *of* the Mediterranean. H362
Isa 24:15 the God of Israel, in the **i** *of* the sea. H362
Isa 40:15 he weighs the **i** as though they were fine H362
Isa 41: 1 silent before me, you **i**! Let the nations H362
Isa 41: 5 The **i** have seen it and fear; the ends of the H362
Isa 42: 4 In his teaching the **i** will put their hope." H362
Isa 42:10 all that is in it, you **i**, and all who live in H362
Isa 42:12 to the LORD and proclaim his praise in the **i**. H362
Isa 42:15 I will turn rivers into **i** and dry up the pools. H362
Isa 49: 1 Listen to me, you **i**; hear this, you distant H362
Isa 51: 5 The **i** will look to me and wait in hope H362
Isa 59:18 to his foes; he will repay the **i** their due. H362
Isa 60: 9 Surely the **i** look to me; in the lead are the H362
Isa 66:19 to the distant **i** that have not heard of H362
Eze 26:18 the **i** in the sea are terrified at your H362

ISMAKIAH (1)
2Ch 31:13 **I**, Mahath and Benaiah were H3577

ISN'T (33) [BE, NOT] See Index of Articles Etc.

ISOLATE (8) [ISOLATED]
Lev 13: 4 the priest *is to* **i** the affected person for H6037
Lev 13: 5 he *is to* **i** them for another seven days. H6037
Lev 13:11 *He* is not *to* **i** them, because they are H6037
Lev 13:21 then the priest *is to* **i** them for seven days. H6037
Lev 13:26 then the priest *is to* **i** them for seven days. H6037
Lev 13:31 then the priest *is to* **i** the affected person H6037
Lev 13:50 affected area and **i** the article for seven H6037
Lev 13:54 Then *he is to* **i** it for another seven days H6037

ISOLATED (1) [ISOLATE]
Lev 13:33 the priest *is to* **keep** them **i** another seven H6037

ISRAEL (1793) [ISRAEL'S, ISRAELITE, ISRAELITE'S, ISRAELITES, ISRAELITES']
Ge 32:28 longer be Jacob, but **I**, because you have H3776
Ge 34: 7 an outrageous thing in **I** by sleeping with H3776
Ge 35:10 be called Jacob; your name will be **I**." H3776
Ge 35:10 name will be Israel." So he named him **I**. H3776
Ge 35:21 **I** moved on again and pitched his tent H3776
Ge 35:22 While **I** was living in that region, Reuben H3776
Ge 35:22 concubine Bilhah, and **I** heard of it. H3776
Ge 37: 3 Now **I** loved Joseph more than any of his H3776
Ge 37:13 **I** said to Joseph, "As you know, your H3776
Ge 43: 6 **I** asked, "Why did you bring this trouble H3776
Ge 43: 8 Then Judah said to **I** his father, "Send the H3776
Ge 43:11 Then their father **I** said to them, "If it must H3776
Ge 45:21 So the sons of **I** did this. Joseph gave H3776
Ge 45:28 And **I** said, "I'm convinced! My son Joseph H3776
Ge 46: 1 So **I** set out with all that was his, and H3776
Ge 46: 2 And God spoke to **I** in a vision at night H3776
Ge 46: 8 These are the names of the sons of **I** H3776
Ge 46:29 went to Goshen to meet his father **I**. H3776
Ge 46:30 **I** said to Joseph, "Now I am ready to die H3776
Ge 47:29 When the time drew near for **I** to die, he H3776
Ge 47:31 **I** worshiped as he leaned on the top H3776
Ge 48: 2 **I** rallied his strength and sat up on the H3776
Ge 48: 8 When **I** saw the sons of Joseph, he asked H3776
Ge 48: 9 Then **I** said, "Bring them to me so I may NDT
Ge 48:11 **I** said to Joseph, "I never expected to see H3776
Ge 48:14 But **I** reached out his right hand and put it H3776
Ge 48:20 "In your name will **I** pronounce this H3776
Ge 48:21 Then **I** said to Joseph, "I am about to die H3776
Ge 49: 2 sons of Jacob; listen to your father **I**. H3776
Ge 49: 7 them in Jacob and disperse them in **I**. H3776
Ge 49:16 his people as one of the tribes of **I**. H3776
Ge 49:24 because of the Shepherd, the Rock of **I**, H3776
Ge 49:28 All these are the twelve tribes of **I**, and H3776
Ge 50: 2 in his service to embalm his father **I**. H3776
Ex 1: 1 names of the sons of **I** who went to Egypt H3776
Ex 3:16 assemble the elders of **I** and say to them H3776
Ex 3:18 "The elders of **I** will listen to you. H3776
Ex 4:22 is what the LORD says: **I** is my firstborn son, H3776
Ex 5: 1 "This is what the LORD, the God of **I**, says: H3776
Ex 5: 2 that I should obey him and let **I** go? H3776
Ex 5: 2 not know the LORD and I will not let **I** go." H3776
Ex 6:14 firstborn son of **I** were Hanok and Pallu H3776
Ex 9: 4 the livestock of **I** and that of Egypt, H3776
Ex 11: 7 makes a distinction between Egypt and **I**. H3776
Ex 12: 3 whole community of **I** that on the tenth H3776
Ex 12: 6 the community of **I** must slaughter them H3776
Ex 12:15 the seventh must be cut off from **I**. H3776
Ex 12:19 it must be cut off from the community of **I**. H3776
Ex 12:21 all the elders of **I** and said to them, H3776
Ex 12:47 whole community of **I** must celebrate it. H3776
Ex 14:20 coming between the armies of Egypt and **I**. H3776
Ex 14:30 day the LORD saved **I** from the hands of the H3776
Ex 14:30 **I** saw the Egyptians lying dead on the H3776
Ex 15:22 Then Moses led **I** from the Red Sea and H3776
Ex 16:31 The people of **I** called the bread manna H3776
Ex 17: 5 of the elders of **I** and take in your hand H3776
Ex 17: 6 did this in the sight of the elders of **I**. H3776
Ex 18: 1 had done for Moses and for his people **I**, H3776
Ex 18: 1 how the LORD had brought **I** out of Egypt. H3776
Ex 18: 9 LORD had done for **I** in rescuing them from H3776
Ex 18:11 to those who had treated **I** arrogantly." H2157S
Ex 18:12 with all the elders of **I** to eat a meal with H3776
Ex 18:25 capable men from all **I** and made them H3776
Ex 19: 2 **I** camped there in the desert in front H3776
Ex 19: 3 what you are to tell the people of **I**: H3776
Ex 24: 1 Abihu, and seventy of the elders of **I**. H3776
Ex 24: 4 pillars representing the twelve tribes of **I**. H3776
Ex 24: 9 the seventy elders of **I** went up H3776
Ex 24:10 saw the God of **I**. Under his feet was H3776
Ex 28: 9 on them the names of the sons of **I** H3776
Ex 28:11 names of the sons of **I** on the two stones H3776
Ex 28:12 as memorial stones for the sons of **I**. H3776
Ex 28:21 one for each of the names of the sons of **I**, H3776
Ex 28:29 names of the sons of **I** over his heart on H3776
Ex 32: 4 are your gods, **I**, who brought you up H3776
Ex 32: 8 are your gods, **I**, who brought you up H3776
Ex 32:13 Abraham, Isaac and **I**, to whom you swore H3776
Ex 32:27 "This is what the LORD, the God of **I**, says: H3776
Ex 34:23 before the Sovereign LORD, the God of **I**. H3776
Ex 34:27 made a covenant with you and with **I**." H3776
Ex 39: 6 a seal with the names of the sons of **I**. H3776
Ex 39: 7 as memorial stones for the sons of **I**, H3776
Ex 39:14 one for each of the names of the sons of **I**, H3776
Lev 9: 1 Aaron and his sons and the elders of **I**. H3776
Lev 16:17 household and the whole community of **I**. H3776
Lev 17: 9 LORD must be cut off from the people of **I**. NDT
Lev 19: 2 assembly of **I** and say to them: H1201+3776
Lev 20: 2 residing in **I** who sacrifices any of H3776
Lev 22:18 an Israelite or a foreigner residing in **I**— H3776
Nu 1: 3 all the men in **I** who are twenty years old H3776
Nu 1:16 They were the heads of the clans of **I**. H3776
Nu 1:20 of Reuben the firstborn son of **I**: H3776
Nu 1:44 Aaron and the twelve leaders of **I**, H3776
Nu 3:13 I set apart for myself every firstborn in **I** H3776
Nu 3:45 in place of all the firstborn of **I**, H1201+3776
Nu 4:46 the leaders of **I** counted all the H3776
Nu 7: 2 Then the leaders of **I**, the heads of H3776
Nu 8:17 Every firstborn male in **I**, whether H1201+3776
Nu 8:18 place of all the firstborn sons in **I**. H1201+3776
Nu 10: 4 the heads of the clans of **I**—are to H3776
Nu 10:29 the LORD has promised good things to **I**." H3776
Nu 10:36 to the countless thousands of **I**. H3776
Nu 11:30 the elders of **I** returned to the camp. H3776
Nu 15:30 must be cut off from the people of **I**. NDT
Nu 16: 9 you that the God of **I** has separated you H3776
Nu 16:25 Abiram, and the elders of **I** followed him. H3776
Nu 18:14 "Everything in **I** that is devoted to the LORD H3776
Nu 18:21 all the tithes in **I** as their inheritance in H3776
Nu 19:13 They must be cut off from **I**. Because the H3776
Nu 20:14 "This is what your brother **I** says: You H3776
Nu 20:21 their territory, **I** turned away from them. H3776
Nu 21: 1 heard that **I** was coming along the road to H3776
Nu 21: 2 Then **I** made this vow to the LORD: "If you H3776
Nu 21:17 Then **I** sang this song: "Spring up, O well H3776
Nu 21:21 **I** sent messengers to say to Sihon king of H3776
Nu 21:23 But Sihon would not let **I** pass through his H3776
Nu 21:23 marched out into the wilderness against **I**. H3776
Nu 21:23 When he reached Jahaz, he fought with **I**. H3776
Nu 21:24 **I**, however, put him to the sword and took H3776
Nu 21:25 **I** captured all the cities of the Amorites H3776
Nu 21:31 So **I** settled in the land of the Amorites. H3776
Nu 22: 2 of Zippor saw all that **I** had done to the H3776
Nu 23: 7 'curse Jacob for me; come, denounce **I**. H3776
Nu 23:10 of Jacob or number even a fourth of **I**? H3776
Nu 23:21 is seen in Jacob, no misery observed in **I**. H3776
Nu 23:23 against Jacob, no evil omens against **I**. H3776
Nu 23:23 It will now be said of Jacob and of **I**, 'See H3776
Nu 24: 1 saw that it pleased the LORD to bless **I**, H3776
Nu 24: 2 looked out and saw **I** encamped tribe by H3776
Nu 24: 5 your tents, Jacob, your dwelling places, **I**! H3776
Nu 24:17 out of Jacob; a scepter will rise out of **I**. H3776
Nu 24:18 will be conquered, but **I** will grow strong. H3776
Nu 25: 1 While **I** was staying in Shittim, the men H3776
Nu 25: 3 So **I** yoked themselves to the Baal of Peor H3776
Nu 25: 4 LORD's fierce anger may turn away from **I**." H3776
Nu 25: 6 assembly of **I** while they were H1201+3776
Nu 26: 2 who are able to serve in the army of **I**." H3776
Nu 26: 5 of Reuben, the firstborn son of **I**, were: H3776
Nu 26:51 number of the men of **I** was 601,730. H3776
Nu 30: 1 said to the heads of the tribes of **I**: H1201+3776
Nu 31: 4 thousand men from each of the tribes of **I**." H3776
Nu 31: 5 were supplied from the clans of **I**. H3776
Nu 32: 4 the LORD subdued before the people of **I**— H3776
Nu 32:13 burned against **I** and he made them H3776
Nu 32:14 making the LORD even more angry with **I**. H3776
Nu 32:22 from your obligation to the LORD and to **I**. H3776
Nu 36: 7 No inheritance in **I** is to pass from H1201+3776
Dt 1: 1 Moses spoke to all **I** in the wilderness H3776
Dt 1:38 because he will lead **I** to inherit it. H3776
Dt 2:12 just as **I** did in the land the LORD gave H3776
Dt 4: 1 **I**, hear the decrees and laws I am H3776
Dt 5: 1 Moses summoned all **I** and said: Hear H3776
Dt 5: 1 **I**, the decrees and laws I declare in H3776
Dt 6: 3 **I**, and be careful to obey so that it H3776
Dt 6: 4 O **I**: The LORD our God, the LORD is H3776
Dt 9: 1 **I**: You are now about to cross the H3776
Dt 10:12 And now, **I**, what does the LORD your God H3776
Dt 11: 6 in the middle of all **I** and swallowed them H3776
Dt 13:11 Then all **I** will hear and be afraid, and no H3776
Dt 17: 4 this detestable thing has been done in **I**, H3776
Dt 17:12 You must purge the evil from **I**. H3776
Dt 17:20 reign a long time over his kingdom in **I**. H3776
Dt 18: 1 to have no allotment or inheritance with **I**. H3776
Dt 18: 6 towns anywhere in **I** where he is living, H3776
Dt 19:13 You must purge from **I** the guilt of H3776
Dt 20: 3 "Hear, **I**: Today you are H3776
Dt 21: 8 Accept this atonement for your people **I** H3776
Dt 21:21 All **I** will hear of it and be afraid. H3776
Dt 22:21 outrageous thing in **I** by being H3776
Dt 22:22 You must purge the evil from **I**. H3776
Dt 25: 6 his name will not be blotted out from **I**. H3776
Dt 25: 7 refuses to carry on his brother's name in **I**. H3776
Dt 25:10 shall be known in **I** as The Family of the H3776
Dt 26:15 bless your people **I** and the land you have H3776
Dt 27: 1 the elders of **I** commanded the H3776
Dt 27: 9 the Levitical priests said to all **I**, H3776
Dt 27: 9 said to all Israel, "Be silent, **I**, and listen! H3776
Dt 27:14 to all the people of **I** in a loud voice: H3776
Dt 29:10 officials, and all the other men of **I**, H3776
Dt 29:21 out from all the tribes of **I** for disaster, H3776
Dt 31: 1 went out and spoke these words to all **I**: H3776
Dt 31: 7 said to him in the presence of all **I**, H3776
Dt 31: 9 of the LORD, and to all the elders of **I**. H3776
Dt 31:11 when all **I** comes to appear before the H3776
Dt 31:30 in the hearing of the whole assembly of **I**: H3776
Dt 32: 8 according to the number of the sons of **I**. H3776
Dt 32:45 finished reciting all these words to all **I**, H3776
Dt 32:52 the land I am giving to the people of **I**." H3776
Dt 33: 5 assembled, along with the tribes of **I**. H3776
Dt 33:10 your precepts to Jacob and your law to **I**. H3776
Dt 33:21 and his judgments concerning **I**. H3776
Dt 33:28 So **I** will live in safety; Jacob will dwell H3776
Dt 33:29 Blessed are you, **I**! Who is like you, H3776
Dt 34:10 no prophet has risen in **I** like Moses H3776
Dt 34:12 deeds that Moses did in the sight of all **I**. H3776
Jos 3: 7 will begin to exalt you in the eyes of all **I**, H3776
Jos 3:12 choose twelve men from the tribes of **I** H3776
Jos 3:17 while all **I** passed by until the whole H3776
Jos 4: 7 be a memorial to the people of **I** forever." H3776
Jos 4:14 LORD exalted Joshua in the sight of all **I**; H3776
Jos 4:22 '**I** crossed the Jordan on dry ground. H3776
Jos 6:18 make the camp of **I** liable to destruction H3776
Jos 6:23 put them in a place outside the camp of **I**. H3776
Jos 7: 1 the LORD's anger burned against **I**. H1201+3776
Jos 7: 6 The elders of **I** did the same, and H3776
Jos 7: 8 now that **I** has been routed by its enemies H3776
Jos 7:11 **I** has sinned; they have violated my H3776
Jos 7:13 this is what the LORD, the God of **I**, says: H3776
Jos 7:13 things among you, **I**. You cannot stand H3776
Jos 7:15 has done an outrageous thing in **I**! H3776
Jos 7:16 morning Joshua had **I** come forward by H3776
Jos 7:19 to the LORD, the God of **I**, and honor him. H3776
Jos 7:20 sinned against the LORD, the God of **I**. H3776
Jos 7:24 together with all **I**, took Achan son of H3776
Jos 7:25 Then all **I** stoned him, and after they had H3776
Jos 8:10 the leaders of **I** marched before them H3776
Jos 8:14 the morning to meet **I** in battle at a H3776
Jos 8:15 Joshua and all **I** let themselves be driven H3776
Jos 8:17 in Ai or Bethel who did not go after **I**. H3776
Jos 8:17 left the city open and went in pursuit of **I**. H3776
Jos 8:21 Joshua and all **I** saw that the ambush H3776
Jos 8:22 **I** cut them down, leaving them neither NDT
Jos 8:24 When **I** had finished killing all the men of H3776
Jos 8:27 But **I** did carry off for themselves the H3776
Jos 8:30 Ebal an altar to the LORD, the God of **I**, H3776
Jos 8:33 gave instructions to bless the people of **I**. H3776
Jos 8:35 did not read to the whole assembly of **I**, H3776
Jos 9: 2 to wage war against Joshua and **I**. H3776
Jos 9:18 an oath to them by the LORD, the God of **I**. H3776

Jos 9:19 the God of I, and we cannot touch H3776
Jos 10: 1 of peace with I and had become their H3776
Jos 10:10 LORD threw them into confusion before I, H3776
Jos 10:10 I pursued them along the road going up to NDT
Jos 10:11 As they fled before I on the road down H3776
Jos 10:12 LORD gave the Amorites over to I, H1201+3776
Jos 10:12 said to the LORD in the presence of I: H3776
Jos 10:14 Surely the LORD was fighting for I! H3776
Jos 10:15 returned with all I to the camp at Gilgal. H3776
Jos 10:24 all the men of I and said to the army H3776
Jos 10:29 Then Joshua and all I with him moved on H3776
Jos 10:31 Then Joshua and all I with him moved on H3776
Jos 10:34 Then Joshua and all I with him moved on H3776
Jos 10:36 Then Joshua and all I with him went up H3776
Jos 10:38 Then Joshua and all I with him turned H3776
Jos 10:40 the LORD, the God of I, had commanded. H3776
Jos 10:42 the LORD, the God of I, fought for Israel. H3776
Jos 10:42 the LORD, the God of Israel, fought for I. H3776
Jos 10:43 returned with all I to the camp at Gilgal. H3776
Jos 11: 5 at the Waters of Merom to fight against I. H3776
Jos 11: 6 I will hand all of them, slain, over to I. H3776
Jos 11: 8 the LORD gave them into the hand of I H3776
Jos 11:13 Yet I did not burn any of the cities built on H3776
Jos 11:16 the mountains of I with their foothills, H3776
Jos 11:20 their hearts to wage war against I, H3776
Jos 11:21 of Judah, and from all the hill country of I. H3776
Jos 11:23 it as an inheritance to I according to their H3776
Jos 12: 7 to the tribes of I according to their tribal H3776
Jos 13: 6 allocate this land to I for an inheritance, H3776
Jos 13:14 the LORD, the God of I, are their H3776
Jos 13:33 the LORD, the God of I, is their inheritance H3776
Jos 14: 1 tribal clans of I allotted to them. H1201+3776
Jos 14:10 while I moved about in the wilderness. H3776
Jos 14:14 the LORD, the God of I, wholeheartedly. H3776
Jos 19:51 tribal clans of I assigned by lot at H1201+3776
Jos 21: 1 of the other tribal families of I H1201+3776
Jos 21:43 So the LORD gave I all the land he had H3776
Jos 21:45 of all the LORD's good promises to I failed; H3776
Jos 22:12 whole assembly of I gathered at H1201+3776
Jos 22:14 one from each of the tribes of I, each the H3776
Jos 22:16 you break faith with the God of I like this? H3776
Jos 22:18 be angry with the whole community of I. H3776
Jos 22:20 wrath come on the whole community of I? H3776
Jos 22:21 replied to the heads of the clans of I: H3776
Jos 22:22 And let I know! If this has been H3776
Jos 22:24 have to do with the LORD, the God of I? H3776
Jos 23: 1 the LORD had given I rest from all their H3776
Jos 23: 2 summoned all I—their elders, leaders H3776
Jos 24: 1 assembled all the tribes of I at Shechem. H3776
Jos 24: 1 judges and officials of I, and they H3776
Jos 24: 2 "This is what the LORD, the God of I, says: H3776
Jos 24: 9 prepared to fight against I, he sent for H3776
Jos 24:23 your hearts to the LORD, the God of I." H3776
Jos 24:31 I served the LORD throughout the lifetime H3776
Jos 24:31 everything the LORD had done for I. H3776
Jdg 1:28 When I became strong, they pressed the H3776
Jdg 2: 7 the great things the LORD had done for I. H3776
Jdg 2:10 the LORD nor what he had done for I. H3776
Jdg 2:14 In his anger against I the LORD gave them H3776
Jdg 2:15 Whenever I went out to fight, the hand of NDT
Jdg 2:20 the LORD was very angry with I and said, H3776
Jdg 2:22 use them to test I and see whether they H3776
Jdg 3: 8 LORD burned against I so that he sold H3776
Jdg 3:12 gave Eglon king of Moab power over I. H3776
Jdg 3:13 Eglon came and attacked I, and they took H3776
Jdg 3:30 That day Moab was made subject to I, and H3776
Jdg 3:31 with an oxgoad. He too saved I. H3776
Jdg 4: 4 of Lappidoth, was leading I at that time. H3776
Jdg 4: 6 "The LORD, the God of I, commands you: H3776
Jdg 5: 2 "When the princes in I take the lead H3776
Jdg 5: 3 will praise the LORD, the God of I, in song. H3776
Jdg 5: 5 of Sinai, before the LORD, the God of I. H3776
Jdg 5: 7 Villagers in I would not fight; they held H3776
Jdg 5: 7 until I arose, a mother in I. H3776
Jdg 5: 8 was seen among forty thousand in I. H3776
Jdg 5:11 the LORD, the victories of his villagers in I. H3776
Jdg 6: 4 did not spare a living thing for I, H3776
Jdg 6: 8 "This is what the LORD, the God of I, says: H3776
Jdg 6:14 you have and save I out of Midian's hand. H3776
Jdg 6:15 Gideon replied, "but how can I save I? H3776
Jdg 6:36 "If you will save I by my hand as you have H3776
Jdg 6:37 will know that you will save I by my hand, H3776
Jdg 7: 2 their hands, or I would boast against me H3776
Jdg 7:15 returned to the camp of I and called out, H3776
Jdg 8:27 All I prostituted themselves by worshiping H3776
Jdg 9:22 Abimelek had governed I three years, H3776
Jdg 10: 1 of Puah, the son of Dodo, rose to save I. H3776
Jdg 10: 2 He led I twenty-three years; then he died H3776
Jdg 10: 3 Jair of Gilead, who led I twenty-two years. H3776
Jdg 10: 9 Ephraim; I was in great distress. H3776
Jdg 11: 4 the Ammonites were fighting against I, H3776
Jdg 11:13 "When I came up out of Egypt H3776
Jdg 11:15 I did not take the land of Moab or the H3776
Jdg 11:16 I went through the wilderness to the Red H3776
Jdg 11:17 Then I sent messengers to the king of H3776
Jdg 11:17 he refused. So I stayed at Kadesh. H3776
Jdg 11:19 "Then I sent messengers to Sihon king of H3776
Jdg 11:20 did not trust I to pass through his territory. H3776
Jdg 11:20 encamped at Jahaz and fought with I. H3776
Jdg 11:21 the LORD, the God of I, gave Sihon and his H3776
Jdg 11:21 I took over all the land of the Amorites H3776
Jdg 11:23 the LORD, the God of I, has driven the H3776
Jdg 11:23 the Amorites out before his people I, H3776
Jdg 11:25 he ever quarrel with I or fight with them? H3776
Jdg 11:26 three hundred years I occupied Heshbon, H3776
Jdg 11:33 Thus I subdued Ammon. H1201+3776
Jdg 11:40 the young women of I go out for four days H3776
Jdg 12: 7 Jephthah led I six years. Then Jephthah H3776
Jdg 12: 8 After him, Ibzan of Bethlehem led I. H3776
Jdg 12: 9 outside his clan. Ibzan led I seven years. H3776
Jdg 12:11 Elon the Zebulunite led I ten years. H3776
Jdg 12:13 Abdon son of Hillel, from Pirathon, led I. H3776
Jdg 12:14 on seventy donkeys. He led I eight years. H3776
Jdg 13: 5 lead in delivering I from the hands of the H3776
Jdg 14: 4 at that time they were ruling over I.) H3776
Jdg 15:20 Samson led I for twenty years in the days H3776
Jdg 16:31 He had led I twenty years. H3776
Jdg 17: 6 In those days I had no king; everyone did H3776
Jdg 18: 1 In those days I had no king. And in those H3776
Jdg 18: 1 into an inheritance among the tribes of I. H3776
Jdg 18:19 a tribe and clan in I as priest rather than H3776
Jdg 18:29 who was born to I—though the city used H3776
Jdg 19: 1 In those days I had no king. Now a Levite H3776
Jdg 19:29 parts and sent them into all the areas of I. H3776
Jdg 20: 1 Then all I from Dan to Beersheba H1201+3776
Jdg 20: 2 of the tribes of I took their places in H3776
Jdg 20: 6 this lewd and outrageous act in I. H3776
Jdg 20:10 of every hundred from all the tribes of I, H3776
Jdg 20:10 deserve for this outrageous act done in I." H3776
Jdg 20:12 The tribes of I sent messengers H3776
Jdg 20:13 them to death and purge the evil from I." H3776
Jdg 20:17 I, apart from Benjamin, mustered H408+3776
Jdg 20:29 Then I set an ambush around Gibeah. H3776
Jdg 20:33 All the men of I moved from their places H3776
Jdg 20:35 The LORD defeated Benjamin before I, and H3776
Jdg 20:36 Now the men of I had given way before H3776
Jdg 20:48 The men of I went back to Benjamin and H3776
Jdg 21: 1 The men of I had taken an oath at H3776
Jdg 21: 3 God of I," they cried, "why has this H3776
Jdg 21: 3 they cried, "why has this happened to I? H3776
Jdg 21: 3 should one tribe be missing from I today?" H3776
Jdg 21: 5 all the tribes of I has failed to assemble H3776
Jdg 21: 6 "Today one tribe is cut off from I," they H3776
Jdg 21: 8 one of the tribes of I failed to assemble H3776
Jdg 21:15 LORD had made a gap in the tribes of I. H3776
Jdg 21:17 "so that a tribe of I will not be wiped out. H3776
Jdg 21:25 In those days I had no king; everyone did H3776
Ru 2:12 the LORD, the God of I, under whose wings H3776
Ru 4: 7 Now in earlier times in I, for the H3776
Ru 4: 7 the method of legalizing transactions in I.) H3776
Ru 4:11 who together built up the family of I. H3776
Ru 4:14 May he become famous throughout I! H3776
1Sa 1:17 may the God of I grant you what you H3776
1Sa 2:22 were doing to all I and how they slept H3776
1Sa 2:28 out of all the tribes of I to be my priest, H3776
1Sa 2:29 of every offering made by my people I? H3776
1Sa 2:30 the LORD, the God of I, declares: H3776
1Sa 2:32 Although good will be done to I, no one H3776
1Sa 3:11 to do something in I that will make the H3776
1Sa 3:20 And all I from Dan to Beersheba H3776
1Sa 4: 1 And Samuel's word came to all I. H3776
1Sa 4: 2 Philistines deployed their forces to meet I, H3776
1Sa 4: 2 I was defeated by the Philistines H3776
1Sa 4: 3 the elders of I asked, "Why did the H3776
1Sa 4: 5 all I raised such a great shout that the H3776
1Sa 4:10 I lost thirty thousand foot soldiers. H3776
1Sa 4:17 news replied, "I fled before the Philistines H3776
1Sa 4:18 he was heavy. He had led I forty years. H3776
1Sa 4:21 "The Glory has departed from I" H3776
1Sa 4:22 "The Glory has departed from I, for the ark H3776
1Sa 5: 7 "The ark of the god of I must not stay here H3776
1Sa 5: 8 shall we do with the ark of the god of I?" H3776
1Sa 5: 8 the ark of the god of I moved to Gath." H3776
1Sa 5: 8 So they moved the ark of the God of I. H3776
1Sa 5:10 the ark of the god of I around to us to kill H3776
1Sa 5:11 "Send the ark of the god of I away; let it H3776
1Sa 6: 3 "If you return the ark of the god of I, do H3776
1Sa 7: 2 all the people of I turned back to the H3776
1Sa 7: 5 "Assemble all I at Mizpah, and I will H3776
1Sa 7: 6 serving as leader of I at Mizpah. H1201+3776
1Sa 7: 7 heard that I had assembled at H1201+3776
1Sa 7:10 drew near to engage I in battle. H3776
1Sa 7:11 The men of I rushed out of Mizpah and H3776
1Sa 7:14 had captured from I were restored to H3776
1Sa 7:14 captured from Israel were restored to I, H3776
1Sa 7:14 I delivered the neighboring territory H3776
1Sa 7:14 was peace between I and the Amorites. H3776
1Sa 7:16 to Mizpah, judging I in all those places. H3776
1Sa 7:17 and there he also held court for I. H3776
1Sa 8: 4 So all the elders of I gathered together H3776
1Sa 9: 2 man as could be found anywhere in I, H3776
1Sa 9: 9 Formerly in I, if someone went to inquire H3776
1Sa 9:16 Anoint him ruler over my people I; he will H3776
1Sa 9:20 And to whom is all the desire of I turned H3776
1Sa 9:21 from the smallest tribe of I, and is not my H3776
1Sa 10:17 the people of I to the LORD at Mizpah NDT
1Sa 10:18 "This is what the LORD, the God of I, says: H3776
1Sa 10:18 'I brought I up out of Egypt, and I H3776
1Sa 10:20 When Samuel had all I come forward by H3776
1Sa 11: 2 one of you and so bring disgrace on all I." H3776
1Sa 11: 3 so we can send messengers throughout I; H3776
1Sa 11: 7 the pieces by messengers throughout I, H3776
1Sa 11: 8 the men of I numbered three hundred H3776
1Sa 11:13 for this day the LORD has rescued I. H3776
1Sa 12: 1 Samuel said to all I, "I have listened to H3776
1Sa 13: 1 he reigned over I forty- two years. H3776
1Sa 13: 2 Saul chose three thousand men from I H3776
1Sa 13: 4 So all I heard the news: "Saul has H3776
1Sa 13: 4 now I has become obnoxious to the H3776
1Sa 13: 5 The Philistines assembled to fight I, with H3776
1Sa 13:13 your kingdom over I for all time. H3776
1Sa 13:19 could be found in the whole land of I, H3776
1Sa 13:20 So all I went down to the Philistines to H3776
1Sa 14:12 LORD has given them into the hand of I." H3776
1Sa 14:23 So on that day the LORD saved I, and the H3776
1Sa 14:39 As surely as the LORD who rescues I lives H3776
1Sa 14:41 the LORD, the God of I, "Why have you not H3776
1Sa 14:41 if the men of I are at fault, respond H3776
1Sa 14:45 brought about this great deliverance in I? H3776
1Sa 14:47 After Saul had assumed rule over I, he H3776
1Sa 14:48 delivering I from the hands of those who H3776
1Sa 15: 1 sent to anoint you king over his people I; H3776
1Sa 15: 2 what they did to I when they waylaid H3776
1Sa 15:17 not become the head of the tribes of I? H3776
1Sa 15:17 The LORD anointed you king over I. H3776
1Sa 15:26 the LORD has rejected you as king over I!" H3776
1Sa 15:28 torn the kingdom of I from you today and H3776
1Sa 15:29 He who is the Glory of I does not lie or H3776
1Sa 15:30 the elders of my people and before I; H3776
1Sa 15:35 that he had made Saul king over I. H3776
1Sa 16: 1 since I have rejected him as king over I? H3776
1Sa 17: 8 stood and shouted to the ranks of I, H3776
1Sa 17:10 "This day I defy the armies of I! H3776
1Sa 17:19 all the men of I in the Valley of Elah, H3776
1Sa 17:21 I and the Philistines were drawing up their H3776
1Sa 17:25 He comes out to defy I. The king will give H3776
1Sa 17:25 will exempt his family from taxes in I." H3776
1Sa 17:26 removes this disgrace from I? H3776
1Sa 17:45 the God of the armies of I, whom you H3776
1Sa 17:46 world will know that there is a God in I. H3776
1Sa 17:52 Then the men of I and Judah surged H3776
1Sa 18: 6 from all the towns of I to meet King Saul H3776
1Sa 18:16 But all I and Judah loved David, because H3776
1Sa 18:18 what is my family or my clan in I, that H3776
1Sa 19: 5 The LORD won a great victory for all I, and H3776
1Sa 20:12 by the LORD, the God of I, that I will surely H3776
1Sa 23:10 God of I, your servant has heard H3776
1Sa 23:11 LORD, God of I, tell your servant. H3776
1Sa 23:17 You will be king over I, and I will be H3776
1Sa 24: 2 young men from all I and set out to look H3776
1Sa 24:14 whom has the king of I come out? H3776
1Sa 24:20 that the kingdom of I will be established H3776
1Sa 25: 1 all I assembled and mourned for him; H3776
1Sa 25:30 him and has appointed him ruler over I, H3776
1Sa 25:32 the LORD, the God of I, who has sent you H3776
1Sa 25:34 the LORD, the God of I, lives, who has kept H3776
1Sa 26:15 And who is like you in I? Why didn't you H3776
1Sa 26:20 The king of I has come out to look for a H3776
1Sa 27: 1 give up searching for me anywhere in I, H3776
1Sa 28: 1 gathered their forces to fight against I. H3776
1Sa 28: 3 all I had mourned for him and buried H3776
1Sa 28: 4 Saul gathered all I and set up camp at H3776
1Sa 28:19 will deliver both I and you into the hands H3776
1Sa 28:19 give the army of I into the hands of the H3776
1Sa 29: 1 I camped by the spring in Jezreel. H3776
1Sa 29: 3 who was an officer of Saul king of I? H3776
1Sa 30:25 ordinance for I from that day to this. H3776
1Sa 31: 1 Now the Philistines fought against I; the H3776
2Sa 1:12 army of the LORD and for the nation of I, H3776
2Sa 1:19 on your heights, I. How the mighty have H3776
2Sa 1:24 "Daughters of I, weep for Saul, who H3776
2Sa 2: 9 also over Ephraim, Benjamin and all I. H3776
2Sa 2:10 years old when he became king over I, H3776
2Sa 2:28 they no longer pursued I, nor did they H3776
2Sa 3:10 David's throne over I and Judah from Dan H3776
2Sa 3:12 I will help you bring all I over to you." H3776
2Sa 3:17 conferred with the elders of I and said, H3776
2Sa 3:18 rescue my people I from the hand of the H3776
2Sa 3:19 everything that I and the whole tribe H3776
2Sa 3:21 assemble all I for my lord the king, H3776
2Sa 3:37 people there and all I knew that the king H3776
2Sa 3:38 a great man has fallen in I this day? H3776
2Sa 4: 1 lost courage, and all I became alarmed. H3776
2Sa 5: 1 All the tribes of I came to David at H3776
2Sa 5: 2 were the one who led I on their military H3776
2Sa 5: 2 'You will shepherd my people I, and you H3776
2Sa 5: 3 all the elders of I had come to King David H3776
2Sa 5: 3 and they anointed David king over I. H3776
2Sa 5: 5 he reigned over all I and Judah H3776
2Sa 5:12 him as king over I and had exalted his H3776
2Sa 5:12 his kingdom for the sake of his people I. H3776
2Sa 5:17 that David had been anointed king over I, H3776
2Sa 6: 1 together all the able young men of I— H3776
2Sa 6: 5 David and all I were celebrating H1074+3776
2Sa 6:15 while he and all I were bringing up H1074+3776
2Sa 6:20 "How the king of I has distinguished H3776
2Sa 6:21 me ruler over the LORD's people I— H3776
2Sa 7: 7 I commanded to shepherd my people I, H3776
2Sa 7: 8 appointed you ruler over my people I. H3776
2Sa 7:10 place for my people I and will plant them H3776
2Sa 7:11 I appointed leaders over my people I. H3776
2Sa 7:23 And who is like your people I—the one H3776
2Sa 7:24 your people I as your very own H3776
2Sa 7:26 say, 'The LORD Almighty is God over I! H3776
2Sa 7:27 Almighty, God of I, you have revealed H3776
2Sa 8:15 David reigned over all I, doing what was H3776

I

2Sa 10: 9 of the best troops in **I** and deployed them H3776
2Sa 10:15 saw that they had been routed by **I**, H3776
2Sa 10:17 he gathered all **I**, crossed the Jordan H3776
2Sa 10:18 But they fled before **I**, and David killed H3776
2Sa 10:19 saw that they had been routed by **I**, H3776
2Sa 11:11 "The ark and **I** and Judah are staying in H3776
2Sa 12: 7 the LORD, the God of **I**, says: 'I anointed H3776
2Sa 12: 7 'I anointed you king over **I**, and I H3776
2Sa 12: 8 I gave you all **I** and Judah. And if H3776
2Sa 12:12 this thing in broad daylight before all **I**. H3776
2Sa 13:12 Such a thing should not be done in **I** H3776
2Sa 13:13 would be like one of the wicked fools in **I**. H3776
2Sa 14:25 In all **I** there was not a man so highly H3776
2Sa 15: 2 "Your servant is from one of the tribes of **I**."H3776
2Sa 15: 6 so he stole the hearts of the people of **I**. H3776
2Sa 15:10 throughout the tribes of **I** to say, H3776
2Sa 15:13 of the people of **I** are with Absalom." H3776
2Sa 16:15 all the men of **I** came to Jerusalem, H3776
2Sa 16:18 by all the men of **I**—his I will be, H3776
2Sa 16:21 Then all **I** will hear that you have made H3776
2Sa 16:22 father's concubines in the sight of all **I**. H3776
2Sa 17: 4 to Absalom and to all the elders of **I**. H3776
2Sa 17:10 all **I** knows that your father is a fighter H3776
2Sa 17:11 Let all **I**, from Dan to Beersheba—as H3776
2Sa 17:13 then all **I** will bring ropes to that city H3776
2Sa 17:14 Absalom and all the men of **I** said, "The H3776
2Sa 17:15 the elders of **I** to do such and such, H3776
2Sa 17:24 crossed the Jordan with all the men of **I**. H3776
2Sa 18: 6 army marched out of the city to fight **I**, H3776
2Sa 18:16 the troops stopped pursuing **I**, for H3776
2Sa 19: 9 Throughout the tribes of **I**, all the people H3776
2Sa 19:11 said throughout **I** has reached the king H3776
2Sa 19:22 Should anyone be put to death in **I** today H3776
2Sa 19:22 Don't I know that today I am king over **I**?" H3776
2Sa 19:40 half the troops of **I** had taken the king H3776
2Sa 19:41 Soon all the men of **I** were coming to the H3776
2Sa 19:42 the men of Judah answered the men of **I**, H3776
2Sa 19:43 Then the men of **I** answered the men of H3776
2Sa 19:43 even more forcefully than the men of **I**. H3776
2Sa 20: 1 in Jesse's son! Every man to his tent, **I**!" H3776
2Sa 20: 2 So all the men of **I** deserted David to H3776
2Sa 20:14 all the tribes of **I** to Abel Beth Maakah H3776
2Sa 20:19 We are the peaceful and faithful in **I**. H3776
2Sa 20:19 to destroy a city that is a mother in **I**. H3776
2Sa 21: 2 not a part of **I** but were survivors H1201+3776
2Sa 21: 2 in his zeal for **I** and Judah had H1201+3776
2Sa 21: 4 have the right to put anyone in **I** to death." H3776
2Sa 21: 5 have no place anywhere in **I**, H3776
2Sa 21:15 a battle between the Philistines and **I**. H3776
2Sa 21:17 so that the lamp of **I** will not be H3776
2Sa 21:21 When he taunted **I**, Jonathan son of H3776
2Sa 23: 3 The God of **I** spoke, the Rock of Israel said H3776
2Sa 23: 3 of Israel spoke, the Rock of **I** said to me: H3776
2Sa 24: 1 the anger of the LORD burned against **I**, H3776
2Sa 24: 1 "Go and take a census of **I** and Judah." H3776
2Sa 24: 2 the tribes of **I** from Dan to Beersheba H3776
2Sa 24: 4 of the king to enroll the fighting men of **I**. H3776
2Sa 24: 9 In **I** there were eight hundred thousand H3776
2Sa 24:15 LORD sent a plague on **I** from that morning H3776
2Sa 24:25 and the plague on **I** was stopped. H3776
1Ki 1: 3 searched throughout **I** for a beautiful H3776
1Ki 1:20 the eyes of all **I** are on you, to learn H3776
1Ki 1:30 I swore to you by the LORD, the God of **I**: H3776
1Ki 1:34 the prophet anoint him king over **I**. H3776
1Ki 1:35 appointed him ruler over **I** and Judah." H3776
1Ki 1:48 the God of **I**, who has allowed my H3776
1Ki 2: 4 fail to have a successor on the throne of **I**. H3776
1Ki 2:11 He had reigned forty years over **I**—seven H3776
1Ki 2:15 All **I** looked to me as their king H3776
1Ki 3:28 When all **I** heard the verdict the king had H3776
1Ki 4: 1 So King Solomon ruled over all **I**. H3776
1Ki 4: 7 had twelve district governors over all **I**, H3776
1Ki 4:20 of Judah and **I** were as numerous as H3776
1Ki 4:25 During Solomon's lifetime Judah and **I** H3776
1Ki 5:13 Solomon conscripted laborers from all **I**— H3776
1Ki 6: 1 the fourth year of Solomon's reign over **I**, H3776
1Ki 6:13 will not abandon my people **I**. H3776
1Ki 8: 1 his presence at Jerusalem the elders of **I**, H3776
1Ki 8: 3 When all the elders of **I** had arrived, the H3776
1Ki 8: 5 the entire assembly of **I** that had gathered H3776
1Ki 8:14 whole assembly of **I** was standing there, H3776
1Ki 8:15 the LORD, the God of **I**, who with his own H3776
1Ki 8:16 day I brought my people **I** out of Egypt, H3776
1Ki 8:16 city in any tribe of **I** to have a temple built H3776
1Ki 8:16 I have chosen David to rule my people **I**. H3776
1Ki 8:17 the Name of the LORD, the God of **I**. H3776
1Ki 8:20 my father and now I sit on the throne of **I**, H3776
1Ki 8:20 the Name of the LORD, the God of **I**. H3776
1Ki 8:22 LORD in front of the whole assembly of **I**, H3776
1Ki 8:23 the God of **I**, there is no God like H3776
1Ki 8:25 "Now LORD, the God of **I**, keep for your H3776
1Ki 8:25 to sit before me on the throne of **I**, H3776
1Ki 8:26 And now, God of **I**, let your word that you H3776
1Ki 8:30 of your people **I** when they pray H3776
1Ki 8:33 "When your people **I** have been defeated H3776
1Ki 8:34 sin of your people **I** and bring them back H3776
1Ki 8:36 the sin of your servants, your people **I**. H3776
1Ki 8:38 made by anyone among your people **I**— H3776
1Ki 8:41 to your people **I** but has come from a H3776
1Ki 8:43 as do your own people **I**, and may know H3776
1Ki 8:52 plea and to the plea of your people **I**, H3776
1Ki 8:55 the whole assembly of **I** in a loud voice, H3776
1Ki 8:56 rest to his people **I** just as he promised. H3776
1Ki 8:59 cause of his people **I** according to each H3776
1Ki 8:62 Then the king and all **I** with him offered H3776
1Ki 8:65 at that time, and all **I** with him—a vast H3776
1Ki 8:66 his servant David and his people **I**. H3776
1Ki 9: 5 establish your royal throne over **I** forever, H3776
1Ki 9: 5 fail to have a successor on the throne of **I**. H3776
1Ki 9: 7 then I will cut off **I** from the land I have H3776
1Ki 9: 7 **I** will then become a byword and an H3776
1Ki 10: 9 in you and placed you on the throne of **I**. H3776
1Ki 10: 9 Because of the LORD's eternal love for **I**, he H3776
1Ki 11: 9 the God of **I**, who had appeared to H3776
1Ki 11:25 ruled in Aram and was hostile toward **I**. H3776
1Ki 11:31 this is what the LORD, the God of **I**, says: H3776
1Ki 11:32 I have chosen out of all the tribes of **I**, H3776
1Ki 11:37 your heart desires; you will be king over **I**. H3776
1Ki 11:38 one I built for David and will give **I** to you. H3776
1Ki 11:42 reigned in Jerusalem over all **I** forty years. H3776
1Ki 12: 1 all **I** had gone there to make him king. H3776
1Ki 12: 3 whole assembly of **I** went to Rehoboam H3776
1Ki 12:16 When all **I** saw that the king refused to H3776
1Ki 12:16 To your tents, **I**! Look after your own H3776
1Ki 12:18 but all **I** stoned him to death. H3776
1Ki 12:19 So **I** has been in rebellion against the H3776
1Ki 12:20 assembly and made him king over all **I**. H3776
1Ki 12:21 to war against **I** and to regain the H1074+3776
1Ki 12:28 Here are your gods, **I**, who brought you up H3776
1Ki 14: 7 this is what the LORD, the God of **I**, says: H3776
1Ki 14: 7 appointed you ruler over my people **I**. H3776
1Ki 14:10 off from Jeroboam every last male in **I**— H3776
1Ki 14:13 All **I** will mourn for him and bury him. H3776
1Ki 14:13 the LORD, the God of **I**, has found anything H3776
1Ki 14:14 himself a king over **I** who will cut off the H3776
1Ki 14:15 And the LORD will strike **I**, so that it will be H3776
1Ki 14:15 He will uproot **I** from this good land that H3776
1Ki 14:16 And he will give **I** up because of the sins H3776
1Ki 14:16 committed and has caused **I** to commit." H3776
1Ki 14:18 buried him, and all **I** mourned for him, as H3776
1Ki 14:19 in the book of the annals of the kings of **I**. H3776
1Ki 14:21 of all the tribes of **I** in which to put his H3776
1Ki 15: 9 the twentieth year of Jeroboam king of **I**, H3776
1Ki 15:16 Asa and Baasha king of **I** throughout their H3776
1Ki 15:17 Baasha king of **I** went up against Judah H3776
1Ki 15:19 with Baasha king of **I** so he will withdraw H3776
1Ki 15:20 of his forces against the towns of **I**. H3776
1Ki 15:25 became king of **I** in the second year of H3776
1Ki 15:25 of Judah, and he reigned over **I** two years. H3776
1Ki 15:26 sin his father had caused **I** to commit. H3776
1Ki 15:27 while Nadab and all **I** were besieging it. H3776
1Ki 15:30 committed and had caused **I** to commit, H3776
1Ki 15:30 the anger of the LORD, the God of **I**. H3776
1Ki 15:31 in the book of the annals of the kings of **I**? H3776
1Ki 15:32 Asa and Baasha king of **I** throughout their H3776
1Ki 15:33 of Ahijah became king of all **I** in Tirzah, H3776
1Ki 15:34 sin Jeroboam had caused **I** to commit. H3776
1Ki 16: 2 appointed you ruler over my people **I**, H3776
1Ki 16: 2 caused my people **I** to sin and to arouse H3776
1Ki 16: 5 in the book of the annals of the kings of **I**? H3776
1Ki 16: 8 Elah son of Baasha became king of **I**, and H3776
1Ki 16:13 committed and had caused **I** to commit, H3776
1Ki 16:13 the LORD, the God of **I**, by their worthless H3776
1Ki 16:14 in the book of the annals of the kings of **I**? H3776
1Ki 16:16 king over **I** that very day there in the camp. H3776
1Ki 16:19 sin Jeroboam had caused **I** to commit. H3776
1Ki 16:20 in the book of the annals of the kings of **I**? H3776
1Ki 16:21 Then the people of **I** were split into two H3776
1Ki 16:23 Omri became king of **I**, and he reigned H3776
1Ki 16:26 sin Jeroboam had caused **I** to commit, H3776
1Ki 16:26 the LORD, the God of **I**, by their worthless H3776
1Ki 16:27 in the book of the annals of the kings of **I**? H3776
1Ki 16:29 Ahab son of Omri became king of **I**, and H3776
1Ki 16:29 in Samaria over **I** twenty-two years. H3776
1Ki 16:33 the LORD, the God of **I**, than did all the H3776
1Ki 16:33 than did all the kings of **I** before him. H3776
1Ki 17: 1 the LORD, the God of **I**, lives, whom I serve, H3776
1Ki 17:14 the LORD, the God of **I**, says: 'The jar of H3776
1Ki 18:17 said to him, "Is that you, you troubler of **I**?" H3776
1Ki 18:18 "I have not made trouble for **I**," Elijah H3776
1Ki 18:19 from all over **I** to meet me on Mount H3776
1Ki 18:20 throughout all **I** and assembled the H1201+3776
1Ki 18:31 had come, saying, "Your name shall be **I**." H3776
1Ki 18:36 of Abraham, Isaac and **I**, let it be known H3776
1Ki 18:36 that you are God in **I** and that I am your H3776
1Ki 19:16 anoint Jehu son of Nimshi king over **I** H3776
1Ki 19:18 Yet I reserve seven thousand in **I**—all H3776
1Ki 20: 2 messengers into the city to Ahab king of **I**, H3776
1Ki 20: 4 The king of **I** answered, "Just as you say H3776
1Ki 20: 7 The king of **I** summoned all the elders of H3776
1Ki 20:11 The king of **I** answered, "Tell him: 'One H3776
1Ki 20:13 came to Ahab king of **I** and announced, H3776
1Ki 20:21 The king of **I** advanced and overpowered H3776
1Ki 20:22 prophet came to the king of **I** and said, H3776
1Ki 20:25 chariot—so we can fight **I** on the plains. H4392S
1Ki 20:26 went up to Aphek to fight against **I**. H3776
1Ki 20:28 of God came up and told the king of **I**, H3776
1Ki 20:31 that the kings of **I** are merciful. H1074+3776
1Ki 20:31 us go to the king of **I** with sackcloth H3776
1Ki 20:32 they went to the king of **I** and said, "Your H3776
1Ki 20:40 "That is your sentence," the king of **I** said. H3776
1Ki 20:41 the king of **I** recognized him as one H3776
1Ki 20:43 the king of **I** went to his palace in H3776
1Ki 21: 7 "Is this how you act as king over **I**? H3776
1Ki 21:18 "Go down to meet Ahab king of **I**, who H3776
1Ki 21:21 cut off from Ahab every last male in **I**— H3776
1Ki 21:22 my anger and have caused **I** to sin. H3776
1Ki 21:26 the LORD drove out before **I**. H1201+3776
1Ki 22: 1 there was no war between Aram and **I**. H3776
1Ki 22: 2 of Judah went down to see the king of **I**. H3776
1Ki 22: 3 The king of **I** had said to his officials H3776
1Ki 22: 4 Jehoshaphat replied to the king of **I**, "I H3776
1Ki 22: 5 But Jehoshaphat also said to the king of **I** H3776
1Ki 22: 6 So the king of **I** brought together the H3776
1Ki 22: 8 The king of **I** answered Jehoshaphat H3776
1Ki 22: 9 So the king of **I** called one of his officials H3776
1Ki 22:10 the king of **I** and Jehoshaphat king of H3776
1Ki 22:17 "I saw all **I** scattered on the hills like H3776
1Ki 22:18 The king of **I** said to Jehoshaphat, "Didn't H3776
1Ki 22:26 The king of **I** then ordered, "Take Micaiah H3776
1Ki 22:29 So the king of **I** and Jehoshaphat king of H3776
1Ki 22:30 The king of **I** said to Jehoshaphat, "I will H3776
1Ki 22:30 So the king of **I** disguised himself and H3776
1Ki 22:31 small or great, except the king of **I**." H3776
1Ki 22:32 they thought, "Surely this is the king of **I**." H3776
1Ki 22:33 was not the king of **I** and stopped H3776
1Ki 22:34 hit the king of **I** between the sections H3776
1Ki 22:39 in the book of the annals of the kings of **I**? H3776
1Ki 22:41 Judah in the fourth year of Ahab king of **I**. H3776
1Ki 22:44 was also at peace with the king of **I**. H3776
1Ki 22:51 Ahab became king of **I** in Samaria in the H3776
1Ki 22:51 of Judah, and he reigned over **I** two years. H3776
1Ki 22:52 son of Nebat, who caused **I** to sin. H3776
1Ki 22:53 the LORD, the God of **I**, just as his father H3776
2Ki 1: 1 Ahab's death, Moab rebelled against **I**. H3776
2Ki 1: 3 there is no God in **I** that you are going off H3776
2Ki 1: 6 there is no God in **I** that you are sending H3776
2Ki 1:16 there is no God in **I** for you to consult that H3776
2Ki 1:18 in the book of the annals of the kings of **I**? H3776
2Ki 2:12 The chariots and horsemen of **I**!" And H3776
2Ki 3: 1 Ahab became king of **I** in Samaria in the H3776
2Ki 3: 3 which he had caused **I** to commit; he did H3776
2Ki 3: 4 to pay the king of **I** a tribute of a hundred H3776
2Ki 3: 5 of Moab rebelled against the king of **I**. H3776
2Ki 3: 6 set out from Samaria and mobilized all **I**. H3776
2Ki 3: 9 So the king of **I** set out with the king of H3776
2Ki 3:10 exclaimed the king of **I**. "Has the LORD H3776
2Ki 3:11 An officer of the king of **I** answered H3776
2Ki 3:12 So the king of **I** and Jehoshaphat and the H3776
2Ki 3:13 Elisha said to the king of **I**, "Why do you H3776
2Ki 3:13 the king of **I** answered, "because it was H3776
2Ki 3:24 the Moabites came to the camp of **I**, H3776
2Ki 3:27 The fury against **I** was great; they H3776
2Ki 5: 2 taken captive a young girl from **I**, H824+3776
2Ki 5: 4 him what the girl from **I** had said. H824+3776
2Ki 5: 5 "I will send a letter to the king of **I**." H3776
2Ki 5: 6 The letter that he took to the king of **I** read: H3776
2Ki 5: 7 As soon as the king of **I** read the letter, he H3776
2Ki 5: 8 heard that the king of **I** had torn his robes, H3776
2Ki 5: 8 he will know that there is a prophet in **I**." H3776
2Ki 5:12 Damascus, better than all the waters of **I**? H3776
2Ki 5:15 is no God in all the world except in **I**. H3776
2Ki 6: 8 Now the king of Aram was at war with **I** H3776
2Ki 6: 9 The man of God sent word to the king of **I**: H3776
2Ki 6:10 So the king of **I** checked on the place H3776
2Ki 6:11 Which of us is on the side of the king of **I**?" H3776
2Ki 6:12 the prophet who is in **I**, tells the king of H3776
2Ki 6:12 tells the king of **I** the very words you speak H3776
2Ki 6:21 When the king of **I** saw them, he asked H3776
2Ki 6:26 As the king of **I** was passing by on the H3776
2Ki 7: 6 the king of **I** has hired the Hittite and H3776
2Ki 8:16 fifth year of Joram son of Ahab king of **I**, H3776
2Ki 8:18 He followed the ways of the kings of **I**, as H3776
2Ki 8:25 year of Joram son of Ahab king of **I**, H3776
2Ki 8:26 a granddaughter of Omri king of **I**. H3776
2Ki 9: 3 I anoint you king over **I**.' Then open the H3776
2Ki 9: 6 "This is what the LORD, the God of **I**, says: H3776
2Ki 9: 6 'I anoint you king over the LORD's people **I** H3776
2Ki 9: 8 cut off from Ahab every last male in **I**— H3776
2Ki 9:12 the LORD says: I anoint you king over **I**.'" H3776
2Ki 9:14 Now Joram and all **I** had been defending H3776
2Ki 9:21 Joram king of **I** and Ahaziah king of H3776
2Ki 10:21 Then he sent word throughout **I**, and all H3776
2Ki 10:28 So Jehu destroyed Baal worship in **I**. H3776
2Ki 10:29 which he had caused **I** to commit—the H3776
2Ki 10:30 sit on the throne of **I** to the fourth H3776
2Ki 10:31 the LORD, the God of **I**, with all his heart. H3776
2Ki 10:31 which he had caused **I** to commit. H3776
2Ki 10:32 the LORD began to reduce the size of **I**. H3776
2Ki 10:34 in the book of the annals of the kings of **I**? H3776
2Ki 10:36 that Jehu reigned over **I** in Samaria was H3776
2Ki 13: 1 son of Jehu became king of **I** in Samaria, H3776
2Ki 13: 2 which he had caused **I** to commit, and he H3776
2Ki 13: 3 So the LORD's anger burned against **I**, and H3776
2Ki 13: 4 the king of Aram was oppressing **I**. H3776
2Ki 13: 5 The LORD provided a deliverer for **I**, and H3776
2Ki 13: 6 which he had caused **I** to commit; they H3776
2Ki 13: 8 in the book of the annals of the kings of **I**? H3776
2Ki 13:10 of Jehoahaz became king of **I** in Samaria, H3776
2Ki 13:11 which he had caused **I** to commit; he H3776
2Ki 13:12 in the book of the annals of the kings of **I**? H3776
2Ki 13:13 was buried in Samaria with the kings of **I**. H3776
2Ki 13:14 Jehoash king of **I** went down to see him H3776
2Ki 13:14 "The chariots and horsemen of **I**!" H3776
2Ki 13:16 in your hands," he said to the king of **I**. H3776
2Ki 13:22 of Aram oppressed **I** throughout the reign H3776

2Ki 14: 1 year of Jehoash son of Jehoahaz king of I, H3776
2Ki 14: 8 son of Jehu, king of I, with the challenge: H3776
2Ki 14: 9 But Jehoash king of I replied to Amaziah H3776
2Ki 14:11 not listen, so Jehoash king of I attacked. H3776
2Ki 14:12 Judah was routed by I, and every man fled H3776
2Ki 14:13 Jehoash king of I captured Amaziah king H3776
2Ki 14:15 in the book of the annals of the kings of I? H3776
2Ki 14:16 was buried in Samaria with the kings of I. H3776
2Ki 14:17 of Jehoash son of Jehoahaz king of I. H3776
2Ki 14:23 of Jehoash king of I became king in H3776
2Ki 14:24 which he had caused I to commit. H3776
2Ki 14:25 the boundaries of I from Lebo Hamath to H3776
2Ki 14:25 the LORD, the God of I, spoken through his H3776
2Ki 14:26 LORD had seen how bitterly everyone in I, H3776
2Ki 14:27 blot out the name of I from under heaven, H3776
2Ki 14:28 he recovered for I both Damascus and H3776
2Ki 14:28 in the book of the annals of the kings of I? H3776
2Ki 14:29 rested with his ancestors, the kings of I. H3776
2Ki 15: 1 year of Jeroboam king of I, H3776
2Ki 15: 8 of Jeroboam became king of I in Samaria, H3776
2Ki 15: 9 which he had caused I to commit. H3776
2Ki 15:11 in the book of the annals of the kings of I. H3776
2Ki 15:12 sit on the throne of I to the fourth H3776
2Ki 15:15 in the book of the annals of the kings of I. H3776
2Ki 15:17 Menahem son of Gadi became king of I H3776
2Ki 15:18 which he had caused I to commit. H3776
2Ki 15:20 Menahem exacted this money from I H3776
2Ki 15:21 in the book of the annals of the kings of I? H3776
2Ki 15:23 Menahem became king of I in Samaria, H3776
2Ki 15:24 which he had caused I to commit. H3776
2Ki 15:26 in the book of the annals of the kings of I. H3776
2Ki 15:27 of Remaliah became king of I in Samaria, H3776
2Ki 15:28 which he had caused I to commit. H3776
2Ki 15:29 In the time of Pekah king of I H3776
2Ki 15:31 in the book of the annals of the kings of I? H3776
2Ki 15:32 year of Pekah son of Remaliah king of I, H3776
2Ki 16: 3 ways of the kings of I and even sacrificed H3776
2Ki 16: 5 of Remaliah king of I marched up to fight H3776
2Ki 16: 7 of the king of Aram and of the king of I, H3776
2Ki 17: 1 son of Elah became king of I in Samaria, H3776
2Ki 17: 2 not like the kings of I who preceded him. H3776
2Ki 17: 8 that the kings of I had introduced. H3776
2Ki 17:13 The LORD warned I and Judah through all H3776
2Ki 17:18 was very angry with I and removed them H3776
2Ki 17:19 followed the practices I had introduced. H3776
2Ki 17:20 the LORD rejected all the people of I; H3776
2Ki 17:21 When he tore I away from the house of H3776
2Ki 17:21 Jeroboam enticed I away from following H3776
2Ki 17:23 So the people of I were taken from their H3776
2Ki 17:34 descendants of Jacob, whom he named I. H3776
2Ki 18: 1 third year of Hoshea son of Elah king of I, H3776
2Ki 18: 5 the LORD, the God of I. There was no one H3776
2Ki 18: 9 year of Hoshea son of Elah king of I, H3776
2Ki 18:10 was the ninth year of Hoshea king of I. H3776
2Ki 18:11 of Assyria deported I to Assyria and H3776
2Ki 19:15 the God of I, enthroned between H3776
2Ki 19:20 the LORD, the God of I, says: I have heard H3776
2Ki 19:22 eyes in pride? Against the Holy One of I! H3776
2Ki 21: 3 as Ahab king of I had done. H3776
2Ki 21: 7 I have chosen out of all the tribes of I, H3776
2Ki 21:12 this is what the LORD, the God of I, says: H3776
2Ki 22:15 "This is what the LORD, the God of I, says: H3776
2Ki 22:18 the LORD, the God of I, says concerning the H3776
2Ki 23:13 ones Solomon king of I had built for H3776
2Ki 23:15 who had caused I to sin—even that H3776
2Ki 23:19 that the kings of I had built in the towns H3776
2Ki 23:22 of the judges who led I nor in the days of H3776
2Ki 23:22 days of the kings of I and the kings of H3776
2Ki 23:27 also from my presence as I removed I, H3776
2Ki 24:13 that Solomon king of I had made for the H3776
1Ch 1:34 The sons of Isaac: Esau and I. H3776
1Ch 2: 1 These were the sons of I: Reuben H3776
1Ch 2: 7 brought trouble on I by violating the ban H3776
1Ch 4:10 Jabez cried out to the God of I, "Oh, that H3776
1Ch 5: 1 The sons of Reuben the firstborn of I (he H3776
1Ch 5: 1 were given to the sons of Joseph son of I; H3776
1Ch 5: 3 the sons of Reuben the firstborn of I H3776
1Ch 5:17 king of Judah and Jeroboam king of I. H3776
1Ch 5:26 So the God of I stirred up the spirit of Pul H3776
1Ch 6:38 of Kohath, the son of Levi, the son of I; H3776
1Ch 6:49 making atonement for I, in accordance H3776
1Ch 7:29 of Joseph son of I lived in these towns. H3776
1Ch 9: 1 All I was listed in the genealogies H3776
1Ch 9: 1 in the book of the kings of I and Judah. H3776
1Ch 10: 1 Now the Philistines fought against I; the H3776
1Ch 11: 1 All I came together to David at Hebron H3776
1Ch 11: 2 were the one who led I on their military H3776
1Ch 11: 2 'You will shepherd my people I, and you H3776
1Ch 11: 3 all the elders of I had come to King David H3776
1Ch 11: 3 they anointed David king over I, as H3776
1Ch 11:10 together with all I, gave his kingship H3776
1Ch 12:32 the times and knew what I should do— H3776
1Ch 12:38 determined to make David king over all I. H3776
1Ch 12:40 cattle and sheep, for there was joy in I. H3776
1Ch 13: 2 He then said to the whole assembly of I H3776
1Ch 13: 2 our people throughout the territories of I, H3776
1Ch 13: 5 So David assembled all I, from the Shihor H3776
1Ch 13: 6 David and all I went to Baalah of Judah H3776
1Ch 14: 2 him as king over I and that his kingdom H3776
1Ch 14: 2 highly exalted for the sake of his people I. H3776
1Ch 14: 8 David had been anointed king over all I, H3776
1Ch 15: 3 David assembled all I in Jerusalem to H3776
1Ch 15:12 the LORD, the God of I, to the place I have H3776
1Ch 15:14 bring up the ark of the LORD, the God of I. H3776
1Ch 15:25 the elders of I and the commanders H3776
1Ch 15:28 So all I brought up the ark of the covenant H3776
1Ch 16: 4 and praise the LORD, the God of I: H3776
1Ch 16:13 the descendants of I, his chosen ones, H3776
1Ch 16:17 a decree, to I as an everlasting covenant: H3776
1Ch 16:36 the LORD, the God of I, from everlasting to H3776
1Ch 16:40 the Law of the LORD, which he had given I. H3776
1Ch 17: 5 from the day I brought I up out of Egypt to H3776
1Ch 17: 7 appointed you ruler over my people I. H3776
1Ch 17: 9 place for my people I and will plant them H3776
1Ch 17:10 I appointed leaders over my people I. H3776
1Ch 17:21 And who is like your people I—the one H3776
1Ch 17:22 You made your people I your very own H3776
1Ch 17:24 Almighty, the God over I, is Israel's God! H3776
1Ch 18:14 David reigned over all I, doing what was H3776
1Ch 19:10 of the best troops in I and deployed them H3776
1Ch 19:16 saw that they had been routed by I, H3776
1Ch 19:17 he gathered all I and crossed the Jordan H3776
1Ch 19:18 But they fled before I, and David killed H3776
1Ch 19:19 saw that they had been routed by I, H3776
1Ch 20: 7 When he taunted I, Jonathan son of H3776
1Ch 21: 1 rose up against I and incited David to H3776
1Ch 21: 1 incited David to take a census of I. H3776
1Ch 21: 3 Why should he bring guilt on I?" H3776
1Ch 21: 4 went throughout I and then came back H3776
1Ch 21: 5 In all I there were one million one H3776
1Ch 21: 7 evil in the sight of God; so he punished I. H3776
1Ch 21:12 angel of the LORD ravaging every part of I. H3776
1Ch 21:14 So the LORD sent a plague on I, and H3776
1Ch 21:14 seventy thousand men of I fell dead. H3776
1Ch 22: 1 also the altar of burnt offering for I." H3776
1Ch 22: 2 the foreigners residing in I, H824+3776
1Ch 22: 6 to build a house for the LORD, the God of I. H3776
1Ch 22: 9 I will grant I peace and quiet during H3776
1Ch 22:10 the throne of his kingdom over I forever. H3776
1Ch 22:12 when he puts you in command over I, H3776
1Ch 22:13 laws that the LORD gave Moses for I. H3776
1Ch 22:17 all the leaders of I to help his son H3776
1Ch 23: 1 he made his son Solomon king over I. H3776
1Ch 23: 2 gathered together all the leaders of I, H3776
1Ch 23:25 the LORD, the God of I, has granted rest to H3776
1Ch 24:19 the God of I, had commanded him. H3776
1Ch 26:29 the temple, as officials and judges over I. H3776
1Ch 26:30 were responsible in I west of the Jordan H3776
1Ch 27:16 The leaders of the tribes of I: over the H3776
1Ch 27:22 These were the leaders of the tribes of I. H3776
1Ch 27:23 promised to make I as numerous as the H3776
1Ch 27:24 God's wrath came on I on account of this H3776
1Ch 28: 1 all the officials of I to assemble at H3776
1Ch 28: 4 the LORD, the God of I, chose me from my H3776
1Ch 28: 4 my whole family to be king over I forever. H3776
1Ch 28: 4 was pleased to make me king over all I. H3776
1Ch 28: 5 throne of the kingdom of the LORD over I. H3776
1Ch 28: 8 in the sight of all I and of the assembly of H3776
1Ch 29: 6 the officers of the tribes of I, the H3776
1Ch 29:10 the God of our father I, from everlasting to H3776
1Ch 29:18 Abraham, Isaac and I, keep these desires H3776
1Ch 29:21 other sacrifices in abundance for all I. H3776
1Ch 29:23 He prospered and all I obeyed him. H3776
1Ch 29:25 in the sight of all I and bestowed on him H3776
1Ch 29:25 such as no king over I ever had before. H3776
1Ch 29:26 David son of Jesse was king over all I. H3776
1Ch 29:27 He ruled over I forty years—seven in H3776
1Ch 29:30 surrounded him and I and the kingdoms H3776
2Ch 1: 2 Then Solomon spoke to all I—to the H3776
2Ch 1: 2 to the judges and to all the leaders in I H3776
2Ch 1:13 tent of meeting. And he reigned over I. H3776
2Ch 2: 4 This is a lasting ordinance for I. H3776
2Ch 2:12 the God of I, who made heaven and H3776
2Ch 2:17 of all the foreigners residing in I, H824+3776
2Ch 5: 2 summoned to Jerusalem the elders of I, H3776
2Ch 5: 4 When all the elders of I had arrived, the H3776
2Ch 5: 6 the entire assembly of I that had gathered H3776
2Ch 6: 3 whole assembly of I was standing there, H3776
2Ch 6: 4 the LORD, the God of I, who with his hands H3776
2Ch 6: 5 city in any tribe of I to have a temple built H3776
2Ch 6: 5 anyone to be ruler over my people I. H3776
2Ch 6: 6 I have chosen David to rule my people I. H3776
2Ch 6: 7 the Name of the LORD, the God of I. H3776
2Ch 6:10 my father and now I sit on the throne of I, H3776
2Ch 6:10 the Name of the LORD, the God of I. H3776
2Ch 6:11 LORD that he made with the people of I." H3776
2Ch 6:12 whole assembly of I and spread out his H3776
2Ch 6:13 whole assembly of I and spread out his H3776
2Ch 6:14 the God of I, there is no God like H3776
2Ch 6:16 the God of I, keep for your servant H3776
2Ch 6:16 to sit before me on the throne of I, H3776
2Ch 6:17 the God of I, let your word that you H3776
2Ch 6:21 of your people I when they pray H3776
2Ch 6:24 "When your people I have been defeated H3776
2Ch 6:25 sin of your people I and bring them back H3776
2Ch 6:27 the sin of your servants, your people I. H3776
2Ch 6:29 made by anyone among your people I— H3776
2Ch 6:32 to your people I but has come from a H3776
2Ch 6:33 as do your own people I, and may know H3776
2Ch 7: 8 seven days, and all I with him—a vast H3776
2Ch 7:10 David and Solomon and for his people I. H3776
2Ch 7:18 fail to have a successor to rule over I. H3776
2Ch 7:20 then I will uproot I from my land, which I H4392S
2Ch 8:11 not live in the palace of David king of I, H3776
2Ch 9: 8 love of your God for I and his desire to H3776
2Ch 9:30 reigned in Jerusalem over all I forty years. H3776
2Ch 10: 1 all I had gone there to make him king. H3776
2Ch 10: 3 he and all I went to Rehoboam and H3776
2Ch 10:16 When all I saw that the king refused to H3776
2Ch 10:16 To your tents, I! Look after your own H3776
2Ch 10:19 So I has been in rebellion against the H3776
2Ch 11: 1 to go to war against I and to regain the H3776
2Ch 11: 3 of Judah and to all I in Judah and H3776
2Ch 11:13 their districts throughout I sided with him. H3776
2Ch 11:16 from every tribe of I who set their hearts H3776
2Ch 11:16 the LORD, the God of I, followed the H3776
2Ch 12: 1 he and all I with him abandoned the law H3776
2Ch 12: 6 The leaders of I and the king humbled H3776
2Ch 12:13 of all the tribes of I in which to put his H3776
2Ch 13: 4 "Jeroboam and all I, listen to me! H3776
2Ch 13: 5 the LORD, the God of I, has given the H3776
2Ch 13: 5 given the kingship of I to David and his H3776
2Ch 13:12 People of I, do not fight against the LORD H3776
2Ch 13:15 Jeroboam and all I before Abijah and H3776
2Ch 15: 3 For a long time I was without the true God H3776
2Ch 15: 4 to the LORD, the God of I, and sought him, H3776
2Ch 15: 9 over to him from I when they saw that H3776
2Ch 15:13 the LORD, the God of I, were to be put to H3776
2Ch 15:17 he did not remove the high places from I, H3776
2Ch 16: 1 reign Baasha king of I went up against H3776
2Ch 16: 3 with Baasha king of I so he will withdraw H3776
2Ch 16: 4 of his forces against the towns of I. H3776
2Ch 16:11 in the book of the kings of Judah and I. H3776
2Ch 17: 1 king and strengthened himself against I. H3776
2Ch 17: 4 commands rather than the practices of I. H3776
2Ch 18: 3 Ahab king of I asked Jehoshaphat king of H3776
2Ch 18: 4 But Jehoshaphat also said to the king of I H3776
2Ch 18: 5 So the king of I brought together the H3776
2Ch 18: 7 The king of I answered Jehoshaphat H3776
2Ch 18: 8 So the king of I called one of his officials H3776
2Ch 18: 9 the king of I and Jehoshaphat king of H3776
2Ch 18:16 "I saw all I scattered on the hills like H3776
2Ch 18:17 The king of I said to Jehoshaphat, "Didn't H3776
2Ch 18:19 entice Ahab king of I into attacking H3776
2Ch 18:25 The king of I then ordered, "Take Micaiah H3776
2Ch 18:28 So the king of I and Jehoshaphat king of H3776
2Ch 18:29 The king of I said to Jehoshaphat, "I will H3776
2Ch 18:29 So the king of I disguised himself and H3776
2Ch 18:30 small or great, except the king of I." H3776
2Ch 18:31 they thought, "This is the king of I. H3776
2Ch 18:32 saw that he was not the king of I, H3776
2Ch 18:33 hit the king of I between the H3776
2Ch 18:34 the king of I propped himself up in H3776
2Ch 20: 7 before your people I and give it forever to H3776
2Ch 20:10 would not allow I to invade when they H3776
2Ch 20:19 the LORD, the God of I, with a very loud H3776
2Ch 20:29 LORD had fought against the enemies of I. H3776
2Ch 20:34 are recorded in the book of the kings of I. H3776
2Ch 20:35 made an alliance with Ahaziah king of I, H3776
2Ch 21: 2 these were sons of Jehoshaphat king of I. H3776
2Ch 21: 4 along with some of the officials of I. H3776
2Ch 21: 6 He followed the ways of the kings of I, as H3776
2Ch 21:13 have followed the ways of the kings of I, H3776
2Ch 22: 5 son of Ahab king of I to wage war against H3776
2Ch 24: 5 collect the money due annually from all I, H3776
2Ch 24: 6 by the assembly of I for the tent of the H3776
2Ch 24: 9 God had required of I in the wilderness. H3776
2Ch 24:16 good he had done in I for God and his H3776
2Ch 25: 6 fighting men from I for a hundred talents H3776
2Ch 25: 7 these troops from I must not march with H3776
2Ch 25: 7 the LORD is not with I—not with any of H3776
2Ch 25:17 of Jehoahaz, the son of Jehu, king of I: H3776
2Ch 25:18 But Jehoash king of I replied to Amaziah H3776
2Ch 25:21 So Jehoash king of I attacked. He and H3776
2Ch 25:22 Judah was routed by I, and every man fled H3776
2Ch 25:23 Jehoash king of I captured Amaziah king H3776
2Ch 25:25 of Jehoash son of Jehoahaz king of I. H3776
2Ch 25:26 in the book of the kings of Judah and I? H3776
2Ch 27: 7 in the book of the kings of I and Judah. H3776
2Ch 28: 2 ways of the kings of I and also made idols H3776
2Ch 28: 5 also given into the hands of the king of I, H3776
2Ch 28: 8 The men of I took captive from their fellow H3776
2Ch 28:13 and his fierce anger rests on I. H3776
2Ch 28:19 Judah because of Ahaz king of I, H3776
2Ch 28:23 his downfall and the downfall of all I. H3776
2Ch 28:26 in the book of the kings of Judah and I. H3776
2Ch 28:27 not placed in the tombs of the kings of I. H3776
2Ch 29: 7 offerings at the sanctuary to the God of I. H3776
2Ch 29:10 the LORD, the God of I, so that his fierce H3776
2Ch 29:24 altar for a sin offering to atone for all I, H3776
2Ch 29:24 burnt offering and the sin offering for all I. H3776
2Ch 29:27 the instruments of David king of I. H3776
2Ch 30: 1 sent word to all I and Judah and also H3776
2Ch 30: 1 the Passover to the LORD, the God of I. H3776
2Ch 30: 5 to send a proclamation throughout I, H3776
2Ch 30: 5 the Passover to the LORD, the God of I. H3776
2Ch 30: 6 went throughout I and Judah with letters H3776
2Ch 30: 6 "People of I, return to the LORD, the God of H3776
2Ch 30: 6 Abraham, Isaac and I, that he may return H3776
2Ch 30:25 all who had assembled from I, H3776
2Ch 30:25 who had come from I and also those H824+3776
2Ch 30:26 son of David king of I there had been H3776
2Ch 31: 6 The people of I and Judah who lived in H3776
2Ch 31: 8 praised the LORD and blessed his people I. H3776
2Ch 32:17 the LORD, the God of I, and saying this H3776
2Ch 32:32 in the book of the kings of Judah and I. H3776

2Ch 33: 7 I have chosen out of all the tribes of **I**, H3776
2Ch 33:16 told Judah to serve the LORD, the God of **I**. H3776
2Ch 33:18 of the LORD, the God of **I**, are written in the H3776
2Ch 33:18 are written in the annals of the kings of **I**. H3776
2Ch 34: 7 all the incense altars throughout **I**. H824+3776
2Ch 34: 9 the entire remnant of **I** and from all the H3776
2Ch 34:21 the remnant in **I** and Judah about H3776
2Ch 34:23 "This is what the LORD, the God of **I**, says: H3776
2Ch 34:26 the LORD, the God of **I**, says concerning the H3776
2Ch 34:33 who were present in **I** serve the LORD their H3776
2Ch 35: 3 who instructed all **I** and who had been H3776
2Ch 35: 3 that Solomon son of David king of **I** built. H3776
2Ch 35: 3 serve the LORD your God and his people **I**. H3776
2Ch 35: 4 by David king of **I** and by his son Solomon H3776
2Ch 35:18 like this in **I** since the days of the H3776
2Ch 35:18 none of the kings of **I** had ever celebrated H3776
2Ch 35:18 all Judah and **I** who were there with H3776
2Ch 35:25 became a tradition in **I** and are written in H3776
2Ch 35:27 in the book of the kings of **I** and Judah. H3776
2Ch 36: 8 in the book of the kings of **I** and Judah. H3776
2Ch 36:13 would not turn to the LORD, the God of **I**. H3776
Ezr 1: 3 the LORD, the God of **I**, the God who is in H3776
Ezr 2: 2 The list of the men of the people of **I**: H3776
Ezr 2:59 that their families were descended from **I**: H3776
Ezr 3: 2 the altar of the God of **I** to sacrifice burnt H3776
Ezr 3:10 the LORD, as prescribed by David king of **I**. H3776
Ezr 3:11 is good; his love toward **I** endures forever." H3776
Ezr 4: 1 a temple for the LORD, the God of **I**, H3776
Ezr 4: 3 the heads of the families of **I** answered, H3776
Ezr 4: 3 for the LORD, the God of **I**, as King Cyrus, H3776
Ezr 5: 1 Jerusalem in the name of the God of **I**, A10335
Ezr 5:11 that a great king of **I** built and finished. A10335
Ezr 6:14 of the God of **I** and the decrees of A10335
Ezr 6:16 Then the people of **I**—the priests, the A10335
Ezr 6:17 as a sin offering for all **I**, twelve male A10335
Ezr 6:17 one for each of the tribes of **I**. A10335
Ezr 6:21 in order to seek the LORD, the God of **I**. H3776
Ezr 6:22 work on the house of God, the God of **I**. H3776
Ezr 7: 6 which the LORD, the God of **I**, had given. H3776
Ezr 7:10 to teaching its decrees and laws in **I**. H3776
Ezr 7:11 commands and decrees of the LORD for **I**: H3776
Ezr 7:15 have freely given to the God of **I**, A10335
Ezr 7:28 gathered leaders from **I** to go up with me. H3776
Ezr 8:18 the son of **I**, and Sherebiah's sons H3776
Ezr 8:25 his officials and all **I** present there had H3776
Ezr 8:29 the Levites and the family heads of **I**." H3776
Ezr 8:35 sacrificed burnt offerings to the God of **I**: H3776
Ezr 8:35 twelve bulls for all **I**, ninety-six rams H3776
Ezr 9: 1 "The people of **I**, including the H3776
Ezr 9: 4 words of the God of **I** gathered around me H3776
Ezr 9:15 the God of **I**, you are righteous! We H3776
Ezr 10: 2 But in spite of this, there is still hope for **I**. H3776
Ezr 10: 5 Levites and all **I** under oath to do H3776
Ne 1: 6 night for your servants, the people of **I**. H3776
Ne 7: 7 Baanah): The list of the men of **I**: H6639+3776
Ne 7:61 that their families were descended from **I**: H3776
Ne 8: 1 which the LORD had commanded for **I**. H3776
Ne 10:33 sin offerings to make atonement for **I** H3776
Ne 10:39 The people of **I**, including the Levites, are H3776
Ne 12:47 all **I** contributed the daily portions for the H3776
Ne 13: 3 they excluded from **I** all who were of H3776
Ne 13:18 more wrath against **I** by desecrating the H3776
Ne 13:26 like these that Solomon king of **I** sinned? H3776
Ne 13:26 God made him king over all **I**, but H3776
Ps 14: 7 that salvation for **I** would come out of H3776
Ps 14: 7 people, let Jacob rejoice and **I** be glad! H3776
Ps 22: 3 the Holy One; you are the one **I** praises. H3776
Ps 22:23 Revere him, all you descendants of **I**! H3776
Ps 25:22 Deliver **I**, O God, from all their troubles! H3776
Ps 41:13 the LORD, the God of **I**, from everlasting to H3776
Ps 50: 7 I will speak; I will testify against you, **I**: H3776
Ps 53: 6 that salvation for **I** would come out of H3776
Ps 53: 6 people, let Jacob rejoice and **I** be glad! H3776
Ps 59: 5 you who are the God of **I**, rouse yourself H3776
Ps 68: 8 One of Sinai, before God, the God of **I**. H3776
Ps 68:26 praise the LORD in the assembly of **I**. H3776
Ps 68:34 whose majesty is over **I**, whose power is H3776
Ps 68:35 the God of **I** gives power and strength to H3776
Ps 69: 6 God of **I**, may those who seek H3776
Ps 71:22 praise to you with the lyre, Holy One of **I**. H3776
Ps 72:18 LORD God, the God of **I**, who alone does H3776
Ps 73: 1 Surely God is good to **I**, to those who are H3776
Ps 76: 1 in Judah; in **I** his name is great. H3776
Ps 78: 5 Jacob and established the law in **I**, H3776
Ps 78:21 and his wrath rose against **I**, H3776
Ps 78:31 cutting down the young men of **I**. H3776
Ps 78:41 to the test; they vexed the Holy One of **I**. H3776
Ps 78:55 he settled the tribes of **I** in their homes. H3776
Ps 78:59 he was furious; he rejected **I** completely. H3776
Ps 78:71 of his people Jacob, of **I** his inheritance. H3776
Ps 80: 1 Shepherd of **I**, you who lead Joseph H3776
Ps 81: 4 this is a decree for **I**, an ordinance of the H3776
Ps 81: 8 if you would only listen to me, **I**! H3776
Ps 81:11 listen to me; **I** would not submit to me. H3776
Ps 81:13 if **I** would only follow my ways H3776
Ps 89:18 to the LORD, our king to the Holy One of **I**. H3776
Ps 98: 3 his love and his faithfulness to **I**; H1074+3776
Ps 99: 8 you were to **I** a forgiving God H2157S
Ps 103: 7 to Moses, his deeds to the people of **I**: H3776
Ps 105:10 a decree, to **I** as an everlasting covenant: H3776
Ps 105:23 Then **I** entered Egypt; Jacob resided as a H3776
Ps 105:37 He brought out **I**, laden with silver and H4392S
Ps 105:38 because dread of **I** had fallen on them. H4392S
Ps 106:48 the LORD, the God of **I**, from everlasting to H3776
Ps 114: 1 When **I** came out of Egypt, Jacob from a H3776
Ps 114: 2 became God's sanctuary, **I** his dominion. H3776
Ps 115:12 He will bless his people **I**, he will bless H3776
Ps 118: 2 Let **I** say: "His love endures forever." H3776
Ps 121: 4 he who watches over **I** will neither H3776
Ps 122: 4 LORD according to the statute given to **I**. H3776
Ps 124: 1 had not been on our side—let **I** say— H3776
Ps 125: 5 banish with the evildoers. Peace be on **I**. H3776
Ps 128: 6 your children's children—peace be on **I**. H3776
Ps 129: 1 oppressed me from my youth," let **I** say; H3776
Ps 130: 7 **I**, put your hope in the LORD, for with the H3776
Ps 130: 8 himself will redeem **I** from all their sins. H3776
Ps 131: 3 **I**, put your hope in the LORD both now and H3776
Ps 135: 4 his own, **I** to be his treasured possession. H3776
Ps 135:12 an inheritance to his people **I**. H3776
Ps 136:11 brought **I** out from among them His H3776
Ps 136:14 brought **I** through the midst of it, His H3776
Ps 136:22 an inheritance to his servant **I**. His love H3776
Ps 147: 2 up Jerusalem; he gathers the exiles of **I**. H3776
Ps 147:19 word to Jacob, his laws and decrees to **I**. H3776
Ps 148:14 servants, of **I**, the people close to H1201+3776
Ps 149: 2 Let **I** rejoice in their Maker; let the people H3776
Pr 1: 1 of Solomon son of David, king of **I**: H3776
Ecc 1:12 the Teacher, was king over **I** in Jerusalem. H3776
SS 3: 7 escorted by sixty warriors, the noblest of **I**, H3776
Isa 1: 3 owner's manger, but **I** does not know, my H3776
Isa 1: 4 the Holy One of **I** and turned their backs H3776
Isa 1:24 Almighty, the Mighty One of **I**, declares: H3776
Isa 4: 2 be the pride and glory of the survivors in **I**. H3776
Isa 5: 7 of the LORD Almighty is the nation of **I**, H3776
Isa 5:19 The plan of the Holy One of **I**—let it H3776
Isa 5:24 spurned the word of the Holy One of **I**. H3776
Isa 7: 1 of Remaliah king of **I** marched up to fight H3776
Isa 8:14 both **I and Judah** he will be a H1074+3776
Isa 8:18 signs and symbols in **I** from the LORD H3776
Isa 9: 8 a message against Jacob; it will fall on **I**. H3776
Isa 9:12 west have devoured **I** with open mouth. H3776
Isa 9:14 LORD will cut off from **I** both head and tail, H3776
Isa 10:17 The Light of **I** will become a fire, their H3776
Isa 10:20 In that day the remnant of **I**, the survivors H3776
Isa 10:20 truly rely on the LORD, the Holy One of **I**. H3776
Isa 10:22 the sand by the sea, **I**, only a remnant will H3776
Isa 11:12 the nations and gather the exiles of **I**; H3776
Isa 11:16 as there was for **I** when they came up H3776
Isa 12: 6 great is the Holy One of **I** among you." H3776
Isa 14: 1 he will choose **I** and will settle them H3776
Isa 14: 2 And **I** will take possession of the H1074+3776
Isa 17: 6 boughs," declares the LORD, the God of **I**. H3776
Isa 17: 7 turn their eyes to the Holy One of **I**. H3776
Isa 19:24 In that day **I** will be the third, along with H3776
Isa 19:25 my handiwork, and **I** my inheritance." H3776
Isa 21:10 from the LORD Almighty, from the God of **I**. H3776
Isa 21:17 The LORD, the God of **I**, has spoken. H3776
Isa 24:15 the LORD, the God of **I**, in the islands of H3776
Isa 27: 6 **I** will bud and blossom and fill all the H3776
Isa 27:12 and you, **I**, will be gathered up one H1201+3776
Isa 29:19 the needy will rejoice in the Holy One of **I**. H3776
Isa 29:23 will stand in awe of the God of **I**. H3776
Isa 30:11 confronting us with the Holy One of **I**!" H3776
Isa 30:12 this is what the Holy One of **I** says: H3776
Isa 30:15 Sovereign LORD, the Holy One of **I**, says: H3776
Isa 30:29 the mountain of the LORD, to the Rock of **I**. H3776
Isa 31: 1 do not look to the Holy One of **I**, or H3776
Isa 37:16 the God of **I**, enthroned between H3776
Isa 37:21 the LORD, the God of **I**, says: Because you H3776
Isa 37:23 eyes in pride? Against the Holy One of **I**! H3776
Isa 40:27 Why do you say, **I**, "My way is hidden H3776
Isa 41: 8 "But you, **I**, my servant, Jacob, whom I H3776
Isa 41:14 you worm Jacob, little **I**, do not fear, for I H3776
Isa 41:14 your Redeemer, the Holy One of **I**. H3776
Isa 41:16 in the LORD and glory in the Holy One of **I**. H3776
Isa 41:17 the God of **I**, will not forsake H3776
Isa 41:20 that the Holy One of **I** has created it. H3776
Isa 42:24 to become loot, and **I** to the plunderers? H3776
Isa 43: 1 created you, Jacob, he who formed you, **I**: H3776
Isa 43: 3 your God, the Holy One of **I**, your Savior; H3776
Isa 43:14 your Redeemer, the Holy One of **I**: H3776
Isa 43:22 you have not wearied yourselves for me, **I**. H3776
Isa 43:28 Jacob to destruction and **I** to scorn. H3776
Isa 44: 1 my servant, **I**, whom I have chosen. H3776
Isa 44: 5 'The LORD's,' and will take the name **I**. H3776
Isa 44:21 Jacob, for you, **I**, are my servant. H3776
Isa 44:21 you are my servant; **I**, I will not forget you. H3776
Isa 44:23 he displays his glory in **I**. H3776
Isa 45: 3 the God of **I**, who summons you by H3776
Isa 45: 4 my servant, of **I** my chosen, I summon H3776
Isa 45:11 the Holy One of **I**, and its Maker: H3776
Isa 45:15 hiding himself, the God and Savior of **I**. H3776
Isa 45:17 But **I** will be saved by the LORD with an H3776
Isa 45:25 the descendants of **I** will find deliverance H3776
Isa 46: 3 all the remnant of the people of **I**, you H3776
Isa 46:13 grant salvation to Zion, my splendor to **I**. H3776
Isa 47: 4 is his name—is the Holy One of **I**. H3776
Isa 48: 1 by the name of **I** and come from the H3776
Isa 48: 1 of the LORD and invoke the God of **I**— H3776
Isa 48: 2 city and claim to rely on the God of **I**— H3776
Isa 48:12 Jacob, **I**, whom I have called: H3776
Isa 48:17 your Redeemer, the Holy One of **I**: H3776
Isa 49: 3 "You are my servant, **I**, in whom I will H3776
Isa 49: 5 Jacob back to him and gather **I** to himself, H3776
Isa 49: 6 bring back those of **I** I have kept. H3776
Isa 49: 7 the Redeemer and Holy One of **I**—to him H3776
Isa 49: 7 the Holy One of **I**, who has chosen you." H3776
Isa 52:12 the God of **I** will be your rear guard. H3776
Isa 54: 5 the Holy One of **I** is your Redeemer; he H3776
Isa 55: 5 the Holy One of **I**, for he has endowed H3776
Isa 56: 8 declares—he who gathers the exiles of **I**: H3776
Isa 60: 9 the Holy One of **I**, for he has endowed H3776
Isa 60:14 of the LORD, Zion of the Holy One of **I**. H3776
Isa 63: 7 good things he has done for **I**, H1074+3776
Isa 63:16 does not know us or **I** acknowledge us; H3776
Jer 2: 3 **I** was holy to the LORD, the firstfruits of his H3776
Jer 2: 4 of Jacob, all you clans of **I**. H1074+3776
Jer 2:14 Is **I** a servant, a slave by birth? Why then H3776
Jer 2:26 so the people of **I** are disgraced—they, H3776
Jer 2:31 I been a desert to **I** or a land of great H3776
Jer 3: 6 "Have you seen what faithless **I** has done? H3776
Jer 3: 8 I gave faithless **I** her certificate of divorce H3776
Jer 3:11 "Faithless **I** is more righteous than H3776
Jer 3:12 " 'Return, faithless **I**,' declares the LORD, 'I H3776
Jer 3:18 people of Judah will join the people of **I**, H3776
Jer 3:20 so you, **I**, have been unfaithful to H1074+3776
Jer 3:21 weeping and pleading of the people of **I**, H3776
Jer 3:23 in the LORD our God is the salvation of **I**. H3776
Jer 4: 1 **I**, will return, then return to me, H3776
Jer 5:11 The people of **I** and the people of Judah H3776
Jer 5:15 People of **I**," declares the LORD, "I am H3776
Jer 6: 9 glean the remnant of **I** as thoroughly as a H3776
Jer 7: 3 the LORD Almighty, the God of **I**, says: H3776
Jer 7:12 of the wickedness of my people **I**. H3776
Jer 7:21 the LORD Almighty, the God of **I**, says: H3776
Jer 9:15 the LORD Almighty, the God of **I**, says: H3776
Jer 9:26 the whole house of **I** is uncircumcised in H3776
Jer 10: 1 what the LORD says to you, people of **I**. H3776
Jer 10:16 of all things, including **I**, the people of his H3776
Jer 11: 3 this is what the LORD, the God of **I**, says: H3776
Jer 11:10 Both **I** and Judah have broken the H1074+3776
Jer 11:17 the people of both **I** and Judah have H3776
Jer 12:14 seize the inheritance I gave my people **I**, H3776
Jer 13:11 all the people of **I** and all the people of H3776
Jer 13:12 the LORD, the God of **I**, says: Every H3776
Jer 14: 8 You who are the hope of **I**, its Savior in H3776
Jer 16: 9 the LORD Almighty, the God of **I**, says: H3776
Jer 17:13 you are the hope of **I**; all who forsake you H3776
Jer 18: 6 I not do with you, **I**, as this potter H1074+3776
Jer 18: 6 potter, so are you in my hand, **I**. H1074+3776
Jer 18:13 horrible thing has been done by Virgin **I**. H3776
Jer 19: 3 the LORD Almighty, the God of **I**, says: H3776
Jer 19:15 the LORD Almighty, the God of **I**, says: H3776
Jer 21: 4 the LORD, the God of **I**, says: I am about to H3776
Jer 23: 2 the LORD, the God of **I**, says to the H3776
Jer 23: 6 will be saved and **I** will live in safety. H3776
Jer 23: 8 descendants of **I** up out of the land H1074+3776
Jer 23:13 by Baal and led my people **I** astray. H3776
Jer 24: 5 the LORD, the God of **I**, says: 'Like these H3776
Jer 25:15 is what the LORD, the God of **I**, said to me: H3776
Jer 25:27 the LORD Almighty, the God of **I**, says: H3776
Jer 27: 4 the LORD Almighty, the God of **I**, says: H3776
Jer 27:21 Almighty, the God of **I**, says about the H3776
Jer 28: 2 the LORD Almighty, the God of **I**, says: H3776
Jer 28:14 the LORD Almighty, the God of **I**, says: H3776
Jer 29: 4 Almighty, the God of **I**, says to all those I H3776
Jer 29: 8 the LORD Almighty, the God of **I**, says: H3776
Jer 29:21 the God of **I**, says about Ahab son H3776
Jer 29:23 For they have done outrageous things in **I** H3776
Jer 29:25 the LORD Almighty, the God of **I**, says: H3776
Jer 30: 2 the LORD, the God of **I**, says: 'Write in a H3776
Jer 30: 3 bring my people **I** and Judah back from H3776
Jer 30: 4 the LORD spoke concerning **I** and Judah: H3776
Jer 30:10 do not be dismayed, **I**,' declares the LORD. H3776
Jer 31: 1 "I will be the God of all the families of **I** H3776
Jer 31: 2 wilderness; I will come to give rest to **I**." H3776
Jer 31: 4 and you, Virgin **I**, will be rebuilt. H3776
Jer 31: 7 save your people, the remnant of **I**. H3776
Jer 31:10 'He who scattered **I** will gather them and H3776
Jer 31:21 Return, Virgin **I**, return to your towns. H3776
Jer 31:22 long will you wander, unfaithful Daughter **I**? NDT
Jer 31:23 the LORD Almighty, the God of **I**, says: H3776
Jer 31:27 the kingdoms of **I** and Judah with the H3776
Jer 31:31 with the people of **I** and with the people H3776
Jer 31:33 make with the people of **I** after that time," H3776
Jer 31:36 "will **I** ever cease being a nation H2446+3776
Jer 31:37 the descendants of **I** because of all they H3776
Jer 32:14 the LORD Almighty, the God of **I**, says: H3776
Jer 32:15 the LORD Almighty, the God of **I**, says: H3776
Jer 32:20 to this day, in **I** and among all mankind H3776
Jer 32:21 brought your people **I** out of Egypt with H3776
Jer 32:30 "The people of **I** and Judah have done H3776
Jer 32:30 the people of **I** have done nothing but H3776
Jer 32:32 The people of **I** and Judah have provoked H3776
Jer 32:36 this is what the LORD, the God of **I**, says: H3776
Jer 33: 4 the LORD, the God of **I**, says about the H3776
Jer 33: 7 I will bring Judah and **I** back from captivity H3776
Jer 33:14 I made to the people of **I** and Judah. H3776
Jer 33:17 a man to sit on the throne of **I**, H1074+3776
Jer 34: 2 the LORD, the God of **I**, says: Go to H3776
Jer 34:13 the LORD, the God of **I**, says: I made a H3776
Jer 35:13 the LORD Almighty, the God of **I**, says: H3776
Jer 35:17 the LORD God Almighty, the God of **I**, says: H3776
Jer 35:18 the LORD Almighty, the God of **I**, says: H3776
Jer 35:19 the LORD Almighty, the God of **I**, says: H3776
Jer 36: 2 words I have spoken to you concerning **I**, H3776

Jer 37: 7 the LORD, the God of I, says: Tell the king H3776
Jer 38:17 the LORD God Almighty, the God of I, says: H3776
Jer 39:16 the LORD Almighty, the God of I, says: H3776
Jer 41: 9 of his defense against Baasha king of I. H3776
Jer 42: 9 the God of I, to whom you sent me H3776
Jer 42:15 the LORD Almighty, the God of I, says: H3776
Jer 42:18 the LORD Almighty, the God of I, says: H3776
Jer 43:10 the LORD Almighty, the God of I, says: H3776
Jer 44: 2 the LORD Almighty, the God of I, says: H3776
Jer 44: 7 the LORD God Almighty, the God of I, says: H3776
Jer 44:11 the LORD Almighty, the God of I, says: H3776
Jer 44:25 the LORD Almighty, the God of I, says: H3776
Jer 45: 2 is what the LORD, the God of I, says to you, H3776
Jer 46:25 Almighty, the God of I, says: "I am about H3776
Jer 46:27 Jacob my servant; do not be dismayed, I. H3776
Jer 48: 1 the LORD Almighty, the God of I, says: H3776
Jer 48:13 as I was ashamed when they H1074+3776
Jer 48:27 Was not I the object of your ridicule? Was H3776
Jer 49: 1 the LORD says: "Has I no sons? Has Israel H3776
Jer 49: 1 Israel no sons? Has I no heir? Why then H2257
Jer 49: 2 Then I will drive out those who drove her H3776
Jer 50: 4 "the people of I and the people of Judah H3776
Jer 50:17 "I is a scattered flock that lions have H3776
Jer 50:18 the LORD Almighty, the God of I, says: H3776
Jer 50:19 But I will bring I back to their own pasture H3776
Jer 50:29 has defied the LORD, the Holy One of I. H3776
Jer 50:33 "The people of I are oppressed, and the H3776
Jer 51: 5 For I and Judah have not been forsaken H3776
Jer 51: 5 is full of guilt before the Holy One of I. H3776
Jer 51:33 the LORD Almighty, the God of I, says: H3776
La 2: 1 the splendor of I from heaven to earth H3776
La 2: 3 fierce anger he has cut off every horn of I. H3776
La 2: 5 is like an enemy; he has swallowed up I. H3776
Eze 3: 1 then go and speak to the people of I." H3776
Eze 3: 4 to the people of I and speak my words H3776
Eze 3: 5 language, but to the people of I— H3776
Eze 3: 7 But the people of I are not willing to listen H3776
Eze 3:17 made you a watchman for the people of I; H3776
Eze 4: 3 This will be a sign to the people of I. H3776
Eze 4: 4 the sin of the people of I upon yourself. H3776
Eze 4: 5 you will bear the sin of the people of I. H3776
Eze 4:13 way the people of I will eat defiled food H3776
Eze 5: 4 A fire will spread from there to all I. H1074+3776
Eze 6: 2 set your face against the mountains of I H3776
Eze 6: 3 'You mountains of I, hear the word of the H3776
Eze 6:11 detestable practices of the people of I, H3776
Eze 7: 2 the Sovereign LORD says to the land of I: H3776
Eze 8: 4 before me was the glory of the God of I, H3776
Eze 8:10 animals and all the idols of I. H1074+3776
Eze 8:11 of them stood seventy elders of I, H1074+3776
Eze 8:12 the elders of I are doing in the H1074+3776
Eze 9: 3 glory of the God of I went up from above H3776
Eze 9: 8 entire remnant of I in this outpouring of H3776
Eze 9: 9 sin of the people of I and Judah is H3776
Eze 10:19 the glory of the God of I was above them. H3776
Eze 10:20 beneath the God of I by the Kebar River, H3776
Eze 11: 5 you leaders in I, but I know what is H3776
Eze 11:10 judgment on you at the borders of I. H3776
Eze 11:11 judgment on you at the borders of I. H3776
Eze 11:13 you completely destroy the remnant of I?" H3776
Eze 11:17 I will give you back the land of I again. H3776
Eze 11:22 the glory of the God of I was above them. H3776
Eze 12:19 living in Jerusalem and in the land of I: H3776
Eze 12:22 is this proverb you have in the land of I: H3776
Eze 12:23 they will no longer quote it in I. H3776
Eze 12:24 divinations among the people of I. H3776
Eze 13: 2 the prophets of I who are now H3776
Eze 13: 4 Your prophets, I, are like jackals among H3776
Eze 13: 5 it for the people of I so that it will stand H3776
Eze 13: 9 be listed in the records of I, H1074+3776
Eze 13: 9 of Israel, nor will they enter the land of I. H3776
Eze 13:16 those prophets of I who prophesied to H3776
Eze 14: 1 of the elders of I came to me and sat H3776
Eze 14: 5 to recapture the hearts of the people of I, H3776
Eze 14: 6 "Therefore say to the people of I, 'This is H3776
Eze 14: 7 residing in I separate themselves H3776
Eze 14: 9 destroy him from among my people I. H3776
Eze 14:11 Then the people of I will no longer stray H3776
Eze 17:23 On the mountain heights of I I will plant it H3776
Eze 18: 2 quoting this proverb about the land of I: H3776
Eze 18: 3 you will no longer quote this proverb in I. H3776
Eze 18: 6 shrines or look to the idols of I. H1074+3776
Eze 18:15 shrines or look to the idols of I. H1074+3776
Eze 18:29 people of I? Is it not your ways H3776
Eze 18:31 Why will you die, people of I? H3776
Eze 19: 1 up a lament concerning the princes of I H3776
Eze 19: 9 heard no longer on the mountains of I. H3776
Eze 20: 1 some of the elders of I came to inquire of H3776
Eze 20: 3 speak to the elders of I and say to them H3776
Eze 20: 5 On the day I chose I, I swore with uplifted H3776
Eze 20:13 " 'Yet the people of I rebelled against me H3776
Eze 20:27 speak to the people of I and say to them H3776
Eze 20:38 yet they will not enter the land of I. H3776
Eze 20:39 " 'As for you, people of I, this is what the H3776
Eze 20:40 the high mountain of I, declares the H3776
Eze 20:40 the land all the people of I will serve me, H3776
Eze 20:42 when I bring you into the land of I, the H3776
Eze 20:44 you people of I, declares the Sovereign H3776
Eze 21: 2 Prophesy against the land of I H3776
Eze 21:12 people; it is against all the princes of I. H3776
Eze 21:25 " 'You profane and wicked prince of I H3776
Eze 22: 6 of the princes of I who are in you uses H3776

Eze 22:18 the people of I have become dross to me H3776
Eze 24:21 Say to the people of I, 'This is what the H3776
Eze 25: 3 over the land of I when it was laid H3776
Eze 25: 6 malice of your heart against the land of I, H3776
Eze 25:14 on Edom by the hand of my people I, H3776
Eze 27:17 " 'Judah and I traded with you; they H824+3776
Eze 28:24 will the people of I have malicious H3776
Eze 28:25 gather the people of I from the nations H3776
Eze 29: 6 been a staff of reed for the people of I. H3776
Eze 29:16 the people of I but will be a reminder H3776
Eze 33: 7 made you a watchman for the people of I; H3776
Eze 33:11 Why will you die, people of I?' H3776
Eze 33:24 in those ruins in the land of I are saying, H3776
Eze 33:28 the mountains of I will become desolate H3776
Eze 34: 2 prophesy against the shepherds of I H3776
Eze 34: 2 to you shepherds of I who only take care H3776
Eze 34:13 I will pasture them on the mountains of I H3776
Eze 34:14 mountain heights of I will be their grazing H3776
Eze 34:14 in a rich pasture on the mountains of I. H3776
Eze 35:12 you have said against the mountains of I. H3776
Eze 35:15 inheritance of I became desolate, H1074+3776
Eze 36: 1 prophesy to the mountains of I and say H3776
Eze 36: 1 'Mountains of I, hear the word of the H3776
Eze 36: 4 mountains of I, hear the word of the H3776
Eze 36: 6 concerning the land of I and say to the H3776
Eze 36: 8 mountains of I, will produce H3776
Eze 36: 8 branches and fruit for my people I, H3776
Eze 36:10 people to live on you—yes, all of I. H1074+3776
Eze 36:12 cause people, my people I, to live on you. H3776
Eze 36:17 when the people of I were living in their H3776
Eze 36:21 the people of I profaned among the H3776
Eze 36:22 your sake, people of I, that I am going to H3776
Eze 36:32 disgraced for your conduct, people of I! H3776
Eze 37:11 of man, these bones are the people of I. H3776
Eze 37:12 I will bring you back to the land of I. H3776
Eze 37:22 nation in the land, on the mountains of I. H3776
Eze 37:28 will know that I the LORD make I holy, H3776
Eze 38: 8 from many nations to the mountains of I, H3776
Eze 38:14 when my people I are living in safety H3776
Eze 38:16 against my people I like a cloud that H3776
Eze 38:17 days by my servants the prophets of I. H3776
Eze 38:18 When Gog attacks the land of I, my hot H3776
Eze 38:19 be a great earthquake in the land of I. H3776
Eze 39: 2 send you against the mountains of I. H3776
Eze 39: 4 On the mountains of I you will fall, you H3776
Eze 39: 7 known my holy name among my people I. H3776
Eze 39: 7 know that I the LORD am the Holy One in I. H3776
Eze 39: 9 live in the towns of I will go out and use H3776
Eze 39:11 that day I will give Gog a burial place in I, H3776
Eze 39:17 the great sacrifice on the mountains of I. H3776
Eze 39:22 the people of I will know that I am H3776
Eze 39:23 that the people of I went into exile for H3776
Eze 39:25 have compassion on all the people of I, H3776
Eze 39:29 will pour out my Spirit on the people of I, H3776
Eze 40: 2 me to the land of I and set me on a very H3776
Eze 40: 4 Tell the people of I everything you see." H3776
Eze 43: 2 glory of the God of I coming from the east H3776
Eze 43: 7 The people of I will never again defile my H3776
Eze 43:10 describe the temple to the people of I H3776
Eze 44: 2 the God of I, has entered through H3776
Eze 44: 6 Say to rebellious I, 'This is what the H1074+3776
Eze 44: 6 of your detestable practices, people of I! H3776
Eze 44:10 far from me when I went astray and who H3776
Eze 44:12 made the people of I fall into sin, H3776
Eze 44:28 You are to give them no possession in I; H3776
Eze 44:29 everything in I devoted to the LORD H3776
Eze 45: 6 portion; it will belong to all I. H1074+3776
Eze 45: 8 This land will be his possession in I. H3776
Eze 45: 8 allow the people of I to possess the land H3776
Eze 45: 9 enough, princes of I! Give up your H3776
Eze 45:15 from the well-watered pastures of I. H3776
Eze 45:16 give this special offering to the prince in I. H3776
Eze 45:17 at all the appointed festivals of I. H1074+3776
Eze 47:13 the twelve tribes of I as their inheritance, H3776
Eze 47:18 Jordan between Gilead and the land of I, H3776
Eze 47:21 yourselves according to the tribes of I. H3776
Eze 47:22 an inheritance among the tribes of I. H3776
Eze 48:19 farm it will come from all the tribes of I. H3776
Eze 48:29 to allot as an inheritance to the tribes of I, H3776
Eze 48:31 the city will be named after the tribes of I. H3776
Da 9: 7 the inhabitants of Jerusalem and all I, H3776
Da 9:11 All I has transgressed your law and turned H3776
Da 9:20 the sin of my people I and making my H3776
Hos 1: 1 of Jeroboam son of Jehoash king of I: H3776
Hos 1: 4 will put an end to the kingdom of I. H1074+3776
Hos 1: 6 I will no longer show love to I H1074+3776
Hos 1:11 the people of I will come together; H3776
Hos 4:15 "Though you, I, commit adultery, do not H3776
Hos 5: 3 about Ephraim; I is not hidden from me. H3776
Hos 5: 3 now turned to prostitution; I is corrupt. H3776
Hos 5: 9 Among the tribes of I I proclaim what is H3776
Hos 6:10 I have seen a horrible thing in I H1074+3776
Hos 6:10 is given to prostitution, I is defiled. H3776
Hos 7: 1 whenever I would heal I, the sins of H3776
Hos 8: 2 I cries out to me, 'Our God, we H3776
Hos 8: 3 But I has rejected what is good; an enemy H3776
Hos 8: 6 They are from I! This calf—a metalworker H3776
Hos 8: 8 I is swallowed up; now she is among the H3776
Hos 8:14 I has forgotten their Maker and built H3776
Hos 9: 1 Do not rejoice, I; do not be jubilant like H3776
Hos 9: 7 Let I know this. Because your H3776
Hos 9:10 "When I found I, it was like finding H3776

Hos 10: 1 I was a spreading vine; he brought forth H3776
Hos 10: 6 I will be ashamed of its foreign alliances. H3776
Hos 10: 8 will be destroyed—it is the sin of I. H3776
Hos 10: 9 you have sinned, I, and there you have H3776
Hos 10:15 the king of I will be completely destroyed. H3776
Hos 11: 1 "When I was a child, I loved him, and out H3776
Hos 11: 8 I hand you over, I? How can I treat you H3776
Hos 11:12 me with lies, I with deceit. H1074+3776
Hos 12:12 the country of Aram; I served to get a wife H3776
Hos 12:13 used a prophet to bring I up from Egypt, H3776
Hos 13: 1 people trembled; he was exalted in I. H3776
Hos 13: 9 "You are destroyed, I, because you are H3776
Hos 14: 1 I, to the LORD your God. Your sins H3776
Hos 14: 5 I will be like the dew to I; he will blossom H3776
Joel 2:27 Then you will know that I am in I, that I H3776
Joel 3: 2 inheritance, my people I, because they H3776
Joel 3:16 people, a stronghold for the people of I. H3776
Am 1: 1 he saw concerning I two years before the H3776
Am 1: 1 Jeroboam son of Jehoash was king of I. H3776
Am 2: 6 "For three sins of I, even for four, I will not H3776
Am 2:11 not true, people of I?" declares the LORD. H3776
Am 3: 1 this word, people of I, the word the LORD H3776
Am 3:14 "On the day I punish I for her sins, I will H3776
Am 4:12 I will do to you, I, and because I will do H3776
Am 4:12 will do this to you, I, prepare to meet your H3776
Am 5: 1 Hear this word, I, this lament I take H1074+3776
Am 5: 2 "Fallen is Virgin I, never to rise again H3776
Am 5: 3 what the Sovereign LORD says to I: H1074+3776
Am 5: 4 This is what the LORD says to I H1074+3776
Am 5:25 forty years in the wilderness, people of I? H3776
Am 6: 1 to whom the people of I come! H3776
Am 6:14 against you, I, that will oppress H1074+3776
Am 7: 8 setting a plumb line among my people I; H3776
Am 7: 9 the sanctuaries of I will be ruined; H3776
Am 7:10 sent a message to Jeroboam king of I: H3776
Am 7:10 against you in the very heart of I. H1074+3776
Am 7:11 the sword, and I will surely go into exile H3776
Am 7:15 said to me, 'Go, prophesy to my people I. H3776
Am 7:16 " 'Do not prophesy against I, and stop H3776
Am 7:17 And I will surely go into exile, away from H3776
Am 8: 2 "The time is ripe for my people I; I will H3776
Am 9: 7 "Did I not bring I up from Egypt, the H3776
Am 9: 9 shake the people of I among all the H3776
Am 9:14 I will bring my people I back from exile. H3776
Am 9:15 I will plant I in their own land, never H4392S
Mic 1: 5 because of the sins of the people of I. H3776
Mic 1:13 the transgressions of I were found in you. H3776
Mic 1:14 will prove deceptive to the kings of I. H3776
Mic 1:15 The nobles of I will flee to Adullam. H3776
Mic 2:12 will surely bring together the remnant of I. H3776
Mic 3: 1 leaders of Jacob, you rulers of I. H1074+3776
Mic 3: 8 to Jacob his transgression, to I his sin. H3776
Mic 3: 9 you rulers of I, who despise justice H1074+3776
Mic 5: 2 come for me one who will be ruler over I, H3776
Mic 5: 3 Therefore I will be abandoned until the H4392S
Mic 6: 2 people; he is lodging a charge against I. H3776
Na 2: 2 splendor of Jacob like the splendor of I, H3776
Zep 2: 9 Almighty, the God of I, "surely Moab will H3776
Zep 3:12 The remnant of I will trust in the name of H3776
Zep 3:14 shout aloud, I! Be glad and rejoice H3776
Zep 3:15 The LORD, the King of I, is with you; never H3776
Zec 1:19 that scattered Judah, I and Jerusalem." H3776
Zec 8:13 as you, Judah and I, have been a H1074+3776
Zec 9: 1 all the tribes of I are on the LORD— H3776
Zec 11:14 the family bond between Judah and I. H3776
Zec 12: 1 The word of the LORD concerning I. H3776
Mal 1: 1 The word of the LORD to I through Malachi. H3776
Mal 1: 5 is the LORD—even beyond the borders of I! H3776
Mal 2:11 been committed in I and in Jerusalem: H3776
Mal 2:16 the LORD, the God of I, "does violence to H3776
Mal 4: 4 laws I gave him at Horeb for all I. H3776
Mt 2: 6 a ruler who will shepherd my people I. G2702
Mt 2:20 his mother and go to the land *of* I, G2702
Mt 2:21 his mother and went to the land *of* I. G2702
Mt 8:10 not found anyone in I with such great G2702
Mt 9:33 "Nothing like this has ever been seen in I." G2702
Mt 10: 6 Go rather to the lost sheep *of* I. G3875+2702
Mt 10:23 through the towns *of* I before the Son of G2702
Mt 15:24 was sent only to the lost sheep *of* I." G3875+2702
Mt 15:31 And they praised the God *of* I. G2702
Mt 19:28 thrones, judging the twelve tribes *of* I. G2702
Mt 27: 9 the price set on him by the people *of* I, G2702
Mt 27:42 He's the king *of* I! Let him come down G2702
Mk 12:29 'Hear, O I: The Lord our God, the G2702
Mk 15:32 Messiah, this king *of* I, come down now G2702
Lk 1:16 many of the people *of* I to the Lord their G2702
Lk 1:54 He has helped his servant I, remembering G2702
Lk 1:68 the Lord, the God *of* I, because he has G2702
Lk 1:80 wilderness until he appeared publicly to I. G2702
Lk 2:25 He was waiting for the consolation *of* I G2702
Lk 2:32 Gentiles, and the glory of your people I." G2702
Lk 2:34 cause the falling and rising of many in I, G2702
Lk 4:25 were many widows in I in Elijah's time, G2702
Lk 4:27 there were many in I with leprosy in the G2702
Lk 7: 9 I have not found such great faith even in I." G2702
Lk 22:30 on thrones, judging the twelve tribes *of* I. G2702
Lk 24:21 was the one who was going to redeem I. G2702
Jn 1:31 water was that he might be revealed *to* I." G2702
Jn 1:49 are the Son of God; you are the king *of* I." G2702
Jn 12:13 "Blessed is the king *of* I!" G2702
Ac 1: 6 time going to restore the kingdom *to* I?" G2702
Ac 2:36 let all I be assured of this G3875+2702

Ac 4:10 then know this, you and all the people of I: G2702
Ac 4:27 Gentiles and the people of I in this city to G2702
Ac 5:21 the full assembly of the elders of I— G5626+2702
Ac 5:31 that he might bring I to repentance and G2702
Ac 5:35 "Men of I, consider carefully what you G2703
Ac 7:42 forty years in the wilderness, people of I? G2702
Ac 9:15 their kings and to the people of I. G2702
Ac 10:36 the message God sent to the people of I, G2702
Ac 13:17 God of the people of I chose our G2702
Ac 13:23 God has brought to I the Savior Jesus, G2702
Ac 13:24 baptism to all the people of I. G2702
Ac 28:20 because of the hope of I that I am bound G2702
Ro 9:4 the people of I. Theirs is the adoption to G2703
Ro 9:6 all who are descended from I are Israel. G2702
Ro 9:6 all who are descended from Israel are I. G2702
Ro 9:27 Isaiah cries out concerning I: "Though the G2702
Ro 9:31 the people of I, who pursued the law G2702
Ro 10:19 Did I not understand? First G2702
Ro 10:21 But concerning I he says, "All day long I G2702
Ro 11:2 how he appealed to God against I: G2702
Ro 11:7 What the people of I sought so earnestly G2702
Ro 11:11 come to the Gentiles to make I envious. G899S
Ro 11:25 I has experienced a hardening in part G2702
Ro 11:26 in this way all I will be saved. As it is G2702
1Co 10:18 Consider the people of I: Do not those G2702
Gal 6:16 all who follow this rule—to the I of God. G2702
Eph 2:12 from citizenship in I and foreigners to the G2702
Eph 3:6 the Gentiles are heirs together with I, NDT
Php 3:5 of the people of I, of the tribe of G2702
Heb 8:8 with the people of I and with the people G2702
Heb 8:10 with the people of I after that time, G2702
Heb 11:28 firstborn would not touch the firstborn of I. G899S
Rev 7:4 144,000 from all the tribes of I. G5626+2702
Rev 21:12 the names of the twelve tribes of I. G5626+2702

ISRAEL'S (54) [ISRAEL]

Ge 42:5 So I sons were among those who went to H3776
Ge 46:5 I sons took their father Jacob and H3776
Ge 48:10 Now I eyes were failing because of old H3776
Ge 48:12 removed them from I knees and bowed H2257S
Ge 48:13 on his right toward I left hand and H3776
Ge 48:13 Manasseh on his left toward I right hand, H3776
Ex 14:19 who had been traveling in front of I army H3776
Ex 18:8 the Egyptians for I sake and about all H3776
Nu 1:45 able to serve in I army were counted H928+3776
Nu 11:16 me seventy of I elders who are known H3776
Nu 21:3 The LORD listened to I plea and gave the H3776
Nu 25:5 So Moses said to I judges, "Each of you H3776
Jos 10:30 gave that city and its king into I hand. H3776
Jos 10:32 The LORD gave Lachish into I hands, and H3776
Jdg 3:10 so that he became I judge and went to H3776
Jdg 5:9 My heart is with I princes, with the willing H3776
Jdg 10:16 And he could bear I misery no longer. H3776
Jdg 11:21 Sihon and his whole army into I hands, H3776
Jdg 20:6 one piece to each region of I inheritance, H3776
Jdg 20:34 ten thousand of I able young men made H3776
1Sa 6:5 the country, and give glory to I god. H3776
1Sa 6:6 When I god dealt harshly with them, did NDT
1Sa 7:9 He cried out to the LORD on I behalf, and H3776
1Sa 7:13 they stopped invading I territory. H3776
1Sa 7:15 Samuel continued as I leader all the days H3776
1Sa 8:1 he appointed his sons as I leaders. H4200+3776
1Sa 14:37 Will you give them into I hand?" But God H3776
2Sa 18:7 There I troops were routed by David's men, H3776
2Sa 20:23 Joab was over I entire army; Benaiah son H3776
2Sa 23:1 by the God of Jacob, the hero of I songs: H3776
2Sa 23:11 full of lentils, I troops fled from them. H2021S
1Ki 2:5 did to the two commanders of I armies, H3776
1Ki 2:32 commander of I army, and Amasa H3776
1Ki 11:25 Rezon was I adversary as long as H4200+3776
2Ki 6:23 from Aram stopped raiding I territory. H3776
1Ch 17:24 the God over Israel, is I God! H4200+3776
2Ch 13:17 thousand casualties among I able men. H3776
Ezr 10:10 married foreign women, adding to I guilt. H3776
Ps 83:4 so that I name is remembered no more." H3776
Isa 43:15 your Holy One, I Creator, your King." H3776
Isa 44:6 the LORD says—I King and Redeemer H3776
Isa 56:10 I watchmen are blind, they all lack H2257S
Isa 57:18 them and restore comfort to I mourners, H2257S
Jer 3:9 Because I immorality mattered so little to H2023S
Jer 31:9 because I am I father, and Ephraim H4200+3776
Jer 50:20 "search will be made for I guilt, but there H3776
Jer 51:49 "Babylon must fall because of I slain, just H3776
Eze 36:37 I will yield to I plea and do this H1074+3776
Hos 1:5 that day I will break I bow in the Valley of H3776
Hos 5:5 I arrogance testifies against them; the H3776
Hos 7:10 I arrogance testifies against him, but H3776
Hos 14:7 I fame will be like the wine of Lebanon. H2257S
Mic 5:1 They will strike I ruler on the cheek with a H3776
Jn 3:10 "You are I teacher," said Jesus, "and do G2702

ISRAELITE (99) [ISRAEL]

Ge 36:31 in Edom before any I king reigned: H1201+3776
Ex 5:14 drivers beat the I overseers they H1201+3776
Ex 5:15 Then the I overseers went and H1201+3776
Ex 5:19 The I overseers realized they were H1201+3776
Ex 12:40 of time the I people lived in Egypt H1201+3776
Ex 16:1 The whole I community set out H1201+3776
Ex 16:9 "Say to the entire I community H1201+3776
Ex 16:10 to the whole I community, H1201+3776
Ex 17:1 The whole I community set out H1201+3776
Ex 24:5 Then he sent young I men, and H1201+3776
Ex 35:1 the whole I community and said H1201+3776
Ex 35:4 said to the whole I community, H1201+3776
Ex 35:20 Then the whole I community H1201+3776
Ex 35:29 All the I men and women who were H1201+3776
Lev 4:13 " 'If the whole I community sins H3776
Lev 16:5 From the I community he is to take H1201+3776
Lev 17:3 Any I who sacrifices an H408+4946+1074+3776
Lev 17:8 'Any I or any foreigner H408+4946+1074+3776
Lev 17:10 against any I or any H408+4946+1074+3776
Lev 17:13 " 'Any I or any foreigner H408+4946+1201+3776
Lev 19:17 " 'Do not hate a fellow I in your heart H278
Lev 20:2 'Any I or any foreigner H408+4946+1201+3776
Lev 22:18 whether an I or a H408+4946+1074+3776
Lev 24:10 Now the son of an I mother and an H3778
Lev 24:10 camp between him and an I. H408+2021+3778
Lev 24:11 The son of the I woman blasphemed the H3778
Nu 1:2 of the whole I community by their H1201+3776
Nu 1:53 will not fall on the I community. H1201+3776
Nu 3:12 male offspring of every I woman. H1201+3776
Nu 3:40 all the firstborn I males who are a H1201+3776
Nu 7:84 were the offerings of the I leaders for the H3776
Nu 8:9 assemble the whole I community. H1201+3776
Nu 8:16 male offspring from every I woman. H1201+3776
Nu 8:20 and the whole I community did H1201+3776
Nu 10:28 of march for the I divisions as they H1201+3776
Nu 13:26 and the whole I community at H1201+3776
Nu 14:5 of the whole I assembly gathered H1201+3776
Nu 14:7 said to the entire I assembly H1201+3776
Nu 15:25 the whole I community, H1201+3776
Nu 15:26 The whole I community and the H1201+3776
Nu 15:29 a native-born I or a foreigner H928+1201+3776
Nu 16:2 With them were 250 I men H1201+3776
Nu 16:9 from the rest of the I community and H3776
Nu 16:41 day the whole I community H1201+3776
Nu 19:9 be kept by the I community for use H1201+3776
Nu 20:1 month the whole I community H1201+3776
Nu 20:22 The whole I community set out H1201+3776
Nu 22:41 he could see the outskirts of the I camp. H6639
Nu 25:6 Then an I man brought into H4946+1201+3776
Nu 25:8 followed the I into the tent. H408+3776
Nu 25:8 right through the I man and into the H3776
Nu 25:14 The name of the I who was killed H408+3776
Nu 26:2 of the whole I community by H1201+3776
Nu 27:20 so the whole I community will obey H1201+3776
Nu 31:12 priest and the I assembly at their H1201+3776
Nu 32:28 to the family heads of the I tribes. H1201+3776
Nu 36:1 the heads of the I families. H1201+3776
Nu 36:3 they marry men from other I tribes; H1201+3776
Nu 36:7 every I shall keep the tribal H1201+3776
Nu 36:8 land in any I tribe must marry H1201+3776
Nu 36:8 so that every I will possess the H1201+3776
Nu 36:9 each I tribe is to keep the land H1201+3776
Dt 1:16 between an I and a foreigner residing H408S
Dt 15:2 any loan they have made to a fellow I. H8276
Dt 15:3 cancel any debt your fellow I owes you. H278
Dt 17:15 a foreigner over you, one who is not an I. H278
Dt 19:18 giving false testimony against a fellow I, H278
Dt 22:19 man has given an I virgin a bad name. H3776
Dt 23:17 No I man or woman is to become a H3776+4946
Dt 23:19 Do not charge a fellow I interest, whether H278
Dt 23:20 interest, but not a fellow I, so that the LORD H278
Dt 24:7 a fellow I and treating or H4946+1201+3776
Dt 24:14 that worker is a fellow I or a foreigner H278
Dt 25:3 your fellow I will be degraded in your eyes. H278
Jos 11:22 No Anakites were left in I territory H1201+3776
Jos 18:2 were still seven I tribes who had H1201+3776
Jos 22:11 near the Jordan on the I side, H1201+3776
Jos 22:14 of a family division among the I clans. H3776
Jdg 7:14 sword of Gideon son of Joash, the I. H408+3776
Jdg 11:39 From this comes the I tradition H928+3776
Jdg 20:33 the I ambush charged out of its place H3776
1Sa 26:2 with his three thousand select I troops, to H3776
1Sa 31:7 Jordan saw that the I army had fled and H3776
2Sa 1:3 "I have escaped from the I camp. H3776
2Sa 11:1 with the king's men and the whole I army. H3776
1Ki 8:1 and the chiefs of the I families, H1201+3776
2Ki 13:25 and so he recovered the I towns. H3776
1Ch 1:43 before any I king reigned: H4200+1201+3776
1Ch 16:3 of raisins to each I man and woman. H408+3776
2Ch 5:2 and the chiefs of the I families, H1201+3776
2Ch 19:8 priests and heads of I families to H3776
2Ch 23:2 the heads of I families from all the H3776
2Ch 25:9 hundred talents I paid for these I troops?" H3776
Ne 9:2 Those of I descent had separated H3776
Eze 37:19 of the I tribes associated with him H3776
Eze 44:22 only virgins of I descent or widows H1074+3776
Ob 20 This company of I exiles who are in H1201+3776
Jn 1:47 "Here truly is an I in whom there is no G2703
Ro 11:1 I am an I myself, a descendant of G2703

ISRAELITE'S (2) [ISRAEL]

Dt 22:1 If you see your fellow I ox or sheep straying, H278
Dt 22:4 If you see your fellow I donkey or ox fallen H278

ISRAELITES (701) [ISRAEL]

Ge 32:32 to this day the I do not eat the H1201+3776
Ge 47:27 Now the I settled in Egypt in the region of H3776
Ge 50:25 Joseph made the I swear an oath H1201+3776
Ex 1:7 the I were exceedingly fruitful H1201+3776
Ex 1:9 "the I have become far too H6639+1201+3776
Ex 1:12 the Egyptians came to dread the I H1201+3776
Ex 2:23 The I groaned in their slavery and H1201+3776
Ex 2:25 looked on the I and was concerned H1201+3776
Ex 3:9 the cry of the I has reached me, H1201+3776
Ex 3:10 bring my people the I out of Egypt." H1201+3776
Ex 3:11 and bring the I out of Egypt? H1201+3776
Ex 3:13 I go to the I and say to them, H1201+3776
Ex 3:14 This is what you are to say to the I H1201+3776
Ex 3:15 to Moses, "Say to the I, 'The LORD, H1201+3776
Ex 4:29 together all the elders of the I, H1201+3776
Ex 6:5 I have heard the groaning of the I H1201+3776
Ex 6:6 say to the I: 'I am the LORD, H1201+3776
Ex 6:9 Moses reported this to the I, but H1201+3776
Ex 6:11 of Egypt to let the I go out of his H1201+3776
Ex 6:12 "If the I will not listen to me H1201+3776
Ex 6:13 Aaron about the I and Pharaoh H1201+3776
Ex 6:13 them to bring the I out of Egypt. H1201+3776
Ex 6:26 "Bring the I out of Egypt by their H1201+3776
Ex 6:27 about bringing the I out of Egypt— H1201+3776
Ex 7:2 Pharaoh to let the I go out of his H1201+3776
Ex 7:4 out my divisions, my people the I. H1201+3776
Ex 7:5 Egypt and bring the I out of it." H1201+3776
Ex 9:4 animal belonging to the I will die. H1201+3776
Ex 9:6 animal belonging to the I died. H1201+3776
Ex 9:7 one of the animals of the I had died. H3776
Ex 9:26 land of Goshen, where the I were. H1201+3776
Ex 9:35 hard and he would not let the I go, H1201+3776
Ex 10:20 and he would not let the I go. H1201+3776
Ex 10:23 Yet all the I had light in the places H1201+3776
Ex 11:7 But among the I not a dog will bark H1201+3776
Ex 11:10 he would not let the I go out of his H1201+3776
Ex 12:27 the houses of the I in Egypt and H1201+3776
Ex 12:28 The I did just what the LORD H1201+3776
Ex 12:31 my people, you and the I! Go, H1201+3776
Ex 12:35 The I did as Moses instructed and H1201+3776
Ex 12:37 The I journeyed from Rameses to H1201+3776
Ex 12:39 With the dough the I had brought from Egypt NDT
Ex 12:42 this night all the I are to keep vigil H1201+3776
Ex 12:50 All the I did just what the LORD had H1201+3776
Ex 12:51 LORD brought the I out of Egypt by H1201+3776
Ex 13:2 womb among the I belongs to me, H1201+3776
Ex 13:18 The I went up out of Egypt ready H1201+3776
Ex 13:19 had made the I swear an oath. H1201+3776
Ex 14:2 "Tell the I to turn back and encamp H1201+3776
Ex 14:3 'The I are wandering around the H1201+3776
Ex 14:4 know that I am the LORD." So the I did this. NDT
Ex 14:5 We have let the I go and have lost their H3776
Ex 14:8 so that he pursued the I, who were H1201+3776
Ex 14:9 pursued the I and overtook them as they H2157S
Ex 14:10 approached, the I looked up, and H1201+3776
Ex 14:15 Tell the I to move on. H1201+3776
Ex 14:16 water so that the I can go through H1201+3776
Ex 14:22 the I went through the sea on H1201+3776
Ex 14:25 Egyptians said, "Let's get away from the I! H3776
Ex 14:28 that had followed the I into the sea. H2157S
Ex 14:29 But the I went through the sea on H1201+3776
Ex 14:31 And when the I saw the mighty hand of H3776
Ex 15:1 Moses and the I sang this song to H1201+3776
Ex 15:19 the I walked through the sea H1201+3776
Ex 16:3 The I said to them, "If only we had H1201+3776
Ex 16:6 Moses and Aaron said to all the I, H1201+3776
Ex 16:12 have heard the grumbling of the I. H1201+3776
Ex 16:15 When the I saw it, they said to each H1201+3776
Ex 16:17 The I did as they were told; some H1201+3776
Ex 16:35 The I ate manna forty years, until H1201+3776
Ex 17:7 because the I quarreled and H1201+3776
Ex 17:8 came and attacked the I at Rephidim. H3776
Ex 17:11 up his hands, the I were winning, but H3776
Ex 19:1 third month after the I left Egypt— H1201+3776
Ex 19:6 the words you are to speak to the I." H1201+3776
Ex 20:22 LORD said to Moses, "Tell the I this: H1201+3776
Ex 24:11 against these leaders of the I; H1201+3776
Ex 24:17 To the I the glory of the LORD looked H1201+3776
Ex 25:2 "Tell the I to bring me an offering H1201+3776
Ex 25:22 you all my commands for the I. H1201+3776
Ex 27:20 "Command the I to bring you clear H1201+3776
Ex 27:21 among the I for the generations H1201+3776
Ex 28:1 brought to you from among the I, H1201+3776
Ex 28:30 decisions for the I over his heart H1201+3776
Ex 28:38 in the sacred gifts the I consecrate, H1201+3776
Ex 29:28 share from the I for Aaron and his H1201+3776
Ex 29:28 contribution the I are to make to H1201+3776
Ex 29:43 there also I will meet with the I H1201+3776
Ex 29:45 dwell among the I and be their H1201+3776
Ex 30:12 a census of the I to count them, H1201+3776
Ex 30:16 money from the I and use it for the H1201+3776
Ex 30:16 memorial for the I before the LORD, H1201+3776
Ex 30:31 Say to the I, 'This is to be my sacred H1201+3776
Ex 31:13 "Say to the I, 'You must observe my H1201+3776
Ex 31:16 The I are to observe the Sabbath H1201+3776
Ex 31:17 sign between me and the I forever, H1201+3776
Ex 32:20 the water and made the I drink it. H1201+3776
Ex 33:5 to Moses, "Tell the I, 'You are a H1201+3776
Ex 33:6 So the I stripped off their ornaments H1201+3776
Ex 34:30 Aaron and all the I saw Moses, H1201+3776
Ex 34:32 Afterward all the I came near him H1201+3776
Ex 34:34 and told the I what he had been H1201+3776
Ex 35:30 Then Moses said to the I, "See, the H1201+3776
Ex 36:3 the offerings the I had brought to H1201+3776
Ex 39:32 The I did everything just as the H1201+3776
Ex 39:42 The I had done all the work just as H1201+3776
Ex 40:36 In all the travels of the I, whenever H1201+3776
Ex 40:38 the sight of all the I during all their H1074+3776
Lev 1:2 "Speak to the I and say to them H1201+3776

Lev 4: 2 “Say to the **I**: ‘When anyone sins H1201+3776
Lev 7:23 “Say to the **I**: ‘Do not eat any of the H1201+3776
Lev 7:29 “Say to the **I**: ‘Anyone who brings a H1201+3776
Lev 7:34 the fellowship offerings of the **I**, H1201+3776
Lev 7:34 as their perpetual share from the **I**. H1201+3776
Lev 7:36 that the **I** give this to them H1201+3776
Lev 7:38 he commanded the **I** to bring their H1201+3776
Lev 9: 3 Then say to the **I**: ‘Take a male H1201+3776
Lev 10: 6 relatives, all the **I**, may mourn for H1074+3776
Lev 10:11 you can teach the **I** all the decrees H1201+3776
Lev 11: 2 “Say to the **I**: ‘Of all the animals H1201+3776
Lev 12: 2 “Say to the **I**: ‘A woman who H1201+3776
Lev 15: 2 “Speak to the **I** and say to them H1201+3776
Lev 15:31 ‘You must keep the **I** separate from H1201+3776
Lev 16:16 uncleanness and rebellion of the **I**, H1201+3776
Lev 16:19 it from the uncleanness of the **I**. H1201+3776
Lev 16:21 wickedness and rebellion of the **I**— H1201+3776
Lev 16:34 once a year for all the sins of the **I**.” H1201+3776
Lev 17: 2 and to all the **I** and say to them: H1201+3776
Lev 17: 5 This is so the **I** will bring to the LORD H1201+3776
Lev 17:12 Therefore I say to the **I**, “None of H1201+3776
Lev 17:14 That is why I have said to the **I** H1201+3776
Lev 18: 2 “Speak to the **I** and say to them: ‘I H1201+3776
Lev 20: 2 “Say to the **I**: ‘Any Israelite or any H1201+3776
Lev 21:24 Aaron and his sons and to all the **I**. H1201+3776
Lev 22: 2 offerings the **I** consecrate to me, H1201+3776
Lev 22: 3 that the **I** consecrate to the H1201+3776
Lev 22:15 offerings the **I** present to the LORD H1201+3776
Lev 22:18 and to all the **I** and say to them: H1201+3776
Lev 22:32 be acknowledged as holy by the **I**. H1201+3776
Lev 23: 2 “Speak to the **I** and say to them H1201+3776
Lev 23:10 “Speak to the **I** and say to them H1201+3776
Lev 23:24 “Say to the **I**: ‘On the first day of the H1201+3776
Lev 23:34 “Say to the **I**: ‘On the fifteenth day H1201+3776
Lev 23:42 All native-born **I** are to live in such H3776
Lev 23:43 that I had the **I** live in temporary H1201+3776
Lev 23:44 announced to the **I** the appointed H1201+3776
Lev 24: 2 “Command the **I** to bring you clear H1201+3776
Lev 24: 8 on behalf of the **I**, as a lasting H1201+3776
Lev 24:10 father went out among the **I**, H1201+3776
Lev 24:15 Say to the **I**: ‘Anyone who curses H1201+3776
Lev 24:23 Then Moses spoke to the **I**, and H1201+3776
Lev 24:23 The **I** did as the LORD commanded H1201+3776
Lev 25: 2 “Speak to the **I** and say to them H1201+3776
Lev 25:25 “ ‘If one of your **fellow I** becomes poor H278
Lev 25:33 are their property among the **I**. H1201+3776
Lev 25:35 “ ‘If any of your **fellow I** become poor and H278
Lev 25:39 “ ‘If any of your **fellow I** become poor and H278
Lev 25:42 Because **the I** are my servants, whom I H2156S
Lev 25:46 rule over your **fellow I** ruthlessly. H1201+3776
Lev 25:47 any of your **fellow I** become poor and H278
Lev 25:55 the **I** belong to me as servants H1201+3776
Lev 26:46 himself and the **I** through Moses. H1201+3776
Lev 27: 2 “Speak to the **I** and say to them: ‘If H1201+3776
Lev 27:34 Moses at Mount Sinai for the **I**. H1201+3776
Nu 1: 1 second year after **the I** came out of Egypt H4392S
Nu 1:45 All the **I** twenty years old or more H1201+3776
Nu 1:49 them in the census of the other **I**. H1201+3776
Nu 1:52 The **I** are to set up their tents by H1201+3776
Nu 1:54 The **I** did all this just as the LORD H1201+3776
Nu 2: 2 “The **I** are to camp around the tent H1201+3776
Nu 2:32 These are the **I**, counted according H1201+3776
Nu 2:33 not counted along with the other **I**, H1201+3776
Nu 2:34 So the **I** did everything the LORD H1201+3776
Nu 3: 8 of the **I** by doing the work H1201+3776
Nu 3: 9 they are the **I** who are to be given H1201+3776
Nu 3:12 from among the **I** in place of the H1201+3776
Nu 3:38 of the sanctuary on behalf of the **I**. H1201+3776
Nu 3:41 in place of all the firstborn of the **I**, H1201+3776
Nu 3:41 firstborn of the livestock of the **I**. H1201+3776
Nu 3:42 counted all the firstborn of the **I**, H1201+3776
Nu 3:46 the 273 firstborn **I** who exceed the H1201+3776
Nu 3:48 of the additional **I** to Aaron and his sons H2157S
Nu 3:50 firstborn of the **I** he collected silver H1201+3776
Nu 5: 2 “Command the **I** to send away from H1201+3776
Nu 5: 4 The **I** did so; they sent them outside H1201+3776
Nu 5: 6 “Say to the **I**: ‘Any man or woman H1201+3776
Nu 5: 9 contributions the **I** bring to a priest H1201+3776
Nu 5:12 “Speak to the **I** and say to them: ‘If H1201+3776
Nu 6: 2 “Speak to the **I** and say to them: ‘If H1201+3776
Nu 6:23 ‘This is how you are to bless the **I**. H1201+3776
Nu 6:27 “So they will put my name on the **I** H1201+3776
Nu 8: 6 from among *all* the **I** and make H1201+3776
Nu 8:10 and the **I** are to lay their hands on H1201+3776
Nu 8:11 LORD as a wave offering from the **I**, H1201+3776
Nu 8:14 the Levites apart from the other **I**, H1201+3776
Nu 8:16 They are the **I** who are to be given H1201+3776
Nu 8:19 From among *all* the **I**, I have given H1201+3776
Nu 8:19 on behalf of the **I** and to make H1201+3776
Nu 8:19 will strike the **I** when they go near H1201+3776
Nu 9: 2 “Have the **I** celebrate the Passover H1201+3776
Nu 9: 4 Moses told the **I** to celebrate the H1201+3776
Nu 9: 5 The **I** did everything just as the H1201+3776
Nu 9: 7 with the other **I** at the appointed H1201+3776
Nu 9:10 “Tell the **I**: ‘When any of you or H1201+3776
Nu 9:17 the tent, the **I** set out; wherever H1201+3776
Nu 9:17 the cloud settled, the **I** encamped. H1201+3776
Nu 9:18 At the LORD's command the **I** set out, H1201+3776
Nu 9:19 the **I** obeyed the LORD's order and H1201+3776
Nu 9:22 the **I** would remain in camp and H1201+3776
Nu 10:12 Then the **I** set out from the Desert H1201+3776
Nu 11: 4 and again the **I** started wailing and H1201+3776
Nu 13: 2 Canaan, which I am giving to the **I**. H1201+3776
Nu 13: 3 All of them were leaders of the **I**. H1201+3776
Nu 13:24 cluster of grapes the **I** cut off there. H1201+3776
Nu 13:32 spread among the **I** a bad report H1201+3776
Nu 14: 2 All the **I** grumbled against Moses H1201+3776
Nu 14:10 at the tent of meeting to all the **I**. H1201+3776
Nu 14:27 complaints of these grumbling **I**. H1201+3776
Nu 14:39 Moses reported this to all the **I**, H1201+3776
Nu 15: 2 “Speak to the **I** and say to them H1201+3776
Nu 15:18 “Speak to the **I** and say to them H1201+3776
Nu 15:32 While the **I** were in the wilderness H1201+3776
Nu 15:38 “Speak to the **I** and say to them H1201+3776
Nu 16:34 At their cries, all the **I** around them fled H3776
Nu 16:38 Let them be a sign to the **I**.” H1201+3776
Nu 16:40 was to remind the **I** that no one H1201+3776
Nu 17: 2 “Speak to the **I** and get twelve staffs H1201+3776
Nu 17: 5 grumbling against you by the **I**.” H1201+3776
Nu 17: 6 So Moses spoke to the **I**, and their H1201+3776
Nu 17: 9 the LORD's presence to all the **I**. H1201+3776
Nu 17:12 The **I** said to Moses, “We will die H1201+3776
Nu 18: 5 wrath will not fall on the **I** again. H1201+3776
Nu 18: 6 from among the **I** as a gift to you, H1201+3776
Nu 18: 8 offerings the **I** give me I give to H1201+3776
Nu 18:11 of all the wave offerings of the **I**. H1201+3776
Nu 18:19 holy offerings the **I** present to the H1201+3776
Nu 18:20 and your inheritance among the **I**. H1201+3776
Nu 18:22 From now on the **I** must not go near H1201+3776
Nu 18:23 no inheritance among the **I**. H1201+3776
Nu 18:24 the tithes that the **I** present as an H1201+3776
Nu 18:24 have no inheritance among the **I**. H1201+3776
Nu 18:26 receive from the **I** the tithe I give H1201+3776
Nu 18:28 all the tithes you receive from the **I**. H1201+3776
Nu 18:32 defile the holy offerings of the **I**, H1201+3776
Nu 19: 2 Tell the **I** to bring you a red heifer H1201+3776
Nu 19:10 both for the **I** and for the foreigners H1201+3776
Nu 20:12 me as holy in the sight of the **I**, H1201+3776
Nu 20:13 where the **I** quarreled with the LORD H1201+3776
Nu 20:19 The **I** replied: “We will go along H1201+3776
Nu 20:24 will not enter the land I give the **I**, H1201+3776
Nu 20:29 all the **I** mourned for him thirty H1074+3776
Nu 21: 1 he attacked the **I** and captured some of H3776
Nu 21: 6 bit the people and many **I** died. H4946+3776
Nu 21:10 The **I** moved on and camped at H1201+3776
Nu 21:32 the **I** captured its surrounding settlements NDT
Nu 22: 1 Then the **I** traveled to the plains of H1201+3776
Nu 22: 3 filled with dread because of the **I**. H1201+3776
Nu 25: 8 plague against the **I** was stopped; H1201+3776
Nu 25:11 turned my anger away from the **I**. H1201+3776
Nu 25:13 and made atonement for the **I**.” H1201+3776
Nu 26: 4 These were the **I** who came out of H1201+3776
Nu 26:62 along with the other **I** because they H1201+3776
Nu 26:63 they counted the **I** on the plains of H1201+3776
Nu 26:64 they counted the **I** in the Desert of H1201+3776
Nu 26:65 LORD had told **those I** they would surely H2157S
Nu 27: 8 “Say to the **I**, ‘If a man dies and H1201+3776
Nu 27:11 is to have the force of law for the **I**, H1201+3776
Nu 27:12 see the land I have given the **I**. H1201+3776
Nu 27:21 community of the **I** will go out, H1201+3776
Nu 28: 2 command to the **I** and say to them: H1201+3776
Nu 29:40 Moses told the **I** all that the LORD H1201+3776
Nu 31: 2 on the Midianites for the **I**. H1201+3776
Nu 31: 9 The **I** captured the Midianite H1201+3776
Nu 31:16 and enticed the **I** to be unfaithful H1201+3776
Nu 31:42 The half belonging to the **I**, which H1201+3776
Nu 31:54 memorial for the **I** before the LORD. H1201+3776
Nu 32: 6 “Should your **fellow I** go to war while you H278
Nu 32: 7 discourage the **I** from crossing over H1201+3776
Nu 32: 9 discouraged the **I** from entering the H1201+3776
Nu 32:17 go ahead of the **I** until we have H1201+3776
Nu 32:18 until each of the **I** has received H1201+3776
Nu 33: 1 journey of the **I** when they came H1201+3776
Nu 33: 3 The **I** set out from Rameses on the H1201+3776
Nu 33: 5 The **I** left Rameses and camped at H1201+3776
Nu 33:38 year after the **I** came out of Egypt. H1201+3776
Nu 33:40 heard that the **I** were coming. H1201+3776
Nu 33:51 “Speak to the **I** and say to them H1201+3776
Nu 34: 2 “Command the **I** and say to them H1201+3776
Nu 34:13 Moses commanded the **I**: “Assign H1201+3776
Nu 34:29 inheritance to the **I** in the land of H1201+3776
Nu 35: 2 “Command the **I** to give the Levites H1201+3776
Nu 35: 2 from the inheritance **the I** will possess. H4392S
Nu 35: 8 the land the **I** possess are to be H1201+3776
Nu 35:10 “Speak to the **I** and say to them H1201+3776
Nu 35:15 of refuge for **I** and for foreigners H1201+3776
Nu 35:34 the LORD, dwell among the **I**. H1201+3776
Nu 36: 2 as an inheritance to the **I** by lot, H1201+3776
Nu 36: 4 the Year of Jubilee for the **I** comes, H1201+3776
Nu 36: 5 Moses gave this order to the **I**: H1201+3776
Nu 36:13 Moses to the **I** on the plains of H1201+3776
Dt 1: 3 proclaimed to the **I** all that the LORD H1201+3776
Dt 1:16 the case is between *two* **I** or between an H278
Dt 3:18 cross over ahead of the other **I**. H1201+3776
Dt 3:20 gives rest to your **fellow I** as he has to you, H278
Dt 4:44 is the law Moses set before the **I**. H1201+3776
Dt 4:46 Moses and the **I** as they came out H1201+3776
Dt 10: 6 The **I** traveled from the wells of H1201+3776
Dt 10: 9 share or inheritance among their **fellow I**; H278
Dt 15: 7 is poor among your **fellow I** in any of the H278
Dt 15: 9 needy among your **fellow I** and give them H278
Dt 15:11 toward your **fellow I** who are poor and H278
Dt 17:15 He must be from among your **fellow I**. H278
Dt 17:20 better than his **fellow I** and turn from the H278
Dt 18: 2 have no inheritance among their **fellow I**; H278
Dt 18:15 me from among you, from your **fellow I**. H278
Dt 18:18 prophet like you from among their **fellow I**, H278
Dt 29: 1 Moses to make with the **I** in Moab, H1201+3776
Dt 29: 2 summoned all the **I** and said to them: H3776
Dt 31:19 teach it to the **I** and have them H1201+3776
Dt 31:22 song that day and taught it to the **I**. H1201+3776
Dt 31:23 you will bring the **I** into the land I H1201+3776
Dt 32:49 land I am giving the **I** as their own H1201+3776
Dt 32:51 presence of the **I** at the waters of H1201+3776
Dt 32:51 uphold my holiness among the **I**. H1201+3776
Dt 33: 1 on the **I** before his death. H1201+3776
Dt 34: 8 The **I** grieved for Moses in the H1201+3776
Dt 34: 9 So the **I** listened to him and did H1201+3776
Jos 1: 2 am about to give to them—to the **I**. H1201+3776
Jos 1:14 must cross over ahead of your **fellow I**. H278
Jos 2: 2 some of the **I** have come here H1201+3776
Jos 3: 1 Joshua and all the **I** set out from H1201+3776
Jos 3: 9 Joshua said to the **I**, “Come here H1201+3776
Jos 4: 4 men he had appointed from the **I**, H1201+3776
Jos 4: 5 to the number of the tribes of the **I**, H1201+3776
Jos 4: 8 So the **I** did as Joshua commanded H1201+3776
Jos 4: 8 to the number of the tribes of the **I**, H1201+3776
Jos 4:12 in front of the **I**, as Moses had H1201+3776
Jos 4:21 He said to the **I**, “In the future when H1201+3776
Jos 5: 1 Jordan before the **I** until they had H1201+3776
Jos 5: 1 had the courage to face the **I**. H1201+3776
Jos 5: 2 knives and circumcise the **I** again.” H1201+3776
Jos 5: 3 and circumcised the **I** at Gibeath H1201+3776
Jos 5: 6 The **I** had moved about in the H1201+3776
Jos 5:10 the **I** celebrated the Passover. H1201+3776
Jos 5:12 was no longer any manna for the **I**, H1201+3776
Jos 6: 1 securely barred because of the **I**. H1201+3776
Jos 6:25 she lives among the **I** to this day. H3776
Jos 7: 1 But the **I** were unfaithful in regard H1201+3776
Jos 7: 5 They chased **the I** from the city gate as H4392S
Jos 7:12 That is why the **I** cannot stand H1201+3776
Jos 7:23 and all the **I** and spread them H1201+3776
Jos 8:20 the **I** who had been fleeing toward the H6639S
Jos 8:22 in the middle, with **I** on both sides. H3776
Jos 8:24 all the **I** returned to Ai and killed those H3776
Jos 8:31 of the LORD had commanded the **I**. H1201+3776
Jos 8:32 in the presence of the **I**, Joshua H1201+3776
Jos 8:33 All the **I**, with their elders, officials and H3776
Jos 9: 6 at Gilgal and said to him and the **I**, H408+3776
Jos 9: 7 The **I** said to the Hivites, “But H408+3776
Jos 9:14 The **I** sampled their provisions but did not H408S
Jos 9:16 the **I** heard that they were neighbors NDT
Jos 9:17 So the **I** set out and on the third day H1201+3776
Jos 9:18 But the **I** did not attack them H1201+3776
Jos 9:26 So Joshua saved them from the **I** H1201+3776
Jos 10: 4 made peace with Joshua and the **I**.” H1201+3776
Jos 10:10 so Joshua and the **I** defeated them NDT
Jos 10:11 were killed by the swords of the **I**. H1201+3776
Jos 10:20 So Joshua and the **I** defeated them H1201+3776
Jos 10:21 one uttered a word against the **I**. H1201+3776
Jos 11:14 The **I** carried off for themselves all H1201+3776
Jos 11:19 made a treaty of peace with the **I**, H1201+3776
Jos 12: 1 land whom the **I** had defeated and H1201+3776
Jos 12: 6 and the **I** conquered them. H1201+3776
Jos 12: 7 Joshua and the **I** conquered on the H1201+3776
Jos 13: 6 will drive them out before the **I**. H1201+3776
Jos 13:13 But the **I** did not drive out the H1201+3776
Jos 13:13 continue to live among the **I** to this day. H3776
Jos 13:22 the **I** had put to the sword Balaam H1201+3776
Jos 14: 1 are the areas the **I** received as an H1201+3776
Jos 14: 5 So the **I** divided the land, just as H1201+3776
Jos 14: 8 my **fellow I** who went up with me made H278
Jos 17:13 However, when the **I** grew stronger H1201+3776
Jos 18: 1 assembly of the **I** gathered at H1201+3776
Jos 18: 3 So Joshua said to the **I**: “How long H1201+3776
Jos 18:10 the land to the **I** according to their H1201+3776
Jos 19:49 the **I** gave Joshua son of Nun an H1201+3776
Jos 20: 2 “Tell the **I** to designate the cities of H1201+3776
Jos 20: 9 Any of the **I** or any foreigner H1201+3776
Jos 21: 3 the **I** gave the Levites the following H1201+3776
Jos 21: 8 So the **I** allotted to the Levites H1201+3776
Jos 21:41 held by the **I** were forty-eight in H1201+3776
Jos 22: 3 not deserted your **fellow I** but have carried H278
Jos 22: 7 side of the Jordan along with their **fellow I**.) H278
Jos 22: 8 from your enemies with your **fellow I**.” H278
Jos 22: 9 Manasseh left the **I** at Shiloh in H1201+3776
Jos 22:11 And when the **I** heard that they had H1201+3776
Jos 22:13 So the **I** sent Phinehas son of H1201+3776
Jos 22:30 the heads of the clans of the **I**—heard H3776
Jos 22:31 have rescued the **I** from the LORD's H1201+3776
Jos 22:32 in Gilead and reported to the **I**. H1201+3776
Jos 24:32 which the **I** had brought up from H1201+3776
Jdg 1: 1 of Joshua, the **I** asked the LORD H1201+3776
Jdg 1: 3 then said to the Simeonites their **fellow I**, H278
Jdg 1:17 Simeonites their **fellow I** and attacked the H278
Jdg 2: 4 spoken these things to all the **I**, H1201+3776
Jdg 2: 6 After Joshua had dismissed the **I** H1201+3776
Jdg 2:11 Then the **I** did evil in the eyes of H1201+3776
Jdg 3: 1 left to test all those **I** who had not H3776
Jdg 3: 2 of the **I** who had not had H1201+3776
Jdg 3: 4 were left to test the **I** to see whether they H3776
Jdg 3: 5 The **I** lived among the Canaanites H1201+3776
Jdg 3: 7 The **I** did evil in the eyes of the H1201+3776
Jdg 3: 8 to whom the **I** were subject for H1201+3776
Jdg 3:12 Again the **I** did evil in the eyes of H1201+3776
Jdg 3:14 The **I** were subject to Eglon king of H1201+3776

Jdg 3:15 Again the I cried out to the LORD H1201+3776
Jdg 3:15 The I sent him with tribute to Eglon H1201+3776
Jdg 3:27 and the I went down with him from H1201+3776
Jdg 4: 1 Again the I did evil in the eyes of H1201+3776
Jdg 4: 3 oppressed the I for twenty years, H1201+3776
Jdg 4: 5 and the I went up to her to have H1201+3776
Jdg 4:23 Jabin king of Canaan before the I. H1201+3776
Jdg 4:24 the hand of the I pressed harder H1201+3776
Jdg 6: 1 The I did evil in the eyes of the H1201+3776
Jdg 6: 2 the I prepared shelters for H1201+3776
Jdg 6: 3 Whenever the I planted their crops, the H3776
Jdg 6: 6 so impoverished the I that they cried out H3776
Jdg 6: 7 When the I cried out to the LORD H1201+3776
Jdg 7: 8 the rest of the I home but kept the H408+3776
Jdg 7:23 I from Naphtali, Asher and all H408+3776
Jdg 8:22 The I said to Gideon, "Rule over us H408+3776
Jdg 8:28 before the I and did not raise H1201+3776
Jdg 8:33 died than the I again prostituted H1201+3776
Jdg 9:55 When the I saw that Abimelek was H408+3776
Jdg 10: 6 Again the I did evil in the eyes of H1201+3776
Jdg 10: 6 And because the I forsook the LORD and no NDT
Jdg 10: 8 oppressed all the I on the east side H1201+3776
Jdg 10:10 Then the I cried out to the LORD H1201+3776
Jdg 10:15 But the I said to the LORD, "We H1201+3776
Jdg 10:17 the I assembled and camped at H1201+3776
Jdg 11:27 day between the I and the H1201+3776
Jdg 13: 1 Again the I did evil in the eyes of H1201+3776
Jdg 19:12 city whose people are not I. H4946+1201+3776
Jdg 19:30 since the day the I came up out of H1201+3776
Jdg 20: 3 heard that the I had gone up to H1201+3776
Jdg 20: 3 Then the I said, "Tell us how this H1201+3776
Jdg 20: 7 all you I, speak up and tell H1201+3776
Jdg 20:11 So all the I got together and united H408+3776
Jdg 20:13 would not listen to their fellow I. H1201+3776
Jdg 20:14 at Gibeah to fight against the I. H1201+3776
Jdg 20:18 The I went up to Bethel and H1201+3776
Jdg 20:19 next morning the I got up and H1201+3776
Jdg 20:20 The I went out to fight the H408+3776
Jdg 20:21 twenty-two thousand I on the battlefield H3776
Jdg 20:22 But the I encouraged one another H408+3776
Jdg 20:23 The I went up and wept before the H1201+3776
Jdg 20:23 fight against the Benjamites, our **fellow** I?" H278
Jdg 20:24 Then the I drew near to Benjamin H1201+3776
Jdg 20:25 down another eighteen thousand I, H1201+3776
Jdg 20:26 Then all the I, the whole army H1201+3776
Jdg 20:27 And the I inquired of the LORD. H1201+3776
Jdg 20:28 the Benjamites, our **fellow** I, or not? H278
Jdg 20:31 to inflict casualties on the I as before, H6639S
Jdg 20:32 the I were saying, "Let's retreat H1201+3776
Jdg 20:35 on that day the I struck down H1201+3776
Jdg 20:38 The I had arranged with the ambush H408+3776
Jdg 20:39 then the I would counterattack H408+3776
Jdg 20:39 begun to inflict casualties on the I H408+3776
Jdg 20:41 Then the I counterattacked, and the H408+3776
Jdg 20:42 fled before the I in the direction of H408+3776
Jdg 20:42 And the I who came out of the towns cut NDT
Jdg 20:45 the I cut down five thousand men along the NDT
Jdg 21: 5 Then the I asked, "Who from all H1201+3776
Jdg 21: 6 Now the I grieved for the tribe of H1201+3776
Jdg 21: 6 the tribe of Benjamin, their **fellow** I. H278
Jdg 21:18 since we I have taken this oath: H1201+3776
Jdg 21:24 At that time the I left that place H1201+3776
1Sa 2:14 they treated all the I who came to Shiloh. H3776
1Sa 2:28 food offerings presented by the I. H1201+3776
1Sa 4: 1 Now the I went out to fight against the H3776
1Sa 4: 1 The I camped at Ebenezer, and the NDT
1Sa 4:10 the I were defeated and every man H3776
1Sa 6: 6 did they not send **the** I out so they could H4392S
1Sa 7: 3 So Samuel said to all the I, "If you H1074+3776
1Sa 7: 4 So the I put away their Baals and H1201+3776
1Sa 7: 7 When the I heard of it, they were H1201+3776
1Sa 7:10 a panic that they were routed before the I. H3776
1Sa 8:22 Then Samuel said to the I H408+3776
1Sa 11:15 and Saul and all the I held a great H408+3776
1Sa 13: 6 When the I saw that their situation H408+3776
1Sa 14:18 At that time it was with the I.) H1201+3776
1Sa 14:21 went over to the I who were with Saul H3776
1Sa 14:22 When all the I who had hidden in H408+3776
1Sa 14:24 Now the I were in distress that day H408+3776
1Sa 14:31 after the I had struck down the H6639S
1Sa 14:40 Saul then said to all the I, "You stand H3776
1Sa 15: 6 to all the I when they came up H1201+3776
1Sa 17: 2 Saul and the I assembled and H408+3776
1Sa 17: 3 occupied one hill and the I another, H3776
1Sa 17:11 Saul and all the I were dismayed and H3776
1Sa 17:24 Whenever the I saw the man, they H408+3776
1Sa 17:25 Now the I had been saying, "Do you H408+3776
1Sa 17:53 When the I returned from chasing H1201+3776
1Sa 27:12 to his people, the I, that he will be my H3776
1Sa 31: 1 against Israel; the I fled before them H408+3776
1Sa 31: 7 When the I along the valley and H408+3776
2Sa 2:17 Abner and the I were defeated by H408+3776
2Sa 2:26 your men to stop pursuing their **fellow** I?" H278
2Sa 6:19 to each person in the whole crowd of I, H3776
2Sa 7: 6 day I brought the I up out of Egypt H1201+3776
2Sa 7: 7 I have moved with all the I, H1201+3776
2Sa 10:19 peace with the I and became subject H3776
2Sa 15: 6 way toward all the I who came to the king H3776
2Sa 16: 3 'Today the I will restore to me my H1074+3776
2Sa 17:26 The I and Absalom camped in the land of H3776
2Sa 18:17 Meanwhile, all the I fled to their homes. H3776
2Sa 19: 8 Meanwhile, the I had fled to their homes H3776
2Sa 21: 2 the I had sworn to spare them H1201+3776
2Sa 23: 9 Then the I retreated, H408+3776
1Ki 6: 1 year after the I came out of Egypt, H1201+3776
1Ki 6:13 will live among the I and will not H1201+3776
1Ki 8: 2 All the I came together to King H408+3776
1Ki 8: 9 covenant with the I after they came H1201+3776
1Ki 8:63 king and all the I dedicated the H1201+3776
1Ki 9:20 these peoples were not I). H1201+3776
1Ki 9:21 whom the I could not exterminate H1201+3776
1Ki 9:22 did not make slaves of any of the I; H1201+3776
1Ki 11: 2 which the LORD had told the I, H1201+3776
1Ki 11:16 Joab and all the I stayed there for six H3776
1Ki 12:16 own house, David!" So the I went home. H3776
1Ki 12:17 But as for the I who were living in H1201+3776
1Ki 12:20 When all the I heard that Jeroboam had H3776
1Ki 12:24 to fight against your brothers, the I. H1201+3776
1Ki 12:33 festival for the I and went up to the H1201+3776
1Ki 14:24 LORD had driven out before the I. H1201+3776
1Ki 16:16 When the I in the camp heard that Zimri H6639S
1Ki 16:17 Then Omri and all the I with him withdrew H3776
1Ki 19:10 The I have rejected your covenant H1201+3776
1Ki 19:14 The I have rejected your covenant H1201+3776
1Ki 20:15 he assembled the rest of the I, H1201+3776
1Ki 20:20 the Arameans fled, with the I in pursuit. H3776
1Ki 20:27 When the I were also mustered and H1201+3776
1Ki 20:27 The I camped opposite them like H1201+3776
1Ki 20:29 The I inflicted a hundred thousand H1201+3776
2Ki 3:24 the I rose up and fought them until they H3776
2Ki 3:24 And the I invaded the land and slaughtered NDT
2Ki 7:13 will be like that of all the I left here— H3776
2Ki 7:13 only be like all these I who are doomed. H3776
2Ki 8:12 know the harm you will do to the I," H1201+3776
2Ki 10:32 overpowered the I throughout their H3776
2Ki 13: 5 So the I lived in their own homes H1201+3776
2Ki 13:21 Once while *some* I were burying a man H2156S
2Ki 16: 3 LORD had driven out before the I. H1201+3776
2Ki 17: 6 Samaria and deported the I to Assyria. H3776
2Ki 17: 7 place because the I had sinned H1201+3776
2Ki 17: 9 The I secretly did things against the H1201+3776
2Ki 17:22 The I persisted in all the sins of H1201+3776
2Ki 17:24 towns of Samaria to replace the I. H1201+3776
2Ki 17:35 the LORD made a covenant with **the** I, H4392S
2Ki 18: 4 to that time the I had been burning H1201+3776
2Ki 21: 2 LORD had driven out before the I. H1201+3776
2Ki 21: 8 the feet of the I wander from the land H3776
2Ki 21: 9 LORD had destroyed before the I. H1201+3776
1Ch 6:64 So the I gave the Levites these H1201+3776
1Ch 6:70 of Manasseh the I gave Aner and Bileam, NDT
1Ch 9: 2 property in their own towns were *some* I, H3776
1Ch 10: 1 against Israel; the I fled before them H408+3776
1Ch 10: 7 When all the I in the valley saw that H408+3776
1Ch 11: 4 David and all the I marched to Jerusalem H3776
1Ch 12:38 All the rest of the I were also of one mind H3776
1Ch 13: 8 David and all the I were celebrating with H3776
1Ch 17: 6 Wherever I have moved with all the I, did H3776
1Ch 21: 2 "Go and count the I from Beersheba to H3776
1Ch 27: 1 This is the list of the I—heads of H1201+3776
1Ch 28: 2 "Listen to me, my **fellow** I, my people. H278
2Ch 5: 3 And all the I came together to the H408+3776
2Ch 5:10 covenant with the I after they came H1201+3776
2Ch 7: 3 When all the I saw the fire coming H1201+3776
2Ch 7: 6 trumpets, and all the I were standing. H3776
2Ch 8: 2 given him, and settled I in them. H1201+3776
2Ch 8: 7 Jebusites (these people were not I). H3776
2Ch 8: 8 whom the I had not destroyed H1201+3776
2Ch 8: 9 make slaves of the I for his work; H1201+3776
2Ch 10:16 So all the I went home. H3776
2Ch 10:17 But as for the I who were living in H1201+3776
2Ch 10:18 the I stoned him to death. H1201+3776
2Ch 11: 4 Do not go up to fight against your **fellow** I H278
2Ch 13:16 The I fled before Judah, and God H1201+3776
2Ch 13:18 The I were subdued on that H1201+3776
2Ch 28: 3 LORD had driven out before the I. H1201+3776
2Ch 28: 8 captive from their **fellow** I who were from H278
2Ch 28:11 Send back your **fellow** I you have taken as H278
2Ch 28:15 took them back to their **fellow** I at Jericho, H278
2Ch 30: 7 not be like your parents and your **fellow** I, H278
2Ch 30: 9 then your **fellow** I and your children will be H278
2Ch 30:21 The I who were present in H1201+3776
2Ch 31: 1 the I who were there went out to the H3776
2Ch 31: 1 the I returned to their own towns H1201+3776
2Ch 31: 5 the I generously gave the firstfruits H1201+3776
2Ch 33: 2 LORD had driven out before the I. H1201+3776
2Ch 33: 8 make the feet of the I leave the land I H3776
2Ch 33: 9 LORD had destroyed before the I. H1201+3776
2Ch 34:33 all the territory belonging to the I, H1201+3776
2Ch 35: 5 subdivision of the families of your **fellow** I, H278
2Ch 35: 6 prepare the lambs for your **fellow** I, H278
2Ch 35:17 The I who were present celebrated H1201+3776
Ezr 2:70 the rest of the I settled in their towns. H3776
Ezr 3: 1 came and the I had settled in H1201+3776
Ezr 6:21 So the I who had returned from the H1201+3776
Ezr 7: 7 Some of the I, including priests H1201+3776
Ezr 7:13 that any of the I in my kingdom, A10553+10335
Ezr 7:18 You and your **fellow** I may then do A10017
Ezr 10: 1 house of God, a large crowd of I—men, H3776
Ezr 10:25 And among the other I: From the H3776
Ne 1: 6 I confess the sins we I, including H1201+3776
Ne 2:10 to promote the welfare of the I. H1201+3776
Ne 7:73 certain of the people and the rest of the I, H3776
Ne 7:73 came and the I had settled in H1201+3776
Ne 8:14 that the I were to live in temporary H1201+3776
Ne 8:17 the I had not celebrated it like this. H1201+3776
Ne 9: 1 month, the I gathered together H1201+3776
Ne 10:29 all these now join their **fellow** I the nobles H278
Ne 11: 3 settled in Jerusalem (now *some* I, priests, H3776
Ne 11:20 The rest of the I, with the priests and H3776
Ne 13: 2 had not met the I with food and H1201+3776
Ps 115: 9 All you I, trust in the LORD—he is their H3776
Ps 135:19 All you I, praise the LORD; house of H1074+3776
Isa 17: 3 Aram will be like the glory of the I," H1201+3776
Isa 17: 9 which they left because of the I H1201+3776
Isa 31: 6 Return, you I, to the One you have H1201+3776
Isa 66:20 as the I bring their grain offerings H1201+3776
Jer 7:15 just as I did all your **fellow** I, the people of H278
Jer 16:14 who brought the I up out of Egypt,' H1201+3776
Jer 16:15 who brought the I up out of the H1201+3776
Jer 23: 7 who brought the I up out of Egypt,' H1201+3776
Jer 23:35 keeps saying to your friends and **other** I: H278
Eze 2: 3 I am sending you to the I, to a H1201+3776
Eze 3: 7 all the I are hardened and H1074+3776
Eze 6: 5 bodies of the I in front of their H1201+3776
Eze 8: 6 things the I are doing here, H1074+3776
Eze 11:15 fellow exiles and all the other I, H1074+3776
Eze 12: 6 I have made you a sign to the I." H1074+3776
Eze 12: 9 did not the I, that rebellious H1074+3776
Eze 12:10 and all the I who are there. H1074+3776
Eze 12:27 "Son of man, the I are saying, 'The H1074+3776
Eze 14: 4 When any of the I set up idols in H1074+3776
Eze 14: 7 'When any of the I or any foreigner H1074+3776
Eze 17: 2 and tell it to the I as a parable. H1074+3776
Eze 18:25 Hear, you I: Is my way unjust? H1074+3776
Eze 18:29 Yet the I say, 'The way of the Lord is H1074+3776
Eze 18:30 "Therefore, you I, I will judge each H1074+3776
Eze 20: 9 sight I had revealed myself to **the** I. H2157S
Eze 20:30 "Therefore say to the I: 'This is H1074+3776
Eze 20:31 I to let you inquire of me, you I? H1074+3776
Eze 29:21 I will make a horn grow for the I, H1074+3776
Eze 33:10 say to the I, 'This is what you H1074+3776
Eze 33:20 Yet you I say, 'The way of the Lord H1074+3776
Eze 34:30 and that they, the I, are my people, H1074+3776
Eze 35: 5 delivered the I over to the sword H1201+3776
Eze 36:22 "Therefore say to the I, 'This is H1074+3776
Eze 37:16 to Judah and the I associated with H1201+3776
Eze 37:16 and all the I associated with him. H1074+3776
Eze 37:21 I will take the I out of the nations H1201+3776
Eze 39:12 seven months the I will be burying H1074+3776
Eze 43: 7 I will live among the I forever. H1201+3776
Eze 44: 9 foreigners who live among the I. H1201+3776
Eze 44:15 when the I went astray from H1201+3776
Eze 45:17 to make atonement for the I. H1074+3776
Eze 47:22 to consider them as native-born I; H1201+3776
Eze 48:11 Levites did when the I went astray. H1201+3776
Da 1: 3 service some of the I from the royal H1201+3776
Hos 1:10 "Yet the I will be like the sand on H1201+3776
Hos 3: 1 Love her as the LORD loves the I H1201+3776
Hos 3: 4 For the I will live many days H1201+3776
Hos 3: 5 Afterward the I will return and seek H1201+3776
Hos 4: 1 of the LORD, you I, because the LORD H1201+3776
Hos 4:16 The I are stubborn, like a stubborn heifer H3776
Hos 5: 1 Pay attention, you I! Listen, H1074+3776
Hos 5: 5 against them; the I, even Ephraim, H3776
Am 3:12 so will the I living in Samaria be H1201+3776
Am 4: 5 about them, you I, for this is what H1201+3776
Am 9: 7 "Are not you I the same to me as H1201+3776
Mic 5: 3 of his brothers return to join the I. H1201+3776
Ac 2:22 "Fellow I, listen to this: Jesus of Nazareth *G2703*
Ac 2:29 "**Fellow** *I*, I can tell you confidently that the AIT
Ac 3:12 "Fellow I, why does this *G2703*
Ac 3:17 **fellow** *I*, I know that you acted in AIT
Ac 7:23 to visit his own people, the I. *G5626+2702*
Ac 7:26 Moses came upon **two** I who were *G899S*
Ac 7:37 "This is the Moses who told the I *G5626+2702*
Ac 13:16 "Fellow I and you Gentiles who worship *G2703*
Ac 21:28 shouting, "Fellow I, help us! This is the *G2703*
Ro 9:27 the number *of* the I be like the *G5626+2702*
Ro 10: 1 prayer to God for **the** I is that they may be *G899S*
Ro 10:16 But not all the I accepted the good news NDT
2Co 3: 7 so that the I could not look steadily *G5626+2702*
2Co 3:13 to prevent the I from seeing the *G5626+2702*
2Co 11:22 Are they I? So am I. Are they *G2703*
Heb 7: 5 *from* their **fellow** I—even though they *G81*
Heb 11:22 the exodus *of* the I from Egypt and *G5626+2702*
Rev 2:14 to entice the I to sin so that they *G5626+2702*

ISRAELITES' (3) [ISRAEL]

Lev 10:14 as your share of the I fellowship H1201+3776
Nu 31:30 From the I half, select one out of H1201+3776
Nu 31:47 From the I half, Moses selected H1201+3776

ISSACHAR (43)

Ge 30:18 to my husband." So she named him I. H3779
Ge 35:23 Simeon, Levi, Judah, I and Zebulun. H3779
Ge 46:13 The sons of I: Tola, Puah, Jashub and H3779
Ge 49:14 "I is a rawboned donkey lying down H3779
Ex 1: 3 I, Zebulun and Benjamin; H3779
Nu 1: 8 from I, Nethanel son of Zuar; H3779
Nu 1:28 From the descendants of I: All the men H3779
Nu 1:29 number from the tribe of I was 54,400. H3779
Nu 2: 5 The tribe of I will camp next to them. H3779
Nu 2: 5 of the people of I is Nethanel son of Zuar H3779
Nu 7:18 the leader of I, brought his offering. H3779
Nu 10:15 over the division of the tribe of I, H1201+3779
Nu 13: 7 from the tribe of I, Igal son of Joseph; H3779

Nu 26:23 The descendants of I by their clans were H3779
Nu 26:25 These were the clans of I; those H3779
Nu 34:26 the leader from the tribe of I; H1201+3779
Dt 27:12 Judah, I, Joseph and Benjamin H3779
Dt 33:18 in your going out, and you, I, in your tents. H3779
Jos 17:10 Asher on the north and I on the east. H3779
Jos 17:11 Within I and Asher, Manasseh also had H3779
Jos 19:17 lot came out for I according to its H1201+3779
Jos 19:23 the inheritance of the tribe of I, H1201+3779
Jos 21: 6 towns from the clans of the tribes of I, H3779
Jos 21:28 from the tribe of I, Kishion, Daberath, H3779
Jdg 5:15 The princes of I were with Deborah; yes H3779
Jdg 5:15 I was with Barak, sent under his H3779
Jdg 10: 1 a man of I named Tola son of Puah H3779
1Ki 4:17 Jehoshaphat son of Paruah—in I; H3779
1Ki 15:27 from the tribe of I plotted against him, H3779
1Ch 2: 1 Reuben, Simeon, Levi, Judah, I, Zebulun, H3779
1Ch 6:62 allotted thirteen towns from the tribes of I, H3779
1Ch 6:72 from the tribe of I they received Kedesh H3779
1Ch 7: 1 The sons of I: Tola, Puah, Jashub and H3779
1Ch 7: 5 men belonging to all the clans of I, H3779
1Ch 12:32 from I, men who understood the times H3779
1Ch 12:40 their neighbors from as far away as I H3779
1Ch 26: 5 I the seventh and Peullethai the eighth. H3779
1Ch 27:18 of David; over I: Omri son of Michael; H3779
2Ch 30:18 I and Zebulun had not purified H3779
Eze 48:25 "I will have one portion; it will border the H3779
Eze 48:26 border the territory of I from east to west. H3779
Eze 48:33 the gate of I and the gate of Zebulun. H3779
Rev 7: 7 of Levi 12,000, from the tribe *of* I 12,000, *G2704*

ISSHIAH (NIV84) ISHIAH

ISSUE (11) [ISSUED, ISSUES]
Ex 22:11 the i between them will be settled by the NDT
2Sa 14: 8 and I *will* i an order in your behalf." H7422
Ezr 4:21 Now i an order *to* these men to stop A10682
Ezr 5:17 see if King Cyrus *did* in fact i a decree to A10682
Est 1:19 *let* him i a royal decree and let it be H3655
Pr 8:15 reign and rulers i decrees that are just; H2980
Isa 10: 1 to *those who* i oppressive decrees, H4180+4180
Da 2:15 "Why did the king i such a harsh A10427+10621
Da 6: 7 that the king *should* i an edict and A10624
Da 6: 8 i the decree and put it in writing so that A10624
Da 6:26 "I i a decree that in every part of my A10682

ISSUED (21) [ISSUE]
Ex 15:25 There the LORD i a ruling and instruction H8492
1Ki 15:22 Then King Asa i an order *to* all Judah—no H9048
2Ch 24: 9 A proclamation *was* then i in Judah and H5989
Ezr 4:19 I i an order and a search was made, and A10682
Ezr 5:13 King Cyrus i a decree to rebuild this A10682
Ezr 6: 1 King Darius then i an order, and they A10682
Ezr 6: 3 the king i a decree concerning the A10682
Ezr 10: 7 A proclamation *was* then i throughout H6296
Est 3: 9 the king, *let* a decree be i to destroy them H4180
Est 3:14 of the edict *was* to be i *as* law in every H5989
Est 3:15 the edict was i in the citadel of Susa. H5989
Est 8:13 of the edict *was* to be i *as* law in every H5989
Est 8:14 the edict was i in the citadel of Susa. H5989
Est 9:14 An edict was i in Susa, and they impaled H5989
Est 9:25 *he* i written orders that the evil scheme H606
Ps 148: 6 *he* i a decree that will never pass away. H5989
Da 2:13 So the decree *was* i to put the wise men A10485
Da 3:10 Your Majesty *has* i a decree that A10682
Da 4:24 the Most High *has* i against my lord the A10413
Jnh 3: 7 This is the proclamation *he* i in Nineveh H2410
Lk 2: 1 days Caesar Augustus i a decree that a *G2002*

ISSUES (1) [ISSUE]
Da 6:15 edict that the king i can be changed." A10624

IT (5230) [IT'S, ITS, ITSELF] See Index of Articles Etc.

IT'S (19) [BE, IT] See Index of Articles Etc.

ITALIAN (1) [ITALY]
Ac 10: 1 in what was known as the I Regiment. *G2713*

ITALY (4) [ITALIAN]
Ac 18: 2 had recently come from I with his wife *G2712*
Ac 27: 1 it was decided that we would sail for I, *G2712*
Ac 27: 6 ship sailing for I and put us on board. *G2712*
Heb 13:24 Those from I send you their greetings *G2712*

ITCH (1) [ITCHING]
Dt 28:27 festering sores and the i, from which you H3063

ITCHING (1) [ITCH]
2Ti 4: 3 *to* say what their i ears want to hear. *G3117+198*

ITHAI (2)
2Sa 23:29 I son of Ribai from Gibeah in Benjamin H915
1Ch 11:31 I son of Ribai from Gibeah in Benjamin H416

ITHAMAR (19) [ITHAMAR'S]
Ex 6:23 bore him Nadab and Abihu, Eleazar and I. H418
Ex 28: 1 Eleazar and I, so they may serve me H418
Ex 38:21 under the direction of I son of Aaron, H418
Lev 10: 6 said to Aaron and his sons Eleazar and I, H418
Lev 10:12 Eleazar and I, "Take the grain H418
Lev 10:16 he was angry with Eleazar and I, Aaron's H418
Nu 3: 2 the firstborn and Abihu, Eleazar and I. H418
Nu 3: 4 so Eleazar and I served as priests during H418
Nu 4:28 to be under the direction of I son of Aaron, H418
Nu 4:33 under the direction of I son of Aaron, H418
Nu 7: 8 all under the direction of I son of Aaron, H418
Nu 26:60 father of Nadab and Abihu, Eleazar and I. H418
1Ch 6: 3 Nadab, Abihu, Eleazar and I. H418
1Ch 24: 1 Aaron were Nadab, Abihu, Eleazar and I. H418
1Ch 24: 2 so Eleazar and I served as the priests. H418
1Ch 24: 3 of Eleazar and Ahimelek a descendant of I, H418
1Ch 24: 5 the descendants of both Eleazar and I. H418
1Ch 24: 6 taken from Eleazar and then one from I. H418
Ezr 8: 2 of the descendants of I, Daniel; of the H418

ITHAMAR'S (2) [ITHAMAR]
1Ch 24: 4 Eleazar's descendants than among I, H418
1Ch 24: 4 eight heads of families from I descendants. H418

ITHIEL (2)
Ne 11: 7 Maaseiah, the son of I, the son of Jeshaiah H417
Pr 30: 1 This man's utterance to I: "I am weary, H417

ITHLAH (1)
Jos 19:42 Shaalabbin, Aijalon, I, H3849

ITHMAH (1)
1Ch 11:46 the sons of Elnaam, I the Moabite, H3850

ITHNAN (1)
Jos 15:23 Kedesh, Hazor, I, H3854

ITHRAN (3)
Ge 36:26 Hemdan, Eshban, I and Keran. H3864
1Ch 1:41 Hemdan, Eshban, I and Keran. H3864
1Ch 7:37 Shamma, Shilshah, I and Beera. H3864

ITHREAM (2)
2Sa 3: 5 the sixth, I the son of David's wife Eglah. H3865
1Ch 3: 3 and the sixth, I, by his wife Eglah. H3865

ITHRITE (4) [ITHRITES]
2Sa 23:38 Ira the I, Gareb the Ithrite H3863
2Sa 23:38 Ira the Ithrite, Gareb the I H3863
1Ch 11:40 Ira the I, Gareb the Ithrite, H3863
1Ch 11:40 Ira the Ithrite, Gareb the I, H3863

ITHRITES (1) [ITHRITE]
1Ch 2:53 the I, Puthites, Shumathites and H3863

ITS (1101) [IT] See Index of Articles Etc.

ITSELF (53) [IT, SELF] See Index of Articles Etc.

ITTAI (7)
2Sa 15:19 The king said to I the Gittite, "Why should H915
2Sa 15:21 But I replied to the king, "As surely as the H915
2Sa 15:22 David said to I, "Go ahead, march on." H915
2Sa 15:22 So I the Gittite marched on with all his H915
2Sa 18: 2 of Zeruiah, and a third under I the Gittite. H915
2Sa 18: 5 Abishai and I, "Be gentle with the H915
2Sa 18:12 king commanded you and Abishai and I, H915

ITUREA (1)
Lk 3: 1 brother Philip tetrarch *of* I and Traconitis, *G2714*

IVORY (13)
1Ki 10:18 throne covered with i and overlaid with H9094
1Ki 10:22 silver and i, and apes and baboons. H9105
1Ki 22:39 the palace he built and *adorned with* i H9094
2Ch 9:17 throne covered with i and overlaid with H9094
2Ch 9:21 silver and i, and apes and baboons. H9105
Ps 45: 8 palaces adorned with i the music of the H9094
SS 5:14 is like polished i decorated with lapis H9094
SS 7: 4 Your neck is like an i tower. Your eyes are H9094
Eze 27: 6 they made your deck, adorned with i. H9094
Eze 27:15 they paid you with i tusks and ebony. H9094
Am 3:15 houses adorned with i will be destroyed H9094
Am 6: 4 beds adorned with i and lounge on your H9094
Rev 18:12 articles of every kind made of i, costly *G1804*

IVVAH (3)
2Ki 18:34 are the gods of Sepharvaim, Hena and I? H6394
2Ki 19:13 kings of Lair, Sepharvaim, Hena and I?" H6394
Isa 37:13 kings of Lair, Sepharvaim, Hena and I?" H6394

IYE ABARIM (3) [ABARIM]
Nu 21:11 out from Oboth and camped in I, H6516
Nu 33:44 They left Oboth and camped at I H6516
Nu 33:45 They left I and camped at Dibon H6517

IYIM (1)
Jos 15:29 Baalah, I, Ezem, H6517

IZAL (1)
Eze 27:19 casks of wine from I in exchange for your H374.5

IZHAR (9) [IZHARITES]
Ex 6:18 were Amram, I, Hebron and Uzziel H3659
Ex 6:21 The sons of I were Korah, Nepheg and H3659
Nu 3:19 Amram, I, Hebron and Uzziel. H3659
Nu 16: 1 Korah son of I, the son of Kohath, the son H3659
1Ch 6: 2 Amram, I, Hebron and Uzziel. H3659
1Ch 6:18 Amram, I, Hebron and Uzziel. H3659
1Ch 6:38 the son of I, the son of Kohath, the son of H3659
1Ch 23:12 Amram, I, Hebron and Uzziel H3659
1Ch 23:18 The sons of I: Shelomith was the first. H3659

IZHARITES (4) [IZHAR]
Nu 3:27 clans of the Amramites, I, Hebronites H3660
1Ch 24:22 From the I: Shelomoth; from the sons of H3660
1Ch 26:23 the Amramites, the I, the Hebronites and H3660
1Ch 26:29 From the I: Kenaniah and his sons were H3660

IZLIAH (1)
1Ch 8:18 I and Jobab were the sons of Elpaal. H3468

IZRAHIAH (2)
1Ch 7: 3 The son of Uzzi: I. The sons of Izrahiah H3474
1Ch 7: 3 The sons of I: Michael, Obadiah H3474

IZRAHITE (1)
1Ch 27: 8 was the commander Shamhuth the I. H3473

IZRI (1)
1Ch 25:11 the fourth to I, his sons and relatives 12 H3673

IZZIAH (1)
Ezr 10:25 Ramiah, I, Malkijah, Mijamin, Eleazar H3466

J

JAAKAN See BENE JAAKAN

JAAKOBAH (1)
1Ch 4:36 also Elioenai, J, Jeshohaiah, Asaiah H3621

JAALA (2)
Ezr 2:56 J, Darkon, Giddel, H3608
Ne 7:58 J, Darkon, Giddel, H3606

JAAN See DAN JAAN

JAAR (1)
Ps 132: 6 we came upon it in the fields of J: H3625

JAARESHIAH (1)
1Ch 8:27 J, Elijah and Zikri were the sons of H3631

JAASIEL (2)
1Ch 11:47 Obed and J the Mezobaite. H3634
1Ch 27:21 over Benjamin: J son of Abner; H3634

JAASU (1)
Ezr 10:37 Mattaniah, Mattenai and J. H3632

JAAZANIAH (5)
2Ki 25:23 Netophathite, J the son of the Maakathite H3280
Jer 35: 3 So I went to get J son of Jeremiah, the H3279
Jer 40: 8 J the son of the Maakathite H3471
Eze 8:11 J son of Shaphan was standing H3280
Eze 11: 1 I saw among them J son of Azzur and H3279

JAAZER (KJV) JAZER

JAAZIAH (2)
1Ch 24:26 Mahli and Mushi. The son of J: Beno. H3596
1Ch 24:27 sons of Merari: from J: Beno, Shoham, H3596

JAAZIEL (3)
1Ch 15:18 Zechariah, J, Shemiramoth, Jehiel, Unni H3595
1Ch 15:20 Zechariah, J, Shemiramoth, Jehiel, Unni H6456
1Ch 16: 5 were Zechariah, then J, Shemiramoth, H3599

JABAL (1)
Ge 4:20 Adah gave birth to J; he was the father of H3299

JABBOK (7)
Ge 32:22 eleven sons and crossed the ford of the J. H3309
Nu 21:24 took over his land from the Arnon to the J, H3309
Dt 2:37 the course of the J nor that around the H3309
Dt 3:16 and out to the J River, which is the H3309
Jos 12: 2 of the gorge—to the J River, which is the H3309
Jdg 11:13 away my land from the Arnon to the J, H3309
Jdg 11:22 the Arnon to the J and from the desert H3309

JABESH (11) [JABESH GILEAD]
1Sa 11: 1 And all the men of J said to him, "Make a H3315
1Sa 11: 3 The elders of J said to him, "Give us H3315
1Sa 11: 5 to him what the men of J had said. H3315
1Sa 11: 9 went and reported this to the men of J, H3315
1Sa 31:12 from the wall of Beth Shan and went to J, H3315
1Sa 31:13 buried them under a tamarisk tree at J, H3315
2Ki 15:10 Shallum son of J conspired against H3314
2Ki 15:13 Shallum son of J became king in the H3314
2Ki 15:14 He attacked Shallum son of J in Samaria H3314
1Ch 10:12 Saul and his sons and brought them to J. H3315
1Ch 10:12 their bones under the great tree in J, H3315

JABESH GILEAD (11) [GILEAD, JABESH]
Jdg 21: 8 no one from J had come to the H3316
Jdg 21: 9 of the people of J were there. H3316
Jdg 21:10 to go to J and put to the sword H3316
Jdg 21:12 people living in J four hundred H3316
Jdg 21:14 the women of J who had been H3316
1Sa 11: 1 went up and besieged J. H3316
1Sa 11: 9 "Say to the men of J, 'By the time H3316
1Sa 31:11 the people of J heard what the H3316
2Sa 2: 4 the men from J who had buried H3316
2Sa 21:12 Jonathan from the citizens of J. H3316

1Ch 10:11 inhabitants of J heard what the H3316

JABEZ (4)
1Ch 2:55 the clans of scribes who lived at J H3583
1Ch 4: 9 J was more honorable than his brothers H3584
1Ch 4: 9 His mother had named him J, saying, "I H3584
1Ch 4:10 J cried out to the God of Israel, "Oh, that H3584

JABIN (6) [JABIN'S]
Jos 11: 1 When J king of Hazor heard of this, he H3296
Jdg 4: 2 them into the hands of J king of Canaan, H3296
Jdg 4:17 an alliance between J king of Hazor and H3296
Jdg 4:23 that day God subdued J king of Canaan H3296
Jdg 4:24 harder against J king of Canaan until H3296
Ps 83: 9 you did to Sisera and J at the river Kishon, H3296

JABIN'S (1) [JABIN]
Jdg 4: 7 the commander of J army, with his H3296

JABNEEL (2)
Jos 15:11 along to Mount Baalah and reached J. H3305
Jos 19:33 Adami Nekeb and J to Lakkum and H3305

JABNEH (1)
2Ch 26: 6 down the walls of Gath, J and Ashdod. H3306

JACAN (NIV84) JAKAN

JACHIN (KJV) JAKIN

JACHINITES (KJV) JAKINITE

JACINTH (3)
Ex 28:19 the third row shall be j, agate and H4385
Ex 39:12 the third row was j, agate and amethyst; H4385
Rev 21:20 turquoise, the eleventh j, and the twelfth *G5611*

JACKAL (2) [JACKALS]
Ne 2:13 Gate toward the J Well and the Dung H9490
Mic 1: 8 I will howl like a j and moan like an owl. H9478

JACKALS (17) [JACKAL]
Job 30:29 I have become a brother of j, H9478
Ps 44:19 you crushed us and made us a haunt for j; H9478
Ps 63:10 over to the sword and become food for j. H8785
Isa 13:21 creatures will lie there, j will fill her houses H280
Isa 13:22 her strongholds, j her luxurious palaces. H9478
Isa 34:13 She will become a haunt for j, a home H9478
Isa 35: 7 In the haunts where j once lay, grass and H9478
Isa 43:20 honor me, the j and the owls, because H9478
Jer 9:11 of ruins, a haunt of j; and I will lay waste H9478
Jer 10:22 the towns of Judah desolate, a haunt of j. H9478
Jer 14: 6 on the barren heights and pant like j; H9478
Jer 49:33 "Hazor will become a haunt of j, H9478
Jer 51:37 of ruins, a haunt of j, an object of horror H9478
La 4: 3 Even j offer their breasts to nurse their H9478
La 5:18 lies desolate, with j prowling over it. H8785
Eze 13: 4 prophets, Israel, are like j among ruins. H8785
Mal 1: 3 left his inheritance to the desert j. H9478

JACOB (363) [JACOB'S]
Ge 25:26 grasping Esau's heel; so he was named J. H3620
Ge 25:27 while J was content to stay at home H3620
Ge 25:28 loved Esau, but Rebekah loved J. H3620
Ge 25:29 Once when J was cooking some stew H3620
Ge 25:30 He said to J, "Quick, let me have some of H3620
Ge 25:31 J replied, "First sell me your birthright." H3620
Ge 25:33 But J said, "Swear to me first." So he H3620
Ge 25:33 an oath to him, selling his birthright to J. H3620
Ge 25:34 Then J gave Esau some bread and some H3620
Ge 27: 6 Rebekah said to her son J, "Look, H3620
Ge 27:11 J said to Rebekah his mother, "But my H3620
Ge 27:15 put them on her younger son J. H3620
Ge 27:17 handed to her son J the tasty food and H3620
Ge 27:19 J said to his father, "I am Esau your H3620
Ge 27:21 Then Isaac said to J, "Come near so I can H3620
Ge 27:22 J went close to his father Isaac, who H3620
Ge 27:22 "The voice is the voice of J, but the hands H3620
Ge 27:25 J brought it to him and he ate; and he NDT
Ge 27:30 J had scarcely left his father's H3620
Ge 27:36 "Isn't he rightly named J? This is the H3620
Ge 27:41 held a grudge against J because of the H3620
Ge 27:41 are near; then I will kill my brother J." H3620
Ge 27:42 her younger son J and said to him, H3620
Ge 27:46 If J takes a wife from among the women H3620
Ge 28: 1 So Isaac called for J and blessed him H3620
Ge 28: 5 Then Isaac sent J on his way, and he went H3620
Ge 28: 5 who was the mother of J and Esau. H3620
Ge 28: 6 Isaac had blessed J and had sent him to H3620
Ge 28: 7 that J had obeyed his father and H3620
Ge 28:10 J left Beersheba and set out for Harran. H3620
Ge 28:16 When J awoke from his sleep, he thought, H3620
Ge 28:18 the next morning J took the stone he had H3620
Ge 28:20 Then J made a vow, saying, "If God will H3620
Ge 29: 1 Then J continued on his journey and H3620
Ge 29: 4 J asked the shepherds, "My brothers H3620
Ge 29: 6 Then J asked them, "Is he well?" "Yes, NDT
Ge 29:10 When J saw Rachel daughter of his uncle H3620
Ge 29:11 Then J kissed Rachel and began to weep H3620
Ge 29:13 As soon as Laban heard the news about J, H3620
Ge 29:13 and there J told him all these things. NDT
Ge 29:14 After J had stayed with him for a whole NDT
Ge 29:18 J was in love with Rachel and said, "I'll H3620
Ge 29:20 So J served seven years to get Rachel, but H3620
Ge 29:21 Then J said to Laban, "Give me my wife H3620
Ge 29:23 his daughter Leah and brought her to J, H2257S
Ge 29:23 her to Jacob, and J made love to her. NDT
Ge 29:25 So J said to Laban, "What is this you have NDT
Ge 29:28 And J did so. He finished the week with H3620
Ge 29:30 J made love to Rachel also, and his love NDT
Ge 30: 1 that she was not bearing J any children, H3620
Ge 30: 1 So she said to J, "Give me children, or I'll H3620
Ge 30: 2 J became angry with her and said, "Am I H3620
Ge 30: 4 servant Bilhah as a wife. J slept with her, H3620
Ge 30: 7 conceived again and bore J a second son. H3620
Ge 30: 9 Zilpah and gave her to J as a wife. H3620
Ge 30:10 Leah's servant Zilpah bore J a son. H3620
Ge 30:12 Leah's servant Zilpah bore J a second son. H3620
Ge 30:16 So when J came in from the fields that H3620
Ge 30:17 became pregnant and bore J a fifth son. H3620
Ge 30:19 conceived again and bore J a sixth son. H3620
Ge 30:25 birth to Joseph, J said to Laban, "Send H3620
Ge 30:29 J said to him, "You know how I have worked NDT
Ge 30:31 give me anything," J replied. "But if you H3620
Ge 30:36 three-day journey between himself and J, H3620
Ge 30:36 while J continued to tend the rest of H3620
Ge 30:37 J, however, took fresh-cut branches from H3620
Ge 30:40 J set apart the young of the flock by H3620
Ge 30:41 J would place the branches in the troughs H3620
Ge 30:42 went to Laban and the strong ones to J. H3620
Ge 31: 1 J heard that Laban's sons were saying NDT
Ge 31: 1 "J has taken everything our father owned H3620
Ge 31: 2 And J noticed that Laban's attitude toward H3620
Ge 31: 3 Then the LORD said to J, "Go back to the H3620
Ge 31: 4 So J sent word to Rachel and Leah to H3620
Ge 31:11 angel of God said to me in the dream, 'J. H3620
Ge 31:17 Then J put his children and his wives on H3620
Ge 31:20 J deceived Laban the Aramean by not H3620
Ge 31:22 third day Laban was told that J had fled. H3620
Ge 31:23 he pursued J for seven days and caught H2257S
Ge 31:24 "Be careful not to say anything to J, either H3620
Ge 31:25 J had pitched his tent in the hill country of H3620
Ge 31:26 Then Laban said to J, "What have you H3620
Ge 31:29 'Be careful not to say anything to J, either H3620
Ge 31:31 J answered Laban, "I was afraid, because H3620
Ge 31:32 Now J did not know that Rachel had H3620
Ge 31:36 J was angry and took Laban to task H3620
Ge 31:43 Laban answered J, "The women are my H3620
Ge 31:45 So J took a stone and set it up as a pillar. H3620
Ge 31:47 Jegar Sahadutha, and J called it Galeed. H3620
Ge 31:51 Laban also said to J, "Here is this heap H3620
Ge 31:53 So J took an oath in the name of the Fear H3620
Ge 32: 1 J also went on his way, and the angels of H3620
Ge 32: 2 When J saw them, he said, "This is the H3620
Ge 32: 3 J sent messengers ahead of him to his H3620
Ge 32: 4 'Your servant J says, I have been staying H3620
Ge 32: 6 When the messengers returned to J, they H3620
Ge 32: 7 fear and distress J divided the people H3620
Ge 32: 9 Then J prayed, "O God of my father H3620
Ge 32:18 are to say, 'They belong to your servant J. H3620
Ge 32:20 'Your servant J is coming behind us. H3620
Ge 32:22 That night J got up and took his two wives NDT
Ge 32:24 So J was left alone, and a man wrestled H3620
Ge 32:26 But J replied, "I will not let you go unless NDT
Ge 32:27 "What is your name?" "J," he answered. H3620
Ge 32:28 "Your name will no longer be J, but Israel H3620
Ge 32:29 J said, "Please tell me your name." But H3620
Ge 32:30 So J called the place Peniel, saying, "It is H3620
Ge 33: 1 J looked up and there was Esau, coming H3620
Ge 33: 4 Esau ran to meet J and embraced him; H2257S
Ge 33: 5 J answered, "They are the children God has NDT
Ge 33:10 said J. "If I have found favor in H3620
Ge 33:11 And because J insisted, Esau NDT
Ge 33:13 But J said to him, "My lord knows that the NDT
Ge 33:15 "But why do that?" J asked. "Just let me find NDT
Ge 33:17 J, however, went to Sukkoth, where he H3620
Ge 33:18 After J came from Paddan Aram, he H3620
Ge 34: 1 the daughter Leah had borne to J, went H3620
Ge 34: 3 heart was drawn to Dinah daughter of J; H3620
Ge 34: 5 When J heard that his daughter Dinah H3620
Ge 34: 6 father Hamor went out to talk with J. H3620
Ge 34:27 The sons of J came upon the dead bodies H3620
Ge 34:30 Then J said to Simeon and Levi, "You H3620
Ge 35: 1 Then God said to J, "Go up to Bethel and H3620
Ge 35: 2 So J said to his household and to all who H3620
Ge 35: 4 So they gave J all the foreign gods they H3620
Ge 35: 4 J buried them under the oak at H3620
Ge 35: 6 J and all the people with him came to Luz H3620
Ge 35: 9 After J returned from Paddan Aram, God H3620
Ge 35:10 "Your name is J, but you will no H3620
Ge 35:10 you will no longer be called J; your H3620
Ge 35:14 J set up a stone pillar at the place where H3620
Ge 35:15 J called the place where God had talked H3620
Ge 35:20 Over her tomb J set up a pillar, and to this H3620
Ge 35:22 Israel heard of it. J had twelve sons: H3620
Ge 35:23 Reuben the firstborn of J, Simeon, Levi H3620
Ge 35:26 These were the sons of J, who were born H3620
Ge 35:27 J came home to his father Isaac in Mamre H3620
Ge 35:29 And his sons Esau and J buried him. H3620
Ge 36: 6 a land some distance from his brother J. H3620
Ge 37: 1 J lived in the land where his father had H3620
Ge 37:34 Then J tore his clothes, put on sackcloth H3620
Ge 42: 1 When J learned that there was grain in H3620
Ge 42: 4 But J did not send Benjamin, Joseph's H3620
Ge 42:29 came to their father J in the land of H3620
Ge 42:36 Their father J said to them, "You have H3620
Ge 42:38 But J said, "My son will not go down there NDT
Ge 45:25 came to their father J in the land of H3620
Ge 45:26 J was stunned; he did not believe them. H2257S
Ge 45:27 the spirit of their father J revived. H3620
Ge 46: 2 to Israel in a vision at night and said, "J! H3620
Ge 46: 2 said, "Jacob! J!" "Here I am," he H3620
Ge 46: 5 Then J left Beersheba, and Israel's sons H3620
Ge 46: 5 took their father J and their children and H3620
Ge 46: 6 So J and all his offspring went to Egypt H3620
Ge 46: 7 J brought with him to Egypt his sons and NDT
Ge 46: 8 the sons of Israel (J and his descendants H3620
Ge 46: 8 went to Egypt: Reuben the firstborn of J. H3620
Ge 46:15 the sons Leah bore to J in Paddan Aram, H3620
Ge 46:18 were the children born to J by Zilpah, H3620
Ge 46:22 the sons of Rachel who were born to J— H3620
Ge 46:25 These were the sons born to J by Bilhah H3620
Ge 46:26 All those who went to Egypt with J—those H3620
Ge 46:28 Now J sent Judah ahead of him to Joseph NDT
Ge 47: 7 brought his father J in and presented him H3620
Ge 47: 7 before Pharaoh. After J blessed Pharaoh, H3620
Ge 47: 9 And J said to Pharaoh, "The years of my H3620
Ge 47:10 Then J blessed Pharaoh and went out H3620
Ge 47:28 J lived in Egypt seventeen years, and the H3620
Ge 48: 2 When J was told, "Your son Joseph has H3620
Ge 48: 3 J said to Joseph, "God Almighty H3620
Ge 49: 1 Then J called for his sons and said H3620
Ge 49: 2 listen, sons of J; listen to your father H3620
Ge 49: 7 scatter them in J and disperse them in H3620
Ge 49:24 of the hand of the Mighty One of J, H3620
Ge 49:33 When J had finished giving instructions to H3620
Ge 50:24 on oath to Abraham, Isaac and J. H3620
Ex 1: 1 sons of Israel who went to Egypt with J, H3620
Ex 1: 5 The descendants of J numbered seventy in H3620
Ex 2:24 with Abraham, with Isaac and with J. H3620
Ex 3: 6 the God of Isaac and the God of J. H3620
Ex 3:15 the God of Isaac and the God of J—has H3620
Ex 3:16 Isaac and J—appeared to me and H3620
Ex 4: 5 the God of Isaac and the God of J—has H3620
Ex 6: 3 to Isaac and to J as God Almighty, but by H3620
Ex 6: 8 to give to Abraham, to Isaac and to J. H3620
Ex 19: 3 the descendants of J and what you are to H3620
Ex 33: 1 on oath to Abraham, Isaac and J, saying, H3620
Lev 26:42 my covenant with J and my covenant with H3620
Nu 23: 7 he said, 'curse J for me; come, denounce H3620
Nu 23:10 can count the dust of J or number even a H3620
Nu 23:21 "No misfortune is seen in J, no misery H3620
Nu 23:23 There is no divination against J, no evil H3620
Nu 23:23 It will now be said of J and of Israel, 'See H3620
Nu 24: 5 are your tents, J, your dwelling places, H3620
Nu 24:17 A star will come out of J; a scepter will H3620
Nu 24:19 A ruler will come out of J and destroy the H3620
Nu 32:11 on oath to Abraham, Isaac and J— H3620
Dt 1: 8 to Abraham, Isaac and J—and to their H3620
Dt 6:10 Abraham, Isaac and J, to give you—a H3620
Dt 9: 5 to your fathers, to Abraham, Isaac and J. H3620
Dt 9:27 your servants Abraham, Isaac and J. H3620
Dt 29:13 to your fathers, Abraham, Isaac and J. H3620
Dt 30:20 to your fathers, Abraham, Isaac and J. H3620
Dt 32: 9 is his people, J his allotted inheritance. H3620
Dt 33: 4 the possession of the assembly of J. H3620
Dt 33:10 your precepts to J and your law to Israel. H3620
Dt 33:28 J will dwell secure in a land of grain and H3620
Dt 34: 4 Abraham, Isaac and J when I said, 'I will H3620
Jos 24: 4 to Isaac I gave J and Esau. I assigned H3620
Jos 24: 4 J and his family went down to Egypt. H3620
Jos 24:32 tract of land that J bought for a hundred H3620
1Sa 12: 8 "After J entered Egypt, they cried to the H3620
2Sa 23: 1 the man anointed by the God of J, the H3620
1Ki 18:31 each of the tribes descended from J, H3620
2Ki 13:23 his covenant with Abraham, Isaac and J. H3620
2Ki 17:34 that the LORD gave the descendants of J, H3620
1Ch 16:13 his chosen ones, the children of J. H3620
1Ch 16:17 He confirmed it to J as a decree, to Israel H3620
Ps 14: 7 people, let J rejoice and Israel be glad! H3620
Ps 20: 1 may the name of the God of J protect you. H3620
Ps 22:23 All you descendants of J, honor him H3620
Ps 24: 6 seek him, who seek your face, God of J. H3620
Ps 44: 4 my God, who decrees victories for J. H3620
Ps 46: 7 is with us; the God of J is our fortress. H3620
Ps 46:11 is with us; the God of J is our fortress. H3620
Ps 47: 4 the pride of J, whom he loved. H3620
Ps 53: 6 people, let J rejoice and Israel be glad! H3620
Ps 59:13 ends of the earth that God rules over J. H3620
Ps 75: 9 I will sing praise to the God of J, H3620
Ps 76: 6 At your rebuke, God of J, both horse and H3620
Ps 77:15 people, the descendants of J and Joseph. H3620
Ps 78: 5 decreed statutes for J and established the H3620
Ps 78:21 his fire broke out against J, and his wrath H3620
Ps 78:71 him to be the shepherd of his people J, H3620
Ps 79: 7 they have devoured J and devastated his H3620
Ps 81: 1 our strength; shout aloud to the God of J! H3620
Ps 81: 4 Israel, an ordinance of the God of J. H3620
Ps 84: 8 LORD God Almighty; listen to me, God of J. H3620
Ps 85: 1 your land; you restored the fortunes of J. H3620
Ps 87: 2 more than all the other dwellings of J. H3620
Ps 94: 7 not see; the God of J takes no notice." H3620
Ps 99: 4 in J you have done what is just and right. H3620
Ps 105: 6 his chosen ones, the children of J. H3620
Ps 105:10 He confirmed it to J as a decree, to Israel H3620
Ps 105:23 J resided as a foreigner in the land of H3620
Ps 114: 1 J from a people of foreign tongue H1074+3620
Ps 114: 7 the Lord, at the presence of the God of J, H3620

Ps 132: 2 he made a vow to the Mighty One of J: H3620
Ps 132: 5 a dwelling for the Mighty One of J." H3620
Ps 135: 4 For the LORD has chosen J to be his own H3620
Ps 146: 5 are those whose help is the God of J, H3620
Ps 147:19 He has revealed his word to J, his laws H3620
Isa 2: 3 of the LORD, to the temple of the God of J. H3620
Isa 2: 5 descendants of J, let us walk in the H3620
Isa 2: 6 your people, the descendants of J. H3620
Isa 8:17 hiding his face from the descendants of J. H3620
Isa 9: 8 The Lord has sent a message against J; it H3620
Isa 10:20 the survivors of J, will no longer H1074+3620
Isa 10:21 a remnant of J will return to the Mighty H3620
Isa 14: 1 The LORD will have compassion on J; once H3620
Isa 14: 1 them and unite with the descendants of J. H3620
Isa 17: 4 "In that day the glory of J will fade; the fat H3620
Isa 27: 6 In days to come J will take root, Israel will H3620
Isa 29:22 Abraham, says to the descendants of J: H3620
Isa 29:22 "No longer will J be ashamed; no longer H3620
Isa 29:23 the holiness of the Holy One of J, H3620
Isa 40:27 Why do you complain, J? Why do you say H3620
Isa 41: 8 my servant, J, whom I have chosen H3620
Isa 41:14 be afraid, you worm J, little Israel, do not H3620
Isa 42:24 Who handed J over to become loot, and H3620
Isa 43: 1 who created you, J, he who formed you, H3620
Isa 43:22 not called on me, J, you have not wearied H3620
Isa 43:28 I consigned J to destruction and Israel to H3620
Isa 44: 1 "But now listen, J, my servant, Israel H3620
Isa 44: 2 Do not be afraid, J, my servant, Jeshurun H3620
Isa 44: 5 will call themselves by the name of J; H3620
Isa 44:21 "Remember these things, J, for you, Israel, H3620
Isa 44:23 the LORD has redeemed J, he displays H3620
Isa 45: 4 For the sake of J my servant, of Israel my H3620
Isa 46: 3 you descendants of J, all the remnant of H3620
Isa 48: 1 you descendants of J, you who are called H3620
Isa 48:12 "Listen to me, J, Israel, whom I have H3620
Isa 48:20 "The LORD has redeemed his servant J." H3620
Isa 49: 5 his servant to bring J back to him and H3620
Isa 49: 6 the tribes of J and bring back those H3620
Isa 49:26 your Redeemer, the Mighty One of J." H3620
Isa 58: 1 to the descendants of J their sins. H3620
Isa 58:14 feast on the inheritance of your father J." H3620
Isa 59:20 to those in J who repent of their sins," H3620
Isa 60:16 your Redeemer, the Mighty One of J. H3620
Isa 65: 9 I will bring forth descendants from J, and H3620
Jer 2: 4 you descendants of J, all you clans of H3620
Jer 5:20 to the descendants of J and proclaim it in H3620
Jer 10:16 who is the Portion of J is not like these, H3620
Jer 10:25 For they have devoured J; they have H3620
Jer 30: 7 It will be a time of trouble for J, but he H3620
Jer 30:10 do not be afraid, J my servant; do not be H3620
Jer 30:10 J will again have peace and security, and H3620
Jer 31: 7 "Sing with joy for J; shout for the foremost H3620
Jer 31:11 LORD will deliver J and redeem them from H3620
Jer 33:26 the descendants of J and David my H3620
Jer 33:26 the descendants of Abraham, Isaac and J. H3620
Jer 46:27 "Do not be afraid, J my servant; do not be H3620
Jer 46:27 J will again have peace and security, and H3620
Jer 46:28 Do not be afraid, J my servant, for I am H3620
Jer 51:19 who is the Portion of J is not like these, H3620
La 1:17 LORD has decreed for J that his neighbors H3620
La 2: 2 has swallowed up all the dwellings of J; H3620
La 2: 3 He has burned in J like a flaming fire that H3620
Eze 20: 5 the descendants of J and revealed H1074+3620
Eze 28:25 own land, which I gave to my servant J. H3620
Eze 37:25 will live in the land I gave to my servant J, H3620
Eze 39:25 restore the fortunes of J and will have H3620
Hos 10:11 and J must break up the ground. H3620
Hos 12: 2 he will punish J according to his ways H3620
Hos 12:12 J fled to the country of Aram; Israel served H3620
Am 3:13 testify against the descendants of J," H3620
Am 6: 8 "I abhor the pride of J and detest his H3620
Am 7: 2 forgive! How can J survive? He is so H3620
Am 7: 5 beg you, stop! How can J survive? He is so H3620
Am 8: 7 LORD has sworn by himself, the Pride of J: H3620
Am 9: 8 not totally destroy the descendants of J," H3620
Ob 10 of the violence against your brother J, H3620
Ob 17 and J will possess his inheritance. H1074+3620
Ob 18 J will be a fire and Joseph a flame H1074+3620
Mic 2: 7 You descendants of J, should it be said H3620
Mic 2:12 gather all of you, J; I will surely bring H3620
Mic 3: 1 you leaders of J, you rulers of Israel. H3620
Mic 3: 8 to declare to J his transgression, to H3620
Mic 3: 9 you leaders of J, you rulers of H1074+3620
Mic 4: 2 of the LORD, to the temple of the God of J. H3620
Mic 5: 7 The remnant of J will be in the midst of H3620
Mic 5: 8 The remnant of J will be among the H3620
Mic 7:20 You will be faithful to J, and show love to H3620
Na 2: 2 the splendor of J like the splendor of H3620
Mal 1: 2 declares the LORD. "Yet I have loved J, H3620
Mal 2:12 the LORD remove him from the tents of J— H3620
Mal 3: 6 the descendants of J, are not destroyed. H3620
Mt 1: 2 Isaac the father of J, Jacob the father of G2609
Mt 1: 2 J the father of Judah and his brothers, G2609
Mt 1:15 of Matthan, Matthan the father of J, G2609
Mt 1:16 J the father of Joseph, the husband G2609
Mt 8:11 Isaac and J in the kingdom of heaven. G2609
Mt 22:32 the God of Isaac, and the God *of* J'? G2609
Mk 12:26 the God of Isaac, and the God *of* J'? G2609
Lk 3:34 the son *of* J, the son of Isaac, the son of G2609
Lk 13:28 Isaac and J and all the prophets in the G2609
Lk 20:37 the God of Isaac, and the God *of* J. G2609
Jn 4: 5 the plot of ground J had given to his son G2609
Jn 4:12 Are you greater than our father J, who G2609
Ac 3:13 of Abraham, Isaac and J, the God of our G2609
Ac 7: 8 Later Isaac became the father of J, and G2609
Ac 7: 8 J became the father of the twelve G2609
Ac 7:12 When J heard that there was grain in G2609
Ac 7:14 sent for his father J and his whole family, G2609
Ac 7:15 Then J went down to Egypt, where he and G2609
Ac 7:32 the God of Abraham, Isaac and J. G2609
Ac 7:46 provide a dwelling place for the God *of* J. G2609
Ro 9:13 Just as it is written: "J I loved, but Esau I G2609
Ro 11:26 he will turn godlessness away from J. G2609
Heb 11: 9 as did Isaac and J, who were heirs with G2609
Heb 11:20 faith Isaac blessed J and Esau in regard G2609
Heb 11:21 By faith J, when he was dying, blessed G2609

JACOB'S (22) [JACOB]
Ge 31:33 So Laban went into J tent and into Leah's H3620
Ge 32:21 So J gifts went on ahead of him, but he H2021S
Ge 32:25 touched the socket of J hip so that his hip H3620
Ge 32:32 the socket of J hip was touched near H3620
Ge 34: 7 J sons had come in from the fields as H3620
Ge 34: 7 in Israel by sleeping with J daughter— H3620
Ge 34:13 J sons replied deceitfully as they spoke to H3620
Ge 34:19 he was delighted with J daughter. H3620
Ge 34:25 in pain, two of J sons, Simeon and Levi H3620
Ge 37: 2 This is the account of J family line H3620
Ge 46:19 The sons of J wife Rachel: Joseph and H3620
Ge 46:27 the members of J family, which went to H3620
Ge 50:12 So J sons did as he had commanded H2257S
Isa 27: 9 will J guilt be atoned for, and this H3620
Isa 41:21 "Set forth your arguments," says J King. H3620
Isa 45:19 I have not said to J descendants, 'Seek H3620
Jer 30:18 restore the fortunes of J tents and have H3620
Mic 1: 5 All this is because of J transgression H3620
Mic 1: 5 What is J transgression? Is it not H3620
Mal 1: 2 "Was not Esau J brother? H4200+3620
Lk 1:33 he will reign over J descendants forever; G2609
Jn 4: 6 J well was there, and Jesus, tired as he G2609

JADA (2)
1Ch 2:28 Shammai and J. The sons of H3360
1Ch 2:32 The sons of J, Shammai's brother: Jether H3360

JADAH (2)
1Ch 9:42 Ahaz was the father of J, Jadah was the H3586
1Ch 9:42 of Jadah, J was the father of Alemeth H3586

JADDAI (1)
Ezr 10:43 Zebina, J, Joel and Benaiah. H3350

JADDUA (3)
Ne 10:21 Meshezabel, Zadok, J, H3348
Ne 12:11 of Jonathan, and Jonathan the father of J. H3348
Ne 12:22 Johanan and J, as well as those H3348

JADON (1)
Ne 3: 7 Melatiah of Gibeon and J of Meronoth H3347

JAEL (6)
Jdg 4:17 fled on foot to the tent of J, the wife of H3605
Jdg 4:18 J went out to meet Sisera and said to him, H3605
Jdg 4:21 But J, Heber's wife, picked up a tent peg H3605
Jdg 4:22 of Sisera, and J went out to meet him. H3605
Jdg 5: 6 in the days of J, the highways were H3605
Jdg 5:24 "Most blessed of women be J, the wife of H3605

JAGGED (1)
Job 41:30 Its undersides are j potsherds, leaving a H2529

JAGUR (1)
Jos 15:21 of Edom were: Kabzeel, Eder, J, H3327

JAH (KJV) LORD*

JAHATH (8)
1Ch 4: 2 Reaiah son of Shobal was the father of J H3511
1Ch 4: 2 J the father of Ahumai and Lahad. H3511
1Ch 6:20 Libni his son, J his son, Zimmah his son H3511
1Ch 6:43 the son of J, the son of Gershon, the son H3511
1Ch 23:10 the sons of Shimei: J, Ziza, Jeush and H3511
1Ch 23:11 J was the first and Ziza the second, but H3511
1Ch 24:22 from the sons of Shelomoth: J. H3511
2Ch 34:12 them to direct them were J and Obadiah, H3511

JAHAZ (7)
Nu 21:23 When he reached J, he fought with Israel. H3403
Dt 2:32 army came out to meet us in battle at J, H3403
Jos 13:18 J, Kedemoth, Mephaath, H3403
Jos 21:36 from the tribe of Reuben, Bezer, J, H3403
Jdg 11:20 encamped at J and fought with Israel H3403
Isa 15: 4 their voices are heard all the way to J. H3403
Jer 48:34 cry rises from Heshbon to Elealeh and J, H3403

JAHAZIEL (6)
1Ch 12: 4 Jeremiah, J, Johanan, Jozabad the H3487
1Ch 16: 6 Benaiah and J the priests were to H3487
1Ch 23:19 J the third and Jekameam the fourth. H3487
1Ch 24:23 J the third and Jekameam the fourth. H3487
2Ch 20:14 of the LORD came on J son of Zechariah, H3487
Ezr 8: 5 Shekaniah son of J, and with him 300 H3487

JAHDAI (1)
1Ch 2:47 The sons of J: Regem, Jotham, Geshan H3367

JAHDIEL (1)
1Ch 5:24 Azriel, Jeremiah, Hodaviah and J. H3484

JAHDO (1)
1Ch 5:14 of Jeshishai, the son of J, the son of Buz. H3482

JAHLEEL (2) [JAHLEELITE]
Ge 46:14 The sons of Zebulun: Sered, Elon and J. H3499
Nu 26:26 through J, the Jahleelite clan. H3499

JAHLEELITE (1) [JAHLEEL]
Nu 26:26 Elonite clan; through Jahleel, the J clan. H3500

JAHMAI (1)
1Ch 7: 2 Rephaiah, Jeriel, J, Ibsam and Samuel H3503

JAHZAH (2)
1Ch 6:78 they received Bezer in the wilderness, J, H3404
Jer 48:21 the plateau—to Holon, J and Mephaath, H3404

JAHZEEL (1) [JAHZEELITE]
Nu 26:48 through J, the Jahzeelite clan; through H3505

JAHZEELITE (1) [JAHZEEL]
Nu 26:48 through Jahzeel, the J clan; through Guni H3506

JAHZEIAH (1)
Ezr 10:15 son of Asahel and J son of Tikvah, H3488

JAHZERAH (1)
1Ch 9:12 of Adiel, the son of J, the son of H3492

JAHZIEL (2)
Ge 46:24 The sons of Naphtali: J, Guni, Jezer and H3505
1Ch 7:13 J, Guni, Jezer and Shillem—the H3507

JAIL (7) [JAILER, JAILERS]
Ac 4: 3 they put them in j until the next day. G5499
Ac 5:18 the apostles and put them in the public j. G5499
Ac 5:19 opened the doors *of* the j and brought G5871
Ac 5:21 Israel—and sent to the j for the apostles. G1303
Ac 5:22 But on arriving at the j, the officers did not G5871
Ac 5:23 "We found the j securely locked, with the G1303
Ac 5:25 The men you put in j are standing in the G5871

JAILER (7) [JAIL]
Ac 16:23 the j was commanded to guard them G1302
Ac 16:27 The j woke up, and when he saw the G1302
Ac 16:29 The j called for lights, rushed in and fell NDT
Ac 16:33 of the night the j took them and washed NDT
Ac 16:34 The j brought them into his house and set a NDT
Ac 16:35 sent their officers to the j with the order: NDT
Ac 16:36 The j told Paul, "The magistrates have G1302

JAILERS (1) [JAIL]
Mt 18:34 handed him over *to* the j to be tortured, G991

JAIR (10) [JAIRITE, HAVVOTH JAIR]
Nu 32:41 J, a descendant of Manasseh, captured H3281
Dt 3:14 J, a descendant of Manasseh, took the H3281
Jos 13:30 all the settlements of J in Bashan, sixty H3281
Jdg 10: 3 He was followed by J of Gilead, who led H3281
Jdg 10: 5 When J died, he was buried in Kamon. H3281
2Sa 21:19 Elhanan son of Jthe Bethlehemite killed H3600
1Ki 4:13 the settlements of J son of Manasseh in H3281
1Ch 2:22 Segub was the father of J, who controlled H3281
1Ch 20: 5 Elhanan son of J killed Lahmi the brother H3600
Est 2: 5 named Mordecai son of J, the son of H3281

JAIRITE (1) [JAIR]
2Sa 20:26 Ira the J was David's priest. H3285

JAIRUS (6)
Mk 5:22 the synagogue leaders, named J, came, G2608
Mk 5:35 some people came from the house of J, the NDT
Lk 8:41 Then a man named J, a synagogue leader G2608
Lk 8:49 someone came from the house of J, the NDT
Lk 8:50 Jesus said *to* J, "Don't be afraid; G899S
Lk 8:51 When he arrived at the house of J, he did NDT

JAKAN (1)
1Ch 5:13 Jorai, J, Zia and Eber—seven in H3602

JAKEH (1)
Pr 30: 1 The sayings of Agur son of J—an inspired H3681

JAKIM (2)
1Ch 8:19 J, Zikri, Zabdi, H3691
1Ch 24:12 the eleventh to Eliashib, the twelfth to J, H3691

JAKIN (8) [JAKINITE]
Ge 46:10 J, Zohar and Shaul the son of a H3520
Ex 6:15 J, Zohar and Shaul the son of a H3520
Nu 26:12 through J, the Jakinite clan; H3520
1Ki 7:21 the south he named J and the one to the H3521
1Ch 9:10 Of the priests: Jedaiah; Jehoiarib; J; H3520
1Ch 24:17 the twenty-first to J, the twenty-second to H3520
2Ch 3:17 the south he named J and the one to the H3521
Ne 11:10 Jedaiah; the son of Joiarib; J; H3520

JAKINITE (1) [JAKIN]
Nu 26:12 Jaminite clan; through Jakin, the J clan; H3522

JALAM (4)
Ge 36: 5 Oholibamah bore Jeush, J and Korah. H3609

Ge 36:14 she bore to Esau: Jeush, J and Korah. H3609
Ge 36:18 Chiefs Jeush, J and Korah. These were H3609
1Ch 1:35 Eliphaz, Reuel, Jeush, J and Korah. H3609

JALON (1)
1Ch 4:17 Epher and J. One of Mered's H3534

JAMBRES (1)
2Ti 3: 8 Just as Jannes and J opposed Moses, so G2612

JAMBS (10)
Eze 40: 9 cubits deep and its j were two cubits thick. H382
Eze 40:24 He measured its j and its portico, and they H382
Eze 40:31 palm trees decorated its j, and eight steps H382
Eze 40:34 palm trees decorated the j on either side H382
Eze 40:37 palm trees decorated the j on either side H382
Eze 40:48 temple and measured the j *of* the portico; H382
Eze 40:49 there were pillars on each side of the j. H382
Eze 41: 1 me to the main hall and measured the j; H382
Eze 41: 1 the width of the j was six cubits on each NDT
Eze 41: 3 measured the j *of* the entrance; H382

JAMES (42)
Mt 4:21 J son of Zebedee and his brother John. G2610
Mt 10: 2 brother Andrew; J son of Zebedee, and G2610
Mt 10: 3 the tax collector; J son of Alphaeus, and G2610
Mt 13:55 and aren't his brothers J, Joseph, G2610
Mt 17: 1 J and John the brother of James G2610
Mt 17: 1 James and John the brother *of* J, and led G899S
Mt 27:56 Mary the mother *of* J and Joseph, and the G2610
Mk 1:19 he saw J son of Zebedee and his brother G2610
Mk 1:29 they went with J and John to the home of G2610
Mk 3:17 J son of Zebedee and his brother John (to G2610
Mk 3:18 Matthew, Thomas, J son of Alphaeus G2610
Mk 5:37 J and John the brother of James. G2610
Mk 5:37 James and John the brother *of* J. G2610
Mk 6: 3 Isn't this Mary's son and the brother *of* J G2610
Mk 9: 2 J and John with him and led them up a G2610
Mk 10:35 Then J and John, the sons of Zebedee G2610
Mk 10:41 they became indignant with J and John. G2610
Mk 13: 3 J, John and Andrew asked him G2610
Mk 14:33 He took Peter, J and John along with him G2610
Mk 15:40 Mary the mother *of* J the younger and of G2610
Mk 16: 1 Mary the mother *of* J, and Salome bought G2610
Lk 5:10 so were J and John, the sons of G2610
Lk 6:14 his brother Andrew, J, John, Philip G2610
Lk 6:15 Thomas, J son of Alphaeus, Simon who G2610
Lk 6:16 Judas *son of* J, and Judas Iscariot, who G2610
Lk 8:51 except Peter, John and J, and the child's G2610
Lk 9:28 John and J with him and went up onto a G2610
Lk 9:54 When the disciples J and John saw this G2610
Lk 24:10 Mary the mother *of* J, and the others with G2610
Ac 1:13 were Peter, John, J and Andrew; Philip G2610
Ac 1:13 J son of Alphaeus and Simon the Zealot G2610
Ac 1:13 Simon the Zealot, and Judas *son of* J. G2610
Ac 12: 2 He had J, the brother of John, put to death G2610
Ac 12:17 "Tell J and the other brothers and sisters G2610
Ac 15:13 When they finished, J spoke up. "Brothers," G2610
Ac 21:18 day Paul and the rest of us went to see J, G2610
1Co 15: 7 Then he appeared *to* J, then to all the G2610
Gal 1:19 other apostles—only J, the Lord's brother. G2610
Gal 2: 9 J, Cephas and John, those esteemed as G2610
Gal 2:12 For before certain men came from J, he G2610
Jas 1: 1 J, a servant of God and of the Lord Jesus G2610
Jude 1 servant of Jesus Christ and a brother *of* J, G2610

JAMIN (6) [JAMINITE]
Ge 46:10 Jemuel, J, Ohad, Jakin, Zohar and Shaul H3546
Ex 6:15 sons of Simeon were Jemuel, J, Ohad, H3546
Nu 26:12 through J, the Jaminite clan; H3546
1Ch 2:27 firstborn of Jerahmeel: Maaz, J and Eker. H3546
1Ch 4:24 Nemuel, J, Jarib, Zerah and H3546
Ne 8: 7 Sherebiah, J, Akkub, Shabbethai H3546

JAMINITE (1) [JAMIN]
Nu 26:12 through Jamin, the J clan; through Jakin H3547

JAMLECH (1)
1Ch 4:34 Meshobab, J, Joshah son of Amaziah, H3552

JAMMED (1)
Ex 14:25 *He* j the wheels of their chariots so that they H673

JANAI (1)
1Ch 5:12 the second, then J and Shaphat, in H3614

JANIM (1)
Jos 15:53 J, Beth Tappuah, Aphekah, H3565

JANNAI (1)
Lk 3:24 of Melki, the son *of* J, the son of Joseph, G2613

JANNES (1)
2Ti 3: 8 Just as J and Jambres opposed Moses, so G2614

JANOAH (3)
Jos 16: 6 passing by it to J on the east. H3562
Jos 16: 7 it went down from J to Ataroth and H3562
2Ki 15:29 Abel Beth Maakah, J, Kedesh and Hazor. H3562

JAPHETH (12) [JAPHETH'S]
Ge 5:32 became the father of Shem, Ham and J. H3651
Ge 6:10 Noah had three sons: Shem, Ham and J. H3651
Ge 7:13 Ham and J, together with his wife H3651
Ge 9:18 out of the ark were Shem, Ham and J. H3651
Ge 9:23 But Shem and J took a garment and laid it H3651
Ge 9:27 may J live in the tents of Shem NDT
Ge 9:27 may Canaan be the slave of J. H4564S
Ge 10: 1 of Shem, Ham and J, Noah's sons, H3651
Ge 10: 2 The sons of J: Gomer, Magog, Madai H3651
Ge 10:21 whose older brother was J; Shem was the H3651
1Ch 1: 4 The sons of Noah: Shem, Ham and J. H3651
1Ch 1: 5 The sons of J: Gomer, Magog, Madai H3651

JAPHETH'S (1) [JAPHETH]
Ge 9:27 May God extend J territory; may H4200+3651

JAPHIA (5)
Jos 10: 3 J king of Lachish and Debir king of Eglon. H3644
Jos 19:12 went on to Daberath and up to J. H3643
2Sa 5:15 Elishua, Nepheg, J, H3644
1Ch 3: 7 Nepheg, J, H3644
1Ch 14: 6 Nepheg, J, H3644

JAPHLET (2) [JAPHLET'S, JAPHLETITES]
1Ch 7:32 Heber was the father of J, Shomer and H3646
1Ch 7:33 The sons of J: Pasak, Bimhal and Ashvath. H3646

JAPHLET'S (1) [JAPHLET]
1Ch 7:33 Bimhal and Ashvath. These were J sons. H3646

JAPHLETITES (1) [JAPHLET]
Jos 16: 3 the territory of the J as far as the region of H3647

JAR (38) [JARS]
Ge 24:14 'Please let down your j that I may have a H3902
Ge 24:15 came out with her j on her shoulder. H3902
Ge 24:16 filled her j and came up again. H3902
Ge 24:17 "Please give me a little water from your j." H3902
Ge 24:18 quickly lowered the j to her hands and H3902
Ge 24:20 she quickly emptied her j into the trough, H3902
Ge 24:43 let me drink a little water from your j," H3902
Ge 24:45 came out, with her j on her shoulder. H3902
Ge 24:46 quickly lowered her j from her shoulder H3902
Ex 16:33 "Take a j and put an omer of manna in it. H7573
Nu 5:17 holy water in a clay j and put some dust H3998
Nu 19:17 offering into a j and pour fresh water over H3998
1Ki 14: 3 some cakes and a j *of* honey, and go to H1318
1Ki 17:10 a little water in a j so I may have a drink?" H3998
1Ki 17:12 handful of flour in a j and a little olive oil H3902
1Ki 17:14 'The j *of* flour will not be used up and the H3902
1Ki 17:16 For the j *of* flour was not used up and the H3902
1Ki 19: 6 baked over hot coals, and a j *of* water. H7608
2Ki 4: 2 she said, "except a small j *of* olive oil." H655
2Ki 4: 6 "There is not a j left." Then the oil H3998
Jer 19: 1 "Go and buy a clay j *from* a potter. H1318
Jer 19:10 "Then break the j while those who go H1318
Jer 19:11 as this potter's j is smashed and cannot H3998
Jer 32:14 put them in a clay j so they will last a H3998
Jer 48:11 not poured from *one* j to another—she H3998
Jer 48:38 broken Moab like a j that no one wants," H3998
Jer 51:34 confusion, he has made us an empty j. H3998
Eze 4: 9 put them in a storage j and use them to H3998
Mt 26: 7 to him with an alabaster j of very expensive G223
Mk 14: 3 came with an alabaster j of very expensive G223
Mk 14: 3 She broke the j and poured the perfume on G223
Mk 14:13 a man carrying a j of water will meet G3040
Lk 7:37 came there with an alabaster j of perfume. G223
Lk 8:16 hides it *in* a clay j or puts it under G5007
Lk 22:10 a man carrying a j of water will meet you. G3040
Jn 4:28 leaving her water j, the woman went G5620
Jn 19:29 A j of wine vinegar was there, so they G5007
Heb 9: 4 This ark contained the gold j of manna G5085

JAREB (KJV) GREAT

JARED (7)
Ge 5:15 lived 65 years, he became the father of J. H3719
Ge 5:16 After he became the father of J, Mahalalel H3719
Ge 5:18 When J had lived 162 years, he became H3719
Ge 5:19 J lived 800 years and had other sons and H3719
Ge 5:20 Altogether, J lived a total of 962 years H3719
1Ch 1: 2 Mahalalel, J, H3719
Lk 3:37 son of Enoch, the son *of* J, the son of G2616

JARHA (2)
1Ch 2:34 He had an Egyptian servant named J. H3739
1Ch 2:35 his daughter in marriage to his servant J, H3739

JARIB (3)
1Ch 4:24 Nemuel, Jamin, J, Zerah and Shaul; H3743
Ezr 8:16 Shemaiah, Elnathan, J, Elnathan, Nathan, H3743
Ezr 10:18 Maaseiah, Eliezer, J and Gedaliah. H3743

JARKON See ME JARKON

JARMUTH (7)
Jos 10: 3 Hebron, Piram king of J, Japhia king of H3754
Jos 10: 5 Jerusalem, Hebron, J, Lachish and Eglon H3754
Jos 10:23 Jerusalem, Hebron, J, Lachish and Eglon. H3754
Jos 12:11 the king of J one the king of Lachish one H3754
Jos 15:35 J, Adullam, Sokoh, Azekah, H3754
Jos 21:29 J and En Gannim, together with their H3754
Ne 11:29 in En Rimmon, in Zorah, in J, H3754

JAROAH (1)
1Ch 5:14 the son of J, the son of Gilead, H3726

JARS (21) [JAR]
Nu 4: 7 bowls, and the j *for* drink offerings H7987
Nu 4: 9 all its j *for* the olive oil used to supply H3998
Jdg 7:16 trumpets and empty j in the hands of all H3902
Jdg 7:19 trumpets and broke the j that were in their H3902
Jdg 7:20 blew the trumpets and smashed the j. H3902
Ru 2: 9 drink from the water j the men have filled." H3998
1Ki 18:33 "Fill four large j with water and pour it on H3902
2Ki 4: 3 ask all your neighbors for empty j. H3998
2Ki 4: 4 Pour oil into all the j, and as each is filled H3998
2Ki 4: 5 They brought the j to her and she kept NDT
2Ki 4: 6 When all the j were full, she said to her H3998
Job 38:37 can tip over the water j *of* the heavens H5574
Ps 33: 7 He gathers the waters of the sea into j; he H5532
Isa 22:24 lesser vessels, from the bowls to all the j. H5574
Jer 14: 3 They return with their j unfilled; dismayed H3998
Jer 40:10 put them in your storage j, and live in H3998
Jer 48:12 will empty her pitchers and smash her j. H5574
Mt 25: 4 however, took oil in j along with their lamps. G31
Jn 2: 6 Nearby stood six stone water j, the kind G5620
Jn 2: 7 servants, "Fill the j with water"; so they G5620
2Co 4: 7 have this treasure in j of clay to show that G5007

JASHAR (2)
Jos 10:13 enemies, as it is written in the Book of J. H3839
2Sa 1:18 of the bow (it is written in the Book of J): H3839

JASHEN (1)
2Sa 23:32 the Shaalbonite, the sons of J, Jonathan H3826

JASHOBEAM (3)
1Ch 11:11 J, a Hakmonite, was chief of the officers H3790
1Ch 12: 6 Joezer and J the Korahites; H3790
1Ch 27: 2 the first month, was J son of Zabdiel. H3790

JASHUB (4) [JASHUBITE]
Ge 46:13 Tola, Puah, J and Shimron. H3793
Nu 26:24 through J, the Jashubite clan; through H3793
1Ch 7: 1 Puah, J and Shimron—four in H3793
Ezr 10:29 Adaiah, J, Sheal and Jeremoth. H3793

JASHUBI LEHEM (1)
1Ch 4:22 Saraph, who ruled in Moab and J. H3788

JASHUBITE (1) [JASHUB]
Nu 26:24 through Jashub, the J clan; through H3795

JASON (4) [JASON'S]
Ac 17: 6 they dragged J and some other believers G2619
Ac 17: 7 J has welcomed them into his house G2619
Ac 17: 9 Then they made J and the others post G2619
Ro 16:21 as do Lucius, J and Sosipater, my fellow G2619

JASON'S (1) [JASON]
Ac 17: 5 They rushed to J house in search of Paul G2619

JASPER (8)
Ex 28:20 be topaz, onyx and j. Mount them in gold H3835
Ex 39:13 onyx and j. They were mounted H3835
Job 28:18 Coral and j are not worthy of mention; the H1486
Eze 28:13 onyx and j, lapis lazuli, turquoise H3835
Rev 4: 3 had the appearance of j and ruby. G3345+2618
Rev 21:11 like a j, clear as crystal. G3345+2618
Rev 21:18 The wall was made of j, and the city of G2618
Rev 21:19 The first foundation was j, the second G2618

JATHNIEL (1)
1Ch 26: 2 second, Zebadiah the third, J the fourth, H3853

JATTIR (4)
Jos 15:48 In the hill country: Shamir, J, Sokoh, H3848
Jos 21:14 J, Eshtemoa, H3848
1Sa 30:27 who were in Bethel, Ramoth Negev and J; H3848
1Ch 6:57 a city of refuge), and Libnah, J, Eshtemoa, H3848

JAVAN (4)
Ge 10: 2 Magog, Madai, J, Tubal, Meshek and H3430
Ge 10: 4 The sons of J: Elishah, Tarshish, the H3430
1Ch 1: 5 Magog, Madai, J, Tubal, Meshek and H3430
1Ch 1: 7 The sons of J: Elishah, Tarshish, the H3430

JAVELIN (7) [JAVELINS]
Jos 8:18 out toward Ai the j that is in your hand, H3959
Jos 8:18 toward the city the j that was in his hand. H3959
Jos 8:26 that held out his j until he had destroyed H3959
1Sa 17: 6 a bronze j was slung on his back. H3959
1Sa 17:45 against me with sword and spear and j, H3959
Job 41:26 does the spear or the dart or the j. H9233
Ps 35: 3 Brandish spear and j against those who H6038

JAVELINS (1) [JAVELIN]
2Sa 18:14 So he took three j in his hand and H8657

JAW (2) [JAWBONE, JAWS]
Job 41: 2 its nose or pierce its j with a hook? H4305
Ps 3: 7 Strike all my enemies on the j; break the H4305

JAWBONE (4) [JAW]
Jdg 15:15 Finding a fresh j *of* a donkey, he grabbed H4305
Jdg 15:16 "With a donkey's j I have made donkeys H4305
Jdg 15:16 With a donkey's j I have killed a thousand H4305
Jdg 15:17 he threw away the j; and the place was H4305

JAWS (6) [JAW]
Job 36:16 is wooing you from the **j** *of* distress to a H7023
Pr 30:14 swords and whose **j** are set with knives H5506
Isa 5:14 Therefore Death expands its **j**, opening H5883
Isa 30:28 he places in the **j** *of* the peoples a bit that H4305
Eze 29: 4 put hooks in your **j** and make the fish of H4305
Eze 38: 4 put hooks in your **j** and bring you out with H4305

JAZER (13)
Nu 21:32 After Moses had sent spies to **J**, the H3597
Nu 32: 1 saw that the lands of **J** and Gilead were H3597
Nu 32: 3 "Ataroth, Dibon, **J**, Nimrah, Heshbon H3597
Nu 32:35 Atroth Shophan, **J**, Jogbehah, H3597
Jos 13:25 The territory of **J**, all the towns of Gilead H3597
Jos 21:39 Heshbon and **J**, together with their H3597
2Sa 24: 5 then went through Gad and on to **J**. H3597
1Ch 6:81 Heshbon and **J**, together with their H3597
1Ch 26:31 the Hebronites were found at **J** *in* Gilead. H3597
Isa 16: 8 which once reached **J** and spread toward H3597
Isa 16: 9 So I weep, as **J** weeps, for the vines of H3597
Jer 48:32 I weep for you, as **J** weeps, you vines of H3597
Jer 48:32 as far as the sea; they reached as far as **J**. H3597

JAZIZ (1)
1Ch 27:31 **J** the Hagrite was in charge of the flocks H3467

JEALOUS (27) [JEALOUSLY, JEALOUSY]
Ge 30: 1 any children, she *became* **j** of her sister. H7861
Ge 37:11 His brothers *were* **j** of him, but his father H7861
Ex 20: 5 LORD your God, am a **j** God, punishing the H7862
Ex 34:14 whose name is **J**, is a jealous God. H7862
Ex 34:14 whose name is Jealous, is a **j** God. H7862
Nu 5:14 if he *is* **j** and suspects H8120+7863+6296+6584
Nu 11:29 Moses replied, "*Are* you **j** for my sake? H7861
Dt 4:24 your God is a consuming fire, a **j** God. H7862
Dt 5: 9 LORD your God, am a **j** God, punishing the H7862
Dt 6:15 is a **j** God and his anger will burn against H7862
Dt 32:16 *They* **made** him **j** with their foreign gods H7861
Dt 32:21 They **made** me **j** by what is no god and H7861
Jos 24:19 is a holy God; he is a **j** God. He will not H7868
1Ki 14:22 *they* **stirred up** his **j** **anger** more H7861
Isa 11:13 Ephraim *will* not be **j** *of* Judah, nor Judah H7861
Eze 16:38 vengeance of my wrath and **j** **anger**. H7863
Eze 16:42 will subside and my **j** **anger** will turn away H7863
Eze 23:25 I will direct my **j** **anger** against you, and H7863
Eze 36: 6 I speak in my **j** wrath because you have H7863
Joel 2:18 Then the LORD *was* **j** for his land and took H7861
Na 1: 2 The LORD is a **j** and avenging God; the H7868
Zep 3: 8 be consumed by the fire of my **j** **anger**. H7863
Zec 1:14 '*I am* very **j** for Jerusalem and Zion H7861+7863
Zec 8: 2 "*I am* very **j** for Zion; I am burning H7861+7863
Ac 7: 9 "Because the patriarchs *were* **j** of Joseph *G2420*
Ac 17: 5 But other Jews *were* **j**; so they rounded up *G2420*
2Co 11: 2 *I am* **j** for you with a godly jealousy. *G2420*

JEALOUSLY (1) [JEALOUS]
Jas 4: 5 reason that he **j** longs for the spirit *G4639+5784*

JEALOUSY (26) [JEALOUS]
Nu 5:14 if feelings of **j** come over her husband H7863
Nu 5:15 because it is a grain offering for **j**, H7863
Nu 5:18 the grain offering for **j**, while he himself H7863
Nu 5:25 from her hands the grain offering for **j**, H7863
Nu 5:29 is the law of **j** when a woman goes astray H7863
Nu 5:30 when feelings of **j** come over a man H7863
Ps 78:58 *they* **aroused** his **j** with their idols. H7861
Ps 79: 5 How long will your **j** burn like fire? H7863
Pr 6:34 For **j** arouses a husband's fury, and he will H7863
Pr 27: 4 who can stand before **j**? H7863
Ecc 9: 6 their hate and their **j** have long since H7863
SS 8: 6 as death, its **j** unyielding as the grave. H7863
Isa 11:13 Ephraim's **j** will vanish, and Judah's H7863
Eze 8: 3 where the idol that **provokes to** **j** stood. H7861
Eze 8: 5 of the gate of the altar I saw this idol of **j**. H7863
Eze 35:11 with the anger and **j** you showed in your H7863
Zep 1:18 In the fire of his **j** the whole earth will be H7863
Zec 8: 2 Zion; *I am* burning with **j** for her. H7861
Ac 5:17 party of the Sadducees, were filled with **j**. *G2419*
Ac 13:45 saw the crowds, they were filled with **j**. *G2419*
Ro 13:13 debauchery, not in dissension and **j**. *G2419*
1Co 3: 3 For since there is **j** and quarreling among *G2419*
1Co 10:22 *Are we trying to* **arouse** the Lord's **j**? Are *G4143*
2Co 11: 2 I am jealous for you *with* a godly **j**. *G2419*
2Co 12:20 that there may be discord, **j**, fits of rage, *G2419*
Gal 5:20 discord, **j**, fits of rage, selfish *G2419*

JEARIM (1) [KESALON, KIRIATH JEARIM]
Jos 15:10 ran along the northern slope of Mount **J** H3630

JEATHERAI (1)
1Ch 6:21 Iddo his son, Zerah his son and **J** his son. H3290

JEBEREKIAH (1)
Isa 8: 2 Zechariah son of **J** as reliable H3310

JEBUS (3) [JEBUSITE, JEBUSITES, JERUSALEM]
Jdg 19:10 the man left and went toward **J** (that is, H3293
Jdg 19:11 When they were near **J** and the day was H3293
1Ch 11: 4 Jerusalem (that is, **J**). The Jebusites who H3293

JEBUSITE (9) [JEBUS]
Jos 15: 8 along the southern slope of the **J** city H3294
Jos 18:16 slope of the **J** *city* and so to En Rogel. H3294
Jos 18:28 Haeleph, the **J** *city* (that is H3294
2Sa 24:16 at the threshing floor of Araunah the **J**. H3294
2Sa 24:18 on the threshing floor of Araunah the **J**." H3294
1Ch 21:15 at the threshing floor of Araunah the **J**. H3294
1Ch 21:18 on the threshing floor of Araunah the **J**. H3294
1Ch 21:28 on the threshing floor of Araunah the **J**, H3294
2Ch 3: 1 on the threshing floor of Araunah the **J**, H3294

JEBUSITES (33) [JEBUS]
Ge 10:16 **J**, Amorites, Girgashites, H3294
Ge 15:21 Amorites, Canaanites, Girgashites and **J**." H3294
Ex 3: 8 Amorites, Perizzites, Hivites and **J**. H3294
Ex 3:17 Hivites and **J**—a land flowing with H3294
Ex 13: 5 Hivites and **J**—the land he swore to H3294
Ex 23:23 Hivites and **J**, and I will wipe them H3294
Ex 33: 2 Hittites, Perizzites, Hivites and **J**. H3294
Ex 34:11 Hittites, Perizzites, Hivites and **J**. H3294
Nu 13:29 **J** and Amorites live in the hill country H3294
Dt 7: 1 Hivites and **J**, seven nations larger H3294
Dt 20:17 Hivites and **J**—as the LORD your God H3294
Jos 3:10 Perizzites, Girgashites, Amorites and **J**. H3294
Jos 9: 1 Canaanites, Perizzites, Hivites and **J**)— H3294
Jos 11: 3 Perizzites and **J** in the hill country; and H3294
Jos 12: 8 Canaanites, Perizzites, Hivites and **J**. H3294
Jos 15:63 Judah could not dislodge the **J**, who were H3294
Jos 15:63 to this day the **J** live there with the people H3294
Jos 24:11 Hivites and **J**, but I gave them into H3294
Jdg 1:21 did not drive out the **J**, who were living in H3294
Jdg 1:21 to this day the **J** live there with the H3294
Jdg 3: 5 Amorites, Perizzites, Hivites and **J**. H3294
Jdg 19:11 at this city of the **J** and spend the night." H3294
2Sa 5: 6 marched to Jerusalem to attack the **J**, H3294
2Sa 5: 6 The **J** said to David, "You will not get in NDT
2Sa 5: 8 who conquers the **J** will have to use the H3294
1Ki 9:20 Hivites and **J** (these peoples were not H3294
1Ch 1:14 **J**, Amorites, Girgashites, H3294
1Ch 11: 4 that is, Jebus). The **J** who lived there H3294
1Ch 11: 6 leads the attack on the **J** will become H3294
2Ch 8: 7 Hivites and **J** (these people were not H3294
Ezr 9: 1 Perizzites, **J**, Ammonites, Moabites, H3294
Ne 9: 8 Amorites, Perizzites, **J** and Girgashites. H3294
Zec 9: 7 in Judah, and Ekron will be like the **J**. H3294

JECHONIAS (KJV) JECONIAH

JECOLIAH (NIV84) JEKONIAH

JECONIAH (2)
Mt 1:11 Josiah the father of **J** and his brothers at *G2651*
Mt 1:12 **J** was the father of Shealtiel, Shealtiel the *G2651*

JEDAIAH (11) [JEDAIAH'S]
1Ch 4:37 of Allon, the son of **J**, the son of Shimri, H3355
1Ch 9:10 Of the priests: **J**; Jehoiarib; Jakin; H3361
1Ch 24: 7 first lot fell to Jehoiarib, the second to **J**, H3361
Ezr 2:36 the descendants of **J** (through the family H3361
Ne 3:10 **J** son of Harumaph made repairs opposite H3355
Ne 7:39 the descendants of **J** (through the family H3361
Ne 11:10 From the priests: **J**; the son of Joiarib H3361
Ne 12: 6 Shemaiah, Joiarib, **J**, H3361
Ne 12: 7 Hilkiah and **J**. These were the H3361
Zec 6:10 Tobijah and **J**, who have arrived H3361
Zec 6:14 **J** and Hen son of Zephaniah as a H3361

JEDAIAH'S (2) [JEDAIAH]
Ne 12:19 of Joiarib's, Mattenai; of **J**, Uzzi; H3361
Ne 12:21 of Hilkiah's, Hashabiah; of **J**, Nethanel. H3361

JEDIAEL (6)
1Ch 7: 6 sons of Benjamin: Bela, Beker and **J**. H3356
1Ch 7:10 The son of **J**: Bilhan. The sons of Bilhan H3356
1Ch 7:11 All these sons of **J** were heads of families. H3356
1Ch 11:45 **J** son of Shimri, his brother Joha the Tizite H3356
1Ch 12:20 Jozabad, **J**, Michael, Jozabad H3356
1Ch 26: 2 the firstborn, **J** the second, Zebadiah the H3356

JEDIDAH (1)
2Ki 22: 1 mother's name was **J** daughter of Adaiah; H3352

JEDIDIAH (1)
2Sa 12:25 Nathan the prophet to name him **J**. H3354

JEDUTHUN (16)
1Ch 9:16 of Galal, the son of **J**; and Berekiah son of H3349
1Ch 16:38 Obed-Edom son of **J**, and also Hosah H3357
1Ch 16:41 them were Heman and **J** and the rest of H3349
1Ch 16:42 Heman and **J** were responsible for the H3349
1Ch 16:42 The sons of **J** were stationed at the gate H3349
1Ch 25: 1 Heman and **J** for the ministry of H3349
1Ch 25: 3 As for **J**, from his sons: Gedaliah, Zeri H3349
1Ch 25: 3 under the supervision of their father **J** H3349
1Ch 25: 6 **J** and Heman were under the supervision H3349
2Ch 5:12 Heman, **J** and their sons and relatives H3349
2Ch 29:14 from the descendants of **J**, Shemaiah H3349
2Ch 35:15 Heman and **J** the king's seer. H3349
Ne 11:17 Shammua, the son of Galal, the son of **J**. H3349
Ps 39: T director of music. For **J**. A psalm of David. H3349
Ps 62: T director of music. For **J**. A psalm of David. H3349
Ps 77: T For **J**. Of Asaph. A psalm. H3349

JEER (1) [JEERED, JEERS]
Job 16:10 People open their mouths to **j** at me; they NDT

JEERED (1) [JEER]
2Ki 2:23 boys came out of the town and **j** at him. H7840

JEERS (1) [JEER]
Heb 11:36 Some faced **j** and flogging, and even *G1849*

JEGAR SAHADUTHA (1)
Ge 31:47 Laban called it **J**, and Jacob H3337

JEHALLELEL (2)
1Ch 4:16 The sons of **J**: Ziph, Ziphah, Tiria and H3401
2Ch 29:12 Kish son of Abdi and Azariah son of **J** H3401

JEHATH (NIV84) JAHATH

JEHDEIAH (2)
1Ch 24:20 Shubael; from the sons of Shubael: **J**. H3485
1Ch 27:30 **J** the Meronothite was in charge of the H3485

JEHEZKEL (1)
1Ch 24:16 to Pethahiah, the twentieth to **J**, H3489

JEHIAH (1)
1Ch 15:24 Obed-Edom and **J** were also to be H3496

JEHIEL (14)
1Ch 15:18 Shemiramoth, **J**, Unni, Eliab, Benaiah H3493
1Ch 15:20 Jaaziel, Shemiramoth, **J**, Unni, Eliab H3493
1Ch 16: 5 Shemiramoth, **J**, Mattithiah, Eliab, H3493
1Ch 23: 8 The sons of Ladan: **J** the first, Zetham H3493
1Ch 27:32 **J** son of Hakmoni took care of the king's H3493
1Ch 29: 8 LORD in the custody of **J** the Gershonite. H3493
2Ch 21: 2 were Azariah, **J**, Zechariah, Azariahu, H3493
2Ch 29:14 of Heman, **J** and Shimei; from the H3493
2Ch 31:13 **J**, Azaziah, Nahath, Asahel, Jerimoth H3493
2Ch 35: 8 Hilkiah, Zechariah and **J**, the officials in H3493
Ezr 8: 9 Obadiah son of **J**, and with him 218 H3493
Ezr 10: 2 Then Shekaniah son of **J**, one of the H3493
Ezr 10:21 Shemaiah, **J** and Uzziah. H3493
Ezr 10:26 Zechariah, **J**, Abdi, Jeremoth and H3493

JEHIELI (2)
1Ch 26:21 to Ladan the Gershonite, were **J**, H3494
1Ch 26:22 the sons of **J**, Zetham and his brother Joel H3494

JEHIZKIAH (1)
2Ch 28:12 of Meshillemoth, **J** son of Shallum, and H3491

JEHOADDAH (2)
1Ch 8:36 Ahaz was the father of **J**, Jehoaddah was H3389
1Ch 8:36 Jehoaddah, **J** was the father of Alemeth H3389

JEHOADDAN (2)
2Ki 14: 2 His mother's name was **J**; she was from H3391
2Ch 25: 1 His mother's name was **J**; she was from H3391

JEHOAHAZ (22)
2Ki 10:35 And **J** his son succeeded him as king H3370
2Ki 13: 1 **J** son of Jehu became king of Israel in H3370
2Ki 13: 4 Then **J** sought the LORD's favor, and the H3370
2Ki 13: 7 left of the army of **J** except fifty horsemen, H3370
2Ki 13: 8 As for the other events of the reign of **J** H3370
2Ki 13: 9 **J** rested with his ancestors and was buried H3370
2Ki 13:10 Jehoash son of **J** became king of Israel in H3370
2Ki 13:22 Israel throughout the reign of **J**. H3370
2Ki 13:25 Then Jehoash son of **J** recaptured from H3370
2Ki 13:25 he had taken in battle from his father **J**. H3370
2Ki 14: 1 year of Jehoash son of **J** king of Israel, H3407
2Ki 14: 8 sent messengers to Jehoash son of **J**, H3370
2Ki 14:17 death of Jehoash son of **J** king of Israel. H3370
2Ki 23:30 of the land took **J** son of Josiah and H3370
2Ki 23:31 **J** was twenty-three years old when he H3370
2Ki 23:34 But he took **J** and carried him off to Egypt H3370
2Ch 25:17 sent this challenge to Jehoash son of **J**, H3370
2Ch 25:25 death of Jehoash son of **J** king of Israel. H3370
2Ch 36: 1 of the land took **J** son of Josiah and made H3370
2Ch 36: 2 **J** was twenty-three years old when he H3407
2Ch 36: 4 a brother of **J**, king over Judah and H2257S
2Ch 36: 4 Eliakim's brother **J** and carried him off to H3407

JEHOASH (28)
2Ki 13: 9 And **J** his son succeeded him as king H3409
2Ki 13:10 **J** son of Jehoahaz became king of Israel H3371
2Ki 13:12 As for the other events of the reign of **J** H3409
2Ki 13:13 **J** rested with his ancestors, and Jeroboam H3409
2Ki 13:13 **J** was buried in Samaria with the kings of H3409
2Ki 13:14 **J** king of Israel went down to see him H3409
2Ki 13:25 Then **J** son of Jehoahaz recaptured from H3371
2Ki 13:25 Three times **J** defeated him, and so he H3409
2Ki 14: 1 the second year of **J** son of Jehoahaz king H3409
2Ki 14: 8 sent messengers to **J** son of Jehoahaz, H3371
2Ki 14: 9 But **J** king of Israel replied to Amaziah H3371
2Ki 14:11 not listen, so **J** king of Israel attacked. H3371
2Ki 14:13 **J** king of Israel captured Amaziah king of H3371
2Ki 14:13 Then **J** went to Jerusalem and broke down NDT
2Ki 14:15 As for the other events of the reign of **J** H3371
2Ki 14:16 **J** rested with his ancestors and was buried H3371
2Ki 14:17 after the death of **J** son of Jehoahaz king H3371
2Ki 14:23 Jeroboam son of **J** king of Israel became H3409
2Ki 14:27 them by the hand of Jeroboam son of **J**. H3409
2Ch 25:17 sent this challenge to **J** son of Jehoahaz, H3409
2Ch 25:18 But **J** king of Israel replied to Amaziah H3409
2Ch 25:20 he might deliver them into the hands of **J**, NDT
2Ch 25:21 So **J** king of Israel attacked. He and H3409

2Ch 25:23 **J** king of Israel captured Amaziah king of H3409
2Ch 25:23 Then **J** brought him to Jerusalem and broke NDT
2Ch 25:25 after the death of **J** son of Jehoahaz king H3409
Hos 1: 1 reign of Jeroboam son of **J** king of Israel: H3409
Am 1: 1 Jeroboam son of **J** was king of Israel. H3409

JEHOHANAN (9)

1Ch 26: 3 **J** the sixth and Eliehoenai the seventh. H3380
2Ch 17:15 **J** the commander, with 280,000; H3380
2Ch 23: 1 Ishmael son of **J**, Azariah son of Obed, H3380
2Ch 28:12 Azariah son of **J**, Berekiah son of H3380
Ezr 10: 6 went to the room of **J** son of Eliashib. H3380
Ezr 10:28 **J**, Hananiah, Zabbai and H3380
Ne 6:18 his son **J** had married the daughter of H3380
Ne 12:13 of Ezra's, Meshullam; of Amariah's, **J**; H3380
Ne 12:42 Eleazar, Uzzi, **J**, Malkijah, Elam and Ezer H3380

JEHOIACHIN (26) [JEHOIACHIN'S]

2Ki 24: 6 And **J** his son succeeded him as king H3382
2Ki 24: 8 **J** was eighteen years old when he H3382
2Ki 24:12 **J** king of Judah, his mother, his attendants, H3382
2Ki 24:12 the king of Babylon, he took **J** prisoner. H2257S
2Ki 24:15 took **J** captive to Babylon. H3382
2Ki 25:27 year of the exile of **J** king of Judah, H3382
2Ki 25:27 he released **J** king of Judah from prison. H3382
2Ki 25:29 So **J** put aside his prison clothes and for the NDT
2Ki 25:30 day the king gave **J** a regular allowance H2257S
1Ch 3:16 of Jehoiakim: **J** his son, and Zedekiah. H3526
1Ch 3:17 The descendants of **J** the captive H3526
2Ch 36: 8 And **J** his son succeeded him as king H3382
2Ch 36: 9 **J** was eighteen years old when he H3382
Est 2: 6 those taken captive with **J** king of Judah. H3526
Jer 22:24 **J** son of Jehoiakim king of Judah H4037
Jer 22:28 Is this man **J** a despised, broken pot, an H4037
Jer 24: 1 After **J** son of Jehoiakim king of Judah H3527
Jer 27:20 away when he carried **J** son of Jehoiakim H3526
Jer 28: 4 back to this place **J** son of Jehoiakim king H3526
Jer 29: 2 This was after King **J** and the queen H3526
Jer 37: 1 he reigned in place of **J** son of Jehoiakim. H4037
Jer 52:31 year of the exile of **J** king of Judah, H3382
Jer 52:31 he released **J** king of Judah and freed H3382
Jer 52:33 So **J** put aside his prison clothes and for the NDT
Jer 52:34 of Babylon gave **J** a regular allowance H2257S
Eze 1: 2 it was the fifth year of the exile of King **J** H3422

JEHOIACHIN'S (2) [JEHOIACHIN]

2Ki 24:17 He made Mattaniah, **J** uncle, king in his H2257S
2Ch 36:10 and he made **J** uncle, Zedekiah, H2257S

JEHOIADA (53)

2Sa 8:18 Benaiah son of **J** was over the Kerethites H3381
2Sa 20:23 Benaiah son of **J** was over the Kerethites H3381
2Sa 23:20 Benaiah son of **J**, a valiant fighter from H3381
2Sa 23:22 Such were the exploits of Benaiah son of **J**; H3381
1Ki 1: 8 Benaiah son of **J**, Nathan the prophet, H3381
1Ki 1:26 Benaiah son of **J**, and your servant H3381
1Ki 1:32 Nathan the prophet and Benaiah son of **J**." H3381
1Ki 1:36 Benaiah son of **J** answered the king H3381
1Ki 1:38 Benaiah son of **J**, the Kerethites and the H3381
1Ki 1:44 Benaiah son of **J**, the Kerethites and the H3381
1Ki 2:25 Solomon gave orders to Benaiah son of **J**, H3381
1Ki 2:29 Then Solomon ordered Benaiah son of **J** H3381
1Ki 2:34 So Benaiah son of **J** went up and struck H3381
1Ki 2:35 put Benaiah son of **J** over the army in H3381
1Ki 2:46 king gave the order to Benaiah son of **J**, H3381
1Ki 4: 4 Benaiah son of **J**—commander in chief H3381
2Ki 11: 4 In the seventh year **J** sent for the H3381
2Ki 11: 9 a hundred did just as **J** the priest ordered. H3381
2Ki 11: 9 going off duty—and came to **J** the priest. H3381
2Ki 11:12 **J** brought out the king's son and put the NDT
2Ki 11:15 **J** the priest ordered the commanders of H3381
2Ki 11:17 **J** then made a covenant between the LORD H3381
2Ki 11:18 Then **J** the priest posted guards at the NDT
2Ki 12: 2 LORD all the years **J** the priest instructed H3381
2Ki 12: 7 Joash summoned **J** the priest and the H3381
2Ki 12: 9 **J** the priest took a chest and bored a hole H3381
1Ch 11:22 Benaiah son of **J**, a valiant fighter from H3381
1Ch 11:24 Such were the exploits of Benaiah son of **J**; H3381
1Ch 12:27 including **J**, leader of the family of Aaron H3381
1Ch 18:17 Benaiah son of **J** was over the Kerethites H3381
1Ch 27: 5 was Benaiah son of **J** the priest. H3381
1Ch 27:34 was succeeded by **J** son of Benaiah and H3381
2Ch 22:11 of King Jehoram and wife of the priest **J**, H3381
2Ch 23: 1 In the seventh year **J** showed his strength H3381
2Ch 23: 3 **J** said to them, "The king's son shall reign NDT
2Ch 23: 8 of Judah did just as **J** the priest ordered. H3381
2Ch 23: 8 **J** the priest had not released any of the H3381
2Ch 23:11 **J** and his sons brought out the king's son H3381
2Ch 23:14 **J** the priest sent out the commanders of H3381
2Ch 23:16 **J** then made a covenant that he, the H3381
2Ch 23:18 Then **J** placed the oversight of the temple H3381
2Ch 24: 2 of the LORD all the years of **J** the priest. H3381
2Ch 24: 3 **J** chose two wives for him, and he had H3381
2Ch 24: 6 the king summoned **J** the chief priest and H3381
2Ch 24:12 The king and **J** gave it to those who H3381
2Ch 24:14 the rest of the money to the king and **J**, H3381
2Ch 24:14 As long as **J** lived, burnt offerings were H3381
2Ch 24:15 Now **J** was old and full of years, and he H3381
2Ch 24:17 After the death of **J**, the officials of Judah H3381
2Ch 24:20 came on Zechariah son of **J** the priest. H3381
2Ch 24:22 Zechariah's father **J** had shown him but H3381
2Ch 24:25 him for murdering the son of **J** the priest, H3381
Jer 29:26 priest in place of **J** to be in charge of the H3381

JEHOIAKIM (34) [JEHOIAKIM'S]

2Ki 23:34 Josiah and changed Eliakim's name to **J**. H3383
2Ki 23:35 **J** paid Pharaoh Necho the silver and gold H3383
2Ki 23:36 **J** was twenty-five years old when he H3383
2Ki 24: 1 **J** became his vassal for three years. H3383
2Ki 24: 6 **J** rested with his ancestors. H3383
2Ki 24:19 the eyes of the LORD, just as **J** had done. H3383
1Ch 3:15 Johanan the firstborn, **J** the second son H3383
1Ch 3:16 The successors of **J**: Jehoiachin his son H3383
2Ch 36: 4 changed Eliakim's name to **J**. H3383
2Ch 36: 5 **J** was twenty-five years old when he H3383
Jer 1: 3 through the reign of **J** son of Josiah king H3383
Jer 22:18 the LORD says about **J** son of Josiah king of H3383
Jer 22:24 Jehoiachin son of **J** king of Judah, were a H3383
Jer 24: 1 Jehoiachin son of **J** king of Judah and the H3383
Jer 25: 1 the fourth year of **J** son of Josiah king of H3383
Jer 26: 1 in the reign of **J** son of Josiah king of H3383
Jer 26:21 When King **J** and all his officers and H3383
Jer 26:22 King **J**, however, sent Elnathan son of H3383
Jer 26:23 Uriah out of Egypt and took him to King **J**, H3383
Jer 27:20 Jehoiachin son of **J** king of Judah into H3383
Jer 28: 4 Jehoiachin son of **J** king of Judah and all H3383
Jer 35: 1 during the reign of **J** son of Josiah king of H3383
Jer 36: 1 the fourth year of **J** son of Josiah king of H3383
Jer 36: 9 of the fifth year of **J** son of Josiah king of H3383
Jer 36:28 which **J** king of Judah burned up. H3383
Jer 36:29 Also tell **J** king of Judah, 'This is what the H3383
Jer 36:30 what the LORD says about **J** king of Judah: H3383
Jer 36:32 of the scroll that **J** king of Judah had H3383
Jer 37: 1 reigned in place of Jehoiachin son of **J**. H3383
Jer 45: 1 the fourth year of **J** son of Josiah king of H3383
Jer 46: 2 the fourth year of **J** son of Josiah king of H3383
Jer 52: 2 the eyes of the LORD, just as **J** had done. H3383
Da 1: 1 third year of the reign of **J** king of Judah, H3383
Da 1: 2 the Lord delivered **J** king of Judah into H3383

JEHOIAKIM'S (3) [JEHOIAKIM]

2Ki 24: 1 During **J** reign, Nebuchadnezzar king of H2257S
2Ki 24: 5 As for the other events of **J** reign, and all H3383
2Ch 36: 8 The other events of **J** reign, the H3383

JEHOIARIB (2)

1Ch 9:10 Of the priests: Jedaiah; **J**; Jakin; H3384
1Ch 24: 7 The first lot fell to **J**, the second to H3384

JEHONADAB (10)

2Ki 10:15 he came upon **J** son of Rekab, who H3386
2Ki 10:15 I am with you?" "I am," **J** answered. "If so," H3386
2Ki 10:23 Then Jehu and **J** son of Rekab went into H3386
Jer 35: 6 our forefather **J** son of Rekab gave us H3432
Jer 35: 8 our forefather **J** son of Rekab commanded H3386
Jer 35:10 our forefather **J** commanded us. H3432
Jer 35:14 '**J** son of Rekab ordered his descendants H3386
Jer 35:16 The descendants of **J** son of Rekab have H3386
Jer 35:18 of your forefather **J** and have followed all H3386
Jer 35:19 '**J** son of Rekab will never fail to have a H3432

JEHONATHAN (2)

2Ch 17: 8 Shemiramoth, **J**, Adonijah, Tobijah H3387
Ne 12:18 of Bilgah's, Shammua; of Shemaiah's, **J**; H3387

JEHORAM (29) [JEHORAM'S]

1Ki 22:50 And **J** his son succeeded him as king H3393
2Ki 1:17 the second year of **J** son of Jehoshaphat H3393
2Ki 8:16 **J** son of Jehoshaphat began his reign as H3393
2Ki 8:20 In the time of **J**, Edom rebelled against H2257S
2Ki 8:21 So **J** went to Zair with all his chariots. H3456
2Ki 8:24 **J** rested with his ancestors and was buried H3456
2Ki 8:25 Ahaziah son of **J** king of Judah began to H3393
2Ki 8:29 Then Ahaziah son of **J** king of Judah went H3393
2Ki 11: 2 the daughter of King **J** and sister of H3456
2Ki 12:18 Jehoshaphat, **J** and Ahaziah, the kings of H3393
1Ch 3:11 **J** his son, Ahaziah his son, Joash his son, H3456
2Ch 17: 8 the priests Elishama and **J**. H3393
2Ch 21: 1 And **J** his son succeeded him as king H3393
2Ch 21: 3 the kingdom to **J** because he was his H3393
2Ch 21: 4 When **J** established himself firmly over H3393
2Ch 21: 5 **J** was thirty-two years old when he H3393
2Ch 21: 8 In the time of **J**, Edom rebelled against H2257S
2Ch 21: 9 So **J** went there with his officers and all his H3393
2Ch 21:10 same time, because **J** had forsaken the LORD NDT
2Ch 21:12 **J** received a letter from Elijah the H2257S
2Ch 21:16 LORD aroused against **J** the hostility of the H3393
2Ch 21:18 the LORD afflicted **J** with an incurable H2257S
2Ch 21:20 **J** was thirty-two years old when he became NDT
2Ch 22: 1 So Ahaziah son of **J** king of Judah began H3393
2Ch 22: 6 Then Ahaziah son of **J** king of Judah went H3393
2Ch 22:11 the daughter of King **J**, took Joash son of NDT
2Ch 22:11 the daughter of King **J** and wife of the H3393
Mt 1: 8 Jehoshaphat the father of **J**, Jehoram the *G2732*
Mt 1: 8 father of Jehoram, **J** the father of Uzziah, *G2732*

JEHORAM'S (3) [JEHORAM]

2Ki 8:23 As for the other events of **J** reign, and all H3456
2Ch 21: 2 **J** brothers, the sons of Jehoshaphat, were H2257S
2Ch 22: 1 made Ahaziah, **J** youngest son, king in H2257S

JEHOSHAPHAT (85) [JEHOSHAPHAT'S]

2Sa 8:16 the army; **J** son of Ahilud was recorder; H3398
2Sa 20:24 forced labor; **J** son of Ahilud was recorder H3398
1Ki 4: 3 Shisha—secretaries; **J** son of Ahilud H3398
1Ki 4:17 **J** son of Paruah—in Issachar; H3398
1Ki 15:24 And **J** his son succeeded him as king H3398
1Ki 22: 2 But in the third year **J** king of Judah went H3398
1Ki 22: 4 So he asked **J**, "Will you go with me to H3398
1Ki 22: 4 **J** replied to the king of Israel, "I am as H3398
1Ki 22: 5 But **J** also said to the king of Israel, "First H3398
1Ki 22: 7 But **J** asked, "Is there no longer a prophet H3398
1Ki 22: 8 The king of Israel answered **J**, "There is H3398
1Ki 22: 8 should not say such a thing," **J** replied. H3398
1Ki 22:10 king of Israel and **J** king of Judah were H3398
1Ki 22:18 The king of Israel said to **J**, "Didn't I tell H3398
1Ki 22:29 king of Israel and **J** king of Judah went up H3398
1Ki 22:30 The king of Israel said to **J**, "I will enter H3398
1Ki 22:32 When the chariot commanders saw **J**, they H3398
1Ki 22:32 to attack him, but when **J** cried out, H3398
1Ki 22:41 **J** son of Asa became king of Judah in the H3398
1Ki 22:42 **J** was thirty-five years old when he H3398
1Ki 22:44 **J** was also at peace with the king of Israel. H3398
1Ki 22:48 Now **J** built a fleet of trading ships to go H3398
1Ki 22:49 that time Ahaziah son of Ahab said to **J**, H3398
1Ki 22:49 my men sail with yours," but **J** refused. H3398
1Ki 22:50 Then **J** rested with his ancestors and was H3398
1Ki 22:51 the seventeenth year of **J** king of Judah, H3398
2Ki 1:17 year of Jehoram son of **J** king of Judah. H3398
2Ki 3: 1 in the eighteenth year of **J** king of Judah, H3398
2Ki 3: 7 also sent this message to **J** king of Judah: H3398
2Ki 3:11 But **J** asked, "Is there no prophet of the H3398
2Ki 3:12 **J** said, "The word of the LORD is with him." H3398
2Ki 3:12 king of Israel and **J** and the king of Edom H3398
2Ki 3:14 the presence of **J** king of Judah, H3398
2Ki 8:16 king of Israel, when **J** was king of Judah H3398
2Ki 8:16 Jehoram son of **J** began his reign as king H3398
2Ki 9: 2 look for Jehu son of **J**, the son of Nimshi. H3398
2Ki 9:14 So Jehu son of **J**, the son of Nimshi H3398
2Ki 12:18 by his predecessors—**J**, Jehoram and H3398
1Ch 3:10 Abijah his son, Asa his son, **J** his son, H3398
1Ch 18:15 the army; **J** son of Ahilud was recorder H3398
2Ch 17: 1 **J** his son succeeded him as king and H3398
2Ch 17: 3 The LORD was with **J** because he followed H3398
2Ch 17: 5 all Judah brought gifts to **J**, so that H3398
2Ch 17:10 so that they did not go to war against **J**. H3398
2Ch 17:11 Philistines brought **J** gifts and silver as H3398
2Ch 17:12 **J** became more and more powerful; he H3398
2Ch 18: 1 Now **J** had great wealth and honor, and H3398
2Ch 18: 3 Ahab king of Israel asked **J** king of Judah H3398
2Ch 18: 3 **J** replied, "I am as you are, and my people NDT
2Ch 18: 4 But **J** also said to the king of Israel, "First H3398
2Ch 18: 6 But **J** asked, "Is there no longer a prophet H3398
2Ch 18: 7 The king of Israel answered **J**, "There is H3398
2Ch 18: 7 should not say such a thing," **J** replied. H3398
2Ch 18: 9 king of Israel and **J** king of Judah were H3398
2Ch 18:17 The king of Israel said to **J**, "Didn't I tell H3398
2Ch 18:28 king of Israel and **J** king of Judah went up H3398
2Ch 18:29 The king of Israel said to **J**, "I will enter H3398
2Ch 18:31 When the chariot commanders saw **J**, they H3398
2Ch 18:31 to attack him, but **J** cried out, and the LORD H3398
2Ch 19: 1 When **J** king of Judah returned safely to H3398
2Ch 19: 4 **J** lived in Jerusalem, and he went out H3398
2Ch 19: 8 **J** appointed some of the Levites H3398
2Ch 20: 1 Meunites came to wage war against **J**. H3398
2Ch 20: 2 Some people came and told **J**, "A vast H3398
2Ch 20: 3 Alarmed, **J** resolved to inquire of the LORD H3398
2Ch 20: 5 Then **J** stood up in the assembly of Judah H3398
2Ch 20:15 King **J** and all who live in Judah and H3398
2Ch 20:18 **J** bowed down with his face to the ground, H3398
2Ch 20:20 As they set out, **J** stood and said, "Listen H3398
2Ch 20:21 **J** appointed men to sing to the LORD and to NDT
2Ch 20:25 So **J** and his men went to carry off their H3398
2Ch 20:27 led by **J**, all the men of Judah and H3398
2Ch 20:30 And the kingdom of **J** was at peace, for his H3398
2Ch 20:31 So **J** reigned over Judah. He was H3398
2Ch 20:35 **J** king of Judah made an alliance with H3398
2Ch 20:37 of Mareshah prophesied against **J**, H3398
2Ch 21: 1 Then **J** rested with his ancestors and was H3398
2Ch 21: 2 brothers, the sons of **J**, were Azariah, H3398
2Ch 21: 2 All these were sons of **J** king of Israel. H3398
2Ch 21:12 ways of your father **J** or of Asa king of H3398
2Ch 22: 9 "He was a son of **J**, who sought the LORD H3398
Joel 3: 2 bring them down to the Valley of **J**. H3399
Joel 3:12 let them advance into the Valley of **J**, for H3399
Mt 1: 8 Asa the father of **J**, Jehoshaphat the *G2734*
Mt 1: 8 of Jehoshaphat, **J** the father of Jehoram *G2734*

JEHOSHAPHAT'S (2) [JEHOSHAPHAT]

1Ki 22:45 As for the other events of **J** reign, the H3398
2Ch 20:34 The other events of **J** reign, from H3398

JEHOSHEBA (3)

2Ki 11: 2 But **J**, the daughter of King Jehoram and H3394
2Ch 22:11 But **J**, the daughter of King Jehoram, took H3395
2Ch 22:11 Because **J**, the daughter of King Jehoram H3395

JEHOSHUA (KJV) JOSHUA

JEHOVAH (KJV) LORD*

JEHOVAH-JIREH (KJV) THE LORD* WILL PROVIDE

JEHOVAH-NISSI (KJV) THE LORD* IS MY BANNER

JEHOVAH-SHALOM (KJV) THE LORD* IS PEACE

JEHOZABAD (4)

2Ki 12:21 son of Shimeath and **J** son of Shomer. H3379
1Ch 26: 4 the firstborn, **J** the second, Joah the H3379

2Ch 17:18 **J**, with 180,000 men armed for H3379
2Ch 24:26 woman, and **J**, son of Shimrith a H3379

JEHOZADAK (NIV84) JOZADAK

JEHU (74) [JEHU'S]
1Ki 16: 1 of the LORD came to **J** son of Hanani H3369
1Ki 16: 7 through the prophet **J** son of Hanani to H3369
1Ki 16:12 against Baasha through the prophet **J**— H3369
1Ki 19:16 anoint **J** son of Nimshi king over Israel H3369
1Ki 19:17 **J** will put to death any who escape the H3369
1Ki 19:17 to death any who escape the sword of **J**. H3369
2Ki 9: 2 get there, look for **J** son of Jehoshaphat H3369
2Ki 9: 5 asked **J**. "For you H3369
2Ki 9: 6 **J** got up and went into the house. Then the NDT
2Ki 9:11 When **J** went out to his fellow officers H3369
2Ki 9:11 the sort of things he says," **J** replied. NDT
2Ki 9:12 **J** said, "Here is what he told me NDT
2Ki 9:13 blew the trumpet and shouted, "**J** is king!" H3369
2Ki 9:14 So **J** son of Jehoshaphat, the son of H3369
2Ki 9:15 **J** said, "If you desire to make me king H3369
2Ki 9:18 horseman rode off to meet **J** and said, H2257S
2Ki 9:18 have to do with peace?" **J** replied. "Fall in H3369
2Ki 9:19 **J** replied, "What do you have to do with H3369
2Ki 9:20 driving is like that of **J** son of Nimshi— H3369
2Ki 9:21 each in his own chariot, to meet **J**. H3369
2Ki 9:22 When Joram saw **J** he asked, "Have you H3369
2Ki 9:22 he asked, "Have you come in peace, **J**?" H3369
2Ki 9:22 **J** replied, "as long as all the idolatry and NDT
2Ki 9:24 Then **J** drew his bow and shot Joram H3369
2Ki 9:25 **J** said to Bidkar, his chariot officer, "Pick NDT
2Ki 9:27 to Beth Haggan. **J** chased him, shouting H3369
2Ki 9:30 Then **J** went to Jezreel. When Jezebel H3369
2Ki 9:31 As **J** entered the gate, she asked, "Have H3369
2Ki 9:33 "Throw her down!" **J** said. So they threw her NDT
2Ki 9:34 **J** went in and ate and drank. "Take care of NDT
2Ki 9:36 They went back and told **J**, who said H2257S
2Ki 10: 1 So **J** wrote letters and sent them to H3369
2Ki 10: 5 the guardians sent this message to **J**: H3369
2Ki 10: 6 Then **J** wrote them a second letter, saying NDT
2Ki 10: 7 in baskets and sent them to **J** in Jezreel. H2257S
2Ki 10: 8 he told **J**, "They have brought H2257S
2Ki 10: 8 Then **J** ordered, "Put them in two piles at NDT
2Ki 10: 9 The next morning **J** went out. He stood NDT
2Ki 10:11 So **J** killed everyone in Jezreel who H3369
2Ki 10:12 **J** then set out and went toward Samaria. NDT
2Ki 10:15 **J** greeted him and said, "Are you in accord NDT
2Ki 10:15 said **J**, "give me your hand. NDT
2Ki 10:15 and **J** helped him up into the chariot. NDT
2Ki 10:16 **J** said, "Come with me and see my zeal for NDT
2Ki 10:17 When **J** came to Samaria, he killed all who NDT
2Ki 10:18 Then **J** brought all the people together H3369
2Ki 10:18 served Baal a little; **J** will serve him much. H3369
2Ki 10:19 But **J** was acting deceptively in order to H3369
2Ki 10:20 **J** said, "Call an assembly in honor of Baal." H3369
2Ki 10:22 And **J** said to the keeper of the wardrobe NDT
2Ki 10:23 Then **J** and Jehonadab son of Rekab went H3369
2Ki 10:23 **J** said to the servants of Baal, "Look around NDT
2Ki 10:24 Now **J** had posted eighty men outside H3369
2Ki 10:25 As soon as **J** had finished making the H3369
2Ki 10:28 So **J** destroyed Baal worship in Israel. H3369
2Ki 10:30 The LORD said to **J**, "Because you have H3369
2Ki 10:31 Yet **J** was not careful to keep the law of H3369
2Ki 10:35 **J** rested with his ancestors and was buried H3369
2Ki 10:36 The time that **J** reigned over Israel in H3369
2Ki 12: 1 In the seventh year of **J**, Joash became H3369
2Ki 13: 1 Jehoahaz son of **J** became king of Israel H3369
2Ki 14: 8 of Jehoahaz, the son of **J**, king of Israel, H3369
2Ki 15:12 word of the LORD spoken to **J** was fulfilled: H3369
1Ch 2:38 Obed the father of **J**, Jehu the father of H3369
1Ch 2:38 the father of Jehu, **J** the father of Azariah H3369
1Ch 4:35 **J** son of Joshibiah, the son of H3369
1Ch 12: 3 of Azmaveth; Berakah, **J** the Anathothite, H3369
2Ch 19: 2 **J** the seer, the son of Hanani, went out to H3369
2Ch 20:34 written in the annals of **J** son of Hanani, H3369
2Ch 22: 7 out with Joram to meet **J** son of Nimshi, H3369
2Ch 22: 8 While **J** was executing judgment on the H3369
2Ch 22: 9 He was brought to **J** and put to death H3369
2Ch 25:17 of Jehoahaz, the son of **J**, king of Israel: H3369
Hos 1: 4 punish the house of **J** for the massacre at H3369

JEHU'S (3) [JEHU]
2Ki 9: 6 poured the oil on **J** head and declared, H2257S
2Ki 9:17 in Jezreel saw **J** troops approaching, H3369
2Ki 10:34 As for the other events of **J** reign, all he H3369

JEHUCAL (NIV84) JEHUKAL

JEHUD (1)
Jos 19:45 **J**, Bene Berak, Gath Rimmon, H3372

JEHUDI (4)
Jer 36:14 all the officials sent **J** son of Nethaniah H3375
Jer 36:21 The king sent **J** to get the scroll, and H3375
Jer 36:21 **J** brought it from the room of H3375
Jer 36:23 Whenever **J** had read three or four H3375

JEHUKAL (2)
Jer 37: 3 sent **J** son of Shelemiah with the priest H3385
Jer 38: 1 son of Pashhur, **J** son of Shelemiah, and H3426

JEIEL (12)
1Ch 5: 7 **J** the chief, Zechariah H3599
1Ch 8:29 **J** the father of Gibeon lived in Gibeon H3599
1Ch 9:35 **J** the father of Gibeon lived in Gibeon H3599
1Ch 11:44 Shama and **J** the sons of Hotham the H3599
1Ch 15:18 Obed-Edom and **J**, the gatekeepers. H3599
1Ch 15:21 **J** and Azaziah were to play the harps H3599
1Ch 16: 5 Benaiah, Obed-Edom and **J**. H3599
2Ch 20:14 Benaiah, the son of **J**, the son of H3599
2Ch 26:11 as mustered by **J** the secretary and H3599
2Ch 29:13 Shimri and **J**; from the descendants H3599
2Ch 35: 9 Hashabiah, **J** and Jozabad, the H3599
Ezr 10:43 **J**, Mattithiah, Zabad, Zebina, Jaddai, Joel H3599

JEKABZEEL (1)
Ne 11:25 its settlements, in **J** and its villages, H3677

JEKAMEAM (2)
1Ch 23:19 Jahaziel the third and **J** the fourth. H3694
1Ch 24:23 Jahaziel the third and **J** the fourth. H3694

JEKAMIAH (3)
1Ch 2:41 Shallum the father of **J**, and Jekamiah the H3693
1Ch 2:41 Jekamiah, and **J** the father of Elishama. H3693
1Ch 3:18 Pedaiah, Shenazzar, **J**, Hoshama and H3693

JEKOLIAH (2)
2Ki 15: 2 His mother's name was **J**; she was from H3525
2Ch 26: 3 His mother's name was **J**; she was from H3524

JEKUTHIEL (1)
1Ch 4:18 of Soko, and **J** the father of Zanoah.) H3688

JEMIMAH (1)
Job 42:14 The first daughter he named **J**, the second H3544

JEMUEL (2)
Ge 46:10 **J**, Jamin, Ohad, Jakin, Zohar and Shaul H3543
Ex 6:15 The sons of Simeon were **J**, Jamin, Ohad H3543

JEOPARDED, JEOPARDY (KJV) DANGER, ENDANGER, RISK, RISKED

JEOPARDY (2)
2Sa 18:13 And if *I had* **put** my life **in j**—and H6913+9214
Job 13:14 Why *do I* **put** myself **in j** H5951+1414+928+9094

JEPHTHAH (23) [JEPHTHAH'S]
Jdg 11: 1 **J** the Gileadite was a mighty warrior. H3653
Jdg 11: 2 they were grown up, they drove **J** away. H3653
Jdg 11: 3 So **J** fled from his brothers and settled in H3653
Jdg 11: 5 Gilead went to get **J** from the land of Tob. H3653
Jdg 11: 7 **J** said to them, "Didn't you hate me and H3653
Jdg 11: 9 **J** answered, "Suppose you take me back H3653
Jdg 11:11 So **J** went with the elders of Gilead, and H3653
Jdg 11:12 Then **J** sent messengers to the Ammonite H3653
Jdg 11:14 **J** sent back messengers to the Ammonite H3653
Jdg 11:15 "This is what **J** says: Israel did not H3653
Jdg 11:28 no attention to the message **J** sent him. H3653
Jdg 11:29 Then the Spirit of the LORD came on **J**. H3653
Jdg 11:30 And **J** made a vow to the LORD: "If you H3653
Jdg 11:32 Then **J** went over to fight the Ammonites H3653
Jdg 11:34 When **J** returned to his home in Mizpah H3653
Jdg 11:40 the daughter of **J** the Gileadite. H3653
Jdg 12: 1 They said to **J**, "Why did you go to fight H3653
Jdg 12: 2 **J** answered, "I and my people were H3653
Jdg 12: 4 **J** then called together the men of Gilead H3653
Jdg 12: 7 **J** led Israel six years. Then Jephthah the H3653
Jdg 12: 7 Then **J** the Gileadite died and was buried H3653
1Sa 12:11 **J** and Samuel, and he delivered H3653
Heb 11:32 Samson and **J**, about David and *G2650*

JEPHTHAH'S (1) [JEPHTHAH]
Jdg 11:13 the Ammonites answered **J** messengers, H3653

JEPHUNNEH (16)
Nu 13: 6 from the tribe of Judah, Caleb son of **J**; H3648
Nu 14: 6 Joshua son of Nun and Caleb son of **J** H3648
Nu 14:30 except Caleb son of **J** and Joshua son of H3648
Nu 14:38 son of Nun and Caleb son of **J** survived. H3648
Nu 26:65 except Caleb son of **J** and Joshua son of H3648
Nu 32:12 except Caleb son of **J** the Kenizzite and H3648
Nu 34:19 Caleb son of **J**, from the tribe of H3648
Dt 1:36 except Caleb son of **J**. He will see it, and I H3648
Jos 14: 6 Caleb son of **J** the Kenizzite said to H3648
Jos 14:13 Caleb son of **J** and gave him Hebron H3648
Jos 14:14 to Caleb son of **J** the Kenizzite ever since H3648
Jos 15:13 to Caleb son of **J** a portion in Judah— H3648
Jos 21:12 given to Caleb son of **J** as his possession. H3648
1Ch 4:15 The sons of Caleb son of **J**: Iru, Elah and H3648
1Ch 6:56 the city were given to Caleb son of **J**. H3648
1Ch 7:38 The sons of Jether: **J**, Pispah and Ara. H3648

JERAH (2)
Ge 10:26 of Almodad, Sheleph, Hazarmaveth, **J**, H3733
1Ch 1:20 of Almodad, Sheleph, Hazarmaveth, **J**, H3733

JERAHMEEL (9) [JERAHMEELITES]
1Sa 27:10 "Against the Negev of **J**" or "Against H3738
1Ch 2: 9 born to Hezron were: **J**, Ram and Caleb. H3737
1Ch 2:25 The sons of **J** the firstborn of Hezron: Ram H3737
1Ch 2:26 **J** had another wife, whose name was H3737
1Ch 2:27 The sons of Ram the firstborn of **J**: Maaz H3737
1Ch 2:33 These were the descendants of **J**. H3737
1Ch 2:42 The sons of Caleb the brother of **J**: Mesha H3737
1Ch 24:29 the son of Kish: **J**. H3737
Jer 36:26 the king commanded **J**, a son of the king, H3737

JERAHMEELITES (1) [JERAHMEEL]
1Sa 30:29 in the towns of the **J** and the Kenites; H3738

JERED (1)
1Ch 4:18 Judah gave birth to **J** the father of Gedor, H3719

JEREMAI (1)
Ezr 10:33 Eliphelet, **J**, Manasseh and H3757

JEREMIAH (145) [JEREMIAH'S]
2Ki 23:31 name was Hamutal daughter of **J**; H3759
2Ki 24:18 name was Hamutal daughter of **J**; H3759
1Ch 5:24 Eliel, Azriel, **J**, Hodaviah and Jahdiel H3758
1Ch 12: 4 was a leader of the Thirty; **J**, Jahaziel, H3758
1Ch 12:10 Mishmannah the fourth, **J** the fifth, H3758
1Ch 12:13 **J** the tenth and Makbannai the eleventh. H3759
2Ch 35:25 **J** composed laments for Josiah, and to H3759
2Ch 36:12 not humble himself before **J** the prophet, H3759
2Ch 36:21 of the word of the LORD spoken by **J**. H3759
2Ch 36:22 to fulfill the word of the LORD spoken by **J**, H3759
Ezr 1: 1 to fulfill the word of the LORD spoken by **J**, H3758
Ne 10: 2 Seraiah, Azariah, **J**, H3758
Ne 12: 1 with Joshua: Seraiah, **J**, Ezra, H3758
Ne 12:34 Benjamin, Shemaiah, **J**, H3758
Jer 1: 1 The words of **J** son of Hilkiah, one of the H3759
Jer 1:11 "What do you see, **J**?" "I see the branch H3759
Jer 7: 1 is the word that came to **J** from the LORD: H3759
Jer 11: 1 is the word that came to **J** from the LORD: H3759
Jer 14: 1 the LORD that came to **J** concerning the H3759
Jer 18: 1 is the word that came to **J** from the LORD: H3759
Jer 18:18 let's make plans against **J**; for the H3759
Jer 19:14 **J** then returned from Topheth, where the H3759
Jer 20: 1 heard **J** prophesying these things H3759
Jer 20: 2 he had **J** the prophet beaten and put in H3759
Jer 20: 3 him from the stocks, **J** said to him, "The H3759
Jer 21: 1 The word came to **J** from the LORD when H3759
Jer 21: 3 But **J** answered them, "Tell Zedekiah, H3759
Jer 24: 3 the LORD asked me, "What do you see, **J**?" H3759
Jer 25: 1 The word came to **J** concerning all the H3759
Jer 25: 2 So **J** the prophet said to all the people of H3759
Jer 25:13 book and prophesied by **J** against all the H3759
Jer 26: 7 the people heard **J** speak these words in H3759
Jer 26: 8 But as soon as **J** finished telling all the H3759
Jer 26: 9 crowded around **J** in the house of the H3759
Jer 26:12 Then **J** said to all the officials and all the H3759
Jer 26:20 against this city and this land as **J** did. H3759
Jer 26:24 Ahikam son of Shaphan supported **J**, and H3759
Jer 27: 1 this word came to **J** from the LORD: H3758
Jer 28: 5 Then the prophet **J** replied to the prophet H3758
Jer 28:10 off the neck of the prophet **J** and broke it, H3758
Jer 28:11 At this, the prophet **J** went on his way. H3758
Jer 28:12 the yoke off the neck of the prophet **J**, H3758
Jer 28:12 Jeremiah, the word of the LORD came to **J**: H3758
Jer 28:15 Then the prophet **J** said to Hananiah the H3758
Jer 29: 1 that the prophet **J** sent from Jerusalem to H3758
Jer 29:27 you not reprimanded **J** from Anathoth, H3759
Jer 29:29 however, read the letter to **J** the prophet. H3759
Jer 29:30 Then the word of the LORD came to **J**: H3759
Jer 30: 1 is the word that came to **J** from the LORD: H3759
Jer 32: 1 word that came to **J** from the LORD in the H3759
Jer 32: 2 **J** the prophet was confined in the H3759
Jer 32: 6 **J** said, "The word of the LORD came to me: H3759
Jer 32:26 Then the word of the LORD came to **J**: H3759
Jer 33: 1 While **J** was still confined in the courtyard H3759
Jer 33:19 The word of the LORD came to **J**: H3759
Jer 33:23 The word of the LORD came to **J**: H3759
Jer 34: 1 this word came to **J** from the LORD: H3759
Jer 34: 6 Then **J** the prophet told all this to H3759
Jer 34: 8 The word came to **J** from the LORD after H3759
Jer 34:12 Then the word of the LORD came to **J**: H3759
Jer 35: 1 word that came to **J** from the LORD during H3759
Jer 35: 3 So I went to get Jaazaniah son of **J**, the H3759
Jer 35:12 Then the word of the LORD came to **J** H3759
Jer 35:18 Then **J** said to the family of the Rekabites H3759
Jer 36: 1 this word came to **J** from the LORD: H3759
Jer 36: 4 So **J** called Baruch son of Neriah, and H3759
Jer 36: 4 while **J** dictated all the words the H3759
Jer 36: 5 Then **J** told Baruch, "I am restricted; I am H3759
Jer 36: 8 did everything **J** the prophet told him H3759
Jer 36:10 temple the words of **J** from the scroll. H3759
Jer 36:17 come to write all this? Did **J** dictate it?" H2257S
Jer 36:19 said to Baruch, "You and **J**, go and hide. H3759
Jer 36:26 arrest Baruch the scribe and **J** the prophet. H3759
Jer 36:27 dictation, the word of the LORD came to **J**: H3759
Jer 36:32 So **J** took another scroll and gave it to the H3759
Jer 36:32 son of Neriah, and as **J** dictated, Baruch H3759
Jer 37: 2 LORD had spoken through **J** the prophet. H3759
Jer 37: 3 son of Maaseiah to **J** the prophet with this H3759
Jer 37: 4 Now **J** was free to come and go among H3759
Jer 37: 6 word of the LORD came to **J** the prophet: H3759
Jer 37:12 **J** started to leave the city to go to the H3759
Jer 37:14 "That's not true!" **J** said. "I am not H3759
Jer 37:14 he arrested **J** and brought him to the H3759
Jer 37:15 were angry with **J** and had him beaten H3759
Jer 37:16 **J** was put into a vaulted cell in a dungeon H3759
Jer 37:17 **J** replied, "you will be delivered into the H3759
Jer 37:18 Then **J** said to King Zedekiah, "What H3759
Jer 37:21 then gave orders for **J** to be placed in the H3759
Jer 37:21 So **J** remained in the courtyard of the H3759
Jer 38: 1 Malkijah heard what **J** was telling all the H3759
Jer 38: 6 So they took **J** and put him into the cistern H3759

Jer 38: 6 They lowered J by ropes into the cistern; it H3759
Jer 38: 6 only mud, and J sank down into the mud. H3759
Jer 38: 7 heard that they had put J into the cistern. H3759
Jer 38: 9 in all they have done to J the prophet. H3759
Jer 38:10 with you and lift J the prophet out of the H3759
Jer 38:11 them down with ropes to J in the cistern. H3759
Jer 38:12 Ebed-Melek the Cushite said to J, "Put H3759
Jer 38:12 your arms to pad the ropes." J did so, H3759
Jer 38:13 And J remained in the courtyard of the H3759
Jer 38:14 Zedekiah sent for J the prophet and had H3759
Jer 38:14 to ask you something," the king said to J. H3759
Jer 38:15 J said to Zedekiah, "If I give you an H3759
Jer 38:16 Zedekiah swore this oath secretly to J: H3759
Jer 38:17 Then J said to Zedekiah, "This is what the H3759
Jer 38:19 King Zedekiah said to J, "I am afraid of H3759
Jer 38:20 not hand you over," J replied. "Obey the H3759
Jer 38:24 Then Zedekiah said to J, "Do not let H3759
Jer 38:27 officials did come to J and question him, H3759
Jer 38:28 And J remained in the courtyard of the H3759
Jer 39:11 these orders about J through H3759
Jer 39:14 sent and had J taken out of the courtyard H3759
Jer 39:15 While J had been confined in the H3759
Jer 40: 1 The word came to J from the LORD after H3759
Jer 40: 1 He had found J bound in chains among H2257S
Jer 40: 2 the commander of the guard found J, H3759
Jer 40: 5 However, before J turned to go H5647S
Jer 40: 6 So J went to Gedaliah son of Ahikam at H3759
Jer 42: 2 J the prophet and said to him, "Please H3759
Jer 42: 4 heard you," replied J the prophet. "I will H3759
Jer 42: 5 Then they said to J, "May the LORD be a H3759
Jer 42: 7 days later the word of the LORD came to J. H3759
Jer 43: 1 When J had finished telling the people H3759
Jer 43: 2 all the arrogant men said to J, H3759
Jer 43: 6 And they took J the prophet and Baruch H3759
Jer 43: 8 the word of the LORD came to J: H3759
Jer 44: 1 This word came to J concerning all the H3759
Jer 44:15 living in Lower and Upper Egypt, said to J, H3759
Jer 44:20 Then J said to all the people, both men H3759
Jer 44:24 Then J said to all the people, including H3759
Jer 45: 1 a scroll the words J the prophet dictated H3759
Jer 45: 1 king of Judah, J said this to Baruch: H3759
Jer 46: 1 the LORD that came to J the prophet H3759
Jer 46:13 the LORD spoke to J the prophet about the H3759
Jer 47: 1 the LORD that came to J the prophet H3759
Jer 49:34 the LORD that came to J the prophet H3759
Jer 50: 1 LORD spoke through J the prophet H3759
Jer 51:59 This is the message J the prophet gave to H3759
Jer 51:60 J had written on a scroll about all the H3759
Jer 51:64 The words of J end here. H3759
Jer 52: 1 name was Hamutal daughter of J; H3759
Da 9: 2 word of the LORD given to J the prophet, H3758
Mt 2:17 said through the prophet J was fulfilled: *G2635*
Mt 16:14 still others, J or one of the prophets." *G2635*
Mt 27: 9 what was spoken by J the prophet was *G2635*

JEREMIAH'S (2) [JEREMIAH]

Ne 12:12 Meraiah; of J, Hananiah; H3758
Jer 36:27 that Baruch had written at J dictation, H3759

JEREMIAS, JEREMY (KJV) JEREMIAH

JEREMOTH (5)

1Ch 7: 8 Elioenai, Omri, J, Abijah, Anathoth and H3756
1Ch 8:14 Shashak, J, H3756
Ezr 10:26 Zechariah, Jehiel, Abdi, J and Elijah. H3756
Ezr 10:27 Eliashib, Mattaniah, J, Zabad and Aziza. H3756
Ezr 10:29 Adaiah, Jashub, Sheal and J. H3756

JERIAH (4)

1Ch 23:19 J the first, Amariah the second, Jahaziel H3746
1Ch 24:23 J the first, Amariah the second, Jahaziel H3746
1Ch 26:31 J was their chief according to the H3745
1Ch 26:32 J had twenty-seven hundred relatives H2257S

JERIBAI (1)

1Ch 11:46 J and Joshaviah the sons of Elnaam H3744

JERICHO (61)

Nu 22: 1 camped along the Jordan across from J. H3735
Nu 26: 3 of Moab by the Jordan across from J, H3735
Nu 26:63 of Moab by the Jordan across from J. H3735
Nu 31:12 of Moab, by the Jordan across from J. H3735
Nu 33:48 of Moab by the Jordan across from J. H3735
Nu 33:50 Jordan across from J the LORD said to H3735
Nu 34:15 east of the Jordan across from J, H3735
Nu 35: 1 of Moab by the Jordan across from J, H3735
Nu 36:13 of Moab by the Jordan across from J. H3735
Dt 32:49 in Moab, across from J, and view Canaan, H3735
Dt 34: 1 Moab to the top of Pisgah, across from J. H3735
Dt 34: 3 the whole region from the Valley of J, H3735
Jos 2: 1 look over the land," he said, "especially J." H3735
Jos 2: 2 The king of J was told, "Look, some of the H3735
Jos 2: 3 So the king of J sent this message to H3735
Jos 3:16 So the people crossed over opposite J. H3735
Jos 4:13 before the LORD to the plains of J for war. H3735
Jos 4:19 at Gilgal on the eastern border of J. H3735
Jos 5:10 while camped at Gilgal on the plains of J H3735
Jos 5:13 Now when Joshua was near J, he looked H3735
Jos 6: 1 Now the *gates of* J were securely barred H3735
Jos 6: 2 I have delivered J into your hands, along H3735
Jos 6:25 the men Joshua had sent as spies to J— H3735
Jos 6:26 one who undertakes to rebuild this city, J: H3735
Jos 7: 2 Now Joshua sent men from J to Ai, which H3735
Jos 8: 2 its king as you did to J and its king, H3735
Jos 9: 3 heard what Joshua had done to J and Ai, H3735
Jos 10: 1 its king as he had done to J and its king, H3735
Jos 10:28 as he had done to the king of J. H3735
Jos 10:30 to its king as he had done to the king of J. H3735
Jos 12: 9 the king of J one the king of Ai (near H3735
Jos 13:32 of Moab across the Jordan east of J. H3735
Jos 16: 1 east of the springs of J, and went up from H3735
Jos 16: 7 touched J and came out at the Jordan. H3735
Jos 18:12 northern slope of J and headed west into H3735
Jos 18:21 following towns: J, Beth Hoglah, Emek H3735
Jos 20: 8 on the other side from J) they designated H3735
Jos 24:11 you crossed the Jordan and came to J. H3735
Jos 24:11 The citizens of J fought against you, as H3735
2Sa 10: 5 "Stay at J till your beards have grown H3735
1Ki 16:34 Hiel of Bethel rebuilt J. He laid its H3735
2Ki 2: 4 Elisha; the LORD has sent me to J. H3735
2Ki 2: 4 I will not leave you." So they went to J. H3735
2Ki 2: 5 of the prophets at J went up to Elisha H3735
2Ki 2:15 The company of the prophets from J, who H3735
2Ki 2:18 who was staying in J, he said to them, H3735
2Ki 25: 5 king and overtook him in the plains of J. H3735
1Ch 6:78 the Jordan east of J they received Bezer in H3735
1Ch 19: 5 "Stay at J till your beards have grown H3735
2Ch 28:15 them back to their fellow Israelites at J, H3735
Ezr 2:34 of J 345 H3735
Ne 3: 2 The men of J built the adjoining section H3735
Ne 7:36 of J 345 H3735
Jer 39: 5 overtook Zedekiah in the plains of J. H3735
Jer 52: 8 overtook him in the plains of J. H3735
Mt 20:29 As Jesus and his disciples were leaving J *G2637*
Mk 10:46 Then they came to J. As Jesus and his *G2637*
Lk 10:30 was going down from Jerusalem to J, *G2637*
Lk 18:35 As Jesus approached J, a blind man was *G2637*
Lk 19: 1 Jesus entered J and was passing through. *G2637*
Heb 11:30 By faith the walls *of* J fell, after the army *G2637*

JERIEL (1)

1Ch 7: 2 Rephaiah, J, Jahmai, Ibsam and H3741

JERIMOTH (9)

1Ch 7: 7 Uzziel, J and Iri, heads of families H3748
1Ch 12: 5 J, Bealiah, Shemariah and H3748
1Ch 23:23 Mahli, Eder and J—three in all. H3756
1Ch 24:30 Mahli, Eder and J. These were the H3748
1Ch 25: 4 Shubael and J; Hananiah, Hanani, H3748
1Ch 25:22 the fifteenth to J, his sons and relatives 12 H3756
1Ch 27:19 Obadiah; over Naphtali: J son of Azriel; H3748
2Ch 11:18 daughter of David's son J and of Abihail, H3748
2Ch 31:13 Nahath, Asahel, J, Jozabad, Eliel H3748

JERIOTH (1)

1Ch 2:18 wife Azubah (and by J). These were her H3750

JEROBOAM (98) [JEROBOAM'S]

1Ki 11:26 J son of Nebat rebelled against the king. H3716
1Ki 11:28 Now J was a man of standing, and when H3716
1Ki 11:29 About that time J was going out of H3716
1Ki 11:31 Then he said to J, "Take ten pieces for H3716
1Ki 11:40 Solomon tried to kill J, but Jeroboam fled H3716
1Ki 11:40 to kill Jeroboam, but J fled to Egypt, to H3716
1Ki 12: 2 When J son of Nebat heard this (he was H3716
1Ki 12: 3 So they sent for J, and he and the whole H3716
1Ki 12:12 Three days later J and all the people H3716
1Ki 12:15 LORD had spoken to J son of Nebat H3716
1Ki 12:20 the Israelites heard that J had returned, H3716
1Ki 12:25 Then J fortified Shechem in the hill H3716
1Ki 12:26 J thought to himself, "The kingdom will H3716
1Ki 12:31 J built shrines on high places and NDT
1Ki 13: 1 as J was standing by the altar to make an H3716
1Ki 13: 4 When King J heard what the man of God H3716
1Ki 13:33 after this, J did not change his evil ways H3716
1Ki 13:34 the sin of the house of J that led to its H3716
1Ki 14: 1 At that time Abijah son of J became ill, H3716
1Ki 14: 2 J said to his wife, "Go, disguise H3716
1Ki 14: 2 you won't be recognized as the wife of J. H3716
1Ki 14: 6 at the door, he said, "Come in, wife of J. H3716
1Ki 14: 7 tell J that this is what the LORD, the H3716
1Ki 14:10 going to bring disaster on the house of J. H3716
1Ki 14:10 I will cut off from J every last male in H3716
1Ki 14:10 up the house of J as one burns dung, H3716
1Ki 14:11 those belonging to J who die in the city, H3716
1Ki 14:13 one belonging to J who will be buried, H3716
1Ki 14:13 one in the house of J in whom the LORD, H3716
1Ki 14:14 over Israel who will cut off the family of J. H3716
1Ki 14:16 because of the sins J has committed and H3716
1Ki 14:30 warfare between Rehoboam and J. H3716
1Ki 15: 1 year of the reign of J son of Nebat, H3716
1Ki 15: 6 between Abijah and J throughout H3716
1Ki 15: 7 There was war between Abijah and J. H3716
1Ki 15: 9 In the twentieth year of J king of Israel H3716
1Ki 15:25 Nadab son of J became king of Israel in H3716
1Ki 15:29 He did not leave J anyone that breathed H3716
1Ki 15:30 because of the sins J had committed and H3716
1Ki 15:34 the ways of J and committing the H3716
1Ki 15:34 the same sin J had caused Israel to NDT
1Ki 16: 2 the ways of J and caused my people H3716
1Ki 16: 3 your house like that of J son of Nebat. H3716
1Ki 16: 7 becoming like the house of J—and also H3716
1Ki 16:19 the ways of J and committing the H3716
1Ki 16:19 the same sin J had caused Israel to NDT
1Ki 16:26 completely the ways of J son of Nebat, H3716
1Ki 16:26 the same sin J had caused Israel to NDT
1Ki 16:31 to commit the sins of J son of Nebat, H3716
1Ki 21:22 house like that of J son of Nebat and that H3716
1Ki 22:52 father and mother and of J son of Nebat, H3716
2Ki 3: 3 he clung to the sins of J son of Nebat, H3716
2Ki 9: 9 like the house of J son of Nebat and like H3716
2Ki 10:29 turn away from the sins of J son of Nebat, H3716
2Ki 10:31 He did not turn away from the sins of J H3716
2Ki 13: 2 by following the sins of J son of Nebat, H3716
2Ki 13: 6 turn away from the sins of the house of J, H3716
2Ki 13:11 from any of the sins of J son of Nebat, H3716
2Ki 13:13 J succeeded him on the throne. H3716
2Ki 14:16 And J his son succeeded him as king H3716
2Ki 14:23 J son of Jehoash king of Israel became H3716
2Ki 14:24 from any of the sins of J son of Nebat, H3716
2Ki 14:27 them by the hand of J son of Jehoash. H3716
2Ki 14:29 J rested with his ancestors, the kings of H3716
2Ki 15: 1 the twenty-seventh year of J king of Israel, H3716
2Ki 15: 8 Zechariah son of J became king of Israel H3716
2Ki 15: 9 turn away from the sins of J son of Nebat, H3716
2Ki 15:18 turn away from the sins of J son of Nebat, H3716
2Ki 15:24 turn away from the sins of J son of Nebat, H3716
2Ki 15:28 turn away from the sins of J son of Nebat, H3716
2Ki 17:21 they made J son of Nebat their king. H3716
2Ki 17:21 J enticed Israel away from following the H3716
2Ki 17:22 in all the sins of J and did not turn away H3716
2Ki 23:15 the high place made by J son of Nebat H3716
1Ch 5:17 Jotham king of Judah and J king of Israel. H3716
2Ch 9:29 Iddo the seer concerning J son of Nebat? H3716
2Ch 10: 2 When J son of Nebat heard this (he was in H3716
2Ch 10: 3 So they sent for J, and he and all Israel H3716
2Ch 10:12 Three days later J and all the people H3716
2Ch 10:15 LORD had spoken to J son of Nebat H3716
2Ch 11: 4 turned back from marching against J. H3716
2Ch 11:14 because J and his sons had rejected them H3716
2Ch 12:15 warfare between Rehoboam and J. H3716
2Ch 13: 1 In the eighteenth year of the reign of J H3716
2Ch 13: 2 There was war between Abijah and J. H3716
2Ch 13: 3 J drew up a battle line against him H3716
2Ch 13: 4 Ephraim, and said, "J and all Israel, listen H3716
2Ch 13: 6 Yet J son of Nebat, an official of Solomon H3716
2Ch 13: 8 golden calves that J made to be your H3716
2Ch 13:13 Now J had sent troops around to the rear H3716
2Ch 13:15 God routed J and all Israel before Abijah H3716
2Ch 13:19 Abijah pursued J and took from him the H3716
2Ch 13:20 J did not regain power during the time of H3716
Hos 1: 1 during the reign of J son of Jehoash king H3716
Am 1: 1 king of Judah and J son of Jehoash was H3716
Am 7: 9 sword I will rise against the house of J." H3716
Am 7:10 Bethel sent a message to J king of Israel: H3716
Am 7:11 " 'J will die by the sword, and Israel will H3716

JEROBOAM'S (6) [JEROBOAM]

1Ki 14: 4 So J wife did what he said and went to H3716
1Ki 14: 5 "J wife is coming to ask you about her son H3716
1Ki 14:17 Then J wife got up and left and went to H3716
1Ki 14:19 The other events of J reign, his wars and H3716
1Ki 15:29 began to reign, he killed J whole family. H3716
2Ki 14:28 As for the other events of J reign, all he H3716

JEROHAM (10)

1Sa 1: 1 whose name was Elkanah son of J, the H3736
1Ch 6:27 Eliab his son, J his son, Elkanah his son H3736
1Ch 6:34 of Elkanah, the son of J, the son of Eliel, H3736
1Ch 8:27 Elijah and Zikri were the sons of J. H3736
1Ch 9: 8 Ibneiah son of J; Elah son of Uzzi, the son H3736
1Ch 9:12 Adaiah son of J, the son of Pashhur, the H3736
1Ch 12: 7 Zebadiah the sons of J from Gedor. H3736
1Ch 27:22 Azarel son of J. These were the H3736
2Ch 23: 1 Azariah son of J, Ishmael son of H3736
Ne 11:12 Adaiah son of J, the son of Pelaliah H3736

JERUB-BAAL (11) [GIDEON, JERUB-BAAL'S]

Jdg 6:32 they gave him the name J that day H3715
Jdg 7: 1 in the morning, J (that is, Gideon) and H3715
Jdg 8:29 J son of Joash went back home to live. H3715
Jdg 8:35 to show any loyalty to the family of J H3715
Jdg 9: 1 Abimelek son of J went to his mother's H3715
Jdg 9: 5 his seventy brothers, the sons of J. H3715
Jdg 9: 5 the youngest son of J, escaped by hiding. H3715
Jdg 9:16 Have you been fair to J and his family H3715
Jdg 9:19 good faith toward J and his family today H3715
Jdg 9:57 curse of Jotham son of J came on them. H3715
1Sa 12:11 Then the LORD sent J, Barak, Jephthah and H3715

JERUB-BAAL'S (3) [JERUB-BAAL]

Jdg 9: 2 to have all seventy of J sons rule over you H3715
Jdg 9:24 that the crime against J seventy sons, H3715
Jdg 9:28 Isn't he J son, and isn't Zebul his H3715

JERUB-BESHETH (1)

2Sa 11:21 Who killed Abimelek son of J? Didn't a H3717

JERUEL (1)

2Ch 20:16 at the end of the gorge in the Desert of J. H3725

JERUSALEM (808) [JEBUS, JERUSALEM'S]

Jos 10: 1 Adoni-Zedek king of J heard that Joshua H3731
Jos 10: 3 king of J appealed to Hoham H3731
Jos 10: 5 of the Amorites—the kings of J, Hebron, H3731
Jos 10:23 out of the cave—the kings of J, Hebron, H3731
Jos 12:10 the king of J one the king of Hebron one H3731
Jos 15: 8 J). From there it climbed to the top H3731
Jos 15:63 who were living in J; to this day the H3731

J

Jos 18:28 that is, **J**), Gibeah and Kiriath H3731
Jdg 1: 7 They brought him to **J**, and he died there. H3731
Jdg 1: 8 men of Judah attacked **J** also and took it. H3731
Jdg 1:21 who were living in **J**; to this day the H3731
Jdg 19:10 **J**), with his two saddled donkeys H3731
1Sa 17:54 the Philistine's head and brought it to **J**; H3731
2Sa 5: 5 in **J** he reigned over all Israel and H3731
2Sa 5: 6 his men marched to **J** to attack the H3731
2Sa 5:13 took more concubines and wives in **J**, H3731
2Sa 8: 7 of Hadadezer and brought them to **J**. H3731
2Sa 9:13 And Mephibosheth lived in **J**, because he H3731
2Sa 10:14 fighting the Ammonites and came to **J**. H3731
2Sa 11: 1 But David remained in **J**. H3731
2Sa 11:12 So Uriah remained in **J** that day and the H3731
2Sa 12:31 Then he and his entire army returned to **J** H3731
2Sa 14:23 to Geshur and brought Absalom back to **J**. H3731
2Sa 14:28 lived two years in **J** without seeing the H3731
2Sa 15: 8 'If the LORD takes me back to **J**, I will H3731
2Sa 15:11 hundred men from **J** had accompanied H3731
2Sa 15:14 to all his officials who were with him in **J**, H3731
2Sa 15:29 the ark of God back to **J** and stayed there. H3731
2Sa 15:37 arrived at **J** as Absalom was entering the H3731
2Sa 16: 3 "He is staying in **J**, because he thinks, H3731
2Sa 16:15 all the men of Israel came to **J**, H3731
2Sa 17:20 found no one, so they returned to **J**. H3731
2Sa 19:19 wrong on the day my lord the king left **J**. H3731
2Sa 19:25 When he came from **J** to meet the king H3731
2Sa 19:33 "Cross over with me and stay with me in **J** H3731
2Sa 19:34 that I should go up to **J** with the king? H3731
2Sa 20: 2 their king all the way from the Jordan to **J**. H3731
2Sa 20: 3 When David returned to his palace in **J** H3731
2Sa 20: 7 marched out from **J** to pursue Sheba son H3731
2Sa 20:22 And Joab went back to the king in **J**. H3731
2Sa 24: 8 they came back to **J** at the end of nine H3731
2Sa 24:16 angel stretched out his hand to destroy **J**, H3731
1Ki 2:11 seven years in Hebron and thirty-three in **J**. H3731
1Ki 2:36 "Build yourself a house in **J** and live there, H3731
1Ki 2:38 And Shimei stayed in **J** for a long time. H3731
1Ki 2:41 Shimei had gone from **J** to Gath and had H3731
1Ki 3: 1 temple of the LORD, and the wall around **J**. H3731
1Ki 3:15 He returned to **J**, stood before the ark of H3731
1Ki 8: 1 into his presence at **J** the elders of Israel, H3731
1Ki 9:15 the wall of **J**, and Hazor, Megiddo H3731
1Ki 9:19 whatever he desired to build in **J**, in H3731
1Ki 10: 2 Arriving at **J** with a very great caravan H3731
1Ki 10:26 the chariot cities and also with him in **J**. H3731
1Ki 10:27 made silver as common in **J** as stones, H3731
1Ki 11: 7 On a hill east of **J**, Solomon built a high H3731
1Ki 11:13 of David my servant and for the sake of **J**, H3731
1Ki 11:29 that time Jeroboam was going out of **J**, H3731
1Ki 11:32 sake of my servant David and the city of **J**, H3731
1Ki 11:36 may always have a lamp before me in **J**, H3731
1Ki 11:42 Solomon reigned in **J** over all Israel forty H3731
1Ki 12:18 to get into his chariot and escape to **J**. H3731
1Ki 12:21 When Rehoboam arrived in **J**, he H3731
1Ki 12:27 sacrifices at the temple of the LORD in **J**, H3731
1Ki 12:28 "It is too much for you to go up to **J**. H3731
1Ki 14:21 he reigned seventeen years in **J**, the H3731
1Ki 14:25 Shishak king of Egypt attacked **J**. H3731
1Ki 15: 2 he reigned in **J** three years. H3731
1Ki 15: 4 gave him a lamp in **J** by raising up a son H3731
1Ki 15: 4 to succeed him and by making **J** strong. H3731
1Ki 15:10 he reigned in **J** forty-one years. H3731
1Ki 22:42 he reigned in **J** twenty-five years. H3731
2Ki 8:17 and he reigned in **J** eight years. H3731
2Ki 8:26 and he reigned in **J** one year. H3731
2Ki 9:28 him by chariot to **J** and buried him with H3731
2Ki 12: 1 and he reigned in **J** forty years. H3731
2Ki 12:17 Then he turned to attack **J**. H3731
2Ki 12:18 king of Aram, who then withdrew from **J**. H3731
2Ki 14: 2 he reigned in **J** twenty-nine years. H3731
2Ki 14: 2 name was Jehoaddan; she was from **J**. H3731
2Ki 14:13 Jehoash went to **J** and broke down the H3731
2Ki 14:13 down the wall of **J** from the Ephraim Gate H3731
2Ki 14:19 They conspired against him in **J**, and he H3731
2Ki 14:20 was buried in **J** with his ancestors, H3731
2Ki 15: 2 and he reigned in **J** fifty-two years. H3731
2Ki 15: 2 name was Jekoliah; she was from **J**. H3731
2Ki 15:33 and he reigned in **J** sixteen years. H3731
2Ki 16: 2 and he reigned in **J** sixteen years. H3731
2Ki 16: 5 up to fight against **J** and besieged Ahaz, H3731
2Ki 18: 2 he reigned in **J** twenty-nine years. H3731
2Ki 18:17 from Lachish to King Hezekiah at **J**. H3731
2Ki 18:17 They came up to **J** and stopped at the H3731
2Ki 18:22 saying to Judah and **J**, "You must worship H3731
2Ki 18:22 "You must worship before this altar in **J**"? H3731
2Ki 18:35 can the LORD deliver **J** from my hand?" H3731
2Ki 19:10 '**J** will not be given into the hands of the H3731
2Ki 19:21 Daughter **J** tosses her head as you flee H3731
2Ki 19:31 For out of **J** will come a remnant, and out H3731
2Ki 21: 1 and he reigned in **J** fifty-five years. H3731
2Ki 21: 4 LORD had said, "In **J** I will put my Name." H3731
2Ki 21: 7 "In this temple and in **J**, which I have H3731
2Ki 21:12 such disaster on **J** and Judah that the H3731
2Ki 21:13 I will stretch out over **J** the measuring line H3731
2Ki 21:13 I will wipe out **J** as one wipes a dish H3731
2Ki 21:16 blood that he filled **J** from end to end— H3731
2Ki 21:19 and he reigned in **J** two years. H3731
2Ki 22: 1 and he reigned in **J** thirty-one years. H3731
2Ki 22:14 She lived in **J**, in the New Quarter. H3731
2Ki 23: 1 together all the elders of Judah and **J**. H3731
2Ki 23: 2 the inhabitants of **J**, the priests and the H3731
2Ki 23: 4 burned them outside **J** in the fields of the H3731
2Ki 23: 5 towns of Judah and on those around **J**— H3731
2Ki 23: 6 Valley outside **J** and burned it there. H3731
2Ki 23: 9 did not serve at the altar of the LORD in **J**, H3731
2Ki 23:13 that were east of **J** on the south of the Hill H3731
2Ki 23:20 bones on them. Then he went back to **J**. H3731
2Ki 23:23 Passover was celebrated to the LORD in **J**. H3731
2Ki 23:24 detestable things seen in Judah and **J**. H3731
2Ki 23:27 and I will reject **J**, the city I chose, H3731
2Ki 23:30 from Megiddo to **J** and buried him in his H3731
2Ki 23:31 and he reigned in **J** three months. H3731
2Ki 23:33 of Hamath so that he might not reign in **J**, H3731
2Ki 23:36 and he reigned in **J** eleven years. H3731
2Ki 24: 4 For he had filled **J** with innocent blood H3731
2Ki 24: 8 and he reigned in **J** three months. H3731
2Ki 24: 8 daughter of Elnathan; she was from **J**. H3731
2Ki 24:10 Babylon advanced on **J** and laid siege to H3731
2Ki 24:14 He carried all **J** into exile: all the officers H3731
2Ki 24:15 He also took from **J** to Babylon the king's H3731
2Ki 24:18 and he reigned in **J** eleven years. H3731
2Ki 24:20 that all this happened to **J** and Judah, H3731
2Ki 25: 1 marched against **J** with his whole army. H3731
2Ki 25: 8 official of the king of Babylon, came to **J**. H3731
2Ki 25: 9 the royal palace and all the houses of **J**. H3731
2Ki 25:10 guard broke down the walls around **J**. H3731
1Ch 3: 4 David reigned in **J** thirty-three years, H3731
1Ch 6:10 as priest in the temple Solomon built in **J**), H3731
1Ch 6:15 LORD sent Judah and **J** into exile by the H3731
1Ch 6:32 Solomon built the temple of the LORD in **J**. H3731
1Ch 8:28 in their genealogy, and they lived in **J**. H3731
1Ch 8:32 They too lived near their relatives in **J**. H3731
1Ch 9: 3 Manasseh who lived in **J** were: H3731
1Ch 9:34 in their genealogy, and they lived in **J**. H3731
1Ch 9:38 They too lived near their relatives in **J**. H3731
1Ch 11: 4 David and all the Israelites marched to **J** H3731
1Ch 14: 3 In **J** David took more wives and became H3731
1Ch 15: 3 all Israel in **J** to bring up the ark of H3731
1Ch 18: 7 of Hadadezer and brought them to **J**. H3731
1Ch 19:15 inside the city. So Joab went back to **J**. H3731
1Ch 20: 1 besieged it, but David remained in **J**. H3731
1Ch 20: 3 David and his entire army returned to **J**. H3731
1Ch 21: 4 Israel and then came back to **J**. H3731
1Ch 21:15 And God sent an angel to destroy **J**. But as H3731
1Ch 21:16 drawn sword in his hand extended over **J**. H3731
1Ch 23:25 has come to dwell in **J** forever, H3731
1Ch 28: 1 all the officials of Israel to assemble at **J**: H3731
1Ch 29:27 seven in Hebron and thirty-three in **J**. H3731
2Ch 1: 4 because he had pitched a tent for it in **J**. H3731
2Ch 1:13 Solomon went to **J** from the high place H3731
2Ch 1:14 the chariot cities and also with him in **J**. H3731
2Ch 1:15 silver and gold as common in **J** as stones, H3731
2Ch 2: 7 to work in Judah and **J** with my skilled H3731
2Ch 2:16 You can then take them up to **J**." H3731
2Ch 3: 1 temple of the LORD in **J** on Mount Moriah, H3731
2Ch 5: 2 Solomon summoned to **J** the elders of H3731
2Ch 6: 6 now I have chosen **J** for my Name to be H3731
2Ch 8: 6 whatever he desired to build in **J**, in H3731
2Ch 9: 1 she came to **J** to test him with hard H3731
2Ch 9:25 the chariot cities and also with him in **J**. H3731
2Ch 9:27 made silver as common in **J** as stones, H3731
2Ch 9:30 Solomon reigned in **J** over all Israel forty H3731
2Ch 10:18 to get into his chariot and escape to **J**. H3731
2Ch 11: 1 When Rehoboam arrived in **J**, he H3731
2Ch 11: 5 Rehoboam lived in **J** and built up towns H3731
2Ch 11:14 property and came to Judah and **J**, H3731
2Ch 11:16 the Levites to **J** to offer sacrifices to H3731
2Ch 12: 2 king of Egypt attacked **J** in the fifth year of H3731
2Ch 12: 4 cities of Judah and came as far as **J**. H3731
2Ch 12: 5 had assembled in **J** for fear of Shishak, H3731
2Ch 12: 7 not be poured out on **J** through Shishak. H3731
2Ch 12: 9 When Shishak king of Egypt attacked **J** H3731
2Ch 12:13 himself firmly in **J** and continued as king. H3731
2Ch 12:13 he reigned seventeen years in **J**, the H3731
2Ch 13: 2 he reigned in **J** three years. H3731
2Ch 14:15 Then they returned to **J**. H3731
2Ch 15:10 They assembled at **J** in the third month of H3731
2Ch 17:13 also kept experienced fighting men in **J**. H3731
2Ch 19: 1 Judah returned safely to his palace in **J**, H3731
2Ch 19: 4 Jehoshaphat lived in **J**, and he went out H3731
2Ch 19: 8 In **J** also, Jehoshaphat appointed some of H3731
2Ch 19: 8 to settle disputes. And they lived in **J**. H3731
2Ch 20: 5 of Judah and **J** at the temple of the H3731
2Ch 20:15 all who live in Judah and **J**! H3731
2Ch 20:17 the LORD will give you, Judah and **J**. H3731
2Ch 20:18 people of Judah and **J** fell down in H3731
2Ch 20:20 "Listen to me, Judah and people of **J**! H3731
2Ch 20:27 men of Judah and **J** returned joyfully to H3731
2Ch 20:27 Jerusalem returned joyfully to **J**, H3731
2Ch 20:28 They entered **J** and went to the temple of H3731
2Ch 20:31 he reigned in **J** twenty-five years. H3731
2Ch 21: 5 and he reigned in **J** eight years. H3731
2Ch 21:11 caused the people of **J** to prostitute H3731
2Ch 21:13 Judah and the people of **J** to prostitute H3731
2Ch 21:20 and he reigned in **J** eight years. H3731
2Ch 22: 1 The people of **J** made Ahaziah H3731
2Ch 22: 2 and he reigned in **J** one year. H3731
2Ch 23: 2 from all the towns. When they came to **J**, H3731
2Ch 24: 1 and he reigned in **J** forty years. H3731
2Ch 24: 6 in from Judah and **J** the tax imposed by H3731
2Ch 24: 9 issued in Judah and **J** that they should H3731
2Ch 24:18 God's anger came on Judah and **J**. H3731
2Ch 24:23 it invaded Judah and **J** and killed all the H3731
2Ch 25: 1 he reigned in **J** twenty-nine years. H3731
2Ch 25: 1 name was Jehoaddan; she was from **J**. H3731
2Ch 25:23 brought him to **J** and broke down the H3731
2Ch 25:23 down the wall of **J** from the Ephraim Gate H3731
2Ch 25:27 against him in **J** and he fled to Lachish, H3731
2Ch 26: 3 and he reigned in **J** fifty-two years. H3731
2Ch 26: 3 name was Jekoliah; she was from **J**. H3731
2Ch 26: 9 built towers in **J** at the Corner Gate, H3731
2Ch 26:15 In **J** he made devices invented for use on H3731
2Ch 27: 1 and he reigned in **J** sixteen years. H3731
2Ch 27: 8 and he reigned in **J** sixteen years. H3731
2Ch 28: 1 and he reigned in **J** sixteen years. H3731
2Ch 28:10 women of Judah and **J** your slaves. H3731
2Ch 28:24 set up altars at every street corner in **J**. H3731
2Ch 28:27 ancestors and was buried in the city of **J**, H3731
2Ch 29: 1 he reigned in **J** twenty-nine years. H3731
2Ch 29: 8 of the LORD has fallen on Judah and **J**; H3731
2Ch 30: 1 temple of the LORD in **J** and celebrate the H3731
2Ch 30: 2 whole assembly in **J** decided to celebrate H3731
2Ch 30: 3 the people had not assembled in **J**. H3731
2Ch 30: 5 the people to come to **J** and celebrate the H3731
2Ch 30:11 humbled themselves and went to **J**. H3731
2Ch 30:13 of people assembled in **J** to celebrate the H3731
2Ch 30:14 the altars in **J** and cleared away the H3731
2Ch 30:21 who were present in **J** celebrated the H3731
2Ch 30:26 There was great joy in **J**, for since the days H3731
2Ch 30:26 there had been nothing like this in **J**. H3731
2Ch 31: 4 the people living in **J** to give the portion H3731
2Ch 32: 2 that he intended to wage war against **J**, H3731
2Ch 32: 9 sent his officers to **J** with this message H3731
2Ch 32:10 that you remain in **J** under siege? H3731
2Ch 32:12 saying to Judah and **J**, 'You must worship H3731
2Ch 32:18 to the people of **J** who were on the wall, H3731
2Ch 32:19 about the God of **J** as they did about the H3731
2Ch 32:22 the people of **J** from the hand of H3731
2Ch 32:23 brought offerings to **J** for the LORD and H3731
2Ch 32:25 wrath was on him and on Judah and **J**. H3731
2Ch 32:26 as did the people of **J**; therefore the H3731
2Ch 32:33 the people of **J** honored him when H3731
2Ch 33: 1 and he reigned in **J** fifty-five years. H3731
2Ch 33: 4 "My Name will remain in **J** forever." H3731
2Ch 33: 7 "In this temple and in **J**, which I have H3731
2Ch 33: 9 led Judah and the people of **J** astray, H3731
2Ch 33:13 brought him back to **J** and to his kingdom. H3731
2Ch 33:15 he had built on the temple hill and in **J**; H3731
2Ch 33:21 and he reigned in **J** two years. H3731
2Ch 34: 1 and he reigned in **J** thirty-one years. H3731
2Ch 34: 3 to purge Judah and **J** of high places, H3731
2Ch 34: 5 and so he purged Judah and **J**. H3731
2Ch 34: 7 Then he went back to **J**. H3731
2Ch 34: 9 Benjamin and the inhabitants of **J**. H3731
2Ch 34:22 She lived in **J**, in the New Quarter. H3731
2Ch 34:29 together all the elders of Judah and **J**. H3731
2Ch 34:30 the inhabitants of **J**, the priests and the H3731
2Ch 34:32 he had everyone in **J** and Benjamin H3731
2Ch 34:32 the people of **J** did this in accordance H3731
2Ch 35: 1 celebrated the Passover to the LORD in **J**, H3731
2Ch 35:18 who were there with the people of **J**. H3731
2Ch 35:24 in his other chariot and brought him to **J**, H3731
2Ch 35:24 all Judah and **J** mourned for him. H3731
2Ch 36: 1 made him king in **J** in place of his H3731
2Ch 36: 2 and he reigned in **J** three months. H3731
2Ch 36: 3 dethroned him in **J** and imposed on H3731
2Ch 36: 4 king over Judah and **J** and changed H3731
2Ch 36: 5 and he reigned in **J** eleven years. H3731
2Ch 36: 9 he reigned in **J** three months and ten H3731
2Ch 36:10 Zedekiah, king over Judah and **J**. H3731
2Ch 36:11 and he reigned in **J** eleven years. H3731
2Ch 36:14 the LORD, which he had consecrated in **J**. H3731
2Ch 36:19 temple and broke down the wall of **J**; H3731
2Ch 36:23 to build a temple for him at **J** in Judah. H3731
Ezr 1: 2 to build a temple for him at **J** in Judah. H3731
Ezr 1: 3 you may go up to **J** in Judah and build H3731
Ezr 1: 3 the God who is in **J**, and may their God H3731
Ezr 1: 4 offerings for the temple of God in **J**. H3731
Ezr 1: 5 up and build the house of the LORD in **J**. H3731
Ezr 1: 7 carried away from **J** and had placed in the H3731
Ezr 1:11 when they came up from Babylon to **J**. H3731
Ezr 2: 1 they returned to **J** and Judah, each to H3731
Ezr 2:68 they arrived at the house of the LORD in **J**, H3731
Ezr 3: 1 people assembled together as one in **J**. H3731
Ezr 3: 8 after their arrival at the house of God in **J**, H3731
Ezr 3: 8 who had returned from the captivity to **J**) H3731
Ezr 4: 6 against the people of Judah and **J**. H3731
Ezr 4: 8 a letter against **J** to Artaxerxes the king A10332
Ezr 4:12 you have gone to **J** and are rebuilding A10332
Ezr 4:20 **J** has had powerful kings ruling over the A10332
Ezr 4:23 to the Jews in **J** and compelled them by A10332
Ezr 4:24 the house of God in **J** came to a A10332
Ezr 5: 1 Jews in Judah and **J** in the name of the A10332
Ezr 5: 2 to work to rebuild the house of God in **J**. A10332
Ezr 5:14 from the temple in **J** and brought to the A10332
Ezr 5:15 go and deposit them in the temple in **J**. A10332
Ezr 5:16 foundations of the house of God in **J**. A10332
Ezr 5:17 decree to rebuild this house of God in **J**. A10332
Ezr 6: 3 concerning the temple of God in **J**: A10332
Ezr 6: 5 from the temple in **J** and brought to A10332
Ezr 6: 5 to their places in the temple in **J**; A10332
Ezr 6: 9 as requested by the priests in **J**—must A10332
Ezr 6:12 this decree or to destroy this temple in **J**. A10332
Ezr 6:18 their groups for the service of God at **J**, A10332
Ezr 7: 7 also came up to **J** in the seventh year of H3731

Ezr 7: 8 Ezra arrived in **J** in the fifth month of the H3731
Ezr 7: 9 he arrived in **J** on the first day of the H3731
Ezr 7:13 who volunteer to go to **J** with you, may A10332
Ezr 7:14 about Judah and **J** with regard to the A10332
Ezr 7:15 God of Israel, whose dwelling is in **J**, A10332
Ezr 7:16 priests for the temple of their God in **J**. A10332
Ezr 7:17 the altar of the temple of your God in **J**. A10332
Ezr 7:19 Deliver to the God of **J** all the articles A10332
Ezr 7:27 to the house of the LORD in **J** in this way H3731
Ezr 8:29 house of the LORD in **J** before the leading H3731
Ezr 8:30 to be taken to the house of our God in **J**. H3731
Ezr 8:31 set out from the Ahava Canal to go to **J**. H3731
Ezr 8:32 So we arrived in **J**, where we rested three H3731
Ezr 9: 9 us a wall of protection in Judah and **J**. H3731
Ezr 10: 7 throughout Judah and **J** for all the exiles H3731
Ezr 10: 7 all the exiles to assemble in **J**. H3731
Ezr 10: 9 Judah and Benjamin had gathered in **J**. H3731
Ne 1: 2 had survived the exile, and also about **J**. H3731
Ne 1: 3 The wall of **J** is broken down, and its H3731
Ne 2:11 I went to **J**, and after staying there three H3731
Ne 2:12 my God had put in my heart to do for **J**. H3731
Ne 2:13 examining the walls of **J**, which had been H3731
Ne 2:17 **J** lies in ruins, and its gates have been H3731
Ne 2:17 let us rebuild the wall of **J**, and we will no H3731
Ne 2:20 you have no share in **J** or any claim or H3731
Ne 3: 8 They restored **J** as far as the Broad Wall. H3731
Ne 3: 9 ruler of a half-district of **J**, repaired the H3731
Ne 3:12 ruler of a half-district of **J**, repaired the H3731
Ne 4: 8 fight against **J** and stir up trouble H3731
Ne 4:22 man and his helper stay inside **J** at night, H3731
Ne 6: 7 to make this proclamation about you in **J**: H3731
Ne 7: 2 I put in charge of **J** my brother Hanani H3731
Ne 7: 3 "The gates of **J** are not to be opened until H3731
Ne 7: 3 Also appoint residents of **J** as guards H3731
Ne 7: 6 they returned to **J** and Judah, each to his H3731
Ne 8:15 spread it throughout their towns and in **J**: H3731
Ne 11: 1 the leaders of the people settled in **J**. H3731
Ne 11: 1 one out of every ten of them to live in **J**, H3731
Ne 11: 2 all who volunteered to live in **J**. H3731
Ne 11: 3 the provincial leaders who settled in **J** H3731
Ne 11: 4 from both Judah and Benjamin lived in **J**): H3731
Ne 11: 6 Perez who lived in **J** totaled 468 men of H3731
Ne 11:22 of the Levites in **J** was Uzzi son of Bani, H3731
Ne 12:27 At the dedication of the wall of **J**, the H3731
Ne 12:27 were brought to **J** to celebrate joyfully H3731
Ne 12:28 together from the region around **J**— H3731
Ne 12:29 built villages for themselves around **J**. H3731
Ne 12:43 sound of rejoicing in **J** could be heard far H3731
Ne 13: 6 going on, I was not in **J**, for in the H3731
Ne 13: 7 came back to **J**. Here I learned about H3731
Ne 13:15 bringing all this into **J** on the Sabbath. H3731
Ne 13:16 Tyre who lived in **J** were bringing in fish H2023S
Ne 13:16 selling them in **J** on the Sabbath to H3731
Ne 13:19 fell on the gates of **J** before the Sabbath, H3731
Ne 13:20 kinds of goods spent the night outside **J**. H3731
Est 2: 6 into exile from **J** by Nebuchadnezzar king H3731
Ps 51:18 to prosper Zion, to build up the walls of **J**. H3731
Ps 68:29 of your temple at **J** kings will bring you H3731
Ps 79: 1 temple, they have reduced **J** to rubble. H3731
Ps 79: 3 poured out blood like water all around **J**, H3731
Ps 102:21 be declared in Zion and his praise in **J** H3731
Ps 116:19 the house of the LORD—in your midst, **J**. H3731
Ps 122: 2 Our feet are standing in your gates, **J**. H3731
Ps 122: 3 **J** is built like a city that is closely H3731
Ps 122: 6 Pray for the peace of **J**: "May those who H3731
Ps 125: 2 As the mountains surround **J**, so the LORD H3731
Ps 128: 5 see the prosperity of **J** all the days of your H3731
Ps 135:21 LORD from Zion, to him who dwells in **J**. H3731
Ps 137: 5 If I forget you, **J**, may my right hand forget H3731
Ps 137: 6 if I do not consider **J** my highest joy. H3731
Ps 137: 7 what the Edomites did on the day **J** fell. H3731
Ps 147: 2 The LORD builds up **J**; he gathers the H3731
Ps 147:12 Extol the LORD, **J**; praise your God, Zion. H3731
Ecc 1: 1 of the Teacher, son of David, king in **J**: H3731
Ecc 1:12 the Teacher, was king over Israel in **J**. H3731
Ecc 1:16 anyone who has ruled over **J** before me; H3731
Ecc 2: 7 flocks than anyone in **J** before me. H3731
Ecc 2: 9 greater by far than anyone in **J** before me. H3731
SS 1: 5 daughters of **J**, dark like the tents H3731
SS 2: 7 Daughters of **J**, I charge you by the H3731
SS 3: 5 Daughters of **J**, I charge you by the H3731
SS 3:10 interior inlaid with love. Daughters of **J**, H3731
SS 5: 8 Daughters of **J**, I charge you—if you find H3731
SS 5:16 beloved, this is my friend, daughters of **J**. H3731
SS 6: 4 darling, as lovely as **J**, as majestic as H3731
SS 8: 4 Daughters of **J**, I charge you: Do not H3731
Isa 1: 1 concerning Judah and **J** that Isaiah son of H3731
Isa 2: 1 son of Amoz saw concerning Judah and **J**: H3731
Isa 2: 3 from Zion, the word of the LORD from **J**. H3731
Isa 3: 1 about to take from **J** and Judah both H3731
Isa 3: 8 **J** staggers, Judah is falling; their words H3731
Isa 4: 3 who remain in **J**, will be called holy, H3731
Isa 4: 3 who are recorded among the living in **J**. H3731
Isa 4: 4 the bloodstains from **J** by a spirit of H3731
Isa 5: 3 you dwellers in **J** and people of Judah, H3731
Isa 7: 1 of Israel marched up to fight against **J**, H3731
Isa 8:14 the people of **J** he will be a trap and H3731
Isa 10:10 excelled those of **J** and Samaria— H3731
Isa 10:11 shall I not deal with **J** and her images as I H3731
Isa 10:12 all his work against Mount Zion and **J**, H3731
Isa 10:32 mount of Daughter Zion, at the hill of **J**. H3731
Isa 22:10 the buildings in **J** and tore down houses H3731
Isa 22:21 those who live in **J** and to the people of H3731
Isa 24:23 will reign on Mount Zion and in **J**, H3731
Isa 27:13 the LORD on the holy mountain in **J**. H3731
Isa 28:14 you scoffers who rule this people in **J**. H3731
Isa 30:19 of Zion, who live in **J**, you will weep no H3731
Isa 31: 5 the LORD Almighty will shield **J**; he will H3731
Isa 31: 9 fire is in Zion, whose furnace is in **J**. H3731
Isa 33:20 your eyes will see **J**, a peaceful abode, H3731
Isa 36: 2 army from Lachish to King Hezekiah at **J**. H3731
Isa 36: 7 saying to Judah and **J**, "You must worship H3731
Isa 36:20 can the LORD deliver **J** from my hand?" H3731
Isa 37:10 '**J** will not be given into the hands of the H3731
Isa 37:22 Daughter **J** tosses her head as you flee H3731
Isa 37:32 For out of **J** will come a remnant, and out H3731
Isa 40: 2 Speak tenderly to **J**, and proclaim to her H3731
Isa 40: 9 You who bring good news to **J**, lift up your H3731
Isa 41:27 I gave to **J** a messenger of good news. H3731
Isa 44:26 who says of **J**, 'It shall be inhabited H3731
Isa 44:28 I please; he will say of **J**, "Let it be rebuilt," H3731
Isa 51:17 Rise up, **J**, you who have drunk from the H3731
Isa 52: 1 your garments of splendor, **J**, the holy city. H3731
Isa 52: 2 off your dust; rise up, sit enthroned, **J**. H3731
Isa 52: 9 together, you ruins of **J**, for the LORD has H3731
Isa 52: 9 his people, he has redeemed **J**. H3731
Isa 62: 6 on your walls, **J**; they will never be H3731
Isa 62: 7 till he establishes **J** and makes her the H3731
Isa 64:10 even Zion is a wasteland, **J** a desolation. H3731
Isa 65:18 I will create **J** to be a delight and its H3731
Isa 65:19 I will rejoice over **J** and take delight in my H3731
Isa 66:10 "Rejoice with **J** and be glad for her, all H3731
Isa 66:13 and you will be comforted over **J**. H3731
Isa 66:20 my holy mountain in **J** as an offering to H3731
Jer 1: 3 when the people of **J** went into exile. H3731
Jer 1:15 thrones in the entrance of the gates of **J**; H3731
Jer 2: 2 "Go and proclaim in the hearing of **J** H3731
Jer 3:17 time they will call **J** The Throne of the H3731
Jer 3:17 will gather in **J** to honor the name of H3731
Jer 4: 3 LORD says to the people of Judah and to **J**: H3731
Jer 4: 4 you people of Judah and inhabitants of **J** H3731
Jer 4: 5 in Judah and proclaim in **J** and say: H3731
Jer 4:10 deceived this people and **J** by saying, H3731
Jer 4:11 At that time this people and **J** will be told, H3731
Jer 4:14 **J**, wash the evil from your heart and be H3731
Jer 4:16 this to the nations, proclaim concerning **J**: H3731
Jer 5: 1 "Go up and down the streets of **J**, look H3731
Jer 6: 1 Flee from **J**! Sound the trumpet H3731
Jer 6: 6 the trees and build siege ramps against **J**. H3731
Jer 6: 8 Take warning, **J**, or I will turn away from H3731
Jer 7:17 the towns of Judah and in the streets of **J**? H3731
Jer 7:34 in the towns of Judah and the streets of **J**, H3731
Jer 8: 1 of the people of **J** will be removed from H3731
Jer 8: 5 Why does **J** always turn away H3731
Jer 9:11 "I will make **J** a heap of ruins, a haunt of H3731
Jer 11: 2 of Judah and to those who live in **J**. H3731
Jer 11: 6 the towns of Judah and in the streets of **J**: H3731
Jer 11: 9 people of Judah and those who live in **J**. H3731
Jer 11:12 the people of **J** will go and cry out to H3731
Jer 11:13 god Baal are as many as the streets of **J**. H3731
Jer 13: 9 pride of Judah and the great pride of **J**. H3731
Jer 13:13 the prophets and all those living in **J**. H3731
Jer 13:27 Woe to you, **J**! How long will you H3731
Jer 14: 2 the land, and a cry goes up from **J**. H3731
Jer 14:16 into the streets of **J** because of the famine H3731
Jer 15: 4 son of Hezekiah king of Judah did in **J**. H3731
Jer 15: 5 have pity on you, **J**? Who will mourn for H3731
Jer 17:19 stand also at all the other gates of **J**. H3731
Jer 17:20 everyone living in **J** who come through H3731
Jer 17:21 day or bring it through the gates of **J**. H3731
Jer 17:25 by the men of Judah and those living in **J**, H3731
Jer 17:26 towns of Judah and the villages around **J**, H3731
Jer 17:27 the gates of **J** on the Sabbath day, H3731
Jer 17:27 fire in the gates of **J** that will consume her H3731
Jer 18:11 the people of Judah and those living in **J**, H3731
Jer 19: 3 you kings of Judah and people of **J**. H3731
Jer 19: 7 place I will ruin the plans of Judah and **J**. H3731
Jer 19:13 The houses in **J** and those of the kings of H3731
Jer 21:13 I am against you, **J**, you who live above this NDT
Jer 22:19 away and thrown outside the gates of **J**." H3731
Jer 23:14 the prophets of **J** I have seen something H3731
Jer 23:14 the people of **J** are like Gomorrah." H2023S
Jer 23:15 from the prophets of **J** ungodliness has H3731
Jer 24: 1 carried into exile from **J** to Babylon by H3731
Jer 24: 8 his officials and the survivors from **J** H3731
Jer 25: 2 of Judah and to all those living in **J**: H3731
Jer 25:18 **J** and the towns of Judah, its kings and H3731
Jer 26:18 **J** will become a heap of rubble H3731
Jer 27: 3 who have come to **J** to Zedekiah king of H3731
Jer 27:18 king of Judah and in **J** not be taken to H3731
Jer 27:20 king of Judah into exile from **J** to Babylon, H3731
Jer 27:20 with all the nobles of Judah and **J**— H3731
Jer 27:21 the palace of the king of Judah and in **J**: H3731
Jer 29: 1 Jeremiah sent from **J** to the surviving H3731
Jer 29: 1 had carried into exile from **J** to Babylon. H3731
Jer 29: 2 officials and the leaders of Judah and **J**, H3731
Jer 29: 2 the artisans had gone into exile from **J**.) H3731
Jer 29: 4 I carried into exile from **J** to Babylon: H3731
Jer 29:20 whom I have sent away from **J** to Babylon. H3731
Jer 29:25 in your own name to all the people in **J**, H3731
Jer 32: 2 the king of Babylon was then besieging **J**, H3731
Jer 32:32 the people of Judah and those living in **J**. H3731
Jer 32:44 in the villages around **J**, in the towns of H3731
Jer 33:10 the streets of **J** that are deserted, H3731
Jer 33:13 the villages around **J** and in the towns of H3731
Jer 33:16 will be saved and **J** will live in safety. H3731
Jer 34: 1 were fighting against **J** and all its H3731
Jer 34: 6 all this to Zedekiah king of Judah, in **J**, H3731
Jer 34: 7 was fighting against **J** and the other cities H3731
Jer 34: 8 all the people in **J** to proclaim freedom H3731
Jer 34:19 The leaders of Judah and **J**, the court H3731
Jer 35:11 we must go to **J** to escape the Babylonian H3731
Jer 35:11 So we have remained in **J**." H3731
Jer 35:13 the people of Judah and those living in **J**, H3731
Jer 35:17 on everyone living in **J** every disaster I H3731
Jer 36: 9 all the people in **J** and those who had H3731
Jer 36:31 those living in **J** and the people of H3731
Jer 37: 5 who were besieging **J** heard the report H3731
Jer 37: 5 report about them, they withdrew from **J**. H3731
Jer 37:11 had withdrawn from **J** because of H3731
Jer 38:28 of the guard until the day **J** was captured. H3731
Jer 38:28 was captured. This is how **J** was taken: H3731
Jer 39: 1 marched against **J** with his whole army H3731
Jer 39: 8 the people and broke down the walls of **J**. H3731
Jer 40: 1 the captives from **J** and Judah who were H3731
Jer 42:18 been poured out on those who lived in **J**, H3731
Jer 44: 2 I brought on **J** and on all the towns H3731
Jer 44: 6 the streets of **J** and made them the H3731
Jer 44: 9 in the land of Judah and the streets of **J**? H3731
Jer 44:13 famine and plague, as I punished **J**. H3731
Jer 44:17 the towns of Judah and in the streets of **J**. H3731
Jer 44:21 Judah and the streets of **J** by you and your H3731
Jer 51:35 on those who live in Babylonia," says **J**. H3731
Jer 51:50 LORD in a distant land, and call to mind **J**." H3731
Jer 52: 1 and he reigned in **J** eleven years. H3731
Jer 52: 3 that all this happened to **J** and Judah, H3731
Jer 52: 4 marched against **J** with his whole army. H3731
Jer 52:12 served the king of Babylon, came to **J**. H3731
Jer 52:13 the royal palace and all the houses of **J**. H3731
Jer 52:14 broke down all the walls around **J**. H3731
Jer 52:29 eighteenth year, 832 people from **J**; H3731
La 1: 7 wandering **J** remembers all the H3731
La 1: 8 **J** has sinned greatly and so has become H3731
La 1:17 **J** has become an unclean thing among H3731
La 2:10 The young women of **J** have bowed their H3731
La 2:13 With what can I compare you, Daughter **J**? H3731
La 2:15 scoff and shake their heads at Daughter **J**: H3731
La 4:12 foes could enter the gates of **J**. H3731
Eze 4: 1 in front of you and draw the city of **J** on it. H3731
Eze 4: 7 toward the siege of **J** and with bared arm H3731
Eze 4:16 I am about to cut off the food supply in **J**. H3731
Eze 5: 5 This is **J**, which I have set in the center of H3731
Eze 5: 8 I myself am against you, **J**, and I will inflict NDT
Eze 8: 3 in visions of God he took me to **J**, H3731
Eze 9: 4 the city of **J** and put a mark on the H3731
Eze 9: 8 in this outpouring of your wrath on **J**?" H3731
Eze 11:15 the people of **J** have said of your fellow H3731
Eze 12:10 the prince in **J** and all the Israelites H3731
Eze 12:19 about those living in **J** and in the land of H3731
Eze 13:16 who prophesied to **J** and saw visions of H3731
Eze 14:21 be when I send against **J** my four dreadful H3731
Eze 14:22 the disaster I have brought on **J**— H3731
Eze 15: 6 so will I treat the people living in **J**. H3731
Eze 16: 2 confront **J** with her detestable practices H3731
Eze 16: 3 'This is what the Sovereign LORD says to **J**: H3731
Eze 17:12 of Babylon went to **J** and carried off her H3731
Eze 21: 2 set your face against **J** and preach against H3731
Eze 21:20 another against Judah and fortified **J**. H3731
Eze 21:22 Into his right hand will come the lot for **J** H3731
Eze 22:19 all become dross, I will gather you into **J**. H3731
Eze 23: 4 Oholah is Samaria, and Oholibah is **J**. H3731
Eze 24: 2 Babylon has laid siege to **J** this very day. H3731
Eze 26: 2 of man, because Tyre has said of **J**, 'Aha! H3731
Eze 33:21 had escaped from **J** came to me and said, H3731
Eze 36:38 offerings at **J** during her appointed H3731
Da 1: 1 of Babylon came to **J** and besieged it. H3731
Da 5: 2 father had taken from the temple in **J**, A10332
Da 5: 3 been taken from the temple of God in **J**, A10332
Da 6:10 where the windows opened toward **J**. A10332
Da 9: 2 that the desolation of **J** would last seventy H3731
Da 9: 7 the inhabitants of **J** and all Israel, H3731
Da 9:12 been done like what has been done to **J**. H3731
Da 9:16 away your anger and your wrath from **J**, H3731
Da 9:16 have made **J** and your people an H3731
Da 9:25 restore and rebuild **J** until the Anointed H3731
Joel 2:32 on Mount Zion and in **J** there will be H3731
Joel 3: 1 I restore the fortunes of Judah and **J**, H3731
Joel 3: 6 the people of Judah and **J** to the Greeks, H3731
Joel 3:16 will roar from Zion and thunder from **J**; H3731
Joel 3:17 **J** will be holy; never again will foreigners H3731
Joel 3:20 inhabited forever and **J** through all H3731
Am 1: 2 LORD roars from Zion and thunders from **J**; H3731
Am 2: 5 that will consume the fortresses of **J**." H3731
Ob 11 entered his gates and cast lots for **J**, H3731
Ob 20 the exiles from **J** who are in Sepharad will H3731
Mic 1: 1 vision he saw concerning Samaria and **J**. H3731
Mic 1: 5 What is Judah's high place? Is it not **J**? H3731
Mic 1: 9 very gate of my people, even to **J** itself. H3731
Mic 1:12 come from the LORD, even to the gate of **J**. H3731
Mic 3:10 with bloodshed, and **J** with wickedness. H3731
Mic 3:12 **J** will become a heap of rubble H3731
Mic 4: 2 from Zion, the word of the LORD from **J**. H3731
Mic 4: 8 kingship will come to Daughter **J**. H3731
Zep 1: 4 Judah and against all who live in **J**. H3731
Zep 1:12 time I will search **J** with lamps and punish H3731
Zep 3: 7 Of **J** I thought, 'Surely you will fear me and NDT

Zep 3:11 On that day you, J, will not be put to shame NDT
Zep 3:14 rejoice with all your heart, Daughter J! H3731
Zep 3:16 On that day they will say to J, "Do not fear H3731
Zec 1:12 withhold mercy from J and from the towns H3731
Zec 1:14 'I am very jealous for J and Zion, H3731
Zec 1:16 'I will return to J with mercy, and there my H3731
Zec 1:16 line will be stretched out over J, H3731
Zec 1:17 will again comfort Zion and choose J. H3731
Zec 1:19 horns that scattered Judah, Israel and J." H3731
Zec 2: 2 "To measure J, to find out how wide H3731
Zec 2: 4 'J will be a city without walls because of H3731
Zec 2:12 in the holy land and will again choose J. H3731
Zec 3: 2 who has chosen J, rebuke you! Is not H3731
Zec 7: 7 prophets when J and its surrounding H3731
Zec 8: 3 "I will return to Zion and dwell in J. H3731
Zec 8: 3 Then J will be called the Faithful City, and H3731
Zec 8: 4 of ripe old age will sit in the streets of J, H3731
Zec 8: 8 I will bring them back to live in J; they will H3731
Zec 8:15 to do good again to J and Judah. H3731
Zec 8:22 nations will come to J to seek the LORD H3731
Zec 9: 9 Daughter J! See, your king comes H3731
Zec 9:10 from Ephraim and the warhorses from J, H3731
Zec 12: 2 "I am going to make J a cup that sends all H3731
Zec 12: 2 Judah will be besieged as well as J. H3731
Zec 12: 3 I will make J an immovable rock for all H3731
Zec 12: 5 'The people of J are strong, because H3731
Zec 12: 6 but J will remain intact in her place. H3731
Zec 12: 8 the LORD will shield those who live in J, H3731
Zec 12: 9 out to destroy all the nations that attack J. H3731
Zec 12:10 the inhabitants of J a spirit of grace and H3731
Zec 12:11 day the weeping in J will be as great as H3731
Zec 13: 1 house of David and the inhabitants of J, H3731
Zec 14: 1 the LORD is coming, J, when your NDT
Zec 14: 2 all the nations to J to fight against it; H3731
Zec 14: 4 of Olives, east of J, and the Mount of H3731
Zec 14: 8 that day living water will flow out from J, H3731
Zec 14:10 to Rimmon, south of J, will become like H3731
Zec 14:10 But J will be raised up high from the NDT
Zec 14:11 will it be destroyed. J will be secure. H3731
Zec 14:12 strike all the nations that fought against J: H3731
Zec 14:14 Judah too will fight at J. The wealth of all H3731
Zec 14:16 that have attacked J will go up year after H3731
Zec 14:17 do not go up to J to worship the King, H3731
Zec 14:21 Every pot in J and Judah will be holy to H3731
Mal 2:11 has been committed in Israel and in J: H3731
Mal 3: 4 of Judah and J will be acceptable to H3731
Mt 2: 1 King Herod, Magi from the east came to J G2642
Mt 2: 3 this he was disturbed, and all J with him. G2642
Mt 3: 5 went out to him *from* J and all Judea and G2642
Mt 4:25 the Decapolis, J, Judea and the region G2642
Mt 5:35 is his footstool; or by J, for it is the city of G2642
Mt 15: 1 the law came to Jesus from J and asked, G2642
Mt 16:21 that he must go to J and suffer many G2642
Mt 20:17 Now Jesus was going up to J. On the way G2642
Mt 20:18 "We are going up to J, and the Son of G2642
Mt 21: 1 As they approached J and came to G2642
Mt 21:10 When Jesus entered J, the whole city was G2642
Mt 23:37 "J, Jerusalem, you who kill the prophets G2642
Mt 23:37 "Jerusalem, J, you who kill the prophets G2642
Mk 1: 5 all the **people of** J went out to him. G2643
Mk 3: 8 came to him from Judea, J, Idumea, G2642
Mk 3:22 of the law who came down from J said, G2642
Mk 7: 1 who had come from J gathered around G2642
Mk 10:32 They were on their way up to J, with Jesus G2642
Mk 10:33 "We are going up to J," he said, "and the G2642
Mk 11: 1 As they approached J and came to G2642
Mk 11:11 Jesus entered J and went into the temple G2642
Mk 11:15 On reaching J, Jesus entered the temple G2642
Mk 11:27 They arrived again in J, and while Jesus G2642
Mk 15:41 come up with him to J were also there. G2642
Lk 2:22 Mary took him to J to present him to G2642
Lk 2:25 Now there was a man in J called Simeon G2642
Lk 2:38 looking forward to the redemption *of* J. G2642
Lk 2:41 Jesus' parents went to J for the Festival of G2642
Lk 2:43 the boy Jesus stayed behind in J, but they G2642
Lk 2:45 they went back to J to look for him. G2642
Lk 4: 9 devil led him to J and had him stand on G2642
Lk 5:17 village of Galilee and from Judea and J. G2642
Lk 6:17 all over Judea, from J, and from the G2642
Lk 9:31 he was about to bring to fulfillment at J. G2642
Lk 9:51 to heaven, Jesus resolutely set out for J. G2642
Lk 9:53 because he was heading for J. G2642
Lk 10:30 "A man was going down from J to Jericho, G2642
Lk 13: 4 more guilty than all the others living *in* J? G2642
Lk 13:22 teaching as he made his way to J. G2642
Lk 13:33 surely no prophet can die outside J! G2642
Lk 13:34 "J, Jerusalem, you who kill the prophets G2642
Lk 13:34 "Jerusalem, J, you who kill the prophets G2642
Lk 17:11 Now on his way to J, Jesus traveled along G2642
Lk 18:31 "We are going up to J, and everything G2642
Lk 19:11 because he was near J and the people G2642
Lk 19:28 he went on ahead, going up to J. G2642
Lk 19:41 As he approached J and saw the city, he NDT
Lk 21:20 "When you see J being surrounded by G2642
Lk 21:24 J will be trampled on by the Gentiles until G2642
Lk 23: 7 to Herod, who was also in J at that time. G2642
Lk 23:28 to them, "Daughters *of* J, do not weep G2642
Lk 24:13 Emmaus, about seven miles from J. G2642
Lk 24:18 only one visiting J who does not know the G2642
Lk 24:33 They got up and returned at once to J G2642
Lk 24:47 in his name to all nations, beginning at J. G2642
Lk 24:52 him and returned to J with great joy. G2642
Jn 1:19 the Jewish leaders in J sent priests and G2642
Jn 2:13 the Jewish Passover, Jesus went up to J. G2642
Jn 2:23 Now while he was in J at the Passover G2642
Jn 4:20 the place where we must worship is in J." G2642
Jn 4:21 Father neither on this mountain nor in J. G2642
Jn 4:45 all that he had done in J at the Passover G2642
Jn 5: 1 Jesus went up to J for one of the Jewish G2642
Jn 5: 2 Now there is in J near the Sheep Gate a G2642
Jn 7:25 some of the **people of** J began to ask, G2643
Jn 10:22 Then came the Festival of Dedication at J G2642
Jn 11:18 Bethany was less than two miles from J, G2642
Jn 11:55 from the country to J for their ceremonial G2642
Jn 12:12 heard that Jesus was on his way to J. G2642
Ac 1: 4 "Do not leave J, but wait for the gift my G2642
Ac 1: 8 you will be my witnesses in J, and in G2642
Ac 1:12 apostles returned to J from the hill called G2642
Ac 1:19 Everyone in J heard about this, so they G2642
Ac 2: 5 were staying in J God-fearing Jews from G2642
Ac 2:14 "Fellow Jews and all of you who live in J G2642
Ac 4: 5 the teachers of the law met in J. G2642
Ac 4:16 "Everyone living *in* J knows they have G2642
Ac 5:16 gathered also from the towns around J, G2642
Ac 5:28 "Yet you have filled J with your teaching G2642
Ac 6: 7 number of disciples in J increased rapidly, G2642
Ac 8: 1 broke out against the church in J, G2642
Ac 8:14 the apostles in J heard that Samaria G2642
Ac 8:25 Peter and John returned to J, preaching G2642
Ac 8:26 that goes down from J to Gaza. G2642
Ac 8:27 This man had gone to J to worship, G2642
Ac 9: 2 he might take them as prisoners to J. G2642
Ac 9:13 he has done to your holy people in J. G2642
Ac 9:21 who raised havoc in J among those who G2642
Ac 9:26 When he came to J, he tried to join the G2642
Ac 9:28 with them and moved about freely in J, G2642
Ac 10:39 he did in the country of the Jews and *in* J. G2642
Ac 11: 2 So when Peter went up to J, the G2642
Ac 11:22 News of this reached the church in J, and G2642
Ac 11:27 prophets came down from J to Antioch. G2642
Ac 12:25 they returned from J, taking with them G2642
Ac 13:13 where John left them to return to J. G2642
Ac 13:27 The people of J and their rulers did not G2642
Ac 13:31 had traveled with him from Galilee to J. G2642
Ac 15: 2 to go up to J to see the apostles and G2642
Ac 15: 4 When they came to J, they were G2642
Ac 16: 4 elders in J for the people to obey G2642
Ac 18:22 *he* **went up** *to J* and greeted the church and AIT
Ac 19:21 Paul decided to go to J, passing through G2642
Ac 20:16 he was in a hurry to reach J, if possible G2642
Ac 20:22 I am going to J, not knowing what G2642
Ac 21: 4 Spirit they urged Paul not to go on to J. G2642
Ac 21:11 Jewish leaders in J will bind the owner G2642
Ac 21:12 there pleaded with Paul not to go up to J. G2642
Ac 21:13 also to die in J for the name of the G2642
Ac 21:15 After this, we started on our way up to J. G2642
Ac 21:17 When we arrived at J, the brothers and G2642
Ac 21:31 that the whole **city of** J was in an uproar. G2642
Ac 22: 5 people as prisoners to J to be punished. G2642
Ac 22:17 "When I returned to J and was praying at G2642
Ac 22:18 'Leave J immediately, because the G2642
Ac 23:11 As you have testified about me in J, so G2642
Ac 24:11 twelve days ago I went up to J to worship. G2642
Ac 24:17 I came to J to bring my people gifts for the NDT
Ac 25: 1 Festus went up from Caesarea to J, G2642
Ac 25: 3 to have Paul transferred to J, for they were G2642
Ac 25: 7 had come down from J stood around him. G2642
Ac 25: 9 willing to go up to J and stand trial before G2642
Ac 25:15 When I went to J, the chief priests and the G2642
Ac 25:20 be willing to go to J and stand trial there G2642
Ac 25:24 me about him in J and here in Caesarea, G2642
Ac 26: 4 my life in my own country, and also in J. G2642
Ac 26:10 And that is just what I did in J. On the G2642
Ac 26:20 then to those *in* J and in all Judea, and G2642
Ac 28:17 I was arrested in J and handed over to the G2642
Ro 15:19 So from J all the way around to Illyricum, G2642
Ro 15:25 I am on my way to J in the service of the G2642
Ro 15:26 the poor among the Lord's people in J. G2642
Ro 15:31 contribution I take to J may be favorably G2642
1Co 16: 3 approve and send them with your gift to J. G2642
Gal 1:17 I did not go up to J to see those who were G2642
Gal 1:18 I went up to J to get acquainted with G2642
Gal 2: 1 I went up again to J, this time with G2642
Gal 4:25 corresponds to the present **city of** J, G2642
Gal 4:26 But the J that is above is free, and she is G2642
Heb 12:22 the city of the living God, the heavenly J. G2642
Rev 3:12 of my God, the new J, which is coming G2642
Rev 21: 2 Holy City, the new J, coming down out of G2642
Rev 21:10 me the Holy City, J, coming down out of G2642

JERUSALEM'S (3) [JERUSALEM]

Ne 4: 7 that the repairs to J walls had gone H3731
Isa 62: 1 for J sake I will not remain quiet H3731
Zec 12: 7 of David and of J inhabitants may not H3731

JERUSHA (2)

2Ki 15:33 mother's name was J daughter of Zadok. H3729
2Ch 27: 1 mother's name was J daughter of Zadok. H3730

JESARELAH (1)

1Ch 25:14 the seventh to J, his sons and relatives 12 H3777

JESHAIAH (7)

1Ch 3:21 Pelatiah and J, and the sons of Rephaiah H3832
1Ch 25: 3 Gedaliah, Zeri, J, Shimei, Hashabiah H3833
1Ch 25:15 the eighth to J, his sons and relatives 12 H3833
1Ch 26:25 Rehabiah his son, J his son, Joram his H3833
Ezr 8: 7 of Elam, J son of Athaliah, and H3832
Ezr 8:19 together with J from the descendants of H3832
Ne 11: 7 Maaseiah, the son of Ithiel, the son of J, H3832

JESHANAH (3)

2Ch 13:19 the towns of Bethel, J and Ephron, with H3827
Ne 3: 6 The J Gate was repaired by Joiada son of H3827
Ne 12:39 of Ephraim, the J Gate, the Fish Gate, H3827

JESHEBEAB (1)

1Ch 24:13 thirteenth to Huppah, the fourteenth to J, H3784

JESHER (1)

1Ch 2:18 were her sons: J, Shobab and Ardon. H3840

JESHIMON (4)

1Sa 23:19 Horesh, on the hill of Hakilah, south of J? H3810
1Sa 23:24 Desert of Maon, in the Arabah south of J. H3810
1Sa 26: 1 on the hill of Hakilah, which faces J?" H3810
1Sa 26: 3 the road on the hill of Hakilah facing J, H3810

JESHIMOTH See BETH JESHIMOTH

JESHISHAI (1)

1Ch 5:14 of Michael, the son of J, the son of Jahdo, H3814

JESHOHAIAH (1)

1Ch 4:36 Elioenai, Jaakobah, J, Asaiah, Adiel H3797

JESHUA (17)

1Ch 24:11 the ninth to J, the tenth to Shekaniah, H3800
2Ch 31:15 Miniamin, J, Shemaiah, Amariah H3800
Ezr 2: 6 through the line of J and Joab) 2,812 H3800
Ezr 2:36 of Jedaiah (through the family of J) 973 H3800
Ezr 2:40 the descendants of J and Kadmiel (of the H3800
Ezr 8:33 Jozabad son of J and Noadiah son of H3800
Ne 3:19 Next to him, Ezer son of J, ruler of Mizpah H3800
Ne 7:11 through the line of J and Joab) 2,818 H3800
Ne 7:39 of Jedaiah (through the family of J) 973 H3800
Ne 7:43 the descendants of J (through Kadmiel H3800
Ne 8: 7 The Levites—J, Bani, Sherebiah, Jamin H3800
Ne 9: 4 on the stairs of the Levites were J, H3800
Ne 9: 5 And the Levites—J, Kadmiel, Bani H3800
Ne 10: 9 J son of Azaniah, Binnui of the sons of H3800
Ne 11:26 in J, in Moladah, in Beth Pelet, H3801
Ne 12: 8 The Levites were J, Binnui, Kadmiel H3800
Ne 12:24 Sherebiah, J son of Kadmiel, and their H3800

JESHURUN (4)

Dt 32:15 J grew fat and kicked; filled with food H3843
Dt 33: 5 He was king over J when the leaders of H3843
Dt 33:26 "There is no one like the God of J, who H3843
Isa 44: 2 my servant, J, whom I have chosen. H3843

JESIMIEL (1)

1Ch 4:36 Jeshohaiah, Asaiah, Adiel, J, Benaiah, H3774

JESSE (42) [JESSE'S]

Ru 4:17 He was the father of J, the father of David. H3805
Ru 4:22 Obed the father of J, and Jesse the father H3805
Ru 4:22 father of Jesse, and J the father of David. H3805
1Sa 16: 1 I am sending you to J of Bethlehem. H3805
1Sa 16: 3 Invite J to the sacrifice, and I will show you H3805
1Sa 16: 5 Then he consecrated J and his sons and H3805
1Sa 16: 8 Then J called Abinadab and had him H3805
1Sa 16: 9 J then had Shammah pass by, but Samuel H3805
1Sa 16:10 J had seven of his sons pass before H3805
1Sa 16:11 So he asked J, "Are these all the sons you H3805
1Sa 16:11 is still the youngest," J answered. "He is NDT
1Sa 16:18 "I have seen a son of J of Bethlehem who H3805
1Sa 16:19 Then Saul sent messengers to J and said H3805
1Sa 16:20 So J took a donkey loaded with bread, H3805
1Sa 16:22 Then Saul sent word to J, saying, "Allow H3805
1Sa 17:12 was the son of an Ephrathite named J, H3805
1Sa 17:12 J had eight sons, and in Saul's time he H2257S
1Sa 17:17 Now J said to his son David, "Take this H3805
1Sa 17:20 loaded up and set out, as J had directed. H3805
1Sa 17:58 the son of your servant J of Bethlehem." H3805
1Sa 20:27 hasn't the son of J come to the meal, H3805
1Sa 20:30 with the son of J to your own shame and H3805
1Sa 20:31 As long as the son of J lives on this earth H3805
1Sa 22: 7 Will the son of J give all of you fields H3805
1Sa 22: 8 son makes a covenant with the son of J. H3805
1Sa 22: 9 "I saw the son of J come to Ahimelek son H3805
1Sa 22:13 you and the son of J, giving him bread H3805
1Sa 25:10 Who is this son of J? Many servants are H3805
2Sa 23: 1 "The inspired utterance of David son of J H3805
1Ch 2:12 father of Obed and Obed the father of J. H3805
1Ch 2:13 J was the father of Eliab his firstborn; the H414
1Ch 10:14 the kingdom over to David son of J. H3805
1Ch 12:18 are with you, son of J! Success, success to H3805
1Ch 29:26 David son of J was king over all Israel. H3805
Ps 72:20 concludes the prayers of David son of J. H3805
Isa 11: 1 A shoot will come up from the stump of J H3805
Isa 11:10 that day the Root of J will stand as a H3805
Mt 1: 5 mother was Ruth, Obed the father of J, G2649
Mt 1: 6 J the father of King David. David was G2649
Lk 3:32 the son *of* J, the son of Obed, the son of G2649
Ac 13:22 'I have found David son *of* J, a man after G2649
Ro 15:12 "The Root *of* J will spring up, one G2649

JESSE'S (5) [JESSE]

1Sa 17:13 J three oldest sons had followed Saul to H3805
2Sa 20: 1 have no share in David, no part in J son! H3805
1Ki 12:16 do we have in David, what part in J son? H3805
2Ch 10:16 do we have in David, what part in J son? H3805
2Ch 11:18 of Abihail, the daughter of J son Eliab. H3805

JESUS (1266) [JESUS']

Mt 1: 1 is the genealogy *of* J the Messiah the son G2652
Mt 1:16 was the mother of J who is called the G2652
Mt 1:18 is how the birth *of* J the Messiah came G2652
Mt 1:21 you are to give him the name J G2652
Mt 1:25 And he gave him the name J. G2652
Mt 2: 1 After J was born in Bethlehem in Judea G2652
Mt 3:13 Then J came from Galilee to the Jordan G2652
Mt 3:15 J replied, "Let it be so now; it is proper G2652
Mt 3:16 As soon as J was baptized, he went up G2652
Mt 4: 1 Then J was led by the Spirit into the G2652
Mt 4: 4 J answered, "It is written: 'Man shall not G3836S
Mt 4: 7 J answered him, "It is also written: 'Do G2652
Mt 4:10 J said to him, "Away from me, Satan! For G2652
Mt 4:12 When J heard that John had been put in NDT
Mt 4:17 From that time on J began to preach G2652
Mt 4:18 As J was walking beside the Sea of Galilee NDT
Mt 4:19 J said, "and I will send you out to fish for NDT
Mt 4:21 preparing their nets. J called them, NDT
Mt 4:23 J went throughout Galilee, teaching in their NDT
Mt 5: 1 Now when J saw the crowds, he went up on NDT
Mt 7:28 When J had finished saying these things G2652
Mt 8: 1 When J came down from the G899S
Mt 8: 3 J reached out his hand and touched the NDT
Mt 8: 4 Then J said to him, "See that you don't G2652
Mt 8: 5 When J had entered Capernaum, G899S
Mt 8: 7 J said to him, "Shall I come and heal him?" NDT
Mt 8:10 When J heard this, he was amazed and G2652
Mt 8:13 Then J said to the centurion, "Go! Let it G2652
Mt 8:14 When J came into Peter's house, he saw G2652
Mt 8:18 When J saw the crowd around him, he G2652
Mt 8:20 J replied, "Foxes have dens and birds G2652
Mt 8:22 But J told him, "Follow me, and let the G2652
Mt 8:24 swept over the boat. But J was sleeping. G899S
Mt 8:31 The demons begged J, "If you drive us out, G899S
Mt 8:34 Then the whole town went out to meet J G2652
Mt 9: 1 J stepped into a boat, crossed over and NDT
Mt 9: 2 When J saw their faith, he said to the G2652
Mt 9: 4 their thoughts, J said, "Why do you G2652
Mt 9: 9 As J went on from there, he saw a man G2652
Mt 9:10 While J was having dinner at Matthew's G899S
Mt 9:12 On hearing this, J said, "It is not the G3836S
Mt 9:15 J answered, "How can the guests of the G2652
Mt 9:19 J got up and went with him, and so did his G2652
Mt 9:22 J turned and saw her. "Take heart G2652
Mt 9:23 When J entered the synagogue leader's G2652
Mt 9:27 As J went on from there, two blind men G2652
Mt 9:30 J warned them sternly, "See that no one G2652
Mt 9:32 could not talk was brought *to* J. G899S
Mt 9:35 J went through all the towns and villages G2652
Mt 10: 1 J called his twelve disciples to him and NDT
Mt 10: 5 These twelve J sent out with the following G2652
Mt 11: 1 After J had finished instructing his twelve G2652
Mt 11: 4 J replied, "Go back and report to John G2652
Mt 11: 7 J began to speak to the crowd about John: G2652
Mt 11:20 Then J began to denounce the towns in NDT
Mt 11:25 At that time J said, "I praise you, Father G2652
Mt 12: 1 At that time J went through the G2652
Mt 12:10 a reason to bring charges against J, G899S
Mt 12:14 out and plotted how they might kill J. G899S
Mt 12:15 Aware of this, J withdrew from that place G2652
Mt 12:22 blind and mute, and J healed him, so that NDT
Mt 12:25 J knew their thoughts and said to them NDT
Mt 12:46 While J was still talking to the crowd, his G899S
Mt 13: 1 That same day J went out of the house G2652
Mt 13:24 J told them another parable: "The kingdom NDT
Mt 13:34 J spoke all these things to the crowd in G2652
Mt 13:51 understood all these things?" J asked. "Yes," NDT
Mt 13:53 When J had finished these parables, he G2652
Mt 13:57 But J said to them, "A prophet is not G2652
Mt 14: 1 the tetrarch heard the reports *about* J, G2652
Mt 14:12 buried it. Then they went and told J. G2652
Mt 14:13 When J heard what had happened, he G2652
Mt 14:14 When J landed and saw a large crowd, he NDT
Mt 14:16 J replied, "They do not need to go away G2652
Mt 14:22 Immediately J made the disciples get into NDT
Mt 14:25 Shortly before dawn J went out to them NDT
Mt 14:27 But J immediately said to them: "Take G2652
Mt 14:29 walked on the water and came toward J. G2652
Mt 14:31 Immediately J reached out his hand and G2652
Mt 14:35 when the men of that place recognized J, G899S
Mt 15: 1 of the law came to J from Jerusalem and G2652
Mt 15: 3 J replied, "And why do you break the G3836S
Mt 15:10 J called the crowd to him and said, "Listen NDT
Mt 15:16 "Are you still so dull?" J asked them. G3836S
Mt 15:21 J withdrew to the region of Tyre and G2652
Mt 15:23 J did not answer a word. So his disciples G3836S
Mt 15:28 Then J said to her, "Woman, you have G2652
Mt 15:29 J left there and went along the Sea of G2652
Mt 15:32 J called his disciples to him and said, "I G2652
Mt 15:34 loaves do you have?" J asked. "Seven," G2652
Mt 15:39 After J had sent the crowd away, he got into NDT
Mt 16: 1 Sadducees came to J and tested him by NDT
Mt 16: 4 J then left them and went away NDT
Mt 16: 6 "Be careful," J said to them. "Be on your G2652
Mt 16: 8 of their discussion, J asked, "You of little G2652
Mt 16:13 When J came to the region of Caesarea G2652
Mt 16:17 J replied, "Blessed are you, Simon son of G2652
Mt 16:21 From that time on J began to explain to G2652
Mt 16:23 J turned and said to Peter, "Get behind G3836S
Mt 16:24 Then J said to his disciples, "Whoever G2652
Mt 17: 1 After six days J took with him Peter G2652
Mt 17: 3 them Moses and Elijah, talking with J. G899S
Mt 17: 4 Peter said *to* J, "Lord, it is good for us to G2652
Mt 17: 7 But J came and touched them. "Get up," G2652
Mt 17: 8 they looked up, they saw no one except J. G2652
Mt 17: 9 down the mountain, J instructed them G2652
Mt 17:11 J replied, "To be sure, Elijah comes and G3836S
Mt 17:14 a man approached J and knelt before him G899S
Mt 17:17 J replied, "how long shall I stay with you? G2652
Mt 17:18 J rebuked the demon, and it came out of G2652
Mt 17:19 disciples came to J in private and asked, G2652
Mt 17:24 After **J and his disciples** arrived in G899S
Mt 17:25 into the house, J was the first to speak. G2652
Mt 17:26 the children are exempt," J said to him. G2652
Mt 18: 1 time the disciples came to J and asked, G2652
Mt 18:21 Then Peter came to J and asked, "Lord G899S
Mt 18:22 J answered, "I tell you, not seven times G2652
Mt 19: 1 When J had finished saying these things G2652
Mt 19: 8 J replied, "Moses permitted you to divorce NDT
Mt 19:11 J replied, "Not everyone can accept this G3836S
Mt 19:13 little children to J for him to place his G899S
Mt 19:14 J said, "Let the little children come to me G2652
Mt 19:16 Just then a man came up to J and asked G899S
Mt 19:17 about what is good?" J replied. "There is G3836S
Mt 19:18 J replied, " 'You shall not murder, you G2652
Mt 19:21 J answered, "If you want to be perfect, go G2652
Mt 19:23 Then J said to his disciples, "Truly I tell G2652
Mt 19:26 J looked at them and said, "With man G2652
Mt 19:28 J said to them, "Truly I tell you, at the G2652
Mt 20:17 Now J was going up to Jerusalem. On the G2652
Mt 20:20 sons came to J with her sons and, G899S
Mt 20:22 what you are asking," J said to them. G2652
Mt 20:23 J said to them, "You will indeed drink from NDT
Mt 20:25 J called them together and said, "You G2652
Mt 20:29 As **J and his disciples** were leaving G899S
Mt 20:30 when they heard that J was going by G2652
Mt 20:32 J stopped and called them. "What do you G2652
Mt 20:34 J had compassion on them and touched G2652
Mt 21: 1 the Mount of Olives, J sent two disciples, G2652
Mt 21: 6 went and did as J had instructed them. G2652
Mt 21: 7 placed their cloaks on them for J to sit on. NDT
Mt 21:10 When J entered Jerusalem, the whole city G899S
Mt 21:11 answered, "This is J, the prophet from G2652
Mt 21:12 J entered the temple courts and drove out G2652
Mt 21:16 replied J, "have you never read, G2652
Mt 21:18 as J was on his way back to the city NDT
Mt 21:21 J replied, "Truly I tell you, if you have G2652
Mt 21:23 J entered the temple courts, and, while G899S
Mt 21:24 J replied, "I will also ask you one G2652
Mt 21:27 So they answered J, "We don't know." G2652
Mt 21:31 J said to them, "Truly I tell you, the tax G2652
Mt 21:42 J said to them, "Have you never read in G2652
Mt 22: 1 J spoke to them again in parables, saying: G2652
Mt 22:18 But J, knowing their evil intent, said, "You G2652
Mt 22:29 J replied, "You are in error because you G2652
Mt 22:34 Hearing that J had silenced the Sadducees NDT
Mt 22:37 J replied: " 'Love the Lord your God with G3836S
Mt 22:41 were gathered together, J asked them, G2652
Mt 23: 1 Then J said to the crowds and to his G2652
Mt 24: 1 J left the temple and was walking away G2652
Mt 24: 3 As J was sitting on the Mount of Olives G899S
Mt 24: 4 J answered: "Watch out that no one G2652
Mt 26: 1 When J had finished saying all these G2652
Mt 26: 4 schemed to arrest J secretly and kill him. G2652
Mt 26: 6 While J was in Bethany in the home of G2652
Mt 26:10 Aware of this, J said to them, "Why are G2652
Mt 26:17 the disciples came to J and asked G2652
Mt 26:19 the disciples did as J had directed them G2652
Mt 26:20 J was reclining at the table with the Twelve. NDT
Mt 26:23 J replied, "The one who has dipped his G3836S
Mt 26:25 mean me, Rabbi?" J answered, "You have NDT
Mt 26:26 they were eating, J took bread, and when G2652
Mt 26:31 Then J told them, "This very night you will G2652
Mt 26:34 "Truly I tell you," J answered, "this very G2652
Mt 26:36 Then J went with his disciples to a place G2652
Mt 26:49 Going at once to J, Judas said, "Greetings G2652
Mt 26:50 J replied, "Do what you came for, friend." G2652
Mt 26:50 forward, seized J and arrested him. G2652
Mt 26:52 J said to him, "for all who draw the G2652
Mt 26:55 In that hour J said to the crowd, "Am I G2652
Mt 26:57 who had arrested J took him to Caiaphas G2652
Mt 26:59 evidence against J so that they could put G2652
Mt 26:62 the high priest stood up and said *to* J, G899S
Mt 26:63 But J remained silent. The high priest said G2652
Mt 26:64 "You have said so," J replied. "But I say to G2652
Mt 26:69 "You also were with J of Galilee," she G2652
Mt 26:71 "This fellow was with J of Nazareth." G2652
Mt 26:75 remembered the word J had spoken: G2652
Mt 27: 1 made their plans how to have J executed. G2652
Mt 27: 3 saw that J was condemned, he was NDT
Mt 27:11 Meanwhile J stood before the governor G2652
Mt 27:11 "You have said so," J replied. G2652
Mt 27:14 But J made no reply, not even to a single NDT
Mt 27:16 prisoner whose name was J Barabbas. G2652
Mt 27:17 J Barabbas, or Jesus who is called the G2652
Mt 27:17 Barabbas, or J who is called the Messiah?" G2652
Mt 27:18 that they had handed J over to him. G899S
Mt 27:20 ask for Barabbas and to have J executed. G2652
Mt 27:22 *with* J who is called the Messiah? G2652
Mt 27:26 But he had J flogged, and handed him G2652
Mt 27:27 soldiers took J into the Praetorium and G2652
Mt 27:34 There they offered J wine to drink, mixed G899S
Mt 27:37 THIS IS J, THE KING OF THE JEWS G2652
Mt 27:46 in the afternoon J cried out in a loud G2652
Mt 27:48 it on a staff, and offered it *to* J to drink. G899S
Mt 27:50 And when J had cried out again in a loud G2652
Mt 27:54 who were guarding J saw the earthquake G2652
Mt 27:55 They had followed J from Galilee to care G2652
Mt 27:57 who had himself become a disciple *of* J. G2652
Mt 28: 5 I know that you are looking for J, who G2652
Mt 28: 9 Suddenly J met them. "Greetings," he said G2652
Mt 28:10 Then J said to them, "Do not be afraid. G2652
Mt 28:16 the mountain where J had told them to G2652
Mt 28:18 Then J came to them and said, "All G2652
Mk 1: 1 of the good news *about* J the Messiah, G2652
Mk 1: 9 At that time J came from Nazareth in G2652
Mk 1:10 Just as J was coming up out of the water, he NDT
Mk 1:14 was put in prison, J went into Galilee G2652
Mk 1:16 As J walked beside the Sea of Galilee, he NDT
Mk 1:17 J said, "and I will send you out to fish G2652
Mk 1:21 J went into the synagogue and began to NDT
Mk 1:24 do you want with us, J of Nazareth? Have G2652
Mk 1:25 said J sternly. "Come out of G2652
Mk 1:30 they immediately told J about her. G899S
Mk 1:32 the people brought to J all the sick and G899S
Mk 1:34 J healed many who had various NDT
Mk 1:35 it was still dark, J got up, left the house NDT
Mk 1:38 J replied, "Let us go somewhere else—to NDT
Mk 1:41 J was indignant. He reached out his hand NDT
Mk 1:43 J sent him away at once with a strong NDT
Mk 1:45 J could no longer enter a town openly G899S
Mk 2: 1 when J again entered Capernaum NDT
Mk 2: 4 not get him to J because of the crowd G899S
Mk 2: 4 in the roof **above** J by digging G3963+1639S
Mk 2: 5 When J saw their faith, he said to the G2652
Mk 2: 8 Immediately J knew in his spirit that this G2652
Mk 2:13 Once again J went out beside the lake. NDT
Mk 2:14 J told him, and Levi got up and followed NDT
Mk 2:15 While J was having dinner at Levi's house G899S
Mk 2:17 On hearing this, J said to them, "It is not G2652
Mk 2:18 Some people came and asked J, "How is G899S
Mk 2:19 J answered, "How can the guests of the G2652
Mk 2:23 One Sabbath J was going through the G899S
Mk 3: 1 Another time J went into the synagogue NDT
Mk 3: 2 were looking for a reason to accuse J, G899S
Mk 3: 3 J said to the man with the shriveled hand NDT
Mk 3: 4 Then J asked them, "Which is lawful on the NDT
Mk 3: 6 with the Herodians how they might kill J. G899S
Mk 3: 7 J withdrew with his disciples to the lake G2652
Mk 3:13 J went up on a mountainside and called to NDT
Mk 3:20 Then J entered a house, and again a crowd NDT
Mk 3:23 So J called them over to him and began to NDT
Mk 4: 1 Again J began to teach by the lake. NDT
Mk 4: 9 Then J said, "Whoever has ears to hear, let NDT
Mk 4:13 Then J said to them, "Don't you understand NDT
Mk 4:33 many similar parables J spoke the word to NDT
Mk 4:38 J was in the stern, sleeping on a cushion G899S
Mk 5: 2 When J got out of the boat, a man with an G899S
Mk 5: 6 When he saw J from a distance, he ran G2652
Mk 5: 7 do you want with me, J, Son of the Most G2652
Mk 5: 8 For J had said to him, "Come out of this man, NDT
Mk 5: 9 Then J asked him, "What is your name?" NDT
Mk 5:10 And he begged J again and again not to G899S
Mk 5:12 The demons begged J, "Send us among G899S
Mk 5:15 When they came to J, they saw the man G2652
Mk 5:17 began to plead with J to leave their G899S
Mk 5:18 As J was getting into the boat, the man G899S
Mk 5:19 J did not let him, but said, "Go home to your NDT
Mk 5:20 Decapolis how much J had done for him. G2652
Mk 5:21 When J had again crossed over by boat to G2652
Mk 5:22 when he saw J, he fell at his feet. G899S
Mk 5:24 So J went with him. A large crowd followed NDT
Mk 5:27 When she heard about J, she came up G2652
Mk 5:30 At once J realized that power had gone G2652
Mk 5:32 But J kept looking around to see who had NDT
Mk 5:35 While J was still speaking, some people G899S
Mk 5:36 what they said, J told him, "Don't be G2652
Mk 5:38 synagogue leader, J saw a commotion, with NDT
Mk 6: 1 J left there and went to his hometown NDT
Mk 6: 4 J said to them, "A prophet is not without G2652
Mk 6: 6 Then J went around teaching from village to NDT
Mk 6:30 gathered around J and reported to him all G2652
Mk 6:34 When J landed and saw a large crowd, he NDT
Mk 6:39 Then J directed them to have all the people NDT
Mk 6:45 Immediately J made his disciples get into NDT
Mk 6:54 got out of the boat, people recognized J. G899S
Mk 7: 1 come from Jerusalem gathered around J G899S
Mk 7: 5 teachers of the law asked J, G899S
Mk 7:14 Again J called the crowd to him and said NDT
Mk 7:19 In saying this, J declared all foods clean.) NDT
Mk 7:24 J left that place and went to the vicinity of NDT
Mk 7:26 She begged J to drive the demon out of G899S
Mk 7:31 Then J left the vicinity of Tyre and went NDT
Mk 7:32 they begged J to place his hand on G899S
Mk 7:33 J put his fingers into the man's ears. NDT
Mk 7:36 J commanded them not to tell anyone. NDT
Mk 8: 1 J called his disciples to him and said, NDT
Mk 8: 5 many loaves do you have?" J asked. "Seven," NDT

Mk 8:11 Pharisees came and began to question **J**. G899S
Mk 8:15 "Be careful," **J** warned them. "Watch out NDT
Mk 8:17 their discussion, **J** asked them: "Why are G2652
Mk 8:22 a blind man and begged **J** to touch him. G899S
Mk 8:23 put his hands on him, **J** asked, "Do you see NDT
Mk 8:25 Once more **J** put his hands on the man's NDT
Mk 8:26 **J** sent him home, saying, "Don't even go NDT
Mk 8:27 **J** and his disciples went on to the villages G2652
Mk 8:30 **J** warned them not to tell anyone about him. NDT
Mk 8:33 But when **J** turned and looked at his G3836S
Mk 9: 2 After six days **J** took Peter, James and G2652
Mk 9: 4 Moses, who were talking with **J**. G2652
Mk 9: 5 Peter said *to* **J**, "Rabbi, it is good for us to G2652
Mk 9: 8 no longer saw anyone with them except **J**. G2652
Mk 9: 9 **J** gave them orders not to tell anyone what NDT
Mk 9:12 **J** replied, "To be sure, Elijah does come G3836S
Mk 9:15 As soon as all the people saw **J**, they were G899S
Mk 9:19 **J** replied, "how long shall I stay with G3836S
Mk 9:20 When the spirit saw **J**, it immediately G899S
Mk 9:21 **J** asked the boy's father, "How long has he NDT
Mk 9:23 " 'If you can'?" said **J**. "Everything is G2652
Mk 9:25 When **J** saw that a crowd was running to G2652
Mk 9:27 But **J** took him by the hand and lifted him G2652
Mk 9:28 After **J** had gone indoors, his disciples G899S
Mk 9:30 **J** did not want anyone to know where they NDT
Mk 9:35 Sitting down, **J** called the Twelve and said NDT
Mk 9:39 "Do not stop him," **J** said. "For no one G2652
Mk 10: 1 **J** then left that place and went into the NDT
Mk 10: 5 that Moses wrote you this law," **J** replied. G2652
Mk 10:10 the disciples asked **J** about this. G899S
Mk 10:13 little children to **J** for him to place his G899S
Mk 10:14 When **J** saw this, he was indignant. G2652
Mk 10:17 As **J** started on his way, a man ran up to G899S
Mk 10:18 you call me good?" **J** answered. "No one G2652
Mk 10:21 **J** looked at him and loved him. "One G2652
Mk 10:23 **J** looked around and said to his disciples G2652
Mk 10:24 But **J** said again, "Children, how hard it is G2652
Mk 10:27 **J** looked at them and said, "With man G2652
Mk 10:29 **J** replied, "no one who has left home G2652
Mk 10:32 to Jerusalem, with **J** leading the way, and G2652
Mk 10:38 don't know what you are asking," **J** said. G2652
Mk 10:39 **J** said to them, "You will drink the cup I G2652
Mk 10:42 **J** called them together and said, "You G2652
Mk 10:46 As **J** and his disciples, together with a G899S
Mk 10:47 When he heard that it was **J** of Nazareth G2652
Mk 10:47 he began to shout, "**J**, Son of David, have G2652
Mk 10:49 **J** stopped and said, "Call him." So they G2652
Mk 10:50 he jumped to his feet and came to **J**. G2652
Mk 10:51 me to do for you?" **J** asked him. The blind G2652
Mk 10:52 said **J**, "your faith has healed you. G2652
Mk 10:52 his sight and followed **J** along the road. G899S
Mk 11: 1 Mount of Olives, **J** sent two of his disciples NDT
Mk 11: 6 They answered as **J** had told them to, and G2652
Mk 11: 7 brought the colt to **J** and threw their G2652
Mk 11:11 **J** entered Jerusalem and went into the NDT
Mk 11:12 as they were leaving Bethany, **J** was hungry. NDT
Mk 11:15 **J** entered the temple courts and began NDT
Mk 11:19 **J** and his disciples went out of the city. NDT
Mk 11:21 Peter remembered and said *to* **J**, "Rabbi G899S
Mk 11:22 "Have faith in God," **J** answered. G2652
Mk 11:27 while **J** was walking in the temple G899S
Mk 11:29 **J** replied, "I will ask you one question G2652
Mk 11:33 So they answered **J**, "We don't know." G2652
Mk 11:33 **J** said, "Neither will I tell you by what G2652
Mk 12: 1 **J** then began to speak to them in parables NDT
Mk 12:13 Herodians to **J** to catch him in his G899S
Mk 12:15 shouldn't we?" But **J** knew their hypocrisy G3836S
Mk 12:17 Then **J** said to them, "Give back to Caesar G2652
Mk 12:24 **J** replied, "Are you not in error because G2652
Mk 12:28 Noticing that **J** had given them a good NDT
Mk 12:29 most important one," answered **J**, "is this: G2652
Mk 12:34 When **J** saw that he had answered wisely G2652
Mk 12:35 While **J** was teaching in the temple courts G2652
Mk 12:38 As he taught, **J** said, "Watch out for the NDT
Mk 12:41 **J** sat down opposite the place where the NDT
Mk 12:43 his disciples to him, **J** said, "Truly I tell you, NDT
Mk 13: 1 As **J** was leaving the temple, one of his G899S
Mk 13: 2 replied **J**. "Not one stone here G2652
Mk 13: 3 As **J** was sitting on the Mount of Olives G899S
Mk 13: 5 **J** said to them: "Watch out that no one G2652
Mk 14: 1 scheming to arrest **J** secretly and kill him. NDT
Mk 14: 6 her alone," said **J**. "Why are you G2652
Mk 14:10 to the chief priests to betray **J** to them. G899S
Mk 14:16 found things just as **J** had told them. NDT
Mk 14:17 evening came, **J** arrived with the Twelve. NDT
Mk 14:22 they were eating, **J** took bread, and when NDT
Mk 14:27 will all fall away," **J** told them, "for it is G2652
Mk 14:30 "Truly I tell you," **J** answered, "today—yes, G2652
Mk 14:32 Gethsemane, and **J** said to his disciples NDT
Mk 14:45 Going at once to **J**, Judas said, "Rabbi!" G899S
Mk 14:46 The men seized **J** and arrested him. G899S
Mk 14:48 said **J**, "that you have come out with G2652
Mk 14:51 a linen garment, was following **J**. G899S
Mk 14:53 They took **J** to the high priest, and all the G2652
Mk 14:55 evidence against **J** so that they could G2652
Mk 14:60 priest stood up before them and asked **J**, G2652
Mk 14:61 But **J** remained silent and gave no G3836S
Mk 14:62 said **J**. "And you will see the Son G2652
Mk 14:67 were with that Nazarene, **J**," she said. G2652
Mk 14:72 the word **J** had spoken to him: G2652
Mk 15: 1 So they bound **J**, led him away and G2652
Mk 15: 2 "You have said so," **J** replied. G3836S
Mk 15: 5 But **J** still made no reply, and Pilate was G2652
Mk 15:10 chief priests had handed **J** over to him. G899S
Mk 15:15 He had **J** flogged, and handed him over G2652
Mk 15:16 The soldiers led **J** away into the palace G899S
Mk 15:22 They brought **J** to the place called G899S
Mk 15:34 in the afternoon **J** cried out in a loud G2652
Mk 15:36 put it on a staff, and offered it *to* **J** to drink. G899
Mk 15:37 With a loud cry, **J** breathed his last. G2652
Mk 15:39 who stood there in front of **J**, saw how he G899S
Mk 15:44 he asked him if **J** had already died. NDT
Mk 16: 6 "You are looking for **J** the Nazarene, who G2652
Mk 16: 9 When **J** rose early on the first day of the NDT
Mk 16:11 When they heard that **J** was alive and that NDT
Mk 16:12 Afterward **J** appeared in a different form to NDT
Mk 16:14 Later **J** appeared to the Eleven as they were NDT
Mk 16:19 After the Lord **J** had spoken to them, he G2652
Lk 1:31 birth to a son, and you are to call him **J**. G2652
Lk 2:21 he was named **J**, the name the angel G2652
Lk 2:27 brought in the child **J** to do for him what G2652
Lk 2:43 the boy **J** stayed behind in Jerusalem G2652
Lk 2:52 And **J** grew in wisdom and stature, and in G2652
Lk 3:21 were being baptized, **J** was baptized too. G2652
Lk 3:23 Now **J** himself was about thirty years old G2652
Lk 4: 1 **J**, full of the Holy Spirit, left the Jordan G2652
Lk 4: 4 **J** answered, "It is written: 'Man shall not G2652
Lk 4: 8 **J** answered, "It is written: 'Worship the G2652
Lk 4:12 **J** answered, "It is said: 'Do not put the G2652
Lk 4:14 **J** returned to Galilee in the power of the G2652
Lk 4:23 **J** said to them, "Surely you will quote this NDT
Lk 4:34 do you want with us, **J** of Nazareth? Have G2652
Lk 4:35 **J** said sternly. "Come out of G2652
Lk 4:38 **J** left the synagogue and went to the home NDT
Lk 4:38 a high fever, and they asked **J** to help her. G899S
Lk 4:40 people brought to **J** all who had various G899S
Lk 4:42 At daybreak, **J** went out to a solitary place NDT
Lk 5: 1 One day as **J** was standing by the Lake of G899S
Lk 5:10 Then **J** said to Simon, "Don't be afraid G2652
Lk 5:12 While **J** was in one of the towns, a man G899S
Lk 5:12 When he saw **J**, he fell with his face to G2652
Lk 5:13 **J** reached out his hand and touched the NDT
Lk 5:14 Then **J** ordered him, "Don't tell anyone G899S
Lk 5:16 But **J** often withdrew to lonely places and G899S
Lk 5:17 One day **J** was teaching, and Pharisees G899S
Lk 5:17 of the Lord was *with* **J** to heal the sick. G899S
Lk 5:18 him into the house to lay him before **J**. G899S
Lk 5:19 the middle of the crowd, right in front of **J**. G2652
Lk 5:20 When **J** saw their faith, he said, "Friend NDT
Lk 5:22 **J** knew what they were thinking and asked G2652
Lk 5:27 **J** went out and saw a tax collector by the NDT
Lk 5:27 at his tax booth. "Follow me," **J** said to him, NDT
Lk 5:29 held a great banquet *for* **J** at his house, G899S
Lk 5:31 **J** answered them, "It is not the healthy G2652
Lk 5:34 **J** answered, "Can you make the friends of G2652
Lk 6: 1 One Sabbath **J** was going through the G899S
Lk 6: 3 **J** answered them, "Have you never read G2652
Lk 6: 5 Then **J** said to them, "The Son of Man is NDT
Lk 6: 7 law were looking for a reason to accuse **J**, G899S
Lk 6: 8 But **J** knew what they were thinking and G899S
Lk 6: 9 Then **J** said to them, "I ask you, which is G2652
Lk 6:11 with one another what they might do *to* **J**. G2652
Lk 6:12 One of those days **J** went out to a G899S
Lk 7: 1 When **J** had finished saying all this to the G899S
Lk 7: 3 centurion heard of **J** and sent some elders G2652
Lk 7: 4 When they came to **J**, they pleaded G2652
Lk 7: 6 So **J** went with them. He was not far from G2652
Lk 7: 9 When **J** heard this, he was amazed at G2652
Lk 7:11 afterward, **J** went to a town called Nain NDT
Lk 7:15 and **J** gave him back to his mother. NDT
Lk 7:17 This news about **J** spread throughout G899S
Lk 7:20 When the men came to **J**, they said G899S
Lk 7:21 At that very time **J** cured many who had NDT
Lk 7:24 **J** began to speak to the crowd about John: NDT
Lk 7:31 **J** went on to say, "To what, then, can I NDT
Lk 7:36 Pharisees invited **J** to have dinner with G899S
Lk 7:37 a sinful life learned that **J** was eating at the NDT
Lk 7:40 **J** answered him, "Simon, I have G2652
Lk 7:43 "You have judged correctly," **J** said. G3836S
Lk 7:48 Then **J** said to her, "Your sins are forgiven." NDT
Lk 7:50 **J** said to the woman, "Your faith has saved NDT
Lk 8: 1 **J** traveled about from one town and G899S
Lk 8: 4 were coming to **J** from town after town, G899S
Lk 8:22 One day **J** said to his disciples, "Let us go G899S
Lk 8:27 When **J** stepped ashore, he was met by a G899S
Lk 8:28 When he saw **J**, he cried out and fell at G2652
Lk 8:28 do you want with me, **J**, Son of the Most G2652
Lk 8:29 For **J** had commanded the impure spirit to NDT
Lk 8:30 **J** asked him, "What is your name? G2652
Lk 8:31 And they begged **J** repeatedly not to order G899S
Lk 8:32 The demons begged **J** to let them go into G899S
Lk 8:35 When they came to **J**, they found the man G2652
Lk 8:37 of the Gerasenes asked **J** to leave them, G899S
Lk 8:38 to go with him, but **J** sent him away, saying, NDT
Lk 8:39 over town how much **J** had done for him. G2652
Lk 8:40 Now when **J** returned, a crowd welcomed G2652
Lk 8:42 As **J** was on his way, the crowds almost G899S
Lk 8:45 "Who touched me?" **J** asked. When they G2652
Lk 8:46 But **J** said, "Someone touched me; I know G2652
Lk 8:49 While **J** was still speaking, someone G899S
Lk 8:50 Hearing this, **J** said to Jairus, "Don't be G2652
Lk 8:52 "Stop wailing," **J** said. "She is not G3836S
Lk 8:55 Then **J** told them to give her something to NDT
Lk 9: 1 When **J** had called the Twelve together, he NDT
Lk 9:10 they reported *to* **J** what they had done. G899S
Lk 9:18 Once when **J** was praying in private and G899S
Lk 9:21 **J** strictly warned them not to tell this to G3836S
Lk 9:28 About eight days after **J** said this, he took NDT
Lk 9:30 in glorious splendor, talking *with* **J**. G899S
Lk 9:33 As the men were leaving **J**, Peter said to G2652
Lk 9:36 had spoken, they found that **J** was alone. G2652
Lk 9:41 **J** replied, "how long shall I stay with you G2652
Lk 9:42 But **J** rebuked the impure spirit, healed G2652
Lk 9:43 everyone was marveling at all that **J** did, NDT
Lk 9:47 **J**, knowing their thoughts, took a little G2652
Lk 9:50 **J** said, "for whoever is not against you is G2652
Lk 9:51 heaven, **J** resolutely set out for Jerusalem. G899S
Lk 9:55 But **J** turned and rebuked them. NDT
Lk 9:58 **J** replied, "Foxes have dens and birds G2652
Lk 9:60 **J** said to him, "Let the dead bury their own NDT
Lk 9:62 **J** replied, "No one who puts a hand to the G2652
Lk 10:21 At that time **J**, full of joy through the Holy NDT
Lk 10:25 an expert in the law stood up to test **J**. G899S
Lk 10:28 answered correctly," **J** replied. "Do this and NDT
Lk 10:29 himself, so he asked **J**, "And who is my G2652
Lk 10:30 In reply **J** said: "A man was going down G2652
Lk 10:37 had mercy on him." **J** told him, "Go and G2652
Lk 10:38 As **J and his disciples** were on their way G899S
Lk 11: 1 One day **J** was praying in a certain place G899S
Lk 11: 5 Then **J** said to them, "Suppose you have a NDT
Lk 11:14 **J** was driving out a demon that was mute NDT
Lk 11:17 **J** knew their thoughts and said to them G899S
Lk 11:27 As **J** was saying these things, a woman in G899S
Lk 11:29 the crowds increased, **J** said, "This is a NDT
Lk 11:37 When **J** had finished speaking, a Pharisee NDT
Lk 11:38 when he noticed that **J** did not first wash NDT
Lk 11:46 **J** replied, "And you experts in the law G3836S
Lk 11:53 When **J** went outside, the Pharisees and G899S
Lk 12: 1 **J** began to speak first to his disciples NDT
Lk 12:14 **J** replied, "Man, who appointed me a G3836S
Lk 12:22 Then **J** said to his disciples: "Therefore I tell NDT
Lk 13: 1 that time who told **J** about the Galileans G899S
Lk 13: 2 **J** answered, "Do you think that these NDT
Lk 13:10 On a Sabbath **J** was teaching in one of the NDT
Lk 13:12 When **J** saw her, he called her forward G2652
Lk 13:14 Indignant because **J** had healed on the G2652
Lk 13:18 Then **J** asked, "What is the kingdom of God NDT
Lk 13:22 Then **J** went through the towns and villages NDT
Lk 13:31 some Pharisees came to **J** and said to him, NDT
Lk 14: 1 when **J** went to eat in the house of a G899S
Lk 14: 3 **J** asked the Pharisees and experts in the G2652
Lk 14:12 Then **J** said to his host, "When you give a NDT
Lk 14:15 heard this, he said *to* **J**, "Blessed is the G899S
Lk 14:16 **J** replied: "A certain man was preparing G3836S
Lk 14:25 Large crowds were traveling with **J**, and G899S
Lk 15: 1 were all gathering around to hear **J**. G899S
Lk 15: 3 Then **J** told them this parable: NDT
Lk 15:11 **J** continued: "There was a man who had NDT
Lk 16: 1 **J** told his disciples: "There was a rich man NDT
Lk 16:14 heard all this and were sneering at **J**. G899S
Lk 17: 1 **J** said to his disciples: "Things that cause NDT
Lk 17:11 **J** traveled along the border between G899S
Lk 17:13 in a loud voice, "**J**, Master, have pity on G2652
Lk 17:17 **J** asked, "Were not all ten cleansed G2652
Lk 17:20 of God would come, **J** replied, "The coming NDT
Lk 18: 1 Then **J** told his disciples a parable to show NDT
Lk 18: 9 down on everyone else, **J** told this parable: NDT
Lk 18:15 bringing babies to **J** for him to place his G899S
Lk 18:16 But **J** called the children to him and said G2652
Lk 18:19 you call me good?" **J** answered. "No one G2652
Lk 18:22 When **J** heard this, he said to him, "You G2652
Lk 18:24 **J** looked at him and said, "How hard it is G2652
Lk 18:27 **J** replied, "What is impossible with man G3836S
Lk 18:29 **J** said to them, "no one who has left G3836S
Lk 18:31 **J** took the Twelve aside and told them, "We NDT
Lk 18:35 As **J** approached Jericho, a blind man G899S
Lk 18:37 told him, "**J** of Nazareth is passing by." G2652
Lk 18:38 He called out, "**J**, Son of David, have G2652
Lk 18:40 **J** stopped and ordered the man to be G2652
Lk 18:40 When he came near, **J** asked him, NDT
Lk 18:42 **J** said to him, "Receive your sight; your G2652
Lk 18:43 he received his sight and followed **J**, G899S
Lk 19: 1 **J** entered Jericho and was passing through. NDT
Lk 19: 3 He wanted to see who **J** was, but because G2652
Lk 19: 4 to see him, since **J** was coming that way. NDT
Lk 19: 5 When **J** reached the spot, he looked up G2652
Lk 19: 9 **J** said to him, "Today salvation has come G2652
Lk 19:28 After **J** had said this, he went on ahead NDT
Lk 19:35 They brought it to **J**, threw their cloaks on G2652
Lk 19:35 their cloaks on the colt and put **J** on it. G2652
Lk 19:39 of the Pharisees in the crowd said to **J**, G899S
Lk 19:45 When **J** entered the temple courts, he NDT
Lk 20: 1 One day as **J** was teaching the people in G899S
Lk 20: 8 **J** said, "Neither will I tell you by what G2652
Lk 20:17 **J** looked directly at them and asked G3836S
Lk 20:20 They hoped to catch **J** in something he G899S
Lk 20:27 resurrection, came to **J** with a question. G899S
Lk 20:34 **J** replied, "The people of this age marry G2652
Lk 20:41 Then **J** said to them, "Why is it said that the NDT
Lk 20:45 people were listening, **J** said to his disciples NDT
Lk 21: 1 As **J** looked up, he saw the rich putting their NDT
Lk 21: 5 with gifts dedicated to God. But **J** said, NDT
Lk 21:37 Each day **J** was teaching at the temple, and NDT
Lk 22: 2 were looking for some way to get rid of **J**, G899S
Lk 22: 4 with them how he might betray **J**. G899S
Lk 22: 6 opportunity to hand **J** over to them when G899S

Book	Ref	Context	Number
Lk	22: 8	**J** sent Peter and John, saying, "Go and make	NDT
Lk	22:13	found things just as **J** had told them.	NDT
Lk	22:14	**J** and his apostles reclined at the table.	G899S
Lk	22:25	**J** said to them, "The kings of the Gentiles	G3836S
Lk	22:34	**J** answered, "I tell you, Peter, before the	G3836S
Lk	22:35	Then **J** asked them, "When I sent you	NDT
Lk	22:39	**J** went out as usual to the Mount of Olives	NDT
Lk	22:47	He approached **J** to kiss him,	G2652
Lk	22:48	**J** asked him, "Judas, are you betraying	G2652
Lk	22:51	But **J** answered, "No more of this!" And	G2652
Lk	22:52	Then **J** said to the chief priests, the	G2652
Lk	22:63	who were guarding **J** began mocking and	G899S
Lk	22:66	met together, and **J** was led before them.	G899S
Lk	22:67	**J** answered, "If I tell you, you will not	NDT
Lk	23: 3	So Pilate asked **J**, "Are you the king of the	G899S
Lk	23: 3	"You have said so," **J** replied.	G3836S
Lk	23: 7	When he learned that **J** was under Herod's	NDT
Lk	23: 8	When Herod saw **J**, he was greatly	G2652
Lk	23: 9	questions, but **J** gave him no answer.	G899S
Lk	23:20	Wanting to release **J**, Pilate appealed to	G2652
Lk	23:25	asked for, and surrendered **J** to their will.	G2652
Lk	23:26	on him and made him carry it behind **J**.	G2652
Lk	23:28	**J** turned and said to them, "Daughters of	G2652
Lk	23:34	**J** said, "Father, forgive them, for they do	G2652
Lk	23:42	Then he said, "**J**, remember me when you	G2652
Lk	23:43	**J** answered him, "Truly I tell you, today you	NDT
Lk	23:46	**J** called out with a loud voice, "Father, into	G2652
Lk	23:55	who had come with **J** from Galilee followed	NDT
Lk	24: 3	they did not find the body of the Lord **J**.	G2652
Lk	24:15	**J** himself came up and walked along with	G2652
Lk	24:19	"About **J** of Nazareth," they	G2652
Lk	24:24	women had said, but they did not see **J**."	G899S
Lk	24:28	**J** continued on as if he were going farther.	G899S
Lk	24:35	how **J** was recognized by them when he	NDT
Lk	24:36	**J himself** stood among them and said to	G899S
Jn	1:17	grace and truth came through **J** Christ.	G2652
Jn	1:29	next day John saw **J** coming toward him	G2652
Jn	1:36	When he saw **J** passing by, he said, "Look	G2652
Jn	1:37	heard him say this, they followed **J**.	G2652
Jn	1:38	around, **J** saw them following and asked	G2652
Jn	1:40	John had said and who had followed **J**.	G899S
Jn	1:42	And he brought him to **J**. Jesus looked at	G2652
Jn	1:42	**J** looked at him and said, "You are Simon	G2652
Jn	1:43	The next day **J** decided to leave for	G2652
Jn	1:45	prophets also wrote—**J** of Nazareth, the	G2652
Jn	1:47	When **J** saw Nathanael approaching, he	G2652
Jn	1:48	**J** answered, "I saw you while you were	G2652
Jn	1:50	**J** said, "You believe because I told you I	G2652
Jn	2: 2	**J** and his disciples had also been	G2652
Jn	2: 4	do you involve me?" **J** replied. "My hour	G2652
Jn	2: 7	**J** said to the servants, "Fill the jars with	G2652
Jn	2:11	What **J** did here in Cana of Galilee was	G2652
Jn	2:13	Jewish Passover, **J** went up to Jerusalem.	G2652
Jn	2:19	**J** answered them, "Destroy this temple	G2652
Jn	2:22	scripture and the words that **J** had spoken.	G2652
Jn	2:24	But **J** would not entrust himself to them	G2652
Jn	3: 2	He came to **J** at night and said, "Rabbi	G899S
Jn	3: 3	**J** replied, "Very truly I tell you, no one can	G2652
Jn	3: 5	**J** answered, "Very truly I tell you, no one	G2652
Jn	3:10	said **J**, "and do you not understand these	G2652
Jn	3:22	**J** and his disciples went out into the	G2652
Jn	4: 1	Now **J** learned that the Pharisees had	G2652
Jn	4: 2	although in fact it was not **J** who baptized	G2652
Jn	4: 6	well was there, and **J**, tired as he was	G2652
Jn	4: 7	came to draw water, **J** said to her, "Will	G2652
Jn	4:10	**J** answered her, "If you knew the gift of	G2652
Jn	4:13	**J** answered, "Everyone who drinks this	G2652
Jn	4:17	**J** said to her, "You are right when you say	G2652
Jn	4:21	"Woman," **J** replied, "believe me, a time	G2652
Jn	4:26	Then **J** declared, "I, the one speaking to	G2652
Jn	4:34	said **J**, "is to do the will of him who sent	G2652
Jn	4:44	Now **J** himself had pointed out that a	G2652
Jn	4:47	this man heard that **J** had arrived in	G2652
Jn	4:48	signs and wonders," **J** told him, "you will	G2652
Jn	4:50	**J** replied, "your son will live." The	G2652
Jn	4:50	The man took **J** at his word and departed.	G2652
Jn	4:53	the exact time at which **J** had said to him,	G2652
Jn	4:54	was the second sign **J** performed after	G2652
Jn	5: 1	**J** went up to Jerusalem for one of the	G2652
Jn	5: 6	When **J** saw him lying there and learned	G2652
Jn	5: 8	Then **J** said to him, "Get up! Pick up your	G2652
Jn	5:13	**J** had slipped away into the crowd that	G2652
Jn	5:14	Later **J** found him at the temple and said	G2652
Jn	5:15	leaders that it was **J** who had made him	G2652
Jn	5:16	because **J** was doing these things on the	G2652
Jn	5:17	In his defense **J** said to them, "My Father is	NDT
Jn	5:19	**J** gave them this answer: "Very truly I tell	G2652
Jn	6: 1	**J** crossed to the far shore of the Sea of	G2652
Jn	6: 3	Then **J** went up on a mountainside and	G2652
Jn	6: 5	When **J** looked up and saw a great crowd	G2652
Jn	6:10	**J** said, "Have the people sit down." There	G2652
Jn	6:11	**J** then took the loaves, gave thanks, and	G2652
Jn	6:14	After the people saw the sign **J** performed	NDT
Jn	6:15	**J**, knowing that they intended to come	G2652
Jn	6:17	was dark, and **J** had not yet joined them.	G2652
Jn	6:19	they saw **J** approaching the boat	G2652
Jn	6:22	that **J** had not entered it with his	G2652
Jn	6:24	realized that neither **J** nor his disciples	G2652
Jn	6:24	went to Capernaum in search of **J**.	G2652
Jn	6:26	**J** answered, "Very truly I tell you, you are	G2652
Jn	6:29	**J** answered, "The work of God is this: to	G2652
Jn	6:32	**J** said to them, "Very truly I tell you, it is	G2652
Jn	6:35	Then **J** declared, "I am the bread of life	G2652
Jn	6:42	They said, "Is this not **J**, the son of Joseph	G2652
Jn	6:43	among yourselves," **J** answered.	G2652
Jn	6:53	**J** said to them, "Very truly I tell you	G2652
Jn	6:61	about this, **J** said to them, "Does	G2652
Jn	6:64	For **J** had known from the beginning	G2652
Jn	6:67	leave too, do you?" **J** asked the Twelve.	G2652
Jn	6:70	Then **J** replied, "Have I not chosen you	G2652
Jn	7: 1	After this, **J** went around in Galilee.	G2652
Jn	7: 6	Therefore **J** told them, "My time is not	G2652
Jn	7:11	leaders were watching for **J** and asking,	G899S
Jn	7:14	the festival did **J** go up to the temple	G2652
Jn	7:16	**J** answered, "My teaching is not my own	G2652
Jn	7:21	**J** said to them, "I did one miracle, and	G2652
Jn	7:28	Then **J**, still teaching in the temple courts	G2652
Jn	7:33	**J** said, "I am with you for only a short time	G2652
Jn	7:37	festival, **J** stood and said in a loud voice	G2652
Jn	7:39	since **J** had not yet been glorified.	G2652
Jn	7:43	the people were divided because of **J**.	G899S
Jn	7:50	who had gone to **J** earlier and who was	G899S
Jn	8: 1	**J** went to the Mount of Olives.	G2652
Jn	8: 4	said *to* **J**, "Teacher, this woman was	G899S
Jn	8: 6	But **J** bent down and started to write on	G2652
Jn	8: 9	ones first, until only **J** was left, with the	NDT
Jn	8:10	**J** straightened up and asked her, "Woman,	G2652
Jn	8:11	neither do I condemn you," **J** declared.	G2652
Jn	8:12	When **J** spoke again to the people, he	G2652
Jn	8:14	**J** answered, "Even if I testify on my own	G2652
Jn	8:19	do not know me or my Father," **J** replied.	G2652
Jn	8:21	Once more **J** said to them, "I am going	NDT
Jn	8:25	telling you from the beginning," **J** replied.	G2652
Jn	8:28	So **J** said, "When you have lifted up the	G2652
Jn	8:31	had believed him, **J** said, "If you hold to	G2652
Jn	8:34	**J** replied, "Very truly I tell you, everyone	G2652
Jn	8:39	said **J**, "then you would do what	G2652
Jn	8:42	**J** said to them, "If God were your Father	G2652
Jn	8:49	said **J**, "but I honor my Father and you	G2652
Jn	8:54	**J** replied, "If I glorify myself, my glory	G2652
Jn	8:58	"Very truly I tell you," **J** answered, "before	G2652
Jn	8:59	to stone him, but **J** hid himself, slipping	G2652
Jn	9: 3	said **J**, "but this happened so that the	G2652
Jn	9:11	man they call **J** made some mud and	G2652
Jn	9:14	the day on which **J** had made the mud	G2652
Jn	9:22	acknowledged that **J** was the Messiah	G899S
Jn	9:35	**J** heard that they had thrown him out, and	G2652
Jn	9:37	**J** said, "You have now seen him; in fact	G2652
Jn	9:39	**J** said, "For judgment I have come into	G2652
Jn	9:41	**J** said, "If you were blind, you would not	G2652
Jn	10: 6	**J** used this figure of speech, but the	G2652
Jn	10: 7	Therefore **J** said again, "Very truly I tell	G2652
Jn	10:23	**J** was in the temple courts walking in	G2652
Jn	10:25	**J** answered, "I did tell you, but you do not	G2652
Jn	10:32	**J** said to them, "I have shown you	G2652
Jn	10:34	**J** answered them, "Is it not written in your	G2652
Jn	10:40	Then **J** went back across the Jordan to the	NDT
Jn	10:42	And in that place many believed in **J**.	G899S
Jn	11: 3	So the sisters sent word to **J**, "Lord, the	G899S
Jn	11: 4	When he heard this, **J** said, "This sickness	G2652
Jn	11: 5	Now **J** loved Martha and her sister and	G2652
Jn	11: 9	**J** answered, "Are there not twelve hours	G2652
Jn	11:13	**J** had been speaking of his death, but his	G2652
Jn	11:17	**J** found that Lazarus had already been in	G2652
Jn	11:20	When Martha heard that **J** was coming	G2652
Jn	11:21	Martha said to **J**, "if you had been here	G2652
Jn	11:23	**J** said to her, "Your brother will rise again."	G2652
Jn	11:25	**J** said to her, "I am the resurrection and	G2652
Jn	11:30	Now **J** had not yet entered the village, but	G2652
Jn	11:32	the place where **J** was and saw him,	G2652
Jn	11:33	When **J** saw her weeping, and the Jews	G2652
Jn	11:35	**J** wept.	G2652
Jn	11:38	**J**, once more deeply moved, came to the	G2652
Jn	11:40	Then **J** said, "Did I not tell you that if you	G2652
Jn	11:41	Then **J** looked up and said, "Father,	G2652
Jn	11:43	he had said this, **J** called in a loud voice	NDT
Jn	11:44	**J** said to them, "Take off the grave clothes	G2652
Jn	11:45	had seen what **J** did, believed in him.	NDT
Jn	11:46	told them what **J** had done.	G2652
Jn	11:51	he prophesied that **J** would die for the	G2652
Jn	11:54	Therefore **J** no longer moved about	G2652
Jn	11:56	They kept looking for **J**, and as they stood	G2652
Jn	11:57	who found out where **J** was should report it	NDT
Jn	12: 1	before the Passover, **J** came to Bethany	G2652
Jn	12: 1	whom **J** had raised from the dead.	G2652
Jn	12: 7	"Leave her alone," **J** replied. "It was	G2652
Jn	12: 9	found out that **J** was there and came,	G2652
Jn	12:11	were going over to **J** and believing in him	G2652
Jn	12:12	the festival heard that **J** was on his way to	G2652
Jn	12:14	**J** found a young donkey and sat on it, as	G2652
Jn	12:16	Only after **J** was glorified did they realize	G2652
Jn	12:21	they said, "we would like to see **J**."	G2652
Jn	12:22	Andrew; Andrew and Philip in turn told **J**.	G2652
Jn	12:23	**J** replied, "The hour has come for the Son	G2652
Jn	12:30	**J** said, "This voice was for your benefit	G2652
Jn	12:35	Then **J** told them, "You are going to have	G2652
Jn	12:36	**J** left and hid himself from them.	G2652
Jn	12:37	Even after **J** had performed so many signs	G899S
Jn	12:44	Then **J** cried out, "Whoever believes in	G2652
Jn	13: 1	**J** knew that the hour had come for him to	G2652
Jn	13: 2	the son of Simon Iscariot, to betray **J**.	G899S
Jn	13: 3	**J** knew that the Father had put all things	NDT
Jn	13: 7	**J** replied, "You do not realize now what I	G2652
Jn	13: 8	**J** answered, "Unless I wash you, you	G2652
Jn	13:10	**J** answered, "Those who have had a bath	G2652
Jn	13:21	**J** was troubled in spirit and testified	G2652
Jn	13:23	the disciple whom **J** loved, was reclining	G2652
Jn	13:25	Leaning back against **J**, he asked him	G2652
Jn	13:26	**J** answered, "It is the one to whom I will	G2652
Jn	13:27	So **J** told him, "What you are about to do	G2652
Jn	13:28	the meal understood why **J** said this to him.	NDT
Jn	13:29	some thought **J** was telling him to buy	G2652
Jn	13:31	When he was gone, **J** said, "Now the Son	G2652
Jn	13:36	**J** replied, "Where I am going, you	G2652
Jn	13:38	Then **J** answered, "Will you really lay	G2652
Jn	14: 6	**J** answered, "I am the way and the truth	G2652
Jn	14: 9	**J** answered: "Don't you know me, Philip	G2652
Jn	14:23	**J** replied, "Anyone who loves me will	G2652
Jn	16:16	**J** went on to say, "In a little while you will	NDT
Jn	16:19	**J** saw that they wanted to ask him about	G2652
Jn	16:31	"Do you now believe?" **J** replied.	G2652
Jn	17: 1	After **J** said this, he looked toward heaven	G2652
Jn	17: 3	only true God, and **J** Christ, whom you	G2652
Jn	18: 1	**J** left with his disciples and crossed the	G2652
Jn	18: 2	because **J** had often met there with his	G2652
Jn	18: 4	**J**, knowing all that was going to happen	G2652
Jn	18: 5	"**J** of Nazareth," they replied. "I am he,"	G2652
Jn	18: 5	"I am he," **J** said. (And Judas the	NDT
Jn	18: 6	When **J** said, "I am he," they drew back and	NDT
Jn	18: 7	is it you want?" "**J** of Nazareth," they	G2652
Jn	18: 8	**J** answered, "I told you that I am he.	G2652
Jn	18:11	**J** commanded Peter, "Put your sword	G2652
Jn	18:12	the Jewish officials arrested **J**.	G2652
Jn	18:15	another disciple were following **J**.	G2652
Jn	18:15	he went with **J** into the high priest's	G2652
Jn	18:19	priest questioned **J** about his disciples	G2652
Jn	18:20	spoken openly to the world," **J** replied.	G2652
Jn	18:22	When **J** said this, one of the officials	G899S
Jn	18:23	something wrong," **J** replied, "testify as	G2652
Jn	18:28	Jewish leaders took **J** from Caiaphas to	G2652
Jn	18:32	place to fulfill what **J** had said about the	G2652
Jn	18:33	summoned **J** and asked him, "Are	G2652
Jn	18:34	**J** asked, "or did others talk to you about	G2652
Jn	18:36	**J** said, "My kingdom is not of this world.	G2652
Jn	18:37	**J** answered, "You say that I	G2652
Jn	19: 1	Then Pilate took **J** and had him flogged.	G2652
Jn	19: 5	When **J** came out wearing the crown of	G2652
Jn	19: 9	he asked **J**, but Jesus gave him no	G2652
Jn	19: 9	asked Jesus, but **J** gave him no answer.	G2652
Jn	19:11	**J** answered, "You would have no power	G2652
Jn	19:12	Pilate tried to set **J** free, but the Jewish	G899S
Jn	19:13	he brought **J** out and sat down on the	G2652
Jn	19:16	So the soldiers took charge of **J**.	G2652
Jn	19:18	one on each side and **J** in the middle.	G2652
Jn	19:19	It read: **J** OF NAZARETH, THE KING	G2652
Jn	19:20	the place where **J** was crucified was	G2652
Jn	19:23	When the soldiers crucified **J**, they took	G2652
Jn	19:25	Near the cross *of* **J** stood his mother, his	G2652
Jn	19:26	When **J** saw his mother there, and the	G2652
Jn	19:28	would be fulfilled, **J** said, "I am thirsty."	G2652
Jn	19:30	received the drink, **J** said, "It is finished."	G2652
Jn	19:32	first man who had been crucified with **J**,	G899S
Jn	19:33	when they came to **J** and found that he	G2652
Jn	19:38	Arimathea asked Pilate for the body *of* **J**.	G2652
Jn	19:38	Now Joseph was a disciple *of* **J**, but	G2652
Jn	19:39	the man who earlier had visited **J** at night.	G899S
Jn	19:41	At the place where **J** was crucified, there was	NDT
Jn	19:42	the tomb was nearby, they laid **J** there.	G2652
Jn	20: 2	other disciple, the one **J** loved, and said,	G2652
Jn	20: 9	from Scripture that **J** had to rise from the	G899S
Jn	20:14	turned around and saw **J** standing there,	G2652
Jn	20:14	but she did not realize that it was **J**.	G2652
Jn	20:16	**J** said to her, "Mary." She turned toward	G2652
Jn	20:17	**J** said, "Do not hold on to me, for I have	G2652
Jn	20:19	**J** came and stood among them and said	G2652
Jn	20:21	Again **J** said, "Peace be with you! As the	G2652
Jn	20:24	was not with the disciples when **J** came.	G2652
Jn	20:26	**J** came and stood among them and said	G2652
Jn	20:29	Then **J** told him, "Because you have seen	G2652
Jn	20:30	**J** performed many other signs in the	G2652
Jn	20:31	you may believe that **J** is the Messiah,	G2652
Jn	21: 1	Afterward **J** appeared again to his	G2652
Jn	21: 4	Early in the morning, **J** stood on the shore	G2652
Jn	21: 4	the disciples did not realize that it was **J**.	G2652
Jn	21: 7	the disciple whom **J** loved said to Peter,	G2652
Jn	21:10	**J** said to them, "Bring some of the fish	G2652
Jn	21:12	**J** said to them, "Come and have breakfast."	G2652
Jn	21:13	**J** came, took the bread and gave it to	G2652
Jn	21:14	was now the third time **J** appeared to his	G2652
Jn	21:15	had finished eating, **J** said to Simon Peter	G2652
Jn	21:15	that I love you." **J** said, "Feed my lambs."	NDT
Jn	21:16	Again **J** said, "Simon son of John, do you	NDT
Jn	21:16	that I love you." **J** said, "Take care of my	NDT
Jn	21:17	was hurt because **J** asked him the third	NDT
Jn	21:17	that I love you." **J** said, "Feed my sheep.	G2652
Jn	21:19	**J** said this to indicate the kind of death by	NDT
Jn	21:20	the disciple whom **J** loved was following	G2652
Jn	21:20	leaned back against **J** at the supper and	G899S
Jn	21:22	**J** answered, "If I want him to remain alive	G2652
Jn	21:23	But **J** did not say that he would not die	G2652
Jn	21:25	**J** did many other things as well. If every	G2652
Ac	1: 1	wrote about all that **J** began to do and to	G2652
Ac	1:11	This same **J**, who has been taken from	G2652
Ac	1:14	the women and Mary the mother *of* **J**,	G2652
Ac	1:16	served as guide for those who arrested **J**.	G2652
Ac	1:21	time the Lord **J** was living among us	G2652

Ac 1:22 to the time when **J** was taken up from us. NDT
Ac 2:22 **J** of Nazareth was a man accredited by G2652
Ac 2:32 God has raised this **J** to life, and we are G2652
Ac 2:36 God has made this **J**, whom you crucified G2652
Ac 2:38 in the name *of* **J** Christ for the forgiveness G2652
Ac 3: 6 In the name *of* **J** Christ of Nazareth G2652
Ac 3:13 of our fathers, has glorified his servant **J**. G2652
Ac 3:16 By faith in the name *of* **J**, this man whom G899S
Ac 3:20 who has been appointed for you—even **J**. G2652
Ac 4: 2 proclaiming in **J** the resurrection of the G2652
Ac 4:10 It is by the name *of* **J** Christ of Nazareth G2652
Ac 4:11 **J** is " 'the stone you builders rejected G4047S
Ac 4:13 note that these men had been with **J**. G2652
Ac 4:18 to speak or teach at all in the name *of* **J**. G2652
Ac 4:27 to conspire against your holy servant **J**, G2652
Ac 4:30 through the name of your holy servant **J**." G2652
Ac 4:33 to testify to the resurrection of the Lord **J**. G2652
Ac 5:30 of our ancestors raised **J** from the dead— G2652
Ac 5:40 them not to speak in the name *of* **J**, G2652
Ac 5:42 the good news that **J** is the Messiah. G2652
Ac 6:14 heard him say that this **J** of Nazareth will G2652
Ac 7:55 **J** standing at the right hand of God. G2652
Ac 7:59 Stephen prayed, "Lord **J**, receive my spirit." G2652
Ac 8:12 kingdom of God and the name *of* **J** Christ, G2652
Ac 8:16 been baptized in the name of the Lord **J**. G2652
Ac 8:25 the word of the Lord and testified about **J**, NDT
Ac 8:35 told him the good news *about* **J**. G2652
Ac 9: 5 "I am **J**, whom you are persecuting," G2652
Ac 9:17 the Lord—**J**, who appeared to you on the G2652
Ac 9:20 the synagogues that **J** is the Son of God. G2652
Ac 9:22 by proving that **J** is the Messiah. G4047S
Ac 9:27 had preached fearlessly in the name *of* **J**. G2652
Ac 9:34 Peter said to him, "**J** Christ heals you. G2652
Ac 10:36 the good news of peace through **J** Christ, G2652
Ac 10:38 how God anointed **J** of Nazareth with the G2652
Ac 10:48 they be baptized in the name *of* **J** Christ. G2652
Ac 11:17 gave us who believed in the Lord **J** Christ, G2652
Ac 11:20 them the good news about the Lord **J**. G2652
Ac 13:23 God has brought to Israel the Savior **J**, G2652
Ac 13:24 Before the coming *of* **J**, John preached G899S
Ac 13:27 their rulers did not recognize **J**, G4047S
Ac 13:33 their children, by raising up **J**. G2652
Ac 13:38 to know that through **J** the forgiveness of G4047S
Ac 15:11 the grace of our Lord **J** that we are saved, G2652
Ac 15:26 lives for the name of our Lord **J** Christ. G2652
Ac 16: 7 the Spirit *of* **J** would not allow them to G2652
Ac 16:18 "In the name *of* **J** Christ I command you to G2652
Ac 16:31 "Believe in the Lord **J**, and you will be G2652
Ac 17: 3 "This **J** I am proclaiming to you is the G2652
Ac 17: 7 that there is another king, one called **J**." G2652
Ac 17:18 the good news *about* **J** and the G2652
Ac 18: 5 to the Jews that **J** was the Messiah. G2652
Ac 18:25 great fervor and taught about **J** accurately, G2652
Ac 18:28 the Scriptures that **J** was the Messiah. G2652
Ac 19: 4 in the one coming after him, that is, in **J**." G2652
Ac 19: 5 were baptized in the name of the Lord **J**. G2652
Ac 19:13 name of the Lord **J** over those who were G2652
Ac 19:13 "In the name *of* the **J** whom Paul G2652
Ac 19:15 answered them, "**J** I know, and Paul I G2652
Ac 19:17 the name of the Lord **J** was held in high G2652
Ac 20:21 repentance and have faith in our Lord **J**. G2652
Ac 20:24 the task the Lord **J** has given me— G2652
Ac 20:35 the words the Lord **J** himself said: G2652
Ac 21:13 in Jerusalem for the name of the Lord **J**." G2652
Ac 22: 8 " 'I am **J** of Nazareth, whom you are G2652
Ac 24:24 to him as he spoke about faith in Christ **J**. G2652
Ac 25:19 a dead man named **J** who Paul claimed G2652
Ac 26: 9 to oppose the name *of* **J** of Nazareth. G2652
Ac 26:15 " 'I am **J**, whom you are persecuting,' the G2652
Ac 28:23 he tried to persuade them about **J**. G2652
Ac 28:31 God and taught about the Lord **J** Christ— G2652
Ro 1: 1 a servant of Christ **J**, called to be an G2652
Ro 1: 4 from the dead: **J** Christ our Lord. G2652
Ro 1: 6 who are called to *belong to* **J** Christ. G2652
Ro 1: 7 God our Father and from the Lord **J** Christ. G2652
Ro 1: 8 thank my God through **J** Christ for all of G2652
Ro 2:16 judges people's secrets through **J** Christ, G2652
Ro 3:22 is given through faith *in* **J** Christ to all who G2652
Ro 3:24 the redemption that came by Christ **J**. G2652
Ro 3:26 who justifies those who have faith *in* **J**. G2652
Ro 4:24 in him who raised **J** our Lord from the G2652
Ro 5: 1 peace with God through our Lord **J** Christ, G2652
Ro 5:11 boast in God through our Lord **J** Christ, G2652
Ro 5:15 grace of the one man, **J** Christ, overflow to G2652
Ro 5:17 in life through the one man, **J** Christ! G2652
Ro 5:21 bring eternal life through **J** Christ our Lord. G2652
Ro 6: 3 baptized into Christ **J** were baptized into G2652
Ro 6:11 dead to sin but alive to God in Christ **J**. G2652
Ro 6:23 of God is eternal life in Christ **J** our Lord. G2652
Ro 7:25 who delivers me through **J** Christ our Lord! G2652
Ro 8: 1 those who are in Christ **J**, G2652
Ro 8: 2 through Christ **J** the law of the Spirit G2652
Ro 8:11 of him who raised **J** from the dead is G2652
Ro 8:34 Christ **J** who died—more than that, who G2652
Ro 8:39 the love of God that is in Christ **J** our Lord. G2652
Ro 10: 9 with your mouth, "**J** is Lord," and believe G2652
Ro 13:14 clothe yourselves with the Lord **J** Christ G2652
Ro 14:14 being fully persuaded in the Lord **J**, that G2652
Ro 15: 5 mind toward each other that Christ **J** had, G2652
Ro 15: 6 the God and Father of our Lord **J** Christ. G2652
Ro 15:16 to be a minister of Christ **J** to the Gentiles G2652
Ro 15:17 I glory in Christ **J** in my service to God. G2652
Ro 15:30 by our Lord **J** Christ and by the love of the G2652
Ro 16: 3 Aquila, my co-workers in Christ **J**. G2652
Ro 16:20 The grace of our Lord **J** be with you. G2652
Ro 16:25 the message I proclaim *about* **J** Christ, in G2652
Ro 16:27 wise God be glory forever through **J** Christ! G2652
1Co 1: 1 an apostle of Christ **J** by the will of God, G2652
1Co 1: 2 sanctified in Christ **J** and called to be his G2652
1Co 1: 2 call on the name of our Lord **J** Christ— G2652
1Co 1: 3 from God our Father and the Lord **J** Christ. G2652
1Co 1: 4 because of his grace given you in Christ **J**. G2652
1Co 1: 7 wait for our Lord **J** Christ to be revealed. G2652
1Co 1: 8 blameless on the day of our Lord **J** Christ. G2652
1Co 1: 9 fellowship with his Son, **J** Christ our Lord. G2652
1Co 1:10 in the name of our Lord **J** Christ, that all of G2652
1Co 1:30 It is because of him that you are in Christ **J**, G2652
1Co 2: 2 I was with you except **J** Christ and him G2652
1Co 3:11 the one already laid, which is **J** Christ. G2652
1Co 4:15 in Christ **J** I became your father G2652
1Co 4:17 remind you of my way of life in Christ **J**, G2652
1Co 5: 3 name of our Lord **J** on the one who has G2652
1Co 5: 4 the power of our Lord **J** is present, G2652
1Co 6:11 the name of the Lord **J** Christ and by the G2652
1Co 8: 6 is but one Lord, **J** Christ, through whom G2652
1Co 9: 1 Have I not seen **J** our Lord? Are you not G2652
1Co 11:23 The Lord **J**, on the night he was betrayed G2652
1Co 12: 3 Spirit of God says, "**J** be cursed," and no G2652
1Co 12: 3 no one can say, "**J** is Lord," except by G2652
1Co 15:31 as I boast about you in Christ **J** our Lord. G2652
1Co 15:57 us the victory through our Lord **J** Christ. G2652
1Co 16:23 The grace of the Lord **J** be with you. G2652
1Co 16:24 My love to all of you in Christ **J**. Amen. G2652
2Co 1: 1 an apostle of Christ **J** by the will of God G2652
2Co 1: 2 from God our Father and the Lord **J** Christ. G2652
2Co 1: 3 to the God and Father of our Lord **J** Christ, G2652
2Co 1:14 will boast of you in the day of the Lord **J**. G2652
2Co 1:19 For the Son of God, **J** Christ, who was G2652
2Co 4: 5 is not ourselves, but **J** Christ as Lord, and G2652
2Co 4:10 carry around in our body the death *of* **J**, G2652
2Co 4:10 so that the life *of* **J** may also be revealed G2652
2Co 4:14 who raised the Lord **J** from the dead will G2652
2Co 4:14 also raise us with **J** and present us with G2652
2Co 8: 9 For you know the grace of our Lord **J** Christ G2652
2Co 11: 4 you and preaches a **J** other than the Jesus G2652
2Co 11: 4 a Jesus other than **the J** we preached, G4005S
2Co 11:31 The God and Father of the Lord **J**, who is G2652
2Co 13: 5 Do you not realize that Christ **J** is in you G2652
2Co 13:14 May the grace of the Lord **J** Christ, and the G2652
Gal 1: 1 but by **J** Christ and God the Father G2652
Gal 1: 3 from God our Father and the Lord **J** Christ, G2652
Gal 1:12 I received it by revelation *from* **J** Christ. G2652
Gal 2: 4 we have in Christ **J** and to make us slaves. G2652
Gal 2:16 works of the law, but by faith *in* **J** Christ. G2652
Gal 2:16 put our faith in Christ **J** that we may be G2652
Gal 3: 1 Before your very eyes **J** Christ was clearly G2652
Gal 3:14 come to the Gentiles through Christ **J**, G2652
Gal 3:22 being given through faith *in* **J** Christ G2652
Gal 3:26 So in Christ **J** you are all children of God G2652
Gal 3:28 female, for you are all one in Christ **J**. G2652
Gal 4:14 angel of God, as if I were Christ **J** himself. G2652
Gal 5: 6 For in Christ **J** neither circumcision nor G2652
Gal 5:24 who belong to Christ **J** have crucified the G2652
Gal 6:14 except in the cross of our Lord **J** Christ, G2652
Gal 6:17 I bear on my body the marks *of* **J**. G2652
Gal 6:18 The grace of our Lord **J** Christ be with your G2652
Eph 1: 1 an apostle of Christ **J** by the will of God G2652
Eph 1: 1 people in Ephesus, the faithful in Christ **J**: G2652
Eph 1: 2 from God our Father and the Lord **J** Christ. G2652
Eph 1: 3 to the God and Father of our Lord **J** Christ, G2652
Eph 1: 5 adoption to sonship through **J** Christ, G2652
Eph 1:15 faith in the Lord **J** and your love for all G2652
Eph 1:17 asking that the God of our Lord **J** Christ, G2652
Eph 2: 6 him in the heavenly realms in Christ **J**, G2652
Eph 2: 7 expressed in his kindness to us in Christ **J**. G2652
Eph 2:10 created in Christ **J** to do good works G2652
Eph 2:13 But now in Christ **J** you who once were far G2652
Eph 2:20 with Christ **J** himself as the chief G2652
Eph 3: 1 the prisoner of Christ **J** for the sake of you G2652
Eph 3: 6 sharers together in the promise in Christ **J**. G2652
Eph 3:11 that he accomplished in Christ **J** our Lord. G2652
Eph 3:21 the church and in Christ **J** throughout all G2652
Eph 4:21 in accordance with the truth that is in **J**. G2652
Eph 5:20 in the name of our Lord **J** Christ. G2652
Eph 6:23 from God the Father and the Lord **J** Christ. G2652
Eph 6:24 all who love our Lord **J** Christ with an G2652
Php 1: 1 servants of Christ **J**, To all God's holy G2652
Php 1: 1 God's holy people in Christ **J** at Philippi, G2652
Php 1: 2 from God our Father and the Lord **J** Christ. G2652
Php 1: 6 on to completion until the day of Christ **J**. G2652
Php 1: 8 all of you with the affection of Christ **J**. G2652
Php 1:11 that comes through **J** Christ— G2652
Php 1:19 provision of the Spirit *of* **J** Christ what has G2652
Php 1:26 boasting in Christ **J** will abound on G2652
Php 2: 5 have the same mindset as Christ **J**: G2652
Php 2:10 that at the name *of* **J** every knee should G2652
Php 2:11 tongue acknowledge that **J** Christ is Lord, G2652
Php 2:19 I hope in the Lord **J** to send Timothy to G2652
Php 2:21 their own interests, not those *of* **J** Christ. G2652
Php 3: 3 who boast in Christ **J**, and who put no G2652
Php 3: 8 worth of knowing Christ **J** my Lord, G2652
Php 3:12 of that for which Christ **J** took hold of me. G2652
Php 3:14 has called me heavenward in Christ **J**. G2652
Php 3:20 a Savior from there, the Lord **J** Christ, G2652
Php 4: 7 your hearts and your minds in Christ **J**. G2652
Php 4:19 to the riches of his glory in Christ **J**. G2652
Php 4:21 Greet all God's people in Christ **J**. G2652
Php 4:23 The grace of the Lord **J** Christ be with your G2652
Col 1: 1 an apostle of Christ **J** by the will of God G2652
Col 1: 3 the Father of our Lord **J** Christ, when we G2652
Col 1: 4 of your faith in Christ **J** and of the love you G2652
Col 2: 6 just as you received Christ **J** as Lord G2652
Col 3:17 do it all in the name of the Lord **J**, giving G2652
Col 4:11 **J**, who is called Justus, also sends G2652
Col 4:12 is one of you and a servant of Christ **J**, G2652
1Th 1: 1 in God the Father and the Lord **J** Christ: G2652
1Th 1: 3 inspired by hope in our Lord **J** Christ. G2652
1Th 1:10 from the dead—**J**, who rescues us from G2652
1Th 2:14 churches in Judea, which are in Christ **J**: G2652
1Th 2:15 who killed the Lord **J** and the prophets G2652
1Th 2:19 presence of our Lord **J** when he comes? G2652
1Th 3:11 himself and our Lord **J** clear the way for us G2652
1Th 3:13 Father when our Lord **J** comes with all his G2652
1Th 4: 1 urge you in the Lord **J** to do this more G2652
1Th 4: 2 we gave you by the authority of the Lord **J**. G2652
1Th 4:14 For we believe that **J** died and rose again G2652
1Th 4:14 God will bring with **J** those who have G2652
1Th 5: 9 receive salvation through our Lord **J** Christ. G2652
1Th 5:18 this is God's will for you in Christ **J**. G2652
1Th 5:23 at the coming of our Lord **J** Christ. G2652
1Th 5:28 The grace of our Lord **J** Christ be with you. G2652
2Th 1: 1 in God our Father and the Lord **J** Christ: G2652
2Th 1: 2 from God the Father and the Lord **J** Christ. G2652
2Th 1: 7 happen when the Lord **J** is revealed from G2652
2Th 1: 8 do not obey the gospel of our Lord **J**. G2652
2Th 1:12 the name of our Lord **J** may be glorified in G2652
2Th 1:12 the grace of our God and the Lord **J** Christ. G2652
2Th 2: 1 coming of our Lord **J** Christ and our being G2652
2Th 2: 8 whom the Lord **J** will overthrow with the G2652
2Th 2:14 share in the glory of our Lord **J** Christ. G2652
2Th 2:16 May our Lord **J** Christ himself and God our G2652
2Th 3: 6 In the name of the Lord **J** Christ, we G2652
2Th 3:12 urge in the Lord **J** Christ to settle G2652
2Th 3:18 The grace of our Lord **J** Christ be with you G2652
1Ti 1: 1 an apostle of Christ **J** by the command of G2652
1Ti 1: 1 God our Savior and of Christ **J** our hope, G2652
1Ti 1: 2 from God the Father and Christ **J** our Lord. G2652
1Ti 1:12 I thank Christ **J** our Lord, who has given G2652
1Ti 1:14 with the faith and love that are in Christ **J**. G2652
1Ti 1:15 Christ **J** came into the world to save G2652
1Ti 1:16 Christ **J** might display his immense G2652
1Ti 2: 5 God and mankind, the man Christ **J**, G2652
1Ti 3:13 great assurance in their faith in Christ **J**. G2652
1Ti 4: 6 you will be a good minister of Christ **J** G2652
1Ti 5:21 of God and Christ **J** and the elect angels, G2652
1Ti 6: 3 of our Lord **J** Christ and to godly G2652
1Ti 6:13 of Christ **J**, who while testifying G2652
1Ti 6:14 until the appearing of our Lord **J** Christ, G2652
2Ti 1: 1 an apostle of Christ **J** by the will of God G2652
2Ti 1: 1 with the promise of life that is in Christ **J**, G2652
2Ti 1: 2 from God the Father and Christ **J** our Lord. G2652
2Ti 1: 9 given us in Christ **J** before the beginning G2652
2Ti 1:10 of our Savior, Christ **J**, who has destroyed G2652
2Ti 1:13 teaching, with faith and love in Christ **J**. G2652
2Ti 2: 1 be strong in the grace that is in Christ **J**. G2652
2Ti 2: 3 in suffering, like a good soldier of Christ **J**. G2652
2Ti 2: 8 Remember **J** Christ, raised from the dead G2652
2Ti 2:10 obtain the salvation that is in Christ **J**, G2652
2Ti 3:12 a godly life in Christ **J** will be persecuted, G2652
2Ti 3:15 wise for salvation through faith in Christ **J**. G2652
2Ti 4: 1 In the presence of God and of Christ **J** G2652
Titus 1: 1 God and an apostle *of* **J** Christ to further G2652
Titus 1: 4 God the Father and Christ **J** our Savior. G2652
Titus 2:13 glory of our great God and Savior, **J** Christ, G2652
Titus 3: 6 us generously through **J** Christ our Savior, G2652
Phm 1 a prisoner of Christ **J**, and Timothy our G2652
Phm 3 from God our Father and the Lord **J** Christ. G2652
Phm 5 holy people and your faith in the Lord **J**. G2652
Phm 9 man and now also a prisoner *of* Christ **J**— G2652
Phm 23 my fellow prisoner in Christ **J**, sends you G2652
Phm 25 The grace of the Lord **J** Christ be with your G2652
Heb 2: 9 But we do see **J**, who was made lower G2652
Heb 2:11 So **J** is not ashamed to call them brothers NDT
Heb 3: 1 fix your thoughts on **J**, whom we G2652
Heb 3: 3 **J** has been found worthy of greater honor G4047S
Heb 4:14 into heaven, **J** the Son of God, let G2652
Heb 6:20 our forerunner, **J**, has entered on our G2652
Heb 7:22 **J** has become the guarantor of a better G2652
Heb 7:24 because **J** lives forever, he has a G899S
Heb 8: 6 But in fact the ministry **J** has received is as NDT
Heb 10:10 of the body *of* **J** Christ once for all. G2652
Heb 10:19 the Most Holy Place by the blood *of* **J**, G2652
Heb 12: 2 fixing our eyes on **J**, the pioneer and G2652
Heb 12:24 *to* **J** the mediator of a new covenant, and G2652
Heb 13: 8 **J** Christ is the same yesterday and today G2652
Heb 13:12 And so **J** also suffered outside the city G2652
Heb 13:15 Through **J**, therefore, let us continually G899S
Heb 13:20 brought back from the dead our Lord **J**, G2652
Heb 13:21 through **J** Christ, to whom be glory G2652
Jas 1: 1 a servant of God and of the Lord **J** Christ G2652
Jas 2: 1 in our glorious Lord **J** Christ must not show G2652
1Pe 1: 1 an apostle *of* **J** Christ, To God's G2652
1Pe 1: 2 to be obedient *to* **J** Christ and sprinkled G2652
1Pe 1: 3 to the God and Father of our Lord **J** Christ! G2652
1Pe 1: 3 the resurrection *of* **J** Christ from the dead, G2652
1Pe 1: 7 glory and honor when **J** Christ is revealed. G2652

1Pe 1:13 brought to you when J Christ is revealed G2652
1Pe 2: 5 acceptable to God through J Christ. G2652
1Pe 3:21 It saves you by the resurrection *of* J Christ, G2652
1Pe 4:11 God may be praised through J Christ. G2652
2Pe 1: 1 a servant and apostle *of* J Christ, To those G2652
2Pe 1: 1 our God and Savior J Christ have received G2652
2Pe 1: 2 the knowledge of God and *of* J our Lord. G2652
2Pe 1: 8 in your knowledge of our Lord J Christ. G2652
2Pe 1:11 kingdom of our Lord and Savior J Christ. G2652
2Pe 1:14 as our Lord J Christ has made clear to me. G2652
2Pe 1:16 the coming of our Lord J Christ in power, G2652
2Pe 2:20 our Lord and Savior J Christ and are again G2652
2Pe 3:18 knowledge of our Lord and Savior J Christ. G2652
1Jn 1: 3 with the Father and with his Son, J Christ. G2652
1Jn 1: 7 one another, and the blood *of* J, his Son, G2652
1Jn 2: 1 with the Father—J Christ, the Righteous G2652
1Jn 2: 6 claims to live in him must live as J did. G1697S
1Jn 2:22 It is whoever denies that J is the Christ G2652
1Jn 3:16 **J Christ** laid down his life for us G1697S
1Jn 3:23 the name of his Son, J Christ, and to love G2652
1Jn 4: 2 acknowledges that J Christ has come in G2652
1Jn 4: 3 does not acknowledge J is not from God. G2652
1Jn 4:15 acknowledges that J is the Son of God, G2652
1Jn 4:17 In this world we are like J. G1697S
1Jn 5: 1 who believes that J is the Christ is born of G2652
1Jn 5: 5 who believes that J is the Son of God. G2652
1Jn 5: 6 who came by water and blood—J Christ. G2652
1Jn 5:20 who is true by being in his Son J Christ. G2652
2Jn 3 from God the Father and from J Christ, G2652
2Jn 7 do not acknowledge J Christ as coming in G2652
Jude 1 a servant *of* J Christ and a brother of G2652
Jude 1 in God the Father and kept *for* J Christ: G2652
Jude 4 immorality and deny J Christ our only G2652
Jude 17 the apostles of our Lord J Christ foretold. G2652
Jude 21 the mercy of our Lord J Christ to bring you G2652
Jude 25 authority, through J Christ our Lord G2652
Rev 1: 1 The revelation *from* J Christ, which God G2652
Rev 1: 2 word of God and the testimony *of* J Christ. G2652
Rev 1: 5 from J Christ, who is the faithful G2652
Rev 1: 9 patient endurance that are ours in J, G2652
Rev 1: 9 of the word of God and the testimony *of* J. G2652
Rev 12:17 hold fast their testimony *about* J. G2652
Rev 14:12 his commands and remain faithful *to* J. G2652
Rev 17: 6 blood of those who bore testimony *to* J. G2652
Rev 19:10 sisters who hold to the testimony *of* J. G2652
Rev 19:10 of prophecy who bears testimony to J." G2652
Rev 20: 4 of their testimony *about* J and because of G2652
Rev 22:16 J, have sent my angel to give you this G2652
Rev 22:20 I am coming soon." Amen. Come, Lord J. G2652
Rev 22:21 grace of the Lord J be with God's people. G2652

JESUS' (34) [JESUS]

Mt 21:45 priests and the Pharisees heard J parables, G899S
Mt 26:51 one of J companions reached for his sword G2652
Mt 27:53 of the tombs after J resurrection and went G899S
Mt 27:58 to Pilate, he asked for J body, and Pilate G2652
Mk 3:31 Then J mother and brothers arrived G899S
Mk 6:14 for J name had become well known. G899S
Mk 14:12 J disciples asked him, "Where do you want G899S
Mk 15:43 went boldly to Pilate and asked for J body. G2652
Mk 16: 1 so that they might go to anoint J body. G899S
Lk 2:41 Every year J parents went to Jerusalem G899S
Lk 5: 8 saw this, he fell at J knees and said, "Go G2652
Lk 7:29 when they heard J words, acknowledged NDT
Lk 8:19 Now J mother and brothers came to see G899S
Lk 8:35 gone out, sitting at J feet, dressed and in G2652
Lk 8:41 came and fell at J feet, pleading with him G2652
Lk 17:16 He threw himself at J feet and thanked him G899S
Lk 22:49 When J followers saw what was going to G899S
Lk 23:52 Going to Pilate, he asked for J body. G2652
Jn 2: 1 at Cana in Galilee. J mother was there, G2652
Jn 2: 3 the wine was gone, J mother said to him G2652
Jn 7: 3 J brothers said to him, "Leave Galilee and G899S
Jn 12: 2 Here a dinner was given in J honor. Martha G899S
Jn 12: 3 she poured it on J feet and wiped his feet G2652
Jn 12:41 this because he saw J glory and spoke G899S
Jn 16:29 Then J disciples said, "Now you are G899S
Jn 19:29 of the hyssop plant, and lifted it to J lips. G3836S
Jn 19:34 of the soldiers pierced J side with a spear, G899S
Jn 19:40 Taking J body, the two of them wrapped it G2652
Jn 20: 7 that had been wrapped around J head. G899S
Jn 20:12 seated where J body had been, one G2652
Ac 3:16 It is J name and the faith that comes G899S
2Co 4: 5 ourselves as your servants for J sake. G2652
2Co 4:11 being given over to death for J sake, G2652
Heb 5: 7 During the days of J life on earth, he G899S

JETHER (10)

Jdg 8:20 Turning to J, his oldest son, he said, "Kill H3858
Jdg 8:20 But J did not draw his sword H2021+5853S
2Sa 17:25 Amasa was the son of J, an Ishmaelite H3859
1Ki 2: 5 Abner son of Ner and Amasa son of J. H3858
1Ki 2:32 Amasa son of J, commander of H3858
1Ch 2:17 whose father was J the Ishmaelite. H3858
1Ch 2:32 Shammai's brother: J and Jonathan H3858
1Ch 2:32 Jonathan. J died without children H3858
1Ch 4:17 The sons of Ezrah: J, Mered, Epher and H3858
1Ch 7:38 The sons of J: Jephunneh, Pispah and H3858

JETHETH (2)

Ge 36:40 their clans and regions: Timna, Alvah, J, H3867
1Ch 1:51 chiefs of Edom were: Timna, Alvah, J, H3867

JETHRO (11)

Ex 3: 1 tending the flock of J his father-in-law, H3861
Ex 4:18 Moses went back to J his father-in-law H3858
Ex 4:18 are still alive." J said, "Go, and I wish H3861
Ex 18: 1 Now J, the priest of Midian and H3861
Ex 18: 2 Zipporah, his father-in-law J received her H3861
Ex 18: 5 J, Moses' father-in-law, together with H3861
Ex 18: 6 J had sent word to him, "I, your father-in-law NDT
Ex 18: 6 your father-in-law J, am coming to you H3861
Ex 18: 9 J was delighted to hear about all the H3861
Ex 18:12 Then J, Moses' father-in-law, brought a H3861
Ex 18:27 and J returned to his own country. H2257S

JETUR (3)

Ge 25:15 Tema, J, Naphish and Kedemah. H3515
1Ch 1:31 J, Naphish and Kedemah. These were the H3515
1Ch 5:19 the Hagrites, J, Naphish and Nodab. H3515

JEUEL (2)

1Ch 9: 6 Of the Zerahites: J. The people from H3590
Ezr 8:13 were Eliphelet, J and Shemaiah, and H3590

JEUSH (9)

Ge 36: 5 Oholibamah bore J, Jalam and Korah H3593
Ge 36:14 she bore to Esau: J, Jalam and Korah. H3593
Ge 36:18 Chiefs J, Jalam and Korah H3593
1Ch 1:35 Eliphaz, Reuel, J, Jalam and Korah. H3593
1Ch 7:10 J, Benjamin, Ehud, Kenaanah, Zethan H3593
1Ch 8:39 J the second son and Eliphelet the third. H3593
1Ch 23:10 Jahath, Ziza, J and Beriah. These H3593
1Ch 23:11 J and Beriah did not have many sons H3593
2Ch 11:19 She bore him sons: J, Shemariah and H3593

JEUZ (1)

1Ch 8:10 J, Sakia and Mirmah. These were his sons H3591

JEW (33) [JEWISH, JEWS, JEWS', JUDAISM]

Est 2: 5 the citadel of Susa a J of the tribe of H3374
Est 3: 4 he had told them he was a J. H3374
Est 5:13 as long as I see that J Mordecai sitting at H3374
Est 6:10 as you have suggested for Mordecai the J, H3374
Est 8: 7 to Queen Esther and to Mordecai the J, H3374
Est 9:29 along with Mordecai the J, wrote with full H3374
Est 9:31 as Mordecai the J and Queen Esther had H3374
Est 10: 3 Mordecai the J was second in rank to King H3374
Zec 8:23 take firm hold of one J by the hem of his H3374
Jn 3:25 disciples and *a certain* J over the matter G2681
Jn 4: 9 "You are a J and I am a Samaritan G2681
Jn 18:35 "Am I a J?" Pilate replied. "Your own G2681
Ac 10:28 against our law *for* a J to associate G467+2681
Ac 18: 2 There he met a J named Aquila, a native G2681
Ac 18:24 Meanwhile a J named Apollos, a native G2681
Ac 19:34 But when they realized he was a J, they all G2681
Ac 21:39 answered, "I am a J, from Tarsus in G476+2681
Ac 22: 3 "I am a J, born in Tarsus of Cilicia G467+2681
Ro 1:16 who believes: first *to* the J, then to the G2681
Ro 2: 9 who does evil: first *for* the J, then for the G2681
Ro 2:10 who does good: first *for* the J, then for the G2681
Ro 2:17 if you call yourself a J; if you rely on the G2681
Ro 2:28 A person is not a J who is one only G2681
Ro 2:29 a person is a J who is one inwardly G2681
Ro 3: 1 is there in being a J, or what value is G2681
Ro 3:22 is no difference between J and Gentile, NDT
Ro 10:12 is no difference *between* J and Gentile— G2681
Ro 16:11 Herodion, my **fellow** J. Greet those in G5150
1Co 9:20 To the Jews I became like a J, to win the G2681
Gal 2:14 them all, "You are a J, yet you live like a G2681
Gal 2:14 you live like a Gentile and not **like a J**. G2680
Gal 3:28 There is neither J nor Gentile, neither G2681
Col 3:11 Here there is no Gentile or J, circumcised G2681

JEWEL (4) [JEWELRY, JEWELS]

Pr 20:15 lips that speak knowledge are a rare j. H3998
SS 4: 9 of your eyes, with one j of your necklace. H6736
Isa 13:19 Babylon, the j *of* kingdoms, the pride and H7382
Rev 21:11 was like that *of* a very precious j, G3345

JEWELRY (13) [JEWEL]

Ge 24:53 out gold and silver j and articles of H3998
Ex 32:24 'Whoever has any gold j, take it off. NDT
Ex 35:22 came and brought gold j *of* all kinds: H3998
Jer 2:32 Does a young woman forget her j, a bride H6344
Eze 7:20 in their **beautiful** j and used it H7382+6344
Eze 16:11 I adorned you with j: I put bracelets on H6344
Eze 16:17 You also took the fine j I gave you, the H3998
Eze 16:17 I gave you, the j made of my gold and silver NDT
Eze 16:39 take your fine j and leave you stark H3998
Eze 23:26 you of your clothes and take your fine j. H3998
Eze 23:40 eye makeup and **put on** *your* j. H6335+6344
Hos 2:13 she decked herself with rings and j, and H2719
1Pe 3: 3 the wearing *of* **gold** *j* or fine clothes. AIT

JEWELS (8) [JEWEL]

Job 28:17 nor can it be had for j *of* gold. H3998
SS 1:10 with earrings, your neck with **strings of** j. H3016
SS 5:12 in milk, **mounted like** j. H3782+6584+4859
SS 7: 1 Your graceful legs are like j, the work of H2717
Isa 54:12 your gates of **sparkling** j, and all your H74+734
Isa 61:10 as a bride adorns herself with her j. H3998
Jer 4:30 yourself in scarlet and put on j *of* gold? H6344
Zec 9:16 They will sparkle in his land like j *in* a crown. H74

JEWISH (51) [JEW]

Ezr 6: 7 of the Jews and the J elders rebuild this A10316
Ne 1: 2 them about the J remnant that had H3374
Est 6:13 has started, is of J origin, you cannot H3374
Jn 1:19 when the **J leaders** in Jerusalem sent G2681
Jn 2:13 it was almost time for the J Passover, G2681
Jn 3: 1 was a member of the J ruling council. G2681
Jn 5: 1 up to Jerusalem for one of the J festivals. G2681
Jn 5:10 so the **J leaders** said to the man who G2681
Jn 5:15 away and told the **J leaders** that it was G2681
Jn 5:16 the **J leaders** began to persecute him. G2681
Jn 6: 4 The J Passover Festival was near. G2681
Jn 7: 1 Judea because the **J leaders** there were G2681
Jn 7: 2 But when the J Festival of Tabernacles was G2681
Jn 7:11 the festival the **J leaders** were watching G2681
Jn 9:22 because they were afraid *of* the **J leaders**, G2681
Jn 10:31 Again his **J opponents** picked up stones G2681
Jn 11:51 that Jesus would die for the J nation, NDT
Jn 11:55 it was almost time for the J Passover, G2681
Jn 18:12 its commander and the J officials arrested G2681
Jn 18:14 had advised the **J leaders** that it would be G2681
Jn 18:28 Then the J leaders took Jesus from NDT
Jn 18:36 fight to prevent my arrest *by* the **J leaders**. G2681
Jn 19: 7 The **J leaders** insisted, "We have a law G2681
Jn 19:12 but the **J leaders** kept shouting, "If G2681
Jn 19:31 Because the **J leaders** did not want the G2681
Jn 19:38 secretly because he feared the **J leaders**. G2681
Jn 19:40 was in accordance with J burial customs. G2681
Jn 19:42 Because it was the J day of Preparation G2681
Jn 20:19 the doors locked for fear *of* the **J leaders**, G2681
Ac 10:22 who is respected by all the J people. G2681
Ac 12:11 from everything the J people were hoping G2681
Ac 13: 5 the word of God in the J synagogues. G2681
Ac 13: 6 There they met a J sorcerer and false G2681
Ac 13:50 But the **J leaders** incited the God-fearing G2681
Ac 14: 1 went as usual into the J synagogue. G2681
Ac 16: 1 whose mother was a J and a believer but G2681
Ac 17: 1 where there was a J synagogue. G2681
Ac 17:10 they went to the J synagogue. G2681
Ac 18:28 refuted his **J opponents** in public debate, G2681
Ac 19:14 Seven sons of Sceva, a J chief priest, were G2681
Ac 20:19 testing by the plots *of* my **J opponents**. G2681
Ac 21:11 'In this way the **J leaders** in Jerusalem G2681
Ac 24:24 came with his wife Drusilla, who was J. G2681
Ac 25: 2 chief priests and the J leaders appeared G2681
Ac 25: 8 wrong against the J law or against the G2681
Ac 25:24 The whole J community has petitioned G2681
Ac 26: 3 acquainted with all the J customs and G2681
Ac 26: 4 "The **J people** all know the way I have G2681
Ac 28:17 he called together the local J leaders. G2681
Gal 2:14 you force Gentiles *to* **follow J customs**? G2678
Titus 1:14 pay no attention to J myths or to the G2679

JEWRY (KJV) JUDAH, JUDEA

JEWS (207) [JEW]

Ezr 4:23 immediately to the J in Jerusalem and A10316
Ezr 5: 1 prophesied to the J in Judah and A10316
Ezr 5: 5 was watching over the elders of the J, A10316
Ezr 6: 7 the governor of the J and the Jewish A10316
Ezr 6: 8 these elders of the J in the construction A10316
Ezr 6:14 So the elders of the J continued to build A10316
Ne 2:16 had said nothing to the J or the priests H3374
Ne 4: 1 was greatly incensed. He ridiculed the J, H3374
Ne 4: 2 he said, "What are those feeble J doing? H3374
Ne 4:12 Then the J who lived near them came H3374
Ne 5: 1 a great outcry against their fellow J. H3374
Ne 5: 5 blood as our **fellow** J and though our H278
Ne 5: 8 back our fellow J who were sold to the H3374
Ne 5:17 a hundred and fifty J and officials ate at H3374
Ne 6: 6 that you and the J are plotting to revolt H3374
Est 3: 6 people, the J, throughout the whole H3374
Est 3:10 the Agagite, the enemy of the J. H3374
Est 3:13 kill and annihilate all the J—young and H3374
Est 4: 3 there was great mourning among the J H3374
Est 4: 7 royal treasury for the destruction of the J. H3374
Est 4:13 house you alone of all the J will escape. H3374
Est 4:14 deliverance for the J will arise from H3374
Est 4:16 gather together all the J who are in Susa H3374
Est 8: 1 the estate of Haman, the enemy of the J. H3374
Est 8: 3 which he had devised against the J. H3374
Est 8: 5 wrote to destroy the J in all the king's H3374
Est 8: 7 "Because Haman attacked the J, I have H3374
Est 8: 8 in behalf of the J as seems best to you, H3374
Est 8: 9 wrote out all Mordecai's orders to the J, H3374
Est 8: 9 also to the J in their own script H3374
Est 8:11 edict granted the J in every city the right H3374
Est 8:12 day appointed for the J to do this in all the NDT
Est 8:13 so that the J would be ready on that H3374
Est 8:16 For the J it was a time of happiness and H3374
Est 8:17 there was joy and gladness among the J H3374
Est 8:17 nationalities **became J** because fear of H3366
Est 8:17 because fear of the J had seized them. H3374
Est 9: 1 the enemies of the J had hoped to H3374
Est 9: 1 were turned and the J got the upper hand H3374
Est 9: 2 The J assembled in their cities in all the H3374
Est 9: 3 the king's administrators helped the J, H3374
Est 9: 5 The J struck down all their enemies with H3374
Est 9: 6 the J killed and destroyed five hundred H3374
Est 9:10 son of Hammedatha, the enemy of the J. H3374
Est 9:12 "The J have killed and destroyed five H3374
Est 9:13 "give the J in Susa permission to carry out H3374

Est 9:15 The J in Susa came together on the H3374
Est 9:16 the remainder of the J who were in the H3374
Est 9:18 The J in Susa, however, had assembled H3374
Est 9:19 That is why rural J—those living in H3374
Est 9:20 sent letters to all the J throughout the H3374
Est 9:22 as the time when the J got relief from their H3374
Est 9:23 So the J agreed to continue the H3374
Est 9:24 the enemy of all the J, had plotted H3374
Est 9:24 plotted against the J to destroy them and H3374
Est 9:25 devised against the J should come back H3374
Est 9:27 the J took it on themselves to establish the H3374
Est 9:28 never fail to be celebrated by the J— H3374
Est 9:30 letters to all the J in the 127 provinces of H3374
Est 10: 3 preeminent among the J, and held in H3374
Est 10: 3 held in high esteem by his many **fellow** J, H278
Est 10: 3 spoke up for the welfare of all the J. H2446S
Jer 32:12 the deed and of all the J sitting in the H3374
Jer 38:19 "I am afraid of the J who have gone over H3374
Jer 40:11 When all the J in Moab, Ammon, Edom H3374
Jer 40:15 life and cause all the J who are gathered H3373
Jer 43: 9 "While the J are watching, take some H3374
Jer 44: 1 concerning all the J living in Lower Egypt H3374
Jer 44:26 word of the LORD, all you J living in Egypt: H3373
Jer 44:27 the J in Egypt will perish by sword and H3373
Jer 52:28 in the seventh year, 3,023 J; H3374
Jer 52:30 745 J taken into exile by Nebuzaradan H3374
Da 3: 8 came forward and denounced the J. A10316
Da 3:12 But there are some J whom you have set A10316
Mt 2: 2 the one who has been born king *of* the J? G2681
Mt 27:11 asked him, "Are you the king *of* the J?" G2681
Mt 27:29 "Hail, king *of* the J!" they said. G2681
Mt 27:37 THIS IS JESUS, THE KING OF THE J. G2681
Mt 28:15 circulated among the J to this very day. G2681
Mk 7: 3 Pharisees and all the J do not eat unless G2681
Mk 15: 2 "Are you the king *of* the J?" asked Pilate G2681
Mk 15: 9 me to release to you the king *of* the J?" G2681
Mk 15:12 with the one you call the king *of* the J?" G2681
Mk 15:18 to call out to him, "Hail, king *of* the J!" G2681
Mk 15:26 charge against him read: THE KING OF THE J. G2681
Lk 7: 3 sent some elders *of* the J to him, G2681
Lk 23: 3 asked Jesus, "Are you the king *of* the J?" G2681
Lk 23:37 "If you are the king *of* the J, save yourself." G2681
Lk 23:38 which read: THIS IS THE KING OF THE J. G2681
Jn 2: 6 the kind used by the J for ceremonial G2681
Jn 2:18 The J then responded to him, "What sign G2681
Jn 4: 9 For J do not associate with Samaritans G2681
Jn 4:20 you J claim that the place where we NDT
Jn 4:22 we do know, for salvation is from the J. G2681
Jn 6:41 At this the J there began to grumble G2681
Jn 6:52 Then the J began to argue sharply among G2681
Jn 7:15 The J there were amazed and asked G2681
Jn 7:35 The J said to one another, "Where does G2681
Jn 8:22 This made the J ask, "Will he kill himself G2681
Jn 8:31 To the J who had believed him, Jesus G2681
Jn 8:48 The J answered him, "Aren't we right in G2681
Jn 10:19 The J who heard these words were again G2681
Jn 10:24 The J who were there gathered around G2681
Jn 11: 8 short while ago the J there tried to stone G2681
Jn 11:19 many J had come to Martha and Mary G2681
Jn 11:31 When the J who had been with Mary in G2681
Jn 11:33 the J who had come along with her G2681
Jn 11:36 Then the J said, "See how he loved him!" G2681
Jn 11:45 many of the J who had come to visit G2681
Jn 12: 9 a large crowd of J found out that Jesus G2681
Jn 12:11 of him many *of* the J were going over to G2681
Jn 13:33 just as I told the J, so I tell you now: G2681
Jn 18:20 temple, where all the J come together. G2681
Jn 18:33 asked him, "Are you the king *of* the J?" G2681
Jn 18:38 out again to the J gathered there and G2681
Jn 18:39 want me to release 'the king *of* the J'?" G2681
Jn 19: 3 again, saying, "Hail, king *of* the J! G2681
Jn 19: 4 out and said *to* **the** J gathered there, G899S
Jn 19:14 "Here is your king," Pilate said *to* the J. G2681
Jn 19:19 JESUS OF NAZARETH, THE KING OF THE J. G2681
Jn 19:20 Many *of* the J read this sign, for the place G2681
Jn 19:21 The chief priests *of* the J protested to G2681
Jn 19:21 "Do not write 'The King *of* the J,' but that G2681
Jn 19:21 that this man claimed to be king *of* the J." G2681
Ac 2: 5 God-fearing J from every nation G2681+467
Ac 2:11 both J and converts to Judaism); Cretans G2681
Ac 2:14 "*Fellow* J and all of you who live in G467+2681
Ac 6: 1 the **Hellenistic** J among them complained G1821
Ac 6: 1 against the **Hebraic** J because their G1578
Ac 6: 9 J of Cyrene and Alexandria as well as the NDT
Ac 9:22 baffled the J living in Damascus by G2681
Ac 9:23 was a conspiracy among the J to kill him, G2681
Ac 9:29 talked and debated with the **Hellenistic** J, G1821
Ac 10:39 in the country *of* the J and in Jerusalem. G2681
Ac 11:19 spreading the word only *among* J. G2681
Ac 12: 3 that this met with approval *among* the J, G2681
Ac 13:43 many *of* the J and devout converts to G2681
Ac 13:45 When the J saw the crowds, they were G2681
Ac 14: 1 that a great number *of* J and Greeks G2681
Ac 14: 2 But the J who refused to believe stirred up G2681
Ac 14: 4 some sided with the J, others with the G2681
Ac 14: 5 a plot afoot among both Gentiles and J, G2681
Ac 14:19 Then *some* J came from Antioch and G2681
Ac 16: 3 him because of the J who lived in that G2681
Ac 16:20 "These men are J, and are throwing G2681
Ac 17: 4 Some of **the** J were persuaded and joined G899S
Ac 17: 5 But other J were jealous; so they rounded G2681
Ac 17:11 Now **the Berean** J were of more noble G4047S
Ac 17:13 But when the J in Thessalonica learned G2681
Ac 17:17 synagogue with both J and God-fearing G2681
Ac 18: 2 Claudius had ordered all J to leave Rome. G2681
Ac 18: 4 trying to persuade J and Greeks. G2681
Ac 18: 5 testifying *to* the J that Jesus was the G2681
Ac 18:12 the J of Corinth made a united attack on G2681
Ac 18:14 "If you J were making a complaint about G2681
Ac 18:19 the synagogue and reasoned with the J. G2681
Ac 19:10 so that all the J and Greeks who lived in G2681
Ac 19:13 Some J who went around driving out evil G2681
Ac 19:17 became known *to* the J and Greeks living G2681
Ac 19:33 The J in the crowd pushed Alexander to G2681
Ac 20: 3 Because some J had plotted against him G2681
Ac 20:21 I have declared *to* both J and Greeks that G2681
Ac 21:20 how many thousands of J have believed G2681
Ac 21:21 you teach all the J who live among the G2681
Ac 21:27 some J from the province of Asia saw G2681
Ac 22:12 highly respected by all the J living there. G2681
Ac 22:30 why Paul was being accused by the J. G2681
Ac 23:12 next morning some J formed a conspiracy G2681
Ac 23:20 "Some J have agreed to ask you to bring G2681
Ac 23:27 was seized by the J and they were about G2681
Ac 24: 5 stirring up riots *among* the J all over the G2681
Ac 24: 9 The other J joined in the accusation G2681
Ac 24:19 But there are some J from the province of G2681
Ac 24:27 Felix wanted to grant a favor *to* the J, G2681
Ac 25: 7 the J who had come down from G2681
Ac 25: 9 wishing to do the J a favor, said to Paul, G2681
Ac 25:10 I have not done any wrong *to* the J, as G2681
Ac 25:11 brought against me by these J are not true, NDT
Ac 25:15 the elders *of* the J brought charges G2681
Ac 26: 2 against all the accusations of the J, G2681
Ac 26: 7 of this hope that these J are accusing me. G2681
Ac 26:21 That is why *some* J seized me in the G2681
Ac 28:19 The J objected, so I was compelled to G2681
Ro 3: 2 the J have been entrusted with the very NDT
Ro 3: 9 made the charge that J and Gentiles alike G2681
Ro 3:29 Or is God the God *of* J only? Is he not the G2681
Ro 9:24 not only from the J but also from the G2681
Ro 15: 8 become a servant *of* the J on behalf of G4364
Ro 15:27 they owe it to the J to share with them their NDT
Ro 16: 7 my **fellow** J who have been in prison with G5150
Ro 16:21 Jason and Sosipater, my **fellow** J. G5150
1Co 1:22 J demand signs and Greeks look for G2681
1Co 1:23 a stumbling block *to* J and foolishness to G2681
1Co 1:24 God has called, both J and Greeks, Christ G2681
1Co 9:20 *To* the J I became like a Jew, to win the G2681
1Co 9:20 Jews I became like a Jew, to win the J. G2681
1Co 10:32 to stumble, whether J, Greeks or the G2681
1Co 12:13 one body—whether J or Gentiles, slave G2681
2Co 11:24 I received from the J the forty lashes G2681
2Co 11:26 in danger from *my* **fellow** J, in danger G1169
Gal 2:13 The other J joined him in his hypocrisy, so G2681
Gal 2:15 "We who are J by birth and not sinful G2681
Gal 2:17 we J find ourselves also among the sinners NDT
Col 4:11 These are the only J among my G1666+4364
1Th 2:14 things those churches suffered from the J G2681
Rev 2: 9 of those who say they are J and are not, G2681
Rev 3: 9 who claim to be J though they are not G2681

JEWS' (1) [JEW]
Ro 15:27 have shared in the J spiritual blessings, G899S

JEZANIAH (1)
Jer 42: 1 son of Kareah and J son of Hoshaiah, H3470

JEZEBEL (19) [JEZEBEL'S]
1Ki 16:31 he also married J daughter of Ethbaal H374
1Ki 18: 4 While J was killing off the LORD's prophets H374
1Ki 18:13 what I did while J was killing the prophets H374
1Ki 19: 1 Now Ahab told J everything Elijah had H374
1Ki 19: 2 So J sent a messenger to Elijah to say H374
1Ki 21: 5 His wife J came in and asked him, "Why H374
1Ki 21: 7 J his wife said, "Is this how you act as king H374
1Ki 21:11 Naboth's city did as J directed in the letters H374
1Ki 21:14 Then they sent word to J: "Naboth has been H374
1Ki 21:15 As soon as J heard that Naboth had been H374
1Ki 21:23 "And also concerning J the LORD says H374
1Ki 21:23 'Dogs will devour J by the wall of Jezreel H374
1Ki 21:25 the eyes of the LORD, urged on by J his wife. H374
2Ki 9: 7 blood of all the LORD's servants shed by J. H374
2Ki 9:10 As for J, dogs will devour her on the plot of H374
2Ki 9:22 witchcraft of your mother J abound? H374
2Ki 9:30 When J heard about it, she put on eye H374
2Ki 9:37 that no one will be able to say, 'This is J. H374
Rev 2:20 You tolerate that woman J, who calls G2630

JEZEBEL'S (3) [JEZEBEL]
1Ki 18:19 prophets of Asherah, who eat at J table." H374
2Ki 9:36 ground at Jezreel dogs will devour J flesh. H374
2Ki 9:37 J body will be like dung on the ground in H374

JEZER (3) [JEZERITE]
Ge 46:24 Jahziel, Guni, J and Shillem. H3672
Nu 26:49 through J, the Jezerite clan; through H3672
1Ch 7:13 J and Shillem—the descendants of H3672

JEZERITE (1) [JEZER]
Nu 26:49 through Jezer, the J clan; through Shillem, H3673

JEZIEL (1)
1Ch 12: 3 J and Pelet the sons of Azmaveth H3465

JEZRAHIAH (1)
Ne 12:42 The choirs sang under the direction of J. H3474

JEZREEL (41) [JEZREELITE]
Jos 15:56 J, Jokdeam, Zanoah, H3476
Jos 17:16 settlements and those in the Valley of J." H3476
Jos 19:18 territory included: J, Kesulloth, Shunem, H3476
Jdg 6:33 the Jordan and camped in the Valley of J. H3476
1Sa 25:43 David had also married Ahinoam of J, and H3476
1Sa 27: 3 Ahinoam **of** J and Abigail of Carmel, the H3477
1Sa 29: 1 Israel camped by the spring in J. H3476
1Sa 29:11 the Philistines went up to J. H3476
1Sa 30: 5 captured—Ahinoam **of** J and Abigail, the H3477
2Sa 2: 2 two wives, Ahinoam **of** J and Abigail, the H3477
2Sa 2: 9 Ashuri and J, and also over H3476
2Sa 3: 2 was Amnon the son of Ahinoam **of** J; H3477
2Sa 4: 4 about Saul and Jonathan came from J. H3476
1Ki 4:12 all of Beth Shan next to Zarethan below J, H3476
1Ki 18:45 rain started falling and Ahab rode off to J. H3476
1Ki 18:46 he ran ahead of Ahab all the way to J. H3476
1Ki 21: 1 The vineyard was in J, close to the palace H3476
1Ki 21:23 'Dogs will devour Jezebel by the wall of J H3476
2Ki 8:29 Joram returned to J to recover from the H3476
2Ki 8:29 Judah went down to J to see Joram son of H3476
2Ki 9:10 will devour her on the plot of ground at J, H3476
2Ki 9:15 had returned to J to recover from the H3476
2Ki 9:15 out of the city to go and tell the news in J." H3476
2Ki 9:16 Then he got into his chariot and rode to J H3476
2Ki 9:17 on the tower in J saw Jehu's troops H3476
2Ki 9:30 Then Jehu went to J. When Jezebel H3476
2Ki 9:36 the plot of ground at J dogs will devour H3476
2Ki 9:37 like dung on the ground in the plot at J, H3476
2Ki 10: 1 to the officials of J, to the elders and to H3476
2Ki 10: 6 come to me in J by this time H3476
2Ki 10: 7 in baskets and sent them to Jehu in J. H3476
2Ki 10:11 killed everyone in J who remained of the H3476
1Ch 3: 1 was Amnon the son of Ahinoam **of** J; H3477
1Ch 4: 3 the sons of Etam: J, Ishma and Idbash H3475
2Ch 22: 6 so he returned to J to recover from the H3476
2Ch 22: 6 Judah went down to J to see Joram son of H3476
Hos 1: 4 to Hosea, "Call him J, because I will soon H3475
Hos 1: 4 the house of Jehu for the massacre at J, H3476
Hos 1: 5 I will break Israel's bow in the Valley of J." H3476
Hos 1:11 of the land, for great will be the day of J. H3476
Hos 2:22 the olive oil, and they will respond to J. H3476

JEZREELITE (7) [JEZREEL]
1Ki 21: 1 a vineyard belonging to Naboth the J. H3477
1Ki 21: 4 angry because Naboth the J had said, H3477
1Ki 21: 6 "Because I said to Naboth the J, 'Sell me H3477
1Ki 21: 7 I'll get you the vineyard of Naboth the J." H3477
1Ki 21:15 of Naboth the J that he refused to H3477
2Ki 9:21 that had belonged to Naboth the J. H3477
2Ki 9:25 the field that belonged to Naboth the J. H3477

JIDLAPH (1)
Ge 22:22 Hazo, Pildash, J and Bethuel." H3358

JINGLING (1)
Isa 3:16 with **ornaments** j on their ankles. H6576

JOAB (141) [JOAB'S, ATROTH BETH JOAB]
2Sa 2:13 J son of Zeruiah and David's men went H3405
2Sa 2:14 Then Abner said to J, "Let's have some of H3405
2Sa 2:14 "All right, let them do it," J said. H3405
2Sa 2:18 J, Abishai and Asahel H3405
2Sa 2:22 could I look your brother J in the face?" H3405
2Sa 2:24 But J and Abishai pursued Abner, and as H3405
2Sa 2:26 Abner called out to J, "Must the sword H3405
2Sa 2:27 J answered, "As surely as God lives, if you H3405
2Sa 2:28 So J blew the trumpet, and all the troops H3405
2Sa 2:30 Then J stopped pursuing Abner and H3405
2Sa 2:32 Then J and his men marched all night H3405
2Sa 3:22 David's men and J returned from a raid H3405
2Sa 3:23 When J and all the soldiers with him H3405
2Sa 3:24 So J went to the king and said, "What H3405
2Sa 3:26 J then left David and sent messengers H3405
2Sa 3:27 J took him aside into an inner chamber H3405
2Sa 3:27 J stabbed him in the stomach NDT
2Sa 3:29 fall on the head of J and on his whole H3405
2Sa 3:30 J and his brother Abishai murdered Abner H3405
2Sa 3:31 Then David said to J and all the people H3405
2Sa 8:16 J son of Zeruiah was over the army H3405
2Sa 10: 7 David sent J out with the entire army of H3405
2Sa 10: 9 J saw that there were battle lines in front H3405
2Sa 10:11 J said, "If the Arameans are too strong for NDT
2Sa 10:13 Then J and the troops with him advanced H3405
2Sa 10:14 So J returned from fighting the H3405
2Sa 11: 1 David sent J out with the king's men and H3405
2Sa 11: 6 So David sent this word to J: "Send me H3405
2Sa 11: 6 And J sent him to David. H3405
2Sa 11: 7 David asked him how J was, how the H3405
2Sa 11:11 my commander J and my lord's men H3405
2Sa 11:14 wrote a letter to J and sent it with Uriah. H3405
2Sa 11:16 So while J had the city under siege, he H3405
2Sa 11:17 of the city came out and fought against J, H3405
2Sa 11:18 J sent David a full account of the battle. H3405
2Sa 11:22 David everything J had sent him to say. H3405
2Sa 11:25 "Say this to J: 'Don't let this upset H3405
2Sa 11:25 destroy it.' Say this to encourage J." H2084S
2Sa 12:26 Meanwhile J fought against Rabbah of H3405
2Sa 12:27 J then sent messengers to David, saying H3405

2Sa 14: 1 J son of Zeruiah knew that the king's H3405
2Sa 14: 2 So J sent someone to Tekoa and had a H3405
2Sa 14: 3 And J put the words in her mouth H3405
2Sa 14:19 "Isn't the hand of J with you in all this?" H3405
2Sa 14:19 it was your servant J who instructed me to H3405
2Sa 14:20 Your servant J did this to change the H3405
2Sa 14:21 The king said to J, "Very well, I will do it H3405
2Sa 14:22 J fell with his face to the ground to pay H3405
2Sa 14:22 J said, "Today your servant knows that he H3405
2Sa 14:23 Then J went to Geshur and brought H3405
2Sa 14:29 Absalom sent for J in order to send him H3405
2Sa 14:29 to the king, but J refused to come to him. NDT
2Sa 14:31 Then J did go to Absalom's house, and H3405
2Sa 14:32 Absalom said to J, "Look, I sent word to H3405
2Sa 14:33 So J went to the king and told him this H3405
2Sa 17:25 Amasa over the army in place of J. H3405
2Sa 17:25 sister of Zeruiah the mother of J. H3405
2Sa 18: 2 a third under the command of J, a third H3405
2Sa 18: 5 The king commanded J, Abishai and Ittai H3405
2Sa 18:10 happened, he told J, "I just saw Absalom H3405
2Sa 18:11 J said to the man who had told him this H3405
2Sa 18:14 J said, "I'm not going to wait like this H3405
2Sa 18:16 Then J sounded the trumpet, and the H3405
2Sa 18:16 pursuing Israel, for J halted them. H3405
2Sa 18:20 one to take the news today," J told him. H3405
2Sa 18:21 Then J said to a Cushite, "Go, tell the H3405
2Sa 18:21 Cushite bowed down before J and ran off. H3405
2Sa 18:22 Ahimaaz son of Zadok again said to J H3405
2Sa 18:22 But J replied, "My son, why do you want H3405
2Sa 18:23 So J said, "Run!" Then NDT
2Sa 18:29 confusion just as J was about to send the H3405
2Sa 19: 1 J was told, "The king is weeping and H3405
2Sa 19: 5 Then J went into the house to the king H3405
2Sa 19:13 of my army for life in place of J. H3405
2Sa 20: 8 J was wearing his military tunic, and H3405
2Sa 20: 9 J said to Amasa, "How are you, my H3405
2Sa 20: 9 Then J took Amasa by the beard with his H3405
2Sa 20:10 Joab's hand, and J plunged it into his belly NDT
2Sa 20:10 Then J and his brother Abishai pursued H3405
2Sa 20:11 "Whoever favors J, and whoever is for H3405
2Sa 20:11 whoever is for David, let him follow J!" H3405
2Sa 20:13 went on with J to pursue Sheba son H3405
2Sa 20:15 All the troops with J came and besieged H3405
2Sa 20:16 Tell J to come here so I can speak to him." H3405
2Sa 20:17 toward her, and she asked, "Are you J?" H3405
2Sa 20:20 J replied, "Far be it from me to swallow H3405
2Sa 20:21 The woman said to J, "His head will be H3405
2Sa 20:22 of Sheba son of Bikri and threw it to J. H3405
2Sa 20:22 And J went back to the king in Jerusalem H3405
2Sa 20:23 J was over Israel's entire army; Benaiah H3405
2Sa 23:18 the brother of J son of Zeruiah was H3405
2Sa 23:24 Asahel the brother of J, Elhanan son of H3405
2Sa 23:37 the armor-bearer of J son of Zeruiah, H3405
2Sa 24: 2 So the king said to J and the army H3405
2Sa 24: 3 But J replied to the king, "May the LORD H3405
2Sa 24: 4 overruled J and the army commanders H3405
2Sa 24: 9 J reported the number of the fighting men H3405
1Ki 1: 7 conferred with J son of Zeruiah and with H3405
1Ki 1:19 the priest and J the commander of the H3405
1Ki 1:41 of the trumpet, J asked, "What's the H3405
1Ki 2: 5 yourself know what J son of Zeruiah did to H3405
1Ki 2:22 Abiathar the priest and J son of Zeruiah!" H3405
1Ki 2:28 When the news reached J, who had H3405
1Ki 2:29 was told that J had fled to the tent H3405
1Ki 2:30 the tent of the LORD and said to J, H2257S
1Ki 2:30 to the king, "This is how J answered me." H3405
1Ki 2:31 guilt of the innocent blood that J shed. H3405
1Ki 2:33 rest on the head of J and his descendants H3405
1Ki 2:34 up and struck down J and killed him, H2257S
1Ki 11:15 with Edom, J the commander of the army H3405
1Ki 11:16 J and all the Israelites stayed there for six H3405
1Ki 11:21 ancestors and that J the commander of H3405
1Ch 2:16 three sons were Abishai, J and Asahel. H3405
1Ch 4:14 Seraiah was the father of J, the father of H3405
1Ch 11: 6 J son of Zeruiah went up first, and so he H3405
1Ch 11: 8 while J restored the rest of the city. H3405
1Ch 11:20 the brother of J was chief of the Three H3405
1Ch 11:26 Asahel the brother of J, Elhanan son of H3405
1Ch 11:39 the armor-bearer of J son of Zeruiah, H3405
1Ch 18:15 J son of Zeruiah was over the army H3405
1Ch 19: 8 David sent J out with the entire army of H3405
1Ch 19:10 J saw that there were battle lines in front H3405
1Ch 19:12 J said, "If the Arameans are too strong for NDT
1Ch 19:14 Then J and the troops with him advanced H3405
1Ch 19:15 So J went back to Jerusalem H3405
1Ch 20: 1 go off to war, J led out the armed forces. H3405
1Ch 20: 1 J attacked Rabbah and left it in ruins. H3405
1Ch 21: 2 So David said to J and the commanders of H3405
1Ch 21: 3 But J replied, "May the LORD multiply his H3405
1Ch 21: 4 however, overruled J; so Joab left and H3405
1Ch 21: 4 so J left and went throughout Israel and H3405
1Ch 21: 5 J reported the number of the fighting men H3405
1Ch 21: 6 But J did not include Levi and Benjamin H3405
1Ch 26:28 Abner son of Ner and J son of Zeruiah H3405
1Ch 27: 7 was Asahel the brother of J; his son H3405
1Ch 27:24 J son of Zeruiah began to count the men H3405
1Ch 27:34 J was the commander of the royal army H3405
Ezr 2: 6 through the line of Jeshua and J) 2,812 H3405
Ezr 8: 9 of the descendants of J, Obadiah son of H3405
Ne 7:11 through the line of Jeshua and J) 2,818 H3405
Ps 60: T when J returned and struck down H3405

JOAB'S (9) [JOAB]
1Sa 26: 6 son of Zeruiah, J brother, "Who will go H3405
2Sa 3:29 May J family never be without someone H3405
2Sa 14:30 J field is next to mine, and he has H3405
2Sa 18: 2 a third under J brother Abishai son of H3405
2Sa 18:15 And ten of J armor-bearers surrounded H3405
2Sa 20: 7 So J men and the Kerethites and H3405
2Sa 20:10 his guard against the dagger in J hand, H3405
2Sa 20:11 One of J men stood beside Amasa and H3405
1Ki 2:35 over the army in J position and replaced H2257S

JOAH (11)
2Ki 18:18 J son of Asaph the recorder went out H3406
2Ki 18:26 Shebna and J said to the field H3406
2Ki 18:37 J son of Asaph the recorder went to H3406
1Ch 6:21 J his son, Iddo his son, Zerah his son and H3406
1Ch 26: 4 the second, J the third, Sakar the H3406
2Ch 29:12 J son of Zimmah and Eden son of Joah H3406
2Ch 29:12 Joah son of Zimmah and Eden son of J; H3406
2Ch 34: 8 ruler of the city, with J son of Joahaz, the H3406
Isa 36: 3 J son of Asaph the recorder went out H3406
Isa 36:11 Shebna and J said to the field H3406
Isa 36:22 the secretary and J son of Asaph the H3406

JOAHAZ (1)
2Ch 34: 8 the city, with Joah son of J, the recorder, H3407

JOANAN (1)
Lk 3:27 the son *of* J, the son of Rhesa, the son of *G2720*

JOANNA (2)
Lk 8: 3 J the wife of Chuza, the manager of *G2721*
Lk 24:10 Mary Magdalene, J, Mary the mother of *G2721*

JOASH (42)
Jdg 6:11 Ophrah that belonged to J the Abiezrite, H3409
Jdg 6:29 they were told, "Gideon son of J did it." H3409
Jdg 6:30 The people of the town demanded of J H3409
Jdg 6:31 But J replied to the hostile crowd around H3409
Jdg 7:14 other than the sword of Gideon son of J, H3409
Jdg 8:13 Gideon son of J then returned from the H3409
Jdg 8:29 Jerub-Baal son of J went back home to H3409
Jdg 8:32 Gideon son of J died at a good old age H3409
Jdg 8:32 the tomb of his father J in Ophrah of the H3409
1Ki 22:26 the ruler of the city and to J the king's son H3409
2Ki 11: 2 took J son of Ahaziah and stole him away H3409
2Ki 11:21 J was seven years old when he began to H3371
2Ki 12: 1 year of Jehu, J became king, and he H3371
2Ki 12: 2 J did what was right in the eyes of the LORD H3371
2Ki 12: 4 J said to the priests, "Collect all the H3371
2Ki 12: 6 year of King J the priests still had not H3371
2Ki 12: 7 Therefore King J summoned Jehoiada the H3371
2Ki 12:18 But J king of Judah took all the sacred H3371
2Ki 12:19 As for the other events of the reign of J H3409
2Ki 13: 1 twenty-third year of J son of Ahaziah king H3409
2Ki 13:10 the thirty-seventh year of J king of Judah, H3409
2Ki 14: 1 Amaziah son of J king of Judah began to H3409
2Ki 14: 3 he followed the example of his father J. H3409
2Ki 14:13 the son of J, the son of Ahaziah, H3371
2Ki 14:17 Amaziah son of J king of Judah lived for H3409
2Ki 14:23 year of Amaziah son of J king of Judah, H3409
1Ch 3:11 his son, Ahaziah his son, J his son, H3409
1Ch 4:22 men of Kozeba, and J and Saraph, who H3409
1Ch 7: 8 Zemirah, J, Eliezer, Elioenai, Omri H3447
1Ch 12: 3 their chief and J the sons of Shemaah the H3409
1Ch 27:28 J was in charge of the supplies of olive oil H3447
2Ch 18:25 ruler of the city and to J the king's son, H3409
2Ch 22:11 took J son of Ahaziah and stole him away H3409
2Ch 24: 1 J was seven years old when he became H3409
2Ch 24: 2 J did what was right in the eyes of the LORD H3409
2Ch 24: 4 Some time later J decided to restore the H3409
2Ch 24:22 King J did not remember the kindness H3409
2Ch 24:23 the army of Aram marched against J; it H2257S
2Ch 24:24 ancestors, judgment was executed on J. H3409
2Ch 24:25 withdrew, they left J severely wounded. H2257S
2Ch 25:23 the son of J, the son of Ahaziah, H3409
2Ch 25:25 Amaziah son of J king of Judah lived for H3409

JOB (56) [JOB'S]
2Ch 34:13 supervised all the workers from j to job. H6275
2Ch 34:13 supervised all the workers from job to j. H6275
Job 1: 1 Uz there lived a man whose name was J. H373
Job 1: 5 J would make arrangements for them to be H373
Job 1: 8 "Have you considered my servant J? H373
Job 1: 9 "Does J fear God for nothing?" Satan H373
Job 1:14 a messenger came to J and said, "The oxen H373
Job 1:20 J got up and tore his robe and shaved his H373
Job 1:22 J did not sin by charging God with H373
Job 2: 3 "Have you considered my servant J? H373
Job 2: 7 the LORD and afflicted J with painful sores H373
Job 2: 8 Then J took a piece of broken pottery H2257S
Job 2:10 In all this, J did not sin in what he said. H373
Job 3: 1 J opened his mouth and cursed the day of H373
Job 6: 1 Then J replied: H373
Job 9: 1 Then J replied: H373
Job 12: 1 Then J replied: H373
Job 16: 1 Then J replied: H373
Job 19: 1 Then J replied: H373
Job 21: 1 Then J replied: H373
Job 23: 1 Then J replied: H373
Job 26: 1 Then J replied: H373
Job 27: 1 And J continued his discourse: H373
Job 29: 1 J continued his discourse: H373
Job 31:40 The words of J are ended. H373
Job 32: 1 So these three men stopped answering J H373
Job 32: 2 very angry with J for justifying himself H373
Job 32: 3 because they had found no way to refute J H373
Job 32: 4 before speaking to J because they were H373
Job 32:12 But not one of you has proved J wrong H373
Job 32:14 But J has not marshaled his words against NDT
Job 33: 1 "But now, J, listen to my words; pay H373
Job 33:31 "Pay attention, J, and listen to me; be H373
Job 34: 5 "J says, 'I am innocent, but God denies me H373
Job 34: 7 Is there anyone like J, who drinks scorn like H373
Job 34:35 'J speaks without knowledge; his words H373
Job 34:36 that J might be tested to the utmost for H373
Job 35:16 So J opens his mouth with empty talk H373
Job 37:14 "Listen to this, J; stop and consider God's H373
Job 38: 1 Then the LORD spoke to J out of the storm H373
Job 40: 1 The LORD said to J: H373
Job 40: 3 Then J answered the LORD: H373
Job 40: 6 Then the LORD spoke to J out of the storm: H373
Job 42: 1 Then J replied to the LORD: H373
Job 42: 7 After the LORD had said these things to J H373
Job 42: 7 the truth about me, as my servant J has. H373
Job 42: 8 go to my servant J and sacrifice a burnt H373
Job 42: 8 My servant J will pray for you, and I will H373
Job 42: 8 the truth about me, as my servant J has." H373
Job 42:10 After J had prayed for his friends, the LORD H373
Job 42:16 After this, J lived a hundred and forty years H373
Job 42:17 And so J died, an old man and full of years. H373
Eze 14:14 Noah, Daniel and J—were in it, they H373
Eze 14:20 if Noah, Daniel and J were in it, they could H373
Lk 16: 3 My master is taking away my j. I'm not *G3873*
Lk 16: 4 when I lose my j here, people will *G3873*

JOB'S (8) [JOB]
Job 1: 5 in their hearts." This was J regular custom. H373
Job 1:13 One day when J sons and daughters H2257S
Job 2:11 When J three friends, Eliphaz the H373
Job 31:31 'Who has not been filled with J meat? H2257S
Job 42: 9 told them; and the LORD accepted J prayer. H373
Job 42:12 the latter part of J life more than the former H373
Job 42:15 found women as beautiful as J daughters, H373
Jas 5:11 You have heard of J perseverance and *G2724*

JOBAB (9)
Ge 10:29 Havilah and J. All these were sons H3411
Ge 36:33 J son of Zerah from Bozrah succeeded H3412
Ge 36:34 When J died, Husham from the land of H3412
Jos 11: 1 he sent word to J king of Madon, to the H3412
1Ch 1:23 Havilah and J. All these were sons H3411
1Ch 1:44 J son of Zerah from Bozrah succeeded H3412
1Ch 1:45 When J died, Husham from the land of H3412
1Ch 8: 9 By his wife Hodesh he had J, Zibia H3412
1Ch 8:18 Izliah and J were the sons of Elpaal. H3412

JOCHEBED (2)
Ex 6:20 Amram married his father's sister J, who H3425
Nu 26:59 the name of Amram's wife was J, H3425

JODA (1)
Lk 3:26 of Semein, the son of Josek, the son *of* J, *G2726*

JOED (1)
Ne 11: 7 the son of J, the son of Pedaiah, H3444

JOEL (21)
1Sa 8: 2 of his firstborn was J and the name of his H3408
1Ch 4:35 J, Jehu son of Joshibiah, the son of H3408
1Ch 5: 4 The descendants of J: Shemaiah his son H3408
1Ch 5: 8 of Azaz, the son of Shema, the son of J. H3408
1Ch 5:12 J was the chief, Shapham the second H3408
1Ch 6:28 J the firstborn and Abijah the second son H3408
1Ch 6:33 musician, the son of J, the son of Samuel, H3408
1Ch 6:36 Elkanah, the son of J, the son of Azariah, H3408
1Ch 7: 3 Michael, Obadiah, J and Ishiah. All five H3408
1Ch 11:38 J the brother of Nathan, Mibhar son of H3408
1Ch 15: 7 Gershon, J the leader and 130 relatives; H3408
1Ch 15:11 Uriel, Asaiah, J, Shemaiah, Eliel and H3408
1Ch 15:17 So the Levites appointed Heman son of J H3408
1Ch 23: 8 the first, Zetham and J—three in all. H3408
1Ch 26:22 sons of Jehieli, Zetham and his brother J. H3408
1Ch 27:20 the tribe of Manasseh: J son of Pedaiah; H3408
2Ch 29:12 son of Amasai and J son of Azariah; H3408
Ezr 10:43 Zebina, Jaddai, J and Benaiah. H3408
Ne 11: 9 J son of Zikri was their chief officer, and H3408
Joel 1: 1 of the LORD that came to J son of Pethuel. H3408
Ac 2:16 this is what was spoken by the prophet J: *G2727*

JOELAH (1)
1Ch 12: 7 J and Zebadiah the sons of Jeroham H3443

JOEZER (1)
1Ch 12: 6 J and Jashobeam the Korahites H3445

JOGBEHAH (2)
Nu 32:35 Atroth Shophan, Jazer, J, H3322
Jdg 8:11 east of Nobah and J and attacked the H3322

JOGLI (1)
Nu 34:22 Bukki son of J, the leader from the tribe of H3332

JOHA (2)
1Ch 8:16 Ishpah and J were the sons of Beriah. H3418
1Ch 11:45 son of Shimri, his brother J the Tizite, H3418

JOHANAN (25)

2Ki 25:23 son of Nethaniah, J son of Kareah H3419
1Ch 3:15 J the firstborn, Jehoiakim the second son H3419
1Ch 3:24 Pelaiah, Akkub, J, Delaiah and Anani H3419
1Ch 6: 9 father of Azariah, Azariah the father of J, H3419
1Ch 6:10 J the father of Azariah (it was he who H3419
1Ch 12: 4 Jeremiah, Jahaziel, J, Jozabad the H3419
1Ch 12:12 J the eighth, Elzabad the ninth, H3419
Ezr 8:12 of Azgad, J son of Hakkatan, and H3419
Ne 12:22 J and Jaddua, as well as those of H3419
Ne 12:23 up to the time of J son of Eliashib were H3419
Jer 40: 8 J and Jonathan the sons of Kareah H3419
Jer 40:13 J son of Kareah and all the army officers H3419
Jer 40:15 Then J son of Kareah said privately to H3419
Jer 40:16 son of Ahikam said to J son of Kareah, H3419
Jer 41:11 When J son of Kareah and all the army H3419
Jer 41:13 had with him saw J son of Kareah and the H3419
Jer 41:14 turned and went over to J son of Kareah. H3419
Jer 41:15 of his men escaped from J and fled to the H3419
Jer 41:16 Then J son of Kareah and all the army H3419
Jer 41:16 whom J had recovered from Ishmael son of NDT
Jer 42: 1 including J son of Kareah and Jezaniah H3419
Jer 42: 8 So he called together J son of Kareah and H3419
Jer 43: 2 son of Hoshaiah and J son of Kareah and H3419
Jer 43: 4 So J son of Kareah and all the army H3419
Jer 43: 5 J son of Kareah and all the army officers H3419

JOHN (139) [JOHN'S]

Mt 3: 1 In those days J the Baptist came G2722
Mt 3:13 Galilee to the Jordan to be baptized by J. G2722
Mt 3:14 But J tried to deter him, saying, "I need to G2722
Mt 3:15 fulfill all righteousness." Then J consented. NDT
Mt 4:12 When Jesus heard that J had been put in G2722
Mt 4:21 James son of Zebedee and his brother J. G2722
Mt 10: 2 James son of Zebedee, and his brother J; G2722
Mt 11: 2 When J, who was in prison, heard about G2722
Mt 11: 4 back and report *to* J what you hear and G2722
Mt 11: 7 began to speak to the crowd about J: G2722
Mt 11:11 risen anyone greater *than* J the Baptist; G2722
Mt 11:12 From the days *of* J the Baptist until now G2722
Mt 11:13 Prophets and the Law prophesied until J. G2722
Mt 11:18 For J came neither eating nor drinking G2722
Mt 14: 2 attendants, "This is J the Baptist; he has G2722
Mt 14: 3 Herod had arrested J and bound him and G2722
Mt 14: 4 J had been saying to him: "It is not G2722
Mt 14: 5 Herod wanted to kill J, but he was afraid G899S
Mt 14: 5 because they considered J a prophet. G899S
Mt 14: 8 on a platter the head *of* J the Baptist." G2722
Mt 14:10 had J beheaded in the prison. G2722
Mt 16:14 replied, "Some say J the Baptist; others G2722
Mt 17: 1 James and J the brother of James G2722
Mt 17:13 was talking to them about J the Baptist. G2722
Mt 21:26 they all hold that J was a prophet." G2722
Mt 21:32 For J came to you to show you the way of G2722
Mk 1: 4 And so J the Baptist appeared in the G2722
Mk 1: 6 J wore clothing made of camel's hair, with G2722
Mk 1: 9 was baptized by J in the Jordan. G2722
Mk 1:14 After J was put in prison, Jesus went into G2722
Mk 1:19 of Zebedee and his brother J in a boat, G2722
Mk 1:29 went with James and J to the home of G2722
Mk 3:17 James son of Zebedee and his brother J G2722
Mk 5:37 James and J the brother of James. G2722
Mk 6:14 "J the Baptist has been raised from the G2722
Mk 6:16 he said, "J, whom I beheaded, has G2722
Mk 6:17 had given orders to have J arrested, G2722
Mk 6:18 For J had been saying to Herod, "It is not G2722
Mk 6:19 a grudge against J and wanted to kill him G899S
Mk 6:20 Herod feared J and protected him, G2722
Mk 6:20 When Herod heard J, he was greatly G899S
Mk 6:24 "The head *of* J the Baptist," she G2722
Mk 6:25 right now the head *of* J the Baptist on a G2722
Mk 6:27 The man went, beheaded J in the prison, G899S
Mk 8:28 replied, "Some say J the Baptist; others G2722
Mk 9: 2 James and J with him and led them up a G2722
Mk 9:38 said J, "we saw someone driving out G2722
Mk 10:35 Then James and J, the sons of Zebedee G2722
Mk 10:41 they became indignant with James and J. G2722
Mk 11:32 everyone held that J really was a prophet.) G2722
Mk 13: 3 J and Andrew asked him privately G2722
Mk 14:33 James and J along with him, and G2722
Lk 1:13 bear you a son, and you are to call him J. G2722
Lk 1:60 up and said, "No! He is to be called J." G2722
Lk 1:63 astonishment he wrote, "His name is J." G2722
Lk 3: 2 of God came to J son of Zechariah in G2722
Lk 3: 7 J said to the crowds coming out to be NDT
Lk 3:11 J answered, "Anyone who has two shirts NDT
Lk 3:15 in their hearts if J might possibly be the G2722
Lk 3:16 J answered them all, "I baptize you with G2722
Lk 3:18 many other words J exhorted the people NDT
Lk 3:19 But when J rebuked Herod the tetrarch G899S
Lk 3:20 this to them all: He locked J up in prison. G2722
Lk 5:10 so were James and J, the sons of G2722
Lk 6:14 Andrew, James, J, Philip, Bartholomew, G2722
Lk 7:20 "J the Baptist sent us to you to ask G2722
Lk 7:22 back and report *to* J what you have seen G2722
Lk 7:24 began to speak to the crowd about J: G2722
Lk 7:28 of women there is no one greater *than* J; G2722
Lk 7:29 because they had been baptized *by* J. G2722
Lk 7:30 because they had not been baptized by J.) G899S
Lk 7:33 For J the Baptist came neither eating G2722
Lk 8:51 him except Peter, J and James, and the G2722
Lk 9: 7 were saying that J had been raised from G2722
Lk 9: 9 "I beheaded J. Who, then, is this I G2722
Lk 9:19 replied, "Some say J the Baptist; others G2722
Lk 9:28 J and James with him and went up onto a G2722
Lk 9:49 said J, "we saw someone driving out G2722
Lk 9:54 When the disciples James and J saw this G2722
Lk 11: 1 us to pray, just as J taught his disciples." G2722
Lk 16:16 the Prophets were proclaimed until J. G2722
Lk 20: 6 they are persuaded that J was a prophet." G2722
Lk 22: 8 Jesus sent Peter and J, saying, "Go and G2722
Jn 1: 6 a man sent from God whose name was J. G2722
Jn 1:15 (J testified concerning him. He cried out G2722
Jn 1:23 J replied in the words of Isaiah the prophet NDT
Jn 1:26 J replied, "but among you stands one G2722
Jn 1:28 side of the Jordan, where J was baptizing. G2722
Jn 1:29 The next day J saw Jesus coming toward NDT
Jn 1:32 Then J gave this testimony: "I saw the G2722
Jn 1:35 The next day J was there again with two G2722
Jn 1:40 two who heard what J had said and who G2722
Jn 1:42 at him and said, "You are Simon son *of* J. G2722
Jn 3:23 Now J also was baptizing at Aenon near G2722
Jn 3:24 This was before J was put in prison.) G2722
Jn 3:26 They came to J and said to him, "Rabbi G2722
Jn 3:27 To this J replied, "A person can receive G2722
Jn 4: 1 baptizing more disciples than J— G2722
Jn 5:33 "You have sent to J and he has testified G2722
Jn 5:35 J was a lamp that burned and gave light G1697S
Jn 5:36 "I have testimony weightier *than* that of J G2722
Jn 10:40 to the place where J had been baptizing G2722
Jn 10:41 "Though J never performed a sign G2722
Jn 10:41 all that J said about this man was true." G2722
Jn 21:15 "Simon *son of* J, do you love me G2722
Jn 21:16 "Simon *son of* J, do you love me? G2722
Jn 21:17 "Simon *son of* J, do you love me? G2722
Ac 1: 5 For J baptized with water, but in a few G2722
Ac 1:13 present were Peter, J, James and Andrew; G2722
Ac 3: 1 One day Peter and J were going up to the G2722
Ac 3: 3 When he saw Peter and J about to enter G2722
Ac 3: 4 straight at him, as did J. Then Peter said, G2722
Ac 3:11 While the man held on to Peter and J, all G2722
Ac 4: 1 came up to **Peter and** J while they were G899S
Ac 4: 3 They seized **Peter and** J and, because it G899S
Ac 4: 6 so were Caiaphas, J, Alexander and G2722
Ac 4: 7 They had **Peter and** J brought before them G899S
Ac 4:13 courage of Peter and J and realized that G2722
Ac 4:19 But Peter and J replied, "Which is right in G2722
Ac 4:23 Peter and J went back to their own people NDT
Ac 8:14 they sent Peter and J to Samaria. G2722
Ac 8:17 Then Peter and J placed their hands on NDT
Ac 8:25 Peter and J returned to Jerusalem NDT
Ac 10:37 after the baptism that J preached— G2722
Ac 11:16 'J baptized with water, but you will be G2722
Ac 12: 2 the brother *of* J, put to death with G2722
Ac 12:12 to the house of Mary the mother *of* J, G2722
Ac 12:25 taking with them J, also called Mark. G2722
Ac 13: 5 J was with them as their helper G2722
Ac 13:13 where J left them to return to Jerusalem. G2722
Ac 13:24 J preached repentance and baptism to all G2722
Ac 13:25 As J was completing his work, he said G2722
Ac 15:37 Barnabas wanted to take J, also called G2722
Ac 18:25 though he knew only the baptism *of* J. G2722
Gal 2: 9 Cephas and J, those esteemed as G2722
Rev 1: 1 by sending his angel to his servant J, G2722
Rev 1: 4 J, To the seven churches in the province G2722
Rev 1: 9 J, your brother and companion in the G2722
Rev 22: 8 J, am the one who heard and saw these G2722

JOHN'S (19) [JOHN]

Mt 3: 4 J clothes were made of camel's hair, and G2722
Mt 9:14 Then J disciples came and asked him G2722
Mt 11: 7 As J **disciples** were leaving, Jesus began G4047S
Mt 14:12 J disciples came and took his body and G899S
Mt 21:25 J baptism—where did it come from? Was G2722
Mk 2:18 Now J disciples and the Pharisees were G2722
Mk 2:18 "How is it that J disciples and the G2722
Mk 6:27 executioner with orders to bring J head. G899S
Mk 6:29 J disciples came and took his body and G899S
Mk 11:30 J baptism—was it from heaven, or of G2722
Lk 5:33 "J disciples often fast and pray G2722
Lk 7:18 J disciples told him about all these things. G2722
Lk 7:24 After J messengers left, Jesus began to G2722
Lk 20: 4 J baptism—was it from heaven, or of G2722
Jn 1:19 Now this was J testimony when the G2722
Jn 3:25 between some of J disciples and a certain G2722
Ac 1:22 beginning from J baptism to the time G2722
Ac 19: 3 did you receive?" "J baptism," they G2722
Ac 19: 4 "J baptism was a baptism of repentance. G2722

JOIADA (5)

Ne 3: 6 Gate was repaired by J son of Paseah H3421
Ne 12:10 father of Eliashib, Eliashib the father of J, H3421
Ne 12:11 J the father of Jonathan, and Jonathan the H3421
Ne 12:22 days of Eliashib, J, Johanan and Jaddua, H3421
Ne 13:28 One of the sons of J son of Eliashib the H3421

JOIAKIM (4)

Ne 12:10 Joshua was the father of J, Joiakim the H3423
Ne 12:10 father of Joiakim, J the father of Eliashib H3423
Ne 12:12 In the days of J, these were the heads of H3423
Ne 12:26 They served in the days of J son of Joshua H3423

JOIARIB (4) [JOIARIB'S]

Ezr 8:16 were leaders, and J and Elnathan, who H3424
Ne 11: 5 Adaiah, the son of J, the son of Zechariah H3424
Ne 11:10 Jedaiah; the son of J; Jakin; H3424
Ne 12: 6 Shemaiah, J, Jedaiah, H3424

JOIARIB'S (1) [JOIARIB]

Ne 12:19 of J, Mattenai; of Jedaiah's, Uzzi; H3424

JOIN (46) [ADJOINING, JOINED, JOINS, JUNCTION, REJOINED]

Ge 34:30 and *if they* j **forces** against me and attack H665
Ge 37:35 to mourn *until I* j my son in the H3718+448
Ge 49: 6 their council, *let* me not j their assembly H3479
Ex 1:10 if war breaks out, *will* j our enemies, fight H3578
Ex 26: 3 J five of the curtains together, and do the H2489
Ex 26: 9 J five of the curtains **together** into one set H2489
Nu 18: 2 your ancestral tribe *to* j you and assist you H4277
Nu 18: 4 *They are to* j you and be responsible for H4277
Nu 34: 5 j the Wadi of Egypt and end at the H2025
Jdg 3:13 *Getting* the Ammonites and Amalekites *to* j H665
Jdg 21:21 of Shiloh come out to j in the dancing, H2565
1Sa 13: 4 people were summoned to j Saul at Gilgal. H339
1Sa 22:20 Abiathar, escaped and fled to j David. H339
2Sa 13:24 *Will* the king and his attendants please j H2143+6640
1Ki 1: 8 David's special guard did not j Adonijah. H6640
1Ch 12:17 I *am ready for* you *to* j H2118+4222+4200+3480
1Ch 13: 2 pasturelands, *to* **come and** j us. H7695
2Ch 18: 3 as your people; we will j you in the war." H6640
Ne 4:20 hear the sound of the trumpet, j us there. H7695
Ne 10:29 all *these* now j their fellow H2616+6584
Est 9:27 all who j them should without H4277
Job 37:18 can you j him in spreading out the skies H6640
Ps 49:19 *they will* j those who have gone H995+6330
Ps 50:18 you see a thief, *you* j with him; you throw H8354
Ps 106: 5 of your nation and j your inheritance in H6640
Ps 118:27 j **in the** festal procession up to the horns of H673
Pr 23:20 *Do* not j those who drink too much H2118+928
Pr 24:21 and *do* not j with rebellious officials H6843
Ecc 9: 3 they live, and afterward they j the dead. H448
Isa 5: 8 house to house and j field to field till no H7928
Isa 14: 1 Foreigners *will* j them and unite with the H4277
Isa 14:20 *you will* not j them in burial, for you have H3479
Jer 3:18 of Judah *will* j the people of H2143+6584
Eze 37:17 J them together into one stick so that they H7928
Eze 37:19 with him, and j it to Judah's stick. H5989
Da 11:34 many who are not sincere *will* j them. H4277
Mic 5: 3 rest of his brothers return to j the Israelites. NDT
Ac 5:13 No one else dared j them, even though G3140
Ac 9:26 Jerusalem, he tried *to* j the disciples, but G3140
Ac 17:15 and Timothy to j him as soon as G2262+4639
Ac 21:24 j **in** their purification rites and pay their G5250
Ro 15:30 *to* j **me in** my **struggle** by praying to God G5253
Php 3:17 J **together in following** my **example** G5213+1181
2Ti 1: 8 j **with** me **in suffering** for the gospel G5155
2Ti 2: 3 J **with** me **in suffering**, like a good soldier G5155
1Pe 4: 4 are surprised *that* you *do* not j them in G5340

JOINED (32) [JOIN]

Ge 14: 3 these latter kings j **forces** in the Valley of H2489
Ex 36:10 *They* j five of the curtains together and did H2489
Ex 36:16 *They* j five of the curtains into one set and H2489
Jos 10: 5 Jarmuth, Lachish and Eglon—j **forces**. H665
Jos 10: 6 the hill country *have* j **forces** against us." H7695
Jos 11: 5 All these kings j **forces** and made camp H3585
Jos 15: 4 along to Azmon and j the Wadi of Egypt, H3655
Jdg 6:33 eastern peoples j **forces** and crossed H665+3481
1Sa 10:10 and he j **in** their prophesying. H928+9348
1Sa 14:22 on the run, they j the battle in hot pursuit. H1815
1Sa 28:23 But his men j the woman in urging H2256+1685
1Ki 20:29 on the seventh day the battle *was* j. H7928
2Ch 5:13 musicians j in unison to give praise H2118
Ezr 3: 9 j **together** in supervising those H6641+3869+285
Job 41:17 *They* **are** j **fast** to one another; they cling H1815
Job 41:23 The folds of its flesh *are* **tightly** j; they are H1815
Ps 48: 4 When the kings j **forces**, when they H3585
Ps 83: 8 Even Assyria *has* j them to reinforce Lot's H4277
Hos 4:17 Ephraim *is* j to idols; leave him alone! H2489
Zec 2:11 "Many nations *will* **be** j with the LORD in H4277
Mt 19: 6 Therefore what God *has* j **together**, let no AIT
Mk 10: 9 Therefore what God *has* j **together**, let no G5183
Jn 6:17 and Jesus *had* not yet j them. G2262+4639
Ac 1:14 They all j together **constantly** in G1639+4674
Ac 12:20 they now j **together** and sought an G3924
Ac 16:22 The crowd j **in the attack** against Paul G5308
Ac 17: 4 were persuaded and j Paul and Silas, G4677
Ac 20: 6 five days later j the others at Troas G2262+4639
Ac 24: 9 The other Jews j **in** the accusation G5298
Gal 2:13 The other Jews j him **in** his **hypocrisy**, so G5347
Eph 2:21 whole building *is* j **together** and rises to G5274
Eph 4:16 j and held together by every supporting G5274

JOINS (2) [JOIN]

Hos 7: 5 and he j hands with the mockers. H5432
1Co 16:16 everyone who j **in the work** and labors at G5300

JOINT (2) [JOINTED, JOINTS]

Job 31:22 the shoulder, let it be broken off at the j. H7866
Ps 22:14 like water, and all my bones *are* **out of** j. H7233

JOINTED (1) [JOINT]

Lev 11:21 those that have j legs for H4946+5087+4200+8079

JOINTS (1) [JOINT]

Heb 4:12 soul and spirit, j and marrow; it judges the G765

JOISTS (1)
2Ch 34:11 timber for j and beams for the H4677

JOKDEAM (1)
Jos 15:56 Jezreel, J, Zanoah, H3680

JOKIM (1)
1Ch 4:22 J, the men of Kozeba, and Joash and H3451

JOKING (3)
Ge 19:14 But his sons-in-law thought he was j. H7464
Pr 26:19 their neighbor and says, "I *was* only j!" H8471
Eph 5:4 foolish talk or **coarse** j, which are out of G2365

JOKMEAM (2)
1Ki 4:12 Beth Shan to Abel Meholah across to J; H3695
1Ch 6:68 J, Beth Horon, H3695

JOKNEAM (4)
Jos 12:22 of Kedesh one the king of J in Carmel one H3696
Jos 19:11 extended to the ravine near J. H3696
Jos 21:34 from the tribe of Zebulun, J, Kartah, H3696
1Ch 6:77 From the tribe of Zebulun they received J H3696

JOKSHAN (4)
Ge 25:2 She bore him Zimran, J, Medan, Midian H3705
Ge 25:3 J was the father of Sheba and Dedan; the H3705
1Ch 1:32 Zimran, J, Medan, Midian, Ishbak and H3705
1Ch 1:32 The sons of J: Sheba and Dedan. H3705

JOKTAN (6)
Ge 10:25 was divided; his brother was named J. H3690
Ge 10:26 J was the father of Almodad, Sheleph H3690
Ge 10:29 All these were sons of J. H3690
1Ch 1:19 was divided; his brother was named J. H3690
1Ch 1:20 J was the father of Almodad, Sheleph H3690
1Ch 1:23 All these were sons of J. H3690

JOKTHEEL (2)
Jos 15:38 Mizpah, J, H3706
2Ki 14:7 in battle, calling it J, the name it has to H3706

JOLTING (1)
Na 3:2 wheels, galloping horses and j chariots! H8376

JONA (KJV) JOHN

JONADAB (5)
2Sa 13:3 had an adviser named J son of Shimeah, H3432
2Sa 13:3 David's brother. J was a very shrewd man. H3432
2Sa 13:5 pretend to be ill," J said. "When your H3386
2Sa 13:32 But J son of Shimeah, David's brother H3432
2Sa 13:35 J said to the king, "See, the king's sons H3432

JONAH (28) [JONAH'S]
2Ki 14:25 through his servant J son of Amittai, H3434
Jnh 1:1 word of the LORD came to J son of Amittai: H3434
Jnh 1:3 But J ran away from the LORD and headed H3434
Jnh 1:5 But J had gone below deck, where he lay H3434
Jnh 1:7 They cast lots and the lot fell on J. H3434
Jnh 1:15 Then they took J and threw him overboard H3434
Jnh 1:17 LORD provided a huge fish to swallow J, H3434
Jnh 1:17 J was in the belly of the fish three H3434
Jnh 2:1 From inside the fish J prayed to the LORD H3434
Jnh 2:10 the fish, and it vomited J onto dry land. H3434
Jnh 3:1 word of the LORD came to J a second time: H3434
Jnh 3:3 J obeyed the word of the LORD and went to H3434
Jnh 3:4 J began by going a day's journey into the H3434
Jnh 4:1 But to J this seemed very wrong, and he H3434
Jnh 4:5 J had gone out and sat down at a place H3434
Jnh 4:6 made it grow up over J to give shade for H3434
Jnh 4:6 J was very happy about the plant. H3434
Jnh 4:9 But God said to J, "Is it right for you to be H3434
Mt 12:39 given it except the sign *of* the prophet J. G2731
Mt 12:40 For as J was three days and three nights in G2731
Mt 12:41 they repented at the preaching *of* J G2731
Mt 12:41 now something greater *than* J is here. G2731
Mt 16:4 none will be given it except the sign *of* J." G2731
Mt 16:17 are you, Simon **son of** J, for this was not G980
Lk 11:29 none will be given it except the sign *of* J. G2731
Lk 11:30 For as J was a sign to the Ninevites, so G2731
Lk 11:32 they repented at the preaching *of* J G2731
Lk 11:32 now something greater *than* J is here. G2731

JONAH'S (2) [JONAH]
Jnh 3:6 When J warning reached the king of H2021S
Jnh 4:8 the sun blazed on J head so that he grew H3434

JONAM (1)
Lk 3:30 of Joseph, the son *of* J, the son of Eliakim G2729

JONAS (KJV) JONAH

JONATHAN (114) [JONATHAN'S]
Jdg 18:30 the idol, and J son of Gershom, the son H3387
1Sa 13:2 a thousand were with J at Gibeah in H3440
1Sa 13:3 J attacked the Philistine outpost at Geba H3440
1Sa 13:16 Saul and his son J and the men with H3440
1Sa 13:22 with Saul and J had a sword or spear H3440
1Sa 13:22 only Saul and his son J had them. H3440
1Sa 14:1 One day J son of Saul said to his young H3440
1Sa 14:3 No one was aware that J had left. H3440
1Sa 14:4 side of the pass that J intended to cross to H3440
1Sa 14:6 J said to his young armor-bearer, "Come H3387
1Sa 14:8 J said, "Come on, then; we will cross over H3387
1Sa 14:12 outpost shouted to J and his armor-bearer H3440
1Sa 14:12 So J said to his armor-bearer, "Climb up H3440
1Sa 14:13 J climbed up, using his hands and feet H3440
1Sa 14:13 The Philistines fell before J, and his H3440
1Sa 14:14 In that first attack J and his armor-bearer H3440
1Sa 14:17 it was J and his armor-bearer who were H3440
1Sa 14:21 the Israelites who were with Saul and J. H3440
1Sa 14:27 But J had not heard that his father had H3440
1Sa 14:29 J said, "My father has made trouble for H3440
1Sa 14:39 even if the guilt lies with my son J, he H3440
1Sa 14:40 I and J my son will stand over here." H3440
1Sa 14:41 If the fault is in me or my son J, respond H3440
1Sa 14:41 J and Saul were taken by lot, and the H3440
1Sa 14:42 "Cast the lot between me and J my son." H3440
1Sa 14:42 Jonathan my son." And J was taken. H3440
1Sa 14:43 Then Saul said to J, "Tell me what you H3440
1Sa 14:43 So J told him, "I tasted a little honey H3440
1Sa 14:44 be it ever so severely, if you do not die, J." H3440
1Sa 14:45 said to Saul, "Should J die—he who has H3440
1Sa 14:45 So the men rescued J, and he was not put H3440
1Sa 14:49 Saul's sons were J, Ishvi and Malki-Shua H3440
1Sa 18:1 J became one in spirit with David H3387
1Sa 18:3 And J made a covenant with David H3387
1Sa 18:4 J took off the robe he was wearing and H3387
1Sa 19:1 Saul told his son J and all the attendants H3440
1Sa 19:1 But J had taken a great liking to David H3387
1Sa 19:4 J spoke well of David to Saul his father H3387
1Sa 19:6 Saul listened to J and took this oath: "As H3387
1Sa 19:7 So J called David and told him the whole H3387
1Sa 20:1 at Ramah and went to J and asked, H3387
1Sa 20:2 J replied. "You are not going to die NDT
1Sa 20:3 'J must not know this or he will be grieved H3387
1Sa 20:4 J said to David, "Whatever you want me H3387
1Sa 20:9 J said. "If I had the least inkling H3387
1Sa 20:11 J said, "let's go out into the field. H3387
1Sa 20:12 Then J said to David, "I swear by the LORD H3387
1Sa 20:13 may the LORD deal with J, be it ever so H3387
1Sa 20:16 So J made a covenant with the house of H3387
1Sa 20:17 And J had David reaffirm his oath out of H3387
1Sa 20:18 Then J said to David, "Tomorrow is the H3387
1Sa 20:25 the wall, opposite J, and Abner sat next H3387
1Sa 20:27 Then Saul said to his son J, "Why hasn't H3387
1Sa 20:28 J answered, "David earnestly asked me H3387
1Sa 20:30 anger flared up at J and he said to him, H3387
1Sa 20:32 What has he done?" J asked his father. H3387
1Sa 20:33 Then J knew that his father intended to H3387
1Sa 20:34 J got up from the table in fierce anger; on H3387
1Sa 20:35 In the morning J went out to the field H3387
1Sa 20:37 arrow had fallen, J called out after him H3387
1Sa 20:39 about all this; only J and David knew.) H3387
1Sa 20:40 Then J gave his weapons to the boy and H3387
1Sa 20:41 bowed down before J three times, NDT
1Sa 20:42 J said to David, "Go in peace, for we have H3387
1Sa 20:42 David left, and J went back to the town. H3387
1Sa 23:16 And Saul's son J went to David at Horesh H3387
1Sa 23:18 Then J went home, but David remained H3387
1Sa 31:2 they killed his sons J, Abinadab and H3387
2Sa 1:4 And Saul and his son J are dead." H3387
2Sa 1:5 know that Saul and his son J are dead?" H3387
2Sa 1:12 fasted till evening for Saul and his son J, H3387
2Sa 1:17 lament concerning Saul and his son J, H3387
2Sa 1:22 the bow of J did not turn back, the H3387
2Sa 1:23 Saul and J—in life they were loved and H3387
2Sa 1:25 J lies slain on your heights H3387
2Sa 1:26 I grieve for you, J my brother; you were H3387
2Sa 4:4 J son of Saul had a son who was lame in H3387
2Sa 4:4 about Saul and J came from Jezreel. H3387
2Sa 9:3 "There is still a son of J; he is lame in H3387
2Sa 9:6 When Mephibosheth son of J, the son of H3387
2Sa 9:7 you kindness for the sake of your father J. H3387
2Sa 15:27 with you, and also Abiathar's son J. H3387
2Sa 15:36 son of Zadok and J son of Abiathar, H3387
2Sa 17:17 J and Ahimaaz were staying at En Rogel H3387
2Sa 17:20 they asked, "Where are Ahimaaz and J?" H3387
2Sa 21:7 The king spared Mephibosheth son of J H3387
2Sa 21:7 LORD between David and J son of Saul. H3387
2Sa 21:12 of Saul and his son J from the citizens of H3387
2Sa 21:13 bones of Saul and his son J from there, H3387
2Sa 21:14 of Saul and his son J in the tomb of H3387
2Sa 21:21 When he taunted Israel, J son of Shimeah H3387
2Sa 23:32 the Shaalbonite, the sons of Jashen, J H3387
1Ki 1:42 J son of Abiathar the priest arrived. H3440
1Ki 1:43 J answered. "Our lord King H3440
1Ch 2:32 Jether and J. Jether died without H3440
1Ch 2:33 The sons of J: Peleth and Zaza. These H3440
1Ch 8:33 Saul the father of J, Malki-Shua, H3387
1Ch 8:34 The son of J: Merib-Baal, who was the H3387
1Ch 9:39 Saul the father of J, Malki-Shua, H3387
1Ch 9:40 The son of J: Merib-Baal, who was the H3387
1Ch 10:2 they killed his sons J, Abinadab and H3440
1Ch 11:34 the Gizonite, J son of Shagee the Hararite H3440
1Ch 20:7 he taunted Israel, J son of Shimea H3387
1Ch 27:25 J son of Uzziah was in charge of the H3387
1Ch 27:32 J, David's uncle, was a counselor, a man H3387
Ezr 8:6 Ebed son of J, and with him 50 H3440
Ezr 10:15 Only J son of Asahel and Jahzeiah son of H3440
Ne 12:11 Joiada the father of J, and Jonathan the H3440
Ne 12:11 of Jonathan, and J the father of Jaddua. H3440
Ne 12:14 of Malluk's, J; of Shekaniah's, Joseph; H3440
Ne 12:35 also Zechariah son of J, the son of H3440
Jer 37:15 in the house of J the secretary, H3387
Jer 37:20 me back to the house of J the secretary, H3387
Jer 40:8 Johanan and J the sons of Kareah H3440

JONATHAN'S (3) [JONATHAN]
1Sa 20:37 to the place where J arrow had fallen, H3387
2Sa 9:1 to whom I can show kindness for J sake?" H3387
Jer 38:26 to send me back to J house to die there. H3387

JOPPA (14)
Jos 19:46 Jarkon and Rakkon, with the area facing J. H3639
2Ch 2:16 will float them as rafts by sea down to J. H3639
Ezr 3:7 cedar logs by sea from Lebanon to J, H3639
Jnh 1:3 He went down to J, where he found a H3639
Ac 9:36 In J there was a disciple named Tabitha G2673
Ac 9:38 Lydda was near J; so when the disciples G2673
Ac 9:42 This became known all over J, and many G2673
Ac 9:43 Peter stayed in J for some time with a G2673
Ac 10:5 Now send men to J to bring back a man G2673
Ac 10:8 that had happened and sent them to J. G2673
Ac 10:23 some of the believers from J went along. G2673
Ac 10:32 Send to J for Simon who is called Peter G2673
Ac 11:5 "I was in the city *of* J praying, and in a G2673
Ac 11:13 'Send to J for Simon who is called Peter. G2673

JORAH (1)
Ezr 2:18 of J 112 H3454

JORAI (1)
1Ch 5:13 Meshullam, Sheba, J, Jakan, Zia and H3455

JORAM (28)
2Sa 8:10 he sent his son J to King David to greet H3456
2Sa 8:10 J brought with him articles of silver, of gold NDT
2Ki 1:17 J succeeded him as king in the second H3393
2Ki 3:1 J son of Ahab became king of Israel in H3393
2Ki 3:6 So at that time King J set out from H3393
2Ki 8:16 In the fifth year of J son of Ahab king of H3456
2Ki 8:25 the twelfth year of J son of Ahab king of H3456
2Ki 8:28 Ahaziah went with J son of Ahab to war H3456
2Ki 8:28 The Arameans wounded J; H3456
2Ki 8:29 so King J returned to Jezreel to recover H3456
2Ki 8:29 down to Jezreel to see J son of Ahab, H3456
2Ki 9:14 the son of Nimshi, conspired against J. H3456
2Ki 9:14 Now J and all Israel had been defending H3456
2Ki 9:15 King J had returned to Jezreel to H3393
2Ki 9:16 because J was resting there and Ahaziah H3456
2Ki 9:17 "Get a horseman," J ordered. "Send him H3393
2Ki 9:21 up my chariot," J ordered. And when it H3393
2Ki 9:21 J king of Israel and Ahaziah king of Judah H3393
2Ki 9:22 When J saw Jehu he asked, "Have you H3393
2Ki 9:23 J turned about and fled, calling out to H3393
2Ki 9:24 his bow and shot J between the shoulders H3393
2Ki 9:29 In the eleventh year of J son of Ahab H3456
1Ch 26:25 Jeshaiah his son, J his son, Zikri his son H3456
2Ch 22:5 when he went with J son of Ahab king of H3393
2Ch 22:5 The Arameans wounded J; H3456
2Ch 22:6 to Jezreel to see J son of Ahab because H3393
2Ch 22:7 Through Ahaziah's visit to J, God brought H3456
2Ch 22:7 he went out with J to meet Jehu son of H3393

JORDAN (193) [JORDAN'S]
Ge 13:10 whole plain of the J toward Zoar was well H3720
Ge 13:11 whole plain of the J and set out toward H3720
Ge 32:10 I had only my staff when I crossed this J H3720
Ge 50:10 of Atad, near the J, they lamented loudly H3720
Ge 50:11 that place near the J is called Abel H3720
Nu 13:29 live near the sea and along the J." H3720
Nu 22:1 camped along the J across from Jericho. H3720
Nu 26:3 of Moab by the J *across from* Jericho, H3720
Nu 26:63 of Moab by the J *across from* Jericho. H3720
Nu 31:12 of Moab, by the J *across from* Jericho. H3720
Nu 32:5 Do not make us cross the J." H3720
Nu 32:19 with them on the other side of the J, H3720
Nu 32:19 has come to us on the east side of the J." H3720
Nu 32:21 armed cross over the J before the LORD H3720
Nu 32:29 cross over the J with you before the LORD H3720
Nu 32:32 we inherit will be on this side of the J." H3720
Nu 33:48 of Moab by the J *across from* Jericho. H3720
Nu 33:49 camped along the J from Beth Jeshimoth H3720
Nu 33:50 of Moab by the J *across from* Jericho the H3720
Nu 33:51 'When you cross the J into Canaan, H3720
Nu 34:12 go down along the J and end at the Dead H3720
Nu 34:15 east of the J across from Jericho, H3720
Nu 35:1 of Moab by the J *across from* Jericho, H3720
Nu 35:10 'When you cross the J into Canaan, H3720
Nu 35:14 on this side of the J and three in Canaan H3720
Nu 36:13 of Moab by the J *across from* Jericho. H3720
Dt 1:1 all Israel in the wilderness east of the J— H3720
Dt 1:5 East of the J in the territory of Moab H3720
Dt 2:29 we cross the J into the land the LORD H3720
Dt 3:8 of the Amorites the territory east of the J, H3720
Dt 3:17 Its western border was the J in the Arabah H3720
Dt 3:20 LORD your God is giving them across the J. H3720
Dt 3:25 see the good land beyond the J— H3720
Dt 3:27 since you are not going to cross this J. H3720
Dt 4:14 you are crossing **the** J to possess. H9004+2025S
Dt 4:21 I would not cross the J and enter the good H3720
Dt 4:22 I will not cross the J; but you are about to H3720
Dt 4:26 that you are crossing the J to possess. H3720
Dt 4:41 Moses set aside three cities east of the J, H3720
Dt 4:46 in the valley near Beth Peor east of the J, H3720
Dt 4:47 the two Amorite kings east of the J. H3720
Dt 4:49 included all the Arabah east of the J H3720

Dt 6: 1 you are crossing **the J** to possess, H9004+2025S
Dt 9: 1 now about to cross the **J** to go in and H3720
Dt 11: 8 you are crossing **the J** to possess, H9004+2025S
Dt 11:11 you are crossing **the J** to take H9004+2025S
Dt 11:30 these mountains are across the **J** H3720
Dt 11:31 are about to cross the **J** to enter and take H3720
Dt 12:10 But you will cross the **J** and settle in the H3720
Dt 27: 2 you have crossed the **J** into the land the H3720
Dt 27: 4 And when you have crossed the **J**, set up H3720
Dt 27:12 When you have crossed the **J**, these tribes H3720
Dt 30:18 are crossing the **J** to enter and possess H3720
Dt 31: 2 has said to me, 'You shall not cross the **J**. H3720
Dt 31:13 the land you are crossing the **J** to possess." H3720
Dt 32:47 the land you are crossing the **J** to possess." H3720
Jos 1: 2 ready to cross the **J** River into the land I H3720
Jos 1:11 you will cross the **J** here to go in and take H3720
Jos 1:14 land that Moses gave you east of the **J**, H3720
Jos 1:15 gave you east of the **J** toward the sunrise." H3720
Jos 2: 7 the road that leads to the fords of the **J**, H3720
Jos 2:10 two kings of the Amorites east of the **J**, H3720
Jos 3: 1 set out from Shittim and went to the **J**, H3720
Jos 3:11 the earth will go into the **J** ahead of you. H3720
Jos 3:13 set foot in the **J**, its waters flowing H3720
Jos 3:14 the people broke camp to cross the **J**, H3720
Jos 3:15 Now the **J** is at flood stage all during H3720
Jos 3:15 the ark reached the **J** and their feet H3720
Jos 3:17 in the middle of the **J** and stood on dry H3720
Jos 4: 1 whole nation had finished crossing the **J**, H3720
Jos 4: 3 up twelve stones from the middle of the **J**, H3720
Jos 4: 5 LORD your God into the middle of the **J**. H3720
Jos 4: 7 that the flow of the **J** was cut off before H3720
Jos 4: 7 When it crossed the **J**, the waters of the H3720
Jos 4: 7 the waters of the **J** were cut off. H3720
Jos 4: 8 twelve stones from the middle of the **J**, H3720
Jos 4: 9 in the middle of the **J** at the spot where H3720
Jos 4:10 in the middle of the **J** until everything the H3720
Jos 4:16 the covenant law to come up out of the **J**." H3720
Jos 4:17 the priests, "Come up out of the **J**." H3720
Jos 4:18 than the waters of the **J** returned to their H3720
Jos 4:19 went up from the **J** and camped at Gilgal H3720
Jos 4:20 twelve stones they had taken out of the **J**. H3720
Jos 4:22 'Israel crossed the **J** on dry ground.' H3720
Jos 4:23 God dried up the **J** before you until you H3720
Jos 4:23 your God did to the **J** what he had done to NDT
Jos 5: 1 kings west of the **J** and all the Canaanite H3720
Jos 5: 1 had dried up the **J** before the Israelites H3720
Jos 7: 7 people across the **J** to deliver us into the H3720
Jos 7: 7 content to stay on the other side of the **J**! H3720
Jos 9: 1 the kings west of the **J** heard about these H3720
Jos 9:10 two kings of the Amorites east of the **J**— H3720
Jos 12: 1 territory they took over east of the **J**, H3720
Jos 12: 7 conquered on the west side of the **J**, H3720
Jos 13: 8 that Moses had given them east of the **J**, H3720
Jos 13:23 of the Reubenites was the bank of the **J**. H3720
Jos 13:27 the east side of the **J**, the territory up to H3720
Jos 13:32 of Moab across the **J** east of Jericho. H3720
Jos 14: 3 east of the **J** but had not granted the H3720
Jos 15: 5 Dead Sea as far as the mouth of the **J**. H3720
Jos 15: 5 the bay of the sea at the mouth of the **J**, H3720
Jos 16: 1 The allotment for Joseph began at the **J** H3720
Jos 16: 7 touched Jericho and came out at the **J**. H3720
Jos 17: 5 besides Gilead and Bashan east of the **J**, H3720
Jos 18: 7 their inheritance on the east side of the **J**. H3720
Jos 18:12 north side their boundary began at the **J**, H3720
Jos 18:19 at the mouth of the **J** in the south. H3720
Jos 18:20 The **J** formed the boundary on the eastern H3720
Jos 19:22 Beth Shemesh, and ended at the **J**. H3720
Jos 19:33 Jabneel to Lakkum and ending at the **J**. H3720
Jos 19:34 Asher on the west and the **J** on the east. H3720
Jos 20: 8 East of the **J** (on the other side from H3720
Jos 22: 4 LORD gave you on the other side of the **J**. H3720
Jos 22: 7 the west side of the **J** along with their H3720
Jos 22:10 to Geliloth near the **J** in the land of H3720
Jos 22:10 built an imposing altar there by the **J**. H3720
Jos 22:11 at Geliloth near the **J** on the Israelite side H3720
Jos 22:25 LORD has made the **J** a boundary between H3720
Jos 23: 4 between the **J** and the Mediterranean Sea H3720
Jos 24: 8 of the Amorites who lived east of the **J**. H3720
Jos 24:11 you crossed the **J** and came to Jericho. H3720
Jdg 3:28 of the fords of the **J** that led to Moab; H3720
Jdg 5:17 Gilead stayed beyond the **J**. And Dan H3720
Jdg 6:33 crossed over the **J** and camped in the NDT
Jdg 7:24 the waters of the **J** ahead of them as far H3720
Jdg 7:24 the waters of the **J** as far as Beth Barah. H3720
Jdg 7:25 Zeeb to Gideon, who was by the **J**. H3720
Jdg 8: 4 the pursuit, came to the **J** and crossed it. H3720
Jdg 10: 8 on the east side of the **J** in Gilead, H3720
Jdg 10: 9 also crossed the **J** to fight against Judah, H3720
Jdg 11:13 Arnon to the Jabbok, all the way to the **J**. H3720
Jdg 11:22 the Jabbok and from the desert to the **J**. H3720
Jdg 12: 5 the fords of the **J** leading to Ephraim, H3720
Jdg 12: 6 him and killed him at the fords of the **J**. H3720
1Sa 13: 7 even crossed the **J** to the land of Gad H3720
1Sa 31: 7 those across the **J** saw that the H3720
2Sa 2:29 They crossed the **J**, continued through the H3720
2Sa 10:17 crossed the **J** and went to Helam. H3720
2Sa 17:22 with him set out and crossed the **J**. H3720
2Sa 17:22 one was left who had not crossed the **J**. H3720
2Sa 17:24 Absalom crossed the **J** with all the men of H3720
2Sa 19:15 the king returned and went as far as the **J**. H3720
2Sa 19:15 meet the king and bring him across the **J**. H3720
2Sa 19:17 They rushed to the **J**, where the king was. H3720
2Sa 19:18 When Shimei son of Gera crossed the **J** H3720
2Sa 19:31 to cross the **J** with the king and to H3720
2Sa 19:36 will cross over the **J** with the king for a H3720
2Sa 19:39 So all the people crossed the **J**, and then H3720
2Sa 19:41 bring him and his household across the **J**, H3720
2Sa 20: 2 king all the way from the **J** to Jerusalem. H3720
2Sa 24: 5 After crossing the **J**, they camped near H3720
1Ki 2: 8 When he came down to meet me at the **J**, H3720
1Ki 7:46 in the plain of the **J** between Sukkoth H3720
1Ki 17: 3 hide in the Kerith Ravine, east of the **J**. H3720
1Ki 17: 5 east of the **J**, and stayed there. H3720
2Ki 2: 6 "Stay here; the LORD has sent me to the **J**." H3720
2Ki 2: 7 Elijah and Elisha had stopped at the **J**. H3720
2Ki 2:13 went back and stood on the bank of the **J**. H3720
2Ki 5:10 wash yourself seven times in the **J**, and H3720
2Ki 5:14 dipped himself in the **J** seven times, H3720
2Ki 6: 2 Let us go to the **J**, where each of us can H3720
2Ki 6: 4 They went to the **J** and began to cut down H3720
2Ki 7:15 They followed them as far as the **J**, and H3720
2Ki 10:33 east of the **J** in all the land of Gilead (the H3720
1Ch 6:78 Reuben across the **J** east of Jericho they H3720
1Ch 12:15 they who crossed the **J** in the first month H3720
1Ch 12:37 from east of the **J**, from Reuben, Gad H3720
1Ch 19:17 he gathered all Israel and crossed the **J** H3720
1Ch 26:30 in Israel west of the **J** for all the work of H3720
2Ch 4:17 in the plain of the **J** between Sukkoth H3720
Job 40:23 though the **J** should surge against its H3720
Ps 42: 6 will remember you from the land of the **J**, H3720
Ps 114: 3 sea looked and fled, the **J** turned back; H3720
Ps 114: 5 that you fled? Why, **J**, did you turn back? H3720
Isa 9: 1 by the Way of the Sea, beyond the **J**— H3720
Jer 12: 5 will you manage in the thickets by the **J**? H3720
Eze 47:18 along the **J** between Gilead and the land H3720
Zec 11: 3 the lush thicket of the **J** is ruined! H3720
Mt 3: 5 all Judea and the whole region *of* the **J**. *G2674*
Mt 3: 6 they were baptized by him in the **J** River. *G2674*
Mt 3:13 from Galilee to the **J** to be baptized by *G2674*
Mt 4:15 of the Sea, beyond the **J**, Galilee of the *G2674*
Mt 4:25 the region across the **J** followed him. *G2674*
Mt 19: 1 region of Judea to the other side *of* the **J**. *G2674*
Mk 1: 5 they were baptized by him in the **J** River. *G2674*
Mk 1: 9 was baptized by John in the **J**. *G2674*
Mk 3: 8 regions across the **J** and around Tyre and *G2674*
Mk 10: 1 into the region of Judea and across the **J**. *G2674*
Lk 3: 3 He went into all the country around the **J** *G2674*
Lk 4: 1 left the **J** and was led by the Spirit into *G2674*
Jn 1:28 at Bethany on the other side of the **J**, *G2674*
Jn 3:26 was with you on the other side of the **J**— *G2674*
Jn 10:40 went back across the **J** to the place where *G2674*

JORDAN'S (3) [JORDAN]

Jos 3: 8 'When you reach the edge of the **J** waters, H3720
Jer 49:19 a lion coming up from **J** thickets to a rich H3720
Jer 50:44 a lion coming up from **J** thickets to a rich H3720

JORIM (1)

Lk 3:29 of Eliezer, the son *of* **J**, the son of Matthat *G2733*

JORKEAM (1)

1Ch 2:44 of Raham, and Raham the father of **J**. H3767

JOSAPHAT (KJV) JEHOSHAPHAT

JOSEDECH (KJV) JEHOZADAK

JOSEK (1)

Lk 3:26 of Semein, the son *of* **J**, the son of Joda, *G2738*

JOSEPH (239) [JOSEPH'S]

Ge 30:24 She named him **J**, and said, "May the LORD H3441
Ge 30:25 After Rachel gave birth to **J**, Jacob said to H3441
Ge 33: 2 and Rachel and **J** in the rear. H3441
Ge 33: 7 Last of all came **J** and Rachel, and they H3441
Ge 35:24 The sons of Rachel: **J** and Benjamin. H3441
Ge 37: 2 **J**, a young man of seventeen, was H3441
Ge 37: 3 Now Israel loved **J** more than any of his H3441
Ge 37: 5 **J** had a dream, and when he told it to his H3441
Ge 37:13 Israel said to **J**, "As you know, your H3441
Ge 37:14 When **J** arrived at Shechem, NDT
Ge 37:17 So **J** went after his brothers and found H3441
Ge 37:23 So when **J** came to his brothers, they H3441
Ge 37:28 his brothers pulled **J** up out of the cistern H3441
Ge 37:29 the cistern and saw that **J** was not there, H3441
Ge 37:33 **J** has surely been torn to pieces." H3441
Ge 37:36 the Midianites sold **J** in Egypt to H2257S
Ge 39: 1 Now **J** had been taken down to Egypt H3441
Ge 39: 2 The LORD was with **J** so that he prospered H3441
Ge 39: 4 **J** found favor in his eyes and became his H3441
Ge 39: 5 household of the Egyptian because of **J**. H3441
Ge 39: 6 Joseph's care; with **J** in charge, he did H2257S
Ge 39: 6 Now **J** was well-built and handsome, H3441
Ge 39: 7 master's wife took notice of **J** and said, H3441
Ge 39:10 And though she spoke to **J** day after day H3441
Ge 39:20 But while **J** was there in the prison NDT
Ge 39:22 So the warden put **J** in charge of all those H3441
Ge 39:23 the LORD was with **J** and gave him H2257S
Ge 40: 3 in the same prison where **J** was confined. H3441
Ge 40: 4 captain of the guard assigned them to **J**, H3441
Ge 40: 6 When **J** came to them the next morning H3441
Ge 40: 8 Then **J** said to them, "Do not H3441
Ge 40: 9 So the chief cupbearer told **J** his dream H3441
Ge 40:12 is what it means," **J** said to him. "The H3441
Ge 40:16 chief baker saw that **J** had given a favorable NDT
Ge 40:16 he said to **J**, "I too had a dream: H3441
Ge 40:18 is what it means," **J** said. "The three H3441
Ge 40:22 just as **J** had said to them in his H3441
Ge 40:23 did not remember **J**; he forgot him. H3441
Ge 41:14 So Pharaoh sent for **J**, and he was quickly H3441
Ge 41:15 Pharaoh said to **J**, "I had a dream, and no H3441
Ge 41:16 **J** replied to Pharaoh, "but God will give H3441
Ge 41:17 Then Pharaoh said to **J**, "In my dream I H3441
Ge 41:25 Then **J** said to Pharaoh, "The dreams of H3441
Ge 41:39 Then Pharaoh said to **J**, "Since God has H3441
Ge 41:41 So Pharaoh said to **J**, "I hereby put you in H3441
Ge 41:44 Then Pharaoh said to **J**, "I am Pharaoh H3441
Ge 41:45 Pharaoh gave **J** the name H3441
Ge 41:45 And **J** went throughout the land of Egypt H3441
Ge 41:46 **J** was thirty years old when he entered the H3441
Ge 41:46 And **J** went out from Pharaoh's presence H3441
Ge 41:48 **J** collected all the food produced in those NDT
Ge 41:49 **J** stored up huge quantities of grain, like H3441
Ge 41:50 sons were born to **J** by Asenath daughter H3441
Ge 41:51 **J** named his firstborn Manasseh and said H3441
Ge 41:54 years of famine began, just as **J** had said. H3441
Ge 41:55 "Go to **J** and do what he tells you." H3441
Ge 41:56 **J** opened all the storehouses and sold H3441
Ge 41:57 world came to Egypt to buy grain from **J**, H3441
Ge 42: 6 Now **J** was the governor of the land, the H3441
Ge 42: 7 As soon as **J** saw his brothers, he H3441
Ge 42: 8 Although **J** recognized his brothers, they H3441
Ge 42:14 **J** said to them, "It is just as I told you: You H3441
Ge 42:18 On the third day, **J** said to them, "Do this H3441
Ge 42:23 did not realize that **J** could understand H3441
Ge 42:25 **J** gave orders to fill their bags with grain H3441
Ge 42:36 **J** is no more and Simeon is no more, and H3441
Ge 43:15 to Egypt and presented themselves to **J**. H3441
Ge 43:16 When **J** saw Benjamin with them, he said H3441
Ge 43:17 The man did as **J** told him and took the H3441
Ge 43:26 When **J** came home, they presented to H3441
Ge 43:30 **J** hurried out and looked for a place to H3441
Ge 44: 1 Now **J** gave these instructions to the steward NDT
Ge 44: 2 silver for his grain." And he did as **J** said. H3441
Ge 44: 4 from the city when **J** said to his steward, H3441
Ge 44:14 **J** was still in the house when Judah and H3441
Ge 44:15 **J** said to them, "What is this you have H3441
Ge 44:17 But **J** said, "Far be it from me to do such a NDT
Ge 45: 1 Then **J** could no longer control himself H3441
Ge 45: 1 was no one with **J** when he made himself H3441
Ge 45: 3 **J** said to his brothers, "I am Joseph! Is my H3441
Ge 45: 3 to his brothers, "I am **J**! Is my father still H3441
Ge 45: 4 Then **J** said to his brothers, "Come close H3441
Ge 45: 4 "I am your brother **J**, the one you sold into H3441
Ge 45: 9 say to him, 'This is what your son **J** says: H3441
Ge 45:17 Pharaoh said to **J**, "Tell your brothers, 'Do H3441
Ge 45:21 **J** gave them carts, as Pharaoh had H3441
Ge 45:26 They told him, "**J** is still alive! In fact, he is H3441
Ge 45:27 told him everything **J** had said to them, H3441
Ge 45:27 he saw the carts **J** had sent to carry him H3441
Ge 45:28 My son **J** is still alive. I will H3441
Ge 46:19 of Jacob's wife Rachel: **J** and Benjamin. H3441
Ge 46:20 were born to **J** by Asenath daughter H3441
Ge 46:27 sons who had been born to **J** in Egypt, H3441
Ge 46:28 ahead of him to **J** to get directions to H3441
Ge 46:29 **J** had his chariot made ready and went to H3441
Ge 46:29 As soon as **J** appeared before him, he threw NDT
Ge 46:30 Israel said to **J**, "Now I am ready to die H3441
Ge 46:31 Then **J** said to his brothers and to his H3441
Ge 47: 1 **J** went and told Pharaoh, "My father and H3441
Ge 47: 5 Pharaoh said to **J**, "Your father and your H3441
Ge 47: 7 Then **J** brought his father Jacob in and H3441
Ge 47:11 So **J** settled his father and his brothers in H3441
Ge 47:12 **J** also provided his father and his brothers H3441
Ge 47:14 **J** collected all the money that was to be H3441
Ge 47:15 all Egypt came to **J** and said, "Give us H3441
Ge 47:16 your livestock," said **J**. "I will sell you food H3441
Ge 47:17 So they brought their livestock to **J**, and he H3441
Ge 47:20 So **J** bought all the land in Egypt for H3441
Ge 47:21 **J** reduced the people to servitude, from NDT
Ge 47:23 **J** said to the people, "Now that I have H3441
Ge 47:26 So **J** established it as a law concerning H3441
Ge 47:29 he called for his son **J** and said to him, "If H3441
Ge 47:31 Then **J** swore to him, and Israel worshiped NDT
Ge 48: 1 Some time later **J** was told, "Your father is H3441
Ge 48: 2 was told, "Your son **J** has come to you," H3441
Ge 48: 3 Jacob said to **J**, "God Almighty appeared H3441
Ge 48: 8 When Israel saw the sons of **J**, he asked H3441
Ge 48: 9 has given me here," **J** said to his father. H3441
Ge 48:10 So **J** brought his sons close to him, and his NDT
Ge 48:11 Israel said to **J**, "I never expected to see H3441
Ge 48:12 Then **J** removed them from Israel's knees H3441
Ge 48:13 And **J** took both of them, Ephraim on his H3441
Ge 48:15 Then he blessed **J** and said, "May the H3441
Ge 48:17 When **J** saw his father placing his right H3441
Ge 48:18 **J** said to him, "No, my father, this one is H3441
Ge 48:21 Then Israel said to **J**, "I am about to die H3441
Ge 49:22 "**J** is a fruitful vine, a fruitful vine near a H3441
Ge 49:26 Let all these rest on the head of **J**, on the H3441
Ge 50: 1 **J** threw himself on his father and wept H3441
Ge 50: 2 Then **J** directed the physicians in his H3441
Ge 50: 4 had passed, **J** said to Pharaoh's court H3441
Ge 50: 7 So **J** went up to bury his father. H3441
Ge 50:10 there **J** observed a seven-day period of NDT
Ge 50:14 After burying his father, **J** returned to Egypt H3441
Ge 50:15 "What if **J** holds a grudge against us and H3441
Ge 50:16 So they sent word to **J**, saying, "Your father H3441

Ge 50:17 'This is what you are to say to **J**: I ask you H3441
Ge 50:17 When their message came to him, **J** wept. H3441
Ge 50:19 But **J** said to them, "Don't be afraid. H3441
Ge 50:22 **J** stayed in Egypt, along with all his H3441
Ge 50:24 Then **J** said to his brothers, "I am about to H3441
Ge 50:25 And **J** made the Israelites swear an oath H3441
Ge 50:26 So **J** died at the age of a hundred and ten H3441
Ex 1: 5 seventy in all; **J** was already in Egypt. H3441
Ex 1: 6 Now **J** and all his brothers and all that H3441
Ex 1: 8 new king, to whom **J** meant nothing H3441
Ex 13:19 took the bones of **J** with him because H3441
Ex 13:19 with him because **J** had made the Israelites NDT
Nu 1:10 from the sons of **J**: from Ephraim H3441
Nu 1:32 From the sons of **J**: From the descendants H3441
Nu 13: 7 from the tribe of Issachar, Igal son of **J**; H3441
Nu 13:11 a tribe of **J**), Gaddi son of Susi; H3441
Nu 26:28 The descendants of **J** by their clans H3441
Nu 26:37 were the descendants of **J** by their clans. H3441
Nu 27: 1 to the clans of Manasseh son of **J**. H3441
Nu 32:33 of Manasseh son of **J** the kingdom of H3441
Nu 34:23 from the tribe of Manasseh son of **J**; H3441
Nu 34:24 leader from the tribe of Ephraim son of **J**; NDT
Nu 36: 1 from the clans of the descendants of **J**, H3441
Nu 36: 5 of the descendants of **J** is saying is right. H3441
Nu 36:12 of the descendants of Manasseh son of **J**, H3441
Dt 27:12 Judah, Issachar, **J** and Benjamin. H3441
Dt 33:13 About **J** he said: "May the LORD bless his H3441
Dt 33:16 Let all these rest on the head of **J**, on the H3441
Jos 16: 1 The allotment for **J** began at the H1201+3441
Jos 16: 4 the descendants of **J**, received their H3441
Jos 17: 2 of Manasseh son of **J** by their clans. H3441
Jos 17:14 The people of **J** said to Joshua, "Why H3441
Jos 17:16 The people of **J** replied, "The hill country H3441
Jos 17:17 But Joshua said to the tribes of **J**—to H3441
Jos 18: 5 the tribes of **J** in their territory on H3441
Jos 18:11 between the tribes of Judah and **J**: H1201+3441
Jdg 1:22 Now the tribes of **J** attacked Bethel, and H3441
Jdg 1:35 the power of the tribes of **J** increased, H3441
2Sa 19:20 from the tribes of **J** to come down and H3441
1Ki 11:28 of the whole labor force of the tribes of **J**. H3441
1Ch 2: 2 **J**, Benjamin, Naphtali, Gad and H3441
1Ch 5: 1 were given to the sons of **J** son of Israel; H3441
1Ch 5: 2 the rights of the firstborn belonged to **J**)— H3441
1Ch 7:29 The descendants of **J** son of Israel lived in H3441
1Ch 25: 2 sons of Asaph: Zakkur, **J**, Nethaniah and H3441
1Ch 25: 9 was for Asaph, fell to **J**, his sons and H3441
Ezr 10:42 Shallum, Amariah and **J**. H3441
Ne 12:14 of Malluk's, Jonathan; of Shekaniah's, **J**; H3441
Ps 77:15 people, the descendants of Jacob and **J**. H3441
Ps 78:67 Then he rejected the tents of **J**, he did not H3441
Ps 80: 1 of Israel, you who lead **J** like a flock. H3441
Ps 81: 5 he established it as a statute for **J**. H3388
Ps 105:17 a man before them—**J**, sold as a slave. H3441
Eze 37:16 'Belonging to **J** (that is, to Ephraim) H3441
Eze 37:19 I am going to take the stick of **J**—which is H3441
Eze 47:13 their inheritance, with two portions for **J**. H3441
Eze 48:32 the gate of **J**, the gate of Benjamin and H3441
Am 5: 6 sweep through the tribes of **J** like a fire; H3441
Am 5:15 will have mercy on the remnant of **J**. H3441
Am 6: 6 you do not grieve over the ruin of **J**. H3441
Ob 18 Jacob will be a fire and **J** a flame H1074+3441
Zec 10: 6 strengthen Judah and save the tribes of **J**. H3441
Mt 1:16 Jacob the father of **J**, the husband of *G2737*
Mt 1:18 Mary was pledged to be married *to* **J**, *G2737*
Mt 1:19 Because **J** her husband was faithful to the *G2737*
Mt 1:20 a dream and said, "**J** son of David, do not *G2737*
Mt 1:24 When **J** woke up, he did what the angel *G2737*
Mt 2:13 of the Lord appeared *to* **J** in a dream. *G2737*
Mt 2:19 Lord appeared in a dream *to* **J** in Egypt *G2737*
Mt 13:55 his brothers James, **J**, Simon and Judas? *G2737*
Mt 27:56 Mary the mother of James and **J**, and the *G2736*
Mt 27:57 Arimathea, named **J**, who had himself *G2737*
Mt 27:59 **J** took the body, wrapped it in a clean *G2737*
Mk 6: 3 brother of James, **J**, Judas and Simon? *G2736*
Mk 15:40 mother of James the younger and *of* **J**, *G2736*
Mk 15:43 **J** of Arimathea, a prominent member of *G2737*
Mk 15:45 that it was so, he gave the body *to* **J**. *G2737*
Mk 15:46 So **J** bought some linen cloth, took down the NDT
Mk 15:47 Mary the mother *of* **J** saw where he was *G2736*
Lk 1:27 pledged to be married to a man named **J**, *G2737*
Lk 2: 4 So **J** also went up from the town of *G2737*
Lk 2:16 So they hurried off and found Mary and **J** *G2737*
Lk 2:22 **J** and Mary took him to Jerusalem to present NDT
Lk 2:39 When **J** and Mary had done everything NDT
Lk 3:23 so it was thought, *of* **J**, the son of Heli, *G2737*
Lk 3:24 of Melki, the son of Jannai, the son *of* **J**, *G2737*
Lk 3:30 of Judah, the son *of* **J**, the son of Jonam, *G2737*
Lk 23:50 Now there was a man named **J**, *G2737*
Lk 23:55 Galilee followed **J** and saw the tomb and *G899S*
Jn 1:45 wrote—Jesus of Nazareth, the son *of* **J**." *G2737*
Jn 4: 5 of ground Jacob had given to his son **J**. *G2737*
Jn 6:42 not Jesus, the son *of* **J**, whose father and *G2737*
Jn 19:38 **J** of Arimathea asked Pilate for the body *G2737*
Jn 19:38 Now **J** was a disciple of Jesus, but secretly NDT
Ac 1:23 **J** called Barsabbas (also known as Justus *G2737*
Ac 4:36 **J**, a Levite from Cyprus, whom the *G2737*
Ac 7: 9 "Because the patriarchs were jealous *of* **J** *G2737*
Ac 7:10 He gave **J** wisdom and enabled him to *G899S*
Ac 7:13 **J** told his brothers who he was *G2737*
Ac 7:14 **J** sent for his father Jacob and his whole *G2737*
Ac 7:18 new king, to whom **J** meant nothing *G2737*
Heb 11:22 By faith **J**, when his end was near, spoke *G2737*
Rev 7: 8 from the tribe *of* **J** 12,000, from the *G2737*

JOSEPH'S (25) [JOSEPH]

Ge 37:31 Then they got **J** robe, slaughtered a goat H3441
Ge 39: 6 Potiphar left everything he had in **J** care; H3441
Ge 39:20 **J** master took him and put him in prison H3441
Ge 39:23 no attention to anything under **J** care, H2257S
Ge 41:42 ring from his finger and put it on **J** finger. H3441
Ge 42: 3 Then ten of **J** brothers went down to buy H3441
Ge 42: 4 did not send Benjamin, **J** brother, with the H3441
Ge 42: 6 So when **J** brothers arrived, they bowed H3441
Ge 43:17 told him and took the men to **J** house. H3441
Ge 43:19 So they went up to **J** steward and spoke to H3441
Ge 43:24 The steward took the men into **J** house H3441
Ge 43:25 prepared their gifts for **J** arrival at noon, H3441
Ge 43:34 were served to them from **J** table, H2257S
Ge 45:16 palace that **J** brothers had come, H3441
Ge 46: 4 And **J** own hand will close your eyes." H3441
Ge 50: 8 all the members of **J** household and his H3441
Ge 50:15 When **J** brothers saw that their father was H3441
Ge 50:23 were placed at birth on **J** knees. H3441
Jos 14: 4 **J** descendants had become two tribes— H3441
Jos 17: 1 the tribe of Manasseh as **J** firstborn, H3441
Jos 24:32 And **J** bones, which the Israelites had H3441
Jos 24:32 became the inheritance of **J** descendants. H3441
Lk 4:22 "Isn't this **J** son?" they asked. *G2737*
Ac 7:13 and Pharaoh learned about **J** family. *G2737*
Heb 11:21 blessed each of **J** sons, and worshiped as *G2737*

JOSES (NIV84) JOSEPH

JOSHAH (1)

1Ch 4:34 Meshobab, Jamlech, **J** son of Amaziah, H3459

JOSHAPHAT (2)

1Ch 11:43 Hanan son of Maakah, **J** the Mithnite, H3461
1Ch 15:24 Shebaniah, **J**, Nethanel, Amasai H3461

JOSHAVIAH (1)

1Ch 11:46 Jeribai and **J** the sons of Elnaam H3460

JOSHBEKASHAH (2)

1Ch 25: 4 Romamti-Ezer; **J**, Mallothi, Hothir H3792
1Ch 25:24 the seventeenth to **J**, his sons and H3792

JOSHEB-BASSHEBETH (1)

2Sa 23: 8 **J**, a Tahkemonite, was chief of the Three H3783

JOSHIBIAH (1)

1Ch 4:35 Jehu son of **J**, the son of Seraiah H3458

JOSHUA (231) [HOSHEA]

Ex 17: 9 Moses said to **J**, "Choose some of our men H3397
Ex 17:10 So **J** fought the Amalekites as Moses had H3397
Ex 17:13 So **J** overcame the Amalekite army with H3397
Ex 17:14 make sure that **J** hears it, H3397
Ex 24:13 Then Moses set out with **J** his aide, and H3397
Ex 32:17 When **J** heard the noise of the people H3397
Ex 33:11 his young aide **J** son of Nun did not H3397
Nu 11:28 **J** son of Nun, who had been Moses' aide H3397
Nu 13:16 gave Hoshea son of Nun the name **J**.) H3397
Nu 14: 6 **J** son of Nun and Caleb son of Jephunneh H3397
Nu 14:30 son of Jephunneh and **J** son of Nun. H3397
Nu 14:38 only **J** son of Nun and Caleb son of H3397
Nu 26:65 son of Jephunneh and **J** son of Nun. H3397
Nu 27:18 to Moses, "Take **J** son of Nun, a man in H3397
Nu 27:22 He took **J** and had him stand before H3397
Nu 32:12 the Kenizzite and **J** son of Nun, H3397
Nu 32:28 the priest and **J** son of Nun and to the H3397
Nu 34:17 Eleazar the priest and **J** son of Nun. H3397
Dt 1:38 But your assistant, **J** son of Nun, will enter H3397
Dt 3:21 At that time I commanded **J**: "You have H3397
Dt 3:28 But commission **J**, and encourage and H3397
Dt 31: 3 **J** also will cross over ahead of you, as the H3397
Dt 31: 7 Moses summoned **J** and said to him in H3397
Dt 31:14 Call **J** and present yourselves at the tent H3397
Dt 31:14 So Moses and **J** came and presented H3397
Dt 31:23 LORD gave this command to **J** son of Nun: H3397
Dt 32:44 Moses came with **J** son of Nun and spoke H2107
Dt 34: 9 Now **J** son of Nun was filled with the spirit H3397
Jos 1: 1 the LORD said to **J** son of Nun, Moses' H3397
Jos 1:10 So **J** ordered the officers of the people: H3397
Jos 1:12 the half-tribe of Manasseh, **J** said, H3397
Jos 1:16 Then they answered **J**, "Whatever you H3397
Jos 2: 1 Then **J** son of Nun secretly sent two spies H3397
Jos 2:23 river and came to **J** son of Nun and told H3397
Jos 2:24 They said to **J**, "The LORD has surely given H3397
Jos 3: 1 Early in the morning **J** and all the H3397
Jos 3: 5 **J** told the people, "Consecrate yourselves H3397
Jos 3: 6 **J** said to the priests, "Take up the ark of H3397
Jos 3: 7 And the LORD said to **J**, "Today I will begin H3397
Jos 3: 9 **J** said to the Israelites, "Come here and H3397
Jos 4: 1 crossing the Jordan, the LORD said to **J**, H3397
Jos 4: 4 So **J** called together the twelve men he H3397
Jos 4: 8 the Israelites did as **J** commanded them. H3397
Jos 4: 8 as the LORD had told **J**; and they carried H3397
Jos 4: 9 **J** set up the twelve stones that had been H3397
Jos 4:10 LORD had commanded **J** was done by the H3397
Jos 4:10 the people, just as Moses had directed **J**. H3397
Jos 4:14 day the LORD exalted **J** in the sight of all H3397
Jos 4:15 Then the LORD said to **J**, H3397
Jos 4:17 So **J** commanded the priests, "Come up H3397
Jos 4:20 And **J** set up at Gilgal the twelve stones H3397
Jos 5: 2 At that time the LORD said to **J**, "Make flint H3397
Jos 5: 3 So **J** made flint knives and circumcised the H3397
Jos 5: 7 these were the ones **J** circumcised. H3397
Jos 5: 9 Then the LORD said to **J**, "Today I have H3397
Jos 5:13 Now when **J** was near Jericho, he looked H3397
Jos 5:13 **J** went up to him and asked, "Are you H3397
Jos 5:14 Then **J** fell facedown to the ground in H3397
Jos 5:15 you are standing is holy." And **J** did so. H3397
Jos 6: 2 Then the LORD said to **J**, "See, I have H3397
Jos 6: 6 So **J** son of Nun called the priests and H3397
Jos 6: 8 When **J** had spoken to the people, the H3397
Jos 6:10 But **J** had commanded the army, "Do not H3397
Jos 6:12 **J** got up early the next morning and the H3397
Jos 6:16 the trumpet blast, **J** commanded the army H3397
Jos 6:22 **J** said to the two men who had spied out H3397
Jos 6:25 But **J** spared Rahab the prostitute, with her H3397
Jos 6:25 she hid the men **J** had sent as spies to H3397
Jos 6:26 At that time **J** pronounced this solemn H3397
Jos 6:27 So the LORD was with **J**, and his fame H3397
Jos 7: 2 Now **J** sent men from Jericho to Ai, which H3397
Jos 7: 3 When they returned to **J**, they said, "Not H3397
Jos 7: 6 Then **J** tore his clothes and fell facedown H3397
Jos 7: 7 And **J** said, "Alas, Sovereign LORD, why H3397
Jos 7:10 The LORD said to **J**, "Stand up! What are H3397
Jos 7:16 Early the next morning **J** had Israel come H3397
Jos 7:18 **J** had his family come forward man by man NDT
Jos 7:19 Then **J** said to Achan, "My son, give glory H3397
Jos 7:22 So **J** sent messengers, and they ran to the H3397
Jos 7:23 brought them to **J** and all the Israelites H3397
Jos 7:24 Then **J**, together with all Israel, took H3397
Jos 7:25 **J** said, "Why have you brought this trouble H3397
Jos 8: 1 Then the LORD said to **J**, "Do not be afraid H3397
Jos 8: 3 So **J** and the whole army moved out to H3397
Jos 8: 9 Then **J** sent them off, and they went to H3397
Jos 8: 9 **J** spent that night with the people. H3397
Jos 8:10 the next morning **J** mustered his army, H3397
Jos 8:12 **J** had taken about five thousand men and NDT
Jos 8:13 That night **J** went into the valley. H3397
Jos 8:15 **J** and all Israel let themselves be driven H3397
Jos 8:16 they pursued **J** and were lured away H3397
Jos 8:18 Then the LORD said to **J**, "Hold out toward H3397
Jos 8:18 So **J** held out toward the city the javelin H3397
Jos 8:21 For when **J** and all Israel saw that the H3397
Jos 8:23 the king of Ai alive and brought him to **J**. H3397
Jos 8:26 For **J** did not draw back the hand that held H3397
Jos 8:27 of this city, as the LORD had instructed **J**. H3397
Jos 8:28 So **J** burned Ai and made it a permanent H3397
Jos 8:29 **J** ordered them to take the body from the H3397
Jos 8:30 Then **J** built on Mount Ebal an altar to the H3397
Jos 8:32 **J** wrote on stones a copy of the law of NDT
Jos 8:34 Afterward, **J** read all the words of the law NDT
Jos 8:35 had commanded that **J** did not read to H3397
Jos 9: 2 together to wage war against **J** and Israel. H3397
Jos 9: 3 Gibeon heard what **J** had done to Jericho H3397
Jos 9: 6 Then they went to **J** in the camp at Gilgal H3397
Jos 9: 8 they said to **J**. But Joshua asked, H3397
Jos 9: 8 But **J** asked, "Who are you and where do H3397
Jos 9:15 Then **J** made a treaty of peace with them H3397
Jos 9:22 Then **J** summoned the Gibeonites and H3397
Jos 9:24 They answered **J**, "Your servants were H3397
Jos 9:26 So **J** saved them from the Israelites, and NDT
Jos 10: 1 Jerusalem heard that **J** had taken Ai and H3397
Jos 10: 4 has made peace with **J** and the Israelites." H3397
Jos 10: 6 then sent word to **J** in the camp at Gilgal: H3397
Jos 10: 7 So **J** marched up from Gilgal with his H3397
Jos 10: 8 The LORD said to **J**, "Do not be afraid of H3397
Jos 10: 9 from Gilgal, **J** took them by surprise. H3397
Jos 10:10 so **J** and the Israelites defeated them NDT
Jos 10:12 **J** said to the LORD in the presence of Israel: H3397
Jos 10:15 Then **J** returned with all Israel to the H3397
Jos 10:17 When **J** was told that the five kings had H3397
Jos 10:20 So **J** and the Israelites defeated them H3397
Jos 10:21 returned safely to **J** in the camp at H3397
Jos 10:22 **J** said, "Open the mouth of the cave and H3397
Jos 10:24 When they had brought these kings to **J** H3397
Jos 10:25 **J** said to them, "Do not be afraid; do not H3397
Jos 10:26 Then **J** put the kings to death and exposed H3397
Jos 10:27 At sunset **J** gave the order and they took H3397
Jos 10:28 That day **J** took Makkedah. He put the city H3397
Jos 10:29 Then **J** and all Israel with him moved on H3397
Jos 10:30 city and everyone in it **J** put to the sword. NDT
Jos 10:31 Then **J** and all Israel with him moved on H3397
Jos 10:32 and **J** took it on the second day. NDT
Jos 10:33 Lachish, but **J** defeated him and his army H3397
Jos 10:34 Then **J** and all Israel with him moved on H3397
Jos 10:36 Then **J** and all Israel with him went up H3397
Jos 10:38 Then **J** and all Israel with him turned H3397
Jos 10:40 So **J** subdued the whole region, including H3397
Jos 10:41 **J** subdued them from Kadesh Barnea to H3397
Jos 10:42 kings and their lands **J** conquered in one H3397
Jos 10:43 Then **J** returned with all Israel to the H3397
Jos 11: 6 The LORD said to **J**, "Do not be afraid of H3397
Jos 11: 7 So **J** and his whole army came against H3397
Jos 11: 9 **J** did to them as the LORD had directed: He H3397
Jos 11:10 At that time **J** turned back and captured H3397
Jos 11:12 **J** took all these royal cities and their kings H3397
Jos 11:13 mounds—except Hazor, which **J** burned. H3397
Jos 11:15 so Moses commanded **J**, and Joshua did H3397
Jos 11:15 commanded Joshua, and **J** did it; he left H3397
Jos 11:16 So **J** took this entire land: the hill country H3397
Jos 11:18 **J** waged war against all these kings for a H3397
Jos 11:21 At that time **J** went and destroyed the H3397

Jos 11:21 **J** totally destroyed them and their towns H3397
Jos 11:23 So **J** took the entire land, just as the LORD H3397
Jos 12: 7 kings of the land that **J** and the Israelites H3397
Jos 12: 7 **J** gave their lands as an inheritance to the H3397
Jos 13: 1 When **J** had grown old, the LORD said to H3397
Jos 14: 1 **J** son of Nun and the heads of the tribal H3397
Jos 14: 6 people of Judah approached **J** at Gilgal, H3397
Jos 14:13 Then **J** blessed Caleb son of Jephunneh H3397
Jos 15:13 **J** gave to Caleb son of Jephunneh a H3397
Jos 17: 4 Eleazar the priest, **J** son of Nun, and the H3397
Jos 17: 4 So **J** gave them an inheritance along with NDT
Jos 17:14 The people of Joseph said to **J**, "Why H3397
Jos 17:15 **J** answered, "and if the hill country of H3397
Jos 17:17 But **J** said to the tribes of Joseph—to H3397
Jos 18: 3 So **J** said to the Israelites: "How long will H3397
Jos 18: 8 map out the land, **J** instructed them, "Go H3397
Jos 18: 9 returned to **J** in the camp at Shiloh. H3397
Jos 18:10 **J** then cast lots for them in Shiloh in the H3397
Jos 19:49 the Israelites gave **J** son of Nun an H3397
Jos 19:51 **J** son of Nun and the heads of the tribal H3397
Jos 20: 1 Then the LORD said to **J**: H3397
Jos 21: 1 Eleazar the priest, **J** son of Nun, and the H3397
Jos 22: 1 Then **J** summoned the Reubenites, the H3397
Jos 22: 6 Then **J** blessed them and sent them away, H3397
Jos 22: 7 half of the tribe **J** gave land on the west H3397
Jos 22: 7 When **J** sent them home, he blessed H3397
Jos 23: 1 around them, **J**, by then a very old H3397
Jos 24: 1 Then **J** assembled all the tribes of Israel H3397
Jos 24: 2 **J** said to all the people, "This is what the H3397
Jos 24:19 **J** said to the people, "You are not able to H3397
Jos 24:21 But the people said to **J**, "No! We will H3397
Jos 24:22 Then **J** said, "You are witnesses against H3397
Jos 24:23 said **J**, "throw away the foreign gods that NDT
Jos 24:24 And the people said to **J**, "We will serve H3397
Jos 24:25 On that day **J** made a covenant for the H3397
Jos 24:26 And **J** recorded these things in the Book of H3397
Jos 24:28 Then **J** dismissed the people, each to H3397
Jos 24:29 After these things, **J** son of Nun, the H3397
Jos 24:31 the lifetime of **J** and of the elders who H3397
Jdg 1: 1 After the death of **J**, the Israelites asked H3397
Jdg 2: 6 After **J** had dismissed the Israelites, they H3397
Jdg 2: 7 the lifetime of **J** and of the elders who H3397
Jdg 2: 8 **J** son of Nun, the servant of the LORD, died H3397
Jdg 2:21 any of the nations **J** left when he died. H3397
Jdg 2:23 once by giving them into the hands of **J**. H3397
1Sa 6:14 came to the field of **J** of Beth Shemesh, H3397
1Sa 6:18 this day in the field of **J** of Beth Shemesh. H3397
1Ki 16:34 word of the LORD spoken by **J** son of Nun. H3397
2Ki 23: 8 gateway at the entrance of the Gate of **J**, H3397
1Ch 7:27 Nun his son and **J** his son. H3397
Ezr 2: 2 company with Zerubbabel, **J**, Nehemiah, H3800
Ezr 3: 2 Then **J** son of Jozadak and his fellow H3800
Ezr 3: 8 **J** son of Jozadak and the rest of the H3800
Ezr 3: 9 **J** and his sons and brothers and Kadmiel H3800
Ezr 4: 3 **J** and the rest of the heads of the families H3800
Ezr 5: 2 son of Shealtiel and **J** son of Jozadak set A10336
Ezr 10:18 From the descendants of **J** son of Jozadak H3800
Ne 7: 7 company with Zerubbabel, **J**, Nehemiah, H3800
Ne 8:17 From the days of **J** son of Nun until that H3800
Ne 12: 1 Zerubbabel son of Shealtiel and with **J**: H3800
Ne 12: 7 their associates in the days of **J**. H3800
Ne 12:10 **J** was the father of Joiakim, Joiakim the H3800
Ne 12:26 served in the days of Joiakim son of **J**, H3800
Hag 1: 1 of Judah, and to **J** son of Jozadak, the H3397
Hag 1:12 son of Shealtiel, **J** son of Jozadak, the H3397
Hag 1:14 the spirit of **J** son of Jozadak, the H3397
Hag 2: 2 of Judah, to **J** son of Jozadak, the H3397
Hag 2: 4 'Be strong, **J** son of Jozadak, the high H3397
Zec 3: 1 Then he showed me **J** the high priest H3397
Zec 3: 3 Now **J** was dressed in filthy clothes as he H3397
Zec 3: 4 Then he said to **J**, "See, I have taken H2257S
Zec 3: 6 angel of the LORD gave this charge to **J**: H3397
Zec 3: 8 " 'Listen, High Priest **J**, you and your H3397
Zec 3: 9 the stone I have set in front of **J**! There H3397
Zec 6:11 head of the high priest, **J** son of Jozadak. H3397
Lk 3:29 the son *of* **J**, the son of Eliezer, the son of G2652
Ac 7:45 our ancestors under **J** brought it with them G2652
Heb 4: 8 For if **J** had given them rest, God would G2652

JOSIAH (56) [JOSIAH'S]

1Ki 13: 2 'A son named **J** will be born to the house H3288
2Ki 21:24 they made **J** his son king in his place. H3288
2Ki 21:26 And **J** his son succeeded him as king H3288
2Ki 22: 1 **J** was eight years old when he became H3288
2Ki 22: 3 year of his reign, King **J** sent the secretary H3288
2Ki 23: 4 **J** brought all the priests from the towns of NDT
2Ki 23:11 **J** then burned the chariots dedicated to the NDT
2Ki 23:14 **J** smashed the sacred stones and cut down NDT
2Ki 23:16 Then **J** looked around, and when he saw H3288
2Ki 23:19 **J** removed all the shrines at the high H3288
2Ki 23:20 **J** slaughtered all the priests of those high NDT
2Ki 23:23 But in the eighteenth year of King **J**, this H3288
2Ki 23:24 **J** got rid of the mediums and spiritists H3288
2Ki 23:25 before nor after **J** was there a king like H2257S
2Ki 23:29 While **J** was king, Pharaoh Necho king H2257S
2Ki 23:29 King **J** marched out to meet him in battle H3288
2Ki 23:30 Jehoahaz son of **J** and anointed him and H3288
2Ki 23:34 made Eliakim son of **J** king in place of his H3288
2Ki 23:34 place of his father **J** and changed H3288
1Ch 3:14 Amon his son, **J** his son. H3288
1Ch 3:15 The sons of **J**: Johanan the firstborn H3288
2Ch 33:25 they made **J** his son king in his place. H3288
2Ch 34: 1 **J** was eight years old when he became H3288
2Ch 34:33 **J** removed all the detestable idols from H3288
2Ch 35: 1 **J** celebrated the Passover to the LORD in H3288
2Ch 35: 7 **J** provided for all the lay people who were H3288
2Ch 35:16 altar of the LORD, as King **J** had ordered. H3288
2Ch 35:18 ever celebrated such a Passover as did **J**, H3288
2Ch 35:20 when **J** had set the temple in order H3288
2Ch 35:20 **J** marched out to meet him in battle. H3288
2Ch 35:22 **J**, however, would not turn away from him, H3288
2Ch 35:23 Archers shot King **J**, and he told his H3288
2Ch 35:25 Jeremiah composed laments for **J**, and to H3288
2Ch 35:25 singers commemorate **J** in the laments. H3288
2Ch 36: 1 Jehoahaz son of **J** and made him king in H3288
Jer 1: 2 year of the reign of **J** son of Amon king of H3288
Jer 1: 3 reign of Jehoiakim son of **J** king of Judah, H3288
Jer 1: 3 year of Zedekiah son of **J** king of Judah, H3288
Jer 3: 6 During the reign of King **J**, the LORD said H3288
Jer 22:11 the LORD says about Shallum son of **J**, H3288
Jer 22:18 about Jehoiakim son of **J** king of Judah: H3288
Jer 25: 1 year of Jehoiakim son of **J** king of Judah, H3288
Jer 25: 3 thirteenth year of **J** son of Amon king of H3288
Jer 26: 1 reign of Jehoiakim son of **J** king of Judah, H3288
Jer 27: 1 reign of Zedekiah son of **J** king of Judah, H3288
Jer 35: 1 reign of Jehoiakim son of **J** king of Judah: H3288
Jer 36: 1 year of Jehoiakim son of **J** king of Judah, H3288
Jer 36: 2 speaking to you in the reign of **J** till now. H3288
Jer 36: 9 year of Jehoiakim son of **J** king of Judah, H3288
Jer 37: 1 Zedekiah son of **J** was made king of H3288
Jer 45: 1 year of Jehoiakim son of **J** king of Judah, H3288
Jer 46: 2 year of Jehoiakim son of **J** king of Judah: H3288
Zep 1: 1 during the reign of **J** son of Amon king of H3288
Zec 6:10 day to the house of **J** son of Zephaniah. H3287
Mt 1:10 the father of Amon, Amon the father of **J**, G2739
Mt 1:11 **J** the father of Jeconiah and his G2739

JOSIAH'S (5) [JOSIAH]

2Ki 23:28 As for the other events of **J** reign, and all H3288
2Ki 23:30 **J** servants brought his body in a chariot H2257S
2Ch 34: 8 In the eighteenth year of **J** reign, to H2257S
2Ch 35:19 in the eighteenth year of **J** reign. H3288
2Ch 35:26 The other events of **J** reign and his acts of H3288

JOSIAS (KJV) JOSIAH

JOSIPHIAH (1)

Ezr 8:10 Shelomith son of **J**, and with him 160 H3442

JOSTLE (1) [JOSTLED]

Joel 2: 8 *They do* not **j** each other; each marches H1895

JOSTLED (1) [JOSTLE]

Ge 25:22 The babies **j each other** within her, and H8368

JOT (KJV) SMALLEST LETTER

JOTBAH (1)

2Ki 21:19 daughter of Haruz; she was from **J**. H3513

JOTBATHAH (3)

Nu 33:33 left Hor Haggidgad and camped at **J**. H3514
Nu 33:34 They left **J** and camped at Abronah. H3514
Dt 10: 7 they traveled to Gudgodah and on to **J**, H3514

JOTHAM (27) [JOTHAM'S]

Jdg 9: 5 But **J**, the youngest son of Jerub-Baal H3462
Jdg 9: 7 When **J** was told about this, he climbed H3462
Jdg 9:21 Then **J** fled, escaping to Beer, and he H3462
Jdg 9:57 The curse of **J** son of Jerub-Baal came on H3462
2Ki 15: 5 **J** the king's son had charge of the palace H3462
2Ki 15: 7 And **J** his son succeeded him as king H3462
2Ki 15:30 in the twentieth year of **J** son of Uzziah. H3462
2Ki 15:32 **J** son of Uzziah king of Judah began to H3462
2Ki 15:35 **J** rebuilt the Upper Gate of the temple of H2085S
2Ki 15:38 **J** rested with his ancestors and was buried H3462
2Ki 16: 1 Ahaz son of **J** king of Judah began to H3462
1Ch 2:47 Regem, **J**, Geshan, Pelet, Ephah and H3462
1Ch 3:12 his son, Azariah his son, **J** his son, H3462
1Ch 5:17 during the reigns of **J** king of Judah and H3462
2Ch 26:21 **J** his son had charge of the palace and H3462
2Ch 26:23 And **J** his son succeeded him as king. H3462
2Ch 27: 1 **J** was twenty-five years old when he H3462
2Ch 27: 3 **J** rebuilt the Upper Gate of the temple of H2085S
2Ch 27: 5 **J** waged war against the king of the H2085S
2Ch 27: 6 **J** grew powerful because he walked H3462
2Ch 27: 9 **J** rested with his ancestors and was buried H3462
Isa 1: 1 reigns of Uzziah, **J**, Ahaz and Hezekiah, H3462
Isa 7: 1 When Ahaz son of **J**, the son of Uzziah H3462
Hos 1: 1 reigns of Uzziah, **J**, Ahaz and Hezekiah, H3462
Mic 1: 1 of Moresheth during the reigns of **J**, H3462
Mt 1: 9 Uzziah the father of **J**, Jotham the father G2718
Mt 1: 9 the father of Jotham, **J** the father of Ahaz G2718

JOTHAM'S (2) [JOTHAM]

2Ki 15:36 As for the other events of **J** reign, and H3462
2Ch 27: 7 The other events in **J** reign, including all H3462

JOURNEY (54) [JOURNEYED, JOURNEYS]

Ge 24:21 not the LORD had made his **j** successful. H2006
Ge 24:27 has led me on the **j** to the house of my H2006
Ge 24:40 angel with you and make your **j** a success, H2006
Ge 24:42 success to the **j** on which I have come H2006
Ge 24:56 that the LORD has granted success to my **j**. H2006
Ge 28:20 over me on this **j** I am taking and will H2006
Ge 29: 1 Jacob **continued on** his **j** and came H5951+8079
Ge 30:36 he put a three-day **j** between himself H2006
Ge 42:25 to give them provisions for their **j**. H2006
Ge 42:38 comes to him on the **j** you are taking, H2006
Ge 45:21 he also gave them provisions for their **j**. H2006
Ge 45:23 bread and other provisions for his **j**. H2006
Ex 3:18 us take a three-day **j** into the wilderness H2006
Ex 5: 3 us take a three-day **j** into the wilderness H2006
Ex 8:27 take a three-day **j** into the wilderness H2006
Nu 9:10 of a dead body or are away on a **j**, H2006
Nu 9:13 clean and not on a **j** fails to celebrate the H2006
Nu 33: 1 Here are the **stages in** the **j** *of* the H5023
Nu 33: 2 Moses recorded the stages in their **j**. H5023
Nu 33: 2 in their journey. This is their **j** by stages: H5023
Dt 1:33 who went ahead of you on your **j**, in fire by H2006
Dt 2: 7 watched over your **j** *through* this vast H2143
Dt 25:18 met you on your **j** and attacked all who H2006
Dt 28:68 in ships to Egypt on a **j** I said you should H2006
Jos 5: 5 during the **j** from Egypt had not. H2006
Jos 9:11 'Take provisions for your **j**; go and meet H2006
Jos 9:13 sandals are worn out by the very long **j**." H2006
Jos 24:17 us on our entire **j** and among all the H2006
Jdg 18: 5 to learn whether our **j** will be successful." H2006
Jdg 18: 6 Your **j** has the LORD's approval. H2006
1Ki 13:26 brought him back from his **j** heard of it, H2006
1Ki 19: 4 himself went a day's **j** into the wilderness. H2006
1Ki 19: 7 up and eat, for the **j** is too much for you." H2006
Ezr 7: 9 He had begun his **j** from Babylon on the H5092
Ezr 8:21 ask him for a safe **j** for us and our H2006
Ne 2: 6 "How long will your **j** take, and when will H4544
Pr 7:19 is not at home; he has gone on a long **j**. H2006
Isa 35: 8 The unclean *will* not **j** *on* it; wicked fools H6296
Am 5: 5 do not go to Gilgal, *do* not **j** *to* Beersheba. H6296
Jnh 3: 4 began by going a day's **j** into the city, H4544
Mic 6: 5 Remember your **j** from Shittim to Gilgal, that NDT
Mt 10:10 no bag for the **j** or extra shirt or sandals G3847
Mt 25:14 it will be like a man **going on a j**, who G623
Mt 25:15 Then *he* **went on** *his* **j**. G623
Mk 6: 8 "Take nothing for the **j** except a staff—no G3847
Lk 9: 3 "Take nothing for the **j**—no staff, no bag G3847
Lk 11: 6 a friend of mine on a **j** has come to me G3847
Jn 4: 6 tired as he was from the **j**, sat down by G3845
Ac 9: 3 As he neared Damascus on his **j**, suddenly G4513
Ac 9:27 them how Saul on his **j** had seen the Lord G3847
Ac 10: 9 following day as *they were* **on** *their* **j** and G3844
Ac 16: 3 Paul wanted *to* **take** him along **on the j**, so G2002
Ro 15:24 and *to have* you **assist** me **on** my **j** there, G4636
1Co 16: 6 so that you *can* **help** me **on** my **j** G4636

JOURNEYED (2) [JOURNEY]

Ex 12:37 The Israelites **j** from Rameses to Sukkoth H5825
Job 38:16 "*Have you* **j** to the springs of the sea or H995

JOURNEYS (1) [JOURNEY]

Ac 26:12 "On **one of these j** I was going to G4005S

JOWLS (NIV84) INTERNAL ORGANS

JOY (218) [ENJOY, ENJOYABLE, ENJOYED, ENJOYING, ENJOYMENT, ENJOYS, JOYFUL, JOYOUS, JOYFULLY, OVERJOYED, REJOICE, REJOICED, REJOICES, REJOICING]

Ge 31:27 send you away with **j** and singing to the H8525
Lev 9:24 *they* **shouted for j** and fell facedown. H8264
Dt 16:15 your hands, and your **j** will be complete. H8524
Jdg 9:19 *may* Abimelek *be your* **j**, and may H8523
1Ch 12:40 cattle and sheep, for there was **j** in Israel. H8525
1Ch 16:27 strength and **j** are in his dwelling place. H2530
1Ch 16:33 *let them* **sing for j** before the LORD H8264
1Ch 29:17 now I have seen with **j** how willingly your H8525
1Ch 29:22 drank with great **j** in the presence of H8525
2Ch 30:26 There was great **j** in Jerusalem, for since H8525
Ezr 3:12 while many others shouted for **j**. H8525
Ezr 3:13 sound of the shouts of **j** from the sound of H8525
Ezr 6:16 dedication of the house of God with **j**. A10250
Ezr 6:22 days they celebrated with **j** the Festival of H8525
Ezr 6:22 the LORD *had* **filled** them **with j** by H8523
Ne 8:10 the **j** *of* the LORD is your strength. H2530
Ne 8:12 of food and to celebrate with great **j**, H8525
Ne 8:17 And their **j** was very great. H8525
Ne 12:43 God *had* **given** them great **j**. H8523+8525
Est 8:16 the Jews it was a time of happiness and **j**, H8525
Est 8:17 there was **j** and gladness among the Jews H8525
Est 9:17 made it a day of feasting and **j**. H8525
Est 9:18 made it a day of feasting and **j**. H8525
Est 9:19 month of Adar as a day of **j** and feasting, H8525
Est 9:22 was turned into **j** and their mourning H8525
Est 9:22 days of feasting and **j** and giving presents H8525
Job 3: 7 may no **shout of j** be heard in it. H8265
Job 6:10 consolation—*my* **j** in unrelenting pain H6134
Job 8:21 laughter and your lips with **shouts of j**. H9558
Job 9:25 they fly away without a glimpse of **j**. H3208
Job 10:20 away from me so *I can* **have** a moment's **j** H1158
Job 20: 5 the **j** *of* the godless lasts but a moment. H8525
Job 33:26 they will see God's face and **shout for j** H9558
Job 38: 7 together and all the angels **shouted for j**? H8131
Ps 4: 7 Fill my heart with **j** when their grain and H8525
Ps 5:11 in you be glad; *let them* ever **sing for j**. H8264
Ps 16:11 you will fill me with **j** in your presence H8525
Ps 19: 8 of the LORD are right, **giving j** *to* the heart. H8523
Ps 20: 5 *May we* **shout for j** over your victory and H8264
Ps 21: 1 How great is *his* **j** in the victories you give! H1635
Ps 21: 6 him glad with the **j** of your presence. H8525

J

Ps 27: 6 sacred tent I will sacrifice with **shouts of j**; H9558
Ps 28: 7 My heart **leaps for j**, and with my song I H6600
Ps 30:11 my sackcloth and clothed me with j, H8525
Ps 33: 3 a new song; play skillfully, and **shout for j**. H9558
Ps 35:27 *May* those who delight in my vindication **shout for j** H8264
Ps 42: 4 One with **shouts of j** and praise H7754+8262
Ps 43: 4 altar of God, to God, my j and my delight. H8525
Ps 45: 7 by anointing you with the oil of j. H8607
Ps 45:15 Led in with j and gladness, they enter the H8525
Ps 47: 1 you nations; shout to God with cries of j. H8262
Ps 47: 5 God has ascended amid **shouts of j**, the H9558
Ps 48: 2 in its loftiness, the j *of* the whole earth H5375
Ps 51: 8 Let me hear j and gladness; let the bones H8607
Ps 51:12 Restore to me the j *of* your salvation and H8607
Ps 65: 8 evening fades, *you* **call forth songs of j**. H8264
Ps 65:13 with grain; *they* **shout for j** and sing. H8131
Ps 66: 1 **Shout for j** to God, all the earth! H8131
Ps 67: 4 May the nations be glad and **sing for j**, for H8264
Ps 71:23 My lips *will* **shout for j** when I sing praise H8264
Ps 81: 1 **Sing for j** to God our strength; shout aloud H8264
Ps 86: 4 **Bring j** *to* your servant, Lord, for I put my H8523
Ps 89:12 Hermon **sing for j** at your name. H8264
Ps 90:14 that *we may* **sing for j** and be glad all our H8264
Ps 92: 4 *I* **sing for j** at what your hands have done. H8264
Ps 94:19 within me, your consolation **brought** me j. H9130
Ps 95: 1 Come, *let us* **sing for j** to the LORD; let us H8264
Ps 96:12 *let* all the trees of the forest **sing for j**. H8264
Ps 97:11 on the righteous and j on the upright in H8525
Ps 98: 4 **Shout for j** to the LORD, all the earth, burst H8131
Ps 98: 6 ram's horn—**shout for j** before the LORD H8131
Ps 98: 8 *let* the mountains **sing** together **for j**; H8264
Ps 100: 1 **Shout for j** to the LORD, all the earth. H8131
Ps 105:43 his chosen ones with **shouts of j**; H8262
Ps 106: 5 that I *may* **share** in the j *of* your H8523+8525
Ps 107:22 tell of his works with **songs of j**. H8262
Ps 118:15 **Shouts of j** and victory resound in the H8262
Ps 119:111 they are the j *of* my heart. H8607
Ps 126: 2 with laughter, our tongues with **songs of j**. H8262
Ps 126: 3 things for us, and we are **filled with j**. H8524
Ps 126: 5 sow with tears will reap with **songs of j**. H8262
Ps 126: 6 will return with **songs of j**, carrying H8262
Ps 132: 9 *may* your faithful people **sing for j**. H8264
Ps 132:16 faithful people *will* **ever sing for j**. H8264+8264
Ps 137: 3 our tormentors demanded songs of j; they H8525
Ps 137: 6 I do not consider Jerusalem my highest j. H8525
Ps 149: 5 in this honor and **sing for j** on their beds. H8264
Pr 10: 1 A wise son **brings j** *to* his father, but a H8523
Pr 10:28 The prospect of the righteous is j, but the H8525
Pr 11:10 the wicked perish, there are **shouts of j**. H8262
Pr 12:20 but those who promote peace have j. H8525
Pr 14:10 no one else can share its j. H8525
Pr 15:20 A wise son **brings j** *to* his father, but a H8523
Pr 15:21 Folly brings j to one who has no sense H8525
Pr 15:23 A person finds j in giving an apt reply H8525
Pr 15:30 a messenger's eyes **brings j** *to* the heart, H8523
Pr 17:21 *there is* no j *for* the parent of a godless H8523
Pr 21:15 it brings j to the righteous but terror to H8525
Pr 23:24 of a righteous child *has* **great j**; H1635+1635
Pr 27: 9 Perfume and incense **bring j** *to* the heart H8523
Pr 27:11 my son, and **bring j** *to* my heart; then I H8523
Pr 29: 3 who loves wisdom **brings j** *to* his father, H8523
Pr 29: 6 the righteous **shout for j** and are glad. H8264
Ecc 8:15 Then j will accompany them in their toil H2085S
Ecc 11: 9 and *let* your heart **give** you j in the days of H3512
Isa 9: 3 enlarged the nation and increased their j; H8525
Isa 12: 3 With j you will draw water from the wells H8607
Isa 12: 6 Shout aloud and **sing for j**, people of Zion H8264
Isa 16: 9 The **shouts of j** over your ripened fruit H2116
Isa 16:10 J and gladness are taken away from the H8525
Isa 22:13 But see, there is j and revelry H8607
Isa 24:11 cry out for wine; all j turns to gloom, all H8525
Isa 24:14 their voices, *they* **shout for j**; from the west H8264
Isa 26:19 in the dust wake up and **shout for j**— H8264
Isa 35: 2 it will rejoice greatly and **shout for j**. H8264
Isa 35: 6 and the mute tongue **shout for j**. H8264
Isa 35:10 everlasting j will crown their heads. H8525
Isa 35:10 Gladness and j will overtake them, and H8525
Isa 42:11 *Let* the people of Sela **sing for j**; let them H8264
Isa 44:23 **Sing for j**, *you* heavens, for the LORD has H8264
Isa 48:20 this with **shouts of j** and proclaim it H7754+8262
Isa 49:13 **Shout for j**, *you* heavens; rejoice, you H8264
Isa 51: 3 J and gladness will be found in her H8607
Isa 51:11 everlasting j will crown their heads. H8525
Isa 51:11 Gladness and j will overtake them, and H8525
Isa 52: 8 up their voices; together *they* **shout for j**. H8264
Isa 52: 9 Burst into **songs of j** together, you ruins of H8264
Isa 54: 1 **shout for j**, *you* who were never in labor H7412
Isa 55:12 You will go out in j and be led forth in H8525
Isa 56: 7 mountain and **give them j** in my house of H8523
Isa 58:14 then *you will* **find** *your* j in the LORD, and I H6695
Isa 60: 5 your heart will throb and **swell with j**; the H8143
Isa 60:15 pride and the j *of* all generations. H5375
Isa 61: 3 of ashes, the oil of j instead of mourning H8607
Isa 61: 7 your land, and everlasting j will be yours. H8525
Isa 65:14 will sing out of the j *of* their hearts, H3206
Isa 65:18 to be a delight and its people a j. H5375
Isa 66: 5 LORD be glorified, that we may see your j! H8525
Jer 7:34 to the sounds of j and gladness and to H8607
Jer 15:16 they were my j and my heart's delight H8607
Jer 16: 9 to the sounds of j and gladness and to H8607
Jer 25:10 from them the sounds of j and gladness, H8607
Jer 31: 7 "Sing with j for Jacob; shout for the H8525
Jer 31:12 will come and **shout for j** on the heights H8264
Jer 31:13 give them comfort and j instead of sorrow. H8523
Jer 33: 9 will bring me renown, j, praise and honor H8607
Jer 33:11 the sounds of j and gladness, the voices of H8607
Jer 48:33 J and gladness are gone from the H8525
Jer 48:33 no one treads them with **shouts of j**. H2116
Jer 48:33 there are shouts, they are not **shouts of j**. H2116
Jer 51:48 is in them *will* **shout for j** over Babylon, H8264
La 2:15 of beauty, the j of the whole earth?" H5375
La 5:15 J is gone from our hearts; our dancing has H5375
Eze 7: 7 There is panic, not j, *on* the mountains. H2059
Eze 24:25 stronghold, their j and glory, the delight H5375
Joel 1:12 Surely the people's j is withered away. H8607
Joel 1:16 j and gladness from the house of our God H8525
Mt 13:20 the word and at once receives it with j. *G5915*
Mt 13:44 then in his j went and sold all he had *G5915*
Mt 28: 8 afraid yet filled with j, and ran to tell his *G5915*
Mk 4:16 the word and at once receive it with j. *G5915*
Lk 1:14 He will be a j and delight to you, and *G5915*
Lk 1:44 my ears, the baby in my womb leaped for j. *G21*
Lk 1:58 her great mercy, and *they* **shared** her j. *G5176*
Lk 2:10 that will cause great j for all the people. *G5915*
Lk 6:23 "Rejoice in that day and **leap for j** *G5015*
Lk 8:13 receive the word with j when they hear it, *G5915*
Lk 10:17 The seventy-two returned with j and said *G5915*
Lk 10:21 time Jesus, **full of j** through the Holy Spirit *G22*
Lk 24:41 believe it because of j and amazement, *G5915*
Lk 24:52 returned to Jerusalem with great j. *G5915*
Jn 3:29 and *is* **full of j** when he hears the *G5915+5897*
Jn 3:29 That j is mine, and it is now *G5915*
Jn 15:11 you this so that my j may be in you and *G5915*
Jn 15:11 in you and that your j may be complete. *G5915*
Jn 16:20 You will grieve, but your grief will turn to j. *G5915*
Jn 16:21 because of her j that a child is born *G5915*
Jn 16:22 and no one will take away your j. *G5915*
Jn 16:24 will receive, and your j will be complete. *G5915*
Jn 17:13 the full measure *of* my j within them. *G5915*
Ac 2:28 you will fill me *with* j in your presence. *G2372*
Ac 8: 8 So there was great j in that city. *G5915*
Ac 13:52 were filled with j and with the Holy Spirit. *G5915*
Ac 14:17 plenty of food and fills your hearts *with* j." *G2372*
Ac 16:34 *he was* **filled with j** because he had come to *G22*
Ro 14:17 peace and j in the Holy Spirit, *G5915*
Ro 15:13 fill you with all j and peace as you trust *G5915*
Ro 15:32 so that I may come to you with j, by God's *G5915*
2Co 1:24 we work with you *for* your j, because it *G5915*
2Co 2: 3 all of you, that you would all share my j. *G5915*
2Co 7: 4 in all our troubles my j knows no bounds. *G5915*
2Co 7: 7 so that my j *was* greater than ever. *G5897*
2Co 8: 2 their overflowing j and their extreme *G5915*
Gal 4:27 bore a child; **shout for j** and cry aloud, you *G4838*
Gal 5:22 of the Spirit is love, j, peace, forbearance, *G5915*
Php 1: 4 prayers for all of you, I always pray with j *G5915*
Php 1:25 of you for your progress and j in the faith, *G5915*
Php 2: 2 then make my j complete by being *G5915*
Php 2:29 welcome him in the Lord with great j, and *G5915*
Php 4: 1 long for, my j and crown, stand firm *G5915*
1Th 1: 6 suffering with the j given by the Holy *G5915*
1Th 2:19 what is our hope, our j, or the crown in *G5915*
1Th 2:20 you are our glory and j. *G5915*
1Th 3: 9 in return for all the j we have in the *G5915*
2Ti 1: 4 to see you, so that I may be filled with j. *G5915*
Phm 7 has given me great j and encouragement, *G5915*
Heb 1: 9 by anointing you with the oil *of* j. *G21*
Heb 12: 2 For the j set before him he endured the *G5915*
Heb 13:17 Do this so that their work will be a j, not a *G5915*
Jas 1: 2 Consider it pure j, my brothers and sisters *G5915*
Jas 4: 9 laughter to mourning and your j to gloom. *G5915*
1Pe 1: 8 *are* **filled with** an inexpressible and glorious j *G22+5915*
1Jn 1: 4 We write this to make our j complete. *G5915*
2Jn 4 *It has* **given** *me* great j to find some of *G5897*
2Jn 12 so that our j may be complete. *G5915*
3Jn 3 It **gave** *me* great j when some believers *G5897*
3Jn 4 I have no greater j than to hear that my *G5915*
Jude 24 presence without fault and with **great j**— *G21*

JOYFUL (19) [JOY]

Dt 16:14 *Be* j at your festival—you, your sons and H8523
1Sa 18: 6 with j **songs** and with timbrels and lyres. H8525
1Ki 8:66 j and glad in heart for all the good things H8524
1Ch 15:16 musicians to make a j sound with musical H8525
2Ch 7:10 j and glad in heart for the good things the H8524
Ps 68: 3 before God; may they be happy and j. H8525
Ps 100: 2 gladness; come before him with j **songs**. H8265
Pr 23:25 *may* she who gave you birth *be* j! H1635
Ecc 9: 7 drink your wine with a j heart, for God H3202
Isa 24: 8 The j timbrels are stilled, the noise of the H5375
Isa 24: 8 revelers has stopped, the j harp is silent. H5375
Isa 24:11 all j **sounds** are banished from the earth. H5375
Jer 31: 4 timbrels and go out to dance with the j. H8471
Hab 3:18 in the LORD, *I will be* j in God my Savior. H1635
Zec 8:19 months will become j and glad occasions H8607
Zec 10: 7 Their children will see it and *be* j; their H8523
Ro 12:12 *Be* j in hope, patient in affliction, faithful *G5897*
Col 1:12 giving j thanks to the Father *G3552+5915*
Heb 12:22 upon thousands of angels *in* j **assembly**, *G4108*

JOYFULLY (10) [JOY]

Dt 28:47 the LORD your God j and gladly in the H928+8525
2Ch 20:27 Jerusalem returned j to Jerusalem, H928+8525
2Ch 30:23 another seven days they celebrated j. H8525
Ne 12:27 to celebrate j the dedication with H8525
Job 39:13 "The wings of the ostrich **flap** j, though H6632
Ps 33: 1 **Sing** j to the LORD, *you* righteous; it is H8264
Ps 145: 7 goodness and j **sing** *of* your righteousness H8264
Lk 15: 5 he finds it, he j puts it on his shoulders *G5897*
Lk 19:37 of disciples began j to praise God in loud *G5897*
Heb 10:34 those in prison and j accepted the *G3552+5915*

JOYOUS (1) [JOY]

Est 8:15 And the city of Susa held a j celebration. H8523

JOZABAD (11)

2Ki 12:21 murdered him were J son of Shimeath H3416
1Ch 12: 4 Jahaziel, Johanan, J the Gederathite, H3416
1Ch 12:20 J, Jediael, Michael, Jozabad H3416
1Ch 12:20 Jediael, Michael, J, Elihu and Zillethai H3416
2Ch 31:13 Asahel, Jerimoth, J, Eliel, Ismakiah H3416
2Ch 35: 9 Hashabiah, Jeiel and J, the leaders of the H3416
Ezr 8:33 so were the Levites J son of Jeshua and H3416
Ezr 10:22 Ishmael, Nethanel, J and Elasah. H3416
Ezr 10:23 J, Shimei, Kelaiah (that is, Kelita) H3416
Ne 8: 7 Azariah, J, Hanan and Pelaiah H3416
Ne 11:16 Shabbethai and J, two of the heads of the H3416

JOZADAK (13)

1Ch 6:14 of Seraiah, and Seraiah the father of J. H3392
1Ch 6:15 J was deported when the LORD sent Judah H3392
Ezr 3: 2 Then Joshua son of J and his fellow H3449
Ezr 3: 8 Joshua son of J and the rest of the people H3449
Ezr 5: 2 Joshua son of J set to work to A10318
Ezr 10:18 From the descendants of Joshua son of J H3449
Ne 12:26 of Joshua, the son of J, and in the days of H3449
Hag 1: 1 to Joshua son of J, the high priest: H3392
Hag 1:12 Shealtiel, Joshua son of J, the high priest, H3392
Hag 1:14 the spirit of Joshua son of J, the high H3392
Hag 2: 2 to Joshua son of J, the high priest, H3392
Hag 2: 4 Joshua son of J, the high priest. H3392
Zec 6:11 head of the high priest, Joshua son of J. H3392

JUBAL (1)

Ge 4:21 His brother's name was J; he was the H3415

JUBILANT (5)

1Ch 16:32 that is in it; *let* the fields *be* j, and H6636
Ps 94: 3 the wicked, how long *will* the wicked *be* j? H6600
Ps 96:12 *Let* the fields *be* j, and everything in them; H6600
Ps 98: 4 all the earth, burst into j **song** with music; H8264
Hos 9: 1 *do* not *be* j like the other nations. H1637

JUBILEE (21)

Lev 25:10 It shall be a j for you; each of you is to H3413
Lev 25:11 The fiftieth year shall be a j for you; do not H3413
Lev 25:12 For it is a j and is to be holy for you; eat H3413
Lev 25:13 " 'In this Year of J everyone is to return to H3413
Lev 25:15 basis of the number of years since the J. H3413
Lev 25:28 of the buyer until the Year of J. H3413
Lev 25:28 It will be returned in the J, and they can H3413
Lev 25:30 It is not to be returned in the J. H3413
Lev 25:31 they are to be returned in the J. H3413
Lev 25:33 is to be returned in the J, because the H3413
Lev 25:40 they are to work for you until the Year of J. H3413
Lev 25:50 they sold themselves up to the Year of J. H3413
Lev 25:52 a few years remain until the Year of J, H3413
Lev 25:54 are to be released in the Year of J, H3413
Lev 27:17 they dedicate a field during the Year of J, H3413
Lev 27:18 But if they dedicate a field after the J, the H3413
Lev 27:18 years that remain until the next Year of J, H3413
Lev 27:21 When the field is released in the J, it will H3413
Lev 27:23 determine its value up to the Year of J, H3413
Lev 27:24 In the Year of J the field will revert to the H3413
Nu 36: 4 When the **Year of J** for the Israelites H3413

JUDAH (835) [JUDAH'S, JUDEA, JUDEAN]

Ge 29:35 So she named him J. Then she stopped H3373
Ge 35:23 Simeon, Levi, J, Issachar and H3373
Ge 37:26 J said to his brothers, "What will we gain H3373
Ge 38: 1 J left his brothers and went down to stay H3373
Ge 38: 2 There J met the daughter of a Canaanite H3373
Ge 38: 6 J got a wife for Er, his firstborn, and her H3373
Ge 38: 8 Then J said to Onan, "Sleep with your H3373
Ge 38:11 J then said to his daughter-in-law Tamar H3373
Ge 38:12 When J had recovered from his grief, he H3373
Ge 38:15 When J saw her, he thought she was a H3373
Ge 38:20 Meanwhile J sent the young goat by his H3373
Ge 38:22 So he went back to J and said, "I didn't H3373
Ge 38:23 Then J said, "Let her keep what she has H3373
Ge 38:24 About three months later J was told H3373
Ge 38:24 J said, "Bring her out and have her H3373
Ge 38:26 J recognized them and said, "She is more H3373
Ge 43: 3 But J said to him, "The man warned us H3373
Ge 43: 8 Then J said to Israel his father, "Send the H3373
Ge 44:14 in the house when J and his brothers H3373
Ge 44:16 we say to my lord?" J replied. "What can H3373
Ge 44:18 Then J went up to him and said: "Pardon H3373
Ge 46:12 The sons of J: Er, Onan, Shelah, Perez H3373
Ge 46:28 Now Jacob sent J ahead of him to Joseph H3373
Ge 49: 8 "J, your brothers will praise you; your H3373
Ge 49: 9 are a lion's cub, J; you return from the H3373
Ge 49:10 The scepter will not depart from J, nor the H3373
Ex 1: 2 Reuben, Simeon, Levi and J; H3373
Ex 31: 2 the son of Hur, of the tribe of J, H3373
Ex 35:30 the son of Hur, of the tribe of J, H3373

Ex 38:22 of the tribe of J, made everything the H3373
Nu 1: 7 from J, Nahshon son of Amminadab; H3373
Nu 1:26 From the descendants of J: All the men H3373
Nu 1:27 number from the tribe of J was 74,600. H3373
Nu 2: 3 of the camp of J are to encamp under H3373
Nu 2: 3 of the people of J is Nahshon son of H3373
Nu 2: 9 All the men assigned to the camp of J H3373
Nu 7:12 son of Amminadab of the tribe of J. H3373
Nu 10:14 of the camp of J went first, H1201+3373
Nu 13: 6 from the tribe of J, Caleb son of H3373
Nu 26:19 Er and Onan were sons of J, but they died H3373
Nu 26:20 The descendants of J by their clans were H3373
Nu 26:22 These were the clans of J; those H3373
Nu 34:19 son of Jephunneh, from the tribe of J; H3373
Dt 27:12 Simeon, Levi, J, Issachar, Joseph and H3373
Dt 33: 7 And this he said about J: "Hear, LORD, the H3373
Dt 33: 7 LORD, the cry of J; bring him to his H3373
Dt 34: 2 all the land of J as far as the H3373
Jos 7: 1 of the tribe of J, took some of them. H3373
Jos 7:16 come forward by tribes, and J was chosen. H3373
Jos 7:17 The clans of J came forward, and the H3373
Jos 7:18 of Zerah, of the tribe of J, was chosen. H3373
Jos 11:21 from all the hill country of J, and from all H3373
Jos 14: 6 Now the people of J approached Joshua H3373
Jos 15: 1 The allotment for the tribe of J H1201+3373
Jos 15:12 around the people of J by their clans. H3373
Jos 15:13 son of Jephunneh a portion in J— H1201+3373
Jos 15:20 is the inheritance of the tribe of J, H1201+3373
Jos 15:21 of the tribe of J in the Negev H1201+3373
Jos 15:63 J could not dislodge the Jebusites H1201+3373
Jos 15:63 Jebusites live there with the people of J. H3373
Jos 18: 5 J is to remain in its territory on the south H3373
Jos 18:11 lay between the tribes of J and Joseph: H3373
Jos 18:14 Kiriath Jearim), a town of the people of J. H3373
Jos 19: 1 lay within the territory of J. H1201+3373
Jos 19: 9 was taken from the share of J, H1201+3373
Jos 19: 9 their inheritance within the territory of J. H4392s
Jos 20: 7 that is, Hebron) in the hill country of J. H3373
Jos 21: 4 thirteen towns from the tribes of J, H3373
Jos 21: 9 the tribes of J and Simeon they H1201+3373
Jos 21:11 pastureland, in the hill country of J. H3373
Jdg 1: 2 The LORD answered, "J shall go up; I have H3373
Jdg 1: 3 The men of J then said to the Simeonites H3373
Jdg 1: 4 When J attacked, the LORD gave the H3373
Jdg 1: 8 The men of J attacked Jerusalem also H3373
Jdg 1: 9 J went down to fight against the H1201+3373
Jdg 1:16 with the people of J to live among the H3373
Jdg 1:16 of the Desert of J in the Negev near Arad. H3373
Jdg 1:17 Then the men of J went with the H3373
Jdg 1:18 J also took Gaza, Ashkelon and Ekron H3373
Jdg 1:19 The LORD was with the men of J. They took H3373
Jdg 10: 9 also crossed the Jordan to fight against J, H3373
Jdg 15: 9 The Philistines went up and camped in J H3373
Jdg 15:10 The people of J asked, "Why have you H3373
Jdg 15:11 thousand men from J went down to the H3373
Jdg 17: 7 A young Levite from Bethlehem in J, who H3373
Jdg 17: 7 who had been living within the clan of J, H3373
Jdg 17: 9 "I'm a Levite from Bethlehem in J," he H3373
Jdg 18:12 they set up camp near Kiriath Jearim in J. H3373
Jdg 19: 1 took a concubine from Bethlehem in J. H3373
Jdg 19: 2 to her parents' home in Bethlehem, J. H3373
Jdg 19:18 from Bethlehem in J to a remote area in H3373
Jdg 19:18 to Bethlehem in J and now I am going H3373
Jdg 20:18 The LORD replied, "J shall go first." H3373
Ru 1: 1 So a man from Bethlehem in J, together H3373
Ru 1: 2 from Bethlehem, J. And they went to H3373
Ru 1: 7 would take them back to the land of J. H3373
Ru 4:12 like that of Perez, whom Tamar bore to J." H3373
1Sa 11: 8 thousand and those of J thirty thousand. H3373
1Sa 15: 4 foot soldiers and ten thousand from J. H3373
1Sa 17: 1 war and assembled at Sokoh in J. H3373
1Sa 17:12 who was from Bethlehem in J. H3373
1Sa 17:52 men of Israel and J surged forward with a H3373
1Sa 18:16 But all Israel and J loved David, because H3373
1Sa 22: 5 Go into the land of J." So David left and H3373
1Sa 23: 3 men said to him, "Here in J we are afraid. H3373
1Sa 23:23 track him down among all the clans of J." H3373
1Sa 27: 6 has belonged to the kings of J ever since. H3373
1Sa 27:10 "Against the Negev of J" or "Against the H3373
1Sa 30:14 belonging to J and the Negev of Caleb H3373
1Sa 30:16 the land of the Philistines and from J. H3373
1Sa 30:26 some of the plunder to the elders of J, H3373
2Sa 1:18 that the people of J be taught this lament H3373
2Sa 2: 1 "Shall I go up to one of the towns of J?" H3373
2Sa 2: 4 Then the men of J came to Hebron, and H3373
2Sa 2: 4 anointed David king over the tribe of J. H3373
2Sa 2: 7 the people of J have anointed me H3373
2Sa 2:10 The tribe of J, however, remained loyal to H3373
2Sa 2:11 in Hebron over J was seven years H1074+3373
2Sa 3:10 over Israel and J from Dan to Beersheba." H3373
2Sa 5: 5 he reigned over J seven years and six H3373
2Sa 5: 5 over all Israel and J thirty-three years. H3373
2Sa 6: 2 men went to Baalah in J to bring up from H3373
2Sa 11:11 ark and Israel and J are staying in tents, H3373
2Sa 12: 8 I gave you all Israel and J. And if all this H3373
2Sa 19:11 "Ask the elders of J, 'Why should you be H3373
2Sa 19:14 hearts of the men of J so that they were H3373
2Sa 19:15 Now the men of J had come to Gilgal to H3373
2Sa 19:16 with the men of J to meet King David. H3373
2Sa 19:40 All the troops of J and half the troops of H3373
2Sa 19:41 the men of J, steal the king away H3373
2Sa 19:42 All the men of J answered the men of H3373
2Sa 19:43 the men of Israel answered the men of J, H3373
2Sa 19:43 But the men of J pressed their claims H3373
2Sa 20: 2 But the men of J stayed by their king all H3373
2Sa 20: 4 "Summon the men of J to come to me H3373
2Sa 20: 5 But when Amasa went to summon J, he H3373
2Sa 21: 2 zeal for Israel and J had tried to H3373
2Sa 24: 1 "Go and take a census of Israel and J." H3373
2Sa 24: 7 went on to Beersheba in the Negev of J. H3373
2Sa 24: 9 a sword, and in J five hundred thousand. H3373
1Ki 1: 9 and all the royal officials of J, H3373
1Ki 1:35 appointed him ruler over Israel and J." H3373
1Ki 4:20 The people of J and Israel were as H3373
1Ki 4:25 During Solomon's lifetime J and Israel H3373
1Ki 12:17 who were living in the towns of J, H3373
1Ki 12:20 Only the tribe of J remained loyal to the H3373
1Ki 12:21 he mustered all J and the tribe of H1074+3373
1Ki 12:23 to Rehoboam son of Solomon king of J, H3373
1Ki 12:23 of Judah, to all J and Benjamin H1074+3373
1Ki 12:27 to their lord, Rehoboam king of J. H3373
1Ki 12:32 like the festival held in J, and offered H3373
1Ki 13: 1 LORD a man of God came from J to Bethel, H3373
1Ki 13:12 road the man of God from J had taken. H3373
1Ki 13:14 you the man of God who came from J?" H3373
1Ki 13:21 to the man of God who had come from J, H3373
1Ki 14:21 Rehoboam son of Solomon was king in J H3373
1Ki 14:22 J did evil in the eyes of the LORD. By the H3373
1Ki 14:29 the book of the annals of the kings of J? H3373
1Ki 15: 1 son of Nebat, Abijah became king of J, H3373
1Ki 15: 7 the book of the annals of the kings of J? H3373
1Ki 15: 9 king of Israel, Asa became king of J, H3373
1Ki 15:17 went up against J and fortified Ramah to H3373
1Ki 15:17 entering the territory of Asa king of J. H3373
1Ki 15:22 Then King Asa issued an order to all J H3373
1Ki 15:23 the book of the annals of the kings of J? H3373
1Ki 15:25 Israel in the second year of Asa king of J, H3373
1Ki 15:28 year of Asa king of J and succeeded him H3373
1Ki 15:33 In the third year of Asa king of J, Baasha H3373
1Ki 16: 8 In the twenty-sixth year of Asa king of J H3373
1Ki 16:10 the twenty-seventh year of Asa king of J. H3373
1Ki 16:15 the twenty-seventh year of Asa king of J H3373
1Ki 16:23 In the thirty-first year of Asa king of J H3373
1Ki 16:29 In the thirty-eighth year of Asa king of J H3373
1Ki 19: 3 When he came to Beersheba in J, he left H3373
1Ki 22: 2 Jehoshaphat king of J went down to see H3373
1Ki 22:10 Jehoshaphat king of J were sitting on H3373
1Ki 22:29 Jehoshaphat king of J went up to Ramoth H3373
1Ki 22:41 Asa became king of J in the fourth year of H3373
1Ki 22:45 the book of the annals of the kings of J? H3373
1Ki 22:51 year of Jehoshaphat king of J, H3373
2Ki 1:17 of Jehoram son of Jehoshaphat king of J. H3373
2Ki 3: 1 eighteenth year of Jehoshaphat king of J, H3373
2Ki 3: 7 this message to Jehoshaphat king of J: H3373
2Ki 3: 9 with the king of J and the king of Edom H3373
2Ki 3:14 the presence of Jehoshaphat king of J, H3373
2Ki 8:16 when Jehoshaphat was king of J H3373
2Ki 8:16 Jehoshaphat began his reign as king of J. H3373
2Ki 8:19 the LORD was not willing to destroy J. H3373
2Ki 8:20 rebelled against J and set up its own H3373
2Ki 8:22 Edom has been in rebellion against J. H3373
2Ki 8:23 the book of the annals of the kings of J? H3373
2Ki 8:25 son of Jehoram king of J began to reign. H3373
2Ki 8:29 of Jehoram king of J went down to Jezreel H3373
2Ki 9:16 Ahaziah king of J had gone down to H3373
2Ki 9:21 of Israel and Ahaziah king of J rode out, H3373
2Ki 9:27 When Ahaziah king of J saw what had H3373
2Ki 9:29 of Ahab, Ahaziah had become king of J.) H3373
2Ki 10:13 relatives of Ahaziah king of J and asked, H3373
2Ki 12:18 But Joash king of J took all the sacred H3373
2Ki 12:18 Ahaziah, the kings of J—and the gifts he H3373
2Ki 12:19 the book of the annals of the kings of J? H3373
2Ki 13: 1 year of Joash son of Ahaziah king of J, H3373
2Ki 13:10 the thirty-seventh year of Joash king of J, H3373
2Ki 13:12 his war against Amaziah king of J, H3373
2Ki 14: 1 son of Joash king of J began to reign. H3373
2Ki 14: 9 of Israel replied to Amaziah king of J: H3373
2Ki 14:10 your own downfall and that of J also?" H3373
2Ki 14:11 Amaziah king of J faced each other at H3373
2Ki 14:11 faced each other at Beth Shemesh in J. H3373
2Ki 14:12 J was routed by Israel, and every man fled H3373
2Ki 14:13 king of Israel captured Amaziah king of J, H3373
2Ki 14:15 his war against Amaziah king of J, H3373
2Ki 14:17 son of Joash king of J lived for fifteen H3373
2Ki 14:18 the book of the annals of the kings of J? H3373
2Ki 14:21 Then all the people of J took Azariah H3373
2Ki 14:22 restored it to J after Amaziah rested H3373
2Ki 14:23 year of Amaziah son of Joash king of J, H3373
2Ki 14:28 which had belonged to J, are they not H3373
2Ki 15: 1 son of Amaziah king of J began to reign. H3373
2Ki 15: 6 the book of the annals of the kings of J? H3373
2Ki 15: 8 the thirty-eighth year of Azariah king of J, H3373
2Ki 15:13 in the thirty-ninth year of Uzziah king of J, H3373
2Ki 15:17 the thirty-ninth year of Azariah king of J, H3373
2Ki 15:23 In the fiftieth year of Azariah king of J H3373
2Ki 15:27 the fifty-second year of Azariah king of J, H3373
2Ki 15:32 son of Uzziah king of J began to reign. H3373
2Ki 15:36 the book of the annals of the kings of J? H3373
2Ki 15:37 Pekah son of Remaliah against J. H3373
2Ki 16: 1 son of Jotham king of J began to reign. H3373
2Ki 16: 6 Aram by driving out the **people of J**. H3374
2Ki 16:19 the book of the annals of the kings of J? H3373
2Ki 17: 1 In the twelfth year of Ahaz king of J H3373
2Ki 17:13 LORD warned Israel and J through all his H3373
2Ki 17:18 Only the tribe of J was left, H3373
2Ki 17:19 even J did not keep the commands of H3373
2Ki 18: 1 son of Ahaz king of J began to reign. H3373
2Ki 18: 5 no one like him among all the kings of J, H3373
2Ki 18:13 the fortified cities of J and captured them. H3373
2Ki 18:14 So Hezekiah king of J sent this message to H3373
2Ki 18:14 Hezekiah king of J three hundred talents H3373
2Ki 18:16 Hezekiah king of J stripped off the gold H3373
2Ki 18:22 removed, saying to J and Jerusalem, "You H3373
2Ki 19:10 "Say to Hezekiah king of J: Do not let the H3373
2Ki 19:30 of the kingdom of J will take root below H3373
2Ki 20:20 the book of the annals of the kings of J? H3373
2Ki 21:11 "Manasseh king of J has committed these H3373
2Ki 21:11 him and has led J into sin with his idols. H3373
2Ki 21:12 on Jerusalem and J that the ears of H3373
2Ki 21:16 the sin that he had caused J to commit, H3373
2Ki 21:17 the book of the annals of the kings of J? H3373
2Ki 21:25 the book of the annals of the kings of J? H3373
2Ki 22:13 people and for all J about what is written H3373
2Ki 22:16 written in the book the king of J has read. H3373
2Ki 22:18 Tell the king of J, who sent you to inquire H3373
2Ki 23: 1 all the elders of J and Jerusalem. H3373
2Ki 23: 2 temple of the LORD with the people of J, H3373
2Ki 23: 5 by the kings of J to burn incense on the H3373
2Ki 23: 5 of the towns of J and on those around H3373
2Ki 23: 8 from the towns of J and desecrated the H3373
2Ki 23:11 that the kings of J had dedicated to the H3373
2Ki 23:12 altars the kings of J had erected on the H3373
2Ki 23:17 of God who came from J and pronounced H3373
2Ki 23:22 the kings of J had any such Passover H3373
2Ki 23:24 things seen in J and Jerusalem. H824+3373
2Ki 23:26 burned against J because of all that H3373
2Ki 23:27 "I will remove J also from my presence as H3373
2Ki 23:28 the book of the annals of the kings of J? H3373
2Ki 23:33 and he imposed on J a levy of a H2021+824s
2Ki 24: 2 raiders against him to destroy J, H3373
2Ki 24: 3 things happened to J according to the H3373
2Ki 24: 5 the book of the annals of the kings of J? H3373
2Ki 24:12 Jehoiachin king of J, his mother, his H3373
2Ki 24:20 all this happened to Jerusalem and J, H3373
2Ki 25:21 So J went into captivity, away from her H3373
2Ki 25:22 the people he had left behind in J. H824+3373
2Ki 25:25 also the **men of J** and the H3374
2Ki 25:27 year of the exile of Jehoiachin king of J, H3373
2Ki 25:27 released Jehoiachin king of J from prison. H3373
1Ch 2: 1 Simeon, Levi, J, Issachar, Zebulun, H3373
1Ch 2: 3 The sons of J: Er, Onan and Shelah H3373
1Ch 2: 4 Tamar bore Perez and Zerah to J. H3373
1Ch 2:10 of Nahshon, the leader of the people of J. H3373
1Ch 4: 1 The descendants of J: Perez, Hezron H3373
1Ch 4:18 His wife from the **tribe of J** gave birth to H3374
1Ch 4:21 The sons of Shelah son of J: Er the father H3373
1Ch 4:27 become as numerous as the people of J. H3373
1Ch 4:41 came in the days of Hezekiah king of J. H3373
1Ch 5: 2 though J was the strongest of his H3373
1Ch 5:17 of Jotham king of J and Jeroboam king of H3373
1Ch 6:15 when the LORD sent J and Jerusalem into H3373
1Ch 6:55 given Hebron in J with its H824+3373
1Ch 6:65 From the tribes of J, Simeon and H1201+3373
1Ch 9: 1 in the book of the kings of Israel and J. H3373
1Ch 9: 3 Those from J, from Benjamin, and H1201+3373
1Ch 9: 4 of Bani, a descendant of Perez son of J. H3373
1Ch 9: 6 The **people from J** numbered 690 H278+2157
1Ch 12:16 some men from J also came to David H3373
1Ch 12:24 *from* J, carrying shield and spear H1201+3373
1Ch 13: 6 David and all Israel went to Baalah of J H3373
1Ch 21: 5 four hundred and seventy thousand in J. H3373
1Ch 27:18 over J: Elihu, a brother of David; over H3373
1Ch 28: 4 He chose J as leader, and from the tribe H3373
1Ch 28: 4 from the tribe of J he chose my family, H3373
2Ch 2: 7 to work in J and Jerusalem with my skilled H3373
2Ch 9:11 like them had ever been seen in J.) H824+3373
2Ch 10:17 who were living in the towns of J, H3373
2Ch 11: 1 he mustered J and Benjamin—a H1074+3373
2Ch 11: 3 of Solomon king of J and to all Israel in H3373
2Ch 11: 3 Judah and to all Israel in J and Benjamin, H3373
2Ch 11: 5 built up towns for defense in J: H3373
2Ch 11:10 were fortified cities in J and Benjamin. H3373
2Ch 11:12 So J and Benjamin were his H3373
2Ch 11:14 property and came to J and Jerusalem, H3373
2Ch 11:17 the kingdom of J and supported H3373
2Ch 11:23 the districts of J and Benjamin, H3373
2Ch 12: 4 the fortified cities of J and came as far as H3373
2Ch 12: 5 to the leaders of J who had assembled in H3373
2Ch 12:12 Indeed, there was some good in J. H3373
2Ch 13: 1 of Jeroboam, Abijah became king of J, H3373
2Ch 13:13 he was in front of J the ambush was H3373
2Ch 13:14 J turned and saw that they were being H3373
2Ch 13:15 the men of J raised the battle cry. H3373
2Ch 13:15 all Israel before Abijah and J. H3373
2Ch 13:16 The Israelites fled before J, and God H3373
2Ch 13:18 the people of J were victorious H3373
2Ch 14: 4 He commanded J to seek the LORD, the H3373
2Ch 14: 5 incense altars in every town in J, H3373
2Ch 14: 6 He built up the fortified cities of J, since H3373
2Ch 14: 7 he said to J, "and put walls around them, H3373
2Ch 14: 8 of three hundred thousand men from J, H3373
2Ch 14:12 down the Cushites before Asa and J. H3373
2Ch 14:13 The men of J carried off a large amount of NDT
2Ch 15: 2 Asa and all J and Benjamin. H3373
2Ch 15: 8 the whole land of J and Benjamin and H3373
2Ch 15: 9 he assembled all J and Benjamin and the H3373

2Ch 15:15 All J rejoiced about the oath because they H3373
2Ch 16: 1 went up against J and fortified Ramah to H3373
2Ch 16: 1 entering the territory of Asa king of J. H3373
2Ch 16: 6 Then King Asa brought all the men of J H3373
2Ch 16: 7 came to Asa king of J and said to him: H3373
2Ch 16:11 in the book of the kings of J and Israel. H3373
2Ch 17: 2 the fortified cities of J and put garrisons in H3373
2Ch 17: 2 put garrisons in J and in the towns H824+3373
2Ch 17: 5 all J brought gifts to Jehoshaphat H3373
2Ch 17: 6 places and the Asherah poles from J. H3373
2Ch 17: 7 Micaiah to teach in the towns of J. H3373
2Ch 17: 9 They taught throughout J, taking with H3373
2Ch 17: 9 to all the towns of J and taught the H3373
2Ch 17:10 the kingdoms of the lands surrounding J, H3373
2Ch 17:12 he built forts and store cities in J H3373
2Ch 17:13 had large supplies in the towns of J H3373
2Ch 17:14 From J, commanders of units H3373
2Ch 17:19 in the fortified cities throughout J. H3373
2Ch 18: 3 of Israel asked Jehoshaphat king of J, H3373
2Ch 18: 9 Jehoshaphat king of J were sitting on H3373
2Ch 18:28 Jehoshaphat king of J went up to Ramoth H3373
2Ch 19: 1 Jehoshaphat king of J returned safely to H3373
2Ch 19: 5 in each of the fortified cities of J. H3373
2Ch 19:11 the leader of the tribe of J, will be over H3373
2Ch 20: 3 and he proclaimed a fast for all J. H3373
2Ch 20: 4 The people of J came together to seek H3373
2Ch 20: 4 came from every town in J to seek him. H3373
2Ch 20: 5 in the assembly of J and Jerusalem at the H3373
2Ch 20:13 All the men of J, with their wives and H3373
2Ch 20:15 all who live in J and Jerusalem! H3373
2Ch 20:17 the LORD will give you, J and Jerusalem. H3373
2Ch 20:18 all the people of J and Jerusalem fell H3373
2Ch 20:20 "Listen to me, J and people of Jerusalem! H3373
2Ch 20:22 Mount Seir who were invading J, H3373
2Ch 20:24 When the men of J came to the place H3373
2Ch 20:27 all the men of J and Jerusalem returned H3373
2Ch 20:31 So Jehoshaphat reigned over J. He was H3373
2Ch 20:31 years old when he became king of J, NDT
2Ch 20:35 Jehoshaphat king of J made an alliance H3373
2Ch 21: 3 as well as fortified cities in J, but he had H3373
2Ch 21: 8 rebelled against J and set up its own H3373
2Ch 21:10 Edom has been in rebellion against J. H3373
2Ch 21:11 on the hills of J and had caused the H3373
2Ch 21:11 themselves and had led J astray. H3373
2Ch 21:12 father Jehoshaphat or of Asa king of J. H3373
2Ch 21:13 you have led J and the people of H3373
2Ch 21:17 They attacked J, invaded it and carried off H3373
2Ch 22: 1 son of Jehoram king of J began to reign. H3373
2Ch 22: 6 of Jehoram king of J went down to Jezreel H3373
2Ch 22: 8 found the officials of J and the sons of H3373
2Ch 22:10 the whole royal family of the house of J. H3373
2Ch 23: 2 They went throughout J and gathered the H3373
2Ch 23: 8 all the men of J did just as Jehoiada H3373
2Ch 24: 5 "Go to the towns of J and collect the H3373
2Ch 24: 6 to bring in from J and Jerusalem the tax H3373
2Ch 24: 9 was then issued in J and Jerusalem that H3373
2Ch 24:17 the officials of J came and paid homage H3373
2Ch 24:18 God's anger came on J and Jerusalem. H3373
2Ch 24:23 it invaded J and Jerusalem and killed all H3373
2Ch 24:24 Because J had forsaken the LORD, the God NDT
2Ch 25: 5 called the people of J together and H3373
2Ch 25: 5 of hundreds for all J and Benjamin. H3373
2Ch 25:10 were furious with J and left for home in a H3373
2Ch 25:12 The army of J also captured ten thousand H3373
2Ch 25:13 towns belonging to J from Samaria to H3373
2Ch 25:17 After Amaziah king of J consulted his H3373
2Ch 25:18 of Israel replied to Amaziah king of J: H3373
2Ch 25:19 your own downfall and that of J also?" H3373
2Ch 25:21 Amaziah king of J faced each other at H3373
2Ch 25:21 faced each other at Beth Shemesh in J. H3373
2Ch 25:22 J was routed by Israel, and every man fled H3373
2Ch 25:23 king of Israel captured Amaziah king of J, H3373
2Ch 25:25 son of Joash king of J lived for fifteen H3373
2Ch 25:26 in the book of the kings of J and Israel? H3373
2Ch 25:28 buried with his ancestors in the City of J. H3373
2Ch 26: 1 Then all the people of J took Uzziah, who H3373
2Ch 26: 2 restored it to J after Amaziah rested H3373
2Ch 27: 4 the hill country of J and forts and towers H3373
2Ch 27: 7 in the book of the kings of Israel and J. H3373
2Ch 28: 6 twenty thousand soldiers in J— H3373
2Ch 28: 6 Judah—because J had forsaken the LORD H4392S
2Ch 28: 8 who were from J two hundred thousand NDT
2Ch 28: 9 was angry with J, he gave them into your H3373
2Ch 28:10 men and women of J and H1201+3373
2Ch 28:17 come and attacked J and carried away H3373
2Ch 28:18 in the foothills and in the Negev of J. H3373
2Ch 28:19 The LORD had humbled J because of Ahaz H3373
2Ch 28:19 wickedness in J and had been most H3373
2Ch 28:25 In every town in J he built high places to H3373
2Ch 28:26 in the book of the kings of J and Israel. H3373
2Ch 29: 8 of the LORD has fallen on J and Jerusalem; H3373
2Ch 29:21 the kingdom, for the sanctuary and for J. H3373
2Ch 30: 1 to all Israel and J and also wrote letters H3373
2Ch 30: 6 Israel and J with letters from the H3373
2Ch 30:12 Also in J the hand of God was on the H3373
2Ch 30:24 Hezekiah king of J provided a thousand H3373
2Ch 30:25 The entire assembly of J rejoiced, along H3373
2Ch 30:25 Israel and also those who resided in J. H3373
2Ch 31: 1 were there went out to the towns of J, H3373
2Ch 31: 1 altars throughout J and Benjamin and in H3373
2Ch 31: 6 people of Israel and J who lived in the H3373
2Ch 31: 6 lived in the towns of J also brought a tithe H3373
2Ch 31:20 This is what Hezekiah did throughout J H3373
2Ch 32: 1 king of Assyria came and invaded J. H3373
2Ch 32: 8 from what Hezekiah the king of J said. H3373
2Ch 32: 9 Hezekiah king of J and for all the H3373
2Ch 32: 9 all the people of J who were there: H3373
2Ch 32:12 saying to J and Jerusalem, 'You H3373
2Ch 32:23 valuable gifts for Hezekiah king of J. H3373
2Ch 32:25 was on him and on J and Jerusalem. H3373
2Ch 32:32 in the book of the kings of J and Israel. H3373
2Ch 32:33 All J and the people of Jerusalem H3373
2Ch 33: 9 But Manasseh led J and the people of H3373
2Ch 33:14 commanders in all the fortified cities in J. H3373
2Ch 33:16 and told J to serve the LORD, the H3373
2Ch 34: 3 he began to purge J and Jerusalem of H3373
2Ch 34: 5 and so he purged J and Jerusalem. H3373
2Ch 34: 9 all the people of J and Benjamin and the H3373
2Ch 34:11 that the kings of J had allowed to fall into H3373
2Ch 34:21 in Israel and J about what is written H3373
2Ch 34:24 read in the presence of the king of J. H3373
2Ch 34:26 Tell the king of J, who sent you to inquire H3373
2Ch 34:29 all the elders of J and Jerusalem. H3373
2Ch 34:30 temple of the LORD with the people of J, H3373
2Ch 35:18 the Levites and all J and Israel who were H3373
2Ch 35:21 "What **quarrel** is there, king of J, between H3373
2Ch 35:24 all J and Jerusalem mourned for him. H3373
2Ch 35:27 in the book of the kings of Israel and J. H3373
2Ch 36: 3 and imposed on J a levy of a H2021+824S
2Ch 36: 4 king over J and Jerusalem and changed H3373
2Ch 36: 8 in the book of the kings of Israel and J. H3373
2Ch 36:10 Zedekiah, king over J and Jerusalem. H3373
2Ch 36:23 build a temple for him at Jerusalem in J. H3373
Ezr 1: 2 build a temple for him at Jerusalem in J. H3373
Ezr 1: 3 up to Jerusalem in J and build the temple H3373
Ezr 1: 5 Then the family heads of J and Benjamin H3373
Ezr 1: 8 them out to Sheshbazzar the prince of J. H3373
Ezr 2: 1 they returned to Jerusalem and J, each to H3373
Ezr 4: 1 the enemies of J and Benjamin heard H3373
Ezr 4: 4 the people of J and make them afraid to H3373
Ezr 4: 6 against the people of J and Jerusalem. H3373
Ezr 5: 1 to the Jews in J and Jerusalem in the A10315
Ezr 5: 8 know that we went to the district of J, A10315
Ezr 7:14 to inquire about J and Jerusalem with A10315
Ezr 9: 9 a wall of protection in J and Jerusalem. H3373
Ezr 10: 7 issued throughout J and Jerusalem for all H3373
Ezr 10: 9 all the men of J and Benjamin had H3373
Ezr 10:23 that is, Kelita), Pethahiah, J and Eliezer. H3373
Ne 1: 2 came from J with some other men H3373
Ne 2: 5 me to the city in J where my ancestors are H3373
Ne 2: 7 me safe-conduct until I arrive in J? H3373
Ne 4:10 the people in J said, "The strength of H3373
Ne 4:16 themselves behind all the people of J H3373
Ne 5:14 to be their governor in the land of J, H3373
Ne 6: 7 'There is a king in J!' Now this report will H3373
Ne 6:17 days the nobles of J were sending many H3373
Ne 6:18 For many in J were under oath to him H3373
Ne 7: 6 they returned to Jerusalem and J, each to H3373
Ne 11: 3 servants lived in the towns of J, H3373
Ne 11: 4 people from both J and Benjamin lived in H3373
Ne 11: 4 From the descendants of J: Athaiah son of H3373
Ne 11: 9 J son of Hassenuah was over the H3373
Ne 11:20 were in all the towns of J, each on their H3373
Ne 11:24 one of the descendants of Zerah son of J H3373
Ne 11:25 of the people of J lived in Kiriath Arba H3373
Ne 11:36 of the Levites of J settled in Benjamin. H3373
Ne 12: 8 Sherebiah, J, and also Mattaniah H3373
Ne 12:31 I had the leaders of J go up on top of the H3373
Ne 12:32 half the leaders of J followed them, H3373
Ne 12:34 J, Benjamin, Shemaiah, Jeremiah, H3373
Ne 12:36 Nethanel, J and Hanani—with musical H3373
Ne 12:44 J was pleased with the ministering H3373
Ne 13:12 All J brought the tithes of grain, new wine H3373
Ne 13:15 I saw people in J treading winepresses H3373
Ne 13:16 on the Sabbath to the people of J. H3373
Ne 13:17 I rebuked the nobles of J and said to them, H3373
Ne 13:23 days I saw **men of** J who had married H3374
Ne 13:24 not know how to speak the **language of** J. H3376
Est 2: 6 taken captive with Jehoiachin king of J. H3373
Ps 48:11 the villages of J are glad because of your H3373
Ps 60: 7 Ephraim is my helmet, J is my scepter. H3373
Ps 63: T When he was in the Desert of J. H3373
Ps 69:35 will save Zion and rebuild the cities of J. H3373
Ps 76: 1 God is renowned in J; in Israel his name H3373
Ps 78:68 he chose the tribe of J, Mount Zion H3373
Ps 97: 8 the villages of J are glad because of H3373
Ps 108: 8 Ephraim is my helmet, J is my scepter. H3373
Ps 114: 2 J became God's sanctuary, Israel his H3373
Pr 25: 1 by the men of Hezekiah king of J: H3373
Isa 1: 1 vision concerning J and Jerusalem that H3373
Isa 1: 1 Jotham, Ahaz and Hezekiah, kings of J. H3373
Isa 2: 1 of Amoz saw concerning J and Jerusalem: H3373
Isa 3: 1 from Jerusalem and J both supply and H3373
Isa 3: 8 Jerusalem staggers, J is falling; their H3373
Isa 5: 3 dwellers in Jerusalem and people of J, H3373
Isa 5: 7 the people of J are the vines he H3373
Isa 7: 1 was king of J, King Rezin of Aram H3373
Isa 7: 6 "Let us invade J; let us tear it apart and H3373
Isa 7:17 any since Ephraim broke away from J— H3373
Isa 8: 8 sweep on into J, swirling over it H3373
Isa 8:14 both **Israel and** J he will be a H1074+3776
Isa 9:21 together they will turn against J. H3373
Isa 11:12 scattered people of J from the four H3373
Isa 11:13 Ephraim will not be jealous of J, nor H3373
Isa 11:13 of Judah, nor J hostile toward Ephraim. H3373
Isa 19:17 And the land of J will bring terror to the H3373
Isa 19:17 everyone to whom J is mentioned will H2023S
Isa 22: 8 The Lord stripped away the defenses of J H3373
Isa 22:21 live in Jerusalem and to the people of J. H3373
Isa 26: 1 this song will be sung in the land of J: H3373
Isa 36: 1 the fortified cities of J and captured them. H3373
Isa 36: 7 removed, saying to J and Jerusalem, "You H3373
Isa 37:10 "Say to Hezekiah king of J: Do not let the H3373
Isa 37:31 of the kingdom of J will take root below H3373
Isa 38: 9 of Hezekiah king of J after his illness and H3373
Isa 40: 9 say to the towns of J, "Here is your God!" H3373
Isa 44:26 of the towns of J, 'They shall be rebuilt, H3373
Isa 48: 1 of Israel and come from the line of J, H3373
Isa 65: 9 from J those who will possess my H3373
Jer 1: 2 the reign of Josiah son of Amon king of J, H3373
Jer 1: 3 reign of Jehoiakim son of Josiah king of J, H3373
Jer 1: 3 year of Zedekiah son of Josiah king of J, H3373
Jer 1:15 walls and against all the towns of J. H3373
Jer 1:18 against the kings of J, its officials, H3373
Jer 2:28 For you, J, have as many gods as you H3373
Jer 3: 7 did not, and her unfaithful sister J saw it. H3373
Jer 3: 8 that her unfaithful sister J had no fear; H3373
Jer 3:10 her unfaithful sister J did not return to me H3373
Jer 3:11 Israel is more righteous than unfaithful J. H3373
Jer 3:18 days the people of J will join the people H3373
Jer 4: 3 says to the people of J and to Jerusalem: H3373
Jer 4: 4 you people of J and inhabitants of H3373
Jer 4: 5 "Announce in J and proclaim in H3373
Jer 4:16 raising a war cry against the cities of J. H3373
Jer 5:11 the people of J have been utterly H3373
Jer 5:20 descendants of Jacob and proclaim it in J: H3373
Jer 7: 2 all you people of J who come through H3373
Jer 7:17 in the towns of J and in the streets of H3373
Jer 7:30 " 'The people of J have done evil in my H3373
Jer 7:34 in the towns of J and the streets of H3373
Jer 8: 1 the bones of the kings and officials of J H3373
Jer 9:11 waste the towns of J so no one can live H3373
Jer 9:26 J, Edom, Ammon, Moab and all H3373
Jer 10:22 It will make the towns of J desolate, H3373
Jer 11: 2 to the people of J and to those who live H3373
Jer 11: 6 in the towns of J and in the streets of H3373
Jer 11: 9 the people of J and those who live H3373
Jer 11:10 **Both** Israel and J have broken the H1074+3373
Jer 11:12 The towns of J and the people of H3373
Jer 11:13 J, have as many gods as you have H3373
Jer 11:17 of both Israel and J have done evil and H3373
Jer 12:14 uproot the people of J from among them. H3373
Jer 13: 9 ruin the pride of J and the great pride of H3373
Jer 13:11 of Israel and all the people of J to me, H3373
Jer 13:19 All J will be carried into exile, carried H3373
Jer 14: 2 "J mourns, her cities languish; they wail H3373
Jer 14:19 Have you rejected J completely? Do you H3373
Jer 15: 4 of Hezekiah king of J did in Jerusalem. H3373
Jer 17:19 which the kings of J go in and out; H3373
Jer 17:20 you kings of J and all people of Judah H3373
Jer 17:20 all people of J and everyone living in H3373
Jer 17:25 by the men of J and those living in H3373
Jer 17:26 come from the towns of J and the villages H3373
Jer 18:11 say to the people of J and those living in H3373
Jer 19: 3 you kings of J and people of Jerusalem. H3373
Jer 19: 4 ancestors nor the kings of J ever knew, H3373
Jer 19: 7 I will ruin the plans of J and Jerusalem. H3373
Jer 19:13 those of the kings of J will be defiled like H3373
Jer 20: 4 I will give all J into the hands of the king H3373
Jer 20: 5 all the treasures of the kings of J. H3373
Jer 21: 7 I will give Zedekiah king of J, his officials H3373
Jer 21:11 say to the royal house of J, 'Hear the word H3373
Jer 22: 1 palace of the king of J and proclaim this H3373
Jer 22: 2 LORD to you, king of J, you who sit on H3373
Jer 22: 6 says about the palace of the king of J: H3373
Jer 22:11 his father as king of J but has gone from H3373
Jer 22:18 about Jehoiakim son of Josiah king of J: H3373
Jer 22:24 Jehoiachin son of Jehoiakim king of J H3373
Jer 22:30 the throne of David or rule anymore in J." H3373
Jer 23: 6 In his days J will be saved and Israel will H3373
Jer 24: 1 of Jehoiakim king of J and the officials, H3373
Jer 24: 1 the artisans of J were carried into H3373
Jer 24: 5 I regard as good the exiles from J, whom I H3373
Jer 24: 8 'so will I deal with Zedekiah king of J, his H3373
Jer 25: 1 all the people of J in the fourth year of H3373
Jer 25: 1 year of Jehoiakim son of Josiah king of J, H3373
Jer 25: 2 to all the people of J and to all those H3373
Jer 25: 3 son of Amon king of J until this very day— H3373
Jer 25:18 Jerusalem and the towns of J, its kings H3373
Jer 26: 1 reign of Jehoiakim son of Josiah king of J, H3373
Jer 26: 2 of the towns of J who come to worship in H3373
Jer 26:10 When the officials of J heard about these H3373
Jer 26:18 in the days of Hezekiah king of J. H3373
Jer 26:18 He told all the people of J, 'This is what H3373
Jer 26:19 "Did Hezekiah king of J or anyone else in H3373
Jer 26:19 anyone else in J put him to death? H3373
Jer 27: 1 reign of Zedekiah son of Josiah king of J, H3373
Jer 27: 3 come to Jerusalem to Zedekiah king of J. H3373
Jer 27:12 the same message to Zedekiah king of J. H3373
Jer 27:18 of the king of J and in Jerusalem not H3373
Jer 27:20 son of Jehoiakim king of J into exile from H3373
Jer 27:20 with all the nobles of J and Jerusalem— H3373
Jer 27:21 palace of the king of J and in Jerusalem: H3373
Jer 28: 1 early in the reign of Zedekiah king of J H3373
Jer 28: 4 of Jehoiakim king of J and all the other H3373
Jer 28: 4 other exiles from J who went to Babylon, H3373

Jer 29: 2 the leaders of J and Jerusalem, H3373
Jer 29: 3 whom Zedekiah king of J sent to King H3373
Jer 29:22 all the exiles from J who are in Babylon H3373
Jer 30: 3 my people Israel and J back from captivity H3373
Jer 30: 4 the LORD spoke concerning Israel and J: H3373
Jer 31:23 in the land of J and in its towns will H3373
Jer 31:24 will live together in J and all its towns— H3373
Jer 31:27 of Israel and J with the offspring of H3373
Jer 31:31 people of Israel and with the people of J. H3373
Jer 32: 1 in the tenth year of Zedekiah king of J, H3373
Jer 32: 2 of the guard in the royal palace of J. H3373
Jer 32: 3 Zedekiah king of J had imprisoned him H3373
Jer 32: 4 Zedekiah king of J will not escape the H3373
Jer 32:30 people of Israel and J have done nothing H3373
Jer 32:32 of Israel and J have provoked me by H3373
Jer 32:32 the people of J and those living in H3373
Jer 32:35 a detestable thing and so make J sin. H3373
Jer 32:44 in the towns of J and in the towns of the H3373
Jer 33: 4 the royal palaces of J that have been torn H3373
Jer 33: 7 I will bring J and Israel back from captivity H3373
Jer 33:10 Yet in the towns of J and the streets of H3373
Jer 33:13 around Jerusalem and in the towns of J, H3373
Jer 33:14 I made to the people of Israel and J. H3373
Jer 33:16 In those days J will be saved and H3373
Jer 34: 2 Go to Zedekiah king of J and tell him H3373
Jer 34: 4 LORD's promise to you, Zedekiah king of J. H3373
Jer 34: 6 prophet told all this to Zedekiah king of J, H3373
Jer 34: 7 the other cities of J that were still holding H3373
Jer 34: 7 were the only fortified cities left in J. H3373
Jer 34:19 The leaders of J and Jerusalem, the court H3373
Jer 34:21 Zedekiah king of J and his officials into H3373
Jer 34:22 waste the towns of J so no one can live H3373
Jer 35: 1 reign of Jehoiakim son of Josiah king of J: H3373
Jer 35:13 tell the people of J and those living in H3373
Jer 35:17 am going to bring on J and on everyone H3373
Jer 36: 1 year of Jehoiakim son of Josiah king of J, H3373
Jer 36: 2 J and all the other nations from the time I H3373
Jer 36: 3 when the people of J hear about every H3373
Jer 36: 6 to all the people of J who come in from H3373
Jer 36: 9 year of Jehoiakim son of Josiah king of J, H3373
Jer 36: 9 those who had come from the towns of J. H3373
Jer 36:28 which Jehoiakim king of J burned up. H3373
Jer 36:29 Also tell Jehoiakim king of J, 'This is what H3373
Jer 36:30 the LORD says about Jehoiakim king of J: H3373
Jer 36:31 the people of J every disaster I H3373
Jer 36:32 Jehoiakim king of J had burned in the fire H3373
Jer 37: 1 was made king of J by H824+3373
Jer 37: 7 Tell the king of J, who sent you to inquire H3373
Jer 38:22 palace of the king of J will be brought out H3373
Jer 39: 1 In the ninth year of Zedekiah king of J, in H3373
Jer 39: 4 Zedekiah king of J and all the soldiers H3373
Jer 39: 6 eyes and also killed all the nobles of J. H3373
Jer 39:10 behind in the land of J some of the poor H3373
Jer 40: 1 from Jerusalem and J who were being H3373
Jer 40: 5 has appointed over the towns of J, H3373
Jer 40:11 left a remnant in J and had appointed H3373
Jer 40:12 they all came back to the land of J, to H3373
Jer 40:15 scattered and the remnant of J to perish?" H3373
Jer 41: 3 also killed all the men of J who were with H3374
Jer 42:15 the word of the LORD, you remnant of J. H3373
Jer 42:19 "Remnant of J, the LORD has told you, 'Do H3373
Jer 43: 4 LORD's command to stay in the land of J. H3373
Jer 43: 5 all the remnant of J who had come back H3373
Jer 43: 5 to live in the land of J from all the nations H3373
Jer 44: 2 on Jerusalem and on all the towns of J. H3373
Jer 44: 6 against the towns of J and the streets of H3373
Jer 44: 7 by cutting off from J the men and women, H3373
Jer 44: 9 kings and queens of J and the wickedness H3373
Jer 44: 9 wives in the land of J and the streets of H3373
Jer 44:11 bring disaster on you and to destroy all J. H3373
Jer 44:12 the remnant of J who were determined H3373
Jer 44:14 of the remnant of J who have gone to live H3373
Jer 44:14 survive to return to the land of J, H3373
Jer 44:17 did in the towns of J and in the streets of H3373
Jer 44:21 burned in the towns of J and the streets of H3373
Jer 44:24 of the LORD, all you people of J in Egypt. H3373
Jer 44:26 'that no one from J living anywhere in H3373
Jer 44:28 return to the land of J from Egypt will be H3373
Jer 44:28 whole remnant of J who came to live in H3373
Jer 44:30 gave Zedekiah king of J into the hands of H3373
Jer 45: 1 year of Jehoiakim son of Josiah king of J, H3373
Jer 46: 2 year of Jehoiakim son of Josiah king of J: H3373
Jer 49:34 early in the reign of Zedekiah king of J: H3373
Jer 50: 4 the people of J together will go in H3373
Jer 50:20 for the sins of J, but none will be H3373
Jer 50:33 oppressed, and the people of J as well. H3373
Jer 51: 5 For Israel and J have not been forsaken by H3373
Jer 51:59 Zedekiah king of J in the fourth year of H3373
Jer 52: 3 all this happened to Jerusalem and J, H3373
Jer 52:10 he also killed all the officials of J. H3373
Jer 52:27 So J went into captivity, away from her H3373
Jer 52:31 year of the exile of Jehoiachin king of J, H3373
Jer 52:31 Jehoiachin king of J and freed him from H3373
La 1: 3 harsh labor, J has gone into exile. H3373
La 1:15 the Lord has trampled Virgin Daughter J. H3373
La 2: 2 torn down the strongholds of Daughter J. H3373
La 2: 5 lamentation for Daughter J. H3373
La 5:11 in Zion, and virgins in the towns of J. H3373
Eze 4: 6 and bear the sin of the people of J. H3373
Eze 8: 1 the elders of J were sitting before me H3373
Eze 8:17 the people of J to do the detestable H3373
Eze 9: 9 of Israel and J is exceedingly great H3373
Eze 21:20 another against J and fortified H3373
Eze 25: 3 over the people of J when they went into H3373
Eze 25: 8 J has become like all the other H1074+3373
Eze 25:12 took revenge on J and became very H1074+3373
Eze 25:15 with ancient hostility sought to destroy J, NDT
Eze 27:17 " 'J and Israel traded with you; they H3373
Eze 37:16 'Belonging to J and the Israelites H3373
Eze 48: 7 "J will have one portion; it will border the H3373
Eze 48: 8 the territory of J from east to west will be H3373
Eze 48:22 between the border of J and the border of H3373
Eze 48:31 the gate of J and the gate of Levi. H3373
Da 1: 1 year of the reign of Jehoiakim king of J, H3373
Da 1: 2 Jehoiakim king of J into his hand, H3373
Da 1: 6 who were chosen were some from J: H3373
Da 2:25 the exiles from J who can tell the king A10315
Da 5:13 exiles my father the king brought from J? A10315
Da 6:13 who is one of the exiles from J, pays no A10315
Da 9: 7 the people of J and the inhabitants of H3373
Hos 1: 1 Hezekiah, kings of J, and during the reign H3373
Hos 1: 7 Yet I will show love to J; and I will H1074+3373
Hos 1:11 The people of J and the people of Israel H3373
Hos 4:15 adultery, do not let J become guilty. H3373
Hos 5: 5 in their sin; J also stumbles with them. H3373
Hos 5:12 to Ephraim, like rot to the people of J. H3373
Hos 5:13 saw his sickness, and J his sores, then H3373
Hos 5:14 to Ephraim, like a great lion to J. H1074+3373
Hos 6: 4 can I do with you, J? Your love is like the H3373
Hos 6:11 "Also for you, J, a harvest is appointed H3373
Hos 8:14 built palaces; J has fortified many towns. H3373
Hos 10:11 will drive Ephraim, J must plow, and H3373
Hos 11:12 And J is unruly against God, even against H3373
Hos 12: 2 The LORD has a charge to bring against J H3373
Joel 2:21 not be afraid, land of J; be glad and rejoice. NDT
Joel 3: 1 I restore the fortunes of J and Jerusalem, H3373
Joel 3: 6 sold the people of J and Jerusalem to the H3373
Joel 3: 8 sons and daughters to the people of J, H3373
Joel 3:18 all the ravines of J will run with water. H3373
Joel 3:19 of violence done to the people of J, H3373
Joel 3:20 J will be inhabited forever and Jerusalem H3373
Am 1: 1 Uzziah was king of J and Jeroboam son of H3373
Am 2: 4 "For three sins of J, even for four, I will not H3373
Am 2: 5 I will send fire on J that will consume the H3373
Am 7:12 Go back to the land of J. Earn your bread H3373
Ob 12 over the people of J in the day of their H3373
Mic 1: 1 Hezekiah, kings of J—the vision he saw H3373
Mic 1: 9 plague is incurable; it has spread to J. H3373
Mic 5: 2 you are small among the clans of J, H3373
Na 1:12 I have afflicted you, J, I will afflict you no NDT
Na 1:15 your festivals, J, and fulfill your vows. H3373
Zep 1: 1 the reign of Josiah son of Amon king of J: H3373
Zep 1: 4 my hand against J and against all who H3373
Zep 2: 7 belong to the remnant of the people of J; H3373
Hag 1: 1 governor of J, and to Joshua son of H3373
Hag 1:14 Shealtiel, governor of J, and the spirit of H3373
Hag 2: 2 Shealtiel, governor of J, to Joshua son of H3373
Hag 2:21 governor of J that I am going to H3373
Zec 1:12 from Jerusalem and from the towns of J, H3373
Zec 1:19 "These are the horns that scattered J H3373
Zec 1:21 that scattered J so that no one could H3373
Zec 1:21 against the land of J to scatter its people." H3373
Zec 2:12 The LORD will inherit J as his portion in the H3373
Zec 8:13 Just as you, J and Israel, have been H1074+3373
Zec 8:15 do good again to Jerusalem and J. H1074+3373
Zec 8:19 occasions and happy festivals for J. H1074+3373
Zec 9: 7 to our God and become a clan in J, H3373
Zec 9:13 I will bend J as I bend my bow and fill it H3373
Zec 10: 3 the people of J, and make them like H3373
Zec 10: 4 From J will come the cornerstone, from H5647S
Zec 10: 6 "I will strengthen J and save the H1074+3373
Zec 11:14 the family bond between J and Israel. H3373
Zec 12: 2 J will be besieged as well as Jerusalem H3373
Zec 12: 4 "I will keep a watchful eye over J H1074+3373
Zec 12: 5 Then the clans of J will say in their hearts H3373
Zec 12: 6 will make the clans of J like a firepot in a H3373
Zec 12: 7 "The LORD will save the dwellings of J first H3373
Zec 12: 7 may not be greater than that of J. H3373
Zec 14: 5 in the days of Uzziah king of J. H3373
Zec 14:14 J too will fight at Jerusalem. The wealth of H3373
Zec 14:21 pot in Jerusalem and J will be holy to the H3373
Mal 2:11 J has been unfaithful. A detestable thing H3373
Mal 2:11 J has desecrated the sanctuary the LORD H3373
Mal 3: 4 the offerings of J and Jerusalem will H3373
Mt 1: 2 Jacob the father of J and his brothers, G2683
Mt 1: 3 J the father of Perez and Zerah, whose G2683
Mt 2: 6 in the land of J, are by no means G2683
Mt 2: 6 by no means least among the rulers of J; G2683
Lk 3:30 of Simeon, the son of J, the son of Joseph G2683
Lk 3:33 of Hezron, the son of Perez, the son of J, G2683
Heb 7:14 it is clear that our Lord descended from J, G2683
Heb 8: 8 people of Israel and with the people of J. G2683
Rev 5: 5 the Lion of the tribe of J, the Root of G2683
Rev 7: 5 From the tribe of J 12,000 were sealed G2683

JUDAH'S (13) [JUDAH]

Ge 38: 7 J firstborn, was wicked in the LORD's H3373
Ge 38:12 After a long time J wife, the daughter of H3373
Jos 19: 9 because J portion was more than H1201+3373
2Sa 3: 8 "Am I a dog's head—on J side? H3373
1Ki 2:32 commander of J army—were better men H3373
1Ch 2: 3 J firstborn, was wicked in the LORD's H3373
1Ch 2: 4 J daughter-in-law Tamar bore Perez H2257S
Ps 68:27 there the great throng of J princes, and H3373
Isa 11:13 and J enemies will be destroyed H3373
Jer 17: 1 "J sin is engraved with an iron tool H3373
Eze 37:19 associated with him, and join it to J stick. H3373
Hos 5:10 J leaders are like those who move H3373
Mic 1: 5 What is J high place? Is it H3373

JUDAISM (5) [JEW]

Ac 2:11 both Jews and converts to J); Cretans and G4670
Ac 6: 5 Nicolas from Antioch, a convert to J. G4670
Ac 13:43 devout converts to J followed Paul G4670
Gal 1:13 have heard of my previous way of life in J, G2682
Gal 1:14 I was advancing in J beyond many of my G2682

JUDAS (41)

Mt 10: 4 Simon the Zealot and J Iscariot, who G2683
Mt 13:55 his brothers James, Joseph, Simon and J? G2683
Mt 26:14 the one called J Iscariot—went to the G2683
Mt 26:16 From then on J watched for an opportunity NDT
Mt 26:25 Then J, the one who would betray him G2683
Mt 26:47 was still speaking, J, one of the Twelve, G2683
Mt 26:49 Going at once to Jesus, J said, "Greetings NDT
Mt 27: 3 When J, who had betrayed him, saw that G2683
Mt 27: 5 So J threw the money into the temple and NDT
Mk 3:19 J Iscariot, who betrayed him. G2683
Mk 6: 3 brother of James, Joseph, J and Simon? G2683
Mk 14:10 Then J Iscariot, one of the Twelve, went G2683
Mk 14:43 as he was speaking, J, one of the Twelve, G2683
Mk 14:45 Going at once to Jesus, J said, "Rabbi!" NDT
Lk 6:16 J son of James, and Judas Iscariot, who G2683
Lk 6:16 son of James, and J Iscariot, who became G2683
Lk 22: 3 Then Satan entered J, called Iscariot, one G2683
Lk 22: 4 And J went to the chief priests and the NDT
Lk 22:47 the man who was called J, one of the G2683
Lk 22:48 Jesus asked him, "J, are you betraying G2683
Jn 6:71 He meant J, the son of Simon Iscariot G2683
Jn 12: 4 one of his disciples, J Iscariot, who was G2683
Jn 13: 2 the devil had already prompted J, the G2683
Jn 13:26 of bread, he gave it to J, the son of Simon G2683
Jn 13:27 As soon as J took the bread, Satan entered NDT
Jn 13:29 Since J had charge of the money, some G2683
Jn 13:30 As soon as J had taken the bread, he G1697S
Jn 14:22 Then J (not Judas Iscariot) said, "But, Lord, G2683
Jn 14:22 Then Judas (not J Iscariot) said, "But, Lord NDT
Jn 18: 2 Now J, who betrayed him, knew the place, G2683
Jn 18: 3 So J came to the garden, guiding a G2683
Jn 18: 5 And J the traitor was standing there with G2683
Ac 1:13 Simon the Zealot, and J son of James. G2683
Ac 1:16 long ago through David concerning J, G2683
Ac 1:18 his wickedness, J bought a field G4047S
Ac 1:25 which J left to go where he belongs." G2683
Ac 5:37 J the Galilean appeared in the days of G2683
Ac 9:11 "Go to the house of J on Straight Street G2683
Ac 15:22 They chose J (called Barsabbas) and Silas, G2683
Ac 15:27 we are sending J and Silas to confirm by G2683
Ac 15:32 J and Silas, who themselves were G2683

JUDE (1)

Jude 1 J, a servant of Jesus Christ and a brother G2683

JUDEA (45) [JUDAH]

Mt 2: 1 After Jesus was born in Bethlehem in J G2677
Mt 2: 5 "In Bethlehem in J," they replied, "for this G2677
Mt 2:22 was reigning in J in place of his father G2677
Mt 3: 1 preaching in the wilderness of J G2677
Mt 3: 5 Jerusalem and all J and the whole region G2677
Mt 4:25 J and the region across the Jordan G2677
Mt 19: 1 into the region of J to the other side of G2677
Mt 24:16 let those who are in J flee to the G2677
Mk 3: 8 many people came to him from J G2677
Mk 10: 1 went into the region of J and across the G2677
Mk 13:14 let those who are in J flee to the G2677
Lk 1: 5 time of Herod king of J there was a priest G2677
Lk 1:39 hurried to a town in the hill country of J, G2683
Lk 1:65 the hill country of J people were talking G2677
Lk 2: 4 from the town of Nazareth in Galilee to J, G2677
Lk 3: 1 when Pontius Pilate was governor of J G2677
Lk 4:44 kept on preaching in the synagogues of J. G2677
Lk 5:17 of Galilee and from J and Jerusalem. G2677
Lk 6:17 a great number of people from all over J, G2677
Lk 7:17 spread throughout J and the surrounding G2677
Lk 21:21 let those who are in J flee to the G2677
Lk 23: 5 up the people all over J by his teaching. G2677
Jn 4: 3 So he left J and went back once more to G2677
Jn 4:47 that Jesus had arrived in Galilee from J, G2677
Jn 4:54 performed after coming from J to Galilee. G2677
Jn 7: 1 want to go about in J because the Jewish G2677
Jn 7: 3 "Leave Galilee and go to J, so that your G2677
Jn 11: 7 said to his disciples, "Let us go back to J." G2677
Jn 11:54 about publicly among the people of J. G2681
Ac 1: 8 in all J and Samaria, and to G2677
Ac 2: 9 of Mesopotamia, J and Cappadocia G2677
Ac 8: 1 throughout J and Samaria. G6001+2677
Ac 9:31 Then the church throughout J, Galilee G2677
Ac 10:37 happened throughout the province of J, G2677
Ac 11: 1 believers throughout J heard that the G2677
Ac 11:29 the brothers and sisters living in J. G2677
Ac 12:19 Then Herod went from J to Caesarea and G2677
Ac 15: 1 came down from J to Antioch and were G2677
Ac 21:10 named Agabus came down from J. G2677
Ac 26:20 then to those in Jerusalem and in all J G2677
Ac 28:21 any letters from J concerning you, G2677
Ro 15:31 from the unbelievers in J and that the G2677
2Co 1:16 then to have you send me on my way to J. G2677

Gal 1:22 to the churches of **J** that are in Christ. G2677
1Th 2:14 became imitators of God's churches in **J** G2677

JUDEAN (3) [JUDAH]

Mk 1:5 The whole **J** countryside and all the G2681
Lk 23:51 He came from the **J** town of Arimathea G2681
Jn 3:22 disciples went out into the **J** countryside, G2681

JUDGE (151) [JUDGE'S, JUDGED, JUDGES, JUDGING, JUDGMENT, JUDGMENTS]

Ge 16:5 May the LORD **j** between you and me." H9149
Ge 18:25 Will not the **J** of all the earth do right?" H9149
Ge 19:9 and now he wants to **play the j**! H9149+9149
Ge 31:37 and let them **j** between the two of us. H3519
Ge 31:53 May the God of Abraham and the God of Nahor, the God of their father, **j** H9149
Ex 2:14 "Who made you ruler and **j** over us? H9149
Ex 5:21 "May the LORD look on you and **j** you! H9149
Ex 18:13 took his seat to **serve as j** for the people, H9149
Ex 18:14 Why do you alone **sit as j**, while all these H3782
Lev 19:15 to the great, but **j** your neighbor fairly. H9149
Lev 27:12 who will **j** its **quality** as good or bad H6885
Lev 27:14 the priest will **j** its **quality** as good or bad. H6885
Nu 35:24 the assembly must **j** between the accused H9149
Dt 1:16 disputes between your people and **j** fairly, H9149
Dt 16:18 and they shall **j** the people fairly. H9149+5477
Dt 17:8 courts that are too difficult for you to **j**— H5477
Dt 17:9 to the **j** who is **in office** at that time. H9149
Dt 17:12 contempt for the **j** or for the priest who H9149
Dt 25:2 the **j** shall make them lie down and have H9149
Dt 25:3 the **j** must not impose more than forty NDT
Jdg 2:18 Whenever the LORD raised up a **j** for them H9149
Jdg 2:18 he was with the **j** and saved them out of H9149
Jdg 2:18 of their enemies as long as the **j** lived; H9149
Jdg 2:19 But when the **j** died, the people returned H9149
Jdg 3:10 so that he became Israel's **j** and went to H9149
Jdg 11:27 Let the LORD, the **J**, decide the dispute this H9149
1Sa 2:10 the LORD will **j** the ends of the earth. H1906
1Sa 3:13 I told him that I would **j** his family forever H9149
1Sa 24:12 May the LORD **j** between you and me. H9149
1Sa 24:15 May the LORD be our **j** and decide between H1908
2Sa 15:4 "If only I were appointed **j** in the land! H9149
1Ki 7:7 where he was to **j**, and he H9149
1Ki 8:32 **J** between your servants, condemning the H9149
1Ch 12:17 the God of our ancestors see it and **j** you." H3519
1Ch 16:33 the LORD, for he comes to **j** the earth. H9149
2Ch 6:23 **J** between your servants, condemning the H9149
2Ch 19:7 **J** carefully, for with the LORD our God H6913S
2Ch 20:12 Our God, will you not **j** them? For we have H9149
Job 9:15 I could only plead with my **J** for mercy. H9149
Job 22:13 Does he **j** through such darkness? H9149
Job 23:7 I would be delivered forever from my **j**. H9149
Ps 7:8 Let the LORD **j** the peoples. Vindicate me H1906
Ps 7:11 God is a righteous **j**, a God who displays H9149
Ps 9:4 sitting enthroned as the righteous **j**. H9149
Ps 50:4 the earth, that he may **j** his people: H1906
Ps 51:4 in your verdict and justified when you **j**. H9149
Ps 58:1 Do you **j** people with equity H9149
Ps 72:2 May he **j** your people in righteousness H1906
Ps 75:2 appointed time; it is I who **j** with equity. H9149
Ps 76:9 rose up to **j**, to save all the afflicted H5477
Ps 82:8 **j** the earth, for all the nations are H9149
Ps 94:2 Rise up, **J** of the earth; pay back to the H9149
Ps 96:10 he will **j** the peoples with equity. H1906
Ps 96:13 he comes, he comes to **j** the earth. H9149
Ps 96:13 He will **j** the world in righteousness and H9149
Ps 98:9 the LORD, for he comes to **j** the earth. H9149
Ps 98:9 He will **j** the world in righteousness and H9149
Ps 110:6 He will **j** the nations, heaping up the H1906
Pr 20:8 When a king sits on his throne to **j**, he H1907
Pr 25:12 is the rebuke of a **wise j** to a listening ear. AIT
Pr 31:9 Speak up and **j** fairly; defend the rights of H9149
Ecc 3:17 every activity, a time to **j** every deed." NDT
Isa 2:4 He will **j** between the nations and will H9149
Isa 3:2 the warrior, the **j** and the prophet, the H9149
Isa 3:13 his place in court; he rises to **j** the people. H1906
Isa 5:3 of Judah, **j** between me and my vineyard. H9149
Isa 11:3 He will not **j** by what he sees with his H9149
Isa 11:4 with righteousness he will **j** the needy, H9149
Isa 33:22 For the LORD is our **j**, the LORD is our H9149
Jer 11:20 who **j** righteously and test the heart and H9149
Eze 7:3 I will **j** you according to your conduct and H9149
Eze 7:8 I will **j** you according to your conduct and H9149
Eze 7:27 by their own standards I will **j** them. H9149
Eze 18:30 I will **j** each of you according to your own H9149
Eze 20:4 "Will you **j** them? Will you judge them H9149
Eze 20:4 you judge them? Will you **j** them, son of H9149
Eze 20:36 land of Egypt, so I will **j** you, declares the H9149
Eze 21:30 in the land of your ancestry, I will **j** you. H9149
Eze 22:2 "Son of man, will you **j** her? Will you H9149
Eze 22:2 Will you **j** this city of bloodshed H9149
Eze 23:36 of man, will you **j** Oholah and Oholibah? H9149
Eze 33:20 But I will **j** each of you according to your H9149
Eze 34:17 I will **j** between one sheep and another H9149
Eze 34:20 I myself will **j** between the fat sheep and H9149
Eze 34:22 I will **j** between one sheep and another. H9149
Eze 35:11 myself known among them when I **j** you. H9149
Joel 3:12 there I will sit to **j** all the nations on H9149
Mic 3:11 Her leaders **j** for a bribe, her priests teach H9149
Mic 4:3 He will **j** between many peoples and will H9149
Mic 7:3 demands gifts, the **j** accepts bribes, the H9149
Mt 5:25 your adversary may hand you over to the **j**, G3216
Mt 5:25 the **j** may hand you over to the officer, G3216
Mt 7:1 "Do not **j**, or you too will be judged. G3212
Mt 7:2 For in the same way you **j** others, you will G3212
Lk 6:37 "Do not **j**, and you will not be judged. G3212
Lk 12:14 who appointed me a **j** or an arbiter G3216
Lk 12:57 "Why don't you **j** for yourselves what is G3212
Lk 12:58 your adversary may drag you off to the **j**, G3216
Lk 12:58 the **j** turn you over to the officer G3216
Lk 18:2 town there was a **j** who neither feared G3216
Lk 18:6 "Listen to what the unjust **j** says. G3216
Lk 19:22 replied, 'I will **j** you by your own words G3212
Jn 5:27 him authority to **j** because he is the G3213+4472
Jn 5:30 I can do nothing; I **j** only as I hear, and G3212
Jn 7:24 mere appearances, but instead **j** correctly." G3212
Jn 8:15 You **j** by human standards; I pass G3212
Jn 8:16 But if I do **j**, my decisions are true G3212
Jn 8:50 there is one who seeks it, and he is the **j**. G3212
Jn 12:47 not keep them, I do not **j** that person. G3212
Jn 12:47 For I did not come to **j** the world, but to G3212
Jn 12:48 There is a **j** for the one who rejects me G3212
Jn 18:31 him yourselves and **j** him by your own law G3212
Ac 7:27 'Who made you ruler and **j** over us? G1471
Ac 7:35 the words, 'Who made you ruler and **j**? G1471
Ac 10:42 God appointed as **j** of the living and G3216
Ac 17:31 a day when he will **j** the world with justice G3212
Ac 18:15 I will not be a **j** of such things." G3216
Ac 23:3 You sit there to **j** me according to the law G3212
Ac 24:10 years you have been a **j** over this nation; G3216
Ro 2:1 at whatever point you **j** another, you G3212
Ro 3:4 when you speak and prevail when you **j**." G3212
Ro 3:6 that were so, how could God **j** the world? G3212
Ro 14:3 eat everything must not **j** the one who G3212
Ro 14:4 Who are you to **j** someone else's servant G3212
Ro 14:10 why do you **j** your brother or sister? G3212
1Co 4:3 indeed, I do not even **j** myself. G373
1Co 4:5 Therefore **j** nothing before the appointed G3212
1Co 5:12 is it of mine to **j** those outside the G3212
1Co 5:12 Are you not to **j** those inside? G3212
1Co 5:13 God will **j** those outside. "Expel the wicked G3212
1Co 6:2 that the Lord's people will **j** the world? G3212
1Co 6:2 And if you are to **j** the world, are you not G3212
1Co 6:2 are you not competent to **j** trivial cases? G3215
1Co 6:3 Do you not know that we will **j** angels G3212
1Co 6:5 you wise enough to **j a dispute** between G1359
1Co 10:15 people; **j** for yourselves what I say. G3212
1Co 11:13 **J** for yourselves: Is it proper for a woman G3212
Col 2:16 Therefore do not let anyone **j** you by what G3212
2Ti 4:1 who will **j** the living and the dead G3212
2Ti 4:8 the righteous **J**, will award to me on G3216
Heb 10:30 and again, "The Lord will **j** his people." G3212
Heb 12:23 have come to God, the **J** of all, to the G3216
Heb 13:4 God will **j** the adulterer and all the G3212
Jas 4:11 When you **j** the law, you are not keeping G3212
Jas 4:12 There is only one Lawgiver and **J**, the one G3216
Jas 4:12 But you—who are you to **j** your neighbor? G3212
Jas 5:9 The **J** is standing at the door! G3216
1Pe 4:5 to him who is ready to **j** the living and the G3212
Jude 15 to **j** everyone, and to convict all of G4472+3213
Rev 6:10 until you **j** the inhabitants of the earth G3212
Rev 20:4 those who had been given authority to **j**. G3210

JUDGE'S (2) [JUDGE]

Mt 27:19 While Pilate was sitting on the **j seat**, his G1037
Jn 19:13 sat down on the **j seat** at a place known G1037

JUDGED (22) [JUDGE]

Job 31:11 would have been wicked, a sin **to be j**. H7132
Job 31:28 then these also would be sins **to be j**, for I H7132
Ps 9:19 let the nations **be j** in your presence. H9149
Eze 20:36 As I **j** your ancestors in the wilderness of H9149
Eze 24:14 You will be **j** according to your conduct H9149
Eze 36:19 I **j** them according to their conduct and H9149
Mt 7:1 "Do not judge, or you too will be **j**. G3212
Mt 7:2 judge others, you will be **j**, and with the G3212
Lk 6:37 not judge, and you will not be **j**. Do not G3212
Lk 7:43 debt forgiven." "You have **j** correctly," G3212
Jn 5:24 life and will not be **j** but has G1650+3213+2262
Ro 2:12 sin under the law will be **j** by the law. G3212
1Co 4:3 I care very little if I am **j** by you or by any G373
1Co 10:29 For why is my freedom being **j** by G3212
1Co 11:32 when we are **j** in this way by the Lord G3212
Jas 2:12 who are going to be **j** by the law that G3212
Jas 3:1 that we who teach will be **j** more G3210+3284
Jas 5:9 brothers and sisters, or you will be **j**. G3212
1Pe 4:6 so that they might be **j** according to G3212
Rev 18:20 For God has **j** her with the judgment she G3212
Rev 20:12 The dead were **j** according to what they G3212
Rev 20:13 each person was **j** according to what G3212

JUDGES (54) [JUDGE]

Ex 18:22 Have them **serve as j** for the people at all H9149
Ex 18:26 They **served as j** for the people at all times H9149
Ex 21:6 then his master must take him before the **j** H466
Ex 22:8 of the house must appear before the **j**, H466
Ex 22:9 parties are to bring their cases before the **j**. H466
Ex 22:9 The one whom the **j** declare guilty must H466
Nu 25:5 So Moses said to Israel's **j**, "Each of you H9149
Dt 1:16 And I charged your **j** at that time, "Hear H9149
Dt 16:18 Appoint **j** and officials for each of your H9149
Dt 19:17 the **j** who are **in office** at the time. H9149
Dt 19:18 The **j** must make a thorough investigation H9149
Dt 21:2 your elders and **j** shall go out and H9149
Dt 25:1 it to court and the **j** will **decide** the case, H9149
Jos 8:33 officials and **j**, were standing on H9149
Jos 23:2 their elders, leaders, **j** and officials—and H9149
Jos 24:1 leaders, **j** and officials of Israel, and they H9149
Jdg 2:16 Then the LORD raised up **j**, who saved H9149
Jdg 2:17 would not listen to their **j** but prostituted H9149
Ru 1:1 In the days when the **j** ruled, there was a H9149
2Ki 23:22 in the days of the **j** who led Israel nor in H9149
1Ch 23:4 six thousand are to be officials and **j**. H9149
1Ch 26:29 the temple, as officials and **j** over Israel. H9149
2Ch 1:2 to the **j** and to all the leaders in Israel H9149
2Ch 19:5 He appointed **j** in the land, in each of the H9149
Ezr 4:9 of their associates—the **j**, officials and A10171
Ezr 7:25 magistrates and **j** to administer justice A10171
Ezr 10:14 along with the elders and **j** of each town H9149
Job 9:24 hands of the wicked, he blindfolds its **j**. H9149
Job 12:17 rulers away stripped and makes fools of **j**. H9149
Job 21:22 since he **j** even the highest? H9149
Ps 9:8 in righteousness and **j** the peoples with H1906
Ps 58:11 surely there is a God who **j** the earth." H9149
Ps 75:7 It is God who **j**: He brings one down, he H9149
Pr 29:14 If a king **j** the poor with fairness, his H9149
Eze 18:8 doing wrong and **j** fairly between H6913+5477
Eze 23:45 But righteous **j** will sentence them to the H408S
Eze 44:24 are to serve as **j** and decide it according H9149
Da 3:2 treasurers, **j**, magistrates and all the A10188
Da 3:3 treasurers, **j**, magistrates and all the A10188
Mt 12:27 So then, they will be your **j**. G3216
Lk 11:19 So then, they will be your **j**. G3216
Jn 5:22 Moreover, the Father **j** no one, but has G3212
Ac 4:19 to listen to you, or to him? You be the **j**! G3212
Ac 13:20 God gave them **j** until the time of Samuel G3216
Ro 2:16 on the day when God **j** people's secrets G3212
1Co 4:4 make me innocent. It is the Lord who **j** me. G373
Heb 4:12 it **j** the thoughts and attitudes of the heart. G3217
Jas 2:4 become **j** with evil thoughts? G3216
Jas 4:11 brother or sister or **j** them speaks against G3212
Jas 4:11 them speaks against the law and **j** it. G3212
1Pe 1:17 call on a Father who **j** each person's work G3212
1Pe 2:23 he entrusted himself to him who **j** justly. G3212
Rev 18:8 for mighty is the Lord God who **j** her. G3212
Rev 19:11 With justice he **j** and wages war. G3212

JUDGING (10) [JUDGE]

Dt 1:17 Do not show partiality in **j**; hear both small H5477
1Sa 7:16 to Mizpah, **j** Israel in all those places. H9149
2Ch 19:6 because you are not **j** for mere mortals H9149
Pr 24:23 To show partiality in **j** is not good: H5477
Isa 16:5 one who in **j** seeks justice and speeds the H9149
Mt 19:28 thrones, **j** the twelve tribes of Israel. G3212
Lk 22:30 sit on thrones, **j** the twelve tribes of Israel. G3212
Jn 7:24 Stop **j** by mere appearances, but instead G3212
2Co 10:7 You are **j** by appearances. If anyone is G1063
Rev 11:18 The time has come for **j** the dead, and G3212

JUDGMENT (121) [JUDGE]

Ex 6:6 arm and with mighty **acts of j**. H9150
Ex 7:4 with mighty **acts of j** I will bring out H9150
Ex 12:12 I will bring **j** on all the gods of Egypt. H9150
Nu 33:4 the LORD had brought **j** on their gods. H9150
Dt 1:17 be afraid of anyone, for **j** belongs to God. H5477
Dt 32:41 flashing sword and my hand grasps it in **j**, H5477
1Sa 25:33 blessed for your **good j** and for keeping H3248
2Ch 20:9 whether the sword of **j**, or plague or H9144
2Ch 22:8 While Jehu was **executing j** on the house H9149
2Ch 24:24 their ancestors, **j** was executed on Joash. H9150
Job 14:3 Will you bring them before you for **j**? H5477
Job 19:29 then you will know that there is **j**. H1907
Job 24:1 "Why does the Almighty not set times for **j** NDT
Job 34:23 that they should come before him for **j**. H5477
Job 36:17 you are laden with the **j** due the wicked; H1907
Job 36:17 **j** and justice have taken hold of you. H1907
Ps 1:5 the wicked will not stand in the **j**, H5477
Ps 9:7 he has established his throne for **j**. H5477
Ps 76:8 From heaven you pronounced **j**, and the H1907
Ps 82:1 assembly; he **renders j** among the "gods": H9149
Ps 94:15 **J** will again be founded on righteousness H5477
Ps 119:66 Teach me knowledge and good **j**, for I H3248
Ps 122:5 There stand the thrones for **j**, the thrones H5477
Ps 143:2 Do not bring your servant into **j**, for no H5477
Pr 3:21 preserve **sound j** and discretion; H9370
Pr 8:14 Counsel and **sound j** are mine; I have H9370
Pr 13:15 Good **j** wins favor, but the way of the H8507
Pr 18:1 against all **sound j** starts quarrels. H9370
Ecc 3:16 In the place of **j**—wickedness was there H5477
Ecc 3:17 "God will **bring into j** both the righteous H9149
Ecc 11:9 all these things God will bring you into **j**. H5477
Ecc 12:14 For God will bring every deed into **j** H5477
Isa 3:14 The LORD enters into **j** against the elders H5477
Isa 4:4 by a spirit of **j** and a spirit of fire. H5477
Isa 28:6 a spirit of justice to the one who sits in **j**, H5477
Isa 34:5 it descends in **j** on Edom, the people H5477
Isa 41:1 let us meet together at the **place of j**. H5477
Isa 53:8 By oppression and **j** he was taken away H5477
Isa 66:16 the LORD will **execute j** on all people, H9149
Jer 2:35 But I will **pass j** on you because you say H9149
Jer 10:15 of mockery; when their **j** comes, they will H7213
Jer 25:31 he will **bring j** on all mankind and put the H9149
Jer 48:21 **J** has come to the plateau—to Holon H5477
Jer 48:47 Here ends the **j** on Moab. H5477
Jer 51:9 own land, for her **j** reaches to the skies H5477
Jer 51:18 of mockery; when their **j** comes, they will H7213

Eze 9: 1 those who are appointed to execute j on H7213
Eze 11:10 and I will execute j on you at the borders H9149
Eze 11:11 I will execute j on you at the borders of H9149
Eze 17:20 to Babylon and execute j on him there H9149
Eze 20:35 face to face, I will execute j upon you. H9149
Eze 38:22 I will execute j on him with plague and H9149
Da 7:22 came and pronounced j in favor of the A10170
Hos 5: 1 This j is against you: You H5477
Hos 5:11 trampled in j, intent on pursuing H5477
Am 7: 4 Sovereign LORD was calling for j by fire; H8189
Hab 1:12 have appointed them to execute j; you, H5477
Zec 8:16 and render true and sound j in your H9149+5477
Mt 5:21 anyone who murders will be subject to j. G3213
Mt 5:22 with a brother or sister will be subject to j. G3213
Mt 10:15 on the day of j than for that town G3213
Mt 11:22 Sidon on the day of j than for you. G3213
Mt 11:24 Sodom on the day of j than for you." G3213
Mt 12:36 account on the day of j for every empty G3213
Mt 12:41 will stand up at the j with this generation G3213
Mt 12:42 will rise at the j with this generation G3213
Lk 10:14 Tyre and Sidon at the j than for you. G3213
Lk 11:31 South will rise at the j with the people of G3213
Lk 11:32 will stand up at the j with this generation G3213
Jn 5:22 no one, but has entrusted all j to the Son, G3213
Jn 5:30 only as I hear, and my j is just, for I seek G3213
Jn 8:15 by human standards; I pass j on no one. G3212
Jn 8:26 "I have much to say in j of you. But he who G3212
Jn 9:39 "For j I have come into this world G3210
Jn 12:31 Now is the time for j on this world; now G3213
Jn 16: 8 wrong about sin and righteousness and j: G3213
Jn 16:11 about j, because the prince of this G3213
Ac 15:19 "It is my j, therefore, that we should not G3212
Ac 18:12 on Paul and brought him to the place of j. G1037
Ac 24:25 self-control and the j to come, Felix was G3210
Ro 2: 1 you who pass j on someone else G3212
Ro 2: 1 because you who pass j do the same G3212
Ro 2: 2 we know that God's j against those who G3210
Ro 2: 3 So when you, a mere human being, pass j G3212
Ro 2: 3 do you think you will escape God's j? G3210
Ro 2: 5 when his righteous j will be revealed. G1464
Ro 5:16 The j followed one sin and brought G3210
Ro 12: 3 rather think of yourself with sober j, in G5404
Ro 13: 2 who do so will bring j on themselves. G3210
Ro 14:10 For we will all stand before God's j seat. G1037
Ro 14:13 Therefore let us stop passing j on one G3212
1Co 5: 3 I have already passed j in the name of G3212
1Co 6: 1 dare to take it before the ungodly for j G3212
1Co 7:25 I give a j as one who by the Lord's G1191
1Co 7:40 In my j, she is happier if she stays as she G1191
1Co 9: 3 is my defense to those who sit in j on me. G373
1Co 11:29 of Christ eat and drink j on themselves. G3210
1Co 11:31 we would not come under such j. G3212
1Co 11:34 you meet together it may not result in j. G3210
1Co 14:24 of sin and are brought under j by all, G373
2Co 5:10 must all appear before the j seat of Christ, G1037
2Co 8:10 And here is my j about what is best for G1191
2Th 1: 5 All this is evidence that God's j is right G3213
1Ti 3: 6 fall under the same j as the devil. G3210
1Ti 5:12 Thus they bring j on themselves, because G3210
1Ti 5:24 reaching the place of j ahead of them G3213
Heb 6: 2 the resurrection of the dead, and eternal j. G3210
Heb 9:27 to die once, and after that to face j, G3213
Heb 10:27 fearful expectation of j and of raging fire G3213
Jas 2:13 because j without mercy will be shown to G3213
Jas 2:13 not been merciful. Mercy triumphs over j. G3213
Jas 4:11 are not keeping it, but sitting in j on it. G3216
1Pe 4:17 For it is time for j to begin with God's G3210
2Pe 2: 4 in chains of darkness to be held for j; G3213
2Pe 2: 9 punishment on the day of j. G3213
2Pe 2:11 beings when bringing j on them from the G3213
2Pe 3: 7 kept for the day of j and destruction of G3213
1Jn 4:17 we will have confidence on the day of j: G3213
Jude 6 everlasting chains for j on the great Day. G3213
Rev 14: 7 because the hour of his j has come. G3213
Rev 18:20 has judged her with the j she imposed on G3210

JUDGMENTS (19) [JUDGE]

Dt 33:21 righteous will, and his j concerning Israel." H5477
1Ch 16:12 his miracles, and the j he pronounced, H5477
1Ch 16:14 the LORD our God; his j are in all the earth. H5477
Ps 48:11 of Judah are glad because of your j. H5477
Ps 97: 8 of Judah are glad because of your j, H5477
Ps 105: 5 his miracles, and the j he pronounced, H5477
Ps 105: 7 the LORD our God; his j are in all the earth. H5477
Isa 26: 9 When your j come upon the earth, the H5477
Jer 1:16 I will pronounce my j on my people H5477
Jer 4:12 Now I pronounce my j against them." H5477
Eze 14:21 against Jerusalem my four dreadful j— H9150
Da 9:11 the curses and sworn j written in the Law H8652
Hos 6: 5 mouth—then my j go forth like the sun. H5477
Ro 11:33 How unsearchable his j, and his paths G3210
1Co 2:15 with the Spirit makes j about all things, G373
1Co 2:15 a person is not subject to merely human j, G373
Rev 16: 5 "You are just in these j, O Holy One, you G3212
Rev 16: 7 God Almighty, true and just are your j." G3213
Rev 19: 2 true and just are his j. He has G3213

JUDITH (1)

Ge 26:34 he married J daughter of Beeri the Hittite H3377

JUG (6)

1Sa 26:11 the spear and water j that are near his H7608
1Sa 26:12 the spear and water j near Saul's head, H7608
1Sa 26:16 spear and water j that were near his H7608
1Ki 17:12 of flour in a jar and a little olive oil in a j. H7608
1Ki 17:14 be used up and the j of oil will not run dry H7608
1Ki 17:16 not used up and the j of oil did not run H7608

JUICE (3)

Nu 6: 3 must not drink grape j or eat grapes or H5489
Nu 18:27 threshing floor or j from the winepress. H4852
Isa 65: 8 "As when j is still found in a cluster of H9408

JULIA (1)

Ro 16:15 Greet Philologus, J, Nereus and his sister G2684

JULIUS (2)

Ac 27: 1 handed over to a centurion named J, G2685
Ac 27: 3 at Sidon; and J, in kindness to Paul G2685

JUMP (1) [JUMPED, JUMPING]

Ac 27:43 who could swim to j overboard first and get G681

JUMPED (5) [JUMP]

Mk 10:50 he j to his feet and came to Jesus. G403
Jn 21: 7 had taken it off) and j into the water. G965+1571
Ac 3: 8 He j to his feet and began to walk. G1982
Ac 14:10 At that, the man j up and began to walk. G256
Ac 19:16 had the evil spirit j on them and G2383

JUMPING (1) [JUMP]

Ac 3: 8 walking and j, and praising God. G256

JUNCTION (1) [JOIN]

Eze 21:21 in the road, at the j of the two roads, to H8031

JUNIA (1)

Ro 16: 7 Greet Andronicus and J, my fellow Jews G2686

JUNIOR (4)

1Ki 20:14 'The j officers under the provincial H5853
1Ki 20:15 the 232 j officers under the provincial H5853
1Ki 20:17 The j officers under the provincial H5853
1Ki 20:19 The j officers under the provincial H5853

JUNIPER (13) [JUNIPERS]

1Ki 5: 8 want in providing the cedar and j logs. H1360
1Ki 5:10 with all the cedar and j logs he wanted, H1360
1Ki 6:15 the floor of the temple with planks of j. H1360
1Ki 6:34 He also made two doors out of j wood H1360
1Ki 9:11 all the cedar and j and gold he wanted. H1360
2Ch 2: 8 j and algum logs from Lebanon H1360
2Ch 3: 5 the main hall with j and covered it H6770+1360
Isa 55:13 Instead of the thornbush will grow the j H1360
Isa 60:13 will come to you, the j, the fir and the H1360
Eze 27: 5 made all your timbers of j from Senir; H1360
Hos 14: 8 I am like a flourishing j; your fruitfulness H1360
Na 2: 3 the spears of j are brandished. H1360
Zec 11: 2 you j, for the cedar has fallen; the H1360

JUNIPERS (6) [JUNIPER]

2Ki 19:23 its tallest cedars, the choicest of its j. H1360
Ps 104:17 their nests; the stork has its home in the j. H1360
Isa 14: 8 Even the j and the cedars of Lebanon H1360
Isa 37:24 its tallest cedars, the choicest of its j. H1360
Isa 41:19 I will set j in the wasteland, the fir and H1360
Eze 31: 8 nor could the j equal its boughs, nor H1360

JUPITER (KJV) HEAVEN, ZEUS

JURISDICTION (1)

Lk 23: 7 learned that Jesus was under Herod's j, G2026

JUSHAB-HESED (1)

1Ch 3:20 Berekiah, Hasadiah and J. H3457

JUST (405) [JUSTICE, JUSTIFICATION, JUSTIFIED, JUSTIFIES, JUSTIFY, JUSTIFYING, JUSTLY]

Ge 6:22 did everything j as God commanded him. H3869
Ge 9: 3 J as I gave you the green plants, I now H3869
Ge 18:19 of the LORD by doing what is right and j, H5477
Ge 18:32 be angry, but let me speak j once more. H421
Ge 26:29 j as we did not harm you but always H3869+889
Ge 27: 9 your father, j the way he likes it. H3869+889
Ge 27:13 curse fall on me. J do what I say; go and H421
Ge 27:14 j the way his father liked it. H3869+889
Ge 27:33 I ate it j before you came and I H928+3270
Ge 29:15 "J because you are a relative of mine H3954
Ge 33:13 If they are driven hard j one day, all the NDT
Ge 33:15 "J let me find favor in the eyes of my lord." AIT
Ge 38:11 "He may die too, j like his brothers." H3869
Ge 40:13 j as you used to do when you were his H3869
Ge 40:22 j as Joseph had said to them in his H3869+889
Ge 41:21 they looked j as ugly as before. H3869+889
Ge 41:28 "It is j as I said to Pharaoh: God has shown H889
Ge 41:54 famine began, j as Joseph had said. H3869+889
Ge 42: 1 "Why do you j keep looking at each other?" AIT
Ge 42:14 said to them, "It is j as I told you: You are H889
Ge 46:34 from our boyhood on, j as our fathers did. H1685
Ge 47: 3 replied to Pharaoh, "j as our fathers were." H1685
Ge 48: 5 mine, j as Reuben and Simeon are mine. H3869
Ex 5:13 each day, j as when you had straw." H3869+889
Ex 7: 6 and Aaron did j as the LORD H3869+889+4027
Ex 7:10 Pharaoh and did j as the LORD H3869+889+4027
Ex 7:13 to them, j as the LORD had said. H889+3869
Ex 7:20 Aaron did j as the LORD had H3869+889+4027
Ex 7:22 and Aaron, j as the LORD had said. H3869+889
Ex 8:15 and Aaron, j as the LORD had said. H3869+889
Ex 8:19 not listen, j as the LORD had said. H3869+889
Ex 9:12 j as the LORD had said to Moses. H3869+889
Ex 9:35 j as the LORD had said through H3869+889
Ex 10:29 "J as you say," Moses replied. "I will H4027
Ex 12:28 Israelites did j what the LORD H3869+889+4027
Ex 12:50 did j what the LORD had H3869+889+4027
Ex 16:18 gathered j as much as they needed H4200+7023
Ex 27: 8 is to be made j as you were H3869+889+4027
Ex 28:27 to the seam j above the waistband H4946+5087
Ex 31:11 make them j as I commanded H3869+3972+889
Ex 36: 1 do the work j as the LORD has H4200+3972+889
Ex 39:20 to the seam j above the waistband H4946+5087
Ex 39:32 did everything j as the LORD H3869+889+4027
Ex 39:42 all the work j as the LORD had H3869+889+4027
Ex 39:43 had done it j as the LORD had H3869+889+4027
Ex 40:15 Anoint them j as you anointed their H3869+889
Ex 40:16 did everything j as the LORD H3869+889+4027
Lev 4:10 j as the fat is removed from the ox H3869+889
Lev 4:20 with this bull j as he did with H3869+889+4027
Lev 4:31 j as the fat is removed from the H3869+889
Lev 4:35 j as the fat is removed from the H3869+889
Lev 12: 2 j as she is unclean during her monthly H3869
Lev 15:25 discharge, j as in the days of her period. H3869
Nu 1:54 did all this j as the LORD H3869+889+4027
Nu 5: 4 They did j as the LORD had H3869+889+4027
Nu 8: 3 j as the LORD commanded Moses. H3869+889
Nu 8:20 the Levites j as the LORD H3869+3972+889+4027
Nu 8:22 with the Levites j as the LORD H3869+889+4027
Nu 9: 5 did everything j as the LORD H3869+889+4027
Nu 11:19 You will not eat it for j one day, or two days NDT
Nu 14:17 displayed, j as you have declared: H3869+889
Nu 14:19 j as you have pardoned them from H3869+889
Nu 15:27 " 'But if j one person sins unintentionally NDT
Nu 17:11 Moses did j as the LORD H3869+889+4027
Nu 18:18 j as the breast of the wave offering and H3869
Nu 20: 9 presence, j as he commanded him. H3869+889
Nu 32:27 before the LORD, j as our lord says." H3869+889
Dt 2:12 j as Israel did in the land the LORD H3869+889
Dt 6: 3 milk and honey, j as the LORD, the H3869+889
Dt 27: 3 milk and honey, j as the LORD, the H3869+889
Dt 28:63 J as it pleased the LORD to make you H3869+889
Dt 30: 9 j as he delighted in your ancestors H3869+889
Dt 32: 4 works are perfect, and all his ways are j. H5477
Dt 32: 4 who does no wrong, upright and j is he. H3838
Dt 32:47 They are not j idle words for you—they are H3954
Dt 32:50 j as your brother Aaron died on H3869+889
Jos 1:17 J as we fully obeyed Moses, so we will H3869
Jos 4:10 j as Moses had directed H3869+3972+889
Jos 4:14 j as they had stood in awe of Moses. H3869+889
Jos 8:34 j as it is written in the Book of the Law. H3869
Jos 10:32 j as he had done to Libnah. H3869+3972+889
Jos 10:35 j as they had done to Lachish. H3869+3972+889
Jos 10:37 J as at Eglon, they totally H3869+3972+889
Jos 10:40 who breathed, j as the LORD, the God H3869+889
Jos 11:23 j as the LORD had directed H3869+3972+889
Jos 14: 5 j as the LORD had commanded H3869+889+4027
Jos 14:10 "Now then, j as the LORD promised H3869+889
Jos 14:11 I'm j as vigorous to go out to battle now H3869
Jos 14:12 I will drive them out j as he said." H3869+889
Jos 21:44 j as he had sworn to their H3869+3972+889
Jos 23:10 God fights for you, j as he promised. H3869+889
Jos 23:15 But j as all the good things the LORD H3869+889
Jdg 2:15 j as he had sworn to them. H3869+889
Jdg 4:22 J then Barak came by in pursuit of H2256+2180
Jdg 6:39 Let me make j one more request H421
Jdg 7:13 Gideon arrived j as a man was telling a H2180
Jdg 7:19 j after they had changed the guard. H421
Jdg 8: 7 replied, "J for that, when the LORD H4200+4027
Jdg 9: 2 sons rule over you, or j one man? NDT
Jdg 9:35 of the city gate j as Abimelek and his H2256
Jdg 11:36 Do to me j as you promised, now H3869+889
Jdg 16:28 strengthen me j once more, and let H421
Jdg 18:19 priest rather than j one man's household?" NDT
Jdg 19:30 J imagine! We must do H8492+4200
Ru 2: 4 J then Boaz arrived from H2256+2180
Ru 4: 1 sat down there j as the H2180
1Sa 4:16 "I have j come from the battle line AIT
1Sa 9:12 he has j come to our town today H3954
1Sa 11: 5 J then Saul was returning from the fields H2180
1Sa 13:10 J as he finished making the offering H3869
1Sa 24:18 You have j now told me about the H2021+3427
1Sa 25:21 David had j said, "It's been useless—all my AIT
1Sa 25:25 He is j like his name—his name H3869+4027
2Sa 3:22 J then David's men and Joab H2256+2180
2Sa 8:15 doing what was j and right for all his H5477
2Sa 10: 2 j as his father showed kindness to H3869+889
2Sa 11:10 "Haven't you j come from a military AIT
2Sa 13:35 it has happened j as your servant H3869+4027
2Sa 16:19 J as I served your father, so I will H3869+889
2Sa 18:10 "I j saw Absalom hanging in an oak tree." H2180
2Sa 18:29 saw great confusion j as Joab was about to NDT
2Sa 19: 5 who have j saved your life and the H2021+3427
2Sa 21: 9 j as the barley harvest was beginning. H928
1Ki 5:12 wisdom, j as he had promised him. H3869+889
1Ki 8:20 of Israel, j as the LORD promised H3869+889
1Ki 8:53 j as you declared through your H3869+889
1Ki 8:56 Israel j as he promised. H3869+3972+889
1Ki 20: 4 Israel answered, "J as you say, my lord H3869
1Ki 22:53 j as his father had done. H3869+3972+889
2Ki 4: 3 empty jars. Don't ask for j a few. H5070

2Ki 4:17 birth to a son, **j as** Elisha had told her. H889
2Ki 5:22 prophets have **j** come to me from H6964+2296
2Ki 7:10 and the tents left **j as** they were." H3869+889
2Ki 7:17 **j as** the man of God had foretold H3869+889
2Ki 8: 5 **J as** Gehazi was telling the king how H2256
2Ki 11: 9 hundred did **j as** Jehoiada H3869+3972+889
2Ki 15: 3 **j as** his father Amaziah had H3869+3972+889
2Ki 15:34 **j as** his father Uzziah had H3869+3972+889
2Ki 16:16 priest did **j as** King Ahaz had H3869+3972+889
2Ki 18: 3 **j as** his father David had H3869+3972+889
2Ki 23:19 **J as** he had done at Bethel, Josiah H3869+3972
2Ki 23:32 **j as** his predecessors had H3869+3972+889
2Ki 23:37 **j as** his predecessors had H3869+3972+889
2Ki 24: 9 **j as** his father had done. H3869+3972+889
2Ki 24:19 **j as** Jehoiakim had done. H3869+3972+889
1Ch 9:19 of the tent **j as** their ancestors had H2256
1Ch 18:14 doing *what* was **j** and right for all his H5477
1Ch 24:31 **j as** their relatives the descendants H4200+6645
1Ch 26:12 of the LORD, **j as** their relatives had. H4200+6645
2Ch 6:10 of Israel, **j as** the LORD promised H3869+889
2Ch 12: 6 themselves and said, "The LORD is **j**." H7404
2Ch 21:13 themselves, **j as** the house of Ahab did. H3869
2Ch 23: 8 of Judah did **j as** Jehoiada H3869+3972+889
2Ch 26: 4 **j as** his father Amaziah had H3869+3972+889
2Ch 27: 2 **j as** his father Uzziah had H3869+3972+889
2Ch 29: 2 **j as** his father David had H3869+3972+889
2Ch 32:17 "**J as** the gods of the peoples of the other H3869
Ne 6: 8 you are **j** making it up out of your head." H3954
Ne 9:13 regulations and laws that are **j** and right, H3838
Est 2:20 and nationality **j as** Mordecai had H3869+889
Est 6: 4 Now Haman *had j* **entered** the outer court of AIT
Est 6:10 horse and do **j as** you have H3869+889+4027
Est 7: 8 **J as** the king returned from the palace H2256
Job 34:17 Will you condemn the **j** and mighty One? H7404
Job 35: 2 "Do you think this is **j**? You say, 'I am in H5477
Ps 17: 1 LORD, my plea is **j**; listen to my cry. H7406
Ps 35:25 let them think, "Aha, **j what** we **wanted**!" H5883
Ps 37:28 the LORD loves the **j** and will not forsake H5477
Ps 37:30 their tongues speak *what* is **j**. H5477
Ps 86:16 because I **serve** you **j as** my **mother** did. H563
Ps 90: 4 your sight are like a day that *has j* **gone by**, AIT
Ps 99: 4 Jacob you have done *what* is **j** and right. H5477
Ps 111: 7 The works of his hands are faithful and **j** H5477
Ps 116:16 I serve you **j as** my **mother did**; you have H563S
Ps 119:121 I have done what is righteous and **j**; do H5477
Pr 1: 3 doing what is right and **j** and fair; H5477
Pr 2: 8 the course of the **j** and protects the way of H5477
Pr 2: 9 understand what is right and **j** and fair— H5477
Pr 8: 8 All the words of my mouth are **j**; none of H7406
Pr 8:15 reign and rulers issue decrees *that* are **j**; H7406
Pr 12: 5 The plans of the righteous are **j**, but the H5477
Pr 21: 3 do what is right and **j** is more acceptable H5477
Pr 25:16 find honey, eat **j enough**—too much of it, H1896
Pr 26: 4 his folly, or *you* yourself *will* **be j like** him. H8750
Ecc 2:13 **j as** light is better than darkness. H3869
Ecc 12:10 Teacher searched to find **j** the **right** words, H2914
SS 4: 2 teeth are like a flock of **sheep j shorn**, H7892
Isa 20: 3 "**J as** my servant Isaiah has gone H3869+889
Isa 28: 9 their milk, to *those j* **taken** from the breast? AIT
Isa 32: 7 even when the plea of the needy is **j**. H5477
Isa 52:14 **J as** there were many who were H3869+889
Isa 58: 2 They ask me for **j** decisions and seem H7406
Jer 3: 4 Have you not **j** called to me: 'My H4946+6964
Jer 4: 2 a truthful, **j** and righteous way you swear H5477
Jer 5:28 do not defend the **j cause** *of* the poor. H5477
Jer 7:15 **j as** I did all your fellow Israelites H3869+889
Jer 7:22 *I did* not *j* **give** them **commands** about burnt AIT
Jer 19:11 and this city **j as** this potter's jar H3869+889
Jer 22: 3 the LORD says: Do *what* is **j** and right H5477
Jer 22:15 He did what was right and **j**, so all went H7407
Jer 23: 5 wisely and do *what* is **j** and right in the H5477
Jer 23:27 **j as** their ancestors forgot my name H3869+889
Jer 31:28 **J as** I watched over them to uproot H3869+889
Jer 32: 8 **j as** the LORD had said, my cousin H3869
Jer 33:15 he will do *what* is **j** and right in the land. H5477
Jer 40: 3 he has done **j as** he said he would. H3869+889
Jer 44:17 offerings to her **j as** we and our H3869+889
Jer 44:30 **j as** I gave Zedekiah king of Judah H3869+889
Jer 51:49 **j as** the slain in all the earth have fallen H1685
Jer 52: 2 **j as** Jehoiakim had done. H3869+3972+889
Eze 18: 5 man who does *what* is **j** and right. H5477
Eze 18:19 the son has done *what* is **j** and right and H5477
Eze 18:21 my decrees and does *what* is **j** and right, H5477
Eze 18:25 'The way of the Lord *is* not **j**.' Hear, H9419
Eze 18:27 committed and does *what* is **j** and right, H5477
Eze 18:29 'The way of the Lord *is* not **j**. H9419
Eze 20:49 are saying of me, 'Isn't he *j* **telling** parables? AIT
Eze 23:18 **j as** I had turned away from her H3869+889
Eze 24:24 you will do **j as** he has done. H3869+3972+889
Eze 33:14 from their sin and do *what* is **j** and right— H5477
Eze 33:16 They have done *what* is **j** and right; they H5477
Eze 33:17 people say, 'The way of the Lord *is* not **j**. H9419
Eze 33:17 But it is their way that *is* not **j**. H9419
Eze 33:19 wickedness and does *what* is **j** and right, H5477
Eze 33:20 'The way of the Lord *is* not **j**. H9419
Eze 40:23 the north gate, **j as** there was on the east. H2256
Eze 45: 9 oppression and do *what* is **j** and right. H5477
Da 2:41 **J as** you saw that the feet and toes were A10168
Da 2:43 And **j as** you saw the iron mixed with A10168
Da 4:37 he does is right and all his ways are **j**. A10170
Da 6:10 **j as** he had done before. A10353+10619+10168
Da 9:13 **J as** it is written in the Law of Moses H3869+889
Am 5:14 with you, **j as** you say he is. H3869+889+4027
Am 7: 1 been harvested and **j as** the late crops H928
Ob 16 **J as** you drank on my holy hill, so all H3869+889
Mic 2:11 that would be **j** the prophet for this people! NDT
Zec 1: 6 deserve, **j as** he determined to do. H3869+889
Zec 7: 6 *were* you not *j* **feasting** *for* yourselves? AIT
Zec 8:13 **J as** you, Judah and Israel, have H3869+889
Zec 8:14 "**J as** I had determined to bring H3869+889
Mal 3:17 **j as** a father has compassion and H3869+889
Mt 8: 8 But **j** say the word, and my servant will be *G3667*
Mt 8:13 Let it be done **j as** you believed it would." *G6055*
Mt 9:18 him and said, "My daughter has **j** died. *G785*
Mt 9:20 **J then** a woman who had been *G2779+2627*
Mt 12:13 restored, **j as** sound as the other. *G6055*
Mt 14:36 him to let the sick **j** touch the edge of his *G3667*
Mt 17: 3 **J then** there appeared before them *G2779+2627*
Mt 18:15 out their fault, **j** between the two of you. *G3668*
Mt 18:33 on your fellow servant **j as** I had on you? *G6055*
Mt 19:16 **J then** a man came up to Jesus *G2779+2627*
Mt 20:28 **j as** the Son of Man did not come to be *G6061*
Mt 26:24 Son of Man will go **j as** it is written about *G2777*
Mt 28: 6 he has risen, **j as** he said. Come and *G2777*
Mk 1:10 **J as** Jesus was coming up out of the water *G2317*
Mk 1:23 **J then** a man in their synagogue who was *G2317*
Mk 4:36 took him along, **j as** he was, in the boat. *G6055*
Mk 5:28 she thought, "If I **j** touch his clothes, I will *G2829*
Mk 5:36 Jesus told him, "Don't be afraid; **j** believe." *G3667*
Mk 9:13 they wished, **j as** it is written about him." *G2777*
Mk 11: 2 ahead of you, and **j as** you enter it, you *G2317*
Mk 13:11 **J** say whatever is given you at the time, for *G247*
Mk 14:16 found things **j as** Jesus had told them *G2777*
Mk 14:21 Son of Man will go **j as** it is written about *G2777*
Mk 14:43 **J as** he was speaking, Judas, one *G2317+2285*
Mk 16: 2 the week, **j after sunrise**, they *G422+3836+2463*
Mk 16: 7 you will see him, **j as** he told you.'" *G2777*
Lk 1: 2 **j as** they were handed down to us by those *G2777*
Lk 1:55 **j as** he promised our ancestors. *G2777*
Lk 2:20 which were **j as** they had been told. *G2777*
Lk 6:36 Be merciful, **j as** your Father is merciful. *G2777*
Lk 8:50 "Don't be afraid; **j** believe, and she will *G3667*
Lk 11: 1 us to pray, **j as** John taught his disciples." *G2777*
Lk 11:36 it will be **j as** full of light as when a lamp *G6055*
Lk 14:18 The first said, '*I have j* **bought** a field, and I AIT
Lk 14:19 '*I have j* **bought** five yoke of oxen AIT
Lk 14:20 another said, '*I j* **got married**, so I can't come AIT
Lk 17:26 "**J as** it was in the days of Noah, so also *G2777*
Lk 17:30 "It will be **j like** this on the day the Son of *G2848*
Lk 19:32 went and found it *j* **as** he had told them. AIT
Lk 22:13 found things **j as** Jesus had told them *G2777*
Lk 22:29 **j as** my Father conferred one on me, *G2777*
Lk 22:60 **J** as he was speaking, the rooster crowed. *G4202*
Lk 24:24 and found it **j as** the women had *G4048+2777*
Jn 3:14 **J as** Moses lifted up the snake in the *G2777*
Jn 4:18 What *you have j* **said** is quite true." AIT
Jn 4:27 **J then** his disciples returned and *G2093+4047*
Jn 4:42 longer believe *j* **because of** what you said; AIT
Jn 5:21 For **j as** the Father raises the dead and *G6061*
Jn 5:23 all may honor the Son **j as** they honor the *G2777*
Jn 5:30 my judgment is **j**, for I seek not to *G1465*
Jn 6:57 **J as** the living Father sent me and I live *G2777*
Jn 8:25 "**J what** I have been telling you *G4005+5516*
Jn 8:28 my own but speak **j what** the Father has *G2777*
Jn 10:15 **j as** the Father knows me and I know the *G2777*
Jn 12:35 going to have the light *j a* **little** while longer. AIT
Jn 12:50 whatever I say is **j what** the Father has *G2777*
Jn 13: 1 It was **j before** the Passover Festival. Jesus *G4574*
Jn 13: 9 "not **j** my feet but my hands and my head *G3667*
Jn 13:33 look for me, and **j as** I told the Jews, so *G2777*
Jn 15:10 **j as** I have kept my Father's commands *G2777*
Jn 17:21 **j as** you are in me and I am in you. *G2777*
Jn 21:10 "Bring some of the fish you have **j** caught." *G3814*
Ac 5: 4 have not lied *j to* **human beings** but to God." AIT
Ac 7:51 You are **j like** your ancestors: You *G6055*
Ac 10:47 received the Holy Spirit **j as** we have." *G6055*
Ac 14:13 whose temple was **j outside** the city *G4574*
Ac 15: 8 the Holy Spirit to them, **j as** he did to us. *G2777*
Ac 15:11 we are saved, **j as** they are." *G2848+4005+5573*
Ac 18:14 *J as* Paul *was* **about to** speak, Gallio said to AIT
Ac 20: 3 against him *j as he was* **about to** sail for AIT
Ac 22: 3 I was **j as** zealous for God as any of you *G2777*
Ac 26:10 And that is *j* **what** I did in Jerusalem. On the AIT
Ac 27:25 happen **j as** he told me *G4048+2848+4005+5573*
Ac 27:33 **J before** dawn Paul urged them all *G948+4005*
Ro 1:13 **j as** I have had among the other Gentiles. *G2777*
Ro 1:17 by faith from first to last, **j as** it is written: *G2777*
Ro 1:28 **j as** they did not think it worthwhile to *G2777*
Ro 3: 8 may result"? Their condemnation is **j**! *G1899*
Ro 3:26 so as to be **j** and the one who justifies *G1465*
Ro 4:18 nations, **j as** it had been said to him *G2848*
Ro 5: 6 You see, **at j the right** time, when we *G2848*
Ro 5:12 **j as** sin entered the world through one *G6061*
Ro 5:18 **j as** one trespass resulted in *G6055*
Ro 5:19 For **j as** through the disobedience of the *G6061*
Ro 5:21 **j as** sin reigned in death, so also *G6061*
Ro 6: 4 **j as** Christ was raised from the dead *G6061*
Ro 6:19 **J as** you used to offer yourselves as slaves *G6061*
Ro 9:13 **J as** it is written: "Jacob I loved, but Esau I *G2777*
Ro 9:29 It is **j as** Isaiah said previously: "Unless *G2777*
Ro 11:30 **J as** you who were at one time *G6061*
Ro 12: 4 For **j as** each of us has one body with *G2749*
Ro 15: 7 **j as** Christ accepted you, in order to *G2777*
1Co 7:17 to them, **j as** God has called them. *G6055*
1Co 9:18 What then is my reward? **J** this: that in NDT
1Co 11: 2 to the traditions **j as** I passed them on to *G2777*
1Co 12:11 them to each one, **j as** he determines. *G2777*
1Co 12:12 **J as** a body, though one, has many parts *G2749*
1Co 12:18 one of them, **j as** he wanted them to be. *G2777*
1Co 14: 9 *You will j* **be** speaking into the air AIT
1Co 15:31 **yes, j as surely as** I boast about you in *G3755*
1Co 15:37 body that will be, but **j** a seed, perhaps of *G1218*
1Co 15:49 And **j as** we have borne the image of the *G2777*
1Co 16:10 carrying on the work of the Lord, **j as** I am. *G6055*
2Co 1: 5 For **j as** we share abundantly in the *G2777*
2Co 1: 7 we know that **j as** you share in our *G6055*
2Co 1:14 you can boast of us **j as** we will boast of *G2749*
2Co 7:14 But **j as** everything we said to you was *G6055*
2Co 8: 6 **j as** he had earlier made a beginning *G2777*
2Co 10: 7 we belong to Christ **j as much as** they do. *G2777*
2Co 11: 3 But I am afraid that **j as** Eve was deceived *G6055*
2Co 11:16 then tolerate me **j as** you would a fool *G6055*
Gal 2: 7 **j as** Peter had been to the circumcised. *G2777*
Gal 3: 2 I would like to learn **j** one thing from you *G4047*
Gal 3:15 **J as** no one can set aside or add to a *G3940*
Gal 4:18 to be so always, not **j** when I am with you. *G3667*
Eph 4: 4 **j as** you were called to one hope when *G2777*
Eph 4:32 each other, **j as** in Christ God forgave you. *G2777*
Eph 5: 2 **j as** Christ loved us and gave himself up *G2777*
Eph 5:25 **j as** Christ loved the church and gave *G2777*
Eph 5:29 their body, **j as** Christ does the church *G2777*
Eph 6: 5 of heart, **j as** you would obey Christ. *G6055*
Php 3:17 and **j as** you have us as a model *G2777*
Col 1: 6 **j as** it has been doing among you since *G2777*
Col 2: 6 **j as** you received Christ Jesus as Lord *G6055*
1Th 2: 7 **J as** a nursing mother cares for her *G6055+1569*
1Th 3: 6 But Timothy has **j now** come to us from you *G785*
1Th 3: 6 to see us, **j as** we also long to see you. *G2749*
1Th 3:12 everyone else, **j as** ours does for you. *G2749*
1Th 4:11 work with your hands, **j as** we told you, *G2777*
1Th 5:11 each other up, **j as** in fact you are doing. *G2777*
2Th 1: 6 God is **j**: He will pay back trouble to those *G1465*
2Th 3: 1 be honored, **j as** it was with you. *G2777*
1Ti 6: 2 them disrespect *j* **because** they are fellow AIT
2Ti 3: 8 **J as** Jannes and Jambres opposed *G4005+5573*
Heb 2: 2 disobedience received its **j** punishment, *G1899*
Heb 3: 2 **j as** Moses was faithful in all God's house. *G6055*
Heb 3: 3 **j as** the builder of a house has *G2848+4012*
Heb 3:15 As *has j been* **said**: "Today, if you hear his AIT
Heb 4: 2 proclaimed to us, **j as** they did; but the *G2749*
Heb 4: 3 enter that rest, **j as** God has said, "So I *G2777*
Heb 4:10 from their works, **j as** God did from his. *G6061*
Heb 4:15 in every way, **j as** we are—yet he *G2848+3928*
Heb 5: 4 it when called by God, **j as** Aaron was. *G2778*
Heb 7: 4 **J** think how great he was: Even the *G1254*
Heb 9:27 **J as** people are destined to die *G2848+4012*
Heb 10:37 "In *j a* **little** while, he who is coming will AIT
Jas 2:10 yet stumbles at *j* **one** *point* is guilty of AIT
1Pe 1:15 But **j as** he who called you is holy, so be *G2848*
2Pe 2: 1 **j as** there will be false teachers among *G6055*
2Pe 2:18 people who are **j** escaping from those *G3903*
2Pe 3:15 **j as** our dear brother Paul also wrote you *G2777*
1Jn 1: 9 he is faithful and **j** and will forgive us our *G1465*
1Jn 2:27 not counterfeit—**j as** it has taught you *G2777*
1Jn 3: 3 in him purify themselves, **j as** he is pure. *G2777*
1Jn 3: 7 is right is righteous, **j as** he is righteous. *G2777*
2Jn 4 the truth, **j as** the Father commanded us. *G2777*
Rev 2:27 **j as** I have received authority from my *G6055*
Rev 3:21 **j as** I was victorious and sat down with my *G6055*
Rev 6:11 were killed **j as** they had been. *G6055*
Rev 10: 7 **j as** he announced to his servants the *G6055*
Rev 15: 3 **J** and true are your ways, King of the *G1465*
Rev 16: 5 "You are **j** in these judgments, O Holy *G1465*
Rev 16: 7 Almighty, true and **j** are your judgments." *G1465*
Rev 19: 2 true and **j** are his judgments. He has *G1465*

JUSTICE (130) [JUST]

Ge 49:16 "Dan *will* **provide j** *for* his people as one H1906
Ex 23: 2 do not pervert **j** by siding with the crowd, NDT
Ex 23: 6 "Do not deny **j** *to* your poor people in H5477
Lev 19:15 "'Do not pervert **j**; do not show partiality H5477
Dt 16:19 Do not pervert **j** or show partiality. Do not H5477
Dt 16:20 Follow **j** and justice alone, so that you may H7406
Dt 16:20 Follow justice and **j** *alone*, so that you may H7406
Dt 24:17 deprive the foreigner or the fatherless of **j**, H5477
Dt 27:19 who withholds **j** *from* the foreigner, H5477
1Sa 8: 3 gain and accepted bribes and perverted **j**. H5477
2Sa 15: 4 to me and *I would* **see that** they **receive j**." H7405
2Sa 15: 6 who came to the king asking for **j**, H5477
1Ki 3:11 for discernment in administering **j**, H5477
1Ki 3:28 he had wisdom from God to administer **j**. H5477
1Ki 7: 7 the Hall of **J**, where he was to judge, H5477
1Ki 10: 9 you king to maintain **j** and righteousness." H5477
2Ch 9: 8 to maintain **j** and righteousness. H5477
Ezr 7:25 judges to **administer j** to all the A10169
Est 1:13 to consult experts in matters of law and **j**, H1907
Job 8: 3 Does God pervert **j**? Does the Almighty H5477
Job 9:19 And if it is a matter of **j**, who can H5477
Job 19: 7 though I call for help, there is no **j**. H5477
Job 27: 2 who has denied me **j**, the Almighty, H5477
Job 29:14 clothing; **j** was my robe and my turban. H5477
Job 31:13 "If I have denied **j** to any of my servants H5477
Job 34: 5 'I am innocent, but God denies me **j**. H5477
Job 34:12 that the Almighty would pervert **j**. H5477
Job 34:17 Can someone who hates **j** govern? Will H5477
Job 36: 3 from afar; I will ascribe **j** to my Maker. H7406

Job 36:17 judgment and **j** have taken hold of you. H5477
Job 37:23 in power; in his **j** and great righteousness H5477
Job 40: 8 "Would you discredit my **j**? Would you H5477
Ps 7: 6 Awake, my God; decree **j**. H5477
Ps 9:16 The LORD is known by his **acts of j**; the H5477
Ps 11: 7 righteous, he loves **j**; the upright will see H7407
Ps 33: 5 The LORD loves righteousness and **j**; the H5477
Ps 36: 6 mountains, your **j** like the great deep. H5477
Ps 45: 4 of truth, humility and **j**; let your right hand H7406
Ps 45: 6 a scepter of **j** will be the scepter of your H4793
Ps 50: 6 his righteousness, for he is a God *of* **j**. H5477
Ps 72: 1 Endow the king with your **j**, O God, the H5477
Ps 72: 2 righteousness, your afflicted ones with **j**. H5477
Ps 89:14 Righteousness and **j** are the foundation of H5477
Ps 97: 2 righteousness and **j** are the foundation of H5477
Ps 99: 4 is mighty, he loves **j**—you have H5477
Ps 101: 1 I will sing of your love and **j**; to you, LORD H5477
Ps 103: 6 righteousness and **j** for all the oppressed. H5477
Ps 112: 5 who conduct their affairs with **j**. H5477
Ps 140:12 the LORD secures **j** *for* the poor and H1907
Pr 8:20 of righteousness, along the paths of **j**, H5477
Pr 16:10 and his mouth does not betray **j**. H5477
Pr 17:23 bribes in secret to pervert the course of **j**. H5477
Pr 18: 5 wicked and so deprive the innocent of **j**. H5477
Pr 19:28 A corrupt witness mocks at **j**, and the H5477
Pr 21:15 When **j** is done, it brings joy to the H5477
Pr 29: 4 By **j** a king gives a country stability, but H5477
Pr 29: 7 The righteous care about **j** *for* the poor H1907
Pr 29:26 it is from the LORD that one gets **j**. H5477
Ecc 3:16 in the place of **j**—wickedness was there. H7406
Ecc 5: 8 in a district, and **j** and rights denied, do H5477
Isa 1:17 to do right; seek **j**. Defend the oppressed. H5477
Isa 1:21 She once was full of **j**; righteousness used H5477
Isa 1:27 Zion will be delivered with **j**, her penitent H5477
Isa 5: 7 And he looked for **j**, but saw bloodshed H5477
Isa 5:16 the LORD Almighty will be exalted by his **j**, H5477
Isa 5:23 a bribe, but deny **j** *to* the innocent. H7407
Isa 9: 7 upholding it with **j** and righteousness H5477
Isa 10: 2 rights and withhold **j** from the oppressed H5477
Isa 11: 4 with **j** he will give decisions for the poor H4793
Isa 16: 5 in judging seeks **j** and speeds the cause H5477
Isa 28: 6 will be a spirit of **j** to the one who sits in H5477
Isa 28:17 I will make **j** the measuring line and H5477
Isa 29:21 false testimony deprive the innocent of **j**. NDT
Isa 30:18 For the LORD is a God of **j**. Blessed are all H5477
Isa 32: 1 righteousness and rulers will rule with **j**. H5477
Isa 32:16 The LORD's **j** will dwell in the desert, his H5477
Isa 33: 5 will fill Zion with his **j** and righteousness. H5477
Isa 42: 1 on him, and he will bring **j** to the nations. H5477
Isa 42: 3 In faithfulness he will bring forth **j**; H5477
Isa 42: 4 discouraged till he establishes **j** on earth. H5477
Isa 51: 4 my **j** will become a light to the nations. H5477
Isa 51: 5 my arm *will* **bring j** *to* the nations. H9149
Isa 56: 1 "Maintain **j** and do what is right, for my H5477
Isa 59: 4 No one calls for **j**; no one pleads a case H7406
Isa 59: 8 do not know; there is no **j** in their paths. H5477
Isa 59: 9 So **j** is far from us, and righteousness H5477
Isa 59:11 We look for **j**, but find none; for H5477
Isa 59:14 So **j** is driven back, and righteousness H5477
Isa 59:15 was displeased that there was no **j**. H5477
Isa 61: 8 the LORD, love **j**; I hate robbery and H5477
Jer 5:28 have no limit; *they do* not **seek j**. H1906+1907
Jer 9:24 kindness, **j** and righteousness on earth H5477
Jer 12: 1 Yet I would speak with you about your **j** H5477
Jer 21:12 " 'Administer **j** every morning; rescue from H5477
La 3:36 to deprive them of **j**—would not the Lord H8190
Eze 22:29 mistreat the foreigner, denying them **j**. H5477
Eze 34:16 I will shepherd the flock with **j**. H5477
Hos 2:19 I will betroth you in righteousness and **j** H5477
Hos 12: 6 maintain love and **j**, and wait for your H5477
Am 2: 7 the ground and deny **j** *to* the oppressed. H2006
Am 5: 7 are those who turn **j** into bitterness and H5477
Am 5:10 who hate the *one who* **upholds j** in court H3519
Am 5:12 bribes and **deprive** the poor **of j** in the H5742
Am 5:15 love good; maintain **j** in the courts. H5477
Am 5:24 But let **j** roll on like a river, righteousness H5477
Am 6:12 But you have turned **j** into poison and the H5477
Mic 3: 1 Should you not embrace **j**, H5477
Mic 3: 8 the LORD, and with **j** and might, to declare H5477
Mic 3: 9 who despise **j** and distort all that is right; H5477
Hab 1: 4 the law is paralyzed, and **j** never prevails. H5477
Hab 1: 4 in the righteous, so that **j** is perverted. H5477
Zep 3: 5 Morning by morning he dispenses his **j** H5477
Zec 7: 9 'Administer true **j**; show mercy and H5477
Mal 2:17 with them" or "Where is the God of **j**?" H5477
Mal 3: 5 **deprive** the foreigners among you **of j**, H5742
Mt 12:18 and he will proclaim **j** to the nations. *G3213*
Mt 12:20 till he has brought **j** through to victory. *G3213*
Mt 23:23 matters of the law—**j**, mercy and *G3213*
Lk 11:42 you neglect **j** and the love of God. *G3213*
Lk 18: 3 '**Grant** me **j** against my adversary. *G1688*
Lk 18: 5 *I will see that* she **gets j**, so that she *G1688*
Lk 18: 7 not God bring about **j** for his chosen ones, *G1689*
Lk 18: 8 he will see that they get **j**, and quickly. *G1689*
Ac 8:33 In his humiliation he was deprived of **j** *G3213*
Ac 17:31 judge the world with **j** by the man he has *G1466*
Ac 28: 4 the **goddess J** has not allowed him to live." *G1472*
2Co 7:11 concern, what **readiness to see j done**. *G1689*
Heb 1: 8 a scepter *of* **j** will be the scepter of your *G2319*
Heb 11:33 administered **j**, and gained what was *G1466*
Rev 19:11 With **j** he judges and wages war. *G1466*

JUSTIFICATION (5) [JUST]

Eze 16:52 for *you have* **furnished** *some* **j** for your H7136
Ac 13:39 a **j** you were not able *to* **obtain** under the *G1467*
Ro 4:25 our sins and was raised to life for our **j**. *G1470*
Ro 5:16 followed many trespasses and brought **j**. *G1468*
Ro 5:18 act resulted in **j** and life for all people. *G1470*

JUSTIFIED (19) [JUST]

Ps 51: 4 right in your verdict and **j** when you judge. H2342
Lk 18:14 than the other, went home **j before God**. *G1467*
Ro 3:24 and *all are* **j** freely by his grace through *G1467*
Ro 3:28 For we maintain *that* a person *is* **j** by faith *G1467*
Ro 4: 2 Abraham *was* **j** by works, he had *G1467*
Ro 5: 1 *since we have been* **j** through faith *G1467*
Ro 5: 9 Since *we have* now *been* **j** by his blood *G1467*
Ro 8:30 those he called, *he* also **j**; those he *G1467*
Ro 8:30 justified; those *he* **j**, he also glorified. *G1467*
Ro 10:10 with your heart that you believe and are **j**, *G1466*
1Co 6:11 *you were* **j** in the name of the Lord Jesus *G1467*
Gal 2:16 know that a person *is* not **j** by the works of *G1467*
Gal 2:16 Christ Jesus that *we may be* **j** by faith in *G1467*
Gal 2:16 by the works of the law no one *will be* **j**. *G1467*
Gal 2:17 in seeking *to be* **j** in Christ, we Jews *G1467*
Gal 3:11 one who relies on the law *is* **j** before God, *G1467*
Gal 3:24 Christ came that *we might be* **j** by faith. *G1467*
Gal 5: 4 *You* who *are trying to be* **j** by the law have *G2934*
Titus 3: 7 *having been* **j** by his grace, we *G1467*

JUSTIFIES (3) [JUST]

Ro 3:26 be just and the *one who* **j** those who have *G1467*
Ro 4: 5 not work but trusts God *who* **j** the ungodly, *G1467*
Ro 8:33 whom God has chosen? It is God who **j**. *G1467*

JUSTIFY (7) [JUST]

Est 7: 4 no such distress *would* **j** disturbing the H8750
Job 40: 8 Would you condemn me to **j** *yourself*? H7405
Isa 53:11 my righteous servant *will* **j** many, H7405
Lk 10:29 But he wanted *to* **j** himself, so he asked *G1467*
Lk 16:15 "You are the *ones who* **j** yourselves in the *G1467*
Ro 3:30 who *will* **j** the circumcised by faith and the *G1467*
Gal 3: 8 foresaw that God *would* **j** the Gentiles by *G1467*

JUSTIFYING (1) [JUST]

Job 32: 2 angry with Job for **j** himself rather than H7405

JUSTLY (6) [JUST]

Ps 58: 1 Do you rulers indeed speak **j**? Do you H7406
Ps 106: 3 Blessed are those who act **j**, who always H5477
Jer 7: 5 your actions and deal with each other **j**, H5477
Mic 6: 8 To act **j** and to love mercy and to walk H5477
Lk 23:41 We are punished **j**, for we are getting *G1469*
1Pe 2:23 he entrusted himself to him who judges **j**. *G1469*

JUSTUS (3) [TITIUS]

Ac 1:23 also known as **J**) and Matthias. *G2688*
Ac 18: 7 went next door to the house of Titius **J**, *G2688*
Col 4:11 who is called **J**, also sends *G2688*

JUTTAH (3)

Jos 15:55 Carmel, Ziph, **J**, H3420
Jos 21:16 **J** and Beth Shemesh, together with H3420
1Ch 6:59 **J** and Beth Shemesh, together H3420

K

KABBON (1)

Jos 15:40 **K**, Lahmas, Kitlish, H3887

KABUL (2)

Jos 19:27 Emek and Neiel, passing **K** on the left. H3886
1Ki 9:13 And he called them the Land of **K**, H3886

KABZEEL (3)

Jos 15:21 boundary of Edom were: **K**, Eder, Jagur, H7696
2Sa 23:20 a valiant fighter from **K**, performed great H7696
1Ch 11:22 a valiant fighter from **K**, performed great H7696

KADESH (14) [EN MISHPAT, KADESH BARNEA, MERIBAH KADESH]

Ge 14: 7 **K**), and they conquered the whole H7729
Ge 16:14 it is still there, between **K** and Bered. H7729
Ge 20: 1 the Negev and lived between **K** and Shur. H7729
Nu 13:26 community at **K** in the Desert of Paran H7729
Nu 20: 1 at the Desert of Zin, and they stayed at **K**. H7729
Nu 20:14 messengers from **K** to the king of Edom, H7729
Nu 20:16 "Now we are here at **K**, a town on the H7729
Nu 20:22 set out from **K** and came to Mount Hor. H7729
Nu 33:36 They left Ezion Geber and camped at **K** H7729
Nu 33:37 They left **K** and camped at Mount Hor, on H7729
Dt 1:46 And so you stayed in **K** many days—all the H7729
Jdg 11:16 wilderness to the Red Sea and on to **K**. H7729
Jdg 11:17 he refused. So Israel stayed at **K**. H7729
Ps 29: 8 the LORD shakes the Desert of **K**. H7729

KADESH BARNEA (10) [KADESH]

Nu 32: 8 I sent them from **K** to look over the H7732
Nu 34: 4 on to Zin and go south of **K**. H7732
Dt 1: 2 go from Horeb to **K** by the Mount H7732
Dt 1:19 have seen, and so we reached **K**. H7732
Dt 2:14 the time we left **K** until we crossed H7732
Dt 9:23 the LORD sent you out from **K**, H7732
Jos 10:41 them from **K** to Gaza and from H7732
Jos 14: 6 man of God at **K** about you and H7732
Jos 14: 7 LORD sent me from **K** to explore the H7732
Jos 15: 3 went over to the south of **K**. H7732

KADMIEL (8)

Ezr 2:40 the descendants of Jeshua and **K** (of the H7718
Ezr 3: 9 his sons and brothers and **K** and his sons H7718
Ne 7:43 through **K** through the line of Hodaviah H7718
Ne 9: 4 were Jeshua, Bani, **K**, Shebaniah, Bunni, H7718
Ne 9: 5 Levites—Jeshua, **K**, Bani, Hashabneiah, H7718
Ne 10: 9 Binnui of the sons of Henadad, **K**, H7718
Ne 12: 8 Jeshua, Binnui, **K**, Sherebiah, Judah, H7718
Ne 12:24 Jeshua son of **K**, and their associates, H7718

KADMONITES (1)

Ge 15:19 the land of the Kenites, Kenizzites, **K**, H7720

KAIN (1)

Jos 15:57 **K**, Gibeah and Timnah—ten towns and H7805

KALKOL (2)

1Ki 4:31 wiser than Heman, **K** and Darda, the sons H4004
1Ch 2: 6 Heman, **K** and Darda—five in H4004

KALLAI (1)

Ne 12:20 of Sallu's, **K**; of Amok's, Eber; H7834

KALNEH (2)

Ge 10:10 Babylon, Uruk, Akkad and **K**, in Shinar. H4011
Am 6: 2 Go to **K** and look at it; go from there to H4011

KALNO (1)

Isa 10: 9 'Has not **K** fared like Carchemish? Is not H4012

KAMAI See LEB KAMAI

KAMON (1)

Jdg 10: 5 When Jair died, he was buried in **K**. H7852

KANAH (3)

Jos 16: 8 went west to the **K** Ravine and ended at H7867
Jos 17: 9 continued south to the **K** Ravine. H7867
Jos 19:28 Hammon and **K**, as far as Greater H7867

KANDAKE (1)

Ac 8:27 in charge of all the treasury *of* the **K** *G2833*

KANNEH (1)

Eze 27:23 **K** and Eden and merchants of Sheba H4034

KAR See BETH KAR

KAREAH (14)

2Ki 25:23 Johanan son of **K**, Seraiah son of H7945
Jer 40: 8 Johanan and Jonathan the sons of **K** H7945
Jer 40:13 Johanan son of **K** and all the army officers H7945
Jer 40:15 Then Johanan son of **K** said privately to H7945
Jer 40:16 son of Ahikam said to Johanan son of **K**, H7945
Jer 41:11 When Johanan son of **K** and all the army H7945
Jer 41:13 saw Johanan son of **K** and the army H7945
Jer 41:14 went over to Johanan son of **K**. H7945
Jer 41:16 Then Johanan son of **K** and all the army H7945
Jer 42: 1 Johanan son of **K** and Jezaniah son of H7945
Jer 42: 8 Johanan son of **K** and all the army H7945
Jer 43: 2 Johanan son of **K** and all the H7945
Jer 43: 4 So Johanan son of **K** and all the army H7945
Jer 43: 5 Johanan son of **K** and all the army officers H7945

KARKA (1)

Jos 15: 3 up to Addar and curved around to **K**. H7978

KARKAS (1)

Est 1:10 Abagtha, Zethar and **K**— H4139

KARKOR (1)

Jdg 8:10 Zalmunna were in **K** with a force of H7980

KARMI (8) [KARMITE]

Ge 46: 9 Hanok, Pallu, Hezron and **K**. H4145
Ex 6:14 were Hanok and Pallu, Hezron and **K**. H4145
Nu 26: 6 through **K**, the Karmite clan. H4145
Jos 7: 1 Achan son of **K**, the son of Zimri, H4145
Jos 7:18 Achan son of **K**, the son of Zimri, H4145
1Ch 2: 7 The son of **K**: Achar, who brought trouble H4145
1Ch 4: 1 Perez, Hezron, **K**, Hur and Shobal. H4145
1Ch 5: 3 Hanok, Pallu, Hezron and **K**. H4145

KARMITE (1) [KARMI]

Nu 26: 6 Hezronite clan; through Karmi, the **K** clan. H4146

KARNAIM (1) [ASHTEROTH KARNAIM]

Am 6:13 "Did we not take **K** by our own strength?" H7969

KARSHENA (1)

Est 1:14 closest to the king—**K**, Shethar, Admatha, H4161

KARTAH (2)

Jos 21:34 from the tribe of Zebulun, Jokneam, **K**, H7985
1Ch 6:77 received Jokneam, **K**, Rimmono and H7985

KARTAN (1)

Jos 21:32 Hammoth Dor and **K**, together with their H7986

K

KASIPHIA (2)
Ezr 8:17 them to go to Iddo, the leader in K. H4085
Ezr 8:17 the temple servants in K, so that they H4085

KASLUHITES (2)
Ge 10:14 Pathrusites, K (from whom the Philistines H4078
1Ch 1:12 Pathrusites, K (from whom the Philistines H4078

KATTATH (1)
Jos 19:15 Included were K, Nahalal, Shimron H7793

KATYDID (1)
Lev 11:22 any kind of locust, k, cricket or H6155

KAZIN See ETH KAZIN

KEBAR (8)
Eze 1: 1 I was among the exiles by the K River, H3894
Eze 1: 3 by the K River in the land of the H3894
Eze 3:15 who lived at Tel Aviv near the K River. H3894
Eze 3:23 like the glory I had seen by the K River H3894
Eze 10:15 living creatures I had seen by the K River. H3894
Eze 10:20 beneath the God of Israel by the K River, H3894
Eze 10:22 as those I had seen by the K River. H3894
Eze 43: 3 like the visions I had seen by the K River, H3894

KEDAR (11) [KEDAR'S]
Ge 25:13 the firstborn of Ishmael, K, Adbeel, H7723
1Ch 1:29 the firstborn of Ishmael, K, Adbeel, H7723
Ps 120: 5 Meshek, that I live among the tents of K! H7723
SS 1: 5 dark like the tents of K, like the tent H7723
Isa 21:16 all the splendor of K will come to an end. H7723
Isa 21:17 the warriors of K, will be few. H1201+7723
Isa 42:11 let the settlements where K lives rejoice. H7723
Jer 2:10 look, send to K and observe closely H7723
Jer 49:28 Concerning K and the kingdoms of Hazor H7723
Jer 49:28 attack K and destroy the people of H7723
Eze 27:21 all the princes of K were your customers; H7723

KEDAR'S (1) [KEDAR]
Isa 60: 7 All K flocks will be gathered to you, the H7723

KEDEMAH (2)
Ge 25:15 Tema, Jetur, Naphish and K. H7715
1Ch 1:31 Naphish and K. These were the H7715

KEDEMOTH (4)
Dt 2:26 From the Desert of K I sent messengers to H7717
Jos 13:18 K, Mephaath, H7717
Jos 21:37 K and Mephaath, together with their H7717
1Ch 6:79 K and Mephaath, together with their H7717

KEDESH (11)
Jos 12:22 the king of K one the king of Jokneam in H7730
Jos 15:23 K, Hazor, Ithnan, H7730
Jos 19:37 K, Edrei, En Hazor, H7730
Jos 20: 7 So they set apart K in Galilee in the hill H7730
Jos 21:32 tribe of Naphtali, K in Galilee (a city of H7730
Jdg 4: 6 of Abinoam from K *in* Naphtali and said H7730
Jdg 4: 9 So Deborah went with Barak to K. H7730
Jdg 4:11 by the great tree in Zaanannim near K. H7730
2Ki 15:29 Abel Beth Maakah, Janoah, K and Hazor. H7730
1Ch 6:72 from the tribe of Issachar they received K H7730
1Ch 6:76 of Naphtali they received K in Galilee, H7730

KEDORLAOMER (5)
Ge 14: 1 K king of Elam and Tidal king of Goyim H3906
Ge 14: 4 twelve years they had been subject to K, H3906
Ge 14: 5 K and the kings allied with him went out H3906
Ge 14: 9 against K king of Elam, Tidal king of H3906
Ge 14:17 from defeating K and the kings allied H3906

KEEN (1)
Da 5:12 found to have a k mind and knowledge A10339

KEEP (342) [KEEPER, KEEPERS, KEEPING, KEEPS, KEPT, SAFEKEEPING]
Ge 6:19 female, to k them **alive** with you. H2649
Ge 7: 3 to k their various kinds **alive** throughout H2649
Ge 14:21 me the people and k the goods for H4374
Ge 17: 9 "As for you, *you must* k my covenant, you H9068
Ge 17:10 after you, the covenant *you are to* k: H9068
Ge 18:19 after him *to* k the way of the LORD H9068
Ge 31:49 "*May* the LORD k **watch** between you and H7595
Ge 32:16 k some space between the herds. H8492
Ge 33: 9 K what you have for yourself. H2118
Ge 38: 9 on the ground to k **from** providing H1194
Ge 38:23 Judah said, "*Let her* k what she has, or H4374
Ge 42: 1 "Why *do you just* k **looking at each other**?" AIT
Ge 47:24 four-fifths you *may* k as seed for H2118+4200
Ex 5: 9 the people so that *they* k **working** and pay no AIT
Ex 5:17 That is why you k **saying**, 'Let us go and AIT
Ex 12:42 the Israelites are to k vigil to honor the H4200
Ex 13:10 *You must* k this ordinance at the H9068
Ex 15:26 to his commands and k all his decrees, H9068
Ex 16:19 "No one *is to* k any of it until morning." H3855
Ex 16:23 whatever is left and k it until morning. H5466
Ex 16:28 will you refuse to k my commands and my H9068
Ex 16:32 an omer of manna and k it for the H5466
Ex 19: 5 if you obey me fully and k my covenant, H9068
Ex 20: 6 who love me and k my commandments. H9068
Ex 20:20 will be with you to k you **from** sinning." H1194
Ex 21:36 the owner *did* not k it **penned up**, the H9068
Ex 27:21 his sons *are to* k the lamps burning H6885
Lev 7: 8 offering for anyone *may* k its hide for H2118
Lev 13:33 the priest *is to* k them **isolated** another H6037
Lev 15:31 " '*You must* k the Israelites **separate** from H5692
Lev 18: 5 K my decrees and laws, for the person who H9068
Lev 18:26 But you *must* k my decrees and my laws H9068
Lev 18:30 K my requirements and do not follow any H9068
Lev 19:19 " 'K my decrees. " 'Do not mate different H9068
Lev 19:37 " 'K all my decrees and all my laws and H9068
Lev 20: 8 K my decrees and follow them. I am the H9068
Lev 20:22 " 'K all my decrees and laws and follow H9068
Lev 22:31 "K my commands and follow them. H9068
Lev 26: 9 and *I will* k my covenant with you. H7756
Nu 6:24 " ' "The LORD bless you and k you; H9068
Nu 11:13 *They* k **wailing** to me, 'Give us AIT
Nu 15:22 unintentionally fail *to* k any of these H6913
Nu 22:16 *Do* not *let anything* k *you* from coming to H4979
Nu 36: 7 every Israelite *shall* k the tribal H1815
Nu 36: 9 each Israelite tribe *is to* k the land it H1815
Dt 4: 2 k the commands of the LORD your God H9068
Dt 4:40 K his decrees and commands, which I am H9068
Dt 5:10 who love me and k my commandments. H9068
Dt 5:29 to fear me and k all my commands always H9068
Dt 6:17 **Be sure to** k the commands of the H9068+9068
Dt 7: 9 who love him and k his commandments. H9068
Dt 7:12 the LORD your God *will* k his covenant of H9068
Dt 7:15 LORD *will* k you **free** from every disease. H6073
Dt 8: 2 not *you would* k his commands. H9068
Dt 11: 1 the LORD your God and k his requirements, H9068
Dt 13: 4 K his commands and obey him; serve him H9068
Dt 22: 2 it home with you and k it until they come H2118
Dt 23: 9 enemies, k away from everything impure. H9068
Dt 26:17 that you *will* k his decrees H9068
Dt 26:18 that you *are to* k all his commands. H9068
Dt 27: 1 "K all these commands that I give you H9068
Dt 28: 9 if *you* k the commands of the LORD your H9068
Dt 28:41 daughters but you *will* not k them, H2118+4200
Dt 30:10 LORD your God and k his commands and H9068
Dt 30:16 and to k his commands, decrees H9068
Jos 1: 8 K this Book of the Law *always* on H4631+4202
Jos 3: 4 But k a distance of about two thousand H2118
Jos 6:18 But k **away** from the devoted things, so H9068
Jos 7:11 covenant, which I commanded them to k. NDT
Jos 22: 5 be very careful to k the commandment H6913
Jos 22: 5 obedience to him, to k his commands, to H9068
Jdg 2:22 see whether they *will* k the way of the H9068
Jdg 6:11 in a winepress to k it from the Midianites. H5674
1Sa 2: 3 "*Do* not k talking so proudly or let your H8049
1Sa 6: 9 but *k* **watching** it. If it goes up to its own AIT
2Sa 7:25 k forever the promise you have made H7756
2Sa 13:13 *he will* not k me from being married to H4979
2Sa 14:18 "Don't k from me the answer to what I am H3948
1Ki 1: 1 he *could* not *k* **warm** even when they put AIT
1Ki 1: 2 him so that our lord the king *may* k **warm**." AIT
1Ki 2: 3 and k his decrees and commands H9068
1Ki 2: 4 that the LORD *may* k his promise to me H7756
1Ki 2:43 Why then *did you* not k your oath to the H9068
1Ki 3:14 in obedience to me and k my decrees H9068
1Ki 6:12 my laws and k all my commands and H9068
1Ki 8:23 you *who* k your covenant of love with your H9068
1Ki 8:25 k for your servant David my father the H9068
1Ki 8:58 obedience to him and k the commands, H9068
1Ki 11:10 Solomon *did* not k the LORD's command. H9068
1Ki 15: 5 LORD and *had* not **failed to** k any of H6073+4946
1Ki 18: 5 *to* k the horses and mules **alive** so we H2649
2Ki 10:31 was not careful to k the law of the H2143+928
2Ki 17:15 the statutes *he had* **warned** them **to** k. H6386
2Ki 17:19 even Judah *did* not k the commands H9068
2Ki 17:37 always be careful to k the decrees and H6913
2Ki 21: 8 them and will k the whole Law that my NDT
2Ki 23: 3 to follow the LORD and k his commands H9068
1Ch 4:10 k me from harm so that I will be free H6913
1Ch 10:13 *he did* not k the word of the LORD and H9068
1Ch 22:12 so that you *may* k the law of the LORD your H9068
1Ch 29:18 k these desires and thoughts in the hearts H9068
1Ch 29:18 and k their hearts **loyal** to you. H3922
1Ch 29:19 devotion to k your commands, H9068
2Ch 2:18 over them to k the people **working**. H6268
2Ch 6:14 you *who* k your covenant of love with your H9068
2Ch 6:16 k for your servant David my father the H9068
2Ch 23: 4 the Sabbath are to k **watch** *at* the doors, H8788
2Ch 34:31 to follow the LORD and k his commands H9068
Ne 1: 5 who love him and k his commandments, H9068
Ne 5:13 anyone who *does* not k this promise. H7756
Ne 9:34 the statutes *you* **warned** them **to** k. H6386
Ne 13:22 gates in order to k the Sabbath day **holy**. H7727
Est 3: 8 your kingdom *who* k *themselves* **separate**. H7233
Est 3:11 "K the money," the king said to Haman H5989
Job 4: 2 But who can k from speaking? H6806
Job 7:11 "Therefore I *will* not k **silent**; I will H3104+7023
Job 13:13 "*K* **silent** and let me speak; then let come to AIT
Job 13:27 *you* k **close watch on** all my paths by H9068
Job 14:16 count my steps but not k **track of** my sin. H9068
Job 16: 3 What ails you that *you k* on **arguing**? AIT
Job 22:15 *Will you* k *to* the old path that the wicked H9068
Job 30:10 They detest me and k *their* **distance**; they H8178
Job 33:17 from wrongdoing and k them from pride, H4059
Job 34:30 to k the godless from ruling, from laying NDT
Job 36: 6 *He does* not k the wicked **alive** but gives H2649
Job 41: 3 *Will it* k begging you for mercy? Will it H8049
Ps 12: 7 *will* k the needy **safe** and will protect us H9068
Ps 16: 1 K me **safe**, my God, for in you I take H9068
Ps 16: 8 *I* k my eyes always *on* the LORD. With him H8751
Ps 17: 8 K me as the apple of your eye; hide me in H9068
Ps 18:28 k my lamp **burning**; my God turns my H239
Ps 19:13 K your servant also from willful sins; may H3104
Ps 22:29 *those who* cannot k themselves **alive**. H2649
Ps 25:10 toward *those who* k the demands of H5915
Ps 27: 5 day of trouble *he will* k me **safe** in his H7621
Ps 31: 4 K me **free** from the trap that is set for me H3655
Ps 31:20 *you* k them **safe** in your dwelling from H7621
Ps 33:19 from death and k them **alive** in famine. H2649
Ps 34:13 k your tongue from evil and your lips from H5915
Ps 37:34 Hope in the LORD and k his way. He will H9068
Ps 39: 1 watch my ways and k my tongue from sin; NDT
Ps 78: 7 his deeds but *would* k his commands. H5915
Ps 78:10 *they did* not k God's covenant and refused H9068
Ps 78:56 the Most High; *they did* not k his statutes. H9068
Ps 89:31 my decrees and fail *to* k my commands, H9068
Ps 103:18 with *those who* k his covenant and H9068
Ps 105:45 that *they might* k his precepts and observe H9068
Ps 106:23 the breach before him to k his wrath from H8740
Ps 119: 2 Blessed are *those who* k his statutes and H5915
Ps 119:22 scorn and contempt, for *I* k your statutes. H5915
Ps 119:29 K me from deceitful ways; be gracious to H6073
Ps 119:34 so that *I may* k your law and obey it with H5915
Ps 119:55 your name, that *I may* k your law. H9068
Ps 119:69 I k your precepts with all my heart. H5915
Ps 119:115 that *I may* k the commands of my God! H5915
Ps 119:146 save me and *I will* k your statutes. H9068
Ps 121: 7 The LORD *will* k you from all harm—he H9068
Ps 132:12 If your sons k my covenant and the H9068
Ps 140: 4 K me **safe**, LORD, from the hands of the H9068
Ps 141: 3 k watch over the door of my lips. NDT
Ps 141: 9 K me **safe** from the traps set by evildoers H9068
Pr 2:20 ways of the good and k *to* the paths of the H9068
Pr 3: 1 but k my commands *in* your heart, H5915
Pr 3:26 be at your side and *will* k your foot from H9068
Pr 4: 4 all your heart; k my commands, and you H9068
Pr 4:21 out of your sight, k them within your heart H9068
Pr 4:24 K your mouth **free** of perversity; keep H6073
Pr 4:24 perversity; k corrupt talk **far** from your lips. H8178
Pr 4:27 the right or the left; k your foot from evil. H6073
Pr 5: 8 K *to* a path **far** from her, do not go near H8178
Pr 6:20 k your father's command and do not H5915
Pr 7: 1 k my words and store up my commands H9068
Pr 7: 2 K my commands and you will live; guard H9068
Pr 7: 5 They *will* k you from the adulterous H9068
Pr 8:32 blessed are *those who* k my ways. H9068
Pr 12:23 prudent k their knowledge *to themselves*, H4059
Pr 15:24 the prudent to k them from going H6073
Pr 17:28 fools are thought wise if *they* k **silent**, H3087
Pr 20:28 Love and faithfulness k a king **safe** H5915
Pr 21:23 their tongues k themselves from H9068
Pr 22: 3 the simple *k* **going** and pay the penalty. AIT
Pr 22:12 eyes of the LORD k **watch over** knowledge, H5915
Pr 22:18 is pleasing when *you* k them in your heart H9068
Pr 27:12 the simple *k* **going** and pay the penalty. AIT
Pr 30: 8 K falsehood and lies **far** from me; give me H8178
Ecc 3: 6 a time to k and a time to throw away H9068
Ecc 4:11 if two lie down together, they will k **warm**. AIT
Ecc 4:11 But how *can* one *k* **warm** alone? AIT
Ecc 12:13 Fear God and k his commandments, for H9068
Isa 7: 4 'Be careful, k **calm** and don't be afraid. AIT
Isa 7:21 a person *will* k **alive** a young cow and two H2649
Isa 19:21 will make vows to the LORD and k them. H8966
Isa 26: 3 *You will* k in perfect peace those whose H5915
Isa 28:24 *Does he k on* **breaking up** and working the AIT
Isa 29:23 my hands, *they will* k my name **holy**; they H7727
Isa 33:15 gain from extortion and k their hands from H5850
Isa 42: 6 *I will* k you and will make you to be a H5915
Isa 46: 8 "Remember this, k it **in mind**, take it to H899
Isa 47:12 "K **on**, then, with your magic spells and H6641
Isa 49: 8 *I will* k you and will make you to be a H5915
Isa 56: 4 "To the eunuchs who k my Sabbaths, who H9068
Isa 56: 6 all *who* k the Sabbath without desecrating H9068
Isa 58:13 "If *you* k your feet from breaking the H8740
Isa 62: 1 For Zion's sake *I will* not k **silent**, for AIT
Isa 64:12 *Will you* k **silent** and punish us beyond AIT
Isa 65: 5 who say, 'K **away**; don't come H7928+448+3870
Isa 65: 6 *I will* not k **silent** but will pay back in full; AIT
Jer 4:19 within me, *I* cannot k **silent**. For I have heard AIT
Jer 11: 8 them to follow but that *they did* not k. H6913
Jer 13:14 compassion to k me **from** destroying them H4946
Jer 14:13 The prophets *k* **telling** them, 'You will not AIT
Jer 15: 6 "*You* k **on** backsliding. H2143
Jer 16:11 They forsook me and *did* not k my law. H9068
Jer 17:15 They *k* **saying** to me, "Where is the word of AIT
Jer 17:18 to shame, but *k* me from **shame**; let them be AIT
Jer 17:18 let them be terrified, but *k* me from **terror**. AIT
Jer 17:22 Sabbath, but k the Sabbath day **holy**, as I H7727
Jer 17:24 k the Sabbath day **holy** by not doing H7727
Jer 17:27 obey me to k the Sabbath day **holy** by not H7727
Jer 23:17 *They* k **saying** to those who despise H606+606
Jer 23:37 This is what *you* k **saying** to a prophet: 'What AIT
Jer 42: 4 says and *will* k nothing **back** from you." H4979
Jer 44:25 do what you promised! K your vows! H7756+7756
Jer 49:11 fatherless children; *I will* k them **alive**. H2649
Jer 50: 2 proclaim it; k nothing **back**, but say, H3948
La 1:11 food to k **themselves alive**. H8740+5883
La 1:19 *to* k **themselves alive**. H8740+906+5883+4392
Eze 11:20 my decrees and be careful *to* k my laws. H6913
Eze 18:19 has been careful *to* k all my decrees, H6913
Eze 20: 9 I did it to k my name **from** being profaned H1194

Eze 20:14 I did what would **k** it **from** being profaned H1194
Eze 20:18 of your parents or **k** their laws or defile H9068
Eze 20:19 my decrees and be careful *to* **k** my laws. H6913
Eze 20:20 **K** my Sabbaths **holy**, that they may be a H7727
Eze 20:21 they were not careful to **k** my laws, of H6913
Eze 20:22 I did what would **k** it **from** being profaned H1194
Eze 24:17 *K* your turban **fastened** and your sandals on AIT
Eze 24:23 You will **k** your turbans on your heads and NDT
Eze 36:27 my decrees and be careful *to* **k** my laws. H6913
Eze 37:24 my laws and be careful *to* **k** my decrees. H6913
Eze 44:20 *they are to* **k** *the* **hair** of their heads **trimmed** H4080+4080
Eze 44:24 *They are to* **k** my laws and my decrees H9068
Eze 44:24 and *they are to* **k** my Sabbaths **holy**. H7727
Eze 46:17 the servant *may* **k** it until the year H2118+4200
Da 5:17 "You *may* **k** your gifts for yourself and A10201
Da 9: 4 who love him and **k** his commandments, H9068
Am 5:13 the prudent **k quiet** in such times, H1957
Am 9: 4 "*I will* **k** my eye on them for harm and not H8492
Hab 1:17 Is he to **k on** emptying his net, destroying H9458
Zec 3: 7 obedience to me and **k** my requirements, H9068
Zec 11:12 give me my pay; but if not, **k** it. H2532
Zec 12: 4 "*I will* **k** a **watchful** eye over Judah, but I H7219
Mt 6: 7 you pray, *do* not **k** *on* **babbling** like pagans AIT
Mt 10:10 a staff, for the worker is worth his **k**. *G5575*
Mt 19:17 want to enter life, **k** the commandments." *G5498*
Mt 24:42 "Therefore **k watch**, because you do not *G1213*
Mt 25:13 "Therefore **k watch**, because you do not *G1213*
Mt 26:38 Stay here and **k watch** with me." *G1213*
Mt 26:40 you men **k watch** with me for one *G1213*
Mt 28:14 will satisfy him and **k** you out of trouble." *G4472*
Mk 3: 9 to **k** the people **from** crowding him. *G3590*
Mk 7:24 yet he could not **k** his presence **secret**. *G3291*
Mk 13:34 tells the one at the door to **k watch**. *G1213*
Mk 13:35 "Therefore **k watch** because you do not *G1213*
Mk 14:34 he said to them. "Stay here and **k watch**." *G1213*
Mk 14:37 Couldn't you **k watch** for one hour? *G1213*
Lk 4:42 *they tried to* **k** him from leaving them. *G2988*
Lk 12:35 ready for service and *k* your lamps **burning**, AIT
Lk 13:32 '*I will* **k** *on* **driving out** demons and healing AIT
Lk 17:33 Whoever tries *to* **k** their life will lose it *G4347*
Lk 18: 7 day and night? *Will he* **k putting** them **off**? AIT
Lk 19:40 he replied, "if they *k* **quiet**, the stones will cry AIT
Jn 4:15 get thirsty and *have to k* **coming** here to draw AIT
Jn 9:16 from God, for *he does* not **k** the Sabbath." *G5498*
Jn 10:24 *will you* **k** us in **suspense**? *G3836+6034+149*
Jn 12:25 life in this world *will* **k** it for eternal life. *G5875*
Jn 12:47 hears my words but *does* not **k** them, *G5875*
Jn 14:15 "If you love me, **k** my commands. *G5498*
Jn 15:10 If *you* **k** my commands, you will remain in *G5498*
Jn 15:18 hates you, **k in mind** that it hated me first. *G1182*
Jn 18:18 around a fire they had made *to* **k warm**. AIT
Ac 2:24 impossible for death *to k its* **hold on** him. AIT
Ac 15: 5 required *to* **k** the law of Moses. *G5498*
Ac 18: 9 not be afraid; *k* **on speaking**, do not be silent AIT
Ac 20:28 **K watch over** yourselves and all the flock *G4668*
Ac 24:16 So I strive always *to* **k** my conscience clear *G2400*
Ac 24:23 centurion *to* **k** Paul **under guard** but to *G5498*
Ac 27:22 But now I urge you *to* **k up** your **courage** *G2313*
Ac 27:25 So **k up** *your* **courage**, men, for I have faith *G2313*
Ro 2:26 are not circumcised **k** the law's *G5875*
Ro 7:19 evil I do not want to do—this *I k* **on doing**. AIT
Ro 12:11 but *k* your spiritual **fervor**, serving the AIT
Ro 14:22 about these things **k** between yourself *G2400*
Ro 16:17 you have learned. **K away** from them. *G1712*
1Co 1: 8 He *will* also **k** you **firm** to the end, so that *G1011*
1Co 5: 8 Therefore *let us* **k the Festival**, not with the *G2037*
1Co 7:30 something, as if it *were* not *theirs to* **k**; *G2988*
1Co 10: 6 as examples to **k** us from setting our *G1639*
1Co 14:28 the speaker *should k* **quiet** in the church AIT
2Co 11:12 And *I will* **k on doing** what I am doing in AIT
2Co 12: 7 in order to **k** me **from** becoming conceited, *G3590*
Gal 5: 7 cut in on you to **k** you **from** obeying the *G3590*
Gal 5:25 the Spirit, *let us* **k in step with** the Spirit. *G5123*
Gal 6:13 even those who are circumcised **k** the law, *G5875*
Eph 1:17 I **k** asking that the God of our Lord Jesus NDT
Eph 4: 3 every effort *to* **k** the unity of the Spirit *G5498*
Eph 6:18 be alert and always **k on** praying for all *G4675*
Php 3:17 **k** *your* **eyes on** those who live as we do. *G5023*
1Th 2:16 *in their effort to* **k** us **from** speaking to the *G3266*
2Th 3: 6 *to* **k away** from every believer who is idle *G5097*
1Ti 3: 9 *They must* **k hold of** the deep truths of the *G2400*
1Ti 5:21 to **k** these instructions without partiality *G5875*
1Ti 5:22 in the sins of others. **K** yourself pure. *G5498*
1Ti 6:14 *to* **k** this command without spot or blame *G5498*
2Ti 1:13 **k** as the pattern of sound teaching *G2400*
2Ti 2:14 **K reminding** God's people of these things AIT
2Ti 4: 5 **k** *your* **head** in all situations *G3768*
Phm 13 I would have liked *to* **k** him with me so *G2988*
Heb 9:20 which God *has* **commanded** you to **k**." *G1948*
Heb 10:26 *If* we deliberately *k* **on sinning** after we have AIT
Heb 13: 1 **K on** loving one another as brothers and *G3531*
Heb 13: 5 **K** your lives free from the love of money NDT
Heb 13:17 because they **k watch** over you as those who *G70*
Jas 1:26 and *yet do* not **k a tight rein on** their *G5902*
Jas 1:27 their distress and *to* **k** oneself from being *G5498*
Jas 2: 8 If *you* really **k** the royal law found in *G5464*
Jas 2:16 "Go in peace; *k* **warm** and well fed," but AIT
Jas 3: 2 able *to* **k** their whole body **in check**. *G5902*
1Pe 3:10 days *must* **k** their tongue **from** evil and *G4264*
2Pe 1: 8 *they will* **k** you from being ineffective and *G2770*
1Jn 2: 3 come to know him if *we* **k** his commands. *G5498*
1Jn 3:22 because *we* **k** his commands and do what *G5498*
1Jn 5: 3 is love for God: to **k** his commands. *G5498*
1Jn 5:21 Dear children, **k** yourselves from idols. *G5875*
Jude 6 the angels who *did* not **k** their positions *G5498*
Jude 21 **k** yourselves in God's love as you wait for *G5498*
Jude 24 To him who is able *to* **k** you from *G5875*
Rev 3:10 I *will* also **k** you from the hour of trial that *G5498*
Rev 12:17 those *who* **k** God's commands and hold *G5498*
Rev 14:12 people of God who **k** his commands and *G5498*
Rev 20: 3 to **k** him **from** deceiving the nations *G3590*
Rev 22: 9 prophets and *with all* who **k** the words of *G5498*

KEEPER (8) [KEEP]

Ge 4: 9 he replied. "Am I my brother's **k**?" H9068
1Sa 17:22 David left his things with the **k** *of* supplies H9068
2Ki 10:22 Jehu said to the **k** *of* the wardrobe, H889+6584[S]
2Ki 22:14 the son of Harhas, **k** *of* the wardrobe. H9068
2Ch 31:14 the Levite, **k of** the East **Gate**, was in H8788
2Ch 34:22 the son of Hasrah, **k** *of* the wardrobe. H9068
Ne 2: 8 a letter to Asaph, **k** *of* the royal park, so H9068
Jn 12: 6 he was a thief; *as* **k** of the money bag, he *G2400*

KEEPERS (1) [KEEP]

Ecc 12: 3 when the **k** *of* the house tremble, and the H9068

KEEPING (42) [KEEP]

Ge 26: 5 I required of him, **k** my commands, my NDT
Ge 41:49 that he stopped **k records** because it was H6218
Ex 20: 8 "Remember the Sabbath day by **k** it **holy**. H7727
Dt 5:12 "Observe the Sabbath day by **k** it **holy**, as H7727
Dt 6: 2 long as you live by **k** all his decrees and H9068
Dt 7: 9 **k** his covenant of love to a thousand H9068
Dt 13:18 the LORD your God by **k** all his commands H9068
Jdg 8: 4 exhausted yet *k up the* **pursuit**, came to the AIT
1Sa 6:12 **k** on the road and lowing **all the way** H2143+2143
1Sa 17:34 servant has been **k** his father's sheep. H8286
1Sa 25:33 judgment and for **k** me from bloodshed H3973
1Ki 17:16 **in k with** the word of the LORD spoken by H3869
2Ki 7: 9 of good news and we *are* **k it to ourselves**. H3120
2Ch 8:14 **In k with** the ordinance of his father David H3869
Est 1: 7 abundant, **in k with** the king's liberality. H3869
Ps 19:11 is warned; in **k** them there is great reward. H9068
Ps 119:112 My heart is set on **k** your decrees to the H6913
Pr 6:24 **k** you from your neighbor's wife, from the H9068
Pr 15: 3 **k watch** *on* the wicked and the good. H7595
Isa 65: 4 spend their nights **k secret vigil**; H5915
Eze 14: 4 answer them myself **in k with** their great H928
Eze 17:14 to rise again, surviving only by **k** his treaty. H9068
Eze 22:26 they shut their eyes to the **k** of my Sabbaths, NDT
Da 9:16 **in k with** all your righteous acts, turn H3869
Zec 9: 8 people, for now *I am* **k watch**. H8011+928+6524
Mt 3: 8 Produce fruit **in k with** repentance. *G545*
Lk 2: 8 **k watch** over their flocks at night. *G5875+5871*
Lk 2:24 offer a sacrifice **in k with** what is said in *G2848*
Lk 3: 8 Produce fruit **in k with** repentance. And do *G545*
Lk 20:20 **K a close watch on** him, they sent spies *G4190*
Ac 14:18 *they had* difficulty **k** the crowd from *G2924*
Ro 16:25 **in k with** the revelation of the mystery *G2848*
1Co 7:19 **K** God's commands is what counts *G5499*
1Co 16: 2 of money **in k with** your *G4005+5516+1569*
Gal 5:14 entire law is fulfilled **in** *k* this one command: AIT
1Ti 1:18 this command **in k with** the prophecies *G2848*
2Ti 1: 1 **in k with** the promise of life that is in *G2848*
Heb 11: 7 of the righteousness that is **in k with** faith. *G2848*
Jas 4:11 the law, you are not **k** it, but sitting in *G4475*
1Pe 3:16 **k** a clear conscience, so that those who *G2400*
2Pe 3: 9 The Lord is not slow *in k* his **promise**, as AIT
2Pe 3:13 But **in k with** his promise we are looking *G2848*

KEEPS (37) [KEEP]

Jdg 5:29 indeed, she **k saying** to herself, H8740+609
1Sa 17:25 "Do you see how this man *k* **coming out**? AIT
2Sa 22:33 me with strength and **k** my way secure. H5989
Ne 1: 5 *who* **k** his covenant of love with those who H9068
Ne 9:32 awesome, *who* **k** his covenant of love H9068
Job 24:15 will see me,' and *he* **k** his face concealed. H8492
Job 33:11 *he* **k close watch** on all my paths. H9068
Job 34: 8 *He* **k company** with evildoers H782+4200+2495
Ps 15: 4 *who* **k an oath** even when it hurts H8678
Ps 18:32 me with strength and **k** my way secure. H5989
Pr 11:13 a trustworthy person **k** a secret. H4059
Pr 15:21 has understanding **k** a **straight** course. H3837
Pr 17:24 A discerning person **k** wisdom in view, but a NDT
Pr 18:18 disputes and **k** strong opponents **apart**. H7233
Pr 19:16 *Whoever* **k** commandments keeps their H9068
Pr 19:16 keeps commandments **k** their life, H9068
Ecc 5:20 because God **k** them **occupied** with H6701
Isa 26: 2 nation may enter, the nation *that* **k** faith. H9068
Isa 56: 2 *who* **k** the Sabbath without desecrating it H9068
Isa 56: 2 and **k** their hands from doing any evil." H9068
Isa 65: 5 in my nostrils, a fire *that* **k burning** all day. AIT
Jer 23:35 is what each of *you* **k saying** to your friends AIT
Jer 48:10 A curse on *anyone who* **k** their sword from H4979
Eze 18: 9 my decrees and faithfully **k** my laws. H9068
Eze 18:17 *He* **k** my laws and follows my decrees H6913
Eze 18:21 have committed and **k** all my decrees H9068
Da 9: 4 *who* **k** his covenant of love with those who H9068
Mt 15:23 "Send her away, for *she k* **crying out** after us." AIT
Lk 18: 5 because this widow *k* **bothering** me, I will AIT
Jn 7:19 Yet not one of you **k** the law. Why are you *G4472*
Jn 14:21 my commands and **k** them is the one who *G5498*
1Co 13: 5 easily angered, *it* **k** no **record** of wrongs. *G3357*
Jas 2:10 For whoever **k** the whole law and yet *G5498*
1Jn 3: 6 No one who lives in him *k on* **sinning**. No one AIT
1Jn 3:24 The *one who* **k** God's commands lives in *G5498*
1Jn 5:18 One who was born of God **k** them **safe**, *G5498*
Rev 22: 7 Blessed is the *one who* **k** the words of the *G5498*

KEHELATHAH (2)

Nu 33:22 They left Rissah and camped at **K**. H7739
Nu 33:23 They left **K** and camped at Mount H7739

KEILAH (18)

Jos 15:44 **K**, Akzib and Mareshah—nine towns and H7881
1Sa 23: 1 are fighting against **K** and are looting the H7881
1Sa 23: 2 attack the Philistines and save **K**. H7881
1Sa 23: 3 if we go to **K** against the Philistine forces!" H7881
1Sa 23: 4 "Go down to **K**, for I am going to H7881
1Sa 23: 5 So David and his men went to **K**, fought H7881
1Sa 23: 5 the Philistines and saved the people of **K**. H7881
1Sa 23: 6 with him when he fled to David at **K**.) H7881
1Sa 23: 7 Saul was told that David had gone to **K** H7881
1Sa 23: 8 to go down to **K** to besiege David and his H7881
1Sa 23:10 plans to come to **K** and destroy the town H7881
1Sa 23:11 Will the citizens of **K** surrender me to him H7881
1Sa 23:12 the citizens of **K** surrender me and my H7881
1Sa 23:13 left **K** and kept moving from place to H7881
1Sa 23:13 was told that David had escaped from **K**, H7881
1Ch 4:19 the father of **K** the Garmite, and H7881
Ne 3:17 ruler of half the district of **K**, carried out H7881
Ne 3:18 ruler of the other half-district of **K**. H7881

KELAIAH (1) [KELITA]

Ezr 10:23 Jozabad, Shimei, **K** (that is, Kelita) H7835

KELAL (1)

Ezr 10:30 **K**, Benaiah, Maaseiah, Mattaniah H4006

KELITA (3) [KELAIAH]

Ezr 10:23 Kelaiah (that is, **K**), Pethahiah, Judah H7836
Ne 8: 7 Hodiah, Maaseiah, **K**, Azariah, Jozabad H7836
Ne 10:10 Shebaniah, Hodiah, **K**, Pelaiah, Hanan, H7836

KELUB (2)

1Ch 4:11 **K**, Shuhah's brother, was the father of H3991
1Ch 27:26 Ezri son of **K** was in charge of the workers H3991

KELUHI (1)

Ezr 10:35 Benaiah, Bedeiah, **K**, H3988

KEMUEL (3)

Ge 22:21 Buz his brother, **K** (the father of Aram), H7851
Nu 34:24 **K** son of Shiphtan, the leader from the H7851
1Ch 27:17 Hashabiah son of **K**; over Aaron: Zadok; H7851

KENAANAH (5)

1Ki 22:11 Now Zedekiah son of **K** had made iron H4049
1Ki 22:24 Zedekiah son of **K** went up and slapped H4049
1Ch 7:10 Benjamin, Ehud, **K**, Zethan, Tarshish and H4049
2Ch 18:10 Now Zedekiah son of **K** had made iron H4049
2Ch 18:23 Zedekiah son of **K** went up and slapped H4049

KENAN (7)

Ge 5: 9 lived 90 years, he became the father of **K**. H7809
Ge 5:10 After he became the father of **K**, Enosh H7809
Ge 5:12 When **K** had lived 70 years, he became H7809
Ge 5:13 **K** lived 840 years and had other sons and H7809
Ge 5:14 Altogether, **K** lived a total of 910 years H7809
1Ch 1: 2 **K**, Mahalalel, Jared, H7809
Lk 3:37 the son of Mahalalel, the son *of* **K**, *G2783*

KENANI (1)

Ne 9: 4 Shebaniah, Bunni, Sherebiah, Bani and **K**. H4039

KENANIAH (3)

1Ch 15:22 **K** the head Levite was in charge of the H4041
1Ch 15:27 the musicians, and **K**, who was in charge H4040
1Ch 26:29 **K** and his sons were assigned duties away H4041

KENATH (2)

Nu 32:42 And Nobah captured **K** and its surrounding H7875
1Ch 2:23 as well as **K** with its surrounding H7875

KENAZ (11)

Ge 36:11 Teman, Omar, Zepho, Gatam and **K**. H7869
Ge 36:15 Chiefs Teman, Omar, Zepho, **K**, H7869
Ge 36:42 **K**, Teman, Mibzar, H7869
Jos 15:17 Othniel son of **K**, Caleb's brother, took it H7869
Jdg 1:13 Othniel son of **K**, Caleb's younger brother H7869
Jdg 3: 9 Othniel son of **K**, Caleb's younger brother, H7869
Jdg 3:11 forty years, until Othniel son of **K** died. H7869
1Ch 1:36 Zepho, Gatam and **K**; by Timna: H7869
1Ch 1:53 **K**, Teman, Mibzar, H7869
1Ch 4:13 The sons of **K**: Othniel and Seraiah. H7869
1Ch 4:15 Elah and Naam. The son of Elah: **K**. H7869

KENITE (5) [KENITES]

Jdg 1:16 father-in-law, the **K**, went up from the City H7808
Jdg 4:11 Now Heber the **K** had left the other H7808
Jdg 4:17 the wife of Heber the **K**, because there H7808
Jdg 4:17 of Hazor and the family of Heber the **K**. H7808
Jdg 5:24 the wife of Heber the **K**, most blessed of H7808

KENITES (9) [KENITE]

Ge 15:19 the land of the **K**, Kenizzites, Kadmonites, H7808
Nu 24:21 Then he saw the **K** and spoke his H7808
Nu 24:22 you **K** will be destroyed when Ashur H7804

K

Jdg 4:11 Heber the Kenite had left the other **K**, H7804
1Sa 15: 6 Then he said to the **K**, "Go away, leave H7808
1Sa 15: 6 So the **K** moved away from the H7808
1Sa 27:10 "Against the Negev of the **K**. H7808
1Sa 30:29 the towns of the Jerahmeelites and the **K**; H7808
1Ch 2:55 These are the **K** who came from H7808

KENIZZITE (3) [KENIZZITES]

Nu 32:12 of Jephunneh the **K** and Joshua son of H7870
Jos 14: 6 son of Jephunneh the **K** said to him, H7870
Jos 14:14 Caleb son of Jephunneh the **K** ever since, H7870

KENIZZITES (1) [KENIZZITE]

Ge 15:19 the land of the Kenites, **K**, Kadmonites, H7870

KEPHAR AMMONI (1)

Jos 18:24 **K**, Ophni and Geba—twelve H4112

KEPHIRAH (4)

Jos 9:17 Gibeon, **K**, Beeroth and Kiriath H4098
Jos 18:26 Mizpah, **K**, Mozah, H4098
Ezr 2:25 of Kiriath Jearim, **K** and Beeroth 743 H4098
Ne 7:29 of Kiriath Jearim, **K** and Beeroth 743 H4098

KEPT (176) [KEEP]

Ge 4: 2 Now Abel **k** flocks, and Cain worked the H8286
Ge 6:20 the ground will come to you to *be* **k alive**. H2649
Ge 7:17 For forty days the flood *k* **coming** on the earth, AIT
Ge 8: 7 and *it k* **flying** back and forth until the water AIT
Ge 16: 2 "The LORD *has* **k** me from having children. H6806
Ge 19: 9 *They* **k bringing pressure** on Lot H7210+4394
Ge 20: 6 so I *have* **k** you from sinning against H3104
Ge 20:18 *had* **k** all **the women** in Abimelek's household **from conceiving** H6806+1237+8167+6806
Ge 30: 2 who *has* **k** you from having children?" H4979
Ge 37:11 but his father **k** the matter **in mind**. H9068
Ge 39:16 *She* **k** his cloak beside her until his master H5663
Ge 41:35 of Pharaoh, *to be* **k** in the cities *for* food. H9068
Ge 42:16 the rest of you *will* **be k in prison**, so that H673
Ex 5:13 The slave drivers *k* **pressing** them, saying AIT
Ex 12:42 Because the LORD **k** vigil that night to bring H4200
Ex 16:20 to Moses; *they* **k** part of it until morning H3855
Ex 16:33 before the LORD to be **k** for the generations H5466
Ex 21:29 warned but *has* not **k** it **penned up** and it H9068
Ex 23:18 offerings *must* not *be* **k** until morning. H4328
Ex 27:20 light so that the lamps may be **k** burning. H9458
Lev 6: 9 the fire *must* **be k burning** on the H3678
Lev 6:12 The fire on the altar *must* **be k burning**; it H3678
Lev 6:13 The fire *must* **be k burning** on the altar H3678
Lev 24: 2 the lamps *may be* **k burning** continually. H6590
Nu 9: 7 but why *should we* **be k from** H1757+4200+1194
Nu 15:34 and *they* **k** him in custody, because it was H5663
Nu 17:10 to be **k** as a sign to the rebellious. H5466
Nu 18: 9 most holy offerings that is **k from** the fire. H4946
Nu 19: 9 *They are to be* **k** by the Israelite H2118
Nu 24:11 the LORD *has* **k** you from being H4979
Dt 6:24 we might always prosper and *be* **k alive**, H2649
Dt 7: 8 LORD loved you and **k** the oath he swore to H9068
Dt 32:34 "*Have* I not **k** this **in reserve** and sealed it H4022
Dt 33:21 the leader's portion **was k** for him. H6211
Jos 6:13 the LORD, while the trumpets **k** sounding. H2143
Jos 9:21 So the leaders' **promise** to them *was k*. AIT
Jos 14:10 *he has* **k** me **alive** for forty-five years since H2649
Jdg 7: 8 Israelites home but **k** the three hundred, H2616
Jdg 20:45 *They* **k pressing** after the Benjamites as far as AIT
1Sa 1: 6 her rival **k provoking** her in H4087+1685+4088
1Sa 1:12 As *she* **k on** praying to the LORD, Eli H8049
1Sa 9:24 "Here is what *has* **been k** for you. H8636
1Sa 10:27 brought him no gifts. But Saul **k** silent. H2118
1Sa 13:13 "*You have* not **k** the command the LORD H9068
1Sa 13:14 because *you have* not **k** the LORD's H9068
1Sa 17:41 of him, **k coming** closer to David. H2143+2143
1Sa 18: 2 From that day Saul **k** David with him and H4374
1Sa 18: 9 that time on Saul **k a close eye on** David. H6523
1Sa 21: 4 the men *have* **k themselves** from women." H9068
1Sa 21: 5 "Indeed women *have* **been k** from us, as H6806
1Sa 23:13 left Keilah and *k* **moving from place to place**. AIT
1Sa 25:26 since the LORD *has* **k** you from bloodshed H4979
1Sa 25:34 who *has* **k** me from harming you, if H4979
1Sa 25:39 *He has* **k** his servant from doing wrong H3104
2Sa 15:12 Absalom's following **k on** increasing. H2143
2Sa 18: 9 while the mule he was riding **k on going**. H6296
2Sa 18:13 *would have* **k** *your* **distance** *from* me." H3656+4946+5584
2Sa 20: 3 They were **k in confinement** till the day of H7674
2Sa 22:22 For *I have* **k** the ways of the LORD; I am not H9068
2Sa 22:24 before him and *have* **k myself** from sin. H9068
1Ki 5:10 way Hiram *k* Solomon **supplied** *with* all the AIT
1Ki 8:20 "The LORD *has* **k** the promise he made: H7756
1Ki 8:24 *You have* **k** your promise to your servant H9068
1Ki 10:26 which *he* **k** in the chariot cities and also H5697
1Ki 11:11 attitude and *you have* not **k** my covenant H9068
1Ki 11:33 nor **k** my decrees and laws as David NDT
1Ki 13:21 of the LORD and *have* not **k** the command H9068
1Ki 14: 8 who **k** my commands and followed me H9068
2Ki 4: 5 brought the jars to her and she *k* **pouring**. AIT
2Ki 13: 3 for a long time *he* **k** them under the H5989
2Ki 18: 6 *he* **k** the commands the LORD had given H9068
2Ki 25: 2 The city *was* **k** under siege until the H995
1Ch 4:33 And they **k a genealogical record**. H3509
2Ch 1:14 which *he* **k** in the chariot cities and also H5663
2Ch 6:10 "The LORD *has* **k** the promise he made. H7756
2Ch 6:15 You *have* **k** your promise to your servant H9068
2Ch 9:25 which *he* **k** in the chariot cities and also H5663
2Ch 17:13 He also **k** experienced fighting men in NDT
2Ch 34:21 gone before us *have* not **k** the word of the H9068
Ezr 9: 1 *have* not **k themselves separate** from the H976
Ne 5: 8 *They k* **quiet**, because they could find AIT
Ne 6:17 replies from Tobiah *k* **coming** to them. AIT
Ne 6:19 *they* **k** reporting to me his good deeds H2118
Ne 9: 8 *You have* **k** your promise because you are H7756
Ne 10:39 gatekeepers and the musicians are also **k**. NDT
Ne 11:19 associates, who **k watch** at the gates H9068
Est 2:20 But Esther *had* **k secret** her family H401+5583
Est 7: 4 *I would have k* **quiet**, because no AIT
Job 21:32 the grave, and **watch** *is* **k** over their tombs. H9193
Job 23:11 *I have* **k** *to* his way without turning aside. H9068
Job 31:17 if *I have* **k** my bread to myself, not sharing H430
Job 31:34 of the clans that *I* **k silent** and would not go AIT
Ps 17: 4 I *have* **k** *myself from* the ways of the H9068
Ps 18:21 For *I have* **k** the ways of the LORD; I am not H9068
Ps 18:23 before him and *have* **k myself** from sin. H9068
Ps 32: 3 When *I k* **silent**, my bones wasted away AIT
Ps 50:21 When you did these things and *I k* **silent**, you AIT
Ps 66: 9 our lives and **k** our feet from slipping. H5989
Ps 73:13 in vain *I have* **k** my heart **pure** and have H2342
Ps 77: 4 *You* **k** my eyes **from closing**; I was H296+9073
Ps 78:32 of all this, they **k on** sinning; in spite of H6388
Ps 99: 7 *they* **k** his statutes and the decrees he H9068
Ps 119:101 *I have* **k** my feet from every evil path so H3973
Ps 130: 3 If *you*, LORD, **k a record** *of* sins, Lord, who H9068
Pr 20: 9 can say, "*I have* **k** my heart **pure**; I am H2342
Pr 28:18 one whose walk is blameless *is* **k safe**, H3828
Pr 28:26 those who walk in wisdom **are k safe**. H4880
Pr 29:25 whoever trusts in the LORD **is k safe**. H8435
Isa 38:17 **In** *your* **love** you **k** me from the pit of H3137
Isa 42:14 "For a long time *I have k* **silent**, I have been AIT
Isa 49: 6 bring back *those of* Israel *I have* **k**. H5915
Isa 57:17 yet *they* **k on** in their willful ways. H2143+8743
Jer 5:25 Your wrongdoings *have* **k** these **away** H5742
Jer 35:14 drink wine and this command *has* **been k**. H7756
Jer 52: 5 The city *was* **k** under siege until the H995
Eze 5: 7 not followed my decrees or **k** my laws. H6913
Eze 11:12 my decrees or **k** my laws but have H6913
Da 7:11 *I* **k** looking until the beast was slain and A10201
Da 7:28 turned pale, but *I* **k** the matter to myself." A10476
Da 9:10 LORD our God or **k** the laws he gave H2143+928
Hos 13:12 is stored up, his sins *are* **k on record**. H7621
Am 2: 4 of the LORD and *have* not **k** his decrees, H9068
Mal 3: 7 from my decrees and *have* not **k** them. H9068
Mt 19:20 "All these *I have* **k**," the young man said *G5875*
Mt 24:43 *he* would have **k watch** and would not *G1213*
Mt 27:36 sitting down, *they* **k watch over** him there. *G5498*
Mk 5:32 But Jesus *k* **looking around** to see who had AIT
Mk 7:36 he did so, the more they *k* **talking about** it. AIT
Mk 9:10 *They* **k** the matter to themselves *G3195*
Mk 9:34 But they **k quiet** because on the way they had AIT
Mk 10:20 "all these *I have* **k** since I was a boy." *G5875*
Lk 1:22 he **k** making signs to them but *G1639*
Lk 4:44 And *he* **k on** preaching in the synagogues *G1639*
Lk 8:29 hand and foot and **k under guard**, *G5875*
Lk 9:36 disciples **k** this **to themselves** and did not *G4967*
Lk 13:16 whom Satan *has k* **bound** for eighteen long AIT
Lk 18: 3 in that town *who k* **coming** to him with the AIT
Lk 18:21 "All these *I have* **k** since I was a boy," *G5875*
Lk 19:20 *I have* **k** it laid away in a piece of cloth. *G2400*
Lk 23:21 they *k* **shouting**, "Crucify him! Crucify him!" AIT
Lk 24:16 they *were* **k from** recognizing *G3195+3590*
Jn 8: 7 When *they* **k on** questioning him, he *G2152*
Jn 11:37 of the blind man *have* **k** this man from *G4472*
Jn 11:56 *They* **k looking for** Jesus, and as they stood in AIT
Jn 15:10 just as I *have* **k** my Father's commands *G5498*
Jn 16:18 *They* **k asking**, "What does he mean by 'a AIT
Jn 17:12 them and **k** them **safe** by that name you *G5875*
Jn 19:12 the Jewish leaders *k* **shouting**, "If you let AIT
Ac 5: 2 *he* **k back** part of the money *for himself*, *G3802*
Ac 5: 3 Spirit and *have* **k** *for yourself* some of the *G3802*
Ac 9:24 night *they* **k close watch** on the city *G4190*
Ac 12: 5 So Peter *was* **k** in prison, but the church *G5498*
Ac 12:15 *When* she **k insisting** *that* it was so, they said, AIT
Ac 12:16 But Peter **k on** knocking, and when they *G2152*
Ac 16: 6 *having been* **k** by the Holy Spirit **from** *G3266*
Ac 16:18 *She* **k** this **up** for many days. Finally Paul *G4472*
Ac 20: 7 the next day, **k on** talking until midnight. *G4189*
Ac 21:36 The crowd that followed *k* **shouting**, "Get rid AIT
Ac 23:35 he ordered *that* Paul *be* **k under guard** in *G5875*
Ac 27:43 life and **k** them **from carrying out** their *G3266*
Ro 15:31 Pray that *I may be* **k safe** from the *G4861*
2Co 11: 9 *I have* **k** myself *from* being a burden to *G5498*
Eph 3: 9 which for ages past *was* **k hidden** in God AIT
Col 1:26 mystery that *has been* **k hidden** for ages AIT
1Th 3: 4 *we k* **telling** you that we would be persecuted AIT
1Th 5:23 *May* your whole spirit, soul and body *be* **k** *G5498*
2Ti 4: 7 I have finished the race, *I have* **k** the faith. *G5498*
Heb 11:28 By faith *he* **k** the Passover and the *G4472*
Heb 13: 4 the marriage bed **k** pure, for God will NDT
1Pe 1: 4 This inheritance *is* **k** in heaven for you, *G5498*
2Pe 3: 7 *being* **k** for the day of judgment and *G5498*
Jude 1 in God the Father and **k** for Jesus Christ: *G5498*
Jude 6 dwelling—these *he has* **k** in darkness *G5498*
Rev 3: 8 yet *you have* **k** my word and have not *G5498*
Rev 3:10 Since *you have* **k** my command to endure *G5498*
Rev 9:15 angels who *had been k* **ready** for this very AIT

KERAMIM See ABEL KERAMIM

KERAN (2)

Ge 36:26 Hemdan, Eshban, Ithran and **K**. H4154
1Ch 1:41 Hemdan, Eshban, Ithran and **K**. H4154

KERCHIEFS (KJV) VEILS

KEREN-HAPPUCH (1)

Job 42:14 the second Keziah and the third **K**. H7968

KERETHITE (1) [KERETHITES]

Zep 2: 5 live by the sea, you **K** people; the word of H4165

KERETHITES (9) [KERETHITE]

1Sa 30:14 We raided the Negev of the **K**, some H4165
2Sa 8:18 Jehoiada was over the **K** and Pelethites; H4165
2Sa 15:18 along with all the **K** and Pelethites; and H4165
2Sa 20: 7 Joab's men and the **K** and Pelethites and H4165
2Sa 20:23 Jehoiada was over the **K** and Pelethites; H4165
1Ki 1:38 the **K** and the Pelethites went down and H4165
1Ki 1:44 son of Jehoiada, the **K** and the Pelethites H4165
1Ch 18:17 Jehoiada was over the **K** and Pelethites; H4165
Eze 25:16 I will wipe out the **K** and destroy those H4165

KERIOTH (3) [KERIOTH HEZRON]

Jer 48:24 to **K** and Bozrah—to all the towns of H7954
Jer 48:41 **K** will be captured and the strongholds H7954
Am 2: 2 that will consume the fortresses of **K**. H7954

KERIOTH HEZRON (1) [HAZOR, HEZRON, KERIOTH]

Jos 15:25 Hazor Hadattah, **K** (that is, Hazor), H7955

KERITH (2)

1Ki 17: 3 turn eastward and hide in the **K** Ravine H4134
1Ki 17: 5 He went to the **K** Ravine, east of the H4134

KERNEL (2) [KERNELS]

Mk 4:28 then the head, then the full **k** in the head. *G4992*
Jn 12:24 unless a **k** of wheat falls to the ground *G3133*

KERNELS (3) [KERNEL]

Dt 23:25 you may pick **k** with your hands, but you H4884
Dt 32:14 rams of Bashan and the finest **k** *of* wheat. H4000
Lk 6: 1 rub them in their hands and eat the **k**. NDT

KEROS (2)

Ezr 2:44 **K**, Siaha, Padon, H7820
Ne 7:47 **K**, Sia, Padon, H7820

KERUB (2)

Ezr 2:59 Tel Harsha, **K**, Addon and Immer H4132
Ne 7:61 Tel Harsha, **K**, Addon and Immer H4132

KESALON (1) [JEARIM]

Jos 15:10 **K**), continued down to Beth H4076

KESED (1)

Ge 22:22 **K**, Hazo, Pildash, Jidlaph and Bethuel." H4168

KESIL (1)

Jos 15:30 Eltolad, **K**, Hormah, H4069

KESULLOTH (1)

Jos 19:18 territory included: Jezreel, **K**, Shunem, H4063

KETTLE (1) [KETTLES]

1Sa 2:14 the fork into the pan or **k** or caldron or pot. H1857

KETTLES (1) [KETTLE]

Mk 7: 4 as the washing of cups, pitchers and **k**. *G5908*

KETURAH (4)

Ge 25: 1 taken another wife, whose name was **K**. H7778
Ge 25: 4 All these were descendants of **K**. H7778
1Ch 1:32 The sons born to **K**, Abraham's concubine: H7778
1Ch 1:33 All these were descendants of **K**. H7778

KEY (8) [KEYS]

Jdg 3:25 they took a **k** and unlocked them. H5158
1Ch 9:27 charge of the **k for opening** it each H5158
Isa 22:22 his shoulder the **k** *to* the house of David H5158
Isa 33: 6 fear of the LORD is **the k** to this treasure. H2085S
Lk 11:52 you have taken away the **k** to knowledge. *G3090*
Rev 3: 7 is holy and true, who holds the **k** of David. *G3090*
Rev 9: 1 star was given the **k** to the shaft of the *G3090*
Rev 20: 1 having the **k** to the Abyss and holding in *G3090*

KEYS (2) [KEY]

Mt 16:19 I will give you the **k** of the kingdom of *G3090*
Rev 1:18 And I hold the **k** of death and Hades. *G3090*

KEZIAH (1)

Job 42:14 the second **K** and the third H7905

KEZIB (1)

Ge 38: 5 It was at **K** that she gave birth to him H3945

KEZIZ See EMEK KEZIZ

KIBROTH HATTAAVAH (5)

Nu 11:34 Therefore the place was named **K**, H7701
Nu 11:35 From **K** the people traveled to Hazeroth H7701
Nu 33:16 the Desert of Sinai and camped at **K**. H7701
Nu 33:17 They left **K** and camped at Hazeroth. H7701
Dt 9:22 angry at Taberah, at Massah and at **K**. H7701

KIBZAIM (1)
Jos 21:22 **K** and Beth Horon, together with their H7698

KICK (1) [KICKED, KICKING]
Ac 26:14 It is hard for you *to* **k** against the goads.' *G3280*

KICKED (1) [KICK]
Dt 32:15 Jeshurun grew fat and **k**; filled with food H1246

KICKING (2) [KICK]
Eze 16: 6 by and saw you **k about** in your blood, H1008
Eze 16:22 naked and bare, **k about** in your blood. H1008

KIDNAPPER (1) [KIDNAPPER'S, KIDNAPPING, KIDNAPS]
Dt 24: 7 selling them as a slave, the **k** must die. H1705

KIDNAPPER'S (1) [KIDNAPPER]
Ex 21:16 been sold or is still in **the k** possession. H2257[S]

KIDNAPPING (1) [KIDNAPPER]
Dt 24: 7 someone is caught **k** a fellow H1704+5883

KIDNAPS (1) [KIDNAPPER]
Ex 21:16 "*Anyone who* **k** someone is to be put to H1704

KIDNEYS (18)
Ex 29:13 the liver, and both **k** with the fat on them H4000
Ex 29:22 of the liver, both **k** with the fat on them H4000
Lev 3: 4 both **k** with the fat on them near the loins H4000
Lev 3: 4 which you will remove with the **k**. H4000
Lev 3:10 both **k** with the fat on them near the loins H4000
Lev 3:10 which you will remove with the **k**. H4000
Lev 3:15 both **k** with the fat on them near the loins H4000
Lev 3:15 which you will remove with the **k**. H4000
Lev 4: 9 both **k** with the fat on them near the loins H4000
Lev 4: 9 which he will remove with the **k**— H4000
Lev 7: 4 both **k** with the fat on them near the loins H4000
Lev 7: 4 which is to be removed with the **k**. H4000
Lev 8:16 of the liver, and both **k** and their fat, and H4000
Lev 8:25 both **k** and their fat and the right thigh. H4000
Lev 9:10 the **k** and the long lobe of the liver from H4000
Lev 9:19 the **k** and the long lobe of the liver H4000
Job 16:13 he pierces my **k** and spills my gall on the H4000
Isa 34: 6 lambs and goats, fat from the **k** *of* rams. H4000

KIDON (1)
1Ch 13: 9 they came to the threshing floor of **K**, H3961

KIDRON (11)
2Sa 15:23 The king also crossed the **K** Valley, and H7724
1Ki 2:37 The day you leave and cross the **K** Valley H7724
1Ki 15:13 cut it down and burned it in the **K** Valley. H7724
2Ki 23: 4 in the fields of the **K** Valley and took the H7724
2Ki 23: 6 of the LORD to the **K** Valley outside H7724
2Ki 23:12 threw the rubble into the **K** Valley. H7724
2Ch 15:16 broke it up and burned it in the **K** Valley. H7724
2Ch 29:16 took it and carried it out to the **K** Valley. H7724
2Ch 30:14 altars and threw them into the **K** Valley. H7724
Jer 31:40 terraces out to the **K** Valley on the east as H7724
Jn 18: 1 his disciples and crossed the **K** Valley. *G3022*

KILEAB (1)
2Sa 3: 3 **K** the son of Abigail the widow of Nabal H3976

KILION (3)
Ru 1: 2 of his two sons were Mahlon and **K**. H4002
Ru 1: 5 both Mahlon and **K** also died, and Naomi H4002
Ru 4: 9 the property of Elimelek, **K** and Mahlon. H4002

KILL (208) [KILLED, KILLER, KILLING, KILLS]
Ge 4:14 and whoever finds me *will* **k** me. H2222
Ge 4:15 that no one who found him *would* **k** him. H5782
Ge 12:12 Then *they will* **k** me but will let you live. H2222
Ge 18:25 to **k** the righteous with the wicked H4637
Ge 20:11 and *they will* **k** me because of my wife. H2222
Ge 26: 7 of this place might **k** me on account of H2222
Ge 27:41 are near; then *I will* **k** my brother Jacob." H2222
Ge 37:18 he reached them, they plotted to **k** him. H4637
Ge 37:20 *let's* **k** him and throw him into one of H2222
Ge 37:26 will we gain if *we* **k** our brother and H2222
Ex 1:16 that the baby is a boy, **k** him; but if it is a H4637
Ex 2:15 he tried to **k** Moses, but Moses H2222
Ex 4:19 who **wanted to k** you are H1335+906+5883
Ex 4:23 to let him go; so I *will* **k** your firstborn son. H2222
Ex 4:24 LORD met Moses and was about to **k** him. H4637
Ex 5:21 have put a sword in their hand to **k** us." H2222
Ex 22:24 aroused, and *I will* **k** you with the sword H2222
Ex 32:12 to **k** them in the mountains and to wipe H2222
Lev 14:50 *He shall* **k** one of the birds over fresh water H8821
Lev 20:15 put to death, and *you must* **k** the animal. H2222
Lev 20:16 **k** both the woman and the animal. H2222
Nu 11:15 please *go ahead and* **k** me—if I H2222+2222
Nu 16:13 milk and honey to **k** us in the wilderness? H4637
Nu 22:29 in my hand, *I would* **k** you right now." H2222
Nu 25: 4 **k** them **and expose** them in broad H3697
Nu 25:17 the Midianites as enemies and **k** them. H5782
Nu 31:17 Now **k** all the boys. And kill every woman H2222
Nu 31:17 And **k** every woman who has slept with a H2222
Nu 35:23 on them a stone heavy enough *to* **k** them, H4637
Nu 35:27 avenger of blood *may* **k** the accused H8357
Dt 19: 5 fly off and hit his neighbor and **k** him. H4637
Dt 19: 6 and **k** him even though he is not H5782+5883
Dt 27:25 a bribe to **k** an innocent person H5782+5883
Jos 9:26 the Israelites, and *they did* not **k** them. H2222
Jdg 8:18 "What kind of men *did you* **k** at Tabor?" H2222
Jdg 8:19 had spared their lives, *I would* not **k** you." H2222
Jdg 8:20 his oldest son, he said, "**K** them! H2222
Jdg 9:54 "Draw your sword and **k** me, so that they H4637
Jdg 13:23 "If the LORD had meant to **k** us, he would H4637
Jdg 15:12 to me that *you* won't **k** me yourselves." H7003
Jdg 15:13 *We will* not **k** you." So H4637+4637
Jdg 16: 2 the night, saying, "At dawn *we'll* **k** him." H2222
Jdg 20: 5 surrounded the house, intending to **k** me. H2222
Jdg 21:11 "**K** every male and every woman who is H3049
1Sa 5:10 around to us to **k** us and our people." H4637
1Sa 5:11 own place, or *it will* **k** us and our people." H4637
1Sa 16: 2 hears about it, *he will* **k** me." The LORD H2222
1Sa 17: 9 If he is able to fight and **k** me, we will H5782
1Sa 17: 9 if I overcome him and **k** him, you will H5782
1Sa 19: 1 all the attendants to **k** David. H4637
1Sa 19: 2 Saul is looking for a chance to **k** you. H4637
1Sa 19:11 to watch it and to **k** him in the morning. H4637
1Sa 19:15 up to me in his bed so that I *may* **k** him." H4637
1Sa 19:17 'Let me get away. Why *should I* **k** you?' " H4637
1Sa 20: 1 father, that *he is* **trying to k** me?" H1335+5883
1Sa 20: 8 If I am guilty, then **k** me yourself! Why H4637
1Sa 20:33 But Saul hurled his spear at him to **k** him H5782
1Sa 20:33 knew that his father intended to **k** David. H4637
1Sa 22:17 "Turn and **k** the priests of the LORD H4637
1Sa 22:23 The man who **wants to k** you is H1335+5883
1Sa 22:23 to kill you *is* **trying to k** me too. H1335+5883
1Sa 24:10 Some urged me to **k** you, but I spared you; H2222
1Sa 24:11 the corner of your robe but *did* not **k** you. H2222
1Sa 24:18 me into your hands, but *you did* not **k** me. H2222
1Sa 24:21 the LORD that *you will* not **k off** my H4162
1Sa 30:15 God that *you will* not **k** me or hand me H4637
2Sa 1: 9 said to me, 'Stand here by me and **k** me! H4637
2Sa 4: 8 your enemy, who **tried to k** you. H1335+5883
2Sa 13:28 'Strike Amnon down,' then **k** him. H4637
2Sa 16:11 flesh and blood, *is* **trying to k** me. H1335+5883
2Sa 21:16 with a new sword, said he *would* **k** David. H5782
1Ki 3:26 living baby! Don't **k** him!" But the H4637+4637
1Ki 3:27 first woman. *Do* not **k** him; she is H4637+4637
1Ki 11:40 Solomon tried to **k** Jeroboam, but H4637
1Ki 12:27 *They will* **k** me and return to King H2222
1Ki 17:18 to remind me of my sin and **k** my son?" H4637
1Ki 18: 5 alive so *we will* not *have to* **k** any of our H4162
1Ki 18:12 he doesn't find you, *he will* **k** me. H2222
1Ki 18:14 'Elijah is here.' *He will* **k** me!" H2222
1Ki 19:10 now they are trying to **k** me too." H4374+5883
1Ki 19:14 now they are trying to **k** me too." H4374+5883
1Ki 20:36 as soon as you leave me a lion *will* **k** you." H5782
2Ki 5: 7 *Can I* **k** and bring back to life H4637
2Ki 6:21 asked Elisha, "*Shall I* **k** them, my father? H5782
2Ki 6:21 I kill them, my father? *Shall I* **k** them?" H5782
2Ki 6:22 "*Do* not **k** them," he answered. "Would H5782
2Ki 6:22 "*Would* you **k** those you have captured H5782
2Ki 7: 4 we live; if *they* **k** us, then we die. H4637
2Ki 8:12 **k** their young men with the sword H2222
2Ki 9:27 shouting, "**K** him too!" They H5782
2Ki 10:25 "Go in and **k** them; let no one H5782
2Ch 22:11 from Athaliah so *she could* not **k** him. H4637
2Ch 30:17 the Levites had to **k** the Passover lambs H8824
Ne 4:11 among them and *will* **k** them and put an H2222
Ne 6:10 because men are coming to **k** you—by H2222
Ne 6:10 by night they are coming to **k** you. H2222
Est 3:13 to destroy, **k** and annihilate all the Jews H2222
Est 8:11 **k** and annihilate the armed men of any H2222
Job 20:16 serpents; the fangs of an adder *will* **k** him. H2222
Ps 38:12 *Those who* **want to k** me set their H1335+5883
Ps 54: 3 ruthless people *are* **trying to k** me— H1335+5883
Ps 59: T to watch David's house in order to **k** him. H4637
Ps 59:11 But *do* not **k** them, Lord our shield, or my H2222
Ps 63: 9 Those *who* **want to k** me will be H1335+5883
Ps 71:10 *those who* **wait to k** me conspire H9068+5883
Ps 86:14 ruthless people are **trying to k** me— H1335+5883
Pr 1:32 waywardness of the simple *will* **k** them, H2222
Pr 29:10 of integrity and seek to **k** the upright. H5883
Ecc 3: 3 a time to **k** and a time to heal, a time to H2222
Jer 4:30 despise you; *they* **want to k** you. H1335+5883
Jer 11:21 who *are* **threatening to k** you, H1335+5883
Jer 15: 3 "the sword to **k** and the dogs to drag away H2222
Jer 18:23 know all their plots to **k** me. Do not H4638
Jer 19: 7 of *those who* **want to k** them, H1335+5883
Jer 20:17 For *he did* not **k** me in the womb, with my H4637
Jer 21: 7 their enemies *who* **want to k** them. H1335+5883
Jer 22:25 hands of *those who* **want to k** you, H1335+5883
Jer 34:20 their enemies *who* **want to k** them. H1335+5883
Jer 34:21 their enemies *who* **want to k** them, H1335+5883
Jer 38:15 you an answer, *will you* not **k** me? H4637+4637
Jer 38:16 *I will* neither **k** you nor hand you over to H4637
Jer 38:16 to those who **want to k** you." H1335+906+5883
Jer 38:25 do not hide it from us or *we will* **k** you,' H4637
Jer 40:15 "Let me go and **k** Ishmael son of H5782
Jer 41: 8 ten of them said to Ishmael, "Don't **k** us! H4637
Jer 41: 8 them alone and *did* not **k** them with the H4637
Jer 43: 3 so they *may* **k** us or carry us into exile to H4637
Jer 44:30 of his enemies *who* **want to k** him, H1335+5883
Jer 44:30 the enemy *who* **wanted to k** him. H1335+5883
Jer 46:26 of *those who* **want to k** them— H1335+5883
Jer 49:37 before *those who* **want to k** them; H1335+5883
Jer 50:21 **k** and completely destroy them, H2991
Jer 50:27 **K** all her young bulls; let them go down to H2991
Eze 9: 5 "Follow him through the city and **k** H5782
Eze 14:13 famine upon it and **k** its people and their H4162
Eze 14:17 and *I* **k** its people and their animals, H4162
Eze 14:21 plague—to **k** its men and their animals! H4162
Eze 22:27 they shed blood and **k** people to make unjust H6
Eze 23:47 *they will* **k** their sons and daughters and H2222
Eze 25:13 against Edom and **k** both man and beast. H4162
Eze 26:11 *he will* **k** your people with the sword H2222
Eze 28: 9 in the presence of *those who* **k** you? H2222
Eze 29: 8 against you and **k** both man and beast. H4162
Am 2: 3 destroy her ruler and **k** all her officials H2222
Am 9: 1 those who are left *I will* **k** with the sword. H2222
Na 2:12 his lairs with the **k** and his dens with the H3272
Mt 2:13 is going to search for the child *to* **k** him." *G660*
Mt 2:16 he gave orders *to* **k** all the boys in *G359*
Mt 10:28 be afraid of those *who* **k** the body but *G650*
Mt 10:28 who kill the body but cannot **k** the soul. *G650*
Mt 12:14 out and plotted how *they might* **k** Jesus. *G660*
Mt 14: 5 Herod wanted *to* **k** John, but he was afraid *G650*
Mt 17:23 *They will* **k** him, and on the third day he will *G650*
Mt 21:38 *let's* **k** him and take his inheritance *G650*
Mt 23:34 Some of them *you will* **k** and crucify; others *G650*
Mt 23:37 you *who* **k** the prophets and stone those *G650*
Mt 26: 4 schemed to arrest Jesus secretly and **k** him. *G650*
Mk 3: 4 to save life or *to* **k**?" But they remained *G650*
Mk 3: 6 with the Herodians how *they might* **k** Jesus. *G660*
Mk 6:19 grudge against John and wanted *to* **k** him. *G650*
Mk 9:22 often thrown him into fire or water to **k** him. *G660*
Mk 9:31 *They will* **k** him, and after three days he *G650*
Mk 10:34 him and spit on him, flog him and **k** him. *G650*
Mk 11:18 this and began looking for a way *to* **k** him, *G660*
Mk 12: 7 *let's* **k** him, and the inheritance will *G650*
Mk 12: 9 He will come and **k** those tenants and give *G660*
Mk 14: 1 to arrest Jesus secretly and **k** him. *G650*
Lk 11:49 some of whom *they will* **k** and others they *G650*
Lk 12: 4 be afraid of those *who* **k** the body and after *G650*
Lk 13:31 somewhere else. Herod wants *to* **k** you." *G650*
Lk 13:34 you who **k** the prophets and stone those *G650*
Lk 15:23 Bring the fattened calf and **k** it. Let's have *G2604*
Lk 15:30 *you* **k** the fattened calf for him! *G2604*
Lk 18:33 they will flog him and **k** him. On the third *G650*
Lk 19:27 bring them here and **k** them in front of me. *G2956*
Lk 19:47 among the people were trying *to* **k** him. *G660*
Lk 20:14 '*Let's* **k** him, and the inheritance will be *G650*
Lk 20:16 He will come and **k** those tenants and give *G660*
Jn 5:18 this reason they tried all the more to **k** him; *G650*
Jn 7: 1 there were looking for a way *to* **k** him. *G650*
Jn 7:19 Why are you trying to **k** me?" *G650*
Jn 7:20 crowd answered. "Who is trying to **k** you?" *G650*
Jn 7:25 "Isn't this the man they are trying to **k**? *G650*
Jn 8:22 made the Jews ask, "*Will he* **k** himself? *G650*
Jn 8:37 Yet you are looking for a way *to* **k** me *G650*
Jn 8:40 you are looking for a way *to* **k** me, a man *G650*
Jn 10:10 comes only to steal and **k** and destroy; *G2604*
Jn 12:10 priests made plans to **k** Lazarus as well, *G650*
Ac 9:23 was a conspiracy among the Jews *to* **k** him, *G359*
Ac 9:24 watch on the city gates in order to **k** him. *G359*
Ac 9:29 Hellenistic Jews, but they tried to **k** him. *G359*
Ac 10:13 voice told him, "Get up, Peter. **K** and eat." *G2604*
Ac 11: 7 telling me, 'Get up, Peter. **K** and eat.' *G2604*
Ac 16:27 was about to **k** himself because he *G359*
Ac 21:31 While they were trying to **k** him, news *G650*
Ac 23:15 We are ready *to* **k** him before he gets here." *G359*
Ac 23:27 by the Jews and they were about to **k** him, *G359*
Ac 25: 3 an ambush *to* **k** him along the way. *G359*
Ac 26:21 me in the temple courts and tried to **k** me. *G1429*
Ac 27:42 The soldiers planned to **k** the prisoners to *G650*
Ro 11: 3 and *they are* **trying to k** me"? *G2426+3836+6034*
1Ti 1: 9 *for those who* **k** their **fathers** or mothers *G4260*
[1Ti 1: 9 *for those who* **k** their fathers or **mothers** *G3618*]
Jas 4: 2 do not have, *so you* **k**. You covet but *G5839*
Rev 6: 4 earth and to make *people* **k** each other. *G5377*
Rev 6: 8 over a fourth of the earth *to* **k** by sword, *G650*
Rev 9: 5 They were not allowed to **k** them but only to *G650*
Rev 9:15 year were released to **k** a third of mankind. *G650*
Rev 11: 7 attack them, and overpower and **k** them. *G650*

KILLED (217) [KILL]
Ge 4: 8 Cain attacked his brother Abel and **k** him. H2222
Ge 4:23 *I have* **k** a man for wounding me, a young H2222
Ge 4:25 child in place of Abel, since Cain **k** him." H2222
Ge 49: 6 for *they have* **k** men in their anger and H2222
Ex 2:12 *he* **k** the Egyptian and hid him in the sand H5782
Ex 2:14 of killing me as *you* **k** the Egyptian?" H2222
Ex 13:15 the LORD **k** the firstborn of both people H2222
Lev 14: 5 one of the birds *be* **k** over fresh water in H8821
Lev 14: 6 of the bird that **was k** over the fresh water. H8821
Nu 16:41 "You *have* **k** the LORD's people, H4637
Nu 19:16 someone *who* has been **k** *with* a sword H2728
Nu 19:18 who has been **k** or anyone who has H2728
Nu 22:33 *I would* certainly *have* **k** you by now H2222
Nu 25:14 the Israelite who *was* **k** with the Midianite H5782
Nu 25:18 the *woman who* **was k** when the plague H5782
Nu 31: 7 commanded Moses, and **k** every man. H2222
Nu 31: 8 *They* also **k** Balaam son of Beor with the H2222
Nu 31:19 "Anyone *who has* **k** someone or touched H2222
Nu 31:19 someone who was **k** must stay outside the H2728
Nu 35: 6 to which a *person who has* **k** someone H8357
Nu 35:11 which a *person who has* **k** H8357+5782
Nu 35:15 so that anyone *who has* **k** another H5782
Dt 4:42 to which *anyone* who *had* **k a person** could H8357
Dt 4:42 had unintentionally **k** a neighbor without H8357
Jos 7: 5 who **k** about thirty-six of them. H5782

K

Jos 8:24 to Ai and **k** those who H5782+4200+7023+2995
Jos 10:11 from the hail than *were* **k** by the swords of H2222
Jos 20: 5 because the fugitive **k** their neighbor H5782
Jos 20: 9 residing among them *who* **k** someone H5782
Jos 20: 9 cities and not *be* **k** by the avenger of H4637
Jdg 7:25 *They* **k** Oreb at the rock of Oreb, and Zeeb H2222
Jdg 8:17 tower of Peniel and **k** the men of the town H2222
Jdg 8:21 So Gideon stepped forward and **k** them H2222
Jdg 9:40 and many *were* **k** as they fled. H5877+2728
Jdg 9:45 until he had captured it and **k** its people. H2222
Jdg 9:54 so that they can't say, 'A woman **k** him.' H2222
Jdg 12: 6 they seized him and **k** him at the fords of H8821
Jdg 12: 6 thousand Ephraimites *were* **k** at that time. H5877
Jdg 15:16 jawbone *I have* **k** a thousand men." H5782
Jdg 16:30 Thus *he* **k** many more when he died than H4637
1Sa 4: 2 *who* **k** about four thousand of them on the H5782
1Sa 14:13 armor-bearer followed and **k** behind him. H4637
1Sa 14:14 his armor-bearer **k** some twenty men in H5782
1Sa 17:35 I seized it by its hair, struck it and **k** it. H4637
1Sa 17:36 Your servant *has* **k** both the lion and the H5782
1Sa 17:50 he struck down the Philistine and **k** him. H4637
1Sa 17:51 After *he* **k** him, he cut off his head with H4637
1Sa 18: 6 home after David *had* **k** the Philistine, H5782
1Sa 18:27 him and went out and **k** two hundred H5782
1Sa 19: 5 life in his hands when *he* **k** the Philistine. H5782
1Sa 19:11 your life tonight, tomorrow you'll **be k**." H4637
1Sa 20:14 as long as I live, so that *I may* not **be k**, H4637
1Sa 21: 9 whom *you* **k** in the Valley of Elah H5782
1Sa 22:18 That day *he* **k** eighty-five men who wore H4637
1Sa 22:21 David that Saul *had* **k** the priests of the H2222
1Sa 30: 2 *They* **k** none of them, but carried them off H4637
1Sa 31: 2 his sons, and they **k** his sons Jonathan H5782
2Sa 1:10 "So I stood beside him and **k** him H4637
2Sa 1:16 when you said, 'I **k** the LORD's anointed.' H4637
2Sa 2:31 David's men *had* **k** three hundred H5782+4637
2Sa 3:30 Abner because *he had* **k** their brother H4637
2Sa 4: 7 After they stabbed and **k** him, they cut off H4637
2Sa 4:11 when wicked men *have* **k** an innocent man H2222
2Sa 4:12 an order to his men, and *they* **k** them. H2222
2Sa 10:18 David **k** seven hundred of their H2222
2Sa 11:21 Who **k** Abimelek son of Jerub-Besheth H5782
2Sa 12: 9 *You* **k** him with the sword of the H2222
2Sa 13:32 not think that *they* **k** all the princes; H4637
2Sa 14: 6 One struck the other and **k** him. H4637
2Sa 14: 7 the life of his brother whom *he* **k**; H2222
2Sa 18:15 Absalom, struck him and **k** him. H4637
2Sa 21: 6 to us *to be* **k and** their bodies **exposed** H3697
2Sa 21: 9 *who* **k** them **and exposed** their bodies on H3697
2Sa 21:13 those *who had* **been k and exposed** were H3697
2Sa 21:17 he struck the Philistine down and **k** him. H4637
2Sa 21:18 that time Sibbekai the Hushathite **k** Saph, H5782
2Sa 21:19 Jairthe Bethlehemite **k** the brother of H5782
2Sa 21:21 son of Shimeah, David's brother, **k** him. H5782
2Sa 23: 8 whom he **k** in one encounter. H2728
2Sa 23:18 whom he **k**, and so he became as H2728
2Sa 23:20 into a pit on a snowy day and **k** a lion. H5782
2Sa 23:21 Egyptian's hand and **k** him with his own H2222
1Ki 2: 5 *He* **k** them, shedding their blood in H2222
1Ki 2:32 two men and **k** them with the sword. H2222
1Ki 2:34 went up and struck down Joab and **k** him, H4637
1Ki 9:16 *He* **k** its Canaanite inhabitants and then H2222
1Ki 13:24 a lion met him on the road and **k** him H4637
1Ki 13:26 which has mauled him and **k** him, as the H4637
1Ki 15:28 Baasha **k** Nadab in the third year of Asa H4637
1Ki 15:29 to reign, *he* **k** Jeroboam's whole family. H5782
1Ki 16:10 struck him down and **k** him in the H4637
1Ki 16:11 *he* **k off** Baasha's whole family. H5782
1Ki 19: 1 had done and how *he had* **k** all the H2222
1Ki 20:36 went away, a lion found him and **k** him. H5782
2Ki 10: 9 conspired against my master and **k** him, H2222
2Ki 10: 9 killed him, but who **k** all these? H5782
2Ki 10:11 So Jehu **k** everyone in Jezreel who H5782
2Ki 10:17 *he* **k** all who were left there of Ahab's H5782
2Ki 11: 2 hide him from Athaliah; so *he* **was** not **k**. H4637
2Ki 11:18 idols to pieces and **k** Mattan the priest of H2222
2Ki 14:19 men after him to Lachish and **k** him there. H4637
2Ki 15:25 So Pekah **k** Pekahiah and succeeded him H4637
2Ki 17:25 among them and *they* **k** some of the H2222
2Ki 19:37 Sharezer **k** him with the sword, H5782
2Ki 21:24 people of the land **k** all who had plotted H5782
2Ki 23:29 Necho faced him and **k** him at Megiddo. H4637
2Ki 25: 7 *They* **k** the sons of Zedekiah before his H8821
1Ch 4:43 *They* **k** the remaining Amalekites who had H5782
1Ch 7:21 Ezer and Elead *were* **k** *by* the native-born H2222
1Ch 10: 2 his sons, and they **k** his sons Jonathan H5782
1Ch 11:11 three hundred *men*, whom he **k** in one H2728
1Ch 11:20 against three hundred *men*, *whom* he **k**, H2728
1Ch 11:22 into a pit on a snowy day and **k** a lion. H5782
1Ch 11:23 Egyptian's hand and **k** him with his own H2222
1Ch 19:18 David **k** seven thousand of their H2222
1Ch 19:18 *He* also **k** Shophak the commander of H4637
1Ch 20: 4 time Sibbekai the Hushathite **k** Sippai, H5782
1Ch 20: 5 Elhanan son of Jair **k** Lahmi the brother of H5782
1Ch 20: 7 son of Shimea, David's brother, **k** him. H5782
2Ch 22: 1 into the camp, *had* **k** all the older sons. H2222
2Ch 22: 8 been attending Ahaziah, and *he* **k** them. H2222
2Ch 23:17 altars and idols and **k** Mattan the priest of H2222
2Ch 24:22 Jehoiada had shown him but **k** his son, H2222
2Ch 24:23 Jerusalem and **k** all the leaders of H8845
2Ch 24:25 the priest, and *they* **k** him in his bed. H2222
2Ch 25:11 where *he* **k** ten thousand men of Seir. H5782
2Ch 25:13 *They* **k** three thousand people and carried H5782
2Ch 25:27 men after him to Lachish and **k** him there. H4637
2Ch 28: 6 son of Remaliah **k** a hundred and twenty H2222
2Ch 28: 7 **k** Maaseiah the king's son H2222
2Ch 33:25 people of the land **k** all who had plotted H5782
2Ch 36:17 *who* **k** their young men with the sword in H2222
Ne 9:26 *They* **k** your prophets, who had warned H2222
Est 7: 4 sold to be destroyed, **k** and annihilated. H2222
Est 9: 6 the Jews **k** and destroyed five hundred H2222
Est 9: 7 *They* also **k** Parshandatha, Dalphon H2222
Est 9:11 The number of those **k** in the citadel of H2222
Est 9:12 "The Jews *have* **k** and destroyed five H2222
Est 9:16 They **k** seventy-five thousand of them H2222
Ps 135:10 down many nations and **k** mighty kings— H2222
Ps 136:18 **k** mighty kings—His love endures H2222
Pr 22:13 *I'll* **be k** in the public square! H8357
Isa 14:20 destroyed your land and **k** your people. H2222
Isa 22: 2 Your slain were not **k** *by* the sword, nor H2728
Isa 27: 7 *Has she* **been k** as those were killed who H2222
Isa 27: 7 killed as those were **k** who killed her? H2223
Isa 27: 7 killed as *those* were killed *who* **k** her? H2222
Isa 37:38 Sharezer **k** him with the sword, H5782
Jer 39: 6 his eyes and also **k** all the nobles of H8821
Jer 41: 3 Ishmael also **k** all the men of Judah who H5782
Jer 41: 9 bodies of the men *he had* **k** along with H5782
Jer 41:18 son of Nethaniah *had* **k** Gedaliah son of H5782
Jer 52:10 the king of Babylon **k** the sons of H8821
Jer 52:10 *he* also **k** all the officials of Judah. H8821
La 2:20 *Should* priest and prophet **be k** in the H2222
La 4: 9 *Those* **k** *by* the sword are better off than H2728
Eze 11: 6 You have **k** many *people* in this city and H2728
Eze 13:19 you *have* **k** those who should not have H4637
Eze 23:10 daughters and **k** her with the sword. H2222
Eze 31:17 of the dead, to *those* **k** *by* the sword H2728
Eze 31:18 uncircumcised, with *those* **k** *by* the sword. H2728
Eze 32:20 They will fall among *those* **k** *by* the sword H2728
Eze 32:21 uncircumcised, with *those* **k** *by* the sword. H2728
Eze 32:25 them are uncircumcised, **k** *by* the sword. H2728
Eze 32:26 **k** *by* the sword because they spread their H2726
Eze 32:28 uncircumcised, with *those* **k** *by* the sword. H2728
Eze 32:29 they are laid with *those* **k** *by* the sword. H2728
Eze 32:30 with *those* **k** *by* the sword and H2728
Eze 32:31 all his hordes *that* were **k** *by* the sword, H2728
Eze 32:32 uncircumcised, with *those* **k** *by* the sword H2728
Eze 35: 8 *those* **k** *by* the sword will fall on your hills H2728
Da 3:22 flames of the fire **k** the soldiers who took A10625
Hos 6: 5 *I* **k** you with the words of my mouth H2222
Am 4:10 *I* **k** your young men with the sword, along H2222
Na 2:12 The lion **k** enough for his cubs and H3271
Mt 16:21 that he must *be* **k** and on the third day *G650*
Mt 21:35 they beat one, **k** another, and stoned a *G650*
Mt 21:39 threw him out of the vineyard and **k** him. *G650*
Mt 22: 6 his servants, mistreated them and **k** them. *G650*
Mk 8:31 and *that* he *must be* **k** and after three days *G650*
Mk 12: 5 that one *they* **k**. He sent many others *G650*
Mk 12: 5 some of them they beat, others *they* **k**. *G650*
Mk 12: 8 So they took him and **k** him, and threw him *G650*
Lk 9:22 and *he must be* **k** and on the third day be *G650*
Lk 11:47 it was your ancestors *who* **k** them. *G650*
Lk 11:48 ancestors did; they **k** the prophets, and you *G650*
Lk 11:51 who *was* **k** between the altar and the *G660*
Lk 12: 5 after your body *has been* **k**, has authority to *G650*
Lk 15:27 'and your father *has* **k** the fattened calf *G2604*
Lk 20:15 threw him out of the vineyard and **k** him. *G650*
Ac 3:13 You **handed** him **over** *to be* **k**, and you AIT
Ac 3:15 *You* **k** the author of life, but God raised him *G650*
Ac 5:30 whom you **k** by hanging him on a cross. *G1429*
Ac 5:36 He *was* **k**, all his followers were dispersed *G359*
Ac 5:37 He too *was* **k**, and all his followers were *G660*
Ac 7:28 of killing me as *you* **k** the Egyptian *G359*
Ac 7:52 *They* even **k** those who predicted the *G650*
Ac 10:39 *They* **k** him by hanging him on a cross, *G359*
Ac 11:19 out when Stephen was **k** traveled as far as NDT
Ac 23:12 not to eat or drink until *they had* **k** Paul. *G650*
Ac 23:14 not to eat anything until *we have* **k** Paul. *G650*
Ac 23:21 not to eat or drink until *they have* **k** him. *G359*
Ro 11: 3 *they have* **k** your prophets and torn down *G650*
1Co 10: 9 some of them did—and *were* **k** by snakes. *G660*
1Co 10:10 and *were* **k** by the destroying angel. *G660*
2Co 6: 9 yet we live on; beaten, and yet not **k**; *G2506*
1Th 2:15 who **k** the Lord Jesus and the prophets and *G650*
Heb 11:31 *was* not **k with** those who were *G5272*
Heb 11:37 *they were* **k** by the sword. *G1877+5840+633*
Rev 6:11 sisters, *were* **k** just as they had been. *G650*
Rev 9:18 A third of mankind *was* **k** by the three *G650*
Rev 9:20 of mankind who *were* not **k** by these *G650*
Rev 11:13 thousand people *were* **k** in the earthquake, *G650*
Rev 13:10 If anyone *is to be* **k** with the sword, with the *G650*
Rev 13:10 the sword, with the sword *they will be* **5**." *G650*
Rev 13:15 who refused to worship the image *to be* **k**. *G650*
Rev 19:21 The rest *were* **k** with the sword coming out *G650*

KILLER (2) [KILL]

Dt 19:12 the **k** shall be sent for by the town elders, be NDT
Dt 21: 1 it is not known who the **k** *was*, H5782

KILLING (22) [KILL]

Ge 27:42 is planning to avenge himself by **k** you. H2222
Ge 34:25 the unsuspecting city, **k** every male. H2222
Ex 2:14 Are you thinking of **k** me as you killed the H2222
Ex 32:27 each **k** his brother and friend and H2222
Jos 8:24 Israel had finished **k** all the men of Ai in H2222
1Sa 17:57 as David returned from **k** the Philistine, H5782
1Sa 19: 5 man like David by **k** him for no reason?" H4637
1Ki 18: 4 While Jezebel *was* **k off** the LORD's H4162
1Ki 18:13 I did while Jezebel *was* **k** the prophets of H2222
2Ki 17:26 which *are* **k** them **off**, because the H4637
Est 3: 6 the idea of **k** only Mordecai. H8938+3338+928
Est 9: 5 with the sword, **k** and destroying them H2223
Isa 22:13 slaughtering of cattle and **k** *of* sheep H8821
Jer 41: 2 **k** the one whom the king of Babylon had H4637
Eze 9: 7 they went out and *began* **k** throughout the H5782
Eze 9: 8 While they *were* **k** and I was left alone, H5782
Eze 14:19 **k** its people and their animals, H4162
Jnh 1:14 us accountable for **k** an innocent man, H1947
Ac 7:24 avenged him *by* **k** the Egyptian. *G4250*
Ac 7:28 Are you thinking of **k** me as you killed the *G359*
Ac 8: 1 And Saul approved *of* their **k** him. On that *G358*
Ac 22:20 the clothes *of* those *who were* **k** him. *G359*

KILLS (20) [KILL]

Ge 4:15 anyone *who* **k** Cain will suffer vengeance H2222
Ex 21:14 anyone schemes and **k** someone H2222
Ex 21:29 it penned up and *it* **k** a man or woman, H4637
Lev 24:21 *Whoever* **k** an animal must make H5782
Lev 24:21 but *whoever* **k** a human being is to be put H5782
Nu 35:30 " 'Anyone *who* **k** a person is to be put to H5782
Dt 19: 3 that a person *who* **k someone** may flee H8357
Dt 19: 4 anyone *who* **k a person** and flees there H8357
Dt 19: 4 *anyone* who **k** a neighbor unintentionally H5782
Dt 19:11 and **k** a neighbor, H5782+5883+2256+4637
Dt 27:24 "Cursed is *anyone who* **k** their neighbor H5782
Jos 20: 3 so that anyone *who* **k** a person H5782
1Sa 17:25 give great wealth to the man who **k** him. H5782
1Sa 17:26 the man who **k** this Philistine and H5782
1Sa 17:27 what will be done for the man who **k** him." H5782
Job 5: 2 Resentment **k** a fool, and envy slays the H2222
Job 24:14 murderer rises up, **k** the poor and needy H7779
Isa 66: 3 a bull is like *one who* **k** a person, H5782
Jn 16: 2 when anyone who **k** you will think they *G650*
2Co 3: 6 for the letter **k**, but the Spirit gives *G650*

KILMAD (1)

Eze 27:23 of Sheba, Ashur and **K** traded with you. H4008

KIMHAM (3) [GERUTH KIMHAM]

2Sa 19:37 But here is your servant **K**. Let him cross H4016
2Sa 19:38 The king said, "**K** shall cross over with me H4016
2Sa 19:40 crossed over to Gilgal, **K** crossed with him. H4016

KINAH (1)

Jos 15:22 **K**, Dimonah, Adadah, H7807

KIND (110) [KINDEST, KINDHEARTED, KINDLY, KINDNESS, KINDNESSES, KINDS]

Ge 1:21 every winged bird according to its **k**. H4786
Ge 1:24 the wild animals, each according to its **k**." H4786
Ge 6:20 Two of every **k** *of* bird, of every kind of H4786
Ge 6:20 of every **k** *of* animal and of every kind of H4786
Ge 6:20 of every **k** *of* creature that moves H4786
Ge 6:21 You are to take **every** *k of* food that is to be AIT
Ge 7: 2 you seven pairs of **every** *k of* clean animal, AIT
Ge 7: 2 one pair of every **k** of unclean animal, NDT
Ge 7: 3 also seven pairs of every **k** of bird, male NDT
Ge 7:14 them every wild animal according to its **k**, H4786
Ge 7:14 ground according to its **k** and every bird H4786
Ge 7:14 its kind and every bird according to its **k**, H4786
Ge 8:17 Bring out **every** *k of* living creature that is AIT
Ge 8:19 the ark, **one k after another**. H4200+5476+2157
Ge 9:15 you and all living creatures of every **k**. H1414
Ge 9:16 all living creatures of every **k** on the earth." H1414
Ge 27: 4 Prepare me the **k** *of* tasty food I like H3869+889
Ge 37: 4 him and could not speak a **k** word to him. H8934
Ex 1:20 So God *was* **k** to the midwives and the H3512
Lev 7:14 They are to bring one of **each** *k* as an offering, AIT
Lev 11:14 the red kite, any **k** *of* black kite, H4786
Lev 11:15 any **k** *of* raven, H4786
Lev 11:16 the screech owl, the gull, any **k** *of* hawk, H4786
Lev 11:19 the stork, any **k** *of* heron, the hoopoe and H4786
Lev 11:22 Of these you may eat any **k** *of* locust H4786
Lev 11:29 the weasel, the rat, any **k** *of* great lizard, H4786
Lev 19:23 enter the land and plant **any** *k of* fruit tree, AIT
Nu 5: 2 defiling skin disease or a discharge *of* **any** *k*, AIT
Nu 13:19 **What** *k of* land do they live in? Is it good AIT
Nu 13:19 good or bad? **What** *k of* towns do they live in AIT
Nu 28: 8 along with the **same** *k of* grain offering and AIT
Dt 4:15 You saw no form *of* **any** *k* the day the LORD AIT
Dt 4:25 become corrupt and make any **k** *of* idol, H9454
Dt 14:13 the red kite, the black kite, any **k** *of* falcon, H4786
Dt 14:14 any **k** *of* raven, H4786
Dt 14:15 the screech owl, the gull, any **k** *of* hawk, H4786
Dt 14:18 the stork, any **k** *of* heron, the hoopoe and H4786
Dt 24:10 make a loan of **any k** to your neighbor, H4399
Dt 28:61 also bring on you **every** *k of* sickness and AIT
Jdg 6:26 Then build a **proper k** of altar to the LORD H5120
Jdg 8:18 "What **k** of men did you kill at Tabor?" NDT
2Sa 13:18 for **this was the k** *of* garment the virgin H4027
1Ki 9:13 "What **k** of towns are these you have given NDT
2Ki 1: 7 "What **k** *of* man was it who came to meet H5477
1Ch 22:15 as well as those skilled in **every** *k of* work AIT
2Ch 10: 7 "If you will be **k** to these people and H3202
2Ch 15: 6 was troubling them with **every** *k of* distress. AIT
Job 6:28 "But now **be so k** as to look at me. H3283
Ps 144:13 with **every** *k of* provision. H4946+2385+448+2385
Pr 11:17 Those who are **k** benefit themselves, but H2876
Pr 12:25 down the heart, but a **k** word cheers it up. H3202

Pr 14:21 blessed is the one *who is* **k** *to* the needy. H2858
Pr 14:31 but *whoever is* **k** *to* the needy honors God. H2858
Pr 19:17 *Whoever is* **k** *to* the poor lends to the LORD, H2858
Pr 23: 7 he is the **k** *of* person who is always H4017
Pr 28: 8 it for *another, who will be* **k** to the poor. H2858
SS 4:14 cinnamon, with **every** *k of* incense tree AIT
Isa 58: 5 Is this the **k** of fast I have chosen, only a H3869
Isa 58: 6 "Is not this the **k** of fasting I have chosen: to NDT
Jer 8: 9 the LORD, **what** *k of* wisdom do they have? H4537
Eze 17:23 Birds *of* **every** *k* will nest in it; they will find AIT
Eze 39:17 Call out to every **k** *of* bird and all the H4053S
Eze 39:20 mighty men and soldiers of **every** *k*, declares AIT
Da 1: 4 showing aptitude for **every** *k of* learning, well AIT
Da 4:27 wickedness by *being* **k** *to* the oppressed. A10274
Jnh 1: 8 What *k of* **work** do you do? Where do AIT
Zep 2:14 will lie down there, creatures of every **k**. H1580
Zec 1:13 So the LORD spoke **k** and comforting words H3202
Mt 8:27 asked, "**What k of** *man* is this? G4534
Mt 12:31 **every** *k of* sin and slander can be forgiven AIT
Mk 9:29 "This **k** can come out only by prayer." G1169
Lk 1:29 wondered **what k of** greeting this G4534
Lk 6:35 because he is **k** to the ungrateful and G5982
Lk 7:39 him and **what k of** woman she is— G4534
Lk 16: 8 with their own **k** than are the people of G1155
Jn 2: 6 the **k** used by the Jews for ceremonial NDT
Jn 4:23 for *they are* **the k of** worshipers the Father G5525
Jn 12:33 said this to show **the k of** death he was G4481
Jn 16:25 longer use **this k** *of* language but G1877+4231S
Jn 18:32 had said about **the k of** death he was G4481
Jn 21:19 this to indicate **the k of** death by which G4481
Ac 7:49 **What k of** house will you build for me G4481
Ac 20:35 showed you that **by this k** of hard work we G4048
Ac 24: 4 that you be **k** *enough* to hear us briefly G2116
Ro 1:29 become filled *with* **every k** of wickedness, AIT
Ro 7: 8 produced in me **every** *k of* coveting. AIT
1Co 5: 1 and **of a k** that even pagans do not G5525
1Co 13: 4 Love is patient, love *is* **k**. It does not envy G5980
1Co 15:35 *With* **what k** of body will they come?" G4481
1Co 15:38 and *to* **each** *k* of seed he gives its own body. AIT
1Co 15:39 People have **one** *k of* flesh, animals have G257
1Co 15:40 splendor of the heavenly bodies is **one k**, G2283
1Co 15:41 The sun has **one** *k of* splendor, the moon G257
Gal 5: 8 **That** *k* of persuasion does not come from the AIT
Eph 4:19 so as to indulge in **every** *k of* impurity, AIT
Eph 4:32 Be **k** and compassionate to one another G5982
Eph 5: 3 immorality, or of **any** *k of* impurity, or of AIT
1Th 1: 9 themselves report **what k** *of* reception you G3961
1Th 5:22 reject every **k** of evil. G1626
2Ti 2:24 quarrelsome but must be **k** to everyone, G2473
2Ti 3: 6 They are **the k** who worm their way into G1666S
Titus 2: 5 busy at home, to be **k**, and to be subject to G19
Jas 1:18 that we might be **a k of** firstfruits of all he G5516
1Pe 2: 1 hypocrisy, envy, and slander *of* **every** *k*. AIT
1Pe 4:15 a murderer or thief or *any other k of* **criminal**, AIT
1Pe 5: 9 world is undergoing the **same** *k* of sufferings. AIT
2Pe 3:11 **what k of** *people* ought you to be? G4534
Rev 11: 6 the earth with **every** *k of* plague as often AIT
Rev 18:12 and articles *of* **every** *k* made of ivory AIT
Rev 21:19 decorated with **every** *k of* precious stone. AIT

KINDEST (1) [KIND]

Pr 12:10 the **k acts** *of* the wicked are cruel. H8171

KINDHEARTED (1) [KIND, HEART]

Pr 11:16 A **k** woman gains honor, but ruthless men H2834

KINDLE (5) [KINDLED, KINDLES, KINDLING]

Jer 15:14 my anger *will* **k** a fire that will burn H7706
Jer 17:27 then *I will* **k** an unquenchable fire in the H3675
Jer 21:14 *I will* **k** a fire in your forests that will H3675
Jer 50:32 *I will* **k** a fire in her towns that will H3675
Eze 24:10 So heap on the wood and **k** the fire. H1944

KINDLED (8) [KINDLE]

Dt 32:22 For a fire *will be* **k** by my wrath, one that H7706
Isa 10:16 his pomp a fire *will be* **k** like a blazing H3678
Jer 17: 4 not know, for *you have* **k** my anger H7706+836
La 4:11 *He* **k** a fire in Zion that consumed her H3675
Eze 20:48 Everyone will see that I the LORD *have* **k** it H1277
Lk 12:49 the earth, and how I wish *it were* already **k**! G409
Lk 22:55 And *when* some there *had* **k** a fire in the G4312
2Co 8: 7 in the love we have **k** in you— G1666S

KINDLES (1) [KINDLE]

Isa 44:15 himself, *he* **k a fire** and bakes bread. H5956

KINDLING (1) [KINDLE]

Pr 26:21 so is a quarrelsome person for **k** strife. H3081

KINDLY (7) [KIND]

Ge 50:21 he reassured them and spoke **k** to them. H4213
Jos 2:14 we will treat you **k** and faithfully when the H2876
Ru 2:13 ease by **speaking k** *to* your H1819+6584+4213
2Ki 25:28 He spoke **k** to him and gave him a seat of H3208
Ps 138: 6 LORD is exalted, *he* **looks k** *on* the lowly H8011
Jer 52:32 He spoke **k** to him and gave him a seat of H3208
1Co 4:13 are slandered, *we* **answer k**. We have G4151

KINDNESS (63) [KIND]

Ge 19:19 have shown great **k** to me in sparing my H2876
Ge 21:23 foreigner the same **k** I have shown to you." H2876
Ge 24:12 and show **k** to my master Abraham. H2876
Ge 24:14 know that you have shown **k** to my master." H2876
Ge 24:27 not abandoned his **k** and faithfulness to H2876
Ge 24:49 Now if you will show **k** and faithfulness to H2876
Ge 32:10 unworthy of all the **k** and faithfulness you H2876
Ge 39:21 he showed him **k** and granted him favor H2876
Ge 40:14 remember me and show me **k**; mention H2876
Ge 47:29 that you will show me **k** and faithfulness. H2876
Jos 2:12 LORD that you will show **k** to my family, H2876
Jos 2:12 my family, because I have shown **k** to you. H2876
Ru 1: 8 May the LORD show you **k**, as you have H2876
Ru 1: 8 as you have shown **k** to your dead husbands NDT
Ru 2:20 stopped showing his **k** to the living and H2876
Ru 3:10 "This **k** is greater than that which you H2876
1Sa 15: 6 you showed **k** to all the Israelites when H2876
1Sa 20: 8 As for you, show **k** to your servant, for you H2876
1Sa 20:14 But show me **unfailing k** *like* the LORD's H2876
1Sa 20:14 kindness like the LORD's **k** as long as I live, NDT
1Sa 20:15 do not ever cut off your **k** from my family H2876
2Sa 2: 5 you for showing this **k** to Saul your master H2876
2Sa 2: 6 the LORD now show you **k** and faithfulness, H2876
2Sa 9: 1 to whom I can show **k** for Jonathan's sake H2876
2Sa 9: 3 of Saul to whom I can show God's **k**?" H2876
2Sa 9: 7 will surely show you **k** for the sake of your H2876
2Sa 10: 2 "I will show **k** to Hanun son of Nahash H2876
2Sa 10: 2 just as his father showed **k** to me. H2876
2Sa 15:20 May the LORD show you **k** and faithfulness H2876
2Sa 22:51 he shows **unfailing k** to his anointed H2876
1Ki 2: 7 "But show **k** to the sons of Barzillai of H2876
1Ki 3: 6 "You have shown great **k** to your servant H2876
1Ki 3: 6 continued this great **k** to him and have H2876
1Ch 19: 2 "I will show **k** to Hanun son of Nahash H2876
1Ch 19: 2 because his father showed **k** to me." H2876
2Ch 1: 8 have shown great **k** to David my father H2876
2Ch 24:22 did not remember the **k** Zechariah's father H2876
2Ch 32:25 he did not respond to the **k** *shown* him; H1691
Ezr 9: 9 He has shown us **k** in the sight of the H2876
Job 6:14 "Anyone who withholds **k** from a friend H2876
Job 10:12 You gave me life and showed me **k**, and H2876
Job 24:21 woman, and *to* the widow *they* **show** no **k**. H3512
Ps 109:12 May no one extend **k** to him or take pity H2876
Ps 109:16 For he never thought of doing a **k**, but H2876
Ps 141: 5 that is a **k**; let him rebuke me— H2876
Isa 54: 8 with everlasting **k** I will have H2876
Jer 9:24 the LORD, who exercises **k**, justice and H2876
Jer 31: 3 I have drawn you with **unfailing k**. H2876
Hos 11: 4 I led them with cords of human **k**, with ties NDT
Ac 4: 9 today for an **act of k** shown to a man who G2307
Ac 14:17 *He has* **shown k** by giving you rain from G14
Ac 27: 3 and Julius, *in* **k** to Paul, allowed G5793+5968
Ac 28: 2 The islanders showed us unusual **k**. G5792
Ro 2: 4 you show contempt for the riches *of* his **k**, G5983
Ro 2: 4 realizing that God's **k** is intended to lead G5982
Ro 11:22 Consider therefore the **k** and sternness of God: G5983
Ro 11:22 those who fell, but **k** to you, provided that G5983
Ro 11:22 provided that you continue *in* his **k**. G5983
2Co 6: 6 patience and **k**; in the Holy Spirit and in G5983
Gal 5:22 forbearance, **k**, goodness G5983
Eph 2: 7 expressed in his **k** to us in Christ Jesus. G5983
Col 3:12 yourselves with compassion, **k**, humility, G5983
Titus 3: 4 But when the **k** and love of God our Savior G5983

KINDNESSES (3) [KIND]

Ps 106: 7 they did not remember your many **k**, and H2876
Isa 63: 7 I will tell of the **k** *of* the LORD, the deeds H2876
Isa 63: 7 according to his compassion and many **k**. H2876

KINDRED, KINDREDS (KJV) CLAN, FAMILIES, FAMILY, NATIVE, PEOPLE, PEOPLES, RELATIVES, TRIBE

KINDS (77) [KIND]

Ge 1:11 seed in it, according to their **various k**." H4786
Ge 1:12 according to their **k** and trees bearing fruit H4786
Ge 1:12 fruit with seed in it according to their **k**. H4786
Ge 1:21 according to their **k**, and every winged H4786
Ge 1:24 living creatures according to their **k**: H4786
Ge 1:25 the wild animals according to their **k**, H4786
Ge 1:25 the livestock according to their **k**, and all H4786
Ge 1:25 along the ground according to their **k**. H4786
Ge 2: 9 The LORD God made **all** *k of* trees grow out of AIT
Ge 4:22 who forged **all** *k of* tools out of bronze and AIT
Ge 7: 3 to keep their **various k** alive throughout H2446
Ge 7:14 all livestock according to their **k**, every H4786
Ge 24:10 camels loaded with **all** *k of* good things from AIT
Ge 40:17 basket were **all k** *of* baked goods H4946+3972
Ex 1:14 mortar and with **all** *k of* work in the fields AIT
Ex 31: 3 with knowledge and with **all** *k of* skills— AIT
Ex 31: 5 in wood, and to engage in **all** *k of* crafts. AIT
Ex 35:22 came and brought gold jewelry of **all** *k*: AIT
Ex 35:31 with knowledge and with **all** *k of* skills— AIT
Ex 35:33 to engage in all **k** *of* artistic crafts. H4856
Ex 35:35 with skill to do **all** *k of* work as engravers, AIT
Lev 19:19 " 'Do not mate **different k** *of* animals. H3977
Lev 19:19 not plant your field with **two k** *of* seed. H3977
Lev 19:19 wear clothing woven of **two k** of material. H3977
Dt 6:11 houses filled with **all** *k of* good things you did AIT
Dt 12:31 they do **all** *k of* detestable things the LORD AIT
Dt 22: 9 Do not plant **two k** of seed in your H3977
1Sa 4: 8 the Egyptians with **all** *k of* plagues in the AIT
1Ki 7:14 with knowledge to do **all** *k of* bronze work. AIT
1Ch 18:10 Hadoram brought **all** *k of* articles of gold, of AIT
1Ch 28:14 used in **various k of service**, H6275+2256+6275
1Ch 28:14 used in **various k of service**: H6275+2256+6275
1Ch 29: 2 and **all** *k of* fine stone and marble AIT
2Ch 2:14 is experienced in **all** *k of* engraving and can AIT
2Ch 32:27 shields and all **k** *of* valuables. H3998
2Ch 32:28 stalls for various **k of cattle**, H989+2256+989
Ne 5:18 ten days an abundant supply of wine of **all** *k*. AIT
Ne 9:25 of houses filled with **all** *k of* good things, AIT
Ne 13:15 grapes, figs and **all** *other k of* loads. AIT
Ne 13:16 bringing in fish and **all** *k of* merchandise AIT
Ne 13:20 sellers of **all** *k of* goods spent the night AIT
Ecc 2: 5 parks and planted **all** *k of* fruit trees in them. AIT
Jer 15: 3 "I will send four **k** of destroyers against H5476
Eze 8:10 over the walls all **k** *of* crawling things and H9322
Eze 27:22 the finest of **all** *k of* spices and precious AIT
Eze 39: 4 you as food to all **k** *of* carrion birds and H4053S
Eze 47:10 The fish will be of many **k**—like the fish of H4786
Eze 47:12 Fruit trees of **all** *k* will grow on both banks of AIT
Da 1:17 understanding of **all** *k of* literature and AIT
Da 1:17 could understand visions and dreams of **all** *k*. AIT
Da 3: 5 pipe and all **k** *of* music, you must A10235
Da 3: 7 harp and all **k** *of* music, all the A10235
Da 3:10 pipe and all **k** *of* music must fall down A10235
Da 3:15 pipe and all **k** *of* music, if you are A10235
Mt 5:11 you and falsely say **all** *k* of evil against you AIT
Mt 13:47 into the lake and caught all **k** *of fish*. G1169
Lk 4:40 to Jesus all who had **various k** of sickness, G4476
Lk 11:42 rue and **all** *other k of* garden herbs, but AIT
Lk 12:15 Be on your guard against **all** *k of* greed; life AIT
Ac 10:12 It contained **all** *k of* four-footed animals, as AIT
Ac 13:10 You are full of **all** *k of* deceit and trickery AIT
1Co 1: 5 with **all** *k of* speech and with all knowledge AIT
1Co 12: 4 There are **different k** of gifts, but the same G1348
1Co 12: 5 There are **different k** of service, but the G1348
1Co 12: 6 There are **different k** of working, but in all G1348
1Co 12:10 speaking in **different k** *of* tongues, G1169
1Co 12:28 of guidance, and *of* **different k** of tongues. G1169
Eph 6:18 all occasions with **all** *k of* prayers and AIT
1Ti 5:10 devoting herself to **all** *k of* good deeds. AIT
1Ti 6:10 For the love of money is a root *of* **all** *k* of evil AIT
2Ti 3: 6 are swayed by **all k** *of* evil desires, G4476
2Ti 3:11 **what k** *of things* happened to me in G3888
Titus 3: 3 enslaved by **all k** *of* passions and G4476
Heb 13: 9 carried away by **all k of** strange teachings G4476
Jas 1: 2 whenever you face trials *of* **many k**, G4476
Jas 3: 7 All **k** of animals, birds, reptiles and sea G5882
1Pe 1: 6 have had to suffer grief in **all k** of trials. G4476

KINE (KJV) COWS, HERD, HERDS

KING (2282) [KING'S, KINGDOM, KINGDOMS, KINGS, KINGS', KINGSHIP]

Ge 14: 1 the time when Amraphel was **k** *of* Shinar, H4889
Ge 14: 1 of Shinar, Arioch **k** *of* Ellasar H4889
Ge 14: 1 Kedorlaomer **k** *of* Elam and Tidal king of H4889
Ge 14: 1 king of Elam and Tidal **k** *of* Goyim, H4889
Ge 14: 2 went to war against Bera **k** *of* Sodom, H4889
Ge 14: 2 of Sodom, Birsha **k** *of* Gomorrah, Shinab H4889
Ge 14: 2 Gomorrah, Shinab **k** *of* Admah, Shemeber H4889
Ge 14: 2 Admah, Shemeber **k** *of* Zeboyim, and the H4889
Ge 14: 2 of Zeboyim, and the **k** *of* Bela (that is, H4889
Ge 14: 8 Then the **k** *of* Sodom, the king of H4889
Ge 14: 8 king of Sodom, the **k** *of* Gomorrah, the H4889
Ge 14: 8 of Gomorrah, the **k** *of* Admah, the king of H4889
Ge 14: 8 the **k** *of* Zeboyim and the king of Bela H4889
Ge 14: 8 the king of Zeboyim and the **k** *of* Bela H4889
Ge 14: 9 against Kedorlaomer **k** *of* Elam, Tidal king H4889
Ge 14: 9 king of Elam, Tidal **k** *of* Goyim, Amraphel H4889
Ge 14: 9 Amraphel **k** *of* Shinar and Arioch king of H4889
Ge 14: 9 king of Shinar and Arioch **k** *of* Ellasar— H4889
Ge 14:17 the **k** *of* Sodom came out to meet him in H4889
Ge 14:18 Then Melchizedek **k** *of* Salem brought out H4889
Ge 14:21 The **k** *of* Sodom said to Abram, "Give me H4889
Ge 14:22 But Abram said to the **k** *of* Sodom, "With H4889
Ge 20: 2 Then Abimelek **k** *of* Gerar sent for Sarah H4889
Ge 26: 1 went to Abimelek **k** *of* the Philistines in H4889
Ge 26: 8 Abimelek **k** *of* the Philistines looked down H4889
Ge 36:31 in Edom before any Israelite **k** reigned: H4889
Ge 36:32 Bela son of Beor *became* **k** of Edom. H4887
Ge 36:33 of Zerah from Bozrah succeeded him *as* **k**. H4887
Ge 36:34 of the Temanites succeeded him *as* **k**. H4887
Ge 36:35 the country of Moab, succeeded him *as* **k**. H4887
Ge 36:36 from Masrekah succeeded him *as* **k**. H4887
Ge 36:37 on the river succeeded him *as* **k**. H4887
Ge 36:38 son of Akbor succeeded him *as* **k**. H4887
Ge 36:39 Akbor died, Hadad succeeded him *as* **k**. H4887
Ge 40: 1 the baker of the **k** *of* Egypt offended H4889
Ge 40: 1 offended their master, the **k** *of* Egypt. H4889
Ge 40: 5 cupbearer and the baker of the **k** *of* Egypt, H4889
Ge 41:46 entered the service of Pharaoh **k** *of* Egypt. H4889
Ge 49:20 he will provide delicacies fit for a **k**. H4889
Ex 1: 8 Then a new **k**, to whom Joseph meant H4889
Ex 1:15 The **k** *of* Egypt said to the Hebrew H4889
Ex 1:17 did not do what the **k** *of* Egypt had told H4889
Ex 1:18 Then the **k** *of* Egypt summoned the H4889
Ex 2:23 that long period, the **k** *of* Egypt died. H4889
Ex 3:18 are to go to the **k** *of* Egypt and say to him, H4889
Ex 3:19 But I know that the **k** *of* Egypt will not let H4889
Ex 5: 4 But the **k** *of* Egypt said, "Moses and Aaron H4889
Ex 6:11 tell Pharaoh **k** *of* Egypt to let the Israelites H4889
Ex 6:13 the Israelites and Pharaoh **k** *of* Egypt, H4889
Ex 6:27 who spoke to Pharaoh **k** *of* Egypt about H4889
Ex 6:29 Tell Pharaoh **k** *of* Egypt everything I tell H4889
Ex 14: 5 When the **k** *of* Egypt was told that the H4889

K

Ex 14: 8 hardened the heart of Pharaoh **k** *of* Egypt, H4889
Nu 20:14 from Kadesh to the **k** *of* Edom, H4889
Nu 21: 1 When the Canaanite **k** *of* Arad, who lived H4889
Nu 21:21 to say to Sihon **k** *of* the Amorites: H4889
Nu 21:26 was the city of Sihon **k** *of* the Amorites, H4889
Nu 21:26 against the former **k** *of* Moab and had H4889
Nu 21:29 as captives to Sihon **k** *of* the Amorites. H4889
Nu 21:33 Og **k** *of* Bashan and his whole army H4889
Nu 21:34 what you did to Sihon **k** *of* the Amorites, H4889
Nu 22: 4 of Zippor, who was **k** of Moab at that time H4889
Nu 22:10 son of Zippor, **k** *of* Moab, sent me this H4889
Nu 23: 7 the **k** *of* Moab from the eastern mountains H4889
Nu 23:21 the shout of the **K** is among them. H4889
Nu 24: 7 "Their **k** will be greater than Agag; their H4889
Nu 32:33 kingdom of Sihon **k** *of* the Amorites and H4889
Nu 32:33 the kingdom of Og **k** *of* Bashan— H4889
Nu 33:40 The Canaanite **k** *of* Arad, who lived in the H4889
Dt 1: 4 he had defeated Sihon **k** *of* the Amorites, H4889
Dt 1: 4 at Edrei had defeated Og **k** *of* Bashan, H4889
Dt 2:24 Sihon the Amorite, **k** *of* Heshbon, and his H4889
Dt 2:26 to Sihon **k** *of* Heshbon offering H4889
Dt 2:30 But Sihon **k** *of* Heshbon refused to let us H4889
Dt 3: 1 Og **k** *of* Bashan with his whole army H4889
Dt 3: 2 what you did to Sihon **k** *of* the Amorites, H4889
Dt 3: 3 into our hands Og **k** *of* Bashan and all his H4889
Dt 3: 6 as we had done with Sihon **k** *of* Heshbon H4889
Dt 3:11 Og **k** *of* Bashan was the last of the H4889
Dt 4:46 in the land of Sihon **k** *of* the Amorites H4889
Dt 4:47 his land and the land of Og **k** *of* Bashan, H4889
Dt 7: 8 from the power of Pharaoh **k** *of* Egypt. H4889
Dt 11: 3 both to Pharaoh **k** *of* Egypt and to his H4889
Dt 17:14 "Let us set a **k** over us like all the nations H4889
Dt 17:15 to appoint over you a **k** the LORD your God H4889
Dt 17:16 The **k**, moreover, must not acquire great NDT
Dt 28:36 drive you and the **k** you set over you to a H4889
Dt 29: 7 Sihon **k** *of* Heshbon and Og king of H4889
Dt 29: 7 of Heshbon and Og **k** *of* Bashan came out H4889
Dt 33: 5 He was **k** over Jeshurun when the leaders H4889
Jos 2: 2 The **k** *of* Jericho was told, "Look, some of H4889
Jos 2: 3 So the **k** *of* Jericho sent this message to H4889
Jos 6: 2 along with its **k** and its fighting men. H4889
Jos 8: 1 delivered into your hands the **k** *of* Ai, H4889
Jos 8: 2 do to Ai and its **k** as you did to Jericho H4889
Jos 8: 2 its king as you did to Jericho and its **k**, H4889
Jos 8:14 When the **k** *of* Ai saw this, he and all the H4889
Jos 8:23 But they took the **k** *of* Ai alive and brought H4889
Jos 8:29 He impaled *the body of* the **k** *of* Ai on a H4889
Jos 9:10 the Jordan—Sihon **k** *of* Heshbon, and Og H4889
Jos 9:10 of Heshbon, and Og **k** *of* Bashan, who H4889
Jos 10: 1 Now Adoni-Zedek **k** *of* Jerusalem heard H4889
Jos 10: 1 doing to Ai and its **k** as he had done to H4889
Jos 10: 1 king as he had done to Jericho and its **k**, H4889
Jos 10: 3 So Adoni-Zedek **k** *of* Jerusalem appealed H4889
Jos 10: 3 appealed to Hoham **k** *of* Hebron, H4889
Jos 10: 3 of Hebron, Piram **k** *of* Jarmuth, Japhia H4889
Jos 10: 3 Japhia **k** *of* Lachish and Debir king of H4889
Jos 10: 3 king of Lachish and Debir **k** *of* Eglon. H4889
Jos 10:28 He put the city and its **k** to the sword and H4889
Jos 10:28 And he did to the **k** *of* Makkedah as he H4889
Jos 10:28 as he had done to the **k** *of* Jericho. H4889
Jos 10:30 gave that city and its **k** into Israel's hand. H4889
Jos 10:30 And he did to its **k** as he had done to the H4889
Jos 10:30 king as he had done to the **k** *of* Jericho. H4889
Jos 10:33 Horam **k** *of* Gezer had come up to help H4889
Jos 10:37 together with its **k**, its villages and H4889
Jos 10:39 took the city, its **k** and its villages, and H4889
Jos 10:39 did to Debir and its **k** as they had done to H4889
Jos 10:39 done to Libnah and its **k** and to Hebron. H4889
Jos 11: 1 When Jabin **k** *of* Hazor heard of this, he H4889
Jos 11: 1 he sent word to Jobab **k** *of* Madon, to the H4889
Jos 11:10 captured Hazor and put its **k** to the sword. H4889
Jos 12: 2 Sihon **k** *of* the Amorites, who reigned in H4889
Jos 12: 4 And the territory of Og **k** *of* Bashan, one of H4889
Jos 12: 5 to the border of Sihon **k** *of* Heshbon. H4889
Jos 12: 9 the **k** *of* Jericho one the king of Ai (near H4889
Jos 12: 9 the king of Jericho one the **k** *of* Ai (near H4889
Jos 12:10 the **k** *of* Jerusalem one the king of Hebron H4889
Jos 12:10 of Jerusalem one the **k** *of* Hebron one H4889
Jos 12:11 the **k** *of* Jarmuth one the king of Lachish H4889
Jos 12:11 king of Jarmuth one the **k** *of* Lachish one H4889
Jos 12:12 the **k** *of* Eglon one the king of Gezer one H4889
Jos 12:12 the king of Eglon one the **k** *of* Gezer one H4889
Jos 12:13 the **k** *of* Debir one the king of Geder one H4889
Jos 12:13 the king of Debir one the **k** *of* Geder one H4889
Jos 12:14 the **k** *of* Hormah one the king of Arad one H4889
Jos 12:14 the king of Hormah one the **k** *of* Arad one H4889
Jos 12:15 the **k** *of* Libnah one the king of Adullam H4889
Jos 12:15 king of Libnah one the **k** *of* Adullam one H4889
Jos 12:16 the **k** *of* Makkedah one the king of Bethel H4889
Jos 12:16 king of Makkedah one the **k** *of* Bethel one H4889
Jos 12:17 the **k** *of* Tappuah one the king of Hepher H4889
Jos 12:17 king of Tappuah one the **k** *of* Hepher one H4889
Jos 12:18 the **k** *of* Aphek one the king of Lasharon H4889
Jos 12:18 king of Aphek one the **k** *of* Lasharon one H4889
Jos 12:19 the **k** *of* Madon one the king of Hazor one H4889
Jos 12:19 the king of Madon one the **k** *of* Hazor one H4889
Jos 12:20 the **k** *of* Shimron Meron one the king of H4889
Jos 12:20 Shimron Meron one the **k** *of* Akshaph one H4889
Jos 12:21 the **k** *of* Taanach one the king of Megiddo H4889
Jos 12:21 of Taanach one the **k** *of* Megiddo one H4889
Jos 12:22 the **k** *of* Kedesh one the king of Jokneam H4889
Jos 12:22 of Kedesh one the **k** *of* Jokneam in H4889
Jos 12:23 the **k** *of* Dor (in Naphoth Dor) one the king H4889
Jos 12:23 one the **k** *of* Goyim in Gilgal one H4889
Jos 12:24 the **k** *of* Tirzah one thirty-one kings in all. H4889
Jos 13:10 all the towns of Sihon **k** *of* the Amorites, H4889
Jos 13:21 entire realm of Sihon **k** *of* the Amorites, H4889
Jos 13:27 rest of the realm of Sihon **k** *of* Heshbon H4889
Jos 13:30 the entire realm of Og **k** *of* Bashan—all H4889
Jos 24: 9 son of Zippor, the **k** *of* Moab, prepared to H4889
Jdg 3: 8 Cushan-Rishathaim **k** *of* Aram Naharaim, H4889
Jdg 3:10 Cushan-Rishathaim **k** *of* Aram into the H4889
Jdg 3:12 the LORD gave Eglon **k** *of* Moab power over H4889
Jdg 3:14 subject to Eglon **k** *of* Moab for eighteen H4889
Jdg 3:15 sent him with tribute to Eglon **k** *of* Moab. H4889
Jdg 3:17 presented the tribute to Eglon **k** *of* Moab, H4889
Jdg 3:19 The **k** said to his attendants NDT
Jdg 3:20 God for you." As the **k** rose from his seat, NDT
Jdg 4: 2 them into the hands of Jabin **k** *of* Canaan, H4889
Jdg 4:17 between Jabin **k** *of* Hazor and the family H4889
Jdg 4:23 God subdued Jabin **k** *of* Canaan before H4889
Jdg 4:24 against Jabin **k** *of* Canaan until they H4889
Jdg 9: 6 pillar in Shechem to crown Abimelek **k**. H4889
Jdg 9: 8 went out to anoint a **k** for themselves. H4889
Jdg 9: 8 They said to the olive tree, '*Be* our **k**.' H4887
Jdg 9:10 said to the fig tree, 'Come and *be* our **k**. H4887
Jdg 9:12 said to the vine, 'Come and *be* our **k**. H4887
Jdg 9:14 to the thornbush, 'Come and *be* our **k**. H4887
Jdg 9:15 'If you really want to anoint me **k** over you, H4889
Jdg 9:16 in good faith *by* **making** Abimelek **k**? H4887
Jdg 9:18 *have* **made** Abimelek, the son of his female slave, **k** H4887
Jdg 11:12 to the Ammonite **k** with the question: H4889
Jdg 11:13 The **k** *of* the Ammonites answered H4889
Jdg 11:14 sent back messengers to the Ammonite **k**, H4889
Jdg 11:17 Israel sent messengers to the **k** *of* Edom, H4889
Jdg 11:17 the **k** *of* Edom would not listen. H4889
Jdg 11:17 They sent also to the **k** *of* Moab, and he H4889
Jdg 11:19 messengers to Sihon **k** *of* the Amorites, H4889
Jdg 11:25 than Balak son of Zippor, **k** *of* Moab? H4889
Jdg 11:28 The **k** *of* Ammon, however, paid no H4889
Jdg 17: 6 In those days Israel had no **k**; everyone did H4889
Jdg 18: 1 In those days Israel had no **k**. And in H4889
Jdg 19: 1 In those days Israel had no **k**. H4889
Jdg 21:25 In those days Israel had no **k**; everyone H4889
1Sa 2:10 give strength to his **k** and exalt the horn of H4889
1Sa 8: 5 now appoint a **k** to lead us, such as H4889
1Sa 8: 6 they said, "Give us a **k** to lead us," this H4889
1Sa 8: 7 they have rejected me as their **k**. H4887
1Sa 8: 9 them know what the **k** who will reign over H4889
1Sa 8:10 the people who were asking him for a **k**. H4889
1Sa 8:11 "This is what the **k** who will reign over you H4889
1Sa 8:18 out for relief from the **k** you have chosen, H4889
1Sa 8:19 they said. "We want a **k** over us. H4889
1Sa 8:20 with a **k** to lead us and to go out before H4889
1Sa 8:22 "Listen to them and **give** them a **k**." H4887+4889
1Sa 10:19 you have said, 'No, appoint a **k** over us. H4889
1Sa 10:24 the people shouted, "Long live the **k**!" H4889
1Sa 11:15 to Gilgal and **made** Saul **k** in the H4887
1Sa 12: 1 to me and *have* **set a k** over you. H4887+4889
1Sa 12: 2 Now you have a **k** as your leader. As for H4889
1Sa 12: 9 of the Philistines and the **k** *of* Moab, H4889
1Sa 12:12 saw that Nahash **k** *of* the Ammonites was H4889
1Sa 12:12 we want a **k** to rule over us'—even H4889
1Sa 12:12 though the LORD your God was your **k**. H4889
1Sa 12:13 Now here is the **k** you have chosen, the H4889
1Sa 12:13 see, the LORD has set a **k** over you. H4889
1Sa 12:14 if both you and the **k** who reigns over you H4889
1Sa 12:17 eyes of the LORD when you asked for a **k**." H4889
1Sa 12:19 all our other sins the evil of asking for a **k**." H4889
1Sa 12:25 both you and your **k** will perish. H4889
1Sa 13: 1 was thirty years old when he *became* **k**, H4887
1Sa 15: 1 sent to anoint you **k** over his people Israel H4889
1Sa 15: 8 He took Agag **k** *of* the Amalekites alive H4889
1Sa 15:11 "I regret that *I have* **made** Saul **k** H4887+4889
1Sa 15:17 The LORD anointed you **k** over Israel. H4889
1Sa 15:20 brought back Agag their **k**. H4889
1Sa 15:23 of the LORD, he has rejected you as **k**." H4889
1Sa 15:26 the LORD has rejected you as **k** over Israel!" H4889
1Sa 15:32 "Bring me Agag **k** *of* the Amalekites." H4889
1Sa 15:35 that *he had* **made** Saul **k** over Israel. H4887
1Sa 16: 1 since I have rejected him as **k** over Israel? H4887
1Sa 16: 1 I have chosen one of his sons to be **k**." H4889
1Sa 17:25 The **k** will give great wealth to the man H4889
1Sa 17:56 The **k** said, "Find out whose son this H4889
1Sa 18: 6 of Israel to meet **K** Saul with singing and H4889
1Sa 18:22 the **k** likes you, and his attendants H4889
1Sa 18:25 'The **k** wants no other price for the bride H4889
1Sa 18:27 full number to the **k** so that David might H4889
1Sa 19: 4 "Let not the **k** do wrong to his servant H4889
1Sa 20: 5 I am supposed to dine with the **k**; but H4889
1Sa 20:24 Moon feast came, the **k** sat down to eat. H4889
1Sa 21: 2 "The **k** sent me on a mission and said to H4889
1Sa 21:10 from Saul and went to Achish **k** *of* Gath. H4889
1Sa 21:11 "Isn't this David, the **k** *of* the land? H4889
1Sa 21:12 was very much afraid of Achish **k** *of* Gath. H4889
1Sa 22: 3 in Moab and said to the **k** *of* Moab, H4889
1Sa 22: 4 So he left them with the **k** *of* Moab, and H4889
1Sa 22:11 Then the **k** sent for the priest Ahimelek H4889
1Sa 22:11 priests at Nob, and they all came to the **k**. H4889
1Sa 22:14 Ahimelek answered the **k**, "Who of all H4889
1Sa 22:15 Let not the **k** accuse your servant or any of H4889
1Sa 22:16 But the **k** said, "You will surely die H4889
1Sa 22:17 Then the **k** ordered the guards at his side H4889
1Sa 22:18 The **k** then ordered Doeg, "You turn and H4889
1Sa 23:17 You *will be* **k** over Israel, and I will be H4887
1Sa 24: 8 called out to Saul, "My lord the **k**! H4889
1Sa 24:14 whom has the **k** *of* Israel come out? H4889
1Sa 24:20 that *you will* **surely be k** and that H4887+4887
1Sa 25:36 house holding a banquet like that of a **k**. H4889
1Sa 26:14 replied, "Who are you who calls to the **k**?" H4889
1Sa 26:15 Why didn't you guard your lord the **k** H4889
1Sa 26:15 Someone came to destroy your lord the **k**. H4889
1Sa 26:17 David replied, "Yes it is, my lord the **k**." H4889
1Sa 26:19 Now let my lord the **k** listen to his servant's H4889
1Sa 26:20 The **k** *of* Israel has come out to look for a H4889
1Sa 27: 2 over to Achish son of Maok **k** *of* Gath. H4889
1Sa 28:13 The **k** said to her, "Don't be afraid. H4889
1Sa 29: 3 who was an officer of Saul **k** *of* Israel? H4889
1Sa 29: 8 against the enemies of my lord the **k**?" H4889
2Sa 2: 4 they anointed David **k** over the tribe of H4889
2Sa 2: 7 of Judah have anointed me **k** over them." H4889
2Sa 2: 9 *He* **made** him **k** over Gilead, Ashuri and H4887
2Sa 2:10 years old when he *became* **k** over Israel, H4887
2Sa 2:11 of time David was **k** in Hebron over Judah H4889
2Sa 3: 3 Maakah daughter of Talmai **k** *of* Geshur; H4889
2Sa 3:17 you have wanted to make David your **k**. H4889
2Sa 3:21 assemble all Israel for my lord the **k**, H4889
2Sa 3:23 Ner had come to the **k** and that the king H4889
2Sa 3:23 king and that the **k** had sent him away and NDT
2Sa 3:24 So Joab went to the **k** and said, "What H4889
2Sa 3:31 **K** David himself walked behind the bier H4889
2Sa 3:32 the **k** wept aloud at Abner's tomb. H4889
2Sa 3:33 The **k** sang this lament for Abner: "Should H4889
2Sa 3:36 everything the **k** did pleased them. H4889
2Sa 3:37 Israel knew that the **k** had no part in the H4889
2Sa 3:38 Then the **k** said to his men, "Do you not H4889
2Sa 3:39 though I am the anointed **k**, I am weak, H4889
2Sa 4: 8 to David at Hebron and said to the **k**, H4889
2Sa 4: 8 avenged my lord the **k** against Saul and H4889
2Sa 5: 2 while Saul was **k** over us, you were H4889
2Sa 5: 3 of Israel had come to **K** David at Hebron, H4889
2Sa 5: 3 the **k** made a covenant with them at H4889
2Sa 5: 3 they anointed David **k** over Israel. H4889
2Sa 5: 4 was thirty years old when he *became* **k**, H4887
2Sa 5: 6 The **k** and his men marched to Jerusalem H4889
2Sa 5:11 Now Hiram **k** *of* Tyre sent envoys to David H4889
2Sa 5:12 established him as **k** over Israel and had H4889
2Sa 5:17 David had been anointed **k** over Israel, H4889
2Sa 6:12 Now **K** David was told, "The LORD has H4889
2Sa 6:16 And when she saw **K** David leaping and H4889
2Sa 6:20 "How the **k** *of* Israel has distinguished H4889
2Sa 7: 1 After the **k** was settled in his palace and H4889
2Sa 7: 3 Nathan replied to the **k**, "Whatever you H4889
2Sa 7:18 Then **K** David went in and sat before the H4889
2Sa 8: 3 son of Rehob, **k** *of* Zobah, when he went H4889
2Sa 8: 5 came to help Hadadezer **k** *of* Zobah, H4889
2Sa 8: 8 **K** David took a great quantity of bronze. H4889
2Sa 8: 9 When Tou **k** *of* Hamath heard that David H4889
2Sa 8:10 his son Joram to **K** David to greet him H4889
2Sa 8:11 **K** David dedicated these articles to the H4889
2Sa 8:12 Hadadezer son of Rehob, **k** *of* Zobah. H4889
2Sa 9: 2 and the **k** said to him, "Are you H4889
2Sa 9: 3 The **k** asked, "Is there no one still alive H4889
2Sa 9: 3 Ziba answered the **k**, "There is still a son H4889
2Sa 9: 4 "Where is he?" the **k** asked. H4889
2Sa 9: 5 So **K** David had him brought from Lo H4889
2Sa 9: 9 Then the **k** summoned Ziba, Saul's H4889
2Sa 9:11 Then Ziba said to the **k**, "Your servant will H4889
2Sa 9:11 my lord the **k** commands his servant H4889
2Sa 10: 1 of time, the **k** *of* the Ammonites died H4889
2Sa 10: 1 his son Hanun succeeded him *as* **k**. H4887
2Sa 10: 5 The **k** said, "Stay at Jericho till your H4889
2Sa 10: 6 as well as the **k** *of* Maakah with a H4889
2Sa 11: 8 a gift from the **k** was sent after him. H4889
2Sa 11:19 finished giving the **k** this account of the H4889
2Sa 12: 7 'I anointed you **k** over Israel, and I H4889
2Sa 13: 6 When the **k** came to see him, Amnon H4889
2Sa 13:13 Please speak to the **k**; he will not keep H4889
2Sa 13:18 the virgin daughters of the **k** wore. H4889
2Sa 13:21 When **K** David heard all this, he was H4889
2Sa 13:24 Absalom went to the **k** and said, "Your H4889
2Sa 13:24 Will the **k** and his attendants please join H4889
2Sa 13:25 my son," the **k** replied. "All of us H4889
2Sa 13:26 The **k** asked him, "Why should he go H4889
2Sa 13:31 The **k** stood up, tore his clothes and lay H4889
2Sa 13:33 My lord the **k** should not be concerned H4889
2Sa 13:34 The watchman went and told the **k**, "I see H4889
2Sa 13:35 Jonadab said to the **k**, "See, the king's H4889
2Sa 13:36 The **k**, too, and all his attendants wept H4889
2Sa 13:37 Talmai son of Ammihud, the **k** *of* Geshur. H4889
2Sa 13:37 But **K** David mourned many days for his son NDT
2Sa 13:39 And **K** David longed to go to Absalom, for H4889
2Sa 14: 3 Then go to the **k** and speak these words to H4889
2Sa 14: 4 the woman from Tekoa went to the **k**, H4889
2Sa 14: 5 The **k** asked her, "What is troubling you?" H4889
2Sa 14: 8 The **k** said to the woman, "Go home, and H4889
2Sa 14: 9 "Let my lord the **k** pardon me and my H4889
2Sa 14: 9 let the **k** and his throne be without H4889
2Sa 14:10 The **k** replied, "If anyone says anything to H4889
2Sa 14:11 "Then let the **k** invoke the LORD his God to H4889
2Sa 14:12 servant speak a word to my lord the **k**." H4889
2Sa 14:13 When the **k** says this, does he not convict H4889
2Sa 14:13 the **k** has not brought back his H4889
2Sa 14:15 this to my lord the **k** because the people H4889
2Sa 14:15 'I will speak to the **k**; perhaps he will H4889

2Sa 14:16 Perhaps the **k** will agree to deliver his H4889
2Sa 14:17 word of my lord the **k** secure my H4889
2Sa 14:17 my lord the **k** is like an angel of God in H4889
2Sa 14:18 Then the **k** said to the woman, "Don't H4889
2Sa 14:18 "Let my lord the **k** speak," the woman H4889
2Sa 14:19 The **k** asked, "Isn't the hand of Joab with H4889
2Sa 14:19 you live, my lord the **k**, no one can turn to H4889
2Sa 14:19 the left from anything my lord the **k** says. H4889
2Sa 14:21 The **k** said to Joab, "Very well, I will do it H4889
2Sa 14:22 to pay him honor, and he blessed the **k**. H4889
2Sa 14:22 my lord the **k**, because the king has H4889
2Sa 14:22 because the **k** has granted his servant's H4889
2Sa 14:24 But the **k** said, "He must go to his own H4889
2Sa 14:24 house and did not see the face of the **k**. H4889
2Sa 14:29 Joab in order to send him to the **k**, H4889
2Sa 14:32 here so I can send you to the **k** to ask, H4889
2Sa 14:33 So Joab went to the **k** and told him this H4889
2Sa 14:33 Then the **k** summoned Absalom, and he H4889
2Sa 14:33 with his face to the ground before the **k**. H4889
2Sa 14:33 And the **k** kissed Absalom. H4889
2Sa 15: 2 to be placed before the **k** for a decision, H4889
2Sa 15: 3 is no representative of the **k** to hear you." H4889
2Sa 15: 6 who came to the **k** asking for justice, H4889
2Sa 15: 7 Absalom said to the **k**, "Let me go to H4889
2Sa 15: 9 The **k** said to him, "Go in peace." So he H4889
2Sa 15:10 then say, 'Absalom *is* **k** in Hebron. H4887
2Sa 15:15 to do whatever our lord the **k** chooses." H4889
2Sa 15:16 The **k** set out, with his entire household H4889
2Sa 15:17 So the **k** set out, with all the people H4889
2Sa 15:18 him from Gath marched before the **k**. H4889
2Sa 15:19 The **k** said to Ittai the Gittite, "Why should H4889
2Sa 15:19 Go back and stay with **K** Absalom. H4889
2Sa 15:21 But Ittai replied to the **k**, "As surely as the H4889
2Sa 15:21 as my lord the **k** lives, wherever my H4889
2Sa 15:21 wherever my lord the **k** may be, whether it H4889
2Sa 15:23 The **k** also crossed the Kidron Valley, and H4889
2Sa 15:25 Then the **k** said to Zadok, "Take the ark of H4889
2Sa 15:27 The **k** also said to Zadok the priest, "Do H4889
2Sa 16: 2 The **k** asked Ziba, "Why have you brought H4889
2Sa 16: 3 The **k** then asked, "Where is your master's H4889
2Sa 16: 4 Then the **k** said to Ziba, "All that H4889
2Sa 16: 4 I find favor in your eyes, my lord the **k**." H4889
2Sa 16: 5 As **K** David approached Bahurim, a man H4889
2Sa 16: 9 Then Abishai son of Zeruiah said to the **k** H4889
2Sa 16: 9 should this dead dog curse my lord the **k**? H4889
2Sa 16:10 But the **k** said, "What does this have to do H4889
2Sa 16:14 The **k** and all the people with him arrived H4889
2Sa 16:16 said to him, "Long live the **k**! H4889
2Sa 16:16 "Long live the king! Long live the **k**!" H4889
2Sa 17: 2 I would strike down only the **k** H4889
2Sa 17:16 the **k** and all the people with him will H4889
2Sa 17:17 they were to go and tell **K** David, for H4889
2Sa 17:21 of the well and went to inform **K** David. H4889
2Sa 18: 2 The **k** told the troops, "I myself will surely H4889
2Sa 18: 4 The **k** answered, "I will do whatever H4889
2Sa 18: 4 So the **k** stood beside the gate while all H4889
2Sa 18: 5 The **k** commanded Joab, Abishai and Ittai H4889
2Sa 18: 5 the troops heard the **k** giving orders H4889
2Sa 18:12 In our hearing the **k** commanded you and H4889
2Sa 18:13 nothing is hidden from the **k**—you H4889
2Sa 18:19 take the news to the **k** that the LORD has H4889
2Sa 18:21 tell the **k** what you have seen. H4889
2Sa 18:25 called out to the **k** and reported it. H4889
2Sa 18:25 The **k** said, "If he is alone, he must have H4889
2Sa 18:26 The **k** said, "He must be bringing good H4889
2Sa 18:27 a good man," the **k** said. "He comes with H4889
2Sa 18:28 Then Ahimaaz called out to the **k**, "All is H4889
2Sa 18:28 down before the **k** with his face to the H4889
2Sa 18:28 lifted their hands against my lord the **k**." H4889
2Sa 18:29 The **k** asked, "Is the young man Absalom H4889
2Sa 18:30 The **k** said, "Stand aside and wait here." H4889
2Sa 18:31 "My lord the **k**, hear the good news! H4889
2Sa 18:32 The **k** asked the Cushite, "Is the young H4889
2Sa 18:32 of my lord the **k** and all who rise up to H4889
2Sa 18:33 The **k** was shaken. He went up to the H4889
2Sa 19: 1 "The **k** is weeping and mourning for H4889
2Sa 19: 2 "The **k** is grieving for his son. H4889
2Sa 19: 4 The **k** covered his face and cried aloud, H4889
2Sa 19: 5 went into the house to the **k** and said, H4889
2Sa 19: 8 So the **k** got up and took his seat in the H4889
2Sa 19: 8 were told, "The **k** is sitting in the gateway," H4889
2Sa 19: 9 "The **k** delivered us from the hand of our H4889
2Sa 19:10 say nothing about bringing the **k** back?" H4889
2Sa 19:11 **K** David sent this message to Zadok and H4889
2Sa 19:11 the last to bring the **k** back to his palace, H4889
2Sa 19:11 Israel has reached the **k** at his quarters? H4889
2Sa 19:12 should you be the last to bring back the **k**? H4889
2Sa 19:14 They sent word to the **k**, "Return, you and H4889
2Sa 19:15 Then the **k** returned and went as far as the H4889
2Sa 19:15 go out and meet the **k** and bring him H4889
2Sa 19:16 with the men of Judah to meet **K** David. H4889
2Sa 19:17 rushed to the Jordan, where the **k** was. H4889
2Sa 19:18 the Jordan, he fell prostrate before the **k** H4889
2Sa 19:19 on the day my lord the **k** left Jerusalem. H4889
2Sa 19:19 May the **k** put it out of his mind H4889
2Sa 19:20 to come down and meet my lord the **k**." H4889
2Sa 19:22 Don't I know that today I am **k** over Israel? H4889
2Sa 19:23 So the **k** said to Shimei, "You shall not die." H4889
2Sa 19:23 And the **k** promised him on oath. H4889
2Sa 19:24 grandson, also went down to meet the **k**. H4889
2Sa 19:24 from the day the **k** left until the day he H4889
2Sa 19:25 he came from Jerusalem to meet the **k**, H4889
2Sa 19:25 to meet the king, the **k** asked him, "Why H4889
2Sa 19:26 "My lord the **k**, since I your servant H4889
2Sa 19:26 will ride on it, so I can go with the **k**. H4889
2Sa 19:27 slandered your servant to my lord the **k**. H4889
2Sa 19:27 My lord the **k** is like an angel of God; so H4889
2Sa 19:28 nothing but death from my lord the **k**, H4889
2Sa 19:28 have to make any more appeals to the **k**?" H4889
2Sa 19:29 The **k** said to him, "Why say more? I order H4889
2Sa 19:30 Mephibosheth said to the **k**, "Let him take H4889
2Sa 19:30 now that my lord the **k** has returned home H4889
2Sa 19:31 the Jordan with the **k** and to send him on H4889
2Sa 19:32 had provided for the **k** during his stay in H4889
2Sa 19:33 The **k** said to Barzillai, "Cross over with me H4889
2Sa 19:34 But Barzillai answered the **k**, "How many H4889
2Sa 19:34 I should go up to Jerusalem with the **k**? H4889
2Sa 19:35 be an added burden to my lord the **k**? H4889
2Sa 19:36 the Jordan with the **k** for a short distance, H4889
2Sa 19:36 why should the **k** reward me in this H4889
2Sa 19:37 Let him cross over with my lord the **k**. H4889
2Sa 19:38 The **k** said, "Kimham shall cross over with H4889
2Sa 19:39 the Jordan, and then the **k** crossed over. H4889
2Sa 19:39 The **k** kissed Barzillai and bid him H4889
2Sa 19:40 When the **k** crossed over to Gilgal H4889
2Sa 19:40 the troops of Israel had taken the **k** over. H4889
2Sa 19:41 were coming to the **k** and saying to him, H4889
2Sa 19:41 steal the **k** away and bring him and his H4889
2Sa 19:42 did this because the **k** is closely related to H4889
2Sa 19:43 "We have ten shares in the **k**; so we have H4889
2Sa 19:43 the first to speak of bringing back our **k**?" H4889
2Sa 20: 2 stayed by their **k** all the way from the H4889
2Sa 20: 4 Then the **k** said to Amasa, "Summon the H4889
2Sa 20: 5 longer than the time the **k** had set for him. NDT
2Sa 20:21 has lifted up his hand against the **k** H4889
2Sa 20:22 And Joab went back to the **k** in Jerusalem. H4889
2Sa 21: 2 The **k** summoned the Gibeonites and H4889
2Sa 21: 5 They answered the **k**, "As for the man H4889
2Sa 21: 6 So the **k** said, "I will give H4889
2Sa 21: 7 The **k** spared Mephibosheth son of H4889
2Sa 21: 8 But the **k** took Armoni and Mephibosheth H4889
2Sa 21:14 did everything the **k** commanded. H4889
2Sa 22:51 "He gives his **k** great victories; he shows H4889
2Sa 24: 2 So the **k** said to Joab and the army H4889
2Sa 24: 3 But Joab replied to the **k**, "May the LORD H4889
2Sa 24: 3 may the eyes of my lord the **k** see it. H4889
2Sa 24: 3 why does my lord the **k** want to do such a H4889
2Sa 24: 4 the presence of the **k** to enroll the fighting H4889
2Sa 24: 9 the number of the fighting men to the **k**: H4889
2Sa 24:20 looked and saw the **k** and his officials H4889
2Sa 24:20 down before the **k** with his face to the H4889
2Sa 24:21 has my lord the **k** come to his servant?" H4889
2Sa 24:22 "Let my lord the **k** take whatever he H4889
2Sa 24:23 Majesty, Araunah gives all this to the **k**." H4889
2Sa 24:24 But the **k** replied to Araunah, "No, I insist H4889
1Ki 1: 1 When **K** David was very old, he could not H4889
1Ki 1: 2 virgin to serve the **k** and take care of him. H4889
1Ki 1: 2 him so that our lord the **k** may keep warm." H4889
1Ki 1: 3 a Shunammite, and brought her to the **k**. H4889
1Ki 1: 4 she took care of the **k** and waited on him H4889
1Ki 1: 4 the **k** had no sexual relations with her. H4889
1Ki 1: 5 put himself forward and said, "I *will be* **k**." H4887
1Ki 1:11 of Haggith, *has become* **k**, and our lord H4887
1Ki 1:13 Go in to **K** David and say to him, 'My lord H4889
1Ki 1:13 'My lord the **k**, did you not swear H4889
1Ki 1:13 Solomon your son *shall be* **k** after me, H4887
1Ki 1:13 Why then *has* Adonijah *become* **k**?' H4887
1Ki 1:14 While you are still there talking to the **k**, H4889
1Ki 1:15 went to see the aged **k** in his room, H4889
1Ki 1:16 prostrating herself before the **k**. H4889
1Ki 1:16 "What is it you want?" the **k** asked. H4889
1Ki 1:17 'Solomon your son *shall be* **k** after me H4887
1Ki 1:18 But now Adonijah *has become* **k**, and you H4887
1Ki 1:18 you, my lord the **k**, do not know about H4889
1Ki 1:20 My lord the **k**, the eyes of all Israel are on H4889
1Ki 1:20 on the throne of my lord the **k** after him. H4889
1Ki 1:21 soon as my lord the **k** is laid to rest with H4889
1Ki 1:22 While she was still speaking with the **k** H4889
1Ki 1:23 And the **k** was told, "Nathan the prophet is H4889
1Ki 1:23 he went before the **k** and bowed with his H4889
1Ki 1:24 "Have you, my lord the **k**, declared that H4889
1Ki 1:24 that Adonijah *shall be* **k** after you, H4887
1Ki 1:25 him and saying, 'Long live **K** Adonijah! H4889
1Ki 1:27 something my lord the **k** has done without H4889
1Ki 1:27 on the throne of my lord the **k** after him?" H4889
1Ki 1:28 Then **K** David said, "Call in Bathsheba." H4889
1Ki 1:29 The **k** then took an oath: "As surely as the H4889
1Ki 1:30 Solomon your son *shall be* **k** after me H4887
1Ki 1:31 prostrating herself before the **k**, and said, H4889
1Ki 1:31 "May my lord **K** David live forever! H4889
1Ki 1:32 **K** David said, "Call in Zadok the priest H4889
1Ki 1:32 When they came before the **k**, H4889
1Ki 1:34 the prophet anoint him **k** over Israel. H4889
1Ki 1:34 trumpet and shout, 'Long live **K** Solomon! H4889
1Ki 1:36 Benaiah son of Jehoiada answered the **k** H4889
1Ki 1:36 the God of my lord the **k**, so declare it. H4889
1Ki 1:37 As the LORD was with my lord the **k**, so H4889
1Ki 1:37 than the throne of my lord **K** David!" H4889
1Ki 1:38 had Solomon mount **K** David's mule, H4889
1Ki 1:39 people shouted, "Long live **K** Solomon!" H4889
1Ki 1:43 "Our lord **K** David has made Solomon H4889
1Ki 1:43 lord King David *has* **made** Solomon **k**. H4887
1Ki 1:44 The **k** has sent with him Zadok the priest H4889
1Ki 1:45 prophet have anointed him **k** at Gihon. H4889
1Ki 1:47 come to congratulate our lord **K** David, H4889
1Ki 1:47 And the **k** bowed in worship on his bed H4889
1Ki 1:51 "Adonijah is afraid of **K** Solomon and is H4889
1Ki 1:51 'Let **K** Solomon swear to me today that he H4889
1Ki 1:53 Then **K** Solomon sent men, and they H4889
1Ki 1:53 came and bowed down to **K** Solomon, H4889
1Ki 2:15 All Israel looked to me as their **k**. H4887
1Ki 2:17 "Please ask **K** Solomon—he will not H4889
1Ki 2:18 replied, "I will speak to the **k** for you." H4889
1Ki 2:19 Bathsheba went to **K** Solomon to speak to H4889
1Ki 2:19 Adonijah, the **k** stood up to meet her H4889
1Ki 2:20 The **k** replied, "Make it, my mother; I will H4889
1Ki 2:22 **K** Solomon answered his mother, "Why H4889
1Ki 2:23 Then **K** Solomon swore by the LORD: "May H4889
1Ki 2:25 So **K** Solomon gave orders to Benaiah son H4889
1Ki 2:26 To Abiathar the priest the **k** said, "Go H4889
1Ki 2:29 **K** Solomon was told that Joab had fled to H4889
1Ki 2:30 said to Joab, "The **k** says, 'Come out! H4889
1Ki 2:30 Benaiah reported to the **k**, "This is how H4889
1Ki 2:31 Then the **k** commanded Benaiah, "Do as H4889
1Ki 2:35 The **k** put Benaiah son of Jehoiada over H4889
1Ki 2:36 Then the **k** sent for Shimei and said to H4889
1Ki 2:38 Shimei answered the **k**, "What you say is H4889
1Ki 2:38 servant will do as my lord the **k** has said." H4889
1Ki 2:39 son of Maakah, **k** *of* Gath, and Shimei H4889
1Ki 2:42 the **k** summoned Shimei and said to him H4889
1Ki 2:44 The **k** also said to Shimei, "You know in H4889
1Ki 2:45 But **K** Solomon will be blessed, and H4889
1Ki 2:46 Then the **k** gave the order to Benaiah son H4889
1Ki 3: 1 with Pharaoh **k** *of* Egypt and married H4889
1Ki 3: 4 The **k** went to Gibeon to offer sacrifices H4889
1Ki 3: 7 you *have* **made** your servant **k** in place of H4887
1Ki 3:16 came to the **k** and stood before him. H4889
1Ki 3:22 And so they argued before the **k**. H4889
1Ki 3:23 The **k** said, "This one says, 'My son is H4889
1Ki 3:24 Then the **k** said, "Bring me a sword." H4889
1Ki 3:24 So they brought a sword for the **k**. H4889
1Ki 3:26 out of love for her son and said to the **k**, H4889
1Ki 3:27 Then the **k** gave his ruling: "Give the H4889
1Ki 3:28 Israel heard the verdict the **k** had given, H4889
1Ki 3:28 they held the **k** in awe, because they H4889
1Ki 4: 1 So **K** Solomon ruled over all Israel. H4889
1Ki 4: 5 of Nathan—a priest and adviser to the **k**; H4889
1Ki 4: 7 provisions for the **k** and the royal H4889
1Ki 4:19 the country of Sihon **k** *of* the Amorites and H4889
1Ki 4:19 the country of Og **k** *of* Bashan). H4889
1Ki 4:27 provisions for **K** Solomon and all who H4889
1Ki 5: 1 When Hiram **k** *of* Tyre heard that H4889
1Ki 5: 1 had been anointed **k** to succeed his father H4889
1Ki 5:13 **K** Solomon conscripted laborers from all H4889
1Ki 6: 2 The temple that **K** Solomon built for the H4889
1Ki 7:13 **K** Solomon sent to Tyre and brought H4889
1Ki 7:14 He came to **K** Solomon and did all the H4889
1Ki 7:40 had undertaken for **K** Solomon in the H4889
1Ki 7:45 that Huram made for **K** Solomon for the H4889
1Ki 7:46 The **k** had them cast in clay molds in the H4889
1Ki 7:51 When all the work **K** Solomon had done H4889
1Ki 8: 1 Then **K** Solomon summoned into his H4889
1Ki 8: 2 came together to **K** Solomon at the time H4889
1Ki 8: 5 **K** Solomon and the entire assembly of H4889
1Ki 8:14 the **k** turned around and blessed them. H4889
1Ki 8:62 Then the **k** and all Israel with him offered H4889
1Ki 8:63 So the **k** and all the Israelites dedicated H4889
1Ki 8:64 On that same day the **k** consecrated the H4889
1Ki 8:66 They blessed the **k** and then went home H4889
1Ki 9:11 **K** Solomon gave twenty towns in Galilee H4889
1Ki 9:11 towns in Galilee to Hiram **k** *of* Tyre, H4889
1Ki 9:14 had sent to the **k** 120 talents of gold. H4889
1Ki 9:15 of the forced labor **K** Solomon conscripted H4889
1Ki 9:16 Pharaoh **k** *of* Egypt had attacked and H4889
1Ki 9:26 **K** Solomon also built ships at Ezion Geber H4889
1Ki 9:28 which they delivered to **K** Solomon. H4889
1Ki 10: 3 was too hard for the **k** to explain to her. H4889
1Ki 10: 6 She said to the **k**, "The report I heard in H4889
1Ki 10: 9 he has made you **k** to maintain justice H4889
1Ki 10:10 And she gave the **k** 120 talents of gold H4889
1Ki 10:10 the queen of Sheba gave to **K** Solomon. H4889
1Ki 10:12 The **k** used the almugwood to make H4889
1Ki 10:13 **K** Solomon gave the queen of Sheba all H4889
1Ki 10:16 **K** Solomon made two hundred large H4889
1Ki 10:17 The **k** put them in the Palace of the Forest H4889
1Ki 10:18 Then the **k** made a great throne covered H4889
1Ki 10:21 All **K** Solomon's goblets were gold, and H4889
1Ki 10:22 The **k** had a fleet of trading ships at sea H4889
1Ki 10:23 **K** Solomon was greater in riches and H4889
1Ki 10:27 The **k** made silver as common in H4889
1Ki 11: 1 **K** Solomon, however, loved many foreign H4889
1Ki 11:18 to Egypt, to Pharaoh **k** *of* Egypt, who gave H4889
1Ki 11:23 from his master, Hadadezer **k** *of* Zobah. H4889
1Ki 11:26 son of Nebat rebelled against the **k**. H4889
1Ki 11:27 account of how he rebelled against the **k**: H4889
1Ki 11:37 heart desires; you will be **k** over Israel. H4889
1Ki 11:40 to Shishak the **k**, and stayed there H4889
1Ki 11:43 Rehoboam his son succeeded him *as* **k**. H4887
1Ki 12: 1 all Israel had gone there to **make** him **k**. H4887
1Ki 12: 2 where he had fled from **K** Solomon), H4889
1Ki 12: 6 Then **K** Rehoboam consulted the elders H4889
1Ki 12:12 to Rehoboam, as the **k** had said, "Come H4889
1Ki 12:13 The **k** answered the people harshly H4889
1Ki 12:15 So the **k** did not listen to the people, for H4889
1Ki 12:16 Israel saw that the **k** refused to listen to H4889
1Ki 12:16 to listen to them, they answered the **k**: H4889

1Ki 12:18 **K** Rehoboam sent out Adoniram, who was H4889
1Ki 12:18 **K** Rehoboam, however, managed to get H4889
1Ki 12:20 assembly and **made** him **k** over all Israel H4887
1Ki 12:23 to Rehoboam son of Solomon **k** *of* Judah, H4889
1Ki 12:27 to their lord, Rehoboam **k** *of* Judah. H4889
1Ki 12:27 will kill me and return to **K** Rehoboam." H4889
1Ki 12:28 the **k** made two golden calves. H4889
1Ki 13: 4 When **K** Jeroboam heard what the man of H4889
1Ki 13: 6 Then the **k** said to the man of God H4889
1Ki 13: 7 The **k** said to the man of God, "Come H4889
1Ki 13: 8 But the man of God answered the **k** H4889
1Ki 13:11 told their father what he had said to the **k**. H4889
1Ki 14: 2 told me I would be **k** over this people. H4889
1Ki 14:14 up for himself a **k** over Israel who will H4889
1Ki 14:20 And Nadab his son succeeded him *as* **k**. H4887
1Ki 14:21 son of Solomon *was* **k** in Judah. H4887
1Ki 14:21 forty-one years old when he *became* **k**, H4887
1Ki 14:25 In the fifth year of **K** Rehoboam, Shishak H4889
1Ki 14:25 Shishak **e** *of* Egypt attacked Jerusalem. H4889
1Ki 14:27 So **K** Rehoboam made bronze shields to H4889
1Ki 14:28 Whenever the **k** went to the LORD's temple H4889
1Ki 14:31 And Abijah his son succeeded him *as* **k**. H4887
1Ki 15: 1 son of Nebat, Abijah *became* **k** of Judah, H4887
1Ki 15: 8 And Asa his son succeeded him *as* **k**. H4887
1Ki 15: 9 the twentieth year of Jeroboam **k** *of* Israel, H4889
1Ki 15: 9 of Israel, Asa *became* **k** *of* Judah, H4887+4889
1Ki 15:16 Asa and Baasha **k** *of* Israel throughout H4889
1Ki 15:17 Baasha **k** *of* Israel went up against Judah H4889
1Ki 15:17 entering the territory of Asa **k** *of* Judah. H4889
1Ki 15:18 son of Hezion, the **k** *of* Aram, who was H4889
1Ki 15:19 treaty with Baasha **k** *of* Israel so he will H4889
1Ki 15:20 agreed with **K** Asa and sent the H4889
1Ki 15:22 Then **K** Asa issued an order to all Judah H4889
1Ki 15:22 With them **K** Asa built up Geba in H4889
1Ki 15:24 Jehoshaphat his son succeeded him *as* **k**. H4887
1Ki 15:25 son of Jeroboam *became* **k** of Israel in the H4887
1Ki 15:25 in the second year of Asa **k** *of* Judah, H4889
1Ki 15:28 third year of Asa **k** *of* Judah and H4889
1Ki 15:28 king of Judah and succeeded him *as* **k**. H4887
1Ki 15:32 Asa and Baasha **k** *of* Israel throughout H4889
1Ki 15:33 In the third year of Asa **k** *of* Judah H4889
1Ki 15:33 son of Ahijah *became* **k** of all Israel in H4887
1Ki 16: 6 And Elah his son succeeded him *as* **k**. H4887
1Ki 16: 8 In the twenty-sixth year of Asa **k** *of* Judah H4889
1Ki 16: 8 Elah son of Baasha *became* **k** of Israel H4887
1Ki 16:10 twenty-seventh year of Asa **k** *of* Judah. H4889
1Ki 16:10 Then *he* succeeded him *as* **k**. H4887
1Ki 16:15 twenty-seventh year of Asa **k** *of* Judah, H4889
1Ki 16:16 plotted against the **k** and murdered him, H4889
1Ki 16:16 **proclaimed** Omri, the commander of the army, **k** H4887
1Ki 16:21 half supported Tibni son of Ginath for **k** H4887
1Ki 16:22 So Tibni died and Omri *became* **k**. H4887
1Ki 16:23 In the thirty-first year of Asa **k** *of* Judah H4889
1Ki 16:23 of Judah, Omri *became* **k** of Israel, and he H4887
1Ki 16:28 And Ahab his son succeeded him *as* **k**. H4887
1Ki 16:29 In the thirty-eighth year of Asa **k** *of* Judah H4889
1Ki 16:29 Ahab son of Omri *became* **k** of Israel, and H4887
1Ki 16:31 daughter of Ethbaal **k** *of* the Sidonians, H4889
1Ki 19:15 you get there, anoint Hazael **k** over Aram. H4889
1Ki 19:16 anoint Jehu son of Nimshi **k** over Israel H4889
1Ki 20: 1 Now Ben-Hadad **k** *of* Aram mustered his H4889
1Ki 20: 2 into the city to Ahab **k** *of* Israel, H4889
1Ki 20: 4 The **k** *of* Israel answered, "Just as you say H4889
1Ki 20: 4 answered, "Just as you say, my lord the **k**. H4889
1Ki 20: 7 The **k** *of* Israel summoned all the elders H4889
1Ki 20: 9 "Tell my lord the **k**, 'Your servant will do H4889
1Ki 20:11 The **k** *of* Israel answered, "Tell him: 'One H4889
1Ki 20:13 prophet came to Ahab **k** *of* Israel and H4889
1Ki 20:20 But Ben-Hadad **k** *of* Aram escaped on H4889
1Ki 20:21 The **k** *of* Israel advanced and overpowered H4889
1Ki 20:22 prophet came to the **k** *of* Israel and said, H4889
1Ki 20:22 next spring the **k** *of* Aram will attack you H4889
1Ki 20:23 the officials of the **k** *of* Aram advised him H4889
1Ki 20:28 of God came up and told the **k** *of* Israel, H4889
1Ki 20:31 Let us go to the **k** *of* Israel with sackcloth H4889
1Ki 20:32 they went to the **k** *of* Israel and said H4889
1Ki 20:32 The **k** answered, "Is he still NDT
1Ki 20:33 get him," the **k** said. When Ben-Hadad NDT
1Ki 20:38 stood by the road waiting for the **k**. H4889
1Ki 20:39 As the **k** passed by, the prophet called out H4889
1Ki 20:40 is your sentence," the **k** *of* Israel said. H4889
1Ki 20:41 the **k** *of* Israel recognized him as one H4889
1Ki 20:42 He said to **the k**, "This is what the LORD H2257
1Ki 20:43 the **k** *of* Israel went to his palace in H4889
1Ki 21: 1 close to the palace of Ahab **k** *of* Samaria. H4889
1Ki 21: 7 "Is this how you act as **k** over Israel? H4867
1Ki 21:10 that he has cursed both God and the **k**. H4889
1Ki 21:13 "Naboth has cursed both God and the **k**." H4889
1Ki 21:18 "Go down to meet Ahab **k** *of* Israel, who H4889
1Ki 22: 2 year Jehoshaphat **k** *of* Judah went down H4889
1Ki 22: 2 of Judah went down to see the **k** *of* Israel. H4889
1Ki 22: 3 The **k** *of* Israel had said to his officials H4889
1Ki 22: 3 nothing to retake it from the **k** *of* Aram?" H4889
1Ki 22: 4 Jehoshaphat replied to the **k** *of* Israel, "I H4889
1Ki 22: 5 Jehoshaphat also said to the **k** *of* Israel, H4889
1Ki 22: 6 So the **k** *of* Israel brought together the H4889
1Ki 22: 8 The **k** *of* Israel answered Jehoshaphat H4889
1Ki 22: 8 "The **k** should not say such a thing," H4889
1Ki 22: 9 So the **k** *of* Israel called one of his H4889
1Ki 22:10 the **k** *of* Israel and Jehoshaphat king of H4889
1Ki 22:10 Jehoshaphat **k** *of* Judah were sitting H4889
1Ki 22:13 exception are predicting success for the **k**. H4889
1Ki 22:15 he arrived, the **k** asked him, "Micaiah, H4889
1Ki 22:16 The **k** said to him, "How many times must H4889
1Ki 22:18 The **k** *of* Israel said to Jehoshaphat H4889
1Ki 22:26 The **k** *of* Israel then ordered, "Take H4889
1Ki 22:27 'This is what the **k** says: Put this fellow H4889
1Ki 22:29 So the **k** *of* Israel and Jehoshaphat king of H4889
1Ki 22:29 Jehoshaphat **k** *of* Judah went up to H4889
1Ki 22:30 The **k** *of* Israel said to Jehoshaphat, "I will H4889
1Ki 22:30 So the **k** *of* Israel disguised himself and H4889
1Ki 22:31 Now the **k** *of* Aram had ordered his H4889
1Ki 22:31 small or great, except the **k** *of* Israel." H4889
1Ki 22:32 they thought, "Surely this is the **k** *of* Israel." H4889
1Ki 22:33 he was not the **k** *of* Israel and stopped H4889
1Ki 22:34 random and hit the **k** *of* Israel between H4889
1Ki 22:34 The **k** told his chariot driver, "Wheel around NDT
1Ki 22:35 the **k** was propped up in his chariot H4889
1Ki 22:37 So the **k** died and was brought to Samaria H4889
1Ki 22:40 And Ahaziah his son succeeded him *as* **k** H4887
1Ki 22:41 son of Asa *became* **k** of Judah in the H4887
1Ki 22:41 in the fourth year of Ahab **k** *of* Israel. H4889
1Ki 22:42 thirty-five years old when he *became* **k**, H4887
1Ki 22:44 was also at peace with the **k** *of* Israel. H4889
1Ki 22:47 There was then no **k** in Edom; a provincial H4889
1Ki 22:50 And Jehoram his son succeeded him *as* **k** H4887
1Ki 22:51 son of Ahab *became* **k** of Israel in H4887
1Ki 22:51 year of Jehoshaphat **k** *of* Judah, H4889
2Ki 1: 3 messengers of the **k** *of* Samaria and ask H4889
2Ki 1: 5 When the messengers returned to **the k** H2257S
2Ki 1: 6 'Go back to the **k** who sent you and tell H4889
2Ki 1: 7 The **k** asked them, "What kind of man was it NDT
2Ki 1: 8 The **k** said, "That was Elijah NDT
2Ki 1: 9 "Man of God, the **k** says, 'Come down! H4889
2Ki 1:11 At this the **k** sent to Elijah another captain NDT
2Ki 1:11 this is what the **k** says, 'Come down at H4889
2Ki 1:13 So the **k** sent a third captain with his fifty NDT
2Ki 1:15 got up and went down with him to the **k**. H4889
2Ki 1:16 told **the k**, "This is what the LORD says: H2257S
2Ki 1:17 succeeded him *as* **k** in the second year H4887
2Ki 1:17 Jehoram son of Jehoshaphat **k** *of* Judah. H4889
2Ki 3: 1 Joram son of Ahab *became* **k** of Israel in H4887
2Ki 3: 1 year of Jehoshaphat **k** *of* Judah, H4889
2Ki 3: 4 Now Mesha **k** *of* Moab raised sheep, and H4889
2Ki 3: 4 he had to pay the **k** *of* Israel a tribute of H4889
2Ki 3: 5 the **k** *of* Moab rebelled against the king of H4889
2Ki 3: 5 of Moab rebelled against the **k** *of* Israel. H4889
2Ki 3: 6 So at that time **K** Joram set out from H4889
2Ki 3: 7 this message to Jehoshaphat **k** *of* Judah: H4889
2Ki 3: 7 "The **k** *of* Moab has rebelled against me H4889
2Ki 3: 9 So the **k** *of* Israel set out with the king of H4889
2Ki 3: 9 set out with the **k** *of* Judah and the king of H4889
2Ki 3: 9 with the king of Judah and the **k** *of* Edom. H4889
2Ki 3:10 exclaimed the **k** *of* Israel. "Has the H4889
2Ki 3:11 An officer of the **k** *of* Israel answered H4889
2Ki 3:12 So the **k** *of* Israel and Jehoshaphat and H4889
2Ki 3:12 the **k** *of* Edom went down to H4889
2Ki 3:13 Elisha said to the **k** *of* Israel, "Why do you H4889
2Ki 3:13 the **k** *of* Israel answered, "because it was H4889
2Ki 3:14 the presence of Jehoshaphat **k** *of* Judah, H4889
2Ki 3:26 When the **k** *of* Moab saw that the battle H4889
2Ki 3:26 to break through to the **k** *of* Edom, H4889
2Ki 3:27 who *was to* succeed him *as* **k**, and H4887
2Ki 4:13 your behalf to the **k** or the commander of H4889
2Ki 5: 1 commander of the army of the **k** *of* Aram. H4889
2Ki 5: 5 all means, go," the **k** *of* Aram replied. "I H4889
2Ki 5: 5 "I will send a letter to the **k** *of* Israel." H4889
2Ki 5: 6 letter that he took to the **k** *of* Israel read: H4889
2Ki 5: 7 As soon as the **k** *of* Israel read the letter H4889
2Ki 5: 8 God heard that the **k** *of* Israel had torn his H4889
2Ki 6: 8 Now the **k** *of* Aram was at war with Israel H4889
2Ki 6: 9 man of God sent word to the **k** *of* Israel: H4889
2Ki 6:10 So the **k** *of* Israel checked on the place H4889
2Ki 6:10 Time and again Elisha warned **the k**, so H2257S
2Ki 6:11 This enraged the **k** *of* Aram. H4889
2Ki 6:11 of us is on the side of the **k** *of* Israel?" H4889
2Ki 6:12 my lord the **k**," said one of his H4889
2Ki 6:12 tells the **k** *of* Israel the very words you H4889
2Ki 6:13 the **k** ordered, "so I can send men and NDT
2Ki 6:21 When the **k** *of* Israel saw them, he asked H4889
2Ki 6:24 Ben-Hadad **k** *of* Aram mobilized his H4889
2Ki 6:26 As the **k** *of* Israel was passing by on the H4889
2Ki 6:26 cried to him, "Help me, my lord the **k**!" H4889
2Ki 6:27 The **k** replied, "If the LORD does not help NDT
2Ki 6:30 When the **k** heard the woman's words, he H4889
2Ki 6:32 **The k** sent a messenger ahead, but H2257S
2Ki 6:33 The **k** said, "This disaster NDT
2Ki 7: 2 on whose arm the **k** was leaning said to H4889
2Ki 7: 6 the **k** *of* Israel has hired the Hittite and H4889
2Ki 7:12 The **k** got up in the night and said to his H4889
2Ki 7:14 the **k** sent them after the Aramean H4889
2Ki 7:15 returned and reported to the **k**. H4889
2Ki 7:17 Now the **k** had put the officer on whose H4889
2Ki 7:17 had foretold when the **k** came down to his H4889
2Ki 7:18 as the man of God had said to the **k**: H4889
2Ki 8: 3 went to appeal to the **k** for her house and H4889
2Ki 8: 4 The **k** was talking to Gehazi, the servant of H4889
2Ki 8: 5 Gehazi was telling the **k** how Elisha had H4889
2Ki 8: 5 came to appeal to the **k** for her house H4889
2Ki 8: 5 woman, my lord the **k**, and this is her son H4889
2Ki 8: 6 The **k** asked the woman about it, and she H4889
2Ki 8: 7 Ben-Hadad **k** *of* Aram was ill. H4889
2Ki 8: 7 When **the k** was told, "The man of God H2257S
2Ki 8: 9 son Ben-Hadad **k** *of* Aram has sent me H4889
2Ki 8:13 me that you will become **k** of Aram," H4889
2Ki 8:15 Then Hazael succeeded him *as* **k**. H4887
2Ki 8:16 fifth year of Joram son of Ahab **k** *of* Israel, H4889
2Ki 8:16 when Jehoshaphat was **k** *of* Judah H4889
2Ki 8:16 began his reign as **k** *of* Judah. H4889
2Ki 8:17 thirty-two years old when he *became* **k**, H4887
2Ki 8:20 against Judah and **set up** its own **k**. H4887+4889
2Ki 8:24 And Ahaziah his son succeeded him *as* **k** H4887
2Ki 8:25 year of Joram son of Ahab **k** *of* Israel, H4889
2Ki 8:25 son of Jehoram **k** *of* Judah began to reign H4889
2Ki 8:26 twenty-two years old when he *became* **k**, H4887
2Ki 8:26 a granddaughter of Omri **k** *of* Israel. H4889
2Ki 8:28 war against Hazael **k** *of* Aram at Ramoth H4889
2Ki 8:29 so **K** Joram returned to Jezreel to recover H4889
2Ki 8:29 in his battle with Hazael **k** *of* Aram. H4889
2Ki 8:29 son of Jehoram **k** *of* Judah went down to H4889
2Ki 9: 3 I anoint you **k** over Israel.' Then H4889
2Ki 9: 6 'I anoint you **k** over the LORD's people H4889
2Ki 9:12 the LORD says: I anoint you **k** over Israel.' " H4889
2Ki 9:13 blew the trumpet and shouted, "Jehu *is* **k**!" H4887
2Ki 9:14 Ramoth Gilead against Hazael **k** *of* Aram, H4889
2Ki 9:15 **K** Joram had returned to Jezreel to H4889
2Ki 9:15 him in the battle with Hazael **k** *of* Aram.) H4889
2Ki 9:15 "If you desire to make me **k**, don't let NDT
2Ki 9:16 there and Ahaziah **k** *of* Judah had gone H4889
2Ki 9:18 Jehu and said, "This is what the **k** says: H4889
2Ki 9:19 So the **k** sent out a second horseman. NDT
2Ki 9:19 to them he said, "This is what the **k** says: H4889
2Ki 9:21 Joram **k** *of* Israel and Ahaziah king of H4889
2Ki 9:21 of Israel and Ahaziah **k** *of* Judah rode out, H4889
2Ki 9:27 When Ahaziah **k** *of* Judah saw what had H4889
2Ki 9:29 Ahaziah *had become* **k** of Judah. H4887
2Ki 10: 5 *We will* not **appoint** anyone **as k**; you do H4887
2Ki 10:13 of Ahaziah **k** *of* Judah and asked, H4889
2Ki 10:13 the families of the **k** and of the queen H4889
2Ki 10:35 Jehoahaz his son succeeded him *as* **k**. H4887
2Ki 11: 2 the daughter of **K** Jehoram and sister of H4889
2Ki 11: 7 duty are all to guard the temple for the **k**. H4889
2Ki 11: 8 Station yourselves around the **k**, each of H4889
2Ki 11: 8 Stay close to the **k** wherever he goes." H4889
2Ki 11:10 had belonged to **K** David and that were H4889
2Ki 11:11 stationed themselves around the **k**—near H4889
2Ki 11:12 of the covenant and **proclaimed** him **k**. H4887
2Ki 11:12 their hands and shouted, "Long live the **k**!" H4889
2Ki 11:14 She looked and there was the **k**, standing H4889
2Ki 11:14 the trumpeters were beside the **k**, H4889
2Ki 11:17 the LORD and the **k** and people that they H4889
2Ki 11:17 covenant between the **k** and the people. H4889
2Ki 11:19 they brought the **k** down from the temple H4889
2Ki 11:19 The **k** then took his place on the royal NDT
2Ki 12: 1 of Jehu, Joash *became* **k**, and he reigned H4887
2Ki 12: 6 twenty-third year of **K** Joash the priests H4889
2Ki 12: 7 Therefore **K** Joash summoned Jehoiada H4889
2Ki 12:17 this time Hazael **k** *of* Aram went up and H4889
2Ki 12:18 But Joash **k** *of* Judah took all the sacred H4889
2Ki 12:18 he sent them to Hazael **k** *of* Aram H4889
2Ki 12:21 And Amaziah his son succeeded him *as* **k**. H4887
2Ki 13: 1 year of Joash son of Ahaziah **k** *of* Judah, H4889
2Ki 13: 1 son of Jehu *became* **k** of Israel in H4887
2Ki 13: 3 power of Hazael **k** *of* Aram and H4889
2Ki 13: 4 how severely the **k** *of* Aram was H4889
2Ki 13: 7 the **k** *of* Aram had destroyed the rest H4889
2Ki 13: 9 And Jehoash his son succeeded him *as* **k** H4887
2Ki 13:10 thirty-seventh year of Joash **k** *of* Judah, H4889
2Ki 13:10 son of Jehoahaz *became* **k** of Israel in H4887
2Ki 13:12 his war against Amaziah **k** *of* Judah, H4889
2Ki 13:14 Jehoash **k** *of* Israel went down to see him H4889
2Ki 13:16 in your hands," he said to the **k** *of* Israel. H4889
2Ki 13:18 "Take the arrows," and the **k** took them. H4889
2Ki 13:22 Hazael **k** *of* Aram oppressed Israel H4889
2Ki 13:24 Hazael **k** *of* Aram died, and Ben-Hadad H4889
2Ki 13:24 Ben-Hadad his son succeeded him *as* **k**. H4887
2Ki 14: 1 of Jehoash son of Jehoahaz **k** *of* Israel, H4889
2Ki 14: 1 son of Joash **k** *of* Judah began to H4889
2Ki 14: 2 twenty-five years old when he *became* **k**, H4887
2Ki 14: 5 who had murdered his father the **k**. H4889
2Ki 14: 8 the son of Jehu, **k** *of* Israel, with the H4889
2Ki 14: 9 But Jehoash **k** *of* Israel replied to H4889
2Ki 14: 9 of Israel replied to Amaziah **k** *of* Judah: H4889
2Ki 14:11 not listen, so Jehoash **k** *of* Israel attacked. H4889
2Ki 14:11 He and Amaziah **k** *of* Judah faced each H4889
2Ki 14:13 Jehoash **k** *of* Israel captured Amaziah king H4889
2Ki 14:13 of Israel captured Amaziah **k** *of* Judah, H4889
2Ki 14:15 his war against Amaziah **k** *of* Judah, H4889
2Ki 14:16 Jeroboam his son succeeded him *as* **k**. H4887
2Ki 14:17 Amaziah son of Joash **k** *of* Judah lived H4889
2Ki 14:17 of Jehoash son of Jehoahaz **k** *of* Israel. H4889
2Ki 14:21 and **made** him **k** in place of his father H4887
2Ki 14:23 year of Amaziah son of Joash **k** *of* Judah, H4889
2Ki 14:23 son of Jehoash **k** *of* Israel became king in H4889
2Ki 14:23 king of Israel *became* **k** in Samaria, H4887
2Ki 14:29 Zechariah his son succeeded him *as* **k**. H4887
2Ki 15: 1 year of Jeroboam **k** *of* Israel, H4889
2Ki 15: 1 son of Amaziah **k** *of* Judah began to reign H4889
2Ki 15: 2 was sixteen years old when he *became* **k**, H4887
2Ki 15: 5 LORD afflicted the **k** with leprosy until the H4889
2Ki 15: 7 And Jotham his son succeeded him *as* **k**. H4887
2Ki 15: 8 thirty-eighth year of Azariah **k** *of* Judah, H4889
2Ki 15: 8 son of Jeroboam *became* **k** of Israel in H4887
2Ki 15:10 him and succeeded him *as* **k**. H4887
2Ki 15:13 son of Jabesh *became* **k** in the thirty-ninth H4887

2Ki 15:13 the thirty-ninth year of Uzziah **k** *of* Judah, H4889
2Ki 15:14 him and succeeded him *as* **k**. H4887
2Ki 15:17 the thirty-ninth year of Azariah **k** *of* Judah, H4889
2Ki 15:17 Menahem son of Gadi *became* **k** of Israel H4887
2Ki 15:19 Then Pul **k** *of* Assyria invaded the land H4889
2Ki 15:20 of silver to be given to the **k** *of* Assyria. H4889
2Ki 15:20 So the **k** *of* Assyria withdrew and stayed in H4889
2Ki 15:22 Pekahiah his son succeeded him *as* **k**. H4887
2Ki 15:23 In the fiftieth year of Azariah **k** *of* Judah H4889
2Ki 15:23 son of Menahem *became* **k** of Israel in H4887
2Ki 15:25 killed Pekahiah and succeeded him *as* **k**. H4887
2Ki 15:27 fifty-second year of Azariah **k** *of* Judah, H4889
2Ki 15:27 son of Remaliah *became* **k** of Israel in H4887
2Ki 15:29 In the time of Pekah **k** *of* Israel H4889
2Ki 15:29 Tiglath-Pileser **k** *of* Assyria came and took H4889
2Ki 15:30 then succeeded him *as* **k** in the twentieth H4887
2Ki 15:32 year of Pekah son of Remaliah **k** *of* Israel, H4889
2Ki 15:32 Jotham son of Uzziah **k** *of* Judah began to H4889
2Ki 15:33 twenty-five years old when he *became* **k**, H4887
2Ki 15:37 to send Rezin **k** *of* Aram and Pekah son H4889
2Ki 15:38 And Ahaz his son succeeded him *as* **k**. H4887
2Ki 16: 1 Ahaz son of Jotham **k** *of* Judah began to H4889
2Ki 16: 2 was twenty years old when he *became* **k**, H4887
2Ki 16: 5 Then Rezin **k** *of* Aram and Pekah son of H4889
2Ki 16: 5 son of Remaliah **k** *of* Israel marched up to H4889
2Ki 16: 6 Rezin **k** *of* Aram recovered Elath for Aram H4889
2Ki 16: 7 to say to Tiglath-Pileser **k** *of* Assyria, H4889
2Ki 16: 7 of the hand of the **k** *of* Aram and of the H4889
2Ki 16: 7 of the king of Aram and of the **k** *of* Israel, H4889
2Ki 16: 8 sent it as a gift to the **k** *of* Assyria. H4889
2Ki 16: 9 The **k** *of* Assyria complied by attacking H4889
2Ki 16:10 Then **K** Ahaz went to Damascus to meet H4889
2Ki 16:10 to meet Tiglath-Pileser **k** *of* Assyria. H4889
2Ki 16:11 all the plans that **K** Ahaz had sent from H4889
2Ki 16:11 finished it before **K** Ahaz returned. H4889
2Ki 16:12 When the **k** came back from Damascus H4889
2Ki 16:15 **K** Ahaz then gave these orders to Uriah H4889
2Ki 16:16 the priest did just as **K** Ahaz had ordered. H4889
2Ki 16:17 **K** Ahaz cut off the side panels and H4889
2Ki 16:18 the LORD, in deference to the **k** *of* Assyria. H4889
2Ki 16:20 Hezekiah his son succeeded him *as* **k**. H4887
2Ki 17: 1 In the twelfth year of Ahaz **k** *of* Judah H4889
2Ki 17: 1 Hoshea son of Elah *became* **k** of Israel in H4887
2Ki 17: 3 Shalmaneser **k** *of* Assyria came up to H4889
2Ki 17: 4 But the **k** *of* Assyria discovered that H4889
2Ki 17: 4 he had sent envoys to So **k** *of* Egypt H4889
2Ki 17: 4 no longer paid tribute to the **k** *of* Assyria, H4889
2Ki 17: 5 The **k** *of* Assyria invaded the entire land H4889
2Ki 17: 6 the **k** *of* Assyria captured Samaria and H4889
2Ki 17: 7 under the power of Pharaoh **k** *of* Egypt. H4889
2Ki 17:21 *they* **made** Jeroboam son of Nebat *their* **k**. H4887
2Ki 17:24 The **k** *of* Assyria brought people from H4889
2Ki 17:26 It was reported to the **k** *of* Assyria: "The H4889
2Ki 17:27 Then the **k** *of* Assyria gave this order H4889
2Ki 18: 1 year of Hoshea son of Elah **k** *of* Israel, H4889
2Ki 18: 1 son of Ahaz **k** *of* Judah began to H4889
2Ki 18: 2 twenty-five years old when he *became* **k**, H4887
2Ki 18: 7 against the **k** *of* Assyria and did not H4889
2Ki 18: 9 In **K** Hezekiah's fourth year, which was the H4889
2Ki 18: 9 year of Hoshea son of Elah **k** *of* Israel, H4889
2Ki 18: 9 Shalmaneser **k** *of* Assyria marched H4889
2Ki 18:10 was the ninth year of Hoshea **k** *of* Israel. H4889
2Ki 18:11 The **k** *of* Assyria deported Israel to Assyria H4889
2Ki 18:13 the fourteenth year of **K** Hezekiah's reign, H4889
2Ki 18:13 Sennacherib **k** *of* Assyria attacked all the H4889
2Ki 18:14 So Hezekiah **k** *of* Judah sent this message H4889
2Ki 18:14 this message to the **k** *of* Assyria at Lachish H4889
2Ki 18:14 The **k** *of* Assyria exacted from Hezekiah H4889
2Ki 18:14 from Hezekiah **k** *of* Judah three hundred H4889
2Ki 18:16 this time Hezekiah **k** *of* Judah stripped off H4889
2Ki 18:16 of the LORD, and gave it to the **k** *of* Assyria. H4889
2Ki 18:17 The **k** *of* Assyria sent his supreme H4889
2Ki 18:17 from Lachish to **K** Hezekiah at Jerusalem. H4889
2Ki 18:18 They called for the **k**; and Eliakim son of H4889
2Ki 18:19 " 'This is what the great **k**, the king of H4889
2Ki 18:19 what the great king, the **k** *of* Assyria, says: H4889
2Ki 18:21 Such is Pharaoh **k** *of* Egypt to all who H4889
2Ki 18:23 bargain with my master, the **k** *of* Assyria: H4889
2Ki 18:28 "Hear the word of the great **k**, the king of H4889
2Ki 18:28 word of the great king, the **k** *of* Assyria! H4889
2Ki 18:29 This is what the **k** says: Do not let H4889
2Ki 18:30 be given into the hand of the **k** *of* Assyria. H4889
2Ki 18:31 This is what the **k** *of* Assyria says: Make H4889
2Ki 18:33 his land from the hand of the **k** *of* Assyria? H4889
2Ki 18:36 because the **k** had commanded, "Do H4889
2Ki 19: 1 When **K** Hezekiah heard this, he tore his H4889
2Ki 19: 4 his master, the **k** *of* Assyria, has sent H4889
2Ki 19: 5 When **K** Hezekiah's officials came to H4889
2Ki 19: 6 the underlings of the **k** *of* Assyria have H4889
2Ki 19: 8 heard that the **k** *of* Assyria had left H4889
2Ki 19: 8 withdrew and found the **k** fighting against NDT
2Ki 19: 9 that Tirhakah, the **k** of Cush, was H4889
2Ki 19:10 "Say to Hezekiah **k** *of* Judah: Do not let H4889
2Ki 19:10 given into the hands of the **k** *of* Assyria. H4889
2Ki 19:13 Where is the **k** *of* Hamath or the king of H4889
2Ki 19:13 is the king of Hamath or the **k** *of* Arpad? H4889
2Ki 19:20 concerning Sennacherib **k** *of* Assyria. H4889
2Ki 19:32 the LORD says concerning the **k** *of* Assyria: H4889
2Ki 19:36 So Sennacherib **k** *of* Assyria broke camp H4889
2Ki 19:37 Esarhaddon his son succeeded him *as* **k**. H4887
2Ki 20: 6 this city from the hand of the **k** *of* Assyria. H4889
2Ki 20:12 son of Baladan **k** *of* Babylon sent H4889
2Ki 20:14 prophet went to **K** Hezekiah and asked, H4889
2Ki 20:18 eunuchs in the palace of the **k** *of* Babylon." H4889
2Ki 20:21 Manasseh his son succeeded him *as* **k**. H4887
2Ki 21: 1 was twelve years old when he *became* **k**, H4887
2Ki 21: 3 as Ahab **k** *of* Israel had done. H4889
2Ki 21:11 "Manasseh **k** *of* Judah has committed H4889
2Ki 21:18 And Amon his son succeeded him *as* **k**. H4887
2Ki 21:19 twenty-two years old when he *became* **k**, H4887
2Ki 21:23 him and assassinated the **k** in his palace. H4889
2Ki 21:24 all who had plotted against **K** Amon, H4889
2Ki 21:24 they **made** Josiah his son **k** in his H4887
2Ki 21:26 And Josiah his son succeeded him *as* **k**. H4887
2Ki 22: 1 was eight years old when he *became* **k**, H4887
2Ki 22: 3 of his reign, **K** Josiah sent the secretary H4889
2Ki 22: 9 went to the **k** and reported to him: H4889
2Ki 22:10 Shaphan the secretary informed the **k**, H4889
2Ki 22:10 read from it in the presence of the **k**. H4889
2Ki 22:11 When the **k** heard the words of the Book H4889
2Ki 22:16 in the book the **k** *of* Judah has read. H4889
2Ki 22:18 Tell the **k** *of* Judah, who sent you to H4889
2Ki 22:20 So they took her answer back to the **k**. H4889
2Ki 23: 1 Then the **k** called together all the elders H4889
2Ki 23: 3 The **k** stood by the pillar and renewed the H4889
2Ki 23: 4 The **k** ordered Hilkiah the high priest, the H4889
2Ki 23:13 The **k** also desecrated the high places that H4889
2Ki 23:13 the ones Solomon **k** *of* Israel had built H4889
2Ki 23:17 The **k** asked, "What is that tombstone I see?" NDT
2Ki 23:21 The **k** gave this order to all the people H4889
2Ki 23:23 But in the eighteenth year of **K** Josiah, this H4889
2Ki 23:25 Josiah was there a **k** like him who turned H4889
2Ki 23:29 While Josiah was **k**, Pharaoh Necho king of NDT
2Ki 23:29 Pharaoh Necho **k** *of* Egypt went up to the H4889
2Ki 23:29 Euphrates River to help the **k** *of* Assyria. H4889
2Ki 23:29 **K** Josiah marched out to meet him in H4889
2Ki 23:30 him and **made** him **k** in place of his H4887
2Ki 23:31 years old when he *became* **k**, H4887
2Ki 23:34 Necho **made** Eliakim son of Josiah **k** in H4887
2Ki 23:36 twenty-five years old when he *became* **k**, H4887
2Ki 24: 1 Nebuchadnezzar **k** *of* Babylon invaded the H4889
2Ki 24: 6 Jehoiachin his son succeeded him *as* **k**. H4887
2Ki 24: 7 The **k** *of* Egypt did not march out from his H4889
2Ki 24: 7 because the **k** *of* Babylon had taken all H4889
2Ki 24: 8 eighteen years old when he *became* **k**, H4887
2Ki 24:10 Nebuchadnezzar **k** *of* Babylon advanced H4889
2Ki 24:12 Jehoiachin **k** *of* Judah, his mother, his H4889
2Ki 24:12 year of the reign of the **k** *of* Babylon, H4889
2Ki 24:13 that Solomon **k** *of* Israel had made for H4889
2Ki 24:16 The **k** *of* Babylon also deported to Babylon H4889
2Ki 24:17 He **made** Mattaniah, Jehoiachin's uncle, **k** H4887
2Ki 24:18 twenty-one years old when he *became* **k**, H4887
2Ki 24:20 rebelled against the **k** *of* Babylon. H4889
2Ki 25: 1 Nebuchadnezzar **k** *of* Babylon marched H4889
2Ki 25: 2 until the eleventh year of **K** Zedekiah. H4889
2Ki 25: 5 army pursued the **k** and overtook him in H4889
2Ki 25: 6 was taken to the **k** *of* Babylon at Riblah, H4889
2Ki 25: 8 year of Nebuchadnezzar **k** *of* Babylon, H4889
2Ki 25: 8 an official of the **k** *of* Babylon, came to H4889
2Ki 25:11 who had deserted to the **k** *of* Babylon. H4889
2Ki 25:20 them to the **k** *of* Babylon at Riblah. H4889
2Ki 25:21 of Hamath, the **k** had them executed. H4889
2Ki 25:22 Nebuchadnezzar **k** *of* Babylon appointed H4889
2Ki 25:23 men heard that the **k** *of* Babylon had H4889
2Ki 25:24 in the land and serve the **k** *of* Babylon, H4889
2Ki 25:27 year of the exile of Jehoiachin **k** *of* Judah, H4889
2Ki 25:27 year Awel-Marduk *became* **k** *of* Babylon, H4887
2Ki 25:27 Jehoiachin **k** *of* Judah from prison. H4889
2Ki 25:30 Day by day the **k** gave Jehoiachin a H4889
1Ch 1:43 in Edom before any Israelite **k** reigned: H4889
1Ch 1:44 of Zerah from Bozrah succeeded him *as* **k**. H4887
1Ch 1:45 of the Temanites succeeded him *as* **k**. H4887
1Ch 1:46 the country of Moab, succeeded him *as* **k**. H4887
1Ch 1:47 from Masrekah succeeded him *as* **k**. H4887
1Ch 1:48 on the river succeeded him *as* **k**. H4887
1Ch 1:49 son of Akbor succeeded him *as* **k**. H4887
1Ch 1:50 Hadad succeeded him *as* **k**. H4887
1Ch 3: 2 Maakah daughter of Talmai **k** *of* Geshur; H4889
1Ch 4:23 they stayed there and worked for the **k**. H4889
1Ch 4:41 came in the days of Hezekiah **k** *of* Judah. H4889
1Ch 5: 6 Tiglath-Pileser **k** *of* Assyria took into H4889
1Ch 5:17 reigns of Jotham **k** *of* Judah and H4889
1Ch 5:17 king of Judah and Jeroboam **k** *of* Israel. H4889
1Ch 5:26 stirred up the spirit of Pul **k** *of* Assyria H4889
1Ch 5:26 Tiglath-Pileser **k** *of* Assyria), who took H4889
1Ch 11: 2 even while Saul was **k**, you were the one H4889
1Ch 11: 3 of Israel had come to **K** David at Hebron, H4889
1Ch 11: 3 they anointed David **k** over Israel, as H4889
1Ch 12:31 by name to come and **make** David **k**— H4887
1Ch 12:38 determined to **make** David **k** over all H4887
1Ch 12:38 were also of one mind to **make** David **k**. H4887
1Ch 14: 1 Now Hiram **k** *of* Tyre sent messengers to H4889
1Ch 14: 2 established him as **k** over Israel and that H4889
1Ch 14: 8 David had been anointed **k** over all Israel, H4889
1Ch 15:29 And when she saw **K** David dancing and H4889
1Ch 17:16 Then **K** David went in and sat before the H4889
1Ch 18: 3 David defeated Hadadezer **k** *of* Zobah, in H4889
1Ch 18: 5 came to help Hadadezer **k** *of* Zobah, H4889
1Ch 18: 9 When Tou **k** *of* Hamath heard that David H4889
1Ch 18: 9 the entire army of Hadadezer **k** *of* Zobah, H4889
1Ch 18:10 his son Hadoram to **K** David to greet him H4889
1Ch 18:11 **K** David dedicated these articles to the H4889
1Ch 19: 1 of time, Nahash **k** *of* the Ammonites died H4889
1Ch 19: 1 and his son succeeded him *as* **k**. H4887
1Ch 19: 5 The **k** said, "Stay at Jericho till your H4889
1Ch 19: 7 as well as the **k** *of* Maakah with his troops, H4889
1Ch 20: 2 took the crown from the head of their **k**— H4889
1Ch 21: 3 My lord the **k**, are they not all my lord's H4889
1Ch 21:23 Let my lord the **k** do whatever pleases him H4889
1Ch 21:24 But **K** David replied to Araunah, "No, H4889
1Ch 23: 1 *he* **made** his son Solomon **k** over Israel. H4887
1Ch 24: 6 the presence of the **k** and of the officials: H4889
1Ch 24:31 in the presence of **K** David and of Zadok H4889
1Ch 25: 6 were under the supervision of the **k**. H4889
1Ch 26:26 the things dedicated by **K** David, H4889
1Ch 26:32 **K** David put them in charge of the H4889
1Ch 26:32 to God and for the affairs of the **k**. H4889
1Ch 27: 1 who served the **k** in all that concerned the H4889
1Ch 27:24 in the book of the annals of **K** David. H4889
1Ch 27:31 officials in charge of **K** David's property. H4889
1Ch 28: 1 of the divisions in the service of the **k**, H4889
1Ch 28: 1 livestock belonging to the **k** and his sons, H4889
1Ch 28: 2 **K** David rose to his feet and said: "Listen H4889
1Ch 28: 4 whole family to be **k** over Israel forever. H4889
1Ch 28: 4 was pleased to **make** me **k** over all Israel. H4887
1Ch 29: 1 Then **K** David said to the whole assembly H4889
1Ch 29: 9 David the **k** also rejoiced greatly H4889
1Ch 29:20 themselves before the LORD and the **k**. H4889
1Ch 29:22 *they* **acknowledged** Solomon son of David **as k** H4887
1Ch 29:23 throne of the LORD as **k** in place of his H4889
1Ch 29:24 as well as all of **K** David's sons, pledged H4889
1Ch 29:24 pledged their submission to **K** Solomon. H4889
1Ch 29:25 splendor such as no **k** over Israel ever had H4889
1Ch 29:26 David son of Jesse *was* **k** over all Israel. H4887
1Ch 29:28 His son Solomon succeeded him *as* **k**. H4887
1Ch 29:29 As for the events of **K** David's reign, from H4889
2Ch 1: 8 father and *have* **made** me **k** in his place H4887
2Ch 1: 9 you *have* **made** me **k** over a people H4887
2Ch 1:11 my people over whom *I have* **made** you **k**, H4887
2Ch 1:12 such as no **k** who was before you ever had H4889
2Ch 1:15 The **k** made silver and gold as common in H4889
2Ch 2: 3 sent this message to Hiram **k** *of* Tyre: H4889
2Ch 2:11 Hiram **k** *of* Tyre replied by letter to H4889
2Ch 2:11 his people, he has made you their **k**." H4889
2Ch 2:12 He has given **K** David a wise son H4889
2Ch 4:11 had undertaken for **K** Solomon in the H4889
2Ch 4:16 Huram-Abi made for **K** Solomon for the H4889
2Ch 4:17 The **k** had them cast in clay molds in the H4889
2Ch 5: 3 came together to the **k** at the time of the H4889
2Ch 5: 6 **K** Solomon and the entire assembly of H4889
2Ch 6: 3 the **k** turned around and blessed them. H4889
2Ch 7: 4 Then the **k** and all the people offered H4889
2Ch 7: 5 And **K** Solomon offered a sacrifice of H4889
2Ch 7: 5 So the **k** and all the people dedicated the H4889
2Ch 7: 6 which **K** David had made for praising the H4889
2Ch 8:10 They were also **K** Solomon's chief officials H4889
2Ch 8:11 not live in the palace of David **k** *of* Israel, H4889
2Ch 8:18 which they delivered to **K** Solomon. H4889
2Ch 9: 5 She said to the **k**, "The report I heard in H4889
2Ch 9: 8 you on his throne as **k** to rule for the LORD H4889
2Ch 9: 8 he has made you **k** over them, to H4889
2Ch 9: 9 Then she gave the **k** 120 talents of gold H4889
2Ch 9: 9 the queen of Sheba gave to **K** Solomon. H4889
2Ch 9:11 The **k** used the algumwood to make steps H4889
2Ch 9:12 **K** Solomon gave the queen of Sheba all H4889
2Ch 9:15 **K** Solomon made two hundred large H4889
2Ch 9:16 The **k** put them in the Palace of the Forest H4889
2Ch 9:17 Then the **k** made a great throne covered H4889
2Ch 9:20 All **K** Solomon's goblets were gold, and H4889
2Ch 9:21 The **k** had a fleet of trading ships manned H4889
2Ch 9:22 **K** Solomon was greater in riches and H4889
2Ch 9:27 The **k** made silver as common in H4889
2Ch 9:31 Rehoboam his son succeeded him *as* **k**. H4887
2Ch 10: 1 all Israel had gone there to **make** him **k**. H4887
2Ch 10: 2 where he had fled from **K** Solomon), H4889
2Ch 10: 6 Then **K** Rehoboam consulted the elders H4889
2Ch 10:12 to Rehoboam, as the **k** had said, "Come H4889
2Ch 10:13 The **k** answered them harshly. Rejecting H4889
2Ch 10:15 So the **k** did not listen to the people, for H4889
2Ch 10:16 Israel saw that the **k** refused to listen to H4889
2Ch 10:16 to listen to them, they answered the **k**: H4889
2Ch 10:18 **K** Rehoboam sent out Adoniram, who was H4889
2Ch 10:18 **K** Rehoboam, however, managed to get H4889
2Ch 11: 3 son of Solomon **k** *of* Judah and to all H4889
2Ch 11:22 his brothers, in order to **make** him **k**. H4887
2Ch 12: 1 Rehoboam's **position as k** was H4895
2Ch 12: 2 Shishak **k** *of* Egypt attacked Jerusalem in H4889
2Ch 12: 2 in the fifth year of **K** Rehoboam. H4889
2Ch 12: 6 of Israel and the **k** humbled themselves H4889
2Ch 12: 9 When Shishak **k** *of* Egypt attacked H4889
2Ch 12:10 So **K** Rehoboam made bronze shields to H4889
2Ch 12:11 Whenever the **k** went to the LORD's temple H4889
2Ch 12:13 **K** Rehoboam established himself firmly in H4889
2Ch 12:13 firmly in Jerusalem and *continued as* **k**. H4887
2Ch 12:13 forty-one years old when he *became* **k**, H4887
2Ch 12:16 And Abijah his son succeeded him *as* **k**. H4887
2Ch 13: 1 of Jeroboam, Abijah *became* **k** of Judah, H4887
2Ch 14: 1 Asa his son succeeded him *as* **k**, and in H4887
2Ch 15:16 **K** Asa also deposed his grandmother H4889
2Ch 16: 1 of Asa's reign Baasha **k** *of* Israel went up H4889
2Ch 16: 1 entering the territory of Asa **k** *of* Judah. H4889
2Ch 16: 2 sent it to Ben-Hadad **k** *of* Aram, H4889
2Ch 16: 3 treaty with Baasha **k** *of* Israel so he will H4889
2Ch 16: 4 agreed with **K** Asa and sent the H4889
2Ch 16: 6 Then **K** Asa brought all the men of Judah H4889

2Ch 16: 7 seer came to Asa **k** *of* Judah and said to H4889
2Ch 16: 7 you relied on the **k** *of* Aram and not on H4889
2Ch 16: 7 the army of the **k** *of* Aram has escaped H4889
2Ch 17: 1 son succeeded him *as* **k** and strengthened H4887
2Ch 17:19 These were the men who served the **k** H4889
2Ch 18: 3 Ahab **k** *of* Israel asked Jehoshaphat king H4889
2Ch 18: 3 of Israel asked Jehoshaphat **k** *of* Judah, H4889
2Ch 18: 4 Jehoshaphat also said to the **k** *of* Israel, H4889
2Ch 18: 5 So the **k** *of* Israel brought together the H4889
2Ch 18: 7 The **k** *of* Israel answered Jehoshaphat H4889
2Ch 18: 7 "The **k** should not say such a thing," H4889
2Ch 18: 8 So the **k** *of* Israel called one of his H4889
2Ch 18: 9 the **k** *of* Israel and Jehoshaphat king of H4889
2Ch 18: 9 Jehoshaphat **k** *of* Judah were sitting H4889
2Ch 18:12 exception are predicting success for the **k**. H4889
2Ch 18:14 he arrived, the **k** asked him, "Micaiah, H4889
2Ch 18:15 The **k** said to him, "How many times must H4889
2Ch 18:17 The **k** *of* Israel said to Jehoshaphat H4889
2Ch 18:19 'Who will entice Ahab **k** *of* Israel into H4889
2Ch 18:25 The **k** *of* Israel then ordered, "Take H4889
2Ch 18:26 'This is what the **k** says: Put this fellow H4889
2Ch 18:28 So the **k** *of* Israel and Jehoshaphat king of H4889
2Ch 18:28 Jehoshaphat **k** *of* Judah went up to H4889
2Ch 18:29 The **k** *of* Israel said to Jehoshaphat, "I will H4889
2Ch 18:29 So the **k** *of* Israel disguised himself and H4889
2Ch 18:30 Now the **k** *of* Aram had ordered his H4889
2Ch 18:30 small or great, except the **k** *of* Israel." H4889
2Ch 18:31 they thought, "This is the **k** *of* Israel." H4889
2Ch 18:32 saw that he was not the **k** *of* Israel, H4889
2Ch 18:33 random and hit the **k** *of* Israel between H4889
2Ch 18:33 The **k** told the chariot driver, "Wheel around NDT
2Ch 18:34 the **k** *of* Israel propped himself up in H4889
2Ch 19: 1 When Jehoshaphat **k** *of* Judah returned H4889
2Ch 19: 2 went out to meet him and said to the **k** H4889
2Ch 19:11 over you in any matter concerning the **k**, H4889
2Ch 20:15 **K** Jehoshaphat and all who live in Judah H4889
2Ch 20:31 years old when he *became* **k** *of* Judah, H4887
2Ch 20:35 Jehoshaphat **k** *of* Judah made an alliance H4889
2Ch 20:35 an alliance with Ahaziah **k** *of* Israel, H4889
2Ch 21: 1 And Jehoram his son succeeded him *as* **k** H4887
2Ch 21: 2 were sons of Jehoshaphat **k** *of* Israel. H4889
2Ch 21: 5 thirty-two years old when he *became* **k**, H4887
2Ch 21: 8 against Judah and **set up** its own **k**. H4887+4889
2Ch 21:12 father Jehoshaphat or of Asa **k** *of* Judah. H4889
2Ch 21:20 thirty-two years old when he *became* **k**, H4887
2Ch 22: 1 **made** Ahaziah, Jehoram's youngest son, **k** H4887
2Ch 22: 1 son of Jehoram **k** *of* Judah began to reign H4889
2Ch 22: 2 twenty-two years old when he *became* **k**, H4887
2Ch 22: 5 Joram son of Ahab **k** *of* Israel to wage war H4889
2Ch 22: 5 war against Hazael **k** *of* Aram at Ramoth H4889
2Ch 22: 6 in his battle with Hazael **k** *of* Aram. H4889
2Ch 22: 6 son of Jehoram **k** *of* Judah went down to H4889
2Ch 22:11 the daughter of **K** Jehoram, took Joash H4889
2Ch 22:11 the daughter of **K** Jehoram and wife of H4889
2Ch 23: 3 a covenant with the **k** at the temple of H4889
2Ch 23: 7 are to station themselves around the **k**, H4889
2Ch 23: 7 Stay close to the **k** wherever he goes." H4889
2Ch 23: 9 had belonged to **K** David and that were H4889
2Ch 23:10 around the **k**—near the altar and H4889
2Ch 23:11 of the covenant and **proclaimed** him **k**. H4887
2Ch 23:11 him and shouted, "Long live the **k**! H4889
2Ch 23:12 of the people running and cheering the **k**, H4889
2Ch 23:13 there was the **k**, standing by his pillar H4889
2Ch 23:13 the trumpeters were beside the **k**, H4889
2Ch 23:16 the people and the **k** would be the LORD's H4889
2Ch 23:20 brought the **k** down from the temple H4889
2Ch 23:20 Gate and seated the **k** on the royal throne H4889
2Ch 24: 1 was seven years old when he *became* **k**, H4887
2Ch 24: 6 Therefore the **k** summoned Jehoiada the H4889
2Ch 24:12 The **k** and Jehoiada gave it to those who H4889
2Ch 24:14 rest of the money to the **k** and Jehoiada, H4889
2Ch 24:17 of Judah came and paid homage to the **k**, H4889
2Ch 24:21 by order of the **k** they stoned him to H4889
2Ch 24:22 **K** Joash did not remember the kindness H4889
2Ch 24:23 all the plunder to their **k** *in* Damascus. H4889
2Ch 24:27 And Amaziah his son succeeded him *as* **k**. H4887
2Ch 25: 1 twenty-five years old *when he became* **k**, H4887
2Ch 25: 3 who had murdered his father the **k**. H4889
2Ch 25:16 still speaking, the **k** said to him, "Have we NDT
2Ch 25:16 we appointed you an adviser to the **k**? H4889
2Ch 25:17 After Amaziah **k** *of* Judah consulted his H4889
2Ch 25:17 of Jehoahaz, the son of Jehu, **k** *of* Israel: H4889
2Ch 25:18 But Jehoash **k** *of* Israel replied to H4889
2Ch 25:18 of Israel replied to Amaziah **k** *of* Judah: H4889
2Ch 25:21 So Jehoash **k** *of* Israel attacked. He and H4889
2Ch 25:21 He and Amaziah **k** *of* Judah faced each H4889
2Ch 25:23 Jehoash **k** *of* Israel captured Amaziah king H4889
2Ch 25:23 of Israel captured Amaziah **k** *of* Judah, H4889
2Ch 25:25 Amaziah son of Joash **k** *of* Judah lived H4889
2Ch 25:25 of Jehoash son of Jehoahaz **k** *of* Israel. H4889
2Ch 26: 1 and **made** him **k** in place of his father H4887
2Ch 26: 3 was sixteen years old when he *became* **k**, H4887
2Ch 26:13 to support the **k** against his enemies. H4889
2Ch 26:18 They confronted **K** Uzziah and said, "It is H4889
2Ch 26:21 **K** Uzziah had leprosy until the day he H4889
2Ch 26:23 And Jotham his son succeeded him *as* **k**. H4887
2Ch 27: 1 twenty-five years old when he *became* **k**, H4887
2Ch 27: 5 war against the **k** *of* the Ammonites and H4889
2Ch 27: 8 twenty-five years old when he *became* **k**, H4887
2Ch 27: 9 And Ahaz his son succeeded him *as* **k**. H4887
2Ch 28: 1 was twenty years old when he *became* **k**, H4887
2Ch 28: 5 him into the hands of the **k** *of* Aram. H4889
2Ch 28: 5 given into the hands of the **k** *of* Israel, H4889
2Ch 28: 7 the palace, and Elkanah, second to the **k**. H4889
2Ch 28:16 At that time **K** Ahaz sent to the kings of H4889
2Ch 28:19 Judah because of Ahaz **k** *of* Israel, H4889
2Ch 28:20 Tiglath-Pileser **k** *of* Assyria came to him H4889
2Ch 28:21 presented them to the **k** *of* Assyria, H4889
2Ch 28:22 his time of trouble **K** Ahaz became even H4889
2Ch 28:27 Hezekiah his son succeeded him *as* **k**. H4887
2Ch 29: 1 twenty-five years old *when he became* **k**, H4887
2Ch 29:15 of the LORD, as the **k** had ordered H4889
2Ch 29:18 Then they went in to **K** Hezekiah and H4889
2Ch 29:19 all the articles that **K** Ahaz removed in his H4889
2Ch 29:19 in his unfaithfulness while he was **k**. H4895
2Ch 29:20 the next morning **K** Hezekiah gathered H4889
2Ch 29:21 The **k** commanded the priests, the NDT
2Ch 29:23 brought before the **k** and the assembly, H4889
2Ch 29:24 because the **k** had ordered the burnt H4889
2Ch 29:27 the instruments of David **k** *of* Israel. H4889
2Ch 29:29 the **k** and everyone present with him knelt H4889
2Ch 29:30 **K** Hezekiah and his officials ordered the H4889
2Ch 30: 2 The **k** and his officials and the whole H4889
2Ch 30: 4 right both to the **k** and to the whole H4889
2Ch 30: 6 with letters from the **k** and from his H4889
2Ch 30:12 carry out what the **k** and his officials had H4889
2Ch 30:24 Hezekiah **k** *of* Judah provided a thousand H4889
2Ch 30:26 son of David **k** *of* Israel there had H4889
2Ch 31: 3 The **k** contributed from his own H4889
2Ch 31:13 by appointment of **K** Hezekiah and H4889
2Ch 32: 1 Sennacherib **k** *of* Assyria came and H4889
2Ch 32: 7 because of the **k** *of* Assyria and the vast H4889
2Ch 32: 8 from what Hezekiah the **k** *of* Judah said. H4889
2Ch 32: 9 when Sennacherib **k** *of* Assyria and all his H4889
2Ch 32: 9 Hezekiah **k** *of* Judah and for all H4889
2Ch 32:10 is what Sennacherib **k** *of* Assyria says: H4889
2Ch 32:11 save us from the hand of the **k** *of* Assyria, H4889
2Ch 32:17 The **k** also wrote letters ridiculing the LORD NDT
2Ch 32:20 **K** Hezekiah and the prophet Isaiah son of H4889
2Ch 32:21 officers in the camp of the Assyrian **k**. H4889
2Ch 32:22 of Sennacherib **k** *of* Assyria and from H4889
2Ch 32:23 valuable gifts for Hezekiah **k** *of* Judah. H4889
2Ch 32:33 Manasseh his son succeeded him *as* **k**. H4887
2Ch 33: 1 was twelve years old when he *became* **k**, H4887
2Ch 33:11 the army commanders of the **k** *of* Assyria, H4889
2Ch 33:20 And Amon his son succeeded him *as* **k**. H4887
2Ch 33:21 twenty-two years old when he *became* **k**, H4887
2Ch 33:25 all who had plotted against **K** Amon, H4889
2Ch 33:25 they **made** Josiah his son **k** in his H4887
2Ch 34: 1 was eight years old when he *became* **k**, H4887
2Ch 34:16 the book to the **k** and reported to him: H4889
2Ch 34:18 Shaphan the secretary informed the **k**, H4889
2Ch 34:18 read from it in the presence of the **k**. H4889
2Ch 34:19 When the **k** heard the words of the Law H4889
2Ch 34:22 Hilkiah and those the **k** had sent with him H4889
2Ch 34:24 read in the presence of the **k** *of* Judah. H4889
2Ch 34:26 Tell the **k** *of* Judah, who sent you to H4889
2Ch 34:28 So they took her answer back to the **k**. H4889
2Ch 34:29 Then the **k** called together all the elders H4889
2Ch 34:31 The **k** stood by his pillar and renewed the H4889
2Ch 35: 3 Solomon son of David **k** *of* Israel built. H4889
2Ch 35: 4 written by David **k** *of* Israel and by his son H4889
2Ch 35:10 in their divisions as the **k** had ordered. H4889
2Ch 35:16 altar of the LORD, as **K** Josiah had ordered. H4889
2Ch 35:20 Necho **k** *of* Egypt went up to fight at H4889
2Ch 35:21 quarrel is there, **k** *of* Judah, between you H4889
2Ch 35:23 Archers shot **K** Josiah, and he told his H4889
2Ch 36: 1 of Josiah and **made** him **k** in Jerusalem in H4887
2Ch 36: 2 years old when he *became* **k**, H4887
2Ch 36: 3 The **k** *of* Egypt dethroned him in H4889
2Ch 36: 4 The **k** *of* Egypt made Eliakim, a brother of H4889
2Ch 36: 4 **made** Eliakim, a brother of Jehoahaz, **k** H4887
2Ch 36: 5 twenty-five years old when he *became* **k**, H4887
2Ch 36: 6 Nebuchadnezzar **k** *of* Babylon attacked H4889
2Ch 36: 8 Jehoiachin his son succeeded him *as* **k**. H4887
2Ch 36: 9 eighteen years old when he *became* **k**, H4887
2Ch 36:10 **K** Nebuchadnezzar sent for him and H4889
2Ch 36:10 *he* **made** Jehoiachin's uncle, Zedekiah, **k** H4887
2Ch 36:11 twenty-one years old when he *became* **k**, H4887
2Ch 36:13 also rebelled against **K** Nebuchadnezzar, H4889
2Ch 36:17 up against them the **k** *of* the Babylonians, H4889
2Ch 36:18 the treasures of the **k** and his officials. H4889
2Ch 36:22 In the first year of Cyrus **k** *of* Persia, in H4889
2Ch 36:22 the heart of Cyrus **k** *of* Persia to make a H4889
2Ch 36:23 "This is what Cyrus **k** *of* Persia says: H4889
Ezr 1: 1 In the first year of Cyrus **k** *of* Persia, in H4889
Ezr 1: 1 the heart of Cyrus **k** *of* Persia to make a H4889
Ezr 1: 2 "This is what Cyrus **k** *of* Persia says: H4889
Ezr 1: 7 **K** Cyrus brought out the articles belonging H4889
Ezr 1: 8 Cyrus **k** *of* Persia had them brought by H4889
Ezr 2: 1 Nebuchadnezzar **k** *of* Babylon had taken H4889
Ezr 3: 7 as authorized by Cyrus **k** *of* Persia. H4889
Ezr 3:10 as prescribed by David **k** *of* Israel. H4889
Ezr 4: 2 since the time of Esarhaddon **k** *of* Assyria, H4889
Ezr 4: 3 the God of Israel, as **K** Cyrus, the king of H4889
Ezr 4: 3 King Cyrus, the **k** *of* Persia, commanded H4889
Ezr 4: 5 reign of Cyrus **k** *of* Persia and down to H4889
Ezr 4: 5 down to the reign of Darius **k** *of* Persia. H4889
Ezr 4: 7 And in the days of Artaxerxes **k** *of* Persia H4889
Ezr 4: 8 Jerusalem to Artaxerxes the **k** as follows: A10421
Ezr 4:11 To **K** Artaxerxes, From your servants in A10421
Ezr 4:12 The **k** should know that the people who A10421
Ezr 4:13 the **k** should know that if this city is built A10421
Ezr 4:14 proper for us to see the **k** dishonored, A10421
Ezr 4:14 sending this message to inform the **k**, A10421
Ezr 4:16 We inform the **k** that if this city is built A10421
Ezr 4:17 The **k** sent this reply: To Rehum the A10421
Ezr 4:23 of the letter of **K** Artaxerxes was read A10421
Ezr 4:24 year of the reign of Darius **k** *of* Persia. A10421
Ezr 5: 6 of Trans-Euphrates, sent to **K** Darius. A10421
Ezr 5: 7 him read as follows: To **K** Darius: Cordial A10421
Ezr 5: 8 The **k** should know that we went to the A10421
Ezr 5:11 one that a great **k** of Israel built and A10421
Ezr 5:12 the Chaldean, **k** *of* Babylon, who A10421
Ezr 5:13 in the first year of Cyrus **k** of Babylon A10421
Ezr 5:13 **K** Cyrus issued a decree to rebuild this A10421
Ezr 5:14 Then **K** Cyrus gave them to a man A10421
Ezr 5:17 Now if it pleases the **k**, let a search be A10421
Ezr 5:17 of Babylon to see if **K** Cyrus did in fact A10421
Ezr 5:17 Then let the **k** send us his decision in A10421
Ezr 6: 1 **K** Darius then issued an order, and they A10421
Ezr 6: 3 In the first year of **K** Cyrus, the king A10421
Ezr 6: 3 the **k** issued a decree concerning the A10421
Ezr 6:10 the well-being of the **k** and his sons. A10421
Ezr 6:12 overthrow any **k** or people who lifts a A10421
Ezr 6:13 because of the decree **K** Darius had sent, A10421
Ezr 6:15 in the sixth year of the reign of **K** Darius. A10421
Ezr 6:22 the attitude of the **k** *of* Assyria so that he H4889
Ezr 7: 1 during the reign of Artaxerxes **k** *of* Persia H4889
Ezr 7: 6 The **k** had granted him everything he H4889
Ezr 7: 7 in the seventh year of **K** Artaxerxes. H4889
Ezr 7: 8 fifth month of the seventh year of the **k**. H4889
Ezr 7:11 a copy of the letter **K** Artaxerxes had given H4889
Ezr 7:12 Artaxerxes, **k** *of* kings, To Ezra the priest A10421
Ezr 7:14 You are sent by the **k** and his seven A10421
Ezr 7:15 gold that the **k** and his advisers A10421
Ezr 7:21 **K** Artaxerxes, decree that all the A10421
Ezr 7:23 on the realm of the **k** and of his sons? A10421
Ezr 7:26 God and the law of the **k** must surely be A10421
Ezr 7:28 to me before the **k** and his advisers and H4889
Ezr 8: 1 Babylon during the reign of **K** Artaxerxes: H4889
Ezr 8:22 was ashamed to ask the **k** for soldiers H4889
Ezr 8:22 because we had told the **k**, "The gracious H4889
Ezr 8:25 silver and gold and the articles that the **k**, H4889
Ne 1:11 I was cupbearer to the **k**. H4889
Ne 2: 1 in the twentieth year of **K** Artaxerxes, H4889
Ne 2: 1 I took the wine and gave it to the **k**. H4889
Ne 2: 2 so the **k** asked me, "Why does your face H4889
Ne 2: 3 I said to the **k**, "May the king live H4889
Ne 2: 3 I said to the king, "May the **k** live forever! H4889
Ne 2: 4 The **k** said to me, "What is it you want?" H4889
Ne 2: 5 I answered the **k**, "If it pleases the H4889
Ne 2: 5 "If it pleases the **k** and if your servant has H4889
Ne 2: 6 Then the **k**, with the queen sitting beside H4889
Ne 2: 6 It pleased the **k** to send me; so I set a H4889
Ne 2: 7 "If it pleases the **k**, may I have letters to H4889
Ne 2: 8 was on me, the **k** granted my requests. H4889
Ne 2: 9 The **k** had also sent army officers and H4889
Ne 2:18 on me and what the **k** had said to me. H4889
Ne 2:19 "Are you rebelling against the **k**?" H4889
Ne 5:14 from the twentieth year of **K** Artaxerxes H4889
Ne 6: 6 reports you are about to become their **k** H4889
Ne 6: 7 'There is a **k** in Judah!' Now this H4889
Ne 6: 7 Now this report will get back to the **k**; so H4889
Ne 7: 6 Nebuchadnezzar **k** *of* Babylon had taken H4889
Ne 9:22 the country of Sihon **k** *of* Heshbon and the H4889
Ne 9:22 the country of Og **k** *of* Bashan. H4889
Ne 13: 6 year of Artaxerxes **k** *of* Babylon I had H4889
Ne 13: 6 king of Babylon I had returned to the **k**. H4889
Ne 13:26 these that Solomon **k** *of* Israel sinned? H4889
Ne 13:26 the many nations there was no **k** like him. H4889
Ne 13:26 God made him **k** over all Israel, but H4889
Est 1: 2 At that time **K** Xerxes reigned from his H4889
Est 1: 5 days were over, the **k** gave a banquet H4889
Est 1: 8 the **k** instructed all the wine stewards H4889
Est 1: 9 women in the royal palace of **K** Xerxes. H4889
Est 1:10 when **K** Xerxes was in high spirits from H4889
Est 1:12 Then the **k** became furious and burned H4889
Est 1:13 customary for the **k** to consult experts in H4889
Est 1:14 were closest to the **k**—Karshena H2257S
Est 1:14 access to the **k** and were highest in H4889
Est 1:15 obeyed the command of **K** Xerxes that the H4889
Est 1:16 in the presence of the **k** and the nobles, H4889
Est 1:16 not only against the **k** but also against all H4889
Est 1:16 peoples of all the provinces of **K** Xerxes. H4889
Est 1:17 '**K** Xerxes commanded Queen Vashti to be H4889
Est 1:19 if it pleases the **k**, let him issue a royal H4889
Est 1:19 again to enter the presence of **K** Xerxes. H4889
Est 1:19 Also let the **k** give her royal position to H4889
Est 1:21 The **k** and his nobles were pleased with H4889
Est 1:21 so the **k** did as Memukan proposed. H4889
Est 2: 1 Later when **K** Xerxes' fury had subsided H4889
Est 2: 2 made for beautiful young virgins for the **k**. H4889
Est 2: 3 Let the **k** appoint commissioners in every H4889
Est 2: 4 who pleases the **k** be queen instead of H4889
Est 2: 4 This advice appealed to the **k**, and he H4889
Est 2: 6 by Nebuchadnezzar **k** *of* Babylon, H4889
Est 2: 6 taken captive with Jehoiachin **k** *of* Judah. H4889
Est 2:12 woman's turn came to go in to **K** Xerxes, H4889
Est 2:13 And this is how she would go to the **k** H4889
Est 2:14 not return to the **k** unless he was pleased H4889
Est 2:15 Abihail) to go to the **k**, she asked for H4889
Est 2:16 She was taken to **K** Xerxes in the royal H4889
Est 2:17 Now the **k** was attracted to Esther more H4889
Est 2:18 And the **k** gave a great banquet, Esther's H4889
Est 2:21 conspired to assassinate **K** Xerxes. H4889

Est	2:22	who in turn reported it to the **k**, giving	H4889
Est	2:23	of the annals in the presence of the **k**.	H4889
Est	3: 1	**K** Xerxes honored Haman son of	H4889
Est	3: 2	the **k** had commanded this concerning	H4889
Est	3: 7	In the twelfth year of **K** Xerxes, in the first	H4889
Est	3: 8	Then Haman said to **K** Xerxes, "There is a	H4889
Est	3: 9	If it pleases the **k**, let a decree be issued	H4889
Est	3:10	So the **k** took his signet ring from his	H4889
Est	3:11	the **k** said to Haman, "and do with the	H4889
Est	3:12	in the name of **K** Xerxes himself and	H4889
Est	3:15	The **k** and Haman sat down to drink, but	H4889
Est	4: 3	which the edict and order of the **k** came,	H4889
Est	4:11	who approaches the **k** in the inner court	H4889
Est	4:11	being summoned **the k** has but one law:	H2257
Est	4:11	put to death unless the **k** extends the gold	H4889
Est	4:11	passed since I was called to go to the **k**."	H4889
Est	4:16	I will go to the **k**, even though it is	H4889
Est	5: 1	The **k** was sitting on his royal throne in	H4889
Est	5: 3	Then the **k** asked, "What is it, Queen	H4889
Est	5: 4	"If it pleases the **k**," replied Esther, "let	H4889
Est	5: 4	"let the **k**, together with Haman,	H4889
Est	5: 5	the **k** said, "so that we may do what	H4889
Est	5: 5	So the **k** and Haman went to the banquet	H4889
Est	5: 6	drinking wine, the **k** again asked Esther	H4889
Est	5: 8	If the **k** regards me with favor and if it	H4889
Est	5: 8	if it pleases the **k** to grant my petition	H4889
Est	5: 8	let the **k** and Haman come tomorrow to	H4889
Est	5:11	all the ways the **k** had honored him and	H4889
Est	5:12	to accompany the **k** to the banquet she	H4889
Est	5:12	has invited me along with the **k** tomorrow.	H4889
Est	5:14	ask the **k** in the morning to have	H4889
Est	5:14	Then go with the **k** to the banquet and	H4889
Est	6: 1	That night the **k** could not sleep; so he	H4889
Est	6: 2	had conspired to assassinate **K** Xerxes.	H4889
Est	6: 3	the **k** asked. "Nothing has	H4889
Est	6: 4	The **k** said, "Who is in the court?" Now	H4889
Est	6: 4	palace to speak to the **k** about impaling	H4889
Est	6: 5	"Bring him in," the **k** ordered.	H4889
Est	6: 6	Haman entered, the **k** asked him, "What	H4889
Est	6: 6	done for the man the **k** delights to honor?"	H4889
Est	6: 6	is there that the **k** would rather honor	H4889
Est	6: 7	So he answered the **k**, "For the man the	H4889
Est	6: 7	"For the man the **k** delights to honor,	H4889
Est	6: 8	a royal robe the **k** has worn and a horse	H4889
Est	6: 8	has worn and a horse the **k** has ridden,	H4889
Est	6: 9	robe the man the **k** delights to honor,	H4889
Est	6: 9	done for the man the **k** delights to honor!	H4889
Est	6:10	"Go at once," the **k** commanded Haman	H4889
Est	6:11	done for the man the **k** delights to honor!"	H4889
Est	7: 1	So the **k** and Haman went to Queen	H4889
Est	7: 2	second day, the **k** again asked, "Queen	H4889
Est	7: 4	distress would justify disturbing the **k**."	H4889
Est	7: 5	**K** Xerxes asked Queen Esther, "Who is he?	H4889
Est	7: 6	was terrified before the **k** and queen.	H4889
Est	7: 7	The **k** got up in a rage, left his wine and	H4889
Est	7: 7	realizing that the **k** had already decided	H4889
Est	7: 8	Just as the **k** returned from the palace	H4889
Est	7: 8	The **k** exclaimed, "Will he even molest	H4889
Est	7: 9	one of the eunuchs attending the **k**, said,	H4889
Est	7: 9	Mordecai, who spoke up to help the **k**."	H4889
Est	7: 9	help the king." The **k** said, "Impale him	H4889
Est	8: 1	That same day **K** Xerxes gave Queen	H4889
Est	8: 1	Mordecai came into the presence of the **k**,	H4889
Est	8: 2	The **k** took off his signet ring, which he	H4889
Est	8: 3	Esther again pleaded with the **k**, falling at	H4889
Est	8: 4	Then the **k** extended the gold scepter to	H4889
Est	8: 5	"If it pleases the **k**," she said, "and if he	H4889
Est	8: 7	**K** Xerxes replied to Queen Esther and to	H4889
Est	8:10	Mordecai wrote in the name of **K** Xerxes	H4889
Est	8:10	rode fast horses especially bred **for** the **k**.	H350
Est	8:12	in all the provinces of **K** Xerxes was the	H4889
Est	8:17	every city to which the edict of the **k** came,	H4889
Est	9: 1	commanded by the **k** was to be carried	H4889
Est	9: 2	all the provinces of **K** Xerxes to attack	H4889
Est	9:11	Susa was reported to the **k** that same day.	H4889
Est	9:12	The **k** said to Queen Esther, "The Jews	H4889
Est	9:13	"If it pleases the **k**," Esther answered	H4889
Est	9:14	So the **k** commanded that this be done	H4889
Est	9:20	throughout the provinces of **K** Xerxes,	H4889
Est	10: 1	**K** Xerxes imposed tribute throughout the	H4889
Est	10: 2	Mordecai, whom the **k** had promoted, are	H4889
Est	10: 3	the Jew was second in rank to **K** Xerxes,	H4889
Job	15:24	overwhelm him, like a **k** poised to attack,	H4889
Job	18:14	tent and marched off to the **k** *of* terrors.	H4889
Job	29:25	I dwelt as a **k** among his troops;	H4889
Job	41:34	are haughty; it is **k** over all that are proud."	H4889
Ps	2: 6	"I have installed my **k** on Zion, my holy	H4889
Ps	5: 2	my cry for help, my **K** and my God, for to	H4889
Ps	10:16	The LORD is **K** for ever and ever; the	H4889
Ps	18:50	He gives his **k** great victories; he shows	H4889
Ps	20: 9	give victory to the **k**! Answer us when we	H4889
Ps	21: 1	The **k** rejoices in your strength, LORD.	H4889
Ps	21: 7	For the **k** trusts in the LORD; through the	H4889
Ps	24: 7	that the **K** *of* glory may come in.	H4889
Ps	24: 8	Who is this **K** *of* glory? The LORD strong	H4889
Ps	24: 9	that the **K** *of* glory may come in.	H4889
Ps	24:10	Who is he, this **e** *of* glory? The LORD	H4889
Ps	24:10	The LORD Almighty—he is the **K** *of* glory.	H4889
Ps	29:10	the LORD is enthroned as **K** forever.	H4889
Ps	33:16	No **k** is saved by the size of his army; no	H4889
Ps	44: 4	You are my **K** and my God, who decrees	H4889
Ps	45: 1	theme as I recite my verses for the **k**;	H4889
Ps	45:11	Let the **k** be enthralled by your beauty	H4889
Ps	45:14	embroidered garments she is led to the **k**;	H4889
Ps	45:15	gladness, they enter the palace of the **k**.	H4889
Ps	47: 2	awesome, the great **K** over all the earth.	H4889
Ps	47: 6	sing praises to our **K**, sing praises.	H4889
Ps	47: 7	For God is the **K** *of* all the earth; sing to	H4889
Ps	48: 2	is Mount Zion, the city of the Great **K**.	H4889
Ps	63:11	But the **k** will rejoice in God; all who	H4889
Ps	68:24	of my God and **K** into the sanctuary.	H4889
Ps	72: 1	Endow the **k** with your justice, O God, the	H4889
Ps	74:12	But God is my **K** from long ago; he brings	H4889
Ps	84: 3	LORD Almighty, my **K** and my God.	H4889
Ps	89:18	the LORD, our **k** to the Holy One of Israel.	H4889
Ps	95: 3	the great God, the great **K** above all gods.	H4889
Ps	98: 6	shout for joy before the LORD, the **K**.	H4889
Ps	99: 4	The **K** is mighty, he loves justice—you	H4889
Ps	105:20	The **k** sent and released him, the ruler of	H4889
Ps	135:11	Sihon **k** *of* the Amorites, Og king of	H4889
Ps	135:11	of the Amorites, Og **k** *of* Bashan, and all	H4889
Ps	136:19	Sihon **k** *of* the Amorites His love endures	H4889
Ps	136:20	Og **k** *of* Bashan—His love endures	H4889
Ps	145: 1	exalt you, my God the **K**; I will praise your	H4889
Ps	149: 2	let the people of Zion be glad in their **K**.	H4889
Pr	1: 1	of Solomon son of David, **k** *of* Israel:	H4889
Pr	14:35	A **k** delights in a wise servant, but a	H4889
Pr	16:10	The lips of a **k** speak as an oracle, and his	H4889
Pr	20: 8	When a **k** sits on his throne to judge, he	H4889
Pr	20:26	A wise **k** winnows out the wicked; he	H4889
Pr	20:28	Love and faithfulness keep a **k** safe	H4889
Pr	22:11	with grace will have the **k** for a friend.	H4889
Pr	24:21	Fear the LORD and the **k**, my son, and do	H4889
Pr	25: 1	by the men of Hezekiah **k** *of* Judah:	H4889
Pr	29: 4	By justice a **k** gives a country stability, but	H4889
Pr	29:14	If a **k** judges the poor with fairness, his	H4889
Pr	30:22	a servant *who becomes* **k**, a godless fool	H4887
Pr	30:27	locusts have no **k**, yet they advance	H4889
Pr	30:31	a he-goat, and a **k** secure against revolt.	H4889
Pr	31: 1	The sayings of **K** Lemuel—an inspired	H4889
Ecc	1: 1	the Teacher, son of David, **k** in Jerusalem:	H4889
Ecc	1:12	Teacher, was **k** over Israel in Jerusalem.	H4889
Ecc	4:13	an old but foolish **k** who no longer knows	H4889
Ecc	5: 9	the **k** himself profits from the fields.	H4889
Ecc	9:14	And a powerful **k** came against it	H4889
Ecc	10:16	to the land whose **k** was a servant and	H4889
Ecc	10:17	is the land whose **k** is of noble birth and	H4889
Ecc	10:20	Do not revile the **k** even in your thoughts	H4889
SS	1: 4	Let the **k** bring me into his chambers	H4889
SS	1:12	While the **k** was at his table, my perfume	H4889
SS	3: 9	**K** Solomon made for himself the carriage	H4889
SS	3:11	Look on **K** Solomon wearing a crown, the	H4889
SS	7: 5	the **k** is held captive by its tresses.	H4889
Isa	6: 1	In the year that **K** Uzziah died, I saw the	H4889
Isa	6: 5	my eyes have seen the **K**, the LORD	H4889
Isa	7: 1	son of Uzziah, was **k** *of* Judah, King Rezin	H4889
Isa	7: 1	**K** Rezin *of* Aram and Pekah son of	H4889
Isa	7: 1	son of Remaliah **k** *of* Israel marched up to	H4889
Isa	7: 6	and **make** the son of Tabeel **k** over	H4887+4889
Isa	7:17	Judah—he will bring the **k** *of* Assyria."	H4889
Isa	7:20	the **k** *of* Assyria—to shave	H4889
Isa	8: 4	will be carried off by the **k** *of* Assyria."	H4889
Isa	8: 7	the **k** *of* Assyria with all his pomp.	H4889
Isa	8:21	upward, will curse their **k** and their God.	H4889
Isa	10:12	"I will punish the **k** *of* Assyria for the	H4889
Isa	14: 4	up this taunt against the **k** *of* Babylon:	H4889
Isa	14:28	prophecy came in the year **K** Ahaz died:	H4889
Isa	19: 4	and a fierce **k** will rule over them,	H4889
Isa	20: 1	sent by Sargon **k** *of* Assyria, came to	H4889
Isa	20: 4	so the **k** *of* Assyria will lead away stripped	H4889
Isa	20: 6	deliverance from the **k** *of* Assyria!	H4889
Isa	30:33	it has been made ready for the **k**.	H4889
Isa	32: 1	a **k** will reign in righteousness and rulers	H4889
Isa	33:17	eyes will see the **k** in his beauty and view	H4889
Isa	33:22	the LORD is our **k**; it is he who will save	H4889
Isa	36: 1	the fourteenth year of **K** Hezekiah's reign,	H4889
Isa	36: 1	Sennacherib **k** *of* Assyria attacked all the	H4889
Isa	36: 2	Then the **k** *of* Assyria sent his field	H4889
Isa	36: 2	army from Lachish to **K** Hezekiah at	H4889
Isa	36: 4	" 'This is what the great **k**, the king of	H4889
Isa	36: 4	what the great king, the **k** *of* Assyria, says:	H4889
Isa	36: 6	Such is Pharaoh **k** *of* Egypt to all who	H4889
Isa	36: 8	bargain with my master, the **k** *of* Assyria:	H4889
Isa	36:13	"Hear the words of the great **k**, the king of	H4889
Isa	36:13	words of the great king, the **k** *of* Assyria!	H4889
Isa	36:14	This is what the **k** says: Do not let	H4889
Isa	36:15	be given into the hand of the **k** *of* Assyria.	H4889
Isa	36:16	This is what the **k** *of* Assyria says: Make	H4889
Isa	36:18	lands from the hand of the **k** *of* Assyria?	H4889
Isa	36:21	because the **k** had commanded, "Do	H4889
Isa	37: 1	When **K** Hezekiah heard this, he tore his	H4889
Isa	37: 4	his master, the **k** *of* Assyria, has sent	H4889
Isa	37: 5	When **K** Hezekiah's officials came to	H4889
Isa	37: 6	the underlings of the **k** *of* Assyria have	H4889
Isa	37: 8	heard that the **k** *of* Assyria had left	H4889
Isa	37: 8	withdrew and found the **k** fighting against	NDT
Isa	37: 9	that Tirhakah, the **k** *of* Cush, was	H4889
Isa	37:10	"Say to Hezekiah **k** *of* Judah: Do not let	H4889
Isa	37:10	given into the hands of the **k** *of* Assyria.	H4889
Isa	37:13	Where is the **k** *of* Hamath or the king of	H4889
Isa	37:13	is the king of Hamath or the **k** *of* Arpad?	H4889
Isa	37:21	me concerning Sennacherib **k** *of* Assyria,	H4889
Isa	37:33	the LORD says concerning the **k** *of* Assyria:	H4889
Isa	37:37	So Sennacherib **k** *of* Assyria broke camp	H4889
Isa	37:38	Esarhaddon his son succeeded him *as* **k**.	H4887
Isa	38: 6	this city from the hand of the **k** *of* Assyria.	H4889
Isa	38: 9	A writing of Hezekiah **k** *of* Judah after his	H4889
Isa	39: 1	son of Baladan **k** *of* Babylon sent	H4889
Isa	39: 3	prophet went to **K** Hezekiah and asked,	H4889
Isa	39: 7	eunuchs in the palace of the **k** *of* Babylon."	H4889
Isa	41:21	"Set forth your arguments," says Jacob's **K**.	H4889
Isa	43:15	your Holy One, Israel's Creator, your **K**."	H4889
Isa	44: 6	LORD says—Israel's **K** and Redeemer, the	H4889
Jer	1: 2	reign of Josiah son of Amon **k** *of* Judah,	H4889
Jer	1: 3	of Jehoiakim son of Josiah **k** *of* Judah,	H4889
Jer	1: 3	year of Zedekiah son of Josiah **k** *of* Judah,	H4889
Jer	3: 6	During the reign of **K** Josiah, the LORD said	H4889
Jer	4: 9	"the **k** and the officials will lose heart	H4889
Jer	8:19	Is her **K** no longer there?	H4889
Jer	10: 7	should not fear you, **K** *of* the nations?	H4889
Jer	10:10	he is the living God, the eternal **K**.	H4889
Jer	13:18	Say to the **k** and to the queen mother	H4889
Jer	15: 4	son of Hezekiah **k** *of* Judah did in	H4889
Jer	20: 4	Judah into the hands of the **k** *of* Babylon,	H4889
Jer	21: 1	from the LORD when **K** Zedekiah sent to	H4889
Jer	21: 2	Nebuchadnezzar **k** *of* Babylon is attacking	H4889
Jer	21: 4	are using to fight the **k** *of* Babylon and the	H4889
Jer	21: 7	I will give Zedekiah **k** *of* Judah, his	H4889
Jer	21: 7	of Nebuchadnezzar **k** *of* Babylon and to	H4889
Jer	21:10	given into the hands of the **k** *of* Babylon,	H4889
Jer	22: 1	the palace of the **k** *of* Judah and proclaim	H4889
Jer	22: 2	of the LORD to you, **k** *of* Judah, you who sit	H4889
Jer	22: 6	says about the palace of the **k** *of* Judah:	H4889
Jer	22:10	not weep for the dead **k** or mourn his loss;	NDT
Jer	22:11	his father *as* **k** *of* Judah but has gone	H4887
Jer	22:15	"*Does it make you a* **k** to have more and	H4887
Jer	22:18	about Jehoiakim son of Josiah **k** *of* Judah:	H4889
Jer	22:24	Jehoiachin son of Jehoiakim **k** *of* Judah	H4889
Jer	22:25	Nebuchadnezzar **k** *of* Babylon and the	H4889
Jer	23: 5	a **K** who will reign wisely and do what is	H4889
Jer	24: 1	son of Jehoiakim **k** *of* Judah and the	H4889
Jer	24: 1	Babylon by Nebuchadnezzar **k** *of* Babylon,	H4889
Jer	24: 8	'so will I deal with Zedekiah **k** *of* Judah	H4889
Jer	25: 1	of Jehoiakim son of Josiah **k** *of* Judah,	H4889
Jer	25: 1	first year of Nebuchadnezzar **k** *of* Babylon.	H4889
Jer	25: 3	Josiah son of Amon **k** *of* Judah until this	H4889
Jer	25: 9	my servant Nebuchadnezzar **k** *of* Babylon,"	H4889
Jer	25:11	will serve the **k** *of* Babylon seventy years	H4889
Jer	25:12	I will punish the **k** *of* Babylon and his	H4889
Jer	25:19	Pharaoh **k** *of* Egypt, his attendants, his	H4889
Jer	25:26	of them, the **k** *of* Sheshak will drink it too.	H4889
Jer	26: 1	of Jehoiakim son of Josiah **k** *of* Judah,	H4889
Jer	26:18	in the days of Hezekiah **k** *of* Judah.	H4889
Jer	26:19	"Did Hezekiah **k** *of* Judah or anyone else	H4889
Jer	26:21	When **K** Jehoiakim and all his officers	H4889
Jer	26:21	the **k** was determined to put him to death.	H4889
Jer	26:22	**K** Jehoiakim, however, sent Elnathan son	H4889
Jer	26:23	out of Egypt and took him to **K** Jehoiakim,	H4889
Jer	27: 1	of Zedekiah son of Josiah **k** *of* Judah,	H4889
Jer	27: 3	to Jerusalem to Zedekiah **k** *of* Judah.	H4889
Jer	27: 6	my servant Nebuchadnezzar **k** *of* Babylon;	H4889
Jer	27: 8	Nebuchadnezzar **k** *of* Babylon or bow its	H4889
Jer	27: 9	'You will not serve the **k** *of* Babylon.	H4889
Jer	27:11	the yoke of the **k** *of* Babylon and serve	H4889
Jer	27:12	same message to Zedekiah **k** *of* Judah.	H4889
Jer	27:12	neck under the yoke of the **k** *of* Babylon;	H4889
Jer	27:13	that will not serve the **k** *of* Babylon?	H4889
Jer	27:14	'You will not serve the **k** *of* Babylon,' for	H4889
Jer	27:17	Serve the **k** *of* Babylon, and you	H4889
Jer	27:18	in the palace of the **k** *of* Judah and in	H4889
Jer	27:20	Nebuchadnezzar **k** *of* Babylon did not	H4889
Jer	27:20	son of Jehoiakim **k** *of* Judah into exile	H4889
Jer	27:21	in the palace of the **k** *of* Judah and in	H4889
Jer	28: 1	early in the reign of Zedekiah **k** *of* Judah	H4889
Jer	28: 2	'I will break the yoke of the **k** *of* Babylon.	H4889
Jer	28: 3	Nebuchadnezzar **k** *of* Babylon removed	H4889
Jer	28: 4	son of Jehoiakim **k** *of* Judah and all the	H4889
Jer	28: 4	I will break the yoke of the **k** *of* Babylon.	H4889
Jer	28:11	of Nebuchadnezzar **k** *of* Babylon off the	H4889
Jer	28:14	them serve Nebuchadnezzar **k** *of* Babylon,	H4889
Jer	29: 2	This was after **K** Jehoiachin and the queen	H4889
Jer	29: 3	whom Zedekiah **k** *of* Judah sent to King	H4889
Jer	29: 3	of Judah sent to **K** Nebuchadnezzar in	H4889
Jer	29:16	LORD says about the **k** who sits on David's	H4889
Jer	29:21	hands of Nebuchadnezzar **k** *of* Babylon,	H4889
Jer	29:22	whom the **k** *of* Babylon burned in the fire.	H4889
Jer	30: 9	the LORD their God and David their **k**,	H4889
Jer	32: 1	in the tenth year of Zedekiah **k** *of* Judah,	H4889
Jer	32: 2	The army of the **k** *of* Babylon was then	H4889
Jer	32: 3	Now Zedekiah **k** *of* Judah had imprisoned	H4889
Jer	32: 3	city into the hands of the **k** *of* Babylon,	H4889
Jer	32: 4	Zedekiah **k** *of* Judah will not escape the	H4889
Jer	32: 4	given into the hands of the **k** *of* Babylon,	H4889
Jer	32:28	to Nebuchadnezzar **k** *of* Babylon,	H4889
Jer	32:36	given into the hands of the **k** *of* Babylon';	H4889
Jer	34: 1	Nebuchadnezzar **k** *of* Babylon and all his	H4889
Jer	34: 2	Go to Zedekiah **k** *of* Judah and tell him	H4889
Jer	34: 2	city into the hands of the **k** *of* Babylon,	H4889
Jer	34: 3	You will see the **k** *of* Babylon with your	H4889
Jer	34: 4	promise to you, Zedekiah **k** *of* Judah.	H4889
Jer	34: 6	told all this to Zedekiah **k** *of* Judah,	H4889
Jer	34: 7	while the army of the **k** *of* Babylon was	H4889
Jer	34: 8	the LORD after **K** Zedekiah had made a	H4889
Jer	34:21	will deliver Zedekiah **k** *of* Judah and his	H4889
Jer	34:21	to the army of the **k** *of* Babylon, which has	H4889
Jer	35: 1	of Jehoiakim son of Josiah **k** *of* Judah:	H4889

Book	Ref	Context	Number
Jer	35:11	Nebuchadnezzar **k** *of* Babylon invaded	H4889
Jer	36: 1	of Jehoiakim son of Josiah **k** *of* Judah,	H4889
Jer	36: 9	of Jehoiakim son of Josiah **k** *of* Judah,	H4889
Jer	36:16	"We must report all these words to the **k**."	H4889
Jer	36:20	they went to the **k** in the courtyard and	H4889
Jer	36:21	The **k** sent Jehudi to get the scroll, and	H4889
Jer	36:21	read it to the **k** and all the officials	H4889
Jer	36:22	ninth month and the **k** was sitting in the	H4889
Jer	36:23	the **k** cut them off with a scribe's knife and	NDT
Jer	36:24	The **k** and all his attendants who heard all	H4889
Jer	36:25	Gemariah urged the **k** not to burn the	H4889
Jer	36:26	the **k** commanded Jerahmeel,	H4889
Jer	36:26	a son of the **k**, Seraiah son of Azriel	H4889
Jer	36:27	After the **k** burned the scroll containing	H4889
Jer	36:28	which Jehoiakim **k** *of* Judah burned up.	H4889
Jer	36:29	Also tell Jehoiakim **k** *of* Judah, 'This is	H4889
Jer	36:29	write on it that the **k** *of* Babylon would	H4889
Jer	36:30	the LORD says about Jehoiakim **k** *of* Judah:	H4889
Jer	36:32	that Jehoiakim **k** *of* Judah had burned in	H4889
Jer	37: 1	son of Josiah *was* **made k** of Judah *by*	H4887
Jer	37: 1	Judah by Nebuchadnezzar **k** *of* Babylon;	H4889
Jer	37: 3	**K** Zedekiah, however, sent Jehukal son of	H4889
Jer	37: 7	Tell the **k** *of* Judah, who sent you to	H4889
Jer	37:17	Then **K** Zedekiah sent for him and had	H4889
Jer	37:17	into the hands of the **k** *of* Babylon.	H4889
Jer	37:18	Then Jeremiah said to **K** Zedekiah, "What	H4889
Jer	37:19	'The **k** *of* Babylon will not attack you or	H4889
Jer	37:20	But now, my lord the **k**, please listen.	H4889
Jer	37:21	**K** Zedekiah then gave orders for Jeremiah	H4889
Jer	38: 3	the hands of the army of the **k** *of* Babylon,	H4889
Jer	38: 4	Then the officials said to the **k**, "This man	H4889
Jer	38: 5	is in your hands," **K** Zedekiah answered.	H4889
Jer	38: 5	"The **k** can do nothing to oppose you."	H4889
Jer	38: 7	While the **k** was sitting in the Benjamin	H4889
Jer	38: 9	"My lord the **k**, these men have acted	H4889
Jer	38:10	Then the **k** commanded Ebed-Melek the	H4889
Jer	38:14	Then **K** Zedekiah sent for Jeremiah the	H4889
Jer	38:14	you something," the **k** said to Jeremiah.	H4889
Jer	38:16	But **K** Zedekiah swore this oath secretly to	H4889
Jer	38:17	to the officers of the **k** *of* Babylon,	H4889
Jer	38:18	to the officers of the **k** *of* Babylon,	H4889
Jer	38:19	**K** Zedekiah said to Jeremiah, "I am afraid	H4889
Jer	38:22	in the palace of the **k** *of* Judah will be	H4889
Jer	38:22	out to the officials of the **k** *of* Babylon.	H4889
Jer	38:23	will be captured by the **k** *of* Babylon;	H4889
Jer	38:25	what you said to the **k** and what the king	H4889
Jer	38:25	to the king and what the **k** said to you;	H4889
Jer	38:26	pleading with the **k** not to send me back	H4889
Jer	38:27	them everything the **k** had ordered him to	H4889
Jer	38:27	one had heard his conversation with the **k**.	NDT
Jer	39: 1	In the ninth year of Zedekiah **k** *of* Judah	H4889
Jer	39: 1	Nebuchadnezzar **k** *of* Babylon marched	H4889
Jer	39: 3	the officials of the **k** *of* Babylon came and	H4889
Jer	39: 3	all the other officials of the **k** *of* Babylon.	H4889
Jer	39: 4	When Zedekiah **k** *of* Judah and all the	H4889
Jer	39: 5	to Nebuchadnezzar **k** *of* Babylon at Riblah	H4889
Jer	39: 6	There at Riblah the **k** *of* Babylon	H4889
Jer	39:11	Nebuchadnezzar **k** *of* Babylon had given	H4889
Jer	39:13	all the other officers of the **k** *of* Babylon	H4889
Jer	40: 5	whom the **k** *of* Babylon has appointed	H4889
Jer	40: 7	heard that the **k** *of* Babylon had	H4889
Jer	40: 9	in the land and serve the **k** *of* Babylon,	H4889
Jer	40:11	heard that the **k** *of* Babylon had left a	H4889
Jer	40:14	know that Baalis **k** *of* the Ammonites has	H4889
Jer	41: 2	the one whom the **k** *of* Babylon had	H4889
Jer	41: 9	was the one **K** Asa had made as part	H4889
Jer	41: 9	of his defense against Baasha **k** *of* Israel.	H4889
Jer	41:18	whom the **k** *of* Babylon had appointed as	H4889
Jer	42:11	Do not be afraid of the **k** *of* Babylon	H4889
Jer	43:10	my servant Nebuchadnezzar **k** *of* Babylon,	H4889
Jer	44:30	Pharaoh Hophra **k** *of* Egypt into the hands	H4889
Jer	44:30	as I gave Zedekiah **k** *of* Judah into the	H4889
Jer	44:30	hands of Nebuchadnezzar **k** *of* Babylon,	H4889
Jer	45: 1	of Jehoiakim son of Josiah **k** *of* Judah,	H4889
Jer	46: 2	the army of Pharaoh Necho **k** *of* Egypt,	H4889
Jer	46: 2	by Nebuchadnezzar **k** *of* Babylon in the	H4889
Jer	46: 2	of Jehoiakim son of Josiah **k** *of* Judah:	H4889
Jer	46:13	of Nebuchadnezzar **k** *of* Babylon to attack	H4889
Jer	46:17	'Pharaoh **k** *of* Egypt is only a loud noise	H4889
Jer	46:18	declares the **K**, whose name is the LORD	H4889
Jer	46:26	Nebuchadnezzar **k** *of* Babylon and his	H4889
Jer	48:15	declares the **K**, whose name is the LORD	H4889
Jer	49:28	Nebuchadnezzar **k** *of* Babylon attacked:	H4889
Jer	49:30	"Nebuchadnezzar **k** *of* Babylon has	H4889
Jer	49:34	early in the reign of Zedekiah **k** *of* Judah:	H4889
Jer	49:38	in Elam and destroy her **k** and officials,"	H4889
Jer	50:17	first to devour them was the **k** *of* Assyria;	H4889
Jer	50:17	bones was Nebuchadnezzar **k** *of* Babylon."	H4889
Jer	50:18	"I will punish the **k** *of* Babylon and his	H4889
Jer	50:18	his land as I punished the **k** *of* Assyria.	H4889
Jer	50:43	The **k** *of* Babylon has heard reports about	H4889
Jer	51:31	to announce to the **k** *of* Babylon that his	H4889
Jer	51:34	"Nebuchadnezzar **k** *of* Babylon has	H4889
Jer	51:57	declares the **K**, whose name is the LORD	H4889
Jer	51:59	with Zedekiah **k** *of* Judah in the fourth	H4889
Jer	52: 1	twenty-one years old when he *became* **k**,	H4887
Jer	52: 3	rebelled against the **k** *of* Babylon.	H4889
Jer	52: 4	Nebuchadnezzar **k** *of* Babylon marched	H4889
Jer	52: 5	until the eleventh year of **K** Zedekiah.	H4889
Jer	52: 8	army pursued **K** Zedekiah and overtook	H4889
Jer	52: 9	was taken to the **k** *of* Babylon at Riblah	H4889
Jer	52:10	There at Riblah the **k** *of* Babylon killed the	H4889
Jer	52:12	year of Nebuchadnezzar **k** *of* Babylon,	H4889
Jer	52:12	who served the **k** *of* Babylon, came to	H4889
Jer	52:15	who had deserted to the **k** *of* Babylon.	H4889
Jer	52:20	which **K** Solomon had made for the	H4889
Jer	52:26	them to the **k** *of* Babylon at Riblah.	H4889
Jer	52:27	of Hamath, the **k** had them executed.	H4889
Jer	52:31	year of the exile of Jehoiachin **k** *of* Judah,	H4889
Jer	52:31	year Awel-Marduk **became k** *of* Babylon,	H4895
Jer	52:31	released Jehoiachin **k** *of* Judah and freed	H4889
Jer	52:34	Day by day the **k** *of* Babylon gave	H4889
La	2: 6	anger he has spurned both **k** and priest.	H4889
La	2: 9	Her **k** and her princes are exiled among	H4889
Eze	1: 2	fifth year of the exile of **K** Jehoiachin—	H4889
Eze	7:27	The **k** will mourn, the prince will be	H4889
Eze	17:12	'The **k** *of* Babylon went to Jerusalem and	H4889
Eze	17:12	carried off her **k** and her nobles,	H4889
Eze	17:15	But the **k** rebelled against him by sending	NDT
Eze	17:16	in the land of the **k** who put him on the	H4889
Eze	19: 9	cage and brought him to the **k** *of* Babylon.	H4889
Eze	21:19	the sword of the **k** *of* Babylon to take,	H4889
Eze	21:21	For the **k** *of* Babylon will stop at the fork in	H4889
Eze	24: 2	because the **k** *of* Babylon has laid siege	H4889
Eze	26: 7	Tyre Nebuchadnezzar **k** *of* Babylon,	H4889
Eze	26: 7	king of Babylon, **k** *of* kings, with horses	H4889
Eze	28:12	concerning the **k** *of* Tyre and say to him:	H4889
Eze	29: 2	against Pharaoh **k** *of* Egypt and prophesy	H4889
Eze	29: 3	against you, Pharaoh **k** *of* Egypt, you great	H4889
Eze	29:18	Nebuchadnezzar **k** *of* Babylon drove his	H4889
Eze	29:19	Egypt to Nebuchadnezzar **k** *of* Babylon,	H4889
Eze	30:10	hand of Nebuchadnezzar **k** *of* Babylon.	H4889
Eze	30:21	broken the arm of Pharaoh **k** *of* Egypt.	H4889
Eze	30:22	I am against Pharaoh **k** *of* Egypt. I will	H4889
Eze	30:24	the arms of the **k** *of* Babylon and put my	H4889
Eze	30:25	strengthen the arms of the **k** *of* Babylon,	H4889
Eze	30:25	into the hand of the **k** *of* Babylon and he	H4889
Eze	31: 2	say to Pharaoh **k** *of* Egypt and to his	H4889
Eze	32: 2	concerning Pharaoh **k** *of* Egypt and say to	H4889
Eze	32:11	" 'The sword of the **k** *of* Babylon will come	H4889
Eze	37:22	There will be one **k** over all of them and	H4889
Eze	37:24	" 'My servant David will be **k** over them	H4889
Da	1: 1	year of the reign of Jehoiakim **k** *of* Judah,	H4889
Da	1: 1	Nebuchadnezzar **k** *of* Babylon came to	H4889
Da	1: 2	delivered Jehoiakim **k** *of* Judah into his	H4889
Da	1: 3	Then the **k** ordered Ashpenaz, chief of his	H4889
Da	1: 5	The **k** assigned them a daily amount of	H4889
Da	1:10	"I am afraid of my lord the **k**, who has	H4889
Da	1:10	The **k** would then have my head because	H4889
Da	1:18	the time set by the **k** to bring them into	H4889
Da	1:19	The **k** talked with them, and he found	H4889
Da	1:20	about which the **k** questioned them,	H4889
Da	1:21	there until the first year of **K** Cyrus.	H4889
Da	2: 2	So the **k** summoned the magicians	H4889
Da	2: 2	they came in and stood before the **k**,	H4889
Da	2: 4	Then the astrologers answered the **k**	H4889
Da	2: 4	the king, "May the **k** live forever!	A10421
Da	2: 5	The **k** replied to the astrologers, "This is	A10421
Da	2: 7	"Let the **k** tell his servants the dream	A10421
Da	2: 8	Then the **k** answered, "I am certain that	A10421
Da	2:10	The astrologers answered the **k**, "There	A10421
Da	2:10	on earth who can do what the **k** asks!	A10421
Da	2:10	No **k**, however great and mighty, has	A10421
Da	2:11	What the **k** asks is too difficult. No one	A10421
Da	2:11	can reveal it to the **k** except the gods,	A10421
Da	2:12	This made the **k** so angry and furious	A10421
Da	2:15	"Why did the **k** issue such a harsh	A10421
Da	2:16	went in to the **k** and asked for time,	A10421
Da	2:23	made known to us the dream of the **k**."	A10421
Da	2:24	whom the **k** had appointed to execute	A10421
Da	2:24	Take me to the **k**, and I will interpret his	A10421
Da	2:25	took Daniel to the **k** at once and said,	A10421
Da	2:25	who can tell the **k** what his dream	A10421
Da	2:26	The **k** asked Daniel (also called	A10421
Da	2:27	can explain to the **k** the mystery he has	A10421
Da	2:28	He has shown **K** Nebuchadnezzar what	A10421
Da	2:36	now we will interpret it to the **k**.	A10421
Da	2:37	you are the **k** *of* kings. The God of	A10421
Da	2:45	God has shown the **k** what will take	A10421
Da	2:46	Then **K** Nebuchadnezzar fell prostrate	A10421
Da	2:47	The **k** said to Daniel, "Surely your God is	A10421
Da	2:48	Then the **k** placed Daniel in a high	A10421
Da	2:49	request the **k** appointed Shadrach,	A10421
Da	3: 1	**K** Nebuchadnezzar made an image of	A10421
Da	3: 3	of the image that **K** Nebuchadnezzar	A10421
Da	3: 5	of gold that **K** Nebuchadnezzar has	A10421
Da	3: 7	of gold that **K** Nebuchadnezzar had	A10421
Da	3: 9	They said to **K** Nebuchadnezzar, "May	A10421
Da	3: 9	Nebuchadnezzar, "May the **k** live forever!	A10421
Da	3:13	So these men were brought before the **k**	A10421
Da	3:16	replied to him, "**K** Nebuchadnezzar, we	A10421
Da	3:24	Then **K** Nebuchadnezzar leaped to his	A10421
Da	3:30	Then the **k** promoted Shadrach	A10421
Da	4: 1	**K** Nebuchadnezzar, To the nations and	A10421
Da	4:18	the dream that I, **K** Nebuchadnezzar	A10421
Da	4:19	So the **k** said, "Belteshazzar, do not let	A10421
Da	4:24	High has issued against my lord the **k**:	A10421
Da	4:28	All this happened to **K** Nebuchadnezzar.	A10421
Da	4:29	as the **k** was walking on the roof of the royal	NDT
Da	4:31	is decreed for you, **K** Nebuchadnezzar:	A10421
Da	4:37	exalt and glorify the **K** *of* heaven,	A10421
Da	5: 1	**K** Belshazzar gave a great banquet for a	A10421
Da	5: 2	so that the **k** and his nobles, his	A10421
Da	5: 3	Jerusalem, and the **k** and his nobles, his	A10421
Da	5: 5	The **k** watched the hand as it wrote	A10421
Da	5: 7	The **k** summoned the enchanters	A10421
Da	5: 8	the writing or tell the **k** what it meant.	A10421
Da	5: 9	So **K** Belshazzar became even more	A10421
Da	5:10	the voices of the **k** and his nobles,	A10421
Da	5:10	"May the **k** live forever!" she	A10421
Da	5:11	Your father, **K** Nebuchadnezzar	A10421
Da	5:12	whom the **k** called Belteshazzar	A10421
Da	5:13	So Daniel was brought before the **k**, and	A10421
Da	5:13	the king, and the **k** said to him, "Are you	A10421
Da	5:13	my father the **k** brought from Judah?	A10421
Da	5:17	Then Daniel answered the **k**, "You may	A10421
Da	5:17	the writing for the **k** and tell him what it	A10421
Da	5:19	Those the **k** wanted to put to death, he put	NDT
Da	5:30	night Belshazzar, **k** *of* the Babylonians	A10421
Da	6: 2	to them so that the **k** might not suffer	A10421
Da	6: 3	qualities that the **k** planned to set him	A10421
Da	6: 6	went as a group to the **k** and said:	A10421
Da	6: 6	"May **K** Darius live forever!	A10421
Da	6: 7	all agreed that the **k** should issue an	A10421
Da	6: 9	So **K** Darius put the decree in writing.	A10421
Da	6:12	So they went to the **k** and spoke to him	A10421
Da	6:12	The **k** answered, "The decree stands	A10421
Da	6:13	Then they said to the **k**, "Daniel, who is	A10421
Da	6:14	When the **k** heard this, he was greatly	A10421
Da	6:15	went as a group to **K** Darius and said to	A10421
Da	6:15	edict that the **k** issues can be changed	A10421
Da	6:16	So the **k** gave the order, and they	A10421
Da	6:16	The **k** said to Daniel, "May your God	A10421
Da	6:17	the **k** sealed it with his own signet	A10421
Da	6:18	Then the **k** returned to his palace and	A10421
Da	6:19	the **k** got up and hurried to the lions'	A10421
Da	6:21	Daniel answered, "May the **k** live forever!	A10421
Da	6:23	The **k** was overjoyed and gave orders to	A10421
Da	6:25	Then **K** Darius wrote to all the nations	A10421
Da	7: 1	the first year of Belshazzar **k** *of* Babylon,	A10421
Da	7:24	After them another **k** will arise, different	NDT
Da	8: 1	In the third year of **K** Belshazzar's reign,	H4889
Da	8:21	The shaggy goat is the **k** *of* Greece, and	H4889
Da	8:21	large horn between its eyes is the first **k**.	H4889
Da	8:23	a fierce-looking **k**, a master of intrigue,	H4889
Da	10: 1	In the third year of Cyrus **k** *of* Persia,	H4889
Da	10:13	I was detained there with the **k** *of* Persia.	H4889
Da	11: 3	Then a mighty **k** will arise, who will rule	H4889
Da	11: 5	"The **k** *of* the South will become strong	H4889
Da	11: 6	The daughter of the **k** *of* the South will go	H4889
Da	11: 6	will go to the **k** *of* the North to make	H4889
Da	11: 7	the forces of the **k** *of* the North and enter	H4889
Da	11: 8	he will leave the **k** *of* the North alone.	H4889
Da	11: 9	Then the **k** of the North will invade the realm	NDT
Da	11: 9	the realm of the **k** *of* the South but will	H4889
Da	11:11	"Then the **k** *of* the South will march out in	H4889
Da	11:11	rage and fight against the **k** *of* the North,	H4889
Da	11:12	**the k of the South** will be filled with	H2257S
Da	11:13	For the **k** *of* the North will muster another	H4889
Da	11:14	many will rise against the **k** *of* the South.	H4889
Da	11:15	Then the **k** *of* the North will come and	H4889
Da	11:17	an alliance with **the k of the South**.	H2257S
Da	11:25	courage against the **k** *of* the South.	H4889
Da	11:25	The **k** *of* the South will wage war with a	H4889
Da	11:28	The **k** of the North will return to his own	NDT
Da	11:36	"The **k** will do as he pleases. He will exalt	H4889
Da	11:40	time of the end the **k** *of* the South will	H4889
Da	11:40	the **k** *of* the North will storm out	H4889
Hos	1: 1	of Jeroboam son of Jehoash **k** *of* Israel:	H4889
Hos	3: 4	will live many days without **k** or prince,	H4889
Hos	3: 5	seek the LORD their God and David their **k**.	H4889
Hos	5:13	Assyria, and sent to the great **k** for help.	H4889
Hos	7: 3	"They delight the **k** with their wickedness	H4889
Hos	7: 5	of the festival of our **k** the princes become	H4889
Hos	8:10	under the oppression of the mighty **k**.	H4889
Hos	10: 3	"We have no **k** because we did not revere	H4889
Hos	10: 3	But even if we had a **k**, what could he do	H4889
Hos	10: 6	carried to Assyria as tribute for the great **k**.	H4889
Hos	10: 7	Samaria's **k** will be destroyed, swept away	H4889
Hos	10:15	the **k** *of* Israel will be completely	H4889
Hos	13:10	Where is your **k**, that he may save you	H4889
Hos	13:10	you said, 'Give me a **k** and princes'?	H4889
Hos	13:11	So in my anger I gave you a **k**, and in my	H4889
Am	1: 1	when Uzziah was **k** *of* Judah and	H4889
Am	1: 1	Jeroboam son of Jehoash was **k** *of* Israel.	H4889
Am	1: 5	I will destroy the **k** *who is* in the Valley of	H3782
Am	1: 8	I will destroy the **k** of Ashdod and the one	H3782
Am	1:15	Her **k** will go into exile, he and his	H4889
Am	2: 1	burned to ashes the bones of Edom's **k**,	H4889
Am	5:26	You have lifted up the shrine of your **k**	H4889
Am	7:10	sent a message to Jeroboam **k** *of* Israel:	H4889
Jnh	3: 6	warning reached the **k** *of* Nineveh,	H4889
Jnh	3: 7	"By the decree of the **k** and his nobles: Do	H4889
Mic	2:13	Their **K** will pass through before them, the	H4889
Mic	4: 9	do you now cry aloud—have you no **k**?	H4889
Mic	6: 5	what Balak **k** *of* Moab plotted and	H4889
Na	3:18	**K** *of* Assyria, your shepherds slumber; your	H4889
Zep	1: 1	reign of Josiah son of Amon **k** *of* Judah:	H4889
Zep	3:15	The LORD, the **K** *of* Israel, is with you	H4889
Hag	1: 1	In the second year of **K** Darius, on the first	H4889
Hag	1:15	In the second year of **K** Darius,	H4889
Zec	7: 1	In the fourth year of **K** Darius, the word of	H4889
Zec	9: 5	Gaza will lose her **k** and Ashkelon will be	H4889
Zec	9: 9	your **k** comes to you, righteous and	H4889
Zec	11: 6	the hands of their neighbors and their **k**.	H4889
Zec	14: 5	in the days of Uzziah **k** *of* Judah.	H4889

Zec 14: 9 The LORD will be k over the whole earth H4889
Zec 14:16 will go up year after year to worship the K, H4889
Zec 14:17 not go up to Jerusalem to worship the K, H4889
Mal 1:14 I am a great k," says the LORD Almighty H4889
Mt 1: 6 Jesse the father of K David. David was G995
Mt 2: 1 during the time *of* K Herod, Magi from the G995
Mt 2: 2 the one who has been born k of the Jews? G995
Mt 2: 3 When K Herod heard this he was disturbed, G995
Mt 2: 9 After they had heard the k, they went on G995
Mt 5:35 Jerusalem, for it is the city *of* the Great K. G995
Mt 14: 9 The k was distressed, but because of his G995
Mt 18:23 of heaven is like a k who wanted to G476+995
Mt 21: 5 your k comes to you, gentle and G995
Mt 22: 2 of heaven is like a k who prepared a G476+995
Mt 22: 7 The k was enraged. He sent his army and G995
Mt 22:11 "But when the k came in to see the guests G995
Mt 22:13 "Then the k told the attendants, 'Tie him G995
Mt 25:34 "Then the K will say to those on his right G995
Mt 25:40 "The K will reply, 'Truly I tell you, whatever G995
Mt 27:11 asked him, "Are you the k of the Jews?" G995
Mt 27:29 "Hail, k of the Jews!" they G995
Mt 27:37 THIS IS JESUS, THE K OF THE JEWS. G995
Mt 27:42 He's the k of Israel! Let him G995
Mk 6:14 K Herod heard about this, for Jesus' name G995
Mk 6:22 The k said to the girl, "Ask me for anything G995
Mk 6:25 the girl hurried in to the k with the request: G995
Mk 6:26 The k was greatly distressed, but because G995
Mk 15: 2 "Are you the k of the Jews?" asked Pilate G995
Mk 15: 9 me to release to you the k of the Jews?" G995
Mk 15:12 with the one you call the k of the Jews?" G995
Mk 15:18 to call out to him, "Hail, k of the Jews!" G995
Mk 15:26 charge against him read: THE K OF THE JEWS. G995
Mk 15:32 Let this Messiah, this k of Israel, come down G995
Lk 1: 5 In the time of Herod k of Judea there was a G995
Lk 14:31 "Or suppose a k is about to go to war G995
Lk 14:31 is about to go to war *against* another k. G995
Lk 19:12 *to have* himself **appointed** k and G3284+993
Lk 19:14 'We don't want this man *to be* our k. G996
Lk 19:15 "*He was* **made** k, however G3284+3836+993
Lk 19:27 who did not want me *to be* k over them— G996
Lk 19:38 "Blessed is the k who comes in the name G995
Lk 23: 2 to Caesar and claims to be Messiah, a k." G995
Lk 23: 3 asked Jesus, "Are you the k of the Jews?" G995
Lk 23:37 "If you are the k of the Jews, save G995
Lk 23:38 which read: THIS IS THE K OF THE JEWS. G995
Jn 1:49 are the Son of God; you are the k of Israel." G995
Jn 6:15 intended to come and make him k by force, G995
Jn 12:13 "Blessed is the k of Israel!" G995
Jn 12:15 your k is coming, seated on a donkey's G995
Jn 18:33 asked him, "Are you the k of the Jews?" G995
Jn 18:37 "You are a k, then!" said Pilate. G995
Jn 18:37 answered, "You say that I am a k. In fact, G995
Jn 18:39 you want me to release 'the k of the Jews'?" G995
Jn 19: 3 again, saying, "Hail, k of the Jews! G995
Jn 19:12 who claims to be a k opposes Caesar." G995
Jn 19:14 "Here is your k," Pilate said to the G995
Jn 19:15 "Shall I crucify your k?" Pilate asked. G995
Jn 19:15 "We have no k but Caesar," the chief G995
Jn 19:19 JESUS OF NAZARETH, THE K OF THE JEWS. G995
Jn 19:21 "Do not write 'The K of the Jews,' but that G995
Jn 19:21 that this man claimed to be k of the Jews." G995
Ac 7:10 to gain the goodwill of Pharaoh k of Egypt. G995
Ac 7:18 Then 'a new k, to whom Joseph meant G995
Ac 12: 1 about this time that K Herod arrested some G995
Ac 12:20 a trusted personal servant *of* the k, they G995
Ac 13:21 Then the people asked *for* a k, and he gave G995
Ac 13:22 he made David their k. God testified G995
Ac 17: 7 saying that there is another k, one called G995
Ac 25:13 A few days later K Agrippa and Bernice G995
Ac 25:14 Festus discussed Paul's case *with* the k. G995
Ac 25:24 "K Agrippa, and all who are present with G995
Ac 25:26 before you, K Agrippa, so that as a G995
Ac 26: 2 "K Agrippa, I consider myself fortunate to G995
Ac 26: 7 K Agrippa, it is because of this hope that G995
Ac 26:13 About noon, K Agrippa, as I was on the G995
Ac 26:19 "So then, K Agrippa, I was not disobedient G995
Ac 26:26 The k is familiar with these things, and I G995
Ac 26:27 K Agrippa, do you believe the prophets? G995
Ac 26:30 The k rose, and with him the governor and G995
2Co 11:32 the governor *under* K Aretas had the city G995
1Ti 1:17 Now *to* the K eternal, immortal, invisible G995
1Ti 6:15 only Ruler, the K of kings and Lord of lords, G995
Heb 7: 1 Melchizedek was k of Salem and priest G995
Heb 7: 2 Melchizedek means "k of righteousness"; G995
Heb 7: 2 then also, "k of Salem" means "king of G995
Heb 7: 2 "king of Salem" means "k of peace." G995
Rev 9:11 They had *as* k over them the angel of the G995
Rev 15: 3 true are your ways, K of the nations. G995
Rev 17:11 once was, and now is not, is an eighth k. NDT
Rev 17:14 he is Lord of lords and K of kings— G995
Rev 19:16 K OF KINGS AND LORD OF LORDS. G995

KING'S (199) [KING]

Ge 14:17 Valley of Shaveh (that is, the K Valley). H4889
Ge 39:20 the place where the k prisoners were H4889
Nu 20:17 travel along the K Highway and not turn H4889
Nu 21:22 travel along the K Highway until we have H4889
Jdg 3:21 right thigh and plunged it into the k belly. H2257
1Sa 18:18 I should become the k son-in-law?" H4200+4889
1Sa 18:23 matter to become the k son-in-law? H928+4889
1Sa 18:26 to become the k son-in-law. H928+4889
1Sa 18:27 might become the k son-in-law. H928+4889
1Sa 20:29 is why he has not come to the k table." H4889
1Sa 21: 8 because the k mission was urgent. H4889
1Sa 22:14 loyal as David, the k son-in-law, captain H4889
1Sa 22:17 But the k officials were unwilling to raise H4889
1Sa 26:16 Where are the k spear and water jug that H4889
1Sa 26:22 "Here is the k spear," David answered H4889
2Sa 9:11 ate at David's table like one of the k sons. H4889
2Sa 9:13 because he always ate at the k table; he H4889
2Sa 11: 1 Joab out with **the** k men and the whole H2257S
2Sa 11:20 the k anger may flare up, and he may ask H4889
2Sa 11:24 the wall, and some of the k men died. H4889
2Sa 12:30 David took the crown from their k head H4889
2Sa 13: 4 "Why do you, the k son, look so haggard H4889
2Sa 13:23 he invited all the k sons to come there. H4889
2Sa 13:27 him Amnon and the rest of the k sons. H4889
2Sa 13:29 Then all the k sons got up, mounted their H4889
2Sa 13:30 "Absalom has struck down all the k sons H4889
2Sa 13:33 the report that all the k sons are dead. H4889
2Sa 13:35 the k sons have come; it has H4889
2Sa 13:36 speaking, the k sons came in, wailing H4889
2Sa 14: 1 Zeruiah knew that the k heart longed for H4889
2Sa 14:28 in Jerusalem without seeing the k face. H4889
2Sa 14:32 I want to see the k face, and if I am H4889
2Sa 15:15 The k officials answered him, "Your H4889
2Sa 15:35 them anything you hear in the k palace. H4889
2Sa 16: 2 donkeys are for the k household to ride on H4889
2Sa 16: 6 David and all the k officials with stones, H4889
2Sa 18:12 I would not lay a hand on the k son. H4889
2Sa 18:18 erected it in the K Valley as a monument H4889
2Sa 18:20 do so today, because the k son is dead." H4889
2Sa 18:29 was about to send the k servant and me, H4889
2Sa 19:18 the ford to take the k household over and H4889
2Sa 19:42 Have we eaten any of the k provisions H4889
2Sa 24: 4 The k word, however, overruled Joab and H4889
1Ki 1: 9 all his brothers, the k sons, and all the H4889
1Ki 1:19 has invited all the k sons, Abiathar H4889
1Ki 1:25 He has invited all the k sons, the H4889
1Ki 1:28 she came into the k presence and stood H4889
1Ki 1:44 they have put him on the k mule, H4889
1Ki 2:19 He had a throne brought for the k mother H4889
1Ki 4:27 Solomon and all who came to the k table. H4889
1Ki 5:17 At the k command they removed from the H4889
1Ki 13: 6 the k hand was restored and became H4889
1Ki 22: 6 "for the Lord will give it into the k hand." H4889
1Ki 22:12 "for the LORD will give it into the k hand." H4889
1Ki 22:15 "for the LORD will give it into the k hand." H4889
1Ki 22:26 the ruler of the city and to Joash the k son H4889
2Ki 8:15 it in water and spread it over **the** k face, H2257S
2Ki 9:34 "and bury her, for she was a k daughter." H4889
2Ki 11: 4 Then he showed them the k son. H4889
2Ki 11:12 brought out the k son and put the crown H4889
2Ki 13:16 Elisha put his hands on the k hands. H4889
2Ki 15: 5 Jotham the k son had charge of the H4889
2Ki 16:15 the k burnt offering and his grain offering H4889
2Ki 22:12 the secretary and Asaiah the k attendant: H4889
2Ki 24:15 from Jerusalem to Babylon the k mother, H4889
2Ki 25: 4 between the two walls near the k garden, H4889
2Ki 25:29 of his life ate regularly at **the** k table. H2257S
1Ch 9:18 being stationed at the K Gate on the east H4889
1Ch 18:17 sons were chief officials at the k side. H4889
1Ch 21: 4 The k word, however, overruled Joab; so H4889
1Ch 21: 6 because the k command was repulsive to H4889
1Ch 25: 2 who prophesied under the k supervision. H4889
1Ch 25: 5 All these were sons of Heman the k seer H4889
1Ch 26:30 the work of the LORD and for the k service. H4889
1Ch 27:32 son of Hakmoni took care of the k sons. H4889
1Ch 27:33 Ahithophel was the k counselor H4200+4889
1Ch 27:33 Hushai the Arkite was the k confidant. H4889
1Ch 29: 6 in charge of the k work gave willingly. H4889
2Ch 8:15 not deviate from the k commands to the H4889
2Ch 18: 5 "for God will give it into the k hand." H4889
2Ch 18:11 "for the LORD will give it into the k hand." H4889
2Ch 18:25 ruler of the city and to Joash the k son, H4889
2Ch 21:17 off all the goods found in the k palace, H4889
2Ch 23: 3 said to them, "The k son shall reign, as H4889
2Ch 23:11 sons brought out the k son and put the H4889
2Ch 24: 8 At the k command, a chest was made H4889
2Ch 24:11 by the Levites to the k officials and they H4889
2Ch 28: 7 killed Maaseiah the k son, Azrikam the H4889
2Ch 29:25 David and Gad the k seer and Nathan the H4889
2Ch 30: 6 At the k command, couriers went H4889
2Ch 34:20 the secretary and Asaiah the k attendant: H4889
2Ch 35: 7 cattle—all from the k *own* possessions. H4889
2Ch 35:15 Heman and Jeduthun the k seer. H4889
Ezr 7:27 has put it into the k heart to bring honor H4889
Ezr 7:28 advisers and all the k powerful officials. H4889
Ezr 8:36 also delivered the k orders to the royal H4889
Ne 2: 9 gave them the k letters. H4889
Ne 2:14 toward the Fountain Gate and the K Pool, H4889
Ne 3:15 of Siloam, by the K Garden, as far as the H4889
Ne 5: 4 money to pay the k tax on our fields and H4889
Ne 11:23 The musicians were under the k orders H4889
Ne 11:24 was the k agent in all affairs relating to H4889
Est 1: 5 in the enclosed garden of the k palace H4889
Est 1: 7 abundant, in keeping with the k liberality. H4889
Est 1: 8 By the k command each guest was allowed NDT
Est 1:12 the attendants delivered the k command, H4889
Est 1:18 respond to all the k nobles in the same H4889
Est 1:20 Then when the k edict is proclaimed H4889
Est 2: 2 Then the k personal attendants proposed H4889
Est 2: 3 the care of Hegai, the k eunuch, who is in H4889
Est 2: 8 When the k order and edict had been H4889
Est 2: 8 was taken to the k palace and entrusted H4889
Est 2: 9 selected from the k palace and moved her H4889
Est 2:13 with her from the harem to the k palace. H4889
Est 2:14 the k eunuch who was in charge of the H4889
Est 2:15 the k eunuch who was in charge of the H4889
Est 2:19 Mordecai was sitting at the k gate. H4889
Est 2:21 time Mordecai was sitting at the k gate, H4889
Est 2:21 two of the k officers who guarded the H4889
Est 3: 2 officials at the k gate knelt down and H4889
Est 3: 3 officials at the k gate asked Mordecai, H4889
Est 3: 3 "Why do you disobey the k command?" H4889
Est 3: 8 they do not obey the k laws; it is not H4889
Est 3: 8 it is not in the k best interest to tolerate H4889
Est 3: 9 of silver to the k administrators for the NDT
Est 3:12 all Haman's orders to the k satraps, H4889
Est 3:13 by couriers to all the k provinces with the H4889
Est 3:15 spurred on by the k command, and the H4889
Est 4: 2 But he went only as far as the k gate H4889
Est 4: 5 one of the k eunuchs assigned to attend H4889
Est 4: 6 square of the city in front of the k gate. H4889
Est 4: 8 her to go into the k presence to beg for H4889
Est 4:11 "All the k officials and the people of the H4889
Est 4:13 you are in the k house you alone of all H4889
Est 5: 1 court of the palace, in front of the k hall. H4889
Est 5: 8 Then I will answer the k question." H4889
Est 5: 9 saw Mordecai at the k gate and observed H4889
Est 5:13 that Jew Mordecai sitting at the k gate." H4889
Est 6: 2 two of the k officers who guarded the H4889
Est 6: 9 to one of the k most noble princes. H4889
Est 6:10 Mordecai the Jew, who sits at the k gate. H4889
Est 6:12 Afterward Mordecai returned to the k gate. H4889
Est 6:14 the k eunuchs arrived and hurried Haman H4889
Est 7: 8 As soon as the word left the k mouth, they H4889
Est 7:10 up for Mordecai. Then the k fury subsided. H4889
Est 8: 5 to destroy the Jews in all the k provinces. H4889
Est 8: 8 decree in the k name in behalf of the H4889
Est 8: 8 seal it with the k signet ring—for no H4889
Est 8: 8 written in the k name and sealed with H4889
Est 8:10 the dispatches with the k signet ring, H4889
Est 8:11 The k edict granted the Jews in every city H4889
Est 8:14 spurred on by the k command, and the H4889
Est 8:15 When Mordecai left the k presence, he H4889
Est 9: 3 governors and the k administrators H4200+4889
Est 9:12 they done in the rest of the k provinces? H4889
Est 9:16 Jews who were in the k provinces also H4889
Est 9:25 But when the plot came to the k attention H4889
Ps 45: 5 arrows pierce the hearts of the k enemies; H4889
Ps 61: 6 Increase the days of the k life, his years H4889
Pr 14:28 A large population is a k glory, but H4889
Pr 16:14 A k wrath is a messenger of death, but H4889
Pr 16:15 When a k face brightens, it means life H4889
Pr 19:12 A k rage is like the roar of a lion, but his H4889
Pr 20: 2 A k wrath strikes terror like the roar of a H4889
Pr 21: 1 the LORD's hand the k heart is a stream of H4889
Pr 25: 5 wicked officials from the k presence, H4889
Pr 25: 6 Do not exalt yourself in the k presence H4889
Ecc 2:12 What more can the k successor do than H4889
Ecc 4:15 sun followed the youth, **the** k successor. H2257S
Ecc 8: 2 Obey the k command, I say, because you H4889
Ecc 8: 3 not be in a hurry to leave **the** k presence. H2257S
Ecc 8: 4 Since a k word is supreme, who can say to H4889
Isa 23:15 seventy years, the span of a k life. H4889
Jer 38: 6 of Malkijah, the k son, which was in the H4889
Jer 39: 4 the city at night by way of the k garden, H4889
Jer 41: 1 blood and had been one of the k officers, H4889
Jer 41:10 the k daughters along with all the others H4889
Jer 43: 6 women, the children and the k daughters. H4889
Jer 52: 7 between the two walls near the k garden, H4889
Jer 52:33 of his life ate regularly at **the** k table. H2257S
Da 1: 3 to bring into the k service some of the NDT
Da 1: 4 qualified to serve in the k palace. H4889
Da 1: 5 of food and wine from the k table. H4889
Da 1: 5 after that they were to enter the k service. H4889
Da 1:19 Azariah; so they entered the k service. H4889
Da 2:14 the commander of the k guard, had A10421
Da 2:15 He asked the k officer, "Why did the king A10421
Da 3:22 The k command was so urgent and the A10421
Da 3:28 defied the k command and were A10421
Da 5: 8 Then all the k wise men came in, but A10421
Da 6:24 At the k command, the men who had A10421
Da 8:27 I got up and went about the k business. H4889
Da 11:26 Those who eat from **the** k provisions will H2257S
Am 7: 1 locusts after the k *share* had been H4889
Am 7:13 because this is the k sanctuary and the H4889
Zep 1: 8 the officials and the k sons and all those H4889
Ac 12:20 depended on the k *country* for their food G997
Heb 11:23 they were not afraid of the k edict. G995
Heb 11:27 not fearing the k anger; he persevered G995

KINGDOM (304) [KING]

Ge 10:10 The first centers of his k were Babylon H4930
Ge 20: 9 such great guilt upon me and my k? H4930
Ex 19: 6 you will be for me a k *of* priests and a holy H4930
Nu 24: 7 greater than Agag; their k will be exalted. H4895
Nu 32:33 son of Joseph the k *of* Sihon king of the H4930
Nu 32:33 Amorites and the k *of* Og king of Bashan H4930
Dt 3: 4 whole region of Argob, Og's k in Bashan. H4930
Dt 3:10 Edrei, towns of Og's k in Bashan. H4930
Dt 3:13 all of Bashan, the k *of* Og, I gave to the H4930
Dt 17:18 When he takes the throne of his k, he is H4930
Dt 17:20 will reign a long time over his k in Israel. H4930
Jos 13:12 the whole k *of* Og in Bashan, who H4931

1Sa 13:13 have established your **k** over Israel for all H4930
1Sa 13:14 But now your **k** will not endure; the LORD H4930
1Sa 15:28 LORD has torn the **k** *of* Israel from you H4931
1Sa 18: 8 What more can he get but the **k**?" H4867
1Sa 20:31 neither you nor your **k** will be established. H4895
1Sa 24:20 be king and that the **k** *of* Israel will be H4930
1Sa 28:17 LORD has torn the **k** out of your hands and H4930
2Sa 3:10 transfer the **k** from the house of Saul H4930
2Sa 3:28 "I and my **k** are forever innocent before H4930
2Sa 5:12 had exalted his **k** for the sake of his H4930
2Sa 7:12 flesh and blood, and I will establish his **k**. H4930
2Sa 7:13 I will establish the throne of his **k** forever. H4930
2Sa 7:16 Your house and your **k** will endure forever H4930
2Sa 8: 6 garrisons in the **Aramean k** *of* Damascus, H806
2Sa 16: 3 will restore to me my grandfather's **k**. H4931
2Sa 16: 8 LORD has given the **k** into the hands of H4867
1Ki 2:15 he said, "the **k** was mine. All Israel H4867
1Ki 2:15 the **k** has gone to my brother H4867
1Ki 2:22 You might as well request the **k** for him H4867
1Ki 2:46 The **k** was now established in Solomon's H4930
1Ki 10:20 it had ever been made for any other **k**. H4930
1Ki 11:11 certainly tear the **k** away from you and H4930
1Ki 11:13 Yet I will not tear the whole **k** from him H4930
1Ki 11:31 am going to tear the **k** out of Solomon's H4930
1Ki 11:34 not take the whole **k** out of Solomon's H4930
1Ki 11:35 I will take the **k** from his son's hands and H4867
1Ki 12:21 to regain the **k** for Rehoboam son of H4867
1Ki 12:26 "The **k** will now likely revert to the house H4930
1Ki 14: 8 I tore the **k** away from the house of David H4930
1Ki 18:10 is not a nation or **k** where my master has H4930
1Ki 18:10 a nation or **k** claimed you were not H4930
2Ki 14: 5 After the **k** was firmly in his grasp, he H4930
2Ki 15:19 strengthen his own hold on the **k**. H4930
2Ki 19:30 a remnant of the **k** *of* Judah will take root H1074
2Ki 20:13 palace or in all his **k** that Hezekiah did H4939
1Ch 10:14 turned the **k** over to David son of H4867
1Ch 12:23 at Hebron to turn Saul's **k** over to him, H4895
1Ch 14: 2 Israel and that his **k** had been highly H4895
1Ch 16:20 nation to nation, from one **k** to another. H4930
1Ch 17:11 your own sons, and I will establish his **k**. H4895
1Ch 17:14 set him over my house and my **k** forever; H4895
1Ch 18: 6 garrisons in the **Aramean k** *of* Damascus, H806
1Ch 22:10 the throne of his **k** over Israel forever. H4895
1Ch 28: 5 on the throne of the **k** *of* the LORD over H4895
1Ch 28: 7 I will establish his **k** forever if he is H4895
1Ch 29:11 is the **k**; you are exalted as head H4930
2Ch 1: 1 established himself firmly over his **k**, H4895
2Ch 9:19 it had ever been made for any other **k**. H4930
2Ch 11: 1 Israel and to regain the **k** for Rehoboam. H4930
2Ch 11:17 strengthened the **k** *of* Judah and H4895
2Ch 13: 8 now you plan to resist the **k** *of* the LORD, H4930
2Ch 14: 5 and the **k** was at peace under him. H4930
2Ch 17: 5 LORD established the **k** under his control; H4930
2Ch 20:30 And the **k** *of* Jehoshaphat was at peace H4895
2Ch 21: 3 he had given the **k** to Jehoram because H4930
2Ch 21: 4 himself firmly over his father's **k**, H4930
2Ch 22: 9 Ahaziah powerful enough to retain the **k**. H4930
2Ch 25: 3 After the **k** was firmly in his control, he H4930
2Ch 29:21 male goats as a sin offering for the **k**, H4930
2Ch 32:15 god of any nation or **k** has been able to H4930
2Ch 33:13 him back to Jerusalem and to his **k**. H4895
2Ch 36:20 successors until the **k** *of* Persia came to H4895
Ezr 7:13 decree that any of the Israelites in my **k**, A10424
Ne 9:35 Even while they were in their **k**, enjoying H4895
Est 1: 4 vast wealth of his **k** and the splendor and H4895
Est 1:14 to the king and were highest in the **k**. H4895
Est 1:22 He sent dispatches to all parts of the **k**, to H4889
Est 3: 6 throughout the whole **k** *of* Xerxes. H4895
Est 3: 8 provinces of your **k** who keep themselves H4895
Est 5: 3 Even up to half the **k**, it will be given you." H4895
Est 5: 6 Even up to half the **k**, it will be granted." H4895
Est 7: 2 Even up to half the **k**, it will be granted." H4895
Est 9:30 Jews in the 127 provinces of Xerxes' **k**— H4895
Ps 45: 6 of justice will be the scepter of your **k**. H4895
Ps 103:19 throne in heaven, and his **k** rules over all. H4895
Ps 105:13 nation to nation, from *one* **k** to another. H4930
Ps 145:11 of the glory of your **k** and speak of your H4895
Ps 145:12 acts and the glorious splendor of your **k**. H4895
Ps 145:13 Your **k** is an everlasting kingdom, and H4895
Ps 145:13 Your kingdom is an everlasting **k**, and H4895
Ecc 4:14 have been born in poverty within his **k**. H4895
Isa 9: 7 reign on David's throne and over his **k**, H4930
Isa 19: 2 city against city, **k** against kingdom. H4930
Isa 19: 2 city against city, kingdom against **k**. H4930
Isa 34:12 will have nothing there to be called a **k**, H4867
Isa 37:31 a remnant of the **k** *of* Judah will take root H1074
Isa 39: 2 palace or in all his **k** that Hezekiah did H4939
Isa 60:12 For the nation or **k** that will not serve you H4930
Jer 18: 7 that a nation or **k** is to be uprooted, H4930
Jer 18: 9 that a nation or **k** is to be built up and H4930
Jer 27: 8 any nation or **k** will not serve H4930
La 2: 2 He has brought her **k** and its princes down H4930
Eze 17:14 so that the **k** would be brought low H4930
Eze 29:14 There they will be a lowly **k**. H4930
Da 1:20 magicians and enchanters in his whole **k**. H4895
Da 2:39 "After you, another **k** will arise, inferior A10424
Da 2:39 a third **k**, one of bronze, will rule A10424
Da 2:40 there will be a fourth **k**, strong as iron— A10424
Da 2:41 so this will be a divided **k**; yet it will A10424
Da 2:42 so this **k** will be partly strong and partly A10424
Da 2:44 heaven will set up a **k** that will never be A10424
Da 4: 3 His **k** is an eternal kingdom; his A10424
Da 4: 3 His kingdom is an eternal **k**; his A10424
Da 4:18 the wise men in my **k** can interpret it A10424
Da 4:26 means that your **k** will be restored to A10424
Da 4:34 his **k** endures from generation to A10424
Da 4:36 returned to me for the glory of my **k**. A10424
Da 5: 7 be made the third highest ruler in the **k**." A10424
Da 5:11 is a man in your **k** who has the spirit of A10424
Da 5:16 be made the third highest ruler in the **k**." A10424
Da 5:28 Your **k** is divided and given to the Medes A10424
Da 5:29 the third highest ruler in the **k**. A10424
Da 5:31 Darius the Mede took over the **k**, at A10424
Da 6: 1 120 satraps to rule throughout the **k**, A10424
Da 6: 3 planned to set him over the whole **k**. A10424
Da 6:26 in every part of my **k** people must fear A10424
Da 6:26 his **k** will not be destroyed A10424
Da 7:14 his **k** is one that will never be A10424
Da 7:18 will receive the **k** and will possess it A10424
Da 7:22 time came when they possessed the **k**. A10424
Da 7:23 beast is a fourth **k** that will appear on A10424
Da 7:24 are ten kings who will come from this **k**. A10424
Da 7:27 His **k** will be an everlasting kingdom A10424
Da 7:27 His kingdom will be an everlasting **k** A10424
Da 9: 1 was made ruler over the Babylonian **k**— H4895
Da 10:13 prince of the Persian **k** resisted me H4895
Da 11: 2 stir up everyone against the **k** *of* Greece. H4895
Da 11: 5 will rule his own **k** with great power. H4939
Da 11:17 the might of his entire **k** and will make an H4895
Da 11:17 in marriage in order to overthrow **the k**, H2023S
Da 11:21 He will invade the **k** when its people feel H4895
Hos 1: 4 I will put an end to the **k** *of* Israel. H4931
Am 7:13 king's sanctuary and the temple of the **k**." H4930
Am 9: 8 of the Sovereign LORD are on the sinful **k**. H4930
Ob 21 And the **k** will be the LORD's. H4867
Mt 3: 2 the **k** of heaven has come near. *G993*
Mt 4:17 the **k** of heaven has come near. *G993*
Mt 4:23 proclaiming the good news *of* the **k**, and *G993*
Mt 5: 3 poor in spirit, for theirs is the **k** of heaven. *G993*
Mt 5:10 righteousness, for theirs is the **k** of heaven. *G993*
Mt 5:19 will be called least in the **k** of heaven, *G993*
Mt 5:19 will be called great in the **k** of heaven. *G993*
Mt 5:20 you will certainly not enter the **k** of heaven. *G993*
Mt 6:10 your **k** come, your will be done, on earth as *G993*
Mt 6:33 But seek first his **k** and his righteousness *G993*
Mt 7:21 will enter the **k** of heaven, but only *G993*
Mt 8:11 Isaac and Jacob in the **k** of heaven. *G993*
Mt 8:12 But the subjects *of* the **k** will be thrown *G993*
Mt 9:35 the good news *of* the **k** and healing every *G993*
Mt 10: 7 'The **k** of heaven has come near *G993*
Mt 11:11 is least in the **k** of heaven is greater *G993*
Mt 11:12 the **k** of heaven has been subjected to *G993*
Mt 12:25 "Every **k** divided against itself will be *G993*
Mt 12:26 against himself. How then can his **k** stand? *G993*
Mt 12:28 then the **k** of God has come upon you. *G993*
Mt 13:11 of the secrets *of* the **k** of heaven has been *G993*
Mt 13:19 the message *about* the **k** and does not *G993*
Mt 13:24 "The **k** of heaven is like a man who sowed *G993*
Mt 13:31 "The **k** of heaven is like a mustard seed *G993*
Mt 13:33 "The **k** of heaven is like yeast that a *G993*
Mt 13:38 good seed stands for the people *of* the **k**. *G993*
Mt 13:41 will weed out of his **k** everything that *G993*
Mt 13:43 shine like the sun in the **k** of their Father. *G993*
Mt 13:44 "The **k** of heaven is like treasure hidden in *G993*
Mt 13:45 the **k** of heaven is like a merchant looking *G993*
Mt 13:47 the **k** of heaven is like a net that was let *G993*
Mt 13:52 become a disciple *in* the **k** of heaven is like *G993*
Mt 16:19 I will give you the keys *of* the **k** of heaven *G993*
Mt 16:28 they see the Son of Man coming in his **k**." *G993*
Mt 18: 1 is the greatest in the **k** of heaven? *G993*
Mt 18: 3 you will never enter the **k** of heaven. *G993*
Mt 18: 4 this child is the greatest in the **k** of heaven. *G993*
Mt 18:23 the **k** of heaven is like a king who wanted *G993*
Mt 19:12 eunuchs for the sake of the **k** of heaven. *G993*
Mt 19:14 the **k** of heaven belongs to such as *G993*
Mt 19:23 who is rich to enter the **k** of heaven. *G993*
Mt 19:24 someone who is rich to enter the **k** of God." *G993*
Mt 20: 1 "For the **k** of heaven is like a landowner *G993*
Mt 20:21 right and the other at your left in your **k**." *G993*
Mt 21:31 are entering the **k** of God ahead of you. *G993*
Mt 21:43 I tell you that the **k** of God will be taken *G993*
Mt 22: 2 "The **k** of heaven is like a king who *G993*
Mt 23:13 You shut the door *of* the **k** of heaven in *G993*
Mt 24: 7 rise against nation, and **k** against kingdom. *G993*
Mt 24: 7 rise against nation, and kingdom against **k**. *G993*
Mt 24:14 And this gospel *of* the **k** will be preached in *G993*
Mt 25: 1 "At that time the **k** of heaven will be like *G993*
Mt 25:34 the **k** prepared for you since the creation of *G993*
Mt 26:29 I drink it new with you in my Father's **k**." *G993*
Mk 1:15 "The **k** of God has come near *G993*
Mk 3:24 If a **k** is divided against itself, that kingdom *G993*
Mk 3:24 divided against itself, that **k** cannot stand. *G993*
Mk 4:11 "The secret *of* the **k** of God has been given *G993*
Mk 4:26 also said, "This is what the **k** of God is like. *G993*
Mk 4:30 "What shall we say the **k** of God is like, or *G993*
Mk 6:23 you ask I will give you, up to half my **k**." *G993*
Mk 9: 1 they see that the **k** of God has come with *G993*
Mk 9:47 you to enter the **k** of God with one eye *G993*
Mk 10:14 the **k** of God belongs to such as these. *G993*
Mk 10:15 will not receive the **k** of God like a little *G993*
Mk 10:23 hard it is for the rich to enter the **k** of God!" *G993*
Mk 10:24 how hard it is to enter the **k** of God! *G993*
Mk 10:25 someone who is rich to enter the **k** of God." *G993*
Mk 11:10 is the coming **k** of our father David! *G993*
Mk 12:34 "You are not far from the **k** of God. *G993*
Mk 13: 8 rise against nation, and **k** against kingdom. *G993*
Mk 13: 8 rise against nation, and kingdom against **k**. *G993*
Mk 14:25 day when I drink it new in the **k** of God." *G993*
Mk 15:43 who was himself waiting *for* the **k** of God *G993*
Lk 1:33 descendants forever; his **k** will never end." *G993*
Lk 4:43 the good news *of* the **k** of God to the other *G993*
Lk 6:20 you who are poor, for yours is the **k** of God. *G993*
Lk 7:28 who is least in the **k** of God is greater than *G993*
Lk 8: 1 proclaiming the good news *of* the **k** of God. *G993*
Lk 8:10 of the secrets *of* the **k** of God has been *G993*
Lk 9: 2 out to proclaim the **k** of God and to heal *G993*
Lk 9:11 spoke to them about the **k** of God, *G993*
Lk 9:27 taste death before they see the **k** of God." *G993*
Lk 9:60 you go and proclaim the **k** of God. *G993*
Lk 9:62 looks back is fit for service *in* the **k** of God." *G993*
Lk 10: 9 'The **k** of God has come near to you. *G993*
Lk 10:11 The **k** of God has come near *G993*
Lk 11: 2 hallowed be your name, your **k** come. *G993*
Lk 11:17 "Any **k** divided against itself will be ruined *G993*
Lk 11:18 against himself, how can his **k** stand? *G993*
Lk 11:20 then the **k** of God has come upon you. *G993*
Lk 12:31 But seek his **k**, and these things will be *G993*
Lk 12:32 Father has been pleased to give you the **k**. *G993*
Lk 13:18 Jesus asked, "What is the **k** of God like? *G993*
Lk 13:20 "What shall I compare the **k** of God to? *G993*
Lk 13:28 Jacob and all the prophets in the **k** of God, *G993*
Lk 13:29 their places at the feast in the **k** of God. *G993*
Lk 14:15 who will eat at the feast in the **k** of God." *G993*
Lk 16:16 the good news *of* the **k** of God is being *G993*
Lk 17:20 Pharisees when the **k** of God would come, *G993*
Lk 17:20 "The coming of the **k** of God is not *G993*
Lk 17:21 because the **k** of God is in your midst." *G993*
Lk 18:16 the **k** of God belongs to such as these. *G993*
Lk 18:17 will not receive the **k** of God like a little *G993*
Lk 18:24 hard it is for the rich to enter the **k** of God! *G993*
Lk 18:25 someone who is rich to enter the **k** of God." *G993*
Lk 18:29 children for the sake of the **k** of God *G993*
Lk 19:11 thought that the **k** of God was going to *G993*
Lk 21:10 rise against nation, and **k** against kingdom. *G993*
Lk 21:10 rise against nation, and kingdom against **k**. *G993*
Lk 21:31 you know that the **k** of God is near. *G993*
Lk 22:16 it finds fulfillment in the **k** of God. *G993*
Lk 22:18 fruit of the vine until the **k** of God comes." *G993*
Lk 22:29 And I confer on you a **k**, just as my Father *G993*
Lk 22:30 at my table in my **k** and sit on thrones, *G993*
Lk 23:42 remember me when you come into your **k**." *G993*
Lk 23:51 he himself was waiting for the **k** of God. *G993*
Jn 3: 3 no one can see the **k** of God unless they *G993*
Jn 3: 5 no one can enter the **k** of God unless they *G993*
Jn 18:36 Jesus said, "My **k** is not of this world. *G993*
Jn 18:36 But now my **k** is from another place." *G993*
Ac 1: 3 of forty days and spoke about the **k** of God. *G993*
Ac 1: 6 at this time going to restore the **k** to Israel?" *G993*
Ac 8:12 good news of the **k** of God and the name *G993*
Ac 14:22 many hardships to enter the **k** of God," *G993*
Ac 19: 8 arguing persuasively about the **k** of God. *G993*
Ac 20:25 about preaching the **k** will ever see me *G993*
Ac 28:23 explaining about the **k** of God, and from *G993*
Ac 28:31 He proclaimed the **k** of God and taught *G993*
Ro 14:17 For the **k** of God is not a matter of eating *G993*
1Co 4:20 For the **k** of God is not a matter of talk but *G993*
1Co 6: 9 wrongdoers will not inherit the **k** of God? *G993*
1Co 6:10 swindlers will inherit the **k** of God. *G993*
1Co 15:24 he hands over the **k** to God the Father *G993*
1Co 15:50 blood cannot inherit the **k** of God, *G993*
Gal 5:21 live like this will not inherit the **k** of God. *G993*
Eph 2: 2 world and of the ruler *of* the **k** of the air, *G2026*
Eph 5: 5 inheritance in the **k** of Christ and of God. *G993*
Col 1:12 of his holy people in the **k** *of* **light**. AIT
Col 1:13 brought us into the **k** of the Son he loves, *G993*
Col 4:11 among my co-workers for the **k** of God, *G993*
1Th 2:12 who calls you into his **k** and glory. *G993*
2Th 1: 5 you will be counted worthy *of* the **k** of God, *G993*
2Ti 4: 1 in view of his appearing and his **k**, *G993*
2Ti 4:18 will bring me safely to his heavenly **k**. *G993*
Heb 1: 8 of justice will be the scepter *of* your **k**. *G993*
Heb 12:28 we are receiving a **k** that cannot be shaken, *G993*
Jas 2: 5 to inherit the **k** he promised those who *G993*
2Pe 1:11 into the eternal **k** of our Lord and Savior *G993*
Rev 1: 6 has made us to be a **k** and priests to serve *G993*
Rev 1: 9 in the suffering and **k** and patient *G993*
Rev 5:10 made them to be a **k** and priests to serve *G993*
Rev 11:15 "The **k** of the world has become the *G993*
Rev 11:15 world has become the **k** of our Lord and of NDT
Rev 12:10 the power and the **k** of our God, *G993*
Rev 16:10 and its **k** was plunged into darkness. *G993*
Rev 17:12 ten kings who have not yet received a **k**, *G993*

KINGDOMS (61) [KING]

Dt 3:21 the same to all the **k** over there where you H4930
Dt 28:25 a thing of horror to all the **k** *on* earth. H4930
Jos 11:10 Hazor had been the head of all these **k**.) H4930
1Sa 10:18 of Egypt and all the **k** that oppressed you. H4930
1Ki 4:21 ruled over all the **k** from the Euphrates H4930
1Ki 4:24 ruled over all the **k** west of the Euphrates H4889
2Ki 19:15 alone are God over all the **k** *of* the earth. H4930
2Ki 19:19 so that all the **k** *of* the earth may know H4930
1Ch 29:30 Israel and the **k** *of* all the other lands. H4930
2Ch 17:10 LORD fell on all the **k** *of* the lands H4930
2Ch 20: 6 You rule over all the **k** *of* the nations H4930
2Ch 20:29 the surrounding **k** when they heard how H4930

2Ch 36:23 has given me all the **k** *of* the earth and he H4930
Ezr 1: 2 has given me all the **k** *of* the earth and he H4930
Ne 9:22 "You gave them **k** and nations, allotting H4930
Ps 46: 6 Nations are in uproar, **k** fall; he lifts his H4930
Ps 68:32 Sing to God, you **k** *of* the earth, sing H4930
Ps 79: 6 on the **k** that do not call on your name; H4930
Ps 102:22 peoples and the **k** assemble to worship H4930
Isa 10:10 As my hand seized the **k** *of* the idols H4930
Isa 10:10 **k** whose images excelled those of NDT
Isa 13: 4 an uproar among the **k**, like nations H4930
Isa 13:19 the jewel of **k**, the pride and glory H4930
Isa 14:16 who shook the earth and made **k** tremble, H4930
Isa 23:11 over the sea and made its **k** tremble. H4930
Isa 23:17 her trade with all the **k** on the face of the H4930
Isa 37:16 alone are God over all the **k** *of* the earth. H4930
Isa 37:20 so that all the **k** *of* the earth may know H4930
Isa 47: 5 no more will you be called queen of **k**. H4930
Jer 1:10 you over nations and **k** to uproot and tear H4930
Jer 1:15 summon all the peoples of the northern **k**," H4930
Jer 10: 7 leaders of the nations and in all their **k**, H4895
Jer 15: 4 abhorrent to all the **k** *of* the earth because H4930
Jer 24: 9 an offense to all the **k** *of* the earth, H4930
Jer 25:26 all the **k** on the face of the earth. H4930
Jer 28: 8 against many countries and great **k**. H4930
Jer 29:18 them abhorrent to all the **k** *of* the earth, H4930
Jer 31:27 I will plant the **k** *of* Israel and Judah with H1074
Jer 33:24 LORD has rejected the two **k** he chose'? H5476
Jer 34: 1 his army and all the **k** and peoples in the H4930
Jer 34:17 you abhorrent to all the **k** *of* the earth. H4930
Jer 49:28 Concerning Kedar and the **k** *of* Hazor H4930
Jer 51:20 you I shatter nations, with you I destroy **k**, H4930
Jer 51:27 against her; summon against her these **k**: H4930
Eze 29:15 be the lowliest of **k** and will never again H4930
Eze 37:22 be two nations or be divided into two **k**. H4930
Da 2:44 crush all those **k** and bring them to an A10424
Da 4:17 is sovereign over *all* **k** on earth and gives A10424
Da 4:25 is sovereign over *all* **k** on earth and gives A10424
Da 4:32 is sovereign over *all* **k** on earth and gives A10424
Da 5:21 is sovereign over *all* **k** on earth and sets A10424
Da 7:23 from all the other **k** and will devour the A10424
Da 7:27 of all the **k** under heaven will be A10424
Da 8:22 off represent four **k** that will emerge from H4895
Am 6: 2 Are they better off than your two **k**? H4930
Na 3: 5 your nakedness and the **k** your shame. H4930
Zep 3: 8 to gather the **k** and to pour out my wrath H4930
Hag 2:22 shatter the power of the foreign **k**. H4930
Mt 4: 8 showed him all the **k** of the world and their *G993*
Lk 4: 5 him in an instant all the **k** of the world. *G993*
Heb 11:33 who through faith conquered **k** *G993*

KINGS (328) [KING]

Ge 14: 2 these **k** went to war against Bera king of NDT
Ge 14: 3 All these latter **k** joined forces in the Valley NDT
Ge 14: 5 Kedorlaomer and the **k** allied with him H4889
Ge 14: 9 Arioch king of Ellasar—four **k** against five. H4889
Ge 14:10 when the **k** *of* Sodom and Gomorrah H4889
Ge 14:11 The four **k** seized all the goods of Sodom NDT
Ge 14:17 Kedorlaomer and the **k** allied with him, H4889
Ge 17: 6 nations of you, and **k** will come from you. H4889
Ge 17:16 nations; **k** *of* peoples will come from her." H4889
Ge 35:11 **k** will be among your descendants. H4889
Ge 36:31 These were the **k** who reigned in Edom H4889
Nu 31: 8 Hur and Reba—the five **k** *of* Midian. H4889
Dt 3: 8 took from these two **k** *of* the Amorites the H4889
Dt 3:21 LORD your God has done to these two **k**. H4889
Dt 4:47 the two Amorite **k** east of the Jordan. H4889
Dt 7:24 He will give their **k** into your hand, and H4889
Dt 31: 4 Sihon and Og, the **k** *of* the Amorites H4889
Jos 2:10 the two **k** *of* the Amorites east of the H4889
Jos 5: 1 when all the Amorite **k** west of the Jordan H4889
Jos 5: 1 all the Canaanite **k** along the coast heard H4889
Jos 9: 1 Now when all the **k** west of the Jordan H4889
Jos 9: 1 about these things—the **k** in the hill country NDT
Jos 9: 1 as far as Lebanon (the **k** of the Hittites NDT
Jos 9:10 he did to the two **k** *of* the Amorites east of H4889
Jos 10: 5 Then the five **k** *of* the Amorites—the kings H4889
Jos 10: 5 the Amorites—the **k** *of* Jerusalem, Hebron H4889
Jos 10: 6 all the Amorite **k** *from* the hill country H4889
Jos 10:16 Now the five **k** had fled and hidden in the H4889
Jos 10:17 told that the five **k** had been found hiding H4889
Jos 10:22 the cave and bring those five **k** out to me." H4889
Jos 10:23 So they brought the five **k** out of the cave— H4889
Jos 10:23 of the cave—the **k** *of* Jerusalem, Hebron, H4889
Jos 10:24 When they had brought these **k** to Joshua H4889
Jos 10:24 put your feet on the necks of these **k**." H4889
Jos 10:26 Then Joshua put **the k** to death and H4392S
Jos 10:40 mountain slopes, together with all their **k**. H4889
Jos 10:42 All these **k** and their lands Joshua H4889
Jos 11: 1 Madon, to the **k** *of* Shimron and Akshaph, H4889
Jos 11: 2 to the northern **k** who were in the H4889
Jos 11: 5 All these **k** joined forces and made camp H4889
Jos 11:12 cities and their **k** and put them to the H4889
Jos 11:17 captured all their **k** and put them to death H4889
Jos 11:18 war against all these **k** for a long time. H4889
Jos 12: 1 These are the **k** *of* the land whom the H4889
Jos 12: 7 is a list of the **k** *of* the land that Joshua H4889
Jos 12: 8 Hivites and Jebusites. These were the **k**: NDT
Jos 12:24 the king of Tirzah one thirty-one **k** in all. H4889
Jos 24:12 out before you—also the two Amorite **k**. H4889
Jdg 1: 7 "Seventy **k** with their thumbs and big toes H4889
Jdg 5: 3 "Hear this, you **k**! Listen, you rulers! H4889
Jdg 5:19 "**K** came, they fought, the kings of Canaan H4889
Jdg 5:19 they fought, the **k** *of* Canaan fought. H4889
Jdg 8: 5 Zebah and Zalmunna, the **k** *of* Midian." H4889
Jdg 8:12 Zalmunna, the two **k** *of* Midian, fled, H4889
Jdg 8:26 garments worn by the **k** *of* Midian or the H4889
1Sa 14:47 the **k** *of* Zobah, and the H4889
1Sa 27: 6 belonged to the **k** *of* Judah ever since. H4889
2Sa 10:19 When all the **k** who were vassals of H4889
2Sa 11: 1 at the time when **k** go off to war, David H4889
1Ki 3:13 lifetime you will have no equal among **k**. H4889
1Ki 4:34 sent by all the **k** *of* the world, who had H4889
1Ki 10:15 all the Arabian **k** and the governors of H4889
1Ki 10:23 wisdom than all the other **k** *of* the earth. H4889
1Ki 10:29 them to all the **k** *of* the Hittites and of the H4889
1Ki 14:19 the book of the annals of the **k** *of* Israel. H4889
1Ki 14:29 the book of the annals of the **k** *of* Judah? H4889
1Ki 15: 7 the book of the annals of the **k** *of* Judah? H4889
1Ki 15:23 the book of the annals of the **k** *of* Judah? H4889
1Ki 15:31 the book of the annals of the **k** *of* Israel? H4889
1Ki 16: 5 the book of the annals of the **k** *of* Israel? H4889
1Ki 16:14 the book of the annals of the **k** *of* Israel? H4889
1Ki 16:20 the book of the annals of the **k** *of* Israel? H4889
1Ki 16:27 the book of the annals of the **k** *of* Israel? H4889
1Ki 16:33 than did all the **k** *of* Israel before him. H4889
1Ki 20: 1 by thirty-two **k** with their horses and H4889
1Ki 20:12 while he and the **k** were drinking in their H4889
1Ki 20:16 the 32 **k** allied with him were H4889
1Ki 20:24 Remove all the **k** from their commands H4889
1Ki 20:31 have heard that the **k** *of* Israel are H4889
1Ki 22:39 the book of the annals of the **k** *of* Israel? H4889
1Ki 22:45 the book of the annals of the **k** *of* Judah? H4889
2Ki 1:18 the book of the annals of the **k** *of* Israel? H4889
2Ki 3:10 LORD called us three **k** together only to H4889
2Ki 3:13 who called us three **k** together to deliver H4889
2Ki 3:21 had heard that the **k** had come to fight H4889
2Ki 3:23 "Those **k** must have fought and H4889
2Ki 7: 6 the Hittite and Egyptian **k** to attack us!" H4889
2Ki 8:18 He followed the ways of the **k** *of* Israel, as H4889
2Ki 8:23 the book of the annals of the **k** *of* Judah? H4889
2Ki 10: 4 said, "If two **k** could not resist him H4889
2Ki 10:34 the book of the annals of the **k** *of* Israel? H4889
2Ki 12:18 Ahaziah, the **k** *of* Judah—and the H4889
2Ki 12:19 the book of the annals of the **k** *of* Judah? H4889
2Ki 13: 8 the book of the annals of the **k** *of* Israel? H4889
2Ki 13:12 the book of the annals of the **k** *of* Israel? H4889
2Ki 13:13 was buried in Samaria with the **k** *of* Israel. H4889
2Ki 14:15 the book of the annals of the **k** *of* Israel? H4889
2Ki 14:16 was buried in Samaria with the **k** *of* Israel. H4889
2Ki 14:18 the book of the annals of the **k** *of* Judah? H4889
2Ki 14:28 the book of the annals of the **k** *of* Israel? H4889
2Ki 14:29 rested with his ancestors, the **k** *of* Israel. H4889
2Ki 15: 6 the book of the annals of the **k** *of* Judah? H4889
2Ki 15:11 the book of the annals of the **k** *of* Israel. H4889
2Ki 15:15 the book of the annals of the **k** *of* Israel. H4889
2Ki 15:21 the book of the annals of the **k** *of* Israel? H4889
2Ki 15:26 the book of the annals of the **k** *of* Israel. H4889
2Ki 15:31 the book of the annals of the **k** *of* Israel? H4889
2Ki 15:36 the book of the annals of the **k** *of* Judah? H4889
2Ki 16: 3 the ways of the **k** *of* Israel and even H4889
2Ki 16:19 the book of the annals of the **k** *of* Judah? H4889
2Ki 17: 2 not like the **k** *of* Israel who preceded H4889
2Ki 17: 8 practices that the **k** *of* Israel had H4889
2Ki 18: 5 no one like him among all the **k** *of* Judah, H4889
2Ki 19:11 heard what the **k** *of* Assyria have done H4889
2Ki 19:13 Where are the **k** *of* Lair, Sepharvaim H4889
2Ki 19:17 that the Assyrian **k** have laid waste these H4889
2Ki 20:20 the book of the annals of the **k** *of* Judah? H4889
2Ki 21:17 the book of the annals of the **k** *of* Judah? H4889
2Ki 21:25 the book of the annals of the **k** *of* Judah? H4889
2Ki 23: 5 appointed by the **k** *of* Judah to burn H4889
2Ki 23:11 the horses that the **k** *of* Judah had H4889
2Ki 23:12 the altars the **k** *of* Judah had erected H4889
2Ki 23:19 places that the **k** *of* Israel had built in H4889
2Ki 23:22 in the days of the **k** *of* Israel and the kings H4889
2Ki 23:22 of Israel and the **k** *of* Judah had any such H4889
2Ki 23:28 the book of the annals of the **k** *of* Judah? H4889
2Ki 24: 5 the book of the annals of the **k** *of* Judah? H4889
2Ki 25:28 those of the other **k** who were with him in H4889
1Ch 1:43 These were the **k** who reigned in Edom H4889
1Ch 9: 1 in the book of the **k** *of* Israel and Judah. H4889
1Ch 16:21 oppress them; for their sake he rebuked **k**: H4889
1Ch 19: 9 while the **k** who had come were by H4889
1Ch 20: 1 at the time when **k** go off to war, Joab led H4889
2Ch 1:17 them to all the **k** *of* the Hittites and of the H4889
2Ch 9:14 Also all the **k** *of* Arabia and the governors H4889
2Ch 9:22 wisdom than all the other **k** *of* the earth. H4889
2Ch 9:23 All the **k** *of* the earth sought audience with H4889
2Ch 9:26 He ruled over all the **k** from the Euphrates H4889
2Ch 12: 8 me and serving the **k** *of* other lands." H4930
2Ch 16:11 in the book of the **k** of Judah and Israel. H4889
2Ch 20:34 are recorded in the book of the **k** *of* Israel. H4889
2Ch 21: 6 He followed the ways of the **k** *of* Israel, as H4889
2Ch 21:13 have followed the ways of the **k** *of* Israel, H4889
2Ch 21:20 of David, but not in the tombs of the **k**. H4889
2Ch 24:16 was buried with the **k** in the City of David, H4889
2Ch 24:25 of David, but not in the tombs of the **k**. H4889
2Ch 24:27 in the annotations on the book of the **k**. H4889
2Ch 25:26 in the book of the **k** *of* Judah and Israel? H4889
2Ch 26:23 in a cemetery that belonged to the **k**, H4889
2Ch 27: 7 in the book of the **k** *of* Israel and Judah. H4889
2Ch 28: 2 the ways of the **k** *of* Israel and also made H4889
2Ch 28:16 Ahaz sent to the **k** *of* Assyria for help. H4889
2Ch 28:23 the gods of the **k** *of* Aram have helped H4889
2Ch 28:26 in the book of the **k** *of* Judah and Israel. H4889
2Ch 28:27 not placed in the tombs of the **k** *of* Israel. H4889
2Ch 30: 6 escaped from the hand of the **k** *of* Assyria. H4889
2Ch 32: 4 "Why should the **k** *of* Assyria come and H4889
2Ch 32:32 in the book of the **k** *of* Judah and Israel. H4889
2Ch 33:18 are written in the annals of the **k** *of* Israel. H4889
2Ch 34:11 buildings that the **k** *of* Judah had allowed H4889
2Ch 35:18 none of the **k** *of* Israel had ever H4889
2Ch 35:27 in the book of the **k** *of* Israel and Judah. H4889
2Ch 36: 8 in the book of the **k** *of* Israel and Judah. H4889
Ezr 4:15 troublesome to **k** and provinces, A10421
Ezr 4:19 of revolt against **k** and has been a place A10421
Ezr 4:20 has had powerful **k** ruling over the whole A10421
Ezr 6:14 Darius and Artaxerxes, **k** *of* Persia. A10421
Ezr 7:12 Artaxerxes, king of **k**, To Ezra the priest A10421
Ezr 9: 7 we and our **k** and our priests have been H4889
Ezr 9: 7 humiliation at the hand of foreign **k**, H4889
Ezr 9: 9 us kindness in the sight of the **k** *of* Persia: H4889
Ne 9:24 along with their **k** and the peoples of the H4889
Ne 9:32 come on us, on our **k** and leaders, on our H4889
Ne 9:32 the days of the **k** *of* Assyria until today H4889
Ne 9:34 Our **k**, our leaders, our priests and our H4889
Ne 9:37 harvest goes to the **k** you have placed H4889
Est 10: 2 the annals of the **k** *of* Media and Persia? H4889
Job 3:14 with **k** and rulers of the earth, who built H4889
Job 12:18 shackles put on by **k** and ties a loincloth H4889
Job 34:18 Is he not the One who says to **k**, 'You are H4889
Job 36: 7 he enthrones them with **k** and exalts them H4889
Ps 2: 2 The **k** *of* the earth rise up and the rulers H4889
Ps 2:10 Therefore, you **k**, be wise; be warned, you H4889
Ps 45: 9 Daughters of **k** are among your honored H4889
Ps 47: 9 the **k** *of* the earth belong to God H4482
Ps 48: 4 When the **k** joined forces, when they H4889
Ps 68:12 "**K** and armies flee in haste; the women H4889
Ps 68:14 the Almighty scattered the **k** in the land, H4889
Ps 68:29 temple at Jerusalem **k** will bring you gifts. H4889
Ps 72:10 May the **k** *of* Tarshish and of distant H4889
Ps 72:10 May the **k** *of* Sheba and Seba present him H4889
Ps 72:11 May all **k** bow down to him and all H4889
Ps 76:12 he is feared by the **k** *of* the earth. H4889
Ps 89:27 the most exalted of the **k** *of* the earth. H4889
Ps 102:15 all the **k** *of* the earth will revere your glory. H4889
Ps 105:14 oppress them; for their sake he rebuked **k**: H4889
Ps 110: 5 he will crush **k** on the day of his wrath. H4889
Ps 119:46 your statutes before **k** and will not be put H4889
Ps 135:10 down many nations and killed mighty **k**— H4889
Ps 135:11 of Bashan, and all the **k** *of* Canaan— H4930
Ps 136:17 to him who struck down great **k**, His love H4889
Ps 136:18 killed mighty **k**—His love endures H4889
Ps 138: 4 May all the **k** *of* the earth praise you, LORD H4889
Ps 144:10 to the One who gives victory to **k**, who H4889
Ps 148:11 **k** *of* the earth and all nations, you princes H4889
Ps 149: 8 to bind their **k** with fetters, their nobles H4889
Pr 8:15 By me **k** reign and rulers issue decrees H4889
Pr 16:12 **K** detest wrongdoing, for a throne is H4889
Pr 16:13 **K** take pleasure in honest lips; they value H4889
Pr 22:29 They will serve before **k**; they will not H4889
Pr 25: 2 to search out a matter is the glory of **k**. H4889
Pr 25: 3 so the hearts of **k** are unsearchable. H4889
Pr 31: 3 women, your vigor on those who ruin **k**. H4889
Pr 31: 4 It is not for **k**, Lemuel—it is not for kings H4889
Pr 31: 4 Lemuel—it is not for **k** to drink wine, not H4889
Ecc 2: 8 the treasure of **k** and provinces. H4889
Isa 1: 1 Jotham, Ahaz and Hezekiah, **k** *of* Judah. H4889
Isa 7:16 the land of the two **k** you dread will be H4889
Isa 10: 8 'Are not my commanders all **k**?' he says. H4889
Isa 10:13 like a mighty one I subdued their **k**. H3782
Isa 14: 9 all *those who* were **k** *over* the nations. H4889
Isa 14:18 All the **k** *of* the nations lie in state, each H4889
Isa 19:11 wise men, a disciple of the ancient **k**"? H4889
Isa 24:21 above and the **k** *on* the earth below. H4889
Isa 37:11 heard what the **k** *of* Assyria have done H4889
Isa 37:13 Where are the **k** *of* Lair, Sepharvaim H4889
Isa 37:18 that the Assyrian **k** have laid waste all H4889
Isa 41: 2 over to him and subdues **k** before him. H4889
Isa 45: 1 before him and to strip **k** of their armor, H4889
Isa 49: 7 "**K** will see you and stand up, princes will H4889
Isa 49:23 **K** will be your foster fathers, and their H4889
Isa 52:15 **k** will shut their mouths because of H4889
Isa 60: 3 **k** to the brightness of your dawn. H4889
Isa 60:10 your walls, and their **k** will serve you. H4889
Isa 60:11 their **k** led in triumphal procession. H4889
Isa 62: 2 vindication, and all **k** your glory; you will H4889
Jer 1:15 "Their **k** will come and set up their H408S
Jer 1:18 against the **k** *of* Judah, its officials, H4889
Jer 2:26 their **k** and their officials, their H4889
Jer 8: 1 the bones of the **k** and officials of Judah H4889
Jer 13:13 including the **k** who sit on David's throne H4889
Jer 17:19 through which the **k** *of* Judah go in and H4889
Jer 17:20 you **k** *of* Judah and all people of Judah H4889
Jer 17:25 then **k** who sit on David's throne will come H4889
Jer 19: 3 you **k** *of* Judah and people of Jerusalem. H4889
Jer 19: 4 ancestors nor the **k** *of* Judah ever knew, H4889
Jer 19:13 those of the **k** *of* Judah will be H4889
Jer 20: 5 all the treasures of the **k** *of* Judah. H4889
Jer 22: 4 then **k** who sit on David's throne will H4889
Jer 25:14 be enslaved by many nations and great **k**; H4889
Jer 25:18 towns of Judah, its **k** and officials, to H4889
Jer 25:20 all the **k** *of* Uz; all the kings of H4889
Jer 25:20 kings of Uz; all the **k** *of* the Philistines H4889
Jer 25:22 all the **k** *of* Tyre and Sidon; the kings of H4889
Jer 25:22 the **k** *of* the coastlands across the sea H4889

K

Jer 25:24 all the **k** *of* Arabia and all the kings of the H4889
Jer 25:24 Arabia and all the **k** *of* the foreign people H4889
Jer 25:25 all the **k** *of* Zimri, Elam and Media; H4889
Jer 25:26 all the **k** *of* the north, near and far H4889
Jer 27: 3 Then send word to the **k** *of* Edom, Moab H4889
Jer 27: 7 nations and great **k** will subjugate him. H4889
Jer 32:32 their **k** and officials, their priests and H4889
Jer 34: 5 predecessors, the **k** who ruled before you H4889
Jer 44: 9 by the **k** and queens *of* Judah and H4889
Jer 44:17 our **k** and our officials did in the towns of H4889
Jer 44:21 your **k** and your officials and the people of H4889
Jer 46:25 on Egypt and her gods and her **k**, and on H4889
Jer 50:41 nation and many **k** are being stirred up H4889
Jer 51:11 LORD has stirred up the **k** *of* the Medes, H4889
Jer 51:28 against her—the **k** *of* the Medes, their H4889
Jer 52:32 those of the other **k** who were with him in H4889
La 4:12 The **k** *of* the earth did not believe, nor did H4889
Eze 26: 7 king of Babylon, king of **k**, with horses H4889
Eze 27:33 wares you enriched the **k** *of* the earth. H4889
Eze 27:35 their **k** shudder with horror and their faces H4889
Eze 28:17 I made a spectacle of you before **k**. H4889
Eze 32:10 their **k** will shudder with horror H4889
Eze 32:29 "Edom is there, her **k** and all her princes H4889
Eze 43: 7 neither they nor their **k**—by their H4889
Eze 43: 7 funeral offerings for their **k** at their death. H4889
Eze 43: 9 the funeral offerings for their **k**, H4889
Da 2:21 he deposes **k** and raises up others. A10421
Da 2:37 you are the king of **k**. The God of heaven A10421
Da 2:44 "In the time of those **k**, the God of A10421
Da 2:47 gods and the Lord of **k** and a revealer of A10421
Da 7:17 great beasts are four **k** that will rise from A10421
Da 7:24 ten horns are ten **k** who will come from A10421
Da 7:24 the earlier ones; he will subdue three **k**. A10421
Da 8:20 saw represents the **k** *of* Media and Persia. H4889
Da 9: 6 who spoke in your name to our **k**, our H4889
Da 9: 8 We and our **k**, our princes and our H4889
Da 11: 2 Three more **k** will arise in Persia, and H4889
Da 11:27 The two **k**, with their hearts bent on evil H4889
Hos 1: 1 Hezekiah, **k** *of* Judah, and during H4889
Hos 7: 7 All their **k** fall, and none of them calls on H4889
Hos 8: 4 They **set up k** without my consent; they H4887
Mic 1: 1 Hezekiah, **k** *of* Judah—the vision H4889
Mic 1:14 will prove deceptive to the **k** *of* Israel. H4889
Hab 1:10 They mock **k** and scoff at rulers. H4889
Mt 10:18 governors and **k** as witnesses to them G995
Mt 17:25 "From whom do the **k** of the earth collect G995
Mk 13: 9 governors and **k** as witnesses to them G995
Lk 10:24 many prophets and **k** wanted to see what G995
Lk 21:12 you will be brought before **k** and governors, G995
Lk 22:25 "The **k** of the Gentiles lord it over them G995
Ac 4:26 The **k** of the earth rise up and the rulers G995
Ac 9:15 Gentiles and their **k** and to the people of G995
1Ti 2: 2 **k** and all those in authority, that we may G995
1Ti 6:15 only Ruler, the King *of* **k** and Lord of lords, G996
Heb 7: 1 from the defeat *of* the **k** and blessed him, G995
Rev 1: 5 and the ruler *of* the **k** of the earth. G995
Rev 6:15 Then the **k** of the earth, the princes, the G995
Rev 10:11 many peoples, nations, languages and **k**." G995
Rev 16:12 to prepare the way *for* the **k** from the East. G995
Rev 16:14 they go out to the **k** of the whole world, G995
Rev 16:16 Then they gathered **the k** together to the G899S
Rev 17: 2 With her the **k** of the earth committed G995
Rev 17:10 They are also seven **k**. Five have fallen, one G995
Rev 17:12 horns you saw are ten **k** who have not yet G995
Rev 17:12 receive authority as **k** along with the beast. G995
Rev 17:14 because he is Lord of lords and King *of* **k**— G995
Rev 17:18 great city that rules over the **k** of the earth." G995
Rev 18: 3 The **k** of the earth committed adultery with G995
Rev 18: 9 "When the **k** of the earth who committed G995
Rev 19:16 KING OF **K** AND LORD OF LORDS. G995
Rev 19:18 so that you may eat the flesh *of* **k**, generals G995
Rev 19:19 saw the beast and the **k** of the earth and G995
Rev 21:24 the **k** of the earth will bring their G995

KINGS' (2) [KING]

Pr 30:28 the hand, yet it is found in **k** palaces. H4889
Mt 11: 8 who wear fine clothes are in **k** palaces. G995

KINGSHIP (7) [KING]

1Sa 10:16 uncle what Samuel had said about the **k**. H4867
1Sa 10:25 to the people the rights and duties of **k**. H4867
1Sa 11:14 let us go to Gilgal and there renew the **k**." H4867
1Ch 11:10 gave his **k** strong support to extend it over H4895
2Ch 13: 5 has given the **k** of Israel to David and his H4930
Ecc 4:14 may have come from prison to the **k**, H4887
Mic 4: 8 **k** will come to Daughter Jerusalem." H4930

KINNERETH (4)

Dt 3:17 Arabah, from **K** to the Sea of the Arabah H4055
Jos 11: 2 in the Arabah south of **K**, in the western H4054
Jos 19:35 were Ziddim, Zer, Hammath, Rakkath, **K**, H4055
1Ki 15:20 Beth Maakah and all **K** in addition to H4054

KIOS (NIV84) CHIOS

KIR (5) [KIR HARESETH]

2Ki 16: 9 its inhabitants to **K** and put Rezin to death H7817
Isa 15: 1 destroyed in a night! **K** *in* Moab is ruined H7816
Isa 22: 6 horses; **K** uncovers the shield. H7817
Am 1: 5 people of Aram will go into exile to **K**," H7817
Am 9: 7 from Caphtor and the Arameans from **K**? H7817

KIR HARESETH (5) [KIR]

2Ki 3:25 Only **K** was left with its stones in H7819
Isa 16: 7 grieve for the raisin cakes of **K**. H7819
Isa 16:11 my inmost being for **K**. H7818
Jer 48:31 I moan for the people of **K**. H7818
Jer 48:36 like a pipe for the people of **K**. H7818

KIRIATH (1)

Jos 18:28 Gibeah and **K**—fourteen towns and their H7956

KIRIATH ARBA (9) [ARBA, HEBRON]

Ge 23: 2 She died at **K** (that is, Hebron) in the H7957
Ge 35:27 Isaac in Mamre, near **K** (that is, H7959
Jos 14:15 used to be called **K** after Arba, H7957
Jos 15:13 a portion in Judah—**K**, that is, H7957
Jos 15:54 Humtah, **K** (that is, Hebron) and Zior H7957
Jos 20: 7 country of Ephraim, and **K** (that is, H7957
Jos 21:11 They gave them **K** (that is, Hebron), H7957
Jdg 1:10 formerly called **K**) and defeated H7957
Ne 11:25 of Judah lived in **K** and its H7959

KIRIATH BAAL (2) [BAAL, KIRIATH JEARIM]

Jos 15:60 **K** (that is, Kiriath Jearim) and H7958
Jos 18:14 the western side and came out at **K** H7958

KIRIATH HUZOTH (1) [HUZOTH]

Nu 22:39 Balaam went with Balak to **K**. H7960

KIRIATH JEARIM (19) [BAALAH, JEARIM, KIRIATH BAAL]

Jos 9:17 Gibeon, Kephirah, Beeroth and **K**. H7961
Jos 15: 9 down toward Baalah (that is, **K**). H7961
Jos 15:60 that is, **K**) and Rabbah—two H7961
Jos 18:14 **K**), a town of the people of H7961
Jos 18:15 at the outskirts of **K** on the west, H7961
Jdg 18:12 they set up camp near **K** in Judah. H7961
Jdg 18:12 the place west of **K** is called H7961
1Sa 6:21 messengers to the people of **K**, H7961
1Sa 7: 1 So the men of **K** came and took up H7961
1Sa 7: 2 ark remained at **K** a long time— H7961
1Ch 2:50 Shobal the father of **K**, H7961
1Ch 2:52 of Shobal the father of **K** were: H7961
1Ch 2:53 the clans of **K**: the Ithrites H7961
1Ch 13: 5 to bring the ark of God from **K**. H7961
1Ch 13: 6 to Baalah of Judah (**K**) to bring up H7961
2Ch 1: 4 ark of God from **K** to the place he H7961
Ezr 2:25 of **K**, Kephirah and Beeroth 743 H7961
Ne 7:29 of **K**, Kephirah and Beeroth 743 H7961
Jer 26:20 Shemaiah from **K** was another H7961

KIRIATH SANNAH (1) [DEBIR, SANNAH]

Jos 15:49 Dannah, **K** (that is, Debir), H7962

KIRIATH SEPHER (4) [SEPHER]

Jos 15:15 living in Debir (formerly called **K**). H7963
Jos 15:16 man who attacks and captures **K**." H7963
Jdg 1:11 living in Debir (formerly called **K**). H7963
Jdg 1:12 man who attacks and captures **K**." H7963

KIRIATHAIM (6) [SHAVEH KIRIATHAIM]

Nu 32:37 rebuilt Heshbon, Elealeh and **K**, H7964
Jos 13:19 **K**, Sibmah, Zereth Shahar on the hill in H7964
1Ch 6:76 Galilee, Hammon and **K**, together with H7964
Jer 48: 1 **K** will be disgraced and captured; the H7964
Jer 48:23 to **K**, Beth Gamul and Beth Meon, H7964
Eze 25: 9 Baal Meon and **K**—the glory of that land. H7964

KIRJATH (KJV) KIRIATH; all compound names in the KJV starting with KIRJATH are KIRIATH in the NIV

KISH (23)

1Sa 9: 1 whose name was **K** son of Abiel, the son H7821
1Sa 9: 2 **K** had a son named Saul, as handsome a H2257S
1Sa 9: 3 belonging to Saul's father **K** were lost, H7821
1Sa 9: 3 Kish were lost, and **K** said to his son Saul H7821
1Sa 10:11 is this that has happened to the son of **K**? H7821
1Sa 10:21 Finally Saul son of **K** was taken. But when H7821
1Sa 14:51 Saul's father **K** and Abner's father Ner H7821
2Sa 21:14 Jonathan in the tomb of Saul's father **K**, H7821
1Ch 8:30 was Abdon, followed by Zur, **K**, Baal, Ner, H7821
1Ch 8:33 Ner was the father of **K**, Kish the father of H7821
1Ch 8:33 the father of Kish, **K** the father of Saul H7821
1Ch 9:36 was Abdon, followed by Zur, **K**, Baal, Ner, H7821
1Ch 9:39 Ner was the father of **K**, Kish the father of H7821
1Ch 9:39 the father of Kish, **K** the father of Saul H7821
1Ch 12: 1 from the presence of Saul son of **K** H7821
1Ch 23:21 The sons of Mahli: Eleazar and **K**. H7821
1Ch 23:22 cousins, the sons of **K**, married them. H7821
1Ch 24:29 From **K**: the son of Kish: Jerahmeel. H7821
1Ch 24:29 the son of **K**: Jerahmeel. H7821
1Ch 26:28 by Samuel the seer and by Saul son of **K**, H7821
2Ch 29:12 **K** son of Abdi and Azariah son of H7821
Est 2: 5 the son of Shimei, the son of **K**, H7821
Ac 13:21 he gave them Saul son *of* **K**, of the G3078

KISHI (1)

1Ch 6:44 Ethan son of **K**, the son of Abdi, the son H7823

KISHION (2)

Jos 19:20 Rabbith, **K**, Ebez, H8002
Jos 21:28 from the tribe of Issachar, **K**, Daberath, H8002

KISHON (6)

Jdg 4: 7 his troops to the **K** River and give him H7822
Jdg 4:13 Haggoyim to the **K** River all his men and H7822
Jdg 5:21 The river **K** swept them away, the age-old H7822
Jdg 5:21 them away, the age-old river, the river **K**. H7822
1Ki 18:40 brought down to the **K** Valley and H7822
Ps 83: 9 you did to Sisera and Jabin at the river **K**, H7822

KISLEV (2)

Ne 1: 1 In the month of **K** in the twentieth year H4075
Zec 7: 1 day of the ninth month, the month of **K**. H4075

KISLON (1)

Nu 34:21 Elidad son of **K**, from the tribe of H4077

KISLOTH TABOR (1) [TABOR]

Jos 19:12 to the territory of **K** and went on to H4079

KISS (22) [KISSED, KISSES, KISSING]

Ge 27:26 "Come here, my son, and **k** me. H5975
Ge 31:28 **k** my grandchildren and my daughters **goodbye** H5975
2Sa 15: 5 out his hand, take hold of him and **k** him. H5975
2Sa 20: 9 by the beard with his right hand to **k** him. H5975
1Ki 19:20 "*Let me* **k** my father and mother **goodbye**," H5975
Job 31:27 **offered** them **a k of homage**, H5975+4200+7023
Ps 2:12 **K** his son, or he will be angry and your H5975
Ps 85:10 righteousness and peace **k** *each other*. H5975
Pr 24:26 An honest answer *is* like *a* **k** *on* the lips. H5975
SS 1: 2 *Let him* **k** me with the kisses of his mouth H5975
SS 8: 1 you outside, *I would* **k** you, and no one H5975
Hos 13: 2 offer human sacrifices! *They* **k** calf-idols!" H5975
Mt 26:48 "The one *I* **k** is the man; arrest G5797
Mk 14:44 "The one *I* **k** is the man; arrest him and G5797
Lk 7:45 You did not give me a **k**, but this woman G5799
Lk 22:47 He approached Jesus *to* **k** him, G5797
Lk 22:48 you betraying the Son of Man *with* a **k**?" G5799
Ro 16:16 Greet one another with a holy **k**. All the G5799
1Co 16:20 Greet one another with a holy **k**. G5799
2Co 13:12 Greet one another with a holy **k**. G5799
1Th 5:26 Greet all God's people with a holy **k**. G5799
1Pe 5:14 Greet one another with a **k** of love. Peace G5799

KISSED (23) [KISS]

Ge 27:27 So he went to him and **k** him. When Isaac H5975
Ge 29:11 Then Jacob **k** Rachel and began to weep H5975
Ge 29:13 embraced him and **k** him and brought H5975
Ge 31:55 next morning Laban **k** his grandchildren H5975
Ge 33: 4 threw his arms around his neck and **k** him. H5975
Ge 45:15 And *he* **k** all his brothers and wept over H5975
Ge 48:10 his father **k** them and embraced them H5975
Ge 50: 1 his father and wept over him and **k** him. H5975
Ex 4:27 Moses at the mountain of God and **k** him. H5975
Ex 18: 7 bowed down and **k** him. H5975
Ru 1: 9 Then *she* **k** them **goodbye** and they wept H5975
Ru 1:14 Then Orpah **k** her mother-in-law **goodbye**, H5975
1Sa 10: 1 poured it on Saul's head and **k** him, H5975
1Sa 20:41 Then *they* **k** each other and wept together H5975
2Sa 14:33 before the king. And the king **k** Absalom. H5975
2Sa 19:39 The king **k** Barzillai and bid him farewell H5975
1Ki 19:18 Baal and whose mouths *have* not **k** him." H5975
Pr 7:13 took hold of him and **k** him and with a H5975
Mt 26:49 "Greetings, Rabbi!" and **k** him. G2968
Mk 14:45 to Jesus, Judas said, "Rabbi!" and **k** him. G2968
Lk 7:38 **k** them and poured perfume on them. G2968
Lk 15:20 threw his arms around him and **k** him. G2968
Ac 20:37 all wept as they embraced him and **k** him. G2968

KISSES (2) [KISS]

Pr 27: 6 can be trusted, but an enemy multiplies **k**. H5965
SS 1: 2 Let him kiss me with the **k** *of* his mouth H5965

KISSING (1) [KISS]

Lk 7:45 time I entered, has not stopped **k** my feet. G2968

KIT (3)

Eze 9: 2 in linen who had a writing **k** at his side. H7879
Eze 9: 3 in linen who had the writing **k** at his side H7879
Eze 9:11 in linen with the **writing k** at his side H7879

KITCHENS (1)

Eze 46:24 "These are the **k** where those who H1074+1418

KITE (4)

Lev 11:14 the **red k**, any kind of black kite, H1798
Lev 11:14 the red kite, any kind of **black k**, H370
Dt 14:13 the **red k**, the black kite, any kind of falcon, H8012
Dt 14:13 the red kite, the **black k**, any kind of falcon, H370

KITLISH (1)

Jos 15:40 Kabbon, Lahmas, **K**, H4186

KITRON (1)

Jdg 1:30 out the Canaanites living in **K** or Nahalol, H7790

KITTITES (2)

Ge 10: 4 Tarshish, the **K** and the Rodanites. H4183
1Ch 1: 7 Tarshish, the **K** and the Rodanites. H4183

KNEAD (2) [KNEADED, KNEADING, WELL-KNEADED]

Ge 18: 6 the finest flour and **k** it and bake some H4297
Jer 7:18 the women **k** the dough and make H4297

KNEADED (2) [KNEAD]
1Sa 28:24 **k** it and baked bread without yeast. H4297
2Sa 13: 8 took some dough, **k** it, made the bread H4297

KNEADING (5) [KNEAD]
Ex 8: 3 into your ovens and **k troughs**. H5400
Ex 12:34 their shoulders in **k troughs** wrapped in H5400
Dt 28: 5 basket and your **k trough** will be blessed. H5400
Dt 28:17 basket and your **k trough** will be cursed. H5400
Hos 7: 4 need not stir from the **k** *of* the dough till it H4297

KNEE (4) [KNEE-DEEP, KNEES]
Isa 45:23 Before me every **k** will bow; by me every H1386
Ro 11: 4 who have not bowed the **k** to Baal." *G1205*
Ro 14:11 says the Lord, 'every **k** will bow before me *G1205*
Php 2:10 at the name of Jesus every **k** should bow, *G1205*

KNEE-DEEP (2) [KNEE]
Eze 47: 4 led me through water that was **k**. H1386
Hos 5: 2 The rebels *are* **k** *in* slaughter. I will H6676

KNEEL (7) [KNEELING, KNELT]
Ge 24:11 *He* **had** the camels **k down** near the well H1384
Jdg 7: 5 dog laps from those who **k** down to drink." H1386
Est 3: 2 Mordecai *would* not **k down** or pay him H4156
Est 3: 5 Mordecai *would* not **k down** or pay him H4156
Ps 22:29 go down to the dust *will* **k** before him— H4156
Ps 95: 6 *let us* **k** before the LORD our Maker; H1384
Eph 3:14 this reason I **k** before the *G2828+3836+1205*

KNEELING (2) [KNEEL]
1Ki 8:54 where *he had been* **k** with H4156+6584+1386
Mt 20:20 her sons and, **k down**, asked a favor of *G4686*

KNEES (28) [KNEE]
Ge 48:12 them from Israel's **k** and bowed down H1386
Ge 50:23 were placed at birth on Joseph's **k**. H1386
Dt 28:35 will afflict your **k** and legs with painful H1386
Jdg 7: 6 All the rest got down on their **k** to drink. H1386
1Ki 18:42 ground and put his face between his **k**. H1386
1Ki 19:18 all whose **k** have not bowed down to Baal H1386
2Ki 1:13 went up and fell on his **k** before Elijah. H1386
Ezr 9: 5 fell on my **k** with my hands spread H1386
Job 3:12 Why were there **k** to receive me and H1386
Job 4: 4 you have strengthened faltering **k**. H1386
Ps 20: 8 They *are* **brought to** *their* **k** and fall, but H4156
Ps 109:24 My **k** give way from fasting; my body is H1386
Isa 35: 3 feeble hands, steady the **k** that give way; H1386
Isa 66:12 carried on her arm and dandled on her **k**. H1386
Da 5: 6 became weak and his **k** were knocking. A10072
Da 6:10 a day he got down on his **k** and prayed, A10123
Da 10:10 set me trembling on my hands and **k**. H1386
Na 2:10 Hearts melt, **k** give way, bodies tremble H1386
Mt 18:26 this the servant fell **on** *his* **k before** him. *G4686*
Mt 18:29 fellow servant fell to his **k** and begged him, NDT
Mk 1:40 came to him and begged him **on** *his* **k**, *G1206*
Mk 5: 6 he ran and **fell on** *his* **k in front of** him. *G4686*
Mk 10:17 up to him and **fell on** *his* **k before** him. *G1206*
Mk 15:19 Falling on their **k**, they paid homage to *G1205*
Lk 5: 8 he fell at Jesus' **k** and said, "Go away *G1205*
Ac 7:60 Then he fell on his **k** and cried out, "Lord *G1205*
Ac 9:40 then he got down on his **k** and prayed. *G1205*
Heb 12:12 strengthen your feeble arms and weak **k**. *G1205*

KNELT (12) [KNEEL]
2Ch 6:13 and then **k down** before the H1384+6584+1386
2Ch 7: 3 *they* **k** on the pavement with their faces to H4156
2Ch 29:29 present with him **k down** and worshiped. H4156
Est 3: 2 the king's gate **k down** and paid honor to H4156
Mt 8: 2 leprosy came and **k before** him and said, *G4686*
Mt 9:18 leader came and **k before** him and said, *G4686*
Mt 15:25 The woman came and **k before** him. "Lord *G4686*
Mt 17:14 man approached Jesus and **k** before him. *G1206*
Mt 27:29 Then *they* **k** in front of him and mocked *G1206*
Lk 22:41 them, **k down** and prayed, *G5502+3836+1205*
Ac 20:36 he **k down** with all of them *G5502+3836+1205*
Ac 21: 5 on the beach *we* **k** to pray. *G5502+3836+1205*

KNEW (82) [KNOW]
Ge 8:11 Then Noah **k** that the water had receded H3359
Ge 16: 4 When *she* **k** she was pregnant, she began H8011
Ge 38: 9 But Onan **k** that the child would not be his H3359
Dt 7:15 you the horrible diseases *you* **k** in Egypt, H3359
Dt 34:10 like Moses, whom the LORD **k** face to face, H3359
Jdg 2:10 grew up who **k** neither the LORD nor H3359
1Sa 3:13 forever because of the sin *he* **k about**; H3359
1Sa 20:33 Then Jonathan **k** that his father intended H3359
1Sa 20:39 The boy **k** nothing **about** all this; only H3359
1Sa 20:39 about all this; only Jonathan and David **k**.) H3359
1Sa 22:17 *They* **k** he was fleeing, yet they did not H3359
1Sa 22:22 *I* **k** he would be sure to tell Saul. H3359
1Sa 26:12 No one saw or **k about** it, nor did anyone H3359
1Sa 28:14 Then Saul **k** it was Samuel, and he H3359
2Sa 1:10 because *I* **k** that after he had fallen he H3359
2Sa 3:37 there and all Israel **k** that the king had no H3359
2Sa 5:12 Then David **k** that the LORD had H3359
2Sa 11:16 Uriah at a place where *he* **k** the strongest H3359
2Sa 14: 1 Joab son of Zeruiah **k** that the king's heart H3359
2Sa 17:19 No *one* **k** anything **about** it. H3359
1Ki 9:27 his men—sailors *who* **k** the sea—to serve H3359
2Ki 4:39 of stew, though no *one* **k** what they were. H3359
1Ch 12:32 the times and **k** what Israel should do— H3359
1Ch 14: 2 And David **k** that the LORD had established H3359
2Ch 8:18 by his own men, sailors *who* **k** the sea. H3359
2Ch 33:13 Then Manasseh **k** that the LORD is God. H3359
Ne 9:10 for *you* **k** how arrogantly the Egyptians H3359
Job 23: 3 If only *I* **k** where to find him; if only I could H3359
Ps 31: 7 saw my affliction and **k** the anguish of my H3359
Ps 90:11 If only we **k** the power of your anger! Your H3359
Pr 24:12 "But *we* **k** nothing **about** this," does H3359
Ecc 6: 5 Though it never saw the sun or **k** anything H3359
Isa 48: 4 For I **k** how stubborn you were; your neck H3359
Isa 48: 7 So you cannot say, 'Yes, *I* **k** *of* them.' H3359
Jer 1: 5 "Before I formed you in the womb *I* **k** you H3359
Jer 11:18 their plot to me, *I* **k** it, for at that time he H3359
Jer 19: 4 ancestors nor the kings of Judah *ever* **k**, H3359
Jer 32: 8 "*I* **k** that this was the word of the LORD H3359
Jer 41: 4 assassination, before anyone **k about** it, H3359
Jer 44: 3 they nor you nor your ancestors *ever* **k**. H3359
Jer 44:15 Then all the men who **k** that their wives H3359
Jer 50:24 you were caught before you **k** it; you H3359
Eze 28:19 All the nations *who* **k** you are appalled at H3359
Da 5:22 humbled yourself, though *you* **k** all this. A10313
Jnh 1:10 They **k** he was running away from the LORD H3359
Jnh 4: 2 *I* **k** that you are a gracious and H3359
Zec 11:11 were watching me **k** it was the word of H3359
Mt 7:23 them plainly, '*I* never **k** you. Away from *G1182*
Mt 12:25 Jesus **k** their thoughts and said to them *G3857*
Mt 21:45 *they* **k** he was talking about them. *G1182*
Mt 24:39 and *they* **k** nothing about what would *G1182*
Mt 25:24 he said, '*I* **k** that you are a hard man *G1182*
Mt 25:26 *So you* **k** that I harvest where I have not *G3857*
Mt 27:18 For *he* **k** it was out of self-interest that they *G3857*
Mk 1:34 speak because *they* **k** who he was. *G3857*
Mk 2: 8 Immediately Jesus **k** in his spirit that this *G2105*
Mk 12:12 him because *they* **k** he had spoken the *G1182*
Mk 12:15 But Jesus **k** their hypocrisy. "Why *G3857*
Lk 4:41 because *they* **k** he was the Messiah. *G3857*
Lk 5:22 Jesus **k** what they were thinking and *G2105*
Lk 6: 8 But Jesus **k** what they were thinking and *G3857*
Lk 11:17 Jesus **k** their thoughts and said to them *G3857*
Lk 19:22 *You* **k**, did you, that I am a hard man *G3857*
Lk 20:19 because *they* **k** he had spoken this *G1182*
Lk 23:49 But all those *who* **k** him, including the *G1196*
Jn 2: 9 the servants who had drawn the water **k**. *G3857*
Jn 2:24 himself to them, for he **k** all people. *G1182*
Jn 2:25 he **k** what was in each person. *G1182*
Jn 4:10 "If *you* **k** the gift of God and who it is that *G3857*
Jn 8:19 "If *you* **k** me, you would know my Father *G3857*
Jn 11:42 I **k** that you always hear me, but I said this *G3857*
Jn 13: 1 Jesus **k** that the hour had come for him to *G3857*
Jn 13: 3 Jesus **k** that the Father had put all things *G3857*
Jn 13:11 For *he* **k** who was going to betray him, and *G3857*
Jn 17: 8 *They* **k** with certainty that I came from you *G1182*
Jn 18: 2 who betrayed him, **k** the place, because *G3857*
Jn 21:12 "Who are you?" *They* **k** it was the Lord. *G3857*
Ac 2:30 he was a prophet and **k** that God had *G3857*
Ac 16: 3 for *they* all **k** that his father was a Greek. *G3857*
Ac 18:25 *though he* **k** only the baptism of John. *G2179*
Ro 1:21 For *although they* **k** God, they neither *G1182*
Heb 10:34 *because you* **k** that you yourselves had *G1182*

KNIFE (6) [KNIVES]
Ge 22: 6 he himself carried the fire and the **k**. H4408
Ge 22:10 his hand and took the **k** to slay his son. H4408
Ex 4:25 Zipporah took a **flint k**, cut off her son's H7644
Jdg 19:29 he took a **k** and cut up his concubine H4408
Pr 23: 2 put a **k** to your throat if you are given H8501
Jer 36:23 off with a scribe's **k** and threw them into H9509

KNIT (2) [CLOSE-KNIT, KNITTED]
Job 10:11 flesh and **k** me **together** with bones H6115
Ps 139:13 *you* **k** me **together** in my mother's womb. H6115

KNITTED (9) [KNIT]
Lev 13:48 any woven or **k material** of linen or wool H6849
Lev 13:49 the woven or **k material**, or any leather H6849
Lev 13:51 the woven or **k material**, or the leather, H6849
Lev 13:52 the woven or **k material** of wool or linen H6849
Lev 13:53 the woven or **k material**, or the leather H6849
Lev 13:56 the leather, or the woven or **k material**. H6849
Lev 13:57 in the woven or **k material**, or in the H6849
Lev 13:58 woven or **k material**, or any leather H6849
Lev 13:59 woven or **k material**, or any leather H6849

KNIVES (4) [KNIFE]
Jos 5: 2 "Make flint **k** and circumcise the Israelites H2995
Jos 5: 3 Joshua made flint **k** and circumcised the H2995
Pr 30:14 jaws are set with **k** to devour the poor H4408
Isa 18: 5 he will cut off the shoots with **pruning k** H4661

KNOCK (3) [KNOCKED, KNOCKING, KNOCKS]
Mt 7: 7 **k** and the door will be opened to you. *G3218*
Lk 11: 9 **k** and the door will be opened to you. *G3218*
Rev 3:20 I stand at the door and **k**. If anyone hears *G3218*

KNOCKED (2) [KNOCK]
Da 8: 7 the goat **k** it to the ground and trampled H8959
Ac 12:13 Peter **k** at the outer entrance, and a *G3218*

KNOCKING (4) [KNOCK]
SS 5: 2 My beloved *is* **k**: "Open to me, my H1985
Da 5: 6 and his knees *were* **k**.
A10491+10154+10378+10154
Lk 13:25 you will stand outside **k** and pleading, 'Sir *G3218*
Ac 12:16 But Peter kept on **k**, and when they *G3218*

KNOCKS (4) [KNOCK]
Ex 21:27 And an owner *who* **k out** the tooth of a H5877
Mt 7: 8 and *to the one who* **k**, the door will *G3218*
Lk 11:10 and *to the one who* **k**, the door will *G3218*
Lk 12:36 when he comes and **k** they can *G3218*

KNOP, KNOPS (KJV) BUD, BUDS, GOURDS

KNOTTED (1) [KNOT]
Eze 27:24 rugs with cords twisted and **tightly k**. H775

KNOW (867) [FOREKNEW, FOREKNOWLEDGE, KNEW, KNOWING, KNOWLEDGE, KNOWN, KNOWS, WELL-KNOWN]
Ge 4: 9 brother Abel?" "*I* don't **k**," he replied H3359
Ge 12:11 "*I* **k** what a beautiful woman you are. H3359
Ge 15: 8 how *can I* **k** that I will gain possession of H3359
Ge 15:13 "**K for certain** that for four hundred H3359+3359
Ge 18:21 that has reached me. If not, *I will* **k**." H3359
Ge 20: 6 I **k** you did this with a clear conscience H3359
Ge 21:26 "*I* don't **k** who has done this. H3359
Ge 22:12 Now *I* **k** that you fear God, because you H3359
Ge 24:14 By this *I will* **k** that you have shown H3359
Ge 24:49 tell me, so *I may* **k** which way *to* **turn**. AIT
Ge 27: 2 old man and don't **k** the day of my death. H3359
Ge 27:21 to **k** whether you really are my son Esau NDT
Ge 29: 5 said to them, "*Do you* **k** Laban, Nahor's H3359
Ge 29: 5 "Yes, *we* **k** him," they H3359
Ge 30:26 You **k** how much work I've done for you." H3359
Ge 30:29 "You **k** how I have worked for you and H3359
Ge 31: 6 You **k** that I've worked for your father with H3359
Ge 31:32 Now Jacob *did* not **k** that Rachel had H3359
Ge 37:13 to Joseph, "**As you k**, your brothers H2022+4202
Ge 42:33 'This is how *I will* **k** whether you are H3359
Ge 42:34 brother to me so *I will* **k** that you are not H3359
Ge 43: 7 *How were we to* **k** he would say H3359+3359
Ge 43:22 *We* don't **k** who put our silver in our sacks." H3359
Ge 44:15 Don't *you* **k** that a man like me can find H3359
Ge 44:27 'You **k** that my wife bore me two sons. H3359
Ge 47: 6 And if *you* **k** *of* any among them with H3359
Ge 48:19 his father refused and said, "*I* **k**, my son, H3359
Ge 48:19 refused and said, "I know, my son, *I* **k**. H3359
Ex 3:19 But I **k** that the king of Egypt will not let H3359
Ex 4:14 Aaron the Levite? *I* **k** he can speak well H3359
Ex 5: 2 *I do* not **k** the LORD and I will not let Israel H3359
Ex 6: 7 Then *you will* **k** that I am the LORD your H3359
Ex 7: 5 And the Egyptians *will* **k** that I am the LORD H3359
Ex 7:17 By this *you will* **k** that I am the LORD H3359
Ex 8:10 so that *you may* **k** there is no one like the H3359
Ex 8:22 be there, so that *you will* **k** that I, the LORD, H3359
Ex 9:14 so *you may* **k** that there is no one like me H3359
Ex 9:29 so *you may* **k** that the earth is the LORD's. H3359
Ex 9:30 But *I* **k** that you and your officials still do H3359
Ex 10: 2 that *you may* **k** that I am the LORD. H3359
Ex 10:26 we get there we *will* not **k** what we are to H3359
Ex 11: 7 Then *you will* **k** that the LORD makes a H3359
Ex 14: 4 the Egyptians *will* **k** that I am the LORD H3359
Ex 14:18 The Egyptians *will* **k** that I am the LORD H3359
Ex 16: 6 "In the evening *you will* **k** that it was the H3359
Ex 16: 8 "You will **k** that it was the LORD when he NDT
Ex 16:12 Then *you will* **k** that I am the LORD your H3359
Ex 16:15 For *they did* not **k** what it was H3359
Ex 18:11 Now *I* **k** that the LORD is greater than all H3359
Ex 23: 9 *you* yourselves **k** how it feels to be H3359
Ex 29:46 *They will* **k** that I am the LORD their God H3359
Ex 31:13 to come, so *you may* **k** that I am the LORD H3359
Ex 32: 1 *we* don't **k** what has happened to him." H3359
Ex 32:22 "You **k** how prone these people are to evil H3359
Ex 32:23 *we* don't **k** what has happened to him. H3359
Ex 33:12 you *have* not **let** me **k** whom you will H3359
Ex 33:12 '*I* **k** you by name and you have found H3359
Ex 33:13 me your ways so *I may* **k** you and continue H3359
Ex 33:16 How *will anyone* **k** that you are pleased H3359
Ex 33:17 pleased with you and *I* **k** you by name." H3359
Ex 36: 1 skill and ability to **k how** to carry out all H3359
Lev 5:17 even though *they do* not **k** it, they are H3359
Lev 23:43 so your descendants *will* **k** that I had the H3359
Nu 10:31 *You* **k** where we should camp in the H3359
Nu 14:34 your sins and **k what it is like** to have me H3359
Nu 16:28 "This is how *you will* **k** that the LORD has H3359
Nu 16:30 then *you will* **k** that these men have H3359
Nu 20:14 You **k about** all the hardships that have H3359
Nu 22: 6 For *I* **k** that whoever you bless is blessed H3359
Dt 1:39 children who *do* not yet **k** good from bad H3359
Dt 3:19 your livestock (*I* **k** you have much livestock H3359
Dt 4:35 things so that *you might* **k** that the LORD is H3359
Dt 7: 9 **K** therefore that the LORD your God is God H3359
Dt 8: 2 test you in order to **k** what was in your H3359
Dt 8: 5 **K** then in your heart that as a man H3359
Dt 9: 2 You **k about** them and have heard it said H3359
Dt 11:30 **As you k**, these mountains are H2022+4202
Dt 18:21 "How *can we* **k** when a message has not H3359
Dt 20:20 cut down trees that *you* **k** are not fruit H3359
Dt 22: 2 near you or if *you do* not **k** who owns it, H3359
Dt 28:33 A people that *you do* not **k** will eat what H3359
Dt 29: 6 I did this so that *you might* **k** that I am the H3359
Dt 29:16 *You* yourselves **k** how we lived in Egypt H3359
Dt 29:26 to them, gods *they did* not **k**, gods he had H3359
Dt 31:13 Their children, who *do* not **k** this law, must H3359
Dt 31:21 *I* **k** what they are disposed to do, even H3359
Dt 31:27 For I **k** how rebellious and stiff-necked you H3359
Dt 31:29 For *I* **k** that after my death you are sure to H3359

K

Jos 2: 4 but *I did* not **k** where they had come from. H3359
Jos 2: 5 *I* don't **k** which way they went H3359
Jos 2: 9 "*I* **k** that the LORD has given you this land H3359
Jos 3: 4 Then *you will* **k** which way to go, since you H3359
Jos 3: 7 so *they may* **k** that I am with you as I was H3359
Jos 3:10 This is how *you will* **k** that the living God is H3359
Jos 4:24 of the earth *might* **k** that the hand of H3359
Jos 8:14 But he *did* not **k** that an ambush had H3359
Jos 14: 6 "You **k** what the LORD said to Moses the H3359
Jos 22:22 And *let* Israel **k**! If this has H3359
Jos 22:31 "Today *we* **k** that the LORD is with us H3359
Jos 23:14 *You* **k** with all your heart and soul that not H3359
Jdg 6:37 then *I will* **k** that you will save Israel by my H3359
Jdg 14: 4 His parents *did* not **k** that this was from the H3359
Jdg 16:20 But he *did* not **k** that the LORD had left him. H3359
Jdg 17:13 "Now *I* **k** that the LORD will be good to me H3359
Jdg 18:14 "*Do you* **k** that one of these houses has H3359
Jdg 18:14 Now *you* **k** what to do." H3359
Ru 2:11 to live with a people *you did* not **k** before. H3359
Ru 3: 3 don't **let** him **k** *you* are there until he H3359
Ru 3:11 people of my town **k** that you are a H3359
Ru 3:14 "No *one must* **k** that a woman came to H3359
Ru 4: 4 tell me, so *I will* **k**. For no one has the H3359
1Sa 3: 7 Now Samuel *did* not yet **k** the LORD: The H3359
1Sa 6: 3 you *will* **k** why his hand has not been H3359
1Sa 6: 9 then *we will* **k** that it was not his hand H3359
1Sa 8: 9 solemnly and **let** them **k** what the king H5583
1Sa 17:28 I **k** how conceited you are and how wicked H3359
1Sa 17:46 the whole world *will* **k** that there is a H3359
1Sa 17:47 those gathered here *will* **k** that it is not by H3359
1Sa 17:55 surely as you live, Your Majesty, *I* don't **k**." H3359
1Sa 20: 2 small, without **letting** me **k**. H1655+906+265
1Sa 20: 3 'Jonathan *must* not **k** this or he will be H3359
1Sa 20:12 send you word and **let** you **k**? H1655+906+265
1Sa 20:13 if *I do* not **let** you **k** and send H1655+906+265
1Sa 20:30 Don't *I* **k** that you have sided with the son H3359
1Sa 21: 2 'No one *is to* **k** anything **about** the H3359
1Sa 24:20 *I* **k** that you will surely be king and that the H3359
1Sa 28: 9 "Surely you **k** what Saul has done. H3359
1Sa 29: 9 "*I* **k** that you have been as pleasing in my H3359
2Sa 1: 5 "How *do you* **k** that Saul and his son H3359
2Sa 3:25 *You* **k** Abner son of Ner; he came to H3359
2Sa 3:26 the cistern at Sirah. But David *did* not **k** it. H3359
2Sa 7:20 For you **k** your servant H3359
2Sa 11:20 Didn't *you* **k** they would shoot arrows from H3359
2Sa 15:20 I **do not k where** I **am going**? H2143+6584+889+2143
2Sa 17: 8 You **k** your father and his men; they are H3359
2Sa 18:29 your servant, but *I* don't **k** what it was." H3359
2Sa 19:20 For I your servant **k** that I have sinned, but H3359
2Sa 19:22 Don't *I* **k** that today I am king over Israel?" H3359
2Sa 22:44 People *I did* not **k** now serve me, H3359
2Sa 24: 2 so that *I may* **k** how many there are." H3359
1Ki 1:18 *you*, my lord the king, *do* not **k about** it. H3359
1Ki 1:27 without **letting** his servants **k** who should H3359
1Ki 2: 5 "Now *you* yourself **k** what Joab son of H3359
1Ki 2: 9 of wisdom; *you will* **k** what to do to him. H3359
1Ki 2:15 "*As* you **k**," he said, "the kingdom was H3359
1Ki 2:44 "You **k** in your heart all the wrong you did H3359
1Ki 3: 7 child and *do* not **k how** to carry out my H3359
1Ki 5: 3 "You **k** that because of the wars waged H3359
1Ki 5: 6 You **k** that we have no one so skilled in H3359
1Ki 8:39 to all they do, since *you* **k** their hearts (for H3359
1Ki 8:39 you alone **k** every human heart), H3359
1Ki 8:43 of the earth *may* **k** your name and fear H3359
1Ki 8:43 *may* **k** that this house I have built H3359
1Ki 8:60 peoples of the earth *may* **k** that the LORD is H3359
1Ki 17:24 "Now *I* **k** that you are a man of God and H3359
1Ki 18:12 *I* don't **k** where the Spirit of the LORD may H3359
1Ki 18:37 so these people *will* **k** that you, LORD, H3359
1Ki 20:13 then *you will* **k** that I am the LORD. H3359
1Ki 20:28 and *you will* **k** that I am the LORD. H3359
1Ki 22: 3 "Don't *you* **k** that Ramoth Gilead belongs H3359
2Ki 2: 3 "*Do you* **k** that the LORD is going to take H3359
2Ki 2: 3 "Yes, I **k**," Elisha replied, "so H3359
2Ki 2: 5 "*Do you* **k** that the LORD is going to take H3359
2Ki 2: 5 "Yes, I **k**," he replied, "so be H3359
2Ki 4: 1 and you **k** that he revered the LORD. H3359
2Ki 4: 9 "*I* **k** that this man who often comes our H3359
2Ki 5: 8 come to me and *he will* **k** that there is a H3359
2Ki 5:15 "Now *I* **k** that there is no God in all the H3359
2Ki 7:12 *They* **k** we are starving; so they have left H3359
2Ki 8:12 "Because *I* **k** the harm you will do to the H3359
2Ki 9:11 "You **k** the man and the sort of things he H3359
2Ki 10:10 **K**, then, that not a word the LORD has H3359
2Ki 17:26 of Samaria *do* not **k** what the god of H3359
2Ki 17:26 the people *do* not **k** what he requires." H3359
2Ki 18:21 **Look, I k** you are depending on H2180+6964
2Ki 19:19 of the earth *may* **k** that you alone, H3359
2Ki 19:27 " 'But *I* **k** where you are and when you H3359
1Ch 17:18 For you **k** your servant, H3359
1Ch 21: 2 to me so that *I may* **k** how many there H3359
1Ch 29:17 *I* **k**, my God, that you test the heart and are H3359
2Ch 2: 8 I **k** that your servants are skilled in H3359
2Ch 6:30 to all they do, since *you* **k** their hearts (for H3359
2Ch 6:30 for you alone **k** the human heart), H3359
2Ch 6:33 of the earth *may* **k** your name and fear H3359
2Ch 6:33 *may* **k** that this house I have built H3359
2Ch 13: 5 Don't you **k** that the LORD, the God of H3359
2Ch 20:12 We *do* not **k** what to do, but our eyes are H3359
2Ch 25:16 "*I* **k** that God has determined to destroy H3359
2Ch 32:13 "*Do you* not **k** what I and my predecessors H3359
2Ch 32:31 to test him and to **k** everything that was in H3359
Ezr 4:12 The king *should* **k** that the people who A10313
Ezr 4:13 the king *should* **k** that if this city is built A10313
Ezr 5: 8 The king *should* **k** that we went to the A10313
Ezr 7:24 You *are* also *to* **k** that you have no A10313
Ezr 7:25 all *who* **k** the laws of your God. A10313
Ezr 7:25 you are to teach any who *do* not **k** them. A10313
Ne 2:16 The officials *did* not **k** where I had gone H3359
Ne 4:11 "Before *they* **k** it or see us, we H3359
Ne 13:24 and *did* not **k how** to speak the language H5795
Est 4:11 the royal provinces **k** that for any man H3359
Job 5:24 *You will* **k** that your tent is secure; you will H3359
Job 5:25 *You will* **k** that your children will be many H3359
Job 7:10 his place *will* **k** him no more. H5795
Job 8: 9 were born only yesterday and **k** nothing, H3359
Job 9: 2 "Indeed, *I* **k** that this is true. But how can H3359
Job 9:28 for *I* **k** you will not hold me innocent. H3359
Job 10: 7 though you **k** that I am not guilty and that H1981
Job 10:13 and *I* **k** that this was in your mind: H3359
Job 11: 6 has two sides. **K** this: God has even H3359
Job 11: 8 than the depths below—what *can you* **k**? H3359
Job 12: 3 Who does not **k** all these things? H907
Job 12: 9 of all these *does* not **k** that the hand of H3359
Job 13: 2 What you **k**, I also know; I am not inferior H1981
Job 13: 2 you know, I also **k**; I am not inferior to H3359
Job 13:18 prepared my case, *I* **k** I will be vindicated. H3359
Job 14:21 are honored, *they do* not **k** it; if their H3359
Job 15: 9 What *do you* **k** that we do not know H3359
Job 15: 9 What do you know that *we do* not **k** H3359
Job 18:21 is the place of *one who does* not **k** God." H3359
Job 19: 6 then **k** that God has wronged me and H3359
Job 19:25 I **k** that my redeemer lives, and that in the H3359
Job 19:29 then *you will* **k** that there is judgment." H3359
Job 20: 4 "Surely *you* **k** how it has been from of old H3359
Job 21:14 We have no desire to **k** your ways. H1981
Job 21:27 "*I* **k** full well what you are thinking, the H3359
Job 22:13 you say, 'What *does* God **k**? Does he H3359
Job 24: 1 Why must *those who* **k** him look in vain H3359
Job 24:13 *who do* not **k** its ways or stay in its paths. H5795
Job 30:23 *I* **k** you will bring me down to death, to H3359
Job 31: 6 honest scales and *he will* **k** that I am H3359
Job 32: 6 was fearful, not daring to tell you **what** I **k**. H1976
Job 32:10 Listen to me; I too will tell you **what** I **k**. H1976
Job 32:17 will have my say; I too will tell **what** I **k**. H1976
Job 33: 3 my lips sincerely speak **what** I **k**. H1981
Job 34:33 must decide, not I; so tell me what *you* **k**. H3359
Job 37: 7 everyone he has made *may* **k** his work, H3359
Job 37:15 *Do you* **k** how God controls the clouds H3359
Job 37:16 *Do you* **k** how the clouds hang poised H3359
Job 38: 5 Surely *you* **k**! Who stretched a H3359
Job 38:18 Tell me, if *you* **k** all this. H3359
Job 38:20 *Do you* **k** the paths to their dwellings H1067
Job 38:21 Surely *you* **k**, for you were already born H3359
Job 38:33 *Do you* **k** the laws of the heavens? Can H3359
Job 39: 1 "*Do you* **k** when the mountain goats give H3359
Job 39: 2 *Do you* **k** the time they give birth? H3359
Job 42: 2 "*I* **k** that you can do all things; no purpose H3359
Job 42: 3 things too wonderful for me *to* **k**. H3359
Ps 4: 3 **K** that the LORD has set apart his faithful H3359
Ps 9:10 *Those who* **k** your name trust in you, for H3359
Ps 9:20 *let* the nations **k** they are only mortal. H3359
Ps 14: 4 Do all these evildoers **k** nothing? They H3359
Ps 18:43 People *I did* not **k** now serve me, H3359
Ps 20: 6 Now this *I* **k**: The LORD gives victory to his H3359
Ps 35:11 question me on things *I* **k** nothing **about**. H3359
Ps 36:10 Continue your love to *those who* **k** you H3359
Ps 39: 4 my days; *let me* **k** how fleeting my life is. H3359
Ps 40: 9 I do not seal my lips, LORD, *as* you **k**. H3359
Ps 41:11 *I* **k** that you are pleased with me, for my H3359
Ps 46:10 "Be still, and **k** that I am God; I will be H3359
Ps 50:11 *I* **k** every bird in the mountains, and the H3359
Ps 51: 3 For I **k** my transgressions, and my sin is H3359
Ps 53: 4 *Do all these* evildoers **k** nothing H7188+3359
Ps 56: 9 By this *I will* **k** that God is for me. H3359
Ps 69: 5 **k** my folly; my guilt is not hidden H3359
Ps 69:19 You **k** how I am scorned, disgraced and H3359
Ps 71:15 though *I* **k** not how to relate them all. H3359
Ps 73:11 They say, "How *would* God **k**? Does the H3359
Ps 73:11 the Most High **k** anything?" H3780+928+1978
Ps 78: 6 so the next generation *would* **k** them H3359
Ps 82: 5 "The 'gods' **k** nothing, they understand H3359
Ps 83:18 *Let them* **k** that you, whose name is the H3359
Ps 92: 6 Senseless people *do* not **k**, fools do not H3359
Ps 100: 3 **K** that the LORD is God. It is he who made H3359
Ps 109:27 *Let them* **k** that it is your hand, that you H3359
Ps 119:75 *I* **k**, LORD, that your laws are righteous, and H3359
Ps 135: 5 I **k** that the LORD is great, that our Lord is H3359
Ps 139: 1 have searched me, LORD, and *you* **k** me. H3359
Ps 139: 2 You **k** when I sit and when I rise; you H3359
Ps 139: 4 is on my tongue you, LORD, **k** it completely. H3359
Ps 139:14 your works are wonderful, I **k** that full well. H3359
Ps 139:23 and **k** my heart; test me and know H3359
Ps 139:23 test me and **k** my anxious thoughts. H3359
Ps 140:12 *I* **k** that the LORD secures justice for the H3359
Ps 145:12 that all people *may* **k** *of* your mighty acts H3359
Ps 147:20 no other nation; *they do* not **k** his laws. H3359
Pr 4:19 *they do* not **k** what makes them stumble. H3359
Pr 5: 6 wander aimlessly, but *she does* not **k** it. H3359
Pr 9:18 But little *do they* **k** that the dead are there, H3359
Pr 10:32 lips of the righteous **k** what finds favor, H3359
Pr 24:12 *Does* not he who guards your life **k** it H3359
Pr 24:14 **K** also that wisdom is like honey for you: If H3359
Pr 27: 1 for *you do* not **k** what a day may bring. H3359
Pr 27:23 **Be sure** *you* **k** the condition of your H3359+3359
Pr 30: 4 is the name of his son? Surely *you* **k**! H3359
Ecc 3:12 *I* **k** that there is nothing better for people H3359
Ecc 3:14 *I* **k** that everything God does will endure H3359
Ecc 5: 1 of fools, who *do* not **k** that they do wrong. H3359
Ecc 7:22 for *you* **k** in your heart that many times H3359
Ecc 8: 5 the wise heart *will* **k** the proper time H3359
Ecc 8:12 I **k** that it will go better with those who H3359
Ecc 8:16 I applied my mind to **k** wisdom and to H3359
Ecc 8:17 Even if the wise claim *they* **k**, they cannot H3359
Ecc 9: 5 For the living **k** that they will die, but the H3359
Ecc 9: 5 but the dead **k** nothing; they have no H3359
Ecc 10:15 *they do* not **k** the way to town. H3359
Ecc 11: 2 *you do* not **k** what disaster may come H3359
Ecc 11: 5 As you *do* not **k** the path of the wind, or H3359
Ecc 11: 6 for you *do* not **k** which will succeed H3359
Ecc 11: 9 **k** that for all these things God will H3359
SS 1: 8 If *you do* not **k**, most beautiful of women H3359
Isa 1: 3 Israel *does* not **k**, my people do not H3359
Isa 5:19 let it come into view, so *we may* **k** it." H3359
Isa 9: 9 All the people *will* **k** it—Ephraim and the H3359
Isa 29:12 will answer, "*I* don't **k how to read**." H3359+6219
Isa 29:15 think, "Who sees us? Who *will* **k**?" H3359
Isa 29:16 pot say to the potter, "*You* **k** nothing"? H1067
Isa 32: 4 The fearful heart *will* **k** and understand H3359
Isa 36: 6 I **k** you are depending on Egypt, that NDT
Isa 37:20 the kingdoms of the earth *may* **k** that you, H3359
Isa 37:28 "But *I* **k** where you are and when you H3359
Isa 40:21 *Do you* not **k**? Have you not heard? Has it H3359
Isa 40:28 *Do you* not **k**? Have you not heard? The H3359
Isa 41:20 so that people may see and **k**, may H3359
Isa 41:22 consider them and **k** their final outcome. H3359
Isa 41:23 so *we may* **k** that you are gods. H3359
Isa 41:26 beginning, so *we could* **k**, or beforehand, H3359
Isa 43:10 so that *you may* **k** and believe me and H3359
Isa 44: 8 there is no other Rock; *I* **k** not one." H3359
Isa 44:18 *They* **k** nothing, they understand nothing H3359
Isa 45: 3 so that *you may* **k** that I am the LORD H3359
Isa 45: 6 of its setting *people may* **k** there is none H3359
Isa 47:11 and *you will* not **k how** to conjure it away. H3359
Isa 48: 8 Well *do I* **k** how treacherous you are; you H3359
Isa 49:23 Then *you will* **k** that I am the LORD; those H3359
Isa 49:26 Then all mankind *will* **k** that I, the LORD H3359
Isa 50: 4 to **k** the word that sustains the weary. H3359
Isa 50: 7 and *I* **k** I will not be put to shame. H3359
Isa 51: 7 "Hear me, *you who* **k** what is right, you H3359
Isa 52: 6 Therefore my people *will* **k** my name H3359
Isa 52: 6 in that day they will **k** that it is I who foretold NDT
Isa 55: 5 Surely you will summon nations *you* **k** not H3359
Isa 55: 5 nations you *do* not **k** will come H3359
Isa 58: 2 they seem eager to **k** my ways, as if they H1981
Isa 59: 8 The way of peace *they do* not **k**; there is H3359
Isa 59: 8 one who walks along them *will* **k** peace. H3359
Isa 60:16 Then *you will* **k** that I, the LORD, am your H3359
Isa 63:16 though Abraham *does* not **k** us or Israel H3359
Jer 1: 6 "*I do* not **k how** to speak; I am too H3359
Jer 2: 8 who deal with the law *did* not **k** me; H3359
Jer 4:22 are fools; *they do* not **k** me. They are H3359
Jer 4:22 in doing evil; *they* **k** not **how** to do good." H3359
Jer 5: 4 for *they do* not **k** the way of the LORD H3359
Jer 5: 5 to them; surely they **k** the way of the LORD H3359
Jer 5:15 a people whose language *you do* not **k** H3359
Jer 6:15 *they do* not even **k how** to blush. H3359
Jer 8: 7 But my people *do* not **k** the requirements H3359
Jer 8:12 *they do* not even **k how** to blush. H3359
Jer 9:24 that they have the understanding *to* **k** me H3359
Jer 10:23 *I* **k** that people's lives are not their own H3359
Jer 12: 3 Yet you **k** me, LORD; you see me and test H3359
Jer 13:12 'Don't *we* **k** that every wineskin H3359+3359
Jer 14:18 priest have gone to a land *they* **k** not. H3359
Jer 15:14 to your enemies in a land *you do* not **k**, H3359
Jer 16:21 Then *they will* **k** that my name is the LORD H3359
Jer 17: 4 to your enemies in a land *you do* not **k**, H3359
Jer 17:16 you **k** I have not desired the day of H3359
Jer 18:23 But you, LORD, **k** all their plots to kill me H3359
Jer 22:16 Is that not what it means to **k** me? H1981
Jer 22:28 hurled out, cast into a land *they do* not **k**? H3359
Jer 24: 7 I will give them a heart to **k** me, that I am H3359
Jer 29:11 For I **k** the plans I have for you," declares H3359
Jer 29:23 I **k** it and am a witness to it," declares the H3359
Jer 31:34 say to one another, '**K** the LORD,' because H3359
Jer 31:34 because they *will* all **k** me, from the least H3359
Jer 33: 3 unsearchable things *you do* not **k**. H3359
Jer 36:19 Don't *let* anyone **k** where you are. H3359
Jer 38:24 "*Do* not *let* anyone **k** about this H3359
Jer 40:14 "Don't *you* **k** that Baalis king of the H3359+3359
Jer 40:15 son of Nethaniah, and no one *will* **k** it. H3359
Jer 44:19 did not our husbands **k** that we were making NDT
Jer 44:28 to live in Egypt *will* **k** whose word will H3359
Jer 44:29 'so that *you will* **k** that my threats of harm H3359
Jer 48:17 live around her, all *who* **k** her fame; say, H3359
Jer 48:30 I **k** her insolence but it is futile," declares H3359
Eze 2: 5 *they will* **k** that a prophet has been among H3359
Eze 5:13 *they will* **k** that I the LORD have spoken in H3359
Eze 6: 7 and *you will* **k** that I am the LORD. H3359
Eze 6:10 And *they will* **k** that I am the LORD; I did H3359
Eze 6:13 And *they will* **k** that I am the LORD, when H3359
Eze 6:14 Then *they will* **k** that I am the LORD H3359
Eze 7: 4 " 'Then *you will* **k** that I am the LORD H3359
Eze 7: 9 " 'Then *you will* **k** that it is I the LORD who H3359
Eze 7:27 " 'Then *they will* **k** that I am the LORD H3359

Eze 11: 5 I **k** what is going through your mind. H3359
Eze 11:10 Then *you will* **k** that I am the LORD H3359
Eze 11:12 And *you will* **k** that I am the LORD, for you H3359
Eze 12:15 "*They will* **k** that I am the LORD, when I H3359
Eze 12:16 Then *they will* **k** that I am the LORD." H3359
Eze 12:20 Then *you will* **k** that I am the LORD H3359
Eze 13: 9 Then *you will* **k** that I am the Sovereign H3359
Eze 13:14 and *you will* **k** that I am the LORD. H3359
Eze 13:21 Then *you will* **k** that I am the LORD. H3359
Eze 13:23 And then *you will* **k** that I am the LORD H3359
Eze 14: 8 Then *you will* **k** that I am the LORD. H3359
Eze 14:23 for *you will* **k** that I have done nothing in H3359
Eze 15: 7 *you will* **k** that I am the LORD. H3359
Eze 16:62 and *you will* **k** that I am the LORD. H3359
Eze 17:12 '*Do you* not **k** what these things mean? H3359
Eze 17:21 Then *you will* **k** that I the LORD have H3359
Eze 17:24 trees of the forest *will* **k** that I the LORD H3359
Eze 20:12 so they *would* **k** that I the LORD made them H3359
Eze 20:20 Then you *will* **k** that I am the LORD your H3359
Eze 20:26 with horror so *they would* **k** that I am the H3359
Eze 20:38 Then *you will* **k** that I am the LORD. H3359
Eze 20:42 Then *you will* **k** that I am the LORD, when I H3359
Eze 20:44 *You will* **k** that I am the LORD, when I deal H3359
Eze 21: 5 Then all people *will* **k** that I the LORD have H3359
Eze 22:16 the nations, *you will* **k** that I am the LORD. H3359
Eze 22:22 and *you will* **k** that I the LORD have poured H3359
Eze 23:49 Then *you will* **k** that I am the Sovereign H3359
Eze 24:24 *you will* **k** that I am the Sovereign LORD. H3359
Eze 24:27 and *they will* **k** that I am the LORD. H3359
Eze 25: 5 Then *you will* **k** that I am the LORD H3359
Eze 25: 7 and *you will* **k** that I am the LORD. H3359
Eze 25:11 Then *they will* **k** that I am the LORD H3359
Eze 25:14 my wrath; *they will* **k** my vengeance H3359
Eze 25:17 Then *they will* **k** that I am the LORD, when I H3359
Eze 26: 6 Then *they will* **k** that I am the LORD H3359
Eze 28:22 *You will* **k** that I am the LORD, when I inflict H3359
Eze 28:23 Then *you will* **k** that I am the LORD. H3359
Eze 28:24 Then *they will* **k** that I am the Sovereign H3359
Eze 28:26 Then *they will* **k** that I am the LORD their H3359
Eze 29: 6 who live in Egypt *will* **k** that I am the LORD.H3359
Eze 29: 9 Then *they will* **k** that I am the LORD H3359
Eze 29:16 Then *they will* **k** that I am the Sovereign H3359
Eze 29:21 Then *they will* **k** that I am the LORD." H3359
Eze 30: 8 Then *they will* **k** that I am the LORD, when I H3359
Eze 30:19 and *they will* **k** that I am the LORD. H3359
Eze 30:25 Then *they will* **k** that I am the LORD, when I H3359
Eze 30:26 Then *they will* **k** that I am the LORD." H3359
Eze 32:15 then *they will* **k** that I am the LORD. H3359
Eze 33:29 Then *they will* **k** that I am the LORD, when I H3359
Eze 33:33 then *they will* **k** that a prophet has been H3359
Eze 34:27 *They will* **k** that I am the LORD, when I H3359
Eze 34:30 Then *they will* **k** that I, the LORD their God H3359
Eze 35: 4 Then *you will* **k** that I am the LORD. H3359
Eze 35: 9 Then *you will* **k** that I am the LORD. H3359
Eze 35:12 Then *you will* **k** that I the LORD have heard H3359
Eze 35:15 Then *they will* **k** that I am the LORD H3359
Eze 36:11 Then *you will* **k** that I am the LORD H3359
Eze 36:23 Then the nations *will* **k** that I am the LORD H3359
Eze 36:32 *I want* you *to* **k** that I am not doing this H3359
Eze 36:36 you that remain *will* **k** that I the LORD have H3359
Eze 36:38 Then *they will* **k** that I am the LORD." H3359
Eze 37: 3 "Sovereign LORD, you alone **k**." H3359
Eze 37: 6 Then *you will* **k** that I am the LORD H3359
Eze 37:13 Then *you*, my people, *will* **k** that I am the H3359
Eze 37:14 Then *you will* **k** that I the LORD have H3359
Eze 37:28 Then the nations *will* **k** that I the LORD H3359
Eze 38:16 so that the nations *may* **k** me when I am H3359
Eze 38:23 Then *they will* **k** that I am the LORD H3359
Eze 39: 6 and *they will* **k** that I am the LORD. H3359
Eze 39: 7 the nations *will* **k** that I the LORD am H3359
Eze 39:22 people of Israel *will* **k** that I am the LORD H3359
Eze 39:23 And the nations *will* **k** that the people of H3359
Eze 39:28 Then *they will* **k** that I am the LORD their H3359
Da 2: 3 me and I want to **k what** it **means**. H3359
Da 2: 9 and *I will* **k** that you can interpret it for A10313
Da 2:30 that Your Majesty *may* **k** the A10313
Da 3:18 does not, we *want* you *to* **k**, Your Majesty A10313
Da 4: 9 I **k** that the spirit of the holy gods is in A10313
Da 4:17 so that the living *may* **k** that the Most A10313
Da 7:19 I wanted to **k the meaning** of the fourth A10326
Da 7:20 I also wanted to **k** about the ten horns on its NDT
Da 9:25 "**K** and understand this: From the time the H3359
Da 10:20 "*Do you* **k** why I have come to you? H3359
Da 11:32 the people *who* **k** their God will firmly H3359
Hos 5: 3 I **k all about** Ephraim; Israel is not hidden H3359
Hos 9: 7 *Let* Israel **k** this. Because your H3359
Joel 2:27 Then *you will* **k** that I am in Israel, that I H3359
Joel 3:17 "Then *you will* **k** that I, the LORD your God H3359
Am 3:10 "*They do* not **k how** to do right," declares H3359
Am 5:12 For *I* **k** how many are your offenses and H3359
Jnh 1:12 I **k** that it is my fault that this great storm H3359
Mic 4:12 But they *do* not **k** the thoughts of the LORD H3359
Mic 6: 5 that *you may* **k** the righteous acts of the H3359
Zep 3: 5 not fail, yet the unrighteous **k** no shame. H3359
Zec 2: 9 Then *you will* **k** that the LORD Almighty has H3359
Zec 2:11 among you and *you will* **k** that the LORD H3359
Zec 4: 5 answered, "*Do you* not **k** what these are?" H3359
Zec 4: 9 Then *you will* **k** that the LORD Almighty has H3359
Zec 4:13 He replied, "*Do you* not **k** what these are?" H3359
Zec 6:15 and *you will* **k** that the LORD Almighty has H3359
Mal 2: 4 And *you will* **k** that I have sent you this H3359
Mt 6: 3 *do* not *let* your left hand **k** what your right *G1182*
Mt 7:11 **k how** to give good gifts to your children *G3857*
Mt 9: 6 But I want *you to* **k** that the Son of Man *G3857*
Mt 15:12 "*Do you* **k** that the Pharisees were *G3857*
Mt 16: 3 *You* **k how** to interpret the appearance of *G1182*
Mt 20:22 "*You* don't **k** what you are asking," Jesus *G3857*
Mt 20:25 "*You* **k** that the rulers of the Gentiles lord *G3857*
Mt 21:27 "*We* don't **k**." Then he said, *G3857*
Mt 22:16 "*we* **k** that you are a man of integrity and *G3857*
Mt 22:29 are in error *because you do* not **k** the *G3857*
Mt 24:32 come out, *you* **k** that summer is near. *G1182*
Mt 24:33 see all these things, *you* **k** that it is near *G1182*
Mt 24:42 because *you do* not **k** on what day your *G3857*
Mt 25:12 he replied, 'Truly I tell you, *I* don't **k** you. *G3857*
Mt 25:13 because *you do* not **k** the day or the hour. *G3857*
Mt 26: 2 "*As you* **k**, the Passover is two days away *G3857*
Mt 26:70 "*I* don't **k** what you're talking about," *G3857*
Mt 26:72 with an oath: "*I* don't **k** the man!" *G3857*
Mt 26:74 he swore to them, "*I* don't **k** the man!" *G3857*
Mt 27:65 make the tomb as secure as *you* **k how**." *G3857*
Mt 28: 5 for *I* **k** that you are looking for Jesus *G3857*
Mk 1:24 come to destroy us? *I* **k** who you are—the *G3857*
Mk 2:10 But I want *you to* **k** that the Son of Man *G3857*
Mk 4:27 grows, though he *does* not **k how**. *G3857*
Mk 5:43 strict orders not to *let* anyone **k** about this, *G1182*
Mk 7:24 a house and did not want anyone *to* **k** it; *G1182*
Mk 9: 6 *He did* not **k** what to say, they were so *G3857*
Mk 9:30 not want anyone to **k** where they were, *G1182*
Mk 10:19 *You* **k** the commandments: 'You shall not *G3857*
Mk 10:38 "*You* don't **k** what you are asking," Jesus *G3857*
Mk 10:42 "*You* **k** that those who are regarded as *G3857*
Mk 11:33 answered Jesus, "*We* don't **k**." Jesus said, *G3857*
Mk 12:14 *we* **k** that you are a man of integrity. *G3857*
Mk 12:24 error because *you do* not **k** the Scriptures *G3857*
Mk 13:28 come out, *you* **k** that summer is near. *G1182*
Mk 13:29 things happening, *you* **k** that it is near *G1182*
Mk 13:33 *You do* not **k** when that time will come. *G3857*
Mk 13:35 watch because *you do* not **k** when the *G3857*
Mk 14:40 *They did* not **k** what to say to him *G3857*
Mk 14:68 "*I* don't **k** or understand what you're *G3857*
Mk 14:71 "*I* don't **k** this man you're talking about." *G3857*
Lk 1: 4 so that *you may* **k** the certainty of the *G2105*
Lk 2:49 "Didn't *you* **k** I had to be in my Father's *G3857*
Lk 4:34 come to destroy us? *I* **k** who you are—the *G3857*
Lk 5:24 But I want you *to* **k** that the Son of Man *G3857*
Lk 7:39 *he* would **k** who is touching him and what *G1182*
Lk 8:46 I **k** *that* power has gone out from me." *G1182*
Lk 9:33 (*He did* not **k** what he was saying.) *G3857*
Lk 11:13 **k how** to give good gifts to your children *G3857*
Lk 12:48 But the *one who does* not **k** and does *G1182*
Lk 12:56 *You* **k how** to interpret the appearance of *G3857*
Lk 12:56 How is it that *you* don't **k how** to interpret *G3857*
Lk 13:25 '*I* don't **k** you or where you come from. *G3857*
Lk 13:27 '*I* don't **k** you or where you come from. *G3857*
Lk 16: 4 *I* **k** what I'll do so that, when I lose my job *G1182*
Lk 18:20 *You* **k** the commandments: 'You shall not *G3857*
Lk 18:34 and *they did* not **k** what he was talking *G1182*
Lk 20: 7 answered, "*We* don't **k** where it was from." *G3857*
Lk 20:21 *we* **k** that you speak and teach what is *G3857*
Lk 21:20 *you will* **k** that its desolation is near. *G1182*
Lk 21:30 yourselves and **k** that summer is near. *G1182*
Lk 21:31 *you* **k** that the kingdom of God is near. *G1182*
Lk 22:34 you will deny three times *that you* **k** me." *G3857*
Lk 22:57 "Woman, *I* don't **k** him," he said. *G3857*
Lk 22:60 *I* don't **k** what you're talking about!" *G3857*
Lk 23:34 for *they do* not **k** what they are doing." *G3857*
Lk 24:18 Jerusalem *who does* not **k** the things that *G1182*
Jn 1:26 "but among you stands one you *do* not **k**. *G3857*
Jn 1:31 *I* myself *did* not **k** him, but the reason I *G3857*
Jn 1:33 And *I* myself *did* not **k** him, but the one *G3857*
Jn 1:48 "How *do you* **k** me?" Nathanael asked *G1182*
Jn 3: 2 *we* **k** that you are a teacher who has come *G3857*
Jn 3:11 we speak of what *we* **k**, and we testify to *G3857*
Jn 4:22 You Samaritans worship what *you do* not **k**; *G3857*
Jn 4:22 we worship what *we do* **k**, for salvation is *G3857*
Jn 4:25 The woman said, "*I* **k** that Messiah" *G3857*
Jn 4:32 have food to eat that you **k** nothing **about**." *G3857*
Jn 4:42 and *we* **k** that this man really is the Savior *G3857*
Jn 5:32 and *I* **k** that his testimony about me is true *G3857*
Jn 5:42 but *I* **k** you. I know that you do not have *G1182*
Jn 5:42 I **k** that you do not have the love of God in NDT
Jn 6:42 of Joseph, whose father and mother we **k**? *G3857*
Jn 6:69 come to believe and *to* **k** that you are the *G1182*
Jn 7:27 But *we* **k** where this man is from; when the *G3857*
Jn 7:27 no one *will* **k** where he is from. *G1182*
Jn 7:28 *you* **k** me, and you know where I am *G3857*
Jn 7:28 you know me, and *you* **k** where I am from. *G3857*
Jn 7:28 he who sent me is true. You *do* not **k** him, *G3857*
Jn 7:29 I **k** him because I am from him and he *G3857*
Jn 8:14 for *I* **k** where I came from and where I am *G3857*
Jn 8:19 "*You do* not **k** me or my Father," Jesus *G3857*
Jn 8:19 you knew me, *you* would **k** my Father also."*G3857*
Jn 8:28 then *you will* **k** that I am he and that I do *G1182*
Jn 8:32 Then *you will* **k** the truth, and the truth will *G1182*
Jn 8:37 *I* **k** that you are Abraham's descendants *G3857*
Jn 8:52 "Now *we* **k** that you are demon-possessed *G1182*
Jn 8:55 Though *you do* not **k** him, I know him. *G1182*
Jn 8:55 do not know him, I **k** him. If I said I did *G3857*
Jn 8:55 but *I do* **k** him and obey his word. *G3857*
Jn 9:12 they asked him. "*I* don't **k**," he said. *G3857*
Jn 9:20 "*We* **k** he is our son," the parents *G3857*
Jn 9:20 answered, "and we **k** he was born blind. NDT
Jn 9:21 or who opened his eyes, we don't **k**. *G3857*
Jn 9:24 "We **k** this man is a sinner." *G3857*
Jn 9:25 "Whether he is a sinner or not, *I* don't **k**. *G3857*
Jn 9:25 One thing *I do* **k**. I was blind but *G3857*
Jn 9:29 We **k** that God spoke to Moses, but as *G3857*
Jn 9:29 *we* don't *even* **k** where he comes from." *G3857*
Jn 9:30 You don't **k** where he comes from, yet he *G3857*
Jn 9:31 *We* **k** that God does not listen to sinners *G3857*
Jn 10: 4 follow him because *they* **k** his voice. *G3857*
Jn 10:14 *I* **k** my sheep and my sheep know me— *G1182*
Jn 10:14 I know my sheep and my sheep **k** me— *G1182*
Jn 10:15 the Father knows me and I **k** the Father— *G1182*
Jn 10:27 to my voice; I **k** them, and they follow *G1182*
Jn 10:38 that *you may* **k** and understand that the *G1182*
Jn 11:22 But *I* **k** that even now God will give you *G3857*
Jn 11:24 "*I* **k** he will rise again in the resurrection *G3857*
Jn 11:49 that year, spoke up, "You **k** nothing at all! *G3857*
Jn 12:35 in the dark *does* not **k** where they are *G3857*
Jn 12:50 *I* **k** that his command leads to eternal life *G3857*
Jn 13:17 *Now* that *you* **k** these things, you will be *G3857*
Jn 13:18 to all of you; *I* **k** those I have chosen. *G3857*
Jn 13:22 **at a loss to k** which of them he meant. *G679*
Jn 13:35 By this everyone *will* **k** that you are my *G1182*
Jn 14: 4 *You* **k** the way to the place where I am *G3857*
Jn 14: 5 *we* don't **k** where you are going, so *G3857*
Jn 14: 5 you are going, so how can we **k** the way?" *G3857*
Jn 14: 7 If *you really* **k** me, you will know my Father *G1182*
Jn 14: 7 know me, *you will* **k** my Father as well. *G1182*
Jn 14: 7 now on, *you do* **k** him and have seen him." *G1182*
Jn 14: 9 "Don't *you* **k** me, Philip, even after I have *G1182*
Jn 14:17 But you **k** him, for he lives with you and *G1182*
Jn 15:15 because a servant *does* not **k** his master's *G3857*
Jn 15:21 for *they do* not **k** the one who sent me. *G3857*
Jn 16:30 Now we can see that *you* **k** all things and *G3857*
Jn 17: 3 that *they* **k** you, the only true God, and *G1182*
Jn 17: 7 Now *they* **k** that everything you have given *G1182*
Jn 17:23 Then the world *will* **k** that you sent me *G1182*
Jn 17:25 though the world *does* not **k** you, I know *G1182*
Jn 17:25 does not know you, I **k** you, and they know *G1182*
Jn 17:25 and *they* **k** that you have sent me. *G1182*
Jn 18:21 Surely they **k** what I said." *G3857*
Jn 19: 4 him out to you to *let you* **k** that I find no *G1182*
Jn 20: 2 and *we* don't **k** where they have put him!" *G3857*
Jn 20:13 "and *I* don't **k** where they have put him." *G3857*
Jn 21:15 Lord," he said, "you **k** that I love you." *G3857*
Jn 21:16 Lord, you **k** that I love you. *G3857*
Jn 21:17 you **k** all things; you know that I *G3857*
Jn 21:17 you know all things; you **k** that I love you." *G1182*
Jn 21:24 *We* **k** that his testimony is true. *G3857*
Ac 1: 7 "It is not for you *to* **k** the times or dates *G1182*
Ac 1:24 they prayed, "Lord, you **k** everyone's **heart**.*G2841*
Ac 2:22 you through him, as *you* yourselves **k**. *G3857*
Ac 3:16 whom you see and **k** was made strong. *G3857*
Ac 3:17 Israelites, *I* **k** that you acted in ignorance *G3857*
Ac 4:10 then **k** *this*, you and all the people *G1196+1639*
Ac 7:40 we don't **k** what has happened to him! *G3857*
Ac 10:36 You **k** the message God sent to the people NDT
Ac 10:37 You **k** what has happened throughout the *G3857*
Ac 12:11 "Now *I* **k** without a doubt that the Lord has *G3857*
Ac 13:38 I *want* you *to* **k** that through Jesus *G1196+1639*
Ac 15: 7 you **k** that some time ago God made a *G2179*
Ac 17:19 "May we **k** what this new teaching is that *G1182*
Ac 17:20 we would like *to* **k** what they mean." *G1182*
Ac 19:15 "Jesus *I* **k**, and Paul I know *G1182*
Ac 19:15 and Paul *I* **k about**, but who are *G2179*
Ac 19:25 "*You* **k**, my friends, that we receive a good *G2179*
Ac 19:32 of the people *did* not even **k** why they *G3857*
Ac 19:35 all the world **k** *that* the city of Ephesus *G1182*
Ac 20:18 "You **k** how I lived the whole time I was *G2179*
Ac 20:20 You **k** that I have not hesitated to preach NDT
Ac 20:23 I only **k** that in every city the Holy Spirit NDT
Ac 20:25 "Now I **k** that none of you among whom I *G3857*
Ac 20:29 I **k** that after I leave, savage wolves will *G3857*
Ac 20:34 *You* yourselves **k** that these hands of mine *G1182*
Ac 21:24 Then everyone *will* **k** there is no truth in *G1182*
Ac 22:14 has chosen you *to* **k** his will and to see *G1182*
Ac 22:19 'these people **k** that I went from one *G2179*
Ac 23:28 I wanted *to* **k** why they were accusing him *G2105*
Ac 24:10 "*I* **k** *that* for a number of years you have *G2179*
Ac 25:10 to the Jews, as *you* yourself **k** very well. *G2105*
Ac 26: 4 Jewish people all **k** the way I have lived *G3857*
Ac 26:27 do you believe the prophets? *I* **k** you do." *G3857*
Ac 28:22 we **k** that people everywhere *G1196+1639*
Ac 28:28 "Therefore *I want* you *to* **k** that *G1196+1639*
Ro 1:32 *Although* they **k** God's righteous decree *G2105*
Ro 2: 2 Now *we* **k** that God's judgment against *G3857*
Ro 2:18 if *you* **k** his will and approve of what is *G1182*
Ro 3:17 the way of peace *they do* not **k**. *G1182*
Ro 3:19 Now *we* **k** that whatever the law says, it *G3857*
Ro 5: 3 *because we* **k** that suffering produces *G3857*
Ro 6: 3 Or **don't** *you* **k** that all of us who were *G51*
Ro 6: 6 *For we* **k** that our old self was crucified with *G1182*
Ro 6: 9 *For we* **k** that since Christ was raised from *G3857*
Ro 6:16 Don't *you* **k** that when you offer yourselves *G3857*
Ro 7: 1 *Do you* **not k**, brothers and sisters—for I am *G51*
Ro 7: 1 I am speaking *to those who* **k** the law *G1182*
Ro 7:14 *We* **k** that the law is spiritual; but I am *G3857*
Ro 7:18 For *I* **k** that good itself does not dwell in *G3857*
Ro 8:22 *We* **k** that the whole creation has been *G3857*
Ro 8:26 *We do* not **k** what we ought to pray for *G3857*
Ro 8:28 And *we* **k** that in all things God works *G3857*
Ro 10: 3 Since *they did* **not k** the righteousness of God *G51*
Ro 11: 2 Don't *you* **k** what Scripture says in the *G3857*

Ro 14:16 do not let what you **k** is good be spoken of NDT
Ro 15:29 *I* **k** that when I come to you, I will come in G3857
1Co 1:21 world through its wisdom *did* not **k** him, G1182
1Co 2: 2 For I resolved *to* **k** nothing while I was with G3857
1Co 3:16 Don't *you* **k** that you yourselves are God's G3857
1Co 5: 6 Don't *you* **k** that a little yeast leavens the G3857
1Co 6: 2 Or *do you* not **k** that the Lord's people will G3857
1Co 6: 3 *Do you* not **k** that we will judge angels G3857
1Co 6: 9 Or *do you* not **k** that wrongdoers will not G3857
1Co 6:15 *Do you* not **k** that your bodies are G3857
1Co 6:16 *Do you* not **k** that he who unites himself G3857
1Co 6:19 *Do you* not **k** that your bodies are temples G3857
1Co 7:16 How *do you* **k**, wife, whether you will save G3857
1Co 7:16 how *do you* **k**, husband, whether you G3857
1Co 8: 1 *We* **k** that "We all possess knowledge." G3857
1Co 8: 2 Those who think *they* **k** something do not G1182
1Co 8: 2 something *do* not yet **k** as they ought G1182
1Co 8: 2 do not yet know as they ought to **k**. G1182
1Co 8: 4 *We* **k** that "An idol is nothing at all in the G3857
1Co 9:13 Don't *you* **k** that those who serve in the G3857
1Co 9:24 *Do you* not **k** that in a race all the runners G3857
1Co 12: 2 *You* **k** that when you were pagans G3857
1Co 12: 3 Therefore *I want* you *to* **k** that no one who G1192
1Co 13: 9 For *we* **k** in part and we prophesy in part, G1182
1Co 13:12 Now *I* **k** in part; then I shall know fully G1182
1Co 13:12 then *I shall* **k fully**, even as I am G2105
1Co 14: 7 how *will anyone* **k** what tune is being G1182
1Co 14: 9 how *will anyone* **k** what you are saying? G1182
1Co 14:16 since *they do* not **k** what you are saying? G3857
1Co 15:58 *because you* **k** that your labor in the Lord G3857
1Co 16:15 *You* **k** that the household of Stephanas G3857
2Co 1: 7 *because we* **k** that just as you share in our G3857
2Co 2: 4 grieve you but to *let you* **k** the depth of my G1182
2Co 4:14 *because we* **k** that the one who raised the G3857
2Co 5: 1 For *we* **k** that if the earthly tent we live in G3857
2Co 5: 6 always confident and **k** that as long as we G3857
2Co 5:11 *Since*, then, *we* **k** what it is to fear the G3857
2Co 8: 1 *we want* you *to* **k** about the grace that G1192
2Co 8: 9 For *you* **k** the grace of our Lord Jesus Christ G1182
2Co 9: 2 For *I* **k** your eagerness to help, and I have G3857
2Co 12: 2 *I* **k** a man in Christ who fourteen years ago G3857
2Co 12: 2 in the body or out of the body *I do* not **k**— G3857
2Co 12: 3 And *I* **k** *that* this man—whether in the G3857
2Co 12: 3 the body or apart from the body *I do* not **k**, G3857
Gal 1:11 *I want* you *to* **k**, brothers and sisters, that G1192
Gal 2:16 **k** that a person is not justified by the works G3857
Gal 4: 8 Formerly, *when you did* not **k** God, you G3857
Gal 4: 9 But now *that you* **k** God—or rather are G1182
Gal 4:13 As *you* **k**, it was because of an illness that G3857
Eph 1:17 revelation, so that you may **k** him **better**. G2106
Eph 1:18 in order that you *may* **k** the hope to which G3857
Eph 3:19 and *to* **k** this love that surpasses G1182
Eph 6: 8 *because you* **k** that the Lord will reward G3857
Eph 6: 9 *since you* **k** that he who is both their G3857
Eph 6:21 so that you also *may* **k** how I am and what G3857
Eph 6:22 purpose, that *you may* **k** how we are, and G1182
Php 1:12 Now I want you *to* **k**, brothers and sisters G1182
Php 1:19 for *I* **k** that through your prayers and God's G3857
Php 1:22 Yet what shall I choose? *I do* not **k**! G1192
Php 1:25 Convinced of this, *I* **k** that I will remain G3857
Php 1:27 I will **k** that you stand firm in the one Spirit NDT
Php 2:22 But *you* **k** that Timothy has proved himself G1182
Php 3:10 I want *to* **k** Christ—yes, to know the power G1182
Php 3:10 to **k** the power of his resurrection and NDT
Php 4:12 *I* **k** what it is to be in need, and I know G3857
Php 4:12 in need, and *I* **k** what it is to have plenty. G3857
Php 4:15 as you Philippians **k**, in the early days of G3857
Col 2: 1 I want you *to* **k** how hard I am contending G3857
Col 2: 2 order that they may **k** the mystery of God, G2106
Col 3:24 *since you* **k** that you will receive an G3857
Col 4: 1 *because you* **k** that you also have a G3857
Col 4: 6 *so that* you *may* **k** how to answer everyone G3857
Col 4: 8 express purpose that *you may* **k** about our G1182
1Th 1: 4 *For we* **k**, brothers and sisters loved by G3857
1Th 1: 5 *You* **k** how we lived among you for your G3857
1Th 2: 1 You **k**, brothers and sisters, that our visit to G3857
1Th 2: 2 in Philippi, as *you* **k**, but with the help of G3857
1Th 2: 5 *You* **k** we never used flattery, nor did we G3857
1Th 2:11 For *you* **k** that we dealt with each of you as G3857
1Th 3: 3 For you **k** *quite well* that we are destined G3857
1Th 3: 4 And it turned out that way, as *you well* **k**. G3857
1Th 4: 2 For *you* **k** what instructions we gave you by G3857
1Th 4: 5 lust like the pagans, who *do* not **k** God; G3857
1Th 5: 2 you **k** very well that the day of the Lord G3857
2Th 1: 8 punish those *who do* not **k** God and do G3857
2Th 2: 6 And now *you* **k** what is holding him back G3857
2Th 3: 7 For *you* yourselves **k** how you ought to G3857
1Ti 1: 7 but *they do* not **k** what they are talking G3783
1Ti 1: 8 *We* **k** that the law is good if one uses it G3857
1Ti 1: 9 *We* also **k** that the law is made not for the G3857
1Ti 3: 5 If anyone *does* not **k how** to manage his G3857
1Ti 3:15 *you will* **k** how people ought to conduct G3857
1Ti 4: 3 by those who believe and *who* **k** the truth. G2105
2Ti 1:12 because *I* **k** whom I have believed G3857
2Ti 1:15 *You* **k** that everyone in the province of G3857
2Ti 1:18 You **k** very well in how many ways he G1182
2Ti 2:23 *because you* **k** they produce quarrels. G3857
2Ti 3:10 however, **k all about** my teaching, my way G4158
2Ti 3:14 *because you* **k** those from whom you G3857
Titus 1:16 They claim *to* **k** God, but by their actions G3857
Heb 8:11 say to one another, '**K** the Lord,' because G1182
Heb 8:11 because *they will* all **k** me, from the G3857
Heb 10:30 For *we* **k** him who said, "It is mine to G3857
Heb 11: 8 *even though he did* not **k** where he was G2179
Heb 12:17 Afterward, *as you* **k**, when he wanted to G3857
Heb 13:23 I *want you to* **k** that our brother Timothy G1182
Jas 1: 3 *because you* **k** that the testing of your faith G1182
Jas 3: 1 *because you* **k** that we who teach will be G3857
Jas 4: 4 don't *you* **k** that friendship with the world G3857
Jas 4:14 you *do* not *even* **k** what will happen G2179
Jas 5:11 **As you k**, we count as blessed those who G2627
1Pe 1:18 *For you* **k** that it was not with perishable G3857
1Pe 5: 9 *because you* **k** *that* the family of believers G3857
2Pe 1:12 even though *you* **k** them and are firmly G3857
2Pe 1:14 *because I* **k** that I will soon put it aside, as G3857
1Jn 2: 3 *We* **k** that we have come to know him if G1182
1Jn 2: 3 know that *we have come to* **k** him if we G1182
1Jn 2: 4 Whoever says, "*I* **k** him," but does not do G1182
1Jn 2: 5 This is how *we* **k** we are in him: G1182
1Jn 2:11 *They do* not **k** where they are going G3857
1Jn 2:13 because *you* **k** him who is from the G1182
1Jn 2:14 dear children, because *you* **k** the Father. G1182
1Jn 2:14 because *you* **k** him who is from the G1182
1Jn 2:18 This is how *we* **k** it is the last hour. G1182
1Jn 2:20 the Holy One, and all of *you* **k** the truth. G3857
1Jn 2:21 to you because *you do* not **k** the truth, G3857
1Jn 2:21 because *you do* **k** it and because no G3857
1Jn 2:29 If *you* **k** that he is righteous, you know that G3857
1Jn 2:29 *you* **k** that everyone who does what is G1182
1Jn 3: 1 reason the world *does* not **k** us is that it G1182
1Jn 3: 1 does not know us is that *it did* not **k** him. G1182
1Jn 3: 2 But *we* **k** that when Christ appears, we G3857
1Jn 3: 5 But *you* **k** that he appeared so that he G3857
1Jn 3:10 This is how we **k** who the children of God G5745
1Jn 3:14 We **k** that we have passed from death to G3857
1Jn 3:15 and *you* **k** that no murderer has eternal G3857
1Jn 3:16 This is how *we* **k** what love is: Jesus Christ G1182
1Jn 3:19 This is how *we* **k** that we belong to the G1182
1Jn 3:20 we **k** that God is greater than our hearts NDT
1Jn 3:24 And this is how *we* **k** that he lives in us G1182
1Jn 3:24 We **k** it by the Spirit he gave us. NDT
1Jn 4: 8 Whoever does not love *does* not **k** God G1182
1Jn 4:13 This is how *we* **k** that we live in him and G1182
1Jn 4:16 And so we **k** and rely on the love God has G1182
1Jn 5: 2 This is how *we* **k** that we love the children G1182
1Jn 5:13 of God so that *you may* **k** that you have G3857
1Jn 5:15 And if *we* **k** that he hears us—whatever we G3857
1Jn 5:15 *we* **k** that we have what we asked of him. G3857
1Jn 5:18 *We* **k** that anyone born of God does not G3857
1Jn 5:19 *We* **k** that we are children of God, and that G3857
1Jn 5:20 *We* **k** also that the Son of God has come G3857
1Jn 5:20 so that *we may* **k** him who is true. G1182
2Jn 1 not I only, but also all who **k** the truth— G1182
3Jn 12 and *you* **k** that our testimony is true. G3857
Jude 5 *Though* you *already* **k** all this, I want to G3857
Rev 2: 2 *I* **k** your deeds, your hard work and your G3857
Rev 2: 2 I **k** that you cannot tolerate wicked people NDT
Rev 2: 9 *I* **k** your afflictions and your poverty—yet G3857
Rev 2: 9 I **k** about the slander of those who say they NDT
Rev 2:13 *I* **k** where you live—where Satan has his G3857
Rev 2:19 *I* **k** your deeds, your love and faith, your G3857
Rev 2:23 all the churches *will* **k** that I am he who G1182
Rev 3: 1 *I* **k** your deeds; you have a reputation of G3857
Rev 3: 3 and *you will* not **k** at what time I will G1182
Rev 3: 8 *I* **k** your deeds. See, I have placed before G3857
Rev 3: 8 I **k** that you have little strength, yet you have NDT
Rev 3:15 *I* **k** your deeds, that you are neither cold G3857
Rev 7:14 answered, "Sir, you **k**." And he said G3857

KNOWING (28) [KNOW]

Ge 3: 5 you will be like God, **k** good and evil." H3359
Ge 3:22 become like one of us, **k** good and evil. H3359
2Sa 15:11 innocently, **k** nothing **about** the matter. H3359
1Ki 2:32 my father David **k** it he attacked two men H3359
Job 9: 5 mountains without *their* **k** it and overturns H3359
Job 31:21 fatherless, **k** that I had influence in court, H8011
Ps 39: 6 up wealth without **k** whose it will finally H3359
Pr 7:23 a snare, little **k** it will cost him his life. H3359
Ecc 6: 8 do the poor gain *by* **k how** to conduct H3359
Mt 9: 4 **K** their thoughts, Jesus said, "Why do you G3857
Mt 22:18 But Jesus, **k** their evil intent, said, "You G1182
Mk 5:33 the woman, **k** what had happened to her G3857
Mk 6:20 **k** him to be a righteous and holy man. G3857
Mk 15:10 **k** it was out of self-interest that the chief G1182
Lk 8:53 laughed at him, **k** that she was dead. G3857
Lk 9:47 **k** their thoughts, took a little child G3857
Lk 11:44 which people walk over without **k** it." G3857
Jn 6:15 **k** that they intended to come and make G1182
Jn 18: 4 **k** all that was going to happen to him G3857
Jn 19:28 **k** that everything had now been finished G3857
Ac 5: 7 wife came in, not **k** what had happened. G3857
Ac 20:22 not **k** what will happen to me there. G3857
Ac 23: 6 **k** that some of them were Sadducees and G1182
Php 1:16 **k** that I am put here for the defense of the G3857
Php 3: 8 surpassing worth *of* **k** Christ Jesus my Lord G1194
Phm 21 **k** that you will do even more than I ask. G3857
Heb 13: 2 shown hospitality to angels **without k it**. G3291
2Pe 2:20 of the world by **k** our Lord and Savior G2106

KNOWLEDGE (132) [KNOW]

Ge 2: 9 life and the tree of the **k** *of* good and evil. H1981
Ge 2:17 from the tree of the **k** *of* good and evil, H1981
Ex 31: 3 with **k** and with all kinds of skills H1981
Ex 35:31 with **k** and with all kinds of skills H1981
Nu 24:16 *who* **has k** *from* the Most High H3359+1981
1Ki 7:14 with **k** to do all kinds of H1981
2Ch 1:10 Give me wisdom and **k**, that I may lead H4529
2Ch 1:11 for wisdom and **k** to govern my people H4529
2Ch 1:12 therefore wisdom and **k** will be given you H4529
Job 21:22 "Can anyone teach **k** to God, since he H1981
Job 34:35 'Job speaks without **k**; his words lack H1981
Job 35:16 empty talk; without **k** he multiplies words." H1981
Job 36: 3 I get my **k** from afar; I will ascribe justice H1976
Job 36: 4 *one who has* perfect **k** is with you. H1978
Job 36:12 will perish by the sword and die without **k**. H1981
Job 37:16 those wonders of *him who* has perfect **k**? H1976
Job 38: 2 obscures my plans with words without **k**? H1981
Job 42: 3 is this that obscures my plans without **k**? H1981
Ps 19: 2 speech; night after night they reveal **k**. H1981
Ps 35:15 gathered against me without *my* **k**. H3359
Ps 94:10 Does he who teaches mankind lack **k**? H1981
Ps 119:66 Teach me **k** and good judgment, for I trust H1981
Ps 139: 6 *Such* **k** is too wonderful for me, too lofty H1981
Pr 1: 4 are simple, **k** and discretion to the young H1981
Pr 1: 7 The fear of the LORD is the beginning of **k** H1981
Pr 1:22 delight in mockery and fools hate **k**? H1981
Pr 1:29 since they hated **k** and did not choose to H1981
Pr 2: 5 the fear of the LORD and find the **k** *of* God. H1981
Pr 2: 6 his mouth come **k** and understanding. H1981
Pr 2:10 and **k** will be pleasant to your soul. H1981
Pr 3:20 by his **k** the watery depths were divided H1981
Pr 5: 2 discretion and your lips may preserve **k**. H1981
Pr 8: 9 are upright to those who have found **k**. H1981
Pr 8:10 of silver, **k** rather than choice gold, H1981
Pr 8:12 with prudence; I possess **k** and discretion. H1981
Pr 9:10 and **k** *of* the Holy One is understanding. H1981
Pr 10:14 The wise store up **k**, but the mouth of a H1981
Pr 11: 9 through **k** the righteous escape. H1981
Pr 12: 1 Whoever loves discipline loves **k**, but H1981
Pr 12:23 The prudent keep their **k** to themselves H1981
Pr 13:16 All who are prudent act with **k**, but fools H1981
Pr 14: 6 **k** comes easily to the discerning. H1981
Pr 14: 7 for you will not find **k** on their lips. H1981
Pr 14:18 but the prudent are crowned with **k**. H1981
Pr 15: 2 The tongue of the wise adorns **k**, but the H1981
Pr 15: 7 The lips of the wise spread **k**, but the H1981
Pr 15:14 The discerning heart seeks **k**, but the H1981
Pr 17:27 The *one who* **has k** uses words with H3359+1981
Pr 18:15 The heart of the discerning acquires **k**, for H1981
Pr 19: 2 Desire without **k** is not good—how much H1981
Pr 19:25 the discerning, and they will gain **k**. H1981
Pr 19:27 you will stray from the words of **k**. H1981
Pr 20:15 lips that speak **k** are a rare jewel. H1981
Pr 21:11 by paying attention to the wise they get **k**. H1981
Pr 22:12 The eyes of the LORD keep watch over **k** H1981
Pr 22:20 sayings for you, sayings of counsel and **k**, H1981
Pr 23:12 to instruction and your ears to words of **k**. H1981
Pr 24: 4 through **k** its rooms are filled with rare H1981
Pr 24: 5 those who have **k** muster their H1981
Pr 28: 2 with discernment and **k** maintains order. H3359
Pr 30: 3 nor *have I* **attained to** the **k** *of* the H3359+1981
Ecc 1:16 have experienced much of wisdom and **k**." H1981
Ecc 1:18 much sorrow; the more **k**, the more grief. H1981
Ecc 2:21 labor with wisdom, **k** and skill, and then H1981
Ecc 2:26 God gives wisdom, **k** and happiness, but H1981
Ecc 7:12 is a shelter, but the advantage of **k** is this: H1981
Ecc 9:10 working nor planning nor **k** nor wisdom. H1981
Ecc 12: 9 he also imparted **k** *to* the people. H1981
Isa 11: 2 the Spirit of the **k** and fear of the LORD— H1981
Isa 11: 9 be filled with the **k** *of* the LORD as the H1978
Isa 33: 6 rich store of salvation and wisdom and **k**; H1981
Isa 40:14 Who was it that taught him **k**, or showed H1981
Isa 44:19 no one has the **k** or understanding to say H1981
Isa 47:10 Your wisdom and **k** mislead you when H1981
Isa 53:11 by his **k** my righteous servant will justify H1981
Isa 56:10 they all lack **k**; they are all mute H3359
Jer 3:15 will lead you with **k** and understanding. H1978
Jer 10:14 Everyone is senseless and without **k**; every H1981
Jer 51:17 "Everyone is senseless and without **k** H1981
Da 1:17 men God gave **k** and understanding H4529
Da 2:21 to the wise and **k** to the discerning. A10430
Da 5:12 a keen mind and **k** and understanding, A10430
Da 12: 4 Many will go here and there to increase **k**." H1981
Hos 4: 6 my people are destroyed from lack of **k** H1981
Hos 4: 6 "Because you have rejected **k**, I also reject H1981
Hab 2:14 be filled with the **k** *of* the glory of the LORD H3359
Mal 2: 7 the lips of a priest ought to preserve **k**, H1981
Mt 13:11 "Because *the* **k** *of* the secrets of the G1182
Lk 1:77 give his people the **k** of salvation through G1194
Lk 8:10 "The **k** of the secrets of the kingdom of G1182
Lk 11:52 because you have taken away the key *to* **k**. G1194
Ac 5: 2 *With* his wife's **full k** he kept back part of G5323
Ac 18:24 with a **thorough k** of the Scriptures. G1543
Ro 1:28 think it worthwhile to retain the **k** of God, G2106
Ro 2:20 the law the embodiment *of* **k** and truth— G1194
Ro 10: 2 God, but their zeal is not based on **k**. G2106
Ro 11:33 of the riches of the wisdom and **k** of God! G1194
Ro 15:14 filled with **k** and competent to instruct one G1194
1Co 1: 5 with all kinds of speech and with all **k**— G1194
1Co 8: 1 We know that "We all possess **k**." But G1194
1Co 8: 1 But **k** puffs up while love builds up G1194
1Co 8: 7 But not everyone possesses this **k**. G1194
1Co 8:10 sees you, with *all* your **k**, eating in an G1194
1Co 8:11 whom Christ died, is destroyed by your **k**. G1194
1Co 12: 8 another a message *of* **k** by means of the G1194
1Co 13: 2 can fathom all mysteries and all **k**, G1194

1Co 13: 8 where there is **k**, it will pass away. *G1194*
1Co 14: 6 some revelation or **k** or prophecy or word *G1194*
2Co 2:14 spread the aroma *of* the **k** of him *G1194*
2Co 4: 6 to give us the light *of* the **k** of God's glory *G1194*
2Co 8: 7 in speech, *in* **k**, in complete earnestness *G1194*
2Co 10: 5 that sets itself up against the **k** of God, *G1194*
2Co 11: 6 untrained as a speaker, but I do *have* **k**. *G1194*
Eph 3:19 to know this love that surpasses **k** *G1194*
Eph 4:13 in the faith and *in* the **k** of the Son of God *G2106*
Php 1: 9 more and more in **k** and depth of insight, *G2106*
Col 1: 9 to fill you with the **k** of his will through all *G2106*
Col 1:10 every good work, growing *in* the **k** of God, *G2106*
Col 2: 3 hidden all the treasures of wisdom and **k**. *G1194*
Col 3:10 is being renewed in **k** in the image of its *G2106*
1Ti 2: 4 be saved and to come to a **k** of the truth. *G2106*
1Ti 6:20 opposing ideas of what is falsely called **k**, *G1194*
2Ti 2:25 leading them to a **k** of the truth, *G2106*
2Ti 3: 7 never able to come to a **k** of the truth. *G2106*
Titus 1: 1 God's elect and their **k** of the truth that *G2106*
Heb 10:26 after we have received the **k** of the truth, *G2106*
2Pe 1: 2 through the **k** of God and of Jesus *G2106*
2Pe 1: 3 life through our **k** of him who called us *G2106*
2Pe 1: 5 your faith goodness; and to goodness, **k**; *G1194*
2Pe 1: 6 to **k**, self-control; and to self-control *G1194*
2Pe 1: 8 unproductive in your **k** of our Lord Jesus *G2106*
2Pe 3:18 grow in the grace and **k** of our Lord and *G1194*

KNOWN (143) [KNOW]

Ge 41:39 "Since God *has* **made** all this **k** *to* you H3359
Ge 45: 1 Joseph when he **made himself k** to his H3359
Ex 2:14 "What I did *must have* **become k**." H3359
Ex 6: 3 LORD *I did* not **make myself fully k** to them H3359
Ex 21:36 if *it* **was k** that the bull had the habit of H3359
Lev 4:14 the sin they committed *becomes* **k** H3359
Lev 4:23 the sin he has committed *becomes* **k** H3359
Lev 4:28 the sin they have committed *becomes* **k**, H3359
Nu 11:16 elders who *are* **k** *to you* as leaders and H3359
Dt 3:13 in Bashan *used to* **be k as** a land of the H7924
Dt 8: 3 neither *you* nor your ancestors *had* **k**, H3359
Dt 8:16 something your ancestors *had* never **k**, to H3359
Dt 9:24 against the LORD ever since I *have* **k** you. H3359
Dt 11:28 other gods, which *you have* not **k**. H3359
Dt 13: 2 gods *you have* not **k**) "and let us worship H3359
Dt 13: 6 that neither you nor your ancestors *have* **k**, H3359
Dt 13:13 other gods" (gods *you have* not **k**), H3359
Dt 21: 1 possess, and *it* is not **k** who the killer was, H3359
Dt 25:10 line *shall* **be k** in Israel **as** The H7924+9005
Dt 28:64 neither you nor your ancestors *have* **k**. H3359
Dt 32:17 not God—gods *they had* not **k**, gods that H3359
1Sa 10:11 When all *those who had* formerly **k** him H3359
1Sa 18:23 I'm only a poor man and **little k**." H7829
1Sa 18:30 and his name *became* **well k**. H3700+4394
2Sa 7:21 great thing and **made** it **k** *to* your servant. H3359
1Ki 18:36 *let it* **be k** today that you are God in Israel H3359
1Ch 16: 8 **make k** among the nations what he has H3359
1Ch 17:19 great thing and **made k** all these great H3359
Ne 8:12 the words that *had been* **made k** to them. H3359
Ne 9:14 *You* **made k** to them your holy Sabbath H3359
Est 1:17 queen's conduct *will* **become k** to all the H3655
Est 2: 7 who was also **k** as Esther, had a NDT
Est 3:14 province and **made k** to the people of H1655
Est 8:13 province and **made k** to the people of H1655
Job 36:33 even the cattle make **k** its approach. NDT
Job 42:11 everyone *who had* **k** him before came H3359
Ps 9:16 The LORD **is k** *by* his acts of justice; the H3359
Ps 16:11 *You* **make k** *to* me the path of life; you H3359
Ps 25:14 he **makes** his covenant **k** *to* them. H3359
Ps 59:13 Then *it will* **be k** to the ends of the earth H3359
Ps 67: 2 so that your ways *may be* **k** on earth, your H3359
Ps 78: 3 things we have heard and **k**, things our H3359
Ps 79:10 **make k** among the nations that you H3359
Ps 88:12 **Are** your wonders **k** in the place of H3359
Ps 89: 1 mouth *I will* **make** your faithfulness **k** H3359
Ps 95:10 go astray, and they *have* not **k** my ways. H3359
Ps 98: 2 The LORD *has* **made** his salvation **k** and H3359
Ps 103: 7 *He* **made k** his ways to Moses, his deeds H3359
Ps 105: 1 **make k** among the nations what he has H3359
Ps 106: 8 name's sake, to **make** his mighty power **k**. H3359
Ps 119:168 statutes, for all my ways are **k to** you. H5584
Pr 1:23 *I will* **make k** to you my teachings. H3359
Pr 14:33 even among fools *she* **lets** *herself* **be k**. H3359
Pr 20:11 Even small children **are k** by their actions H5795
Pr 24: 8 Whoever plots evil *will be* **k as** a schemer. H7924
Ecc 6:10 what humanity is *has* **been k**; no one H3359
Isa 12: 4 **make k** among the nations what he has H3359
Isa 12: 5 *let* this **be k** to all the world. H3359
Isa 19:12 them show you and **make k** what the LORD H3359
Isa 19:21 So the LORD *will* **make himself k** to the H3359
Isa 42:16 lead the blind by ways *they have* not **k**, H3359
Isa 46:10 I **make k** the end from the beginning H5583
Isa 48: 3 announced them and *I* **made** them **k**; H9048
Isa 61: 9 Their descendants *will* **be k** among the H3359
Isa 64: 2 come down to **make** your name **k** to your H3359
Isa 66:14 of the LORD *will* **be made k** *to* his servants, H3359
Jer 7: 9 follow other gods *you have* not **k**, H3359
Jer 9:16 neither they nor their ancestors *have* **k**, H3359
Jer 16:13 neither you nor your ancestors *have* **k**, H3359
Eze 20:11 my decrees and **made k** *to* them my laws, H3359
Eze 32: 9 the nations, among lands *you have* not **k**. H3359
Eze 35:11 them and *I will* **make myself k** among H3359
Eze 38:23 and *I will* **make myself k** in the sight of H3359
Eze 39: 7 " '*I will* **make k** my holy name among my H3359
Eze 43:11 **make k** *to* them the design of the temple H3359
Da 2:23 *you have* **made k** *to* me what we asked A10313
Da 2:23 *you have* **made k** *to* us the dream of the A10313
Hab 3: 2 in our time **make** them **k**; in wrath H3359
Zec 14: 7 a unique day—a day **k** only to the LORD H3359
Mt 10:26 hidden that *will* not *be* **made k**. *G1182*
Mt 12: 7 If *you had* **k** what these words mean, 'I *G1182*
Mt 24:43 owner of the house *had* **k** at what time of *G3857*
Mk 6:14 for Jesus' name had become **well k**. *G5745*
Lk 8:17 concealed that *will* not *be* **k** or brought *G1182*
Lk 12: 2 hidden that *will* not *be* **made k**. *G1182*
Lk 12:39 of the house *had* **k** at what hour the *G3857*
Lk 19:42 "If *you*, even you, *had* only **k** on this day *G1182*
Jn 1:18 with the Father, *has* **made** him **k**. *G2007*
Jn 6:64 For Jesus *had* **k** from the beginning which *G3857*
Jn 11:16 Then Thomas (also **k as** Didymus) said to *G3306*
Jn 15:15 from my Father *I have* **made k** to you. *G1192*
Jn 16: 3 because *they have* not **k** the Father or *G1182*
Jn 16:14 he will receive what *he will* **make k** to you. *G334*
Jn 16:15 from me what *he will* **make k** to you." *G334*
Jn 17:26 *I have* **made** you **k** to them, and will *G1192*
Jn 17:26 and *will continue to* **make** you **k** in order *G1192*
Jn 18:15 this disciple was **k** to the high priest, *G1196*
Jn 18:16 disciple, who was **k** to the high priest *G1196*
Jn 19:13 seat at a place **k as** the Stone Pavement *G3306*
Jn 20:24 Now Thomas (also **k as** Didymus), one of *G3306*
Jn 21: 2 Thomas (also **k as** Didymus), Nathanael *G3306*
Ac 1:23 Barsabbas (also *k* **as** Justus) and Matthias. AIT
Ac 2:28 *You have* **made k** to me the paths of life *G1192*
Ac 6: 3 among you *who are* **k** *to be* full of the *G3455*
Ac 9:42 This became **k** all over Joppa, and many *G1196*
Ac 10: 1 a centurion in what *was* **k as** the Italian *G2813*
Ac 10:18 if Simon who *was* **k as** Peter was staying *G2126*
Ac 15:18 things **k** from long ago. *G1196*
Ac 19:17 When this became **k** to the Jews and *G1196*
Ac 26: 5 *They have* **k** me for a long time and can *G4589*
Ro 1:19 since what may be **k** about God is plain to *G1196*
Ro 3:21 righteousness of God *has been* **made k**, *G5746*
Ro 7: 7 *I would* not *have* **k** what sin was had it not *G1182*
Ro 7: 7 For *I would* not *have* **k** what coveting *G3857*
Ro 9:22 to show his wrath and **make** his power **k**, *G1192*
Ro 9:23 this to **make** the riches of his glory **k** to the *G1192*
Ro 11:34 "Who *has* **k** the mind of the Lord? Or who *G1182*
Ro 15:20 preach the gospel where Christ *was* not **k**, *G3951*
Ro 16:26 now revealed and **made k** through the *G1192*
1Co 2:16 "Who *has* **k** the mind of the Lord so as to *G1182*
1Co 8: 3 But whoever loves God *is* **k** by God. *G1182*
1Co 13:12 I shall know fully, even as *I am* **fully k**. *G2105*
2Co 3: 2 on our hearts, **k** and read by everyone. *G1182*
2Co 6: 9 **k**, yet regarded as unknown; dying, and *G2105*
2Co 11:27 I have **k** hunger and thirst and have often NDT
Gal 4: 9 or rather *are* **k** by God—how is it *G1182*
Eph 1: 9 *he* **made k** to us the mystery of his will *G1192*
Eph 3: 3 the mystery **made k** to me by revelation *G1192*
Eph 3: 5 which *was* not **made k** to people in other *G1192*
Eph 3:10 wisdom of God *should be* **made k** to the *G1192*
Eph 6:19 me *so that* I *will* fearlessly **make k** the *G1192*
Col 1:27 God has chosen *to* **make k** among the *G1192*
1Th 1: 8 faith in God *has become* **k** everywhere. *G2002*
1Ti 5:10 and *is* **well k** for her good deeds, such as *G3455*
2Ti 3:15 how from infancy *you have* **k** the Holy *G3857*
Heb 3:10 and they *have* not **k** my ways. *G1182*
Heb 11:24 refused *to be* **k as** the son of Pharaoh's *G3306*
2Pe 2:21 better for them not *to have* **k** the way of *G2105*
2Pe 2:21 than *to have* **k** it and then to turn their *G2105*
1Jn 3: 2 what we will be *has* not yet *been* **made k**. *G5746*
1Jn 3: 6 to sin has either seen him or **k** him. *G1182*
Rev 1: 1 *He* **made** it **k** by sending his angel to his *G4955*
Rev 2:17 **k** only to the one who receives it. *G3857*

KNOWS (84) [KNOW]

Ge 3: 5 "For God **k** that when you eat from it your H3359
Ge 16: 5 and now that *she* **k** she is pregnant H8011
Ge 33:13 "My lord **k** that the children are tender H3359
Dt 34: 6 to this day no one **k** where his grave is. H3359
Jos 22:22 the LORD! He **k**! And let Israel know! H3359
1Sa 2: 3 the LORD is a God who **k**, and by him H1978
1Sa 16:18 of Bethlehem *who* **k how** to play the lyre. H3359
1Sa 20: 3 "Your father **k very well** that I have H3359+3359
1Sa 22:15 your servant **k** nothing at all about this H3359
1Sa 23:17 Even my father Saul **k** this." H3359
1Sa 25:11 give it to men coming from who **k** where?" H3359
2Sa 12:22 I thought, 'Who **k**? The LORD may be H3359
2Sa 14:20 he **k** everything that happens in the land." H3359
2Sa 14:22 "Today your servant **k** that he has found H3359
2Sa 17:10 all Israel **k** that your father is a fighter H3359
1Ki 1:11 our lord David **k** nothing *about it*? H3359
Est 4:14 And who **k** but that you have come to your H3359
Job 15:23 *he* **k** the day of darkness is at hand. H3359
Job 23:10 But *he* **k** the way that I take; when he has H3359
Job 28: 7 No bird of prey **k** that hidden path, no H3359
Job 28:23 way to it and he alone **k** where it dwells, H3359
Ps 37:13 at the wicked, for *he* **k** their day is coming. H8011
Ps 44:21 since he **k** the secrets of the heart? H3359
Ps 74: 9 none of us **k** how long this will be. H3359
Ps 94:11 The LORD **k** all human plans; he knows H3359
Ps 94:11 all human plans; he **k** that they are futile. NDT
Ps 103:14 he **k how** we are formed, he H3359
Ps 104:19 seasons, and the sun **k** when to go down. H3359
Pr 9:13 woman; she is simple and **k** nothing. H3359
Pr 14:10 Each heart **k** its own bitterness, and no H3359
Pr 24:22 who **k** what calamities they can bring? H3359
Ecc 2:19 And who **k** whether that person will be H3359
Ecc 3:21 Who **k** if the human spirit rises upward H3359
Ecc 4:13 who no longer **k how** to heed a warning H3359
Ecc 6:12 For who **k** what is good for a person in life, H3359
Ecc 8: 1 Who **k** the explanation of things H3359
Ecc 8: 7 Since no one **k** the future, who can tell H3359
Ecc 9: 1 no one **k** whether love or hate awaits H3359
Ecc 9:12 no one **k** when their hour will come: H3359
Ecc 10:14 No one **k** what is coming—who can tell H3359
Isa 1: 3 The ox **k** its master, the donkey its owner's H3359
Isa 7:15 honey when he **k** *enough* to reject the H3359
Isa 7:16 before the boy **k** *enough* to reject the H3359
Isa 8: 4 For before the boy **k how** to say 'My father' H3359
Jer 8: 7 the stork in the sky **k** her appointed H3359
Da 2:22 hidden things; *he* **k** what lies in darkness A10313
Joel 2:14 Who **k**? He may turn and relent and leave H3359
Jnh 3: 9 Who **k**? God may yet relent and with H3359
Na 3:17 they fly away, and no *one* **k** where. H3359
Mt 6: 8 your Father **k** what you need before *G3857*
Mt 6:32 heavenly Father **k** that you need them. *G3857*
Mt 9:30 "See that no one **k about** this. *G1182*
Mt 11:27 No one **k** the Son except the Father, and *G2105*
Mt 11:27 no *one* **k** the Father except the Son *G2105*
Mt 24:36 "But about that day or hour no one **k**, not *G3857*
Mk 13:32 "But about that day or hour no one **k**, not *G3857*
Lk 10:22 No one **k** who the Son is except the Father *G1182*
Lk 10:22 no one **k** who the Father is except the NDT
Lk 12:30 your Father **k** that you need them. *G3857*
Lk 12:47 "The servant who **k** the master's will and *G1182*
Lk 16:15 the eyes of others, but God **k** your hearts. *G1182*
Jn 7:49 But this mob that **k** nothing of the law *G1182*
Jn 10:15 just as the Father **k** me and I know the *G1182*
Jn 14:17 because it neither sees him nor **k** him. *G1182*
Jn 19:35 He **k** that he tells the truth, and he *G3857*
Ac 4:16 living in Jerusalem **k** they have performed *G5745*
Ac 15: 8 *who* **k the heart**, showed that he *G2841*
Ro 8:27 searches our hearts **k** the mind of the *G3857*
1Co 2:11 For who **k** a person's thoughts except their *G3857*
1Co 2:11 same way no one **k** the thoughts of God *G1182*
1Co 3:20 "The Lord **k** that the thoughts of the wise *G1182*
2Co 7: 4 in all our troubles my joy **k no bounds**. *G5668*
2Co 11:11 Because I do not love you? God **k** I do! *G3857*
2Co 11:31 be praised forever, **k** that I am not lying. *G3857*
2Co 12: 2 out of the body I do not know—God **k**. *G3857*
2Co 12: 3 from the body I do not know, but God **k**— *G3857*
2Ti 2:19 "The Lord **k** those who are his," and *G1182*
Jas 4:17 *If anyone*, then, **k** the good they ought to *G3857*
2Pe 2: 9 then the Lord **k how** to rescue the godly *G3857*
1Jn 3:20 than our hearts, and *he* **k** everything. *G1182*
1Jn 4: 6 and whoever **k** God listens to us *G1182*
1Jn 4: 7 loves has been born of God and **k** God. *G1182*
Rev 12:12 *because he* **k** that his time is short." *G3857*
Rev 19:12 on him that no one **k** but he himself. *G3857*

KOA (1)

Eze 23:23 the men of Pekod and Shoa and **K**, and H7760

KOHATH (19) [KOHATH'S, KOHATHITE, KOHATHITES]

Ge 46:11 The sons of Levi: Gershon, **K** and Merari. H7740
Ex 6:16 Gershon, **K** and Merari. Levi lived H7740
Ex 6:18 The sons of **K** were Amram, Izhar, Hebron H7740
Ex 6:18 Hebron and Uzziel. **K** lived 133 years. H7740
Nu 3:17 the sons of Levi: Gershon, **K** and Merari. H7740
Nu 3:27 To **K** belonged the clans of the H7740
Nu 16: 1 son of Izhar, the son of **K**, the son of Levi, H7740
Nu 26:57 through **K**, the Kohathite clan; H7740
Nu 26:58 (**K** was the forefather of Amram; H7740
1Ch 6: 1 The sons of Levi: Gershon, **K** and Merari. H7740
1Ch 6: 2 The sons of **K**: Amram, Izhar, Hebron and H7740
1Ch 6:16 The sons of Levi: Gershon, **K** and Merari. H7740
1Ch 6:18 The sons of **K**: Amram, Izhar, Hebron and H7740
1Ch 6:22 The descendants of **K**: Amminadab his H7740
1Ch 6:38 son of Izhar, the son of **K**, the son of Levi, H7740
1Ch 15: 5 From the descendants of **K**, Uriel the H7740
1Ch 23: 6 the sons of Levi: Gershon, **K** and Merari. H7740
1Ch 23:12 The sons of **K**: Amram, Izhar, Hebron and H7740
2Ch 34:12 Meshullam, descended from **K**. H7741

KOHATH'S (2) [KOHATH]

Jos 21: 5 The rest of **K** descendants were allotted H7740
1Ch 6:61 The rest of **K** descendants were allotted H7740

KOHATHITE (15) [KOHATH]

Nu 3:19 The **K** clans: Amram, Izhar, Hebron H1201+7740
Nu 3:27 Uzzielites; these were the **K** clans. H7741
Nu 3:29 The **K** clans were to camp on the H1201+7740
Nu 3:30 the families of the **K** clans was Elizaphan H7741
Nu 4: 2 a census of the **K** branch of the H1201+7740
Nu 4:18 "See that the **K** tribal clans are not H7741
Nu 4:37 of all those in the **K** clans who served at H7741
Nu 26:57 through Kohath, the **K** clan; through H7741
Jos 21:10 who were from the **K** clans of the Levites, H7741
Jos 21:20 The rest of the **K** clans of the H1201+7740
Jos 21:26 given to the rest of the **K** clans. H1201+7740
1Ch 6:54 of Aaron who were from the **K** clan, H7741
1Ch 6:60 distributed among the **K** clans came to H2157S
1Ch 6:66 Some of the **K** clans were given as H1201+7740
1Ch 6:70 to the rest of the **K** clans. H1201+7740

KOHATHITES (13) [KOHATH]

Nu 3:28 The **K** were responsible for the care of the NDT
Nu 4: 4 is the work of the **K** at the tent of H1201+7740
Nu 4:15 only then are the **K** to come and do H1201+7740

Nu 4:15 The **K** are to carry those things that H1201+7740
Nu 4:20 But the **K** must not go in to look at the holy NDT
Nu 4:34 counted the **K** by their clans and H1201+7741
Nu 7: 9 But Moses did not give any to the **K** H1201+7740
Nu 10:21 Then the **K** set out, carrying the holy things H7741
Jos 21: 4 The first lot came out for the **K**, according H7741
1Ch 6:33 with their sons: From the **K**: Heman, H7741
1Ch 9:32 Some of the **K**, their fellow Levites H1201+7741
2Ch 20:19 Levites from the **K** and Korahites H1201+7741
2Ch 29:12 from the **K**, Mahath son of Amasai H1201+7741

KOL-HOZEH (2)
Ne 3:15 Gate was repaired by Shallun son of **K**, H3997
Ne 11: 5 the son of **K**, the son of Hazaiah, H3997

KOLAIAH (2)
Ne 11: 7 Pedaiah, the son of **K**, the son of H7755
Jer 29:21 about Ahab son of **K** and Zedekiah son of H7755

KONANIAH (3)
2Ch 31:12 **K**, a Levite, was the overseer in charge of H4042
2Ch 31:13 were assistants of **K** and Shimei his H4042
2Ch 35: 9 Also **K** along with Shemaiah and H4042

KORAH (36) [KORAH'S, KORAHITE, KORAHITES]
Ge 36: 5 Oholibamah bore Jeush, Jalam and **K**. H7946
Ge 36:14 she bore to Esau: Jeush, Jalam and **K**. H7946
Ge 36:16 **K**, Gatam and Amalek. These were the H7946
Ge 36:18 Jalam and **K**. These were the H7946
Ex 6:21 The sons of Izhar were **K**, Nepheg and H7946
Ex 6:24 The sons of **K** were Assir, Elkanah and H7946
Nu 16: 1 **K** son of Izhar, the son of Kohath, the son H7946
Nu 16: 5 Then he said to **K** and all his followers: "In H7946
Nu 16: 6 **K**, and all your followers are to do H7946
Nu 16: 8 Moses also said to **K**, "Now listen, you H7946
Nu 16:16 Moses said to **K**, "You and all your H7946
Nu 16:19 When **K** had gathered all his followers in H7946
Nu 16:24 'Move away from the tents of **K**, Dathan H7946
Nu 16:27 So they moved away from the tents of **K** H7946
Nu 16:32 all those associated with **K**, together H7946
Nu 16:40 would become like **K** and his followers. H7946
Nu 16:49 to those who had died because of **K**. H7946
Nu 26:10 mouth and swallowed them along with **K**, H7946
Nu 26:11 The line of **K**, however, did not die out. H7946
1Ch 1:35 Eliphaz, Reuel, Jeush, Jalam and **K**. H7946
1Ch 2:43 sons of Hebron: **K**, Tappuah, Rekem and H7946
1Ch 6:22 Amminadab his son, **K** his son, Assir his H7946
1Ch 6:37 the son of Ebiasaph, the son of **K**, H7946
1Ch 9:19 of Ebiasaph, the son of **K**, and his fellow H7946
1Ch 26:19 who were descendants of **K** and Merari. H7948
Ps 42: T A maskil of the Sons of **K**. H7946
Ps 44: T Of the Sons of **K**. A maskil. H7946
Ps 45: T Of the Sons of **K**. A maskil. H7946
Ps 46: T Of the Sons of **K**. According to alamoth H7946
Ps 47: T Of the Sons of **K**. A psalm. H7946
Ps 48: T A psalm of the Sons of **K**. H7946
Ps 49: T Of the Sons of **K**. A psalm. H7946
Ps 84: T Of the Sons of **K**. A psalm. H7946
Ps 85: T Of the Sons of **K**. A psalm. H7946
Ps 87: T Of the Sons of **K**. A psalm. A song. H7946
Ps 88: T A psalm of the Sons of **K**. For the director H7946

KORAH'S (3) [KORAH]
Nu 26: 9 were among **K** followers when they H7946
Nu 27: 3 He was not among **K** followers, who H7946
Jude 11 they have been destroyed in **K** rebellion. *G3169*

KORAHITE (3) [KORAH]
Ex 6:24 Abiasaph. These were the **K** clans. H7948
Nu 26:58 the Mushite clan, the **K** clan. H7948
1Ch 9:31 the firstborn son of Shallum the **K**, was H7948

KORAHITES (4) [KORAH]
1Ch 9:19 from his family (the **K**) were responsible H7948
1Ch 12: 6 Joezer and Jashobeam the **K**; H7948
1Ch 26: 1 From the **K**: Meshelemiah son of H7948
2Ch 20:19 the Kohathites and **K** stood up and H1201+7948

KORAZIN (NIV84) CHORAZIN

KORE (3)
1Ch 9:19 Shallum son of **K**, the son of Ebiasaph H7927
1Ch 26: 1 Meshelemiah son of **K**, one of the sons of H7927
2Ch 31:14 **K** son of Imnah the Levite, keeper of the H7927

KOS (1)
Ac 21: 1 we put out to sea and sailed straight to **K**. *G3271*

KOUM (1)
Mk 5:41 by the hand and said to her, "Talitha **k**!" *G3182*

KOZ (1)
1Ch 4: 8 **K**, who was the father of Anub and H7766

KOZBI (2)
Nu 25:15 was put to death was **K** daughter of Zur, H3944
Nu 25:18 the Peor incident involving their sister **K**, H3944

KOZEBA (1)
1Ch 4:22 the men of **K**, and Joash and H3943

KUB (1)
Eze 30: 5 **K** and the people of the covenant land H3915

KUE (4)
1Ki 10:28 were imported from Egypt and from **K**— H7750
1Ki 10:28 purchased them from **K** at the current H7750
2Ch 1:16 were imported from Egypt and from **K**— H7745
2Ch 1:16 purchased them from **K** at the current H7745

KUN (1)
1Ch 18: 8 From Tebah and **K**, towns that belonged to H3923

KUSHAIAH (1)
1Ch 15:17 relatives the Merarites, Ethan son of **K**; H7773

KUTHAH (2)
2Ki 17:24 brought people from Babylon, **K**, Avva, H3940
2Ki 17:30 Benoth, those from **K** made Nergal, and H3939

L

LAADAH (1)
1Ch 4:21 **L** the father of Mareshah and the clans of H4355

LAADAN (KJV) LADAN

LABAN (49) [LABAN'S]
Ge 24:29 Now Rebekah had a brother named **L**, and H4238
Ge 24:33 what I have to say." "Then tell us," **L** said. NDT
Ge 24:50 **L** and Bethuel answered, "This is from the H4238
Ge 25:20 Aram and sister of **L** the Aramean. H4238
Ge 27:43 Flee at once to my brother **L** in Harran. H4238
Ge 28: 2 from among the daughters of **L**, your H4238
Ge 28: 5 to **L** son of Bethuel the Aramean H4238
Ge 29: 5 "Do you know **L**, Nahor's grandson?" H4238
Ge 29:10 Jacob saw Rachel daughter of his uncle **L**, H4238
Ge 29:13 As soon as **L** heard the news about Jacob H4238
Ge 29:14 **L** said to him, "You are my own flesh H4238
Ge 29:15 **L** said to him, "Just because you are a H4238
Ge 29:16 Now **L** had two daughters; the name of H4238
Ge 29:19 **L** said, "It's better that I give her to you H4238
Ge 29:21 Then Jacob said to **L**, "Give me my wife H4238
Ge 29:22 So **L** brought together all the people of H4238
Ge 29:24 And **L** gave his servant Zilpah to his H4238
Ge 29:25 So Jacob said to **L**, "What is this you have H4238
Ge 29:26 **L** replied, "It is not our custom here to H4238
Ge 29:28 then **L** gave him his daughter Rachel to NDT
Ge 29:29 **L** gave his servant Bilhah to his daughter H4238
Ge 29:30 And he worked for **L** another seven years. H2257S
Ge 30:25 Jacob said to **L**, "Send me on my way H4238
Ge 30:27 But **L** said to him, "If I have found favor in H4238
Ge 30:34 "Agreed," said **L**. "Let it be as you have H4238
Ge 30:40 dark-colored animals that belonged to **L**. H4238
Ge 30:42 animals went to **L** and the strong ones H4238
Ge 31:12 I have seen all that **L** has been doing to H4238
Ge 31:19 When **L** had gone to shear his sheep H4238
Ge 31:20 Jacob deceived **L** the Aramean by not H4238
Ge 31:22 On the third day **L** was told that Jacob had H4238
Ge 31:24 Then God came to **L** the Aramean in a H4238
Ge 31:25 country of Gilead when **L** overtook him, H4238
Ge 31:25 **L** and his relatives camped there too. H4238
Ge 31:26 Then **L** said to Jacob, "What have you H4238
Ge 31:31 Jacob answered **L**, "I was afraid, because H4238
Ge 31:33 So **L** went into Jacob's tent and into H4238
Ge 31:34 **L** searched through everything in the tent H4238
Ge 31:36 Jacob was angry and took **L** to task. "What H4238
Ge 31:36 he asked **L**. "How have I H4238
Ge 31:43 **L** answered Jacob, "The women are my H4238
Ge 31:47 **L** called it Jegar Sahadutha, and Jacob H4238
Ge 31:48 **L** said, "This heap is a witness between H4238
Ge 31:51 **L** also said to Jacob, "Here is this heap H4238
Ge 31:55 Early the next morning **L** kissed his H4238
Ge 32: 4 been staying with **L** and have remained H4238
Ge 46:18 whom **L** had given to his daughter Leah H4238
Ge 46:25 whom **L** had given to his daughter Rachel H4238
Dt 1: 1 Paran and Tophel, **L**, Hazeroth and H4239

LABAN'S (5) [LABAN]
Ge 29:10 uncle Laban, and **L** sheep, he went over H4238
Ge 30:36 continued to tend the rest of **L** flocks. H4238
Ge 30:40 did not put them with **L** animals. H4238
Ge 31: 1 Jacob heard that **L** sons were saying H4238
Ge 31: 2 Jacob noticed that **L** attitude toward him H4238

LABOR (97) [LABORED, LABORER, LABORERS, LABORING, LABORS]
Ge 3:16 with **painful l** you will give birth to H6776
Ge 5:29 will comfort us in the **l** and painful toil of H5126
Ge 49:15 to the burden and submit to **forced l**. H4989
Ex 1:11 over them to oppress them with **forced l**, H6026
Ex 1:14 bitter with harsh **l** in brick and mortar and H6275
Ex 1:14 in all their harsh **l** the Egyptians worked H6275
Ex 2:11 were and watched them at their **hard l**. H6026
Ex 5: 4 you taking the people away from their **l**? H5126
Ex 6: 9 of their discouragement and harsh **l**. H6275
Ex 20: 9 Six days *you shall* **l** and do all your work, H6268
Ex 34:21 "Six days *you shall* **l**, but on the seventh H6268
Dt 5:13 Six days *you shall* **l** and do all your work, H6268
Dt 20:11 be subject to **forced l** and shall work for H4989
Dt 26: 6 made us suffer, subjecting us to harsh **l**. H6275
Dt 28:33 will eat what your land and **l** produce, H3330
Jos 16:10 of Ephraim but are required to do **forced l**. H4989
Jos 17:13 the Canaanites to **forced l** but did not H4989
Jdg 1:28 Canaanites into **forced l** but never drove H4989
Jdg 1:30 Zebulun did subject them to **forced l**. H4989
Jdg 1:35 they too were pressed into **forced l**. H4989
1Sa 4:19 were dead, *she* **went into l** and gave birth H4156
1Sa 4:19 but was overcome by her **l pains**. H7496
2Sa 12:31 **consigning** them to **l** with saws and with H8492
2Sa 20:24 Adoniram was in charge of **forced l** H4989
1Ki 4: 6 son of Abda—in charge of **forced l**. H4989
1Ki 5:14 Adoniram was in charge of the **forced l**. H4989
1Ki 9:15 the account of the **forced l** King Solomon H4989
1Ki 9:21 to serve as slave **l**, as it is to this day. H4989
1Ki 11:28 charge of the whole **l force** *of* the tribes of H6023
1Ki 12: 4 lighten the harsh **l** and the heavy yoke he H6275
1Ki 12:18 who was in charge of **forced l**, but all H4989
1Ch 20: 3 **consigning** them to **l** with saws and with H8492
2Ch 8: 8 to serve as **slave l**, as it is to this H4989
2Ch 10: 4 lighten the harsh **l** and the heavy yoke he H6275
2Ch 10:18 who was in charge of **forced l**, but the H4989
Job 24: 5 the poor go about their **l** of foraging food H7189
Job 37: 7 his work, he stops all people from their **l**. H3338
Job 39: 3 forth their young; their **l pains** are ended. H2477
Job 39:16 she cares not that her **l** was in vain, H3330
Ps 48: 6 pain like that of a *woman* **in l**. H3528
Ps 104:23 out to their work, to their **l** until evening. H6275
Ps 107:12 So he subjected them to **bitter l**; they H6662
Ps 109:11 may strangers plunder the **fruits of** his **l**. H3330
Ps 127: 1 builds the house, the builders **l** in vain. H6661
Ps 128: 2 You will eat the **fruit of** your **l** H3330+4090
Pr 12:24 will rule, but laziness ends in **forced l**. H4989
Ecc 2:10 My heart took delight in all my **l**, and this H6662
Ecc 2:20 over all my toilsome **l** under the sun. H6661
Ecc 2:21 For a person may **l** with wisdom H6662
Ecc 2:22 striving with which they **l** under the sun? H6665
Ecc 4: 9 they have a good return for their **l**: H6662
Ecc 5:18 in their toilsome **l** under the sun during H6661
Ecc 8:16 to observe the **l** that is done on earth H6721
Ecc 9: 9 life and in your toilsome **l** under the sun. H6662
SS 8: 5 there *she who was* **in l** gave you birth. H2473
Isa 13: 8 they will writhe like a *woman* **in l**. H3528
Isa 14: 3 from the harsh **l** forced on you, H6275
Isa 21: 3 like those of a *woman* **in l**; I am H3528
Isa 23: 4 "*I have* neither *been* **in l** nor given birth; H2655
Isa 26:18 with child, *we* **writhed in l**, but we gave H2655
Isa 31: 8 their young men will be put to **forced l**. H4989
Isa 54: 1 joy, you *who were* never **in l**; because H2655
Isa 55: 2 your **l** on what does not satisfy? H3330
Isa 65:23 *They will* not **l** in vain, nor will they bear H3333
Isa 66: 7 "Before *she* **goes into l**, she gives birth H2655
Isa 66: 8 Yet no sooner *is* Zion **in l** than she gives H2655
Jer 3:24 consumed the **fruits of** our ancestors' **l**— H3330
Jer 4:31 I hear a cry as of a *woman* **in l**, a groan as H2655
Jer 6:24 gripped us, pain like that of a *woman* **in l**. H3528
Jer 13:21 pain grip you like that of a woman **in l**? H4256
Jer 22:13 nothing, not paying them for their **l**. H7189
Jer 22:23 upon you, pain like that of a *woman* **in l**! H3528
Jer 30: 6 hands on his stomach like a *woman* **in l**, H3528
Jer 31: 8 expectant mothers and *women* **in l**; H3528
Jer 48:41 will be like the heart of a woman **in l**. H7674
Jer 49:22 will be like the heart of a woman **in l**. H7674
Jer 49:24 seized her, pain like that of a *woman* **in l**. H3528
Jer 50:43 pain like that of a *woman* **in l**. H3528
Jer 51:58 the nations' **l** is only fuel for the flames." H3615
La 1: 3 After affliction and harsh **l**, Judah has H6275
Mic 4: 9 pain seizes you like that of a *woman* **in l**? H3528
Mic 4:10 like a *woman* **in l**, for now you must H3528
Mic 5: 3 time when *she who is* **in l** bears a son, H3528
Hab 2:13 that the people's **l** is only fuel for the fire, H3333
Hag 1:11 livestock, and on all the **l** *of* your hands." H3330
Mt 6:28 of the field grow. *They do* not **l** or spin. *G3159*
Lk 12:27 *They do* not **l** or spin. Yet I *G3159*
Jn 4:38 you have reaped the benefits of their **l**." *G3160*
1Co 3: 8 be rewarded according to their own **l**. *G3160*
1Co 15:58 you know that your **l** in the Lord is not in *G3160*
Gal 4:27 you *who were* never **in l**; because *G6048*
Php 1:22 the body, this will mean fruitful **l** for me. *G2240*
Php 2:16 day of Christ that I did not run or **l** in vain. *G3159*
1Th 1: 3 by faith, your **l** prompted by love, and *G3160*
1Th 5: 3 as **l pains** on a pregnant woman *G6047*
1Ti 4:10 That is why *we* **l** and strive, because we *G3159*
Rev 14:13 "they will rest from their **l**, for their deeds *G3160*

LABORED (5) [LABOR]
2Ch 34:12 The workers **l** faithfully. Over them to H4856
Isa 47:12 which *you have* **l** at since childhood. H3333
Isa 47:15 dealt with and **l** *with* since childhood. H6086
Isa 49: 4 But I said, "*I have* **l** in vain; I have spent H3333
2Co 11:27 I have **l** and toiled and have often gone *G3160*

LABORER (3) [LABOR]
Job 7: 2 shadows, or a **hired l** waiting to be paid, H8502
Job 14: 6 till he has put in his time like a **hired l**. H8502
Ecc 5:12 The sleep of a **l** is sweet, whether they H6268

LABORERS (7) [LABOR]
Jdg 1:33 Beth Anath became **forced l** for them. H4989
1Ki 5:13 Solomon conscripted **l** from all Israel— H4989
2Ch 34:13 had charge of the **l** and supervised all the H6025
Ne 4:10 "The strength of the **l** is giving out, and H6025
Job 7: 1 Are not their days like those of **hired l**? H8502
Pr 16:26 The appetite of **l** works for them; their H6664
Mal 3: 5 those who defraud **l** of their wages, H8502

LABORING (1) [LABOR]
2Th 3: 8 **l** and toiling so that we would not be a *G3160*

LABORS (3) [LABOR]
Ecc 1: 3 gain from all their **l** at which they toil H6662
1Co 16:16 everyone who joins in the work and **l** at it. *G3159*
1Th 3: 5 you and that our **l** might have been in *G3160*

LACE (KJV) CORD

LACHISH (24)
Jos 10: 3 Japhia king of **L** and Debir king of Eglon. H4337
Jos 10: 5 Hebron, Jarmuth, **L** and Eglon—joined H4337
Jos 10:23 Jerusalem, Hebron, Jarmuth, **L** and Eglon. H4337
Jos 10:31 with him moved on from Libnah to **L**; H4337
Jos 10:32 The LORD gave **L** into Israel's hands, and H4337
Jos 10:33 king of Gezer had come up to help **L**, H4337
Jos 10:34 Israel with him moved on from **L** to Eglon; H4337
Jos 10:35 everyone in it, just as they had done to **L**. H4337
Jos 12:11 the king of Jarmuth one the king of **L** one H4337
Jos 15:39 **L**, Bozkath, Eglon, H4337
2Ki 14:19 he fled to **L**, but they sent men after H4337
2Ki 14:19 men after him to **L** and killed him there. H4337
2Ki 18:14 this message to the king of Assyria at **L**: H4337
2Ki 18:17 from **L** to King Hezekiah at Jerusalem. H4337
2Ki 19: 8 heard that the king of Assyria had left **L**, H4337
2Ch 11: 9 Adoraim, **L**, Azekah, H4337
2Ch 25:27 him in Jerusalem and he fled to **L**, H4337
2Ch 25:27 men after him to **L** and killed him there. H4337
2Ch 32: 9 all his forces were laying siege to **L**, H4337
Ne 11:30 their villages, in **L** and its fields, and in H4337
Isa 36: 2 a large army from **L** to King Hezekiah at H4337
Isa 37: 8 heard that the king of Assyria had left **L**, H4337
Jer 34: 7 that were still holding out—**L** and Azekah. H4337
Mic 1:13 You who live in **L**, harness fast horses to H4337

LACK (43) [LACKED, LACKING, LACKS]
Ge 18:28 destroy the whole city **for l of** five people?" H928
Dt 8: 9 will not be scarce and *you will* **l** nothing; H2893
Job 4:11 The lion perishes for **l** *of* prey, and the H1172
Job 24: 8 rains and hug the rocks for **l** *of* shelter. H1172
Job 31:19 seen anyone perishing for **l** *of* clothing, H1172
Job 34:35 knowledge; his words **l** insight. H4202+928
Job 38:41 to God and wander about for **l** *of* food? H1172
Ps 23: 1 The LORD is my shepherd, *I* **l** nothing. H2893
Ps 34: 9 people, for those who fear him **l** nothing. H4728
Ps 34:10 those who seek the LORD **l** no good thing. H2893
Ps 49:20 who have wealth but **l** understanding are H4202
Ps 94:10 Does he who teaches mankind **l** knowledge? NDT
Pr 5:23 For **l** *of* discipline they will die, led astray H401
Pr 10:21 nourish many, but fools die for **l** *of* sense. H2894
Pr 11:14 For **l** *of* guidance a nation falls, but victory H401
Pr 15:22 Plans fail for **l** *of* counsel, but with many H401
Pr 22:27 if you **l** the means to pay, your very H401+4200
Pr 28:27 Those who give to the poor will **l** nothing H4728
Ecc 6: 2 so that they **l** nothing their hearts desire H2894
Ecc 10: 3 *they* **l** sense and show everyone how H2893
Isa 5:13 will go into exile for **l** *of* understanding; H1172
Isa 34:16 will be missing, not one *will* **l** her mate. H7212
Isa 50: 2 Do I **l** the strength to rescue you H401+928
Isa 50: 2 their fish rot for **l** *of* water and die of thirst. H401
Isa 51:14 in their dungeon, nor *will they* **l** bread. H2893
Isa 56:10 are blind, they all **l** knowledge; they are H4202
Isa 56:11 They are shepherds who **l** understanding H4202
Jer 14: 6 like jackals; their eyes fail for **l** *of* food." H401
La 4: 9 they waste away **for l of** food from the H4946
Hos 4: 6 are destroyed from **l** *of* knowledge. H1172
Am 4: 6 in every city and **l** *of* bread in every town, H2896
Zec 10: 2 like sheep oppressed for **l** *of* a shepherd. H401
Mt 13:58 miracles there because of their **l of faith**. *G602*
Mt 19:20 the young man said. "What *do I* still **l**?" *G5728*
Mk 6: 6 He was amazed at their **l of faith**. *G602*
Mk 10:21 "One thing you **l**," he said. "Go, *G5728*
Mk 16:14 rebuked them *for* their **l of faith** and their *G602*
Lk 18:22 he said to him, "You still **l** one thing. *G3309*
Lk 22:35 bag or sandals, *did* you **l** anything?" *G5728*
1Co 1: 7 Therefore you *do* not **l** any spiritual gift as *G5728*
1Co 7: 5 tempt you because of your **l of self-control**. *G202*
1Co 9: 6 I and Barnabas *who* **l** the right to *G4024+2400*
Col 2:23 they **l** any value in restraining sensual *G4024*

LACKED (5) [LACK]
Dt 2: 7 with you, and *you have* not **l** anything. H2893
Jdg 18: 7 And since their land **l** nothing, they were H4007
1Ki 11:22 "What *have* you **l** here that you want to H2894
Ne 9:21 in the wilderness; *they* **l** nothing, their H2893
1Co 12:24 giving greater honor *to* the parts that **l** it, *G5728*

LACKING (9) [LACK]
1Ki 4:27 *They* **saw to it that** nothing **was l**. H6372
Job 24: 7 **L** clothes, they spend the night H4946+1172
Job 24:10 **L** clothes, they go about naked; they carry H1172
Ecc 1:15 straightened; *what* is **l** cannot be counted. H2898
Ro 12:11 Never be **l** in zeal, but keep your spiritual *G3891*
1Co 16:17 they have supplied what was **l** from you. *G5729*
Col 1:24 my flesh what is still **l** in regard to Christ's *G5729*
1Th 3:10 again and supply what *is* **l** in your faith. *G5729*
Jas 1: 4 be mature and complete, not **l** anything. *G3309*

LACKS (7) [LACK]
Jdg 18:10 a land that **l** nothing whatever. H4728
2Sa 3:29 who falls by the sword or who **l** food." H2894
Pr 25:28 through is a person who **l** self-control. H401
Pr 31:11 confidence in her and **l** nothing of value. H2893
SS 7: 2 goblet *that* never **l** blended wine. H2893
Eze 34: 8 because my flock **l** a shepherd and so has H401
Jas 1: 5 If any of you **l** wisdom, you should ask *G3309*

LADAN (7)
1Ch 7:26 **L** his son, Ammihud his son, Elishama his H4356
1Ch 23: 7 to the Gershonites: **L** and Shimei. H4356
1Ch 23: 8 The sons of **L**: Jehiel the first, Zetham H4356
1Ch 23: 9 These were the heads of the families of **L** H4356
1Ch 26:21 The descendants of **L**, who were H4356
1Ch 26:21 through **L** and who were heads H4356
1Ch 26:21 of families belonging to **L** the Gershonite, H4356

LADE, LADED, LADEN, LADING (KJV)
BURDENED, CARGO, FURNISHED, LAID, LOAD, LOADED, LOADING

LADEN (3) [LOAD]
Job 36:16 comfort of your table **l with** choice food. H4848
Job 36:17 But now *you are* **l with** the judgment due H4848
Ps 105:37 brought out Israel, **l with** silver and gold H928

LADIES (1) [LADY]
Jdg 5:29 The wisest of her **l** answer her; indeed H8576

LADY (2) [LADIES]
2Jn 1 *To* the **l** chosen by God and to her *G3257*
2Jn 5 And now, **dear l**, I am not writing you a *G3257*

LAEL (1)
Nu 3:24 of the Gershonites was Eliasaph son of **L**. H4210

LAGGING (1)
Dt 25:18 attacked all who *were* **l** behind; H3129

LAHAD (1)
1Ch 4: 2 Jahath the father of Ahumai and **L**. H4262

LAHAI See BEER LAHAI ROI

LAHMAS (1)
Jos 15:40 Kabbon, **L**, Kitlish, H4314

LAHMI (1)
1Ch 20: 5 son of Jair killed **L** the brother of Goliath H4313

LAID (143) [LAY]
Ge 9:23 took a garment and **l** it across their H8492
Ge 22: 9 his son Isaac and **l** him on the altar, H8492
Ex 19:13 not a hand *is to be* **l** on them. H5595
Ex 22: 8 owner of the house *has* **l** hands on the H8938
Lev 8:14 Aaron and his sons **l** their hands on its H6164
Lev 8:18 Aaron and his sons **l** their hands on its H6164
Lev 8:22 Aaron and his sons **l** their hands on its H6164
Lev 9:20 these *they* **l** on the breasts, and then H8492
Lev 26:33 Your land will be **l waste**, and your cities H9039
Nu 27:23 Then *he* **l** his hands on him and H6164
Dt 24: 5 to war or *have* any other duty **l** on him. H6296
Dt 34: 9 because Moses *had* **l** his hands on him. H6164
Jos 2: 6 the stalks of flax she *had* **l out** on the roof.) H6885
Jos 2:19 will be on our head if a hand is **l** on them. NDT
Jdg 16:24 the *one who* **l waste** our land and H2990
1Sa 19:13 Michal took an idol and **l** it on the bed, H8492
2Sa 22:16 of the earth **l bare** at the rebuke of the H1655
1Ki 1:21 my lord the king *is* **l to rest** with his H8886
1Ki 6:37 **The foundation** of the temple of the LORD **was l** H3569
1Ki 7:10 **The foundations were l** *with* large stones H3569
1Ki 12:11 My father **l** on you a heavy yoke; I will H6673
1Ki 13:29 of the man of God, **l** it on the donkey, and H5663
1Ki 13:30 Then *he* **l** the body in his own tomb, and H5663
1Ki 16:17 from Gibbethon and **l siege** to Tirzah. H7443
1Ki 16:34 *He* **l** its **foundations** at the cost of his H3569
1Ki 17:19 he was staying, and **l** him on his bed. H8886
1Ki 18:33 the bull into pieces and **l** it on the wood. H8492
2Ki 4:21 She went up and **l** him on the bed of the H8886
2Ki 4:31 went on ahead and **l** the staff on the H8492
2Ki 6:24 marched up and **l siege** to Samaria. H7443
2Ki 17: 5 against Samaria and **l siege** to it for three H7443
2Ki 18: 9 against Samaria and **l siege** to it. H7443
2Ki 19:17 Assyrian kings *have* **l waste** these nations H2990
2Ki 22:19 would become a curse and *be* **l waste**— H9014
2Ki 24:10 and **l siege** *to* it, H995+928+2021+5189
1Ch 6:32 according to the **regulations** *l down* for them. AIT
1Ch 20: 1 *He* **l waste** the land of the Ammonites H8845
2Ch 3: 3 **The foundation** Solomon **l** for building H3569
2Ch 8:16 **foundation** *of* the temple of the LORD was **l** H4586
2Ch 10:11 My father **l** on you a heavy yoke; I will H6673
2Ch 16:14 *They* **l** him on a bier covered with spices H8886
2Ch 29:23 assembly, and *they* **l** their hands on them. H6164
2Ch 32: 1 *He* **l siege to** the fortified cities H2837+6584
Ezr 3: 6 **the foundation** of the LORD's temple *had* not *yet* **been l** H3569
Ezr 3:10 builders **l the foundation** *of* the temple H3569
Ezr 3:11 **the foundation** *of* the house of the LORD **was l** H3569
Ezr 3:12 saw **the foundation** *of* this temple *being* **l**, H3569
Ezr 5:16 came and **l** the foundations of A10314
Ezr 6: 3 sacrifices, and *let* its foundations **be l**. A10502
Ne 3: 3 They **l** its **beams** and put its doors and H7936
Ne 3: 6 They **l** its **beams** and put its doors with H7936
Job 14:10 But a man dies and *is* **l low**; he breathes H2764
Job 16:18 my blood; may my cry never be **l** to rest! NDT
Job 38: 4 were you when I **l the** earth's **foundation**? H3569
Job 38: 6 its footings set, or who **l** its cornerstone— H3721
Ps 18:15 of the earth **l bare** at your rebuke, H1655
Ps 66:11 us into prison and **l** burdens on our backs. H8492
Ps 102:25 beginning *you* **l the foundations** *of* the H3569
Ps 119: 4 You *have* **l down** precepts that are to be H7422
Ps 119:25 I *am* **l low** in the dust; preserve my life H1815
Ps 119:138 The statutes *you have* **l down** are H7422
Ps 141: 9 from the snares *they have* **l** for me. H3704
Pr 3:19 the LORD **l the** earth's **foundations**, H3569
Ecc 1:13 a heavy burden God *has* **l** on mankind! H5989
Ecc 3:10 the burden God *has* **l** on the human race. H5989
Isa 1: 7 **l waste** as when overthrown by strangers. H9039
Isa 6:13 in the land, it will again be **l waste**. H1278
Isa 7:16 of the two kings you dread *will* **be l waste**. H6440
Isa 14: 8 "Now that *you have been* **l low**, no one H8886
Isa 14:12 the earth, *you who once* **l low** the nations! H2765
Isa 24: 3 *will* **be completely l waste** and H1327+1327
Isa 28: 1 that city, the pride of *those* **l low** *by* wine! H2150
Isa 37:18 Assyrian kings *have* **l waste** all these H2990
Isa 44:28 of the temple, "*Let its* **foundations be l**." H3569
Isa 47: 6 Even on the aged *you* **l** a very **heavy** yoke. H3877
Isa 48:13 own hand **l the foundations** *of* the earth, H3569
Isa 49:17 and *those who* **l** you **waste** H2990+2256+2238
Isa 49:19 made desolate and your land **l** waste, NDT
Isa 51:16 *who* **l the foundations** *of* the earth H3569
Isa 53: 6 the LORD *has* **l** on him the iniquity of H7003
Jer 2:15 *They have* **l** waste his land; his towns are H8883
Jer 9:12 been ruined and **l waste** like a desert that H5898
Jer 12:11 whole land *will* **be l waste** because there H9037
Jer 25:37 meadows **will be l waste** because of the H1959
Jer 39: 1 with his whole army and **l siege** to it. H7443
Jer 46:15 Why *will* your warriors **be l low**? They H6085
Jer 46:19 Memphis will be **l waste** and lie in ruins H9014
Jer 48: 9 Moab, for *she will be* **l waste**; her H5898+5898
La 1:10 The enemy **l** hands on all her treasures H7298
La 2: 6 *He has* **l waste** his dwelling like a garden H2803
La 3:28 in silence, for the LORD *has* **l** it on him. H5747
Eze 6: 6 the towns *will be* **l waste** and the high H2990
Eze 6: 6 your altars *will be* **l waste** and devastated, H2990
Eze 12:20 towns *will be* **l waste** and the land H2990
Eze 13:14 so that its foundation *will be* **l bare**. H1655
Eze 21:29 it *will be* **l** on the necks of the wicked who H5989
Eze 24: 2 king of Babylon *has* **l siege** to Jerusalem H6164
Eze 25: 3 of Israel when *it* **was l waste** and over the H9037
Eze 32:19 Go down and **be l** among the H8886
Eze 32:25 to the pit; *they* **are l** among the slain. H5989
Eze 32:29 *they are* **l** with those killed by the sword. H5989
Eze 32:32 all his hordes *will* **be l** among the H8886
Eze 35:12 "*They have been* **l waste** and have been H9037
Eze 36:35 "This land that **was l waste** has become H9037
Hos 5: 9 Ephraim will be **l waste** on the day of H9014
Joel 1: 7 *It has* **l** waste my vines and ruined my fig H8492
Mic 5: 1 city of troops, for a siege *is* **l** against us. H8492
Na 2: 2 destroyers *have* **l** them **waste** and have H1327
Zep 3: 6 Their cities **are l waste**; they are deserted H7400
Hag 2:15 before one stone *was* **l** on another in the H8492
Hag 2:18 **the foundation** of the LORD's temple **was l**. H3569
Zec 4: 9 Zerubbabel *have* **l the foundation** *of* this H3569
Zec 8: 9 when **the foundation was l** *for* the house H3569
Mt 15:30 many others, and **l** them at his feet *G4849*
Mt 22:15 went out and **l** plans to trap him in *G3284*
Mk 6:29 took his body and **l** it in a tomb. *G5502*
Mk 15:47 the mother of Joseph saw where *he was* **l**. *G5502*
Mk 16: 6 See the place where *they* **l** him. *G5502*
Lk 6:48 dug down deep and **l** the foundation on *G5502*
Lk 12:19 have plenty of grain **l up** for many years. *G3023*
Lk 16:20 At his gate *was* **l** a beggar named Lazarus *G965*
Lk 19:20 I have kept it **l away** in a piece of cloth. *G641*
Lk 23:53 one in which no one had yet been **l**. *G3023*
Lk 23:55 the tomb and how his body *was* **l** in it. *G5502*
Jn 7:30 seize him, but no one **l** a hand on him *G2095*
Jn 7:44 to seize him, but no one **l** a hand on him. *G2095*
Jn 11:34 "Where *have you* **l** him?" he asked. "Come *G5502*
Jn 11:38 a cave with a stone **l across** the entrance. *G2130*
Jn 19:41 in which no one had ever been **l**. *G5502*
Jn 19:42 the tomb was nearby, *they* **l** Jesus there. *G5502*
Ac 5:15 into the streets and **l** them on beds and *G5502*
Ac 6: 6 who prayed and **l** their hands **on** them. *G2202*
Ac 7:58 the witnesses **l** their coats at the feet of a *G700*
Ac 13:29 down from the cross and **l** him in a tomb. *G5502*
1Co 3:10 me, *I* **l** a foundation as a wise builder *G5502*
1Co 3:11 foundation other than the *one already* **l**, *G3023*
1Co 14:25 as the secrets of their hearts are **l bare**. *G5745*
1Ti 4:14 the body of elders **l** their hands **on** you. *G2120*
Heb 1:10 you **l the foundations** of the earth *G2530*
Heb 4:13 is uncovered and **l bare** before the eyes of *G5548*
2Pe 3:10 everything done in it *will be* **l bare**. *G2351*
1Jn 3:16 Jesus Christ **l down** his life for us. *G5502*
Rev 21:16 The city *was* **l out** like a square, as long as *G3023*

LAIN (1) [LAY]
1Sa 26: 5 the commander of the army, *had* **l down**. H8886

LAIR (6) [LAIRS]
2Ki 19:13 Where are the kings of **L**, Sepharvaim H4359
Isa 37:13 Where are the kings of **L**, Sepharvaim H4359
Jer 4: 7 A lion has come out of his **l**; a destroyer H6020
Jer 25:38 Like a lion he will leave his **l**, and their H6108
Hos 5:15 I will return to my **l** until they have borne H5226
Zep 2:15 ruin she has become, a **l** for wild beasts! H5271

L

LAIRS (1) [LAIR]

Na 2:12 filling his **l** with the kill and his dens with H2986

LAISH (6)

Jdg 18: 7 So the five men left and came to **L**, where H4332
Jdg 18:14 spied out the land of **L** said to their fellow H4332
Jdg 18:27 went on to **L**, against a people at H4332
Jdg 18:29 though the city used to be called **L**. H4332
1Sa 25:44 to Paltiel son of **L**, who was from Gallim. H4331
2Sa 3:15 away from her husband Paltiel son of **L**. H4331

LAISHAH (1)

Isa 10:30 Gallim! Listen, **L**! Poor Anathoth! H4333

LAKE (40)

Dt 33:23 he will inherit southward to the **l**. H3542
Job 14:11 As the water of a **l** dries up or a riverbed H3542
Mt 4:13 which was **by the l** in the area of Zebulun *G4144*
Mt 4:18 They were casting a net into the **l**, for they *G2498*
Mt 8:18 orders to cross to the **other side of the l**. *G4305*
Mt 8:24 Suddenly a furious storm came up on the **l**, *G2498*
Mt 8:32 steep bank into the **l** and died in the *G2498*
Mt 13: 1 went out of the house and sat by the **l**. *G2498*
Mt 13:47 let down into the **l** and caught all kinds *G2498*
Mt 14:25 Jesus went out to them, walking on the **l**. *G2498*
Mt 14:26 the disciples saw him walking on the **l**, *G2498*
Mt 16: 5 When they went **across the l**, *G1650+3836+4305*
Mt 17:27 go to the **l** and throw out your line. *G2498*
Mk 1:16 brother Andrew casting a net into the **l**, *G2498*
Mk 2:13 Once again Jesus went out beside the **l** *G2498*
Mk 3: 7 Jesus withdrew with his disciples to the **l** *G2498*
Mk 4: 1 Again Jesus began to teach by the **l**. *G2498*
Mk 4: 1 got into a boat and sat in it out on the **l**, *G2498*
Mk 5: 1 They went across the **l** to the region of the *G2498*
Mk 5:13 steep bank into the **l** and were drowned. *G2498*
Mk 5:21 over by boat to the **other side of the l**, *G4305*
Mk 5:21 around him while he was by the **l**. *G2498*
Mk 6:47 the boat was in the middle *of* the **l**, and *G2498*
Mk 6:48 he went out to them, walking on the **l**. *G2498*
Mk 6:49 when they saw him walking on the **l** *G2498*
Lk 5: 1 was standing by the **L** of Gennesaret, *G3349*
Lk 8:22 "Let us go over to the other side *of* the **l**." *G3349*
Lk 8:23 A squall came down on the **l**, so that the *G3349*
Lk 8:26 which is **across** *the l* **from** Galilee. AIT
Lk 8:33 steep bank into the **l** and was drowned. *G3349*
Jn 6:16 his disciples went down to the **l**, *G2498*
Jn 6:17 set off across the **l** for Capernaum. *G2498*
Jn 6:22 the opposite shore *of* the **l** realized that *G2498*
Jn 6:25 they found him on the other side *of* the **l**, *G2498*
Rev 19:20 alive into the fiery **l** of burning sulfur. *G3349*
Rev 20:10 was thrown into the **l** of burning sulfur *G3349*
Rev 20:14 Hades were thrown into the **l** of fire. *G3349*
Rev 20:14 The **l** of fire is the second death. *G3349*
Rev 20:15 book of life was thrown into the **l** of fire. *G3349*
Rev 21: 8 consigned to the fiery **l** of burning sulfur. *G3349*

LAKKUM (1)

Jos 19:33 Jabneel to **L** and ending at the H4373

LAMA (NIV84) LEMA

LAMB (104) [LAMB'S, LAMBS]

Ge 22: 7 "but where is the **l** for the burnt offering?" H8445
Ge 22: 8 will provide the **l** for the burnt offering, H8445
Ge 30:32 dark-colored **l** and every H8445+928+2021+4166
Ge 30:33 spotted, or any **l** that is not dark-colored H4166
Ex 12: 3 each man is to take a **l** for his family, H8445
Ex 12: 4 If any household is too small for a *whole* **l** H8445
Ex 12: 4 the amount of **l** needed in accordance H8445
Ex 12:21 families and slaughter the **Passover l**. H7175
Ex 13:13 Redeem with a **l** every firstborn donkey H8445
Ex 29:40 With the first **l** offer a tenth of an ephah of H3897
Ex 29:41 Sacrifice the other **l** at twilight with the H3897
Ex 34:20 Redeem the firstborn donkey with a **l**, but H8445
Lev 3: 7 If you offer a **l**, you are to present it before H4166
Lev 4:32 'If someone brings a **l** as their sin offering H3897
Lev 4:35 fat is removed from the **l** *of* the fellowship H4166
Lev 5: 6 to the LORD a female **l** or goat from the H4167
Lev 5: 7 who cannot afford a **l** is to bring two H8445
Lev 9: 3 a calf and a **l**—both a year old and H3897
Lev 12: 6 meeting a year-old **l** for a burnt offering H3897
Lev 12: 8 But if she cannot afford a **l**, she is to bring H8445
Lev 14:10 male lambs and one **ewe l** a year old, H3898
Lev 14:13 is to slaughter the **l** in the sanctuary area H3897
Lev 14:21 they must take one **male l** as a guilt H3897
Lev 14:24 priest is to take the **l** *for* the guilt offering, H3897
Lev 14:25 shall slaughter the **l** *for* the guilt offering H3897
Lev 17: 3 a **l** or a goat in the camp or outside of it H4166
Lev 22:27 "When a calf, a **l** or a goat is born, it is to H4166
Lev 23:12 offering to the LORD a **l** a year old without H3897
Nu 6:12 bring a year-old **male l** as a guilt offering. H3897
Nu 6:14 a year-old **male l** without defect for a H3897
Nu 6:14 a year-old **ewe l** without defect for a sin H3898
Nu 7:15 one ram and one **male l** a year old for a H3897
Nu 7:21 one ram and one **male l** a year old for a H3897
Nu 7:27 one ram and one **male l** a year old for a H3897
Nu 7:33 one ram and one **male l** a year old for a H3897
Nu 7:39 one ram and one **male l** a year old for a H3897
Nu 7:45 one ram and one **male l** a year old for a H3897
Nu 7:51 one ram and one **male l** a year old for a H3897
Nu 7:57 one ram and one **male l** a year old for a H3897
Nu 7:63 one ram and one **male l** a year old for a H3897
Nu 7:69 one ram and one **male l** a year old for a H3897
Nu 7:75 one ram and one **male l** a year old for a H3897
Nu 7:81 one ram and one **male l** a year old for a H3897
Nu 9:11 They are to eat **the l**, together with H2084S
Nu 15: 5 With each **l** for the burnt offering or the H3897
Nu 15:11 each **l** or young goat H8445+928+2021+3897
Nu 28: 4 Offer one **l** in the morning and the other at H3897
Nu 28: 7 of a hin of fermented drink with each **l**. H3897
Nu 28: 8 Offer the second **l** at twilight, along with H3897
Nu 28:13 with each **l**, a grain offering of a tenth H3897
Nu 28:14 and with each **l**, a quarter of a hin. H3897
1Sa 7: 9 took a suckling **l** and sacrificed it as a H3231
2Sa 12: 3 except one little **ewe l** he had bought. H3898
2Sa 12: 4 took the **ewe l** *that belonged to* the poor H3898
2Sa 12: 6 He must pay for that **l** four times over H3898
2Ch 30:15 slaughtered the **Passover l** on the H7175
2Ch 35: 1 the **Passover l** was slaughtered on H7175
Ezr 6:20 slaughtered the **Passover l** for all the H7175
Isa 11: 6 The wolf will live with the **l**, the leopard H3897
Isa 53: 7 he was led like a **l** to the slaughter, and H8445
Isa 65:25 The wolf and the **l** will feed together, and H3231
Isa 66: 3 whoever offers a **l** is like one who H8445
Jer 11:19 been like a gentle **l** led to the slaughter; H3897
Eze 46:13 to provide a year-old **l** without defect for a H3897
Eze 46:15 So the **l** and the grain offering and the oil H3897
Mk 14:12 was customary to sacrifice the **Passover l**, *G4247*
Lk 22: 7 Bread on which the **Passover l** had to be *G4247*
Jn 1:29 the **L** of God, who takes away the sin *G303*
Jn 1:36 passing by, he said, "Look, the **L** of God!" *G303*
Ac 8:32 as a **l** before its shearer is silent *G303*
1Co 5: 7 For Christ, our **Passover l**, has been *G4247*
1Pe 1:19 of Christ, a **l** without blemish or defect. *G303*
Rev 5: 6 Then I saw a **L**, looking as if it had been *G768*
Rev 5: 6 The **L** had seven horns and seven eyes NDT
Rev 5: 8 twenty-four elders fell down before the **L**. *G768*
Rev 5:12 "Worthy is the **L**, who was slain, to receive *G768*
Rev 5:13 on the throne and *to* the **L** be praise and *G768*
Rev 6: 1 I watched as the **L** opened the first of the *G768*
Rev 6: 3 When the **L** opened the second seal, NDT
Rev 6: 5 When the **L** opened the third seal, I heard NDT
Rev 6: 7 When the **L** opened the fourth seal, I heard NDT
Rev 6:16 on the throne and from the wrath *of* the **L**! *G768*
Rev 7: 9 before the throne and before the **L**. *G768*
Rev 7:10 who sits on the throne, and *to* the **L**." *G768*
Rev 7:14 made them white in the blood *of* the **L**. *G768*
Rev 7:17 For the **L** at the center of the throne will be *G768*
Rev 12:11 him by the blood *of* the **L** and by the word *G768*
Rev 13: 8 the **L** who was slain from the creation of the NDT
Rev 13:11 It had two horns like a **l**, but it spoke like a *G768*
Rev 14: 1 there before me was the **L**, standing *G768*
Rev 14: 4 They follow the **L** wherever he goes. *G768*
Rev 14: 4 offered as firstfruits to God and the **L**. *G768*
Rev 14:10 presence of the holy angels and of the **L**. *G768*
Rev 15: 3 song of God's servant Moses and *of* the **L**: *G768*
Rev 17:14 They will wage war against the **L**, but the *G768*
Rev 17:14 the **L** will triumph over them because *G768*
Rev 19: 7 For the wedding *of* the **L** has come, and his *G768*
Rev 19: 9 are invited to the wedding supper *of* the **L**!" *G768*
Rev 21: 9 I will show you the bride, the wife *of* the **L**." *G768*
Rev 21:14 the names of the twelve apostles *of* the **L**. *G768*
Rev 21:22 God Almighty and the **L** are its temple. *G768*
Rev 21:23 of God gives it light, and the **L** is its lamp. *G768*
Rev 22: 1 flowing from the throne of God and *of* the **L** *G768*
Rev 22: 3 throne of God and *of* the **L** will be in the *G768*

LAMB'S (2) [LAMB]

Rev 13: 8 have not been written in the **L** book of life, *G768*
Rev 21:27 names are written in the **L** book of life. *G768*

LAMBS (93) [LAMB]

Ge 21:28 set apart seven **ewe l** *from* the flock, H3898
Ge 21:29 of these seven **ewe l** you have set apart H3898
Ge 21:30 "Accept these seven **l** from my hand as a H3898
Ge 30:35 all the dark-colored **l**, and he placed H4166
Ex 12: 7 of the houses where they eat **the l**. H2257S
Ex 29:38 altar regularly each day: two **l** a year old. H3897
Lev 14:10 must bring two **male l** and one ewe lamb H3897
Lev 14:12 to take one of the **male l** and offer it as a H3897
Lev 23:18 Present with this bread seven **male l**, each H3897
Lev 23:19 male goat for a sin offering and two **l**, H3897
Lev 23:20 is to wave the two **l** before the LORD as a H3897
Nu 7:17 goats and five **male l** a year old to be H3897
Nu 7:23 goats and five **male l** a year old to be H3897
Nu 7:29 goats and five **male l** a year old to be H3897
Nu 7:35 goats and five **male l** a year old to be H3897
Nu 7:41 goats and five **male l** a year old to be H3897
Nu 7:47 goats and five **male l** a year old to be H3897
Nu 7:53 goats and five **male l** a year old to be H3897
Nu 7:59 goats and five **male l** a year old to be H3897
Nu 7:65 goats and five **male l** a year old to be H3897
Nu 7:71 goats and five **male l** a year old to be H3897
Nu 7:77 goats and five **male l** a year old to be H3897
Nu 7:83 goats and five **male l** a year old to be H3897
Nu 7:87 twelve rams and twelve **male l** a year old H3897
Nu 7:88 male goats and sixty **male l** a year old. H3897
Nu 28: 3 two **l** a year old without defect, as a H3897
Nu 28: 9 an offering of two **l** a year old without H3897
Nu 28:11 one ram and seven **male l** a year old, all H3897
Nu 28:19 one ram and seven **male l** a year old, all H3897
Nu 28:21 with each of the seven **l**, one-tenth. H3897
Nu 28:27 ram and seven **male l** a year old as an H3897
Nu 28:29 with each of the seven **l**, one-tenth. H3897
Nu 29: 2 one ram and seven **male l** a year old, all H3897
Nu 29: 4 with each of the seven **l**, one-tenth. H3897
Nu 29: 8 one ram and seven **male l** a year old, all H3897
Nu 29:10 with each of the seven **l**, one-tenth. H3897
Nu 29:13 two rams and fourteen **male l** a year old H3897
Nu 29:15 with each of the fourteen **l**, one-tenth. H3897
Nu 29:17 two rams and fourteen **male l** a year old H3897
Nu 29:18 With the bulls, rams and **l**, offer their grain H3897
Nu 29:20 two rams and fourteen **male l** a year old H3897
Nu 29:21 With the bulls, rams and **l**, offer their grain H3897
Nu 29:23 two rams and fourteen **male l** a year old H3897
Nu 29:24 With the bulls, rams and **l**, offer their grain H3897
Nu 29:26 two rams and fourteen **male l** a year old H3897
Nu 29:27 With the bulls, rams and **l**, offer their grain H3897
Nu 29:29 two rams and fourteen **male l** a year old H3897
Nu 29:30 With the bulls, rams and **l**, offer their grain H3897
Nu 29:32 two rams and fourteen **male l** a year old H3897
Nu 29:33 With the bulls, rams and **l**, offer their grain H3897
Nu 29:36 one ram and seven **male l** a year old, all H3897
Nu 29:37 the ram and the **l**, offer their grain H3897
Dt 7:13 your herds and the **l** *of* your flocks in the H6957
Dt 28: 4 of your herds and the **l** *of* your flocks. H6957
Dt 28:18 of your herds and the **l** *of* your flocks. H6957
Dt 28:51 of your herds or **l** *of* your flocks until you H6957
Dt 32:14 flock and with fattened **l** and goats, H4119
1Sa 15: 9 the fat calves and **l**—everything that was H4119
2Ki 3: 4 a hundred thousand **l** and the wool of a H4119
1Ch 29:21 a thousand rams and a thousand **male l** H3897
2Ch 29:21 seven **male l** and seven male goats as a H3897
2Ch 29:22 they slaughtered the **l** and splashed their H3897
2Ch 29:32 hundred rams and two hundred **male l**— H3897
2Ch 30:17 had to kill the **Passover l** for all those who H7175
2Ch 30:17 could not consecrate their **l** to the LORD. NDT
2Ch 35: 6 Slaughter the **Passover l**, consecrate H7175
2Ch 35: 6 prepare the **l** for your fellow Israelites NDT
2Ch 35: 7 thirty thousand **l** and goats for the H7366+3897
2Ch 35:11 The **Passover l** were slaughtered, and the H7175
Ezr 6: 9 **male l** for burnt offerings to the God of A10043
Ezr 6:17 four hundred **male l** and, as a sin A10043
Ezr 7:17 rams and **male l**, together with A10043
Ezr 8:35 seventy-seven **male l** and, as a sin H3897
Ps 114: 4 leaped like rams, the hills like **l**. H1201+7366
Ps 114: 6 you leap like rams, you hills, like **l**? H1201+7366
Pr 27:26 the **l** will provide you with clothing, and H3897
Isa 1:11 in the blood of bulls and **l** and goats. H3897
Isa 5:17 **l** will feed among the ruins of the rich. H1531
Isa 16: 1 Send **l** as tribute to the ruler of the land H4119
Isa 34: 6 the blood of **l** and goats, fat from H4119
Isa 40:11 He gathers the **l** in his arms and carries H3231
Jer 51:40 bring them down like **l** to the slaughter, H4119
Eze 27:21 they did business with you in **l**, rams and H4119
Eze 39:18 of the earth as if they were rams and **l**, H4119
Eze 46: 4 day is to be six **male l** and a ram, H3897
Eze 46: 5 offering with the **l** is to be as much as he H3897
Eze 46: 6 a young bull, six **l** and a ram, all without H3897
Eze 46: 7 with the **l** as much as he wants to H3897
Eze 46:11 with the **l** as much as he pleases H3897
Hos 4:16 the LORD pasture them like **l** in a meadow? H3897
Am 6: 4 You dine on **choice l** and H4946+7366+4119
Lk 10: 3 I am sending you out like **l** among wolves. *G748*
Jn 21:15 that I love you." Jesus said, "Feed my **l**." *G768*

LAME (33)

Lev 21:18 no man who is blind or **l**, disfigured or H7177
Dt 15:21 has a defect, is **l** or blind, or has any H7177
2Sa 4: 4 of Saul had a son who was **l** *in* both feet. H5783
2Sa 5: 6 even the blind and the **l** can ward you off." H7177
2Sa 5: 8 shaft to reach those '**l** and blind' who are H7177
2Sa 5: 8 "The 'blind and **l**' will not enter the H7177
2Sa 9: 3 a son of Jonathan; he is **l** *in* both feet." H5783
2Sa 9:13 at the king's table; he was **l** *in* both feet. H7177
2Sa 19:26 the king, since I your servant am **l**, I said, H7177
Job 29:15 I was eyes to the blind and feet to the **l**. H7177
Pr 25:19 a broken tooth or a **l** foot is reliance on H5048
Pr 26: 7 useless legs of *one who* is **l** is a proverb H7177
Isa 33:23 divided and even the **l** will carry off H7177
Isa 35: 6 Then will the **l** leap like a deer, and the H7177
Jer 31: 8 Among them will be the blind and the **l** H7177
Mic 4: 6 "I will gather the **l**; I will assemble the H7519
Mic 4: 7 I will make the **l** my remnant, those driven H7519
Zep 3:19 I will rescue the **l**; I will gather the H7519
Mal 1: 8 When you sacrifice **l** or diseased animals H7177
Mal 1:13 **l** or diseased animals and offer them as H7177
Mt 11: 5 receive sight, the **l** walk, those who have *G6000*
Mt 15:30 came to him, bringing the **l**, the blind, *G6000*
Mt 15:31 the **l** walking and the blind seeing. *G6000*
Mt 21:14 The blind and the **l** came to him at the *G6000*
Lk 7:22 receive sight, the **l** walk, those who have *G6000*
Lk 14:13 the poor, the crippled, the **l**, the blind, *G6000*
Lk 14:21 the poor, the crippled, the blind and the **l**. *G6000*
Jn 5: 3 the blind, the **l**, the paralyzed. *G6000*
Ac 3: 2 Now a man who was **l** from birth was *G6000*
Ac 4: 9 to a man who was **l** and are being asked *G822*
Ac 8: 7 who were paralyzed or **l** were healed. *G6000*
Ac 14: 8 there sat a man who was **l**. *G105+3836+4546*
Heb 12:13 so that the **l** may not be disabled, but *G6000*

LAMECH (12)

Ge 4:18 Methushael was the father of **L**. H4347
Ge 4:19 **L** married two women, one named Adah H4347
Ge 4:23 **L** said to his wives, "Adah and Zillah H4347
Ge 4:23 listen to me; wives of **L**, hear my words. H4347
Ge 4:24 seven times, then **L** seventy-seven times." H4347

Ge 5:25 187 years, he became the father of L. H4347
Ge 5:26 After he became the father of L H4347
Ge 5:28 When L had lived 182 years, he had a H4347
Ge 5:30 L lived 595 years and had other sons and H4347
Ge 5:31 Altogether, L lived a total of 777 years H4347
1Ch 1: 3 Methuselah, L, Noah. H4347
Lk 3:36 of Shem, the son of Noah, the son *of* L, *G3285*

LAMENT (29) [LAMENTATION, LAMENTED, LAMENTS]

2Sa 1:17 David **took up** this l concerning H7801+7806
2Sa 1:18 of Judah be taught this l of the bow NDT
2Sa 3:33 The king **sang** *this* l for Abner: "Should H7801
Ps 5: 1 Listen to my words, LORD, consider my l. H2052
Ps 102: T weak and pours out a l before the LORD. H8490
Isa 3:26 The gates of Zion *will* l and mourn H627
Isa 15: 5 road to Horonaim *they* l their H6424+2411
Isa 16: 7 L and grieve for the raisin cakes of Kir H2047
Isa 19: 8 The fishermen will groan and l, all who cast H61
Isa 29: 2 she will mourn and l, she will be to me like H640
Jer 4: 8 So put on sackcloth, l and wail, for the H6199
Jer 7:29 it away; take up a l on the barren heights H7806
Jer 9:10 mountains and take up a l concerning the H7806
Jer 9:20 how to wail; teach one another a l. H7806
Jer 34: 5 they will make a fire in your honor and l, H6199
La 2: 8 *He* **made** ramparts and walls l; together they H61
Eze 2:10 written words of l and mourning and woe. H7806
Eze 9: 4 those who grieve and l over all the H650
Eze 19: 1 "Take up a l concerning the princes of H7806
Eze 19:14 "This is a l and is to be used as a lament." H7806
Eze 19:14 "This is a lament and is to be used as a l." H7806
Eze 24:16 Yet *do* not l or weep or shed any tears. H6199
Eze 26:17 they will take up a l concerning you and H7806
Eze 27: 2 "Son of man, take up a l concerning Tyre. H7806
Eze 27:32 *they will* **take up a** l concerning you: H7801
Eze 28:12 take up a l concerning the king of Tyre H7806
Eze 32: 2 take up a l concerning Pharaoh king of H7806
Eze 32:16 "This is the l they will chant for her. H7806
Am 5: 1 this l I take up concerning you: H7806

LAMENTATION (3) [LAMENT]

Est 9:31 in regard to their times of fasting and l. H2411
Isa 15: 8 far as Eglaim, their l as far as Beer Elim. H3538
La 2: 5 mourning and l for Daughter Judah. H640

LAMENTED (1) [LAMENT]

Ge 50:10 Jordan, *they* l loudly and bitterly H6199+5027

LAMENTS (6) [LAMENT]

2Ch 35:25 Jeremiah **composed** l for Josiah, and to H7801
2Ch 35:25 singers commemorate Josiah in the l. H7806
2Ch 35:25 tradition in Israel and are written in the L. H7806
Isa 16:11 My heart l for Moab like a harp, my H2159
Jer 48:36 "So my heart l for Moab like the music of H2159
Jer 48:36 it l like a pipe for the people of Kir H2159

LAMP (34) [LAMPS, LAMPSTAND, LAMPSTANDS]

1Sa 3: 3 The l *of* God had not yet gone out, and H5944
2Sa 21:17 so that the l *of* Israel will not be H5944
2Sa 22:29 are my l; the LORD turns my darkness H5944
1Ki 11:36 may always have a l before me in H5775
1Ki 15: 4 his God gave him a l in Jerusalem by H5775
2Ki 4:10 a bed and a table, a chair and a l for him. H4963
2Ki 8:19 to maintain a l for David and his H5775
2Ch 21: 7 promised to maintain a l for him and his H5775
Job 18: 5 "The l *of* a wicked man is snuffed out; the H240
Job 18: 6 becomes dark; the l beside him goes out. H5944
Job 21:17 how often is the l *of* the wicked snuffed H5944
Job 29: 3 when his l shone on my head and by his H5944
Ps 18:28 keep my l burning; my God turns my H5944
Ps 119:105 Your word is a l for my feet, a light on H5944
Ps 132:17 David and set up a l for my anointed one. H5944
Pr 6:23 For this command is a l, this teaching is a H5944
Pr 13: 9 the l *of* the wicked is snuffed out. H5944
Pr 20:20 their l will be snuffed out in pitch H5944
Pr 20:27 human spirit is the l *of* the LORD that sheds H5944
Pr 24:20 the l *of* the wicked will be snuffed out H5944
Pr 31:18 her l does not go out at night. H5944
Jer 25:10 sound of millstones and the light of the l. H5944
Mt 5:15 do people light a l and put it under a *G3394*
Mt 6:22 "The eye is the l of the body. If your eyes *G3394*
Mk 4:21 "Do you bring in a l to put it under a bowl *G3394*
Lk 8:16 "No one lights a l and hides it in a clay *G3394*
Lk 11:33 "No one lights a l and puts it in a place *G3394*
Lk 11:34 Your eye is the l of your body. When your *G3394*
Lk 11:36 of light as when a l shines its light on you *G3394*
Lk 15: 8 Doesn't she light a l, sweep the house *G3394*
Jn 5:35 John was a l that burned and gave light *G3394*
Rev 18:23 The light *of* a l will never shine in you *G3394*
Rev 21:23 of God gives it light, and the Lamb is its l. *G3394*
Rev 22: 5 not need the light *of* a l or the light of the *G3394*

LAMPS (35) [LAMP]

Ex 25:37 make its seven l and set them up on H5944
Ex 27:20 light so that the l may be kept burning. H5944
Ex 27:21 sons are to keep **the** l burning before the H2257S
Ex 30: 7 altar every morning when he tends the l. H5944
Ex 30: 8 when he lights the l at twilight so incense H5944
Ex 35:14 with its accessories, l and oil for the light; H5944
Ex 37:23 They made its seven l, as well as its wick H5944
Ex 39:37 lampstand with its row *of* l and all its H5944
Ex 40: 4 bring in the lampstand and set up its l. H5944
Ex 40:25 set up the l before the LORD, as the H5944
Lev 24: 2 the light so that the l may be kept burning H5944
Lev 24: 3 Aaron is to tend **the** l before the LORD H2257S
Lev 24: 4 The l on the pure gold lampstand before H5944
Nu 4: 9 together with its l, its wick trimmers and H5944
Nu 8: 2 'When you set up the l, see that all seven H5944
Nu 8: 3 he set up the l so that they faced forward H5944
1Ki 7:49 the gold floral work and l and tongs; H5944
1Ch 28:15 gold for the gold lampstands and their l, H5944
1Ch 28:15 the weight for each lampstand and its l; H5944
1Ch 28:15 silver for each silver lampstand and its l, H5944
2Ch 4:20 the lampstands of pure gold with their l H5944
2Ch 4:21 the gold floral work and l and tongs (they H5944
2Ch 13:11 table and light the l on the gold H5944
2Ch 29: 7 the doors of the portico and put out the l. H5944
Zep 1:12 Jerusalem with l and punish those who H5944
Zec 4: 2 with a bowl at the top and seven l on it, H5944
Zec 4: 2 lamps on it, with seven channels to the l. H5944
Mt 25: 1 who took their l and went out to meet *G3286*
Mt 25: 3 ones took their l but did not take any *G3286*
Mt 25: 4 however, took oil in jars along with their l. *G3286*
Mt 25: 7 the virgins woke up and trimmed their l. *G3286*
Mt 25: 8 us some of your oil; our l are going out. *G3286*
Lk 12:35 ready for service and keep your l burning, *G3394*
Ac 20: 8 There were many l in the upstairs room *G3286*
Rev 4: 5 of the throne, seven l were blazing. *G3286+4786*

LAMPSTAND (37) [LAMP]

Ex 25:31 "Make a l of pure gold. Hammer out its H4963
Ex 25:32 are to extend from the sides of the l— H4963
Ex 25:33 all six branches extending from the l. H4963
Ex 25:34 And on the l there are to be four cups H4963
Ex 25:35 first pair of branches extending from the l, H4963
Ex 25:36 shall all be of one piece with **the** l, H5626S
Ex 25:39 is to be used for the l and all these NDT
Ex 26:35 put the l opposite it on the H4963
Ex 30:27 all its articles, the l and its accessories H4963
Ex 31: 8 the pure gold l and all its accessories H4963
Ex 35:14 the l that is *for* light with its accessories H4963
Ex 37:17 They made the l of pure gold. H4963
Ex 37:18 extended from the sides of the l— H4963
Ex 37:19 all six branches extending from the l. H4963
Ex 37:20 And on the l were four cups shaped like H4963
Ex 37:21 pair of branches extending from **the** l, H5626S
Ex 37:22 were all of one piece with **the** l, H5626S
Ex 37:24 They made **the** l and all its accessories H2023S
Ex 39:37 the pure gold l with its row of lamps and H4963
Ex 40: 4 Then bring in the l and set up its lamps H4963
Ex 40:24 He placed the l in the tent of meeting H4963
Lev 24: 4 on the pure gold l before the LORD must H4963
Nu 3:31 the table, the l, the altars, the H4963
Nu 4: 9 blue cloth and cover the l that is *for* light, H4963
Nu 8: 2 seven light up the area in front of the l. H4963
Nu 8: 3 lamps so that they faced forward on the l, H4963
Nu 8: 4 This is how the l was made: It was made H4963
Nu 8: 4 The l was made exactly like the pattern H4963
1Ch 28:15 weight for **each** l and its H4963+2256+4963
1Ch 28:15 of silver for **each** silver l and its H4963+4963
1Ch 28:15 to the use of **each** l; H4963+2256+4963
2Ch 13:11 the lamps on the gold l every evening. H4963
Da 5: 5 the wall, near the l in the royal palace. A10456
Zec 4: 2 "I see a solid gold l with a bowl at the top H4963
Zec 4:11 trees on the right and the left of the l?" H4963
Heb 9: 2 first room were the l and the table with its *G3393*
Rev 2: 5 to you and remove your l from its place. *G3393*

LAMPSTANDS (11) [LAMP]

1Ki 7:49 the l of pure gold (five on the right and H4963
1Ch 28:15 of gold for the gold l and their lamps, H4963
2Ch 4: 7 He made ten gold l according to the H4963
2Ch 4:20 the l of pure gold with their lamps, to H4963
Jer 52:19 l, dishes and bowls used for drink H4963
Rev 1:12 And when I turned I saw seven golden l, *G3393*
Rev 1:13 among the l was someone like a son *G3393*
Rev 1:20 hand and *of* the seven golden l is this: *G3393*
Rev 1:20 the seven l are the seven churches. *G3393*
Rev 2: 1 walks among the seven golden l. *G3393*
Rev 11: 4 and the two l, and "they stand *G3393*

LANCE (2)

Job 39:23 along with the flashing spear and l. H3959
Job 41:29 of straw; it laughs at the rattling of the l. H3959

LANCETS (KJV) SPEARS

LAND (1464) [BORDERLAND, FARMLANDS, GRASSLANDS, LAND'S, LANDED, LANDOWNER, LANDS, MAINLAND, SHORELANDS, WASTELAND, WASTELANDS]

Ge 1:10 God called the dry ground "l," and the H824
Ge 1:11 God said, "Let the l produce vegetation: H824
Ge 1:11 plants and trees on the l that bear fruit with H824
Ge 1:12 The l produced vegetation: plants bearing H824
Ge 1:24 "Let the l produce living creatures H824
Ge 2:11 it winds through the entire l of Havilah H824
Ge 2:12 The gold of that l is good; aromatic resin H824
Ge 2:13 it winds through the entire l *of* Cush. H824
Ge 4:14 Today you are driving me from the l, and I H141
Ge 4:16 LORD's presence and lived in the l *of* Nod, H824
Ge 7:21 living thing that moved on l perished— H824
Ge 7:22 Everything on **dry** l that had the breath of H3000
Ge 8:19 everything that moves on l—came out of H824
Ge 10:11 From that l he went to Assyria, where he H824
Ge 11:28 in Ur of the Chaldeans, in the l *of* his birth. H824
Ge 12: 1 father's household to the l I will show you. H824
Ge 12: 5 they set out for the l *of* Canaan, and H824
Ge 12: 6 traveled through the l as far as the site of H824
Ge 12: 6 At that time the Canaanites were in the l. H824
Ge 12: 7 "To your offspring I will give this l. H824
Ge 12:10 Now there was a famine in the l, and H824
Ge 13: 6 But the l could not support them while they H824
Ge 13: 7 were also living in the l at that time. H824
Ge 13: 9 Is not the whole l before you? Let's part H824
Ge 13:10 the garden of the LORD, like the l *of* Egypt. H824
Ge 13:12 Abram lived in the l *of* Canaan, while Lot H824
Ge 13:15 All the l that you see I will give to you and H824
Ge 13:17 through the length and breadth of the l, H824
Ge 15: 7 to give you this l to take possession of it." H824
Ge 15:18 "To your descendants I give this l, from the H824
Ge 15:19 the l of the Kenites, Kenizzites, Kadmonites, NDT
Ge 17: 8 The whole l *of* Canaan, where you now H824
Ge 19:23 reached Zoar, the sun had risen over the l. H824
Ge 19:25 the cities—and also the vegetation in the l. H141
Ge 19:28 toward all the l *of* the plain, and he saw H824
Ge 19:28 he saw dense smoke rising from the l H824
Ge 20:15 Abimelek said, "My l is before you; live H824
Ge 21:32 forces returned to the l *of* the Philistines. H824
Ge 21:34 stayed in the l *of* the Philistines for H824
Ge 23: 2 Hebron) in the l *of* Canaan, and Abraham H824
Ge 23: 7 bowed down before the people of the l, H824
Ge 23:12 bowed down before the people of the l H824
Ge 23:15 the l is worth four hundred shekels of silver H824
Ge 23:19 which is at Hebron) in the l *of* Canaan. H824
Ge 24: 5 is unwilling to come back with me to this l? H824
Ge 24: 7 my native l and who spoke to me and H824
Ge 24: 7 'To your offspring I will give this l'—he H824
Ge 24:37 of the Canaanites, in whose l I live, H824
Ge 25: 6 away from his son Isaac to the l *of* the east. H824
Ge 26: 1 Now there was a famine in the l—besides H824
Ge 26: 2 live in the l where I tell you to live. H824
Ge 26: 3 Stay in this l for a while, and I will be with H824
Ge 26:12 planted crops in that l and the same year H824
Ge 26:22 given us room and we will flourish in the l." H824
Ge 27:46 a wife from among the women of this l, H824
Ge 28: 4 possession of the l *where* you now reside H824
Ge 28: 4 a foreigner, **the** l God gave to Abraham." H889S
Ge 28:13 your descendants the l on which you are H824
Ge 28:15 and I will bring you back to this l. H141
Ge 29: 1 came to the l *of* the eastern peoples. H824
Ge 31: 3 "Go back to the l *of* your fathers and to your H824
Ge 31:13 Now leave this l at once and go back to H824
Ge 31:13 land at once and go back to your native l. H824
Ge 31:18 to go to his father Isaac in the l *of* Canaan. H824
Ge 32: 3 of him to his brother Esau in the l *of* Seir, H824
Ge 34: 1 went out to visit the women of the l. H824
Ge 34:10 can settle among us; the l is open to you. H824
Ge 34:21 "Let them live in our l and trade in it; the H824
Ge 34:21 the l has plenty of room for them. H824
Ge 34:30 Perizzites, the people living in this l. H824
Ge 35: 6 that is, Bethel) in the l *of* Canaan. H824
Ge 35:12 The l I gave to Abraham and Isaac I also H824
Ge 35:12 I will give this l to your descendants H824
Ge 36: 6 moved to a l some distance from his H824
Ge 36: 7 the l *where* they were staying could not H824
Ge 36:30 according to their divisions, in the l *of* Seir. H824
Ge 36:34 Husham from the l *of* the Temanites H824
Ge 36:43 to their settlements in the l they occupied. H824
Ge 37: 1 Jacob lived in the l *where* his father had H824
Ge 37: 1 his father had stayed, the l *of* Canaan. H824
Ge 40:15 carried off from the l *of* the Hebrews, H824
Ge 41:19 seen such ugly cows in all the l *of* Egypt. H824
Ge 41:29 are coming throughout the l *of* Egypt, H824
Ge 41:30 forgotten, and the famine will ravage the l. H824
Ge 41:31 The abundance in the l will not be H824
Ge 41:33 put him in charge of the l *of* Egypt. H824
Ge 41:34 over the l to take a fifth of the H824
Ge 41:41 put you in charge of the whole l *of* Egypt." H824
Ge 41:43 put him in charge of the whole l *of* Egypt. H824
Ge 41:45 And Joseph went throughout the l *of* Egypt H824
Ge 41:47 of abundance the l produced plentifully. H824
Ge 41:52 made me fruitful in the l *of* my suffering." H824
Ge 41:54 in the whole l *of* Egypt there was food. H824
Ge 42: 5 there was famine in the l *of* Canaan also. H824
Ge 42: 6 Now Joseph was the governor of the l, the H824
Ge 42: 7 "From the l *of* Canaan," they replied, "to H824
Ge 42: 9 come to see where our l is unprotected." H824
Ge 42:12 come to see where our l is unprotected." H824
Ge 42:13 of one man, who lives in the l *of* Canaan. H824
Ge 42:29 to their father Jacob in the l *of* Canaan, H824
Ge 42:30 who is lord over the l spoke harshly to us H824
Ge 42:30 us as though we were spying on the l. H824
Ge 42:33 the man who is lord over the l said to us, H824
Ge 42:34 back to you, and you can trade in the l. H824
Ge 43: 1 Now the famine was still severe in the l. H824
Ge 43:11 best products of the l in your bags and take H824
Ge 44: 8 back to you from the l *of* Canaan the silver H824
Ge 45: 6 years now there has been famine in the l, H824
Ge 45:17 your animals and return to the l *of* Canaan, H824
Ge 45:18 you the best of the l *of* Egypt and you can H824
Ge 45:18 of Egypt and you can enjoy the fat of the l. H824
Ge 45:25 to their father Jacob in the l *of* Canaan. H824
Ge 46:12 Er and Onan had died in the l *of* Canaan). H824
Ge 46:31 who were living in the l *of* Canaan, have H824
Ge 47: 1 have come from the l *of* Canaan and are H824
Ge 47: 6 the l *of* Egypt is before you; settle your H824

L

Ge 47: 6 your brothers in the best part of the **l**. H824
Ge 47:11 gave them property in the best part of the **l**, H824
Ge 47:18 left for our lord except our bodies and our **l**. H141
Ge 47:19 before your eyes—we and our **l** as well? H141
Ge 47:19 Buy us and our **l** in exchange for food, and H141
Ge 47:19 we with our **l** will be in bondage to H141
Ge 47:19 that the **l** may not become desolate." H141
Ge 47:20 bought all the **l** *in* Egypt for Pharaoh. H141
Ge 47:20 severe for them. The **l** became Pharaoh's, H824
Ge 47:22 he did not buy the **l** *of* the priests, because H141
Ge 47:22 That is why they did not sell their **l**. H141
Ge 47:23 bought you and your **l** today for Pharaoh, H141
Ge 47:26 it as a law concerning **l** *in* Egypt— H141
Ge 47:26 It was only the **l** *of* the priests that did not H141
Ge 48: 3 appeared to me at Luz in the **l** *of* Canaan, H824
Ge 48: 4 I will give this **l** as an everlasting H824
Ge 48: 7 Rachel died in the **l** *of* Canaan while we H824
Ge 48:21 take you back to the **l** *of* your fathers. H824
Ge 48:22 I give one more **ridge of l** than to your H8900
Ge 49:15 his resting place and how pleasant is his **l**, H824
Ge 50: 5 tomb I dug for myself in the **l** *of* Canaan." H824
Ge 50:13 carried him to the **l** *of* Canaan and buried H824
Ge 50:24 you up out of this **l** to the land he promised H824
Ge 50:24 of this land to the **l** he promised on oath to H824
Ex 1: 7 so numerous that the **l** was filled with them H824
Ex 2:22 "I have become a foreigner in a foreign **l**." H824
Ex 3: 8 them up out of that **l** into a good and H824
Ex 3: 8 out of that land into a good and spacious **l**, H824
Ex 3: 8 a **l** flowing with milk and honey H824
Ex 3:17 in Egypt into the **l** *of* the Canaanites, H824
Ex 3:17 a **l** flowing with milk and honey. H824
Ex 5: 5 the people of the **l** are now numerous, and H824
Ex 6: 4 with them to give them the **l** *of* Canaan, H824
Ex 6: 8 will bring you to the **l** I swore with uplifted H824
Ex 8: 5 make frogs come up on the **l** *of* Egypt. H824
Ex 8: 6 the frogs came up and covered the **l**. H824
Ex 8: 7 also made frogs come up on the **l** *of* Egypt. H824
Ex 8:14 piled into heaps, and the **l** reeked of them. H824
Ex 8:16 throughout the **l** *of* Egypt the dust will H824
Ex 8:17 throughout the **l** *of* Egypt became gnats H824
Ex 8:22 I will deal differently with the **l** *of* Goshen, H824
Ex 8:22 you will know that I, the LORD, am in this **l**. H824
Ex 8:24 throughout Egypt the **l** was ruined by the H824
Ex 8:25 sacrifice to your God here in the **l**. H824
Ex 9: 5 "Tomorrow the LORD will do this in the **l**." H824
Ex 9: 9 become fine dust over the whole **l** *of* Egypt, H824
Ex 9: 9 on people and animals throughout the **l**." H824
Ex 9:23 So the LORD rained hail on the **l** *of* Egypt; H824
Ex 9:24 worst storm in all the **l** *of* Egypt since it had H824
Ex 9:26 place it did not hail was the **l** *of* Goshen, H824
Ex 9:33 the rain no longer poured down on the **l**. H824
Ex 10: 6 from the day they settled in this **l** till now. H141
Ex 10:12 swarm over the **l** and devour everything H824
Ex 10:13 wind blow across the **l** all that day and all H824
Ex 10:15 on tree or plant in all the **l** *of* Egypt. H824
Ex 12:23 LORD goes through the **l** to strike down the NDT
Ex 12:25 When you enter the **l** that the LORD will H824
Ex 12:48 he may take part like one born in the **l**. H824
Ex 13: 3 of Egypt, out of the **l** *of* slavery, because H1074
Ex 13: 5 brings you into the **l** *of* the Canaanites, H824
Ex 13: 5 **the l** he swore to your ancestors to give H889S
Ex 13: 5 give you, a **l** flowing with milk and honey H824
Ex 13:11 brings you into the **l** *of* the Canaanites H824
Ex 13:14 us out of Egypt, out of the **l** *of* slavery. H1074
Ex 14: 3 are wandering around the **l** in confusion, H824
Ex 14:21 a strong east wind and turned it into **dry l**. H3000
Ex 16:35 they came to a **l** that was settled; they H824
Ex 18: 3 "I have become a foreigner in a foreign **l**"; H824
Ex 20: 2 you out of Egypt, out of the **l** *of* slavery. H1074
Ex 20:12 may live long in the **l** the LORD your God is H141
Ex 23:11 seventh year let **the l** lie unplowed and H5626S
Ex 23:23 you and bring you into the **l** of the Amorites, NDT
Ex 23:26 none will miscarry or be barren in your **l**. H824
Ex 23:29 because the **l** would become desolate H824
Ex 23:30 enough to take possession of the **l**. H824
Ex 23:31 your hands the people who live in the **l**, H824
Ex 23:33 let them live in your **l** or they will cause you H824
Ex 32:13 descendants all this **l** I promised them, H824
Ex 33: 1 go up to the **l** I promised on oath to H824
Ex 33: 3 Go up to the **l** flowing with milk and honey H824
Ex 34:12 who live in the **l** where you are going, H824
Ex 34:15 make a treaty with those who live in the **l**; H824
Ex 34:24 one will covet your **l** when you go up three H824
Lev 11: 2 'Of all the animals that live on **l**, these are H824
Lev 14:34 "When you enter the **l** *of* Canaan, which I H824
Lev 14:34 I put a spreading mold in a house in that **l**, H824
Lev 18: 3 must not do as they do in the **l** *of* Canaan, H824
Lev 18:25 Even the **l** was defiled; so I punished it H824
Lev 18:25 and the **l** vomited out its inhabitants. H824
Lev 18:27 the people who lived in the **l** before you, H824
Lev 18:27 land before you, and the **l** became defiled. H824
Lev 18:28 And if you defile the **l**, it will vomit you out H824
Lev 19: 9 " 'When you reap the harvest of your **l**, do H824
Lev 19:23 'When you enter the **l** and plant any kind H824
Lev 19:29 the **l** will turn to prostitution and be H824
Lev 19:33 a foreigner resides among you in your **l**, H824
Lev 20:22 so that the **l** where I am bringing you to H824
Lev 20:24 "You will possess their **l**; I will give it to you H141
Lev 20:24 a **l** flowing with milk and honey. H824
Lev 22:24 You must not do this in your own **l**, H824
Lev 23:10 'When you enter the **l** I am going to give H824
Lev 23:22 " 'When you reap the harvest of your **l**, do H824

Lev 23:39 after you have gathered the crops of the **l** H824
Lev 25: 2 'When you enter the **l** I am going to give H824
Lev 25: 2 the **l** itself must observe a sabbath to the H824
Lev 25: 4 the seventh year the **l** is to have a year of H824
Lev 25: 5 The **l** is to have a year of rest H824
Lev 25: 6 Whatever the **l** yields during the sabbath H824
Lev 25: 7 livestock and the wild animals in your **l**. H824
Lev 25: 7 Whatever **the l** produces may be eaten H2023S
Lev 25: 9 sound the trumpet throughout your **l**. H824
Lev 25:10 liberty throughout the **l** to all its inhabitants H824
Lev 25:14 " 'If *you* **sell l** to any of your own H4835+4928
Lev 25:14 any of your own people or buy **l** from them, NDT
Lev 25:18 my laws, and you will live safely in the **l**. H824
Lev 25:19 Then the **l** will yield its fruit, and you will H824
Lev 25:21 the sixth year that the **l** will yield enough NDT
Lev 25:23 " 'The **l** must not be sold permanently H824
Lev 25:23 because the **l** is mine and you reside in my H824
Lev 25:23 you reside in my **l** as foreigners and NDT
Lev 25:24 Throughout the **l** *that* you hold as a H824
Lev 25:24 must provide for the redemption of the **l**. H824
Lev 25:38 Egypt to give you the **l** *of* Canaan and to be H824
Lev 26: 1 carved stone in your **l** to bow down before H824
Lev 26: 5 food you want and live in safety in your **l**. H824
Lev 26: 6 " 'I will grant peace in the **l**, and you will H824
Lev 26: 6 I will remove wild beasts from the **l**, and H824
Lev 26:20 will the trees of your **l** yield their fruit. H824
Lev 26:32 I myself will lay waste the **l**, so that your H824
Lev 26:33 Your **l** will be laid waste, and your cities H824
Lev 26:34 Then the **l** will enjoy its sabbath years all H824
Lev 26:34 then the **l** will rest and enjoy its sabbaths. H824
Lev 26:35 the **l** will have the rest it did not have during NDT
Lev 26:38 the **l** *of* your enemies will devour you. H824
Lev 26:41 I sent them into the **l** *of* their enemies— H824
Lev 26:42 with Abraham, and I will remember the **l**. H824
Lev 26:43 For the **l** will be deserted by them and will H824
Lev 26:44 when they are in the **l** *of* their enemies, H824
Lev 27:16 to the LORD part of their **family l**, H8441+299
Lev 27:22 which is not part of their **family l**, H8441+299
Lev 27:24 it was bought, the one whose **l** it was. H299+824
Lev 27:28 being or an animal or **family l**— H8441+299
Lev 27:30 " 'A tithe of everything from the **l**, whether H824
Nu 10: 9 battle in your own **l** against an enemy who H824
Nu 10:30 back to my own **l** and my own people." H824
Nu 11:12 to the **l** you promised on oath to their H141
Nu 13: 2 some men to explore the **l** *of* Canaan, H824
Nu 13:16 of the men Moses sent to explore the **l**. H824
Nu 13:18 See what the **l** is like and whether the H824
Nu 13:19 What kind of **l** do they live in? Is it good H824
Nu 13:20 best to bring back some of the fruit of the **l**." H824
Nu 13:21 up and explored the **l** from the Desert of H824
Nu 13:25 days they returned from exploring the **l**. H824
Nu 13:26 showed them the fruit of the **l**. H824
Nu 13:27 "We went into the **l** to which you sent us H824
Nu 13:30 go up and take possession of **the l**, H2023S
Nu 13:32 a bad report about the **l** they had explored. H824
Nu 13:32 "The **l** we explored devours those living in H824
Nu 14: 3 bringing us to this **l** only to let us fall by H824
Nu 14: 6 were among those who had explored the **l**, H824
Nu 14: 7 "The **l** we passed through and explored is H824
Nu 14: 8 he will lead us into that **l**, a land flowing H824
Nu 14: 8 that land, a **l** flowing with milk and honey H824
Nu 14: 9 And do not be afraid of the people of the **l** H824
Nu 14:14 will tell the inhabitants of this **l** about it. H824
Nu 14:16 people into the **l** he promised them on H824
Nu 14:23 will ever see the **l** I promised on oath to H824
Nu 14:24 I will bring him into the **l** he went to, and H824
Nu 14:30 of you will enter the **l** I swore with uplifted H824
Nu 14:31 them in to enjoy the **l** you have rejected. H824
Nu 14:34 each of the forty days you explored the **l**— H824
Nu 14:36 the men Moses had sent to explore the **l**, H824
Nu 14:37 report about the **l** were struck down and H824
Nu 14:38 Of the men who went to explore the **l**, only H824
Nu 14:40 ready to go up to the **l** the LORD promised. H5226
Nu 15: 2 'After you enter the **l** I am giving you as a H824
Nu 15:18 'When you enter the **l** to which I am taking H824
Nu 15:19 you eat the food of the **l**, present a H824
Nu 16:13 us up out of a **l** flowing with milk and H824
Nu 16:14 brought us into a **l** flowing with milk and H824
Nu 18:20 "You will have no inheritance in their **l**, nor H824
Nu 20:12 bring this community into the **l** I give them." H824
Nu 20:24 He will not enter the **l** I give the Israelites H824
Nu 21:24 took over his **l** from the Arnon to the H824
Nu 21:26 taken from him all his **l** as far as the Arnon. H824
Nu 21:31 So Israel settled in the **l** *of* the Amorites. H824
Nu 21:34 along with his whole army and his **l**. H824
Nu 21:35 And they took possession of his **l**. H824
Nu 22: 5 near the Euphrates River, in his native **l**. H824
Nu 22: 5 the face of the **l** and have settled next H824
Nu 22: 6 to defeat them and drive them out of the **l**. H824
Nu 22:11 come out of Egypt covers the face of the **l**. H824
Nu 26:53 "The **l** is to be allotted to them as an H824
Nu 26:55 Be sure that the **l** is distributed by lot. H824
Nu 27:12 Range and see the **l** I have given the H824
Nu 32: 4 the **l** the LORD subdued before the people of H824
Nu 32: 5 "let this **l** be given to your servants as our H824
Nu 32: 7 crossing over into the **l** the LORD has given H824
Nu 32: 8 from Kadesh Barnea to look over the **l**. H824
Nu 32: 9 up to the Valley of Eshkol and viewed the **l**, H824
Nu 32: 9 from entering the **l** the LORD had given H824
Nu 32:11 Egypt will see the **l** I promised on oath to H141
Nu 32:17 protection from the inhabitants of the **l**. H824
Nu 32:22 then when the **l** is subdued before the LORD H824

Nu 32:22 And this **l** will be your possession before H824
Nu 32:29 then when the **l** is subdued before you H824
Nu 32:29 you must give them the **l** *of* Gilead as their H824
Nu 32:33 the whole **l** with its cities and the territory H824
Nu 33:52 out all the inhabitants of the **l** before you. H824
Nu 33:53 Take possession of the **l** and settle in it, for H824
Nu 33:53 for I have given you the **l** to possess. H824
Nu 33:54 Distribute the **l** by lot, according to your H824
Nu 33:55 do not drive out the inhabitants of the **l**, H824
Nu 33:55 you trouble in the **l** where you will live. H824
Nu 34: 2 the **l** that will be allotted to you as an H824
Nu 34:12 " 'This will be your **l**, with its boundaries H824
Nu 34:13 "Assign this **l** by lot as an inheritance H824
Nu 34:17 who are to assign the **l** for you as an H824
Nu 34:18 leader from each tribe to help assign the **l**. H824
Nu 34:29 to the Israelites in the **l** *of* Canaan. H824
Nu 35: 8 the Levites from the **l** the Israelites possess NDT
Nu 35:32 live on their own **l** before the death of H824
Nu 35:33 " 'Do not pollute the **l** where you are H824
Nu 35:33 Bloodshed pollutes the **l**, and atonement H824
Nu 35:33 be made for the **l** on which blood has H824
Nu 35:34 Do not defile the **l** where you live and H824
Nu 36: 2 my lord to give the **l** as an inheritance to H824
Nu 36: 8 daughter who inherits **l** in any Israelite H5709
Nu 36: 9 Israelite tribe is to keep the **l** it **inherits**." H5709
Dt 1: 7 to the **l** *of* the Canaanites and to Lebanon H824
Dt 1: 8 I have given you this **l**. Go in and take H824
Dt 1: 8 take possession of the **l** the LORD swore he H824
Dt 1:21 the LORD your God has given you the **l**. H824
Dt 1:22 ahead to spy out the **l** for us and bring back H824
Dt 1:25 Taking with them some of the fruit of the **l** H824
Dt 1:25 "It is a good **l** that the LORD our God is H824
Dt 1:35 shall see the good **l** I swore to give your H824
Dt 1:36 his descendants the **l** he set his feet on, H824
Dt 1:39 from bad—they will enter **the l**. H2025+9004S
Dt 2: 5 I will not give you any of their **l**, not H824
Dt 2: 9 I will not give you any part of their **l**. H824
Dt 2:12 as Israel did in the **l** the LORD gave them as H824
Dt 2:19 of any **l** *belonging to* the Ammonites. H824
Dt 2:20 too was considered a **l** *of* the Rephaites, H824
Dt 2:29 the Jordan into the **l** the LORD our God is H824
Dt 2:31 Now begin to conquer and possess his **l**." H824
Dt 2:37 encroach on any of the **l** *of* the Ammonites, H824
Dt 2:37 neither the **l** along the course of the Jabbok NDT
Dt 3: 2 along with his whole army and his **l**. H824
Dt 3:12 Of the **l** that we took over at that time, H824
Dt 3:13 used to be known as a **l** *of* the Rephaites. H824
Dt 3:18 has given you this **l** to take possession of H824
Dt 3:20 have taken over the **l** that the LORD your H824
Dt 3:25 see the good **l** beyond the Jordan— H824
Dt 3:27 Look at the **l** with your own eyes, since you NDT
Dt 3:28 them to inherit the **l** that you will see." H824
Dt 4: 1 go in and take possession of the **l** the LORD, H824
Dt 4: 5 follow them in the **l** you are entering to H824
Dt 4:10 as they live in the **l** and may teach them to H141
Dt 4:14 are to follow in the **l** that you are crossing H824
Dt 4:21 enter the good **l** the LORD your God is H824
Dt 4:22 I will die in this **l**; I will not cross the Jordan H824
Dt 4:22 over and take possession of that good **l**. H824
Dt 4:25 have lived in the **l** a long time— H824
Dt 4:26 perish from the **l** that you are crossing H824
Dt 4:38 to bring you into their **l** to give it to you H824
Dt 4:40 may live long in the **l** the LORD your God H141
Dt 4:46 in the **l** *of* Sihon king of the Amorites H824
Dt 4:47 took possession of his **l** and the land of Og H824
Dt 4:47 of his land and the **l** *of* Og king of Bashan, H824
Dt 4:48 This **l** extended from Aroer on the rim of the NDT
Dt 5: 6 you out of Egypt, out of the **l** *of* slavery. H1074
Dt 5:16 well with you in the **l** the LORD your God is H141
Dt 5:21 your desire on your neighbor's house or **l**, H8441
Dt 5:31 them to follow in the **l** I am giving them to H824
Dt 5:33 your days in the **l** that you will possess. H824
Dt 6: 1 you to observe in the **l** that you are crossing H824
Dt 6: 3 greatly in a **l** flowing with milk and H824
Dt 6:10 God brings you into the **l** he swore to your H824
Dt 6:10 to give you—a **l** with large, flourishing cities NDT
Dt 6:12 you out of Egypt, out of the **l** *of* slavery. H1074
Dt 6:15 he will destroy you from the face of the **l**. H141
Dt 6:18 take over the good **l** the LORD promised on H824
Dt 6:23 in and give us the **l** he promised on oath H824
Dt 7: 1 brings you into the **l** you are entering to H824
Dt 7: 8 redeemed you from the **l** *of* slavery, H1074
Dt 7:13 your womb, the crops of your **l**—your grain, H141
Dt 7:13 of your flocks in the **l** he swore to your H141
Dt 8: 1 possess the **l** the LORD promised on H824
Dt 8: 7 your God is bringing you into a good **l**— H824
Dt 8: 7 into a good land—a **l** *with* brooks, streams, H824
Dt 8: 8 a **l** *with* wheat and barley, vines and fig H824
Dt 8: 9 a **l** where bread will not be scarce and you H824
Dt 8: 9 a **l** where the rocks are iron and you can H824
Dt 8:10 your God for the good **l** he has given you. H824
Dt 8:14 you out of Egypt, out of the **l** *of* slavery. H1074
Dt 8:15 that thirsty and waterless **l**, with its NDT
Dt 9: 4 to take possession of this **l** because of my H824
Dt 9: 5 are going in to take possession of their **l**; H824
Dt 9: 6 God is giving you this good **l** to possess, H824
Dt 9:23 take possession of the **l** I have given you." H824
Dt 9:28 take them into the **l** he had promised them H824
Dt 10: 7 on to Jotbathah, a **l** *with* streams of water. H824
Dt 10:11 may enter and possess the **l** I swore to their H824
Dt 11: 8 in and take over the **l** that you are crossing H824
Dt 11: 9 may live long in the **l** the LORD swore to H141

Dt 11: 9 a l flowing with milk and honey. H824
Dt 11:10 The l you are entering to take over is not H824
Dt 11:10 to take over is not like the l *of* Egypt, H824
Dt 11:11 But the l you are crossing the Jordan to take H824
Dt 11:11 possession of is a l *of* mountains and H824
Dt 11:12 It is a l the LORD your God cares for; H824
Dt 11:14 then I will send rain on your l in its season H824
Dt 11:17 perish from the good l the LORD is giving H824
Dt 11:21 may be many in the l the LORD swore to H141
Dt 11:25 the terror and fear of you on the whole l, H824
Dt 11:29 brought you into the l you are entering to H824
Dt 11:31 possession of the l the LORD your God is H824
Dt 12: 1 be careful to follow in the l that the LORD, H824
Dt 12: 1 to possess—as long as you live in the l. H141
Dt 12:10 settle in the l the LORD your God is H824
Dt 12:19 the Levites as long as you live in your l. H141
Dt 12:29 have driven them out and settled in their l, H824
Dt 13: 5 redeemed you from the l *of* slavery. H1074
Dt 13: 7 from one end of the l to the other), H824
Dt 13:10 you out of Egypt, out of the l *of* slavery. H1074
Dt 15: 4 in the l the LORD your God is giving you H824
Dt 15: 7 of the towns of the l the LORD your God is H824
Dt 15:11 There will always be poor people in the l H824
Dt 15:11 Israelites who are poor and needy in your l. H824
Dt 16: 4 possession in all your l for seven days. H1473
Dt 16:20 live and possess the l the LORD your God is H824
Dt 17:14 When you enter the l the LORD your God is H824
Dt 18: 9 When you enter the l the LORD your God is H824
Dt 19: 1 the nations whose l he is giving you, H824
Dt 19: 2 three cities in the l the LORD your God is H824
Dt 19: 3 into three parts the l the LORD your God is H824
Dt 19: 8 gives you the whole l he promised them, H824
Dt 19:10 innocent blood will not be shed in your l, H824
Dt 19:14 you receive in the l the LORD your God is H824
Dt 21: 1 lying in a field in the l the LORD your God is H141
Dt 21:23 not desecrate the l the LORD your God is H141
Dt 23:20 your hand to in the l you are entering to H824
Dt 24: 4 bring sin upon the l the LORD your God is H824
Dt 25:15 may live long in the l the LORD your God is H141
Dt 25:19 around you in the l he is giving you to H824
Dt 26: 1 you have entered the l the LORD your God is H824
Dt 26: 2 from the soil of the l the LORD your God is H824
Dt 26: 3 I have come to the l the LORD swore to our H824
Dt 26: 9 brought us to this place and gave us this l, H824
Dt 26: 9 this land, a l flowing with milk and honey; H824
Dt 26:15 Israel and the l you have given us as H141
Dt 26:15 ancestors, a l flowing with milk and honey." H824
Dt 27: 2 the Jordan into the l the LORD your God is H824
Dt 27: 3 over to enter the l the LORD your God is H824
Dt 27: 3 giving you, a l flowing with milk and honey H824
Dt 28: 4 the crops of your l and the young of your H141
Dt 28: 8 God will bless you in the l he is giving you. H824
Dt 28:11 in the l he swore to your ancestors to give H141
Dt 28:12 to send rain on your l in season and to H824
Dt 28:18 the crops of your l, and the calves of H141
Dt 28:21 you from the l you are entering to H141
Dt 28:33 will eat what your l and labor produce, H141
Dt 28:42 over all your trees and the crops of your l. H141
Dt 28:51 the crops of your l until you are H141
Dt 28:52 cities throughout your l until the high H824
Dt 28:52 cities throughout the l the LORD your God is H824
Dt 28:63 be uprooted from the l you are entering to H141
Dt 29: 2 Pharaoh, to all his officials and to all his l. H824
Dt 29: 8 We took their l and gave it as an H824
Dt 29:19 disaster on the **watered** l as well as the H8116
Dt 29:22 have fallen on the l and the diseases with H824
Dt 29:23 The whole l will be a burning waste of salt H824
Dt 29:24 "Why has the LORD done this to this l? Why H824
Dt 29:27 the LORD's anger burned against this l, H824
Dt 29:28 them from their l and thrust them into H141
Dt 29:28 their land and thrust them into another l, H824
Dt 30: 4 to the **most distant** l *under* the heavens, H7895
Dt 30: 5 will bring you to the l that belonged to your H824
Dt 30: 9 of your livestock and the crops of your l. H141
Dt 30:16 will bless you in the l you are entering to H824
Dt 30:18 not live long in the l you are crossing the H141
Dt 30:20 you many years in the l he swore to give to H141
Dt 31: 3 and you will take possession of their l. NDT
Dt 31: 4 whom he destroyed along with their l. H824
Dt 31: 7 this people into the l that the LORD swore to H824
Dt 31:13 as you live in the l you are crossing the H141
Dt 31:16 the foreign gods of the l they are entering. H824
Dt 31:20 them into the l flowing with milk and H141
Dt 31:20 **the** l I promised on oath to their ancestors, H889S
Dt 31:21 I bring them into the l I promised them on H824
Dt 31:23 Israelites into the l I promised them on H824
Dt 32:10 In a desert l he found him, in a barren H824
Dt 32:13 the heights of the l and fed him with the H824
Dt 32:43 make atonement for his l and people. H141
Dt 32:47 will live long in the l you are crossing the H141
Dt 32:49 the l I am giving the Israelites as their own H824
Dt 32:52 you will see the l only from a distance; you H824
Dt 32:52 you will not enter the l I am giving to the H824
Dt 33:13 the LORD bless his l with the precious dew H824
Dt 33:21 He chose the best l for himself; the leader's NDT
Dt 33:28 dwell secure in a l *of* grain and new wine, H824
Dt 34: 1 There the LORD showed him the whole l H824
Dt 34: 2 all the l *of* Judah as far as the H824
Dt 34: 4 "This is the l I promised on oath to H824
Dt 34:11 to all his officials and to his whole l. H824
Jos 1: 2 Jordan River into the l I am about to give to H824
Jos 1: 6 people to inherit the l I swore to their H824
Jos 1:11 possession of the l the LORD your God is H824
Jos 1:13 God will give you rest by giving you this l. H824
Jos 1:14 may stay in the l that Moses gave you east H824
Jos 1:15 possession of the l the LORD your God is H824
Jos 1:15 you may go back and occupy your own l H824
Jos 2: 1 look over the l," he said, "especially H824
Jos 2: 2 have come here tonight to spy out the l." H824
Jos 2: 3 they have come to spy out the whole l." H824
Jos 2: 9 has given you this l and that a great fear H824
Jos 2:14 faithfully when the LORD gives us the l." H824
Jos 2:18 when we enter the l, you have tied this H824
Jos 2:24 surely given the whole l into our hands; H824
Jos 5: 6 they would not see the l he had solemnly H824
Jos 5: 6 to give us, a l flowing with milk and honey. H824
Jos 5:11 they ate some of the produce of the l: H824
Jos 5:12 the day after they ate this food from the l; H824
Jos 6:22 to the two men who had spied out the l, H824
Jos 6:27 his fame spread throughout the l. H824
Jos 8: 1 the king of Ai, his people, his city and his l. H824
Jos 9:24 to give you the whole l and to wipe out all H824
Jos 11:16 So Joshua took this entire l: the hill country, H824
Jos 11:23 So Joshua took the entire l, just as the LORD H824
Jos 11:23 Then the l had rest from war. H824
Jos 12: 1 are the kings of the l whom the Israelites H824
Jos 12: 6 of the LORD gave **their** l to the Reubenites H2023S
Jos 12: 7 list of the kings of the l that Joshua and the H824
Jos 13: 1 still very large **areas of** l to be taken over. H824
Jos 13: 2 "This is the l that remains: all the regions H824
Jos 13: 4 the south; all the l *of* the Canaanites, from H824
Jos 13: 6 Be sure to allocate **this** l to Israel for an H2023S
Jos 13:12 had defeated them and taken over their l. NDT
Jos 14: 1 as an inheritance in the l *of* Canaan, H824
Jos 14: 4 no share of the l but only towns to live H824
Jos 14: 5 So the Israelites divided the l, just as the H824
Jos 14: 7 me from Kadesh Barnea to explore the l. H824
Jos 14: 9 'The l on which your feet have walked will H824
Jos 14:15 Then the l had rest from war. H824
Jos 15:19 Since you have given me l *in* the Negev H824
Jos 17: 5 consisted of ten **tracts of** l besides Gilead H824
Jos 17: 6 The l *of* Gilead belonged to the rest of the H824
Jos 17: 8 Manasseh had the l *of* Tappuah, but H824
Jos 17:10 On the south the l belonged to Ephraim, on NDT
Jos 17:15 into the forest and **clear** l for yourselves H1345
Jos 17:15 there in the l *of* the Perizzites and H824
Jos 18: 3 to take possession of the l that the LORD, H824
Jos 18: 4 to make a survey of the l and to write a H824
Jos 18: 5 You are to divide **the** l into seven parts H2023S
Jos 18: 6 descriptions of the seven parts of the l, H824
Jos 18: 8 men started on their way to map out the l, H824
Jos 18: 8 make a survey of the l and write a H824
Jos 18: 9 So the men left and went through the l H824
Jos 18:10 there he distributed the l to the Israelites H824
Jos 19:49 had finished dividing the l into its allotted H824
Jos 19:51 And so they finished dividing the l. H824
Jos 21:43 gave Israel all the l he had sworn to give H824
Jos 22: 4 to your homes in the l that Moses the H824+299
Jos 22: 7 of Manasseh Moses had given l in Bashan, NDT
Jos 22: 7 the tribe Joshua gave l on the west side of NDT
Jos 22: 9 to Gilead, their own l, which they had H824+299
Jos 22:10 near the Jordan in the l *of* Canaan, H824
Jos 22:13 the priest, to the l *of* Gilead—to Reuben H824
Jos 22:19 If the l you possess is defiled, come over to H824
Jos 22:19 come over to the LORD's l, where the H824+299
Jos 22:19 tabernacle stands, and share the l with us. NDT
Jos 23: 4 your tribes all the l of the nations that NDT
Jos 23: 5 you will take possession of their l, as H824
Jos 23:13 you perish from this good l, which the H141
Jos 23:15 you from this good l he has given you. H141
Jos 23:16 perish from the good l he has given you." H824
Jos 24: 3 Abraham from the l **beyond** the Euphrates H6298
Jos 24: 8 'I brought you to the l *of* the Amorites who H824
Jos 24: 8 and you took possession of their l. H824
Jos 24:13 So I gave you a l on which you did not toil H824
Jos 24:15 of the Amorites, in whose l you are living. H824
Jos 24:17 of Egypt, from that l *of* slavery, and H1074
Jos 24:18 including the Amorites, who lived in the l. H824
Jos 24:30 they buried him in the l *of* his inheritance, H1473
Jos 24:32 in the tract of l that Jacob bought for a H8441
Jdg 1: 2 I have given the l into their hands. H824
Jdg 1:15 Since you have given me l in the Negev H824
Jdg 1:26 He then went to the l *of* the Hittites, where H824
Jdg 1:27 were determined to live in that l. H824
Jdg 1:32 inhabitants of the l because they did not H824
Jdg 1:33 among the Canaanite inhabitants of the l, H824
Jdg 2: 1 led you into the l I swore to give to H824
Jdg 2: 2 make a covenant with the people of this l, H824
Jdg 2: 6 they went to take possession of the l, each H824
Jdg 2: 9 they buried him in the l *of* his inheritance, H1473
Jdg 3:11 So the l had peace for forty years, until H824
Jdg 3:30 and the l had peace for eighty years. H824
Jdg 5: 4 when you marched from the l *of* Edom H8441
Jdg 5:31 Then the l had peace forty years H824
Jdg 6: 4 They camped on the l and ruined the crops H824
Jdg 6: 5 they invaded the l to ravage it. H824
Jdg 6: 8 you up out of Egypt, out of the l *of* slavery. H1074
Jdg 6: 9 them out before you and gave you their l. H824
Jdg 6:10 gods of the Amorites, in whose l you live. H824
Jdg 8:28 lifetime, the l had peace forty years. H824
Jdg 10: 8 the Jordan in Gilead, the l *of* the Amorites. H824
Jdg 11: 3 his brothers and settled in the l *of* Tob, H824
Jdg 11: 5 went to get Jephthah from the l *of* Tob. H824
Jdg 11:13 they took away my l from the Arnon to the H824
Jdg 11:15 did not take the l *of* Moab or the land of H824
Jdg 11:15 land of Moab or the l *of* the Ammonites. H824
Jdg 11:21 took over all the l *of* the Amorites who H824
Jdg 12:12 was buried in Aijalon in the l *of* Zebulun. H824
Jdg 16:24 who laid waste our l and multiplied our H824
Jdg 18: 2 Eshtaol to spy out the l and explore it. H824
Jdg 18: 2 explore the l." So they entered the H824
Jdg 18: 7 And since their l lacked nothing, they were H824
Jdg 18: 9 We have seen the l, and it is very good H824
Jdg 18:10 a spacious l that God has put into H824
Jdg 18:10 a l that lacks nothing whatever. H5226
Jdg 18:14 had spied out the l *of* Laish said to their H824
Jdg 18:17 had spied out the l went inside and took H824
Jdg 18:30 Dan until the time of the captivity of the l. H824
Jdg 20: 1 from the l *of* Gilead came together H824
Jdg 21:21 Then return to the l *of* Benjamin. H824
Ru 1: 1 judges ruled, there was a famine in the l. H824
Ru 1: 7 would take them back to the l *of* Judah. H824
Ru 4: 3 selling the piece of l that belonged to our H8441
Ru 4: 5 "On the day you buy the l from Naomi H8441
1Sa 6: 5 hand from you and your gods and your l. H824
1Sa 9:16 send you a man from the l *of* Benjamin. H824
1Sa 13: 3 trumpet blown throughout the l and said, H824
1Sa 13: 7 the Jordan to the l *of* Gad and Gilead. H824
1Sa 13:19 could be found in the whole l *of* Israel, H824
1Sa 14:46 they withdrew to their own l. H5226
1Sa 21:11 "Isn't this David, the king of the l? H824
1Sa 22: 5 Go into the l *of* Judah." So David left H824
1Sa 23:27 The Philistines are raiding the l." H824
1Sa 27: 1 do is to escape to the l *of* the Philistines. H824
1Sa 27: 8 had lived in the l extending to Shur and H824
1Sa 28: 3 the mediums and spiritists from the l. H824
1Sa 28: 9 off the mediums and spiritists from the l. H824
1Sa 29:11 to go back to the l *of* the Philistines, H824
1Sa 30:16 had taken from the l *of* the Philistines and H824
1Sa 31: 9 throughout the l *of* the Philistines to H824
2Sa 3:12 his behalf to say to David, "Whose l is it? H824
2Sa 9: 7 to you all the l *that belonged to* your H8441
2Sa 9:10 are to farm the l for him and bring in the H141
2Sa 10: 2 men came to the l *of* the Ammonites, H824
2Sa 14:20 he knows everything that happens in the l." H824
2Sa 15: 4 "If only I were appointed judge in the l! H824
2Sa 17:26 Absalom camped in the l *of* Gilead. H824
2Sa 19:29 I order you and Ziba to divide the l." H8441
2Sa 21:14 God answered prayer in behalf of the l. H824
2Sa 24: 8 After they had gone through the entire l H824
2Sa 24:13 on you three years of famine in your l? H824
2Sa 24:13 Or three days of plague in your l? Now then H824
2Sa 24:25 LORD answered his prayer in behalf of the l, H824
1Ki 4:10 Sokoh and all the l *of* Hepher were his); H824
1Ki 4:21 Euphrates River to the l *of* the Philistines, H824
1Ki 8:34 bring them back to the l you gave to their H141
1Ki 8:36 send rain on the l you gave your people H824
1Ki 8:37 "When famine or plague comes to the l, or H824
1Ki 8:40 time they live in the l you gave our H141
1Ki 8:41 come from a distant l because of your H824
1Ki 8:47 of heart in the l where they are held H824
1Ki 8:47 plead with you in the l *of* their captors and H824
1Ki 8:48 soul in the l *of* their enemies who H824
1Ki 8:48 pray to you toward the l you gave their H824
1Ki 9: 7 off Israel from the l I have given them and H141
1Ki 9: 8 such a thing to this l and to this temple? H824
1Ki 9:13 And he called them the L *of* Kabul, a name H824
1Ki 9:18 Tadmor in the desert, within his l, H824
1Ki 9:21 of all these peoples remaining in the l— H824
1Ki 11:18 Hadad a house and l and provided him H824
1Ki 14:15 Israel from this good l that he gave to their H141
1Ki 14:24 were even male shrine prostitutes in the l; H824
1Ki 15:12 prostitutes from the l and got rid of all the H824
1Ki 17: 7 because there had been no rain in the l. H824
1Ki 17:14 the day the LORD sends rain on the l. H141
1Ki 18: 1 to Ahab, and I will send rain on the l." H141
1Ki 18: 5 "Go through the l to all the springs and H824
1Ki 18: 6 So they divided the l they were to cover H824
1Ki 20: 7 all the elders of the l and said to them, H824
1Ki 22:36 man to his town. Every man to his l!" H824
1Ki 22:46 He rid the l of the rest of the male shrine H824
2Ki 2:19 the water is bad and the l is unproductive." H824
2Ki 2:21 it cause death or make the l unproductive. NDT
2Ki 3:20 And the l was filled with water. H824
2Ki 3:24 Israelites invaded **the** l and slaughtered H2023S
2Ki 3:27 they withdrew and returned to their own l. H824
2Ki 8: 1 a famine in the l that will last seven H824
2Ki 8: 2 stayed in the l *of* the Philistines seven H824
2Ki 8: 3 came back from the l *of* the Philistines H824
2Ki 8: 3 to appeal to the king for her house and l. H8441
2Ki 8: 5 to appeal to the king for her house and l. H8441
2Ki 8: 6 the income from her l from the day she H8441
2Ki 10:33 east of the Jordan in all the l *of* Gilead (the H824
2Ki 11: 3 for six years while Athaliah ruled the l. H824
2Ki 11:14 all the people of the l were rejoicing and H824
2Ki 11:18 All the people of the l went to the temple H824
2Ki 11:19 the guards and all the people of the l, and H824
2Ki 11:20 All the people of the l rejoiced, and the city H824
2Ki 15: 5 palace and governed the people of the l. H824
2Ki 15:19 Then Pul king of Assyria invaded the l, and H824
2Ki 15:20 withdrew and stayed in the l no longer. H824
2Ki 15:29 including all the l *of* Naphtali, and H824
2Ki 16:15 the burnt offering of all the people of the l, H824
2Ki 17: 5 The king of Assyria invaded the entire l H824
2Ki 17:27 the people what the god of the l requires." H824
2Ki 18:32 I come and take you to a l like your own— H824

2Ki 18:32 like your own—a l *of* grain and new wine H824
2Ki 18:32 new wine, a l *of* bread and vineyards H824
2Ki 18:32 vineyards, a l *of* olive trees and honey. H824
2Ki 18:33 ever delivered his l from the hand of the H824
2Ki 18:35 has been able to save his l from me? H824
2Ki 19:37 and they escaped to the l *of* Ararat. H824
2Ki 20:14 "From a distant l," Hezekiah replied H824
2Ki 21: 8 wander from the l I gave their ancestors, H141
2Ki 21:24 Then the people of the l killed all who had H824
2Ki 23:30 the people of the l took Jehoahaz son of H824
2Ki 23:33 at Riblah in the l *of* Hamath so that he H824
2Ki 23:35 he taxed the l and exacted the silver and H824
2Ki 23:35 from the people of the l according to their H824
2Ki 24: 1 king of Babylon invaded the l, NDT
2Ki 24:14 Only the poorest people of the l were left. H824
2Ki 24:15 officials and the prominent people of the l. H824
2Ki 25:12 people of the l to work the vineyards H824
2Ki 25:19 the people of the l and sixty of the H824
2Ki 25:21 at Riblah, in the l *of* Hamath, the king had H824
2Ki 25:21 Judah went into captivity, away from her l. H141
2Ki 25:24 "Settle down in the l and serve the king of H824
1Ch 1:45 Husham from the l *of* the Temanites H824
1Ch 4:40 good pasture, and the l was spacious H824
1Ch 5: 9 they occupied the l up to the edge of the NDT
1Ch 5:22 And they occupied the l until the exile. H9393S
1Ch 5:23 they settled in the l from Bashan to Baal H824
1Ch 5:25 to the gods of the peoples of the l, H824
1Ch 10: 9 throughout the l *of* the Philistines to H824
1Ch 11:10 support to extend it over **the whole** l, H3776S
1Ch 14:17 So David's fame spread throughout every l H824
1Ch 16:18 you I will give the l *of* Canaan as the H824
1Ch 19: 2 to Hanun in the l *of* the Ammonites to H824
1Ch 20: 1 He laid waste the l *of* the Ammonites and H824
1Ch 21:12 days of plague in the l, with the angel of H824
1Ch 22:18 the inhabitants of the l into my hands, H824
1Ch 22:18 the l is subject to the LORD and to his H824
1Ch 27:26 in charge of the workers who farmed the l. H141
1Ch 28: 8 possess this good l and pass it on as an H824
2Ch 6:25 them back to the l you gave to them and H141
2Ch 6:27 send rain on the l you gave your people H824
2Ch 6:28 "When famine or plague comes to the l, or H824
2Ch 6:31 time they live in the l you gave our H141
2Ch 6:32 come from a distant l because of your great H824
2Ch 6:36 takes them captive to a l far away or near; H824
2Ch 6:37 of heart in the l where they are held H824
2Ch 6:37 plead with you in the l *of* their captivity H824
2Ch 6:38 heart and soul in the l *of* their captivity H824
2Ch 6:38 pray toward the l you gave their H824
2Ch 7:13 locusts to devour the l or send a plague H824
2Ch 7:14 I will forgive their sin and will heal their l. H824
2Ch 7:20 then I will uproot Israel from my l, which I H141
2Ch 7:21 such a thing to this l and to this temple? H824
2Ch 8: 8 of all these people remaining in the l— H824
2Ch 9:26 Euphrates River to the l *of* the Philistines, H824
2Ch 14: 6 cities of Judah, since the l was at peace. H824
2Ch 14: 7 The l is still ours, because we have sought H824
2Ch 15: 8 from the whole l *of* Judah and Benjamin H824
2Ch 19: 3 you have rid the l of the Asherah poles H824
2Ch 19: 5 He appointed judges in the l, in each of the H824
2Ch 20: 7 the inhabitants of this l before your people H824
2Ch 22:12 God for six years while Athaliah ruled the l. H824
2Ch 23:13 all the people of the l were rejoicing and H824
2Ch 23:20 all the people of the l and brought the king H824
2Ch 23:21 All the people of the l rejoiced, and the city H824
2Ch 26:21 palace and governed the people of the l. H824
2Ch 30: 9 by their captors and will return to this l, H824
2Ch 32: 4 the stream that flowed through the l. H824
2Ch 32:13 ever able to deliver their l from my hand? H824
2Ch 32:21 So he withdrew to his own l in disgrace H824
2Ch 32:31 miraculous sign that had occurred in the l, H824
2Ch 33: 8 the Israelites leave the l I assigned to your H141
2Ch 33:25 Then the people of the l killed all who had H824
2Ch 34: 8 to purify the l and the temple, he H824
2Ch 36: 1 the people of the l took Jehoahaz son of H824
2Ch 36:21 The l enjoyed its sabbath rests; all the time H824
Ezr 9:11 'The l you are entering to possess is a land H824
Ezr 9:11 entering to possess is a l polluted by the H824
Ezr 9:12 the good things of the l and leave it to your H824
Ne 4: 4 them over as plunder in a l *of* captivity. H824
Ne 5:14 to be their governor in the l *of* Judah, H824
Ne 5:16 the work; we did not acquire *any* l. H8441
Ne 9: 8 to his descendants the l *of* the Canaanites, H824
Ne 9:10 all his officials and all the people of his l, H824
Ne 9:15 take possession of the l you had sworn with H824
Ne 9:23 brought them into the l that you told their H824
Ne 9:24 went in and took possession of the l. H824
Ne 9:24 who lived in the l; you gave the Canaanites H824
Ne 9:24 with their kings and the peoples of the l, H824
Ne 9:25 They captured fortified cities and fertile l H141
Ne 9:35 in the spacious and fertile l you gave them, H824
Ne 9:36 slaves in the l you gave our ancestors so H824
Ne 10:31 will forgo working the l and will cancel all NDT
Job 1: 1 In the l *of* Uz there lived a man whose H824
Job 1:10 herds are spread throughout the l. H824
Job 9:24 When a l falls into the hands of the wicked, H824
Job 10:21 to the l *of* gloom and utter darkness, H824
Job 10:22 to the l *of* deepest night, of utter darkness H824
Job 12:15 if he lets them loose, they devastate the l. H824
Job 15:19 to whom alone the l was given when no H824
Job 15:29 will his possessions spread over the l. H824
Job 18:17 from the earth; he has no name in the l. H2575
Job 22: 8 owning l—an honored man, H824
Job 24: 4 force all the poor of the l into hiding. H824
Job 24:18 their portion of the l is cursed, so that no H824
Job 28:13 it cannot be found in the l *of* the living. H824
Job 30: 3 they roamed the **parched** l in desolate H7480
Job 30: 8 they were driven out of the l. H824
Job 31:38 "if my l cries out against me and all its H141
Job 37:17 clothes when the l lies hushed under the H824
Job 38:26 to water a l where no one lives, an H824
Job 42:15 Nowhere in all the l were there found H824
Ps 10:16 ever; the nations will perish from his l. H824
Ps 16: 3 I say of the holy people who are in the l H824
Ps 25:13 their descendants will inherit the l. H824
Ps 27:13 goodness of the LORD in the l *of* the living. H824
Ps 35:20 against those who live quietly in the l. H824
Ps 37: 3 dwell in the l and enjoy safe pasture. H824
Ps 37: 9 who hope in the LORD will inherit the l. H824
Ps 37:11 will inherit the l and enjoy peace and H824
Ps 37:22 those the LORD blesses will inherit the l, but H824
Ps 37:27 do good; then you will dwell in the l forever. NDT
Ps 37:29 will inherit the l and dwell in it forever. H824
Ps 37:34 He will exalt you to inherit the l; when the H824
Ps 41: 2 are counted among the blessed in the l— H824
Ps 42: 6 will remember you from the l *of* the Jordan, H824
Ps 44: 3 was not by their sword that they won the l, H824
Ps 45:16 will make them princes throughout the l. H824
Ps 52: 5 he will uproot you from the l *of* the living. H824
Ps 60: 2 You have shaken the l and torn it open H824
Ps 63: 1 in a dry and parched l where there is no H824
Ps 65: 9 You care for the l and water it; you enrich it H824
Ps 66: 6 He turned the sea into **dry** l, they passed H3317
Ps 67: 6 The l yields its harvest; God, our God H824
Ps 68: 6 the rebellious live in a **sun-scorched** l. H7461
Ps 68:14 the Almighty scattered the kings in **the** l, H2023S
Ps 72:16 May grain abound throughout the l; on the H824
Ps 74: 8 place where God was worshiped in the l. H824
Ps 74:20 of violence fill the dark places of the l. H824
Ps 76: 8 judgment, and the l feared and was quiet H824
Ps 76: 9 to judge, to save all the afflicted of the l. H824
Ps 78:12 the sight of their ancestors in the l *of* Egypt, H824
Ps 78:54 he brought them to the border of his holy l, NDT
Ps 80: 9 and it took root and filled the l. H824
Ps 85: 1 showed favor to your l; you restored the H824
Ps 85: 9 fear him, that his glory may dwell in our l. H824
Ps 85:12 is good, and our l will yield its harvest. H824
Ps 88:12 your righteous deeds in the l *of* oblivion? H824
Ps 95: 5 made it, and his hands formed the **dry** l. H3318
Ps 101: 6 My eyes will be on the faithful in the l, that H824
Ps 101: 8 I will put to silence all the wicked in the l; H824
Ps 104:13 the l is satisfied by the fruit of his work. H824
Ps 105:11 you I will give the l *of* Canaan as the H824
Ps 105:16 down famine on the l and destroyed all H824
Ps 105:23 resided as a foreigner in the l *of* Ham. H824
Ps 105:27 among them, his wonders in the l *of* Ham. H824
Ps 105:28 He sent darkness and made the l dark—for NDT
Ps 105:30 Their l teemed with frogs, which went up H824
Ps 105:32 into hail, with lightning throughout their l; H824
Ps 105:35 they ate up every green thing in their l, ate H824
Ps 105:36 he struck down all the firstborn in their l, H824
Ps 106:22 miracles in the l *of* Ham and awesome H824
Ps 106:24 Then they despised the pleasant l; they did H824
Ps 106:38 the l was desecrated by their blood. H824
Ps 107:34 fruitful l into a salt waste, because of H824
Ps 112: 2 Their children will be mighty in the l; the H824
Ps 116: 9 walk before the LORD in the l *of* the living. H824
Ps 125: 3 remain over the *l* **allotted** *to* the righteous, AIT
Ps 135:12 he gave their l as an inheritance, an H824
Ps 136:21 gave their l as an inheritance, His love H824
Ps 137: 4 the songs of the LORD while in a foreign l? H141
Ps 140:11 May slanderers not be established in the l H824
Ps 142: 5 my refuge, my portion in the l *of* the living." H824
Ps 143: 6 I thirst for you like a parched l. H824
Pr 2:21 For the upright will live in the l, and the H824
Pr 2:22 the wicked will be cut off from the l H824
Pr 10:30 the wicked will not remain in the l. H824
Pr 12:11 Those who work their l will have abundant H141
Pr 25:25 a weary soul is good news from a distant l. H824
Pr 28:19 Those who work their l will have abundant H141
Pr 30:16 the barren womb, l, which is never satisfied H824
Pr 31:23 he takes his seat among the elders of the l. H824
Ecc 5: 9 The increase from the l is taken by all; the H824
Ecc 10:16 Woe to the l whose king is a servant H824
Ecc 10:17 Blessed is the l whose king is of noble birth H824
Ecc 11: 2 know what disaster may come upon the l. H824
SS 2:12 the cooing of doves is heard in our l. H824
Isa 1:19 you will eat the good things of the l; H824
Isa 2: 7 Their l is full of silver and gold; there is no H824
Isa 2: 7 Their l is full of horses; there is no end to H824
Isa 2: 8 Their l is full of idols; they bow down to the H824
Isa 4: 2 the fruit of the l will be the pride and H824
Isa 5: 8 no space is left and you live alone in the l. H824
Isa 5:30 And if one looks at the l, there is only H824
Isa 6:12 far away and the l is utterly forsaken. H824
Isa 6:13 And though a tenth remains in **the** l, it H2023S
Isa 6:13 the holy seed will be the stump in **the** l." H2023S
Isa 7:16 the l of the two kings you dread will be laid H141
Isa 7:18 in Egypt and for bees from the l *of* Assyria. H824
Isa 7:22 All who remain in the l will eat curds and H824
Isa 7:24 the l will be covered with briers and H824
Isa 8: 8 wings will cover the breadth of your l, H824
Isa 8:21 they will roam through **the** l; when they H2023S
Isa 9: 1 past he humbled the l *of* Zebulun and the H824
Isa 9: 1 the land of Zebulun and the l *of* Naphtali, H824
Isa 9: 2 those living in the l *of* deep darkness a H824
Isa 9:19 LORD Almighty the l will be scorched and H824
Isa 10:23 the destruction decreed upon the whole l. H824
Isa 13: 9 to make the l desolate and destroy the H824
Isa 13:14 own people, they will flee to their **native** l. H824
Isa 14: 1 Israel and will settle them in their own l. H141
Isa 14: 2 male and female servants in the LORD's l. H141
Isa 14:20 have destroyed your l and killed your H824
Isa 14:21 to rise to inherit the l and cover the earth H824
Isa 14:25 I will crush the Assyrian in my l; on my H824
Isa 15: 9 Moab and upon those who remain in the l. H141
Isa 16: 1 Send lambs as tribute to the ruler of the l H824
Isa 16: 4 the aggressor will vanish from the l. H824
Isa 18: 1 Woe to the l *of* whirring wings along the H824
Isa 18: 2 whose l is divided by rivers. H824
Isa 18: 7 strange speech, whose l is divided by rivers H824
Isa 19:17 And the l *of* Judah will bring terror to the H141
Isa 19:20 to the LORD Almighty in the l *of* Egypt. H824
Isa 21: 1 comes from the desert, from a l *of* terror. H824
Isa 23: 1 From the l *of* Cyprus word has come to H824
Isa 23:10 Till your l as they do along the Nile H824
Isa 23:13 Look at the l *of* the Babylonians, this H824
Isa 25:10 will be trampled **in** their l as straw is H9393
Isa 26: 1 this song will be sung in the l *of* Judah: H824
Isa 26:10 even in a l *of* uprightness they go on doing H824
Isa 26:15 you have extended all the borders of the l. H824
Isa 28:22 destruction decreed against the whole l. H824
Isa 30: 6 Through a l *of* hardship and distress, of H824
Isa 30:23 food that comes from the l will be rich and H141
Isa 32: 2 the shadow of a great rock in a thirsty l. H824
Isa 32:13 for the l *of* my people, a land H141
Isa 32:13 a l overgrown with thorns and briers NDT
Isa 33: 9 The l dries up and wastes away, Lebanon H824
Isa 33:17 his beauty and view a l *that* stretches afar. H824
Isa 34: 6 a great slaughter in the l *of* Edom. H824
Isa 34: 7 Their l will be drenched with blood, and H824
Isa 34: 9 her l will become blazing pitch! H824
Isa 35: 1 The desert and the **parched** l will be glad H7480
Isa 36:10 attack and destroy this l without the LORD? H824
Isa 36:17 I come and take you to a l like your own— H824
Isa 36:17 like your own—a l *of* grain and new wine H824
Isa 36:17 new wine, a l *of* bread and vineyards. H824
Isa 37:38 and they escaped to the l *of* Ararat. H824
Isa 38:11 see the LORD himself in the l *of* the living; H824
Isa 39: 3 "From a distant l," Hezekiah replied H824
Isa 44: 3 For I will pour water on the thirsty l, and NDT
Isa 45:19 from somewhere in a l *of* darkness; I have H824
Isa 46:11 from a far-off l, a man to fulfill my H824
Isa 49: 8 to restore the l and to reassign its desolate H824
Isa 49:19 made desolate and your l laid waste, H824
Isa 53: 8 For he was cut off from the l *of* the living H824
Isa 57:13 in me will inherit the l and possess my holy H824
Isa 58:11 your needs in a **sun-scorched** l and will H7463
Isa 58:14 on the heights of the l and to feast on the H824
Isa 60: 6 Herds of camels will cover your l, young NDT
Isa 60:18 No longer will violence be heard in your l H824
Isa 60:21 they will possess the l forever. H824
Isa 61: 7 you will inherit a double portion in your l, H824
Isa 62: 4 call you Deserted, or name your l Desolate. H824
Isa 62: 4 Hephzibah, and your l Beulah; for the LORD H824
Isa 62: 4 delight in you, and your l will be married. H824
Isa 65:16 a blessing in the l will do so by the one H824
Isa 65:16 takes an oath in the l will swear by the one H824
Jer 1:14 will be poured out on all who live in the l. H824
Jer 1:18 bronze wall to stand against the whole l— H824
Jer 1:18 officials, its priests and the people of the l. H824
Jer 2: 2 the wilderness, through a l not sown. H824
Jer 2: 6 through a l *of* deserts and ravines H824
Jer 2: 6 a l *of* drought and utter darkness H824
Jer 2: 6 a l where no one travels and no one lives? H824
Jer 2: 7 you into a fertile l to eat its fruit and rich H824
Jer 2: 7 came and defiled my l and made my H824
Jer 2:15 They have laid waste his l; his towns are H824
Jer 2:31 a desert to Israel or a l *of* great darkness? H824
Jer 3: 1 Would not the l be completely defiled H824
Jer 3: 2 You have defiled the l with your H824
Jer 3: 9 she defiled the l and committed adultery H824
Jer 3:16 numbers have increased greatly in the l," H824
Jer 3:18 come from a northern l to the land I gave H824
Jer 3:18 northern land to the l I gave your ancestors H824
Jer 3:19 like my children and give you a pleasant l, H824
Jer 4: 5 'Sound the trumpet throughout the l!' Cry H824
Jer 4: 7 He has left his place to lay waste your l H824
Jer 4:16 besieging army is coming from a distant l, H824
Jer 4:20 follows disaster; the whole l lies in ruins. H824
Jer 4:26 I looked, and the **fruitful** l was a desert H4149
Jer 4:27 "The whole l will be ruined, though I will H824
Jer 5:19 me and served foreign gods in your own l, H824
Jer 5:19 will serve foreigners in a l not your own. H824
Jer 5:30 shocking thing has happened in the l: H824
Jer 6: 8 you and make your l desolate so no one H824
Jer 6:12 my hand against those who live in the l," H824
Jer 6:20 Sheba or sweet calamus from a distant l? H824
Jer 6:22 an army is coming from the l *of* the north; H824
Jer 7: 7 in the l I gave your ancestors for ever and H824
Jer 7:20 of the field and on the crops of your l— H141
Jer 7:34 Jerusalem, for the l will become desolate. H824
Jer 8:16 of their stallions the whole l trembles. H824
Jer 8:16 come to devour the l and everything in it, H824
Jer 8:19 to the cry of my people from a l far away: H824
Jer 9: 3 it is not by truth that they triumph in the l. H824
Jer 9:12 Why has the l been ruined and laid waste H824

Jer 9:19 We must leave our l because our houses H824
Jer 10:17 Gather up your belongings to leave the l H824
Jer 10:18 time I will hurl out those who live in this l; H824
Jer 10:22 a great commotion from the l of the north! H824
Jer 11: 5 to give them a l flowing with milk and H824
Jer 11: 5 milk and honey'—the l you possess today." NDT
Jer 11:19 let us cut him off from the l of the living H824
Jer 12: 4 How long will the l lie parched and the H824
Jer 12:11 the whole l will be laid waste because H824
Jer 12:12 devour from one end of the l to the other; H824
Jer 13:13 fill with drunkenness all who live in this l, H824
Jer 14: 2 they wail for the l, and a cry goes up from H824
Jer 14: 4 is cracked because there is no rain in the l; H824
Jer 14: 8 why are you like a stranger in the l, like a H824
Jer 14:15 'No sword or famine will touch this l. H824
Jer 14:18 priest have gone to a l they know not. H824
Jer 15: 7 a winnowing fork at the city gates of the l. H824
Jer 15:10 with whom the whole l strives and H824
Jer 15:14 to your enemies in a l you do not know, H824
Jer 16: 3 born in this l and about the women H5226
Jer 16: 6 "Both high and low will die in this l. H824
Jer 16:13 throw you out of this l into a land neither H824
Jer 16:13 out of this land into a l neither you nor your H824
Jer 16:15 up out of the l of the north and out of H824
Jer 16:15 restore them to the l I gave their ancestors. H141
Jer 16:18 they have defiled my l with the lifeless H824
Jer 17: 3 My mountain in the l and your wealth H8441
Jer 17: 4 to your enemies in a l you do not know, H824
Jer 17: 6 of the desert, in a salt l where no one lives. H824
Jer 18:16 Their l will be an object of horror and of H824
Jer 22:10 will never return nor see his native l again. H824
Jer 22:12 him captive; he will not see this l again." H824
Jer 22:27 come back to the l you long to return to." H824
Jer 22:28 hurled out, cast into a l they do not know? H824
Jer 22:29 O l, land, land, hear the word of the LORD! H824
Jer 22:29 l, land, hear the word of the LORD! H824
Jer 22:29 land, l, hear the word of the LORD! H824
Jer 23: 5 do what is just and right in the l. H824
Jer 23: 8 Israel up out of the l of the north and out of H824
Jer 23: 8 Then they will live in their own l." H141
Jer 23:10 The l is full of adulterers; because of the H824
Jer 23:10 of the curse the l lies parched and the H824
Jer 23:15 ungodliness has spread throughout the l." H824
Jer 24: 5 from this place to the l of the Babylonians. H824
Jer 24: 6 and I will bring them back to this l. H824
Jer 24: 8 they remain in this l or live in Egypt. H824
Jer 24:10 are destroyed from the l I gave to them H141
Jer 25: 5 you can stay in the l the LORD gave to you H141
Jer 25: 9 them against this l and its inhabitants and H824
Jer 25:12 his nation, the l of the Babylonians, for H824
Jer 25:13 I will bring on that l all the things I have H824
Jer 25:30 dwelling and roar mightily against his l. H5659
Jer 25:38 their l will become desolate because H824
Jer 26:17 of the elders of the l stepped forward and H824
Jer 26:20 against this city and this l as Jeremiah did. H824
Jer 27: 7 his grandson until the time for his l comes; H824
Jer 27:11 remain in its own l to till it and to live H141
Jer 30: 3 restore them to the l I gave their ancestors H824
Jer 30:10 your descendants from the l of their exile. H824
Jer 31: 8 bring them from the l of the north and H824
Jer 31:16 "They will return from the l of the enemy. H824
Jer 31:17 "Your children will return to their own l. H1473
Jer 31:23 the people in the l of Judah and in its H824
Jer 32:15 vineyards will again be bought in this l. H824
Jer 32:22 You gave them this l you had sworn to give H824
Jer 32:22 ancestors, a l flowing with milk and honey. H824
Jer 32:41 plant them in this l with all my heart and H824
Jer 32:43 will be bought in this l of which you say, H824
Jer 33:11 the fortunes of the l as they were before, H824
Jer 33:15 he will do what is just and right in the l. H824
Jer 34:13 them out of Egypt, out of the l of slavery. H1074
Jer 34:19 the people of the l who walked between H824
Jer 35: 7 a long time in the l where you are nomads. H141
Jer 35:11 king of Babylon invaded this l, H824
Jer 35:15 you will live in the l I have given to you H141
Jer 36:29 destroy this l and wipe from it both H824
Jer 37: 2 the people of the l paid any attention to H824
Jer 37: 7 will go back to its own l, to Egypt. H824
Jer 37:19 of Babylon will not attack you or this l'? H824
Jer 39: 5 of Babylon at Riblah in the l of Hamath, H824
Jer 39:10 left behind in the l of Judah some of the H824
Jer 40: 6 the people who were left behind in the l. H824
Jer 40: 7 as governor over the l and had put him in H824
Jer 40: 7 the poorest in the l and who had not been H824
Jer 40: 9 "Settle down in the l and serve the king of H824
Jer 40:12 they all came back to the l of Judah, to H824
Jer 41: 2 had appointed as governor over the l. H824
Jer 41:18 had appointed as governor over the l. H824
Jer 42:10 'If you stay in this l, I will build you up and H824
Jer 42:12 on you and restore you to your l. H141
Jer 42:13 'We will not stay in this l,' and so disobey H824
Jer 43: 4 LORD's command to stay in the l of Judah. H824
Jer 43: 5 back to live in the l of Judah from all the H824
Jer 44: 9 your wives in the l of Judah and the H824
Jer 44:14 survive to return to the l of Judah, H824
Jer 44:21 your officials and the people of the l? H824
Jer 44:22 your l became a curse and a desolate H824
Jer 44:28 return to the l of Judah from Egypt will H824
Jer 46:10 offer sacrifice in the l of the north by the H824
Jer 46:27 your descendants from the l of their exile. H824
Jer 47: 2 They will overflow the l and everything in H824
Jer 47: 2 will cry out; all who dwell in the l will wail H824
Jer 49:19 I will chase Edom from its l in an instant. H2023S
Jer 50: 1 Babylon and the l of the Babylonians: H824
Jer 50: 3 north will attack her and lay waste her l. H824
Jer 50: 8 Babylon; leave the l of the Babylonians H824
Jer 50: 9 of great nations from the l of the north. H824
Jer 50:12 nations—a wilderness, a dry l, a desert. H7480
Jer 50:16 let everyone flee to their own l. H824
Jer 50:18 of Babylon and his l as I punished the king H824
Jer 50:21 "Attack the l of Merathaim and those who H824
Jer 50:22 The noise of battle is in the l, the noise of H824
Jer 50:25 has work to do in the l of the Babylonians. H824
Jer 50:34 cause so that he may bring rest to their l, H824
Jer 50:38 For it is a l of idols, idols that will go mad H824
Jer 50:44 chase Babylon from its l in an instant. H2023S
Jer 50:45 purposed against the l of the Babylonians: H824
Jer 51: 2 to winnow her and to devastate her l; H824
Jer 51: 5 though their l is full of guilt before the Holy H824
Jer 51: 9 let us leave her and each go to our own l H824
Jer 51:27 "Lift up a banner in the l! Blow the trumpet H824
Jer 51:29 The l trembles and writhes, for the LORD's H824
Jer 51:29 to lay waste the l of Babylon so that no one H824
Jer 51:43 a dry and desert l, a land where no one H824
Jer 51:43 dry and desert land, a l where no one lives NDT
Jer 51:46 be afraid when rumors are heard in the l; H824
Jer 51:46 of violence in the l and of ruler against H824
Jer 51:47 her whole l will be disgraced and her slain H824
Jer 51:50 Remember the LORD in a distant l, and call AIT
Jer 51:52 throughout her l the wounded will H824
Jer 51:54 destruction from the l of the Babylonians. H824
Jer 52: 9 of Babylon at Riblah in the l of Hamath, H824
Jer 52:16 people of the l to work the vineyards H824
Jer 52:25 charge of conscripting the people of the l, H824
Jer 52:27 at Riblah, in the l of Hamath, the king had H824
Jer 52:27 Judah went into captivity, away from her l. H141
La 3:34 To crush underfoot all prisoners in the l, H824
La 4:21 Daughter Edom, you who live in the l of Uz. H824
Eze 1: 3 the Kebar River in the l of the Babylonians. H824
Eze 6:14 them and make the l a desolate waste H824
Eze 7: 2 the Sovereign LORD says to the l of Israel: H141
Eze 7: 2 has come upon the four corners of the l! H824
Eze 7: 7 upon you, upon you who dwell in the l. H824
Eze 7:23 For the l is full of bloodshed, and the city is H824
Eze 7:27 hands of the people of the l will tremble. H824
Eze 8:12 not see us; the LORD has forsaken the l. H824
Eze 8:17 Must they also fill the l with violence and H824
Eze 9: 9 the l is full of bloodshed and the city is full H824
Eze 9: 9 'The LORD has forsaken the l; the LORD H824
Eze 11:15 this l was given to us as our possession. H824
Eze 11:17 I will give you back the l of Israel again. H141
Eze 12: 6 your face so that you cannot see the l, H824
Eze 12:12 cover his face so that he cannot see the l. H824
Eze 12:13 to Babylonia, the l of the Chaldeans, but H824
Eze 12:19 Say to the people of the l: 'This is what the H824
Eze 12:19 living in Jerusalem and in the l of Israel: H141
Eze 12:19 their l will be stripped of everything in it H824
Eze 12:20 be laid waste and the l will be desolate. H824
Eze 12:22 is this proverb you have in the l of Israel: H141
Eze 13: 9 of Israel, nor will they enter the l of Israel. H141
Eze 14:16 be saved, but the l would be desolate. H824
Eze 14:17 'Let the sword pass throughout the l,' and I H824
Eze 14:19 a plague into that l and pour out my wrath H824
Eze 15: 8 I will make the l desolate because they H824
Eze 16: 3 birth were in the l of the Canaanites; H824
Eze 16:29 Babylonia, a l of merchants, but even H824
Eze 17: 4 carried it away to a l of merchants, H824
Eze 17: 5 of the seedlings of the l and put it in fertile H824
Eze 17:13 also carried away the leading men of the l, H824
Eze 17:16 in the l of the king who put him on the H5226
Eze 18: 2 quoting this proverb about the l of Israel: H141
Eze 19: 4 They led him with hooks to the l of Egypt. H824
Eze 19: 7 The l and all who were in it were terrified H824
Eze 19:13 planted in the desert, in a dry and thirsty l. H824
Eze 20: 6 out of Egypt into a l I had searched out H824
Eze 20: 6 them, a l flowing with milk and honey NDT
Eze 20:15 bring them into the l I had given them— H824
Eze 20:15 a l flowing with milk and honey NDT
Eze 20:28 brought them into the l I had sworn to give H824
Eze 20:36 in the wilderness of the l of Egypt, H824
Eze 20:38 them out of the l where they are living, H824
Eze 20:38 yet they will not enter the l of Israel. H141
Eze 20:40 there in the l all the people of Israel will H824
Eze 20:42 when I bring you into the l of Israel, the H141
Eze 20:42 the l I had sworn with uplifted hand to give H824
Eze 21: 2 Prophesy against the l of Israel H141
Eze 21:30 created, in the l of your ancestry, I will H824
Eze 21:32 your blood will be shed in your l, you will H824
Eze 22:24 "Son of man, say to the l, 'You are a land H2023S
Eze 22:24 'You are a l that has not been cleansed H824
Eze 22:29 The people of the l practice extortion and H824
Eze 22:30 gap on behalf of the l so I would not have H824
Eze 23: 3 In that l their breasts were fondled and H9004S
Eze 23:48 "So I will put an end to lewdness in the l H824
Eze 25: 3 over the l of Israel when it was H141
Eze 25: 6 malice of your heart against the l of Israel, H141
Eze 25: 9 Meon and Kiriathaim—the glory of that l. H824
Eze 26:20 take your place in the l of the living. H824
Eze 28:25 Then they will live in their own l, which I H141
Eze 29:10 I will make the l of Egypt a ruin and a H824
Eze 29:12 I will make the l of Egypt desolate among H824
Eze 29:14 them to Upper Egypt, the l of their ancestry. H824
Eze 29:19 loot and plunder the l as pay for his H2023S
Eze 30: 5 of the covenant l will fall by the sword H824
Eze 30:11 will be brought in to destroy the l. H824
Eze 30:11 against Egypt and fill the l with the slain. H824
Eze 30:12 of the Nile and sell the l to an evil nation; H824
Eze 30:12 I will lay waste the l and everything in it. H824
Eze 30:13 I will spread fear throughout the l. H824
Eze 31:12 lay broken in all the ravines of the l. H824
Eze 32: 4 will throw you on the l and hurl you on the H824
Eze 32: 6 I will drench the l with your flowing blood H824
Eze 32: 8 I will bring darkness over your l, declares H824
Eze 32:15 desolate and strip the l of everything in it, H824
Eze 32:23 spread terror in the l of the living are slain, H824
Eze 32:24 spread terror in the l of the living went H824
Eze 32:25 their terror had spread in the l of the living, H824
Eze 32:26 they spread their terror in the l of the living. H824
Eze 32:27 also had terrorized the l of the living. H824
Eze 32:32 had him spread terror in the l of the living, H824
Eze 33: 2 'When I bring the sword against a l, and H824
Eze 33: 2 the people of the l choose one of their H824
Eze 33: 3 coming against the l and blows the H824
Eze 33:24 in those ruins in the l of Israel are saying, H141
Eze 33:24 was only one man, yet he possessed the l. H824
Eze 33:24 surely the l has been given to us as our H824
Eze 33:25 shed blood, should you then possess the l? H824
Eze 33:26 Should you then possess the l?' H824
Eze 33:28 I will make the l a desolate waste, and her H824
Eze 33:29 when I have made the l a desolate waste H824
Eze 34:13 I will bring them into their own l. H141
Eze 34:13 ravines and in all the settlements in the l. H824
Eze 34:14 heights of Israel will be their grazing l. H5659
Eze 34:14 There they will lie down in good grazing l, H5659
Eze 34:25 with them and rid the l of savage beasts so H824
Eze 34:27 the people will be secure in their l. H141
Eze 34:29 them a l renowned for its crops, H4760
Eze 34:29 of famine in the l or bear the scorn of the H824
Eze 36: 5 hearts they made my l their own H824
Eze 36: 6 concerning the l of Israel and say to the H141
Eze 36:17 people of Israel were living in their own l, H141
Eze 36:18 shed blood in the l and because they had H824
Eze 36:20 and yet they had to leave his l. H824
Eze 36:24 bring you back into your own l. H141
Eze 36:28 you will live in the l I gave your ancestors; H824
Eze 36:34 The desolate l will be cultivated instead of H824
Eze 36:35 "This l that was laid waste has become like H824
Eze 37:12 I will bring you back to the l of Israel. H141
Eze 37:14 will live, and I will settle you in your own l. H141
Eze 37:21 bring them back into their own l. H141
Eze 37:22 I will make them one nation in the l, on the H824
Eze 37:25 They will live in the l I gave to my servant H824
Eze 37:25 the l where your ancestors lived. H2023S
Eze 38: 2 against Gog, of the l of Magog, the chief H824
Eze 38: 8 you will invade a l that has recovered from H824
Eze 38: 9 you will be like a cloud covering the l. H824
Eze 38:11 "I will invade a l of unwalled villages; H824
Eze 38:12 goods, living at the center of the l. H824
Eze 38:16 people Israel like a cloud that covers the l. H824
Eze 38:16 I will bring you against my l, so that the H824
Eze 38:18 When Gog attacks the l of Israel, my hot H141
Eze 38:19 be a great earthquake in the l of Israel. H141
Eze 39:12 be burying them in order to cleanse the l. H824
Eze 39:13 All the people of the l will bury them, and H824
Eze 39:14 continually employed in cleansing the l. H2023S
Eze 39:14 They will spread out across the l and H824
Eze 39:15 As they go through the l, anyone who sees H824
Eze 39:16 And so they will cleanse the l.' H824
Eze 39:26 in safety in their l with no one to make H141
Eze 39:28 I will gather them to their own l, not H141
Eze 40: 2 he took me to the l of Israel and set me on H824
Eze 43: 2 and the l was radiant with his glory. H824
Eze 45: 1 " 'When you allot the l as an inheritance H824
Eze 45: 1 LORD a portion of the l as a sacred district, H824
Eze 45: 2 with 50 cubits around it for open l. H4494
Eze 45: 4 the sacred portion of the l for the priests, H824
Eze 45: 7 prince will have the l bordering each side of NDT
Eze 45: 8 This l will be his possession in Israel. H824
Eze 45: 8 of Israel to possess the l according to their H824
Eze 45:16 All the people of the l will be required to H824
Eze 45:22 himself and for all the people of the l. H824
Eze 46: 3 the people of the l are to worship in the H824
Eze 46: 9 the people of the l come before the LORD at H824
Eze 47:13 the boundaries of the l that you will divide H824
Eze 47:14 this l will become your inheritance. H824
Eze 47:15 "This is to be the boundary of the l: "On H824
Eze 47:18 Jordan between Gilead and the l of Israel, H824
Eze 47:21 are to distribute this l among yourselves H824
Eze 48:12 to them from the sacred portion of the l, H824
Eze 48:14 is the best of the l and must not pass into H824
Eze 48:29 "This is the l you are to allot as an H824
Da 4:10 me stood a tree in the middle of the l. A10075
Da 8: 9 to the east and toward the Beautiful L. NDT
Da 9: 6 ancestors, and to all the people of the l. H824
Da 11:16 in the Beautiful L and will have the power H824
Da 11:39 people and will distribute the l at a price. H141
Da 11:41 He will also invade the Beautiful L. H824
Hos 1: 2 an adulterous wife this l is guilty of H824
Hos 1:11 one leader and will come up out of the l, H824
Hos 2: 3 turn her into a parched l, and slay her with H824
Hos 2:18 sword and battle I will abolish from the l, H824
Hos 2:23 I will plant her for myself in the l; I will H824
Hos 4: 1 to bring against you who live in the l: H824
Hos 4: 1 no acknowledgment of God in the l. H824
Hos 4: 3 Because of this the l dries up, and all who H824
Hos 7:16 this they will be ridiculed in the l of Egypt. H824

Hos 9: 3 They will not remain in the LORD's **l** H824
Hos 10: 1 more altars; as his **l** prospered, he adorned H824
Hos 13: 5 in the wilderness, in the **l** *of* burning heat. H824
Joel 1: 2 you elders; listen, all who live in the **l**. H824
Joel 1: 6 A nation has invaded my **l**, a mighty army H824
Joel 1:14 all who live in the **l** to the house of the H824
Joel 2: 1 Let all who live in the **l** tremble, for the day H824
Joel 2: 3 Before them the **l** is like the garden of H824
Joel 2:18 was jealous for his **l** and took pity on his H824
Joel 2:20 pushing it into a parched and barren **l**; its H824
Joel 2:21 Do not be afraid, **l** of Judah; be glad and H141
Joel 3: 2 among the nations and divided up my **l**. H824
Joel 3:19 in whose **l** they shed innocent blood. H824
Am 1:11 slaughtered the women of **the l**, H2257S
Am 2:10 to give you the **l** *of* the Amorites. H824
Am 3:11 "An enemy will overrun your **l**, pull down H824
Am 5: 2 deserted in her own **l**, with no one to lift H141
Am 5: 8 pours them out over the face of the **l**— H824
Am 6: 2 two kingdoms? Is their **l** larger than yours? H1473
Am 7: 2 When they had stripped the **l** clean, I cried H824
Am 7: 4 up the great deep and devoured the **l**. H2750
Am 7:10 The **l** cannot bear all his words. H824
Am 7:11 go into exile, away from their **native l**. H141
Am 7:12 Go back to the **l** *of* Judah. Earn your H824
Am 7:17 Your **l** will be measured and divided up H141
Am 7:17 go into exile, away from their **native l**. H141
Am 8: 4 needy and do away with the poor of the **l**, H824
Am 8: 8 "Will not the **l** tremble for this, and all who H824
Am 8: 8 The whole **l** will rise like the Nile; it will H2023S
Am 8:11 "when I will send a famine through the **l** H824
Am 9: 5 it mourn; the whole **l** rises like the Nile H2023S
Am 9: 6 pours them out over the face of the **l**— H824
Am 9:15 I will plant Israel in their own **l**, never H141
Am 9:15 be uprooted from the **l** I have given them," H141
Ob 19 foothills will possess the **l** of the Philistines. NDT
Ob 20 will possess the **l** as far as Zarephath; NDT
Jnh 1: 9 heaven, who made the sea and the **dry l**." H3317
Jnh 1:13 the men did their best to row back to **l**. H3317
Jnh 2:10 the fish, and it vomited Jonah onto **dry l**. H3317
Mic 2: 5 assembly of the LORD to divide the **l** by lot. H2475
Mic 5: 5 Assyrians invade our **l** and march through H824
Mic 5: 6 who will rule the **l** *of* Assyria with the sword H824
Mic 5: 6 the **l** *of* Nimrod with drawn sword. H824
Mic 5: 6 they invade our **l** and march across our H824
Mic 5:11 the cities of your **l** and tear down all your H824
Mic 6: 4 redeemed you from the **l** *of* slavery. H1074
Mic 7: 2 The faithful have been swept from the **l** H824
Na 3:13 The gates of your **l** are wide open to your H824
Na 3:16 locusts they strip the **l** and then fly away. NDT
Hab 3:13 crushed the leader of the **l** *of* wickedness, H1074
Zep 2: 3 all you humble of the **l**, you who do what H824
Zep 2: 5 is against you, Canaan, **l** *of* the Philistines. H824
Zep 2: 6 The **l** *by* the sea will become pastures H2475
Zep 2: 7 That **l** will belong to the remnant of the H2475
Zep 2: 8 people and made threats against their **l**. H1473
Zep 2: 9 survivors of my nation *will* **inherit** their **l**." H5706
Zep 3:19 honor in every **l** *where* they have suffered H824
Hag 2: 4 all you people of the **l**,' declares the LORD, H824
Hag 2: 6 the earth, the sea and the **dry l**. H3000
Zec 1:21 horns against the **l** *of* Judah to scatter its H824
Zec 2: 6 Flee from the **l** *of* the north," declares the H824
Zec 2:12 portion in the holy **l** and will again choose H141
Zec 3: 9 will remove the sin of this **l** in a single day. H824
Zec 5: 3 the curse that is going out over the whole **l**; H824
Zec 5: 6 the iniquity of the people throughout the **l**." H824
Zec 6: 8 given my Spirit rest in the **l** *of* the north." H824
Zec 7: 5 "Ask all the people of the **l** and the priests H824
Zec 7:14 The **l** they left behind them was so H824
Zec 7:14 is how they made the pleasant **l** desolate. H824
Zec 9: 1 LORD is against the **l** *of* Hadrak and will H824
Zec 9:16 will sparkle in his **l** like jewels in a crown. H141
Zec 11: 6 no longer have pity on the people of the **l**," H824
Zec 11: 6 They will devastate the **l**, and I will not H824
Zec 11:16 a shepherd over the **l** who will not care H824
Zec 12:12 The **l** will mourn, each clan by itself, with H824
Zec 13: 2 banish the names of the idols from the **l**, H824
Zec 13: 2 the spirit of impurity from the **l**. H824
Zec 13: 5 the **l** has been my livelihood since my H141
Zec 13: 8 In the whole **l**," declares the LORD H824
Zec 14:10 The whole **l**, from Geba to Rimmon, south H824
Mal 1: 4 They will be called the Wicked **L**, H1473
Mal 3:12 yours will be a delightful **l**," says the H824
Mal 4: 6 come and strike the **l** with total destruction." H824
Mt 2: 6 Bethlehem, *in* the **l** of Judah, are by no G1178
Mt 2:20 his mother and go to the **l** of Israel, G1178
Mt 2:21 his mother and went to the **l** of Israel. G1178
Mt 4:15 "**L** of Zebulun and land of Naphtali, the G1178
Mt 4:15 "Land of Zebulun and **l** of Naphtali, the G1178
Mt 4:16 those living in the **l** of the shadow of G6001
Mt 14:24 already a considerable distance from **l**, G1178
Mt 23:15 You travel over **l** and sea to win a single G3831
Mt 27:45 afternoon darkness came over all the **l**. G1178
Mk 6:47 of the lake, and he was alone on **l**. G1178
Mk 15:33 came over the whole **l** until three in the G1178
Lk 4:25 was a severe famine throughout the **l**. G1178
Lk 21:23 great distress in the **l** and wrath against G1178
Lk 23:44 came over the whole **l** until three in the G1178
Ac 4:34 those who owned **l** or houses sold them, G6005
Ac 5: 3 some of the money you received *for* the **l**? G6005
Ac 5: 8 the price you and Ananias got *for* the **l**?" G6005
Ac 7: 3 God said, 'and go to the **l** I will show you. G1178
Ac 7: 4 "So he left the **l** of the Chaldeans and G1178
Ac 7: 4 God sent him to this **l** where you are now G1178
Ac 7: 5 after him would possess **the l**, G899S
Ac 7:45 when they took the **l** from the nations God NDT
Ac 7:45 It remained in the **l** until the time of David, NDT
Ac 13:19 giving their **l** to his people as their G1178
Ac 27:27 sailors sensed they were approaching **l**. G6001
Ac 27:39 they did not recognize the **l**, but they saw G1178
Ac 27:43 swim to jump overboard first and get to **l**. G1178
Ac 27:44 In this way everyone reached **l** safely. G1178
Heb 6: 7 **L** that drinks in the rain often falling on it G1178
Heb 6: 8 But **l** that produces thorns and thistles is NDT
Heb 11: 9 in the promised **l** like a stranger in a G1178
Heb 11:29 passed through the Red Sea as on dry **l**; G1178
Jas 5: 7 farmer waits for the **l** to yield its valuable G1178
Jas 5:17 it did not rain on the **l** for three and a half G1178
Rev 7: 1 from blowing on the **l** or on the sea or on G1178
Rev 7: 2 given power to harm the **l** and the sea: G1178
Rev 7: 3 "Do not harm the **l** or the sea or the trees G1178
Rev 10: 2 foot on the sea and his left foot on the **l**, G1178
Rev 10: 5 the sea and on the **l** raised his right hand G1178
Rev 10: 8 who is standing on the sea and on the **l**." G1178
Rev 16: 2 went and poured out his bowl on the **l**, G1178

LAND'S (1) [LAND]

Nu 18:13 All the **l** firstfruits that they bring to the H928+824

LANDED (11) [LAND]

Mt 14:14 *When* Jesus **l** and saw a large crowd, he G2002
Mt 14:34 *they* **l** at Gennesaret. G2262+2093+3836+1178
Mk 6:34 *When* Jesus **l** and saw a large crowd, he G2002
Mk 6:53 *they* **l** at Gennesaret and G2093+3836+1178+2262
Jn 6:23 boats from Tiberias **l** near the place G2262
Jn 21: 9 When *they* **l**, they saw a G609+1650+3836+1178
Ac 18:22 *When he* **l** at Caesarea, he went up to G2982
Ac 21: 3 *We* **l** at Tyre, where our ship was to G2982
Ac 21: 7 our voyage from Tyre and **l** at Ptolemais, G2918
Ac 27: 3 The next day *we* **l** at Sidon; and Julius, in G2864
Ac 27: 5 Pamphylia, *we* **l** at Myra in Lycia. G2982

LANDMARK, LANDMARKS (KJV) BOUNDARY STONE, BOUNDARY STONES

LANDOWNER (3) [LAND]

Mt 20: 1 heaven is like a **l** who went out early G476+3867
Mt 20:11 they began to grumble against the **l**. G3867
Mt 21:33 There was a **l** who planted a G476+3867

LANDS (54) [LAND]

Ge 26: 3 I will give all these **l** and will confirm the H824
Ge 26: 4 in the sky and will give them all these **l**, H824
Ge 41:54 There was famine in all the other **l**, but in H824
Lev 26:36 so fearful in the **l** *of* their enemies that the H824
Lev 26:39 waste away in the **l** *of* their enemies H824
Nu 32: 1 saw that the **l** *of* Jazer and Gilead were H824
Dt 29:22 who come from distant **l** will see the H824
Jos 10:42 kings and their **l** Joshua conquered in H824
Jos 12: 7 Joshua gave **their l** as an inheritance to H2023S
Jos 12: 8 The **l** included the hill country, the western NDT
Jos 12: 8 These were the **l** of the Hittites, Amorites NDT
Jdg 11:18 skirted the **l** *of* Edom and Moab, passed H824
1Ki 8:46 who take them captive to their own **l**, far H824
2Ki 19:17 have laid waste these nations and their **l**. H824
2Ki 19:24 I have dug wells in **foreign** *l* and drunk the AIT
1Ch 7:28 Their **l** and settlements included Bethel H299
1Ch 29:30 Israel and the kingdoms of all the other **l**. H824
2Ch 12: 8 serving me and serving the kings of other **l**." H824
2Ch 13: 9 of your own as the peoples of other **l** do? H824
2Ch 15: 5 inhabitants of the **l** were in great turmoil. H824
2Ch 17:10 the kingdoms of the **l** surrounding Judah, H824
2Ch 26:10 vineyards in the hills and in the **fertile l**, H4149
2Ch 32:13 have done to all the peoples of the other **l**? H824
2Ch 32:17 peoples of the other **l** did not rescue their H824
Ps 49:11 though they had named **l** after themselves. H141
Ps 76:11 let all the **neighboring** *l* bring gifts to the AIT
Ps 78:55 them and allotted their **l** to them as an H2475
Ps 105:44 he gave them the **l** *of* the nations, and they H824
Ps 106:27 nations and scatter them throughout the **l**. H824
Ps 107: 3 those he gathered from the **l**, from east H824
Ps 111: 6 giving them the **l** *of* other nations. H5709
Isa 8: 9 all you distant **l**. Prepare for battle, H824
Isa 13: 5 They come from faraway **l**, from the ends H824
Isa 14: 7 All the **l** are at rest and at peace; they H824
Isa 23: 7 feet have taken her to settle in far-off **l**? NDT
Isa 36:18 ever delivered their **l** from the hand of the H824
Isa 36:20 have been able to save their **l** from me? H824
Isa 37:18 laid waste all these peoples and their **l**. H824
Isa 37:25 I have dug wells in **foreign** *l* and drunk the AIT
Jer 12:14 them from their **l** and I will uproot the H141
Jer 27:10 only serve to remove you far from your **l**; H141
Jer 32:37 them from all the **l** where I banish them in H824
Jer 46:16 back to our own people and our native **l**, H824
Eze 6: 8 you are scattered among the **l** and nations. H824
Eze 20: 6 milk and honey, the most beautiful of all **l**. H824
Eze 20:15 honey, the most beautiful of all **l**— H824
Eze 29:12 of Egypt desolate among devastated **l**, H824
Eze 30: 7 " 'They will be desolate among desolate **l** H824
Eze 32: 9 the nations, among **l** you have not known. H824
Hab 2: 8 you have destroyed **l** and cities and H824
Hab 2:17 you have destroyed **l** and cities and H824
Zep 2:11 down to him, all of them in their own **l**. H5226
Zec 10: 9 in **distant l** they will remember me. H5305
Ac 17:26 in history and the boundaries *of* their **l**. G3000

LANES (1)

Lk 14:23 the roads and **country l** and compel them G5850

LANGUAGE (40) [LANGUAGES]

Ge 10: 5 within their nations, each with its own **l**.) H4383
Ge 11: 1 world had one **l** and a common speech H8557
Ge 11: 6 speaking the same **l** they have begun to H8557
Ge 11: 7 down and confuse their **l** so they will not H8557
Ge 11: 9 LORD confused the **l** *of* the whole world. H8557
Dt 28:49 a nation whose **l** you will not understand, H4383
Ezr 4: 7 in Aramaic script and in the Aramaic **l**. H9553
Ne 13:24 spoke the **l of Ashdod** or the language H848
Ne 13:24 of Ashdod or the **l** *of* one of the other H4383
Ne 13:24 did not know how to speak the **l of Judah**. H3376
Est 1:22 script and to each people in their own **l**, H4383
Est 3:12 province and in the **l** *of* each people all H4383
Est 8: 9 province and the **l** *of* each people and H4383
Est 8: 9 also to the Jews in their own script and **l**. H4383
Isa 19:18 will speak the **l** *of* Canaan and swear H8557
Isa 33:19 whose **l** is strange and incomprehensible. H4383
Jer 5:15 a people whose **l** you do not know, whose H4383
Eze 3: 5 a people of obscure speech and strange **l**, H4383
Eze 3: 6 peoples of obscure speech and strange **l**, H4383
Da 1: 4 to teach them the **l** and literature of the H4383
Da 3: 4 "Nations and peoples *of every* **l**, this is A10392
Da 3: 7 peoples *of every* **l** fell down and A10392
Da 3:29 of any nation or **l** who say anything A10392
Da 4: 1 To the nations and peoples *of every* **l** A10392
Da 5:19 peoples *of every* **l** dreaded and A10392
Da 6:25 peoples *of every* **l** in all the earth: A10392
Da 7:14 peoples *of every* **l** worshiped him. A10392
Jn 8:43 Why is my **l** not clear to you? Because you G3282
Jn 8:44 he speaks **his native l**, for he G1666+3836+2625
Jn 16:25 when *I will* no longer **use** this kind of **l** G3281
Ac 1:19 they called that field *in* their **l** Akeldama, G1365
Ac 2: 6 each one heard their own **l** being spoken. G1365
Ac 2: 8 that each of us hears them *in* our native **l**? G1365
Ac 14:11 they shouted **in the Lycaonian l**, "The G3378
Col 3: 8 slander, and **filthy l** from your lips. G155
Rev 5: 9 from every tribe and **l** and people and G1185
Rev 7: 9 people and **l**, standing before the G1185
Rev 11: 9 **l** and nation will gaze on their bodies G1185
Rev 13: 7 over every tribe, people, **l** and nation. G1185
Rev 14: 6 to every nation, tribe, **l** and people. G1185

LANGUAGES (7) [LANGUAGE]

Ge 10:20 are the sons of Ham by their clans and **l**, H4383
Ge 10:31 are the sons of Shem by their clans and **l**, H4383
Isa 66:18 gather the people of all nations and **l**, H4383
Zec 8:23 ten people from all **l** and nations will take H4383
1Co 14:10 there are all sorts *of* **l** in the world, G5889
Rev 10:11 about many peoples, nations, **l** and kings." G1185
Rev 17:15 are peoples, multitudes, nations and **l**. G1185

LANGUISH (2) [LANGUISHES]

Isa 24: 4 withers, the heavens **l** with the earth. H581
Jer 14: 2 mourns, her cities **l**; they wail for the land, H581

LANGUISHES (1) [LANGUISH]

Isa 24: 4 withers, the world **l** and withers, the H581

LANTERNS (1)

Jn 18: 3 were carrying torches, **l** and weapons. G3286

LAODICEA (6) [LAODICEANS]

Col 2: 1 am contending for you and for those at **L**, G3293
Col 4:13 you and for those at **L** and Hierapolis. G3293
Col 4:15 greetings to the brothers and sisters at **L**, G3293
Col 4:16 that you in turn read the letter from **L**. G3293
Rev 1:11 Thyatira, Sardis, Philadelphia and **L**." G3293
Rev 3:14 "To the angel of the church in **L** write G3293

LAODICEANS (1) [LAODICEA]

Col 4:16 read in the church *of* the **L** and that you in G3294

LAP (7) [LAPPED, LAPPING, LAPS]

Jdg 7: 5 "Separate those who **l** the water with their H4379
Jdg 16:19 After putting him to sleep on her **l**, she H1386
2Ki 4:20 the boy sat on her **l** until noon, and then H1386
Pr 6:27 scoop fire into his **l** without his clothes H2668
Pr 16:33 The lot is cast into the **l**, but its every H2668
Ecc 7: 9 for anger resides in the **l** *of* fools. H2668
Lk 6:38 running over, will be poured into your **l**. G3146

LAPIS (11)

Ex 24:10 like a pavement made of **l lazuli**, H6209
Ex 28:18 shall be turquoise, **l lazuli** and emerald; H6209
Ex 39:11 row was turquoise, **l lazuli** and emerald; H6209
Job 28: 6 **l lazuli** comes from its rocks, and its dust H6209
Job 28:16 of Ophir, with precious onyx or **l lazuli**. H6209
SS 5:14 like polished ivory decorated with **l lazuli**. H6209
Isa 54:11 turquoise, your foundations with **l lazuli**. H6209
La 4: 7 than rubies, their appearance like **l lazuli**. H6209
Eze 1:26 what looked like a throne of **l lazuli**, H74+6209
Eze 10: 1 of a throne of **l lazuli** above the vault H74+6209
Eze 28:13 onyx and jasper, **l lazuli**, turquoise and H6209

LAPPED (1) [LAP]

Jdg 7: 7 hundred men that **l** I will save you and H4379

LAPPIDOTH (1)

Jdg 4: 4 prophet, the wife of **L**, was leading Israel H4366

LAPPING (1) [LAP]
Jdg 7: 6 of them drank from cupped hands, l like H4379

LAPS (5) [LAP]
Jdg 7: 5 tongues as a dog l from those who kneel H4379
Ps 79:12 Pay back into the l of our neighbors seven H2668
Isa 65: 6 back in full; I will pay it back into their l— H2668
Isa 65: 7 measure into their l the full payment for H2668
Jer 32:18 sins into the l of their children after H2668

LAPWING (KJV) HOOPOE

LARGE (156) [ENLARGE, ENLARGED, ENLARGES, LARGER, LARGEST]
Ge 29: 2 stone over the mouth of the well was l. H1524
Ge 30:43 prosperous and came to own l flocks, H8041
Ge 50: 9 It was a very l company. H3878
Ex 12:38 and also l droves of livestock H3878+4394
Nu 13:28 the cities are fortified and very l. H1524
Nu 20:20 against them with a l and powerful army. H3878
Nu 32: 1 who had very l herds and flocks, saw H8041
Dt 1:28 the cities are l, with walls up to the H1524
Dt 6:10 give you—a land with l, flourishing cities H1524
Dt 8:13 herds and flocks grow l and your silver H8049
Dt 9: 1 with l cities that have walls up to the sky. H1524
Dt 17:17 He must not accumulate l amounts of H8049+4394
Dt 25:14 in your house—one l, one small. H1524
Dt 27: 2 set up some l stones and coat them with H1524
Jos 7:26 Achan they heaped up a l pile of rocks, H1524
Jos 8:29 And they raised a l pile of rocks over it H1524
Jos 10:11 the LORD hurled l hailstones down on H1524
Jos 10:18 "Roll l rocks up to the mouth of the cave H1524
Jos 10:27 the mouth of the cave they placed l rocks, H1524
Jos 11: 4 their troops and a l number of horses and H4394
Jos 13: 1 there are still very l areas of land to be H2221
Jos 14:12 there and their cities were l and fortified, H1524
Jos 19:33 from Heleph and the l tree in Zaanannim, H471
Jos 22: 8 wealth—with l herds of livestock H8041+4394
Jos 24:26 Then he took a l stone and set it up there H1524
1Sa 6:14 there it stopped beside a l rock. H1524
1Sa 6:15 objects, and placed them on the l rock. H1524
1Sa 6:18 The l rock on which the Levites set the ark H1524
1Sa 14:33 "Roll a l stone over here at once. H1524
2Sa 12: 2 man had a very l number of sheep and H2221
2Sa 18: 9 went under the thick branches of a l oak, H1524
2Sa 18:17 and piled up a l heap of rocks over H1524+4394
1Ki 4:13 in Bashan and its sixty l walled cities with H1524
1Ki 5:17 from the quarry l blocks of high-grade H1524
1Ki 7:10 were laid with l stones of good quality, H1524
1Ki 10: 2 carrying spices, l quantities of gold, and H4394
1Ki 10:10 120 talents of gold, l quantities of spices H4394
1Ki 10:16 made two hundred l shields of hammered H7558
1Ki 18:32 trench around it l enough to hold two H3869
1Ki 18:33 "Fill four l jars with water and pour it on H3902
2Ki 4:38 "Put on the l pot and cook some stew H1524
2Ki 12:10 that there was a l amount of money in the H8041
2Ki 16:15 "On the l new altar, offer the morning H1524
2Ki 18:17 his field commander with a l army, H3878
1Ch 22: 3 He provided a l amount of iron to H4200+8044
1Ch 22: 4 had brought l numbers of them to H4200+8044
1Ch 29: 2 all of these in l quantities. H4200+8044
2Ch 2: 9 temple I build must be l and magnificent. H1524
2Ch 4: 9 the l court and the doors for the court H1524
2Ch 9: 1 spices, l quantities of gold, and H4200+8044
2Ch 9: 9 120 talents of gold, l quantities of spices H4394
2Ch 9:15 made two hundred l shields of hammered H7558
2Ch 14: 8 equipped with l shields and with spears H7558
2Ch 14:13 carried off a l amount of plunder. H2221+4394
2Ch 15: 9 for l numbers had come over to H4200+8044
2Ch 17:13 had l supplies in the towns of Judah H8041
2Ch 23: 9 the spears and the l and small shields H4482S
2Ch 24:11 saw that there was a l amount of money, H8041
2Ch 26:15 arrows and hurl l stones from the walls H1524
2Ch 30: 5 celebrated in l numbers according H4200+8044
2Ch 30:13 A very l crowd of people assembled in H8041
2Ch 32: 4 They gathered a l group of people who H8041
2Ch 32: 5 also made l numbers of weapons H4200+8044
2Ch 36:18 temple of God, both l and small, and the H1524
Ezr 5: 8 it with l stones and placing the A10006+10146
Ezr 6: 4 courses of l stones and one of A10006+10146
Ezr 10: 1 of God, a l crowd of Israelites H8041+4394
Ne 5: 7 I called together a l meeting to deal with H1524
Ne 7: 4 Now the city was l and spacious, but there H1524
Ne 12:31 I also assigned two l choirs to give thanks H1524
Ne 13: 5 provided him with a l room formerly used H1524
Est 8:15 a l crown of gold and a purple robe of H1524
Job 1: 3 donkeys, and had a l number of servants. H4394
Job 36:18 do not let a l bribe turn you aside. H8044
Ps 104:25 number—living things both l and small. H1524
Pr 14:28 A l population is a king's glory, but H8044
Isa 8: 1 "Take a l scroll and write on it with an H1524
Isa 22:18 ball and throw you into a l country. H8146+3338
Isa 36: 2 commander with a l army from Lachish to H3878
Jer 22:14 So he makes l windows in it, panels it H7973
Jer 43: 9 take some l stones with you and bury H1524
Jer 44:15 who were present—a l assembly—and all H1524
Jer 46: 3 your shields, both l and small, and H7558S
Jer 49:32 their l herds will be spoils of war. H2162
Eze 16:26 your neighbors with l genitals, and H1541
Eze 17:15 to Egypt to get horses and a l army. H8041
Eze 23:24 on every side with l and small shields H7558S
Eze 23:32 sister's cup, a cup l and deep; it will bring H8146
Eze 38: 4 a great horde with l and small shields, H7558S
Eze 39: 9 the small and l shields, the bows H7558S
Eze 47: 9 There will be l numbers of fish, because H4394
Da 2:31 there before you stood a l statue A10678
Da 4:11 The tree grew l and strong and its top A10648
Da 4:20 you saw, which grew l and strong, with A10648
Da 7: 7 It had l iron teeth; it crushed and A10647
Da 8: 8 of its power the l horn was broken off, H1524
Da 8:21 the l horn between its eyes is the first H1524
Da 11:11 who will raise a l army, but it will be H8041
Da 11:25 "With a l army he will stir up his strength H1524
Da 11:25 will wage war with a l and very powerful H1524
Joel 2: 2 the mountains a l and mighty army comes H8041
Jnh 3: 3 Now Nineveh was a very l city; it took H1524
Mt 4:25 L crowds from Galilee, the Decapolis G4498
Mt 8: 1 the mountainside, l crowds followed him. G4498
Mt 8:30 distance from them a l herd of pigs was G4498
Mt 12:15 A l crowd followed him, and he healed G4498
Mt 13: 2 Such l crowds gathered around him that G4498
Mt 14:14 When Jesus landed and saw a l crowd, he G4498
Mt 18: 6 to have a l millstone hung around G3685+3948
Mt 19: 2 L crowds followed him, and he healed G4498
Mt 20:29 leaving Jericho, a l crowd followed him. G4498
Mt 21: 8 A very l crowd spread their cloaks on the G4498
Mt 26:47 With him was a l crowd armed with G4498
Mt 28:12 they gave the soldiers a l sum of money, G2653
Mk 2: 2 gathered in such l numbers that there G4498
Mk 2:13 A l crowd came to him, and he began to G4246
Mk 3: 7 and a l crowd from Galilee followed. G4498
Mk 4: 1 around him was so l that he got into a G4498
Mk 5:11 A l herd of pigs was feeding on the G3489
Mk 5:21 a l crowd gathered around him while he G4498
Mk 5:24 A l crowd followed and pressed around G4498
Mk 6:34 When Jesus landed and saw a l crowd, he G4498
Mk 8: 1 those days another l crowd gathered. G4498
Mk 9:14 they saw a l crowd around them and the G4498
Mk 9:42 them if a l millstone were hung G3685+3948
Mk 10:46 together with a l crowd, were leaving the G2653
Mk 12:37 The l crowd listened to him with delight G4498
Mk 12:41 Many rich people threw in l amounts. G4498
Mk 14:15 He will show you a l room upstairs G3489
Mk 16: 4 which was very l, had been rolled away G3489
Lk 5: 6 they caught such a l number of fish that G4498
Lk 5:29 a l crowd of tax collectors and others G4498
Lk 6:17 A l crowd of his disciples was there and a G4498
Lk 7:11 his disciples and a l crowd went along G4498
Lk 7:12 And a l crowd from the town was with her G2653
Lk 8: 4 While a l crowd was gathering and G4498
Lk 8:32 A l herd of pigs was feeding there on the G2653
Lk 9:37 from the mountain, a l crowd met him. G4498
Lk 14:25 L crowds were traveling with Jesus, and G4498
Lk 22:12 He will show you a l room upstairs, all G3489
Lk 23:27 A l number of people followed him G4498
Jn 12: 9 Meanwhile a l crowd of Jews found out G4498
Jn 21: 6 the net in because of the l number of fish. G4436
Jn 21:11 It was full of l fish, 153, but even with so G3489
Ac 6: 7 a l number of priests became G4498
Ac 10:11 something like a l sheet being let down G3489
Ac 10:27 inside and found a l gathering of people. G4498
Ac 11: 5 something like a l sheet being let down G3489
Ac 14:21 that city and won a l number of disciples. G2653
Ac 17: 4 as did a l number of God-fearing Greeks G4498
Ac 19:26 led astray l numbers of people here G2653
Gal 6:11 See what l letters I use as I write to you G4383
2Ti 2:20 In a l house there are articles not only of G3489
Jas 3: 4 Although they are so l and are driven by G5496
Rev 6: 4 To him was given a l sword. G3489
Rev 18:21 the size of a l millstone and threw G3489

LARGER (14) [LARGE]
Lev 25:51 redemption a l share of the price paid H4946
Nu 26:54 To a l group give a larger inheritance, and H8041
Nu 26:54 To a larger group give a l inheritance, and H8049
Nu 26:56 by lot among the l and smaller groups." H8041
Nu 33:54 To a l group give a larger inheritance H8041
Nu 33:54 To a larger group give a l inheritance H8049
Dt 7: 1 seven nations l and stronger than you— H8041
Dt 11:23 dispossess nations l and stronger than H1524
Jos 10: 2 royal cities; it was l than Ai, and all its H1524
1Ch 24: 4 A l number of leaders were found among H8041
2Ch 24:24 into their hands a much l army. H4200+8044
Da 11:13 muster another army, l than the first; and H8041
Am 6: 2 two kingdoms? Is their land l than yours? H8041
Ac 28:23 came in even l numbers to the place G4498

LARGEST (2) [LARGE]
Mt 13:32 it is the l of garden plants and becomes a G3505
Mk 4:32 becomes the l of all garden plants, G3505

LASCIVIOUSNESS (KJV) DEBAUCHERY, IMMORALITY, LEWDNESS, SENSUALITY

LASEA (1)
Ac 27: 8 called Fair Havens, near the town of L. G3297

LASH (2) [LASHED, LASHES]
Job 5:21 will be protected from the l of the tongue, H8765
Isa 10:26 LORD Almighty will l them with a whip, H6424

LASHA (1)
Ge 10:19 Admah and Zeboyim, as far as L. H4388

LASHARON (1)
Jos 12:18 the king of Aphek one the king of L one H4389

LASHED (1) [LASH]
Isa 54:11 l by storms and not comforted H6192

LASHES (5) [LASH]
Dt 25: 2 with the number of l the crime deserves, NDT
Dt 25: 3 judge must not impose more than forty l. H5782
Pr 14: 3 A fool's mouth l out with pride, but the H2643
Pr 17:10 person more than a hundred l a fool. H5782
2Co 11:24 received from the Jews the forty l minus one. AIT

LAST (113) [LASTED, LASTING, LASTS, LATTER]
Ge 19:34 the younger, "L night I slept with my father. H621
Ge 25: 8 Then Abraham breathed his l and died at H1588
Ge 25:17 He breathed his l and died, and he was H1588
Ge 29:34 "Now at l my husband will become H2021+7193
Ge 31:29 but l night the God of your father said to H621
Ge 31:42 of my hands, and l night he rebuked you." H621
Ge 33: 7 L of all came Joseph and Rachel, and they H339
Ge 35:18 As she breathed her l—for she was H5883+3655
Ge 35:29 Then he breathed his l and died and was H1588
Ge 49:33 breathed his l and was gathered to his H1588
Ex 14:24 the l watch of the night the LORD H874+1332
Lev 8:33 your ordination will l seven days. NDT
Lev 15:19 of her monthly period will l seven days, H2118
Lev 26:10 be eating l year's harvest when you H3824+3823
Nu 2:31 They will set out l, under their standards. H340
Nu 14:33 until the l of your bodies lies in the H9462
Dt 2:16 Now when the l of these fighting men H9462
Dt 3:11 of Bashan was the l of the H8636+4946+3856
Jos 12: 4 Bashan, one of the l of the Rephaites H3856
Jos 13:12 He was the l of the H8636+4946+3856
1Sa 11:11 the l watch of the night they H874+2021+1332
1Sa 15:16 what the LORD said to me l night." H2021+4326
2Sa 19:11 should you be the l to bring the king back H340
2Sa 19:12 why should you be the l to bring back the H340
2Sa 23: 1 These are the l words of David: "The H340
1Ki 14:10 Jeroboam every l male in H8874+928+7815
1Ki 21:21 from Ahab every l male in H8874+928+7815
2Ki 8: 1 a famine in the land that will l seven years." H995
2Ki 9: 8 from Ahab every l male in H8874+928+7815
1Ch 23:27 According to the l instructions of David, H340
Ezr 8:13 of Adonikam, the l ones, whose names H340
Ne 8:18 from the first day to the l, Ezra read from H340
Job 14:10 he breathes his l and is no more. H1588
Ps 45: 6 will l for ever and ever; a scepter of NDT
Ps 76: 5 they sleep their l sleep; not one of the AIT
Ps 81:15 their punishment would l forever. H2118
Ps 119:152 that you established them to l forever. NDT
Isa 2: 2 In the l days the mountain of the LORD's H344
Isa 41: 4 with the first of them and with the l—I am H340
Isa 44: 6 I am the first and I am the l; apart from me H340
Isa 48:12 I am he; I am the first and I am the l. H340
Isa 51: 6 But my salvation will l forever, my H2118
Isa 51: 8 But my righteousness will l forever, my H2118
Jer 15: 9 will grow faint and breathe her l. H5870+5883
Jer 32:14 in a clay jar so they will l a long time. H6641
Jer 50:17 the l to crush their bones was H340
Da 9: 2 of Jerusalem would l seventy years. H4848
Da 11: 6 and he and his power will not l. H6641
Hos 3: 5 the LORD and to his blessings in the l days. H344
Am 1: 8 till the l of the Philistines are dead," H8642
Am 4: 2 with hooks, the l of you with fishhooks. H344
Mic 4: 1 In the l days the mountain of the LORD's H344
Mt 5:26 get out until you have paid the l penny. G2274
Mt 13:21 they have no root, they l only a short time. G1639
Mt 19:30 But many who are first will be l, and many G2274
Mt 19:30 and many who are l will be first. G2274
Mt 20: 8 with the l ones hired and going G2274
Mt 20:12 who were hired l worked only one hour G2274
Mt 20:14 one who was hired l the same as I gave G2274
Mt 20:16 "So the l will be first, and the first will be G2274
Mt 20:16 the last will be first, and the first will be l." G2274
Mt 21:37 L of all, he sent his son to them. 'They G5731
Mt 27:64 This l deception will be worse than the G2274
Mk 4:17 they have no root, they l only a short time. G1639
Mk 9:35 who wants to be first must be the very l, G2274
Mk 10:31 But many who are first will be l, and the G2274
Mk 10:31 who are first will be last, and the l first." G2274
Mk 12: 6 He sent him l of all, saying, 'They will G2274
Mk 12:22 left any children. L of all, the woman died G2274
Mk 15:37 With a loud cry, Jesus breathed his l. G1743
Lk 12:59 get out until you have paid the l penny." G2274
Lk 13:30 there are those who are l who will be G2274
Lk 13:30 who will be first, and first who will be l." G2274
Lk 23:46 When he had said this, he breathed his l. G1743
Jn 6:39 given me, but raise them up at the l day. G2274
Jn 6:40 and I will raise them up at the l day." G2274
Jn 6:44 I will raise them up at the l day. G2274
Jn 6:54 and I will raise them up at the l day. G2274
Jn 7:37 On the l and greatest day of the festival G2274
Jn 11:24 rise again in the resurrection at the l day." G2274
Jn 12:48 spoken will condemn them at the l day. G2274
Jn 15:16 bear fruit—fruit that will l—and so that G3531
Ac 2:17 " 'In the l days, God says, I will pour out G2274
Ac 27:23 L night an angel of the God to whom I G4047
Ac 27:33 "For the l fourteen days," he said G4958+2465
Ro 1:10 I pray that now at l by God's will G2453+4537
Ro 1:17 that is by faith from first to l, G1666+4411+1650+4411

1Co 9:25 They do it to get a crown **that will not l** G5778
1Co 9:25 we do it to get a crown **that will l forever**. G915
1Co 15: 8 **l** of all he appeared to me also, as to G2274
1Co 15:26 The **l** enemy to be destroyed is death. G2274
1Co 15:45 a living being"; the **l** Adam, a life-giving G2274
1Co 15:52 the twinkling of an eye, at the **l** trumpet. G2274
2Co 8:10 **L year** you were the first not only to give G4373
2Co 9: 2 them that since **l year** you in Achaia were G4373
Php 4:10 in the Lord that **at l** you renewed G2453+4537
1Th 2:16 wrath of God has come upon them at **l**. G5465
2Ti 3: 1 There will be terrible times in the **l** days. G2274
Heb 1: 2 in these **l** days he has spoken to us by G2274
Heb 1: 8 will **l** for ever and ever; a scepter of NDT
Jas 5: 3 You have hoarded wealth in the **l** days. G2274
1Pe 1: 5 that is ready to be revealed in the **l** time. G2274
1Pe 1:20 revealed in these **l** times for your sake. G2274
2Pe 3: 3 understand that in the **l** days scoffers will G2274
1Jn 2:18 this is the **l** hour; and as you have G2274
1Jn 2:18 This is how we know it is the **l** hour. G2274
Jude 18 "In the **l** times there will be scoffers who G2274
Rev 1:17 "Do not be afraid. I am the First and the **L**. G2274
Rev 2: 8 words of him who is the First and the **L**, G2274
Rev 15: 1 seven angels with the seven **l** plagues G2274
Rev 15: 1 seven last plagues—**l**, because with them NDT
Rev 21: 9 full of the seven **l** plagues came and said G2274
Rev 22:13 the First and the **L**, the Beginning and the G2274

LASTED (2) [LAST]

2Sa 3: 1 the house of David **l** a long time. H2118
2Ki 6:25 the siege **l so long** that a donkey's head H6330

LASTING (36) [LAST]

Ex 12:14 it as a festival to the LORD—a **l** ordinance. H6409
Ex 12:17 Celebrate this day as a **l** ordinance for the H6409
Ex 12:24 instructions as a **l** ordinance for you H6330+6409
Ex 27:21 This is to be a **l** ordinance among the H6409
Ex 28:43 "This is to be a **l** ordinance for Aaron and H6409
Ex 29: 9 The priesthood is theirs by a **l** ordinance H6409
Ex 30:21 This is to be a **l** ordinance for Aaron and H6409
Ex 31:16 the generations to come as a **l** covenant. H6409
Lev 3:17 " 'This is a **l** ordinance for the generations H6409
Lev 10: 9 This is a **l** ordinance for the generations H6409
Lev 16:29 "This is to be a **l** ordinance for you: On H6409
Lev 16:31 must deny yourselves; it is a **l** ordinance. H6409
Lev 16:34 "This is to be a **l** ordinance for you H6409
Lev 17: 7 This is to be a **l** ordinance for them and H6409
Lev 23:14 This is to be a **l** ordinance for the H6409
Lev 23:21 This is to be a **l** ordinance for the H6409
Lev 23:31 This is to be a **l** ordinance for the H6409
Lev 23:41 This is to be a **l** ordinance for the H6409
Lev 24: 3 This is to be a **l** ordinance for the H6409
Lev 24: 8 behalf of the Israelites, as a **l** covenant. H6409
Nu 10: 8 This is to be a **l** ordinance for you and the H6409
Nu 15:15 this is a **l** ordinance for the generations to H6409
Nu 18:23 This is a **l** ordinance for the generations H6409
Nu 19:10 This will be a **l** ordinance both for the H6409
Nu 19:21 This is a **l** ordinance for them. "The man H6409
Nu 25:13 will have a covenant of a **l** priesthood, H6409
Dt 11: 4 the LORD brought **l** ruin on them.
H6330+2021+3427+2021+2296
1Sa 25:28 will certainly make a **l** dynasty for my lord, H586
2Ch 2: 4 This is a **l** ordinance for Israel H4200+6409
Est 1: 5 king gave a banquet, **l** seven days, in the NDT
Pr 10: 2 Ill-gotten treasures **have** no **l value**, but H3603
Jer 14:13 I will give you **l** peace in this place. H622
Jer 18:16 will be an object of horror and of **l** scorn; H6409
Eze 45:21 the Passover, a **festival** *l* seven days, during AIT
Eze 46:14 to the LORD is a **l** ordinance. H6409+9458
Heb 10:34 yourselves had better and **l** possessions. G3531

LASTS (6) [LAST]

Lev 23:34 Tabernacles begins, and it **l** for seven days. NDT
Job 20: 5 the joy of the godless **l** but a moment. H6330
Ps 30: 5 For his anger **l** only a moment, but his favor NDT
Ps 30: 5 moment, but his favor **l** a lifetime; weeping NDT
Pr 12:19 a lying tongue **l** only a moment. H6330
2Co 3:11 much greater is the glory *of* that which **l**! G3531

LATCH-OPENING (1)

SS 5: 4 My beloved thrust his hand through the **l** H2986

LATCHET (KJV) STRAP, STRAPS

LATE (8) [LATELY, LATER, LATEST]

Ps 127: 2 In vain you rise early and stay up **l**, toiling H336
Isa 5:11 *who* **stay up l** at night till they are inflamed H336
Am 7: 1 just as the **l crops** were coming up. H4381
Mt 14:15 and *it's* already **getting l**. G3836+6052+4216
Mk 6:35 By this time it was **l in the day**, so G6052+4498
Mk 6:35 they said, "and it's already **very l**. G6052+4498
Mk 11:11 but since it was already **l**, he G4070+3836+6052
Lk 9:12 **L in the afternoon** the G3836+2465+806+3111

LATELY (2) [LATE]

Isa 52: 4 to Egypt to live; **l**, Assyria has H928+700
Mic 2: 8 **L** my people have risen up like an enemy H919

LATER (82) [LATE]

Ge 4: 2 **L** she gave birth to his brother Abel. H3578
Ge 10:18 **L** the Canaanite clans scattered H339
Ge 22: 1 **Some time l** God tested Abraham.
H339+2021+1821+2021+465
Ge 22:20 **Some time l** Abraham was told,
H339+2021+1821+2021+465
Ge 30:21 **Some time l** she gave birth to a daughter H339
Ge 32:20 on ahead; **l**, when I see him, H339+4027
Ge 34:25 Three days **l**, while all of them were still in H928
Ge 38:24 About three months **l** Judah was told H4946
Ge 40: 1 **Some time l**, the H339+2021+1821+2021+465
Ge 48: 1 **Some time l** Joseph was told,
H339+2021+1821+2021+465
Ex 9:32 were not destroyed, because they **ripen l**.) H689
Lev 25:26 them but *l on* they **prosper** and acquire AIT
Dt 4:30 then in **l** days you will return to the LORD H344
Dt 29:22 who follow you in **l** generations and H340
Jdg 11: 4 **Some time l**, when the Ammonites H4946+3427
Jdg 14: 8 **Some time l**, when he went back to H4946+3427
Jdg 15: 1 **L on**, at the time of wheat harvest H4946+3427
Jdg 16: 4 **Some time l**, he fell in love with a H339+4027
1Sa 25:38 About ten days **l**, the LORD struck Nabal and NDT
2Sa 3:28 **L**, when David heard about H4946+339+4027
2Sa 13:23 Two years **l**, when Absalom's H4200
1Ki 2:39 But three years **l**, two of Shimei's H4946+7891
1Ki 12:12 Three days **l** Jeroboam and all the people H928
1Ki 17: 7 Some time **l** the brook dried up H4946+7891
1Ki 17:17 **Some time l** the son of the woman
H339+2021+1821+2021+465
1Ki 21: 1 **Some time l** there was an incident
H339+2021+1821+2021+465
2Ki 6:24 **Some time l**, Ben-Hadad king of H339+4027
1Ch 2:21 **L**, Hezron, when he was sixty years old H339
2Ch 10:12 Three days **l** Jeroboam and all the people H928
2Ch 18: 2 **Some years l** he went down H4200+7891+9102
2Ch 20:35 **L**, Jehoshaphat king of Judah made H339+4027
2Ch 24: 4 **Some time l** Joash decided to H339+4027
2Ch 32: 9 **L**, when Sennacherib king of Assyria H339+2296
Ne 13: 6 Some time **l** I asked his permission H4200+7891
Est 2: 1 **L** when King Xerxes' fury
H339+2021+1821+2021+465
Pr 20:25 rashly and only **l** to consider one's vows. H339
Ecc 4:16 But those *who* came **l** were not pleased H340
Jer 13: 6 Many days **l** the LORD said to me H4946+7891
Jer 42: 7 Ten days **l** the word of the LORD H4946+7891
Jer 46:26 **L**, however, Egypt will be inhabited H339+4027
Eze 16: 8 " '**L** I passed by, and when I looked at you H2256
Da 4:29 Twelve months **l**, as the king A10378+10636
Da 8: 3 than the other but grew up **l**. H928+2021+340
Da 8:19 will happen **l in the time** *of* wrath, H928+344
Mt 14:23 by himself to pray. **L** that night, he was G1181
Mt 21:29 **l** he changed his mind and went. G5731
Mt 25:11 "**L** the others also came. 'Lord, Lord,' they G5731
Mk 2: 1 **A few days l**, when Jesus again G1328+2465
Mk 6:47 **L** that night, the boat was in the middle of G1181
Mk 10:34 Three days **l** he will rise." G3552
Mk 12:13 **L** they sent some of the Pharisees and G2779
Mk 16:14 **L** Jesus appeared to the Eleven as they G5731
Lk 22:58 A little **l** someone else saw him and said G3552
Lk 22:59 About an hour **l** another asserted G1460
Jn 5: 1 **Some time l**, Jesus went up to G3552+4047
Jn 5:14 **L** Jesus found him at the temple G3552+4047
Jn 6:71 one of the Twelve, *was* **l to** betray him.) G3516
Jn 7:39 who believed in him *were* **l** to receive. G3516
Jn 12: 4 Judas Iscariot, who *was* **l** to betray him G3516
Jn 13: 7 doing, but **l** you will understand." G3552+4047
Jn 13:36 cannot follow now, but you will follow **l**." G5731
Jn 19:28 **L**, knowing that everything had now G3552+4047
Jn 19:38 **L**, Joseph of Arimathea asked G3552+4047
Jn 20:26 **A week l** his disciples were G3552+2465+3893
Ac 5: 7 About three hours **l** his wife came in, not G1404
Ac 7: 8 **L** Isaac became the father of Jacob, and G2779
Ac 15:36 Some time **l** Paul said to Barnabas, "Let G3552
Ac 20: 6 five days **l** joined the others at Troas G948
Ac 24: 1 Five days **l** the high priest Ananias went G3552
Ac 24:24 Several days **l** Felix came with his wife G3552
Ac 25:13 A few days **l** King Agrippa and Bernice G1335
Ac 27:28 A short time **l** they took soundings again G1460
Ac 28:17 Three days **l** he called together the local G3552
Gal 1:17 **L** I returned to Damascus. G4099
Gal 3:17 introduced 430 years **l**, does not set aside G3552
1Ti 4: 1 clearly says that in **l** times some will G5731
Heb 4: 7 This he did **when** a long time **l** he spoke G3552
Heb 4: 8 not have spoken **l** about another G3552+4047
Heb 11: 8 to go to a place *he would* **l** receive as his G3516
Heb 12:11 **L on**, however, it produces a harvest of G5731
Jude 5 **l** destroyed those who did not G3836+1309
Rev 1:19 is now and what will take place **l**. G3552+4047

LATEST (1) [LATE]

Ac 17:21 talking about and listening to the **l** *ideas*.) G2785

LATIN (1)

Jn 19:20 sign was written in Aramaic, **L** and Greek. G4872

LATRINE (1)

2Ki 10:27 people have used it for a **l** to this day. H4738

LATTER (7) [LAST]

Ge 14: 3 All these **l** kings joined forces in the Valley NDT
Job 42:12 blessed the **l part of** Job's **life** more than H344
Da 8:23 "In the **l part** *of* their reign, when rebels H344
Mt 23:23 You should have practiced **the l**, without G4047S
Lk 11:42 have practiced **the l** without leaving the G4047S
Php 1:16 **The l** do so out of love, knowing G3836+3525
2Ti 2:21 themselves from **the l** will be G4047S

LATTICE (4)

Jdg 5:28 behind the **l** she cried out, 'Why is H876
2Ki 1: 2 fallen through the **l** of his upper room in H8422
Pr 7: 6 of my house I looked down through the **l**. H876
SS 2: 9 the windows, peering through the **l**. H3048

LAUGH (13) [LAUGHED, LAUGHINGSTOCK, LAUGHS, LAUGHTER]

Ge 18:13 Abraham, "Why *did* Sarah **l** and say, 'Will H7464
Ge 18:15 so she lied and said, "*I did* not **l**. H7464
Ge 18:15 But he said, "Yes, *you did* **l**." H7464
Ge 21: 6 who hears about this *will* **l** with me." H7464
Job 5:22 *You will* **l** at destruction and famine, and H8471
Ps 52: 6 see and fear; *they will* **l** at you, saying, H8471
Ps 59: 8 But you **l** at them, LORD; you scoff at all H8471
Pr 1:26 I in turn *will* **l** when disaster strikes you; H8471
Pr 31:25 *she can* **l** at the days to come. H8471
Ecc 3: 4 a time to weep and a time to **l**, a time to H8471
Hab 1:10 They **l** at all fortified cities; by building H8471
Lk 6:21 are you who weep now, for *you will* **l**. G1151
Lk 6:25 Woe to you who **l** now, for you will mourn G1151

LAUGHED (6) [LAUGH]

Ge 17:17 fell facedown; *he* **l** and said to himself H7464
Ge 18:12 So Sarah **l** to herself as she thought, "After H7464
La 1: 7 looked at her and **l** at her destruction. H8471
Mt 9:24 not dead but asleep." But *they* **l** at him. G2860
Mk 5:40 But *they* **l** at him. After he put them all out, G2860
Lk 8:53 *They* **l** at him, knowing that she was dead. G2860

LAUGHINGSTOCK (6) [LAUGH]

Ge 38:23 keep what she has, or we will become a **l**. H997
Ex 32:25 so become a **l** to their enemies. H9067
Job 12: 4 "I have become a **l** to my friends, though I H8468
Job 12: 4 answered—a mere **l**, though righteous H8468
La 3:14 I became the **l** of all my people; they H8468
Eze 22: 4 to the nations and a **l** to all the countries. H7842

LAUGHS (6) [LAUGH]

Job 39: 7 *It* **l** at the commotion in the town; it does H8471
Job 39:18 feathers to run, *she* **l** at horse and rider. H8471
Job 39:22 *It* **l** at fear, afraid of nothing; it does not H8471
Job 41:29 of straw; *it* **l** at the rattling of the lance. H8471
Ps 2: 4 The One enthroned in heaven **l**; the Lord H8471
Ps 37:13 the Lord **l** at the wicked, for he knows H8471

LAUGHTER (10) [LAUGH]

Ge 21: 6 "God has brought me **l**, and everyone H7465
Job 8:21 fill your mouth with **l** and your lips with H8468
Ps 126: 2 Our mouths were filled with **l**, our tongues H8468
Pr 14:13 Even in **l** the heart may ache, and H8468
Ecc 2: 2 "**L**," I said, "is madness. And what does H8468
Ecc 7: 3 Frustration is better than **l**, because a sad H8468
Ecc 7: 6 thorns under the pot, so is the **l** *of* fools. H8468
Ecc 10:19 A feast is made for **l**, wine makes life H8468
Jer 51:39 so that *they* **shout with l**—then sleep H6600
Jas 4: 9 Change your **l** to mourning and your joy to G1152

LAUNDERER'S (3)

Isa 7: 3 the Upper Pool, on the road to the **L** Field. H3891
Isa 36: 2 the Upper Pool, on the road to the **L** Field, H3891
Mal 3: 2 he will be like a refiner's fire or a **l** soap. H3891

LAVER, LAVERS (KJV) BASIN, BASINS

LAVISHED (6)

Isa 43:24 or **l on** me the fat of your sacrifices. H8115
Eze 16:15 *You* **l** your favors on anyone who passed H9161
Da 2:48 a high position and **l** many gifts on him. A10314
Hos 2: 8 oil, *who* **l** on her the silver and gold H8049
Eph 1: 8 that *he* **l** on us. With all wisdom and G4355
1Jn 3: 1 what great love the Father *has* **l** on us, G1443

LAW (507) [LAW'S, LAWFUL, LAWGIVER, LAWS, LAWYER]

Ge 47:26 established it as a **l** concerning land in H2976
Ex 12:49 The same **l** applies both to the H9368
Ex 13: 9 forehead that this **l** *of* the LORD is to be on H9368
Ex 16:34 manna with the **tablets of the covenant l**, H6343
Ex 21:31 This **l** also applies if the bull gores a son H5477
Ex 24:12 of stone with the **l** and commandments I H9368
Ex 25:16 in the ark the **tablets of the covenant l**, H6343
Ex 25:21 the ark the **tablets of the covenant l** that I H6343
Ex 25:22 that are over the ark of the **covenant l**, H6343
Ex 26:33 the ark of the **covenant l** behind the H6343
Ex 26:34 the ark of the **covenant l** in the Most Holy H6343
Ex 27:21 that shields the ark of the **covenant l**, H6343
Ex 30: 6 that shields the ark of the **covenant l**— H6343
Ex 30: 6 that is over the **tablets of the covenant l** H6343
Ex 30:26 tent of meeting, the ark of the *covenant l*, H6343
Ex 30:36 of the ark of the **covenant l** in the tent of H6343
Ex 31: 7 the ark of the **covenant l** with the H6343
Ex 31:18 him the two tablets of the **covenant l**, H6343
Ex 32:15 two tablets of the **covenant l** in his hands. H6343
Ex 34:29 two tablets of the **covenant l** in his hands, H6343
Ex 38:21 the tabernacle of the **covenant l**, which H6343
Ex 39:35 the ark of the **covenant l** with its poles H6343
Ex 40: 3 the ark of the **covenant l** in it and shield H6343
Ex 40: 5 of the ark of the **covenant l** and put the H6343
Ex 40:20 took the **tablets of the covenant l** and H6343
Ex 40:21 shielded the ark of the **covenant l**, H6343
Lev 7: 7 " 'The same **l** applies to both the sin H9368
Lev 16:13 cover above the **tablets of the covenant l**, H6343

Lev 24: 3 the ark of the **covenant l** in the tent of H6343
Lev 24:22 are to have the same **l** for the foreigner H5477
Nu 1:50 of the tabernacle of the **covenant l**— H6343
Nu 1:53 of the **covenant l** so that my wrath H6343
Nu 1:53 care of the tabernacle of the **covenant l**." H6343
Nu 4: 5 put it over the ark of the **covenant l**. H6343
Nu 5:29 is the **l** *of* jealousy when a woman goes H9368
Nu 5:30 LORD and is to apply this entire **l** to her. H9368
Nu 6:13 " 'Now this is the **l** *of* the Nazirite when H9368
Nu 6:21 " 'This is the **l** *of* the Nazirite who vows H9368
Nu 6:21 according to the **l** *of* the Nazirite. H9368
Nu 7:89 cover on the ark of the **covenant l**. H6343
Nu 9:15 the tent of the **covenant l**, was set up, H6343
Nu 10:11 above the tabernacle of the **covenant l**. H6343
Nu 15:29 One and the same **l** applies to everyone H9368
Nu 17: 4 in front of the ark of the **covenant l**, H6343
Nu 17: 7 the LORD in the tent of the **covenant l**. H6343
Nu 17:10 staff in front of the ark of the **covenant l**, H6343
Nu 18: 2 minister before the tent of the **covenant l**. H6343
Nu 19: 2 is a requirement of the **l** that the LORD has H9368
Nu 19:14 "This is the **l** that applies when a person H9368
Nu 27:11 is to have the **force of l** for the H5477+2978
Nu 31:21 is required by the **l** that the LORD gave H9368
Nu 35:29 is to have the **force of l** for you H5477+2978
Dt 1: 5 Moses began to expound this **l**, saying: H9368
Dt 4:44 This is the **l** Moses set before the H9368
Dt 6:25 to obey all this **l** before the LORD our God, H5184
Dt 17:18 himself on a scroll a copy of this **l**, H9368
Dt 17:19 all the words of this **l** and these decrees H9368
Dt 17:20 turn from the **l** to the right or to the H5184
Dt 27: 3 the words of this **l** when you have crossed H9368
Dt 27: 8 all the words of this **l** on these stones you H9368
Dt 27:26 the words of this **l** by carrying them out." H9368
Dt 28:58 not carefully follow all the words of this **l**, H9368
Dt 28:61 disaster not recorded in this Book of the **L**, H9368
Dt 29:21 the covenant written in this Book of the **L**. H9368
Dt 29:29 that we may follow all the words of this **l**. H9368
Dt 30:10 in this Book of the **L** and turn to the LORD H9368
Dt 31: 9 wrote down this **l** and gave it to the H9368
Dt 31:11 you shall read this **l** before them in their H9368
Dt 31:12 follow carefully all the words of this **l**. H9368
Dt 31:13 who do not know this **l**, must hear it and NDT
Dt 31:24 the words of this **l** from beginning to end, H9368
Dt 31:26 this Book of the **L** and place it beside H9368
Dt 32:46 to obey carefully all the words of this **l**. H9368
Dt 33: 4 the **l** that Moses gave us, the possession H9368
Dt 33:10 your precepts to Jacob and your **l** to Israel. H9368
Jos 1: 7 to obey all the **l** my servant Moses gave H9368
Jos 1: 8 this Book of the **L** always on your lips; H9368
Jos 4:16 the ark of the **covenant l** to come up out H6343
Jos 8:31 is written in the Book of the **L** *of* Moses— H9368
Jos 8:32 wrote on stones a copy of the **l** *of* Moses. H9368
Jos 8:34 Joshua read all the words of the **l**—the H9368
Jos 8:34 just as it is written in the Book of the **L**. H9368
Jos 22: 5 commandment and the **l** that Moses the H9368
Jos 23: 6 is written in the Book of the **L** *of* Moses, H9368
Jos 24:26 these things in the Book of the **L** *of* God. H9368
1Ki 2: 3 regulations, as written in the **L** *of* Moses. H9368
2Ki 10:31 was not careful to keep the **l** *of* the LORD, H9368
2Ki 14: 6 in the Book of the **L** *of* Moses where the H9368
2Ki 17:13 with the entire **L** that I commanded your H9368
2Ki 21: 8 will keep the whole **L** that my servant H9368
2Ki 22: 8 the Book of the **L** in the temple of the H9368
2Ki 22:11 king heard the words of the Book of the **L**, H9368
2Ki 23:24 requirements of the **l** written in the book H9368
2Ki 23:25 in accordance with all the **L** *of* Moses. H9368
1Ch 16:40 everything written in the **L** *of* the LORD, H9368
1Ch 22:12 you may keep the **l** *of* the LORD your God. H9368
2Ch 6:16 do to walk before me according to my **l**, H9368
2Ch 12: 1 with him abandoned the **l** *of* the LORD. H9368
2Ch 15: 3 without a priest to teach and without the **l**. H9368
2Ch 17: 9 with them the Book of the **L** *of* the LORD; H9368
2Ch 19: 8 to administer the **l** *of* the LORD and to H5477
2Ch 19:10 bloodshed or other concerns of the **l**, H9368
2Ch 23:18 of the LORD as written in the **L** *of* Moses, H9368
2Ch 24: 6 of Israel for the tent of the **covenant l**?" H6343
2Ch 25: 4 accordance with what is written in the **L**, H9368
2Ch 30:16 prescribed in the **L** *of* Moses the man of H9368
2Ch 31: 3 festivals as written in the **L** *of* the LORD. H9368
2Ch 31: 4 devote themselves to the **L** *of* the LORD. H9368
2Ch 31:21 in obedience to the **l** and the commands, H9368
2Ch 34:14 the Book of the **L** *of* the LORD that had H9368
2Ch 34:15 the Book of the **L** in the temple of the H9368
2Ch 34:19 When the king heard the words of the **L** H9368
2Ch 35:26 with what is written in the **L** *of* the LORD— H9368
Ezr 3: 2 is written in the **L** *of* Moses the man of H9368
Ezr 7: 6 a teacher well versed in the **L** *of* Moses, H9368
Ezr 7:10 study and observance of the **L** *of* the LORD, H9368
Ezr 7:11 the priest, a **teacher of the L**, a man H6221
Ezr 7:12 teacher of the **L** of the God of heaven: A10186
Ezr 7:14 with regard to the **L** *of* your God, A10186
Ezr 7:21 the teacher of the **L** of the God of A10186
Ezr 7:26 does not obey the **l** of your God and the A10186
Ezr 7:26 of your God and the **l** of the king must A10186
Ezr 10: 3 Let it be done according to the **L**. H9368
Ne 8: 1 told Ezra the **teacher of the L** to bring out H6221
Ne 8: 1 to bring out the Book of the **L** *of* Moses, H9368
Ne 8: 2 priest brought the **L** before the assembly, H9368
Ne 8: 3 listened attentively to the Book of the **L**. H9368
Ne 8: 4 Ezra the **teacher of the L** stood on a high H6221
Ne 8: 7 the people in the **L** while the people were H9368
Ne 8: 8 They read from the Book of the **L** *of* God H9368
Ne 8: 9 Ezra the priest and **teacher of the L**, and H6221
Ne 8: 9 as they listened to the words of the **L**. H9368
Ne 8:13 to give attention to the words of the **L**. H9368
Ne 8:14 found written in the **L**, which the LORD H9368
Ne 8:18 Ezra read from the Book of the **L** *of* God. H9368
Ne 9: 3 the Book of the **L** *of* the LORD their God H9368
Ne 9:26 they turned their backs on your **l**. H9368
Ne 9:29 them in order to turn them back to your **l**, H9368
Ne 9:34 our ancestors did not follow your **l**; H9368
Ne 10:28 peoples for the sake of the **L** *of* God, H9368
Ne 10:29 oath to follow the **L** *of* God given through H9368
Ne 10:34 the LORD our God, as it is written in the **L**. H9368
Ne 10:36 "As it is also written in the **L**, we will H9368
Ne 12:26 of Ezra the priest, the **teacher of the L**. H6221
Ne 12:36 Ezra the **teacher of the L** led the H6221
Ne 12:44 required by the **L** for the priests and the H9368
Ne 13: 3 When the people heard this **l**, they H9368
Est 1:13 consult experts in *matters of* **l** and justice, H2017
Est 1:15 "According to **l**, what must be done to H2017
Est 3:14 was to be issued as **l** in every province H2017
Est 4:11 being summoned the king has but one **l**: H2017
Est 4:16 the king, even though it is against the **l**. H2017
Est 8:13 was to be issued as **l** in every province H2017
Ps 1: 2 whose delight is in the **l** *of* the LORD H9368
Ps 1: 2 who meditates on his **l** day and night. H9368
Ps 19: 7 The **l** *of* the LORD is perfect, refreshing the H9368
Ps 37:31 The **l** *of* their God is in their hearts; their H9368
Ps 40: 8 my God; your **l** is within my heart. H9368
Ps 78: 5 Jacob and established the **l** in Israel, H9368
Ps 78:10 covenant and refused to live by his **l**. H9368
Ps 89:30 his sons forsake my **l** and do not follow H9368
Ps 94:12 the one you teach from your **l**; H9368
Ps 119: 1 who walk according to the **l** *of* the LORD. H9368
Ps 119:18 that I may see wonderful things in your **l**. H9368
Ps 119:29 be gracious to me and teach me your **l**. H9368
Ps 119:34 that I may keep your **l** and obey it with all H9368
Ps 119:44 I will always obey your **l**, for ever and ever. H9368
Ps 119:51 unmercifully, but I do not turn from your **l**. H9368
Ps 119:53 of the wicked, who have forsaken your **l**. H9368
Ps 119:55 your name, that I may keep your **l**. H9368
Ps 119:61 me with ropes, I will not forget your **l**. H9368
Ps 119:70 unfeeling, but I delight in your **l**. H9368
Ps 119:72 The **l** *from* your mouth is more precious to H9368
Ps 119:77 me that I may live, for your **l** is my delight. H9368
Ps 119:85 dig pits to trap me, contrary to your **l**. H9368
Ps 119:92 If your **l** had not been my delight, I would H9368
Ps 119:97 how I love your **l**! I meditate on it all H9368
Ps 119:109 life in my hands, I will not forget your **l**. H9368
Ps 119:113 double-minded people, but I love your **l**. H9368
Ps 119:126 you to act, LORD; your **l** is being broken. H9368
Ps 119:136 from my eyes, for your **l** is not obeyed. H9368
Ps 119:142 is everlasting and your **l** is true. H9368
Ps 119:150 are near, but they are far from your **l**. H9368
Ps 119:153 me, for I have not forgotten your **l**. H9368
Ps 119:163 detest falsehood but I love your **l**. H9368
Ps 119:165 Great peace have those who love your **l** H9368
Ps 119:174 and your **l** gives me delight. H9368
Isa 2: 3 The **l** will go out from Zion, the word of H9368
Isa 5:24 have rejected the **l** *of* the LORD Almighty H9368
Isa 42:21 to make his **l** great and glorious. H9368
Isa 42:24 follow his ways; they did not obey his **l**. H9368
Jer 2: 8 who deal with the **l** did not know me; H9368
Jer 6:19 to my words and have rejected my **l**. H9368
Jer 8: 8 for we have the **l** *of* the LORD," when H9368
Jer 9:13 "It is because they have forsaken my **l** H9368
Jer 9:13 have not obeyed me or followed **my l**. H2023[S]
Jer 16:11 They forsook me and did not keep my **l**. H9368
Jer 18:18 the **teaching of** the **l** by the priest will H9368
Jer 26: 4 If you do not listen to me and follow my **l** H9368
Jer 31:33 "I will put my **l** in their minds and write it H9368
Jer 32:23 they did not obey you or follow your **l** H9368
Jer 44:10 they followed my **l** and the decrees I set H9368
Jer 44:23 him or followed his **l** or his decrees or his H9368
La 2: 9 the nations, the **l** is no more, and her H9368
Eze 7:26 priestly **instruction in the l** will cease, H9368
Eze 22:26 do violence to my **l** and profane my holy H9368
Eze 43:12 "This is the **l** *of* the temple: All the H9368
Eze 43:12 be most holy. Such is the **l** *of* the temple. H9368
Da 6: 5 something to do with the **l** *of* his God." A10186
Da 6: 8 accordance with the **l** *of* the Medes and A10186
Da 6:12 accordance with the **l** *of* the Medes and A10186
Da 6:15 that according to the **l** of the Medes and A10186
Da 9:11 has transgressed your **l** and turned away, H9368
Da 9:11 judgments written in the **L** *of* Moses, H9368
Da 9:13 Just as it is written in the **L** *of* Moses, all H9368
Hos 4: 6 you have ignored the **l** *of* your God, H9368
Hos 8: 1 my covenant and rebelled against my **l**. H9368
Hos 8:12 I wrote for them the many things of my **l** H9368
Am 2: 4 have rejected the **l** *of* the LORD and have H9368
Mic 4: 2 The **l** will go out from Zion, the word of H9368
Hab 1: 4 Therefore the **l** is paralyzed, and justice H9368
Hab 1: 7 they are a **l** to themselves and promote H5477
Zep 3: 4 the sanctuary and do violence to the **l**. H9368
Hag 2:11 'Ask the priests what the **l** says: H9368
Zec 7:12 not listen to the **l** or to the words that H9368
Mal 2: 9 have shown partiality in **matters of** the **l**." H9368
Mal 4: 4 "Remember the **l** *of* my servant Moses H9368
Mt 1:19 Joseph her husband was **faithful to the l**, *G1465*
Mt 2: 4 chief priests and **teachers of the l**, *G1208*
Mt 5:17 come to abolish the **L** or the Prophets; *G3795*
Mt 5:18 disappear from the **L** until everything is *G3795*
Mt 5:20 of the Pharisees and the **teachers of the l**, *G1208*
Mt 7:12 this sums up the **L** and the Prophets. *G3795*
Mt 7:29 not as their **teachers of the l**. *G1208*
Mt 8:19 Then a **teacher of the l** came to him and *G1208*
Mt 9: 3 some *of* the **teachers of the l** said to *G1208*
Mt 11:13 the Prophets and the **L** prophesied until *G3795*
Mt 12: 5 you read in the **L** that the priests on *G3795*
Mt 12:38 and **teachers of the l** said to him, *G1208*
Mt 13:52 every **teacher of the l** who has become *G1208*
Mt 15: 1 Pharisees and **teachers of the l** came to *G1208*
Mt 16:21 the chief priests and the **teachers of the l** *G1208*
Mt 17:10 then do the **teachers of the l** say that *G1208*
Mt 20:18 the chief priests and the **teachers of the l**. *G1208*
Mt 21:15 priests and the **teachers of the l** saw the *G1208*
Mt 22:35 One of them, an **expert in the l**, tested him *G3788*
Mt 22:36 is the greatest commandment in the **L**?" *G3795*
Mt 22:40 All the **L** and the Prophets hang on these *G3795*
Mt 23: 2 "The **teachers of the l** and the Pharisees *G1208*
Mt 23:13 **teachers of the l** and Pharisees *G1208*
Mt 23:15 **teachers of the l** and Pharisees *G1208*
Mt 23:23 **teachers of the l** and Pharisees *G1208*
Mt 23:23 the more important matters *of* the **l**— *G3795*
Mt 23:25 **teachers of the l** and Pharisees *G1208*
Mt 23:27 **teachers of the l** and Pharisees *G1208*
Mt 23:29 **teachers of the l** and Pharisees *G1208*
Mt 26:57 where the **teachers of the l** and the elders *G1208*
Mt 27: 6 "*It is* against *the* **l** to put this into the *G2003*
Mt 27:41 the **teachers of the l** and the elders *G1208*
Mk 1:22 had authority, not as the **teachers of the l**. *G1208*
Mk 2: 6 Now some **teachers of the l** were sitting *G1208*
Mk 2:16 When the **teachers of the l** who were *G1208*
Mk 3:22 And the **teachers of the l** who came down *G1208*
Mk 7: 1 some *of* the **teachers of the l** who had *G1208*
Mk 7: 5 **teachers of the l** asked Jesus, *G1208*
Mk 8:31 the chief priests and the **teachers of the l** *G1208*
Mk 9:11 "Why do the **teachers of the l** say that *G1208*
Mk 9:14 them and the **teachers of the l** arguing *G1208*
Mk 10: 5 were hard that Moses wrote you this **l**," *G1953*
Mk 10:33 the chief priests and the **teachers of the l**. *G1208*
Mk 11:18 the **teachers of the l** heard this and *G1208*
Mk 11:27 the **teachers of the l** and the elders came *G1208*
Mk 12:12 the teachers of the **l** and the elders looked NDT
Mk 12:28 One *of* the **teachers of the l** came and *G1208*
Mk 12:35 "Why do the **teachers of the l** say that the *G1208*
Mk 12:38 "Watch out for the **teachers of the l**. *G1208*
Mk 14: 1 the **teachers of the l** were scheming *G1208*
Mk 14:43 the **teachers of the l**, and the *G1208*
Mk 14:53 the **teachers of the l** came together *G1208*
Mk 15: 1 the **teachers of the l** and the whole *G1208*
Mk 15:31 the **teachers of the l** mocked him *G1208*
Lk 2:22 rites required by the **L** of Moses, *G3795*
Lk 2:23 as it is written in the **L** of the Lord, "Every *G3795*
Lk 2:24 with what is said in the **L** of the Lord: *G3795*
Lk 2:27 him what the custom *of* the **L** required, *G3795*
Lk 2:39 everything required by the **L** of the Lord, *G3795*
Lk 5:17 and **teachers of the l** were sitting *G3791*
Lk 5:21 the **teachers of the l** began thinking *G1208*
Lk 5:30 the **teachers of the l** who belonged to *G1208*
Lk 6: 7 the **teachers of the l** were looking for *G1208*
Lk 6:11 **the Pharisees and the teachers of the l** *G899*[S]
Lk 7:30 the **experts in the l** rejected God's *G3788*
Lk 9:22 the chief priests and the **teachers of the l** *G1208*
Lk 10:25 occasion an **expert in the l** stood up to *G3788*
Lk 10:26 "What is written in the **L**?" he replied *G3795*
Lk 10:37 **The expert in the l** replied, "The one *G3836*[S]
Lk 11:45 One *of* the **experts in the l** answered him *G3788*
Lk 11:46 "And you **experts in the l**, woe *to* you *G3788*
Lk 11:52 "Woe to you **experts in the l**, because you *G3788*
Lk 11:53 the **teachers of the l** began to oppose *G1208*
Lk 14: 3 asked the Pharisees and **experts in the l**, *G3788*
Lk 15: 2 the **teachers of the l** muttered, *G1208*
Lk 16:16 "The **L** and the Prophets were proclaimed *G3795*
Lk 16:17 least stroke of a pen to drop out of the **L**. *G3795*
Lk 19:47 the **teachers of the l** and the leaders *G1208*
Lk 20: 1 the chief priests and the **teachers of the l** *G1208*
Lk 20:19 The **teachers of the l** and the chief priests *G1208*
Lk 20:39 Some *of* the **teachers of the l** responded *G1208*
Lk 20:46 "Beware of the **teachers of the l**. *G1208*
Lk 22: 2 the **teachers of the l** were looking *G1208*
Lk 22:66 the chief priests and the **teachers of the l**, *G1208*
Lk 23:10 the **teachers of the l** were standing *G1208*
Lk 24:44 that is written about me in the **L** of Moses, *G3795*
Jn 1:17 For the **l** was given through Moses; grace *G3795*
Jn 1:45 the one Moses wrote about in the **L**, *G3795*
Jn 5:10 **the l forbids** you to carry your mat." *G4024+2003*
Jn 7:19 Has not Moses given you the **l**? Yet not *G3795*
Jn 7:19 Yet not one of you keeps the **l**. Why are *G3795*
Jn 7:23 so that the **l** of Moses may not be *G3795*
Jn 7:49 But this mob that knows nothing *of* the **l** *G3795*
Jn 7:51 "Does our **l** condemn a man without first *G3795*
Jn 8: 3 The **teachers of the l** and the Pharisees *G1208*
Jn 8: 5 In the **L** Moses commanded us to stone *G3795*
Jn 8:17 In your own **L** it is written that the *G3795*
Jn 10:34 "Is it not written in your **L**, 'I have said *G3795*
Jn 12:34 have heard from the **L** that the Messiah *G3795*
Jn 15:25 this is to fulfill what is written in their **L**: *G3795*
Jn 18:31 yourselves and judge him by your own **l**." *G3795*
Jn 19: 7 insisted, "We have a **l**, and according to *G3795*
Jn 19: 7 according to that **l** he must die *G3795*
Ac 4: 5 elders and the **teachers of the l** met in *G1208*
Ac 5:34 Gamaliel, a **teacher of the l**, who was *G3791*
Ac 6:12 the elders and the **teachers of the l**. *G1208*
Ac 6:13 against this holy place and against the **l**. *G3795*

Ac 7:44 tabernacle *of* the **covenant l** with them in G3457
Ac 7:53 who have received the **l** that was given G3795
Ac 10:28 aware that it is **against** our **l** for a Jew to G116
Ac 13:15 After the reading *from* the **L** and the G3795
Ac 13:39 not able to obtain under the **l** of Moses. G3795
Ac 15: 5 required to keep the **l** of Moses. G3795
Ac 15:21 For *the l of* Moses has been preached in every AIT
Ac 18:13 to worship God in ways contrary to the **l**." G3795
Ac 18:15 about words and names and your own **l**— G3795
Ac 21:20 all of them are zealous *for* the **l**. G3795
Ac 21:24 yourself are living in obedience to the **l**. G3795
Ac 21:28 our people and our **l** and this place. G3795
Ac 22: 3 trained *in* the **l** of our ancestors. G3795
Ac 22:12 observer of the **l** and highly respected G3795
Ac 23: 3 sit there to judge me according to the **l**, G3795
Ac 23: 3 yet *you yourself* **violate the l** by G4174
Ac 23: 9 some *of* the **teachers of the l** who G1208
Ac 23:29 had to do with questions *about* their **l**, G3795
Ac 24:14 accordance with the **L** and that is written G3795
Ac 25: 8 against the Jewish **l** or against the temple G3795
Ac 28:23 from the **L** of Moses and from the G3795
Ro 2:12 All who sin **apart from the l** will also G492
Ro 2:12 the law will also perish **apart from the l**, G492
Ro 2:12 who sin under the **l** will be judged by the G3795
Ro 2:12 sin under the law will be judged by the **l**. G3795
Ro 2:13 those who hear the **l** who are righteous in G3795
Ro 2:13 those who obey the **l** who will be G3795
Ro 2:14 who do not have the **l**, do by nature G3795
Ro 2:14 do by nature things *required by* the **l**, they G3795
Ro 2:14 the law, they are a **l** for themselves, even G3795
Ro 2:14 even though they do not have the **l**. G3795
Ro 2:15 the requirements *of* the **l** are written on G3795
Ro 2:17 if you rely on the **l** and boast in God; G3795
Ro 2:18 because you are instructed by the **l**; G3795
Ro 2:20 you have in the **l** the embodiment of G3795
Ro 2:23 You who boast in the **l**, do you dishonor G3795
Ro 2:23 do you dishonor God by breaking the **l**? G3795
Ro 2:25 has value if you observe the **l**, G3795
Ro 2:25 if you break the **l**, you have become G3795
Ro 2:27 yet obeys the **l** will condemn you who G3795
Ro 3:19 Now we know that whatever the **l** says, it G3795
Ro 3:19 it says to those who are under the **l**, so G3795
Ro 3:20 in God's sight by the works *of* the **l**; G3795
Ro 3:20 through the **l** we become conscious of our G3795
Ro 3:21 now apart from the **l** the righteousness of G3795
Ro 3:21 to which the **L** and the Prophets testify. G3795
Ro 3:27 Because of what **l**? The law that requires G3795
Ro 3:27 The **l** that requires works? No, NDT
Ro 3:27 because of the **l** that requires faith. G3795
Ro 3:28 by faith apart from the works *of* the **l**. G3795
Ro 3:31 then, nullify the **l** by this faith? Not at G3795
Ro 3:31 Not at all! Rather, we uphold the **l**. G3795
Ro 4:13 was not through the **l** that Abraham and G3795
Ro 4:14 For if those who depend on the **l** are heirs G3795
Ro 4:15 because the **l** brings wrath. And where G3795
Ro 4:15 And where there is no **l** there is no G3795
Ro 4:16 those who are of the **l** but also to those G3795
Ro 5:13 was in the world before the **l** was given, G3795
Ro 5:13 anyone's account where there is no **l**. G3795
Ro 5:20 The **l** was brought in so that the trespass G3795
Ro 6:14 because you are not under the **l**, but G3795
Ro 6:15 we are not under the **l** but under grace? G3795
Ro 7: 1 I am speaking to those who know the **l**— G3795
Ro 7: 1 that the **l** has authority over someone only G3795
Ro 7: 2 *by* **l** a married woman is bound to her G3795
Ro 7: 2 is released from the **l** that binds her to G3795
Ro 7: 3 is released from that **l** and is not an G3795
Ro 7: 4 you also died *to* the **l** through the body of G3795
Ro 7: 5 aroused by the **l** were at work in us, G3795
Ro 7: 6 released from the **l** so that we serve in G3795
Ro 7: 7 Is the **l** sinful? Certainly not! G3795
Ro 7: 7 what sin was had it not been for the **l**. G3795
Ro 7: 7 coveting really was if the **l** had not said, G3795
Ro 7: 8 For apart from the **l**, sin was dead. G3795
Ro 7: 9 Once I was alive apart from the **l**; but G3795
Ro 7:12 So then, the **l** is holy, and the G3795
Ro 7:14 We know that the **l** is spiritual; but I am G3795
Ro 7:16 not want to do, I agree that the **l** is good. G3795
Ro 7:21 So I find this **l** at work: Although I want to G3795
Ro 7:22 For in my inner being I delight in God's **l**; G3795
Ro 7:23 I see another **l** at work in me, waging G3795
Ro 7:23 war against the **l** of my mind and making G3795
Ro 7:23 me a prisoner of the **l** of sin at work within G3795
Ro 7:25 I myself in my mind am a slave *to* God's **l** G3795
Ro 7:25 in my sinful nature a slave *to* the **l** of sin. G3795
Ro 8: 2 Christ Jesus the **l** of the Spirit who gives G3795
Ro 8: 2 set you free from the **l** of sin and death. G3795
Ro 8: 3 For what the **l** was powerless to do G3795
Ro 8: 4 requirement *of* the **l** might be fully met G3795
Ro 8: 7 it does not submit *to* God's **l**, nor can it do G3795
Ro 9: 4 the **receiving of the l**, the temple G3792
Ro 9:31 who pursued the **l** as the way of G3795
Ro 10: 4 the culmination *of* the **l** so that there may G3795
Ro 10: 5 about the righteousness that is by the **l**: G3795
Ro 13: 8 whoever loves others has fulfilled the **l**. G3795
Ro 13:10 Therefore love is the fulfillment *of* the **l**. G3795
1Co 1:20 Where is the **teacher of the l**? Where is G1208
1Co 9: 8 Doesn't the **L** say the same thing? G3795
1Co 9: 9 For it is written in the **L** of Moses: "Do not G3795
1Co 9:20 To those under the **l** I became like one G3795
1Co 9:20 the law I became like one under the **l** G3795
1Co 9:20 though I myself am not under the **l**), G3795
1Co 9:20 the law), so as to win those under the **l**. G3795
1Co 9:21 To those **not having the l** I became like one G491
1Co 9:21 law I became like *one* **not having the l** G491
1Co 9:21 I am not **free from** God's **l** but am under G491
1Co 9:21 from God's law but am **under** Christ's **l**), G1937
1Co 9:21 so as to win those **not having the l**. G491
1Co 14:21 In the **L** it is written: "With other tongues G3795
1Co 14:34 must be in submission, as the **l** says. G3795
1Co 15:56 death is sin, and the power of sin is the **l**. G3795
Gal 2:16 is not justified by the works *of* the **l**, G3795
Gal 2:16 in Christ and not by the works *of* the **l**, G3795
Gal 2:16 by the works *of* the **l** no one will be G3795
Gal 2:19 "For through the **l** I died to the law so that G3795
Gal 2:19 the law I died *to* the **l** so that I might live G3795
Gal 2:21 could be gained through the **l**, G3795
Gal 3: 2 you receive the Spirit by the works *of* the **l**, G3795
Gal 3: 5 miracles among you by the works *of* the **l**, G3795
Gal 3:10 rely on the works *of* the **l** are under a G3795
Gal 3:10 do everything written in the Book *of* the **L**." G3795
Gal 3:11 one who relies on the **l** is justified before G3795
Gal 3:12 The **l** is not based on faith; on the contrary, G3795
Gal 3:13 us from the curse *of* the **l** by becoming a G3795
Gal 3:17 The **l**, introduced 430 years later, does G3795
Gal 3:18 For if the inheritance depends on the **l** G3795
Gal 3:19 then, was the **l** given at all? It was G3795
Gal 3:19 The **l** was given through angels and NDT
Gal 3:21 Is the **l**, therefore, opposed to the G3795
Gal 3:21 For if a **l** had been given that could impart G3795
Gal 3:21 would certainly have come by the **l**. G3795
Gal 3:23 we were held in custody under the **l** G3795
Gal 3:24 So the **l** was our guardian until Christ G3795
Gal 4: 4 born of a woman, born under the **l**, G3795
Gal 4: 5 to redeem those under the **l**, that we G3795
Gal 4:21 you who want to be under the **l**, are you G3795
Gal 4:21 are you not aware of what the **l** says? G3795
Gal 5: 3 that he is obligated to obey the whole **l**. G3795
Gal 5: 4 be justified by the **l** have been alienated G3795
Gal 5:14 For the entire **l** is fulfilled in keeping this G3795
Gal 5:18 led by the Spirit, you are not under the **l**. G3795
Gal 5:23 Against such things there is no **l**. G3795
Gal 6: 2 in this way you will fulfill the **l** of Christ. G3795
Gal 6:13 those who are circumcised keep the **l**, G3795
Eph 2:15 in his flesh the **l** with its commands and G3795
Php 3: 5 of Hebrews; in regard to the **l**, a Pharisee; G3795
Php 3: 6 as for righteousness based on the **l** G3795
Php 3: 9 of my own that comes from the **l**, G3795
1Ti 1: 7 They want to be **teachers of the l**, but they G3791
1Ti 1: 8 We know that the **l** is good if one uses it G3795
1Ti 1: 9 also know that the **l** is made not for the G3795
Titus 3: 9 arguments and quarrels **about** *the* **l**, G3788
Heb 7: 5 Now the **l** requires the descendants of Levi G3795
Heb 7:11 indeed *the* **l given** *to* the people G3793
Heb 7:12 is changed, the **l** must be changed also. G3795
Heb 7:19 the **l** made nothing perfect), and a G3795
Heb 7:28 For the **l** appoints as high priests men in G3795
Heb 7:28 which came after the **l**, appointed the Son G3795
Heb 8: 4 who offer the gifts prescribed by the **l**. G3795
Heb 9:19 every command of the **l** to all the people, G3795
Heb 9:22 the **l** requires that nearly everything be G3795
Heb 10: 1 The **l** is only a shadow of the good things G3795
Heb 10: 8 were offered in accordance with the **l**. G3795
Heb 10:28 who rejected the **l** of Moses died without G3795
Jas 1:25 into the perfect **l** that gives freedom, G3795
Jas 2: 8 really keep the royal **l** found in Scripture, G3795
Jas 2: 9 are convicted by the **l** as lawbreakers. G3795
Jas 2:10 keeps the whole **l** and yet stumbles at G3795
Jas 2:12 to be judged by the **l** that gives freedom, G3795
Jas 4:11 them speaks against the **l** and judges it. G3795
Jas 4:11 When you judge the **l**, you are not G3795
1Jn 3: 4 Everyone who sins **breaks** the **l**; in G490+4472
Rev 15: 5 the tabernacle *of* the **covenant l**—and it G3457

LAW'S (1) [LAW]

Ro 2:26 not circumcised keep the **l** requirements, G3795

LAWBREAKER (3) [BREAK]

Ro 2:27 code and circumcision, are a **l**. G4127+3795
Gal 2:18 I destroyed, then I really would be a **l**. G4127
Jas 2:11 murder, you have become a **l**. G4127+3795

LAWBREAKERS (2) [BREAK]

1Ti 1: 9 not for the righteous but *for* **l** and rebels, G491
Jas 2: 9 you sin and are convicted by the law as **l**. G4127

LAWFUL (12) [LAW]

Mt 12: 4 which was not **l** for them to do, but G2003
Mt 12:10 asked him, "*Is it* **l** to heal on the Sabbath?" G2003
Mt 12:12 Therefore *it is* **l** to do good on the G2003
Mt 14: 4 "*It is* not **l** for you to have her. G2003
Mt 19: 3 "*Is it* **l** *for* a man to divorce his wife for any G2003
Mk 2:26 which *is* **l** only for priests to eat. G2003
Mk 3: 4 asked them, "*Which is* **l** on the Sabbath: G2003
Mk 6:18 "*It is* not **l** for you to have your brother's G2003
Mk 10: 2 "*Is it* **l** for a man to divorce his wife?" G2003
Lk 6: 4 he ate what *is* **l** only for priests to eat. G2003
Lk 6: 9 "I ask you, which *is* **l** on the Sabbath: G2003
Lk 14: 3 "*Is it* **l** to heal on the Sabbath or not?" G2003

LAWGIVER (2) [LAW]

Isa 33:22 our judge, the LORD *is* our **l**, the LORD is H2980
Jas 4:12 There is only one **L** and Judge, the one G3794

LAWLESS (7) [LAWLESSNESS]

2Sa 3:33 "Should Abner have died as the **l** die? H5572
2Th 2: 8 And then the **l** *one* will be revealed, whom G491
2Th 2: 9 The coming *of* **the l one** will be in G4005S
Heb 10:17 "Their sins and **l acts** I will remember no G490
2Pe 2: 7 distressed by the depraved conduct *of* the **l** G118
2Pe 2: 8 righteous soul by the **l** deeds he saw and G491
2Pe 3:17 away by the error *of* the **l** and fall from your G118

LAWLESSNESS (3) [LAWLESS]

2Th 2: 3 occurs and the man *of* **l** is revealed, G490
2Th 2: 7 For the secret power *of* **l** is already at work G490
1Jn 3: 4 who sins breaks the law; in fact, sin is **l**. G490

LAWS (109) [LAW]

Ex 21: 1 "These are the **l** you are to set before H5477
Ex 24: 3 told the people all the LORD's words and **l**, H5477
Lev 18: 4 You must obey my **l** and be careful to H5477
Lev 18: 5 Keep my decrees and **l**, for the person who H5477
Lev 18:26 But you must keep my decrees and my **l** H5477
Lev 19:37 my decrees and all my **l** and follow them. H5477
Lev 20:22 all my decrees and **l** and follow them, H5477
Lev 25:18 my decrees and be careful to obey my **l**, H5477
Lev 26:15 decrees and abhor my **l** and fail to carry H5477
Lev 26:43 they rejected my **l** and abhorred my H5477
Lev 26:46 the **l** and the regulations that the LORD H5477
Nu 15:16 The same **l** and regulations will apply H9368
Dt 4: 1 the decrees and **l** I am about to teach H5477
Dt 4: 5 you decrees and **l** as the LORD my God H5477
Dt 4: 8 decrees and **l** as this body of laws H5477
Dt 4: 8 laws as this body of **l** I am setting before H9368
Dt 4:14 you the decrees and **l** you are to follow in H5477
Dt 4:45 decrees and **l** Moses gave them when H5477
Dt 5: 1 the decrees and **l** I declare in your H5477
Dt 5:31 decrees and **l** you are to teach them to H5477
Dt 6: 1 decrees and **l** the LORD your God directed H5477
Dt 6:20 decrees and **l** the LORD our God has H5477
Dt 7:11 decrees and **l** I give you today. H5477
Dt 7:12 pay attention to these **l** and are careful to H5477
Dt 8:11 his **l** and his decrees that I am giving you H5477
Dt 11: 1 decrees, his **l** and his commands always. H5477
Dt 11:32 all the decrees and **l** I am setting before H5477
Dt 12: 1 are the decrees and **l** you must be careful H5477
Dt 19: 9 follow all these **l** I command you today— H5184
Dt 26:16 you this day to follow these decrees and **l**; H5477
Dt 26:17 commands and **l**—that you will listen H5477
Dt 30:16 decrees and **l**; then you will live H5477
Jos 24:25 he reaffirmed for them decrees and **l**. H5477
2Sa 22:23 All his **l** are before me; I have not turned H5477
1Ki 2: 3 commands, his **l** and regulations, as H5477
1Ki 6:12 observe my **l** and keep all my commands H5477
1Ki 8:58 decrees and **l** he gave our ancestors. H5477
1Ki 9: 4 command and observe my decrees and **l**, H5477
1Ki 11:33 kept my decrees and **l** as David H5477
2Ki 17:34 the **l** and commands that the LORD gave H9368
2Ki 17:37 the **l** and commands he wrote for you. H9368
1Ch 22:13 the decrees and **l** that the LORD gave H5477
1Ch 28: 7 in carrying out my commands and **l**, H5477
2Ch 7:17 command, and observe my decrees and **l**, H5477
2Ch 14: 4 to obey his **l** and commands. H9368
2Ch 33: 8 I commanded them concerning all the **l**, H9368
Ezr 7:10 to teaching its decrees and **l** in Israel. H5477
Ezr 7:25 all who know the **l** *of* your God. A10186
Ne 1: 7 decrees and **l** you gave your servant H5477
Ne 9:13 them regulations and **l** that are just and H9368
Ne 9:14 decrees and **l** through your servant Moses. H9368
Est 1:19 it be written in the **l** *of* Persia and Media, H2017
Est 3: 8 they do not obey the king's **l**; it is not H2017
Job 38:33 Do you know the **l** *of* the heavens? Can H2978
Ps 10: 5 prosperous; your **l** are rejected by him; he H5477
Ps 18:22 All his **l** are before me; I have not turned H5477
Ps 50:16 you to recite my **l** or take my covenant H2976
Ps 105:45 might keep his precepts and observe his **l**. H9368
Ps 119: 7 upright heart as I learn your righteous **l**. H5477
Ps 119:13 all the **l** *that come from* your mouth. H5477
Ps 119:20 with longing for your **l** at all times. H5477
Ps 119:30 faithfulness; I have set my heart on your **l**. H5477
Ps 119:39 the disgrace I dread, for your **l** are good. H5477
Ps 119:43 for I have put my hope in your **l**. H5477
Ps 119:52 your ancient **l**, and I find comfort in H5477
Ps 119:62 to give you thanks for your righteous **l**. H5477
Ps 119:75 that your **l** are righteous, and that in H5477
Ps 119:91 Your **l** endure to this day, for all things H5477
Ps 119:102 I have not departed from your **l**, for you H5477
Ps 119:106 that I will follow your righteous **l**. H5477
Ps 119:108 praise of my mouth, and teach me your **l**. H5477
Ps 119:120 in fear of you; I stand in awe of your **l**. H5477
Ps 119:137 are righteous, LORD, and your **l** are right. H5477
Ps 119:149 my life, LORD, according to your **l**. H5477
Ps 119:156 preserve my life according to your **l**. H5477
Ps 119:160 are true; all your righteous **l** are eternal. H5477
Ps 119:164 a day I praise you for your righteous **l**. H5477
Ps 119:175 praise you, and may your **l** sustain me. H5477
Ps 147:19 word to Jacob, his **l** and decrees to Israel. H5477
Ps 147:20 no other nation; they do not know his **l**. H5477
Isa 10: 1 Woe to those *who* **make** unjust **l** H2980+2976
Isa 24: 5 they have disobeyed the **l**, violated the H9368
Isa 26: 8 walking in the way of your **l**, we wait for H5477
Jer 33:25 established the **l** *of* heaven and earth, H2978
Eze 5: 6 rebelled against my **l** and decrees more H5477
Eze 5: 6 She has rejected my **l** and has not H5477
Eze 5: 7 not followed my decrees or kept my **l**. H5477

Eze 11:12 decrees or kept my **l** but have conformed H5477
Eze 11:20 my decrees and be careful to keep my **l**. H5477
Eze 18: 9 my decrees and faithfully keeps my **l**. H5477
Eze 18:17 He keeps my **l** and follows my decrees H5477
Eze 20:11 decrees and made known to them my **l**, H5477
Eze 20:13 not follow my decrees but rejected my **l**— H5477
Eze 20:16 they rejected my **l** and did not follow my H5477
Eze 20:18 parents or keep their **l** or defile yourselves H5477
Eze 20:19 my decrees and be careful to keep my **l**. H5477
Eze 20:21 they were not careful to keep my **l**, of H5477
Eze 20:24 had not obeyed my **l** but had rejected my H5477
Eze 20:25 were not good and **l** through which they H5477
Eze 36:27 my decrees and be careful to keep my **l**. H5477
Eze 37:24 They will follow my **l** and be careful to H5477
Eze 43:11 design and all its regulations and **l**. H9368
Eze 44:24 They are to keep my **l** and my decrees H9368
Da 7:25 try to change the set times and the **l**. A10186
Da 9: 5 turned away from your commands and **l**. H5477
Da 9:10 our God or kept the **l** he gave us through H9368
Mal 4: 4 the decrees and **l** I gave him at Horeb H5477
Heb 8:10 I will put my **l** in their minds and write *G3795*
Heb 10:16 I will put my **l** in their hearts, and I will *G3795*

LAWSUIT (3) [LAWSUITS]

Ex 23: 2 When you give testimony in a **l**, do not H8190
Ex 23: 3 show favoritism to a poor person in a **l**. H8190
Pr 18:17 In a **l** the first to speak seems right, until H8190

LAWSUITS (4) [LAWSUIT]

Ex 23: 6 deny justice to your poor people in their **l**. H8190
Dt 17: 8 bloodshed, **l** or assaults H1907+4200+1907
Hos 10: 4 therefore **l** spring up like poisonous H5477
1Co 6: 7 fact that you have **l** among you means *G3210*

LAWYER (2) [LAW]

Ac 24: 1 of the elders and a **l** named Tertullus, *G4842*
Titus 3:13 to help Zenas the **l** and Apollos on their *G3788*

LAX (1)

Jer 48:10 on anyone who is **l** in doing the LORD's H8244

LAY (150) [LAID, LAIN, LAYER, LAYING, LAYS]

Ge 9:21 drunk and *l* **uncovered** inside his tent AIT
Ge 19:33 of it when she **l down** or when she got up. H8886
Ge 19:35 of it when she **l down** or when she got up. H8886
Ge 22:12 "*Do* not **l** a hand on the boy," he said H8938
Ge 28:11 put it under his head and **l down to sleep**. H8886
Ge 37:22 the wilderness, but don't **l** a hand on him." H8938
Ge 37:27 Ishmaelites and not **l** our hands on him; H2118
Ex 7: 4 Then *I will* **l** my hand on Egypt and with H5989
Ex 22:11 that the neighbor *did* not **l** hands on the H8938
Ex 29:10 Aaron and his sons *shall* **l** their hands on H6164
Ex 29:15 Aaron and his sons *shall* **l** their hands on H6164
Ex 29:19 Aaron and his sons *shall* **l** their hands on H6164
Lev 1: 4 *You are to* **l** your hand on the head of the H6164
Lev 3: 2 *You are to* **l** your hand on the head of your H6164
Lev 3: 8 **l** your hand on its head and slaughter it in H6164
Lev 3:13 **l** your hand on its head and slaughter it in H6164
Lev 4: 4 *He is to* **l** his hand on its head and H6164
Lev 4:15 of the community *are to* **l** their hands on H6164
Lev 4:24 *He is to* **l** his hand on the goat's head H6164
Lev 4:29 *They are to* **l** their hand on the head of the H6164
Lev 4:33 *They are to* **l** their hand on its head and H6164
Lev 16:21 He *is to* **l** both hands on the head of the H6164
Lev 24:14 who heard him *are to* **l** their hands on his H6164
Lev 26:31 into ruins and **l waste** your sanctuaries, H9037
Lev 26:32 *I* myself *will* **l waste** the land, so that your H9037
Nu 8:10 the Israelites *are to* **l** their hands on H6164
Nu 8:12 "Then the Levites *are to* **l** their hands on H6164
Nu 22:27 of the LORD, *it* **l down** under Balaam, and H8069
Nu 27:18 of leadership, and **l** your hand on him. H6164
Dt 9:25 *I* **l prostrate** before the LORD those forty H5877
Dt 20:12 engage you in battle, **l siege** to that city. H7443
Dt 20:19 When *you* **l siege** to a city for a long time H7443
Dt 28:52 *They will* **l siege** to all the cities H7674
Jos 2: 8 Before the spies **l down** for the night, she H8886
Jos 6:26 his firstborn son *he will* **l** its **foundations**; H3569
Jos 8: 9 of ambush and **l in wait** between Bethel H3782
Jos 18:11 allotted territory **l** between the tribes of H3655
Jos 19: 1 Their inheritance **l** within the territory of H2118
Jdg 4:21 went quietly to him while he **l fast asleep**, H8101
Jdg 4:22 there **l** Sisera with the tent peg H5877
Jdg 5:27 he fell; there *he* **l**. At her feet he H8886
Jdg 7: 8 the camp of Midian **l** below him in the H2118
Jdg 16: 2 the place and **l in wait** for him all night at H741
Jdg 16: 3 But Samson **l** there only until the middle H8886
Jdg 19:26 down at the door and **l** there until daylight. NDT
Jdg 19:27 on his way, there **l** his concubine, fallen in NDT
Ru 2: 9 have told the men not *to* **l a hand on** you. H5595
Ru 3: 7 uncovered his feet and **l down**. H8886
Ru 3:14 So *she* **l** at his feet until morning, but got H8886
1Sa 3: 5 lie down." So he went and **l down**. H8886
1Sa 3: 9 So Samuel went and **l down** in his place. H8886
1Sa 3:15 Samuel **l down** until morning and then H8886
1Sa 9:23 I gave you, the one I told you *to* **l** aside." H8492
1Sa 19:24 *He* **l** naked all that day and all that night H5877
1Sa 23:17 "My father Saul *will* not **l** a hand on you H5162
1Sa 24: 6 LORD's anointed, or **l** my hand on him; for H8938
1Sa 24:10 '*I will* not **l** my hand on my lord H8938
1Sa 26: 9 Who *can* **l** a hand on the LORD's anointed H8938
1Sa 26:11 LORD forbid that I *should* **l** a hand on the H8938
1Sa 26:23 I would not **l** a hand on the LORD's H8938
2Sa 13: 6 So Amnon **l down** and pretended to be ill. H8886
2Sa 13:31 tore his clothes and **l down** on the ground; H8886
2Sa 18:12 *I would* not **l** a hand on the king's son. H8938
2Sa 20:12 Amasa **l wallowing** in his blood in the H1670
1Ki 3:19 woman's son died because *she* **l** on him. H8886
1Ki 13:31 is buried; **l** my bones beside his bones. H5663
1Ki 19: 5 Then *he* **l down** under the bush and fell H8886
1Ki 19: 6 He ate and drank and then **l down** again. H8886
1Ki 21: 4 *He* **l** on his bed sulking and refused to eat H8886
1Ki 21:27 *He* **l** in sackcloth and went around meekly. H8886
2Ki 4:11 he went up to his room and **l down** there. H8886
2Ki 4:29 **L** my staff on the boy's face. H8492
2Ki 4:34 Then he got on the bed and **l** on the boy H8886
2Ch 24:22 who said as he **l** dying, "May the LORD NDT
2Ch 35: 5 your fellow Israelites, the **l people**. H1201+6639
2Ch 35: 7 all the **l people** who were there H1201+6639
Est 4: 3 Many **l** *in* sackcloth and ashes H3667
Est 9:10 But *they did* not **l** their hands on the H8938
Est 9:15 but *they did* not **l** their hands on the H8938
Est 9:16 of them but *did* not **l** their hands on the H8938
Job 1:12 on the man himself *do* not **l** a finger." H8938
Job 5: 8 *I would* **l** my cause before him. H8492
Job 22:22 from his mouth and **l up** his words in your H8492
Job 28: 9 their hands and **l bare** the roots of the H2200
Job 30:12 *they* **l snares** *for* my feet, they H8938
Job 41: 8 If *you* **l** a hand on it, you will remember H8492
Ps 5: 3 in the morning *I* **l** my requests before you H6885
Ps 21: 8 Your hand *will* **l hold** on all your enemies H5162
Ps 22:15 my mouth; *you* **l** me in the dust of death. H9189
Ps 73: 9 Their mouths **l claim** to heaven, and their H9286
Ps 139: 5 and *you* **l** your hand upon me. H8883
Ecc 10: 4 calmness *can* **l** great offenses **to rest**. H5663
Isa 21: 2 Media, **l siege**! I will bring to an H7443
Isa 24: 1 the LORD *is going to* **l waste** the earth and H1327
Isa 25:12 your high fortified walls and **l** *them* **low**; H9164
Isa 28:16 I **l** a stone in Zion, a tested stone, H3569
Isa 34:15 The owl will nest there and **l eggs**, she H4880
Isa 35: 7 In the haunts **where** jackals once **l**, grass H8070
Isa 42:15 *I will* **l waste** the mountains and hills and H2990
Isa 43:17 together, and *they* **l** there, never to rise H8886
Isa 44: 7 him declare and **l out** before me what has H6885
Isa 52:10 The LORD *will* **l bare** his holy arm in the H3106
Isa 64: 7 on your name or strives to **l hold** of you; H2616
Jer 2:20 spreading tree you **l down** as a prostitute. H7579
Jer 4: 7 He has left his place to **l** waste your land H8492
Jer 4:26 all its towns **l in ruins** before the LORD H5997
Jer 9:11 and *I will* **l** waste the towns of Judah so H5989
Jer 17:11 hatches eggs *it did* not **l** are those who H3528
Jer 34:22 And *I will* **l** waste the towns of Judah so H5989
Jer 50: 3 north will attack her and **l** waste her land. H8883
Jer 51:29 to **l** waste the land of Babylon so that no H8492
La 4:19 the mountains and **l in wait** for us in the H741
Eze 4: 2 Then **l** siege to it: Erect siege works H5989
Eze 6: 5 *I will* **l** the dead bodies of the Israelites in H5989
Eze 16: 6 as you **l** there in your blood I said to NDT
Eze 19: 2 *She* **l down** among them and reared her H8069
Eze 25:13 *I will* **l** it waste, and from Teman to H5989
Eze 26:16 their thrones and **l aside** their robes and H6073
Eze 30:12 of foreigners *I will* **l waste** the land and H9037
Eze 30:14 *I will* **l waste** Upper Egypt, set fire to Zoan H9037
Eze 31:12 its branches *l* **broken** in all the ravines of the AIT
Eze 39:21 I inflict and the hand *I* **l** on them. H8492
Da 8:27 *I* **l exhausted** for several days H2703
Jnh 1: 5 where *he* **l down** and fell into a deep H8886
Mic 1: 6 into the valley and **l bare** her foundations. H1655
Mt 8:20 Son of Man has no place *to* **l** his head." *G3111*
Mt 28: 6 Come and see the place where *he* **l**. *G3023*
Mk 6: 5 except **l** his hands **on** a few sick people *G2202*
Lk 5:18 him into the house *to* **l** him before Jesus. *G5502*
Lk 9:58 Son of Man has no place *to* **l** his head." *G3111*
Lk 14:29 For if you **l** the foundation and are not *G5502*
Lk 22:53 and *you did* not **l** a hand on me. *G1753*
Jn 4:46 royal official whose son *l* **sick** at Capernaum. AIT
Jn 10:15 and *I* **l down** my life for the sheep. *G5502*
Jn 10:17 Father loves me is that I **l down** my life— *G5502*
Jn 10:18 from me, but I **l** it **down** of my own accord. *G5502*
Jn 10:18 I have authority *to* **l** it **down** and authority *G5502*
Jn 11: 2 whose brother Lazarus *now l* **sick**, was the AIT
Jn 13:37 *I will* **l down** my life for you. *G5502*
Jn 13:38 "*Will you really* **l down** your life for me? *G5502*
Jn 15:13 to **l down** one's life for one's friends. *G5502*
Ac 8:19 that everyone **on** whom *I* **l** my hands may *G2202*
Ro 9:33 *I* **l** in Zion a stone that causes people to *G5502*
1Co 3:11 For no one can **l** any foundation other than *G5502*
1Co 7:17 This *is* **the rule** *I* **l down** in all the *G1411*
1Ti 6:19 In this way *they will* **l up treasure** for *G631*
1Pe 2: 6 *I* **l** a stone in Zion, a chosen and *G5502*
1Jn 3:16 And we ought *to* **l down** our lives for our *G5502*
Rev 4:10 *They* **l** their crowns before the throne and *G965*
Rev 10: 2 a little scroll, *which l* **open** in his hand. AIT

LAYER (2) [LAY]

Ex 16:13 morning there was a **l** *of* dew around the H8887
Lev 9:19 the fat tail, the **l of fat**, the kidneys and the H4833

LAYING (8) [LAY]

2Ch 32: 9 all his forces were **l** siege to Lachish, NDT
Job 34:30 from ruling, from **l** snares for the people. NDT
Lk 4:40 sickness, and **l** his hands **on** each one, he *G2202*
Ac 8:18 was given at the **l on** of the apostles' *G2120*
1Ti 5:22 Do not be hasty *in the* **l on** of hands, and *G2202*
2Ti 1: 6 is in you through the **l on** of my hands. *G2120*
Heb 6: 1 not **l** again the foundation of repentance *G2850*
Heb 6: 2 cleansing rites, the **l on** of hands, the *G2120*

LAYS (9) [LAY]

Job 27:17 what *he* **l up** the righteous will wear, and H3922
Job 30:24 "Surely no *one* **l** a hand on a broken man H8938
Job 39:14 *She* **l** her eggs on the ground and lets H6440
Ps 104: 3 **l** *the* **beams** *of* his upper chambers H7936
Isa 26: 5 on high, *he* **l** the lofty city **low**; he levels it H9164
Isa 30:32 the LORD **l** on them *with* his punishing H5663
Isa 51:13 and *who* **l the foundations** *of* the earth, H3569
Zec 12: 1 *who* **l the foundation** *of* the earth H3569
Jn 10:11 The good shepherd **l down** his life for the *G5502*

LAZARUS (18)

Lk 16:20 At his gate was laid a beggar named **L** *G3276*
Lk 16:23 saw Abraham far away, with **L** by his side. *G3276*
Lk 16:24 pity on me and send **L** to dip the tip of his *G3276*
Lk 16:25 good things, while **L** received bad things *G3276*
Lk 16:27 I beg you, father, send **L** to my family, *G899S*
Jn 11: 1 Now a man named **L** was sick. He was *G3276*
Jn 11: 2 whose brother **L** now lay sick, was *G3276*
Jn 11: 5 Jesus loved Martha and her sister and **L**. *G3276*
Jn 11: 6 when he heard that **L** was sick, he stayed NDT
Jn 11:11 "Our friend **L** has fallen asleep; but *G3276*
Jn 11:14 So then he told them plainly, "**L** is dead, *G3276*
Jn 11:17 Jesus found *that* **L** had already been in *G899S*
Jn 11:43 Jesus called in a loud voice, "**L**, come out!" *G3276*
Jn 12: 1 to Bethany, where **L** lived, whom Jesus *G3276*
Jn 12: 2 while **L** was among those reclining at the *G3276*
Jn 12: 9 not only because of him but also to see **L** *G3276*
Jn 12:10 chief priests made plans to kill **L** as well, *G3276*
Jn 12:17 him when he called **L** from the tomb and *G3276*

LAZINESS (3) [LAZY]

Pr 12:24 hands will rule, but **l** ends in forced labor. H8244
Pr 19:15 **L** brings on deep sleep, and the shiftless H6790
Ecc 10:18 Through **l**, the rafters sag; because of idle H6792

LAZULI (11)

Ex 24:10 like a pavement made of **lapis l**, H6209
Ex 28:18 shall be turquoise, **lapis l** and emerald; H6209
Ex 39:11 row was turquoise, **lapis l** and emerald; H6209
Job 28: 6 **lapis l** comes from its rocks, and its dust H6209
Job 28:16 of Ophir, with precious onyx or **lapis l**. H6209
SS 5:14 like polished ivory decorated with **lapis l**. H6209
Isa 54:11 of turquoise, your foundations with **lapis l**. H6209
La 4: 7 than rubies, their appearance like **lapis l**. H6209
Eze 1:26 what looked like a throne of **lapis l**, H74+6209
Eze 10: 1 of a throne of **lapis l** above the vault H74+6209
Eze 28:13 onyx and jasper, **lapis l**, turquoise and H6209

LAZY (9) [LAZINESS]

Ex 5: 8 They *are* **l**; that is why they are crying out H8332
Ex 5:17 Pharaoh said, "**L**, that's what you are H8332
Ex 5:17 "Lazy, that's what you are—**l**! H8332
Pr 10: 4 **L** hands make for poverty, but diligent H8244
Pr 12:27 The **l** do not roast any game, but the H8244
Pr 26:15 *he is too* **l** to bring it back to his mouth. H4206
Mt 25:26 master replied, 'You wicked, **l** servant! *G3891*
Titus 1:12 are always liars, evil brutes, **l** gluttons." *G734*
Heb 6:12 We do not want you to become **l**, but to *G3821*

LEAD (99) [LEADER, LEADER'S, LEADERS, LEADERS', LEADERSHIP, LEADING, LEADS, LED, RINGLEADER]

Ge 32:17 He instructed the **one in the l**: "When my H8037
Ex 13:17 God *did* not **l** them *on* the road through H5697
Ex 15:10 They sank like **l** in the mighty waters. H6769
Ex 15:13 unfailing love *you will* **l** the people you H5697
Ex 32:34 **l** the people to the place I spoke of H5697
Ex 33:12 been telling me, '**L** these people,' but you H6590
Ex 34:16 *they will* **l** your sons **to do the same** H2388+339+466+2177S
Nu 14: 8 pleased with us, *he will* **l** us into that land H995
Nu 21:15 of the ravines that **l** to the settlement of H5742
Nu 27:17 *one* who *will* **l** them **out** and bring them H3655
Nu 31:22 silver, bronze, iron, tin, **l** H6769
Dt 1:38 because he *will* **l** Israel **to inherit** it. H5706
Dt 3:28 he *will* **l** this people **across** H6296+4200+7156
Dt 10:11 "and **l** the people on their H2143+4200+7156
Dt 21: 4 and **l** it **down** to a valley that has not been H3718
Dt 31: 2 I am no longer able to **l** you. H3655+2256+995
Jos 1: 6 you *will* **l** these people **to inherit** the land H5706
Jdg 4: 6 Zebulun and **l** them **up** to Mount Tabor H5432
Jdg 4: 7 *I will* **l** Sisera, the commander of Jabin's H5432
Jdg 5: 2 "When the princes in Israel **take the l** H7276
Jdg 7:17 "**Follow** my **l**. When I get H6913+4027
Jdg 10:18 "Whoever *will* **take the l** in attacking the H2725
Jdg 13: 5 He *will* **take the l** in delivering Israel from H2725
1Sa 8: 5 now appoint a king to **l** us, such as all the H9149
1Sa 8: 6 "Give us a king to **l** us," this displeased H9149
1Sa 8:20 with a king *to* **l** us and to go out before us H9149
1Sa 30:15 "*Can you* **l** me **down** to this raiding party?" H3718
2Ki 4:24 servant, "**L on**; don't slow H5627+2256+2143
2Ki 6:19 and *I will* **l** you to the man you are H2143
2Ch 1:10 that *I may* **l** this people H3655+4200+7156+2256+995
2Ch 8:14 the Levites to **l** the praise and to H5466
Est 6: 9 **l** him on the horse through the city H8206
Job 19:24 they were inscribed with an iron tool on **l**, H6769
Job 38:32 in their seasons or **l out** the Bear with its H5697
Ps 2:12 angry and your way *will* **l** *to your* **destruction**, H6
Ps 5: 8 **L** me, LORD, in your righteousness because H5697
Ps 26:11 I **l** a blameless **life**; deliver me and H2143+928

Ps 27:11 l me in a straight path because of my H5697
Ps 31: 3 the sake of your name l and guide me. H5697
Ps 43: 3 faithful care, let them l me; let them bring H5697
Ps 60: 9 the fortified city? Who will l me to Edom? H5697
Ps 61: 2 l me to the rock that is higher than I. H5697
Ps 80: 1 of Israel, you who l Joseph like a flock. H5627
Ps 101: 2 I will be careful to l a blameless life—when NDT
Ps 108:10 the fortified city? Who will l me to Edom? H5697
Ps 139:24 and l me in the way everlasting. H5697
Ps 143:10 may your good Spirit l me on level ground H5697
Pr 4:11 way of wisdom and l you along straight H2005
Pr 5: 5 to death; her steps l straight to the grave. H9461
Pr 20: 7 The righteous l blameless lives; blessed H2143
Pr 21: 5 plans of the diligent l to profit as surely as H4200
Ecc 5: 6 Do not let your mouth l you into sin. H2627
SS 2: 4 Let him l me to the banquet hall, and let H995
SS 8: 2 I would l you and bring you to my H5627
Isa 3:12 your guides l you astray; they turn you H9494
Isa 11: 6 together; and a little child will l them. H5627
Isa 20: 4 king of Assyria will l away stripped and H5627
Isa 42:16 I will l the blind by ways they have not H2143
Isa 43: 8 L out those who have eyes but are blind H3655
Isa 49:10 guide them and l them beside springs H5633
Isa 60: 9 in the l are the ships of Tarshish H8037
Jer 3:15 who will l you with knowledge and H8286
Jer 6:29 blow fiercely to burn away the l with fire, H6769
Jer 23:32 them and l my people astray with their H9494
Jer 31: 9 I will l them beside streams of water on a H2143
Jer 31:32 them by the hand to l them out of Egypt, H3655
Jer 50: 8 be like the goats that l the flock. H4200+7156
Eze 13:10 " 'Because they l my people astray, saying H3246
Eze 22:18 iron and l left inside a furnace. H6769
Eze 22:20 l and tin are gathered into a furnace to be H6769
Eze 27:12 iron, tin and l for your merchandise. H6769
Da 12: 3 and those who l many to righteousness H7405
Hos 2:14 I will l her into the wilderness and speak H2143
Hos 5: 8 cry in Beth Aven; l on, Benjamin. H339+3870
Mic 3: 5 the prophets who l my people astray, H9494
Mic 6: 4 I sent Moses to l you, also Aaron and H7156
Zec 5: 7 Then the cover of l was raised, and there H6769
Zec 5: 8 basket and pushed its l cover down on it. H6769
Mt 6:13 And l us not into temptation, but deliver G1662
Mt 15:14 If the blind l the blind, both will fall into a G3842
Mk 14:44 arrest him and l him away under guard." G552
Lk 6:39 "Can the blind l the blind? Will they G3842
Lk 11: 4 And l us not into temptation. G1662
Lk 13:15 from the stall and l it out to give it water? G552
Jn 21:18 will dress you and l you where you do not G5770
Ac 5:24 at a loss, wondering what this might l to. G1181
Ac 13:11 seeking someone to l him by the hand. G5933
Ro 2: 4 God's kindness is intended to l you to G72
Ro 12: 8 generously; if it is to l, do it diligently; G4613
1Th 4:11 to make it your ambition to l a quiet life: G2483
Heb 6: 1 of repentance from acts that l to death, AIT
Heb 8: 9 them by the hand to l them out of Egypt, G1974
Heb 9:14 our consciences from acts that l to death, AIT
1Jn 2:26 about those who are trying to l you astray. G4414
1Jn 3: 7 children, do not let anyone l you astray. G4414
1Jn 5:16 commit a sin that does not l to death, G4639
1Jn 5:16 to those whose sin does not l to death. G4639
1Jn 5:17 there is sin that does not l to death. G4639
Rev 7:17 'he will l them to springs of living water. G3842

LEADER (78) [LEAD]

Lev 4:22 " 'When a l sins unintentionally and does H5954
Nu 2: 3 The l of the people of Judah is Nahshon H5954
Nu 2: 5 The l of the people of Issachar is H5954
Nu 2: 7 The l of the people of Zebulun is Eliab H5954
Nu 2:10 The l of the people of Reuben is Elizur H5954
Nu 2:12 The l of the people of Simeon is H5954
Nu 2:14 The l of the people of Gad is Eliasaph H5954
Nu 2:18 The l of the people of Ephraim is H5954
Nu 2:20 The l of the people of Manasseh is H5954
Nu 2:22 The l of the people of Benjamin is H5954
Nu 2:25 The l of the people of Dan is Ahiezer son H5954
Nu 2:27 The l of the people of Asher is Pagiel son H5954
Nu 2:29 The l of the people of Naphtali is Ahira H5954
Nu 3:24 The l of the families of the Gershonites H5954
Nu 3:30 The l of the families of the Kohathite clans H5954
Nu 3:32 The chief l of the Levites was H5954+5954
Nu 3:35 The l of the families of the Merarite clans H5954
Nu 7: 3 an ox from each l and a cart from every H5954
Nu 7:11 "Each day one l is to bring his offering H5954
Nu 7:18 son of Zuar, the l of Issachar, brought his H5954
Nu 7:24 of Helon, the l of the people of Zebulun H5954
Nu 7:30 of Shedeur, the l of the people of Reuben H5954
Nu 7:36 the l of the people of Simeon H5954
Nu 7:42 son of Deuel, the l of the people of Gad H5954
Nu 7:48 Ammihud, the l of the people of Ephraim H5954
Nu 7:54 the l of the people of Manasseh H5954
Nu 7:60 Gideoni, the l of the people of Benjamin H5954
Nu 7:66 Ammishaddai, the l of the people of Dan H5954
Nu 7:72 son of Okran, the l of the people of Asher H5954
Nu 7:78 of Enan, the l of the people of Naphtali H5954
Nu 14: 4 "We should choose a l and go back to H8031
Nu 17: 2 one from the l of each of their ancestral H5954
Nu 17: 6 one for the l of each of their ancestral H5954
Nu 25:14 son of Salu, the l of a Simeonite family. H5954
Nu 25:18 the daughter of a Midianite l, the woman H5954
Nu 34:18 And appoint one l from each tribe to help H5954
Nu 34:22 son of Jogli, the l from the tribe of Dan; H5954
Nu 34:23 the l from the tribe of Manasseh son of H5954
Nu 34:24 the l from the tribe of Ephraim son of H5954
Nu 34:25 of Parnak, the l from the tribe of Zebulun; H5954
Nu 34:26 of Azzan, the l from the tribe of Issachar H5954
Nu 34:27 of Shelomi, the l from the tribe of Asher; H5954
Nu 34:28 the l from the tribe of Naphtali. H5954
1Sa 7: 6 Now Samuel was serving as l of Israel at H9149
1Sa 7:15 Samuel continued as Israel's l all the H9149
1Sa 12: 2 you have a king as your l. H2143+4200+7156
1Sa 12: 2 I have been your l from my H2143+4200+7156
1Sa 19:20 with Samuel standing there as their l, the H5893
1Ki 11:24 of men around him and became their l; H8569
1Ch 2:10 of Nahshon, the l of the people of Judah. H5954
1Ch 5: 6 Beerah was a l of the Reubenites. H5954
1Ch 12: 4 who was a l of the Thirty; Jeremiah H6584
1Ch 12:27 Jehoiada, l of the family of Aaron H5592
1Ch 15: 5 of Kohath, Uriel the l and 120 relatives; H8569
1Ch 15: 6 of Merari, Asaiah the l and 220 relatives; H8569
1Ch 15: 7 of Gershon, Joel the l and 130 relatives; H8569
1Ch 15: 8 Shemaiah the l and 200 relatives; H8569
1Ch 15: 9 of Hebron, Eliel the l and 80 relatives; H8569
1Ch 15:10 Amminadab the l and 112 relatives. H8569
1Ch 27: 4 Ahohite; Mikloth was the l of his division. H5592
1Ch 28: 4 He chose Judah as l, and from the tribe of H5592
2Ch 13:12 is with us; he is our l. His priests with their H8031
2Ch 19:11 son of Ishmael, the l of the tribe of Judah H5592
Ezr 8:17 them to go to Iddo, the l in Kasiphia. H8031
Ne 9:17 appointed a l in order to return to H8031
Isa 3: 6 a cloak, you be our l; take charge of this H7903
Isa 3: 7 do not make me the l of the people." H7903
Jer 30:21 Their l will be one of their own; their ruler H129
Hos 1:11 will appoint one l and will come up out H8031
Hab 3:13 You crushed the l of the land of H8031
Mt 9:18 a synagogue l came and knelt before him G807
Mk 5:35 from the house of Jairus, the synagogue l. G801
Mk 5:38 they came to the home of the synagogue l, G801
Lk 8:41 a synagogue l, came and fell at G807
Lk 8:49 from the house of Jairus, the synagogue l. G801
Lk 13:14 the synagogue l said to the people G801
Ac 18: 8 the synagogue l, and his entire G801
Ac 18:17 Sosthenes the synagogue l and beat him G801

LEADER'S (3) [LEAD]

Lev 4:26 priest will make atonement for the l sin, H2257S
Dt 33:21 himself; the l portion was kept for him. H2980
Mt 9:23 entered the synagogue l house and saw G807

LEADERS (147) [LEAD]

Ex 15:15 the l of Moab will be seized with trembling, H380
Ex 16:22 the l of the community came and H5954
Ex 18:25 all Israel and made them l of the people, H8031
Ex 24:11 his hand against these l of the Israelites; H722
Ex 34:31 so Aaron and all the l of the community H5954
Ex 35:27 The l brought onyx stones and other gems H5954
Nu 1:16 community, the l of their ancestral tribes. H5954
Nu 1:44 Aaron and the twelve l of Israel, H5954
Nu 4:34 Aaron and the l of the community H5954
Nu 4:46 Aaron and the l of Israel counted all the H5954
Nu 7: 2 Then the l of Israel, the heads of families H5954
Nu 7: 2 who were the tribal l in charge of those H5954
Nu 7:10 the l brought their offerings for its H5954
Nu 7:84 of the Israelite l for the dedication of the H5954
Nu 10: 4 one is sounded, the l—the heads of the H5954
Nu 11:16 are known to you as l and officials among H2418
Nu 13: 2 From each ancestral tribe send one of its l." H5954
Nu 13: 3 All of them were l of the Israelites. H408+8031
Nu 16: 2 well-known community l who had been H5954
Nu 17: 6 their l gave him twelve staffs H5954
Nu 17: 9 and each of the l took his own staff. H408S
Nu 25: 4 "Take all the l of these people, kill H8031
Nu 27: 2 the l and the whole assembly at the H5954
Nu 31:13 priest and all the l of the community went H5954
Nu 32: 2 the priest and to the l of the community, H5954
Nu 36: 1 came and spoke before Moses and the l H5954
Dt 5:23 all the l of your tribes and your elders H8031
Dt 29:10 LORD your God—your l and chief men, H8031
Dt 32:42 the captives, the heads of the enemy l." H7278
Dt 33: 5 Jeshurun when the l of the people H8031
Jos 8:10 he and the l of Israel marched before H2418
Jos 9:15 the l of the assembly ratified it by H5954
Jos 9:18 because the l of the assembly had sworn H5954
Jos 9:18 whole assembly grumbled against the l, H5954
Jos 9:19 all the l answered, "We have given H5954
Jos 17: 4 son of Nun, and the l and said, "The LORD H5954
Jos 22:30 the priest and the l of the community— H5954
Jos 22:32 the l returned to Canaan from their H5954
Jos 23: 2 Israel—their elders, l, judges and officials H8031
Jos 24: 1 summoned the elders, l, judges and H8031
Jdg 5: 8 God chose new l when war came to the city NDT
Jdg 7:25 They also captured two of the Midianite l H8569
Jdg 8: 3 the Midianite l, into your hands. H8569
Jdg 10:18 The l of the people of Gilead said to each H8569
Jdg 20: 2 The l of all the people of the tribes of H7157
1Sa 8: 1 he appointed his sons as Israel's l. H9149
1Sa 14:38 all you who are l of the army, and let us H7157
2Sa 4: 2 two men who were l of raiding bands. H8569
2Sa 7:11 the time I appointed l over my people H9149
1Ch 4:38 above by name were l of their clans. H5954
1Ch 7:40 brave warriors and outstanding l. H5954
1Ch 12:18 made them l of his raiding bands. H8031
1Ch 12:20 l of units of a thousand in Manasseh. H8031
1Ch 15:16 David told the l of the Levites to appoint H8569
1Ch 17: 6 to any of their l whom I commanded to H9149
1Ch 17:10 the time I appointed l over my people H9149
1Ch 22:17 ordered all the l of Israel to help his H8569
1Ch 23: 2 also gathered together all the l of Israel, H8569
1Ch 24: 4 A larger number of l were found among H8031
1Ch 26: 6 who were l in their father's family H4938
1Ch 26:12 through their l, had duties for H8031+1505
1Ch 27:16 The l of the tribes of Israel: over the H5592
1Ch 27:22 These were the l of the tribes of Israel. H8569
1Ch 29: 6 Then the l of families, the officers of the H8569
1Ch 29: 9 at the willing response of their l, H4392S
2Ch 1: 2 to the judges and to all the l in Israel, the H5954
2Ch 12: 5 Rehoboam and to the l of Judah who had H8569
2Ch 12: 6 The l of Israel and the king humbled H8569
2Ch 24:23 killed all the l of the people. H8569
2Ch 26:12 number of family l over the fighting men H8031
2Ch 28:12 Then some of the l in Ephraim—Azariah H8031
2Ch 35: 9 Jozabad, the l of the Levites H8569
2Ch 36:14 all the l of the priests and the people H8569
Ezr 5:10 the names of their l for your information. A10646
Ezr 7:28 gathered l from Israel to go up H8031
Ezr 8:16 Meshullam, who were l, and Joiarib H8031
Ezr 9: 1 been done, the l came to me and said H8569
Ezr 9: 2 And the l and officials have led the way H8569
Ne 9:32 on our kings and l, on our priests and H8569
Ne 9:34 Our kings, our l, our priests and our H8569
Ne 9:38 it in writing, and our l, our Levites and our H8569
Ne 10:14 The l of the people: Parosh H8031
Ne 11: 1 Now the l of the people settled in H8569
Ne 11: 3 are the provincial l who settled in H8031
Ne 12: 7 These were the l of the priests and their H8031
Ne 12:24 And the l of the Levites were Hashabiah H8031
Ne 12:31 I had the l of Judah go up on top of the H8569
Ne 12:32 half the l of Judah followed them H8569
Est 1: 3 The military l of Persia and Media, the H2657
Job 12:24 He deprives the l of the earth of H8031+6639
Isa 1:26 I will restore your l as in days of old, your H9149
Isa 3:14 against the elders and l of his people: H8569
Isa 14: 9 all those who were l in the world; it H6966
Isa 19:13 the l of Memphis are deceived H8569
Isa 22: 3 All your l have fled together; they have H7903
Jer 2: 8 not know me; the l rebelled against me. H8286
Jer 5: 5 So I will go to the l and speak to them H1524
Jer 10: 7 Among all the wise l of the nations and in AIT
Jer 25:34 roll in the dust, you l of the flock. H129
Jer 25:35 the l of the flock no place to escape. H129
Jer 25:36 wailing of the l of the flock, for the LORD H129
Jer 29: 2 officials and the l of Judah and Jerusalem H8569
Jer 34:19 The l of Judah and Jerusalem, the court H8569
Eze 11: 1 Pelatiah son of Benaiah, l of the people. H8569
Eze 11: 5 you are saying, you l in Israel, but I know H1074
Eze 32:21 the dead the mighty l will say of Egypt H1475
Da 11:41 Moab and the l of Ammon will be H8040
Hos 5:10 Judah's l are like those who move H8569
Hos 7:16 Their l will fall by the sword because of H8569
Hos 9:15 love them; all their l are rebellious. H8569
Mic 3: 1 "Listen, you l of Jacob, you rulers of H8031
Mic 3: 9 Hear this, you l of Jacob, you rulers of H8031
Mic 3:11 Her l judge for a bribe, her priests teach H8031
Zec 10: 3 I will punish the l; for the LORD H6966
Mk 5:22 Then one of the synagogue l, named Jairus, G801
Lk 19:47 of the law and the l among the people G4755
Jn 1:19 when the Jewish l in Jerusalem sent G2681
Jn 5:10 so the Jewish l said to the man who G2681
Jn 5:15 away and told the Jewish l that it was G2681
Jn 5:16 the Jewish l began to persecute him. G2681
Jn 7: 1 Judea because the Jewish l there were G2681
Jn 7:11 the festival the Jewish l were watching G2681
Jn 7:13 publicly about him for fear of the l. G2681S
Jn 9:22 because they were afraid of the Jewish l, G2681
Jn 12:42 many even among the l believed in him. G807
Jn 18:14 had advised the Jewish l that it would be G2681
Jn 18:28 Then the Jewish l took Jesus from Caiaphas NDT
Jn 18:36 fight to prevent my arrest by the Jewish l. G2681
Jn 19: 7 The Jewish l insisted, "We have a law G2681
Jn 19:12 but the Jewish l kept shouting, "If G2681
Jn 19:31 Because the Jewish l did not want the G2681
Jn 19:38 secretly because he feared the Jewish l. G2681
Jn 20:19 the doors locked for fear of the Jewish l, G2681
Ac 3:17 that you acted in ignorance, as did your l. G807
Ac 13:15 the l of the synagogue sent word to them G801
Ac 13:50 But the Jewish l incited the God-fearing G2681
Ac 14: 5 together with their l, to mistreat them and G807
Ac 15:22 men who were l among the believers. G2451
Ac 21:11 'In this way the Jewish l in Jerusalem will G2681
Ac 25: 2 the Jewish l appeared before him G4755
Ac 25: 5 Let some of your l come with me, and if G1543
Ac 28:17 later he called together the local Jewish l. G4755
1Co 3:21 no more boasting about human l! All things AIT
Gal 2: 2 privately with those esteemed as l, G1506
Heb 13: 7 Remember your l, who spoke the word of G2451
Heb 13:17 Have confidence in your l and submit to G2451
Heb 13:24 Greet all your l and all the Lord's people G2451

LEADERS' (1) [LEAD]

Jos 9:21 So the l promise to them was kept H5954

LEADERSHIP (4) [LEAD]

Nu 27:18 a man in whom is the spirit of l, and lay H8120
Nu 33: 1 divisions under the l of Moses and Aaron. H3338
Ps 109: 8 may another take his place of l. H7213
Ac 1:20 and, " 'May another take his place of l. G2175

LEADING (34) [LEAD]
Dt 1:15 So I took the l *men of* your tribes, wise H8031
Jdg 3:27 him from the hills, with him l them. H4200+7156
Jdg 4: 4 of Lappidoth, *was* l Israel at that time. H9149
Jdg 12: 5 the fords of the Jordan l to Ephraim, H4200
Jdg 18: 2 five of their l men from Zorah and H1201+2657
Jdg 20:31 the one l to Bethel and the other to H6590
2Sa 10:16 of Hadadezer's army l them. H4200+7156
2Sa 15: 2 by the side of the road *l to* the city gate. AIT
2Sa 17:11 with you yourself l them into battle. H2143
2Ki 10: 6 were with the l *men of* the city, who were H1524
2Ki 19: 2 Shebna the secretary and the l priests, all H2418
1Ch 19:16 of Hadadezer's army l them. H4200+7156
2Ch 23:13 with their instruments *were* l the praises. H3359
Ezr 8:24 Then I set apart twelve of the l priests H8569
Ezr 8:29 Jerusalem before the l priests and the H8569
Ezr 10: 5 rose up and put the l priests and Levites H8569
Ps 68:27 tribe of Benjamin, l them, there the great H8097
Pr 7:27 l down to the chambers of death. H3718
Pr 8: 3 beside the gate l into the city, at H4200+7023
Isa 37: 2 secretary, and the l priests, all wearing H2418
Eze 17:13 He also carried away the l men *of* the land H380
Eze 40:20 of the north gate, l into the outer court. H4200
Mt 26:55 "Am I l a rebellion, that you have G3334
Mk 6:21 commanders and the l *men* of Galilee. G4755
Mk 10:32 with Jesus l the way, and the G1639+4575
Mk 14:48 "Am I l a rebellion," said Jesus, "that you G3334
Lk 22:47 one of the Twelve, *was* l them. G4601
Lk 22:52 "Am I l a rebellion, that you G6055+2093+3334
Ac 12:10 came to the iron gate l to the city. G5770
Ac 13:50 of high standing and the l *men* of the city. G4755
Ac 16:12 Roman colony and the l city of that district G4755
Ro 6:19 as slaves to righteousness l to holiness. G1650
Ro 15:18 through me *in* l the Gentiles to obey God G1650
2Ti 2:25 repentance l them to a knowledge of G1650

LEADS (40) [LEAD]
Dt 27:18 is *anyone who* l the blind astray on the H8706
Jos 2: 7 spies on the road that l to the fords of the H6584
1Ch 11: 6 "Whoever l the attack on the H928+2021+8037
Job 12:17 *He* l rulers away stripped and makes fools H2143
Job 12:19 *He* l priests away stripped and overthrows H2143
Ps 1: 6 the way of the wicked l to destruction. H6
Ps 23: 2 pastures, *he* l me beside quiet waters, H5633
Ps 37: 8 from wrath; do not fret—it l only to evil. H8317
Ps 68: 6 he l out the prisoners with singing H3655
Pr 2:18 Surely her house l down to death and her H8755
Pr 10:17 whoever ignores correction l others astray. H9494
Pr 12:26 the way of the wicked l them astray. H9494
Pr 13:15 way of the unfaithful l to their destruction. NDT
Pr 14:12 to be right, but in the end it l to death. H2006
Pr 14:23 a profit, but mere talk l only to poverty. H4200
Pr 15:24 The path of life l upward for the prudent to NDT
Pr 16:25 to be right, but in the end it l to death. H2006
Pr 16:29 their neighbor and l them down a path H2143
Pr 19: 3 A person's own folly l *to* their ruin, yet H2006
Pr 19:23 The fear of the LORD l to life; then one H4200
Pr 21: 5 to profit as surely as haste l to poverty. H4200
Pr 28:10 *Whoever* l the upright along an evil path H8706
Isa 30:28 of the peoples a bit *that* l them astray. H9494
Isa 40:11 *he* gently l those that have young. H5633
Hos 4:12 A spirit of prostitution l them astray; they H9494
Mt 7:13 broad is the road that l to destruction, G552
Mt 7:14 the gate and narrow the road that l to life, G552
Jn 10: 3 his own sheep by name and l them out. G1974
Jn 12:50 I know that his command l to eternal life G1639
Ac 11:18 God has granted repentance that l to life." G1650
Ro 6:16 slaves to sin, which l to death, or to G1650
Ro 6:16 to obedience, which l to righteousness? G1650
Ro 6:22 the benefit you reap l to holiness, and the G1650
Ro 14:19 effort to do what *l to* peace and to mutual AIT
2Co 2:14 l us as captives in Christ's triumphal procession G2581
2Co 7:10 repentance that *l* to salvation and leaves AIT
Eph 5:18 on wine, which l to debauchery. G1877+1639
Titus 1: 1 of the truth that l to godliness— G2848
1Jn 5:16 There is a sin that l to death. I am not G4639
Rev 12: 9 Satan, who l the whole world astray. G4414

LEAF (7) [LEAFY, LEAVES]
Ge 8:11 in its beak was a freshly plucked olive l! H6591
Lev 26:36 sound of a windblown l will put them to H6591
Job 13:25 Will you torment a windblown l? Will you H6591
Ps 1: 3 in season and whose l does not wither— H6591
Pr 11:28 the righteous will thrive like a green l. H6591
Isa 64: 6 we all shrivel up like a l, and like the H6591
Mk 11:13 Seeing in the distance a fig tree in l, he G5877

LEAFY (5) [LEAF]
Lev 23:40 willows and other l trees—and rejoice H6290
Eze 6:13 every spreading tree and every l oak— H6290
Eze 17: 6 produced branches and put out l boughs. H6997
Eze 20:28 they saw any high hill or any l tree, H6290
Jnh 4: 6 God provided a l plant and made it grow H7813

LEAGUE (KJV) AGREEMENT, COVENANT, TREATY

LEAH (29) [LEAH'S]
Ge 29:16 the name of the older was L, and the H4207
Ge 29:17 L *had* weak eyes, but Rachel had a lovely H4207
Ge 29:23 he took his daughter L and brought her to H4207
Ge 29:25 there was L! So Jacob said to H4207
Ge 29:28 He finished the week with L, and then H2296S
Ge 29:30 Rachel was greater than his love for L. H4207
Ge 29:31 When the LORD saw that L was not loved H4207
Ge 29:32 L became pregnant and gave birth to a H4207
Ge 30: 9 When L saw that she had stopped having H4207
Ge 30:11 Then L said, "What good fortune!" So she H4207
Ge 30:13 Then L said, "How happy I am! The H4207
Ge 30:14 which he brought to his mother L. H4207
Ge 30:14 Rachel said to L, "Please give me some of H4207
Ge 30:16 that evening, L went out to meet him. H4207
Ge 30:17 God listened to L, and she became H4207
Ge 30:18 Then L said, "God has rewarded me for H4207
Ge 30:19 L conceived again and bore Jacob a sixth H4207
Ge 30:20 Then L said, "God has presented me with H4207
Ge 31: 4 word to Rachel and L to come out to the H4207
Ge 31:14 Then Rachel and L replied, "Do we still H4207
Ge 33: 1 so he divided the children among L H4207
Ge 33: 2 children in front, L and her children next H4207
Ge 33: 7 L and her children came and bowed down H4207
Ge 34: 1 the daughter L had borne to Jacob H4207
Ge 35:23 The sons of L: Reuben the firstborn of H4207
Ge 46:15 These were the sons L bore to Jacob in H4207
Ge 46:18 Laban had given to his daughter L— H4207
Ge 49:31 were buried, and there I buried L. H4207
Ru 4:11 coming into your home like Rachel and L, H4207

LEAH'S (5) [LEAH]
Ge 30:10 L servant Zilpah bore Jacob a son. H4207
Ge 30:12 L servant Zilpah bore Jacob a second son. H4207
Ge 31:33 Jacob's tent and into L tent and into the H4207
Ge 31:33 After he came out of L tent, he entered H4207
Ge 35:26 The sons of L servant Zilpah: Gad and H4207

LEAKS (1) [LEAKY]
Ecc 10:18 because of idle hands, the house l. H1940

LEAKY (2) [LEAKS]
Pr 19:13 is like the constant dripping of a l roof. H1942
Pr 27:15 like the dripping of a l roof in a rainstorm; H1942

LEAN (7) [LEANED, LEANING, LEANS]
Ge 41:19 scrawny and very ugly and l. H8369+1414
Ge 41:20 The l, ugly cows ate up the seven fat cows H8369
Ge 41:27 The seven l, ugly cows that came up H8369
Jdg 16:26 the temple, so that *I may* l against them." H9128
Job 8:15 *They* l on the web, but it gives way; they H9128
Pr 3: 5 with all your heart and l not on your own H9128
Eze 34:20 between the fat sheep and the l sheep. H8136

LEANED (5) [LEAN]
Ge 47:31 Israel worshiped *as he* l on the top of H2556
2Ki 7:17 officer on whose arm *he* l in charge of the H9128
Eze 29: 7 shoulders; when they l on you, you broke H9128
Jn 21:20 was the one who *had* l back against Jesus G404
Heb 11:21 worshiped as he *l* on the top of his staff. AIT

LEANFLESHED (KJV) GAUNT, LEAN

LEANING (6) [LEAN]
2Sa 1: 6 "and there was Saul, l on his spear, with H9128
2Ki 5:18 to bow down and he *is* l on my arm and I H9128
2Ki 7: 2 whose arm the king *was* l said to the man H9128
Ps 62: 3 throw me down—this l wall, this tottering H5742
SS 8: 5 up from the wilderness l on her beloved? H8345
Jn 13:25 L back against Jesus, he asked him, "Lord G404

LEANNOTH (1)
Ps 88: T According to mahalath l. A maskil of H4361

LEANS (3) [LEAN]
2Sa 3:29 sore or leprosy or *who* l on a crutch or who H2616
2Ki 18:21 pierces the hand of anyone who l on it! H6164
Isa 36: 6 pierces the hand of anyone who l on it! H6164

LEAP (7) [LEAPED, LEAPING, LEAPS]
Job 39:20 *Do you* make it l like a locust, striking H8321
Ps 29: 6 *He* makes Lebanon l like a calf, Sirion like H8376
Ps 114: 6 mountains, *did you* l like rams, you H8376
Isa 13:21 there the wild goats *will* l about. H8376
Isa 35: 6 Then *will* the lame l like a deer, and the H1925
Joel 2: 5 that of chariots *they* l over the H8376
Lk 6:23 "Rejoice in that day and l for joy, because G5015

LEAPED (4) [LEAP]
Ps 114: 4 the mountains l like rams, the hills like H8376
Da 3:24 l to *his* feet in amazement A10624
Lk 1:41 greeting, the baby l in her womb, and G5015
Lk 1:44 my ears, the baby in my womb l for joy. G5015

LEAPING (2) [LEAP]
2Sa 6:16 she saw King David l and dancing before H7060
SS 2: 8 Here he comes, l across the mountains H1925

LEAPS (2) [LEAP]
Job 37: 1 this my heart pounds and l from its place. H6001
Ps 28: 7 My heart l for joy, and with my song I H6600

LEARN (41) [LEARNED, LEARNING]
Ge 24:21 her closely to l whether or not the H3359
Lev 5: 3 then they l of it and realize their guilt H3359
Lev 5: 4 then they l of it and realize their guilt H3359
Dt 4:10 words so that *they may* l to revere me as H4340
Dt 5: 1 L them and be sure to follow them H4340
Dt 14:23 so that *you may* l to revere the LORD your H4340
Dt 17:19 his life so that *he may* l to revere the LORD H4340
Dt 18: 9 *do* not l to imitate the detestable ways of H4340
Dt 31:12 they can listen and l to fear the LORD your H4340
Dt 31:13 must hear it and l to fear the LORD your H4340
Jdg 18: 5 inquire of God *to* l whether our journey H3359
1Sa 22: 3 stay with you until *I* l what God will do H3359
1Ki 1:20 to l from you who will sit on the throne of H5583
2Ch 12: 8 so that *they may* l the difference between H3359
Job 34: 4 *let* us l together what is good. H3359
Ps 119: 7 an upright heart as I l your righteous laws. H4340
Ps 119:71 be afflicted so that *I might* l your decrees. H4340
Ps 119:73 me understanding *to* l your commands. H4340
Ps 141: 6 the wicked *will* l that my words were H9048
Pr 19:25 the simple *will* l prudence; rebuke H6891
Pr 22:25 or *you may* l their ways and get yourself H544
Isa 1:17 L to do right; seek justice. Defend the H4340
Isa 26: 9 the people of the world l righteousness. H4340
Isa 26:10 to the wicked, *they do* not l righteousness H4340
Jer 2:33 the worst of women *can* l *from* your ways. H4340
Jer 10: 2 "*Do* not l the ways of the nations or be H4340
Jer 12:16 And if *they* l well the ways of my H4340+4340
Jer 35:13 '*Will you* not l a lesson and obey my H4374
Mt 9:13 But go and l what this means: 'I desire G3443
Mt 11:29 Take my yoke upon you and l from me, for G3443
Mt 24:32 "Now l this lesson from the fig tree: As G3443
Mk 13:28 "Now l this lesson from the fig tree: As G3443
Jn 14:31 so that the world *may* l that I love the G1182
Ac 24: 8 will be able *to* l the truth about all these G2105
1Co 4: 6 so that *you may* l from us the meaning of G3443
Gal 3: 2 I would like *to* l just one thing from you G3443
1Th 4: 4 *that* each of you *should* l to control your G3857
1Ti 2:11 A woman *should* l in quietness and full G3443
1Ti 5: 4 *these should* l first of all to put their G3443
Titus 3:14 Our people *must* l to devote themselves to G3443
Rev 14: 3 No one could l the song except the G3443

LEARNED (51) [LEARN]
Ge 28: 6 Now Esau l that Isaac had blessed Jacob H8011
Ge 30:27 *I have* l by divination that the LORD has H5727
Ge 42: 1 When Jacob l that there was grain in H8011
Lev 5: 1 something they have seen or l about, H3359
Nu 20:29 whole community l that Aaron had died H8011
1Sa 4: 6 When *they* l that the ark of the LORD had H3359
1Sa 23: 9 When David l that Saul was plotting H3359
1Sa 23:15 he l that Saul had come out to take his H8011
1Sa 26: 4 he sent out scouts and l that Saul had H3359
Ezr 7:11 a man l *in* matters concerning the H6221
Ne 13: 7 Here *I* l about the evil thing Eliashib had H1067
Ne 13:10 *I* also l that the portions assigned to the H3359
Est 3: 6 Yet *having* l who Mordecai's people H5583+4200
Est 4: 1 When Mordecai l *of* all that had been H3359
Job 8: 8 find out what their ancestors l, H2984
Ps 89:15 are those who *have* l to acclaim you, H3359
Ps 119:152 Long ago *I* l from your statutes that you H3359
Pr 24:32 what I observed and l a lesson from what H4374
Pr 30: 3 *I have* not l wisdom, nor have I attained H4340
Ecc 1:17 of madness and folly, but *I* l that this, too, H3359
Ecc 9:11 wealth to the brilliant or favor to the l; H3359
Eze 19: 3 *He* l to tear the prey and he became a H4340
Eze 19: 6 *He* l to tear the prey and he became a H4340
Da 6:10 Now when Daniel l that the decree had A10313
Mt 2:16 with the time *he had* l from the Magi. G208
Mt 11:25 hidden these things from the wise and l, G5305
Mk 15:45 *When he* l from the centurion *that it was so* G1182
Lk 7:37 lived a sinful life l that Jesus was eating G2105
Lk 9:11 the crowds l about it and followed him. G1182
Lk 10:21 hidden these things from the wise and l, G5305
Lk 23: 7 *When he* l that Jesus was under Herod's G2105
Jn 4: 1 Now Jesus l that the Pharisees had heard G1182
Jn 5: 6 him lying there and l that he had been in G1182
Jn 6:45 the Father and l from him comes to me G3443
Jn 15:15 everything that *I* l from my Father I have G201
Ac 7:13 and Pharaoh l about Joseph's G5745+1181
Ac 9:24 Saul l *of* their plan. Day and night they G1182
Ac 9:30 *When* the believers l *of* this, they took him G2105
Ac 17:13 Jews in Thessalonica l that Paul was G1182
Ac 18:24 He was a l man, with a thorough G3360
Ac 23:27 him, *for I had* l that he is a Roman citizen. G3443
Ro 16:17 are contrary to the teaching you *have* l. G3443
Eph 4:20 however, is not the way of life you l G3443
Php 4: 9 Whatever *you have* l or received or heard G3443
Php 4:11 I *have* l to be content whatever the G3443
Php 4:12 *I have* l the secret of being content in any G3679
Col 1: 7 *You* l it from Epaphras, our dear fellow G3443
2Ti 3:14 in what *you have* l and have become G3443
2Ti 3:14 you know those from whom *you* l it, G3443
Heb 5: 8 *he* l obedience from what he suffered G3443
Rev 2:24 her teaching and *have* not l Satan's G1182

LEARNING (12) [LEARN]
Ezr 8:16 Joiarib and Elnathan, *who were men of* l, H1067
Job 34: 2 you wise men; listen to me, you *men of* l. H3359
Pr 1: 5 let the wise listen and add to their l, and H4375
Pr 4: 2 I give you sound l, so do not forsake my H4375
Pr 9: 9 the righteous and they will add to their l. H4375
Isa 44:25 who overthrows the l *of* the wise and turns H1981
Da 1: 4 showing aptitude for every kind of l, well H2683
Da 1:17 of all kinds of literature and l. H2683
Jn 7:15 "How *did* this man get *such* l G1207+3857
Ac 23:34 L that he was from Cilicia, G4785
Ac 26:24 "Your great l is driving you insane. G1207
2Ti 3: 7 always l but never able to come to a G3443

LEASH (1)
Job 41: 5 it like a bird or **put** it **on a l** for the young H8003

LEASING (KJV) FALSE GODS, LIES

LEAST (41) [LESS]
Jdg 6:15 in Manasseh, and I am the **l** in my family." H7582
1Sa 9:21 is not my clan the **l** of all the clans of H7582
1Sa 20: 9 "If *I* **had the l inkling** that my father H3359+3359
2Ki 18:24 one officer of the **l** of my master's officials H7783
2Ki 23: 2 all the people from the **l** to the greatest. H7785
2Ki 25:26 all the people from the **l** to the greatest H7785
1Ch 12:14 the **l** was a match for a hundred H7783
2Ch 34:30 all the people from the **l** to the greatest. H7783
Est 1: 5 the people from the **l** to the greatest who H7783
Est 1:20 their husbands, from the **l** to the greatest." H7783
Job 14: 7 "**At l** there is hope for a tree: If it is cut H3954
Job 35:15 does not take the **l** notice of wickedness H4394
Isa 36: 9 one officer of the **l** of my master's officials H7783
Isa 60:22 The **l** of you will become a thousand, the H7785
Jer 6:13 "From the **l** to the greatest, all are greedy H7783
Jer 8:10 From the **l** to the greatest, all are greedy H7785
Jer 23:32 *They do* not **benefit** these people **in the l** H3603+3603
Jer 31:34 from the **l** *of* them to the greatest, H7783
Jer 42: 1 all the people from the **l** to the greatest H7785
Jer 42: 8 all the people from the **l** to the greatest. H7785
Jer 44:12 From the **l** to the greatest, they will die by H7785
Jer 50:12 She will be the **l** *of* the nations—a H344
Jnh 3: 5 from the greatest to the **l**, put on sackcloth H7783
Mt 2: 6 are by no means **l** among the rulers of *G1788*
Mt 5:18 not the **l stroke of a pen**, will by any *G3037*
Mt 5:19 sets aside one *of* the **l** of these *G1788*
Mt 5:19 will be called **l** in the kingdom of heaven, *G1788*
Mt 11:11 whoever is **l** in the kingdom of heaven *G3625*
Mt 25:40 you did for one *of* the **l** of these brothers *G1788*
Mt 25:45 you did not do for one *of* the **l** of these, *G1788*
Lk 7:28 the *one who is* **l** in the kingdom of *G3625*
Lk 9:48 is the one who is **l** among you all who is *G3625*
Lk 14: 9 will have to take the **l important** place. *G2274*
Lk 16:17 than *for* the **l stroke of a pen** to drop out *G3037*
Jn 14:11 or **at l** believe on the evidence of *G1623+3590*
Ac 5:15 mats so that **at l** Peter's shadow *G2829*
1Co 15: 9 For I am the **l** of the apostles and do not *G1788*
2Co 11: 5 I do **not** think I am **in the l** inferior to *G3594*
2Co 12:11 I am **not in the l** inferior to the *G4029*
Eph 3: 8 Although I am **less than the l** of all the *G1788*
Heb 8:11 from the **l** of them to the greatest. *G3625*

LEATHER (30)
Ex 25: 5 dyed red and another type of **durable l**; H6425
Ex 26:14 over that a covering of the other **durable l**. H6425
Ex 35: 7 dyed red and another type of **durable l**; H6425
Ex 35:23 red or the other **durable l** brought them. H6425
Ex 36:19 over that a covering of the other **durable l**. H6425
Ex 39:34 of another **durable l** and the shielding H6425
Lev 13:48 wool, any **l** or anything made of leather H6425
Lev 13:48 any leather or anything made of **l**— H6425
Lev 13:49 in the fabric, the **l**, the woven or knitted H6425
Lev 13:49 material, or any **l** article, is greenish or H6425
Lev 13:51 knitted material, or the **l**, whatever its use, H6425
Lev 13:52 any **l** article that has been spoiled H6425
Lev 13:53 woven or knitted material, or the **l** article, H6425
Lev 13:56 out of the fabric, the **l**, or the woven or H6425
Lev 13:57 material, or in the **l** article, it is a H6425
Lev 13:58 any **l** article that has been washed and H6425
Lev 13:59 material, or any **l** article, for pronouncing H6425
Lev 15:17 Any clothing or **l** that has semen on it H6425
Nu 4: 6 are to cover the curtain with a durable **l**, H6425
Nu 4: 8 with the durable **l** and put the poles in H6425
Nu 4:10 covering of the durable **l** and put it on a H6425
Nu 4:11 with the durable **l** and put the poles in H6425
Nu 4:12 that with the durable **l** and put them on a H6425
Nu 4:14 of the durable **l** and put the poles in H6425
Nu 4:25 its outer covering of **durable l**, H9391S
Nu 31:20 garment as well as everything made of **l**, H6425
2Ki 1: 8 of hair and had a **l** belt around his waist." H6425
Eze 16:10 dress and put sandals *of* **fine l** on you. H9391
Mt 3: 4 and he had a **l** belt around his waist. *G1294*
Mk 1: 6 with a **l** belt around his waist *G1294*

LEAVE (206) [LEAVES, LEAVING]
Ge 18:16 When the men got up to **l**, they H4946+9004
Ge 28:15 *I will* not **l** you until I have done what I H6440
Ge 31:13 Now **l** this land at once and go back to H3655
Ge 33:15 "Then *let me* **l** some of my men with you." H3657
Ge 42:15 *you will* not **l** this place unless your H3655
Ge 42:33 **L** one of your brothers here with me, and H5663
Ge 44:22 'The boy cannot **l** his father; if he H6440
Ge 45: 1 cried out, "**Have** everyone **l** my presence!" H3655
Ex 1:10 fight against us and **l** the country." H6590+4946
Ex 2:20 "Why *did you* **l** him? Invite him H6440
Ex 3:21 so that when *you* **l** you will not go H2143
Ex 8: 9 "**I l** *to you* **the honor** *of* setting the time H6995
Ex 8:11 The frogs *will* **l** you and your houses, your H6073
Ex 8:29 "As soon as **I l** you, I will pray to the H3655
Ex 8:29 tomorrow the flies *will* **l** Pharaoh and his H6073
Ex 10:24 only **l** your flocks and herds **behind**." H3657
Ex 11: 8 After that *I will* **l**." Then Moses, H3655
Ex 12:10 *Do* not **l** any of it till morning; if some is H3855
Ex 12:31 **L** my people, you and the Israelites H3655
Ex 12:33 the people to hurry and **l** the country. H8938
Ex 14:12 in Egypt, '**L** us **alone**; let us serve H2532+4946
Ex 23: 5 its load, do not **l** it there; be sure you H6440
Ex 32:10 Now **l** me **alone** so that my anger may H5663
Ex 33: 1 said to Moses, "**L** this place, you H2143+4946
Ex 33:11 aide Joshua son of Nun *did* not **l** the tent. H4631
Ex 34: 7 *he does* not **l the guilty unpunished** H5927+5927
Lev 2:13 *Do* not **l** the salt of the covenant of your H8697
Lev 7:15 *they must* **l** none of it till morning. H5663
Lev 8:33 *Do* not **l** the entrance to the tent of H3655
Lev 10: 7 *Do* not **l** the entrance to the tent of H3655
Lev 16:23 Holy Place, and *he is to* **l** them there. H5663
Lev 19:10 **L** them for the poor and the foreigner H6440
Lev 21:12 **l** the sanctuary of his God or desecrate H3655
Lev 22:30 that same day; **l** none of it till morning. H3855
Lev 23:22 **L** them for the poor and for the foreigner H6440
Nu 9:12 *They must* not **l** any of it till morning or H8636
Nu 10:31 "Please *do* not **l** us. You know where H6440
Nu 11:20 saying, "Why *did we ever* **l** Egypt? H3655
Nu 14:18 *he does* not **l the guilty unpunished** H5927+5927
Nu 24:11 Now **l at once** and go home! I said I would H1368
Nu 32:15 he will again **l** all this people in the H5663
Dt 15:16 "*I do* not *want to* **l** you," because H3655
Dt 20:16 *do* not **l alive** anything that breathes. H2649
Dt 21:23 *you must* not **l** the body hanging on the **pole** H6770
Dt 24:19 **L** it for the foreigner, the fatherless and H2118
Dt 24:20 **L** what remains for the foreigner, the H2118
Dt 24:21 **L** what remains for the foreigner, the H2118
Dt 28:51 *They will* **l** you no grain, new wine or H8636
Dt 31: 6 you; *he will* never **l** you nor forsake you." H8332
Dt 31: 8 you; *he will* never **l** you nor forsake you. H8332
Jos 1: 5 *I will* never **l** you nor forsake you. H8332
Jdg 3:19 to his attendants, "**L** us!" And they all left. H2187
Jdg 7: 3 fear may turn back and **l** Mount Gilead. H7629
Jdg 16:17 my strength *would* **l** me, and I would H6073
Jdg 19: 5 they got up early and he prepared to **l**, H2143
Jdg 19: 9 his servant, got up to **l**, his father-in-law, H2143
Ru 1:16 "Don't urge me to **l** you or to turn back H6440
Ru 2:16 the bundles and **l** them for her to pick H6440
1Sa 10: 2 When you **l** me today, you H2143+4946+6643
1Sa 10: 9 As Saul turned to **l** Samuel H2143+4946+6640
1Sa 14:36 and *let us* not **l** one of them **alive**. H8636
1Sa 15: 6 **l** the Amalekites so that I do H3718+4946+9348
1Sa 15:27 As Samuel turned to **l**, Saul caught hold H2143
1Sa 16:23 feel better, and the evil spirit *would* **l** him. H6073
1Sa 17:28 And with whom *did you* **l** those few sheep H5759
1Sa 25:22 if by morning *I* **l alive** one male of all who H8636
1Sa 27: 9 *he did* not **l** a man or woman **alive**, but H2649
1Sa 27:11 He *did* not **l** a man or woman **alive** to be H2649
1Sa 29:10 **l** in the morning as soon as it is light." H2143
2Sa 4: 4 as she hurried to **l**, he fell and H5674
2Sa 15:14 We must **l** immediately, or he will move H2143
2Sa 16:11 **L** him **alone**; let him curse, for the LORD H5663
1Ki 2:37 The day you **l** and cross the Kidron Valley H3655
1Ki 2:42 'On the day you **l** to go anywhere else H3655
1Ki 8:57 *may he* never **l** us nor forsake us. H6440
1Ki 15:29 *He did* not **l** Jeroboam anyone that H8636
1Ki 17: 3 "**L** here, turn eastward and hide in H2143+4946
1Ki 18:12 may carry you when **I l** you. H2143+4946+907
1Ki 20:36 soon as you **l** me a lion will H2143+4946+907
2Ki 1: 4 '*You will* not **l** the bed you are H3718+4946
2Ki 1: 6 Therefore *you will* not **l** the bed H3718+4946
2Ki 1:16 *you will* never **l** the bed you are H3718+4946
2Ki 2: 2 LORD lives and as you live, *I will* not **l** you. H6440
2Ki 2: 4 LORD lives and as you live, *I will* not **l** you. H6440
2Ki 2: 6 LORD lives and as you live, *I will* not **l** you. H6440
2Ki 4:27 the man of God said, "**L** her **alone**! H8332
2Ki 4:30 LORD lives and as you live, *I will* not **l** you. H6440
2Ki 23:18 "**L** it **alone**," he said. "Don't let anyone H5663
2Ch 26:18 **L** the sanctuary, for you have been H3655
2Ch 26:20 he himself was eager to **l**, because the H3655
2Ch 33: 8 again **make** the feet of the Israelites **l** the H6073
2Ch 35:15 at each gate *did* not *need to* **l** their posts, H6073
Ezr 9:12 **l** it to your children **as an** everlasting **inheritance** H3769
Ne 6: 3 the work stop while *I* **l** it and go down to H8332
Job 21:14 to God, '**L** us **alone**! We have no H6073+4946
Job 21:21 the families they **l behind** when their H339
Job 22:17 to God, '**L** us **alone**! What can the H6073+4946
Job 39: 4 in the wilds; *they* **l** and do not return. H3655
Job 39:11 *Will you* **l** your heavy work to it H6440
Ps 35:12 evil for good and **l** me like one bereaved H4200
Ps 37:33 the LORD *will* not **l** them in the power H6440
Ps 55:11 the city; threats and lies never **l** its streets. H4631
Ps 119:121 just; *do* not **l** me to my oppressors. H5663
Pr 3: 3 *Let* love and faithfulness never **l** you; bind H6440
Pr 9: 6 **L** your simple ways and you will live; walk H6440
Pr 17:13 Evil *will* never **l** the house of one who H4631
Ecc 2:18 because *I must* **l** them to the one who H5663
Ecc 2:21 then *they must* **l** all they own to H5989
Ecc 8: 3 Do not be in a hurry *to* **l** the king's H2143+4946
Ecc 10: 4 rises against you, *do* not **l** your post H5663
Isa 6:13 terebinth and oak **l** stumps when they are H928
Isa 10: 3 Where *will you* **l** your riches? H6440
Isa 30:11 **L** this way, get off this path, and stop H6073
Isa 32: 6 the hungry they **l empty** and from the H8197
Isa 48:20 **L** Babylon, flee from the Babylonians H3655
Isa 52:12 But *you will* not **l** in haste or go in flight H3655
Isa 65:15 *You will* **l** your name for my chosen ones H5663
Jer 2:37 *You will* also **l** that place with your hands H3655
Jer 9: 2 so that *I might* **l** my people and go away H6440
Jer 9:19 *We must* **l** our land because our houses H6440
Jer 10:17 Gather up your belongings to **l** the land H4946
Jer 25:38 Like a lion *he will* **l** his lair, and their land H6440
Jer 37: 9 *will* **surely l** us. H2143+4946+6584+2143
Jer 37:12 Jeremiah *started to* **l** the city to go to the H3655
Jer 44: 7 so **l** yourselves without a remnant? H3855
Jer 49: 9 *would they* not **l** a few grapes? H8636
Jer 49:11 '**L** your fatherless children; I will keep H6440
Jer 50: 8 of Babylon; **l** the land of the Babylonians H3655
Jer 50:26 destroy her and **l** her no remnant. H2118
Jer 51: 9 *let us* **l** her and each go to our own land H6440
Jer 51:50 escaped the sword, **l** and do not linger! H2143
Eze 5:17 against you, and *they will* **l** you **childless**. H8897
Eze 10:16 the wheels *did* not **l** their side. H6015+4946
Eze 12:12 his things on his shoulder at dusk and **l**, H3655
Eze 14:15 country and *they* **l** it **childless** and it H8897
Eze 16:39 your fine jewelry and **l** you stark naked. H5663
Eze 23:29 *They will* **l** you stark naked, and the H6440
Eze 29: 5 *I will* **l** you in the desert, you and all the H5759
Eze 36:20 people, and yet *they had to* **l** his land. H3655
Eze 39:15 sees a human bone *will* **l** a marker beside H1215
Eze 42:14 outer court until *they* **l** behind the H5663
Eze 44:19 ministering in and *are to* **l** them in the H5663
Da 4:23 destroy it, but **l** the stump, bound A10697
Da 4:26 The command to **l** the stump of the tree A10697
Da 11: 8 *will* **l** the king of the North **alone**. H6641+4946
Hos 4:17 Ephraim is joined to idols; **l** him **alone**! H5663
Hos 12:14 his Lord *will* **l** on him the guilt of his H5759
Joel 2:14 turn and relent and **l** behind a blessing— H8636
Joel 2:16 *Let* the bridegroom **l** his room and the H3655
Joel 3:21 Shall *I* **l** their innocent blood **unavenged** H5927
Ob 5 *would they* not **l** a few grapes? H8636
Mic 4:10 now *you must* **l** the city to camp in the H3655
Na 1: 3 *will* not **l the guilty unpunished**. H5927+5927
Na 2:13 *I will* **l** you **no** prey on the earth H4162
Zep 3: 3 *who* **l** nothing for the morning. H1750
Zep 3:12 But *I will* **l** within you the meek and H8636
Mt 5:24 **l** your gift there in front of the altar. First go *G918*
Mt 8:34 they pleaded with him to **l** their region. *G3553*
Mt 10:11 person and stay at their house until *you* **l**. *G2002*
Mt 10:14 **l** that home or town and shake the *G2002+2032*
Mt 15:14 **L** them; they are blind guides. If the blind *G918*
Mt 18:12 *will he* not **l** the ninety-nine on the hills *G918*
Mt 19: 5 this reason a man *will* **l** his father and *G2901*
Mt 27:49 The rest said, "*Now* **l** him **alone**. Let's see if *G918*
Mk 5:17 began to plead with Jesus *to* **l** their region. *G599*
Mk 6:10 a house, stay there until *you* **l** that town. *G2002*
Mk 6:11 **l** that place and shake the dust off your *G1744*
Mk 10: 7 'For this reason a man *will* **l** his father and *G2901*
Mk 14: 6 "**L** her **alone**," said Jesus. "Why are you *G918*
Mk 15:36 "Now **l** *him* **alone**. Let's see if *G918*
Lk 8:37 of the Gerasenes asked Jesus *to* **l** them, *G599*
Lk 9: 4 you enter, stay there until *you* **l** that town. *G2002*
Lk 9: 5 **l** their town and shake the dust off your *G2002*
Lk 13: 8 man replied, '**l** it **alone** for one more year *G918*
Lk 13:31 "**L** this place and go somewhere else. *G2002*
Lk 15: 4 Doesn't *he* **l** the ninety-nine in the open *G2901*
Lk 19:44 *They will* not **l** one stone on another *G918*
Jn 1:43 next day Jesus decided *to* **l** for Galilee. *G2002*
Jn 6:67 "You do not want *to* **l** too, do you?" Jesus *G5632*
Jn 7: 3 said to him, "**L** Galilee and go to Judea *G3553*
Jn 8:11 "Go now and **l** *your* **life of sin**."—— *G3600+279*
Jn 12: 7 "**L** her **alone**," Jesus replied. "It was *G918*
Jn 13: 1 had come for him to **l** this world and go to *G3553*
Jn 14:18 *I will* not **l** you *as* orphans; I will come to *G918*
Jn 14:27 Peace *I* **l** with you; my peace I give you. *G918*
Jn 14:31 commanded me. "Come now; *let us* **l**. *G72+1949*
Jn 16:32 your own home. *You will* **l** me all alone *G918*
Ac 1: 4 "*Do* not **l** Jerusalem, but wait for the gift *G6004*
Ac 5:38 **L** these men **alone**! Let them *G923*
Ac 7: 3 '**L** your country and your people,' God said *G2002*
Ac 16:10 we got ready at once *to* **l** for Macedonia *G2002*
Ac 16:36 Now *you can* **l**. Go in peace. *G2002*
Ac 16:39 the prison, requesting them *to* **l** the city. *G599*
Ac 18: 2 Claudius had ordered all Jews *to* **l** Rome. *G6004*
Ac 20: 7 because he intended to **l** the next day *G1996*
Ac 20:29 I know that after **I** l, savage wolves will *G922*
Ac 21: 5 When it was time *to* **l**, we left and *G1992*
Ac 22:18 '**L** Jerusalem immediately, because the *G2002*
Ac 24:25 enough for now! *You may* **l**. When I find it *G4513*
Ac 28:25 themselves and *began to* **l** after Paul had *G668*
Ro 12:19 dear friends, but **l** room for God's wrath *G1443*
1Co 5:10 that case you would have to **l** this world. *G2002*
Eph 5:31 "For this reason a man *will* **l** his father *G2901*
Heb 13: 5 has said, "Never *will I* **l** you; never will I *G479*
Rev 3:12 Never again *will they* **l** it. I will write *G2002*
Rev 17:16 They will bring her to ruin and **l** her naked NDT

LEAVEN (KJV) YEAST

LEAVENED (2) [LEAVENS]
Am 4: 5 Burn **l bread** as a thank offering and brag H2809
1Co 5: 8 not with the old bread **l** with malice and *G2434*

LEAVENS (1) [LEAVENED]
1Co 5: 6 that a little yeast **l** the whole batch of *G2435*

LEAVES (35) [LEAF, LEAVE]
Ge 2:24 That is why a man **l** his father and mother H6440
Ge 3: 7 so they sewed fig **l** together and made H6591
Ge 44:22 leave his father; if *he* **l** him, his father will H6440
Nu 27: 8 'If a man dies and **l** no son, give his H4200
Dt 24: 2 if after *she* **l** his house she becomes H3655
1Ki 6:34 each having two **l** that turned in sockets. H7521
Job 41:32 *It* **l** a **glistening** wake behind it; one would H239

Pr 13:22 A good person **l an inheritance** *for* their H5706
Pr 15:10 discipline awaits *anyone who* l the path; H6440
Pr 28:3 the poor is like a driving rain that l no crops. NDT
Isa 1:30 You will be like an oak with fading l, like H6591
Isa 33:9 Bashan and Carmel **drop** *their* l. H5850
Isa 34:4 host will fall like withered l from the vine, H6591
Jer 3:1 his wife and *she* l him and H2143+4946+907
Jer 8:13 no figs on the tree, and their l will wither. H6591
Jer 17:8 when heat comes; its l are always green. H6591
Eze 41:24 Each door had two l—two hinged leaves H1946
Eze 41:24 two leaves—two hinged l for each door. H1946
Eze 47:12 Their l will not wither, nor will their fruit H6591
Eze 47:12 will serve for food and their l for healing." H6591
Da 4:12 Its l were beautiful, its fruit abundant A10564
Da 4:14 strip off its l and scatter its fruit. A10564
Da 4:21 with beautiful l and abundant fruit A10564
Mt 21:19 up to it but found nothing on it except l. G5877
Mt 24:32 as its twigs get tender and its l come out, G5877
Mk 11:13 he found nothing but l, because it was G5877
Mk 12:19 brother dies and l a wife but no children G2901
Mk 13:28 as its twigs get tender and its l come out, G5877
Mk 13:34 *He* l his house and puts his servants in G918
Lk 9:39 *It* scarcely ever l him and is destroying him G713
Lk 20:28 brother dies and l a wife but no children G2400
Lk 21:30 When *they* **sprout** l, you can see for G4582
1Co 7:15 But if the unbeliever l, let it be so. G6004
2Co 7:10 that leads to salvation and l no regret, NDT
Rev 22:2 And the l of the tree are for the healing of G5877

LEAVING (49) [LEAVE]

Ge 6:16 l *below* the roof *an opening* one cubit H3983
Ge 45:24 and *as they were* l he said to them H2143
Ex 13:4 in the month of Aviv, you *are* l. H3655
Ex 13:20 After l Sukkoth they camped at H5825+4946
Nu 14:15 to death, **l none alive**, the H3869+408+285
Nu 21:35 his whole army, l them no survivors. H8636
Dt 3:3 We struck them down, l no survivors. H8636
Jos 5:4 in the wilderness on the way after l Egypt. H3655
Jos 8:22 l them neither survivors nor fugitives. H8636
Jdg 6:16 the Midianites, **l none alive**." H3869+408+285
2Sa 14:7 l my husband neither name nor H8492
2Sa 15:24 the people had finished l the city. H6296+4946
1Ki 15:17 to prevent *anyone* from l or entering the H3655
2Ki 10:11 friends and his priests, l him no survivor. H8636
2Ch 16:1 to prevent *anyone* from l or entering the H3655
Ezr 9:8 has been gracious in l us a remnant and H8636
Ezr 9:14 us to destroy us, l us no remnant or survivor? NDT
Job 22:6 people of their clothing, l them naked. NDT
Job 41:30 **l a trail** in the mud like a threshing sledge H8331
Ps 49:10 also perish, l their wealth to others. H6440
Isa 17:6 l two or three olives on the topmost NDT
Eze 39:28 them to their own land, not l any behind. H3855
Da 2:35 wind swept them away without l a trace. A10708
Joel 1:7 thrown it away, l their branches **white**. H4235
Zep 2:13 l Nineveh utterly desolate and dry as the H8492
Zec 2:3 the angel who was speaking to me *was* l, H3655
Mt 4:13 L Nazareth, he went and lived in G2901
Mt 11:7 *As* John's disciples *were* l, Jesus began to G4513
Mt 15:21 L that place, Jesus withdrew to the region G2002
Mt 20:29 *As* Jesus and his disciples *were* l Jericho G1744
Mk 4:36 L the crowd **behind**, they took him along G918
Mk 6:33 many who saw them l recognized them G5632
Mk 6:46 *After* l them, he went up on a mountainside G698
Mk 10:46 *As* Jesus and his disciples, together with a large crowd, *were* l G1744
Mk 11:12 The next day *as* they *were* l Bethany G2002
Mk 12:20 married and died without l any children. G918
Mk 12:21 the widow, but he also died, l no child. G2901
Mk 13:1 *As* Jesus *was* l the temple, one of his G1744
Mk 14:52 he fled naked, l his garment **behind**. G2901
Lk 4:42 they tried to keep him from l them. G4513+608
Lk 9:33 As the men *were* l Jesus, Peter said to him G1431
Lk 10:30 beat him and went away, l him half dead. G918
Lk 11:42 the latter without l the former **undone**. G4223
Lk 20:31 same way the seven died, l no children. G2901
Jn 4:28 l her water jar, the woman went back G918
Jn 16:28 now *I am* l the world and going back to the G918
Ac 13:42 *As* Paul and Barnabas *were* l the G1996
Ac 21:8 L the next day, we reached Caesarea and G2002
1Pe 2:21 suffered for you, l you an example, that G5701

LEB KAMAI (1)

Jer 51:1 Babylon and the people of L. H4214

LEBANA (1)

Ne 7:48 L, Hagaba, Shalmai, H4245

LEBANAH (1)

Ezr 2:45 L, Hagabah, Akkub, H4245

LEBANON (70)

Dt 1:7 to the land of the Canaanites and to L, as H4248
Dt 3:25 the Jordan—that fine hill country and L." H4248
Dt 11:24 territory will extend from the desert to L, H4248
Jos 1:4 territory will extend from the desert to L, H4248
Jos 9:1 of the Mediterranean Sea as far as L H4248
Jos 11:17 in the Valley of L below Mount Hermon. H4248
Jos 12:7 Gad in the Valley of L to Mount Halak, H4248
Jos 13:5 of Byblos; and all L to the east, from Baal H4248
Jos 13:6 regions from L to Misrephoth Maim, H4248
Jdg 3:3 living in the L mountains from Mount H4248
Jdg 9:15 thornbush and consume the cedars of L! H4248
1Ki 4:33 from the cedar of L to the hyssop that H4248
1Ki 5:6 give orders that cedars of L be cut for me. H4248
1Ki 5:9 haul them down from L to the H4248
1Ki 5:14 He sent them off to L in shifts of ten H4248
1Ki 5:14 spent one month in L and two months at H4248
1Ki 7:2 of the Forest of L a hundred cubits long, H4248
1Ki 9:19 in L and throughout all the territory he H4248
1Ki 10:17 put them in the Palace of the Forest of L. H4248
1Ki 10:21 Palace of the Forest of L were pure gold. H4248
2Ki 14:9 "A thistle in L sent a message to a cedar H4248
2Ki 14:9 Lebanon sent a message to a cedar in L, H4248
2Ki 14:9 Then a wild beast in L came along and H4248
2Ki 19:23 of the mountains, the utmost heights of L. H4248
2Ch 2:8 juniper and algum logs from L, for I know H4248
2Ch 2:16 cut all the logs from L that you need and H4248
2Ch 8:6 in L and throughout all the territory he H4248
2Ch 9:16 put them in the Palace of the Forest of L. H4248
2Ch 9:20 Palace of the Forest of L were pure gold. H4248
2Ch 25:18 "A thistle in L sent a message to a cedar H4248
2Ch 25:18 Lebanon sent a message to a cedar in L, H4248
2Ch 25:18 Then a wild beast in L came along and H4248
Ezr 3:7 bring cedar logs by sea from L to Joppa, H4248
Ps 29:5 the LORD breaks in pieces the cedars of L. H4248
Ps 29:6 He makes L leap like a calf, Sirion like a H4248
Ps 72:16 the crops flourish like L and thrive like the H4248
Ps 92:12 palm tree, they will grow like a cedar of L; H4248
Ps 104:16 watered, the cedars of L that he planted. H4248
SS 3:9 the carriage; he made it of wood from L. H4248
SS 4:8 Come with me from L, my bride, come H4248
SS 4:8 Lebanon, my bride, come with me from L. H4248
SS 4:11 of your garments is like the fragrance of L. H4248
SS 4:15 of flowing water streaming down from L. H4248
SS 5:15 His appearance is like L, choice as its H4248
SS 7:4 is like the tower of L looking toward H4248
Isa 2:13 all the cedars of L, tall and lofty, and H4248
Isa 10:34 L will fall before the Mighty One. H4248
Isa 14:8 the cedars of L gloat over you and say H4248
Isa 29:17 will not L be turned into a fertile field H4248
Isa 33:9 wastes away, L is ashamed and withers H4248
Isa 35:2 The glory of L will be given to it, the H4248
Isa 37:24 of the mountains, the utmost heights of L. H4248
Isa 40:16 L is not sufficient for altar fires, nor its H4248
Isa 60:13 "The glory of L will come to you, the H4248
Jer 18:14 Does the snow of L ever vanish from its H4248
Jer 22:6 like the summit of L, I will surely make H4248
Jer 22:20 "Go up to L and cry out, let your voice be H4248
Jer 22:23 You who live in 'L,' who are nestled in H4248
Eze 17:3 full plumage of varied colors came to L. H4248
Eze 27:5 took a cedar from L to make a mast for H4248
Eze 31:3 once a cedar in L, with beautiful branches H4248
Eze 31:15 Because of it I clothed L with gloom, and H4248
Eze 31:16 the choicest and best of L, the H4248
Hos 14:5 Like a **cedar of L** he will send down his H4248
Hos 14:6 olive tree, his fragrance like a **cedar of L**. H4248
Hos 14:7 Israel's fame will be like the wine of L. H4248
Na 1:4 Carmel wither and the blossoms of L fade. H4248
Hab 2:17 you have done to L will overwhelm you, H4248
Zec 10:10 I will bring them to Gilead and L, and H4248
Zec 11:1 Open your doors, L, so that fire may H4248

LEBAOTH (1) [BETH LEBAOTH]

Jos 15:32 L, Shilhim, Ain and Rimmon—a total of H4219

LEBBAEUS (KJV) THADDAEUS

LEBO HAMATH (12)

Nu 13:21 of Zin as far as Rehob, toward L. H4217
Nu 34:8 from Mount Hor to L. H4217
Jos 13:5 Gad below Mount Hermon to L. H4217
Jdg 3:3 from Mount Baal Hermon to L. H4217
1Ki 8:65 people from L to the Wadi of H4217
2Ki 14:25 of Israel from L to the Dead Sea, H4217
1Ch 13:5 the Shihor River in Egypt to L, H4217
2Ch 7:8 people from L to the Wadi of H4217
Eze 47:15 Hethlon road past L to Zedad, H4217
Eze 47:20 boundary to a point opposite L. H4217
Eze 48:1 will follow the Hethlon road to L; H4217
Am 6:14 all the way from L to the valley of H4217

LEBONAH (1)

Jdg 21:19 from Bethel to Shechem, and south of L." H4228

LECAH (NIV84) LEKAH

LECTURE (2)

Jn 9:34 steeped in sin at birth; *how dare* you l us!" G1438
Ac 19:9 discussions daily in the **l hall** of Tyrannus. G5391

LED (148) [LEAD]

Ge 19:16 his two daughters and l them safely out of H3655
Ge 24:27 the LORD *has* l me on the journey *to* the H5697
Ge 24:48 who *had* l me on the right road to get the H5697
Ex 3:1 and *he* l the flock *to* the far side of the H5627
Ex 13:18 l the people **around** *by* the desert road *toward* H6015
Ex 15:22 Then Moses l Israel from the Red Sea H5825
Ex 19:17 Then Moses l the people **out** of the camp H3655
Ex 32:21 that *you* l them **into** such great sin? H995
Dt 8:2 how the LORD your God l you all the way H2143
Dt 8:15 He l you through the vast and dreadful H2143
Dt 13:13 *have* l the people of their town **astray**, H5615
Dt 17:17 many wives, or his heart *will be* **l astray**. H6073
Dt 29:5 the forty years that *I* l you through the H2143
Dt 32:12 The LORD alone l him; no foreign god was H5697
Jos 24:3 the Euphrates and l him throughout H2143
Jdg 2:1 up out of Egypt and l you into the land I H995
Jdg 3:28 of the fords of the Jordan that **l to** Moab; H4200
Jdg 9:39 So Gaal **l out** the citizens of H3655+4200+7156
Jdg 10:2 He l Israel twenty-three years; then he H9149
Jdg 10:3 of Gilead, *who* l Israel twenty-two years. H9149
Jdg 12:7 Jephthah l Israel six years. Then Jephthah H9149
Jdg 12:8 After him, Ibzan of Bethlehem l Israel. H9149
Jdg 12:9 Ibzan l Israel seven years. H9149
Jdg 12:11 Elon the Zebulunite l Israel ten years. H9149
Jdg 12:13 son of Hillel, from Pirathon, l Israel. H9149
Jdg 12:14 seventy donkeys. *He* l Israel eight years H9149
Jdg 15:13 two new ropes and l him **up** from the rock. H6590
Jdg 15:20 Samson l Israel for twenty years in the H9149
Jdg 16:31 He *had* l Israel twenty years. H9149
1Sa 4:18 he was heavy. He *had* l Israel forty years. H9149
1Sa 18:13 l the troops **in** their **campaigns** H3655+2256+995+4200+7156
1Sa 18:16 l them **in** their **campaigns** H3655+2256+995+4200+7156
1Sa 30:16 *He* l David **down**, and there they were H3718
2Sa 5:2 *one who* l Israel **on** their **military campaigns** H3655+2256+995
1Ki 6:8 a stairway *l* **up** to the middle level and from AIT
1Ki 11:3 and his wives l him **astray**. H5742+4213
1Ki 13:34 Jeroboam that **l to** its **downfall** and to its H3948
2Ki 6:19 And *he* l them to Samaria. H2143
2Ki 15:15 and the **conspiracy** he l, are written H8004+8003
2Ki 21:9 Manasseh l them **astray**, so that they did H9494
2Ki 21:11 him and *has* l Judah **into sin** with his H2627
2Ki 23:22 of the judges who l Israel nor in the days H9149
1Ch 4:42 Simeonites, **l by** Pelatiah, Neariah H928+8031
1Ch 11:2 *one who* l Israel **on** their **military campaigns** H3655+2256+995
1Ch 20:1 go off to war, Joab **l out** the armed forces. H5627
2Ch 20:27 **l by** Jehoshaphat, all the men H928+8031
2Ch 21:11 themselves and *had* l Judah **astray**. H5615
2Ch 21:13 *you have* l Judah and the people of Jerusalem **to prostitute themselves** H2388
2Ch 25:11 his strength and l his army to the Valley of H5627
2Ch 26:16 powerful, his pride **l to** his downfall. H6330
2Ch 33:9 l Judah and the people of Jerusalem **astray** H9494
Ezr 9:2 *have* **l the way** in this H3338+2118+8037
Ne 9:12 By day *you* l them with a pillar of cloud H5697
Ne 11:17 director *who* **l in thanksgiving** and H3344+9378
Ne 12:36 teacher of the Law l the procession. H4200+7156
Ne 13:26 even he *was* **l into sin** *by* foreign H2627
Est 6:11 and l him **on horseback** through the city H8206
Job 31:7 if my heart *has been* l *by* my eyes, or H2143+339
Ps 26:1 *I have* l a blameless **life**; I have H2143+928
Ps 45:14 garments *she is* l to the king; H3297
Ps 45:15 L in with joy and gladness, they enter the H3297
Ps 77:19 Your path l through the sea, your way NDT
Ps 77:20 *You* l your people like a flock by the hand H5697
Ps 78:13 He divided the sea and l them **through** H6296
Ps 78:52 *he* l them like sheep through the H5627
Ps 78:72 of heart; with skillful hands *he* l them. H5697
Ps 106:9 *he* l them through the depths as through H2143
Ps 107:7 *He* l them by a straight way to a city H2005
Ps 136:16 to *him who* l his people through the H2143
Pr 5:23 will die, **l astray** by their own great folly. H8706
Pr 7:21 With persuasive words *she* l him **astray** H5742
Pr 20:1 whoever *is* **l astray** by them is not wise. H8706
Pr 24:11 Rescue *those* **being l away** to death; hold H4374
Isa 9:16 those who are guided **are l astray**. H1182
Isa 19:13 of her peoples *have* l Egypt **astray**. H9494
Isa 48:21 did not thirst *when he* l them through the H2143
Isa 53:7 *he* **was** l like a lamb to the slaughter H3297
Isa 55:12 will go out in joy and **be l forth** in peace; H3297
Isa 60:11 their kings **l in triumphal procession**. H5627
Isa 63:13 *who* l them through the depths? Like a H2143
Jer 2:6 up out of Egypt and l us through the H2143
Jer 2:17 LORD your God when *he* l you in the way? H2143
Jer 11:19 like a gentle lamb l to the slaughter; H3297
Jer 22:12 the place where *they have* l him **captive**; H1655
Jer 23:13 by Baal and l my people Israel **astray**. H9494
Jer 41:16 who were with him **l away** all the people H4374
Jer 43:5 the army officers **l away** all the remnant of H4374
Jer 43:6 They also l away all those whom NDT
Jer 50:6 shepherds *have* l them **astray** and caused H9494
Eze 19:4 *They* l him with hooks to the land of Egypt. H995
Eze 20:10 Therefore *I* l them **out** of Egypt and H3655
Eze 29:18 from the campaign *he* l against Tyre. H6268
Eze 37:2 *He* l me back and forth among them, and I H6296
Eze 40:22 Seven steps **l up** to it, with its portico H6590
Eze 40:24 Then *he* l me *to* the south side and I saw H2143
Eze 40:26 Seven steps **l up** *to* it, with its portico H6590
Eze 40:31 its jambs, and eight steps **l up** *to* it. H6590
Eze 40:34 on either side, and eight steps **l up** *to* it. H6590
Eze 40:37 on either side, and eight steps **l up** *to* it. H6590
Eze 42:1 Then the man l me northward into the H3655
Eze 42:15 *he* l me **out** by the east gate and H3655
Eze 46:21 the outer court and l me **around** to its four H6296
Eze 47:2 north gate and l me **around** the outside to H6015
Eze 47:3 cubits and then l me through water that H6296
Eze 47:4 thousand cubits and l me through water H6296
Eze 47:4 thousand and l me **through** water that H6296
Eze 47:6 Then *he* l me back to the bank of the river. H2143
Da 7:13 of Days and *was* l into his presence. A10638
Hos 11:4 *I* l them with cords of human kindness H5432
Am 2:4 they *have been* **l astray** *by* false gods, H9494
Am 2:10 up out of Egypt and l you forty years in the H2143

Mt 4: 1 Then Jesus was l by the Spirit into the G343
Mt 17: 1 and l them up a high mountain by G429
Mt 27: 2 l him away and handed him over to Pilate G552
Mt 27:31 Then they l him away to crucify him. G552
Mk 8:23 man by the hand and l him outside the G1766
Mk 9: 2 with him and l them up a high mountain, G429
Mk 15: 1 l him away and handed him over to Pilate. G708
Mk 15:16 The soldiers l Jesus away into the palace G552
Mk 15:20 Then they l him out to crucify him G1974
Lk 4: 1 left the Jordan and was l by the Spirit into G72
Lk 4: 5 The devil l him up to a high place and G343
Lk 4: 9 The devil l him to Jerusalem and had him G72
Lk 18:39 Those who l the way rebuked him and G4575
Lk 22:54 they l him away and took him into the house G72
Lk 22:66 met together, and Jesus was l before them. G552
Lk 23: 1 whole assembly rose and l him off to Pilate. G72
Lk 23:26 As the soldiers l him away, they seized G552
Lk 23:32 were also l out with him to be executed. G72
Lk 24:50 When he had l them out to the vicinity of G1974
Ac 5:37 and l a band of people in revolt. G923+3958
Ac 7:36 He l them out of Egypt and performed G1974
Ac 7:40 this fellow Moses who l us out of Egypt— G1974
Ac 8:32 "He was l like a sheep to the slaughter, and G72
Ac 9: 8 So they l him by the hand into Damascus G1652
Ac 13:17 mighty power he l them out of that G1974
Ac 19:26 convinced and l astray large numbers of G3496
Ac 21:38 and l four thousand terrorists out into the G1974
Ac 22:11 My companions l me by the hand into G5932
Ro 8:14 For those who are l by the Spirit of God are G72
1Co 12: 2 were influenced and l astray to mute idols. G552
2Co 7: 9 because your sorrow l you to repentance. G1650
2Co 11: 3 minds may somehow be l astray from your G5780
2Co 11:29 Who is l into sin, and I do not inwardly G4997
Gal 2:13 hypocrisy even Barnabas was l astray. G5270
Gal 5:18 But if you are l by the Spirit, you are not G72
Heb 3:16 they not all those Moses l out of Egypt? G2002
Rev 18:23 magic spell all the nations were l astray. G4414

LEDGE (12) [LEDGES]

Ex 27: 5 Put it under the l of the altar so that it is H4136
Ex 38: 4 to be under its l, halfway up the altar. H4136
Eze 43:14 to the lower l that goes around the altar it H6478
Eze 43:14 is two cubits high, and the l is a cubit wide. NDT
Eze 43:14 From this lower l to the upper ledge that H6478
Eze 43:14 to the upper l that goes around the altar it H6478
Eze 43:14 cubits high, and that l is also a cubit wide. NDT
Eze 43:17 The upper l also is square, fourteen cubits H6478
Eze 43:20 corners of the upper l and all around the H6478
Eze 45:19 corners of the upper l of the altar and on H6478
Eze 46:23 of each of the four courts was a l of stone, H3215
Eze 46:23 places for fire built all around under the l. H3227

LEDGES (2) [LEDGE]

1Ki 6: 6 He made offset l around the outside of H4492
Eze 41: 6 There were l all around the wall of the H995

LEE (3)

Ac 27: 4 sea again and passed to the l of Cyprus G5709
Ac 27: 7 our course, we sailed to the l of Crete G5709
Ac 27:16 As we passed to the l of a small island G5720

LEECH (1)

Pr 30:15 "The l has two daughters. 'Give! Give!' H6598

LEEKS (1)

Nu 11: 5 cucumbers, melons, l, onions and garlic. H2946

LEES (KJV) AGED, DREGS, FINEST

LEFT (551) [LEFT-HANDED, LEFTOVER, LEFTOVERS]

Ge 7:23 Only Noah was l, and those with him in H8636
Ge 13: 9 If you go to the l, I'll go to the right; if you H8520
Ge 13: 9 if you go to the right, I'll go to the l." H8521
Ge 18:33 with Abraham, he l, and Abraham H2143
Ge 19:30 two daughters l Zoar and settled H6590+4946
Ge 24:10 Then the servant l, taking with him ten of H2143
Ge 24:61 So the servant took Rebekah and l. H2143
Ge 25: 5 Abraham l everything he owned to Isaac. H5989
Ge 25:34 then got up and l. So Esau despised H2143
Ge 27: 5 When Esau l for the open country to hunt H2143
Ge 27:30 and Jacob had scarcely l his H3655+3655
Ge 28:10 Jacob l Beersheba and set out for Harran. H3655
Ge 31:55 Then he l and returned home. H2143
Ge 32: 8 the group that is l may escape. H8636
Ge 32:24 So Jacob was l alone, and a man wrestled H3855
Ge 34:26 took Dinah from Shechem's house and l. H3655
Ge 38: 1 Judah l his brothers and went down H4946+907
Ge 38:19 After she l, she took off her veil and put on H2143
Ge 39: 6 So Potiphar l everything he had in H6440
Ge 39:12 But he l his cloak in her hand and ran out H6440
Ge 39:13 she saw that he had l his cloak in her H6440
Ge 39:15 he l his cloak beside me and ran out of H6440
Ge 39:18 he l his cloak beside me and ran out of H6440
Ge 42:26 loaded their grain on their donkeys and l. H2143
Ge 42:38 brother is dead and he is the only one l. H8636
Ge 44:20 he is the only one of his mother's sons l, H3855
Ge 46: 5 Then Jacob l Beersheba, and H7756+4946
Ge 47:18 there is nothing l for our lord except our H8636
Ge 48:13 toward Israel's l hand and Manasseh on H8520
Ge 48:13 Manasseh on his l toward Israel's H8520
Ge 48:14 he put his l hand on Manasseh's head H8520
Ge 50: 8 their flocks and herds were l in Goshen. H6440
Ge 50:16 "Your father l these instructions before he H7422
Ex 5:20 When they l Pharaoh, they found Moses H3655
Ex 8:12 After Moses and Aaron l Pharaoh, Moses H3655
Ex 8:30 Then Moses l Pharaoh and prayed to the H3655
Ex 8:31 The flies l Pharaoh and his officials and H6073
Ex 9:21 the word of the LORD l their slaves and H6440
Ex 9:33 Then Moses l Pharaoh and went out of H3655
Ex 10: 5 what little you have l after H3856+7129+8636
Ex 10: 6 Then Moses turned and l Pharaoh. H3655
Ex 10:12 in the fields, everything l by the hail." H8636
Ex 10:15 devoured all that was l after the hail— H3855
Ex 10:18 Moses then l Pharaoh and prayed to the H3655
Ex 10:19 Not a locust was l anywhere in Egypt H8636
Ex 10:26 go with us; not a hoof is to be l behind. H8636
Ex 11: 8 Then Moses, hot with anger, l Pharaoh. H3655
Ex 12:10 till morning; if some is l till morning, you H3855
Ex 12:41 very day, all the LORD's divisions l Egypt. H3655
Ex 13:22 of fire by night l its place in front of the H4631
Ex 14:22 wall of water on their right and on their l. H8520
Ex 14:29 wall of water on their right and on their l. H8520
Ex 16:23 Save whatever is l and keep it until H6369
Ex 19: 1 third month after the Israelites l Egypt— H3655
Ex 23:11 and the wild animals may eat what is l. H3856
Ex 26:12 half curtain that is l over is to hang down H6369
Ex 26:13 what is l will hang over the sides of the H6369
Ex 29:34 ram or any bread is l over till morning, H3855
Ex 36: 4 on the sanctuary l what they were H995+4946
Lev 6: 2 to them or l in their care or about H9582
Lev 7:16 anything l over may be eaten on the H3855
Lev 7:17 of the sacrifice l over till the third day H3855
Lev 10:12 the grain offering l over from the food H3855
Lev 14:15 pour it in the palm of his own l hand, H8522
Lev 14:26 of the oil into the palm of his own l hand, H8522
Lev 19: 6 anything l over until the third day must be H3855
Lev 25:15 of the number of years l for harvesting crops. AIT
Lev 26:36 " 'As for those of you who are l, I will H8636
Lev 26:39 Those of you who are l will waste away in H8636
Nu 12: 9 LORD burned against them, and he l them. H2143
Nu 12:16 the people l Hazeroth and H5825+4946
Nu 14:19 them from the time they l Egypt until now." NDT
Nu 20:17 the right or to the l until we have passed H8520
Nu 22: 7 The elders of Moab and Midian l, taking H2143
Nu 22:26 room to turn, either to the right or to the l. H8520
Nu 25: 7 saw this, he l the assembly H7756+4946+9348
Nu 26:65 not one of them was l except Caleb son H3855
Nu 27: 3 died for his own sin and l no sons. H2118+4200
Nu 33: 5 The Israelites l Rameses and camped at H5825
Nu 33: 6 They l Sukkoth and camped at Etham, on H5825
Nu 33: 7 They l Etham, turned back to Pi Hahiroth H5825
Nu 33: 8 They l Pi Hahiroth and passed through H5825
Nu 33: 9 They l Marah and went to Elim, where H5825
Nu 33:10 They l Elim and camped by the Red Sea. H5825
Nu 33:11 They l the Red Sea and camped in the H5825
Nu 33:12 They l the Desert of Sin and camped at H5825
Nu 33:13 They l Dophkah and camped at Alush. H5825
Nu 33:14 They l Alush and camped at Rephidim H5825
Nu 33:15 They l Rephidim and camped in the H5825
Nu 33:16 They l the Desert of Sinai and camped at H5825
Nu 33:17 They l Kibroth Hattaavah and camped at H5825
Nu 33:18 They l Hazeroth and camped at Rithmah. H5825
Nu 33:19 They l Rithmah and camped at Rimmon H5825
Nu 33:20 They l Rimmon Perez and camped at H5825
Nu 33:21 They l Libnah and camped at Rissah. H5825
Nu 33:22 They l Rissah and camped at Kehelathah. H5825
Nu 33:23 They l Kehelathah and camped at Mount H5825
Nu 33:24 They l Mount Shepher and camped at H5825
Nu 33:25 They l Haradah and camped at H5825
Nu 33:26 They l Makheloth and camped at Tahath. H5825
Nu 33:27 They l Tahath and camped at Terah. H5825
Nu 33:28 They l Terah and camped at Mithkah. H5825
Nu 33:29 They l Mithkah and camped at H5825
Nu 33:30 They l Hashmonah and camped at H5825
Nu 33:31 They l Moseroth and camped at Bene H5825
Nu 33:32 They l Bene Jaakan and camped at Hor H5825
Nu 33:33 They l Hor Haggidgad and camped at H5825
Nu 33:34 They l Jotbathah and camped at Abronah. H5825
Nu 33:35 They l Abronah and camped at Ezion H5825
Nu 33:36 They l Ezion Geber and camped at H5825
Nu 33:37 They l Kadesh and camped at Mount Hor H5825
Nu 33:41 They l Mount Hor and camped at H5825
Nu 33:42 They l Zalmonah and camped at Punon. H5825
Nu 33:43 They l Punon and camped at Oboth. H5825
Nu 33:44 They l Oboth and camped at Iye Abarim H5825
Nu 33:45 They l Iye Abarim and camped at Dibon H5825
Nu 33:46 They l Dibon Gad and camped at Almon H5825
Nu 33:47 They l Almon Diblathaim and camped in H5825
Nu 33:48 They l the mountains of Abarim and H5825
Dt 1:24 They l and went up into the hill country H7155
Dt 2:14 from the time we l Kadesh Barnea H2143+4946
Dt 2:27 will not turn aside to the right or to the l. H8520
Dt 2:34 women and children. We l no survivors. H8636
Dt 5:32 do not turn aside to the right or to the l. H8520
Dt 9: 7 From the day you l Egypt until you arrived H3655
Dt 16: 3 because you l Egypt in haste—so H3655
Dt 17:11 what they tell you, to the right or to the l. H8520
Dt 17:20 turn from the law to the right or to the l. H8520
Dt 28:14 to the right or to the l, following other H8520
Dt 28:55 It will be all he has l because of the H8636
Dt 28:62 stars in the sky will be l but few in number H8636
Dt 32:36 sees their strength is gone and no one is l, NDT
Jos 1: 7 do not turn from it to the right or to the l H8520
Jos 2: 5 it was time to close the city gate, they l. H3655
Jos 2:22 When they l, they went into the hills and H2143
Jos 5: 6 military age when they l Egypt had died H3655
Jos 8:17 They l the city open and went in pursuit of H6440
Jos 8:29 of Ai on a pole and l it there until evening. NDT
Jos 9:12 at home on the day we l to come to you. H3655
Jos 10:26 they were l hanging on the poles until AIT
Jos 10:28 everyone in it. He l no survivors. And he H8636
Jos 10:30 put to the sword. He l no survivors there H8636
Jos 10:33 his army—until no survivors were l. H8636
Jos 10:37 everyone in it. They l no survivors. H8636
Jos 10:39 totally destroyed. They l no survivors. H8636
Jos 10:40 with all their kings. He l no survivors. H8636
Jos 11: 8 on the east, until no survivors were l. H8636
Jos 11:15 he l nothing undone of all that the LORD H6073
Jos 11:22 No Anakites were l in Israelite territory H3855
Jos 18: 9 So the men l and went through the land H2143
Jos 19:27 Emek and Neiel, passing Kabul on the l. H8520
Jos 22: 9 of Manasseh l the Israelites H2143+4946+907
Jos 23: 6 turning aside to the right or to the l. H8520
Jdg 2:21 any of the nations Joshua l when he died. H6440
Jdg 3: 1 are the nations the LORD l to test all those H5663
Jdg 3: 4 They were l to test the Israelites to see H2118
Jdg 3:19 his attendants, "Leave us!" And they all l. H3655
Jdg 3:21 Ehud reached with his l hand, drew the H8520
Jdg 4:11 Heber the Kenite had l the other Kenites, H7233
Jdg 4:16 troops fell by the sword; not a man was l. H8636
Jdg 7: 3 So twenty-two thousand men l, while ten H8740
Jdg 7:20 the torches in their l hands and holding in H8520
Jdg 8:10 all that were l of the armies of the eastern H3855
Jdg 16:19 to subdue him. And his strength l him. H6073
Jdg 16:20 he did not know that the LORD had l him. H6073
Jdg 16:29 on the one and his l hand on the other, H8520
Jdg 17: 8 l that town in search of some other H2143+4946
Jdg 18: 7 So the five men l and came to Laish H2143
Jdg 18:21 in front of them, they turned away and l. H2143
Jdg 19: 2 She l him and went back to H2143+4946+907
Jdg 19:10 the man l and went toward Jebus H2143
Jdg 21: 7 can we provide wives for those who are l, H3855
Jdg 21:16 we provide wives for the men who are l? H3855
Jdg 21:24 the Israelites l that place and went H2143+4946
Ru 1: 3 and she was l with her two sons. H8636
Ru 1: 5 Naomi was l without her two sons H8636
Ru 1: 7 daughters-in-law she l the place where H3655
Ru 2:11 how you l your father and mother and your H6440
Ru 2:14 ate all she wanted and had some l over. H3855
Ru 2:18 gave her what she had l over after she H3855
Ru 4:14 who this day has not l you without a H8697
1Sa 2:36 Then everyone l in your family line will H3855
1Sa 6:12 they did not turn to the right or to the l. H8520
1Sa 11:11 so that no two of them were l together. H8636
1Sa 13:15 Then Samuel l Gilgal and went up H7756+4946
1Sa 14: 3 No one was aware that Jonathan had l. H2143
1Sa 14:17 forces and see who has l us." H2143+4946+6640
1Sa 15:34 Then Samuel l for Ramah, but Saul went H2143
1Sa 17:20 in the morning David l the flock in the H5759
1Sa 17:22 David l his things with the keeper of H5759
1Sa 19:22 he himself l for Ramah and went to the H2143
1Sa 20:42 Then David l, and Jonathan went back H2143
1Sa 22: 1 David l Gath and escaped to the H2143+4946
1Sa 22: 4 So he l them with the king of Moab, and H5697
1Sa 22: 5 So David l and went to the forest of H2143
1Sa 23:13 l Keilah and kept moving from place to H3655
1Sa 24: 7 And Saul l the cave and went his H7756+4946
1Sa 25:34 to Nabal would have been l alive by H3855
1Sa 26:12 water jug near Saul's head, and they l. H2143
1Sa 27: 2 hundred men with him l and went over to H7756
1Sa 28:25 That same night they got up and l. H2143
1Sa 29: 3 from the day he l Saul until now, H5877
1Sa 30: 4 aloud until they had no strength l to weep. NDT
1Sa 30:21 him and who were l behind at the Besor H3782
2Sa 2:12 of Saul, l Mahanaim and went to Gibeon. H3655
2Sa 2:19 the right nor to the l as he pursued him. H8520
2Sa 2:21 "Turn aside to the right or to the l; take on H8520
2Sa 3:26 Joab then l David and sent messengers H3655
2Sa 5:13 After he l Hebron, David took more H995+4946
2Sa 9: 1 there anyone still l of the house of Saul H3855
2Sa 11: 8 So Uriah l the palace, and a gift from the H3655
2Sa 13: 9 of here," Amnon said. So everyone l him. H3655
2Sa 13:30 all the king's sons; not one of them is l." H3855
2Sa 14: 7 put out the only burning coal I have l, H8636
2Sa 14:19 to the right or to the l from anything my H8521
2Sa 15:16 he l ten concubines to take care of the H6440
2Sa 16: 6 special guard were on David's right and l. H8520
2Sa 16:21 concubines whom he l to take care of the H5663
2Sa 17:12 he nor any of his men will be l alive. H3855
2Sa 17:13 valley until not so much as a pebble is l." H5162
2Sa 17:18 So the two of them l at once and went to H2143
2Sa 17:22 no one was l who had not crossed the H6372
2Sa 18: 9 He was l hanging in midair, while the H5989
2Sa 19: 7 not a man will be l with you by nightfall. H4328
2Sa 19:19 on the day my lord the king l Jerusalem. H3655
2Sa 19:24 from the day the king l until the day he H2143
2Sa 20: 3 ten concubines he had l to take care of H5663
2Sa 24: 4 so they l the presence of the king to enroll H3655
1Ki 7:47 Solomon l all these things unweighed H5663
1Ki 7:49 five on the right and five on the l, in front H8520
1Ki 9:20 There were still people l from the H3855
1Ki 10:13 Then she l and returned with her retinue H7155
1Ki 13:24 his body was l lying on the road, with H8959
1Ki 14:17 wife got up and l and went to Tirzah. H2143
1Ki 15:18 silver and gold that was l in the treasuries H3855
1Ki 18:22 am the only one of the LORD's prophets l, H3855
1Ki 19: 3 in Judah, he l his servant there, H5663

1Ki 19:10 I *am* the only one l, and now they are H3855
1Ki 19:14 I *am* the only one l, and now they are H3855
1Ki 19:20 Elisha then l his oxen and ran after Elijah H6440
1Ki 19:21 So Elisha l him and went back. H4946+339
1Ki 20: 9 They l and took the answer back to H2143
1Ki 22:19 around him on his right and on his l. H8520
2Ki 2: 8 water divided to the right and *to the* l, H2178S
2Ki 2:14 it divided to the right and *to the* l, and H2178S
2Ki 3:25 Only Kir Hareseth *was* l with its stones in H8636
2Ki 4: 5 *She* l him and shut the door H2143+4946+907
2Ki 4: 6 "There is not a jar l." Then the oil H6388
2Ki 4: 7 You and your sons can live on what *is* l." H3855
2Ki 4:43 'They will eat and **have** *some* l **over**.'" H3855
2Ki 4:44 they ate and **had** *some* l **over** H3855
2Ki 5: 5 So Naaman l, taking with him ten talents H2143
2Ki 5:24 He sent the men away and *they* l. H2143
2Ki 7: 7 They l the camp as it was and ran for their NDT
2Ki 7:10 donkeys, and the tents l just as they were." NDT
2Ki 7:12 so *they have* l the camp to hide in the H3655
2Ki 7:13 five of the horses that *are* l in the city. H8636
2Ki 7:13 be like that of all the Israelites l here— H8636
2Ki 8: 6 land from the day *she* l the country until H6440
2Ki 8:14 Then Hazael l Elisha and H2143+4946+907
2Ki 10:14 forty-two of them. *He* l no **survivor**. H8636
2Ki 10:15 After *he* l there, he came upon H2143+4946
2Ki 10:17 he killed all who *were* l there of Ahab's H8636
2Ki 13: 7 Nothing *had been* l *of* the army of H8636
2Ki 17:18 Only the tribe of Judah *was* l, H8636
2Ki 19: 8 that the king of Assyria *had* l Lachish, H5825
2Ki 20: 4 Before Isaiah *had* l the middle court, the H3655
2Ki 20:17 Nothing *will* **be** l, says the LORD. H3855
2Ki 22: 2 not turning aside to the right or to the l. H8520
2Ki 23: 8 which was on the l of the city gate. H8520
2Ki 24:14 the poorest people of the land *were* l. H8636
2Ki 25:12 But the commander l **behind** some of the H8636
2Ki 25:22 the people *he had* l **behind** in Judah. H8636
1Ch 6:44 associates, the Merarites, at his l hand: H8520
1Ch 16:37 David l Asaph and his associates before H6440
1Ch 16:38 He also l Obed-Edom and his sixty-eight NDT
1Ch 16:39 David l Zadok the priest and his fellow NDT
1Ch 16:43 Then all the people l, each for their own H2143
1Ch 20: 1 Joab attacked Rabbah and l it **in ruins**. H2238
1Ch 21: 4 so Joab l and went throughout Israel and H3655
1Ch 21:21 *he* l the threshing floor and bowed down H3655
2Ch 8: 7 There were **still** people l from the Hittites H3855
2Ch 9:12 Then she l and returned with her retinue H2200
2Ch 18:18 heaven standing on his right and on his l. H8520
2Ch 20:20 in the morning *they* l for the Desert of H3655
2Ch 21:17 Not a son *was* l to him except Ahaziah H8636
2Ch 24:25 withdrew, *they* l Joash severely wounded. H6440
2Ch 25:10 with Judah and l for home in a great H8740
2Ch 30: 6 that he may return to you who *are* l, who H8636
2Ch 31:10 people, and this great amount *is* l **over**." H3855
2Ch 32:31 God l him to test him and to know H6440
2Ch 34: 2 not turning aside to the right or to the l. H8520
Ezr 4:16 you **will be** l **with** nothing in A10029+10378
Ezr 9:15 *We are* l this day as a remnant H8636
Ne 6: 1 the wall and not a gap **was** l in it— H3855
Ne 8: 4 Maaseiah; and on his l were Pedaiah H8520
Est 7: 7 l his wine and went out into the palace H4946
Est 7: 8 As soon as the word l the king's mouth H3655
Est 8:15 When Mordecai l the king's presence, he H3655
Job 20:19 oppressed the poor and l them **destitute**; H6440
Job 20:21 Nothing is l for him to devour; his H8586
Job 20:26 him and devour *what* is l in his tent. H8586
Job 21:34 Nothing *is* l of your answers but falsehood H8636
Ps 34: T Abimelek, who drove him away, and *he* l. H2143
Ps 69:20 has broken my heart and *has l me* **helpless**; AIT
Ps 74: 9 no prophets are l, and none of us H6388
Ps 79: 2 *They have* l the dead bodies of your H5989
Ps 105:38 Egypt was glad when they l, because H3655
Pr 2:13 who *have* l the straight paths to walk in H6440
Pr 2:17 who *has* l the partner of her youth and H6440
Pr 3:16 in her l hand are riches and honor. H8520
Pr 4:27 Do not turn to the right or the l; keep your H8520
Pr 29:15 a child l **undisciplined** disgraces its H8938
Ecc 5:14 there is nothing l for them *to inherit*. H928+3338
Ecc 10: 2 the right, but the heart of the fool to the l. H8520
SS 2: 6 His l arm is under my head, and his right H8520
SS 5: 6 my beloved *had* l; he was gone. H2811
SS 8: 3 His l arm is under my head and his right H8520
Isa 1: 8 Daughter Zion *is* l like a shelter in a H3855
Isa 1: 9 LORD Almighty *had* l us some survivors, H3855
Isa 4: 3 Those *who are* l in Zion, who remain in H8636
Isa 5: 8 field till no space is l and you live alone in NDT
Isa 5: 9 the fine mansions l without occupants. NDT
Isa 6:11 the houses are l deserted and the NDT
Isa 9:20 be hungry; on the l they will eat, but not H8520
Isa 11:16 of his people that *is* l from Assyria, H8636
Isa 15: 6 vegetation is gone and nothing green *is* l. H2118
Isa 17: 2 of Aroer will be deserted and l to flocks, H2118
Isa 17: 9 which *they* l because of the Israelites H6440
Isa 18: 6 *They will* all **be** l to the mountain birds of H6440
Isa 21:11 "Watchman, what is l **of** the night? H4946
Isa 21:11 Watchman, what is l **of the night**?" H4946
Isa 23: 1 Tyre is destroyed and l without house or NDT
Isa 24: 6 are burned up, and very few *are* l. H8636
Isa 24:12 The city *is* l in ruins, its gate is battered to H8636
Isa 24:13 as when gleanings are l after the grape NDT
Isa 27: 9 poles or incense altars *will be l* **standing**. AIT
Isa 30:17 till *you are* l like a flagstaff on a H3855
Isa 30:21 Whether you turn to the right or **to the** l H8521
Isa 37: 8 that the king of Assyria *had* l Lachish, H5825
Isa 39: 6 Nothing *will* **be** l, says the LORD. H3855
Isa 44:19 I make a detestable thing from *what* is l? H3856
Isa 49:21 I *was* l all alone, but these—where have H8636
Isa 54: 3 will spread out to the right and to the l; H8520
Jer 4: 7 *He has* l his place to lay waste your land H3655
Jer 7:25 the time your ancestors l Egypt until now, H3655
Jer 10:20 no one is l **now** to pitch my tent or to set H6388
Jer 11:23 Not even a remnant *will be* l to them H2118
Jer 25:20 and the *people* l *at* Ashdod); H8642
Jer 27:19 the other articles that *are* l in this city, H3855
Jer 27:21 the things that *are* l in the house of the H3855
Jer 29:32 He will have no one l among this people H3782
Jer 34: 7 These *were* the only fortified cities l in H8636
Jer 37:10 only wounded men *were* l in their tents, H8636
Jer 38: 4 the soldiers who *are* l in this city, H8636
Jer 38:22 All the women l in the palace of the king H8636
Jer 39: 4 *they* l the city at night by way of the king's H3655
Jer 39:10 of the guard l **behind** in the land of Judah H8636
Jer 40: 6 people who *were* l **behind** in the land. H8636
Jer 40:11 king of Babylon *had* l a remnant in Judah H5989
Jer 41:10 with all the others who *were* l there, H8636
Jer 42: 2 we were once many, now only a few *are* l. H8636
Jer 43: 6 imperial guard *had* l with Gedaliah son H5663
Jer 48:11 from youth, like wine l on its dregs, not H9200
Jer 52: 7 *They* l the city at night through the gate H3655
Jer 52:16 But Nebuzaradan l **behind** the rest of the H8636
La 3:11 mangled me and l me without help. H8492
Eze 1:10 of a lion, and on the l the face of an ox H8520
Eze 4: 4 "Then lie on your l side and put the sin of H8522
Eze 7:11 None of the people will be l, none of that NDT
Eze 9: 8 While they were killing and I *was* l **alone** H8636
Eze 19:14 No strong branch *is* l on it fit for a ruler's H2118
Eze 21:16 you sword, then **to the** l, wherever your H8521
Eze 22:18 tin, iron and lead l inside a furnace. NDT
Eze 23:25 and *those of* you *who* are l will fall by the H344
Eze 23:25 and *those of* you *who* are l will be H344
Eze 24:21 daughters *you* l **behind** will fall by H6440
Eze 31:12 of foreign nations cut it down and l it. H5759
Eze 31:12 came out from under its shade and l it. H5759
Eze 33:27 those who are l in the ruins will fall by the NDT
Eze 39: 3 your bow from your l hand and make your H8520
Eze 47:11 not become fresh; *they will* **be** l for salt. H5989
Da 2:44 nor *will* it **be** l to another people. A10697
Da 7: 7 trampled underfoot *whatever* was l. A10692
Da 7:19 trampled underfoot *whatever* was l. A10692
Da 10: 8 So I *was* l alone, gazing at this great H8636
Da 10: 8 I had no strength l, my face turned H8636
Da 12: 7 right hand and his l hand toward heaven, H8520
Joel 1: 4 *What* the locust swarm has l the great H3856
Joel 1: 4 *what* the great locusts have l the young H3856
Joel 1: 4 *what* the young locusts have l other H3856
Am 5: 3 strong *will* **have** only a hundred l; H8636
Am 5: 3 out a hundred strong *will* **have** only ten l." H8636
Am 6: 9 If ten people **are** l in one house, they too H3855
Am 9: 1 those who are l I will kill with the sword. H344
Jnh 4:11 cannot tell their right hand from their l— H8520
Hab 2: 8 the peoples who are l will plunder you. H3856
Zep 1:12 who are like wine l on its dregs, who think, NDT
Zep 2: 4 will be abandoned and Ashkelon l in ruins. NDT
Zep 2: 5 "I will destroy you, and none *will be* l." H3782
Zep 3: 6 *I have* l their streets **deserted**, with no one H2990
Hag 2: 3 'Who of you *is* l who saw this house in its H8636
Hag 2:19 Is there yet any seed l in the barn? NDT
Zec 4: 3 right of the bowl and the other on its l." H8520
Zec 4:11 on the right and the l *of* the lampstand?" H8520
Zec 7:14 The land they l **behind** them was so H339
Zec 9: 7 Those *who are* l will belong to our God H8636
Zec 11: 9 Let those *who are* l eat one another's H8636
Zec 12: 6 all the surrounding peoples right and l, H8520
Zec 13: 8 perish; yet one-third *will* **be** l in it. H3855
Mal 1: 3 into a wasteland and l his inheritance to the NDT
Mal 4: 1 "Not a root or a branch *will be* l to them. H6440
Mt 2:14 his mother during the night and l for Egypt, G432
Mt 4:11 Then the devil l him, and angels came G918
Mt 4:20 At once they l their nets and followed him. G918
Mt 4:22 immediately they l the boat and their G918
Mt 6: 3 do not let your l **hand** know what your right G754
Mt 8:15 He touched her hand and the fever l her G918
Mt 12:44 'I will return to the house *I* l.' When it G2002
Mt 13:36 Then *he* l the crowd and went into the G918
Mt 14:20 of broken pieces that *were* l **over**. G4355
Mt 15:29 Jesus l there and went along the Sea of G3553
Mt 15:37 of broken pieces that *were* l **over**. G4355
Mt 16: 4 Jesus then l them and went away G2901
Mt 19: 1 *he* l Galilee and went into the region of G3558
Mt 19:27 "We *have* l everything to follow you! G918
Mt 19:29 And everyone who *has* l houses or brothers G918
Mt 20:21 the other at your l in your kingdom." G2381
Mt 20:23 to sit at my right or l is not for me to grant. G2381
Mt 21:17 And *he* l them and went out of the city to G2901
Mt 22:22 So *they* l him and went away. G918
Mt 22:25 no children, *he* l his wife to his brother. G918
Mt 23:38 your house *is* l to you desolate. G918
Mt 24: 1 Jesus l the temple and was walking away G2002
Mt 24: 2 not one stone here *will be* l on another G918
Mt 24:40 the field; one will be taken and the other l. G918
Mt 24:41 one will be taken and the other l. G918
Mt 25:33 sheep on his right and the goats on his l. G2381
Mt 25:41 "Then he will say to those on his l G2381
Mt 26:44 So *he* l them and went away once more G918
Mt 27: 5 threw the money into the temple and l. G432
Mt 27:38 one on his right and one on his l. G2381
Mk 1:18 At once *they* l their nets and followed him. G918
Mk 1:20 and *they* l their father Zebedee in the boat G918
Mk 1:29 As soon as *they* l the synagogue, they G2002
Mk 1:31 The fever l her and she began to wait on G918
Mk 1:35 l the house and went off to a solitary G2002
Mk 1:42 Immediately the leprosy l him and he was G599
Mk 2: 2 such large numbers that *there was* no **room** *l*, AIT
Mk 6: 1 Jesus l there and went to his hometown G2002
Mk 7:17 After he had l the crowd and entered the G608
Mk 7:24 Jesus l that place and went to the vicinity G482
Mk 7:29 may go; the demon *has* l your daughter." G2002
Mk 7:31 Then Jesus l the vicinity of Tyre and went G2002
Mk 8: 8 of broken pieces *that were* l **over**. G4354
Mk 8:13 Then *he* l them, got back into the boat and G918
Mk 9:30 *They* l that place and passed through G2002
Mk 10: 1 Jesus then l that place and went into the G482
Mk 10:28 "We *have* l everything to follow you!" G918
Mk 10:29 "no one who *has* l home or brothers or G918
Mk 10:37 right and the other at your l in your glory." G754
Mk 10:40 to sit at my right or l is not for me to grant. G2381
Mk 12: 6 "He had one l to send, a son, whom he G2285
Mk 12:12 of the crowd; so *they* l him and went away. G918
Mk 12:22 none of the seven l any children. Last of G918
Mk 13: 2 "Not one stone here *will be* l on another G918
Mk 14:16 The disciples l, went into the city and G2002
Mk 15:27 one on his right and one on his l. G2381
Lk 1:38 to me be fulfilled." Then the angel l her. G599
Lk 2:15 When the angels *had* l them and gone G599
Lk 2:37 She never l the temple but worshiped night G923
Lk 4: 1 l the Jordan and was led by the Spirit into G5715
Lk 4:13 *he* l him until an opportune time. G923
Lk 4:38 Jesus l the synagogue and went to G482+608
Lk 4:39 over her and rebuked the fever, and *it* l her. G918
Lk 5: 2 edge two boats, l there by the fishermen G609
Lk 5:11 on shore, l everything and followed him. G918
Lk 5:13 And immediately the leprosy l him. G599
Lk 5:28 l everything and followed him. G2901
Lk 7:24 *After* John's messengers l, Jesus began to G599
Lk 8:37 So he got into the boat and l. G5715
Lk 9:17 of broken pieces that *were* l **over**. G4355
Lk 10:40 care that my sister *has* l me to do the work G2901
Lk 11:14 *When* the demon l, the man who had G2002
Lk 11:24 Then it says, 'I will return to the house *I* l.' G2002
Lk 13:35 your house *is* l to you desolate. I tell G918
Lk 17:29 But the day Lot l Sodom, fire and sulfur G2002
Lk 17:34 one bed; one will be taken and the other l. G918
Lk 17:35 together; one will be taken and the other l." G918
Lk 18:28 "We *have* l all we had to follow you!" G918
Lk 18:29 "no one who *has* l home or wife or brothers G918
Lk 21: 6 when not one stone *will be* l on another; G918
Lk 22:13 *They* l and found things just as Jesus had G599
Lk 23:33 one on his right, the other on his l. G754
Lk 24:51 *he* l them and was taken up into heaven. G1460
Jn 4: 3 So *he* l Judea and went back once more to G918
Jn 4:43 After the two days *he* l for Galilee. G2002
Jn 4:52 at one in the afternoon, the fever l him." G918
Jn 6:12 "Gather the pieces *that are* l **over**. G4355
Jn 6:13 five barley loaves l **over** by those who had G4355
Jn 7:10 after his brothers *had* l for the festival, he G326
Jn 8: 9 until only Jesus *was* l, with the woman G2901
Jn 8:29 me is with me; *he has* not l me alone, for I G918
Jn 12:36 Jesus l and hid himself from them. G599
Jn 18: 1 Jesus l with his disciples and crossed the G2002
Jn 19:31 not want the bodies l on the crosses G3531
Ac 1:25 which Judas l to go where he belongs." G4124
Ac 5:41 The apostles l the Sanhedrin G4513+608+4725
Ac 7: 4 "So *he* l the land of the Chaldeans and G2002
Ac 12:10 of one street, suddenly the angel l him. G923
Ac 12:17 he said, and then *he* l for another place. G2002
Ac 13:13 where John l them to return to Jerusalem. G713
Ac 14:17 Yet *he has* not l himself without testimony G918
Ac 14:20 The next day *he* and Barnabas l for Derbe. G2002
Ac 15:40 Paul chose Silas and l, commended by G2002
Ac 16:18 At that moment the spirit l her. G2002
Ac 16:40 encouraged them. Then *they* l. G2002
Ac 17:15 to Athens and then l with instructions G1996
Ac 17:33 Paul l the Council. G2002
Ac 18: 1 Paul l Athens and went to Corinth. G6004
Ac 18: 7 Then Paul l the synagogue and went next G3553
Ac 18:18 Then *he* l the brothers and sisters and G698
Ac 18:19 where Paul l Priscilla and Aquila. G2901
Ac 18:21 But *as he* l, he promised, "I will come back G698
Ac 19: 9 So Paul l them. He took the G923
Ac 19:12 were cured and the evil spirits l them. G1744
Ac 20:11 After talking until daylight, *he* l. G2002
Ac 21: 5 to leave, *we* l and continued on our way. G2002
Ac 24:27 a favor to the Jews, *he* l Paul in prison. G2901
Ac 25:14 is a man here *whom* Felix l as a prisoner. G2901
Ac 26:31 *After they* l the room, they began saying to G432
Ac 27:40 *they* l them in the sea and at the same G1572
Ro 3:25 l the sins committed beforehand **unpunished** G4217
Ro 9:29 the Lord Almighty *had* l us descendants, G1593
Ro 11: 3 I *am* the only one l, and they are G5699
2Co 2: 2 who is l to make me glad but you whom I NDT
2Co 6: 7 in the right hand and *in* the l; G754
1Th 3: 1 we thought it best *to be* l by ourselves in G2901
1Th 4:15 who *are* l until the coming of the Lord G4335
1Th 4:17 are still alive and *are* l will be caught up G4335
1Ti 5: 5 in need and l **all alone** puts her hope in G3670
2Ti 4:13 bring the cloak that *I* l with Carpus at Troas G657

2Ti 4:20 and *I* **l** Trophimus sick in Miletus. *G657*
Titus 1: 5 The reason *I* **l** you in Crete was that you *G657*
Titus 1: 5 order what *was* **l** *unfinished* and appoint *G3309*
Heb 2: 8 God **l** nothing that is not subject to them. *G918*
Heb 10:26 of the truth, no sacrifice for sins *is* **l**, *G657*
Heb 11:15 been thinking of the country *they had* **l**, *G1674*
Heb 11:27 By faith *he* **l** Egypt, not fearing the king's *G2901*
2Pe 2:15 *They have* **l** the straight way and *G2901*
Rev 10: 2 foot on the sea and his **l** foot on the land, *G2381*

LEFT-HANDED (3) [HAND]
Jdg 3:15 a **l** man, the son of H360+3338+3545
Jdg 20:16 select troops who were **l**, H360+3338+3545
1Ch 12: 2 to sling stones right-handed or **l**; H8521

LEFTOVER (1) [LEFT]
Ru 2: 2 pick up the **l grain** behind anyone in H8672

LEFTOVERS (1) [LEFT]
Ps 17:14 and may there be **l** for their little ones. H3856

LEG (4) [LEGS]
Eze 7:17 go limp; every **l** will be wet with urine. H1386
Eze 21: 7 faint and every **l** will be wet with urine H1386
Eze 24: 4 choice pieces—the **l** and the shoulder. H3751
Am 3:12 mouth only two **l bones** or a piece of an H4157

LEGAL (3) [ILLEGAL, LEGALIZING]
Ac 19:39 it must be settled in a **l** assembly. *G1937*
Ac 22:25 "*Is it* **l** for you to flog a Roman citizen who *G2003*
Col 2:14 the charge of our **l** indebtedness, *G1504*

LEGALIZING (1) [LEGAL]
Ru 4: 7 the **method of l transactions** in Israel.) H9496

LEGION (3) [LEGIONS]
Mk 5: 9 "My name is **L**," he replied, "for we are *G3305*
Mk 5:15 had been possessed by the **l** of demons, *G3305*
Lk 8:30 "**L**," he replied, because many demons *G3305*

LEGIONS (1) [LEGION]
Mt 26:53 my disposal more than twelve **l** of angels? *G3305*

LEGITIMATE (1)
Heb 12: 8 then you are **not l**, not true sons and *G3785*

LEGS (28) [LEG]
Ex 12: 9 with the head, **l** and internal organs. H4157
Ex 25:26 to the four corners, where the four **l** are. H8079
Ex 29:17 wash the internal organs and the **l**, H4157
Ex 37:13 to the four corners, where the four **l** were. H8079
Lev 1: 9 the internal organs and the **l** with water, H4157
Lev 1:13 the internal organs and the **l** with water, H4157
Lev 4:11 as well as the head and **l**, the internal H4157
Lev 8:21 organs and the **l** with water and burned H4157
Lev 9:14 organs and the **l** and burned them on top H4157
Lev 11:21 that have jointed **l** for hopping on the H4157
Lev 11:23 that have four **l** you are to regard as H8079
Dt 28:35 afflict your knees and **l** with painful boils H8797
1Sa 17: 6 on his **l** he wore bronze greaves, and a H8079
Ps 147:10 his delight in the **l** *of* the warrior; H8797
Pr 26: 7 Like the useless **l** of one who is lame is a H8797
SS 5:15 His **l** are pillars of marble set on bases of H8797
SS 7: 1 Your graceful **l** are like jewels, the work of H3751
Isa 47: 2 bare your **l**, and wade through the H8797
Eze 1: 7 Their **l** were straight; their feet were like H8079
Eze 16:25 spreading your **l** with increasing H8079
Da 2:33 its **l** of iron, its feet partly of iron and A10741
Da 5: 6 that his **l** became weak and his A10626+10284
Da 10: 6 his arms and **l** like the gleam of H5274
Hab 3:16 crept into my bones, and my **l** trembled. H9393
Jn 19:31 Pilate to have the **l** broken and the bodies *G5003*
Jn 19:32 came and broke the **l** of the first man who *G5003*
Jn 19:33 already dead, they did not break his **l**. *G5003*
Rev 10: 1 the sun, and his **l** were like fiery pillars. *G4546*

LEHABITES (2)
Ge 10:13 of the Ludites, Anamites, **L**, Naphtuhites, H4260
1Ch 1:11 of the Ludites, Anamites, **L**, Naphtuhites, H4260

LEHEM See JASHUBI LEHEM

LEHI (4) [RAMATH LEHI]
Jdg 15: 9 camped in Judah, spreading out near **L**. H4306
Jdg 15:14 As he approached **L**, the Philistines came H4306
Jdg 15:19 God opened up the hollow place in **L**, H4306
Jdg 15:19 called En Hakkore, and it is still there in **L**. H4306

LEKAH (1)
1Ch 4:21 Er the father of **L**, Laadah the father of H4336

LEMA (2)
Mt 27:46 in a loud voice, "Eli, Eli, **l** sabachthani?" *G3316*
Mk 15:34 in a loud voice, "Eloi, Eloi, **l** sabachthani?" *G3316*

LEMUEL (2)
Pr 31: 1 The sayings of King **L**—an inspired H4345
Pr 31: 4 It is not for kings, **L**—it is not for kings to H4345

LEND (14) [LENDER, LENDING, LENDS, LENT, MONEYLENDER]
Ex 22:25 "If *you* **l** money *to* one of my people H4278
Lev 25:37 *You must* not **l** them money at interest H5989
Dt 15: 6 you *will* **l** *to* many nations but will H6292
Dt 15: 8 and **freely l** them whatever H6292+6292
Dt 28:12 *You will* **l** *to* many nations but will borrow H4278
Dt 28:44 They *will* **l** *to* you, but you will not lend to H4278
Dt 28:44 lend to you, but you *will* not **l** *to* them. H4278
Ps 37:26 They are always generous and **l freely** H4278
Ps 112: 5 to those who are generous and **l freely**, H4278
Eze 18: 8 *He does* not **l** to them at interest or take a H5989
Lk 6:34 And if *you* **l** to those from whom you *G1247*
Lk 6:34 Even sinners **l** to sinners, expecting to be *G1247*
Lk 6:35 **l** to them without expecting to get *G1247*
Lk 11: 5 'Friend, **l** me three loaves of bread; *G3079*

LENDER (2) [LEND]
Pr 22: 7 and the borrower is slave to the **l**. H4278
Isa 24: 2 borrower as for **l**, for debtor as for H4278

LENDING (1) [LEND]
Ne 5:10 my men *are* also **l** the people money H5957

LENDS (3) [LEND]
Ps 15: 5 *who* **l** money to the poor without interest H5989
Pr 19:17 Whoever is kind to the poor **l** *to* the LORD H4278
Eze 18:13 *He* **l** at interest and takes a profit. H5989

LENGTH (26) [LONG]
Ge 13:17 walk through the **l** and breadth of the land H802
Ex 12:40 Now the **l of time** the Israelite people H4632
Ex 26:12 As for the additional **l** of the tent curtains H6245
Lev 19:35 dishonest standards when measuring **l**, H4500
1Sa 28:20 Immediately Saul fell full **l** on the ground H7757
2Sa 2:11 The **l** *of* time David was king in Hebron H5031
2Sa 8: 2 measured them off with a **l of cord**. H2475
2Sa 8: 2 and the third **l** was allowed to live. H2475
2Ch 3: 8 its **l** corresponding to the width of the H802
Ps 21: 4 you gave it to him—**l** *of* days, for ever and H802
Pr 10:27 The fear of the LORD **adds l** *to* life, but the H3578
Eze 40: 5 The **l** of the measuring rod in the man's NDT
Eze 40:11 was ten cubits and its **l** was thirteen cubits. H802
Eze 40:20 Then he measured the **l** and width of the H802
Eze 41: 4 And he measured the **l** *of* the inner H802
Eze 41: 8 It was the **l** *of* the rod, six long H4850
Eze 41:12 thick all around, and its **l** was ninety cubits. H802
Eze 41:15 he measured the **l** *of* the building facing H802
Eze 42:10 south side along the **l** *of* the wall of the H8145
Eze 42:11 they had the same **l** and width, with similar H802
Eze 48: 8 its **l** from east to west will equal one of H802
Eze 48:13 Its total **l** will be 25,000 cubits and its H802
Eze 48:18 the sacred portion and running the **l** of it, H802
Eze 48:21 areas running the **l** *of* the tribal H4200+6645
Ac 12:10 *When they had* **walked the l** *of* one street *G4601*
Rev 21:16 rod and found it to be 12,000 stadia *in* **l**, *G3601*

LENGTHEN (2) [LONG]
Ecc 8:13 their days *will* not **l** like a shadow. H799
Isa 54: 2 do not hold back; **l** your cords, strengthen H799

LENGTHS (2) [LONG]
2Sa 8: 2 Every two **l** of them were put to death H2475
Eze 13:18 make veils of various **l** for their heads in H7757

LENGTHWISE (1) [LONG]
Eze 45: 7 running **l** from the western to the eastern H802

LENGTHY (2) [LONG]
Mk 12:40 houses and for a show make **l** prayers. *G3431*
Lk 20:47 houses and for a show make **l** prayers. *G3431*

LENT (1) [LEND]
Jer 15:10 *I have* neither **l** nor borrowed, yet H5957

LENTIL (1) [LENTILS]
Ge 25:34 gave Esau some bread and some **l** stew. H6378

LENTILS (3) [LENTIL]
2Sa 17:28 flour and roasted grain, beans and **l**, H6378
2Sa 23:11 a place where there was a field full of **l**, H6378
Eze 4: 9 barley, beans and **l**, millet and spelt; H6378

LEOPARD (6) [LEOPARDS]
Isa 11: 6 the lamb, the **l** will lie down with the goat H5807
Jer 5: 6 a **l** will lie in wait near their towns to tear H5807
Jer 13:23 Ethiopian change his skin or a **l** its spots? H5807
Da 7: 6 another beast, one that looked like a **l**. A10480
Hos 13: 7 to them, like a **l** I will lurk by the path. H5807
Rev 13: 2 The beast I saw resembled a **l**, but had *G4203*

LEOPARDS (2) [LEOPARD]
SS 4: 8 lions' dens and the mountain haunts of **l**. H5807
Hab 1: 8 Their horses are swifter than **l**, fiercer than H5807

LEPER (2) [LEPROSY]
Mt 26: 6 in Bethany in the home of Simon the **L**, *G3320*
Mk 14: 3 at the table in the home of Simon the **L**, *G3320*

LEPROSY (25) [LEPER, LEPROUS]
2Sa 3:29 has a running sore or **l** or who leans on a H7665
2Ki 5: 1 He was a valiant soldier, but *he* **had l**. H7665
2Ki 5: 3 He would cure him of his **l**. H7669
2Ki 5: 6 to you so that you may cure him of his **l**." H7669
2Ki 5: 7 send someone to me to be cured of his **l**? H7669
2Ki 5:11 hand over the spot and cure me of my **l**. H7665
2Ki 5:27 Naaman's **l** will cling to you and to your H7669
2Ki 7: 3 were four men *with* **l** at the entrance of H7665
2Ki 7: 8 The *men who* **had l** reached the edge of H7665
2Ki 15: 5 the king with **l** until the day he died, H7665
2Ch 26:19 temple, **l** broke out on his forehead. H7669
2Ch 26:20 they saw that he **had l** on his forehead, so H7665
2Ch 26:21 King Uzziah **had l** until the day he died H7665
2Ch 26:23 to the kings, for people said, "He **had l**." H7665
Mt 8: 2 A **man with l** came and knelt before him *G3320*
Mt 8: 3 Immediately he was cleansed *of* his **l**. *G3319*
Mt 10: 8 cleanse **those who have l**, drive out *G3320*
Mt 11: 5 lame walk, **those who have l** are cleansed *G3320*
Mk 1:40 A **man with l** came to him and begged *G3320*
Mk 1:42 Immediately the **l** left him and he was *G3319*
Lk 4:27 were many in Israel **with l** in the time of *G3320*
Lk 5:12 man came along who was covered with **l**. *G3319*
Lk 5:13 And immediately the **l** left him. *G3319*
Lk 7:22 lame walk, *those who* **have l** are cleansed *G3320*
Lk 17:12 a village, ten men *who* **had l** met him. *G3320*

LEPROUS (4) [LEPROSY]
Ex 4: 6 the skin *was* **l**—it had become as H7665
Nu 12:10 Miriam's skin *was* **l**—it became as H7665
2Ki 5:27 Elisha's presence and *his* **skin was l**— H7665
2Ch 26:21 in a separate house—**l**, and banned from H7665

LESHEM (2)
Jos 19:47 they went up and attacked **L**, took it, H4386
Jos 19:47 They settled in **L** and named it Dan after H4386

LESS (22) [LEAST, LESSER]
Ge 18:28 the **number** of the righteous **is** five **l than** H2893
Ex 30:15 the poor *are* not *to* **give l** when you H5070
Nu 11:32 **No** one gathered **l than** ten homers H5070
1Ki 8:27 **How much l** this temple I have built H677+3954
1Ch 27:23 number of the men twenty years old or **l**, H4752
2Ch 6:18 **How much l** this temple I have built H677+3954
2Ch 32:15 **How much l** will your god H677+3954+4202
Ezr 9:13 you *have* **punished** us **l** than H3104+4200+4752
Job 15:16 **how much l** mortals, who are vile H677+3954
Job 25: 6 **how much l** a mortal, who is but a H677+3954
Job 35:14 **How much l**, then, will he listen H677+3954
Ecc 6:11 words, the **l** the **meaning**, and how H8049+2039
Isa 40:17 by him as worthless and **l than** nothing. H4946
Isa 41:24 But you are **l than** nothing and your works H4946
Eze 15: 5 **how much l** can it be made into H677+3954
Jn 3:30 He must become greater; I *must become* **l**." *G1783*
Jn 11:18 was **l than two miles** from *G6055+5084+1278*
1Co 12:23 that we think are **l honorable** we treat with *G872*
2Co 12:15 If I love you more, will you love me **l**? *G2482*
Eph 3: 8 Although I am **l than the least** of all the *G1788*
Php 2:28 you may be glad and I may have **l anxiety**. *G267*
Heb 12:25 on earth, how much **l** will we, if we turn *G3437*

LESSER (3) [LESS]
Ge 1:16 the day and the **l** light to govern the H7785
Isa 22:24 offshoots—all its **l** vessels, from the H7783
Heb 7: 7 And without doubt the **l** is blessed by the *G1781*

LESSON (6)
Jdg 8:16 and **taught** the men of Sukkoth **a l** by H3359
1Sa 14:12 "Come up to us and we'll teach you a **l**." H1821
Pr 24:32 observed and learned a **l** from what I saw: H4592
Jer 35:13 you not learn a **l** and obey my words? H4592
Mt 24:32 "Now learn this **l** from the fig tree: As *G4130*
Mk 13:28 "Now learn this **l** from the fig tree: As *G4130*

LEST (7)
Dt 32:27 **l** the adversary misunderstand and say H7153
2Sa 1:20 **l** the daughters of the Philistines be glad H7153
2Sa 1:20 **l** the daughters of the uncircumcised H7153
Pr 5: 9 **l** you lose your honor to others and your H7153
Pr 5:10 **l** strangers feast on your wealth and your H7153
Pr 31: 5 **l** they drink and forget what has been H7153
1Co 1:17 **l** the cross of Christ be emptied of *G2671+3590*

LET (1042) [LET'S, LETS, LETTING]
Ge 1: 3 And God said, "*L there* **be** light," and there AIT
Ge 1: 6 "*L there* **be** a vault between the waters to AIT
Ge 1: 9 "*L* the water under the sky **be gathered** to AIT
Ge 1: 9 to one place, and *l* dry ground **appear**." AIT
Ge 1:11 God said, "*L* the land **produce** vegetation: AIT
Ge 1:14 "*L there* **be** lights in the vault of the sky to AIT
Ge 1:14 and *l them* **serve** as signs to mark sacred AIT
Ge 1:15 and *l them* **be** lights in the vault of the sky to AIT
Ge 1:20 "*L* the water **teem** *with* living creatures AIT
Ge 1:20 and *l* birds **fly** above the earth across the AIT
Ge 1:22 and *l* the birds **increase** on the earth. AIT
Ge 1:24 "*L* the land **produce** living creatures AIT
Ge 1:26 God said, "*L us* **make** mankind in our image AIT
Ge 11: 4 *l us* **build** ourselves a city, with a AIT
Ge 11: 7 *l us* **go down** and confuse their language so AIT
Ge 12:12 Then they will kill me but *will* **l** you **live**. H2649
Ge 14:24 Eshkol and Mamre. *L* them **have** their share." AIT
Ge 18: 4 *L* a little water **be brought**, and then you may AIT
Ge 18: 5 *L me* **get** you something to eat, so you can be AIT
Ge 18:30 "May the Lord not be angry, but *l me* **speak**. AIT
Ge 18:32 not be angry, but *l me* **speak** just once more. AIT
Ge 19: 8 *L me* **bring** them **out** to you, and you can do AIT
Ge 19:20 *L me* **flee** to it—it is very AIT
Ge 20: 6 That is why *I did* not **l** you touch her. H5989
Ge 23: 8 "If you are willing to *l me* **bury** my dead, AIT
Ge 24:14 'Please **l down** your jar that I may have a H5742
Ge 24:14 **l** her be the one you have chosen for your NDT
Ge 24:43 "Please **l** me **drink** a little water from your H9197
Ge 24:44 **l** her be the one the LORD has chosen for my NDT

Ge 24:51 and *l her* **become** the wife of your master's AIT
Ge 24:55 "*L* the young woman **remain** with us ten days AIT
Ge 25:30 **l** me **have** some of that red stew! H4358
Ge 26:28 us and you. *L us* **make** a treaty with you AIT
Ge 27:13 said to him, "My son, **l** the curse fall on me. NDT
Ge 30:32 *L me* **go** through all your flocks today and AIT
Ge 30:34 "**L** it be as you have said. H4273
Ge 31:28 *You* didn't even **l** me kiss my H5759
Ge 31:37 and *l them* **judge** between the two of us. AIT
Ge 31:44 and *l it* **serve** as a witness between us." AIT
Ge 32:26 Then the man said, "**L** me **go**, for it is H8938
Ge 32:26 "*I will* not **l** you go unless you bless me." H8938
Ge 33:12 Esau said, "*L us* **be on** *our* **way**; I'll AIT
Ge 33:14 So *l* my lord **go on** ahead of his servant, while AIT
Ge 33:15 "Then *l me* **leave** some of my men with you." AIT
Ge 33:15 "*Just l me* **find** favor in the eyes of my lord." AIT
Ge 34:11 brothers, "*L me* **find** favor in your eyes AIT
Ge 34:21 "*L them* **live** in our land and trade in it; the AIT
Ge 34:23 So *l us* **agree** to their **terms**, and they will AIT
Ge 35: 3 Then come, *l us* **go up** *to* Bethel, where I will AIT
Ge 38:16 said, "Come now, *l me* **sleep with** you." AIT
Ge 38:23 Judah said, "*L her* **keep** what she has, or AIT
Ge 41:33 "And now *l* Pharaoh **look for** a discerning AIT
Ge 41:34 *L* Pharaoh **appoint** commissioners over the AIT
Ge 42:19 *l* one of your brothers **stay** here in prison AIT
Ge 43:14 *he will l* your other brother and Benjamin **come back** AIT
Ge 44:10 he said, "**l** it **be** as you say. H4027+2085
Ge 44:18 my lord, *l* me **speak** a word to my lord. AIT
Ge 44:33 please *l* your servant **remain** here as my AIT
Ge 44:33 and *l* the boy **return** with his brothers. AIT
Ge 44:34 *Do* not *l me* **see** the misery that would come AIT
Ge 47: 4 please *l* your servants **settle** in Goshen." AIT
Ge 47: 6 part of the land. *L them* **live** in Goshen. AIT
Ge 49: 6 *L* me not **enter** their council, let me not join AIT
Ge 49: 6 their council, *l* me not **join** their assembly, for AIT
Ge 49:26 *L all these* **rest** on the head of Joseph, on the AIT
Ge 50: 5 Now *l me* **go up** and bury my father; then I AIT
Ex 1:16 is a boy, kill him; but if it is a girl, *l her* **live**." AIT
Ex 1:17 had told them to do; *they* **l** the boys **live**. H2649
Ex 1:18 Why *have you* **l** the boys **live**?" H2649
Ex 1:22 throw into the Nile, but **l** every girl **live**." H2649
Ex 3:18 *L us* **take** a three-day journey into the AIT
Ex 3:19 king of Egypt *will* not **l** you go unless a H5989
Ex 3:20 among them. After that, *he will* **l** you **go**. H8938
Ex 4:18 "*L me* **return** to my own people in Egypt to AIT
Ex 4:21 heart so that *he will* not **l** the people **go**. H8938
Ex 4:23 I told you, "**L** my son **go**, so he may H8938
Ex 4:23 But you refused to **l** him **go**; so I will kill H8938
Ex 4:26 So the LORD **l** him **alone**. (At that time she H8332
Ex 5: 1 '**L** my people **go**, so that they may hold a H8938
Ex 5: 2 that I should obey him and **l** Israel **go**? H8938
Ex 5: 2 know the LORD and *I will* not **l** Israel **go**." H8938
Ex 5: 3 Now *l us* **take** a three-day journey into the AIT
Ex 5: 7 *l* them **go** and gather their own straw. AIT
Ex 5: 8 crying out, '*L us* **go** and sacrifice to our God. AIT
Ex 5:17 '*L us* **go** and sacrifice to the LORD. AIT
Ex 6: 1 of my mighty hand *he will* **l** them **go**; H8938
Ex 6:11 of Egypt *to* **l** the Israelites **go** out of his H8938
Ex 7: 2 Pharaoh *to* **l** the Israelites **go** out of his H8938
Ex 7:14 unyielding; he refuses to **l** the people **go**. H8938
Ex 7:16 **L** my people **go**, so that they may worship H8938
Ex 8: 1 **L** my people **go**, so that they may worship H8938
Ex 8: 2 If you refuse to **l** them **go**, I will send a H8938
Ex 8: 8 and *I will* **l** your people **go** to offer H8938
Ex 8:20 **L** my people **go**, so that they may worship H8938
Ex 8:21 If you *do* not **l** my people **go**, I will send H8938
Ex 8:28 "*I will* **l** you **go** to offer sacrifices to the H8938
Ex 8:29 *l* Pharaoh *be sure that he does* not **act deceitfully** AIT
Ex 8:32 his heart and *would* not **l** the people **go**. H8938
Ex 9: 1 "**L** my people **go**, so that they may H8938
Ex 9: 2 If you refuse to **l** them **go** and continue to H8938
Ex 9: 7 and *he would* not **l** the people **go**. H8938
Ex 9:13 **L** my people **go**, so that they may worship H8938
Ex 9:17 against my people and *will* not **l** them **go**. H8938
Ex 9:28 *I will* **l** you **go**; you don't have to stay any H8938
Ex 9:35 hard and *he would* not **l** the Israelites **go**, H8938
Ex 10: 3 **L** my people **go**, so that they may worship H8938
Ex 10: 4 If you refuse to **l** them **go**, I will bring H8938
Ex 10: 7 **L** the people **go**, so that they may worship H8938
Ex 10:10 be with you—if *I* **l** you **go**, along with your H8938
Ex 10:20 and *he would* not **l** the Israelites **go**. H8938
Ex 10:27 he was not willing to **l** them **go**. H8938
Ex 11: 1 After that, *he will* **l** you **go** from here, and H8938
Ex 11:10 and *he would* not **l** the Israelites **go** out of H8938
Ex 13:15 Pharaoh stubbornly refused to **l** us **go**, H8938
Ex 13:17 When Pharaoh **l** the people **go**, God did H8938
Ex 14: 5 *We have* **l** the Israelites **go** and have lost H8938
Ex 14:12 'Leave us alone; *l us* **serve** the Egyptians'? AIT
Ex 21: 8 himself, *he must* **l** her **be redeemed**. H7009
Ex 21:26 destroys it *must* **l** the slave **go** free to H8938
Ex 21:27 female slave *must* **l** the slave **go** free to H8938
Ex 22:30 *L them* **stay** with their mothers for seven days AIT
Ex 23:11 year *l* the land **lie unplowed** and unused. AIT
Ex 23:13 gods; *do* not *l them* **be heard** on your lips. AIT
Ex 23:33 *Do* not *l them* **live** in your land or they will AIT
Ex 32:25 Aaron *had l* them **get out of control** and so AIT
Ex 33:12 you *have* not **l** me **know** whom you H3359
Ex 34: 9 favor in your eyes, then *l* the Lord **go** with us. AIT
Ex 34:25 *do* not *l* any of the sacrifice from the Passover Festival **remain** AIT

Lev 10: 6 "*Do* not *l* your hair *become* **unkempt** and do AIT
Lev 13:45 torn clothes, *l* their hair **be** unkempt, cover AIT
Lev 21:10 *must* not *l* his hair *become* **unkempt** or tear AIT
Nu 6: 5 LORD is over; *they must l* their hair **grow long**. AIT
Nu 11:15 and *do* not *l me* **face** my own ruin. AIT
Nu 12:12 *Do* not *l her* **be** like a stillborn infant coming AIT
Nu 14: 3 us to this land only to *l us* **fall** by the sword? AIT
Nu 16:38 *L them* **be** a sign to the Israelites. AIT
Nu 20:17 Please *l us* **pass** through your country. AIT
Nu 20:21 Since Edom refused *to* **l** them go through H5989
Nu 21:22 "*L us* **pass** through your country. We will not AIT
Nu 21:23 But Sihon *would* not **l** Israel pass through H5989
Nu 21:27 "Come to Heshbon and *l it* **be rebuilt**; let AIT
Nu 21:27 let it be rebuilt; *l* Sihon's city **be restored**. AIT
Nu 22:13 the LORD has refused to **l** me go with you." H5989
Nu 22:16 *Do* not *l anything* **keep** *you* from coming to AIT
Nu 23:10 *L* me **die** the death of the righteous, and may AIT
Nu 23:27 *l me* **take** you to another place. AIT
Nu 23:27 will please God *to l you* **curse** them for me AIT
Nu 24:14 *l me* **warn** you of what this people will do to AIT
Nu 32: 5 "*l* this land **be given** to your servants as our AIT
Dt 1:22 "*L us* **send** men ahead to spy out the land AIT
Dt 2:27 "*L us* **pass** through your country. We will stay AIT
Dt 2:28 Only *l us* **pass through** on foot— AIT
Dt 2:30 of Heshbon refused *to* **l** us **pass** through. H6296
Dt 3:25 *L* me **go over** and see the good land beyond AIT
Dt 4: 9 have seen or *l them* **fade** from your heart AIT
Dt 9:14 **L** me **alone**, so that I may destroy them H8332
Dt 13: 2 the prophet says, "*L us* **follow** other gods" AIT
Dt 13: 2 have not known) "and *l us* **worship** them," AIT
Dt 13: 6 saying, "*L us* **go** and worship other gods AIT
Dt 13:13 "*L us* **go** and worship other gods AIT
Dt 15:12 the seventh year *you must* **l** them **go** free. H8938
Dt 16: 4 *L* no yeast **be found** in your possession in all AIT
Dt 16: 4 *Do* not *l* any of the meat you sacrifice on the evening of the first day **remain** AIT
Dt 17:14 "*L us* **set** a king over us like all the nations AIT
Dt 18:10 *L* no *one* **be found** among you who sacrifices AIT
Dt 18:16 "*L us* not **hear** the voice of the LORD our God AIT
Dt 20: 5 *L him* **go** home, or he may die in battle and AIT
Dt 20: 6 *L him* **go** home, or he may die in battle and AIT
Dt 20: 7 *L him* **go** home, or he may die in battle and AIT
Dt 20: 8 *L him* **go** home so that his fellow soldiers will AIT
Dt 21:14 with her, **l** her **go** wherever she wishes. H8938
Dt 22: 7 but **be sure to l** the mother **go**, so H8938+8938
Dt 23:16 *L them* **live** among you wherever they like AIT
Dt 24:11 *l* the neighbor to whom you are making the loan **bring** the pledge **out** AIT
Dt 32: 2 *L* my teaching **fall** like rain and my words AIT
Dt 32:38 *L them* **rise up** to help you! Let AIT
Dt 32:38 rise up to help you! *L them* **give** you **shelter**! AIT
Dt 33: 6 "*L* Reuben **live** and not die, nor his people AIT
Dt 33:12 "*L* the beloved of the LORD **rest** secure in him AIT
Dt 33:16 *L all these* **rest** on the head of Joseph, on the AIT
Dt 33:24 is Asher; *l him* **be** favored by his brothers AIT
Dt 33:24 his brothers, and *l him* **bathe** his feet in oil. AIT
Dt 34: 4 *I have* **l** you **see** it with your eyes, but you H8011
Jos 2:15 So *she* **l** them **down** by a rope through the H3718
Jos 2:18 the window through which *you* **l** us **down**, H3718
Jos 2:21 "**L** it be as you say." So she sent NDT
Jos 8:15 Israel **l themselves be driven back** before H5595
Jos 9:15 a treaty of peace with them to **l** them **live**, H2649
Jos 9:20 *We will* **l** them **live**, so that God's wrath H2649
Jos 9:21 They continued, "*L them* **live**, but let them be AIT
Jos 9:21 but *l them* **be** woodcutters and water carriers AIT
Jos 10:19 the rear and don't **l** them reach their cities H5989
Jos 22:22 And *l* Israel **know**! If this has been AIT
Jos 22:26 we said, '*L us* **get ready** and build an altar AIT
Jdg 6:32 that day, saying, "*L* Baal **contend** with him." AIT
Jdg 6:39 *L me* **make** just one more **request**. Allow AIT
Jdg 6:39 fleece dry and *l* the ground **be** covered with AIT
Jdg 7: 7 into your hands. *L* all the others **go** home." AIT
Jdg 9:15 then *l* fire **come out** of the thornbush and AIT
Jdg 9:20 *l* fire **come out** from Abimelek and consume AIT
Jdg 9:20 Beth Millo, and *l* fire **come out** from you, the AIT
Jdg 10:14 *L* them **save** you when you are in trouble!" AIT
Jdg 11:19 '*L us* **pass** through your country to our own AIT
Jdg 11:27 *L* the LORD, the Judge, **decide** *the* **dispute** this AIT
Jdg 11:38 And *he* **l** her **go** for two months H8938
Jdg 12: 5 Ephraim said, "*L me* **cross over**," the men of AIT
Jdg 13: 8 you *to l* the man of God you sent to us **come** AIT
Jdg 14:12 "*L me* **tell** you a riddle," Samson said to AIT
Jdg 15: 1 But her father *would* not **l** him go in. H5989
Jdg 15: 5 the torches and **l** the foxes **loose** in the H8938
Jdg 16:28 and *l me with* one blow **get revenge** on the AIT
Jdg 16:30 Samson said, "*L* me **die** with the Philistines!" AIT
Jdg 19:20 "**L** me supply whatever you need NDT
Jdg 19:25 the night, and at dawn *they* **l** her **go**. H8938
Ru 2: 2 "*L me* **go** *to* the fields and pick up the AIT
Ru 2: 7 'Please *l me* **glean** and gather among the AIT
Ru 2:15 "*L her* **gather** among the sheaves and don't AIT
Ru 3: 3 don't **l** him **know** *you* are there until H3359
Ru 3:13 *l him* **redeem** you. AIT
1Sa 2: 3 so proudly or *l* your mouth **speak** such AIT
1Sa 2:16 said to him, "*L* the fat *be* **burned** first, and AIT
1Sa 3:18 the LORD; *l him* **do** what is good in his eyes." AIT
1Sa 3:19 and *he* **l** none of Samuel's words **fall to** H5877
1Sa 4: 3 *L us* **bring** the ark of the LORD's covenant AIT
1Sa 5:11 of Israel away; *l it* **go back** to its own place AIT
1Sa 8: 9 solemnly and **l** them **know** what the king H5583
1Sa 9: 9 *l us* **go** to the seer," because the AIT
1Sa 11:14 *l us* **go** *to* Gilgal and there renew the AIT

1Sa 13: 3 the land and said, "*L* the Hebrews **hear**!" AIT
1Sa 14: 8 cross over toward them and **l** them **see** *us*. H1655
1Sa 14:36 "*L us* **go down** and pursue the Philistines by AIT
1Sa 14:36 and *l us* not **leave** one of them **alive**. AIT
1Sa 14:36 the priest said, "*L us* **inquire of** God here." AIT
1Sa 14:38 and *l us* **find out** what sin has been AIT
1Sa 15:16 "*L me* **tell** you what the LORD said to me last AIT
1Sa 16:16 *L* our lord **command** his servants here to AIT
1Sa 17:10 Give me a man and *l us* **fight** each other." AIT
1Sa 17:32 "*L* no one **lose** heart on account of this AIT
1Sa 18: 2 with him and *did* not **l** him return home H5989
1Sa 18:17 hand against him. *L* the Philistines **do that!**" AIT
1Sa 19: 4 "*L* not the king **do wrong** to his servant David AIT
1Sa 19:12 Michal **l** David **down** through a window, H3718
1Sa 19:17 told him, "He said to me, '**L** me **get away**. H8938
1Sa 20: 5 but **l** me **go** and hide in the field until the H8938
1Sa 20:12 send you word and **l** you **know**? H1655+906+265
1Sa 20:13 if *I do* not **l** you **know** and send H1655+906+265
1Sa 20:29 He said, '**L** me **go**, because our family is H8938
1Sa 20:29 **l** me **get away** to see my brothers. H4880
1Sa 22: 3 "*Would you l* my father and mother **come** AIT
1Sa 22:15 *L* not the king **accuse** your servant or any of AIT
1Sa 24:19 *does he* **l** him **get away** H8938+928+2006
1Sa 25:24 and *l* me **speak** to you; hear what AIT
1Sa 25:27 *l* this gift, which your servant has brought to my lord, **be given** AIT
1Sa 26: 8 Now *l me* **pin** him to the ground with one AIT
1Sa 26:19 Now *l* my lord the king **listen** *to* his servant's AIT
1Sa 26:20 Now *do* not *l* my blood **fall** to the ground far AIT
1Sa 26:22 "*L* one of your young men **come over** and get AIT
1Sa 27: 5 *l* a place *be* **assigned** to me in one of the AIT
1Sa 28:22 your servant and *l me* **give** you some food so AIT
2Sa 2:14 "**All right**, *l them* **do it**," Joab said. AIT
2Sa 3:21 "*L me* **go** at once and assemble all Israel AIT
2Sa 3:24 Why *did you* **l** him **go**? Now he is H8938
2Sa 10:12 and *l us* **fight bravely** for our people and the AIT
2Sa 11:25 'Don't *l* this **upset** you; the sword devours AIT
2Sa 12:22 may be gracious to me and *l* the child **live**. AIT
2Sa 13: 5 *L her* **prepare** the food in my sight so I may AIT
2Sa 13:26 please *l* my brother Amnon **come** with us." AIT
2Sa 14: 9 "**L** my lord the king pardon me and my NDT
2Sa 14: 9 **l** the king and his throne be without NDT
2Sa 14:11 "Then *l* the king **invoke** the LORD his God to AIT
2Sa 14:12 "*L* your servant **speak** a word to my lord the AIT
2Sa 14:18 "*L* my lord the king **speak**," the AIT
2Sa 14:32 guilty of anything, *l him* **put** me **to death**." AIT
2Sa 15: 7 "*L me* **go** to Hebron and fulfill a vow I made AIT
2Sa 15:25 bring me back and **l** me **see** it and his H8011
2Sa 15:26 *l him* **do** to me whatever seems good to him." AIT
2Sa 16: 9 *L me* **go over** and cut off his head. AIT
2Sa 16:11 Leave him alone; *l* him **curse**, for the LORD AIT
2Sa 17:11 *L* all Israel, ... **be gathered** AIT
2Sa 18:19 "*L me* **run** and take the news to the king that AIT
2Sa 18:22 please *l me* **run** behind the Cushite. AIT
2Sa 19:30 said to the king, "*L him* **take** everything, now AIT
2Sa 19:37 *L* your servant **return**, that I may die in my AIT
2Sa 19:37 *L him* **cross over** with my lord the king AIT
2Sa 20:11 whoever is for David, **l** him follow Joab!" NDT
2Sa 21: 6 *l* seven of his male descendants **be given** to AIT
2Sa 21:10 *she did* not **l** the birds touch them by day H5989
2Sa 24:14 *L us* **fall** into the hands of the LORD, for his AIT
2Sa 24:14 but *do* not *l me* **fall** into human hands." AIT
2Sa 24:17 done? *L* your hand **fall** on me and my family." AIT
2Sa 24:22 "*L* my lord the king **take** whatever he wishes AIT
1Ki 1: 2 "*L us* **look for** a young virgin to serve the AIT
1Ki 1:12 *l me* **advise** you how you can save your own AIT
1Ki 1:51 '*L* King Solomon **swear** to me today that he AIT
1Ki 2: 6 but *do* not **l** his gray head **go down** *to* the H3718
1Ki 2: 7 of Gilead and *l them* **be** among those who AIT
1Ki 2:21 *L* Abishag the Shunammite **be given in marriage** AIT
1Ki 8:26 *l* your word that you promised your servant David my father **come true** AIT
1Ki 11:21 said to Pharaoh, "**L** me **go**, that I may H8938
1Ki 11:22 Hadad replied, "but **do l** me **go**!" H8938+8938
1Ki 15:19 "**L** there be a treaty between me and you," NDT
1Ki 17:21 my God, *l* this boy's life **return** to him!" AIT
1Ki 18:23 *L* Baal's prophets **choose** one for themselves AIT
1Ki 18:23 and *l them* **cut** it **into pieces** and put it on the AIT
1Ki 18:36 *l it* **be known** today that you are God in Israel AIT
1Ki 18:40 Don't **l** anyone **get away**!" They H4880
1Ki 19:20 "*L me* **kiss** my father and mother **goodbye**," AIT
1Ki 20:31 *L us* **go** to the king of Israel with sackcloth AIT
1Ki 20:32 servant Ben-Hadad says: 'Please *l me* **live**.' " AIT
1Ki 20:34 he made a treaty with him, and **l** him **go**. H8938
1Ki 21: 2 "**L** me **have** your vineyard to use for a H5989
1Ki 22:13 *L* your word **agree** with theirs, and speak AIT
1Ki 22:17 *L* each one **go** home in peace.' AIT
1Ki 22:49 Jehoshaphat, "*L* my men **sail** with yours," AIT
2Ki 2: 9 "*L me* **inherit** a double portion of your spirit," AIT
2Ki 2:16 *L them* **go** and look for your master AIT
2Ki 5:17 "please *l me*, your servant, **be given** as much AIT
2Ki 6: 2 *L us* **go** to the Jordan, where each of us can AIT
2Ki 6: 2 and *l us* **build** a place there for us to meet." AIT
2Ki 7:13 So *l us* **send** them to find out what happened AIT
2Ki 9:15 don't *l* anyone **slip out** of the city to go and AIT
2Ki 10:25 kill them; *l* no one **escape**." So they cut AIT
2Ki 12: 5 *L* every priest **receive** the money from one of AIT
2Ki 14: 8 *l us* **face each other in battle**." AIT
2Ki 18:29 *Do* not **l** Hezekiah **deceive** you. H5958
2Ki 18:30 *Do* not **l** Hezekiah **persuade** you **to trust** in H1053
2Ki 19:10 *Do* not **l** the god you depend on **deceive** H5958

L

2Ki 23:18 "Don't *l* anyone **disturb** his bones." So AIT
1Ch 4:10 *L* your hand **be** with me, and keep me from AIT
1Ch 13: 2 *l us* **send word** far and wide to the rest of our AIT
1Ch 13: 3 *L us* **bring** the ark of our God **back** to us, for AIT
1Ch 16:10 *l* the hearts of those who seek the LORD **rejoice** AIT
1Ch 16:31 *L* the heavens **rejoice**, let the earth be glad AIT
1Ch 16:31 *l* the earth *be* **glad**; let them say AIT
1Ch 16:31 earth be glad; *l them* **say** among the nations AIT
1Ch 16:32 *L* the sea **resound**, and all that is in it; let the AIT
1Ch 16:32 that is in it; *l* the fields *be* **jubilant**, and AIT
1Ch 16:33 **L** the trees of the forest sing, let them sing NDT
1Ch 16:33 sing, *l them* **sing for joy** before the LORD AIT
1Ch 17:23 *l* the promise you have made concerning your servant and his house **be established** AIT
1Ch 19:13 and *l us* **fight bravely** for our people and the AIT
1Ch 21:13 *L me* **fall** into the hands of the LORD, for his AIT
1Ch 21:13 but *do* not *l me* **fall** into human hands." AIT
1Ch 21:17 *l* your hand **fall** on me and my family AIT
1Ch 21:17 do not **l** this plague remain on your NDT
1Ch 21:22 "*L* me **have** the site of your threshing floor so AIT
1Ch 21:23 *L* my lord the king **do** whatever pleases him AIT
2Ch 1: 9 *l* your promise to my father David **be confirmed** AIT
2Ch 2:15 "Now *l* my lord **send** his servants the wheat AIT
2Ch 6:17 *l* your word that you promised your servant David **come true** AIT
2Ch 14: 7 "*L us* **build up** these towns," he said to Judah AIT
2Ch 14:11 *do* not *l* mere mortals **prevail** against you." AIT
2Ch 16: 3 "**L** there be a treaty between me and you," NDT
2Ch 18:12 *L* your word **agree** with theirs, and speak AIT
2Ch 18:16 *L* each one **go** home in peace.' AIT
2Ch 19: 7 Now *l* the fear of the LORD **be** on you. Judge AIT
2Ch 25:17 *l us* **face each other in battle**." AIT
2Ch 32:11 to **l** you die of hunger and thirst. H5989
2Ch 32:15 Now *do* not *l* Hezekiah **deceive** you and AIT
Ezr 4: 2 "*L us* help you **build** because, like AIT
Ezr 4:22 Why *l* this threat **grow**, to the detriment of AIT
Ezr 5:17 *l* **a search be made** in the royal archives of AIT
Ezr 5:17 Then *l* the king **send** us his decision in this AIT
Ezr 6: 3 *L* the temple **be rebuilt** as a place to present AIT
Ezr 6: 3 sacrifices, and *l* its foundations **be laid**. AIT
Ezr 6: 7 *L* the governor of the Jews and the Jewish elders **rebuild** AIT
Ezr 6:12 *L it* **be carried out** with diligence. AIT
Ezr 7:23 *l it* **be done** with diligence for the temple of AIT
Ezr 10: 3 Now *l us* **make** a covenant before our God to AIT
Ezr 10: 3 *L it* **be done** according to the Law AIT
Ezr 10:14 *L* our officials **act** for the whole assembly AIT
Ezr 10:14 *l* everyone in our towns who has married a foreign woman **come** AIT
Ne 1: 6 *l* your ear **be** attentive and your eyes open to AIT
Ne 1:11 *l* your ear **be** attentive to the prayer of this AIT
Ne 2: 5 *l him* **send** me to the city in Judah where my AIT
Ne 2:17 *l us* **rebuild** the wall of Jerusalem AIT
Ne 2:18 They replied, "*L us* **start** rebuilding." So AIT
Ne 5:10 But *l us* **stop** charging interest! AIT
Ne 6: 2 *l us* **meet** together in one of the villages on AIT
Ne 6: 7 to the king; so come, *l us* **meet** together." AIT
Ne 6:10 He said, "*L us* **meet** in the house of God AIT
Ne 6:10 the temple, and *l us* **close** the temple doors AIT
Ne 9:32 *do* not *l* all this hardship *seem* **trifling** in your AIT
Est 1:19 *l* him **issue** a royal decree and let it be AIT
Est 1:19 royal decree and *l it* **be written** in the laws of AIT
Est 1:19 Also *l* the king **give** her royal position to AIT
Est 2: 2 "*L a* **search** *be* **made for** beautiful young AIT
Est 2: 3 *L* the king **appoint** commissioners in every AIT
Est 2: 3 **L** them be placed under the care of Hegai NDT
Est 2: 3 and *l* beauty treatments *be* **given** *to* them. AIT
Est 2: 4 *l* the young woman who pleases the king *be* **queen** AIT
Est 3: 9 *l a* **decree be issued** to destroy them AIT
Est 5: 4 "*l* the king, together with Haman, **come** AIT
Est 5: 8 *l* the king and Haman **come** tomorrow to the AIT
Est 6: 9 Then *l* the robe and horse *be* **entrusted** to AIT
Est 6: 9 *L them* **robe** the man the king delights to AIT
Est 8: 5 *l an* **order be written** overruling the AIT
Est 9:13 and *l* Haman's ten sons *be* **impaled** on poles AIT
Job 6: 9 *to* **l loose** his hand and cut off my life! H6000
Job 7:16 **L** me **alone**; my days have no H2532
Job 7:19 or **l** me **alone** even for an instant? H8332
Job 9:18 *He would* not **l** me catch my breath but H5989
Job 10:14 *would* not **l** my offense **go unpunished**. H5927
Job 12: 8 teach you, or *l* the fish in the sea **inform** you. AIT
Job 13:13 "Keep silent and *l* me **speak**; then let come AIT
Job 13:13 let me speak; then *l* **come** to me what may. AIT
Job 13:17 to what I say; **l** my words ring in your ears. NDT
Job 13:22 I will answer, or *l me* **speak**, and you reply to AIT
Job 14: 6 So look away from him and **l** him **alone** H2532
Job 15:17 *l me* **tell** you what I have seen, AIT
Job 15:31 *L him* not **deceive himself** by trusting what is AIT
Job 17: 4 therefore *you will* not **l** them **triumph**. H8123
Job 20:13 he cannot bear *to l it* **go** and lets it linger in AIT
Job 21: 2 *l* this **be** the consolation you give me. AIT
Job 21:19 *L him* **repay** the wicked, so that they AIT
Job 21:20 *L* their own eyes **see** *their destruction; let* AIT
Job 21:20 *l them* **drink** the cup of the wrath of the AIT
Job 24:23 *He may* **l** them rest in a feeling of security, H5989
Job 27: 6 my innocence and never **l go** *of* it; H8332
Job 31: 6 *l* God **weigh** me in honest scales and he will AIT
Job 31:16 poor or *l* the eyes of the widow **grow weary**, AIT
Job 31:22 then *l* my arm **fall** from the shoulder, let it be AIT
Job 31:22 the shoulder, *l it* **be broken off** at the joint. AIT
Job 31:35 defense—*l* the Almighty **answer** me; let my AIT
Job 31:35 *l* my accuser **put** *his* indictment **in writing**. AIT
Job 31:40 then *l* briers **come up** instead of wheat and AIT
Job 32:13 found wisdom; *l* God, **not** a man, refute him. AIT
Job 33:25 *l* their flesh **be renewed** like a child's; let AIT
Job 33:25 *l them* **be restored** as in the days of their AIT
Job 34: 4 *L us* **discern** for ourselves what is right; let us AIT
Job 34: 4 *l us* **learn** together what is good. AIT
Job 36:18 *do* not *l* a large bribe **turn** you **aside**. AIT
Job 39: 5 "Who **l** the wild donkey **go** free? Who H8938
Job 40: 2 *L him* who accuses God **answer** him!" AIT
Ps 2: 3 "*L us* **break** their chains and throw off their AIT
Ps 4: 6 **L** the light of your face **shine** on us. H5951
Ps 5:10 *L* their intrigues *be their* **downfall** AIT
Ps 5:11 But *l* all who take refuge in you *be* **glad**; let AIT
Ps 5:11 in you be glad; *l them* ever **sing for joy**. AIT
Ps 7: 5 then *l* my enemy **pursue** and overtake me; let AIT
Ps 7: 5 *l him* **trample** my life to the ground and AIT
Ps 7: 7 *L* the assembled peoples **gather around** you AIT
Ps 7: 8 *L* the LORD **judge** the peoples. Vindicate me AIT
Ps 9:19 *do* not *l* mortals **triumph**; let the nations AIT
Ps 9:19 *l* the nations **be judged** in your presence. AIT
Ps 9:20 *l* the nations **know** they are only mortal. AIT
Ps 14: 7 *l* Jacob **rejoice** and Israel be glad! AIT
Ps 16:10 nor *will you* **l** your faithful one see decay. H5989
Ps 17: 2 *L* my vindication **come** from you; may your AIT
Ps 22: 8 the LORD," they say, "*l* the LORD **rescue** him. AIT
Ps 22: 8 LORD rescue him. *L him* **deliver** him, since he AIT
Ps 25: 2 *do* not *l me be* **put to shame**, nor let AIT
Ps 25: 2 nor *l* my enemies **triumph** over me. AIT
Ps 25:20 rescue me; *do* not *l me be* **put to shame**, for I AIT
Ps 30: 1 and *did* not **l** my enemies **gloat** over me. H8523
Ps 31: 1 *l me* never *be* **put to shame**; deliver AIT
Ps 31:16 *L* your face **shine** on your servant; save me in AIT
Ps 31:17 *L me* not *be* **put to shame**, LORD, for I have AIT
Ps 31:17 but *l* the wicked *be* **put to shame** and be AIT
Ps 31:18 *L* their lying lips **be silenced**, for with pride AIT
Ps 32: 6 Therefore *l* all the faithful pray **to** you while AIT
Ps 33: 8 *L* all the earth **fear** the LORD; let all the AIT
Ps 33: 8 *l* all the people of the world **revere** him. AIT
Ps 34: 2 in the LORD; *l* the afflicted **hear** and rejoice. AIT
Ps 34: 3 LORD with me; *l us* **exalt** his name together. AIT
Ps 35:19 *Do* not *l those* **gloat** over me who are my AIT
Ps 35:19 *do* not *l* those who hate me without reason **maliciously wink** AIT
Ps 35:24 LORD my God; *do* not *l them* **gloat** over me. AIT
Ps 35:25 *Do* not *l them* **think**, "Aha, just what we AIT
Ps 37:33 wicked or **l** them **be condemned** when H8399
Ps 38:16 "*Do* not *l them* **gloat** or exalt themselves over AIT
Ps 39: 4 my days; *l me* **know** how fleeting my life is. AIT
Ps 43: 3 faithful care, *l* them **lead** me; let them bring AIT
Ps 43: 3 *l them* **bring** me to your holy mountain AIT
Ps 45: 4 *l* your right hand **achieve** awesome deeds. AIT
Ps 45: 5 **L** your sharp arrows pierce the hearts of the NDT
Ps 45: 5 enemies; *l* the nations **fall** beneath your feet. AIT
Ps 45:11 *L* the king *be* **enthralled** *by* your beauty AIT
Ps 51: 8 **L** me **hear** joy and gladness; let the bones H9048
Ps 51: 8 *l* the bones you have crushed **rejoice**. AIT
Ps 53: 6 *l* Jacob **rejoice** and Israel be glad! AIT
Ps 54: 5 *L* evil **recoil** on those who slander me; in your AIT
Ps 55:15 *L* death **take** my enemies **by surprise**; let AIT
Ps 55:15 *l them* **go down** alive *to* the realm of the AIT
Ps 55:22 *he will* never **l** the righteous be shaken. H5989
Ps 56: 7 of their wickedness *do* not **l** them **escape**; H7117
Ps 57: 5 heavens; **l** your glory be over all the earth. NDT
Ps 57:11 heavens; **l** your glory be over all the earth. NDT
Ps 58: 7 *L them* **vanish** like water that flows away AIT
Ps 58: 7 they draw the bow, *l* their arrows **fall short**. AIT
Ps 59:10 before me and *will* **l** me **gloat** over those H8011
Ps 59:12 of their lips, *l them* **be caught** in their pride. AIT
Ps 66: 6 waters on foot—*come, l us* **rejoice** in him. AIT
Ps 66: 7 *l* not the rebellious **rise up** against him. AIT
Ps 66: 8 **l** the sound of his praise **be heard**; H9048
Ps 66:12 *You* **l** people **ride** over our heads; we H8206
Ps 66:16 *l me* **tell** you what he has done for me. AIT
Ps 69:14 from the mire, *do* not *l me* **sink**; deliver me AIT
Ps 69:15 *Do* not *l* the floodwaters **engulf** me or the AIT
Ps 69:24 on them; *l* your fierce anger **overtake** them. AIT
Ps 69:25 *l there* **be** no one to dwell in their tents. AIT
Ps 69:27 *do* not *l them* **share** in your salvation. AIT
Ps 69:34 *L* heaven and earth **praise** him, the seas AIT
Ps 71: 1 taken refuge; *l me* never **be put to shame**. AIT
Ps 74:21 *Do* not *l* the oppressed **retreat** in disgrace AIT
Ps 76:11 *l* all the neighboring lands **bring** gifts to the AIT
Ps 78:26 *He* **l loose** the east wind from the H5825
Ps 80:17 *L* your hand **rest** on the man at your right AIT
Ps 83: 4 they say, "*l us* **destroy** them as a nation, so AIT
Ps 83:12 "*L us* **take possession** *of* the pasturelands of AIT
Ps 83:18 *L them* **know** that you, whose name is the AIT
Ps 85: 8 faithful servants—but *l them* not **turn** to folly. AIT
Ps 95: 1 Come, *l us* **sing for joy** to the LORD; let us AIT
Ps 95: 1 *l us* **shout aloud** to the Rock of our salvation. AIT
Ps 95: 2 *L us* **come** before him with thanksgiving and AIT
Ps 95: 6 *l us* **bow down** in worship, let us kneel AIT
Ps 95: 6 *l us* **kneel** before the LORD our Maker; AIT
Ps 96:11 *L* the heavens **rejoice**, let the earth be glad AIT
Ps 96:11 *l* the earth *be* **glad**; let the sea AIT
Ps 96:11 earth be glad; *l* the sea **resound**, and all that AIT
Ps 96:12 *L* the fields *be* **jubilant**, and everything in AIT
Ps 96:12 *l* all the trees of the forest **sing for joy**. AIT
Ps 96:13 **L** all creation rejoice before the LORD, for he NDT
Ps 97: 1 The LORD reigns, *l* the earth *be* **glad**; let the AIT
Ps 97: 1 earth be glad; *l* the distant shores **rejoice**. AIT
Ps 97:10 *L those who* **love** the LORD hate evil, for he AIT
Ps 98: 7 *L* the sea **resound**, and everything in it, the AIT
Ps 98: 8 *L* the rivers **clap** their hands, let the AIT
Ps 98: 8 *l* the mountains **sing** together **for joy**; AIT
Ps 98: 9 **l** them sing before the LORD, for he comes to NDT
Ps 99: 1 The LORD reigns, *l* the nations **tremble**; he sits AIT
Ps 99: 1 between the cherubim, *l* the earth **shake**. AIT
Ps 99: 3 *L them* **praise** your great and awesome name AIT
Ps 102: 1 LORD; *l* my cry for help **come** to you. AIT
Ps 102:18 *L* this **be written** for a future generation, that AIT
Ps 105: 3 *l* the hearts of those who seek the LORD **rejoice** AIT
Ps 106:48 *L* all the people **say**, "Amen! AIT
Ps 107: 2 *L* the redeemed of the LORD **tell** their **story** AIT
Ps 107: 8 *L them* **give thanks** to the LORD *for* his AIT
Ps 107:15 *L them* **give thanks** to the LORD *for* his AIT
Ps 107:21 *L them* **give thanks** to the LORD *for* his AIT
Ps 107:22 *L them* **sacrifice** thank offerings and tell of his AIT
Ps 107:31 *L them* **give thanks** to the LORD *for* his AIT
Ps 107:32 *L them* **exalt** him in the assembly of the AIT
Ps 107:38 and *he did* not **l** their herds **diminish**. H5070
Ps 107:43 *L* the one who is wise **heed** these things AIT
Ps 108: 5 heavens; **l** your glory be over all the earth. NDT
Ps 109: 6 *l* an accuser **stand** at his right hand. AIT
Ps 109: 7 he is tried, *l him be* **found** guilty, and may AIT
Ps 109:27 *L them* **know** that it is your hand, that you AIT
Ps 113: 2 *L* the name of the LORD **be** praised, both now AIT
Ps 118: 2 *L* Israel **say**: "His love endures forever." AIT
Ps 118: 3 *L* the house of Aaron **say**: "His love endures AIT
Ps 118: 4 *L* those who fear the LORD **say**: "His love AIT
Ps 118:24 this very day; *l us* **rejoice** today and be glad. AIT
Ps 119:10 *do* not **l** me **stray** from your commands. H8706
Ps 119:31 *do* not **l** me **be put to shame**. H1017
Ps 119:77 *L* your compassion **come** *to* me that I may AIT
Ps 119:116 I will live; *do* not **l** my hopes **be dashed**. H1017
Ps 119:122 *do* not *l* the arrogant **oppress** me. AIT
Ps 119:133 to your word; **l** no sin **rule** over me. H8948
Ps 119:175 *L* me **live** that I may praise you, and may AIT
Ps 121: 3 *He will* not **l** your foot slip—he who H5989
Ps 122: 1 said to me, "*L us* **go** *to* the house of the LORD." AIT
Ps 124: 1 had not been on our side—*l* Israel **say**— AIT
Ps 124: 6 who *has* not **l** us be torn by their teeth. H5989
Ps 129: 1 oppressed me from my youth," *l* Israel **say**; AIT
Ps 130: 2 *L* your ears **be** attentive to my cry for mercy. AIT
Ps 132: 7 "*L us* **go** *to* his dwelling place, let us worship AIT
Ps 132: 7 dwelling place, *l us* **worship** at his footstool AIT
Ps 140: 8 desires, LORD; *do* not **l** their plans **succeed**. H7049
Ps 141: 4 **Do** not **l** my heart **be drawn** to what is evil H5742
Ps 141: 4 evildoers; *do* not *l me* **eat** their delicacies. AIT
Ps 141: 5 *L* a righteous man **strike** me—that is a AIT
Ps 141: 5 is a kindness; *l him* **rebuke** me—that is oil on AIT
Ps 141:10 *L* the wicked **fall** into their own nets, while I AIT
Ps 143: 8 *L* the morning **bring** me **word** *of* your AIT
Ps 145:21 *L* every creature **praise** his holy name for AIT
Ps 148: 5 *L them* **praise** the name of the LORD, for at AIT
Ps 148:13 *L them* **praise** the name of the LORD, for his AIT
Ps 149: 2 *L* Israel **rejoice** in their Maker; let the people AIT
Ps 149: 2 *l* the people of Zion *be* **glad** in their King. AIT
Ps 149: 3 *L them* **praise** his name with dancing and AIT
Ps 149: 5 *L* his faithful people **rejoice** in this honor AIT
Ps 150: 6 *L* everything that has breath **praise** the LORD AIT
Pr 1: 5 *l* the wise **listen** and add to their learning AIT
Pr 1: 5 and *l* the discerning **get** guidance— AIT
Pr 3: 3 *L* love and faithfulness never **leave** you; bind AIT
Pr 3:20 divided, and the clouds **l drop** the dew. H8319
Pr 3:21 *do* not **l** wisdom and understanding **out** of H4279
Pr 4:13 to instruction, *do* not **l** it **go**; guard it well, H8332
Pr 4:21 *Do* not **l** *them* **out** of your sight, keep H4279
Pr 4:25 **L** your eyes **look** straight ahead; fix your H5564
Pr 5:17 *L them* **be** yours alone, never to be shared AIT
Pr 6:25 her beauty or *l her* **captivate** you with her AIT
Pr 7:25 *Do* not *l* your heart **turn** to her ways or stray AIT
Pr 9: 4 "*L all* who are simple **come** to my house!" AIT
Pr 9:16 "*L all* who are simple **come** to my house!" AIT
Pr 10: 3 LORD *does* not **l** the righteous **go hungry**, H8279
Pr 23:17 *Do* not *l* your heart **envy** sinners, but always AIT
Pr 23:26 heart and *l* your eyes **delight** *in* my ways, AIT
Pr 24:17 they stumble, *do* not *l* your heart **rejoice**, AIT
Pr 27: 2 *L* someone else **praise** you, and not your own AIT
Pr 28:17 refuge in the grave; *l* no *one* **hold** them **back**. AIT
Pr 31: 6 **L** beer be for those who are perishing H5989
Pr 31: 7 *L them* **drink** and forget their poverty and AIT
Pr 31:31 and *l* her works **bring** her **praise** at the city AIT
Ecc 5: 2 you are on earth, so *l* your words **be** few. AIT
Ecc 5: 6 *Do* not **l** your mouth lead you into sin. H5989
Ecc 7:18 one and not **l go** of the other. H5663+906+3338
Ecc 11: 6 at evening **l** your hands not **be idle** H5663
Ecc 11: 8 anyone may live, *l them* **enjoy** them all. AIT
Ecc 11: 8 But *l them* **remember** the days of darkness AIT
Ecc 11: 9 and *l* your heart **give** you **joy** in the days of AIT
SS 1: 2 *L him* **kiss** me with the kisses of his mouth AIT
SS 1: 4 me away with you—*l us* **hurry**! Let the king AIT
SS 1: 4 *L* the king **bring** me **into** his chambers AIT
SS 2: 4 *L him* **lead** me to the banquet hall, and let AIT
SS 2: 4 and **l** his banner over me be love. NDT
SS 2:14 me your face, **l** me **hear** your voice; for H9048
SS 3: 4 held him and *would* not **l** him **go** till I had H8332
SS 4:16 *L* my beloved **come** into his garden and taste AIT
SS 7:11 my beloved, *l us* **go** *to* the countryside, let us AIT
SS 7:11 *l us* **spend the night** in the villages. AIT

SS 7:12 L us go early to the vineyards to see if the AIT
SS 8:11 Hamon; he l out his vineyard to tenants. H5989
SS 8:13 in attendance, l me hear your voice! H9048
Isa 1:18 "Come now, l us settle the matter," says the AIT
Isa 2: 3 l us go up to the mountain of the LORD AIT
Isa 2: 5 of Jacob, l us walk in the light of the LORD. AIT
Isa 4: 1 only l us be called by your name. AIT
Isa 5:19 those who say, "L God hurry; let him hasten AIT
Isa 5:19 l him hasten his work so we may see it. AIT
Isa 5:19 One of Israel—l it approach, let it come into AIT
Isa 5:19 it approach, l it come into view, so we may AIT
Isa 7: 6 "L us invade Judah; let us tear it apart and AIT
Isa 7: 6 l us tear it apart and divide it among AIT
Isa 12: 5 l this be known to all the world. AIT
Isa 14:17 cities and would not l his captives go home?" AIT
Isa 14:20 L the offspring of the wicked never be mentioned AIT
Isa 16: 4 L the Moabite fugitives stay with you; be their AIT
Isa 19:12 L them show you and make known what the AIT
Isa 21: 7 riders on camels, l him be alert, fully alert." AIT
Isa 22: 4 "Turn away from me; l me weep bitterly. AIT
Isa 22:13 "L us eat and drink," you say, "for tomorrow AIT
Isa 25: 9 l us rejoice and be glad in his salvation." AIT
Isa 26:11 L them see your zeal for your people and be AIT
Isa 26:11 l the fire reserved for your enemies consume AIT
Isa 26:19 l those who dwell in the dust wake up and AIT
Isa 27: 5 Or else l them come to me for refuge; let AIT
Isa 27: 5 to me for refuge; l them make peace with me AIT
Isa 27: 5 with me, yes, l them make peace with me." AIT
Isa 28:12 is the resting place, l the weary rest"; and, AIT
Isa 29: 1 to year and l your cycle of festivals go on. AIT
Isa 34: 1 L the earth hear, and all that is in it, the AIT
Isa 36:14 Do not l Hezekiah deceive you. H5958
Isa 36:15 Do not l Hezekiah persuade you to trust H1053
Isa 36:18 "Do not l Hezekiah mislead you when he H6077
Isa 37:10 Do not l the god you depend on deceive H1053
Isa 38:16 You restored me to health and l me live. H2649
Isa 41: 1 L the nations renew their strength H2736
Isa 41: 1 L them come forward and speak; let us meet AIT
Isa 41: 1 l us meet together at the place of judgment. AIT
Isa 42:11 L the wilderness and its towns raise their AIT
Isa 42:11 l the settlements where Kedar lives rejoice. NDT
Isa 42:11 L the people of Sela sing for joy; let them AIT
Isa 42:11 l them shout from the mountaintops. AIT
Isa 42:12 L them give glory to the LORD and proclaim AIT
Isa 43: 9 L them bring in their witnesses to prove they AIT
Isa 43:26 past for me, l us argue the matter together AIT
Isa 44: 7 then is like me? L him proclaim it. Let him AIT
Isa 44: 7 L him declare and lay out before me what AIT
Isa 44: 7 yes, l them foretell what will come. AIT
Isa 44:11 L them all come together and take their AIT
Isa 44:14 He l it grow among the trees of the forest H599
Isa 44:28 say of Jerusalem, "L it be rebuilt," and of the AIT
Isa 44:28 of the temple, "L its foundations be laid." AIT
Isa 45: 8 righteousness; l the clouds shower it down. AIT
Isa 45: 8 L the earth open wide, let salvation spring up AIT
Isa 45: 8 earth open wide, l salvation spring up, let AIT
Isa 45: 8 spring up, l righteousness flourish with it; I, AIT
Isa 45:21 present it—l them take counsel together. AIT
Isa 47:13 L your astrologers come forward, those AIT
Isa 47:13 l them save you from what is coming upon AIT
Isa 48:11 How can I l myself be defamed? I will AIT
Isa 50: 8 L us face each other! Who is AIT
Isa 50: 8 Who is my accuser? L him confront me! AIT
Isa 50:10 L the one who walks in the dark, ... trust AIT
Isa 55: 7 L the wicked forsake their ways and the AIT
Isa 55: 7 L them turn to the LORD, and he will have AIT
Isa 56: 3 L no foreigner who is bound to the LORD say, AIT
Isa 56: 3 And l no eunuch complain, "I am only a dry AIT
Isa 56:12 each one cries, "l me get wine! Let us drink AIT
Isa 56:12 L us drink our fill of beer! And AIT
Isa 57:13 l your collection of idols save you! AIT
Isa 66: 5 have said, 'L the LORD be glorified, that we AIT
Jer 2:28 L them come if they can save you when you AIT
Jer 3:25 L us lie down in our shame, and let our AIT
Jer 3:25 in our shame, and l our disgrace cover us. AIT
Jer 4: 5 L us flee to the fortified cities AIT
Jer 5:13 in them; so l what they say be done to them." AIT
Jer 5:24 to themselves, 'L us fear the LORD our God AIT
Jer 6: 4 Arise, l us attack at noon! But, AIT
Jer 6: 5 l us attack at night and destroy her fortresses! AIT
Jer 6: 9 L them glean the remnant of Israel as thoroughly AIT
Jer 7: 3 actions, and I will l you live in this place. H8905
Jer 7: 7 then I will l you live in this place, in the H8905
Jer 8:14 L us flee to the fortified cities and perish AIT
Jer 9:18 L them come quickly and wail over us till our AIT
Jer 9:23 "L not the wise boast of their wisdom or the AIT
Jer 9:24 but l the one who boasts boast about this AIT
Jer 11:19 "L us destroy the tree and its fruit; let AIT
Jer 11:19 l us cut him off from the land of the living AIT
Jer 11:20 mind, l me see your vengeance on them AIT
Jer 13: 1 your waist, but do not l it touch water." H995+928
Jer 14:17 "'L my eyes overflow with tears night and AIT
Jer 15: 1 them away from my presence! L them go! AIT
Jer 15:19 L this people turn to you, but you must not AIT
Jer 17:15 the word of the LORD? L it now be fulfilled!" AIT
Jer 17:18 L my persecutors be put to shame, but keep AIT
Jer 17:18 from shame; l them be terrified, but keep me AIT
Jer 18:21 L their wives be made childless and widows AIT
Jer 18:21 widows; l their men be put to death AIT
Jer 18:22 L a cry be heard from their houses when you AIT
Jer 18:23 L them be overthrown before you; deal with AIT
Jer 20:12 mind, l me see your vengeance on them AIT
Jer 22:20 l your voice be heard in Bashan H5989
Jer 23:28 L the prophet who has a dream recount the AIT
Jer 23:28 but l the one who has my word speak it AIT
Jer 27:11 I will l that nation remain in its own land H5663
Jer 27:18 l them plead with the LORD Almighty that the AIT
Jer 29: 8 Do not l the prophets and diviners among you deceive AIT
Jer 30:11 I will not l you go entirely unpunished H5927+5927
Jer 31: 6 l us go up to Zion, to the LORD our AIT
Jer 32:37 to this place and l them live in safety. H3782
Jer 33: 6 people and will l them enjoy abundant H1655
Jer 34:14 you six years, you must l them go free. H8938
Jer 36:19 Don't l anyone know where you are. AIT
Jer 37:20 L me bring my petition before you AIT
Jer 38:11 from there and l them down with ropes to H8938
Jer 38:24 "Do not l anyone know about this AIT
Jer 40: 5 provisions and a present and l him go. H8938
Jer 40:15 "L me go and kill Ishmael son of Nethaniah AIT
Jer 41: 8 So he l them alone and did not kill them H2532
Jer 45: 5 wherever you go I will l you escape with H5989
Jer 46:16 l us go back to our own people and our AIT
Jer 46:28 I will not l you go entirely unpunished H5927+5927
Jer 48: 2 l us put an end to that nation.' AIT
Jer 48:26 L Moab wallow in her vomit; let her be an AIT
Jer 48:26 in her vomit; l her be an object of ridicule. AIT
Jer 50:16 the oppressor l everyone return to their own AIT
Jer 50:16 l everyone flee to their own land. AIT
Jer 50:27 l them go down to the slaughter! AIT
Jer 50:29 all around her; l no one escape. Repay H2118
Jer 50:33 hold them fast, refusing to l them go. H8938
Jer 51: 3 L not the archer string his bow, nor let him AIT
Jer 51: 3 string his bow, nor l him put on his armor. AIT
Jer 51: 9 l us leave her and each go to our own land AIT
Jer 51:10 l us tell in Zion what the LORD our God has AIT
La 1:22 "L all their wickedness come before you; deal AIT
La 2:17 he has l the enemy gloat over you H8523
La 2:18 l your tears flow like a river day and night H3718
La 3:28 L him sit alone in silence, for the LORD has AIT
La 3:29 L him bury his face in the dust—there may AIT
La 3:30 L him offer his cheek to one who would strike AIT
La 3:30 strike him, and l him be filled with disgrace. AIT
La 3:40 L us examine our ways and test them, and let AIT
La 3:40 test them, and l us return to the LORD. AIT
La 3:41 L us lift up our hearts and our hands to God AIT
Eze 3:27 Whoever will listen l them listen, and AIT
Eze 3:27 whoever will refuse l them refuse; for AIT
Eze 4:15 "I will l you bake your bread over cow H5989
Eze 7:12 L not the buyer rejoice nor the seller grieve AIT
Eze 14: 3 Should I l them inquire of me at all H2011+4200+2011
Eze 14:17 'L the sword pass throughout the land AIT
Eze 20: 3 I will not l you inquire of me H2011
Eze 20:31 Am I to l you inquire of me, you H2011+4200
Eze 20:31 I will not l you inquire of me. H2011+4200
Eze 21:14 L the sword strike twice, even three AIT
Eze 21:30 "'L the sword return to its sheath. In the AIT
Eze 23:43 'Now l them use her as a prostitute, for that AIT
Eze 24:10 in the spices; and l the bones be charred. AIT
Eze 32: 4 I will l all the birds of the sky settle on you H8905
Eze 32:14 Then I will l her waters settle and make H9205
Eze 32:20 l her be dragged off with all her hordes. AIT
Eze 39: 7 I will no longer l my holy name be profaned H2725
Eze 43: 9 Now l them put away from me their AIT
Eze 43:10 L them consider its perfection, AIT
Eze 44:20 their heads or l their hair grow long, H8938
Da 2: 7 "L the king tell his servants the dream AIT
Da 4:14 L the animals flee from under it and the birds AIT
Da 4:15 l the stump and its roots, ... remain AIT
Da 4:15 "'L him be drenched with the dew of heaven, AIT
Da 4:15 l him live with the animals among the NDT
Da 4:16 L his mind be changed from that of a man AIT
Da 4:16 of a man and l him be given the mind of an AIT
Da 4:19 do not l the dream or its meaning alarm you." AIT
Da 4:23 L him be drenched with the dew of heaven AIT
Da 4:23 of heaven; l him live with the wild animals NDT
Hos 2: 2 L her remove the adulterous look from her AIT
Hos 4: 4 "But l no one bring a charge, let no one AIT
Hos 4: 4 bring a charge, l no one accuse another, for AIT
Hos 4:15 adultery, do not l Judah become guilty. AIT
Hos 6: 1 l us return to the LORD. He has torn us AIT
Hos 6: 3 L us acknowledge the LORD; let us press on AIT
Hos 6: 3 the LORD; l us press on to acknowledge him. AIT
Hos 9: 7 L Israel know this. Because your AIT
Hos 14: 9 L them realize these things AIT
Hos 14: 9 L them understand. The ways of AIT
Joel 1: 3 l your children tell it to their children NDT
Joel 2: 1 L all who live in the land tremble, for the day AIT
Joel 2:16 L the bridegroom leave his room and the AIT
Joel 2:17 L the priests, who minister ..., weep AIT
Joel 2:17 L them say, "Spare your people AIT
Joel 3: 9 L all the fighting men draw near and attack AIT
Joel 3:10 L the weakling say, "I am strong! AIT
Joel 3:12 "L the nations be roused; let them advance AIT
Joel 3:12 l them advance into the Valley of AIT
Am 5:24 But l justice roll on like a river, righteousness AIT
Ob 1 "Rise, l us go against her for battle" AIT
Jnh 1: 7 l us cast lots to find out who is responsible AIT
Jnh 1:14 do not l us die for taking this man's life. AIT
Jnh 3: 7 Do not l people or animals, herds ..., taste AIT
Jnh 3: 7 taste anything; do not l them eat or drink. AIT
Jnh 3: 8 But l people and animals be covered with AIT
Jnh 3: 8 L everyone call urgently on God AIT
Jnh 3: 8 L them give up their evil ways and their AIT
Mic 4: 2 l us go up to the mountain of the LORD AIT
Mic 4:11 They say, "L her be defiled, let our eyes gloat AIT
Mic 4:11 her be defiled, l our eyes gloat over Zion!" AIT
Mic 6: 1 l the hills hear what you have to say. AIT
Mic 7:14 L them feed in Bashan and Gilead as in days AIT
Hab 2:16 Drink and l your nakedness be exposed! AIT
Hab 2:20 l all the earth be silent before him. AIT
Zep 3:16 Zion; do not l your hands hang limp. AIT
Zec 8: 9 'L your hands be strong so that the temple AIT
Zec 8:13 not be afraid, but l your hands be strong." AIT
Zec 8:21 'L us go at once to entreat the LORD and seek AIT
Zec 8:23 his robe and say, 'L us go with you, because AIT
Zec 11: 9 be your shepherd. L the dying die, and the AIT
Zec 11: 9 L those who are left eat one another's flesh." AIT
Mt 3:15 Jesus replied, "L it be so now; it is proper G918
Mt 5:16 same way, l your light shine before others AIT
Mt 6: 3 do not l your left hand know what your right AIT
Mt 7: 4 'L me take the speck out of your eye G918
Mt 8:13 L it be done just as you believed it would." AIT
Mt 8:21 first l me go and bury my father. G2205
Mt 8:22 and l the dead bury their own dead." G918
Mt 9:29 "According to your faith l it be done to you"; AIT
Mt 10:13 is deserving, l your peace rest on it; if it is AIT
Mt 10:13 if it is not, l your peace return to you. AIT
Mt 11:15 Whoever has ears, l them hear. AIT
Mt 13: 9 Whoever has ears, l them hear. AIT
Mt 13:30 L both grow together until the harvest. G918
Mt 13:43 Whoever has ears, l them hear. AIT
Mt 13:47 is like a net that was l down into the lake G965
Mt 14:36 him to l the sick just touch the edge of AIT
Mt 18:27 canceled the debt and l him go. G918
Mt 19: 6 God has joined together, l no one separate." AIT
Mt 19:14 "L the little children come to me G918
Mt 23:13 nor will you l those enter who are trying to. G918
Mt 24:15 prophet Daniel—l the reader understand— AIT
Mt 24:16 then l those who are in Judea flee to the AIT
Mt 24:17 L no one on the housetop go down to take AIT
Mt 24:18 L no one in the field go back to get their cloak AIT
Mt 24:43 would not have l his house be broken G1572
Mt 26:46 L us go! Here comes my betrayer! AIT
Mt 27:42 L him come down now from the cross, and AIT
Mt 27:43 L God rescue him now if he wants him, for AIT
Mk 1:34 but he would not l the demons speak G918
Mk 1:38 Jesus replied, "L us go somewhere else—to AIT
Mk 4: 9 "Whoever has ears to hear, l them hear." AIT
Mk 4:23 If anyone has ears to hear, l them hear." AIT
Mk 4:35 his disciples, "L us go over to the other side." AIT
Mk 5:19 Jesus did not l him, but said, "Go home to G918
Mk 5:37 He did not l anyone follow him except G918
Mk 5:43 strict orders not to l anyone know about this, AIT
Mk 6:56 They begged him to l them touch even G2671
Mk 7: 8 You have l go of the commands of God G918
Mk 7:12 then you no longer l them do anything for G918
Mk 7:27 "First l the children eat all they want," G918
Mk 9: 5 L us put up three shelters—one for you, one AIT
Mk 10: 9 God has joined together, l no one separate." AIT
Mk 10:14 to them, "L the little children come to me G918
Mk 10:37 "L one of us sit at your right and the other G1443
Mk 11: 6 told them to, and the people l them go. G918
Mk 12:15 "Bring me a denarius and l me look at it." G2671
Mk 13:14 belong—l the reader understand—then let AIT
Mk 13:14 then l those who are in Judea flee to the AIT
Mk 13:15 L no one on the housetop go down or enter AIT
Mk 13:16 L no one in the field go back to get their cloak AIT
Mk 13:36 suddenly, do not l him find you sleeping. AIT
Mk 14:42 L us go! Here comes my betrayer! AIT
Mk 15:32 L this Messiah, this king of Israel, come down AIT
Lk 5: 4 and l down the nets for a catch. G5899
Lk 5: 5 because you say so, I will l down the nets." G5899
Lk 6:42 l me take the speck out of your eye G918
Lk 8: 8 "Whoever has ears to hear, l them hear." AIT
Lk 8:22 "L us go over to the other side of the lake." AIT
Lk 8:32 begged Jesus to l them go into the pigs, G2205
Lk 8:51 he did not l anyone go in with him except G918
Lk 9:33 L us put up three shelters—one for you, one AIT
Lk 9:59 first l me go and bury my father. G2205
Lk 9:60 "L the dead bury their own dead G918
Lk 9:61 first l me go back and say goodbye to G2205
Lk 12:39 he would not have l his house be broken G918
Lk 14:35 "Whoever has ears to hear, l them hear." AIT
Lk 16:28 L him warn them, so that they will not G3968
Lk 16:29 the Prophets; l them listen to them. AIT
Lk 18:16 said, "L the little children come to me G918
Lk 21:21 Then l those who are in Judea flee to the AIT
Lk 21:21 mountains, l those in the city get out, and let AIT
Lk 21:21 and l those in the country not enter the city. AIT
Lk 23:35 l him save himself if he is God's Messiah AIT
Jn 6:12 that are left over. L nothing be wasted." G2671
Jn 7:37 "L anyone who is thirsty come to me and AIT
Jn 8: 7 L any one of you who is without sin be the first to throw AIT
Jn 11: 7 said to his disciples, "L us go back to Judea." AIT
Jn 11:15 so that you may believe. But l us go to him." AIT
Jn 11:16 the disciples, "L us also go, that we may die AIT
Jn 11:44 "Take off the grave clothes and l him go." G918
Jn 11:48 If we l him go on like this, everyone will G918

Jn 14: 1 "*Do* not *l* your hearts *be* **troubled**. AIT
Jn 14:27 *Do* not *l* your hearts *be* **troubled** and do not AIT
Jn 14:31 has commanded me. "Come now; *l us* **leave**. AIT
Jn 18: 8 are looking for me, then **l** these men go." *G918*
Jn 19: 4 him out to you to *l you* **know** that I find no AIT
Jn 19:12 shouting, "If *you* **l** this man **go**, you are no *G668*
Ac 1:20 be deserted; *l there* **be** no one to dwell in it AIT
Ac 2:14 live in Jerusalem, *l me* **explain** this to you AIT
Ac 2:27 *you will* not **l** your holy one see decay. *G1443*
Ac 2:36 "Therefore *l* all Israel **be** assured of this: God AIT
Ac 3:13 though he had decided *to* **l** him **go**. *G668*
Ac 4:21 After further threats *they* **l** them **go**. *G668*
Ac 5:38 these men alone! **L** them **go**! For if their *G918*
Ac 5:40 speak in the name of Jesus, and **l** them **go**. *G668*
Ac 10:11 a large sheet *being* **l down** to earth by its *G2768*
Ac 11: 5 a large sheet *being* **l down** from heaven *G2768*
Ac 13:35 " '*You will* not **l** your holy one see decay *G1443*
Ac 14:16 he **l** all nations go their own way. *G1572*
Ac 15:36 "*L us* **go back** and visit the believers in all the AIT
Ac 16:37 *L them* **come** themselves and escort us out." AIT
Ac 17: 9 the others post bond and **l** them **go**. *G668*
Ac 19:30 but the disciples *would* not **l** him. *G1572*
Ac 21:39 Please **l** me speak to the people. *G2205*
Ac 23:32 The next day *they* **l** the cavalry go on with *G1572*
Ac 25: 5 *L* some of your leaders **come with** me, and if AIT
Ac 27:17 sea anchor and *l* the ship *be* **driven along**. AIT
Ac 27:30 the sailors **l** the lifeboat **down** into the *G5899*
Ac 27:32 that held the lifeboat and **l** it drift away. *G1572*
Ro 3: 4 *L* God **be** true, and every human AIT
Ro 3: 8 we say—"*L us* **do** evil that good may result"? AIT
Ro 6:12 Therefore *do* not *l* sin **reign** in your mortal AIT
Ro 13: 1 *L* everyone *be* **subject** to the governing AIT
Ro 13: 8 *L* no **debt remain outstanding**, except the AIT
Ro 13:12 So *l us* **put aside** the deeds of darkness and AIT
Ro 13:13 *L us* **behave** decently, as in the daytime, not AIT
Ro 14:13 Therefore *l us* stop **passing judgment** on one AIT
Ro 14:16 *do* not *l* what you know is good *be* **spoken of as evil** AIT
Ro 14:19 *L us* therefore **make every effort** to do what AIT
Ro 15:11 all you Gentiles; *l* all the peoples **extol** him." AIT
1Co 1:31 "*L* the one who boasts **boast** in the Lord." AIT
1Co 5: 8 Therefore *l us* **keep the Festival**, not with the AIT
1Co 7:15 unbeliever leaves, *l it be* **so**. The brother AIT
1Co 7:21 Don't *l* it **trouble** you—although if you can AIT
1Co 10:13 he *will* not **l** you be tempted beyond what *G1572*
1Co 14:37 *l them* **acknowledge** that what I am writing to AIT
1Co 15:32 dead are not raised, "*L us* **eat** and drink, for AIT
1Co 15:58 **L** nothing move you. Always give NDT
1Co 16:22 not love the Lord, *l that person* **be** cursed! AIT
2Co 2: 4 grieve you but to *l you* **know** the depth of my AIT
2Co 4: 6 who said, "*L* light **shine** out of darkness," AIT
2Co 7: 1 *l us* **purify** ourselves from everything that AIT
2Co 10:17 "*L* the one who boasts **boast** in the Lord." AIT
2Co 11:16 *L* no one **take** me **for** a fool. But if AIT
Gal 1: 8 to you, *l them* **be** under God's curse! AIT
Gal 1: 9 you accepted, *l them* **be** under God's curse! AIT
Gal 3:15 *l me* **take an example** from everyday life. AIT
Gal 5: 1 and *do* not *l yourselves be* **burdened** again AIT
Gal 5: 2 you that if *you l yourselves be* **circumcised**, AIT
Gal 5:25 by the Spirit, *l us* **keep in step with** the Spirit. AIT
Gal 5:26 *L us* not **become** conceited, provoking and AIT
Gal 6: 9 *L us* not *become* **weary** in doing good, for at AIT
Gal 6:10 have opportunity, *l us* **do** good to all people AIT
Gal 6:17 From now on, *l* no one **cause** me trouble, for AIT
Eph 4:26 *Do* not *l* the sun **go down** while you are still AIT
Eph 4:29 *Do* not *l* any unwholesome talk **come out** of AIT
Eph 5: 6 *L* no one **deceive** you with empty words, for AIT
Php 3:16 Only *l us* **live up to** what we have already AIT
Php 4: 5 *L* your gentleness *be* **evident** to all. The Lord AIT
Col 2:16 Therefore *do* not *l* anyone **judge** you by what AIT
Col 2:18 *Do* not *l* anyone who delights in false humility and the worship of angels **disqualify** AIT
Col 3:15 *L* the peace of Christ **rule** in your hearts, AIT
Col 3:16 *L* the message of Christ **dwell** among you AIT
Col 4: 6 **L** your conversation be always full of grace NDT
1Th 5: 6 *l us* not *be* like others, *who are* **asleep**, but AIT
1Th 5: 6 who are asleep, but *l us be* **awake** and sober. AIT
1Th 5: 8 to the day, *l us be* **sober**, putting on faith AIT
2Th 2: 3 Don't *l* anyone **deceive** you in any way, for AIT
1Ti 3:10 against them, *l them* **serve as deacons**. AIT
1Ti 4:12 Don't *l* anyone **look down on** you because AIT
1Ti 5:16 not *l* the church *be* **burdened** with them, AIT
Titus 2:15 *Do* not *l* anyone **despise** you. AIT
Heb 1: 6 "*L* all God's angels **worship** him. AIT
Heb 4: 1 *l us be* **careful** that none of you be found to AIT
Heb 4:11 *L us*, therefore, **make every effort** to enter AIT
Heb 4:14 God, *l us* **hold firmly** to the faith we profess. AIT
Heb 4:16 *L us* then **approach** God's throne of grace AIT
Heb 6: 1 Therefore *l us* **move beyond** the elementary AIT
Heb 10:22 *l us* **draw near** to God with a sincere heart AIT
Heb 10:23 *L us* **hold** unswervingly to the hope we AIT
Heb 10:24 And *l us* **consider** how we may spur one AIT
Heb 12: 1 *l us* **throw off** everything that hinders and the AIT
Heb 12: 1 And *l us* **run** with perseverance the race AIT
Heb 12:28 cannot be shaken, *l us be* thankful, and so AIT
Heb 13:13 *L us*, then, **go** to him outside the camp AIT
Heb 13:15 *l us* continually **offer** to God a sacrifice of AIT
Jas 1: 4 *L* perseverance **finish** its work so that you AIT
Jas 3:13 *L them* **show** it by their good life, by deeds AIT
Jas 5:13 you in trouble? *L them* **pray**. Is anyone happy AIT
Jas 5:13 anyone happy? *L them* **sing songs of praise**. AIT
Jas 5:14 *L them* **call** the elders of the church to pray AIT
1Jn 3: 7 children, *do* not *l* anyone **lead** you **astray**. AIT
1Jn 3:18 *l us* not **love** with words or speech but with AIT
1Jn 4: 7 Dear friends, *l us* **love** one another, for love AIT
Rev 2: 7 *l them* **hear** what the Spirit says to the AIT
Rev 2:11 *l them* **hear** what the Spirit says to the AIT
Rev 2:17 *l them* **hear** what the Spirit says to the AIT
Rev 2:29 *l them* **hear** what the Spirit says to the AIT
Rev 3: 6 *l them* **hear** what the Spirit says to the AIT
Rev 3:13 *l them* **hear** what the Spirit says to the AIT
Rev 3:22 *l them* **hear** what the Spirit says to the AIT
Rev 13: 9 Whoever has ears, *l them* **hear**. AIT
Rev 13:18 *L* the person who has insight **calculate** the AIT
Rev 19: 7 *L us* **rejoice** and be glad and give him glory AIT
Rev 22:11 *L* the one who does wrong continue *to* **do wrong** AIT
Rev 22:11 *l* the vile person continue *to be* **vile**; let AIT
Rev 22:11 *l* the one who does right continue *to* **do** right AIT
Rev 22:11 and *l* the holy person continue *to be* **holy**." AIT
Rev 22:17 And *l* the one who hears **say**, "Come!" AIT
Rev 22:17 *L* the one who is thirsty **come**; and let the AIT
Rev 22:17 and *l* the one who wishes **take** the free gift of AIT

LET'S (47) [LET, WE]

Ge 4: 8 to his brother Abel, "*L* **go out** *to* the field." AIT
Ge 11: 3 *l* **make bricks** and bake them thoroughly." AIT
Ge 13: 8 "*L* not **have** any quarreling between you AIT
Ge 13: 9 land before you? *L* **part company**. If you go AIT
Ge 19:32 *L* **get** our father **to drink** wine and then sleep AIT
Ge 19:34 *L* **get** him **to drink** wine again tonight, and AIT
Ge 24:57 "*L* **call** the young woman and ask her about it AIT
Ge 31:44 Come now, *l* **make** a covenant, you and I, and AIT
Ge 37:17 "I heard them say, '*L* **go** to Dothan.' " AIT
Ge 37:20 *l* **kill** him and throw him into one of these AIT
Ge 37:21 from their hands. "*L* not **take** his life," he said AIT
Ge 37:27 *l* **sell** him to the Ishmaelites and not lay our AIT
Ex 14:25 "*L* **get away** from the Israelites! AIT
Jdg 14:13 "Tell us your riddle," they said. "*L* **hear** it." AIT
Jdg 18: 9 "Come on, *l* **attack** them! We have seen AIT
Jdg 19:11 *l* **stop** at this city of the Jebusites and spend AIT
Jdg 19:13 *l try to* **reach** Gibeah or Ramah and spend AIT
Jdg 19:28 said to her, "Get up; *l* **go**." But there was no AIT
Jdg 20:32 "*L* **retreat** and draw them away from the city AIT
1Sa 9: 5 *l* **go back**, or my father will stop AIT
1Sa 9: 6 he says comes true. *L* **go** there now. Perhaps AIT
1Sa 9:10 "Come, *l* **go**." So they set out for AIT
1Sa 14: 1 *l* **go over** to the Philistine outpost on the AIT
1Sa 14: 6 *l* **go over** to the outpost of those AIT
1Sa 20:11 Jonathan said, "*l* **go out** *into* the field." AIT
1Sa 26:11 water jug that are near his head, and *l* **go**." AIT
2Sa 2:14 "*L have* some of the young men **get up** and AIT
2Ki 4:10 *L* **make** a small room on the roof and put in it AIT
2Ki 7: 4 So *l* **go over** to the camp of the Arameans AIT
2Ki 7: 9 *L* **go at once** and report this to the royal AIT
Pr 1:11 along with us; *l* **lie in wait** for innocent blood AIT
Pr 1:11 *l* **ambush** some harmless soul AIT
Pr 1:12 *l* **swallow** them alive, like the grave, and AIT
Pr 7:18 *l* **drink deeply** *of* love till morning AIT
Pr 7:18 till morning; *l* **enjoy ourselves** with love! AIT
Jer 18:18 *l* **make plans** against Jeremiah; for AIT
Jer 18:18 *l* **attack** him with our tongues and pay no AIT
Jer 20:10 Denounce him! *L* **denounce** him!" All my AIT
Mt 21:38 *l* **kill** him and take his inheritance AIT
Mt 27:49 *L* **see** if Elijah comes to save him. AIT
Mk 12: 7 *l* **kill** him, and the inheritance will be AIT
Mk 15:36 *L* **see** if Elijah comes to take him down," AIT
Lk 2:15 "*L* **go** to Bethlehem and see this thing that AIT
Lk 15:23 calf and kill it. *L* **have a feast** and celebrate. AIT
Lk 20:14 '*L* **kill** him, and the inheritance AIT
Jn 19:24 "*L* not **tear** it," they said to one another AIT
Jn 19:24 "*L* **decide by lot** who will get it. AIT

LETHEK (1)

Hos 3: 2 about a homer and a **l** *of* barley. H4390

LETS (8) [LET]

Ex 21:13 but God **l** *it* **happen**, they are H628+4200+3338
Ex 22: 5 vineyard and **l** them **stray** and they graze H8938
2Ki 10:24 "If one of you **l** any of the men I am placing NDT
Job 12:15 is drought; if *he* **l** them **loose**, they H8938
Job 20:13 bear to let it go and *l* it **linger** in his mouth, AIT
Job 39:14 the ground and **l** them **warm** in the sand, H2801
Pr 14:33 even among fools *she* **l** *herself* **be known**. H3359
Gal 5: 3 man *who* **l** *himself* **be circumcised** that he AIT

LETTER (48) [LETTERS]

2Sa 11:14 David wrote a **l** to Joab and sent it H6219
2Ki 5: 5 "I will send a **l** to the king of Israel." H6219
2Ki 5: 6 The **l** that he took to the king of Israel read H6219
2Ki 5: 6 "With this **l** I am sending my servant H6219
2Ki 5: 7 As soon as the king of Israel read the **l** H6219
2Ki 10: 2 Now as soon as this **l** reaches you, H6219
2Ki 10: 6 Then Jehu wrote them a second **l**, saying H6219
2Ki 10: 7 When the **l** arrived, these men took the H6219
2Ki 19:14 received the **l** from the messengers H6219
2Ch 2:11 king of Tyre replied by **l** to Solomon: H4181
2Ch 21:12 Jehoram received a **l** from Elijah the H4844
Ezr 4: 7 rest of his associates wrote a **l** to Artaxerxes. NDT
Ezr 4: 7 The **l** was written in Aramaic script and in H5981
Ezr 4: 8 secretary wrote a **l** against Jerusalem to A10007
Ezr 4:11 This is a copy of the **l** they sent him.) A10007
Ezr 4:18 The **l** you sent us has been read and A10496
Ezr 4:23 as the copy of the **l** of King Artaxerxes A10496
Ezr 5: 6 This is a copy of the **l** that Tattenai A10007
Ezr 7:11 This is a copy of the **l** King Artaxerxes had H5981
Ne 2: 8 And may I have a **l** to Asaph, keeper of the H115
Ne 6: 5 in his hand was an unsealed **l** H115
Est 9:26 written in this **l** and because of what they H115
Est 9:29 to confirm this second **l** *concerning* Purim. H115
Isa 37:14 received the **l** from the messengers H6219
Jer 29: 1 This is the text of the **l** that the prophet H6219
Jer 29: 3 He entrusted the **l** to Elasah son of Shaphan NDT
Jer 29:29 read the **l** to Jeremiah the prophet. H6219
Mt 5:18 not the **smallest l**, not the least *G2740*
Ac 15:23 With them *they* **sent** *the following* **l**: The *G1211*
Ac 15:30 the church together and delivered the **l**. *G2186*
Ac 23:25 He wrote a **l** as follows: *G2186*
Ac 23:33 they delivered the **l** to the governor and *G2186*
Ac 23:34 The governor read the **l** and asked what NDT
Ro 16:22 who wrote down this **l**, greet you in the *G2186*
1Co 5: 9 I wrote to you in my **l** not to associate with *G2186*
2Co 3: 2 You yourselves are our **l**, written on our *G2186*
2Co 3: 3 You show that you are a **l** from Christ, the *G2186*
2Co 3: 6 covenant—not *of* the **l** but of the Spirit *G1207*
2Co 3: 6 of the Spirit; for the **l** kills, but the Spirit *G1207*
2Co 7: 8 Even if I caused you sorrow by my **l**, I do *G2186*
2Co 7: 8 I see that my **l** hurt you, but only for *G2186*
Col 4:16 After this **l** has been read to you, see that *G2186*
Col 4:16 that you in turn read the **l** from Laodicea. NDT
1Th 5:27 the Lord to have this **l** read to all the *G2186*
2Th 2: 2 a prophecy or by word of mouth or by **l**— *G2186*
2Th 2:15 whether by word of mouth or by **l**. *G2186*
2Th 3:14 does not obey our instruction in this **l**. *G2186*
2Pe 3: 1 this is now my second **l** to you. *G2186*

LETTERS (29) [LETTER]

1Ki 21: 8 So she wrote **l** in Ahab's name, placed H6219
1Ki 21: 9 In those **l** she wrote: "Proclaim a day of H6219
1Ki 21:11 directed in the **l** she had written to them H6219
2Ki 10: 1 So Jehu wrote **l** and sent them to Samaria H6219
2Ki 20:12 of Babylon sent Hezekiah **l** and a gift, H6219
2Ch 30: 1 Judah and also wrote **l** to Ephraim and H115
2Ch 30: 6 Israel and Judah with **l** from the king and H115
2Ch 32:17 The king also wrote **l** ridiculing the LORD H6219
Ne 2: 7 may I have **l** to the governors of H115
Ne 2: 9 gave them the king's **l**. H115
Ne 6:17 of Judah were sending many **l** to Tobiah, H115
Ne 6:19 And Tobiah sent **l** to intimidate me. H115
Est 9:20 he sent **l** to all the Jews throughout H6219
Est 9:30 And Mordecai sent **l** to all the Jews in the H6219
Isa 39: 1 of Babylon sent Hezekiah **l** and a gift, H6219
Jer 29:25 You sent **l** in your own name to all the H6219
Ac 9: 2 asked him for **l** to the synagogues in *G2186*
Ac 22: 5 I even obtained **l** from them to their *G2186*
Ac 28:21 not received any **l** from Judea concerning *G1207*
1Co 16: 3 I will give **l of introduction** to the men *G2186*
2Co 3: 1 **l** of recommendation to you or from you? *G2186*
2Co 3: 7 which was engraved in **l** on stone, came *G1207*
2Co 10: 9 to be trying to frighten you with my **l**. *G2186*
2Co 10:10 some say, "His **l** are weighty and forceful *G2186*
2Co 10:11 what we are in our **l** when we are absent, *G2186*
Gal 6:11 See what large **l** I use as I write to you *G1207*
2Th 3:17 is the distinguishing mark in all my **l**. *G2186*
2Pe 3:16 He writes the same way in all his **l** *G2186*
2Pe 3:16 **His l** contain some things that are hard *G4005S*

LETTING (5) [LET]

Ex 8:29 again by not **l** the people **go** to offer H8938
1Sa 20: 2 small, without **l** me **know**. H1655+906+265
1Sa 21:13 the gate and **l** saliva **run down** his beard. H3718
1Ki 1:27 without **l** his servants **know** who should H3359
Isa 32:20 **l** your cattle and donkeys **range free** H8938+8079

LETUSHITES (1)

Ge 25: 3 the Ashurites, the **L** and the Leummites. H4322

LEUMMITES (1)

Ge 25: 3 the Ashurites, the Letushites and the **L**. H4212

LEVEL (14) [LEVELED, LEVELS]

1Ki 6: 8 led up to the **middle** *l* and from there to the AIT
Ps 26:12 My feet stand on **l ground**; in the great H4793
Ps 65:10 You drench its furrows and **l** its ridges; H5737
Ps 143:10 may your good Spirit lead me on **l** ground. H4793
Isa 26: 7 The path of the righteous is **l**; you, the H4797
Isa 40: 4 the rough ground shall become **l**, the H4793
Isa 45: 2 go before you and *will* **l** the mountains; H3837
Jer 31: 9 of water on a **l** path where they will H3838
Eze 13:14 with whitewash and *will* **l** it to the ground H5595
Eze 41: 6 one above another, thirty on *each* **l**. H7193
Eze 41: 7 were wider **at each successive l**. H4200+5087+2025+4200+5087+2025
Zec 4: 7 Zerubbabel you will become **l ground**. H4793
Lk 6:17 down with them and stood on a **l** place. *G4268*
Heb 12:13 "Make **l** paths for your feet," so that the *G3981*

LEVELED (3) [LEVEL]

Isa 28:25 When *he has* **l** the surface, does he not H8750
Isa 32:19 the city *is* **l completely**, H9164+928+2021+9168
Jer 51:58 thick wall *will* **be l** and her high H6910+6910

LEVELS (3) [LEVEL]

Isa 26: 5 *he* **l** it to the ground and casts it down to H9164
Eze 41: 6 The side rooms were on three **l**, one above NDT
Eze 42: 3 gallery faced gallery at the **three** *l*. AIT

LEVI (56) [LEVI'S, LEVITE, LEVITES, LEVITICAL]
Ge 29:34 him three sons." So he was named **L**. H4290
Ge 34:25 Simeon and L, Dinah's brothers, H4290
Ge 34:30 Then Jacob said to Simeon and L, "You H4290
Ge 35:23 of Jacob, Simeon, L, Judah, Issachar and H4290
Ge 46:11 The sons of L: Gershon, Kohath and H4290
Ge 49: 5 "Simeon and L are brothers—their swords H4290
Ex 1: 2 Reuben, Simeon, L and Judah; H4290
Ex 2: 1 a man of the tribe of L married a Levite H4290
Ex 6:16 names of the sons of L according to their H4290
Ex 6:16 Kohath and Merari. L lived 137 years. H4290
Ex 6:19 were the clans of L according to their H4290
Nu 1:49 count the tribe of L or include them in the H4290
Nu 3: 6 "Bring the tribe of L and present them to H4290
Nu 3:17 These were the names of the sons of L H4290
Nu 16: 1 of Kohath, the son of L, and certain H4290
Nu 17: 3 On the staff of L write Aaron's name, for H4290
Nu 17: 8 which represented the tribe of L, had not H4290
Nu 26:59 a descendant of L, who was born to the H4290
Dt 10: 8 set apart the tribe of L to carry the ark of H4290
Dt 18: 1 the whole tribe of L—are to have no H4290
Dt 27:12 Simeon, L, Judah, Issachar, Joseph and H4290
Dt 33: 8 About L he said: "Your Thummim and H4290
Jos 13:14 But to the tribe of L he gave no H4291
Jos 13:33 But to the tribe of L, Moses had given no H4291
1Ch 2: 1 Reuben, Simeon, L, Judah, Issachar H4290
1Ch 6: 1 The sons of L: Gershon, Kohath and H4290
1Ch 6:16 The sons of L: Gershon, Kohath and H4290
1Ch 6:38 of Kohath, the son of L, the son of Israel; H4290
1Ch 6:43 the son of Gershon, the son of L; H4290
1Ch 6:47 of Mushi, the son of Merari, the son of L. H4290
1Ch 12:26 from L—4,600, H1201+4291
1Ch 21: 6 did not include L and Benjamin in the H4290
1Ch 23: 6 divisions corresponding to the sons of L: H4290
1Ch 23:14 God were counted as part of the tribe of L. H4290
1Ch 23:24 the descendants of L by their families— H4290
1Ch 24:20 As for the rest of the descendants of L H4290
1Ch 27:17 over L: Hashabiah son of Kemuel; over H4290
Ezr 8:18 from the descendants of Mahli son of L H4291
Ne 12:23 the descendants of L up to the time of H4290
Ps 135:20 house of L, praise the LORD; you who fear H4290
Eze 48:31 the gate of Judah and the gate of L. H4290
Zec 12:13 the clan of the house of L and their wives H4290
Mal 2: 4 so that my covenant with L may continue," H4290
Mal 2: 8 you have violated the covenant with L," H4290
Mk 2:14 he saw L son of Alphaeus sitting at the G3322
Mk 2:14 told him, and L got up and followed him. NDT
Lk 3:24 of Matthat, the son *of* L, the son of Melki, G3322
Lk 3:29 of Jorim, the son of Matthat, the son *of* L, G3322
Lk 5:27 by the name of L sitting at his tax booth G3322
Lk 5:28 L got up, left everything and followed NDT
Lk 5:29 Then L held a great banquet for Jesus at G3322
Heb 7: 5 the descendants *of* L who become priests G3322
Heb 7: 6 did not trace his descent from L, yet he G899S
Heb 7: 9 One might even say that L, who collects G3322
Heb 7:10 L was still in the body of his ancestor. NDT
Rev 7: 7 from the tribe *of* L 12,000, from the G3322

LEVI'S (1) [LEVI]
Mk 2:15 Jesus was having dinner at L house, G899S

LEVIATHAN (6) [LEVIATHAN'S]
Job 3: 8 that day, those who are ready to rouse L. H4293
Job 41: 1 "Can you pull in L with a fishhook or tie H4293
Ps 74:14 the heads of L and gave it as food H4293
Ps 104:26 go to and fro, and L, which you formed to H4293
Isa 27: 1 powerful sword—L the gliding serpent H4293
Isa 27: 1 the gliding serpent, L the coiling serpent H4293

LEVIATHAN'S (1) [LEVIATHAN]
Job 41:12 "I will not fail to speak of L limbs, its H2257S

LEVITE (30) [LEVI]
Ex 2: 1 of the tribe of Levi married a L woman, H4290
Ex 4:14 "What about your brother, Aaron the L? H4291
Ex 6:25 These were the heads of the L families H4291
Nu 3:20 These were the L clans, according to their H4291
Nu 26:58 These also were L clans: the Libnite clan H4290
Dt 18: 6 If a L moves from one of your towns H4291
Dt 26:12 you shall give it to the L, the foreigner, H4291
Dt 26:13 sacred portion and have given it to the L, H4291
Jos 21:27 The L clans of the Gershonites were given: H4291
Jdg 17: 7 A young L from Bethlehem in Judah, who H4291
Jdg 17: 9 "I'm a L from Bethlehem in Judah," he H4291
Jdg 17:11 So the L agreed to live with him, and the H4291
Jdg 17:12 Then Micah installed the L, and the young H4291
Jdg 17:13 since this L has become my priest. H4291
Jdg 18: 3 they recognized the voice of the young L H4291
Jdg 18:15 of the young L *at* Micah's place and H4291
Jdg 19: 1 Now a L who lived in a remote area in the H4291
Jdg 20: 4 So the L, the husband of the murdered H4291
1Ch 9:31 A L named Mattithiah, the firstborn son of H4291
1Ch 9:33 musicians, heads of L families, stayed in H4291
1Ch 9:34 All these were heads of L families, chiefs H4291
1Ch 15:22 Kenaniah the head L was in charge of the H4291
1Ch 24: 6 son of Nethanel, a L, recorded their H4291
2Ch 20:14 Mattaniah, a L and descendant of Asaph H4291
2Ch 31:12 Konaniah, a L, was the overseer in charge H4291
2Ch 31:14 Kore son of Imnah the L, keeper of the H4291
Ezr 10:15 by Meshullam and Shabbethai the L, H4291
Ne 13:13 a L named Pedaiah in charge of the H4291
Lk 10:32 a L, when he came to the place G3324
Ac 4:36 Joseph, a L from Cyprus, whom the G3324

LEVITES (280) [LEVI]
Ex 32:26 And all the L rallied to him. H1201+4290
Ex 32:28 The L did as Moses commanded H1201+4290
Ex 38:21 command by the L under the direction H4291
Lev 25:32 " 'The L always have the right to redeem H4291
Lev 25:33 So the property of the L is redeemable H4291
Lev 25:33 in the towns of the L are their property H4291
Nu 1:47 The ancestral tribe of the L, however, was H4291
Nu 1:50 appoint the L to be in charge of the H4291
Nu 1:51 is to move, the L are to take it down, and H4291
Nu 1:51 is to be set up, the L shall do it. H4291
Nu 1:53 The L, however, are to set up their tents H4291
Nu 1:53 The L are to be responsible for the care of H4291
Nu 2:17 the camp of the L will set out in the H4291
Nu 2:33 The L, however, were not counted along H4291
Nu 3: 9 Give the L to Aaron and his sons; they are H4291
Nu 3:12 "I have taken the L from among the H4291
Nu 3:12 of every Israelite woman. The L are mine, H4291
Nu 3:15 "Count the L by their families and H1201+4290
Nu 3:32 chief leader of the L was Eleazar son of H4291
Nu 3:39 The total number of L counted at the H4291
Nu 3:41 Take the L for me in place of all the H4291
Nu 3:41 the livestock of the L in place of all the H4291
Nu 3:45 "Take the L in place of all the firstborn of H4291
Nu 3:45 the livestock of the L in place of their H4291
Nu 3:45 their livestock. The L are to be mine. H4291
Nu 3:46 who exceed the number of the L, H4291
Nu 3:49 exceeded the number redeemed by the L. H4291
Nu 4: 2 branch of the L by their clans and H1201+4290
Nu 4:18 clans are not destroyed from among the L. H4291
Nu 4:46 Israel counted all the L by their clans and H4291
Nu 7: 5 Give them to the L as each man's work H4291
Nu 7: 6 carts and oxen and gave them to the L. H4291
Nu 8: 6 "Take the L from among all the Israelites H4291
Nu 8: 9 Bring the L to the front of the tent of H4291
Nu 8:10 You are to bring the L before the LORD, H4291
Nu 8:11 is to present the L before the LORD as a H4291
Nu 8:12 "Then the L are to lay their hands on the H4291
Nu 8:12 offering, to make atonement for the L. H4291
Nu 8:13 Have the L stand in front of Aaron and his H4291
Nu 8:14 you are to set the L apart from the other H4291
Nu 8:14 other Israelites, and the L will be mine. H4291
Nu 8:15 have purified the L and presented them H4291
Nu 8:18 And I have taken the L in place of all the H4291
Nu 8:19 I have given the L as gifts to Aaron and H4291
Nu 8:20 community did with the L just as the LORD H4291
Nu 8:21 The L purified themselves and washed H4291
Nu 8:22 the L came to do their work at the tent of H4291
Nu 8:22 They did with the L just as the LORD H4291
Nu 8:24 "This applies to the L: Men twenty-five H4291
Nu 8:26 are to assign the responsibilities of the L." H4291
Nu 16: 7 You L have gone too far! H1201+4290
Nu 16: 8 said to Korah, "Now listen, you L! H1201+4290
Nu 16:10 and all your fellow L near himself, H1201+4290
Nu 18: 2 Bring your fellow L from your H4751+4290
Nu 18: 6 selected your fellow L from among the H4291
Nu 18:21 "I give to the L all the tithes in H1201+4290
Nu 18:23 It is the L who are to do the work at the H4291
Nu 18:24 I give to the L as their inheritance the H4291
Nu 18:26 "Speak to the L and say to them: 'When H4291
Nu 18:30 "Say to the L: 'When you present the best H4291
Nu 26:57 These were the L who were counted by H4291
Nu 26:59 who was born to the L in Egypt. H4290
Nu 26:62 All the male L a month old or more NDT
Nu 31:30 Give them to the L, who are responsible H4291
Nu 31:47 gave them to the L, who were H4291
Nu 35: 2 to give the L towns to live in from H4291
Nu 35: 4 that you give the L will extend a thousand H4291
Nu 35: 6 the towns you give the L will be cities of H4291
Nu 35: 7 In all you must give the L forty-eight towns H4291
Nu 35: 8 The towns you give the L from the land the H4291
Dt 10: 9 That is why the L have no share or H4290
Dt 12:12 the L from your towns who have no H4291
Dt 12:18 servants, and the L from your towns—and H4291
Dt 12:19 not to neglect the L as long as you live in H4291
Dt 14:27 do not neglect the L living in your towns, H4291
Dt 14:29 so that the L (who have no allotment or H4291
Dt 16:11 female servants, the L in your towns, and H4291
Dt 16:14 female servants, and the L, the foreigners, H4291
Dt 18: 7 like all his fellow L who serve there in the H4291
Dt 26:11 Then you and the L and the foreigners H4291
Dt 27:14 The L shall recite to all the people of H4291
Dt 31:25 this command to the L who carried the ark H4291
Jos 14: 3 had not granted the L an inheritance H4291
Jos 14: 4 The L received no share of the land but H4291
Jos 18: 7 The L, however, do not get a portion H4291
Jos 21: 1 family heads of the L approached Eleazar H4291
Jos 21: 3 Israelites gave the L the following towns H4291
Jos 21: 4 The L who were descendants of Aaron the H4291
Jos 21: 8 allotted to the L these towns and their H4291
Jos 21:10 from the Kohathite clans of the L, H1201+4290
Jos 21:20 clans of the L were allotted towns H4291
Jos 21:34 the rest of the L) were given: H4291
Jos 21:40 who were the rest of the L, came to H5476+4291
Jos 21:41 The towns of the L in the territory held by H4291
1Sa 6:15 The L took down the ark of the LORD H4291
1Sa 6:18 rock on which the L set the ark of the LORD NDT
2Sa 15:24 all the L who were with him were H4291
1Ki 8: 4 The priests and L carried them up, H4291
1Ki 12:31 even though they were not L. H1201+4290
1Ch 6:19 are the clans of the L listed according to H4291
1Ch 6:48 Their fellow L were assigned to all the H4291
1Ch 6:64 Israelites gave the L these towns and their H4291
1Ch 6:77 the rest of the L) received the following: NDT
1Ch 9: 2 Israelites, priests, L and temple servants. H4291
1Ch 9:14 Of the L: Shemaiah son of Hasshub, the H4291
1Ch 9:17 Ahiman and their **fellow** L, Shallum their H278
1Ch 9:18 belonging to the camp of the L. H1201+4290
1Ch 9:25 Their **fellow** L in their villages had to come H278
1Ch 9:26 who were L, were entrusted with H4291
1Ch 9:32 Kohathites, their **fellow** L, were in charge of H278
1Ch 13: 2 to the priests and L who are with them in H4291
1Ch 15: 2 "No one but the L may carry the ark of H4291
1Ch 15: 4 the descendants of Aaron and the L: H4291
1Ch 15:11 Shemaiah, Eliel and Amminadab the L. H4291
1Ch 15:12 you and your **fellow** L are to consecrate H278
1Ch 15:13 It was because you, the L, did not bring it NDT
1Ch 15:14 So the priests and L consecrated H4291
1Ch 15:15 And the L carried the ark of God H1201+4291
1Ch 15:16 the leaders of the L to appoint their fellow H4291
1Ch 15:16 to appoint their **fellow** L as musicians to H278
1Ch 15:17 So the L appointed Heman son of Joel H4291
1Ch 15:26 God had helped the L who were carrying H4291
1Ch 15:27 as were all the L who were carrying the H4291
1Ch 16: 4 some of the L to minister before H4291
1Ch 23: 2 of Israel, as well as the priests and L. H4291
1Ch 23: 3 The L thirty years old or more were H4291
1Ch 23: 6 David separated **the** L into divisions H4392S
1Ch 23:26 the L no longer need to carry the H4291
1Ch 23:27 the L were counted from those H1201+4290
1Ch 23:28 The duty of **the** L was to help Aaron's H4392S
1Ch 23:32 And so the L carried out their NDT
1Ch 24: 6 of families of the priests and of the L— H4291
1Ch 24:30 These were the L, according to H1201+4290
1Ch 24:31 of families of the priests and of the L. H4291
1Ch 26:17 There were six L a day on the east, four a H4291
1Ch 26:20 Their fellow L were in charge of the H4291
1Ch 28:13 the divisions of the priests and L, H4291
1Ch 28:21 of the priests and L are ready for all the H4291
2Ch 5: 4 Israel had arrived, the L took up the ark, H4291
2Ch 5:12 All the L who were musicians—Asaph H4291
2Ch 7: 6 as did the L with the LORD's musical H4291
2Ch 7: 6 Opposite **the** L, the priests blew their H4392S
2Ch 8:14 the L to lead the praise and to assist H4291
2Ch 8:15 to the priests or to the L in any matter, H4291
2Ch 11:13 The priests and L from all their districts H4291
2Ch 11:14 The L even abandoned their pasturelands H4291
2Ch 11:16 followed **the** L to Jerusalem to offer H2157S
2Ch 13: 9 of Aaron, and the L, and make priests of H4291
2Ch 13:10 are sons of Aaron, and the L assist them. H4291
2Ch 17: 8 With them were certain L—Shemaiah H4291
2Ch 19: 8 Jehoshaphat appointed some of the L H4291
2Ch 19:11 the L will serve as officials before you. H4291
2Ch 20:19 Then some L from the Kohathites and H4291
2Ch 23: 2 gathered the L and the heads of H4291
2Ch 23: 4 of you priests and L who are going on H4291
2Ch 23: 6 the LORD except the priests and L on duty; H4291
2Ch 23: 7 The L are to station themselves around the H4291
2Ch 23: 8 The L and all the men of Judah did just H4291
2Ch 24: 5 the priests and L and said to them, H4291
2Ch 24: 5 But the L did not act at once. H4291
2Ch 24: 6 you required the L to bring in from Judah H4291
2Ch 24:11 was brought in by the L to the king's H4291
2Ch 29: 4 He brought in the priests and the L H4291
2Ch 29: 5 "Listen to me, L! Consecrate H4291
2Ch 29:12 Then these L set to work: from the H4291
2Ch 29:15 assembled their **fellow** L and consecrated H278
2Ch 29:16 The L took it and carried it out to the H4291
2Ch 29:25 He stationed the L in the temple of the H4291
2Ch 29:26 So the L stood ready with David's H4291
2Ch 29:30 officials ordered the L to praise the LORD H4291
2Ch 29:34 their relatives the L helped them until the H4291
2Ch 29:34 the L had been more conscientious in H4291
2Ch 30:15 The priests and the L were ashamed and H4291
2Ch 30:16 altar the blood handed to them by the L. H4291
2Ch 30:17 the L had to kill the Passover lambs for all H4291
2Ch 30:21 while the L and priests praised the LORD H4291
2Ch 30:22 Hezekiah spoke encouragingly to all the L, H4291
2Ch 30:25 with the priests and L and all who had H4291
2Ch 30:27 The priests and the L stood to bless the H4291
2Ch 31: 2 assigned the priests and L to divisions— H4291
2Ch 31: 2 according to their duties as priests or L— H4291
2Ch 31: 4 due the priests and L so they could devote H4291
2Ch 31: 9 asked the priests and L about the heaps; H4291
2Ch 31:17 likewise to the L twenty years old or H4291
2Ch 31:19 recorded in the genealogies of the L. H4291
2Ch 34: 9 which the L who were the gatekeepers H4291
2Ch 34:12 Obadiah, L descended from Merari H4291
2Ch 34:12 The L—all who were skilled in playing H4291
2Ch 34:13 Some of the L were secretaries, scribes H4291
2Ch 34:30 the priests and the L—all the people from H4291
2Ch 35: 3 He said to the L, who instructed all Israel H4291
2Ch 35: 5 with a group of L for each subdivision H4291
2Ch 35: 8 to the people and the priests and L. H4291
2Ch 35: 9 the leaders of the L, provided five H4291
2Ch 35: 9 five hundred head of cattle for the L. H4291
2Ch 35:10 their places with the L in their divisions as H4291
2Ch 35:11 to them, while the L skinned the animals. H4291
2Ch 35:14 So the L made preparations for H4291
2Ch 35:15 because their fellow L made the H4291
2Ch 35:18 the L and all Judah and Israel who were H4291
Ezr 1: 5 the priests and L—everyone whose H4291

Ezr 2:40 The L: the descendants of Jeshua and H4291
Ezr 2:70 The priests, the L, the musicians, the H4291
Ezr 3: 8 the priests and the L and all who had H4291
Ezr 3: 8 They appointed L twenty years old and H4291
Ezr 3: 9 brothers—all L—joined together in H4291
Ezr 3:10 trumpets, and the L (the sons of Asaph) H4291
Ezr 3:12 the older priests and L and family heads, H4291
Ezr 6:16 the L and the rest of the exiles A10387
Ezr 6:18 divisions and the L in their groups for the A10387
Ezr 6:20 The priests and L had purified themselves H4291
Ezr 6:20 The L slaughtered the Passover lamb for all NDT
Ezr 7: 7 including priests, L, musicians H4291
Ezr 7:13 including priests and L, who volunteer to A10387
Ezr 7:24 duty on any of the priests, L, musicians, A10387
Ezr 8:15 and the priests, I found no L there. H1201+4291
Ezr 8:17 them what to say to Iddo and his **fellow** L, H278
Ezr 8:20 officials had established to assist the L. H4291
Ezr 8:29 priests and the L and the family heads of H4291
Ezr 8:30 Then the priests and L received the silver H4291
Ezr 8:33 so were the L Jozabad son of Jeshua H4291
Ezr 9: 1 including the priests and the L, have not H4291
Ezr 10: 5 leading priests and L and all Israel under H4291
Ezr 10:23 Among the L: Jozabad, Shimei, Kelaiah H4291
Ne 3:17 were made by the L under Rehum son of H4291
Ne 3:18 made by their **fellow** L under Binnui son H278
Ne 7: 1 the musicians and the L were appointed. H4291
Ne 7:43 The L: the descendants of Jeshua H4291
Ne 7:73 The priests, the L, the gatekeepers, the H4291
Ne 8: 7 The L—Jeshua, Bani, Sherebiah, Jamin H4291
Ne 8: 9 the L who were instructing the people H4291
Ne 8:11 The L calmed all the people, saying, "Be H4291
Ne 8:13 along with the priests and the L, gathered H4291
Ne 9: 4 on the stairs of the L were Jeshua, H4291
Ne 9: 5 And the L—Jeshua, Kadmiel, Bani H4291
Ne 9:38 our L and our priests are affixing their H4291
Ne 10: 9 The L: Jeshua son of Azaniah, Binnui of H4291
Ne 10:28 of the people—priests, L, gatekeepers H4291
Ne 10:34 the priests, the L and the people—have H4291
Ne 10:37 we will bring a tithe of our crops to the L, H4291
Ne 10:37 it is the L who collect the tithes in all H4291
Ne 10:38 is to accompany the L when they receive H4291
Ne 10:38 the L are to bring a tenth of the tithes H4291
Ne 10:39 including the L, are to bring their H1201+4291
Ne 11: 3 L, temple servants and H4291
Ne 11:15 From the L: Shemaiah son of Hasshub H4291
Ne 11:16 two of the heads of the L, who had charge H4291
Ne 11:18 The L in the holy city totaled 284. H4291
Ne 11:20 with the priests and L, were in all the H4291
Ne 11:22 chief officer of the L in Jerusalem was H4291
Ne 11:36 the divisions of the L *of* Judah settled in H4291
Ne 12: 1 were the priests and L who returned with H4291
Ne 12: 8 The L were Jeshua, Binnui, Kadmiel H4291
Ne 12:22 family heads of the L in the days of H4291
Ne 12:24 And the leaders of the L were Hashabiah H4291
Ne 12:27 the L were sought out from where they H4291
Ne 12:30 When the priests and L had purified H4291
Ne 12:44 by the Law for the priests and the L, H4291
Ne 12:44 with the ministering priests and L. H4291
Ne 12:47 also set aside the portion for the other L, H4291
Ne 12:47 the L set aside the portion for the H4291
Ne 13: 5 wine and olive oil prescribed for the L, H4291
Ne 13:10 assigned to the L had not been given to H4291
Ne 13:10 that all the L and musicians H4291
Ne 13:13 distributing the supplies to their **fellow** L. H278
Ne 13:22 Then I commanded the L to purify H4291
Ne 13:29 covenant of the priesthood and of the L. H4291
Ne 13:30 the priests and the L of everything foreign, H4291
Isa 66:21 some of them also to be priests and L," H4291
Jer 33:21 my covenant with the L who are priests H4291
Jer 33:22 my servant and the L who minister before H4291
Eze 40:46 who are the only L who may draw H1201+4290
Eze 44:10 " 'The L who went far from me when H4291
Eze 45: 5 10,000 cubits wide will belong to the L, H4291
Eze 48:11 not go astray as the L did when the H4291
Eze 48:12 portion, bordering the territory of the L. H4291
Eze 48:13 the L will have an allotment 25,000 cubits H4291
Eze 48:22 So the property of the L and the property H4291
Mal 3: 3 he will purify the L and refine them H1201+4290
Jn 1:19 sent priests and L to ask him who he was. *G3324*

LEVITICAL (17) [LEVI]

Lev 25:32 to redeem their houses in the L towns, H4291
Dt 17: 9 Go to the L priests and to the judge who is H4291
Dt 17:18 this law, taken from that of the L priests. H4291
Dt 18: 1 The L priests—indeed, the whole tribe of H4291
Dt 21: 5 The L priests shall step forward, for H1201+4290
Dt 24: 8 to do exactly as the L priests instruct you. H4291
Dt 27: 9 Then Moses and the L priests said to all H4291
Dt 31: 9 this law and gave it to the L priests, H1201+4290
Jos 3: 3 your God, and the L priests carrying it H4291
Jos 8:33 facing the L priests who carried it. H4291
1Ch 15:12 "You are the heads of the L families; you H4291
2Ch 5: 5 The L priests carried them up; H4291
2Ch 23:18 of the LORD in the hands of the L priests, H4291
Jer 33:18 will the L priests ever fail to have a H4291
Eze 43:19 a sin offering to the L priests of the family H4291
Eze 44:15 " 'But the L priests, who are descendants H4291
Heb 7:11 been attained through the L priesthood— *G3325*

LEVY (3)

2Ki 23:33 imposed on Judah a l of a hundred H6741
2Ch 36: 3 and **imposed** *on* Judah a l *of* a hundred H6740

Am 5:11 You **l a straw tax** on the poor and impose H1424

LEWD (4) [LEWDNESS]

Jdg 20: 6 this l and outrageous **act** in Israel. H2365
Eze 16:27 who were shocked by your l conduct. H2365
Eze 22: 9 the mountain shrines and commit l **acts**. H2365
Eze 23:44 so they slept with those l women, Oholah H2365

LEWDNESS (11) [LEWD]

Eze 16:43 Did you not add l to all your other H2365
Eze 16:58 bear the **consequences of** your l and your H2365
Eze 23:21 So you longed for the l *of* your youth H2365
Eze 23:27 put a stop to the l and prostitution you H2365
Eze 23:29 will be exposed. Your l and promiscuity H2365
Eze 23:35 must bear the **consequences of** your l H2365
Eze 23:48 "So I will put an end to l in the land, that H2365
Eze 23:49 suffer the **penalty for** your l and bear the H2365
Eze 24:13 " 'Now your impurity is l. Because I tried H2365
Hos 2:10 now I will expose her l before the eyes of H5578
Mk 7:22 malice, deceit, l, envy, slander *G816*

LIABLE (3)

Ex 21:19 the blow *will* **not be held** l if the other H5927
Jos 6:18 the camp of Israel l **to** destruction and H4200
Jos 7:12 they have been made l **to** destruction. H4200

LIAR (15) [LIE]

Dt 19:18 if the witness proves to be a l, giving H9214
Job 34: 6 I am right, *I am* **considered a** l; although I H3941
Ps 116:11 in my alarm I said, "Everyone *is a* l." H3941
Pr 17: 4 a l pays attention to a destructive tongue. H9214
Pr 19:22 better to be poor than a l. H408+3942
Pr 30: 6 he will rebuke you and **prove** *you* **a** l. H3941
Mic 2:11 If a l and deceiver comes and says H3941+8120
Jn 8:44 he is a l and the father of lies. *G6026*
Jn 8:55 did not, I would be a l like you, but I do *G6026*
Ro 3: 4 God be true, and every human being a l. *G6026*
1Jn 1:10 him out to be a l and his word is not *G6026*
1Jn 2: 4 does not do what he commands is a l *G6026*
1Jn 2:22 Who is the l? It is whoever denies that *G6026*
1Jn 4:20 God yet hates a brother or sister is a l. *G6026*
1Jn 5:10 believe God has made him out to be a l, *G6026*

LIARS (8) [LIE]

Ps 63:11 the mouths of l will be silenced. H1819+9214
Isa 57: 4 not a brood of rebels, the offspring of l? H9214
Mic 6:12 your inhabitants *are* l and their H9214+1819
1Ti 1:10 slave traders and l and perjurers—and *G6026*
1Ti 4: 2 teachings come through hypocritical l, *G6016*
Titus 1:12 "Cretans are always l, evil brutes, lazy *G6026*
Rev 3: 9 they are not, but *are* l—I will make them *G6017*
Rev 21: 8 the idolaters and all l—they will be *G6014*

LIBATIONS (1)

Ps 16: 4 I will not pour out l of blood to such gods H5821

LIBERAL (1) [LIBERALITY, LIBERALLY]

2Co 8:20 of the way we administer this l **gift**. *G103*

LIBERALITY (2) [LIBERAL]

Est 1: 7 abundant, in keeping with the king's l. H3338
Est 2:18 provinces and distributed gifts with royal l. H3338

LIBERALLY (1) [LIBERAL]

Dt 15:14 **Supply** them l from your flock, your H6735+6735

LIBERATED (1) [LIBERTY]

Ro 8:21 creation itself *will be* l from its bondage *G1802*

LIBERTINES (KJV) FREEDMEN

LIBERTY (1) [LIBERATED]

Lev 25:10 year and proclaim l throughout the land H2002

LIBNAH (17) [LIBNITE, LIBNITES]

Nu 33:20 They left Rimmon Perez and camped at L. H4243
Nu 33:21 They left L and camped at Rissah. H4243
Jos 10:29 on from Makkedah to L and attacked it. H4243
Jos 10:31 with him moved on from L to Lachish; H4243
Jos 10:32 put to the sword, just as he had done to L. H4243
Jos 10:39 as they had done to L and its king and to H4243
Jos 12:15 the king of L one the king of Adullam one H4243
Jos 15:42 L, Ether, Ashan, H4243
Jos 21:13 of refuge for one accused of murder), L, H4243
2Ki 8:22 L revolted at the same time H4243
2Ki 19: 8 found the king fighting against L. H4243
2Ki 23:31 daughter of Jeremiah; she was from L. H4243
2Ki 24:18 daughter of Jeremiah; she was from L. H4243
1Ch 6:57 a city of refuge), and L, Jattir, Eshtemoa, H4243
2Ch 21:10 L revolted at the same time, because H4243
Isa 37: 8 found the king fighting against L. H4243
Jer 52: 1 daughter of Jeremiah; she was from L. H4243

LIBNATH See SHIHOR LIBNATH

LIBNI (5)

Ex 6:17 of Gershon, by clans, were L and Shimei. H4249
Nu 3:18 of the Gershonite clans: L and Shimei. H4249
1Ch 6:17 of the sons of Gershon: L and Shimei. H4249
1Ch 6:20 L his son, Jahath his son, Zimmah his son, H4249
1Ch 6:29 L his son, Shimei his son, Uzzah H4249

LIBNITE (1) [LIBNAH]

Nu 26:58 the L clan, the Hebronite clan, the H4250

LIBNITES (1) [LIBNAH]

Nu 3:21 the clans of the L and Shimeites; H4250

LIBYA (3) [LIBYANS]

Eze 30: 5 Cush and L, Lydia and all Arabia, Kub H7033
Na 3: 9 Put and L were among her allies. H4275
Ac 2:10 Egypt and the parts of L near Cyrene *G3340*

LIBYANS (4) [LIBYA]

2Ch 12: 3 the innumerable troops of L, H4275
2Ch 16: 8 not the Cushites and L a mighty army with H4275
Isa 66:19 to Tarshish, to the L and Lydians (famous H7033
Da 11:43 with the L and Cushites in submission. H4275

LICE (KJV) GNATS

LICE (1)

Jer 43:12 a shepherd **picks** his garment **clean of** l, H6487

LICENSE (1)

Jude 4 our God into a l **for immorality** and deny *G816*

LICK (6) [LICKED, LICKS]

Nu 22: 4 "This horde *is* going to l up everything H4308
1Ki 21:19 dogs *will* l up your blood—yes, H4379
Ps 72: 9 before him and his enemies l the dust. H4308
Isa 5:24 as tongues of fire l up straw and as dry H430
Isa 49:23 ground; *they will* l the dust at your feet. H4308
Mic 7:17 *They will* l dust like a snake, like creatures H4308

LICKED (4) [LICK]

1Ki 18:38 and also l up the water in the trench. H4308
1Ki 21:19 place where dogs l up Naboth's blood, H4379
1Ki 22:38 and the dogs l up his blood, as the word H4379
Lk 16:21 Even the dogs came and l his sores. *G2143*

LICKS (1) [LICK]

Nu 22: 4 as an ox l up the grass of the field." H4308

LID (2)

Nu 19:15 container without a l fastened on it will H7544
2Ki 12: 9 took a chest and bored a hole in its l. H1946

LIE (127) [LIAR, LIARS, LIED, LIES, LYING]

Ex 23:11 year *let* the land l **unplowed** and unused. H9023
Lev 6: 3 if they find lost property and l about it H3950
Lev 19:11 'Do not steal. " '*Do* not l. " 'Do not H3950
Lev 26: 6 and *you will* l **down** and no one will make H8886
Lev 26:33 laid waste, and your cities *will* l in ruins. H2118
Nu 21:15 settlement of Ar and l along the border of H9128
Nu 23:19 not human, that *he should* l, not a human H3941
Nu 24: 9 Like a lion they crouch and l **down**, like a H8886
Dt 6: 7 when you l **down** and when you get up. H8886
Dt 11:19 when you l **down** and when you get up. H8886
Dt 25: 2 judge *shall* **make** them l **down** and have H5877
Dt 33:13 with the deep waters *that* l below; H8069
Jdg 9:32 should come and l **in wait** in the fields. H741
Ru 3: 4 Then go and uncover his feet and l **down** H8886
Ru 3: 7 he went over to l **down** at the far end of H8886
Ru 3:13 lives I will do it. L here until morning." H8886
1Sa 3: 5 "I did not call; go back and l **down**." H8886
1Sa 3: 6 "I did not call; go back and l **down**." H8886
1Sa 3: 9 Samuel, "Go and l **down**, and if he calls H8886
1Sa 15:29 Glory of Israel *does* not l or change his H9213
1Sa 22: 8 has incited my servant to l **in wait** for me, H741
2Sa 8: 2 *He* **made** them l **down** on the ground H8886
2Sa 23: 7 a spear; they are burned up where they l." H8699
1Ki 1: 2 *She can* l beside him so that our lord the H8886
Job 6:28 as to look at me. *Would I* l to your face? H3941
Job 7: 4 When *I* l **down** I think, 'How long before I H8886
Job 7:21 For *I will* soon l **down** in the dust; you will H8886
Job 11:19 *You will* l **down**, with no one to make you H8069
Job 20:11 fills his bones *will* l with him in the dust H8886
Job 21:26 Side by side *they* l in the dust, and worms H8886
Job 29:19 the dew *will* l **all night** on my H4328
Job 38:40 in their dens or l in wait in a thicket? H3782
Ps 3: 5 I l **down** and sleep; I wake again H8886
Ps 4: 8 In peace *I will* l **down** and sleep, for you H8886
Ps 23: 2 *He* **makes** me l **down** in green pastures H8069
Ps 36:12 See how the evildoers l **fallen**—thrown H5877
Ps 37:32 The wicked l **in wait** for the righteous H7595
Ps 38: 9 All my longings l open before you, Lord; NDT
Ps 38:12 my ruin; all day long they scheme and l. H5327
Ps 59: 3 See how *they* l **in wait** for me! Fierce men H741
Ps 62: 9 are but a breath, the highborn are *but a* l. H3942
Ps 76: 5 The valiant *l* **plundered**, they sleep their last AIT
Ps 76: 6 of Jacob, both horse and chariot l **still**. H8101
Ps 88: 5 like the slain *who* l in the grave, whom H8905
Ps 89:35 my holiness—and *I will* not l to David— H3941
Ps 102: 7 *I* l **awake**; I have become like a bird alone H9193
Ps 104:22 they return and l **down** in their dens. H8069
Pr 1:11 *let's* l **in wait** for innocent blood H741
Pr 1:18 These men l **in wait** for their own blood H741
Pr 3:24 When *you* l **down**, you will not be afraid H8886
Pr 3:24 be afraid; when *you* l **down**, your sleep H8886
Pr 6: 9 How long *will you* l there, you sluggard H8886
Pr 12: 6 The words of the wicked l **in wait** *for* blood H741
Pr 15:11 Destruction l open before the LORD— NDT
Ecc 4:11 if two l **down** *together*, they will H8886
Ecc 11: 3 in the place where it falls, there *it will* l. H2093
Isa 6:11 "Until the cities l **ruined** and without H8615
Isa 11: 6 the leopard *will* l **down** with the goat H8069
Isa 11: 7 their young *will* l **down** together, and H8069

Isa 13:21 But desert creatures *will* **l** there, jackals H8069
Isa 14:18 kings of the nations **l in state,** H8886+928+3883
Isa 14:30 the needy *will* **l down** in safety. H8069
Isa 17: 2 to flocks, *which will* **l down,** with no one H8069
Isa 21: 9 images of its gods *l* **shattered** on the ground! AIT
Isa 27:10 there *they* **l down;** they strip its H8069
Isa 28:15 we have made a **l** our refuge and H3942
Isa 28:17 away your refuge, the **l,** and water will H3942
Isa 34:10 generation to generation *it will l* **desolate;** AIT
Isa 34:14 creatures *will* also **l down** and find for H8089
Isa 44:20 "Is not this thing in my right hand a **l**?" H9214
Isa 50:11 from my hand: *You will* **l down** in torment. H8886
Isa 51:20 have fainted; *they* **l** at every street corner H8886
Isa 56:10 cannot bark; *they* **l around** and dream H8886
Isa 57: 2 they find rest as they **l in death.** H5435
Jer 3:25 *Let us* **l down** in our shame, and let our H8886
Jer 4: 7 Your towns *will* **l in ruins** without H5898
Jer 5: 6 a leopard *will* **l in wait** near their towns to H9193
Jer 5:26 are the wicked *who* **l in wait** like men who H8800
Jer 9: 5 They have taught their tongues *to* **l;** H1819+9214
Jer 9:22 " 'Dead bodies *will* **l** like dung on the H5877
Jer 12: 4 How long *will* the land *l* **parched** and the AIT
Jer 23:14 They commit adultery and live a **l.** H9214
Jer 44: 2 Today they *l* **deserted** and in ruins AIT
Jer 46:19 be laid waste and **l in ruins** without H5898
Jer 51:47 her slain *will* all **l fallen** within her. H5877
La 2:21 "Young and old **l** *together* in the dust of H8886
La 4: 5 up in royal purple now **l** *on* ash heaps. H2485
Eze 4: 4 "Then **l** on your left side and put the sin H8886
Eze 4: 4 the number of days *you* **l** on your side. H8886
Eze 4: 6 finished this, **l down** again, this time on H8886
Eze 4: 9 it during the 390 days you **l** on your side. H8886
Eze 6:13 when their people **l** slain among their H2118
Eze 13: 6 visions are false and their divinations a **l.** H3942
Eze 29:12 her cities *will* **l** desolate forty years H2118
Eze 30: 7 their cities *will* **l** among ruined cities. H2118
Eze 31:18 *you will* **l** among the uncircumcised H8886
Eze 32:21 and *they* **l** *with* the uncircumcised, *with* H8886
Eze 32:27 But *they do* not **l** with the fallen warriors of H8886
Eze 32:28 will be broken and *will* **l** among the H8886
Eze 32:29 They **l** with the uncircumcised, with those H8886
Eze 32:30 They **l** uncircumcised with those killed by H8886
Eze 34:14 There *they will* **l down** in good grazing H8069
Eze 34:15 tend my sheep and **have** them **l down,** H8069
Eze 48:22 property of the city *will* **l** in the center of H2118
Eze 48:22 to the prince *will* **l** between the border of H2118
Da 11:27 the same table and **l** *to each other,* H1819+3942
Hos 2:18 the land, so that all *may* **l down** in safety. H8886
Hos 6: 9 As marauders **l in ambush** *for* a victim, so H2675
Am 2: 8 *They* **l down** beside every altar on H5742
Am 6: 4 *You* **l** on beds adorned with ivory and H8886
Na 3:18 slumber; your nobles **l down to rest.** H8905
Zep 2: 7 the evening *they will* **l down** in the H8069
Zep 2:14 Flocks and herds *will* **l down** there H8069
Zep 3:13 They will eat and **l down** and no one will H8069
Zec 10: 2 diviners see visions that **l;** they tell H9214
Jn 5: 3 number of disabled people *used to* **l**— *G2879*
Ro 1:25 exchanged the truth about God for a **l,** *G6022*
Gal 1:20 God that what I am writing you *is* no **l.** *G6017*
Col 3: 9 *Do* not **l** to each other, since you have *G6017*
2Th 2: 9 signs and wonders that *serve* the **l,** *G6022*
2Th 2:11 delusion so that they will believe the **l** *G6022*
Titus 1: 2 who does **not l,** promised before *G950*
Heb 6:18 in which it is impossible for God *to* **l,** *G6017*
1Jn 1: 6 *we* **l** and do not live out the truth. *G6017*
1Jn 2:21 it and because no **l** comes from the truth. *G6022*
Rev 11: 8 Their bodies will *l* **in** the public square of the AIT
Rev 14: 5 No **l** was found in their mouths; they are *G6022*

LIED (6) [LIE]

Ge 18:15 Sarah was afraid, so *she* **l** and said, "I did H3950
Jos 7:11 have stolen, *they have* **l,** they have put H3950
Jdg 16:10 made a fool of me; *you* **l** to me. H1819+3942
Jer 5:12 *They have* **l** about the LORD; they said, "He H3950
Ac 5: 3 your heart *that* you *have* **l** to the Holy *G6017*
Ac 5: 4 *You have* not **l** just to human beings but *G6017*

LIEN (KJV) SLEEP, SLEPT, RAVISHED

LIES (100) [LIE]

Ge 21:17 God has heard the boy crying as he **l** there. NDT
Ge 49: 9 Like a lion he crouches and **l down,** like a H8069
Ex 5: 9 working and pay no attention to **l.**" H1821+9214
Lev 15: 4 with a discharge **l** on will be unclean, H8886
Lev 15:20 " 'Anything *she* **l** on during her period will H8886
Lev 15:24 any bed *he* **l** on will be unclean. H8886
Lev 15:26 Any bed *she* **l** on while her discharge H8886
Lev 26:34 the time that *it* **l desolate** and you are in H9037
Lev 26:35 All the time *that it* **l desolate,** the land will H9037
Lev 26:43 sabbaths while *it* **l desolate** without them. H9037
Nu 14:33 the last of your bodies **l** in the wilderness. NDT
Dt 19:11 But if out of hate someone **l in wait** H741
Jdg 21:19 LORD in Shiloh, which **l** north of Bethel, NDT
Ru 3: 4 When he **l down,** note the place where he H8886
1Sa 14:39 even if the guilt **l** with my son Jonathan H3780
1Sa 22:13 rebelled against me and **l in wait** for me, H741
2Sa 1:19 "A gazelle **l** slain on your heights, Israel NDT
2Sa 1:25 Jonathan **l** slain on your heights. NDT
Ne 2: 3 city where my ancestors are buried **l** in ruins, NDT
Ne 2:17 Jerusalem **l** in ruins, and its gates have NDT
Job 13: 4 smear me with **l;** you are worthless H9214
Job 14:12 so he **l down** and does not rise; till the H8886
Job 18:10 him on the ground; a trap **l** in his path. NDT
Job 19:28 since the root of the trouble **l** in him, H5162
Job 20:26 total darkness **l in wait** for his treasures. H3243
Job 26: 6 naked before God; Destruction **l** uncovered. NDT
Job 27: 4 and my tongue will not utter **l.** H8245
Job 27:19 *He* **l down** wealthy, but will do so no H8886
Job 37:17 when the land **l hushed** under the south H9200
Job 40:21 Under the lotus plants *it* **l,** hidden among H8886
Ps 5: 6 you destroy those who tell **l.** H3942
Ps 5: 9 open grave; *with* their tongues *they* **tell l.** H2744
Ps 10: 7 His mouth is full of **l** and threats; trouble H5327
Ps 10: 8 *He* **l** in wait near the villages; from H3782
Ps 10: 9 lion in cover *he* **l in wait.** H741+928+2021+5041
Ps 10: 9 *He* **l in wait** to catch the helpless; he H741
Ps 12: 2 Everyone **l** to their neighbor; they H1819+8736
Ps 34:13 from evil and your lips from telling **l.** H5327
Ps 41: 8 never get up from the place where *he* **l.**" H8886
Ps 55:11 threats and **l** never leave its streets. H5327
Ps 58: 3 the womb they are wayward, spreading **l.** H3942
Ps 59:12 For the curses and **l** they utter, H3951
Ps 62: 4 from my lofty place; they take delight in **l.** H3942
Ps 88: 7 Your wrath **l heavily** on me; you have H6164
Ps 119:69 the arrogant have smeared me with **l,** H9214
Ps 144: 8 whose mouths are full of **l,** whose right H8736
Ps 144:11 of foreigners whose mouths are full of **l,** H8736
Pr 6:19 witness who pours out **l** and a person who H3942
Pr 12:17 tells the truth, but a false witness tells **l.** H5327
Pr 14: 5 deceive, but a false witness pours out **l.** H3942
Pr 19: 5 whoever pours out **l** will not go free. H3942
Pr 19: 9 whoever pours out **l** will perish. H3942
Pr 23:28 Like a bandit she **l in wait** and multiplies H741
Pr 29:12 If a ruler listens to **l,** all his officials H1821+9214
Pr 30: 8 Keep falsehood and **l** far from me H1821+3942
Isa 9:15 the prophets who teach **l** are the tail. H9214
Isa 24:10 The ruined city *l* **desolate;** the entrance to AIT
Isa 32: 7 schemes to destroy the poor with **l,** H609+9214
Isa 59: 4 arguments, they utter **l;** they conceive H8736
Isa 59:13 uttering **l** our hearts have H1821+9214
Isa 64:11 and all that we treasured **l** in ruins. H2118
Jer 4:20 follows disaster; the whole land **l in ruins.** H8720
Jer 5:31 The prophets prophesy **l,** the priests rule H9214
Jer 9: 3 like a bow, to shoot **l;** it is not by truth that H9214
Jer 14:14 prophets are prophesying **l** in my name. H9214
Jer 20: 6 friends to whom you have prophesied **l.** H9214
Jer 23:10 the curse the land *l* **parched** and the pastures AIT
Jer 23:25 prophets say who prophesy **l** in my name. H9214
Jer 23:32 my people astray with their reckless **l,** H9214
Jer 27:10 They prophesy **l** to you that will only serve H9214
Jer 27:14 they are prophesying **l** to you. H9214
Jer 27:15 'They are prophesying **l** in my name H9214
Jer 27:16 They are prophesying **l** to you. H9214
Jer 28:15 have persuaded this nation to trust in **l.** H9214
Jer 29: 9 are prophesying **l** to you in my name. H9214
Jer 29:21 who are prophesying **l** to you in my name: H9214
Jer 29:23 in my name they have uttered **l** H9214
Jer 29:31 and has persuaded you to trust in **l,** H9214
Jer 40: 4 the whole country **l** before you; go wherever NDT
La 1: 1 How deserted **l** the city, once so full of H3782
La 5:18 Mount Zion, which **l desolate,** with jackals H9037
Eze 13:19 people, who listen to **l,** you have killed H3942
Eze 13:22 disheartened the righteous with your **l,** H9214
Eze 26: 2 now that *she* **l in ruins** I will prosper H2990
Eze 32:23 the pit and her army **l** around her grave. H2118
Eze 47:16 which **l** on the border between Damascus NDT
Da 2:22 he knows what **l** in darkness, and NDT
Hos 7: 3 their wickedness, the princes with their **l.** H3951
Hos 11:12 Ephraim has surrounded me with **l,** Israel H3951
Hos 12: 1 all day and multiplies **l** and violence. H3942
Mic 7: 2 Everyone **l in wait** to shed blood; they hunt H741
Mic 7: 5 with the *woman who* **l** *in* your embrace H8886
Na 3: 1 the city of blood, full of **l,** full of plunder, H3951
Hab 2:18 Or an image that teaches **l**? For the one H9214
Zep 3:13 they will tell no **l.** A deceitful tongue will H3942
Zec 13: 3 you have told **l** in the LORD's name. H9214
Mt 8: 6 he said, "my servant **l** at home paralyzed *G965*
Jn 8:44 When *he* **l,** he speaks his *G3281+3836+6022*
Jn 8:44 he is a liar and the father *of* **l.** *G899*
Rev 10: 8 take the scroll that *l* **open** in the hand of the AIT

LIEUTENANTS (KJV) SATRAPS

LIFE (565) [LIVE]

Ge 1:30 everything that has the breath of **l** in it—I H2645
Ge 2: 7 breathed into his nostrils the breath of **l,** H2644
Ge 2: 9 were the tree of **l** and the tree of the H2644
Ge 3:14 you will eat dust all the days of your **l.** H2644
Ge 3:17 will eat food from it all the days of your **l.** H2644
Ge 3:22 take also from the tree of **l** and eat, H2644
Ge 3:24 forth to guard the way to the tree of **l.** H2644
Ge 6:17 earth to destroy all **l** under the heavens, H1414
Ge 6:17 every creature that has the breath of **l** in it. H2644
Ge 7:11 In the six hundredth year of Noah's **l,** on H2644
Ge 7:15 have the breath of **l** in them came to H2644
Ge 7:22 that had the breath of **l** in its nostrils died. H2644
Ge 9: 5 accounting for the **l** *of* another human H5883
Ge 9:11 Never again will all **l** be destroyed by the H1414
Ge 9:15 the waters become a flood to destroy all **l.** H1414
Ge 9:17 between me and all **l** on the earth." H1414
Ge 12:13 your sake and my **l** will be spared H5883
Ge 19:19 great kindness to me in sparing my **l.** H5883
Ge 19:20 isn't it? Then my **l** will be spared." H5883
Ge 26: 9 I thought *I* might **lose** *my* **l** on account of H4637
Ge 27:46 my **l will not be worth living.**" H2644+4200+4537
Ge 32:30 face to face, and yet my **l** was spared." H5883
Ge 37:21 "Let's not take his **l,**" he said. H5883
Ge 42:21 he was when he pleaded with us for his **l,** H5883
Ge 43: 9 I will bear the blame before you all my **l.** H3427
Ge 44:30 whose **l** is closely bound up with the boy's H5883
Ge 44:30 life is closely bound up with the boy's **l,** H5883
Ge 44:32 the blame before you, my father, all my **l!** H3427
Ge 47:28 the years of his **l** were a hundred and H2644
Ge 48:15 my shepherd **all** my **l** to this day, H4946+6388
Ex 21: 6 Then he will be his servant **for l.** H4200+6409
Ex 21:23 is serious injury, you are to take **l** for life, H5883
Ex 21:23 is serious injury, you are to take life for **l,** H5883
Ex 21:30 may redeem his **l** by the payment of H5883
Ex 23:26 I will give you a full **l span.** H5031+3427
Ex 30:12 LORD a ransom for his **l** at the time he is H5883
Lev 17:11 For the **l** *of* a creature is in the blood, and I H5883
Lev 17:11 blood that makes atonement for one's **l.** H5883
Lev 17:14 because the **l** *of* every creature is its blood H5883
Lev 17:14 because the **l** *of* every creature is its blood H5883
Lev 19:16 *Do* not **do anything that endangers** your neighbor's **l** H6641+6584+1947
Lev 24:17 *who* **takes** the **l** *of* a human H5782+5883
Lev 24:18 *Anyone who* **takes** the **l** *of* H5782+5883
Lev 24:18 animal must make restitution—**l** for life. H5883
Lev 24:18 animal must make restitution—life for **l.** H5883
Lev 25:46 property and can make them slaves for **l,** H6409
Nu 35:31 accept a ransom for the **l** *of* a murderer, H5883
Dt 4:42 into one of these cities and **save** *their* **l.** H2649
Dt 6: 2 and so that you *may* **enjoy long l.** H799+3427
Dt 12:23 because the blood is the **l,** and you must H5883
Dt 12:23 you must not eat the **l** with the meat. H5883
Dt 15:17 he will become your servant **for l.** H6409
Dt 16: 3 the days of your **l** you may remember the H2644
Dt 17:19 it all the days of his **l** so that he may learn H2644
Dt 19: 5 flee to one of these cities and **save** *his* **l.** H2649
Dt 19:21 **l** for life, eye for eye, tooth for tooth, hand H5883
Dt 19:21 life for **l,** eye for eye, tooth for tooth, hand H5883
Dt 22: 7 well with you and you may have a long **l.** H3427
Dt 28:66 both night and day, never sure of your **l.** H2644
Dt 30:15 I set before you today **l** and prosperity H2644
Dt 30:19 that I have set before you **l** and death, H2644
Dt 30:19 Now choose **l,** so that you and your H2644
Dt 30:20 the LORD is your **l,** and he will give you H2644
Dt 32:39 I put to death and *I* **bring to l,** I have H2649
Dt 32:47 just idle words for you—they are your **l.** H2644
Jos 1: 5 to stand against you all the days of your **l.** H2644
Jos 4:14 stood in awe of him all the days of his **l,** H2644
Jdg 9:17 you and risked his **l** to rescue you from the H5883
Jdg 12: 3 I took my **l** in my hands and crossed over H5883
Jdg 13:12 the rule that governs the boy's **l** and work?" NDT
Ru 1:20 the Almighty has made **my l** very bitter. H3276
Ru 4:15 He will renew your **l** and sustain you in H5883
1Sa 1:11 him to the LORD for all the days of his **l,** H2644
1Sa 1:28 *For* his whole **l** he will be H3427+889+2118
1Sa 2:33 your descendants will die **in the prime of l.** H408
1Sa 7:15 as Israel's leader all the days of his **l.** H2644
1Sa 19: 5 He took his **l** in his hands when he killed H5883
1Sa 19:11 "If you don't run for your **l** tonight H5883
1Sa 23:15 that Saul had come out to take his **l.** H5883
1Sa 24:11 you are hunting me down to take my **l.** H5883
1Sa 25: 6 Say to him: '**Long l** to you H4200+2021+2644
1Sa 25:29 someone is pursuing you to take your **l,** H5883
1Sa 25:29 the **l** *of* my lord will be bound securely in H5883
1Sa 26:21 you considered my **l** precious today, H5883
1Sa 26:24 As surely as I valued your **l** today, so may H5883
1Sa 26:24 the LORD value my **l** and deliver me from H5883
1Sa 27:12 Israelites, that he will be my servant **for l.**" H6409
1Sa 28: 2 you my bodyguard **for l.** H3972+2021+3427
1Sa 28: 9 you set a trap for my **l** to bring about my H5883
1Sa 28:21 I took my **l** in my hands and did what you H5883
2Sa 1:23 in **l** they were loved and admired H2644
2Sa 14: 7 to death for the **l** *of* his brother whom he H5883
2Sa 15:21 whether it means **l** or death, there will H2644
2Sa 18:13 And if I had put my **l** in jeopardy—and H5883
2Sa 19: 5 have just saved your **l** and the lives of H5883
2Sa 19:13 of my army **for l** in place of H3972+2021+3427
1Ki 1:12 can save your own **l** and the life of your H5883
1Ki 1:12 own life and the **l** *of* your son Solomon. H5883
1Ki 2:23 does not pay with his **l** for this request! H5883
1Ki 3:11 this and not for long **l** or wealth for H3427
1Ki 3:14 your father did, I will give you a long **l.**" H3427
1Ki 4:21 were Solomon's subjects all his **l.** H2644
1Ki 4:33 He spoke about **plant l,** from the cedar of H6770
1Ki 11:34 all the days of his **l** for the sake of David H2644
1Ki 15: 5 LORD's commands all the days of his **l**— H2644
1Ki 15:14 was fully committed to the LORD all his **l.** H3427
1Ki 17:21 my God, let this boy's **l** return to him!" H5883
1Ki 17:22 and the boy's **l** returned to him, and H5883
1Ki 19: 2 I do not make your **l** like that of one of H5883
1Ki 19: 3 Elijah was afraid and ran for his **l.** H5883
1Ki 19: 4 "Take my **l;** I am no better than my H5883
1Ki 20:31 Perhaps he will spare your **l.**" H5883
1Ki 20:39 missing, it will be your **l** for his life, or you H5883
1Ki 20:39 it will be your life for his **l,** or you must H5883
1Ki 20:42 Therefore it is your **l** for his life, your H5883
1Ki 20:42 Therefore it is your life for his **l,** your H5883
2Ki 1:13 have respect for my **l** and the lives of H5883
2Ki 1:14 But now have respect for my **l!**" H5883
2Ki 5: 7 Can I kill and **bring back to l**? Why does H2649
2Ki 8: 1 woman whose son *he had* **restored to l,** H2649
2Ki 8: 5 how Elisha *had* **restored** the dead to **l,** H2649
2Ki 8: 5 son Elisha *had* **brought back to l** came to H2649

L

2Ki 8: 5 this is her son whom Elisha **restored to l.**” H2649
2Ki 10:24 hands escape, it will be your l for his life.” H5883
2Ki 10:24 hands escape, it will be your life for his l.” H5883
2Ki 13:21 the man **came to l** and stood up on his H2649
2Ki 18:32 trees and honey. **Choose l** and not death H2649
2Ki 20: 6 I will add fifteen years to your l. And I will H3427
2Ki 25:29 for the rest of his l ate regularly at the H2644
1Ch 29:28 having **enjoyed long l**, wealth H8428+3427
2Ch 1:11 not asked for a long l but for wisdom and H3427
2Ch 15:17 was fully committed to the LORD all his l. H3427
Ezr 9: 9 He has granted us **new l** to rebuild the H4695
Ne 4: 2 *Can they* **bring** the stones **back to l** from H2649
Ne 6:11 like me go into the temple *to* **save** *his* l? H2649
Ne 9: 6 You **give l** *to* everything, and the H2649
Est 7: 3 grant me my l—this is my petition. H5883
Est 7: 7 behind to beg Queen Esther for his l. H5883
Job 2: 4 “A man will give all he has for his own l. H5883
Job 2: 6 is in your hands; but you must spare his l.” H5883
Job 3:20 those in misery, and l to the bitter of soul, H2644
Job 3:23 Why is l given to a man whose way is NDT
Job 6: 9 to let loose his hand and cut off **my l**! H5761
Job 7: 7 that my l is but a breath; my eyes H2644
Job 7:16 I despise my l; I would not live forever. NDT
Job 8:19 Surely its l withers away, and from the soil H2006
Job 9:21 no concern for myself; I despise my own l. H2644
Job 10: 1 “I loathe my very l; therefore I will give H2644
Job 10:12 You gave me l and showed me kindness H2644
Job 11:17 **L** will be brighter than noonday, and H2698
Job 12:10 In his hand is the l *of* every creature and H5883
Job 12:12 Does not long l bring understanding? H3427
Job 13:14 in jeopardy and take my l in my hands? H5883
Job 24:22 established, they have no assurance of l. H2644
Job 27: 2 the Almighty, who has made my l bitter, H5883
Job 27: 3 as long as I have l within me, the breath H5972
Job 27: 8 are cut off, when God takes away their l? H5883
Job 30:16 “And now my l ebbs away; days of H5883
Job 31:30 to sin by invoking a curse against their l— H5883
Job 33: 4 the breath of the Almighty **gives** me l. H2649
Job 33:22 their l to the messengers of death. H2652
Job 33:28 and I shall live to enjoy the **light** *of l*. AIT
Job 33:30 that the light of l may shine on them. H2644
Job 41: 4 you for you to take it as your slave **for l**? H6409
Job 42:12 blessed the **latter part of** Job’s l more than H344
Ps 7: 5 let him trample my l to the ground and H2644
Ps 16:11 You make known to me the path of l; you H2644
Ps 17:14 of this world whose reward is in this l. H2645
Ps 21: 4 He asked you for l, and you gave it to him H2644
Ps 22:20 my **precious l** from the power of the dogs. H3495
Ps 23: 6 love will follow me all the days of my l, H2644
Ps 25:20 Guard my l and rescue me; do not let me H5883
Ps 26: 1 I *have* **led** a blameless l; I have H2143+928
Ps 26: 9 my l with those who are bloodthirsty, H2644
Ps 26:11 I **lead** a blameless l; deliver me and H2143+928
Ps 27: 1 The LORD is the stronghold of my l—of H2644
Ps 27: 4 the house of the LORD all the days of my l, H2644
Ps 31:10 My l is consumed by anguish and my H2644
Ps 31:13 conspire against me and plot to take my l. H5883
Ps 34:12 Whoever of you loves l and desires to see H2644
Ps 35: 4 those who seek my l be disgraced and put H5883
Ps 35:17 ravages, my **precious l** from these lions. H3495
Ps 36: 9 For with you is the fountain of l; in your H2644
Ps 39: 4 my days; let me know how fleeting **my l** is. H638
Ps 39:13 that *I may* **enjoy l** *again* before I depart H1158
Ps 40:14 want to take my l be put to shame and H5883
Ps 42: 8 is with me—a prayer to the God of my l. H2644
Ps 49: 7 one can redeem the l of another or give to NDT
Ps 49: 8 the ransom for a l is costly, no payment is H5883
Ps 49:19 who will never again see the **light** *of l*. AIT
Ps 56: 6 they watch my steps, hoping to take my l. H5883
Ps 56:13 I may walk before God in the light of l. H2644
Ps 61: 6 Increase the **days of** the king’s l, his years H3427
Ps 63: 3 Because your love is better than l, my lips H2644
Ps 64: 1 protect my l from the threat of the enemy. H2644
Ps 69:28 out of the book of l and not be listed with H2644
Ps 70: 2 want to take my l be put to shame and H5883
Ps 71:20 *you will* **restore** my l again; from H2649
Ps 74:19 not hand over the l *of* your dove to wild H5883
Ps 86: 2 Guard my l, for I am faithful to you; save H5883
Ps 88: 3 troubles and my l draws near to death. H2644
Ps 89:47 Remember how **fleeting** is my l. For what H2698
Ps 91:16 With long l I will satisfy him and show H3427
Ps 101: 2 I will be careful to lead a blameless l H2006
Ps 102:23 In the **course of** my l he broke my strength; H2006
Ps 103: 4 who redeems your l from the pit and H2644
Ps 103:15 The l *of* mortals is like grass, they flourish H3427
Ps 104:33 I will sing to the LORD all my l; I will sing H2644
Ps 119:25 **preserve** my l according to your word. H2649
Ps 119:37 **preserve** my l according to your word. H2649
Ps 119:40 In your righteousness **preserve** my l. H2649
Ps 119:50 Your promise **preserves** my l. H2649
Ps 119:88 In your unfailing love **preserve** my l, that I H2649
Ps 119:93 by them *you have* **preserved** my l. H2649
Ps 119:107 suffered much; **preserve** my l, LORD H2649
Ps 119:109 I constantly take my l in my hands, H5883
Ps 119:149 with your love; **preserve** my l, LORD, H2649
Ps 119:154 **preserve** my l according to your promise. H2649
Ps 119:156 **preserve** my l according to your laws. H2649
Ps 119:159 I love your precepts; **preserve** my l, H2649
Ps 121: 7 from all harm—he will watch over your l; H5883
Ps 128: 5 of Jerusalem all the days of your l. H2644
Ps 133: 3 bestows his blessing, even l forevermore. H2644
Ps 138: 7 in the midst of trouble, *you* **preserve** my l. H2649
Ps 142: 4 I have no refuge; no one cares for my l. H5883
Ps 143: 8 way I should go, for to you I entrust my l. H5883
Ps 143:11 name’s sake, LORD, **preserve** my l; in your H2649
Ps 146: 2 I will praise the LORD all my l; I will sing H2644
Pr 1:19 it takes away the l *of* those who get it. H5883
Pr 2:19 go to her return or attain the paths of l. H2644
Pr 3: 2 will prolong your l many years and bring H2644
Pr 3:16 Long l is in her right hand; in her left H3427
Pr 3:18 She is a tree of l to those who take hold H2644
Pr 3:22 they will be l for you, an ornament to H2644
Pr 4:10 and the years of your l will be many. H2644
Pr 4:13 not let it go; guard it well, for it is your l. H2644
Pr 4:22 they are l to those who find them and H2644
Pr 5: 6 She gives no thought to the way of l; her H2644
Pr 5:11 At the **end of** your l you will groan, when H344
Pr 6:23 correction and instruction are the way to l, H2644
Pr 6:26 another man’s wife preys on your very l. H5883
Pr 7:23 little knowing it will cost him his l. H5883
Pr 8:35 who find me find l and receive favor from H2644
Pr 9:11 and years will be added to your l. H2644
Pr 10:11 mouth of the righteous is a fountain of l, H2644
Pr 10:16 The wages of the righteous is l, but the H2644
Pr 10:17 heeds discipline shows the way to l, H2644
Pr 10:27 The fear of the LORD adds length to l, but H3427
Pr 11:19 Truly the righteous attain l, but whoever H2644
Pr 11:30 The fruit of the righteous is a tree of l H2644
Pr 12:28 In the way of righteousness there is l H2644
Pr 13: 8 A person’s riches may ransom their l, but H5883
Pr 13:12 but a longing fulfilled is a tree of l. H2644
Pr 13:14 The teaching of the wise is a fountain of l, H2644
Pr 14:27 The fear of the LORD is a fountain of l H2644
Pr 14:30 A heart at peace gives l *to* the body, but H2644
Pr 15: 4 The soothing tongue is a tree of l, but a H2644
Pr 15:24 The path of l leads upward for the H2644
Pr 16:15 brightens, it means l; his favor is like a H2644
Pr 16:22 Prudence is a fountain of l to the prudent H2644
Pr 18:21 The tongue has the power of l and death H2644
Pr 19: 8 The one who gets wisdom loves l; the H5883
Pr 19:16 keeps commandments keeps their l, H5883
Pr 19:23 The fear of the LORD leads to l; then one H2644
Pr 21:21 pursues righteousness and love finds l, H2644
Pr 22: 4 its wages are riches and honor and l. H2644
Pr 22: 5 would preserve their l stay far from them. H5883
Pr 22:23 take up their case and will exact l *for life*. H5883
Pr 22:23 will take up their case and will exact **life** *for l*. AIT
Pr 23:22 to your father, who **gave** you l, and do not H3528
Pr 24:12 Does not he who guards your l know it H5883
Pr 27:19 the face, so one’s l reflects the heart. H132
Pr 31:12 him good, not harm, all the days of her l. H2644
Ecc 2:17 So I hated l, because the work that is H2644
Ecc 5:18 the few days of l God has given them— H2644
Ecc 5:20 They seldom reflect on the days of their l H2644
Ecc 6:12 who knows what is good for a person in l, H2644
Ecc 7:15 In this meaningless l *of* mine I have seen H3427
Ecc 8:15 So I commend the enjoyment of l, because NDT
Ecc 8:15 all the days of the l God has given them H2644
Ecc 9: 9 Enjoy l with your wife, whom you love, all H2644
Ecc 9: 9 of this meaningless l that God has given H2644
Ecc 9: 9 this is your lot in l and in your toilsome H2644
Ecc 10:19 wine makes l merry, and money is H2644
Isa 23:15 seventy years, the **span of** a king’s l. H3427
Isa 26:18 people of the world *have* not **come to l**. H5877
Isa 38: 5 I will add fifteen years to your l. H3427
Isa 38:10 “In the prime of my l must I go through H3427
Isa 38:12 Like a weaver I have rolled up my l, and H2644
Isa 38:16 and my spirit finds l in them too. H2644
Isa 42: 5 its people, and l to those who walk on it: H8120
Isa 43: 4 you, nations in exchange for your l. H5883
Isa 53:10 the LORD makes his l an offering for sin, H5883
Isa 53:11 he will see the **light** *of l* and be satisfied; by AIT
Isa 53:12 because he poured out his l unto death H5883
Jer 4:31 fainting; my l is given over to murderers.” H5883
Jer 8: 3 of this evil nation will prefer death to l, H2644
Jer 20:13 He rescues the l *of* the needy from the H5883
Jer 21: 8 you the way of l and the way of death. H2644
Jer 38:17 your l will be spared and this city will not H5883
Jer 38:20 well with you, and your l will be spared. H5883
Jer 39:18 by the sword but will escape with your l, H5883
Jer 40:14 Ishmael son of Nethaniah to take your l?” H5883
Jer 40:15 should he take your l and cause all the H5883
Jer 45: 5 you go I will let you escape with your l. H5883
Jer 52:33 for the rest of his l ate regularly at the H2644
La 3:53 They tried to end my l in a pit and threw H2644
La 3:58 took up my case; you redeemed my l. H2644
La 4:20 our very **l breath**, was caught in H8120+678
Eze 3:18 their evil ways in order to **save** their l, H2649
Eze 7:13 not one of them will preserve their l. H2652
Eze 18:27 is just and right, they will save their l. H5883
Eze 32:10 them will tremble every moment for his l. H5883
Eze 33: 4 the sword comes and **takes** their l, H4374
Eze 33: 6 the sword comes and takes someone’s l, H5883
Eze 33: 6 **that person’s** l will be taken because of H2085S
Eze 33:15 follow the decrees that give l, and do no H2644
Eze 37: 5 breath enter you, and *you will* **come to l**. H2649
Eze 37: 6 put breath in you, and *you will* **come to l**. H2649
Eze 37:10 *they* **came to l** and stood up on their feet H2649
Da 5:23 in his hand your l and all your ways. A10494
Da 12: 2 some to everlasting l, others to shame H2644
Am 2:14 the warrior will not save his l. H5883
Am 2:15 the horseman will not save his l. H5883
Jnh 1:14 do not let us die for taking this man’s l. H5883
Jnh 2: 6 my God, brought my l up from the pit. H2644
Jnh 2: 7 “When my l was ebbing away, H5883
Jnh 4: 3 take away my l, for it is better for me H5883
Hab 2:10 your own house and forfeiting your l. H5883
Hab 2:19 Woe to him who says to wood, ‘**Come to l**! H7810
Mal 2: 5 a covenant of l and peace, and I H2644
Mt 2:20 were trying to take the child’s l are dead.” *G6034*
Mt 6:25 do not worry about your l, what you will *G6034*
Mt 6:25 Is not l more than food, and the body *G6034*
Mt 6:27 by worrying add a single hour to your l? *G2461*
Mt 7:14 gate and narrow the road that leads to l, *G2437*
Mt 10:39 Whoever finds their l will lose it, and *G6034*
Mt 10:39 whoever loses their l for my sake will find *G6034*
Mt 13:22 the worries *of* this l and the *G172*
Mt 16:21 killed and on the third day *be* **raised to l**. *G1586*
Mt 16:25 whoever wants to save their l will lose it, *G6034*
Mt 16:25 whoever loses their l for me will find it. *G6034*
Mt 17:23 on the third day *he will be* **raised to l**.” *G1586*
Mt 18: 8 you to enter l maimed or crippled than *G2437*
Mt 18: 9 you to enter l with one eye than to *G2437*
Mt 19:16 good thing must I do to get eternal l?” *G2437*
Mt 19:17 If you want to enter l, keep the *G2437*
Mt 19:29 times as much and will inherit eternal l. *G2437*
Mt 20:19 On the third day *he will be* **raised to l**!” *G1586*
Mt 20:28 to give his l as a ransom for many. *G6034*
Mt 25:46 the righteous to eternal l. *G2437*
Mt 27:52 people who had died *were* **raised to l**. *G1586*
Mk 3: 4 do good or to do evil, to save l or to kill?” *G6034*
Mk 4:19 the worries *of* this l, the deceitfulness of *G172*
Mk 8:35 whoever wants to save their l will lose it, *G6034*
Mk 8:35 whoever loses their l for me and for the *G6034*
Mk 9:43 you to enter l maimed than with two *G2437*
Mk 9:45 you to enter l crippled than to have *G2437*
Mk 10:17 “what must I do to inherit eternal l?” *G2437*
Mk 10:30 in the age to come eternal l. *G2437*
Mk 10:45 to give his l as a ransom for many. *G6034*
Lk 6: 9 to do evil, to save l or to destroy it? *G6034*
Lk 7:37 town who lived a **sinful l** learned that Jesus *G283*
Lk 9: 8 prophets of long ago *had* **come back to l**. *G482*
Lk 9:19 prophets of long ago *has* **come back to l**.” *G482*
Lk 9:22 killed and on the third day *be* **raised to l**.” *G1586*
Lk 9:24 whoever wants to save their l will lose it, *G6034*
Lk 9:24 whoever loses their l for me will save it. *G6034*
Lk 10:25 “what must I do to inherit eternal l?” *G2437*
Lk 12:15 l does not consist in an abundance of *G2437*
Lk 12:19 many years. **Take l easy**; eat, drink and *G399*
Lk 12:20 This very night your l will be demanded *G6034*
Lk 12:22 do not worry about your l, what you will *G6034*
Lk 12:23 For l is more than food, and the body more *G6034*
Lk 12:25 worrying can add a single hour to your l? *G2461*
Lk 14:26 even their own l—such a person *G6034*
Lk 17:33 Whoever tries to keep their l will lose it *G6034*
Lk 17:33 and whoever loses their l will preserve it. NDT
Lk 18:18 what must I do to inherit eternal l? *G2437*
Lk 18:30 and in the age to come eternal l. *G2437*
Lk 21:19 Stand firm, and you will win l. *G6034*
Lk 21:34 drunkenness and the anxieties **of l**, and *G1053*
Jn 1: 4 In him was l, and that life was the light of *G2437*
Jn 1: 4 that l was the light of all mankind. *G2437*
Jn 3:15 who believes may have eternal l in him.” *G2437*
Jn 3:16 in him shall not perish but have eternal l. *G2437*
Jn 3:36 Whoever believes in the Son has eternal l *G2437*
Jn 3:36 whoever rejects the Son will not see l *G2437*
Jn 4:14 a spring of water welling up to eternal l.” *G2437*
Jn 4:36 a wage and harvests a crop for eternal l, *G2437*
Jn 5:21 Father raises the dead and **gives** them l, *G2443*
Jn 5:21 even so the Son **gives** l to whom he is *G2443*
Jn 5:24 sent me has eternal l and will not be *G2437*
Jn 5:24 has crossed over from death to l. *G2437*
Jn 5:26 For as the Father has l in himself, so he *G2437*
Jn 5:26 granted the Son also to have l in himself. *G2437*
Jn 5:39 you think that in them you have eternal l. *G2437*
Jn 5:40 you refuse to come to me to have l. *G2437*
Jn 6:27 for food that endures to eternal l *G2437*
Jn 6:33 from heaven and gives l to the world.” *G2437*
Jn 6:35 “I am the bread *of* l. Whoever comes to *G2437*
Jn 6:40 believes in him shall have eternal l, *G2437*
Jn 6:47 the one who believes has eternal l. *G2437*
Jn 6:48 I am the bread *of* l. *G2437*
Jn 6:51 which I will give for the l of the world.” *G2437*
Jn 6:53 drink his blood, you have no l in you. *G2437*
Jn 6:54 flesh and drinks my blood has eternal l, *G2437*
Jn 6:63 The Spirit **gives** l; the flesh counts for *G2443*
Jn 6:63 to you—they are full of the Spirit and l. *G2437*
Jn 6:68 You have the words of eternal l. *G2437*
Jn 8:11 “Go now and **leave** *your* **l of sin**.” *G3600+279*
Jn 8:12 in darkness, but will have the light *of* l.” *G2437*
Jn 10:10 I have come that they may have l, and *G2437*
Jn 10:11 shepherd lays down his l for the sheep. *G6034*
Jn 10:15 I lay down my l for the sheep. *G6034*
Jn 10:17 Father loves me is that I lay down my l— *G6034*
Jn 10:28 I give them eternal l, and they shall never *G2437*
Jn 11:25 “I am the resurrection and the l. *G2437*
Jn 11:53 from that day on they plotted to **take** his l. *G650*
Jn 12:25 Anyone who loves their l will lose it, while *G6034*
Jn 12:25 anyone who hates their l in this world will *G6034*
Jn 12:25 life in this world will keep it for eternal l. *G2437*
Jn 12:50 know that his command leads to eternal l. *G2437*
Jn 13:37 I will lay down my l for you.” *G6034*
Jn 13:38 “Will you really lay down your l for me? *G6034*
Jn 14: 6 “I am the way and the truth and the l. *G2437*
Jn 15:13 to lay down one’s l for one’s friends. *G6034*
Jn 17: 2 might give eternal l to all those you have *G2437*

Jn 17: 3 Now this is eternal l: that they know you G2437
Jn 20:31 by believing you may have l in his name. G2437
Ac 2:28 have made known to me the paths of l; G2437
Ac 2:32 God has raised this Jesus to l, and we are G482
Ac 3:15 You killed the author of l, but God raised G2437
Ac 5:20 "and tell the people all about this new l." G2437
Ac 8:33 For his l was taken from the earth. G2437
Ac 11:18 has granted repentance that leads to l." G2437
Ac 13:46 consider yourselves worthy of eternal l, G2437
Ac 13:48 were appointed for eternal l believed. G2437
Ac 17:25 himself gives everyone l and breath and G2437
Ac 20:24 I consider my l worth nothing to me G6034
Ac 26: 4 the beginning of my l in my own country G1181
Ac 27:43 wanted to spare Paul's l and kept them G1407
Ro 1: 3 who as to his earthly l was a descendant G4922
Ro 2: 7 immortality, he will give eternal l. G2437
Ro 4:17 the God who gives l to the dead and calls G2443
Ro 4:25 our sins and was raised to l for our G1586
Ro 5:10 shall we be saved through his l! G2437
Ro 5:17 reign in l through the one man, G2437
Ro 5:18 in justification and l for all people. G2437
Ro 5:21 to bring eternal l through Jesus Christ our G2437
Ro 6: 4 of the Father, we too may live a new l. G2437
Ro 6:10 once for all; but the l he lives, he lives G4005S
Ro 6:13 those who have been brought from death to l G2409
Ro 6:19 an example from everyday l because of G474
Ro 6:22 to holiness, and the result is eternal l. G2437
Ro 6:23 gift of God is eternal l in Christ Jesus our G2437
Ro 7: 9 sin sprang to l and I died. G348
Ro 7:10 was intended to bring l actually brought G2437
Ro 8: 2 of the Spirit who gives l has set you free G2437
Ro 8: 6 governed by the Spirit is l and peace. G2437
Ro 8:10 the Spirit gives l because of righteousness G2437
Ro 8:11 from the dead will also give l to your G2443
Ro 8:34 than that, who was raised to l—is at the G1586
Ro 8:38 For I am convinced that neither death nor l, G2437
Ro 11:15 their acceptance be but l from the dead? G2437
Ro 14: 9 Christ died and returned to l so that he G2409
1Co 3:22 Cephas or the world or l or death or the G2437
1Co 4:17 remind you of my way of l in Christ Jesus G3847
1Co 6: 3 How much more the things of this l! G1053
1Co 6: 4 from those whose way of l is scorned in the NDT
1Co 7:28 marry will face many troubles in this l, G4922
1Co 15:19 If only for this l we have hope in Christ, G2437
1Co 15:36 you sow does not come to l unless it G2443
2Co 1: 8 to endure, so that we despaired of l itself. G2409
2Co 1:23 I stake my l on it—that it was in G6034
2Co 2:16 an aroma that brings l. G1666+2437+1650+2437
2Co 3: 6 the letter kills, but the Spirit gives l. G2443
2Co 4:10 so that the l of Jesus may also be G2437
2Co 4:11 so that his l may also be revealed in our G2437
2Co 4:12 is at work in us, but l is at work in you. G2437
2Co 5: 4 what is mortal may be swallowed up by l. G2437
Gal 1:13 have heard of my previous way of l in G419
Gal 2:20 The l I now live in the body, I live by G4005S
Gal 3:15 take an example from everyday l. G2848+476
Gal 3:21 a law had been given that could impart l, G2443
Gal 6: 8 from the Spirit will reap eternal l. G2437
Eph 4: 1 I urge you to live a l worthy of the calling G4344
Eph 4:18 separated from the l of God because G2437
Eph 4:20 however, is not the way of l you learned G4048S
Eph 4:22 with regard to your former way of l, to put G419
Eph 6: 3 that you may enjoy long l on the earth." G3432
Php 1:20 in my body, whether by l or by death. G2437
Php 2:16 as you hold firmly to the word of l. G2437
Php 2:30 He risked his l to make up for the help G6034
Php 4: 3 whose names are in the book of l. G2437
Col 1:10 so that you may live a l worthy of the Lord G4344
Col 3: 3 your l is now hidden with Christ in G2437
Col 3: 4 who is your l, appears, then you G2437
Col 3: 7 in these ways, in the l you once lived. G4047S
1Th 4: 7 not call us to be impure, but to live a holy l. AIT
1Th 4:11 to make it your ambition to lead a quiet l: G2483
1Th 4:12 so that your daily l may win the respect of G4344
1Ti 1:16 believe in him and receive eternal l. G2437
1Ti 4: 8 promise for both the present l and the life G2437
1Ti 4: 8 both the present life and the l to come. NDT
1Ti 4:16 Watch your l and doctrine closely G4932
1Ti 6:12 hold of the eternal l to which you were G2437
1Ti 6:13 sight of God, who gives l to everything G2441
1Ti 6:19 may take hold of the l that is truly life. G2437
1Ti 6:19 they may take hold of the life that is truly l. NDT
2Ti 1: 1 with the promise of l that is in Christ Jesus G2437
2Ti 1: 9 has saved us and called us to a holy l— G3104
2Ti 1:10 has brought l and immortality to G2437
2Ti 3:10 about my teaching, my way of l, my purpose, G73
2Ti 3:12 who wants to live a godly l in Christ Jesus G2409
Titus 1: 2 in the hope of eternal l, which God, who G2437
Titus 3: 7 heirs having the hope of eternal l. G2437
Heb 5: 7 During the days of Jesus' l on earth, he G4922
Heb 7: 3 without beginning of days or end of l G2437
Heb 7:16 basis of the power of an indestructible l. G2437
Heb 11: 5 By faith Enoch was taken from this l, so that AIT
Heb 11:35 received back their dead, raised to l again. G414
Heb 13: 7 the outcome of their way of l and imitate G419
Jas 1:12 receive the crown of l that the Lord has G2437
Jas 3: 6 sets the whole course of one's l on fire G1161
Jas 3:13 Let them show it by their good l, by deeds G419
Jas 4:14 What is your l? You are a mist that G2437
1Pe 1:18 from the empty way of l handed down to G419
1Pe 3: 7 as heirs with you of the gracious gift of l, G2437
1Pe 3:10 would love l and see good days G2437
2Pe 1: 3 we need for a godly l through our G2437
1Jn 1: 1 this we proclaim concerning the Word of l. G2437
1Jn 1: 2 The l appeared; we have seen it and G2437
1Jn 1: 2 we proclaim to you the eternal l G2437
1Jn 2:16 the pride of l—comes not from the G1050
1Jn 2:25 this is what he promised us—eternal l. G2437
1Jn 3:14 that we have passed from death to l, G2437
1Jn 3:15 no murderer has eternal l residing in him. G2437
1Jn 3:16 Jesus Christ laid down his l for us. And we G6034
1Jn 5:11 God has given us eternal l, and this life is G2437
1Jn 5:11 us eternal life, and this l is in his Son. G2437
1Jn 5:12 Whoever has the Son has l; whoever does G2437
1Jn 5:12 not have the Son of God does not have l. G2437
1Jn 5:13 you may know that you have eternal l. G2437
1Jn 5:16 you should pray and God will give them l. G2437
1Jn 5:20 He is the true God and eternal l. G2437
Jude 21 Lord Jesus Christ to bring you to eternal l. G2437
Rev 2: 7 will give the right to eat from the tree of l, G2437
Rev 2: 8 the Last, who died and came to l again. G2409
Rev 2:10 I will give you l as your victor's crown. G2437
Rev 3: 5 name of that person from the book of l, G2437
Rev 11:11 half days the breath of l from God entered G2437
Rev 13: 8 not been written in the Lamb's book of l, G2437
Rev 17: 8 written in the book of l from the creation G2437
Rev 20: 4 They came to l and reigned with Christ a G2409
Rev 20: 5 of the dead did not come to l until the G2409
Rev 20:12 book was opened, which is the book of l. G2437
Rev 20:15 in the book of l was thrown into the G2437
Rev 21: 6 cost from the spring of the water of l. G2437
Rev 21:27 names are written in the Lamb's book of l. G2437
Rev 22: 1 showed me the river of the water of l, G2437
Rev 22: 2 each side of the river stood the tree of l, G2437
Rev 22:14 right to the tree of l and may go through G2437
Rev 22:17 wishes take the free gift of the water of l. G2437
Rev 22:19 share in the tree of l and in the Holy City, G2437

LIFE'S (2) [LIVE]

Ps 39: 4 my l end and the number of my days H3276
Lk 8:14 on their way they are choked by l worries, G1050

LIFE-GIVING (2) [GIVE]

Pr 15:31 Whoever heeds l correction will be at H2644
1Co 15:45 a living being"; the last Adam, a l spirit. G2443

LIFEBLOOD (3) [BLOOD]

Ge 9: 4 not eat meat that has its l still in it. H1947+5883
Ge 9: 5 And for your l I will surely demand H1947+5883
Jer 2:34 is found the l of the innocent poor, H1947+5883

LIFEBOAT (3) [BOAT]

Ac 27:16 we were hardly able to make the l secure G5002
Ac 27:30 the sailors let the l down into the sea G5002
Ac 27:32 cut the ropes that held the l and let it drift G5002

LIFELESS (5) [LIVE]

Lev 26:30 dead bodies on the l forms of your idols, H7007
Ps 106:28 Peor and ate sacrifices offered to l gods; H4637
Jer 16:18 my land with the l forms of their vile H5577
Hab 2:19 Or to l stone, 'Wake up!' Can H1876
1Co 14: 7 in the case of l things that make sounds, G953

LIFETIME (17) [LIVE]

Nu 3: 4 priests during the l of their father Aaron. H7156
Jos 24:31 LORD throughout the l of Joshua and of the H3427
Jdg 2: 7 LORD throughout the l of Joshua and of the H3427
Jdg 8:28 During Gideon's l, the land had peace H3427
1Sa 7:13 Throughout Samuel's l, the hand of the H3427
2Sa 18:18 During his l Absalom had taken a pillar H2644
1Ki 3:13 so that in your l you will have no H3972+3427
1Ki 4:25 During Solomon's l Judah and Israel, from H3427
1Ki 11:12 your father, I will not do it during your l. H3427
1Ki 12: 6 served his father Solomon during his l. H2645
1Ki 15: 6 Jeroboam throughout Abijah's l. H3427+2644
2Ki 20:19 there not be peace and security in my l?" H3427
2Ch 10: 6 served his father Solomon during his l. H2645
Ps 30: 5 his favor lasts a l; weeping may stay H2644
Isa 39: 8 "There will be peace and security in my l." H3427
Jer 22:30 a man who will not prosper in his l, for H3427
Lk 16:25 remember that in your l you received your G2437

LIFT (61) [LIFTED, LIFTING, LIFTS, UPLIFTED]

Ge 21:18 L the boy up and take him by the hand, for H5951
Ge 40:13 days Pharaoh will l up your head and H5951
Ge 40:19 days Pharaoh will l off your head and H5951
Ge 41:44 your word no one will l hand or foot in all H8123
Ex 40:37 if the cloud did not l, they did not set H6590
Dt 28:32 them day after day, powerless to l a hand. NDT
Dt 32:40 I l my hand to heaven and solemnly H5951
1Sa 6: 5 Perhaps he will l his hand from you and H7837
2Sa 1:14 you afraid to l your hand to destroy H8938
2Ki 6: 7 "L it out," he said. Then the man reached H8123
Ezr 9: 6 my God, to l up my face to you, because H8123
Job 10:15 I am innocent, I cannot l my head, for I H5951
Job 11:15 free of fault, you will l up your face; you H5951
Job 22:26 the Almighty and will l up your face to H5951
Job 22:29 are brought low and you say, 'L them up! H1575
Ps 9:13 Have mercy and l me up from the gates of H8123
Ps 10:12 L up your hand, O God. Do not H5951
Ps 20: 5 victory and l up our banners in the name H1839
Ps 24: 7 L up your heads, you gates; be lifted up H5951
Ps 24: 9 L up your heads, you gates; lift them up H5951
Ps 24: 9 you gates; l them up, you ancient doors H5951
Ps 28: 2 as I l up my hands toward your Most Holy H5951
Ps 63: 4 in your name I will l up my hands. H5951
Ps 75: 4 to the wicked, 'Do not l up your horns. H8123
Ps 75: 5 Do not l your horns against heaven; do H8123
Ps 76: 5 not one of the warriors can l his hands. H5162
Ps 91:12 they will l you up in their hands, so that H5951
Ps 110: 7 the way, and so he will l his head high. H8123
Ps 116:13 I will l up the cup of salvation and call on H5951
Ps 121: 1 I l up my eyes to the mountains—where H5951
Ps 123: 1 I l up my eyes to you, to you who sit H5951
Ps 134: 2 L up your hands in the sanctuary and H5951
Ps 142: 1 I l up my voice to the LORD for mercy. H2858
Isa 10:24 you with a rod and l up a club against you H5951
Isa 40: 9 to Jerusalem, l up your voice with a shout H8123
Isa 40: 9 voice with a shout, l it up, do not be H8123
Isa 40:26 L up your eyes and look to the heavens H5951
Isa 46: 7 They l it to their shoulders and carry it H5951
Isa 47: 2 L up your skirts, bare your legs, and wade H3106
Isa 49:18 L up your eyes and look around; all your H5951
Isa 49:22 I will l up my banner to the peoples H8123
Isa 51: 6 L up your eyes to the heavens, look at the H5951
Isa 52: 8 Your watchmen l up their voices; together H5951
Isa 60: 4 "L up your eyes and look about you: All H5951
Jer 38:10 here with you and l Jeremiah the prophet H6590
Jer 50: 2 the nations, l up a banner and proclaim it H5951
Jer 51:12 L up a banner against the walls of H5951
Jer 51:27 "L up a banner in the land! Blow the H5951
La 2:19 L up your hands to him for the lives of H5951
La 3:41 Let us l up our hearts and our hands to H5951
Da 6:23 gave orders to l Daniel out of the den. A10513
Am 5: 2 in her own land, with no one to l her up." H7756
Na 3: 5 "I will l your skirts over your face H1655
Mt 4: 6 and they will l you up in their hands G149
Mt 12:11 will you not take hold of it and l it out? G1586
Mt 23: 4 are not willing to l a finger to move them. AIT
Lk 4:11 they will l you up in their hands, so that G149
Lk 11:46 you yourselves will not l one finger to help G4718+3836+5845
Lk 21:28 stand up and l up your heads G2048
Jas 4:10 before the Lord, and he will l you up. G5738
1Pe 5: 6 that he may l you up in due time. G5738

LIFTED (66) [LIFT]

Ge 7:17 waters increased they l the ark high above H5951
Ge 40:20 He l up the heads of the chief cupbearer H5951
Ex 17:16 "Because hands were l up against the NDT
Ex 40:36 whenever the cloud l from above the H6590
Ex 40:37 they did not set out—until the day it l. H6590
Lev 9:22 Then Aaron l his hands toward the H5951
Nu 9:17 Whenever the cloud l from above the tent H6590
Nu 9:21 when it l in the morning, they H6590
Nu 9:21 whenever the cloud l, they set out. H6590
Nu 9:22 but when it l, they would set out. H6590
Nu 10:11 the cloud l from above the tabernacle of H6590
Nu 12:10 When the cloud l from above the tent H6073
Jdg 9:48 branches, which he l to his shoulders. H5951
Jdg 16: 3 He l them to his shoulders and carried H8492
1Sa 2: 1 in the LORD; in the LORD my horn is l high. H8123
1Sa 6: 3 why his hand has not been l from you." H6073
2Sa 18:28 up those who l their hands against my H5951
2Sa 20:21 has l up his hand against the king H5951
1Ki 16: 2 "I l you up from the dust and appointed H8123
2Ki 4:20 the servant had l him up and carried him H5951
2Ki 19:22 raised your voice and l your eyes in pride? H5951
Ne 8: 6 all the people l their hands and H5089
Job 5:11 those who mourn are l to safety. H8435
Ps 24: 7 you gates; be l up, you ancient doors, that H5951
Ps 30: 1 for you l me out of the depths and did not H1926
Ps 40: 2 He l me out of the slimy pit, out of the H6590
Ps 75:10 the horns of the righteous will be l up." H8123
Ps 93: 3 The seas have l up, LORD, the seas have H5951
Ps 93: 3 the seas have l up their voice; the H5951
Ps 93: 3 the seas have l up their pounding waves. H5951
Ps 107:25 stirred up a tempest that l high the waves. H8123
Ps 107:41 But he l the needy out of their affliction H8435
Ps 112: 9 their horn will be l high in honor. H8123
Ps 118:16 The LORD's right hand is l high; the LORD's H8123
Isa 10:27 day their burden will be l from your H6073
Isa 26:11 your hand is l high, but they do not H8123
Isa 33:10 "Now will I be exalted; now will I be l up. H5951
Isa 37:23 raised your voice and l your eyes in pride? H5951
Isa 52:13 will be raised and l up and highly exalted H5951
Isa 63: 9 he l them up and carried them all the H5747
Jer 38:13 up with the ropes and l him out of the H6590
Eze 3:12 Then the Spirit l me up, and I heard H5951
Eze 3:14 The Spirit then l me up and took me away H5951
Eze 8: 3 The Spirit l me up between earth and H5951
Eze 11: 1 Then the Spirit l me up and brought me H5951
Eze 11:24 The Spirit l me up and brought me to the H5951
Eze 43: 5 Then the Spirit l me up and brought me H5951
Da 6:23 And when Daniel was l from the den, no A10513
Da 7: 4 torn off and it was l from the ground A10475
Da 12: 7 l his right hand and his left hand toward H8123
Am 5:26 You have l up the shrine of your king, the H5951
Mic 5: 9 Your hand will be l up in triumph over H8123
Hab 3:10 the deep roared and l its waves on high. H5951
Zec 1:21 of the nations who l up their horns H5951
Zec 5: 9 and they l up the basket between heaven H5951
Mt 11:23 Capernaum, will you be l to the heavens? G5738
Mk 9:27 him by the hand and l him to his feet, G1586
Lk 1:52 their thrones but has l up the humble. G5738
Lk 10:15 Capernaum, will you be l to the heavens? G5738

Lk 24:50 he l up his hands and blessed them. G2048
Jn 3:14 Just as Moses l up the snake in the G5738
Jn 3:14 so the Son of Man must be l up, G5738
Jn 8:28 "When you have l up the Son of Man G5738
Jn 12:32 when I am l up from the earth, will G5738
Jn 12:34 you say, 'The Son of Man must be l up'? G5738
Jn 19:29 of the hyssop plant, and l it to Jesus' lips. G4712

LIFTING (3) [LIFT]

Ps 141: 2 may the l up of my hands be like the H5368
Eze 31:14 l their tops above the thick foliage. H5989
1Ti 2: 8 l up holy hands without anger or G2048

LIFTS (10) [LIFT]

1Sa 2: 8 from the dust and l the needy from the H8123
Ezr 6:12 king or people who l a hand to change A10714
Ps 3: 3 my glory, the One who l my head high. H8123
Ps 46: 6 kingdoms fall; he l his voice, the earth H5989
Ps 113: 7 from the dust and l the needy from the H8123
Ps 145:14 all who fall and l up all who are bowed H2422
Ps 146: 8 the LORD l up those who are bowed down H2422
Isa 5:26 He l up a banner for the distant nations H5951
Isa 10:15 rod were to wield the person who l it up, H8123
Hos 11: 4 them I was like one who l a little child to H8123

LIGAMENT (1) [LIGAMENTS]

Eph 4:16 held together by every supporting l, G913

LIGAMENTS (1) [LIGAMENT]

Col 2:19 held together by its l and sinews, G913

LIGHT (232) [DAYLIGHT, ENLIGHTEN, ENLIGHTENED, LIGHTEN, LIGHTENED, LIGHTER, LIGHTS, LIT, SUNLIGHT, TWILIGHT]

Ge 1: 3 "Let there be l," and there was light. H240
Ge 1: 3 "Let there be light," and there was l. H240
Ge 1: 4 God saw that the l was good, and he H240
Ge 1: 4 he separated the l from the darkness. H240
Ge 1: 5 God called the l "day," and the darkness he H240
Ge 1:15 in the vault of the sky to give l on the earth." H239
Ge 1:16 the greater l to govern the day and the H4401
Ge 1:16 day and the lesser l to govern the night. H4401
Ge 1:17 in the vault of the sky to give l on the earth, H239
Ge 1:18 the night, and to separate l from darkness. H240
Ex 10:23 all the Israelites had l in the places where H240
Ex 13:21 by night in a pillar of fire to give them l, H239
Ex 14:20 to the one side and l to the other side; H239
Ex 25: 6 olive oil for the l; spices for the anointing H4401
Ex 25:37 up on it so that they l the space in front H239
Ex 27:20 olives for the l so that the lamps may H4401
Ex 35: 3 Do not l a fire in any of your dwellings on H1277
Ex 35: 8 olive oil for the l; spices for the anointing H4401
Ex 35:14 lampstand that is for l with its accessories, H4401
Ex 35:14 its accessories, lamps and oil for the l; H4401
Ex 35:28 olive oil for the l and for the anointing H4401
Ex 39:37 its accessories, and the olive oil for the l; H4401
Lev 24: 2 olives for the l so that the lamps may H4401
Nu 4: 9 cloth and cover the lampstand that is for l, H4401
Nu 4:16 is to have charge of the oil for the l, the H4401
Nu 8: 2 see that all seven l up the area in front of H239
Dt 25:13 weights in your bag—one heavy, one l. H7783
1Sa 29:10 leave in the morning as soon as it is l." H239
2Sa 22:29 the LORD turns my darkness into l. H5585
2Sa 23: 4 he is like the l of morning at sunrise on a H240
1Ki 3:21 I looked at him closely in the morning l, H1332
1Ki 18:25 name of your god, but do not l the fire." H8492
2Ch 13:11 clean table and l the lamps on the gold H1277
Ezr 9: 8 so our God gives l to our eyes and a H239
Ne 4:21 from the first l of dawn till the stars H6590+8840
Ne 9:12 pillar of fire to give them l on the way they H239
Job 3: 4 not care about it; may no l shine on it. H5644
Job 3:16 like an infant who never saw the l of day? H240
Job 3:20 "Why is l given to those in misery, and life H240
Job 9: 7 not shine; he seals off the l of the stars. NDT
Job 10:22 where even the l is like darkness. H3649
Job 12:22 brings utter darkness into the l. H240
Job 12:25 They grope in darkness with no l; he makes H240
Job 17:12 in the face of the darkness l is near. H240
Job 18: 6 The l in his tent becomes dark; the lamp H240
Job 18:18 He is driven from l into the realm of H240
Job 22:28 will be done, and l will shine on your ways. H240
Job 24:13 "There are those who rebel against the l H240
Job 24:16 they want nothing to do with the l. H240
Job 25: 3 On whom does his l not rise? H240
Job 26:10 a boundary between l and darkness. H240
Job 28:11 of the rivers and bring hidden things to l. H240
Job 29: 3 on my head and by his l I walked through H240
Job 29:24 the l of my face was precious to them. H240
Job 30:26 when I looked for l, then came darkness. H240
Job 33:28 and I shall live to enjoy the l of life. H240
Job 33:30 that the l of life may shine on them. H240
Job 38:15 The wicked are denied their l, and their H240
Job 38:19 "What is the way to the abode of l? And H240
Job 41:18 Its snorting throws out flashes of l; its eyes H240
Ps 4: 6 Let the l of your face shine on us. H240
Ps 13: 3 Give l to my eyes, or I will H239
Ps 18:28 burning; my God turns my darkness into l. H5585
Ps 19: 8 of the LORD are radiant, giving l to the eyes. H239
Ps 27: 1 The LORD is my l and my salvation—whom H240
Ps 36: 9 the fountain of life; in your l we see light. H240
Ps 36: 9 the fountain of life; in your light we see l. H240
Ps 38:10 even the l has gone from my eyes. H240
Ps 43: 3 Send me your l and your faithful care, let H240
Ps 44: 3 your arm, and the l of your face, for you H240
Ps 49:19 who will never again see the l of life. H240
Ps 56:13 that I may walk before God in the l of life. H240
Ps 76: 4 You are radiant with l, more majestic than H239
Ps 78:14 by day and with l from the fire all night. H240
Ps 89:15 who walk in the l of your presence, LORD H240
Ps 90: 8 our secret sins in the l of your presence. H4401
Ps 97:11 L shines on the righteous and joy on the H240
Ps 104: 2 LORD wraps himself in l as with a garment; H240
Ps 105:39 as a covering, and a fire to give l at night. H239
Ps 112: 4 Even in darkness l dawns for the upright H240
Ps 118:27 and he has made his l shine on us. H239
Ps 119:105 word is a lamp for my feet, a l on my path. H240
Ps 119:130 The unfolding of your words gives l; H239
Ps 139:11 hide me and the l become night around H240
Ps 139:12 like the day, for darkness is as l to you. H245
Pr 4:18 shining ever brighter till the full l of day. NDT
Pr 6:23 this teaching is a l, and correction and H240
Pr 13: 9 The l of the righteous shines brightly, but H240
Pr 15:30 L in a messenger's eyes brings joy to the H4401
Pr 20:27 of the LORD that sheds l on one's inmost H2924
Ecc 2:13 than folly, just as l is better than darkness. H240
Ecc 11: 7 L is sweet, and it pleases the eyes to see H240
Ecc 12: 2 the sun and the l and the moon and the H240
Isa 2: 5 of Jacob, let us walk in the l of the LORD. H240
Isa 5:20 who put darkness for l and light for H240
Isa 5:20 put darkness for light and l for darkness, H240
Isa 8:20 to this word, they have no l of dawn. H8840
Isa 9: 2 walking in darkness have seen a great l; H240
Isa 9: 2 the land of deep darkness a l has dawned. H240
Isa 10:17 The L of Israel will become a fire, their H240
Isa 13:10 their constellations will not show their l. H240
Isa 13:10 darkened and the moon will not give its l. H240
Isa 30:26 brighter, like the l of seven full days, when H240
Isa 42: 6 the people and a l for the Gentiles, H240
Isa 42:16 the darkness into l before them and make H240
Isa 45: 7 I form the l and create darkness, I bring H240
Isa 49: 6 I will also make you a l for the Gentiles H240
Isa 50:10 the dark, who has no l, trust in the name H5586
Isa 50:11 all you who l fires and provide yourselves H7706
Isa 50:11 walk in the l of your fires and of the torches H241
Isa 51: 4 my justice will become a l to the nations. H240
Isa 53:11 he will see the l of life and be satisfied; by H240
Isa 58: 8 Then your l will break forth like the dawn H240
Isa 58:10 then your l will rise in the darkness H240
Isa 59: 9 We look for l, but all is darkness; for H240
Isa 60: 1 for your l has come, and the glory of H240
Isa 60: 3 Nations will come to your l, and kings to H240
Isa 60:19 The sun will no more be your l by day, nor H240
Isa 60:19 the LORD will be your everlasting l, and H240
Isa 60:20 the LORD will be your everlasting l, and H240
Jer 4:23 at the heavens, and their l was gone. H240
Jer 7:18 the fathers l the fire, and the H1277
Jer 13:16 You hope for l, but he will turn it to utter H240
Jer 25:10 sound of millstones and the l of the lamp. H240
La 3: 2 made me walk in darkness rather than l; H240
Eze 1: 4 lightning and surrounded by brilliant l. H5586
Eze 1:27 like fire; and brilliant l surrounded him. H5586
Eze 32: 7 the moon will not give its l. H239+240
Da 2:22 lies in darkness, and l dwells with him. A10466
Da 6:19 At the first l of dawn, the king got up A10459
Am 5:18 That day will be darkness, not l. H240
Am 5:20 of the LORD be darkness, not l—pitch-dark, H240
Mic 2: 1 At morning's l they carry it out because it is H240
Mic 7: 8 I sit in darkness, the LORD will be my l. H240
Mic 7: 9 He will bring me out into the l; I will see H240
Zec 14: 7 When evening comes, there will be l. H240
Mal 1:10 so that you would not l useless fires on my H239
Mt 4:16 living in darkness have seen a great l; G5890
Mt 4:16 of the shadow of death a l has dawned." G5890
Mt 5:14 "You are the l of the world. A town built G5890
Mt 5:15 Neither do people l a lamp and put it G2794
Mt 5:15 and it gives l to everyone in the house. G3290
Mt 5:16 same way, let your l shine before others G5890
Mt 6:22 healthy, your whole body will be full of l. G5893
Mt 6:23 If then the l within you is darkness, how G5890
Mt 11:30 For my yoke is easy and my burden is l." G1787
Mt 17: 2 his clothes became as white as the l. G5890
Mt 24:29 the moon will not give its l; the stars G5766
Mk 13:24 the moon will not give its l; G5766
Lk 2:32 a l for revelation to the Gentiles, and the G5890
Lk 8:16 so that those who come in can see the l. G5890
Lk 11:33 so that those who come in may see the l. G5890
Lk 11:34 healthy, your whole body also is full of l. G5893
Lk 11:35 that the l within you is not darkness. G5890
Lk 11:36 if your whole body is full of l, and no part G5893
Lk 11:36 be just as full of l as when a lamp shines G5893
Lk 11:36 of light as when a lamp shines its l on you." G847
Lk 15: 8 Doesn't she l a lamp, sweep the house G721
Lk 16: 8 own kind than are the people of the l. G5890
Jn 1: 4 and that life was the l of all mankind. G5890
Jn 1: 5 The l shines in the darkness, and the G5890
Jn 1: 7 as a witness to testify concerning that l, G5890
Jn 1: 8 He himself was not the l; he came only as G5890
Jn 1: 8 he came only as a witness to the l. G5890
Jn 1: 9 The true l that gives light to everyone was G5890
Jn 1: 9 The true light that gives l to everyone was G5894
Jn 3:19 L has come into the world, but people G5890
Jn 3:19 darkness instead of l because their deeds G5890
Jn 3:20 Everyone who does evil hates the l, and G5890
Jn 3:20 will not come into the l for fear that their G5890
Jn 3:21 lives by the truth comes into the l, G5890
Jn 5:35 John was a lamp that burned and gave l G5743
Jn 5:35 you chose for a time to enjoy his l. G5890
Jn 8:12 people, he said, "I am the l of the world. G5890
Jn 8:12 in darkness, but will have the l of life." G5890
Jn 9: 5 I am in the world, I am the l of the world." G5890
Jn 11: 9 not stumble, for they see by this world's l. G5890
Jn 11:10 that they stumble, for they have no l." G5890
Jn 12:35 are going to have the l just a little while G5890
Jn 12:35 Walk while you have the l, before G5890
Jn 12:36 Believe in the l while you have the light G5890
Jn 12:36 Believe in the light while you have the l G5890
Jn 12:36 so that you may become children of l." G5890
Jn 12:46 I have come into the world as a l, so that G5890
Ac 9: 3 suddenly a l from heaven flashed around G5890
Ac 12: 7 Lord appeared and a l shone in the cell. G5890
Ac 13:11 not even able to see the l of the sun." G2463
Ac 13:47 " 'I have made you a l for the Gentiles G5890
Ac 22: 6 suddenly a bright l from heaven flashed G5890
Ac 22: 9 My companions saw the l, but they did not G5890
Ac 22:11 the brilliance of the l had blinded me. G5890
Ac 26:13 on the road, I saw a l from heaven G5890
Ac 26:18 eyes and turn them from darkness to l, G5890
Ac 26:23 bring the message of l to his own people G5890
Ro 2:19 the blind, a l for those who are in the dark G5890
Ro 13:12 of darkness and put on the armor of l. G5890
1Co 3:13 because the Day will bring it to l. G1317
1Co 4: 5 He will bring to l what is hidden in G5894
2Co 4: 4 they cannot see the l of the gospel that G5895
2Co 4: 6 who said, "Let l shine out of darkness," G5890
2Co 4: 6 made his l shine in our hearts to give us the NDT
2Co 4: 6 in our hearts to give us the l of the G5895
2Co 4:17 For our l and momentary troubles are G1787
2Co 6:14 what fellowship can l have with darkness? G5890
2Co 11:14 himself masquerades as an angel of l. G5890
Eph 5: 8 darkness, but now you are l in the Lord. G5890
Eph 5: 8 are light in the Lord. Live as children of l G5890
Eph 5: 9 the fruit of the l consists in all G5890
Eph 5:13 exposed by the l becomes visible— G5890
Eph 5:13 that is illuminated becomes a l. G5890
Col 1:12 of his holy people in the kingdom of l. G5890
1Th 5: 5 are all children of the l and children of G5890
1Ti 6:16 who lives in unapproachable l, G5890
2Ti 1:10 and has brought life and immortality to l G5894
Titus 1: 3 now at his appointed season he has brought to l G5746
Heb 10:32 earlier days after you had received the l, G5894
Heb 12: 5 do not make l of the Lord's discipline G3902
1Pe 2: 9 you out of darkness into his wonderful l. G5890
2Pe 1:19 as to a l shining in a dark place G3394
1Jn 1: 5 God is l; in him there is no darkness at all. G5890
1Jn 1: 7 But if we walk in the l, as he is in the light G5890
1Jn 1: 7 as he is in the l, we have fellowship G5890
1Jn 2: 8 passing and the true l is already shining. G5890
1Jn 2: 9 claims to be in the l but hates a brother G5890
1Jn 2:10 loves their brother and sister lives in the l, G5890
Rev 8:12 A third of the day was without l, and also G5743
Rev 18:23 The l of a lamp will never shine in you G5890
Rev 21:23 the glory of God gives it l, and the G5894
Rev 21:24 The nations will walk by its l, and the G5890
Rev 22: 5 will not need the l of a lamp or the light G5890
Rev 22: 5 the light of a lamp or the l of the sun, G5890
Rev 22: 5 the sun, for the Lord God will give them l. G5894

LIGHTEN (5) [LIGHT]

1Ki 12: 4 now l the harsh labor and the heavy H7837
1Ki 12: 9 'L the yoke your father put on us'? H7837
2Ch 10: 4 now l the harsh labor and the heavy H7837
2Ch 10: 9 'L the yoke your father put on us'? H7837
Jnh 1: 5 threw the cargo into the sea to l the ship. H7837

LIGHTENED (1) [LIGHT]

Ac 27:38 they l the ship by throwing the grain into G3185

LIGHTER (3) [LIGHT]

Ex 18:22 That will make your load l, because they H7837
1Ki 12:10 a heavy yoke on us, but make our yoke l. H7837
2Ch 10:10 a heavy yoke on us, but make our yoke l. H7837

LIGHTNING (45)

Ex 9:23 and l flashed down to the ground. H836
Ex 9:24 hail fell and l flashed back and forth. It was H836
Ex 19:16 of the third day there was thunder and l, H1398
Ex 20:18 saw the thunder and l and heard the H4365
2Sa 22:13 of his presence bolts of l blazed forth. H836
2Sa 22:15 with great bolts of l he routed them. H1398
Job 36:30 See how he scatters his l about him H240
Job 36:32 fills his hands with l and commands it to H240
Job 37: 3 He unleashes his l beneath the whole H240
Job 37:11 moisture; he scatters his l through them. H240
Job 37:15 controls the clouds and makes his l flash? H240
Job 38:24 way to the place where the l is dispersed, H240
Job 38:35 Do you send the l bolts on their way? Do H1398
Ps 18:12 advanced, with hailstones and bolts of l. H836
Ps 18:14 with great bolts of l he routed them. H1398
Ps 29: 7 voice of the LORD strikes with flashes of l. H836
Ps 77:18 the whirlwind, your l lit up the world; the H1398
Ps 78:48 to the hail, their livestock to bolts of l. H8404
Ps 97: 4 His l lights up the world; the earth sees H1398
Ps 105:32 with l throughout their land H836+4259
Ps 135: 7 he sends l with the rain and brings out H1398
Ps 144: 6 Send forth l and scatter the enemy H1397+1398
Ps 148: 8 l and hail, snow and clouds, stormy winds H836

Jer 10:13 He sends l with the rain and brings out H1398
Jer 51:16 He sends l with the rain and brings out H1398
Eze 1: 4 cloud with flashing l and surrounded by H836
Eze 1:13 it was bright, and l flashed out of it. H1398
Eze 1:14 sped back and forth like **flashes of l**. H1027
Eze 21:10 the slaughter, polished to **flash like l**! H1398
Eze 21:15 It is forged to **strike like l**, it is grasped H1398
Eze 21:28 polished to consume and to **flash like l**! H1398
Da 10: 6 his face like l, his eyes like flaming H1398
Na 2: 4 like flaming torches; they dart about like l. H1398
Hab 3:11 at the l *of* your flashing spear. H1398
Zec 9:14 over them; his arrow will flash like l. H1398
Mt 24:27 For as l that comes from the east is visible *G847*
Mt 28: 3 His appearance was like l, and his clothes *G847*
Lk 9:29 clothes became as bright as a **flash of l**. *G1993*
Lk 10:18 "I saw Satan fall like l from heaven. *G847*
Lk 17:24 the Son of Man in his day will be like the l, *G847*
Lk 24: 4 in clothes *that* **gleamed like l** stood beside *G848*
Rev 4: 5 From the throne came **flashes of l** *G847*
Rev 8: 5 rumblings, **flashes of l** and an earthquake. *G847*
Rev 11:19 And there came **flashes of l**, rumblings *G847*
Rev 16:18 Then there came **flashes of l**, rumblings *G847*

LIGHTS (12) [LIGHT]

Ge 1:14 "Let there be l in the vault of the sky to H4401
Ge 1:15 let them be l in the vault of the sky to H4401
Ge 1:16 God made two great l—the greater light to H4401
Ex 30: 8 again when he l the lamps at twilight H6590
Ps 97: 4 His lightning **l up** the world; the earth sees H239
Ps 136: 7 who made the great l—His love endures H240
Eze 32: 8 All the shining l in the heavens I will H4401
Lk 8:16 "No one l a lamp and hides it in a clay jar *G721*
Lk 11:33 "No one l a lamp and puts it in a place *G721*
Lk 17:24 which flashes and **l up** the sky from one *G3290*
Ac 16:29 The jailer called for l, rushed in and fell *G5890*
Jas 1:17 down from the Father *of* the *heavenly* l, *G5890*

LIGURE (KJV) JACINTH

LIKE (1530) [ALIKE, LIKE-MINDED, LIKED, LIKELY, LIKEN, LIKING, LIKENESS, LIKES, LIKEWISE]

Ge 3: 5 you will be l God, knowing good and H3869
Ge 3:22 "The man has now become l one of us H3869
Ge 10: 9 is why it is said, "L Nimrod, a mighty H3869
Ge 13:10 was well watered, l the garden of the LORD H3869
Ge 13:10 garden of the LORD, l the land of Egypt. H3869
Ge 13:16 make your offspring l the dust of the earth H3869
Ge 19: 8 can do what you l with them. H3202+928+6524
Ge 19:28 from the land, l smoke from a furnace. H3869
Ge 20:15 live wherever you l. H3202+928+6524
Ge 25:25 his whole body was l a hairy garment; H3869
Ge 27: 4 kind of tasty food *I* l and bring it to me to H170
Ge 27:23 his hands were hairy l those of his brother H3869
Ge 27:27 smell of my son is l the smell of a field H3869
Ge 27:46 from Hittite women l these, my life will H3869
Ge 28:14 descendants will be l the dust of the earth H3869
Ge 29:20 they seemed l only a few days to him H3869
Ge 31:26 carried off my daughters l captives in war. H3869
Ge 31:41 It was *l* **this** for the twenty years I was in your AIT
Ge 32:12 your descendants l the sand of the sea, H3869
Ge 33:10 to see your face is l seeing the face of H3869
Ge 34:12 **Make** the price for the bride and the gift I am to bring **as great as you l** H8049+4394
Ge 34:15 that you become l us by circumcising all H4017
Ge 34:31 he have treated our sister l a prostitute?" H3869
Ge 38:11 "He may die too, **just l** his brothers." H3869
Ge 41:38 "Can we find anyone l this man, one in H3869
Ge 41:49 quantities of grain, l the sand of the sea H3869
Ge 44: 7 it from your servants to do anything l that! H3869
Ge 44:15 you know that a man l me can find things H4017
Ge 48:20 'May God make you l Ephraim and H3869
Ge 49: 9 **L** a lion he crouches and lies down, like a H3869
Ge 49: 9 lies down, l a lioness—who dares to H3869
Ex 1:19 women are not l Egyptian women; H3869
Ex 4: 7 it was restored, l the rest of his flesh. H3869
Ex 7: 1 I have made you l God to Pharaoh, and NDT
Ex 8:10 know there is no one l the LORD our God. H3869
Ex 9:14 that there is no one l me in all the earth. H4017
Ex 12:48 he may take part l one born in the land. H3869
Ex 13: 9 will be for you l a sign on your hand and H4200
Ex 13:16 And it will be l a sign on your hand and a H4200
Ex 15: 5 they sank to the depths l a stone. H4017
Ex 15: 7 it consumed them l stubble. H3869
Ex 15: 8 The surging waters stood up l a wall; the H4017
Ex 15:10 They sank l lead in the mighty waters. H3869
Ex 15:11 Who among the gods is l you, LORD? Who H4017
Ex 15:11 Who is l you—majestic in holiness H4017
Ex 16:14 thin flakes l frost on the ground appeared H3869
Ex 16:31 It was white l coriander seed and tasted H3869
Ex 16:31 seed and tasted l wafers made with H3869
Ex 19:18 billowed up from it l smoke from a H3869
Ex 22:25 do not treat it l a business deal H3869
Ex 24:10 was something l a pavement made of H3869
Ex 24:17 of the LORD looked l a consuming fire on H3869
Ex 25: 9 furnishings **exactly l** the H3869+3972+889+4027
Ex 25:33 Three cups **shaped l almond flowers** with H5481
Ex 25:34 four cups **shaped l almond flowers** with H5481
Ex 26:24 into a single ring; both shall be l **that**. H4027
Ex 28: 8 woven waistband is to be l it— H3869+5126
Ex 28:14 chains of pure gold, l a rope, and attach H5126
Ex 28:15 Make it l the ephod: of gold H3869+5126
Ex 28:21 each **engraved** *l* a seal with the name of one AIT
Ex 28:22 braided chains of pure gold, l a rope. H5126
Ex 28:32 be a woven edge l a collar around this H3869
Ex 30:33 Whoever makes perfume l it and puts it on H4017
Ex 30:38 Whoever makes incense l it to enjoy its H4017
Ex 34: 1 out two stone tablets l the first ones, H3869
Ex 34: 4 out two stone tablets l the first ones and H3869
Ex 37:19 Three cups **shaped l almond flowers** with H5481
Ex 37:20 four cups **shaped l almond flowers** with H5481
Ex 38:18 l the curtains of the courtyard H4200+6645
Ex 39: 5 woven waistband was l it— H3869+5126
Ex 39: 6 settings and **engraved** them *l* a seal with the AIT
Ex 39: 8 They made it l the ephod: of gold, H3869
Ex 39:14 each **engraved** *l* a seal with the name of one AIT
Ex 39:15 braided chains of pure gold, l a rope. H5126
Ex 39:23 the center of the robe l the opening of a H3869
Ex 39:30 engraved on it, l an inscription on a seal: NDT
Lev 6:17 **L** the sin offering and the guilt offering, it H3869
Lev 13:43 is reddish-white l a defiling skin H3869+5260
Lev 14:13 **L** the sin offering, the guilt offering H3869
Lev 14:35 something that looks l a defiling mold in H3869
Lev 26:19 the sky above you l iron and the ground H3869
Lev 26:19 the ground beneath you l bronze. H3869
Lev 27:21 become holy, l a field devoted to the LORD H3869
Nu 8: 4 was made **exactly l** the pattern the H3869+4027
Nu 9:15 cloud above the tabernacle looked l fire. H3869
Nu 9:16 cloud covered it, and at night it **looked** *l* fire. AIT
Nu 11: 7 The manna was l coriander seed and H3869
Nu 11: 7 like coriander seed and looked l resin. H3869
Nu 11: 8 And it tasted l something made with olive H3869
Nu 12:12 Do not let her be l a stillborn infant H3869
Nu 13:18 See **what** the land is l and whether the H4537
Nu 13:33 We seemed l grasshoppers in our own H3869
Nu 14:34 your sins and **know what it is l** to have me H3359
Nu 16:14 *Do you want to* **treat** these men **l slaves** H5941+6524
Nu 16:40 he would become l Korah and his H3869
Nu 23:10 may my final end be l theirs! H4017
Nu 23:24 The people rise l a lioness; they rouse H3869
Nu 23:24 rouse themselves l a lion that does not H3869
Nu 24: 6 "**L** valleys they spread out, like gardens H3869
Nu 24: 6 they spread out, l gardens beside a river H3869
Nu 24: 6 beside a river, l aloes planted by the LORD H3869
Nu 24: 6 by the LORD, l cedars beside the waters. H3869
Nu 24: 9 **L** a lion they crouch and lie down, like a H3869
Nu 24: 9 lie down, l a lioness—who dares H3869
Nu 27:17 people will not be l sheep without a H3869
Nu 32:16 "*We would l to* **build** pens here for our AIT
Dt 1:44 they chased you l a swarm of bees H3869+889
Dt 2:11 **L** the Anakites, they too were considered H3869
Dt 4:16 whether **formed** *l* a man or a woman AIT
Dt 4:17 l any animal on earth or any bird that flies NDT
Dt 4:18 l any creature that moves along the NDT
Dt 4:32 has anything l it ever been heard of? H4017
Dt 4:34 l all the things the LORD your God did for H3869
Dt 7:26 your house or you, l it, will be set apart H4017
Dt 8:20 **L** the nations the LORD destroyed before H3869
Dt 9: 3 goes across ahead of you l a devouring fire. NDT
Dt 10: 1 out two stone tablets l the first ones and H3869
Dt 10: 3 out two stone tablets l the first ones, H3869
Dt 11:10 to take over is not l the land of Egypt, H3869
Dt 12:16 pour it out on the ground l water. H3869
Dt 12:20 meat and say, "*I would* l some meat," H430
Dt 12:24 pour it out on the ground l water. H3869
Dt 14:26 Use the silver to buy whatever you l: cattle H203
Dt 15:23 pour it out on the ground l water. H3869
Dt 17:14 us set a king over us l all the nations H3869
Dt 18: 7 of the LORD his God l all his fellow Levites H3869
Dt 18:15 you a prophet l me from among you, H4017
Dt 18:18 them a prophet l you from among their H4017
Dt 22:26 This case is l that of someone H3869+889+4027
Dt 23:16 wherever they l and in H928+2021+3202+4200
Dt 28:29 will grope about l a blind person in H3869+889
Dt 28:49 l an eagle swooping down H3869+889
Dt 29:23 It will be l the destruction of Sodom and H3869
Dt 32: 2 Let my teaching fall l rain and my words H3869
Dt 32: 2 fall like rain and my words descend l dew, H3869
Dt 32: 2 descend like dew, l showers on new grass H3869
Dt 32: 2 l abundant rain on tender plants. H3869
Dt 32:11 l an eagle that stirs up its nest and hovers H3869
Dt 32:31 For their rock is not l our Rock, as even H3869
Dt 33:17 In majesty he is l a firstborn bull; his horns NDT
Dt 33:20 Gad lives there l a lion, tearing at arm H3869
Dt 33:26 "There is no one l the God of Jeshurun H3869
Dt 33:29 Who is l you, a people saved by H4017
Dt 34:10 no prophet has risen in Israel l Moses H3869
Jos 7: 5 melted in fear and became l water. H4200
Jos 10: 2 an important city, l one of the royal cities H3869
Jos 10:14 has never been a day l it before or since, H3869
Jos 22:16 you break faith with the God of Israel l this? H889
Jdg 5:31 all who love you be l the sun when it rises H3869
Jdg 6: 5 their tents l swarms of locusts. H3869
Jdg 7: 6 drank from cupped hands, lapping l dogs. NDT
Jdg 8: 1 "Why have you treated us l this? NDT
Jdg 8:18 "Men l you," they answered, "each one H4017
Jdg 13: 6 He looked l an angel of God, very H3869
Jdg 13:15 "*We would l* you *to* **stay** until we prepare a AIT
Jdg 15: 7 "Since you've acted l this, I swear that I H3869
Jdg 15:14 on his arms became l charred flax, H3869+889
Jdg 17:11 young man became l one of his sons to H3869
Jdg 18: 7 living in safety, l the Sidonians, at H3869+5477
Ru 4:11 into your home l Rachel and Leah, H3869
Ru 4:12 may your family be l that of Perez, whom H3869
1Sa 2: 2 "There is no one holy l the LORD; there is H3869
1Sa 2: 2 besides you; there is no Rock l our God. H3869
1Sa 4: 7 Nothing l this has happened before H3869
1Sa 8:20 Then we will be l all the other nations H3869
1Sa 10:24 There is no one l him among all the H4017
1Sa 11:10 can do to us whatever you l." H3202+928+6524
1Sa 15:23 For rebellion is l the sin of divination, and NDT
1Sa 15:23 arrogance l the evil of idolatry. NDT
1Sa 17: 7 His spear shaft was l a weaver's rod, and H3869
1Sa 17:36 Philistine will be l one of them, H3869
1Sa 19: 5 to an innocent man l David by killing him NDT
1Sa 19:17 you deceive me **l this** and send my enemy H3970
1Sa 20:14 But show me **unfailing kindness** *l* the LORD's AIT
1Sa 21: 9 "There is none l it; give it to me. H4017
1Sa 21:13 was in their hands *he* **acted l a madman**, H2147
1Sa 21:15 fellow here to carry on l this in front of me? NDT
1Sa 25:25 He is **just** l his name—his name H3869+4027
1Sa 25:26 are intent on harming my lord be l Nabal. H3869
1Sa 25:36 house holding a banquet l that of a king. H3869
1Sa 25:37 failed him and he became l a stone. H4200
1Sa 26:15 And who is l you in Israel? Why H4017
1Sa 26:21 Surely *I have* **acted l a fool** and have H6118
1Sa 28:14 "What does he **look l**?" he asked. "An old H9307
2Sa 7: 9 l the names of the greatest men on earth. H3869
2Sa 7:22 There is no one l you, and there is no H4017
2Sa 7:23 And who is l your people Israel—the one H3869
2Sa 9: 8 that you should notice a dead dog l me?" H4017
2Sa 9:11 ate at David's table l one of the king's H3869
2Sa 12: 3 It was l a daughter to him. H3869
2Sa 13: 5 '**I would l** my sister Tamar to come and H5528
2Sa 13: 6 "**I would l** my sister Tamar to come and H5528
2Sa 13:13 You would be l one of the wicked fools in H3869
2Sa 14: 2 Act l a woman who has spent many days H3869
2Sa 14:13 you devised a thing l this against the H3869
2Sa 14:14 **L** water spilled on the ground, which H3869
2Sa 14:17 my lord the king is l an angel of God in H3869
2Sa 14:20 My lord has wisdom l that of an angel of H3869
2Sa 16:23 Ahithophel gave was l that of one who H3869
2Sa 17:10 whose heart is l the heart of a lion H3869
2Sa 18:14 "I'm not going to wait **l this** for you." H4027
2Sa 18:27 the first one runs l Ahimaaz son of Zadok." H3869
2Sa 18:32 rise up to harm you be l that young man." H3869
2Sa 19:27 My lord the king is l an angel of God; so H3869
2Sa 21:19 had a spear with a shaft l a weaver's rod. H3869
2Sa 22:34 He makes my feet l the feet of a deer; he H3869
2Sa 22:43 trampled them l mud in the streets. H3869
2Sa 23: 4 he is l the light of morning at sunrise on a H3869
2Sa 23: 4 l the brightness after rain that brings grass H4946
2Sa 23: 6 evil men are all to be cast aside l thorns, H3869
1Ki 1:42 A worthy man l you must be bringing good NDT
1Ki 2: 2 he said. "So be strong, **act** *l* a man, AIT
1Ki 3:12 there will never have been anyone l you, H4017
1Ki 7: 8 also made a palace l this hall for H3869
1Ki 7:26 and its rim was l the rim of a cup H3869+5126
1Ki 7:26 was like the rim of a cup, l a lily blossom. NDT
1Ki 7:33 were made l chariot wheels; H3869+5126
1Ki 8:23 there is no God l you in heaven above H4017
1Ki 10:20 Nothing l it had ever been made for any H4027
1Ki 12:32 eighth month, l the festival held in Judah H3869
1Ki 14: 8 you have not been l my servant David H3869
1Ki 14:15 so that it will be l a reed swaying in H3869+889
1Ki 16: 3 make your house l that of Jeroboam son H3869
1Ki 16: 7 becoming l the house of Jeroboam H3869
1Ki 19: 2 not make your life l that of one of them." H3869
1Ki 20:11 should not boast l one who takes it off. H3869
1Ki 20:25 also raise an army l the one you lost— H3869
1Ki 20:27 opposite them l two small flocks of H3869
1Ki 21:22 make your house l that of Jeroboam son H3869
1Ki 21:25 There was never anyone l Ahab, who sold H3869
1Ki 21:26 l the Amorites the LORD drove H3869+3972+889
1Ki 22:17 scattered on the hills l sheep without a H3869
2Ki 3:22 the way, the water looked red—l blood. H3869
2Ki 5:14 became clean l that of a young boy. H3869
2Ki 7:13 Their plight will be l that of all the H3869
2Ki 7:13 they will only be l all these Israelites who H3869
2Ki 9: 9 the house of Ahab l the house of H3869
2Ki 9: 9 son of Nebat and l the house of Baasha H3869
2Ki 9:20 The driving is l that of Jehu son of Nimshi H3869
2Ki 9:20 Jehu son of Nimshi—he drives l a maniac." H928
2Ki 9:37 body will be l dung on the ground in H3869
2Ki 13: 7 rest and made them l the dust at H3869
2Ki 17: 2 not l the kings of Israel who preceded H3869
2Ki 18: 5 There was no one l him among all the H4017
2Ki 18:27 l you, will have to eat their own H6640
2Ki 18:32 come and take you to a land l your own— H3869
2Ki 19:26 They are l plants in the field, like tender NDT
2Ki 19:26 plants in the field, l tender green shoots NDT
2Ki 19:26 green shoots, l grass sprouting on the roof NDT
2Ki 23:25 was there a king l him who turned to the H4017
1Ch 11:23 Egyptian had a spear l a weaver's rod in H3869
1Ch 12:22 he had a great army, l the army of God. H3869
1Ch 17: 8 I will make your name l the names of the H3869
1Ch 17:20 "There is no one l you, LORD, and there is H4017
1Ch 17:21 And who is l your people Israel—the one H3869
1Ch 20: 5 had a spear with a shaft l a weaver's rod. H3869
1Ch 29:15 Our days on earth are l a shadow, without H3869
2Ch 4: 5 and its rim was l the rim of a cup H3869+5126
2Ch 4: 5 was like the rim of a cup, l a lily blossom. NDT
2Ch 6:14 there is no God l you in heaven or on H4017
2Ch 9:11 Nothing l them had ever been seen in H3869
2Ch 9:19 Nothing l it had ever been made for any H4027
2Ch 14:11 there is no one l you to help the H6640

2Ch 18:16 scattered on the hills l sheep without a H3869
2Ch 30: 7 Do not be l your parents and your fellow H3869
2Ch 30:26 had been nothing l this in Jerusalem. H3869
2Ch 32:15 deceive you and mislead you l this. H3869
2Ch 35:18 not been observed l this in Israel since H4017
Ezr 4: 2 you build because, l you, we seek your H3869
Ezr 9: 1 practices, l those of the Canaanites H4200
Ezr 9:13 have given us a remnant l this. H3869
Ne 5:15 of reverence for God I did not act **l that**. H4027
Ne 6: 8 "Nothing l what you are saying is H3869
Ne 6:11 "Should a man l me run away? Or H4017
Ne 6:11 Or should someone l me go into the H4017
Ne 8:17 the Israelites had not celebrated it **l this**. H4027
Ne 9:11 the depths, l a stone into mighty waters. H4017
Ne 13:26 because of marriages l these that Solomon NDT
Ne 13:26 the many nations there was no king l him. H4017
Job 1: 8 There is no one on earth l him; he is H4017
Job 2: 3 There is no one on earth l him; he is H4017
Job 2:10 "You are talking l a foolish woman. H3869
Job 3:16 away in the ground l a stillborn child, H3869
Job 3:16 l an infant who never saw the light of day? H3869
Job 3:24 my daily food; my groans pour out l water. H3869
Job 5:25 your descendants l the grass of the H3869
Job 5:26 full vigor, l sheaves gathered in season. H3869
Job 7: 1 Are not their days l those of hired laborers H3869
Job 7: 2 L a slave longing for the evening shadows H3869
Job 8:16 They are l a well-watered plant in the NDT
Job 9:26 They skim past l boats of papyrus, like H6640
Job 9:26 l eagles swooping down on their prey. H3869
Job 9:32 is not a mere mortal l me that I might H4017
Job 10: 5 Are your days l those of a mortal or your H3869
Job 10: 5 mortal or your years l those of a strong H3869
Job 10: 9 Remember that you molded me l clay H3869
Job 10:10 you not pour me out l milk and curdle me H3869
Job 10:10 me out like milk and curdle me l cheese, H3869
Job 10:16 you stalk me l a lion and again display H3869
Job 10:22 where even the light is l darkness. H4017
Job 11:17 darkness will become l morning. H3869
Job 12:25 he makes them stagger l drunkards. H3869
Job 13:28 "So man wastes away l something rotten H3869
Job 13:28 l a garment eaten by moths. H3869
Job 14: 2 They spring up l flowers and wither away H3869
Job 14: 2 wither away; l fleeting shadows, they H3869
Job 14: 6 till he has put in his time l a hired laborer. H3869
Job 14: 9 it will bud and put forth shoots l a plant. H4017
Job 15:16 vile and corrupt, who drink up evil l water! H3869
Job 15:23 He wanders about for food l a vulture; he NDT
Job 15:24 overwhelm him, l a king poised to attack H3869
Job 15:33 He will be l a vine stripped of its unripe H3869
Job 15:33 l an olive tree shedding its blossoms. H3869
Job 16: 2 "I have heard many things l these; you H3869
Job 16: 4 I also could speak l you, if you were in my H3869
Job 16:14 upon me; he rushes at me l a warrior. H3869
Job 19:10 I am gone; he uproots my hope l a tree. H3869
Job 20: 7 will perish forever, l his own dung; those H3869
Job 20: 8 L a dream he flies away, no more to be H3869
Job 20: 8 be found, banished l a vision of the night. H3869
Job 21:18 How often are they l straw before the H3869
Job 21:18 the wind, l chaff swept away by a gale? H3869
Job 24: 5 L wild donkeys in the desert, the poor go NDT
Job 24:14 in the night steals forth l a thief. H3869
Job 24:20 remembered but are broken l a tree. H3869
Job 24:24 brought low and gathered up l all others; H3869
Job 24:24 they are cut off l heads of grain. H3869
Job 27: 7 "May my enemy be l the wicked, my H3869
Job 27: 7 like the wicked, my adversary l the unjust! H3869
Job 27:16 he heaps up silver l dust and clothes like H3869
Job 27:16 silver like dust and clothes l piles of clay, H3869
Job 27:18 The house he builds is l a moth's cocoon H3869
Job 27:18 cocoon, l a hut made by a watchman. H3869
Job 27:20 Terrors overtake him l a flood; a tempest H3869
Job 29:25 I was l one who comforts mourners. H3869+889
Job 30:15 by the wind, my safety vanishes l a cloud. H3869
Job 30:18 power God **becomes** l clothing to me H2924
Job 30:18 he binds me l the neck of my garment. H3869
Job 31:36 on my shoulder, I would put it on l a crown. NDT
Job 32:19 inside I am l bottled-up wine, like new H3869
Job 32:19 l new wineskins ready to burst. H3869
Job 33:25 let their flesh be renewed l a child's; let H4946
Job 34: 7 Is there anyone l Job, who drinks scorn H3869
Job 34: 7 anyone like Job, who drinks scorn l water? H3869
Job 34:36 the utmost for answering l a wicked man! H928
Job 35: 4 "I *would l to* **reply** *to* you and to your friends AIT
Job 35: 8 wickedness only affects humans l yourself, H4017
Job 36:22 Who is a teacher l him? H4017
Job 38: 3 Brace yourself l a man; I will question you, H3869
Job 38:14 The earth takes shape l clay under a seal H3869
Job 38:14 its features stand out l those of a garment. H4017
Job 39:20 Do you make it leap l a locust, striking H3869
Job 40: 7 "Brace yourself l a man; I will question H3869
Job 40: 9 Do you have an arm l God's, and can your H3869
Job 40: 9 and can your voice thunder l his? H4017
Job 40:15 you and which feeds on grass l an ox. H3869
Job 40:17 Its tail sways l a cedar; the sinews of its H4017
Job 40:18 tubes of bronze, its limbs l rods of iron. H3869
Job 41: 5 you make a pet of it l a bird or put it on a H3869
Job 41:18 of light; its eyes are l the rays of dawn. H3869
Job 41:27 Iron it treats l straw and bronze like rotten H4200
Job 41:27 treats like straw and bronze l rotten wood. H4200
Job 41:28 make it flee; slingstones are l chaff to it. H4200
Job 41:30 a trail in the mud l a threshing sledge. NDT
Job 41:31 the depths churn l a boiling caldron and H3869
Job 41:31 stirs up the sea l a pot of ointment. H3869
Ps 1: 3 That person is l a tree planted by streams H3869
Ps 1: 4 They are l chaff that the wind blows away. H3869
Ps 2: 9 you will dash them to pieces l pottery." H3869
Ps 7: 2 will tear me apart l a lion and rip me to H3869
Ps 10: 9 l a lion in cover he lies in wait. He lies in H3869
Ps 11: 1 "Flee l a bird to your mountain. NDT
Ps 12: 6 are flawless, l silver purified in a crucible NDT
Ps 12: 6 in a crucible, l gold refined seven times. NDT
Ps 17:12 They are l a lion hungry for prey, like a H1955
Ps 17:12 prey, l a fierce lion crouching in cover. H3869
Ps 18:33 He makes my feet l the feet of a deer; he H3869
Ps 18:42 I trampled them l mud in the streets. H3869
Ps 19: 5 It is l a bridegroom coming out of his H3869
Ps 19: 5 l a champion rejoicing to run his course. H3869
Ps 22:14 I am poured out l water, and all my bones H3869
Ps 22:15 My mouth is dried up l a potsherd, and H3869
Ps 28: 1 *I will* **be** l those who go down to the pit. H5439
Ps 29: 6 He makes Lebanon leap l a calf, Sirion H4017
Ps 29: 6 leap like a calf, Sirion l a young wild ox. H4017
Ps 31:12 I have become l broken pottery. H3869
Ps 32: 9 Do not be l the horse or the mule, which H3869
Ps 35: 5 May they be l chaff before the wind, with H3869
Ps 35:10 being will exclaim, "Who is l you, LORD? H4017
Ps 35:12 evil for good and leave me l one bereaved. NDT
Ps 35:16 L the ungodly they maliciously mocked H3869
Ps 36: 6 righteousness is l the highest mountains H3869
Ps 36: 6 mountains, your justice l the great deep. NDT
Ps 37: 2 l the grass they will soon wither, like H3869
Ps 37: 2 l green plants they will soon die away. H3869
Ps 37: 6 your righteous reward shine l the dawn, H3869
Ps 37: 6 your vindication l the noonday sun. H3869
Ps 37:20 the LORD's enemies are l the flowers of the H3869
Ps 37:35 man flourishing l a luxuriant native tree, H3869
Ps 38: 4 overwhelmed me l a burden too heavy H3869
Ps 38:13 I am l the deaf, who cannot hear, like the H3869
Ps 38:13 who cannot hear, l the mute, who cannot H3869
Ps 38:14 I have become l one who does not hear H3869
Ps 39: 6 everyone goes around l a mere phantom; H928
Ps 39:11 you consume their wealth l a moth H3869
Ps 44:11 us up to be devoured l sheep and have H3869
Ps 48: 2 l the heights of Zaphon is Mount Zion NDT
Ps 48: 6 pain l that of a woman in labor. H3869
Ps 48: 7 You destroyed them l ships of Tarshish NDT
Ps 48:10 L your name, O God, your praise reaches H3869
Ps 49:12 endure; *they* **are** l the beasts that perish. H5439
Ps 49:14 They are l sheep and are destined to die H3869
Ps 49:20 lack understanding **are** l the beasts that H5439
Ps 50:21 you thought I was exactly l you. H4017
Ps 52: 2 plots destruction; it is l a sharpened razor. H3869
Ps 52: 8 But I am l an olive tree flourishing in the H3869
Ps 55:13 it is you, a man l myself, my H3869+6886
Ps 58: 4 Their venom is l the venom of a H3869+1952
Ps 58: 4 l that of a cobra that has stopped its ears H4017
Ps 58: 7 Let them vanish l water that flows away H4017
Ps 58: 8 May they be l a slug that melts away as it H4017
Ps 58: 8 l a stillborn child that never sees the sun. NDT
Ps 59: 6 at evening, snarling l dogs, and prowl H3869
Ps 59:14 at evening, snarling l dogs, and prowl H3869
Ps 64: 3 their tongues l swords and aim cruel H3869
Ps 64: 3 swords and aim cruel words l deadly arrows. NDT
Ps 66:10 tested us; you refined us l silver. H3869
Ps 68: 2 May you blow them away l smoke—as H3869
Ps 68:14 *it was l* **snow fallen** on Mount Zalmon. AIT
Ps 71:19 done great things. Who is l you, God? H4017
Ps 72: 6 May he be l rain falling on a mown field H3869
Ps 72: 6 mown field, l showers watering the earth. H3869
Ps 72:16 the crops flourish l Lebanon and thrive H3869
Ps 72:16 Lebanon and thrive l the grass of the field H3869
Ps 73:12 This is what the wicked are l—always free NDT
Ps 73:15 If I had spoken out **l that**, I would have H4017
Ps 73:20 They are l a dream when one awakes H3869
Ps 74: 5 They behaved l men wielding axes to cut H3869
Ps 77:20 You led your people l a flock by the hand H3869
Ps 78: 8 They would not be l their ancestors—a H3869
Ps 78:13 he made the water stand up l a wall. H4017
Ps 78:16 crag and made water flow down l rivers. H3869
Ps 78:27 He rained meat down on them l dust H3869
Ps 78:27 like dust, birds l sand on the seashore. H3869
Ps 78:52 But he brought his people out l a flock; he H3869
Ps 78:52 he led them l sheep through the H3869
Ps 78:57 L their ancestors they were disloyal and H3869
Ps 78:69 He built his sanctuary l the heights, like H4017
Ps 78:69 l the earth that he established forever. H3869
Ps 79: 3 have poured out blood l water all around H3869
Ps 79: 5 How long will your jealousy burn l fire? H4017
Ps 80: 1 of Israel, you who lead Joseph l a flock. H3869
Ps 82: 7 But you will die l mere mortals; you will H3869
Ps 82: 7 mortals; you will fall l every other ruler." H3869
Ps 83:10 at Endor and became l dung on the ground. NDT
Ps 83:11 Make their nobles l Oreb and Zeeb, all H3869
Ps 83:11 all their princes l Zebah and Zalmunna, H3869
Ps 83:13 Make them l tumbleweed, my God, like H3869
Ps 83:13 my God, l chaff before the wind. H3869
Ps 86: 8 Among the gods there is none l you, Lord H4017
Ps 88: 4 to the pit; I am l one without strength. H3869
Ps 88: 5 the dead, l the slain who lie in the grave H4017
Ps 88:17 All day long they surround me l a flood H3869
Ps 89: 6 *Who* **is** l the LORD among the heavenly H1948
Ps 89: 8 Who is l you, LORD God Almighty? You H4017
Ps 89:10 You crushed Rahab l one of the slain H3869
Ps 89:36 his throne endure before me l the sun; H3869
Ps 89:37 it will be established forever l the moon H3869
Ps 89:46 How long will your wrath burn l fire? H4017
Ps 90: 4 years in your sight are l a day that has just H3869
Ps 90: 4 has just gone by, or l a watch in the night. NDT
Ps 90: 5 they are l the new grass of the morning: H3869
Ps 92: 7 the wicked spring up l grass and all H4017
Ps 92:10 have exalted my horn l that of a wild ox; H3869
Ps 92:12 The righteous will flourish l a palm tree H3869
Ps 92:12 they will grow l a cedar of Lebanon; H3869
Ps 97: 5 mountains melt l wax before the LORD, H3869
Ps 102: 3 my days vanish l smoke; my bones burn H928
Ps 102: 3 my bones burn l glowing embers. H3869
Ps 102: 4 My heart is blighted and withered l grass H3869
Ps 102: 6 *I* **am** l a desert owl, like an owl among H1948
Ps 102: 6 a desert owl, l an owl among the ruins. H3869
Ps 102: 7 I have become l a bird alone on a roof. H3869
Ps 102:11 My days are l the evening shadow; H3869
Ps 102:11 evening shadow; I wither away l grass. H3869
Ps 102:26 remain; they will all wear out l a garment. H3869
Ps 102:26 L clothing you will change them and they H3869
Ps 103: 5 that your youth is renewed l the eagle's. H3869
Ps 103:15 The life of mortals is l grass, they flourish H3869
Ps 103:15 they flourish l a flower of the field; H3869
Ps 104: 2 he stretches out the heavens l a tent H3869
Ps 105:41 gushed out; it flowed l a river in the desert. NDT
Ps 107:27 They reeled and staggered l drunkards H3869
Ps 107:41 increased their families l flocks. H3869
Ps 109:18 it entered into his body l water, into his H3869
Ps 109:18 his body like water, into his bones l oil. H3869
Ps 109:19 May it be l a cloak wrapped about him H3869
Ps 109:19 l a belt tied forever around him. H4200
Ps 109:23 I fade away l an evening shadow; I am H3869
Ps 109:23 shadow; I am shaken off l a locust. H3869
Ps 110: 3 men will come to you l dew from the NDT
Ps 113: 5 Who is l the LORD our God, the One who H3869
Ps 114: 4 the mountains leaped l rams, the hills H3869
Ps 114: 4 leaped like rams, the hills l lambs. H3869
Ps 114: 6 did you leap l rams, you hills, like H3869
Ps 114: 6 did you leap like rams, you hills, l lambs? H3869
Ps 115: 8 Those who make them will be l them H4017
Ps 118:12 They swarmed around me l bees, but they H3869
Ps 119:83 Though I am l a wineskin in the smoke, H3869
Ps 119:119 the wicked of the earth you discard l dross; NDT
Ps 119:162 in your promise l one who finds great H3869
Ps 119:176 I have strayed l a lost sheep. Seek your H3869
Ps 122: 3 Jerusalem is built l a city that is closely H3869
Ps 124: 7 We have escaped l a bird from the H3869
Ps 125: 1 who trust in the LORD are l Mount Zion, H3869
Ps 126: 1 of Zion, we were l those who dreamed. H3869
Ps 126: 4 our fortunes, LORD, l streams in the Negev. H3869
Ps 127: 4 L arrows in the hands of a warrior are H3869
Ps 128: 3 Your wife will be l a fruitful vine within H3869
Ps 128: 3 your children will be l olive shoots around H3869
Ps 129: 6 May they be l grass on the roof, which H3869
Ps 131: 2 I am l a weaned child with its mother H3869
Ps 131: 2 its mother; l a weaned child I am content. H3869
Ps 133: 2 It is l precious oil poured on the head H3869
Ps 135:18 Those who make them will be l them H4017
Ps 139:12 the night will shine l the day, for darkness H3869
Ps 141: 2 May my prayer be set before you l incense NDT
Ps 141: 2 up of my hands be l the evening sacrifice. NDT
Ps 143: 3 dwell in the darkness l those long dead. H3869
Ps 143: 6 I thirst for you l a parched land. H3869
Ps 143: 7 face from me or *I will* **be** l those who go H5439
Ps 144: 4 They *are* l a breath; their days are like a H1948
Ps 144: 4 their days are l a fleeting shadow. H3869
Ps 144:12 their youth will be l well-nurtured plants, H3869
Ps 144:12 our daughters will be l pillars carved to H3869
Ps 147:16 He spreads the snow l wool and scatters H3869
Ps 147:16 like wool and scatters the frost l ashes. H3869
Ps 147:17 He hurls down his hail l pebbles. H3869
Pr 1:12 swallow them alive, l the grave, and H3869
Pr 1:12 l those who go down to the pit; H3869
Pr 1:27 when calamity overtakes you l a storm H3869
Pr 1:27 disaster sweeps over you l a whirlwind, H3869
Pr 4:18 path of the righteous is l the morning sun, H3869
Pr 4:19 the way of the wicked is l deep darkness; H3869
Pr 6: 5 l a gazelle from the hand of the hunter H3869
Pr 6: 5 l a bird from the snare of the fowler. H3869
Pr 6:11 will come on you l a thief and scarcity H3869
Pr 6:11 like a thief and scarcity l an armed man. H3869
Pr 7:10 **dressed** *l* a prostitute and with crafty intent. AIT
Pr 7:22 once he followed her l an ox going to the H3869
Pr 7:22 slaughter, l a deer stepping into a noose H3869
Pr 7:23 his liver, l a bird darting into a snare H3869
Pr 11:22 L a gold ring in a pig's snout is a beautiful NDT
Pr 11:28 the righteous will thrive l a green leaf. H3869
Pr 12: 4 a disgraceful wife is l decay in his bones. H3869
Pr 12:18 The words of the reckless pierce l swords H3869
Pr 16:15 his favor is l a rain cloud in spring. H3869
Pr 16:27 on their lips it is l a scorching fire. H3869
Pr 17:14 Starting a quarrel is l breaching a dam; so NDT
Pr 18: 8 words of a gossip are l choice morsels; H3869
Pr 18:19 disputes are l the barred gates of a H3869
Pr 19:12 A king's rage is l the roar of a lion, but his H3869
Pr 19:12 but his favor is l dew on the grass. H3869
Pr 19:13 quarrelsome wife is l the constant dripping NDT
Pr 20: 2 wrath strikes terror l the roar of a lion; H3869
Pr 23: 5 wings and fly off to the sky l an eagle. H3869
Pr 23:28 L a bandit she lies in wait and multiplies H3869
Pr 23:32 In the end it bites l a snake and poisons H3869
Pr 23:32 it bites like a snake and poisons l a viper. H3869

Book	Ref	Context	Code
Pr	23:34	You will be **l** one sleeping on the high	H3869
Pr	24:14	Know also that wisdom is **l** *honey* for you	H4027
Pr	24:15	Do not lurk **l** a thief near the house of the	NDT
Pr	24:26	An honest answer is **l** a kiss on the lips.	NDT
Pr	24:34	will come on you **l** a thief and scarcity	NDT
Pr	24:34	like a thief and scarcity **l** an armed man.	H3869
Pr	25:11	**L** apples of gold in settings of silver is a	NDT
Pr	25:12	**L** an earring of gold or an ornament of fine	NDT
Pr	25:13	**L** a snow-cooled drink at harvest time is a	H3869
Pr	25:14	**L** clouds and wind without rain is one who	NDT
Pr	25:18	**L** a club or a sword or a sharp arrow is one	NDT
Pr	25:19	**L** a broken tooth or a lame foot is reliance	NDT
Pr	25:20	**L** one who takes away a garment on a cold	NDT
Pr	25:20	a cold day, or **l** vinegar poured on a wound	NDT
Pr	25:23	**L** a north wind that brings unexpected rain is	NDT
Pr	25:25	**L** cold water to a weary soul is good news	NDT
Pr	25:26	**L** a muddied spring or a polluted well are	NDT
Pr	25:28	**L** a city whose walls are broken through is a	NDT
Pr	26: 1	**L** snow in summer or rain in harvest	H3869
Pr	26: 2	**L** a fluttering sparrow or a darting swallow,	H3869
Pr	26: 4	his folly, or *you* yourself *will* **be just l** him.	H8750
Pr	26: 6	the hands of a fool is **l** cutting off one's feet	NDT
Pr	26: 7	**L** the useless legs of one who is lame is a	NDT
Pr	26: 8	**L** tying a stone in a sling is the giving of	H3869
Pr	26: 9	**L** a thornbush in a drunkard's hand is a	NDT
Pr	26:10	**L** an archer who wounds at random is one	NDT
Pr	26:17	**L** one who grabs a stray dog by the ears is	NDT
Pr	26:18	**L** a maniac shooting flaming arrows of	H3869
Pr	26:22	words of a gossip are **l** choice morsels;	H3869
Pr	26:23	**L** a coating of silver dross on earthenware	NDT
Pr	27: 8	**L** a bird that flees its nest is anyone who	H3869
Pr	27:15	A quarrelsome wife **is l** the dripping of a	H8750
Pr	27:16	restraining her is **l** restraining the wind or	NDT
Pr	27:22	grinding them **l** grain with a pestle	H928+9348
Pr	28: 3	oppresses the poor is **l** a driving rain that	NDT
Pr	28:15	**L** a roaring lion or a charging bear is a	NDT
Pr	31:14	She is **l** the merchant ships, bringing her	H3869
Ecc	2:16	For the wise, **l** the fool, will not be long	H6640
Ecc	2:16	have been forgotten. **L** the fool, the wise	H6640
Ecc	3:18	they may see that they are **l** the animals.	H4200
Ecc	3:19	of human beings is **l** that of the animals;	NDT
Ecc	6:12	days they pass through **l** a shadow?	H3869
Ecc	7: 6	**L** the crackling of thorns under the pot, so	H3869
Ecc	7:11	Wisdom, **l** an inheritance, is a good thing	H6640
Ecc	8: 1	Who is **l** the wise? Who knows the	H3869
Ecc	8:13	their days will not lengthen **l** a shadow.	H3869
Ecc	10: 7	while princes go on foot **l** slaves.	H3869
Ecc	12:11	The words of the wise are **l** goads, their	H3869
Ecc	12:11	collected sayings **l** firmly embedded nails	H3869
SS	1: 3	your name is **l** perfume poured out.	NDT
SS	1: 5	of Jerusalem, dark **l** the tents of Kedar	H3869
SS	1: 5	of Kedar, **l** the tent curtains of Solomon.	H3869
SS	1: 7	Why should I be **l** a veiled woman beside	H3869
SS	2: 2	**L** a lily among thorns is my darling among	H3869
SS	2: 3	**L** an apple tree among the trees of the	H3869
SS	2: 9	My beloved **is l** a gazelle or a young stag	H1948
SS	2:17	and **be l** a gazelle or like a young stag on	H1948
SS	2:17	be like a gazelle or **l** a young stag on the	NDT
SS	3: 6	from the wilderness **l** a column of smoke,	H3869
SS	4: 1	Your hair is **l** a flock of goats descending	H3869
SS	4: 2	Your teeth are **l** a flock of sheep just shorn	H3869
SS	4: 3	Your lips are **l** a scarlet ribbon; your	H3869
SS	4: 3	behind your veil are **l** the halves of a	H3869
SS	4: 4	Your neck is **l** the tower of David, built	H3869
SS	4: 5	Your breasts are **l** two fawns, like twin	H3869
SS	4: 5	**l** twin fawns of a gazelle that browse among	NDT
SS	4:11	of your garments is **l** the fragrance of	H3869
SS	5:12	His eyes are **l** doves by the water streams	H3869
SS	5:12	in milk, **mounted l jewels.**	H3782+6584+4859
SS	5:13	His cheeks are **l** beds of spice yielding	H3869
SS	5:13	His lips are **l** lilies dripping with myrrh.	NDT
SS	5:14	His body is **l** polished ivory decorated with	NDT
SS	5:15	His appearance is **l** Lebanon, choice as its	H3869
SS	6: 5	Your hair is **l** a flock of goats descending	H3869
SS	6: 6	Your teeth are **l** a flock of sheep coming	H3869
SS	6: 7	behind your veil are **l** the halves of a	H3869
SS	6:10	Who is this that appears **l** the dawn, fair	H4017
SS	7: 1	Your graceful legs are **l** jewels, the work	H4017
SS	7: 3	Your breasts are **l** two fawns, like twin	H3869
SS	7: 3	are like two fawns, **l** twin fawns of a gazelle.	NDT
SS	7: 4	Your neck is **l** an ivory tower. Your eyes	H3869
SS	7: 4	Your nose is **l** the tower of Lebanon	H3869
SS	7: 5	Your head crowns you **l** Mount Carmel	H3869
SS	7: 5	Your hair is **l** royal tapestry; the king is	H3869
SS	7: 7	Your stature **is l** that of the palm, and your	H1948
SS	7: 7	the palm, and your breasts **l** clusters of fruit.	NDT
SS	7: 8	May your breasts be **l** clusters of grapes	H3869
SS	7: 8	the fragrance of your breath **l** apples,	H3869
SS	7: 9	your mouth **l** the best wine. May the	H3869
SS	8: 1	If only you were to me **l** a brother, who	H3869
SS	8: 6	Place me **l** a seal over your heart, like a	H3869
SS	8: 6	seal over your heart, **l** a seal on your arm	H3869
SS	8: 6	It burns **l** blazing fire, like a	NDT
SS	8: 6	It burns like blazing fire, **l** a mighty flame.	NDT
SS	8:10	my breasts are **l** towers. Thus I have	H3869
SS	8:10	have become in his eyes **l** one bringing	H3869
SS	8:14	and **be l** a gazelle or like a young stag on	H1948
SS	8:14	be like a gazelle or **l** a young stag on the	NDT
Isa	1: 8	Daughter Zion is left **l** a shelter in a	H3869
Isa	1: 8	in a vineyard, **l** a hut in a cucumber field	H3869
Isa	1: 8	in a cucumber field, **l** a city under siege.	H3869
Isa	1: 9	we would have become **l** Sodom, we	H3869
Isa	1: 9	Sodom, *we would have* **been l** Gomorrah.	H1948
Isa	1:18	"Though your sins are **l** scarlet, they shall	H3869
Isa	1:18	are red as crimson, they shall be **l** wool.	H3869
Isa	1:30	You will be **l** an oak with fading leaves	H3869
Isa	1:30	fading leaves, **l** a garden without water.	H3869
Isa	2: 6	practice divination **l** the Philistines and	H3869
Isa	3: 9	they parade their sin **l** Sodom; they do not	H3869
Isa	5:24	decay and their flowers blow away **l** dust;	H3869
Isa	5:25	the dead bodies are **l** refuse in the streets	H3869
Isa	5:28	their horses' hooves seem **l** flint, their	H3869
Isa	5:28	their chariot wheels **l** a whirlwind.	H3869
Isa	5:29	Their roar is **l** that of the lion, they roar	H3869
Isa	5:29	of the lion, they roar **l** young lions; they	H3869
Isa	5:30	will roar over it **l** the roaring of the sea	H3869
Isa	9:18	Surely wickedness burns **l** a fire; it	H3869
Isa	10: 6	trample them down **l** mud in the streets.	H3869
Isa	10: 9	'Has not Kalno **fared l** Carchemish? Is not	H3869
Isa	10: 9	Is not Hamath **l** Arpad, and Samaria like	H3869
Isa	10: 9	like Arpad, and Samaria **l** Damascus?	H3869
Isa	10:13	**l** a mighty one I subdued their kings.	H3869
Isa	10:16	a fire will be kindled **l** a blazing flame.	H3869
Isa	10:22	your people be **l** the sand by the sea,	H3869
Isa	11: 7	the lion will eat straw **l** the ox.	H3869
Isa	13: 4	the mountains, **l** *that of* a great multitude!	H1952
Isa	13: 4	the kingdoms, **l** nations massing together!	NDT
Isa	13: 6	it will come **l** destruction from the	H3869
Isa	13: 8	they will writhe **l** a woman in labor.	H3869
Isa	13:14	**L** a hunted gazelle, like sheep without a	H3869
Isa	13:14	gazelle, **l** sheep without a shepherd	H3869
Isa	13:19	overthrown by God **l** Sodom and	H3869
Isa	14:10	as we are; *you have* **become l** us.	H5439
Isa	14:14	*I will* **make myself l** the Most High."	H1948
Isa	14:19	cast out of your tomb **l** a rejected branch;	H3869
Isa	14:19	**L** a corpse trampled underfoot	H3869
Isa	16: 2	**L** fluttering birds pushed from the nest, so	H3869
Isa	16: 3	Make your shadow **l** night—at high noon	H3869
Isa	16:11	My heart laments for Moab **l** a harp, my	H3869
Isa	17: 3	remnant of Aram will be **l** the glory of the	H3869
Isa	17: 9	will be **l** places abandoned to thickets	H3869
Isa	17:12	that rage—they rage **l** the raging sea!	H3869
Isa	17:12	they roar **l** the roaring of great waters!	H3869
Isa	17:13	the peoples roar **l** the roar of surging	H3869
Isa	17:13	driven before the wind **l** chaff on the hills	H3869
Isa	17:13	on the hills, **l** tumbleweed before a gale.	H3869
Isa	18: 4	**l** shimmering heat in the sunshine	H3869
Isa	18: 4	**l** a cloud of dew in the heat of harvest."	H3869
Isa	21: 1	**L** whirlwinds sweeping through the	H3869
Isa	21: 3	seize me, **l** those of a woman in labor	H3869
Isa	22:18	roll you up tightly **l** a ball and throw you	H3869
Isa	22:23	I will drive him **l** a peg into a firm place;	NDT
Isa	24:20	The earth reels **l** a drunkard, it sways like	H3869
Isa	24:20	a drunkard, it sways **l** a hut in the wind; so	H3869
Isa	24:22	be herded together **l** prisoners bound in a	NDT
Isa	25: 4	of the ruthless is **l** a storm driving against	H3869
Isa	25: 5	**l** the heat of the desert. You silence	H3869
Isa	26:19	your dew is **l** the dew of the morning	NDT
Isa	27: 9	altar stones to be **l** limestone crushed to	H3869
Isa	27:10	settlement, forsaken **l** the wilderness	H3869
Isa	28: 2	**L** a hailstorm and a destructive wind, like	H3869
Isa	28: 2	**l** a driving rain and a flooding downpour	H3869
Isa	28: 4	will be **l** figs ripe before harvest	H3869
Isa	29: 2	she will be to me **l** an altar hearth.	H3869
Isa	29: 5	many enemies will become **l** fine dust,	H3869
Isa	29: 5	the ruthless hordes **l** blown chaff.	H3869
Isa	29:16	if the potter were thought to be **l** the clay!	H3869
Isa	29:17	field and the fertile field seem **l** a forest?	H4200
Isa	30:13	this sin will become for you **l** a high wall	H3869
Isa	30:14	It will break in pieces **l** pottery, shattered	H3869
Isa	30:17	till you are left **l** a flagstaff on a	H3869
Isa	30:17	on a mountaintop, **l** a banner on a hill."	H3869
Isa	30:22	will throw them away **l** a menstrual cloth	H4017
Isa	30:26	The moon will shine **l** the sun, and the	H3869
Isa	30:26	brighter, **l** the light of seven full days	H3869
Isa	30:28	His breath is **l** a rushing torrent, rising up	H3869
Isa	30:33	of the LORD, **l** a stream of burning sulfur	H3869
Isa	31: 5	**L** birds hovering overhead, the LORD	H3869
Isa	32: 2	Each one will be **l** a shelter from the wind	H3869
Isa	32: 2	**l** streams of water in the desert and the	H3869
Isa	32:15	and the fertile field seems **l** a forest.	H4200
Isa	33: 4	**l** a swarm of locusts people pounce on it.	H3869
Isa	33: 9	withers; Sharon is **l** the Arabah, and	H3869
Isa	33:12	**l** cut thornbushes they will be set ablaze."	NDT
Isa	33:21	It will be **l** a place of broad rivers and	NDT
Isa	34: 4	the heavens rolled up **l** a scroll;	H3869
Isa	34: 4	starry host will fall **l** withered leaves from	H3869
Isa	34: 4	the vine, **l** shriveled figs from the fig tree.	H3869
Isa	35: 1	will rejoice and blossom. **L** the crocus,	H3869
Isa	35: 6	Then will the lame leap **l** a deer, and the	H3869
Isa	36:12	**l** you, will have to eat their own	H6640
Isa	36:17	come and take you to a land **l** your own—	H3869
Isa	37:27	They are **l** plants in the field, like tender	NDT
Isa	37:27	plants in the field, **l** tender green shoots	NDT
Isa	37:27	green shoots, **l** grass sprouting on the roof	NDT
Isa	38:12	**L** a shepherd's tent my house has been	H3869
Isa	38:12	**L** a weaver I have rolled up my life, and	H3869
Isa	38:13	but **l** a lion he broke all my bones	H3869
Isa	38:14	I cried **l** a swift or thrush, I moaned like a	H3869
Isa	38:14	thrush, I moaned **l** a mourning dove.	H3869
Isa	40: 6	"All people are **l** grass, and all their	NDT
Isa	40: 6	their faithfulness is **l** the flowers of the	H3869
Isa	40:11	He tends his flock **l** a shepherd: He	H3869
Isa	40:15	Surely the nations are **l** a drop in a bucket;	H3869
Isa	40:22	and its people are **l** grasshoppers.	H3869
Isa	40:22	He stretches out the heavens **l** a canopy	H3869
Isa	40:22	spreads them out **l** a tent to live in.	H3869
Isa	40:24	a whirlwind sweeps them away **l** chaff.	H3869
Isa	40:31	They will soar on wings **l** eagles; they will	H3869
Isa	42:13	The LORD will march out **l** a champion,	H3869
Isa	42:13	**l** a warrior he will stir up his zeal	H3869
Isa	42:14	But now, **l** a woman in childbirth, I cry out	H3869
Isa	42:19	servant, and deaf **l** the messenger I send?	H3869
Isa	42:19	Who is blind **l** the one in covenant with	H3869
Isa	42:19	with me, blind **l** the servant of the LORD?	H3869
Isa	43:17	extinguished, snuffed out **l** a wick:	H3869
Isa	44: 4	They will spring up **l** grass in a meadow	NDT
Isa	44: 4	**l** poplar trees by flowing streams.	H3869
Isa	44: 7	Who then is **l** me? Let him proclaim it.	H4017
Isa	44:22	I have swept away your offenses **l** a cloud	H3869
Isa	44:22	like a cloud, your sins **l** the morning mist.	H3869
Isa	46: 9	I am God, and there is none **l** me.	H4017
Isa	47:14	Surely they are **l** stubble; the fire will burn	H3869
Isa	48:18	your peace would have been **l** a river	H3869
Isa	48:18	your well-being **l** the waves of the sea.	H3869
Isa	48:19	descendants would have been **l** the sand,	H3869
Isa	48:19	your children **l** its numberless grains	H3869
Isa	49: 2	He made my mouth **l** a sharpened sword	H3869
Isa	49:18	you will put them on, **l** a bride.	H3869
Isa	50: 4	my ear to listen **l** one being instructed.	H3869
Isa	50: 7	Therefore have I set my face **l** flint, and I	H3869
Isa	50: 9	They will all wear out **l** a garment; the	H3869
Isa	51: 3	he will make her deserts **l** Eden, her	H3869
Isa	51: 3	her wastelands **l** the garden of the LORD.	H3869
Isa	51: 6	the heavens will vanish **l** smoke, the earth	H3869
Isa	51: 6	the earth will wear out **l** a garment and its	H3869
Isa	51: 6	a garment and its inhabitants die **l** flies.	H4017
Isa	51: 8	For the moth will eat them up **l** a garment;	H3869
Isa	51: 8	the worm will devour them **l** wool.	H3869
Isa	51:20	street corner, **l** antelope caught in a net.	H3869
Isa	51:23	And you made your back **l** the ground	H3869
Isa	51:23	the ground, **l** a street to be walked on."	H3869
Isa	53: 2	He grew up before him **l** a tender shoot	H3869
Isa	53: 2	and **l** a root out of dry ground.	H3869
Isa	53: 3	**L** one from whom people hide their faces	H3869
Isa	53: 6	**l** sheep, have gone astray, each	H3869
Isa	53: 7	he was led **l** a lamb to the slaughter	H3869
Isa	54: 9	"To me this is **l** the days of Noah, when I	H3869
Isa	56:12	And tomorrow will be **l** today, or even far	H3869
Isa	57:20	But the wicked are **l** the tossing sea	H3869
Isa	58: 1	Raise your voice **l** a trumpet. Declare to	H3869
Isa	58: 5	bowing one's head **l** a reed and for lying	H3869
Isa	58: 8	Then your light will break forth **l** the dawn,	H3869
Isa	58:10	your night will become **l** the noonday.	H3869
Isa	58:11	You will be **l** a well-watered garden, like	H3869
Isa	58:11	**l** a spring whose waters never fail.	H3869
Isa	59:10	**L** the blind we grope along the wall	H3869
Isa	59:10	feeling our way **l** people without eyes.	H3869
Isa	59:10	among the strong, we are **l** the dead.	H3869
Isa	59:11	We all growl **l** bears; we moan mournfully	H3869
Isa	59:11	like bears; we moan mournfully **l** doves.	H3869
Isa	59:19	For he will come **l** a pent-up flood that	H3869
Isa	60: 8	"Who are these that fly along **l** clouds	H3869
Isa	60: 8	along like clouds, **l** doves to their nests?	H3869
Isa	61:10	as a bridegroom adorns his head *l a* **priest**	AIT
Isa	62: 1	till her vindication shines out **l** the dawn	H3869
Isa	62: 1	the dawn, her salvation **l** a blazing torch.	H3869
Isa	63: 2	**l** those *of* one treading the winepress?	H3869
Isa	63:13	**L** a horse in open country, they did not	H3869
Isa	63:14	**l** cattle that go down to the plain, they	H3869
Isa	64: 6	of us have become **l** one who is unclean,	H3869
Isa	64: 6	all our righteous acts are **l** filthy rags	H3869
Isa	64: 6	we all shrivel up **l** a leaf, and like the	H3869
Isa	64: 6	**l** the wind our sins sweep us away.	H3869
Isa	65:25	the lion will eat straw **l** the ox, and	H3869
Isa	66: 3	sacrifices a bull is **l** one who kills a person,	NDT
Isa	66: 3	offers a lamb is **l** one who breaks a dog's	NDT
Isa	66: 3	a grain offering is **l** one who presents pig's	NDT
Isa	66: 3	memorial incense is **l** one who worships an	NDT
Isa	66: 8	Who has ever seen things **l** this? Can a	H3869
Isa	66:12	"I will extend peace to her **l** a river, and	H3869
Isa	66:12	the wealth of nations **l** a flooding stream;	H3869
Isa	66:14	will rejoice and you will flourish **l** grass;	H3869
Isa	66:15	his chariots are **l** a whirlwind; he will	H3869
Jer	2:10	see if there has ever been anything **l** this:	H3869
Jer	2:21	I had planted you **l** a choice vine of sound	NDT
Jer	2:30	devoured your prophets **l** a ravenous lion.	H3869
Jer	3: 2	lovers, sat **l** a nomad in the desert.	H3869
Jer	3:19	would I treat you **l** my children and give	H928
Jer	3:20	But **l** a woman unfaithful to her husband, so	NDT
Jer	4: 4	will flare up and burn **l** fire because of the	H3869
Jer	4:13	He advances **l** the clouds, his chariots	H3869
Jer	4:13	his chariots come **l** a whirlwind, his horses	H3869
Jer	4:17	They surround her **l** men guarding a field	H3869
Jer	5:16	Their quivers are **l** an open grave; all of	H3869
Jer	5:26	who lie in wait **l** men who snare birds	H3869
Jer	5:26	who snare birds and **l** those who set traps to	NDT
Jer	5:27	**L** cages full of birds, their houses are full	H3869
Jer	6: 9	branches again, **l** one gathering grapes."	H3869
Jer	6:23	They sound **l** the roaring sea as they ride	H3869
Jer	6:23	they come **l** men in battle formation to	H3869
Jer	6:24	pain **l** that of a woman in labor.	H3869
Jer	8: 2	will be **l** dung lying on the ground.	H4200
Jer	8: 6	their own course **l** a horse charging into	H3869
Jer	9: 3	"They make ready their tongue **l** a bow, to	NDT
Jer	9:12	laid waste **l** a desert that no one	H3869

Jer 9:22 'Dead bodies will lie l dung on the open H3869
Jer 9:22 open field, l cut grain behind the reaper H3869
Jer 10: 5 L a scarecrow in a cucumber field, their H3869
Jer 10: 6 No one is l you, LORD; you are great, and H4017
Jer 10: 7 all their kingdoms, there is no one l you. H4017
Jer 10:16 who is the Portion of Jacob is not l these, H3869
Jer 11:19 I had been l a gentle lamb led to the H3869
Jer 12: 3 Drag them off l sheep to be butchered H3869
Jer 12: 8 has become to me l a lion in the forest. H3869
Jer 12: 9 become to me l a speckled bird of prey NDT
Jer 13:10 will be l this belt—completely H3869
Jer 13:21 not pain grip you l that of a woman in H4017
Jer 13:24 "I will scatter you l chaff driven by the H3869
Jer 14: 6 on the barren heights and pant l jackals; H3869
Jer 14: 8 why are you l a stranger in the land H3869
Jer 14: 8 l a traveler who stays only a night? H3869
Jer 14: 9 Why are you l a man taken by surprise H3869
Jer 14: 9 by surprise, l a warrior powerless to save? H3869
Jer 15:18 You are to me l a deceptive brook, like a H4017
Jer 15:18 like a deceptive brook, l a spring that fails. NDT
Jer 16: 4 buried but will be l dung lying on the H4200
Jer 17: 6 That person will be l a bush in the H3869
Jer 17: 8 They will be l a tree planted by the water H3869
Jer 17:11 L a partridge that hatches eggs it did not lay NDT
Jer 18: 6 "L clay in the hand of the potter, so are H3869
Jer 18:13 Who has ever heard anything l this? H3869
Jer 18:17 L a wind from the east, I will scatter them H3869
Jer 19:12 I will make this city l Topheth. H3869
Jer 19:13 kings of Judah will be defiled l this place, H3869
Jer 20: 9 his word is in my heart l a fire, a fire shut H3869
Jer 20:11 But the LORD is with me l a mighty warrior H3869
Jer 20:16 May that man be l the towns the LORD H3869
Jer 21:12 break out and burn l fire because of the H3869
Jer 22: 6 "Though you are l Gilead to me, like the NDT
Jer 22: 6 like Gilead to me, l the summit of Lebanon NDT
Jer 22: 6 I will surely make you l a wasteland, like NDT
Jer 22: 6 you like a wasteland, l towns not inhabited. NDT
Jer 22:23 pain l that of a woman in labor! H3869
Jer 23: 9 I am l a drunken man, like a strong man H3869
Jer 23: 9 l a strong man overcome by wine H3869
Jer 23:14 They are all l Sodom to me; the people of H3869
Jer 23:14 the people of Jerusalem are l Gomorrah." H3869
Jer 23:29 "Is not my word l fire," declares the LORD H3869
Jer 23:29 "and l a hammer that breaks a rock in H3869
Jer 24: 2 had very good figs, l those that ripen early H3869
Jer 24: 5 'L these good figs, I regard as good the H3869
Jer 24: 8 " 'But l the bad figs, which are so bad H3869
Jer 25:30 He will shout l those who tread the H3869
Jer 25:33 will be l dung lying on the ground. H4200
Jer 25:34 you will fall l the best of the rams. H3869
Jer 25:38 L a lion he will leave his lair, and their H3869
Jer 26: 6 will make this house l Shiloh and this city H3869
Jer 26: 9 this house will be l Shiloh and this city H3869
Jer 26:18 " 'Zion will be plowed l a field, Jerusalem NDT
Jer 29:17 I will make them l figs that are so bad H3869
Jer 29:22 the LORD treat you l Zedekiah and Ahab, H3869
Jer 29:26 any maniac *who* **acts l a prophet** into the H5547
Jer 30: 6 hands on his stomach l a woman in labor, H3869
Jer 30: 7 No other will be l it. It will be a time H4017
Jer 31:10 will watch over his flock l a shepherd. H3869
Jer 31:12 They will be l a well-watered garden, and H3869
Jer 31:18 'You disciplined me l an unruly calf, and I H3869
Jer 31:32 It will not be l the covenant I made with H3869
Jer 34:18 *I will* **treat** *l* the calf they cut in two and then AIT
Jer 40: 4 Babylon, if you l, and I will H3202+928+6524
Jer 46: 7 "Who is this that rises l the Nile, like H3869
Jer 46: 7 like the Nile, l rivers of surging waters? H3869
Jer 46: 8 Egypt rises l the Nile, like rivers of surging H3869
Jer 46: 8 like the Nile, l rivers of surging waters. H3869
Jer 46:18 "one will come who is l Tabor among the H3869
Jer 46:18 the mountains, l Carmel by the sea. H3869
Jer 46:21 in her ranks are l fattened calves. H3869
Jer 46:22 Egypt will hiss l a fleeing serpent as the H3869
Jer 46:22 her with axes, l men who cut down trees. H3869
Jer 48: 6 your lives; become l a bush in the desert. H3869
Jer 48:11 at rest from youth, l wine left on its dregs NDT
Jer 48:28 Be l a dove that makes its nest at the H3869
Jer 48:36 laments for Moab l the music of a pipe; H3869
Jer 48:36 it laments l a pipe for the people of Kir H3869
Jer 48:38 I have broken Moab l a jar that no one H3869
Jer 48:41 warriors will be l the heart of a woman in H3869
Jer 49:19 "L a lion coming up from Jordan's thickets H3869
Jer 49:19 Who is l me and who can challenge me H4017
Jer 49:22 warriors will be l the heart of a woman in H3869
Jer 49:23 disheartened, troubled l the restless sea. H3869
Jer 49:24 pain l that of a woman in labor. H3869
Jer 50: 8 be l the goats that lead the flock. H3869
Jer 50: 9 Their arrows will be l skilled warriors who H3869
Jer 50:11 because you frolic l a heifer threshing H3869
Jer 50:11 threshing grain and neigh l stallions, H3869
Jer 50:26 granaries; pile her up l heaps of grain. H4017
Jer 50:42 They sound l the roaring sea as they ride H3869
Jer 50:42 they come l men in battle formation to H3869
Jer 50:43 pain l that of a woman in labor. H3869
Jer 50:44 L a lion coming up from Jordan's thickets H3869
Jer 50:44 Who is l me and who can challenge me H4017
Jer 51:19 who is the Portion of Jacob is not l these, H3869
Jer 51:27 send up horses l a swarm of locusts. H3869
Jer 51:33 "Daughter Babylon is l a threshing floor at H3869
Jer 51:34 L a serpent he has swallowed us and H3869
Jer 51:38 Her people all roar l young lions, they H3869
Jer 51:38 like young lions, they growl l lion cubs. H3869
Jer 51:40 will bring them down l lambs to the H3869
Jer 51:40 lambs to the slaughter, l rams and goats. H3869
Jer 51:55 of enemies will rage l great waters; H3869
La 1: 1 How l a widow is she, who once was H3869
La 1: 6 Her princes are l deer that find no pasture; H3869
La 1:12 Is any suffering l my suffering that was H3869
La 1:21 announced so they may become l me. H4017
La 2: 3 has burned in Jacob l a flaming fire that H3869
La 2: 4 L an enemy he has strung his bow; his H3869
La 2: 4 L a foe he has slain all who were H3869
La 2: 4 poured out his wrath l fire on the tent of H3869
La 2: 5 The Lord is l an enemy; he has swallowed H3869
La 2: 6 He has laid waste his dwelling l a garden; H3869
La 2:12 as they faint l the wounded in the streets H3869
La 2:18 let your tears flow l a river day and night H3869
La 2:19 pour out your heart l water in the H3869
La 2:20 Whom have you ever treated l **this** H3907
La 3: 6 me dwell in darkness l those long dead. H3869
La 3:10 L a bear lying in wait, like a lion in hiding, NDT
La 3:10 Like a bear lying in wait, l a lion in hiding, NDT
La 3:52 without cause hunted me l a bird. H3869
La 4: 3 have become heartless l ostriches in the H3869
La 4: 7 than rubies, their appearance l lapis lazuli. NDT
Eze 1: 4 center of the fire looked l glowing metal, H3869
Eze 1: 5 in the fire was *what* **looked** l four living H1952
Eze 1: 7 their feet were l those of a calf and H3869
Eze 1: 7 and gleamed l burnished bronze H3869+6524
Eze 1:10 Their faces **looked** l this: Each of the four H1952
Eze 1:13 living creatures was l burning coals of fire H1952
Eze 1:13 was like burning coals of fire or l torches. H3869
Eze 1:14 sped back and forth l flashes of lightning. H3869
Eze 1:16 They sparkled l topaz, and all four looked H3869
Eze 1:16 appeared to be made l a wheel H3869+889
Eze 1:22 was *what* **looked something** l a vault, H1952
Eze 1:22 sparkling l crystal, and awesome. H3869
Eze 1:24 of their wings, l the roar of rushing waters H3869
Eze 1:24 rushing waters, l the voice of the Almighty H3869
Eze 1:24 of the Almighty, l the tumult of an army. NDT
Eze 1:26 heads was what looked l a throne of lapis H1952
Eze 1:26 the throne was a figure l that of a man. H3869
Eze 1:27 his waist up he looked l glowing metal, H3869
Eze 1:27 that from there down he looked l fire H3869
Eze 1:28 L the appearance of a rainbow in the H3869
Eze 2: 8 Do not rebel l that rebellious people H3869
Eze 3: 9 make your forehead l the hardest stone, H3869
Eze 3:23 l the glory I had seen by the Kebar River H3869
Eze 7:16 L doves of the valleys, they will all moan H3869
Eze 8: 2 and I saw a figure l that of a man. H3869
Eze 8: 2 appeared to be his waist down he was l fire, NDT
Eze 8: 3 He stretched out *what* **looked** l a hand H9322
Eze 10: 5 l the voice of God Almighty when he H3869
Eze 10: 8 be seen *what* **looked** l human hands.) H9322
Eze 10: 9 cherubim; the wheels sparkled l topaz. H3869
Eze 10:10 each was l a wheel intersecting a H3869+889
Eze 10:21 wings was *what* **looked** l human hands. H1952
Eze 12: 4 go out l those who go into exile. H3869
Eze 13: 4 are l jackals among ruins. H3869
Eze 13:20 you ensnare people l birds and I will tear H4200
Eze 13:20 free the people that you ensnare l birds. H4200
Eze 16: 7 I made you grow l a plant of the field. H3869
Eze 16:30 all these things, **acting** *l* a brazen prostitute! AIT
Eze 16:44 proverb about you: "L mother, like H3869
Eze 16:44 "Like mother, l daughter." NDT
Eze 17: 5 He planted it l a willow by abundant water, NDT
Eze 19:10 " 'Your mother was l a vine in your H3869
Eze 20:32 "We want to be l the nations, like the H3869
Eze 20:32 the nations, l the peoples of the world H3869
Eze 21:10 slaughter, polished to **flash l lightning**! H1398
Eze 21:15 It is forged to **strike l lightning**, it is H1398
Eze 21:23 It will seem l a false omen to those who H3869
Eze 21:28 to consume and to **flash l lightning**! H1398
Eze 22:25 princes within her l a roaring lion tearing H3869
Eze 22:27 within her are l wolves tearing their H3869
Eze 23:15 all of them looked l Babylonian chariot H1952
Eze 23:20 whose genitals were l those of donkeys NDT
Eze 23:20 whose emission was l that of horses. NDT
Eze 24:19 Why are you acting l this?" NDT
Eze 25: 8 Judah has become l all the other nations," H3869
Eze 26: 3 l the sea casting up its waves. H3869
Eze 26:19 desolate city, l cities no longer inhabited H3869
Eze 27:32 "Who was ever silenced l Tyre H3869
Eze 30:24 will groan before him l a mortally wounded NDT
Eze 31:17 They too, l the great cedar, had gone down H907
Eze 32: 2 " '*You* **are** l a lion among the nations; you H1948
Eze 32: 2 you are l a monster in the seas thrashing H3869
Eze 32:14 settle and make her streams flow l oil, H3869
Eze 36:17 Their conduct was l a woman's monthly H3869
Eze 36:35 waste has become l the garden of Eden; H3869
Eze 38: 9 advancing l a storm; you will be H3869
Eze 38: 9 you will be l a cloud covering the land. H3869
Eze 38:16 my people Israel l a cloud that covers the H3869
Eze 40: 2 were some buildings that looked l a city. H3869
Eze 40: 3 a man whose appearance was l bronze; H3869
Eze 40:25 all around, l the openings of the others. H3869
Eze 41:25 and palm trees l those carved on the H3869+889
Eze 42:11 These were l the rooms on the H3869+5260
Eze 43: 2 His voice was l the roar of rushing waters H3869
Eze 43: 3 The vision I saw was l the vision I had H3869
Eze 43: 3 destroy the city and l the visions I had H3869
Eze 47:10 l the fish of the Mediterranean Sea. H3869
Da 2:35 pieces and became l chaff on a A10341
Da 3:25 the fourth looks l a son of the gods." A10179
Da 4:25 you will eat grass l the ox and be A10341
Da 4:32 wild animals; you will eat grass l the ox. A10341
Da 4:33 away from people and ate grass l the ox. A10341
Da 4:33 until his hair grew l the feathers of an A10341
Da 4:33 eagle and his nails l the claws of a bird. A10341
Da 5:11 wisdom l that of the gods. A10341
Da 5:21 the wild donkeys and ate grass l the ox; A10341
Da 7: 4 "The first was l a lion, and it had the A10341
Da 7: 4 it stood on two feet l a human being, A10341
Da 7: 5 a second beast, which **looked** l a bear. A10179
Da 7: 6 one that looked l a leopard. A10341
Da 7: 6 its back it had four wings l those of a bird. NDT
Da 7: 8 This horn had eyes l the eyes of a A10341
Da 7: 9 the hair of his head was white l wool. A10341
Da 7:13 there before me was one l a son of man, A10341
Da 8:15 before me stood one who looked l a man. H3869
Da 9:12 ever been done l what has been done H3869
Da 9:26 The end will come l a flood: War will H928
Da 10: 6 His body was l topaz, his face like H3869
Da 10: 6 his face l lightning, his eyes H3869+5260
Da 10: 6 lightning, his eyes l flaming torches, his H3869
Da 10: 6 his arms and legs l the gleam of H3869
Da 10: 6 his voice l the sound of a multitude. H3869
Da 10:16 Then one who looked l a man touched my H3869
Da 10:18 the one who looked l a man touched me H3869
Da 11:10 which will sweep on l an irresistible flood NDT
Da 11:40 countries and sweep through them l a flood. NDT
Da 12: 3 are wise will shine l the brightness of the H3869
Da 12: 3 l the stars for ever and ever. H3869
Hos 1: 2 for *l an* **adulterous** *wife* this land is guilty of AIT
Hos 1:10 the Israelites will be l the sand on the H3869
Hos 2: 3 I will make her l a desert, turn her H3869
Hos 4: 4 your people are l those who bring H3869
Hos 4: 9 And it will be: L people, like priests. I will H3869
Hos 4: 9 Like people, l priests. I will punish H3869
Hos 4:16 are stubborn, l a stubborn heifer. H3869
Hos 4:16 LORD pasture them l lambs in a meadow? H3869
Hos 5:10 Judah's leaders are l those who move H3869
Hos 5:10 out my wrath on them l a flood of water. H3869
Hos 5:12 I am l a moth to Ephraim, like rot to the H3869
Hos 5:12 to Ephraim, l rot to the people of Judah. H3869
Hos 5:14 For I will be l a lion to Ephraim, like a H3869
Hos 5:14 a lion to Ephraim, l a great lion to Judah. H3869
Hos 6: 3 he will come to us l the winter rains, like H3869
Hos 6: 3 l the spring rains that water the earth." H3869
Hos 6: 4 Your love is l the morning mist, like the H3869
Hos 6: 4 l the early dew that disappears. H3869
Hos 6: 5 then my judgments go forth l the sun. H3869
Hos 7: 4 burning l an oven whose fire the baker H4017
Hos 7: 6 Their hearts are l an oven; they approach H3869
Hos 7: 6 in the morning it blazes l a flaming fire. H3869
Hos 7:11 "Ephraim is l a dove, easily deceived and H3869
Hos 7:12 I will pull them down l the birds in the sky. H3869
Hos 7:16 to the Most High; they are l a faulty bow. H3869
Hos 8: 8 is among the nations l something no one H3869
Hos 8: 9 gone up to Assyria l a wild donkey NDT
Hos 9: 1 do not be jubilant l the other nations. H3869
Hos 9: 4 will be to them l the bread of mourners; H3869
Hos 9:10 it was l finding grapes in the desert H3869
Hos 9:10 it was l seeing the early fruit on the fig H3869
Hos 9:11 Ephraim's glory will fly away l a bird—no H3869
Hos 9:13 seen Ephraim, l Tyre, planted in a H3869+889
Hos 10: 4 lawsuits spring up l poisonous weeds in a H3869
Hos 10: 7 swept away l a twig on the surface of the H3869
Hos 11: 4 To them I was l one who lifts a little child H3869
Hos 11: 8 How can I treat you l Admah? How can I H3869
Hos 11: 8 How can I make you l Zeboyim? My heart H3869
Hos 11:10 will follow the LORD; he will roar l a lion. H3869
Hos 11:11 from Egypt, trembling l sparrows, from H3869
Hos 11:11 sparrows, from Assyria, fluttering l doves. H3869
Hos 12:11 Their altars will be l piles of stones on a H3869
Hos 13: 3 Therefore they will be l the morning mist H3869
Hos 13: 3 l the early dew that disappears H3869
Hos 13: 3 l chaff swirling from a threshing floor H3869
Hos 13: 3 l smoke escaping through a window. H3869
Hos 13: 7 So I will be l a lion to them, like a H4017
Hos 13: 7 to them, l a leopard I will lurk by the path. H3869
Hos 13: 8 L a bear robbed of her cubs, I will attack H3869
Hos 13: 8 rip them open; l a lion I will devour them H3869
Hos 14: 5 I will be l the dew to Israel; he will H3869
Hos 14: 5 the dew to Israel; he will blossom l a lily. H3869
Hos 14: 5 L a cedar of Lebanon he will send down H3869
Hos 14: 6 His splendor will be l an olive tree, his H3869
Hos 14: 6 his fragrance l a cedar of Lebanon. H3869
Hos 14: 7 they will flourish l the grain, they will NDT
Hos 14: 7 they will blossom l the vine—Israel's H3869
Hos 14: 7 fame will be l the wine of Lebanon. H3869
Hos 14: 8 I am l a flourishing juniper; your H3869
Joel 1: 2 Has anything l this ever happened in your NDT
Joel 1: 8 Mourn l a virgin in sackcloth grieving for H3869
Joel 1:15 it will come l destruction from the H3869
Joel 2: 2 L dawn spreading across the mountains a H3869
Joel 2: 3 them the land is l the garden of Eden, H3869
Joel 2: 4 of horses; they gallop along l cavalry. H3869
Joel 2: 5 With a noise l that of chariots they leap H3869
Joel 2: 5 l a crackling fire consuming stubble H3869
Joel 2: 5 l a mighty army drawn up for battle. H3869
Joel 2: 7 They charge l warriors; they scale walls H3869
Joel 2: 7 like warriors; they scale walls l soldiers. H3869
Joel 2: 9 l thieves they enter through the windows. H3869
Am 4:11 You were l a burning stick snatched from H3869
Am 5: 6 through the tribes of Joseph l a fire; H3869

Am 5:24 But let justice roll on l a river H3869
Am 5:24 righteousness l a never-failing stream! H3869
Am 6: 5 away on your harps l David and improvise H3869
Am 8: 8 The whole land will rise l the Nile; it will H3869
Am 8: 8 up and then sink l the river of Egypt. H3869
Am 8:10 will make that time l mourning for an only H3869
Am 8:10 only son and the end of it l a bitter day. H3869
Am 9: 5 the whole land rises l the Nile, then sinks H3869
Am 9: 5 the Nile, then sinks l the river of Egypt; H3869
Ob 4 Though you soar l the eagle and make H3869
Ob 11 Jerusalem, you were l one of them. H3869
Mic 1: 4 valleys split apart, l wax before the fire H3869
Mic 1: 4 the fire, l water rushing down a slope. H3869
Mic 1: 8 I will howl l a jackal and moan like an H3869
Mic 1: 8 will howl like a jackal and moan l an owl. H3869
Mic 2: 8 my people have risen up l an enemy. H4200
Mic 2: 8 without a care, l men returning from battle. NDT
Mic 2:12 will bring them together l sheep in a pen, H3869
Mic 2:12 like sheep in a pen, l a flock in its pasture H3869
Mic 3: 3 chop them up l meat for the pan H3869+889
Mic 3: 3 like meat for the pan, l flesh for the pot?" H3869
Mic 3:12 Zion will be plowed l a field, Jerusalem will NDT
Mic 4: 9 that pain seizes you l that of a woman in H3869
Mic 4:10 Daughter Zion, l a woman in labor, for H3869
Mic 4:12 he has gathered them l sheaves to the H3869
Mic 5: 7 of many peoples l dew from the LORD, H3869
Mic 5: 7 dew from the LORD, l showers on the grass H3869
Mic 5: 8 l a lion among the beasts of the forest H3869
Mic 5: 8 l a young lion among flocks of sheep H3869
Mic 7: 1 I am l one who gathers summer fruit at H3869
Mic 7: 4 The best of them is l a brier, the most H3869
Mic 7:10 trampled underfoot l mire in the streets. H3869
Mic 7:17 They will lick dust l a snake, like creatures H3869
Mic 7:17 l creatures that crawl on the ground. H3869
Mic 7:18 Who is a God l you, who pardons sin and H4017
Na 1: 6 His wrath is poured out l fire; the rocks are H3869
Na 1:10 they will be consumed l dry stubble. H3869
Na 2: 2 the splendor of Jacob l the splendor of H3869
Na 2: 4 They look l flaming torches; they dart H3869
Na 2: 4 torches; they dart about l lightning. H3869
Na 2: 7 female slaves moan l doves and beat on H3869
Na 2: 8 Nineveh is l a pool whose water is H3869
Na 3:12 All your fortresses are l fig trees with their NDT
Na 3:15 they will devour you l a swarm of locusts. H3869
Na 3:15 Multiply l grasshoppers, multiply like H3869
Na 3:15 like grasshoppers, multiply l locusts! H3869
Na 3:16 l locusts they strip the land and then fly NDT
Na 3:17 Your guards are l locusts, your officials H3869
Na 3:17 your officials l swarms of locusts that H3869
Hab 1: 8 They fly l an eagle swooping to devour H3869
Hab 1: 9 Their hordes advance l a desert wind and NDT
Hab 1: 9 a desert wind and gather prisoners l sand. H3869
Hab 1:11 they sweep past l the wind and go on— NDT
Hab 1:14 have made people l the fish in the sea, H3869
Hab 1:14 l the sea creatures that have no ruler. H3869
Hab 2: 5 greedy as the grave and l death is never H3869
Hab 3: 4 His splendor was l the sunrise; rays H3869
Hab 3:19 he makes my feet l the feet of a deer, he H3869
Zep 1:12 complacent, who are l wine left on its dregs NDT
Zep 1:17 will grope about l those who are blind, H3869
Zep 1:17 will be poured out l dust and their entrails H3869
Zep 1:17 out like dust and their entrails l dung. H3869
Zep 2: 2 that day passes l windblown chaff, H3869
Zep 2: 9 "surely Moab will become l Sodom, the H3869
Zep 2: 9 the Ammonites l Gomorrah—a place of H3869
Hag 2: 3 Does it not seem to you l nothing? H3869
Hag 2:23 'and I will make you l my signet ring, for I H3869
Zec 1: 4 Do not be l your ancestors, to whom the H3869
Zec 4: 1 l someone awakened from sleep. H3869
Zec 5: 9 They had wings l those of a stork, and H3869
Zec 9: 3 she has heaped up silver l dust, and gold H3869
Zec 9: 3 like dust, and gold l the dirt of the streets. H3869
Zec 9: 7 and Ekron will be l the Jebusites. H3869
Zec 9:13 Greece, and make you l a warrior's sword. H3869
Zec 9:14 over them; his arrow will flash l lightning. H3869
Zec 9:15 they will be full l a bowl used for H3869
Zec 9:16 will sparkle in his land l jewels in a crown. NDT
Zec 10: 2 the people wander l sheep oppressed H4017
Zec 10: 3 make them l a proud horse in battle. H3869
Zec 10: 5 Together they will be l warriors in battle H3869
Zec 10: 7 The Ephraimites will become l warriors H3869
Zec 12: 6 the clans of Judah l a firepot in a H3869
Zec 12: 6 l a flaming torch among sheaves. H3869
Zec 12: 8 the feeblest among them will be l David, H3869
Zec 12: 8 the house of David will be l God, like H3869
Zec 12: 8 l the angel of the LORD going before them. H3869
Zec 13: 9 I will refine them l silver and test them H3869
Zec 13: 9 them like silver and test them l gold. H3869
Zec 14:10 of Jerusalem, will become l the Arabah. H3869
Zec 14:20 LORD's house will be l the sacred bowls in H3869
Mal 3: 2 For he will be l a refiner's fire or a H3869
Mal 3: 3 Levites and refine them l gold and silver. H3869
Mal 3:14 going about l mourners before the LORD NDT
Mal 4: 1 the day is coming; it will burn l a furnace. H3869
Mal 4: 2 will go out and frolic l well-fed calves. H3869
Mt 3:16 of God descending l a dove and alighting *G6059*
Mt 6: 5 you pray, do not be l the hypocrites, for *G6055*
Mt 6: 7 do not keep on babbling l pagans, for *G6061*
Mt 6: 8 *Do* not *be* l them, for your Father knows *G3929*
Mt 6:29 his splendor was dressed l one of these. *G6055*
Mt 7:24 them into practice *is* l a wise man who *G3929*
Mt 7:26 them into practice *is* l a foolish man who *G3929*
Mt 9:33 "Nothing **l this** has ever been seen in *G4048*
Mt 9:36 helpless, l sheep without a shepherd. *G6059*
Mt 10:16 sending you out l sheep among wolves *G6055*
Mt 10:25 enough for students to be l their teachers, *G6055*
Mt 10:25 teachers, and servants l their masters. *G6055*
Mt 11:16 They are l children sitting in the *G3927*
Mt 13:24 kingdom of heaven *is* l a man who sowed *G3929*
Mt 13:31 kingdom of heaven is l a mustard seed, *G3927*
Mt 13:33 of heaven is l yeast that a woman *G3927*
Mt 13:43 righteous will shine l the sun in the *G6055*
Mt 13:44 of heaven is l treasure hidden in a *G3927*
Mt 13:45 of heaven is l a merchant looking *G3927*
Mt 13:47 kingdom of heaven is l a net that was let *G3927*
Mt 13:52 of heaven is l the owner of a house *G3927*
Mt 17: 2 His face shone l the sun, and his clothes *G6055*
Mt 18: 3 you change and become l little children, *G6055*
Mt 18:23 kingdom of heaven *is* l a king who *G3929*
Mt 19:12 those who **choose to live l eunuchs** for the *G2335*
Mt 20: 1 of heaven is l a landowner who went *G3927*
Mt 22: 2 kingdom of heaven *is* l a king who *G3929*
Mt 22:30 they will be l the angels in heaven. *G6055*
Mt 22:39 And the second is l it: 'Love your neighbor *G3927*
Mt 23:27 *You are* l whitewashed tombs, which look *G4234*
Mt 25: 1 of heaven *will be* l ten virgins who *G3929*
Mt 25:14 it will be l a man going on a journey *G6061*
Mt 28: 3 His appearance was l lightning, and his *G6055*
Mt 28: 4 that they shook and became l dead men. *G6055*
Mk 1:10 the Spirit descending on him l a dove. *G6055*
Mk 2: 7 "Why does this fellow talk **l that**? He's *G4048*
Mk 2:12 "We have never seen anything **l this**!" *G4048*
Mk 4:15 Some people *are* l seed along the path *G1639*
Mk 4:16 l seed sown on rocky places, hear *G3931*
Mk 4:18 Still others, l seed sown among thorns *G1639S*
Mk 4:20 l seed sown on good soil, hear *G1639S*
Mk 4:26 "This is what the kingdom of God is l. *G6055*
Mk 4:30 *shall we* **say** the kingdom of God **is l**, *G3929*
Mk 4:31 It is l a mustard seed, which is the *G6055*
Mk 6:15 l one of the prophets of long ago. *G6055*
Mk 6:34 because they were l sheep without a *G6055*
Mk 7:13 And you do many things l that." *G4235*
Mk 8:24 people; they look l trees walking around." *G6055*
Mk 9:21 "How long has he been l this? *G6055*
Mk 9:26 The boy **looked so much** l a corpse *G1181+6059*
Mk 10:15 the kingdom of God l a little child will *G6055*
Mk 12:25 they will be l the angels in heaven. *G6055*
Mk 12:38 *They* l to walk around in flowing robes *G2527*
Mk 13:34 It's l a man going away: He leaves his *G6055*
Lk 1:62 to find out what *he* would l to name the *G2527*
Lk 2:48 "Son, why have you treated us **l this**? *G4048*
Lk 3:22 on him in bodily form l a dove. *G6055*
Lk 6:40 who is fully trained will be l their teacher. *G6055*
Lk 6:47 practice, I will show you what they are l. *G3927*
Lk 6:48 They are l a man building a house, who *G3927*
Lk 6:49 them into practice is l a man who built a *G3927*
Lk 7:31 of this generation? What are they l? *G3927*
Lk 7:32 They are l children sitting in the *G3927*
Lk 10: 3 sending you out l lambs among wolves *G6055*
Lk 10:18 "I saw Satan fall l lightning from heaven. *G6055*
Lk 11:44 because you are l unmarked graves *G6055*
Lk 12:27 his splendor was dressed l one of these. *G6055*
Lk 12:36 l servants waiting for their master to return *G3927*
Lk 13:18 "What is the kingdom of God l? *G3927*
Lk 13:19 It is l a mustard seed, which a man took *G3927*
Lk 13:21 It is l yeast that a woman took and mixed *G3927*
Lk 15:19 make me l one of your hired servants. *G6055*
Lk 17:24 of Man in his day will be l the lightning, *G6061*
Lk 17:30 "It will be **just** l this on the day the Son of *G2848*
Lk 18:11 I thank you that I am not l other people *G6061*
Lk 18:11 adulterers—or even l this tax collector. *G6055*
Lk 18:17 the kingdom of God l a little child will *G6055*
Lk 20:36 no longer die; for they are l *the* **angels**. *G2694*
Lk 20:46 They l to walk around in flowing robes *G2527*
Lk 21:34 day will close on you suddenly l a trap. *G6055*
Lk 22:26 But you are not to be **l that**. Instead, the *G4048*
Lk 22:26 among you should be l the youngest, *G6055*
Lk 22:26 the one who rules l the one who serves. *G6055*
Lk 22:44 his sweat was l drops of blood falling *G6059*
Lk 24: 4 in clothes *that* **gleamed l lightning** stood *G848*
Lk 24:11 their words seemed to them l nonsense. *G6059*
Jn 1:44 *l* **Andrew** and Peter, was from the AIT
Jn 8:55 I would be a liar l you, but I do know him *G3927*
Jn 9: 9 he only looks l him." But he himself *G3927*
Jn 11:48 If we let him go on **l this**, everyone will *G4048*
Jn 12:21 they said, "*we would* l to see Jesus." *G2527*
Jn 15: 6 you are l a branch that is thrown away *G6055*
Ac 2: 2 Suddenly a sound l the blowing of a *G6061*
Ac 3:22 you a prophet l me from among your *G6055*
Ac 6:15 that his face was l the face of an angel. *G6059*
Ac 7:37 up for you a prophet l me from your own *G6055*
Ac 7:51 You are **just** l your ancestors: You *G6055*
Ac 8:32 "He was led l a sheep to the slaughter *G6055*
Ac 9:18 *something* l scales fell from Saul's eyes *G6055*
Ac 10:11 something l a large sheet being *G6055*
Ac 11: 5 I saw something l a large sheet being let *G6055*
Ac 14:15 too are only human, l you. We are *G3926*
Ac 17:20 and *we would* l to know what they mean." *G1089*
Ac 17:29 the divine being is l gold or silver or stone *G3927*
Ac 22:24 the people were shouting at him **l this**. *G4048*
Ac 25:22 "*I would* l to hear this man myself. *G1089*
Ro 1:23 God for images **made to look** l a mortal *G3930*
Ro 5:15 But the gift is not l the trespass. For if the *G6055*
Ro 6: 5 been united with him *in* a death l his, *G3930*
Ro 6: 5 be united with him in a resurrection l his. NDT
Ro 9:20 formed it, 'Why did you make me **l this**? *G4048*
Ro 9:27 of the Israelites be l the sand by the sea, *G6055*
Ro 9:29 we would have become l Sodom, we *G6055*
Ro 9:29 Sodom, *we* would have *been* l Gomorrah." *G3929*
1Co 3: 3 Are you not acting l mere humans? *G2848*
1Co 4: 9 l those condemned to die in the arena. *G6055*
1Co 7:32 *I would* l you to be free from concern. *G2527*
1Co 9:20 To the Jews I became l a Jew, to win the *G6055*
1Co 9:20 the law I became l one under the law *G6055*
1Co 9:21 the law I became l one not having the *G6055*
1Co 9:26 Therefore I do not run l someone running *G6055*
1Co 9:26 I do not fight l a boxer beating the air. *G6055*
1Co 13:11 was a child, I talked l a child, I thought *G6055*
1Co 13:11 like a child, I thought l a child, I reasoned *G6055*
1Co 13:11 I thought like a child, I reasoned l a child. *G6055*
1Co 14: 5 *I would* l every one of you to speak in *G2527*
1Co 14:20 stop thinking *l* **children**. In regard to evil be AIT
2Co 3: 1 Or do we need, l some people, letters of *G6055*
2Co 3:13 We are not l Moses, who would put a veil *G2749*
2Co 11:23 I am out of my mind to talk l this.) I am NDT
2Co 12: 5 I will boast about a *man* **l that**, but I will *G5525*
Gal 2:14 you live **l a Gentile** and not like a Jew. *G1619*
Gal 2:14 you live like a Gentile and not **l a Jew**. *G2680*
Gal 3: 2 *I would* l to learn just one thing from you *G2527*
Gal 4:12 sisters, become l me, for I became *G6055*
Gal 4:12 become like me, for I became l you. *G6055*
Gal 4:28 brothers and sisters, l Isaac, are children *G2848*
Gal 5:21 and the l. I warn you, *G3927*
Gal 5:21 that those who live **l this** will not inherit *G5525*
Eph 2: 3 **L** the rest, we were by nature deserving of *G6055*
Eph 4:24 created to be l God in true righteousness *G2848*
Php 2:15 will shine among them l stars in the sky *G6055*
Php 2:17 *I am being* **poured out l a drink offering** *G5064*
Php 2:20 I have no one else l him, who will show *G2701*
Php 2:29 with great joy, and honor *people* **l him**, *G5525*
Php 3:10 sufferings, **becoming** l him in his death, *G5214*
Php 3:21 so that they will **be** l his glorious body. *G5215*
1Th 2: 7 we were l young children among you. NDT
1Th 4: 5 not in passionate lust l the pagans, who *G2749*
1Th 4:13 you do not grieve l the rest of mankind, *G2777*
1Th 5: 2 of the Lord will come l a thief in the night. *G6055*
1Th 5: 4 of this day should surprise you l a thief. *G6055*
1Th 5: 6 So then, let us not be l others, who are *G6055*
2Ti 2: 3 suffering, l a good soldier of Christ Jesus. *G6055*
2Ti 2: 9 to the point of being chained l a criminal. *G6055*
2Ti 2:17 Their teaching will spread l gangrene *G6055*
2Ti 4: 6 *am* already *being* **poured out l a drink offering** *G5064*
Heb 1:11 remain; they will all wear out l a garment. *G6055*
Heb 1:12 You will roll them up l a robe; like a *G6059*
Heb 1:12 l a garment they will be changed. *G6055*
Heb 2:17 For this reason he had to *be* **made** l them *G3929*
Heb 6: 9 Even though we speak **l this**, dear friends *G4048*
Heb 7:15 another priest l Melchizedek *G2848+3836+3928*
Heb 8: 9 It will not be l the covenant I made with *G2848*
Heb 9: 6 everything had been arranged **l this**, *G4048*
Heb 11: 9 in the promised land l a stranger in a *G6055*
Heb 12:16 is godless l Esau, who for a single *G6055*
Jas 1: 6 the one who doubts *is* l a wave of the sea *G2036*
Jas 1:10 since they will pass away l a wild flower. *G6055*
Jas 1:17 who does not change l shifting shadows. NDT
Jas 1:23 do what it says *is* l someone who looks *G2036*
Jas 1:24 forgets **what** *he* **looks l**. *G3961+1639*
Jas 5: 3 against you and eat your flesh l fire. *G6055*
1Pe 1:24 "All people are l grass, and all their *G6055*
1Pe 1:24 all their glory is l the flowers of the *G6055*
1Pe 2: 2 **L** newborn babies, crave pure spiritual milk *G6055*
1Pe 2: 5 you also, l living stones, are being built *G6055*
1Pe 2:25 For "you were l sheep going astray," but *G6055*
1Pe 3: 6 l Sarah, who obeyed Abraham and called *G6055*
1Pe 5: 8 devil prowls around l a roaring lion *G6055*
2Pe 2:12 They are l unreasoning animals, creatures *G6055*
2Pe 2:12 l animals they too will perish. NDT
2Pe 3: 8 With the Lord a day is l a thousand years *G6055*
2Pe 3: 8 and a thousand years are l a day. *G6055*
2Pe 3:10 But the day of the Lord will come l a thief *G6055*
1Jn 3: 2 appears, we shall be l him, for we shall *G3927*
1Jn 3:12 Do not be l Cain, who belonged to the evil *G2777*
1Jn 4:17 In this world we are l Jesus. *G2777*
Rev 1:10 behind me a loud voice l a trumpet, *G6055*
Rev 1:13 lampstands was someone l a son of man, *G3927*
Rev 1:14 The hair on his head was white l wool, as *G6055*
Rev 1:14 as snow, and his eyes were l blazing fire. *G6055*
Rev 1:15 His feet were l bronze glowing in a *G3927*
Rev 1:15 his voice was l the sound of rushing *G6055*
Rev 1:16 His face was l the sun shining in all its *G6055*
Rev 2:18 whose eyes are l blazing fire and whose *G6055*
Rev 2:18 whose feet are l burnished bronze. *G3927*
Rev 2:27 will dash them to pieces l pottery'— *G6055*
Rev 3: 3 wake up, I will come l a thief, and you *G6055*
Rev 3: 5 is victorious will, l them, be dressed in *G4048*
Rev 4: 1 heard speaking to me l a trumpet said, *G6055*
Rev 4: 3 rainbow that shone l an emerald *G3927*
Rev 4: 6 there was what *looked* l a sea of glass, *G6055*
Rev 4: 7 The first living creature was l a lion, the *G3927*
Rev 4: 7 the second was l an ox, the third had *G3927*
Rev 4: 7 the third had a face l a man, the fourth *G6055*
Rev 4: 7 the fourth was l a flying eagle. *G3927*
Rev 6: 1 living creatures say in a voice l thunder, *G6055*
Rev 6: 6 I heard what *sounded* l a voice among *G6055*
Rev 6:12 The sun turned black l sackcloth made of *G6055*

Rev 6:14 The heavens receded **l** a scroll being G6055
Rev 8: 8 and *something* **l** a huge mountain G6055
Rev 8:10 a great star, blazing **l** a torch, fell from the G6055
Rev 9: 2 smoke rose from it **l** the smoke from a G6055
Rev 9: 3 were given power **l** that of scorpions of G6055
Rev 9: 5 they suffered was **l** that of the sting of a G6055
Rev 9: 7 The locusts **looked l** horses prepared for G3930
Rev 9: 7 they wore *something* **l** crowns of gold G6055
Rev 9: 8 Their hair was **l** women's hair, and their G6055
Rev 9: 8 and their teeth were **l** lions' teeth. G6055
Rev 9: 9 had breastplates **l** breastplates of iron G6055
Rev 9: 9 of their wings was **l** the thundering of G6055
Rev 9:10 tails with stingers, **l** scorpions, and in their G3927
Rev 9:17 riders I saw in my vision looked **l this**: G4048
Rev 9:19 their tails were **l** snakes, having heads G3927
Rev 10: 1 his face was **l** the sun, and his legs G6055
Rev 10: 1 the sun, and his legs were **l** fiery pillars. G6055
Rev 10: 3 he gave a loud shout **l** the roar of a lion. G6061
Rev 11: 1 I was given a reed **l** a measuring rod and G3927
Rev 12:15 mouth the serpent spewed water **l** a river, G6055
Rev 13: 2 had feet **l** those of a bear and a G6055
Rev 13: 2 of a bear and a mouth **l** that of a lion. G6055
Rev 13: 4 the beast and asked, "Who is **l** the beast? G3927
Rev 13:11 It had two horns **l** a lamb, but it spoke **l**ike G3927
Rev 13:11 horns like a lamb, but it spoke **l** a dragon. G6055
Rev 14: 2 a sound from heaven **l** the roar of rushing G6055
Rev 14: 2 of rushing waters and **l** a loud peal of G6055
Rev 14: 2 The sound I heard was **l** that of harpists G6055
Rev 14:14 the cloud was one **l** a son of man with a G3927
Rev 15: 2 And I saw what **looked l** a sea of glass G6055
Rev 16: 3 it turned into blood **l** that of a dead G6055
Rev 16:13 three impure spirits that **looked l** frogs; G6055
Rev 16:15 I come **l** a thief! Blessed is the one G6055
Rev 16:18 No earthquake **l** it has ever occurred since G3888
Rev 18:18 'Was there ever a city **l** this great city? G3927
Rev 19: 1 this I heard what *sounded* **l** the roar of a G6055
Rev 19: 6 I heard what sounded **l** a great multitude, G6055
Rev 19: 6 **l** the roar of rushing waters and like loud G6055
Rev 19: 6 rushing waters and **l** loud peals of G6055
Rev 19:12 His eyes are **l** blazing fire, and on his G6055
Rev 20: 8 In number they are **l** the sand on the G6055
Rev 21:11 its brilliance was **l** that of a very G3927
Rev 21:11 a very precious jewel, **l** a jasper, clear as G6055
Rev 21:16 The city was laid out *l* a **square**, as long as it AIT

LIKE-MINDED (2) [LIKE, MIND]

Php 2: 2 my joy complete by *being* **l**, G3836+899+5858
1Pe 3: 8 all of you, be **l**, be sympathetic, love G3939

LIKED (5) [LIKE]

Ge 27:14 some tasty food, just the way his father **l** it. H170
Jdg 14: 7 the woman, and he **l** her. H3837+928+6524
1Sa 16:21 Saul **l** him very much, and David became H170
Mk 6:20 greatly puzzled; yet he **l to** listen to him. G2452
Phm 13 I *would have* **l** to keep him with me so that G1089

LIKELY (1) [LIKE]

1Ki 12:26 "The kingdom *will* now *l* revert to the house AIT

LIKEN (4) [LIKE]

SS 1: 9 *I* **l** you, my darling, to a mare among H1948
Isa 40:18 To what image *will you* **l** him? H6885
Isa 46: 5 To whom *will you* **l** me that we may be H5439
La 2:13 To what *can I* **l** you, that I may comfort H8750

LIKENESS (10) [LIKE]

Ge 1:26 in our image, in our **l**, so that they may H1952
Ge 5: 1 mankind, he made them in the **l** *of* God. H1952
Ge 5: 3 he had a son in his own **l**, in his own H1952
Ps 17:15 I will be satisfied with seeing your **l**. H9454
Isa 52:14 his form marred beyond human **l**— NDT
Eze 1:28 the appearance of the **l** *of* the glory of the H1952
Eze 10: 1 I saw the **l** *of* a throne of lapis lazuli H1952
Ro 8: 3 his own Son in the **l** of sinful flesh to be a G3930
Php 2: 7 of a servant, being made in human **l**. G3930
Jas 3: 9 who have been made in God's **l**. G3932

LIKES (2) [LIKE]

Ge 27: 9 food for your father, just the way *he* **l** it. H170
1Sa 18:22 the king **l** you, and his attendants H2911

LIKEWISE (10) [LIKE]

Jdg 11:24 **L**, whatever the LORD our God has given H2256
2Ch 31:17 genealogical records **and l** to the Levites H2256
Mt 7:17 **L**, every good tree bears good fruit, but a G4048
Lk 10:37 Jesus told him, "Go and do **l**." G3931
Lk 17:31 **L**, no one in the field should go back for G3931
1Co 7: 3 to his wife, and **l** the wife to her husband. G3931
2Co 13: 4 **L**, we are weak in him, yet by God's power G2779
Titus 2: 3 **L**, teach the older women to be reverent G6058
Jas 3: 5 **L**, the tongue is a small part of the body G4048
Rev 2:15 **L**, you also have those who hold to the G4048

LIKHI (1)

1Ch 7:19 Ahian, Shechem, **L** and Aniam. H4376

LIKING (1) [LIKE]

1Sa 19: 1 But Jonathan *had* **taken a** great **l** to David H2911

LILIES (11) [LILY]

1Ki 7:19 in the portico were in the shape of **l**, H8808
1Ki 7:22 The capitals on top were in the shape of **l** H8808
Ps 45: T To the tune of "**L**." Of the Sons of Korah H8808
Ps 69: T To the tune of "**L**." Of David. H8808
Ps 80: T To the tune of "The **L** *of* the Covenant." H8808
SS 2:16 I am his; he browses among the **l**. H8808
SS 4: 5 of a gazelle that browse among the **l**. H8808
SS 5:13 His lips are like **l** dripping with myrrh. H8808
SS 6: 2 to browse in the gardens and to gather **l**. H8808
SS 6: 3 beloved is mine; he browses among the **l**. H8808
SS 7: 2 waist is a mound of wheat encircled by **l**. H8808

LILY (6) [LILIES]

1Ki 7:26 was like the rim of a cup, like a **l** blossom. H8808
2Ch 4: 5 was like the rim of a cup, like a **l** blossom. H8808
Ps 60: T To the tune of "The **L** *of* the Covenant." H8808
SS 2: 1 I am a rose of Sharon, a **l** *of* the valleys. H8808
SS 2: 2 Like a **l** among thorns is my darling H8808
Hos 14: 5 the dew to Israel; he will blossom like a **l**. H8808

LIMB (2) [LIMBS]

Jdg 19:29 cut up his concubine, **l** by limb, into twelve NDT
Jdg 19:29 concubine, limb by **l**, into twelve parts H6795

LIMBER (1)

Ge 49:24 his strong arms *stayed* **l**, because of the H7060

LIMBS (3) [LIMB]

Job 18:13 of his skin; death's firstborn devours his **l**. H963
Job 40:18 are tubes of bronze, its **l** like rods of iron. H1752
Job 41:12 "I will not fail to speak of Leviathan's **l**, its H963

LIMESTONE (1)

Isa 27: 9 stones to be like **l** crushed to pieces, H1732+74

LIMIT (6) [LIMITATIONS, LIMITS]

Ezr 7:22 baths of olive oil, and salt without **l**. A10375
Ps 119:96 To all perfection I see a **l**, but your H7891
Ps 147: 5 in power; his understanding has no **l**. H5031
Jer 5:28 Their evil deeds **have no l**; they do not H6296
Jn 3:34 for God gives the Spirit without **l**. G3586
1Th 2:16 way they always **heap up** their sins **to the l**. G405

LIMITATIONS (1) [LIMIT]

Ro 6:19 everyday life because of your human **l**. G819

LIMITS (10) [LIMIT]

Ex 19:12 **Put l** *for* the people around the mountain H1487
Ex 19:23 '**Put l around** the mountain and set it H1487
Nu 35:26 goes outside the **l** *of* the city of refuge H1473
Jos 17:18 Clear it, and its **farthest l** will be yours H9362
Job 11: 7 Can you probe the **l** *of* the Almighty? H9417
Job 14: 5 months and have set **l** he cannot exceed. H2976
Job 38:10 when I fixed **l** for it and set its doors and H2976
Ps 73: 7 iniquity; their evil imaginations **have no l**. H6296
2Co 10:13 will not boast beyond *proper* **l**, but will G296
2Co 10:15 do we go beyond our **l** by boasting of work G296

LIMP (8) [LIMPING]

Isa 13: 7 all hands *will* **go l**, every heart will H8332
Jer 6:24 about them, and our hands **hang l**. H8332
Jer 47: 3 their children; their hands will **hang l**. H8342
Jer 50:43 reports about them, and his hands **hang l**. H8332
Eze 7:17 Every hand *will* **go l**; every leg will be wet H8332
Eze 21: 7 will melt with fear and every hand **go l**; H8332
Eze 30:25 the arms of Pharaoh *will* **fall l**. H5877
Zep 3:16 Zion; *do* not *let* your hands **hang l**. H8332

LIMPING (1) [LIMP]

Ge 32:31 and he *was* **l** because of his hip. H7519

LINE (60) [LINED, LINES]

Ge 5: 1 is the written **account of** Adam's **family l**. H9352
Ge 11:10 This is the **account** of Shem's **family l** H9352
Ge 11:27 This is the **account** of Terah's **family l** H9352
Ge 19:32 preserve our **family l** through our H2446
Ge 19:34 can preserve our **family l** through our H2446
Ge 25:12 is the **account of the family l** of H9352
Ge 25:19 is the **account of the family l** *of* H9352
Ge 36: 1 This is the **account of the family l** *of* Esau H9352
Ge 36: 9 is the **account of the family l** *of* Esau the H9352
Ge 36:43 This is the family **l** of Esau, the father of the NDT
Ge 37: 2 This is the **account** of Jacob's **family l** H9352
Nu 26:11 The **l** *of* Korah, however, did not die out. H1201
Nu 34: 7 **run a l** from the Mediterranean Sea to H9292
Nu 34:10 **run a l** from Hazar Enan to Shepham. H204
Dt 25: 9 will not build up his brother's **family l**." H1074
Dt 25:10 **That man's l** shall be known in Israel as H2257s
Ru 4: 4 right to do it except you, and I am **next in l**." H339
Ru 4:18 is the **family l** *of* Perez: Perez was H9352
1Sa 2:32 no one in your **family l** will ever reach old H1074
1Sa 2:36 left in your **family l** will come and bow H1074
1Sa 4:12 ran from the **battle l** and went to Shiloh H5120
1Sa 4:16 "I have just come from the **battle l**; I fled H5120
1Sa 9:20 if not to you and your whole **family l**?" H1074+3
1Sa 17: 2 of Elah and **drew up** their battle **l** to meet H6885
1Sa 17: 8 "Why do you come out and **l up** *for* battle? H6885
1Sa 17:48 quickly toward the **battle l** to meet him. H5120
1Ki 7:23 It took a **l** of thirty cubits to measure H7742
1Ki 11:14 the Edomite, from the royal **l** of Edom. H2446
2Ki 21:13 the **measuring l** *used against* Samaria H7742
2Ki 21:13 the **plumb l** *used against* the house H5487
2Ch 4: 2 It took a **l** of thirty cubits to measure H7742
2Ch 13: 3 Jeroboam **drew up** *a* battle **l** against him H6885
Ezr 2: 6 through the **l** *of* Jeshua and Joab) 2,812 H1201
Ezr 2:40 Kadmiel (of the **l** *of* Hodaviah) 74 H1201
Ne 7:11 through the **l** *of* Jeshua and Joab) 2,818 H1201
Ne 7:43 Kadmiel through the **l** of Hodaviah) H1201
Job 38: 5 Who stretched a **measuring l** across it? H7742
Ps 89: 4 will establish your **l** forever and make your H2446
Ps 89:29 I will establish his **l** forever, his throne as H2446
Ps 89:36 that his **l** will continue forever and his H2446
Isa 28:17 make justice the **measuring l** and H7742
Isa 28:17 line and righteousness the **plumb l**; H5487
Isa 34:11 over Edom the **measuring l** *of* chaos and H7742
Isa 34:11 line of chaos and the **plumb l** *of* desolation. H74
Isa 44:13 measures with a **l** and makes an outline H7742
Isa 48: 1 of Israel and come from the **l** *of* Judah, H5055
Jer 31:39 The measuring **l** will stretch from there H7742
Jer 33:15 a righteous Branch sprout from **David's l**; H1858
La 2: 8 stretched out a **measuring l** and did not H7742
Eze 47: 3 eastward with a **measuring l** in his hand, H7742
Da 11: 7 "One from her **family l** will arise to H5916+9247
Joel 2: 7 They all march in **l**, not swerving from H2006
Am 7: 7 true to plumb, with a **plumb l** in his hand. H643
Am 7: 8 "A **plumb l**," I replied. Then the H643
Am 7: 8 I am setting a **plumb l** among my people H643
Zec 1:16 And the **measuring l** will be stretched out H7742
Zec 2: 1 a man with a measuring **l** in his hand. H2475
Mt 17:27 go to the lake and throw out your **l**. G45
Lk 2: 4 he belonged to the house and **l** of David. G4255
Gal 2:14 saw that *they were* not **acting in l** with the G3980

LINED (1) [LINE]

1Ki 6:15 *He* **l** its interior walls with cedar boards H1215

LINEN (105) [LINENS]

Ge 41:42 him in robes of **fine l** and put a gold H9254
Ex 25: 4 purple and scarlet yarn and **fine l**; goat H9254
Ex 26: 1 ten curtains of finely twisted **l** and blue, H9254
Ex 26:31 scarlet yarn and finely twisted **l**, H9254
Ex 26:36 scarlet yarn and finely twisted **l**— H9254
Ex 27: 9 is to have curtains of finely twisted **l**, H9254
Ex 27:16 scarlet yarn and finely twisted **l**— H9254
Ex 27:18 curtains of finely twisted **l** five cubits high, H9254
Ex 28: 5 purple and scarlet yarn, and **fine l**. H9254
Ex 28: 6 of finely twisted **l**—the work of skilled H9254
Ex 28: 8 scarlet yarn, and with finely twisted **l**. H9254
Ex 28:15 scarlet yarn, and of finely twisted **l**. H9254
Ex 28:39 "Weave the tunic of **fine l** and make the H9254
Ex 28:39 fine linen and make the turban of **fine l**. H9254
Ex 28:42 "Make **l** undergarments as a covering for H965
Ex 35: 6 purple and scarlet yarn and **fine l**; goat H9254
Ex 35:23 purple or scarlet yarn or **fine l**, or goat hair H9254
Ex 35:25 purple or scarlet yarn or **fine l**. H9254
Ex 35:35 purple and scarlet yarn and **fine l**, and H9254
Ex 36: 8 ten curtains of finely twisted **l** and blue, H9254
Ex 36:35 scarlet yarn and finely twisted **l**, H9254
Ex 36:37 scarlet yarn and finely twisted **l**— H9254
Ex 38: 9 long and had curtains of finely twisted **l**, H9254
Ex 38:16 the courtyard were of finely twisted **l**. H9254
Ex 38:18 scarlet yarn and finely twisted **l**— H9254
Ex 38:23 in blue, purple and scarlet yarn and **fine l**.) H9254
Ex 39: 2 scarlet yarn, and of finely twisted **l**. H9254
Ex 39: 3 purple and scarlet yarn and **fine l**—the H9254
Ex 39: 5 with finely twisted **l**, as the LORD H9254
Ex 39: 8 scarlet yarn, and of finely twisted **l**. H9254
Ex 39:24 finely twisted **l** around the hem of the NDT
Ex 39:27 they made tunics of **fine l**—the work of a H9254
Ex 39:28 the turban of **fine l**, the linen caps H9254
Ex 39:28 the **l** caps and the undergarments of H9254
Ex 39:28 the undergarments of finely twisted **l**. H9254
Ex 39:29 was made of finely twisted **l** and blue, H9254
Lev 6:10 The priest shall then put on his **l** clothes H965
Lev 6:10 with **l** undergarments next to his body H965
Lev 13:47 defiling mold—any woolen or **l** clothing, H7324
Lev 13:48 any woven or knitted material of **l** or wool H7324
Lev 13:52 the woven or knitted material of wool or **l** H7324
Lev 13:59 defiling molds in woolen or **l** clothing, H7324
Lev 16: 4 He is to put on the sacred **l** tunic, with linen H965
Lev 16: 4 with **l** undergarments next to his body H965
Lev 16: 4 he is to tie the **l** sash around him and put H965
Lev 16: 4 sash around him and put on the **l** turban. H965
Lev 16:23 take off the **l** garments he put on H965
Lev 16:32 He is to put on the sacred **l** garments H965
Dt 22:11 clothes of wool and **l** woven together. H7324
Jdg 14:12 give you thirty **l garments** and thirty sets H6041
Jdg 14:13 give me thirty **l garments** and thirty sets H6041
1Sa 2:18 before the LORD—a boy wearing a **l** ephod. H965
1Sa 22:18 eighty-five men who wore the **l** ephod. H965
2Sa 6:14 Wearing a **l** ephod, David was dancing H965
1Ch 4:21 the clans of the **l** workers at Beth H1009
1Ch 15:27 Now David was clothed in a robe of **fine l** H1009
1Ch 15:27 David also wore a **l** ephod. H965
2Ch 2:14 blue and crimson yarn and **fine l**. H1009
2Ch 3:14 purple and crimson yarn and **fine l**, with H1009
2Ch 5:12 dressed in **fine l** and playing cymbals H1009
Est 1: 6 garden had **hangings of** white and blue **l**, H4158
Est 1: 6 with cords of **white l** and purple material H1009
Est 8:15 crown of gold and a purple robe of **fine l**. H1009
Pr 31:22 she is clothed in **fine l** and purple. H9254
Pr 31:24 She makes **l garments** and sells them H6041
Isa 3:23 the **l garments** and tiaras and shawls. H6041
Isa 19: 9 the weavers of **fine l** will lose hope. H2583
Jer 13: 1 "Go and buy a **l** belt and put it around H7324
Eze 9: 2 was a man clothed in **l** who had a writing H965
Eze 9: 3 to the man clothed in **l** who had the writing H965
Eze 9:11 Then the man in **l** with the writing kit at his H965
Eze 10: 2 The LORD said to the man clothed in **l**, "Go H965

Eze 10: 6 When the LORD commanded the man in l H965
Eze 10: 7 it and put it into the hands of the man in l, H965
Eze 16:10 I dressed you in **fine l** and covered you H9254
Eze 16:13 clothes were of **fine l** and costly fabric H9254
Eze 27: 7 **Fine** embroidered l from Egypt was your H9254
Eze 27:16 embroidered work, **fine l**, coral and rubies H1009
Eze 40: 3 the gateway with a l cord and a H7324
Eze 44:17 they are to wear l clothes; they must not H7324
Eze 44:18 They are to wear l turbans on their heads H7324
Eze 44:18 on their heads and l undergarments H7324
Da 10: 5 there before me was a man dressed in l, H965
Da 12: 6 One of them said to the man clothed in l H965
Da 12: 7 The man clothed in l, who was above the H965
Hos 2: 5 my wool and my l, my olive oil and my H7324
Hos 2: 9 I will take back my wool and my l H7324
Mt 27:59 the body, wrapped it in a clean **l cloth**, G4984
Mk 14:51 wearing nothing but a **l garment**, was G4984
Mk 15:46 So Joseph bought *some* **l cloth**, took down G4984
Mk 15:46 wrapped it in the l, and placed it in a G4984
Lk 16:19 in purple and **fine l** and lived in luxury G1116
Lk 23:53 wrapped it in **l cloth** and placed it in a G4984
Lk 24:12 he saw the **strips of l** lying by themselves G3856
Jn 11:44 hands and feet wrapped *with* **strips of l**, G3024
Jn 19:40 wrapped it, with the spices, *in* **strips of l**. G3856
Jn 20: 5 looked in *at* the **strips of l** lying there G3856
Jn 20: 6 He saw the **strips of l** lying there, G3856
Jn 20: 7 still lying in its place, separate from the l. G3856
Rev 15: 6 shining l and wore golden sashes around G3351
Rev 18:12 stones and pearls; **fine l**, purple, silk and G1115
Rev 18:16 dressed in **fine l**, purple and scarlet, G1115
Rev 19: 8 **Fine l**, bright and clean, was given her to G1115
Rev 19: 8 **Fine l** stands for the righteous acts of G1115
Rev 19:14 on white horses and dressed in **fine l**, G1115

LINENS (1) [LINEN]
Pr 7:16 covered my bed with colored l *from* Egypt. H355

LINES (13) [LINE]
Ge 10:32 according to their **l of descent**, within their H9352
Ge 14: 8 out and **drew up** their battle l in the H6885
1Sa 17:21 were drawing up their l facing each other. H5120
1Sa 17:22 ran to the **battle l** and asked his brothers H5120
1Sa 17:23 stepped out from his l and shouted his H5120
2Sa 10: 9 that there were **battle l** in front of him H4878
2Sa 10:17 Arameans **formed** *their* **battle l** to meet H6885
2Sa 23:16 warriors broke through the Philistine l, H4722
1Ch 11:18 So the Three broke through the Philistine l, H4722
1Ch 19:10 that there were **battle l** in front of him H4878
1Ch 19:17 them and **formed** his **battle l** opposite H6885
1Ch 19:17 David **formed** *his* l to meet the Arameans H6885
Ps 16: 6 The **boundary l** have fallen for me in H2475

LINGER (5) [LINGERING]
Jdg 5:17 And Dan, why *did he* l *by* the ships H1591
Job 20:13 bear to let it go and *lets* it l in his mouth, H4979
Pr 23:30 Those *who* l over wine, who go to sample H336
Jer 51:50 escaped the sword, leave and *do* not l! H6641
Hab 2: 3 Though *it* l, wait for it; it will certainly H4538

LINGERING (2) [LINGER]
Dt 28:59 disasters, and severe and l illnesses. H586
2Ch 21:15 ill with a l disease of the H3427+6584+3427

LINTEL (KJV) COLUMNS, TOP, TOPS

LINUS (1)
2Ti 4:21 so do Pudens, L, Claudia and all the G3352

LION (86) [LION'S, LIONESS, LIONESSES, LIONS, LIONS']
Ge 49: 9 Like a l he crouches and lies down, like a H793
Nu 23:24 themselves like a l that does not rest till H787
Nu 24: 9 Like a l they crouch and lie down, like a H787
Dt 33:20 Gad lives there like a l, tearing at arm H4233
Jdg 14: 5 suddenly a **young l** came roaring H4097+787
Jdg 14: 6 him so that he tore **the l** apart with his H2084S
Jdg 14:18 What is stronger than a l?" Samson said to H787
1Sa 17:34 When a l or a bear came and carried off a H787
1Sa 17:36 servant has killed both the l and the bear; H787
1Sa 17:37 from the paw of the l and the paw of the H787
2Sa 17:10 whose heart is like the heart of a l, will H793
2Sa 23:20 into a pit on a snowy day and killed a l. H787
1Ki 10:19 with a l standing beside each of them. H787
1Ki 13:24 a l met him on the road and killed him H793
1Ki 13:24 the donkey and the l standing beside it. H793
1Ki 13:25 with the l standing beside the body H793
1Ki 13:26 The LORD has given him over to the l, H793
1Ki 13:28 the donkey and the l standing beside it. H793
1Ki 13:28 The l had neither eaten the body nor H793
1Ki 20:36 as soon as you leave me a l will kill you." H793
1Ki 20:36 went away, a l found him and killed him. H793
1Ch 11:22 into a pit on a snowy day and killed a l. H787
2Ch 9:18 with a l standing beside each of them. H787
Job 4:11 The l perishes for lack of prey, and the H4330
Job 10:16 you stalk me like a l and again display H8828
Job 28: 8 not set foot on it, and no l prowls there. H8828
Ps 7: 2 tear me apart like a l and rip me to pieces H793
Ps 10: 9 like a l in cover he lies in wait. He lies in H793
Ps 17:12 They are like a l hungry for prey, like a H793
Ps 17:12 prey, like a **fierce l** crouching in cover. H4097
Ps 91:13 You will tread on the l and the cobra; you H8828
Ps 91:13 will trample the **great l** and the serpent. H4097
Pr 19:12 A king's rage is like the roar of a l, but his H4097
Pr 20: 2 wrath strikes terror like the roar of a l; H4097
Pr 22:13 "There's a l outside! I'll be killed H787
Pr 26:13 "There's a l in the road, a fierce H8828
Pr 26:13 in the road, a **fierce l** roaming the streets!" H787
Pr 28: 1 the righteous are as bold as a l. H4097
Pr 28:15 Like a roaring l or a charging bear is a H787
Pr 30:30 a l, mighty among beasts, who retreats H4330
Ecc 9: 4 even a live dog is better off than a dead l! H793
Isa 5:29 Their roar is like that of the l, they roar H4233
Isa 11: 6 the calf and the l and the yearling H4097
Isa 11: 7 the l will eat straw like the ox. H793
Isa 15: 9 a l upon the fugitives of Moab and upon H793
Isa 31: 4 "As a l growls, a great lion over its prey H793
Isa 31: 4 a lion growls, a **great l** over its prey—and H4097
Isa 35: 9 No l will be there, nor any ravenous beast H793
Isa 38:13 till dawn, but like a l he broke all my bones H787
Isa 65:25 together, and the l will eat straw like the ox H793
Jer 2:30 devoured your prophets like a ravenous l. H793
Jer 4: 7 A l has come out of his lair; a destroyer of H793
Jer 5: 6 Therefore a l from the forest will attack H793
Jer 12: 8 has become to me like a l in the forest. H793
Jer 25:38 Like a l he will leave his lair, and their H4097
Jer 49:19 "Like a l coming up from Jordan's thickets H793
Jer 50:44 Like a l coming up from Jordan's thickets to H793
Jer 51:38 roar like young lions, they growl like l cubs. H787
La 3:10 Like a bear lying in wait, like a l in hiding, H787
Eze 1:10 on the right side each had the face of a l, H793
Eze 10:14 the third the face of a l, and the fourth the H793
Eze 19: 3 of her cubs, and he became a **strong l**. H4097
Eze 19: 5 of her cubs and made him a **strong l**. H4097
Eze 19: 6 the lions, for he was now a **strong l**. H4097
Eze 22:25 within her like a roaring l tearing its prey; H787
Eze 32: 2 " 'You are like a l *among* the nations; you H4097
Eze 41:19 the face of a l toward the palm tree H4097
Da 7: 4 "The first was like a l, and it had the A10069
Hos 5:14 For I will be like a l to Ephraim, like a H8828
Hos 5:14 a lion to Ephraim, like a **great l** to Judah. H4097
Hos 11:10 will follow the LORD; he will roar like a l. H793
Hos 13: 7 So I will be like a l to them, like a leopard H8828
Hos 13: 8 them open; like a l I will devour them—a H4233
Joel 1: 6 it has the teeth of a l, the fangs of a H793
Am 3: 4 Does a l roar in the thicket when it has no H793
Am 3: 8 The l has roared—who will not fear? The H793
Am 5:19 a man fled from a l only to meet a bear, H787
Mic 5: 8 like a l among the beasts of the forest H793
Mic 5: 8 like a **young l** among flocks of sheep H4097
Na 2:11 where the l and lioness went, and H793
Na 2:12 The l killed enough for his cubs and H793
1Pe 5: 8 like a roaring l looking for someone G3329
Rev 4: 7 The first living creature was like a l, the G3329
Rev 5: 5 the L of the tribe of Judah, the Root G3329
Rev 10: 3 he gave a loud shout like the roar *of* a l. G3329
Rev 13: 2 of a bear and a mouth like that *of* a l. G3329

LION'S (6) [LION]
Ge 49: 9 You are a l cub, Judah; you return from the H793
Dt 33:22 "Dan is a l cub, springing out of H793
Jdg 14: 8 he turned aside to look at the l carcass H793
Jdg 14: 9 he had taken the honey from the l carcass. H793
Am 3:12 rescues from the l mouth only two leg H787
2Ti 4:17 And I was delivered from the l mouth. G3329

LIONESS (8) [LION]
Ge 49: 9 lies down, like a l—who dares to rouse H4233
Nu 23:24 The people rise like a l; they rouse H4233
Nu 24: 9 lie down, like a l—who dares to rouse H4233
Job 4:11 and the cubs of the l are scattered. H4233
Job 38:39 hunt the prey for the l and satisfy the H4233
Eze 19: 2 " 'What a l was your mother among the H4234
Joel 1: 6 it has the teeth of a lion, the fangs of a l. H4233
Na 2:11 where the lion and l went, and the cubs, H4233

LIONESSES (1) [LION]
Isa 30: 6 of lions and l, of adders and darting H4233

LIONLIKE (KJV) MIGHTIEST

LIONS (35) [LION]
2Sa 1:23 than eagles, they were stronger than l. H787
1Ki 7:29 On the panels between the uprights were l H787
1Ki 7:29 Above and below the l and bulls were H787
1Ki 7:36 l and palm trees on the surfaces of the H787
1Ki 10:20 Twelve l stood on the six steps, one at H787
2Ki 17:25 so he sent l among them and they killed H787
2Ki 17:26 He has sent l among them, which are H787
1Ch 12: 8 Their faces were the faces of l, and they H793
2Ch 9:19 Twelve l stood on the six steps, one at H787
Job 4:10 The l may roar and growl, yet the teeth of H793
Job 4:10 the teeth of the **great l** are broken. H4097
Job 38:39 the lioness and satisfy the hunger of the l H4097
Ps 22:13 Roaring l that tear their prey open their H793
Ps 22:21 Rescue me from the mouth of the l; save H793
Ps 34:10 The l may grow weak and hungry, but H4097
Ps 35:17 ravages, my precious life from these l. H4097
Ps 57: 4 I am in the midst of l; I am forced to dwell H4216
Ps 58: 6 LORD, tear out the fangs of those l! H4097
Ps 104:21 The l roar for their prey and seek their H4097
Isa 5:29 they roar like **young l**; they growl as they H4097
Isa 30: 6 distress, of l and lionesses, of adders H4330
Jer 2:15 L have roared; they have growled at him H4097
Jer 50:17 a scattered flock that l have chased away. H787
Jer 51:38 Her people all roar like **young l**, they H4097
Eze 19: 2 a lioness was your mother among the l! H787
Eze 19: 6 He prowled among the l, for he was now a H787
Da 6:20 been able to rescue you from the l?" A10069
Da 6:22 and he shut the mouths of the l. A10069
Da 6:24 the l overpowered them and crushed all A10069
Da 6:27 rescued Daniel from the power of the l." A10069
Na 2:13 the sword will devour your **young l**. H4097
Zep 3: 3 Her officials within her are roaring l; her H787
Zec 11: 3 Listen to the roar of the l; the lush thicket H4097
Heb 11:33 was promised; who shut the mouths *of* l, G3329
Rev 9:17 of the horses resembled the heads *of* l, G3329

LIONS' (8) [LION]
SS 4: 8 from the l dens and the mountain haunts H787
Da 6: 7 Majesty, shall be thrown into the l den. A10069
Da 6:12 would be thrown into the l den? A10069
Da 6:16 Daniel and threw him into the l den. A10069
Da 6:19 the king got up and hurried to the l den. A10069
Da 6:24 brought in and thrown into the l den, A10069
Na 2:11 Where now is the l den, the place where H787
Rev 9: 8 and their teeth were like l teeth. G3329

LIPS (130)
Ex 6:12 listen to me, since I speak with faltering l?" H8557
Ex 6:30 "Since I speak with faltering l, why would H8557
Ex 13: 9 that this law of the LORD is to be on your l. H7023
Ex 23:13 do not let them be heard on your l. H7023
Nu 30: 6 a vow or after her l utter a rash promise by H8557
Nu 30:12 pledges that came from her l will stand. H8557
Dt 23:23 Whatever your l utter you must be sure to H8557
Jos 1: 8 this Book of the Law always on your l; H7023
1Sa 1:13 her l were moving but her voice was H8557
Job 6:30 Is there any wickedness on my l? Can my H4383
Job 8:21 laughter and your l with shouts of joy. H8557
Job 11: 5 that he would open his l against you H8557
Job 12:20 He silences the l of trusted advisers and H8557
Job 13: 6 my argument; listen to the pleas of my l. H8557
Job 15: 6 not mine; your own l testify against you. H8557
Job 16: 5 comfort from my l would bring you relief. H8557
Job 23:12 not departed from the commands of his l; H8557
Job 27: 4 my l will not say anything wicked, and my H8557
Job 32:20 find relief; I must open my l and reply. H8557
Job 33: 3 my l sincerely speak what I know. H8557
Ps 12: 2 they flatter *with* their l but harbor H8557
Ps 12: 3 silence all flattering l and every boastful H8557
Ps 12: 4 our own l will defend us—who is H8557
Ps 16: 4 such gods or take up their names on my l. H8557
Ps 17: 1 prayer—it does not rise from deceitful l. H8557
Ps 17: 4 through what your l have commanded. H8557
Ps 21: 2 have not withheld the request of his l. H8557
Ps 31:18 Let their lying l be silenced, for with pride H8557
Ps 34: 1 his praise will always be on my l. H7023
Ps 34:13 from evil and your l from telling lies. H8557
Ps 40: 9 great assembly; I do not seal my l, LORD, H8557
Ps 45: 2 of men and your l have been anointed H8557
Ps 50:16 my laws or take my covenant on your l? H7023
Ps 51:15 Open my l, Lord, and my mouth will H8557
Ps 59: 7 the words from their l are sharp as swords H8557
Ps 59:12 the words of their l, let them be caught H8557
Ps 63: 3 is better than life, my l will glorify you. H8557
Ps 63: 5 with singing l my mouth will praise you. H8557
Ps 66:14 vows my l promised and my mouth spoke H8557
Ps 71:23 My l will shout for joy when I sing praise H8557
Ps 89:34 covenant or alter what my l have uttered. H8557
Ps 106:33 and rash words came from Moses' l. H8557
Ps 119:13 With my l I recount all the laws that come H8557
Ps 119:171 May my l overflow with praise, for you H8557
Ps 120: 2 from lying l and from deceitful tongues. H8557
Ps 140: 3 the poison of vipers is on their l. H8557
Ps 140: 9 may the mischief of their l engulf them. H8557
Ps 141: 3 keep watch over the door of my l. H8557
Pr 4:24 keep corrupt talk far from your l. H8557
Pr 5: 2 discretion and your l may preserve H8557
Pr 5: 3 For the l *of* the adulterous woman drip H8557
Pr 8: 6 I open my l to speak what is right. H8557
Pr 8: 7 what is true, for my l detest wickedness. H8557
Pr 10:13 is found on the l *of* the discerning, H8557
Pr 10:18 conceals hatred *with* lying l and spreads H8557
Pr 10:21 The l *of* the righteous nourish many, but H8557
Pr 10:32 The l *of* the righteous know what finds H8557
Pr 12:14 the fruit of their l people are filled with H7023
Pr 12:19 Truthful l endure forever, but a lying H8557
Pr 12:22 The LORD detests lying l, but he delights in H8557
Pr 13: 2 From the fruit of their l people enjoy good H7023
Pr 13: 3 who guard their l preserve their lives, H7023
Pr 14: 3 but the l *of* the wise protect them. H8557
Pr 14: 7 you will not find knowledge on their l. H8557
Pr 15: 7 The l *of* the wise spread knowledge, but H8557
Pr 16:10 The l *of* a king speak as an oracle, and H8557
Pr 16:13 Kings take pleasure in honest l; they H8557
Pr 16:23 prudent, and their l promote instruction. H8557
Pr 16:27 on their l it is like a scorching fire. H8557
Pr 16:30 whose purses their l is bent on evil. H8557
Pr 17: 4 A wicked person listens to deceitful l; H8557
Pr 17: 7 Eloquent l are unsuited to a godless fool H8557
Pr 17: 7 how much worse lying l to a ruler! H8557
Pr 18: 6 The l *of* fools bring them strife, and their H8557
Pr 18: 7 their l are a snare to their very lives. H8557
Pr 18:20 the harvest of their l they are satisfied. H8557
Pr 19: 1 than a fool whose l are perverse. H8557
Pr 20:15 but l *that speak* knowledge are a rare H8557
Pr 22:18 have all of them ready on your l. H8557
Pr 23:16 rejoice when your l speak what is right. H8557

Pr 24: 2 their l talk about making trouble. H8557
Pr 24:26 An honest answer is like a kiss on the l. H8557
Pr 24:28 cause—would you use your l to mislead? H8557
Pr 26:23 are fervent l with an evil heart. H8557
Pr 26:24 Enemies disguise themselves with their l H8557
Pr 27: 2 an outsider, and not your own l. H8557
Ecc 10:12 fools are consumed by their own l. H8557
SS 4: 3 Your l are like a scarlet ribbon; your H8557
SS 4:11 Your l drop sweetness as the honeycomb H8557
SS 5:13 His l are like lilies dripping with myrrh. H8557
SS 7: 9 beloved, flowing gently over l and teeth. H8557
Isa 6: 5 For I am a man of unclean l, and I live H8557
Isa 6: 5 I live among a people of unclean l H8557
Isa 6: 7 this has touched your l; your guilt is taken H8557
Isa 11: 4 with the breath of his l he will slay the H8557
Isa 28:11 with foreign l and strange tongues God H8557
Isa 29:13 their mouth and honor me with their l, H8557
Isa 30:27 clouds of smoke; his l are full of wrath H8557
Isa 57:19 creating praise on their l. Peace, peace H8557
Isa 59: 3 Your l have spoken falsely, and your H8557
Isa 59:21 in your mouth will always be on your l, H7023
Isa 59:21 on the l of your children and on the lips of H7023
Isa 59:21 on the l of their descendants— H7023
Jer 7:28 has perished; it has vanished from their l. H7023
Jer 12: 2 You are always on their l but far from their H7023
Jer 17:16 What passes my l is open before you. H8557
Da 4:31 Even as the words were on his l, a voice A10588
Da 10: 3 no meat or wine touched my l; and I used H7023
Da 10:16 one who looked like a man touched my l, H8557
Hos 2:17 remove the names of the Baals from her l; H7023
Hos 8: 1 "Put the trumpet to your l! An eagle is H2674
Hos 14: 2 that we may offer the fruit of our l. H8557
Joel 1: 5 for it has been snatched from your l. H7023
Mic 7: 5 in your embrace guard the words of your l. H7023
Hab 3:16 pounded, my l quivered at the sound H8557
Zep 3: 9 "Then I will purify the l of the peoples H8557
Mal 2: 6 nothing false was found on his l. H8557
Mal 2: 7 "For the l of a priest ought to preserve H8557
Mt 15: 8 " 'These people honor me with their l, but G5927
Mt 21:16 " 'From the l of children and infants you G5125
Mk 7: 6 " 'These people honor me with their l, but G5927
Lk 4:22 the gracious words that came from his l. G5125
Lk 22:71 We have heard it from his own l." G5125
Jn 19:29 the hyssop plant, and lifted it to Jesus' l. G5125
Ac 15: 7 might hear from my l the message of the G5125
Ro 3:13 "The poison of vipers is on their l." G5927
1Co 14:21 through the l of foreigners I will G5927
Col 3: 8 slander, and filthy language from your l. G5125
Heb 13:15 the fruit of l that openly profess his name. G5927
1Pe 3:10 from evil and their l from deceitful speech G5927

LIQUID (2)

Ex 30:23 500 shekels of l myrrh, half as much (that H2001
Lev 11:34 any l that is drunk from such a pot is H5482

LIQUOR, LIQUORS (KJV) BLENDED WINE, JUICE, VATS

LIST (11) [LISTED, LISTING]

Nu 3:40 old or more and make a l of their names. H5031
Jos 12: 7 **Here is a l of** the kings of the land that H4655
Jos 17:11 settlements (the third in the l is Naphoth). NDT
1Ch 11:11 this is the l of David's mighty warriors H5031
1Ch 25: 1 Here is the l of the men who performed H5031
1Ch 27: 1 This is the l of the Israelites—heads of H5031
Ezr 2: 2 The l of the men of the people of Israel H5031
Ne 7: 7 Baanah): The l of the men of Israel: H5031
Ps 56: 8 my misery; l my tears on your scroll H8492
1Ti 5: 9 No widow may be **put on the l** of widows G2899
1Ti 5:11 do not put them on such a l. NDT

LISTED (35) [LIST]

Ge 25:13 sons of Ishmael, l in the order of their birth: AIT
Nu 1:18 twenty years old or more were l by name, H5031
Nu 1:20 able to serve in the army were l by name, H5031
Nu 1:22 in the army were counted and l by name, H5031
Nu 1:24 able to serve in the army were l by name, H5031
Nu 1:26 able to serve in the army were l by name, H5031
Nu 1:28 able to serve in the army were l by name, H5031
Nu 1:30 able to serve in the army were l by name, H5031
Nu 1:32 able to serve in the army were l by name, H5031
Nu 1:34 able to serve in the army were l by name, H5031
Nu 1:36 able to serve in the army were l by name, H5031
Nu 1:38 able to serve in the army were l by name, H5031
Nu 1:40 able to serve in the army were l by name, H5031
Nu 1:42 able to serve in the army were l by name, H5031
Nu 3:43 month old or more, l by name, was H5031
Nu 11:26 They **were l** among the elders, but did not H4180
Nu 26:54 according to the number of those l. H7212
1Ch 4:38 The men l above by name were leaders of H995
1Ch 4:41 men whose names were l came in the H4180
1Ch 5: 1 could not **be l in the genealogical record** H3509
1Ch 5: 7 l according to their genealogical records: H3509
1Ch 6:19 the clans of the Levites l according to their NDT
1Ch 7: 2 descendants of Tola l as fighting men in H5031
1Ch 7: 5 Issachar, as **l in** their **genealogy**, were H3509
1Ch 7: 7 Their **genealogical record l** 22,034 H3509
1Ch 7: 9 genealogical record l the heads of H3509
1Ch 7:40 as **l in** their **genealogy**, was H3509
1Ch 8:28 chiefs as l in their **genealogy**, and they H9352
1Ch 9: 1 Israel **was l in the genealogies** recorded H3509
1Ch 9: 9 as l in their **genealogy**, numbered H9352
1Ch 9:34 chiefs as l in their **genealogy**, and they H9352
2Ch 31:18 **l in** these **genealogical records**. H3509
Ps 69:28 of life and not **be l** with the righteous. H4180
Eze 13: 9 of my people or **be l** in the records of H4180
Eze 48: 1 "These are the tribes, l by name: At the NDT

LISTEN (354) [LISTENED, LISTENER, LISTENING, LISTENS]

Ge 4:10 "What have you done? L! Your brother's H7754
Ge 4:23 "Adah and Zillah, l to me; wives of H9048
Ge 21:12 L to whatever Sarah tells you, because it H9048
Ge 23: 6 l to us. You are a mighty prince H9048
Ge 23: 8 then l to me and intercede with Ephron H9048
Ge 23:11 "L to me; I give you the field, and I give H9048
Ge 23:13 in their hearing, "L to me, if you will. H9048
Ge 23:15 "L to me, my lord; the land is worth four H9048
Ge 27: 8 **l carefully** and do what I tell H9048+928+7754
Ge 37: 6 He said to them, "L to this dream I had: H9048
Ge 37: 9 "L," he said, "I had another dream, and H2180
Ge 42:21 but we would not l; that's why this H9048
Ge 42:22 But you wouldn't l! Now we must H9048
Ge 49: 2 "Assemble and l, sons of Jacob; listen to H9048
Ge 49: 2 sons of Jacob; l to your father Israel. H9048
Ex 3:18 "The elders of Israel will l to you. H9048
Ex 4: 1 do not believe me or l to me and say, H9048
Ex 4: 9 do not believe these two signs or l to you, H9048
Ex 6: 9 but they did not l to him because of their H9048
Ex 6:12 "If the Israelites will not l to me, why H9048
Ex 6:12 why would Pharaoh l to me, since I H9048
Ex 6:30 faltering lips, why would Pharaoh l to me?" H9048
Ex 7: 4 he will not l to you. Then I will lay my H9048
Ex 7:13 became hard and he would not l to them, H9048
Ex 7:22 he would not l to Moses and Aaron H9048
Ex 8:15 his heart and would not l to Moses and H9048
Ex 8:19 heart was hard and he would not l, H9048
Ex 9:12 heart and he would not l to Moses and H9048
Ex 11: 9 "Pharaoh will refuse to l to you—so that H9048
Ex 15:26 "If you **l carefully** to the LORD your H9048+9048
Ex 18:19 L now to me and I will give you some H9048
Ex 20:19 "Speak to us yourself and we will l. H9048
Ex 23:21 Pay attention to him and l to what he says H9048
Ex 23:22 If you **l carefully** to what he says H9048+9048
Lev 26:14 " 'But if you will not l to me and carry out H9048
Lev 26:18 " 'If after all this you will not l to me, I will H9048
Lev 26:21 hostile toward me and refuse to l to me, H9048
Lev 26:27 in spite of this you still do not l to me H9048
Nu 12: 6 "L to my words: "When there is a H9048
Nu 16: 8 also said to Korah, "Now l, you Levites! H9048
Nu 20:10 Moses said to them, "L, you rebels, H9048
Nu 23:18 Balak, and l; hear me, son of H9048
Dt 1:43 told you, but you would not l. H9048
Dt 3:26 was angry with me and would not l to me. H9048
Dt 5:27 Go near and l to all that the LORD our God H9048
Dt 5:27 our God tells you. We will l and obey." H9048
Dt 13: 3 you must not l to the words of that prophet H9048
Dt 13: 8 do not yield to them or l to them. H9048
Dt 18:14 you will dispossess l to those who practice H9048
Dt 18:15 your fellow Israelites. You must l to him. H9048
Dt 18:19 anyone who does not l to my words H9048
Dt 21:18 mother and will not l to them when H9048
Dt 23: 5 your God would not l to Balaam but H9048
Dt 26:17 laws—that you will l to him. H9048
Dt 27: 9 said to all Israel, "Be silent, Israel, and l! H9048
Dt 30:20 the LORD your God, l to his voice, and hold H9048
Dt 31:12 so they can l and learn to fear the LORD H9048
Dt 32: 1 L, you heavens, and I will speak; hear, you H263
Jos 3: 9 "Come here and l to the words of the LORD H9048
Jos 8: 4 "**L carefully**. You are to set H8011
Jos 24:10 But I would not l to Balaam, so he blessed H9048
Jdg 2:17 Yet they would not l to their judges but H9048
Jdg 5: 3 "Hear this, you kings! L, you rulers! H263
Jdg 7:11 and l to what they are saying. Afterward H9048
Jdg 9: 7 shouted to them, "L to me, citizens of H9048
Jdg 9: 7 of Shechem, so that God may l to you. H9048
Jdg 11:17 the king of Edom would not l. H9048
Jdg 19:25 But the men would not l to him. So the H9048
Jdg 20:13 the Benjamites would not l to their fellow H9048
Ru 2: 8 Boaz said to Ruth, "My daughter, l to me. H9048
1Sa 2:25 however, did not l to their father's rebuke H9048
1Sa 8: 7 "L to all that the people are saying to you H9048
1Sa 8: 9 Now l to them; but warn them solemnly H9048
1Sa 8:19 But the people refused to l to Samuel H9048
1Sa 8:22 "L to them and give them a king." H9048
1Sa 15: 1 so l now to the message from the LORD. H9048
1Sa 22: 7 He said to them, "L, men of Benjamin H9048
1Sa 22:12 Saul said, "L now, son of Ahitub." "Yes H9048
1Sa 24: 9 to Saul, "Why do you l when men say H9048
1Sa 26:19 Now let my lord the king l to his servant's H9048
1Sa 28:22 Now please l to your servant and let me H9048
1Sa 30:24 Who will l to what you say? The share of H9048
2Sa 12:18 he wouldn't l to us when we spoke to him. H9048
2Sa 13:14 But he refused to l to her, and since he H9048
2Sa 13:16 But he refused to l to her. H9048
2Sa 13:28 ordered his men, "L! When Amnon is in H8011
2Sa 20:16 woman called from the city, "L! Listen! H9048
2Sa 20:16 L! Tell Joab to come here so I can H9048
2Sa 20:17 "L to what your servant has to say. H9048
1Ki 4:34 all nations people came to l to Solomon's H9048
1Ki 8:52 may you l to them whenever they cry H9048
1Ki 12:15 So the king did not l to the people, for this H9048
1Ki 12:16 saw that the king refused to l to them, H9048
1Ki 20: 8 "Don't l to him or agree to his demands." H9048
2Ki 14:11 however, would not l, so Jehoash king of H9048
2Ki 17:14 But they would not l and were as H9048
2Ki 17:40 They would not l, however, but persisted H9048
2Ki 18:31 "Do not l to Hezekiah. This is what the H9048
2Ki 18:32 "Do not l to Hezekiah, for he is H9048
2Ki 19: 7 L! When he hears a certain report, I will H2180
2Ki 19:16 l to the words Sennacherib has sent to H9048
2Ki 21: 9 But the people did not l. Manasseh led H9048
1Ch 28: 2 to his feet and said: "L to me, my fellow H9048
2Ch 10:15 So the king did not l to the people, for this H9048
2Ch 10:16 saw that the king refused to l to them, H9048
2Ch 13: 4 "Jeroboam and all Israel, l to me! H9048
2Ch 15: 2 said to him, "L to me, Asa and all H9048
2Ch 20:15 "L, King Jehoshaphat and all who live in H7992
2Ch 20:20 stood and said, "L to me, Judah and H9048
2Ch 24:19 testified against them, they would not l. H263
2Ch 25:20 however, would not l, for God so worked H9048
2Ch 28:11 Now l to me! Send back your fellow H9048
2Ch 29: 5 "L to me, Levites! Consecrate H9048
2Ch 35:22 He would not l to what Necho had said at H9048
Ne 9:17 They refused to l and failed to remember H9048
Ne 9:29 became stiff-necked and refused to l. H9048
Job 13: 6 my argument; l to the pleas of my lips. H7992
Job 13:17 **L carefully** to what I say; let my H9048+9048
Job 15: 8 Do you **l in** on God's council? Do you H9048
Job 15:17 "L to me and I will explain to you; let me H9048
Job 21: 2 "**L carefully** to my words; let this be H9048+9048
Job 27: 9 Does God l to their cry when distress H9048
Job 32:10 "Therefore I say: L to me; I too will tell H9048
Job 33: 1 l to my words; pay attention to H9048
Job 33:31 attention, Job, and l to me; be silent, and H9048
Job 33:33 But if not, then l to me; be silent, and I H9048
Job 34: 2 you wise men; l to me, you men of H263
Job 34:10 "So l to me, you men of understanding H9048
Job 34:16 understanding, hear this; l to what I say. H263
Job 35:13 God does not l to their empty plea H9048
Job 35:14 will he l when you say that you do not see NDT
Job 36:10 He **makes** them l to correction and H1655+265
Job 36:12 But if they do not l, they will perish by the H9048
Job 37: 2 L! Listen to the roar of his voice, to the H9048
Job 37: 2 L to the roar of his voice, to the rumbling H9048
Job 37:14 "L to this, Job; stop and consider God's H263
Job 42: 4 "You said, 'L now, and I will speak; I will H9048
Ps 5: 1 L to my words, LORD, consider my lament. H263
Ps 10:17 and you l to their cry, H7992+265
Ps 17: 1 my plea is just; l to my cry. Hear my prayer H7992
Ps 34:11 my children, l to me; I will teach you the H9048
Ps 39:12 l to my cry for help; do not be deaf to H263
Ps 45:10 L, daughter, and pay careful attention H9048
Ps 49: 1 all you peoples; l, all who live in this world, H263
Ps 50: 7 "L, my people, and I will speak; I will H9048
Ps 54: 2 O God; l to the words of my mouth. H263
Ps 55: 1 L to my prayer, O God, do not ignore my H263
Ps 61: 1 Hear my cry, O God; l to my prayer. H7992
Ps 78: 1 l to the words of my mouth. H5742+265
Ps 81: 8 warn you—if you would only l to me H9048
Ps 81:11 "But my people would not l to me; Israel H9048
Ps 81:13 "If my people would only l to me, if Israel H9048
Ps 84: 8 LORD God Almighty; l to me, God of Jacob. H263
Ps 85: 8 I will l to what God the LORD says; he H9048
Ps 86: 6 my prayer, LORD; l to my cry for mercy. H7992
Ps 142: 6 L to my cry, for I am in desperate need H7992
Ps 143: 1 hear my prayer, l to my cry for mercy; in H263
Pr 1: 5 let the wise l and add to their learning H9048
Pr 1: 8 L, my son, to your father's instruction and H9048
Pr 1:24 But since you **refuse to** l when I call and no AIT
Pr 4: 1 L, my sons, to a father's instruction; pay H9048
Pr 4:10 L, my son, accept what I say, and the H9048
Pr 5: 7 my sons, l to me; do not turn aside from H9048
Pr 7:24 my sons, l to me; pay attention to what I H9048
Pr 8: 6 L, for I have trustworthy things to say; H9048
Pr 8:32 my children, l to me; blessed are those H9048
Pr 8:33 L to my instruction and be wise; do not H9048
Pr 8:34 Blessed are those who l to me, watching H9048
Pr 12:15 right to them, but the wise l to advice. H9048
Pr 19:20 L to advice and accept discipline, and at H9048
Pr 23:19 L, my son, and be wise, and set your heart H9048
Pr 23:22 L to your father, who gave you life, and do H9048
Pr 31: 2 L, my son! Listen, son of my womb! H4537
Pr 31: 2 my son! L, son of my womb! Listen H4537
Pr 31: 2 son of my womb! L, my son, the answer to H4537
Ecc 5: 1 Go near to l rather than to offer the H9048
Ecc 7: 5 wise person than to l to the song of fools. H9048
SS 2: 8 L! My beloved! Look! Here he comes H7754
SS 5: 2 my heart was awake. L! My beloved is H7754
Isa 1: 2 L, earth! For the LORD has H263
Isa 1:10 of Sodom; l to the instruction of our God H263
Isa 8: 9 be shattered! L, all you distant lands H263
Isa 10:30 Daughter Gallim! L, Laishah! Poor H7992
Isa 13: 4 L, a noise on the mountains, like that of a H7754
Isa 13: 4 L, an uproar among the kingdoms, like H7754
Isa 28:12 place of repose"—but they would not l. H9048
Isa 28:23 L and hear my voice; pay attention and H263
Isa 30: 9 children unwilling to l to the LORD's H9048
Isa 32: 3 the ears of those who hear will l. H7992
Isa 32: 9 rise up and l to me; you daughters H9048+7754
Isa 34: 1 you nations, and l; pay attention, you H9048
Isa 36:16 "Do not l to Hezekiah. This is what the H9048
Isa 37: 7 L! When he hears a certain report, I will H2180
Isa 37:17 l to all the words Sennacherib has sent to H9048
Isa 42:20 your ears are open, but you do not l." H9048
Isa 42:23 Which of you will l to this or pay close H263
Isa 44: 1 "But now l, Jacob, my servant, Israel H9048

Isa 46: 3 "L to me, you descendants of Jacob, all H9048
Isa 46:12 L to me, you stubborn-hearted, you who H9048
Isa 47: 8 "Now then, l, you lover of pleasure H9048
Isa 48: 1 "L to this, you descendants of Jacob, you H9048
Isa 48:12 "L to me, Jacob, Israel, whom I have H9048
Isa 48:14 all of you, and l: Which of the idols has H9048
Isa 48:16 "Come near me and l to this: "From the H9048
Isa 49: 1 L to me, you islands; hear this, you distant H9048
Isa 50: 4 wakens my ear to l like one being H9048
Isa 51: 1 "L to me, you who pursue righteousness H9048
Isa 51: 4 "L to me, my people; hear me, my nation H7992
Isa 52: 8 L! Your watchmen lift up their voices H7754
Isa 55: 2 L, listen to me, and eat what is good, and H9048
Isa 55: 2 l to me, and eat what is good, and H9048
Isa 55: 3 ear and come to me; l, that you may live. H9048
Isa 65:12 did not answer, I spoke but you did not l. H9048
Jer 6:10 give warning? Who will l to me? Their H9048
Jer 6:17 said, 'L to the sound of the trumpet! H7992
Jer 6:17 But you said, 'We will not l.' H7992
Jer 7:13 again, but you did not l; I called you, H9048
Jer 7:16 not plead with me, for I will not l to you. H9048
Jer 7:24 But they did not l or pay attention; instead H9048
Jer 7:26 But they did not l to me or pay attention H9048
Jer 7:27 them all this, they will not l to you; when H9048
Jer 8:19 L to the cry of my people from a land far H7754
Jer 10:22 L! The report is coming—a great H7754
Jer 11: 2 "L to the terms of this covenant and tell H9048
Jer 11: 6 'L to the terms of this covenant and follow H9048
Jer 11: 8 But they did not l or pay attention; instead H9048
Jer 11:10 ancestors, who refused to l to my words. H9048
Jer 11:11 they cry out to me, I will not l to them. H9048
Jer 11:14 because I will not l when they call to me H9048
Jer 12:17 But if any nation does not l, I will H9048
Jer 13:10 who refuse to l to my words, who follow H9048
Jer 13:17 If you do not l, I will weep in secret H9048
Jer 14:12 Although they fast, I will not l to their cry H9048
Jer 17:23 Yet they did not l or pay attention; they H9048
Jer 17:23 stiff-necked and would not l or respond to H9048
Jer 18:19 L to me, LORD; hear what my accusers are H7992
Jer 19: 3 L! I am going to bring a disaster on H2180
Jer 19:15 'L! I am going to bring on this city H2180
Jer 19:15 stiff-necked and would not l to my words. H9048
Jer 22:21 you felt secure, but you said, 'I will not l! H9048
Jer 23:16 "Do not l to what the prophets are H9048
Jer 25: 7 "But you did not l to me," declares the H9048
Jer 26: 3 Perhaps they will l and each will turn from H9048
Jer 26: 4 If you do not l to me and follow my law H9048
Jer 26: 5 if you do not l to the words of my H9048
Jer 27: 9 So do not l to your prophets, your diviners H9048
Jer 27:14 Do not l to the words of the prophets who H9048
Jer 27:16 Do not l to the prophets who say, 'Very H9048
Jer 27:17 Do not l to them. Serve the king of H9048
Jer 28: 7 l to what I have to say in your hearing H9048
Jer 28:15 to Hananiah the prophet, "L, Hananiah! H9048
Jer 29: 8 Do not l to the dreams you encourage H9048
Jer 29:12 come and pray to me, and I will l to you. H9048
Jer 32:33 they would not l or respond to discipline. H9048
Jer 34:14 did not l to me or pay attention to me. H9048
Jer 35:17 'L! I am going to bring on Judah and H2180
Jer 35:17 to them, but they did not l; I called to H9048
Jer 36:25 to burn the scroll, he would not l to them. H9048
Jer 37:14 But Irijah would not l to him; instead, he H9048
Jer 37:20 lord the king, please l. Let me bring my H9048
Jer 38:15 give you counsel, you would not l to me." H9048
Jer 44: 5 But they did not l or pay attention; they did H9048
Jer 44:16 "We will not l to the message you have H9048
Jer 50:28 L to the fugitives and refugees from H7754
La 1:18 against his command. L, all you peoples H9048
Eze 2: 5 And whether they l or fail to listen—for H9048
Eze 2: 5 And whether they listen or fail to l—for they NDT
Eze 2: 7 to them, whether they l or fail to listen H9048
Eze 2: 7 whether they listen or fail to l, for they are NDT
Eze 2: 8 son of man, l to what I say to you H9048
Eze 3: 7 are not willing to l to you because they H9048
Eze 3: 7 because they are not willing to l to me, H9048
Eze 3:10 l carefully and take to heart all H928+265+9048
Eze 3:11 LORD says,' whether they l or fail to listen." H9048
Eze 3:11 LORD says,' whether they listen or fail to l." NDT
Eze 3:27 Whoever will l let them listen, and H9048
Eze 3:27 Whoever will listen let them l, and H9048
Eze 8:18 they shout in my ears, I will not l to them." H9048
Eze 13:19 to my people, who l to lies, you have H9048
Eze 20: 8 against me and would not l to me; H9048
Eze 20:39 afterward you will surely l to me and no H9048
Eze 40: 4 carefully and l closely and pay H9048+928+265
Eze 44: 5 l closely and give attention to H9048+928+265
Da 9:19 l! Lord, forgive! Lord, hear and act H9048
Hos 5: 1 L, royal house! This H263
Joel 1: 2 Hear this, you elders; l, all who live in the H263
Am 5:23 I will not l to the music of your harps. H9048
Mic 1: 2 peoples, all of you, l, earth and all who H7992
Mic 3: 1 Then I said, "L, you leaders of Jacob, you H9048
Mic 6: 1 L to what the LORD says: "Stand up, plead H9048
Mic 6: 2 the LORD's accusation; l, you everlasting NDT
Mic 6: 9 L! The LORD is calling to the city—and to NDT
Hab 1: 2 must I call for help, but you do not l? H9048
Zec 1: 4 But they would not l or pay attention to H9048
Zec 3: 8 "'L, High Priest Joshua, you and your H9048
Zec 7:12 flint and would not l to the law or to the H9048
Zec 7:13 I called, they did not l; so when they H9048
Zec 7:13 they called, I would not l,' says the LORD H9048
Zec 11: 3 L to the wail of the shepherds; their rich H7754
Zec 11: 3 L to the roar of the lions; the lush thicket H7754
Mal 2: 2 If you do not l, and if you do not resolve to H9048
Mt 10:14 will not welcome you or l to your words, G201
Mt 12:42 ends of the earth to l to Solomon's wisdom G201
Mt 13:18 L then to what the parable of the sower means G201
Mt 15:10 crowd to him and said, "L and understand. G201
Mt 17: 5 with him I am well pleased. L to him!" G201
Mt 18:15 the two of you. If they l to you, you have G201
Mt 18:16 But if they will not l, take one or two others G201
Mt 18:17 If they still refuse to l, tell it to the church NDT
Mt 18:17 if they refuse to l even to the church NDT
Mt 21:33 "L to another parable: There was a G201
Mk 4: 3 "L! A farmer went out to sow his seed. G201
Mk 6:11 any place will not welcome you or l to you, G201
Mk 6:20 greatly puzzled; yet he liked to l to him. G201
Mk 7:14 crowd to him and said, "L to me, everyone, G201
Mk 9: 7 "This is my Son, whom I love. L to him!" G201
Mk 15:35 they said, "L, he's calling Elijah. G2623
Lk 8:18 Therefore consider carefully how you l G201
Lk 9:35 is my Son, whom I have chosen; l to him." G201
Lk 9:44 "L carefully to what I am G5502+1650+3836+4044
Lk 11:31 ends of the earth to l to Solomon's wisdom G201
Lk 16:29 the Prophets; let them l to them. G201
Lk 16:31 'If they do not l to Moses and the Prophets G201
Lk 18: 6 Lord said, "L to what the unjust judge says. G201
Jn 9:27 "I have told you already and you did not l. G201
Jn 9:31 We know that God does not l to sinners. G201
Jn 10: 3 gate for him, and the sheep l to his voice. G201
Jn 10:16 They too will l to my voice, and there shall G201
Jn 10:20 raving mad. Why l to him?" G201
Jn 10:27 My sheep l to my voice; I know them, and G201
Ac 2:14 this to you; l carefully to what I say. G1969
Ac 2:22 "Fellow Israelites, l to this: Jesus of G201
Ac 3:22 you must l to everything he tells you. G201
Ac 3:23 Anyone who does not l to him will be G201
Ac 4:19 right in God's eyes: to l to you, or to him G201
Ac 5: 9 Spirit of the Lord? L! The feet of the men G2627
Ac 7: 2 "Brothers and fathers, l to me! The God of G201
Ac 10:33 the presence of God to l to everything the G201
Ac 13:16 you Gentiles who worship God, l to me! G201
Ac 15:13 "Brothers," he said, "l to me. G201
Ac 18:14 it would be reasonable for me to l to you. G462
Ac 22: 1 "Brothers and fathers, l now to my defense." G201
Ac 26: 3 Therefore, I beg you to l to me patiently. G201
Ac 28:28 been sent to the Gentiles, and they will l!" G201
1Co 14:21 even then they will not l to me, says G1653
1Co 15:51 L, I tell you a mystery: We will not all G2627
Eph 4:29 that it may benefit those who l. G201
2Ti 2:14 it is of no value, and only ruins those who l. G201
Jas 1:19 Everyone should be quick to l, slow to G201
Jas 1:22 Do not merely l to the word, and so G212
Jas 2: 5 L, my dear brothers and sisters: Has not G201
Jas 4:13 Now l, you who say, "Today or tomorrow we G72
Jas 5: 1 Now l, you rich people, weep and wail G72
1Jn 4: 6 whoever is not from God does not l to us. G201

LISTENED (53) [LISTEN]

Ge 3:17 "Because you l to your wife and ate fruit H9048
Ge 30: 6 he has l to my plea and given me a son." H9048
Ge 30:17 God l to Leah, and she became pregnant H9048
Ge 30:22 he l to her and enabled her to conceive. H9048
Ex 7:16 But until now you have not l. H9048
Ex 18:24 Moses l to his father-in-law and did H9048
Nu 21: 3 The LORD l to Israel's plea and gave the H9048
Dt 9:19 to destroy you. But again the LORD l to me. H9048
Dt 10:10 the LORD l to me at this time also. H9048
Dt 34: 9 So the Israelites l to him and did what the H9048
Jos 10:14 a day when the LORD l to a human being. H9048
Jdg 2:20 their ancestors and has not l to me, H9048
Jdg 6:10 land you live.' But you have not l to me." H9048
1Sa 12: 1 "I have l to everything you said to me H9048
1Sa 19: 6 Saul l to Jonathan and took this oath: "As H9048
1Sa 28:23 woman in urging him, and he l to them. H9048
2Ki 13: 4 and the LORD l to him, for he saw H9048
2Ki 18:12 They neither l to the commands nor H9048
2Ch 24:17 homage to the king, and he l to them. H9048
2Ch 25:16 done this and have not l to my counsel." H9048
2Ch 33:13 moved by his entreaty and l to his plea; H9048
Ne 8: 3 the people l attentively to the Book of H265+448
Ne 8: 9 weeping as they l to the words of the H9048
Job 29:21 "People l to me expectantly, waiting in H9048
Job 32:11 while you spoke, I l to your reasoning H263
Ps 22:24 face from him but has l to his cry for help. H9048
Ps 66:18 sin in my heart, the Lord would not have l; H9048
Ps 66:19 God has surely l and has heard my H9048
Isa 66: 4 no one answered, when I spoke, no one l. H9048
Jer 6:19 because they have not l to my words and H7992
Jer 8: 6 I have l attentively, but they do not say H9048
Jer 13:11 praise and honor. But they have not l.' H9048
Jer 23:18 Who has l and heard his word H7992
Jer 25: 3 you again and again, but you have not l. H9048
Jer 25: 4 you have not l or paid any attention. H9048
Jer 25: 8 "Because you have not l to my words, H9048
Jer 26: 5 again and again (though you have not l), H9048
Jer 29:19 For they have not l to my words," declares H9048
Jer 29:19 And you exiles have not l either," H9048
Jer 35:15 But you have not paid attention or l to me. H9048
Jer 36:31 against them, because they have not l. H9048
Eze 3: 6 you to them, they would have l to you. H9048
Eze 9: 5 As I l, he said to the others, "Follow H928+265
Da 9: 6 We have not l to your servants the H9048
Da 10: 9 speaking, and as I l to him, I fell into a H9048
Jnh 2: 2 dead I called for help, and you l to my cry. H9048
Mal 3:16 with each other, and the LORD l and heard. H7992
Mk 12:37 The large crowd l to him with delight. G201
Jn 10: 8 robbers, but the sheep have not l to them. G201
Ac 14: 9 He l to Paul as he was speaking. G201
Ac 15:12 became silent as they l to Barnabas and G201
Ac 22:22 The crowd l to Paul until he said this. G201
Ac 24:24 He sent for Paul and l to him as he spoke G201

LISTENER (1) [LISTEN]

Pr 21:28 a careful l will testify successfully H408+9048

LISTENING (21) [LISTEN]

Ge 18:10 Now Sarah was l at the entrance to the H9048
Ge 27: 5 Now Rebekah was l as Isaac spoke to his H9048
1Sa 3: 9 say, 'Speak, LORD, for your servant is l. H9048
1Sa 3:10 Samuel said, "Speak, for your servant is l." H9048
2Sa 20:17 your servant has to say." "I'm l," he said. H9048
Pr 18:13 To answer before l—that is folly and H9048
Pr 19:27 Stop l to instruction, my son, and you will H9048
Pr 25:12 is the rebuke of a wise judge to a l ear. H9048
Isa 1:15 when you offer many prayers, I am not l. H9048
Lk 2:46 l to them and asking them questions. G201
Lk 5: 1 around him and l to the word of God. G201
Lk 6:27 "But to you who are l I say: Love your G201
Lk 7: 1 saying all this to the people who were l, G198
Lk 10:39 who sat at the Lord's feet l to what he said. G201
Lk 19:11 While they were l to this, he went on to tell G201
Lk 20:45 While all the people were l, Jesus said to G201
Ac 16:14 One of those l was a woman from the city G201
Ac 16:25 the other prisoners were l to them. G2053
Ac 17:21 talking about and l to the latest ideas.) G201
Ac 26:29 only you but all who are l to me today may G201
Ac 27:11 the centurion, instead of l to what Paul said NDT

LISTENS (11) [LISTEN]

Pr 1:33 but whoever l to me will live in safety H9048
Pr 17: 4 A wicked person l to deceitful lips; a liar H7992
Pr 29:12 If a ruler l to lies, all his officials become H7992
Lk 10:16 "Whoever l to you listens to me; whoever G201
Lk 10:16 "Whoever listens to you l to me; whoever G201
Jn 3:29 attends the bridegroom waits and l for him, G201
Jn 9:31 He l to the godly person who does his will. G201
Jn 18:37 Everyone on the side of truth l to me." G201
Jas 1:23 Anyone who l to the word but does not do G212
1Jn 4: 5 of the world, and the world l to them. G201
1Jn 4: 6 whoever knows God l to us; but G201

LISTETH (KJV) PLEASES, WANTS

LISTING (1) [LIST]

Nu 1: 2 clans and families, l every man by name H5031

LIT (2) [LIGHT]

Jdg 15: 5 l the torches and let the foxes loose H1277+836
Ps 77:18 your lightning l up the world; the earth H239

LITERATURE (2)

Da 1: 4 the language and l of the Babylonians. H6219
Da 1:17 of all kinds of l and learning. H6219

LITTLE (170)

Ge 18: 4 Let a l water be brought, and then you H5071
Ge 24:17 "Please give me a l water from your jar." H5071
Ge 24:43 let me drink a l water from your jar," H5071
Ge 30:30 The l you had before I came has increased H5071
Ge 43: 2 "Go back and buy us a l more food." H5071
Ge 43:11 man as a gift—a l balm and a little honey H5071
Ge 43:11 a little balm and a l honey, some spices H5071
Ge 44:25 'Go back and buy a l more food. H5071
Ge 48: 7 the way, a l distance from Ephrath. H3896+824
Ex 10: 5 what l you have left after the H3856+7129+8636
Ex 16:17 were told; some gathered much, some l. H5070
Ex 16:18 the one who gathered l did not have H5070
Ex 16:18 who gathered little did not have too l. H2893
Ex 23:30 L by little I will drive them out before you H5071
Ex 23:30 Little by l I will drive them out before you H5071
Lev 11:17 the l owl, the cormorant, the great owl, H3927
Nu 16:27 children and l ones at the entrances to H3251
Dt 1:39 And the l ones that you said would be H3251
Dt 7:22 out those nations before you, l by little. H5071
Dt 7:22 out those nations before you, little by l. H5071
Dt 14:16 the l owl, the great owl, the white owl, H3927
Dt 28:38 seed in the field but you will harvest l, H5071
Jdg 18:21 Putting their l children, their livestock and H3251
1Sa 2:19 mother made him a l robe and took it to H7785
1Sa 14:29 when I tasted a l of this honey. H5071
1Sa 14:43 "I tasted a l honey with the end of my H5071
1Sa 17:42 over and saw that he was l more than a boy, NDT
1Sa 18:23 I'm only a poor man and l known." H7829
2Sa 12: 3 nothing except one l ewe lamb he had H7783
2Sa 12: 8 And if all this had been too l, I would H5071
1Ki 3: 7 But I am only a l child and do not know H7785
1Ki 10:21 considered of l value in Solomon's H4202+4399
1Ki 12:10 'My l finger is thicker than my father's H7782
1Ki 17:10 you bring me a l water in a jar so I H5071
1Ki 17:12 of flour in a jar and a l olive oil in a jug. H5071
2Ki 8:12 dash their l children to the ground H6407
2Ki 10:18 "Ahab served Baal a l; Jehu will serve H5071
2Ch 9:20 considered of l value in Solomon's day H4399
2Ch 10:10 'My l finger is thicker than my father's H7782

2Ch 20:13 with their wives and children and l ones H3251
2Ch 31:18 They included all the l ones, the wives H3251
Ezr 9: 8 to our eyes and a l relief in our bondage. H5071
Job 19:18 Even the l boys scorn me; when I appear H6396
Job 21:11 as a flock; their l ones dance about. H3529
Job 24:24 For a l while they are exalted, and then H5071
Job 36: 2 "Bear with me a l longer and I will show H2402
Ps 8: 5 You have made them a l lower than the H5071
Ps 17:14 may there be leftovers for their l ones. H6407
Ps 37:10 A l while, and the wicked will be H6388+5071
Ps 37:16 Better the l that the righteous have than H5071
Ps 68:27 There is the l tribe of Benjamin, leading H7582
Pr 6:10 A l sleep, a little slumber, a little folding H5071
Pr 6:10 A little sleep, a l slumber, a little folding H5071
Pr 6:10 slumber, a l folding of the hands to rest H5071
Pr 7:23 a snare, l knowing it will cost him his life. H4202
Pr 9:18 But l do they know that the dead are there H4202
Pr 10:20 heart of the wicked is of l value. H3869+5071
Pr 13:11 gathers money l by little makes it H6584+3338
Pr 13:11 gathers money little by l makes it H6584+3338
Pr 15:16 Better a l with the fear of the LORD than H5071
Pr 16: 8 Better a l with righteousness than much H5071
Pr 23: 8 will vomit up the l you have eaten and H7326
Pr 24:33 A l sleep, a little slumber, a little folding H5071
Pr 24:33 A little sleep, a l slumber, a little folding H5071
Pr 24:33 slumber, a l folding of the hands to rest H5071
Pr 30:25 Ants are creatures of l strength, yet they H4202
Pr 30:26 hyraxes are creatures of l power, yet they H4202
Ecc 5:12 whether they eat l or much, but as for the H5071
Ecc 10: 1 so a l folly outweighs wisdom and honor. H5071
SS 2:15 the l foxes that ruin the vineyards H7783
SS 8: 8 We have a l sister, and her breasts are H7783
Isa 11: 6 together; and a l child will lead them. H7785
Isa 26:20 a l while until his wrath H5071+8092
Isa 28:10 a rule for that; a l here, a little there." H2402
Isa 28:10 a rule for that; a little here, a l there." H2402
Isa 28:13 a rule for that; a l here, a little there—so H2402
Isa 28:13 a little here, a l there—so that as they go H2402
Isa 32:10 In l more than a year you who feel H3427+6584
Isa 41:14 you worm Jacob, l Israel, do not fear H5493
Isa 63:18 For a l while your people possessed your H5203
Jer 3: 9 Israel's immorality mattered so l to her, H7825
Jer 48: 4 will be broken; her l ones will cry out. H7582
Eze 11:16 yet for a l while I have been a sanctuary H5071
Da 7: 8 another horn, a l one, which came up A10236
Da 11:34 they will receive a l help, and many who H5071
Hos 11: 4 like one who lifts a l child to the cheek, H6403
Hos 13:16 their l ones will be dashed to the ground H6407
Hag 1: 6 planted much, but harvested l. You eat, H5071
Hag 1: 9 but see, it turned out to be l. H5071
Hag 2: 6 'In a l while I will once more shake the H5071
Zec 1:15 I was only a l angry, but they went too far H5071
Zec 13: 7 I will turn my hand against the l ones. H7592
Mt 6:30 not much more clothe you—you of l faith? G3899
Mt 8:26 He replied, "You of l faith, why are you so G3899
Mt 10:42 water to one of these l ones who is my G3625
Mt 11:25 learned, and revealed them to l children. G3758
Mt 14:31 "You of l faith," he said, "why did you G3899
Mt 16: 8 Jesus asked, "You of l faith, why are you G3899
Mt 17:20 "Because you have so l faith. Truly I tell G3898
Mt 18: 2 He called a l child to him, and placed the G4086
Mt 18: 3 you change and become like l children, G4086
Mt 18: 6 "If anyone causes one of these l ones G3625
Mt 18:10 you do not despise one of these l ones. G3625
Mt 18:14 that any of these l ones should perish. G3625
Mt 19:13 people brought l children to Jesus for him G4086
Mt 19:14 "Let the l children come to me, and G4086
Mt 26:39 Going a l farther, he fell with his face to G3625
Mt 26:73 After a l while, those standing there went G3625
Mk 1:19 When he had gone a l farther, he saw G3900
Mk 5:23 with him, "My l daughter is dying. G2589
Mk 5:41 which means "L girl, I say to you, get G3166
Mk 7:25 woman whose l daughter was possessed G2589
Mk 9:36 He took a l child whom he placed among G4086
Mk 9:37 one of these l children in my name G4086
Mk 9:42 "If anyone causes one of these l ones G3625
Mk 10:13 were bringing l children to Jesus for him G4086
Mk 10:14 "Let the l children come to me, and G4086
Mk 10:15 of God like a l child will never enter it." G4086
Mk 14:35 Going a l farther, he fell to the ground G3625
Mk 14:70 After a l while, those standing near said G3625
Lk 5: 3 asked him to put out a l from shore. G3900
Lk 7:47 whoever has been forgiven l loves little." G3900
Lk 7:47 whoever has been forgiven little loves l." G3900
Lk 9:47 took a l child and had him stand beside G4086
Lk 9:48 welcomes this l child in my name G4086
Lk 10:21 learned, and revealed them to l children. G3758
Lk 12:26 Since you cannot do this very l thing, why G1788
Lk 12:28 more will he clothe you—you of l faith! G3899
Lk 12:32 "Do not be afraid, l flock, for your Father G3625
Lk 16:10 can be trusted with very l can also be G1788
Lk 16:10 is dishonest with very l will also be G1788
Lk 17: 2 to cause one of these l ones to stumble. G3625
Lk 18:16 "Let the l children come to me, and G4086
Lk 18:17 of God like a l child will never enter it." G4086
Lk 22:58 A l later someone else saw him and said G1099
Jn 12:35 to have the light just a l while longer. G3625
Jn 13:33 children, I will be with you only a l longer. G3625
Jn 16:16 "In a l while you will see me no more G3625
Jn 16:16 then after a l while you will see me." G3625
Jn 16:17 'In a l while you will see me no more G3625
Jn 16:17 then after a l while you will see me G3625
Jn 16:18 "What does he mean by 'a l while'? G3625
Jn 16:19 'In a l while you will see me no more G3625
Jn 16:19 then after a l while you will see me'? G3625
Ac 5:34 that the men be put outside for a l while. G1099
Ac 19:22 he stayed in the province of Asia a l longer. AIT
Ro 2:20 a teacher of l children, because you have G3758
1Co 4: 3 I care very l if I am judged by G1650+1788+1639
1Co 5: 6 Don't you know that a l yeast leavens the G3625
2Co 7: 8 my letter hurt you, but only for a l while— G6052
2Co 8:15 the one who gathered l did not have too G3900
2Co 8:15 who gathered little did not have too l." G1782
2Co 11: 1 you will put up with me in a l foolishness. G3625
2Co 11:16 so that I may do a l boasting. G3625
Gal 5: 9 "A l yeast works through the whole batch G3625
1Ti 5:23 use a l wine because of your stomach G3900
Phm 15 from you for a l while was that you might G6052
Heb 2: 7 You made them a l lower than the angels; G1099
Heb 2: 9 made lower than the angels for a l while, G1099
Heb 10:37 "In just a l while, he who is coming G3625
Heb 12:10 disciplined us for a l while as they G3900
Jas 4:14 appears for a l while and then vanishes G3900
1Pe 1: 6 though now for a l while you may have G3900
1Pe 5:10 after you have suffered a l while, will G3900
Rev 3: 8 I know that you have l strength, yet you G3625
Rev 6:11 they were told to wait a l longer, until G3625
Rev 10: 2 He was holding a l scroll, which lay open G1044
Rev 10: 9 asked him to give me the l scroll. G1044
Rev 10:10 I took the l scroll from the angel's hand G1044
Rev 17:10 he must remain for only a l while. G3900

LIVE (654) [ALIVE, LIFE, LIFE'S, LIFELESS, LIFETIME, LIVED, LIVES, LIVING, OUTLIVED]

Ge 3:22 from the tree of life and eat, and l forever." H2649
Ge 4:20 the father of those who l in tents and H3782
Ge 9:27 may Japheth l in the tents of Shem H8905
Ge 12:10 to Egypt to l there for a while because the H1591
Ge 12:12 Then they will kill me but will let you l. H2649
Ge 13:18 So Abram went to l near the great trees of H3782
Ge 16:12 and he will l in hostility toward all his H8905
Ge 17:18 "If only Ishmael might l under your H2649
Ge 20: 7 he will pray for you and you will l. H2649
Ge 20:15 land is before you; l wherever you like." H3782
Ge 24:37 of the Canaanites, in whose land I l, H3782
Ge 26: 2 l in the land where I tell you to live. H8905
Ge 26: 2 live in the land where I tell you to l. NDT
Ge 27:40 You will l by the sword and you will serve H2649
Ge 31:32 has your gods, that person shall not l. H2649
Ge 34:10 L in it, trade in it, and acquire property in H3782
Ge 34:21 "Let them l in our land and trade in it; the H3782
Ge 34:22 men will agree to l with us as one people H3782
Ge 38:11 "L as a widow in your father's household H3782
Ge 38:11 So Tamar went to l in her father's H3782
Ge 42: 2 some for us, so that we may l and not die." H2649
Ge 42:18 "Do this and you will l, for I fear God: H2649
Ge 43: 8 you and our children may l and not die. H2649
Ge 45:10 You shall l in the region of Goshen and be H3782
Ge 47: 4 "We have come to l here for a while H1591
Ge 47: 6 of the land. Let them l in Goshen. H3782
Ge 47:19 us seed so that we may l and not die, H2649
Ge 49:13 "Zebulun will l by the seashore and H8905
Ex 1:16 kill him; but if it is a girl, let her l. H2649
Ex 1:17 had told them to do; they let the boys l. H2649
Ex 1:18 Why have you let the boys l?" H2649
Ex 1:22 throw into the Nile, but let every girl l." H2649
Ex 2:15 from Pharaoh and went to l in Midian, H3782
Ex 8:22 where my people l; no swarms of flies H6641
Ex 12:20 Wherever you l, you must eat unleavened H4632
Ex 18:20 them the way they are to l and how they H2143
Ex 19:13 person or animal shall be permitted to l. H2649
Ex 20:12 so that you may l long in the land H799+3427
Ex 21:35 are to sell the l one and divide both the H2645
Ex 22:18 "Do not allow a sorceress to l. H2649
Ex 23:31 your hands the people who l in the land, H3782
Ex 23:33 Do not let them l in your land or they will H3782
Ex 33:20 my face, for no one may see me and l." H2649
Ex 34:10 The people you l among will see how NDT
Ex 34:12 a treaty with those who l in the land H3782
Ex 34:15 a treaty with those who l in the land; H3782
Lev 3:17 the generations to come, wherever you l: H4632
Lev 7:26 And wherever you l, you must not eat the H4632
Lev 11: 2 'Of all the animals that l on land, these are NDT
Lev 13:46 They must l alone; they must live outside H3782
Lev 13:46 live alone; they must l outside the camp. H4632
Lev 14: 4 order that two l clean birds and some H2645
Lev 14: 6 He is then to take the l bird and dip it H2645
Lev 14: 7 he is to release the l bird in the open H2645
Lev 14:51 the scarlet yarn and the l bird, dip them H2645
Lev 14:52 the fresh water, the l bird, the cedar wood, H2645
Lev 14:53 he is to release the l bird in the open H2645
Lev 16:20 he shall bring forward the l goat. H2645
Lev 16:21 on the head of the l goat and confess H2645
Lev 18: 3 where you used to l, and you must H3782
Lev 18: 5 person who obeys them will l by them. H2649
Lev 20:22 I am bringing you to l may not vomit you H3782
Lev 20:23 You must not l according to the customs of H2143
Lev 22:13 she returns to l in her father's NDT
Lev 23: 3 wherever you l, it is a sabbath to H4632
Lev 23:14 the generations to come, wherever you l. H4632
Lev 23:17 From wherever you l, bring two loaves H4632
Lev 23:21 the generations to come, wherever you l. H4632
Lev 23:31 the generations to come, wherever you l. H4632
Lev 23:42 L in temporary shelters for seven days: H3782
Lev 23:42 Israelites are to l in such shelters H3782
Lev 23:43 know that I had the Israelites l in H3782
Lev 25: 6 temporary resident who l among you, H1591
Lev 25:18 my laws, and you will l safely in the land. H3782
Lev 25:19 you will eat your fill and l there in safety. H3782
Lev 25:35 so they can continue to l among you. H2649
Lev 25:36 so that they may continue to l among you. H2649
Lev 26: 5 the food you want and l in safety in your H3782
Lev 26:32 that your enemies who l there will be H3782
Nu 4:19 So that they may l and not die when they H2649
Nu 13:18 the people who l there are strong or H3782
Nu 13:19 What kind of land do they l in? Is it good H3782
Nu 13:19 What kind of towns do they l in? Are they H3782
Nu 13:28 But the people who l there are powerful H3782
Nu 13:29 The Amalekites l in the Negev; the Hittites H3782
Nu 13:29 Amorites l in the hill country; H3782
Nu 13:29 the Canaanites l near the sea and H3782
Nu 14:21 as surely as I l and as surely as the glory H2644
Nu 14:28 So tell them, 'As surely as I l, declares the H2644
Nu 21: 8 anyone who is bitten can look at it and l." H2649
Nu 23: 9 I see a people who l apart and do not H8905
Nu 24:23 Who can l when God does this? H2649
Nu 31:15 "Have you allowed all the women to l?" H2649
Nu 32:17 women and children will l in fortified H3782
Nu 33:55 you trouble in the land where you will l. H3782
Nu 35: 2 the Levites towns to l in from the H3782
Nu 35: 3 will have towns to l in and pasturelands H3782
Nu 35:29 the generations to come, wherever you l. H4632
Nu 35:32 them to go back and l on their own land H3782
Nu 35:34 the land where you l and where I dwell, H3782
Dt 2: 4 the descendants of Esau, who l in Seir. H3782
Dt 2: 8 the descendants of Esau, who l in Seir. H3782
Dt 2:10 The Emites used to l there—a people H3782
Dt 2:12 Horites used to l in Seir, but the H3782
Dt 2:20 Rephaites, who used to l there; but the H3782
Dt 2:29 of Esau, who l in Seir, and the H3782
Dt 2:29 the Moabites, who l in Ar, did for us— H3782
Dt 4: 1 them so that you may l and may go in H2649
Dt 4: 9 fade from your heart as long as you l. H2644
Dt 4:10 me as long as they l in the land and may H2645
Dt 4:26 You will not l there long but will H799+3427
Dt 4:40 and that you may l long in the land H799+3427
Dt 5:16 so that you may l long and that it H799+3427
Dt 5:24 that a person can l even if God speaks H2649
Dt 5:33 so that you may l and prosper and H2649
Dt 6: 2 God as long as you l by keeping all his H2644
Dt 8: 1 so that you may l and increase and may H2649
Dt 8: 3 you that man does not l on bread alone H2649
Dt 11: 9 so that you may l long in the H799+3427
Dt 12: 1 to possess—as long as you l in the land. H2645
Dt 12:10 around you so that you will l in safety. H3782
Dt 12:19 the Levites as long as you l in your H3972+3427
Dt 13:12 the LORD your God is giving you to l in H3782
Dt 13:15 put to the sword all who l in that town. H3782
Dt 14:29 the widows who l in your towns may NDT
Dt 16:14 the widows who l in your towns. NDT
Dt 16:20 so that you may l and possess the land H2649
Dt 18: 1 They shall l on the food offerings H430
Dt 20: 5 a new house and not yet begun to l in it? H2852
Dt 20: 5 someone else may begin to l in it. H2852
Dt 22: 2 If they do not l near you or if you do not NDT
Dt 23: 6 them as long as you l. H3972+3427+4200+6409
Dt 23:16 Let them l among you wherever they like H3782
Dt 25:15 so that you may l long in the land H799+3427
Dt 28:30 will build a house, but you will not l in it. H3782
Dt 28:66 You will l in constant suspense, filled with H2644
Dt 30: 6 your heart and with all your soul, and l. H2644
Dt 30:16 laws; then you will l and increase H2649
Dt 30:18 You will not l long in the land you H799+3427
Dt 30:19 so that you and your children may l H2649
Dt 31:13 God as long as you l in the land you are H2645
Dt 32:40 solemnly swear: As surely as I l forever, H2645
Dt 32:47 By them you will l long in the land H799+3427
Dt 33: 6 "Let Reuben l and not die, nor his people H2649
Dt 33:28 So Israel will l in safety; Jacob will dwell H8905
Jos 2: 9 so that all who l in this country are H3782
Jos 7: 3 whole army, for only a few people l there." NDT
Jos 9: 7 "But perhaps you l near us, so how can H3782
Jos 9:15 a treaty of peace with them to let them l, H2649
Jos 9:20 We will let them l, so that God's wrath H2649
Jos 9:21 They continued, "Let them l, but let them H2649
Jos 9:22 us by saying, 'We l a long way from you,' H3782
Jos 9:22 way from you,' while actually you l near us? NDT
Jos 13:13 so they continue to l among the Israelites H3782
Jos 14: 4 share of the land but only towns to l in, H3782
Jos 15:63 day the Jebusites l there with the people H3782
Jos 16:10 day the Canaanites l among the people H3782
Jos 17:12 were determined to l in that region. H3782
Jos 17:16 all the Canaanites who l in the plain have H3782
Jos 20: 4 city and provide a place to l among them. H3782
Jos 21: 2 Moses that you give us towns to l in, H3782
Jos 24:13 and you l in them and eat from vineyards H3782
Jdg 1:16 the people of Judah to l among the H3782
Jdg 1:21 this day the Jebusites l there with the H3782
Jdg 1:27 were determined to l in that land. H3782
Jdg 1:29 Canaanites continued to l there among H3782
Jdg 6:10 of the Amorites, in whose land you l. H3782
Jdg 8:29 son of Joash went back home to l. H3782
Jdg 10:18 will be head over all who l in Gilead." H3782
Jdg 11: 8 be head over all of us who l in Gilead." H3782
Jdg 17:10 "L with me and be my father and priest H3782
Jdg 17:11 So the Levite agreed to l with him, and the H3782

Jdg 19:18 area in the hill country of Ephraim where I l. NDT
Ru 1: 1 went to l for a while in the country of H1591
Ru 2:11 homeland and came to l with a people you NDT
1Sa 1:22 the LORD, and he will l there always." H3782
1Sa 1:26 As surely as you l, I am the woman H2644+5883
1Sa 10:24 the people shouted, "Long l the king!" H2649
1Sa 17:55 replied, "As surely as you l, Your Majesty, H2644
1Sa 20: 3 as surely as the LORD lives and as you l, H2644
1Sa 20:14 like the LORD's kindness as long as I l, H2644
1Sa 25:26 as the LORD your God lives and as you l, H2644
1Sa 25:28 will be found in you as long as you l. H3427
1Sa 27: 5 of the country towns, that I may l there. H3782
1Sa 27: 5 Why should your servant l in the royal city H3782
2Sa 8: 2 the third length was allowed to l. H2649
2Sa 11:11 As surely as you l, I H2644+2256+2644+5883
2Sa 12:22 may be gracious to me and let the child l. H2649
2Sa 14:19 "As surely as you l, my lord H2644+5883
2Sa 16:16 said to him, "Long l the king! H2649
2Sa 16:16 "Long live the king! Long l the king!" H2649
2Sa 19:34 "How many more years will I l, that I H2644
1Ki 1:25 him and saying, 'Long l King Adonijah! H2649
1Ki 1:31 "May my lord King David l forever! H2649
1Ki 1:34 trumpet and shout, 'Long l King Solomon! H2649
1Ki 1:39 people shouted, "Long l King Solomon!" H2649
1Ki 2: 4 'If your descendants watch how they l H2006
1Ki 2:36 yourself a house in Jerusalem and l there, H3782
1Ki 3:17 This woman and I l in the same house H3782
1Ki 6:13 And I will l among the Israelites and will H8905
1Ki 7: 8 And the palace in which he was to l, set H3782
1Ki 8:36 Teach them the right way to l, and send H2143
1Ki 8:40 all the time they l in the land you gave H2645
1Ki 8:61 to l by his decrees and obey his H2143
1Ki 20:32 Ben-Hadad says: 'Please let me l.'" H2649
2Ki 2: 2 "As surely as the LORD lives and as you l, H2644
2Ki 2: 4 "As surely as the LORD lives and as you l, H2644
2Ki 2: 6 "As surely as the LORD lives and as you l, H2644
2Ki 4: 7 You and your sons can l on what is left." H2649
2Ki 4:30 "As surely as the LORD lives and as you l, H2644
2Ki 7: 4 If they spare us, we l; if they kill us, then H2649
2Ki 10:19 Anyone who fails to come will no longer l. H2649
2Ki 11:12 their hands and shouted, "Long l the king! H2649
2Ki 17:27 Samaria go back to l there and teach the H3782
2Ki 17:28 from Samaria came to l in Bethel and H3782
2Ch 2: 3 sent him cedar to build a palace to l in. H3782
2Ch 6:27 Teach them the right way to l, and send H2143
2Ch 6:31 all the time they l in the land you gave H2645
2Ch 8:11 "My wife must not l in the palace of David H3782
2Ch 19:10 you from your people who l in the cities— H3782
2Ch 20:15 Jehoshaphat and all who l in Judah and H3782
2Ch 23:11 him and shouted, "Long l the king!" H2649
2Ch 34:28 on this place and on those who l here. H3782
Ne 2: 3 I said to the king, "May the king l forever! H2649
Ne 8:14 that the Israelites were to l in temporary H3782
Ne 9:29 person who obeys them will l by them. H2649
Ne 11: 1 out of every ten of them to l in Jerusalem, H3782
Ne 11: 2 all who volunteered to l in Jerusalem. H3782
Job 4:19 how much more those who l in houses of H8905
Job 7:16 my life; I would not l forever. Let me H2649
Job 14:14 will they l again? All the days H2649
Job 21: 7 Why do the wicked l on, growing old and H2649
Job 26: 5 beneath the waters and all that l in them. H8905
Job 27: 6 will not reproach me as long as I l. H4946+3427
Job 30: 6 They were forced to l in the dry stream H8905
Job 33:28 and I shall l to enjoy the light of life. H2652
Ps 15: 1 Who may l on your holy mountain? H8905
Ps 22:26 praise him—may your hearts l forever! H2649
Ps 24: 1 the world, and all who l in it; H3782
Ps 26: 8 I love the house where you l, the place H5061
Ps 33:14 place he watches all who l on earth— H3782
Ps 35:20 against those who l quietly in the land. H8091
Ps 44:15 I l in disgrace all day long, and my face is H5584
Ps 49: 1 peoples; listen, all who l in this world, H3782
Ps 49: 9 so that they should l on forever and not H2649
Ps 49:18 Though while they l they count H2644
Ps 55:23 deceitful will not l out half their days. H2936
Ps 63: 4 I will praise you as long as I l, and in your H2644
Ps 65: 4 choose and bring near to l in your courts! H8905
Ps 68: 6 the rebellious l in a sun-scorched H8905
Ps 69:32 you who seek God, may your hearts l! H2649
Ps 72:15 Long may he l! May gold from Sheba be H2649
Ps 78:10 covenant and refused to l by his law. H2143
Ps 89:48 Who can l and not see death, or who can H2649
Ps 98: 7 the world, and all who l in it. H3782
Ps 102:28 of your servants will l in your presence; H8905
Ps 104:33 sing praise to my God as long as I l. H928+6388
Ps 107:36 there he brought the hungry to l, and they H3782
Ps 116: 2 ear to me, I will call on him as long as I l. H3427
Ps 118:17 I will not die but l, and will proclaim what H2649
Ps 119:17 Be good to your servant while I l, that I H2649
Ps 119:77 your compassion come to me that I may l, H2649
Ps 119:116 to your promise, and I will l; do not let H2649
Ps 119:144 give me understanding that I may l. H2649
Ps 119:175 Let me l that I may praise you, and may H2649
Ps 120: 5 Meshek, that I l among the tents of Kedar! H8905
Ps 128: 6 May you l to see your children's children NDT
Ps 133: 1 it is when God's people l together in H3782
Ps 140:13 the upright will l in your presence. H3782
Ps 146: 2 sing praise to my God as long as I l. H928+6388
Pr 1:33 listens to me will l in safety and be at H8905
Pr 2:21 For the upright will l in the land, and the H8905
Pr 4: 4 keep my commands, and you will l. H2649
Pr 7: 2 Keep my commands and you will l; guard H2649
Pr 9: 6 Leave your simple ways and you will l H2649
Pr 15:27 the one who hates bribes will l. H2649
Pr 19:10 It is not fitting for a fool to l in luxury H9503
Pr 21: 9 Better to l on a corner of the roof than H3782
Pr 21:19 Better to l in a desert than with a H3782
Pr 25:24 Better to l on a corner of the roof than H3782
Ecc 3:12 to be happy and to do good while they l. H2644
Ecc 6: 3 a hundred children and l many years; H2649
Ecc 8:12 a hundred crimes may l a long time, H799
Ecc 9: 3 is madness in their hearts while they l, H2644
Ecc 9: 4 even a l dog is better off than a dead lion! H2645
Ecc 11: 8 However many years anyone may l, let H2649
Isa 5: 8 space is left and you l alone in the land. H3782
Isa 6: 5 I l among a people of unclean lips H3782
Isa 6: 6 flew to me with a l coal in his hand, H8365
Isa 10:24 "My people who l in Zion, do not be H3782
Isa 11: 6 The wolf will l with the lamb, the leopard H1591
Isa 18: 3 the world, you who l on the earth, when H8905
Isa 20: 6 In that day the people who l on this coast H3782
Isa 21:14 the thirsty; you who l in Tema, bring food H3782
Isa 22:21 a father to those who l in Jerusalem and H3782
Isa 23:18 will go to those who l before the LORD, H3782
Isa 26:14 They are now dead, they l no more; their H2649
Isa 26:19 But your dead will l, LORD; their bodies H2649
Isa 30:19 People of Zion, who l in Jerusalem, you H3782
Isa 32:16 his righteousness l in the fertile field. H3782
Isa 32:18 My people will l in peaceful dwelling H3782
Isa 38:16 by such things people l; and my spirit H2649
Isa 38:16 You restored me to health and let me l. H2649
Isa 40:22 spreads them out like a tent to l in. H3782
Isa 42:10 you islands, and all who l in them. H3782
Isa 49:18 As surely as I l," declares the LORD, "you H2644
Isa 49:20 small for us; give us more space to l in. H3782
Isa 51:13 that you l in constant terror every day H7064
Isa 52: 4 first my people went down to Egypt to l; H1591
Isa 55: 3 come to me; listen, that you may l. H2649
Isa 57:15 "I l in a high and holy place, but also with H8905
Isa 65: 9 inherit them, and there will my servants l. H8905
Isa 65:20 an old man who does not l out his years; H4848
Isa 65:22 they build houses and others l in them, H3782
Jer 1:14 be poured out on all who l in the land. H3782
Jer 6: 8 your land desolate so no one can l in it." H3782
Jer 6:12 my hand against those who l in the land," H3782
Jer 7: 3 actions, and I will let you l in this place. H8905
Jer 7: 7 then I will let you l in this place, in the H8905
Jer 8:16 the city and all who l there. H3782
Jer 9: 6 You l in the midst of deception; in their H3782
Jer 9:11 the towns of Judah so no one can l there." H3782
Jer 9:26 Moab and all who l in the wilderness in H3782
Jer 10:17 to leave the land, you who l under siege. H3782
Jer 10:18 I will hurl out those who l in this land; H3782
Jer 11: 2 of Judah and to those who l in Jerusalem. H3782
Jer 11: 9 of Judah and those who l in Jerusalem. H3782
Jer 12: 1 Why do all the faithless l at ease? H8922
Jer 12: 4 Because those who l in it are wicked, the H3782
Jer 13:13 with drunkenness all who l in this land, H3782
Jer 19:12 do to this place and to those who l here, H3782
Jer 20: 6 all who l in your house will go into H3782
Jer 21: 6 I will strike down those who l in this city H3782
Jer 21: 9 Babylonians who are besieging you will l; H2649
Jer 21:13 you who l above this valley on the rocky H3782
Jer 22:23 You who l in 'Lebanon,' who are nestled H3782
Jer 22:24 "As surely as I l," declares the LORD, H2644
Jer 23: 6 will be saved and Israel will l in safety. H8905
Jer 23: 8 Then they will l in their own land." H3782
Jer 23:14 They commit adultery and l a lie H2143+928
Jer 24: 8 they remain in this land or l in Egypt. H3782
Jer 25:24 foreign people who l in the wilderness; H8905
Jer 25:29 down a sword on all who l on the earth, H3782
Jer 25:30 shout against all who l on the earth. H3782
Jer 26:15 on this city and on those who l in it, H3782
Jer 27:11 in its own land to till it and to l there, H3782
Jer 27:12 serve him and his people, and you will l. H2649
Jer 27:17 of Babylon, and you will l. Why should H2649
Jer 31:24 People will l together in Judah and all its H3782
Jer 32:37 back to this place and let them l in safety. H3782
Jer 33:16 be saved and Jerusalem will l in safety. H8905
Jer 34:22 the towns of Judah so no one can l there." H3782
Jer 35: 7 of these things, but must always l in tents. H3782
Jer 35: 7 Then you will l a long time in the land H2649
Jer 35: 9 built houses to l in or had vineyards H3782
Jer 35:15 Then you will l in the land I have given to H3782
Jer 38: 2 goes over to the Babylonians will l. H2649
Jer 38: 2 will escape with their lives; they will l. H2649
Jer 38:17 burned down; you and your family will l. H2649
Jer 40: 5 and l with him among the people H3782
Jer 40:10 l in the towns you have taken over." H3782
Jer 42:14 we will go and l in Egypt, where we H3782
Jer 43: 5 had come back to l in the land of Judah H1591
Jer 44: 8 gods in Egypt, where you have come to l? H1591
Jer 44:13 I will punish those who l in Egypt with the H3782
Jer 44:14 who have gone to l in Egypt will escape H1591
Jer 44:14 to which they long to return and l; none H3782
Jer 44:28 of Judah who came to l in Egypt will know H1591
Jer 46:18 "As surely as I l," declares the King H2644
Jer 46:19 exile, you who l in Egypt, for Memphis H3782
Jer 47: 2 the towns and those who l in them. H3782
Jer 48: 9 desolate, with no one to l in them. H3782
Jer 48:17 Mourn for her, all who l around her, all who NDT
Jer 48:19 the road and watch, you who l in Aroer. H3782
Jer 48:28 among the rocks, you who l in Moab. H3782
Jer 49: 1 Why do his people l in its towns? H3782
Jer 49: 8 deep caves, you who l in Dedan, for I will H3782
Jer 49:16 you who l in the clefts of the rocks H8905
Jer 49:18 "so no one will l there; no people H3782
Jer 49:20 purposed against those who l in Teman: H3782
Jer 49:30 deep caves, you who l in Hazor," declares H3782
Jer 49:31 bars; its people l far from danger. H8905
Jer 49:33 No one will l there; no people will dwell H3782
Jer 50: 3 No one will l in it; both people and H3782
Jer 50:21 of Merathaim and those who l in Pekod. H3782
Jer 50:34 unrest to those who l in Babylon. H3782
Jer 50:35 "against those who l in Babylon and H3782
Jer 50:39 desert creatures and hyenas will l there, H3782
Jer 50:40 "so no one will l there; no people H3782
Jer 51:13 You who l by many waters and are rich in H8905
Jer 51:24 Babylon and all who l in Babylonia for all H3782
Jer 51:29 of Babylon so that no one will l there. H3782
Jer 51:35 our blood be on those who l in Babylonia," H3782
Jer 51:62 neither people nor animals will l in it; H3782
La 4:20 under his shadow we would l among the H2649
La 4:21 you who l in the land of Uz. H3782
Eze 2: 6 around you and you l among scorpions. H3782
Eze 3:21 they will surely l because they took H2649+2649
Eze 5:11 Therefore as surely as I l, declares the H2644
Eze 6: 6 Wherever you l, the towns will be laid H4632
Eze 6:14 the desert to Diblah—wherever they l. H4632
Eze 7:13 as both buyer and seller l. H928+2021+2644
Eze 12:19 because of the violence of all who l there. H3782
Eze 13:19 have spared those who should not l. H2649
Eze 14:16 as surely as I l, declares the Sovereign H2644
Eze 14:18 as surely as I l, declares the Sovereign H2644
Eze 14:20 as surely as I l, declares the Sovereign H2644
Eze 16: 6 lay there in your blood I said to you, "L!" H2649
Eze 16:48 As surely as I l, declares the Sovereign H2644
Eze 17:16 " 'As surely as I l, declares the Sovereign H2644
Eze 17:19 As surely as I l, I will repay him for H2644
Eze 18: 3 "As surely as I l, declares the Sovereign H2644
Eze 18: 9 righteous; he will surely l, declares H2649+2649
Eze 18:13 Will such a man l? He will not! H2649
Eze 18:17 his father's sin; he will surely l. H2649+2649
Eze 18:19 all my decrees, he will surely l. H2649+2649
Eze 18:21 that person will surely l; they H2649+2649
Eze 18:22 things they have done, they will l. H2649
Eze 18:23 when they turn from their ways and l? H2649
Eze 18:24 things the wicked person does, will they l? H2649
Eze 18:28 that person will surely l; they H2649+2649
Eze 18:32 the Sovereign LORD. Repent and l! H2649
Eze 20: 3 As surely as I l, I will not let you inquire H2644
Eze 20:11 which the person who obeys them will l. H2649
Eze 20:13 which the person who obeys them will l— H2649
Eze 20:21 person who obeys them will l by them," H2649
Eze 20:25 laws through which they could not l; H2649
Eze 20:31 As surely as I l, declares the Sovereign H2644
Eze 20:33 As surely as I l, declares the Sovereign H2644
Eze 27:35 All who l in the coastlands are appalled H3782
Eze 28:25 Then they will l in their own land, which I H3782
Eze 28:26 They will l there in safety and will build H3782
Eze 28:26 they will l in safety when I inflict H3782
Eze 29: 6 Then all who l in Egypt will know that I H3782
Eze 29:11 no one will l there for forty years. H3782
Eze 32:15 when I strike down all who l there, then H3782
Eze 33:10 because of them. How then can we l?" H2649
Eze 33:11 Say to them, 'As surely as I l, declares the H2644
Eze 33:11 rather that they turn from their ways and l. H2649
Eze 33:12 not be allowed to l even though they H2649
Eze 33:13 person that they will surely l, H2649+2649
Eze 33:15 evil—that person will surely l; they H2649+2649
Eze 33:16 is just and right; they will surely l. H2649+2649
Eze 33:19 is just and right, they will l by doing so. H2649
Eze 33:27 As surely as I l, those who are left in the H2644
Eze 34: 8 As surely as I l, declares the Sovereign H2644
Eze 34:25 beasts so that they may l in the H3782
Eze 34:28 They will l in safety, and no one will H3782
Eze 35: 6 therefore as surely as I l, declares the H2644
Eze 35:11 therefore as surely as I l, declares the H2644
Eze 36:10 I will cause many people to l on you NDT
Eze 36:12 I will cause people, my people Israel, to l H2143
Eze 36:28 Then you will l in the land I gave your H3782
Eze 37: 3 "Son of man, can these bones l? H2649
Eze 37: 9 breathe into these slain, that they may l. H2649
Eze 37:14 I will put my Spirit in you and you will l H2649
Eze 37:25 They will l in the land I gave to my servant H3782
Eze 37:25 children's children will l there forever, H3782
Eze 38: 8 nations, and now all of them l in safety. H3782
Eze 39: 6 on those who l in safety in the H3782
Eze 39: 9 " 'Then those who l in the towns of Israel H3782
Eze 43: 7 This is where I will l among the Israelites H8905
Eze 43: 9 and I will l among them forever. H8905
Eze 44: 9 the foreigners who l among the Israelites. NDT
Eze 45: 5 as their possession for towns to l in. H3782
Eze 47: 9 of living creatures will l wherever the river H2649
Eze 47: 9 so where the river flows everything will l. H2644
Da 2: 4 the king, "May the king l forever! A10262
Da 2:11 and they do not l among humans." A10407
Da 2:38 Wherever they l, he has made you ruler A10163
Da 3: 9 "May the king l forever! A10262
Da 4: 1 of every language, who l in all the earth: A10163
Da 4:15 let him l with the animals among A10269
Da 4:23 heaven; let him l with the wild animals A10269
Da 4:25 from people and will l with the wild A10403
Da 4:32 from people and will l with the wild A10403
Da 5:10 "May the king l forever!" she A10262
Da 6: 6 "May King Darius l forever! A10262

L

Da 6:21 answered, "May the king l forever! A10262
Da 7:12 allowed to l for a period A10073+10089+10261
Hos 3: 3 told her, "You are to l with me many days H3782
Hos 3: 4 For the Israelites will l many days without H3782
Hos 4: 1 to bring against you who l in the land: H3782
Hos 4: 3 dries up, and all who l in it waste away H3782
Hos 6: 2 restore us, that we may l in his presence. H2649
Hos 10: 5 The people who l in Samaria fear for the H8907
Hos 12: 9 of Egypt; I will make you l in tents again H3782
Joel 1: 2 you elders; listen, all who l in the land. H3782
Joel 1:14 the elders and all who l in the land to the H3782
Joel 2: 1 Let all who l in the land tremble, for the H3782
Am 5: 4 the LORD says to Israel: "Seek me and l; H2649
Am 5: 6 Seek the LORD and l, or he will sweep H2649
Am 5:11 mansions, you will not l in them; though H3782
Am 5:14 not evil, that you may l. Then the LORD H2649
Am 8: 8 tremble for this, and all who l in it mourn? H3782
Am 9: 5 it melts, and all who l in it mourn; the H3782
Am 9:14 rebuild the ruined cities and l in them. H3782
Ob 3 you who l in the clefts of the rocks and H8905
Jnh 4: 3 for it is better for me to die than to l." H2644
Jnh 4: 8 "It would be better for me to die than to l." H2644
Mic 1: 2 earth and all who l in it, that the H4850
Mic 1:11 in shame, you who l in Shaphir. H3782
Mic 1:11 Those who l in Zaanan will not come out H3782
Mic 1:12 Those who l in Maroth writhe in pain H3782
Mic 1:13 You who l in Lachish, harness fast horses H3782
Mic 1:15 conqueror against you who l in Mareshah. H3782
Mic 5: 4 And they will l securely, for then his H3782
Na 1: 5 his presence, the world and all who l in it. H3782
Hab 2: 4 righteous person will l by his faithfulness H2649
Zep 1: 4 Judah and against all who l in Jerusalem. H3782
Zep 1:11 Wail, you who l in the market district; all H3782
Zep 1:13 houses, they will not l in them; though H3782
Zep 1:18 a sudden end of all who l on the earth. H3782
Zep 2: 5 Woe to you who l by the sea, you H3782
Zep 2: 9 Therefore, as surely as I l," declares the H2644
Zec 1: 5 And the prophets, do they l forever? H2649
Zec 2: 7 Escape, you who l in Daughter Babylon!" H3782
Zec 2:10 For I am coming, and I will l among you," H8905
Zec 2:11 I will l among you and you will know that H8905
Zec 8: 8 I will bring them back to l in Jerusalem H8905
Zec 10:12 LORD and in his name they will l securely," H2143
Zec 12: 8 LORD will shield those who l in Jerusalem, H3782
Mt 4: 4 'Man shall not l on bread alone, but on G2409
Mt 9:18 put your hand on her, and she will l." G2409
Mt 12:45 than itself, and they go in and l there. G2997
Mt 19:12 those who choose to l like eunuchs for the G2335
Mk 5:23 on her so that she will be healed and l." G2409
Mk 7: 5 don't your disciples l according to the G4344
Mk 12:44 put in everything—all she had to l on." G1050
Lk 4: 4 'Man shall not l on bread alone G2409
Lk 10:28 Jesus replied. "Do this and you will l." G2409
Lk 11:26 than itself, and they go in and l there. G2997
Lk 21: 4 of her poverty put in all she had to l on." G1050
Lk 21:35 come on all those who l on the face of G2764
Jn 4:50 replied, "your son will l." The man took G2409
Jn 4:53 Jesus had said to him, "Your son will l." G2409
Jn 5:25 the Son of God and those who hear will l. G2409
Jn 5:29 who have done what is good will rise to l, G2437
Jn 6:51 Whoever eats this bread will l forever G2409
Jn 6:57 Father sent me and I l because of the G2409
Jn 6:57 who feeds on me will l because of me. G2409
Jn 6:58 whoever feeds on this bread will l forever." G2409
Jn 7:35 where our people l scattered G3836+1402
Jn 11:25 The one who believes in me will l, even G2409
Jn 14:19 Because I l, you also will live. G2409
Jn 14:19 Because I live, you also will l. G2409
Ac 2:14 Jews and all of you who l in Jerusalem, G2997
Ac 7:48 the Most High does not l in houses made G2997
Ac 17:24 earth and does not l in temples built G2997
Ac 17:28 'For in him we l and move and have our G2409
Ac 21:21 all the Jews who l among the Gentiles to AIT
Ac 21:21 their children or l according to our G4344
Ac 22:22 "Rid the earth of him! He's not fit to l!" G2409
Ac 25:24 shouting that he ought not to l any longer. G2409
Ac 28: 4 goddess Justice has not allowed him to l." G2409
Ac 28:16 Paul was allowed to l by himself, with a G3531
Ro 1:17 "The righteous will l by faith." G2409
Ro 6: 2 died to sin; how can we l in it any longer? G2409
Ro 6: 4 of the Father, we too may l a new life. G4344
Ro 6: 8 we believe that we will also l with him. G5182
Ro 8: 4 who do not l according to the flesh but G4344
Ro 8: 5 Those who l according to the flesh have G1639
Ro 8: 5 those who l in accordance with the Spirit NDT
Ro 8:12 it is not to the flesh, to l according to it. G2409
Ro 8:13 For if you l according to the flesh, you will G2409
Ro 8:13 the misdeeds of the body, you will l. G2409
Ro 8:15 you slaves, so that you l in fear again; rather, AIT
Ro 10: 5 who does these things will l by them." G2409
Ro 12:16 L in harmony with one another G3836+899+5858
Ro 12:18 l at peace with everyone. G1644
Ro 14: 8 If we l, we live for the Lord; and if we die G2409
Ro 14: 8 If we live, we l for the Lord; and if we die G2409
Ro 14: 8 whether we l or die, we belong to the G2409
Ro 14:11 " 'As surely as I l,' says the Lord, 'every G2409
1Co 3: 1 you as people who l by the Spirit but as G4461
1Co 7:12 a believer and she is willing to l with him, G3861
1Co 7:13 a believer and he is willing to l with her, G3861
1Co 7:15 God has called us to l in peace. NDT
1Co 7:17 each person should l as a believer in G4344
1Co 7:29 who have wives should l as if they do not; G1639
1Co 7:35 that you may l in a right way in undivided AIT
1Co 8: 6 whom all things came and for whom we l; NDT
1Co 8: 6 all things came and through whom we l. NDT
2Co 5: 1 that if the earthly tent we l in is destroyed, G3864
2Co 5: 7 For we l by faith, not by sight. G4344
2Co 5:15 that those who l should no longer live G2409
2Co 5:15 those who live should no longer l for G2409
2Co 6: 9 and yet we l on; beaten, and yet G2409
2Co 6:16 "I will l with them and walk among them G1940
2Co 7: 3 our hearts that we would l or die with you. G5182
2Co 10: 2 people who think that we l by the G4344
2Co 10: 3 For though we l in the world, we do not G4344
2Co 13: 4 by God's power we will l with him in our G2409
2Co 13:11 one another, be of one mind, l in peace. G1644
Gal 1: 6 one who called you to l in the grace of Christ AIT
Gal 2:14 yet you l like a Gentile and not like a Jew. G2409
Gal 2:19 I died to the law so that I might l for God. G2409
Gal 2:20 crucified with Christ and I no longer l, G2409
Gal 2:20 The life I now l in the body, I live by faith G2409
Gal 2:20 in the body, I l by faith in the Son of God G2409
Gal 3:11 because "the righteous will l by faith." G2409
Gal 3:12 who does these things will l by them." G2409
Gal 5:21 that those who l like this will not inherit G4556
Gal 5:25 Since we l by the Spirit, let us keep in step G2409
Gal 6: 1 you who l by the Spirit should restore that G4461
Eph 2: 2 in which you used to l when you followed G4344
Eph 4: 1 I urge you to l a life worthy of the calling G4344
Eph 4:17 that you must no longer l as the Gentiles G4344
Eph 5: 8 are light in the Lord. L as children of light G4344
Eph 5:15 how you l—not as unwise but as G4344
Php 1:21 For to me, to l is Christ and to die is gain. G2409
Php 3:16 Only let us l up to what we have already G5123
Php 3:17 keep your eyes on those who l as we do. G4344
Php 3:18 many l as enemies of the cross of Christ. G4344
Col 1:10 so that you may l a life worthy of the Lord G4344
Col 2: 6 as Lord, continue to l your lives in him, G4344
1Th 2:12 urging you to l lives worthy of God, G4344
1Th 3: 8 For now we really l, since you are standing G2409
1Th 4: 1 instructed you how to l in order to please G4344
1Th 4: 7 not call us to be impure, but to l a holy life. NDT
1Th 5:10 asleep, we may l together with him. G2409
1Th 5:13 L in peace with each other. G1644
2Th 3: 6 disruptive and does not l according to the G4344
1Ti 2: 2 that we may l peaceful and quiet lives in G1341
2Ti 2:11 we died with him, we will also l with him; G5182
2Ti 3:12 who wants to l a godly life in Christ Jesus G2409
Titus 2: 3 women to be reverent in the way they l, G2949
Titus 2:12 to l self-controlled, upright and godly lives G2409
Titus 3:14 urgent needs and not l unproductive lives. G1639
Heb 10:38 "But my righteous one will l by faith. G2409
Heb 12: 9 we submit to the Father of spirits and l! G2409
Heb 12:14 Make every effort to l in peace with AIT
Heb 13:18 desire to l honorably in every G418
Jas 4:15 Lord's will, we will l and do this or that." G2409
1Pe 1:17 l out your time as foreigners here in G418
1Pe 2:12 L such good lives among the pagans that G2400
1Pe 2:16 L as free people, but do not use your NDT
1Pe 2:16 as a cover-up for evil; l as God's slaves. NDT
1Pe 2:24 might die to sins and l for righteousness; G2409
1Pe 3: 7 be considerate as you l with your wives, G5324
1Pe 4: 2 they do not l the rest of their earthly lives G1051
1Pe 4: 6 l according to God in regard to the G2409
2Pe 1:13 memory as long as I l in the tent of this G1639
2Pe 2:18 are just escaping from those who l in error. G418
2Pe 3:11 You ought to l holy and godly lives G419
1Jn 1: 6 we lie and do not l out the truth. G4472
1Jn 2: 6 Whoever claims to l in him must live as G3531
1Jn 2: 6 claims to live in him must l as Jesus did. G4344
1Jn 4: 9 the world that we might l through him. G2409
1Jn 4:13 how we know that we l in him and he in G3531
Rev 2:13 I know where you l—where Satan has his G2997
Rev 11:10 had tormented those who l on the earth. G2997
Rev 13: 6 place and those who l in heaven. G5012
Rev 14: 6 to proclaim to those who l on the earth— G2764

LIVED (243) [LIVE]

Ge 4:16 LORD's presence and l in the land of Nod, H3782
Ge 5: 3 When Adam had l 130 years, he had a H2649
Ge 5: 4 Adam l 800 years and had other H2118+3427
Ge 5: 5 Altogether, Adam l a total of 930 years H2649
Ge 5: 6 When Seth had l 105 years, he became H2649
Ge 5: 7 Seth l 807 years and had other sons and H2649
Ge 5: 8 Seth l a total of 912 years H2118+3427
Ge 5: 9 When Enosh had l 90 years, he became H2649
Ge 5:10 Enosh l 815 years and had other sons H2649
Ge 5:11 Enosh l a total of 905 years H2118+3427
Ge 5:12 When Kenan had l 70 years, he became H2649
Ge 5:13 Kenan l 840 years and had other sons H2649
Ge 5:14 Kenan l a total of 910 years H2118+3427
Ge 5:15 When Mahalalel had l 65 years, he H2649
Ge 5:16 Mahalalel l 830 years and had other sons H2649
Ge 5:17 Mahalalel l a total of 895 years H2118+3427
Ge 5:18 When Jared had l 162 years, he became H2649
Ge 5:19 Jared l 800 years and had other sons and H2649
Ge 5:20 Jared l a total of 962 years H2118+3427
Ge 5:21 When Enoch had l 65 years, he became H2649
Ge 5:23 Enoch l a total of 365 years. H2118+3427
Ge 5:25 When Methuselah had l 187 years, he H2649
Ge 5:26 Methuselah l 782 years and had other H2649
Ge 5:27 Methuselah l a total of 969 years H2118+3427
Ge 5:28 When Lamech had l 182 years, he had a H2649
Ge 5:30 Lamech l 595 years and had other sons H2649
Ge 5:31 Lamech l a total of 777 years H2118+3427
Ge 9:28 After the flood Noah l 350 years. H2649
Ge 9:29 Noah l a total of 950 years, and H2118+3427
Ge 10:30 The region where they l stretched from H4632
Ge 11:11 Shem l 500 years and had other sons H2649
Ge 11:12 When Arphaxad had l 35 years, he H2649
Ge 11:13 Arphaxad l 403 years and had other sons H2649
Ge 11:14 When Shelah had l 30 years, he became H2649
Ge 11:15 Shelah l 403 years and had other sons H2649
Ge 11:16 When Eber had l 34 years, he became H2649
Ge 11:17 Eber l 430 years and had other sons and H2649
Ge 11:18 When Peleg had l 30 years, he became H2649
Ge 11:19 Peleg l 209 years and had other sons H2649
Ge 11:20 When Reu had l 32 years, he became the H2649
Ge 11:21 Reu l 207 years and had other sons and H2649
Ge 11:22 When Serug had l 30 years, he became H2649
Ge 11:23 Serug l 200 years and had other sons H2649
Ge 11:24 When Nahor had l 29 years, he became H2649
Ge 11:25 Nahor l 119 years and had other sons H2649
Ge 11:26 After Terah had l 70 years, he became H2649
Ge 11:32 Terah l 205 years, and he died in H2118+3427
Ge 13:12 Abram l in the land of Canaan, while Lot H3782
Ge 13:12 while Lot l among the cities of the plain H3782
Ge 19:29 that overthrew the cities where Lot had l. H3782
Ge 19:30 He and his two daughters l in a cave. H3782
Ge 20: 1 of the Negev and l between Kadesh and H3782
Ge 21:20 He l in the desert and became an archer H3782
Ge 23: 1 Sarah l to be a hundred and twenty-seven H2644
Ge 25: 7 Abraham l a hundred and seventy-five H2649
Ge 25:11 son Isaac, who then l near Beer Lahai Roi. H3782
Ge 25:17 Ishmael l a hundred and thirty-seven years H2644
Ge 25:18 And they l in hostility toward H5877+6584+7156
Ge 35:28 Isaac l a hundred and eighty years. H2118+3427
Ge 37: 1 Jacob l in the land where his father had H3782
Ge 38:21 He asked the men who l there, "Where is the AIT
Ge 38:22 Besides, the men who l there said, 'There AIT
Ge 39: 2 and he l in the house of his Egyptian H2118
Ge 47:28 Jacob l in Egypt seventeen years, and the H2649
Ge 50:11 When the Canaanites who l there saw the H3782
Ge 50:22 He l a hundred and ten years H2649
Ex 6:16 Kohath and Merari. Levi l 137 years. H2644
Ex 6:18 Hebron and Uzziel. Kohath l 133 years. H2644
Ex 6:20 Aaron and Moses. Amram l 137 years. H2644
Ex 10:23 had light in the places where they l. H4632
Ex 12:40 the Israelite people l in Egypt was 430 H3782
Lev 18:27 by the people who l in the land before you NDT
Lev 26:35 not have during the sabbaths you l in it. H3782
Nu 13:22 Talmai, the descendants of Anak, l. NDT
Nu 14:45 the Canaanites who l in that hill country H3782
Nu 20:15 into Egypt, and we l there many years. H3782
Nu 21: 1 king of Arad, who l in the Negev, heard H3782
Nu 21: 9 looked at the bronze snake, they l. H2649
Nu 33:40 of Arad, who l in the Negev of Canaan H3782
Dt 1:44 The Amorites who l in those hills came H3782
Dt 2:22 of Esau, who l in Seir, when he H3782
Dt 2:22 them out and have l in their place to H3782
Dt 2:23 the Avvites who l in villages as far as H3782
Dt 4:25 and have l in the land a long time— H3823
Dt 4:33 speaking out of fire, as you have, and l? H2649
Dt 21:13 After she has l in your house and H3782
Dt 26: 5 a few people and l there and became a H1591
Dt 29:16 know how we l in Egypt and how H3782
Jos 2:15 the house she l in was part of the city H3782
Jos 8:26 until he had destroyed all who l in Ai. H3782
Jos 8:35 the foreigners who l among them. H2143
Jos 13:21 allied with Sihon—who l in that country. H3782
Jos 22:33 where the Reubenites and the Gadites l. H3782
Jos 24: 2 l beyond the Euphrates River and H3782
Jos 24: 7 Then you l in the wilderness for a long H3782
Jos 24: 8 of the Amorites who l east of the Jordan. H3782
Jos 24:18 including the Amorites, who l in the land. H3782
Jdg 1:30 so these Canaanites l among them, but H3782
Jdg 1:32 The Asherites l among the Canaanite H3782
Jdg 1:33 Naphtalites too l among the Canaanite H3782
Jdg 2:18 of their enemies as long as the judge l; H3427
Jdg 3: 5 The Israelites l among the Canaanites H3782
Jdg 8:31 His concubine, who l in Shechem, also bore NDT
Jdg 9:21 and he l there because he was afraid of H3782
Jdg 10: 1 He l in Shamir, in the hill country of H3782
Jdg 11:21 land of the Amorites who l in that country, H3782
Jdg 16:30 many more when he died than while he l. H2644
Jdg 17:12 man became his priest and l in his house. H2118
Jdg 18: 7 they l a long way from the Sidonians and NDT
Jdg 18:22 the men who l near Micah H928+2021+1074
Jdg 18:28 them because they l a long way from Sidon NDT
Jdg 19: 1 Now a Levite who l in a remote area in H1591
Ru 1: 2 And they went to Moab and l there. H2118
Ru 1: 4 After they had l there about ten years H3782
Ru 2:23 And she l with her mother-in-law H3782
1Sa 10:12 A man who l there answered, "And who H4946
1Sa 12:11 all around you, so that you l in safety. H3782
1Sa 23:29 up from there and l in the strongholds of H3782
1Sa 27: 7 David l in Philistine territory a year and H3782
1Sa 27: 8 these peoples had l in the land extending H3782
1Sa 27:11 practice as long as he l in Philistine H3782
2Sa 5: 6 to attack the Jebusites, who l there. H3782
2Sa 9:13 And Mephibosheth l in Jerusalem H3782
2Sa 13:20 And Tamar l in her brother Absalom's H3782
2Sa 14:28 Absalom l two years in Jerusalem without H3782
1Ki 4:25 Dan to Beersheba, l in safety, everyone H3782
1Ki 11:20 There Genubath l with Pharaoh's own H2118
1Ki 11:25 adversary as long as Solomon l, H3972+3427

1Ki 12:25 in the hill country of Ephraim and l there. H3782
1Ki 13:25 it in the city where the old prophet l. H3782
1Ki 14: 9 done more evil than all who l before you. H2118
1Ki 17:22 the boy's life returned to him, and *he* l. H2649
1Ki 21: 8 nobles who l in Naboth's city with H3782
1Ki 21:11 nobles who l in Naboth's city did H3782
2Ki 13: 5 So the Israelites l in their own homes as H3782
2Ki 14:17 of Joash king of Judah l for fifteen years H2649
2Ki 15: 5 he died, and *he* l in a separate house. H3782
2Ki 16: 6 into Elath and *have* l there to this day. H3782
2Ki 17:24 They took over Samaria and l in its towns H3782
2Ki 17:25 When they first l there, they did not H3782
2Ki 22:14 the wardrobe. She l in Jerusalem, in the H3782
2Ki 25:30 a regular allowance as long as he l. H2644
1Ch 2:55 the clans of scribes *who* l **at** Jabez H3782
1Ch 4:23 were the potters *who* l **at** Netaim and H3782
1Ch 4:28 *They* l in Beersheba, Moladah, Hazar H3782
1Ch 4:40 Some Hamites *had* l there formerly. H3782
1Ch 4:43 and *they have* l there to this day. H3782
1Ch 5:11 The Gadites l next to them in Bashan, as H3782
1Ch 5:16 The Gadites l in Gilead, in Bashan and its H3782
1Ch 7:29 of Joseph son of Israel l in these towns. H3782
1Ch 8:28 their genealogy, and they l in Jerusalem. H3782
1Ch 8:29 Jeiel the father of Gibeon l in Gibeon. H3782
1Ch 8:32 They too l near their relatives in H3782
1Ch 9: 3 *Those* from Judah, from Benjamin, and from Ephraim and Manasseh *who* l H3782
1Ch 9:16 who l in the villages of the Netophathites. H3782
1Ch 9:34 their genealogy, and they l in Jerusalem. H3782
1Ch 9:35 Jeiel the father of Gibeon l in Gibeon. H3782
1Ch 9:38 They too l near their relatives in H3782
1Ch 11: 4 that is, Jebus). The Jebusites *who* l there H3782
2Ch 11: 5 Rehoboam l in Jerusalem and built up H3782
2Ch 19: 4 Jehoshaphat l in Jerusalem, and he went H3782
2Ch 19: 8 settle disputes. And *they* l **in** Jerusalem. H3782
2Ch 20: 8 *They have* l in it and have built in it a H3782
2Ch 21:16 of the Arabs who l near the Cushites. NDT
2Ch 24:14 **As long as** Jehoiada l, burnt H3972+3427
2Ch 25:25 of Joash king of Judah l for fifteen years H2649
2Ch 26: 7 against the Arabs who l in Gur Baal and H3782
2Ch 26:21 *He* l **in** a separate house—leprous, and H3782
2Ch 31: 6 Israel and Judah who l in the towns of H3782
2Ch 31:19 who l on the farmlands around their towns NDT
2Ch 34:22 the wardrobe. She l in Jerusalem, in the H3782
2Ch 34:33 **As long as** he l, they did not fail to H3972+3427
Ne 4:12 Then the Jews who l near them came H3782
Ne 8:17 built temporary shelters and l in them. H3782
Ne 9:24 the Canaanites, *who* l **in** the land; you H3782
Ne 11: 3 Solomon's servants l in the towns of H3782
Ne 11: 4 both Judah and Benjamin l in Jerusalem): H3782
Ne 11: 6 of Perez who l in Jerusalem totaled 468 H3782
Ne 11:21 The temple servants l on the hill of Ophel, H3782
Ne 11:25 the people of Judah l in Kiriath Arba and H3782
Ne 11:31 of the Benjamites from Geba l in Mikmash, NDT
Ne 12:27 sought out from **where** they l and were H5226
Ne 13:16 People from Tyre *who* l in Jerusalem were H3782
Job 1: 1 the land of Uz *there* l a man whose name H2118
Job 18:19 his people, no survivor where once he l. H4472
Job 21:28 of the great, the tents where the wicked l? H5438
Job 38:21 You have l so many years! NDT
Job 42:16 After this, Job l a hundred and forty years H2649
Ps 3: 3 unfailing love and *have* l in reliance on H2143
Ps 107:34 of the wickedness of *those who* l there. H3782
Ps 120: 6 Too long *have* I l among those who hate H8905
Ecc 4:15 I saw that all who l and walked under the H2645
Ecc 9:15 Now *there* l in that city a man poor but H5162
Isa 13:20 never be inhabited or l **in** through all H8905
Jer 3: 1 But you *have* l *as a* **prostitute** with many AIT
Jer 35:10 *We have* l in tents and have fully obeyed H3782
Jer 42:18 poured out on *those who* l **in** Jerusalem, H3782
Jer 50:39 be inhabited or l **in** from generation to H8905
Jer 52:34 a regular allowance as long as he l, H2644
La 2:16 we have waited for; *we have* l to see it." H5162
Eze 3:15 to the exiles who l at Tel Aviv near the H3782
Eze 16:46 who l to the north of you with her H3782
Eze 16:46 who l to the south of you with her H3782
Eze 20: 9 among whom they l and in whose sight I NDT
Eze 26:17 you put your terror on all *who* l there. H3782
Eze 31: 6 all the great nations l in its shade. H3782
Eze 31:13 all the wild animals l among its branches. H2118
Eze 31:17 with the armed men *who* l in its shade H3782
Eze 37:25 the land where your ancestors l. H3782
Eze 39:26 toward me when they l in safety in their H3782
Da 4:12 the birds l in its branches; from A10163
Da 5:21 he l with the wild donkeys and ate grass A10403
Zep 2:15 This is the city of revelry that l in safety H3782
Mt 2:23 he went and l in a town called G2997
Mt 4:13 he went and l in Capernaum, which G2997
Mt 23:30 'If *we had* l in the days of our ancestors G1639
Mk 5: 3 This man l in the tombs, and G3836+2998+2400
Lk 1:80 and *he* l in the wilderness until he G1639
Lk 2:36 *she had* l with her husband seven years G2409
Lk 7:37 in that town who l a sinful life learned G1639
Lk 8:27 man had not worn clothes or l in a house, G3531
Lk 8:27 lived in a house, but had l in the tombs. NDT
Lk 16:19 fine linen and **l in luxury** every day. G2370+3289
Jn 7:42 from Bethlehem, the town where David l?" G1639
Jn 12: 1 where Lazarus l, whom Jesus had raised G1639
Ac 7: 2 in Mesopotamia, before he l in Harran. G2997
Ac 9:32 to visit the Lord's people who l in Lydda. G2997
Ac 9:35 All those *who* l in Lydda and Sharon saw G2997
Ac 16: 1 where a disciple named Timothy l, whose G1639
Ac 16: 3 because of the Jews who l in that area, G1639
Ac 17:21 the foreigners *who* l **there** spent their time G2111
Ac 19:10 Jews and Greeks who l **in** the province of G2997
Ac 20:18 "You know how *I* l the whole time I was G1181
Ac 26: 4 all know the **way** I *have* l ever since I was G1052
Eph 2: 3 All of us also l among them at one time G418
Col 3: 7 walk in these ways, in the life *you* once l. G2409
1Th 1: 5 You know how *we* l among you for your G1181
2Ti 1: 5 which first l **in** your grandmother Lois and G1940
Titus 3: 3 *We* l in malice and envy, being hated G1341
Heb 11: 9 a foreign country; *he* l **in** tents, as did G2997
Jas 5: 5 *You have* l on earth in **luxury** and G5587
1Pe 1:14 evil desires you had when you *l* **in** ignorance. AIT
Rev 13:14 who was wounded by the sword and yet l. G2409

LIVELIHOOD (2)

Dt 24: 6 would be taking a person's l as security. H5883
Zec 13: 5 the land has been my l since my youth. H7871

LIVELY (KJV) LIVING, MANY, VIGOROUS

LIVER (14)

Ex 29:13 the long lobe of the l, and both kidneys H3879
Ex 29:22 the long lobe of the l, both kidneys with H3879
Lev 3: 4 the long lobe of the l, which you will H3879
Lev 3:10 the long lobe of the l, which you will H3879
Lev 3:15 the long lobe of the l, which you will H3879
Lev 4: 9 the long lobe of the l, which he will H3879
Lev 7: 4 the long lobe of the l, which is to be H3879
Lev 8:16 the long lobe of the l, and both kidneys H3879
Lev 8:25 the long lobe of the l, both kidneys and H3879
Lev 9:10 the long lobe of the l from the sin offering H3879
Lev 9:19 the kidneys and the long lobe of the l— H3879
Job 20:25 his back, the gleaming point out of his l. H5355
Pr 7:23 till an arrow pierces his l, like a bird H3879
Eze 21:21 consult his idols, he will examine the l. H3879

LIVES (188) [LIVE]

Ge 9: 3 Everything that l and moves about will be H2645
Ge 19:17 one of them said, "Flee for your l! H5883
Ge 42:13 of one man, who l in the land of Canaan. NDT
Ge 42:15 **As surely as** Pharaoh l, you will not leave H2644
Ge 42:16 then **as surely as** Pharaoh l, you are H2644
Ge 45: 5 because it was to **save** l that God sent me H4695
Ge 45: 7 on earth and to **save** your l by a great H2649
Ge 47:25 "*You have* **saved** our l," they said. "May H2649
Ge 50:20 is now being done, the saving of many l. H6639
Ex 1:14 They made their l bitter with harsh labor in H2644
Ex 30:15 offering to the LORD to atone for your l. H5883
Ex 30:16 the LORD, making atonement for your l." H5883
Nu 16:38 the men who sinned at the cost of their l. H5883
Dt 22:19 not divorce her **as long as** he l. H3972+3427
Dt 22:29 never divorce her **as long as** he l. H3972+3427
Dt 33:20 Gad l there like a lion, tearing at arm H8905
Jos 2:13 that *you will* **spare** *the* l *of* my father and H2649
Jos 2:14 "Our l for your lives!" the men assured her. H5883
Jos 2:14 "Our lives for your l!" the men assured her NDT
Jos 6:25 and *she* l among the Israelites to this day. H3782
Jos 9:24 So we feared for our l because of you H5883
Jdg 5:18 The people of Zebulun risked their very l H5883
Jdg 8:19 **As surely as** the LORD l, if you had spared H2644
Jdg 8:19 if *you had* **spared** their l, I would not H2649
Jdg 18:25 you and your family will lose your l." H5883
Ru 3:13 **as surely as** the LORD l I will do it. H2644
1Sa 14:39 **As surely as** the LORD who rescues Israel l H2644
1Sa 14:45 **As surely as** the LORD l, not a hair of his H2644
1Sa 19: 6 "**As surely as** the LORD l, David will not be H2644
1Sa 20: 3 Yet **as surely as** the LORD l and as you live, H2644
1Sa 20:21 because, **as surely as** the LORD l, you are H2644
1Sa 20:31 As long as the son of Jesse l on this earth H2644
1Sa 25:26 **as surely as** the LORD your God l and as H2644
1Sa 25:29 the l *of* your enemies he will hurl H5883
1Sa 25:34 **as surely as** the LORD, the God of Israel, l H2644
1Sa 26:10 **As surely as** the LORD l," he said, "the H2644
1Sa 26:16 **As surely as** the LORD l, you and your men H2644
1Sa 28:10 the LORD, "**As surely as** the LORD l, you H2644
1Sa 29: 6 "**As surely as** the LORD l, you have H2644
2Sa 2:27 answered, "**As surely as** God l, if you had H2644
2Sa 4: 9 "**As surely as** the LORD l, who has H2644
2Sa 12: 5 Nathan, "**As surely as** the LORD l, the man H2644
2Sa 14:11 "**As surely as** the LORD l," he said, "not H2644
2Sa 15:21 "**As surely as** the LORD l, and as my H2644
2Sa 15:21 and **as** my lord the king l, wherever H2644
2Sa 19: 5 saved your life and the l *of* your sons and H5883
2Sa 19: 5 daughters and the l *of* your wives and H5883
2Sa 22:47 "The LORD l! Praise be to my Rock! H2644
2Sa 23:17 of men who went at the risk of their l?" H5883
1Ki 1:29 "**As surely as** the LORD l, who has H2644
1Ki 2:24 And now, **as surely as** the LORD l—he who H2644
1Ki 17: 1 "**As** the LORD, the God of Israel, l, whom H2644
1Ki 17:12 "**As surely as** the LORD your God l," she H2644
1Ki 18:10 **As surely as** the LORD your God l, there is H2644
1Ki 18:15 "**As** the LORD Almighty l, whom I H2644
1Ki 22:14 "**As surely as** the LORD l, I can tell H2644
2Ki 1:13 my life and the l *of* these fifty men, H5883
2Ki 2: 2 "**As surely as** the LORD l and as you live H2644
2Ki 2: 4 "**As surely as** the LORD l and as you live H2644
2Ki 2: 6 "**As surely as** the LORD l and as you live H2644
2Ki 3:14 "**As surely as** the LORD Almighty l, whom H2644
2Ki 4:30 "**As surely as** the LORD l and as you live H2644
2Ki 5:16 "**As surely as** the LORD l, whom I H2644
2Ki 5:20 **As surely as** the LORD l, I will run after H2644
2Ki 7: 7 left the camp as it was and ran for their l. H5883
1Ch 11:19 these men who went at the risk of their l?" H5883
1Ch 11:19 Because they risked their l to bring it back H5883
2Ch 18:13 "**As surely as** the LORD l, I can tell H2644
Est 4:11 gold scepter to them and **spares** *their* l. H2649
Job 15:28 ruined towns and houses where no *one* l, H3782
Job 19:25 I know that my redeemer l, and that in the H2645
Job 27: 2 "**As surely as** God l, who has denied me H2644
Job 33:18 their l from perishing by the sword. H2652
Job 38:26 to water a land where no one l, an NDT
Ps 18:46 The LORD l! Praise be to my Rock! H2644
Ps 66: 9 he has preserved our l and kept our feet H5883
Ps 74:19 do not forget the l *of* your afflicted people H2652
Ps 97:10 he guards the l *of* his faithful ones and H5883
Ps 107: 5 thirsty, and their l ebbed away. H5883
Ps 109:31 to save their l from those who would H5883
Pr 3:29 your neighbor, who l trustfully near you. H3782
Pr 11:30 and the one who is wise saves l. H5883
Pr 13: 3 who guard their lips preserve their l, H5883
Pr 14:25 A truthful witness saves l, but a false H5883
Pr 16:17 who guard their ways preserve their l. H5883
Pr 18: 7 their lips are a snare to their very l. H5883
Pr 20: 2 those who anger him forfeit their l. H5883
Pr 20: 7 The righteous **lead** blameless l; blessed H2143
Ecc 2: 3 the heavens during the few days of their l. H2644
Ecc 6: 3 no matter how long he l, if he H3427+9102
Ecc 6: 6 even if *he* l a thousand years twice over H2649
Isa 38:20 all the days of our l in the temple of the H2644
Isa 42:11 let the settlements where Kedar l rejoice. H3782
Isa 57:15 One says—*he who* l forever, whose H8905
Isa 65:20 there be in it an infant who l but a few days, NDT
Jer 2: 6 a land where no one travels and no one l? H3782
Jer 4: 2 '**As surely as** the LORD l,' then the H2644
Jer 4:29 the towns are deserted; no one l in them. H3782
Jer 5: 2 they say, '**As surely as** the LORD l,' still H2644
Jer 10:23 I know that people's l are not their own; H2006
Jer 12:16 '**As surely as** the LORD l'—even as H2644
Jer 16:14 be said, '**As surely as** the LORD l, who H2644
Jer 16:15 be said, '**As surely as** the LORD l, who H2644
Jer 17: 6 the desert, in a salt land where no *one* l. H3782
Jer 17:11 When their l are half gone, their riches H3427
Jer 21: 9 you will live; they will escape with their l. H5883
Jer 23: 7 '**As surely as** the LORD l, who brought H2644
Jer 23: 8 will say, '**As surely as** the LORD l, who H2644
Jer 38: 2 They will escape with their l; they will live. H5883
Jer 38:16 "**As surely as** the LORD l, who has given H2644
Jer 44:26 "**As surely as** the Sovereign LORD l." H2644
Jer 48: 6 Run for your l; become like a bush in the H5883
Jer 49:31 a nation at ease, *which* l in confidence," H3782
Jer 51: 6 Run for your l! Do not be destroyed H5883
Jer 51:37 horror and scorn, a place where no *one* l. H3782
Jer 51:43 a land where no one l, through which no H3782
Jer 51:45 Run for your l! Run from the fierce H5883
La 2:12 as their l ebb away in their mothers' arms. H5883
La 2:19 hands to him for the l *of* your children, H5883
La 5: 9 at the risk of our l because of the sword in H5883
Eze 13:18 Will you ensnare the l of my people but H5883
Eze 13:22 from their evil ways and so **save** their l, H2649
Eze 17:17 siege works erected to destroy many l. H5883
Da 3:28 to give up their l rather than serve or A10151
Da 4:34 honored and glorified *him who* l forever. A10261
Da 12: 7 I heard him swear by *him who* l forever, H2645
Hos 4:15 do not swear, '**As surely as** the LORD l!' H2644
Am 8:14 who say, '**As surely as** your god l, Dan,' H2644
Am 8:14 '**As surely as** the god of Beersheba l' H2644
Mic 7:14 inheritance, *which* l by itself **in** a forest, H8905
Hab 1:16 by his net he l in luxury and enjoys the H2750
Jn 3:21 But whoever l **by** the truth comes into the G4472
Jn 11:26 whoever l by believing in me will G2409
Jn 14:17 for *he* l with you and will be in you. G3531
Ac 10:32 of Simon the tanner, who l by the sea. NDT
Ac 15:26 have risked their l for the name of our G6034
Ac 27:10 to ship and cargo, and *to* our own l also." G6034
Ac 27:24 given you the l of all who sail with you NDT
Ro 6:10 but the life *he* l, he lives to God. G2409
Ro 6:10 but the life he lives, *he* l to God. G2409
Ro 7: 1 someone only as long as *that person* l? G2409
Ro 8: 9 if indeed the Spirit of God l in you. G3861
Ro 8:11 bodies because of his Spirit *who* l **in** you. G1940
Ro 14: 7 For none of us l for ourselves alone, and G2409
Ro 16: 4 They risked their l for me. Not only I but G5549
1Co 7:39 is bound to her husband as long as *he* l. G2409
2Co 13: 4 in weakness, yet *he* l by God's power. G2409
Gal 2:20 I no longer live, but Christ l in me. G2409
Eph 2:22 to become a **dwelling** *in which* God *l* by his AIT
Col 2: 6 as Lord, *continue to* **live** *your* l in him, G4344
Col 2: 9 the fullness of the Deity l in bodily form, G2997
1Th 2: 8 only the gospel of God but our l as well. G6034
1Th 2:12 urging you to **live** l worthy of God, G4344
1Ti 2: 2 peaceful and quiet l in all godliness and G1050
1Ti 5: 6 But the widow *who* l **for pleasure** is dead G5059
1Ti 5: 6 pleasure is dead *even while she* l. G2409
1Ti 6:16 is immortal and *who* l **in** unapproachable G3861
2Ti 1: 5 I am persuaded, now l in you also. NDT
2Ti 1:14 the help of the Holy Spirit who l **in** us. G1940
Titus 2:12 *to* **live** self-controlled, upright and godly l G2409
Titus 3:14 urgent needs and not **live** unproductive l. G1639
Heb 2:15 those who all their l were held in slavery G2409
Heb 5:13 Anyone who l **on** milk, being still an infant G3576
Heb 7:24 because Jesus l forever, he has a G3531
Heb 7:25 *because he* always l to intercede for them. G2409
Heb 13: 5 Keep your l free from the love of money G5573
1Pe 2:12 Live such good l among the pagans that G419

1Pe 3: 2 they see the purity and reverence *of* your **l**. *G419*
1Pe 4: 2 live the rest *of* their earthly **l** for evil *G5989*
2Pe 3:11 You ought to live holy and **godly** *l* AIT
1Jn 2:10 loves their brother and sister **l** in the light, *G3531*
1Jn 2:14 the word of God **l** in you, and you *G3531*
1Jn 2:17 whoever does the will of God **l** forever. *G3531*
1Jn 3: 6 No one who **l** in him keeps on sinning. *G3531*
1Jn 3:16 to lay down our **l** for our brothers and *G6034*
1Jn 3:24 one who keeps God's commands **l** in him, *G3531*
1Jn 3:24 And this is how we know that *he* **l** in us *G3531*
1Jn 4:12 God **l** in us and his love is made *G3531*
1Jn 4:15 God **l** in them and they in God. *G3531*
1Jn 4:16 Whoever **l** in love lives in God, and God *G3531*
1Jn 4:16 Whoever lives in love **l** in God, and God *G3531*
2Jn 2 which **l** in us and will be with us forever: *G3531*
Rev 2:13 put to death in your city—where Satan **l**. *G2997*
Rev 4: 9 on the throne and who **l** for ever and ever, *G2409*
Rev 4:10 worship him *who* **l** for ever and ever. *G2409*
Rev 10: 6 he swore by him *who* **l** for ever and ever *G2409*
Rev 12:11 did not love their **l** so much as to shrink *G6034*
Rev 15: 7 the wrath of God, who **l** for ever and ever. *G2409*

LIVESTOCK (87)

Ge 1:24 the **l**, the creatures that move along the H989
Ge 1:25 to their kinds, the **l** according to their kinds H989
Ge 1:26 over the **l** and all the wild animals H989
Ge 2:20 So the man gave names to all the **l**, the H989
Ge 3:14 are you above all **l** and all wild animals! H989
Ge 4:20 of those who live in tents and raise **l**. H5238
Ge 7:14 to its kind, all **l** according to their kinds H989
Ge 7:21 land perished—birds, **l**, wild animals, all H989
Ge 8: 1 wild animals and the **l** that were with him H989
Ge 9:10 the birds, the **l** and all the wild animals, all H989
Ge 13: 2 very wealthy in **l** and in silver and gold H5238
Ge 30:29 you and how your **l** has fared under my H5238
Ge 31: 9 away your father's **l** and has given them H5238
Ge 31:18 he drove all his **l** ahead of him, along H5238
Ge 33:17 himself and made shelters for his **l**. H5238
Ge 34: 5 his sons were in the fields with his **l**; so H5238
Ge 34:23 Won't their **l**, their property and all their H5238
Ge 36: 6 as well as his **l** and all his other animals H5238
Ge 36: 7 not support them both because of their **l**. H5238
Ge 46: 6 with them their **l** and the possessions H5238
Ge 46:32 *they* **tend l**, and they H408+5238+2118
Ge 46:34 servants *have* **tended l** from H408+5238+2118
Ge 47: 6 put them in charge of my own **l**. H5238
Ge 47:16 "Then bring your **l**," said Joseph. "I will H5238
Ge 47:16 "I will sell you food in exchange for your **l** H5238
Ge 47:17 So they brought their **l** to Joseph, and he H5238
Ge 47:17 year with food in exchange for all their **l**. H5238
Ge 47:18 is gone and our **l** belongs to you, H5238+989
Ex 9: 3 a terrible plague on your **l** in the field— H5238
Ex 9: 4 between the **l** *of* Israel and that of H5238
Ex 9: 6 All the **l** *of* the Egyptians died, but not H5238
Ex 9:19 now to bring your **l** and everything you H5238
Ex 9:20 to bring their slaves and their **l** inside. H5238
Ex 9:21 the LORD left their slaves and **l** in the field. H5238
Ex 10:26 Our **l** too must go with us; not a hoof is to H5238
Ex 12:29 the firstborn of all the **l** as well. H989
Ex 12:38 also large **droves of l**, both flocks and H5238
Ex 13:12 firstborn males of your **l** belong to the LORD. H989
Ex 17: 3 us and our children and **l** die of thirst?" H5238
Ex 22: 5 anyone grazes their **l** in a field or vineyard H1248
Ex 34:19 including all the firstborn males of your **l** H5238
Lev 25: 7 as well as for your **l** and the wild animals in H989
Nu 3:41 the **l** *of* the Levites in place of all the H989
Nu 3:41 of all the firstborn of the **l** *of* the Israelites. H989
Nu 3:45 the **l** *of* the Levites in place of their H989
Nu 3:45 livestock of the Levites in place of their **l**. H989
Nu 20: 4 that we and our **l** should die here? H1248
Nu 20: 8 community so they and their **l** can drink." H1248
Nu 20:11 and the community and their **l** drank. H1248
Nu 20:19 if we or our **l** drink any of your water H5238
Nu 32: 1 of Jazer and Gilead were suitable for **l**. H5238
Nu 32: 4 are suitable for **l**, and your servants have H5238
Nu 32: 4 livestock, and your servants have **l**. H5238
Nu 32:16 build pens here for our **l** and cities for our H5238
Dt 2:35 But the **l** and the plunder from the towns H989
Dt 3: 7 But all the **l** and the plunder from their H989
Dt 3:19 your children and your **l** (I know you have H5238
Dt 3:19 I know you have much **l**) may stay in the H5238
Dt 7:14 will any of your **l** be without young. H989
Dt 13:15 it completely, both its people and its **l**. H989
Dt 20:14 the **l** and everything else in the city H989
Dt 28: 4 of your land and the young of your **l**— H989
Dt 28:11 the young of your **l** and the crops of your H989
Dt 28:51 the young of your **l** and the crops of your H989
Dt 30: 9 the young of your **l** and the crops of your H989
Jos 1:14 children and your **l** may stay in the land H5238
Jos 8: 2 carry off their plunder and **l** for yourselves. H989
Jos 8:27 off for themselves the **l** and plunder of this H989
Jos 11:14 all the plunder and **l** of these cities, H989
Jos 21: 2 to live in, with pasturelands for our **l**." H989
Jos 22: 8 wealth—with large **herds of l**, with silver, H5238
Jdg 6: 5 came up with their **l** and their tents like H5238
Jdg 18:21 their **l** and their possessions in front of H5238
1Sa 23: 5 the Philistines and carried off their **l**. H5238
1Sa 30:20 his men drove them ahead of the other **l**, H5238
1Ch 5: 9 because their **l** had increased in Gilead. H5238
1Ch 5:21 They seized the **l** *of* the Hagrites—fifty H5238
1Ch 7:21 when they went down to seize their **l**." H5238
1Ch 28: 1 all the property and **l** belonging to the H5238
2Ch 26:10 because he had much **l** in the foothills H5238
Ezr 1: 4 with goods and **l**, and with freewill H989
Ezr 1: 6 with goods and **l**, and with valuable H989
Ps 78:48 to the hail, their **l** to bolts of lightning. H5238
Eze 38:12 the nations, rich in **l** and goods, living at H5238
Eze 38:13 to take away **l** and goods and to seize H5238
Hag 1:11 on people and **l**, and on all the labor H989
Jn 4:12 it himself, as did also his sons and his **l**? *G2576*

LIVING (304) [LIVE]

Ge 1:20 "Let the water teem with **l** creatures, and H2645
Ge 1:21 the sea and every **l** thing with which the H2645
Ge 1:24 the land produce **l** creatures according H2645
Ge 1:28 over every **l creature** that moves on H2651
Ge 2: 7 and the man became a **l** being. H2645
Ge 2:19 whatever the man called each **l** creature, H2645
Ge 3:20 she would become the mother of all the **l**. H2645
Ge 6:19 to bring into the ark two of all **l** creatures, H2644
Ge 7: 4 of the earth every **l creature** I have made." H3685
Ge 7:16 in were male and female of every **l thing**, H1414
Ge 7:21 Every **l thing** that moved on land perished H1414
Ge 7:23 Every **l thing** on the face of the earth was H3685
Ge 8:17 out every kind of **l** creature that is with H2651
Ge 8:21 never again will I destroy all **l creatures**, H2645
Ge 9:10 with every **l** creature that was with you H2651
Ge 9:10 ark with you—every **l creature** *on* earth. H2651
Ge 9:12 me and you and every **l** creature with you, H2651
Ge 9:15 me and you and all **l** creatures of every H2651
Ge 9:16 between God and all **l** creatures of every H2651
Ge 13: 7 Perizzites *were* also **l** in the land at H3782
Ge 14: 7 the Amorites who *were* **l** in Hazezon H3782
Ge 14:12 his possessions, since he *was* **l** in Sodom. H3782
Ge 14:13 Now Abram *was* **l** near the great trees of H8905
Ge 16: 3 So after Abram *had been* **l** in Canaan ten H3782
Ge 19:25 destroying all *those* **l in** the cities—and H3782
Ge 21:21 While *he was* **l** in the Desert of Paran, his H3782
Ge 24: 3 of the Canaanites, among whom I *am* **l**, H3782
Ge 24:62 Beer Lahai Roi, for he *was* **l** in the Negev. H3782
Ge 25: 6 But while he was still **l**, he gave gifts to H2645
Ge 27:46 "I'm disgusted with **l** because of these H2644
Ge 27:46 my **life will not be worth l**." H2644+4200+4537
Ge 34:30 Perizzites, the *people* **l in** this land. H3782
Ge 35:22 While Israel *was* **l** in that region, Reuben H8905
Ge 36:20 Seir the Horite, *who were* **l in** the region: H3782
Ge 43: 7 'Is your father still **l**?' he asked us. H2645
Ge 43:27 father you told me about? Is he still **l**?" H2645
Ge 45: 3 Is my father still **l**?" But his brothers were H2645
Ge 46:31 household, who were *l* **in** the land of Canaan AIT
Ex 3:22 neighbor and *any woman* **l** *in* her house H1591
Ex 23:12 the **foreigner l among** you may be H1731
Lev 11: 9 " 'Of all the creatures **l** in the water of the NDT
Lev 11:10 among all the other **l** creatures in the H2651
Lev 11:12 Anything **l** in the water that does not have NDT
Lev 11:46 every **l** thing that moves about in the H2651
Lev 11:47 between **l creatures** that may be eaten H2651
Lev 18:18 relations with her while your wife is **l**. H2644
Lev 25:45 temporary residents **l** among you and H1591
Nu 13:32 land we explored devours *those* **l in** it. H3782
Nu 14:25 the Canaanites *are* **l** in the valleys, H3782
Nu 15:14 anyone else **l** among you presents a H1591
Nu 16:22 the God who gives breath to all **l things** H1414
Nu 16:48 He stood between the **l** and the dead, and H2645
Nu 27:16 *May* the LORD, the God who gives breath to all **l things** H1414
Nu 30: 3 a young woman still **l** in her father's NDT
Nu 30:10 "If a woman **l with** her husband makes a H1074
Nu 30:16 his young daughter still **l** at home. NDT
Dt 5:26 the voice of the **l** God speaking out of H2645
Dt 11: 6 tents and every **l thing** that belonged to H3685
Dt 11:30 of those Canaanites **l** in the Arabah in the H3782
Dt 11:31 you have taken it over and *are* **l** there, H3782
Dt 14: 9 Of all the creatures **l** in the water, you may NDT
Dt 14:27 do not neglect the Levites **l** in your towns, NDT
Dt 16:11 the fatherless and the widows **l** among you. NDT
Dt 17: 2 If a man or woman **l** among you in one of NDT
Dt 18: 6 towns anywhere in Israel where he *is* **l**, H1591
Dt 25: 5 If brothers *are* **l** together and one of them H3782
Dt 29:11 the foreigners **l** in your camps who chop NDT
Jos 3:10 will know that the **l** God is among you H2645
Jos 6:21 with the sword every **l thing** in it— H889S
Jos 8:33 Both the **foreigners l among** them and the H1731
Jos 9:11 elders and all *those* **l in** our country said H3782
Jos 9:16 that they were neighbors, **l** near them. H3782
Jos 11:19 Except for the Hivites **l in** Gibeon, not one H3782
Jos 15:15 marched against the *people* **l in** Debir H3782
Jos 15:63 the Jebusites, *who were* **l in** Jerusalem; to H3782
Jos 16:10 not dislodge the Canaanites **l** in Gezer; H3782
Jos 17: 7 to include the *people* **l at** En Tappuah. H3782
Jos 24:15 of the Amorites, in whose land you *are* **l**. H3782
Jdg 1: 9 the Canaanites **l in** the hill country, H3782
Jdg 1:10 against the Canaanites **l** in Hebron H3782
Jdg 1:11 advanced against the *people* **l in** Debir H3782
Jdg 1:17 attacked the Canaanites **l in** Zephath, H3782
Jdg 1:21 the Jebusites, *who were* **l in** Jerusalem; to H3782
Jdg 1:29 drive out the Canaanites **l** in Gezer, H3782
Jdg 1:30 out the Canaanites **l in** Kitron or Nahalol, H3782
Jdg 1:31 Asher drive out *those* **l in** Akko or Sidon H3782
Jdg 1:33 drive out *those* **l in** Beth Shemesh or H3782
Jdg 1:33 and *those* **l** in Beth Shemesh and Beth H3782
Jdg 3: 3 the Hivites **l in** the Lebanon H3782
Jdg 6: 4 did not spare a **l thing** for Israel, H4695
Jdg 17: 7 who *had been* **l** within the clan of Judah H1591
Jdg 18: 7 they saw that the people *were* **l** in safety, H3782
Jdg 19:16 of Ephraim, who *was* **l** in Gibeah (the H1591
Jdg 20:15 able young men from *those* **l in** Gibeah. H3782
Jdg 21:10 Gilead and put to the sword *those* **l** there, H3782
Jdg 21:12 among the *people* **l in** Jabesh Gilead H3782
Ru 1: 7 place where *she had been* **l** and set out H2118
Ru 2:20 his kindness to the **l** and the dead." H2645
Ru 4:17 The *women* **l** there said, "Naomi has a H8907
1Sa 17:26 he should defy the armies of the **l** God?" H2645
1Sa 17:36 he has defied the armies of the **l** God. H2645
1Sa 25:29 the bundle of the **l** by the LORD your God H2645
2Sa 7: 2 "Here I am, **l** in a house of cedar, while H3782
2Sa 12:18 "While the child was still **l**, he wouldn't H2645
2Sa 15: 8 While your servant *was* **l** at Geshur in H3782
2Sa 20: 3 till the day of their death, **l** *as* widows. H2654
1Ki 3:22 The **l** *one* is my son; the dead one is H2645
1Ki 3:22 the dead one is yours; the **l** *one* is mine." And so H2645
1Ki 3:25 "Cut the **l** child in two and give half to H2645
1Ki 3:26 "Please, my lord, give her the **l** baby! H2645
1Ki 3:27 "Give the **l** baby to the first woman H2645
1Ki 12:17 the Israelites who *were* **l** in the towns of H3782
1Ki 13:11 Now *there was* a certain old prophet **l** in H3782
2Ki 19: 4 has sent to ridicule the **l** God, and that he H2645
2Ki 19:16 has sent to ridicule the **l** God. H2645
1Ch 8: 6 of families of *those* **l in** Geba and were H3782
1Ch 8:13 of families of *those* **l in** Aijalon and who H3782
1Ch 12:15 they put to flight **everyone** *l* in the valleys, AIT
1Ch 17: 1 "Here I am, **l** in a house of cedar, while H3782
2Ch 10:17 the Israelites who *were* **l** in the towns of H3782
2Ch 31: 4 ordered the people **l in** Jerusalem to give H3782
Ezr 1: 4 any locality where survivors *may now be* **l**, H1591
Ezr 4:17 of their associates **l** in Samaria and A10338
Ne 3:26 the temple servants **l** on the hill of Ophel H3782
Ne 3:30 made repairs opposite his **l quarters**. H5969
Ne 11:30 So *they were* **l** all the way from Beersheba H2837
Est 9:19 rural Jews—those **l** in villages—observe H3782
Job 22: 8 owning land—an honored man, **l** on it. H3782
Job 28:13 it cannot be found in the land of the **l**. H2645
Job 28:21 It is hidden from the eyes of every **l thing** H2645
Job 30:23 to the place appointed for all the **l**. H2645
Ps 27:13 goodness of the LORD in the land of the **l**. H2645
Ps 42: 2 God, for the **l** God. When can I go and H2645
Ps 52: 5 he will uproot you from the land of the **l**. H2645
Ps 84: 2 heart and my flesh cry out for the **l** God. H2645
Ps 104:25 number—**l things** both large and small. H2651
Ps 116: 9 walk before the LORD in the land of the **l**. H2645
Ps 119: 9 of purity? *By* **l** according to your word. H9068
Ps 142: 5 my refuge, my portion in the land of the **l**." H2645
Ps 143: 2 no one **l** is righteous before you. H2645
Ps 145:16 satisfy the desires of every **l** *thing*. H2645
Ecc 4: 2 are happier than the **l**, who are still alive. H2645
Ecc 7: 2 everyone; the **l** should take this to heart. H2645
Ecc 7:15 the wicked **l long** in their wickedness. H799
Ecc 9: 4 Anyone who is among the **l** has hope H2645
Ecc 9: 5 For the **l** know that they will die, but the H2645
Isa 4: 3 are recorded among the **l** in Jerusalem. H2645
Isa 8:19 Why consult the dead on behalf of the **l**? H2645
Isa 9: 2 on *those* **l** in the land of deep darkness a H3782
Isa 33:24 No **one l in** Zion will say, "I am ill"; and H8907
Isa 37: 4 has sent to ridicule the **l** God, and that he H2645
Isa 37:17 has sent to ridicule the **l** God. H2645
Isa 38:11 see the LORD himself in the land of the **l**; H2645
Isa 38:19 The **l**, the living—they praise you, as I am H2645
Isa 38:19 The living, the **l**—they praise you, as I am H2645
Isa 53: 8 For he was cut off from the land of the **l** H2645
Jer 2:13 the spring of **l** water, and have dug H2645
Jer 10:10 true God; he is the **l** God, the eternal King H2645
Jer 11:19 let us cut him off from the land of the **l** H2645
Jer 13:13 the prophets and all *those* **l in** Jerusalem. H3782
Jer 17:13 forsaken the LORD, the spring of **l** water. H2645
Jer 17:20 Judah and everyone **l in** Jerusalem who H3782
Jer 17:25 men of Judah and *those* **l in** Jerusalem, H3782
Jer 18:11 of Judah and *those* **l in** Jerusalem, H3782
Jer 23:36 So you distort the words of the **l** God, the H2645
Jer 25: 2 of Judah and to all *those* **l in** Jerusalem: H3782
Jer 32:32 of Judah and *those* **l** *in* Jerusalem. H3782
Jer 35:13 of Judah and *those* **l** in Jerusalem, H3782
Jer 35:17 on everyone **l in** Jerusalem every H3782
Jer 36:31 on them and *those* **l in** Jerusalem and the H3782
Jer 44: 1 concerning all the Jews **l** in Lower Egypt— H3782
Jer 44:15 all the people **l** in Lower and Upper H3782
Jer 44:26 word of the LORD, all you Jews **l** in Egypt: H3782
Jer 44:26 no one from Judah **l** anywhere in Egypt will NDT
La 3:39 Why should the **l** complain when H2645+132
Eze 1: 5 fire was what looked like four **l creatures**. H2651
Eze 1:13 of the **l creatures** was like burning H2651
Eze 1:15 As I looked at the **l creatures**, I saw a H2651
Eze 1:19 When the **l creatures** moved, the wheels H2651
Eze 1:19 when the **l creatures** rose from the H2651
Eze 1:20 the spirit of the **l creatures** was in the H2651
Eze 1:21 the spirit of the **l creatures** was in the H2651
Eze 1:22 heads of the **l creatures** was what looked H2651
Eze 3:13 the wings of the **l creatures** brushing H2651
Eze 3:15 where they *were* **l**, I sat among H3782
Eze 10:15 These were the **l creatures** I had seen by H2651
Eze 10:17 the spirit of the **l creatures** was in them. H2651
Eze 10:20 These were the **l creatures** I had seen H2651
Eze 12: 2 you *are* **l** among a rebellious people. H3782
Eze 12:19 LORD says about *those* **l in** Jerusalem and H3782
Eze 15: 6 so will I treat the *people* **l in** Jerusalem. H3782
Eze 20:38 them out of the land where they are **l**, H4472
Eze 26:20 take your place in the land of the **l**. H2645

Eze 32:23 spread terror in the land of the **l** are slain, H2645
Eze 32:24 in the land of the **l** went down H2645
Eze 32:25 their terror had spread in the land of the **l**, H2645
Eze 32:26 spread their terror in the land of the **l**. H2645
Eze 32:27 also had terrorized the land of the **l**. H2645
Eze 32:32 had him spread terror in the land of the **l**, H2645
Eze 33:24 the *people* **l in** those ruins in the land of H3782
Eze 36:11 the number of people and animals **l** on you, NDT
Eze 36:17 *when* the people of Israel *were* **l** in their H3782
Eze 38:11 all of them **l** without walls and without H3782
Eze 38:12 goods, **l** at the center of the land. H3782
Eze 38:14 when my people Israel *are* **l** in safety, will H3782
Eze 47: 9 Swarms of **l** creatures will live wherever H2651
Da 4:17 so that the **l** may know that the Most A10261
Da 6:20 servant of the **l** God, has your God, A10261
Da 6:26 "For he is the **l** God and he endures A10261
Hos 1:10 they will be called 'children of the **l** God. H2645
Am 3:12 will the Israelites **l** in Samaria be rescued, H3782
Hag 1: 4 you yourselves to *be* **l** in your paneled H3782
Zec 14: 8 On that day **l** water will flow out from H2645
Mt 4:16 the people **l** in darkness have seen a *G2764*
Mt 4:16 on those **l** in the land of the shadow of *G2764*
Mt 16:16 are the Messiah, the Son of the **l** God." *G2409*
Mt 22:32 He is not the God of the dead but *of* the **l**." *G2409*
Mt 26:63 "I charge you under oath by the **l** God: *G2409*
Mk 12:27 of the dead, but *of* the **l**. You are badly *G2409*
Lk 1:79 to shine on those **l** in darkness and in the *G2764*
Lk 2: 8 there were shepherds **l out** in the fields *G64*
Lk 13: 4 guilty than all the others **l** in Jerusalem? *G2997*
Lk 15:13 there squandered his wealth *in* wild **l**. *G2409*
Lk 20:38 of the dead, but *of* the **l**, for to him all are *G2409*
Lk 24: 5 do you look for the **l** among the dead? *G2409*
Jn 4:10 him and he would have given you **l** water." *G2409*
Jn 4:11 Where can you get this **l** water? *G2409*
Jn 4:51 met him with the news that his boy *was* **l**. *G2409*
Jn 6:51 I am the **l** bread that came down from *G2409*
Jn 6:57 Just as the **l** Father sent me and I live *G2409*
Jn 7:38 rivers of **l** water will flow from within them *G2409*
Jn 14:10 it is the Father, **l** in me, who is doing his *G3531*
Ac 1:21 Lord Jesus *was* **l** among us, *G1656+2779+2002*
Ac 4:16 "Everyone **l** in Jerusalem knows they have *G2997*
Ac 7: 4 sent him to this land where you *are* now **l**. *G2997*
Ac 7:38 he received **l** words to pass on to us. *G2409*
Ac 9:22 baffled the Jews **l** in Damascus by *G2997*
Ac 9:31 **L** in the fear of the Lord and encouraged *G4513*
Ac 10:42 appointed as judge *of* the **l** and the dead. *G2409*
Ac 11:29 the brothers and sisters **l** in Judea. *G2997*
Ac 14:15 from these worthless things to the **l** God, *G2409*
Ac 19:17 to the Jews and Greeks **l in** Ephesus, *G2997*
Ac 21:24 but *that you* yourself *are* **l** in obedience to *G5123*
Ac 22:12 highly respected by all the Jews **l** there. *G2997*
Ac 26: 5 *I* conformed to the strictest sect of our religion, **l** *G2409*
Ro 7:17 I myself who do it, but it is sin **l** in me. *G3861*
Ro 7:20 who do it, but it is sin **l** in me that does it. *G3861*
Ro 8:11 raised Jesus from the dead *is* **l** in you, *G3861*
Ro 9:26 they will be called 'children of the **l** God. *G2409*
Ro 12: 1 to offer your bodies as a **l** sacrifice, holy *G2409*
Ro 14: 9 be the Lord of both the dead and the **l**. *G2409*
1Co 9: 6 who lack the right *to* not **work for a l**? *G2237*
1Co 9:14 *that* those who preach the gospel *should* **receive** *their* **l** *G2409*
1Co 15: 6 most of whom *are* still **l**, though some *G3531*
1Co 15:45 "The first man Adam became a **l** being"; *G2409*
2Co 3: 3 with ink but with the Spirit of the **l** God, *G2409*
2Co 6:16 For we are the temple of the **l** God. *G2409*
Php 1:22 If I am *to go on* **l** in the body, this will *G2409*
Php 4:12 hungry, whether **l in plenty** or in want. *G4355*
1Th 1: 9 from idols to serve the **l** and true God, *G2409*
1Th 4: 1 order to please God, as in fact *you are* **l**. *G4344*
1Ti 3:15 which is the church of the **l** God, the pillar *G2409*
1Ti 4:10 we have put our hope in the **l** God, *G2409*
2Ti 4: 1 who will judge the **l** and the dead, and in *G2409*
Heb 3:12 heart that turns away from the **l** God. *G2409*
Heb 7: 8 by him who is declared to *be* **l**. *G2409*
Heb 9:14 to death, so that we may serve the **l** God! *G2409*
Heb 9:17 effect while the one who made it *is* **l**. *G2409*
Heb 10:20 by a new and **l** way opened for us through *G2409*
Heb 10:31 thing to fall into the hands of the **l** God. *G2409*
Heb 11:13 people were still *l* **by** faith when they died. AIT
Heb 11:38 **l** in caves and in holes in the ground. NDT
Heb 12:22 to the city of the **l** God, the heavenly *G2409*
1Pe 1: 3 us new birth into a **l** hope through the *G2409*
1Pe 1:23 through the **l** and enduring word of God. *G2409*
1Pe 2: 4 you come to him, the **l** Stone—rejected by *G2409*
1Pe 2: 5 you also, like **l** stones, are being built into *G2409*
1Pe 4: 3 choose to do—**l** in debauchery, lust *G4513*
1Pe 4: 4 in their reckless, **wild l**, and they heap *G861*
1Pe 4: 5 who is ready to judge the **l** and the dead. *G2409*
2Pe 2: 8 man, **l among** them day after day *G1594*
Rev 1:18 I am the **L** *One*; I was dead, and now look *G2409*
Rev 4: 6 were four **l creatures**, and they were *G2442*
Rev 4: 7 The first **l creature** was like a lion, the *G2442*
Rev 4: 8 Each of the four **l creatures** had six wings *G2442*
Rev 4: 9 Whenever the **l creatures** give glory *G2442*
Rev 5: 6 by the four **l creatures** and the elders. *G2442*
Rev 5: 8 the four **l creatures** and the twenty-four *G2442*
Rev 5:11 throne and the **l creatures** and the elders. *G2442*
Rev 5:14 The four **l creatures** said, "Amen," and *G2442*
Rev 6: 1 one of the four **l creatures** say in a voice *G2442*
Rev 6: 3 I heard the second **l creature** say, "Come!" *G2442*
Rev 6: 5 I heard the third **l creature** say, "Come!" *G2442*
Rev 6: 6 like a voice among the four **l creatures**, *G2442*
Rev 6: 7 the voice *of* the fourth **l creature** say, *G2442*
Rev 7: 2 the east, having the seal of the **l** God. *G2409*
Rev 7:11 around the elders and the four **l creatures**. *G2442*
Rev 7:17 'he will lead them to springs of **l** water. *G2437*
Rev 8: 9 a third of the **l** creatures in the sea *G2400+6034*
Rev 14: 3 before the four **l creatures** and the elders. *G2442*
Rev 15: 7 one of the four **l creatures** gave to the *G2442*
Rev 16: 3 and every **l thing** in the sea died. *G6034+2437*
Rev 18:17 all *who* **earn** *their* **l** from the sea *G2237*
Rev 19: 4 the four **l creatures** fell down and *G2442*

LIZARD (4)

Lev 11:29 the weasel, the rat, any kind of **great l**, H7370
Lev 11:30 the gecko, the **monitor l**, the wall lizard H3947
Lev 11:30 the **wall l**, the skink and the H4321
Pr 30:28 a **l** can be caught with the hand, yet it is H8532

LO DEBAR (4)

2Sa 9: 4 house of Makir son of Ammiel in **L**." H4274
2Sa 9: 5 David had him brought from **L**, H4274
2Sa 17:27 Makir son of Ammiel from **L** H4203
Am 6:13 in the conquest of **L** and say, H4203

LO-AMMI (1)

Hos 1: 9 him **L** (*which means "not my people"*) H4204

LO-RUHAMAH (2)

Hos 1: 6 "Call her **L** (*which means "not loved"*) H4205
Hos 1: 8 After she had weaned **L**, Gomer had H4205

LOAD (12) [CAMEL-LOADS, LADEN, LOADED, LOADING, LOADS, SPICE-LADEN]

Ge 45:17 **L** your animals and return to the land of H3250
Ex 18:22 That will make your **l** lighter, because H6584
Ex 23: 5 who hates you fallen down under its **l**, H5362
Ne 13:19 the gates so that no **l** could be brought in H5362
Job 35: 9 "People cry out under a **l** *of* oppression H8044
Isa 22:25 the **l** hanging on it will be cut down." H5362
Jer 17:21 not to carry a **l** on the Sabbath day or H5362
Jer 17:22 Do not bring a **l** out of your houses or do H5362
Jer 17:24 bring no **l** through the gates of this H5362
Jer 17:27 by not carrying any **l** as you come through H5362
Lk 11:46 because *you* **l** people **down** with burdens *G5844*
Gal 6: 5 each one should carry their own **l**. *G5845*

LOADED (14) [LOAD]

Ge 22: 3 Abraham got up and **l** his donkey. H2502
Ge 24:10 master's camels **l with** all kinds of good H2256
Ge 37:25 Their camels *were* **l** *with* spices, balm H5951
Ge 42:26 *they* **l** their grain on their donkeys and left. H5951
Ge 44:13 Then *they* all **l** their donkeys and returned H6673
Ge 45:23 ten donkeys **l** with the best things of Egypt H5951
Ge 45:23 female donkeys **l** *with* grain and bread H5951
Jos 9: 4 whose donkeys *were* **l** *with* worn-out sacks H4374
1Sa 16:20 So Jesse took a **donkey** *l with* bread, a skin AIT
1Sa 17:20 care of a shepherd, **l up** and set out, as H5951
1Sa 25:18 of pressed figs, and **l** them on donkeys. H8492
2Sa 16: 1 saddled and **l with** two hundred loaves H6584
Am 2:13 you as a cart crushes when **l** *with* grain. H4849
2Ti 3: 6 *who are* **l down with** sins and are swayed *G5397*

LOADING (1) [LOAD]

Ne 13:15 bringing in grain and **l** it on donkeys, H6673

LOADS (5) [LOAD]

Ne 13:15 grapes, figs and all other kinds of **l**. H5362
Job 37:11 *He* **l** the clouds with moisture; he scatters H3267
Ps 144:14 our oxen *will* **draw heavy l**. There will be H6022
La 5:13 millstones; boys stagger under **l of wood**. H6770
Mt 23: 4 cumbersome **l** and put them on other *G5845*

LOAF (22) [LOAVES]

Ex 29:23 take one round **l**, one thick loaf with H4312
Ex 29:23 one **thick l** *with* olive oil *mixed in* H2705+4312
Ex 29:23 with olive oil mixed in, and one **thin l**. H8386
Lev 8:26 he took one **thick l**, one thick loaf H2705
Lev 8:26 one **thick l** *with* olive oil *mixed in*, and H2705
Lev 8:26 mixed in, and one **thin l**, and he put H8386
Lev 24: 5 using two-tenths of an ephah for each **l**. H2705
Nu 6:19 one **thick l** and one thin loaf from the H2705
Nu 6:19 thick loaf and one **thin l** from the basket, H8386
Nu 15:20 Present a **l** from the first of your ground H2705
Jdg 7:13 "A **round l** *of* barley bread came tumbling H7501
1Sa 2:36 piece of silver and a **l** *of* bread and plead, H3971
2Sa 6:19 Then he gave a **l** *of* bread, a cake of dates H2705
1Ki 17:13 make a small **l of bread** for me from what H6314
1Ch 16: 3 Then he gave a **l** *of* bread, a cake of dates H3971
Pr 6:26 a prostitute can be had for a **l** *of* bread, H3971
Jer 37:21 the guard and given a **l** *of* bread from the H3971
Eze 4:12 the food as you would a **l of barley bread**; H6314
Hos 7: 8 Ephraim is a **flat l** not turned over. H6314
Mk 8:14 except for one **l** they had with them in the *G788*
1Co 10:17 Because there is one **l**, we, who are many *G788*
1Co 10:17 are one body, for we all share the one **l**. *G788*

LOAN (6)

Dt 15: 2 cancel *any* **l** *they have* **made** to a fellow H5957
Dt 24:10 When *you* **make a l** of any kind to H5957+5394
Dt 24:11 to whom you *are* **making** *the* **l** bring the H5957
Eze 18: 7 returns what he took in pledge for a **l**. H2550
Eze 18:16 anyone or **require a pledge for a l**. H2471+2478
Eze 33:15 back **what** they **took in pledge for a l**, H2478

LOATHE (5) [LOATHED, LOATHES, LOATHING, LOATHSOME]

Nu 11:20 it comes out of your nostrils and you **l** it— H2426
Job 10: 1 "I **l** my very life; therefore I will give free H7752
Eze 6: 9 *They will* **l** themselves for the evil they H7752
Eze 20:43 and *you will* **l** yourselves for all the evil H7752
Eze 36:31 and *you will* **l** yourselves for your sins and H7752

LOATHED (1) [LOATHE]

Ps 107:18 They **l** all food and drew near the gates of H9493

LOATHES (2) [LOATHE]

Job 33:20 repulsive and their soul **l** the choicest meal. NDT
Pr 27: 7 One who is full **l** honey from the comb H1008

LOATHING (1) [LOATHE]

Ps 119:158 I look on the faithless *with* **l**, for they do H7752

LOATHSOME (3) [LOATHE]

Job 19:17 to my wife; *I am* **l** to my own family. H2859
Ps 38: 5 My wounds fester and *are* **l** because of my H944
Isa 66:24 they will be **l** to all mankind. H1994

LOAVES (46) [LOAF]

Ex 12:39 they baked **l** *of* unleavened bread. H6314
Ex 29: 2 wheat flour make **round l** without yeast, H4312
Ex 29: 2 **thick l** without yeast and with olive oil H2705
Ex 29: 2 and **thin l** without yeast and brushed with H8386
Lev 2: 4 either **thick l** *made* without yeast and with H2705
Lev 2: 4 oil mixed in or **thin l** *made* without yeast H8386
Lev 7:12 they are to offer **thick l** made without H2705
Lev 7:12 **thin l** made without yeast and brushed H8386
Lev 7:12 and **thick l** *of* the finest flour H2705
Lev 7:13 offering with **thick l** *of* bread made with H2705
Lev 23:17 bring two **l** made of two-tenths of an H4312
Lev 24: 5 finest flour and bake twelve **l of bread**, H2705
Nu 6:15 yeast—**thick l** with olive oil mixed in H2705
Nu 6:15 and **thin l** brushed with olive oil. H8386
Nu 11: 8 They cooked it in a pot or made it into **l** H6314
1Sa 10: 3 another three **l** *of* bread, and another H3971
1Sa 10: 4 will greet you and offer you two **l** of bread, NDT
1Sa 17:17 these ten **l of bread** for your brothers H4312
1Sa 21: 3 Give me five **l of bread**, or whatever you H4312
1Sa 25:18 She took two hundred **l of bread**, two H4312
2Sa 16: 1 loaded with two hundred **l of bread**, H4312
1Ki 14: 3 Take ten **l of bread** with you, some cakes H4312
2Ki 4:42 God twenty **l** of barley **bread** baked from H4312
1Ch 23:29 offerings, the **thin l** made without yeast H8386
Mt 14:17 have here only five **l of bread** and two fish, *G788*
Mt 14:19 Taking the five **l** and the two fish and *G788*
Mt 14:19 to heaven, he gave thanks and broke the **l**. *G788*
Mt 15:34 "How many **l** do you have?" Jesus asked *G788*
Mt 15:36 Then he took the seven **l** and the fish, and *G788*
Mt 16: 9 remember the five **l** for the five thousand *G788*
Mt 16:10 Or the seven **l** for the four thousand, and *G788*
Mk 6:38 "How many **l** do you have?" he asked. "Go *G788*
Mk 6:41 Taking the five **l** and the two fish and *G788*
Mk 6:41 to heaven, he gave thanks and broke the **l**. *G788*
Mk 6:52 they had not understood about the **l** *G788*
Mk 8: 5 "How many **l** do you have?" Jesus asked *G788*
Mk 8: 6 he had taken the seven **l** and given thanks, *G788*
Mk 8:19 When I broke the five **l** for the five thousand *G788*
Mk 8:20 I broke the seven **l** for the four thousand, NDT
Lk 9:13 have only five **l of bread** and two fish— *G788*
Lk 9:16 Taking the five **l** and the two fish and *G788*
Lk 11: 5 'Friend, lend me three **l of bread**; *G788*
Jn 6: 9 a boy with five **small** barley **l** and two small *G788*
Jn 6:11 Jesus then took the **l**, gave thanks, and *G788*
Jn 6:13 of the five barley **l** left over by those who *G788*
Jn 6:26 because you ate the **l** and had your fill. *G788*

LOBE (16) [LOBES]

Ex 29:13 the **long l** of the liver, and H3866
Ex 29:22 the **long l** *of* the liver, both H3866
Lev 3: 4 the loins, and the **long l** of the liver H3866
Lev 3:10 the loins, and the **long l** of the liver H3866
Lev 3:15 the loins, and the **long l** of the liver H3866
Lev 4: 9 the loins, and the **long l** of the liver H3866
Lev 7: 4 the loins, and the **long l** of the liver H3866
Lev 8:16 the **long l** *of* the liver, and both H3866
Lev 8:23 put it on the **l** *of* Aaron's right ear, H9483
Lev 8:25 the **long l** *of* the liver, both H3866
Lev 9:10 kidneys and the **long l** of the liver from H3866
Lev 9:19 the kidneys and the **long l** *of* the liver— H3866
Lev 14:14 put it on the **l** *of* the right ear of the H9483
Lev 14:17 in his palm on the **l** *of* the right ear of the H9483
Lev 14:25 put it on the **l** *of* the right ear of the H9483
Lev 14:28 on the **l** *of* the right ear of the one to be H9483

LOBES (2) [LOBE]

Ex 29:20 put it on the **l** *of* the right ears of H9483
Lev 8:24 of the blood on the **l** *of* their right ears, H9483

LOCAL (3) [LOCALITY]

Mt 10:17 over to the **l councils** and be flogged in *G5284*
Mk 13: 9 over to the **l councils** and flogged in *G5284*
Ac 28:17 he called together the **l** Jewish leaders. *G1639*

LOCALITY (1) [LOCAL]

Ezr 1: 4 And in any **l** where survivors may now be H5226

LOCATIONS (1)

1Ch 6:54 These were the **l** *of* their settlements H3227

LOCKED (12)
Jdg 3:23 the upper room behind him and **l** them. H5835
Jdg 3:24 found the doors of the upper room **l**. H5835
Jdg 9:51 *They had* **l** themselves in and climbed up H6037
SS 4:12 You are a garden **l up**, my sister, my bride; H5835
Lk 3:20 this to them all: *He* **l** John **up** in prison. G2881
Lk 11: 7 The door *is* already **l**, and my children G3091
Jn 20:19 with the doors **l** for fear of the Jewish G3091
Jn 20:26 *Though* the doors *were* **l**, Jesus came G3091
Ac 5:23 "We found the jail securely **l**, with the G3091
Gal 3:22 But Scripture *has* **l up** everything under G5168
Gal 3:23 **l up** until the faith that was to come G5168
Rev 20: 3 the Abyss, and **l** and sealed it over him G3091

LOCKS (KJV) BRAIDS, BOLTS, HAIR

LOCUST (9) [LOCUSTS]
Ex 10:19 Not a **l** was left anywhere in Egypt H746
Lev 11:22 Of these you may eat any kind of **l**, katydid H746
Job 39:20 Do you make it leap like a **l**, striking terror H746
Ps 78:46 to the grasshopper, their produce to the **l**. H746
Ps 109:23 evening shadow; I am shaken off like a **l**. H746
Joel 1: 4 What the **l swarm** has left the great H1612
Joel 2:25 eaten—the **great l** and the young locust H746
Joel 2:25 the great locust and the **young l**, the other H3540
Joel 2:25 the other locusts and the **l swarm**—my H1612

LOCUSTS (37) [LOCUST]
Ex 10: 4 I will bring **l** into your country tomorrow. H746
Ex 10:12 over Egypt so that **l** swarm over the land H746
Ex 10:13 By morning the wind had brought the **l**; H746
Ex 10:14 before had there been such a plague of **l**, H746
Ex 10:19 which caught up the **l** and carried them H746
Dt 28:38 will harvest little, because **l** will devour it. H746
Dt 28:42 **Swarms of l** will take over all your trees H7526
Jdg 6: 5 livestock and their tents like swarms of **l**. H746
Jdg 7:12 peoples had settled in the valley, thick as **l**. H746
1Ki 8:37 blight or mildew, **l** or grasshoppers, or H746
2Ch 6:28 blight or mildew, **l** or grasshoppers, or H746
2Ch 7:13 command **l** to devour the land or send H2506
Ps 105:34 He spoke, and the **l** came, grasshoppers H746
Pr 30:27 **l** have no king, yet they advance together H746
Isa 33: 4 is harvested as by **young l**; like a swarm H2885
Isa 33: 4 like a swarm of **l** people pounce on it. H1466
Jer 46:23 They are more numerous than **l**, they H746
Jer 51:14 as with a **swarm of l**, and they will H3540
Jer 51:27 send up horses like a swarm of **l**. H3540
Joel 1: 4 swarm has left the **great l** have eaten; H746
Joel 1: 4 what the **great l** have left the young locusts H746
Joel 1: 4 locusts have left the **young l** have eaten; H3540
Joel 1: 4 what the **young l** have left other locusts H3540
Joel 1: 4 locusts have left other **l** have eaten. H2885
Joel 2:25 repay you for the years the **l** have eaten— NDT
Joel 2:25 the other **l** and the locust swarm H2885
Am 4: 9 **L** devoured your fig and olive trees, yet H1612
Am 7: 1 He was preparing **swarms of l** after the H1479
Na 3:15 they will devour you like a **swarm of l**. H3540
Na 3:15 Multiply like grasshoppers, multiply like **l**! H746
Na 3:16 like **l** they strip the land and then fly H3540
Na 3:17 Your guards are like **l**, your officials like H746
Na 3:17 like swarms of **l** that settle in the walls H1479
Mt 3: 4 His food was **l** and wild honey. G210
Mk 1: 6 his waist, and he ate **l** and wild honey. G210
Rev 9: 3 And out of the smoke **l** came down on the G210
Rev 9: 7 The **l** looked like horses prepared for battle. G210

LOD (4)
1Ch 8:12 who built Ono and **L** with its surrounding H4254
Ezr 2:33 of **L**, Hadid and Ono 725 H4254
Ne 7:37 of **L**, Hadid and Ono 721 H4254
Ne 11:35 in **L** and Ono, and in Ge Harashim. H4254

LODGE (2) [LODGED, LODGING]
Ps 38:20 good with evil **l accusations against** me, H8476
Ps 119:54 the theme of my song wherever **I l**. H1074+4472

LODGED (1) [LODGE]
Ezr 4: 6 *they* **l** an accusation against the people of H4180

LODGING (6) [LODGE]
Ex 4:24 At a **l place** on the way, the LORD met H4869
Ps 55:15 of the dead, for evil finds **l** among them. H4472
Jer 9: 2 I had in the desert a **l place** *for* travelers, H4869
Mic 6: 2 his people; *he is* **l a charge** against Israel. H3519
Lk 9:12 countryside and find food and **l**, G2907
Jas 2:25 what she did *when she* **gave l** to the spies G5685

LOFT (KJV) STORY, UPPER ROOM

LOFTINESS (1) [LOFTY]
Ps 48: 2 Beautiful in its **l**, the joy of the whole H5679

LOFTY (19) [LOFTINESS]
Job 22:12 And see how **l** *are* the highest stars H8123
Ps 62: 4 they intend to topple me from my **l place**; H8420
Ps 138: 6 on the lowly; though **l**, he sees them from H1469
Ps 139: 6 wonderful for me, too **l** for me to attain. H8435
Isa 2:12 has a day in store for all the proud and **l**, H8123
Isa 2:13 of Lebanon, tall and **l**, and all the oaks of H5951
Isa 2:15 every **l** tower and every fortified wall, H1469
Isa 10:33 The **l trees** will be felled, the tall H8123+7757
Isa 26: 5 on high, he lays the **l** city low; he levels it H8435
Isa 30:25 on every high mountain and every **l** hill. H5951
Isa 57: 7 have made your bed on a high and **l** hill; H5951
Isa 63:15 from your **l throne**, holy and H2292
Jer 51:53 the heavens and fortifies her **l** stronghold, H5294
Eze 16:24 made a **l shrine** in every public H8229
Eze 16:25 you built your **l shrines** and degraded your H8229
Eze 16:31 made your **l shrines** in every public H8229
Eze 16:39 your mounds and destroy your **l shrines**. H8229
Eze 17:22 plant it on a high and **l** mountain. H9435
Am 9: 6 he builds his **l palace** in the heavens and H5092

LOG (5) [LOGS]
Lev 14:10 oil for a grain offering, and one **l** *of* oil. H4253
Lev 14:12 along with the **l** *of* oil; he shall wave H4253
Lev 14:15 priest shall then take some of the **l** *of* oil, H4253
Lev 14:21 olive oil for a grain offering, a **l** *of* oil, H4253
Lev 14:24 together with the **l** *of* oil, and wave them H4253

LOGS (10) [LOG]
2Sa 5:11 along with cedar **l** and carpenters and H6770
1Ki 5: 8 want in providing the cedar and juniper **l**. H6770
1Ki 5:10 all the cedar and juniper **l** he wanted, H6770
1Ch 14: 1 along with cedar **l**, stonemasons and H6770
1Ch 22: 4 provided more cedar **l** than could be H6770
2Ch 2: 3 "Send me cedar **l** as you did for my father NDT
2Ch 2: 8 juniper and algum **l** from Lebanon, for I H6770
2Ch 2:16 we will cut all the **l** from Lebanon that you H6770
Ezr 3: 7 would bring cedar **l** by sea from Lebanon H6770
Ecc 10: 9 whoever splits **l** may be endangered by H6770

LOINCLOTH (1)
Job 12:18 on by kings and ties a **l** around their waist. H258

LOINS (6)
Lev 3: 4 kidneys with the fat on them near the **l**, H4072
Lev 3:10 kidneys with the fat on them near the **l**, H4072
Lev 3:15 kidneys with the fat on them near the **l**, H4072
Lev 4: 9 kidneys with the fat on them near the **l**, H4072
Lev 7: 4 kidneys with the fat on them near the **l**, H4072
Job 40:16 What strength it has in its **l**, what power H5516

LOIS (1)
2Ti 1: 5 in your grandmother **L** and in your mother G3396

LONELY (4) [ALONE]
Ps 25:16 be gracious to me, for I am **l** and afflicted. H3495
Ps 68: 6 God sets the **l** in families, he leads out H3495
Mk 1:45 openly but stayed outside in **l** places. G2245
Lk 5:16 often withdrew to **l places** and prayed. G2245

LONG (451) [LENGTH, LENGTHEN, LENGTHS, LENGTHWISE, LENGTHY, LONGED, LONGER, LONGING, LONGINGS, LONGS]
Ge 6:15 The ark is to be three hundred cubits **l**, fifty H802
Ge 8:22 "**As l as** the earth endures H6388+3972
Ge 21:34 in the land of the Philistines for a **l** time. H8041
Ge 26: 8 When Isaac *had* **been** there *a* **l** time H799
Ge 38:12 After a **l** time Judah's wife, the daughter H8049
Ge 46:29 around his father and wept *for a* **l time**. H6388
Ex 2:23 During that **l** period, the king of Egypt H8041
Ex 10: 3 '**How l** will you refuse to humble H6330+5503
Ex 10: 7 "**How l** will this man be a snare to H6330+5503
Ex 14:20 so neither went near the other **all** night *l*. AIT
Ex 16:28 "**How l** will you refuse to keep H6330+625+2025
Ex 17:11 **As l as** Moses held up his hands, the H3869+889
Ex 19:13 the ram's horn **sounds a l blast** may they H5432
Ex 20:12 so that you *may* **live l** in the land the H799+3427
Ex 25:10 two and a half cubits **l**, a cubit and a half H802
Ex 25:17 two and a half cubits **l** and a cubit and a H802
Ex 25:23 two cubits **l**, a cubit wide and a H802
Ex 26: 2 twenty-eight cubits **l** and four cubits wide. H802
Ex 26: 8 thirty cubits **l** and four cubits wide. H802
Ex 26:16 is to be ten cubits **l** and a cubit and a half H802
Ex 27: 1 five cubits **l** and five cubits wide. H802
Ex 27: 9 be a hundred cubits **l** and is to have H802
Ex 27:11 be a hundred cubits **l** and is to have H802
Ex 27:14 Curtains fifteen cubits **l** are to be on one side NDT
Ex 27:15 fifteen cubits **l** are to be on the other NDT
Ex 27:16 provide a curtain twenty cubits **l**, of blue, NDT
Ex 27:18 be a hundred cubits **l** and fifty cubits wide, H802
Ex 28:16 be square—a span **l** and a span wide H802
Ex 29:13 the **l lobe** of the liver, and H3866
Ex 29:22 the **l lobe** *of* the liver, both H3866
Ex 30: 2 be square, a cubit **l** and a cubit wide, and H802
Ex 32: 1 saw that Moses *was so* **l** in coming down H1018
Ex 36: 9 twenty-eight cubits **l** and four cubits wide. H802
Ex 36:15 thirty cubits **l** and four cubits wide. H802
Ex 36:21 frame was ten cubits **l** and a cubit and a H802
Ex 37: 1 two and a half cubits **l**, a cubit and a half H802
Ex 37: 6 two and a half cubits **l** and a cubit and a H802
Ex 37:10 two cubits **l**, a cubit wide and a H802
Ex 37:25 a cubit **l** and a cubit wide and two cubits H802
Ex 38: 1 five cubits **l** and five cubits wide. H802
Ex 38: 9 was a hundred cubits **l** and had curtains of NDT
Ex 38:11 a hundred cubits **l** and had twenty posts NDT
Ex 38:14 Curtains fifteen cubits **l** were on one side of NDT
Ex 38:15 fifteen cubits **l** were on the other side NDT
Ex 38:18 It was twenty cubits **l**, and, like the curtains H802
Ex 39: 9 was square—a span **l** and a span wide H802
Lev 3: 4 the loins, and the **l lobe** of the liver H3866
Lev 3:10 the loins, and the **l lobe** of the liver H3866
Lev 3:15 the loins, and the **l lobe** of the liver H3866
Lev 4: 9 the loins, and the **l lobe** of the liver H3866
Lev 7: 4 the loins, and the **l lobe** of the liver H3866
Lev 8:16 the **l lobe** *of* the liver, and both H3866
Lev 8:25 the **l lobe** *of* the liver, both H3866
Lev 9:10 kidneys and the **l lobe** of the liver from H3866
Lev 9:19 the kidneys and the **l lobe** *of* the liver— H3866
Lev 13:46 **As l as** they have the disease they H3972+3427
Lev 15:25 will be unclean **as l as** she has the H3972+3427
Nu 6: 4 **As l as** they remain under their H3427+3972
Nu 6: 5 *they must let* their hair **grow l**. H1540
Nu 9:18 **As l as** the cloud stayed over the H3972+3427
Nu 9:19 remained over the tabernacle a **l** time, H8041
Nu 14:11 "**How l** will these people treat H6330+625+2025
Nu 14:11 **How l** will they refuse to H6330+625+2025
Nu 14:27 "**How l** will this wicked community H6330+5503
Nu 36: 6 they please **as l as** they marry within H421
Dt 1: 6 "You have stayed **l enough** at this H8041
Dt 2: 1 For a **l** time we made our way around the H8041
Dt 2: 3 way around this hill country **l enough**; H8041
Dt 3:11 than nine cubits **l** and four cubits wide. H802
Dt 4: 9 from your heart **as l as** you live. H3972+3427
Dt 4:10 to revere me **as l as** they live H3972+2021+3427
Dt 4:25 and *have* **lived** in the land **a l time**— H3823
Dt 4:26 *You will* not **live** there **l** but will H799+3427
Dt 4:32 the former days, **l** before your time, from NDT
Dt 4:40 and that *you may* **live l** in the land H799+3427
Dt 5:16 so that you *may* **live l** and that it H799+3427
Dt 6: 2 LORD your God **as l as** you live by H3972+3427
Dt 6: 2 and so that you *may* **enjoy l life**. H799+3427
Dt 11: 9 so that *you may* **live l** in the land H799+3427
Dt 12: 1 **as l as** you live in the land. H3972+2021+3427
Dt 12:19 the Levites **as l as** you **live** in your H3972+3427
Dt 17:20 his descendants *will* reign a **l** time over his H799
Dt 20:19 When you lay siege to a city for a **l** time H8041
Dt 22: 7 go well with you and *you may* **have** *a* **l** life. H799
Dt 22:19 not divorce her **as l as** he **lives**. H3972+3427
Dt 22:29 never divorce her **as l as** he **lives**. H3972+3427
Dt 23: 6 them **as l as** you **live**. H3972+3427+4200+6409
Dt 25:15 so that you *may* **live l** in the land the H799+3427
Dt 30:18 *You will* not **live l** in the land you H799+3427
Dt 31:13 your God **as l as** you live in H3972+2021+3427
Dt 32: 7 the **generations l past**. H9102+1887+2256+1887
Dt 32:47 By them *you will* **live l** in the land H799+3427
Dt 33:12 he shields him all **day** *l*, and the one the AIT
Jos 6: 5 you hear them **sound** a **l** blast on the H5432
Jos 9:13 sandals are worn out by the very **l** journey." H8044
Jos 9:22 'We live a **l way** from you,' while H8158+4394
Jos 11:18 war against all these kings for a **l** time. H8041
Jos 18: 3 "**How l** will you wait before H6330+625+2025
Jos 22: 3 For a **l** time now—to this very day—you H8041
Jos 23: 1 After a **l** time had passed and the LORD H8041
Jos 24: 2 '**L ago** your ancestors, including H4946+6409
Jos 24: 7 you lived in the wilderness for a **l** time. H8041
Jdg 2:18 of their enemies **as l as** the judge lived; H3972
Jdg 3:16 a double-edged sword about a cubit **l**, H802
Jdg 5:28 'Why *is* his chariot **so l** in coming? H1018
Jdg 18: 7 they lived a **l way** from the Sidonians and H8158
Jdg 18:28 they lived a **l way** from Sidon and had H8158
1Sa 1:14 "**How l** are you going to stay drunk? H6330+5503
1Sa 7: 2 ark remained at Kiriath Jearim a **l** time— H8049
1Sa 10:24 Then the people shouted, "**L live** the king!" H2649
1Sa 16: 1 "**How l** will you mourn for Saul H6330+5503
1Sa 20:14 like the LORD's kindness **as l as** I live, H561+6388
1Sa 20:31 **As l as** the son of Jesse lives H3972+2021+3427
1Sa 22: 4 with him **as l as** David was in H3972+3427
1Sa 25: 6 Say to him: '**L life** to you H4200+2021+2644
1Sa 25:28 will be found in you **as l as** you live. H4946
1Sa 27:11 practice **as l as** he lived in H3972+2021+3427
2Sa 2:26 **How l** before you order your men to H6330+5503
2Sa 3: 1 the house of David lasted a **l time**. H801
2Sa 16:16 Absalom and said to him, "**L live** the king! H2649
2Sa 16:16 "Long live the king! **L live** the king!" H2649
2Sa 20:18 "**L ago** they used to say H928+2021+8037
1Ki 1:25 him and saying, '**L live** King Adonijah! H2649
1Ki 1:34 trumpet and shout, '**L live** King Solomon! H2649
1Ki 1:39 people shouted, "**L live** King Solomon!" H2649
1Ki 2:38 Shimei stayed in Jerusalem for a **l** time. H8041
1Ki 3:11 this and not for **l** life or wealth for H8041
1Ki 3:14 your father did, *I will* **give** you a **l** life." H799
1Ki 6: 2 built for the LORD was sixty cubits **l**, H802
1Ki 6:17 hall in front of this room was forty cubits **l**. NDT
1Ki 6:20 The inner sanctuary was twenty cubits **l** H802
1Ki 6:24 wing of the first cherub was five cubits **l** NDT
1Ki 7: 2 of the Forest of Lebanon a hundred cubits **l**, H802
1Ki 7: 6 a colonnade fifty cubits **l** and thirty wide. H802
1Ki 7:27 each was four cubits **l**, four wide and three H802
1Ki 8: 8 These poles *were so* **l** that their ends could H799
1Ki 11:25 adversary **as l as** Solomon **lived**, H3972+3427
1Ki 18: 1 After a **l** time, in the third year, the word H8041
1Ki 18:21 "**How l** will you waver between two H6330+5503
1Ki 22:35 **All day l** the battle raged, H928+2021+3427+2021+2085
2Ki 6:25 the siege **lasted so l** that a donkey's head H6330
2Ki 9:22 "**as l as** all the idolatry and witchcraft of H6330
2Ki 11:12 their hands and shouted, "**L live** the king!" H2649
2Ki 13: 3 for a **l** time he kept them under the H3972
2Ki 14:13 a section about four hundred cubits **l**. NDT
2Ki 19:25 **L ago** I ordained it H4200+4946+8158
2Ki 25:30 regular allowance **as l as** he lived. H3972+3427
1Ch 29:28 having **enjoyed l life**, wealth H8428+3427
2Ch 1:11 have not asked for a **l** life but for wisdom H8041
2Ch 3: 3 God was sixty cubits **l** and twenty cubits H802
2Ch 3: 4 was twenty cubits **l** across the width of the H802
2Ch 3: 8 twenty cubits **l** and twenty cubits wide. NDT

2Ch 3:11 was five cubits **l** and touched the temple NDT
2Ch 3:11 also five cubits **l**, touched the wing of NDT
2Ch 3:12 was five cubits **l** and touched the other NDT
2Ch 3:12 also five cubits **l**, touched the wing of NDT
2Ch 3:15 which together were thirty-five cubits **l** H802
2Ch 4: 1 He made a bronze altar twenty cubits **l** H802
2Ch 5: 9 These poles *were so* **l** that their ends H799
2Ch 6:13 platform, five cubits **l**, five cubits wide and H802
2Ch 15: 3 For a **l** time Israel was without the true H8041
2Ch 18:34 **All day l** the battle raged, H928+2021+3427+2021+2085
2Ch 23:11 him and shouted, "**L live** the king! H2649
2Ch 24:14 **As l as** Jehoiada **lived**, burnt H3972+3427
2Ch 25:23 a section about four hundred cubits **l**. NDT
2Ch 26: 5 **As l as** he sought the LORD, God H928+3427
2Ch 34:33 **As l as** he **lived**, they did not fail to H3972+3427
Ezr 4:15 a place with a **l** history of sedition. A10550
Ezr 4:19 has a **l history** of revolt A10427+10317+10550
Ne 2: 6 "**How l** will your journey take H6330+5503
Ne 12:46 For **l ago**, in the days of David and H4946+7710
Est 5:13 satisfaction **as l as** I see that H928+3972+6961
Job 3:21 to those *who* **l for** death that does not H2675
Job 7: 4 I lie down I think, '**How l** *before* I get up? H5503
Job 8: 2 "**How l** will you say such things H6330+625
Job 12:12 Does not **l** life bring understanding? H802
Job 12:19 overthrows *officials* **l established**. H419
Job 14:15 *you will* **l for** the creature your hands have H4083
Job 19: 2 "**How l** will you torment me H6330+625+2025
Job 27: 3 **as l as** I have life within me, the H3972+6388
Job 27: 6 will not reproach me **as l as** I **live**. H4946+3427
Job 29: 2 "**How I l for** the months H4769+5989+5761
Job 36:20 *Do* not **l for** the night, to drag people H8634
Ps 4: 2 **How l** will you people turn my glory H6330+4537
Ps 4: 2 How **l** will you love delusions and seek false NDT
Ps 6: 3 deep anguish. **How l**, LORD, how H6330+5503
Ps 6: 3 is in deep anguish. How long, LORD, how **l**? NDT
Ps 6: 6 **All** night *l* I flood my bed with weeping and AIT
Ps 13: 1 **How l**, LORD? Will you forget H6330+625+2025
Ps 13: 1 **How l** will you hide your face H6330+625+2025
Ps 13: 2 **How l** must I wrestle with my H6330+625+2025
Ps 13: 2 **How l** will my enemy triumph H6330+625+2025
Ps 25: 5 my Savior, and my hope is in you all **day l**. AIT
Ps 32: 3 wasted away through my groaning all **day** *l*. AIT
Ps 35:17 **How l**, Lord, will you look on H3869+4537
Ps 35:28 your righteousness, your praises all **day** *l*. AIT
Ps 38: 6 very low; all **day** *l* I go about mourning. AIT
Ps 38:12 talk of my ruin; all **day** *l* they scheme and lie. AIT
Ps 40:16 may *those who* **l for** your saving help H170
Ps 42: 3 while people say to me all **day** *l*, "Where is AIT
Ps 42:10 saying to me all **day** *l*, "Where is your God?" AIT
Ps 44: 1 what you did in their days, in days **l ago**. H7710
Ps 44: 8 In God we make our boast all **day** *l*, and we AIT
Ps 44:15 I live in disgrace all **day** *l*, and my face is AIT
Ps 44:22 Yet for your sake we face death all **day** *l*; we AIT
Ps 52: 1 Why do you boast all **day** *l*, you who are a AIT
Ps 56: 1 in hot pursuit; all **day** *l* they press their attack. AIT
Ps 56: 2 My adversaries pursue me all **day** *l*; in their AIT
Ps 56: 5 All **day** *l* they twist my words; all their AIT
Ps 61: 4 *I l to* **dwell** in your tent forever and take AIT
Ps 62: 3 **How l** will you assault me H6330+625+2025
Ps 63: 4 I will praise you **as l as** I live, and in your H928
Ps 70: 4 may *those who* **l for** your saving help H170
Ps 71: 8 your praise, declaring your splendor all **day** *l*. AIT
Ps 71:15 of your saving acts all **day** *l*—though I know AIT
Ps 71:24 will tell of your righteous acts all **day** *l*, AIT
Ps 72: 5 May he endure **as l as** the sun, as long as H6640
Ps 72: 5 long as the sun, **as l as** the moon H4200+7156
Ps 72:15 **L** *may he* **live**! May gold from Sheba be H2649
Ps 72:15 ever pray for him and bless him all **day** *l*. AIT
Ps 72:17 may it continue **as l as** the sun. H4200+7156
Ps 73:14 All **day** *l* I have been afflicted, and every AIT
Ps 74: 2 the nation you purchased **l ago**, H7710
Ps 74: 9 of us knows **how l** this will be. H6330+4537
Ps 74:10 **How l** will the enemy mock you H6330+5503
Ps 74:12 But God is my King from **l ago**; he brings H7710
Ps 74:22 remember how fools mock you all **day** *l*. AIT
Ps 77: 5 about the former days, the years of **l ago**; H6409
Ps 77:11 I will remember your miracles of **l ago**. H7710
Ps 79: 5 **How l**, LORD? Will you be angry H6330+4537
Ps 79: 5 How **l** will your jealousy burn like fire? NDT
Ps 80: 4 **How l**, LORD God Almighty, will your H6330+5503
Ps 82: 2 "**How l** will you defend the unjust H6330+5503
Ps 86: 3 mercy on me, Lord, for I call to you all **day** *l*. AIT
Ps 88:17 All **day** *l* they surround me like a flood; they AIT
Ps 89:16 They rejoice in your name all **day** *l*; they AIT
Ps 89:29 throne **as l as** the heavens **endure**. H3869+3427
Ps 89:46 **How l**, LORD? Will you hide H6330+4537
Ps 89:46 How **l** will your wrath burn like fire? NDT
Ps 90:13 **How l** will it be? Have H6330+5503
Ps 91:16 With **l** life I will satisfy him and show him H802
Ps 93: 2 Your throne was established **l ago** H4946+255
Ps 94: 3 **How l**, LORD, will the wicked, how H6330+5503
Ps 94: 3 **how l** will the wicked be jubilant? H6330+5503
Ps 102: 8 All **day** *l* my enemies taunt me; those who AIT
Ps 104:33 sing praise to my God **as l as** I **live**. H928+6388
Ps 116: 2 ear to me, I will call on him **as l as** I live. H928
Ps 119:40 How *I* **l for** your precepts! In your H9289
Ps 119:84 **How l must** your servant **wait** H3869+4537+3427
Ps 119:97 I love your law! I meditate on it all **day** *l*. AIT
Ps 119:152 **L ago** I learned from your statutes that H7710
Ps 119:174 *I* **l for** your salvation, LORD, and your H9289
Ps 120: 6 **Too l** have I lived among those who hate H8041
Ps 129: 3 plowed my back and **made** their furrows **l**. H799
Ps 143: 3 dwell in the darkness like those **l** dead. H6409
Ps 143: 5 I remember the days of **l** ago; I meditate H7710
Ps 146: 2 sing praise to my God **as l as** I **live**. H928+6388
Pr 1:22 "**How l** will you who are simple H6330+5503
Pr 1:22 How **l** will mockers delight in mockery and NDT
Pr 3:16 **L** life is in her right hand; in her left hand H802
Pr 6: 9 **How l** will you lie there, you H6330+5503
Pr 7:19 home; he has gone on a **l** journey. H4946+8158
Pr 8:23 I was formed **l ages ago**, at the H4946+6409
Pr 21:26 All day *l* he craves for more, but the AIT
Pr 28:16 ill-gotten gain *will* **enjoy a l reign**. H799+3427
Ecc 1:10 here already, **l ago**; it was here H4200+6409
Ecc 2:16 will not be **l** remembered; the H4200+6409
Ecc 6: 3 no matter how **l** he lives, if he cannot H8041
Ecc 7:15 the wicked **living l** in their wickedness. H799
Ecc 8:12 a hundred crimes *may* **live a l time**, H799
Ecc 9: 6 their jealousy have **l since** vanished; H3893
SS 3: 1 **All night l** on my bed I looked H928+2021+4326
Isa 6:11 Then I said, "**For how l**, Lord?" H6330+5503
Isa 22:11 the One who planned it **l ago**. H4946+8158
Isa 25: 1 things, things planned **l ago**. H4946+8158
Isa 30:33 Topheth has **l** been prepared; it has H4946+919
Isa 33: 2 be gracious to us; **we l for** you. Be our H7747
Isa 37:26 **L ago** I ordained it H4200+4946+8158
Isa 42:14 "For a **l time** I have kept silent, I have H6409
Isa 44: 8 proclaim this and foretell it **l ago**? H4946+255
Isa 45:21 Who foretold this **l ago**, who H4946+7710
Isa 46: 9 former things, those of **l ago**; I am God, H6409
Isa 48: 3 I foretold the former things **l ago**, my H4946+255
Isa 48: 5 I told you these things **l ago**; H4946+255
Isa 48: 7 and not **l ago**; you have not H4946+255
Isa 52: 5 "And all **day** *l* my name is constantly AIT
Isa 57:11 because I have **l** been silent that H4946+6409
Isa 61: 4 ruins and restore the places **l** devastated; H8037
Isa 65: 2 All **day** *l* I have held out my hands to an AIT
Isa 65:22 my chosen ones *will* **l enjoy** the work of H1162
Jer 2:20 "**L ago** you broke off your yoke and H4946+6409
Jer 4:14 **How l** will you harbor wicked H6330+5503
Jer 4:21 **How l** must I see the battle H6330+5503
Jer 6: 4 the shadows of evening **grow l**. H5742
Jer 12: 4 **How l** will the land lie parched and H6330+5503
Jer 13:27 **How l** will you be unclean?" H339+5503+6388
Jer 20: 7 I am ridiculed all **day** *l*; everyone mocks me. AIT
Jer 20: 8 has brought me insult and reproach all **day** *l*. AIT
Jer 22:27 back to the land you **l** to return to." H5951+5883
Jer 23:26 **How l** will this continue in the H6330+5503
Jer 29:28 It will be a **l time**. Therefore build H801
Jer 31:22 **How l** will you wander, unfaithful H6330+5503
Jer 32:14 in a clay jar so they will last a **l** time. H8041
Jer 35: 7 Then you will live a **l** time in the land H8041
Jer 37:16 a dungeon, where he remained a **l** time. H8041
Jer 44:14 to which they **l** to return and live H5951+5883
Jer 47: 5 **how l** will you cut yourselves? H6330+5503
Jer 47: 6 the LORD, **how l** till you rest? H6330+625+2025
Jer 52:34 regular allowance **as l as** he lived, H3972+3427
La 1:13 He made me desolate, faint all the **day** *l*. AIT
La 2:17 which he decreed **l ago**. H4946+3427+7710
La 3: 3 hand against me again and again, all **day** *l*. AIT
La 3: 6 me dwell in darkness like those **l** dead. H6409
La 3:14 my people; they mock me in song all **day** *l*. AIT
La 3:62 whisper and mutter against me all **day** *l*. AIT
La 5:20 Why do you forsake us **so l**? H802+3427
Eze 7:13 **as l as** both buyer and seller live. H6388
Eze 17: 3 **l** feathers and full plumage of varied colors H800
Eze 26:20 go down to the pit, to the people of **l ago**. H6409
Eze 31: 5 boughs increased and its branches *grew* **l**, H799
Eze 38: 8 of Israel, which had **l** been desolate. H9458
Eze 40: 5 rod in the man's hand was six **l cubits**, H564
Eze 40: 7 guards were one rod **l** and one rod wide, H802
Eze 40:18 gateways and was as wide as they were **l**; H802
Eze 40:21 It was fifty cubits **l** and twenty-five cubits H802
Eze 40:25 It was fifty cubits **l** and twenty-five cubits H802
Eze 40:29 It was fifty cubits **l** and twenty-five cubits H802
Eze 40:33 It was fifty cubits **l** and twenty-five cubits H802
Eze 40:36 It was fifty cubits **l** and twenty-five cubits H802
Eze 40:42 each a cubit and a half **l**, a cubit and a half H802
Eze 40:43 each a handbreadth **l**, were attached to the NDT
Eze 40:47 a hundred cubits **l** and a hundred cubits H802
Eze 41: 2 it was forty cubits **l** and twenty cubits wide. H802
Eze 41: 8 It was the length of the rod, six **l** cubits. H723
Eze 41:13 it was a hundred cubits **l**, and the temple H802
Eze 41:13 with its walls were also a hundred cubits **l**. H802
Eze 42: 2 was a hundred cubits **l** and fifty cubits wide H802
Eze 42: 4 ten cubits wide and a hundred cubits **l**. H2006
Eze 42: 8 next to the outer court was fifty cubits **l**, H802
Eze 42: 8 the sanctuary was a hundred cubits **l**. NDT
Eze 42:20 five hundred cubits **l** and five hundred H802
Eze 43:13 the measurements of the altar in **l cubits**, H564
Eze 43:16 twelve cubits **l** and twelve cubits wide. H802
Eze 43:17 fourteen cubits **l** and fourteen cubits wide. H802
Eze 44:20 shave their heads or let their **hair** grow **l**, H7279
Eze 45: 1 25,000 cubits **l** and 20,000 cubits wide H802
Eze 45: 3 section 25,000 cubits **l** and 10,000 cubits H802
Eze 45: 5 An area 25,000 cubits **l** and 10,000 cubits H802
Eze 45: 6 area 5,000 cubits wide and 25,000 cubits **l**, H802
Eze 46:22 forty cubits **l** and thirty cubits wide H802
Eze 48: 9 will be 25,000 cubits **l** and 10,000 cubits H802
Eze 48:10 It will be 25,000 cubits **l** on the north side NDT
Eze 48:10 side and 25,000 cubits **l** on the south side. H802
Eze 48:13 25,000 cubits **l** and 10,000 cubits wide. H802
Eze 48:15 5,000 cubits wide and 25,000 cubits **l**, will NDT
Eze 48:30 on the north side, which is 4,500 cubits **l**, H4500
Eze 48:32 which is 4,500 cubits **l**, will be three gates: NDT
Eze 48:34 which is 4,500 cubits **l**, will be three gates: NDT
Da 8: 3 beside the canal, and the horns were **l**. H1469
Da 8:13 "**How l** will it take *for* the vision to H6330+5503
Da 12: 6 "**How l** will it be before these H6330+5503
Hos 7:13 I *l to* **redeem** them but they speak about me AIT
Hos 8: 5 **How l** will they be incapable of purity? H5503
Am 5:18 Woe to *you who* **l for** the day of the LORD H203
Am 5:18 Why *do* you **l for** the day of the LORD H2296S
Mic 7:14 in Bashan and Gilead as in days **l ago**. H6409
Mic 7:20 on oath to our ancestors in days **l ago**. H7710
Hab 1: 2 **How l**, LORD, must I call for H6330+625+2025
Hab 2: 6 by extortion! **How l** must this go on H5503+6330
Zec 1:12 **how l** will you withhold mercy from H6330+5503
Zec 2: 2 to find out how wide and how **l** it is." H802
Zec 5: 2 twenty cubits **l** and ten cubits wide. H802
Mt 5:21 heard that it was said *to* the **people l ago**, *G792*
Mt 5:33 heard that it was said *to* the **people l ago**, *G792*
Mt 11:21 have repented **l ago** in sackcloth and *G4093*
Mt 17:17 "**how l** shall I stay with you? *G2401+4536*
Mt 17:17 **How l** shall I put up with you *G2401+4536*
Mt 20: 6 been standing here **all** day *l* doing nothing? AIT
Mt 23: 5 wide and the tassels on their garments **l**; *G3486*
Mt 24:48 'My master *is* **staying away a l time**,' *G5988*
Mt 25: 5 The bridegroom *was* **a l time in coming** *G5988*
Mt 25:19 "After a **l** time the master of those *G4498*
Mk 2:19 **so l as** they have him with them. *G4012+5989*
Mk 6:15 a prophet, like one *of* the **prophets** *of l ago*." AIT
Mk 8: 3 some of them have come a **l distance**." *G3427*
Mk 9:19 "**how l** shall I stay with you? *G2401+4536*
Mk 9:19 **How l** shall I put up with you *G2401+4536*
Mk 9:21 boy's father, "How **l** has he been like this?" *G5989*
Lk 1:21 why he **stayed so l** in the temple. *G5988*
Lk 1:70 he said through his holy prophets of **l ago**), *G172*
Lk 8:27 For a **l** time this man had not worn clothes *G2653*
Lk 9: 8 of the prophets *of* **l ago** had come back to *G792*
Lk 9:19 of the prophets *of* **l ago** has come back to *G792*
Lk 9:41 "**how l** shall I stay with you and put *G2401+4536*
Lk 10:13 they would have repented **l ago**, sitting in *G4093*
Lk 12:45 'My master *is* **taking a l time** in coming,' *G5988*
Lk 13:16 Satan has kept bound for eighteen *l* **years**, AIT
Lk 14:32 the other is still a **l way off** and will ask *G4522*
Lk 15:13 "**Not l** after that, the younger son *G4498+2465*
Lk 15:20 "But while he was still a **l** way off, his *G3426*
Lk 17:22 is coming when *you will* **l** to see one of *G2121*
Lk 20: 9 some farmers and went away for a **l** time. *G2653*
Lk 23: 8 because for a **l** time he had been wanting *G2653*
Jn 5: 6 he had been in this condition for a **l** time, *G4498*
Jn 9: 4 **As l as** it is day, we must do the works of *G2401*
Jn 10:24 "**How l** will you keep us in *G2401+4536*
Jn 14: 9 I have been among you **such a l** time? *G5537*
Jn 14:19 **Before l**, the world will not see me *G2285+3625*
Ac 1:16 the Holy Spirit **spoke l ago** through David *G4625*
Ac 3:21 as he promised **l ago** through his holy *G608+172*
Ac 8:11 amazed them for a **l** time with his sorcery *G2653*
Ac 14:28 they stayed there a **l** time with the *G4024+3900*
Ac 15:18 things known from **l ago**. *G172*
Ac 24: 2 have enjoyed a **l period** of peace under *G4498*
Ac 26: 5 have known me **for a l time** and can testify, *G540*
Ac 26:29 "Short time or **l**—I pray to God that not *G3489*
Ac 27:14 **Before very l**, a wind of *G3552+4024+4498*
Ac 27:21 After they had gone a **l** *time* without food *G4498*
Ac 28: 6 after waiting a **l** *time* and seeing nothing *G4498*
Ro 1:11 *I* **l** to see you so that I may impart to you *G2160*
Ro 7: 1 someone **only as l as** that *G2093+4012+5989*
Ro 7: 2 is bound to her husband *as l as he is* **alive**, AIT
Ro 8:36 "For your sake we face death **all day** *l*; we are AIT
Ro 10:21 "**All** day *l* I have held out my hands to a AIT
Ro 16:25 of the mystery hidden for **l** ages past, *G5989*
1Co 7:39 her husband **as l as** he lives. *G2093+4012+5989*
1Co 11:14 things teach you that if a man **has l hair**, *G3150*
1Co 11:15 that if a woman **has l hair**, it is her *G3150*
1Co 11:15 For **l hair** is given to her as a covering *G3151*
2Co 5: 6 know that *as l as we are* **at home** in the body AIT
Gal 4: 1 is that **as l as** an heir is *G2093+4012+5989*
Eph 3:18 grasp how wide and **l** and high and deep *G3601*
Eph 6: 3 that you may enjoy **l life** on the earth." *G3432*
Php 1: 8 God can testify how *I* **l for** all of you with *G2160*
Php 4: 1 you whom I love and **l for**, my joy and *G2162*
1Th 3: 6 memories of us and *that you* **l** to see us, *G2160*
1Th 3: 6 long to see us, just as we also **l** to see you. NDT
2Ti 1: 4 Recalling your tears, *I* **l** to see you, so that *G2160*
Heb 3:13 daily, **as l as** it is called "Today," *G948+4005*
Heb 4: 7 This he did when a **l** time later he spoke *G5537*
Heb 9: 8 **as l as** the first tabernacle was **still** *G2285*
1Pe 1:12 Even angels **l** to look into these things *G2121*
1Pe 3:20 were disobedient **l ago** when God waited *G4537*
2Pe 1:13 your memory **as l as** I live in the *G2093+4012*
2Pe 2: 3 condemnation has **l** been hanging over *G1732*
2Pe 3: 5 forget that **l ago** by God's word the *G1732*
Jude 4 was written about **l ago** have secretly *G4093*
Rev 6:10 a loud voice, "**How l**, Sovereign *G2401+4536*
Rev 9: 6 will not find it; *they will* **l to** die, but death *G2121*
Rev 21:16 laid out like a square, as **l** as it was wide. *G3601*
Rev 21:16 in length, and as wide and high as it is **l**. NDT

LONG-SUFFERING (1) [SUFFER]

Jer 15:15 You are **l**—do not take me away H800+678

LONG-WINDED (1) [WIND]

Job 16: 3 Will your **l** speeches never end? What ails H8120

LONGED (13) [LONG]

Ge 31:30 off because *you* **l** *to return* to your H4083+4083
2Sa 13:39 And King David **l** to go to Absalom, for he H3983
2Sa 14: 1 knew that the king's heart **l for** Absalom. H6584
2Sa 23:15 David **l for** water and said, "Oh, that H203
1Ch 11:17 David **l for** water and said, "Oh, that H203
Isa 21: 4 the twilight I **l for** has become a horror to H3139
Eze 23:21 So *you* **l for** the lewdness of your youth H7212
Mt 13:17 righteous people **l** to see what you see *G2121*
Mt 23:37 how often *I have* **l** to gather your children *G2527*
Lk 13:34 how often *I have* **l** to gather your children *G2527*
Lk 15:16 *He* **l** to fill his stomach with the pods that *G2121*
2Ti 4: 8 also to all who *have* **l for** his appearing. *G26*
Rev 18:14 fruit you **l for** is gone from *G2123+3836+6034*

LONGER (198) [LONG]

Ge 4:12 ground, it will no **l** yield its crops for you. H3578
Ge 17: 5 No **l** will you be called Abram; your name H6388
Ge 17:15 your wife, you are no *l* to call her Sarai; her AIT
Ge 27: 1 his eyes were so weak *that* he could **no** *l* see, AIT
Ge 27:45 When your brother *is* **no** *l* angry with you H8740
Ge 32:28 "Your name will no **l** be Jacob, but Israel, H6388
Ge 35:10 you will no **l** be called Jacob; your H6388
Ge 45: 1 Then Joseph could **no** *l* control himself AIT
Ge 49: 4 the waters, you will **no** *l* excel, for you went AIT
Ex 2: 3 But when she could hide him no **l**, she got H6388
Ex 5: 7 "*You are* no **l** to supply the people with H3578
Ex 9:28 let you go; you don't have to stay **any l**." H3578
Ex 9:33 the rain no *l* **poured down** on the land. AIT
Ex 26:13 tent curtains will be a cubit **l** on both sides; H802
Lev 17: 7 They must no **l** offer any of their sacrifices H6388
Lev 26:13 out of Egypt **so that** you would **no** *l* be slaves AIT
Nu 8:25 from their regular service and work no **l**. H6388
Dt 5:25 the voice of the LORD our God **any l**. H3578+6388
Dt 10:16 do not be stiff-necked **any l**. H6388
Dt 31: 2 years old and I am no **l** able to lead you. H6388
Jos 5: 1 in fear and they no **l** had the courage to H6388
Jos 5:12 there was no **l** any manna for the H6388
Jos 23:13 LORD your God *will* no **l** drive out these H3578
Jdg 2:14 whom they were no **l** able to resist. H6388
Jdg 2:21 I *will* no **l** drive out before them any of the H3578
Jdg 10: 6 forsook the LORD and **no** *l* served him, AIT
Jdg 10:13 served other gods, so *I will* no **l** save you. H3578
Jdg 10:16 And he *could* **bear** Israel's misery **no l**. H7918
1Sa 1:18 her face was no **l** downcast. H6388
1Sa 27: 4 to Gath, *he* no **l** searched for him. H3578+6388
1Sa 28:15 He no **l** answers me, either by prophets H6388
2Sa 1:21 the shield of Saul—**no l** rubbed with oil. H1172
2Sa 2:28 came to a halt; *they* no **l** pursued Israel H6388
2Sa 3:22 But Abner **was no** *l* with David in Hebron AIT
2Sa 7:10 home of their own and no **l** be disturbed. H6388
2Sa 20: 5 *he* **took l** than the time the king had set H336
1Ki 21:15 He **is no** *l* alive, but dead." AIT
1Ki 22: 7 "**Is there no l** a prophet of the LORD here H401
2Ki 6:33 Why should I wait for the LORD **any l**?" H6388
2Ki 10:19 Anyone who fails to come *will* no *l* **live**." AIT
2Ki 15:20 Assyria withdrew and **stayed** in the land no *l*. AIT
2Ki 17: 4 and *he* no *l* **paid** tribute to the king of Assyria AIT
1Ch 17: 9 home of their own and no **l** be disturbed. H6388
1Ch 23:26 the Levites no *l* **need** to **carry** the tabernacle AIT
2Ch 18: 6 "**Is there no l** a prophet of the LORD here H401
Ne 2:17 we will no **l** be in disgrace. H6388
Ne 13:21 that time on they **no** *l* came on the Sabbath. AIT
Job 3:18 they **no** *l* hear the slave driver's shout. AIT
Job 7: 8 The eye that now sees me will see me **no** *l* AIT
Job 11: 9 Their measure is **l** than the earth and wider H801
Job 15:29 He will **no** *l* be rich and his wealth will not AIT
Job 24:20 the wicked are no **l** remembered but are H6388
Job 36: 2 "Bear with me a **little l** and I will show H2402
Ps 44: 9 humbled us; *you* **no** *l* **go out** with our armies. AIT
Ps 60:10 now rejected us and **no** *l* go out with our AIT
Ps 108:11 have rejected us and **no** *l* go out with our AIT
Ecc 4:13 king who no **l** knows how to heed a H6388
Ecc 9:16 is despised, and his words are **no** *l* heeded. AIT
Ecc 12: 5 itself along and desire **no l** *is* **stirred**. H7296
Isa 7:25 you will **no** *l* go there for fear of the briers AIT
Isa 10:20 *will* no **l** rely on him who struck H3578+6388
Isa 17: 1 Damascus *will* **no l be** a city but H6073+4946
Isa 23:10 Tarshish, for you no **l** have a harbor. H6388
Isa 24: 9 **No** *l* do they drink wine with a song; the beer AIT
Isa 26:21 the earth will conceal its slain no **l**. H6388
Isa 29:22 "No **l** will Jacob be ashamed; no longer H6964
Isa 29:22 ashamed; no **l** will their faces grow pale. H6964
Isa 32: 3 eyes of those who see *will* no *l* **be closed**, AIT
Isa 32: 5 No **l** will the fool be called noble nor the H6388
Isa 38:11 no **l** will I look on my fellow man H6388
Isa 60:18 No **l** will violence be heard in your land H6388
Isa 62: 4 No **l** will they call you Deserted, or name H6388
Isa 62:12 called Sought After, the City No *L* **Deserted**. AIT
Isa 65:22 **No** *l* will they build houses and others live in AIT
Jer 3:12 'I will frown on you **no** *l*, for I am faithful, AIT
Jer 3:16 "people will no **l** say, 'The ark of the H6388
Jer 3:17 No **l** will they follow the stubbornness of H6388
Jer 4: 1 idols out of my sight and **no** *l* go astray, AIT
Jer 7:32 when people will no **l** call it Topheth or H6388
Jer 8:19 **Is** her King **no** *l* there?" "Why AIT
Jer 16:14 "when it will no **l** be said, 'As surely as H6388
Jer 19: 6 when people will no **l** call this place H6388
Jer 23: 4 they will no **l** be afraid or terrified H6388
Jer 23: 7 "when people will no **l** say, 'As surely as H6388
Jer 30: 8 no **l** will foreigners enslave them. H6388
Jer 31:29 "In those days people will no **l** say, 'The H6388
Jer 31:34 No **l** will they teach their neighbor, or say H6388
Jer 33:20 day and night no *l* **come** at their appointed AIT
Jer 33:21 David will **no** *l* have a descendant to AIT
Jer 33:24 my people and no **l** regard them as a H6388
Jer 34:10 slaves and no **l** hold them in bondage H6388
Jer 38: 9 when there is no **l** any bread in the city." H6388
Jer 44:22 the LORD could no **l** endure your wicked H6388
Jer 49: 7 "Is there no **l** wisdom in Teman H6388
Jer 51:44 The nations will no **l** stream to him. H6388
La 2: 9 her prophets **no** *l* find visions from the AIT
La 4:15 the nations say, "They can stay here no **l**." H3578
La 4:16 *he* no **l** watches over them. H3578
Eze 12:23 they will no **l** quote it in Israel. H6388
Eze 12:28 None of my words will be delayed **any l** H6388
Eze 13:21 they will no **l** fall prey to your power. H6388
Eze 13:23 therefore you will no **l** see false visions H6388
Eze 14:11 people of Israel will no **l** stray from me, H6388
Eze 16:41 you will no **l** pay your lovers. H6388
Eze 16:42 from you; I will be calm and no **l** angry. H6388
Eze 18: 3 you will no **l** quote this proverb in Israel. H6388
Eze 19: 9 roar was heard no **l** on the mountains of H6388
Eze 20:39 listen to me and no **l** profane my holy H6388
Eze 24:27 speak with him and will no **l** be silent. H6388
Eze 26:19 like cities **no** *l* inhabited, and when I AIT
Eze 28:24 " 'No **l** will the people of Israel have H6388
Eze 29:16 Egypt will no **l** be a source of confidence H6388
Eze 30:13 No **l** will there be a prince in Egypt, and I H6388
Eze 32:13 abundant waters no **l** to be stirred by the H6388
Eze 33:22 mouth was opened and I was no **l** silent. H6388
Eze 34:10 the shepherds can no **l** feed themselves. H6388
Eze 34:10 and it will **no** *l* be food for them. AIT
Eze 34:22 my flock, and they will no **l** be plundered. H6388
Eze 34:28 They will no **l** be plundered by the nations, H6388
Eze 34:29 they will no **l** be victims of famine in H6388
Eze 36:14 therefore you will no **l** devour people or H6388
Eze 36:15 No **l** will I make you hear the taunts of the H6388
Eze 36:15 no **l** will you suffer the scorn of the H6388
Eze 36:30 so that you will no **l** suffer disgrace H6388
Eze 37:23 They will no **l** defile themselves with their H6388
Eze 39: 7 I will no **l** let my holy name be profaned H6388
Eze 39:29 I will no **l** hide my face from them, for I H6388
Eze 45: 8 my princes will no **l** oppress my people H6388
Da 8: 3 One of the horns was **l** than the other H1469
Hos 1: 6 I will no **l** show love to Israel H6388+3578
Hos 2:16 you will no **l** call me 'my master. H6388
Hos 2:17 her lips; no **l** will their names be invoked. H6388
Hos 9:15 I will no **l** love them; all their leaders are H3578
Joel 2:10 darkened, and the stars **no l shine**. H665+5586
Joel 3:15 darkened, and the stars **no l shine**. H665+5586
Am 7: 8 I will spare them no **l**. H6388+3578
Am 8: 2 I will spare them no **l**. H6388+3578
Mic 1:11 is in mourning; it **no l** protects you. H4374+4946
Mic 2: 3 You will **no** *l* walk proudly, for it will be a AIT
Mic 5:12 your witchcraft and you will no **l** cast spells. NDT
Mic 5:13 will no **l** bow down to the work of your H6388
Na 2:13 of your messengers will no **l** be heard." H6388
Zep 3:17 in his love *he will* **no l rebuke** you, but H3087
Zec 11: 6 For I will no **l** have pity on the people of H6388
Zec 14:21 day there will no **l** be a Canaanite in the H6388
Mal 2:13 wail because he no **l** looks with favor on H6388
Mt 5:13 It is no **l** good for anything, except to be *G2285*
Mt 19: 6 So they are **no l** two, but one flesh *G4033*
Mk 1:45 Jesus could no **l** enter a town openly but *G3600*
Mk 7:12 then you **no l** let them do anything for *G4033*
Mk 9: 8 they **no l** saw anyone with them except *G4033*
Mk 10: 8 So they are **no l** two, but one flesh. *G4033*
Lk 15:19 I am **no l** worthy to be called your son *G4033*
Lk 15:21 I am **no l** worthy to be called your son *G4033*
Lk 16: 2 because you cannot be manager **any l**. *G2285*
Lk 20:36 they can no **l** die; for they are like the *G2285*
Jn 4:42 "We **no l** believe just because of what *G4033*
Jn 6:66 turned back and **no l** followed him. *G4033*
Jn 11:54 Therefore Jesus **no l** moved about *G4033*
Jn 12:35 going to have the light just a little while **l**. *G2285*
Jn 13:33 children, I will be with you only a little **l**. *G2285*
Jn 15:15 I **no l** call you servants, because a servant *G4033*
Jn 16:10 to the Father, where you can see me **no l**; *G4033*
Jn 16:23 In that day you will **no** *l* ask me anything. AIT
Jn 16:25 is coming when I will **no l** use this kind of *G4033*
Jn 17:11 I will remain in the world **no l**, but they *G4033*
Ac 4:17 warn them to speak **no l** to anyone in this *G3600*
Ac 19:22 he stayed in the province of Asia a *little* **l**. *G5989*
Ac 25:24 shouting that he ought not to live **any l**. *G3600*
Ro 6: 2 died to sin; how can we live in it **any l**? *G2285*
Ro 6: 6 that we should **no l** be slaves to sin— *G3600*
Ro 6: 9 death **no l** has mastery over him. *G4033*
Ro 6:14 For sin *shall* no *l be* your **master**, because AIT
Ro 7:17 it is **no l** I myself who do it, but it *G4033*
Ro 7:20 not want to do, it is **no l** I who do it, but it *G4033*
Ro 11: 6 if it were, grace would **no l** be grace. *G4033*
Ro 14:15 what you eat, you are **no l** acting in love. *G4033*
2Co 5:15 who live should **no l** live for themselves *G3600*
2Co 5:16 regarded Christ in this way, we do so **no l**. *G4033*
Gal 2:20 been crucified with Christ and I **no l** live, *G4033*
Gal 3:18 then it **no l** depends on the promise *G4033*
Gal 3:25 has come, we are **no l** under a guardian. *G4033*
Gal 4: 7 So you are **no l** a slave, but God's child *G4033*
Eph 2:19 you are **no l** foreigners and strangers *G4033*
Eph 4:14 Then we will **no l** be infants, tossed back *G3600*
Eph 4:17 that you must **no l** live as the Gentiles do *G3600*
Eph 4:28 who has been stealing must steal **no l**, *G3600*
1Th 3: 1 So when we could stand it **no l**, we *G3600*
1Th 3: 5 when I could stand it **no l**, I sent to find *G3600*
1Ti 1: 3 people not *to* **teach false doctrines** *any l* AIT
Phm 16 **no l** as a slave, but better than a slave, as *G4033*
Heb 5:11 you because *you* **no l try** to *G3821+1181*
Heb 8:11 **No l** will they teach their neighbor *G4024+3590*
Heb 10: 2 would no **l** have felt guilty for their *G2285*
Heb 10:18 forgiven, sacrifice for sin is **no l** *necessary*. *G4033*
Rev 6:11 and they were told to wait a little **l** *G2285+5989*
Rev 21: 1 passed away, and there was no **l** any sea. *G2285*
Rev 22: 3 No **l** will there be any curse. The throne of *G2285*

LONGING (15) [LONG]

Dt 28:65 eyes **weary with l**, and a despairing H4001
Job 7: 2 Like a slave **l for** the evening shadows, or H8634
Ps 119:20 is consumed with **l** for your laws at all H9291
Ps 119:81 My soul **faints with l** for your salvation, H3983
Ps 119:131 mouth and pant, **l for** your commands. H3277
Pr 13:12 heart sick, but a **l** fulfilled is a tree of life. H9294
Pr 13:19 A **l** fulfilled is sweet to the soul, but fools H9294
Eze 23:27 *will* not **look** on these things with **l** H5951+6524
Lk 16:21 **l** to eat what fell from the rich man's *G2121*
Ro 15:23 since I have been **l** for many years to *G2163*
2Co 5: 2 **l** to be clothed instead with our heavenly *G2160*
2Co 7: 7 He told us about your **l** for me, your deep *G2161*
2Co 7:11 what alarm, what **l**, what concern, what *G2161*
1Th 2:17 out of our intense **l** we made every effort *G2123*
Heb 11:16 *they were* **l for** a better country—a *G3977*

LONGINGS (2) [LONG]

Ps 38: 9 All my **l** lie open before you, Lord; my H9294
Ps 112:10 the **l** *of* the wicked will come to nothing. H9294

LONGS (5) [LONG]

Ps 63: 1 my whole being **l for** you, in a dry and H4014
Isa 26: 9 in the morning my spirit **l for** you. H8838
Isa 30:18 Yet the LORD **l** to be gracious to you H2675
Php 2:26 For *he* **l for** all of you and is *G2160+1639*
Jas 4: 5 reason that *he* jealously **l for** the spirit he *G2160*

LONGSUFFERING (KJV) FORBEARANCE, PATIENCE, PATIENT, SLOW TO ANGER

LOOK (333) [FINE-LOOKING, LOOKED, LOOKING, LOOKOUT, LOOKOUTS, LOOKS]

Ge 4: 5 his offering *he did* not **l with favor**. H9120
Ge 13:14 "**L around** from where H5951+6524+2256+8011
Ge 15: 5 "**L up** at the sky and count the stars H5564
Ge 19: 8 **L**, I have two daughters who have never H2180
Ge 19:17 Don't **l** back, and don't stop anywhere in H5564
Ge 19:20 **L**, here is a town near enough to run to H2180
Ge 25:32 "**L**, I am about to die," Esau said. "What H2180
Ge 27: 6 said to her son Jacob, "**L**, I overheard your H2180
Ge 29: 7 "**L**," he said, "the sun is still high; it is not H2176
Ge 31:12 '**L** up and see that all the male goats H6524
Ge 39:14 "**L**," she said to them, "this Hebrew has H8011
Ge 40: 7 "Why do you **l** so sad today? H7156
Ge 41:33 "And now *let* Pharaoh **l for** a discerning H8011
Ge 49:18 "*I* **l** for your deliverance, LORD. H7747
Ex 1: 9 "**L**," he said to his people, "the Israelites H2180
Ex 3: 4 the LORD saw that he had gone over to **l**, H8011
Ex 3: 6 because he was afraid *to* **l** at God. H5564
Ex 5: 5 Then Pharaoh said, "**L**, the people of the H2176
Ex 5:21 "*May* the LORD **l** on you and judge you! H8011
Lev 13:36 he *does* not *need to* **l** for yellow hair H1329
Lev 26: 9 " '*I will* **l** on you **with favor** and make you H7155
Nu 4:20 must not go in to **l** *at* the holy things, H8011
Nu 15:39 have these tassels *to* **l** *at* and so you will H8011
Nu 21: 8 anyone who is bitten *can* **l** *at* it and live." H8011
Nu 32: 8 from Kadesh Barnea to **l over** the land. H8011
Dt 3:27 top of Pisgah and **l** west and north H5951+6524
Dt 3:27 **L** at the land with your own eyes, since H8011
Dt 4:19 And when you **l** up to the sky and see the H6524
Dt 7:16 *Do* not **l** on them **with pity** and do H2571+6524
Dt 26:15 **L down** from heaven, your holy dwelling H9207
Jos 2: 1 **l over** the land," he said, "especially H8011
Jos 2: 2 of Jericho was told, "**L**, some of the H2180
Jos 22:28 **L** *at* the replica of the LORD's altar, which H8011
Jdg 6:37 **l**, I will place a wool fleece on the H2180
Jdg 9:36 he said to Zebul, "**L**, people are coming H2180
Jdg 9:37 "**L**, people are coming down from the H2180
Jdg 14: 8 he turned aside to **l** *at* the lion's carcass H8011
Jdg 19: 9 said, "Now **l**, it's almost evening. H2180
Jdg 19:24 **L**, here is my virgin daughter, and his H2180
Jdg 21:19 But **l**, there is the annual festival of the H2180
Ru 1:15 "**L**," said Naomi, "your sister-in-law is H2180
1Sa 1:11 if *you will* **only l** on your servant's H8011+8011
1Sa 9: 3 with you and go and **l for** the donkeys." H1335
1Sa 9: 6 the servant replied, "**L**, in this town there H2180
1Sa 9: 8 "**L**," he said, "I have a quarter of a shekel H2180
1Sa 10: 2 you set out to **l for** have been found. H1335
1Sa 14:11 Philistine outpost. "**L**!" said the Philistines H2180
1Sa 14:33 said to Saul, "**L**, the men are sinning H2180
1Sa 16: 7 The LORD does not **l** at the things people NDT
1Sa 16: 7 does not look at the things people **l** *at*. H8011
1Sa 16: 7 People **l** at the outward appearance, but H8011
1Sa 18:22 privately and say, '**L**, the king likes you, H2180
1Sa 20: 2 **L**, my father doesn't do anything, great H2180
1Sa 20: 5 So David said, "**L**, tomorrow is the New H2180
1Sa 20:21 If I say to him, '**L**, the arrows are on this H2180
1Sa 20:22 if I say to the boy, '**L**, the arrows are H2180

1Sa 21:14 to his servants, "L at the man! He is H8011
1Sa 23: 1 David was told, "L, the Philistines are H2180
1Sa 24: 2 set out to l for David and his men H1335
1Sa 24:11 l at this piece of your robe in my hand! H8011
1Sa 26:16 LORD's anointed. L around you. Where H8011
1Sa 26:20 of Israel has come out to l for a flea— H1335
1Sa 28:14 "What does he l like?" he asked. "An old H9307
1Sa 28:21 shaken, she said, "L, your servant has H2180
2Sa 2:22 could I l your brother Joab in the face H5951+7156+448
2Sa 3:24 have you done? L, Abner came to you H2180
2Sa 13: 4 l so haggard morning after morning? NDT
2Sa 14:30 said to his servants, "L, Joab's field is next H8011
2Sa 14:32 said to Joab, "L, I sent word to you H2180
2Sa 15: 3 say to him, "L, your claims are valid H8011
2Sa 16:12 be that the LORD will l upon my misery H8011
2Sa 18:26 to the gatekeeper, "L, another man H2180
1Ki 1: 2 "Let us l for a young virgin to serve the H1335
1Ki 12:16 L after your own house, David!" So H8011
1Ki 17:23 his mother and said, "L, your son is alive!" H8011
1Ki 18:10 master has not sent someone to l for you. H1335
1Ki 18:43 "Go and l toward the sea," he told his H5564
1Ki 20:31 said to him, "L, we have heard that the H2180
1Ki 22:13 said to him, "L, the other prophets H2180
2Ki 2:16 "L," they said, "we your servants have H2180
2Ki 2:16 Let them go and l for your master H1335
2Ki 2:19 of the city said to Elisha, "L, our lord, H2180
2Ki 4:25 man of God said to his servant Gehazi, "L! H2180
2Ki 6: 1 said to Elisha, "L, the place where we H2180
2Ki 6:32 L, when the messenger comes, shut the H8011
2Ki 7: 2 to the man of God, "L, even if the LORD H2180
2Ki 7: 6 said to one another, "L, the king of Israel H2180
2Ki 7:19 to the man of God, "L, even if the LORD H2180
2Ki 9: 2 get there, l for Jehu son of Jehoshaphat H8011
2Ki 10:23 "L around and see that no one who serves H2924
2Ki 18:21 L, I know you are depending on H2180+6964
1Ch 16:11 L to the LORD and his strength; seek his H2011
1Ch 21:23 L, I will give the oxen for the burnt H8011
2Ch 10:16 L after your own house, David!" So H8011
2Ch 18:12 said to him, "L, the other prophets H2180
Ne 2: 2 does your face l so sad when you are not H8273
Ne 2: 3 Why should my face not l sad when the H8317
Est 1:11 nobles, for she was lovely to l at. H5260
Job 6:19 The caravans of Tema l for water, the H5564
Job 6:19 traveling merchants of Sheba l in hope. H7747
Job 6:28 "But now be so kind as to l at me. Would H7155
Job 7: 8 no longer; you will l for me, but I will be H6524
Job 7:19 Will you never l away from me, or let me H9120
Job 11:18 you will l about you and take your rest in H2916
Job 14: 6 So l away from him and let him alone, till H9120
Job 19:15 they l on me as on a stranger. H928+6524
Job 20: 9 his place will l on him no more. H8800
Job 21: 5 L at me and be appalled; clap your hand H7155
Job 24: 1 must those who know him l in vain for H2600
Job 30:20 I stand up, but you merely l at me. H1067
Job 31: 1 with my eyes not to l lustfully at a young H1067
Job 35: 5 L up at the heavens and see; gaze at the H5564
Job 37:21 Now no one can l at the sun, bright as it H8011
Job 40:11 l at all who are proud and bring them low, H8011
Job 40:12 l at all who are proud and humble them H8011
Job 40:15 "L at Behemoth, which I made along with H2180
Ps 11: 2 For l, the wicked bend their bows; they set H2180
Ps 13: 3 L on me and answer, LORD my God. H5564
Ps 25:18 L on my affliction and my distress and H8011
Ps 34: 5 Those who l to him are radiant; their H5564
Ps 35:17 Lord, will you l on? Rescue me from H8011
Ps 37:10 be no more; though you l for them, they H1067
Ps 39: 7 Lord, what do I l for? My hope is in H7747
Ps 39:13 L away from me, that I may enjoy life H9120
Ps 40: 4 in the LORD, who does not l to the proud H7155
Ps 59: 4 Arise to help me; l on my plight! H8011
Ps 80:14 L down from heaven and see H5564
Ps 84: 9 L on our shield, O God; look with favor on H8011
Ps 84: 9 l with favor on your anointed one. H5564+7156
Ps 101: 3 not l with approval on H8883+4200+5584+6524
Ps 104:27 All creatures l to you to give them their H8432
Ps 105: 4 L to the LORD and his strength; seek his H2011
Ps 112: 8 in the end they will l in triumph on their H8011
Ps 113: 6 who stoops down to l on the heavens H8011
Ps 118: 7 I l in triumph on my enemies. H8011
Ps 119:153 L on my suffering and deliver me, for I H8011
Ps 119:158 I l on the faithless with loathing, for they H8011
Ps 123: 2 As the eyes of slaves l to the hand of their AIT
Ps 123: 2 eyes of a female slave l to the hand of her AIT
Ps 123: 2 mistress, so our eyes l to the LORD our God AIT
Ps 142: 4 L and see, there is no one at my right H5564
Ps 145:15 The eyes of all l to you, and you give H8432
Pr 1:28 they will l for me but will not find me, H8838
Pr 2: 4 if you l for it as for silver and search H1335
Pr 4:25 Let your eyes l straight ahead; fix your H5564
Pr 20: 4 so at harvest time they l but find nothing. H8626
Pr 25:23 sly tongue—which provokes a horrified l. H7156
Ecc 1:10 which one can say, "L! This is something H8011
Ecc 1:16 I said to myself, "L, I have increased in H2180
Ecc 7:27 "L," says the Teacher, "this is what I have H8011
SS 2: 8 L! Here he comes, leaping H2180
SS 2: 9 a young stag. L! There he stands H2180
SS 3: 7 L! It is Solomon's carriage, escorted by H2180
SS 3:11 come out, and l, you daughters of Zion H8011
SS 3:11 L on King Solomon wearing a crown, the NDT
SS 6: 1 that we may l for him with you? H1335
SS 6:11 of nut trees to l at the new growth in H8011
Isa 3: 9 The l on their faces testifies against them H2129
Isa 8:22 Then they will l toward the earth and see H5564
Isa 10:12 of his heart and the haughty l in his eyes. H9514
Isa 13: 8 They will l aghast at each other, their H9449
Isa 13:18 nor will they l with compassion on H2571+6524
Isa 17: 7 In that day people will l to their Maker H9120
Isa 17: 8 They will not l to the altars, the work of H9120
Isa 18: 4 remain quiet and will l on from my H5564
Isa 21: 9 L, here comes a man in a chariot with a H2180
Isa 22:11 but you did not l to the One who made it H5564
Isa 23:13 L at the land of the Babylonians, this H2176
Isa 30: 2 who l for help to Pharaoh's protection H6395
Isa 31: 1 but do not l to the Holy One of Israel H9120
Isa 33: 7 L, their brave men cry aloud in the streets H2176
Isa 33:20 L on Zion, the city of our festivals; your H2600
Isa 34:16 L in the scroll of the LORD and read: None H2011
Isa 36: 6 L, I know you are depending on Egypt H2180
Isa 38:11 no longer will I l on my fellow man H5564
Isa 40:20 they l for a skilled worker to set up an idol H1335
Isa 40:26 Lift up your eyes and l to the heavens H8011
Isa 41:27 was the first to tell Zion, 'L, here they are! H2180
Isa 41:28 I l but there is no one—no one among H8011
Isa 42:18 you deaf; l, you blind, and see! H5564
Isa 48: 6 have heard these things; l at them all. H2600
Isa 49:18 Lift up your eyes and l around; all your H8011
Isa 51: 1 L to the rock from which you were cut and H5564
Isa 51: 2 l to Abraham, your father, and to Sarah H5564
Isa 51: 3 Zion and will l with compassion on all her H5714
Isa 51: 5 The islands will l to me and wait in hope H7747
Isa 51: 6 to the heavens, l at the earth beneath H5564
Isa 59: 9 We l for light, but all is darkness; for H7747
Isa 59:11 We l for justice, but find none; for H7747
Isa 60: 4 "Lift up your eyes and l about you: All H8011
Isa 60: 5 Then you will l and be radiant, your heart H8011
Isa 60: 9 Surely the islands l to me; in the lead are H7747
Isa 63:15 L down from heaven and see, from your H5564
Isa 64: 9 l on us, we pray, for we are all your H5564
Isa 66: 2 "These are the ones I l on with favor H5564
Isa 66:24 they will go out and l on the dead bodies H8011
Jer 2:10 Cross over to the coasts of Cyprus and l H8011
Jer 3: 2 "L up to the barren heights and see. H6524
Jer 3: 3 Yet you have the brazen l of a prostitute H5195
Jer 4:13 L! He advances like the clouds, his H2180
Jer 5: 1 of Jerusalem, l around and consider H8011
Jer 5: 3 do not your eyes l for truth? You struck NDT
Jer 6:16 "Stand at the crossroads and l; ask for the H8011
Jer 6:22 "L, an army is coming from the land of the H2180
Jer 7: 8 But l, you are trusting in deceptive words H2180
Jer 13:20 L up and see those who are H5951+6524
Jer 18:11 is what the LORD says: L! I am preparing H2180
Jer 25:32 LORD Almighty says: "L! Disaster is H2180
Jer 39:12 "Take him and l after him H8492+6524+6584
Jer 40: 4 and I will l after you; but H8492+6524+6584
Jer 40: 4 L, the whole country lies before you; go H8011
Jer 48:40 what the LORD says: "L! An eagle is H2180
Jer 49:22 L! An eagle will soar and swoop down H2180
Jer 50:41 "L! An army is coming from the north; H2180
La 1: 9 "L, LORD, on my affliction, for the enemy H8011
La 1:11 themselves alive. "L, LORD, and consider H8011
La 1:12 L around and see. Is any H5564
La 1:18 all you peoples; l on my suffering. H8011
La 2:20 "L, LORD, and consider: Whom have you H8011
La 3:63 L at them! Sitting or standing, they mock H5564
La 5: 1 has happened to us; l, and see our H5564
Eze 5:11 I will not l on you with pity or spare H2571+6524
Eze 7: 4 I will not l on you with pity; I will H2571+6524
Eze 7: 9 I will not l on you with pity; I will H2571+6524
Eze 8: 5 "Son of man, l toward the north." H5951+6524
Eze 8:17 L at them putting the branch to their nose H2180
Eze 8:18 I will not l on them with pity or H2571+6524
Eze 9:10 So I will not l on them with pity or H2571+6524
Eze 18: 6 shrines or l to the idols of H5951+6524
Eze 18:15 shrines or l to the idols of H5951+6524
Eze 21:15 at all their gates. L! It is forged to strike like H277
Eze 23:27 will not l on these things with longing H5951+6524
Eze 25: 8 Seir said, "L, Judah has become H2180
Eze 33:25 still in it and l to your idols and H5951+6524
Eze 34:11 will search for my sheep and l after them. H1329
Eze 34:12 he is with them, so will I l after my sheep. H1329
Eze 36: 9 you and will l on you with favor; H7155
Eze 40: 4 l carefully and listen closely H8011+928+6524
Eze 44: 5 of man, l carefully, listen H8011+928+6524
Da 2:13 and men were sent to l for Daniel and A10114
Da 3:25 He said, "L! I see four men walking A10194
Da 5:10 be alarmed! Don't l so pale! A10731+10228
Da 9:17 l with favor on your desolate H239+7156
Hos 2: 2 her remove the adulterous l from her face H2393
Hos 2: 7 she will l for them but not find them. H1335
Am 6: 2 Go to Kalneh and l at it; go from there to H8011
Am 7: 8 Then the Lord said, "L, I am setting a H2180
Jnh 2: 4 I will l again toward your holy temple. H5564
Mic 1: 3 L! The LORD is coming from his dwelling H2180
Mic 3:11 Yet they l for the LORD's support and say H9128
Na 1:15 L, there on the mountains, the feet of one H2180
Na 2: 4 They l like flaming torches; they dart H5260
Na 3:13 L at your troops—they are all weaklings H2180
Hab 1: 3 Why do you make me l at injustice? Why H8011
Hab 1: 5 "L at the nations and watch—and be H8011
Hab 1:13 Your eyes are too pure to l on evil; you H8011
Hab 2: 1 I will l to see what he will say to me H7595
Hag 2: 3 How does it l to you now? Does H8011
Zec 5: 5 "L up and see what is appearing. H6524
Zec 6: 8 he called to me, "L, those going toward H8011
Zec 12:10 They will l on me, the one they have H5564
Mt 6:16 fast, do not l somber as the hypocrites do G1181
Mt 6:26 L at the birds of the air; they do not sow G1838
Mt 7: 3 "Why do you l at the speck of sawdust in G1063
Mt 12: 2 Pharisees saw this, they said to him, "L! G2627
Mt 18:12 on the hills and go to l for the one that G2426
Mt 23:27 which l beautiful on the outside but on G5743
Mt 23:38 L, your house is left to you desolate. G2627
Mt 24:23 says to you, 'L, here is the Messiah G2627
Mt 25:43 in prison and you did not l after me. G2170
Mt 26:45 L, the hour has come, and the Son of Man G2627
Mt 26:65 more witnesses? L, now you have heard G2623
Mt 28: 1 the other Mary went to l at the tomb. G2555
Mk 1:36 his companions went to l for him, G2870
Mk 2:24 said to him, "L, why are they doing G2623
Mk 8:24 people; they l like trees walking around." G3972
Mk 11:21 remembered and said to Jesus, "Rabbi, l! G2623
Mk 12:15 "Bring me a denarius and let me l at it." G3972
Mk 13: 1 of his disciples said to him, "L, Teacher! G2623
Mk 13:21 says to you, 'L, here is the Messiah G2623
Mk 13:21 is the Messiah!' or, 'L, there he is!' do not G2623
Mk 14:41 L, the Son of Man is delivered into the G2627
Lk 2:45 they went back to Jerusalem to l for him. G349
Lk 6:41 "Why do you l at the speck of sawdust in G1063
Lk 9:38 I beg you to l at my son, for he is G2098
Lk 10:35 'L after him,' he said, 'and when I return, G2150
Lk 13: 6 he went to l for fruit on it but did not G2426
Lk 13: 7 I've been coming to l for fruit on this fig G2426
Lk 13:35 L, your house is left to you desolate. I tell G2627
Lk 15:29 his father, 'L! All these years I've G2627
Lk 18:13 not even l up to heaven, G3836+4057+2048
Lk 19: 8 stood up and said to the Lord, "L, Lord! G2627
Lk 21:29 "L at the fig tree and all the trees. G3972
Lk 24: 5 "Why do you l for the living among the G2426
Lk 24:39 L at my hands and my feet. It is I myself G3972
Jn 1:29 him and said, "L, the Lamb of God, G2623
Jn 1:36 passing by, he said, "L, the Lamb of God!" G2623
Jn 3:26 you testified about—l, he is baptizing, G2623
Jn 4:35 open your eyes and l at the fields! G2517
Jn 7:34 You will l for me, but you will not find me G2426
Jn 7:36 when he said, 'You will l for me, but you G2426
Jn 7:52 L into it, and you will find that a prophet G2236
Jn 8:21 and you will l for me, and you G2426
Jn 12:19 L how the whole world has gone after him G2623
Jn 13:33 You will l for me, and just as I told the G2426
Jn 19: 4 gathered there, "L, I am bringing him G2623
Jn 19:37 "They will l on the one they have pierced." G3972
Jn 20:11 she wept, she bent over to l into the tomb G4160
Ac 3: 4 Then Peter said, "L at us!" G1063
Ac 5:25 came and said, "L! The men you put in G2627
Ac 7:31 As he went over to get a closer l, he G2917
Ac 7:32 trembled with fear and did not dare to l. G2917
Ac 7:56 "L," he said, "I see heaven open and the G2627
Ac 8:36 the eunuch said, "L, here is water. G2627
Ac 11:25 Then Barnabas went to Tarsus to l for Saul, G349
Ac 13:41 " 'L, you scoffers, wonder and perish, for I G3972
Ro 1:23 God for images made to l like a mortal G3930
1Co 1:22 demand signs and Greeks l for wisdom, G2426
1Co 7:27 such a commitment? Do not l for a wife. G2426
2Co 3: 7 Israelites could not l steadily at the face of G867
1Ti 4:12 Don't let anyone l down on you because G2969
Jas 1:27 to l after orphans and widows in their G2170
Jas 5: 4 L! The wages you failed to pay the workers G2627
1Pe 1:12 Even angels long to l into these things. G4160
2Pe 3:12 as you l forward to the day of God and G4659
Rev 1: 7 "L, he is coming with the clouds," and G2627
Rev 1:18 I was dead, and now l, I am alive for ever G2627
Rev 5: 3 could open the scroll or even l inside it. G1063
Rev 5: 4 was worthy to open the scroll or l inside. G1063
Rev 16:15 "L, I come like a thief! Blessed is the one G2627
Rev 21: 3 a loud voice from the throne saying, "L! G2627
Rev 22: 7 "L, I am coming soon! Blessed is the one G2627
Rev 22:12 "L, I am coming soon! My reward is with G2627

LOOKED (208) [LOOK]

Ge 4: 4 The LORD l with favor on Abel and his H9120
Ge 13:10 Lot l around and saw that the whole plain H6524
Ge 18: 2 Abraham l up and saw three men H6524
Ge 18:16 up to leave, they l down toward Sodom H9207
Ge 19:26 But Lot's wife l back, and she became a H5564
Ge 19:28 He l down toward Sodom and Gomorrah H9207
Ge 22: 4 third day Abraham l up and saw the place H6524
Ge 22:13 Abraham l up and there in a thicket he H6524
Ge 24:63 to meditate, and as he l up, he saw H6524
Ge 24:64 Rebekah also l up and saw Isaac. She got H6524
Ge 26: 8 the Philistines l down from a window and H9207
Ge 31:10 a dream in which I l up and saw that the H6524
Ge 33: 1 Jacob l up and there was Esau, coming H6524
Ge 33: 5 Then Esau l up and saw the women and H6524
Ge 37:25 they l up and saw a caravan of H6524
Ge 41:21 had done so; they l just as ugly as before. H5260
Ge 43:29 As he l about and saw his brother H6524+5951
Ge 43:30 hurried out and l for a place to weep. H1335
Ge 43:33 they l at each other in astonishment. H9449
Ex 2:25 So God l on the Israelites and was H8011
Ex 14:10 the Israelites l up, and there were the H6524
Ex 14:24 the night the LORD l down from the pillar H9207
Ex 16:10 community, they l toward the desert H7155
Ex 24:17 glory of the LORD l like a consuming fire H5260
Nu 9:15 the cloud above the tabernacle l like fire. H5260

L

Nu 9:16 cloud covered it, and at night it **l** *like* fire. H5260
Nu 11: 7 was like coriander seed and **l** like resin. H6524
Nu 13:33 and *we* **l** the same *to* them." H2118+928+6524
Nu 17: 9 *They* **l** *at* them, and each of the leaders H8011
Nu 21: 9 by a snake and **l** at the bronze snake, H5564
Nu 24: 2 When Balaam **l** out and saw Israel H6524
Dt 9:16 When *I* **l**, I saw that you had sinned H8011
Jos 5:13 he **l** up and saw a man standing in front H6524
Jos 8:20 The men of Ai **l** back and saw the smoke H8011
Jdg 13: 6 He **l** like an angel of God H5260
Jdg 19:17 When *he* **l** and saw the traveler in H5951+6524
1Sa 6:13 when they **l** up and saw the ark H6524
1Sa 6:19 to death because *they* **l** into the ark of the H8011
1Sa 9:16 *I have* **l** *on* my people, for their cry has H8011
1Sa 10:21 But when *they* **l for** him, he was not to be H1335
1Sa 17:42 He **l** David **over** and saw that he was little H5564
1Sa 24: 8 When Saul **l** behind him, David bowed H5564
2Sa 2:20 Abner **l** behind him and asked, "Is that H7155
2Sa 13:34 standing watch **l** up and saw many H6524+906
2Sa 18:24 As he **l** out, he saw a man H6524
2Sa 24:20 When Araunah **l** and saw the king and his H9207
1Ki 2:15 All Israel **l** to me as their king H8492+7156
1Ki 3:21 But when *I* **l** at him **closely** in the morning H1067
1Ki 18:43 And he went up and **l**. "There is nothing H5564
1Ki 19: 6 *He* **l around**, and there by his head was H5564
2Ki 2:24 **l** *at* them and called down a curse on H8011
2Ki 3:22 the way, the water **l** red—like blood. H8011
2Ki 6:17 and *he* **l** and saw the hills full of horses H8011
2Ki 6:20 the LORD opened their eyes and *they* **l**, H8011
2Ki 6:30 the wall, the people **l**, and they saw that, H8011
2Ki 9:30 arranged her hair and **l out** of a window. H9207
2Ki 9:32 He **l** up at the window and called out H7156
2Ki 9:32 Two or three eunuchs **l down** at him. H9207
2Ki 11:14 *She* **l** and there was the king, standing by H8011
2Ki 23:16 Then Josiah **l around**, and when he saw H7155
1Ch 17:17 *You*, LORD God, *have* **l** *on* me as though I H8011
1Ch 21:16 David **l** up and saw the angel of the LORD H6524
1Ch 21:21 when Araunah **l** and saw him, he left H5564
2Ch 20:24 the desert and **l** toward the vast army, H7155
2Ch 23:13 *She* **l**, and there was the king, standing by H8011
2Ch 26:20 priest and all the other priests **l** at him, H7155
Ne 4:14 After *I* **l things over**, I stood up and said H8011
Est 3: 6 Instead Haman **l for** a way to destroy all H1335
Job 28:27 then *he* **l** *at* wisdom and appraised it; he H8011
Job 30:26 evil came; when *I* **l** for light, then came H3498
Ps 37:36 no more; though *I* **l for** him, he could not H1335
Ps 54: 7 my eyes *have* **l** in triumph on my foes. H8011
Ps 69:20 left me helpless; *I* **l for** sympathy, but H7747
Ps 102:19 "The LORD **l down** from his sanctuary on H9207
Ps 114: 3 The sea **l** and fled, the Jordan turned H8011
Pr 7: 6 window of my house *I* **l down** through the H9207
Pr 7:15 meet you; I **l for** you and have found you! H8838
Ecc 4: 1 Again I **l** and saw all the oppression that NDT
SS 3: 1 long on my bed *I* **l for** the one my heart H1335
SS 3: 1 *I* **l for** him but did not find him. H1335
SS 3: 2 So *I* **l for** him but did not find him. H1335
SS 5: 6 *I* **l for** him but did not find him H1335
Isa 5: 2 Then *he* **l for** a crop of good grapes, but it H7747
Isa 5: 4 *When I* **l for** good grapes, why did it yield H7747
Isa 5: 7 And *he* **l for** justice, but saw bloodshed H7747
Isa 22: 8 and *you* **l** in that day to the weapons in H5564
Isa 38:14 My eyes grew weak as I **l** to the heavens. NDT
Isa 57: 8 and *you* **l with lust** *on* their naked bodies. H2600
Isa 59:15 The LORD **l** and was displeased that there H8011
Isa 63: 5 *I* **l**, but there was no one to help, I was H5564
Jer 4:23 *I* **l** *at* the earth, and it was formless and H8011
Jer 4:24 *I* **l** *at* the mountains, and they were H8011
Jer 4:25 *I* **l**, and there were no people; every bird H8011
Jer 4:26 *I* **l**, and the fruitful land was a desert; all H8011
Jer 31:26 At this I awoke and **l** *around*. My sleep H8011
Jer 36:16 *they* **l** at each other **in fear** and said to H7064
La 1: 7 Her enemies **l** *at* her and laughed at her H8011
Eze 1: 4 *I* **l**, and I saw a windstorm coming out of H8011
Eze 1: 4 The center of the fire **l** like glowing metal, H6524
Eze 1: 5 in the fire was *what* **l like** four living H1952
Eze 1:10 Their faces **l like** this: Each of the four had H1952
Eze 1:15 As *I* **l** *at* the living creatures, I saw a H8011
Eze 1:16 sparkled like topaz, and all four **l** alike. H1952
Eze 1:22 was *what* **l something like** a vault, H1952
Eze 1:26 their heads was what **l** like a throne of H5260
Eze 1:27 to be his waist up he **l** like glowing metal, H6524
Eze 1:27 that from there down he **l** like fire H5260
Eze 2: 9 Then *I* **l**, and I saw a hand stretched out H8011
Eze 8: 2 *I* **l**, and I saw a figure like that of a man H8011
Eze 8: 3 He stretched out *what* **l like** a hand and H9322
Eze 8: 5 So I **l**, and in the entrance north of H5951+6524
Eze 8: 7 *I* **l**, and I saw a hole in H8011
Eze 8:10 So I went in and **l**, and I saw portrayed all H8011
Eze 10: 1 *I* **l**, and I saw the likeness of a throne of H8011
Eze 10: 8 could be seen *what* **l like** human hands.) H9322
Eze 10: 9 *I* **l**, and I saw beside the cherubim four H8011
Eze 10:10 the four of them **l** alike; each was like a H1952
Eze 10:21 their wings was *what* **l like** human hands. H1952
Eze 16: 5 No *one* **l** on you **with pity** or had H2571+6524
Eze 16: 8 when *I* **l** *at* you and saw that you H8011
Eze 20:17 Yet I **l** on them **with pity** and did not H2571+6524
Eze 22:30 "*I* **l for** someone among them who would H1335
Eze 23:15 all of them **l** like Babylonian chariot H5260
Eze 34: 6 and no one searched or **l for** them. H1335
Eze 37: 8 *I* **l**, and tendons and flesh appeared on H8011
Eze 40: 2 side were some buildings that **l** like a city. NDT
Eze 44: 4 *I* **l** and saw the glory of the LORD filling H8011
Da 1:15 the ten days they **l** healthier and H8011+5260
Da 2:31 "Your Majesty **l**, and there before you A10255
Da 4:10 I **l**, and there before me stood a tree in A10255
Da 4:13 lying in bed, I **l**, and there before me A10255
Da 7: 2 "In my vision at night *I* **l**, and there A10255
Da 7: 5 was a second beast, which **l like** a bear. A10179
Da 7: 6 "After that, I **l**, and there before me was A10255
Da 7: 6 was another beast, one that **l** like a leopard. NDT
Da 7: 7 in my vision at night I **l**, and there before A10255
Da 7: 9 "As I **l**, "thrones were set in place, and A10255
Da 7:13 "In my vision at night I **l**, and there A10255
Da 7:20 the horn that **l** more imposing than the A10256
Da 8: 3 I **l** up, and there before me was a ram with H6524
Da 8:15 before me stood one who **l** like a man. H5260
Da 10: 5 I **l** up and there before me was a man H6524
Da 10:16 Then one who **l** like a man touched my H1952
Da 10:18 Again the one who **l** like a man touched H5260
Da 12: 5 **l**, and there before me stood two H8011
Hab 3: 6 shook the earth; *he* **l**, and made the H8011
Zec 1:18 Then I **l** up, and there before me were H6524
Zec 2: 1 Then I **l** up, and there before me was a H6524
Zec 5: 1 I **l** again, and there before me was H6524+5951
Zec 5: 9 Then I **l** up—and there before me were H6524
Zec 6: 1 I **l** up again, and there before me were H6524
Mt 17: 8 *When* they **l up**, they saw no G2048+3836+4057
Mt 19:26 Jesus **l at** them and said, "With man this G1838
Mt 21:46 *They* **l for a way** to arrest him, but they G2426
Mt 25:36 I was sick and *you* **l after** me, I was in G2170
Mk 3: 5 *He* **l around** at them in anger and, deeply G4315
Mk 3:34 Then *he* **l at** those seated in a circle G4315
Mk 7:34 *He* **l up** to heaven and with a deep sigh G329
Mk 8:24 *He* **l up** and said, "I see people; they look G329
Mk 8:33 when Jesus turned and **l at** his disciples, G3972
Mk 9: 8 Suddenly, *when they* **l around**, they no G4315
Mk 9:26 The boy **l so much like** a corpse G1181+6059
Mk 10:21 Jesus **l at** him and loved him. "One thing G1838
Mk 10:23 Jesus **l around** and said to his disciples G4315
Mk 10:27 Jesus **l at** them and said, "With man this G1838
Mk 11:11 *He* **l around** at everything, but since it was G4315
Mk 12:12 the elders **l for a way** to arrest him G2426
Mk 14:67 warming himself, *she* **l closely at** him. G1838
Mk 16: 4 But *when they* **l up**, they saw that the stone, G329
Lk 6:10 *He* **l around** at them all, and then said to G4315
Lk 16:23 he **l up** and saw Abraham G2048+3836+4057
Lk 18: 9 and **l down on** everyone else, G2024
Lk 18:24 Jesus **l** at him and said, "How hard it is G3972
Lk 19: 5 reached the spot, *he* **l up** and said to him G329
Lk 20:17 Jesus **l directly at** them and asked, "Then G1838
Lk 20:19 the chief priests **l for a way** to arrest him G2426
Lk 21: 1 *As* Jesus **l up**, he saw the rich putting their G329
Lk 22:56 *She* **l closely at** him and said, "This man G867
Lk 22:61 The Lord turned and **l straight at** Peter G1838
Jn 1:42 Jesus **l at** him and said, "You are Simon G1838
Jn 6: 5 *When* Jesus **l up** and saw a G2048+3836+4057
Jn 11:41 Then Jesus **l up** and said G149+3836+4057
Jn 17: 1 he **l** toward heaven and G2048+3836+4057
Jn 20: 5 He bent over and **l in** at the strips of linen G1063
Ac 3: 4 Peter **l straight** at him, as did John. G867
Ac 6:15 in the Sanhedrin **l intently** at Stephen, G867
Ac 7:55 **l** up to heaven and saw the glory of God G867
Ac 11: 6 *I* **l** into it and saw four-footed G867+2917
Ac 13: 9 Holy Spirit, **l straight at** Elymas and said G867
Ac 14: 9 Paul **l directly at** him, saw that he had faith G867
Ac 17:23 around and **l carefully at** your objects of G355
Ac 23: 1 Paul **l straight at** the Sanhedrin and said G867
1Jn 1: 1 which *we have* **l** at and our hands have G2517
Rev 4: 1 After this *I* **l**, and there before me was a G3972
Rev 4: 6 throne there was what *l* **like** a sea of glass, AIT
Rev 5:11 Then *I* **l** and heard the voice of many G3972
Rev 6: 2 *I* **l**, and there before me was a white horse! G3972
Rev 6: 5 *I* **l**, and there before me was a black G3972
Rev 6: 8 *I* **l**, and there before me was a pale horse G3972
Rev 7: 9 After this *I* **l**, and there before me was a G3972
Rev 9: 7 The locusts **l like** horses prepared for G3930
Rev 9:17 riders I saw in my vision **l** like this: NDT
Rev 11:12 in a cloud, while their enemies **l on**. G2555
Rev 14: 1 Then *I* **l**, and there before me was the G3972
Rev 14:14 *I* **l**, and there before me was a white G3972
Rev 15: 2 And I saw what **l like** a sea of glass G6055
Rev 15: 5 After this *I* **l**, and I saw in heaven the G3972
Rev 16:13 I saw three impure spirits that **l like** frogs; G6055

LOOKING (69) [LOOK]

Ge 37:15 and asked him, "What *are you* **l for**?" H1335
Ge 37:16 He replied, "I'm **l for** my brothers. Can H1335
Ge 42: 1 "Why *do you just keep* **l at each other**?" H8011
Ex 2:12 **L** this way and that and seeing no one, he H7155
Ex 22:10 injured or is taken away *while* no *one is* **l**, H8011
Ex 25:20 are to face each other, **l** toward the cover. H7156
Ex 37: 9 faced each other, **l** toward the cover. H7156
Dt 22: 2 you and keep it until they **come l for** it. H2011
Jdg 4:22 "I will show you the man you're **l for**." H1335
Jdg 17: 9 he said, "and I'm **l for** a place to stay." H5162
1Sa 10:14 have you been?" "**L for** the donkeys," H1335
1Sa 19: 2 father Saul *is* **l for a chance** to kill you. H1335
1Ki 20: 7 "See how this man *is* **l for** trouble! H1335
2Ki 6:19 I will lead you to the man *you are* **l for**." H1335
Ps 69: 3 My eyes fail, **l** for my God. H3498
Ps 119:82 My eyes fail, **l** for your promise; I say NDT
Ps 119:123 My eyes fail, **l** for your salvation, looking NDT
Ps 119:123 your salvation, **l** for your righteous promise. NDT
Ecc 12: 3 those **l** through the windows grow H8011
SS 7: 4 the tower of Lebanon **l** toward Damascus. H7595
Isa 8:21 become enraged and, **l** upward, will curse H7155
Jer 46: 5 They flee in haste without **l back**, and H7155
La 4:17 our eyes failed, **l** in vain for help; from our NDT
Da 1:10 should he see you **l worse** than the other H2407
Da 7:11 I kept **l** until the beast was slain and its A10255
Mt 12:10 *L* for a reason *to* **bring charges against** Jesus AIT
Mt 13:45 heaven is like a merchant **l for** fine pearls. G2426
Mt 14:19 loaves and the two fish and **l up** to heaven, G329
Mt 26:59 whole Sanhedrin *were* **l for** false evidence G2426
Mt 28: 5 I know that *you are* **l for** Jesus, who G2426
Mk 1:37 they exclaimed: "Everyone *is* **l for** you!" G2426
Mk 3: 2 *Some* of them *were l* for a reason *to* **accuse** AIT
Mk 3:32 mother and brothers *are* outside **l for** you." G2426
Mk 5:32 But Jesus *kept* **l around** to see who had G4315
Mk 6:41 loaves and the two fish and **l up** to heaven, G329
Mk 11:18 heard this and *began* **l for** a way to kill G2426
Mk 14:55 whole Sanhedrin *were* **l for** evidence G2426
Mk 16: 6 "*You are* **l for** Jesus the Nazarene, who G2426
Lk 2:38 to all who *were* **l forward to the** G4657
Lk 2:44 Then *they began* **l for** him among their G349
Lk 4:42 The people *were* **l for** him and when they G2118
Lk 6: 7 of the law *were* **l for** a reason to accuse G2351
Lk 6:20 **L** at his disciples, he said G2048+3836+4057
Lk 9:16 loaves and the two fish and **l up** to heaven, G329
Lk 17: 7 has a servant plowing or **l after the sheep**. G4477
Lk 22: 2 of the law *were* **l for** some way to get G2426
Jn 6:26 I tell you, *you are* **l for** me, not because G2426
Jn 7: 1 leaders there *were* **l for a way** to kill him. G2426
Jn 8:37 Yet *you are* **l for a way** to kill me, because G2426
Jn 8:40 *you are* **l for a way** to kill me, G2426
Jn 11:56 *They kept* **l for** Jesus, and as they stood in G2426
Jn 18: 8 If *you are* **l for** me, then let G2426
Jn 20:15 Who is it *you are* **l for**?" Thinking he G2426
Ac 1:10 They were **l intently up** into the sky as he G867
Ac 1:11 "why do you stand here **l** into the sky? G1838
Ac 10:19 "Simon, three men *are* **l for** you. G2426
Ac 10:21 said to the men, "I'm the one *you're* **l for**. G2426
Ac 13:25 I am not the one you are **l** for. But there is NDT
Php 2: 4 not **l to** your own interests but each of you G5023
1Th 2: 6 *We were* not **l for** praise from people, not G2426
Heb 11:10 For *he was* **l forward to** the city with G1683
Heb 11:14 things show that *they are* **l for** a country of G2118
Heb 11:26 because *he was* **l ahead** to his reward. G611
Heb 13:14 but *we are* **l for** the city that is to come. G2118
Jas 1:24 *after* **l at** himself, goes away and G2917
1Pe 5: 8 a roaring lion **l for** someone to devour. G2426
2Pe 3:13 his promise *we are* **l forward to** a new G4659
2Pe 3:14 *since you are* **l forward to** this G4659
Rev 5: 6 Then I saw a Lamb, *l* **as if** it had been slain AIT

LOOKOUT (5) [LOOK]

2Ki 9:17 When the **l** standing on the tower in H7595
2Ki 9:18 The **l** reported, "The messenger has H7595
2Ki 9:20 The **l** reported, "He has reached them H7595
Isa 21: 6 post a **l** and have him report what he sees H7595
Isa 21: 8 And the **l** shouted, "Day after day, my lord H8011

LOOKOUTS (1) [LOOK]

1Sa 14:16 Saul's **l** at Gibeah in Benjamin saw the H7595

LOOKS (29) [LOOK]

Lev 14:35 seen something that **l** like a defiling mold NDT
1Sa 16: 7 appearance, but the LORD **l** at the heart." H8011
Ezr 8:22 of our God is on everyone *who* **l** to him, H1335
Job 8:17 pile of rocks and **l** *for* a place among the H2600
Job 39:29 From there *it* **l** for food; its eyes detect it H2916
Job 41:34 *It* **l down on** all that are haughty; it is king H8011
Ps 14: 2 The LORD **l down** from heaven on all H9207
Ps 33:13 From heaven the LORD **l down** and sees all H5564
Ps 53: 2 God **l down** from heaven on all mankind H9207
Ps 85:11 righteousness **l down** from heaven. H9207
Ps 104:32 he *who* **l** at the earth, and it trembles H5564
Ps 138: 6 LORD is exalted, *he* **l kindly** *on* the lowly H8011
Ecc 11: 4 *whoever* **l** at the clouds will not reap. H8011
Isa 5:30 And if *one* **l** at the land, there is only H5564
La 3:50 until the LORD **l down** from heaven and H9207
Eze 18:12 He **l** to the idols. H5951+6524
Eze 34:12 As a shepherd **l after** his scattered flock H1333
Da 3:25 the fourth **l** like a son of the gods." A10657
Mal 2:13 because *he* no longer **l with favor** on your H7155
Mt 5:28 that anyone who **l at** a woman lustfully G1063
Mt 16: 4 adulterous generation **l for** a sign, G2118
Lk 9:62 a hand to the plow and **l** back is fit for G1063
Jn 6:40 is that everyone who **l to** the Son and G2555
Jn 9: 9 "No, he only **l like** him." But he G1639
Jn 12:45 The *one who* **l at** me is seeing the one G2555
Php 2:21 For everyone **l out for** their own interests G2426
Jas 1:23 says is like someone *who* **l** at his face in a G2917
Jas 1:24 immediately forgets **what** *he* **l like**. G3961+1639
Jas 1:25 But whoever **l intently** into the perfect law G4160

LOOM (3) [LOOMS]

Jdg 16:13 into the fabric on the **l** and tighten it with NDT
Jdg 16:14 his sleep and pulled up the pin and the **l**, H756
Isa 38:12 he has cut me off from the **l**; day and H1929

LOOMS (1) [LOOM]

Jer 6: 1 For disaster **l** out of the north, even H9207

LOOPS (11)

Ex 26: 4 Make **l** *of* blue material along the edge of H4339
Ex 26: 5 Make fifty **l** on one curtain and fifty loops H4339

Ex 26: 5 curtain and fifty l on the end curtain of H4339
Ex 26: 5 other set, with the l opposite each other. H4339
Ex 26:10 Make fifty l along the edge of the end H4339
Ex 26:11 put them in the l to fasten the tent H4339
Ex 36:11 Then they made l *of* blue material along H4339
Ex 36:12 They also made fifty l on one curtain and H4339
Ex 36:12 curtain and fifty l on the end curtain of H4339
Ex 36:12 other set, with the l opposite each other. H4339
Ex 36:17 Then they made fifty l along the edge of H4339

LOOSE (12) [LOOSED, LOOSEN, LOOSENED]

Jdg 15: 5 the torches and **let** the foxes l in the H8938
Jdg 16: 3 two posts, and **tore** them l, bar and all. H5825
Job 6: 9 *to* **let** l his hand and cut off my life! H6000
Job 12:15 is drought; if *he* **lets** them l, they H8938
Ps 78:26 *He* **let** l the east wind from the heavens H5825
Isa 7:25 **places where** cattle are **turned** l and H5448
Isa 33:23 Your rigging **hangs** l: The mast is not held H5759
Isa 58: 6 *to* l the chains of injustice and untie the H7337
Mt 16:19 whatever *you* l on earth will be *G3395*
Mt 18:18 whatever *you* l on earth will be *G3395*
Ac 16:26 flew open, and everyone's chains **came** l. *G479*
Ac 27:40 **Cutting** l the anchors, they left them in the *G4311*

LOOSED (2) [LOOSE]

Mt 16:19 you loose on earth will be l in heaven." *G3395*
Mt 18:18 you loose on earth will be l in heaven. *G3395*

LOOSEN (2) [LOOSE]

Nu 5:18 *he shall* l her hair and place in her hands H7277
Job 38:31 of the Pleiades? *Can you* l Orion's belt? H7337

LOOSENED (2) [LOOSE]

Isa 5:27 sleeps; not a belt *is* l at the waist, not a H7337
Mk 7:35 his tongue *was* l and he began to speak *G3395*

LOOT (13) [LOOTED, LOOTER, LOOTING]

Pr 1:14 cast lots with us; we will all share the l"— H3967
Isa 10: 6 anger me, to seize l and snatch plunder H8965
Isa 17:14 This is the portion of *those who* l us, the H9115
Isa 21: 2 traitor betrays, the looter **takes** l. Elam, H8720
Isa 42:22 they have been made l, with no one to H5468
Isa 42:24 Who handed Jacob over to become l, and H5468
Eze 7:21 to foreigners and as l to the wicked of the H8965
Eze 26:12 your wealth and l your merchandise; H1024
Eze 29:19 *He will* l and plunder the land as H8964+8965
Eze 38:12 plunder and l and turn my hand H1024+1020
Eze 38:13 Have you gathered your hordes to l, H1024+1020
Eze 39:10 plundered them and l those who looted H1024
Da 11:24 l and wealth among his followers. H8965

LOOTED (7) [LOOT]

Ge 34:27 the dead bodies and l the city where their H1024
2Ki 21:14 They will be l and plundered by all their H1020
2Ch 14:14 *They* l all these villages, since there was H1024
Isa 13:16 their houses *will* **be** l and their wives H9116
Isa 42:22 But this is a people plundered and l, all H9115
Eze 39:10 them and loot *those who* l them, H1024
Am 3:10 what they have plundered and l. H8719

LOOTER (1) [LOOT]

Isa 21: 2 The traitor betrays, the l takes loot. Elam, H8720

LOOTING (1) [LOOT]

1Sa 23: 1 against Keilah and *are* l the threshing H9115

LOP (1)

Isa 10:33 *will* l **off** the boughs with great power. H6188

LORD (952) [LORD'S, LORDED, LORDING, LORDS]

Ge 18: 3 favor in your eyes, my l, do not pass your H123
Ge 18:12 "After I am worn out and my l is old, will I H123
Ge 18:27 I have been so bold as to speak to **the** L, H151
Ge 18:30 Then he said, "May **the** L not be angry, but H151
Ge 18:31 I have been so bold as to speak to **the** L, H151
Ge 18:32 Then he said, "May **the** L not be angry, but H151
Ge 20: 4 so he said, "L, will you destroy an innocent H151
Ge 23:11 my l," he said. "Listen to me; I give H123
Ge 23:15 "Listen to me, my l; the land is worth four H123
Ge 24:18 my l," she said, and quickly lowered H123
Ge 27:29 Be l over your brothers, and may the sons H1484
Ge 27:37 "I have made him l over you and have H1484
Ge 31:35 "Don't be angry, my l, that I cannot stand H123
Ge 32: 4 "This is what you are to say to my l Esau H123
Ge 32: 5 Now I am sending this message to my l H123
Ge 32:18 They are a gift sent to my l Esau, and he is H123
Ge 33: 8 "To find favor in your eyes, my l," he said. H123
Ge 33:13 "My l knows that the children are tender H123
Ge 33:14 So let my l go on ahead of his servant H123
Ge 33:14 of the children, until I come to my l in Seir." H123
Ge 33:15 "Just let me find favor in the eyes of my l." H123
Ge 42:10 my l," they answered. "Your servants H123
Ge 42:30 "The man who is l *over* the land spoke H123
Ge 42:33 the man who is l *over* the land said to us H123
Ge 43:20 beg your pardon, our l," they said, "we H123
Ge 44: 7 "Why does my l say such things? H123
Ge 44:16 "What can we say to my l?" Judah replied H123
Ge 44:18 your servant, my l, let me speak a word to H123
Ge 44:18 my lord, let me speak a word to my l. H123
Ge 44:19 My l asked his servants, 'Do you have a H123
Ge 44:22 And we said to my l, 'The boy cannot leave H123
Ge 44:24 my father, we told him what my l had said. H123
Ge 45: 8 l of his entire household and ruler of all H123
Ge 45: 9 God has made me l of all Egypt. H123
Ge 47:18 cannot hide from our l the fact that since H123
Ge 47:18 nothing left for our l except our bodies H123
Ge 47:25 "May we find favor in the eyes of our l; we H123
Ex 4:10 said to the LORD, "Pardon your servant, L. H151
Ex 4:13 your servant, L. Please send someone H151
Ex 5:22 L, why have you brought trouble on H151
Ex 15:17 the sanctuary, L, your hands established. H151
Ex 32:22 "Do not be angry, my l," Aaron answered H123
Ex 34: 9 "L," he said, "if I have found favor in your H151
Ex 34: 9 favor in your eyes, then let **the** L go with us. H151
Nu 11:28 up and said, "Moses, my l, stop them!" H123
Nu 12:11 "Please, my l, I ask you not to hold against H123
Nu 16:13 And now *you* also *want to* l **it** over H8606+8606
Nu 32:25 your servants will do as our l commands. H123
Nu 32:27 to fight before the LORD, just as our l says." H123
Nu 36: 2 LORD commanded my l to give the land as H123
Dt 10:17 your God is God of gods and L *of* lords, H123
Jos 3:11 the covenant of the L *of* all the earth will H123
Jos 3:13 ark of the LORD—the L *of* all the earth—set H123
Jos 5:14 message does my L have for his servant?" H123
Jos 7: 8 Pardon your servant, L. What can I say, now H151
Jdg 3:25 There they saw their l fallen to the floor H123
Jdg 4:18 said to him, "Come, my l, come right in. H123
Jdg 6:13 "Pardon me, my l," Gideon replied, "but if H123
Jdg 6:15 "Pardon me, my l," Gideon replied, "but H123
Jdg 13: 8 "Pardon your servant, L. I beg you to let the H151
Ru 2:13 to find favor in your eyes, my l," she said. H123
1Sa 1:15 "Not so, my l," Hannah replied, "I am a H123
1Sa 1:26 "Pardon me, my l. As surely as you H123
1Sa 16:16 Let our l command his servants here to H123
1Sa 22:12 son of Ahitub." "Yes, my l," he answered. H123
1Sa 24: 8 cave and called out to Saul, "My l the king!" H123
1Sa 24:10 'I will not lay my hand on my l, because he H123
1Sa 25:24 your servant, my l, and let me speak to you H123
1Sa 25:25 pay no attention, my l, to that wicked man H123
1Sa 25:25 I did not see the men my l sent. H123
1Sa 25:26 And now, my l, as surely as the LORD your H123
1Sa 25:26 are intent on harming my l be like Nabal. H123
1Sa 25:27 which your servant has brought to my l, be H123
1Sa 25:28 certainly make a lasting dynasty for my l, H123
1Sa 25:29 the life of my l will be bound securely in H123
1Sa 25:30 has fulfilled for my l every good thing he H123
1Sa 25:31 my l will not have on his conscience the H123
1Sa 25:31 LORD your God has brought my l success, H123
1Sa 26:15 Why didn't you guard your l the king H123
1Sa 26:15 Someone came to destroy your l the king. H123
1Sa 26:17 David replied, "Yes it is, my l the king." H123
1Sa 26:18 "Why is my l pursuing his servant? H123
1Sa 26:19 Now let my l the king listen to his servant's H123
1Sa 29: 8 fight against the enemies of my l the king?" H123
2Sa 1:10 arm and have brought them here to my l." H123
2Sa 3:21 assemble all Israel for my l the king, H123
2Sa 4: 8 LORD has avenged my l the king against H123
2Sa 9:11 will do whatever my l the king commands H123
2Sa 10: 3 commanders said to Hanun their l, H123
2Sa 13:32 "My l should not think that they killed all H123
2Sa 13:33 My l the king should not be concerned H123
2Sa 14: 9 "Let my l the king pardon me and my H123
2Sa 14:12 your servant speak a word to my l the king." H123
2Sa 14:15 to say this to my l the king because the H123
2Sa 14:17 'May the word of my l the king secure my H123
2Sa 14:17 my l the king is like an angel of God in H123
2Sa 14:18 "Let my l the king speak," the woman said. H123
2Sa 14:19 as you live, my l the king, no one can H123
2Sa 14:19 to the left from anything my l the king says. H123
2Sa 14:20 My l has wisdom like that of an angel of H123
2Sa 14:22 in your eyes, my l the king, because the H123
2Sa 15:15 to do whatever our l the king chooses." H123
2Sa 15:21 LORD lives, and as my l the king lives H123
2Sa 15:21 king lives, wherever my l the king may be H123
2Sa 16: 4 May I find favor in your eyes, my l the king. H123
2Sa 16: 9 should this dead dog curse my l the king? H123
2Sa 18:28 lifted their hands against my l the king." H123
2Sa 18:31 arrived and said, "My l the king, hear the H123
2Sa 18:32 the enemies of my l the king and all who H123
2Sa 19:19 said to him, "May my l not hold me guilty. H123
2Sa 19:19 wrong on the day my l the king left H123
2Sa 19:20 to come down and meet my l the king." H123
2Sa 19:26 He said, "My l the king, since I your servant H123
2Sa 19:27 has slandered your servant to my l the king. H123
2Sa 19:27 My l the king is like an angel of God; so do H123
2Sa 19:28 nothing but death from my l the king, H123
2Sa 19:30 now that my l the king has returned home H123
2Sa 19:35 be an added burden to my l the king? H123
2Sa 19:37 Let him cross over with my l the king. H123
2Sa 24: 3 may the eyes of my l the king see it. H123
2Sa 24: 3 But why does my l the king want to do such H123
2Sa 24:21 "Why has my l the king come to his servant H123
2Sa 24:22 "Let my l the king take whatever he wishes H123
1Ki 1: 2 him so that our l the king may keep warm H123
1Ki 1:11 our l David knows nothing about it? H123
1Ki 1:13 say to him, 'My l the king, did you not H123
1Ki 1:17 She said to him, "My l, you yourself swore H123
1Ki 1:18 you, my l the king, do not know about H123
1Ki 1:20 My l the king, the eyes of all Israel are on H123
1Ki 1:20 sit on the throne of my l the king after him. H123
1Ki 1:21 as soon as my l the king is laid to rest with H123
1Ki 1:24 "Have you, my l the king, declared that H123
1Ki 1:27 Is this something my l the king has done H123
1Ki 1:27 sit on the throne of my l the king after him?" H123
1Ki 1:31 said, "May my l King David live forever!" H123
1Ki 1:36 the God of my l the king, so declare it H123
1Ki 1:37 As the LORD was with my l the king, so may H123
1Ki 1:37 greater than the throne of my l King David!" H123
1Ki 1:43 "Our l King David has made Solomon king. H123
1Ki 1:47 come to congratulate our l King David, H123
1Ki 2:38 servant will do as my l the king has said." H123
1Ki 3:10 **The** L was pleased that Solomon had H151
1Ki 3:17 "Pardon me, my l. This woman and I H123
1Ki 3:26 the king, "Please, my l, give her the living H123
1Ki 12:27 will again give their allegiance to their l, H123
1Ki 18: 7 said, "Is it really you, my l Elijah? H123
1Ki 18:13 Haven't you heard, my l, what I did while H123
1Ki 20: 4 answered, "Just as you say, my l the king. H123
1Ki 20: 9 messengers, "Tell my l the king, 'Your H123
1Ki 22: 6 "for **the** L will give it into the king's hand." H151
2Ki 2:19 to Elisha, "Look, our l, this town is well H123
2Ki 4:16 "No, my l!" she objected. H123
2Ki 4:28 ask you for a son, my l?" she said. "Didn't I H123
2Ki 6: 5 into the water. "Oh no, my l!" he cried out. H123
2Ki 6:12 "None of us, my l the king," said one of his H123
2Ki 6:15 "Oh no, my l! What shall we do? H123
2Ki 6:26 cried to him, "Help me, my l the king!" H123
2Ki 7: 6 for **the** L had caused the Arameans to hear H151
2Ki 8: 5 is the woman, my l the king, and this is H123
2Ki 8:12 "Why is my l weeping?" asked Hazael H123
2Ki 19:23 your messengers you have ridiculed **the** L. H151
1Ch 21: 3 My l the king, are they not all my lord's H123
1Ch 21: 3 Why does my l want to do this? Why H123
1Ch 21:23 Let my l the king do whatever pleases him H123
2Ch 2:14 your skilled workers and with those of my l, H123
2Ch 2:15 "Now let my l send his servants the wheat H123
Ezr 10: 3 the counsel of my l and of those who fear H123
Ne 1:11 L, let your ear be attentive to the prayer of H151
Ne 4:14 Remember **the** L, who is great and H151
Ne 8:10 This day is holy to our L. Do not grieve, H151
Ne 10:29 regulations and decrees of the LORD our L. H151
Job 28:28 "The fear of **the** L—that is wisdom, H151
Ps 2: 4 in heaven laughs; **the** L scoffs at them. H151
Ps 8: 1 our L, how majestic is your name in H123
Ps 8: 9 our L, how majestic is your name in H123
Ps 12: 4 own lips will defend us—who is l over us?" H123
Ps 16: 2 the LORD, "You are my L; apart from you I H151
Ps 22:30 future generations will be told about **the** L. H151
Ps 30: 8 LORD, I called; to **the** L I cried for mercy: H151
Ps 35:17 How long, L, will you look on? Rescue me H151
Ps 35:22 do not be silent. Do not be far from me, L. H151
Ps 35:23 Contend for me, my God and L. H151
Ps 37:13 but **the** L laughs at the wicked, for he H151
Ps 38: 9 lie open before you, L; my sighing is not H151
Ps 38:15 I wait for you; you will answer, L my God. H151
Ps 38:22 quickly to help me, my L and my Savior. H151
Ps 39: 7 "But now, L, what do I look for? My hope H151
Ps 40:17 am poor and needy; may **the** L think of me. H151
Ps 44:23 L! Why do you sleep? Rouse H151
Ps 45:11 by your beauty; honor him, for he is your l. H123
Ps 51:15 Open my lips, L, and my mouth will declare H151
Ps 54: 4 my help; **the** L is the one who sustains me. H151
Ps 55: 9 L, confuse the wicked, confound their H151
Ps 57: 9 I will praise you, L, among the nations; H151
Ps 59:11 But do not kill them, L our shield, or my H151
Ps 62:12 with you, L, is unfailing love"; and H151
Ps 66:18 in my heart, **the** L would not have listened; H151
Ps 68:11 **The** L announces the word, and the women H151
Ps 68:17 **the** L has come from Sinai into his H151
Ps 68:19 Praise be to **the** L, to God our Savior, who H151
Ps 68:22 **The** L says, "I will bring them from Bashan H151
Ps 68:32 kingdoms of the earth, sing praise to **the** L, H151
Ps 69: 6 L, the LORD Almighty, may those who hope H151
Ps 73:20 when you arise, L, you will despise them as H151
Ps 77: 2 in distress, I sought **the** L; at night I H151
Ps 77: 7 "Will **the** L reject forever? Will he never H151
Ps 78:65 Then **the** L awoke as from sleep, as a H151
Ps 79:12 the contempt they have hurled at you, L. H151
Ps 86: 3 have mercy on me, L, for I call to you all H151
Ps 86: 4 joy to your servant, L, for I put my trust in H151
Ps 86: 5 L, are forgiving and good, abounding H151
Ps 86: 8 is none like you, L; no deeds can compare H151
Ps 86: 9 worship before you, L; they will bring glory H151
Ps 86:12 I will praise you, L my God, with all my H151
Ps 86:15 But you, L, are a compassionate and H151
Ps 89:49 L, where is your former great love, which in H151
Ps 89:50 Remember, L, how your servant has been H151
Ps 90: 1 L, you have been our dwelling place H151
Ps 90:17 May the favor of **the** L our God rest on us H151
Ps 97: 5 the LORD, before the L *of* all the earth. H123
Ps 110: 1 The LORD says to my l: "Sit at my right H123
Ps 110: 5 **The** L is at your right hand; he will crush H151
Ps 114: 7 at the presence of **the** L, at the presence of H151
Ps 130: 2 L, hear my voice. Let your ears be attentive H151
Ps 130: 3 kept a record of sins, L, who could stand? H151
Ps 130: 6 I wait for **the** L more than watchmen wait H151
Ps 135: 5 is great, that our L is greater than all gods. H151
Ps 136: 3 Give thanks to the L *of* lords: His love H151
Ps 147: 5 Great is our L and mighty in power; his H151
Isa 1:24 Therefore the L, the LORD Almighty, the H123
Isa 3: 1 See now, the L, the LORD Almighty, is about H123
Isa 3:15 declares **the** L, the LORD Almighty H151
Isa 3:17 Therefore **the** L will bring sores on the H151
Isa 3:18 In that day **the** L will snatch away their H151
Isa 4: 4 **The** L will wash away the filth of the H151
Isa 6: 1 Uzziah died, I saw **the** L, high and exalted, H151
Isa 6: 8 Then I heard the voice of **the** L saying H151

Isa 6:11 "For how long, L?" And he answered: H151
Isa 7:14 Therefore **the L** himself will give you a sign H151
Isa 7:20 In that day **the L** will use a razor hired from H151
Isa 8: 7 therefore **the L** is about to bring against H151
Isa 9: 8 **The L** has sent a message against Jacob; it H151
Isa 9:17 Therefore **the L** will take no pleasure in the H151
Isa 10:12 When **the L** has finished all his work H151
Isa 10:16 Therefore, the L, the LORD Almighty, will H123
Isa 10:23 **The L**, the LORD Almighty, will carry out H151
Isa 10:24 Therefore this is what **the L**, the LORD H151
Isa 10:33 the L, the LORD Almighty, will lop off H123
Isa 11:11 In that day **the L** will reach out his hand a H151
Isa 19: 4 declares the L, the LORD Almighty. H123
Isa 21: 6 This is what **the L** says to me: "Go, post a H151
Isa 21: 8 "Day after day, my **l**, I stand on the H123
Isa 21:16 This is what **the L** says to me: "Within one H151
Isa 22: 5 **The L**, the LORD Almighty, has a day of H151
Isa 22: 8 The L stripped away the defenses of Judah NDT
Isa 22:12 **The L**, the LORD Almighty, called you on H151
Isa 22:14 atoned for," says **the L**, the LORD Almighty. H151
Isa 22:15 This is what **the L**, the LORD Almighty, says H151
Isa 28: 2 **the L** has one who is powerful and strong. H151
Isa 28:22 become heavier; **the L**, the LORD Almighty, H151
Isa 29:13 **The L** says: "These people come near to H151
Isa 30:20 Although **the L** gives you the bread of H151
Isa 37:24 your messengers you have ridiculed **the L**. H151
Isa 38:14 am being threatened; **L**, come to my aid!" H151
Isa 38:16 **L**, by such things people live; and my spirit H151
Isa 49:14 has forsaken me, **the L** has forgotten me." H151
Jer 2:19 declares **the L**, the LORD Almighty. H151
Jer 37:20 But now, my **l** the king, please listen. H123
Jer 38: 9 "My **l** the king, these men have acted H123
Jer 46:10 But that day belongs to **the L**, the LORD H151
Jer 46:10 For **the L**, the LORD Almighty, will offer H151
Jer 49: 5 declares **the L**, the LORD Almighty. H151
Jer 50:31 declares **the L**, the LORD Almighty H151
La 1:14 and **the L** has sapped my strength. H151
La 1:15 "**The L** has rejected all the warriors in my H151
La 1:15 In his winepress **the L** has trampled Virgin H151
La 2: 1 How **the L** has covered Daughter Zion with H151
La 2: 2 Without pity **the L** has swallowed up all the H151
La 2: 5 **The L** is like an enemy; he has swallowed H151
La 2: 7 **The L** has rejected his altar and H151
La 2:18 The hearts of the people cry out to **the L** H151
La 2:19 heart like water in the presence of **the L**. H151
La 2:20 prophet be killed in the sanctuary of **the L**? H151
La 3:31 For no one is cast off by **the L** forever. H151
La 3:36 justice—would not **the L** see such things? H151
La 3:37 have it happen if **the L** has not decreed it? H151
La 3:58 **L**, took up my case; you redeemed my H151
Eze 18:25 you say, 'The way of **the L** is not just.' Hear, H151
Eze 18:29 Israelites say, 'The way of **the L** is not just. H151
Eze 21: 9 prophesy and say, 'This is what **the L** says: H151
Eze 33:17 people say, 'The way of **the L** is not just. H151
Eze 33:20 Israelites say, 'The way of **the L** is not just. H151
Da 1: 2 And **the L** delivered Jehoiakim king of H151
Da 1:10 "I am afraid of my **l** the king, who has H123
Da 2:47 God of gods and the L *of* kings and a A10437
Da 4:19 answered, "My **l**, if only the dream A10437
Da 4:24 High has issued against my **l** the king: A10437
Da 5:23 set yourself up against the L *of* heaven. A10437
Da 9: 3 So I turned to **the L** God and pleaded with H151
Da 9: 4 "**L**, the great and awesome God, who H151
Da 9: 7 "**L**, you are righteous, but this day we are H151
Da 9: 9 **The L** our God is merciful and forgiving H151
Da 9:15 **L** our God, who brought your people H151
Da 9:16 **L**, in keeping with all your righteous acts H151
Da 9:17 For your sake, **L**, look with favor on your H151
Da 9:19 **L**, listen! Lord, forgive! Lord, hear and act H151
Da 9:19 **L**, forgive! Lord, hear and act H151
Da 9:19 **L**, hear and act! For your sake H151
Da 10:16 of the vision, my **l**, and I feel very weak. H123
Da 10:17 talk with you, my **l**? My strength is gone H123
Da 10:19 my **l**, since you have given me H123
Da 12: 8 So I asked, "My **l**, what will the outcome of H123
Hos 12:14 his **L** will leave on him the guilt of his H151
Am 3:13 of Jacob," declares **the L**, the LORD God H151
Am 5:16 Therefore this is what **the L**, the LORD God H151
Am 7: 7 **The L** was standing by a wall that had H151
Am 7: 8 Then **the L** said, "Look, I am setting a H151
Am 9: 1 I saw **the L** standing by the altar, and he H151
Am 9: 5 **The L**, the LORD Almighty—he touches the H151
Mic 1: 2 against you, **the L** from his holy temple. H151
Mic 4:13 their wealth to the L *of* all the earth. H123
Zec 1: 9 are these, my **l**?" The angel who was H123
Zec 4: 4 talked with me, "What are these, my **l**?" H123
Zec 4: 5 what these are?" "No, my **l**," I replied. H123
Zec 4:13 know what these are?" "No, my **l**," I said. H123
Zec 4:14 are anointed to serve the L *of* all the earth." H123
Zec 6: 4 speaking to me, "What are these, my **l**?" H123
Zec 6: 5 in the presence of the L *of* the whole world. H123
Zec 9: 4 But **the L** will take away her possessions H151
Mal 1:14 sacrifices a blemished animal to **the L**. H151
Mal 3: 1 Then suddenly the L you are seeking will H123
Mt 1:20 an angel *of* the L appeared to him in a *G3261*
Mt 1:22 to fulfill what the L had said through the *G3261*
Mt 1:24 what the angel *of* the L had commanded *G3261*
Mt 2:13 an angel *of* the L appeared to Joseph in a *G3261*
Mt 2:15 fulfilled what the L had said through the *G3261*
Mt 2:19 an angel *of* the L appeared in a dream to *G3261*
Mt 3: 3 'Prepare the way *for* the L, make straight *G3261*
Mt 4: 7 'Do not put the L your God to the test.'" *G3261*
Mt 4:10 'Worship the L your God, and serve him *G3261*
Mt 5:33 fulfill *to* the L the vows you have *G3261*
Mt 7:21 who says to me, 'L, Lord,' will enter the *G3261*
Mt 7:21 L,' will enter the kingdom of heaven *G3261*
Mt 7:22 say to me on that day, 'L, Lord, did we not *G3261*
Mt 7:22 L, did we not prophesy in your *G3261*
Mt 8: 2 before him and said, "L, if you are willing, *G3261*
Mt 8: 6 "L," he said, "my servant lies at home *G3261*
Mt 8: 8 centurion replied, "L, I do not deserve to *G3261*
Mt 8:21 said to him, "L, first let me go and *G3261*
Mt 8:25 went and woke him, saying, "L, save us! *G3261*
Mt 9:28 able to do this?" "Yes, L," they replied. *G3261*
Mt 9:38 Ask the L of the harvest, therefore, to send *G3261*
Mt 11:25 L of heaven and earth, because *G3261*
Mt 12: 8 For the Son of Man is L of the Sabbath." *G3261*
Mt 14:28 "L, if it's you," Peter replied, "tell me to *G3261*
Mt 14:30 beginning to sink, cried out, "L, save me!" *G3261*
Mt 15:22 crying out, "L, Son of David, have *G3261*
Mt 15:25 knelt before him. "L, help me!" she said. *G3261*
Mt 15:27 "Yes it is, L," she said. "Even the dogs eat *G3261*
Mt 16:22 began to rebuke him. "Never, L!" he said. *G3261*
Mt 17: 4 Peter said to Jesus, "L, it is good for us to *G3261*
Mt 17:15 "L, have mercy on my son," he said. "He *G3261*
Mt 18:21 to Jesus and asked, "L, how many times *G3261*
Mt 20:25 the rulers of the Gentiles **l it over** them, *G2894*
Mt 20:30 they shouted, "L, Son of David, have *G3261*
Mt 20:31 shouted all the louder, "L, Son of David, *G3261*
Mt 20:33 "L," they answered, "we want our sight." *G3261*
Mt 21: 3 say that the L needs them, and he *G3261*
Mt 21: 9 is he who comes in the name *of* the L!" *G3261*
Mt 21:16 infants you, L, have called forth your NDT
Mt 21:42 the cornerstone; the L has done this, and *G3261*
Mt 22:37 " 'Love the L your God with all your heart *G3261*
Mt 22:43 speaking by the Spirit, calls him 'L'? *G3261*
Mt 22:44 " 'The L said to my Lord: "Sit at my right *G3261*
Mt 22:44 " 'The Lord said *to* my L: "Sit at my right *G3261*
Mt 22:45 If then David calls him 'L,' how can he be *G3261*
Mt 23:39 is he who comes in the name *of* the L. *G3261*
Mt 24:42 not know on what day your L will come. *G3261*
Mt 25:11 the others also came. 'L, Lord,' they said *G3261*
Mt 25:11 'Lord, L,' they said, 'open the *G3261*
Mt 25:37 will answer him, 'L, when did we see you *G3261*
Mt 25:44 also will answer, 'L, when did we see you *G3261*
Mt 26:22 the other, "Surely you don't mean me, L?" *G3261*
Mt 27:10 potter's field, as the L commanded me." *G3261*
Mt 28: 2 an angel *of* the L came down from *G3261*
Mk 1: 3 'Prepare the way *for* the L, make straight *G3261*
Mk 2:28 the Son of Man is L even of the Sabbath *G3261*
Mk 5:19 them how much the L has done for you, *G3261*
Mk 7:28 "L," she replied, "even the dogs under the *G3261*
Mk 10:42 as rulers of the Gentiles **l it over** them, *G2894*
Mk 11: 3 'The L needs it and will send it back here *G3261*
Mk 11: 9 is he who comes in the name *of* the L!" *G3261*
Mk 12:11 the L has done this, and it is marvelous in *G3261*
Mk 12:29 O Israel: The L our God, the Lord is *G3261*
Mk 12:29 The Lord our God, the L is one. *G3261*
Mk 12:30 Love the L your God with all your heart *G3261*
Mk 12:36 " 'The L said to my Lord: "Sit at *G3261*
Mk 12:36 " 'The Lord said *to* my L: "Sit at my right *G3261*
Mk 12:37 David himself calls him 'L.' How then can *G3261*
Mk 13:20 "If the L had not cut short those days, no *G3261*
Mk 16:19 After the L Jesus had spoken to them, he *G3261*
Mk 16:20 the L worked with them and *G3261*
Lk 1: 9 into the temple *of* the L and burn incense. *G3261*
Lk 1:11 Then an angel *of* the L appeared to him *G3261*
Lk 1:15 he will be great in the sight of the L *G3261*
Lk 1:16 of the people of Israel to the L their God. *G3261*
Lk 1:17 And he will go on before **the L**, in the *G899S*
Lk 1:17 to make ready a people prepared *for* the L. *G3261*
Lk 1:25 "The L has done this for me," she said. *G3261*
Lk 1:28 are highly favored! The L is with you." *G3261*
Lk 1:32 The L God will give him the throne of his *G3261*
Lk 1:43 that the mother *of* my L should come to *G3261*
Lk 1:45 has believed that the L would fulfill his *G3261*
Lk 1:46 And Mary said: "My soul glorifies the L *G3261*
Lk 1:58 heard that the L had shown her great *G3261*
Lk 1:68 "Praise be *to* the L, the God of Israel *G3261*
Lk 1:76 will go on before the L to prepare the way *G3261*
Lk 2: 9 An angel *of* the L appeared to them, and *G3261*
Lk 2: 9 the glory *of* the L shone around them *G3261*
Lk 2:11 born to you; he is the Messiah, the L. *G3261*
Lk 2:15 happened, which the L has told us about." *G3261*
Lk 2:22 him to Jerusalem to present him *to* the L *G3261*
Lk 2:23 as it is written in the Law *of* the L, "Every *G3261*
Lk 2:23 male is to be consecrated *to* the L" *G3261*
Lk 2:24 with what is said in the Law *of* the L: *G3261*
Lk 2:29 "**Sovereign** L, as you have promised, you *G1305*
Lk 2:39 everything required by the Law *of* the L, *G3261*
Lk 3: 4 'Prepare the way *for* the L, make straight *G3261*
Lk 4: 8 'Worship the L your God and serve him *G3261*
Lk 4:12 'Do not put the L your God to the test *G3261*
Lk 4:18 "The Spirit *of* the L is on me, because he *G3261*
Lk 5: 8 "Go away from me, L; I am a sinful man!" *G3261*
Lk 5:12 begged him, "L, if you are willing, *G3261*
Lk 5:17 And the power *of* the L was with Jesus to *G3261*
Lk 6: 5 "The Son of Man is L of the Sabbath." *G3261*
Lk 6:46 do you call me, 'L, Lord,' and do not do *G3261*
Lk 6:46 you call me, 'Lord, L,' and do not do what *G3261*
Lk 7: 6 "L, don't trouble yourself, for I do not *G3261*
Lk 7:13 When the L saw her, his heart went out to *G3261*
Lk 7:19 he sent them to the L to ask, "Are you the *G3261*
Lk 9:54 they asked, "L, do you want us to call fire *G3261*
Lk 9:59 But he replied, "L, first let me go and bury *G3261*
Lk 9:61 "I will follow you, L; but first let me go *G3261*
Lk 10: 1 After this the L appointed seventy-two *G3261*
Lk 10: 2 Ask the L of the harvest, therefore, to send *G3261*
Lk 10:17 with joy and said, "L, even the demons *G3261*
Lk 10:21 L of heaven and earth, because *G3261*
Lk 10:27 " 'Love the L your God with all your heart *G3261*
Lk 10:40 to him and asked, "L, don't you care that *G3261*
Lk 10:41 the L answered, "you are worried and *G3261*
Lk 11: 1 disciples said to him, "L, teach us to pray, *G3261*
Lk 11:39 Then the L said to him, "Now then, you *G3261*
Lk 12:41 Peter asked, "L, are you telling this *G3261*
Lk 12:42 The L answered, "Who then is the faithful *G3261*
Lk 13:15 The L answered him, "You hypocrites *G3261*
Lk 13:23 Someone asked him, "L, are only a few *G3261*
Lk 13:35 is he who comes in the name *of* the L. *G3261*
Lk 17: 5 The apostles said *to* the L, "Increase our *G3261*
Lk 17:37 "Where, L?" they asked. He replied *G3261*
Lk 18: 6 And the L said, "Listen to what the unjust *G3261*
Lk 18:41 me to do for you?" "L, I want to see," *G3261*
Lk 19: 8 But Zacchaeus stood up and said to the L *G3261*
Lk 19: 8 stood up and said to the Lord, "Look, L! *G3261*
Lk 19:31 are you untying it?' say, 'The L needs it.' " *G3261*
Lk 19:34 They replied, "The L needs it." *G3261*
Lk 19:38 the king who comes in the name *of* the L!" *G3261*
Lk 20:37 he calls the L 'the God of Abraham *G3261*
Lk 20:42 " 'The L said to my Lord: "Sit *G3261*
Lk 20:42 " 'The Lord said *to* my L: "Sit at my right *G3261*
Lk 20:44 David calls him 'L.' How then can he be *G3261*
Lk 22:25 "The kings of the Gentiles **l it over** them *G3259*
Lk 22:33 But he replied, "L, I am ready to go with *G3261*
Lk 22:38 "See, L, here are two swords. *G3261*
Lk 22:49 they said, "L, should we strike with our *G3261*
Lk 22:61 The L turned and looked straight at Peter *G3261*
Lk 22:61 the word the L had spoken to him: *G3261*
Lk 24: 3 they did not find the body *of* the L Jesus. *G3261*
Lk 24:34 The L has risen and has appeared to *G3261*
Jn 1:23 'Make straight the way *for* the L. *G3261*
Jn 6:23 the bread after the L had given thanks. *G3261*
Jn 6:68 answered him, "L, to whom shall we go *G3261*
Jn 9:38 Then the man said, "L, I believe," and he *G3261*
Jn 11: 2 perfume on the L and wiped his feet *G3261*
Jn 11: 3 sent word to Jesus, "L, the one you love is *G3261*
Jn 11:12 disciples replied, "L, if he sleeps, he will *G3261*
Jn 11:21 "L," Martha said to Jesus, "if you had *G3261*
Jn 11:27 L," she replied, "I believe that you *G3261*
Jn 11:32 his feet and said, "L, if you had been here *G3261*
Jn 11:34 "Come and see, L," they replied. *G3261*
Jn 11:39 L," said Martha, the sister of the *G3261*
Jn 12:13 is he who comes in the name *of* the L!" *G3261*
Jn 12:38 "L, who has believed our message and to *G3261*
Jn 12:38 has the arm *of* the L been revealed?" *G3261*
Jn 13: 6 who said to him, "L, are you going to *G3261*
Jn 13: 9 L," Simon Peter replied, "not just *G3261*
Jn 13:13 "You call me 'Teacher' and 'L,' and rightly *G3261*
Jn 13:14 Now that I, your L and Teacher, have *G3261*
Jn 13:25 against Jesus, he asked him, "L, who is it?" *G3261*
Jn 13:36 Peter asked him, "L, where are you going?" *G3261*
Jn 13:37 Peter asked, "L, why can't I follow you *G3261*
Jn 14: 5 said to him, "L, we don't know where *G3261*
Jn 14: 8 Philip said, "L, show us the Father and *G3261*
Jn 14:22 L, why do you intend to show *G3261*
Jn 20: 2 "They have taken the L out of the tomb *G3261*
Jn 20:13 "They have taken my L away," she said *G3261*
Jn 20:18 "I have seen the L!" And she told them *G3261*
Jn 20:20 were overjoyed when they saw the L. *G3261*
Jn 20:25 disciples told him, "We have seen the L!" *G3261*
Jn 20:28 Thomas said to him, "My L and my God!" *G3261*
Jn 21: 7 Jesus loved said to Peter, "It is the L!" *G3261*
Jn 21: 7 him say, "It is the L," he wrapped his *G3261*
Jn 21:12 "Who are you?" They knew it was the L. *G3261*
Jn 21:15 L," he said, "you know that I love *G3261*
Jn 21:16 He answered, "Yes, L, you know that I *G3261*
Jn 21:17 He said, "L, you know all things; you *G3261*
Jn 21:20 supper and had said, "L, who is going to *G3261*
Jn 21:21 saw him, he asked, "L, what about him?" *G3261*
Ac 1: 6 him and asked him, "L, are you at this *G3261*
Ac 1:21 us the whole time the L Jesus was living *G3261*
Ac 1:24 they prayed, "L, you know everyone's *G3261*
Ac 2:20 of the great and glorious day *of* the L. *G3261*
Ac 2:21 calls on the name *of* the L will be saved. *G3261*
Ac 2:25 " 'I saw the L always before me *G3261*
Ac 2:34 yet he said, " 'The L said to my Lord: *G3261*
Ac 2:34 yet he said, " 'The Lord said *to* my L: *G3261*
Ac 2:36 whom you crucified, both L and Messiah." *G3261*
Ac 2:39 for all whom the L our God will call." *G3261*
Ac 2:47 And the L added to their number daily *G3261*
Ac 3:19 times of refreshing may come from the L, *G3261*
Ac 3:22 'The L your God will raise up for you a *G3261*
Ac 4:24 "**Sovereign** L," they said, "you made the *G1305*
Ac 4:26 together against the L and against his *G3261*
Ac 4:29 L, consider their threats and enable *G3261*
Ac 4:33 to testify to the resurrection *of* the L Jesus. *G3261*
Ac 5: 9 you conspire to test the Spirit *of* the L? *G3261*
Ac 5:14 women believed *in* the L and were added *G3261*
Ac 5:19 night an angel *of* the L opened the doors *G3261*
Ac 7:31 to get a closer look, he heard the L say: *G3261*
Ac 7:33 "Then the L said to him, 'Take off your *G3261*
Ac 7:49 build for me? says the L. Or where will my *G3261*
Ac 7:59 Stephen prayed, "L Jesus, receive my *G3261*
Ac 7:60 cried out, "L, do not hold this sin *G3261*
Ac 8:16 been baptized in the name *of* the L Jesus. *G3261*

Ac 8:22 pray *to* the L in the hope that *G3261*
Ac 8:24 "Pray to the L for me so that nothing you *G3261*
Ac 8:25 proclaimed the word *of* the L and testified *G3261*
Ac 8:26 Now an angel *of* the L said to Philip, "Go *G3261*
Ac 8:39 the Spirit *of* the L suddenly took Philip *G3261*
Ac 9: 5 "Who are you, L?" Saul asked. "I am *G3261*
Ac 9:10 The L called to him in a vision *G3261*
Ac 9:10 "Ananias!" "Yes, L," he answered. *G3261*
Ac 9:11 The L told him, "Go to the house of Judas *G3261*
Ac 9:13 "L," Ananias answered, "I have heard *G3261*
Ac 9:15 But the L said to Ananias, "Go! This man *G3261*
Ac 9:17 "Brother Saul, the L—Jesus, who *G3261*
Ac 9:27 journey had seen the L and that the Lord *G3261*
Ac 9:27 the Lord and that the L had spoken to him, NDT
Ac 9:28 speaking boldly in the name *of* the L. *G3261*
Ac 9:31 in the fear *of* the L and encouraged by *G3261*
Ac 9:35 Sharon saw him and turned to the L. *G3261*
Ac 9:42 many people believed in the L. *G3261*
Ac 10: 4 at him in fear. "What is it, L?" he asked. *G3261*
Ac 10:14 "Surely not, L!" Peter replied. "I have *G3261*
Ac 10:33 to everything the L has commanded you *G3261*
Ac 10:36 through Jesus Christ, who is L of all. *G3261*
Ac 11: 8 replied, 'Surely not, L! Nothing impure *G3261*
Ac 11:16 Then I remembered what the L had said *G3261*
Ac 11:17 us who believed in the L Jesus Christ, *G3261*
Ac 11:20 them the good news *about* the L Jesus. *G3261*
Ac 11:21 of people believed and turned to the L. *G3261*
Ac 11:23 all to remain true *to* the L with all their *G3261*
Ac 11:24 number of people were brought to the L. *G3261*
Ac 12: 7 an angel *of* the L appeared and a *G3261*
Ac 12:11 a doubt that the L has sent his angel and *G3261*
Ac 12:17 described how the L had brought him out *G3261*
Ac 12:23 an angel *of* the L struck him down *G3261*
Ac 13: 2 they were worshiping the L and fasting, *G3261*
Ac 13:10 stop perverting the right ways *of* the L? *G3261*
Ac 13:11 Now the hand *of* the L is against you. *G3261*
Ac 13:12 was amazed at the teaching *about* the L. *G3261*
Ac 13:44 city gathered to hear the word *of* the L. *G3261*
Ac 13:47 For this is what the L has commanded us: *G3261*
Ac 13:48 were glad and honored the word *of* the L; *G3261*
Ac 13:49 The word *of* the L spread through the *G3261*
Ac 14: 3 speaking boldly for the L, who confirmed *G3261*
Ac 14:23 committed them *to* the L, in whom they *G3261*
Ac 15:11 through the grace *of* our L Jesus that we *G3261*
Ac 15:17 that the rest of mankind may seek the L *G3261*
Ac 15:17 my name, says the L, who does these *G3261*
Ac 15:26 lives for the name *of* our L Jesus Christ. *G3261*
Ac 15:35 taught and preached the word *of* the L. *G3261*
Ac 15:36 the word *of* the L and see how they *G3261*
Ac 15:40 by the believers to the grace *of* the L. *G3261*
Ac 16:14 The L opened her heart to respond to *G3261*
Ac 16:15 "If you consider me a believer *in* the L," *G3261*
Ac 16:31 "Believe in the L Jesus, and you will be *G3261*
Ac 16:32 spoke the word *of* the L to him and to all *G3261*
Ac 17:24 in it is the L of heaven and earth and *G3261*
Ac 18: 8 his entire household believed *in* the L; *G3261*
Ac 18: 9 One night the L spoke to Paul in a vision *G3261*
Ac 18:25 He had been instructed in the way *of* the L, *G3261*
Ac 19: 5 were baptized in the name *of* the L Jesus. *G3261*
Ac 19:10 province of Asia heard the word *of* the L. *G3261*
Ac 19:13 invoke the name *of* the L Jesus over those *G3261*
Ac 19:17 the name *of* the L Jesus was held in *G3261*
Ac 19:20 this way the word *of* the L spread widely *G3261*
Ac 20:19 I served the L with great humility and with *G3261*
Ac 20:21 repentance and have faith in our L Jesus. *G3261*
Ac 20:24 the task the L Jesus has given me— *G3261*
Ac 20:35 the words the L Jesus himself said: *G3261*
Ac 21:13 in Jerusalem for the name *of* the L Jesus." *G3261*
Ac 22: 8 " 'Who are you, L?' I asked. " 'I am Jesus *G3261*
Ac 22:10 " 'What shall I do, L?' I asked. " 'Get up,' *G3261*
Ac 22:10 " 'Get up,' the L said, 'and go into *G3261*
Ac 22:18 saw **the** L speaking to me. 'Quick!' he *G899S*
Ac 22:19 " 'L,' I replied, 'these people know that I *G3261*
Ac 22:21 "Then the L said to me, 'Go; I will send you NDT
Ac 23:11 following night the L stood near Paul and *G3261*
Ac 26:15 I asked, 'Who are you, L?' " 'I am Jesus, *G3261*
Ac 26:15 whom you are persecuting,' the L replied. *G3261*
Ac 28:31 God and taught about the L Jesus Christ— *G3261*
Ro 1: 4 from the dead: Jesus Christ our L. *G3261*
Ro 1: 7 our Father and from the L Jesus Christ. *G3261*
Ro 4: 8 the one whose sin the L will never count *G3261*
Ro 4:24 who raised Jesus our L from the dead. *G3261*
Ro 5: 1 with God through our L Jesus Christ, *G3261*
Ro 5:11 boast in God through our L Jesus Christ, *G3261*
Ro 5:21 eternal life through Jesus Christ our L. *G3261*
Ro 6:23 of God is eternal life in Christ Jesus our L. *G3261*
Ro 7:25 delivers me through Jesus Christ our L! *G3261*
Ro 8:39 love of God that is in Christ Jesus our L. *G3261*
Ro 9:28 For the L will carry out his sentence on *G3261*
Ro 9:29 "Unless the L Almighty had left us *G3261*
Ro 10: 9 "Jesus is L," and believe in your *G3261*
Ro 10:12 the same L is Lord of all and richly blesses NDT
Ro 10:12 the same Lord is L of all and richly blesses *G3261*
Ro 10:13 calls on the name *of* the L will be saved." *G3261*
Ro 10:16 For Isaiah says, "L, who has believed our *G3261*
Ro 11: 3 "L, they have killed your prophets and torn *G3261*
Ro 11:34 "Who has known the mind *of* the L? Or *G3261*
Ro 12:11 keep your spiritual fervor, serving the L. *G3261*
Ro 12:19 mine to avenge; I will repay," says the L. *G3261*
Ro 13:14 clothe yourselves with the L Jesus Christ *G3261*
Ro 14: 4 the L is able to make them stand. *G3261*
Ro 14: 6 one day as special does so *to* the L. *G3261*
Ro 14: 6 Whoever eats meat does so *to* the L, for *G3261*
Ro 14: 6 abstains does so *to* the L and gives thanks *G3261*
Ro 14: 8 If we live, we live *for* the L; and if we die *G3261*
Ro 14: 8 the Lord; and if we die, we die *for* the L. *G3261*
Ro 14: 8 we live or die, we belong *to* the L. *G3261*
Ro 14: 9 life so that *he might be the* L of both the *G3259*
Ro 14:11 as I live,' says the L, 'every knee will bow *G3261*
Ro 14:14 being fully persuaded in the L Jesus, that *G3261*
Ro 15: 6 the God and Father *of* our L Jesus Christ. *G3261*
Ro 15:11 "Praise the L, all you Gentiles; let *G3261*
Ro 15:30 by our L Jesus Christ and by the love of *G3261*
Ro 16: 2 to receive her in the L in a way worthy of *G3261*
Ro 16: 8 Greet Ampliatus, my dear friend in the L. *G3261*
Ro 16:11 household of Narcissus who are in the L. *G3261*
Ro 16:12 those women who work hard in the L. *G3261*
Ro 16:12 who has worked very hard in the L. *G3261*
Ro 16:13 chosen in the L, and his mother, *G3261*
Ro 16:18 such people are not serving our L Christ, *G3261*
Ro 16:20 The grace *of* our L Jesus be with you. *G3261*
Ro 16:22 wrote down this letter, greet you in the L. *G3261*
1Co 1: 2 call on the name *of* our L Jesus Christ— *G3261*
1Co 1: 2 of our Lord Jesus Christ—their L and ours: NDT
1Co 1: 3 God our Father and the L Jesus Christ. *G3261*
1Co 1: 7 eagerly wait for our L Jesus Christ to be *G3261*
1Co 1: 8 on the day *of* our L Jesus Christ. *G3261*
1Co 1: 9 fellowship with his Son, Jesus Christ our L. *G3261*
1Co 1:10 in the name *of* our L Jesus Christ, that *G3261*
1Co 1:31 "Let the one who boasts boast in the L." *G3261*
1Co 2: 8 would not have crucified the L of glory. *G3261*
1Co 2:16 known the mind *of* the L so as to instruct *G3261*
1Co 3: 5 as the L has assigned to each his task. *G3261*
1Co 3:20 "The L knows that the thoughts of the *G3261*
1Co 4: 4 It is the L who judges me. *G3261*
1Co 4: 5 appointed time; wait until the L comes. *G3261*
1Co 4:17 son whom I love, who is faithful in the L. *G3261*
1Co 4:19 you very soon, if the L is willing, and then *G3261*
1Co 5: 3 in the name *of* our L Jesus on the one *G3261*
1Co 5: 4 the power *of* our L Jesus is present, *G3261*
1Co 5: 5 spirit may be saved on the day *of* the L. *G3261*
1Co 6:11 in the name *of* the L Jesus Christ and by *G3261*
1Co 6:13 meant for sexual immorality but *for* the L, *G3261*
1Co 6:13 for the Lord, and the L for the body. *G3261*
1Co 6:14 his power God raised the L from the dead, *G3261*
1Co 6:17 is united with the L is one with him in *G3261*
1Co 7:10 but the L): A wife must not separate *G3261*
1Co 7:12 not the L): If any brother has a wife who *G3261*
1Co 7:17 situation the L has assigned to them, *G3261*
1Co 7:22 called to faith in the L is the Lord's freed *G3261*
1Co 7:25 I have no command *from* the L, but I give *G3261*
1Co 7:32 Lord's affairs—how he can please the L. *G3261*
1Co 7:34 aim is to be **devoted to the** L in both body *G41*
1Co 7:35 a right way in undivided devotion *to* the L. *G3261*
1Co 7:39 she wishes, but he must belong to the L. *G3261*
1Co 8: 6 and there is but one L, Jesus Christ, *G3261*
1Co 9: 1 Have I not seen Jesus our L? Are you not *G3261*
1Co 9: 1 Are you not the result of my work in the L? *G3261*
1Co 9: 2 are the seal of my apostleship in the L. *G3261*
1Co 9:14 the L has commanded that those who *G3261*
1Co 10:21 drink the cup *of* the L and the cup of *G3261*
1Co 11:11 in the L woman is not independent of *G3261*
1Co 11:23 I received from the L what I also passed *G3261*
1Co 11:23 The L Jesus, on the night he was betrayed *G3261*
1Co 11:27 drinks the cup *of* the L in an unworthy *G3261*
1Co 11:27 against the body and blood *of* the L. *G3261*
1Co 11:32 when we are judged in this way by the L *G3261*
1Co 12: 3 can say, "Jesus is L," except by the Holy *G3261*
1Co 12: 5 different kinds of service, but the same L. *G3261*
1Co 14:21 then they will not listen to me, says the L." *G3261*
1Co 15:31 as I boast about you in Christ Jesus our L. *G3261*
1Co 15:57 us the victory through our L Jesus Christ. *G3261*
1Co 15:58 give yourselves fully to the work *of* the L, *G3261*
1Co 15:58 that your labor in the L is not in vain. *G3261*
1Co 16: 7 some time with you, if the L permits. *G3261*
1Co 16:10 he is carrying on the work *of* the L, just *G3261*
1Co 16:19 Priscilla greet you warmly in the L, *G3261*
1Co 16:22 If anyone does not love the L, let that *G3261*
1Co 16:22 let that person be cursed! **Come,** L! *G3448*
1Co 16:23 The grace *of* the L Jesus be with you. *G3261*
2Co 1: 2 God our Father and the L Jesus Christ. *G3261*
2Co 1: 3 the God and Father *of* our L Jesus Christ, *G3261*
2Co 1:14 will boast of you in the day *of* the L Jesus. *G3261*
2Co 1:24 Not that *we* **l it over** your faith, but we *G3259*
2Co 2:12 found that the L had opened a door *G3261*
2Co 3:16 But whenever anyone turns to the L, the *G3261*
2Co 3:17 Now the L is the Spirit, and where the *G3261*
2Co 3:17 where the Spirit *of* the L is, there is *G3261*
2Co 3:18 which comes from the L, who is the Spirit. *G3261*
2Co 4: 5 Jesus Christ *as* L, and ourselves as *G3261*
2Co 4:14 one who raised the L Jesus from the dead *G3261*
2Co 5: 6 home in the body we are away from the L. *G3261*
2Co 5: 8 from the body and at home with the L. *G3261*
2Co 5:11 we know what it is to fear the L, we try to *G3261*
2Co 6:17 from them and be separate, says the L. *G3261*
2Co 6:18 sons and daughters, says the L Almighty." *G3261*
2Co 8: 5 They gave themselves first of all *to* the L *G3261*
2Co 8: 9 you know the grace *of* our L Jesus Christ, *G3261*
2Co 8:19 order to honor the L himself and to show *G3261*
2Co 8:21 in the eyes of the L but also in the eyes of *G3261*
2Co 10: 8 the authority the L gave us for building *G3261*
2Co 10:17 "Let the one who boasts boast in the L." *G3261*
2Co 10:18 the one whom the L commends. *G3261*
2Co 11:17 boasting I am not talking as the L would, *G3261*
2Co 11:31 The God and Father *of* the L Jesus, who is *G3261*
2Co 12: 1 on to visions and revelations *from* the L. *G3261*
2Co 12: 8 I pleaded with the L to take it away from *G3261*
2Co 13:10 the authority the L gave me for building *G3261*
2Co 13:14 May the grace *of* the L Jesus Christ, and *G3261*
Gal 1: 3 God our Father and the L Jesus Christ, *G3261*
Gal 5:10 I am confident in the L that you will take *G3261*
Gal 6:14 except in the cross *of* our L Jesus Christ, *G3261*
Gal 6:18 The grace *of* our L Jesus Christ be with *G3261*
Eph 1: 2 God our Father and the L Jesus Christ. *G3261*
Eph 1: 3 the God and Father *of* our L Jesus Christ, *G3261*
Eph 1:15 your faith in the L Jesus and your love *G3261*
Eph 1:17 asking that the God *of* our L Jesus Christ, *G3261*
Eph 2:21 rises to become a holy temple in the L. *G3261*
Eph 3:11 he accomplished in Christ Jesus our L. *G3261*
Eph 4: 1 As a prisoner for the L, then, I urge you to *G3261*
Eph 4: 5 one L, one faith, one baptism; *G3261*
Eph 4:17 insist on it in the L, that you must no *G3261*
Eph 5: 8 darkness, but now you are light in the L. *G3261*
Eph 5:10 find out what pleases the L. *G3261*
Eph 5:19 make music from your heart *to* the L, *G3261*
Eph 5:20 in the name *of* our L Jesus Christ. *G3261*
Eph 5:22 to your own husbands as you do *to* the L. *G3261*
Eph 6: 1 obey your parents in the L, for this is right. *G3261*
Eph 6: 4 up in the training and instruction *of* the L. *G3261*
Eph 6: 7 as if you were serving the L, not people, *G3261*
Eph 6: 8 you know that the L will reward each one *G3261*
Eph 6:10 be strong in the L and in his mighty power *G3261*
Eph 6:21 dear brother and faithful servant in the L, *G3261*
Eph 6:23 God the Father and the L Jesus Christ. *G3261*
Eph 6:24 to all who love our L Jesus Christ with an *G3261*
Php 1: 2 God our Father and the L Jesus Christ. *G3261*
Php 1:14 confident in the L and dare all the more *G3261*
Php 2:11 tongue acknowledge that Jesus Christ is L, *G3261*
Php 2:19 I hope in the L Jesus to send Timothy to *G3261*
Php 2:24 I am confident in the L that I myself will *G3261*
Php 2:29 welcome him in the L with great joy, and *G3261*
Php 3: 1 my brothers and sisters, rejoice in the L! *G3261*
Php 3: 8 worth of knowing Christ Jesus my L, *G3261*
Php 3:20 a Savior from there, the L Jesus Christ, *G3261*
Php 4: 1 stand firm in the L in this way, dear *G3261*
Php 4: 2 Syntyche to be of the same mind in the L. *G3261*
Php 4: 4 Rejoice in the L always. I will say it again *G3261*
Php 4: 5 be evident to all. The L is near. *G3261*
Php 4:10 rejoiced greatly in the L that at last you *G3261*
Php 4:23 The grace *of* the L Jesus Christ be with *G3261*
Col 1: 3 the Father *of* our L Jesus Christ *G3261*
Col 1:10 a life worthy *of* the L and please him in *G3261*
Col 2: 6 just as you received Christ Jesus *as* L *G3261*
Col 3:13 Forgive as the L forgave you. *G3261*
Col 3:17 do it all in the name *of* the L Jesus, giving *G3261*
Col 3:18 to your husbands, as is fitting in the L. *G3261*
Col 3:20 in everything, for this pleases the L. *G3261*
Col 3:22 sincerity of heart and reverence *for* the L. *G3261*
Col 3:23 as working *for* the L, not for human *G3261*
Col 3:24 an inheritance from the L as a reward. *G3261*
Col 3:24 It is the L Christ you are serving *G3261*
Col 4: 7 minister and fellow servant in the L. *G3261*
Col 4:17 the ministry you have received in the L." *G3261*
1Th 1: 1 in God the Father and the L Jesus Christ: *G3261*
1Th 1: 3 inspired by hope *in* our L Jesus Christ. *G3261*
1Th 1: 6 You became imitators of us and *of* the L *G3261*
1Th 2:15 who killed the L Jesus and the prophets *G3261*
1Th 2:19 presence of our L Jesus when he comes *G3261*
1Th 3: 8 since you are standing firm in the L. *G3261*
1Th 3:11 himself and our L Jesus clear the way *G3261*
1Th 3:12 May the L make your love increase and *G3261*
1Th 3:13 Father when our L Jesus comes with *G3261*
1Th 4: 1 urge you in the L Jesus to do this *G3261*
1Th 4: 2 gave you by the authority of the L Jesus. *G3261*
1Th 4: 6 The L will punish all those who commit *G3261*
1Th 4:15 who are left until the coming *of* the L, will *G3261*
1Th 4:16 For the L himself will come down from *G3261*
1Th 4:17 in the clouds to meet the L in the air. *G3261*
1Th 4:17 And so we will be with the L forever. *G3261*
1Th 5: 2 well that the day *of* the L will come like a *G3261*
1Th 5: 9 salvation through our L Jesus Christ. *G3261*
1Th 5:12 care for you in the L and who admonish *G3261*
1Th 5:23 at the coming *of* our L Jesus Christ. *G3261*
1Th 5:27 I charge you *before* the L to have this letter *G3261*
1Th 5:28 The grace *of* our L Jesus Christ be with *G3261*
2Th 1: 1 in God our Father and the L Jesus Christ: *G3261*
2Th 1: 2 God the Father and the L Jesus Christ. *G3261*
2Th 1: 7 will happen when the L Jesus is revealed *G3261*
2Th 1: 8 do not obey the gospel *of* our L Jesus. *G3261*
2Th 1: 9 from the presence *of* the L and from the *G3261*
2Th 1:12 so that the name *of* our L Jesus may be *G3261*
2Th 1:12 grace of our God and the L Jesus Christ. *G3261*
2Th 2: 1 the coming *of* our L Jesus Christ and our *G3261*
2Th 2: 2 that the day *of* the L has already come. *G3261*
2Th 2: 8 whom the L Jesus will overthrow with the *G3261*
2Th 2:13 brothers and sisters loved by the L *G3261*
2Th 2:14 share in the glory *of* our L Jesus Christ. *G3261*
2Th 2:16 May our L Jesus Christ himself and God *G3261*
2Th 3: 1 that the message *of* the L may spread *G3261*
2Th 3: 3 But the L is faithful, and he will strengthen *G3261*
2Th 3: 4 confidence in the L that you are doing *G3261*
2Th 3: 5 May the L direct your hearts into God's *G3261*
2Th 3: 6 In the name *of* the L Jesus Christ, we *G3261*
2Th 3:12 urge in the L Jesus Christ to settle *G3261*
2Th 3:16 Now may the L of peace himself give you *G3261*
2Th 3:16 in every way. The L be with all of you. *G3261*

2Th 3:18 The grace *of* our L Jesus Christ be with *G3261*
1Ti 1: 2 God the Father and Christ Jesus our L. *G3261*
1Ti 1:12 I thank Christ Jesus our L, who has given *G3261*
1Ti 1:14 The grace *of* our L was poured out on me *G3261*
1Ti 6: 3 sound instruction *of* our L Jesus Christ *G3261*
1Ti 6:14 until the appearing *of* our L Jesus Christ, *G3261*
1Ti 6:15 the King of kings and L of lords, *G3261*
2Ti 1: 2 God the Father and Christ Jesus our L. *G3261*
2Ti 1: 8 of the testimony *about* our L or of me his *G3261*
2Ti 1:16 May the L show mercy to the household of *G3261*
2Ti 1:18 May the L grant that he will find mercy *G3261*
2Ti 1:18 he will find mercy from the L on that day! *G3261*
2Ti 2: 7 the L will give you insight into all this. *G3261*
2Ti 2:19 "The L knows those who are his," and *G3261*
2Ti 2:19 the name *of* the L must turn away *G3261*
2Ti 2:22 who call on the L out of a pure heart. *G3261*
2Ti 3:11 Yet the L rescued me from all of them. *G3261*
2Ti 4: 8 which the L, the righteous Judge, *G3261*
2Ti 4:14 The L will repay him for what he has done *G3261*
2Ti 4:17 But the L stood at my side and gave me *G3261*
2Ti 4:18 The L will rescue me from every evil attack *G3261*
2Ti 4:22 The L be with your spirit. Grace be with *G3261*
Phm 3 God our Father and the L Jesus Christ. *G3261*
Phm 5 holy people and your faith in the L Jesus. *G3261*
Phm 16 as a fellow man and as a brother in the L. *G3261*
Phm 20 may have some benefit from you in the L; *G3261*
Phm 25 The grace *of* the L Jesus Christ be with *G3261*
Heb 1:10 "In the beginning, L, you laid the *G3261*
Heb 2: 3 which was first announced by the L, was *G3261*
Heb 7:14 is clear that our L descended from Judah *G3261*
Heb 7:21 "The L has sworn and will not change his *G3261*
Heb 8: 2 the true tabernacle set up by the L, not by *G3261*
Heb 8: 8 declares the L, when I will make a *G3261*
Heb 8: 9 I turned away from them, declares the L. *G3261*
Heb 8:10 of Israel after that time, declares the L. *G3261*
Heb 8:11 another, 'Know the L,' because they will *G3261*
Heb 10:16 with them after that time, says the L. *G3261*
Heb 10:30 and again, "The L will judge his people." *G3261*
Heb 12: 6 because the L disciplines the one he *G3261*
Heb 12:14 without holiness no one will see the L. *G3261*
Heb 13: 6 confidence, "The L is my helper; I will *G3261*
Heb 13:20 brought back from the dead our L Jesus, *G3261*
Jas 1: 1 a servant of God and *of* the L Jesus Christ *G3261*
Jas 1: 7 not expect to receive anything from the L. *G3261*
Jas 1:12 of life that the L has promised to those NDT
Jas 2: 1 believers *in* our glorious L Jesus Christ *G3261*
Jas 3: 9 the tongue we praise our L and Father, *G3261*
Jas 4:10 Humble yourselves before the L, and he *G3261*
Jas 5: 4 have reached the ears *of* the L Almighty. *G3261*
Jas 5:10 prophets who spoke in the name *of* the L. *G3261*
Jas 5:11 have seen what the L finally brought *G3261*
Jas 5:11 The L is full of compassion and mercy. *G3261*
Jas 5:14 anoint them with oil in the name *of* the L. *G3261*
Jas 5:15 sick person well; the L will raise them up. *G3261*
1Pe 1: 3 the God and Father *of* our L Jesus Christ! *G3261*
1Pe 1:25 the word *of* the L endures forever. *G3261*
1Pe 2: 3 that you have tasted that the L is good. *G3261*
1Pe 3: 6 obeyed Abraham and called him her l. *G3261*
1Pe 3:12 For the eyes *of* the L are on the righteous *G3261*
1Pe 3:12 the face *of* the L is against those who *G3261*
1Pe 3:15 But in your hearts revere Christ *as* L *G3261*
2Pe 1: 2 the knowledge of God and of Jesus our L. *G3261*
2Pe 1: 8 in your knowledge *of* our L Jesus Christ. *G3261*
2Pe 1:11 eternal kingdom *of* our L and Savior Jesus *G3261*
2Pe 1:14 as our L Jesus Christ has made clear to *G3261*
2Pe 1:16 about the coming *of* our L Jesus Christ in *G3261*
2Pe 2: 1 denying the **sovereign** L who bought them *G1305*
2Pe 2: 9 then the L knows how to rescue the godly *G3261*
2Pe 2:11 bringing judgment on them from the L. *G3261*
2Pe 2:20 world by knowing our L and Savior Jesus *G3261*
2Pe 3: 2 the command *given by* our L and Savior *G3261*
2Pe 3: 8 With the L a day is like a thousand years *G3261*
2Pe 3: 9 The L is not slow in keeping his promise *G3261*
2Pe 3:10 But the day *of* the L will come like a thief *G3261*
2Pe 3:18 knowledge *of* our L and Savior Jesus *G3261*
Jude 4 Jesus Christ our only Sovereign and L. *G3261*
Jude 5 remind you that the L at one time *G3261*
Jude 9 slander but said, "The L rebuke you!" *G3261*
Jude 14 the L is coming with thousands upon *G3261*
Jude 17 what the apostles *of* our L Jesus Christ *G3261*
Jude 21 wait for the mercy *of* our L Jesus Christ to *G3261*
Jude 25 through Jesus Christ our L, before all ages *G3261*
Rev 1: 8 the Omega," says the L God, "who is, and *G3261*
Rev 4: 8 holy is the L God Almighty,' who *G3261*
Rev 4:11 "You are worthy, our L and God, to receive *G3261*
Rev 6:10 "How long, **Sovereign** L, holy and true *G1305*
Rev 11: 4 "they stand before the L of the earth." *G3261*
Rev 11: 8 Egypt—where also their L was crucified. *G3261*
Rev 11:15 the kingdom *of* our L and of his Messiah *G3261*
Rev 11:17 give thanks to you, L God Almighty, the *G3261*
Rev 14:13 the dead who die in the L from now on." *G3261*
Rev 15: 3 are your deeds, L God Almighty. *G3261*
Rev 15: 4 Who will not fear *you*, L, and bring glory *G3261*
Rev 16: 7 L God Almighty, true and just are *G3261*
Rev 17:14 them because he is L of lords and King of *G3261*
Rev 18: 8 mighty is the L God who judges her. *G3261*
Rev 19: 6 For our L God Almighty reigns. *G3261*
Rev 19:16 written: KING OF KINGS AND L OF LORDS. *G3261*
Rev 21:22 because the L God Almighty and the *G3261*
Rev 22: 5 the sun, for the L God will give them light. *G3261*
Rev 22: 6 The L, the God who inspires the prophets *G3261*
Rev 22:20 am coming soon." Amen. Come, L Jesus. *G3261*
Rev 22:21 The grace *of* the L Jesus be with God's *G3261*

LORD* (6542) [LORD'S* (YAHWEH'S); see introduction, page xiv]

Ge 2: 4 when **the L** God made the earth and the H3378
Ge 2: 5 for **the L** God had not sent rain on the H3378
Ge 2: 7 Then **the L** God formed a man from the H3378
Ge 2: 8 Now **the L** God had planted a garden in H3378
Ge 2: 9 **The L** God made all kinds of trees grow H3378
Ge 2:15 **The L** God took the man and put him in H3378
Ge 2:16 And **the L** God commanded the man, "You H3378
Ge 2:18 **The L** God said, "It is not good for the H3378
Ge 2:19 Now **the L** God had formed out of the H3378
Ge 2:21 So **the L** God caused the man to fall into a H3378
Ge 2:22 Then **the L** God made a woman from the H3378
Ge 3: 1 of the wild animals **the L** God had made. H3378
Ge 3: 8 heard the sound of **the L** God as he was H3378
Ge 3: 8 they hid from **the L** God among the H3378
Ge 3: 9 But **the L** God called to the man, "Where H3378
Ge 3:13 Then **the L** God said to the woman H3378
Ge 3:14 So **the L** God said to the serpent H3378
Ge 3:21 **The L** God made garments of skin for H3378
Ge 3:22 And **the L** God said, "The man has now H3378
Ge 3:23 So **the L** God banished him from the H3378
Ge 4: 1 "With the help of **the L** I have brought H3378
Ge 4: 3 fruits of the soil as an offering to **the L**. H3378
Ge 4: 4 **The L** looked with favor on Abel and his H3378
Ge 4: 6 Then **the L** said to Cain, "Why are you H3378
Ge 4: 9 Then **the L** said to Cain, "Where is your H3378
Ge 4:10 The L said, "What have you done? Listen NDT
Ge 4:13 Cain said to **the L**, "My punishment is H3378
Ge 4:15 But **the L** said to him, "Not so; anyone H3378
Ge 4:15 Then **the L** put a mark on Cain so that no H3378
Ge 4:26 began to call on the name of **the L**. H3378
Ge 5:29 caused by the ground **the L** has cursed." H3378
Ge 6: 3 Then **the L** said, "My Spirit will not H3378
Ge 6: 5 **The L** saw how great the wickedness of H3378
Ge 6: 6 **The L** regretted that he had made human H3378
Ge 6: 7 So **the L** said, "I will wipe from the face of H3378
Ge 6: 8 But Noah found favor in the eyes of **the L**. H3378
Ge 7: 1 **The L** then said to Noah, "Go into the ark H3378
Ge 7: 5 Noah did all that **the L** commanded him. H3378
Ge 7:16 Then **the L** shut him in. H3378
Ge 8:20 Then Noah built an altar to **the L** and H3378
Ge 8:21 **The L** smelled the pleasing aroma and H3378
Ge 9:26 "Praise be *to* **the L**, the God of Shem H3378
Ge 10: 9 He was a mighty hunter before **the L**; that H3378
Ge 10: 9 Nimrod, a mighty hunter before **the L**." H3378
Ge 11: 5 But **the L** came down to see the city and H3378
Ge 11: 6 **The L** said, "If as one people speaking the H3378
Ge 11: 8 So **the L** scattered them from there over H3378
Ge 11: 9 because there **the L** confused the H3378
Ge 11: 9 From there **the L** scattered them over the H3378
Ge 12: 1 **The L** had said to Abram, "Go from your H3378
Ge 12: 4 So Abram went, as **the L** had told him H3378
Ge 12: 7 **The L** appeared to Abram and said, "To H3378
Ge 12: 7 So he built an altar there to **the L**, who H3378
Ge 12: 8 built an altar to **the L** and called on the H3378
Ge 12: 8 the LORD and called on the name of **the L**. H3378
Ge 12:17 But **the L** inflicted serious diseases on H3378
Ge 13: 4 There Abram called on the name of **the L**. H3378
Ge 13:10 like the garden of **the L**, like the land of H3378
Ge 13:10 This was before **the L** destroyed Sodom H3378
Ge 13:13 were sinning greatly against **the L**. H3378
Ge 13:14 **The L** said to Abram after Lot had parted H3378
Ge 13:18 There he built an altar to **the L**. H3378
Ge 14:22 raised hand I have sworn an oath to **the L**, H3378
Ge 15: 1 the word of **the L** came to Abram in a H3378
Ge 15: 2 "Sovereign **L**, what can you give me H3378
Ge 15: 4 Then the word of **the L** came to him: H3378
Ge 15: 6 Abram believed **the L**, and he credited it H3378
Ge 15: 7 said to him, "I am **the L**, who brought you H3378
Ge 15: 8 "Sovereign **L**, how can I know that I H3378
Ge 15: 9 So the L said to him, "Bring me a heifer, NDT
Ge 15:13 Then the L said to him, "Know for certain NDT
Ge 15:18 On that day **the L** made a covenant with H3378
Ge 16: 2 "**The L** has kept me from having children. H3378
Ge 16: 5 May **the L** judge between you and me." H3378
Ge 16: 7 The angel of **the L** found Hagar near a H3378
Ge 16: 9 Then the angel of **the L** told her, "Go back H3378
Ge 16:11 The angel of **the L** also said to her: "You H3378
Ge 16:11 for **the L** has heard of your misery. H3378
Ge 16:13 gave this name to **the L** who spoke to her: H3378
Ge 17: 1 years old, **the L** appeared to him and said H3378
Ge 18: 1 **The L** appeared to Abraham near the H3378
Ge 18:13 Then **the L** said to Abraham, "Why did H3378
Ge 18:14 Is anything too hard for **the L**? I will H3378
Ge 18:17 Then **the L** said, "Shall I hide from H3378
Ge 18:19 to keep the way of **the L** by doing what is H3378
Ge 18:19 so that **the L** will bring about for Abraham H3378
Ge 18:20 Then **the L** said, "The outcry against H3378
Ge 18:22 Abraham remained standing before **the L**. H3378
Ge 18:26 **The L** said, "If I find fifty righteous H3378
Ge 18:33 When **the L** had finished speaking with H3378
Ge 19:13 The outcry to **the L** against its people is so H3378
Ge 19:14 because **the L** is about to destroy the city!" H3378
Ge 19:16 of the city, for **the L** was merciful to them. H3378
Ge 19:24 Then **the L** rained down burning sulfur on H3378
Ge 19:24 Gomorrah—from **the L** out of the heavens. H3378
Ge 19:27 place where he had stood before **the L**. H3378
Ge 20:18 for **the L** had kept all the women in H3378
Ge 21: 1 Now **the L** was gracious to Sarah as he H3378
Ge 21: 1 and **the L** did for Sarah what he had H3378
Ge 21:33 there he called on the name of **the L** H3378
Ge 22:11 But the angel of **the L** called out to him H3378
Ge 22:14 called that place **The L** Will Provide. H3378
Ge 22:14 "On the mountain of **the L** it will be H3378
Ge 22:15 The angel of **the L** called to Abraham H3378
Ge 22:16 declares **the L**, that because you H3378
Ge 24: 1 and **the L** had blessed him in every way. H3378
Ge 24: 3 I want you to swear by **the L**, the God of H3378
Ge 24: 7 "**The L**, the God of heaven, who brought H3378
Ge 24:12 Then he prayed, "**L**, God of my master H3378
Ge 24:21 learn whether or not **the L** had made his H3378
Ge 24:26 man bowed down and worshiped **the L**, H3378
Ge 24:27 "Praise be to **the L**, the God of my H3378
Ge 24:27 **the L** has led me on the journey to the H3378
Ge 24:31 you who are blessed by **the L**," he said. H3378
Ge 24:35 **The L** has blessed my master abundantly H3378
Ge 24:40 "He replied, '**The L**, before whom I have H3378
Ge 24:42 spring today, I said, '**L**, God of my master H3378
Ge 24:44 let her be the one **the L** has chosen for my H3378
Ge 24:48 I bowed down and worshiped **the L**. H3378
Ge 24:48 I praised **the L**, the God of my master H3378
Ge 24:50 "This is from **the L**; we can say nothing to H3378
Ge 24:51 your master's son, as **the L** has directed." H3378
Ge 24:52 bowed down to the ground before **the L**. H3378
Ge 24:56 now that **the L** has granted success to my H3378
Ge 25:21 Isaac prayed to **the L** on behalf of his wife, H3378
Ge 25:21 **The L** answered his prayer, and his wife H3378
Ge 25:22 So she went to inquire of **the L**. H3378
Ge 25:23 **The L** said to her, "Two nations are in H3378
Ge 26: 2 **The L** appeared to Isaac and said, "Do not H3378
Ge 26:12 hundredfold, because **the L** blessed him. H3378
Ge 26:22 "Now **the L** has given us room and we H3378
Ge 26:24 That night **the L** appeared to him and said, H3378
Ge 26:25 there and called on the name of **the L**. H3378
Ge 26:28 "We saw clearly that **the L** was with you H3378
Ge 26:29 And now you are blessed by **the L**." H3378
Ge 27: 7 in the presence of **the L** before I die. H3378
Ge 27:20 "**The L** your God gave me success," he H3378
Ge 27:27 the smell of a field that **the L** has blessed. H3378
Ge 28:13 There above it stood **the L**, and he said: "I H3378
Ge 28:13 "I am **the L**, the God of your father H3378
Ge 28:16 he thought, "Surely **the L** is in this place H3378
Ge 28:21 household, then **the L** will be my God H3378
Ge 29:31 When **the L** saw that Leah was not loved H3378
Ge 29:32 "It is because **the L** has seen my misery. H3378
Ge 29:33 "Because **the L** heard that I am not loved H3378
Ge 29:35 she said, "This time I will praise **the L**." H3378
Ge 30:24 "May **the L** add to me another son." H3378
Ge 30:27 by divination that **the L** has blessed me H3378
Ge 30:30 and **the L** has blessed you wherever I H3378
Ge 31: 3 Then **the L** said to Jacob, "Go back to the H3378
Ge 31:49 "May **the L** keep watch between you and H3378
Ge 32: 9 of my father Isaac, **L**, you who said to me, H3378
Ge 38: 7 the LORD's sight; so **the L** put him to death. H3378
Ge 38:10 LORD's sight; so the L put him to death. NDT
Ge 39: 2 **The L** was with Joseph so that he H3378
Ge 39: 3 master saw that **the L** was with him and H3378
Ge 39: 3 with him and that **the L** gave him success H3378
Ge 39: 5 **the L** blessed the household of the H3378
Ge 39: 5 The blessing of **the L** was on everything H3378
Ge 39:21 **the L** was with him; he showed him H3378
Ge 39:23 because **the L** was with Joseph and gave H3378
Ge 49:18 "I look for your deliverance, **L**. H3378
Ex 3: 2 There the angel of **the L** appeared to him H3378
Ex 3: 4 When **the L** saw that he had gone over to H3378
Ex 3: 7 **The L** said, "I have indeed seen the H3378
Ex 3:15 to the Israelites, '**The L**, the God of your H3378
Ex 3:16 say to them, '**The L**, the God of your H3378
Ex 3:18 say to him, '**The L**, the God of the H3378
Ex 3:18 to offer sacrifices to **the L** our God. H3378
Ex 4: 1 say, '**The L** did not appear to you'? H3378
Ex 4: 2 Then **the L** said to him, "What is that in H3378
Ex 4: 3 The L said, "Throw it on the ground." NDT
Ex 4: 4 Then **the L** said to him, "Reach out your H3378
Ex 4: 5 said the L, "is so that they may believe that NDT
Ex 4: 5 "is so that they may believe that **the L**, the H3378
Ex 4: 6 Then **the L** said, "Put your hand inside H3378
Ex 4: 8 Then the L said, "If they do not believe you NDT
Ex 4:10 Moses said to **the L**, "Pardon your servant H3378
Ex 4:11 **The L** said to him, "Who gave human H3378
Ex 4:11 makes them blind? Is it not I, **the L**? H3378
Ex 4:19 Now **the L** had said to Moses in Midian H3378
Ex 4:21 **The L** said to Moses, "When you return to H3378
Ex 4:22 say to Pharaoh, 'This is what **the L** says: H3378
Ex 4:24 **the L** met Moses and was about to kill H3378
Ex 4:26 So the L let him alone. (At that time she NDT
Ex 4:27 **The L** said to Aaron, "Go into the H3378
Ex 4:28 Aaron everything **the L** had sent him to H3378
Ex 4:30 them everything **the L** had said to Moses. H3378
Ex 4:31 they heard that **the L** was concerned H3378
Ex 5: 1 "This is what **the L**, the God of Israel H3378
Ex 5: 2 "Who is **the L**, that I should obey H3378
Ex 5: 2 I do not know **the L** and I will not let Israel H3378
Ex 5: 3 to offer sacrifices to **the L** our God, H3378
Ex 5:17 'Let us go and sacrifice to **the L**. H3378
Ex 5:21 "May **the L** look on you and judge you! H3378
Ex 5:22 Moses returned to **the L** and said, "Why H3378
Ex 6: 1 Then **the L** said to Moses, "Now you will H3378
Ex 6: 2 God also said to Moses, "I am **the L**. H3378
Ex 6: 3 by my name **the L** I did not make H3378
Ex 6: 6 'I am **the L**, and I will bring you out from H3378

Book	Ref	Context	Number
Ex	6: 7	you will know that I am **the L** your God,	H3378
Ex	6: 8	it to you as a possession. I am **the L**.' "	H3378
Ex	6:10	Then **the L** said to Moses,	H3378
Ex	6:12	But Moses said to **the L**, "If the Israelites	H3378
Ex	6:13	Now **the L** spoke to Moses and Aaron	H3378
Ex	6:26	this Aaron and Moses to whom **the L** said,	H3378
Ex	6:28	Now when **the L** spoke to Moses in Egypt,	H3378
Ex	6:29	said to him, "I am **the L**. Tell Pharaoh	H3378
Ex	6:30	But Moses said to **the L**, "Since I speak	H3378
Ex	7: 1	Then **the L** said to Moses, "See, I have	H3378
Ex	7: 5	know that I am **the L** when I stretch out	H3378
Ex	7: 6	Aaron did just as **the L** commanded them.	H3378
Ex	7: 8	**The L** said to Moses and Aaron,	H3378
Ex	7:10	did just as **the L** commanded.	H3378
Ex	7:13	not listen to them, just as **the L** had said.	H3378
Ex	7:14	Then **the L** said to Moses, "Pharaoh's	H3378
Ex	7:16	Then say to him, '**The L**, the God of the	H3378
Ex	7:17	This is what **the L** says: By this you will	H3378
Ex	7:17	By this you will know that I am **the L**:	H3378
Ex	7:19	**The L** said to Moses, "Tell Aaron, 'Take	H3378
Ex	7:20	Aaron did just as **the L** had commanded.	H3378
Ex	7:22	Moses and Aaron, just as **the L** had said.	H3378
Ex	7:25	days passed after **the L** struck the Nile.	H3378
Ex	8: 1	Then **the L** said to Moses, "Go to Pharaoh	H3378
Ex	8: 1	say to him, 'This is what **the L** says:	H3378
Ex	8: 5	Then **the L** said to Moses, "Tell Aaron	H3378
Ex	8: 8	"Pray to **the L** to take the frogs away from	H3378
Ex	8: 8	your people go to offer sacrifices to **the L**."	H3378
Ex	8:10	know there is no one like **the L** our God.	H3378
Ex	8:12	Moses cried out to **the L** about the frogs	H3378
Ex	8:13	And **the L** did what Moses asked.	H3378
Ex	8:15	Moses and Aaron, just as **the L** had said.	H3378
Ex	8:16	Then **the L** said to Moses, "Tell Aaron	H3378
Ex	8:19	would not listen, just as **the L** had said.	H3378
Ex	8:20	Then **the L** said to Moses, "Get up early in	H3378
Ex	8:20	say to him, 'This is what **the L** says:	H3378
Ex	8:22	will know that I, **the L**, am in this land.	H3378
Ex	8:24	And **the L** did this. Dense swarms of flies	H3378
Ex	8:26	sacrifices we offer **the L** our God would be	H3378
Ex	8:27	to offer sacrifices to **the L** our God,	H3378
Ex	8:28	to offer sacrifices to **the L** your God in the	H3378
Ex	8:29	I will pray to **the L**, and tomorrow the	H3378
Ex	8:29	the people go to offer sacrifices to **the L**."	H3378
Ex	8:30	Moses left Pharaoh and prayed to **the L**,	H3378
Ex	8:31	and **the L** did what Moses asked. The flies	H3378
Ex	9: 1	Then **the L** said to Moses, "Go to Pharaoh	H3378
Ex	9: 1	'This is what **the L**, the God of the	H3378
Ex	9: 3	the hand of **the L** will bring a terrible	H3378
Ex	9: 4	But **the L** will make a distinction between	H3378
Ex	9: 5	**The L** set a time and said, "Tomorrow the	H3378
Ex	9: 5	"Tomorrow **the L** will do this in the land."	H3378
Ex	9: 6	And the next day **the L** did it: All the	H3378
Ex	9: 8	Then **the L** said to Moses and Aaron	H3378
Ex	9:12	But **the L** hardened Pharaoh's heart and	H3378
Ex	9:12	just as **the L** had said to Moses.	H3378
Ex	9:13	Then **the L** said to Moses, "Get up early in	H3378
Ex	9:13	'This is what **the L**, the God of the	H3378
Ex	9:20	feared the word of **the L** hurried to bring	H3378
Ex	9:21	ignored the word of **the L** left their slaves	H3378
Ex	9:22	Then **the L** said to Moses, "Stretch out	H3378
Ex	9:23	**the L** sent thunder and hail	H3378
Ex	9:23	So **the L** rained hail on the land of Egypt	H3378
Ex	9:27	"**The L** is in the right, and I and my	H3378
Ex	9:28	Pray to **the L**, for we have had enough	H3378
Ex	9:29	spread out my hands in prayer to **the L**.	H3378
Ex	9:30	your officials still do not fear **the L** God."	H3378
Ex	9:33	He spread out his hands toward **the L**; the	H3378
Ex	9:35	just as **the L** had said through Moses.	H3378
Ex	10: 1	Then **the L** said to Moses, "Go to Pharaoh,	H3378
Ex	10: 2	that you may know that I am **the L**.	H3378
Ex	10: 3	"This is what **the L**, the God of the	H3378
Ex	10: 7	so that they may worship **the L** their God.	H3378
Ex	10: 8	worship **the L** your God," he said	H3378
Ex	10: 9	we are to celebrate a festival to **the L**."	H3378
Ex	10:10	Pharaoh said, "**The L** be with you—if I let	H3378
Ex	10:11	Have only the men go and worship **the L**	H3378
Ex	10:12	And **the L** said to Moses, "Stretch out your	H3378
Ex	10:13	and **the L** made an east wind blow across	H3378
Ex	10:16	have sinned against **the L** your God and	H3378
Ex	10:17	more and pray to **the L** your God to take	H3378
Ex	10:18	then left Pharaoh and prayed to **the L**.	H3378
Ex	10:19	And **the L** changed the wind to a very	H3378
Ex	10:20	But **the L** hardened Pharaoh's heart, and	H3378
Ex	10:21	Then **the L** said to Moses, "Stretch out	H3378
Ex	10:24	Moses and said, "Go, worship **the L**.	H3378
Ex	10:25	offerings to present to **the L** our God.	H3378
Ex	10:26	of them in worshiping **the L** our God,	H3378
Ex	10:26	know what we are to use to worship **the L**."	H3378
Ex	10:27	But **the L** hardened Pharaoh's heart, and	H3378
Ex	11: 1	Now **the L** had said to Moses, "I will bring	H3378
Ex	11: 3	**The L** made the Egyptians favorably	H3378
Ex	11: 4	"This is what **the L** says: 'About	H3378
Ex	11: 7	you will know that **the L** makes a	H3378
Ex	11: 9	**The L** had said to Moses, "Pharaoh will	H3378
Ex	11:10	but **the L** hardened Pharaoh's heart	H3378
Ex	12: 1	**The L** said to Moses and Aaron in Egypt,	H3378
Ex	12:12	on all the gods of Egypt. I am **the L**.	H3378
Ex	12:14	shall celebrate it as a festival to **the L**—	H3378
Ex	12:23	When **the L** goes through the land to strike	H3378
Ex	12:25	enter the land that **the L** will give you as	H3378
Ex	12:27	'It is the Passover sacrifice to **the L**, who	H3378
Ex	12:28	did just what **the L** commanded Moses	H3378
Ex	12:29	At midnight **the L** struck down all the	H3378
Ex	12:31	worship **the L** as you have requested.	H3378
Ex	12:36	**The L** had made the Egyptians favorably	H3378
Ex	12:42	Because **the L** kept vigil that night to bring	H3378
Ex	12:42	keep vigil to honor **the L** for the	H3378
Ex	12:43	**The L** said to Moses and Aaron, "These	H3378
Ex	12:50	did just what **the L** had commanded	H3378
Ex	12:51	And on that very day **the L** brought the	H3378
Ex	13: 1	**The L** said to Moses,	H3378
Ex	13: 3	because **the L** brought you out of it with a	H3378
Ex	13: 5	When **the L** brings you into the land of the	H3378
Ex	13: 6	the seventh day hold a festival to **the L**.	H3378
Ex	13: 8	because of what **the L** did for me when I	H3378
Ex	13: 9	that this law of **the L** is to be on your lips.	H3378
Ex	13: 9	For **the L** brought you out of Egypt with	H3378
Ex	13:11	"After **the L** brings you into the land of	H3378
Ex	13:12	are to give over to **the L** the first offspring	H3378
Ex	13:12	males of your livestock belong to **the L**.	H3378
Ex	13:14	a mighty hand **the L** brought us out of	H3378
Ex	13:15	**the L** killed the firstborn of both people	H3378
Ex	13:15	is why I sacrifice to **the L** the first male	H3378
Ex	13:16	your forehead that **the L** brought us out of	H3378
Ex	13:21	By day **the L** went ahead of them in a	H3378
Ex	14: 1	Then **the L** said to Moses,	H3378
Ex	14: 4	the Egyptians will know that I am **the L**."	H3378
Ex	14: 8	**The L** hardened the heart of Pharaoh king	H3378
Ex	14:10	They were terrified and cried out to **the L**.	H3378
Ex	14:13	see the deliverance **the L** will bring you	H3378
Ex	14:14	**The L** will fight for you; you need only to	H3378
Ex	14:15	Then **the L** said to Moses, "Why are you	H3378
Ex	14:18	know that I am **the L** when I gain glory	H3378
Ex	14:21	all that night **the L** drove the sea back	H3378
Ex	14:24	watch of the night **the L** looked down from	H3378
Ex	14:25	**The L** is fighting for them against Egypt."	H3378
Ex	14:26	Then **the L** said to Moses, "Stretch out	H3378
Ex	14:27	and **the L** swept them into the sea.	H3378
Ex	14:30	That day **the L** saved Israel from the hands	H3378
Ex	14:31	mighty hand of **the L** displayed against	H3378
Ex	14:31	the people feared **the L** and put their trust	H3378
Ex	15: 1	the Israelites sang this song to **the L**:	H3378
Ex	15: 1	"I will sing to **the L**, for he is highly	H3378
Ex	15: 2	"**The L** is my strength and my defense; he	H3363
Ex	15: 3	**The L** is a warrior; the LORD is his name.	H3378
Ex	15: 3	The LORD is a warrior; **the L** is his name.	H3378
Ex	15: 6	Your right hand, **L**, was majestic in power	H3378
Ex	15: 6	Your right hand, **L**, shattered the enemy.	H3378
Ex	15:11	the gods is like you, **L**? Who is like you—	H3378
Ex	15:16	your people pass by, **L**, until the people	H3378
Ex	15:17	the place, **L**, you made for your	H3378
Ex	15:18	"**The L** reigns for ever and ever."	H3378
Ex	15:19	**the L** brought the waters of the sea back	H3378
Ex	15:21	"Sing to **the L**, for he is highly	H3378
Ex	15:25	Then Moses cried out to **the L**, and the	H3378
Ex	15:25	and **the L** showed him a piece of wood.	H3378
Ex	15:25	There the L issued a ruling and instruction	NDT
Ex	15:26	listen carefully to **the L** your God and do	H3378
Ex	15:26	Egyptians, for I am **the L**, who heals you."	H3378
Ex	16: 4	Then **the L** said to Moses, "I will rain	H3378
Ex	16: 6	know that it was **the L** who brought you	H3378
Ex	16: 7	morning you will see the glory of **the L**,	H3378
Ex	16: 8	know that it was **the L** when he gives you	H3378
Ex	16: 8	grumbling against us, but against **the L**."	H3378
Ex	16: 9	'Come before **the L**, for he has heard your	H3378
Ex	16:10	was the glory of **the L** appearing in the	H3378
Ex	16:11	**The L** said to Moses,	H3378
Ex	16:12	you will know that I am **the L** your God.	H3378
Ex	16:15	"It is the bread **the L** has given you to eat.	H3378
Ex	16:16	This is what **the L** has commanded	H3378
Ex	16:23	to them, "This is what **the L** commanded:	H3378
Ex	16:23	of sabbath rest, a holy sabbath to **the L**.	H3378
Ex	16:25	"because today is a sabbath to **the L**.	H3378
Ex	16:28	Then **the L** said to Moses, "How long will	H3378
Ex	16:29	Bear in mind that **the L** has given you the	H3378
Ex	16:32	"This is what **the L** has commanded:	H3378
Ex	16:33	place it before **the L** to be kept for the	H3378
Ex	16:34	As **the L** commanded Moses, Aaron put	H3378
Ex	17: 1	from place to place as **the L** commanded.	H3378
Ex	17: 2	Why do you put **the L** to the test?"	H3378
Ex	17: 4	Then Moses cried out to **the L**, "What am	H3378
Ex	17: 5	**The L** answered Moses, "Go out in front	H3378
Ex	17: 7	because they tested **the L** saying,	H3378
Ex	17: 7	LORD saying, "Is **the L** among us or not?"	H3378
Ex	17:14	Then **the L** said to Moses, "Write this on a	H3378
Ex	17:15	an altar and called it **The L** is my Banner.	H3378
Ex	17:16	were lifted up against the throne of **the L**,	H3363
Ex	17:16	**the L** will be at war against the	H3378
Ex	18: 1	how **the L** had brought Israel out of	H3378
Ex	18: 8	about everything **the L** had done to	H3378
Ex	18: 8	the way and how **the L** had saved them.	H3378
Ex	18: 9	the good things **the L** had done for Israel	H3378
Ex	18:10	"Praise be to **the L**, who rescued you	H3378
Ex	18:11	Now I know that **the L** is greater than all	H3378
Ex	19: 3	and **the L** called to him from the	H3378
Ex	19: 7	all the words **the L** had commanded him	H3378
Ex	19: 8	"We will do everything **the L** has said."	H3378
Ex	19: 8	Moses brought their answer back to **the L**.	H3378
Ex	19: 9	**The L** said to Moses, "I am going to come	H3378
Ex	19: 9	Then Moses told **the L** what the people	H3378
Ex	19:10	And **the L** said to Moses, "Go to the	H3378
Ex	19:11	on that day **the L** will come down on	H3378
Ex	19:18	because **the L** descended on it in fire.	H3378
Ex	19:20	**The L** descended to the top of Mount	H3378
Ex	19:21	and **the L** said to him, "Go down and warn	H3378
Ex	19:21	through to see **the L** and many of them	H3378
Ex	19:22	who approach **the L**, must consecrate	H3378
Ex	19:22	or **the L** will break out against them."	H3378
Ex	19:23	Moses said to **the L**, "The people cannot	H3378
Ex	19:24	**The L** replied, "Go down and bring Aaron	H3378
Ex	19:24	their way through to come up to **the L**,	H3378
Ex	20: 2	"I am **the L** your God, who brought you	H3378
Ex	20: 5	worship them; for I, **the L** your God, am a	H3378
Ex	20: 7	not misuse the name of **the L** your God,	H3378
Ex	20: 7	for **the L** will not hold anyone guiltless	H3378
Ex	20:10	day is a sabbath to **the L** your God.	H3378
Ex	20:11	For in six days **the L** made the heavens	H3378
Ex	20:11	Therefore **the L** blessed the Sabbath day	H3378
Ex	20:12	long in the land **the L** your God is giving	H3378
Ex	20:22	Then **the L** said to Moses, "Tell the	H3378
Ex	22:11	of an oath before **the L** that the neighbor	H3378
Ex	22:20	god other than **the L** must be destroyed.	H3378
Ex	23:17	are to appear before the Sovereign **L**.	H3378
Ex	23:19	your soil to the house of **the L** your God.	H3378
Ex	23:25	Worship **the L** your God, and his blessing	H3378
Ex	24: 1	Then the L said to Moses, "Come up to the	NDT
Ex	24: 1	"Come up to **the L**, you and Aaron,	H3378
Ex	24: 2	Moses alone is to approach **the L**; the	H3378
Ex	24: 3	"Everything **the L** has said we will do."	H3378
Ex	24: 4	wrote down everything **the L** had said.	H3378
Ex	24: 5	bulls as fellowship offerings to **the L**.	H3378
Ex	24: 7	"We will do everything **the L** has said; we	H3378
Ex	24: 8	the covenant that **the L** has made with	H3378
Ex	24:12	**The L** said to Moses, "Come up to me on	H3378
Ex	24:16	the glory of **the L** settled on Mount	H3378
Ex	24:16	the seventh day the L called to Moses from	NDT
Ex	24:17	Israelites the glory of **the L** looked like a	H3378
Ex	25: 1	**The L** said to Moses,	H3378
Ex	27:21	burning before **the L** from evening till	H3378
Ex	28:12	his shoulders as a memorial before **the L**.	H3378
Ex	28:29	as a continuing memorial before **the L**.	H3378
Ex	28:30	whenever he enters the presence of **the L**.	H3378
Ex	28:30	the Israelites over his heart before **the L**.	H3378
Ex	28:35	Holy Place before **the L** and when he	H3378
Ex	28:36	engrave on it as on a seal: HOLY TO THE **L**.	H3378
Ex	28:38	so that they will be acceptable to **the L**.	H3378
Ex	29:18	It is a burnt offering to **the L**, a pleasing	H3378
Ex	29:18	a food offering presented to **the L**.	H3378
Ex	29:23	which is before **the L**, take one round loaf,	H3378
Ex	29:24	wave them before **the L** as a wave	H3378
Ex	29:25	offering for a pleasing aroma to **the L**,	H3378
Ex	29:25	a food offering presented to **the L**.	H3378
Ex	29:26	wave it before **the L** as a wave offering	H3378
Ex	29:28	are to make to **the L** from their fellowship	H3378
Ex	29:41	a food offering presented to **the L**.	H3378
Ex	29:42	to the tent of meeting, before **the L**.	H3378
Ex	29:46	They will know that I am **the L** their God	H3378
Ex	29:46	dwell among them. I am **the L** their God.	H3378
Ex	30: 8	regularly before **the L** for the generations	H3378
Ex	30:10	It is most holy to **the L**."	H3378
Ex	30:11	Then **the L** said to Moses,	H3378
Ex	30:12	each one must pay **the L** a ransom for his	H3378
Ex	30:13	This half shekel is an offering to **the L**.	H3378
Ex	30:14	more, are to give an offering to **the L**.	H3378
Ex	30:15	the offering to **the L** to atone for your	H3378
Ex	30:16	a memorial for the Israelites before **the L**,	H3378
Ex	30:17	Then **the L** said to Moses,	H3378
Ex	30:20	by presenting a food offering to **the L**,	H3378
Ex	30:22	Then **the L** said to Moses,	H3378
Ex	30:34	Then **the L** said to Moses, "Take fragrant	H3378
Ex	30:37	yourselves; consider it holy to **the L**.	H3378
Ex	31: 1	Then **the L** said to Moses,	H3378
Ex	31:12	Then **the L** said to Moses,	H3378
Ex	31:13	so you may know that I am **the L**, who	H3378
Ex	31:15	day is a day of sabbath rest, holy to **the L**.	H3378
Ex	31:17	in six days **the L** made the heavens	H3378
Ex	31:18	When **the L** finished speaking to Moses	H2257S
Ex	32: 5	Tomorrow there will be a festival to **the L**.	H3378
Ex	32: 7	Then **the L** said to Moses, "Go down	H3378
Ex	32: 9	**the L** said to Moses, "and they are a	H3378
Ex	32:11	Moses sought the favor of **the L** his God.	H3378
Ex	32:11	"**L**," he said, "why should your anger burn	H3378
Ex	32:14	Then **the L** relented and did not bring on	H3378
Ex	32:26	"Whoever is for **the L**, come to me."	H3378
Ex	32:27	"This is what **the L**, the God of Israel	H3378
Ex	32:29	"You have been set apart to **the L** today	H3378
Ex	32:30	But now I will go up to **the L**; perhaps I	H3378
Ex	32:31	So Moses went back to **the L** and said	H3378
Ex	32:33	**The L** replied to Moses, "Whoever has	H3378
Ex	32:35	And **the L** struck the people with a plague	H3378
Ex	33: 1	Then **the L** said to Moses, "Leave this	H3378
Ex	33: 5	For **the L** had said to Moses, "Tell the	H3378
Ex	33: 7	Anyone inquiring of **the L** would go to the	H3378
Ex	33: 9	the entrance, while the L spoke with Moses.	NDT
Ex	33:11	**The L** would speak to Moses face to face	H3378
Ex	33:12	Moses said to **the L**, "You have been	H3378
Ex	33:14	The L replied, "My Presence will go with you	NDT
Ex	33:17	And **the L** said to Moses, "I will do the	H3378
Ex	33:19	And the L said, "I will cause all my	NDT
Ex	33:19	proclaim my name, **the L**, in your	H3378
Ex	33:21	Then **the L** said, "There is a place near	H3378
Ex	34: 1	**The L** said to Moses, "Chisel out two	H3378
Ex	34: 4	morning, as **the L** had commanded him	H3378
Ex	34: 5	Then **the L** came down in the cloud and	H3378
Ex	34: 5	with him and proclaimed his name, **the L**.	H3378
Ex	34: 6	proclaiming, "**The L**, the LORD, the	H3378

Ex 34: 6 "The LORD, **the L**, the compassionate and H3378
Ex 34:10 Then **the L** said: "I am making a covenant NDT
Ex 34:10 is the work that I, **the L**, will do for you. H3378
Ex 34:14 any other god, for **the L**, whose name is H3378
Ex 34:23 are to appear before the Sovereign **L**, H3378
Ex 34:24 year to appear before **the L** your God. H3378
Ex 34:26 your soil to the house of **the L** your God. H3378
Ex 34:27 Then **the L** said to Moses, "Write down H3378
Ex 34:28 Moses was there with **the L** forty days and H3378
Ex 34:29 because he had spoken with **the L**. H2257S
Ex 34:32 all the commands **the L** had given him on H3378
Ex 34:35 face until he went in to speak with **the L**. H2257S
Ex 35: 1 are the things **the L** has commanded you H3378
Ex 35: 2 holy day, a day of sabbath rest to **the L**. H3378
Ex 35: 4 "This is what **the L** has commanded: H3378
Ex 35: 5 what you have, take an offering for **the L**. H3378
Ex 35: 5 is to bring to **the L** an offering of gold, H3378
Ex 35:10 make everything **the L** has commanded: H3378
Ex 35:21 an offering to **the L** for the work on the H3378
Ex 35:22 their gold as a wave offering to **the L**. H3378
Ex 35:24 bronze brought it as an offering to **the L**, H3378
Ex 35:29 willing brought to **the L** freewill offerings H3378
Ex 35:29 all the work **the L** through Moses had H3378
Ex 35:30 **the L** has chosen Bezalel son of Uri H3378
Ex 36: 1 person to whom **the L** has given skill and H3378
Ex 36: 1 do the work just as **the L** has commanded." H3378
Ex 36: 2 person to whom **the L** had given ability H3378
Ex 36: 5 doing the work **the L** commanded to be H3378
Ex 38:22 everything **the L** commanded Moses H3378
Ex 39: 1 Aaron, as **the L** commanded Moses. H3378
Ex 39: 5 as **the L** commanded Moses. H3378
Ex 39: 7 of Israel, as **the L** commanded Moses. H3378
Ex 39:21 the ephod—as **the L** commanded Moses. H3378
Ex 39:26 ministering, as **the L** commanded Moses. H3378
Ex 39:29 as **the L** commanded Moses. H3378
Ex 39:30 an inscription on a seal: HOLY TO THE **L**. H3378
Ex 39:31 the turban, as **the L** commanded Moses. H3378
Ex 39:32 just as **the L** commanded Moses. H3378
Ex 39:42 the work just as **the L** had commanded H3378
Ex 39:43 done it just as **the L** had commanded. H3378
Ex 40: 1 Then **the L** said to Moses: H3378
Ex 40:16 everything just as **the L** commanded him. H3378
Ex 40:19 over the tent, as **the L** commanded him. H3378
Ex 40:21 covenant law, as **the L** commanded him. H3378
Ex 40:23 set out the bread on it before **the L**, as H3378
Ex 40:23 the LORD, as **the L** commanded him. H3378
Ex 40:25 set up the lamps before **the L**, as the H3378
Ex 40:25 the LORD, as **the L** commanded him. H3378
Ex 40:27 incense on it, as **the L** commanded him. H3378
Ex 40:29 grain offerings, as **the L** commanded him. H3378
Ex 40:32 the altar, as **the L** commanded Moses. H3378
Ex 40:34 the glory of **the L** filled the tabernacle H3378
Ex 40:35 the glory of **the L** filled the tabernacle H3378
Ex 40:38 So the cloud of **the L** was over the H3378
Lev 1: 1 **The L** called to Moses and spoke to him H3378
Lev 1: 2 among you brings an offering to **the L**, H3378
Lev 1: 3 so that it will be acceptable to **the L**. H3378
Lev 1: 5 to slaughter the young bull before **the L**, H3378
Lev 1: 9 food offering, an aroma pleasing to **the L**. H3378
Lev 1:11 at the north side of the altar before **the L**, H3378
Lev 1:13 food offering, an aroma pleasing to **the L**. H3378
Lev 1:14 'If the offering to **the L** is a burnt offering H3378
Lev 1:17 food offering, an aroma pleasing to **the L**. H3378
Lev 2: 1 anyone brings a grain offering to **the L**, H3378
Lev 2: 2 food offering, an aroma pleasing to **the L**. H3378
Lev 2: 3 of the food offerings presented to **the L**. H3378
Lev 2: 8 offering made of these things to **the L**; H3378
Lev 2: 9 food offering, an aroma pleasing to **the L**. H3378
Lev 2:10 of the food offerings presented to **the L**. H3378
Lev 2:11 you bring to **the L** must be made without H3378
Lev 2:11 in a food offering presented to **the L**. H3378
Lev 2:12 may bring them to **the L** as an offering of H3378
Lev 2:14 bring a grain offering of firstfruits to **the L**, H3378
Lev 2:16 as a food offering presented to **the L**. H3378
Lev 3: 1 to present before **the L** an animal without H3378
Lev 3: 3 you are to bring a food offering to **the L**: H3378
Lev 3: 5 food offering, an aroma pleasing to **the L**. H3378
Lev 3: 6 the flock as a fellowship offering to **the L**, H3378
Lev 3: 7 a lamb, you are to present it before **the L**, H3378
Lev 3: 9 you are to bring a food offering to **the L**: H3378
Lev 3:11 altar as a food offering presented to **the L**. H3378
Lev 3:12 you are to present it before **the L**, H3378
Lev 3:14 are to present this food offering to **the L**: H3378
Lev 4: 1 **The L** said to Moses, H3378
Lev 4: 3 he must bring to **the L** a young bull H3378
Lev 4: 4 to the tent of meeting before **the L**. H3378
Lev 4: 4 head and slaughter it there before **the L**. H3378
Lev 4: 6 some of it seven times before **the L**, H3378
Lev 4: 7 incense that is before **the L** in the tent of H3378
Lev 4:15 hands on the bull's head before **the L**, H3378
Lev 4:15 the bull shall be slaughtered before **the L**. H3378
Lev 4:17 sprinkle it before **the L** seven times in H3378
Lev 4:18 altar that is before **the L** in the tent of H3378
Lev 4:22 in any of the commands of **the L** his God, H3378
Lev 4:24 burnt offering is slaughtered before **the L**. H3378
Lev 4:31 the altar as an aroma pleasing to **the L**. H3378
Lev 4:35 of the food offerings presented to **the L**. H3378
Lev 5: 6 they must bring to **the L** a female lamb H3378
Lev 5: 7 young pigeons to **the L** as a penalty for H3378
Lev 5:12 of the food offerings presented to **the L**. H3378
Lev 5:14 **The L** said to Moses: H3378
Lev 5:15 is unfaithful to **the L** by sinning NDT
Lev 5:15 are to bring to **the L** as a penalty a ram H3378
Lev 5:19 been guilty of wrongdoing against **the L**." H3378
Lev 6: 1 **The L** said to Moses: H3378
Lev 6: 2 is unfaithful to **the L** by deceiving a H3378
Lev 6: 6 that is, to **the L**, their guilt offering H3378
Lev 6: 7 make atonement for them before **the L**, H3378
Lev 6: 8 **The L** said to Moses: H3378
Lev 6:14 Aaron's sons are to bring it before **the L** H3378
Lev 6:15 the altar as an aroma pleasing to **the L**. H3378
Lev 6:18 of the food offerings presented to **the L**. H3378
Lev 6:19 **The L** also said to Moses, H3378
Lev 6:20 sons are to bring to **the L** on the day he is H3378
Lev 6:21 in pieces as an aroma pleasing to **the L**. H3378
Lev 6:24 **The L** said to Moses, H3378
Lev 6:25 slaughtered before **the L** in the place the H3378
Lev 7: 5 altar as a food offering presented to **the L**. H3378
Lev 7:11 offering anyone may present to **the L**: H3378
Lev 7:14 a contribution to **the L**; it belongs to the H3378
Lev 7:20 the fellowship offering belonging to **the L**, H3378
Lev 7:21 belonging to **the L** must be cut off from H3378
Lev 7:22 **The L** said to Moses, H3378
Lev 7:25 may be presented to **the L** must be cut off H3378
Lev 7:28 **The L** said to Moses, H3378
Lev 7:29 offering to **the L** is to bring part of H3378
Lev 7:29 to bring part of it as their sacrifice to **the L**. H3378
Lev 7:30 are to present the food offering to **the L**; H3378
Lev 7:30 the breast before **the L** as a wave offering. H3378
Lev 7:35 presented to **the L** that were allotted to H3378
Lev 7:35 were presented to serve **the L** as priests. H3378
Lev 7:36 **the L** commanded that the Israelites give H3378
Lev 7:38 which **the L** gave Moses at Mount Sinai in H3378
Lev 7:38 Israelites to bring their offerings to **the L**. H3378
Lev 8: 1 **Theon** said to Moses, H3378
Lev 8: 4 Moses did as **the L** commanded him, and H3378
Lev 8: 5 "This is what **the L** has commanded to be H3378
Lev 8: 9 front of it, as **the L** commanded Moses. H3378
Lev 8:13 on them, as **the L** commanded Moses. H3378
Lev 8:17 the camp, as **the L** commanded Moses. H3378
Lev 8:21 a food offering presented to **the L**, as the H3378
Lev 8:21 to the LORD, as **the L** commanded Moses. H3378
Lev 8:26 which was before **the L**, he took one thick H3378
Lev 8:27 waved them before **the L** as a wave H3378
Lev 8:28 a food offering presented to **the L**. H3378
Lev 8:29 waved it before **the L** as a wave offering H3378
Lev 8:29 offering, as **the L** commanded Moses. H3378
Lev 8:34 was commanded by **the L** to make H3378
Lev 8:35 seven days and do what **the L** requires, H3378
Lev 8:36 did everything **the L** commanded through H3378
Lev 9: 2 and present them before **the L**. H3378
Lev 9: 4 offering to sacrifice before **the L**, H3378
Lev 9: 4 For today **the L** will appear to you H3378
Lev 9: 5 came near and stood before **the L**. H3378
Lev 9: 6 "This is what **the L** has commanded you H3378
Lev 9: 6 that the glory of **the L** may appear to you." H3378
Lev 9: 7 them, as **the L** has commanded. H3378
Lev 9:10 sin offering, as **the L** commanded Moses; H3378
Lev 9:21 right thigh before **the L** as a wave offering H3378
Lev 9:23 the glory of **the L** appeared to all the H3378
Lev 9:24 the presence of **the L** and consumed the H3378
Lev 10: 1 offered unauthorized fire before **the L**, H3378
Lev 10: 2 the presence of **the L** and consumed them H3378
Lev 10: 2 and they died before **the L**. H3378
Lev 10: 3 "This is what **the L** spoke of when he said: H3378
Lev 10: 6 you will die and **the L** will be angry with the NDT
Lev 10: 6 mourn for those **the L** has destroyed by H3378
Lev 10: 8 Then **the L** said to Aaron, H3378
Lev 10:11 all the decrees **the L** has given them H3378
Lev 10:12 presented to **the L** and eat it beside H3378
Lev 10:13 of the food offerings presented to **the L**; H3378
Lev 10:15 to be waved before **the L** as a wave H3378
Lev 10:15 your children, as **the L** has commanded." H3378
Lev 10:17 making atonement for them before **the L**. H3378
Lev 10:19 their burnt offering before **the L**, H3378
Lev 10:19 Would **the L** have been pleased if I had H3378
Lev 11: 1 **The L** said to Moses and Aaron, H3378
Lev 11:44 I am **the L** your God; consecrate H3378
Lev 11:45 I am **the L**, who brought you up out of H3378
Lev 12: 1 **The L** said to Moses, H3378
Lev 12: 7 offer them before **the L** to make H3378
Lev 13: 1 **The L** said to Moses and Aaron, H3378
Lev 14: 1 **The L** said to Moses, H3378
Lev 14:11 offerings before **the L** at the entrance to H3378
Lev 14:12 wave them before **the L** as a wave H3378
Lev 14:16 some of it before **the L** seven times. H3378
Lev 14:18 make atonement for them before **the L**. H3378
Lev 14:23 to the tent of meeting, before **the L**. H3378
Lev 14:24 wave them before **the L** as a wave H3378
Lev 14:27 from his palm seven times before **the L**. H3378
Lev 14:29 to make atonement for them before **the L**. H3378
Lev 14:31 atonement before **the L** on behalf of the H3378
Lev 14:33 **The L** said to Moses and Aaron, H3378
Lev 15: 1 **The L** said to Moses and Aaron, H3378
Lev 15:14 come before **the L** to the entrance to H3378
Lev 15:15 atonement before **the L** for the man H3378
Lev 15:30 her before **the L** for the uncleanness of H3378
Lev 16: 1 **The L** spoke to Moses after the death of H3378
Lev 16: 1 who died when they approached **the L**. H3378
Lev 16: 2 **The L** said to Moses: "Tell your brother H3378
Lev 16: 7 them before **the L** at the entrance to H3378
Lev 16: 8 one lot for **the L** and the other for the H3378
Lev 16: 9 whose lot falls to **the L** and sacrifice it H3378
Lev 16:10 alive before **the L** to be used for making H3378
Lev 16:12 the altar before **the L** and two handfuls of H3378
Lev 16:13 to put the incense on the fire before **the L**, H3378
Lev 16:18 that is before **the L** and make atonement H3378
Lev 16:30 before **the L**, you will be clean from H3378
Lev 16:34 it was done, as **the L** commanded Moses. H3378
Lev 17: 1 **The L** said to Moses, H3378
Lev 17: 2 'This is what **the L** has commanded: H3378
Lev 17: 4 it as an offering to **the L** in front of the H3378
Lev 17: 4 LORD in front of the tabernacle of **the L**— H3378
Lev 17: 5 will bring to **the L** the sacrifices they are H3378
Lev 17: 5 to **the L**, at the entrance to the tent H3378
Lev 17: 6 the altar of **the L** at the entrance to H3378
Lev 17: 6 the fat as an aroma pleasing to **the L**. H3378
Lev 17: 9 to sacrifice it to **the L** must be cut off from H3378
Lev 18: 1 **The L** said to Moses, H3378
Lev 18: 2 say to them: 'I am **the L** your God. H3378
Lev 18: 4 follow my decrees. I am **the L** your God. H3378
Lev 18: 5 obeys them will live by them. I am **the L**. H3378
Lev 18: 6 to have sexual relations. I am **the L**. H3378
Lev 18:21 profane the name of your God. I am **the L**. H3378
Lev 18:30 I am **the L** your God.' " H3378
Lev 19: 1 **The L** said to Moses, H3378
Lev 19: 2 holy because I, **the L** your God, am holy. H3378
Lev 19: 3 my Sabbaths. I am **the L** your God. H3378
Lev 19: 4 gods for yourselves. I am **the L** your God. H3378
Lev 19: 5 sacrifice a fellowship offering to **the L**, H3378
Lev 19: 8 have desecrated what is holy to **the L**; H3378
Lev 19:10 the foreigner. I am **the L** your God. H3378
Lev 19:12 the name of your God. I am **the L**. H3378
Lev 19:14 the blind, but fear your God. I am **the L**. H3378
Lev 19:16 your neighbor's life. I am **the L**. H3378
Lev 19:18 your neighbor as yourself. I am **the L**. H3378
Lev 19:21 of meeting for a guilt offering to **the L**. H3378
Lev 19:22 him before **the L** for the sin he has H3378
Lev 19:24 will be holy, an offering of praise to **the L**. H3378
Lev 19:25 will be increased. I am **the L** your God. H3378
Lev 19:28 tattoo marks on yourselves. I am **the L**. H3378
Lev 19:30 reverence for my sanctuary. I am **the L**. H3378
Lev 19:31 be defiled by them. I am **the L** your God. H3378
Lev 19:32 elderly and revere your God. I am **the L**. H3378
Lev 19:34 foreigners in Egypt. I am **the L** your God. H3378
Lev 19:36 I am **the L** your God, who brought you out H3378
Lev 19:37 my laws and follow them. I am **the L**.' " H3378
Lev 20: 1 **The L** said to Moses, H3378
Lev 20: 7 be holy, because I am **the L** your God. H3378
Lev 20: 8 I am **the L**, who makes you H3378
Lev 20:24 I am **the L** your God, who has set you H3378
Lev 20:26 be holy to me because I, **the L**, am holy, H3378
Lev 21: 1 **The L** said to Moses, "Speak to the priests, H3378
Lev 21: 6 they present the food offerings to **the L**, H3378
Lev 21: 8 because I **the L** am holy—I who H3378
Lev 21:12 the anointing oil of his God. I am **the L**. H3378
Lev 21:15 I am **the L**, who makes him H3378
Lev 21:16 **The L** said to Moses, H3378
Lev 21:21 near to present the food offerings to **the L**. H3378
Lev 21:23 I am **the L**, who makes them H3378
Lev 22: 1 **The L** said to Moses, H3378
Lev 22: 2 not profane my holy name. I am **the L**. H3378
Lev 22: 3 that the Israelites consecrate to **the L**, H3378
Lev 22: 3 be cut off from my presence. I am **the L**. H3378
Lev 22: 8 so become unclean through it. I am **the L**. H3378
Lev 22: 9 I am **the L**, who makes them H3378
Lev 22:15 offerings the Israelites present to **the L** H3378
Lev 22:16 I am **the L**, who makes them H3378
Lev 22:17 **The L** said to Moses, H3378
Lev 22:18 presents a gift for a burnt offering to **the L** H3378
Lev 22:21 offering to **the L** to fulfill a special H3378
Lev 22:22 Do not offer to **the L** the blind, the injured H3378
Lev 22:22 altar as a food offering presented to **the L**. H3378
Lev 22:24 must not offer to **the L** an animal whose H3378
Lev 22:26 **The L** said to Moses, H3378
Lev 22:27 as a food offering presented to **the L**. H3378
Lev 22:29 you sacrifice a thank offering to **the L**, H3378
Lev 22:30 leave none of it till morning. I am **the L**. H3378
Lev 22:31 commands and follow them. I am **the L**. H3378
Lev 22:32 I am **the L**, who made you holy H3378
Lev 22:33 out of Egypt to be your God. I am **the L**." H3378
Lev 23: 1 **The L** said to Moses, H3378
Lev 23: 2 the appointed festivals of **the L**, which you H3378
Lev 23: 3 wherever you live, it is a sabbath to **the L**. H3378
Lev 23: 8 days present a food offering to **the L**. H3378
Lev 23: 9 **The L** said to Moses, H3378
Lev 23:11 wave the sheaf before **the L** so it will be H3378
Lev 23:12 a burnt offering to **the L** a lamb a year old H3378
Lev 23:13 a food offering presented to **the L**, H3378
Lev 23:16 present an offering of new grain to **the L**. H3378
Lev 23:17 as a wave offering of firstfruits to **the L**. H3378
Lev 23:18 They will be a burnt offering to **the L** H3378
Lev 23:18 food offering, an aroma pleasing to **the L**. H3378
Lev 23:20 two lambs before **the L** as a wave offering H3378
Lev 23:20 a sacred offering to **the L** for the priest. H3378
Lev 23:22 I am **the L** your God.' " H3378
Lev 23:23 **The L** said to Moses, H3378
Lev 23:25 but present a food offering to **the L**. H3378
Lev 23:26 **The L** said to Moses, H3378
Lev 23:27 present a food offering to **the L**. H3378
Lev 23:28 is made for you before **the L** your God. H3378
Lev 23:33 **The L** said to Moses, H3378
Lev 23:36 seven days present food offerings to **the L**, H3378
Lev 23:36 present a food offering to **the L**. H3378
Lev 23:37 bringing food offerings to **the L**— H3378
Lev 23:38 the freewill offerings you give to **the L**.) H3378

Lev 23:39 the festival to **the L** for seven days; H3378
Lev 23:40 rejoice before **the L** your God for H3378
Lev 23:41 as a festival to **the L** for seven days each H3378
Lev 23:43 them out of Egypt. I am **the L** your God.' " H3378
Lev 23:44 Israelites the appointed festivals of **the L.** H3378
Lev 24: 1 **The L** said to Moses, H3378
Lev 24: 3 the lamps before **the L** from evening till H3378
Lev 24: 4 lampstand before **the L** must be tended H3378
Lev 24: 6 on the table of pure gold before **the L.** H3378
Lev 24: 7 to be a food offering presented to **the L.** H3378
Lev 24: 8 is to be set out before **the L** regularly, H3378
Lev 24: 9 of the food offerings presented to **the L.**" H3378
Lev 24:12 until the will of **the L** should be made H3378
Lev 24:13 Then **the L** said to Moses: H3378
Lev 24:16 the name of **the L** is to be put to death H3378
Lev 24:22 the native-born. I am **the L** your God.' " H3378
Lev 24:23 Israelites did as **the L** commanded Moses. H3378
Lev 25: 1 **The L** said to Moses at Mount Sinai, H3378
Lev 25: 2 itself must observe a sabbath to **the L.** H3378
Lev 25: 4 a year of sabbath rest, a sabbath to **the L.** H3378
Lev 25:17 fear your God. I am **the L** your God. H3378
Lev 25:38 I am **the L** your God, who brought you out H3378
Lev 25:55 brought out of Egypt. I am **the L** your God. H3378
Lev 26: 1 bow down before it. I am **the L** your God. H3378
Lev 26: 2 reverence for my sanctuary. I am **the L.** H3378
Lev 26:13 I am **the L** your God, who brought you out H3378
Lev 26:44 covenant with them. I am **the L** their God. H3378
Lev 26:45 the nations to be their God. I am **the L.**' " H3378
Lev 26:46 the regulations that **the L** established at H3378
Lev 27: 1 **The L** said to Moses, H3378
Lev 27: 2 to dedicate a person to **the L** by giving the H3378
Lev 27: 9 that is acceptable as an offering to **the L,** H3378
Lev 27: 9 an animal given to **the L** becomes holy. H3378
Lev 27:11 is not acceptable as an offering to **the L**— H3378
Lev 27:14 their house as something holy to **the L,** H3378
Lev 27:16 anyone dedicates to **the L** part of their H3378
Lev 27:21 like a field devoted to **the L;** it will H3378
Lev 27:22 dedicates to **the L** a field they have H3378
Lev 27:23 on that day as something holy to **the L.** H3378
Lev 27:26 the firstborn already belongs to **the L;** H3378
Lev 27:28 that a person owns and devotes to **the L**— H3378
Lev 27:28 so devoted is most holy to **the L.** H3378
Lev 27:30 the trees, belongs to **the L;** it is holy to the H3378
Lev 27:30 belongs to the LORD; it is holy to **the L.** H3378
Lev 27:32 the shepherd's rod—will be holy to **the L.** H3378
Lev 27:34 are the commands **the L** gave Moses at H3378
Nu 1: 1 **The L** spoke to Moses in the tent of H3378
Nu 1:19 as **the L** commanded Moses. And so he H3378
Nu 1:48 **The L** had said to Moses: H3378
Nu 1:54 all this just as **the L** commanded Moses. H3378
Nu 2: 1 **The L** said to Moses and Aaron: H3378
Nu 2:33 Israelites, as **the L** commanded Moses. H3378
Nu 2:34 did everything **the L** commanded Moses; H3378
Nu 3: 1 Moses at the time **the L** spoke to Moses at H3378
Nu 3: 4 died before **the L** when they made an H3378
Nu 3: 5 **The L** said to Moses, H3378
Nu 3:11 **The L** also said to Moses, H3378
Nu 3:13 They are to be mine. I am **the L.**" H3378
Nu 3:14 **The L** said to Moses in the Desert of Sinai, H3378
Nu 3:16 he was commanded by the word of **the L.** H3378
Nu 3:40 **The L** said to Moses, "Count all the H3378
Nu 3:41 the livestock of the Israelites. I am **the L.**" H3378
Nu 3:42 the Israelites, as **the L** commanded him. H3378
Nu 3:44 **The L** also said to Moses, H3378
Nu 3:45 The Levites are to be mine. I am **the L.** H3378
Nu 3:51 he was commanded by the word of **the L.** H3378
Nu 4: 1 **The L** said to Moses and Aaron: H3378
Nu 4:17 **The L** said to Moses and Aaron, H3378
Nu 4:21 **The L** said to Moses, H3378
Nu 4:49 counted, as **the L** commanded Moses. H3378
Nu 5: 1 **The L** said to Moses, H3378
Nu 5: 4 They did just as **the L** had instructed H3378
Nu 5: 5 **The L** said to Moses, H3378
Nu 5: 6 way and so is unfaithful to **the L** is guilty H3378
Nu 5: 8 belongs to **the L** and must be given to H3378
Nu 5:11 Then **the L** said to Moses, H3378
Nu 5:16 bring her and have her stand before **the L.** H3378
Nu 5:18 has had the woman stand before **the L,** H3378
Nu 5:21 "may **the L** cause you to become a curse H3378
Nu 5:25 wave it before **the L** and bring it to the H3378
Nu 5:30 her stand before **the L** and is to apply this H3378
Nu 6: 1 **The L** said to Moses, H3378
Nu 6: 2 a vow of dedication to **the L** as a Nazirite, H3378
Nu 6: 5 period of their dedication to **the L** is over; H3378
Nu 6: 6 the period of their dedication to **the L,** H3378
Nu 6: 8 dedication, they are consecrated to **the L.** H3378
Nu 6:12 themselves to **the L** for the same period of H3378
Nu 6:14 they are to present their offerings to **the L:** H3378
Nu 6:16 all these before **the L** and make the sin H3378
Nu 6:17 the ram as a fellowship offering to **the L,** H3378
Nu 6:20 wave these before **the L** as a wave H3378
Nu 6:21 vows offerings to **the L** in accordance with H3378
Nu 6:22 **The L** said to Moses, H3378
Nu 6:24 " ' "**The L** bless you and keep you; H3378
Nu 6:25 **the L** make his face shine on you and be H3378
Nu 6:26 **the L** turn his face toward you and give H3378
Nu 7: 3 as their gifts before **the L** six covered carts H3378
Nu 7: 4 **The L** said to Moses, H3378
Nu 7:11 For **the L** had said to Moses, "Each day H3378
Nu 7:89 the tent of meeting to speak with **the L,** H2257S
Nu 7:89 In this way **the L** spoke to him. NDT
Nu 8: 1 **The L** said to Moses, H3378
Nu 8: 3 just as **the L** commanded Moses. H3378
Nu 8: 4 like the pattern **the L** had shown Moses. H3378
Nu 8: 5 **The L** said to Moses: H3378
Nu 8:10 You are to bring the Levites before **the L** H3378
Nu 8:11 the Levites before **the L** as a wave offering H3378
Nu 8:11 they may be ready to do the work of **the L.** H3378
Nu 8:12 a sin offering to **the L** and the other for a H3378
Nu 8:13 present them as a wave offering to **the L.** H3378
Nu 8:20 Levites just as **the L** commanded Moses. H3378
Nu 8:21 offering before **the L** and made H3378
Nu 8:22 Levites just as **the L** commanded Moses. H3378
Nu 8:23 **The L** said to Moses, H3378
Nu 9: 1 **The L** spoke to Moses in the Desert of H3378
Nu 9: 5 just as **the L** commanded Moses. H3378
Nu 9: 8 I find out what **the L** commands H3378
Nu 9: 9 Then **the L** said to Moses, H3378
Nu 10: 1 **The L** said to Moses: H3378
Nu 10: 9 be remembered by **the L** your God and H3378
Nu 10:10 before your God. I am **the L** your God." H3378
Nu 10:29 out for the place about which **the L** said, H3378
Nu 10:29 for **the L** has promised good things to H3378
Nu 10:32 you whatever good things **the L** gives us." H3378
Nu 10:33 the mountain of **the L** and traveled for H3378
Nu 10:33 of the covenant of **the L** went before them H3378
Nu 10:34 The cloud of **the L** was over them by day H3378
Nu 10:35 the ark set out, Moses said, "Rise up, **L!** H3378
Nu 10:36 "Return, **L,** to the countless thousands of H3378
Nu 11: 1 their hardships in the hearing of **the L,** H3378
Nu 11: 1 Then fire from **the L** burned among them H3378
Nu 11: 2 he prayed to **the L** and the fire died down. H3378
Nu 11: 3 fire from **the L** had burned among H3378
Nu 11:10 **The L** became exceedingly angry, and H3378
Nu 11:11 He asked **the L,** "Why have you brought H3378
Nu 11:16 **The L** said to Moses: "Bring me seventy H3378
Nu 11:18 **The L** heard you when you wailed, "If H3378
Nu 11:18 Now **the L** will give you meat, and you H3378
Nu 11:20 because you have rejected **the L,** who is H3378
Nu 11:23 **The L** answered Moses, "Is the LORD's H3378
Nu 11:24 told the people what **the L** had said. H3378
Nu 11:25 Then **the L** came down in the cloud and H3378
Nu 11:29 prophets and that **the L** would put his H3378
Nu 11:31 wind went out from **the L** and drove quail H3378
Nu 11:33 the anger of **the L** burned against the H3378
Nu 12: 2 "Has **the L** spoken only through Moses?" H3378
Nu 12: 2 spoken through us?" And **the L** heard this. H3378
Nu 12: 4 At once **the L** said to Moses, Aaron and H3378
Nu 12: 5 Then **the L** came down in a pillar of cloud H3378
Nu 12: 6 among you, I, **the L,** reveal myself to H3378
Nu 12: 8 not in riddles; he sees the form of **the L.** H3378
Nu 12: 9 The anger of **the L** burned against them H3378
Nu 12:13 So Moses cried out to **the L,** "Please, God H3378
Nu 12:14 **The L** replied to Moses, "If her father had H3378
Nu 13: 1 **The L** said to Moses, H3378
Nu 14: 3 Why is **the L** bringing us to this land only H3378
Nu 14: 8 If **the L** is pleased with us, he will lead us H3378
Nu 14: 9 Only do not rebel against **the L.** And do H3378
Nu 14: 9 protection is gone, but **the L** is with us. H3378
Nu 14:10 Then the glory of **the L** appeared at the H3378
Nu 14:11 **The L** said to Moses, "How long will these H3378
Nu 14:13 Moses said to **the L,** "Then the Egyptians H3378
Nu 14:14 heard that you, **L,** are with these people H3378
Nu 14:14 that you, **L,** have been seen face H3378
Nu 14:16 '**The L** was not able to bring these people H3378
Nu 14:18 '**The L** is slow to anger, abounding in love H3378
Nu 14:20 **The L** replied, "I have forgiven them, as H3378
Nu 14:21 as the glory of **the L** fills the whole earth H3378
Nu 14:26 **The L** said to Moses and Aaron: H3378
Nu 14:28 as I live, declares **the L,** I will do to you H3378
Nu 14:35 **the L,** have spoken, and I will surely do H3378
Nu 14:37 down and died of a plague before **the L.** H3378
Nu 14:40 ready to go up to the land **the L** promised. H3378
Nu 14:42 not go up, because **the L** is not with you. H3378
Nu 14:43 Because you have turned away from **the L** H3378
Nu 15: 1 **The L** said to Moses, H3378
Nu 15: 3 you present to **the L** food offerings H3378
Nu 15: 3 as an aroma pleasing to **the L**—whether H3378
Nu 15: 4 shall present to **the L** a grain offering of a H3378
Nu 15: 7 Offer it as an aroma pleasing to **the L.** H3378
Nu 15: 8 vow or a fellowship offering to **the L,** H3378
Nu 15:10 food offering, an aroma pleasing to **the L.** H3378
Nu 15:13 offering as an aroma pleasing to **the L.** H3378
Nu 15:14 offering as an aroma pleasing to **the L,** H3378
Nu 15:15 foreigner shall be the same before **the L:** H3378
Nu 15:17 **The L** said to Moses, H3378
Nu 15:19 present a portion as an offering to **the L.** H3378
Nu 15:21 give this offering to **the L** from the first of H3378
Nu 15:22 of these commands **the L** gave Moses— H3378
Nu 15:23 from the day **the L** gave them and H3378
Nu 15:24 offering as an aroma pleasing to **the L,** H3378
Nu 15:25 have presented to **the L** for their wrong a H3378
Nu 15:28 atonement before **the L** for the one who H3378
Nu 15:30 blasphemes **the L** and must be cut off H3378
Nu 15:35 Then **the L** said to Moses, "The man must H3378
Nu 15:36 to death, as **the L** commanded Moses. H3378
Nu 15:37 **The L** said to Moses, H3378
Nu 15:39 will remember all the commands of **the L,** H3378
Nu 15:41 I am **the L** your God, who brought you out H3378
Nu 15:41 to be your God. I am **the L** your God.' " H3378
Nu 16: 3 every one of them, and **the L** is with them. H3378
Nu 16: 5 "In the morning **the L** will show who H3378
Nu 16: 7 coals and incense in them before **the L.** H3378
Nu 16: 7 The man **the L** chooses will be the one H3378
Nu 16:11 It is against **the L** that you and all your H3378
Nu 16:15 became very angry and said to **the L,** H3378
Nu 16:16 are to appear before **the L** tomorrow— H3378
Nu 16:17 and present it before **the L.** H3378
Nu 16:19 the glory of **the L** appeared to the entire H3378
Nu 16:20 **The L** said to Moses and Aaron, H3378
Nu 16:23 Then **the L** said to Moses, H3378
Nu 16:28 you will know that **the L** has sent me to do H3378
Nu 16:29 all mankind, then **the L** has not sent me. H3378
Nu 16:30 But if **the L** brings about something totally H3378
Nu 16:30 men have treated **the L** with contempt." H3378
Nu 16:35 came out from **the L** and consumed the H3378
Nu 16:36 **The L** said to Moses, H3378
Nu 16:38 presented before **the L** and have become H3378
Nu 16:40 as **the L** directed him through Moses. H3378
Nu 16:40 should come to burn incense before **the L,** H3378
Nu 16:42 it and the glory of **the L** appeared. H3378
Nu 16:44 and **the L** said to Moses, H3378
Nu 16:46 Wrath has come out from **the L;** the H3378
Nu 17: 1 **The L** said to Moses, H3378
Nu 17: 7 the staffs before **the L** in the tent of the H3378
Nu 17:10 **The L** said to Moses, "Put back Aaron's H3378
Nu 17:11 Moses did just as **the L** commanded him. H3378
Nu 17:13 near the tabernacle of **the L** will die. H3378
Nu 18: 1 **The L** said to Aaron, "You, your sons and H3378
Nu 18: 6 dedicated to **the L** to do the work at the H3378
Nu 18: 8 Then **the L** said to Aaron, "I myself have H3378
Nu 18:12 grain they give **the L** as the firstfruits H3378
Nu 18:13 that they bring to **the L** will be yours. H3378
Nu 18:14 in Israel that is **devoted to the L** is yours. H3051
Nu 18:15 animal, that is offered to **the L** is yours. H3378
Nu 18:17 food offering, an aroma pleasing to **the L.** H3378
Nu 18:19 present to **the L** I give to you and H3378
Nu 18:19 of salt before **the L** for both you and your H3378
Nu 18:20 **The L** said to Aaron, "You will have no H3378
Nu 18:24 Israelites present as an offering to **the L.** H3378
Nu 18:25 **The L** said to Moses, H3378
Nu 18:28 an offering to **the L** from all the tithes H3378
Nu 19: 1 **The L** said to Moses and Aaron: H3378
Nu 19: 2 of the law that **the L** has commanded: H3378
Nu 19:20 they have defiled the sanctuary of **the L.** H3378
Nu 20: 3 when our brothers fell dead before **the L!** H3378
Nu 20: 6 the glory of **the L** appeared to them. H3378
Nu 20: 7 **The L** said to Moses, H3378
Nu 20:12 But **the L** said to Moses and Aaron H3378
Nu 20:13 quarreled with **the L** and where he was H3378
Nu 20:16 when we cried out to **the L,** he heard H3378
Nu 20:23 of Edom, **the L** said to Moses and Aaron, H3378
Nu 20:27 Moses did as **the L** commanded: They H3378
Nu 21: 2 Then Israel made this vow to **the L:** "If H3378
Nu 21: 3 **The L** listened to Israel's plea and gave H3378
Nu 21: 6 Then **the L** sent venomous snakes among H3378
Nu 21: 7 we spoke against **the L** and against you. H3378
Nu 21: 7 Pray that **the L** will take the snakes away H3378
Nu 21: 8 **The L** said to Moses, "Make a snake and H3378
Nu 21:14 is why the Book of the Wars of **the L** says: H3378
Nu 21:16 the well where **the L** said to Moses H3378
Nu 21:34 **The L** said to Moses, "Do not be afraid of H3378
Nu 22: 8 to you with the answer **the L** gives me." H3378
Nu 22:13 for **the L** has refused to let me go with you H3378
Nu 22:18 go beyond the command of **the L** my God. H3378
Nu 22:19 I can find out what else **the L** will tell me." H3378
Nu 22:22 the angel of **the L** stood in the road H3378
Nu 22:23 saw the angel of **the L** standing in the H3378
Nu 22:24 Then the angel of **the L** stood in a narrow H3378
Nu 22:25 When the donkey saw the angel of **the L** H3378
Nu 22:26 Then the angel of **the L** moved on ahead H3378
Nu 22:27 When the donkey saw the angel of **the L** H3378
Nu 22:28 Then **the L** opened the donkey's mouth H3378
Nu 22:31 Then **the L** opened Balaam's eyes, and H3378
Nu 22:31 he saw the angel of **the L** standing in the H3378
Nu 22:32 The angel of **the L** asked him, "Why have H3378
Nu 22:34 Balaam said to the angel of **the L,** "I have H3378
Nu 22:35 The angel of **the L** said to Balaam, "Go H3378
Nu 23: 3 Perhaps **the L** will come to meet with me H3378
Nu 23: 5 **The L** put a word in Balaam's mouth and H3378
Nu 23: 8 those whom **the L** has not denounced? H3378
Nu 23:12 I not speak what **the L** puts in my mouth?" H3378
Nu 23:16 **The L** met with Balaam and put a word in H3378
Nu 23:17 Balak asked him, "What did **the L** say?" H3378
Nu 23:21 **The L** their God is with them; the shout of H3378
Nu 23:26 tell you I must do whatever **the L** says?" H3378
Nu 24: 1 saw that it pleased **the L** to bless Israel, H3378
Nu 24: 6 like aloes planted by **the L,** like cedars H3378
Nu 24:11 **the L** has kept you from being H3378
Nu 24:13 to go beyond the command of **the L**—and H3378
Nu 24:13 I must say only what **the L** says'? H3378
Nu 25: 4 **The L** said to Moses, "Take all the leaders H3378
Nu 25: 4 them in broad daylight before **the L,** H3378
Nu 25:10 **The L** said to Moses, H3378
Nu 25:16 **The L** said to Moses, H3378
Nu 26: 1 After the plague **the L** said to Moses and H3378
Nu 26: 4 old or more, as **the L** commanded Moses." H3378
Nu 26: 9 when they rebelled against **the L.** H3378
Nu 26:52 **The L** said to Moses, H3378
Nu 26:61 an offering before **the L** with unauthorized H3378
Nu 26:65 For **the L** had told those Israelites they H3378
Nu 27: 3 who banded together against **the L,** but H3378
Nu 27: 5 So Moses brought their case before **the L,** H3378
Nu 27: 6 and **the L** said to him, H3378
Nu 27:11 Israelites, as **the L** commanded Moses. H3378
Nu 27:12 Then **the L** said to Moses, "Go up this H3378

Nu 27:15 Moses said to **the L**, H3378
Nu 27:16 "May **the L**, the God who gives breath to H3378
Nu 27:18 So **the L** said to Moses, "Take Joshua son H3378
Nu 27:21 him by inquiring of the Urim before **the L**. H3378
Nu 27:22 Moses did as **the L** commanded him. H3378
Nu 27:23 as **the L** instructed through Moses. H3378
Nu 28: 1 **The L** said to Moses, H3378
Nu 28: 3 food offering you are to present to **the L**: H3378
Nu 28: 6 a food offering presented to **the L**. H3378
Nu 28: 7 the drink offering to **the L** at the sanctuary. H3378
Nu 28: 8 food offering, an aroma pleasing to **the L**. H3378
Nu 28:11 present to **the L** a burnt offering of two H3378
Nu 28:13 a food offering presented to **the L**. H3378
Nu 28:15 to be presented to **the L** as a sin offering. H3378
Nu 28:19 Present to **the L** a food offering consisting H3378
Nu 28:24 seven days as an aroma pleasing to **the L**; H3378
Nu 28:26 you present to **the L** an offering of new H3378
Nu 28:27 a year old as an aroma pleasing to **the L**. H3378
Nu 29: 2 As an aroma pleasing to **the L**, offer a H3378
Nu 29: 6 They are food offerings presented to **the L**, H3378
Nu 29: 8 aroma pleasing to **the L** a burnt offering H3378
Nu 29:12 a festival to **the L** for seven days. H3378
Nu 29:13 aroma pleasing to **the L** a food offering H3378
Nu 29:36 aroma pleasing to **the L** a food offering H3378
Nu 29:39 offer these to **the L** at your appointed H3378
Nu 29:40 Israelites all that **the L** commanded him. H3378
Nu 30: 1 "This is what **the L** commands: H3378
Nu 30: 2 makes a vow to **the L** or takes an oath H3378
Nu 30: 3 makes a vow to **the L** or obligates herself H3378
Nu 30: 5 **the L** will release her because her father H3378
Nu 30: 8 and **the L** will release her. H3378
Nu 30:12 nullified them, and **the L** will release her. H3378
Nu 30:16 are the regulations **the L** gave Moses H3378
Nu 31: 1 **The L** said to Moses, H3378
Nu 31: 7 Midian, as **the L** commanded Moses H3378
Nu 31:16 to be unfaithful to **the L** in the Peor H3378
Nu 31:21 by the law that **the L** gave Moses: H3378
Nu 31:25 **The L** said to Moses, H3378
Nu 31:28 apart as tribute for **the L** one out of every H3378
Nu 31:31 priest did as **the L** commanded Moses. H3378
Nu 31:37 of which the tribute for **the L** was 675; H3378
Nu 31:38 of which the tribute for **the L** was 72; H3378
Nu 31:39 of which the tribute for **the L** was 61; H3378
Nu 31:40 of whom the tribute for **the L** was 32. H3378
Nu 31:41 LORD's part, as **the L** commanded Moses. H3378
Nu 31:47 animals, as **the L** commanded him H3378
Nu 31:50 as an offering to **the L** the gold articles H3378
Nu 31:50 atonement for ourselves before **the L**." H3378
Nu 31:52 as a gift to **the L** weighed 16,750 H3378
Nu 31:54 a memorial for the Israelites before **the L**. H3378
Nu 32: 4 the land **the L** subdued before the people H3378
Nu 32: 7 over into the land **the L** has given them? H3378
Nu 32: 9 entering the land **the L** had given them. H3378
Nu 32:12 they followed **the L** wholeheartedly. H3378
Nu 32:14 fathers and making **the L** even more angry H3378
Nu 32:20 will arm yourselves before **the L** for battle H3378
Nu 32:21 the Jordan before **the L** until he has H3378
Nu 32:22 when the land is subdued before **the L**, H3378
Nu 32:22 from your obligation to **the L** and to Israel. H3378
Nu 32:22 land will be your possession before **the L**. H3378
Nu 32:23 you will be sinning against **the L**; and you H3378
Nu 32:27 will cross over to fight before **the L**, just H3378
Nu 32:29 over the Jordan with you before **the L**, H3378
Nu 32:31 "Your servants will do what **the L** has said. H3378
Nu 32:32 cross over before **the L** into Canaan armed H3378
Nu 33: 4 whom **the L** had struck down among them; H3378
Nu 33: 4 for **the L** had brought judgment on their H3378
Nu 33:50 across from Jericho **the L** said to Moses, H3378
Nu 34: 1 **The L** said to Moses, H3378
Nu 34:13 **The L** has ordered that it be given to the H3378
Nu 34:16 **The L** said to Moses, H3378
Nu 34:29 These are the men **the L** commanded to H3378
Nu 35: 1 across from Jericho, **the L** said to Moses, H3378
Nu 35: 9 Then **the L** said to Moses: H3378
Nu 35:34 for I, **the L**, dwell among the H3378
Nu 36: 2 "When **the L** commanded my lord to give H3378
Nu 36: 6 This is what **the L** commands for H3378
Nu 36:10 did as **the L** commanded Moses H3378
Nu 36:13 regulations **the L** gave through Moses H3378
Dt 1: 3 all that **the L** had commanded him H3378
Dt 1: 6 **The L** our God said to us at Horeb, "You H3378
Dt 1: 8 of the land **the L** swore he would give to H3378
Dt 1:10 **The L** your God has increased your H3378
Dt 1:11 May **the L**, the God of your ancestors H3378
Dt 1:19 as **the L** our God commanded us H3378
Dt 1:20 which **the L** our God is giving us. H3378
Dt 1:21 **the L** your God has given you the land. H3378
Dt 1:21 Go up and take possession of it as **the L** H3378
Dt 1:25 is a good land that **the L** our God is giving H3378
Dt 1:26 against the command of **the L** your God. H3378
Dt 1:27 tents and said, "**The L** hates us; so he H3378
Dt 1:30 **The L** your God, who is going before you H3378
Dt 1:31 There you saw how **the L** your God carried H3378
Dt 1:32 you did not trust in **the L** your God, H3378
Dt 1:34 When **the L** heard what you said, he was H3378
Dt 1:36 he followed **the L** wholeheartedly. H3378
Dt 1:37 Because of you **the L** became angry with H3378
Dt 1:41 replied, "We have sinned against **the L**. H3378
Dt 1:41 as **the L** our God commanded us. H3378
Dt 1:42 But **the L** said to me, "Tell them, 'Do not H3378
Dt 1:45 You came back and wept before **the L**, but H3378
Dt 2: 1 to the Red Sea, as **the L** had directed me. H3378
Dt 2: 2 Then **the L** said to me, H3378
Dt 2: 7 **The L** your God has blessed you in all the H3378
Dt 2: 7 These forty years **the L** your God has been H3378
Dt 2: 9 Then **the L** said to me, "Do not harass the H3378
Dt 2:12 did in the land **the L** gave them as their H3378
Dt 2:13 And the L said, "Now get up and cross the NDT
Dt 2:14 the camp, as **the L** had sworn to them. H3378
Dt 2:17 **the L** said to me, H3378
Dt 2:21 **The L** destroyed them from before the H3378
Dt 2:22 The L had done the same for the NDT
Dt 2:29 into the land **the L** our God is giving us H3378
Dt 2:30 For **the L** your God had made his spirit H3378
Dt 2:31 **The L** said to me, "See, I have begun to H3378
Dt 2:33 **the L** our God delivered him over to us H3378
Dt 2:36 **The L** our God gave us all of them H3378
Dt 2:37 with the command of **the L** our God, H3378
Dt 3: 2 **The L** said to me, "Do not be afraid of him H3378
Dt 3: 3 So **the L** our God also gave into our hands H3378
Dt 3:18 "**The L** your God has given you this land H3378
Dt 3:20 until **the L** gives rest to your fellow H3378
Dt 3:20 over the land that **the L** your God is giving H3378
Dt 3:21 own eyes all that **the L** your God has done H3378
Dt 3:21 **The L** will do the same to all the H3378
Dt 3:22 **the L** your God himself will fight for you." H3378
Dt 3:23 At that time I pleaded with **the L**: H3378
Dt 3:24 "Sovereign **L**, you have begun to show to H3378
Dt 3:26 because of you **the L** was angry with me H3378
Dt 3:26 "That is enough," **the L** said. "Do not H3378
Dt 4: 1 in and take possession of the land **the L**, H3378
Dt 4: 2 the commands of **the L** your God that I H3378
Dt 4: 3 own eyes what **the L** did at Baal Peor. H3378
Dt 4: 3 **The L** your God destroyed from among H3378
Dt 4: 4 who held fast to **the L** your God are still H3378
Dt 4: 5 laws as **the L** my God commanded H3378
Dt 4: 7 near them the way **the L** our God is near H3378
Dt 4:10 you stood before **the L** your God at Horeb, H3378
Dt 4:12 Then **the L** spoke to you out of the fire H3378
Dt 4:14 And **the L** directed me at that time to H3378
Dt 4:15 of any kind the day **the L** spoke to you at H3378
Dt 4:19 worshiping things **the L** your God has H3378
Dt 4:20 **the L** took you and brought you out of the H3378
Dt 4:21 **The L** was angry with me because of you H3378
Dt 4:21 the good land **the L** your God is giving H3378
Dt 4:23 the covenant of **the L** your God that he H3378
Dt 4:23 the form of anything **the L** your God has H3378
Dt 4:24 For **the L** your God is a consuming fire, H3378
Dt 4:25 evil in the eyes of **the L** your God and H3378
Dt 4:27 **The L** will scatter you among the peoples H3378
Dt 4:27 the nations to which **the L** will drive you. H3378
Dt 4:29 But if from there you seek **the L** your God H3378
Dt 4:30 you will return to **the L** your God and obey H3378
Dt 4:31 For **the L** your God is a merciful God; he H3378
Dt 4:34 like all the things **the L** your God did for H3378
Dt 4:35 so that you might know that **the L** is God; H3378
Dt 4:39 heart this day that **the L** is God in heaven H3378
Dt 4:40 long in the land **the L** your God gives you H3378
Dt 5: 2 **The L** our God made a covenant with us H3378
Dt 5: 3 our ancestors that **the L** made this H3378
Dt 5: 4 **The L** spoke to you face to face out of the H3378
Dt 5: 5 I stood between **the L** and you to declare H3378
Dt 5: 5 you to declare to you the word of **the L**, H3378
Dt 5: 6 "I am **the L** your God, who brought you H3378
Dt 5: 9 worship them; for I, **the L** your God, am a H3378
Dt 5:11 not misuse the name of **the L** your God, H3378
Dt 5:11 for **the L** will not hold anyone guiltless H3378
Dt 5:12 as **the L** your God has commanded you. H3378
Dt 5:14 day is a sabbath to **the L** your God. H3378
Dt 5:15 in Egypt and that **the L** your God brought H3378
Dt 5:15 Therefore **the L** your God has commanded H3378
Dt 5:16 as **the L** your God has commanded you H3378
Dt 5:16 you in the land **the L** your God is giving H3378
Dt 5:22 the commandments **the L** proclaimed in a H3378
Dt 5:24 "**The L** our God has shown us his glory H3378
Dt 5:25 hear the voice of **the L** our God any longer H3378
Dt 5:27 listen to all that **the L** our God says. H3378
Dt 5:27 tell us whatever **the L** our God tells you. H3378
Dt 5:28 **The L** heard you when you spoke to me H3378
Dt 5:28 spoke to me, and **the L** said to me, "I H3378
Dt 5:32 be careful to do what **the L** your God has H3378
Dt 5:33 obedience to all that **the L** your God has H3378
Dt 6: 1 decrees and laws **the L** your God directed H3378
Dt 6: 2 them may fear **the L** your God as long as H3378
Dt 6: 3 honey, just as **the L**, the God of your H3378
Dt 6: 4 O Israel: **The L** our God, the LORD is H3378
Dt 6: 4 The LORD our God, **the L** is one. H3378
Dt 6: 5 Love **the L** your God with all your heart H3378
Dt 6:10 When **the L** your God brings you into the H3378
Dt 6:12 be careful that you do not forget **the L** H3378
Dt 6:13 Fear **the L** your God, serve him only and H3378
Dt 6:15 for **the L** your God, who is among you, is H3378
Dt 6:16 Do not put **the L** your God to the test as H3378
Dt 6:17 the commands of **the L** your God and the H3378
Dt 6:18 the good land **the L** promised on oath H3378
Dt 6:19 your enemies before you, as **the L** said. H3378
Dt 6:20 decrees and laws **the L** our God has H3378
Dt 6:21 but **the L** brought us out of Egypt with a H3378
Dt 6:22 Before our eyes **the L** sent signs and H3378
Dt 6:24 **The L** commanded us to obey all these H3378
Dt 6:24 these decrees and to fear **the L** our God, H3378
Dt 6:25 to obey all this law before **the L** our God, H3378
Dt 7: 1 When **the L** your God brings you into the H3378
Dt 7: 2 when **the L** your God has delivered H3378
Dt 7: 6 you are a people holy to **the L** your God. H3378
Dt 7: 6 **The L** your God has chosen you out of all H3378
Dt 7: 7 **The L** did not set his affection on you and H3378
Dt 7: 8 But it was because **the L** loved you and H3378
Dt 7: 9 Know therefore that **the L** your God is H3378
Dt 7:12 then **the L** your God will keep his H3378
Dt 7:15 **The L** will keep you free from every H3378
Dt 7:16 all the peoples **the L** your God gives over H3378
Dt 7:18 remember well what **the L** your God did H3378
Dt 7:19 with which **the L** your God brought you H3378
Dt 7:19 **The L** your God will do the same to all the H3378
Dt 7:20 **the L** your God will send the hornet H3378
Dt 7:21 by them, for **the L** your God, who is H3378
Dt 7:22 **The L** your God will drive out those H3378
Dt 7:23 But **the L** your God will deliver them over H3378
Dt 7:25 for it is detestable to **the L** your God. H3378
Dt 8: 1 possess the land **the L** promised on oath H3378
Dt 8: 2 Remember how **the L** your God led you H3378
Dt 8: 3 word that comes from the mouth of **the L**. H3378
Dt 8: 5 his son, so **the L** your God disciplines you. H3378
Dt 8: 6 Observe the commands of **the L** your God H3378
Dt 8: 7 For **the L** your God is bringing you into a H3378
Dt 8:10 praise **the L** your God for the good land H3378
Dt 8:11 that you do not forget **the L** your God, H3378
Dt 8:14 proud and you will forget **the L** your God, H3378
Dt 8:18 But remember **the L** your God, for it is he H3378
Dt 8:19 If you ever forget **the L** your God and H3378
Dt 8:20 Like the nations **the L** destroyed before H3378
Dt 8:20 destroyed for not obeying **the L** your God. H3378
Dt 9: 3 assured today that **the L** your God is the H3378
Dt 9: 3 them quickly, as **the L** has promised you. H3378
Dt 9: 4 After **the L** your God *has* driven them out H3378
Dt 9: 4 "**The L** has brought me here to take H3378
Dt 9: 4 these nations that **the L** is going to drive H3378
Dt 9: 5 **the L** your God will drive them out before H3378
Dt 9: 6 righteousness that **the L** your God is H3378
Dt 9: 7 how *you* aroused the anger of **the L** your H3378
Dt 9: 7 you have been rebellious against **the L**. H3378
Dt 9: 9 the covenant that **the L** had made with H3378
Dt 9:10 **The L** gave me two stone tablets inscribed H3378
Dt 9:10 the commandments **the L** proclaimed to H3378
Dt 9:11 **the L** gave me the two stone tablets H3378
Dt 9:12 Then **the L** told me, "Go down from here H3378
Dt 9:13 And **the L** said to me, "I have seen this H3378
Dt 9:16 you had sinned against **the L** your God; H3378
Dt 9:16 from the way that **the L** had commanded H3378
Dt 9:18 prostrate before **the L** for forty days and H3378
Dt 9:19 I feared the anger and wrath of **the L**, for H3378
Dt 9:19 But again **the L** listened to me. H3378
Dt 9:20 And **the L** was angry enough with Aaron H3378
Dt 9:22 You also made **the L** angry at Taberah, at H3378
Dt 9:23 And when **the L** sent you out from Kadesh H3378
Dt 9:23 against the command of **the L** your God. H3378
Dt 9:24 rebellious against **the L** ever since I have H3378
Dt 9:25 lay prostrate before **the L** those forty days H3378
Dt 9:25 nights because **the L** had said he would H3378
Dt 9:26 I prayed to **the L** and said, "Sovereign H3378
Dt 9:26 "Sovereign **L**, do not destroy your H3378
Dt 9:28 'Because **the L** was not able to take them H3378
Dt 10: 1 At that time **the L** said to me, "Chisel out H3378
Dt 10: 4 **The L** wrote on these tablets what he had H3378
Dt 10: 4 the assembly. And **the L** gave them to me H3378
Dt 10: 5 I had made, as **the L** commanded me H3378
Dt 10: 8 that time **the L** set apart the tribe of Levi H3378
Dt 10: 8 to carry the ark of the covenant of **the L**, H3378
Dt 10: 8 to stand before **the L** to minister and to H3378
Dt 10: 9 fellow Israelites; **the L** is their inheritance H3378
Dt 10: 9 inheritance, as **the L** your God told them.) H3378
Dt 10:10 and **the L** listened to me at this time also. H3378
Dt 10:11 **the L** said to me, "and lead the people H3378
Dt 10:12 what does **the L** your God ask of you but H3378
Dt 10:12 God ask of you but to fear **the L** your God, H3378
Dt 10:12 to serve **the L** your God with all your heart H3378
Dt 10:14 To **the L** your God belong the heavens H3378
Dt 10:15 Yet **the L** set his affection on your H3378
Dt 10:17 For **the L** your God is God of gods and H3378
Dt 10:20 Fear **the L** your God and serve him. H3378
Dt 10:22 now **the L** your God has made you as H3378
Dt 11: 1 Love **the L** your God and keep his H3378
Dt 11: 2 the discipline of **the L** your God: H3378
Dt 11: 4 how **the L** brought lasting ruin on H3378
Dt 11: 7 saw all these great things **the L** has done. H3378
Dt 11: 9 live long in the land **the L** swore to your H3378
Dt 11:12 It is a land **the L** your God cares for; the H3378
Dt 11:12 the eyes of **the L** your God are continually H3378
Dt 11:13 to love **the L** your God and to serve him H3378
Dt 11:17 from the good land **the L** is giving you. H3378
Dt 11:21 many in the land **the L** swore to give your H3378
Dt 11:22 to follow—to love **the L** your God, to walk H3378
Dt 11:23 then **the L** will drive out all these nations H3378
Dt 11:25 **The L** your God, as he promised you, will H3378
Dt 11:27 the commands of **the L** your God that I am H3378
Dt 11:28 the commands of **the L** your God and turn H3378
Dt 11:29 When **the L** your God has brought you H3378
Dt 11:31 of the land **the L** your God is giving you H3378
Dt 12: 1 be careful to follow in the land that **the L**, H3378
Dt 12: 4 must not worship **the L** your God in their H3378
Dt 12: 5 to seek the place **the L** your God will H3378
Dt 12: 7 in the presence of **the L** your God, you H3378
Dt 12: 7 because **the L** your God has blessed you. H3378
Dt 12: 9 the inheritance **the L** your God is giving H3378
Dt 12:10 settle in the land **the L** your God is giving H3378

Dt 12:11 Then to the place **the L** your God will H3378
Dt 12:11 possessions you have vowed to **the L**. H3378
Dt 12:12 And there rejoice before **the L** your God H3378
Dt 12:14 only at the place **the L** will choose in one H3378
Dt 12:15 to the blessing **the L** your God gives you. H3378
Dt 12:18 in the presence of **the L** your God at the H3378
Dt 12:18 God at the place **the L** your God will H3378
Dt 12:18 are to rejoice before **the L** your God in H3378
Dt 12:20 When **the L** your God has enlarged your H3378
Dt 12:21 If the place where **the L** your God chooses H3378
Dt 12:21 the herds and flocks **the L** has given you, H3378
Dt 12:25 be doing what is right in the eyes of **the L**. H3378
Dt 12:26 go to the place **the L** will choose. H3378
Dt 12:27 offerings on the altar of **the L** your God, H3378
Dt 12:27 poured beside the altar of **the L** your God, H3378
Dt 12:28 right in the eyes of **the L** your God. H3378
Dt 12:29 **The L** your God will cut off before you the H3378
Dt 12:31 must not worship **the L** your God in their H3378
Dt 12:31 all kinds of detestable things **the L** hates. H3378
Dt 13: 3 **The L** your God is testing you to find out H3378
Dt 13: 4 It is **the L** your God you must follow, and H3378
Dt 13: 5 inciting rebellion against **the L** your God, H3378
Dt 13: 5 you from the way **the L** your God H3378
Dt 13:10 to turn you away from **the L** your God, H3378
Dt 13:12 one of the towns **the L** your God is giving H3378
Dt 13:16 a whole burnt offering to **the L** your God. H3378
Dt 13:17 Then **the L** will turn from his fierce anger H3378
Dt 13:18 because you obey **the L** your God by H3378
Dt 14: 1 You are the children of **the L** your God. H3378
Dt 14: 2 you are a people holy to **the L** your God. H3378
Dt 14: 2 **the L** has chosen you to be his treasured H3378
Dt 14:21 you are a people holy to **the L** your God. H3378
Dt 14:23 in the presence of **the L** your God at the H3378
Dt 14:23 learn to revere **the L** your God always. H3378
Dt 14:24 been blessed by **the L** your God and H3378
Dt 14:24 the place where **the L** will choose to put H3378
Dt 14:25 go to the place **the L** your God will H3378
Dt 14:26 in the presence of **the L** your God and H3378
Dt 14:29 so that **the L** your God may bless you H3378
Dt 15: 4 in the land **the L** your God is giving H3378
Dt 15: 5 only you fully obey **the L** your God and H3378
Dt 15: 6 For **the L** your God will bless you as he H3378
Dt 15: 7 towns of the land **the L** your God is giving H3378
Dt 15: 9 may then appeal to **the L** against you, H3378
Dt 15:10 because of this **the L** your God will bless H3378
Dt 15:14 Give to them as **the L** your God has H3378
Dt 15:15 in Egypt and **the L** your God redeemed H3378
Dt 15:18 And **the L** your God will bless you in H3378
Dt 15:19 Set apart for **the L** your God every H3378
Dt 15:20 in the presence of **the L** your God at the H3378
Dt 15:21 you must not sacrifice it to **the L** your God. H3378
Dt 16: 1 celebrate the Passover of **the L** your God, H3378
Dt 16: 2 as the Passover to **the L** your God an H3378
Dt 16: 2 herd at the place **the L** will choose as a H3378
Dt 16: 5 in any town **the L** your God gives you H3378
Dt 16: 7 eat it at the place **the L** your God will H3378
Dt 16: 8 an assembly to **the L** your God and do no H3378
Dt 16:10 of Weeks to **the L** your God by giving H3378
Dt 16:10 to the blessings **the L** your God has given H3378
Dt 16:11 And rejoice before **the L** your God at the H3378
Dt 16:15 the festival to **the L** your God at the place H3378
Dt 16:15 your God at the place **the L** will choose. H3378
Dt 16:15 For **the L** your God will bless you in all H3378
Dt 16:16 must appear before **the L** your God at the H3378
Dt 16:16 appear before **the L** empty-handed: H3378
Dt 16:17 to the way **the L** your God has blessed H3378
Dt 16:18 in every town **the L** your God is giving H3378
Dt 16:20 possess the land **the L** your God is giving H3378
Dt 16:21 the altar you build to **the L** your God, H3378
Dt 16:22 for these **the L** your God hates. H3378
Dt 17: 1 Do not sacrifice to **the L** your God an ox H3378
Dt 17: 2 one of the towns **the L** gives you is found H3378
Dt 17: 2 evil in the eyes of **the L** your God in H3378
Dt 17: 8 them to the place **the L** your God will H3378
Dt 17:10 give you at the place **the L** will choose. H3378
Dt 17:12 there to **the L** your God is to be H3378
Dt 17:14 enter the land **the L** your God is giving H3378
Dt 17:15 over you a king **the L** your God chooses. H3378
Dt 17:16 more of them, for **the L** has told you, "You H3378
Dt 17:19 learn to revere **the L** his God and follow H3378
Dt 18: 1 on the food offerings presented to **the L**, H3378
Dt 18: 2 fellow Israelites; **the L** is their inheritance H3378
Dt 18: 5 for **the L** your God has chosen them and H3378
Dt 18: 6 to the place **the L** will choose, H3378
Dt 18: 7 in the name of **the L** his God like all his H3378
Dt 18: 7 who serve there in the presence of **the L**. H3378
Dt 18: 9 enter the land **the L** your God is giving H3378
Dt 18:12 does these things is detestable to **the L**; H3378
Dt 18:12 practices **the L** your God will drive H3378
Dt 18:13 must be blameless before **the L** your God. H3378
Dt 18:14 **the L** your God has not permitted you to H3378
Dt 18:15 **The L** your God will raise up for you a H3378
Dt 18:16 what you asked of **the L** your God at H3378
Dt 18:16 hear the voice of **the L** our God nor see H3378
Dt 18:17 **The L** said to me: "What they say is good. H3378
Dt 18:21 a message has not been spoken by **the L**?" H3378
Dt 18:22 in the name of **the L** does not take place H3378
Dt 18:22 that is a message **the L** has not spoken. H3378
Dt 19: 1 When **the L** your God has destroyed the H3378
Dt 19: 2 cities in the land **the L** your God is giving H3378
Dt 19: 3 parts the land **the L** your God is giving H3378
Dt 19: 8 If **the L** your God enlarges your territory, H3378
Dt 19: 9 to love **the L** your God and to walk always H3378
Dt 19:10 which **the L** your God is giving you as H3378
Dt 19:14 in the land **the L** your God is giving H3378
Dt 19:17 in the presence of **the L** before the priests H3378
Dt 20: 1 of them, because **the L** your God, who H3378
Dt 20: 4 For **the L** your God is the one who goes H3378
Dt 20:13 When **the L** your God delivers it into your H3378
Dt 20:14 use the plunder **the L** your God gives you H3378
Dt 20:16 of the nations **the L** your God is giving H3378
Dt 20:17 as **the L** your God has commanded you. H3378
Dt 20:18 you will sin against **the L** your God. H3378
Dt 21: 1 a field in the land **the L** your God is giving H3378
Dt 21: 5 for **the L** your God has chosen them to H3378
Dt 21: 5 in the name of **the L** and to decide all H3378
Dt 21: 8 you have redeemed, **L**, and do not hold H3378
Dt 21: 9 done what is right in the eyes of **the L**. H3378
Dt 21:10 your enemies and **the L** your God delivers H3378
Dt 21:23 the land **the L** your God is giving H3378
Dt 22: 5 for **the L** your God detests anyone who H3378
Dt 23: 1 cutting may enter the assembly of **the L**. H3378
Dt 23: 2 may enter the assembly of **the L**, H3378
Dt 23: 3 may enter the assembly of **the L**, H3378
Dt 23: 5 **the L** your God would not listen to Balaam H3378
Dt 23: 5 you, because **the L** your God loves you. H3378
Dt 23: 8 to them may enter the assembly of **the L**. H3378
Dt 23:14 For **the L** your God moves about in your H3378
Dt 23:18 into the house of **the L** your God to pay H3378
Dt 23:18 because **the L** your God detests them both H3378
Dt 23:20 so that **the L** your God may bless you in H3378
Dt 23:21 If you make a vow to **the L** your God, do H3378
Dt 23:21 for **the L** your God will certainly demand H3378
Dt 23:23 your vow freely to **the L** your God with H3378
Dt 24: 4 would be detestable in the eyes of **the L**. H3378
Dt 24: 4 sin upon the land **the L** your God is giving H3378
Dt 24: 9 Remember what **the L** your God did to H3378
Dt 24:13 act in the sight of **the L** your God. H3378
Dt 24:15 they may cry to **the L** against you, H3378
Dt 24:18 in Egypt and **the L** your God redeemed H3378
Dt 24:19 so that **the L** your God may bless you in H3378
Dt 25:15 long in the land **the L** your God is giving H3378
Dt 25:16 For **the L** your God detests anyone who H3378
Dt 25:19 When **the L** your God gives you rest from H3378
Dt 26: 1 entered the land **the L** your God is giving H3378
Dt 26: 2 soil of the land **the L** your God is giving H3378
Dt 26: 2 go to the place **the L** your God will choose H3378
Dt 26: 3 "I declare today to **the L** your God that I H3378
Dt 26: 3 have come to the land **the L** swore to our H3378
Dt 26: 4 in front of the altar of **the L** your God. H3378
Dt 26: 5 you shall declare before **the L** your God: H3378
Dt 26: 7 Then we cried out to **the L**, the God of our H3378
Dt 26: 7 and **the L** heard our voice and saw our H3378
Dt 26: 8 So **the L** brought us out of Egypt with a H3378
Dt 26:10 of the soil that you, **L**, have given me." H3378
Dt 26:10 the basket before **the L** your God and bow H3378
Dt 26:11 the good things **the L** your God has given H3378
Dt 26:13 Then say to **the L** your God: "I have H3378
Dt 26:14 I have obeyed **the L** my God; I have done H3378
Dt 26:16 **The L** your God commands you this day to H3378
Dt 26:17 this day that **the L** is your God and that H3378
Dt 26:18 And **the L** has declared this day that you H3378
Dt 26:19 will be a people holy to **the L** your God, H3378
Dt 27: 2 into the land **the L** your God is giving H3378
Dt 27: 3 to enter the land **the L** your God is giving H3378
Dt 27: 3 honey, just as **the L**, the God of your H3378
Dt 27: 5 Build there an altar to **the L** your God, an H3378
Dt 27: 6 Build the altar of **the L** your God with H3378
Dt 27: 6 burnt offerings on it to **the L** your God. H3378
Dt 27: 7 in the presence of **the L** your God. H3378
Dt 27: 9 become the people of **the L** your God. H3378
Dt 27:10 Obey **the L** your God and follow his H3378
Dt 27:15 a thing detestable to **the L**, the work of H3378
Dt 28: 1 If you fully obey **the L** your God and H3378
Dt 28: 1 **the L** your God will set you high above all H3378
Dt 28: 2 you if you obey **the L** your God: H3378
Dt 28: 7 **The L** will grant that the enemies who rise H3378
Dt 28: 8 **The L** will send a blessing on your barns H3378
Dt 28: 8 **The L** your God will bless you in the land H3378
Dt 28: 9 **The L** will establish you as his holy H3378
Dt 28: 9 the commands of **the L** your God and walk H3378
Dt 28:10 that you are called by the name of **the L**, H3378
Dt 28:11 **The L** will grant you abundant prosperity H3378
Dt 28:12 **The L** will open the heavens, the H3378
Dt 28:13 **The L** will make you the head, not the tail H3378
Dt 28:13 to the commands of **the L** your God that I H3378
Dt 28:15 if you do not obey **the L** your God and do H3378
Dt 28:20 **The L** will send on you curses, confusion H3378
Dt 28:21 **The L** will plague you with diseases until H3378
Dt 28:22 **The L** will strike you with wasting disease H3378
Dt 28:24 **The L** will turn the rain of your country H3378
Dt 28:25 **The L** will cause you to be defeated H3378
Dt 28:27 **The L** will afflict you with the boils of H3378
Dt 28:28 **The L** will afflict you with madness H3378
Dt 28:35 **The L** will afflict your knees and legs with H3378
Dt 28:36 **The L** will drive you and the king you set H3378
Dt 28:37 all the peoples where **the L** will drive you. H3378
Dt 28:45 you did not obey **the L** your God and H3378
Dt 28:47 you did not serve **the L** your God joyfully H3378
Dt 28:48 the enemies **the L** sends against you H3378
Dt 28:49 **The L** will bring a nation against you from H3378
Dt 28:52 the land **the L** your God is giving H3378
Dt 28:53 daughters **the L** your God has given H3378
Dt 28:58 awesome name—**the L** your God— H3378
Dt 28:59 **the L** will send fearful plagues on you H3378
Dt 28:61 **The L** will also bring on you every kind H3378
Dt 28:62 because you did not obey **the L** your God. H3378
Dt 28:63 Just as it pleased **the L** to make you H3378
Dt 28:64 Then **the L** will scatter you among all H3378
Dt 28:65 There **the L** will give you an anxious mind H3378
Dt 28:68 **The L** will send you back in ships to Egypt H3378
Dt 29: 1 of the covenant **the L** commanded Moses H3378
Dt 29: 2 have seen all that **the L** did in Egypt to H3378
Dt 29: 4 But to this day **the L** has not given you a H3378
Dt 29: 5 Yet **the L** says, "During the forty years that NDT
Dt 29: 6 you might know that I am **the L** your God. H3378
Dt 29:10 today in the presence of **the L** your God— H3378
Dt 29:12 enter into a covenant with **the L** your God, H3378
Dt 29:12 a covenant **the L** is making with you this H3378
Dt 29:15 in the presence of **the L** our God but also H3378
Dt 29:18 turns away from **the L** our God to go and H3378
Dt 29:20 **The L** will never be willing to forgive H3378
Dt 29:20 and **the L** will blot out their names from H3378
Dt 29:21 **The L** will single them out from all the H3378
Dt 29:22 diseases with which **the L** has afflicted it. H3378
Dt 29:23 which **the L** overthrew in fierce anger. H3378
Dt 29:24 "Why has **the L** done this to this land H3378
Dt 29:25 people abandoned the covenant of **the L**, H3378
Dt 29:28 in great wrath **the L** uprooted them H3378
Dt 29:29 The secret things belong to **the L** our God H3378
Dt 30: 1 to heart wherever **the L** your God H3378
Dt 30: 2 children return to **the L** your God and obey H3378
Dt 30: 3 then **the L** your God will restore your H3378
Dt 30: 4 from there **the L** your God will gather you H3378
Dt 30: 6 **The L** your God will circumcise your H3378
Dt 30: 7 **The L** your God will put all these curses H3378
Dt 30: 8 will again obey **the L** and follow all his H3378
Dt 30: 9 Then **the L** your God will make you most H3378
Dt 30: 9 **The L** will again delight in you and make H3378
Dt 30:10 if you obey **the L** your God and keep his H3378
Dt 30:10 Law and turn to **the L** your God with all H3378
Dt 30:16 you today to love **the L** your God, H3378
Dt 30:16 and **the L** your God will bless you in the H3378
Dt 30:20 that you may love **the L** your God H3378
Dt 30:20 For **the L** is your life, and he will give you H3378
Dt 31: 2 **The L** has said to me, 'You shall not cross H3378
Dt 31: 3 **The L** your God himself will cross over H3378
Dt 31: 3 will cross over ahead of you, as **the L** said. H3378
Dt 31: 4 And **the L** will do to them what he did to H3378
Dt 31: 5 **The L** will deliver them to you, and you H3378
Dt 31: 6 of them, for **the L** your God goes with you H3378
Dt 31: 7 into the land that **the L** swore to their H3378
Dt 31: 8 **The L** himself goes before you and will be H3378
Dt 31: 9 carried the ark of the covenant of **the L**, H3378
Dt 31:11 to appear before **the L** your God at the H3378
Dt 31:12 learn to fear **the L** your God and H3378
Dt 31:13 learn to fear **the L** your God as long H3378
Dt 31:14 **The L** said to Moses, "Now the day of H3378
Dt 31:15 Then **the L** appeared at the tent in a pillar H3378
Dt 31:16 And **the L** said to Moses: "You are going H3378
Dt 31:23 **The L** gave this command to Joshua son of NDT
Dt 31:25 carried the ark of the covenant of **the L**: H3378
Dt 31:26 the ark of the covenant of **the L** your God. H3378
Dt 31:27 rebellious against **the L** while I am still H3378
Dt 31:29 evil in the sight of **the L** and arouse his H3378
Dt 32: 3 I will proclaim the name of **the L**. H3378
Dt 32: 6 Is this the way you repay **the L**, you H3378
Dt 32:12 **The L** alone led him; no foreign god was H3378
Dt 32:19 **The L** saw this and rejected them because H3378
Dt 32:27 triumphed; **the L** has not done all this. H3378
Dt 32:30 unless **the L** had given them up? H3378
Dt 32:36 **The L** will vindicate his people and relent H3378
Dt 32:48 On that same day **the L** told Moses, H3378
Dt 33: 2 "**The L** came from Sinai and dawned over H3378
Dt 33: 7 **L**, the cry of Judah; bring him to his H3378
Dt 33:11 Bless all his skills, **L**, and be pleased with H3378
Dt 33:12 the beloved of **the L** rest secure in him H3378
Dt 33:12 the one **the L** loves rests between his NDT
Dt 33:13 "May **the L** bless his land with the H3378
Dt 33:23 with the favor of **the L** and is full of his H3378
Dt 33:29 a people saved by **the L**? He is your shield H3378
Dt 34: 1 There **the L** showed him the whole land H3378
Dt 34: 4 Then **the L** said to him, "This is the land I H3378
Dt 34: 5 the servant of **the L** died there in Moab, H3378
Dt 34: 5 died there in Moab, as **the L** had said. H3378
Dt 34: 9 him and did what **the L** had commanded H3378
Dt 34:10 like Moses, whom **the L** knew face to face, H3378
Dt 34:11 signs and wonders **the L** sent him to do in H3378
Jos 1: 1 the death of Moses the servant of **the L**, H3378
Jos 1: 1 the LORD, **the L** said to Joshua son of Nun H3378
Jos 1: 9 for **the L** your God will be with you H3378
Jos 1:11 of the land **the L** your God is giving you H3378
Jos 1:13 the servant of **the L** gave you after he H3378
Jos 1:13 '**The L** your God will give you rest by H3378
Jos 1:15 until **the L** gives them rest, as he has done H3378
Jos 1:15 of the land **the L** your God is giving H3378
Jos 1:15 the servant of **the L** gave you east of H3378
Jos 1:17 Only may **the L** your God be with you as H3378
Jos 2: 9 "I know that **the L** has given you this land H3378
Jos 2:10 We have heard how **the L** dried up the H3378
Jos 2:11 for **the L** your God is God in heaven above H3378
Jos 2:12 swear to me by **the L** that you will show H3378
Jos 2:14 faithfully when **the L** gives us the land." H3378
Jos 2:24 "**The L** has surely given the whole land H3378
Jos 3: 3 the ark of the covenant of **the L** your God, H3378
Jos 3: 5 tomorrow **the L** will do amazing things H3378

Book	Ref	Context	Code
Jos	3: 7	And **the L** said to Joshua, "Today I will	H3378
Jos	3: 9	listen to the words of **the L** your God.	H3378
Jos	3:13	as the priests who carry the ark of **the L**—	H3378
Jos	3:17	of the covenant of **the L** stopped in the	H3378
Jos	4: 1	crossing the Jordan, **the L** said to Joshua,	H3378
Jos	4: 5	before the ark of **the L** your God into the	H3378
Jos	4: 7	off before the ark of the covenant of **the L**.	H3378
Jos	4: 8	the Israelites, as **the L** had told Joshua	H3378
Jos	4:10	until everything **the L** had commanded	H3378
Jos	4:11	the ark of **the L** and the priests came to	H3378
Jos	4:13	crossed over before **the L** to the plains of	H3378
Jos	4:14	That day **the L** exalted Joshua in the sight	H3378
Jos	4:15	Then **the L** said to Joshua,	H3378
Jos	4:18	carrying the ark of the covenant of **the L**.	H3378
Jos	4:23	For **the L** your God dried up the Jordan	H3378
Jos	4:23	**The L** your God did to the Jordan what he	H3378
Jos	4:24	that the hand of **the L** is powerful and so	H3378
Jos	4:24	you might always fear **the L** your God."	H3378
Jos	5: 1	coast heard how **the L** had dried up the	H3378
Jos	5: 2	At that time **the L** said to Joshua, "Make	H3378
Jos	5: 6	since they had not obeyed **the L**.	H3378
Jos	5: 6	For **the L** had sworn to them that they	H3378
Jos	5: 9	Then **the L** said to Joshua, "Today I have	H3378
Jos	5:14	of the army of **the L** I have now come."	H3378
Jos	6: 2	Then **the L** said to Joshua, "See, I have	H3378
Jos	6: 6	of the covenant of **the L** and have seven	H3378
Jos	6: 7	guard going ahead of the ark of **the L**."	H3378
Jos	6: 8	seven trumpets before **the L** went forward,	H3378
Jos	6:11	he had the ark of **the L** carried around the	H3378
Jos	6:12	the priests took up the ark of **the L**.	H3378
Jos	6:13	before the ark of **the L** and blowing the	H3378
Jos	6:13	the rear guard followed the ark of **the L**,	H3378
Jos	6:16	For **the L** has given you the city!	H3378
Jos	6:17	all that is in it are to be devoted to **the L**.	H3378
Jos	6:19	iron are sacred to **the L** and must go into	H3378
Jos	6:21	the city to the L and destroyed with the	NDT
Jos	6:26	"Cursed before **the L** is the one who	H3378
Jos	6:27	So **the L** was with Joshua, and his fame	H3378
Jos	7: 6	to the ground before the ark of **the L**,	H3378
Jos	7: 7	Sovereign L, why did you ever bring	H3378
Jos	7:10	**The L** said to Joshua, "Stand up! What	H3378
Jos	7:13	this is what **the L**, the God of Israel,	H3378
Jos	7:14	The tribe **the L** chooses shall come	H3378
Jos	7:14	the clan **the L** chooses shall come forward	H3378
Jos	7:14	the family **the L** chooses shall come	H3378
Jos	7:15	the covenant of **the L** and has done an	H3378
Jos	7:19	give glory to **the L**, the God of Israel,	H3378
Jos	7:20	I have sinned against **the L**, the God of	H3378
Jos	7:23	spread them out before **the L**.	H3378
Jos	7:25	**The L** will bring trouble on you today."	H3378
Jos	7:26	Then **the L** turned from his fierce anger	H3378
Jos	8: 1	Then **the L** said to Joshua, "Do not be	H3378
Jos	8: 7	**The L** your God will give it into your hand.	H3378
Jos	8: 8	Do what **the L** has commanded	H3378
Jos	8:18	Then **the L** said to Joshua, "Hold out	H3378
Jos	8:27	of this city, as **the L** had instructed Joshua.	H3378
Jos	8:30	built on Mount Ebal an altar to **the L**,	H3378
Jos	8:31	the servant of **the L** had commanded the	H3378
Jos	8:31	it they offered to **the L** burnt offerings and	H3378
Jos	8:33	sides of the ark of the covenant of **the L**,	H3378
Jos	8:33	Moses the servant of **the L** had formerly	H3378
Jos	9: 9	because of the fame of **the L** your God.	H3378
Jos	9:14	provisions but did not inquire of **the L**.	H3378
Jos	9:18	had sworn an oath to them by **the L**,	H3378
Jos	9:19	"We have given them our oath by **the L**	H3378
Jos	9:24	were clearly told how **the L** your God had	H3378
Jos	9:27	needs of the altar of **the L** at the place the	H3378
Jos	9:27	of the LORD at the place the L would choose.	NDT
Jos	10: 8	**The L** said to Joshua, "Do not be afraid of	H3378
Jos	10:10	**The L** threw them into confusion before	H3378
Jos	10:11	**the L** hurled large hailstones down on	H3378
Jos	10:12	On the day **the L** gave the Amorites over	H3378
Jos	10:12	Joshua said to **the L** in the presence of	H3378
Jos	10:14	a day when **the L** listened to a human	H3378
Jos	10:14	Surely **the L** was fighting for Israel	H3378
Jos	10:19	for **the L** your God has given them into	H3378
Jos	10:25	This is what **the L** will do to all the	H3378
Jos	10:30	**The L** also gave that city and its king into	H3378
Jos	10:32	**The L** gave Lachish into Israel's hands	H3378
Jos	10:40	breathed, just as **the L**, the God of Israel,	H3378
Jos	10:42	campaign, because **the L**, the God of	H3378
Jos	11: 6	**The L** said to Joshua, "Do not be afraid of	H3378
Jos	11: 8	and **the L** gave them into the hand of	H3378
Jos	11: 9	Joshua did to them as **the L** had directed	H3378
Jos	11:12	the servant of **the L** had commanded.	H3378
Jos	11:15	As **the L** commanded his servant Moses	H3378
Jos	11:15	of all that **the L** commanded Moses.	H3378
Jos	11:20	For it was **the L** *himself* who hardened	H3378
Jos	11:20	as **the L** had commanded Moses.	H3378
Jos	11:23	just as **the L** had directed Moses	H3378
Jos	12: 6	the servant of **the L**, and the Israelites	H3378
Jos	12: 6	the servant of **the L** gave their land to	H3378
Jos	13: 1	had grown old, **the L** said to him, "You	H3378
Jos	13: 8	the servant of **the L**, had assigned it to	H3378
Jos	13:14	the food offerings presented to **the L**,	H3378
Jos	13:33	no inheritance; **the L**, the God of Israel,	H3378
Jos	14: 2	as **the L** had commanded through Moses.	H3378
Jos	14: 5	just as **the L** had commanded Moses.	H3378
Jos	14: 6	"You know what **the L** said to Moses the	H3378
Jos	14: 7	the servant of **the L** sent me from Kadesh	H3378
Jos	14: 8	followed **the L** my God wholeheartedly.	H3378
Jos	14: 9	you have followed **the L** my God	H3378
Jos	14:10	"Now then, just as **the L** promised, he has	H3378
Jos	14:12	hill country that **the L** promised me that	H3378
Jos	14:12	**the L** helping me, I will drive them	H3378
Jos	14:14	because he followed **the L**, the God of	H3378
Jos	17: 4	"**The L** commanded Moses to give us an	H3378
Jos	17:14	and **the L** has blessed us abundantly."	H3378
Jos	18: 3	to take possession of the land that **the L**,	H3378
Jos	18: 6	you in the presence of **the L** our God.	H3378
Jos	18: 7	priestly service of **the L** is their inheritance	H3378
Jos	18: 7	Moses the servant of **the L** gave it to them.	H3378
Jos	18: 8	here at Shiloh in the presence of **the L**."	H3378
Jos	18:10	them in Shiloh in the presence of **the L**,	H3378
Jos	19:50	as **the L** had commanded. They gave him	H3378
Jos	19:51	in the presence of **the L** at the entrance to	H3378
Jos	20: 1	Then **the L** said to Joshua:	H3378
Jos	21: 2	"**The L** commanded through Moses that	H3378
Jos	21: 3	as **the L** had commanded, the	H3378
Jos	21: 8	as **the L** had commanded through Moses.	H3378
Jos	21:43	So **the L** gave Israel all the land he had	H3378
Jos	21:44	**The L** gave them rest on every side, just as	H3378
Jos	21:44	**the L** gave all their enemies into their	H3378
Jos	22: 2	Moses the servant of **the L** commanded,	H3378
Jos	22: 3	out the mission **the L** your God gave you.	H3378
Jos	22: 4	Now that **the L** your God has given them	H3378
Jos	22: 4	the servant of **the L** gave you on the	H3378
Jos	22: 5	that Moses the servant of **the L** gave you:	H3378
Jos	22: 5	to love **the L** your God, to walk in	H3378
Jos	22: 9	the command of **the L** through Moses.	H3378
Jos	22:16	"The whole assembly of **the L** says: 'How	H3378
Jos	22:16	you turn away from **the L** and build	H3378
Jos	22:17	a plague fell on the community of **the L**!	H3378
Jos	22:18	And are you now turning away from **the L**	H3378
Jos	22:18	" 'If you rebel against **the L** today	H3378
Jos	22:19	do not rebel against **the L** or against us by	H3378
Jos	22:19	other than the altar of **the L** our God.	H3378
Jos	22:22	Mighty One, God, **the L**! The Mighty One,	H3378
Jos	22:22	The Mighty One, God, **the L**! He knows!	H3378
Jos	22:22	in rebellion or disobedience to **the L**,	H3378
Jos	22:23	to turn away from **the L** and to offer burnt	H3378
Jos	22:23	may **the L** himself call us to account.	H3378
Jos	22:24	'What do you have to do with **the L**, the	H3378
Jos	22:25	**The L** has made the Jordan a boundary	H3378
Jos	22:25	You have no share in **the L**.' So your	H3378
Jos	22:25	might cause ours to stop fearing **the L**.	H3378
Jos	22:27	that we will worship **the L** at his sanctuary	H3378
Jos	22:27	say to ours, 'You have no share in **the L**.	H3378
Jos	22:29	to rebel against **the L** and turn away from	H3378
Jos	22:29	than the altar of **the L** our God that stands	H3378
Jos	22:31	"Today we know that **the L** is with us	H3378
Jos	22:31	not been unfaithful to **the L** in this matter.	H3378
Jos	22:34	A Witness Between Us—that **the L** is God.	H3378
Jos	23: 1	had passed and **the L** had given Israel	H3378
Jos	23: 3	seen everything **the L** your God has done	H3378
Jos	23: 3	it was **the L** your God who fought for you.	H3378
Jos	23: 5	**The L** your God himself will push them	H3378
Jos	23: 5	as **the L** your God promised you.	H3378
Jos	23: 8	But you are to hold fast to **the L** your God	H3378
Jos	23: 9	"**The L** has driven out before you great	H3378
Jos	23:10	because **the L** your God fights for you	H3378
Jos	23:11	So be very careful to love **the L** your God.	H3378
Jos	23:13	may be sure that **the L** your God will no	H3378
Jos	23:13	which **the L** your God has given you.	H3378
Jos	23:14	good promises **the L** your God gave you	H3378
Jos	23:15	all the good things **the L** your God has	H3378
Jos	23:15	until **the L** your God has destroyed you	H3378
Jos	23:16	violate the covenant of **the L** your God,	H3378
Jos	24: 2	"This is what **the L**, the God of Israel,	H3378
Jos	24: 7	But they cried to **the L** for help, and he put	H3378
Jos	24:14	"Now fear **the L** and serve him with all	H3378
Jos	24:14	River and in Egypt, and serve **the L**.	H3378
Jos	24:15	But if serving **the L** seems undesirable to	H3378
Jos	24:15	my household, we will serve **the L**.	H3378
Jos	24:16	from us to forsake **the L** to serve other	H3378
Jos	24:17	It was **the L** our God himself who brought	H3378
Jos	24:18	And **the L** drove out before us all the	H3378
Jos	24:18	We too will serve **the L**, because he is our	H3378
Jos	24:19	people, "You are not able to serve **the L**.	H3378
Jos	24:20	If you forsake **the L** and serve foreign gods	H3378
Jos	24:21	said to Joshua, "No! We will serve **the L**."	H3378
Jos	24:22	that you have chosen to serve **the L**."	H3378
Jos	24:23	among you and yield your hearts to **the L**,	H3378
Jos	24:24	"We will serve **the L** our God and obey	H3378
Jos	24:26	the oak near the holy place of **the L**.	H3378
Jos	24:27	heard all the words **the L** has said to us.	H3378
Jos	24:29	the servant of **the L**, died at the age	H3378
Jos	24:31	Israel served **the L** throughout the lifetime	H3378
Jos	24:31	everything **the L** had done for Israel.	H3378
Jdg	1: 1	the Israelites asked **the L**, "Who of us is to	H3378
Jdg	1: 2	**The L** answered, "Judah shall go up;	H3378
Jdg	1: 4	**the L** gave the Canaanites and Perizzites	H3378
Jdg	1:19	**The L** was with the men of Judah.	H3378
Jdg	1:22	attacked Bethel, and **the L** was with them.	H3378
Jdg	2: 1	The angel of **the L** went up from Gilgal to	H3378
Jdg	2: 4	the angel of **the L** had spoken these	H3378
Jdg	2: 5	There they offered sacrifices to **the L**.	H3378
Jdg	2: 7	The people served **the L** throughout the	H3378
Jdg	2: 7	the great things **the L** had done for Israel	H3378
Jdg	2: 8	the servant of **the L**, died at the age	H3378
Jdg	2:10	who knew neither **the L** nor what he had	H3378
Jdg	2:11	evil in the eyes of **the L** and served the	H3378
Jdg	2:12	They forsook **the L**, the God of their	H3378
Jdg	2:14	against Israel **the L** gave them into the	H3378
Jdg	2:15	the hand of **the L** was against them to	H3378
Jdg	2:16	Then **the L** raised up judges, who saved	H3378
Jdg	2:18	Whenever **the L** raised up a judge for	H3378
Jdg	2:18	for **the L** relented because of their	H3378
Jdg	2:20	Therefore **the L** was very angry with Israel	H3378
Jdg	2:22	keep the way of **the L** and walk in it as	H3378
Jdg	2:23	**The L** had allowed those nations to	H3378
Jdg	3: 1	These are the nations **the L** left to test all	H3378
Jdg	3: 7	The Israelites did evil in the eyes of **the L**	H3378
Jdg	3: 7	they forgot **the L** their God and served the	H3378
Jdg	3: 8	The anger of **the L** burned against Israel	H3378
Jdg	3: 9	But when they cried out to **the L**, he raised	H3378
Jdg	3:10	The Spirit of **the L** came on him, so that	H3378
Jdg	3:10	**The L** gave Cushan-Rishathaim king of	H3378
Jdg	3:12	the Israelites did evil in the eyes of **the L**,	H3378
Jdg	3:12	they did this evil **the L** gave Eglon king of	H3378
Jdg	3:15	Again the Israelites cried out to **the L**, and	H3378
Jdg	3:28	he ordered, "for **the L** has given Moab	H3378
Jdg	4: 1	the Israelites did evil in the eyes of **the L**,	H3378
Jdg	4: 2	So **the L** sold them into the hands of Jabin	H3378
Jdg	4: 3	twenty years, they cried to **the L** for help.	H3378
Jdg	4: 6	said to him, "**The L**, the God of Israel,	H3378
Jdg	4: 9	for **the L** will deliver Sisera into the hands	H3378
Jdg	4:14	This is the day **the L** has given Sisera into	H3378
Jdg	4:14	Has not **the L** gone ahead of you?	H3378
Jdg	4:15	**the L** routed Sisera and all his chariots	H3378
Jdg	5: 2	willingly offer themselves—praise **the L**!	H3378
Jdg	5: 3	will sing to **the L**; I will praise the	H3378
Jdg	5: 3	I will praise **the L**, the God of Israel,	H3378
Jdg	5: 4	"When you, L, went out from Seir, when	H3378
Jdg	5: 5	The mountains quaked before **the L**, the	H3378
Jdg	5: 5	of Sinai, before **the L**, the God of Israel.	H3378
Jdg	5: 9	among the people. Praise **the L**!	H3378
Jdg	5:11	They recite the victories of **the L**, the	H3378
Jdg	5:11	the people of **the L** went down to the	H3378
Jdg	5:13	the people of **the L** came down to me	H3378
Jdg	5:23	said the angel of **the L**. 'Curse its people	H3378
Jdg	5:23	because they did not come to help **the L**	H3378
Jdg	5:23	the LORD, to help **the L** against the mighty.	H3378
Jdg	5:31	your enemies perish, L! But may all who	H3378
Jdg	6: 1	The Israelites did evil in the eyes of **the L**	H3378
Jdg	6: 6	that they cried out to **the L** for help.	H3378
Jdg	6: 7	cried out to **the L** because of Midian,	H3378
Jdg	6: 8	"This is what **the L**, the God of Israel	H3378
Jdg	6:10	I said to you, 'I am **the L** your God; do not	H3378
Jdg	6:11	The angel of **the L** came and sat down	H3378
Jdg	6:12	When the angel of **the L** appeared to	H3378
Jdg	6:12	said, "**The L** is with you, mighty warrior."	H3378
Jdg	6:13	replied, "but if **the L** is with us, why has	H3378
Jdg	6:13	'Did not **the L** bring us up out of Egypt?	H3378
Jdg	6:13	But now **the L** has abandoned us and	H3378
Jdg	6:14	**The L** turned to him and said, "Go in the	H3378
Jdg	6:16	**The L** answered, "I will be with you, and	H3378
Jdg	6:18	And the L said, "I will wait	NDT
Jdg	6:21	Then the angel of **the L** touched the meat	H3378
Jdg	6:21	And the angel of **the L** disappeared.	H3378
Jdg	6:22	realized that it was the angel of **the L**,	H3378
Jdg	6:22	he exclaimed, "Alas, Sovereign L!	H3378
Jdg	6:22	have seen the angel of **the L** face to face!"	H3378
Jdg	6:23	But **the L** said to him, "Peace! Do not be	H3378
Jdg	6:24	built an altar to **the L** there and called it	H3378
Jdg	6:24	LORD there and called it **The L** Is Peace.	H3378
Jdg	6:25	That same night **the L** said to him, "Take	H3378
Jdg	6:26	kind of altar to **the L** your God on the top	H3378
Jdg	6:27	of his servants and did as **the L** told him.	H3378
Jdg	6:34	Then the Spirit of **the L** came on Gideon	H3378
Jdg	7: 2	**The L** said to Gideon, "You have too many	H3378
Jdg	7: 4	But **the L** said to Gideon, "There are still	H3378
Jdg	7: 5	There **the L** told him, "Separate those	H3378
Jdg	7: 7	**The L** said to Gideon, "With the three	H3378
Jdg	7: 9	During that night **the L** said to Gideon	H3378
Jdg	7:15	**The L** has given the Midianite camp into	H3378
Jdg	7:18	shout, 'For **the L** and for Gideon.	H3378
Jdg	7:20	"A sword for **the L** and for Gideon!	H3378
Jdg	7:22	**the L** caused the men throughout the	H3378
Jdg	8: 7	when **the L** has given Zebah and	H3378
Jdg	8:19	As surely as **the L** lives, if you had spared	H3378
Jdg	8:23	rule over you. **The L** will rule over you."	H3378
Jdg	8:34	did not remember **the L** their God	H3378
Jdg	10: 6	the Israelites did evil in the eyes of **the L**.	H3378
Jdg	10: 6	Israelites forsook **the L** and no longer	H3378
Jdg	10:10	Then the Israelites cried out to **the L**, "We	H3378
Jdg	10:11	**The L** replied, "When the Egyptians, the	H3378
Jdg	10:15	But the Israelites said to **the L**, "We have	H3378
Jdg	10:16	gods among them and served **the L**.	H3378
Jdg	11: 9	Ammonites and **the L** gives them to me	H3378
Jdg	11:10	Gilead replied, "**The L** is our witness; we	H3378
Jdg	11:11	all his words before **the L** in Mizpah.	H3378
Jdg	11:21	"Then **the L**, the God of Israel, gave Sihon	H3378
Jdg	11:23	"Now since **the L**, the God of Israel, has	H3378
Jdg	11:24	whatever **the L** our God has given us	H3378
Jdg	11:27	Let **the L**, the Judge, decide the dispute	H3378
Jdg	11:29	the Spirit of **the L** came on Jephthah.	H3378
Jdg	11:30	And Jephthah made a vow to **the L**: "If	H3378
Jdg	11:32	and **the L** gave them into his hands.	H3378
Jdg	11:35	have made a vow to **the L** that I cannot	H3378
Jdg	11:36	"you have given your word to **the L**.	H3378
Jdg	11:36	now that **the L** has avenged you of your	H3378
Jdg	12: 3	and **the L** gave me the victory over them.	H3378
Jdg	13: 1	the Israelites did evil in the eyes of **the L**,	H3378
Jdg	13: 1	so **the L** delivered them into the hands of	H3378
Jdg	13: 3	The angel of **the L** appeared to her and	H3378

Jdg 13: 8 Then Manoah prayed to **the L**: "Pardon H3378
Jdg 13:13 The angel of **the L** answered, "Your wife H3378
Jdg 13:15 Manoah said to the angel of **the L**, "We H3378
Jdg 13:16 The angel of **the L** replied, "Even though H3378
Jdg 13:16 prepare a burnt offering, offer it to **the L**." H3378
Jdg 13:16 not realize that it was the angel of **the L**.) H3378
Jdg 13:17 Manoah inquired of the angel of **the L**, H3378
Jdg 13:19 sacrificed it on a rock to **the L**. H3378
Jdg 13:19 And the L did an amazing thing while NDT
Jdg 13:20 the angel of **the L** ascended in the flame. H3378
Jdg 13:21 When the angel of **the L** did not show H3378
Jdg 13:21 realized that it was the angel of **the L**. H3378
Jdg 13:23 answered, "If **the L** had meant to kill us H3378
Jdg 13:24 He grew and **the L** blessed him, H3378
Jdg 13:25 the Spirit of **the L** began to stir him H3378
Jdg 14: 4 did not know that this was from **the L**, H3378
Jdg 14: 6 The Spirit of **the L** came powerfully upon H3378
Jdg 14:19 Then the Spirit of **the L** came powerfully H3378
Jdg 15:14 The Spirit of **the L** came powerfully upon H3378
Jdg 15:18 he cried out to **the L**, "You have given H3378
Jdg 16:20 he did not know that **the L** had left him. H3378
Jdg 16:28 Then Samson prayed to **the L**, "Sovereign H3378
Jdg 16:28 to the LORD, "Sovereign **L**, remember me. H3378
Jdg 17: 2 mother said, "**The L** bless you, my son!" H3378
Jdg 17: 3 my silver to **the L** for my son to make an H3378
Jdg 17:13 Now I know that **the L** will be good to me H3378
Jdg 19:18 now I am going to the house of **the L**. H3378
Jdg 20: 1 assembled before **the L** in Mizpah. H3378
Jdg 20:18 the Benjamites?" **The L** replied, "Judah H3378
Jdg 20:23 up and wept before **the L** until evening, H3378
Jdg 20:23 until evening, and they inquired of **the L**. H3378
Jdg 20:23 **The L** answered, "Go up H3378
Jdg 20:26 there they sat weeping before **the L**. H3378
Jdg 20:26 offerings and fellowship offerings to **the L**. H3378
Jdg 20:27 And the Israelites inquired of **the L**. H3378
Jdg 20:28 **The L** responded, "Go, for tomorrow I will H3378
Jdg 20:35 **The L** defeated Benjamin before Israel H3378
Jdg 21: 3 "**L**, God of Israel," they cried, "why has H3378
Jdg 21: 5 has failed to assemble before **the L**?" H3378
Jdg 21: 5 assemble before **the L** at Mizpah was to H3378
Jdg 21: 7 taken an oath by **the L** not to give them H3378
Jdg 21: 8 to assemble before **the L** at Mizpah?" H3378
Jdg 21:15 because **the L** had made a gap in the H3378
Jdg 21:19 is the annual festival of **the L** in Shiloh, H3378
Ru 1: 6 heard in Moab that **the L** had come to the H3378
Ru 1: 8 May **the L** show you kindness, as you H3378
Ru 1: 9 May **the L** grant that each of you will find H3378
Ru 1:17 May **the L** deal with me, be it ever so H3378
Ru 1:21 but **the L** has brought me back empty. H3378
Ru 1:21 **The L** has afflicted me; the Almighty has H3378
Ru 2: 4 the harvesters, "**The L** be with you! H3378
Ru 2: 4 LORD be with you!" "**The L** bless you!" H3378
Ru 2:12 May **the L** repay you for what you have H3378
Ru 2:12 May you be richly rewarded by **the L**, the H3378
Ru 2:20 "**The L** bless him!" Naomi said to her H3378
Ru 3:10 "**The L** bless you, my daughter," he H3378
Ru 3:13 as surely as **the L** lives I will do it. H3378
Ru 4:11 May **the L** make the woman who is H3378
Ru 4:12 the offspring **the L** gives you by this H3378
Ru 4:13 love to her, **the L** enabled her to conceive H3378
Ru 4:14 "Praise be to **the L**, who this day has not H3378
1Sa 1: 3 sacrifice to **the L** Almighty at Shiloh, H3378
1Sa 1: 3 the two sons of Eli, were priests of **the L**. H3378
1Sa 1: 5 and **the L** had closed her womb. H3378
1Sa 1: 6 Because **the L** had closed Hannah's womb, H3378
1Sa 1: 7 Hannah went up to the house of **the L**, H3378
1Sa 1:10 deep anguish Hannah prayed to **the L**, H3378
1Sa 1:11 "**L** Almighty, if you will only look H3378
1Sa 1:11 I will give him to **the L** for all the days of H3378
1Sa 1:12 As she kept on praying to **the L**, Eli H3378
1Sa 1:15 I was pouring out my soul to **the L**. H3378
1Sa 1:19 worshiped before **the L** and then went H3378
1Sa 1:19 wife Hannah, and **the L** remembered her. H3378
1Sa 1:20 "Because I asked **the L** for him. H3378
1Sa 1:21 annual sacrifice to **the L** and to fulfill his H3378
1Sa 1:22 take him and present him before **the L**, H3378
1Sa 1:23 only may **the L** make good his word." H3378
1Sa 1:24 him to the house of **the L** at Shiloh. H3378
1Sa 1:26 stood here beside you praying to **the L**. H3378
1Sa 1:27 and **the L** has granted me what I asked of H3378
1Sa 1:28 So now I give him to **the L**. For his whole H3378
1Sa 1:28 whole life he will be given over to **the L**." H3378
1Sa 1:28 And he worshiped **the L** there. H3378
1Sa 2: 1 "My heart rejoices in **the L**; in the LORD H3378
1Sa 2: 1 the LORD; in **the L** my horn is lifted high. H3378
1Sa 2: 2 "There is no one holy like **the L**; there is H3378
1Sa 2: 3 arrogance, for **the L** is a God who knows H3378
1Sa 2: 6 "**The L** brings death and makes alive; he H3378
1Sa 2: 7 **The L** sends poverty and wealth; he H3378
1Sa 2:10 those who oppose **the L** will be broken H3378
1Sa 2:10 **the L** will judge the ends of the earth. H3378
1Sa 2:11 ministered before **the L** under Eli the H3378
1Sa 2:12 scoundrels; they had no regard for **the L**. H3378
1Sa 2:18 Samuel was ministering before **the L**— H3378
1Sa 2:20 "May **the L** give you children by this H3378
1Sa 2:20 the one she prayed for and gave to **the L**." H3378
1Sa 2:21 And **the L** was gracious to Hannah; she H3378
1Sa 2:21 Samuel grew up in the presence of **the L**. H3378
1Sa 2:25 if anyone sins against **the L**, who will H3378
1Sa 2:26 in favor with **the L** and with people. H3378
1Sa 2:27 said to him, "This is what **the L** says: H3378
1Sa 2:30 "Therefore **the L**, the God of Israel H3378
1Sa 2:30 But now **the L** declares: 'Far be H3378
1Sa 3: 1 Samuel ministered before **the L** under Eli. H3378
1Sa 3: 1 In those days the word of **the L** was rare H3378
1Sa 3: 3 was lying down in the house of **the L**, H3378
1Sa 3: 4 Then **the L** called Samuel. Samuel H3378
1Sa 3: 6 Again **the L** called, "Samuel!" And H3378
1Sa 3: 7 Now Samuel did not yet know **the L**: H3378
1Sa 3: 7 The word of **the L** had not yet been H3378
1Sa 3: 8 A third time **the L** called, "Samuel!" H3378
1Sa 3: 8 Eli realized that **the L** was calling the boy. H3378
1Sa 3: 9 calls you, say, 'Speak, **L**, for your servant H3378
1Sa 3:10 **The L** came and stood there, calling as at H3378
1Sa 3:11 And **the L** said to Samuel: "See, I am H3378
1Sa 3:15 opened the doors of the house of **the L**. H3378
1Sa 3:18 Eli said, "He is **the L**; let him do what is H3378
1Sa 3:19 **The L** was with Samuel as he grew up H3378
1Sa 3:20 was attested as a prophet of **the L**. H3378
1Sa 3:21 **The L** continued to appear at Shiloh, and H3378
1Sa 4: 3 "Why did **the L** bring defeat on us today H3378
1Sa 4: 4 the ark of the covenant of **the L** Almighty, H3378
1Sa 4: 6 that the ark of **the L** had come into the H3378
1Sa 5: 3 face on the ground before the ark of **the L**! H3378
1Sa 5: 4 face on the ground before the ark of **the L**! H3378
1Sa 6: 1 When the ark of **the L** had been in H3378
1Sa 6: 2 "What shall we do with the ark of **the L**? H3378
1Sa 6: 8 Take the ark of **the L** and put it on the cart H3378
1Sa 6: 9 then **the L** has brought this great disaster H2085S
1Sa 6:11 placed the ark of **the L** on the cart and H3378
1Sa 6:14 the cows as a burnt offering to **the L**. H3378
1Sa 6:15 The Levites took down the ark of **the L** H3378
1Sa 6:15 offerings and made sacrifices to **the L**. H3378
1Sa 6:17 sent as a guilt offering to **the L**— H3378
1Sa 6:18 set the ark of **the L** is a witness to this H3378
1Sa 6:19 because they looked into the ark of **the L**. H3378
1Sa 6:19 of the heavy blow **the L** had dealt them. H3378
1Sa 6:20 "Who can stand in the presence of **the L** H3378
1Sa 6:21 Philistines have returned the ark of **the L**. H3378
1Sa 7: 1 Jearim came and took up the ark of **the L**. H3378
1Sa 7: 1 Eleazar his son to guard the ark of **the L**. H3378
1Sa 7: 2 the people of Israel turned back to **the L**. H3378
1Sa 7: 3 you are returning to **the L** with all your H3378
1Sa 7: 3 yourselves to **the L** and serve him only, H3378
1Sa 7: 4 Ashtoreths, and served **the L** only. H3378
1Sa 7: 5 I will intercede with **the L** for you. H3378
1Sa 7: 6 drew water and poured it out before **the L**. H3378
1Sa 7: 6 "We have sinned against **the L**. H3378
1Sa 7: 8 not stop crying out to **the L** our God for us, H3378
1Sa 7: 9 it as a whole burnt offering to **the L**. H3378
1Sa 7: 9 He cried out to **the L** on Israel's behalf H3378
1Sa 7: 9 Israel's behalf, and **the L** answered him. H3378
1Sa 7:10 But that day **the L** thundered with loud H3378
1Sa 7:12 "Thus far **the L** has helped us. H3378
1Sa 7:13 the hand of **the L** was against the H3378
1Sa 7:17 And he built an altar there to **the L**. H3378
1Sa 8: 6 displeased Samuel; so he prayed to **the L**. H3378
1Sa 8: 7 And **the L** told him: "Listen to all that the H3378
1Sa 8:10 all the words of **the L** to the people who H3378
1Sa 8:18 but **the L** will not answer you in that day." H3378
1Sa 8:21 people said, he repeated it before **the L**. H3378
1Sa 8:22 **The L** answered, "Listen to them and give H3378
1Sa 9:15 **the L** had revealed this to Samuel: H3378
1Sa 9:17 sight of Saul, **the L** said to him, "This is H3378
1Sa 10: 1 "Has not **the L** anointed you ruler over his H3378
1Sa 10: 6 The Spirit of **the L** will come powerfully H3378
1Sa 10:17 the people of Israel to **the L** at Mizpah H3378
1Sa 10:18 "This is what **the L**, the God of Israel H3378
1Sa 10:19 yourselves before **the L** by your tribes and H3378
1Sa 10:22 So they inquired further of **the L**, "Has the H3378
1Sa 10:22 And **the L** said, "Yes, he has hidden H3378
1Sa 10:24 "Do you see the man **the L** has chosen? H3378
1Sa 10:25 on a scroll and deposited it before **the L**. H3378
1Sa 11: 7 Then the terror of **the L** fell on the people H3378
1Sa 11:13 this day **the L** has rescued Israel. H3378
1Sa 11:15 made Saul king in the presence of **the L**. H3378
1Sa 11:15 fellowship offerings before **the L**, H3378
1Sa 12: 3 in the presence of **the L** and his anointed. H3378
1Sa 12: 5 to them, "**The L** is witness against you H3378
1Sa 12: 6 "It is **the L** who appointed Moses and H3378
1Sa 12: 7 with evidence before **the L** as to all the H3378
1Sa 12: 7 acts performed by **the L** for you and your H3378
1Sa 12: 8 they cried to **the L** for help, and the H3378
1Sa 12: 8 help, and **the L** sent Moses and Aaron H3378
1Sa 12: 9 "But they forgot **the L** their God; so he H3378
1Sa 12:10 They cried out to **the L** and said, 'We have H3378
1Sa 12:10 we have forsaken **the L** and served the H3378
1Sa 12:11 Then **the L** sent Jerub-Baal, Barak H3378
1Sa 12:12 though **the L** your God was your king. H3378
1Sa 12:13 see, **the L** has set a king over you. H3378
1Sa 12:14 If you fear **the L** and serve and obey him H3378
1Sa 12:14 reigns over you follow **the L** your God— H3378
1Sa 12:15 But if you do not obey **the L**, and if you H3378
1Sa 12:16 see this great thing **the L** is about to do H3378
1Sa 12:17 I will call on **the L** to send thunder and H3378
1Sa 12:17 did in the eyes of **the L** when you asked H3378
1Sa 12:18 Then Samuel called on **the L**, and that H3378
1Sa 12:18 that same day **the L** sent thunder and H3378
1Sa 12:18 stood in awe of **the L** and of Samuel. H3378
1Sa 12:19 "Pray to **the L** your God for your servants H3378
1Sa 12:20 do not turn away from **the L**, but serve H3378
1Sa 12:20 but serve **the L** with all your heart. H3378
1Sa 12:22 of his great name **the L** will not reject his H3378
1Sa 12:22 because **the L** was pleased to make you H3378
1Sa 12:23 should sin against **the L** by failing to pray H3378
1Sa 12:24 But be sure to fear **the L** and serve him H3378
1Sa 13:13 kept the command **the L** your God gave H3378
1Sa 13:14 **the L** has sought out a man after his own H3378
1Sa 14: 6 Perhaps **the L** will act in our behalf H3378
1Sa 14: 6 Nothing can hinder **the L** from saving H3378
1Sa 14:10 be our sign that **the L** has given them into H3378
1Sa 14:12 **the L** has given them into the hand of H3378
1Sa 14:23 So on that day **the L** saved Israel, and the H3378
1Sa 14:33 are sinning against **the L** by eating meat H3378
1Sa 14:34 Do not sin against **the L** by eating meat H3378
1Sa 14:35 Then Saul built an altar to **the L**; it was the H3378
1Sa 14:39 As surely as **the L** who rescues Israel lives H3378
1Sa 14:41 Then Saul prayed to **the L**, the God of H3378
1Sa 14:45 As surely as **the L** lives, not a hair of his H3378
1Sa 15: 1 "I am the one **the L** sent to anoint you H3378
1Sa 15: 1 so listen now to the message from **the L**. H3378
1Sa 15: 2 This is what **the L** Almighty says: 'I will H3378
1Sa 15:10 Then the word of **the L** came to Samuel: H3378
1Sa 15:11 he cried out to **the L** all that night. H3378
1Sa 15:13 reached him, Saul said, "**The L** bless you! H3378
1Sa 15:15 cattle to sacrifice to **the L** your God, H3378
1Sa 15:16 "Let me tell you what **the L** said to me last H3378
1Sa 15:17 **The L** anointed you king over Israel H3378
1Sa 15:19 Why did you not obey **the L**? Why did you H3378
1Sa 15:19 plunder and do evil in the eyes of **the L**?" H3378
1Sa 15:20 "But I did obey **the L**," Saul said. "I went H3378
1Sa 15:20 "I went on the mission **the L** assigned me H3378
1Sa 15:21 sacrifice them to **the L** your God at Gilgal." H3378
1Sa 15:22 "Does **the L** delight in burnt offerings and H3378
1Sa 15:22 sacrifices as much as in obeying **the L**? H3378
1Sa 15:23 you have rejected the word of **the L**, H3378
1Sa 15:25 back with me, so that I may worship **the L**." H3378
1Sa 15:26 You have rejected the word of **the L**, and H3378
1Sa 15:26 and **the L** has rejected you as king over H3378
1Sa 15:28 "**The L** has torn the kingdom of Israel from H3378
1Sa 15:30 so that I may worship **the L** your God." H3378
1Sa 15:31 back with Saul, and Saul worshiped **the L**. H3378
1Sa 15:33 put Agag to death before **the L** at Gilgal. H3378
1Sa 15:35 And **the L** regretted that he had made H3378
1Sa 16: 1 **The L** said to Samuel, "How long will you H3378
1Sa 16: 2 **The L** said, "Take a heifer with you and H3378
1Sa 16: 2 'I have come to sacrifice to **the L**. H3378
1Sa 16: 4 Samuel did what **the L** said. When he H3378
1Sa 16: 5 in peace; I have come to sacrifice to **the L**. H3378
1Sa 16: 6 LORD's anointed stands here before **the L**." H3378
1Sa 16: 7 But **the L** said to Samuel, "Do not H3378
1Sa 16: 7 The L does not look at the things people NDT
1Sa 16: 7 appearance, but **the L** looks at the heart." H3378
1Sa 16: 8 "**The L** has not chosen this one either." H3378
1Sa 16: 9 "Nor has **the L** chosen this one. H3378
1Sa 16:10 said to him, "**The L** has not chosen these." H3378
1Sa 16:12 Then **the L** said, "Rise and anoint him H3378
1Sa 16:13 day on the Spirit of **the L** came powerfully H3378
1Sa 16:14 Now the Spirit of **the L** had departed from H3378
1Sa 16:14 an evil spirit from **the L** tormented him. H3378
1Sa 16:18 fine-looking man. And **the L** is with him." H3378
1Sa 17:37 **The L** who rescued me from the paw of H3378
1Sa 17:37 said to David, "Go, and **the L** be with you. H3378
1Sa 17:45 you in the name of **the L** Almighty, H3378
1Sa 17:46 This day **the L** will deliver you into my H3378
1Sa 17:47 it is not by sword or spear that **the L** saves; H3378
1Sa 18:12 because **the L** was with David but had H3378
1Sa 18:14 success, because **the L** was with him. H3378
1Sa 18:17 me bravely and fight the battles of **the L**." H3378
1Sa 18:28 Saul realized that **the L** was with David H3378
1Sa 19: 5 **The L** won a great victory for all Israel H3378
1Sa 19: 6 "As surely as **the L** lives, David will not H3378
1Sa 19: 9 evil spirit from **the L** came on Saul as he H3378
1Sa 20: 3 Yet as surely as **the L** lives and as you H3378
1Sa 20: 8 him into a covenant with you before **the L**. H3378
1Sa 20:12 to David, "I *swear by* **the L**, the God of H3378
1Sa 20:13 harm you, may **the L** deal with Jonathan H3378
1Sa 20:13 May **the L** be with you as he has been H3378
1Sa 20:15 not even when **the L** has cut off every one H3378
1Sa 20:16 "May **the L** call David's enemies to H3378
1Sa 20:21 as surely as **the L** lives, you are safe; H3378
1Sa 20:22 because **the L** has sent you away. H3378
1Sa 20:23 **the L** is witness between you and me H3378
1Sa 20:42 with each other in the name of **the L**, H3378
1Sa 20:42 '**The L** is witness between you and me H3378
1Sa 21: 6 from before **the L** and replaced by H3378
1Sa 21: 7 detained before **the L**; he was Doeg the H3378
1Sa 22:10 Ahimelek inquired of **the L** for him; he H3378
1Sa 22:17 "Turn and kill the priests of **the L**, because H3378
1Sa 22:17 raise a hand to strike the priests of **the L**. H3378
1Sa 22:21 that Saul had killed the priests of **the L**. H3378
1Sa 23: 2 he inquired of **the L**, saying, "Shall I go H3378
1Sa 23: 2 **The L** answered him, "Go, attack the H3378
1Sa 23: 4 Once again David inquired of **the L**, and H3378
1Sa 23: 4 of the LORD, and **the L** answered him, "Go H3378
1Sa 23:10 David said, "**L**, God of Israel, your servant H3378
1Sa 23:11 servant has heard? **L**, God of Israel, tell H3378
1Sa 23:11 And **the L** said, "He will." H3378
1Sa 23:12 And **the L** said, "They will. H3378
1Sa 23:18 of them made a covenant before **the L**. H3378
1Sa 23:21 "**The L** bless you for your concern for me. H3378
1Sa 24: 4 "This is the day **the L** spoke of when he H3378
1Sa 24: 6 "**The L** forbid that I should do such a thing H3378
1Sa 24: 6 on him; for he is the anointed of **the L**." H3378
1Sa 24:10 your own eyes how **the L** delivered you H3378
1Sa 24:12 May **the L** judge between you and me H3378

1Sa 24:12 And may the L avenge the wrongs you H3378
1Sa 24:15 May the L be our judge and decide H3378
1Sa 24:18 the L delivered me into your hands H3378
1Sa 24:19 May the L reward you well for the way H3378
1Sa 24:21 Now swear to me by the L that you will H3378
1Sa 25:26 as surely as the L your God lives and as H3378
1Sa 25:26 since the L has kept you from bloodshed H3378
1Sa 25:28 The L your God will certainly make a H3378
1Sa 25:29 the bundle of the living by the L your God, H3378
1Sa 25:30 When the L has fulfilled for my lord every H3378
1Sa 25:31 And when the L your God has brought my H3378
1Sa 25:32 "Praise be to the L, the God of Israel, H3378
1Sa 25:34 as surely as the L, the God of Israel, H3378
1Sa 25:38 days later, the L struck Nabal and he died. H3378
1Sa 25:39 "Praise be to the L, who has upheld my H3378
1Sa 26:10 As surely as the L lives," he said, "the H3378
1Sa 26:10 he said, "the L himself will strike him, or H3378
1Sa 26:11 But the L forbid that I should lay a hand H3378
1Sa 26:12 because the L had put them into a deep H3378
1Sa 26:16 As surely as the L lives, you and your men H3378
1Sa 26:19 If the L has incited you against me, then H3378
1Sa 26:19 done it, may they be cursed before the L! H3378
1Sa 26:20 the ground far from the presence of the L. H3378
1Sa 26:23 The L rewards everyone for their H3378
1Sa 26:23 The L delivered you into my hands today H3378
1Sa 26:24 so may the L value my life and deliver me H3378
1Sa 28: 6 He inquired of the L, but the LORD did not H3378
1Sa 28: 6 but the L did not answer him by dreams H3378
1Sa 28:10 Saul swore to her by the L, "As surely as H3378
1Sa 28:10 "As surely as the L lives, you will not H3378
1Sa 28:16 now that the L has departed from you H3378
1Sa 28:17 The L has done what he predicted through H3378
1Sa 28:17 The L has torn the kingdom out of your H3378
1Sa 28:18 you did not obey the L or carry out his H3378
1Sa 28:18 the L has done this to you today. H3378
1Sa 28:19 The L will deliver both Israel and you into H3378
1Sa 28:19 The L will also give the army of Israel into H3378
1Sa 29: 6 "As surely as the L lives, you have H3378
1Sa 30: 6 But David found strength in the L his God H3378
1Sa 30: 8 David inquired of the L, "Shall I H3378
1Sa 30:23 not do that with what the L has given us. H3378
2Sa 1:12 the army of the L and for the nation H3378
2Sa 2: 1 course of time, David inquired of the L. H3378
2Sa 2: 1 The L said, "Go up." David H3378
2Sa 2: 1 "To Hebron," the L answered. NDT
2Sa 2: 5 "The L bless you for showing this H3378
2Sa 2: 6 May the L now show you kindness and H3378
2Sa 3: 9 do for David what the L promised him on H3378
2Sa 3:18 For the L promised David, 'By my servant H3378
2Sa 3:28 innocent before the L concerning the H3378
2Sa 3:39 May the L repay the evildoer according to H3378
2Sa 4: 8 This day the L has avenged my lord the H3378
2Sa 4: 9 "As surely as the L lives, who has H3378
2Sa 5: 2 And the L said to you, 'You will shepherd H3378
2Sa 5: 3 with them at Hebron before the L, H3378
2Sa 5:10 because the L God Almighty was with him H3378
2Sa 5:12 David knew that the L had established H3378
2Sa 5:19 so David inquired of the L, "Shall I go and H3378
2Sa 5:19 The L answered him, "Go, for I will surely H3378
2Sa 5:20 the L has broken out against my enemies H3378
2Sa 5:23 so David inquired of the L, and he H3378
2Sa 5:24 that will mean the L has gone out in front H3378
2Sa 5:25 So David did as the L commanded him H3378
2Sa 6: 2 the name of the L Almighty, who is H3378
2Sa 6: 5 with all their might before the L, H3378
2Sa 6: 9 was afraid of the L that day and said, H3378
2Sa 6: 9 can the ark of the L ever come to me?" H3378
2Sa 6:10 to take the ark of the L to be with him in H3378
2Sa 6:11 The ark of the L remained in the house of H3378
2Sa 6:11 and the L blessed him and his entire H3378
2Sa 6:12 "The L has blessed the household of H3378
2Sa 6:13 carrying the ark of the L had taken six H3378
2Sa 6:14 was dancing before the L with all his H3378
2Sa 6:15 up the ark of the L with shouts and the H3378
2Sa 6:16 As the ark of the L was entering the City H3378
2Sa 6:16 David leaping and dancing before the L, H3378
2Sa 6:17 brought the ark of the L and set it in its H3378
2Sa 6:17 fellowship offerings before the L. H3378
2Sa 6:18 the people in the name of the L Almighty. H3378
2Sa 6:21 "It was before the L, who chose me rather H3378
2Sa 6:21 Israel—I will celebrate before the L. H3378
2Sa 7: 1 in his palace and the L had given him rest H3378
2Sa 7: 3 go ahead and do it, for the L is with you." H3378
2Sa 7: 4 night the word of the L came to Nathan, H3378
2Sa 7: 5 servant David, 'This is what the L says: H3378
2Sa 7: 8 'This is what the L Almighty says: H3378
2Sa 7:11 " 'The L declares to you that the LORD H3378
2Sa 7:11 declares to you that the L himself will H3378
2Sa 7:18 King David went in and sat before the L, H3378
2Sa 7:18 "Who am I, Sovereign L, and what is my H3378
2Sa 7:19 Sovereign L, you have also spoken H3378
2Sa 7:19 Sovereign L, is for a mere human! H3378
2Sa 7:20 For you know your servant, Sovereign L. H3378
2Sa 7:22 you are, Sovereign L! There is no one like H3378
2Sa 7:24 and you, L, have become their H3378
2Sa 7:25 "And now, L God, keep forever the H3378
2Sa 7:26 'The L Almighty is God over Israel! H3378
2Sa 7:27 "L Almighty, God of Israel, you have H3378
2Sa 7:28 Sovereign L, you are God! Your covenant H3378
2Sa 7:29 you, Sovereign L, have spoken, and H3378
2Sa 8: 6 The L gave David victory wherever he H3378
2Sa 8:11 David dedicated these articles to the L, H3378
2Sa 8:14 The L gave David victory wherever he H3378
2Sa 10:12 The L will do what is good in his sight." H3378
2Sa 11:27 thing David had done displeased the L. H3378
2Sa 12: 1 The L sent Nathan to David. When he H3378
2Sa 12: 5 "As surely as the L lives, the man who H3378
2Sa 12: 7 This is what the L, the God of Israel H3378
2Sa 12: 9 despise the word of the L by doing what is H3378
2Sa 12:11 "This is what the L says: 'Out of your own H3378
2Sa 12:13 to Nathan, "I have sinned against the L." H3378
2Sa 12:13 replied, "The L has taken away your sin. H3378
2Sa 12:14 you have shown utter contempt for the L, H3378
2Sa 12:15 the L struck the child that Uriah's wife had H3378
2Sa 12:20 into the house of the L and worshiped. H3378
2Sa 12:22 The L may be gracious to me and let the H3378
2Sa 12:24 named him Solomon. The L loved him; H3378
2Sa 12:25 because the L loved him, he sent H3378
2Sa 14:11 the king invoke the L his God to prevent H3378
2Sa 14:11 "As surely as the L lives," he said, "not H3378
2Sa 14:17 May the L your God be with you H3378
2Sa 15: 7 Hebron and fulfill a vow I made to the L. H3378
2Sa 15: 8 'If the L takes me back to Jerusalem, I will H3378
2Sa 15: 8 Jerusalem, I will worship the L in Hebron. H3378
2Sa 15:20 May the L show you kindness and H3378
2Sa 15:21 "As surely as the L lives, and as my H3378
2Sa 15:31 So David prayed, "L, turn Ahithophel's H3378
2Sa 16: 8 The L has repaid you for all the blood you H3378
2Sa 16: 8 The L has given the kingdom into the H3378
2Sa 16:10 If he is cursing because the L said to him H3378
2Sa 16:11 let him curse, for the L has told him to. H3378
2Sa 16:12 It may be that the L will look upon my H3378
2Sa 16:18 the one chosen by the L, by these people, H3378
2Sa 17:14 For the L had determined to frustrate the H3378
2Sa 18:19 to the king that the L has vindicated him H3378
2Sa 18:28 said, "Praise be to the L your God! H3378
2Sa 18:31 The L has vindicated you today by H3378
2Sa 19: 7 I swear by the L that if you don't go out H3378
2Sa 21: 1 so David sought the face of the L. H3378
2Sa 21: 1 The L said, "It is on account of Saul and H3378
2Sa 21: 6 exposed before the L at Gibeah of Saul— H3378
2Sa 21: 7 the oath before the L between David and H3378
2Sa 21: 9 their bodies on a hill before the L. H3378
2Sa 22: 1 David sang to the L the words of this song H3378
2Sa 22: 1 of this song when the L delivered him H3378
2Sa 22: 2 "The L is my rock, my fortress and my H3378
2Sa 22: 4 "I called to the L, who is worthy of praise H3378
2Sa 22: 7 "In my distress I called to the L; I called H3378
2Sa 22:14 The L thundered from heaven; the voice H3378
2Sa 22:16 the earth laid bare at the rebuke of the L, H3378
2Sa 22:19 of my disaster, but the L was my support. H3378
2Sa 22:21 "The L has dealt with me according to my H3378
2Sa 22:22 For I have kept the ways of the L; I am not H3378
2Sa 22:25 The L has rewarded me according to my H3378
2Sa 22:29 L, are my lamp; the LORD turns my H3378
2Sa 22:29 the L turns my darkness into light. H3378
2Sa 22:32 For who is God besides the L? And who is H3378
2Sa 22:42 to save them—to the L, but he did not H3378
2Sa 22:47 "The L lives! Praise be to my Rock! H3378
2Sa 22:50 I will praise you, L, among the nations; H3378
2Sa 23: 2 "The Spirit of the L spoke through me; H3378
2Sa 23:10 The L brought about a great victory that H3378
2Sa 23:12 and the L brought about a great victory. H3378
2Sa 23:16 instead, he poured it out before the L. H3378
2Sa 23:17 "Far be it from me, L, to do this!" he said H3378
2Sa 24: 1 Again the anger of the L burned against H3378
2Sa 24: 3 "May the L your God multiply the troops H3378
2Sa 24:10 and he said to the L, "I have sinned H3378
2Sa 24:10 L, I beg you, take away the guilt of H3378
2Sa 24:11 the word of the L had come to Gad the H3378
2Sa 24:12 tell David, 'This is what the L says: H3378
2Sa 24:14 Let us fall into the hands of the L, for his H3378
2Sa 24:15 So the L sent a plague on Israel from that H3378
2Sa 24:16 the L relented concerning the disaster H3378
2Sa 24:16 The angel of the L was then at the H3378
2Sa 24:17 people, he said to the L, "I have sinned; H3378
2Sa 24:18 build an altar to the L on the threshing H3378
2Sa 24:19 as the L had commanded through Gad. H3378
2Sa 24:21 "so I can build an altar to the L, that the H3378
2Sa 24:23 "May the L your God accept you. H3378
2Sa 24:24 will not sacrifice to the L my God burnt H3378
2Sa 24:25 built an altar to the L there and sacrificed H3378
2Sa 24:25 Then the L answered his prayer in behalf H3378
1Ki 1:17 to me your servant by the L your God: H3378
1Ki 1:29 "As surely as the L lives, who has H3378
1Ki 1:30 this very day what I swore to you by the L, H3378
1Ki 1:36 May the L, the God of my lord the king, H3378
1Ki 1:37 As the L was with my lord the king, so H3378
1Ki 1:48 'Praise be to the L, the God of Israel, H3378
1Ki 2: 3 observe what the L your God requires H3378
1Ki 2: 4 that the L may keep his promise to me H3378
1Ki 2: 8 me at the Jordan, I swore to him by the L: H3378
1Ki 2:15 brother; for it has come to him from the L. H3378
1Ki 2:23 Then King Solomon swore by the L: H3378
1Ki 2:24 as surely as the L lives—he who has H3378
1Ki 2:26 the ark of the Sovereign L before my H3378
1Ki 2:27 Abiathar from the priesthood of the L, H3378
1Ki 2:27 fulfilling the word the L had spoken at H3378
1Ki 2:28 fled to the tent of the L and took hold of H3378
1Ki 2:29 to the tent of the L and was beside the H3378
1Ki 2:30 entered the tent of the L and said to Joab, H3378
1Ki 2:32 The L will repay him for the blood he H3378
1Ki 2:42 make you swear by the L and warn you, H3378
1Ki 2:43 keep your oath to the L and obey the H3378
1Ki 2:44 Now the L will repay you for your H3378
1Ki 2:45 will remain secure before the L forever." H3378
1Ki 3: 1 his palace and the temple of the L, H3378
1Ki 3: 2 not yet been built for the Name of the L. H3378
1Ki 3: 3 showed his love for the L by walking H3378
1Ki 3: 5 At Gibeon the L appeared to Solomon H3378
1Ki 3: 7 L my God, you have made your H3378
1Ki 5: 3 the Name of the L his God until the H3378
1Ki 5: 3 LORD his God until the L put his enemies H3378
1Ki 5: 4 But now the L my God has given me rest H3378
1Ki 5: 5 a temple for the Name of the L my God, H3378
1Ki 5: 5 my God, as the L told my father David H3378
1Ki 5: 7 "Praise be to the L today, for he has H3378
1Ki 5:12 The L gave Solomon wisdom, just as he H3378
1Ki 6: 1 he began to build the temple of the L. H3378
1Ki 6: 2 Solomon built for the L was sixty cubits H3378
1Ki 6:11 The word of the L came to Solomon: H3378
1Ki 6:19 set the ark of the covenant of the L there. H3378
1Ki 6:37 of the temple of the L was laid in the H3378
1Ki 7:12 of the temple of the L with its portico. H3378
1Ki 7:40 King Solomon in the temple of the L: H3378
1Ki 7:45 the temple of the L were of burnished H3378
1Ki 7:51 done for the temple of the L was finished, H3378
1Ki 8: 4 brought up the ark of the L and the tent of H3378
1Ki 8: 9 where the L made a covenant with the H3378
1Ki 8:10 the cloud filled the temple of the L. H3378
1Ki 8:11 the glory of the L filled his temple. H3378
1Ki 8:12 "The L has said that he would dwell in a H3378
1Ki 8:15 "Praise be to the L, the God of Israel, who H3378
1Ki 8:17 to build a temple for the Name of the L, H3378
1Ki 8:18 But the L said to my father David, 'You H3378
1Ki 8:20 "The L has kept the promise he made: H3378
1Ki 8:20 of Israel, just as the L promised, and I H3378
1Ki 8:20 built the temple for the Name of the L, H3378
1Ki 8:21 is the covenant of the L that he made with H3378
1Ki 8:22 before the altar of the L in front of the H3378
1Ki 8:23 "L, the God of Israel, there is no God like H3378
1Ki 8:25 "Now L, the God of Israel, keep for your H3378
1Ki 8:28 prayer and his plea for mercy, L my God. H3378
1Ki 8:44 when they pray to the L toward the city H3378
1Ki 8:53 when you, Sovereign L, brought our H3378
1Ki 8:54 these prayers and supplications to the L, H3378
1Ki 8:54 he rose from before the altar of the L H3378
1Ki 8:56 "Praise be to the L, who has given rest to H3378
1Ki 8:57 May the L our God be with us as he was H3378
1Ki 8:59 which I have prayed before the L, be near H3378
1Ki 8:59 be near to the L our God day and night H3378
1Ki 8:60 earth may know that the L is God and that H3378
1Ki 8:61 be fully committed to the L our God, H3378
1Ki 8:62 with him offered sacrifices before the L. H3378
1Ki 8:63 a sacrifice of fellowship offerings to the L: H3378
1Ki 8:63 Israelites dedicated the temple of the L. H3378
1Ki 8:64 courtyard in front of the temple of the L, H3378
1Ki 8:64 that stood before the L was too small to H3378
1Ki 8:65 it before the L our God for seven H3378
1Ki 8:66 all the good things the L had done for his H3378
1Ki 9: 1 the temple of the L and the royal palace, H3378
1Ki 9: 2 the L appeared to him a second time, as H3378
1Ki 9: 3 The L said to him: "I have heard the prayer H3378
1Ki 9: 8 'Why has the L done such a thing to this H3378
1Ki 9: 9 they have forsaken the L their God, H3378
1Ki 9: 9 that is why the L brought all this disaster H3378
1Ki 9:10 the temple of the L and the royal palace H3378
1Ki 9:25 on the altar he had built for the L, H3378
1Ki 9:25 incense before the L along with them, H3378
1Ki 10: 1 and his relationship to the L, H9005+3378
1Ki 10: 5 offerings he made at the temple of the L, H3378
1Ki 10: 9 Praise be to the L your God, who has H3378
1Ki 10:12 the temple of the L and for the royal H3378
1Ki 11: 2 nations about which the L had told the H3378
1Ki 11: 4 was not fully devoted to the L his God, H3378
1Ki 11: 6 So Solomon did evil in the eyes of the L H3378
1Ki 11: 6 he did not follow the L completely, as H3378
1Ki 11: 9 The L became angry with Solomon H3378
1Ki 11: 9 his heart had turned away from the L, H3378
1Ki 11:11 So the L said to Solomon, "Since this is H3378
1Ki 11:14 Then the L raised up against Solomon an H3378
1Ki 11:31 this is what the L, the God of Israel, H3378
1Ki 12:15 this turn of events was from the L, to H3378
1Ki 12:15 to fulfill the word the L had spoken to H3378
1Ki 12:24 'This is what the L says: Do not go up to H3378
1Ki 12:24 obeyed the word of the L and went home H3378
1Ki 12:24 went home again, as the L had ordered. H3378
1Ki 12:27 at the temple of the L in Jerusalem, H3378
1Ki 13: 1 By the word of the L a man of God came H3378
1Ki 13: 2 By the word of the L he cried out against H3378
1Ki 13: 2 This is what the L says: 'A son named H3378
1Ki 13: 3 "This is the sign the L has declared: The H3378
1Ki 13: 5 by the man of God by the word of the L. H3378
1Ki 13: 6 "Intercede with the L your God and pray H3378
1Ki 13: 6 So the man of God interceded with the L H3378
1Ki 13: 9 I was commanded by the word of the L H3378
1Ki 13:17 I have been told by the word of the L: H3378
1Ki 13:18 an angel said to me by the word of the L: H3378
1Ki 13:20 the word of the L came to the old prophet H3378
1Ki 13:21 from Judah, "This is what the L says: H3378
1Ki 13:21 the word of the L and have not kept H3378
1Ki 13:21 kept the command the L your God gave H3378
1Ki 13:26 man of God who defied the word of the L. H3378
1Ki 13:26 The L has given him over to the lion H3378
1Ki 13:26 as the word of the L had warned him." H3378
1Ki 13:32 by the word of the L against the altar in H3378

1Ki 14: 5 But **the L** had told Ahijah, “Jeroboam’s H3378
1Ki 14: 7 tell Jeroboam that this is what **the L**, the H3378
1Ki 14:11 die in the country. **The L** has spoken!’ H3378
1Ki 14:13 in the house of Jeroboam in whom **the L**, H3378
1Ki 14:14 “**The L** will raise up for himself a king H3378
1Ki 14:15 And **the L** will strike Israel, so that it will H3378
1Ki 14:18 as **the L** had said through his servant the H3378
1Ki 14:21 the city **the L** had chosen out of all the H3378
1Ki 14:22 Judah did evil in the eyes of **the L**. By the H3378
1Ki 14:24 of the nations **the L** had driven out before H3378
1Ki 14:26 of the temple of **the L** and the treasures of H3378
1Ki 15: 3 was not fully devoted to **the L** his God, H3378
1Ki 15: 4 David’s sake **the L** his God gave him a H3378
1Ki 15: 5 in the eyes of **the L** and had not failed H3378
1Ki 15:11 did what was right in the eyes of **the L**, H3378
1Ki 15:14 was fully committed to **the L** all his life. H3378
1Ki 15:15 into the temple of **the L** the silver and H3378
1Ki 15:26 He did evil in the eyes of **the L**, following H3378
1Ki 15:29 to the word of **the L** given through his H3378
1Ki 15:30 because he aroused the anger of **the L**, H3378
1Ki 15:34 He did evil in the eyes of **the L**, following H3378
1Ki 16: 1 Then the word of **the L** came to Jehu son H3378
1Ki 16: 7 the word of **the L** came through the H3378
1Ki 16: 7 the evil he had done in the eyes of **the L**, H3378
1Ki 16:12 with the word of **the L** spoken against H3378
1Ki 16:13 so that they aroused the anger of **the L** H3378
1Ki 16:19 evil in the eyes of **the L** and following the H3378
1Ki 16:25 evil in the eyes of **the L** and sinned more H3378
1Ki 16:26 so that they aroused the anger of **the L** H3378
1Ki 16:30 evil in the eyes of **the L** than any of those H3378
1Ki 16:33 did more to arouse the anger of **the L**, H3378
1Ki 16:34 with the word of **the L** spoken by Joshua H3378
1Ki 17: 1 said to Ahab, “As **the L**, the God of Israel H3378
1Ki 17: 2 Then the word of **the L** came to Elijah: H3378
1Ki 17: 5 So he did what **the L** had told him. H3378
1Ki 17: 8 Then the word of **the L** came to him: H3378
1Ki 17:12 “As surely as **the L** your God lives,” she H3378
1Ki 17:14 For this is what **the L**, the God of Israel H3378
1Ki 17:14 dry until the day **the L** sends rain on the H3378
1Ki 17:16 with the word of **the L** spoken by Elijah. H3378
1Ki 17:20 Then he cried out to **the L**, “LORD my God H3378
1Ki 17:20 cried out to the LORD, “**L** my God, have H3378
1Ki 17:21 the boy three times and cried out to **the L**, H3378
1Ki 17:21 out to the LORD, “**L** my God, let this boy’s H3378
1Ki 17:22 **The L** heard Elijah’s cry, and the boy’s life H3378
1Ki 17:24 that the word of **the L** from your mouth is H3378
1Ki 18: 1 the word of **the L** came to Elijah: H3378
1Ki 18: 3 Obadiah was a devout believer in **the L**. H3378
1Ki 18:10 As surely as **the L** your God lives, there is H3378
1Ki 18:12 the Spirit of **the L** may carry you when H3378
1Ki 18:12 have worshiped **the L** since my youth. H3378
1Ki 18:13 Jezebel was killing the prophets of **the L**? H3378
1Ki 18:15 Elijah said, “As **the L** Almighty lives H3378
1Ki 18:21 If **the L** is God, follow him; but if Baal is H3378
1Ki 18:24 and I will call on the name of **the L**. H3378
1Ki 18:30 he repaired the altar of **the L**, which H3378
1Ki 18:31 to whom the word of **the L** had come H3378
1Ki 18:32 he built an altar in the name of **the L**, H3378
1Ki 18:36 “**L**, the God of Abraham, Isaac and Israel H3378
1Ki 18:37 Answer me, **L**, answer me, so these H3378
1Ki 18:37 people will know that you, **L**, are God, H3378
1Ki 18:38 Then the fire of **the L** fell and burned up H3378
1Ki 18:39 prostrate and cried, “**The L**—he is God! H3378
1Ki 18:39 he is God! **The L**—he is God!” H3378
1Ki 18:46 The power of **the L** came on Elijah and H3378
1Ki 19: 4 have had enough, **L**,” he said. “Take my H3378
1Ki 19: 7 The angel of **the L** came back a second H3378
1Ki 19: 9 And the word of **the L** came to him H3378
1Ki 19:10 been very zealous for **the L** God Almighty. H3378
1Ki 19:11 The **L** said, “Go out and stand on the NDT
1Ki 19:11 on the mountain in the presence of **the L**, H3378
1Ki 19:11 of the LORD, for **the L** is about to pass by.” H3378
1Ki 19:11 apart and shattered the rocks before **the L**, H3378
1Ki 19:11 the LORD, but **the L** was not in the wind. H3378
1Ki 19:11 but **the L** was not in the earthquake. H3378
1Ki 19:12 came a fire, but **the L** was not in the fire. H3378
1Ki 19:14 been very zealous for **the L** God Almighty. H3378
1Ki 19:15 **The L** said to him, “Go back the way you H3378
1Ki 20:13 announced, “This is what **the L** says: H3378
1Ki 20:13 then you will know that I am **the L**. H3378
1Ki 20:14 prophet replied, “This is what **the L** says: H3378
1Ki 20:28 the king of Israel, “This is what **the L** says: H3378
1Ki 20:28 the Arameans think **the L** is a god of the H3378
1Ki 20:28 and you will know that I am **the L**. H3378
1Ki 20:35 By the word of **the L** one of the company H3378
1Ki 20:36 “Because you have not obeyed **the L**, as H3378
1Ki 20:42 said to the king, “This is what **the L** says: H3378
1Ki 21: 3 “**The L** forbid that I should give you the H3378
1Ki 21:17 Then the word of **the L** came to Elijah the H3378
1Ki 21:19 ‘This is what **the L** says: Have you H3378
1Ki 21:19 ‘This is what **the L** says: In the place H3378
1Ki 21:20 yourself to do evil in the eyes of **the L**. H3378
1Ki 21:23 “And also concerning Jezebel **the L** says H3378
1Ki 21:25 himself to do evil in the eyes of **the L**, H3378
1Ki 21:26 like the Amorites **the L** drove out before H3378
1Ki 21:28 Then the word of **the L** came to Elijah the H3378
1Ki 22: 5 of Israel, “First seek the counsel of **the L**.” H3378
1Ki 22: 7 a prophet of **the L** here whom we can H3378
1Ki 22: 8 through whom we can inquire of **the L**, H3378
1Ki 22:11 he declared, “This is what **the L** says: H3378
1Ki 22:12 “for **the L** will give it into the king’s hand. H3378
1Ki 22:14 “As surely as **the L** lives, I can tell H3378
1Ki 22:14 I can tell him only what **the L** tells me.” H3378
1Ki 22:15 “for **the L** will give it into the king’s hand. H3378
1Ki 22:16 the truth in the name of **the L**? H3378
1Ki 22:17 a shepherd, and **the L** said, ‘These H3378
1Ki 22:19 “Therefore hear the word of **the L**: H3378
1Ki 22:19 I saw **the L** sitting on his throne with all H3378
1Ki 22:20 And **the L** said, ‘Who will entice Ahab H3378
1Ki 22:21 stood before **the L** and said, ‘I will H3378
1Ki 22:22 “ ‘By what means?’ **the L** asked. “ ‘I will H3378
1Ki 22:22 will succeed in enticing him,’ said **the L**. NDT
1Ki 22:23 “So now **the L** has put a deceiving spirit in H3378
1Ki 22:23 **The L** has decreed disaster for you.” H3378
1Ki 22:24 did the spirit from **the L** go when he went H3378
1Ki 22:28 **the L** has not spoken through me. H3378
1Ki 22:38 as the word of **the L** had declared. H3378
1Ki 22:43 he did what was right in the eyes of **the L**. H3378
1Ki 22:52 He did evil in the eyes of **the L**, because H3378
1Ki 22:53 Baal and aroused the anger of **the L**, H3378
2Ki 1: 3 But the angel of **the L** said to Elijah the H3378
2Ki 1: 4 Therefore this is what **the L** says: ‘You H3378
2Ki 1: 6 you and tell him, “This is what **the L** says: H3378
2Ki 1:15 The angel of **the L** said to Elijah, “Go H3378
2Ki 1:16 “This is what **the L** says: Is it H3378
2Ki 1:17 to the word of **the L** that Elijah had H3378
2Ki 2: 1 When **the L** was about to take Elijah up to H3378
2Ki 2: 2 “Stay here; **the L** has sent me to Bethel.” H3378
2Ki 2: 2 “As surely as **the L** lives and as you live H3378
2Ki 2: 3 “Do you know that **the L** is going to take H3378
2Ki 2: 4 Elisha; **the L** has sent me to Jericho.” H3378
2Ki 2: 4 “As surely as **the L** lives and as you live H3378
2Ki 2: 5 “Do you know that **the L** is going to take H3378
2Ki 2: 6 **the L** has sent me to the Jordan. H3378
2Ki 2: 6 “As surely as **the L** lives and as you live H3378
2Ki 2:14 “Where now is **the L**, the God of Elijah?” H3378
2Ki 2:16 the Spirit of **the L** has picked him up H3378
2Ki 2:21 saying, “This is what **the L** says: H3378
2Ki 2:24 a curse on them in the name of **the L**. H3378
2Ki 3: 2 He did evil in the eyes of **the L**, but not as H3378
2Ki 3:10 “Has **the L** called us three kings together H3378
2Ki 3:11 “Is there no prophet of **the L** here, through H3378
2Ki 3:11 through whom we may inquire of **the L**?” H3378
2Ki 3:12 “The word of **the L** is with him. H3378
2Ki 3:13 “because it was **the L** who called us three H3378
2Ki 3:14 “As surely as **the L** Almighty lives H3378
2Ki 3:15 playing, the hand of **the L** came on Elisha H3378
2Ki 3:16 he said, “This is what **the L** says: I will fill H3378
2Ki 3:17 For this is what **the L** says: You will see H3378
2Ki 3:18 This is an easy thing in the eyes of **the L** H3378
2Ki 4: 1 and you know that he revered **the L**. H3378
2Ki 4:27 but **the L** has hidden it from me and has H3378
2Ki 4:30 “As surely as **the L** lives and as you live H3378
2Ki 4:33 on the two of them and prayed to **the L**. H3378
2Ki 4:43 For this is what **the L** says: ‘They will eat H3378
2Ki 4:44 left over, according to the word of **the L**. H3378
2Ki 5: 1 through him **the L** had given victory H3378
2Ki 5:11 call on the name of **the L** his God, H3378
2Ki 5:16 “As surely as **the L** lives, whom I serve, H3378
2Ki 5:17 sacrifices to any other god but **the L**. H3378
2Ki 5:18 may **the L** forgive your servant for this H3378
2Ki 5:18 may **the L** forgive your servant for this.” H3378
2Ki 5:20 As surely as **the L** lives, I will run after H3378
2Ki 6:17 “Open his eyes, **L**, so that he may see.” H3378
2Ki 6:17 Then **the L** opened the servant’s eyes H3378
2Ki 6:18 Elisha prayed to **the L**, “Strike this army H3378
2Ki 6:20 Elisha said, “**L**, open the eyes of these H3378
2Ki 6:20 Then **the L** opened their eyes and they H3378
2Ki 6:27 king replied, “If **the L** does not help you H3378
2Ki 6:33 “This disaster is from **the L**. Why should I H3378
2Ki 6:33 Why should I wait for **the L** any longer?” H3378
2Ki 7: 1 “Hear the word of **the L**. This is what the H3378
2Ki 7: 1 This is what **the L** says: About this H3378
2Ki 7: 2 even if **the L** should open the floodgates H3378
2Ki 7:16 barley sold for a shekel, as **the L** had said. H3378
2Ki 7:19 even if **the L** should open the floodgates H3378
2Ki 8: 1 because **the L** has decreed a famine in H3378
2Ki 8: 8 Consult **the L** through him; ask him, ‘Will H3378
2Ki 8:10 **the L** has revealed to me that he will in H3378
2Ki 8:13 “**The L** has shown me that you will H3378
2Ki 8:18 He did evil in the eyes of **the L**. H3378
2Ki 8:19 **the L** was not willing to destroy Judah. H3378
2Ki 8:27 of Ahab and did evil in the eyes of **the L**, H3378
2Ki 9: 3 declare, ‘This is what **the L** says: H3378
2Ki 9: 6 “This is what **the L**, the God of Israel, H3378
2Ki 9:12 ‘This is what **the L** says: I anoint you H3378
2Ki 9:25 his father when **the L** spoke this prophecy H3378
2Ki 9:26 his sons, declares **the L**, and I will surely H3378
2Ki 9:26 it on this plot of ground, declares **the L**. H3378
2Ki 9:26 in accordance with the word of **the L**.” H3378
2Ki 9:36 “This is the word of **the L** that he spoke H3378
2Ki 10:10 that not a word **the L** has spoken against H3378
2Ki 10:10 **The L** has done what he announced H3378
2Ki 10:16 with me and see my zeal for **the L**.” H3378
2Ki 10:17 to the word of **the L** spoken to Elijah. H3378
2Ki 10:23 no one who serves **the L** is here with you H3378
2Ki 10:30 **The L** said to Jehu, “Because you have H3378
2Ki 10:31 was not careful to keep the law of **the L**, H3378
2Ki 10:32 In those days **the L** began to reduce the H3378
2Ki 11: 3 at the temple of **the L** for six years while H3378
2Ki 11: 4 brought to him at the temple of **the L**. He H3378
2Ki 11: 4 them under oath at the temple of **the L**. H3378
2Ki 11:10 that were in the temple of **the L**. H3378
2Ki 11:13 went to the people at the temple of **the L**. H3378
2Ki 11:15 not be put to death in the temple of **the L**.” H3378
2Ki 11:17 covenant between **the L** and the king and H3378
2Ki 11:18 posted guards at the temple of **the L**. H3378
2Ki 11:19 the temple of **the L** and went into the H3378
2Ki 12: 2 right in the eyes of **the L** all the years H3378
2Ki 12: 4 sacred offerings to the temple of **the L**— H3378
2Ki 12: 9 side as one enters the temple of **the L**. H3378
2Ki 12: 9 that was brought to the temple of **the L**. H3378
2Ki 12:10 into the temple of **the L** and put it into H3378
2Ki 12:11 who worked on the temple of **the L**— H3378
2Ki 12:12 stone for the repair of the temple of **the L**, H3378
2Ki 12:13 of gold or silver for the temple of **the L**; H3378
2Ki 12:16 was not brought into the temple of **the L**; H3378
2Ki 12:18 of the temple of **the L** and of the royal H3378
2Ki 13: 2 evil in the eyes of **the L** by following the H3378
2Ki 13: 4 LORD’s favor, and **the L** listened to him, H3378
2Ki 13: 5 **The L** provided a deliverer for Israel, and H3378
2Ki 13:11 evil in the eyes of **the L** and did not turn H3378
2Ki 13:23 But **the L** was gracious to them and had H3378
2Ki 14: 3 He did what was right in the eyes of **the L** H3378
2Ki 14: 6 Law of Moses where **the L** commanded: H3378
2Ki 14:14 in the temple of **the L** and in the H3378
2Ki 14:24 evil in the eyes of **the L** and did not turn H3378
2Ki 14:25 in accordance with the word of **the L**, the H3378
2Ki 14:26 **The L** had seen how bitterly everyone in H3378
2Ki 14:27 And since **the L** had not said he would H3378
2Ki 15: 3 He did what was right in the eyes of **the L** H3378
2Ki 15: 5 **The L** afflicted the king with leprosy until H3378
2Ki 15: 9 He did evil in the eyes of **the L**, as his H3378
2Ki 15:12 So the word of **the L** spoken to Jehu was H3378
2Ki 15:18 He did evil in the eyes of **the L**. During his H3378
2Ki 15:24 Pekahiah did evil in the eyes of **the L**. H3378
2Ki 15:28 He did evil in the eyes of **the L**. He did H3378
2Ki 15:34 He did what was right in the eyes of **the L** H3378
2Ki 15:35 the Upper Gate of the temple of **the L**. H3378
2Ki 15:37 In those days **the L** began to send Rezin H3378
2Ki 16: 2 was right in the eyes of **the L** his God. H3378
2Ki 16: 3 of the nations **the L** had driven out before H3378
2Ki 16: 8 in the temple of **the L** and in the H3378
2Ki 16:14 the bronze altar that stood before **the L**, H3378
2Ki 16:14 the new altar and the temple of **the L**— H3378
2Ki 16:18 entryway outside the temple of **the L**, H3378
2Ki 17: 2 He did evil in the eyes of **the L**, but not H3378
2Ki 17: 7 had sinned against **the L** their God, H3378
2Ki 17: 8 of the nations **the L** had driven out before H3378
2Ki 17: 9 did things against **the L** their God that H3378
2Ki 17:11 as the nations whom **the L** had driven out H3378
2Ki 17:12 though **the L** had said, “You shall H3378
2Ki 17:13 **The L** warned Israel and Judah through all H3378
2Ki 17:14 who did not trust in **the L** their God. H3378
2Ki 17:15 them although **the L** had ordered them, H3378
2Ki 17:16 the commands of **the L** their God and H3378
2Ki 17:17 themselves to do evil in the eyes of **the L**, H3378
2Ki 17:18 So **the L** was very angry with Israel and H3378
2Ki 17:19 keep the commands of **the L** their God. H3378
2Ki 17:20 Therefore **the L** rejected all the people of H3378
2Ki 17:21 from following **the L** and caused them to H3378
2Ki 17:23 until **the L** removed them from his H3378
2Ki 17:25 they did not worship **the L**; so he sent H3378
2Ki 17:28 taught them how to worship **the L**. H3378
2Ki 17:32 They worshiped **the L**, but they also H3378
2Ki 17:33 They worshiped **the L**, but they also H3378
2Ki 17:34 neither worship **the L** nor adhere to the H3378
2Ki 17:34 commands that **the L** gave the H3378
2Ki 17:35 When **the L** made a covenant with the H3378
2Ki 17:36 **the L**, who brought you up out of Egypt H3378
2Ki 17:39 worship **the L** your God; it is he H3378
2Ki 17:41 these people were worshiping **the L**, H3378
2Ki 18: 3 He did what was right in the eyes of **the L** H3378
2Ki 18: 5 Hezekiah trusted in **the L**, the God of H3378
2Ki 18: 6 He held fast to **the L** and did not stop H3378
2Ki 18: 6 the commands **the L** had given Moses. H3378
2Ki 18: 7 **the L** was with him; he was successful H3378
2Ki 18:12 they had not obeyed **the L** their God, H3378
2Ki 18:12 Moses the servant of **the L** commanded. H3378
2Ki 18:15 in the temple of **the L** and in the H3378
2Ki 18:16 doorposts of the temple of **the L**, H3378
2Ki 18:22 “We are depending on **the L** our God”— H3378
2Ki 18:25 this place without word from **the L**? H3378
2Ki 18:25 **The L** himself told me to march against H3378
2Ki 18:30 you to trust in **the L** when he says, H3378
2Ki 18:30 he says, ‘**The L** will surely deliver us H3378
2Ki 18:32 you when he says, ‘**The L** will deliver us. H3378
2Ki 18:35 How then can **the L** deliver Jerusalem H3378
2Ki 19: 1 went into the temple of **the L**. H3378
2Ki 19: 4 It may be that **the L** your God will hear all H3378
2Ki 19: 4 him for the words **the L** your God has H3378
2Ki 19: 6 “Tell your master, ‘This is what **the L** says: H3378
2Ki 19:14 to the temple of **the L** and spread it out H3378
2Ki 19:14 of the LORD and spread it out before **the L**. H3378
2Ki 19:15 And Hezekiah prayed to **the L**: “LORD, the H3378
2Ki 19:15 “**L**, the God of Israel, enthroned between H3378
2Ki 19:16 Give ear, **L**, and hear; open your eyes, H3378
2Ki 19:16 open your eyes, **L**, and see; listen to H3378
2Ki 19:17 “It is true, **L**, that the Assyrian kings have H3378
2Ki 19:19 **L** our God, deliver us from his hand H3378
2Ki 19:19 may know that you alone, **L**, are God.” H3378
2Ki 19:20 “This is what **the L**, the God of Israel, H3378
2Ki 19:21 is the word that **the L** has spoken against H3378
2Ki 19:31 “The zeal of **the L** Almighty will H3378
2Ki 19:32 this is what **the L** says concerning the H3378
2Ki 19:33 he will not enter this city, declares **the L**. H3378

Ref	Context	No.
2Ki 19:35	night the angel of **the L** went out and put	H3378
2Ki 20: 1	to him and said, "This is what **the L** says:	H3378
2Ki 20: 2	his face to the wall and prayed to **the L**,	H3378
2Ki 20: 3	"Remember, L, how I have walked before	H3378
2Ki 20: 4	the word of **the L** came to him:	H3378
2Ki 20: 5	'This is what **the L**, the God of your	H3378
2Ki 20: 5	now you will go up to the temple of **the L**.	H3378
2Ki 20: 8	be the sign that **the L** will heal me and	H3378
2Ki 20: 8	up to the temple of **the L** on the third day	H3378
2Ki 20: 9	sign to you that **the L** will do what he has	H3378
2Ki 20:11	Then the prophet Isaiah called on **the L**	H3378
2Ki 20:11	the L made the shadow go back the ten	NDT
2Ki 20:16	said to Hezekiah, "Hear the word of **the L**:	H3378
2Ki 20:17	Nothing will be left, says **the L**.	H3378
2Ki 20:19	"The word of **the L** you have spoken is	H3378
2Ki 21: 2	He did evil in the eyes of **the L**, following	H3378
2Ki 21: 2	of the nations **the L** had driven out before	H3378
2Ki 21: 4	He built altars in the temple of **the L**, of	H3378
2Ki 21: 4	of the LORD, of which **the L** had said, "In	H3378
2Ki 21: 5	In the two courts of the temple of **the L**,	H3378
2Ki 21: 6	He did much evil in the eyes of **the L**	H3378
2Ki 21: 7	of which **the L** had said to David and to	H3378
2Ki 21: 9	than the nations **the L** had destroyed	H3378
2Ki 21:10	**The L** said through his servants the	H3378
2Ki 21:12	Therefore this is what **the L**, the God of	H3378
2Ki 21:16	so that they did evil in the eyes of **the L**.	H3378
2Ki 21:20	He did evil in the eyes of **the L**, as his	H3378
2Ki 21:22	He forsook **the L**, the God of his ancestors	H3378
2Ki 22: 2	right in the eyes of **the L** and followed	H3378
2Ki 22: 3	son of Meshullam, to the temple of **the L**.	H3378
2Ki 22: 4	been brought into the temple of **the L**,	H3378
2Ki 22: 5	workers who repair the temple of **the L**—	H3378
2Ki 22: 8	Book of the Law in the temple of **the L**."	H3378
2Ki 22: 9	in the temple of **the L** and have entrusted	H3378
2Ki 22:13	"Go and inquire of **the L** for me and for	H3378
2Ki 22:15	"This is what **the L**, the God of Israel	H3378
2Ki 22:16	'This is what **the L** says: I am going to	H3378
2Ki 22:18	who sent you to inquire of **the L**, 'This is	H3378
2Ki 22:18	'This is what **the L**, the God of Israel,	H3378
2Ki 22:19	yourself before **the L** when you heard	H3378
2Ki 22:19	I also have heard you, declares **the L**.	H3378
2Ki 23: 2	to the temple of **the L** with the people of	H3378
2Ki 23: 2	had been found in the temple of **the L**.	H3378
2Ki 23: 3	the covenant in the presence of **the L**—	H3378
2Ki 23: 3	to follow **the L** and keep his commands	H3378
2Ki 23: 4	from the temple of **the L** all the articles	H3378
2Ki 23: 6	from the temple of **the L** to the Kidron	H3378
2Ki 23: 7	that were in the temple of **the L**,	H3378
2Ki 23: 9	serve at the altar of **the L** in Jerusalem,	H3378
2Ki 23:11	to the temple of **the L** the horses that the	H3378
2Ki 23:12	in the two courts of the temple of **the L**.	H3378
2Ki 23:16	with the word of **the L** proclaimed by the	H3378
2Ki 23:21	Celebrate the Passover to **the L** your God	H3378
2Ki 23:23	was celebrated to **the L** in Jerusalem.	H3378
2Ki 23:24	had discovered in the temple of **the L**.	H3378
2Ki 23:25	like him who turned to **the L** as he did—	H3378
2Ki 23:26	**the L** did not turn away from the heat of	H3378
2Ki 23:27	So **the L** said, "I will remove Judah also	H3378
2Ki 23:32	He did evil in the eyes of **the L**, just as his	H3378
2Ki 23:37	And he did evil in the eyes of **the L**, just as	H3378
2Ki 24: 2	**The L** sent Babylonian, Aramean, Moabite	H3378
2Ki 24: 2	with the word of **the L** proclaimed by his	H3378
2Ki 24: 4	and **the L** was not willing to forgive.	H3378
2Ki 24: 9	He did evil in the eyes of **the L**, just as his	H3378
2Ki 24:13	As **the L** had declared, Nebuchadnezzar	H3378
2Ki 24:13	from the temple of **the L** and from the	H3378
2Ki 24:13	Israel had made for the temple of **the L**.	H3378
2Ki 24:19	He did evil in the eyes of **the L**, just as	H3378
2Ki 25: 9	He set fire to the temple of **the L**, the royal	H3378
2Ki 25:13	at the temple of **the L** and they carried the	H3378
2Ki 25:16	had made for the temple of **the L**,	H3378
1Ch 2: 3	the LORD's sight; so the L put him to death.	NDT
1Ch 6:15	was deported when **the L** sent Judah and	H3378
1Ch 6:31	in the house of **the L** after the ark came	H3378
1Ch 6:32	built the temple of **the L** in Jerusalem.	H3378
1Ch 9:19	the entrance to the dwelling of **the L**.	H3378
1Ch 9:20	the gatekeepers, and **the L** was with him.	H3378
1Ch 9:23	the gates of the house of **the L**—	H3378
1Ch 10:13	died because he was unfaithful to **the L**;	H3378
1Ch 10:13	keep the word of **the L** and even	H3378
1Ch 10:14	did not inquire of **the L**. So the LORD	H3378
1Ch 10:14	So the L put him to death and turned the	NDT
1Ch 11: 2	And **the L** your God said to you, 'You will	H3378
1Ch 11: 3	with them at Hebron before **the L**,	H3378
1Ch 11: 3	as **the L** had promised through Samuel.	H3378
1Ch 11: 9	because **the L** Almighty was with him.	H3378
1Ch 11:10	the whole land, as **the L** had promised—	H3378
1Ch 11:14	and **the L** brought about a great victory.	H3378
1Ch 11:18	instead, he poured it out to **the L**.	H3378
1Ch 12:23	kingdom over to him, as **the L** had said:	H3378
1Ch 13: 2	to you and if it is the will of **the L** our God,	H3378
1Ch 13: 6	bring up from there the ark of God **the L**,	H3378
1Ch 13:14	and **the L** blessed his household and	H3378
1Ch 14: 2	David knew that **the L** had established	H3378
1Ch 14:10	**The L** answered him, "Go, I will deliver	H3378
1Ch 14:17	and **the L** made all the nations fear him.	H3378
1Ch 15: 2	because **the L** chose them to carry the ark	H3378
1Ch 15: 2	to carry the ark of **the L** and to minister	H3378
1Ch 15: 3	bring up the ark of **the L** to the place he	H3378
1Ch 15:12	yourselves and bring up the ark of **the L**,	H3378
1Ch 15:13	the first time that **the L** our God broke out	H3378
1Ch 15:14	in order to bring up the ark of **the L**,	H3378
1Ch 15:15	in accordance with the word of **the L**.	H3378
1Ch 15:25	of the covenant of **the L** from the house of	H3378
1Ch 15:26	carrying the ark of the covenant of **the L**,	H3378
1Ch 15:28	ark of the covenant of **the L** with shouts,	H3378
1Ch 15:29	of the covenant of **the L** was entering the	H3378
1Ch 16: 2	blessed the people in the name of **the L**.	H3378
1Ch 16: 4	Levites to minister before the ark of **the L**,	H3378
1Ch 16: 4	and praise **the L**, the God of Israel:	H3378
1Ch 16: 7	to give praise to **the L** in this manner:	H3378
1Ch 16: 8	Give praise to **the L**, proclaim his name	H3378
1Ch 16:10	the hearts of those who seek **the L** rejoice.	H3378
1Ch 16:11	Look to **the L** and his strength; seek his	H3378
1Ch 16:14	He is **the L** our God; his judgments are in	H3378
1Ch 16:23	Sing to **the L**, all the earth; proclaim his	H3378
1Ch 16:25	For great is **the L** and most worthy of	H3378
1Ch 16:26	are idols, but **the L** made the heavens.	H3378
1Ch 16:28	Ascribe to **the L**, all you families of	H3378
1Ch 16:28	ascribe to **the L** glory and strength.	H3378
1Ch 16:29	Ascribe to **the L** the glory due his name	H3378
1Ch 16:29	Worship **the L** in the splendor of his	H3378
1Ch 16:31	say among the nations, "**The L** reigns!"	H3378
1Ch 16:33	let them sing for joy before **the L**, for he	H3378
1Ch 16:34	Give thanks to **the L**, for he is good; his	H3378
1Ch 16:36	Praise be to **the L**, the God of Israel, from	H3378
1Ch 16:36	people said "Amen" and "Praise **the L**."	H3378
1Ch 16:37	of the covenant of **the L** to minister there	H3378
1Ch 16:39	the tabernacle of **the L** at the high place	H3378
1Ch 16:40	burnt offerings to **the L** on the altar of	H3378
1Ch 16:40	everything written in the Law of **the L**,	H3378
1Ch 16:41	by name to give thanks to **the L**,	H3378
1Ch 17: 1	of the covenant of **the L** is under a tent."	H3378
1Ch 17: 4	servant David, 'This is what **the L** says:	H3378
1Ch 17: 7	'This is what **the L** Almighty says:	H3378
1Ch 17:10	to you that **the L** will build a house	H3378
1Ch 17:16	King David went in and sat before **the L**,	H3378
1Ch 17:16	"Who am I, **L** God, and what is my family	H3378
1Ch 17:17	**L** God, have looked on me as though	H3378
1Ch 17:19	**L**. For the sake of your servant and	H3378
1Ch 17:20	is no one like you, **L**, and there is no God	H3378
1Ch 17:22	and you, **L**, have become their	H3378
1Ch 17:23	"And now, **L**, let the promise you have	H3378
1Ch 17:24	people will say, '**The L** Almighty, the God	H3378
1Ch 17:26	**L**, are God! You have promised these	H3378
1Ch 17:27	your sight; for you, **L**, have blessed it, and	H3378
1Ch 18: 6	**The L** gave David victory wherever he	H3378
1Ch 18:11	David dedicated these articles to **the L**,	H3378
1Ch 18:13	**The L** gave David victory wherever he	H3378
1Ch 19:13	**The L** will do what is good in his sight."	H3378
1Ch 21: 3	"May **the L** multiply his troops a hundred	H3378
1Ch 21: 9	**The L** said to Gad, David's seer,	H3378
1Ch 21:10	tell David, 'This is what **the L** says:	H3378
1Ch 21:11	said to him, "This is what **the L** says:	H3378
1Ch 21:12	three days of the sword of **the L**—days	H3378
1Ch 21:12	with the angel of **the L** ravaging every part	H3378
1Ch 21:13	Let me fall into the hands of **the L**, for his	H3378
1Ch 21:14	So **the L** sent a plague on Israel, and	H3378
1Ch 21:15	**the L** saw it and relented concerning the	H3378
1Ch 21:15	The angel of **the L** was then standing at	H3378
1Ch 21:16	saw the angel of **the L** standing between	H3378
1Ch 21:17	**L** my God, let your hand fall on me and	H3378
1Ch 21:18	Then the angel of **the L** ordered Gad to	H3378
1Ch 21:18	build an altar to **the L** on the threshing	H3378
1Ch 21:19	Gad had spoken in the name of **the L**.	H3378
1Ch 21:22	floor so I can build an altar to **the L**,	H3378
1Ch 21:24	I will not take for **the L** what is yours, or	H3378
1Ch 21:26	built an altar to **the L** there and sacrificed	H3378
1Ch 21:26	He called on **the L**, and the LORD	H3378
1Ch 21:26	the L answered him with fire from	NDT
1Ch 21:27	Then **the L** spoke to the angel, and he put	H3378
1Ch 21:28	David saw that **the L** had answered him	H3378
1Ch 21:29	The tabernacle of **the L**, which Moses had	H3378
1Ch 21:30	afraid of the sword of the angel of **the L**.	H3378
1Ch 22: 1	"The house of **the L** God is to be here	H3378
1Ch 22: 5	to be built for **the L** should be of great	H3378
1Ch 22: 6	charged him to build a house for **the L**,	H3378
1Ch 22: 7	a house for the Name of **the L** my God.	H3378
1Ch 22: 8	But this word of **the L** came to me: 'You	H3378
1Ch 22:11	my son, **the L** be with you, and may you	H3378
1Ch 22:11	build the house of **the L** your God,	H3378
1Ch 22:12	May **the L** give you discretion and	H3378
1Ch 22:12	you may keep the law of **the L** your God.	H3378
1Ch 22:13	laws that **the L** gave Moses for	H3378
1Ch 22:14	the temple of **the L** a hundred	H3378
1Ch 22:16	begin the work, and **the L** be with you."	H3378
1Ch 22:18	to them, "Is not **the L** your God with you?	H3378
1Ch 22:18	land is subject to **the L** and to his people.	H3378
1Ch 22:19	heart and soul to seeking **the L** your God.	H3378
1Ch 22:19	Begin to build the sanctuary of **the L** God	H3378
1Ch 22:19	of the covenant of **the L** and the sacred	H3378
1Ch 22:19	that will be built for the Name of **the L**."	H3378
1Ch 23: 4	of the temple of **the L** and six thousand	H3378
1Ch 23: 5	are to praise **the L** with the musical	H3378
1Ch 23:13	to offer sacrifices before **the L**, to minister	H3378
1Ch 23:24	more who served in the temple of **the L**.	H3378
1Ch 23:25	had said, "Since **the L**, the God of Israel,	H3378
1Ch 23:28	in the service of the temple of **the L**:	H3378
1Ch 23:30	every morning to thank and praise **the L**.	H3378
1Ch 23:31	were presented to **the L** on the Sabbaths,	H3378
1Ch 23:31	were to serve before **the L** regularly in the	H3378
1Ch 23:32	the service of the temple of **the L**.	H3378
1Ch 24:19	when they entered the temple of **the L**,	H3378
1Ch 24:19	ancestor Aaron, as **the L**, the God of Israel	H3378
1Ch 25: 3	the harp in thanking and praising **the L**.	H3378
1Ch 25: 6	father for the music of the temple of **the L**,	H3378
1Ch 25: 7	trained and skilled in music for **the L**—	H3378
1Ch 26:12	ministering in the temple of **the L**,	H3378
1Ch 26:22	of the treasuries of the temple of **the L**.	H3378
1Ch 26:27	the repair of the temple of **the L**.	H3378
1Ch 26:30	all the work of **the L** and for the king's	H3378
1Ch 27:23	because **the L** had promised to make	H3378
1Ch 28: 2	of rest for the ark of the covenant of **the L**,	H3378
1Ch 28: 4	"Yet **the L**, the God of Israel, chose me	H3378
1Ch 28: 5	my sons—and **the L** has given me many	H3378
1Ch 28: 5	throne of the kingdom of **the L** over Israel.	H3378
1Ch 28: 8	of all Israel and of the assembly of **the L**,	H3378
1Ch 28: 8	all the commands of **the L** your God,	H3378
1Ch 28: 9	for **the L** searches every heart and	H3378
1Ch 28:10	for **the L** has chosen you to build a house	H3378
1Ch 28:12	courts of the temple of **the L** and all the	H3378
1Ch 28:13	the work of serving in the temple of **the L**,	H3378
1Ch 28:18	the ark of the covenant of **the L**.	H3378
1Ch 28:20	discouraged, for **the L** God, my God,	H3378
1Ch 28:20	service of the temple of **the L** is finished.	H3378
1Ch 29: 1	structure is not for man but for **the L** God.	H3378
1Ch 29: 5	to consecrate themselves to **the L** today?"	H3378
1Ch 29: 8	of the temple of **the L** in the custody of	H3378
1Ch 29: 9	given freely and wholeheartedly to **the L**.	H3378
1Ch 29:10	David praised **the L** in the presence of the	H3378
1Ch 29:10	"Praise be to you, **L**, the God of our father	H3378
1Ch 29:11	**L**, is the greatness and the power	H3378
1Ch 29:11	**L**, is the kingdom; you are exalted	H3378
1Ch 29:16	**L** our God, all this abundance that we	H3378
1Ch 29:18	**L**, the God of our fathers Abraham, Isaac	H3378
1Ch 29:20	whole assembly, "Praise **the L** your God."	H3378
1Ch 29:20	So they all praised **the L**, the God of their	H3378
1Ch 29:20	themselves before **the L** and the king.	H3378
1Ch 29:21	made sacrifices to **the L** and presented	H3378
1Ch 29:22	great joy in the presence of **the L** that day.	H3378
1Ch 29:22	anointing him before **the L** to be ruler	H3378
1Ch 29:23	on the throne of **the L** as king in place of	H3378
1Ch 29:25	**The L** highly exalted Solomon in the sight	H3378
2Ch 1: 1	for **the L** his God was with him and made	H3378
2Ch 1: 5	Gibeon in front of the tabernacle of **the L**;	H3378
2Ch 1: 6	bronze altar before **the L** in the tent of	H3378
2Ch 1: 9	**L** God, let your promise to my father	H3378
2Ch 2: 1	the Name of **the L** and a royal palace	H3378
2Ch 2: 4	the Name of **the L** my God and to	H3378
2Ch 2: 4	the appointed festivals of **the L** our God.	H3378
2Ch 2:11	"Because **the L** loves his people, he has	H3378
2Ch 2:12	"Praise be to **the L**, the God of Israel, who	H3378
2Ch 2:12	build a temple for **the L** and a palace	H3378
2Ch 3: 1	build the temple of **the L** in Jerusalem on	H3378
2Ch 3: 1	where the L had appeared to his father	NDT
2Ch 4:16	the temple of **the L** were of polished	H3378
2Ch 5: 1	done for the temple of **the L** was finished,	H3378
2Ch 5:10	where **the L** made a covenant with the	H3378
2Ch 5:13	unison to give praise and thanks to **the L**.	H3378
2Ch 5:13	their voices in praise to **the L** and sang:	H3378
2Ch 5:13	Then the temple of **the L** was filled with	H3378
2Ch 5:14	the glory of **the L** filled the temple of	H3378
2Ch 6: 1	"**The L** has said that he would dwell in a	H3378
2Ch 6: 4	"Praise be to **the L**, the God of Israel, who	H3378
2Ch 6: 7	to build a temple for the Name of **the L**,	H3378
2Ch 6: 8	**the L** said to my father David, 'You did	H3378
2Ch 6:10	"**The L** has kept the promise he made.	H3378
2Ch 6:10	of Israel, just as **the L** promised, and I	H3378
2Ch 6:10	built the temple for the Name of **the L**,	H3378
2Ch 6:11	is the covenant of **the L** that he made with	H3378
2Ch 6:12	before the altar of **the L** in front of the	H3378
2Ch 6:14	"**L**, the God of Israel, there is no God like	H3378
2Ch 6:16	**L**, the God of Israel, keep for your	H3378
2Ch 6:17	And now, **L**, the God of Israel, let your	H3378
2Ch 6:19	**L** my God, give attention to your	H3378
2Ch 6:41	"Now arise, **L** God, and come to your	H3378
2Ch 6:41	May your priests, **L** God, be clothed with	H3378
2Ch 6:42	**L** God, do not reject your anointed one	H3378
2Ch 7: 1	the glory of **the L** filled the temple.	H3378
2Ch 7: 2	the temple of **the L** because the glory	H3378
2Ch 7: 2	LORD because the glory of **the L** filled it.	H3378
2Ch 7: 3	the glory of **the L** above the temple,	H3378
2Ch 7: 3	they worshiped and gave thanks to **the L**,	H3378
2Ch 7: 4	the people offered sacrifices before **the L**.	H3378
2Ch 7: 6	made for praising **the L** and which were	H3378
2Ch 7: 7	courtyard in front of the temple of **the L**,	H3378
2Ch 7:10	the good things **the L** had done for David	H3378
2Ch 7:11	the temple of **the L** and the royal palace,	H3378
2Ch 7:11	do in the temple of **the L** and in his own	H3378
2Ch 7:12	**the L** appeared to him at night and said:	H3378
2Ch 7:21	'Why has **the L** done such a thing to this	H3378
2Ch 7:22	'Because they have forsaken **the L**, the	H3378
2Ch 8: 1	the temple of **the L** and his own palace	H3378
2Ch 8:11	places the ark of **the L** has entered are	H3378
2Ch 8:12	On the altar of **the L** that he had built in	H3378
2Ch 8:12	sacrificed burnt offerings to **the L**,	H3378
2Ch 8:16	of the temple of **the L** was laid until its	H3378
2Ch 8:16	So the temple of **the L** was finished.	H3378
2Ch 9: 4	offerings he made at the temple of **the L**,	H3378
2Ch 9: 8	Praise be to **the L** your God, who has	H3378
2Ch 9: 8	throne as king to rule for **the L** your God.	H3378
2Ch 9:11	the temple of **the L** and for the royal	H3378
2Ch 10:15	to fulfill the word **the L** had spoken to	H3378
2Ch 11: 2	But this word of **the L** came to Shemaiah	H3378
2Ch 11: 4	'This is what **the L** says: Do not go up to	H3378
2Ch 11: 4	the words of **the L** and turned back	H3378

2Ch 11:14 sons had rejected them as priests of **the L** H3378
2Ch 11:16 who set their hearts on seeking **the L**, H3378
2Ch 11:16 to Jerusalem to offer sacrifices to **the L**, H3378
2Ch 12: 1 with him abandoned the law of **the L**. H3378
2Ch 12: 2 Because they had been unfaithful to **the L** H3378
2Ch 12: 5 “This is what **the L** says, ‘You have H3378
2Ch 12: 6 themselves and said, “**The L** is just.” H3378
2Ch 12: 7 When **the L** saw that they humbled H3378
2Ch 12: 7 this word of **the L** came to Shemaiah: H3378
2Ch 12: 9 of the temple of **the L** and the treasures of H3378
2Ch 12:13 the city **the L** had chosen out of all the H3378
2Ch 12:14 he had not set his heart on seeking **the L**. H3378
2Ch 13: 5 Don’t you know that **the L**, the God of H3378
2Ch 13: 8 you plan to resist the kingdom of **the L**, H3378
2Ch 13: 9 didn’t you drive out the priests of **the L** H3378
2Ch 13:10 “As for us, **the L** is our God, and we have H3378
2Ch 13:10 priests who serve **the L** are sons of Aaron, H3378
2Ch 13:11 offerings and fragrant incense to **the L**. H3378
2Ch 13:11 the requirements of **the L** our God. H3378
2Ch 13:12 do not fight against **the L**, the God of your H3378
2Ch 13:14 Then they cried out to **the L**. The priests H3378
2Ch 13:18 victorious because they relied on **the L**, H3378
2Ch 13:20 And **the L** struck him down and he died H3378
2Ch 14: 2 right in the eyes of **the L** his God. H3378
2Ch 14: 4 He commanded Judah to seek **the L**, the H3378
2Ch 14: 6 those years, for **the L** gave him rest. H3378
2Ch 14: 7 because we have sought **the L** our God H3378
2Ch 14:11 Asa called to **the L** his God and said, H3378
2Ch 14:11 his God and said, “**L**, there is no one like H3378
2Ch 14:11 Help us, **L** our God, for we rely on you H3378
2Ch 14:11 **L**, you are our God; do not let mere H3378
2Ch 14:12 **The L** struck down the Cushites before Asa H3378
2Ch 14:13 were crushed before **the L** and his forces. H3378
2Ch 14:14 the terror of **the L** had fallen on them. H3378
2Ch 15: 2 **The L** is with you when you are with him H3378
2Ch 15: 4 But in their distress they turned to **the L** H3378
2Ch 15: 8 the altar of **the L** that was in front of H3378
2Ch 15: 9 they saw that **the L** his God was with H3378
2Ch 15:11 they sacrificed to **the L** seven hundred H3378
2Ch 15:12 They entered into a covenant to seek **the L**, H3378
2Ch 15:13 All who would not seek **the L**, the God of H3378
2Ch 15:14 They took an oath to **the L** with loud H3378
2Ch 15:15 So **the L** gave them rest on every side H3378
2Ch 15:17 was fully committed to the L all his life. NDT
2Ch 16: 7 king of Aram and not on **the L** your God, H3378
2Ch 16: 8 Yet when you relied on **the L**, he H3378
2Ch 16: 9 For the eyes of **the L** range throughout the H3378
2Ch 16:12 illness he did not seek help from **the L**, H3378
2Ch 17: 3 **The L** was with Jehoshaphat because he H3378
2Ch 17: 5 **The L** established the kingdom under his H3378
2Ch 17: 6 His heart was devoted to the ways of **the L** H3378
2Ch 17: 9 with them the Book of the Law of **the L**; H3378
2Ch 17:10 The fear of **the L** fell on all the kingdoms H3378
2Ch 17:16 himself for the service of **the L**, H3378
2Ch 18: 4 of Israel, “First seek the counsel of **the L**.” H3378
2Ch 18: 6 a prophet of **the L** here whom we can H3378
2Ch 18: 7 through whom we can inquire of **the L**, H3378
2Ch 18:10 he declared, “This is what **the L** says: H3378
2Ch 18:11 “for **the L** will give it into the king’s hand. H3378
2Ch 18:13 “As surely as **the L** lives, I can tell H3378
2Ch 18:15 the truth in the name of **the L**? H3378
2Ch 18:16 a shepherd, and **the L** said, ‘These H3378
2Ch 18:18 “Therefore hear the word of **the L**: H3378
2Ch 18:18 I saw **the L** sitting on his throne with all H3378
2Ch 18:19 And **the L** said, ‘Who will entice Ahab H3378
2Ch 18:20 stood before **the L** and said, ‘I will H3378
2Ch 18:20 “ ‘By what means?’ **the L** asked. H3378
2Ch 18:21 will succeed in enticing him,’ said the L. NDT
2Ch 18:22 “So now **the L** has put a deceiving spirit in H3378
2Ch 18:22 **The L** has decreed disaster for you.” H3378
2Ch 18:23 did the spirit from **the L** go when he went H3378
2Ch 18:27 **the L** has not spoken through me. H3378
2Ch 18:31 cried out, and **the L** helped him. H3378
2Ch 19: 2 wicked and love those who hate **the L**? H3378
2Ch 19: 2 the wrath of **the L** is on you. H3378
2Ch 19: 4 of Ephraim and turned them back to **the L**, H3378
2Ch 19: 6 not judging for mere mortals but for **the L**, H3378
2Ch 19: 7 Now let the fear of **the L** be on you. Judge H3378
2Ch 19: 7 with **the L** our God there is no injustice H3378
2Ch 19: 8 administer the law of **the L** and to settle H3378
2Ch 19: 9 wholeheartedly in the fear of **the L**. H3378
2Ch 19:10 are to warn them not to sin against **the L**; H3378
2Ch 19:11 over you in any matter concerning **the L**, H3378
2Ch 19:11 may **the L** be with those who do well.” H3378
2Ch 20: 3 Jehoshaphat resolved to inquire of **the L** H3378
2Ch 20: 4 came together to seek help from **the L**; H3378
2Ch 20: 5 at the temple of **the L** in the front of the H3378
2Ch 20: 6 “**L**, the God of our ancestors, are you not H3378
2Ch 20:13 little ones, stood there before **the L**. H3378
2Ch 20:14 Then the Spirit of **the L** came on Jahaziel H3378
2Ch 20:15 This is what **the L** says to you: ‘Do not H3378
2Ch 20:17 see the deliverance **the L** will give you, H3378
2Ch 20:17 tomorrow, and **the L** will be with you. H3378
2Ch 20:18 fell down in worship before **the L**. H3378
2Ch 20:19 Korahites stood up and praised **the L**, H3378
2Ch 20:20 Have faith in **the L** your God and you will H3378
2Ch 20:21 men to sing to **the L** and to praise him H3378
2Ch 20:21 “Give thanks to **the L**, for his love endures H3378
2Ch 20:22 **the L** set ambushes against the men of H3378
2Ch 20:26 of Berakah, where they praised **the L**. H3378
2Ch 20:27 for **the L** had given them cause to rejoice H3378
2Ch 20:28 to the temple of **the L** with harps and lyres H3378
2Ch 20:29 they heard how **the L** had fought against H3378
2Ch 20:32 he did what was right in the eyes of **the L**. H3378
2Ch 20:37 **the L** will destroy what you have made.” H3378
2Ch 21: 6 He did evil in the eyes of **the L**. H3378
2Ch 21: 7 of the covenant **the L** had made with H3378
2Ch 21: 7 the L was not willing to destroy the house of NDT
2Ch 21:10 because Jehoram had forsaken **the L**, the H3378
2Ch 21:12 “This is what **the L**, the God of your father H3378
2Ch 21:14 So now **the L** is about to strike your H3378
2Ch 21:16 **The L** aroused against Jehoram the H3378
2Ch 21:18 **the L** afflicted Jehoram with an incurable H3378
2Ch 22: 4 He did evil in the eyes of **the L**, as the H3378
2Ch 22: 7 whom **the L** had anointed to destroy the H3378
2Ch 22: 9 who sought **the L** with all his heart.” H3378
2Ch 23: 3 as **the L** promised concerning the H3378
2Ch 23: 5 in the courtyards of the temple of **the L**. H3378
2Ch 23: 6 the temple of **the L** except the priests H3378
2Ch 23:12 she went to them at the temple of **the L**. H3378
2Ch 23:14 put her to death at the temple of **the L**.” H3378
2Ch 23:18 of the temple of **the L** in the hands of the H3378
2Ch 23:18 burnt offerings of **the L** as written in the H3378
2Ch 23:20 the king down from the temple of **the L**. H3378
2Ch 24: 2 right in the eyes of **the L** all the years of H3378
2Ch 24: 4 decided to restore the temple of **the L**. H3378
2Ch 24: 6 the servant of **the L** and by the assembly H3378
2Ch 24: 8 at the gate of the temple of **the L**. H3378
2Ch 24: 9 should bring to **the L** the tax that Moses H3378
2Ch 24:12 the work required for the temple of **the L**. H3378
2Ch 24:14 continually in the temple of **the L**. H3378
2Ch 24:18 They abandoned the temple of **the L**, the H3378
2Ch 24:19 Although **the L** sent prophets to the H3378
2Ch 24:20 Because you have forsaken **the L**, he has H3378
2Ch 24:22 “May **the L** see this and call you to H3378
2Ch 24:24 **the L** delivered into their hands a much H3378
2Ch 24:24 Because Judah had forsaken **the L**, the H3378
2Ch 25: 2 He did what was right in the eyes of **the L** H3378
2Ch 25: 4 Book of Moses, where **the L** commanded: H3378
2Ch 25: 7 with you, for **the L** is not with Israel H3378
2Ch 25: 9 “**The L** can give you much more than that. H3378
2Ch 25:15 The anger of **the L** burned against H3378
2Ch 25:27 turned away from following **the L**, H3378
2Ch 26: 4 He did what was right in the eyes of **the L** H3378
2Ch 26: 5 As long as he sought **the L**, God gave him H3378
2Ch 26:16 He was unfaithful to **the L** his God, and H3378
2Ch 26:16 the temple of **the L** to burn incense on H3378
2Ch 26:17 priests of **the L** followed him in. H3378
2Ch 26:18 you, Uzziah, to burn incense to **the L**. H3378
2Ch 26:18 you will not be honored by **the L** God.” H3378
2Ch 26:20 to leave, because **the L** had afflicted him. H3378
2Ch 26:21 banned from the temple of **the L**. H3378
2Ch 27: 2 He did what was right in the eyes of **the L** H3378
2Ch 27: 2 him he did not enter the temple of **the L**. H3378
2Ch 27: 3 of the temple of **the L** and did extensive H3378
2Ch 27: 6 walked steadfastly before **the L** his God. H3378
2Ch 28: 1 not do what was right in the eyes of **the L**. H3378
2Ch 28: 3 of the nations **the L** had driven out before H3378
2Ch 28: 5 Therefore **the L** his God delivered him H3378
2Ch 28: 6 because Judah had forsaken **the L**, the H3378
2Ch 28: 9 But a prophet of **the L** named Oded was H3378
2Ch 28: 9 to them, “Because **the L**, the God of your H3378
2Ch 28:10 also guilty of sins against **the L** your God? H3378
2Ch 28:13 “or we will be guilty before **the L**. H3378
2Ch 28:19 **The L** had humbled Judah because of H3378
2Ch 28:19 had been most unfaithful to **the L**. H3378
2Ch 28:21 from the temple of **the L** and from the H3378
2Ch 28:22 became even more unfaithful to **the L**. H3378
2Ch 28:25 gods and aroused the anger of **the L**, H3378
2Ch 29: 2 He did what was right in the eyes of **the L** H3378
2Ch 29: 3 of the temple of **the L** and repaired them. H3378
2Ch 29: 5 now and consecrate the temple of **the L**, H3378
2Ch 29: 6 evil in the eyes of **the L** our God and H3378
2Ch 29: 8 the anger of **the L** has fallen on Judah H3378
2Ch 29:10 I intend to make a covenant with **the L**, H3378
2Ch 29:11 for **the L** has chosen you to stand before H3378
2Ch 29:15 they went in to purify the temple of **the L** H3378
2Ch 29:15 had ordered, following the word of **the L**. H3378
2Ch 29:16 into the sanctuary of **the L** to purify it. H3378
2Ch 29:16 that they found in the temple of **the L**. H3378
2Ch 29:17 month they reached the portico of **the L**. H3378
2Ch 29:17 consecrated the temple of **the L** itself, H3378
2Ch 29:18 have purified the entire temple of **the L**, H3378
2Ch 29:20 went up to the temple of **the L**. H3378
2Ch 29:21 to offer these on the altar of **the L**. H3378
2Ch 29:25 in the temple of **the L** with cymbals, H3378
2Ch 29:25 was commanded by **the L** through his H3378
2Ch 29:27 singing to **the L** began also H3378
2Ch 29:30 Levites to praise **the L** with the words of H3378
2Ch 29:31 have now dedicated yourselves to **the L**. H3378
2Ch 29:31 thank offerings to the temple of **the L**.” H3378
2Ch 29:32 all of them for burnt offerings to **the L**. H3378
2Ch 29:35 of the temple of **the L** was reestablished. H3378
2Ch 30: 1 to the temple of **the L** in Jerusalem and H3378
2Ch 30: 1 celebrate the Passover to **the L**, H3378
2Ch 30: 5 celebrate the Passover to **the L**, H3378
2Ch 30: 6 return to **the L**, the God of H3378
2Ch 30: 7 who were unfaithful to **the L**, the God of H3378
2Ch 30: 8 as your ancestors were; submit to **the L**. H3378
2Ch 30: 8 Serve **the L** your God, so that his fierce H3378
2Ch 30: 9 If you return to **the L**, then your fellow H3378
2Ch 30: 9 for **the L** your God is gracious and H3378
2Ch 30:12 had ordered, following the word of **the L**. H3378
2Ch 30:15 burnt offerings to the temple of **the L**. H3378
2Ch 30:17 could not consecrate their lambs to **the L**. H3378
2Ch 30:18 saying, “May **the L**, who is good H3378
2Ch 30:19 on seeking God—**the L**, the God of their H3378
2Ch 30:20 And **the L** heard Hezekiah and healed the H3378
2Ch 30:21 priests praised **the L** every day with H3378
2Ch 30:21 instruments dedicated to **the L**. H3378
2Ch 30:22 understanding of the service of **the L**. H3378
2Ch 30:22 fellowship offerings and praised **the L**, H3378
2Ch 31: 3 festivals as written in the Law of **the L**. H3378
2Ch 31: 4 devote themselves to the Law of **the L**. H3378
2Ch 31: 6 holy things dedicated to **the L** their God, H3378
2Ch 31: 8 they praised **the L** and blessed his people H3378
2Ch 31:10 their contributions to the temple of **the L**, H3378
2Ch 31:10 because **the L** has blessed his people H3378
2Ch 31:11 prepare storerooms in the temple of **the L**, H3378
2Ch 31:14 contributions made to **the L** and also the H3378
2Ch 31:16 enter the temple of **the L** to perform the H3378
2Ch 31:20 right and faithful before **the L** his God. H3378
2Ch 32: 8 with us is **the L** our God to help us H3378
2Ch 32:11 ‘**The L** our God will save us from the hand H3378
2Ch 32:16 further against **the L** God and against his H3378
2Ch 32:17 The king also wrote letters ridiculing **the L** H3378
2Ch 32:21 And **the L** sent an angel, who annihilated H3378
2Ch 32:22 So **the L** saved Hezekiah and the people H3378
2Ch 32:23 to Jerusalem for **the L** and valuable gifts H3378
2Ch 32:24 He prayed to **the L**, who answered him H3378
2Ch 33: 2 He did evil in the eyes of **the L**, following H3378
2Ch 33: 2 of the nations **the L** had driven out before H3378
2Ch 33: 4 He built altars in the temple of **the L**, of H3378
2Ch 33: 4 the LORD, of which **the L** had said, “My H3378
2Ch 33: 5 In both courts of the temple of **the L**, he H3378
2Ch 33: 6 He did much evil in the eyes of **the L** H3378
2Ch 33: 9 than the nations **the L** had destroyed H3378
2Ch 33:10 **The L** spoke to Manasseh and his people H3378
2Ch 33:11 So **the L** brought against them the army H3378
2Ch 33:12 sought the favor of **the L** his God and H3378
2Ch 33:13 the L was moved by his entreaty and NDT
2Ch 33:13 Then Manasseh knew that **the L** is God. H3378
2Ch 33:15 the image from the temple of **the L**, H3378
2Ch 33:16 restored the altar of **the L** and sacrificed H3378
2Ch 33:16 told Judah to serve **the L**, the God of H3378
2Ch 33:17 high places, but only to **the L** their God. H3378
2Ch 33:18 seers spoke to him in the name of **the L**, H3378
2Ch 33:22 He did evil in the eyes of **the L**, as his H3378
2Ch 33:23 he did not humble himself before **the L** H3378
2Ch 34: 2 right in the eyes of **the L** and followed the H3378
2Ch 34: 8 to repair the temple of **the L** his God. H3378
2Ch 34:14 had been taken into the temple of **the L**, H3378
2Ch 34:14 Book of the Law of **the L** that had been H3378
2Ch 34:15 Book of the Law in the temple of **the L**.” H3378
2Ch 34:17 in the temple of **the L** and have entrusted H3378
2Ch 34:21 “Go and inquire of **the L** for me and for H3378
2Ch 34:21 before us have not kept the word of **the L**; H3378
2Ch 34:23 “This is what **the L**, the God of Israel H3378
2Ch 34:24 ‘This is what **the L** says: I am going to H3378
2Ch 34:26 who sent you to inquire of **the L**, ‘This is H3378
2Ch 34:26 ‘This is what **the L**, the God of Israel, H3378
2Ch 34:27 I have heard you, declares **the L**. H3378
2Ch 34:30 to the temple of **the L** with the people of H3378
2Ch 34:30 had been found in the temple of **the L**. H3378
2Ch 34:31 the covenant in the presence of **the L**— H3378
2Ch 34:31 to follow **the L** and keep his commands H3378
2Ch 34:33 present in Israel serve **the L** their God. H3378
2Ch 34:33 they did not fail to follow **the L**, the God H3378
2Ch 35: 1 the Passover to **the L** in Jerusalem, H3378
2Ch 35: 3 who had been consecrated to **the L**: H3378
2Ch 35: 3 Now serve **the L** your God and his people H3378
2Ch 35: 6 doing what **the L** commanded through H3378
2Ch 35:12 families of the people to offer to **the L**, H3378
2Ch 35:16 entire service of **the L** was carried out for H3378
2Ch 35:16 of burnt offerings on the altar of **the L**, H3378
2Ch 35:26 with what is written in the Law of **the L**— H3378
2Ch 36: 5 He did evil in the eyes of **the L** his God. H3378
2Ch 36: 7 from the temple of **the L** and put them in H3378
2Ch 36: 9 He did evil in the eyes of **the L**. H3378
2Ch 36:10 articles of value from the temple of **the L**, H3378
2Ch 36:12 evil in the eyes of **the L** his God and did H3378
2Ch 36:12 the prophet, who spoke the word of **the L**. H3378
2Ch 36:13 his heart and would not turn to **the L**, H3378
2Ch 36:14 nations and defiling the temple of **the L**, H3378
2Ch 36:15 **The L**, the God of their ancestors, sent H3378
2Ch 36:16 until the wrath of **the L** was aroused H3378
2Ch 36:21 of the word of **the L** spoken by Jeremiah. H3378
2Ch 36:22 the word of **the L** spoken by Jeremiah H3378
2Ch 36:22 **the L** moved the heart of Cyrus king of H3378
2Ch 36:23 “ ‘**The L**, the God of heaven, has given H3378
2Ch 36:23 may **the L** their God be with them. H3378
Ezr 1: 1 the word of **the L** spoken by Jeremiah H3378
Ezr 1: 1 **the L** moved the heart of Cyrus king of H3378
Ezr 1: 2 “ ‘**The L**, the God of heaven, has given H3378
Ezr 1: 3 in Judah and build the temple of **the L**, H3378
Ezr 1: 5 build the house of **the L** in Jerusalem. H3378
Ezr 1: 7 articles belonging to the temple of **the L**, H3378
Ezr 2:68 arrived at the house of **the L** in Jerusalem, H3378
Ezr 3: 3 sacrificed burnt offerings on it to **the L**, H3378
Ezr 3: 5 all the appointed sacred festivals of **the L**, H3378
Ezr 3: 5 brought as freewill offerings to **the L**. H3378
Ezr 3: 6 began to offer burnt offerings to **the L**, H3378
Ezr 3: 8 the building of the house of **the L**. H3378
Ezr 3:10 laid the foundation of the temple of **the L**, H3378
Ezr 3:10 took their places to praise **the L**, as H3378
Ezr 3:11 thanksgiving they sang to **the L**: H3378

Book	Ref	Context	Code
Ezr	3:11	gave a great shout of praise to **the L**,	H3378
Ezr	3:11	foundation of the house of **the L** was laid.	H3378
Ezr	4: 1	exiles were building a temple for **the L**,	H3378
Ezr	4: 3	We alone will build it for **the L**, the God	H3378
Ezr	6:21	Gentile neighbors in order to seek **the L**,	H3378
Ezr	6:22	because **the L** had filled them with joy by	H3378
Ezr	7: 6	of Moses, which **the L**, the God of Israel	H3378
Ezr	7: 6	the hand of **the L** his God was on him.	H3378
Ezr	7:10	study and observance of the Law of **the L**,	H3378
Ezr	7:11	commands and decrees of **the L** for Israel:	H3378
Ezr	7:27	Praise be to **the L**, the God of our	H3378
Ezr	7:27	to the house of **the L** in Jerusalem in this	H3378
Ezr	7:28	the hand of **the L** my God was on me,	H3378
Ezr	8:28	as these articles are consecrated to **the L**.	H3378
Ezr	8:28	gold are a freewill offering to **the L**,	H3378
Ezr	8:29	of the house of **the L** in Jerusalem before	H3378
Ezr	8:35	All this was a burnt offering to **the L**.	H3378
Ezr	9: 5	with my hands spread out to **the L** my God	H3378
Ezr	9: 8	**the L** our God has been gracious in	H3378
Ezr	9:15	L, the God of Israel, you are righteous	H3378
Ezr	10:11	Now honor **the L**, the God of your	H3378
Ne	1: 5	"L, the God of heaven, the great and	H3378
Ne	5:13	"Amen," and praised **the L**.	H3378
Ne	8: 1	which **the L** had commanded for Israel.	H3378
Ne	8: 6	Ezra praised **the L**, the great God; and all	H3378
Ne	8: 6	down and worshiped **the L** with their faces	H3378
Ne	8: 9	"This day is holy to **the L** your God.	H3378
Ne	8:10	for the joy of **the L** is your strength.	H3378
Ne	8:14	which **the L** had commanded through	H3378
Ne	9: 3	Book of the Law of **the L** their God for a	H3378
Ne	9: 3	in worshiping **the L** their God.	H3378
Ne	9: 4	out with loud voices to **the L** their God.	H3378
Ne	9: 5	"Stand up and praise **the L** your God, who	H3378
Ne	9: 6	You alone are **the L**. You made the	H3378
Ne	9: 7	"You are **the L** God, who chose Abram	H3378
Ne	10:29	regulations and decrees of **the L** our Lord.	H3378
Ne	10:34	to burn on the altar of **the L** our God,	H3378
Ne	10:35	to the house of **the L** each year the	H3378
Job	1: 6	came to present themselves before **the L**,	H3378
Job	1: 7	**The L** said to Satan, "Where have you	H3378
Job	1: 7	Satan answered **the L**, "From roaming	H3378
Job	1: 8	Then **the L** said to Satan, "Have you	H3378
Job	1:12	**The L** said to Satan, "Very well, then	H3378
Job	1:12	went out from the presence of **the L**.	H3378
Job	1:21	**The L** gave and the LORD has taken away	H3378
Job	1:21	The LORD gave and **the L** has taken away	H3378
Job	1:21	may the name of **the L** be praised.	H3378
Job	2: 1	came to present themselves before **the L**,	H3378
Job	2: 2	And **the L** said to Satan, "Where have you	H3378
Job	2: 2	Satan answered **the L**, "From roaming	H3378
Job	2: 3	Then **the L** said to Satan, "Have you	H3378
Job	2: 6	**The L** said to Satan, "Very well, then, he	H3378
Job	2: 7	the presence of **the L** and afflicted Job	H3378
Job	12: 9	that the hand of **the L** has done this?	H3378
Job	38: 1	Then **the L** spoke to Job out of the storm	H3378
Job	40: 1	**The L** said to Job:	H3378
Job	40: 3	Then Job answered **the L**:	H3378
Job	40: 6	Then **the L** spoke to Job out of the storm:	H3378
Job	42: 1	Then Job replied to **the L**:	H3378
Job	42: 7	After **the L** had said these things to Job	H3378
Job	42: 9	the Naamathite did what **the L** told them;	H3378
Job	42: 9	and **the L** accepted Job's prayer.	H3378
Job	42:10	**the L** restored his fortunes and gave him	H3378
Job	42:11	all the trouble **the L** had brought on him,	H3378
Job	42:12	**The L** blessed the latter part of Job's life	H3378
Ps	1: 2	whose delight is in the law of **the L**	H3378
Ps	1: 6	For **the L** watches over the way of the	H3378
Ps	2: 2	together against **the L** and against his	H3378
Ps	2:11	Serve **the L** with fear and celebrate his	H3378
Ps	3: 1	L, how many are my foes! How many rise	H3378
Ps	3: 3	But you, L, are a shield around me, my	H3378
Ps	3: 4	I call out to **the L**, and he answers me	H3378
Ps	3: 5	I wake again, because **the L** sustains me.	H3378
Ps	3: 7	L! Deliver me, my God! Strike all my	H3378
Ps	3: 8	From **the L** comes deliverance. May your	H3378
Ps	4: 3	Know that **the L** has set apart his faithful	H3378
Ps	4: 3	himself; **the L** hears when I call to him.	H3378
Ps	4: 5	of the righteous and trust in **the L**.	H3378
Ps	4: 6	L, are asking, "Who will bring us	H3378
Ps	4: 8	for you alone, L, make me dwell in	H3378
Ps	5: 1	Listen to my words, L, consider my lament.	H3378
Ps	5: 3	In the morning, L, you hear my voice; in	H3378
Ps	5: 6	bloodthirsty and deceitful you, L, detest.	H3378
Ps	5: 8	Lead me, L, in your righteousness	H3378
Ps	5:12	L, you bless the righteous; you	H3378
Ps	6: 1	L, do not rebuke me in your anger or	H3378
Ps	6: 2	Have mercy on me, L, for I am faint; heal	H3378
Ps	6: 2	I am faint; heal me, L, for my bones are in	H3378
Ps	6: 3	in deep anguish. How long, L, how long?	H3378
Ps	6: 4	L, and deliver me; save me because	H3378
Ps	6: 8	for **the L** has heard my weeping.	H3378
Ps	6: 9	**The L** has heard my cry for mercy;	H3378
Ps	6: 9	my cry for mercy; **the L** accepts my prayer.	H3378
Ps	7: T	which he sang to **the L** concerning Cush,	H3378
Ps	7: 1	L my God, I take refuge in you; save and	H3378
Ps	7: 3	L my God, if I have done this and there is	H3378
Ps	7: 6	L, in your anger; rise up against the	H3378
Ps	7: 8	Let **the L** judge the peoples. Vindicate me,	H3378
Ps	7: 8	Vindicate me, L, according to my	H3378
Ps	7:17	I will give thanks to **the L** because of his	H3378
Ps	7:17	praises of the name of **the L** Most High.	H3378
Ps	8: 1	L, our Lord, how majestic is your name in	H3378
Ps	8: 9	L, our Lord, how majestic is your name in	H3378
Ps	9: 1	I give thanks to you, L, with all my heart;	H3378
Ps	9: 7	**The L** reigns forever; he has established	H3378
Ps	9: 9	**The L** is a refuge for the oppressed,	H3378
Ps	9:10	L, have never forsaken those who	H3378
Ps	9:11	Sing the praises of **the L**, enthroned in	H3378
Ps	9:13	L, see how my enemies persecute me	H3378
Ps	9:16	**The L** is known by his acts of justice; the	H3378
Ps	9:19	L, do not let mortals triumph; let	H3378
Ps	9:20	them with terror, L; let the nations know	H3378
Ps	10: 1	L, do you stand far off? Why do you	H3378
Ps	10: 3	he blesses the greedy and reviles **the L**.	H3378
Ps	10:12	L! Lift up your hand, O God. Do not	H3378
Ps	10:16	**The L** is King for ever and ever; the	H3378
Ps	10:17	*You*, L, hear the desire of the afflicted	H3378
Ps	11: 1	In **the L** I take refuge. How then can you	H3378
Ps	11: 4	**The L** is in his holy temple; the LORD is	H3378
Ps	11: 4	temple; **the L** is on his heavenly throne.	H3378
Ps	11: 5	**The L** examines the righteous, but the	H3378
Ps	11: 7	For **the L** is righteous, he loves justice;	H3378
Ps	12: 1	L, for no one is faithful anymore	H3378
Ps	12: 3	May **the L** silence all flattering lips and	H3378
Ps	12: 5	needy groan, I will now arise," says **the L**.	H3378
Ps	12: 6	And the words of **the L** are flawless, like	H3378
Ps	12: 7	L, will keep the needy safe and will	H3378
Ps	13: 1	How long, L? Will you forget me forever	H3378
Ps	13: 3	on me and answer, L my God. Give light	H3378
Ps	14: 2	**The L** looks down from heaven on all	H3378
Ps	14: 4	eating bread; they never call on **the L**.	H3378
Ps	14: 6	plans of the poor, but **the L** is their refuge.	H3378
Ps	14: 7	When **the L** restores his people, let Jacob	H3378
Ps	15: 1	L, who may dwell in your sacred tent	H3378
Ps	15: 4	person but honors those who fear **the L**;	H3378
Ps	16: 2	I say to **the L**, "You are my Lord; apart	H3378
Ps	16: 5	L, you alone are my portion and my cup	H3378
Ps	16: 7	I will praise **the L**, who counsels me; even	H3378
Ps	16: 8	I keep my eyes always on **the L**. With him	H3378
Ps	17: 1	Hear me, L, my plea is just; listen to my	H3378
Ps	17:13	Rise up, L, confront them, bring them	H3378
Ps	17:14	me from such people, L, from those of this	H3378
Ps	18: T	Of David the servant of **the L**. He sang to	H3378
Ps	18: T	He sang to **the L** the words of this song	H3378
Ps	18: T	of this song when **the L** delivered him	H3378
Ps	18: 1	I love you, L, my strength.	H3378
Ps	18: 2	**The L** is my rock, my fortress and my	H3378
Ps	18: 3	I called to **the L**, who is worthy of praise	H3378
Ps	18: 6	In my distress I called to **the L**; I cried to	H3378
Ps	18:13	**The L** thundered from heaven; the voice	H3378
Ps	18:15	bare at your rebuke, L, at the blast of	H3378
Ps	18:18	of my disaster, but **the L** was my support.	H3378
Ps	18:20	**The L** has dealt with me according to my	H3378
Ps	18:21	For I have kept the ways of **the L**; I am not	H3378
Ps	18:24	**The L** has rewarded me according to my	H3378
Ps	18:28	L, keep my lamp burning; my God	H3378
Ps	18:31	For who is God besides **the L**? And who is	H3378
Ps	18:41	to save them—to **the L**, but he did not	H3378
Ps	18:46	**The L** lives! Praise be to my Rock! Exalted	H3378
Ps	18:49	I will praise you, L, among the nations;	H3378
Ps	19: 7	The law of **the L** is perfect, refreshing the	H3378
Ps	19: 7	The statutes of **the L** are trustworthy	H3378
Ps	19: 8	The precepts of **the L** are right, giving joy	H3378
Ps	19: 8	The commands of **the L** are radiant	H3378
Ps	19: 9	The fear of **the L** is pure, enduring forever	H3378
Ps	19: 9	The decrees of **the L** are firm, and all of	H3378
Ps	19:14	pleasing in your sight, L, my Rock and my	H3378
Ps	20: 1	May **the L** answer you when you are in	H3378
Ps	20: 5	May **the L** grant all your requests.	H3378
Ps	20: 6	**The L** gives victory to his anointed	H3378
Ps	20: 7	we trust in the name of **the L** our God.	H3378
Ps	20: 9	L, give victory to the king! Answer us	H3378
Ps	21: 1	in your strength, L. How great is his joy in	H3378
Ps	21: 7	For the king trusts in **the L**; through the	H3378
Ps	21: 9	**The L** will swallow them up in his wrath	H3378
Ps	21:13	in your strength, L; we will sing and praise	H3378
Ps	22: 8	"He trusts in **the L**," they say, "let the	H3378
Ps	22: 8	the LORD," they say, "let **the L** rescue him.	NDT
Ps	22:19	But you, L, do not be far from me. You are	H3378
Ps	22:23	You who fear **the L**, praise him! All you	H3378
Ps	22:26	those who seek **the L** will praise him	H3378
Ps	22:27	the earth will remember and turn to **the L**,	H3378
Ps	22:28	belongs to **the L** and he rules over	H3378
Ps	23: 1	**The L** is my shepherd, I lack nothing.	H3378
Ps	23: 6	I will dwell in the house of **the L** forever.	H3378
Ps	24: 3	Who may ascend the mountain of **the L**	H3378
Ps	24: 5	blessing from **the L** and vindication from	H3378
Ps	24: 8	**The L** strong and mighty, the LORD mighty	H3378
Ps	24: 8	strong and mighty, **the L** mighty in battle.	H3378
Ps	24:10	King of glory? **The L** Almighty—he is the	H3378
Ps	25: 1	L my God, I put my trust.	H3378
Ps	25: 4	Show me your ways, L, teach me your	H3378
Ps	25: 6	Remember, L, your great mercy and love	H3378
Ps	25: 7	love remember me, for you, L, are good.	H3378
Ps	25: 8	Good and upright is **the L**; therefore he	H3378
Ps	25:10	All the ways of **the L** are loving and	H3378
Ps	25:11	sake of your name, L, forgive my iniquity,	H3378
Ps	25:12	are those who fear **the L**? He will instruct	H3378
Ps	25:14	**The L** confides in those who fear him; he	H3378
Ps	25:15	My eyes are ever on **the L**, for only he will	H3378
Ps	25:21	protect me, because my hope, L, is in you.	H3378
Ps	26: 1	Vindicate me, L, for I have led a	H3378
Ps	26: 1	I have trusted in **the L** and have not	H3378
Ps	26: 2	Test me, L, and try me, examine my heart	H3378
Ps	26: 6	in innocence, and go about your altar, L,	H3378
Ps	26: 8	L, I love the house where you live, the	H3378
Ps	26:12	the great congregation I will praise **the L**.	H3378
Ps	27: 1	**The L** is my light and my salvation	H3378
Ps	27: 1	**The L** is the stronghold of my life—of	H3378
Ps	27: 4	One thing I ask from **the L**, this only do I	H3378
Ps	27: 4	in the house of **the L** all the days of my	H3378
Ps	27: 4	on the beauty of **the L** and to seek him in	H3378
Ps	27: 6	I will sing and make music to **the L**.	H3378
Ps	27: 7	my voice when I call, L; be merciful to me	H3378
Ps	27: 8	"Seek his face!" Your face, L, I will seek.	H3378
Ps	27:10	mother forsake me, **the L** will receive me.	H3378
Ps	27:11	Teach me your way, L; lead me in a	H3378
Ps	27:13	the goodness of **the L** in the land of the	H3378
Ps	27:14	Wait for **the L**; be strong and take heart	H3378
Ps	27:14	strong and take heart and wait for **the L**.	H3378
Ps	28: 1	L, I call; you are my Rock, do not	H3378
Ps	28: 5	the deeds of **the L** and what his hands	H3378
Ps	28: 6	Praise be to **the L**, for he has heard my cry	H3378
Ps	28: 7	**The L** is my strength and my shield; my	H3378
Ps	28: 8	**The L** is the strength of his people,	H3378
Ps	29: 1	Ascribe to **the L**, you heavenly beings	H3378
Ps	29: 1	ascribe to **the L** glory and strength.	H3378
Ps	29: 2	Ascribe to **the L** the glory due his name	H3378
Ps	29: 2	worship **the L** in the splendor of his	H3378
Ps	29: 3	The voice of **the L** is over the waters; the	H3378
Ps	29: 3	**the L** thunders over the mighty waters.	H3378
Ps	29: 4	The voice of **the L** is powerful; the voice	H3378
Ps	29: 4	is powerful; the voice of **the L** is majestic.	H3378
Ps	29: 5	The voice of **the L** breaks the cedars; the	H3378
Ps	29: 5	**the L** breaks in pieces the cedars of	H3378
Ps	29: 7	The voice of **the L** strikes with flashes of	H3378
Ps	29: 8	The voice of **the L** shakes the desert; the	H3378
Ps	29: 8	**the L** shakes the Desert of Kadesh.	H3378
Ps	29: 9	The voice of **the L** twists the oaks and	H3378
Ps	29:10	**The L** sits enthroned over the flood; the	H3378
Ps	29:10	**the L** is enthroned as King forever.	H3378
Ps	29:11	**The L** gives strength to his people; the	H3378
Ps	29:11	**the L** blesses his people with peace.	H3378
Ps	30: 1	I will exalt you, L, for you lifted me out of	H3378
Ps	30: 2	L my God, I called to you for help, and	H3378
Ps	30: 3	L, brought me up from the realm of	H3378
Ps	30: 4	Sing the praises of **the L**, you his faithful	H3378
Ps	30: 7	L, when you favored me, you made my	H3378
Ps	30: 8	L, I called; to the Lord I cried for	H3378
Ps	30:10	L, and be merciful to me; LORD, be	H3378
Ps	30:10	be merciful to me; L, be my help.	H3378
Ps	30:12	not be silent. L my God, I will praise	H3378
Ps	31: 1	L, I have taken refuge; let me	H3378
Ps	31: 5	my spirit; deliver me, L, my faithful God.	H3378
Ps	31: 6	worthless idols; as for me, I trust in **the L**.	H3378
Ps	31: 9	Be merciful to me, L, for I am in distress	H3378
Ps	31:14	But I trust in you, L; I say, "You are my	H3378
Ps	31:17	not be put to shame, L, for I have cried	H3378
Ps	31:21	Praise be to **the L**, for he showed me the	H3378
Ps	31:23	Love **the L**, all his faithful people! The	H3378
Ps	31:23	**The L** preserves those who are true to him,	H3378
Ps	31:24	take heart, all you who hope in **the L**.	H3378
Ps	32: 2	is the one whose sin **the L** does not count	H3378
Ps	32: 5	"I will confess my transgressions to **the L**.	H3378
Ps	32:11	Rejoice in **the L** and be glad, you	H3378
Ps	33: 1	Sing joyfully to **the L**, you righteous; it is	H3378
Ps	33: 2	Praise **the L** with the harp; make music to	H3378
Ps	33: 4	For the word of **the L** is right and true; he	H3378
Ps	33: 5	**The L** loves righteousness and justice; the	H3378
Ps	33: 6	By the word of **the L** the heavens were	H3378
Ps	33: 8	Let all the earth fear **the L**; let all the	H3378
Ps	33:10	**The L** foils the plans of the nations; he	H3378
Ps	33:11	But the plans of **the L** stand firm forever	H3378
Ps	33:12	Blessed is the nation whose God is **the L**	H3378
Ps	33:13	From heaven **the L** looks down and sees	H3378
Ps	33:18	But the eyes of **the L** are on those who	H3378
Ps	33:20	We wait in hope for **the L**; he is our help	H3378
Ps	33:22	love be with us, L, even as we put our	H3378
Ps	34: 1	I will extol **the L** at all times; his praise	H3378
Ps	34: 2	I will glory in **the L**; let the afflicted hear	H3378
Ps	34: 3	Glorify **the L** with me; let us exalt his	H3378
Ps	34: 4	I sought **the L**, and he answered me; he	H3378
Ps	34: 6	man called, and **the L** heard him; he	H3378
Ps	34: 7	The angel of **the L** encamps around those	H3378
Ps	34: 8	Taste and see that **the L** is good; blessed	H3378
Ps	34: 9	Fear **the L**, you his holy people, for those	H3378
Ps	34:10	those who seek **the L** lack no good	H3378
Ps	34:11	I will teach you the fear of **the L**.	H3378
Ps	34:15	The eyes of **the L** are on the righteous	H3378
Ps	34:16	the face of **the L** is against those who	H3378
Ps	34:17	and **the L** hears them;	H3378
Ps	34:18	**The L** is close to the brokenhearted and	H3378
Ps	34:19	but **the L** delivers him from them all;	H3378
Ps	34:22	**The L** will rescue his servants; no one who	H3378
Ps	35: 1	Contend, L, with those who contend with	H3378
Ps	35: 5	with the angel of **the L** driving them away	H3378
Ps	35: 6	with the angel of **the L** pursuing them.	H3378
Ps	35: 9	soul will rejoice in **the L** and delight in his	H3378
Ps	35:10	being will exclaim, "Who is like you, L?	H3378
Ps	35:22	L, you have seen this; do not be silent.	H3378
Ps	35:24	your righteousness, L my God; do not let	H3378
Ps	35:27	they always say, "**The L** be exalted, who	H3378
Ps	36: T	Of David the servant of **the L**.	H3378
Ps	36: 5	Your love, L, reaches to the heavens, your	H3378
Ps	36: 6	L, preserve both people and animals.	H3378
Ps	37: 3	Trust in **the L** and do good; dwell in the	H3378

Ps 37: 4 Take delight in **the L**, and he will give you H3378
Ps 37: 5 Commit your way to **the L**; trust in him H3378
Ps 37: 7 Be still before **the L** and wait patiently H3378
Ps 37: 9 those who hope in **the L** will inherit the H3378
Ps 37:17 but **the L** upholds the righteous. H3378
Ps 37:22 those **the L** blesses will inherit the land H2257
Ps 37:23 **The L** makes firm the steps of the one H3378
Ps 37:24 for **the L** upholds him with his hand. H3378
Ps 37:28 For **the L** loves the just and will not H3378
Ps 37:33 but **the L** will not leave them in the power H3378
Ps 37:34 Hope in **the L** and keep his way. He will H3378
Ps 37:39 of the righteous comes from **the L**; H3378
Ps 37:40 **The L** helps them and delivers them; he H3378
Ps 38: 1 **L**, do not rebuke me in your anger or H3378
Ps 38:15 **L**, I wait for you; you will answer, Lord my H3378
Ps 38:21 **L**, do not forsake me; do not be far from H3378
Ps 39: 4 "Show me, **L**, my life's end and the H3378
Ps 39:12 "Hear my prayer, **L**, listen to my cry for H3378
Ps 40: 1 I waited patiently for **the L**; he turned to H3378
Ps 40: 3 will see and fear **the L** and put their trust H3378
Ps 40: 4 Blessed is the one who trusts in **the L** H3378
Ps 40: 5 **L** my God, are the wonders you H3378
Ps 40: 9 I do not seal my lips, **L**, as you know. H3378
Ps 40:11 your mercy from me, **L**; may your love and H3378
Ps 40:13 pleased to save me, **L**; come quickly, LORD, H3378
Ps 40:13 LORD; come quickly, **L**, to help me. H3378
Ps 40:16 saving help always say, "**The L** is great!" H3378
Ps 41: 1 **the L** delivers them in times of trouble. H3378
Ps 41: 2 **The L** protects and preserves them—they H3378
Ps 41: 3 **The L** sustains them on their sickbed and H3378
Ps 41: 4 "Have mercy on me, **L**; heal me, for I have H3378
Ps 41:10 you have mercy on me, **L**; raise me up, H3378
Ps 41:13 Praise be to **the L**, the God of Israel, from H3378
Ps 42: 8 By day **the L** directs his love, at night his H3378
Ps 46: 7 **The L** Almighty is with us; the God of H3378
Ps 46: 8 Come and see what **the L** has done, the H3378
Ps 46:11 **The L** Almighty is with us; the God of H3378
Ps 47: 2 For **the L** Most High is awesome, the great H3378
Ps 47: 5 **the L** amid the sounding of trumpets. H3378
Ps 48: 1 Great is **the L**, and most worthy of praise H3378
Ps 48: 8 have seen in the city of **the L** Almighty, H3378
Ps 50: 1 **the L**, speaks and summons the H3378
Ps 54: 6 I will praise your name, **L**, for it is good. H3378
Ps 55:16 I call to God, and **the L** saves me. H3378
Ps 55:22 Cast your cares on **the L** and he will H3378
Ps 56:10 word I praise, in **the L**, whose word I H3378
Ps 58: 6 **L**, tear out the fangs of those lions! H3378
Ps 59: 3 me for no offense or sin of mine, **L**. H3378
Ps 59: 5 **L** God Almighty, you who are the H3378
Ps 59: 8 But you laugh at them, **L**; you scoff at all H3378
Ps 64:10 will rejoice in **the L** and take refuge in H3378
Ps 68: 4 rejoice before him—his name is **the L**. H3363
Ps 68:16 where **the L** *himself* will dwell forever? H3378
Ps 68:18 rebellious—that you, **L** God, might dwell H3363
Ps 68:20 from **the** Sovereign **L** comes escape from H3378
Ps 68:26 praise **the L** in the assembly of Israel. H3378
Ps 69: 6 **the L** Almighty, may those who hope H3378
Ps 69:13 But I pray to you, **L**, in the time of your H3378
Ps 69:16 Answer me, **L**, out of the goodness of your H3378
Ps 69:31 This will please **the L** more than an ox H3378
Ps 69:33 **The L** hears the needy and does not H3378
Ps 70: 1 to save me; come quickly, **L**, to help me. H3378
Ps 70: 4 saving help always say, "*The* **L** is great!" H3378
Ps 70: 5 my help and my deliverer; **L**, do not delay. H3378
Ps 71: 1 **L**, I have taken refuge; let me H3378
Ps 71: 5 my hope, Sovereign **L**, my confidence H3378
Ps 71:16 Sovereign **L**; I will proclaim your H3378
Ps 72:18 Praise be to **the L** God, the God of Israel H3378
Ps 73:28 I have made **the** Sovereign **L** my refuge; H3378
Ps 74:18 has mocked you, **L**, how foolish people H3378
Ps 75: 8 In the hand of **the L** is a cup full of H3378
Ps 76:11 Make vows to **the L** your God and fulfill H3378
Ps 77:11 I will remember the deeds of **the L**; yes, H3363
Ps 78: 4 the praiseworthy deeds of **the L**, H3378
Ps 78:21 When **the L** heard them, he was furious H3378
Ps 79: 5 How long, **L**? Will you be angry forever H3378
Ps 80: 4 How long, **L** God Almighty, will your H3378
Ps 80:19 Restore us, **L** God Almighty; make your H3378
Ps 81:10 I am **the L** your God, who brought you up H3378
Ps 81:15 Those who hate **the L** would cringe before H3378
Ps 83:16 faces with shame, **L**, so that they will seek H3378
Ps 83:18 whose name is **the L**—that you alone H3378
Ps 84: 1 lovely is your dwelling place, **L** Almighty! H3378
Ps 84: 2 the courts of **the L**; my heart and my H3378
Ps 84: 3 near your altar, **L** Almighty, my King and H3378
Ps 84: 8 Hear my prayer, **L** God Almighty; listen to H3378
Ps 84:11 For **the L** God is a sun and shield; H3378
Ps 84:11 shield; **the L** bestows favor and honor H3378
Ps 84:12 **L** Almighty, blessed is the one who trusts H3378
Ps 85: 1 **L**, showed favor to your land; you H3378
Ps 85: 7 your unfailing love, **L**, and grant us your H3378
Ps 85: 8 I will listen to what God **the L** says; he H3378
Ps 85:12 **The L** will indeed give what is good, and H3378
Ps 86: 1 Hear me, **L**, and answer me, for I am poor H3378
Ps 86: 6 Hear my prayer, **L**; listen to my cry for H3378
Ps 86:11 Teach me your way, **L**, that I may rely on H3378
Ps 86:17 **L**, have helped me and comforted H3378
Ps 87: 2 **The L** loves the gates of Zion more than H3378
Ps 87: 6 **The L** will write in the register of the H3378
Ps 88: 1 **L**, you are the God who saves me; day H3378
Ps 88: 9 I call to you, **L**, every day; I spread out my H3378
Ps 88:13 I cry to you for help, **L**; in the morning my H3378
Ps 88:14 **L**, do you reject me and hide your H3378
Ps 89: 5 praise your wonders, **L**, your faithfulness H3378
Ps 89: 6 the skies above can compare with **the L**? H3378
Ps 89: 6 Who is like **the L** among the heavenly H3378
Ps 89: 8 Who is like you, **L** God Almighty? You H3378
Ps 89: 8 **L**, are mighty, and your faithfulness H3363
Ps 89:15 who walk in the light of your presence, **L**. H3378
Ps 89:18 our shield belongs to **the L**, our king to H3378
Ps 89:46 How long, **L**? Will you hide yourself H3378
Ps 89:51 with which your enemies, **L**, have mocked, H3378
Ps 89:52 Praise be to **the L** forever! Amen and H3378
Ps 90:13 **L**! How long will it be? Have H3378
Ps 91: 2 I will say of **the L**, "He is my refuge and H3378
Ps 91: 9 If you say, "**The L** is my refuge," and you H3378
Ps 91:14 loves me," says the **L**, "I will rescue him; NDT
Ps 92: 1 is good to praise **the L** and make music to H3378
Ps 92: 4 me glad by your deeds, **L**; I sing for joy at H3378
Ps 92: 5 great are your works, **L**, how profound H3378
Ps 92: 8 But you, **L**, are forever exalted. H3378
Ps 92: 9 your enemies, **L**, surely your enemies H3378
Ps 92:13 planted in the house of **the L**, they will H3378
Ps 92:15 proclaiming, "**The L** is upright; he is my H3378
Ps 93: 1 **The L** reigns, he is robed in majesty; the H3378
Ps 93: 1 **the L** is robed in majesty and armed with H3378
Ps 93: 3 seas have lifted up, **L**, the seas have lifted H3378
Ps 93: 4 of the sea—**the L** on high is mighty. H3378
Ps 93: 5 Your statutes, **L**, stand firm; holiness H3378
Ps 94: 1 **The L** is a God who avenges. O God who H3378
Ps 94: 3 How long, **L**, will the wicked, how long H3378
Ps 94: 5 crush your people, **L**; they oppress your H3378
Ps 94: 7 They say, "**The L** does not see; the God of H3363
Ps 94:11 **The L** knows all human plans; he knows H3378
Ps 94:12 one you discipline, **L**, the one you teach H3363
Ps 94:14 For **the L** will not reject his people; he will H3378
Ps 94:17 Unless **the L** had given me help, I would H3378
Ps 94:18 your unfailing love, **L**, supported me. H3378
Ps 94:22 But **the L** has become my fortress, and my H3378
Ps 94:23 **the L** our God will destroy them. H3378
Ps 95: 1 let us sing for joy to **the L**; let us shout H3378
Ps 95: 3 For **the L** is the great God, the great King H3378
Ps 95: 6 let us kneel before **the L** our Maker; H3378
Ps 96: 1 Sing to **the L** a new song; sing to the LORD H3378
Ps 96: 1 a new song; sing to **the L**, all the earth. H3378
Ps 96: 2 Sing to **the L**, praise his name; proclaim H3378
Ps 96: 4 For great is **the L** and most worthy of H3378
Ps 96: 5 are idols, but **the L** made the heavens. H3378
Ps 96: 7 Ascribe to **the L**, all you families of H3378
Ps 96: 7 ascribe to **the L** glory and strength. H3378
Ps 96: 8 Ascribe to **the L** the glory due his name H3378
Ps 96: 9 Worship **the L** in the splendor of his H3378
Ps 96:10 the nations, "**The L** reigns." The world H3378
Ps 96:13 Let all creation rejoice before **the L**, for he H3378
Ps 97: 1 **The L** reigns, let the earth be glad; let the H3378
Ps 97: 5 The mountains melt like wax before **the L** H3378
Ps 97: 8 are glad because of your judgments, **L**. H3378
Ps 97: 9 For you, **L**, are the Most High over all the H3378
Ps 97:10 Let those who love **the L** hate evil, for he H3378
Ps 97:12 Rejoice in **the L**, you who are righteous H3378
Ps 98: 1 Sing to **the L** a new song, for he has done H3378
Ps 98: 2 **The L** has made his salvation known and H3378
Ps 98: 4 Shout for joy to **the L**, all the earth, burst H3378
Ps 98: 5 make music to **the L** with the harp, with H3378
Ps 98: 6 shout for joy before **the L**, the King. H3378
Ps 98: 9 let them sing before **the L**, for he comes H3378
Ps 99: 1 **The L** reigns, let the nations tremble; he H3378
Ps 99: 2 Great is **the L** in Zion; he is exalted over H3378
Ps 99: 5 Exalt **the L** our God and worship at his H3378
Ps 99: 6 they called on **the L** and he answered H3378
Ps 99: 8 **L** our God, you answered them; you were H3378
Ps 99: 9 Exalt **the L** our God and worship at his H3378
Ps 99: 9 holy mountain, for **the L** our God is holy. H3378
Ps 100: 1 Shout for joy to **the L**, all the earth. H3378
Ps 100: 2 Worship **the L** with gladness; come before H3378
Ps 100: 3 Know that **the L** is God. It is he who made H3378
Ps 100: 5 For **the L** is good and his love endures H3378
Ps 101: 1 justice; to you, **L**, I will sing praise. H3378
Ps 101: 8 off every evildoer from the city of **the L**. H3378
Ps 102: T pours out a lament before **the L**. H3378
Ps 102: 1 Hear my prayer, **L**; let my cry for help H3378
Ps 102:12 But you, **L**, sit enthroned forever; your H3378
Ps 102:15 The nations will fear the name of **the L** H3378
Ps 102:16 For **the L** will rebuild Zion and appear in H3378
Ps 102:18 a people not yet created may praise **the L**: H3363
Ps 102:19 "**The L** looked down from his sanctuary on H3378
Ps 102:21 So the name of **the L** will be declared in H3378
Ps 102:22 the kingdoms assemble to worship **the L**. H3378
Ps 103: 1 Praise **the L**, my soul; all my inmost being, H3378
Ps 103: 2 Praise **the L**, my soul, and forget not all H3378
Ps 103: 6 **The L** works righteousness and justice H3378
Ps 103: 8 **The L** is compassionate and gracious H3378
Ps 103:13 so **the L** has compassion on those who H3378
Ps 103:19 **The L** has established his throne in H3378
Ps 103:20 Praise **the L**, you his angels, you mighty H3378
Ps 103:21 Praise **the L**, all his heavenly hosts, you H3378
Ps 103:22 Praise **the L**, all his works everywhere in H3378
Ps 103:22 in his dominion. Praise **the L**, my soul. H3378
Ps 104: 1 Praise **the L**, my soul. LORD my God, you H3378
Ps 104: 1 **L** my God, you are very great; you are H3378
Ps 104: 2 The **L** wraps himself in light as with a NDT
Ps 104:16 The trees of **the L** are well watered, the H3378
Ps 104:24 are your works, **L**! In wisdom you made H3378
Ps 104:31 May the glory of **the L** endure forever; H3378
Ps 104:31 may **the L** rejoice in his works H3378
Ps 104:33 I will sing to **the L** all my life; I will sing H3378
Ps 104:34 be pleasing to him, as I rejoice in **the L**. H3378
Ps 104:35 Praise **the L**, my soul. Praise H3378
Ps 104:35 Praise the LORD, my soul. Praise **the L**. H3363
Ps 105: 1 Give praise to **the L**, proclaim his name H3378
Ps 105: 3 the hearts of those who seek **the L** rejoice. H3378
Ps 105: 4 Look to **the L** and his strength; seek his H3378
Ps 105: 7 He is **the L** our God; his judgments are in H3378
Ps 105:19 till the word of **the L** proved him true. H3378
Ps 105:24 **The L** made his people very fruitful; he NDT
Ps 105:45 observe his laws. Praise **the L**. H3363
Ps 106: 1 Praise **the L**. Give thanks to the LORD, for H3363
Ps 106: 1 Give thanks to **the L**, for he is good; his H3378
Ps 106: 2 the mighty acts of **the L** or fully declare H3378
Ps 106: 4 Remember me, **L**, when you show favor H3378
Ps 106:16 of Aaron, who was consecrated to **the L**. H3378
Ps 106:25 in their tents and did not obey **the L**. H3378
Ps 106:32 the waters of Meribah they angered the **L**, NDT
Ps 106:34 the peoples as **the L** had commanded H3378
Ps 106:40 Therefore **the L** was angry with his people H3378
Ps 106:47 Save us, **L** our God, and gather us from H3378
Ps 106:48 Praise be to **the L**, the God of Israel, from H3378
Ps 106:48 all the people say, "Amen!" Praise **the L**. H3363
Ps 107: 1 Give thanks to **the L**, for he is good; his H3378
Ps 107: 2 Let the redeemed of **the L** tell their story H3378
Ps 107: 6 they cried out to **the L** in their trouble, H3378
Ps 107: 8 them give thanks to **the L** for his unfailing H3378
Ps 107:13 Then they cried to **the L** in their trouble H3378
Ps 107:15 them give thanks to **the L** for his unfailing H3378
Ps 107:19 Then they cried to **the L** in their trouble H3378
Ps 107:21 them give thanks to **the L** for his unfailing H3378
Ps 107:24 saw the works of **the L**, his wonderful H3378
Ps 107:28 they cried out to **the L** in their trouble, H3378
Ps 107:31 them give thanks to **the L** for his unfailing H3378
Ps 107:43 ponder the loving deeds of **the L**. H3378
Ps 108: 3 I will praise you, **L**, among the nations; H3378
Ps 109:14 his fathers be remembered before **the L**; H3378
Ps 109:15 May their sins always remain before **the L** H3378
Ps 109:21 But you, Sovereign **L**, help me for your H3378
Ps 109:26 Help me, **L** my God; save me according to H3378
Ps 109:27 it is your hand, that you, **L**, have done it. H3378
Ps 109:30 With my mouth I will greatly extol **the L** H3378
Ps 110: 1 **The L** says to my lord: "Sit at my right H3378
Ps 110: 2 **The L** will extend your mighty scepter H3378
Ps 110: 4 **The L** has sworn and will not change his H3378
Ps 111: 1 Praise **the L**. I will extol the LORD with all H3363
Ps 111: 1 I will extol **the L** with all my heart in the H3378
Ps 111: 2 Great are the works of **the L**; they are H3378
Ps 111: 4 **the L** is gracious and compassionate. H3378
Ps 111:10 The fear of **the L** is the beginning of H3378
Ps 112: 1 Praise **the L**. Blessed are those who fear H3363
Ps 112: 1 Blessed are those who fear **the L**, who H3378
Ps 112: 7 their hearts are steadfast, trusting in **the L**. H3378
Ps 113: 1 Praise **the L**. Praise the LORD, you his H3363
Ps 113: 1 Praise **the L**, you his servants; praise the H3378
Ps 113: 1 you his servants; praise the name of **the L**. H3378
Ps 113: 2 Let the name of **the L** be praised, both H3378
Ps 113: 3 the name of **the L** is to be praised. H3378
Ps 113: 4 **The L** is exalted over all the nations, his H3378
Ps 113: 5 Who is like **the L** our God, the One who H3378
Ps 113: 9 a happy mother of children. Praise **the L**. H3363
Ps 115: 1 Not to us, **L**, not to us but to your name be H3378
Ps 115: 9 Israelites, trust in **the L**—he is their help H3378
Ps 115:10 of Aaron, trust in **the L**—he is their help H3378
Ps 115:11 fear him, trust in **the L**—he is their help H3378
Ps 115:12 **The L** remembers us and will bless us: He H3378
Ps 115:13 he will bless those who fear **the L**—small H3378
Ps 115:14 May **the L** cause you to flourish, both you H3378
Ps 115:15 May you be blessed by **the L**, the Maker H3378
Ps 115:16 The highest heavens belong to **the L**, but H3378
Ps 115:17 It is not the dead who praise **the L**, those H3363
Ps 115:18 it is we who extol **the L**, both now and H3363
Ps 115:18 both now and forevermore. Praise **the L**. H3363
Ps 116: 1 I love **the L**, for he heard my voice; he H3378
Ps 116: 4 Then I called on the name of **the L**: H3378
Ps 116: 4 on the name of the LORD: "**L**, save me!" H3378
Ps 116: 5 **The L** is gracious and righteous; our God H3378
Ps 116: 6 **The L** protects the unwary; when I was H3378
Ps 116: 7 my soul, for **the L** has been good to you. H3378
Ps 116: 8 **L**, have delivered me from death NDT
Ps 116: 9 I may walk before **the L** in the land of the H3378
Ps 116:10 I trusted in **the L** when I said, "I am greatly NDT
Ps 116:12 shall I return to **the L** for all his goodness H3378
Ps 116:13 salvation and call on the name of **the L**. H3378
Ps 116:14 fulfill my vows to **the L** in the presence of H3378
Ps 116:15 in the sight of **the L** is the death of his H3378
Ps 116:16 I am your servant, **L**; I serve you just as H3378
Ps 116:17 to you and call on the name of **the L**. H3378
Ps 116:18 fulfill my vows to **the L** in the presence of H3378
Ps 116:19 in the courts of the house of **the L**—in H3378
Ps 116:19 in your midst, Jerusalem. Praise **the L**. H3363
Ps 117: 1 Praise **the L**, all you nations; extol him, all H3378
Ps 117: 2 the faithfulness of **the L** endures forever. H3378
Ps 117: 2 of the LORD endures forever. Praise **the L**. H3363
Ps 118: 1 Give thanks to **the L**, for he is good; his H3378
Ps 118: 4 Let those who fear **the L** say: "His love H3378
Ps 118: 5 pressed, I cried to **the L**; he brought me H3363
Ps 118: 6 **The L** is with me; I will not be afraid H3378
Ps 118: 7 **The L** is with me; he is my helper. I look H3378
Ps 118: 8 to take refuge in **the L** than to trust in H3378
Ps 118: 9 to take refuge in **the L** than to trust in H3378

Ps 118:10 in the name of **the L** I cut them down. H3378
Ps 118:11 in the name of **the L** I cut them down. H3378
Ps 118:12 in the name of **the L** I cut them down. H3378
Ps 118:13 about to fall, but **the L** helped me. H3378
Ps 118:14 **The L** is my strength and my defense; he H3363
Ps 118:17 will proclaim what **the L** has done. H3363
Ps 118:18 **The L** has chastened me severely, but he H3363
Ps 118:19 I will enter and give thanks to **the L**. H3363
Ps 118:20 This is the gate of **the L** through which the H3378
Ps 118:23 **the L** has done this, and it is marvelous in H3378
Ps 118:24 **The L** has done it this very day; let us H3378
Ps 118:25 **L**, save us! LORD, grant us success! H3378
Ps 118:25 **L**, grant us success! H3378
Ps 118:26 is he who comes in the name of **the L**. H3378
Ps 118:26 From the house of **the L** we bless you. H3378
Ps 118:27 **The L** is God, and he has made his light H3378
Ps 118:29 Give thanks to **the L**, for he is good; his H3378
Ps 119: 1 who walk according to the law of **the L**. H3378
Ps 119:12 Praise be to you, **L**; teach me your decrees H3378
Ps 119:31 to your statutes, **L**; do not let me be put H3378
Ps 119:33 Teach me, **L**, the way of your decrees, that H3378
Ps 119:41 love come to me, **L**, your salvation, H3378
Ps 119:52 I remember, **L**, your ancient laws, and I H3378
Ps 119:55 In the night, **L**, I remember your name H3378
Ps 119:57 You are my portion, **L**; I have promised to H3378
Ps 119:64 with your love, **L**; teach me your decrees H3378
Ps 119:65 to your servant according to your word, **L**. H3378
Ps 119:75 **L**, that your laws are righteous H3378
Ps 119:89 Your word, **L**, is eternal; it stands firm in H3378
Ps 119:107 preserve my life, **L**, according to your H3378
Ps 119:108 **L**, the willing praise of my mouth H3378
Ps 119:126 is time for you to act, **L**; your law is H3378
Ps 119:137 You are righteous, **L**, and your laws are H3378
Ps 119:145 answer me, **L**, and I will obey your H3378
Ps 119:149 preserve my life, **L**, according to your H3378
Ps 119:151 Yet you are near, **L**, and all your H3378
Ps 119:156 Your compassion, **L**, is great; preserve H3378
Ps 119:159 preserve my life, **L**, in accordance with H3378
Ps 119:166 wait for your salvation, **L**, and I follow H3378
Ps 119:169 cry come before you, **L**; give me H3378
Ps 119:174 your salvation, **L**, and your law gives H3378
Ps 120: 1 I call on **the L** in my distress, and he H3378
Ps 120: 2 Save me, **L**, from lying lips and from H3378
Ps 121: 2 My help comes from **the L**, the Maker of H3378
Ps 121: 5 **The L** watches over you—the LORD is H3378
Ps 121: 5 **the L** is your shade at your right hand H3378
Ps 121: 7 **The L** will keep you from all harm—he H3378
Ps 121: 8 **the L** will watch over your coming and H3378
Ps 122: 1 "Let us go to the house of **the L**. H3378
Ps 122: 4 the tribes of **the L**—to praise the H3363
Ps 122: 4 praise the name of **the L** according to the H3378
Ps 122: 9 For the sake of the house of **the L** our God, H3378
Ps 123: 2 so our eyes look to **the L** our God, till he H3378
Ps 123: 3 Have mercy on us, **L**, have mercy on us H3378
Ps 124: 1 If **the L** had not been on our side—let H3378
Ps 124: 2 if **the L** had not been on our side when H3378
Ps 124: 6 Praise be to **the L**, who has not let us be H3378
Ps 124: 8 Our help is in the name of **the L**, the H3378
Ps 125: 1 Those who trust in **the L** are like Mount H3378
Ps 125: 2 so **the L** surrounds his people both now H3378
Ps 125: 4 **L**, do good to those who are good, to H3378
Ps 125: 5 to crooked ways **the L** will banish with the H3378
Ps 126: 1 When **the L** restored the fortunes of Zion H3378
Ps 126: 2 "**The L** has done great things for them." H3378
Ps 126: 3 **The L** has done great things for us, and H3378
Ps 126: 4 Restore our fortunes, **L**, like streams in the H3378
Ps 127: 1 Unless **the L** builds the house, the H3378
Ps 127: 1 Unless **the L** watches over the city, the H3378
Ps 127: 3 Children are a heritage from **the L** H3378
Ps 128: 1 Blessed are all who fear **the L**, who walk H3378
Ps 128: 4 the blessing for the man who fears **the L**. H3378
Ps 128: 5 May **the L** bless you from Zion; may you H3378
Ps 129: 4 But **the L** is righteous; he has cut me free H3378
Ps 129: 8 "The blessing of **the L** be on you; we H3378
Ps 129: 8 we bless you in the name of **the L**. H3378
Ps 130: 1 Out of the depths I cry to you, **L**; H3378
Ps 130: 3 **L**, kept a record of sins, Lord, who H3363
Ps 130: 5 I wait for **the L**, my whole being waits H3378
Ps 130: 7 put your hope in **the L**, for with the LORD H3378
Ps 130: 7 with **the L** is unfailing love and with H3378
Ps 131: 1 My heart is not proud, **L**, my eyes are not H3378
Ps 131: 3 put your hope in **the L** both now and H3378
Ps 132: 1 **L**, remember David and all his self-denial. H3378
Ps 132: 2 He swore an oath to **the L**, he made a H3378
Ps 132: 5 till I find a place for **the L**, a dwelling for H3378
Ps 132: 8 **L**, and come to your resting place H3378
Ps 132:11 **The L** swore an oath to David, a sure oath H3378
Ps 132:13 For **the L** has chosen Zion, he has desired H3378
Ps 133: 3 For there **the L** bestows his blessing, even H3378
Ps 134: 1 Praise **the L**, all you servants of the LORD H3378
Ps 134: 1 all you servants of **the L** who minister by H3378
Ps 134: 1 minister by night in the house of **the L**. H3378
Ps 134: 2 hands in the sanctuary and praise **the L**. H3378
Ps 134: 3 May **the L** bless you from Zion, he who is H3378
Ps 135: 1 Praise **the L**. Praise the name of the LORD H3363
Ps 135: 1 Praise the name of **the L**; praise him, you H3378
Ps 135: 1 praise him, you servants of **the L**, H3378
Ps 135: 2 you who minister in the house of **the L**, in H3378
Ps 135: 3 Praise **the L**, for the LORD is good; sing H3363
Ps 135: 3 Praise the LORD, for **the L** is good; sing H3378
Ps 135: 4 For **the L** has chosen Jacob to be his own H3363
Ps 135: 5 I know that **the L** is great, that our Lord is H3378
Ps 135: 6 **The L** does whatever pleases him, in the H3378
Ps 135:13 Your name, **L**, endures forever, your H3378
Ps 135:13 your renown, **L**, through all H3378
Ps 135:14 For **the L** will vindicate his people and H3378
Ps 135:19 Israelites, praise **the L**; house of Aaron, H3378
Ps 135:19 the LORD; house of Aaron, praise **the L**; H3378
Ps 135:20 praise **the L**; you who fear him, H3378
Ps 135:20 the LORD; you who fear him, praise **the L**. H3378
Ps 135:21 Praise be to **the L** from Zion, to him who H3378
Ps 135:21 who dwells in Jerusalem. Praise **the L**. H3363
Ps 136: 1 Give thanks to **the L**, for he is good. H3378
Ps 137: 4 sing the songs of **the L** while in a foreign H3378
Ps 137: 7 Remember, **L**, what the Edomites did on H3378
Ps 138: 1 I will praise you, **L**, with all my heart; NDT
Ps 138: 4 earth praise you, **L**, when they hear what H3378
Ps 138: 5 May they sing of the ways of **the L**, for the H3378
Ps 138: 5 of the LORD, for the glory of **the L** is great. H3378
Ps 138: 6 Though **the L** is exalted, he looks kindly H3378
Ps 138: 8 **The L** will vindicate me; your love, LORD H3378
Ps 138: 8 your love, **L**, endures forever—do not H3378
Ps 139: 1 have searched me, **L**, and you know me. H3378
Ps 139: 4 Before a word is on my tongue *you*, **L** H3378
Ps 139:21 those who hate you, **L**, and abhor those H3378
Ps 140: 1 Rescue me, **L**, from evildoers; protect me H3378
Ps 140: 4 Keep me safe, **L**, from the hands of the H3378
Ps 140: 6 I say to **the L**, "You are my God." Hear H3378
Ps 140: 6 Hear, **L**, my cry for mercy. H3378
Ps 140: 7 Sovereign **L**, my strong deliverer, you H3378
Ps 140: 8 wicked their desires, **L**; do not let their H3378
Ps 140:12 I know that **the L** secures justice for the H3378
Ps 141: 1 I call to you, **L**, come quickly to me; hear H3378
Ps 141: 3 over my mouth, **L**; keep watch over the H3378
Ps 141: 8 Sovereign **L**; in you I take refuge H3378
Ps 142: 1 I cry aloud to **the L**; I lift up my voice to H3378
Ps 142: 1 I lift up my voice to **the L** for mercy. H3378
Ps 142: 5 I cry to you, **L**; I say, "You are my refuge H3378
Ps 143: 1 **L**, hear my prayer, listen to my cry for H3378
Ps 143: 7 Answer me quickly, **L**; my spirit fails. H3378
Ps 143: 9 me from my enemies, **L**, for I hide myself H3378
Ps 143:11 your name's sake, **L**, preserve my life; in H3378
Ps 144: 1 Praise be to **the L** my Rock, who trains my H3378
Ps 144: 3 **L**, what are human beings that you care H3378
Ps 144: 5 Part your heavens, **L**, and come down H3378
Ps 144:15 blessed is the people whose God is **the L**. H3378
Ps 145: 3 Great is **the L** and most worthy of praise H3378
Ps 145: 8 **The L** is gracious and compassionate H3378
Ps 145: 9 **The L** is good to all; he has compassion H3378
Ps 145:10 works praise you, **L**; your faithful people H3378
Ps 145:13 **The L** is trustworthy in all he promises H3378
Ps 145:14 **The L** upholds all who fall and lifts up all H3378
Ps 145:17 **The L** is righteous in all his ways and H3378
Ps 145:18 **The L** is near to all who call on him, to all H3378
Ps 145:20 **The L** watches over all who love him, but H3378
Ps 145:21 My mouth will speak in praise of **the L**. H3378
Ps 146: 1 Praise **the L**. Praise the LORD, my soul. H3363
Ps 146: 1 Praise the LORD. Praise **the L**, my soul. H3378
Ps 146: 2 I will praise **the L** all my life; I will sing H3378
Ps 146: 5 whose hope is in **the L** their God. H3378
Ps 146: 7 to the hungry. **The L** sets prisoners free, H3378
Ps 146: 8 **the L** gives sight to the blind, the LORD H3378
Ps 146: 8 **the L** lifts up those who are bowed down H3378
Ps 146: 8 bowed down, **the L** loves the righteous. H3378
Ps 146: 9 **The L** watches over the foreigner and H3378
Ps 146:10 **The L** reigns forever, your God, O Zion, H3378
Ps 146:10 for all generations. Praise **the L**. H3363
Ps 147: 1 Praise **the L**. How good it is to sing H3363
Ps 147: 2 **The L** builds up Jerusalem; he gathers the H3378
Ps 147: 6 **The L** sustains the humble but casts the H3378
Ps 147: 7 Sing to **the L** with grateful praise; make H3378
Ps 147:11 **the L** delights in those who fear him, who H3378
Ps 147:12 Extol **the L**, Jerusalem; praise your God H3378
Ps 147:20 they do not know his laws. Praise **the L**. H3363
Ps 148: 1 Praise **the L**. Praise the LORD from the H3363
Ps 148: 1 Praise **the L** from the heavens; praise him H3378
Ps 148: 5 Let them praise the name of **the L**, for at H3378
Ps 148: 7 Praise **the L** from the earth, you great sea H3378
Ps 148:13 Let them praise the name of **the L**, for his H3378
Ps 148:14 people close to his heart. Praise **the L**. H3363
Ps 149: 1 Praise **the L**. Sing to the LORD a new song H3363
Ps 149: 1 Sing to **the L** a new song, his praise in the H3378
Ps 149: 4 For **the L** takes delight in his people; he H3378
Ps 149: 9 of all his faithful people. Praise **the L**. H3363
Ps 150: 1 Praise **the L**. Praise God in his sanctuary H3363
Ps 150: 6 Let everything that has breath praise **the L**. H3363
Ps 150: 6 has breath praise the LORD. Praise **the L**. H3363
Pr 1: 7 The fear of **the L** is the beginning of H3378
Pr 1:29 did not choose to fear **the L**. H3378
Pr 2: 5 understand the fear of **the L** and find the H3378
Pr 2: 6 For **the L** gives wisdom; from his mouth H3378
Pr 3: 5 Trust in **the L** with all your heart and lean H3378
Pr 3: 7 in your own eyes; fear **the L** and shun evil. H3378
Pr 3: 9 Honor **the L** with your wealth, with the H3378
Pr 3:12 because **the L** disciplines those he loves H3378
Pr 3:19 By wisdom **the L** laid the earth's H3378
Pr 3:26 for **the L** will be at your side and will keep H3378
Pr 3:32 For **the L** detests the perverse but takes H3378
Pr 5:21 For your ways are in full view of **the L**, H3378
Pr 6:16 There are six things **the L** hates, seven H3378
Pr 8:13 To fear **the L** is to hate evil; I hate pride H3378
Pr 8:22 "**The L** brought me forth as the first of his H3378
Pr 8:35 me find life and receive favor from **the L**. H3378
Pr 9:10 The fear of **the L** is the beginning of H3378
Pr 10: 3 **The L** does not let the righteous go H3378
Pr 10:22 The blessing of **the L** brings wealth H3378
Pr 10:27 The fear of **the L** adds length to life, but H3378
Pr 10:29 The way of **the L** is a refuge for the H3378
Pr 11: 1 **The L** detests dishonest scales, but H3378
Pr 11:20 **The L** detests those whose hearts are H3378
Pr 12: 2 Good people obtain favor from **the L**, but H3378
Pr 12:22 **The L** detests lying lips, but he delights in H3378
Pr 14: 2 Whoever fears **the L** walks uprightly, but H3378
Pr 14:16 The wise fear the L and shun evil, but a fool NDT
Pr 14:26 Whoever fears **the L** has a secure fortress H3378
Pr 14:27 The fear of **the L** is a fountain of life H3378
Pr 15: 3 The eyes of **the L** are everywhere, keeping H3378
Pr 15: 8 **The L** detests the sacrifice of the wicked H3378
Pr 15: 9 **The L** detests the way of the wicked, but H3378
Pr 15:11 Destruction lie open before **the L**— H3378
Pr 15:16 with the fear of **the L** than great wealth H3378
Pr 15:25 **The L** tears down the house of the proud H3378
Pr 15:26 **The L** detests the thoughts of the wicked H3378
Pr 15:29 **The L** is far from the wicked, but he hears H3378
Pr 15:33 Wisdom's instruction is to fear **the L**, and H3378
Pr 16: 1 from **the L** comes the proper answer of H3378
Pr 16: 2 but motives are weighed by **the L**. H3378
Pr 16: 3 Commit to **the L** whatever you do, and he H3378
Pr 16: 4 **The L** works out everything to its proper H3378
Pr 16: 5 **The L** detests all the proud of heart. H3378
Pr 16: 6 through the fear of **the L** evil is avoided. H3378
Pr 16: 7 When **the L** takes pleasure in anyone's H3378
Pr 16: 9 but **the L** establishes their steps. H3378
Pr 16:11 scales and balances belong to **the L**; H3378
Pr 16:20 blessed is the one who trusts in **the L**. H3378
Pr 16:33 but its every decision is from **the L**. H3378
Pr 17: 3 furnace for gold, but **the L** tests the heart. H3378
Pr 17:15 the innocent—**the L** detests them both. H3378
Pr 18:10 The name of **the L** is a fortified tower; the H3378
Pr 18:22 is good and receives favor from **the L**. H3378
Pr 19: 3 yet their heart rages against **the L**. H3378
Pr 19:14 parents, but a prudent wife is from **the L**. H3378
Pr 19:17 Whoever is kind to the poor lends to **the L**, H3378
Pr 19:23 The fear of **the L** leads to life; then one H3378
Pr 20:10 measures—**the L** detests them both. H3378
Pr 20:12 that see—**the L** has made them both. H3378
Pr 20:22 Wait for **the L**, and he will H3378
Pr 20:23 **The L** detests differing weights, and H3378
Pr 20:24 A person's steps are directed by **the L**. H3378
Pr 20:27 is the lamp of **the L** that sheds light on H3378
Pr 21: 2 ways are right, but **the L** weighs the heart. H3378
Pr 21: 3 is more acceptable to **the L** than sacrifice. H3378
Pr 21:30 no plan that can succeed against **the L**. H3378
Pr 21:31 day of battle, but victory rests with **the L**. H3378
Pr 22: 2 **The L** is the Maker of them all. H3378
Pr 22: 4 Humility is the fear of **the L**; its wages are H3378
Pr 22:12 The eyes of **the L** keep watch over H3378
Pr 22:19 So that your trust may be in **the L**, I teach H3378
Pr 22:23 for **the L** will take up their case and will H3378
Pr 23:17 always be zealous for the fear of **the L**. H3378
Pr 24:18 or **the L** will see and disapprove and turn H3378
Pr 24:21 Fear **the L** and the king, my son, and do H3378
Pr 25:22 on his head, and **the L** will reward you. H3378
Pr 28: 5 those who seek **the L** understand it H3378
Pr 28:25 those who trust in **the L** will prosper. H3378
Pr 29:13 **The L** gives sight to the eyes of both H3378
Pr 29:25 whoever trusts in **the L** is kept safe. H3378
Pr 29:26 it is from **the L** that one gets justice. H3378
Pr 30: 7 things I ask of you, **L**; do not refuse me NDT
Pr 30: 9 disown you and say, 'Who is **the L**? H3378
Pr 31:30 a woman who fears **the L** is to be praised. H3378
Isa 1: 2 For **the L** has spoken: "I reared H3378
Isa 1: 4 They have forsaken **the L**; they have H3378
Isa 1: 9 Unless **the L** Almighty had left us some H3378
Isa 1:10 Hear the word of **the L**, you rulers of H3378
Isa 1:11 says **the L**. "I have more than H3378
Isa 1:18 let us settle the matter," says **the L**. H3378
Isa 1:20 For the mouth of **the L** has spoken. H3378
Isa 1:24 Therefore the Lord, **the L** Almighty, the H3378
Isa 1:28 those who forsake **the L** will perish. H3378
Isa 2: 3 let us go up to the mountain of **the L**, to H3378
Isa 2: 3 the word of **the L** from Jerusalem. H3378
Isa 2: 5 of Jacob, let us walk in the light of **the L**. H3378
Isa 2: 6 **L**, have abandoned your people, the NDT
Isa 2:10 fearful presence of **the L** and the splendor H3378
Isa 2:11 **the L** alone will be exalted in that day. H3378
Isa 2:12 **The L** Almighty has a day in store for all H3378
Isa 2:17 **the L** alone will be exalted in that day, H3378
Isa 2:19 fearful presence of **the L** and the splendor H3378
Isa 2:21 fearful presence of **the L** and the splendor H3378
Isa 3: 1 the Lord, **the L** Almighty, is about to take H3378
Isa 3: 8 their words and deeds are against **the L** H3378
Isa 3:13 **The L** takes his place in court; he rises to H3378
Isa 3:14 **The L** enters into judgment against the H3378
Isa 3:15 declares the Lord, **the L** Almighty. H3378
Isa 3:16 **The L** says, "The women of Zion are H3378
Isa 3:17 of Zion; **the L** will make their scalps bald." H3378
Isa 4: 2 day the Branch of **the L** will be beautiful H3378
Isa 4: 5 Then **the L** will create over all of Mount H3378
Isa 5: 7 The vineyard of **the L** Almighty is the H3378
Isa 5: 9 **The L** Almighty has declared in my H3378
Isa 5:12 have no regard for the deeds of **the L**, H3378
Isa 5:16 But **the L** Almighty will be exalted by his H3378
Isa 5:24 rejected the law of **the L** Almighty and H3378
Isa 6: 3 holy is **the L** Almighty; the whole H3378
Isa 6: 5 eyes have seen the King, **the L** Almighty." H3378

Isa 6:12 until **the L** has sent everyone far away H3378
Isa 7: 3 Then **the L** said to Isaiah, "Go out, you H3378
Isa 7: 7 Yet this is what **the** Sovereign **L** says: H3378
Isa 7:10 Again **the L** spoke to Ahaz, H3378
Isa 7:11 "Ask **the L** your God for a sign, whether H3378
Isa 7:12 not ask; I will not put **the L** to the test." H3378
Isa 7:17 **The L** will bring on you and on your H3378
Isa 7:18 In that day **the L** will whistle for flies from H3378
Isa 8: 1 **The L** said to me, "Take a large scroll H3378
Isa 8: 3 And **the L** said to me, "Name him H3378
Isa 8: 5 **The L** spoke to me again: H3378
Isa 8:11 This is what **the L** says to me with his H3378
Isa 8:13 **The L** Almighty is the one you are to H3378
Isa 8:17 I will wait for **the L**, who is hiding his face H3378
Isa 8:18 and the children **the L** has given me. H3378
Isa 8:18 symbols in Israel from **the L** Almighty, H3378
Isa 9: 7 The zeal of **the L** Almighty will H3378
Isa 9:11 But **the L** has strengthened Rezin's foes H3378
Isa 9:13 have they sought **the L** Almighty. H3378
Isa 9:14 So **the L** will cut off from Israel both head H3378
Isa 9:19 By the wrath of **the L** Almighty the land H3378
Isa 10:16 the Lord, **the L** Almighty, will send a H3378
Isa 10:20 them down but will truly rely on **the L**, H3378
Isa 10:23 The Lord, **the L** Almighty, will carry out H3378
Isa 10:24 this is what the Lord, **the L** Almighty, says: H3378
Isa 10:26 **The L** Almighty will lash them with a whip H3378
Isa 10:33 the Lord, **the L** Almighty, will lop off the H3378
Isa 11: 2 The Spirit of **the L** will rest on him—the H3378
Isa 11: 2 of the knowledge and fear of **the L**— H3378
Isa 11: 3 he will delight in the fear of **the L**. H3378
Isa 11: 9 the knowledge of **the L** as the waters H3378
Isa 11:15 **The L** will dry up the gulf of the Egyptian H3378
Isa 12: 1 "I will praise you, **L**. Although you were H3378
Isa 12: 2 **The L**, the LORD himself, is my strength H3363
Isa 12: 2 The LORD, **the L** *himself*, is my strength H3378
Isa 12: 4 "Give praise to **the L**, proclaim his name H3378
Isa 12: 5 Sing to **the L**, for he has done glorious H3378
Isa 13: 4 **The L** Almighty is mustering an army for H3378
Isa 13: 5 **the L** and the weapons of his wrath H3378
Isa 13: 6 for the day of **the L** is near; it will H3378
Isa 13: 9 the day of **the L** is coming—a cruel H3378
Isa 13:13 its place at the wrath of **the L** Almighty, H3378
Isa 14: 1 **The L** will have compassion on Jacob H3378
Isa 14: 3 On the day **the L** gives you relief from H3378
Isa 14: 5 **The L** has broken the rod of the wicked H3378
Isa 14:22 against them," declares **the L** Almighty. H3378
Isa 14:22 descendants," declares **the L**. H3378
Isa 14:23 of destruction," declares **the L** Almighty. H3378
Isa 14:24 **The L** Almighty has sworn, "Surely, as I H3378
Isa 14:27 For **the L** Almighty has purposed, and who H3378
Isa 14:32 "**The L** has established Zion, and in her H3378
Isa 16:13 This is the word **the L** has already spoken H3378
Isa 16:14 But now **the L** says: "Within three years, H3378
Isa 17: 3 of the Israelites," declares **the L** Almighty. H3378
Isa 17: 6 boughs," declares **the L**, the God of Israel. H3378
Isa 18: 4 This is what **the L** says to me: "I will H3378
Isa 18: 7 will be brought to **the L** Almighty from a H3378
Isa 18: 7 the place of the Name of **the L** Almighty. H3378
Isa 19: 1 **the L** rides on a swift cloud and is coming H3378
Isa 19: 4 declares the Lord, **the L** Almighty. H3378
Isa 19:12 make known what **the L** Almighty has H3378
Isa 19:14 **The L** has poured into them a spirit of H3378
Isa 19:16 uplifted hand that **the L** Almighty raises H3378
Isa 19:17 because of what **the L** Almighty is H3378
Isa 19:18 swear allegiance to **the L** Almighty. H3378
Isa 19:19 will be an altar to **the L** in the heart of H3378
Isa 19:19 a monument to **the L** at its border. H3378
Isa 19:20 sign and witness to **the L** Almighty in the H3378
Isa 19:20 they cry out to **the L** because of their H3378
Isa 19:21 So **the L** will make himself known to the H3378
Isa 19:21 in that day they will acknowledge **the L**. H3378
Isa 19:21 will make vows to **the L** and keep them. H3378
Isa 19:22 **The L** will strike Egypt with a plague; he H3378
Isa 19:22 They will turn to **the L**, and he will H3378
Isa 19:25 **The L** Almighty will bless them, saying H3378
Isa 20: 2 at that time **the L** spoke through Isaiah son H3378
Isa 20: 3 Then **the L** said, "Just as my servant H3378
Isa 21:10 what I have heard from **the L** Almighty, H3378
Isa 21:17 **The L**, the God of Israel, has H3378
Isa 22: 5 The Lord, **the L** Almighty, has a day of H3378
Isa 22:12 The Lord, **the L** Almighty, called you on H3378
Isa 22:14 **The L** Almighty has revealed this in my H3378
Isa 22:14 atoned for," says the Lord, **the L** Almighty. H3378
Isa 22:15 This is what the Lord, **the L** Almighty, says: H3378
Isa 22:17 **the L** is about to take firm hold of you H3378
Isa 22:25 declares **the L** Almighty, "the peg driven H3378
Isa 22:25 on it will be cut down." **The L** has spoken. H3378
Isa 23: 9 **The L** Almighty planned it, to bring down H3378
Isa 23:11 **The L** has stretched out his hand over the H3378
Isa 23:17 of seventy years, **the L** will deal with Tyre. H3378
Isa 23:18 her earnings will be set apart for **the L**; H3378
Isa 23:18 will go to those who live before **the L**, H3378
Isa 24: 1 **the L** is going to lay waste the earth and H3378
Isa 24: 3 **The L** has spoken this word H3378
Isa 24:15 Therefore in the east give glory to **the L** H3378
Isa 24:15 exalt the name of **the L**, the God of Israel, H3378
Isa 24:21 In that day **the L** will punish the powers in H3378
Isa 24:23 for **the L** Almighty will reign on Mount H3378
Isa 25: 1 **L**, you are my God; I will exalt you and H3378
Isa 25: 6 On this mountain **the L** Almighty will H3378
Isa 25: 8 **The** Sovereign **L** will wipe away the tears H3378
Isa 25: 8 from all the earth. **The L** has spoken. H3378
Isa 25: 9 This is **the L**, we trusted in him; let us H3378
Isa 25:10 The hand of **the L** will rest on this H3378
Isa 26: 4 Trust in **the L** forever, for the LORD, H3378
Isa 26: 4 LORD forever, for **the L**, the LORD himself, H3363
Isa 26: 4 the LORD, **the L** *himself*, is the Rock H3378
Isa 26: 8 **L**, walking in the way of your laws H3378
Isa 26:10 do not regard the majesty of **the L**. H3378
Isa 26:11 **L**, your hand is lifted high, but they do not H3378
Isa 26:12 **L**, you establish peace for us; all that we H3378
Isa 26:13 **L** our God, other lords besides you have H3378
Isa 26:15 enlarged the nation, **L**; you have enlarged H3378
Isa 26:16 **L**, they came to you in their distress; when H3378
Isa 26:17 her pain, so were we in your presence, **L**. H3378
Isa 26:19 your dead will live, **L**; their bodies will rise NDT
Isa 26:21 **the L** is coming out of his dwelling to H3378
Isa 27: 1 that day, **the L** will punish with his sword H3378
Isa 27: 3 **the L**, watch over it; I water it continually H3378
Isa 27: 7 Has the L struck her as he struck down NDT
Isa 27:12 In that day **the L** will thresh from the H3378
Isa 27:13 come and worship **the L** on the holy H3378
Isa 28: 5 In that day **the L** Almighty will be a H3378
Isa 28:13 the word of **the L** to them will become: H3378
Isa 28:14 Therefore hear the word of **the L**, you H3378
Isa 28:16 So this is what **the** Sovereign **L** says: H3378
Isa 28:21 **The L** will rise up as he did at Mount H3378
Isa 28:22 the Lord, **the L** Almighty, has told me of H3378
Isa 28:29 All this also comes from **the L** Almighty H3378
Isa 29: 6 **the L** Almighty will come with thunder H3378
Isa 29:10 **The L** has brought over you a deep sleep H3378
Isa 29:15 depths to hide their plans from **the L**, H3378
Isa 29:19 more the humble will rejoice in **the L**; H3378
Isa 29:22 Therefore this is what **the L**, who H3378
Isa 30: 1 declares **the L**, "to those who carry out H3378
Isa 30:15 This is what **the** Sovereign **L**, the Holy H3378
Isa 30:18 Yet **the L** longs to be gracious to you H3378
Isa 30:18 For **the L** is a God of justice H3378
Isa 30:26 when **the L** binds up the bruises of his H3378
Isa 30:27 the Name of **the L** comes from afar H3378
Isa 30:29 pipes go up to the mountain of **the L**, H3378
Isa 30:30 **The L** will cause people to hear his H3378
Isa 30:31 The voice of **the L** will shatter Assyria H3378
Isa 30:32 Every stroke **the L** lays on them with his H3378
Isa 30:33 the breath of **the L**, like a stream of H3378
Isa 31: 1 One of Israel, or seek help from **the L**. H3378
Isa 31: 3 When **the L** stretches out his hand, those H3378
Isa 31: 4 This is what **the L** says to me: "As a lion H3378
Isa 31: 4 so **the L** Almighty will come down to do H3378
Isa 31: 5 **the L** Almighty will shield Jerusalem H3378
Isa 31: 9 will panic," declares **the L**, whose fire is H3378
Isa 32: 6 spread error concerning **the L**; H3378
Isa 33: 2 **L**, be gracious to us; we long for you. H3378
Isa 33: 5 **The L** is exalted, for he dwells on high; he H3378
Isa 33: 6 the fear of **the L** is the key to this treasure. H3378
Isa 33:10 will I arise," says **the L**. "Now will I be H3378
Isa 33:21 There **the L** will be our Mighty One. H3378
Isa 33:22 For **the L** is our judge, the LORD is our H3378
Isa 33:22 LORD is our judge, **the L** is our lawgiver H3378
Isa 33:22 is our lawgiver, **the L** is our king; it is he H3378
Isa 34: 2 **The L** is angry with all nations; his wrath H3378
Isa 34: 6 The sword of **the L** is bathed in blood, it is H3378
Isa 34: 6 For **the L** has a sacrifice in Bozrah and a H3378
Isa 34: 8 For **the L** has a day of vengeance, a year H3378
Isa 34:16 Look in the scroll of **the L** and read: None H3378
Isa 35: 2 they will see the glory of **the L**, the H3378
Isa 35:10 those **the L** has rescued will return H3378
Isa 36: 7 "We are depending on **the L** our God"— H3378
Isa 36:10 attack and destroy this land without **the L**? H3378
Isa 36:10 **The L** himself told me to march against H3378
Isa 36:15 you to trust in **the L** when he says, H3378
Isa 36:15 he says, '**The L** will surely deliver us H3378
Isa 36:18 you when he says, '**The L** will deliver us. H3378
Isa 36:20 How then can **the L** deliver Jerusalem H3378
Isa 37: 1 went into the temple of **the L**. H3378
Isa 37: 4 It may be that **the L** your God will hear the H3378
Isa 37: 4 him for the words **the L** your God has H3378
Isa 37: 6 "Tell your master, 'This is what **the L** says: H3378
Isa 37:14 to the temple of **the L** and spread it out H3378
Isa 37:14 of the LORD and spread it out before **the L**. H3378
Isa 37:15 And Hezekiah prayed to **the L**: H3378
Isa 37:16 "**L** Almighty, the God of Israel, enthroned H3378
Isa 37:17 Give ear, **L**, and hear; open your eyes, H3378
Isa 37:17 open your eyes, **L**, and see; listen to H3378
Isa 37:18 "It is true, **L**, that the Assyrian kings have H3378
Isa 37:20 **L** our God, deliver us from his hand H3378
Isa 37:20 may know that you, **L**, are the only God." H3378
Isa 37:21 "This is what **the L**, the God of Israel, says: H3378
Isa 37:22 this is the word **the L** has spoken against H3378
Isa 37:32 The zeal of **the L** Almighty will H3378
Isa 37:33 this is what **the L** says concerning the H3378
Isa 37:34 he will not enter this city," declares **the L**. H3378
Isa 37:36 Then the angel of **the L** went out and put H3378
Isa 38: 1 to him and said, "This is what **the L** says: H3378
Isa 38: 2 his face to the wall and prayed to **the L**, H3378
Isa 38: 3 "Remember, **L**, how I have walked before H3378
Isa 38: 4 Then the word of **the L** came to Isaiah: H3378
Isa 38: 5 'This is what **the L**, the God of your H3378
Isa 38: 7 sign to you that **the L** will do what he has H3378
Isa 38:11 again see **the L himself** in the land H3363+3363
Isa 38:20 **The L** will save me, and we will sing with H3378
Isa 38:20 days of our lives in the temple of **the L**. H3378
Isa 38:22 that I will go up to the temple of **the L**?" H3378
Isa 39: 5 "Hear the word of **the L** Almighty: H3378
Isa 39: 6 Nothing will be left, says **the L**. H3378
Isa 39: 8 "The word of **the L** you have spoken is H3378
Isa 40: 3 the wilderness prepare the way for **the L**; H3378
Isa 40: 5 And the glory of **the L** will be revealed H3378
Isa 40: 5 For the mouth of **the L** has spoken." H3378
Isa 40: 7 the breath of **the L** blows on them. H3378
Isa 40:10 **the** Sovereign **L** comes with power H3378
Isa 40:13 Who can fathom the Spirit of **the L**, or H3378
Isa 40:13 or instruct **the L** as his counselor? H5647S
Isa 40:14 Whom did the L consult to enlighten him NDT
Isa 40:27 "My way is hidden from **the L**; my caus H3378
Isa 40:28 **The L** is the everlasting God, the Creator H3378
Isa 40:31 those who hope in **the L** will renew their H3378
Isa 41: 4 **the L**—with the first of them and with H3378
Isa 41:13 For I am **the L** your God who takes hold H3378
Isa 41:14 help you," declares **the L**, your Redeemer H3378
Isa 41:16 you will rejoice in **the L** and glory in the H3378
Isa 41:17 But I **the L** will answer them; I, the God H3378
Isa 41:20 that the hand of **the L** has done this, that H3378
Isa 41:21 your case," says **the L**. "Set forth your H3378
Isa 42: 5 This is what God **the L** says—the Creator H3378
Isa 42: 6 **the L**, have called you in righteousness; H3378
Isa 42: 8 "I am **the L**; that is my name! I will not H3378
Isa 42:10 Sing to **the L** a new song, his praise from H3378
Isa 42:12 them give glory to **the L** and proclaim his H3378
Isa 42:13 **The L** will march out like a champion, like H3378
Isa 42:19 with me, blind like the servant of **the L**? H3378
Isa 42:21 It pleased **the L** for the sake of his H3378
Isa 42:24 Was it not **the L**, against whom we have H3378
Isa 43: 1 this is what **the L** says—he who H3378
Isa 43: 3 For I am **the L** your God, the Holy One of H3378
Isa 43:10 declares **the L**, "and my servant whom I H3378
Isa 43:11 am **the L**, and apart from me there H3378
Isa 43:12 declares **the L**, "that I am God. H3378
Isa 43:14 This is what **the L** says—your Redeemer H3378
Isa 43:15 I am **the L**, your Holy One, Israel's Creator H3378
Isa 43:16 This is what **the L** says—he who made a H3378
Isa 44: 2 This is what **the L** says—he who made H3378
Isa 44: 5 will say, 'I belong to **the L**'; others will H3378
Isa 44: 6 "This is what **the L** says—Israel's King H3378
Isa 44: 6 King and Redeemer, **the L** Almighty: H3378
Isa 44:23 you heavens, for **the L** has done this H3378
Isa 44:23 your trees, for **the L** has redeemed Jacob H3378
Isa 44:24 "This is what **the L** says—your Redeemer H3378
Isa 44:24 I am **the L**, the Maker of all things, who H3378
Isa 45: 1 "This is what **the L** says to his anointed, to H3378
Isa 45: 3 so that you may know that I am **the L**, the H3378
Isa 45: 5 I am **the L**, and there is no other; apart H3378
Isa 45: 6 I am **the L**, and there is no H3378
Isa 45: 7 create disaster; I, **the L**, do all these H3378
Isa 45: 8 flourish with it; I, **the L**, have created it. H3378
Isa 45:11 "This is what **the L** says—the Holy One H3378
Isa 45:13 a price or reward, says **the L** Almighty." H3378
Isa 45:14 This is what **the L** says: "The products of H3378
Isa 45:17 will be saved by **the L** with an everlasting H3378
Isa 45:18 For this is what **the L** says—he who H3378
Isa 45:18 "I am **the L**, and there is no other. H3378
Isa 45:19 **the L**, speak the truth; I declare what is H3378
Isa 45:21 Was it not I, **the L**? And there is no H3378
Isa 45:24 'In **the L** alone are deliverance and H3378
Isa 45:25 find deliverance in **the L** and will make H3378
Isa 47: 4 Redeemer—**the L** Almighty is his name H3378
Isa 48: 1 in the name of **the L** and invoke the God H3378
Isa 48: 2 of Israel—**the L** Almighty is his name: H3378
Isa 48:16 And now **the** Sovereign **L** has sent me H3378
Isa 48:17 This is what **the L** says—your Redeemer H3378
Isa 48:17 "I am **the L** your God, who teaches you H3378
Isa 48:20 "**The L** has redeemed his servant Jacob." H3378
Isa 48:22 is no peace," says **the L**, "for the wicked." H3378
Isa 49: 1 Before I was born **the L** called me; from H3378
Isa 49: 5 And now **the L** says—he who formed me H3378
Isa 49: 5 in the eyes of **the L** and my God has been H3378
Isa 49: 7 This is what **the L** says—the Redeemer H3378
Isa 49: 7 because of **the L**, who is faithful, H3378
Isa 49: 8 This is what **the L** says: "In the time of my H3378
Isa 49:13 For **the L** comforts his people and will H3378
Isa 49:14 But Zion said, "**The L** has forsaken me H3378
Isa 49:18 declares **the L**, "you will wear them all as H3378
Isa 49:22 This is what **the** Sovereign **L** says: "See, H3378
Isa 49:23 Then you will know that I am **the L**; those H3378
Isa 49:25 But this is what **the L** says: "Yes, captives H3378
Isa 49:26 will know that I, **the L**, am your Savior, H3378
Isa 50: 1 This is what **the L** says: "Where is your H3378
Isa 50: 4 **The** Sovereign **L** has given me a H3378
Isa 50: 5 **The** Sovereign **L** has opened my ears; H3378
Isa 50: 7 Because **the** Sovereign **L** helps me, I will H3378
Isa 50: 9 It is **the** Sovereign **L** who helps me. H3378
Isa 50:10 among you fears **the L** and obeys the H3378
Isa 50:10 trust in the name of **the L** and rely on their H3378
Isa 51: 1 pursue righteousness and who seek **the L**: H3378
Isa 51: 3 **The L** will surely comfort Zion and will H3378
Isa 51: 3 her wastelands like the garden of **the L**. H3378
Isa 51: 9 arm of **the L**, clothe yourself with H3378
Isa 51:11 Those **the L** has rescued will return. H3378
Isa 51:13 that you forget **the L** your Maker, who H3378
Isa 51:15 For I am **the L** your God, who stirs up the H3378
Isa 51:15 waves roar—**the L** Almighty is his name. H3378
Isa 51:17 from the hand of **the L** the cup of his H3378
Isa 51:20 They are filled with the wrath of **the L** H3378
Isa 51:22 This is what your Sovereign **L** says, your H3378
Isa 52: 3 For this is what **the L** says: "You were sold H3378
Isa 52: 4 For this is what **the** Sovereign **L** says: "At H3378

Book	Ref	Context	Number
Isa	52: 5	declares **the L**. "For my people	H3378
Isa	52: 5	who rule them mock," declares **the L**.	H3378
Isa	52: 8	When **the L** returns to Zion, they will see	H3378
Isa	52: 9	for **the L** has comforted his people	H3378
Isa	52:10	**The L** will lay bare his holy arm in the	H3378
Isa	52:12	go in flight; for **the L** will go before you	H3378
Isa	53: 1	has the arm of **the L** been revealed?	H3378
Isa	53: 6	and **the L** has laid on him the iniquity of	H3378
Isa	53:10	though the L makes his life an offering	NDT
Isa	53:10	the will of **the L** will prosper in his	H3378
Isa	54: 1	of her who has a husband," says **the L**.	H3378
Isa	54: 5	husband—**the L** Almighty is his name	H3378
Isa	54: 6	**The L** will call you back as if you were a	H3378
Isa	54: 8	says **the L** your Redeemer.	H3378
Isa	54:10	be removed," says **the L**, who has	H3378
Isa	54:13	All your children will be taught by **the L**	H3378
Isa	54:17	is the heritage of the servants of the L,	H3378
Isa	54:17	their vindication from me," declares **the L**.	H3378
Isa	55: 5	because of **the L** your God, the	H3378
Isa	55: 6	Seek **the L** while he may be found; call on	H3378
Isa	55: 7	Let them turn to **the L**, and he will have	H3378
Isa	55: 8	are your ways my ways," declares **the L**.	H3378
Isa	56: 1	This is what **the L** says: "Maintain justice	H3378
Isa	56: 3	Let no foreigner who is bound to **the L**	H3378
Isa	56: 3	"**The L** will surely exclude me from his	H3378
Isa	56: 4	For this is what **the L** says: "To the	H3378
Isa	56: 6	bind themselves to **the L** to minister to	H3378
Isa	56: 6	to love the name of **the L**, and to be his	H3378
Isa	56: 8	**The** Sovereign **L** declares—he who	H3378
Isa	57:19	to those far and near," says **the L**.	H3378
Isa	58: 5	you call a fast, a day acceptable to **the L**?	H3378
Isa	58: 8	the glory of **the L** will be your rear	H3378
Isa	58: 9	you will call, and **the L** will answer; you	H3378
Isa	58:11	**The L** will guide you always; he will	H3378
Isa	58:14	then you will find your joy in **the L**, and I	H3378
Isa	58:14	For the mouth of **the L** has spoken.	H3378
Isa	59: 1	Surely the arm of **the L** is not too short to	H3378
Isa	59:13	rebellion and treachery against **the L**	H3378
Isa	59:15	**The L** looked and was displeased that	H3378
Isa	59:19	people will fear the name of **the L**, and	H3378
Isa	59:19	flood that the breath of **the L** drives along.	H3378
Isa	59:20	who repent of their sins," declares **the L**.	H3378
Isa	59:21	this is my covenant with them," says **the L**.	H3378
Isa	59:21	from this time on and forever," says **the L**.	H3378
Isa	60: 1	the glory of **the L** rises upon you.	H3378
Isa	60: 2	but **the L** rises upon you and his glory	H3378
Isa	60: 6	proclaiming the praise of **the L**.	H3378
Isa	60: 9	to the honor of **the L** your God, the Holy	H3378
Isa	60:14	feet and will call you the City of **the L**,	H3378
Isa	60:16	will know that I, **the L**, am your Savior,	H3378
Isa	60:19	for **the L** will be your everlasting light	H3378
Isa	60:20	**the L** will be your everlasting light	H3378
Isa	60:22	mighty nation. I am **the L**; in its time I will	H3378
Isa	61: 1	The Spirit of **the** Sovereign **L** is on me	H3378
Isa	61: 1	because **the L** has anointed me to	H3378
Isa	61: 3	a planting of **the L** for the display of his	H3378
Isa	61: 6	And you will be called priests of **the L**	H3378
Isa	61: 8	**the L**, love justice; I hate robbery	H3378
Isa	61: 9	that they are a people **the L** has blessed."	H3378
Isa	61:10	I delight greatly in **the L**; my soul rejoices	H3378
Isa	61:11	so **the** Sovereign **L** will make	H3378
Isa	62: 2	name that the mouth of **the L** will bestow.	H3378
Isa	62: 4	Beulah; for **the L** will take delight in you	H3378
Isa	62: 6	You who call on **the L**, give yourselves no	H3378
Isa	62: 8	**The L** has sworn by his right hand and by	H3378
Isa	62: 9	who harvest it will eat it and praise **the L**,	H3378
Isa	62:11	**The L** has made proclamation to the ends	H3378
Isa	62:12	the Redeemed of **the L**; and you will be	H3378
Isa	63: 7	I will tell of the kindnesses of **the L**, the	H3378
Isa	63: 7	according to all **the L** has done for us	H3378
Isa	63:14	they were given rest by the Spirit of **the L**.	H3378
Isa	63:16	**L**, are our Father, our	H3378
Isa	63:17	**L**, do you make us wander from your	H3378
Isa	64: 8	Yet you, **L**, are our Father. We are the clay,	H3378
Isa	64: 9	beyond measure, **L**; do not remember our	H3378
Isa	64:12	After all this, **L**, will you hold yourself	H3378
Isa	65: 7	the sins of your ancestors," says **the L**.	H3378
Isa	65: 8	This is what **the L** says: "As when juice is	H3378
Isa	65:11	you who forsake **the L** and forget my holy	H3378
Isa	65:13	this is what **the** Sovereign **L** says:	H3378
Isa	65:15	**the** Sovereign **L** will put you to death	H3378
Isa	65:23	they will be a people blessed by **the L**	H3378
Isa	65:25	on all my holy mountain," says **the L**.	H3378
Isa	66: 1	This is what **the L** says: "Heaven is my	H3378
Isa	66: 2	declares **the L**. "These are the	H3378
Isa	66: 5	Hear the word of **the L**, you who tremble	H3378
Isa	66: 5	have said, 'Let **the L** be glorified, that we	H3378
Isa	66: 6	It is the sound of **the L** repaying his	H3378
Isa	66: 9	says **the L**. "Do I close up the	H3378
Isa	66:12	For this is what **the L** says: "I will extend	H3378
Isa	66:14	the hand of **the L** will be made known to	H3378
Isa	66:15	**the L** is coming with fire, and his	H3378
Isa	66:16	with his sword **the L** will execute	H3378
Isa	66:16	many will be those slain by **the L**.	H3378
Isa	66:17	with the one they follow," declares **the L**.	H3378
Isa	66:20	in Jerusalem as an offering to **the L**—	H3378
Isa	66:20	on mules and camels," says **the L**.	H3378
Isa	66:20	to the temple of **the L** in ceremonially	H3378
Isa	66:21	also to be priests and Levites," says **the L**.	H3378
Isa	66:22	declares **the L**, "so will your name and	H3378
Isa	66:23	bow down before me," says **the L**.	H3378
Jer	1: 2	The word of **the L** came to him in the	H3378
Jer	1: 4	The word of **the L** came to me, saying,	H3378
Jer	1: 6	Sovereign **L**," I said, "I do not know	H3378
Jer	1: 7	But **the L** said to me, "Do not say, 'I am	H3378
Jer	1: 8	you and will rescue you," declares **the L**.	H3378
Jer	1: 9	Then **the L** reached out his hand and	H3378
Jer	1:11	The word of **the L** came to me: "What do	H3378
Jer	1:12	**The L** said to me, "You have seen	H3378
Jer	1:13	The word of **the L** came to me again	H3378
Jer	1:14	**The L** said to me, "From the north disaster	H3378
Jer	1:15	of the northern kingdoms," declares **the L**.	H3378
Jer	1:19	you and will rescue you," declares **the L**.	H3378
Jer	2: 1	The word of **the L** came to me:	H3378
Jer	2: 2	"This is what **the L** says: " 'I remember	H3378
Jer	2: 3	Israel was holy to **the L**, the firstfruits of	H3378
Jer	2: 3	disaster overtook them,' " declares **the L**.	H3378
Jer	2: 4	Hear the word of **the L**, you descendants	H3378
Jer	2: 5	This is what **the L** says: "What fault did	H3378
Jer	2: 6	not ask, 'Where is **the L**, who brought us	H3378
Jer	2: 8	not ask, 'Where is **the L**?' Those who deal	H3378
Jer	2: 9	against you again," declares **the L**.	H3378
Jer	2:12	shudder with great horror," declares **the L**.	H3378
Jer	2:17	by forsaking **the L** your God when he led	H3378
Jer	2:19	when you forsake **the L** your God and	H3378
Jer	2:19	declares the Lord, **the L** Almighty.	H3378
Jer	2:22	still before me," declares the Sovereign **L**.	H3378
Jer	2:29	all rebelled against me," declares **the L**.	H3378
Jer	2:31	generation, consider the word of **the L**:	H3378
Jer	2:37	for **the L** has rejected those you trust	H3378
Jer	3: 1	you now return to me?" declares **the L**.	H3378
Jer	3: 6	of King Josiah, **the L** said to me, "Have	H3378
Jer	3:10	only in pretense," declares **the L**.	H3378
Jer	3:11	**The L** said to me, "Faithless Israel is more	H3378
Jer	3:12	declares **the L**, 'I will frown on you	H3378
Jer	3:12	faithful,' declares **the L**, 'I will not be	H3378
Jer	3:13	you have rebelled against **the L** your God	H3378
Jer	3:13	have not obeyed me,' " declares **the L**.	H3378
Jer	3:14	people," declares **the L**, "for I am your	H3378
Jer	3:16	declares **the L**, "people will no longer	H3378
Jer	3:16	'The ark of the covenant of **the L**.'	H3378
Jer	3:17	will call Jerusalem The Throne of **the L**,	H3378
Jer	3:17	in Jerusalem to honor the name of **the L**.	H3378
Jer	3:20	been unfaithful to me," declares **the L**.	H3378
Jer	3:21	ways and have forgotten **the L** their God.	H3378
Jer	3:22	come to you, for you are **the L** our God.	H3378
Jer	3:23	surely in **the L** our God is the salvation of	H3378
Jer	3:25	We have sinned against **the L** our God	H3378
Jer	3:25	day we have not obeyed **the L** our God."	H3378
Jer	4: 1	then return to me," declares **the L**.	H3378
Jer	4: 2	'As surely as **the L** lives,' then the	H3378
Jer	4: 3	This is what **the L** says to the people of	H3378
Jer	4: 4	Circumcise yourselves to **the L**,	H3378
Jer	4: 8	the fierce anger of **the L** has not turned	H3378
Jer	4: 9	declares **the L**, "the king and the officials	H3378
Jer	4:10	Sovereign **L**! How completely you	H3378
Jer	4:17	rebelled against me,' " declares **the L**.	H3378
Jer	4:26	all its towns lay in ruins before **the L**	H3378
Jer	4:27	This is what **the L** says: "The whole land	H3378
Jer	5: 2	'As surely as **the L** lives,' still they are	H3378
Jer	5: 3	**L**, do not your eyes look for truth? You	H3378
Jer	5: 4	they do not know the way of **the L**, the	H3378
Jer	5: 5	surely they know the way of **the L**, the	H3378
Jer	5: 9	declares **the L**. "Should I not	H3378
Jer	5:10	these people do not belong to **the L**.	H3378
Jer	5:11	utterly unfaithful to me," declares **the L**.	H3378
Jer	5:12	They have lied about **the L**; they said,	H3378
Jer	5:14	this is what **the L** God Almighty says:	H3378
Jer	5:15	declares **the L**, "I am bringing a distant	H3378
Jer	5:18	declares **the L**, "I will not destroy you	H3378
Jer	5:19	'Why has **the L** our God done all this to us	H3378
Jer	5:22	declares **the L**. "Should you not	H3378
Jer	5:24	'Let us fear **the L** our God, who gives	H3378
Jer	5:29	declares **the L**. "Should I not	H3378
Jer	6: 6	This is what **the L** Almighty says: "Cut	H3378
Jer	6: 9	This is what **the L** Almighty says: "Let	H3378
Jer	6:10	The word of **the L** is offensive to them	H3378
Jer	6:11	But I am full of the wrath of **the L**, and I	H3378
Jer	6:12	who live in the land," declares **the L**.	H3378
Jer	6:15	down when I punish them," says **the L**.	H3378
Jer	6:16	This is what **the L** says: "Stand at the	H3378
Jer	6:21	Therefore this is what **the L** says: "I will	H3378
Jer	6:22	This is what **the L** says: "Look, an army is	H3378
Jer	6:30	because **the L** has rejected them.	H3378
Jer	7: 1	word that came to Jeremiah from **the L**:	H3378
Jer	7: 2	" 'Hear the word of **the L**, all you people	H3378
Jer	7: 2	through these gates to worship **the L**.	H3378
Jer	7: 3	This is what **the L** Almighty, the God of	H3378
Jer	7: 4	"This is the temple of **the L**, the temple of	H3378
Jer	7: 4	the temple of LORD, **the L**, the temple of the	H3378
Jer	7: 4	temple of the LORD, the temple of **the L**!"	H3378
Jer	7:11	But I have been watching! declares **the L**.	H3378
Jer	7:13	declares **the L**, I spoke to you	H3378
Jer	7:19	declares **the L**. Are they not	H3378
Jer	7:20	this is what **the** Sovereign **L** says:	H3378
Jer	7:21	" 'This is what **the L** Almighty, the God of	H3378
Jer	7:28	that has not obeyed **the L** its God or	H3378
Jer	7:29	for **the L** has rejected and abandoned this	H3378
Jer	7:30	have done evil in my eyes, declares **the L**.	H3378
Jer	7:32	coming, declares **the L**, when people will	H3378
Jer	8: 1	that time, declares **the L**, the bones of the	H3378
Jer	8: 3	death to life, declares **the L** Almighty.	H3378
Jer	8: 4	'This is what **the L** says: " 'When	H3378
Jer	8: 7	do not know the requirements of **the L**.	H3378
Jer	8: 8	we have the law of **the L**," when	H3378
Jer	8: 9	Since they have rejected the word of **the L**,	H3378
Jer	8:12	down when they are punished, says **the L**.	H3378
Jer	8:13	take away their harvest, declares **the L**.	H3378
Jer	8:14	For **the L** our God has doomed us to	H3378
Jer	8:17	they will bite you," declares **the L**.	H3378
Jer	8:19	land far away: "Is **the L** not in Zion? Is her	H3378
Jer	9: 3	do not acknowledge me," declares **the L**.	H3378
Jer	9: 6	to acknowledge me," declares **the L**.	H3378
Jer	9: 7	Therefore this is what **the L** Almighty says	H3378
Jer	9: 9	declares **the L**. "Should I not	H3378
Jer	9:12	instructed by **the L** and can explain it	H3378
Jer	9:13	**The L** said, "It is because they have	H3378
Jer	9:15	Therefore this is what **the L** Almighty, the	H3378
Jer	9:17	This is what **the L** Almighty says	H3378
Jer	9:20	hear the word of **the L**; open your ears to	H3378
Jer	9:22	"This is what **the L** declares: " 'Dead	H3378
Jer	9:23	This is what **the L** says: "Let not the wise	H3378
Jer	9:24	know me, that I am **the L**, who exercises	H3378
Jer	9:24	in these I delight," declares **the L**.	H3378
Jer	9:25	declares **the L**, "when I will punish all	H3378
Jer	10: 1	Hear what **the L** says to you, people of	H3378
Jer	10: 2	This is what **the L** says: "Do not learn the	H3378
Jer	10: 6	No one is like you, **L**; you are great, and	H3378
Jer	10:10	But **the L** is the true God; he is the living	H3378
Jer	10:16	inheritance—**the L** Almighty is his name.	H3378
Jer	10:18	For this is what **the L** says: "At this time I	H3378
Jer	10:21	are senseless and do not inquire of **the L**;	H3378
Jer	10:23	**L**, I know that people's lives are not their	H3378
Jer	10:24	Discipline me, **L**, but only in due measure	H3378
Jer	11: 1	word that came to Jeremiah from **the L**:	H3378
Jer	11: 3	Tell them that this is what **the L**, the God	H3378
Jer	11: 5	possess today." I answered, "Amen, **L**."	H3378
Jer	11: 6	**The L** said to me, "Proclaim all these	H3378
Jer	11: 9	Then **the L** said to me, "There is a	H3378
Jer	11:11	Therefore this is what **the L** says: 'I will	H3378
Jer	11:16	**The L** called you a thriving olive tree with	H3378
Jer	11:17	**The L** Almighty, who planted you, has	H3378
Jer	11:18	Because **the L** revealed their plot to me,	H3378
Jer	11:20	But you, **L** Almighty, who judge	H3378
Jer	11:21	this is what **the L** says about the people	H3378
Jer	11:21	in the name of **the L** or you will die by our	H3378
Jer	11:22	therefore this is what **the L** Almighty says	H3378
Jer	12: 1	always righteous, **L**, when I bring a case	H3378
Jer	12: 3	Yet you know me, **L**; you see me and test	H3378
Jer	12:12	the sword of **the L** will devour from one	H3378
Jer	12:14	This is what **the L** says: "As for all my	H3378
Jer	12:16	'As surely as **the L** lives'—even as they	H3378
Jer	12:17	uproot and destroy it," declares **the L**.	H3378
Jer	13: 1	This is what **the L** said to me: "Go and	H3378
Jer	13: 2	I bought a belt, as **the L** directed, and put	H3378
Jer	13: 3	Then the word of **the L** came to me a	H3378
Jer	13: 5	hid it at Perath, as **the L** told me.	H3378
Jer	13: 6	Many days later **the L** said to me, "Go	H3378
Jer	13: 8	Then the word of **the L** came to me:	H3378
Jer	13: 9	"This is what **the L** says: 'In the same way	H3378
Jer	13:11	declares **the L**, 'to be my people	H3378
Jer	13:12	'This is what **the L**, the God of Israel	H3378
Jer	13:13	'This is what **the L** says: I am going	H3378
Jer	13:14	parents and children alike, declares **the L**.	H3378
Jer	13:15	do not be arrogant, for **the L** has spoken.	H3378
Jer	13:16	Give glory to **the L** your God before he	H3378
Jer	13:21	will you say when the L sets over you those	NDT
Jer	13:25	declares **the L**, "because you have	H3378
Jer	14: 1	This is the word of **the L** that came to	H3378
Jer	14: 7	do something, **L**, for the sake of your	H3378
Jer	14: 9	You are among us, **L**, and we bear your	H3378
Jer	14:10	This is what **the L** says about this people	H3378
Jer	14:10	So **the L** does not accept them; he will	H3378
Jer	14:11	Then **the L** said to me, "Do not pray for	H3378
Jer	14:13	Sovereign **L**! The prophets keep	H3378
Jer	14:14	Then **the L** said to me, "The prophets are	H3378
Jer	14:15	Therefore this is what **the L** says about the	H3378
Jer	14:20	our wickedness, **L**, and the guilt of our	H3378
Jer	14:22	it is you, **L** our God. Therefore our	H3378
Jer	15: 1	Then **the L** said to me: "Even if Moses	H3378
Jer	15: 2	'This is what **the L** says: " 'Those	H3378
Jer	15: 3	declares **the L**, "the sword to kill and the	H3378
Jer	15: 6	declares **the L**. "You keep on	H3378
Jer	15: 9	before their enemies," declares **the L**.	H3378
Jer	15:11	**The L** said, "Surely I will deliver you for	H3378
Jer	15:15	**L**, you understand; remember me and	H3378
Jer	15:16	I bear your name, **L** God Almighty.	H3378
Jer	15:19	Therefore this is what **the L** says: "If you	H3378
Jer	15:20	to rescue and save you," declares **the L**.	H3378
Jer	16: 1	Then the word of **the L** came to me:	H3378
Jer	16: 3	For this is what **the L** says about the sons	H3378
Jer	16: 5	For this is what **the L** says: "Do not enter	H3378
Jer	16: 5	my pity from this people," declares **the L**.	H3378
Jer	16: 9	For this is what **the L** Almighty, the God	H3378
Jer	16:10	'Why has **the L** decreed such a great	H3378
Jer	16:10	we committed against **the L** our God?	H3378
Jer	16:11	declares **the L**, 'and followed other	H3378
Jer	16:14	declares **the L**, "when it will no longer be	H3378
Jer	16:14	'As surely as **the L** lives, who brought	H3378
Jer	16:15	'As surely as **the L** lives, who brought	H3378
Jer	16:16	fishermen," declares **the L**, "and they will	H3378
Jer	16:19	**L**, my strength and my fortress, my refuge	H3378
Jer	16:21	they will know that my name is **the L**.	H3378
Jer	17: 5	This is what **the L** says: "Cursed is the one	H3378
Jer	17: 5	whose heart turns away from **the L**.	H3378
Jer	17: 7	"But blessed is the one who trusts in **the L**,	H3378

Jer	17:10	“I **the L** search the heart and examine the	H3378
Jer	17:13	**L**, you are the hope of Israel; all who	H3378
Jer	17:13	dust because they have forsaken **the L**,	H3378
Jer	17:14	Heal me, **L**, and I will be healed; save me	H3378
Jer	17:15	“Where is the word of **the L**?	H3378
Jer	17:19	This is what **the L** said to me: “Go and	H3378
Jer	17:20	‘Hear the word of **the L**, you kings of	H3378
Jer	17:21	This is what **the L** says: Be careful not to	H3378
Jer	17:24	obey me, declares **the L**, and bring no	H3378
Jer	17:26	thank offerings to the house of **the L**.	H3378
Jer	18: 1	word that came to Jeremiah from **the L**:	H3378
Jer	18: 5	Then the word of **the L** came to me.	H3378
Jer	18: 6	declares **the L**. “Like clay in the	H3378
Jer	18:11	in Jerusalem, ‘This is what **the L** says:	H3378
Jer	18:13	Therefore this is what **the L** says: “Inquire	H3378
Jer	18:19	Listen to me, **L**; hear what my accusers are	H3378
Jer	18:23	But you, **L**, know all their plots to kill me	H3378
Jer	19: 1	This is what **the L** says: “Go and buy a	H3378
Jer	19: 3	‘Hear the word of **the L**, you kings of	H3378
Jer	19: 3	This is what **the L** Almighty, the God of	H3378
Jer	19: 6	coming, declares **the L**, when people will	H3378
Jer	19:11	to them, ‘This is what **the L** Almighty says:	H3378
Jer	19:12	to those who live here, declares **the L**.	H3378
Jer	19:14	where **the L** had sent him to prophesy	H3378
Jer	19:15	“This is what **the L** Almighty, the God of	H3378
Jer	20: 1	official in charge of the temple of **the L**,	H3378
Jer	20: 4	For this is what **the L** says: ‘I will make	H3378
Jer	20: 7	You deceived me, **L**, and I was deceived	H3378
Jer	20: 8	So the word of **the L** has brought me	H3378
Jer	20:11	But **the L** is with me like a mighty warrior	H3378
Jer	20:12	**L** Almighty, you who examine the	H3378
Jer	20:13	Sing to **the L**! Give praise to the LORD!	H3378
Jer	20:13	Give praise to **the L**! He rescues the life	H3378
Jer	20:16	be like the towns **the L** overthrew without	H3378
Jer	21: 1	to Jeremiah from **the L** when King	H3378
Jer	21: 2	“Inquire now of **the L** for us because	H3378
Jer	21: 2	Perhaps **the L** will perform wonders for us	H3378
Jer	21: 4	‘This is what **the L**, the God of Israel, says	H3378
Jer	21: 7	After that, declares **the L**, I will give	H3378
Jer	21: 8	tell the people, ‘This is what **the L** says:	H3378
Jer	21:10	city harm and not good, declares **the L**.	H3378
Jer	21:11	house of Judah, ‘Hear the word of **the L**.	H3378
Jer	21:12	This is what **the L** says to you, house of	H3378
Jer	21:13	plateau, declares **the L**—you who say,	H3378
Jer	21:14	you as your deeds deserve, declares **the L**.	H3378
Jer	22: 1	This is what **the L** says: “Go down to the	H3378
Jer	22: 2	‘Hear the word of **the L** to you, king of	H3378
Jer	22: 3	This is what **the L** says: Do what is just	H3378
Jer	22: 5	commands, declares **the L**, I swear by	H3378
Jer	22: 6	For this is what **the L** says about the	H3378
Jer	22: 8	‘Why has **the L** done such a thing to this	H3378
Jer	22: 9	the covenant of **the L** their God and have	H3378
Jer	22:11	For this is what **the L** says about Shallum	H3378
Jer	22:16	it means to know me?” declares **the L**.	H3378
Jer	22:18	this is what **the L** says about Jehoiakim	H3378
Jer	22:24	as I live,” declares **the L**, “even if you	H3378
Jer	22:29	land, land, hear the word of **the L**!	H3378
Jer	22:30	This is what **the L** says: “Record this man	H3378
Jer	23: 1	the sheep of my pasture!” declares **the L**.	H3378
Jer	23: 2	Therefore this is what **the L**, the God of	H3378
Jer	23: 2	the evil you have done,” declares **the L**.	H3378
Jer	23: 4	will any be missing,” declares **the L**.	H3378
Jer	23: 5	declares **the L**, “when I will raise up for	H3378
Jer	23: 6	**The L** Our Righteous Savior.	H3378
Jer	23: 7	declares **the L**, “when people will no	H3378
Jer	23: 7	‘As surely as **the L** lives, who brought	H3378
Jer	23: 8	‘As surely as **the L** lives, who brought	H3378
Jer	23: 9	because of **the L** and his holy words.	H3378
Jer	23:11	I find their wickedness,” declares **the L**.	H3378
Jer	23:12	year they are punished,” declares **the L**.	H3378
Jer	23:15	Therefore this is what **the L** Almighty says	H3378
Jer	23:16	This is what **the L** Almighty says: “Do not	H3378
Jer	23:16	own minds, not from the mouth of **the L**.	H3378
Jer	23:17	to those who despise me, ‘**The L** says:	H3378
Jer	23:18	in the council of **the L** to see or to hear his	H3378
Jer	23:19	the storm of **the L** will burst out in wrath	H3378
Jer	23:20	The anger of **the L** will not turn back until	H3378
Jer	23:23	declares **the L**, “and not a God	H3378
Jer	23:24	declares **the L**. “Do not I fill	H3378
Jer	23:24	I fill heaven and earth?” declares **the L**.	H3378
Jer	23:28	straw to do with grain?” declares **the L**.	H3378
Jer	23:29	declares **the L**, “and like a hammer that	H3378
Jer	23:30	declares **the L**, “I am against the	H3378
Jer	23:31	declares **the L**, “I am against the	H3378
Jer	23:31	tongues and yet declare, ‘The L declares.	NDT
Jer	23:32	prophesy false dreams,” declares **the L**.	H3378
Jer	23:32	these people in the least,” declares **the L**.	H3378
Jer	23:33	ask you, ‘What is the message from **the L**?	H3378
Jer	23:33	I will forsake you, declares **the L**.’	H3378
Jer	23:34	‘This is a message from **the L**,’ I will	H3378
Jer	23:35	or ‘What has **the L** spoken?’	H3378
Jer	23:36	mention ‘a message from **the L**’ again,	H3378
Jer	23:36	the living God, **the L** Almighty, our God	H3378
Jer	23:37	or ‘What has **the L** spoken?’	H3378
Jer	23:38	‘This is a message from **the L**,’ this is	H3378
Jer	23:38	from the LORD,’ this is what **the L** says:	H3378
Jer	23:38	‘This is a message from **the L**,’ even	H3378
Jer	23:38	not claim, ‘This is a message from **the L**.	H3378
Jer	24: 1	**the L** showed me two baskets of figs	H3378
Jer	24: 1	figs placed in front of the temple of **the L**.	H3378
Jer	24: 3	Then **the L** asked me, “What do you see	H3378
Jer	24: 4	Then the word of **the L** came to me:	H3378
Jer	24: 5	“This is what **the L**, the God of Israel, says	H3378
Jer	24: 7	them a heart to know me, that I am **the L**.	H3378
Jer	24: 8	be eaten,’ says **the L**, ‘so will I deal with	H3378
Jer	25: 3	the word of **the L** has come to me and I	H3378
Jer	25: 4	And though **the L** has sent all his servants	H3378
Jer	25: 5	stay in the land **the L** gave to you and	H3378
Jer	25: 7	declares **the L**, “and you have aroused	H3378
Jer	25: 8	Therefore **the L** Almighty says this	H3378
Jer	25: 9	declares **the L**, “and I will bring them	H3378
Jer	25:12	declares **the L**, “and will make it	H3378
Jer	25:15	This is what **the L**, the God of Israel, said	H3378
Jer	25:27	‘This is what **the L** Almighty, the God	H3378
Jer	25:28	‘This is what **the L** Almighty says:	H3378
Jer	25:29	live on the earth, declares **the L** Almighty.	H3378
Jer	25:30	“ ‘**The L** will roar from on high; he will	H3378
Jer	25:31	**the L** will bring charges against the	H3378
Jer	25:31	the wicked to the sword,’ ” declares **the L**.	H3378
Jer	25:32	This is what **the L** Almighty says: “Look	H3378
Jer	25:33	those slain by **the L** will be everywhere	H3378
Jer	25:36	for **the L** is destroying their pasture.	H3378
Jer	25:37	because of the fierce anger of **the L**.	H3378
Jer	26: 1	king of Judah, this word came from **the L**:	H3378
Jer	26: 2	“This is what **the L** says: Stand in the	H3378
Jer	26: 2	come to worship in the house of **the L**.	H3378
Jer	26: 4	‘This is what **the L** says: If you do	H3378
Jer	26: 7	speak these words in the house of **the L**.	H3378
Jer	26: 8	everything **the L** had commanded him	H3378
Jer	26: 9	around Jeremiah in the house of **the L**.	H3378
Jer	26:10	to the house of **the L** and took their places	H3378
Jer	26:12	“**The L** sent me to prophesy against this	H3378
Jer	26:13	your actions and obey **the L** your God.	H3378
Jer	26:13	Then **the L** will relent and not bring the	H3378
Jer	26:15	in truth **the L** has sent me to you to	H3378
Jer	26:16	to us in the name of **the L** our God.”	H3378
Jer	26:18	‘This is what **the L** Almighty says:	H3378
Jer	26:19	not Hezekiah fear **the L** and seek his favor	H3378
Jer	26:19	And did not **the L** relent, so that he did	H3378
Jer	26:20	who prophesied in the name of **the L**;	H3378
Jer	27: 1	this word came to Jeremiah from **the L**:	H3378
Jer	27: 2	This is what **the L** said to me: “Make a	H3378
Jer	27: 4	‘This is what **the L** Almighty, the God	H3378
Jer	27: 8	plague, declares **the L**, until I destroy it	H3378
Jer	27:11	to till it and to live there, declares **the L**.”	H3378
Jer	27:13	plague with which **the L** has threatened	H3378
Jer	27:15	sent them,’ declares **the L**. ‘They are	H3378
Jer	27:16	all these people, “This is what **the L** says:	H3378
Jer	27:18	are prophets and have the word of **the L**,	H3378
Jer	27:18	them plead with **the L** Almighty that the	H3378
Jer	27:18	in the house of **the L** and in the palace of	H3378
Jer	27:19	For this is what **the L** Almighty says about	H3378
Jer	27:21	this is what **the L** Almighty, the God of	H3378
Jer	27:21	in the house of **the L** and in the palace	H3378
Jer	27:22	the day I come for them,’ declares **the L**.	H3378
Jer	28: 1	me in the house of **the L** in the presence	H3378
Jer	28: 2	“This is what **the L** Almighty, the God of	H3378
Jer	28: 4	Babylon,’ declares **the L**, ‘for I will break	H3378
Jer	28: 5	who were standing in the house of **the L**.	H3378
Jer	28: 6	May **the L** do so! May the LORD	H3378
Jer	28: 6	May **the L** fulfill the words you have	H3378
Jer	28: 9	as one truly sent by **the L** only if his	H3378
Jer	28:11	all the people, “This is what **the L** says:	H3378
Jer	28:12	the word of **the L** came to Jeremiah:	H3378
Jer	28:13	tell Hananiah, ‘This is what **the L** says:	H3378
Jer	28:14	This is what **the L** Almighty, the God of	H3378
Jer	28:15	**The L** has not sent you, yet you have	H3378
Jer	28:16	Therefore this is what **the L** says: ‘I am	H3378
Jer	28:16	have preached rebellion against **the L**.	H3378
Jer	29: 4	This is what **the L** Almighty, the God of	H3378
Jer	29: 7	Pray to **the L** for it, because if it prospers	H3378
Jer	29: 8	this is what **the L** Almighty, the God	H3378
Jer	29: 9	I have not sent them,” declares **the L**.	H3378
Jer	29:10	This is what **the L** says: “When seventy	H3378
Jer	29:11	declares **the L**, “plans to prosper you and	H3378
Jer	29:14	declares **the L**, “and will bring you back	H3378
Jer	29:14	declares **the L**, “and will bring you back	H3378
Jer	29:15	“**The L** has raised up prophets for us in	H3378
Jer	29:16	this is what **the L** says about the king	H3378
Jer	29:17	this is what **the L** Almighty says: “I	H3378
Jer	29:19	declares **the L**, “words that I sent to them	H3378
Jer	29:19	have not listened either,” declares **the L**.	H3378
Jer	29:20	hear the word of **the L**, all you exiles	H3378
Jer	29:21	This is what **the L** Almighty, the God of	H3378
Jer	29:22	‘May **the L** treat you like Zedekiah and	H3378
Jer	29:23	it and am a witness to it,” declares **the L**.	H3378
Jer	29:25	“This is what **the L** Almighty, the God of	H3378
Jer	29:26	‘**The L** has appointed you priest in place	H3378
Jer	29:26	to be in charge of the house of **the L**;	H3378
Jer	29:30	Then the word of **the L** came to Jeremiah:	H3378
Jer	29:31	‘This is what **the L** says about Shemaiah	H3378
Jer	29:32	this is what **the L** says: I will surely punish	H3378
Jer	29:32	people, declares **the L**, because he has	H3378
Jer	30: 1	word that came to Jeremiah from **the L**:	H3378
Jer	30: 2	“This is what **the L**, the God of Israel, says	H3378
Jer	30: 3	coming,’ declares **the L**, ‘when I will bring	H3378
Jer	30: 3	their ancestors to possess,’ says **the L**.”	H3378
Jer	30: 4	are the words **the L** spoke concerning	H3378
Jer	30: 5	“This is what **the L** says: “ ‘Cries of fear	H3378
Jer	30: 8	that day,’ declares **the L** Almighty, ‘I will	H3378
Jer	30: 9	they will serve **the L** their God and David	H3378
Jer	30:10	not be dismayed, Israel,’ declares **the L**.	H3378
Jer	30:11	you and will save you,’ declares **the L**.	H3378
Jer	30:12	“This is what **the L** says: “ ‘Your wound is	H3378
Jer	30:17	wounds,’ declares **the L**, ‘because you are	H3378
Jer	30:18	“This is what **the L** says: “ ‘I will restore	H3378
Jer	30:21	to be close to me?’ declares **the L**.	H3378
Jer	30:23	the storm of **the L** will burst out in wrath	H3378
Jer	30:24	The fierce anger of **the L** will not turn back	H3378
Jer	31: 1	declares **the L**, “I will be the God of all	H3378
Jer	31: 2	This is what **the L** says: “The people who	H3378
Jer	31: 3	**The L** appeared to us in the past, saying	H3378
Jer	31: 6	let us go up to Zion, to **the L** our God.	H3378
Jer	31: 7	This is what **the L** says: “Sing with joy	H3378
Jer	31: 7	and say, ‘**L**, save your people, the	H3378
Jer	31:10	“Hear the word of **the L**, you nations	H3378
Jer	31:11	For **the L** will deliver Jacob and redeem	H3378
Jer	31:12	they will rejoice in the bounty of **the L**	H3378
Jer	31:14	be filled with my bounty,” declares **the L**.	H3378
Jer	31:15	This is what **the L** says: “A voice is heard	H3378
Jer	31:16	This is what **the L** says: “Restrain your	H3378
Jer	31:16	work will be rewarded,” declares **the L**.	H3378
Jer	31:17	your descendants,” declares **the L**.	H3378
Jer	31:18	will return, because you are **the L** my God.	H3378
Jer	31:20	great compassion for him,” declares **the L**.	H3378
Jer	31:22	**The L** will create a new thing on earth	H3378
Jer	31:23	This is what **the L** Almighty, the God of	H3378
Jer	31:23	‘**The L** bless you, you prosperous city, you	H3378
Jer	31:27	declares **the L**, “when I will plant the	H3378
Jer	31:28	to build and to plant,” declares **the L**.	H3378
Jer	31:31	declares **the L**, “when I will make a new	H3378
Jer	31:32	I was a husband to them,” declares **the L**.	H3378
Jer	31:33	of Israel after that time,” declares **the L**.	H3378
Jer	31:34	one another, ‘Know **the L**,’ because they	H3378
Jer	31:34	of them to the greatest,” declares **the L**.	H3378
Jer	31:35	This is what **the L** says, he who appoints	H3378
Jer	31:35	waves roar—**the L** Almighty is his name:	H3378
Jer	31:36	declares **the L**, “will Israel ever cease	H3378
Jer	31:37	This is what **the L** says: “Only if the	H3378
Jer	31:37	of all they have done,” declares **the L**.	H3378
Jer	31:38	declares **the L**, “when this city will be	H3378
Jer	31:40	of the Horse Gate, will be holy to **the L**.	H3378
Jer	32: 1	to Jeremiah from **the L** in the tenth year of	H3378
Jer	32: 3	‘This is what **the L** says: I am about to	H3378
Jer	32: 5	until I deal with him, declares **the L**.	H3378
Jer	32: 6	“The word of **the L** came to me:	H3378
Jer	32: 8	just as **the L** had said, my cousin	H3378
Jer	32: 8	“I knew that this was the word of **the L**;	H3378
Jer	32:14	‘This is what **the L** Almighty, the God of	H3378
Jer	32:15	For this is what **the L** Almighty, the God	H3378
Jer	32:16	to Baruch son of Neriah, I prayed to **the L**:	H3378
Jer	32:17	Sovereign **L**, you have made the	H3378
Jer	32:18	whose name is **the L** Almighty,	H3378
Jer	32:25	Sovereign **L**, say to me, ‘Buy the field	H3378
Jer	32:26	Then the word of **the L** came to Jeremiah:	H3378
Jer	32:27	“I am **the L**, the God of all mankind.	H3378
Jer	32:28	Therefore this is what **the L** says: I am	H3378
Jer	32:30	their hands have made, declares **the L**.	H3378
Jer	32:36	this is what **the L**, the God of Israel,	H3378
Jer	32:42	“This is what **the L** says: As I have	H3378
Jer	32:44	will restore their fortunes, declares **the L**.”	H3378
Jer	33: 1	the word of **the L** came to him a second	H3378
Jer	33: 2	“This is what **the L** says, he who made the	H3378
Jer	33: 2	**the L** who formed it and established it	H3378
Jer	33: 2	it and established it—**the L** is his name:	H3378
Jer	33: 4	For this is what **the L**, the God of Israel	H3378
Jer	33:10	“This is what **the L** says: ‘You say about	H3378
Jer	33:11	thank offerings to the house of **the L**,	H3378
Jer	33:11	“Give thanks to **the L** Almighty, for the	H3378
Jer	33:11	LORD Almighty, for **the L** is good; his love	H3378
Jer	33:11	the land as they were before,’ says **the L**.	H3378
Jer	33:12	“This is what **the L** Almighty says: ‘In this	H3378
Jer	33:13	of the one who counts them,’ says **the L**.	H3378
Jer	33:14	are coming,’ declares **the L**, ‘when I will	H3378
Jer	33:16	will be called: **The L** Our Righteous Savior	H3378
Jer	33:17	For this is what **the L** says: ‘David will	H3378
Jer	33:19	The word of **the L** came to Jeremiah:	H3378
Jer	33:20	“This is what **the L** says: ‘If you can break	H3378
Jer	33:23	The word of **the L** came to Jeremiah:	H3378
Jer	33:24	‘**The L** has rejected the two kingdoms he	H3378
Jer	33:25	This is what **the L** says: ‘If I have not	H3378
Jer	34: 1	this word came to Jeremiah from **the L**:	H3378
Jer	34: 2	“This is what **the L**, the God of Israel, says	H3378
Jer	34: 2	tell him, ‘This is what **the L** says:	H3378
Jer	34: 4	This is what **the L** says concerning you	H3378
Jer	34: 5	I myself make this promise, declares **the L**.	H3378
Jer	34: 8	to Jeremiah from **the L** after King	H3378
Jer	34:12	Then the word of **the L** came to Jeremiah:	H3378
Jer	34:13	“This is what **the L**, the God of Israel, says	H3378
Jer	34:17	“Therefore this is what **the L** says: You	H3378
Jer	34:17	you, declares **the L**—‘freedom’ to fall	H3378
Jer	34:22	the order, declares **the L**, and I will bring	H3378
Jer	35: 1	to Jeremiah from **the L** during the reign of	H3378
Jer	35: 2	of the house of **the L** and give them wine	H3378
Jer	35: 4	I brought them into the house of **the L**	H3378
Jer	35:12	Then the word of **the L** came to Jeremiah	H3378
Jer	35:13	“This is what **the L** Almighty, the God of	H3378
Jer	35:13	obey my words?’ declares **the L**.	H3378
Jer	35:17	this is what **the L** God Almighty,	H3378
Jer	35:18	“This is what **the L** Almighty, the God of	H3378
Jer	35:19	Therefore this is what **the L** Almighty, the	H3378
Jer	36: 1	this word came to Jeremiah from **the L**:	H3378
Jer	36: 4	all the words **the L** had spoken to him,	H3378
Jer	36: 6	go to the house of **the L** on a day of	H3378
Jer	36: 6	scroll the words of **the L** that you wrote as	H3378
Jer	36: 7	petition before **the L** and will each turn	H3378

Jer 36: 7 against this people by **the L** are great." H3378
Jer 36: 8 he read the words of **the L** from the scroll. H3378
Jer 36: 9 of fasting before **the L** was proclaimed H3378
Jer 36:11 all the words of **the L** from the scroll, H3378
Jer 36:26 But **the L** had hidden them. H3378
Jer 36:27 the word of **the L** came to Jeremiah: H3378
Jer 36:29 king of Judah, 'This is what **the L** says: H3378
Jer 36:30 this is what **the L** says about Jehoiakim H3378
Jer 37: 2 to the words **the L** had spoken through H3378
Jer 37: 3 "Please pray to **the L** our God for us." H3378
Jer 37: 6 Then the word of **the L** came to Jeremiah H3378
Jer 37: 7 "This is what **the L**, the God of Israel, says H3378
Jer 37: 9 "This is what **the L** says: Do not deceive H3378
Jer 37:17 privately, "Is there any word from **the L**?" H3378
Jer 38: 2 "This is what **the L** says: 'Whoever stays H3378
Jer 38: 3 And this is what **the L** says: 'This city will H3378
Jer 38:14 the third entrance to the temple of **the L**. H3378
Jer 38:16 "As surely as **the L** lives, who has given us H3378
Jer 38:17 "This is what **the L** God Almighty, the God H3378
Jer 38:20 "Obey **the L** by doing what I tell you H3378
Jer 38:21 this is what **the L** has revealed to me: H3378
Jer 39:15 the guard, the word of **the L** came to him: H3378
Jer 39:16 'This is what **the L** Almighty, the God of H3378
Jer 39:17 that day, declares **the L**; you will not be H3378
Jer 39:18 because you trust in me, declares **the L**. H3378
Jer 40: 1 to Jeremiah from **the L** after Nebuzaradan H3378
Jer 40: 2 "**The L** your God decreed this disaster H3378
Jer 40: 3 And now **the L** has brought it about; he H3378
Jer 40: 3 sinned against **the L** and did not obey H3378
Jer 41: 5 incense with them to the house of **the L**. H3378
Jer 42: 2 petition and pray to **the L** your God for H3378
Jer 42: 3 Pray that **the L** your God will tell us where H3378
Jer 42: 4 certainly pray to **the L** your God as you H3378
Jer 42: 4 you everything **the L** says and will keep H3378
Jer 42: 5 "May **the L** be a true and faithful witness H3378
Jer 42: 5 with everything **the L** your God sends you H3378
Jer 42: 6 we will obey **the L** our God, to whom we H3378
Jer 42: 6 with us, for we will obey **the L** our God." H3378
Jer 42: 7 later the word of **the L** came to Jeremiah. H3378
Jer 42: 9 "This is what **the L**, the God of Israel H3378
Jer 42:11 declares **the L**, for I am with you H3378
Jer 42:13 this land,' and so disobey **the L** your God, H3378
Jer 42:15 then hear the word of **the L**, you remnant H3378
Jer 42:15 This is what **the L** Almighty, the God of H3378
Jer 42:18 This is what **the L** Almighty, the God of H3378
Jer 42:19 of Judah, **the L** has told you, 'Do H3378
Jer 42:20 you sent me to **the L** your God and said, H3378
Jer 42:20 said, 'Pray to **the L** our God for us; tell H3378
Jer 42:21 have not obeyed **the L** your God in all he H3378
Jer 43: 1 people all the words of **the L** their God— H3378
Jer 43: 1 everything **the L** had sent him to tell them H3378
Jer 43: 2 **The L** our God has not sent you to say H3378
Jer 43: 7 in disobedience to **the L** and went as far H3378
Jer 43: 8 the word of **the L** came to Jeremiah: H3378
Jer 43:10 'This is what **the L** Almighty, the God H3378
Jer 44: 2 "This is what **the L** Almighty, the God of H3378
Jer 44: 7 "Now this is what **the L** God Almighty, H3378
Jer 44:11 "Therefore this is what **the L** Almighty, H3378
Jer 44:16 have spoken to us in the name of **the L**! H3378
Jer 44:21 "Did not **the L** remember and call to mind H3378
Jer 44:22 When **the L** could no longer endure your H3378
Jer 44:23 have sinned against **the L** and have not H3378
Jer 44:24 "Hear the word of **the L**, all you people of H3378
Jer 44:25 This is what **the L** Almighty, the God of H3378
Jer 44:26 But hear the word of **the L**, all you Jews H3378
Jer 44:26 great name,' says **the L**, 'that no one from H3378
Jer 44:26 "As surely as **the** Sovereign **L** lives." H3378
Jer 44:29 declares **the L**, 'so that you will H3378
Jer 44:30 This is what **the L** says: 'I am going to H3378
Jer 45: 2 "This is what **the L**, the God of Israel, says H3378
Jer 45: 3 **The L** has added sorrow to my pain; I am H3378
Jer 45: 4 But the **L** has told me to say to you, 'This is NDT
Jer 45: 4 me to say to you, 'This is what **the L** says: H3378
Jer 45: 5 people, declares **the L**, but wherever you H3378
Jer 46: 1 This is the word of **the L** that came to H3378
Jer 46: 5 is terror on every side," declares **the L**. H3378
Jer 46:10 to the Lord, **the L** Almighty—a day of H3378
Jer 46:10 For the Lord, **the L** Almighty, will offer H3378
Jer 46:13 is the message **the L** spoke to Jeremiah H3378
Jer 46:15 for **the L** will push them down. H3378
Jer 46:18 whose name is **the L** Almighty, "one H3378
Jer 46:23 declares **the L**, "dense though it H3378
Jer 46:25 **The L** Almighty, the God of Israel, says: H3378
Jer 46:26 as in times past," declares **the L**. H3378
Jer 46:28 servant, for I am with you," declares **the L**. H3378
Jer 47: 1 This is the word of **the L** that came to H3378
Jer 47: 2 This is what **the L** says: "See how the H3378
Jer 47: 4 **The L** is about to destroy the Philistines H3378
Jer 47: 6 sword of **the L**, how long till you H3378
Jer 47: 7 can it rest when **the L** has commanded it, H3378
Jer 48: 1 This is what **the L** Almighty, the God of H3378
Jer 48: 8 destroyed, because **the L** has spoken. H3378
Jer 48:12 declares **the L**, "when I will send men H3378
Jer 48:15 the King, whose name is **the L** Almighty. H3378
Jer 48:25 her arm is broken," declares **the L**. H3378
Jer 48:26 she has defied **the L**. Let Moab wallow H3378
Jer 48:30 declares **the L**, "and her boasts H3378
Jer 48:35 incense to their gods," declares **the L**. H3378
Jer 48:38 a jar that no one wants," declares **the L**. H3378
Jer 48:40 This is what **the L** says: "Look! An eagle H3378
Jer 48:42 as a nation because she defied **the L**. H3378
Jer 48:43 you people of Moab," declares **the L**. H3378

Jer 48:44 year of her punishment," declares **the L**. H3378
Jer 48:47 of Moab in days to come," declares **the L**. H3378
Jer 49: 1 This is what **the L** says: "Has Israel no H3378
Jer 49: 2 declares **the L**, "when I will sound the H3378
Jer 49: 2 out those who drove her out," says **the L**. H3378
Jer 49: 5 declares the Lord, **the L** Almighty. H3378
Jer 49: 6 of the Ammonites," declares **the L**. H3378
Jer 49: 7 This is what **the L** Almighty says H3378
Jer 49:12 This is what **the L** says: "If those who do H3378
Jer 49:13 declares **the L**, "that Bozrah will become H3378
Jer 49:14 I have heard a message from **the L**; an H3378
Jer 49:16 I will bring you down," declares **the L**. H3378
Jer 49:18 says **the L**, "so no one will live H3378
Jer 49:20 hear what **the L** has planned against H3378
Jer 49:26 in that day," declares **the L** Almighty. H3378
Jer 49:28 This is what **the L** says: "Arise, H3378
Jer 49:30 you who live in Hazor," declares **the L**. H3378
Jer 49:31 declares **the L**, "a nation that has neither H3378
Jer 49:32 on them from every side," declares **the L**. H3378
Jer 49:34 This is the word of **the L** that came to H3378
Jer 49:35 This is what **the L** Almighty says: "See, H3378
Jer 49:37 even my fierce anger," declares **the L**. H3378
Jer 49:38 her king and officials," declares **the L**. H3378
Jer 49:39 of Elam in days to come," declares **the L**. H3378
Jer 50: 1 This is the word **the L** spoke through H3378
Jer 50: 4 declares **the L**, "the people of Israel and H3378
Jer 50: 4 will go in tears to seek **the L** their God. H3378
Jer 50: 5 bind themselves to **the L** in an everlasting H3378
Jer 50: 7 they sinned against **the L**, their verdant H3378
Jer 50: 7 verdant pasture, **the L**, the hope of their H3378
Jer 50:10 her will have their fill," declares **the L**. H3378
Jer 50:14 for she has sinned against **the L**. H3378
Jer 50:15 Since this is the vengeance of **the L**, take H3378
Jer 50:18 Therefore this is what **the L** Almighty, the H3378
Jer 50:20 declares **the L**, "search will be made for H3378
Jer 50:21 completely destroy them," declares **the L**. H3378
Jer 50:24 captured because you opposed **the L**. H3378
Jer 50:25 **The L** has opened his arsenal and H3378
Jer 50:25 for the Sovereign **L** Almighty has work to H3378
Jer 50:28 in Zion how **the L** our God has taken H3378
Jer 50:29 For she has defied **the L**, the Holy One of H3378
Jer 50:30 be silenced in that day," declares **the L**. H3378
Jer 50:31 declares the Lord, **the L** Almighty, "for H3378
Jer 50:33 This is what **the L** Almighty says: "The H3378
Jer 50:34 is strong; **the L** Almighty is his name. H3378
Jer 50:35 declares **the L**—"against those who live H3378
Jer 50:40 declares **the L**, "so no one will H3378
Jer 50:45 hear what **the L** has planned against H3378
Jer 51: 1 This is what **the L** says: "See, I will stir up H3378
Jer 51: 5 by their God, **the L** Almighty, though their H3378
Jer 51:10 " '**The L** has vindicated us; come, let us H3378
Jer 51:10 tell in Zion what **the L** our God has done. H3378
Jer 51:11 **The L** has stirred up the kings of the H3378
Jer 51:11 **The L** will take vengeance, vengeance H3378
Jer 51:12 **The L** will carry out his purpose, his H3378
Jer 51:14 **The L** Almighty has sworn by himself: H3378
Jer 51:19 inheritance—**the L** Almighty is his name. H3378
Jer 51:24 they have done in Zion," declares **the L**. H3378
Jer 51:25 destroy the whole earth," declares **the L**. H3378
Jer 51:26 will be desolate forever," declares **the L**. H3378
Jer 51:33 This is what **the L** Almighty, the God of H3378
Jer 51:36 Therefore this is what **the L** says: "See, H3378
Jer 51:39 forever and not awake," declares **the L**. H3378
Jer 51:45 Run from the fierce anger of **the L**. H3378
Jer 51:48 destroyers will attack her," declares **the L**. H3378
Jer 51:50 Remember **the L** in a distant land, and H3378
Jer 51:52 declares **the L**, "when I will punish her H3378
Jer 51:53 destroyers against her," declares **the L**. H3378
Jer 51:55 **The L** will destroy Babylon; he will H3378
Jer 51:56 For **the L** is a God of retribution; he will H3378
Jer 51:57 the King, whose name is **the L** Almighty. H3378
Jer 51:58 This is what **the L** Almighty says H3378
Jer 51:62 Then say, '**L**, you have said you will H3378
Jer 52: 2 He did evil in the eyes of **the L**, just as H3378
Jer 52:13 He set fire to the temple of **the L**, the royal H3378
Jer 52:17 at the temple of **the L** and they carried all H3378
Jer 52:20 had made for the temple of **the L**, H3378
La 1: 5 **The L** has brought her grief because of H3378
La 1: 9 **L**, on my affliction, for the enemy H3378
La 1:11 "Look, **L**, and consider, for I am H3378
La 1:12 that **the L** brought on me in the day of his H3378
La 1:17 **The L** has decreed for Jacob that his H3378
La 1:18 "**The L** is righteous, yet I rebelled against H3378
La 1:20 **L**, how distressed I am! I am in H3378
La 2: 6 **The L** has made Zion forget her H3378
La 2: 7 in the house of **the L** as on the day of an H3378
La 2: 8 **The L** determined to tear down the wall H3378
La 2: 9 prophets no longer find visions from **the L**. H3378
La 2:17 **The L** has done what he planned; he has H3378
La 2:20 **L**, and consider: Whom have you H3378
La 3:18 gone and all that I had hoped from **the L**." H3378
La 3:24 I say to myself, "**The L** is my portion H3378
La 3:25 **The L** is good to those whose hope is in H3378
La 3:26 to wait quietly for the salvation of **the L**. H3378
La 3:28 alone in silence, for the L has laid it on him. NDT
La 3:40 test them, and let us return to **the L**. H3378
La 3:50 until **the L** looks down from heaven and H3378
La 3:55 on your name, **L**, from the depths of H3378
La 3:59 **L**, you have seen the wrong done to me H3378
La 3:61 **L**, you have heard their insults, all their H3378
La 3:64 what they deserve, **L**, for what their hands H3378
La 3:66 them from under the heavens of **the L**. H3378

La 4:11 **The L** has given full vent to his wrath; he H3378
La 4:16 **The L himself** has scattered them H7156+3378
La 5: 1 Remember, **L**, what has happened to us H3378
La 5:19 **L**, reign forever; your throne endures H3378
La 5:21 us to yourself, **L**, that we may return; H3378
Eze 1: 3 the word of **the L** came to Ezekiel the H3378
Eze 1: 3 There the hand of **the L** was on him. H3378
Eze 1:28 of the likeness of the glory of **the L**. H3378
Eze 2: 4 'This is what **the** Sovereign **L** says.' H3378
Eze 3:11 'This is what **the** Sovereign **L** says,' H3378
Eze 3:12 as the glory of **the L** rose from the place H3378
Eze 3:14 with the strong hand of **the L** on me. H3378
Eze 3:16 seven days the word of **the L** came to me: H3378
Eze 3:22 The hand of **the L** was on me there, and H3378
Eze 3:23 And the glory of **the L** was standing there H3378
Eze 3:27 'This is what **the** Sovereign **L** says.' H3378
Eze 4:13 **The L** said, "In this way the people of H3378
Eze 4:14 "Not so, Sovereign **L**! I have never defiled H3378
Eze 5: 5 "This is what **the** Sovereign **L** says: This H3378
Eze 5: 7 this is what **the** Sovereign **L** says: H3378
Eze 5: 8 this is what **the** Sovereign **L** says: H3378
Eze 5:11 declares **the** Sovereign **L**, because you H3378
Eze 5:13 will know that I **the L** have spoken in my H3378
Eze 5:15 with stinging rebuke. I **the L** have spoken. H3378
Eze 5:17 sword against you. I **the L** have spoken." H3378
Eze 6: 1 The word of **the L** came to me: H3378
Eze 6: 3 hear the word of **the** Sovereign **L**. H3378
Eze 6: 3 This is what **the** Sovereign **L** says to the H3378
Eze 6: 7 and you will know that I am **the L**. H3378
Eze 6:10 And they will know that I am **the L**; I did H3378
Eze 6:11 " 'This is what **the** Sovereign **L** says: H3378
Eze 6:13 And they will know that I am **the L**, when H3378
Eze 6:14 Then they will know that I am **the L**.' " H3378
Eze 7: 1 The word of **the L** came to me: H3378
Eze 7: 2 this is what **the** Sovereign **L** says to the H3378
Eze 7: 4 " 'Then you will know that I am **the L**.' H3378
Eze 7: 5 "This is what **the** Sovereign **L** says: H3378
Eze 7: 9 will know that it is I **the L** who strikes you. H3378
Eze 7:27 " 'Then they will know that I am **the L**.' " H3378
Eze 8: 1 the hand of the Sovereign **L** came on me H3378
Eze 8:12 say, '**The L** does not see us; the LORD H3378
Eze 8:12 not see us; **the L** has forsaken the land. H3378
Eze 8:14 of the north gate of the house of **the L**, H3378
Eze 8:16 into the inner court of the house of **the L**, H3378
Eze 8:16 toward the temple of **the L** and their faces H3378
Eze 9: 3 Then the L called to the man clothed in NDT
Eze 9: 8 facedown, crying out, "Alas, Sovereign **L**! H3378
Eze 9: 9 They say, '**The L** has forsaken the land H3378
Eze 9: 9 has forsaken the land; **the L** does not see. H3378
Eze 10: 2 The L said to the man clothed in linen, "Go NDT
Eze 10: 4 Then the glory of **the L** rose from above H3378
Eze 10: 4 full of the radiance of the glory of **the L**. H3378
Eze 10: 6 When **the L** commanded the man in H2257S
Eze 10:18 Then the glory of **the L** departed from over H3378
Eze 11: 1 gate of the house of **the L** that faces east. H3378
Eze 11: 2 The L said to me, "Son of man, these are NDT
Eze 11: 5 Then the Spirit of **the L** came on me, and H3378
Eze 11: 5 "This is what **the L** says: That is what H3378
Eze 11: 7 this is what **the** Sovereign **L** says: H3378
Eze 11: 8 against you, declares **the** Sovereign **L**. H3378
Eze 11:10 Then you will know that I am **the L**. H3378
Eze 11:12 And you will know that I am **the L**, for H3378
Eze 11:13 out in a loud voice, "Alas, Sovereign **L**! H3378
Eze 11:14 The word of **the L** came to me: H3378
Eze 11:15 'They are far away from **the L**; this land H3378
Eze 11:16 'This is what **the** Sovereign **L** says H3378
Eze 11:17 'This is what **the** Sovereign **L** says: I will H3378
Eze 11:21 they have done, declares **the** Sovereign **L**." H3378
Eze 11:23 The glory of **the L** went up from within H3378
Eze 11:25 the exiles everything **the L** had shown me. H3378
Eze 12: 1 The word of **the L** came to me: H3378
Eze 12: 8 morning the word of **the L** came to me: H3378
Eze 12:10 'This is what **the** Sovereign **L** says: H3378
Eze 12:15 "They will know that I am **the L**, when I H3378
Eze 12:16 Then they will know that I am **the L**." H3378
Eze 12:17 The word of **the L** came to me: H3378
Eze 12:19 'This is what **the** Sovereign **L** says about H3378
Eze 12:20 Then you will know that I am **the L**.' " H3378
Eze 12:21 The word of **the L** came to me: H3378
Eze 12:23 'This is what **the** Sovereign **L** says: H3378
Eze 12:25 But I **the L** will speak what I will, and it H3378
Eze 12:25 whatever I say, declares **the** Sovereign **L**. H3378
Eze 12:26 The word of **the L** came to me: H3378
Eze 12:28 'This is what **the** Sovereign **L** says: H3378
Eze 12:28 will be fulfilled, declares **the** Sovereign **L**. H3378
Eze 13: 1 The word of **the L** came to me: H3378
Eze 13: 2 own imagination: 'Hear the word of **the L**! H3378
Eze 13: 3 This is what **the** Sovereign **L** says: Woe to H3378
Eze 13: 5 firm in the battle on the day of **the L**. H3378
Eze 13: 6 Even though **the L** has not sent them, they H3378
Eze 13: 6 they say, "**The L** declares," and expect H3378
Eze 13: 7 when you say, "**The L** declares," though I H3378
Eze 13: 8 this is what **the** Sovereign **L** says: H3378
Eze 13: 8 am against you, declares **the** Sovereign **L**. H3378
Eze 13: 9 you will know that I am **the** Sovereign **L**. H3378
Eze 13:13 this is what **the** Sovereign **L** says: H3378
Eze 13:14 and you will know that I am **the L**. H3378
Eze 13:16 was no peace, declares **the** Sovereign **L**." H3378
Eze 13:18 'This is what **the** Sovereign **L** says: H3378
Eze 13:20 this is what **the** Sovereign **L** says: H3378
Eze 13:21 Then you will know that I am **the L**. H3378
Eze 13:23 And then you will know that I am **the L**.' " H3378

Book	Ref	Context	Number
Eze	14: 2	Then the word of **the L** came to me:	H3378
Eze	14: 4	'This is what **the** Sovereign **L** says:	H3378
Eze	14: 4	I **the L** will answer them myself in keeping	H3378
Eze	14: 6	'This is what **the** Sovereign **L** says:	H3378
Eze	14: 7	I **the L** will answer them myself.	H3378
Eze	14: 8	Then you will know that I am **the L**.	H3378
Eze	14: 9	I **the L** have enticed that prophet	H3378
Eze	14:11	be their God, declares **the** Sovereign **L**.	H3378
Eze	14:12	The word of **the L** came to me:	H3378
Eze	14:14	righteousness, declares **the** Sovereign **L**.	H3378
Eze	14:16	declares **the** Sovereign **L**, even if	H3378
Eze	14:18	declares **the** Sovereign **L**, even if	H3378
Eze	14:20	declares **the** Sovereign **L**, even if Noah	H3378
Eze	14:21	"For this is what **the** Sovereign **L** says	H3378
Eze	14:23	it without cause, declares **the** Sovereign **L**."	H3378
Eze	15: 1	The word of **the L** came to me:	H3378
Eze	15: 6	this is what **the** Sovereign **L** says:	H3378
Eze	15: 7	you will know that I am **the L**.	H3378
Eze	15: 8	been unfaithful, declares **the** Sovereign **L**."	H3378
Eze	16: 1	The word of **the L** came to me:	H3378
Eze	16: 3	'This is what **the** Sovereign **L** says to	H3378
Eze	16: 8	declares **the** Sovereign **L**, and you	H3378
Eze	16:14	beauty perfect, declares **the** Sovereign **L**.	H3378
Eze	16:19	what happened, declares **the** Sovereign **L**.	H3378
Eze	16:23	declares **the** Sovereign **L**. In addition	H3378
Eze	16:30	declares **the** Sovereign **L**, when you do	H3378
Eze	16:35	you prostitute, hear the word of **the L**!	H3378
Eze	16:36	This is what **the** Sovereign **L** says:	H3378
Eze	16:43	you have done, declares **the** Sovereign **L**.	H3378
Eze	16:48	declares **the** Sovereign **L**, your sister	H3378
Eze	16:58	your detestable practices, declares **the L**.	H3378
Eze	16:59	" 'This is what **the** Sovereign **L** says: I will	H3378
Eze	16:62	and you will know that I am **the L**.	H3378
Eze	16:63	humiliation, declares **the** Sovereign **L**.	H3378
Eze	17: 1	The word of **the L** came to me:	H3378
Eze	17: 3	'This is what **the** Sovereign **L** says:	H3378
Eze	17: 9	'This is what **the** Sovereign **L** says:	H3378
Eze	17:11	Then the word of **the L** came to me:	H3378
Eze	17:16	declares **the** Sovereign **L**, he shall die	H3378
Eze	17:19	this is what **the** Sovereign **L** says:	H3378
Eze	17:21	you will know that I **the L** have spoken.	H3378
Eze	17:22	" 'This is what **the** Sovereign **L** says:	H3378
Eze	17:24	will know that I **the L** bring down the tall	H3378
Eze	17:24	" 'I **the L** have spoken, and I	H3378
Eze	18: 1	The word of **the L** came to me:	H3378
Eze	18: 3	declares **the** Sovereign **L**, you will no	H3378
Eze	18: 9	will surely live, declares **the** Sovereign **L**.	H3378
Eze	18:23	declares **the** Sovereign **L**. Rather,	H3378
Eze	18:30	your own ways, declares **the** Sovereign **L**.	H3378
Eze	18:32	of anyone, declares **the** Sovereign **L**.	H3378
Eze	20: 1	elders of Israel came to inquire of **the L**,	H3378
Eze	20: 2	Then the word of **the L** came to me:	H3378
Eze	20: 3	'This is what **the** Sovereign **L** says:	H3378
Eze	20: 3	inquire of me, declares **the** Sovereign **L**.	H3378
Eze	20: 5	'This is what **the** Sovereign **L** says: On the	H3378
Eze	20: 5	I said to them, "I am **the L** your God."	H3378
Eze	20: 7	the idols of Egypt. I am **the L** your God."	H3378
Eze	20:12	would know that I **the L** made them holy.	H3378
Eze	20:19	I am **the L** your God; follow my decrees	H3378
Eze	20:20	you will know that I am **the L** your God."	H3378
Eze	20:26	horror so they would know that I am **the L**.	H3378
Eze	20:27	'This is what **the** Sovereign **L** says:	H3378
Eze	20:30	'This is what **the** Sovereign **L** says: Will	H3378
Eze	20:31	declares **the** Sovereign **L**, I will not	H3378
Eze	20:33	declares **the** Sovereign **L**, I will reign	H3378
Eze	20:36	I will judge you, declares **the** Sovereign **L**.	H3378
Eze	20:38	Then you will know that I am **the L**.	H3378
Eze	20:39	of Israel, this is what **the** Sovereign **L** says:	H3378
Eze	20:40	declares **the** Sovereign **L**, there in the	H3378
Eze	20:42	Then you will know that I am **the L**, when	H3378
Eze	20:44	You will know that I am **the L**, when I deal	H3378
Eze	20:44	people of Israel, declares **the** Sovereign **L**.	H3378
Eze	20:45	The word of **the L** came to me:	H3378
Eze	20:47	'Hear the word of **the L**. This is what the	H3378
Eze	20:47	This is what the Sovereign **L** says: I am	H3378
Eze	20:48	will see that I **the L** have kindled it;	H3378
Eze	20:49	"Sovereign **L**, they are saying of me	H3378
Eze	21: 1	The word of **the L** came to me:	H3378
Eze	21: 3	'This is what **the L** says: I am against	H3378
Eze	21: 5	will know that I **the L** have drawn my	H3378
Eze	21: 7	take place, declares **the** Sovereign **L**."	H3378
Eze	21: 8	The word of **the L** came to me:	H3378
Eze	21:13	not continue? declares **the** Sovereign **L**.'	H3378
Eze	21:17	wrath will subside. I **the L** have spoken."	H3378
Eze	21:18	The word of **the L** came to me:	H3378
Eze	21:24	this is what **the** Sovereign **L** says:	H3378
Eze	21:26	this is what **the** Sovereign **L** says: Take off	H3378
Eze	21:28	'This is what **the** Sovereign **L** says about	H3378
Eze	21:32	no more; for I **the L** have spoken.	H3378
Eze	22: 1	The word of **the L** came to me:	H3378
Eze	22: 3	'This is what **the** Sovereign **L** says: You	H3378
Eze	22:12	forgotten me, declares **the** Sovereign **L**.	H3378
Eze	22:14	I deal with you? I **the L** have spoken, and	H3378
Eze	22:16	the nations, you will know that I am **the L**.	H3378
Eze	22:17	Then the word of **the L** came to me:	H3378
Eze	22:19	Therefore this is what **the** Sovereign **L** says:	H3378
Eze	22:22	will know that I **the L** have poured out my	H3378
Eze	22:23	Again the word of **the L** came to me:	H3378
Eze	22:28	'This is what **the** Sovereign **L** says'—	H3378
Eze	22:28	LORD says'—when **the L** has not spoken.	H3378
Eze	22:31	they have done, declares **the** Sovereign **L**."	H3378
Eze	23: 1	The word of **the L** came to me:	H3378
Eze	23:22	this is what **the** Sovereign **L** says:	H3378
Eze	23:28	"For this is what **the** Sovereign **L** says:	H3378
Eze	23:32	"This is what **the** Sovereign **L** says: "You	H3378
Eze	23:34	I have spoken, declares **the** Sovereign **L**.	H3378
Eze	23:35	this is what **the** Sovereign **L** says:	H3378
Eze	23:36	**The L** said to me: "Son of man, will you	H3378
Eze	23:46	"This is what **the** Sovereign **L** says: Bring	H3378
Eze	23:49	you will know that I am **the** Sovereign **L**."	H3378
Eze	24: 1	tenth day, the word of **the L** came to me:	H3378
Eze	24: 3	'This is what **the** Sovereign **L** says: " 'Put	H3378
Eze	24: 6	" 'For this is what **the** Sovereign **L** says:	H3378
Eze	24: 9	this is what **the** Sovereign **L** says:	H3378
Eze	24:14	" 'I **the L** have spoken. The time has come	H3378
Eze	24:14	your actions, declares **the** Sovereign **L**.	H3378
Eze	24:15	The word of **the L** came to me:	H3378
Eze	24:20	to them, "The word of **the L** came to me:	H3378
Eze	24:21	'This is what **the** Sovereign **L** says:	H3378
Eze	24:24	you will know that I am **the** Sovereign **L**.	H3378
Eze	24:27	and they will know that I am **the L**.	H3378
Eze	25: 1	The word of **the L** came to me:	H3378
Eze	25: 3	'Hear the word of **the** Sovereign **L**.	H3378
Eze	25: 3	This is what **the** Sovereign **L** says	H3378
Eze	25: 5	Then you will know that I am **the L**.	H3378
Eze	25: 6	For this is what **the** Sovereign **L** says	H3378
Eze	25: 7	and you will know that I am **the L**.	H3378
Eze	25: 8	"This is what **the** Sovereign **L** says	H3378
Eze	25:11	Then they will know that I am **the L**.' "	H3378
Eze	25:12	"This is what **the** Sovereign **L** says	H3378
Eze	25:13	therefore this is what **the** Sovereign **L** says	H3378
Eze	25:14	my vengeance, declares **the** Sovereign **L**.	H3378
Eze	25:15	"This is what **the** Sovereign **L** says	H3378
Eze	25:16	therefore this is what **the** Sovereign **L** says	H3378
Eze	25:17	Then they will know that I am **the L**, when	H3378
Eze	26: 1	the month, the word of **the L** came to me:	H3378
Eze	26: 3	therefore this is what **the** Sovereign **L** says	H3378
Eze	26: 5	I have spoken, declares **the** Sovereign **L**.	H3378
Eze	26: 6	Then they will know that I am **the L**.	H3378
Eze	26: 7	"For this is what **the** Sovereign **L** says	H3378
Eze	26:14	be rebuilt, for I **the L** have spoken	H3378
Eze	26:14	have spoken, declares **the** Sovereign **L**.	H3378
Eze	26:15	"This is what **the** Sovereign **L** says to Tyre	H3378
Eze	26:19	"This is what **the** Sovereign **L** says: When	H3378
Eze	26:21	again be found, declares **the** Sovereign **L**."	H3378
Eze	27: 1	The word of **the L** came to me:	H3378
Eze	27: 3	'This is what **the** Sovereign **L** says:	H3378
Eze	28: 1	The word of **the L** came to me:	H3378
Eze	28: 2	'This is what **the** Sovereign **L** says:	H3378
Eze	28: 6	this is what **the** Sovereign **L** says:	H3378
Eze	28:10	have spoken, declares **the** Sovereign **L**.' "	H3378
Eze	28:11	The word of **the L** came to me:	H3378
Eze	28:12	'This is what **the** Sovereign **L** says: " 'You	H3378
Eze	28:20	The word of **the L** came to me:	H3378
Eze	28:22	'This is what **the** Sovereign **L** says: " 'I am	H3378
Eze	28:22	You will know that I am **the L**, when I	H3378
Eze	28:23	Then you will know that I am **the L**.	H3378
Eze	28:24	they will know that I am **the** Sovereign **L**.	H3378
Eze	28:25	" 'This is what **the** Sovereign **L** says	H3378
Eze	28:26	they will know that I am **the L** their God.	H3378
Eze	29: 1	twelfth day, the word of **the L** came to me:	H3378
Eze	29: 3	'This is what **the** Sovereign **L** says: " 'I am	H3378
Eze	29: 6	live in Egypt will know that I am **the L**.	H3378
Eze	29: 8	this is what **the** Sovereign **L** says:	H3378
Eze	29: 9	Then they will know that I am **the L**.	H3378
Eze	29:13	" 'Yet this is what **the** Sovereign **L** says:	H3378
Eze	29:16	they will know that I am **the** Sovereign **L**.	H3378
Eze	29:17	first day, the word of **the L** came to me:	H3378
Eze	29:19	Therefore this is what **the** Sovereign **L** says:	H3378
Eze	29:20	did it for me, declares **the** Sovereign **L**.	H3378
Eze	29:21	Then they will know that I am **the L**."	H3378
Eze	30: 1	The word of **the L** came to me:	H3378
Eze	30: 2	'This is what **the** Sovereign **L** says: " 'Wail	H3378
Eze	30: 3	the day of **the L** is near—a day of	H3378
Eze	30: 6	" 'This is what **the L** says: " 'The allies of	H3378
Eze	30: 6	within her, declares **the** Sovereign **L**.	H3378
Eze	30: 8	Then they will know that I am **the L**, when	H3378
Eze	30:10	" 'This is what **the** Sovereign **L** says: " 'I	H3378
Eze	30:12	everything in it. I **the L** have spoken.	H3378
Eze	30:13	" 'This is what **the** Sovereign **L** says: " 'I	H3378
Eze	30:19	and they will know that I am **the L**.	H3378
Eze	30:20	the word of **the L** came to me:	H3378
Eze	30:22	Therefore this is what **the** Sovereign **L** says:	H3378
Eze	30:25	Then they will know that I am **the L**, when	H3378
Eze	30:26	Then they will know that I am **the L**."	H3378
Eze	31: 1	first day, the word of **the L** came to me:	H3378
Eze	31:10	this is what **the** Sovereign **L** says:	H3378
Eze	31:15	" 'This is what **the** Sovereign **L** says: On	H3378
Eze	31:18	all his hordes, declares **the** Sovereign **L**.	H3378
Eze	32: 1	first day, the word of **the L** came to me:	H3378
Eze	32: 3	" 'This is what **the** Sovereign **L** says:	H3378
Eze	32: 8	over your land, declares **the** Sovereign **L**.	H3378
Eze	32:11	" 'For this is what **the** Sovereign **L** says:	H3378
Eze	32:14	flow like oil, declares **the** Sovereign **L**.	H3378
Eze	32:15	then they will know that I am **the L**.	H3378
Eze	32:16	will chant it, declares **the** Sovereign **L**."	H3378
Eze	32:17	the month, the word of **the L** came to me:	H3378
Eze	32:31	by the sword, declares **the** Sovereign **L**.	H3378
Eze	32:32	by the sword, declares **the** Sovereign **L**."	H3378
Eze	33: 1	The word of **the L** came to me:	H3378
Eze	33:11	declares **the** Sovereign **L**, I take no	H3378
Eze	33:22	the hand of **the L** was on me, and he	H3378
Eze	33:23	Then the word of **the L** came to me:	H3378
Eze	33:25	'This is what **the** Sovereign **L** says:	H3378
Eze	33:27	'This is what **the** Sovereign **L** says: As	H3378
Eze	33:29	Then they will know that I am **the L**, when	H3378
Eze	33:30	the message that has come from **the L**.	H3378
Eze	34: 1	The word of **the L** came to me:	H3378
Eze	34: 2	'This is what **the** Sovereign **L** says: Woe to	H3378
Eze	34: 7	you shepherds, hear the word of **the L**:	H3378
Eze	34: 8	declares **the** Sovereign **L**, because my	H3378
Eze	34: 9	you shepherds, hear the word of **the L**:	H3378
Eze	34:10	This is what **the** Sovereign **L** says: I am	H3378
Eze	34:11	" 'For this is what **the** Sovereign **L** says:	H3378
Eze	34:15	them lie down, declares **the** Sovereign **L**.	H3378
Eze	34:17	flock, this is what **the** Sovereign **L** says:	H3378
Eze	34:20	this is what **the** Sovereign **L** says to them:	H3378
Eze	34:24	I **the L** will be their God, and my servant	H3378
Eze	34:24	prince among them. I **the L** have spoken.	H3378
Eze	34:27	They will know that I am **the L**, when I	H3378
Eze	34:30	will know that I, **the L** their God, am with	H3378
Eze	34:30	are my people, declares **the** Sovereign **L**.	H3378
Eze	34:31	I am your God, declares **the** Sovereign **L**.	H3378
Eze	35: 1	The word of **the L** came to me:	H3378
Eze	35: 3	'This is what **the** Sovereign **L** says: I am	H3378
Eze	35: 4	Then you will know that I am **the L**.	H3378
Eze	35: 6	declares **the** Sovereign **L**, I will give	H3378
Eze	35: 9	Then you will know that I am **the L**.	H3378
Eze	35:10	of them," even though I **the L** was there,	H3378
Eze	35:11	declares **the** Sovereign **L**, I will treat	H3378
Eze	35:12	will know that I **the L** have heard all the	H3378
Eze	35:14	This is what **the** Sovereign **L** says: While	H3378
Eze	35:15	Then they will know that I am **the L**.' "	H3378
Eze	36: 1	of Israel, hear the word of **the L**.	H3378
Eze	36: 2	This is what **the** Sovereign **L** says: The	H3378
Eze	36: 3	'This is what **the** Sovereign **L** says:	H3378
Eze	36: 4	hear the word of **the** Sovereign **L**:	H3378
Eze	36: 4	This is what **the** Sovereign **L** says to the	H3378
Eze	36: 5	this is what **the** Sovereign **L** says: In my	H3378
Eze	36: 6	'This is what **the** Sovereign **L** says: I speak	H3378
Eze	36: 7	Therefore this is what **the** Sovereign **L** says:	H3378
Eze	36:11	Then you will know that I am **the L**.	H3378
Eze	36:13	" 'This is what **the** Sovereign **L** says	H3378
Eze	36:14	nation childless, declares **the** Sovereign **L**.	H3378
Eze	36:15	nation to fall, declares **the** Sovereign **L**.	H3378
Eze	36:16	Again the word of **the L** came to me:	H3378
Eze	36:22	'This is what **the** Sovereign **L** says:	H3378
Eze	36:23	the nations will know that I am **the L**,	H3378
Eze	36:23	declares **the** Sovereign **L**, when I am	H3378
Eze	36:32	your sake, declares **the** Sovereign **L**.	H3378
Eze	36:33	" 'This is what **the** Sovereign **L** says: On	H3378
Eze	36:36	will know that I **the L** have rebuilt what	H3378
Eze	36:36	was desolate. I **the L** have spoken, and I	H3378
Eze	36:37	"This is what **the** Sovereign **L** says: Once	H3378
Eze	36:38	Then they will know that I am **the L**."	H3378
Eze	37: 1	The hand of **the L** was on me, and he	H3378
Eze	37: 1	out by the Spirit of **the L** and set me in the	H3378
Eze	37: 3	"Sovereign **L**, you alone know."	H3378
Eze	37: 4	'Dry bones, hear the word of **the L**!	H3378
Eze	37: 5	This is what **the** Sovereign **L** says to these	H3378
Eze	37: 6	Then you will know that I am **the L**.' "	H3378
Eze	37: 9	'This is what **the** Sovereign **L** says:	H3378
Eze	37:12	'This is what **the** Sovereign **L** says: My	H3378
Eze	37:13	will know that I am **the L**, when I open	H3378
Eze	37:14	you will know that I **the L** have spoken,	H3378
Eze	37:14	I have done it, declares **the L**.	H3378
Eze	37:15	The word of **the L** came to me:	H3378
Eze	37:19	'This is what **the** Sovereign **L** says:	H3378
Eze	37:21	'This is what **the** Sovereign **L** says:	H3378
Eze	37:28	will know that I **the L** make Israel holy,	H3378
Eze	38: 1	The word of **the L** came to me:	H3378
Eze	38: 3	'This is what **the** Sovereign **L** says: I am	H3378
Eze	38:10	" 'This is what **the** Sovereign **L** says: On	H3378
Eze	38:14	'This is what **the** Sovereign **L** says: In that	H3378
Eze	38:17	" 'This is what **the** Sovereign **L** says: You	H3378
Eze	38:18	will be aroused, declares **the** Sovereign **L**.	H3378
Eze	38:21	my mountains, declares **the** Sovereign **L**.	H3378
Eze	38:23	Then they will know that I am **the L**.'	H3378
Eze	39: 1	'This is what **the** Sovereign **L** says: I am	H3378
Eze	39: 5	I have spoken, declares **the** Sovereign **L**.	H3378
Eze	39: 6	they will know that I am **the L**.	H3378
Eze	39: 7	will know that I **the L** am the Holy One in	H3378
Eze	39: 8	take place, declares **the** Sovereign **L**.	H3378
Eze	39:10	looted them, declares **the** Sovereign **L**.	H3378
Eze	39:13	day for them, declares **the** Sovereign **L**.	H3378
Eze	39:17	of man, this is what **the** Sovereign **L** says:	H3378
Eze	39:20	of every kind,' declares **the** Sovereign **L**.	H3378
Eze	39:22	Israel will know that I am **the L** their God.	H3378
Eze	39:25	this is what **the** Sovereign **L** says:	H3378
Eze	39:28	they will know that I am **the L** their God,	H3378
Eze	39:29	people of Israel, declares **the** Sovereign **L**."	H3378
Eze	40: 1	day the hand of **the L** was on me and he	H3378
Eze	40:46	may draw near to **the L** to minister before	H3378
Eze	41:22	"This is the table that is before **the L**."	H3378
Eze	42:13	who approach **the L** will eat the most	H3378
Eze	43: 4	The glory of **the L** entered the temple	H3378
Eze	43: 5	the glory of **the L** filled the temple.	H3378
Eze	43:18	of man, this is what **the** Sovereign **L** says:	H3378
Eze	43:19	before me, declares **the** Sovereign **L**.	H3378
Eze	43:24	You are to offer them before **the L**, and the	H3378
Eze	43:24	sacrifice them as a burnt offering to **the L**.	H3378
Eze	43:27	will accept you, declares **the** Sovereign **L**."	H3378
Eze	44: 2	**The L** said to me, "This gate is to remain	H3378
Eze	44: 2	It is to remain shut because **the L**, the	H3378
Eze	44: 3	gateway to eat in the presence of **the L**.	H3378
Eze	44: 4	saw the glory of **the L** filling the temple	H3378

Book	Ref	Context	Number
Eze	44: 4	of the LORD filling the temple of **the L**,	H3378
Eze	44: 5	**The L** said to me, "Son of man, look	H3378
Eze	44: 5	instructions regarding the temple of **the L**.	H3378
Eze	44: 6	'This is what **the** Sovereign **L** says:	H3378
Eze	44: 9	This is what **the** Sovereign **L** says: No	H3378
Eze	44:12	of their sin, declares **the** Sovereign **L**.	H3378
Eze	44:15	fat and blood, declares **the** Sovereign **L**.	H3378
Eze	44:27	himself, declares **the** Sovereign **L**.	H3378
Eze	44:29	Israel devoted to **the L** will belong to them.	NDT
Eze	45: 1	you are to present to **the L** a portion of the	H3378
Eze	45: 4	who draw near to minister before **the L**.	H3378
Eze	45: 9	" 'This is what **the** Sovereign **L** says: You	H3378
Eze	45: 9	my people, declares **the** Sovereign **L**.	H3378
Eze	45:15	the people, declares **the** Sovereign **L**.	H3378
Eze	45:18	" 'This is what **the** Sovereign **L** says: In the	H3378
Eze	45:23	without defect as a burnt offering to **the L**,	H3378
Eze	46: 1	" 'This is what **the** Sovereign **L** says: The	H3378
Eze	46: 3	in the presence of **the L** at the entrance of	H3378
Eze	46: 4	prince brings to **the L** on the Sabbath day	H3378
Eze	46: 9	land come before **the L** at the appointed	H3378
Eze	46:12	provides a freewill offering to **the L**—	H3378
Eze	46:13	without defect for a burnt offering to **the L**;	H3378
Eze	46:14	this grain offering to **the L** is a lasting	H3378
Eze	46:16	" 'This is what **the** Sovereign **L** says: If the	H3378
Eze	47:13	This is what **the** Sovereign **L** says: "These	H3378
Eze	47:23	inheritance," declares **the** Sovereign **L**.	H3378
Eze	48: 9	you are to offer to **the L** will be 25,000	H3378
Eze	48:10	center of it will be the sanctuary of **the L**.	H3378
Eze	48:14	other hands, because it is holy to **the L**.	H3378
Eze	48:29	their portions," declares **the** Sovereign **L**.	H3378
Eze	48:35	from that time on will be: THE L IS THERE."	H3378
Da	8:11	as the commander of the army of the L;	NDT
Da	8:11	took away the daily sacrifice from **the L**,	H5647S
Da	9: 2	to the word of **the L** given to Jeremiah the	H3378
Da	9: 4	I prayed to **the L** my God and confessed	H3378
Da	9: 8	covered with shame, **L**, because we have	H3378
Da	9:10	we have not obeyed **the L** our God or kept	H3378
Da	9:13	the favor of **the L** our God by turning	H3378
Da	9:14	**The L** did not hesitate to bring the	H3378
Da	9:14	for **the L** our God is righteous in	H3378
Da	9:20	my request to **the L** my God for his holy	H3378
Hos	1: 1	The word of **the L** that came to Hosea son	H3378
Hos	1: 2	When **the L** began to speak through	H3378
Hos	1: 2	through Hosea, **the L** said to him, "Go,	H3378
Hos	1: 2	land is guilty of unfaithfulness to **the L**."	H3378
Hos	1: 4	Then **the L** said to Hosea, "Call him	H3378
Hos	1: 6	Then the L said to Hosea, "Call her	NDT
Hos	1: 7	but I, **the L** their God, will save	H3378
Hos	1: 9	Then the L said, "Call him Lo-Ammi	NDT
Hos	2:13	but me she forgot," declares **the L**.	H3378
Hos	2:16	declares **the L**, "you will call me 'my	H3378
Hos	2:20	you will acknowledge **the L**.	H3378
Hos	2:21	declares **the L**—"I will respond to the	H3378
Hos	3: 1	**The L** said to me, "Go, show your love to	H3378
Hos	3: 1	Love her as **the L** loves the Israelites	H3378
Hos	3: 5	return and seek **the L** their God and David	H3378
Hos	3: 5	come trembling to **the L** and to his	H3378
Hos	4: 1	Hear the word of **the L**, you Israelites	H3378
Hos	4: 1	because **the L** has a charge to bring	H3378
Hos	4:10	have deserted **the L** to give themselves	H3378
Hos	4:15	do not swear, 'As surely as **the L** lives!	H3378
Hos	4:16	How then can **the L** pasture them like	H3378
Hos	5: 4	they do not acknowledge **the L**.	H3378
Hos	5: 6	with their flocks and herds to seek **the L**,	H3378
Hos	5: 7	They are unfaithful to **the L**; they give	H3378
Hos	6: 1	let us return to **the L**. He has torn us to	H3378
Hos	6: 3	Let us acknowledge **the L**; let us press on	H3378
Hos	7:10	does not return to **the L** his God or search	H3378
Hos	8: 1	over the house of **the L** because the	H3378
Hos	8:13	the meat, **the L** is not pleased with them.	H3378
Hos	9: 4	will not pour out wine offerings to **the L**,	H3378
Hos	9: 4	it will not come into the temple of **the L**.	H3378
Hos	9: 5	festivals, on the feast days of **the L**?	H3378
Hos	9:14	Give them, **L**—what will you give them	H3378
Hos	10: 2	**The L** will demolish their altars and	H2085S
Hos	10: 3	no king because we did not revere **the L**.	H3378
Hos	10:12	it is time to seek **the L**, until he comes	H3378
Hos	11:10	They will follow **the L**; he will roar like a	H3378
Hos	11:11	them in their homes," declares **the L**.	H3378
Hos	12: 2	**The L** has a charge to bring against Judah	H3378
Hos	12: 5	**the L** God Almighty, the LORD is his name!	H3378
Hos	12: 5	the LORD God Almighty, **the L** is his name!	H3378
Hos	12: 9	"I have been **the L** your God ever since	H3378
Hos	12:13	**The L** used a prophet to bring Israel up	H3378
Hos	13: 4	"But I have been **the L** your God ever	H3378
Hos	13:15	An east wind from **the L** will come	H3378
Hos	14: 1	Israel, to **the L** your God. Your sins	H3378
Hos	14: 2	Take words with you and return to **the L**	H3378
Hos	14: 9	The ways of **the L** are right; the righteous	H3378
Joel	1: 1	The word of **the L** that came to Joel son of	H3378
Joel	1: 9	are cut off from the house of **the L**.	H3378
Joel	1: 9	those who minister before **the L**.	H3378
Joel	1:14	the land to the house of **the L** your God,	H3378
Joel	1:14	the LORD your God, and cry out to **the L**.	H3378
Joel	1:15	For the day of **the L** is near; it will come	H3378
Joel	1:19	**L**, I call, for fire has devoured the	H3378
Joel	2: 1	tremble, for the day of **the L** is coming.	H3378
Joel	2:11	**The L** thunders at the head of his army	H3378
Joel	2:11	The day of **the L** is great; it is	H3378
Joel	2:12	declares **the L**, "return to me with all your	H3378
Joel	2:13	Return to **the L** your God, for he is	H3378
Joel	2:14	drink offerings for **the L** your God.	H3378
Joel	2:17	who minister before **the L**, weep between	H3378
Joel	2:17	"Spare your people, **L**. Do not make your	H3378
Joel	2:18	Then **the L** was jealous for his land and	H3378
Joel	2:19	**The L** replied to them: "I am sending you	H3378
Joel	2:21	Surely **the L** has done great things!	H3378
Joel	2:23	of Zion, rejoice in **the L** your God, for he	H3378
Joel	2:26	will praise the name of **the L** your God,	H3378
Joel	2:27	that I am **the L** your God, and that	H3378
Joel	2:31	of the great and dreadful day of **the L**.	H3378
Joel	2:32	calls on the name of **the L** will be saved;	H3378
Joel	2:32	be deliverance, as **the L** has said, even	H3378
Joel	2:32	among the survivors whom **the L** calls.	H3378
Joel	3: 8	a nation far away." **The L** has spoken.	H3378
Joel	3:11	Bring down your warriors, **L**!	H3378
Joel	3:14	For the day of **the L** is near in the valley of	H3378
Joel	3:16	**The L** will roar from Zion and thunder	H3378
Joel	3:16	But **the L** will be a refuge for his people,	H3378
Joel	3:17	will know that I, **the L** your God, dwell in	H3378
Joel	3:21	I will not." **The L** dwells in Zion!	H3378
Am	1: 2	"**The L** roars from Zion and thunders from	H3378
Am	1: 3	This is what **the L** says: "For three sins of	H3378
Am	1: 5	Aram will go into exile to Kir," says **the L**.	H3378
Am	1: 6	This is what **the L** says: "For three sins of	H3378
Am	1: 8	are dead," says **the** Sovereign **L**.	H3378
Am	1: 9	This is what **the L** says: "For three sins of	H3378
Am	1:11	This is what **the L** says: "For three sins of	H3378
Am	1:13	This is what **the L** says: "For three sins of	H3378
Am	1:15	he and his officials together," says **the L**.	H3378
Am	2: 1	This is what **the L** says: "For three sins of	H3378
Am	2: 3	kill all her officials with him," says **the L**.	H3378
Am	2: 4	This is what **the L** says: "For three sins of	H3378
Am	2: 4	the law of **the L** and have not kept	H3378
Am	2: 6	This is what **the L** says: "For three sins of	H3378
Am	2:11	people of Israel?" declares **the L**.	H3378
Am	2:16	flee naked on that day," declares **the L**.	H3378
Am	3: 1	the word **the L** has spoken against you	H3378
Am	3: 6	comes to a city, has not **the L** caused it?	H3378
Am	3: 7	Surely **the** Sovereign **L** does nothing	H3378
Am	3: 8	**The** Sovereign **L** has spoken—who can	H3378
Am	3:10	declares **the L**, "who store up in their	H3378
Am	3:11	this is what **the** Sovereign **L** says:	H3378
Am	3:12	This is what **the L** says: "As a shepherd	H3378
Am	3:13	declares the Lord, **the L** God Almighty.	H3378
Am	3:15	will be demolished," declares **the L**.	H3378
Am	4: 2	**The** Sovereign **L** has sworn by his holiness	H3378
Am	4: 3	cast out toward Harmon," declares **the L**.	H3378
Am	4: 5	you love to do," declares **the** Sovereign **L**.	H3378
Am	4: 6	have not returned to me," declares **the L**.	H3378
Am	4: 8	have not returned to me," declares **the L**.	H3378
Am	4: 9	have not returned to me," declares **the L**.	H3378
Am	4:10	have not returned to me," declares **the L**.	H3378
Am	4:11	have not returned to me," declares **the L**.	H3378
Am	4:13	**the L** God Almighty is his name.	H3378
Am	5: 3	This is what **the** Sovereign **L** says to Israel	H3378
Am	5: 4	This is what **the L** says to Israel: "Seek me	H3378
Am	5: 6	Seek **the L** and live, or he will sweep	H3378
Am	5: 8	the face of the land—**the L** is his name.	H3378
Am	5:14	Then **the L** God Almighty will be with you	H3378
Am	5:15	Perhaps **the L** God Almighty will have	H3378
Am	5:16	is what the Lord, **the L** God Almighty, says	H3378
Am	5:17	I will pass through your midst," says **the L**.	H3378
Am	5:18	Woe to you who long for the day of **the L**	H3378
Am	5:18	Why do you long for the day of **the L**	H3378
Am	5:20	Will not the day of **the L** be darkness, not	H3378
Am	5:27	Damascus," says **the L**, whose name is	H3378
Am	6: 8	**The** Sovereign **L** has sworn by himself	H3378
Am	6: 8	by himself—**the L** God Almighty declares:	H3378
Am	6:10	We must not mention the name of **the L**."	H3378
Am	6:11	For **the L** has given the command, and he	H3378
Am	6:14	For **the L** God Almighty declares, "I will	H3378
Am	7: 1	This is what **the** Sovereign **L** showed me	H3378
Am	7: 2	I cried out, "Sovereign **L**, forgive!	H3378
Am	7: 3	So **the L** relented. "This will not happen,"	H3378
Am	7: 3	"This will not happen," **the L** said.	H3378
Am	7: 4	This is what **the** Sovereign **L** showed me	H3378
Am	7: 4	**The** Sovereign **L** was calling for judgment	H3378
Am	7: 5	I cried out, "Sovereign **L**, I beg you, stop!	H3378
Am	7: 6	So **the L** relented. "This will not happen	H3378
Am	7: 6	not happen either," **the** Sovereign **L** said.	H3378
Am	7: 8	And **the L** asked me, "What do you see	H3378
Am	7:15	But **the L** took me from tending the flock	H3378
Am	7:16	hear the word of **the L**. You say, " 'Do not	H3378
Am	7:17	"Therefore this is what **the L** says: " 'Your	H3378
Am	8: 1	This is what **the** Sovereign **L** showed me	H3378
Am	8: 2	Then **the L** said to me, "The time is ripe	H3378
Am	8: 3	declares **the** Sovereign **L**, "the songs in	H3378
Am	8: 7	**The L** has sworn by himself, the Pride of	H3378
Am	8: 9	declares **the** Sovereign **L**, "I will make	H3378
Am	8:11	declares **the** Sovereign **L**, "when I will	H3378
Am	8:11	a famine of hearing the words of **the L**.	H3378
Am	8:12	searching for the word of **the L**, but they	H3378
Am	9: 5	The Lord, **the L** Almighty—he touches the	H3378
Am	9: 6	the face of the land—**the L** is his name.	H3378
Am	9: 7	declares **the L**. "Did I not bring	H3378
Am	9: 8	the eyes of the Sovereign **L** are on the	H3378
Am	9: 8	the descendants of Jacob," declares **the L**.	H3378
Am	9:12	my name," declares **the L**, who will do	H3378
Am	9:13	declares **the L**, "when the reaper will be	H3378
Am	9:15	I have given them," says **the L** your God.	H3378
Ob	1	This is what **the** Sovereign **L** says about	H3378
Ob	1	We have heard a message from **the L**:	H3378
Ob	4	I will bring you down," declares **the L**.	H3378
Ob	8	declares **the L**, "will I not destroy the	H3378
Ob	15	"The day of **the L** is near for all nations	H3378
Ob	18	survivors from Esau." **The L** has spoken.	H3378
Jnh	1: 1	The word of **the L** came to Jonah son of	H3378
Jnh	1: 3	ran away from **the L** and headed for	H3378
Jnh	1: 3	sailed for Tarshish to flee from **the L**.	H3378
Jnh	1: 4	Then **the L** sent a great wind on the sea	H3378
Jnh	1: 9	"I am a Hebrew and I worship **the L**, the	H3378
Jnh	1:10	knew he was running away from **the L**,	H3378
Jnh	1:14	they cried out to **the L**, "Please, LORD	H3378
Jnh	1:14	"Please, **L**, do not let us die for taking this	H3378
Jnh	1:14	for you, **L**, have done as you	H3378
Jnh	1:16	At this the men greatly feared **the L**, and	H3378
Jnh	1:16	a sacrifice to **the L** and made vows to him.	H3378
Jnh	1:17	Now **the L** provided a huge fish to	H3378
Jnh	2: 1	the fish Jonah prayed to **the L** his God.	H3378
Jnh	2: 2	"In my distress I called to **the L**, and he	H3378
Jnh	2: 6	But you, **L** my God, brought my life up	H3378
Jnh	2: 7	I remembered you, **L**, and my prayer rose	H3378
Jnh	2: 9	I will say, 'Salvation comes from **the L**.' "	H3378
Jnh	2:10	And **the L** commanded the fish, and it	H3378
Jnh	3: 1	Then the word of **the L** came to Jonah a	H3378
Jnh	3: 3	obeyed the word of **the L** and went to	H3378
Jnh	4: 2	He prayed to **the L**, "Isn't this what I said	H3378
Jnh	4: 2	this what I said, **L**, when I was still at	H3378
Jnh	4: 3	**L**, take away my life, for it is better	H3378
Jnh	4: 4	But **the L** replied, "Is it right for you to be	H3378
Jnh	4: 6	Then **the L** God provided a leafy plant	H3378
Jnh	4:10	But **the L** said, "You have been concerned	H3378
Mic	1: 1	The word of **the L** that came to Micah of	H3378
Mic	1: 2	that **the** Sovereign **L** may bear witness	H3378
Mic	1: 3	**The L** is coming from his dwelling place	H3378
Mic	1:12	because disaster has come from **the L**	H3378
Mic	2: 3	Therefore, **the L** says: "I am planning	H3378
Mic	2: 5	in the assembly of **the L** to divide the land	H3378
Mic	2: 7	it be said, "Does **the L** become impatient?	H3378
Mic	2:13	through before them, **the L** at their head."	H3378
Mic	3: 4	Then they will cry out to **the L**, but he will	H3378
Mic	3: 5	This is what **the L** says: "As for the	H3378
Mic	3: 8	with the Spirit of **the L**, and with justice	H3378
Mic	3:11	support and say, "Is not **the L** among us?	H3378
Mic	4: 2	let us go up to the mountain of **the L**, to	H3378
Mic	4: 2	the word of **the L** from Jerusalem.	H3378
Mic	4: 4	for **the L** Almighty has spoken.	H3378
Mic	4: 5	walk in the name of **the L** our God for ever	H3378
Mic	4: 6	that day," declares **the L**, "I will gather the	H3378
Mic	4: 7	**The L** will rule over them in Mount Zion	H3378
Mic	4:10	There **the L** will redeem you out of the	H3378
Mic	4:12	they do not know the thoughts of **the L**;	H3378
Mic	4:13	will devote their ill-gotten gains to **the L**,	H3378
Mic	5: 4	shepherd his flock in the strength of **the L**,	H3378
Mic	5: 4	the majesty of the name of **the L** his God.	H3378
Mic	5: 7	of many peoples like dew from **the L**,	H3378
Mic	5:10	declares **the L**, "I will destroy your horses	H3378
Mic	6: 1	Listen to what **the L** says: "Stand up	H3378
Mic	6: 2	For **the L** has a case against his people	H3378
Mic	6: 5	you may know the righteous acts of **the L**."	H3378
Mic	6: 6	shall I come before **the L** and bow down	H3378
Mic	6: 7	Will **the L** be pleased with thousands of	H3378
Mic	6: 8	And what does **the L** require of you? To	H3378
Mic	6: 9	**The L** is calling to the city—and to fear	H3378
Mic	7: 7	I watch in hope for **the L**, I wait for God	H3378
Mic	7: 8	I sit in darkness, **the L** will be my light.	H3378
Mic	7:10	said to me, "Where is **the L** your God?"	H3378
Mic	7:17	turn in fear to **the L** our God and will be	H3378
Na	1: 2	**The L** is a jealous and avenging God; the	H3378
Na	1: 2	**the L** takes vengeance and is filled with	H3378
Na	1: 2	**The L** takes vengeance on his foes and	H3378
Na	1: 3	**The L** is slow to anger but great in power	H3378
Na	1: 3	**the L** will not leave the guilty unpunished.	H3378
Na	1: 7	**The L** is good, a refuge in times of trouble	H3378
Na	1: 9	they plot against **the L** he will bring to an	H3378
Na	1:11	plots evil against **the L** and devises	H3378
Na	1:12	This is what **the L** says: "Although they	H3378
Na	1:14	**The L** has given a command concerning	H3378
Na	2: 2	**The L** will restore the splendor of Jacob	H3378
Na	2:13	am against you," declares **the L** Almighty.	H3378
Na	3: 5	am against you," declares **the L** Almighty.	H3378
Hab	1: 2	How long, **L**, must I call for help, but you	H3378
Hab	1:12	**L**, are you not from everlasting? My God	H3378
Hab	1:12	**L**, have appointed them to execute	H3378
Hab	2: 2	Then **the L** replied: "Write down the	H3378
Hab	2:13	Has not **the L** Almighty determined that	H3378
Hab	2:14	of the glory of **the L** as the waters cover	H3378
Hab	2:20	**The L** is in his holy temple; let all the	H3378
Hab	3: 2	**L**, I have heard of your fame; I stand in	H3378
Hab	3: 2	I stand in awe of your deeds, **L**.	H3378
Hab	3: 8	angry with the rivers, **L**? Was your wrath	H3378
Hab	3:18	I will rejoice in **the L**, I will be joyful in	H3378
Hab	3:19	**The** Sovereign **L** is my strength; he makes	H3378
Zep	1: 1	The word of **the L** that came to Zephaniah	H3378
Zep	1: 2	from the face of the earth," declares **the L**.	H3378
Zep	1: 3	on the face of the earth," declares **the L**,	H3378
Zep	1: 5	down and swear by **the L** and who also	H3378
Zep	1: 6	from following **the L** and neither seek	H3378
Zep	1: 6	neither seek **the L** nor inquire of him."	H3378
Zep	1: 7	Be silent before **the** Sovereign **L**, for the	H3378
Zep	1: 7	for the day of **the L** is near.	H3378
Zep	1: 7	**The L** has prepared a sacrifice; he has	H3378
Zep	1:10	declares **the L**, "a cry will go up from the	H3378
Zep	1:12	who think, '**The L** will do nothing, either	H3378
Zep	1:14	The great day of **the L** is near—near and	H3378

Zep 1:14 The cry on the day of **the L** is bitter; the H3378
Zep 1:17 because they have sinned against **the L**. H3378
Zep 2: 3 Seek **the L**, all you humble of the land H3378
Zep 2: 5 people; the word of **the L** is against you H3378
Zep 2: 7 **The L** their God will care for them; he will H3378
Zep 2: 9 declares **the L** Almighty, the God of H3378
Zep 2:10 mocking the people of **the L** Almighty. H3378
Zep 2:11 **The L** will be awesome to them when he H3378
Zep 3: 2 She does not trust in **the L**, she does not H3378
Zep 3: 5 **The L** within her is righteous; he does no H3378
Zep 3: 8 declares **the L**, "for the day I will stand H3378
Zep 3: 9 call on the name of **the L** and serve him H3378
Zep 3:12 of Israel will trust in the name of **the L**. H3378
Zep 3:15 **The L** has taken away your punishment H3378
Zep 3:15 **The L**, the King of Israel, is with you H3378
Zep 3:17 **The L** your God is with you, the Mighty H3378
Zep 3:20 fortunes before your very eyes," says **the L**. H3378
Hag 1: 1 the word of **the L** came through the H3378
Hag 1: 2 This is what **the L** Almighty says: "These H3378
Hag 1: 3 Then the word of **the L** came through the H3378
Hag 1: 5 Now this is what **the L** Almighty says H3378
Hag 1: 7 This is what **the L** Almighty says: "Give H3378
Hag 1: 8 in it and be honored," says **the L**. H3378
Hag 1: 9 declares **the L** Almighty. "Because H3378
Hag 1:12 the voice of **the L** their God and the H3378
Hag 1:12 because **the L** their God had sent him. H3378
Hag 1:12 And the people feared **the L**. H3378
Hag 1:13 gave this message of **the L** to the people: H3378
Hag 1:13 "I am with you," declares **the L**. H3378
Hag 1:14 So **the L** stirred up the spirit of Zerubbabel H3378
Hag 1:14 to work on the house of **the L** Almighty, H3378
Hag 2: 1 the word of **the L** came through the H3378
Hag 2: 4 be strong, Zerubbabel,' declares **the L**. H3378
Hag 2: 4 of the land,' declares **the L**, 'and work. H3378
Hag 2: 4 I am with you,' declares **the L** Almighty. H3378
Hag 2: 6 "This is what **the L** Almighty says: 'In a H3378
Hag 2: 7 house with glory,' says **the L** Almighty. H3378
Hag 2: 8 gold is mine,' declares **the L** Almighty. H3378
Hag 2: 9 of the former house,' says **the L** Almighty. H3378
Hag 2: 9 will grant peace,' declares **the L** Almighty. H3378
Hag 2:10 the word of **the L** came to the prophet H3378
Hag 2:11 "This is what **the L** Almighty says: 'Ask H3378
Hag 2:14 this nation in my sight,' declares **the L**. H3378
Hag 2:17 you did not return to me,' declares **the L**. H3378
Hag 2:20 The word of **the L** came to Haggai a H3378
Hag 2:23 that day,' declares **the L** Almighty, 'I will H3378
Hag 2:23 Shealtiel,' declares **the L**, 'and I will make H3378
Hag 2:23 chosen you,' declares **the L** Almighty." H3378
Zec 1: 1 the word of **the L** came to the prophet H3378
Zec 1: 2 "**The L** was very angry with your ancestors. H3378
Zec 1: 3 This is what **the L** Almighty says H3378
Zec 1: 3 declares **the L** Almighty, 'and I H3378
Zec 1: 3 I will return to you,' says **the L** Almighty. H3378
Zec 1: 4 This is what **the L** Almighty says: 'Turn H3378
Zec 1: 4 pay attention to me, declares **the L**. H3378
Zec 1: 6 '**The L** Almighty has done to us what our H3378
Zec 1: 7 the word of **the L** came to the prophet H3378
Zec 1:10 "They are the ones **the L** has sent to go H3378
Zec 1:11 to the angel of **the L** who was standing H3378
Zec 1:12 Then the angel of **the L** said, "LORD H3378
Zec 1:12 of the LORD said, "**L** Almighty, how long H3378
Zec 1:13 So **the L** spoke kind and comforting words H3378
Zec 1:14 This is what **the L** Almighty says: 'I H3378
Zec 1:16 "Therefore this is what **the L** says: 'I will H3378
Zec 1:16 over Jerusalem,' declares **the L** Almighty. H3378
Zec 1:17 This is what **the L** Almighty says: 'My H3378
Zec 1:17 and **the L** will again comfort Zion and H3378
Zec 1:20 Then **the L** showed me four craftsmen. H3378
Zec 2: 5 around it,' declares **the L**, 'and I will be its H3378
Zec 2: 6 declares **the L**, "for I have scattered you H3378
Zec 2: 6 the four winds of heaven," declares **the L**. H3378
Zec 2: 8 For this is what **the L** Almighty says: H3378
Zec 2: 9 you will know that **the L** Almighty has H3378
Zec 2:10 I will live among you," declares **the L**. H3378
Zec 2:11 will be joined with **the L** in that day and H3378
Zec 2:11 you will know that **the L** Almighty has H3378
Zec 2:12 **The L** will inherit Judah as his portion in H3378
Zec 2:13 Be still before **the L**, all mankind, because H3378
Zec 3: 1 priest standing before the angel of **the L**, H3378
Zec 3: 2 **The L** said to Satan, "The LORD rebuke H3378
Zec 3: 2 said to Satan, "**The L** rebuke you, Satan! H3378
Zec 3: 2 **The L**, who has chosen Jerusalem, rebuke H3378
Zec 3: 5 while the angel of **the L** stood by. H3378
Zec 3: 6 The angel of **the L** gave this charge to H3378
Zec 3: 7 "This is what **the L** Almighty says: 'If you H3378
Zec 3: 9 says **the L** Almighty, 'and I will H3378
Zec 3:10 fig tree,' declares **the L** Almighty. H3378
Zec 4: 6 "This is the word of **the L** to Zerubbabel: H3378
Zec 4: 6 by my Spirit,' says **the L** Almighty. H3378
Zec 4: 8 Then the word of **the L** came to me: H3378
Zec 4: 9 you will know that **the L** Almighty has H3378
Zec 4:10 the seven eyes of **the L** that range H3378
Zec 5: 4 **The L** Almighty declares, 'I will send it H3378
Zec 6: 9 The word of **the L** came to me: H3378
Zec 6:12 Tell him this is what **the L** Almighty says H3378
Zec 6:12 his place and build the temple of **the L**. H3378
Zec 6:13 It is he who will build the temple of **the L** H3378
Zec 6:14 as a memorial in the temple of **the L**. H3378
Zec 6:15 help to build the temple of **the L**, H3378
Zec 6:15 you will know that **the L** Almighty has H3378
Zec 6:15 if you diligently obey **the L** your God." H3378
Zec 7: 1 the word of **the L** came to Zechariah on H3378
Zec 7: 2 together with their men, to entreat **the L** H3378
Zec 7: 3 of the house of **the L** Almighty and the H3378
Zec 7: 4 Then the word of **the L** Almighty came to H3378
Zec 7: 7 not the words **the L** proclaimed through H3378
Zec 7: 8 And the word of **the L** came again to H3378
Zec 7: 9 "This is what **the L** Almighty said H3378
Zec 7:12 to the words that **the L** Almighty had sent H3378
Zec 7:12 So **the L** Almighty was very angry. H3378
Zec 7:13 I would not listen,' says **the L** Almighty. H3378
Zec 8: 1 The word of **the L** Almighty came to me. H3378
Zec 8: 2 This is what **the L** Almighty says: "I am H3378
Zec 8: 3 This is what **the L** says: "I will return to H3378
Zec 8: 3 the mountain of **the L** Almighty will be H3378
Zec 8: 4 This is what **the L** Almighty says: "Once H3378
Zec 8: 6 This is what **the L** Almighty says: "It may H3378
Zec 8: 6 declares **the L** Almighty. H3378
Zec 8: 7 This is what **the L** Almighty says: "I will H3378
Zec 8: 9 This is what **the L** Almighty says: "Now H3378
Zec 8: 9 was laid for the house of **the L** Almighty. H3378
Zec 8:11 I did in the past," declares **the L** Almighty. H3378
Zec 8:14 This is what **the L** Almighty says: "Just as H3378
Zec 8:14 angered me," says **the L** Almighty, H3378
Zec 8:17 I hate all this," declares **the L**. H3378
Zec 8:18 The word of **the L** Almighty came to me. H3378
Zec 8:19 This is what **the L** Almighty says: "The H3378
Zec 8:20 This is what **the L** Almighty says: "Many H3378
Zec 8:21 at once to entreat **the L** and seek the LORD H3378
Zec 8:21 entreat the LORD and seek **the L** Almighty. H3378
Zec 8:22 Jerusalem to seek **the L** Almighty and to H3378
Zec 8:23 This is what **the L** Almighty says: "In H3378
Zec 9: 1 The word of **the L** is against the land of H3378
Zec 9: 1 all the tribes of Israel are on **the L**— H3378
Zec 9:14 Then **the L** will appear over them; his H3378
Zec 9:14 The Sovereign **L** will sound the trumpet H3378
Zec 9:15 and **the L** Almighty will shield them. H3378
Zec 9:16 **The L** their God will save his people on H3378
Zec 10: 1 Ask **the L** for rain in the springtime; it is H3378
Zec 10: 1 it is **the L** who sends the thunderstorms. H3378
Zec 10: 3 for **the L** Almighty will care for his flock H3378
Zec 10: 5 They will fight because **the L** is with them H3378
Zec 10: 6 I am **the L** their God and I will answer H3378
Zec 10: 7 be joyful; their hearts will rejoice in **the L**. H3378
Zec 10:12 strengthen them in **the L** and in his name H3378
Zec 10:12 they will live securely," declares **the L**. H3378
Zec 11: 4 This is what **the L** my God says H3378
Zec 11: 5 who sell them say, 'Praise **the L**, I am rich! H3378
Zec 11: 6 the people of the land," declares **the L**. H3378
Zec 11:11 me knew it was the word of **the L**. H3378
Zec 11:13 And **the L** said to me, "Throw it to the H3378
Zec 11:13 them to the potter at the house of **the L**. H3378
Zec 11:15 Then **the L** said to me, "Take again the H3378
Zec 12: 1 The word of **the L** concerning Israel H3378
Zec 12: 1 **The L**, who stretches out the heavens H3378
Zec 12: 4 its rider with madness," declares **the L**. H3378
Zec 12: 5 because **the L** Almighty is their God. H3378
Zec 12: 7 "**The L** will save the dwellings of Judah H3378
Zec 12: 8 On that day **the L** will shield those who H3378
Zec 12: 8 like the angel of **the L** going before them. H3378
Zec 13: 2 no more," declares **the L** Almighty. H3378
Zec 13: 7 declares **the L** Almighty. "Strike H3378
Zec 13: 8 declares **the L**, "two-thirds will be struck H3378
Zec 13: 9 and they will say, '**The L** is our God. H3378
Zec 14: 1 A day of **the L** is coming, Jerusalem H3378
Zec 14: 3 Then **the L** will go out and fight against H3378
Zec 14: 5 Then **the L** my God will come, and all the H3378
Zec 14: 7 a day known only to **the L**—with no H3378
Zec 14: 9 **The L** will be king over the whole earth H3378
Zec 14: 9 On that day there will be one **L**, and his H3378
Zec 14:12 plague with which **the L** will strike all the H3378
Zec 14:13 will be stricken by **the L** with great panic. H3378
Zec 14:16 worship the King, **the L** Almighty, and to H3378
Zec 14:17 worship the King, **the L** Almighty, they H3378
Zec 14:18 **The L** will bring on them the plague he H3378
Zec 14:20 that day HOLY TO THE L will be inscribed H3378
Zec 14:21 Judah will be holy to **the L** Almighty, H3378
Zec 14:21 Canaanite in the house of **the L** Almighty. H3378
Mal 1: 1 The word of **the L** to Israel through H3378
Mal 1: 2 have loved you," says **the L**. "But you ask, H3378
Mal 1: 2 declares **the L**. "Yet I have loved H3378
Mal 1: 4 But this is what **the L** Almighty says H3378
Mal 1: 4 a people always under the wrath of **the L**. H3378
Mal 1: 5 'Great is **the L**—even beyond the H3378
Mal 1: 6 says **the L** Almighty. "It is you H3378
Mal 1: 8 he accept you?" says **the L** Almighty. H3378
Mal 1: 9 he accept you?"—says **the L** Almighty. H3378
Mal 1:10 says **the L** Almighty, "and I will accept no H3378
Mal 1:11 among the nations," says **the L** Almighty. H3378
Mal 1:13 it contemptuously," says **the L** Almighty. H3378
Mal 1:13 them from your hands?" says **the L**. H3378
Mal 1:14 says **the L** Almighty, "and my name is to H3378
Mal 2: 2 says **the L** Almighty, "I will send a curse H3378
Mal 2: 4 Levi may continue," says **the L** Almighty. H3378
Mal 2: 7 is the messenger of **the L** Almighty and H3378
Mal 2: 8 covenant with Levi," says **the L** Almighty. H3378
Mal 2:11 the sanctuary **the L** loves by marrying H3378
Mal 2:12 may **the L** remove him from the tents of H3378
Mal 2:12 he brings an offering to **the L** Almighty. H3378
Mal 2:14 It is because **the L** is the witness between H3378
Mal 2:16 his wife," says **the L**, the God of Israel H3378
Mal 2:16 he should protect," says **the L** Almighty. H3378
Mal 2:17 You have wearied **the L** with your words H3378
Mal 2:17 who do evil are good in the eyes of **the L**, H3378
Mal 3: 1 will come," says **the L** Almighty. H3378
Mal 3: 3 Then **the L** will have men who will bring H3378
Mal 3: 4 Jerusalem will be acceptable to **the L**, H3378
Mal 3: 5 do not fear me," says **the L** Almighty. H3378
Mal 3: 6 "I **the L** do not change. So you, the H3378
Mal 3: 7 I will return to you," says **the L** Almighty. H3378
Mal 3:10 says **the L** Almighty, "and see if I will not H3378
Mal 3:11 fruit before it is ripe," says **the L** Almighty. H3378
Mal 3:12 be a delightful land," says **the L** Almighty. H3378
Mal 3:13 spoken arrogantly against me," says **the L**. H3378
Mal 3:14 like mourners before **the L** Almighty? H3378
Mal 3:16 those who feared **the L** talked with each H3378
Mal 3:16 each other, and **the L** listened and heard. H3378
Mal 3:16 those who feared **the L** and honored his H3378
Mal 3:17 says **the L** Almighty, "they will be my H3378
Mal 4: 1 will set them on fire," says **the L** Almighty. H3378
Mal 4: 3 the day when I act," says **the L** Almighty. H3378
Mal 4: 5 great and dreadful day of **the L** comes. H3378

LORD'S (65) [LORD]

Ge 44: 9 rest of us will become my **l** slaves." H4200+123
Ge 44:16 We are now my **l** slaves—we H4200+123
Ge 44:33 here as my **l** slave in place of H4200+123
Nu 14:17 "Now may **the L** strength be displayed, H151
1Sa 25:41 you and wash the feet of my **l** servants." H123
2Sa 11:11 Joab and my **l** men are camped in the H123
1Ki 1:33 "Take your **l** servants with you and have H123
1Ki 3:15 stood before the ark of **the L** covenant and H151
1Ch 21: 3 are they not all my **l** subjects? H4200+123
Mal 1:12 it by saying, '**The L** table is defiled,' and H151
Lk 1: 6 observing all **the L** commands and *G3261*
Lk 1:38 "I am **the L** servant," Mary answered *G3261*
Lk 1:66 For **the L** hand was with him. *G3261*
Lk 2:26 die before he had seen **the L** Messiah. *G3261*
Lk 4:19 to proclaim the year *of* **the L** favor. *G3261*
Lk 10:39 who sat at **the L** feet listening to what he *G3261*
Ac 9: 1 murderous threats against **the L** disciples. *G3261*
Ac 9:32 went to visit **the L people** who lived in Lydda *G41*
Ac 11:21 **The L** hand was with them, and a great *G3261*
Ac 21:14 we gave up and said, "**The L** will be done." *G3261*
Ac 26:10 priests I put many *of* **the L people** in prison, *G41*
Ro 12:13 Share *with* **the L people** who are in need *G41*
Ro 15:25 in the service *of* **the L people** there. *G41*
Ro 15:26 the poor *among* **the L people** in Jerusalem *G41*
Ro 15:31 be favorably received *by* **the L people** there, *G41*
Ro 16:15 Olympas and all **the L people** who are with *G41*
1Co 6: 1 judgment instead of before **the L people**? *G41*
1Co 6: 2 not know that **the L people** will judge the *G41*
1Co 7:22 to faith in the Lord is **the L** freed person; *G3261*
1Co 7:25 as one who by **the L** mercy is trustworthy. *G3261*
1Co 7:32 man is concerned about **the L** affairs— *G3261*
1Co 7:34 virgin is concerned about **the L** affairs: *G3261*
1Co 9: 5 apostles and **the L** brothers and Cephas? *G3261*
1Co 10:21 a part in both **the L** table and the table of *G3261*
1Co 10:22 Are we trying to arouse **the L** jealousy? *G3261*
1Co 10:26 "The earth is **the L**, and everything in it *G3261*
1Co 11:20 together, it is not **the L** Supper you eat, *G3258*
1Co 11:26 you proclaim **the L** death until he comes. *G3261*
1Co 14:33 as in all the congregations *of* **the L people**. *G41*
1Co 14:37 I am writing to you is **the L** command. *G3261*
1Co 16: 1 Now about the collection for **the L people** *G41*
1Co 16:15 themselves to the service *of* **the L people**. *G41*
2Co 3:18 unveiled faces contemplate **the L** glory, *G3261*
2Co 8: 4 of sharing in this service to **the L people**. *G41*
2Co 9: 1 to you about this service to **the L people**. *G41*
2Co 9:12 the needs *of* **the L people** but is also *G41*
Gal 1:19 other apostles—only James, **the L** brother. *G3261*
Eph 3: 8 I am less than the least of all **the L people**, *G41*
Eph 3:18 together with all **the L holy people**, to grasp *G41*
Eph 5:17 but understand what **the L** will is. *G3261*
Eph 6:18 always keep on praying for all **the L people**. *G41*
Col 1:26 is now disclosed *to* **the L people**. *G41*
1Th 1: 8 **The L** message rang out from you not only *G3261*
1Th 4:15 According to **the L** word, we tell you that *G3261*
1Ti 5:10 washing the feet *of* **the L people**, helping *G41*
2Ti 2:24 And **the L** servant must not be *G3261*
Phm 7 have refreshed the hearts *of* **the L people**. *G41*
Heb 12: 5 do not make light of **the L** discipline, and *G3261*
Heb 13:24 Greet all your leaders and all **the L people** *G41*
Jas 4:15 "If it is **the L** will, we will live and *G3261*
Jas 5: 7 brothers and sisters, until **the L** coming. *G3261*
Jas 5: 8 stand firm, because **the L** coming is near. *G3261*
1Pe 2:13 yourselves for **the L** sake to every human *G3261*
2Pe 3:15 Bear in mind that our **L** patience means *G3261*
Rev 1:10 On **the L** Day I was in the Spirit, and I *G3258*

LORD'S* (299) [LORD* (YAHWEH); see introduction, page xiv]

Ge 4:16 Cain went out from **the L** presence and H3378
Ge 38: 7 was wicked in **the L** sight; so the LORD H3378
Ge 38:10 What he did was wicked in **the L** sight; so H3378
Ex 4:14 Then **the L** anger burned against Moses H3378
Ex 9:29 may know that the earth is **the L**. H4200+3378
Ex 12:11 Eat it in haste; it is **the L** Passover. H4200+3378
Ex 12:41 the very day, all **the L** divisions left Egypt. H3378
Ex 12:48 to celebrate **the L** Passover must H4200+3378
Ex 16: 3 only we had died by **the L** hand in Egypt! H3378
Ex 24: 3 told the people all **the L** words and laws, H3378
Ex 29:11 Slaughter it in **the L** presence at the H3378
Ex 34:34 he entered **the L** presence to speak H3378
Lev 3:16 pleasing aroma. All the fat is **the L**. H4200+3378
Lev 4: 2 is forbidden in any of **the L** commands— H3378

L

Lev 4:13 is forbidden in any of **the L** commands, H3378
Lev 4:27 is forbidden in any of **the L** commands, H3378
Lev 5:15 in regard to any of **the L** holy things, H3378
Lev 5:17 is forbidden in any of **the L** commands, H3378
Lev 6:22 It is **the L** perpetual share and is to H4200+3378
Lev 10: 7 because **the L** anointing oil is on you." H3378
Lev 23: 4 " 'These are **the L** appointed festivals, the H3378
Lev 23: 5 **The L** Passover begins at twilight on H4200+3378
Lev 23: 6 day of that month **the L** Festival of H4200+3378
Lev 23:34 the seventh month **the L** Festival of H4200+3378
Lev 23:37 " 'These are **the L** appointed festivals H3378
Lev 23:38 to those for **the L** Sabbaths and in H3378
Lev 27:26 an ox or a sheep, it is **the L**. H4200+3378
Nu 3:39 counted at **the L** command by Moses H3378
Nu 4:37 according to **the L** command through H3378
Nu 4:41 them according to **the L** command. H3378
Nu 4:45 according to **the L** command through H3378
Nu 4:49 At **the L** command through Moses, each H3378
Nu 9: 7 from presenting **the L** offering with the H3378
Nu 9:10 are still to celebrate **the L** Passover, H4200+3378
Nu 9:13 not presenting **the L** offering at the H3378
Nu 9:14 also to celebrate **the L** Passover in H4200+3378
Nu 9:18 At **the L** command the Israelites set out H3378
Nu 9:19 Israelites obeyed **the L** order and did not H3378
Nu 9:20 at **the L** command they would encamp H3378
Nu 9:23 At **the L** command they encamped, and at H3378
Nu 9:23 at **the L** command they set out. H3378
Nu 9:23 They obeyed **the L** order, in accordance H3378
Nu 10:13 at **the L** command through Moses. H3378
Nu 11:23 answered Moses, "Is **the L** arm too short? H3378
Nu 11:29 I wish that all **the L** people were prophets H3378
Nu 13: 3 So at **the L** command Moses sent them H3378
Nu 14:41 "Why are you disobeying **the L** command? H3378
Nu 14:44 the ark of **the L** covenant moved from H3378
Nu 15:23 any of **the L** commands to you through H3378
Nu 15:31 they have despised **the L** word and broken H3378
Nu 16: 3 you set yourselves above **the L** assembly?" H3378
Nu 16: 9 to do the work at **the L** tabernacle and to H3378
Nu 16:41 "You have killed **the L** people," they said. H3378
Nu 17: 9 all the staffs from **the L** presence to all the H3378
Nu 18:26 a tenth of that tithe as **the L** offering. H3378
Nu 18:28 you must give **the L** portion to Aaron the H3378
Nu 18:29 You must present as **the L** portion the best H3378
Nu 19:13 they defile **the L** tabernacle. H3378
Nu 20: 4 Why did you bring **the L** community into H3378
Nu 20: 9 Moses took the staff from **the L** presence, H3378
Nu 25: 3 And **the L** anger burned against them H3378
Nu 25: 4 so that **the L** fierce anger may turn away H3378
Nu 27:17 so **the L** people will not be like sheep H3378
Nu 28:16 the first month **the L** Passover is to H4200+3378
Nu 31: 3 may carry out **the L** vengeance on them H3378
Nu 31:16 so that a plague struck **the L** people. H3378
Nu 31:29 give it to Eleazar the priest as **the L** part. H3378
Nu 31:30 the care of **the L** tabernacle. H3378
Nu 31:41 tribute to Eleazar the priest as **the L** part, H3378
Nu 31:47 the care of **the L** tabernacle. H3378
Nu 32:10 **The L** anger was aroused that day and he H3378
Nu 32:13 **The L** anger burned against Israel and he H3378
Nu 33: 2 At **the L** command Moses recorded the H3378
Nu 33:38 At **the L** command Aaron the priest went H3378
Nu 36: 5 Then at **the L** command Moses gave this H3378
Dt 1:43 rebelled against **the L** command and in H3378
Dt 2:15 **The L** hand was against them until he had H3378
Dt 6:18 Do what is right and good in **the L** sight H3378
Dt 7: 4 and **the L** anger will burn against you H3378
Dt 9: 8 Horeb you aroused **the L** wrath so that he H3378
Dt 9:18 what was evil in **the L** sight and so H3378
Dt 10:13 to observe **the L** commands and H3378
Dt 11:17 Then **the L** anger will burn against you H3378
Dt 15: 2 because **the L** time for canceling H4200+3378
Dt 18: 5 stand and minister in **the L** name always. H3378
Dt 29:27 Therefore **the L** anger burned against this H3378
Dt 32: 9 For **the L** portion is his people, Jacob his H3378
Dt 33:21 he carried out **the L** righteous will, and his H3378
Jos 5:15 The commander of **the L** army replied H3378
Jos 6: 8 the ark of **the L** covenant followed H3378
Jos 6:24 iron into the treasury of **the L** house. H3378
Jos 7: 1 So **the L** anger burned against Israel. H3378
Jos 15:13 In accordance with **the L** command to him, H3378
Jos 17: 4 their father, according to **the L** command. H3378
Jos 21:45 Not one of all **the L** good promises to H3378
Jos 22:19 come over to **the L** land, where the H3378
Jos 22:19 LORD's land, where **the L** tabernacle stands H3378
Jos 22:28 Look at the replica of **the L** altar, which H3378
Jos 22:31 rescued the Israelites from **the L** hand." H3378
Jos 23:16 to them, **the L** anger will burn against you H3378
Jdg 2:12 around them. They aroused **the L** anger H3378
Jdg 2:17 had been obedient to **the L** commands. H3378
Jdg 3: 4 they would obey **the L** commands, H3378
Jdg 11:31 from the Ammonites will be **the L**, H4200+3378
Jdg 18: 6 Your journey has **the L** approval." H3378
Ru 1:13 because **the L** hand has turned against H3378
1Sa 1: 9 his chair by the doorpost of **the L** house. H3378
1Sa 2: 8 foundations of the earth are **the L**; H4200+3378
1Sa 2:17 young men was very great in **the L** sight, H3378
1Sa 2:17 they were treating **the L** offering with H3378
1Sa 2:24 spreading among **the L** people is not H3378
1Sa 2:25 it was **the L** will to put them to death. H3378
1Sa 4: 3 the ark of **the L** covenant from Shiloh H3378
1Sa 4: 5 When the ark of **the L** covenant came into H3378
1Sa 5: 6 **The L** hand was heavy on the people of H3378
1Sa 5: 9 moved it, **the L** hand was against that city H3378
1Sa 13:12 and I have not sought **the L** favor. H3378
1Sa 13:14 you have not kept **the L** command. H3378
1Sa 14: 3 the son of Eli, **the L** priest in Shiloh. H3378
1Sa 15:13 I have carried out **the L** instructions." H3378
1Sa 15:24 I violated **the L** command and your H3378
1Sa 16: 6 "Surely **the L** anointed stands here H2257S
1Sa 17:47 the battle is **the L**, and he will H4200+3378
1Sa 20:14 kindness like **the L** kindness as long as I H3378
1Sa 24: 6 to my master, **the L** anointed, or lay my H3378
1Sa 24:10 on my lord, because he is **the L** anointed. H3378
1Sa 25:28 because you fight **the L** battles, and no H3378
1Sa 26: 9 can lay a hand on **the L** anointed and be H3378
1Sa 26:11 I should lay a hand on **the L** anointed. H3378
1Sa 26:16 did not guard your master, **the L** anointed. H3378
1Sa 26:19 from my share in **the L** inheritance and H3378
1Sa 26:23 I would not lay a hand on **the L** anointed. H3378
1Sa 30:26 you from the plunder of **the L** enemies." H3378
2Sa 1:14 lift your hand to destroy **the L** anointed?" H3378
2Sa 1:16 when you said, 'I killed **the L** anointed.' H3378
2Sa 6: 7 **The L** anger burned against Uzzah H3378
2Sa 6: 8 angry because **the L** wrath had broken H3378
2Sa 6:21 me ruler over **the L** people Israel— H3378
2Sa 15:25 If I find favor in **the L** eyes, he will bring H3378
2Sa 19:21 He cursed **the L** anointed." H3378
2Sa 20:19 want to swallow up **the L** inheritance?" H3378
2Sa 21: 3 so that you will bless **the L** inheritance?" H3378
2Sa 21: 6 at Gibeah of Saul—**the L** chosen one." H3378
2Sa 22:31 **The L** word is flawless; he shields all who H3378
1Ki 2:33 may there be **the L** peace H4946+6640+3378
1Ki 7:48 the furnishings that were in **the L** temple: H3378
1Ki 7:51 them in the treasuries of **the L** temple. H3378
1Ki 8: 1 up the ark of **the L** covenant from Zion H3378
1Ki 8: 6 brought the ark of **the L** covenant to its H3378
1Ki 9:15 conscripted to build **the L** temple, H3378
1Ki 10: 9 Because of **the L** eternal love for Israel, H3378
1Ki 11:10 Solomon did not keep **the L** command. H3378
1Ki 14:15 they aroused **the L** anger by making H3378
1Ki 14:28 Whenever the king went to **the L** temple H3378
1Ki 15: 5 to keep any of **the L** commands all the days NDT
1Ki 15:18 the treasuries of **the L** temple and of his H3378
1Ki 18: 4 Jezebel was killing off **the L** prophets, H3378
1Ki 18:13 I hid a hundred of **the L** prophets in two H3378
1Ki 18:18 have abandoned **the L** commands and H3378
1Ki 18:22 the only one of **the L** prophets left, H4200+3378
2Ki 9: 6 'I anoint you king over **the L** people Israel H3378
2Ki 9: 7 the blood of all **the L** servants shed by H3378
2Ki 11:17 that they would be **the L** people. H4200+3378
2Ki 13: 3 So **the L** anger burned against Israel, and H3378
2Ki 13: 4 Then Jehoahaz sought **the L** favor, and H3378
2Ki 13:17 "**The L** arrow of victory, the arrow H4200+3378
2Ki 17:11 wicked things that aroused **the L** anger. H3378
2Ki 20: 9 "This is **the L** sign to you that H4946+907+3378
2Ki 22:13 Great is **the L** anger that burns against us H3378
2Ki 23:19 Samaria and that had aroused **the L** anger. NDT
2Ki 24: 3 to Judah according to **the L** command, H3378
2Ki 24:20 It was because of **the L** anger that all this H3378
1Ch 2: 3 was wicked in **the L** sight; so the LORD put H3378
1Ch 13:10 **The L** anger burned against Uzzah, and he H3378
1Ch 13:11 angry because **the L** wrath had broken H3378
1Ch 28:19 in writing as a result of **the L** hand on me, H3378
2Ch 1: 3 which Moses **the L** servant had made in H3378
2Ch 5: 2 up the ark of **the L** covenant from Zion H3378
2Ch 5: 7 brought the ark of **the L** covenant to its H3378
2Ch 7: 6 the Levites with **the L** musical instruments H3378
2Ch 12:11 Whenever the king went to **the L** temple H3378
2Ch 12:12 himself, **the L** anger turned from him H3378
2Ch 15: 8 was in front of the portico of **the L** temple. H3378
2Ch 16: 2 the treasuries of **the L** temple and of his H3378
2Ch 23: 6 are to observe **the L** command not to H3378
2Ch 23:16 the king would be **the L** people. H4200+3378
2Ch 23:19 at the gates of **the L** temple so that no H3378
2Ch 24:12 carpenters to restore **the L** temple, H3378
2Ch 24:14 it were made articles for **the L** temple: H3378
2Ch 24:20 'Why do you disobey **the L** commands H3378
2Ch 24:21 to death in the courtyard of **the L** temple. H3378
2Ch 26:19 before the incense altar in **the L** temple, H3378
2Ch 28:11 for **the L** fierce anger rests on you. H3378
2Ch 28:24 shut the doors of **the L** temple and set up H3378
2Ch 29: 6 faces away from **the L** dwelling place and H3378
2Ch 29:16 to the courtyard of **the L** temple everything H3378
2Ch 29:19 They are now in front of **the L** altar." H3378
2Ch 31: 2 praises at the gates of **the L** dwelling. H3378
2Ch 32:25 therefore the L wrath was on him and on NDT
2Ch 32:26 therefore **the L** wrath did not come on H3378
2Ch 34:10 to supervise the work on **the L** temple. H3378
2Ch 34:21 Great is **the L** anger that is poured out on H3378
2Ch 35: 2 them in the service of **the L** temple. H3378
2Ch 36:18 the treasures of **the L** temple and the H3378
Ezr 3: 6 the foundation of **the L** temple had not H3378
Ps 2: 7 I will proclaim **the L** decree: He said to H3378
Ps 13: 6 I will sing **the L** praise, for he has been H3378
Ps 18:30 **The L** word is flawless; he shields all who H3378
Ps 24: 1 The earth is **the L**, and everything H4200+3378
Ps 32:10 but **the L** unfailing love surrounds the one H3378
Ps 37:18 spend their days under **the L** care, H3378
Ps 37:20 Though **the L** enemies are like the flowers H3378
Ps 89: 1 I will sing of **the L** great love forever; with H3378
Ps 103:17 to everlasting **the L** love is with those who H3378
Ps 106:29 they aroused the L anger by their wicked NDT
Ps 109:20 May this be **the L** payment to H4946+907+3378
Ps 118:15 "**The L** right hand has done mighty things! H3378
Ps 118:16 **The L** right hand is lifted high; the LORD's H3378
Ps 118:16 **the L** right hand has done mighty things!" H3378
Pr 3:11 do not despise **the L** discipline, and do H3378
Pr 3:33 **The L** curse is on the house of the wicked H3378
Pr 19:21 but it is **the L** purpose that prevails. H3378
Pr 21: 1 In **the L** hand the king's heart is a stream H3378
Pr 22:14 a man who is under **the L** wrath falls into H3378
Isa 2: 2 days the mountain of **the L** temple will be H3378
Isa 5:25 Therefore **the L** anger burns against his H3378
Isa 14: 2 male and female servants in **the L** land. H3378
Isa 24:14 from the west they acclaim **the L** majesty. H3378
Isa 30: 9 unwilling to listen to **the L** instruction. H3378
Isa 32:16 The L justice will dwell in the desert, his NDT
Isa 38: 7 " 'This is **the L** sign to you H4946+907+3378
Isa 40: 2 has received from **the L** hand double for H3378
Isa 44: 5 their hand, '**The L**,' and will take H4200+3378
Isa 48:14 **The L** chosen ally will carry out his H3378
Isa 49: 4 Yet what is due me is in **the L** hand, and H3378
Isa 52:11 you who carry the articles of **the L** house. H3378
Isa 53:10 Yet it was **the L** will to crush him and H3378
Isa 55:13 This will be for **the L** renown, for an H4200+3378
Isa 58:13 a delight and **the L** holy day honorable, H3378
Isa 61: 2 the year of **the L** favor and the day H4200+3378
Isa 62: 3 will be a crown of splendor in **the L** hand, H3378
Jer 7: 2 at the gate of **the L** house and there H3378
Jer 12:13 harvest because of **the L** fierce anger." H3378
Jer 13:17 because **the L** flock will be taken captive. H3378
Jer 19:14 in the court of **the L** temple and said to H3378
Jer 20: 2 Upper Gate of Benjamin at **the L** temple. H3378
Jer 20: 3 "**The L** name for you is not Pashhur H3378
Jer 23:35 'What is **the L** answer?' or 'What H3378
Jer 23:37 'What is **the L** answer to you?' or H3378
Jer 25:17 took the cup from **the L** hand and made H3378
Jer 25:38 because of **the L** fierce anger. H2257S
Jer 26: 2 the courtyard of **the L** house and speak to H3378
Jer 26: 9 do you prophesy in **the L** name that this H3378
Jer 26:10 entrance of the New Gate of **the L** house. H3378
Jer 27:16 now the articles from **the L** house will be H3378
Jer 28: 3 place all the articles of **the L** house that H3378
Jer 28: 6 the articles of **the L** house and all the H3378
Jer 34: 4 " 'Yet hear **the L** promise to you, Zedekiah H3378
Jer 36: 5 I am not allowed to go to **the L** temple. H3378
Jer 36: 8 at **the L** temple he read the words of the H3378
Jer 36:10 all the people at **the L** temple the words H3378
Jer 43: 4 people disobeyed **the L** command to stay H3378
Jer 48:10 on anyone who is lax in doing **the L** work! H3378
Jer 50:13 Because of **the L** anger she will not be H3378
Jer 51: 6 It is time for **the L** vengeance; he H4200+3378
Jer 51: 7 Babylon was a gold cup in **the L** hand H3378
Jer 51:29 for **the L** purposes against Babylon stand H3378
Jer 51:51 entered the holy places of **the L** house." H3378
Jer 52: 3 It was because of **the L** anger that all this H3378
La 2:22 In the day of **the L** anger no one escaped H3378
La 3: 1 seen affliction by the rod of **the L** wrath. H2257S
La 3:22 Because of **the L** great love we are not H3378
La 4:20 **The L** anointed, our very life breath, was H3378
Eze 7:19 to deliver them in the day of **the L** wrath. H3378
Eze 10:19 entrance of the east gate of **the L** house, H3378
Eze 36:20 of them, 'These are **the L** people, and H3378
Da 8:12 **the L people** and the daily sacrifice were H7372
Da 8:13 the trampling underfoot of **the L people**?" H7372
Hos 9: 3 They will not remain in **the L** land H3378
Joel 3:18 will flow out of **the L** house and will water H3378
Ob 21 And the kingdom will be **the L**. H4200+3378
Mic 3:11 Yet they look for **the L** support and say, "Is H3378
Mic 4: 1 days the mountain of **the L** temple will be H3378
Mic 6: 2 you mountains, **the L** accusation; listen H3378
Mic 7: 9 I will bear **the L** wrath, until he H3378
Hab 2:16 The cup from **the L** right hand is coming H3378
Zep 1: 8 "On the day of **the L** sacrifice I will punish H3378
Zep 1:18 to save them on the day of **the L** wrath." H3378
Zep 2: 2 before **the L** fierce anger comes upon you H3378
Zep 2: 2 before the day of **the L** wrath comes upon H3378
Zep 2: 3 be sheltered on the day of **the L** anger. H3378
Hag 1: 2 has not yet come to rebuild **the L** house. H3378
Hag 1:13 Then Haggai, **the L** messenger, gave this H3378
Hag 2:15 was laid on another in **the L** temple. H3378
Hag 2:18 the foundation of **the L** temple was laid. H3378
Zec 13: 3 because you have told lies in **the L** name. H3378
Zec 14:20 cooking pots in **the L** house will be like H3378
Mal 1: 7 "By saying that **the L** table is H3378
Mal 2:13 You flood **the L** altar with tears H3378

LORDED (1) [LORD]

Ne 5:15 Their assistants also **l it over** the people H8948

LORDING (1) [LORD]

1Pe 5: 3 not **l it over** those entrusted to you, but *G2894*

LORDS (10) [LORD]

Ge 19: 2 "My **l**," he said, "please turn aside to your H123
Ge 19:18 But Lot said to them, "No, my **l**, please! H123
Dt 10:17 LORD your God is God of gods and Lord of **l**, H123
Ps 136: 3 Give thanks to the Lord of **l**: His love H123
Ecc 8: 9 a time when a man **l it over** others to his H8948
Isa 26:13 other **l** besides you have ruled over us H123
1Co 8: 5 there are many "gods" and many "**l**") *G3261*
1Ti 6:15 only Ruler, the King of kings and Lord *of* **l**, *G3259*
Rev 17:14 because he is Lord *of* **l** and King of kings *G3261*
Rev 19:16 written: KING OF KINGS AND LORD OF **L**. *G3261*

LORDSHIP (KJV) LORD IT OVER

LOSE (35) [LOSES, LOSS, LOSSES, LOST]

Ge 26: 9 I thought *I* might **l** *my* **life** on account of H4637
Ge 27:45 Why *should I* **l** both of you in one day?" H8897
Jdg 18:25 and *you* and your family *will* **l** your lives." H665
1Sa 17:32 "*Let* no one **l** heart on account of this H5877
2Sa 22:46 They all **l heart**; they come trembling from H5570
Ps 18:45 They all **l heart**; they come trembling from H5570
Pr 5: 9 lest *you* **l** your honor to others and your H5989
Isa 7: 4 *Do* not **l** heart because of these two H8216
Isa 19: 3 Egyptians *will* **l heart**, H1327+8120+928+7931
Isa 19: 9 the weavers of fine linen will **l** hope. NDT
Jer 4: 9 "the king and the officials *will* **l** heart, the H6
Jer 17: 4 your own fault *you will* **l** the inheritance I H9023
Jer 51:46 *Do* not **l** heart or be afraid when rumors H8216
Da 11:30 will oppose him, and *he will* **l heart**. H3874
Zec 9: 5 Gaza *will* **l** her king and Ashkelon will be H6
Mt 5:29 It is better for you to **l** one part of your body G660
Mt 5:30 It is better for you to **l** one part of your body G660
Mt 10:39 Whoever finds their life *will* **l** it, and G660
Mt 10:42 *that person will* certainly not **l** their reward." G660
Mt 16:25 For whoever wants to save their life *will* **l** it G660
Mk 8:35 For whoever wants to save their life *will* **l** it G660
Mk 9:41 the Messiah *will* certainly not **l** their reward G660
Lk 9:24 For whoever wants to save their life *will* **l** it G660
Lk 9:25 and yet **l** or forfeit their very self? G660
Lk 16: 4 do so that, when *I* **l** my job here G3496+1666
Lk 17:33 Whoever tries to keep their life *will* **l** it, and G660
Jn 6:39 that *I shall* **l** none of all those he has given G660
Jn 12:25 Anyone who loves their life *will* **l** it, while G660
Ac 19:27 *that* our trade *will* **l** *its* **good name** G1650+591+2262
Ac 27:34 Not one of you *will* **l** a single hair from his G660
2Co 4: 1 we have this ministry, *we do* not **l heart**. G1591
2Co 4:16 Therefore *we do* not **l heart**. Though G1591
Heb 12: 3 that you will not grow weary and **l** heart. G1725
Heb 12: 5 and *do* not **l heart** when he rebukes you G1725
2Jn 8 Watch out that *you do* not **l** what we have G660

LOSES (12) [LOSE]

1Sa 20: 7 But if *he* **l** his **temper**, you can be H3013+3013
Isa 44:12 He gets hungry and **l** his strength; he drinks H401
Mt 5:13 But if the salt **l** *its* **saltiness**, how can it be G3701
Mt 10:39 whoever **l** their life for my sake will G660
Mt 16:25 but whoever **l** their life for me will find it. G660
Mk 8:35 whoever **l** their life for me and for the G660
Mk 9:50 if it **l** its **saltiness**, how can you G383+1181
Lk 9:24 whoever **l** their life for me will save it. G660
Lk 14:34 but if it **l** *its* **saltiness**, how can it be G3701
Lk 15: 4 has a hundred sheep and **l** one of them. G660
Lk 15: 8 a woman has ten silver coins and **l** one. G660
Lk 17:33 and whoever **l** their life will preserve it. G660

LOSS (20) [LOSE]

Ge 31:39 torn by wild beasts; I **bore the l** myself. H2627
Ex 21:19 person for any **l of time** and see that the H8700
Ex 21:34 pit *must* **pay** the owner **for the l** H8966+4084
Ex 22:15 the money paid for the hire covers the **l**. NDT
Isa 47: 8 be a widow or suffer the **l of children**. H8890
Isa 47: 9 **l of children** and widowhood H8890
Jer 22:10 not weep for the dead king or **mourn** his **l**; H5653
Da 6: 2 them so that the king *might* not **suffer l**. A10472
Zep 3:18 who mourn over the **l** *of* your appointed H4946
Jn 11:19 Mary to comfort them **in** *the l of* their brother. AIT
Jn 13:22 **at a l to know** which of them he meant. G679
Ac 5:24 guard and the chief priests *were* **at a l**, G1389
Ac 25:20 I *was* **at a l** how to investigate such matters G679
Ac 27:10 bring great **l** to ship and cargo, G2422
Ac 27:21 spared yourselves this damage and **l**. G2422
Ro 11:12 their **l** means riches for the Gentiles G2488
1Co 3:15 the builder *will* **suffer l** but yet will be G2423
Php 3: 7 to me I now consider **l** for the sake of G2422
Php 3: 8 I consider everything a **l** because of the G2422
Heb 6: 6 *To* **their** *l* they are crucifying the Son of God AIT

LOSSES (4) [LOSE]

1Sa 4:17 the army has suffered heavy **l**. H4487
1Sa 23: 5 He inflicted heavy **l** on the Philistines H4804
1Ki 20:21 inflicted heavy **l** on the Arameans. H4804
2Ch 13:17 his troops inflicted heavy **l** on them, H4804

LOST (43) [LOSE]

Ge 34:19 **l** no **time** in doing what they said H336
Ex 14: 5 the Israelites go and have **l** their services!" H4946
Ex 22: 9 any other **l** *property* about which somebody H8
Lev 6: 3 if they find **l property** and lie about it, or if H8
Lev 6: 4 or the **l property** they found, H8
Lev 13:40 "A man *who has* **l** his **hair** and is H5307+8031
Lev 13:41 If *he has* **l** his **hair** from the front of H5307+8031
Nu 11: 6 But now we *have* **l** our appetite; we never H3313
Nu 17:12 *We are* **l**, we are all lost! H6
Nu 17:12 We are lost, we *are* all **l**! H6
Dt 22: 3 cloak or anything else they *have* **l**. H6+8
Jos 19:47 the territory of the Danites *was* **l** to them, H3655
1Sa 4:10 Israel **l** thirty thousand foot soldiers. H5877+4946
1Sa 9: 3 belonging to Saul's father Kish *were* **l**, H6
1Sa 9:20 As for the donkeys you **l** three days ago, do H6
2Sa 4: 1 in Hebron, he **l courage**, and all H8332+3338
1Ki 20:25 an army like the one you **l**— H5877+4946+907
Ne 6:16 **l** their **self-confidence**, H5877+4394+928+6524
Ps 73: 2 slipped; I *had* nearly **l** my foothold. H9161
Ps 119:176 I have strayed like a **l** sheep. Seek your H6
Ecc 5:14 wealth **l** through some misfortune, so that H6
Jer 50: 6 "My people have been **l** sheep; their H6
La 4: 1 How the gold *has* **l** *its* **luster**, the fine gold H6670
Eze 34: 4 brought back the strays or searched for the **l**. H6
Eze 34:16 I will search for the **l** and bring back the strays H6
Zec 11:16 over the land who will not care for the **l**, H3948
Mt 10: 6 Go rather to the **l** sheep of Israel. G660
Mt 15:24 "I was sent only to the **l** sheep of Israel." G660
Lk 15: 4 go after the **l** sheep until he finds it? G660
Lk 15: 6 'Rejoice with me; I have found my **l** sheep. G660
Lk 15: 9 'Rejoice with me; I have found my **l** coin. G660
Lk 15:24 is alive again; he was **l** and is found. G660
Lk 15:32 is alive again; *he was* **l** and is found. G660
Lk 19:10 Son of Man came to seek and to save the **l**." G660
Jn 17:12 None *has been* **l** except the one doomed G660
Jn 18: 9 "*I have* not **l** one of those you gave me." G660
Ac 27: 9 Much time *had been* **l**, and sailing had G1335
Ac 27:22 because not one of you will be **l**; only the G613
1Co 15:18 also who have fallen asleep in Christ *are* **l**. G660
Eph 4:19 *Having* **l all sensitivity**, they have given G556
Php 3: 8 for whose sake *I have* **l** all things. G2423
Col 2:19 They have **l** connection with the head G4024
Rev 12: 8 **and** they **l** their place in heaven. G4028+2351

LOT (86) [LOT'S, LOTS, PUR]

Ge 11:27 And Haran became the father of **L**. H4288
Ge 11:31 his grandson **L** son of Haran, and H4288
Ge 12: 4 LORD had told him; and **L** went with him. H4288
Ge 12: 5 his nephew **L**, all the possessions H4288
Ge 13: 1 everything he had, and **L** went with him. H4288
Ge 13: 5 Now **L**, who was moving about with H4288
Ge 13: 8 So Abram said to **L**, "Let's not have any H4288
Ge 13:10 **L** looked around and saw that the whole H4288
Ge 13:11 So **L** chose for himself the whole plain of H4288
Ge 13:12 while **L** lived among the cities of the plain H4288
Ge 13:14 said to Abram after **L** had parted from him H4288
Ge 14:12 off Abram's nephew **L** and his H4288
Ge 14:16 back his relative **L** and his possessions, H4288
Ge 19: 1 **L** was sitting in the gateway of the H4288
Ge 19: 5 They called to **L**, "Where are the men who H4288
Ge 19: 6 **L** went outside to meet them and shut the H4288
Ge 19: 9 pressure on **L** and moved forward to H4288
Ge 19:10 out and pulled **L** back into the house H4288
Ge 19:12 The two men said to **L**, "Do you have H4288
Ge 19:14 So **L** went out and spoke to his H4288
Ge 19:15 of dawn, the angels urged **L**, saying, H4288
Ge 19:18 But **L** said to them, "No, my lords, please! H4288
Ge 19:23 By the time **L** reached Zoar, the sun had H4288
Ge 19:29 he brought **L** out of the catastrophe H4288
Ge 19:29 overthrew the cities where **L** had lived. H4288
Ge 19:30 **L** and his two daughters left Zoar and H4288
Lev 16: 8 one **l** for the LORD and the other for the H1598
Lev 16: 9 bring the goat whose **l** falls to the LORD H1598
Lev 16:10 But the goat chosen by **l** as the scapegoat H1598
Nu 26:55 Be sure that the land is distributed by **l** H1598
Nu 26:56 be distributed by **l** among the larger and H1598
Nu 33:54 Distribute the land by **l**, according to your H1598
Nu 33:54 Whatever falls to them by **l** will be theirs H1598
Nu 34:13 "Assign this land by **l** as an inheritance H1598
Nu 36: 2 as an inheritance to the Israelites by **l**, H1598
Dt 2: 9 to the descendants of **L** as a possession." H4288
Dt 2:19 it as a possession to the descendants of **L**." H4288
Jos 14: 2 were assigned by **l** to the nine and a half H1598
Jos 18:11 The first **l** came up *for* the tribe of H1598
Jos 19: 1 The second **l** came out for the tribe of H1598
Jos 19:10 The third **l** came up for Zebulun according H1598
Jos 19:17 The fourth **l** came out for Issachar H1598
Jos 19:24 The fifth **l** came out for the tribe of Asher H1598
Jos 19:32 The sixth **l** came out for Naphtali H1598
Jos 19:40 The seventh **l** came out for the tribe of H1598
Jos 19:51 of Israel assigned by **l** at Shiloh in the H1598
Jos 21: 4 The first **l** came out for the Kohathites H1598
Jos 21:10 because the first **l** fell to them): H1598
1Sa 10:20 the tribe of Benjamin **was taken by l**. H4334
1Sa 14:41 Jonathan and Saul were taken by **l**, and the NDT
1Sa 14:42 "Cast the **l** between me and Jonathan my NDT
1Ch 6:54 because the first **l** was for them): H1598
1Ch 24: 7 The first **l** fell to Jehoiarib, the second to H1598
1Ch 25: 9 The first **l**, which was for Asaph, fell to H1598
1Ch 26:14 The **l** for the East Gate fell to Shelemiah H1598
1Ch 26:14 the **l** for the North Gate fell to him. H1598
1Ch 26:15 The **l** for the South Gate fell to Obed-Edom NDT
1Ch 26:15 the **l** for the storehouse fell to his sons. NDT
Est 3: 7 the **l**) was cast in the presence of H1598
Est 3: 7 And the **l** fell on the twelfth month, the H1598
Est 9:24 the pur (that is, the **l**) for their ruin and H1598
Job 31: 2 For what is our **l** *from* God above, our H2750
Ps 11: 6 a scorching wind will be their **l**. H4987+3926
Ps 16: 5 my cup; you make my **l** secure. H1598
Ps 50:18 you throw in your **l** with adulterers. H2750
Pr 6:33 Blows and disgrace are *his* **l**, and his H5162
Pr 16:33 The **l** is cast into the lap, but its every H1598
Pr 18:18 Casting the **l** settles disputes and keeps H1598
Ecc 3:22 to enjoy their work, because that is their **l**. H2750
Ecc 5:18 God has given them—for this is their **l**. H2750
Ecc 5:19 to accept their **l** and be happy in their toil H2750
Ecc 9: 9 For this is your **l** in life and in your H2750
Isa 17:14 the **l** of those who plunder us. H1598
Isa 57: 6 are your portion; indeed, they are your **l**. H1598
Jer 13:25 This is your **l**, the portion I have decreed H1598
Eze 21:22 right hand will come the **l** *for* Jerusalem, H7877
Jnh 1: 7 They cast lots and the **l** fell on Jonah. H1598
Mic 2: 5 of the LORD to divide the land by **l**. H1598
Lk 1: 9 *he was* **chosen by l**, according to the G3275
Lk 17:28 "It was the same in the days *of* **L**. People G3397
Lk 17:29 But the day **L** left Sodom, fire and sulfur G3397
Jn 19:24 "*Let's* **decide by l** who will get it. G3275
Ac 1:26 cast lots, and the **l** fell to Matthias; so he G3102
Ac 19:24 brought in **a l of** business for the G4024+3900
Ac 22:28 "I had to pay **a l of** money for my G4498
2Pe 2: 7 if he rescued **L**, a righteous man, who G3397

LOT'S (5) [LOT]

Ge 13: 7 arose between Abram's herders and **L**. H4288
Ge 19:26 But **L** wife looked back, and she became H2257S
Ge 19:36 So both of **L** daughters became pregnant H4288
Ps 83: 8 joined them to reinforce **L** descendants. H4288
Lk 17:32 Remember **L** wife! G3397

LOTAN (5) [LOTAN'S]

Ge 36:20 in the region: **L**, Shobal, Zibeon, Anah H4289
Ge 36:22 The sons of **L**: Hori and Homam. Timna H4289
Ge 36:29 the Horite chiefs: **L**, Shobal, Zibeon, Anah H4289
1Ch 1:38 **L**, Shobal, Zibeon, Anah, Dishon, Ezer H4289
1Ch 1:39 The sons of **L**: Hori and Homam. Timna H4289

LOTAN'S (2) [LOTAN]

Ge 36:22 Hori and Homam. Timna was **L** sister. H4289
1Ch 1:39 Hori and Homam. Timna was **L** sister. H4289

LOTHE, LOTHED, LOTHETH (KJV) DESPISED, LOATHE, NOT ABLE, REJECTED, WEARY

LOTIONS (4)

2Sa 12:20 washed, **put on l** and changed his clothes H6057
2Sa 14: 2 clothes, and don't use any **cosmetic l**. H9043
Da 10: 3 and *I* **used** no **l at all** until the H6057+6057
Am 6: 6 wine by the bowlful and use the finest **l**, H9043

LOTS (27) [LOT]

Lev 16: 8 He is to cast **l** for the two goats—one lot H1598
Jos 18: 6 to me and I will cast **l** for you in the H1598
Jos 18: 8 I will cast **l** for you here at Shiloh in H1598
Jos 18:10 Joshua then cast **l** for them in Shiloh in H1598
Jdg 20: 9 it in the order *decided by casting* **l**. H1598
1Ch 24: 5 They divided them impartially by **casting l** H1598
1Ch 24:31 They also cast **l**, just as their relatives the H1598
1Ch 25: 8 as well as student, cast **l** for their duties. H1598
1Ch 26:13 **L** were cast for each gate, according to H1598
1Ch 26:14 Then **l** were cast for his son Zechariah, H1598
1Ch 26:16 The **l** for the West Gate and the Shalleketh NDT
Ne 10:34 have cast **l** to determine when each of our H1598
Ne 11: 1 of the people cast **l** to bring one out of H1598
Job 6:27 You would even cast **l** for the fatherless NDT
Ps 22:18 among them and cast **l** for my garment. H1598
Pr 1:14 cast **l** with us; we will all share the loot"— H1598
Eze 21:21 *He will* **cast l** with arrows, he will consult H7837
Joel 3: 3 They cast **l** for my people and traded boys H1598
Ob 11 his gates and cast **l** for Jerusalem, H1598
Jnh 1: 7 let us cast **l** to find out who is responsible H1598
Jnh 1: 7 They cast **l** and the lot fell on Jonah. H1598
Na 3:10 **L** were cast for her nobles, and all her H1598
Mt 27:35 they divided up his clothes by casting **l**. G3102
Mk 15:24 they cast **l** to see what each would get. G3102
Lk 23:34 they divided up his clothes by casting **l**. G3102
Jn 19:24 among them and cast **l** for my garment." G3102
Ac 1:26 Then they cast **l**, and the lot fell to G3102

LOTUS (1) [LOTUSES]

Job 40:21 Under the **l plants** it lies, hidden among H7365

LOTUSES (1) [LOTUS]

Job 40:22 The **l** conceal it in their shadow; the H7365

LOUD (57) [ALOUD, LOUDER, LOUDLY]

Ge 27:34 out with a **l** and bitter cry H1524+6330+4394
Ex 11: 6 There will be **l** wailing throughout Egypt H1524
Ex 12:30 and there was **l** wailing in Egypt H1524
Ex 19:16 the mountain, and a very **l** trumpet blast. H2617
Dt 5:22 LORD proclaimed in a **l** voice to your H1524
Dt 27:14 to all the people of Israel in a **l** voice: H8123
Jos 6: 5 have the whole army give a **l** shout; then H1524
Jos 6:20 when the men gave a **l** shout, the wall H1524
1Sa 7:10 LORD thundered with **l** thunder against the H1524
1Ki 8:55 the whole assembly of Israel in a **l** voice, H1524
2Ch 15:14 an oath to the LORD with **l** acclamation, H1524
2Ch 20:19 the God of Israel, with a very **l** voice. H1524
Ezr 10:12 whole assembly responded with a **l** voice: H1524
Ne 9: 4 They cried out with **l** voices to the LORD H1524
Jer 12: 6 they have raised a **l** cry against you. H4849
Jer 46:17 'Pharaoh king of Egypt is only a **l noise** H8623
Eze 3:12 I heard behind me a **l** rumbling sound as H1524
Eze 3:13 wheels beside them, a **l** rumbling sound. H1524
Eze 9: 1 Then I heard him call out in a **l** voice H1524
Eze 11:13 I fell facedown and cried out in a **l** voice, H1524
Da 4:14 He called in a **l** *voice*: 'Cut down the tree A10264
Zep 1:10 New Quarter, and a **l** crash from the hills. H1524
Mt 24:31 will send his angels with a **l** trumpet call, G3489
Mt 27:46 the afternoon Jesus cried out in a **l** voice, G3489
Mt 27:50 Jesus had cried out again in a **l** voice, G3489
Mk 15:34 the afternoon Jesus cried out in a **l** voice, G3489
Mk 15:37 With a **l** cry, Jesus breathed his last. G3489
Lk 1:42 In a **l** voice she exclaimed: "Blessed are G3489
Lk 17:13 called out **in a l voice**, "Jesus G149+5889
Lk 17:15 came back, praising God in a **l** voice. G3489
Lk 19:37 joyfully to praise God in **l** voices for all the G3489

Lk 23:23 But with l shouts they insistently G3489
Lk 23:46 Jesus called out with a l voice, "Father G3489
Jn 7:37 Jesus stood and said **in a l voice,** "Let G3189
Jn 11:43 Jesus called in a l voice, "Lazarus, G3489
1Th 4:16 heaven, with a l **command,** with the voice G3026
Rev 1:10 I heard behind me a l voice like a trumpet G3489
Rev 5: 2 a mighty angel proclaiming in a l voice, G3489
Rev 5:12 In a l voice they were saying: "Worthy is G3489
Rev 6:10 They called out in a l voice, "How long G3489
Rev 7: 2 He called out in a l voice to the four G3489
Rev 7:10 And they cried out in a l voice: "Salvation G3489
Rev 8:13 was flying in midair call out in a l voice: G3489
Rev 10: 3 he gave a l shout like the roar of a G3489
Rev 11:12 Then they heard a l voice from heaven G3489
Rev 11:15 there were l voices in heaven, which G3489
Rev 12:10 Then I heard a l voice in heaven say G3489
Rev 14: 2 waters and like a l peal of thunder. G3489
Rev 14: 7 He said in a l voice, "Fear God and give G3489
Rev 14: 9 followed them and said in a l voice: G3489
Rev 14:15 called in a l voice to him who was G3489
Rev 14:18 called in a l voice to him who had G3489
Rev 16: 1 Then I heard a l voice from the temple G3489
Rev 16:17 of the temple came a l voice from the G3489
Rev 19: 6 rushing waters and like l peals of thunder, G2708
Rev 19:17 who cried in a l voice to all the birds G3489
Rev 21: 3 And I heard a l voice from the throne G3489

LOUDER (7) [LOUD]

Ex 19:19 *As* the sound of the trumpet **grew l and louder** H2143+2256+2618+4394
Ex 19:19 *As* the sound of the trumpet **grew louder and l** H2143+2256+2618+4394
1Ki 18:27 began to taunt them. "Shout l!" he said. H1524
1Ki 18:28 So they shouted l and slashed themselves H1524
Mt 20:31 be quiet, but they shouted **all the l,** "Lord, G3505
Mt 27:23 But they shouted **all the l,** "Crucify him!" G4360
Mk 15:14 But they shouted **all the l,** "Crucify him!" G4360

LOUDLY (7) [LOUD]

Ge 45: 2 And he **wept so l** that the Egyptians H1140+5989+906+7754+928
Ge 50:10 they lamented l and bitterly; and H1524
2Sa 13:36 the king's sons came in, wailing l. H5951+7754
Est 4: 1 out into the city, wailing l and bitterly. H1524
Pr 27:14 If anyone l blesses their H928+7754+1524
Da 3: 4 Then the herald l proclaimed A10089+10264
Mk 5:38 with people crying and wailing l. G4498

LOUNGE (1) [LOUNGING]

Am 6: 4 adorned with ivory and l on your couches. H6242

LOUNGING (2) [LOUNGE]

Isa 47: 8 l in your security and saying to yourself H3782
Am 6: 7 go into exile; your feasting and l will end. H6242

LOVE (574) [BELOVED, BELOVED'S, LOVED, LOVELY, LOVER, LOVERS, LOVES, LOVING]

Ge 4: 1 Adam **made l to** his wife Eve, and she H3359
Ge 4:17 Cain **made l to** his wife, and she became H3359
Ge 4:25 Adam **made l to** his wife again, and she H3359
Ge 20:13 'This is how you can show your l to me: H2876
Ge 22: 2 only son, whom *you* l—Isaac—and go to H170
Ge 29:18 Jacob *was* **in l with** Rachel and said, "I'll H170
Ge 29:20 a few days to him because of his l *for* her. H173
Ge 29:21 and *I want to* **make l to** her. H995+448
Ge 29:23 to Jacob, and Jacob **made l to** her. H995+448
Ge 29:30 Jacob **made l to** Rachel also, and his H995+448
Ge 29:30 and *his* l *for* Rachel *was* greater than his H170
Ge 29:30 Rachel was greater than his l for Leah. NDT
Ge 29:32 Surely my husband *will* l me now." H170
Ge 38: 2 He married her and **made l to** her; H995+448
Ex 15:13 In your **unfailing l** you will lead the H2876
Ex 20: 6 showing l to a thousand generations H2876
Ex 20: 6 generations of *those who* l me and keep H170
Ex 21: 5 '*I* l my master and my wife and children H170
Ex 34: 6 to anger, abounding in l and faithfulness, H2876
Ex 34: 7 maintaining l to thousands, and forgiving H2876
Lev 19:18 but l your neighbor as yourself. H170
Lev 19:34 L them as yourself, for you were foreigners H170
Nu 14:18 abounding in l and forgiving sin and H2876
Nu 14:19 In accordance with your great l, forgive the H2876
Dt 5:10 showing l to a thousand generations H2876
Dt 5:10 generations of *those who* l me and keep H170
Dt 6: 5 L the LORD your God with all your heart H170
Dt 7: 9 keeping his covenant of l to a thousand H2876
Dt 7: 9 generations of *those who* l him and keep H170
Dt 7:12 God will keep his covenant of l with you, H2876
Dt 7:13 *He will* l you and bless you and increase H170
Dt 10:12 obedience to him, to l him, to serve the H170
Dt 10:19 And *you are to* l those who are foreigners H170
Dt 11: 1 L the LORD your God and keep his H170
Dt 11:13 to l the LORD your God and to serve him H170
Dt 11:22 you to follow—to l the LORD your God, to H170
Dt 13: 3 find out whether you l him with all your H170
Dt 13: 6 the wife you l, or your closest friend H2668
Dt 19: 9 to l the LORD your God and to walk always H170
Dt 21:15 is the son of the wife *he does* **not** l, H8535
Dt 21:16 the son of the wife *he does* **not** l. H8533
Dt 30: 6 so that you *may* l him with all your heart H170
Dt 30:16 command you today to l the LORD your God H170
Dt 30:20 that you *may* l the LORD your God, listen H170
Dt 33: 3 Surely it is you *who* l the people; all the H2462
Jos 22: 5 to l the LORD your God, to walk in H170
Jos 23:11 So be very careful to l the LORD your God. H170
Jdg 5:31 But *may all who* l you be like the sun when H170
Jdg 14:16 *You* don't really l me. You've H170
Jdg 16: 4 *he* **fell in l with** a woman in the Valley of H170
Jdg 16:15 "How can you say, '*I* l you,' when you H170
Ru 4:13 When *he* **made l to** her, the LORD H995+448
1Sa 1:19 Elkanah **made l to** his wife Hannah, and H3359
1Sa 18:20 Saul's daughter Michal *was* **in l with** David, H170
1Sa 18:22 his attendants all l you; now become H170
1Sa 20:17 had David reaffirm his oath out of l *for* him, H170
2Sa 1:26 Your l for me was wonderful, more H173
2Sa 7:15 But my l will never be taken away from H2876
2Sa 11:11 and drink and **make l to** my wife? H8886+6640
2Sa 12:24 he went to her and **made l to** her. H8886+6640
2Sa 13: 1 Amnon son of David **fell in l with** Tamar H170
2Sa 13: 4 said to him, "I'm **in l with** Tamar, my H170
2Sa 16:17 "So this is the l you show your friend? H2876
2Sa 19: 6 You l those who hate you and hate those H170
2Sa 19: 6 who hate you and hate *those who* l you. H170
1Ki 3: 3 Solomon **showed** *his* l *for* the LORD by H170
1Ki 3:26 deeply moved out of l for her son and H8171
1Ki 8:23 keep your covenant of l with your servants H2876
1Ki 10: 9 Because of the LORD's eternal l *for* Israel, H173
1Ki 11: 2 Solomon held fast to them in l. H173
1Ch 2:21 *He* **made l to** her, and she bore him H995+448
1Ch 7:23 Then *he* **made l to** his wife again H995+448
1Ch 16:34 for he is good; his l endures forever. H2876
1Ch 16:41 to the LORD, "for his l endures forever." H2876
1Ch 17:13 I will never take my l away from him, as I H2876
2Ch 5:13 "He is good; his l endures forever." Then H2876
2Ch 6:14 keep your covenant of l with your servants H2876
2Ch 6:42 the **great** l *promised to* David your H2876
2Ch 7: 3 "He is good; his l endures forever." H2876
2Ch 7: 6 saying, "His l endures forever." H2876
2Ch 9: 8 Because of the l *of* your God *for* Israel and H170
2Ch 19: 2 help the wicked and l those who hate the H170
2Ch 20:21 to the LORD, for his l endures forever." H2876
Ezr 3:11 his l toward Israel endures forever. H2876
Ne 1: 5 his covenant of l with those who love H2876
Ne 1: 5 of love with *those who* l him and keep his H170
Ne 9:17 slow to anger and abounding in l. H2876
Ne 9:32 who keeps his covenant of l, do not let all H2876
Ne 13:22 mercy to me according to your great l. H2876
Job 15:34 consume the tents of **those who l bribes.** H8816
Job 19:19 those *I* l have turned against me. H170
Job 37:13 to water his earth and show his l. H2876
Ps 4: 2 How long *will you* l delusions and seek H170
Ps 5: 7 by your great l, can come into your H2876
Ps 5:11 that *those who* l your name may rejoice in H170
Ps 6: 4 save me because of your **unfailing l.** H2876
Ps 11: 5 the wicked, *those who* l violence, he H170
Ps 13: 5 But I trust in your **unfailing l;** my heart H2876
Ps 17: 7 Show me the wonders of your **great l,** you H2876
Ps 18: 1 *I* l you, LORD, my strength. H8163
Ps 18:50 he shows **unfailing l** to his anointed H2876
Ps 21: 7 through the **unfailing l** *of* the Most High H2876
Ps 23: 6 your goodness and l will follow me all the H2876
Ps 25: 6 your great mercy and l, for they are from H2876
Ps 25: 7 according to your l remember me, for you, H2876
Ps 26: 3 mindful of your **unfailing l** and have lived H2876
Ps 26: 8 *I* l the house where you live, the H170
Ps 31: 7 I will be glad and rejoice in your l, for you H2876
Ps 31:16 your servant; save me in your **unfailing l.** H2876
Ps 31:21 the wonders of his l when I was in a city H2876
Ps 31:23 L the LORD, all his faithful people! H170
Ps 32:10 the LORD's **unfailing l** surrounds the H2876
Ps 33: 5 the earth is full of his **unfailing l.** H2876
Ps 33:18 on those whose hope is in his **unfailing l,** H2876
Ps 33:22 May your **unfailing l** be with us, LORD H2876
Ps 36: 5 Your l, LORD, reaches to the heavens, your H2876
Ps 36: 7 How priceless is your **unfailing l,** O God H2876
Ps 36:10 Continue your l to those who know you H2876
Ps 40:10 do not conceal your l and your H2876
Ps 40:11 may your l and faithfulness always protect H2876
Ps 42: 8 By day the LORD directs his l, at night his H2876
Ps 44:26 rescue us because of your **unfailing l.** H2876
Ps 45: 7 *You* l righteousness and hate wickedness H170
Ps 48: 9 we meditate on your **unfailing l.** H2876
Ps 51: 1 according to your **unfailing l;** according to H2876
Ps 52: 3 *You* l evil rather than good, falsehood H170
Ps 52: 4 *You* l every harmful word, you deceitful H170
Ps 52: 8 I trust in God's **unfailing l** for ever and H2876
Ps 57: 3 God sends forth his l and his faithfulness. H2876
Ps 57:10 For great is your l, reaching to the H2876
Ps 59:16 in the morning I will sing of your l; for you H2876
Ps 60: 5 that *those* you l may be delivered. H3351
Ps 61: 7 appoint your l and faithfulness to protect H2876
Ps 62:12 with you, Lord, is **unfailing l**"; and, "You H2876
Ps 63: 3 Because your l is better than life, my lips H2876
Ps 66:20 my prayer or withheld his l from me! H2876
Ps 69:13 time of your favor; in your great l, O God, H2876
Ps 69:16 out of the goodness of your l; in your H2876
Ps 69:36 and *those who* l his name will dwell there. H170
Ps 77: 8 Has his **unfailing l** vanished forever? Has H2876
Ps 85: 7 Show us your **unfailing l,** LORD, and grant H2876
Ps 85:10 L and faithfulness meet together H2876
Ps 86: 5 abounding in l to all who call to you. H2876
Ps 86:13 For great is your l toward me; you have H2876
Ps 86:15 to anger, abounding in l and faithfulness. H2876
Ps 88:11 Is your l declared in the grave, your H2876
Ps 89: 1 I will sing of the LORD's **great l** forever H2876
Ps 89: 2 will declare that your l stands firm forever, H2876
Ps 89:14 l and faithfulness go before you. H2876
Ps 89:24 My faithful l will be with him, and through H2876
Ps 89:28 I will maintain my l to him forever, and H2876
Ps 89:33 I will not take my l from him, nor will I H2876
Ps 89:49 where is your former **great l,** which in H2876
Ps 90:14 us in the morning with your **unfailing l,** H2876
Ps 92: 2 proclaiming your l in the morning and H2876
Ps 94:18 your **unfailing l,** LORD, supported H2876
Ps 97:10 *Let those who* l the LORD hate evil, for he H170
Ps 98: 3 has remembered his l and his faithfulness H2876
Ps 100: 5 the LORD is good and his l endures forever; H2876
Ps 101: 1 I will sing of your l and justice; to you H2876
Ps 103: 4 crowns you with l and compassion, H2876
Ps 103: 8 gracious, slow to anger, abounding in l. H2876
Ps 103:11 so great is his l for those who fear him; H2876
Ps 103:17 the LORD's l is with those who fear H2876
Ps 106: 1 for he is good; his l endures forever. H2876
Ps 106:45 out of his great l he relented. H2876
Ps 107: 1 for he is good; his l endures forever. H2876
Ps 107: 8 the LORD for his **unfailing l** and his H2876
Ps 107:15 the LORD for his **unfailing l** and his H2876
Ps 107:21 the LORD for his **unfailing l** and his H2876
Ps 107:31 the LORD for his **unfailing l** and his H2876
Ps 108: 4 For great is your l, higher than the H2876
Ps 108: 6 that *those* you l may be delivered. H3351
Ps 109:21 out of the goodness of your l, deliver me. H2876
Ps 109:26 save me according to your **unfailing l.** H2876
Ps 115: 1 because of your l and faithfulness. H2876
Ps 116: 1 *I* l the LORD, for he heard my voice; he H170
Ps 117: 2 For great is his l toward us, and the H2876
Ps 118: 1 for he is good; his l endures forever. H2876
Ps 118: 2 Let Israel say: "His l endures forever." H2876
Ps 118: 3 "His l endures forever." H2876
Ps 118: 4 fear the LORD say: "His l endures forever." H2876
Ps 118:29 for he is good; his l endures forever. H2876
Ps 119:41 May your **unfailing l** come to me, LORD H2876
Ps 119:47 in your commands because *I* l them. H170
Ps 119:48 your commands, which *I* l, that I may H170
Ps 119:64 The earth is filled with your l, LORD; teach H2876
Ps 119:76 May your **unfailing l** be my comfort H2876
Ps 119:88 In your **unfailing l** preserve my life, that I H2876
Ps 119:97 how *I* l your law! I meditate on it all H170
Ps 119:113 double-minded people, but *I* l your law. H170
Ps 119:119 like dross; therefore *I* l your statutes. H170
Ps 119:124 according to your l and teach me your H2876
Ps 119:127 *I* l your commands more than gold H170
Ps 119:132 you always do to *those who* l your name. H170
Ps 119:149 Hear my voice in accordance with your l H2876
Ps 119:159 See how *I* l your precepts; preserve my H170
Ps 119:159 LORD, in accordance with your l. H2876
Ps 119:163 hate and detest falsehood but *I* l your law. H170
Ps 119:165 Great peace have *those who* l your law H170
Ps 119:167 I obey your statutes, for *I* l them greatly. H170
Ps 122: 6 "May *those who* l you be secure H170
Ps 130: 7 with the LORD is **unfailing l** and with him H2876
Ps 136: 1 he is good. His l endures forever. H2876
Ps 136: 2 to the God of gods. His l endures forever. H2876
Ps 136: 3 to the Lord of lords: His l endures forever. H2876
Ps 136: 4 does great wonders, His l endures forever. H2876
Ps 136: 5 made the heavens, His l endures forever. H2876
Ps 136: 6 upon the waters, His l endures forever. H2876
Ps 136: 7 the great lights—His l endures forever. H2876
Ps 136: 8 to govern the day, His l endures forever. H2876
Ps 136: 9 to govern the night; His l endures forever. H2876
Ps 136:10 firstborn of Egypt His l endures forever. H2876
Ps 136:11 from among them His l endures forever. H2876
Ps 136:12 outstretched arm; His l endures forever. H2876
Ps 136:13 Red Sea asunder His l endures forever. H2876
Ps 136:14 the midst of it, His l endures forever. H2876
Ps 136:15 into the Red Sea; His l endures forever. H2876
Ps 136:16 the wilderness; His l endures forever. H2876
Ps 136:17 down great kings, His l endures forever. H2876
Ps 136:18 mighty kings—His l endures forever. H2876
Ps 136:19 king of the Amorites His l endures forever. H2876
Ps 136:20 king of Bashan—His l endures forever. H2876
Ps 136:21 as an inheritance, His l endures forever. H2876
Ps 136:22 to his servant Israel. His l endures forever. H2876
Ps 136:23 us in our low estate His l endures forever. H2876
Ps 136:24 from our enemies. His l endures forever. H2876
Ps 136:25 to every creature. His l endures forever. H2876
Ps 136:26 the God of heaven. His l endures forever. H2876
Ps 138: 2 your name for your **unfailing l** and your H2876
Ps 138: 8 vindicate me; your l, LORD, endures forever H2876
Ps 143: 8 bring me word of your **unfailing l,** H2876
Ps 143:12 In your **unfailing l,** silence my enemies H2876
Ps 145: 8 slow to anger and rich in l. H2876
Ps 145:20 The LORD watches over all *who* l him, but H170
Ps 147:11 who put their hope in his **unfailing l.** H2876
Pr 1:22 "How long *will you* who are simple l your H170
Pr 3: 3 Let l and faithfulness never leave you H2876
Pr 4: 6 she will protect you; l her, and she will H170
Pr 5:19 may you ever be intoxicated with her l. H173
Pr 7:18 let's drink deeply of l till morning; let's H1856
Pr 7:18 till morning; let's enjoy ourselves with l! H171
Pr 8:17 I l those who love me, and those who seek H170
Pr 8:17 I love *those who* l me, and those who seek H170
Pr 8:21 inheritance on *those who* l me and making H170
Pr 8:36 harm themselves; all who hate me l death." H170
Pr 9: 8 rebuke the wise and *they will* l you. H170
Pr 10:12 up conflict, but l covers over all wrongs. H173
Pr 14:22 plan what is good find l and faithfulness. H2876
Pr 15:17 of vegetables with l than a fattened calf H173

Pr 16: 6 Through l and faithfulness sin is atoned H2876
Pr 17: 9 Whoever would foster l covers over an H173
Pr 18:21 and *those who* l it will eat its fruit. H170
Pr 19:22 What a person desires is **unfailing** l H2876
Pr 20: 6 Many claim to have **unfailing** l, but a H2876
Pr 20:13 *Do* not l sleep or you will grow poor; stay H170
Pr 20:28 L and faithfulness keep a king safe H2876
Pr 20:28 through l his throne is made secure. H2876
Pr 21:21 pursues righteousness and l finds life, H2876
Pr 27: 5 Better is open rebuke than hidden l. H173
Ecc 3: 8 a time to l and a time to hate, a time for H170
Ecc 9: 1 one knows whether l or hate awaits them. H173
Ecc 9: 6 Their l, their hate and their jealousy have H173
Ecc 9: 9 with your wife, whom *you* l, all the days of H170
SS 1: 2 your l is more delightful than wine. H1856
SS 1: 3 No wonder the young women l you! H170
SS 1: 4 we will praise your l more than wine. H1856
SS 1: 7 Tell me, you whom I l, where you graze H170
SS 2: 4 and let his banner over me be l. H173
SS 2: 5 refresh me with apples, for I am faint with l. H173
SS 2: 7 not arouse or awaken l until it so desires. H173
SS 3: 5 not arouse or awaken l until it so desires. H173
SS 3:10 with purple, its interior inlaid with l. H173
SS 4:10 How delightful is your l, my sister, my H1856
SS 4:10 much more pleasing is your l than wine, H1856
SS 5: 1 friends, and drink; drink your fill of l. H1856
SS 5: 8 will you tell him? Tell him I am faint with l. H173
SS 7: 6 how pleasing, my l, with your delights! H173
SS 7:12 are in bloom—there I will give you my l. H1856
SS 8: 4 not arouse or awaken l until it so desires. H173
SS 8: 6 seal on your arm; for l is as strong as death H173
SS 8: 7 Many waters cannot quench l; rivers cannot H173
SS 8: 7 to give all the wealth of one's house for l, H173
Isa 1:23 they all l bribes and chase after gifts. H170
Isa 5: 1 I will sing for the *one* I l a song about his H3351
Isa 8: 3 Then *I* **made** l **to** the prophetess, and H7928+448
Isa 16: 5 In l a throne will be established; in H2876
Isa 38:17 **In** *your* l you **kept** me from the pit of H3137
Isa 43: 4 and because I l you, I will give H170
Isa 54:10 my **unfailing** l for you will not be H2876
Isa 55: 3 with you, my faithful l *promised to* David. H2876
Isa 56: 6 minister to him, to l the name of the LORD H170
Isa 56:10 they lie around and dream, *they* l to sleep. H170
Isa 57: 8 made a pact with those whose beds *you* l, H170
Isa 61: 8 the LORD, l justice; I hate robbery and H170
Isa 63: 9 In his l and mercy he redeemed them; he H173
Isa 66:10 all you *who* l her; rejoice greatly H170
Jer 2:25 *I* l foreign gods, and I must go H170
Jer 2:33 How skilled you are at pursuing l! Even the H173
Jer 5:31 own authority, and my people l it this way. H170
Jer 12: 7 I will give the *one* I l into the hands of her H3342
Jer 14:10 "*They* greatly l to wander; they do not H170
Jer 16: 5 my l and my pity from this people, H2876
Jer 31: 3 "I have loved you with an everlasting l; H173
Jer 32:18 You show l to thousands but bring the H2876
Jer 33:11 the LORD is good; his l endures forever." H2876
La 3:22 of the LORD's **great** l we are not consumed, H2876
La 3:32 compassion, so great is his **unfailing** l. H2876
Eze 16: 8 saw that you were old enough for l, H1856
Eze 23:17 to the bed of l, and in their lust H1856
Eze 33:31 Their mouths speak of l, but their hearts H6313
Eze 33:32 than one who sings l songs with a H6312
Da 9: 4 his covenant of l with those who love H2876
Da 9: 4 of love with *those who* l him and keep his H170
Hos 1: 6 for *I will* no longer **show** l *to* Israel, that I H8163
Hos 1: 7 Yet *I will* **show** l *to* Judah; and I will save H8163
Hos 2: 4 *I will* not **show** *my* l *to* her children H8163
Hos 2:19 justice, in l and compassion. H2876
Hos 2:23 *I will* **show** *my* l to the one I called 'Not H8163
Hos 3: 1 **show** *your* l *to* your wife again, though H170
Hos 3: 1 L her as the LORD loves the Israelites, NDT
Hos 3: 1 turn to other gods and l the sacred raisin H170
Hos 4: 1 no faithfulness, no l, no acknowledgment H2876
Hos 4:18 their rulers dearly l shameful ways. H170
Hos 6: 4 Your l is like the morning mist, like the H2876
Hos 9: 1 *you* l the wages of a prostitute at every H170
Hos 9:15 *I will* no longer l them; all their leaders are H170
Hos 10:12 reap the fruit of **unfailing** l, and break up H2876
Hos 11: 4 cords of human kindness, with ties of l. H173
Hos 12: 6 your God; maintain l and justice, and wait H2876
Hos 14: 4 heal their waywardness and l them freely, H170
Joel 2:13 slow to anger and abounding in l, and he H2876
Am 4: 5 this is what *you* l to do," declares the H170
Am 5:15 Hate evil, l good; maintain justice in the H170
Jnh 2: 8 idols turn away from **God's** l *for* them. H2876
Jnh 4: 2 slow to anger and abounding in l, a God H2876
Mic 3: 2 you who hate good and l evil; who tear the H170
Mic 6: 8 To act justly and *to* l mercy and to walk H170
Mic 7:20 to Jacob, and show l to Abraham, as you H2876
Zep 3:17 in his l he will no longer rebuke you H173
Zec 8:17 each other, and *do* not l to swear falsely. H170
Zec 8:19 Therefore l truth and peace." H170
Mt 3:17 is my Son, whom I l; with him I am well G28
Mt 5:43 'L your neighbor and hate your enemy. G26
Mt 5:44 l your enemies and pray for those who G26
Mt 5:46 If *you* l those who love you, what reward will G26
Mt 5:46 If you love those *who* l you, what reward will G26
Mt 6: 5 for *they* l to pray standing in the G5797
Mt 6:24 Either you will hate the one and l the other G26
Mt 12:18 I have chosen, the *one* I l, in whom I delight G28
Mt 17: 5 is my Son, whom I l; with him I am well G28
Mt 19:19 and 'l your neighbor as yourself. G26
Mt 22:37 " 'L the Lord your God with all your heart G26
Mt 22:39 second is like it: 'L your neighbor as yourself G26
Mt 23: 6 *they* l the place of honor at banquets and G5797
Mt 23: 7 they l to be greeted with respect in the NDT
Mt 24:12 of wickedness, the l of most will grow cold, G27
Mk 1:11 are my Son, whom I l; with you I am well G28
Mk 9: 7 "This is my Son, whom I l. Listen to him!" G28
Mk 12:30 L the Lord your God with all your heart and G26
Mk 12:31 'L your neighbor as yourself G26
Mk 12:33 *To* l him with all your heart, with all your G26
Mk 12:33 *to* l your neighbor as yourself is more G26
Lk 3:22 are my Son, whom I l; with you I am well G28
Lk 6:27 L your enemies, do good to those who hate G26
Lk 6:32 "If *you* l those who love you, what credit is G26
Lk 6:32 "If you love those *who* l you, what credit is G26
Lk 6:32 Even sinners l those who love them. G26
Lk 6:32 Even sinners love those *who* l them. G26
Lk 6:35 But l your enemies, do good to them, and G26
Lk 7:42 Now which of them *will* l him more?" G26
Lk 7:47 been forgiven—as *her* great l *has* **shown**. G26
Lk 10:27 " 'L the Lord your God with all your heart G26
Lk 10:27 and, 'L your neighbor as yourself. NDT
Lk 11:42 you neglect justice and the l of God. G27
Lk 11:43 because *you* l the most important seats in G26
Lk 16:13 Either you will hate the one and l the other G26
Lk 20:13 send my son, whom I l; perhaps they will G28
Lk 20:46 in flowing robes and l to be greeted with G5797
Jn 5:42 you do not have the l of God in your hearts. G27
Jn 8:42 were your Father, *you* would l me, for I have G26
Jn 11: 3 word to Jesus, "Lord, the one *you* l is sick." G5797
Jn 13:34 command I give you: L one another. G26
Jn 13:34 I have loved you, so you *must* l one another. G26
Jn 13:35 are my disciples, if *you* l one another." G27+2400
Jn 14:15 "If *you* l me, keep my commands. G26
Jn 14:21 I too *will* l them and show myself to G26
Jn 14:23 My Father *will* l them, and we will come to G26
Jn 14:24 Anyone *who does* not l me will not obey my G26
Jn 14:31 world may learn that *I* l the Father and do G26
Jn 15: 9 so have I loved you. Now remain in my l. G27
Jn 15:10 you will remain in my l, just as I have kept G27
Jn 15:10 my Father's commands and remain in his l. G27
Jn 15:12 L each other as I have loved you. G26
Jn 15:13 Greater l has no one than this: to lay down G27
Jn 15:17 This is my command: L each other. G26
Jn 15:19 to the world, it would l you *as* its own. G5797
Jn 17:26 in order that the l you have for me may be G27
Jn 21:15 son of John, *do you* l me more than these?" G26
Jn 21:15 he said, "you know that *I* l you. G5797
Jn 21:16 "Simon son of John, *do you* l me? G26
Jn 21:16 Lord, you know that *I* l you. G5797
Jn 21:17 "Simon son of John, *do you* l me? G5797
Jn 21:17 asked him the third time, "*Do you* l me?" G5797
Jn 21:17 know all things; you know that *I* l you." G5797
Ro 1:31 understanding, no fidelity, **no** l, no mercy. G845
Ro 5: 5 because God's l has been poured out into G27
Ro 5: 8 But God demonstrates his own l for us in this G27
Ro 8:28 God works for the good *of* those *who* l him, G26
Ro 8:35 Who shall separate us from the l of Christ G27
Ro 8:39 to separate us from the l of God that is in G27
Ro 12: 9 L must be sincere. Hate what is evil; cling to G27
Ro 12:10 Be devoted to one another *in* l. Honor one G5789
Ro 13: 8 except the continuing debt *to* l one another G26
Ro 13: 9 one command: "L your neighbor as yourself." G26
Ro 13:10 L does no harm to a neighbor. Therefore love G27
Ro 13:10 Therefore l is the fulfillment of the law. G27
Ro 14:15 what you eat, you are no longer acting in l. G27
Ro 15:30 Lord Jesus Christ and by the l of the Spirit, G27
1Co 2: 9 God has prepared for those *who* l him— G26
1Co 4:17 Timothy, my son whom I l, who is faithful in G28
1Co 4:21 shall I come in l and with a gentle spirit? G27
1Co 8: 1 But knowledge puffs up while l builds up. G27
1Co 13: 1 do not have l, I am only a resounding G27
1Co 13: 2 mountains, but do not have l, I am nothing. G27
1Co 13: 3 may boast, but do not have l, I gain nothing. G27
1Co 13: 4 L is patient, love is kind. It does not envy, it G27
1Co 13: 4 Love is patient, l is kind. It does not envy, it G27
1Co 13: 6 L does not delight in evil but rejoices with NDT
1Co 13: 8 L never fails. But where there are prophecies, G27
1Co 13:13 faith, hope and l. But the greatest of G27
1Co 13:13 But the greatest of these is l. G27
1Co 14: 1 Follow the *way of* l and eagerly desire gifts G27
1Co 16:14 Do everything in l. G27
1Co 16:22 If anyone *does* not l the Lord, let that G5797
1Co 16:24 My l to all of you in Christ Jesus. Amen. G27
2Co 2: 4 to let you know the depth *of* my l for you. G27
2Co 2: 8 therefore, to reaffirm your l for him. G27
2Co 5:14 For Christ's l compels us, because we are G27
2Co 6: 6 kindness; in the Holy Spirit and in sincere l; G27
2Co 8: 7 earnestness and *in* the l we have kindled in G27
2Co 8: 8 test the sincerity *of* your l by comparing it G27
2Co 8:24 men the proof *of* your l and the reason for G27
2Co 11:11 Because *I do* not l you? God knows I do G26
2Co 12:15 myself as well. If *I* l you more, will you love G26
2Co 12:15 If I love you more, *will* you l *me* less? G26
2Co 13:11 And the God *of* l and peace will be with you. G27
2Co 13:14 Jesus Christ, and the l of God, and the G27
Gal 5: 6 counts is faith expressing itself through l. G27
Gal 5:13 rather, serve one another humbly in l. G27
Gal 5:14 command: "L your neighbor as yourself." G26
Gal 5:22 But the fruit of the Spirit is l, joy, peace G27
Eph 1: 4 to be holy and blameless in his sight. In l G27
Eph 1:15 Lord Jesus and your l for all God's people, G27
Eph 2: 4 But because of his great l for us, God, who is G27
Eph 3:17 that you, being rooted and established in l, G27
Eph 3:18 long and high and deep is the l of Christ, NDT
Eph 3:19 to know this l that surpasses knowledge G27
Eph 4: 2 be patient, bearing with one another in l. G27
Eph 4:15 speaking the truth in l, we will grow to G27
Eph 4:16 grows and builds itself up in l, as each part G27
Eph 5: 2 walk in the way of l, just as Christ loved G27
Eph 5:25 Husbands, l your wives, just as Christ loved G26
Eph 5:28 husbands ought to l their wives as their own G26
Eph 5:33 each one of you also *must* l his wife as he G26
Eph 6:23 l with faith from God the Father and the G27
Eph 6:24 Grace to all who l our Lord Jesus Christ with G26
Eph 6:24 love our Lord Jesus Christ with an undying l. NDT
Php 1: 9 that your l may abound more and more in G27
Php 1:16 The latter do so out of l, knowing that I am G27
Php 2: 1 if any comfort *from* his l, if any common G27
Php 2: 2 having the same l, being one in spirit and of G27
Php 4: 1 you whom I l and long for, my joy G28
Col 1: 4 in Christ Jesus and *of* the l you have for all G27
Col 1: 5 the faith and l that spring from the hope NDT
Col 1: 8 who also told us *of* your l in the Spirit. G27
Col 2: 2 may be encouraged in heart and united in l, G27
Col 3:14 And over all these virtues put on l, which G27
Col 3:19 l your wives and do not be harsh with them. G26
1Th 1: 3 your labor *prompted by* l, and your G27
1Th 3: 6 brought good news about your faith and l. G27
1Th 3:12 the Lord make your l increase and overflow G27
1Th 4: 9 about your l **for one another** we do not G5789
1Th 4: 9 have been taught by God to l each other. G26
1Th 4:10 you do l all of God's family throughout G899S
1Th 5: 8 putting on faith and l as a breastplate, and G27
1Th 5:13 the highest regard in l because of their work. G27
2Th 1: 3 the l all of you have for one another is G27
2Th 2:10 because they refused to l the truth and so be G27
2Th 3: 5 your hearts into God's l and Christ's G27
1Ti 1: 5 The goal of this command is l, which comes G27
1Ti 1:14 with the faith and l that are in Christ Jesus G27
1Ti 2:15 l and holiness with propriety. G27
1Ti 4:12 in conduct, in l, in faith and in purity G27
1Ti 6:10 For the **l of money** is a root of all kinds of G5794
1Ti 6:11 godliness, faith, l, endurance and G27
2Ti 1: 7 gives us power, l and self-discipline. G27
2Ti 1:13 teaching, with faith and l in Christ Jesus. G27
2Ti 2:22 l and peace, along with those who call G27
2Ti 3: 3 **without** l, unforgiving, slanderous, without G845
2Ti 3:10 my purpose, faith, patience, l, endurance, G27
Titus 2: 2 sound in faith, *in* l and in endurance. G27
Titus 2: 4 women *to* l their **husbands** and G5791+1639
[Titus 2: 4 *to* l their husbands and **children** G5817+1639]
Titus 3: 4 the kindness and l of God our Savior G5792
Titus 3:15 Greet those *who* l us in the faith G5797
Phm 5 because I hear *about* your l for all his holy G27
Phm 7 Your l has given me great joy and G27
Phm 9 I prefer to appeal to you on the basis of l G27
Heb 6:10 your work and the l you have shown him as G27
Heb 10:24 one another on *toward* l and good deeds, G27
Heb 13: 5 your lives **free from the** l **of money** and be G921
Jas 1:12 the Lord has promised *to* those *who* l him. G26
Jas 2: 5 the kingdom he promised those *who* l him? G26
Jas 2: 8 in Scripture, "L your neighbor as yourself," G26
1Pe 1: 8 have not seen him, you l him; and even G26
1Pe 1:22 so that you have sincere l **for each other**, G5789
1Pe 1:22 love for each other, l one another deeply G26
1Pe 2:17 respect to everyone, l the family of believers G26
1Pe 3: 8 be sympathetic, l **one another**, be G5790
1Pe 3:10 "Whoever would l life and see good days G26
1Pe 4: 8 Above all, l each other deeply G27+2400
1Pe 4: 8 because l covers over a multitude of sins. G27
1Pe 5:14 Greet one another with a kiss *of* l. Peace to G27
2Pe 1: 7 mutual affection; and to mutual affection, l. G27
2Pe 1:17 is my Son, whom I l; with him I am well G28
1Jn 2: 5 l for God is truly made complete in them. G27
1Jn 2:15 *Do* not l the world or anything in the world G26
1Jn 2:15 the world, l for the Father is not in them. G27
1Jn 3: 1 See what great l the Father has lavished on G27
1Jn 3:10 is anyone *who does* not l their brother G26
1Jn 3:11 the beginning: *We should* l one another. G26
1Jn 3:14 from death to life, because *we* l each other. G26
1Jn 3:14 Anyone *who does* not l remains in death. G26
1Jn 3:16 This is how we know what l is: Jesus Christ G27
1Jn 3:17 how can the l of God be in that person? G27
1Jn 3:18 *let us* not l with words or speech but with G26
1Jn 3:23 and *to* l one another as he commanded us. G26
1Jn 4: 7 Dear friends, *let us* l one another, for love G26
1Jn 4: 7 us love one another, for l comes from God. G27
1Jn 4: 8 Whoever *does* not l does not know God G26
1Jn 4: 8 love does not know God, because God is l. G27
1Jn 4: 9 This is how God showed his l among us: He G27
1Jn 4:10 This is l: not that we loved God, but that he G27
1Jn 4:11 so loved us, we also ought *to* l one another. G26
1Jn 4:12 ever seen God; but if *we* l one another, God G26
1Jn 4:12 lives in us and his l is made complete in us. G27
1Jn 4:16 so we know and rely on the l God has for us. G27
1Jn 4:16 has for us. God is l. Whoever lives in love G27
1Jn 4:16 Whoever lives in l lives in God, and God in G27
1Jn 4:17 This is how l is made complete among us so G27
1Jn 4:18 There is no fear in l. But perfect love drives G27
1Jn 4:18 But perfect l drives out fear, because fear G27
1Jn 4:18 The one who fears is not made perfect in l. G27
1Jn 4:19 We l because he first loved us. G26
1Jn 4:20 Whoever claims *to* l God yet hates a brother G26

1Jn 4:20 For whoever *does* not l their brother and G26
1Jn 4:20 have seen, cannot l God, whom they have G26
1Jn 4:21 who loves God *must* also l their brother and G26
1Jn 5: 2 is how we know that *we* l the children of G26
1Jn 5: 3 this is l for God: to keep his G27
2Jn 1 her children, whom I l in the truth—and not I G26
2Jn 3 Father's Son, will be with us in truth and l. G27
2Jn 5 the beginning. I ask that *we* l one another. G26
2Jn 6 And this is l: that we walk in obedience to G27
2Jn 6 his command is that you walk in l. G899S
3Jn 1 my dear friend Gaius, whom I l in the truth. G26
3Jn 6 They have told the church about your l G27
Jude 2 peace and l be yours in abundance. G27
Jude 12 These people are blemishes at your **l feasts** G27
Jude 21 keep yourselves in God's l as you wait for G27
Rev 2: 4 You have forsaken the l you had at first. G27
Rev 2:19 know your deeds, your l and faith, your G27
Rev 3:19 Those whom I l I rebuke and discipline G5797
Rev 12:11 *they did* not l their lives so much as to shrink G26

LOVED (93) [LOVE]

Ge 24:67 his wife, and *he* l her; and Isaac was H170
Ge 25:28 a taste for wild game, l Esau, but Rebekah H170
Ge 25:28 loved Esau, but Rebekah l Jacob. H170
Ge 29:31 When the LORD saw that Leah *was* **not l** H8533
Ge 29:33 "Because the LORD heard that I **am not l** H8533
Ge 34: 3 *he* l the young woman and spoke tenderly H170
Ge 37: 3 Now Israel l Joseph more than any of his H170
Ge 37: 4 saw that their father l him more than any of H170
Dt 4:37 Because *he* l your ancestors and chose their H170
Dt 7: 8 was because the LORD l you and kept the H170
Dt 10:15 his affection on your ancestors and l them, H170
1Sa 1: 5 he gave a double portion because *he* l her, H170
1Sa 18: 1 spirit with David, and he l him as himself. H170
1Sa 18: 3 with David because he l him as himself. H170
1Sa 18:16 But all Israel and Judah l David, because H170
1Sa 18:28 that his daughter Michal l David, H170
1Sa 20:17 because *he* l him as he loved himself. H170
1Sa 20:17 because he loved him as he l himself. H173
2Sa 1:23 in life they **were** l and admired, and in H170
2Sa 12:24 they named him Solomon. The LORD l him; H170
2Sa 12:25 because the LORD l him, he sent word NDT
2Sa 13:15 he hated her more than *he had* l her. H170
1Ki 11: 1 l many foreign women besides Pharaoh's H170
2Ch 11:21 Rehoboam l Maakah daughter of Absalom H170
2Ch 26:10 in the fertile lands, for *he* l the soil. H170
Ne 13:26 *He* **was** l by his God, and God made him H170
Ps 44: 3 the light of your face, for *you* l them. H8354
Ps 47: 4 the pride of Jacob, whom *he* l. H170
Ps 78:68 the tribe of Judah, Mount Zion, which *he* l. H170
Ps 109:17 *He* l to pronounce a curse—may it come H170
Isa 5: 1 My **l one** had a vineyard on a fertile H3351
Jer 2: 2 how as a bride you l me and followed me H173
Jer 8: 2 which *they have* l and served and which H170
Jer 31: 3 "*I have* l you *with* an everlasting love; H170
Eze 16:37 those *you* l as well as those you hated. H170
Hos 1: 6 Call her **Lo-Ruhamah** (*which means "not l"*) AIT
Hos 2: 1 'My people,' and of your sisters, 'My l *one*. H8163
Hos 2:23 my love to the one I called 'Not my l *one*. H8163
Hos 3: 1 though *she is* l *by* another man and is an H170
Hos 9:10 idol and became as vile as the **thing** they l. H171
Hos 11: 1 Israel was a child, *I* l him, and out of Egypt H170
Mal 1: 2 "*I have* l you," says the LORD. "But you ask H170
Mal 1: 2 you ask, 'How *have you* l us?' "Was not H170
Mal 1: 2 declares the LORD. "Yet *I have* l Jacob, H170
Mk 10:21 Jesus looked at him and l him. "One thing G26
Mk 12: 6 a son, *whom* he l. He sent him last G28
Lk 16:14 Pharisees, *who* l **money**, heard all G5795+5639
Jn 3:16 For God so l the world that he gave his one G26
Jn 3:19 people l darkness instead of light G26
Jn 11: 5 Now Jesus l Martha and her sister and G26
Jn 11:36 Then the Jews said, "See how *he* l him!" G5797
Jn 12:43 for *they* l human praise more than praise G26
Jn 13: 1 *Having* l his own who were in the world, he G26
Jn 13: 1 who were in the world, *he* l them to the end. G26
Jn 13:23 the disciple whom Jesus l, was reclining G26
Jn 13:34 As *I have* l you, so you must love one G26
Jn 14:21 one who loves me *will be* l by my Father, G26
Jn 14:28 If *you* l me, you would be glad that I am G26
Jn 15: 9 "As the Father *has* l me, so have I loved you G26
Jn 15: 9 has loved me, so *have* I l you. Now remain G26
Jn 15:12 Love each other as *I have* l you. G26
Jn 16:27 you because you *have* l me and have G5797
Jn 17:23 you sent me and *have* l them even as you G26
Jn 17:23 have loved them even as *you have* l me. G26
Jn 17:24 have given me because *you* l me before the G26
Jn 19:26 the disciple whom *he* l standing nearby G26
Jn 20: 2 other disciple, the one Jesus l, and said, G5797
Jn 21: 7 the disciple whom Jesus l said to Peter, G26
Jn 21:20 disciple whom Jesus l was following them. G26
Ro 1: 7 all in Rome who are l by God and called to G28
Ro 8:37 more than conquerors through him *who* l us. G26
Ro 9:13 as it is written: "Jacob *I* l, but Esau I hated." G26
Ro 9:25 I will call her 'my l *one*' who is not my loved G26
Ro 9:25 call her 'my loved one' who is not my l *one*," G26
Ro 11:28 they are l on account of the patriarchs, G28
Gal 2:20 who l me and gave himself for me. G26
Eph 5: 1 example, therefore, as **dearly** l children G28
Eph 5: 2 just as Christ l us and gave himself up for us G26
Eph 5:25 just as Christ l the church and gave himself G26
Col 3:12 holy and **dearly** l, clothe yourselves G26
1Th 1: 4 brothers and sisters l by God, that he has G26
1Th 2: 8 Because we l *you* **so much**, we were G28+1181
2Th 2:13 brothers and sisters l by the Lord, because G26
2Th 2:16 who l us and by his grace gave us eternal G26
2Ti 4:10 Demas, *because he* l this world, has G26
Heb 1: 9 *You have* l righteousness and hated G26
2Pe 2:15 of Bezer, who l the wages of wickedness. G26
1Jn 4:10 not that we l God, but that he loved us and G26
1Jn 4:10 that he l us and sent his Son as an G26
1Jn 4:11 since God so l us, we also ought to G26
1Jn 4:19 We love because he first l us. G26
Jude 1 *who are* l in God the Father and kept for G26
Rev 3: 9 your feet and acknowledge that I *have* l you. G26

LOVELY (11) [LOVE]

Ge 29:17 Rachel had a l figure and was H3637
Est 1:11 nobles, for she was l to look at. H3202
Est 2: 7 had a l figure and was beautiful. H3637
Ps 84: 1 How l is your dwelling place, LORD H3351
SS 1: 5 Dark am I, yet l, daughters of Jerusalem H5534
SS 2:14 your voice is sweet, and your face is l. H5534
SS 4: 3 are like a scarlet ribbon; your mouth is l. H5534
SS 5:16 is sweetness itself; he is altogether l. H4718
SS 6: 4 my darling, as l as Jerusalem, as majestic H5534
Am 8:13 "In that day "the l young women and H3637
Php 4: 8 whatever is l, whatever is G4713

LOVER (2) [LOVE]

Isa 47: 8 you **l of pleasure**, lounging in your H6349
1Ti 3: 3 not quarrelsome, **not a l of money**. G921

LOVERS (24) [LOVE]

Jer 3: 1 have lived as a prostitute with many l— H8276
Jer 3: 2 By the roadside you sat waiting for l, sat H2157S
Jer 4:30 Your l despise you; they want H6311
La 1: 2 Among all her l there is no one to comfort H170
Eze 16:33 you give gifts to all your l, bribing them H170
Eze 16:36 naked body in your promiscuity with your l, H170
Eze 16:37 therefore I am going to gather all your l H170
Eze 16:39 I will deliver you into the hands of **your l**, H4392S
Eze 16:41 you will no longer pay your l. NDT
Eze 23: 5 she lusted after her l, the Assyrians— H170
Eze 23: 9 I delivered her into the hands of her l, H170
Eze 23:20 There she lusted after her l, whose H7108
Eze 23:22 I will stir up your l against you, those you H170
Hos 2: 5 'I will go after my l, who give me my food H170
Hos 2: 7 will chase after her l but not catch them; H170
Hos 2:10 her lewdness before the eyes of her l; H170
Hos 2:12 which she said were her pay from her l; H170
Hos 2:13 went after her l, but me she forgot, H170
Hos 8: 9 Ephraim has sold herself to l. H172
2Ti 3: 2 People will be **l of themselves**, lovers of G5796
2Ti 3: 2 lovers of themselves, **l of money**, boastful, G5795
2Ti 3: 3 self-control, brutal, **not l of the good**, G920
2Ti 3: 4 **l of pleasure** rather than lovers of God G5798
2Ti 3: 4 lovers of pleasure rather than **l of God**— G5806

LOVES (76) [LOVE]

Ge 44:20 his mother's sons left, and his father l him. H170
Dt 10:18 l the foreigner residing among you H170
Dt 15:16 because *he* l you and your family and is H170
Dt 21:15 two wives, and he l one but not the other H170
Dt 21:16 the son of the wife *he* l in preference to his H170
Dt 23: 5 you, because the LORD your God l you. H170
Dt 28:54 brother or the wife he l or his surviving H2668
Dt 28:56 the husband she l and her own son or H2668
Dt 33:12 the one the LORD l rests between his NDT
Ru 4:15 who l you and who is better to you than H170
2Ch 2:11 "Because the LORD l his people, he has H170
Ps 11: 7 LORD is righteous, *he* l justice; the upright H170
Ps 33: 5 The LORD l righteousness and justice; the H170
Ps 34:12 Whoever of you l life and desires to see H2913
Ps 37:28 For the LORD l the just and will not forsake H170
Ps 87: 2 The LORD l the gates of Zion more than all H170
Ps 91:14 "Because *he* l me," says the LORD, "I will H3137
Ps 99: 4 The King is mighty, *he* l justice—you have H170
Ps 119:140 thoroughly tested, and your servant l them. H170
Ps 127: 2 to eat—for he grants sleep to *those* he l. H3351
Ps 146: 8 are bowed down, the LORD l the righteous. H170
Pr 3:12 because the LORD disciplines those *he* l, as H170
Pr 12: 1 *Whoever* l discipline loves knowledge, but H170
Pr 12: 1 Whoever loves discipline l knowledge, but H170
Pr 13:24 the *one who* l their children is careful H170
Pr 15: 9 but *he* l those who pursue righteousness. H170
Pr 17:17 A friend l at all times, and a brother is born H170
Pr 17:19 *Whoever* l a quarrel loves sin; whoever H170
Pr 17:19 Whoever loves a quarrel l sin; whoever H170
Pr 19: 8 The one who gets wisdom l life; the one H170
Pr 21:17 Whoever l pleasure will become poor H170
Pr 21:17 *whoever* l wine and olive oil will never be H170
Pr 22:11 *One who* l a pure heart and who speaks H170
Pr 29: 3 A man *who* l wisdom brings joy to his H170
Ecc 5:10 *Whoever* l money never has enough H170
Ecc 5:10 whoever l wealth is never satisfied with H170
SS 3: 1 on my bed I looked for the one my heart l; H170
SS 3: 2 I will search for the one my heart l. H170
SS 3: 3 "Have you seen the one my heart l?" H170
SS 3: 4 them when I found the one my heart l. H170
Hos 3: 1 Love her as the LORD l the Israelites, though H170
Hos 10:11 Ephraim is a trained heifer *that* l to thresh H170
Hos 12: 7 uses dishonest scales and l to defraud. H170
Mal 2:11 sanctuary the LORD l by marrying women H170
Mt 10:37 "Anyone *who* l their father or mother G5797
Mt 10:37 anyone *who* l their son or daughter more G5797
Lk 7: 5 because *he* l our nation and has built our G26
Lk 7:47 But whoever has been forgiven little l little." G26
Jn 3:35 The Father l the Son and has placed G26
Jn 5:20 For the Father l the Son and shows him all G5797
Jn 10:17 The reason my Father l me is that I lay down G26
Jn 12:25 Anyone *who* l their life will lose it, while G5797
Jn 14:21 keeps them is the *one who* l me. G26
Jn 14:21 The *one who* l me will be loved by my G26
Jn 14:23 "Anyone *who* l me will obey my teaching. G26
Jn 16:27 the Father himself l you because you have G5797
Ro 13: 8 whoever l others has fulfilled the law. G26
1Co 8: 3 But whoever l God is known by God. G26
2Co 9: 7 under compulsion, for God l a cheerful giver. G26
Eph 1: 6 which he has freely given us in the One *he* l. G26
Eph 5:28 He *who* l his wife loves himself G26
Eph 5:28 He who loves his wife l himself. G26
Eph 5:33 you also must love his wife as he l himself, NDT
Col 1:13 brought us into the kingdom of the Son he l, G27
Titus 1: 8 one who **l what is good**, who is G5787
Heb 12: 6 because the Lord disciplines the one *he* l G26
1Jn 2:10 Anyone *who* l their brother and sister lives in G26
1Jn 2:15 If anyone l the world, love for the Father is G26
1Jn 4: 7 Everyone who l has been born of God and G26
1Jn 4:21 Anyone *who* l God must also love their G26
1Jn 5: 1 everyone who l the father loves his child G26
1Jn 5: 1 who loves the father l his child as well. G26
3Jn 9 Diotrephes, who **l to be first**, will not G5812
Rev 1: 5 *To* him *who* l us and has freed us from our G26
Rev 20: 9 the camp of God's people, the city *he* l. G26
Rev 22:15 everyone *who* l and practices G5797

LOVING (7) [LOVE]

Ps 25:10 ways of the LORD are l and faithful toward H2876
Ps 32: 8 I will counsel you with my *l eye* on you. AIT
Ps 107:43 things and ponder the **l deeds** *of* the LORD. H2876
Ps 144: 2 He is my l God and my fortress, my H2876
Pr 5:19 A l doe, a graceful deer—may her breasts H172
Heb 13: 1 on **l one another as brothers and sisters**. G5789
1Jn 5: 2 by l God and carrying out his commands G26

LOVINGKINDNESS, LOVINGKINDNESSES (KJV)

KINDNESS, KINDNESSES, (UNFAILING) LOVE

LOW (40) [BELOW, LOWBORN, LOWER, LOWERED, LOWEST, LOWLIEST, LOWLY]

Ge 18: 2 to meet them and **bowed** l to the ground. H2556
Nu 22:31 So *he* **bowed** l and fell facedown. H7702
2Sa 22:28 eyes are on the haughty *to* **bring** them l. H9164
Job 14:10 But a man dies and *is* **laid** l; he breathes H2764
Job 14:21 if their offspring *are* **brought** l, they do not H7592
Job 22:29 When *people are* **brought** l and you say H9164
Job 24:24 *they* **are brought** l and gathered up like H4812
Job 40:11 at all who are proud and **bring** them l, H9164
Ps 18:27 the humble but **bring** l those whose eyes H9164
Ps 38: 6 I am bowed down and **brought** very l; all H8820
Ps 49: 2 both l and high, rich and poor alike: H1201+132
Ps 116: 6 unwary; *when I was* **brought** l, he saved H1937
Ps 119:25 I *am* **laid** l in the dust; preserve my life H1815
Ps 136:23 us in our **l estate** His love endures H9165
Pr 22:29 will not serve before **officials of l rank**. H3126
Pr 29:23 Pride **brings** a person l, but the lowly in H9164
Ecc 10: 6 while the rich occupy the l *ones*. H9165
Isa 2: 9 So people *will* **be brought** l and everyone H8820
Isa 2:11 be humbled and human pride **brought l**; H8820
Isa 2:17 of man *will be* **brought** l and human pride H8820
Isa 5:15 So people *will* **be brought** l and everyone H8820
Isa 10:33 be felled, the tall ones *will be* **brought l**. H9164
Isa 14: 8 "Now that *you have been* **laid** l, no one H8886
Isa 14:12 *you who once* **laid** l the nations! H2765
Isa 25:12 your high fortified walls and **lay** *them* l; H9164
Isa 26: 5 on high, *he* **lays** the lofty city l; he levels it H9164
Isa 28: 1 that city, the pride of *those* **laid** l *by* wine! H2150
Isa 29: 4 **Brought** l, you will speak from the ground H9164
Isa 40: 4 every mountain and hill *made* l; the H9164
Isa 46: 1 bows down, Nebo **stoops** l; their idols are H7970
Isa 53: 3 despised, and we held him in l esteem. H4202
Jer 16: 6 "Both high and l will die in this land. H7783
Jer 46:15 Why *will* your warriors **be laid** l? They H6085
Eze 17: 6 it sprouted and became a l H9166+7757
Eze 17:14 so that the kingdom would be *brought* l H9166
Eze 17:24 the tall tree and make the l tree grow tall. H9166
Eze 21:26 exalted and the exalted *will be* **brought l**. H9164
Lk 3: 5 filled in, every mountain and hill **made** l. G5427
Ac 8:10 people, both high and l, gave him their G3625
Ro 12:16 to associate with people **of l position**. G5424

LOWBORN (1) [BEAR, LOW]

Ps 62: 9 Surely the l are but a breath, the H1201+132

LOWER (29) [LOW]

Ge 6:16 a door in the side of the ark and make l, H9397
Lev 13:45 cover the **l part** of their **face** and cry out H8559
Dt 28:43 higher, but you will sink l and lower. H4752
Dt 28:43 higher, but you will sink lower and l. H4752
Jos 15:19 Caleb gave her the upper and l springs. H9397
Jos 16: 3 as the region of L Beth Horon and on to H9396
Jos 18:13 Addar on the hill south of L Beth Horon. H9396
Jdg 1:15 Caleb gave her the upper and l springs. H9397
1Ki 9:17 rebuilt Gezer.) He built up L Beth Horon, H9396
1Ch 7:24 who built L and Upper Beth Horon as well H9396
2Ch 8: 5 Upper Beth Horon and L Beth Horon as H9396
Job 41:24 is hard as rock, hard as a l millstone. H9397
Ps 8: 5 *You have* **made** them a little l than the H2893

Isa 11:11 Assyria, from **L Egypt**, from Upper Egypt H5213
Isa 22: 9 you stored up water in the L Pool. H9396
Jer 44: 1 all the Jews living in **L Egypt**— H824+5213
Jer 44:15 people living in **L** and Upper **Egypt**, H824+5213
Eze 40:18 they were long; this was the l pavement. H9396
Eze 40:19 the inside of the l gateway to the outside H9396
Eze 42: 5 the rooms on the l and middle floors of H9396
Eze 42: 6 space than those *on* the l and middle H9396
Eze 42: 9 The l rooms had an entrance on the H4946+9393
Eze 43:14 the ground up to the l ledge that goes H9396
Eze 43:14 From this l ledge to the upper ledge that H7783
Ac 27:30 they were going to l some anchors from *G1753*
2Co 11: 7 Was it a sin for me *to* l myself in order to *G5427*
Eph 4: 9 except that he also descended to the l, *G3005*
Heb 2: 7 *You* **made** them a little l than the angels *G1783*
Heb 2: 9 who *was* **made** l than the angels for a *G1783*

LOWERED (12) [LOW]

Ge 24:18 quickly l the jar to her hands and H3718
Ge 24:46 "*She* quickly l her jar from her shoulder H3718
Ge 44:11 Each of them quickly l his sack to the H3718
Ex 17:11 winning, but whenever *he* l his hands, the H5663
Jer 38: 6 *They* l Jeremiah by ropes into the cistern H8938
Eze 1:24 When they stood still, *they* l their wings. H8332
Eze 1:25 their heads as they stood with l wings. H8332
Mk 2: 4 it and then l the mat the man was *G5899*
Lk 5:19 up on the roof and l him on his mat *G2768*
Ac 9:25 him by night and l him in a basket *G2768+5899*
Ac 27:17 *they* l the sea anchor and let the ship be *G5899*
2Co 11:33 But *I was* l in a basket from a window in *G5899*

LOWEST (7) [LOW]

Ge 9:25 The **l of slaves** will he be to his H6269+6269
1Ki 6: 6 The l floor was five cubits wide, the H9396
1Ki 6: 8 The entrance to the l floor was on the H9396
Ne 4:13 people behind the l points of the wall at H9397
Ps 88: 6 You have put me in the l pit, in the H9397
Eze 41: 7 went up from the l *floor* to the top floor H9396
Lk 14:10 are invited, take the l place, so that when *G2274*

LOWING (3)

1Sa 6:12 keeping on the road and l all the way H1716
1Sa 15:14 What is this l *of* cattle that I hear? H7754
Jer 9:10 the l *of* cattle is not heard. H7754

LOWLIEST (2) [LOW]

Eze 29:15 It will be the l of kingdoms and will never H9166
Da 4:17 sets over them the l *of* people. A10738

LOWLY (13) [LOW]

Job 5:11 The l he sets on high, and those who H9166
Ps 119:141 Though I am l and despised, I do not H7582
Ps 138: 6 he looks kindly on the l; though lofty, H9166
Pr 16:19 Better to be l *in* spirit along with the H9166
Pr 29:23 person low, but the l *in* spirit gain honor. H9166
Isa 57:15 with the one who is contrite and l *in* spirit, H9166
Isa 57:15 the spirit of the l and to revive the heart H9166
Eze 21:26 The l will be exalted and the exalted will H9166
Eze 29:14 There they will be a l kingdom. H9166
Zec 9: 9 victorious, l and riding on a donkey H6714
Mt 18: 4 whoever **takes the l position** of this child *G5427*
1Co 1:28 God chose the l *things* of this world and the *G38*
Php 3:21 will transform our l bodies so that they *G5428*

LOYAL (9) [LOYALTY]

1Sa 22:14 "Who of all your servants *is* as l as David H586
2Sa 2:10 of Judah, however, remained l to David. H339
2Sa 3: 8 This very day I am l to the house of your H2876
1Ki 12:20 of Judah remained l **to** the house of David. H339
1Ch 12:29 of whom *had remained* l *to* Saul's H9068+5466
1Ch 29:18 and **keep** their hearts l to you. H3922
Ps 12: 1 *those who* are l have vanished from the H574
Ps 78: 8 whose hearts *were* not l to God, whose H3922
Ps 78:37 their hearts *were* not l to him, they were H3922

LOYALTY (2) [LOYAL]

Jdg 8:35 also failed to show *any* l to the family of H2876
1Ch 12:33 to help David with **undivided l**— H4202+4213+2256+4213

LUBIM, LUBIMS (KJV) LIBYA, LIBYANS

LUCAS (KJV) LUKE

LUCIFER (KJV) MORNING STAR

LUCIUS (2)

Ac 13: 1 called Niger, L of Cyrene, Manaen *G3372*
Ro 16:21 as do L, Jason and Sosipater, *G3372*

LUCRATIVE (1)

Isa 23:17 return to her **l prostitution** and will ply her H924

LUCRE (KJV) DISHONEST GAIN, MONEY

LUD (2) [LUDITES]

Ge 10:22 Ashur, Arphaxad, L and Aram. H4276
1Ch 1:17 Arphaxad, L and Aram. The sons H4276

LUDITES (2) [LUD]

Ge 10:13 Egypt was the father of the L, Anamites H4276
1Ch 1:11 Egypt was the father of the L, Anamites H4276

LUHITH (2)

Isa 15: 5 They go up the hill to L, weeping as they H4284
Jer 48: 5 They go up the hill to L, weeping bitterly H4284

LUKE (3)

Col 4:14 Our dear friend L, the doctor, and Demas *G3371*
2Ti 4:11 Only L is with me. Get Mark and bring *G3371*
Phm 24 Demas and L, my fellow workers. *G3371*

LUKEWARM (1) [WARM]

Rev 3:16 because you are l—neither hot nor *G5950*

LUMBER (1)

2Ch 2: 9 to provide me with plenty of l, because H6770

LUMP (1)

Ro 9:21 out of the same l of clay some pottery *G5878*

LUNATICK (KJV) SEIZURES

LUNCHEON (1)

Lk 14:12 "When you give a l or dinner, do not *G756*

LURE (1) [LURED]

Jdg 16: 5 "*See if you can* l him *into* showing you H7331

LURED (2) [LURE]

Jos 8: 6 us until *we have* l them **away** from the city H5998
Jos 8:16 Joshua and **were l away** from the city. H5998

LURK (3) [LURKED, LURKS]

Ps 56: 6 They conspire, they l, they watch my steps, H7621
Pr 24:15 *Do* not l like a thief near the house of the H741
Hos 13: 7 to them, like a leopard *I will* l by the path. H8800

LURKED (1) [LURK]

Job 31: 9 woman, or if *I have* l at my neighbor's door H741

LURKS (1) [LURK]

Pr 7:12 now in the squares, at every corner *she* l.) H741

LUSH (2)

Am 5:11 though you have planted l vineyards, you H2774
Zec 11: 3 the l **thicket** *of* the Jordan is ruined! H1454

LUST (15) [LUSTED, LUSTFUL, LUSTFULLY, LUSTS, LUSTY]

Pr 6:25 *Do* not l in your heart **after** her beauty H2773
Isa 57: 5 You **burn with** l among the oaks and H2801
Isa 57: 8 and *you* **looked with** l **on** their naked H2600
Eze 16:36 you poured out your l and exposed your H5733
Eze 20:30 did and l **after** their vile images H2388+339
Eze 23: 8 bosom and poured out their l on her. H9373
Eze 23:11 yet *in* her l and prostitution she was more H6312
Eze 23:17 and in their l they defiled her. H9373
Na 3: 4 all because of the **wanton** l *of* a prostitute, H2393
Ro 1:27 were inflamed with l for one another. *G3979*
Col 3: 5 immorality, impurity, l, evil desires and *G4079*
1Th 4: 5 not in passionate l like the pagans, who *G2123*
1Pe 4: 3 in debauchery, l, drunkenness, orgies *G2123*
1Jn 2:16 in the world—the l of the flesh, the lust of *G2123*
1Jn 2:16 lust of the flesh, the l of the eyes, and the *G2123*

LUSTED (9) [LUST]

Eze 6: 9 their eyes, which *have* l after their idols. H2388
Eze 20:24 their eyes l after their parents' idols. H2118S
Eze 23: 5 still mine; and *she* l **after** her lovers H6311+6584
Eze 23: 7 with all the idols of everyone *she* l **after**. H6311
Eze 23: 9 her lovers, the Assyrians, for whom *she* l. H6311
Eze 23:12 *She* too l **after** the Assyrians H6311+448
Eze 23:16 *she* l **after** them and sent H6311+6584
Eze 23:20 There *she* l **after** her lovers, whose H6311+6584
Eze 23:30 because you l **after** the nations and H2388+339

LUSTER (1)

La 4: 1 How the gold *has* **lost** *its* l, the fine gold H6670

LUSTFUL (2) [LUST]

Jer 13:27 your adulteries and l **neighings**, your H5177
2Pe 2:18 by appealing to the l desires of the flesh *G816*

LUSTFULLY (2) [LUST]

Job 31: 1 with my eyes not *to* **look** l at a young H1067
Mt 5:28 at a woman l has already *G4639+3836+2121*

LUSTS (2) [LUST]

Nu 15:39 by chasing after the l of your own hearts NDT
Ro 1:26 God gave them over to shameful l. *G4079*

LUSTY (1) [LUST]

Jer 5: 8 They are well-fed, l stallions, each H3469

LUTES (NIV84) LYRES

LUXURIANT (2) [LUXURY]

Lev 23:40 you are to take branches from l trees— H2077
Ps 37:35 man flourishing like a l native **tree**, H8316

LUXURIES (1) [LUXURY]

Rev 18: 3 the earth grew rich from her excessive l." *G5140*

LUXURIOUS (1) [LUXURY]

Isa 13:22 her strongholds, jackals her l palaces. H6696

LUXURY (8) [LUXURIANT, LUXURIES, LUXURIOUS]

Pr 19:10 It is not fitting for a fool to **live in l**—how H9503
Hab 1:16 by his net he lives in l and enjoys the H9045
Lk 7:25 clothes and indulge in l are in palaces. *G5588*
Lk 16:19 fine linen and **lived in l** every day. *G2370+3289*
Jas 5: 5 *You have* **lived** on earth **in l** and *G5587*
Rev 18: 7 grief as the glory and l she gave herself. *G5139*
Rev 18: 9 with her and **shared** her l see the smoke *G5139*
Rev 18:14 All your l and splendor have vanished *G3353*

LUZ (7) [BETHEL]

Ge 28:19 though the city used to be called L. H4281
Ge 35: 6 all the people with him came to L H4281
Ge 48: 3 appeared to me at L in the land of H4281
Jos 16: 2 L), crossed over to the territory of H4281
Jos 18:13 there it crossed to the south slope of L H4281
Jdg 1:23 men to spy out Bethel (formerly called L), H4281
Jdg 1:26 where he built a city and called it L, which H4281

LYCAONIAN (2)

Ac 14: 6 it and fled to the L cities of Lystra and *G3377*
Ac 14:11 they shouted **in the L language**, "The *G3378*

LYCIA (1)

Ac 27: 5 Pamphylia, we landed at Myra *in* L. *G3379*

LYDDA (4)

Ac 9:32 to visit the Lord's people who lived in L. *G3375*
Ac 9:35 those who lived in L and Sharon saw him *G3375*
Ac 9:38 L was near Joppa; so when the disciples *G3375*
Ac 9:38 the disciples heard that Peter was in L, *G899S*

LYDIA (4) [LYDIA'S, LYDIANS]

Jer 46: 9 carry shields, **men of L** who draw the bow. H4276
Eze 27:10 L and Put served as soldiers in your army. H4276
Eze 30: 5 Cush and Libya, L and all Arabia, Kub H4276
Ac 16:14 woman from the city of Thyatira named L, *G3376*

LYDIA'S (1) [LYDIA]

Ac 16:40 they went to L house, where they *G3376*

LYDIANS (1) [LYDIA]

Isa 66:19 to the Libyans and L (famous as archers), H4276

LYING (83) [LIE]

Ge 28:13 descendants the land on which you *are* l. H8886
Ge 29: 2 three flocks of sheep l near it because the H8069
Ge 49:14 donkey **l down** among the sheep H8069
Ex 14:30 Israel saw the Egyptians *l* **dead** on the shore. AIT
Lev 3: 5 offering that is **l on** the burning wood; H6584
Dt 21: 1 l in a field in the land the LORD your God H5877
Jos 17: 9 belonging to Ephraim l among the towns of NDT
Jdg 16:13 making a fool of me and l to me. H1819+3942
Ru 3: 4 lies down, note the place where *he is* l. H8886
Ru 3: 8 there was a woman l *at* his feet! H8886
1Sa 3: 2 barely see, *was* **l down** in his usual place. H8886
1Sa 3: 3 Samuel *was* **l down** in the house of H8886
1Sa 5: 4 broken off and were **l on** the threshold; H448
1Sa 26: 5 Saul *was* l inside the camp, with the army H8886
1Sa 26: 7 l asleep inside the camp with his spear H8886
1Sa 26: 7 Abner and the soldiers *were* l around him. H8886
2Sa 4: 7 house while he *was* l on the bed in his H8886
2Sa 12:16 spent the nights l in sackcloth on the H8886
2Sa 13: 8 of her brother Amnon, who *was* **l down**. H8886
1Ki 13:18 drink water.'" (But *he was* l to him.) H3950
1Ki 13:24 his body was **left** l on the road, with H8959
1Ki 13:25 who passed by saw the body l there, H8959
1Ki 13:28 out and found the body l on the road, H8959
2Ki 1: 4 'You will not leave the bed *you are* **l on** H6590
2Ki 1: 6 you will not leave the bed *you are* **l on**. H6590
2Ki 1:16 you will never leave the bed *you are* **l on**. H6590
2Ki 4:32 there was the boy l dead on his couch. H8886
2Ch 20:24 saw only dead bodies l on the ground; H5877
Job 3:13 For now *I would be* **l down** in peace; H8886
Job 3:14 built for themselves **places** now **l in ruins**, H2999
Ps 31:18 Let their l lips be silenced, for with pride H9214
Ps 78:36 their mouths, l to him with their tongues H3941
Ps 109: 2 have spoken against me with l tongues. H9214
Ps 120: 2 from l lips and from deceitful tongues. H9214
Ps 139: 3 You discern my going out and my **l down** H8061
Pr 6:17 haughty eyes, a l tongue, hands that shed H9214
Pr 10:18 conceals hatred with l lips and spreads H9214
Pr 12:19 a l tongue lasts only a moment. H9214
Pr 12:22 The LORD detests l lips, but he delights in H9214
Pr 17: 7 how much worse l lips to a ruler! H9214
Pr 21: 6 A fortune made by a l tongue is a fleeting H9214
Pr 23:34 on the high seas, l on top of the rigging. H8886
Pr 26:28 A l tongue hates those it hurts, and a H9214
Isa 58: 5 like a reed and for l *in* sackcloth and H3667
Jer 8: 2 will be like dung **l on** the ground. H6584+7156
Jer 8: 8 when actually the l pen of the scribes has H9214
Jer 16: 4 will be like dung l on the ground. H2118
Jer 23:26 continue in the hearts of these l prophets, H9214
Jer 25:33 will be like dung **l on** the ground. H6584+7156
Jer 43: 2 men said to Jeremiah, "You *are* l! H1819+9214
La 3:10 Like a bear **l in wait**, like a lion in hiding, H741
Eze 13: 7 visions and uttered l divinations when you H3942
Eze 13: 8 Because of your false words and l visions H3942
Eze 13: 9 see false visions and utter l divinations. H3942
Eze 13:19 By l to my people, who listen to lies, you H3941
Eze 21:29 concerning you and l divinations about H3942
Eze 22:28 them by false visions and l divinations. H3942
Eze 29: 3 you great monster l among your streams. H8069
Eze 36:34 instead of l desolate in the sight H2118
Eze 36:35 the cities that were l in ruins, desolate and NDT
Eze 39:14 bury any bodies that *are* l on the ground. H3855
Da 2:28 your mind as you were *l* **in** bed are these: AIT

Da 2:29 "As Your Majesty was **l** there, your mind A10542
Da 4: 5 As I was **l in** bed, the images and A10542
Da 4:10 are the visions I saw while **l in** bed: A10542
Da 4:13 "In the visions I saw while **l in** bed, A10542
Da 7: 1 through his mind as he was **l in** bed. A10542
Hos 4: 2 is only cursing, **l** and murder, stealing H3950
Mt 8:14 Peter's mother-in-law **l** *in bed* with a fever. *G965*
Mt 9: 2 to him a paralyzed man, **l** on a mat. *G965*
Mk 2: 4 then lowered the mat the man *was* **l** on. *G2879*
Mk 7:30 home and found her child **l** on the bed, *G965*
Lk 2:12 wrapped in cloths and **l** in a manger." *G3023*
Lk 2:16 the baby, *who was* **l** in the manger. *G3023*
Lk 5:25 took what *he had been* **l** on and went *G2879*
Lk 24:12 he saw the strips of linen **l** by themselves NDT
Jn 5: 6 When Jesus saw him **l** there and learned *G2879*
Jn 20: 5 at the strips of linen **l** there but did not go *G3023*
Jn 20: 6 He saw the strips of linen **l** there, *G3023*
Jn 20: 7 The cloth *was still* **l** in its place, separate *G3023*
Ro 9: 1 truth in Christ—*I am* not **l**, my conscience *G6017*
2Co 11:31 be praised forever, knows that *I am* not **l**. *G6017*
1Ti 2: 7 the truth, *I am* not **l**—and a true and *G6017*

LYRE (20) [LYRES]
1Sa 16:16 to search for someone who can play the **l**. H4036
1Sa 16:18 Bethlehem who knows how *to* **play the l**. H5594
1Sa 16:23 David would take up his **l** and play. H4036
1Sa 18:10 while David *was* **playing the l**, H5594+928+3338
1Sa 19: 9 David *was* **playing the l**, H5594+928+3338
Job 21:12 They sing to the music of timbrel and **l** H4036
Job 30:31 My **l** is tuned to mourning, and my pipe to H4036
Ps 33: 2 make music to him on the ten-stringed **l**. H5575
Ps 43: 4 I will praise you with the **l**, O God, my H4036
Ps 57: 8 Awake, harp and **l**! I will awaken the H5575
Ps 71:22 I will sing praise to you with the **l**, Holy H4036
Ps 81: 2 timbrel, play the melodious harp and **l**. H5575
Ps 92: 3 of the ten-stringed **l** and the melody of H5575
Ps 108: 2 harp and **l**! I will awaken the H5575
Ps 144: 9 on the ten-stringed **l** I will make music to H5575
Ps 150: 3 trumpet, praise him with the harp and **l**, H5575
Da 3: 5 zither, **l**, harp, pipe and all kinds of A10676
Da 3: 7 zither, **l**, harp and all kinds of A10676
Da 3:10 zither, **l**, harp, pipe and all kinds of A10676
Da 3:15 zither, **l**, harp, pipe and all kinds of A10676

LYRES (17) [LYRE]
1Sa 10: 5 coming down from the high place with **l**, H5575
1Sa 18: 6 with joyful songs and with timbrels and **l**. H8956
2Sa 6: 5 with castanets, harps, **l**, timbrels, sistrums H5575
1Ki 10:12 to make harps and **l** for the musicians. H5575
1Ch 13: 8 songs and with harps, **l**, timbrels, cymbals H5575
1Ch 15:16 **l**, harps and cymbals. H5575
1Ch 15:20 were to play the **l** according to alamoth, H5575
1Ch 15:28 cymbals, and the playing of **l** and harps. H5575
1Ch 16: 5 They were to play the **l** and harps, Asaph H5575
1Ch 25: 1 accompanied by harps, **l** and cymbals. H5575
1Ch 25: 6 with cymbals, **l** and harps, for the ministry H5575
2Ch 5:12 linen and playing cymbals, harps and **l**. H5575
2Ch 9:11 to make harps and **l** for the musicians. H5575
2Ch 20:28 of the LORD with harps and **l** and trumpets. H4036
2Ch 29:25 harps and **l** in the way prescribed by H5575
Ne 12:27 with the music of cymbals, harps and **l**. H5575
Isa 5:12 They have harps and **l** at their banquets H5575

LYSANIAS (1)
Lk 3: 1 Traconitis, and **L** tetrarch of Abilene *G3384*

LYSIAS (2)
Ac 23:26 Claudius **L**, To His Excellency, Governor *G3385*
Ac 24:22 "When **L** the commander comes," he said, *G3385*

LYSTRA (6)
Ac 14: 6 the Lycaonian cities *of* **L** and Derbe and to *G3388*
Ac 14: 8 In **L** there sat a man who was lame. *G3388*
Ac 14:21 Then they returned to **L**, Iconium and *G3388*
Ac 16: 1 Paul came to Derbe and then to **L**, where *G3388*
Ac 16: 2 The believers at **L** and Iconium spoke well *G3388*
2Ti 3:11 Antioch, Iconium and **L**, the persecutions I *G3388*

M

MAACAH (NIV84) MAAKAH

MAACATHITE (NIV84) MAAKATHITE

MAACHAH (KJV) MAAKAH

MAACHATHITE, MAACHATHITES (KJV) MAAKAH, MAAKATHITE, MAACATHITES

MAADAI (1)
Ezr 10:34 the descendants of Bani: **M**, Amram, Uel, H5049

MAAI (1)
Ne 12:36 Milalai, Gilalai, **M**, Nethanel, Judah and H5076

MAAKAH (25) [MAAKATHITE, MAAKATHITES, ABEL BETH MAAKAH, ARAM MAAKAH]
Ge 22:24 Tebah, Gaham, Tahash and **M**. H5082
Jos 12: 5 border of the people of Geshur and **M**, H5084
Jos 13:11 territory of the people of Geshur and **M**, H5084
Jos 13:13 not drive out the people of Geshur and **M**, H5084
2Sa 3: 3 Absalom the son of **M** daughter of Talmai H5082
2Sa 10: 6 as the king of **M** with a thousand men H5081
2Sa 10: 8 men of Tob and **M** were by themselves H5081
1Ki 2:39 slaves ran off to Achish son of **M**, H5082
1Ki 15: 2 mother's name was **M** daughter of H5082
1Ki 15:10 name was **M** daughter of Abishalom. H5082
1Ki 15:13 his grandmother **M** from her position as H5082
1Ch 2:48 Caleb's concubine **M** was the mother of H5082
1Ch 3: 2 Absalom the son of **M** daughter of Talmai H5082
1Ch 7:15 His sister's name was **M**. Another H5082
1Ch 7:16 Makir's wife **M** gave birth to a son and H5082
1Ch 8:29 lived in Gibeon. His wife's name was **M**, H5082
1Ch 9:35 lived in Gibeon. His wife's name was **M**, H5082
1Ch 11:43 Hanan son of **M**, Joshaphat the Mithnite, H5082
1Ch 19: 7 as well as the king of **M** with his troops H5081
1Ch 27:16 the Simeonites: Shephatiah son of **M**; H5082
2Ch 11:20 Then he married **M** daughter of Absalom H5082
2Ch 11:21 Rehoboam loved **M** daughter of Absalom H5082
2Ch 11:22 Abijah son of **M** as crown prince among H5082
2Ch 13: 2 His mother's name was **M**, a daughter of H5082
2Ch 15:16 his grandmother **M** from her position as H5082

MAAKATHITE (4) [MAAKAH]
2Sa 23:34 Eliphelet son of Ahasbai the **M** H1201+5084
2Ki 25:23 Jaazaniah the son of the **M**, and their H5084
1Ch 4:19 Keilah the Garmite, and Eshtemoa the **M**. H5084
Jer 40: 8 Jaazaniah the son of the **M**, and their H5084

MAAKATHITES (1) [MAAKAH]
Dt 3:14 the border of the Geshurites and the **M**; H5084

MAARATH (1)
Jos 15:59 **M**, Beth Anoth and Eltekon—six towns H5125

MAASAI (1)
1Ch 9:12 son of Malkijah; and **M** son of Adiel, the H5127

MAASEIAH (23)
1Ch 15:18 Benaiah, **M**, Mattithiah, Eliphelehu, H5129
1Ch 15:20 **M** and Benaiah were to play the lyres H5129
2Ch 23: 1 son of Obed, **M** son of Adaiah, and H5129
2Ch 26:11 the secretary and **M** the officer under the H5129
2Ch 28: 7 killed **M** the king's son, Azrikam H5129
2Ch 34: 8 son of Azaliah and **M** the ruler of the city, H5129
Ezr 10:18 his brothers: **M**, Eliezer, Jarib and H5128
Ezr 10:21 **M**, Elijah, Shemaiah H5128
Ezr 10:22 Elioenai, **M**, Ishmael, Nethanel, Jozabad H5128
Ezr 10:30 Benaiah, **M**, Mattaniah, Bezalel H5128
Ne 3:23 Azariah son of **M**, the son of Ananiah, H5128
Ne 8: 4 Hilkiah and **M**; and on his left were H5128
Ne 8: 7 Shabbethai, Hodiah, **M**, Kelita, Azariah H5128
Ne 10:25 Rehum, Hashabnah, **M**, H5128
Ne 11: 5 **M** son of Baruch, the son of H5128
Ne 11: 7 of Kolaiah, the son of **M**, the son of Ithiel, H5128
Ne 12:41 priests—Eliakim, **M**, Miniamin, Micaiah, H5128
Ne 12:42 also **M**, Shemaiah, Eleazar, Uzzi H5128
Jer 21: 1 the priest Zephaniah son of **M**. H5128
Jer 29:21 son of Kolaiah and Zedekiah son of **M**, H5128
Jer 29:25 to the priest Zephaniah son of **M**, and to H5128
Jer 35: 4 was over that of **M** son of Shallum the H5129
Jer 37: 3 Zephaniah son of **M** to Jeremiah the H5128

MAATH (1)
Lk 3:26 the son *of* **M**, the son of Mattathias, the *G3399*

MAAZ (1)
1Ch 2:27 of Jerahmeel: **M**, Jamin and Eker. H5106

MAAZIAH (2)
1Ch 24:18 to Delaiah and the twenty-fourth to **M**. H5069
Ne 10: 8 **M**, Bilgai and Shemaiah. These were the H5068

MACBANNAI (NIV84) MAKBANNAI

MACBENAH (NIV84) MAKBENAH

MACEDONIA (23) [MACEDONIAN, MACEDONIANS]
Ac 16: 9 a vision of a man **of M** standing and *G3424*
Ac 16: 9 "Come over to **M** and help us. *G3423*
Ac 16:10 we got ready at once to leave for **M** *G3423*
Ac 16:12 the leading city of that district *of* **M**. *G3423*
Ac 18: 5 When Silas and Timothy came from **M** *G3423*
Ac 19:21 passing through **M** and Achaia. *G3423*
Ac 19:22 Erastus, to **M**, while he stayed in the *G3423*
Ac 19:29 Paul's traveling companions **from M**, and *G3424*
Ac 20: 1 said goodbye and set out for **M**. *G3423*
Ac 20: 3 he decided to go back through **M**. *G3423*
Ro 15:26 For **M** and Achaia were pleased to make a *G3423*
1Co 16: 5 After I go through **M**, I will come to you *G3423*
1Co 16: 5 to you—for I will be going through **M**. *G3423*
2Co 1:16 you on my way to **M** and to come back to *G3423*
2Co 1:16 to come back to you from **M**, *G3423*
2Co 2:13 I said goodbye to them and went on to **M**. *G3423*
2Co 7: 5 For when we came into **M**, we had no rest, *G3423*
2Co 11: 9 who came from **M** supplied what I *G3423*
Php 4:15 when I set out from **M**, not one church *G3423*
1Th 1: 7 to all the believers in **M** and Achaia. *G3423*
1Th 1: 8 out from you not only in **M** and Achaia— *G3423*
1Th 4:10 do love all of God's family throughout **M**. *G3423*
1Ti 1: 3 As I urged you when I went into **M**, stay *G3423*

MACEDONIAN (2) [MACEDONIA]
Ac 27: 2 Aristarchus, a **M** from Thessalonica, was *G3424*
2Co 8: 1 grace that God has given the **M** churches. *G3423*

MACEDONIANS (2) [MACEDONIA]
2Co 9: 2 I have been boasting about it *to* the **M**, *G3424*
2Co 9: 4 For if any **M** come with me and find you *G3424*

MACHIR, MACHIRITES (KJV) MAKIR, MAKIRITE, MAKIRITES

MACHPELAH (6)
Ge 23: 9 so he will sell me the cave of **M**, which H4834
Ge 23:17 So Ephron's field in **M** near Mamre—both H4834
Ge 23:19 in the cave in the field of **M** near Mamre H4834
Ge 25: 9 buried him in the cave of **M** near Mamre, H4834
Ge 49:30 the cave in the field of **M**, near Mamre in H4834
Ge 50:13 buried him in the cave in the field of **M**, H4834

MACNADEBAI (NIV84) MAKNADEBAI

MAD (5) [MADDENING, MADMAN, MADMEN, MADNESS]
Dt 28:34 The sights you see will **drive** you **m**. H8713
Jer 25:16 will stagger and **go m** because of the H2147
Jer 50:38 of idols, idols *that will* **go m** with terror. H2147
Jer 51: 7 therefore they *have now* **gone m**. H2147
Jn 10:20 "He is demon-possessed and **raving m**. *G3419*

MADAI (2)
Ge 10: 2 Magog, **M**, Javan, Tubal, Meshek H4512
1Ch 1: 5 Magog, **M**, Javan, Tubal, Meshek H4512

MADDENING (2) [MAD]
Rev 14: 8 the nations drink the **m** wine of her *G2596*
Rev 18: 3 have drunk the **m** wine of her adulteries *G2596*

MADE (1043) [MAKE]
Ge 1: 7 So God **m** the vault and separated the H6913
Ge 1:16 God **m** two great lights—the greater light H6913
Ge 1:16 to govern the night. He also **m** the stars. NDT
Ge 1:25 God **m** the wild animals according to their H6913
Ge 1:31 God saw all that *he had* **m**, and it was H6913
Ge 2: 3 blessed the seventh day and **m** it **holy**, H7727
Ge 2: 4 when the LORD God **m** the earth and the H6913
Ge 2: 9 LORD God **m** all kinds of trees **grow** out of H7541
Ge 2:22 the LORD God **m** a woman *from* the rib he H1215
Ge 3: 1 of the wild animals the LORD God *had* **m**. H6913
Ge 3: 7 fig leaves together and **m** coverings for H6913
Ge 3:21 The LORD God **m** garments of skin for H6913
Ge 4: 1 Adam **m love to** his wife Eve, and she H3359
Ge 4:17 Cain **m love to** his wife, and she became H3359
Ge 4:25 Adam **m love to** his wife again, and she H3359
Ge 5: 1 *he* **m** them in the likeness of God. H6913
Ge 6: 6 regretted that *he had* **m** human beings on H6913
Ge 6: 7 ground—for I regret that *I have* **m** them." H6913
Ge 7: 4 the earth every living creature *I have* **m**." H6913
Ge 8: 6 opened a window *he had* **m** in the ark H6913
Ge 9: 6 in the image of God *has* God **m** mankind. H6913
Ge 14:23 will never be able to say, 'I **m** Abram **rich**. H6947
Ge 15:18 On that day the LORD **m** a covenant with H4162
Ge 17: 5 for *I have* **m** you a father of many nations. H5989
Ge 21:27 to Abimelek, and the two men **m** a treaty. H4162
Ge 21:32 After the treaty *had been* **m** at Beersheba H4162
Ge 24:10 Naharaim and **m** *his* **way** to the town of H2143
Ge 24:21 not the LORD *had* **m** his journey **successful**. H7503
Ge 24:37 And my master **m** me **swear an oath**, and H8678
Ge 26:30 Isaac then **m** a feast for them, and they H6913
Ge 27:17 the tasty food and the bread *she had* **m**. H6913
Ge 27:37 "*I have* **m** him lord over you and have H8492
Ge 27:37 lord over you and *have* **m** all his relatives H5989
Ge 28:20 Then Jacob **m** a **vow**, saying, "If H5623+5624
Ge 29:23 to Jacob, and Jacob **m love to** her. H995+448
Ge 29:30 Jacob **m love to** Rachel also, and his H995+448
Ge 30:37 *m* white stripes on them *by* **peeling** *the bark* AIT
Ge 30:40 but **m** the rest **face** the streaked H7156+5989
Ge 30:40 Thus *he* **m** separate flocks for himself H8883
Ge 31:13 and where *you* **m** a **vow** to me. H5623+5624
Ge 33:17 a place for himself and **m** shelters for his H6913
Ge 37: 3 and *he* **m** an ornate robe for him. H6913
Ge 38: 2 He married her and **m love to** her; H995+448
Ge 39:22 he was *m* **responsible** *for* all that was AIT
Ge 41:39 "Since God *has* **m** all this **known** *to* you H3359
Ge 41:51 is because God *has* **m** me **forget** all my H5960
Ge 41:52 because God *has* **m** me **fruitful** in the H7238
Ge 45: 1 Joseph when he **m himself known** to his H3359
Ge 45: 8 *He* **m** me father to Pharaoh, lord of his H8492
Ge 45: 9 God *has* **m** me lord of all Egypt H8492
Ge 46:29 Joseph *had* his chariot **m ready** and went to H673
Ge 50: 5 'My father **m** me **swear an oath** and said H8678
Ge 50: 6 bury your father, as *he* **m** you **swear** *to do*." H8678
Ge 50:25 **m** the Israelites **swear an oath** and H8678
Ex 1:14 *They* **m** their lives **bitter** with harsh labor H5352
Ex 2:14 "Who **m** you ruler and judge over us? H8492
Ex 5:21 *You have* **m** us **obnoxious** to H944+8194
Ex 7: 1 *I have* **m** you like God to Pharaoh H5989
Ex 8: 7 *they* also **m** frogs **come up** on the land of H6590
Ex 10:13 the LORD **m** an east wind **blow** across the H5627
Ex 11: 3 The LORD **m** the Egyptians favorably H5989
Ex 12: 8 bitter herbs, and **bread m without yeast**. H5174
Ex 12:15 you are to eat **bread m without yeast**. H5174
Ex 12:18 you are to eat **bread m without yeast**, H5174
Ex 12:20 Eat nothing **m with yeast**. Wherever you H4721
Ex 12:36 The LORD *had* **m** the Egyptians favorably H5989
Ex 13: 6 days eat **bread m without yeast** and on H5174
Ex 13:19 *had* **m** the Israelites **swear an oath**. H8678+8678
Ex 14: 6 So *he* **had** his chariot **m ready** and took his H673

Ex 15:17 *you* **m** for your dwelling, the H7188
Ex 16:31 seed and tasted like wafers **m with** honey. H928
Ex 18:25 from all Israel and **m** them leaders of the H5989
Ex 20:11 six days the LORD **m** the heavens and the H6913
Ex 20:11 blessed the Sabbath day and **m** it **holy**. H7727
Ex 22:12 **restitution** *must be* **m** to the owner. H8966
Ex 23:15 seven days eat **bread m without yeast** H5174
Ex 24: 8 covenant that the LORD *has* **m** with you in H4162
Ex 24:10 was *something* like a pavement **m** *of* H5126
Ex 27: 8 *It is to be* **m** just as you were shown on H6913
Ex 28: 8 ephod and **m** *with* gold, and *with* blue, H2118
Ex 29:23 From the basket of **bread m without yeast** H5174
Ex 29:33 by which **atonement was m** for their H4105
Ex 29:42 burnt offering is to be **m** regularly at the NDT
Ex 30:10 annual **atonement** *must be* **m** with the H4105
Ex 31:17 six days the LORD **m** the heavens and the H6913
Ex 32: 4 handed him and **m** it *into* an idol cast in H6913
Ex 32: 8 them and *have* **m** themselves an H6913
Ex 32:20 calf the people *had* **m** and burned it in H6913
Ex 32:20 on the water and **m** the Israelites **drink** it. H9197
Ex 32:31 *They have* **m** themselves gods of gold. H6913
Ex 32:35 what they did with the calf Aaron *had* **m**. H6913
Ex 34:18 For seven days eat **bread m without yeast** H5174
Ex 34:27 these words *I have* **m** a covenant with H4162
Ex 36: 8 among the workers **m** the tabernacle with H6913
Ex 36:11 Then *they* **m** loops of blue material along H6913
Ex 36:12 *They* also **m** fifty loops on one curtain and H6913
Ex 36:13 Then *they* **m** fifty gold clasps and used H6913
Ex 36:14 *They* **m** curtains of goat hair for the tent H6913
Ex 36:17 Then *they* **m** fifty loops along the edge of H6913
Ex 36:18 *They* **m** fifty bronze clasps to fasten the H6913
Ex 36:19 Then *they* **m** for the tent a covering of ram H6913
Ex 36:20 *They* **m** upright frames of acacia wood H6913
Ex 36:22 *They* **m** all the frames of the tabernacle in H6913
Ex 36:23 *They* **m** twenty frames for the south side of H6913
Ex 36:24 **m** forty silver bases to go under them H6913
Ex 36:25 of the tabernacle, *they* **m** twenty frames H6913
Ex 36:27 *They* **m** six frames for the far end, that is H6913
Ex 36:28 two frames *were* **m** for the corners of H6913
Ex 36:29 into a single ring; both *were* **m** alike. H6913
Ex 36:31 *They* also **m** crossbars of acacia wood H6913
Ex 36:33 *They* **m** the center crossbar so that it H6913
Ex 36:34 frames with gold and **m** gold rings to hold H6913
Ex 36:35 *They* **m** the curtain *of* blue, purple and H6913
Ex 36:36 *They* **m** four posts of acacia wood for it H6913
Ex 36:36 They **m** gold hooks for them and cast their NDT
Ex 36:37 to the tent *they* **m** a curtain of blue, H6913
Ex 36:38 they **m** five posts with hooks for them NDT
Ex 36:38 bands with gold and **m** their five bases of NDT
Ex 37: 1 Bezalel **m** the ark *of* acacia wood—two H6913
Ex 37: 2 out, and **m** a gold molding around it. H6913
Ex 37: 4 Then *he* **m** poles of acacia wood and H6913
Ex 37: 6 *He* **m** the atonement cover *of* pure gold H6913
Ex 37: 7 Then *he* **m** two cherubim *out of* H6913
Ex 37: 8 He **m** one cherub on one end and the NDT
Ex 37: 8 at the two ends *he* **m** them of one piece H6913
Ex 37:10 *They* **m** the table *of* acacia wood—two H6913
Ex 37:11 with pure gold and **m** a gold molding H6913
Ex 37:12 *They* also **m** around it a rim a H6913
Ex 37:15 the table *were* **m** *of* acacia wood and H6913
Ex 37:16 And *they* **m** *from* pure gold the articles H6913
Ex 37:17 *They* **m** the lampstand *of* pure gold. H6913
Ex 37:17 base and shaft, and **m** its flowerlike cups H6913
Ex 37:23 *They* **m** its seven lamps, as well as its H6913
Ex 37:24 *They* **m** the lampstand and all its H6913
Ex 37:25 *They* **m** the altar of incense *out of* acacia H6913
Ex 37:26 and **m** a gold molding around it. H6913
Ex 37:27 *They* **m** two gold rings below the molding H6913
Ex 37:28 *They* **m** the poles of acacia wood and H6913
Ex 37:29 *They* also **m** the sacred anointing oil and H6913
Ex 38: 2 *They* **m** a horn at each of the four corners H6913
Ex 38: 3 *They* **m** all its utensils of bronze—its pots H6913
Ex 38: 4 *They* **m** a grating for the altar, a bronze H6913
Ex 38: 6 *They* **m** the poles *of* acacia wood and H6913
Ex 38: 7 carrying it. *They* **m** it hollow, out of H6913
Ex 38: 8 *They* **m** the bronze basin and its bronze H6913
Ex 38: 9 Next *they* **m** the courtyard. The south side H6913
Ex 38:18 the entrance to the courtyard was **m** of blue, NDT
Ex 38:22 **m** everything the LORD commanded Moses H6913
Ex 39: 1 scarlet yarn *they* **m** woven garments H6913
Ex 39: 1 *They* also **m** sacred garments for Aaron H6913
Ex 39: 2 *They* **m** the ephod *of* gold, and of blue H6913
Ex 39: 4 *They* **m** shoulder pieces for the ephod H6913
Ex 39: 5 one piece with the ephod and **m** with gold, NDT
Ex 39: 8 They **m** it like the ephod: of H5126
Ex 39:15 *they* **m** braided chains *of* pure gold, H6913
Ex 39:16 *They* **m** two gold filigree settings and two H6913
Ex 39:19 *They* **m** two gold rings and attached them H6913
Ex 39:20 Then *they* **m** two more gold rings and H6913
Ex 39:22 *They* **m** the robe of the ephod entirely of H6913
Ex 39:24 *They* **m** pomegranates of blue, purple H6913
Ex 39:25 And *they* **m** bells of pure gold and H6913
Ex 39:27 his sons, *they* **m** tunics of fine linen H6913
Ex 39:29 The sash was **m** of finely twisted linen and NDT
Ex 39:30 *They* **m** the plate, the sacred emblem, *out of* H6913
Lev 2: 4 either **thick loaves** *m* without yeast and with AIT
Lev 2: 4 oil mixed in or **thin loaves** *m* without yeast AIT
Lev 2: 5 is to be **m** of the finest flour mixed with oil NDT
Lev 2: 7 *it is to* **be m** *of* the finest flour and some H6913
Lev 2: 8 the grain offering **m** of these things to the H6913
Lev 2:11 bring to the LORD *must* **be m** without yeast, H6913
Lev 6: 7 of the things they did that **m** them guilty." H928
Lev 7:12 thick loaves **m without yeast** and with H5174
Lev 7:12 thin loaves **m without yeast** and brushed H5174
Lev 7:13 with thick loaves of bread **m with yeast**. H2809
Lev 8: 2 basket containing **bread m without yeast**, H5174
Lev 8:26 from the basket of **bread m without yeast**, H5174
Lev 11:32 unclean, whether it is **m of** wood, cloth, H4946
Lev 11:43 means of them or **be m unclean** by them. H3237
Lev 13:48 any leather or anything **m** *of* leather— H4856
Lev 15:32 for *anyone* **m unclean** by an emission of AIT
Lev 16:17 *having* **m atonement** for himself H4105
Lev 16:30 on this day **atonement** *will be* **m** for you, H4105
Lev 16:34 **Atonement** *is to be* **m** once a year for all H4105
Lev 22:32 I am the LORD, *who* **m** you **holy** H7727
Lev 23: 6 days you must eat **bread m without yeast**. H5174
Lev 23:17 bring two loaves **m** *of* two-tenths of an H2118
Lev 23:28 when **atonement** *is* **m** for you before the H4105
Lev 24:12 of the LORD *should be* **m clear** to them. H7300
Lev 26:41 which **m** me hostile toward them so that I NDT
Nu 3: 4 when they **m an offering** *with* H7928
Nu 5: 8 to whom **restitution** *can be* **m** *for* the H8740
Nu 5: 8 with which **atonement** *is* **m** for the H4113+4105
Nu 5:20 *you have* **m yourself impure** by H3237
Nu 5:27 If *she has* **m herself impure** and been H3237
Nu 5:27 When she *is* **m to drink** the water that H9197
Nu 5:28 the woman *has* not **m herself impure**, but H3237
Nu 6: 3 must not drink **vinegar** *m from* wine or other AIT
Nu 6:15 **bread** *m with* the finest flour and **without yeast** AIT
Nu 6:19 from the basket, both **m without yeast**. H5174
Nu 6:21 must fulfill the **vows** *they have* **m**, H5624+5623
Nu 7: 2 of those who were counted, **m offerings**. H7928
Nu 8: 4 This is how the lampstand was **m**: It was H5126
Nu 8: 4 It was **m** of hammered gold—from its base NDT
Nu 8: 4 The lampstand *was* **m** exactly like the H6913
Nu 8:21 the LORD and **m atonement** for them to H4105
Nu 11: 8 They cooked it in a pot or **m** it *into* loaves H6913
Nu 11: 8 it tasted like **something m** *with* olive oil. H4382
Nu 14:36 and **m** the whole community **grumble** H4296
Nu 15:28 when **atonement** *has been* **m**, that H4105
Nu 16:47 the incense and **m atonement** for them. H4105
Nu 21: 2 Then Israel **m** *this* **vow** to the LORD H5623+5624
Nu 21: 9 So Moses **m** a bronze snake and put it up H6913
Nu 22:29 the donkey, "*You have* **m a fool of** me! H6618
Nu 25:13 of his God and **m atonement** for the H4105
Nu 26:61 they **m an offering** before the LORD *with* H7928
Nu 28:14 burnt offering to be **m** at each new moon NDT
Nu 28:17 seven days eat **bread m without yeast**. H5174
Nu 31:20 as well as everything **m of** leather, H5126
Nu 32:13 Israel and *he* **m** them **wander** in the H5675
Nu 35:33 and **atonement** cannot **be m** for the land H4105
Dt 1:28 Our brothers *have* **m** our **hearts** melt in H4222
Dt 2: 1 a long time *we* **m** *our* **way around** the hill H6015
Dt 2: 3 "You *have* **m** *your* **way around** this hill H6015
Dt 2:30 God *had* **m** his spirit **stubborn** and his H7996
Dt 4:23 of the LORD your God that *he* **m** with you; H4162
Dt 4:36 From heaven *he* **m** you **hear** his voice to H9048
Dt 5: 2 The LORD our God **m** a covenant with us H4162
Dt 5: 3 ancestors that the LORD **m** this covenant, H4162
Dt 9: 9 covenant that the LORD *had* **m** with you, H4162
Dt 9:12 commanded them and *have* **m** an idol H6913
Dt 9:16 *you had* **m** for yourselves an idol cast in H6913
Dt 9:21 the calf *you had* **m**, and burned it H6913
Dt 9:22 *You* also **m** the LORD **angry** at H2118+7911
Dt 10: 3 So *I* **m** the ark *out of* acacia wood and H6913
Dt 10: 5 put the tablets in the ark *I had* **m**, H6913
Dt 10:22 LORD your God has **m** you as numerous H8492
Dt 15: 2 cancel *any* **loan** *they have* **m** to a fellow H5957
Dt 16: 3 Do not eat it with **bread m with yeast**, H2809
Dt 23:23 *you* **m** *your* **vow** freely to the LORD H5623
Dt 26: 6 Egyptians mistreated us and **m** us **suffer**, H6700
Dt 26:19 all the nations *he has* **m** and that you will H6913
Dt 29: 1 to the covenant *he had* **m** with them at H4162
Dt 29:25 the covenant *he* **m** with them when he H4162
Dt 31:16 break the covenant *I* **m** with them. H4162
Dt 31:29 his anger by **what** your hands have **m**." H5126
Dt 32: 6 your Creator, who **m** you and formed you? H6913
Dt 32:13 *He* **m** him **ride** on the heights of the land H8206
Dt 32:15 abandoned the God *who* **m** them and H6913
Dt 32:16 *They* **m** him **jealous** with their foreign H7861
Dt 32:21 They **m** me **jealous** by what is no god H7861
Jos 2:17 "This oath *you* **m** us **swear** will not be H8678
Jos 2:20 released from the oath *you* **m** us **swear**." H8678
Jos 5: 3 So Joshua **m** flint knives and circumcised H6913
Jos 7:12 run because *they have been* **m** liable to H2118
Jos 8:28 burned Ai and **m** it a permanent heap H8492
Jos 9:15 Then Joshua **m** a treaty of peace with H4162
Jos 9:16 Three days after *they* **m** the treaty with the H4162
Jos 9:27 That day he **m** the Gibeonites woodcutters H5989
Jos 10: 1 of Gibeon *had* **m a treaty of peace** with H8966
Jos 10: 4 "because *it has* **m peace** with Joshua H8966
Jos 11: 5 joined forces and **m camp** together at the H2837
Jos 11:19 not one city **m a treaty of peace** with the H8966
Jos 14: 8 **m** the hearts of the people **melt in fear**. H4998
Jos 22:25 The LORD *has* **m** the Jordan a boundary H5989
Jos 24:25 On that day Joshua **m** a covenant for the H4162
Jdg 3:16 Now Ehud *had* **m** a double-edged sword H6913
Jdg 3:30 Moab *was* **m subject to** H4044+9393+3338
Jdg 6:19 an ephah of flour he **m** bread without yeast. NDT
Jdg 8: 8 Peniel and **m** *the* same **request** of them, H1819
Jdg 8:27 Gideon **m** the gold into an ephod, which H6913
Jdg 9:18 and *have* **m** Abimelek, ... **king** H4887
Jdg 9:57 **m** the people of Shechem **pay for** H8740+928+8031
Jdg 11:11 the people **m** him head and H8492
Jdg 11:30 And Jephthah **m a vow** to the LORD H5623+5624
Jdg 11:35 I *have* **m a vow** to the LORD that I H7198+7023
Jdg 15:16 jawbone I have **m** donkeys of them. NDT
Jdg 16: 2 *They* **m no move** during the night, saying H3087
Jdg 16:10 Samson, "*You have* **m a fool of** me; you H9438
Jdg 16:15 third time *you have* **m a fool of** me and H9438
Jdg 17: 5 and *he* **m** an ephod and some household H6913
Jdg 18:24 "You took the gods *I* **m**, and my priest, H6913
Jdg 18:27 Then they took what Micah *had* **m**, and H6913
Jdg 18:31 continued to use the idol Micah *had* **m**, H6913
Jdg 20:34 young men **m** a frontal **attack** on Gibeah. H995
Jdg 20:37 in ambush **m** a sudden **dash** into Gibeah, H7320
Jdg 21:15 because the LORD *had* **m** a gap in the H6913
Ru 1:20 the Almighty *has* **m** my life very **bitter**. H5352
Ru 4:13 When *he* **m love to** her, the LORD H995+448
1Sa 1:11 And *she* **m a vow**, saying, "LORD H5623+5624
1Sa 1:19 Elkanah **m love to** his wife Hannah, and H3359
1Sa 2:19 Each year his mother **m** him a little robe H6913
1Sa 2:29 of every **offering m** by my people Israel? AIT
1Sa 6:15 and **m sacrifices** to the LORD. H2284+2285
1Sa 11:15 to Gilgal and **m** Saul **king** in the presence H4887
1Sa 14:29 "My father *has* **m trouble** *for* the country. H6579
1Sa 15:11 "I regret that *I have* **m** Saul **king** H4887+4889
1Sa 15:33 "As your sword *has* **m** women **childless** H8897
1Sa 15:35 that *he had* **m** Saul **king** over Israel. H4887
1Sa 18: 3 And Jonathan **m** a covenant with David H4162
1Sa 19:10 David **m good** *his* **escape**. H5674+2256+4880
1Sa 19:18 When David had fled and **m** *his* **escape** H4880
1Sa 20: 6 sacrifice is being **m** there for his whole clan. NDT
1Sa 20:16 So Jonathan **m a covenant** with the house H4162
1Sa 23:18 The two of them **m** a covenant before the H4162
1Sa 26: 3 Saul **m** *his* **camp** beside the road on the H2837
1Sa 30:25 David **m** this a statute and ordinance for H8492
2Sa 2: 9 *He* **m** him **king** over Gilead, Ashuri and H4887
2Sa 5: 3 the king **m** a covenant with them at H4162
2Sa 7:21 thing and **m** it **known** *to* your servant. H3359
2Sa 7:25 the promise *you have* **m** concerning your H1819
2Sa 8: 2 *He* **m** them **lie down** on the ground and H8886
2Sa 10:19 *they* **m peace** with the Israelites and H8966
2Sa 11:13 drank with him, and David **m** him **drunk**. H8910
2Sa 12:24 he went to her and **m love to** her. H8886+6640
2Sa 12:31 and *he* **m** them **work** at brickmaking. H6268
2Sa 13: 2 with his sister Tamar that *he* **m himself ill**. H2703
2Sa 13: 8 **m** *the* **bread** in his sight and baked it. H4221
2Sa 14:15 because the people *have* **m** me **afraid**. H3707
2Sa 15: 7 and fulfill a **vow** *I* **m** to the LORD. H5624+5623
2Sa 15: 8 at Geshur in Aram, *I* **m** *this* **vow**: H5623+5624
2Sa 16:21 that *you have* **m yourself obnoxious** to your H944
2Sa 19: 6 *You have* **m** *it* **clear** today that the H5583
2Sa 22:12 *He* **m** darkness his canopy around him H8883
2Sa 22:36 my shield; your help *has* **m** me **great**. H8049
2Sa 22:41 *You* **m** my enemies **turn** their backs in H5989
2Sa 23: 5 surely *he would* not *have* **m** with me an H8492
1Ki 1:43 "Our lord King David *has* **m** Solomon **king**.H4887
1Ki 3: 1 Solomon **m an alliance** with Pharaoh king H3161
1Ki 3: 7 you *have* **m** your servant **king** in place of H4887
1Ki 5:12 Solomon, and the two of them **m** a treaty. H4162
1Ki 6: 4 *He* **m** narrow windows high up in the H6913
1Ki 6: 6 *He* **m** offset ledges around the outside of H5989
1Ki 6:23 inner sanctuary *he* **m** a pair of cherubim H6913
1Ki 6:31 inner sanctuary *he* **m** doors out of olive H6913
1Ki 6:33 to the main hall *he* **m** doorframes out of H6913
1Ki 6:34 He also **m** two doors out of juniper wood NDT
1Ki 7: 6 *He* **m** a colonnade fifty cubits long and H6913
1Ki 7: 8 Solomon also **m** a palace like this hall H6913
1Ki 7: 9 were **m** of blocks of high-grade stone cut to NDT
1Ki 7:16 *He* also **m** two capitals of cast bronze to H6913
1Ki 7:18 *He* **m** pomegranates in two rows encircling H6913
1Ki 7:23 *He* **m** the Sea of cast metal, circular in H6913
1Ki 7:27 *He* also **m** ten movable stands of bronze H6913
1Ki 7:28 This is **how** the stands were **m**: They had H5126
1Ki 7:33 The wheels were **m** like chariot wheels H5126
1Ki 7:37 This is the way *he* **m** the ten stands. H6913
1Ki 7:38 *He* then **m** ten bronze basins, each H6913
1Ki 7:40 He also **m** the pots and shovels and H6913
1Ki 7:45 objects that Huram **m** for King Solomon H6913
1Ki 7:48 Solomon also **m** all the furnishings that H6913
1Ki 8: 9 where the LORD **m a covenant** with the H4162
1Ki 8:20 "The LORD has kept the promise *he* **m**: H1819
1Ki 8:21 of the LORD that *he* **m** with our ancestors H4162
1Ki 8:25 my father *the* **promises** *you* **m** to him H1819
1Ki 8:38 a prayer or plea *is* **m** by anyone among H2118
1Ki 9: 3 prayer and plea *you have* **m** before me; H2858S
1Ki 10: 5 the burnt offerings *he* **m** at the temple of H6590S
1Ki 10: 9 *he has* **m** you king to maintain justice H8492
1Ki 10:16 King Solomon **m** two hundred large H6913
1Ki 10:17 He also **m** three hundred small shields of NDT
1Ki 10:18 Then the king **m** a great throne covered H6913
1Ki 10:20 like it *had ever* **been m** for any other H6913
1Ki 10:21 Nothing was **m** of silver, because silver was NDT
1Ki 10:27 The king **m** silver as common in Jerusalem H5989
1Ki 11:34 *I have* **m** him ruler all the days of his life H8883
1Ki 12:14 "My father **m** your yoke **heavy**; I will H3877
1Ki 12:20 assembly and **m** him **king** over all Israel H4887
1Ki 12:28 the king **m** two golden calves. H6913
1Ki 12:32 sacrificing to the calves *he had* **m**. H6913
1Ki 12:32 priests at the high places *he had* **m**. H6913
1Ki 14: 9 *You have* **m** for yourself other gods, idols H6913
1Ki 14: 9 other gods, **idols m of metal**; you have H5011

1Ki 14:26 all the gold shields Solomon *had* **m**. H6913
1Ki 14:27 So King Rehoboam **m** bronze shields to H6913
1Ki 15:12 rid of all the idols his ancestors *had* **m**. H6913
1Ki 15:13 because *she had* **m** a repulsive image H6913
1Ki 16:33 Ahab also **m** an Asherah pole and did H6913
1Ki 18:10 *he* **m** them **swear** they could not find you. H8678
1Ki 18:18 "*I have* not **m trouble** *for* Israel," Elijah H6579
1Ki 18:26 they danced around the altar *they had* **m**. H6913
1Ki 20:34 So *he* **m** a treaty with him, and let him H4162
1Ki 22:11 son of Kenaanah *had* **m** iron horns and H6913
2Ki 3: 2 stone of Baal that his father *had* **m**. H6913
2Ki 6: 6 threw it there, and **m** the iron **float**. H7429
2Ki 11: 4 *He* **m** a covenant with them and put them H4162
2Ki 11:13 heard the **noise** *m by* the guards and AIT
2Ki 11:17 Jehoiada then **m** a covenant between the H4162
2Ki 11:17 He also **m** a covenant between the king NDT
2Ki 13: 7 the rest and **m** them like the dust at H8492
2Ki 14:21 and **m** him **king** in place of his father H4887
2Ki 17:15 the covenant *he had* **m** with their H4162
2Ki 17:16 LORD their God and **m** for themselves two H6913
2Ki 17:21 *they* **m** Jeroboam son of Nebat *their* **king**. H4887
2Ki 17:29 national group **m** its own gods in the H6913
2Ki 17:29 people of Samaria *had* **m** at the high H6913
2Ki 17:30 people from Babylon **m** Sukkoth Benoth, H6913
2Ki 17:30 those from Kuthah **m** Nergal, and those H6913
2Ki 17:30 those from Hamath **m** Ashima; H6913
2Ki 17:31 the Avvites **m** Nibhaz and Tartak, and the H6913
2Ki 17:35 When the LORD **m** a covenant with the H4162
2Ki 17:38 not forget the covenant *I have* **m** with you, H4162
2Ki 18: 4 pieces the bronze snake Moses *had* **m**, H6913
2Ki 19:15 You *have* **m** heaven and earth H6913
2Ki 20:11 the LORD **m** the shadow **go back** the ten H8740
2Ki 20:20 how *he* **m** the pool and the H6913
2Ki 21: 3 altars to Baal and **m** an Asherah pole, H6913
2Ki 21: 7 Asherah pole *he had* **m** and put it in the H6913
2Ki 21:24 they **m** Josiah his son **king** in his H4887
2Ki 22:17 anger by all the **idols** their hands have **m**, H5126
2Ki 23: 4 all the articles **m** for Baal and Asherah H6913
2Ki 23:15 the high place **m** *by* Jeroboam son of H6913
2Ki 23:30 him and **m** him **king** in place of his H4887
2Ki 23:34 Necho **m** Eliakim son of Josiah **king** in H4887
2Ki 24:13 king of Israel *had* **m** for the temple of the H6913
2Ki 24:17 He **m** Mattaniah, Jehoiachin's uncle, **king** H4887
2Ki 25:15 all that were **m** of pure gold or silver. NDT
2Ki 25:16 which Solomon *had* **m** for the temple of H6913
1Ch 2:21 *He* **m love to** her, and she bore him H995+448
1Ch 7:23 Then *he* **m love to** his wife again H995+448
1Ch 11: 3 *he* **m** a covenant with them at Hebron H4162
1Ch 12:18 received them and **m** them leaders of his H5989
1Ch 14:17 the LORD **m** all the nations fear him. H5989
1Ch 16:15 the promise *he* **m**, for a thousand H7422[S]
1Ch 16:16 the covenant *he* **m** with Abraham, the H4162
1Ch 16:26 are idols, but the LORD **m** the heavens. H6913
1Ch 17:19 great thing and **m known** all these great H3359
1Ch 17:22 *You* **m** your people Israel your very own H5989
1Ch 17:23 the promise *you have* **m** concerning your H1819
1Ch 19:19 *they* **m peace** with David and became H8966
1Ch 21:29 which Moses *had* **m** in the wilderness H6913
1Ch 22: 5 So David **m** extensive **preparations** before H3922
1Ch 23: 1 *he* **m** his son Solomon **king** over Israel. H4887
1Ch 23:29 the thin loaves **m without yeast**, the H5174
1Ch 26:31 David's reign *a* **search was m** in the H2011
1Ch 28: 2 of our God, and *I* **m plans** to build it. H3922
1Ch 29:21 next day *they* **m sacrifices** to the H2284+2285
2Ch 1: 1 with him and **m** him exceedingly **great**. H1540
2Ch 1: 3 the LORD's servant *had* **m** in the wilderness H6913
2Ch 1: 5 *had* **m** was in Gibeon in front of the H6913
2Ch 1: 8 father and *have* **m** me **king** in his place H4887
2Ch 1: 9 you *have* **m** me **king** over a people H4887
2Ch 1:11 my people over whom *I have* **m** you **king**, H4887
2Ch 1:15 The king **m** silver and gold as common in H5989
2Ch 2:11 loves his people, *he has* **m** you their king." H5989
2Ch 2:12 God of Israel, who **m** heaven and earth! H6913
2Ch 3:10 the Most Holy Place *he* **m** a pair of H6913
2Ch 3:14 *He* **m** the curtain of blue, purple and H6913
2Ch 3:15 the front of the temple *he* **m** two pillars, H6913
2Ch 3:16 *He* **m** interwoven chains and put them on H6913
2Ch 3:16 *He* also **m** a hundred pomegranates and H6913
2Ch 4: 1 *He* **m** a bronze altar twenty cubits long H6913
2Ch 4: 2 *He* **m** the Sea of cast metal, circular in H6913
2Ch 4: 6 *He* then **m** ten basins for washing and H6913
2Ch 4: 7 *He* **m** ten gold lampstands according to H6913
2Ch 4: 8 *He* **m** ten tables and placed them in the H6913
2Ch 4: 8 *He* also **m** a hundred gold sprinkling H6913
2Ch 4: 9 *He* **m** the courtyard of the priests, and the H6913
2Ch 4:11 And Huram also **m** the pots and shovels H6913
2Ch 4:16 that Huram-Abi **m** for King Solomon for H6913
2Ch 4:18 that Solomon **m** amounted to so much H6913
2Ch 4:19 Solomon also **m** all the furnishings that H6913
2Ch 5:10 where the LORD **m a covenant** with the H4162
2Ch 6:10 "The LORD has kept the promise *he* **m**. H1819
2Ch 6:11 of the LORD that *he* **m** with the people of H4162
2Ch 6:13 Now he *had* **m** a bronze platform, five H6913
2Ch 6:16 my father *the* **promises** *you* **m** to him H1819
2Ch 6:29 a prayer or plea *is* **m** by anyone among H2118
2Ch 7: 6 which King David *had* **m** for praising the H6913
2Ch 7: 7 bronze altar he *had* **m** could not hold the H6913
2Ch 9: 4 the burnt offerings *he* **m** at the temple of H6590
2Ch 9: 8 *he has* **m** you king over them H5989
2Ch 9:15 King Solomon **m** two hundred large H6913
2Ch 9:16 He also **m** three hundred small shields of NDT
2Ch 9:17 Then the king **m** a great throne covered H6913
2Ch 9:19 like it *had ever* **been m** for any other H6913
2Ch 9:20 Nothing was **m** of silver, because silver was NDT
2Ch 9:27 The king **m** silver as common in Jerusalem H5989
2Ch 10:14 "My father **m** your yoke **heavy**; I will H3877
2Ch 11:12 in all the cities, and **m** them very **strong**. H2616
2Ch 11:15 for the goat and calf idols *he had* **m**. H6913
2Ch 12: 9 the gold shields Solomon *had* **m**. H6913
2Ch 12:10 So King Rehoboam **m** bronze shields to H6913
2Ch 13: 8 calves that Jeroboam **m** to be your gods. H6913
2Ch 15:16 because *she had* **m** a repulsive image H6913
2Ch 16:14 and *they* **m** a huge fire in his honor. H8596
2Ch 18:10 son of Kenaanah *had* **m** iron horns, H6913
2Ch 20:35 king of Judah **m an alliance** with Ahaziah H2489
2Ch 20:37 "Because you *have* **m an alliance** with H2489
2Ch 20:37 the LORD will destroy **what** you have **m**." H5126
2Ch 21: 7 the covenant the LORD *had* **m** with David, H4162
2Ch 21:19 His people **m** no funeral fire in his honor H6913
2Ch 22: 1 **m** Ahaziah, Jehoram's youngest son, **king** H4887
2Ch 23: 1 *He* **m** a covenant *with* the H4374+928
2Ch 23: 3 the whole assembly **m** a covenant with the H4162
2Ch 23:16 Jehoiada then **m** a covenant that he, the H4162
2Ch 23:18 *to* whom David *had* **m assignments** in the H2745
2Ch 24: 8 a chest *was* **m** and placed outside H6913
2Ch 24:14 and *with* it *were* **m** articles for the LORD's H6913
2Ch 26: 1 and **m** him **king** in place of his father H4887
2Ch 26:15 In Jerusalem *he* **m** devices invented for H6913
2Ch 28: 2 of Israel and also **m** idols for worshiping H6913
2Ch 29: 8 *he has* **m** them an object of dread and H5989
2Ch 30: 7 so that *he* **m** them an object of horror H5989
2Ch 31:14 the **contributions** *m to* the LORD and AIT
2Ch 32: 5 *He* also **m** large numbers of weapons H6913
2Ch 32:27 and *he* **m** treasuries for his silver and gold H6913
2Ch 32:28 He also **m** buildings to store the harvest of NDT
2Ch 32:28 he **m** stalls for various kinds of cattle NDT
2Ch 33: 3 altars to the Baals and **m** Asherah poles. H6913
2Ch 33: 7 He took the image *he had* **m** and put it in H6913
2Ch 33:14 hill of Ophel; *he* also **m** it much **higher**. H1467
2Ch 33:22 to all the idols Manasseh *had* **m**. H6913
2Ch 33:25 they **m** Josiah his son **king** in his H4887
2Ch 34:25 my anger by all **that** their hands have **m**, H5126
2Ch 35:14 *they* **m preparations** for themselves and H3922
2Ch 35:14 So the Levites **m preparations** for H3922
2Ch 35:15 Levites **m** *the* **preparations** for them. H3922
2Ch 36: 1 of Josiah and **m** him **king** in Jerusalem in H4887
2Ch 36: 4 **m** Eliakim, a brother of Jehoahaz, **king** H4887
2Ch 36:10 *he* **m** Jehoiachin's uncle, Zedekiah, **king** H4887
2Ch 36:13 who *had* **m** him **take an oath** in God's H8678
Ezr 3:13 the people **m** so much **noise**. H8131+9558
Ezr 4:15 so that **a search** *may be* **m** in the A10118
Ezr 4:19 I issued an order and **a search** *was* **m** A10118
Ezr 5:17 *let* **a search be m** in the royal archives of A10118
Ezr 6:11 their house *is to* **be m** a pile of rubble A10522
Ne 3: 4 of Meshezabel, **m repairs**, and next to H2616
Ne 3: 4 him Zadok son of Baana also **m repairs**. H2616
Ne 3: 7 **repairs** *were* **m** *by* men from Gibeon and H2616
Ne 3: 8 perfume-makers, **m repairs** next to that. H2616
Ne 3:10 son of Harumaph **m repairs** opposite his H2616
Ne 3:10 of Hashabneiah **m repairs** next to him. H2616
Ne 3:16 **m repairs** up to a point opposite the H2616
Ne 3:17 *the* **repairs** *were* **m** *by* the Levites under H2616
Ne 3:18 *the* **repairs** *were* **m** *by* their fellow Levites H2616
Ne 3:22 *The* **repairs** next to him *were* **m** *by* the H2616
Ne 3:23 Hasshub **m repairs** in front of their H2616
Ne 3:23 of Ananiah, **m repairs** beside his house. H2616
Ne 3:26 on the hill of Ophel **m** repairs up to a point NDT
Ne 3:28 the priests **m repairs**, each in front H2616
Ne 3:29 son of Immer **m repairs** opposite his H2616
Ne 3:29 the guard at the East Gate, **m repairs**. H2616
Ne 3:30 son of Berekiah **m repairs** opposite his H2616
Ne 3:31 **m repairs** as far as the house of the H2616
Ne 3:32 the goldsmiths and merchants **m repairs**. H2616
Ne 5:12 **m** the nobles and officials **take an oath** to H8678
Ne 8: 2 which was **m up of** men and women and H4946
Ne 8:12 words that *had been* **m known** to them. H3359
Ne 9: 6 You **m** the heavens, even the highest H6913
Ne 9: 8 you **m** a covenant with him to give to H4162
Ne 9:10 *You* **m** a name for yourself, which remains H6913
Ne 9:14 *You* **m known** to them your holy Sabbath H3359
Ne 9:23 *You* **m** their children as **numerous** as the H8049
Ne 13:13 the storerooms and **m** Hanan son of Zakkur, NDT
Ne 13:13 They were **m** responsible for distributing the NDT
Ne 13:25 *I* **m** them **take an oath** in God's name H8678
Ne 13:26 and God **m** him king over all Israel H5989
Ne 13:31 I also **m** provision for contributions of wood NDT
Est 2: 2 "*Let a* **search** *be* **m for** beautiful young H1335
Est 2:17 on her head and **m** her **queen** instead of H4887
Est 3:14 province and **m known** to the people of H1655
Est 8:13 province and **m known** to the people of H1655
Est 9:17 they rested and **m** it a day of feasting H6913
Est 9:18 they rested and **m** it a day of feasting H6913
Job 1:15 Sabeans attacked and **m off with** them. H4374
Job 1:17 on your camels and **m off with** them. H4374
Job 4:14 seized me and **m** all my bones **shake**. H7064
Job 7:20 Why *have you* **m** me your target H8492
Job 10: 8 "Your hands shaped me and **m** me. H6913
Job 14:15 long for the **creature** your hands have **m**. H5126
Job 16:12 crushed me. *He has* **m** me his target; H7756
Job 17: 6 "God *has* **m** me a byword *to* everyone, H3657
Job 23:16 God *has* **m** my heart **faint**; the Almighty H8216
Job 27: 2 the Almighty, *who has* **m** my life **bitter**, H5352
Job 27:18 cocoon, like a hut **m** *by* a watchman. H6913
Job 28:26 when he **m** a decree for the rain and a H6913
Job 29:13 blessed me; *I* **m** the widow's heart **sing**. H8264
Job 31: 1 "*I* **m** a covenant with my eyes not to look H4162
Job 31:15 Did not *he who* **m** me in the womb make H6913
Job 33: 4 The Spirit of God *has* **m** me; the breath of H6913
Job 37: 7 everyone he has **m** may know his work, H5126
Job 38: 9 when I **m** the clouds its garment and H8492
Job 40:15 which *I* **m** along with you and which feeds H6913
Ps 7:15 it out falls into the pit *they have* **m**. H7188
Ps 8: 5 *You have* **m** them a little **lower** than the H2893
Ps 8: 6 *You* **m** them **rulers** over the works of your H5440
Ps 18:11 *He* **m** darkness his covering, his canopy H8883
Ps 18:35 sustains me; your help *has* **m** me **great**. H8049
Ps 18:40 *You* **m** my enemies **turn** their backs in H5989
Ps 18:43 *you have* **m** me the head of nations. H8492
Ps 21: 6 blessings and **m** him **glad** with the joy of H2525
Ps 22: 9 the womb; you **m** me **trust** in you, even at H1053
Ps 30: 7 *you* **m** my royal **mountain** stand firm H2215
Ps 33: 6 the word of the LORD the heavens **were m**, H6913
Ps 39: 5 *You have* **m** my days a mere handbreadth; H5989
Ps 44: 2 the peoples and **m** our ancestors **flourish**. H8938
Ps 44:10 *You* **m** us **retreat** before the enemy H8740+294
Ps 44:13 *You have* **m** us a reproach to our H8492
Ps 44:14 *You have* **m** us a byword among the H8492
Ps 44:19 you crushed us and **m** us a haunt for H928
Ps 50: 5 *who* **m** a covenant with me by sacrifice." H4162
Ps 71:20 Though *you have* **m** me **see** troubles H8011
Ps 73:28 *I have* **m** the Sovereign LORD my refuge; H8883
Ps 74:17 the earth; you **m** both summer and winter. H3670
Ps 78:13 *he* **m** the water **stand up** like a wall. H5893
Ps 78:16 crag and **m** water **flow down** like rivers. H3718
Ps 78:26 by his power **m** the south wind **blow**. H5627
Ps 78:28 *He* **m** them **come down** inside their camp H5877
Ps 80: 5 *you have* **m** them **drink** tears by the H9197
Ps 80: 6 *You have* **m** us an object of derision to H8492
Ps 86: 9 All the nations *you have* **m** will come H6913
Ps 88: 8 friends and *have* **m** me repulsive to H8883
Ps 89: 3 "*I have* **m** a covenant with my chosen one, H4162
Ps 89:42 *you have* **m** all his enemies **rejoice**. H8523
Ps 95: 5 The sea is his, for he **m** it, and his hands H6913
Ps 96: 5 are idols, but the LORD **m** the heavens. H6913
Ps 98: 2 The LORD *has* **m** his salvation **known** and H3359
Ps 100: 3 It is *he who* **m** us, and we are his; we are H6913
Ps 103: 7 *He* **m known** his ways to Moses, his deeds H3359
Ps 104:19 *He* **m** the moon to mark the seasons, and H6913
Ps 104:24 In wisdom *you* **m** them all; the earth is H6913
Ps 105: 8 the promise *he* **m**, for a thousand H7422[S]
Ps 105: 9 the covenant *he* **m** with Abraham, the H4162
Ps 105:21 *He* **m** him master of his household, ruler H8492
Ps 105:24 The LORD **m** his people very **fruitful**; he H7238
Ps 105:24 *he* **m** them too **numerous** for their foes H6793
Ps 105:28 He sent darkness and **m** the land **dark** H3124
Ps 106:19 At Horeb *they* **m** a calf and worshiped an H6913
Ps 107:40 on nobles **m** them **wander** in a trackless H9494
Ps 115: 4 are silver and gold, **m** *by* human hands. H5126
Ps 118:27 and *he has* **m** *his* **light shine** on us. H239
Ps 119:73 Your hands **m** me and formed me; give H6913
Ps 129: 3 plowed my back and **m** their furrows **long**. H799
Ps 132: 2 *he* **m a vow** to the Mighty One of Jacob: H5623
Ps 135:15 are silver and gold, **m** *by* human hands. H5126
Ps 136: 5 *who* by his understanding **m** the heavens H6913
Ps 136: 7 *who* **m** the great lights—His love endures H6913
Ps 139:14 because **I am** fearfully and **wonderfully m**; H7098
Ps 139:15 from you when *I* **was m** in the secret place H6913
Ps 145: 9 he has compassion on all he has **m**. H5126
Pr 2:17 ignored the **covenant** she **m** *before* God. AIT
Pr 8:26 before *he* **m** the world or its fields or any H6913
Pr 20:12 that see—the LORD *has* **m** them both. H6913
Pr 20:28 through love his throne *is* **m secure**. H6184
Pr 21: 6 A fortune **m** by a lying tongue is a H7189
Pr 21:31 The horse **is m ready** for the day of battle H3922
Ecc 2: 5 *I* **m** gardens and parks and planted all H6913
Ecc 2: 6 *I* **m** reservoirs to water groves of H6913
Ecc 3:11 *He has* **m** everything beautiful in its time H6913
Ecc 7:13 can straighten what *he has* **m crooked**? H6430
Ecc 7:14 God *has* **m** the one as well as the other H6913
Ecc 10:19 A feast *is* **m** for laughter, wine makes life H6913
SS 1: 6 angry with me and **m** me take care of the H8492
SS 3: 3 found me *as* they **m** *their* **rounds** in the H6015
SS 3: 6 incense **m from** all the spices of H4946
SS 3: 9 King Solomon **m** for himself the carriage H6913
SS 3: 9 the carriage; he **m** it of wood from Lebanon. NDT
SS 3:10 Its posts *he* **m** *of* silver, its base of gold H6913
SS 5: 7 found me *as* they **m** *their* **rounds** in the H6015
Isa 2: 8 their hands, to what their fingers *have* **m**. H6913
Isa 2:20 idols of gold, which *they* **m** to worship. H6913
Isa 8: 3 Then *I* **m love to** the prophetess, and H7928+448
Isa 14:16 shook the earth and **m** kingdoms **tremble**, H8321
Isa 14:17 *the man who* **m** the world a wilderness H8492
Isa 17: 8 the incense altars their fingers *have* **m**. H6913
Isa 22:11 you did not look to the *One who* **m** it H6913
Isa 23:11 over the sea and **m** its kingdoms **tremble**. H8074
Isa 23:13 The Assyrians *have* **m** it **a place** for desert H3569
Isa 25: 2 *You have* **m** the city a heap of rubble, the H8492
Isa 28:15 of the dead *we have* **m** an agreement. H6913
Isa 28:15 for *we have* **m** a lie our refuge and H8492
Isa 30:33 it *has* **been m ready** for the king. H3922
Isa 30:33 Its fire pit *has been* **m deep** and wide H6676
Isa 31: 7 silver and gold your sinful hands *have* **m**. H6913
Isa 37:16 You *have* **m** heaven and earth. H6913
Isa 38:12 day and night *you* **m an end** *of* me. H8966
Isa 38:13 day and night *you* **m an end** *of* me. H8966
Isa 40: 4 every mountain and hill *m* **low**; the rough AIT

Isa 42:22 they have been **m** loot, with no one to NDT
Isa 43: 7 my glory, whom I formed and **m**. H6913
Isa 43:16 he who **m** a way through the sea H5989
Isa 44: 2 the LORD says—he who **m** you, who H6913
Isa 44:14 planted a pine, and the rain **m** it grow. H1540
Isa 44:21 I have **m** you, you are my servant; Israel, H3670
Isa 45:12 It is I who **m** the earth and created H6913
Isa 45:18 he who fashioned and **m** the earth, he H6913
Isa 46: 4 I have **m** you and I will carry you; I will H6913
Isa 48: 3 announced them and I **m** them known; H9048
Isa 48:21 he **m** water flow for them from the rock H5688
Isa 49: 2 He **m** my mouth like a sharpened sword H8492
Isa 49: 2 he **m** me into a polished arrow and H8492
Isa 49:19 ruined and **m** desolate and your land H9037
Isa 51: 2 and I blessed him and **m** him many. H8049
Isa 51:10 who **m** a road in the depths of the sea so H8492
Isa 51:21 afflicted one, **m** drunk, but not with wine H8912
Isa 51:22 of your hand the cup that **m** you stagger; H9570
Isa 51:23 And you **m** your back like the ground, like H8492
Isa 53:12 and **m** intercession for the transgressors. H7003
Isa 55: 4 I have **m** him a witness to the peoples H5989
Isa 57: 7 You have **m** your bed on a high and lofty H8492
Isa 57: 8 you **m** a pact with those whose beds you H4162
Isa 62:11 The LORD has **m** proclamation to the ends H9048
Isa 63: 6 in my wrath I **m** them drunk and poured H8910
Isa 66: 2 Has not my hand **m** all these things, and H6913
Isa 66:14 of the LORD will be **m** known to his H3359
Jer 1:16 in worshiping what their hands have **m**. H5126
Jer 1:18 Today I have **m** you a fortified city, an iron H5989
Jer 2: 7 defiled my land and **m** my inheritance H8492
Jer 2:28 then are the gods you **m** for yourselves? H6913
Jer 3:16 not be missed, nor will another one be **m**. H6913
Jer 5: 3 They **m** their faces harder than stone and H2616
Jer 5:22 I **m** the sand a boundary for the sea, an H8492
Jer 6:27 "I have **m** you a tester of metals and my H5989
Jer 7:12 where I first **m** a dwelling for my Name, H8905
Jer 9:16 the sword until I have **m** an end of them." H3983
Jer 10: 9 What the craftsman and goldsmith have **m** H5126
Jer 10: 9 purple—all **m** by skilled workers. H5126
Jer 10:12 But God **m** the earth by his power; he H6913
Jer 11:10 broken the covenant I **m** with their H4162
Jer 12:11 It will be **m** a wasteland, parched and H8492
Jer 15:17 revelers, never **m** merry with them; I sat H6600
Jer 18:15 which **m** them stumble in their ways H4173
Jer 18:15 They m them walk in byways, on roads not AIT
Jer 18:21 Let their wives be m childless and widows AIT
Jer 19: 4 me and **m** this a place of foreign gods; H5796
Jer 20:15 who **m** him very glad, saying H8523+8523
Jer 25: 6 my anger with what your hands have **m**. H5126
Jer 25: 7 my anger with what your hands have **m**, H5126
Jer 25:17 **m** all the nations to whom he sent me drink H9197
Jer 27: 5 outstretched arm I **m** the earth and its H6913
Jer 31:32 like the covenant I **m** with their ancestors H4162
Jer 32:17 you have **m** the heavens and the earth by H6913
Jer 32:30 my anger with what their hands have **m**, H5126
Jer 33: 2 the LORD says, he who **m** the earth, the H6913
Jer 33:14 the good promise I **m** to the people of H1819
Jer 33:25 'If I have not **m** my covenant with day H8492
Jer 34: 5 As people **m** a funeral fire in honor of your NDT
Jer 34: 8 King Zedekiah had **m** a covenant with H4162
Jer 34:13 I **m** a covenant with your ancestors when I H4162
Jer 34:15 You even **m** a covenant before me in the H4162
Jer 34:18 terms of the covenant they **m** before me, H4162
Jer 37: 1 son of Josiah was **m** king of Judah by H4887
Jer 37:15 secretary, which they had **m** into a prison. H6913
Jer 41: 9 the one King Asa had **m** as part of his H6913
Jer 41:10 Ishmael **m** captives of all the rest of the H8647
Jer 42:20 that you **m** a fatal mistake H9494+928+5883
Jer 44: 6 of Jerusalem and **m** them the desolate ruins NDT
Jer 44: 8 my anger with what your hands have **m**, H5126
Jer 44:25 carry out the vows we **m** to burn H5623+5624
Jer 49:37 the sword until I have **m** an end of them. H3983
Jer 50:20 "search will be **m** for Israel's guilt H1335
Jer 51: 7 LORD's hand; she **m** the whole earth drunk. H8910
Jer 51:15 "He **m** the earth by his power; he founded H6913
Jer 51:34 into confusion, he has **m** us an empty jar. H3657
Jer 52:19 all that were **m** of pure gold or silver. NDT
Jer 52:20 King Solomon had **m** for the temple of H6913
La 1:13 turned me back. He **m** me desolate, faint H5989
La 2: 6 The LORD has **m** Zion forget her appointed H8894
La 2: 8 He **m** ramparts and walls lament; together H61
La 3: 2 me away and **m** me walk in darkness H2143
La 3: 4 He has **m** my skin and my flesh grow old H1162
La 3: 6 He has **m** me dwell in darkness like those H3782
La 3: 9 of stone; he has **m** my paths crooked. H6390
La 3:12 He drew his bow and **m** me the target H5893
La 3:45 You have **m** us scum and refuse among H8492
Eze 1:16 Each appeared to be **m** like a wheel H5126
Eze 3:17 I have **m** you a watchman for the people H5989
Eze 6: 6 and what you have **m** wiped out. H5126
Eze 7:14 they have **m** all things ready, but no H3922
Eze 7:20 They **m** it into vile images; therefore I will NDT
Eze 12: 6 for I have **m** you a sign to the Israelites." H5989
Eze 15: 5 how much less can it be **m** into H6913
Eze 16: 7 I **m** you grow like a plant of the field. H5989
Eze 16:14 I had given you **m** your beauty perfect, NDT
Eze 16:17 the jewelry **m** of my gold and silver H4946
Eze 16:17 and you **m** for yourself male idols and H6913
Eze 16:24 mound for yourself and **m** a lofty shrine in H6913
Eze 16:31 street corner and **m** your lofty shrines in H6913
Eze 16:51 have **m** your sisters seem righteous by H7405
Eze 16:52 you have **m** your sisters appear righteous. H7405
Eze 16:60 the covenant I **m** with you in the days of NDT
Eze 17:13 the royal family and **m** a treaty with him, H4162
Eze 19: 5 of her cubs and **m** him a strong lion. H8492
Eze 19:12 The east wind **m** it shrivel, it was stripped H3312
Eze 20:11 decrees and **m** known to them my laws, H3359
Eze 20:12 would know that I the LORD **m** them holy. H7727
Eze 20:28 **m** offerings that aroused my anger H5989
Eze 21:11 **m** ready for the hand of the slayer. H5989
Eze 22: 4 become defiled by the idols you have **m**. H6913
Eze 22:13 the unjust gain you have **m** and at the H6913
Eze 27: 5 They **m** all your timbers of juniper from H1215
Eze 27: 6 Of oaks from Bashan they **m** your oars; H6913
Eze 27: 6 the coasts of Cyprus they **m** your deck, H6913
Eze 28:13 settings and mountings were **m** of gold; NDT
Eze 28:17 I **m** a spectacle of you before kings. H5989
Eze 28:18 So I **m** a fire come out from you, and it H3655
Eze 29: 3 The Nile belongs to me; I **m** it for myself. H6913
Eze 29: 9 you said, "The Nile is mine; I **m** it," H6913
Eze 29:18 rubbed bare and every shoulder **m** raw. H5307
Eze 31: 4 deep springs **m** it grow tall; their streams H8123
Eze 31: 9 I **m** it beautiful with abundant branches H6913
Eze 31:16 I **m** the nations tremble at the sound of its H8321
Eze 32:25 A bed is **m** for her among the slain, with H5989
Eze 33: 7 I have **m** you a watchman for the people H5989
Eze 33:29 when I have **m** the land a desolate waste H5989
Eze 36: 5 in their hearts they **m** my land their own H5989
Eze 44:12 **m** the people of Israel fall into H2118+4200+4842
Eze 45:21 you shall eat bread **m** without yeast. H5174
Da 2:12 This **m** the king so angry A10353+10619+10180
Da 2:23 you have **m** known to me what we asked A10313
Da 2:23 you have **m** known to us the dream of A10313
Da 2:32 The head of the statue was **m** of pure gold NDT
Da 2:38 he has **m** you ruler over them all. A10715
Da 2:48 He **m** him ruler over the entire province A10715
Da 3: 1 Nebuchadnezzar **m** an image of gold, A10522
Da 3:15 to fall down and worship the image I **m**, A10522
Da 4: 5 I had a dream that **m** me afraid. A10167
Da 5: 7 and he will be **m** the third highest ruler in AIT
Da 5:16 and you will be **m** the third highest ruler in AIT
Da 6: 2 The satraps were **m** accountable to them A10314
Da 6:14 Daniel and **m** every effort until sundown A10700
Da 9: 1 who was **m** ruler over the Babylonian H4887
Da 9:15 a mighty hand and who **m** for yourself a H6913
Da 9:16 our ancestors have **m** Jerusalem and your H928
Da 11:35 purified and **m** spotless until the time of H4235
Da 12:10 be purified, **m** spotless and refined, but H4235
Hos 8: 6 a metalworker has **m** it; it is not God H6913
Hos 14: 3 gods' to what our own hands have **m**, H5126
Am 2:12 "But you **m** the Nazirites drink wine and H9197
Am 5: 8 He who **m** the Pleiades and Orion, who H6913
Am 5:26 of your god—which you **m** for yourselves. H6913
Jnh 1: 9 heaven, who **m** the sea and the dry land." H6913
Jnh 1:16 to the LORD and **m** vows to him. H5623+5624
Jnh 4: 5 There he **m** himself a shelter, sat in its H6913
Jnh 4: 6 plant and **m** it grow up over Jonah to H6590
Na 2: 3 flashes on the day they are **m** ready; H3922
Hab 1:14 You have **m** people like the fish in the H6913
Hab 3: 6 he looked, and **m** the nations tremble. H6001
Zep 2: 8 my people and **m** threats against their H1540
Zec 7:12 They **m** their hearts as hard as flint and H8492
Zec 7:14 This is how they **m** the pleasant land H8492
Zec 11:10 the covenant I had **m** with all the nations. H4162
Mal 2:15 Has not the one God **m** you? You belong H6913
Mt 3: 4 John's clothes were **m** of camel's hair G2400
Mt 5:13 its saltiness, how can it be **m** salty again? G245
Mt 5:33 fulfill to the Lord the vows you have **m**. NDT
Mt 10:26 hidden that will not be **m** known. G1182
Mt 14:22 Immediately Jesus **m** the disciples get into G337
Mt 15:31 the crippled **m** well, the lame walking G5618
Mt 19: 4 the Creator '**m** them male and female, G4472
Mt 19:12 who have been **m** eunuchs by others— G2335
Mt 20:12 'and you have **m** them equal to us who G4472
Mt 27: 1 of the people **m** their plans how to have G3284
Mt 27:14 But Jesus **m** no reply, not even to a single G646
Mt 27:64 the tomb to be **m** secure until the third G856
Mt 27:66 went and **m** the tomb secure by putting a G856
Mk 1: 6 John wore clothing m of camel's hair, with a AIT
Mk 2: 4 they **m** an opening in the roof above Jesus G689
Mk 2:27 "The Sabbath was **m** for man, not man G1181
Mk 6:45 Immediately Jesus **m** his disciples get into G337
Mk 10: 6 of creation God '**m** them male and G4472
Mk 11:17 But you have **m** it 'a den of robbers G4472
Mk 14: 3 of very expensive perfume, m of pure nard. AIT
Mk 14:58 this temple **m** with human hands and in G5935
Mk 14:58 days will build another, not **m** with hands. G942
Mk 15: 1 the whole Sanhedrin, **m** their plans. G4472
Mk 15: 5 But Jesus still **m** no reply, and Pilate was G646
Lk 1:62 they **m** signs to his father, to find out G1935
Lk 3: 5 filled in, every mountain and hill **m** low. G5427
Lk 10:40 by all the preparations that had to be **m**. G1355
Lk 11:40 Did not the one who **m** the outside make G4472
Lk 12: 2 hidden that will not be **m** known. G1182
Lk 13:22 teaching as he **m** his way to Jerusalem. G4472
Lk 14:34 its saltiness, how can it be **m** salty again? G789
Lk 17:19 "Rise and go; your faith has **m** you well." G5392
Lk 19:15 "He was **m** king, however G3284+3836+993
Lk 19:46 you have **m** it 'a den of robbers.' G4472
Lk 23:26 cross on him and m him carry it behind Jesus AIT
Jn 1: 3 Through him all things were **m**; without G1181
Jn 1: 3 him nothing was **m** that has been made G1181
Jn 1: 3 him nothing was made that has been **m**. G1181
Jn 1:10 and though the world was **m** through him G1181
Jn 1:14 flesh and **m** his dwelling among us. G5012
Jn 1:18 with the Father, has **m** him known. G2007
Jn 2:15 So he **m** a whip out of cords, and drove all G4472
Jn 4:30 of the town and **m** their way toward him. G2262
Jn 5:11 "The man who **m** me well said to me G4472
Jn 5:15 that it was Jesus who had **m** him well. G4472
Jn 8: 3 They **m** her stand before the group G2705
Jn 8:22 This **m** the Jews ask, "Will he kill himself G4036
Jn 9: 6 the ground, **m** some mud with the saliva G4472
Jn 9:11 they call Jesus **m** some mud and put it G4472
Jn 9:14 day on which Jesus had **m** the mud and G4472
Jn 12:10 the chief priests **m** plans to kill Lazarus as G1086
Jn 15:15 from my Father I have **m** known to you. G1192
Jn 17:26 I have **m** you known to them, and will G1192
Jn 18:18 around a fire they had **m** to keep warm. G4472
Ac 2:13 however, **m** fun of them and said, "They G1430
Ac 2:28 You have **m** known to me the paths of life; G1192
Ac 2:36 God has **m** this Jesus, whom you crucified, G4472
Ac 3:12 godliness we had **m** this man walk? G4472
Ac 3:16 whom you see and know was **m** strong. G5105
Ac 3:25 of the covenant God **m** with your fathers. G1416
Ac 4:24 "you **m** the heavens and the earth and G4472
Ac 5: 4 What **m** you think of G5502+1877+3836+2840
Ac 5:27 were brought in and m to appear before the AIT
Ac 7:10 So Pharaoh **m** him ruler over Egypt and G2770
Ac 7:27 'Who **m** you ruler and judge over us? G2770
Ac 7:35 the words, 'Who **m** you ruler and judge?' G2770
Ac 7:41 time they **m** an idol in the form of a calf. G3674
Ac 7:41 reveled in what their own hands had **m**. G2240
Ac 7:43 god Rephan, the idols you **m** to worship. G4472
Ac 7:44 It had been **m** as God directed Moses G4472
Ac 7:48 not live in houses **m** by human hands. G5935
Ac 7:50 Has not my hand **m** all these things? G4472
Ac 9:39 that Dorcas had **m** while she was still G4472
Ac 10:15 anything impure that God has **m** clean." G2751
Ac 10:26 But Peter m him get up. "Stand up," he said AIT
Ac 11: 9 call anything impure that God has m clean. AIT
Ac 12:19 After Herod had a thorough search **m** for G2118
Ac 13:17 he **m** the people prosper during their stay G5738
Ac 13:22 removing Saul, he **m** David their king. G1586
Ac 13:47 " 'I have **m** you a light for the Gentiles G5502
Ac 14:15 who **m** the heavens and the earth and the G4472
Ac 15: 3 This news **m** all the believers very glad G4472
Ac 15: 7 time ago God **m** a choice among you that G1721
Ac 17: 9 they **m** Jason and the others post bond
G3284+3836+2653+4123
Ac 17:24 "The God who **m** the world and G4472
Ac 17:26 From one man he **m** all the nations, that G4472
Ac 17:29 an image m by human design and skill. AIT
Ac 18:12 of Corinth **m** a united attack on Paul and G2987
Ac 19:24 who **m** silver shrines of Artemis G4472
Ac 19:26 He says that gods **m** by human hands are G1181
Ac 20:13 He had **m** this arrangement because he G1411
Ac 20:28 which the Holy Spirit has **m** you overseers. G5502
Ac 21:23 men with us who have **m** a vow. G2400+2093
Ac 21:26 the offering would be **m** for each of G4712
Ac 25: 8 Then Paul **m** his defense: "I have done G664
Ac 25:21 But when Paul **m** his appeal to be held G2126
Ac 25:25 but because he **m** his appeal to the G2126
Ac 27: 7 We **m** slow headway for many days and G1095
Ac 27:40 foresail to the wind and **m** for the beach. G2988
Ac 28:25 after Paul had **m** this final statement G3306+4839
Ro 1:19 because God has **m** it plain to them. G5746
Ro 1:20 being understood from what has been **m** G4473
Ro 1:23 God for images **m** to look like a mortal G3930
Ro 3: 9 For we have already **m** the charge that G4577
Ro 3:21 righteousness of God has been **m** known, G5746
Ro 4:17 "I have **m** you a father of many nations." G5502
Ro 5:19 of the one man the many were **m** sinners, G2770
Ro 5:19 one man the many will be **m** righteous. G2770
Ro 15: 8 the promises m to the patriarchs might be AIT
Ro 15:28 and have **m** sure that they have received G5381
Ro 16:26 now revealed and **m** known through the G1192
1Co 1:20 Has not God **m** foolish the wisdom of the G3701
1Co 4: 9 We have been **m** a spectacle to the G1181
1Co 7:37 who has **m** up his mind not to marry G3212
1Co 9:19 I have **m** myself a slave to everyone G1530
1Co 12:14 so the body is not **m** up of one part but G1639
1Co 15:22 so in Christ all will be **m** alive. G2443
1Co 15:28 Son himself will be **m** subject to him who G5718
1Co 16: 2 I come no collections will have to be **m**. G1181
2Co 1:20 no matter how many promises God has **m**, NDT
2Co 2: 1 So I **m** up my mind that I would not make G3212
2Co 2: 3 by those who should have m me rejoice. AIT
2Co 3: 6 He has **m** us competent as ministers of a G2655
2Co 3:14 But their minds were **m** dull, for to this day G4800
2Co 4: 6 **m** his light shine in our hearts to give us G3290
2Co 5:21 God **m** him who had no sin to be sin for us G4472
2Co 7: 9 not because you were **m** sorry, but G3382
2Co 8: 6 just as he had earlier **m** a beginning, to G4599
2Co 11: 6 We have **m** this perfectly clear to you in G5746
2Co 12: 9 my power is **m** perfect in weakness." G5464
2Co 12:11 I have **m** a fool of myself, but you drove G1181
Gal 4: 7 are his child, God has **m** you also an heir. G1328
Eph 1: 9 he **m** known to us the mystery of his will G1192
Eph 2: 5 **m** us alive with Christ even when we were G5188
Eph 2:14 who has **m** the two groups one and has G4472
Eph 3: 3 the mystery **m** known to me by revelation G1192
Eph 3: 5 which was not **m** known to people in other G1192
Eph 3:10 wisdom of God should be **m** known to the G1192
Eph 4:23 to be **m** new in the attitude of your minds; G391
Php 2: 7 he **m** himself nothing by taking the very G3033

Php 2: 7 of a servant, *being* m in human likeness. G1181
Col 2:13 of your flesh, God m you alive with Christ. G5188
Col 2:15 *he* m a public spectacle of them G1258
1Th 2:17 longing *we* m every effort to see you. G5079
1Ti 1: 9 know that the law *is* m not for the G3023
1Ti 1:18 with the prophecies once m about you, G4575
1Ti 2: 1 *that* petitions, prayers, intercession and thanksgiving *be* m G4472
1Ti 6:12 *when you* m your good confession G3933+3934
1Ti 6:13 Pontius Pilate m the good confession, NDT
2Ti 2:21 special purposes, m holy, useful to the G39
Heb 1: 2 through whom also *he* m the universe. G4472
Heb 2: 7 *You* m them a little lower than the angels; G1783
Heb 2: 9 who *was* m lower than the angels for a G1783
Heb 2:11 those who *are* m holy are of the same G39
Heb 2:17 For this reason he had to *be* m like them G3929
Heb 5: 9 *once* m perfect, he became the G5457
Heb 6:13 *When* God m *his* promise to Abraham G2040
Heb 7:19 the law m nothing perfect), and a G5457
Heb 7:28 the Son, *who has been* m perfect forever. G5457
Heb 8: 9 like the covenant *I* m with their ancestors G4472
Heb 8:13 " *he has* m the first one obsolete; and G4096
Heb 9:11 that is not m with human hands, G5935
Heb 9:16 to prove the death *of* the *one who* m it, G1416
Heb 9:17 effect while the *one who* m it is living. G1416
Heb 9:24 a sanctuary m with human hands that was G5935
Heb 10:10 we have been m holy through the sacrifice G39
Heb 10:13 his enemies *to be* m his footstool. G5502
Heb 10:14 one sacrifice *he has* m perfect forever G5457
Heb 10:14 perfect forever those *who are being* m holy. G39
Heb 11: 3 what is seen *was* not m out of what was G1181
Heb 11: 9 By faith *he* m *his* home in the promised G4228
Heb 11:11 him faithful who *had* m *the* promise. G2040
Heb 11:40 together with us *would they be* m perfect. G5457
Heb 12:23 to the spirits of the righteous m perfect, G5457
Jas 2:22 his faith *was* m complete by what he G5457
Jas 3: 9 who *have been* m in God's likeness. G1181
1Pe 2:23 when he suffered, *he* m no threats. G580
1Pe 3:18 in the body but m alive in the Spirit. G2443
1Pe 3:19 *After being* m alive, he went and G1877+4005
1Pe 3:19 he went and m proclamation to the G3062
2Pe 1:14 as our Lord Jesus Christ *has* m clear to me. G1317
2Pe 2: 6 m them an example of what is going G5502
1Jn 2: 5 love for God *is* truly m complete in them. G5457
1Jn 3: 2 we will be *has* not yet *been* m known. G5746
1Jn 4:12 in us and his love is m complete in us. G5457
1Jn 4:17 is how love *is* m complete among us so G5457
1Jn 4:18 one who fears *is* not m perfect in love. G5457
1Jn 5:10 believe God *has* m him out to be a liar, G4472
Rev 1: 1 *He* m it known by sending his angel to his G4955
Rev 1: 6 and *has* m us to be a kingdom and priests G4472
Rev 5:10 *You have* m them to be a kingdom and G4472
Rev 6:12 turned black like sackcloth m of goat hair, G5570
Rev 7:14 robes and m them white in the blood G3326
Rev 13:12 m the earth and its inhabitants G4472
Rev 14: 7 Worship him *who* m the heavens, the G4472
Rev 14: 8 which m all the nations drink the G4540
Rev 18:12 articles of every kind m of ivory, costly G1804
Rev 19: 7 and his bride *has* m herself ready. G2286
Rev 21:18 The wall was m of jasper, and the city of G1908
Rev 21:21 each gate m of a single pearl. G1639

MADMAN (1) [MAD]
1Sa 21:13 he was in their hands *he* acted like a m, H2147

MADMANNAH (2)
Jos 15:31 M, Sansannah, H4526
1Ch 2:49 Shaaph the father of M and to Sheva the H4525

MADMEN (2) [MAD]
1Sa 21:15 Am I so short of m that you have to bring H8713
Jer 48: 2 the people of M, will also be H4522

MADMENAH (1)
Isa 10:31 M is in flight; the people of Gebim take H4524

MADNESS (9) [MAD]
Dt 28:28 The LORD will afflict you with m, H8714
Ecc 1:17 of wisdom, and also of m and folly, but I H2099
Ecc 2: 2 "Laughter," I said, "*is* m. And what does H2147
Ecc 2:12 to consider wisdom, and also m and folly. H2099
Ecc 7:25 stupidity of wickedness and the m of folly. H2099
Ecc 9: 3 of evil and there is m in their hearts while H2099
Ecc 10:13 are folly; at the end they are wicked m— H2100
Zec 12: 4 horse with panic and its rider with m," H8714
2Pe 2:16 voice and restrained the prophet's m. G4197

MADON (2)
Jos 11: 1 he sent word to Jobab king of M, to the H4507
Jos 12:19 the king of M one the king of Hazor one H4507

MAGADAN (1)
Mt 15:39 the boat and went to the vicinity *of* M. G3400

MAGBISH (1)
Ezr 2:30 of M 156 H4455

MAGDALA (KJV) MAGADAN

MAGDALENE (12)
Mt 27:56 Among them were Mary M, Mary the G3402
Mt 27:61 Mary M and the other Mary were sitting G3402
Mt 28: 1 Mary M and the other Mary went to look G3402
Mk 15:40 Among them were Mary M, Mary the G3402
Mk 15:47 Mary M and Mary the mother of Joseph G3402
Mk 16: 1 was over, Mary M, Mary the mother of G3402
Mk 16: 9 he appeared first to Mary M, out of whom G3402
Lk 8: 2 called M) from whom seven G3402
Lk 24:10 It was Mary M, Joanna, Mary the mother G3402
Jn 19:25 Mary the wife of Clopas, and Mary M. G3402
Jn 20: 1 Mary M went to the tomb and saw that G3402
Jn 20:18 Mary M went to the disciples with the G3402

MAGDIEL (2)
Ge 36:43 M and Iram. These were the chiefs of H4462
1Ch 1:54 M and Iram. These were the chiefs of H4462

MAGGOT (1) [MAGGOTS]
Job 25: 6 who is but a m—a human being, H8231

MAGGOTS (3) [MAGGOT]
Ex 16:20 it was full of m and began to smell. H9357
Ex 16:24 it did not stink or get m in it. H8231
Isa 14:11 m are spread out beneath you and worms H8231

MAGI (4)
Mt 2: 1 M from the east came to Jerusalem G3407
Mt 2: 7 Herod called the M secretly and found G3407
Mt 2:16 that he had been outwitted by the M, G3407
Mt 2:16 with the time he had learned from the M. G3407

MAGIC (7) [MAGICIAN, MAGICIANS]
Isa 47:12 with your m spells and with your many H2490
Eze 13:18 women who sew m charms on all their H4086
Eze 13:20 against your m charms with which you H4086
Rev 9:21 of their murders, their m arts, their sexual G5760
Rev 18:23 By your m spell all the nations were led G5758
Rev 21: 8 immoral, those who practice m arts, the G5761
Rev 22:15 those who practice m arts, the G5761

MAGICIAN (2) [MAGIC]
Da 2:10 such a thing of any m or enchanter or A10282
Da 2:27 m or diviner can explain to the king the A10282

MAGICIANS (13) [MAGIC]
Ge 41: 8 he sent for all the m and wise men of H3033
Ge 41:24 I told this to the m, but none of them H3033
Ex 7:11 the Egyptian m also did the same H3033
Ex 7:22 But the Egyptian m did the same things H3033
Ex 8: 7 But the m did the same things by their H3033
Ex 8:18 But when the m tried to produce gnats by H3033
Ex 8:19 the m said to Pharaoh, "This is the finger H3033
Ex 9:11 The m could not stand before Moses H3033
Da 1:20 better than all the m and enchanters in H3033
Da 2: 2 So the king summoned the m, enchanters H3033
Da 4: 7 When the m, enchanters, astrologers A10282
Da 4: 9 chief of the m, I know that the spirit of A10282
Da 5:11 appointed him chief of the m A10282

MAGISTRATE (1) [MAGISTRATES]
Lk 12:58 you are going with your adversary to the m, G807

MAGISTRATES (8) [MAGISTRATE]
Ezr 7:25 appoint m and judges to administer A10735
Da 3: 2 m and all the other provincial officials to A10767
Da 3: 3 m and all the other provincial officials A10767
Ac 16:20 They brought them before the m and said G5130
Ac 16:22 the m ordered them to be stripped G5130
Ac 16:35 the m sent their officers to the jailer with G5130
Ac 16:36 "The m have ordered that you and Silas G5130
Ac 16:38 The officers reported this *to* the m, and G5130

MAGNIFICENCE (1) [MAGNIFY]
1Ch 22: 5 be of great m and fame and H5087+2025

MAGNIFICENT (5) [MAGNIFY]
1Ki 8:13 I have indeed built a m temple for you, H2292
2Ch 2: 9 the temple I build *must be* large and m. H7098
2Ch 6: 2 I have built a m temple for you, a place H2292
Isa 28:29 plan is wonderful, whose wisdom *is* m. H1540
Mk 13: 1 massive stones! What m buildings!" G4534

MAGNIFY (1) [MAGNIFICENCE, MAGNIFICENT]
Da 11:36 He will exalt and m himself above every H1540

MAGOG (5)
Ge 10: 2 M, Madai, Javan, Tubal, Meshek H4470
1Ch 1: 5 M, Madai, Javan, Tubal, Meshek H4470
Eze 38: 2 of the land of M, the chief prince of H4470
Eze 39: 6 I will send fire on M and on those who live H4470
Rev 20: 8 the earth—Gog and M—and to gather G3408

MAGOR-MISSABIB (NIV84) TERROR ON EVERY SIDE

MAGPIASH (1)
Ne 10:20 M, Meshullam, Hezir, H4488

MAHALALEL (8)
Ge 5:12 70 years, he became the father of M. H4546
Ge 5:13 After he became the father of M, Kenan H4546
Ge 5:15 When M had lived 65 years, he became H4546
Ge 5:16 M lived 830 years and had other sons H4546
Ge 5:17 Altogether, M lived a total of 895 years H4546
1Ch 1: 2 Kenan, M, Jared, H4546
Ne 11: 4 the son of M, a descendant of Perez H4546
Lk 3:37 of Jared, the son *of* M, the son of Kenan, G3435

MAHALATH (4)
Ge 28: 9 so he went to Ishmael and married M, the H4715
2Ch 11:18 Rehoboam married M, who was the H4715
Ps 53: T According to m. A maskil of David. H4714
Ps 88: T According to m leannoth. A maskil H4714

MAHANAIM (14)
Ge 32: 2 So he named that place M. H4724
Jos 13:26 from M to the territory of Debir; H4724
Jos 13:30 extending from M and including all of H4724
Jos 21:38 of refuge for one accused of murder), M, H4724
2Sa 2: 8 son of Saul and brought him over to M. H4724
2Sa 2:12 son of Saul, left M and went to Gibeon. H4724
2Sa 2:29 the morning hours and came to M. H4724
2Sa 17:24 David went to M, and Absalom crossed H4724
2Sa 17:27 When David came to M, Shobi son of H4724
2Sa 19:32 provided for the king during his stay in M, H4724
1Ki 2: 8 bitter curses on me the day I went to M. H4724
1Ki 4:14 Ahinadab son of Iddo—in M; H4724
1Ch 6:80 Gad they received Ramoth in Gilead, M, H4724
SS 6:13 on the Shulammite as on the dance of M? H4724

MAHANEH DAN (2) [DAN]
Jdg 13:25 began to stir him while he was in M, H4723
Jdg 18:12 Kiriath Jearim is called M to this day. H4723

MAHARAI (3)
2Sa 23:28 Zalmon the Ahohite, M the Netophathite, H4560
1Ch 11:30 M the Netophathite, Heled son of Baanah H4560
1Ch 27:13 tenth month, was M the Netophathite, H4560

MAHATH (3)
1Ch 6:35 Elkanah, the son of M, the son of Amasai, H4744
2Ch 29:12 M son of Amasai and Joel son of Azariah H4744
2Ch 31:13 M and Benaiah were assistants of H4744

MAHAVITE (1)
1Ch 11:46 Eliel the M, Jeribai and Joshaviah the H4687

MAHAZIOTH (2)
1Ch 25: 4 Joshbekashah, Mallothi, Hothir and M. H4692
1Ch 25:30 the twenty-third to M, his sons and H4692

MAHER-SHALAL-HASH-BAZ (2)
Isa 8: 1 write on it with an ordinary pen: M." H4561
Isa 8: 3 And the LORD said to me, "Name him M. H4561

MAHLAH (5) [MAHLITE, MAHLITES]
Nu 26:33 daughters, whose names were M, Noah, H4702
Nu 27: 1 The names of the daughters were M H4702
Nu 36:11 daughters—M, Tirzah, Hoglah, H4702
Jos 17: 3 daughters, whose names were M, Noah, H4702
1Ch 7:18 gave birth to Ishhod, Abiezer and M. H4702

MAHLI (12)
Ex 6:19 The sons of Merari were M and Mushi H4706
Nu 3:20 The Merarite clans: M and Mushi. These H4706
1Ch 6:19 The sons of Merari: M and Mushi. These H4706
1Ch 6:29 M, Libni his son, Shimei his son, Uzzah H4706
1Ch 6:47 the son of M, the son of Mushi, the son of H4706
1Ch 23:21 sons of Merari: M and Mushi. The sons H4706
1Ch 23:21 The sons of M: Eleazar and Kish. H4706
1Ch 23:23 The sons of Mushi: M, Eder and Jerimoth H4706
1Ch 24:26 sons of Merari: M and Mushi. The son H4706
1Ch 24:28 From M: Eleazar, who had no sons. H4706
1Ch 24:30 the sons of Mushi: M, Eder and Jerimoth H4706
Ezr 8:18 from the descendants of M son of Levi H4706

MAHLITE (1) [MAHLAH]
Nu 26:58 Hebronite clan, the M clan, the Mushite H4707

MAHLITES (1) [MAHLAH]
Nu 3:33 the clans of the M and the Mushites; H4707

MAHLON (3) [MAHLON'S]
Ru 1: 2 names of his two sons were M and Kilion. H4705
Ru 1: 5 both M and Kilion also died, and Naomi H4705
Ru 4: 9 all the property of Elimelek, Kilion and M. H4705

MAHLON'S (1) [MAHLON]
Ru 4:10 Ruth the Moabite, M widow, as my wife, H4705

MAHOL (1)
1Ki 4:31 Heman, Kalkol and Darda, the sons of M. H4689

MAHSEIAH (2)
Jer 32:12 the son of M, in the presence of H4729
Jer 51:59 of Neriah, the son of M, when he went to H4729

MAID, MAIDS (NIV84) (FEMALE) SERVANT, SERVANTS; (FEMALE) SLAVE, SLAVES

MAIDEN, MAIDENS (NIV84) YOUNG WOMAN, YOUNG WOMEN

MAIDSERVANT, MAIDSERVANTS (NIV84) (FEMALE) SERVANT, SERVANTS; (FEMALE) SLAVE, SLAVES

MAIL (KJV) ARMOR

MAIM See ABEL MAIM, MISREPOTH MAIM

MAIMED (3)
Lev 22:22 the injured or the m, or anything with H3024
Mt 18: 8 you to enter life m or crippled than to G3245
Mk 9:43 you to enter life m than with two hands G3245

M

MAIN (21)
Nu 20:19 "We will go along the m road, and if we H5019
Dt 2:27 We will stay on the m road; we will H2006+2006
Jos 8:13 with the m camp to the north of the city H3972
1Ki 6: 3 at the front of the m hall of the temple H2121
1Ki 6: 5 the walls of the m hall and inner H2121
1Ki 6:17 The m hall in front of this room was forty H2121
1Ki 6:33 entrance to the m hall he made H2121
1Ki 7:50 the doors of the m hall of the temple. H2121
2Ch 3: 5 He paneled the m hall with juniper and H1524
2Ch 3:13 stood on their feet, facing the m hall. H1074
2Ch 4:22 Holy Place and the doors of the m hall. H2121
Eze 19:14 one of its m branches and H4751+964
Eze 41: 1 me to the m hall and measured the H2121
Eze 41: 2 He also measured the m hall; it was forty NDT
Eze 41: 4 twenty cubits across the end of the m hall. H2121
Eze 41:15 The m hall, the inner sanctuary and the H2121
Eze 41:20 were carved on the wall of the m hall. H2121
Eze 41:21 The m hall had a rectangular doorframe H2121
Eze 41:23 Both the m hall and the Most Holy Place H2121
Eze 41:25 on the doors of the m hall were carved H2121
Heb 8: 1 Now the m point of what we are saying is G3049

MAINLAND (2) [LAND]
Eze 26: 6 settlements on the m will be ravaged by H8441
Eze 26: 8 your settlements on the m with the sword; H8441

MAINSTAY (1)
Jer 49:35 the bow of Elam, the m of their might. H8040

MAINTAIN (14) [MAINTAINED, MAINTAINING, MAINTAINS]
Ru 4: 5 in order to m the name of the dead with H7756
Ru 4:10 in order to m the name of the dead with H7756
1Ki 10: 9 he has made you king to m justice and H6913
2Ki 8:19 He had promised to m a lamp for David H5989
2Ch 9: 8 to m justice and righteousness. H6913
2Ch 21: 7 had promised to m a lamp for him and H5989
Job 27: 6 I will m my innocence and never let go of H2616
Ps 89:28 I will m my love to him forever, and my H9068
Pr 5: 2 that you may m discretion and your lips H9068
Isa 56: 1 "M justice and do what is right, for my H9068
Da 11:20 out a tax collector to m the royal splendor. NDT
Hos 12: 6 return to your God; m love and justice H9068
Am 5:15 love good; m justice in the courts. H3657
Ro 3:28 For we m that a person is justified by faith G3357

MAINTAINED (1) [MAINTAIN]
Rev 6: 9 of God and the testimony they had m. G2400

MAINTAINING (2) [MAINTAIN]
Ex 34: 7 m love to thousands, and forgiving H5915
Job 2: 9 "Are you still m your integrity? H2616

MAINTAINS (2) [MAINTAIN]
Job 2: 3 And he still m his integrity, though you H2616
Pr 28: 2 with discernment and knowledge m order. H799

MAJESTIC (14) [MAJESTY]
Ex 15: 6 right hand, LORD, was m in power. H158
Ex 15:11 Who is like you—m in holiness, awesome H158
Job 37: 4 of his roar; he thunders with his m voice. H1454
Ps 8: 1 how m is your name in all the earth! H129
Ps 8: 9 how m is your name in all the earth! H129
Ps 29: 4 is powerful; the voice of the LORD is m. H2077
Ps 68:15 Mount Bashan, m mountain, Mount H466
Ps 76: 4 more m than mountains rich with game. H129
Ps 111: 3 Glorious and m are his deeds, and his H2077
SS 6: 4 as Jerusalem, as m as troops with banners. H398
SS 6:10 as the sun, m as the stars in procession? H398
Isa 30:30 people to hear his m voice and will make H2086
Eze 31: 7 It was m in beauty, with its spreading H3636
2Pe 1:17 the voice came to him from the M Glory, G3485

MAJESTY (63) [MAJESTIC, MAJESTY'S]
Ex 15: 7 greatness of your m you threw down those H1454
Dt 5:24 God has shown us his glory and his m, H1542
Dt 11: 2 his m, his mighty hand, his outstretched H1542
Dt 33:17 In m he is like a firstborn bull; his horns H2077
Dt 33:26 to help you and on the clouds in his m. H1452
Jdg 3:19 and said, "Your M, I have a secret H2021+4889
1Sa 17:55 as you live, Your M, I don't know." H2021+4889
1Sa 23:20 Your M, come down whenever H2021+4889
2Sa 14: 4 and she said, "Help me, Your M!" H2021+4889
2Sa 15:34 to Absalom, 'Your M, I will be your H2021+4889
2Sa 24:23 Your M, Araunah gives all this to the king." NDT
1Ch 16:27 Splendor and m are before him; strength H2077
1Ch 29:11 the glory and the m and the splendor, H5905
2Ch 25: 7 and said, "Your M, these troops H2021+4889
Est 1: 4 the splendor and glory of his m. H1525
Est 7: 3 favor with you, Your M, and if it H2021+4889
Job 37:22 splendor; God comes in awesome m. H2086
Job 40:10 clothe yourself in honor and m. H2077
Ps 21: 5 have bestowed on him splendor and m. H2077
Ps 45: 3 clothe yourself with splendor and m. H2077
Ps 45: 4 In your m ride forth victoriously in the H2077
Ps 68:34 power of God, whose m is over Israel H1452
Ps 93: 1 he is robed in m; the LORD is robed in H1455
Ps 93: 1 the LORD is robed in m and armed with NDT
Ps 96: 6 Splendor and m are before him; strength H2077
Ps 104: 1 you are clothed with splendor and m. H2077
Ps 145: 5 of the glorious splendor of your m— H2086
Isa 2:10 of the LORD and the splendor of his m! H1454
Isa 2:19 of the LORD and the splendor of his m, H1454
Isa 2:21 of the LORD and the splendor of his m, H1454
Isa 24:14 from the west they acclaim the LORD's m. H1454
Isa 26:10 evil and do not regard the m of the LORD. H1455
Isa 53: 2 He had no beauty or m to attract us to H2077
Eze 31: 2 " 'Who can be compared with you in m? H1542
Eze 31:18 be compared with you in splendor and m? H1542
Da 2:29 "As Your M was lying there, A10002+10421
Da 2:30 so that Your M may know the A10002+10421
Da 2:31 "Your M looked, and there A10002+10421
Da 2:37 Your M, you are the king of kings A10002+10421
Da 3:10 Your M has issued a decree that A10002+10421
Da 3:12 pay no attention to you, Your M. A10002+10421
Da 3:18 you to know, Your M, that we A10002+10421
Da 3:24 replied, "Certainly, Your M." A10002+10421
Da 4:22 Your M, you are that tree! You A10002+10421
Da 4:23 "Your M saw a holy one, A10002+10421
Da 4:24 Your M, and this is A10002+10421
Da 4:27 Therefore, Your M, be pleased A10002+10421
Da 4:30 mighty power and for the glory of my m?" A10199
Da 5:18 "Your M, the Most High God A10002+10421
Da 6: 7 except to you, Your M, shall be A10002+10421
Da 6: 8 Your M, issue the decree A10002+10421
Da 6:12 except to you, Your M, would be A10002+10421
Da 6:13 to you, Your M, or to the decree A10002+10421
Da 6:15 "Remember, Your M, that A10002+10421
Da 6:22 any wrong before you, Your M." A10002+10421
Mic 5: 4 in the m of the name of the LORD his God. H1454
Zec 6:13 will be clothed with m and will sit and H2086
Ac 19:27 the world, will be robbed of her divine m." G3484
Ac 25:26 definite to write to His M about him. G3261
Heb 1: 3 at the right hand of the M in heaven. G3488
Heb 8: 1 hand of the throne of the M in heaven, G3488
2Pe 1:16 we were eyewitnesses of his m. G3484
Jude 25 Savior be glory, m, power and authority G3488

MAJESTY'S (1) [MAJESTY]
Da 3:17 deliver us from Your M hand. A10002+10421

MAJOR (1) [MAJORITY]
2Ki 3:19 every fortified city and every m town. H4435

MAJORITY (2) [MAJOR]
Ac 27:12 the m decided that we should sail on G4498
2Co 2: 6 inflicted on him by the m is sufficient. G4498

MAKAZ (1)
1Ki 4: 9 Ben-Deker—in M, Shaalbim, Beth H5242

MAKBANNAI (1)
1Ch 12:13 Jeremiah the tenth and M the eleventh. H4801

MAKBENAH (1)
1Ch 2:49 to Sheva the father of M and Gibea. H4800

MAKE (842) [MADE, MAKER, MAKERS, MAKES, MAKING, MAN-MADE]
Ge 1:26 "Let us m mankind in our image H6913
Ge 2:18 I will m a helper suitable for him. H6913
Ge 3:16 I will m your pains in childbearing very severe H8049+8049
Ge 6:14 So m yourself an ark of cypress wood H6913
Ge 6:14 m rooms in it and coat it with pitch inside H6913
Ge 6:16 M a roof for it, leaving below the roof an H6913
Ge 6:16 a door in the side of the ark and m lower, H6913
Ge 11: 3 let's m bricks and bake them H4236+4246
Ge 11: 4 so that we may m a name for ourselves H6913
Ge 12: 2 "I will m you into a great nation, and I H6913
Ge 12: 2 I will m your name great, and you H1540
Ge 13:16 I will m your offspring like the dust of the H8492
Ge 17: 2 Then I will m my covenant between me H5989
Ge 17: 6 I will m you very fruitful; I will make H7238
Ge 17: 6 I will m nations of you, and kings H5989
Ge 17:20 I will m him fruitful and will greatly H7238
Ge 17:20 and I will m him into a great nation. H5989
Ge 21:13 I will m the son of the slave into a nation H8492
Ge 21:18 for I will m him into a great nation." H8492
Ge 22:17 m your descendants as numerous H8049+8049
Ge 24: 6 "M sure that you do not take my son back H9068
Ge 24:12 Abraham, m me successful today, and H7936
Ge 24:40 with you and m your journey a success, H7503
Ge 26: 4 I will m your descendants as numerous as H8049
Ge 26:28 us and you. Let us m a treaty with you H4162
Ge 28: 3 bless you and m you fruitful and increase H7238
Ge 29:21 and I want to m love to her. H995+448
Ge 31:44 Come now, let's m a covenant, you and I H4162
Ge 32: 9 your relatives, and I will m you prosper,' H3512
Ge 32:12 'I will surely m you prosper and H3512+3512
Ge 32:12 you prosper and will m your descendants H8492
Ge 34:12 M the price for the bride and the gift I am to bring as great as you like H8049+4394
Ge 39:14 has been brought to us to m sport of us! H7464
Ge 39:17 brought us came to me to m sport of me. H7464
Ge 41:43 people shouted before him, "M way!" H91
Ge 46: 3 for I will m you into a great nation there. H8492
Ge 48: 4 'I am going to m you fruitful and increase H7238
Ge 48: 4 I will m you a community of peoples, and H5989
Ge 48:20 'May God m you like Ephraim and H8492
Ex 3:21 "And I will m the Egyptians favorably H5989
Ex 5: 8 But require them to m the same number of H6913
Ex 5: 9 M the work harder for the people so that AIT
Ex 5:16 given no straw, yet we are told, 'M bricks! H6913
Ex 6: 3 LORD I did not m myself fully known to H3359
Ex 8: 5 and m frogs come up on the land of Egypt H6590
Ex 8:23 I will m a distinction between my people H8492
Ex 9: 4 But the LORD will m a distinction between H7111
Ex 10:28 M sure you do not appear before me H9068
Ex 17: 3 to m us and our children and livestock die H4637
Ex 17:14 m sure that Joshua hears it H8492+928+265
Ex 18:22 That will m your load lighter, because H7837
Ex 20: 4 "You shall not m for yourself an image in H6913
Ex 20:23 Do not m any gods to be alongside me H6913
Ex 20:23 do not m for yourselves gods of silver or H6913
Ex 20:24 " 'M an altar of earth for me and sacrifice H6913
Ex 20:25 If you m an altar of stones for me, do not H6913
Ex 22: 3 steals must certainly m restitution, H8966+8966
Ex 22: 5 offender must m restitution from the best H8966
Ex 22: 6 started the fire must m restitution. H8966+8966
Ex 22:14 present, they must m restitution. H8966+8966
Ex 23:27 I will m all your enemies turn their H5989+448
Ex 23:32 Do not m a covenant with them or with H4162
Ex 25: 8 "Then have them m a sanctuary for me H6913
Ex 25: 9 M this tabernacle and all its furnishings H6913
Ex 25:10 "Have them m an ark of acacia wood H6913
Ex 25:11 out, and m a gold molding around it. H6913
Ex 25:13 Then m poles of acacia wood and overlay H6913
Ex 25:17 "M an atonement cover of pure gold—two H6913
Ex 25:18 And m two cherubim out of hammered H6913
Ex 25:19 M one cherub on one end and the second H6913
Ex 25:19 m the cherubim of one piece with the H6913
Ex 25:23 "M a table of acacia wood—two cubits H6913
Ex 25:24 with pure gold and m a gold molding H6913
Ex 25:25 Also m around it a rim a handbreadth H6913
Ex 25:26 M four gold rings for the table and fasten H6913
Ex 25:28 M the poles of acacia wood, overlay them H6913
Ex 25:29 And m its plates and dishes of pure gold H6913
Ex 25:31 "M a lampstand of pure gold. Hammer H6913
Ex 25:31 base and shaft, and m its flowerlike cups H2118
Ex 25:37 "Then m its seven lamps and set them up H6913
Ex 25:40 See that you m them according to the H6913
Ex 26: 1 "M the tabernacle with ten curtains of H6913
Ex 26: 4 M loops of blue material along the edge H6913
Ex 26: 5 M fifty loops on one curtain and fifty loops H6913
Ex 26: 6 Then m fifty gold clasps and use them to H6913
Ex 26: 7 "M curtains of goat hair for the tent over H6913
Ex 26:10 M fifty loops along the edge of the end H6913
Ex 26:11 Then m fifty bronze clasps and put them in H6913
Ex 26:14 M for the tent a covering of ram skins dyed H6913
Ex 26:15 "M upright frames of acacia wood for the H6913
Ex 26:17 M all the frames of the tabernacle in this H6913
Ex 26:18 M twenty frames for the south side of the H6913
Ex 26:19 m forty silver bases to go under them H6913
Ex 26:20 side of the tabernacle, m twenty frames NDT
Ex 26:22 M six frames for the far end, that is, the H6913
Ex 26:23 m two frames for the corners at the far H6913
Ex 26:26 "Also m crossbars of acacia wood: five H6913
Ex 26:29 frames with gold and m gold rings to hold H6913
Ex 26:31 "M a curtain of blue, purple and scarlet H6913
Ex 26:36 entrance to the tent m a curtain of blue, H6913
Ex 26:37 M gold hooks for this curtain and five H6913
Ex 27: 2 M a horn at each of the four corners, so H6913
Ex 27: 3 M all its utensils of bronze—its pots to H6913
Ex 27: 4 M a grating for it, a bronze network, and H6913
Ex 27: 4 m a bronze ring at each of the four H6913
Ex 27: 6 M poles of acacia wood for the altar and H6913
Ex 27: 8 M the altar hollow, out of boards. It is to H6913
Ex 27: 9 "M a courtyard for the tabernacle. H6913
Ex 28: 2 M sacred garments for your brother Aaron H6913
Ex 28: 3 matters that they are to m garments for H6913
Ex 28: 4 These are the garments they are to m: H6913
Ex 28: 4 They are to m these sacred garments for H6913
Ex 28: 6 "M the ephod of gold, and of blue, purple H6913
Ex 28:13 M gold filigree settings H6913
Ex 28:15 of skilled hands. M it like the ephod: of H6913
Ex 28:22 "For the breastpiece m braided chains of H6913
Ex 28:23 M two gold rings for it and fasten them to H6913
Ex 28:26 M two gold rings and attach them to the H6913
Ex 28:27 M two more gold rings and attach them to H6913
Ex 28:31 "M the robe of the ephod entirely of blue H6913
Ex 28:33 M pomegranates of blue, purple and H6913
Ex 28:36 "M a plate of pure gold and engrave on it H6913
Ex 28:39 of fine linen and m the turban of fine H6913
Ex 28:40 M tunics, sashes and caps for Aaron's sons H6913
Ex 28:42 "M linen undergarments as a covering H6913
Ex 29: 2 And from the finest wheat flour m round H6913
Ex 29:28 the Israelites are to m to the LORD from H2118
Ex 29:36 each day as a sin offering to m atonement. NDT
Ex 29:37 For seven days m atonement for the altar H4105
Ex 30: 1 "M an altar of acacia wood for burning H6913
Ex 30: 3 and m a gold molding around it. H6913
Ex 30: 4 M two gold rings for the altar below the H6913
Ex 30: 5 M the poles of acacia wood and overlay H6913
Ex 30:10 a year Aaron shall m atonement on its H4105
Ex 30:15 to give less when you m the offering to H5989
Ex 30:18 "M a bronze basin, with its bronze stand H6913
Ex 30:25 M these into a sacred anointing oil, H6913
Ex 30:32 else's body and do not m any other oil H6913
Ex 30:35 m a fragrant blend of incense, the H6913
Ex 30:37 Do not m any incense with this formula H6913
Ex 31: 4 to m artistic designs for work in gold, H3108
Ex 31: 6 the skilled workers to m everything I have H6913
Ex 31:11 They are to m them just as I commanded H6913
Ex 32: 1 m us gods who will go before us. H6913
Ex 32:10 Then I will m you into a great nation." H6913
Ex 32:13 'I will m your descendants as numerous H8049

M

Ex 32:23 '**M** us gods who will go before us. H6913
Ex 32:30 perhaps *I can* **m atonement** for your sin." H4105
Ex 34:12 Be careful not *to* **m** a treaty with those H4162
Ex 34:15 "Be careful not *to* **m** a treaty with those H4162
Ex 34:17 "*Do* not **m** any idols. H6913
Ex 35:10 are to come and **m** everything the LORD H6913
Ex 35:32 to **m** artistic designs for work in gold, H3108
Ex 36: 6 "No man or woman *is to* **m** anything else H6913
Ex 38:28 *They* **used** the 1,775 shekels **to m** the H6913
Ex 38:28 tops of the posts, and *to* **m** their **bands**. H3138
Ex 38:30 *They* used it *to* **m** the bases for the H6913
Lev 1: 4 on your behalf to **m atonement** for you. H4105
Lev 4:20 way the priest *will* **m atonement** for the H4105
Lev 4:26 way the priest *will* **m atonement** for the H4105
Lev 4:31 way the priest *will* **m atonement** for them, H4105
Lev 4:35 the priest *will* **m atonement** for them for H4105
Lev 5: 3 anything that *would* **m** *them* **unclean**) even AIT
Lev 5: 6 the priest *shall* **m atonement** for them H4105
Lev 5:10 way and **m atonement** for them for the H4105
Lev 5:13 the priest *will* **m atonement** for them for H4105
Lev 5:16 *They must* **m restitution** *for* what they H8966
Lev 5:16 The priest *will* **m atonement** for them with H4105
Lev 5:18 the priest *will* **m atonement** for them for H4105
Lev 6: 5 *They must* **m restitution** in full, add a fifth H8966
Lev 6: 7 way the priest *will* **m atonement** for them H4105
Lev 6:30 of meeting to **m atonement** in the Holy H4105
Lev 8:15 he consecrated it to **m atonement** for it. H4105
Lev 8:34 by the LORD to **m** atonement for you. H6913
Lev 9: 7 offering and **m atonement** for yourself H4105
Lev 9: 7 the people and **m atonement** for them, H4105
Lev 11:24 " '*You will* **m yourselves unclean** by these H3237
Lev 11:43 *Do* not **m yourselves unclean** by means of H3237
Lev 11:44 *Do* not **m** yourselves **unclean** by any H3237
Lev 12: 7 before the LORD *to* **m atonement** for her, H4105
Lev 12: 8 way the priest *will* **m atonement** for her, H4105
Lev 14:18 be cleansed and **m atonement** for them H4105
Lev 14:19 offering and **m atonement** for the one to H4105
Lev 14:20 offering, and **m atonement** for them, and H4105
Lev 14:21 to be waved to **m atonement** for them, H4105
Lev 14:29 to **m atonement** for them before the LORD. H4105
Lev 14:31 the priest *will* **m atonement** before the H4105
Lev 14:53 In this way *he will* **m atonement** for the H4105
Lev 15: 3 body or is blocked, it will **m** him unclean. NDT
Lev 15:15 this way he *will* **m atonement** before the H4105
Lev 15:30 In this way he *will* **m atonement** for her H4105
Lev 15:31 from **things that m** them **unclean**, H3240
Lev 16: 6 sin offering *to* **m atonement** for himself H4105
Lev 16:11 sin offering *to* **m atonement** for himself H4105
Lev 16:16 In this way *he will* **m atonement** for the H4105
Lev 16:17 goes in to **m atonement** in the Most H4105
Lev 16:18 is before the LORD and **m atonement** for it. H4105
Lev 16:24 *to* **m atonement** for himself and for the H4105
Lev 16:27 into the Most Holy Place to **m atonement**, H4105
Lev 16:32 father as high priest *is to* **m atonement**. H4105
Lev 16:33 and **m atonement** *for* the Most Holy Place H4105
Lev 17:11 it to you to **m atonement** for yourselves on H4105
Lev 19: 4 'Do not turn to idols or **m** metal gods for H6913
Lev 19:22 the priest *is to* **m atonement** for him H4105
Lev 20:25 " '*You must* therefore **m a distinction** H976
Lev 21: 1 *must* not **m himself ceremonially unclean** H3237
Lev 21: 3 her *he may* **m himself unclean**. H3237
Lev 21: 4 *He must* not **m himself unclean** for people H3237
Lev 21: 8 I the LORD am holy—I *who* **m** you **holy**. H7727
Lev 21:11 *He must* not **m himself unclean**, even H3237
Lev 22:14 *must* **m restitution** to the priest *for* the H5989
Lev 24:18 of someone's animal *must* **m restitution**— H8966
Lev 24:21 kills an animal *must* **m restitution**, H8966
Lev 25:39 *do* not **m** them **work** as slaves. H6268
Lev 25:46 property and *can* **m** them **slaves** for life, H6268
Lev 26: 1 " '*Do* not **m** idols or set up an image or a H6913
Lev 26: 6 lie down and no *one will* **m** you **afraid**. H3006
Lev 26: 9 with favor and **m** you **fruitful** and increase H7238
Lev 26:10 move it out to **m room for** the new. H4946+7156
Lev 26:19 stubborn pride and **m** the sky above you H5989
Lev 26:22 and **m** you *so* **few in number** that your H5070
Lev 26:36 *I will* **m** their hearts so fearful in the lands H995
Lev 27:33 good from the bad or **m** any **substitution**. H4614
Lev 27:33 If *anyone does* **m a substitution** H4614+4614
Nu 3:40 old or more and **m** a list of their names H5951
Nu 5: 7 *They must* **m full restitution** *for* H8740+928+8031
Nu 5:24 *He shall* **m** the woman **drink** the bitter H9197
Nu 6: 2 woman *wants* to **m a special vow**, H5623+7098
Nu 6: 7 *they must* not **m themselves ceremonially unclean** H3237
Nu 6:11 burnt offering *to* **m atonement** for the H4105
Nu 6:16 before the LORD and **m** the sin offering H6913
Nu 6:25 the LORD **m** his face **shine** on you and be H239
Nu 8: 6 Israelites and **m** them **ceremonially clean**. H3197
Nu 8:12 offering, to **m atonement** for the Levites. H4105
Nu 8:19 to **m atonement** for them so that H4105
Nu 10: 2 "**M** two trumpets of hammered silver, and H6913
Nu 14:12 but *I will* **m** you into a nation greater and H6913
Nu 14:30 swore with uplifted hand to **m** your **home**, H8905
Nu 15:25 The priest is *to* **m atonement** for the whole H4105
Nu 15:28 The priest *is to* **m atonement** before the H4105
Nu 15:38 to come *you are to* **m** tassels on the H6913
Nu 16:46 to the assembly *to* **m atonement** for them. H4105
Nu 21: 8 "**M** a snake and put it up on a pole H6913
Nu 22:28 I done to you *to* **m** *you* **beat** me these three AIT
Nu 28: 2 '**M sure** that you present to me at the H9068
Nu 28: 9 **m** an offering of two lambs a year old NDT
Nu 28:22 as a sin offering to **m atonement** for you. H4105
Nu 28:30 one male goat to **m atonement** for you. H4105
Nu 29: 5 as a sin offering to **m atonement** for you. H4105
Nu 31:50 to **m atonement** for ourselves before the H4105
Nu 32: 5 *Do* not **m** us **cross** the Jordan. H6296
Dt 4:16 become corrupt and **m** for yourselves an H6913
Dt 4:23 *do* not **m** for yourselves an idol in the H6913
Dt 4:25 become corrupt and **m** any kind of idol, H6913
Dt 5: 8 "*You shall* not **m** for yourself an image in H6913
Dt 7: 2 **M** no treaty with them, and show them no H4162
Dt 9:14 And *I will* **m** you into a nation stronger H6913
Dt 10: 1 on the mountain. Also **m** a wooden ark. H6913
Dt 17:16 himself or **m** the people **return** to Egypt to H8740
Dt 19:18 judges *must* **m** *a* thorough **investigation**, H2011
Dt 20:10 **m** its people **an offer** of peace. H7924
Dt 20:12 If *they* refuse *to* **m peace** and they engage H8966
Dt 22: 8 **m** a parapet around your roof so that you H6913
Dt 22:12 **M** tassels on the four corners of the cloak H6913
Dt 23:21 If *you* **m a vow** to the LORD your H5623+5624
Dt 24:10 When *you* **m a loan** of any kind to H5957+5394
Dt 25: 2 judge *shall* **m** them **lie down** and have H5877
Dt 28:13 The LORD *will* **m** you the head, not the tail H5989
Dt 28:63 the LORD to **m** you **prosper** and increase H3512
Dt 28:68 I said you *should* never **m again**. H3578+6388
Dt 29: 1 commanded Moses to **m** with the H4162
Dt 29:18 **M** sure there is no man or woman, clan or NDT
Dt 29:18 **m** sure there is no root among you that NDT
Dt 30: 5 *He will* **m** you **more prosperous** and H3512
Dt 30: 9 LORD your God *will* **m** you **most** prosperous AIT
Dt 30: 9 again delight in you and **m** you prosperous, NDT
Dt 32:21 *I will* **m** them **envious** by those who are H7861
Dt 32:21 *I will* **m** them **angry** by a nation that has H4087
Dt 32:25 the street the sword *will* **m** them **childless**; H8897
Dt 32:42 *I will* **m** my arrows **drunk** with blood, H8910
Dt 32:43 enemies and **m atonement** *for* his land H4105
Jos 5: 2 "**M** flint knives and circumcise the H6913
Jos 6:18 Otherwise *you will* **m** the camp of Israel H8492
Jos 9: 6 from a distant country; **m** a treaty with us." H4162
Jos 9: 7 so how *can we* **m** a treaty with you?" H4162
Jos 9:11 "We are your servants; **m** a treaty with us." H4162
Jos 18: 4 them out *to* **m a survey of** the land H2143+928
Jos 18: 8 "Go and **m a survey of** the land and H2143+928
Jos 24:20 disaster on you and **m an end** *of* you, H3983
Jdg 2: 2 you *shall* not **m** a covenant with the H4162
Jdg 6:39 *Let me* **m** just one more **request** H1819
Jdg 6:39 this time **m** the fleece dry and let the H2118
Jdg 17: 3 LORD for my son to **m** an image overlaid H6913
Jdg 17: 4 silversmith, *who* **used** them **to m** the idol. H6913
Ru 4:11 *May* the LORD **m** the woman who is H5989
1Sa 1:23 only *may* the LORD **m good** his word." H7756
1Sa 3:11 *will* **m** the ears of everyone who hears about it **tingle** AIT
1Sa 6: 5 **M** models of the tumors and of the rats H6913
1Sa 8:11 sons and **m** them **serve** with his H8492+4200
1Sa 8:12 still others to **m** weapons of war and H6913
1Sa 11: 1 Jabesh said to him, "**M** a treaty with us H4162
1Sa 11: 2 "*I will* **m a treaty** with you only on the H4162
1Sa 12: 3 I accepted a bribe *to* **m** *me* **shut** my eyes? H6623
1Sa 12: 3 done any of these things, *I will* **m** it **right**." H8740
1Sa 12:22 the LORD was pleased to **m** you his own. H6913
1Sa 13:19 the Hebrews *will* **m** swords or spears!" H6913
1Sa 20:26 happened to David to **m** him ceremonially NDT
1Sa 22: 7 *Will he* **m** all of you commanders of H8492
1Sa 25:28 your God *will* **certainly m** a lasting H6913+6913
1Sa 28: 2 *I will* **m** you my bodyguard for life. H8492
2Sa 3:12 **M** an agreement with me, and I will help H4162
2Sa 3:13 "I *will* **m** an agreement with you H4162
2Sa 3:17 time *you have* **wanted to m** David H1335+4200
2Sa 3:21 so that *they may* **m** a covenant with you H4162
2Sa 7: 9 Now *I will* **m** your name great, like the H6913
2Sa 7:23 himself, and to **m** a name for himself H8492
2Sa 11:11 and drink and **m love to** my wife? H8886+6640
2Sa 13: 6 and **m** some **special bread** in my H4221+4223
2Sa 15:20 today *shall I* **m** you **wander about** with us, H5675
2Sa 19:28 I have to **m** any more **appeals** to the king H2410
2Sa 21: 3 How *shall I* **m atonement** so that you will H4105
2Sa 22:36 *You* **m** your saving help my shield; your H5989
1Ki 1:37 to **m** his throne *even* **greater** than H1540
1Ki 1:47 *May* your God **m** Solomon's name more **famous** H3512
1Ki 2:16 I **have** one **request to m** of you. H8626+8629
1Ki 2:16 not refuse me." "*You may* **m** it," she said. H1819
1Ki 2:20 "I **have** one small **request to m** of H8626+8629
1Ki 2:20 The king replied, "**M** it, my mother; H8626S
1Ki 2:42 "*Did I* not **m** you **swear** by the LORD and H8678
1Ki 9:22 But Solomon did not **m** slaves of any of H5989
1Ki 10:12 The king **used** the almugwood **to m** H6913
1Ki 10:12 to **m** harps and lyres for the musicians. NDT
1Ki 12: 1 all Israel had gone there to **m** him **king**. H4887
1Ki 12:10 heavy yoke on us, but **m** our yoke **lighter**. H7837
1Ki 12:11 you a heavy yoke; I *will* **m** it **even heavier**. H3578
1Ki 12:14 your yoke heavy; I *will* **m** it **even heavier**. H3578
1Ki 12:33 went up to the altar to **m offerings**. H7787
1Ki 13: 1 standing by the altar to **m** *an* **offering**. H7787
1Ki 13: 2 of the high places who **m offerings** here, H7787
1Ki 16: 3 and *I will* **m** your house like that of H5989
1Ki 17:12 to take home and **m** a meal for myself H6913
1Ki 17:13 But first **m** a small loaf of bread for me H6913
1Ki 17:13 then **m** something for yourself and H6913
1Ki 19: 2 time tomorrow *I do* not **m** your life like H8492
1Ki 21:22 *I will* **m** your house like that of Jeroboam H5989
1Ki 22:16 many times *must* I **m** you **swear** to tell me H8678
2Ki 2:21 cause death or **m** the land **unproductive**. H8897
2Ki 4:10 *Let's* **m** a small room on the roof and put H6913
2Ki 5:17 your servant *will* never again **m** burnt H6913
2Ki 9: 9 *I will* **m** the house of Ahab like the house H5989
2Ki 9:15 "If you desire to **m** me king, don't let NDT
2Ki 9:26 and *I will* surely **m** you **pay** *for* it on this H8966
2Ki 10:24 So they went in to **m** sacrifices and burnt H6913
2Ki 18:23 Come now, **m a bargain** with my master H6842
2Ki 18:31 **M** peace with me and come out to me H6913
2Ki 19: 7 I *will* **m** him **want to** return to H5989+8120+928
2Ki 19:28 and *I will* **m** you **return** by the way you H8740
2Ki 21: 8 **m** the feet of the Israelites **wander** from H5653
1Ch 12:31 by name to come and **m** David **king**— H4887
1Ch 12:38 determined to **m** David **king** over all Israel H4887
1Ch 12:38 were also of one mind to **m** David **king**. H4887
1Ch 15:16 as musicians to **m** a joyful sound with H8123
1Ch 16: 8 **m known** among the nations what he has H3359
1Ch 17: 8 Now *I will* **m** your name like the names of H6913
1Ch 17:21 himself, and to **m** a name for yourself H8492
1Ch 18: 8 which Solomon used *to* **m** the bronze Sea, H6913
1Ch 22: 3 amount of iron to **m** nails for the doors of NDT
1Ch 22: 5 Therefore *I will* **m preparations** for it." H3922
1Ch 27:23 promised to **m** Israel as **numerous** as the H8049
1Ch 28: 4 was pleased to **m** me **king** over all Israel. H4887
2Ch 7:20 *I will* **m** it a byword and an object of H5989
2Ch 8: 9 But Solomon *did* not **m** slaves of the H5989
2Ch 9:11 The king **used** the algumwood **to m** steps H6913
2Ch 9:11 to **m** harps and lyres for the musicians. NDT
2Ch 10: 1 all Israel had gone there to **m** him **king**. H4887
2Ch 10:10 heavy yoke on us, but **m** our yoke **lighter**. H7837
2Ch 10:11 you a heavy yoke; I *will* **m** it **even heavier**. H3578
2Ch 10:14 your yoke heavy; I *will* **m** it **even heavier**. H3578
2Ch 11:22 his brothers, in order to **m** him **king**. H4887
2Ch 13: 9 **m** priests of your own as the peoples H6913
2Ch 18:15 many times *must* I **m** you **swear** to tell me H8678
2Ch 28:10 **m** the **men** and women of Judah and Jerusalem your **slaves** H3899+6269
2Ch 29:10 Now I intend to **m** a covenant with the H4162
2Ch 32:18 terrify them and **m** them **afraid** in order to H987
2Ch 33: 8 **m** the feet of the Israelites **leave** the H6073
2Ch 36:22 Cyrus king of Persia *to* **m** a proclamation H6296
Ezr 1: 1 Cyrus king of Persia *to* **m** a proclamation H6296
Ezr 4: 4 of Judah and **m** them **afraid** to go on H987
Ezr 10: 3 Now *let us* **m** a covenant before our God H4162
Ne 2: 8 me timber to **m beams** *for* the gates of H7936
Ne 6: 7 to **m** *this* **proclamation** about you H7924
Ne 8:15 shade trees, to **m** temporary shelters"— H6913
Ne 10:33 sin offerings to **m atonement** for Israel H4105
Job 1: 5 Job *would* **m arrangements** *for* them to be H8938
Job 7:17 is mankind that *you* **m so much of** them, H1540
Job 11:19 with no *one* to **m** you **afraid**, and many H3006
Job 13:26 against me and **m** me **reap** the sins of my H3769
Job 16: 4 *I could* **m fine speeches** H2488+928+4863
Job 20:10 His children *must* **m amends** *to* the poor H8355
Job 20:15 God *will* **m** his stomach **vomit** them **up**. H3769
Job 21:12 *they* **m merry** to the sound of the pipe. H8523
Job 24:17 *they* **m friends with** the terrors of darkness. H5795
Job 31:15 *Did* not he who made me in the womb **m** H6913
Job 36:33 even the cattle **m** it known its approach. NDT
Job 38:27 wasteland and **m** it **sprout** *with* grass? H7541
Job 39:20 *Do you* **m** it **leap** like a locust, striking H8321
Job 41: 4 *Will it* **m** an agreement with you for you H4162
Job 41: 5 *Can you* **m** a **pet** of it like a bird or put it H8471
Job 41:28 Arrows *do* not **m** it **flee**; slingstones are H1368
Ps 2: 8 and *I will* **m** the nations your inheritance H5989
Ps 4: 8 you alone, LORD, **m** me **dwell** in safety. H3782
Ps 5: 8 **m** your way **straight** before me. H3837
Ps 7: 5 the ground and **m** me **sleep** in the dust. H8905
Ps 7: 9 the wicked and **m** the righteous **secure**— H3922
Ps 16: 5 portion and my cup; you **m** my lot **secure**. H9461
Ps 16:11 *You* **m known** to me the path of life; you H3359
Ps 18:35 *You* **m** your saving help my shield, and H5989
Ps 20: 4 your heart and **m** all your plans **succeed**. H4848
Ps 21:12 *You will* **m** them **turn** their backs when H8883
Ps 27: 6 I will sing and **m music** to the LORD. H2376
Ps 33: 2 **m music** to him on the ten-stringed lyre. H2376
Ps 37: 6 *He will* **m** your righteous reward **shine** like H3655
Ps 39: 8 *do* not **m** me the scorn of fools. H8492
Ps 44: 8 In God *we* **m** *our* **boast** all day long, and H2146
Ps 45:16 *you will* **m** them princes throughout the H8883
Ps 46: 4 whose streams **m glad** the city of God, H8523
Ps 52: 7 now is the man *who did* not **m** God his H8492
Ps 57: 7 heart is steadfast; I will sing and **m music**. H2376
Ps 66: 2 glory of his name; **m** his praise glorious. H8492
Ps 67: 1 bless us and **m** his face **shine** on us— H239
Ps 69:11 people **m sport of** *me*. H2118+4200+5442
Ps 76:11 **M vows** to the LORD your God and fulfill H5623
Ps 79:10 **m known** among the nations that you H3359
Ps 80: 3 **m** your face **shine** on us, that we H239
Ps 80: 7 Almighty; **m** your face **shine** on us, that H239
Ps 80:19 Almighty; **m** your face **shine** on us, that H239
Ps 83:11 **M** their nobles like Oreb and Zeeb, all H8883
Ps 83:13 **M** them like tumbleweed, my God, like H8883
Ps 84: 6 of Baka, *they* **m** it a place of springs H8883
Ps 87: 7 As *they* **m music** they will sing, "All my H2727
Ps 89: 1 mouth *I will* **m** your faithfulness **known** H3359
Ps 89: 4 forever and **m** your throne **firm** through all H1215
Ps 90:15 **M** us **glad** for as many days as you have H8523
Ps 91: 9 and you **m** the Most High your dwelling H8492
Ps 92: 1 the LORD and **m music** to your name, H2376
Ps 92: 4 For *you* **m** me **glad** by your deeds, LORD; H8523
Ps 98: 5 **m music** to the LORD with the harp, with H2376
Ps 104:15 oil to **m** their faces **shine**, and bread H7413

M

Ps 104:17 There the birds **m** *their* **nests**; the stork H7873
Ps 105: 1 **m known** among the nations what he has H3359
Ps 106: 8 to **m** his mighty power **known**. H3359
Ps 106:26 hand that he *would* **m** them **fall** in the H5877
Ps 106:27 **m** their descendants **fall** among the H5877
Ps 108: 1 I will sing and **m music** *with* all my soul. H2376
Ps 110: 1 at my right hand until *I* **m** your enemies a H8883
Ps 115: 8 *Those who* **m** them will be like them, and H6913
Ps 119:98 with me and **m** me **wiser** than my H2681
Ps 119:135 **M** your face **shine** on your servant and H239
Ps 119:165 and nothing can **m** them **stumble**. H4842
Ps 132:17 "Here *I will* **m** a horn **grow** for David and H7541
Ps 135:18 *Those who* **m** them will be like them, and H6913
Ps 139: 8 are there; if *I* **m** *my* **bed** *in* the depths, you H3667
Ps 140: 3 *They* **m** their tongues as **sharp** as a H9111
Ps 144: 9 the ten-stringed lyre *I will* **m music** to you, H2376
Ps 147: 7 **m music** to our God on the harp. H2376
Ps 149: 3 with dancing and **m music** to him with H2376
Pr 1:23 *I will* **m known** *to* you my teachings. H3359
Pr 3: 6 and he *will* **m** your paths **straight**. H3837
Pr 4:16 of sleep till *they* **m** someone **stumble**. H4173
Pr 10: 4 Lazy hands **m** for poverty, but diligent H6913
Pr 13: 5 wicked **m** *themselves* **a stench** and bring H944
Pr 16: 7 *he* **causes** their enemies **to m peace** with H8966
Pr 16:23 of the wise **m** their mouths **prudent**, H8505
Pr 22:24 *Do* not **m friends** with a hot-tempered H8287
Pr 30:26 yet *they* **m** their home in the crags H8492
Ecc 5: 4 When *you* **m a vow** to God, do not H5623+5624
Ecc 5: 5 It is better not *to* **m a vow** than to make H5623
Ecc 5: 5 make a vow than *to* **m one** and not fulfill H5623S
SS 1:11 *We will* **m** you earrings of gold, studded H6913
Isa 1:16 Wash and **m yourselves clean**. Take your H2342
Isa 3: 4 "*I will* **m** mere youths their officials H5989
Isa 3: 7 *do* not **m** me the leader of the people." H8492
Isa 3:17 of Zion; the LORD *will* **m** their scalps **bald**." H6867
Isa 5: 6 *I will* **m** it a wasteland, neither pruned H8883
Isa 6:10 **M** the heart of this people **calloused** H9042
Isa 6:10 **m** their ears **dull** and close their eyes. H3877
Isa 7: 6 and **m** the son of Tabeel **king** over H4887+4889
Isa 10: 1 Woe to those *who* **m** unjust **laws** H2980+2976
Isa 12: 4 **m known** among the nations what he has H3359
Isa 13: 9 to **m** the land desolate and destroy the H8492
Isa 13:12 *I will* **m** people **scarcer** than pure gold H3700
Isa 13:13 Therefore *I will* **m** the heavens **tremble** H8074
Isa 14: 2 of the nations and **m** them male and H4200
Isa 14: 2 *They will* **m captives** of their captors and H8647
Isa 14:14 *I will* **m myself like** the Most High. H1948
Isa 16: 3 "**M up** *your* **mind**," Moab says H995+6783
Isa 16: 3 **M** your shadow like night H8883
Isa 17: 2 lie down, with no *one to* **m** them **afraid**. H3006
Isa 17:11 them out, *you* **m** them **grow**, and on the H8451
Isa 19:12 show you and **m known** what the LORD H3359
Isa 19:14 *they* **m** Egypt **stagger** in all that she does H9494
Isa 19:21 So the LORD *will* **m himself known** to the H3359
Isa 19:21 *they will* **m vows** to the LORD and H5623+5624
Isa 26: 7 *you*, ... **m** the way of the righteous **smooth** H7142
Isa 27: 5 me for refuge; *let them* **m** peace with me H6913
Isa 27: 5 with me, yes, *let them* **m** peace with me." H6913
Isa 27:11 women come and **m fires** *with* them. H239
Isa 28:17 *I will* **m** justice the measuring line and H8492
Isa 28:28 Grain must be ground to **m** bread; so one NDT
Isa 29:16 formed it, "*You did* not **m** me"? H6913
Isa 29:21 *those who* with a word **m** someone **out to be guilty** H2627
Isa 30:30 voice and *will* **m** them **see** his arm H8011
Isa 32: 7 they **m up** evil schemes to destroy the H3619
Isa 32: 8 But the noble **m** noble **plans**, and by H3619
Isa 36: 8 " 'Come now, **m a bargain** with my master H6842
Isa 36:16 **M** peace with me and come out to me H6913
Isa 37: 7 *I will* **m** him **want to** return to H5989+928+8120
Isa 37:29 and *I will* **m** you **return** by the way you H8740
Isa 38: 8 I *will* **m** the shadow cast by the sun **go** H8740
Isa 40: 3 **m straight** in the desert a highway for our H3837
Isa 41:15 *I will* **m** you into a threshing sledge H8492
Isa 41:18 *I will* **m** rivers **flow** on barren heights, and H7337
Isa 42: 6 I will keep you and *will* **m** you to be a H5989
Isa 42:16 light before them and **m** the rough places NDT
Isa 42:21 *to* **m** *his* law **great** and glorious. H1540
Isa 44: 9 All who **m** idols are nothing, and the H3670
Isa 44:19 *Shall I* **m** a detestable thing *from* what is H6913
Isa 45:13 *I will* **m** all his ways **straight**. He will H3837
Isa 45:25 in the LORD and *will* **m** *their* **boast** *in* him. H2146
Isa 46: 6 they hire a goldsmith *to* **m** it *into* a god H6913
Isa 46:10 **I m known** the end from the beginning H5583
Isa 47:13 stargazers *who* **m predictions** month by H3359
Isa 49: 6 *I will* also **m** you a light for the Gentiles H5989
Isa 49: 8 I will keep you and *will* **m** you to be a H5989
Isa 49:26 *I will* **m** your oppressors **eat** their own flesh H430
Isa 50: 3 with darkness and **m** sackcloth its covering H8492
Isa 51: 3 her ruins; *he will* **m** her deserts like Eden H8492
Isa 54:12 *I will* **m** your battlements *of* rubies, your H8492
Isa 55: 3 *I will* **m** an everlasting covenant with you H4162
Isa 59: 6 cover themselves with **what** they **m**. H5126
Isa 60:15 *I will* **m** you the everlasting pride and the H8492
Isa 60:17 *I will* **m** peace your governor and H8492
Isa 61: 8 reward my people and **m** an everlasting H4162
Isa 61:11 *will* **m** righteousness and praise **spring up** H7541
Isa 63:14 guided your people to **m** for yourself a H6913
Isa 63:17 *do you* **m** us **wander** from your ways and H9494
Isa 64: 2 down to **m** your name **known** to your H3359
Isa 66:22 the new earth that I **m** will endure before H6913
Jer 5:14 I *will* **m** my words in your mouth a fire H5989
Jer 6: 8 away from you and **m** your land desolate H8492
Jer 7:18 knead the dough and **m** cakes to offer to H6913
Jer 9: 3 *They* **m ready** their tongue like a bow, **to shoot** H2005
Jer 9:11 "*I will* **m** Jerusalem a heap of ruins, H5989
Jer 9:15 *I will* **m** this people **eat** bitter **food** and H430
Jer 10:11 who *did* not **m** the heavens and the A10522
Jer 10:22 *It will* **m** the towns of Judah desolate, H8492
Jer 15: 4 *I will* **m** them abhorrent to all the H5989
Jer 15: 8 *I will m* their widows more **numerous** than AIT
Jer 15:11 surely *I will* **m** your enemies **plead** with H7003
Jer 15:20 *I will* **m** you a wall to this people, H5989
Jer 16:20 *Do* people **m** their own gods? Yes, but H6913
Jer 18:18 *let's* **m** *plans* against Jeremiah H3108+4742
Jer 19: 3 *will* **m** the ears of everyone who hears of it **tingle** H7509
Jer 19: 7 *I will* **m** them **fall** by the sword before H5877
Jer 19: 8 *I will* devastate this city and **m** it an object H8492
Jer 19: 9 *I will* **m** them **eat** the flesh of their sons H430
Jer 19:12 *I will* **m** this city like Topheth H5989
Jer 20: 4 'I *will* **m** you a terror to yourself and to all H5989
Jer 22: 6 *I will* surely **m** you like a wasteland H8883
Jer 22:15 "*Does it m you a* **king** to have more and AIT
Jer 23:15 "I *will* **m** them eat bitter **food** and drink H430
Jer 23:27 another *will* **m** my people **forget** my name H8894
Jer 24: 9 *I will* **m** them abhorrent and an offense to H5989
Jer 25: 9 destroy them and **m** them an object of H8492
Jer 25:12 the LORD, "and *will* **m** it desolate forever. H8492
Jer 25:15 **m** all the nations to whom I send you **drink** H9197
Jer 25:18 to **m** them a ruin and an object of horror H5989
Jer 26: 6 then *I will* **m** this house like Shiloh and H5989
Jer 27: 2 "**M** a yoke out of straps and crossbars and H6913
Jer 27: 6 *I will* **m** even the wild animals subject to H5989
Jer 28:14 nations to *m* them **serve** Nebuchadnezzar AIT
Jer 29:17 against them and *I will* **m** them like figs H5989
Jer 29:18 plague and *will* **m** them abhorrent to H5989
Jer 30:10 security, and no *one will* **m** him **afraid**. H3006
Jer 30:16 all *who* **m spoil** *of* you I will despoil. H1024
Jer 31: 7 **M** your praises **heard**, and say, 'LORD, save H9048
Jer 31:31 "when *I will* **m** a new covenant with the H4162
Jer 31:33 is the covenant *I will* **m** with the people of H4162
Jer 32:35 a detestable thing and so **m** Judah **sin**. H2627
Jer 32:40 *I will* **m** an everlasting covenant with them: H4162
Jer 33:15 *I will* **m** a righteous Branch **sprout** from H7541
Jer 33:22 *I will* **m** the descendants of David ... as **countless** H8049+889+4202+6218
Jer 34: 5 so *they will* **m a fire** in your honor and H8596
Jer 34: 5 *I* myself **m** *this* **promise**, declares H1819+1821
Jer 34:17 *I will* **m** you abhorrent to all the kingdoms H5989
Jer 44: 8 yourselves and **m** yourselves a curse and H2118
Jer 46:27 security, and no *one will* **m** him **afraid**. H3006
Jer 48:26 "**M** her **drunk**, for she has defied the LORD H8910
Jer 48:35 end to *those who* **m offerings** *on* the high H6590
Jer 49:15 "Now *I will* **m** you small among the H5989
Jer 51:25 and **m** you a burned-out mountain. H5989
Jer 51:36 I will dry up her sea and **m** her springs **dry**. H3312
Jer 51:39 out a feast for them and **m** them **drunk**, H8910
Jer 51:44 and **m** him **spew out** what H3655+4946+7023
Jer 51:57 *I will* **m** her officials and wise men **drunk** H8910
Eze 3: 8 But *I will* **m** you as unyielding and H5989
Eze 3: 9 *I will* **m** your forehead like the hardest H5989
Eze 3:26 *I will* **m** your tongue **stick** to the roof of H1815
Eze 4: 9 a storage jar and **use** them **to m** bread H6913
Eze 5:14 "*I will* **m** you a ruin and a reproach H5989
Eze 6:14 against them and **m** the land a desolate H5989
Eze 7:20 jewelry and used it *to* **m** their detestable H6913
Eze 7:20 therefore *I will* **m** it a thing unclean for H5989
Eze 13:18 on all their wrists and **m** veils of various H6913
Eze 14: 8 against them and **m** them an example H8492
Eze 15: 3 ever taken from it to **m** anything useful? H6913
Eze 15: 3 *Do they* **m** pegs from it to hang things on? H4374
Eze 15: 8 *I will* **m** the land desolate because they H5989
Eze 16: 4 you washed with water to **m** you **clean**, H5470
Eze 16:16 of your garments to **m** gaudy high places, H6913
Eze 16:63 when I **m atonement** for you for all you H4105
Eze 17:24 the tall tree and **m** the low tree **grow tall**. H1467
Eze 17:24 the green tree and **m** the dry tree **flourish**. H7255
Eze 21:19 **M** a signpost where the road branches off H1345
Eze 21:27 *I will* **m** it a ruin! The crown will H8492
Eze 22: 4 Therefore *I will* **m** you an object of scorn H5989
Eze 22:12 you take interest and **m** a profit from the NDT
Eze 22:25 things and **m many** widows within her. H8049
Eze 22:27 and kill people to **m unjust gain**. H1298+1299
Eze 26: 4 away her rubble and **m** her a bare rock. H5989
Eze 26:14 *I will* **m** you a bare rock, and you will H5989
Eze 26:19 When I **m** you a desolate city, like cities H5989
Eze 26:20 *I will* **m** you **dwell** in the earth below, as H3782
Eze 27: 5 cedar from Lebanon to **m** a mast for you. H6913
Eze 28:23 plague upon you and **m** blood flow in your NDT
Eze 29: 4 and **m** the fish of your streams **stick** to H1815
Eze 29:10 and *I will* **m** the land of Egypt a ruin and H5989
Eze 29:12 *I will* **m** the land of Egypt desolate among H5989
Eze 29:15 *I will* **m** it *so* **weak** that it will never again H5070
Eze 29:21 "On that day *I will* **m** a horn **grow** for the H7541
Eze 30:22 and **m** the sword **fall** from his hand. H5877
Eze 32:14 settle and **m** her streams **flow** like oil, H2143
Eze 32:15 When I **m** Egypt desolate and strip the H5989
Eze 33: 2 of their men and **m** him their watchman, H5989
Eze 33:28 *I will* **m** the land a desolate waste, and H5989
Eze 34:25 " '*I will* **m** a covenant of peace with them H4162
Eze 34:26 *I will* **m** them and the places surrounding H5989
Eze 34:28 in safety, and no *one will* **m** them **afraid**. H3006
Eze 35: 3 against you and **m** you a desolate waste H5989
Eze 35: 7 *I will* **m** Mount Seir a desolate waste and H5989
Eze 35: 9 *I will* **m** you desolate forever; your towns H5989
Eze 35:11 them and *I will* **m myself known** among H3359
Eze 35:14 earth rejoices, *I will* **m** you desolate. H6913
Eze 36:11 past and *will* **m** you **prosper** more than H3201
Eze 36:14 devour people or **m** your nation **childless**, H8897
Eze 36:15 No longer *will I* **m** you **hear** the taunts of H9048
Eze 36:29 the grain and **m** it **plentiful** and will not H8049
Eze 36:37 *I will* **m** their people as **numerous** as H8049
Eze 37: 5 I *will* **m** breath **enter** you, and you will H995+928
Eze 37: 6 to you and **m** flesh **come** upon you and H6590
Eze 37:19 *I will* **m** them into a single stick of wood H6913
Eze 37:22 *I will* **m** them one nation in the land, on H6913
Eze 37:26 *I will* **m** a covenant of peace with them; it H4162
Eze 37:28 will know that I the LORD **m** Israel **holy**, H7727
Eze 38:23 and *I will* **m myself known** in the sight of H3359
Eze 39: 3 hand and **m** your arrows **drop** from your H5877
Eze 39: 7 " '*I will* **m known** my holy name among H3359
Eze 39:26 their land with no *one to* **m** them **afraid**. H3006
Eze 43:11 **m known** *to* them the design of the H3359
Eze 43:20 so purify the altar and **m atonement** *for* it. H4105
Eze 43:26 days *they are to* **m atonement** *for* the altar H4105
Eze 45:15 offerings to **m atonement** for the people, H4105
Eze 45:17 offerings to **m atonement** for the Israelites H4105
Eze 45:20 so *you are to* **m atonement** *for* the temple. H4105
Eze 45:25 *he is to* **m** the same **provision** *for* sin H6913
Da 9:18 We *do* not **m** requests of you because we H5877
Da 11: 6 to the king of the North to **m** an alliance, H6913
Da 11:17 kingdom and *will* **m** an alliance with H6913
Da 11:39 *He will* **m** them **rulers** over many people H5440
Hos 2: 3 her naked and **m** her as **bare** as on the H3657
Hos 2: 3 she was born; *I will* **m** her like a desert H8492
Hos 2:12 from her lovers; *I will* **m** them a thicket H8492
Hos 2:15 will **m** the Valley of Achor a door of NDT
Hos 2:18 In that day *I will* **m** a covenant for them H4162
Hos 8: 4 silver and gold *they* **m** idols for H6913
Hos 10: 4 *They* **m many promises**, take false H1819+1821
Hos 10: 4 take false oaths and **m** agreements H4162
Hos 11: 8 How *can I* **m** you like Zeboyim H8492
Hos 12: 9 of Egypt; *I will* **m** you **live** in tents again H3782
Hos 13: 2 *they* **m** idols for themselves from their H6913
Joel 2:17 *Do* not **m** your inheritance an object of H5989
Joel 2:19 never again *will I* **m** you an object of H5989
Am 8: 9 "*I will* **m** the sun **go down** at noon and H995
Am 8:10 *I will* **m** all of you **wear** H6590+6584+5516
Am 8:10 *I will* **m** that time like mourning for an H8492
Am 9:14 *they will* **m** gardens and eat their fruit. H6913
Ob 2 *I will* **m** you small among the nations H5989
Ob 3 clefts of the rocks and **m** your home on the NDT
Ob 4 like the eagle and **m** your nest among the H8492
Jnh 1:11 we do to you *to* **m** the sea **calm down** for us?" AIT
Jnh 2: 9 What I have vowed *I will* **m good**. I will H8966
Jnh 4:10 though you did not tend it or **m** it **grow**. H1540
Mic 1: 6 "Therefore *I will* **m** Samaria a heap of H8492
Mic 1:16 **m** yourself as **bald** as the vulture H8143+7947
Mic 4: 4 no *one will* **m** them **afraid**, for the H3006
Mic 4: 7 *I will* **m** the lame my remnant, those H8492
Na 1: 8 flood *he will* **m** an end of Nineveh; H6913
Na 3: 6 you with contempt and **m** you a spectacle. H8492
Hab 1: 3 Why *do you* **m** me **look** *at* injustice? Why H8011
Hab 2: 2 the revelation and **m** it **plain** on tablets so H930
Hab 2: 7 Will they not wake up and **m** you **tremble**? H2316
Hab 3: 2 in our time **m** them **known**; in wrath H3359
Zep 1:18 for *he will* **m** a sudden end *of* all who live H6913
Zep 3:13 lie down and no *one will* **m** them **afraid**." H3006
Hag 2:23 'and *I will* **m** you like my signet ring H8492
Zec 6:11 Take the silver and gold and **m** a crown H6913
Zec 9:13 Greece, and **m** you like a warrior's sword. H8492
Zec 9:17 Grain *will* **m** the young men **thrive**, and H5649
Zec 10: 3 **m** them like a proud horse in battle. H8492
Zec 12: 2 "*I am going to* **m** Jerusalem a cup that H8492
Zec 12: 3 *I will* **m** Jerusalem an immovable rock H8492
Zec 12: 6 "On that day *I will* **m** the clans of Judah H8492
Mt 3: 3 way for the Lord, **m** straight paths for him. *G4472*
Mt 5:36 you cannot **m** even one hair white or *G4472*
Mt 8: 2 if you are willing, you can **m** me **clean**." *G2751*
Mt 12:33 "**M** a tree good and its fruit will be good *G4472*
Mt 12:33 **m** a tree bad and its fruit will be bad *G4472*
Mt 23: 5 *They* **m** their phylacteries **wide** and the *G4425*
Mt 23:15 *you* **m** them twice as much a child of hell *G4472*
Mt 26:17 you want *us to* **m preparations** for you to *G2286*
Mt 27:65 **m** the tomb as **secure** as you know how." *G856*
Mt 28:19 go and **m disciples** of all nations *G3411*
Mk 1: 3 way for the Lord, **m** straight paths for him. *G4472*
Mk 1:40 "If you are willing, you can **m** me **clean**." *G2751*
Mk 9:50 its saltiness, how *can you* **m** it **salty** again? *G789*
Mk 12:40 houses and for a show **m** lengthy **prayers**. *G4667*
Mk 14:12 us to go and **m preparations** for you to eat *G2286*
Mk 14:15 **M preparations** for us there." *G2286*
Lk 1:17 *to* **m ready** a people prepared for the Lord." *G2286*
Lk 3: 4 way for the Lord, **m** straight paths for him. *G4472*
Lk 5:12 if you are willing, *you* can **m** me **clean**." *G2751*
Lk 5:34 "Can *you* **m** the friends of the bridegroom *G4472*
Lk 11:40 *Did* not the one who made the outside **m** *G4472*
Lk 13:24 "**M every effort** to enter through the narrow *G76*
Lk 14:18 "But they all alike began *to* **m excuses** *G4148*
Lk 15:19 **m** me like one of your hired servants. *G4472*
Lk 16: 6 and **m** it four hundred and fifty. *G1211S*
Lk 16: 7 'Take your bill and **m** it eight hundred. *G1211S*
Lk 20:43 until *I* **m** your enemies a footstool for your *G5502*
Lk 20:47 houses and for a show **m** lengthy **prayers**. *G4667*

Lk 21:14 But **m up** your **mind** not to worry G5502+1877+3836+2840
Lk 22: 8 "Go and **m preparations** for us to eat the G2286
Lk 22:12 **M preparations** there." G2286
Jn 1:23 '**M straight** the way for the Lord. G2316
Jn 6:15 to come and **m** him king by force, G4472
Jn 11:52 to bring them together and **m** them one. G1650
Jn 14:23 come to them and **m** our home with them G4472
Jn 16:14 will receive what *he will* **m known** to you. G334
Jn 16:15 from me what *he will* **m known** to you." G334
Jn 17:26 and *will continue to* **m** you **known** in order G1192
Ac 2:35 until *I* **m** your enemies a footstool for your G5502
Ac 5:28 determined *to* **m** us **guilty of** this man's G2042
Ac 7:40 '**M** us gods who will go before us. G4472
Ac 15:19 *that we should* not **m** it **difficult** for the G4214
Ac 19:33 in order to **m** a **defense** before the people. G664
Ac 24:10 over this nation; so *I* gladly **m** my **defense**. G664
Ac 26: 2 you today as *I* **m** *my* **defense** against all G664
Ac 27:16 we were hardly able *to* **m** the lifeboat G1181
Ac 28:19 was compelled *to* **m** an **appeal** to Caesar. G2126
Ro 1:11 you some spiritual gift to **m** you **strong**— G5114
Ro 8:15 Spirit you received does not **m** you **slaves**, G1525
Ro 9:20 formed it, 'Why *did you* **m** me like this? G4472
Ro 9:21 have the right *to* **m** out of the same lump G4472
Ro 9:22 show his wrath and **m** his power **known**, G1192
Ro 9:23 to **m** the riches of his glory **known** to the G1192
Ro 10:19 "I *will* **m** you **envious** by those who are G4143
Ro 10:19 *I will* **m** you **angry** by a nation that has no G4239
Ro 11:11 come to the Gentiles to **m** Israel **envious**. G4143
Ro 14: 4 the Lord is able *to* **m** them **stand**. G2705
Ro 14:13 **m up** *your* **mind** not to put any stumbling G3212
Ro 14:19 *Let us* therefore **m every effort** to do what G1503
Ro 15:26 were pleased *to* **m** a contribution for G4472
1Co 4: 4 is clear, but that *does* not **m** *me* **innocent**. G1467
1Co 9:18 so not **m full use** of my rights as a G2974
1Co 9:27 to my body and **m** it *my* **slave** so that after G1524
1Co 14: 7 the case of lifeless things *that* **m** sounds, G1443
1Co 16: 7 to see you now and **m** only a passing visit G1877
2Co 1:17 Or *do I* **m** *my* **plans** in a worldly manner G1086
2Co 2: 1 that I *would* not **m** another painful **visit** to G2262
2Co 2: 2 who is left *to* **m** me **glad** but you whom I G2370
2Co 5: 9 So *we* **m** it *our* **goal** to please him G5818
2Co 7: 2 **M room** for us in your hearts. We have G6003
2Co 10: 5 captive every thought to *m* it obedient to AIT
Gal 2: 4 have in Christ Jesus and to **m** us **slaves**. G2871
Eph 3: 9 and *to* **m plain** to everyone the G5894
Eph 4: 3 **M every effort** to keep the unity of the G5079
Eph 5:19 Sing and **m music** from your heart to the G6010
Eph 5:26 to **m** her **holy**, cleansing her by the washing G39
Eph 6:19 me *so that* I *will* fearlessly **m known** the G1192
Php 2: 2 then **m** my joy **complete** by being G4444
Php 2:30 He risked his life to **m up for** the help you G405
Php 3:15 differently, that too God *will* **m clear** to you. G636
Col 1:27 God has chosen *to* **m known** among the G1192
Col 4: 5 **m the most of** every opportunity. G1973
1Th 2: 3 For the appeal we **m** does not spring from NDT
1Th 3:12 *May* the Lord **m** your love **increase** and G4429
1Th 4:11 and *to* **m** it *your* **ambition** to lead a quiet G5818
1Th 5:15 **M sure** that nobody pays back wrong for G3972
2Th 1:11 that our God *may* **m** you **worthy** of his G546
2Ti 1: 7 the Spirit God gave us does not **m** us timid, NDT
2Ti 3:15 which are able *to* **m** you **wise** for salvation G5054
Titus 2:10 *they will* **m** the teaching about God our Savior **attractive** G3175
Heb 1:13 at my right hand until *I* **m** your enemies a G5502
Heb 2:10 *should* **m** the pioneer of their salvation **perfect** G5457
Heb 2:17 that *he might* **m atonement** for the G2661
Heb 4:11 *Let us*, therefore, **m every effort** to enter G5079
Heb 5:11 but *it is* **hard** to **m** it **clear** to you G1549+3306
Heb 6:17 *to* **m** the unchanging nature of his purpose very **clear** G2109
Heb 8: 5 "See to it *that you* **m** everything according G4472
Heb 8: 8 when *I will* **m** a new covenant with the G5334
Heb 10: 1 **m perfect** those who draw near to worship. G5457
Heb 10:16 is the covenant *I will* **m** with them after G1416
Heb 12: 5 *do* not **m light of** the Lord's discipline G3902
Heb 12:13 "**M** level paths for your feet," so that the G4472
Heb 12:14 **M every effort** *to live* in peace with G1503
Heb 13:12 city gate to **m** the people **holy** through his G39
Jas 3: 3 the mouths of horses to **m** them **obey** us, G4275
Jas 4:13 carry on business and **m money**. G3045
Jas 5:15 in faith *will* **m** the sick person **well**; G5392
1Pe 5:10 will himself restore you and **m** you **strong** G5114
2Pe 1: 5 **m** every effort to add to your faith G4210
2Pe 1:10 **m** every **effort** to confirm your calling and G5079
2Pe 1:15 And *I will* **m every effort** *to see that* after G5079
2Pe 3:14 **m every effort** to be found spotless G5079
1Jn 1: 4 We write this to **m** our joy **complete**. G1639+4444
1Jn 1:10 *we* **m** him **out to be** a liar and his word is G4472
1Jn 2:10 is nothing in them *to* **m** them **stumble**. G4998
Rev 2:22 I will **m** those who commit adultery G1650
Rev 3: 9 *I will* **m** those who are of the synagogue G1442
Rev 3: 9 *I will* **m** them come and fall down at your G4472
Rev 3:12 who is victorious *I will* **m** a pillar in the G4472
Rev 6: 4 from the earth and *to* **m** people kill each G2671

MAKER (27) [MAKE]

Job 4:17 a strong man be more pure than his **M**? H6913
Job 9: 9 *He is* the **M** *of* the Bear and Orion, the H6913
Job 32:22 my **M** would soon take me away. H6913
Job 35:10 'Where is God my **M**, who gives songs in H6913
Job 36: 3 from afar; I will ascribe justice to my **M**. H7188
Job 40:19 its **M** can approach it with his sword. H6913
Ps 95: 6 let us kneel before the LORD our **M**; H6913
Ps 115:15 by the LORD, the **M** *of* heaven and earth. H6913
Ps 121: 2 from the LORD, the **M** *of* heaven and earth. H6913
Ps 124: 8 of the LORD, the **M** *of* heaven and earth. H6913
Ps 134: 3 *he who is* the **M** *of* heaven and earth. H6913
Ps 146: 6 *He is* the **M** *of* heaven and earth, the sea H6913
Ps 149: 2 Let Israel rejoice in their **M**; let the people H6913
Pr 14:31 the poor shows contempt for their **M**, H6913
Pr 17: 5 the poor shows contempt for their **M**; H6913
Pr 22: 2 The LORD *is* the **M** *of* them all. H6913
Ecc 11: 5 the work of God, the **M** *of* all things. H6913
Isa 17: 7 will look to their **M** and turn their eyes to H6913
Isa 27:11 so their **M** has no compassion on them H6913
Isa 44:24 I am the LORD, the **M** *of* all things, who H6913
Isa 45: 9 "Woe to those who quarrel with their **M** H3670
Isa 45:11 the Holy One of Israel, and its **M**: H3670
Isa 51:13 that you forget the LORD your **M**, who H6913
Isa 54: 5 For your **M** is your husband—the LORD H6913
Jer 10:16 like these, for he *is* the **M** *of* all things H3670
Jer 51:19 like these, for he *is* the **M** *of* all things H3670
Hos 8:14 has forgotten their **M** and built palaces; H6913

MAKERS (1) [MAKE]

Isa 45:16 All the **m** *of* idols will be put to shame H3093

MAKES (110) [MAKE]

Ex 4:11 their mouths? Who **m** them deaf or mute H8492
Ex 4:11 Who gives them sight or **m** them blind? Is it NDT
Ex 11: 7 that the LORD **m a distinction** between H7111
Ex 30:33 Whoever **m perfume** like it and puts it on H8379
Ex 30:38 Whoever **m** incense like it to enjoy its H6913
Ex 31:13 know that I am the LORD, *who* **m** you **holy**. H7727
Lev 7: 7 to the priest who **m atonement** with them. H4105
Lev 17:11 is the blood *that* **m atonement** for one's H4105
Lev 20: 8 I am the LORD, *who* **m** you **holy**. H7727
Lev 21:15 I am the LORD, *who* **m** him **holy**.'" H7727
Lev 21:23 I am the LORD, *who* **m** them **holy**.'" H7727
Lev 22: 5 any crawling thing that *m* him **unclean**, AIT
Lev 22: 5 any person who *m* him **unclean**, whatever AIT
Lev 22: 9 I am the LORD, *who* **m** them **holy**. H7727
Lev 22:16 I am the LORD, *who* **m** them **holy**.'" H7727
Lev 27: 2 **m a special vow to dedicate** a H7098+5624
Nu 5:21 people when he **m** your womb miscarry H5989
Nu 5:29 astray and **m herself impure** while H3237
Nu 30: 2 When a man **m a vow** to the LORD H5623+5624
Nu 30: 3 household **m a vow** to the LORD or H5623+5624
Nu 30: 6 she marries after she **m** a vow or after her NDT
Nu 30:10 with her husband **m a vow** or obligates H5623
Nu 30:13 nullify any vow she **m** or any sworn pledge NDT
Dt 27:15 "Cursed is anyone who **m** an idol—a H6913
1Sa 2: 6 "The LORD brings death and **m alive**; he H2649
1Sa 22: 8 when my son **m a covenant** with the son H4162
2Sa 22:34 *He* **m** my feet like the feet of a deer; he H8751
Job 6: 7 I refuse to touch it; such food **m** me ill. NDT
Job 9: 6 from its place and **m** its pillars **tremble**. H7145
Job 12:17 away stripped and **m fools of** judges. H2147
Job 12:23 *He* **m** nations **great**, and destroys them H8434
Job 12:24 *he* **m** them **wander** in a trackless waste. H9494
Job 12:25 *he* **m** them **stagger** like drunkards. H9494
Job 35:11 of the earth and **m** us **wiser** than the birds H2681
Job 36:10 *He* **m** them **listen** to correction and H1655+265
Job 37:15 the clouds and **m** his lightning **flash**? H3649
Job 41:31 *It* **m** the depths **churn** like a boiling H8409
Ps 7:13 weapons; *he* **m ready** his flaming arrows. H7188
Ps 18:33 *He* **m** my feet like the feet of a deer; he H8751
Ps 19: 6 end of the heavens and **m** its circuit to the NDT
Ps 23: 2 *He* **m** me **lie down** in green pastures, he H8069
Ps 25:14 he **m** his covenant **known** *to* them. H3359
Ps 29: 6 *He* **m** Lebanon **leap** like a calf, Sirion like H8376
Ps 37:23 The LORD **m firm** the steps of the one who H3922
Ps 45: 8 ivory the music of the strings **m** you **glad**. H8523
Ps 46: 9 *He* **m** wars **cease** to the ends of the earth H8697
Ps 48: 8 city of our God: God **m** her **secure** forever. H3922
Ps 60: 3 you have given us wine *that* **m** us **stagger**. H9570
Ps 104: 3 He **m** the clouds his chariot and rides on H8492
Ps 104: 4 *He* **m** winds his messengers, flames of H6913
Ps 104:10 He **m** springs **pour** water into the ravines H8938
Ps 104:14 *He* **m** grass **grow** for the cattle, and plants H7541
Ps 135: 7 *He* **m** clouds **rise** from the ends of the H6590
Ps 143: 3 *he* **m** me **dwell** in the darkness like those H3782
Ps 147: 8 with rain and **m** grass **grow** *on* the hills. H7541
Pr 1:21 at the city gate *she* **m** her **speech**: H606+609
Pr 4:19 they do not know what *m them* **stumble**. AIT
Pr 11: 5 of the blameless **m** their paths **straight**, H3837
Pr 13:11 gathers money little by little **m** it **grow**. H8049
Pr 13:12 Hope deferred **m** the heart **sick**, but a H2703
Pr 15:13 A happy heart **m** the face **cheerful**, but H3512
Pr 31:22 *She* **m** coverings for her bed; she is H6913
Pr 31:24 *She* **m** linen garments and sells them H6913
Ecc 7:19 **m** one wise person more **powerful** than H6451
Ecc 10:19 laughter, wine **m** life **merry**, and money is H8523
Isa 8:14 to stumble and a rock that **m** them **fall**. H4842
Isa 14: 9 *it* **m** them **rise** from their thrones H7756
Isa 21: 4 fear **m** me **tremble**; the twilight I H1286
Isa 26: 1 God **m** salvation its walls and ramparts. H8883
Isa 27: 9 When he **m** all the altar stones to be like H8492
Isa 44:13 a line and **m** an **outline** with a marker; H9306
Isa 44:15 *he* **m** an idol and bows down to it. H6913
Isa 44:17 *From* the rest *he* **m** a god, his idol; he H6913
Isa 44:25 of false prophets and **m fools of** diviners, H2147
Isa 51:17 dregs the goblet that **m** people **stagger**. H9570
Isa 53:10 though the LORD **m** his life an offering H8492
Isa 61:11 as the soil **m** the sprout **come up** and a H3655
Isa 62: 7 Jerusalem and **m** her the praise of the H8492
Isa 66: 3 *whoever* **m** a grain **offering** is like one H6590
Jer 10:13 *he* **m** clouds **rise** from the ends of the H6590
Jer 10:14 The images he **m** are a fraud; they have no NDT
Jer 22:14 So *he* **m large** windows in it, panels it H7973
Jer 48:28 like a dove *that* **m** *its* **nest** at the mouth H7873
Jer 51:16 *he* **m** clouds **rise** from the ends of the H6590
Jer 51:17 The images he **m** are a fraud; they have no NDT
Eze 44:18 not wear anything that **m** them perspire. H928
Eze 46:16 If the prince **m** a gift *from* his inheritance H5989
Eze 46:17 *he* **m** a gift from his inheritance to one of H5989
Eze 47: 9 flows there and **m** the salt water **fresh**; H8324
Hos 12: 1 *He* **m** a treaty with Assyria and sends H4162
Na 1: 4 dries it up; *he* **m** all the rivers **run dry**. H2990
Hab 2: 6 goods and **m** himself **wealthy** by extortion H3877
Hab 2:18 For the *one who* **m** it trusts in his own H3670
Hab 2:18 creation; *he* **m** idols that cannot speak. H6913
Hab 3:19 *he* **m** my feet like the feet of a deer H8492
Mt 5:32 immorality, **m** her the victim of adultery G4472
Mt 23:17 or the temple that **m** the gold **sacred**? G39
Mt 23:19 or the altar that **m** the gift **sacred**? G39
Mk 7:37 "*He* even **m** the deaf hear and the mute G4472
Jn 16:30 **This m** us believe that you came G1877+4047
Ro 9:33 to stumble and a rock that **m** them **fall**, G4998
1Co 2:15 the Spirit **m judgments about** all things, G373
1Co 3: 7 only God, who **m** things **grow**. G889
1Co 4: 7 For who **m** you **different** from anyone else G1359
2Co 1:21 God who **m** both us and you **stand firm** in G1011
Gal 2: 6 whatever they were **m** no **difference** to me G1422
Heb 1: 7 angels he says, "He **m** his angels spirits G4472
Heb 2:11 Both the *one who* **m** people **holy** and those G39
Jas 3: 5 part of the body, but *it* **m** great **boasts**. G902
1Pe 2: 8 to stumble and a rock that **m** them **fall**." G4998

MAKEUP (3)

2Ki 9:30 *she* **put on** eye **m** H6167+928+2021+7037
Jer 4:30 Why highlight your eyes with **m**? You H7037
Eze 23:40 **applied** eye **m** and put on your jewelry. H3949

MAKHELOTH (2)

Nu 33:25 They left Haradah and camped at **M**. H5221
Nu 33:26 They left **M** and camped at Tahath. H5221

MAKI (1)

Nu 13:15 from the tribe of Gad, Geuel son of **M**. H4809

MAKING (70) [MAKE]

Ge 9:12 of the covenant I *am* **m** between me and H5989
Ge 34:30 trouble on me by **m** me **obnoxious** to the H944
Ex 5: 7 the people with straw for **m bricks**; H4236+4246
Ex 28:15 "Fashion a breastpiece for **m decisions** H5477
Ex 28:30 bear the **means of m decisions** *for* the H5477
Ex 29:36 Purify the altar by **m atonement** for it, H4105
Ex 30:16 the LORD, **m atonement** for your lives." H4105
Ex 34:10 "*I am* **m** a covenant with you H4162
Lev 10:17 community by **m atonement** for them H4105
Lev 16:10 to be used for **m atonement** by sending it H4105
Lev 16:20 has finished **m atonement** *for* the Most H4105
Lev 17: 5 sacrifices they *are now* **m** in the open H2284
Lev 19:29 your daughter by **m** her a **prostitute**, H2388
Lev 27: 8 If anyone **m** the vow is too poor to pay the NDT
Lev 27: 8 to what the *one* **m** *the* **vow** can afford. H5623
Nu 25:12 Therefore tell him I *am* **m** my covenant of H5989
Nu 32:14 **m** the LORD even **more** angry with H3578
Dt 23:22 But if you refrain from **m** a **vow**, you will H5623
Dt 24:11 to whom you *are* **m** *the* **loan** bring the H5957
Dt 29:12 a covenant the LORD *is* **m** with you this day H4162
Dt 29:14 I *am* **m** this covenant, with its oath, not H4162
Jdg 9:16 in good faith *by* **m** Abimelek **king**? H4887
Jdg 16:13 time *you have been* **m** a **fool of** me and H9438
1Sa 13:10 Just as he finished **m** the offering, Samuel H6590
1Sa 21:13 **m marks** on the doors of the gate and H9344
1Ki 8:33 praying and **m supplication** to you in this H2858
1Ki 14:15 the LORD's anger *by* **m** Asherah poles. H6913
1Ki 15: 4 succeed him and by **m** Jerusalem **strong**. H6641
2Ki 10:25 as Jehu had finished **m** the burnt offering, H6913
2Ki 12:13 temple **was not spent for m** silver H6913+4946
1Ch 6:49 Holy Place, **m atonement** for Israel, in H4105
2Ch 2: 4 for **m** burnt offerings every morning and NDT
2Ch 6:24 praying and **m supplication** before you in H2858
Ezr 5: 8 and *is* **m rapid progress** under their A10613
Ne 6: 8 you *are* just **m** it **up** out of your head." H968
Ne 8: 8 **m** it **clear** and giving the meaning so that H7300
Ne 9:38 of all this, we *are* **m** a binding agreement H4162
Ps 19: 7 LORD are trustworthy, **m wise** the simple. H2681
Pr 8:21 who love me and **m** their treasuries **full**. H4848
Pr 14: 9 Fools mock at **m amends for sin**, but H871
Pr 16:11 all the weights in the bag are of his **m**. H5126
Pr 24: 2 their lips talk about **m trouble**. H6662
Ecc 12:12 Of **m** many books there is no end, and H6913
Isa 10: 2 **m** widows their prey and robbing the H2118
Isa 43:19 *I am* **m** a way in the wilderness and H8492
Isa 45: 9 clay say to the potter, 'What *are you* **m**? H6913
Isa 55:10 the earth and **m** it **bud** and flourish, H3528
Jer 22:13 **m** his **own people** work for nothing H8276
Jer 44:19 know that *we were* **m** cakes impressed H6913
Eze 22: 3 her midst and defiles herself by **m** idols, H6913
Da 9:20 my people Israel and **m** my request to the H5877
Jnh 1: 8 who is responsible for **m** all this trouble NDT
Mt 9:16 away from the garment, **m** the tear worse. G1181

Mt 13:22 of wealth choke the word, **m** *it* unfruitful. *G1181*
Mt 21:13 but you *are* **m** it 'a den of robbers. *G4472*
Mk 2:21 pull away from the old, **m** the tear worse. *G1181*
Mk 4:19 in and choke the word, **m** *it* unfruitful. *G1181*
Lk 1:22 he kept **m signs** to them but remained *G1377*
Jn 5:18 own Father, **m** himself equal with God. *G4472*
Ac 16:19 that their hope *of* **m money** was gone, *G2238*
Ac 18:14 Jews *were* **m a complaint** *about* some *G1639S*
Ac 24:13 you the **charges** *they are* now **m** against *G2989*
Ro 7:23 my mind and **m** me **a prisoner** of the law of *G170*
1Co 3:6 watered it, but God *has been* **m** it **grow**. *G889*
2Co 5:20 though God *were* **m** *his* **appeal** through *G4151*
2Co 6:10 yet **m** many **rich**; having nothing *G4457*
Eph 2:15 humanity out of the two, *thus* **m** peace, *G4472*
Eph 5:16 **m the most of** every opportunity, because *G1973*
Col 1:20 in heaven, *by* **m peace** through his blood *G1647*
Rev 21:5 the throne said, "*I am* **m** everything new!" *G4472*

MAKIR (21) [MAKIR'S, MAKIRITE, MAKIRITES]

Ge 50:23 the children of **M** son of Manasseh were H4810
Nu 26:29 through **M**, the Makirite clan (Makir was H4810
Nu 26:29 Makirite clan (**M** was the father of Gilead); H4810
Nu 27:1 the son of **M**, the son of H4810
Nu 32:39 The descendants of **M** son of Manasseh H4810
Nu 36:1 heads of the clan of Gilead son of **M**, H4810
Dt 3:15 And I gave Gilead to **M**. H4810
Jos 13:31 the descendants of **M** son of Manasseh— H4810
Jos 13:31 half of the sons of **M**, according to their H4810
Jos 17:1 for **M**, Manasseh's firstborn. H4810
Jos 17:1 **M** was the ancestor of the Gileadites, who NDT
Jos 17:3 the son of **M**, the son of H4810
Jdg 5:14 From **M** captains came down, from H4810
2Sa 9:4 is at the house of **M** son of Ammiel in Lo H4810
2Sa 9:5 from the house of **M** son of Ammiel. H4810
2Sa 17:27 **M** son of Ammiel from Lo Debar H4810
1Ch 2:21 the daughter of **M** the father of Gilead. H4810
1Ch 2:23 were descendants of **M** the father of H4810
1Ch 7:14 She gave birth to **M** the father of Gilead. H4810
1Ch 7:15 **M** took a wife from among the Huppites H4810
1Ch 7:17 These were the sons of Gilead son of **M** H4810

MAKIR'S (1) [MAKIR]

1Ch 7:16 **M** wife Maakah gave birth to a son and H4810

MAKIRITE (1) [MAKIR]

Nu 26:29 through Makir, the **M** clan (Makir was the H4811

MAKIRITES (2) [MAKIR]

Nu 32:40 So Moses gave Gilead to the **M**, the H4810
Jos 17:1 Bashan because **the M** were great H2085S

MAKKEDAH (9)

Jos 10:10 them down all the way to Azekah and **M**. H5218
Jos 10:16 had fled and hidden in the cave at **M**. H5218
Jos 10:17 had been found hiding in the cave at **M**, H5218
Jos 10:21 safely to Joshua in the camp at **M**, H5218
Jos 10:28 That day Joshua took **M**. He put the city H5218
Jos 10:28 did to the king of **M** as he had done to H5218
Jos 10:29 him moved on from **M** to Libnah and H5218
Jos 12:16 the king of **M** one the king of Bethel one H5218
Jos 15:41 Naamah and **M**—sixteen towns and H5218

MAKNADEBAI (1)

Ezr 10:40 **M**, Shashai, Sharai, H4827

MALACHI (1)

Mal 1:1 The word of the LORD to Israel through **M**. H4858

MALCAM (NIV84) MALKAM

MALCHAM (KJV) MALKAM, MOLEK

MALCHI-SHUA (KJV) MALKI-SHUA

MALCHIAH, MALCHIJAH (KJV) MALKIJAH

MALCHUS (1)

Jn 18:10 (The servant's name was **M**.) *G3438*

MALE (211) [MALES]

Ge 1:27 **m** and female he created them. H2351
Ge 5:2 He created them **m** and female and H2351
Ge 6:19 living creatures, **m** and female, to keep H2351
Ge 7:2 of clean animal, a **m** and its mate, and H408
Ge 7:2 kind of unclean animal, a **m** and its mate, H408
Ge 7:3 every kind of bird, **m** and female, to keep H2351
Ge 7:9 **m** and female, came to Noah and entered H2351
Ge 7:16 going in were **m** and female of every H2351
Ge 12:16 **m** and female **donkeys**, male and H2789
Ge 12:16 donkeys, **m** and female **servants**, and H6269
Ge 17:10 Every **m** among you shall be circumcised. H2351
Ge 17:12 to come every **m** among you who is eight H2351
Ge 17:14 Any uncircumcised **m**, who has not been H2351
Ge 17:23 his money, every **m** in his household, and H2351
Ge 17:27 And every **m** *in* Abraham's household H408
Ge 20:14 cattle and **m** and female **slaves** and gave H6269
Ge 24:35 gold, **m** and female **servants**, and H6269
Ge 30:35 he removed all the **m goats** that were H9411
Ge 30:43 female and **m servants**, and camels H6269
Ge 31:10 saw that the **m goats** mating with the H6966
Ge 31:12 see that all the **m goats** mating with the H6966
Ge 32:5 sheep and goats, **m** and female **servants**. H6269
Ge 32:14 female goats and twenty **m goats**, H9411
Ge 32:15 female donkeys and ten **m donkeys**. H6555
Ge 34:24 every **m** in the city was circumcised. H2351
Ge 34:25 the unsuspecting city, killing every **m**. H2351
Ex 12:48 No **uncircumcised** *m* may eat it. AIT
Ex 13:2 "Consecrate to me every **firstborn** *m*. AIT
Ex 13:15 to the LORD the first **m** offspring of every H2351
Ex 20:10 your **m** or female **servant**, nor your H6269
Ex 20:17 or his **m** or female **servant**, his ox or H6269
Ex 21:7 she is not to go free as **m servants** do. H6269
Ex 21:20 beats their **m** or female **slave** with a rod H6269
Ex 21:26 who hits a **m** or female **slave** in the eye H6269
Ex 21:27 tooth of a **m** or female **slave** must let the H6269
Ex 21:32 If the bull gores a **m** or female **slave**, the H6269
Lev 1:3 you are to offer a **m** without defect. H2351
Lev 1:10 you are to offer a **m** without defect. H2351
Lev 3:1 the herd, whether **m** or female, you are to H2351
Lev 3:6 you are to offer a **m** or female without H2351
Lev 4:23 as his offering a **m** goat without defect. H2351
Lev 6:18 Any **m** descendant of Aaron may eat it. H2351
Lev 6:29 Any **m** in a priest's family may eat it; it is H2351
Lev 7:6 Any **m** in a priest's family may eat it, but it H2351
Lev 9:3 'Take a **m goat** for a sin offering, H8538+6436
Lev 14:10 must bring two **m lambs** and one ewe H3897
Lev 14:12 take one of the **m lambs** and offer it as a H3897
Lev 14:21 they must take one **m lamb** as a guilt H3897
Lev 16:5 he is to take two **m goats** for a sin H8538+6436
Lev 22:19 you must present a **m** without defect from H2351
Lev 23:18 Present with this bread seven **m lambs** H3897
Lev 23:19 Then sacrifice one **m goat** for a sin H8538+6436
Lev 25:6 your **m** and female **servants**, and the H6269
Lev 25:44 " 'Your **m** and female **slaves** are to come H6269
Lev 27:3 set the value of a **m** between the ages of H2351
Lev 27:5 set the value of a **m** at twenty shekels H2351
Lev 27:6 set the value of a **m** at five shekels of H2351
Lev 27:7 set the value of a **m** at fifteen shekels H2351
Nu 3:12 of the **first m offspring** of H1147+7081+8167
Nu 3:15 Count every **m** a month old or more." H2351
Nu 3:39 including every **m** a month old or more H2351
Nu 5:3 Send away **m** and female alike; send H2351
Nu 6:12 bring a year-old **m lamb** as a guilt H3897
Nu 6:14 a year-old **m lamb** without defect for a H3897
Nu 7:15 one ram and one **m lamb** a year old for a H3897
Nu 7:16 one **m goat** for a sin offering; H8538+6436
Nu 7:17 five **m goats** and five male lambs a year H6966
Nu 7:17 goats and five **m lambs** a year old to be H3897
Nu 7:21 one ram and one **m lamb** a year old for a H3897
Nu 7:22 one **m goat** for a sin offering; H8538+6436
Nu 7:23 five **m goats** and five male lambs a year H6966
Nu 7:23 goats and five **m lambs** a year old to be H3897
Nu 7:27 one ram and one **m lamb** a year old for a H3897
Nu 7:28 one **m goat** for a sin offering; H8538+6436
Nu 7:29 five **m goats** and five male lambs a year H6966
Nu 7:29 goats and five **m lambs** a year old to be H3897
Nu 7:33 one ram and one **m lamb** a year old for a H3897
Nu 7:34 one **m goat** for a sin offering; H8538+6436
Nu 7:35 five **m goats** and five male lambs a year H6966
Nu 7:35 goats and five **m lambs** a year old to be H3897
Nu 7:39 one ram and one **m lamb** a year old for a H3897
Nu 7:40 one **m goat** for a sin offering; H8538+6436
Nu 7:41 five **m goats** and five male lambs a year H6966
Nu 7:41 goats and five **m lambs** a year old to be H3897
Nu 7:45 one ram and one **m lamb** a year old for a H3897
Nu 7:46 one **m goat** for a sin offering; H8538+6436
Nu 7:47 five **m goats** and five male lambs a year H6966
Nu 7:47 goats and five **m lambs** a year old to be H3897
Nu 7:51 one ram and one **m lamb** a year old for a H3897
Nu 7:52 one **m goat** for a sin offering; H8538+6436
Nu 7:53 five **m goats** and five male lambs a year H6966
Nu 7:53 goats and five **m lambs** a year old to be H3897
Nu 7:57 one ram and one **m lamb** a year old for a H3897
Nu 7:58 one **m goat** for a sin offering; H8538+6436
Nu 7:59 five **m goats** and five male lambs a year H6966
Nu 7:59 goats and five **m lambs** a year old to be H3897
Nu 7:63 one ram and one **m lamb** a year old for a H3897
Nu 7:64 one **m goat** for a sin offering; H8538+6436
Nu 7:65 five **m goats** and five male lambs a year H6966
Nu 7:65 goats and five **m lambs** a year old to be H3897
Nu 7:69 one ram and one **m lamb** a year old for a H3897
Nu 7:70 one **m goat** for a sin offering; H8538+6436
Nu 7:71 five **m goats** and five male lambs a year H6966
Nu 7:71 goats and five **m lambs** a year old to be H3897
Nu 7:75 one ram and one **m lamb** a year old for a H3897
Nu 7:76 one **m goat** for a sin offering; H8538+6436
Nu 7:77 five **m goats** and five male lambs a year H6966
Nu 7:77 goats and five **m lambs** a year old to be H3897
Nu 7:81 one ram and one **m lamb** a year old for a H3897
Nu 7:82 one **m goat** for a sin offering; H8538+6436
Nu 7:83 five **m goats** and five male lambs a year H6966
Nu 7:83 goats and five **m lambs** a year old to be H3897
Nu 7:87 rams and twelve **m lambs** a year old, H3897
Nu 7:87 Twelve **m goats** were used for the H8538+6436
Nu 7:88 sixty **m goats** and sixty male lambs a year H6966
Nu 7:88 male goats and sixty **m lambs** a year old. H3897
Nu 8:16 the **first m offspring** from every Israelite H1147
Nu 8:17 Every **firstborn m** in Israel, whether H1147
Nu 15:24 and a **m goat** for a sin offering. H8538+6436
Nu 18:10 something most holy; every **m** shall eat it. H2351
Nu 18:15 son and every **firstborn m** *of* unclean H1147
Nu 26:62 All the **m** Levites a month old or more H2351
Nu 28:11 one ram and seven **m lambs** a year old H3897
Nu 28:15 one **m goat** is to be presented to H8538+6436
Nu 28:19 one ram and seven **m lambs** a year old H3897
Nu 28:22 Include one **m goat** as a sin offering to H8538
Nu 28:27 ram and seven **m lambs** a year old as an H3897
Nu 28:30 Include one **m goat** to make H8538+6436
Nu 29:2 one ram and seven **m lambs** a year old H3897
Nu 29:5 Include one **m goat** as a sin H8538+6436
Nu 29:8 one ram and seven **m lambs** a year old H3897
Nu 29:11 Include one **m goat** as a sin H8538+6436
Nu 29:13 rams and fourteen **m lambs** a year old, H3897
Nu 29:16 Include one **m goat** as a sin H8538+6436
Nu 29:17 rams and fourteen **m lambs** a year old, H3897
Nu 29:19 Include one **m goat** as a sin H8538+6436
Nu 29:20 rams and fourteen **m lambs** a year old, H3897
Nu 29:22 Include one **m goat** as a sin offering, in H8538
Nu 29:23 rams and fourteen **m lambs** a year old, H3897
Nu 29:25 Include one **m goat** as a sin H8538+6436
Nu 29:26 rams and fourteen **m lambs** a year old, H3897
Nu 29:28 Include one **m goat** as a sin offering, in H8538
Nu 29:29 rams and fourteen **m lambs** a year old, H3897
Nu 29:31 Include one **m goat** as a sin offering, in H8538
Nu 29:32 rams and fourteen **m lambs** a year old, H3897
Nu 29:34 Include one **m goat** as a sin offering, in H8538
Nu 29:36 one ram and seven **m lambs** a year old H3897
Nu 29:38 Include one **m goat** as a sin offering, in H8538
Dt 5:14 your **m** or female **servant**, nor your ox, H6269
Dt 5:14 that your **m** and female **servants** may rest, H6269
Dt 5:21 land, his **m** or female **servant**, his ox or H6269
Dt 12:12 your **m** and female **servants**, and the H6269
Dt 12:18 your **m** and female **servants**, and the H6269
Dt 15:19 God every firstborn **m** of your herds and H2351
Dt 16:11 your **m** and female **servants**, the Levites H6269
Dt 16:14 your **m** and female **servants**, and the H6269
Dt 23:18 of a **m prostitute** into the house of H3978
Dt 28:68 to your enemies as **m** and female **slaves**, H6269
Jos 17:2 These are the other **m** descendants of H2351
Jdg 21:11 "Kill every **m** and every woman who is not H2351
1Sa 8:16 Your **m** and female **servants** and the best H6269
1Sa 25:22 I leave alive *one* **m** of all who H8874+928+7815
1Sa 25:34 not *one* **m** belonging to H8874+928+7815
2Sa 19:35 still hear the voices of *m* and female **singers**? AIT
2Sa 21:6 let seven of his **m** descendants be given to H408
1Ki 14:10 Jeroboam **every last m** in H8874+928+7815
1Ki 14:24 were even *m* **shrine prostitutes** in the land; AIT
1Ki 15:12 expelled the *m* **shrine prostitutes** from the AIT
1Ki 16:11 He did not spare a *single* **m** H8874+928+7815
1Ki 21:21 from Ahab **every last m** in H8874+928+7815
1Ki 22:46 rest of the *m* **shrine prostitutes** who remained AIT
2Ki 5:26 flocks and herds, or **m** and female **slaves**? H6269
2Ki 9:8 from Ahab **every last m** in H8874+928+7815
2Ki 23:7 of the *m* **shrine prostitutes** that were in AIT
1Ch 29:21 thousand rams and a thousand **m lambs**, H3897
2Ch 29:21 seven **m lambs** and seven male goats as H3897
2Ch 29:21 lambs and seven **m goats** as a sin H7618+6436
2Ch 29:32 rams and two hundred **m lambs**— H3897
2Ch 31:19 portions to every **m** among them and to H2351
2Ch 35:25 day all the *m* and female **singers** AIT
Ezr 2:65 besides their 7,337 **m** and female **slaves** H6269
Ezr 2:65 they also had 200 *m* and female **singers**. AIT
Ezr 6:9 **m lambs** for burnt offerings to the God A10043
Ezr 6:17 four hundred **m lambs** and, as a sin A10043
Ezr 6:17 twelve **m goats**, one for each A10615+10535
Ezr 7:17 rams and **m lambs**, together with A10043
Ezr 8:35 seventy-seven **m lambs** and, as a sin H3897
Ezr 8:35 as a sin offering, twelve **m goats**. H7618
Ne 7:67 besides their 7,337 **m** and female **slaves** H6269
Ne 7:67 they also had 245 *m* and female **singers**. AIT
Est 7:4 been sold as **m** and female **slaves**, H6269
Job 31:13 any of my **servants**, whether **m** or female, H6269
Job 36:14 among *m* **prostitutes of the shrines**. AIT
Ecc 2:7 I bought **m** and female **slaves** and had H6269
Ecc 2:8 I acquired *m* and female **singers**, and a AIT
Isa 14:2 make them **m** and female **servants** in the H6269
Jer 34:9 their Hebrew **slaves**, both **m** and female; H6269
Jer 34:10 free their **m** and female **slaves** and no H6269
Jer 34:16 back the **m** and female **slaves** you had set H6269
Eze 16:17 made for yourself **m** idols and engaged in H2351
Eze 43:22 are to offer a **m goat** without defect H8538+6436
Eze 43:25 you are to provide a **m goat** daily for a sin H8538
Eze 45:23 and a **m goat** for a sin offering. H6436+8538
Eze 46:4 day is to be six **m lambs** and a ram, H3897
Mal 1:14 has an acceptable **m** in his flock and vows H2351
Mt 19:4 the Creator 'made them **m** and female, *G781*
Mk 10:6 creation God 'made them **m** and female. *G781*
Lk 2:23 "Every firstborn **m** is to be consecrated to *G781*
Gal 3:28 free, nor is there **m** and female, for you *G781*
Rev 12:5 birth to a son, a **m** *child*, who "will rule all *G781*
Rev 12:13 woman who had given birth *to* the **m** *child*. *G781*

MALEFACTOR, MALEFACTORS (KJV) CRIMINAL, CRIMINALS

MALES (13) [MALE]

Ge 34:15 become like us by circumcising all your **m**. H2351
Ge 34:22 the condition that our **m** be circumcised, H2351
Ex 12:5 must be year-old **m** without defect, H2351
Ex 12:48 must have all the **m** in his household H2351
Ex 13:12 All the firstborn **m** of your livestock H2351
Ex 34:19 all the firstborn **m** of your livestock, H2350
Nu 3:22 number of all the **m** a month old or more H2351
Nu 3:28 number of all the **m** a month old or more H2351
Nu 3:34 number of all the **m** a month old or more H2351
Nu 3:40 firstborn Israelite **m** who are a month old H2351
Nu 3:43 of firstborn **m** a month old or more H2351
2Ch 31:16 distributed to the **m** three years old or H2351

Jer 2:24 Any *m that* **pursue** her need not tire AIT

MALICE (22) [MALICIOUS, MALICIOUSLY]

Nu 35:20 If anyone with **m aforethought** shoves H8534
Dt 4:42 killed ... without **m aforethought**. H8533+4946+9453+8997
Dt 19: 4 kills ... without **m aforethought**. H8533+4946+9453+8997
Dt 19: 6 did it ... without **m aforethought**. H8533+4946+9453+8997
Jos 20: 5 killed ... without **m aforethought**. H8533+4946+9453+8997
Job 6:30 Can my mouth not discern **m**? H2095
Ps 5: 9 can be trusted; their heart is filled with **m**. H2095
Ps 28: 3 neighbors but harbor **m** in their hearts. H8288
Ps 41: 5 My enemies say of me *in* **m**, "When will H8273
Ps 55:10 on its walls; **m** and abuse are within it. H224
Ps 73: 8 speak with **m**; with arrogance they H8273
Pr 26:26 Their **m** may be concealed by deception H8534
Eze 25: 6 with all the **m** of your heart against H8624
Eze 25:15 took revenge with **m** in their hearts, H8624
Eze 36: 5 with glee and with **m** in their hearts they H8624
Mk 7:22 adultery, greed, **m**, deceit, lewdness, envy *G4504*
Ro 1:29 full of envy, murder, strife, deceit and **m**. *G2799*
1Co 5: 8 bread leavened with **m** and wickedness, *G2798*
Eph 4:31 slander, along with every form of **m**. *G2798*
Col 3: 8 rage, **m**, slander, and filthy *G2798*
Titus 3: 3 We lived in **m** and envy, being hated *G2798*
1Pe 2: 1 rid yourselves of all **m** and all deceit *G2798*

MALICIOUS (9) [MALICE]

Ex 23: 1 a guilty person by being a **m** witness. H2805
Dt 19:16 If a **m** witness takes the stand to accuse H2805
Ps 27:12 up against me, spouting **m** accusations. H2805
Isa 58: 9 with the pointing finger and **m** talk, H224
Eze 28:24 of Israel have **m** neighbors who are H8764
Eze 36: 3 *the* **object of** people's **m talk** H6590+6584+8557+4383
1Ti 3:11 not **m talkers** but temperate and *G1333*
1Ti 6: 4 in envy, strife, **m talk**, evil suspicions *G1060*
3Jn 10 is doing, spreading **m** nonsense about us. *G4505*

MALICIOUSLY (5) [MALICE]

Ps 35:16 Like the ungodly *they* **m mocked** H4352+4352
Ps 35:19 *do* not *let* those who hate me without reason **m wink** H7975
Pr 6:13 *who* **winks m** with his eye, signals with his H7975
Pr 10:10 *Whoever* **winks m** causes grief, and H7975+6524
1Pe 3:16 those *who* **speak m against** your good *G2092*

MALIGN (2) [MALIGNED]

Ps 12: 5 will protect them from *those who* **m** them." H7032
Titus 2: 5 so that no *one will* **m** the word of God. *G1059*

MALIGNED (2) [MALIGN]

Eze 28:26 on all their neighbors who **m** them. H8764
Ac 19: 9 to believe and publicly **m** the Way. *G2800*

MALKAM (1)

1Ch 8: 9 Hodesh he had Jobab, Zibia, Mesha, **M**, H4903

MALKI-SHUA (5)

1Sa 14:49 Jonathan, Ishvi and **M**. The name of his H4902
1Sa 31: 2 his sons Jonathan, Abinadab and **M**. H4902
1Ch 8:33 father of Jonathan, **M**, Abinadab and H4902
1Ch 9:39 father of Jonathan, **M**, Abinadab and H4902
1Ch 10: 2 his sons Jonathan, Abinadab and **M**. H4902

MALKIEL (3) [MALKIELITE]

Ge 46:17 The sons of Beriah: Heber and **M**. H4896
Nu 26:45 through **M**, the Malkielite clan. H4896
1Ch 7:31 Heber and **M**, who was the father of H4896

MALKIELITE (1) [MALKIEL]

Nu 26:45 through Malkiel, the **M** clan. H4897

MALKIJAH (16)

1Ch 6:40 the son of Baaseiah, the son of **M**, H4898
1Ch 9:12 Pashhur, the son of **M**; and Maasai son of H4898
1Ch 24: 9 the fifth to **M**, the sixth to Mijamin, H4898
Ezr 10:25 Ramiah, Izziah, **M**, Mijamin, Eleazar H4898
Ezr 10:25 Mijamin, Eleazar, **M** and Benaiah. H4898
Ezr 10:31 Ishijah, **M**, Shemaiah, Shimeon, H4898
Ne 3:11 **M** son of Harim and Hasshub son of H4898
Ne 3:14 Gate was repaired by **M** son of Rekab, H4898
Ne 3:31 Next to him, **M**, one of the goldsmiths H4898
Ne 8: 4 Pedaiah, Mishael, **M**, Hashum H4898
Ne 10: 3 Pashhur, Amariah, **M**, H4898
Ne 11:12 the son of Pashhur, the son of **M**, H4898
Ne 12:42 Jehohanan, **M**, Elam and Ezer. H4898
Jer 21: 1 to him Pashhur son of **M** and the priest H4898
Jer 38: 1 Pashhur son of **M** heard what H4898
Jer 38: 6 put him into the cistern of **M**, H4899

MALKIRAM (1)

1Ch 3:18 **M**, Pedaiah, Shenazzar, Jekamiah H4901

MALLOTH (2)

1Ch 25: 4 Joshbekashah, **M**, Hothir and Mahazioth. H4871
1Ch 25:26 the nineteenth to **M**, his sons and H4871

MALLOW (1)

Job 6: 6 or is there flavor in the sap of the **m**? H2733

MALLUK (6) [MALLUK'S]

1Ch 6:44 of Kishi, the son of Abdi, the son of **M**, H4866
Ezr 10:29 Meshullam, **M**, Adaiah, Jashub, Sheal H4866
Ezr 10:32 Benjamin, **M** and Shemariah. H4866
Ne 10: 4 Hattush, Shebaniah, **M**, H4866
Ne 10:27 **M**, Harim and Baanah. H4866
Ne 12: 2 Amariah, **M**, Hattush, H4866

MALLUK'S (1) [MALLUK]

Ne 12:14 of **M**, Jonathan; of Shekaniah's, Joseph; H4868

MALTA (1)

Ac 28: 1 found out that the island was called **M**. *G3514*

MAMMON (KJV) MONEY, WEALTH

MAMRE (10)

Ge 13:18 live near the great trees of **M** at Hebron, H4934
Ge 14:13 near the great trees of **M** the Amorite, H4935
Ge 14:24 went with me—to Aner, Eshkol and **M**. H4935
Ge 18: 1 the great trees of **M** while he was sitting H4934
Ge 23:17 So Ephron's field in Machpelah near **M** H4934
Ge 23:19 cave in the field of Machpelah near **M** H4934
Ge 25: 9 him in the cave of Machpelah near **M**, H4934
Ge 35:27 Jacob came home to his father Isaac in **M**, H4934
Ge 49:30 of Machpelah, near **M** in Canaan, which H4934
Ge 50:13 Machpelah, near **M**, which Abraham had H4934

MAN (1290) [HORSEMAN, HORSEMEN, MAN'S, MAN-EATER, MAN-MADE, MANHOOD, MANKIND, MANNED, MEN, MEN'S, SPOKESMAN, WOODSMEN, WORKMAN'S]

Ge 2: 7 LORD God formed a **m** from the dust of the H132
Ge 2: 7 and the **m** became a living being. H132
Ge 2: 8 there he put the **m** he had formed. H132
Ge 2:15 LORD God took the **m** and put him in the H132
Ge 2:16 And the LORD God commanded the **m**, H132
Ge 2:18 "It is not good for the **m** to be alone. H132
Ge 2:19 brought them to the **m** to see what he H132
Ge 2:19 whatever the **m** called each living H132
Ge 2:20 So the **m** gave names to all the livestock H132
Ge 2:21 LORD God caused the **m** to fall into a deep H132
Ge 2:22 from the rib he had taken out of the **m**, H132
Ge 2:22 of the man, and he brought her to the **m**. H132
Ge 2:23 The **m** said, "This is now bone of my bones H132
Ge 2:23 'woman,' for she was taken out of **m**." H408
Ge 2:24 That is why a **m** leaves his father and H408
Ge 3: 8 Then the **m** and his wife heard the sound H132
Ge 3: 9 But the LORD God called to the **m**, "Where H132
Ge 3:12 The **m** said, "The woman you put here with H132
Ge 3:22 "The **m** has now become like one of us H132
Ge 3:24 After he drove the **m** out, he placed on the H132
Ge 4: 1 help of the LORD I have brought forth a **m**." H408
Ge 4:23 I have killed a **m** for wounding me, H408
Ge 4:23 wounding me, a **young m** for injuring me. H3529
Ge 6: 9 Noah was a righteous **m**, blameless H408
Ge 9:20 A **m** *of* the soil, proceeded to plant a H408
Ge 14:13 *A m* who had escaped **came** and reported AIT
Ge 15: 4 "**This** *m* will not be your heir, but a son who AIT
Ge 16:12 He will be a wild donkey of a **m**; his hand H132
Ge 17:17 a son be born to a *m* a hundred years **old**? AIT
Ge 19: 8 daughters who have never slept with a **m**. H408
Ge 19:31 there is no **m** around here to give us H408
Ge 24:16 a virgin; no **m** had ever slept with her. H408
Ge 24:21 the **m** watched her closely to learn whether H408
Ge 24:22 the **m** took out a gold nose ring weighing a H408
Ge 24:26 Then the **m** bowed down and worshiped H408
Ge 24:29 he hurried out to the **m** at the spring. H408
Ge 24:30 heard Rebekah tell what the **m** said to her, H408
Ge 24:30 he went out to the **m** and found him H408
Ge 24:32 So the **m** went to the house, and the H408
Ge 24:58 asked her, "Will you go with this **m**?" H408
Ge 24:61 the camels and went back with the **m**. H408
Ge 24:65 "Who is that **m** in the field coming to meet H408
Ge 25: 8 at a good old age, an **old** *m* and full of years AIT
Ge 25:27 a skillful hunter, a **m** *of* the open country H408
Ge 26:11 "Anyone who harms this **m** or his wife shall H408
Ge 26:13 The **m** became rich, and his wealth H408
Ge 27: 2 "*I am* now *an* **old** *m* and don't know the day AIT
Ge 27:11 Esau is a hairy **m** while I have smooth H408
Ge 29:19 that I give her to you than to some other **m**. H408
Ge 30:43 In this way the **m** grew exceedingly H408
Ge 32:24 a **m** wrestled with him till daybreak. H408
Ge 32:25 When the **m** saw that he could not NDT
Ge 32:25 wrenched as he wrestled with **the m**. H2257S
Ge 32:26 Then the **m** said, "Let me go, for it is NDT
Ge 32:27 The **m** asked him, "What is your name?" NDT
Ge 32:28 Then the **m** said, "Your name will no longer NDT
Ge 34:14 give our sister to a **m** who is not H408
Ge 34:19 The **young m**, who was the most honored H5853
Ge 37: 2 Joseph, a **young m** of seventeen, was H5853
Ge 37:15 a **m** found him wandering around in the H408
Ge 37:17 moved on from here," the **m** answered. H408
Ge 38: 1 down to stay with a **m** of Adullam named H408
Ge 38: 2 daughter of a Canaanite **m** named Shua. H408
Ge 38:25 "I am pregnant by the **m** who owns these," H408
Ge 41:12 giving *each* **m** the interpretation of his H408
Ge 41:13 position, and **the other m** was impaled." H2257S
Ge 41:33 discerning and wise **m** and put him in H408
Ge 41:38 "Can we find anyone like this **m**, one in H408
Ge 42:11 We are all the sons of one **m**. Your servants H408
Ge 42:13 the sons of one **m**, who lives in the land of H408
Ge 42:30 "The **m** who is lord over the land spoke H408
Ge 42:33 "Then the **m** who is lord over the land said H408
Ge 43: 3 said to him, "The **m** warned us solemnly H408
Ge 43: 5 go down, because the **m** said to us, 'You H408
Ge 43: 6 on me by telling the **m** you had another H408
Ge 43: 7 "The **m** questioned us closely about H408
Ge 43:11 take them down to the **m** as a gift— H408
Ge 43:13 brother also and go back to the **m** at once. H408
Ge 43:14 you mercy before the **m** so that he will let H408
Ge 43:17 The **m** did as Joseph told him and took the H408
Ge 44:15 Don't you know that a **m** like me can find H408
Ge 44:17 Only the **m** who was found to have the cup H408
Ex 2: 1 Now a **m** of the tribe of Levi married a H408
Ex 2:14 *The m* **said**, "Who made you ruler and judge AIT
Ex 2:21 Moses agreed to stay with the **m**, who gave H408
Ex 10: 7 "How long will **this** *m* be a snare to us? AIT
Ex 12: 3 day of this month *each* **m** is to take a lamb H408
Ex 21: 4 her master, and only **the m** shall go free. H2085S
Ex 21: 7 "If a **m** sells his daughter as a servant, she H408
Ex 21:28 "If a bull gores a **m** or woman to death, the H408
Ex 21:29 it penned up and it kills a **m** or woman, H408
Ex 22:16 "If a **m** seduces a virgin who is not pledged H408
Ex 32:27 '**Each** *m* strap a sword to his side. AIT
Ex 36: 6 "No **m** or woman is to make anything else H408
Lev 13:29 "If a **m** or woman has a sore on their head H408
Lev 13:33 then *the m or woman must* **shave themselves** AIT
Lev 13:38 "When a **m** or woman has white spots on H408
Lev 13:40 "A **m** who has lost his hair and is bald is H408
Lev 13:44 the **m** is diseased and is unclean. H408
Lev 15: 2 'When **any m** has an unusual bodily H408+408
Lev 15: 4 'Any bed the *m with a* **discharge** lies on will AIT
Lev 15: 6 that the *m with a* **discharge** sat on must wash AIT
Lev 15: 7 the *m who has a* **discharge** must wash AIT
Lev 15: 8 " 'If the *m with the* **discharge** spits on anyone AIT
Lev 15: 9 " 'Everything the **m** sits on when riding H2307S
Lev 15:11 " 'Anyone the *m with a* **discharge** touches AIT
Lev 15:12 'A clay pot that the **m** touches must be H2307S
Lev 15:13 " 'When a **m** is cleansed from his H2307S
Lev 15:15 before the LORD for **the m** because of his H2257S
Lev 15:16 " 'When a **m** has an emission of semen H408
Lev 15:18 When a **m** has sexual relations with a H408
Lev 15:24 " 'If a **m** has sexual relations with her and H408
Lev 15:32 are the regulations for a *m with a* **discharge**, AIT
Lev 15:33 a **m** or a woman with a discharge H2351
Lev 15:33 for a **m** who has sexual relations with H408
Lev 16:22 the **m** shall release it in the wilderness. NDT
Lev 16:26 "The *m who* **releases** the goat as a AIT
Lev 16:28 The *m who* **burns** them must wash his clothes AIT
Lev 18:22 relations with a **m** as one does with a H2351
Lev 19:20 " 'If a **m** sleeps with a female slave who is H408
Lev 19:20 promised to another **m** but who has not H408
Lev 19:21 **The m**, however, must bring a ram to the H2257S
Lev 20: 4 their eyes when that **m** sacrifices one of his H408
Lev 20:10 " 'If a **m** commits adultery with another H408
Lev 20:11 " 'If a **m** has sexual relations with his H408
Lev 20:11 Both **the m and the womli** are to be put H2157S
Lev 20:12 " 'If a **m** has sexual relations with his H408
Lev 20:13 " 'If a **m** has sexual relations with a man as H408
Lev 20:13 relations with a **m** as one does with a H2351
Lev 20:14 " 'If a **m** marries both a woman and her H408
Lev 20:15 " 'If a **m** has sexual relations with an H408
Lev 20:17 " 'If a **m** marries his sister, the daughter of H408
Lev 20:18 " 'If a **m** has sexual relations with a woman H408
Lev 20:20 " 'If a **m** has sexual relations with his aunt H408
Lev 20:21 " 'If a **m** marries his brother's wife, it is an H408
Lev 20:27 " 'A **m** or woman who is a medium or H408
Lev 21:18 No **m** who has any defect may come near H408
Lev 21:18 no **m** who is blind or lame, disfigured or H408
Lev 21:19 no **m** with a crippled foot or hand, H408
Nu 1: 2 listing every **m** by name, one by one. H2351
Nu 1: 4 One **m** from each tribe, each of them the H408
Nu 4:19 assign to each **m** his work and what he H408
Nu 4:32 Assign **to each m** the specific things H928+9005
Nu 5: 6 '*Any* **m** or woman who wrongs another in H408
Nu 5:13 so that another **m** has sexual relations with H408
Nu 5:19 "If no other **m** has had sexual relations H408
Nu 5:20 relations with a **m** other than your husband H408
Nu 5:30 come over a **m** because he suspects H408
Nu 6: 2 'If a **m** or woman wants to make a special H408
Nu 11:27 A **young m** ran and told Moses, "Eldad H5853
Nu 12: 3 Now Moses was a very humble **m**, more H408
Nu 15:32 a **m** was found gathering wood on the H408
Nu 15:35 the LORD said to Moses, "The **m** must die. H408
Nu 16: 5 **The m** he chooses he will cause to come H2257S
Nu 16: 7 The **m** the LORD chooses will be the one H408
Nu 16:17 *Each* **m** is to take his censer and put H408
Nu 16:22 the entire assembly when only one **m** sins?" H408
Nu 17: 2 Write the name of *each* **m** on his staff. H408
Nu 17: 5 belonging to the **m** I choose will sprout, H408
Nu 19: 8 The *m who* **burns** it must also wash his AIT
Nu 19: 9 "A **m** who is clean shall gather up the H408
Nu 19:10 The *m who* **gathers up** the ashes of the heifer AIT
Nu 19:18 Then a **m** who is ceremonially clean is to H408
Nu 19:19 The *m who* is **clean** is to sprinkle those who AIT
Nu 19:21 "The *m who* **sprinkles** the water of cleansing AIT
Nu 25: 6 Then an Israelite **m** brought into the camp H408
Nu 25: 8 the Israelite **m** and into the woman's H408
Nu 27: 8 Israelites, 'If a **m** dies and leaves no son H408
Nu 27:18 a **m** in whom is the spirit of leadership H408
Nu 30: 2 When a **m** makes a vow to the LORD or H408
Nu 30:16 relationships between a **m** and his wife, H408
Nu 31: 7 commanded Moses, and killed every **m**. H2351

Nu 31:17 kill every woman who has slept with a m, H2351
Nu 31:18 every girl who has never slept with a m. H2351
Nu 31:35 women who had never slept with a m. H5883
Nu 32:27 every m who is armed for battle, will AIT
Nu 32:29 Reubenites, every m armed for battle, cross AIT
Dt 1:23 twelve of you, one m from each tribe. H408
Dt 4:16 whether formed like a m or a woman, H2351
Dt 8: 3 to teach you that m does not live on bread H132
Dt 8: 5 your heart that as a m disciplines his son, H408
Dt 17: 2 If a m or woman living among you in one H408
Dt 17: 5 take the m or woman who has done this H408
Dt 19: 5 a m may go into the forest with his H889S
Dt 19: 5 That m may flee to one of these cities H2085S
Dt 21:15 If a m has two wives, and he loves one H408
Dt 22: 5 clothing, nor a m wear women's clothing H1505
Dt 22:13 If a m takes a wife and, after sleeping with H408
Dt 22:16 "I gave my daughter in marriage to this m H408
Dt 22:18 elders shall take the m and punish him. H408
Dt 22:19 because this m has given an Israelite virgin NDT
Dt 22:22 If a m is found sleeping with another H408
Dt 22:22 both the m who slept with her and the H408
Dt 22:23 If a m happens to meet in a town a virgin H408
Dt 22:24 the m because he violated another H408
Dt 22:25 out in the country a m happens to meet a H408
Dt 22:25 only the m who has done this shall die. H408
Dt 22:27 the m found the young woman out in the NDT
Dt 22:28 If a m happens to meet a virgin who is not H408
Dt 22:30 A m is not to marry his father's wife; he H408
Dt 23:17 No Israelite m or woman is to become a H1201
Dt 24: 1 If a m marries a woman who becomes H408
Dt 24: 2 house she becomes the wife of another m, H408
Dt 24: 5 If a m has recently married, he must not be H408
Dt 25: 7 if a m does not want to marry his brother's H408
Dt 25: 9 what is done to the m who will not build H408
Dt 28:54 sensitive m among you will have H408
Dt 29:18 Make sure there is no m or woman, clan H408
Dt 32:30 How could one m chase a thousand, or two AIT
Dt 33: 1 that Moses the m of God pronounced on H408
Jos 5:13 looked up and saw a m standing in front of H408
Jos 7:14 chooses shall come forward m by man. NDT
Jos 7:14 chooses shall come forward man by m. H1505
Jos 7:18 had his family come forward m by man, NDT
Jos 7:18 had his family come forward man by m, H1505
Jos 8:17 Not a m remained in Ai or Bethel who did H408
Jos 14: 6 said to Moses the m of God at Kadesh H408
Jos 14:15 was the greatest m among the Anakites.) H132
Jos 15:16 in marriage to the m who attacks and H2257S
Jos 23: 1 around them, Joshua, by then a very old m, AIT
Jdg 1:12 in marriage to the m who attacks and H2257S
Jdg 1:24 the spies saw a m coming out of the city H408
Jdg 1:25 spared the m and his whole family H408
Jdg 3:15 a left-handed m, the son of Gera the H408
Jdg 3:17 Eglon king of Moab, who was a very fat m. H408
Jdg 4:16 troops fell by the sword; not a m was left. H285S
Jdg 4:22 "I will show you the m you're looking for." H408
Jdg 5:30 a woman or two for each m, colorful H1505
Jdg 7:13 arrived just as a m was telling a friend his H408
Jdg 7:21 While each m held his position around the H408
Jdg 8:14 He caught a young m of Sukkoth and H408
Jdg 8:14 the young m wrote down for him the NDT
Jdg 8:21 'As is the m, so is his strength.'" H408
Jdg 9: 2 sons rule over you, or just one m? H408
Jdg 10: 1 a m of Issachar named Tola son of Puah H408
Jdg 13: 2 A certain m of Zorah, named Manoah H408
Jdg 13: 6 told him, "A m of God came to me. H408
Jdg 13: 8 I beg you to let the m of God you sent to us H408
Jdg 13:10 The m who appeared to me the other day!" H408
Jdg 13:11 When he came to the m, he said, "Are you H408
Jdg 13:11 "Are you the m who talked to my wife?" H408
Jdg 16: 7 I'll become as weak as any other m." H132
Jdg 16:11 I'll become as weak as any other m." H132
Jdg 16:13 I'll become as weak as any other m." H132
Jdg 16:17 I would become as weak as any other m." H132
Jdg 17: 1 Now a m named Micah from the hill H408
Jdg 17: 5 Now this m Micah had a shrine, and he H408
Jdg 17:11 the young m became like one of his H5853
Jdg 17:12 the young m became his priest and H5853
Jdg 19: 7 And when the m got up to go, his H408
Jdg 19: 9 Then when the m, with his concubine and H408
Jdg 19:10 the m left and went toward Jebus H408
Jdg 19:16 That evening an old m from the hill country H408
Jdg 19:17 city square, the old m asked, "Where are H408
Jdg 19:19 the woman and the young m with us. H5853
Jdg 19:20 are welcome at my house," the old m said. H408
Jdg 19:22 shouted to the old m who owned the H408
Jdg 19:22 "Bring out the m who came to your house H408
Jdg 19:23 Since this m is my guest, don't do this H408
Jdg 19:24 But as for this m, don't do such an H408
Jdg 19:25 So the m took his concubine and sent her H408
Jdg 19:28 Then the m put her on his donkey and set H408
Jdg 21:12 women who had never slept with a m, H408
Jdg 21:23 each m caught one and carried her off to H4392S
Ru 1: 1 So a m from Bethlehem in Judah, together H408
Ru 2: 1 a m of standing from the clan of Elimelek H408
Ru 2:19 Blessed be the m who took notice of you!" AIT
Ru 2:19 "The name of the m I worked with today is H408
Ru 2:20 She added, "That m is our close relative H408
Ru 3: 8 of the night something startled the m; H408
Ru 3:18 For the m will not rest until the matter is H408
1Sa 1: 1 There was a certain m from Ramathaim, H408
1Sa 1: 3 Year after year this m went up from his H408
1Sa 2:27 Now a m of God came to Eli and said to H408
1Sa 4:10 were defeated and every m fled to his tent. H408
1Sa 4:13 When the m entered the town and told H408
1Sa 4:14 of this uproar?" The m hurried over to Eli, H408
1Sa 4:17 The m who brought the news replied, "Israel AIT
1Sa 4:18 he was an old m, and he was heavy. H408
1Sa 9: 1 was a Benjamite, a m of standing, whose H1475
1Sa 9: 2 as handsome a young m as could be H1033
1Sa 9: 6 in this town there is a m of God; he is H408
1Sa 9: 7 "If we go, what can we give the m? H408
1Sa 9: 7 We have no gift to take to the m of God H408
1Sa 9: 8 I will give it to the m of God so that he will H408
1Sa 9:10 out for the town where the m of God was. H408
1Sa 9:16 I will send you a m from the land of H408
1Sa 9:17 "This is the m I spoke to you about H408
1Sa 10:12 A m who lived there answered, "And who H408
1Sa 10:22 of the LORD, "Has the m come here yet?" H408
1Sa 10:24 "Do you see the m the LORD has chosen? H889S
1Sa 13:14 LORD has sought out a m after his own heart H408
1Sa 14:52 whenever Saul saw a mighty or brave m, H408
1Sa 16:18 He is a brave m and a warrior H1475+2657
1Sa 16:18 He speaks well and is a fine-looking m H408
1Sa 17: 8 Choose a m and have him come down to H408
1Sa 17:10 Give me a m and let us fight each other." H408
1Sa 17:24 Whenever the Israelites saw the m, they all H408
1Sa 17:25 "Do you see how this m keeps coming out? H408
1Sa 17:25 give great wealth to the m who kills him. H408
1Sa 17:26 will be done for the m who kills this H408
1Sa 17:27 what will be done for the m who kills him." H408
1Sa 17:33 you are only a young m, and he has been H5853
1Sa 17:55 "Abner, whose son is that young m?" H5853
1Sa 17:56 "Find out whose son this young m is." H6624
1Sa 17:58 son are you, young m?" Saul asked him. H5853
1Sa 18:23 I'm only a poor m and little known." H408
1Sa 19: 5 wrong to an innocent m like David H5929+1947
1Sa 21:14 his servants, "Look at the m! He is insane! H408
1Sa 21:15 Must this m come into my house? AIT
1Sa 22:23 The m who wants to kill you is trying to kill AIT
1Sa 24:19 When a m finds his enemy, does he let him H408
1Sa 25: 2 A certain m in Maon, who had property H408
1Sa 25:17 He is such a wicked m that no one can H1201
1Sa 25:25 attention, my lord, to that wicked m Nabal. H408
1Sa 26:15 "You're a m, aren't you? And who H408
1Sa 27: 3 Each m had his family with him, and David H408
1Sa 27: 9 he did not leave a m or woman alive, but H408
1Sa 27:11 He did not leave a m or woman alive to be H408
1Sa 28:14 "An old m wearing a robe is coming up," H408
1Sa 29: 4 said, "Send the m back, that he may H408
1Sa 30:22 each m may take his wife and children H408
1Sa 30:24 The share of the m who stayed with the AIT
2Sa 1: 2 On the third day a m arrived from Saul's H408
2Sa 1: 5 said to the young m who brought him H5853
2Sa 1: 6 the young m said, "and there H5853
2Sa 1:13 said to the young m who brought him H5853
2Sa 2:16 Then each m grabbed his opponent by the H408
2Sa 2:23 And every m stopped when he came to the AIT
2Sa 3:38 a commander and a great m has fallen in AIT
2Sa 4:11 killed an innocent m in his own house H408
2Sa 11: 3 The m said, "She is Bathsheba, the daughter AIT
2Sa 12: 2 The rich m had a very large number of sheep AIT
2Sa 12: 3 the poor m had nothing except one little AIT
2Sa 12: 4 "Now a traveler came to the rich m, but the H408
2Sa 12: 4 the rich m refrained from taking one of NDT
2Sa 12: 4 belonged to the poor m and prepared it H408
2Sa 12: 5 anger against the m and said to Nathan, H408
2Sa 12: 5 the LORD lives, the m who did this must die! H408
2Sa 12: 7 Nathan said to David, "You are the m! H408
2Sa 13: 3 Jonadab was a very shrewd m. H408
2Sa 13:34 Now the m standing watch looked up H5853
2Sa 14:16 from the hand of the m who is trying to cut H408
2Sa 14:21 bring back the young m Absalom." H5853
2Sa 14:25 there was not a m so highly praised for H408
2Sa 16: 5 a m from the same clan as Saul's family H408
2Sa 17: 3 The death of the m you seek will mean the H408
2Sa 17:18 But a young m saw them and told H5853
2Sa 17:18 went to the house of a m in Bahurim. H408
2Sa 18: 5 gentle with the young m Absalom for my H5853
2Sa 18:11 Joab said to the m who had told him this H408
2Sa 18:12 But the m replied, "Even if a thousand H408
2Sa 18:12 'Protect the young m Absalom for my sake H5853
2Sa 18:24 he looked out, he saw a m running alone. H408
2Sa 18:26 another m running alone! H408
2Sa 18:27 "He's a good m," the king said. "He H408
2Sa 18:29 "Is the young m Absalom safe? H5853
2Sa 18:32 Cushite, "Is the young m Absalom safe?" H5853
2Sa 18:32 rise up to harm you be like that young m." H5853
2Sa 19: 7 not a m will be left with you by nightfall. H408
2Sa 19:32 in Mahanaim, for he was a very wealthy m. H408
2Sa 20: 1 in Jesse's son! Every m to his tent, Israel!" H408
2Sa 20:12 the m saw that all the troops came to H408
2Sa 20:21 A m named Sheba son of Bikri, from the H408
2Sa 20:21 Hand over this one m, and I'll withdraw H2257S
2Sa 21: 5 "As for the m who destroyed us and plotted H408
2Sa 21:20 there was a huge m with six fingers on H408
2Sa 22:49 my foes; from a violent m you rescued me. H408
2Sa 23: 1 utterance of the m exalted by the Most H1505
2Sa 23: 1 the m anointed by the God of Jacob NDT
1Ki 1:42 A worthy m like you must be bringing good H408
1Ki 2: 2 "So be strong, act like a m, H408
1Ki 2: 9 You are a m of wisdom; you will know what H408
1Ki 11:28 Now Jeroboam was a m of standing, and H408
1Ki 11:28 saw how well the young m did his work, H5853
1Ki 12:22 of God came to Shemaiah the m of God: H408
1Ki 13: 1 word of the LORD a m of God came from H408
1Ki 13: 3 That same day the m of God gave a sign NDT
1Ki 13: 4 heard what the m of God cried out against H408
1Ki 13: 4 stretched out toward the m shriveled up, H2257S
1Ki 13: 5 sign given by the m of God by the word of H408
1Ki 13: 6 Then the king said to the m of God H408
1Ki 13: 6 So the m of God interceded with the LORD H408
1Ki 13: 7 The king said to the m of God, "Come H408
1Ki 13: 8 But the m of God answered the king, "Even H408
1Ki 13:11 him all that the m of God had done there H408
1Ki 13:12 him which road the m of God from Judah H408
1Ki 13:14 rode after the m of God. He found him H408
1Ki 13:14 "Are you the m of God who came from H408
1Ki 13:16 The m of God said, "I cannot turn back and NDT
1Ki 13:19 So the m of God returned with him and ate NDT
1Ki 13:21 He cried out to the m of God who had come H408
1Ki 13:23 When the m of God had finished eating NDT
1Ki 13:26 "It is the m of God who defied the word of H408
1Ki 13:29 picked up the body of the m of God, H408
1Ki 13:31 in the grave where the m of God is buried; H408
1Ki 17:18 "What do you have against me, m of God? H408
1Ki 17:24 know that you are a m of God and that the H408
1Ki 20: 7 "See how this m is looking for trouble! AIT
1Ki 20:28 The m of God came up and told the king of H408
1Ki 20:36 And after the m went away, a lion found NDT
1Ki 20:37 The prophet found another m and said H408
1Ki 20:37 So the m struck him and wounded him H408
1Ki 20:39 me with a captive and said, 'Guard this m. H408
1Ki 20:40 busy here and there, the m disappeared." H2085S
1Ki 20:42 'You have set free a m I had determined H408
1Ki 21:19 you not murdered a m and seized his NDT
1Ki 22:36 "Every m to his town. Every H408
1Ki 22:36 man to his town. Every m to his land!" H408
2Ki 1: 6 "A m came to meet us," they replied. "And H408
2Ki 1: 7 "What kind of m was it who came to meet H408
2Ki 1: 9 said to him, "M of God, the king says H408
2Ki 1:10 captain, "If I am a m of God, may fire come H408
2Ki 1:11 said to him, "M of God, this is what the H408
2Ki 1:12 "If I am a m of God," Elijah replied, "may H408
2Ki 1:13 "M of God," he begged, "please have H408
2Ki 3:21 against them; so every m, young and old, AIT
2Ki 3:25 and each m threw a stone on every good H408
2Ki 4: 1 The wife of a m from the company of the NDT
2Ki 4: 7 She went and told the m of God, and he H408
2Ki 4: 9 "I know that this m who often comes our H2085S
2Ki 4: 9 often comes our way is a holy m of God. H408
2Ki 4:16 "Please, m of God, don't mislead your H408
2Ki 4:21 laid him on the bed of the m of God, H408
2Ki 4:22 so I can go to the m of God quickly and H408
2Ki 4:25 out and came to the m of God at Mount H408
2Ki 4:25 the m of God said to his servant Gehazi H408
2Ki 4:27 she reached the m of God at the mountain H408
2Ki 4:27 her away, but the m of God said, "Leave H408
2Ki 4:40 they cried out, "M of God, there is death in H408
2Ki 4:42 A m came from Baal Shalishah, bringing H408
2Ki 4:42 bringing the m of God twenty loaves of H408
2Ki 5: 1 He was a great m in the sight of his master H408
2Ki 5: 8 When Elisha the m of God heard that the H408
2Ki 5: 8 Have the m come to me and he will know NDT
2Ki 5:14 seven times, as the m of God had told him H408
2Ki 5:15 his attendants went back to the m of God. H408
2Ki 5:20 the servant of Elisha the m of God, said to H408
2Ki 5:26 with you when the m got down from his H408
2Ki 6: 6 The m of God asked, "Where did it fall?" H408
2Ki 6: 7 Then the m reached out his hand and took NDT
2Ki 6: 9 The m of God sent word to the king of H408
2Ki 6:10 on the place indicated by the m of God. H408
2Ki 6:15 the servant of the m of God got up and H408
2Ki 6:19 I will lead you to the m you are looking for." H408
2Ki 7: 2 the king was leaning said to the m of God, H408
2Ki 7:17 just as the m of God had foretold when the H408
2Ki 7:18 It happened as the m of God had said to H408
2Ki 7:19 The officer had said to the m of God, "Look, H408
2Ki 7:19 The m of God had replied, "You will see it NDT
2Ki 8: 2 proceeded to do as the m of God said. H408
2Ki 8: 4 the servant of the m of God, and had said, H408
2Ki 8: 7 "The m of God has come all the way up H408
2Ki 8: 8 gift with you and go to meet the m of God. H408
2Ki 8:11 Then the m of God began to weep. H408
2Ki 9: 1 Elisha summoned a m from the company H285S
2Ki 9:11 "You know the m and the sort of things he H408
2Ki 13:19 The m of God was angry with him and said H408
2Ki 13:21 while some Israelites were burying a m, H408
2Ki 13:21 the m came to life and stood up on his feet H408
2Ki 14:12 by Israel, and every m fled to his home. H408
2Ki 22:15 Tell the m who sent you to me, H408
2Ki 23:16 proclaimed by the m of God who foretold H408
2Ki 23:17 the tomb of the m of God who came from H408
1Ch 16: 3 of raisins to each Israelite m and woman. H408
1Ch 20: 6 there was a huge m with six fingers on H408
1Ch 22: 9 a son who will be a m of peace and rest, H408
1Ch 23:14 sons of Moses the m of God were counted H408
1Ch 27:32 a counselor, a m of insight and a scribe. H408
1Ch 29: 1 structure is not for m but for the LORD God. H132
2Ch 2: 7 a m skilled to work in gold and silver H408
2Ch 2:13 sending you Huram-Abi, a m of great skill, H408
2Ch 8:14 was what David the m of God had ordered. H408
2Ch 11: 2 the LORD came to Shemaiah the m of God: H408
2Ch 15:13 whether small or great, m or woman. H408
2Ch 25: 7 But a m of God came to him and said H408
2Ch 25: 9 Amaziah asked the m of God, "But what H408
2Ch 25: 9 The m of God replied, "The LORD can give H408

M

2Ch 25:22 by Israel, and *every* **m** fled to his home. H408
2Ch 30:16 in the Law of Moses the **m** *of* God. H408
2Ch 34:23 Tell the **m** who sent you to me, H408
Ezr 2:61 a **m** who had married a daughter of Barzillai NDT
Ezr 3: 2 written in the Law of Moses the **m** *of* God. H408
Ezr 5:14 gave them to a **m** named Sheshbazzar, A10192S
Ezr 7:11 a **m learned** *in* matters concerning the H6221
Ezr 8:18 Sherebiah, a capable **m**, from the H408
Ne 1:11 him favor in the presence of this **m**. H408
Ne 4:18 But the *m who* **sounded** the trumpet stayed AIT
Ne 4:22 "Have *every* **m** and his helper stay inside H408
Ne 6:11 "Should a **m** like me run away? Or H408
Ne 7: 2 because he was a **m** *of* integrity and feared H408
Ne 7:63 a **m** who had married a daughter of Barzillai NDT
Ne 12:24 as prescribed by David the **m** *of* God. H408
Ne 12:36 prescribed by David the **m** *of* God. H408
Est 1: 8 to serve *each* **m** what he H408+2256+408
Est 1:22 that every **m** should be ruler over H408
Est 4:11 know that for any **m** or woman who H408
Est 6: 6 be done for the **m** the king delights to H408
Est 6: 7 "For the **m** the king delights to honor, H408
Est 6: 9 Let them robe the **m** the king delights to H408
Est 6: 9 what is done for the **m** the king delights to H408
Est 6:11 what is done for the **m** the king delights to H408
Est 7: 5 **the m** who has dared to do such a thing?" H2085S
Job 1: 1 Uz there lived a **m** whose name was Job. H408
Job 1: 1 This **m** was blameless and upright; he H408
Job 1: 3 He was the greatest **m** among all the H408
Job 1: 8 a **m** who fears God and shuns evil. H408
Job 1:12 on **the m himself** do not lay a finger." H2257
Job 2: 3 a **m** who fears God and shuns evil. H408
Job 2: 4 "A **m** will give all he has for his own life H408
Job 3:23 is life given to a **m** whose way is hidden, H1505
Job 4:17 Can even a **strong m** be more pure than H1505
Job 5: 7 Yet **m** is born to trouble as surely as sparks H132
Job 10: 5 your years like those of a **strong m**, H1505
Job 13:28 "So **m** wastes away like something H2085S
Job 14:10 But a **m** dies and is laid low; he breathes H1505
Job 15: 7 "Are you the first **m** ever born? Were you H132
Job 15:20 All his days the **wicked** *m* suffers torment, the AIT
Job 15:20 the **ruthless** *m* through all the years stored up AIT
Job 16:21 on behalf of a **m** he pleads with God as H1505
Job 17: 6 to everyone, a **m** in whose face people spit. NDT
Job 17:10 I will not find a **wise** *m* among you. AIT
Job 18: 5 "The lamp of a **wicked** *m* is snuffed out; the AIT
Job 18:21 Surely such is the dwelling of an **evil m** H6405
Job 22: 2 "Can a **m** be of benefit to God? Can even H1505
Job 22: 8 though you were a powerful **m**, owning H408
Job 22: 8 owning land—an **honored** *m*, living on it. AIT
Job 27:13 the heritage a **ruthless** *m* receives from the AIT
Job 30:24 lays a hand on a **broken m** when he cries H6505
Job 32:13 wisdom; let God, not a **m**, refute him. H408
Job 34:36 the utmost for answering like a wicked **m**! H408
Job 38: 3 Brace yourself like a **m**; I will question you H1505
Job 40: 7 "Brace yourself like a **m**; I will question H1505
Job 42:17 And so Job died, an **old** *m* and full of years. AIT
Ps 10: 2 his arrogance the **wicked** *m* hunts down the AIT
Ps 10: 4 In his pride the **wicked** *m* does not seek him AIT
Ps 10:13 Why does the **wicked** *m* revile God? Why AIT
Ps 10:15 Break the arm of the **wicked** *m*; call the AIT
Ps 18:48 my foes; from a violent **m** you rescued me. H408
Ps 22: 6 But I am a worm and not a **m**, scorned by H408
Ps 34: 6 This **poor** *m* called, and the LORD heard him AIT
Ps 37:35 seen a wicked and **ruthless** *m* flourishing like AIT
Ps 52: 7 "Here now is the **m** who did not make H1505
Ps 55:13 But it is you, a **m** like myself, my H632
Ps 56:11 am not afraid. What can **m** do to me? H132
Ps 80:17 your hand rest on the **m** *at* your right hand, H408
Ps 80:17 the son of **m** you have raised up for H132
Ps 89:19 raised up a **young m** from among the H1033
Ps 90: T A prayer of Moses the **m** *of* God. H408
Ps 105:17 he sent a **m** before them—Joseph H408
Ps 109: 4 they accuse me, but I am a **m** of prayer. NDT
Ps 127: 5 Blessed is the **m** whose quiver is full of H1505
Ps 128: 4 the blessing for the **m** who fears the LORD. H1505
Ps 141: 5 Let a **righteous m** strike me—that is a AIT
Pr 3: 4 a good name in the sight of God and **m**. H132
Pr 6:11 like a thief and scarcity like an armed **m**. H408
Pr 6:27 Can a **m** scoop fire into his lap without his H408
Pr 6:28 *Can a* **m** walk on hot coals without his feet H408
Pr 6:32 But *a m who* **commits adultery** has no sense AIT
Pr 15:20 but a foolish **m** despises his mother. H132
Pr 22:14 *a m who is* **under** the LORD's **wrath** falls into AIT
Pr 23:24 a *m who* **fathers** a wise **son** rejoices in H3528
Pr 24:34 like a thief and scarcity like an armed **m**. H408
Pr 29: 3 A **m** who loves wisdom brings joy to his H408
Pr 29:25 Fear of **m** will prove to be a snare, but H132
Pr 30: 2 only a brute, not a **m**; I do not have human H408
Pr 30:19 the way of a **m** with a young woman. H1505
Ecc 4: 8 There was a **m** all alone; he had neither H285S
Ecc 6: 3 A **m** may have a hundred children and live H408
Ecc 6: 5 it has more rest than does **that** *m*— AIT
Ecc 7:26 The *m who* **pleases** God will escape her, but AIT
Ecc 7:28 I found one upright **m** among a thousand H132
Ecc 8: 9 is a time when a **m** lords it over others H132
Ecc 9:15 there lived in that city a **m** poor but wise, H408
Ecc 9:15 But nobody remembered that poor **m**. H408
Isa 1:31 The **mighty** *m* will become tinder and his AIT
Isa 2:17 The arrogance of **m** will be brought low H132
Isa 3: 3 captain of fifty and the **m of rank**, H5951+7156
Isa 3: 5 oppress each other—**m** against man H408
Isa 3: 5 man against **m**, neighbor against H408
Isa 3: 6 A **m** will seize one of his brothers in his H408
Isa 4: 1 women will take hold of one **m** and say, H408
Isa 6: 5 For I am a **m** *of* unclean lips, and I live H408
Isa 14:16 "Is this the **m** who shook the earth and H408
Isa 14:17 *the m who* **made** the world a wilderness AIT
Isa 16: 5 in faithfulness *a m will* **sit** on it—one from AIT
Isa 21: 9 here comes a **m** in a chariot *with* a team of H408
Isa 22:17 of you and hurl you away, you **mighty m**. H1505
Isa 38:11 no longer will I look on my **fellow m**, or be H132
Isa 46:11 a far-off land, a **m** *to fulfill* my purpose. H408
Isa 51: 2 When I called him he was *only* **one** *m*, and I AIT
Isa 53: 3 rejected by mankind, a **m** *of* suffering, and H408
Isa 62: 5 As a **young m** marries a young woman, so H1033
Isa 65:20 an **old** *m* who does not live out his years AIT
Jer 3: 1 "If a **m** divorces his wife and she leaves H408
Jer 3: 1 she leaves him and marries another **m**, H408
Jer 7:20 out on this place—on **m** and beast, on the H132
Jer 14: 9 Why are you like a **m** taken by surprise, like H408
Jer 15:10 a **m** with whom the whole land strives and H408
Jer 15:12 "*Can a m* **break** iron—iron from the north AIT
Jer 17: 5 "Cursed is the one who trusts in **m**, who H132
Jer 20:15 Cursed be the **m** who brought my father the H408
Jer 20:16 May that **m** be like the towns the LORD H408
Jer 21: 6 in this city—both **m** and beast—and they H132
Jer 22: 7 against you, *each* **m** with his weapons, and H408
Jer 22:28 Is this **m** Jehoiachin a despised, broken pot H408
Jer 22:30 "Record this **m** as if childless, a man who H408
Jer 22:30 a **m** who will not prosper in his lifetime H1505
Jer 23: 9 I am like a drunken **m**, like a strong man H408
Jer 23: 9 like a **strong m** overcome by wine H1505
Jer 26:11 "This **m** should be sentenced to death H408
Jer 26:16 "This **m** should not be sentenced to death! H408
Jer 26:20 Jearim was another **m** who prophesied in H408
Jer 30: 6 Ask and see: Can a **m** bear children H2351
Jer 30: 6 do I see every **strong m** with his hands on H1505
Jer 31:22 the woman will return to the **m**. H1505
Jer 33:17 never fail to have a **m** to sit on the throne H408
Jer 33:18 ever fail to have a **m** to stand before me H408
Jer 35: 4 of Hanan son of Igdaliah the **m** *of* God. H408
Jer 36:29 land and wipe from it both **m** and beast?" H132
Jer 38: 4 the king, "This **m** should be put to death. H408
Jer 38: 4 This **m** is not seeking the good of these H408
Jer 48:19 Ask the *m* **fleeing** and the woman escaping AIT
Jer 51:22 with you I shatter **m** and woman, with you I H408
Jer 51:22 with you I shatter **old** *m* and youth, with you AIT
Jer 51:22 you I shatter **young m** and young woman, H1033
La 3: 1 I am the **m** who has seen affliction by the H1505
La 3:27 It is good for a **m** to bear the yoke while H1505
Eze 1:26 on the throne was a figure like that of a **m**. H132
Eze 2: 1 said to me, "Son of **m**, stand up on your H132
Eze 2: 3 "Son of **m**, I am sending you to the H132
Eze 2: 6 And you, son of **m**, do not be afraid of them H132
Eze 2: 8 son of **m**, listen to what I say to you H132
Eze 3: 1 said to me, "Son of **m**, eat what is before H132
Eze 3: 3 said to me, "Son of **m**, eat this scroll I am H132
Eze 3: 4 "Son of **m**, go now to the people of Israel H132
Eze 3:10 said to me, "Son of **m**, listen carefully and H132
Eze 3:17 "Son of **m**, I have made you a watchman H132
Eze 3:25 And you, son of **m**, they will tie with ropes H132
Eze 4: 1 son of **m**, take a block of clay, put it H132
Eze 4:16 "Son of **m**, I am about to cut off the food H132
Eze 5: 1 son of **m**, take a sharp sword and H132
Eze 6: 2 "Son of **m**, set your face against the H132
Eze 7: 2 "Son of **m**, this is what the Sovereign LORD H132
Eze 8: 2 I saw a figure like that of a **m**. H408
Eze 8: 5 said to me, "Son of **m**, look toward the H132
Eze 8: 6 said to me, "Son of **m**, do you see what H132
Eze 8: 8 He said to me, "Son of **m**, now dig into the H132
Eze 8:12 said to me, "Son of **m**, have you seen what H132
Eze 8:15 you see this, son of **m**? You will see things H132
Eze 8:17 said to me, "Have you seen this, son of **m**? H132
Eze 9: 2 With them was a **m** clothed in linen who H408
Eze 9: 3 LORD called to the **m** clothed in linen who H408
Eze 9:11 Then the **m** in linen with the writing kit at H408
Eze 10: 2 The LORD said to the **m** clothed in linen, H408
Eze 10: 3 side of the temple when the **m** went in, H408
Eze 10: 6 When the LORD commanded the **m** in linen H408
Eze 10: 6 the **m** went in and stood beside a wheel. NDT
Eze 10: 7 put it into the hands of the **m** in linen, NDT
Eze 11: 2 said to me, "Son of **m**, these are the men H132
Eze 11: 4 against them; prophesy, son of **m**. H132
Eze 11:15 "Son of **m**, the people of Jerusalem have H132
Eze 12: 2 "Son of **m**, you are living among a H132
Eze 12: 3 "Therefore, son of **m**, pack your belongings H132
Eze 12: 9 "Son of **m**, did not the Israelites, that H132
Eze 12:18 "Son of **m**, tremble as you eat your food H132
Eze 12:22 "Son of **m**, what is this proverb you have in H132
Eze 12:27 "Son of **m**, the Israelites are saying, 'The H132
Eze 13: 2 "Son of **m**, prophesy against the prophets of H132
Eze 13:17 son of **m**, set your face against the H132
Eze 14: 3 "Son of **m**, these men have set up idols in H132
Eze 14:13 "Son of **m**, if a country sins against me by H132
Eze 15: 2 "Son of **m**, how is the wood of a vine H132
Eze 16: 2 "Son of **m**, confront Jerusalem with her H132
Eze 17: 2 "Son of **m**, set forth an allegory and tell it H132
Eze 18: 5 there is a righteous **m** who does what is H408
Eze 18: 9 **That** *m* is righteous; he will surely live AIT
Eze 18:13 *Will such a m* **live**? He will not! AIT
Eze 20: 3 "Son of **m**, speak to the elders of Israel H132
Eze 20: 4 judge them, son of **m**? Then confront them H132
Eze 20:27 "Therefore, son of **m**, speak to the people H132
Eze 20:46 "Son of **m**, set your face toward the south H132
Eze 21: 2 "Son of **m**, set your face against Jerusalem H132
Eze 21: 6 son of **m**! Groan before them with H132
Eze 21: 9 "Son of **m**, prophesy and say, 'This is what H132
Eze 21:12 out and wail, son of **m**, for it is against my H132
Eze 21:14 "So then, son of **m**, prophesy and strike H132
Eze 21:19 "Son of **m**, mark out two roads for the sword H132
Eze 21:28 "And you, son of **m**, prophesy and say H132
Eze 22: 2 "Son of **m**, will you judge her? Will you H132
Eze 22:11 In you *one* **m** commits a detestable offense H408
Eze 22:18 "Son of **m**, the people of Israel have H132
Eze 22:24 "Son of **m**, say to the land, 'You are a land H132
Eze 23: 2 "Son of **m**, there were two women H132
Eze 23:36 "Son of **m**, will you judge Oholah and H132
Eze 24: 2 "Son of **m**, record this date, this very date H132
Eze 24:16 "Son of **m**, with one blow I am about to H132
Eze 24:25 "And you, son of **m**, on the day I take away H132
Eze 25: 2 "Son of **m**, set your face against the H132
Eze 25:13 against Edom and kill both **m** and beast. H132
Eze 26: 2 "Son of **m**, because Tyre has said of H132
Eze 27: 2 "Son of **m**, take up a lament concerning H132
Eze 28: 2 "Son of **m**, say to the ruler of Tyre, 'This is H132
Eze 28:12 "Son of **m**, take up a lament concerning the H132
Eze 28:21 "Son of **m**, set your face against Sidon H132
Eze 29: 2 "Son of **m**, set your face against Pharaoh H132
Eze 29: 8 against you and kill both **m** and beast. H132
Eze 29:11 The foot of neither **m** nor beast will pass H132
Eze 29:18 "Son of **m**, Nebuchadnezzar king of H132
Eze 30: 2 "Son of **m**, prophesy and say: 'This is what H132
Eze 30:21 "Son of **m**, I have broken the arm of H132
Eze 30:24 before him like a **mortally wounded m**. H2728
Eze 31: 2 "Son of **m**, say to Pharaoh king of Egypt H132
Eze 32: 2 "Son of **m**, take up a lament concerning H132
Eze 32:13 stirred by the foot of **m** or muddied by the H132
Eze 32:18 "Son of **m**, wail for the hordes of Egypt and H132
Eze 33: 2 "Son of **m**, speak to your people and say to H132
Eze 33: 7 "Son of **m**, I have made you a watchman H132
Eze 33:10 "Son of **m**, say to the Israelites, 'This is H132
Eze 33:12 "Therefore, son of **m**, say to your people, 'If H132
Eze 33:21 a **m who** *had* **escaped** from Jerusalem H7127
Eze 33:22 Now the evening before the **m** arrived H7127S
Eze 33:22 my mouth before the **m** came to me in the NDT
Eze 33:24 "Son of **m**, the people living in those ruins H132
Eze 33:24 'Abraham was only **one** *m*, yet he possessed AIT
Eze 33:30 "As for you, son of **m**, your people are H132
Eze 34: 2 "Son of **m**, prophesy against the shepherds H132
Eze 35: 2 "Son of **m**, set your face against Mount Seir H132
Eze 36: 1 "Son of **m**, prophesy to the mountains of H132
Eze 36:17 "Son of **m**, when the people of Israel were H132
Eze 37: 3 He asked me, "Son of **m**, can these bones H132
Eze 37: 9 prophesy, son of **m**, and say to it, 'This is H132
Eze 37:11 "Son of **m**, these bones are the people of H132
Eze 37:16 "Son of **m**, take a stick of wood and write H132
Eze 38: 2 "Son of **m**, set your face against Gog, of the H132
Eze 38:14 "Therefore, son of **m**, prophesy and say to H132
Eze 39: 1 "Son of **m**, prophesy against Gog and say H132
Eze 39:17 "Son of **m**, this is what the Sovereign LORD H132
Eze 40: 3 I saw a **m** whose appearance was like H408
Eze 40: 4 The **m** said to me, "Son of man, look H408
Eze 40: 4 said to me, "Son of **m**, look carefully and H132
Eze 41: 1 Then the **m** brought me to the main hall NDT
Eze 41:22 The **m** said to me, "This is the table that is NDT
Eze 42: 1 Then the **m** led me northward into the outer NDT
Eze 43: 1 Then the **m** brought me to the gate facing NDT
Eze 43: 6 While the **m** was standing beside me, H408
Eze 43: 7 "Son of **m**, this is the place of my throne H132
Eze 43:10 "Son of **m**, describe the temple to the H132
Eze 43:18 he said to me, "Son of **m**, this is what the H132
Eze 44: 1 Then the **m** brought me back to the outer NDT
Eze 44: 4 Then the **m** brought me by way of the north NDT
Eze 44: 5 LORD said to me, "Son of **m**, look carefully, H132
Eze 46:19 Then the **m** brought me through the NDT
Eze 47: 1 The **m** brought me back to the entrance to NDT
Eze 47: 3 As the **m** went eastward with a measuring H408
Eze 47: 6 He asked me, "Son of **m**, do you see this?" H132
Da 2:25 "I have found a **m** among the exiles A10131
Da 2:27 Daniel replied, "No **wise** *m*, enchanter AIT
Da 4:16 from that of a **m** and let him be given A10050
Da 5:11 There is a **m** in your kingdom who has A10131
Da 6: 5 charges against **this** *m* Daniel unless it AIT
Da 7:13 before me was one like a son of **m**, A10050
Da 8:15 me stood one who looked like a **m**. H1505
Da 8:16 tell **this** *m* the meaning of the vision. AIT
Da 8:17 "Son of **m**," he said to me, "understand H132
Da 9:21 the **m** I had seen in the earlier vision H408
Da 10: 5 there before me was a **m** dressed in linen, H408
Da 10:16 looked like a **m** touched my lips, H1201+132
Da 10:18 who looked like a **m** touched me and gave H132
Da 12: 6 One of them said to the **m** clothed in linen H408
Da 12: 7 The **m** clothed in linen, who was above the H408
Hos 3: 1 she is loved by **another** *m* and is an AIT
Hos 3: 3 be a prostitute or be intimate with any **m**, H408
Hos 11: 9 am God, and not a **m**—the Holy One H408
Hos 12: 3 as a **m** he struggled with God. H226
Am 5:19 will be as though a **m** fled from a lion only H408
Jnh 1:14 us accountable for killing an **innocent** *m*, AIT
Mic 5: 7 not wait for anyone or depend on **m**. H1201+132
Zep 1: 3 "I will sweep away both **m** and beast; I will H132
Zec 1: 8 before me was a **m** mounted on a red H408
Zec 1:10 Then the **m** standing among the myrtle H408
Zec 2: 1 before me was a **m** with a measuring line H408
Zec 2: 4 tell that **young m**, 'Jerusalem will H5853
Zec 3: 2 Is not **this** *m* a burning stick snatched from AIT

Zec 6:12 'Here is the m whose name is the Branch H408
Zec 13: 7 against the m who is close to me! H1505
Mal 2:12 As for the m who does this, whoever he H408
Mal 2:16 "The m who hates and divorces his wife," AIT
Mt 4: 4 'M shall not live on bread alone, but on G476
Mt 7:24 is like a wise m who built his house on G467
Mt 7:26 is like a foolish m who built his house on G467
Mt 8: 2 A m with leprosy came and knelt before G3320
Mt 8: 3 reached out his hand and touched the m. G899S
Mt 8: 9 For I myself am a m under authority, with G476
Mt 8:20 the Son of M has no place to lay his G476
Mt 8:27 amazed and asked, "What kind of m is this? AIT
Mt 9: 2 Some men brought to him a paralyzed m AIT
Mt 9: 2 their faith, he said to the m, "Take heart, G4166S
Mt 9: 6 to know that the Son of M has authority on G476
Mt 9: 6 So he said to the paralyzed m, "Get up, take AIT
Mt 9: 7 Then the m got up and went home. NDT
Mt 9: 8 who had given such authority to m. G476
Mt 9: 9 he saw a m named Matthew sitting at the G476
Mt 9:32 a m who was demon-possessed and could G476
Mt 9:33 driven out, the m who had been mute spoke. AIT
Mt 10:23 towns of Israel before the Son of M comes. G476
Mt 10:35 have come to turn " 'a m against his father, G476
Mt 11: 8 go out to see? A m dressed in fine clothes G476
Mt 11:19 The Son of M came eating and drinking G476
Mt 12: 8 For the Son of M is Lord of the Sabbath." G476
Mt 12:10 a m with a shriveled hand was there G476
Mt 12:13 Then he said to the m, "Stretch out your G476
Mt 12:22 brought him a demon-possessed m who was AIT
Mt 12:29 unless he first ties up the strong m? AIT
Mt 12:32 word against the Son of M will be forgiven, G476
Mt 12:35 A good m brings good things out of the G476
Mt 12:35 an evil m brings evil things out of the G476
Mt 12:40 so the Son of M will be three days and G476
Mt 13:24 heaven is like a m who sowed good seed G476
Mt 13:31 which a m took and planted in his field. G476
Mt 13:37 who sowed the good seed is the Son of M. G476
Mt 13:41 The Son of M will send out his angels, and G476
Mt 13:44 When a m found it, he hid it again, and G476
Mt 13:54 "Where did this m get this wisdom and these AIT
Mt 13:56 Where then did this m get all these things?" AIT
Mt 16:13 "Who do people say the Son of M is?" G476
Mt 16:27 For the Son of M is going to come in his G476
Mt 16:28 they see the Son of M coming in his G476
Mt 17: 9 the Son of M has been raised from G476
Mt 17:12 same way the Son of M is going to suffer G476
Mt 17:14 a m approached Jesus and knelt before G476
Mt 17:22 "The Son of M is going to be delivered into G476
Mt 18:12 If a m owns a hundred sheep, and one of G476
Mt 18:24 a m who owed him ten thousand bags of AIT
Mt 18:30 went off and had the m thrown into prison G899S
Mt 19: 3 "Is it lawful for a m to divorce his wife for G476
Mt 19: 5 'For this reason a m will leave his father G476
Mt 19: 7 Moses command that a m give his wife a NDT
Mt 19:16 Just then a m came up to Jesus and G1651
Mt 19:20 have kept," the young m said. "What do I G3734
Mt 19:22 When the young m heard this, he went G3734
Mt 19:26 them and said, "With m this is impossible G476
Mt 19:28 when the Son of M sits on his glorious G476
Mt 20:18 the Son of M will be delivered over to G476
Mt 20:28 just as the Son of M did not come to be G476
Mt 21:28 There was a m who had two sons G476
Mt 22:11 he noticed a m there who was not wearing G476
Mt 22:12 clothes, friend?' The m was speechless. G3836S
Mt 22:16 that you are a m of integrity and that you AIT
Mt 22:24 told us that if a m dies without having AIT
Mt 24:27 so will be the coming of the Son of M. G476
Mt 24:30 appear the sign of the Son of M in heaven. G476
Mt 24:30 they see the Son of M coming on the G476
Mt 24:37 so it will be at the coming of the Son of M. G476
Mt 24:39 it will be at the coming of the Son of M. G476
Mt 24:44 because the Son of M will come at an hour G476
Mt 25:14 it will be like a m going on a journey, who G476
Mt 25:16 The m who had received five bags of gold AIT
Mt 25:18 But the m who had received one bag went off, AIT
Mt 25:20 The m who had received five bags of gold AIT
Mt 25:22 "The m with two bags of gold also came AIT
Mt 25:24 "Then the m who had received one bag of AIT
Mt 25:24 'I knew that you are a hard m, harvesting G476
Mt 25:31 "When the Son of M comes in his glory G476
Mt 26: 2 the Son of M will be handed over to be G476
Mt 26:18 "Go into the city to a certain m and tell him AIT
Mt 26:24 The Son of M will go just as it is written G476
Mt 26:24 But woe to that m who betrays the Son of G476
Mt 26:24 woe to that man who betrays the Son of M! G476
Mt 26:45 the Son of M is delivered into the G476
Mt 26:48 "The one I kiss is the m; arrest him." G899S
Mt 26:64 will see the Son of M sitting at the right G476
Mt 26:72 with an oath: "I don't know the m!" G476
Mt 26:74 he swore to them, "I don't know the m!" G476
Mt 27:19 have anything to do with that innocent m, AIT
Mt 27:32 they met a m from Cyrene, named G476
Mt 27:57 there came a rich m from Arimathea G476
Mk 1:23 Just then a m in their synagogue who was G476
Mk 1:26 spirit shook the m violently and came G899S
Mk 1:40 A m with leprosy came to him and G3320
Mk 1:41 reached out his hand and touched the m. G899S
Mk 2: 3 bringing to him a paralyzed m, carried by AIT
Mk 2: 4 lowered the mat the m was lying on. G4166S
Mk 2: 5 their faith, he said to the paralyzed m, "Son, AIT
Mk 2: 9 to say to this paralyzed m, 'Your sins are AIT
Mk 2:10 to know that the Son of M has authority on G476
Mk 2:10 to forgive sins." So he said to the m, G4166S
Mk 2:27 "The Sabbath was made for m, not man G476
Mk 2:27 was made for man, not m for the Sabbath. G476
Mk 2:28 So the Son of M is Lord even of the Sabbath G476
Mk 3: 1 a m with a shriveled hand was there. G476
Mk 3: 3 Jesus said to the m with the shriveled hand G476
Mk 3: 5 said to the m, "Stretch out your G476
Mk 4:26 A m scatters seed on the ground. G476
Mk 5: 2 a m with an impure spirit came from the G476
Mk 5: 3 This m lived in the tombs, and no one could AIT
Mk 5: 8 "Come out of this m, you impure spirit!" G476
Mk 5:15 they saw the m who had been possessed by AIT
Mk 5:16 had happened to the demon-possessed m— AIT
Mk 5:18 the m who had been demon-possessed AIT
Mk 5:20 So the m went away and began to tell in the AIT
Mk 6: 2 "Where did this m get these things? AIT
Mk 6:20 knowing him to be a righteous and holy m. G467
Mk 6:27 The m went, beheaded John in AIT
Mk 7:32 to him a m who was deaf and could G3273
Mk 8:22 people brought a blind m and begged Jesus AIT
Mk 8:23 He took the blind m by the hand and led him AIT
Mk 8:31 them that the Son of M must suffer many G476
Mk 8:38 the Son of M will be ashamed of them G476
Mk 9: 9 seen until the Son of M had risen from the G476
Mk 9:12 that the Son of M must suffer much and G476
Mk 9:17 A m in the crowd answered, "Teacher, G1651
Mk 9:31 "The Son of M is going to be delivered into G476
Mk 10: 2 "Is it lawful for a m to divorce his wife?" G467
Mk 10: 4 "Moses permitted a m to write a certificate NDT
Mk 10: 7 'For this reason a m will leave his father G476
Mk 10:12 divorces her husband and marries another m, AIT
Mk 10:17 a m ran up to him and fell on his knees G1651
Mk 10:27 them and said, "With m this is impossible G476
Mk 10:33 "and the Son of M will be delivered over to G476
Mk 10:45 For even the Son of M did not come to be G476
Mk 10:46 a blind m, Bartimaeus (which AIT
Mk 10:49 So they called to the blind m, "Cheer up! On AIT
Mk 10:51 The blind m said, "Rabbi, I want AIT
Mk 12: 1 them in parables: "A m planted a vineyard G476
Mk 12: 4 they struck this m on the head and treated AIT
Mk 12:14 we know that you are a m of integrity. AIT
Mk 12:19 the m must marry the widow and raise up G81
Mk 12:32 teacher," the m replied. "You are G1208S
Mk 13:26 will see the Son of M coming in clouds G476
Mk 13:34 It's like a m going away: He leaves his G476
Mk 14:13 a m carrying a jar of water will meet G476
Mk 14:21 The Son of M will go just as it is written G476
Mk 14:21 But woe to that m who betrays the Son of G476
Mk 14:21 woe to that man who betrays the Son of M! G476
Mk 14:41 the Son of M is delivered into the hands of G476
Mk 14:44 "The one I kiss is the m; arrest him and G899S
Mk 14:51 A young m, wearing nothing but a linen G3734
Mk 14:62 will see the Son of M sitting at the right G476
Mk 14:71 "I don't know this m you're talking about." G476
Mk 15: 7 A m called Barabbas was in prison with G3836S
Mk 15:21 A certain m from Cyrene, Simon, the father AIT
Mk 15:39 he said, "Surely this m was the Son of God!" G476
Mk 16: 5 they saw a young m dressed in a white G3734
Lk 1:18 I am an old m and my wife is well along G4566
Lk 1:27 to be married to a m named Joseph, G467
Lk 2:25 Now there was a m in Jerusalem called G476
Lk 2:52 stature, and in favor with God and m. G476
Lk 4: 4 'M shall not live on bread alone G476
Lk 4:33 there was a m possessed by a demon, G476
Lk 4:35 the demon threw the m down before G899S
Lk 5: 8 "Go away from me, Lord; I am a sinful m!" G467
Lk 5:12 a m came along who was covered with G467
Lk 5:13 reached out his hand and touched the m. G899S
Lk 5:18 carrying a paralyzed m on a mat and tried G476
Lk 5:24 to know that the Son of M has authority on G476
Lk 5:24 So he said to the paralyzed m, "I tell you AIT
Lk 6: 5 "The Son of M is Lord of the Sabbath." G476
Lk 6: 6 a m was there whose right hand was G476
Lk 6: 8 thinking and said to the m with the G467
Lk 6:10 and then said to the m, "Stretch out G899S
Lk 6:22 name as evil, because of the Son of M. G476
Lk 6:45 A good m brings good things out of the G476
Lk 6:45 an evil m brings evil things out of the AIT
Lk 6:48 They are like a m building a house, who G476
Lk 6:49 practice is like a m who built a house on G476
Lk 7: 4 "This m deserves to have you do this AIT
Lk 7: 8 For I myself am a m under authority, with G476
Lk 7:14 He said, "Young m, I say to you, get G3734
Lk 7:15 The dead m sat up and began to talk, and AIT
Lk 7:25 go out to see? A m dressed in fine clothes G476
Lk 7:34 The Son of M came eating and drinking G476
Lk 7:39 said to himself, "If this m were a prophet, he AIT
Lk 8:27 by a demon-possessed m from the town. G467
Lk 8:27 a long time this m had not worn clothes AIT
Lk 8:29 the impure spirit to come out of the m. G476
Lk 8:33 When the demons came out of the m, they G476
Lk 8:35 they found the m from whom the demons G476
Lk 8:36 how the demon-possessed m had been AIT
Lk 8:38 The m from whom the demons had gone G467
Lk 8:39 So the m went away and told all over town AIT
Lk 8:41 Then a m named Jairus, a synagogue G467
Lk 9:22 "The Son of M must suffer many things G476
Lk 9:26 the Son of M will be ashamed of them G476
Lk 9:38 A m in the crowd called out, "Teacher, G467
Lk 9:44 The Son of M is going to be delivered into G476
Lk 9:57 along the road, a m said to him, "I will AIT
Lk 9:58 the Son of M has no place to lay his G476
Lk 9:59 He said to another m, "Follow me." But he AIT
Lk 10:30 "A m was going down from Jerusalem to G476
Lk 10:31 when he saw the m, he passed by on G899S
Lk 10:33 came where the m was; and when he G899S
Lk 10:34 Then he put the m on his own donkey G899S
Lk 10:36 to the m who fell into the hands of robbers?" AIT
Lk 11:14 the m who had been mute spoke, and AIT
Lk 11:21 "When a strong m, fully armed, guards his AIT
Lk 11:22 the armor in which the m trusted and G899S
Lk 11:30 so also will the Son of M be to this G476
Lk 12: 8 the Son of M will also acknowledge before G476
Lk 12:10 word against the Son of M will be forgiven, G476
Lk 12:14 Jesus replied, "M, who appointed me a G476
Lk 12:16 "The ground of a certain rich m yielded an G476
Lk 12:40 because the Son of M will come at an hour G476
Lk 13: 6 "A m had a fig tree growing in his vineyard AIT
Lk 13: 7 to the m who took care of the vineyard, G307
Lk 13: 8 the m replied, 'leave it alone for one AIT
Lk 13:19 which a m took and planted in his garden. G476
Lk 14: 2 in front of him was a m suffering from G476
Lk 14: 4 So taking hold of the m, he healed him NDT
Lk 14:16 "A certain m was preparing a great G476
Lk 15: 2 "This m welcomes sinners and eats with AIT
Lk 15:11 "There was a m who had two sons. G476
Lk 16: 1 "There was a rich m whose manager was G476
Lk 16:18 the m who marries a divorced woman AIT
Lk 16:19 "There was a rich m who was dressed in G476
Lk 16:22 The rich m also died and was buried. AIT
Lk 17:22 to see one of the days of the Son of M, G476
Lk 17:24 For the Son of M in his day will be like the G476
Lk 17:26 also will it be in the days of the Son of M. G476
Lk 17:30 this on the day the Son of M is revealed. G476
Lk 18: 8 when the Son of M comes, will he find G476
Lk 18:14 "I tell you that this m, rather than the other AIT
Lk 18:27 is impossible with m is possible with God." G476
Lk 18:31 about the Son of M will be fulfilled. G476
Lk 18:35 a blind m was sitting by the roadside AIT
Lk 18:40 ordered the m to be brought to G899S
Lk 19: 2 A m was there by the name of Zacchaeus G467
Lk 19: 9 has come to this house, because this m, too, AIT
Lk 19:10 For the Son of M came to seek and to save G476
Lk 19:12 "A m of noble birth went to a distant G476
Lk 19:14 'We don't want this m to be our king. AIT
Lk 19:21 afraid of you, because you are a hard m. G476
Lk 19:22 that I am a hard m, taking out what I G476
Lk 20: 9 "A m planted a vineyard, rented it to some G476
Lk 20:28 the m must marry the widow and raise up G81
Lk 21:27 will see the Son of M coming in a cloud G476
Lk 21:36 may be able to stand before the Son of M." G476
Lk 22:10 a m carrying a jar of water will meet you. G476
Lk 22:22 The Son of M will go as it has been G476
Lk 22:22 But woe to that m who betrays him! G476
Lk 22:47 and the m who was called Judas, one of AIT
Lk 22:48 are you betraying the Son of M with a kiss?" G476
Lk 22:56 at him and said, "This m was with him." AIT
Lk 22:58 also are one of them." "M, I am not!" G476
Lk 22:60 Peter replied, "M, I don't know what you're G476
Lk 22:69 the Son of M will be seated at the right G476
Lk 23: 2 "We have found this m subverting our nation. AIT
Lk 23: 4 "I find no basis for a charge against this m." G476
Lk 23: 6 Pilate asked if the m was a Galilean. G476
Lk 23:14 "You brought me this m as one who was G476
Lk 23:18 the whole crowd shouted, "Away with this m! AIT
Lk 23:22 What crime has this m committed? I have AIT
Lk 23:25 the m who had been thrown into prison AIT
Lk 23:41 But this m has done nothing wrong. AIT
Lk 23:47 said, "Surely this was a righteous m." G476
Lk 23:50 Now there was a m named Joseph, G467
Lk 23:50 of the Council, a good and upright m, G467
Lk 24: 7 'The Son of M must be delivered over to the G476
Jn 1: 6 There was a m sent from God whose name G476
Jn 1:30 'A m who comes after me has surpassed G467
Jn 1:33 'The m on whom you see the Spirit come G899S
Jn 1:51 descending on' the Son of M. G476
Jn 3: 1 a m named Nicodemus who was a G476
Jn 3:13 who came from heaven—the Son of M. G476
Jn 3:14 so the Son of M must be lifted up, G476
Jn 3:26 that m who was with you on the other side of AIT
Jn 4:18 and the m you now have is not your G4005S
Jn 4:29 see a m who told me everything I ever did. G476
Jn 4:42 we know that this m really is the Savior AIT
Jn 4:47 When this m heard that Jesus had arrived in AIT
Jn 4:50 The m took Jesus at his word and departed. G476
Jn 5: 9 At once the m was cured; he picked up his G476
Jn 5:10 leaders said to the m who had been healed, AIT
Jn 5:11 "The m who made me well said to me AIT
Jn 5:13 The m who was healed had no idea who it AIT
Jn 5:15 The m went away and told the Jewish G476
Jn 5:27 to judge because he is the Son of M. G476
Jn 6:27 which the Son of M will give you. G476
Jn 6:52 "How can this m give us his flesh to eat?" AIT
Jn 6:53 flesh of the Son of M and drink his blood, G476
Jn 6:62 if you see the Son of M ascend to where he G476
Jn 7:12 Some said, "He is a good m." Others replied, AIT
Jn 7:15 "How did this m get such learning without AIT
Jn 7:18 of the one who sent him is a m of truth; G4047S
Jn 7:25 "Isn't this the m they are trying to kill? G4005S
Jn 7:27 But we know where this m is from; when the AIT
Jn 7:31 will he perform more signs than this m?" AIT
Jn 7:35 "Where does this m intend to go that we AIT
Jn 7:40 people said, "Surely this m is the Prophet." AIT
Jn 7:46 "No one ever spoke the way this m does," G476

Jn 7:51 our law condemn a **m** without first hearing G476
Jn 8:28 "When you have lifted up the Son *of* **M** G476
Jn 8:40 a **m** who has told you the truth that I heard G476
Jn 9:1 went along, he saw a **m** blind from birth. G476
Jn 9:2 who sinned, **this** *m* or his parents, that he AIT
Jn 9:3 "Neither **this** *m* nor his parents sinned," AIT
Jn 9:7 So the **m** went and washed, and came NDT
Jn 9:8 "Isn't **this** *the same m* who used to sit and AIT
Jn 9:9 But he himself insisted, "I am the **m**." NDT
Jn 9:11 "The **m** they call Jesus made some mud G476
Jn 9:12 "Where is **this** *m*?" they asked him. "I don't AIT
Jn 9:13 to the Pharisees **the m** who had been G899S
Jn 9:15 mud on my eyes," **the m** replied, "and I G3836S
Jn 9:16 Pharisees said, "This **m** is not from God, for G476
Jn 9:17 Then they turned again *to* the **blind** *m* AIT
Jn 9:17 eyes he opened." **The** *m* replied, "He is a AIT
Jn 9:24 they summoned the **m** who had been blind G476
Jn 9:24 "We know this **m** is a sinner." G476
Jn 9:30 The **m** answered, "Now that is remarkable G476
Jn 9:32 heard of opening the eyes *of* a *m* born **blind**. AIT
Jn 9:33 If **this** *m* were not from God, he could do AIT
Jn 9:35 he said, "Do you believe in the Son *of* **M**?" G476
Jn 9:36 **the m** asked. "Tell me so that I may G1697S
Jn 9:38 Then **the** *m* said, "Lord, I believe," and he AIT
Jn 10:13 The **m** runs away because he is a hired hand NDT
Jn 10:21 the sayings *of* a *m* **possessed by a demon.** AIT
Jn 10:33 because you, a *mere* **m**, claim to be God." G476
Jn 10:41 all that John said about **this** *m* was true." AIT
Jn 11:1 Now a *m* named Lazarus was sick. He was AIT
Jn 11:37 the eyes *of* the **blind** *m* have kept this AIT
Jn 11:37 the blind man have kept **this** *m* from dying?" AIT
Jn 11:39 the sister *of* the **dead** *m*, "by this time AIT
Jn 11:44 The **dead** *m* came out, his hands and feet AIT
Jn 11:47 "Here is this **m** performing many signs. G476
Jn 11:50 you that one **m** die for the people than G476
Jn 12:23 has come for the Son *of* **M** to be glorified. G476
Jn 12:34 you say, 'The Son *of* **M** must be lifted up'? G476
Jn 12:34 Who is this 'Son *of* **M**'?" G476
Jn 13:31 "Now the Son *of* **M** is glorified and God is G476
Jn 18:14 be good if one **m** died for the people. G476
Jn 18:26 a relative *of the m* **whose** ear Peter had cut AIT
Jn 18:29 charges are you bringing against this **m**?" G476
Jn 19:5 Pilate said to them, "Here is the **m**!" G476
Jn 19:12 shouting, "If you let **this** *m* go, you are no AIT
Jn 19:21 that **this** *m* claimed to be king of the AIT
Jn 19:32 broke the legs *of* the **first** *m* who had been AIT
Jn 19:35 The *m who* **saw** it has given testimony, and AIT
Jn 19:39 the *m who* earlier *had* **visited** Jesus at night. AIT
Ac 2:22 of Nazareth was a **m** accredited by God to G467
Ac 2:23 **This** *m* was handed over to you by God's AIT
Ac 3:2 Now a **m** who was lame from birth was G467
Ac 3:5 So **the** *m* gave them his attention, expecting AIT
Ac 3:10 him as *the* **same** *m* who used to sit AIT
Ac 3:11 While the **m** held on to Peter and John G899S
Ac 3:12 godliness we had made **this m** walk? G899S
Ac 3:16 **this** *m* whom you see and know was made AIT
Ac 4:9 of kindness *shown to* a **m** who was lame G476
Ac 4:10 that **this** *m* stands before you healed. AIT
Ac 4:14 they could see the **m** who had been G476
Ac 4:22 For the **m** who was miraculously healed G476
Ac 5:1 Now a **m** named Ananias, together with G467
Ac 6:5 a **m** full of faith and of the Holy Spirit G467
Ac 6:8 Stephen, a **m** full of God's grace and power NDT
Ac 7:27 "But the *m who was* **mistreating** the other AIT
Ac 7:56 open and the Son *of* **M** standing at the G476
Ac 7:58 at the feet *of* a **young m** named Saul. G3733
Ac 8:9 Now for some time a **m** named Simon had G467
Ac 8:10 "**This** *m* is rightly called the Great Power of AIT
Ac 8:27 **This m** had gone to Jerusalem to G4005S
Ac 8:30 chariot and heard **the m** reading Isaiah G899S
Ac 9:11 ask for a *m* **from Tarsus** named Saul, AIT
Ac 9:12 he has seen a **m** named Ananias come G467
Ac 9:13 reports about this **m** and all the harm he G467
Ac 9:15 **This** *m* is my chosen instrument to proclaim AIT
Ac 9:21 he the *m who* **raised havoc** in Jerusalem AIT
Ac 9:33 There he found a **m** named Aeneas, who G476
Ac 10:1 Caesarea there was a **m** named Cornelius, G467
Ac 10:5 to bring back a *m* named Simon who is AIT
Ac 10:22 He is a righteous and God-fearing **m**, who G467
Ac 10:26 he said, "I am *only a* **m** myself." G476
Ac 10:30 Suddenly a **m** in shining clothes stood G467
Ac 11:24 He was a good **m**, full of the Holy Spirit G467
Ac 12:22 "This is the voice of a god, not *of* a **m**." G476
Ac 13:7 an intelligent **m**, sent for Barnabas and G467
Ac 13:22 David son of Jesse, a **m** after my own heart G467
Ac 14:8 In Lystra there sat a **m** who was lame. G467
Ac 14:10 the **m** jumped up and began to walk. NDT
Ac 16:9 Paul had a vision *of* a **m** of Macedonia G467
Ac 17:26 From **one** *m* he made all the nations, that AIT
Ac 17:31 with justice by the **m** he has appointed. G467
Ac 18:13 "This **m**," they charged, "is persuading the G476
Ac 18:24 He was a learned **m**, with a thorough G467
Ac 19:16 Then the **m** who had the evil spirit jumped G476
Ac 20:9 a window was a **young m** named G3733
Ac 20:10 himself on the **young m** and put his arms G899S
Ac 20:12 The people took the **young** *m* home alive AIT
Ac 21:16 He was a *m* **from Cyprus** and one of the early AIT
Ac 21:28 This is the **m** who teaches everyone G476
Ac 22:12 "A **m** named Ananias came to see me. G467
Ac 22:26 he asked. "This **m** is a Roman citizen." G476
Ac 23:9 "We find nothing wrong with this **m**," G476
Ac 23:17 "Take this **young m** to the commander G3733
Ac 23:18 me to bring this **young m** to you because G3734
Ac 23:19 took the **young m** by the hand, G899S
Ac 23:22 dismissed the **young m** with this warning: G3734
Ac 23:27 This **m** was seized by the Jews and they G467
Ac 23:30 of a plot to be carried out against the **m**, G467
Ac 24:5 "We have found this **m** to be a G467
Ac 24:16 my conscience clear before God and **m**. G476
Ac 25:5 and if the **m** has done anything wrong G467
Ac 25:14 "There is a **m** here whom Felix left as a G467
Ac 25:17 day and ordered the **m** to be brought in. G467
Ac 25:19 about a **dead** *m* named Jesus who AIT
Ac 25:22 "I would like to hear this **m** myself. G476
Ac 25:24 all who are present with us, you see this **m**! G467
Ac 26:31 "This **m** is not doing anything that deserves G467
Ac 26:32 "This **m** could have been set free if he had G476
Ac 28:4 to each other, "This **m** must be a murderer G476
Ro 5:12 as sin entered the world through one **m**, G476
Ro 5:15 the many died by the trespass *of* the **one** *m*, AIT
Ro 5:15 gift that came by the grace of the one **m**, G476
Ro 5:17 by the trespass *of* the **one** *m*, death reigned AIT
Ro 5:17 death reigned through that **one** *m*, how AIT
Ro 5:17 reign in life through the **one** *m*, AIT
Ro 5:19 of the one **m** the many were made G476
Ro 5:19 the obedience *of* the **one** *m* the many will be AIT
Ro 7:3 with another **m** while her husband is G467
Ro 7:3 not an adulteress if she marries another **m**. G467
Ro 7:24 What a wretched **m** I am! Who will rescue G476
1Co 5:1 **A** *m* is sleeping with his father's wife. AIT
1Co 5:2 of your fellowship **the** *m* who has been doing AIT
1Co 5:5 hand **this** *m* over to Satan for the destruction AIT
1Co 7:1 "It is good *for* a **m** not to have sexual G476
1Co 7:2 **each** *m* should have sexual relations with his AIT
1Co 7:18 Was a *m* already circumcised when he was AIT
1Co 7:18 Was a *m* uncircumcised when he was called AIT
1Co 7:26 that it is good *for* a **m** to remain as he is. G476
1Co 7:32 An **unmarried** *m* is concerned about the AIT
1Co 7:33 But a **married** *m* is concerned about the AIT
1Co 7:37 But *the m* **who** has settled the matter in his AIT
1Co 7:37 the virgin—this **m** also does the right thing. NDT
1Co 11:3 to realize that the head *of* every **m** is Christ, G467
1Co 11:3 the head of the woman is **m**, and the G467
1Co 11:4 Every **m** who prays or prophesies with his G467
1Co 11:7 A **m** ought not to cover his head, since he G467
1Co 11:7 glory of God; but woman is the glory *of* **m**. G467
1Co 11:8 For **m** did not come from woman, but G467
1Co 11:8 not come from woman, but woman from **m**; G467
1Co 11:9 neither was **m** created for woman, but G467
1Co 11:9 man created for woman, but woman for **m**. G467
1Co 11:11 the Lord woman is not independent of **m**, G467
1Co 11:11 nor is **m** independent of woman. G467
1Co 11:12 For as woman came from **m**, so also man is G467
1Co 11:12 from man, so also **m** is born of woman. G467
1Co 11:14 things teach you that if a **m** has long hair, G467
1Co 13:11 When I became a **m**, I put the ways of G467
1Co 15:21 For since death came through a **m**, the G476
1Co 15:21 of the dead comes also through a **m**. G476
1Co 15:45 "The first **m** Adam became a living being"; G476
1Co 15:47 The first **m** was of the dust of the earth; the G476
1Co 15:47 of the earth; the second **m** is of heaven. G476
1Co 15:48 As was the **earthly** *m*, so are those who are AIT
1Co 15:48 as is the **heavenly** *m*, so also are those AIT
1Co 15:49 we have borne the image *of* the **earthly** *m*, AIT
1Co 15:49 shall we bear the image *of* the **heavenly** *m*. AIT
2Co 8:21 eyes of the Lord but also in the eyes of **m**. G476
2Co 12:2 I know a **m** in Christ who fourteen years ago G476
2Co 12:3 And I know that this **m**—whether in the G476
2Co 12:5 I will boast about a *m* **like that**, but I will not AIT
Gal 1:1 sent not from men nor by a **m**, but by Jesus G476
Gal 1:12 I did not receive it from any **m**, nor was I G476
Gal 1:23 "**The** *m* who formerly persecuted us is now AIT
Gal 3:9 blessed along with Abraham, the *m of* **faith**. AIT
Gal 5:3 I declare to every **m** who lets himself be G476
Gal 6:7 A **m** reaps what he sows. G476
Eph 5:31 "For this reason a **m** will leave his father G476
Php 2:8 And being found in appearance as a **m**, he G476
2Th 2:3 occurs and the **m** of lawlessness is G476
2Th 2:3 is revealed, the **m** doomed to destruction. G5626
1Ti 1:13 a persecutor and a **violent** *m*, AIT
1Ti 2:5 God and mankind, the **m** Christ Jesus, G476
1Ti 2:12 to teach or to assume authority over a **m**; G467
1Ti 5:1 Do not rebuke an **older** *m* harshly, but exhort AIT
1Ti 6:11 But you, **m** of God, flee from all this, and G476
Titus 1:6 *a m* **whose** children believe and are not AIT
Phm 9 an **old m** and now also a prisoner of Christ G4566
Phm 16 both as a **fellow m** and as a brother in the G4922
Heb 2:6 of them, a son *of* **m** that you care for him? G476
Heb 7:6 **This** *m*, however, did not trace his descent AIT
Heb 11:12 And so from this **one** *m*, and he as good as AIT
Jas 2:2 Suppose a **m** comes into your meeting G467
Jas 2:2 a **poor** *m* in filthy old clothes also comes AIT
Jas 2:3 attention to the *m* **wearing** fine clothes and AIT
Jas 2:3 you," but say *to* the **poor** *m*, "You stand AIT
2Pe 2:7 he rescued Lot, a **righteous** *m*, who was AIT
2Pe 2:8 that **righteous** *m*, living among them day AIT
Rev 1:13 lampstands was someone like a son *of* **m**, G476
Rev 4:7 the third had a face like a **m**, the fourth G476
Rev 13:18 of the beast, for it is the number *of* a **m**. G476
Rev 14:14 was one like a son *of* **m** with a crown of G476

MAN'S (56) [MAN]

Ge 2:21 he took one of **the m** ribs and then H2257S
Ge 20:7 Now return the **m** wife, for he is a prophet H408
Ge 42:25 to put each **m** silver back in his sack H2157S
Ge 42:35 there in each **m** sack was his pouch of H2257S
Ge 44:1 put *each* **m** silver in the mouth of his H408
Ge 44:26 We cannot see the **m** face unless our H408
Lev 20:10 commits adultery with another **m** wife— H408
Nu 5:12 'If a **m** wife goes astray and is unfaithful to H408
Nu 7:5 to the Levites as *each* **m** work requires." H408
Dt 22:22 is found sleeping with another **m** wife, H1251
Dt 22:24 man because he violated **another** *m* wife. AIT
Dt 25:10 **That m line** shall be known in Israel as H2257S
Jdg 18:19 as priest rather than just one **m** household?" H408
Ru 1:2 The **m** name was Elimelek, his wife's name H408
Ru 4:5 the Moabite, the **dead** *m* widow, in order to AIT
2Sa 10:4 shaved off half of *each* **m** beard, cut off H4392S
1Ki 18:44 cloud as small as a **m** hand is rising from H408
2Ki 13:21 so they threw the **m body** into Elisha's H408
Job 31:10 then may my wife grind **another** *m* grain, and AIT
Pr 5:20 be intoxicated with **another** *m wife*? AIT
Pr 6:26 but *another* **m** wife preys on your very life. H408
Pr 6:29 So is he who sleeps with **another** *m* wife; AIT
Pr 30:1 This **m** utterance to Ithiel: "I H1505
Ecc 2:8 the delights of a **m** heart. H1201+2021+132
Ecc 9:16 But the **poor** *m* wisdom is despised, and his AIT
Jer 5:8 stallions, each neighing for **another** *m* wife. AIT
Eze 38:21 *Every* **m** sword will be against his brother. H408
Eze 40:5 measuring rod in the **m** hand was six long H408
Da 8:16 And I heard a **m** voice from the Ulai calling H132
Jnh 1:14 do not let us die for taking this **m** life. H408
Mic 7:6 a **m** enemies are the members of his own H408
Mt 10:36 a **m** enemies will be the members of his G476
Mt 12:29 can anyone enter a **strong** *m* house and carry AIT
Mt 27:24 "I am innocent of **this** *m* blood," he said. "It AIT
Mk 3:27 no one can enter a **strong** *m* house without AIT
Mk 3:27 Then he can plunder the **strong m** house. G899S
Mk 7:33 Jesus put his fingers into **the m** ears. G899S
Mk 7:33 Then he spit and touched **the m** tongue. G899S
Mk 7:35 **the m** ears were opened, his G899S
Mk 8:23 he had spit on **the m** eyes and put his G899S
Mk 8:25 more Jesus put his hands on **the m** eyes. G899S
Mk 10:22 At this **the m** face fell. He went away G3836S
Mk 12:19 wrote for us that if a **m** brother dies and G5516S
Lk 16:21 to eat what fell from the **rich** *m* table. AIT
Lk 20:28 wrote for us that if **a** *m* brother dies and AIT
Lk 22:51 And he touched the **m** ear and healed him. NDT
Jn 7:23 with me for healing a **m** whole body on the G476
Jn 9:6 with the saliva, and put it on **the m** eyes. G899S
Jn 9:14 the mud and opened **the m** eyes was a G899S
Jn 9:18 his sight until they sent for the **m** parents. G329
Jn 18:17 "You aren't one of this **m** disciples too, are G476
Ac 3:7 instantly **the m** feet and ankles G899S
Ac 5:28 to make us guilty of this **m** blood. G476
Ac 11:12 with me, and we entered the **m** house. G467
Ac 13:23 "From **this** *m* descendants God has brought AIT
Ro 5:16 be compared with the result *of* **one** *m* sin: AIT

MAN-EATER (2) [EAT, MAN]

Eze 19:3 to tear the prey and *he became* a **m**. H430+132
Eze 19:6 to tear the prey and *he became* a **m**. H430+132

MAN-MADE (1) [MAN, MAKE]

Dt 4:28 will worship **m** gods of wood H5126+3338+132

MANAEN (1)

Ac 13:1 Lucius of Cyrene, **M** (who had been G3441

MANAGE (5) [MANAGED, MANAGES, MANAGEMENT, MANAGER]

Jer 12:5 how *will you* **m** in the thickets by the H6913
1Ti 3:4 *He must* **m** his own family well and see G4613
1Ti 3:5 does not know how *to* **m** his own family, G4613
1Ti 3:12 to his wife and *must* **m** his children and G4613
1Ti 5:14 *to* **m** *their* **homes** and to give the enemy G3866

MANAGED (3) [MANAGE]

Jos 10:20 a few survivors *m to* **reach** their fortified AIT
1Ki 12:18 **m** to get into his chariot and escape to H599
2Ch 10:18 **m** to get into his chariot and escape to H599

MANAGEMENT (1) [MANAGE]

Lk 16:2 Give an account *of* your **m**, because you G3873

MANAGER (7) [MANAGE]

Lk 8:3 the **m** of Herod's **household**; Susanna; G2208
Lk 12:42 "Who then is the faithful and wise **m** G3874
Lk 16:1 was a rich man whose **m** was accused of G3874
Lk 16:2 because you cannot *be* **m** any longer. G3872
Lk 16:3 "The **m** said to himself, 'What shall I do G3874
Lk 16:6 "**The m** told him, 'Take your bill, sit G3836S
Lk 16:8 the dishonest **m** because he had acted G3874

MANAGES (1) [MANAGE]

Titus 1:7 Since an overseer **m** God's **household**, he G3874

MANAHATH (3) [MANAHATHITES]

Ge 36:23 Alvan, **M**, Ebal, Shepho and H4969
1Ch 1:40 Alvan, **M**, Ebal, Shepho and H4969
1Ch 8:6 living in Geba and were deported to **M**: H4970

MANAHATHITES (2) [MANAHATH]

1Ch 2:52 Kiriath Jearim were: Haroeh, half the **M**, H4971
1Ch 2:54 Atroth Beth Joab, half the **M**, the Zorites, H4971

MANASSEH (144) [MANASSEH'S, MANASSITES]

Ge 41:51 Joseph named his firstborn **M** and said, "It H4985
Ge 46:20 **M** and Ephraim were born to Joseph by H4985
Ge 48: 1 took his two sons **M** and Ephraim along H4985
Ge 48: 5 Ephraim and **M** will be mine, just H4985
Ge 48:13 Israel's left hand and **M** on his left toward H4985
Ge 48:14 even though **M** was the firstborn. H4985
Ge 48:20 'May God make you like Ephraim and **M**.' H4985
Ge 48:20 So he put Ephraim ahead of **M**. H4985
Ge 50:23 of Makir son of **M** were placed at birth on H4985
Nu 1:10 of Ammihud; from **M**, Gamaliel son of H4985
Nu 1:34 From the descendants of **M**: All the men H4985
Nu 1:35 number from the tribe of **M** was 32,200. H4985
Nu 2:20 The tribe of **M** will be next to them. H4985
Nu 2:20 of the people of **M** is Gamaliel son of H4985
Nu 7:54 the leader of the people of **M**, brought his H4985
Nu 10:23 over the division of the tribe of **M**, H1201+4985
Nu 13:11 from the tribe of **M** (a tribe of Joseph), H4985
Nu 26:28 their clans through **M** and Ephraim were: H4985
Nu 26:29 The descendants of **M**: through Makir, the H4985
Nu 26:34 These were the clans of **M**; those H4985
Nu 27: 1 of Makir, the son of **M**, belonged to the H4985
Nu 27: 1 belonged to the clans of **M** son of Joseph. H4985
Nu 32:33 the half-tribe of **M** son of Joseph the H4985
Nu 32:39 of Makir son of **M** went to Gilead, H4985
Nu 32:40 the descendants of **M**, and they settled H4985
Nu 32:41 a descendant of **M**, captured their H4985
Nu 34:14 the half-tribe of **M** have received their H4985
Nu 34:23 from the tribe of **M** son of Joseph; H1201+4985
Nu 36: 1 of Makir, the son of **M**, who were from the H4985
Nu 36:12 of the descendants of **M** son of Joseph, H4985
Dt 3:13 I gave to the half-tribe of **M**. H4985
Dt 3:14 a descendant of **M**, took the whole H4985
Dt 29: 8 the Gadites and the half-tribe of **M**. H4986
Dt 33:17 of Ephraim; such are the thousands of **M**." H4985
Dt 34: 2 the territory of Ephraim and **M**, all the H4985
Jos 1:12 the Gadites and the half-tribe of **M** H4985
Jos 4:12 Gad and the half-tribe of **M** crossed over H4985
Jos 12: 6 the half-tribe of **M** to be their H4985
Jos 13: 7 the nine tribes and half of the tribe of **M**." H4985
Jos 13: 8 **The other half of M**, the Reubenites and H2257S
Jos 13:29 Moses had given to the half-tribe of **M**, H4985
Jos 13:29 to half the family of the descendants of **M**, H4985
Jos 13:31 the descendants of Makir son of **M**— H4985
Jos 14: 4 had become two tribes—**M** and Ephraim. H4985
Jos 16: 4 So **M** and Ephraim, the descendants of H4985
Jos 17: 1 the tribe of **M** as Joseph's firstborn, H4985
Jos 17: 2 was for the rest of the people of **M**— H4985
Jos 17: 2 male descendants of **M** son of Joseph by H4985
Jos 17: 3 of Makir, the son of **M**, had no sons but H4985
Jos 17: 6 daughters of the **tribe of M** received an H4985
Jos 17: 6 to the rest of the descendants of **M**. H4985
Jos 17: 7 The territory of **M** extended from Asher to H4985
Jos 17: 8 (**M** had the land of Tappuah, but H4985
Jos 17: 8 on the boundary of **M**, belonged to the H4985
Jos 17: 9 to Ephraim lying among the towns of **M**, H4985
Jos 17: 9 the boundary of **M** was the northern H4985
Jos 17:10 belonged to Ephraim, on the north to **M**. H4985
Jos 17:10 The territory of **M** reached the H2257S
Jos 17:11 Asher, **M** also had Beth Shan H4985
Jos 17:17 to Ephraim and **M**—"You are numerous H4985
Jos 18: 7 the half-tribe of **M** have already received H4985
Jos 20: 8 Golan in Bashan in the tribe of **M**. H4985
Jos 21: 5 the tribes of Ephraim, Dan and half of **M**. H4985
Jos 21: 6 the half-tribe of **M** in Bashan. H4985
Jos 21:25 half the tribe of **M** they received Taanach H4985
Jos 21:27 from the half-tribe of **M**, Golan in Bashan H4985
Jos 22: 1 the Gadites and the half-tribe of **M** H4985
Jos 22: 7 To the half-tribe of **M** Moses had given H4985
Jos 22: 9 the half-tribe of **M** left the Israelites H4985
Jos 22:10 the half-tribe of **M** built an imposing H4985
Jos 22:13 to Reuben, Gad and the half-tribe of **M**. H4985
Jos 22:15 Gad and the half-tribe of **M**—they said to H4985
Jos 22:21 the half-tribe of **M** replied to the heads H4985
Jos 22:30 Reuben, Gad and **M** had to say H1201+4985
Jos 22:31 Gad and **M**, "Today we know H1201+4985
Jdg 1:27 But **M** did not drive out the people of Beth H4985
Jdg 6:15 My clan is the weakest in **M**, and I am the H4985
Jdg 6:35 He sent messengers throughout **M**, calling H4985
Jdg 7:23 Asher and all **M** were called out, and H4985
Jdg 11:29 He crossed Gilead and **M**, passed through H4985
Jdg 12: 4 are renegades from Ephraim and **M**." H4985
1Ki 4:13 of Jair son of **M** in Gilead were his, H4985
2Ki 10:33 Reuben and **M**), from Aroer by the H4986
2Ki 20:21 And **M** his son succeeded him as king H4985
2Ki 21: 1 **M** was twelve years old when he became H4985
2Ki 21: 9 **M** led them astray, so that they did more H4985
2Ki 21:11 "**M** king of Judah has committed these H4985
2Ki 21:16 **M** also shed so much innocent blood that H4985
2Ki 21:18 **M** rested with his ancestors and was H4985
2Ki 21:20 of the LORD, as his father **M** had done. H4985
2Ki 23:12 the altars **M** had built in the two H4985
2Ki 23:26 because of all that **M** had done to arouse H4985
2Ki 24: 3 of the sins of **M** and all he had done, H4985
1Ch 3:13 his son, Hezekiah his son, **M** his son, H4985
1Ch 5:18 the half-tribe of **M** had 44,760 men ready H4985
1Ch 5:23 of the half-tribe of **M** were numerous; H4985
1Ch 5:26 Gadites and the half-tribe of **M** into exile. H4985
1Ch 6:61 from the clans of half the tribe of **M**. H4985
1Ch 6:62 part of the tribe of **M** that is in Bashan. H4985
1Ch 6:70 from half the tribe of **M** the Israelites gave H4985
1Ch 6:71 of the half-tribe of **M** they received Golan H4985
1Ch 7:14 The descendants of **M**: Asriel was his H4985
1Ch 7:17 sons of Gilead son of Makir, the son of **M**. H4985
1Ch 7:29 the borders of **M** were Beth Shan, H1201+4985
1Ch 9: 3 from Ephraim and **M** who lived in H4985
1Ch 12:19 Some of the **tribe of M** defected to David H4985
1Ch 12:20 were the men of **M** who defected to him: H4985
1Ch 12:20 leaders of units of a thousand in **M**. H4985
1Ch 12:31 from half the tribe of **M**, designated by H4985
1Ch 12:37 Gad and the half-tribe of **M**, armed with H4985
1Ch 26:32 the half-tribe of **M** for every matter H4986
1Ch 27:20 son of Azaziah; over half the tribe of **M**: H4985
1Ch 27:21 over the half-tribe of **M** in Gilead: Iddo H4985
2Ch 15: 9 **M** and Simeon who had settled among H4985
2Ch 30: 1 also wrote letters to Ephraim and **M**, H4985
2Ch 30:10 from town to town in Ephraim and **M**, H4985
2Ch 30:11 **M** and Zebulun humbled themselves and H4985
2Ch 30:18 came from Ephraim, **M**, Issachar and H4985
2Ch 31: 1 Benjamin and in Ephraim and **M**. H4985
2Ch 32:33 And **M** his son succeeded him as king H4985
2Ch 33: 1 **M** was twelve years old when he became H4985
2Ch 33: 9 But **M** led Judah and the people of H4985
2Ch 33:10 The LORD spoke to **M** and his people, but H4985
2Ch 33:11 Assyria, who took **M** prisoner, put a hook H4985
2Ch 33:13 Then **M** knew that the LORD is God H4985
2Ch 33:20 **M** rested with his ancestors and was H4985
2Ch 33:22 of the LORD, as his father **M** had done. H4985
2Ch 33:22 sacrifices to all the idols **M** had made. H4985
2Ch 33:23 But unlike his father **M**, he did not humble H4985
2Ch 34: 6 In the towns of **M**, Ephraim and Simeon H4985
2Ch 34: 9 had collected from the people of **M**, H4985
Ezr 10:30 Mattaniah, Bezalel, Binnui and **M**. H4985
Ezr 10:33 Eliphelet, Jeremai, **M** and Shimei. H4985
Ps 60: 7 is mine, and **M** is mine; Ephraim is H4985
Ps 80: 2 Benjamin and **M**. Awaken your might; H4985
Ps 108: 8 Gilead is mine, **M** is mine; Ephraim is my H4985
Isa 9:21 **M** will feed on Ephraim, and Ephraim on H4985
Isa 9:21 Ephraim on **M**; together they will H4985
Jer 15: 4 because of what **M** son of Hezekiah king H4985
Eze 48: 4 "**M** will have one portion; it will border H4985
Eze 48: 5 border the territory of **M** from east to west. H4985
Mt 1:10 Hezekiah the father of **M**, Manasseh the *G3442*
Mt 1:10 father of Manasseh, **M** the father of Amon *G3442*
Rev 7: 6 12,000, from the tribe *of* **M** 12,000, *G3442*

MANASSEH'S (6) [MANASSEH]

Ge 48:14 he put his left hand on **M** head, even H4985
Ge 48:17 move it from Ephraim's head to **M** head. H4985
Jos 17: 1 firstborn, that is, for Makir, **M** firstborn. H4985
Jos 17: 5 **M** share consisted of ten tracts of land H4985
2Ki 21:17 As for the other events of **M** reign, and all H4985
2Ch 33:18 The other events of **M** reign, including his H4985

MANASSITES (3) [MANASSEH]

Dt 4:43 Gadites; and Golan in Bashan, for the **M**. H4986
Jos 16: 9 within the inheritance of the **M**. H1201+4985
Jos 17:12 Yet the **M** were not able to occupy H1201+4985

MANDRAKE (1) [MANDRAKES]

Ge 30:14 into the fields and found *some* **m plants**, H1859

MANDRAKES (5) [MANDRAKE]

Ge 30:14 "Please give me some of your son's **m**." H1859
Ge 30:15 Will you take my son's **m** too?" H1859
Ge 30:15 you tonight in return for your son's **m**." H1859
Ge 30:16 "I have hired you with my son's **m**." So he H1859
SS 7:13 The **m** send out their fragrance, and at H1859

MANE (1)

Job 39:19 clothe its neck with a **flowing m**? H8310

MANGER (6)

Job 39: 9 Will it stay by your **m** at night? H17
Pr 14: 4 are no oxen, the **m** is empty, but from the H17
Isa 1: 3 the donkey its owner's **m**, but Israel does not H17
Lk 2: 7 him in cloths and placed him in a **m**, *G5764*
Lk 2:12 baby wrapped in cloths and lying in a **m**." *G5764*
Lk 2:16 the baby, who was lying in the **m**. *G5764*

MANGLED (1) [MANGLES]

La 3:11 me from the path and **m** me and left me H7318

MANGLES (1) [MANGLED]

Mic 5: 8 which mauls and **m** as it goes, and no H3271

MANHOOD (2) [MAN]

Ps 78:51 the firstfruits of **m** in the tents of Ham. H226
Ps 105:36 in their land, the firstfruits of all their **m**. H226

MANIAC (5)

2Ki 9:11 Why did this **m** come to you?" "You H8713
2Ki 9:20 Jehu son of Nimshi—he drives like a **m**." H8714
Pr 26:18 Like a **m** shooting flaming arrows of death H4263
Jer 29:26 should put any **m** who acts like a H408+8713
Hos 9: 7 the inspired person a **m**. H8713

MANIFESTATION (1)

1Co 12: 7 Now to each one the **m** of the Spirit is *G5748*

MANIFOLD (1)

Eph 3:10 the **m** wisdom of God should be made *G4497*

MANKIND (61) [MAN]

Ge 1:26 "Let us make **m** in our image, in our H132
Ge 1:27 So God created **m** in his own image, in the H132
Ge 5: 1 When God created **m**, he made them in H132
Ge 5: 2 And he named them "**M**" when they were H132
Ge 7:21 that swarm over the earth, and all **m**. H132
Ge 9: 6 in the image of God has God made **m**. H132
Nu 16:29 a natural death and suffer the fate of all **m**, H132
Dt 32: 8 when he divided all **m**, he set up H1201+132
Job 7:17 "What is **m** that you make so much of them H632
Job 12:10 creature and the breath of all **m**. H1414+408
Job 20: 4 ever since **m** was placed on the earth H132
Job 34:15 perish together and **m** would return to the H132
Job 36:28 moisture and abundant showers fall on **m**. H132
Ps 8: 4 what is **m** that you are mindful of them H632
Ps 14: 2 from heaven on *all* **m** to see if there H1201+132
Ps 21:10 the earth, their posterity from **m**. H1201+132
Ps 33:13 the LORD looks down and sees all **m**; H1201+132
Ps 53: 2 from heaven on *all* **m** to see if there H1201+132
Ps 66: 5 his awesome deeds for **m**! H1201+132
Ps 76:10 your wrath against **m** brings you praise, H132
Ps 94:10 Does he who teaches **m** lack knowledge? H132
Ps 107: 8 love and his wonderful deeds for **m**, H1201+132
Ps 107:15 love and his wonderful deeds for **m**, H1201+132
Ps 107:21 love and his wonderful deeds for **m**. H1201+132
Ps 107:31 love and his wonderful deeds for **m**. H1201+132
Ps 115:16 the earth he has given to **m**. H1201+132
Pr 8: 4 I call out; I raise my voice to **all m**. H1201+132
Pr 8:31 whole world and delighting in **m**. H1201+132
Pr 30:14 the earth and the needy from among **m**. H132
Ecc 1:13 burden God has laid on **m**! H1201+2021+132
Ecc 6: 1 under the sun, and it weighs heavily on **m**: H132
Ecc 7:29 God created **m** upright, but they have gone H132
Ecc 12:13 this is the duty of all **m**. H132
Isa 45:12 I who made the earth and created **m** on it. H132
Isa 49:26 Then all **m** will know that I, the LORD, am H1414
Isa 53: 3 He was despised and rejected by **m**, a man H408
Isa 66:23 all **m** will come and bow down before me," H1414
Isa 66:24 they will be loathsome to all **m**. H1414
Jer 25:31 judgment on all **m** and put the wicked to H1414
Jer 32:19 eyes are open to the ways of all **m**; H1201+132
Jer 32:20 in Israel and among all **m**, and have H132
Jer 32:27 the God of all **m**. Is anything too H1414
Jer 49:15 small among the nations, despised by **m**. H132
Da 2:38 he has placed **all m** and the A10120+10050
Am 4:13 who reveals his thoughts to **m**, who H132
Zep 1: 3 "When I destroy all **m** on the face of the H132
Zec 2:13 before the LORD, all **m**, because he has H1414
Jn 1: 4 and that life was the light *of all* **m**. *G476*
Jn 2:25 He did not need any testimony about **m**, for *G476*
Ac 4:12 heaven given to **m** by which we must be *G476*
Ac 15:17 that the rest *of* **m** may seek the Lord, even *G476*
1Co 10:13 you except **what is common to m**. *G474*
1Th 4:13 so that you do not grieve like the **rest** *of m* AIT
1Ti 2: 5 one mediator between God and **m**, *G476*
Heb 2: 6 "What is **m** that you are mindful of them, *G476*
Jas 3: 7 and have been tamed *by* **m**, *G5882+3836+474*
Rev 9:15 year were released to kill a third *of* **m**. *G476*
Rev 9:18 A third *of* **m** was killed by the three plagues *G476*
Rev 9:20 The rest *of* **m** who were not killed by these *G476*
Rev 14: 4 purchased from among **m** and offered as *G476*
Rev 16:18 ever occurred since **m** has been on earth, *G476*

MANNA (20)

Ex 16:31 The people of Israel called the bread **m** H4942
Ex 16:32 'Take an omer of **m** and keep it for the H5647S
Ex 16:33 "Take a jar and put an omer of **m** in it. H4942
Ex 16:34 Aaron put **the m** with the tablets of the H2084S
Ex 16:35 The Israelites ate **m** forty years, until they H4942
Ex 16:35 they ate **m** until they reached the border H4942
Nu 11: 6 we never see anything but this **m**! H4942
Nu 11: 7 The **m** was like coriander seed and H4942
Nu 11: 9 camp at night, the **m** also came down. H4942
Dt 8: 3 to hunger and then feeding you with **m**, H4942
Dt 8:16 He gave you **m** to eat in the wilderness H4942
Jos 5:12 The **m** stopped the day after they ate this H4942
Jos 5:12 was no longer any **m** for the Israelites, H4942
Ne 9:20 not withhold your **m** from their mouths, H4942
Ps 78:24 he rained down **m** for the people to eat H4942
Jn 6:31 Our ancestors ate the **m** in the wilderness *G3445*
Jn 6:49 Your ancestors ate the **m** in the wilderness, *G3445*
Jn 6:58 Your ancestors ate **m** and died, but whoever NDT
Heb 9: 4 This ark contained the gold jar *of* **m** *G3445*
Rev 2:17 I will give *some of* the hidden **m**. *G3445*

MANNED (1) [MAN]

2Ch 9:21 of trading ships **m by** Hiram's servants. H6640

MANNER (11)

Lev 24:19 is to be injured **in the same m**: H3869+889
Nu 15:11 young goat, is to be prepared **in this m**. H3970
Jos 6:15 the city seven times in the same **m**, H5477
1Ki 21:26 *He* **behaved in the vilest m by** H9493+4394
1Ch 16: 7 to give praise to the LORD **in this m**: H255
1Co 11:27 of the Lord **in an unworthy m** will be guilty *G397*
2Co 1:17 make my plans **in a worldly m** so that in *G2848*
Php 1:27 yourselves **in a m worthy** of the gospel of *G547*
1Ti 3: 4 must do so **in a m worthy of** full respect *G3552*
Heb 11:19 and so **in a m of speaking** he did *G1877+4130*
3Jn 6 them on their way **in a m that honors** God. *G547*

MANOAH (15)

Jdg 13: 2 man of Zorah, named **M**, from the clan of H4956
Jdg 13: 8 Then **M** prayed to the LORD: "Pardon your H4956
Jdg 13: 9 God heard **M**, and the angel of God came H4956
Jdg 13: 9 her husband **M** was not with her. H4956

M

Jdg 13:11 **M** got up and followed his wife. When he H4956
Jdg 13:12 So **M** asked him, "When your words are H4956
Jdg 13:15 **M** said to the angel of the LORD, "We H4956
Jdg 13:16 **M** did not realize that it was the angel of H4956
Jdg 13:17 Then **M** inquired of the angel of the LORD H4956
Jdg 13:19 Then **M** took a young goat, together with H4956
Jdg 13:19 amazing thing while **M** and his wife H4956
Jdg 13:20 **M** and his wife fell with their faces to the H4956
Jdg 13:21 not show himself again to **M** and his wife, H4956
Jdg 13:21 **M** realized that it was the angel of the H4956
Jdg 16:31 Eshtaol in the tomb of **M** his father. H4956

MANSERVANT (NIV84) (MALE) SERVANT, SLAVE

MANSIONS (4)

Ps 49:14 in the grave, far from their **princely m**. H2292
Isa 5: 9 desolate, the fine **m** left without occupants. NDT
Am 3:15 destroyed and the **m** will be H8041+1074
Am 5:11 though you have built stone **m**, you will H1074

MANSLAYER, MANSLAYERS (KJV) ACCUSED OF MURDER, MURDERERS, PERSON WHO HAS KILLED

MANTLE (1) [MANTLED]

Ps 89:45 *you have* **covered** him **with a m** *of* shame. H6486

MANTLED (1) [MANTLE]

Ps 65:13 flocks and the valleys *are* **m** *with* grain; H6493

MANURE (2)

Isa 25:10 land as straw is trampled down in the **m**. H4523
Lk 14:35 is fit neither for the soil nor for the **m pile**; *G3161*

MANY (518)

Ge 17: 4 You will be the father of **m** nations. H2162
Ge 17: 5 I have made you a father of **m** nations. H2162
Ge 26:14 He had **so m** flocks and herds and servants H8041
Ge 37:34 mourned for his son **m** days. H8041
Ge 50:20 is now being done, the saving of **m** lives. H8041
Ex 12:38 **M** other people went up with them, and H8041
Ex 19:21 to see the LORD and **m** of them perish. H8041
Lev 11:42 its belly or walks on all fours or on **m** feet; H8049
Lev 15:25 of blood for **m** days at a time other H8041
Lev 25:16 When the years are **m**, you are to increase H8044
Lev 25:51 If **m** years remain, they must pay for their H8041
Nu 13:18 live there are strong or weak, few or **m**. H8041
Nu 15:12 this for each one, for as **m** as you prepare. H5031
Nu 20:15 into Egypt, and we lived there **m** years. H8041
Nu 21: 6 they bit the people and **m** Israelites died. H8041
Nu 22: 3 terrified because there were so **m** people. H8041
Nu 35: 8 **Take m** towns from a tribe that has many H8049
Nu 35: 8 Take many towns from a tribe that has **m** H8041
Dt 1:46 And so you stayed in Kadesh **m** days—all H8041
Dt 3: 5 were also a great **m** unwalled villages. H2221
Dt 7: 1 drives out before you **m** nations— H8041
Dt 11:21 of your children *may be* **m** in the land the H8049
Dt 11:21 **as m as** the days that the heavens are H3869
Dt 15: 6 you will lend to **m** nations but will H8041
Dt 15: 6 You will rule over **m** nations but none will H8041
Dt 17:17 *He must* not **take m** wives, or his heart will H8049
Dt 28:12 You will lend to **m** nations but will borrow H8041
Dt 30:20 will give you **m years** in the land he H802+3427
Dt 31:17 **M** disasters and calamities will come on H8041
Dt 31:21 And when **m** disasters and calamities H8041
Jos 24: 3 Canaan and **gave** him **m** descendants. H8049
Jdg 7: 2 said to Gideon, "You have *too* **m** men. H8041
Jdg 7: 4 to Gideon, "There are still too **m** men. H8041
Jdg 8:30 sons of his own, for he had **m** wives. H8041
Jdg 9:40 the gate, and **m** were killed as they fled. H8041
Jdg 15: 8 viciously and slaughtered **m** of them. H1524
Jdg 16:30 Thus he killed **m** more when he died than H8041
1Sa 2: 5 but *she who has had* **m** sons pines away. H8041
1Sa 3: 1 LORD was rare; there were not **m** visions. H7287
1Sa 14: 6 from saving, whether by **m** or by few." H8041
1Sa 25:10 **M** servants are breaking away from their H8045
1Sa 31: 1 and *m* **fell** dead on Mount Gilboa. AIT
2Sa 1: 4 "**M** of them fell and died. H2221
2Sa 13:34 looked up and saw **m** people on the road H8041
2Sa 13:37 King David mourned **m** days for his son. H3972
2Sa 14: 2 woman who has spent **m** days grieving H8041
2Sa 19:34 "**How m more** years will I live H3869+4537
2Sa 24: 2 so that I may know **how m** there are." H5031
1Ki 7:47 because there were so **m**; the weight of H8041
1Ki 8: 5 sacrificing **so m** sheep and cattle H4946+8044
1Ki 10:10 again were **so m** spices brought H4200+8044
1Ki 11: 1 loved **m** foreign women besides H8041
1Ki 18:25 since there are **so m** of you. H8041
1Ki 22:16 "**How m** times must I make H6330+3869+4537
2Ki 4:39 **as m** of its gourds **as** his garment **could hold** H4850
2Ki 19:23 "With my **m** chariots I have ascended the H8044
1Ch 4:27 his brothers did not have **m** children H8041
1Ch 5:22 and **m** *others* fell slain, because the battle H8041
1Ch 7: 4 for *they* **had m** wives and children. H8049
1Ch 7:22 father Ephraim mourned for them **m** days, H8041
1Ch 8:40 *They* **had m** sons and grandsons—150 in H8049
1Ch 10: 1 and *m* **fell** dead on Mount Gilboa. AIT
1Ch 21: 2 me so that I may know **how m** there are." H5031
1Ch 22: 8 much blood and have fought **m** wars. H1524
1Ch 22:15 You have **m** workers: stonecutters H4200+8044
1Ch 23:11 Jeush and Beriah *did* not **have m** sons; H8049
1Ch 28: 5 the LORD has given me **m**—he has H8041
2Ch 5: 6 sacrificing **so m** sheep and cattle H4946+8044
2Ch 11:23 provisions and took **m** wives for them. H2162
2Ch 18: 2 slaughtered **m** sheep and cattle H4200+8044
2Ch 18:15 "**How m** times must I make H6330+3869+4537
2Ch 21: 3 had given them **m** gifts of silver and H8041
2Ch 24:27 of his sons, the **m** prophecies about him H8044
2Ch 26:10 in the wilderness and dug **m** cisterns, H8041
2Ch 28: 5 him and took **m** of his *people* as prisoners H1524
2Ch 30:17 Since **m** in the crowd had not consecrated H8041
2Ch 30:18 Although most of the **m** people who came H8041
2Ch 32:23 **M** brought offerings to Jerusalem for the H8041
Ezr 3:12 But **m** of the older priests and Levites and H8041
Ezr 3:12 while **m** *others* shouted for joy. H8041
Ezr 5:11 the temple that was built **m** years ago, A10678
Ezr 10:13 But there are **m** people here and it is the H8041
Ne 6:17 nobles of Judah *were* sending **m** letters to H8049
Ne 6:18 For **m** in Judah were under oath to him H8041
Ne 9:30 For **m** years you were patient with them H8041
Ne 13:26 Among the **m** nations there was no king H8041
Est 2: 8 **m** young women were brought to the H8041
Est 4: 3 **M** lay in sackcloth and ashes H8041
Est 5:11 his vast wealth, his **m** sons, and all the H8044
Est 8:17 And **m** *people* of other nationalities H8041
Est 10: 3 held in high esteem by his **m** fellow Jews, H8044
Job 4: 3 Think how you have instructed **m**, how H8041
Job 5:25 will know that your children will be **m**, H8041
Job 11:19 you afraid, and **m** will court your favor. H8041
Job 13:23 **How m** wrongs and sins have I H3869+4537
Job 16: 2 "I have heard **m** *things* like these; you are H8041
Job 23:14 **m** such plans he still has in store. H8041
Job 27:14 However **m** his children, their fate is the H8049
Job 35: 6 If your sins *are* **m**, what does that do to H8045
Job 38:21 You have lived **so m** years! H5031+8041
Ps 3: 1 how **m** *are* my foes! How many rise H8045
Ps 3: 1 How **m** rise up against me! H8041
Ps 3: 2 **M** are saying of me, "God will not deliver H8041
Ps 4: 6 **M**, LORD, are asking, "Who will bring us H8041
Ps 5:10 Banish them for their **m** sins, for they have H8044
Ps 22:12 **M** bulls surround me; strong bulls of H8041
Ps 31:13 For I hear **m** whispering, "Terror on every H8041
Ps 32:10 **M** are the woes of the wicked, but the H8041
Ps 34:12 loves life and desires to see *m* good **days**, AIT
Ps 34:19 righteous person may have **m** troubles, H8041
Ps 37:16 have than the wealth of **m** wicked; H8041
Ps 38:19 **M** *have become* my enemies without H6793
Ps 40: 3 **M** will see and fear the LORD and put their H8041
Ps 40: 5 **M**, LORD my God, are the wonders you H8041
Ps 40: 5 *they would be* too **m** to declare. H6793
Ps 55:18 against me, even though **m** oppose me. H8041
Ps 56: 2 in their pride **m** are attacking me. H8041
Ps 61: 6 his years for **m generations**. H1887+2256+1887
Ps 68:18 on high, *you* **took m captives**; you H8647+8660
Ps 69: 4 **m** *are* my enemies without cause H6793
Ps 71: 7 I have become a sign to **m**; you are my H8041
Ps 71:20 me see troubles, **m** and bitter, you will H8041
Ps 90:15 Make us glad for **as m** days as you have H3869
Ps 90:15 for as **m** years as we have seen trouble. NDT
Ps 104:24 How **m** *are* your works, LORD! In wisdom H8045
Ps 106: 7 they did not remember your **m** kindnesses, H8044
Ps 106:43 **M** times he delivered them, but they were H8041
Ps 119:157 **M** are the foes who persecute me, but I H8041
Ps 135:10 He struck down **m** nations and killed H8041
Pr 3: 2 your life **m years** and bring H3427+2256+9102
Pr 4:10 and the years of your life *will be* **m**. H8049
Pr 7:26 **M** are the victims she has brought down H8041
Pr 9:11 For through wisdom your days *will be* **m** H8049
Pr 10:21 The lips of the righteous nourish **m**, but H8041
Pr 11:14 victory is won through **m** advisers. H8044
Pr 14:20 neighbors, but the rich have **m** friends. H8041
Pr 15:22 with **m** advisers they succeed. H8044
Pr 19: 4 Wealth attracts **m** friends, but even the H8041
Pr 19: 6 **M** curry favor with a ruler, and everyone is H8041
Pr 19:21 **M** are the plans in a person's heart, but it H8041
Pr 20: 6 **M** claim to have unfailing love, but a H8044
Pr 24: 6 victory is won through **m** advisers. H8044
Pr 28: 2 is rebellious, it has **m** rulers, but a ruler H8041
Pr 28:27 close their eyes to them receive **m** curses. H8041
Pr 29: 1 stiff-necked after **m** rebukes will suddenly NDT
Pr 29:22 a hot-tempered person commits **m** sins. H8041
Pr 29:26 **M** seek an audience with a ruler, but it is H8041
Pr 31:29 "**M** women do noble things, but you H8041
Ecc 5: 3 A dream comes when there are **m** cares H8044
Ecc 5: 3 **m** words mark the speech of a fool. H8044
Ecc 5: 7 Much dreaming and **m** words are H2221
Ecc 6: 3 have a hundred children and live **m** years; H8041
Ecc 7:22 in your heart that **m** times you yourself H8041
Ecc 7:29 they have gone in search of **m** schemes." H8041
Ecc 10: 6 Fools are put in **m** high positions, while H8041
Ecc 11: 1 after **m** days you may receive a return. H8044
Ecc 11: 8 However **m** years anyone may live, let H2221
Ecc 11: 8 the days of darkness, for there will be **m**. H2221
Ecc 12: 9 searched out and set in order **m** proverbs. H2221
Ecc 12:12 Of making **m** books there is no end, and H2221
SS 8: 7 **M** waters cannot quench love; rivers H8041
Isa 1:15 even when *you* **offer m** prayers, I am H8049
Isa 2: 3 **M** peoples will come and say, "Come, let H8041
Isa 2: 4 will settle disputes for **m** peoples. H8041
Isa 8:15 **M** of them will stumble; they will fall and H8041
Isa 10: 7 to put an end to **m** nations. H4202+5071
Isa 16:14 splendor and all her **m** people will be H8041
Isa 17:12 Woe to the **m** nations that rage—they H8041
Isa 22: 9 David were broken through *in m places*; H8045
Isa 23:16 the harp well, sing **m** a song, so that you H8049
Isa 24:22 in prison and be punished after **m** days. H8044
Isa 29: 5 But your **m** enemies will become like fine H2162
Isa 37:24 'With my **m** chariots I have ascended the H8044
Isa 41:15 new and sharp, with **m teeth**. H7092
Isa 42:20 You have seen **m** *things*, but you pay no H8041
Isa 47: 9 in spite of your **m** sorceries and all your H8044
Isa 47:12 magic spells and with your **m** sorceries, H8044
Isa 51: 2 I blessed him and **made** him **m**. H8049
Isa 52:14 Just as there were **m** who were appalled H8041
Isa 52:15 so he will sprinkle **m** nations, and kings H8041
Isa 53:11 my righteous servant will justify **m**, H8041
Isa 53:12 For he bore the sin of **m**, and made H8041
Isa 59:12 For our offenses *are* **m** in your sight, and H8045
Isa 63: 7 the **m** good things he has done for Israel H8044
Isa 63: 7 to his compassion and **m** kindnesses. H8044
Isa 66:16 and **m** *will be* those slain by the LORD. H8045
Jer 2:28 have **as m** gods **as** you have towns. H5031
Jer 3: 1 have lived as a prostitute with **m** lovers— H8041
Jer 5: 6 is great and their backslidings **m**. H6793
Jer 11:13 have **as m** gods **as** you have towns H5031
Jer 11:13 god Baal are **as m as** the streets of H5031
Jer 11:15 with **m** *others*, works out her evil H8041
Jer 12:10 **M** shepherds will ruin my vineyard and H8041
Jer 13: 6 **M** days later the LORD said to me, "Go H8041
Jer 13:22 it is because of your **m** sins that your skirts H8044
Jer 16:16 "But now I will send for **m** fishermen," H8041
Jer 16:16 After that I will send for **m** hunters, and H8041
Jer 20:10 I hear **m** whispering, "Terror on every H8041
Jer 22: 8 "People from **m** nations will pass by this H8041
Jer 25:14 will be enslaved by **m** nations and great H8041
Jer 27: 7 then **m** nations and great kings will H8041
Jer 28: 8 plague against **m** countries and great H8041
Jer 30:14 your guilt is so great and your sins *so* **m**. H6793
Jer 30:15 your great guilt and **m** sins I have done H6793
Jer 36:32 And **m** similar words were added to them H8041
Jer 42: 2 though we were once **m**, now only a few H2221
Jer 46:11 But you **try m** medicines in vain; there is H8049
Jer 50:41 a great nation and **m** kings are being H8041
Jer 51:13 You who live by **m** waters and are rich in H8041
La 1: 5 brought her grief because of her **m** sins. H8044
La 1:22 My groans are **m** and my heart is faint." H8041
Eze 3: 6 not to **m** peoples of obscure speech and H8041
Eze 11: 6 *You have* killed **m** people in this city and H8049
Eze 12:27 vision he sees is for **m** years from now, H8041
Eze 16:41 on you in the sight of **m** women. H8041
Eze 17: 9 a strong arm or **m** people to pull it up H8041
Eze 17:17 siege works erected to destroy **m** lives. H8041
Eze 19:11 its height and for its **m** branches. H8044
Eze 21:15 may melt with fear and the fallen *be* **m**, H8049
Eze 22:25 things and **make m** widows within her. H8049
Eze 26: 3 I will bring **m** nations against you H8041
Eze 26:10 His horses will be so **m** that they will H9180
Eze 27: 3 merchant of peoples on **m** coasts, 'This is H8041
Eze 27:15 **m** coastlands were your customers H8041
Eze 27:16 with you because of your **m** products; H8044
Eze 27:18 you because of your **m** products and great H8044
Eze 27:33 you satisfied **m** nations; with your H8041
Eze 28:18 By your **m** sins and dishonest trade you H8044
Eze 32: 9 the hearts of **m** peoples when I bring H8041
Eze 32:10 I will cause **m** peoples to be appalled at H8041
Eze 33:24 But we are **m**; surely the land has been H8041
Eze 36:10 and *I will* **cause m** people to live on you H8049
Eze 37: 2 I saw a great **m** bones on the floor of H8041
Eze 38: 6 all its troops—the **m** nations with you. H8041
Eze 38: 8 After **m** days you will be called to arms. H8041
Eze 38: 8 were gathered from **m** nations to the H8041
Eze 38: 9 your troops and the **m** nations with you H8041
Eze 38:15 far north, you and **m** nations with you, all H8041
Eze 38:22 his troops and on the **m** nations with him. H8041
Eze 38:23 myself known in the sight of **m** nations. H8041
Eze 39:27 through them in the sight of **m** nations. H8041
Eze 47:10 The fish will be of **m** kinds—like H8041+4394
Da 2:48 and lavished **m** gifts on him. A10647+10678
Da 8:25 he will destroy **m** and take his stand H8041
Da 9:27 confirm a covenant with **m** for one 'seven. H8041
Da 11:12 pride and will slaughter **m thousands**, H8052
Da 11:14 "In those times **m** will rise against the H8041
Da 11:18 to the coastlands and will take **m** of them, H8041
Da 11:26 be swept away, and **m** will fall in battle. H8041
Da 11:33 "Those who are wise will instruct **m** H8041
Da 11:34 **m** who are not sincere will join them. H8041
Da 11:39 them rulers over **m** *people* and will H8041
Da 11:40 He will invade *m* **countries** and sweep AIT
Da 11:41 **M** *countries* will fall, but Edom, Moab H8041
Da 11:42 He will extend his power over *m* **countries** AIT
Da 11:44 a great rage to destroy and annihilate **m**. H8041
Da 12: 3 those who lead **m** to righteousness H8041
Da 12: 4 **M** will go here and there to increase H8041
Da 12:10 **M** will be purified, made spotless and H8041
Hos 3: 3 "You are to live with me **m** days; you must H8041
Hos 3: 4 Israelites will live **m** days without king H8041
Hos 8:11 "Though Ephraim **built m** altars for sin H8049
Hos 8:12 I wrote for them the **m** *things of* my law H8044
Hos 8:14 palaces; Judah *has* fortified **m** towns. H8049
Hos 9: 7 your sins are **so m** and your hostility H8044
Hos 10: 4 *They* **make m promises**, take false H1819+1821
Hos 10:13 your own strength and on your **m** warriors, H8044
Hos 12:10 **gave** them **m** visions and told parables H8049
Am 4: 9 "**M times** I struck your gardens and H8049
Am 5:12 For I know how **m** are your offenses and H8041
Am 8: 3 turn to wailing. **M**, many bodies—flung H8041
Am 8: 3 turn to wailing. Many, **m** bodies—flung NDT

Jnh 4:11 from their left—and also **m** animals?" H8041
Mic 4: 2 **M** nations will come and say, "Come, let H8041
Mic 4: 3 will judge between **m** peoples and will H8041
Mic 4:11 But now **m** nations are gathered against H8041
Mic 4:13 you will break to pieces **m** nations." H8041
Mic 5: 7 be in the midst of **m** peoples like dew H8041
Mic 5: 8 in the midst of **m** peoples, like a lion H8041
Na 3: 3 **M** casualties, piles of dead, bodies H8044
Hab 2: 8 Because you have plundered **m** nations H8041
Hab 2:10 You have plotted the ruin of **m** peoples H8041
Hab 3: 9 your bow, you called for **m** arrows. H8679
Zec 2:11 "**M** nations will be joined with the LORD in H8041
Zec 7: 3 as I have done for **so m** years?" H3869+4537
Zec 8:20 "**M** peoples and the inhabitants of many NDT
Zec 8:20 the inhabitants of **m** cities will yet come, H8041
Zec 8:22 And **m** peoples and powerful nations will H8041
Mal 2: 6 uprightness, and turned **m** from sin. H8041
Mal 2: 8 your teaching have caused **m** to stumble; H8041
Mt 3: 7 But when he saw **m** of the Pharisees and *G4498*
Mt 6: 7 will be heard because of their **m words**. *G4494*
Mt 7:13 to destruction, and **m** enter through it. *G4498*
Mt 7:22 **M** will say to me on that day, 'Lord, Lord *G4498*
Mt 7:22 in your name perform **m** miracles? *G4498*
Mt 8:11 I say to you that **m** will come from the east *G4498*
Mt 8:16 **m** who were demon-possessed were *G4498*
Mt 9:10 **m** tax collectors and sinners came and ate *G4498*
Mt 10:31 you are worth more than **m** sparrows. *G4498*
Mt 13: 3 Then he told them **m** *things* in parables *G4498*
Mt 13:17 **m** prophets and righteous people longed *G4498*
Mt 13:58 And he did not do **m** miracles there *G4498*
Mt 15:30 the mute and **m** others, and laid them *G4498*
Mt 15:34 "**How m** loaves do you have?" Jesus *G4531*
Mt 16: 9 and **how m** basketfuls you gathered? *G4531*
Mt 16:10 and **how m** basketfuls you gathered? *G4531*
Mt 16:21 suffer **m** *things* at the hands of the *G4498*
Mt 18:21 **how m times** shall I forgive my brother *G4529*
Mt 19:30 But **m** who are first will be last, and many *G4498*
Mt 19:30 will be last, and **m** who are last will be first. NDT
Mt 20:28 to give his life as a ransom for **m**. *G4498*
Mt 22:14 "For **m** are invited, but few are chosen." *G4498*
Mt 24: 5 For **m** will come in my name, claiming, 'I *G4498*
Mt 24: 5 'I am the Messiah,' and will deceive **m**. *G4498*
Mt 24:10 At that time **m** will turn away from the *G4498*
Mt 24:11 **m** false prophets will appear and *G4498*
Mt 24:11 will appear and deceive **m** *people*. *G4498*
Mt 25:21 I will put you in charge of **m** *things*. *G4498*
Mt 25:23 I will put you in charge of **m** *things*. *G4498*
Mt 26:28 is poured out for **m** for the forgiveness of *G4498*
Mt 26:60 though **m** false witnesses came forward. *G4498*
Mt 27:52 The bodies of **m** holy people who had *G4498*
Mt 27:53 the holy city and appeared *to* **m** *people*. *G4498*
Mt 27:55 **M** women were there, watching from a *G4498*
Mk 1:34 Jesus healed **m** who had various *G4498*
Mk 1:34 He also drove out **m** demons, but he *G4498*
Mk 2:15 **m** tax collectors and sinners were eating *G4498*
Mk 2:15 there were **m** who followed him. *G4498*
Mk 3: 8 **m** people came to him from Judea *G4498*
Mk 3:10 For he had healed **m**, so that those with *G4498*
Mk 4: 2 He taught them **m** *things* by parables, and *G4498*
Mk 4:33 With **m** similar parables Jesus spoke the *G4498*
Mk 5: 9 is Legion," he replied, "for we are **m**." *G4498*
Mk 5:26 under the care of **m** doctors and had *G4498*
Mk 6: 2 **m** who heard him were amazed. *G4498*
Mk 6:13 They drove out **m** demons and anointed *G4498*
Mk 6:13 demons and anointed **m** sick people with *G4498*
Mk 6:31 because **so m** people were coming and *G4498*
Mk 6:33 But **m** who saw them leaving recognized *G4498*
Mk 6:34 So he began teaching them **m** *things*. *G4498*
Mk 6:38 "**How m** loaves do you have?" he asked *G4531*
Mk 7: 4 And they observe **m** other traditions, such *G4498*
Mk 7:13 And you do **m** *things* like that." *G4498*
Mk 8: 5 "**How m** loaves do you have?" Jesus *G4531*
Mk 8:19 **how m** basketfuls of pieces did you pick *G4531*
Mk 8:20 **how m** basketfuls of pieces did you pick *G4531*
Mk 8:31 Man must suffer **m** *things* and be rejected *G4498*
Mk 9:26 looked so much like a corpse that **m** said, *G4498*
Mk 10:31 But **m** who are first will be last, and the *G4498*
Mk 10:45 to give his life as a ransom for **m**. *G4498*
Mk 10:48 **M** rebuked him and told him to be quiet *G4498*
Mk 11: 8 **M** *people* spread their cloaks on the road *G4498*
Mk 12: 5 He sent **m** others; some of them they beat *G4498*
Mk 12:41 **M** rich people threw in large amounts *G4498*
Mk 13: 6 **M** will come in my name, claiming, 'I am *G4498*
Mk 13: 6 claiming, 'I am he,' and will deceive **m**. *G4498*
Mk 14:24 which is poured out for **m**," he said to *G4498*
Mk 14:56 **M** testified falsely against him, but their *G4498*
Mk 15: 3 The chief priests accused him *of* **m** *things*. *G4498*
Mk 15: 4 See **how m** *things* they are accusing you *G4531*
Mk 15:41 **M** other women who had come up with *G4498*
Lk 1: 1 **M** have undertaken to draw up an account *G4498*
Lk 1:14 **m** will rejoice because of his birth, *G4498*
Lk 1:16 He will bring back **m** of the people of *G4498*
Lk 2:34 cause the falling and rising *of* **m** in Israel, *G4498*
Lk 2:35 so that the thoughts of **m** hearts will be *G4498*
Lk 3:18 And *with* **m** other words John exhorted the *G4498*
Lk 4:25 you that there were **m** widows in Israel in *G4498*
Lk 4:27 And there were **m** in Israel with leprosy in *G4498*
Lk 4:41 demons came out of **m** *people*, shouting, *G4498*
Lk 7:21 time Jesus cured **m** who had diseases, *G4498*
Lk 7:21 gave sight to **m** who were blind. *G4498*
Lk 7:47 I tell you, her **m** sins have been forgiven *G4498*
Lk 8: 3 household; Susanna; and **m** others. *G4498*
Lk 8:29 **M** times it had seized him, and though he *G4498*
Lk 8:30 because **m** demons had gone into him. *G4498*
Lk 9:22 Man must suffer **m** *things* and be rejected *G4498*
Lk 10:24 For I tell you that **m** prophets and kings *G4498*
Lk 10:41 are worried and upset about **m** *things*, *G4498*
Lk 12: 1 a crowd *of* **m thousands** had gathered *G3689*
Lk 12: 7 you are worth more than **m** sparrows. *G4498*
Lk 12:19 have plenty of grain laid up for **m** years. *G4498*
Lk 12:47 wants will be beaten with **m** blows. *G4498*
Lk 13:24 the narrow door, because **m**, I tell you, *G4498*
Lk 14:16 a great banquet and invited **m** *guests*. *G4498*
Lk 15:17 '**How m** of my father's hired servants have *G4531*
Lk 17:25 he must suffer **m** *things* and be rejected *G4498*
Lk 18:30 to receive **m times as much** in this age, *G4491*
Lk 21: 8 For **m** will come in my name, claiming, 'I *G4498*
Lk 22:65 And they said **m** other insulting things to *G4498*
Lk 23: 9 He plied him with **m** questions, but Jesus *G2653*
Jn 2:23 **m** *people* saw the signs he was *G4498*
Jn 4:39 **M** of the Samaritans from that town *G4498*
Jn 4:41 because of his words **m** more became *G4498*
Jn 6: 9 how far will they go among **so m**? *G5537*
Jn 6:60 On hearing it, **m** of his disciples said *G4498*
Jn 6:66 From this time **m** of his disciples turned *G4498*
Jn 7:31 **m** in the crowd believed in him. *G4498*
Jn 8:30 Even as he spoke, **m** believed in him. *G4498*
Jn 10:20 **M** of them said, "He is demon-possessed *G4498*
Jn 10:32 "I have shown you **m** good works from the *G4498*
Jn 10:41 and **m** *people* came to him. They said *G4498*
Jn 10:42 And in that place **m** believed in Jesus. *G4498*
Jn 11:19 **m** Jews had come to Martha and Mary *G4498*
Jn 11:45 Therefore **m** of the Jews who had come to *G4498*
Jn 11:47 "Here is this man performing **m** signs. *G4498*
Jn 11:55 **m** went up from the country to Jerusalem *G4498*
Jn 12:11 on account of him **m** of the Jews were *G4498*
Jn 12:18 **M people**, because they had heard that he *G4063*
Jn 12:24 But if it dies, it produces **m** seeds. *G4498*
Jn 12:37 Jesus had performed **so m** signs in their *G5537*
Jn 12:42 Yet at the same time **m** even among the *G4498*
Jn 14: 2 My Father's house has **m** rooms; if that *G4498*
Jn 19:20 **M** of the Jews read this sign, for the place *G4498*
Jn 20:30 Jesus performed **m** other signs in the *G4498*
Jn 21:11 even with **so m** the net was not torn. *G5537*
Jn 21:25 Jesus did **m** other things as well. If every *G4498*
Ac 1: 3 to them and gave **m** convincing proofs *G4498*
Ac 2:40 With **m** other words he warned them; and *G4498*
Ac 2:43 with awe at the **m** wonders and signs *G4498*
Ac 4: 4 But **m** who heard the message believed *G4498*
Ac 5:12 apostles performed **m** signs and wonders *G4498*
Ac 8: 7 impure spirits came out of **m**, and many *G4498*
Ac 8: 7 **m** who were paralyzed or lame were *G4498*
Ac 8:25 the gospel in **m** Samaritan villages. *G4498*
Ac 9:13 "I have heard **m** *reports* about this man *G4498*
Ac 9:23 After **m** days had gone by, there was a *G2653*
Ac 9:42 and **m** *people* believed in the Lord. *G4498*
Ac 12:12 where **m** *people* had gathered and were *G2653*
Ac 13:31 for **m** days he was seen by those who *G4498*
Ac 13:43 **m** of the Jews and devout converts to *G4498*
Ac 14:22 must go through **m** hardships to enter *G4498*
Ac 15:35 where they and **m** others taught and *G4498*
Ac 16:18 She kept this up for **m** days. Finally Paul *G4498*
Ac 17:12 As a result, **m** of them believed, as did *G4498*
Ac 17:12 Greek women and **m** Greek men. *G4024+3900*
Ac 18: 8 **m** of the Corinthians who heard Paul *G4498*
Ac 18:10 because I have **m** people in this city." *G4498*
Ac 19:18 **M** of those who believed now came and *G4498*
Ac 20: 2 speaking **m** words of encouragement to *G4498*
Ac 20: 8 There were **m** lamps in the upstairs room *G2653*
Ac 21:20 **how m** thousands of Jews have believed *G4531*
Ac 25: 7 They brought **m** serious charges against *G4498*
Ac 25:14 Since they were spending **m** days there *G4498*
Ac 26:10 chief priests I put **m** of the Lord's people *G4498*
Ac 26:11 **M a time** I went from one synagogue to *G4490*
Ac 27: 7 made slow headway for **m** days and had *G2653*
Ac 27:20 stars appeared for **m** days and the storm *G4498*
Ac 28:10 They honored us *in* **m** *ways*; and when we *G4498*
Ro 1:13 that I planned **m times** to come to you *G4490*
Ro 4:17 "I have made you a father *of* **m** nations." *G4498*
Ro 4:18 so became the father *of* **m** nations, *G4498*
Ro 5:15 For if the **m** died by the trespass of the *G4498*
Ro 5:15 one man, Jesus Christ, overflow to the **m**! *G4498*
Ro 5:16 the gift followed **m** trespasses and *G4498*
Ro 5:19 of the one man the **m** were made sinners, *G4498*
Ro 5:19 of the one man the **m** will be made *G4498*
Ro 8:29 the firstborn among **m** brothers and sisters *G4498*
Ro 12: 4 of us has one body *with* **m** members, *G4498*
Ro 12: 5 Christ we, though **m**, form one body, and *G4498*
Ro 15:23 been longing for **m** years to visit you, *G4498*
Ro 16: 2 she has been the benefactor *of* **m** *people*, *G4498*
1Co 1:26 Not **m** of you were wise by human *G4498*
1Co 1:26 human standards; not **m** were influential *G4498*
1Co 1:26 influential; not **m** were of noble birth. *G4498*
1Co 4:15 you do not have **m** fathers, for in Christ *G4498*
1Co 7:28 who marry will face *m* **troubles** in this life, AIT
1Co 8: 5 as indeed there are **m** "gods" and many *G4498*
1Co 8: 5 there are many "gods" and **m** "lords") *G4498*
1Co 9:19 to everyone, to win *as* **m** *as possible*. *G4498*
1Co 10:17 we, who are **m**, are one body, for we *G4498*
1Co 10:33 seeking my own good but the good *of* **m**, *G4498*
1Co 11:30 That is why **m** among you are weak and *G4498*
1Co 12:12 though one, has **m** parts, but all its many *G4498*
1Co 12:12 but all its **m** parts form one body, so *G4498*
1Co 12:14 body is not made up of one part but of **m**. *G4498*
1Co 12:20 there are **m** parts, but one body. *G4498*
1Co 16: 9 and there are **m** who oppose me. *G4498*
2Co 1:11 Then **m** will give thanks on our *G4498+4725*
2Co 1:11 granted us in answer to the prayers *of* **m**. *G4498*
2Co 1:20 For **no matter how m** promises God has *G4012*
2Co 2: 4 anguish of heart and with **m** tears, *G4498*
2Co 2:17 Unlike *so* **m**, we do not peddle the word of *G4498*
2Co 6:10 yet making **m** rich; having nothing *G4498*
2Co 8:22 proved to us in **m** *ways* that he is zealous, *G4498*
2Co 9:12 also overflowing in **m** expressions of *G4498*
2Co 11:18 Since **m** are boasting in the way the world *G4498*
2Co 12:21 I will be grieved *over* **m** who have sinned *G4498*
Gal 1:14 in Judaism beyond **m** of my own age *G4498*
Gal 3:16 meaning **m** *people*, but "and to your *G4498*
Eph 4: 8 *he* **took m captives** and gave gifts to *G169+168*
Php 3:18 **m** live as enemies of the cross of Christ. *G4498*
1Ti 6: 9 a trap and into **m** foolish and harmful *G4498*
1Ti 6:10 pierced themselves with **m** griefs. *G4498*
1Ti 6:12 in the presence of **m** witnesses. *G4498*
2Ti 1:18 very well *in* **how m** *ways* he helped me *G4012*
2Ti 2: 2 in the presence of **m** witnesses entrust to *G4498*
Titus 1:10 For there are **m** rebellious people, full of *G4498*
Heb 1: 1 the prophets **at m times** and in various *G4495*
Heb 2:10 In bringing **m** sons and daughters to glory, *G4498*
Heb 6:14 you and **give** you **m descendants**." *G4437+4437*
Heb 7:23 Now there have been **m** of those priests *G4498*
Heb 9:26 have had to suffer **m times** since the *G4490*
Heb 9:28 sacrificed once to take away the sins *of* **m**; *G4498*
Heb 12:15 grows up to cause trouble and defile **m**. *G4498*
Jas 1: 2 whenever you face trials *of* **m kinds**, *G4476*
Jas 3: 1 Not **m** of you should become teachers, my *G4498*
Jas 3: 2 We all stumble *in* **m** *ways*. Anyone who is *G4498*
2Pe 2: 2 **M** will follow their depraved conduct and *G4498*
1Jn 2:18 even now **m** antichrists have come. *G4498*
1Jn 4: 1 because **m** false prophets have gone out *G4498*
2Jn 7 I say this because **m** deceivers, who do *G4498*
Rev 5:11 I looked and heard the voice of **m** angels, *G4498*
Rev 8:11 **m** people died from the waters that *G4498*
Rev 9: 9 the thundering of **m** horses and chariots *G4498*
Rev 10:11 must prophesy again about **m** peoples, *G4498*
Rev 17: 1 the great prostitute, who sits by **m** waters. *G4498*
Rev 19:12 and on his head are **m** crowns. *G4498*

MAOK (1)

1Sa 27: 2 over to Achish son of **M** king of Gath. H5059

MAON (7) [MAONITES]

Jos 15:55 **M**, Carmel, Ziph, Juttah, H5063
1Sa 23:24 his men were in the Desert of **M**, H5063
1Sa 23:25 to the rock and stayed in the Desert of **M**. H5063
1Sa 23:25 into the Desert of **M** in pursuit of David. H5063
1Sa 25: 2 A certain man in **M**, who had property H5063
1Ch 2:45 The son of Shammai was **M**, and Maon H5062
1Ch 2:45 and **M** was the father of Beth Zur. H5062

MAONITES (1) [MAON]

Jdg 10:12 Amalekites and the **M** oppressed you H5062

MAP (1)

Jos 18: 8 started on their way to **m out** the land, H4180

MARA (1)

Ru 1:20 "Call me **M**, because the Almighty has H5259

MARAH (4)

Ex 15:23 When they came to **M**, they could not H5288
Ex 15:23 (That is why the place is called **M**.) H5288
Nu 33: 8 the Desert of Etham, they camped at **M**. H5288
Nu 33: 9 They left **M** and went to Elim, where there H5288

MARALAH (1)

Jos 19:11 Going west it ran to **M**, touched H5339

MARAN-ATHA (KJV) COME, LORD

MARAUDERS (3) [MARAUDING]

Job 12: 6 The tents of **m** are undisturbed, and those H8720
Job 15:21 when all seems well, **m** attack him. H8720
Hos 6: 9 As **m** lie in ambush for a victim, so do H1522

MARAUDING (1) [MARAUDERS]

Zec 9: 8 to guard it against **m forces**. H6296+2256+8740

MARBLE (5)

1Ch 29: 2 all kinds of fine stone and **m**—all H74+8880
Est 1: 6 material to silver rings on **m** pillars. H9253
Est 1: 6 of porphyry, **m**, mother-of-pearl and H9253
SS 5:15 legs are pillars of **m** set on bases of pure H9253
Rev 18:12 of ivory, costly wood, bronze, iron and **m**; *G3454*

MARCABOTH See BETH MARKABOTH

MARCH (26) [MARCHED, MARCHES, MARCHING]

Nu 10:28 This was the **order of m** for the Israelite H5023
Nu 20:18 *we will* **m out** and attack you with the H3655
Dt 20:10 When *you* **m up** to attack a city, make its H7928
Jos 6: 3 **M around** the city once with all the H5938+6015
Jos 6: 4 **m around** the city seven times H6015
Jos 6: 7 **M around** the city, with an armed guard H6015
Jos 10: 9 After an all-night **m** from Gilgal, Joshua H6590
Jdg 5:21 the river Kishon. **M on**, my soul; be strong! H2005
2Sa 15:22 "Go ahead, **m on**." So Ittai the H6296
2Sa 18: 2 *I* myself *will* **surely m out** with you. H3655+3655
2Ki 3: 9 After a roundabout **m** *of* seven days, the H2006

2Ki 18:25 LORD himself told me *to* m against this H6590
2Ki 24: 7 king of Egypt *did* not m out from his own H3655
2Ch 20:16 Tomorrow m down against them. They will H3718
2Ch 25: 7 troops from Israel *must* not m with you, H995
Isa 27: 4 *I would* m against them in battle; I would H7314
Isa 36:10 LORD himself told me *to* m against this H6590
Isa 42:13 The LORD *will* m out like a champion, like H3655
Jer 46: 3 large and small, and m out for battle! H5602
Jer 46: 9 M on, you warriors—men of Cush and Put H3655
Da 11:11 king of the South *will* m out in a rage H3655
Joel 2: 7 They all m in line, not swerving from their H2143
Ob 13 *You should* not m through the gates of my H995
Mic 5: 5 invade our land and m through our H2005
Mic 5: 6 invade our land and m across our borders. H2005
Zec 9:14 *he will* m in the storms of the south H2143

MARCHED (46) [MARCH]

Ge 14: 8 m out and drew up their battle lines in H3655
Nu 21:23 his entire army and m out into the H3655
Nu 21:33 his whole army m out to meet them in H3655
Nu 33: 3 *They* m out defiantly in full view of all the H3655
Dt 1:43 in your arrogance *you* m up into the hill H6590
Dt 3: 1 with his whole army m out to meet us in H3655
Jos 6: 9 The armed guard m ahead of the priests H2143
Jos 6:14 second day *they* m around the city once H6015
Jos 6:15 at daybreak and m around the city seven H6015
Jos 8:10 the leaders of Israel m before them to Ai. H6590
Jos 8:11 that was with him m up and approached H6590
Jos 10: 7 So Joshua m up from Gilgal with his H6590
Jos 15:15 From there *he* m against the people living H6590
Jdg 5: 4 when you m from the land of Edom H7575
1Sa 29: 2 the Philistine rulers m with their units of H6296
1Sa 31:12 their valiant men m through the night to H2143
2Sa 2:29 Abner and his men m through the Arabah H2143
2Sa 2:32 Joab and his men m all night and arrived H2143
2Sa 5: 6 king and his men m *to* Jerusalem to H2143
2Sa 15:18 All his men m past him H6296+6584+3338
2Sa 15:18 him from Gath m before the king. H6296
2Sa 15:22 So Ittai the Gittite m on with all his men H6296
2Sa 18: 4 while all his men m out in units of H3655
2Sa 18: 6 David's army m out *of* the city to fight H3655
2Sa 20: 7 *They* m out from Jerusalem to pursue H3655
1Ki 20:19 commanders m out of the city with the H3655
1Ki 20:27 provisions, *they* m out to meet them. H2143
2Ki 6:24 entire army and m up and laid siege to H6590
2Ki 16: 5 of Israel m up to fight *against* Jerusalem H6590
2Ki 17: 5 m *against* Samaria and laid siege to it H6590
2Ki 18: 9 king of Assyria m against Samaria and H6590
2Ki 23:29 King Josiah m out to meet him in battle H2143
2Ki 25: 1 king of Babylon m against Jerusalem with H995
1Ch 11: 4 all the Israelites m *to* Jerusalem H2143
2Ch 14: 9 Zerah the Cushite m out against them H3655
2Ch 24:23 the army of Aram m against Joash; it H6590
2Ch 35:20 Josiah m out to meet him in battle. H3655
Job 18:14 of his tent and m off to the king of terrors. H7575
Ps 68: 7 when you m through the wilderness, H7575
Isa 7: 1 king of Israel m up to fight against H6590
Jer 37: 5 Pharaoh's army *had* m out of Egypt, and H3655
Jer 37: 7 which *has* m out to support you, will H3655
Jer 39: 1 king of Babylon m against Jerusalem with H995
Jer 52: 4 king of Babylon m against Jerusalem with H995
Heb 11:30 *after the army had* m around them for *G3240*
Rev 20: 9 *They* m across the breadth of the earth and *G326*

MARCHES (4) [MARCH]

Joel 2: 8 jostle each other; each m straight ahead. H2143
Am 5: 3 "Your city that m out a thousand strong H3655
Am 5: 3 your town that m out a hundred strong H3655
Hab 3: 6 hills collapsed—but he m on forever. H2142

MARCHING (9) [MARCH]

Ex 14: 8 the Israelites, who *were* m out boldly. H3655
Ex 14:10 there were the Egyptians, m after them. H5825
Jos 6:13 m before the ark of the LORD and blowing H2143
1Sa 29: 2 his men *were* m at the rear with H6296
2Sa 5:24 you hear the sound of m in the tops of the H7577
2Ki 19: 9 of Cush, *was* m out to fight against him. H3655
1Ch 14:15 you hear the sound of m in the tops of the H7577
2Ch 11: 4 turned back from m against Jeroboam. H2143
Isa 37: 9 of Cush, *was* m out to fight against him. H3655

MARCUS (KJV) MARK

MARDUK (1) [AWEL-MARDUK, MARDUK-BALADAN]

Jer 50: 2 will be put to shame, M filled with terror. H5281

MARDUK-BALADAN (2) [MARDUK]

2Ki 20:12 At that time M son of Baladan king of H5282
Isa 39: 1 At that time M son of Baladan king of H5282

MARE (1)

SS 1: 9 to a m among Pharaoh's chariot horses. H6063

MARESHAH (8)

Jos 15:44 Akzib and M—nine towns and H5358
1Ch 2:42 and his son M, who was the father H5359
1Ch 4:21 the father of M and the clans of the H5359
2Ch 11: 8 M, Ziph, H5358
2Ch 14: 9 hundred chariots, and came as far as M. H5358
2Ch 14:10 in the Valley of Zephathah near M. H5358
2Ch 20:37 son of Dodavahu of M prophesied against H5358
Mic 1:15 a conqueror against you who live in M. H5358

MARINERS (2) [MARITIME]

Eze 27:27 wares, your m, sailors and H4876
Eze 27:29 the m and all the sailors will stand on the H4876

MARITAL (2) [MARRY]

Ex 21:10 one of her food, clothing and m rights. H6703
1Co 7: 3 husband should fulfill his *m* duty to his wife, AIT

MARITIME (1) [MARINERS]

Ge 10: 5 From these the m peoples spread out into H362

MARK (31) [MARKED, MARKER, MARKS]

Ge 1:14 let them serve as signs to *m* sacred times, AIT
Ge 4:15 Then the LORD put a m on Cain so that no H253
1Ki 22:28 he added, "M my words, all you people H9048
2Ch 18:27 he added, "M my words, all you people H9048
Job 36:32 lightning and commands it *to* strike its m. H7003
Ps 104:19 He made the moon to m the seasons H4200
Ecc 5: 3 many words m the speech of a fool. H928
Isa 59: 7 evil schemes; acts of violence m their ways. H928
Eze 9: 4 of Jerusalem and put a m on the H9344+9338
Eze 9: 6 do not touch anyone who has the m. H9338
Eze 21:19 m out two roads *for* the sword of the king H8492
Eze 21:20 M out one road for the sword to come H8492
Ac 12:12 also called M, where many people *G3453*
Ac 12:25 taking with them John, also called M. *G3453*
Ac 15:37 to take John, also called M, with them, *G3453*
Ac 15:39 Barnabas took M and sailed for Cyprus *G3453*
Ro 3:16 ruin and misery m their ways, *G1877*
Gal 5: 2 M my words! I, Paul, tell you that if you let *G2623*
Col 4:10 his greetings, as does M, the cousin of *G3453*
2Th 3:17 which is the distinguishing m in all my *G4956*
2Ti 3: 1 But m this: There will be terrible times in *G1182*
2Ti 4:11 Get M and bring him with you, because *G3453*
Phm 24 And so do M, Aristarchus, Demas and *G3453*
1Pe 5:13 you her greetings, and so does my son M. *G3453*
Rev 13:16 to receive a m on their right hands or on *G5916*
Rev 13:17 not buy or sell unless they had the m, *G5916*
Rev 14: 9 receives its m on their forehead or *G5916*
Rev 14:11 anyone who receives the m of its name." *G5916*
Rev 16: 2 people who had the m of the beast and *G5916*
Rev 19:20 who had received the m of the beast and *G5916*
Rev 20: 4 had not received its m on their foreheads *G5916*

MARKABOTH See BETH MARKABOTH

MARKED (11) [MARK]

Jos 18:20 the boundaries that m out the inheritance of NDT
Job 15:22 realm of darkness; he *is* m for the sword. H7595
Job 38: 5 Who m off its dimensions? Surely you H8492
Pr 8:27 when he m out the horizon on the face of H2980
Pr 8:29 when he m out the foundations of H2980
Isa 40:12 breadth of his hand m off the heavens? H9419
Zec 11: 4 "Shepherd the flock *m for* slaughter. AIT
Zec 11: 7 So I shepherded the flock *m for* slaughter AIT
Ac 17:26 and *he* m out their appointed times in *G3988*
Eph 1:13 *you were* m in him with a seal, the *G5381*
Heb 12: 1 with perseverance the race m out for us, *G4618*

MARKER (2) [MARK]

Isa 44:13 a line and makes an outline with a m; H8574
Eze 39:15 bone will leave a m beside it until the H7483

MARKET (5) [MARKETPLACE, MARKETPLACES]

1Ki 20:34 set up your own m areas in Damascus, H2575
Am 8: 5 Sabbath be ended that *we may* m wheat?" H7337
Zep 1:11 you who live in the m district; all your H4847
Jn 2:16 turning my Father's house into a m! *G3875+1866*
1Co 10:25 sold in the meat m without raising *G3425*

MARKETPLACE (8) [MARKET]

Isa 23: 3 she became the m *of* the nations. H6087
Eze 27:24 In your m they traded with you beautiful H5326
Mt 20: 3 saw others standing in the m doing nothing. *G59*
Mk 7: 4 they come from the m they do not eat unless *G59*
Lk 7:32 sitting in the m and calling out to each *G59*
Ac 16:19 dragged them into the m to face the *G59*
Ac 17: 5 up some bad characters *from* the m, *G61*
Ac 17:17 as well as in the m day by day with those *G59*

MARKETPLACES (6) [MARKET]

Mt 11:16 children sitting in the m and calling out to *G59*
Mt 23: 7 with respect in the m and to be called *G59*
Mk 6:56 countryside—they placed the sick in the m. *G59*
Mk 12:38 robes and be greeted with respect in the m, *G59*
Lk 11:43 respectful greetings in the m. *G59*
Lk 20:46 with respect in the m and have the most *G59*

MARKS (10) [MARK]

Ge 35:20 to this day that pillar m Rachel's tomb. NDT
Lev 19:28 the dead or put tattoo m on yourselves. H4182
1Sa 21:13 making m on the doors of the gate and H9344
2Ki 23:17 "It m the tomb of the man of God who came NDT
Job 13:27 all my paths *by* putting m on the soles of H2977
Job 26:10 *He* m out the horizon on the face of the H2552
Isa 44:13 out with chisels and m it with compasses. H9306
Jn 20:25 I see the nail m in his hands and put *G5596*
2Co 12:12 among you the m of a true apostle, *G4956*
Gal 6:17 I bear on my body the m of Jesus. *G5116*

MAROTH (1)

Mic 1:12 Those who live in M writhe in pain H5300

MARRED (2)

Isa 52:14 being and his form m beyond human NDT
Jer 18: 4 shaping from the clay was m in his hands; H8845

MARRIAGE (43) [MARRY]

Ge 29:26 to give the younger daughter in m before H5989
Ex 2:21 *who* gave his daughter Zipporah to Moses in m H5989
Lev 21: 4 unclean for people related *to* him by m, H1251
Dt 22:16 "*I* gave my daughter in m to H5989+4200+851
Dt 23: 2 No one born of a forbidden m nor any of H4927
Jos 15:16 *I will* give my daughter Aksah in m H5989+4200+851
Jos 15:17 gave his daughter Aksah to him in m H5989+4200+851
Jdg 1:12 *I will* give my daughter Aksah in m H5989+4200+851
Jdg 1:13 gave his daughter Aksah to him in m H5989+4200+851
Jdg 3: 6 *They* took their daughters in m H4374+4200+851
Jdg 12: 9 *He* gave his daughters away in m to those H8938
Jdg 21: 1 us *will* give his daughter in m H5989+4200+851
Jdg 21: 7 to give them any of our daughters in m?" H1426
1Sa 17:25 *He will* also give him his daughter in m H5989
1Sa 18:17 *I will* give her to you in m H5989+4200+851
1Sa 18:19 she was given in m to Adriel H5989+4200+851
1Sa 18:27 gave him his daughter Michal in m H5989+4200+851
1Ki 2:21 *Let* Abishag the Shunammite be given in m H5989+4200+851
1Ki 11:19 *he* gave him a sister of his own wife, Queen Tahpenes, in m H5989+851
2Ki 8:27 he was related by m *to* Ahab's family. H3163
2Ki 14: 9 Give your daughter to my son in m H5989+4200+851
1Ch 2:35 gave his daughter in m to his H5989+4200+851
1Ch 5: 1 when he defiled his father's m bed H3661
2Ch 18: 1 and *he* allied himself with Ahab by m. H3161
2Ch 25:18 Give your daughter to my son in m H5989+4200+851
Ezr 9:12 *do* not give your daughters in m to their H5989
Ne 10:30 not *to* give our daughters in m to the H5989
Ne 13:25 "*You are* not *to* give your daughters in m H5989
Ne 13:25 nor *are you to* take their daughters in m H5951
Jer 29: 6 and give your daughters in m, H5989+4200+408
Da 11:17 *he will* give him a daughter in m H5989+2021+851
Mal 2:14 your partner, the wife of your m covenant. H1382
Mt 1:25 But *he did* not consummate *their* m until *G1182*
Mt 22:30 will neither marry nor *be* given in m; *G1139*
Mt 24:38 marrying and giving in m, up to the day *G1139*
Mk 12:25 they will neither marry nor *be* given in m *G1139*
Lk 2:36 with her husband seven years after her m, *G4220*
Lk 3:19 the tetrarch because of his m to Herodias, NDT
Lk 17:27 marrying and *being* given in m up to the *G1139*
Lk 20:34 of this age marry and *are* given in m. *G1140*
Lk 20:35 dead will neither marry nor *be* given in m, *G1139*
Heb 13: 4 M should be honored by all, and the *G1141*
Heb 13: 4 and the m bed kept pure, for God NDT

MARRIAGES (1) [MARRY]

Ne 13:26 Was it not because of m like these that NDT

MARRIED (77) [MARRY]

Ge 4:19 Lamech m two women, one named Adah H4374
Ge 6: 2 and *they* m any of them they chose. H4374+851
Ge 11:29 Abram and Nahor both m. The name H4374+851
Ge 20: 3 you have taken; she *is a* m *woman*." H1249+1251
Ge 24:67 of his mother Sarah, and *he* m Rebekah. H4374
Ge 25:20 old when he m Rebekah H4374+4200+2257+4200+851
Ge 26:34 *he* m Judith daughter of Beeri the H4374+851
Ge 28: 9 went to Ishmael and m Mahalath, H4374+851
Ge 38: 2 *He* m her and made love to her H4374
Ex 2: 1 of the tribe of Levi m a Levite woman, H4374
Ex 6:20 Amram m his father's sister H4374+4200+851
Ex 6:23 Aaron m Elisheba, daughter H4374+4200+851
Ex 6:25 son of Aaron m one of the H4374+4200+851
Ex 22:16 virgin who is not pledged to be m and H829
Nu 5:19 become impure while m to your husband, H9393
Nu 5:20 gone astray while m to your husband H9393
Nu 5:29 herself impure while m to her husband, H9393
Nu 12: 1 for *he had* m a Cushite. H4374+851
Nu 36:11 m their cousins on their H2118+4200+851
Nu 36:12 *They* m within the clans of the H2118+4200+851
Dt 20: 7 pledged to a woman and not m her? H4374
Dt 22:14 "*I* m this woman, but when I H4374
Dt 22:23 a virgin pledged to be m and he sleeps H829
Dt 22:25 young woman pledged to be m and rapes H829
Dt 22:28 who is not pledged to be m and rapes H829
Dt 24: 5 If a man *has* recently m, he must not H4374+851
Dt 24: 5 bring happiness to the wife *he has* m. H4374
Dt 28:30 *You will be* pledged to be m to a woman H829
Ru 1: 4 *They* m Moabite women, one named H5951+851
1Sa 25:43 David *had* also m Ahinoam of Jezreel H4374
2Sa 13:13 he will not keep me from being m to you." NDT
2Sa 17:25 an Ishmaelite who *had* m Abigail H995+448
1Ki 3: 1 king of Egypt and m his daughter. H4374
1Ki 4:11 he *was* m to Taphath H2118+4200+851
1Ki 4:15 he *had* m Basemath daughter H4374+4200+851
1Ki 7: 8 Pharaoh's daughter, whom *he had* m. H4374
1Ki 16:31 but *he* also m Jezebel daughter of H4374+851
2Ki 8:18 for *he* m a daughter of Ahab. H2118+4200+851

1Ch 2:19 Azubah died, Caleb **m** Ephrath, who bore H4374
1Ch 2:21 **m** the daughter of Makir the father of H4374
1Ch 4:18 daughter Bithiah, whom Mered *had* **m**. H4374
1Ch 23:22 Their cousins, the sons of Kish, **m** them. H5951
2Ch 11:18 Rehoboam **m** Mahalath, who was H4374+851
2Ch 11:20 Then *he* **m** Maakah daughter of Absalom H4374
2Ch 13:21 *He* **m** fourteen wives and had twenty-two H5951
2Ch 21: 6 for he **m** a daughter of Ahab. H2118+851
Ezr 2:61 a man who *had* **m** a daughter of H4374+851
Ezr 10:10 unfaithful; *you have* **m** foreign women H3782
Ezr 10:14 in our towns who *has* **m** a foreign woman H3782
Ezr 10:17 all the men who *had* **m** foreign women. H3782
Ezr 10:18 the following *had* **m** foreign women: H3782
Ezr 10:44 All these *had* **m** foreign women, and H5951
Ne 6:18 his son Jehohanan *had* **m** the daughter of H4374
Ne 7:63 a man who *had* **m** a daughter of H4374+851
Ne 13:23 men of Judah *who had* **m** women from H3782
Pr 30:23 a contemptible woman *who gets* **m**, and H1249
Isa 54: 6 in spirit—a **wife** *who m* young, only to be AIT
Isa 62: 4 delight in you, and your land *will* **be m**. H1249
Hos 1: 3 So *he* **m** Gomer daughter of Diblaim, and H4374
Mt 1:18 Mary *was* **pledged to be m** to Joseph, G3650
Mt 22:25 The first one **m** and died, and since he G1138
Mt 22:28 since all of them *were* **m to** her? G2400
Mk 6:17 his brother Philip's wife, whom *he had* **m**. G1138
Mk 12:20 The first one **m** and died without G3284+1222
Mk 12:21 The second one **m** the widow, but he also G3284
Mk 12:23 since the seven **were m** to her?" G2400+1222
Lk 1:27 to a virgin **pledged to be m** to a man G3650
Lk 2: 5 who *was* **pledged to be m** to him and was G3650
Lk 14:20 '*I just* **got m**, so I can't G1222+1138
Lk 20:29 The first one **m** a woman and died G3284
Lk 20:31 then the third **m** her, and in the same G3284
Lk 20:33 since the seven *were* **m** to her?" G2400+1222
Ro 7: 2 by law a **m** woman is bound to her G5635
1Co 7:10 *To* the **m** I give this command (not I, but G1138
1Co 7:33 But a **m** *man* is concerned about the G1138
1Co 7:34 But a **m** *woman* is concerned about the G1138
1Co 7:36 He is not sinning. *They should get* **m**. G1138

MARRIES (19) [MARRY]

Ex 21:10 If *he* **m** another woman, he must not H4374
Lev 20:14 " 'If a man **m** both a woman and her H4374
Lev 20:17 " 'If a man **m** his sister, the daughter of H4374
Lev 20:21 " 'If a man **m** his brother's wife, it is an H4374
Lev 21:13 " 'The woman he **m** must be a virgin. H4374
Lev 22:12 daughter **m** anyone other H2118+4200+408
Nu 30: 6 "If *she* **m** after she H2118+4200+408+2118
Dt 24: 1 If a man **m** a woman who H4374+2256+1249
Isa 62: 5 As a young man **m** a young woman, so H1249
Jer 3: 1 leaves him and **m** another man, H2118+4200
Mt 5:32 anyone *who* **m** a divorced woman G1138
Mt 19: 9 **m** another woman commits adultery." G1138
Mk 10:11 his wife and **m** another woman commits G1138
Mk 10:12 her husband and **m** another man, G1138
Lk 16:18 his wife and **m** another woman commits G1138
Lk 16:18 the *man who* **m** a divorced woman G1138
Ro 7: 3 not an adulteress *if she* **m** another man. G1181
1Co 7:28 if a virgin **m**, she has not sinned. G1138
1Co 7:38 So then, he *who* **m** the virgin does right G1139

MARROW (2)

Job 21:24 well nourished in body, bones rich with **m**. H4672
Heb 4:12 spirit, joints and **m**; it judges the G3678

MARRY (49) [INTERMARRY, MARITAL, MARRIAGE, MARRIAGES, MARRIED, MARRIES, MARRYING]

Ge 19:14 *who were* **pledged to m** his daughters. H4374
Ge 28: 1 "*Do* not **m** a Canaanite woman. H4374+851
Ge 28: 6 "*Do* not **m** a Canaanite woman," H4374+851
Ge 34:21 We *can* **m** their daughters H4374+4200+851
Ge 34:21 their daughters and they *can* **m** ours. H5989
Lev 21: 7 " '*They must* not **m** women defiled by H4374
Lev 21:14 *He must* not **m** a widow, a divorced H4374
Nu 36: 3 suppose *they* **m** men from H2118+4200+851
Nu 36: 3 to that of the tribe *they* **m into**. H2118+4200
Nu 36: 4 that of the tribe **into** which *they* **m**, H2118+4200
Nu 36: 6 *They may* **m** anyone they H2118+4200+851
Nu 36: 6 as long as *they* **m** within their H2118+4200+851
Nu 36: 8 tribe *must* **m** someone in her H2118+4200+851
Dt 20: 7 die in battle and someone else **m** her." H4374
Dt 22:29 He *must* **m** the young woman, H2118+4200+851
Dt 22:30 A man *is* not *to* **m** his father's wife; he H4374
Dt 24: 4 not allowed to **m** her again H4374+4200+851
Dt 25: 5 his widow *must* not **m** outside H2118+4200+408
Dt 25: 5 take her and **m** her and fulfill H4374+4200+851
Dt 25: 7 does not want to **m** his brother's wife, H4374
Dt 25: 8 in saying, "I do not want to **m** her," H4374
Jdg 11:37 with my friends, because I will **never m**." H1436
Jdg 11:38 wept because she would **never m**. H1436
Jdg 14: 8 when he went back to **m** her, he turned H4374
Isa 62: 5 woman, so *will* your Builder **m** you; as a H1249
Jer 16: 2 "*You must* not **m** and have sons or H4374+851
Jer 29: 6 **M** and have sons and daughters H4374+851
Eze 44:22 *They must* not **m** widows or H4374+851+4200
Eze 44:22 *they may* **m** only virgins of Israelite H4374
Hos 1: 2 **m** a promiscuous woman and have H4374+4200
Mt 19:10 a husband and wife, it is better not *to* **m**." G1138
Mt 22:24 his brother *must* **m** the widow and raise G2102
Mt 22:30 resurrection *people will* neither **m** nor be G1138
Mk 12:19 the man *must* **m** the widow and raise up G3284
Mk 12:25 *they will* neither **m** nor be given in G1138
Lk 20:28 the man *must* **m** the widow and raise up G3284
Lk 20:34 people of this age **m** and are given in G1138
Lk 20:35 from the dead *will* neither **m** nor be given G1138
1Co 7: 9 themselves, *they should* **m**, for it is better G1138
1Co 7: 9 it is better *to* **m** than to burn with G1138
1Co 7:28 But if *you do* **m**, you have not sinned; and G1138
1Co 7:28 But those *who* **m** will face many troubles G5525S
1Co 7:36 and he feels he ought *to* **m**, G4048+1181S
1Co 7:37 made up his mind **not** *to* **m** the virgin— G5498
1Co 7:38 he *who does* not **m** her does better. G1139
1Co 7:39 she is free *to* **m** anyone she wishes G1138
1Ti 4: 3 They forbid people *to* **m** and order them to G1138
1Ti 5:11 their dedication to Christ, they want *to* **m**. G1138
1Ti 5:14 So I counsel younger widows *to* **m**, to have G1138

MARRYING (5) [MARRY]

Ezr 10: 2 to our God *by* **m** foreign women from H3782
Ne 13:27 to our God by **m** foreign women? H3782
Mal 2:11 the LORD loves *by* **m** women who worship H1249
Mt 24:38 drinking, **m** and giving in marriage G1138
Lk 17:27 **m** and being given in marriage up to the G1138

MARS' HILL (KJV) MEETING OF THE AREOPAGUS

MARSENA (1)

Est 1:14 **M** and Memukan, the seven H5333

MARSH (2)

Job 8:11 papyrus grow tall where there is no **m**? H1289
Job 40:21 hidden among the reeds in the **m**. H1289

MARSHAL (2) [MARSHALED]

Mic 5: 1 **M** *your* **troops** now, city of troops, for a H1518
Na 2: 1 brace yourselves, **m** all your strength! H599

MARSHALED (4) [MARSHAL]

2Ch 25:11 Amaziah then **m** *his* **strength** and led his H2616
Job 6: 4 God's terrors *are* **m** *against* me. H6885
Job 32:14 But Job *has* not **m** his words against me H6885
Isa 45:12 out the heavens; *I* **m** their starry hosts. H7422

MARSHES (2)

Jer 51:32 crossings seized, the **m** set on fire, and the H106
Eze 47:11 But the swamps and **m** will not become H1465

MARTHA (13)

Lk 10:38 a woman named **M** opened her home to G3450
Lk 10:40 But **M** was distracted by all the G3450
Lk 10:41 "**M**, Martha," the Lord answered, "you are G3450
Lk 10:41 "Martha, **M**," the Lord answered, "you are G3450
Jn 11: 1 the village of Mary and her sister **M**. G3450
Jn 11: 5 Now Jesus loved **M** and her sister and G3450
Jn 11:19 Jews had come to **M** and Mary to comfort G3450
Jn 11:20 When **M** heard that Jesus was coming G3450
Jn 11:21 **M** said to Jesus, "if you had been G3450
Jn 11:24 **M** answered, "I know he will rise again in G3450
Jn 11:30 still at the place where **M** had met him. G3450
Jn 11:39 said **M**, the sister of the dead man G3450
Jn 12: 2 **M** served, while Lazarus was among those G3450

MARTYR (1)

Ac 22:20 when the blood *of* your **m** Stephen was G3459

MARVELED (2) [MARVELOUS]

Lk 2:33 and mother **m** at what was said G1639+2513
2Th 1:10 holy people and *to be* **m at** among all G2513

MARVELING (1) [MARVELOUS]

Lk 9:43 *While* everyone *was* **m** at all that Jesus G2513

MARVELOUS (14) [MARVELED, MARVELING]

1Ch 16:24 nations, his **m** *deeds* among all peoples. H7098
Job 37: 5 God's voice thunders *in* **m** *ways*; he does H7098
Ps 71:17 to this day I declare your **m** *deeds*. H7098
Ps 72:18 God of Israel, who alone does **m** *deeds*. H7098
Ps 86:10 For you are great and do **m** *deeds*; you H7098
Ps 96: 3 nations, his **m** *deeds* among all peoples. H7098
Ps 98: 1 he has done **m** *things*; his right hand H7098
Ps 118:23 has done this, and it *is* **m** in our eyes. H7098
Zec 8: 6 "*It may* seem **m** to the remnant of this H7098
Zec 8: 6 at that time, but *will it* seem **m** to me?" H7098
Mt 21:42 has done this, and it is **m** in our eyes'? G2515
Mk 12:11 has done this, and it is **m** in our eyes'?" G2515
Rev 15: 1 I saw in heaven another great and **m** sign: G2515
Rev 15: 3 "Great and **m** are your deeds, Lord God G2515

MARY (58) [MARY'S]

Mt 1:16 the husband *of* **M**, and Mary was the G3451
Mt 1:16 **M** was the mother of Jesus who is G4005S
Mt 1:18 His mother **M** was pledged to be married G3451
Mt 1:20 be afraid to take **M** home as your wife, G3451
Mt 1:24 him and took **M** home as his wife. NDT
Mt 2:11 they saw the child with his mother **M**, and G3451
Mt 13:55 Isn't his mother's name **M**, and aren't his G3451
Mt 27:56 Among them were **M** Magdalene, Mary G3451
Mt 27:56 **M** the mother of James and Joseph G3451
Mt 27:61 **M** Magdalene and the other Mary were G3451
Mt 27:61 the other **M** were sitting there G3451
Mt 28: 1 **M** Magdalene and the other Mary went to G3451
Mt 28: 1 the other **M** went to look at the G3451
Mk 15:40 Among them were **M** Magdalene, Mary G3451
Mk 15:40 **M** the mother of James the younger and G3451
Mk 15:47 **M** Magdalene and Mary the mother of G3451
Mk 15:47 Mary Magdalene and **M** the mother of G3451
Mk 16: 1 Sabbath was over, **M** Magdalene, Mary G3451
Mk 16: 1 Mary Magdalene, **M** the mother of James G3451
Mk 16: 9 he appeared first *to* **M** Magdalene, out of G3451
Lk 1:27 The virgin's name was **M**. G3451
Lk 1:29 **M** was greatly troubled at his words and G3836S
Lk 1:30 "Do not be afraid, **M**; you have found G3451
Lk 1:34 "How will this be," **M** asked the angel G3451
Lk 1:38 Lord's servant," **M** answered. "May your G3451
Lk 1:39 At that time **M** got ready and hurried to a G3451
Lk 1:46 And **M** said: "My soul glorifies the Lord G3451
Lk 1:56 **M** stayed with Elizabeth for about three G3451
Lk 2: 5 He went there to register with **M**, who was G3451
Lk 2:16 they hurried off and found **M** and Joseph, G3451
Lk 2:19 But **M** treasured up all these things and G3451
Lk 2:22 Joseph and **M** took him to Jerusalem to NDT
Lk 2:34 Then Simeon blessed them and said to **M** G3451
Lk 2:39 When Joseph and **M** had done everything NDT
Lk 8: 2 **M** (called Magdalene) from whom seven G3451
Lk 10:39 She had a sister called **M**, who sat at the G3451
Lk 10:42 **M** has chosen what is better, and it will G3451
Lk 24:10 It was **M** Magdalene, Joanna, Mary the G3451
Lk 24:10 Joanna, **M** the mother of James, and the G3451
Jn 11: 1 the village *of* **M** and her sister Martha. G3451
Jn 11: 2 **M**, whose brother Lazarus now lay sick G3451
Jn 11:19 come to Martha and **M** to comfort them in G3451
Jn 11:20 out to meet him, but **M** stayed at home. G3451
Jn 11:28 went back and called her sister **M** aside. G3451
Jn 11:29 When **M** heard this, she got up quickly G1697S
Jn 11:31 Jews who had been with **M** in the house, G3451
Jn 11:32 When **M** reached the place where Jesus G3451
Jn 11:45 of the Jews who had come to visit **M**, G3451
Jn 12: 3 Then **M** took about a pint of pure nard, an G3451
Jn 19:25 his mother's sister, **M** the wife of Clopas G3451
Jn 19:25 the wife of Clopas, and **M** Magdalene. G3451
Jn 20: 1 **M** Magdalene went to the tomb and saw G3451
Jn 20:11 Now **M** stood outside the tomb crying. G3451
Jn 20:16 Jesus said to her, "**M**." She turned toward G3451
Jn 20:18 **M** Magdalene went to the disciples with G3451
Ac 1:14 with the women and **M** the mother of G3451
Ac 12:12 went to the house *of* **M** the mother of G3451
Ro 16: 6 Greet **M**, who worked very hard for you. G3451

MARY'S (2) [MARY]

Mk 6: 3 Isn't this **M** son and the brother of James G3451
Lk 1:41 When Elizabeth heard **M** greeting, the G3451

MASH (1)

Isa 30:24 that work the soil will eat fodder and **m**, H2796

MASHAL (1)

1Ch 6:74 from the tribe of Asher they received **M** H5443

MASK (1)

1Th 2: 5 did we put on a **m to cover up** greed— G4733

MASKIL (13)

Ps 32: T A **m**. H5380
Ps 42: T A **m** of the Sons of Korah H5380
Ps 44: T Of the Sons of Korah. A **m**. H5380
Ps 45: T the Sons of Korah. A **m**. A wedding song. H5380
Ps 52: T A **m** of David. When Doeg H5380
Ps 53: T According to mahalath. A **m** of David. H5380
Ps 54: T A **m** of David. When the H5380
Ps 55: T With stringed instruments. A **m** of David. H5380
Ps 74: T A **m** of Asaph. H5380
Ps 78: T A **m** of Asaph. H5380
Ps 88: T A **m** of Heman the Ezrahite H5380
Ps 89: T A **m** of Ethan the Ezrahite. H5380
Ps 142: T A **m** of David. When he was in the cave H5380

MASONS (5)

2Ki 12:12 the **m** and stonecutters. They purchased H1553
2Ki 22: 6 the builders and the **m**. Also have them H1553
1Ch 22:15 stonecutters, **m** and carpenters, as H3093+74
2Ch 24:12 They hired **m** and carpenters to restore H2935
Ezr 3: 7 they gave money to the **m** and carpenters, H2935

MASQUERADE (1) [MASQUERADES, MASQUERADING]

2Co 11:15 if his servants also **m** as servants of G3571

MASQUERADES (1) [MASQUERADE]

2Co 11:14 Satan himself **m** as an angel of light. G3571

MASQUERADING (1) [MASQUERADE]

2Co 11:13 deceitful workers, **m** as apostles of Christ. G3571

MASREKAH (2)

Ge 36:36 Samlah from **M** succeeded him as king. H5388
1Ch 1:47 Samlah from **M** succeeded him as king. H5388

MASSA (2)

Ge 25:14 Mishma, Dumah, **M**, H5364
1Ch 1:30 Mishma, Dumah, **M**, Hadad, Tema, H5364

MASSACRE (1)

Hos 1: 4 the house of Jehu for the **m** *at* Jezreel, H1947

MASSAH (5)

Ex 17: 7 called the place **M** and Meribah because H5001
Dt 6:16 LORD your God to the test as you did at **M**. H5001
Dt 9:22 Taberah, at **M** and at Kibroth Hattaavah. H5001
Dt 33: 8 You tested him at **M**; you contended with H5001
Ps 95: 8 as you did that day at **M** in the wilderness, H5001

MASSES (1) [MASSING]
Isa 5:14 their nobles and **m** with all their brawlers H2162

MASSING (1) [MASSES]
Isa 13: 4 the kingdoms, like nations **m together**! H665

MASSIVE (1)
Mk 13: 1 **What m** stones! What magnificent G4534

MAST (2)
Isa 33:23 The **m** is not held secure, the sail H4029+9568
Eze 27: 5 cedar from Lebanon to make a **m** for you. H9568

MASTER (145) [MASTER'S, MASTERED, MASTERS, MASTERY]
Ge 24: 9 the thigh of his **m** Abraham and swore an H123
Ge 24:10 with all kinds of good things from his **m**. H123
Ge 24:12 God of my **m** Abraham, make me H123
Ge 24:12 show kindness to my **m** Abraham. H123
Ge 24:14 that you have shown kindness to my **m**." H123
Ge 24:27 the God of my **m** Abraham, who has H123
Ge 24:27 his kindness and faithfulness to my **m**. H123
Ge 24:35 The LORD has blessed my **m** abundantly H123
Ge 24:37 And my **m** made me swear an oath, and H123
Ge 24:39 "Then I asked my **m**, 'What if the woman H123
Ge 24:42 God of my **m** Abraham, if you will H123
Ge 24:48 the God of my **m** Abraham, who had H123
Ge 24:49 show kindness and faithfulness to my **m**, H123
Ge 24:54 he said, "Send me on my way to my **m**." H123
Ge 24:56 Send me on my way so I may go to my **m**." H123
Ge 24:65 "He is my **m**," the servant H123
Ge 39: 2 he lived in the house of his Egyptian **m**. H123
Ge 39: 3 his **m** saw that the LORD was with him H123
Ge 39: 8 "my **m** does not concern himself with H123
Ge 39: 9 My **m** has withheld nothing from me except NDT
Ge 39:16 cloak beside her until his **m** came home. H123
Ge 39:19 When his **m** heard the story his wife told H123
Ge 39:20 Joseph's **m** took him and put him in prison H123
Ge 40: 1 baker of the king of Egypt offended their **m**, H123
Ge 44: 5 Isn't this the cup my **m** drinks from and also H123
Ex 21: 4 If his **m** gives him a wife and she bears him H123
Ex 21: 4 her children shall belong to her **m**, H123
Ex 21: 5 'I love my **m** and my wife and children H123
Ex 21: 6 then his **m** must take him before the judges. H123
Ex 21: 8 does not please the **m** who has selected H123
Ex 21:32 thirty shekels of silver to the **m** *of* the slave, H123
Dt 23:15 with you, do not hand them over to their **m**. H123
Jdg 19:11 the servant said to his **m**, "Come, H123
Jdg 19:12 His **m** replied, "No. We won't go into any H123
Jdg 19:26 to the house where her **m** was staying, H123
Jdg 19:27 When her **m** got up in the morning and H123
1Sa 20:38 picked up the arrow and returned to his **m**. H123
1Sa 24: 6 that I should do such a thing to my **m**, H123
1Sa 25:14 the wilderness to give our **m** his greetings, H123
1Sa 25:17 is hanging over our **m** and his whole H123
1Sa 26:16 because you did not guard your **m**, the H123
1Sa 30:13 My **m** abandoned me when I became ill H123
1Sa 30:15 will not kill me or hand me over to my **m**, H123
2Sa 2: 5 kindness to Saul your **m** by burying him. H123
2Sa 2: 7 for Saul your **m** is dead, and the H123
2Sa 9:10 grandson of your **m**, will always eat at my H123
1Ki 11:23 who had fled from his **m**, Hadadezer king H123
1Ki 18: 8 "Go tell your **m**, 'Elijah is here.'" H123
1Ki 18:10 kingdom where my **m** has not sent H123
1Ki 18:11 But now you tell me to go to my **m** and say H123
1Ki 18:14 And now you tell me to go to my **m** and say, H123
1Ki 22:17 the LORD said, 'These people have no **m**. H123
2Ki 2: 3 is going to take your **m** from you today?" H123
2Ki 2: 5 is going to take your **m** from you today?" H123
2Ki 2:16 Let them go and look for your **m**. Perhaps H123
2Ki 5: 1 in the sight of his **m** and highly regarded, H123
2Ki 5: 3 "If only my **m** would see the prophet who is H123
2Ki 5: 4 Naaman went to his **m** and told him what H123
2Ki 5:18 When my **m** enters the temple of Rimmon H123
2Ki 5:20 himself, "My **m** was too easy on Naaman H123
2Ki 5:22 "My **m** sent me to say, 'Two young men H123
2Ki 5:25 When he went in and stood before his **m** H123
2Ki 6:22 eat and drink and then go back to their **m**." H123
2Ki 6:23 them away, and they returned to their **m**. H123
2Ki 8:14 Hazael left Elisha and returned to his **m**. H123
2Ki 9: 7 are to destroy the house of Ahab your **m**, H123
2Ki 9:31 you Zimri, you murderer of your **m**? H123
2Ki 10: 9 conspired against my **m** and killed him, H123
2Ki 18:23 make a bargain with my **m**, the king of H123
2Ki 18:27 "Was it only to your **m** and you that my H123
2Ki 18:27 you that my **m** sent me to say these H123
2Ki 19: 4 commander, whom his **m**, the king of H123
2Ki 19: 6 to them, "Tell your **m**, 'This is what the H123
1Ch 12:19 us our heads if he deserts to his **m** Saul." H123
2Ch 13: 6 son of David, rebelled against his **m**. H123
2Ch 18:16 the LORD said, 'These people have no **m**. H123
Ps 105:21 He made him **m** of his household, ruler H123
Ps 123: 2 eyes of slaves look to the hand of their **m**, H123
Pr 25:13 sends him; he refreshes the spirit of his **m**. H123
Pr 27:18 whoever protects their **m** will be honored. H123
Pr 30:10 "Do not slander a servant to their **m**, or H123
Isa 1: 3 The ox knows its **m**, the donkey its H7864
Isa 19: 4 Egyptians over to the power of a cruel **m**, H123
Isa 24: 2 as for people, for the **m** as for his servant H123
Isa 36: 8 make a bargain with my **m**, the king of H123
Isa 36:12 "Was it only to your **m** and you that my H123
Isa 36:12 you that my **m** sent me to say these H123
Isa 37: 4 commander, whom his **m**, the king of H123
Isa 37: 6 to them, "Tell your **m**, 'This is what the H123
Jer 22:18 will not mourn for him: 'Alas, my **m**! Alas, H123
Jer 34: 5 a fire in your honor and lament, "Alas, **m**!" H123
Da 8:23 a **m** *of* intrigue, will arise. H1067
Hos 2:16 you will no longer call me 'my **m**. H1251
Mal 1: 6 "A son honors his father, and a slave his **m**. H123
Mal 1: 6 If I am a **m**, where is the respect H123
Mt 10:24 the teacher, nor a servant above his **m**. G3261
Mt 18:25 the **m** ordered that he and his wife and G3261
Mt 18:27 The servant's **m** took pity on him, canceled G3261
Mt 18:31 went and told their **m** everything that had G3261
Mt 18:32 "Then the **m** called the servant in. 'You G3261
Mt 18:34 In anger his **m** handed him over to the G3261
Mt 24:45 whom the **m** has put in charge of the G3261
Mt 24:46 that servant whose **m** finds him doing so G3261
Mt 24:48 'My **m** is staying away a long time G3261
Mt 24:50 The **m** of that servant will come on a day G3261
Mt 25:19 "After a long time the **m** of those servants G3261
Mt 25:20 '**M**,' he said, 'you entrusted me with five G3261
Mt 25:21 "His **m** replied, 'Well done, good and G3261
Mt 25:22 '**M**,' he said, 'you entrusted me with two G3261
Mt 25:23 "His **m** replied, 'Well done, good and G3261
Mt 25:24 '**M**,' he said, 'I knew that you are a hard G3261
Mt 25:26 "His **m** replied, 'You wicked, lazy servant G3261
Lk 5: 5 Simon answered, "**M**, we've worked hard G2181
Lk 7: 2 servant, whom **his m** valued highly, was G899S
Lk 8:24 woke him, saying, "**M**, Master, we're G2181
Lk 8:24 "Master, **M**, we're going to drown G2181
Lk 8:45 Peter said, "**M**, the people are crowding G2181
Lk 9:33 Peter said to him, "**M**, it is good for us to G2181
Lk 9:49 "**M**," said John, "we saw someone driving G2181
Lk 12:36 waiting for their **m** to return from a G3261
Lk 12:37 servants whose **m** finds them watching G3261
Lk 12:38 those servants whose **m** finds them ready, NDT
Lk 12:42 whom the **m** puts in charge of his servants G3261
Lk 12:43 servant whom the **m** finds doing so when G3261
Lk 12:45 'My **m** is taking a long time in coming G3261
Lk 12:46 The **m** of that servant will come on a day G3261
Lk 12:47 does not do what the **m** wants will be G899S
Lk 14:21 came back and reported this *to* his **m**. G3261
Lk 14:23 "Then the **m** told his servant, 'Go out to G3261
Lk 16: 3 My **m** is taking away my job G3261
Lk 16: 5 the first, 'How much do you owe my **m**?' G3261
Lk 16: 8 "The **m** commended the dishonest G3261
Lk 17:13 a loud voice, "Jesus, **M**, have pity on us!" G2181
Lk 19:17 his **m** replied. 'Because you NDT
Lk 19:19 "His **m** answered, 'You take charge of five NDT
Lk 19:22 "His **m** replied, 'I will judge you by your NDT
Jn 2: 8 out and take it *to* the **m of the banquet**." G804
Jn 2: 9 the **m of the banquet** tasted the water G804
Jn 13:16 no servant is greater *than* his **m**, nor is a G3261
Jn 15:20 'A servant is not greater *than* his **m**.' If G3261
Ro 6:14 For sin *shall* no *longer be* your **m**, because G3259
Ro 14: 4 To their own **m**, servants stand or G3261
Eph 6: 9 he who is both their **M** and yours is in G3261
Col 4: 1 know that you also have a **M** in heaven. G3261
2Ti 2:21 useful *to* the **M** and prepared to do any G1305

MASTER'S (34) [MASTER]
Ge 24:10 with him ten of his **m** camels loaded with H123
Ge 24:27 the journey to the house of my **m** relatives." H123
Ge 24:36 My **m** wife Sarah has borne him a son in H123
Ge 24:44 the one the LORD has chosen for my **m** son. H123
Ge 24:48 granddaughter of my **m** brother for his son. H123
Ge 24:51 let her become the wife of your **m** son H123
Ge 39: 7 after a while his **m** wife took notice of H123
Ge 40: 7 were in custody with him in his **m** house, H123
Ge 44: 8 we steal silver or gold from your **m** house? H123
1Sa 29: 4 could he regain his **m** favor than by taking H123
1Sa 29:10 along with your **m** servants who have come H123
2Sa 9: 9 "I have given your **m** grandson everything H123
2Sa 9:10 so that your **m** grandson may be provided H123
2Sa 11: 9 palace with all his **m** servants and did not H123
2Sa 11:13 to sleep on his mat among his **m** servants; H123
2Sa 12: 8 I gave your **m** house to you, and your H123
2Sa 12: 8 and your **m** wives into your arms. H123
2Sa 16: 3 then asked, "Where is your **m** grandson?" H123
2Sa 20: 6 Take your **m** men and pursue him, or he H123
2Ki 6:32 the sound of his **m** footsteps behind him H123
2Ki 10: 2 "You have your **m** sons with you and you H123
2Ki 10: 3 most worthy of your **m** sons and set him on H123
2Ki 10: 3 Then fight for your **m** house." H123
2Ki 10: 6 the heads of your **m** sons and come to me H123
2Ki 18:24 one officer of the least of my **m** officials, H123
Isa 22:18 of will become a disgrace to your **m** house. H123
Isa 36: 9 one officer of the least of my **m** officials, H123
Mt 15:27 the crumbs that fall from their **m** table." G3261
Mt 25:18 hole in the ground and hid his **m** money. G3261
Mt 25:21 Come and share your **m** happiness!' G3261
Mt 25:23 Come and share your **m** happiness!' G3261
Lk 12:47 who knows the **m** will and does not get G3261
Lk 16: 5 he called in each one of his **m** debtors. G3261
Jn 15:15 a servant does not know his **m** business. G3261

MASTERED (2) [MASTER]
1Co 6:12 I *will* not *be* **m** by anything. G2027
2Pe 2:19 are slaves to whatever *has* **m** them." G2487

MASTERS (18) [MASTER]
Ex 1:11 So they put slave **m** over them to oppress H8569
1Sa 25:10 are breaking away from their **m** these days. H123
Jer 27: 4 Give them a message for their **m** and say H123
Jer 27: 4 the God of Israel, says: "Tell this to your **m**: H123
La 1: 5 Her foes have become her **m**; her H8031
Mt 6:24 "No one can serve two **m**. Either you will G3261
Mt 10:25 their teachers, and servants like their **m**. G3261
Lk 16:13 "No one can serve two **m**. Either you will G3261
Eph 6: 5 obey your earthly **m** with respect and fear G3261
Eph 6: 9 And **m**, treat your slaves in the same way G3261
Col 3:22 obey your earthly **m** in everything; and do G3261
Col 3:23 as working for the Lord, not for human **m**, NDT
Col 4: 1 **M**, provide your slaves with what is right G3261
1Ti 6: 1 should consider their **m** worthy of full G1305
1Ti 6: 2 who have believing **m** should not show G1305
1Ti 6: 2 better because their **m** are dear to them as NDT
Titus 2: 9 to be subject *to* their **m** in everything, G1305
1Pe 2:18 fear of God submit yourselves *to* your **m**, G1305

MASTERY (1) [MASTER]
Ro 6: 9 death no longer **has m over** him. G3259

MAT (15) [MATS]
2Sa 11:13 out to sleep on his **m** among his master's H5435
Mt 9: 2 to him a paralyzed man, lying on a **m**. G3109
Mt 9: 6 "Get up, take your **m** and go home." G3109
Mk 2: 4 then lowered the **m** the man was lying on G3187
Mk 2: 9 to say, 'Get up, take your **m** and walk'? G3187
Mk 2:11 get up, take your **m** and go home. G3187
Mk 2:12 took his **m** and walked out in full view of G3187
Lk 5:18 a paralyzed man on a **m** and tried to take G3109
Lk 5:19 lowered him on his **m** through the tiles G3110
Lk 5:24 get up, take your **m** and go home. G3110
Jn 5: 8 Pick up your **m** and walk." G3187
Jn 5: 9 he picked up his **m** and walked. G3187
Jn 5:10 the law forbids you to carry your **m**." G3187
Jn 5:11 well said to me, 'Pick up your **m** and walk. G3187
Ac 9:34 Get up and **roll up** your **m**." Immediately G5143

MATCH (3) [MATCHED, MATCHING]
1Ch 12:14 the least was a **m for** a hundred, and the H4200
Eze 31: 8 in the garden of God *could* **m** its beauty. H1948
Lk 5:36 the patch from the new *will* not **m** the old. G5244

MATCHED (1) [MATCH]
2Co 8:11 to do it may be **m by** your completion of it G4048

MATCHING (1) [MATCH]
Ezr 1:10 gold bowls 30 **m** silver bowls 410 other H5467

MATE (7) [MATED, MATING]
Ge 7: 2 a male and its **m**, and one pair of every H851
Ge 7: 2 kind of unclean animal, a male and its **m**, H851
Ge 30:41 animals so they *would* **m** near the H3501
Lev 19:19 "'*Do* not **m** different kinds of animals H8061
Isa 34:15 the falcons will gather, each with its **m**. H8295
Isa 34:16 will be missing, not one will lack her **m**. H8295
Na 2:12 his cubs and strangled the prey for his **m**, H4218

MATED (1) [MATE]
Ge 30:39 they **m** in front of the branches. And they H3501

MATERIAL (17) [MATERIALS]
Ex 26: 4 Make loops of **blue m** along the edge of H9418
Ex 36:11 made loops of **blue m** along the edge of H9418
Lev 13:48 any woven or **knitted m** of linen or wool H6849
Lev 13:49 the woven or **knitted m**, or any leather H6849
Lev 13:51 the woven or **knitted m**, or the leather, H6849
Lev 13:52 the woven or **knitted m** of wool or linen H6849
Lev 13:53 the woven or **knitted m**, or the leather H6849
Lev 13:56 the leather, or the woven or **knitted m**. H6849
Lev 13:57 in the woven or **knitted m**, or in the H6849
Lev 13:58 woven or **knitted m**, or any leather H6849
Lev 13:59 woven or **knitted m**, or any leather H6849
Lev 14:41 scraped and the **m** that is scraped off H6760
Lev 19:19 wear clothing **woven** of two kinds of **m**. H9122
Est 1: 6 of white linen and **purple m** to silver rings H763
Ro 15:27 to share with them their **m** *blessings*. G4920
1Co 9:11 much if we reap a **m** harvest from you? G4920
1Jn 3:17 If anyone has **m** possessions and sees a G3180

MATERIALS (2) [MATERIAL]
Ex 38:21 are the amounts of the **m** used for the NDT
Ne 4:17 Those who carried **m** did their work with H6023

MATING (3) [MATE]
Ge 31:10 male goats **m with** the flock were H6590+6584
Ge 31:12 the male goats **m with** the flock are H6590+6584
Jer 2:24 themselves; at **m time** they will find her. H2544

MATRED (2)
Ge 36:39 name was Mehetabel daughter of **M**, H4765
1Ch 1:50 name was Mehetabel daughter of **M**, H4765

MATRI'S (1)
1Sa 10:21 clan by clan, and **M** clan was taken. H4767

MATRIX (KJV) WOMB

MATS (2) [MAT]
Mk 6:55 carried the sick on **m** to wherever they G3187
Ac 5:15 laid them on beds and **m** so that at least G3187

MATTAN (3)
2Ki 11:18 to pieces and killed **M** the priest of Baal H5509
2Ch 23:17 idols and killed **M** the priest of Baal H5509

Jer 38: 1 Shephatiah son of **M**, Gedaliah son of H5509

MATTANAH (2)

Nu 21:18 Then they went from the wilderness to **M**, H5511
Nu 21:19 from **M** to Nahaliel, from Nahaliel to H5511

MATTANIAH (16)

2Ki 24:17 He made **M**, Jehoiachin's uncle, king in H5514
1Ch 9:15 Heresh, Galal and **M** son of Mika, the son H5514
1Ch 25: 4 Bukkiah, **M**, Uzziel, Shubael and Jerimoth; H5515
1Ch 25:16 the ninth to **M**, his sons and relatives 12 H5515
2Ch 20:14 of Jeiel, the son of **M**, a Levite and H5514
2Ch 29:13 descendants of Asaph, Zechariah and **M**; H5515
Ezr 10:26 **M**, Zechariah, Jehiel, Abdi, Jeremoth H5514
Ezr 10:27 Elioenai, Eliashib, **M**, Jeremoth, Zabad H5514
Ezr 10:30 Benaiah, Maaseiah, **M**, Bezalel, Binnui H5514
Ezr 10:37 **M**, Mattenai and Jaasu. H5514
Ne 11:17 **M** son of Mika, the son of Zabdi, the son H5514
Ne 11:22 Hashabiah, the son of **M**, the son of Mika. H5514
Ne 12: 8 and also **M**, who, together with his H5514
Ne 12:25 **M**, Bakbukiah, Obadiah, Meshullam H5514
Ne 12:35 the son of **M**, the son of Micaiah, H5514
Ne 13:13 of Zakkur, the son of **M**, their assistant, H5514

MATTATHA (1)

Lk 3:31 of Menna, the son *of* **M**, the son of G3477

MATTATHIAS (2)

Lk 3:25 the son *of* **M**, the son of Amos, the son of G3478
Lk 3:26 of Maath, the son *of* **M**, the son of G3478

MATTATTAH (1)

Ezr 10:33 Mattenai, **M**, Zabad, Eliphelet, Jeremai H5523

MATTENAI (3)

Ezr 10:33 **M**, Mattattah, Zabad, Eliphelet, Jeremai H5513
Ezr 10:37 Mattaniah, **M** and Jaasu. H5513
Ne 12:19 of Joiarib's, **M**; of Jedaiah's, Uzzi; H5513

MATTER (73) [MATTERED, MATTERS]

Ge 21:11 The **m** distressed Abraham greatly H1821
Ge 21:17 **"What is the m**, Hagar? H4537+4200+3871
Ge 24: 9 swore an oath to him concerning this **m**. H1821
Ge 37:11 but his father kept the **m** in mind. H1821
Ge 41:32 two forms is that the **m** has been firmly H1821
Lev 4:13 the community is unaware of the **m**, H1821
Lev 5: 4 in any **m** one might carelessly swear about H889S
Lev 13:55 **no m** which side of the fabric has been H196
Nu 18:32 part of it you will not be guilty in **this m**; H2257S
Dt 3:26 not speak to me anymore about this **m**. H1821
Dt 19:15 A **m** must be established by the testimony H1821
Jos 22:31 not been unfaithful to the LORD in this **m**. H5086
Jdg 18:23 **"What's the m** with you that you called H4537
Jdg 18:24 can you ask, **'What's the m** with you?'" H4537
Ru 3:18 will not rest until the **m** is settled today." H1821
Ru 4: 4 I should bring the **m** to your attention and NDT
1Sa 17:30 else and brought up the same **m**, H1821
1Sa 18:23 *"Do you think it is a* **small m** to become the AIT
1Sa 20:23 And about the **m** you and I discussed H1821
2Sa 15:11 innocently, knowing nothing about the **m**. H1821
2Ki 6:28 asked her, **"What's the m?"** She answered H4537
2Ki 20:10 *"It is a* **simple m** for the shadow to go AIT
1Ch 26:32 every **m** *pertaining to* God and for the H1821
2Ch 8:15 to the priests or to the Levites in any **m**, H1821
2Ch 19:11 over you in any **m** *concerning* the LORD, H1821
2Ch 19:11 be over you in any **m** *concerning* the king, H1821
Ezr 4:22 Be careful not to neglect **this** *m*. Why let this AIT
Ezr 5:17 let the king send us his decision in **this** *m*. AIT
Ezr 10: 4 this **m** is in your hands. We will H1821
Ezr 10:13 this **m** cannot be taken care of in a day H4856
Ezr 10:14 of our God in this **m** is turned away from H1821
Job 9:19 If it is **a m of** strength, he is mighty! And if H4200
Job 9:19 And if it is **a m of** justice, who can H4200
Job 12: 2 "Doubtless you are the only people who **m** NDT
Pr 17: 9 whoever repeats the **m** separates close H1821
Pr 17:14 so drop the **m** before a dispute breaks out. NDT
Pr 25: 2 It is the glory of God to conceal a **m**; to H1821
Pr 25: 2 to search out a **m** is the glory of kings. H1821
Ecc 6: 3 many years; yet no **m** how long he lives, if NDT
Ecc 7: 8 The end of a **m** is better than its H1821
Ecc 8: 6 a proper time and procedure for every **m**, H2914
Ecc 12:13 here is the conclusion of the **m**: H1821
Isa 1:18 "Come now, *let us* **settle the m**," says the H3519
Isa 43:26 past for me, *let us* **argue** *the m* together AIT
Eze 8:17 *Is it a* **trivial** *m* for the people of Judah to do AIT
Da 1:20 In every **m** *of* wisdom and understanding H1821
Da 2:15 Arioch then explained the **m** to Daniel. A10418
Da 2:17 explained the **m** to his friends A10418
Da 3:16 to defend ourselves before you in **this** *m*. AIT
Da 7:28 "This is the end of the **m**. I, Daniel, was A10418
Da 7:28 turned pale, but I kept the **m** to myself." A10418
Mt 18:16 so that 'every **m** may be established by G4839
Mk 9:10 They kept the **m** to themselves, discussing G3364
Lk 19:17 you have been trustworthy in a **very small** *m*, AIT
Lk 20:14 *they* **talked the m over**. G1368+4639+253
Jn 3:25 a certain Jew **over the m of** ceremonial G4309
Ac 18:15 your own law—**settle the m** yourselves. G3972
Ro 4: 1 according to the flesh, discovered in this **m**? NDT
Ro 13: 5 also **as a m of** conscience. G1328
Ro 14:17 of God is not a **m** *of* **eating** and drinking, AIT
1Co 4:20 of God is not **a m of** talk but of power. G1877
1Co 7:37 man who *has* **settled the m** in his G2705+1612
1Co 11:22 Shall I praise you? Certainly not in **this** *m*! AIT
2Co 1:20 For **no m how many** promises God has G4012
2Co 7:11 yourselves to be innocent *in* this **m**. G4547
2Co 8:10 about what is best for you in **this** *m*. AIT
2Co 9: 3 about you in this **m** should not prove G3538
2Co 13: 1 "Every **m** must be established by the G4839
Gal 2: 4 This **m** arose because some false believers NDT
Php 1:18 But **what does it m**? The important G5515+5516
Php 4:15 shared with me in the **m** of giving and G3364
1Th 4: 6 that in this **m** no one should wrong or G4547
Heb 9:10 They are only **a m of** food and drink and G2093

MATTERED (1) [MATTER]

Jer 3: 9 Israel's immorality **m** so little to her, H2118

MATTERS (19) [MATTER]

Ex 28: 3 given wisdom in such **m** that they are to NDT
Lev 5: 5 aware that they are guilty in any of **these** *m*, AIT
Ezr 7:11 learned in **m** *concerning* the commands H1821
Est 1:13 to consult experts in *m of* **law** and justice, AIT
Ps 131: 1 not concern myself with **great** *m* or things AIT
Pr 25:27 to search out **m** that are too deep. H4392S
Mal 2: 9 have shown partiality in **m of the law**." H9368
Mt 5:25 **"Settle m** quickly with your G1639+2333
Mt 23:23 the **more important m** of the law— G987
Ac 25:20 I was at a loss how to investigate **such** *m*; AIT
Ro 14: 1 without quarreling over **disputable m**. G1360
1Co 6: 4 if you have disputes *about* **such m**, do G1053S
1Co 7: 1 Now *for the* **m** you wrote about: "It is G4005
1Th 4: 1 As for **other** *m*, brothers and sisters, we AIT
2Th 3: 1 As for **other** *m*, brothers and sisters, pray AIT
1Ti 4:15 Be diligent in **these** *m*; give yourself wholly AIT
Heb 5: 1 represent the people *in* **m** related to God, G3836
2Pe 2:12 people blaspheme in **m** they do not G4005
2Pe 3:16 all his letters, speaking in them of **these** *m*. AIT

MATTHAN (2)

Mt 1:15 Eleazar the father of **M**, Matthan the G3474
Mt 1:15 father of Matthan, **M** the father of Jacob, G3474

MATTHAT (2)

Lk 3:24 the son *of* **M**, the son of Levi, the son of G3415
Lk 3:29 of Jorim, the son *of* **M**, the son of Levi, G3415

MATTHEW (6) [MATTHEW'S]

Mt 9: 9 he saw a man named **M** sitting at the tax G3414
Mt 9: 9 told him, and **M** got up and followed him. NDT
Mt 10: 3 Thomas and **M** the tax collector G3414
Mk 3:18 Bartholomew, **M**, Thomas, James son G3414
Lk 6:15 **M**, Thomas, James son of Alphaeus G3414
Ac 1:13 Bartholomew and **M**; James son of G3414

MATTHEW'S (1) [MATTHEW]

Mt 9:10 While Jesus was having dinner at **M** house NDT

MATTHIAS (2)

Ac 1:23 Barsabbas (also known as Justus) and **M**. G3416
Ac 1:26 the lot fell to **M**; so he was added to G3416

MATTITHIAH (8)

1Ch 9:31 A Levite named **M**, the firstborn son of H5524
1Ch 15:18 Benaiah, Maaseiah, **M**, Eliphelehu H5525
1Ch 15:21 **M**, Eliphelehu, Mikneiah, Obed-Edom H5525
1Ch 16: 5 Shemiramoth, Jehiel, **M**, Eliab, Benaiah H5524
1Ch 25: 3 Hashabiah and **M**, six in all, under H5525
1Ch 25:21 the fourteenth to **M**, his sons and relatives H5525
Ezr 10:43 **M**, Zabad, Zebina, Jaddai, Joel and H5524
Ne 8: 4 Beside him on his right stood **M**, Shema H5524

MATTOCKS (2)

1Sa 13:20 have their plow points, **m**, axes and sickles H908
1Sa 13:21 a shekel for sharpening plow points and **m**, H908

MATURE (9) [MATURITY, PREMATURELY]

Lk 8:14 riches and pleasures, and *they do* not **m**. G5461
1Co 2: 6 a message of wisdom among the **m**, G5455
Eph 4:13 of the Son of God and become **m**, G467+5455
Eph 4:15 *we will* **grow to become** in every respect the **m** G889
Php 3:15 *who* are **m** should take such a view of G5455
Col 1:28 we may present everyone **fully m** in Christ. G5455
Col 4:12 in all the will of God, **m** and fully assured. G5455
Heb 5:14 But solid food is *for* the **m**, who by G5455
Jas 1: 4 work so that you may be **m** and complete, G5455

MATURITY (1) [MATURE]

Heb 6: 1 about Christ and be taken forward to **m**, G5456

MAULED (3) [MAULS]

1Ki 13:26 the lion, *which has* **m** him and killed him H8689
1Ki 13:28 neither eaten the body nor **m** the donkey. H8689
2Ki 2:24 out of the woods and **m** forty-two of the H1324

MAULS (1) [MAULED]

Mic 5: 8 which **m** and mangles as it goes H8252

MAXIMS (1)

Job 13:12 Your **m** are proverbs of ashes; your H2355

MAY (1262) See Index of Articles Etc.

MAYBE (3)

1Ki 18: 5 **M** we can find some grass to keep the H218
1Ki 18:27 **M** he is sleeping and must be awakened." H218
Jnh 1: 6 **M** he will take notice of us so that we will H218

ME (4036) [I] See Index of Articles Etc.

ME JARKON (1)

Jos 19:46 **M** and Rakkon, with the area H4770

ME-ZAHAB (2)

Ge 36:39 daughter of Matred, the daughter of **M**. H4771
1Ch 1:50 daughter of Matred, the daughter of **M**. H4771

MEADOW (2) [MEADOWS]

Isa 44: 4 They will spring up like grass in a **m**, like NDT
Hos 4:16 the LORD pasture them like lambs in a **m**? H5303

MEADOWS (3) [MEADOW]

Ps 65:13 The **m** are covered with flocks and the H4120
Isa 30:23 that day your cattle will graze in broad **m**. H4120
Jer 25:37 The peaceful **m** will be laid waste H5661

MEAH (KJV) HUNDRED

MEAL (29) [MEALTIME]

Ge 19: 3 He prepared a **m** for them, baking bread H5492
Ge 31:54 and invited his relatives to a **m**. H430+4312
Ge 37:25 As they sat down to eat their **m**, they H4312
Ge 43:16 slaughter an animal and prepare a **m**; they NDT
Ex 12:43 are the regulations for the **Passover m**: H7175
Ex 18:12 of Israel to eat a **m** with Moses' H4312
Nu 15:20 the first of your **ground m** and present it H6881
Nu 15:21 the LORD from the first of your **ground m**. H6881
Nu 25: 2 ate the sacrificial **m** and bowed down NDT
1Sa 20:27 hasn't the son of Jesse come to the **m**, H4312
2Sa 12: 4 cattle to prepare a **m** for the traveler who NDT
1Ki 4:22 cors of the finest flour and sixty cors of **m**, H7854
1Ki 13: 7 "Come home with me **for a m**, and I will H6184
1Ki 17:12 home and make a **m** for myself and my H2084S
2Ki 4: 8 who urged him to **stay for a m**. H430+4312
Ne 10:37 the first of our **ground m**, of our grain H6881
Job 33:20 their soul loathes the choicest **m**. H4407
Isa 44:16 over it he prepares his **m**, he roasts his H1414
Jer 16: 5 enter a house where there is a **funeral m**; H5301
Eze 44:30 portion of your **ground m** so that a H6881
Lk 11:38 that Jesus did not first wash before the **m**. G756
Jn 13: 2 The **evening m** was in progress, and the G1270
Jn 13: 4 so he got up from the **m**, took off his outer G1270
Jn 13:28 But no one **at the m** understood why Jesus G367
Ac 10:10 and while the **m** was being prepared NDT
Ac 16:34 house and **set a m before** them; G4192+5544
1Co 10:27 invites you to a **m** and you want to go, NDT
1Co 10:30 If I take part in the **m** with thankfulness, why NDT
Heb 12:16 who for a single **m** sold his inheritance G1111

MEALTIME (1) [MEAL]

Ru 2:14 At **m** Boaz said to her, "Come H6961+2021+431

MEAN (33) [MEANING, MEANINGLESS, MEANS, MEANT]

Ex 12:26 'What does this ceremony **m to** you? H4200
Ex 13:14 your son asks you, '**What** does this **m**? H4537
Jos 4: 6 ask you, '**What** do these stones **m**? H4537
Jos 4:21 their parents, '**What** do these stones **m**? H4537
1Sa 1: 8 Don't I **m more** to you than ten sons?" H3202
1Sa 25: 3 was surly and **m** in his dealings— H8273
2Sa 5:24 because **that will m** the LORD has gone out H255
2Sa 17: 3 of the man you seek will **m** the return of all; NDT
2Sa 19: 6 their men **m** nothing **to** you. H4200
1Ch 14:15 **because that will m** God has gone out in H3954
Job 6:26 *Do you* **m** to correct what I say, and treat H3108
Isa 3:15 What do you **m by** crushing my people H4200
Eze 17:12 'Do you not know **what** these things **m**? H4537
Eze 18: 2 **"What do you** people **m** by H4537+4200+4013
Eze 37:18 'Won't you tell us what you **m by** this? H4200
Da 5:26 "Here is what these words **m**: Mene A10600
Mt 12: 7 If you had known what *these words* **m**, 'I G1639
Mt 26:22 the other, "Surely you don't **m** me, Lord?" NDT
Mt 26:25 said, "Surely you don't **m** me, Rabbi?" NDT
Mk 14:19 they said to him, "Surely you don't **m** me?" NDT
Jn 7:36 What *did he* **m** when he G1639+3836+3364+4047
Jn 7:47 **"You m** he has deceived you also?" the G3590
Jn 16:17 another, "What *does he* **m** by saying, 'In G1639
Jn 16:18 "What *does he* **m** by 'a little while'? G1639
Ac 2:12 one another, "What *does* this **m**?" G2527+1639
Ac 17:20 would like to know what they **m**." G2527+1639
1Co 1:12 What *I* **m** is this: One of you says, "I follow G3306
1Co 7:29 What *I* **m**, brothers and sisters, is that the G5774
1Co 10:19 *Do I* **m** then that food sacrificed to an idol G5774
Gal 2:17 **doesn't that m that** Christ promotes sin? G727
Gal 3:17 What *I* **m** is this: The law, introduced 430 G3306
Eph 4: 9 What *does* "he ascended" **m** except that G1639
Php 1:22 in the body, this will **m** fruitful labor for me. NDT

MEANING (28) [MEAN]

Ge 21:29 **"What is the m** *of* these seven ewe H4537+2179
Ge 33: 8 **"What's the m of** all these flocks H4769+4200
Ge 40: 5 each dream had a **m** *of* its own. H7355
Ge 41:11 each dream had a **m** *of* its own. H7355
Dt 6:20 **"What is the m of** the stipulations H4537
1Sa 4:14 asked, **"What is the m** *of* this uproar?" H4537
1Ki 1:41 **"What's the m of** all the noise in the city?" H4508
Ne 8: 8 clear and giving the **m** so that the people H8507
Job 7:16 Let me alone; my days have **no m**. H2039
Ecc 6: 4 It comes **without m**, it departs H928+2021+2039
Ecc 6:11 words, the **less** the **m**, and how H8049+2039
Ecc 8:17 to search it out, no one *can* **discover** *its* **m**. H5162

M

Da 2:45 **This is the m** *of* the A10353+10619+10168
Da 4:19 do not let the dream or its **m** alarm you." A10600
Da 4:19 enemies and its **m** to your adversaries! A10600
Da 7:16 there and asked him the **m** of all this. A10327
Da 7:19 I wanted to **know the m** of the fourth A10326
Da 8:16 "Gabriel, **tell** this man the **m** *of* the vision." H1067
Lk 8:11 "This *is the* **m** *of* the parable: The seed is G1639
Lk 18:34 Its **m** was hidden from them, and they did G4839
Lk 20:17 "Then what *is the* **m** *of* that which is G1639
Ac 10:17 wondering *about the* **m** of the G5515+323+1639
1Co 4:6 you may learn from us the **m** of the saying, NDT
1Co 5:10 not at all **m** the people of this world who are NDT
1Co 14:10 the world, yet none of them is **without m**. G936
1Co 14:11 I do not grasp the **m** of what someone is G1539
Gal 3:16 **m** many people, but "and to your G6055+2093
Gal 3:16 to your seed," **m** one person, who G6055+2093

MEANINGLESS (39) [MEAN]

Job 27:12 Why then this **m talk**? H2038+2039
Ecc 1:2 "**M**! Meaningless!" says the Teacher H2039
Ecc 1:2 "Meaningless! **M**!" says the Teacher H2039
Ecc 1:2 the Teacher. "**Utterly m**! Everything H2039+2039
Ecc 1:2 "Utterly meaningless! Everything is **m**." H2039
Ecc 1:14 all of them are **m**, a chasing after the H2039
Ecc 2:1 But that also proved to be **m**. H2039
Ecc 2:11 everything was **m**, a chasing after the H2039
Ecc 2:15 I said to myself, "This too is **m**." H2039
Ecc 2:17 All of it is **m**, a chasing after the H2039
Ecc 2:19 skill under the sun. This too is **m**. H2039
Ecc 2:21 This too is **m** and a great misfortune H2039
Ecc 2:23 their minds do not rest. This too is **m**. H2039
Ecc 2:26 This too is **m**, a chasing after the H2039
Ecc 3:19 advantage over animals. Everything is **m**. H2039
Ecc 4:4 This too is **m**, a chasing after the H2039
Ecc 4:7 Again I saw *something* **m** under the sun: H2039
Ecc 4:8 This too is **m**—a miserable business! H2039
Ecc 4:16 This too is **m**, a chasing after the H2039
Ecc 5:7 Much dreaming and many words are **m** H2039
Ecc 5:10 satisfied with their income. This too is **m**. H2039
Ecc 6:2 them instead. This is **m**, a grievous evil. H2039
Ecc 6:9 This too is **m**, a chasing after the H2039
Ecc 6:12 during the few and **m** days they pass H2039
Ecc 7:6 so is the laughter of fools. This too is **m**. H2039
Ecc 7:15 In this **m** life of mine I have seen both of H2039
Ecc 8:10 the city where they did this. This too is **m**. H2039
Ecc 8:14 is something else **m** that occurs on earth: H2039
Ecc 8:14 righteous deserve. This too, I say, is **m**. H2039
Ecc 9:9 all the days of this **m** life that God has H2039
Ecc 9:9 given you under the sun—all your **m** days. H2039
Ecc 11:8 will be many. Everything to come is **m**. H2039
Ecc 11:10 of your body, for youth and vigor are **m**. H2039
Ecc 12:8 "**M**! Meaningless!" says the Teacher H2039
Ecc 12:8 "Meaningless! **M**!" says the Teacher H2039
Ecc 12:8 says the Teacher. "Everything is **m**!" H2039
Isa 1:13 Stop bringing **m** offerings! Your incense is H8736
1Ti 1:6 from these and have turned to **m talk**. G3467
Titus 1:10 people, **full of m talk** and deception G3468

MEANS (74) [MEAN]

Ge 40:12 "This is *what* it **m**," Joseph said to him H7355
Ge 40:18 "This is *what* it **m**," Joseph said. "The H7355
Ex 28:30 bear the **m of making decisions** *for* the H5477
Lev 11:43 unclean **by m of** them or be made H928
Lev 25:26 acquire **sufficient m** *to* redeem it H3869+1896
Lev 25:28 But if they do not acquire the **m** to repay H1896
1Sa 6:3 **by all m send** a guilt offering to H8740+8740
1Sa 25:25 his name—his name **m** Fool, and folly goes NDT
2Sa 15:21 king may be, whether **it m** life or death H4200
1Ki 22:22 " '**By what m**?' the LORD asked. " 'I H928+4537
2Ki 5:5 "**By all m, go**," the king of Aram H2143+995
2Ki 5:23 "**By all m**, take two talents," said Naaman. H3283
2Ch 18:20 " '**By what m**?' the LORD H928+4537
Pr 16:15 face brightens, it **m** life; his favor is like a NDT
Pr 22:27 if you lack the **m** to pay, your very bed will NDT
Jer 17:11 lay are those who gain riches **by** unjust **m**. H928
Jer 22:16 Is that not what it **m** to know me?" declares NDT
Da 2:3 troubles me and I want to **know what** it **m**. H3359
Da 2:25 who can tell the king *what* his dream **m**." A10600
Da 4:18 tell me *what* it **m**, for none of the A10600
Da 4:26 tree with its roots **m** that your kingdom will NDT
Da 5:7 tells me *what* it **m** will be clothed in A10600
Da 5:12 he will tell you *what* the writing **m**." A10600
Da 5:15 read this writing and tell me *what* it **m**, A10600
Da 5:16 read this writing and tell me *what* it **m**, A10600
Da 5:17 the king and tell him *what* it **m**. A10600
Hos 1:6 Call her **Lo-Ruhamah** (*which m* "*not loved*") AIT
Hos 1:9 him **Lo-Ammi** (*which m* "*not my people*") AIT
Hos 11:7 I will **by no m** exalt them. H4202+3480
Mt 1:23 (which **m** "God with us"). G1639+3493
Mt 2:6 are **by no m** least among the rulers of G4027
Mt 5:18 **not** the least stroke of a pen, will **by any m** G4024+3590
Mt 9:13 But go and learn what *this* **m**: 'I desire G1639
Mt 13:18 **Listen** then *to what* the parable of the sower *m* AIT
Mt 23:16 by the temple, *it* **m** nothing; but anyone G1639
Mt 23:18 by the altar, *it* **m** nothing; but anyone G1639
Mt 27:33 which **m** "the place of the skull") G1639+3306
Mt 27:46 which **m** "My God, my God, why have G1639
Mk 3:17 Boanerges, which **m** "sons of thunder") G1639
Mk 5:41 which **m** "Little girl, I say to you G1639+3493
Mk 7:34 "Ephphatha!" (which **m** "Be opened!"). G1639
Mk 10:46 Bartimaeus (which **m** "son of Timaeus") NDT
Mk 15:22 which **m** "the place of the skull") G1639+3493
Mk 15:34 which **m** "My God, my God, why G1639+3493
Lk 8:3 to support them out of their own **m**. G5639
Jn 1:38 "Rabbi" (which **m** "Teacher") G3306+3493
Jn 8:54 "If I glorify myself, my glory **m** nothing. G1639
Jn 9:7 the Pool of Siloam" (this word **m** "Sent") G2257
Jn 13:24 said, "Ask him which one *he* **m**." G3306
Jn 20:16 "Rabboni!" (which **m** "Teacher"). G3306
Ac 4:36 which **m** "son of encouragement") G1639+3493
Ac 8:27 which **m** "queen of the Ethiopians" NDT
Ac 13:8 that is what his name **m**) opposed G3493
Ro 4:14 faith **m nothing** and the promise is G3033
Ro 6:2 **By no m**! We are those who have G3590+1181
Ro 6:15 the law but under grace? **By no m**! G3590+1181
Ro 7:13 death to me? **By no m** G3590+1181
Ro 11:1 his people? **By no m**! I am an G3590+1181
Ro 11:12 if their transgression **m** riches for the world, NDT
Ro 11:12 their loss **m** riches for the Gentiles NDT
1Co 6:7 lawsuits among you **m** you have been G4036
1Co 9:22 so that **by all possible m** I might save G4122
1Co 12:8 of knowledge **by m of** the same Spirit, G2848
2Co 8:11 your completion of it, according to your **m**. G2400
Gal 3:3 After beginning *by m of* the **Spirit**, are you AIT
Gal 3:3 are you now trying to finish *by m of* the **flesh**? AIT
Gal 6:12 to impress people **by m of** the flesh are G1877
Gal 6:15 uncircumcision **m** anything; G1639
1Ti 6:5 that godliness is a **m to financial gain**. G4516
Heb 7:2 the name Melchizedek **m** "king of G2257
Heb 7:2 "king of Salem" **m** "king of peace. G1639
Heb 9:12 He did not enter **by m of** the blood of G1328
Jas 4:4 with the world **m** enmity against God? G1639
2Pe 3:15 mind that our Lord's patience **m** salvation, NDT

MEANT (17) [MEAN]

Ex 1:8 to whom Joseph **m** nothing, came to H3359
Jdg 13:23 "If the LORD *had* **m** to kill us, he would H2911
Da 5:8 the writing or tell the king *what* it **m**. A10600
Mk 4:22 whatever is hidden is **m to** be disclosed, G2671
Mk 4:22 is concealed is **m** to be brought out into G2671
Mk 9:10 discussing what "rising from the dead" **m**. G1639
Mk 9:32 understand what he **m** and were afraid to G4839
Lk 8:9 disciples asked him what this parable **m**. G1639
Lk 9:45 But they did not understand what this **m**. G4839
Jn 1:30 This is **the one** I **m** when I said, 'A G5642+4005
Jn 6:71 *He* **m** Judas, the son of Simon Iscariot G3306
Jn 7:39 By this *he* **m** the Spirit, whom those G3306+4309
Jn 11:13 his disciples thought *he* **m** natural sleep. G3306
Jn 13:22 at a loss to know which of them *he* **m**. G3306
Jn 16:19 one another **what I m** when I said G4309+4047S
Ac 7:18 'a new king, *to* whom Joseph **m** nothing G3857
1Co 6:13 is not *m for* **sexual immorality** but for the AIT

MEANWHILE (35) [WHILE]

Ge 26:26 **M**, Abimelek had come to him from Gerar, H2256
Ge 34:7 **M**, Jacob's sons had come in from the H2256
Ge 37:36 **M**, the Midianites sold Joseph in Egypt to H2256
Ge 38:20 **M** Judah sent the young goat by his friend H2256
Nu 32:17 **M** our women and children will live in H2256
Jos 10:33 **M**, Horam king of Gezer had come up to H255
Jdg 4:17 **m**, fled on foot to the tent of Jael H2256
Ru 4:1 **M** Boaz went up to the town gate and sat H2256
1Sa 2:21 **M**, the boy Samuel grew up in the H2256
1Sa 17:41 **M**, the Philistine, with his shield bearer in H2256
2Sa 2:8 **M**, Abner son of Ner, the commander of H2256
2Sa 12:26 **M** Joab fought against Rabbah of the H2256
2Sa 13:34 **M**, Absalom had fled. Now the man H2256
2Sa 16:15 **M**, Absalom and all the men of Israel H2256
2Sa 18:17 of rocks over him. **M**, all the Israelites H2256
2Sa 19:8 all came before him. **M**, the Israelites had H2256
1Ki 18:45 **M**, the sky grew black H6330+3907+2256+6330+3907
1Ki 20:13 **M** a prophet came to Ahab king of Israel H2180
1Ki 20:23 **M**, the officials of the king of Aram H2256
2Ch 25:13 **M** the troops that Amaziah had sent back H2256
Ne 4:10 **M**, the people in Judah said, "The H2256
Est 9:16 **M**, the remainder of the Jews who were in H2256
Mt 27:11 **M** Jesus stood before the governor, and G1254
Lk 1:21 **M**, the people were waiting for Zechariah G2779
Lk 8:52 **M**, all the people were wailing and G1254
Lk 12:1 **M**, when a crowd of many G1877+4005
Lk 15:25 "**M**, the older son was in the field. G1254
Jn 4:31 **M** his disciples urged him G1877+3836+3568
Jn 12:9 **M** a large crowd of Jews found out that G4036
Jn 18:19 **M**, the high priest questioned Jesus about G4036
Jn 18:25 **M**, Simon Peter was still standing there G1254
Ac 7:58 **M**, the witnesses laid their coats at the G2779
Ac 9:1 **M**, Saul was still breathing out murderous G1254
Ac 18:24 **M** a Jew named Apollos, a native of G1254
2Co 5:2 **M** we groan, longing to be clothed G1877+4047

MEASURE (36) [IMMEASURABLY, MEASURED, MEASURELESS, MEASUREMENT, MEASUREMENTS, MEASURES, MEASURING]

Ge 15:16 Amorites has not yet reached its **full m**." H8969
Ge 41:49 records because it was beyond **m**. H5031
Nu 35:5 **m** two thousand cubits on the east side H4499
Dt 21:2 go out and **m** *the* **distance** from the body H4499
1Ki 7:23 line of thirty cubits *to* **m around** it. H6015+6017
2Ch 4:2 line of thirty cubits *to* **m around** it. H6015+6017
Job 11:9 Their **m** is longer than the earth and H4500
Ps 60:6 out Shechem and **m off** the Valley of H4499
Ps 108:7 out Shechem and **m off** the Valley of H4499
Isa 34:17 portions; his hand distributes them by **m**. H7742
Isa 47:9 They will come upon you in **full m**, in H9448
Isa 64:9 Do not be angry **beyond m**, LORD H6330+4394
Isa 64:12 silent and punish us **beyond m**? H6330+4394
Isa 65:7 *I will* **m** into their laps **the full payment** *for* H4499
Jer 10:24 but only in **due m**—not in your H5477
Jer 30:11 I will discipline you but only in **due m**; H5477
Jer 46:28 I will discipline you but only in **due m**; H5477
La 5:22 and are angry with us **beyond m**. H6330+4394
Eze 4:11 Also **m out** a sixth of a hin of water and H5374
Eze 45:3 **m off** a section 25,000 cubits long and H4499
Eze 45:11 homer is to be the **standard m** *for* both. H5504
Am 8:5 skimping on the **m**, boosting the price H406
Zec 2:2 answered me, "To **m** Jerusalem, to find H4499
Mt 7:2 judged, and with the **m** you use, it will be G3586
Mk 4:24 "With the **m** you use, it will be measured G3586
Lk 6:38 A good **m**, pressed down, shaken G3586
Lk 6:38 For *with* the **m** you use, it will be G3586
Jn 17:13 they may have the **full** *m* of my joy within AIT
Ro 15:29 I will come in *the* **full m** of the blessing of G4445
2Co 10:12 *When* they **m** themselves by themselves G3582
Eph 3:19 you may be filled **to the m** of all the G1650
Eph 4:13 attaining to the whole **m** of the fullness of G3586
2Pe 1:8 possess these qualities *in* **increasing m**, G4429
Rev 11:1 "Go and **m** the temple of God and the G3582
Rev 11:2 the outer court; *do* not **m** it, because it G3582
Rev 21:15 had a measuring rod of gold to **m** the city, G3582

MEASURED (48) [MEASURE]

Ex 16:18 And when *they* **m** it by the omer, the one H4499
2Sa 8:2 the ground and **m** them **off** with a length H4499
1Ki 6:25 The second cherub also **m** ten cubits, for the NDT
1Ki 7:31 with its basework it **m** a cubit and a half. NDT
Job 28:25 wind and **m out** the waters, H9419+928+4500
Isa 40:12 Who *has* **m** the waters in the hollow of H4499
Jer 31:37 the heavens above *can* **be m** and the H4499
Eze 40:5 *He* **m** the wall; it was one measuring rod H4499
Eze 40:6 its steps and **m** the threshold of the H4499
Eze 40:8 Then *he* **m** the portico of the gateway; H4499
Eze 40:11 Then *he* **m** the width of the entrance of H4499
Eze 40:13 Then *he* **m** the gateway from the top of H4499
Eze 40:14 *He* **m** *along* the faces of the projecting H6913
Eze 40:19 Then *he* **m** the distance from the inside of H4499
Eze 40:20 Then *he* **m** the length and width of the H4499
Eze 40:23 *He* **m** from one gate to the opposite one H4499
Eze 40:24 *He* **m** its jambs and its portico, and they H4499
Eze 40:27 and *he* **m** from this gate to the outer gate H4499
Eze 40:28 south gate, and *he* **m** the south gate; it H4499
Eze 40:32 the east side, and *he* **m** the gateway; it H4499
Eze 40:35 he brought me to the north gate and **m** it. H4499
Eze 40:47 Then *he* **m** the court: It was square—a H4499
Eze 40:48 of the temple and **m** the jambs of the H4499
Eze 41:1 me to the main hall and **m** the jambs; H4499
Eze 41:2 *He* also **m** the main hall; it was forty H4499
Eze 41:3 inner sanctuary and **m** the jambs of the H4499
Eze 41:4 And *he* **m** the length of the inner H4499
Eze 41:5 Then *he* **m** the wall of the temple; it was H4499
Eze 41:13 Then *he* **m** the temple; it was a hundred H4499
Eze 41:15 Then *he* **m** the length of the building H4499
Eze 42:15 the east gate and **m** the area all around: H4499
Eze 42:16 *He* **m** the east side with the measuring rod H4499
Eze 42:17 *He* **m** the north side; it was five hundred H4499
Eze 42:18 *He* **m** the south side; it was five hundred H4499
Eze 42:19 Then he turned to the west side and **m**; it H4499
Eze 42:20 So *he* **m** the area on all four sides. It had H4499
Eze 45:14 portion of olive oil, **m** by the bath, is a tenth NDT
Eze 47:3 *he* **m off** a thousand cubits and then led H4499
Eze 47:4 *He* **m off** another thousand cubits and led H4499
Eze 47:4 *He* **m off** another thousand and led me H4499
Eze 47:5 *He* **m off** another thousand, but now it was H4499
Hos 1:10 seashore, which cannot **be m** or counted. H4499
Am 7:17 Your land will be **m** and divided up, and H2475
Mt 7:2 the measure you use, *it will be* **m** to you. G3582
Mk 4:24 you use, *it will be* **m** to you—and even G3582
Lk 6:38 the measure you use, *it will be* **m** to you." G520
Rev 21:16 *He* **m** the city with the rod and found it to G3582
Rev 21:17 The angel **m** the wall using human G3582

MEASURELESS (2) [MEASURE]

1Ki 4:29 of understanding **as m as** the sand on the H3869
Jer 33:22 in the sky and as **m** as the sand on H4202+4499

MEASUREMENT (2) [MEASURE]

Eze 40:14 The **m** was up to the portico facing the NDT
Rev 21:17 angel measured the wall using human **m**, G3586

MEASUREMENTS (13) [MEASURE]

1Ch 23:29 and all **m of quantity** and size. H5374
Eze 40:10 the three had the same **m**, and the faces H4500
Eze 40:10 walls on each side had the same **m**. H4500
Eze 40:21 portico had the same **m** as those of the H4500
Eze 40:22 had the same **m** as those of the gate H4500
Eze 40:24 they had the same **m** as the others. H4500
Eze 40:28 it had the same **m** as the others. H4500
Eze 40:29 its portico had the same **m** as the others. H4500
Eze 40:32 gateway; it had the same **m** as the others. H4500
Eze 40:33 its portico had the same **m** as the others. H4500
Eze 40:35 It had the same **m** as the others, H4500
Eze 43:13 "These are the **m** *of* the altar in long H4500
Eze 48:16 will have these **m**: the north side H4500

MEASURES (9) [MEASURE]

Dt 25:14 have **two differing m** in your H406+2256+406

Dt 25:15 have accurate and honest weights and m, H406
Ru 3:15 *he* poured into it six m of barley and H4499
Ru 3:17 "He gave me these six m of barley, saying, NDT
Pr 20:10 weights and differing m— H406+2256+406
Isa 44:13 The carpenter m *with* a line and makes H5742
Eze 48:33 south side, which m 4,500 cubits, will be H4500
Hag 2:16 When anyone came to a heap of twenty m NDT
Hag 2:16 anyone went to a wine vat to draw fifty m, H7053

MEASURING (24) [MEASURE]

Lev 19:35 use dishonest standards when m length, H5477
1Ki 7:10 some m ten cubits and some eight. NDT
1Ki 7:23 m ten cubits from rim to rim and five cubits NDT
1Ki 7:38 holding forty baths and m four cubits across, NDT
2Ki 21:13 the m line *used against* Samaria and H7742
2Ch 4: 2 m ten cubits from rim to rim and five cubits NDT
Job 38: 5 Who stretched a m line across it? H7742
Isa 28:17 make justice the m line and H7742
Isa 34:11 over Edom the m line *of* chaos and the H7742
Jer 31:39 The m line will stretch from there straight H4500
La 2: 8 He stretched out a m line and did not H7742
Eze 40: 3 with a linen cord and a m rod in his hand. H4500
Eze 40: 5 The length of the m rod in the man's H4500
Eze 40: 5 it was one m rod thick and one rod high. H7866
Eze 42:15 he had finished m what was inside the H4500
Eze 42:16 He measured the east side with the m rod H4500
Eze 42:17 it was five hundred cubits by the m rod. H4500
Eze 42:18 it was five hundred cubits by the m rod. H4500
Eze 42:19 it was five hundred cubits by the m rod. H4500
Eze 47: 3 went eastward with a m line in his hand, H7742
Zec 1:16 And the m line will be stretched out over H7742
Zec 2: 1 me was a man with a m line in his hand. H4500
Rev 11: 1 given a reed like a m rod and was told, G4811
Rev 21:15 talked with me had a m rod of gold to G3586

MEAT (93) [MEATS]

Ge 9: 4 "But you must not eat m that has its H1414
Ex 12: 8 they are to eat the m roasted over the fire, H1414
Ex 12: 9 Do not eat the m raw or boiled in water H5647S
Ex 12:46 take none of the m outside the house. H1414
Ex 16: 3 sat around pots of m and ate all the food H1414
Ex 16: 8 when he gives you m to eat in the H1414
Ex 16:12 'At twilight you will eat m, and in the H1414
Ex 21:28 to death, and its m must not be eaten. H1414
Ex 22:31 So do not eat the m of an animal torn by H1414
Ex 27: 3 sprinkling bowls, m forks and firepans. H4657
Ex 29:31 cook the m in a sacred place. H1414
Ex 29:32 sons are to eat the m *of* the ram and the H1414
Ex 29:34 And if any of the m *of* the ordination ram H1414
Ex 38: 3 sprinkling bowls, m forks and firepans. H4657
Lev 6:28 The clay pot the m is cooked in must be NDT
Lev 7:15 The m *of* their fellowship offering of H1414
Lev 7:17 Any m *of* the sacrifice left over till the H1414
Lev 7:18 If any m *of* the fellowship offering is eaten H1414
Lev 7:19 " 'M that touches anything ceremonially H1414
Lev 7:19 As for other m, anyone ceremonially H1414
Lev 7:20 is unclean eats any m of the fellowship H1414
Lev 7:21 then eats any of the m *of* the fellowship H1414
Lev 8:31 "Cook the m at the entrance to the tent of H1414
Lev 8:32 burn up the rest of the m and the bread. H1414
Lev 11: 8 You must not eat their m or touch their H1414
Lev 11:11 you must not eat their m; you must regard H1414
Lev 19:26 " 'Do not eat any m with the blood still in it NDT
Nu 4:14 the firepans, m forks, shovels and H4657
Nu 11: 4 said, "If only we had m to eat! H1414
Nu 11:13 Where can I get m for all these people H1414
Nu 11:13 keep wailing to me, 'Give us m to eat! H1414
Nu 11:18 tomorrow, when you will eat m. H1414
Nu 11:18 you wailed, "If only we had m to eat! H1414
Nu 11:18 Now the LORD will give you m, and you H1414
Nu 11:21 'I will give them m to eat for a whole H1414
Nu 11:33 But while the m was still between their H1414
Nu 18:18 Their m is to be yours, just as the breast of H1414
Dt 12:15 eat as much of the m as you want, H1414
Dt 12:20 and you crave m and say, "I would H1414
Dt 12:20 "I would like *some* m," then you may H1414
Dt 12:23 you must not eat the life with the m. H1414
Dt 12:27 LORD your God, both the m and the blood. H1414
Dt 12:27 the LORD your God, but you may eat the m. H1414
Dt 14: 8 are not to eat their m or touch their H1414
Dt 16: 4 not let any of the m you sacrifice on the H1414
Dt 18: 3 internal organs and the m from the head. H4305
Jdg 6:19 Putting the m in a basket and its broth in H1414
Jdg 6:20 "Take the m and the unleavened bread H1414
Jdg 6:21 LORD touched the m and the unleavened H1414
Jdg 6:21 the rock, consuming the m and the bread. H1414
1Sa 1: 4 would give portions of the m to his wife H4950
1Sa 2:13 in his hand while the m was being boiled H1414
1Sa 2:15 "Give the priest *some* m to roast; he won't H1414
1Sa 2:15 he won't accept boiled m from you, but H1414
1Sa 9:23 "Bring the piece of m I gave you, the H4950
1Sa 14:33 the LORD by eating m that has blood in it." NDT
1Sa 14:34 the LORD by eating m with blood still in it. NDT
1Sa 25:11 the m I have slaughtered for my H3186
1Ki 17: 6 him bread and m in the morning and H1414
1Ki 17: 6 morning and bread and m in the evening, H1414
1Ki 19:21 to cook the m and gave it to the H1414
2Ch 4:16 shovels, m forks and all related articles. H4657
Job 31:31 'Who has not been filled with Job's m? H1414
Ps 78:20 Can he supply m for his people?" H8638
Ps 78:27 He rained m down on them like dust H8638
Pr 9: 2 has prepared her m and mixed her wine; H3181
Pr 23:20 too much wine or gorge themselves on m, H1414
Isa 22:13 eating of m and drinking of wine! H1414
Isa 44:16 his meal, he roasts his m and eats his fill. H7507
Isa 44:19 bread over its coals, I roasted m and I ate. H1414
Isa 65: 4 whose pots hold broth of impure m; H7002
Jer 7:21 other sacrifices and eat the m yourselves! H1414
Jer 11:15 Can consecrated m avert your punishment H1414
Eze 4:14 No impure m has ever entered my mouth." H1414
Eze 11: 3 This city is a pot, and we are the m in it.' H1414
Eze 11: 7 thrown there are the m and this city is the H1414
Eze 11:11 will you be the m in it; I will execute H1414
Eze 24: 4 Put into it the pieces of m, all the choice H5984
Eze 24: 6 Take the m out piece by piece in whatever NDT
Eze 24:10 Cook the m well, mixing in the spices H1414
Eze 33:25 Since you eat m with the blood still in it NDT
Da 10: 3 no m or wine touched my lips H1414
Hos 8:13 though they eat the m, the LORD is not H1414
Mic 3: 3 who chop them up like m for the pan, like NDT
Hag 2:12 carries consecrated m in the fold of their H1414
Zec 11:16 will eat the m *of* the choice sheep H1414
Ac 15:20 *from* the m *of* strangled *animals* and from AIT
Ac 15:29 *from the* m *of* strangled *animals* and from AIT
Ac 21:25 *from the* m *of* strangled *animals* and from AIT
Ro 14: 6 Whoever eats m does so to the Lord, for NDT
Ro 14:21 is better not to eat m or drink wine or to G3200
1Co 8:13 I will never eat m again, so that I will G3200
1Co 10:25 sold in the m market without raising G3425

MEATS (1) [MEAT]

Isa 25: 6 the best of m and the finest of wines. H4683

MEBUNNAI (NIV84) SIBBEKAI

MECONAH (NIV84) MEKONAH

MEDAD (2)

Nu 11:26 whose names were Eldad and M, had H4773
Nu 11:27 "Eldad and M are prophesying in the H4773

MEDAN (2)

Ge 25: 2 Zimran, Jokshan, M, Midian, Ishbak and H4527
1Ch 1:32 Zimran, Jokshan, M, Midian, Ishbak and H4527

MEDDLER (1)

1Pe 4:15 any other kind of criminal, or even as a m. G258

MEDE (3) [MEDIA]

Da 5:31 Darius the M took over the kingdom A10404
Da 9: 1 son of Xerxes (a M by descent), who was H4512
Da 11: 1 And in the first year of Darius the M, H4513

MEDEBA (5)

Nu 21:30 as far as Nophah, which extends to M." H4772
Jos 13: 9 the whole plateau of M as far as Dibon, H4772
Jos 13:16 the gorge, and the whole plateau past M H4772
1Ch 19: 7 who came and camped near M, while the H4772
Isa 15: 2 to weep; Moab wails over Nebo and M. H4772

MEDES (10) [MEDIA]

2Ki 17: 6 Habor River and in the towns of the M. H4512
2Ki 18:11 on the Habor River and in towns of the M. H4512
Isa 13:17 I will stir up against them the M, who do H4512
Jer 51:11 LORD has stirred up the kings of the M H4512
Jer 51:28 the kings of the M, their governors and H4512
Da 5:28 given to the M and Persians. A10404
Da 6: 8 with the law of the M and Persians, A10404
Da 6:12 with the law of the M and Persians, A10404
Da 6:15 to the law of the M and Persians no A10404
Ac 2: 9 Parthians, M and Elamites; residents of G3597

MEDIA (8) [MEDE, MEDES, MEDIAN]

Ezr 6: 2 citadel of Ecbatana in the province of M, A10404
Est 1: 3 The military leaders of Persia and M, the H4512
Est 1:14 nobles of Persia and M who had special H4512
Est 1:19 it be written in the laws of Persia and M, H4512
Est 10: 2 the annals of the kings of M and Persia? H4512
Isa 21: 2 M, lay siege! I will bring to an end H4512
Jer 25:25 all the kings of Zimri, Elam and M; H4512
Da 8:20 saw represents the kings of M and Persia. H4512

MEDIAN (1) [MEDIA]

Est 1:18 day the Persian and M women of the H4512

MEDIATE (2) [MEDIATOR]

1Sa 2:25 another, God *may* m *for* the offender; but H7136
Job 9:33 there were *someone to* m between us, H3519

MEDIATOR (6) [MEDIATE]

Gal 3:19 through angels and entrusted to a m. G3542
Gal 3:20 A m, however, implies more than one G3542
1Ti 2: 5 is one God and one m between God and G3542
Heb 8: 6 of which he is m is superior to the old G3542
Heb 9:15 reason Christ is the m of a new covenant, G3542
Heb 12:24 to Jesus the m of a new covenant, and to G3542

MEDICINE (1) [MEDICINES]

Pr 17:22 A cheerful heart is good m, but a crushed H1565

MEDICINES (1) [MEDICINE]

Jer 46:11 But you try many m in vain; there is no H8337

MEDITATE (14) [MEDITATED, MEDITATES, MEDITATION]

Ge 24:63 He went out to the field one evening to m H8452
Jos 1: 8 always on your lips; m on it day and night H2047
Ps 48: 9 *we* m *on* your unfailing love. H1948
Ps 77:12 all your works and m on all your mighty H8488
Ps 119:15 *I* m on your precepts and consider your H8488
Ps 119:23 your servant *will* m on your decrees. H8488
Ps 119:27 that *I may* m on your wonderful deeds. H8488
Ps 119:48 that *I may* m on your decrees. H8488
Ps 119:78 but I *will* m on your precepts. H8488
Ps 119:97 I love your law! I m *on* it all day long. H8491
Ps 119:99 all my teachers, for I m *on* your statutes. H8491
Ps 119:148 the night, that I *may* m on your promises. H8488
Ps 143: 5 *I* m on all your works and consider what H2047
Ps 145: 5 and *I will* m on your wonderful works. H8488

MEDITATED (3) [MEDITATE]

Ps 39: 3 While I m, the fire burned; then I spoke H2052
Ps 77: 3 I groaned; *I* m, and my spirit grew H8488
Ps 77: 6 My heart m and my spirit asked H8488

MEDITATES (1) [MEDITATE]

Ps 1: 2 and *who* m on his law day and night. H2047

MEDITATION (3) [MEDITATE]

Ps 19:14 of my mouth and this m *of* my heart be H2053
Ps 49: 3 the m *of* my heart will give you H2050
Ps 104:34 May my m be pleasing to him, as I rejoice H8490

MEDITERRANEAN (27)

Ex 23:31 from the Red Sea to the M Sea, H3542+7149
Nu 34: 5 the Wadi of Egypt and end at the M Sea. H3542
Nu 34: 6 boundary will be the coast of the M Sea. H1524S
Nu 34: 7 run a line from the M Sea to Mount Hor H1524S
Dt 11:24 from the Euphrates River to the M Sea. H340S
Dt 34: 2 all the land of Judah as far as the M Sea, H340S
Jos 1: 4 country—to the M Sea in the west. H1524S
Jos 9: 1 entire coast of the M Sea as far as H1524S
Jos 15: 4 the Wadi of Egypt, ending at the M Sea. H3542
Jos 15:12 boundary is the coastline of the M Sea. H1524S
Jos 15:47 of Egypt and the coastline of the M Sea. H1524S
Jos 16: 3 on to Gezer, ending at the M Sea. H3542
Jos 16: 6 continued to the M Sea. H3542
Jos 16: 8 Kanah Ravine and ended at the M Sea. H3542
Jos 17: 9 of the ravine and ended at the M Sea. H3542
Jos 17:10 reached the M Sea and bordered Asher H3542
Jos 19:29 came out at the M Sea in the region of H3542
Jos 23: 4 the Jordan and the M Sea in the west. H1524S
1Ki 5: 9 them down from Lebanon to the M Sea, H3542
Isa 11:11 Hamath and from the islands of the M. H3542S
Eze 47:10 many kinds—like the fish of the M Sea. H1524S
Eze 47:15 it will run from the M Sea by the Hethlon H1524S
Eze 47:19 along the Wadi of Egypt to the M Sea. H1524S
Eze 47:20 the M Sea will be the boundary to a H1524S
Eze 48:28 along the Wadi of Egypt to the M Sea. H1524S
Joel 2:20 Sea and its western ranks in the M Sea. H340S
Zec 14: 8 Dead Sea and half of it west to the *M Sea*, AIT

MEDIUM (4) [MEDIUMS]

Lev 20:27 woman who is a m or spiritist among H200
Dt 18:11 or *who is a* m or spiritist or who H200+8626
1Sa 28: 7 "Find me a woman who is a m, so I H1266+200
1Ch 10:13 LORD and even consulted a m for guidance, H200

MEDIUMS (10) [MEDIUM]

Lev 19:31 " 'Do not turn to m or seek out spiritists, for H200
Lev 20: 6 anyone who turns to m and spiritists to H200
1Sa 28: 3 Saul had expelled the m and spiritists from H200
1Sa 28: 9 He has cut off the m and spiritists from the H200
2Ki 21: 6 and consulted m and spiritists. H200
2Ki 23:24 Josiah got rid of the m and spiritists, the H200
2Ch 33: 6 and consulted m and spiritists. H200
Isa 8:19 tells you to consult m and spiritists, H200
Isa 19: 3 spirits of the dead, the m and the spiritists. H200
Jer 27: 9 your m or your sorcerers who tell you H6726

MEEK (3) [MEEKLY]

Ps 37:11 But the m will inherit the land and enjoy H6705
Zep 3:12 I will leave within you the m and humble. H6714
Mt 5: 5 Blessed are the m, for they will inherit the G4558

MEEKLY (1) [MEEK]

1Ki 21:27 He lay in sackcloth and went around m. H351

MEET (144) [MEETING, MEETINGS, MEETS, MET]

Ge 14:17 Sodom came out to m him in the Valley H7925
Ge 18: 2 of his tent to m them and bowed low to H7925
Ge 19: 1 he got up to m them and bowed down H7925
Ge 19: 6 Lot went outside to m them and shut the NDT
Ge 24:17 The servant hurried to m her and said H7925
Ge 24:65 is that man in the field coming to m us?" H7925
Ge 29:13 his sister's son, he hurried to m him. H7925
Ge 30:16 that evening, Leah went out to m him. H7925
Ge 32: 6 now he is coming to m you, and four H7925
Ge 32:19 the same thing to Esau when you m him. H5162
Ge 33: 4 But Esau ran to m Jacob and embraced H7925
Ge 46:29 went to Goshen to m his father Israel. H7925
Ex 4:14 He is already on his way to m you, and he H7925
Ex 4:27 "Go into the wilderness to m Moses." H7925
Ex 5:20 Moses and Aaron waiting to m them, H7925
Ex 18: 7 So Moses went out to m his father-in-law H7925
Ex 19:17 people out of the camp to m *with* God, H7925
Ex 25:22 *I will* m with you and give you all my H3585
Ex 29:42 There *I will* m you and speak to you; H3585
Ex 29:43 there also *I will* m with the Israelites, and H3585

M

Ex 30: 6 covenant law—where *I will* **m** with you. H3585
Ex 30:36 tent of meeting, where *I will* **m** with you. H3585
Nu 14:35 *They will* **m** their **end** in this wilderness H9462
Nu 17: 4 of the covenant law, where *I* **m** with you. H3585
Nu 21:33 army marched out to **m** them in battle at H7925
Nu 22:36 he went out to **m** him at the Moabite H7925
Nu 23: 3 Perhaps the LORD will come to **m** *with* me H7925
Nu 23:15 offering while I **m** *with* him over there." H7936
Nu 31:13 community went to **m** them outside the H7925
Nu 35:21 put the murderer to death when they **m**. H7003
Dt 2:32 his army came out to **m** us in battle at H7925
Dt 3: 1 army marched out to **m** us in battle at H7925
Dt 22:23 If a man *happens to* **m** in a town a virgin H5162
Dt 22:25 country a man *happens to* **m** a young H5162
Dt 22:28 If a man *happens to* **m** a virgin who is not H5162
Dt 23: 4 For *they did* not **come to m** you with bread H7709
Jos 8:14 in the morning to **m** Israel in battle at a H7925
Jos 9:11 journey; go and **m** them and say to them H7925
Jdg 4:18 Jael went out to **m** Sisera and said to him, H7925
Jdg 4:22 of Sisera, and Jael went out to **m** him. H7925
Jdg 6:35 so that they too went up to **m** them. H7925
Jdg 11:31 of my house to **m** me when I return in H7925
Jdg 11:34 should come out to **m** him but his H7925
Jdg 20:31 came out to **m** them and were drawn H7925
1Sa 4: 2 deployed their forces to **m** Israel, H7925
1Sa 10: 2 *you will* **m** two men near Rachel's tomb H5162
1Sa 10: 3 to worship God at Bethel *will* **m** you there. H5162
1Sa 10: 5 *you will* **m** a procession of prophets H7003
1Sa 15:12 Samuel got up and **went to m** Saul, H7925
1Sa 17: 2 up their battle line to **m** the Philistines. H7925
1Sa 17:48 quickly toward the battle line to **m** him. H7925
1Sa 17:55 David going out to **m** the Philistine, H7925
1Sa 18: 6 towns of Israel to **m** King Saul with H7925
1Sa 21: 2 I have told them to **m** me at a certain place. NDT
1Sa 23:28 of David and went to **m** the Philistines. H7925
1Sa 25:32 who has sent you today to **m** me. H7925
1Sa 25:34 if you had not come quickly to **m** me, not H7925
1Sa 30:21 They came out to **m** David and the men H7925
2Sa 6:20 of Saul came out to **m** him and said, H7925
2Sa 10: 5 he sent messengers to **m** the men, for H7925
2Sa 10:17 their battle lines to **m** David and fought H7925
2Sa 15:32 Hushai the Arkite was there to **m** him, his H7925
2Sa 16: 1 of Mephibosheth, waiting to **m** him. H7925
2Sa 18: 9 happened to **m** David's men. H4200+7156
2Sa 19:15 Gilgal to go out and **m** the king and bring H7925
2Sa 19:16 with the men of Judah to **m** King David. H7925
2Sa 19:20 to come down and **m** my lord the king." H7925
2Sa 19:24 grandson, also went down to **m** the king. H7925
2Sa 19:25 he came from Jerusalem to **m** the king, H7925
2Sa 20: 8 Gibeon, Amasa came to **m** them. H4200+7156
1Ki 2: 8 he came down to **m** me *at* the Jordan, H7925
1Ki 2:19 the king stood up to **m** her, bowed down H7925
1Ki 18:16 Obadiah went to **m** Ahab and told him, H7925
1Ki 18:16 told him, and Ahab went to **m** Elijah. H7925
1Ki 18:19 all over Israel to **m** me on Mount Carmel. NDT
1Ki 20: 9 the first time, but this demand I cannot **m**. H6913
1Ki 20:27 provisions, they marched out to **m** them. H7925
1Ki 21:18 "Go down to **m** Ahab king of Israel, who H7925
2Ki 1: 3 "Go up and **m** the messengers of the king H7925
2Ki 1: 6 "A man came to **m** us," they replied H7925
2Ki 1: 7 was it who came to **m** you and told you H7925
2Ki 2:15 And they went to **m** him and bowed to H7925
2Ki 4:26 Run to **m** her and ask her, 'Are you all H7925
2Ki 4:29 Don't greet anyone *you* **m**, and if anyone H5162
2Ki 4:31 went back to **m** Elisha and told him H7925
2Ki 5:21 he got down from the chariot to **m** him. H7925
2Ki 5:26 man got down from his chariot to **m** you? H7925
2Ki 6: 1 the place where we **m** with you is too H3782
2Ki 6: 2 let us build a place there for us to **m**." H3782
2Ki 8: 8 gift with you and go to **m** the man of God. H7925
2Ki 8: 9 Hazael went to **m** Elisha, taking with him H7925
2Ki 9:17 "Send him to **m** them and ask, 'Do you H7925
2Ki 9:18 horseman rode off to **m** Jehu and said, H7925
2Ki 9:21 each in his own chariot, to **m** Jehu. H7925
2Ki 10:15 of Rekab, *who was on his way* to **m** him. H7925
2Ki 16:10 went to Damascus to **m** Tiglath-Pileser H7925
2Ki 23:29 Josiah marched out to **m** him **in battle**, H7925
1Ch 12:17 went out to **m** them and said to H4200+7156
1Ch 14: 8 about it and went out to **m** them. H4200+7156
1Ch 19: 5 he sent messengers to **m** them, for they H7925
1Ch 19:17 formed his lines to **m** the Arameans in H7925
2Ch 14:10 Asa went out to **m** him, and they H4200+7156
2Ch 15: 2 He went out to **m** Asa and said to H4200+7156
2Ch 19: 2 went out to **m** him and said to the H448+7156
2Ch 22: 7 out with Joram to **m** Jehu son of Nimshi, H448
2Ch 28: 9 he went out to **m** the army when it H4200+7156
2Ch 35:20 Josiah marched out to **m** him **in battle**. H7925
Ne 4: 9 day and night to **m** this threat. H4946+7156
Ne 6: 2 *let us* **m** together in one of the villages on H3585
Ne 6: 7 to the king; so come, *let us* **m** together." H3619
Ne 6:10 He said, "*Let us* **m** in the house of God H3585
Ps 42: 2 When can I go and **m with** God? H8011+7156
Ps 79: 8 *may* your mercy **come** quickly **to m** us, for H7709
Ps 85:10 Love and faithfulness **m together** H7008
Pr 7:10 Then **out came** a woman **to m** him H7925
Pr 7:15 So I came out to **m** you; I looked for you H7925
Pr 8: 2 where the paths **m**, she takes her stand H1075
Pr 17:12 Better *to* **m** a bear robbed of her cubs H7008
Isa 7: 3 to **m** Ahaz at the end of the aqueduct of H7925
Isa 14: 9 below is all astir to **m** you at your coming; H7925
Isa 34:14 Desert creatures *will* **m** with hyenas, and H7008
Isa 41: 1 *let us* **m** together at the place of H7928
Isa 66:17 *they will* **m** *their* **end** together with the one H6066
Jer 41: 6 went out from Mizpah to **m** them, H7925
Am 4:12 this to you, Israel, prepare to **m** your God." H7925
Am 5:19 a man fled from a lion only *to* **m** a bear, H7003
Am 9:10 'Disaster will not overtake or **m** us. H7709
Zec 2: 3 leaving, another angel came to **m** him H7925
Mt 8:34 Then the whole town went out to **m** Jesus *G5637*
Mt 25: 1 lamps and went out to **m** the bridegroom. *G5637*
Mt 25: 6 the bridegroom! Come out to **m** him!' *G561*
Mk 5: 2 spirit came from the tombs *to* **m** him. *G5636*
Mk 14:13 a man carrying a jar of water *will* **m** you. *G560*
Lk 22:10 a man carrying a jar of water *will* **m** you. *G5267*
Jn 11:20 was coming, *she* **went out to m** him, but *G5636*
Jn 12:13 palm branches and went out to **m** him, *G5637*
Jn 12:18 performed this sign, **went out to m** him. *G5636*
Ac 2:46 Every day *they* **continued** *to m* together in the AIT
Ac 5:12 all the believers *used to* **m** together in *G1639*
Ac 28:15 of Appius and the Three Taverns to **m** us. *G561*
Ac 28:23 *They* **arranged** *to m* Paul on a certain day AIT
1Co 11:34 so that *when you* **m together** it may not *G5302*
Php 4:19 And my God *will* **m** all your needs *G4444*
1Th 4:17 them in the clouds to **m** the Lord in the air. *G561*

MEETING (159) [MEET]

Ex 27:21 In the tent of **m**, outside the curtain that H4595
Ex 28:43 enter the tent of **m** or approach the altar H4595
Ex 29: 4 to the tent of **m** and wash them with H4595
Ex 29:10 the bull to the front of the tent of **m**, H4595
Ex 29:11 presence at the entrance to the tent of **m**. H4595
Ex 29:30 comes to the tent of **m** to minister in the H4595
Ex 29:32 At the entrance to the tent of **m**, Aaron H4595
Ex 29:42 regularly at the entrance to the tent of **m**, H4595
Ex 29:44 the tent of **m** and the altar and will H4595
Ex 30:16 use it for the service of the tent of **m**. H4595
Ex 30:18 it between the tent of **m** and the altar, H4595
Ex 30:20 Whenever they enter the tent of **m**, they H4595
Ex 30:26 Then use it to anoint the tent of **m**, the ark H4595
Ex 30:36 ark of the covenant law in the tent of **m**, H4595
Ex 31: 7 the tent of **m**, the ark of the covenant law H4595
Ex 33: 7 distance away, calling it the "tent of **m**." H4595
Ex 33: 7 go to the tent of **m** outside the camp. H4595
Ex 35:21 to the LORD for the work on the tent of **m**, H4595
Ex 38: 8 served at the entrance to the tent of **m**. H4595
Ex 38:30 bases for the entrance to the tent of **m**, H4595
Ex 39:32 tabernacle, the tent of **m**, was completed. H4595
Ex 39:40 the tabernacle, the tent of **m**; H4595
Ex 40: 2 the tent of **m**, on the first day of H4595
Ex 40: 6 entrance to the tabernacle, the tent of **m**; H4595
Ex 40: 7 between the tent of **m** and the altar and H4595
Ex 40:12 to the tent of **m** and wash them with H4595
Ex 40:22 table in the tent of **m** on the north side of H4595
Ex 40:24 in the tent of **m** opposite the table on H4595
Ex 40:26 altar in the tent of **m** in front of the curtain H4595
Ex 40:29 the tent of **m**, and offered on it H4595
Ex 40:30 between the tent of **m** and the altar and H4595
Ex 40:32 entered the tent of **m** or approached the H4595
Ex 40:34 Then the cloud covered the tent of **m**, and H4595
Ex 40:35 enter the tent of **m** because the cloud had H4595
Lev 1: 1 spoke to him from the tent of **m**. H4595
Lev 1: 3 entrance to the tent of **m** so that it will be H4595
Lev 1: 5 the altar at the entrance to the tent of **m**. H4595
Lev 3: 2 it at the entrance to the tent of **m**. H4595
Lev 3: 8 slaughter it in front of the tent of **m**. H4595
Lev 3:13 slaughter it in front of the tent of **m**. H4595
Lev 4: 4 entrance to the tent of **m** before the LORD. H4595
Lev 4: 5 bull's blood and carry it into the tent of **m**. H4595
Lev 4: 7 that is before the LORD in the tent of **m**. H4595
Lev 4: 7 offering at the entrance to the tent of **m**. H4595
Lev 4:14 present it before the tent of **m**. H4595
Lev 4:16 of the bull's blood into the tent of **m**. H4595
Lev 4:18 that is before the LORD in the tent of **m**. H4595
Lev 4:18 offering at the entrance to the tent of **m**. H4595
Lev 6:16 to eat it in the courtyard of the tent of **m**. H4595
Lev 6:26 in the courtyard of the tent of **m**. H4595
Lev 6:30 into the tent of **m** to make atonement in H4595
Lev 8: 3 assembly at the entrance to the tent of **m**." H4595
Lev 8: 4 gathered at the entrance to the tent of **m**. H4595
Lev 8:31 to the tent of **m** and eat it there with H4595
Lev 8:33 entrance to the tent of **m** for seven days, H4595
Lev 8:35 to the tent of **m** day and night for seven H4595
Lev 9: 5 commanded to the front of the tent of **m**, H4595
Lev 9:23 Aaron then went into the tent of **m**. H4595
Lev 10: 7 entrance to the tent of **m** or you will die, H4595
Lev 10: 9 drink whenever you go into the tent of **m**, H4595
Lev 12: 6 to the tent of **m** a year-old lamb for a H4595
Lev 14:11 the LORD at the entrance to the tent of **m**. H4595
Lev 14:23 the priest at the entrance to the tent of **m**, H4595
Lev 15:14 to the tent of **m** and give them to the H4595
Lev 15:29 the priest at the entrance to the tent of **m**. H4595
Lev 16: 7 the LORD at the entrance to the tent of **m**. H4595
Lev 16:16 He is to do the same for the tent of **m** H4595
Lev 16:17 to be in the tent of **m** from the time Aaron H4595
Lev 16:20 the tent of **m** and the altar, he H4595
Lev 16:23 go into the tent of **m** and take off the H4595
Lev 16:33 the tent of **m** and the altar, and for H4595
Lev 17: 4 to the tent of **m** to present it as an H4595
Lev 17: 5 to the tent of **m** and sacrifice them as H4595
Lev 17: 6 to the tent of **m** and burn the fat as an H4595
Lev 17: 9 to the tent of **m** to sacrifice it to the H4595
Lev 19:21 to the tent of **m** for a guilt offering to H4595
Lev 24: 3 ark of the covenant law in the tent of **m**, H4595
Nu 1: 1 Moses in the tent of **m** in the Desert of H4595
Nu 2: 2 around the tent of **m** some distance from H4595
Nu 2:17 Then the tent of **m** and the camp of the H4595
Nu 3: 7 at the tent of **m** by doing the work of the H4595
Nu 3: 8 care of all the furnishings of the tent of **m**, H4595
Nu 3:25 At the tent of **m** the Gershonites were H4595
Nu 3:25 curtain at the entrance to the tent of **m**, H4595
Nu 3:38 the sunrise, in front of the tent of **m**. H4595
Nu 4: 3 come to serve in the work at the tent of **m**. H4595
Nu 4: 4 work of the Kohathites at the tent of **m**: H4595
Nu 4:15 those things that are in the tent of **m**. H4595
Nu 4:23 come to serve in the work at the tent of **m**. H4595
Nu 4:25 the tent of **m**, its covering and its H4595
Nu 4:25 curtains for the entrance to the tent of **m**, H4595
Nu 4:28 of the Gershonite clans at the tent of **m**. H4595
Nu 4:30 come to serve in the work at the tent of **m**. H4595
Nu 4:33 work at the tent of **m** under the direction H4595
Nu 4:35 came to serve in the work at the tent of **m**, H4595
Nu 4:37 clans who served at the tent of **m**. H4595
Nu 4:39 came to serve in the work at the tent of **m**, H4595
Nu 4:41 clans who served at the tent of **m**. H4595
Nu 4:43 came to serve in the work at the tent of **m**, H4595
Nu 4:47 work of serving and carrying the tent of **m** H4595
Nu 6:10 the priest at the entrance to the tent of **m**. H4595
Nu 6:13 brought to the entrance to the tent of **m**. H4595
Nu 6:18 " 'Then at the entrance to the tent of **m** H4595
Nu 7: 5 may be used in the work at the tent of **m**. H4595
Nu 7:89 entered the tent of **m** to speak with the H4595
Nu 8: 9 front of the tent of **m** and assemble the H4595
Nu 8:15 to come to do their work at the tent of **m**. H4595
Nu 8:19 the work at the tent of **m** on behalf of the H4595
Nu 8:22 work at the tent of **m** under the H4595
Nu 8:24 to take part in the work at the tent of **m**, H4595
Nu 8:26 in performing their duties at the tent of **m**, H4595
Nu 10: 3 you at the entrance to the tent of **m**. H4595
Nu 11:16 Have them come to the tent of **m**, that H4595
Nu 12: 4 "Come out to the tent of **m**, all three of H4595
Nu 14:10 at the tent of **m** to all the Israelites. H4595
Nu 16:18 Aaron at the entrance to the tent of **m**. H4595
Nu 16:19 to them at the entrance to the tent of **m**, H4595
Nu 16:42 Aaron and turned toward the tent of **m**, H4595
Nu 16:43 Aaron went to the front of the tent of **m**, H4595
Nu 16:50 to Moses at the entrance to the tent of **m**, H4595
Nu 17: 4 them in the tent of **m** in front of the ark of H4595
Nu 18: 4 responsible for the care of the tent of **m**— H4595
Nu 18: 6 the LORD to do the work at the tent of **m**. H4595
Nu 18:21 they do while serving at the tent of **m**. H4595
Nu 18:22 Israelites must not go near the tent of **m**, H4595
Nu 18:23 do the work at the tent of **m** and bear the H4595
Nu 18:31 your wages for your work at the tent of **m**. H4595
Nu 19: 4 times toward the front of the tent of **m**. H4595
Nu 20: 6 to the tent of **m** and fell facedown, H4595
Nu 25: 6 weeping at the entrance to the tent of **m**. H4595
Nu 27: 2 at the entrance to the tent of **m** and said, H4595
Nu 31:54 it into the tent of **m** as a memorial for the H4595
Dt 31:14 present yourselves at the tent of **m**, H4595
Dt 31:14 presented themselves at the tent of **m**. H4595
Jos 18: 1 at Shiloh and set up the tent of **m** there. H4595
Jos 19:51 the LORD at the entrance to the tent of **m**. H4595
Jos 22:32 to Canaan from their **m** with the Reubenites NDT
1Sa 2:22 served at the entrance to the tent of **m**. H4595
1Sa 20:35 went out to the field for his **m** *with* David. H4595
1Ki 8: 4 LORD and the tent of **m** and all the sacred H4595
2Ki 4:38 company of the prophets *was* **m** with him, H3782
1Ch 6:32 the tent of **m**, until Solomon built H4595
1Ch 9:21 at the entrance to the tent of **m**. H4595
1Ch 9:23 of the LORD—the house called the tent of **m**. NDT
1Ch 23:32 out their responsibilities for the tent of **m**, H4595
2Ch 1: 3 God's tent of **m** was there, which H4595
2Ch 1: 6 LORD in the tent of **m** and offered a H4595
2Ch 1:13 at Gibeon, from before the tent of **m**. H4595
2Ch 5: 5 ark and the tent of **m** and all the sacred H4595
Ne 5: 7 together a large **m** to deal with them H7737
La 2: 6 garden; he has destroyed his **place of m**. H4595
Jn 11:47 the Pharisees **called a m** of the Sanhedrin *G5251*
Ac 4:31 the place where they were **m** was shaken. *G5251*
Ac 17:19 brought him to a **m of the Areopagus**, *G740*
Ac 17:22 up in the **m of the Areopagus** and said: *G740*
Ac 20: 8 in the upstairs room where we were **m**. *G5251*
Gal 2: 2 **m** privately with those esteemed as leaders NDT
Heb 10:25 not giving up **m together**, as some are in *G2191*
Jas 2: 2 comes into your **m** wearing a gold ring *G5252*

MEETINGS (1) [MEET]

1Co 11:17 for *your* **m** do more harm than good. *G5302*

MEETS (5) [MEET]

Ge 32:17 "When my brother Esau **m** you and asks H7008
Ro 16: 5 also the church that **m at** their house. *G2848*
1Co 16:19 so does the church that **m at** their house. *G2848*
Phm 2 to the church that **m in** your home: *G2848*
Heb 7:26 Such a high priest truly **m** our **need**—one *G4560*

MEGIDDO (12)

Jos 12:21 king of Taanach one the king of **M** one H4459
Jos 17:11 Taanach and **M**, together with H4459
Jdg 1:27 Dor or Ibleam or **M** and their H4459
Jdg 5:19 by the waters of **M**, they took no plunder H4459
1Ki 4:12 in Taanach and **M**, and in all of Beth H4459
1Ki 9:15 of Jerusalem, and Hazor, **M** and Gezer. H4459
2Ki 9:27 he escaped to **M** and died there. H4459
2Ki 23:29 Necho faced him and killed him at **M**. H4459
2Ki 23:30 in a chariot from **M** to Jerusalem and H4459

1Ch 7:29 Taanach, **M** and Dor, together with their H4459
2Ch 35:22 went to fight him on the plain of **M**. H4459
Zec 12:11 of Hadad Rimmon in the plain of **M**. H4461

MEHETABEL (3)
Ge 36:39 wife's name was **M** daughter of Matred, H4541
1Ch 1:50 wife's name was **M** daughter of Matred, H4541
Ne 6:10 Delaiah, the son of **M**, who was shut in at H4541

MEHIDA (2)
Ezr 2:52 Bazluth, **M**, Harsha, H4694
Ne 7:54 Bazluth, **M**, Harsha, H4694

MEHIR (1)
1Ch 4:11 was the father of **M**, who was the father of H4698

MEHOLAH (1) [MEHOLATHITE]
1Sa 18:19 she was given in marriage to Adriel **of M**. H4716

MEHOLATHITE (1) [MEHOLAH]
2Sa 21:8 had borne to Adriel son of Barzillai the **M**. H4716

MEHUJAEL (2)
Ge 4:18 Irad was the father of **M**, and H4686
Ge 4:18 **M** was the father of Methushael H4686

MEHUMAN (1)
Est 1:10 eunuchs who served him—**M**, Biztha, H4540

MEKERATHITE (1)
1Ch 11:36 Hepher the **M**, Ahijah the Pelonite, H4841

MEKONAH (1)
Ne 11:28 in Ziklag, in **M** and its settlements, H4828

MELAH See TEL MELAH

MELATIAH (1)
Ne 3:7 **M** of Gibeon and Jadon of Meronoth H4882

MELCHISEDEC (KJV) MELCHIZEDEK

MELCHIZEDEK (11)
Ge 14:18 Then **M** king of Salem brought out bread H4900
Ps 110:4 are a priest forever, in the order of **M**." H4900
Heb 5:6 are a priest forever, in the order *of* **M**." *G3519*
Heb 5:10 by God to be high priest in the order *of* **M**. *G3519*
Heb 6:20 a high priest forever, in the order *of* **M**. *G3519*
Heb 7:1 This **M** was king of Salem and priest of *G3519*
Heb 7:2 the name **M** means "king of righteousness"; NDT
Heb 7:10 because when **M** met Abraham, Levi was *G3519*
Heb 7:11 one in the order *of* **M**, not in the order of *G3519*
Heb 7:15 clear if another priest like **M** appears, *G3519*
Heb 7:17 are a priest forever, in the order *of* **M**." *G3519*

MELEA (1)
Lk 3:31 the son *of* **M**, the son of Menna, the son *G3507*

MELEK (2)
1Ch 8:35 Pithon, **M**, Tarea and Ahaz. H4890
1Ch 9:41 Pithon, **M**, Tahrea and Ahaz. H4890

MELITA (KJV) MALTA

MELKI (2)
Lk 3:24 the son *of* **M**, the son of Jannai, *G3518*
Lk 3:28 the son *of* **M**, the son of Addi, the son of *G3518*

MELODIOUS (1) [MELODY]
Ps 81:2 the timbrel, play the **m** harp and lyre. H5834

MELODY (1) [MELODIOUS]
Ps 92:3 ten-stringed lyre and the **m** of the harp. H2053

MELONS (1)
Nu 11:5 also the cucumbers, **m**, leeks, onions and H19

MELT (15) [MELTED, MELTING, MELTS]
Ex 15:15 the people of Canaan *will* **m away**; H4570
Dt 1:28 brothers have made our hearts **m in fear**. H5022
Jos 14:8 **made** the hearts of the people **m in fear**. H4998
2Sa 17:10 of a lion, *will* **m with fear**, for all H5022+5022
Ps 97:5 The mountains **m** like wax before the LORD H5022
Isa 13:7 will go limp, every heart *will* **m with fear**. H5022
Isa 14:31 **M away**, all you Philistines! H4570
Isa 19:1 the hearts of the Egyptians **m with fear**. H5022
Eze 21:7 Every heart *will* **m with fear** and every H5022
Eze 21:15 that hearts *may* **m with fear** and the fallen H4570
Eze 22:20 put you inside the city and **m** you. H5988
Mic 1:4 The mountains **m** beneath him and the H5022
Na 1:5 quake before him and the hills **m away**. H4570
Na 2:10 Hearts **m**, knees give way, bodies tremble, H5022
2Pe 3:12 and the elements *will* **m** in the heat. *G5494*

MELTED (12) [MELT]
Ex 16:21 when the sun grew hot, *it* **m away**. H5022
Jos 2:11 our hearts **m in fear** and everyone's H5022
Jos 5:1 their hearts **m in fear** and they no longer H5022
Jos 7:5 of the people **m in fear** and became like H5022
Job 24:19 drought snatch away the **m** snow, H4784
Ps 22:14 has turned to wax; *it has* **m** within me. H5022
Ps 107:26 in their peril their courage **m away**. H4570
Eze 22:20 into a furnace to *be* **m** with a fiery blast, H5988
Eze 22:21 fiery wrath, and *you will* **be m** inside her. H5988
Eze 22:22 As silver is **m** in a furnace, so you will be H2247
Eze 22:22 a furnace, so *you will* **be m** inside her H5988

Eze 24:11 its impurities *may* **be m** and its deposit H5988

MELTING (4) [MELT]
Jos 2:9 this country *are* **m in fear** because of you H4570
Jos 2:24 the people *are* **m in fear** because of us." H4570
1Sa 14:16 saw the army **m away** in all H4570+2256+2143
Job 6:16 by thawing ice and swollen with **m** snow, NDT

MELTS (5) [MELT]
Ps 46:6 he lifts his voice, the earth **m**. H4570
Ps 58:8 be like a slug *that* **m away** as it moves H9468
Ps 68:2 like smoke—as wax **m** before the fire H5022
Ps 147:18 He sends his word and **m** them; he stirs H4998
Am 9:5 he touches the earth and *it* **m**, and all H4570

MELZAR (KJV) GUARD

MEMBER (8) [MEMBERS]
Lev 4:27 " 'If any **m** of the community sins H5883
Lev 25:47 foreigner or to a **m** *of* the foreigner's clan H6830
Eze 17:13 Then he took a **m** *of* the royal family and H4946
Mk 15:43 a prominent **m of the Council**, who was *G1085*
Lk 23:50 Joseph, a **m of the Council**, a good and *G1085*
Jn 3:1 *who was a* **m** *of* the Jewish **ruling council**. AIT
Ac 17:34 Dionysius, a **m of the Areopagus**, also a *G741*
Ro 12:5 each **m** belongs to all the others. *G3517*

MEMBERS (31) [MEMBER]
Ge 36:6 daughters and all the **m** *of* his household, H5883
Ge 46:27 Joseph in Egypt, the **m** of Jacob's family H5883
Ge 50:8 besides **all** *the* **m** *of* Joseph's household AIT
Ex 12:6 when all the **m** *of* the community of Israel H7736
Lev 16:33 priests and all the **m** *of* the community. H6639
Lev 20:2 The **m** *of* the community are to stone him. H6639
Lev 20:4 If the **m** *of* the community close their eyes H6639
Lev 25:45 among you and **m** *of* their clans born in H1201
Nu 14:1 That night all the **m** of the community H6639
Nu 16:2 leaders *who* had been **appointed** *m of* the AIT
1Sa 2:30 that **m** of your **family** H1074+2256+1074+3
2Sa 9:12 all the **m** *of* Ziba's household were H4632
2Ch 21:13 brothers, *m of* your own **family**, men who AIT
Jer 12:6 **m of** your own **family**—even they H1074+3
Mic 7:6 enemies are the **m** *of* his own household. H408
Mt 10:25 how much more the **m of** his **household!** *G3865*
Mt 10:36 will be the **m** of his own **household**. *G3865*
Ac 5:17 who were *m of* the **party** of the Sadducees AIT
Ac 6:9 *from* **m** of the Synagogue of the *G5516*
Ac 7:54 When the **m** of the Sanhedrin heard this NDT
Ac 16:15 she and the **m of** her **household** were *G3875*
Ac 22:30 all the **m of the Sanhedrin** to *G5284*
Ro 12:4 as each of us has one body with many **m**, *G3517*
Ro 12:4 these **m** do not all have the same *G3517*
1Co 6:15 that your bodies are **m** of Christ himself? *G3517*
1Co 6:15 Shall I then take the **m** of Christ and unite *G3517*
Eph 2:19 people and also **m of** his **household**, *G3858*
Eph 3:6 **m together of one body**, and *G5362*
Eph 4:25 neighbor, for we are all **m** of one body. *G3517*
Eph 5:30 we are **m** of his body. *G3517*
Col 3:15 since *as* **m of** one body you were called to *G1877*

MEMORABLE (1) [MEMORY]
Eze 39:13 display my glory will be a **m** day for them, H9005

MEMORANDUM (1)
Ezr 6:2 of Media, and this was written on it: **M**: A10176

MEMORIAL (19) [MEMORY]
Ex 28:12 of the ephod as **m** stones for the sons of H2355
Ex 28:12 on his shoulders as a **m** before the LORD. H2355
Ex 28:29 as a continuing **m** before the LORD. H2355
Ex 30:16 It will be a **m** for the Israelites before the H2355
Ex 39:7 of the ephod as **m** stones for the sons of H2355
Lev 2:2 burn this as a **m portion** on the altar, H260
Lev 2:9 shall take out the **m portion** from the grain H260
Lev 2:16 shall burn the **m portion** of the crushed H260
Lev 5:12 handful of it as a **m portion** and burn it on H260
Lev 6:15 burn the **m portion** on the altar as an H260
Lev 24:7 incense as a **m portion** to represent the H260
Nu 5:26 offering as a **m offering** and burn it on the H260
Nu 10:10 they will be a **m** for you before your H2355
Nu 31:54 tent of meeting as a **m** for the Israelites H2355
Jos 4:7 stones are to be a **m** to the people of H2355
Isa 56:5 its walls a **m** and a name better than H3338
Isa 66:3 and *whoever* **burns m** incense is like one H2349
Zec 6:14 of Zephaniah as a **m** in the temple of the H2355
Ac 10:4 come up as a **m offering** before God. *G3649*

MEMORIES (1) [MEMORY]
1Th 3:6 have pleasant **m** of us and that you *G3644*

MEMORY (10) [MEMORABLE, MEMORIAL, MEMORIES]
Dt 32:26 erase their **name** from human **m**, H2352
2Sa 18:18 no son to **carry on the m** *of* my name." H2349
Est 9:28 should the **m** *of* these days die out H2352
Job 18:17 The **m** *of* him perishes from the earth; he H2352
Ps 9:6 even the **m** *of* them has perished. H2352
Ps 45:17 *I will* **perpetuate** your **m** through all H2349+9005
Isa 26:14 you wiped out all **m** of them. H2352
Mt 26:13 has done will also be told, in **m** of her." *G3649*
Mk 14:9 has done will also be told, in **m** of her." *G3649*
2Pe 1:13 right to refresh your **m** as long as I live in *G5704*

MEMPHIS (8)
Isa 19:13 the leaders of **M** are deceived; the H5862
Jer 2:16 the men of **M** and Tahpanhes have H5862
Jer 44:1 Tahpanhes and **M**—and in Upper Egypt: H5862
Jer 46:14 proclaim it also in **M** and Tahpanhes: H5862
Jer 46:19 **M** will be laid waste and lie in ruins H5862
Eze 30:13 idols and put an end to the images in **M**. H5862
Eze 30:16 by storm; **M** will be in constant distress. H5862
Hos 9:6 will gather them, and **M** will bury them. H5132

MEMUKAN (3)
Est 1:14 Marsena and **M**, the seven nobles H4925
Est 1:16 Then **M** replied in the presence of the H4925
Est 1:21 so the king did as **M** proposed. H4925

MEN (1078) [MAN]
Ge 6:4 They were the heroes of old, **m** *of* renown. H408
Ge 12:20 gave orders about Abram to his **m**, H408
Ge 13:11 The two **m** parted company: H408
Ge 14:10 *some of the m* **fell** into them and the rest AIT
Ge 14:14 called out the 318 **trained m** born in his H2849
Ge 14:15 Abram divided his **m** to attack them and H6269
Ge 14:24 what my **m** have eaten and the H5853
Ge 14:24 that belongs to the **m** who went with me— H408
Ge 18:2 up and saw three **m** standing nearby. H408
Ge 18:16 When the **m** got up to leave, they looked H408
Ge 18:22 The **m** turned away and went toward H408
Ge 19:4 all the **m** from every part of the city of H408
Ge 19:5 "Where are the **m** who came to you tonight H408
Ge 19:8 But don't do anything to these **m**, for they H408
Ge 19:10 But the **m** inside reached out and pulled H408
Ge 19:11 Then they struck the **m** who were at the H408
Ge 19:12 The two **m** said to Lot, "Do you have H408
Ge 19:16 the **m** grasped his hand and the hands of H408
Ge 21:27 Abimelek, and the two **m** made a treaty. H2157S
Ge 21:31 because the two **m** swore an oath there. H2157S
Ge 24:32 water for him and his **m** to wash their feet. H408
Ge 24:54 Then he and the **m** who were with him ate H408
Ge 24:59 nurse and Abraham's servant and his **m**. H408
Ge 26:7 When the **m** *of* that place asked him about H408
Ge 26:7 "The **m** *of* this place might kill me on H408
Ge 26:10 One of the **m** might well have slept with H6639
Ge 26:31 next morning *the m* **swore an oath** to each AIT
Ge 32:6 and four hundred **m** are with him. H408
Ge 33:1 coming with his four hundred **m**; so he H408
Ge 33:15 let me leave some of my **m** with you." H6639
Ge 34:20 of their city to speak to the **m** *of* their city. H408
Ge 34:21 "These **m** are friendly toward us," they said H408
Ge 34:22 But the **m** will agree to live with us as one H408
Ge 34:24 All the *m who* **went out** *of* the city gate AIT
Ge 38:12 to the *m who were* **shearing** his sheep AIT
Ge 38:21 He asked the **m** *who lived* there, "Where is H408
Ge 38:22 Besides, the **m** *who lived* there said, 'There H408
Ge 40:5 each of the two **m**—the cupbearer and H2157S
Ge 41:8 all the magicians and **wise** *m of* Egypt. AIT
Ge 42:11 Your servants are **honest** *m*, not spies." AIT
Ge 42:19 If you are **honest** *m*, let one of your brothers AIT
Ge 42:31 'We are **honest** *m*; we are not spies. AIT
Ge 42:33 is how I will know whether you are **honest** *m*: AIT
Ge 42:34 know that you are not spies but **honest** *m*. AIT
Ge 43:15 So the **m** took the gifts and double the H408
Ge 43:16 "Take these **m** to my house H408
Ge 43:17 told him and took the **m** to Joseph's house. H408
Ge 43:18 Now the **m** were frightened when they were H408
Ge 43:24 steward took the **m** into Joseph's house, H408
Ge 43:33 The **m** had been seated before him in the NDT
Ge 44:3 the **m** were sent on their way with their H408
Ge 44:4 "Go after those **m** at once, and when you H408
Ge 46:32 The **m** are shepherds; they tend livestock H408
Ge 49:6 they have killed **m** in their anger and H408
Ex 7:11 then summoned **wise** *m* and sorcerers, AIT
Ex 10:11 Have only the **m** go and worship the LORD H1505
Ex 11:2 the people that **m** and women alike are H408
Ex 12:37 about six hundred thousand **m** on foot, H1505
Ex 17:9 "Choose *some of* our **m** and go out to fight H408
Ex 18:21 But select capable **m** from all the people H408
Ex 18:21 all the people—*m who* **fear** God, trustworthy AIT
Ex 18:21 trustworthy **m** who hate dishonest gain H408
Ex 18:25 He chose capable **m** from all Israel and H408
Ex 23:17 a year all the **m** are to appear before H2344
Ex 24:5 Then he sent **young** Israelite **m**, and they H5853
Ex 34:23 a year all your **m** are to appear before H2344
Ex 35:22 All who were willing, **m** and women alike H408
Ex 35:29 All the Israelite **m** and women who were H408
Ex 38:26 years old or more, a total of 603,550 **m**. NDT
Nu 1:3 their divisions all the **m** in Israel who are NDT
Nu 1:5 are the names of the **m** who are to assist H408
Nu 1:16 These **were** the *m* **appointed** *from* the AIT
Nu 1:17 Aaron took these **m** whose names had H408
Nu 1:18 the **m** twenty years old or more were NDT
Nu 1:20 All the **m** twenty years old or more who H2351
Nu 1:22 All the **m** twenty years old or more who H2351
Nu 1:24 All the **m** twenty years old or more who NDT
Nu 1:26 All the **m** twenty years old or more who NDT
Nu 1:28 All the **m** twenty years old or more who NDT
Nu 1:30 All the **m** twenty years old or more who NDT
Nu 1:32 All the **m** twenty years old or more who NDT
Nu 1:34 All the **m** twenty years old or more who NDT
Nu 1:36 All the **m** twenty years old or more who NDT
Nu 1:38 All the **m** twenty years old or more who NDT
Nu 1:40 All the **m** twenty years old or more who NDT
Nu 1:42 All the **m** twenty years old or more who NDT

Nu 1:44 These were the *m* **counted** by Moses and AIT
Nu 2: 9 All the *m* **assigned** to the camp of Judah AIT
Nu 2:16 All the *m* **assigned** to the camp of Reuben AIT
Nu 2:24 All the *m* **assigned** to the camp of Ephraim AIT
Nu 2:31 All the *m* **assigned** to the camp of Dan AIT
Nu 2:32 **All** *the m in* the camps, by their divisions AIT
Nu 4: 3 Count all the **m** from thirty to fifty years of NDT
Nu 4:23 Count all the **m** from thirty to fifty years of NDT
Nu 4:30 Count all the **m** from thirty to fifty years of NDT
Nu 4:35 All the **m** from thirty to fifty years of age NDT
Nu 4:39 All the **m** from thirty to fifty years of age NDT
Nu 4:43 All the **m** from thirty to fifty years of age NDT
Nu 4:47 All the **m** from thirty to fifty years of age NDT
Nu 8:24 **M** twenty-five years old or more shall come NDT
Nu 11:21 among six hundred thousand **m** on foot, H6639
Nu 11:26 However, two **m**, whose names were Eldad H408
Nu 13: 2 "Send *some* **m** to explore the land of H408
Nu 13:16 are the names of the **m** Moses sent to H408
Nu 13:31 But the **m** who had gone up with him said H408
Nu 14:36 So the **m** Moses had sent to explore the H408
Nu 14:37 these **m** who were responsible for H408
Nu 14:38 Of the **m** who went to explore the land, only H408
Nu 16: 2 With them were 250 Israelite **m** H408
Nu 16:14 Do you want to treat these **m** like slaves H408
Nu 16:26 back from the tents of these wicked **m**! H408
Nu 16:29 If **these** *m* die a natural death and suffer the AIT
Nu 16:30 will know that these **m** have treated the H408
Nu 16:35 consumed the 250 **m** who were offering H408
Nu 16:38 the censers of the **m** who sinned at the H465S
Nu 22: 9 asked, "Who are these **m** with you? H408
Nu 22:20 "Since these **m** have come to summon you H408
Nu 22:35 "Go with the **m**, but speak only what H408
Nu 25: 1 the **m** began to indulge in sexual H6639
Nu 26: 4 a census of the *m* twenty years **old** or more, AIT
Nu 26:10 died when the fire devoured the 250 **m**. H408
Nu 26:51 number of the **m** *of* Israel was 601,730 H1201
Nu 31: 3 "Arm some of your **m** to go to war against H408
Nu 31: 4 into battle a **thousand** *m* from each of the AIT
Nu 31: 5 So twelve thousand *m* **armed** *for* battle, AIT
Nu 31:42 set apart from that of the fighting **m**— H408
Nu 34:17 are the names of the **m** who are to assign H408
Nu 34:29 These are **the m** the LORD commanded to H889S
Nu 36: 3 suppose they marry **m** from other Israelite H1201
Dt 1:13 respected **m** from each of your tribes, H408
Dt 1:15 So I took the **leading** *m of* your tribes, wise AIT
Dt 1:15 wise and respected **m**, and appointed H408
Dt 1:22 "Let us send **m** ahead to spy out the land H408
Dt 2:14 of fighting **m** had perished from the H408
Dt 2:16 of these fighting **m** among the people had H408
Dt 2:34 destroyed them—**m**, women and children. H5493
Dt 3: 6 every city—**m**, women and children. H5493
Dt 3:18 But all your able-bodied **m**, armed for H1201
Dt 7:14 none of your *m* or *women* will be **childless** AIT
Dt 15:12 of your people—**Hebrew** *m* or women—sell AIT
Dt 16:16 a year all your **m** must appear before H2344
Dt 20:13 your hand, put to the sword all the **m** *in* it. H2344
Dt 21:21 Then all the **m** *of* his town are to stone him H408
Dt 22:21 house and there the **m** *of* her town shall H408
Dt 23:10 If one of your **m** is unclean because of a H408
Dt 25:11 If **two m** are fighting and H408+2256+278+3481
Dt 29:10 your leaders and **chief m**, your elders and H8657
Dt 29:10 officials, and all the other **m** *of* Israel, H408
Dt 31:12 Assemble the people—**m**, women and H408
Dt 32:25 The **young m** and young women will H1033
Jos 1:14 all your **fighting m**, ready for H2657+1475
Jos 2: 3 "Bring out the **m** who came to you and H408
Jos 2: 4 had taken the two **m** and hidden them. H408
Jos 2: 4 the **m** came to me, but I did not know H408
Jos 2: 7 So the **m** set out in pursuit of the spies on H408
Jos 2:14 the **m** assured her. "If you H408
Jos 2:17 Now the **m** had said to her, "This oath you H408
Jos 2:23 Then the two **m** started back. They went H408
Jos 3:12 choose twelve **m** from the tribes of Israel H408
Jos 4: 2 "Choose twelve **m** from among the people H408
Jos 4: 4 together the twelve **m** he had appointed H408
Jos 4:12 The **m** *of* Reuben, Gad and the half-tribe H1201
Jos 5: 4 of Egypt—all the **m** of military age—died H2351
Jos 5: 6 all the **m** who were *of* military age H408
Jos 6: 2 with its king and its **fighting m**. H2657+1475
Jos 6: 3 around the city once with all the armed **m**. H408
Jos 6:13 The **armed** *m* went ahead of them and the AIT
Jos 6:20 trumpet, when the **m** gave a loud shout H6639
Jos 6:21 living thing in it—**m** and women, young H408
Jos 6:22 said to the two **m** who had spied out the H408
Jos 6:23 So the **young m** who had done the spying H5853
Jos 6:25 she hid the **m** Joshua had sent as H4855S
Jos 7: 2 Now Joshua sent **m** from Jericho to Ai H408
Jos 7: 2 So the **m** went up and spied out Ai H408
Jos 7: 3 three thousand **m** to take it and do not H408
Jos 7: 4 but they were routed by the **m** *of* Ai, H408
Jos 8: 3 of his **best fighting m** and sent H2657+1475
Jos 8: 5 and when the **m** come out against us NDT
Jos 8:12 about five thousand **m** and set them in H408
Jos 8:14 he and all the **m** *of* the city hurried out H408
Jos 8:16 All the **m** of Ai were called to pursue them H6639
Jos 8:19 the *m* **in** *the* **ambush** rose quickly from their AIT
Jos 8:20 The **m** *of* Ai looked back and saw the H408
Jos 8:21 turned around and attacked the **m** *of* Ai. H408
Jos 8:24 killing all the **m** *of* Ai in the fields and in H3782
Jos 8:25 Twelve thousand **m** and women fell that H408
Jos 10: 2 than Ai, and all its **m** were good fighters. H408
Jos 10: 7 including all the **best fighting m**. H1475+2657
Jos 10:18 and post *some* **m** there to guard it. H408
Jos 10:24 summoned all the **m** *of* Israel and said to H408
Jos 18: 4 Appoint three **m** from each tribe. I will send H408
Jos 18: 8 As the **m** started on their way to map out H408
Jos 18: 9 So the **m** left and went through the land H408
Jos 22:14 With him they sent ten of the **chief** *m*, one AIT
Jdg 1: 3 The **m** of Judah then said to the Simeonites NDT
Jdg 1: 4 they struck down ten thousand **m** at Bezek. H408
Jdg 1: 8 The **m** *of* Judah attacked Jerusalem also H1201
Jdg 1:17 Then the **m** of Judah went with the NDT
Jdg 1:19 The LORD was with the **m** of Judah. NDT
Jdg 1:23 When they **sent** *m* **to spy out** Bethel AIT
Jdg 4: 6 with you ten thousand **m** of Naphtali and H408
Jdg 4:10 ten thousand **m** went up under his H408
Jdg 4:13 River all his **m** and his nine hundred H6639
Jdg 4:14 with ten thousand **m** following him. H408
Jdg 7: 1 all his **m** camped at the spring of H6639
Jdg 7: 2 said to Gideon, "You have too many **m**. H6639
Jdg 7: 3 So twenty-two thousand **m** left, while ten H6639
Jdg 7: 4 to Gideon, "There are still too many **m**. H6639
Jdg 7: 5 So Gideon took the **m** down to the water H6639
Jdg 7: 7 the three hundred **m** that lapped I will save H408
Jdg 7:16 the three hundred **m** into three companies, H408
Jdg 7:19 the hundred **m** with him reached the H408
Jdg 7:22 LORD caused the **m** throughout the camp H408
Jdg 7:24 So all the **m** *of* Ephraim were called out H408
Jdg 8: 4 Gideon and his three hundred **m** H408
Jdg 8: 5 He said to the **m** *of* Sukkoth, "Give my H408
Jdg 8: 8 they answered as the **m** *of* Sukkoth had. H408
Jdg 8: 9 So he said to the **m** *of* Peniel, "When I H408
Jdg 8:10 with a force of about fifteen thousand **m**, NDT
Jdg 8:15 Gideon came and said to the **m** *of* Sukkoth, H408
Jdg 8:15 should we give bread to your exhausted **m**? H408
Jdg 8:16 town and taught the **m** *of* Sukkoth a lesson H408
Jdg 8:17 of Peniel and killed the **m** *of* the town. H408
Jdg 8:18 "What kind of **m** did you kill at Tabor?" H408
Jdg 8:18 "**M** like you," they answered, "each one H2157S
Jdg 9:25 citizens of Shechem set **m** on the hilltops to NDT
Jdg 9:32 night you and your **m** should come and H6639
Jdg 9:33 When Gaal and his **m** come out against H6639
Jdg 9:36 the shadows of the mountains for **m**." H408
Jdg 9:38 Aren't these the **m** you ridiculed? Go out H6639
Jdg 9:43 So he took his **m**, divided them into three H6639
Jdg 9:48 he and all his **m** went up Mount Zalmon H6639
Jdg 9:48 He ordered the **m** with him, "Quick! Do H6639
Jdg 9:49 So all the **m** cut branches and followed H6639
Jdg 9:49 about a thousand **m** and women, also died H408
Jdg 9:51 to which all the **m** and women—all the H408
Jdg 12: 4 called together the **m** *of* Gilead and fought H408
Jdg 12: 5 the **m** *of* Gilead asked him, "Are you an H408
Jdg 14:10 as was customary for **young m**. H1033
Jdg 14:11 they chose **thirty** *m* to be his companions. AIT
Jdg 14:18 the seventh day the **m** *of* the town said to H408
Jdg 14:19 struck down thirty of their **m**, stripped them H408
Jdg 15:11 Then three thousand **m** from Judah went H408
Jdg 15:15 grabbed it and struck down a thousand **m**. H408
Jdg 15:16 jawbone I have killed a thousand **m**." H408
Jdg 16: 9 With **m** hidden in the room, she called to H2021S
Jdg 16:12 with **m** hidden in the room, she H2021S
Jdg 16:27 temple was crowded with **m** and women; H408
Jdg 16:27 three thousand **m** and women watching H408
Jdg 18: 2 five of their leading **m** from Zorah and H408
Jdg 18: 2 These **m** represented all the Danites H408
Jdg 18: 7 So the five **m** left and came to Laish, where H408
Jdg 18:11 Then six hundred **m** of the Danites, armed H408
Jdg 18:14 Then the five **m** who had spied out the H408
Jdg 18:17 The five **m** who had spied out the land H408
Jdg 18:17 six hundred armed **m** stood at the entrance H408
Jdg 18:18 When **the five m** went into Micah's house H465S
Jdg 18:22 the **m** who lived near Micah were called H408
Jdg 18:23 you that you called out your **m** to fight?" NDT
Jdg 18:25 or *some of* the **m** may get angry and attack H408
Jdg 19:22 some of the wicked **m** *of* the city H408
Jdg 19:25 But the **m** would not listen to him. So the H408
Jdg 20: 2 hundred thousand **m** armed with H408+8081
Jdg 20: 5 the night the **m** *of* Gibeah came after H1251
Jdg 20: 8 All the **m** rose up together as one, saying H6639
Jdg 20:10 We'll take ten **m** out of every hundred from H408
Jdg 20:13 turn those wicked **m** of Gibeah over to us H408
Jdg 20:15 hundred able young **m** from those living in H408
Jdg 20:31 so that about thirty **m** fell in the open field H408
Jdg 20:33 All the **m** *of* Israel moved from their places H408
Jdg 20:34 Israel's able young **m** made a frontal attack H408
Jdg 20:36 Now the **m** *of* Israel had given way before H408
Jdg 20:45 cut down five thousand **m** along the roads. H408
Jdg 20:48 The **m** *of* Israel went back to Benjamin and H408
Jdg 21: 1 The **m** *of* Israel had taken an oath at H408
Jdg 21:10 thousand fighting **m** with instructions to go H408
Jdg 21:16 we provide wives for the *m who are* **left**? AIT
Ru 2: 9 Watch the field where *the m are* **harvesting** AIT
Ru 2: 9 I have told the **m** not to lay a hand on you H5853
Ru 2: 9 from the water jars the **m** have filled." H5853
Ru 2:15 Boaz gave orders to his **m**, "Let her gather H5853
Ru 3:10 You have not run after the **younger m** H1033
1Sa 2:17 This sin of the **young m** was very great in H5853
1Sa 4: 4 So the people sent **m** to Shiloh, and they NDT
1Sa 4: 9 Be **m**, or you will be subject to the Hebrews H408
1Sa 4: 9 they have been to you. Be **m**, and fight!" H408
1Sa 7: 1 So the **m** *of* Kiriath Jearim came and took H408
1Sa 7:11 The **m** *of* Israel rushed out of Mizpah and H408
1Sa 10: 2 you will meet two **m** near Rachel's tomb, at H408
1Sa 10: 3 Three **m** going up to worship God at Bethel H408
1Sa 10:26 accompanied by **valiant** *m* whose hearts God AIT
1Sa 11: 1 And all the **m** *of* Jabesh said to him H408
1Sa 11: 5 to him what the **m** *of* Jabesh had said. H408
1Sa 11: 8 the **m** *of* Israel numbered three hundred H1201
1Sa 11: 9 "Say to the **m** *of* Jabesh Gilead, 'By H408
1Sa 11: 9 went and reported this to the **m** *of* Jabesh, H408
1Sa 11:11 Saul separated his **m** into three divisions; H6639
1Sa 11:12 Turn these **m** over to us so that we may H408
1Sa 13: 2 Saul chose three **thousand** *m* from Israel; AIT
1Sa 13: 2 The rest of the **m** he sent back to their H6639
1Sa 13: 8 to Gilgal, and Saul's **m** began to scatter. H6639
1Sa 13:11 "When I saw that the **m** were scattering H6639
1Sa 13:15 Saul counted the **m** who were with him. H6639
1Sa 13:16 son Jonathan and the **m** with them were H6639
1Sa 14: 2 With him were about six hundred **m**, H408
1Sa 14: 6 to the outpost of those **uncircumcised** *m*. AIT
1Sa 14:12 The **m** *of* the outpost shouted to Jonathan H408
1Sa 14:14 killed some twenty **m** in an area of about H408
1Sa 14:17 Saul said to the **m** who were with him, H6639
1Sa 14:20 Saul and all his **m** assembled and went H6639
1Sa 14:28 That is why the **m** are faint." H6639
1Sa 14:30 have been if the **m** had eaten today some H6639
1Sa 14:33 the **m** are sinning against the LORD by H6639
1Sa 14:34 "Go out among the **m** and tell them H6639
1Sa 14:41 but if the **m** *of* Israel are at fault H6639
1Sa 14:41 taken by lot, and the **m** were cleared. H6639
1Sa 14:45 But the **m** said to Saul, "Should Jonathan H6639
1Sa 14:45 So the **m** rescued Jonathan, and he was H6639
1Sa 15: 3 put to death **m** and women, children H408
1Sa 15: 4 summoned the **m** and mustered them H6639
1Sa 15:24 I was afraid of the **m** and so I gave in to H6639
1Sa 17:19 Saul and all the **m** *of* Israel in the Valley H408
1Sa 17:26 David asked the **m** standing near him H408
1Sa 17:28 heard him speaking with the **m**, he burned H408
1Sa 17:30 the **m** answered him as before. H6639
1Sa 17:52 Then the **m** *of* Israel and Judah surged H408
1Sa 18: 6 When **the m** were returning home after H4392S
1Sa 18:13 gave him command over a **thousand** *m*, AIT
1Sa 18:27 David took his **m** with him and went out H408
1Sa 19:11 Saul sent **m** to David's house to watch it H4855
1Sa 19:14 When Saul sent the **m** to capture David H4855
1Sa 19:15 Then Saul sent the **m** back to see David H4855
1Sa 19:16 But when the **m** entered, there was the H4855
1Sa 19:20 so he sent **m** to capture him. But when H4855
1Sa 19:20 the Spirit of God came on Saul's **m**, and H4855
1Sa 19:21 he sent more **m**, and they prophesied H4855
1Sa 19:21 Saul sent **m** a third time, and they also H4855
1Sa 21: 2 As for my **m**, I have told them to meet H5853
1Sa 21: 4 provided the **m** have kept themselves from H5853
1Sa 22: 2 About four hundred **m** were with him. H408
1Sa 22: 6 that David and his **m** had been discovered. H408
1Sa 22: 7 "Listen, **m of Benjamin**! Will the son H1229
1Sa 22:11 son of Ahitub and **all** *the m of* his family, AIT
1Sa 22:18 he killed eighty-five **m** who wore the linen H408
1Sa 22:19 the priests, with its **m** and women, its H408
1Sa 23: 3 But David's **m** said to him, "Here in Judah H408
1Sa 23: 5 So David and his **m** went to Keilah, fought H408
1Sa 23: 8 to Keilah to besiege David and his **m**. H408
1Sa 23:12 of Keilah surrender me and my **m** to Saul?" H408
1Sa 23:13 So David and his **m**, about six hundred in H408
1Sa 23:24 Now David and his **m** were in the Desert of H408
1Sa 23:25 Saul and his **m** began the search, and H408
1Sa 23:26 David and his **m** were on the other H408
1Sa 23:26 in on David and his **m** to capture them, H408
1Sa 24: 2 thousand able young **m** from all Israel H408
1Sa 24: 2 David and his **m** near the Crags of the H408
1Sa 24: 3 David and his **m** were far back in the cave H408
1Sa 24: 4 The **m** said, "This is the day the LORD spoke H408
1Sa 24: 6 He said to his **m**, "The LORD forbid that I H408
1Sa 24: 7 sharply rebuked his **m** and did not allow H408
1Sa 24: 9 "Why do you listen when **m** say, 'David is H132
1Sa 24:22 David and his **m** went up to the H408
1Sa 25: 5 So he sent ten **young m** and said to them H5853
1Sa 25: 8 Therefore be favorable toward my **m** H5853
1Sa 25: 9 When David's **m** arrived, they gave Nabal H5853
1Sa 25:11 give it to **m** coming from who knows H408
1Sa 25:12 David's **m** turned around and went back H5853
1Sa 25:13 David said to his **m**, "Each of you strap on H408
1Sa 25:13 About four hundred **m** went up with David H408
1Sa 25:15 Yet these **m** were very good to us. They did H408
1Sa 25:20 were David and his **m** descending toward H408
1Sa 25:25 servant, I did not see the **m** my lord sent. H5853
1Sa 25:27 be given to the **m** who follow you. H5853
1Sa 26:16 the LORD lives, **you and your m** must die H917
1Sa 26:22 "Let one of your **young m** come over and H5853
1Sa 27: 2 the six hundred **m** with him left and H408
1Sa 27: 3 David and his **m** settled in Gath with Achish H408
1Sa 27: 8 Now David and his **m** went up and raided H408
1Sa 28: 1 that you and your **m** will accompany me in H408
1Sa 28: 8 at night he and two **m** went to the woman. H408
1Sa 28:23 But his **m** joined the woman in urging H6269
1Sa 28:25 Then she set it before Saul and his **m**, and H6269
1Sa 29: 2 David and his **m** were marching at the rear H408
1Sa 29: 4 than by taking the heads of our own **m**? H408
1Sa 29:11 So David and his **m** got up early in the H408
1Sa 30: 1 David and his **m** reached Ziklag on the H408
1Sa 30: 3 When David and his **m** reached Ziklag H408
1Sa 30: 4 So David and his **m** wept aloud until they H6639
1Sa 30: 6 distressed because the **m** were talking of H6639
1Sa 30: 9 the six hundred **m** with him came to H408
1Sa 30:17 four hundred young **m** who rode off on H408
1Sa 30:20 his **m** drove them ahead of the other NDT

1Sa 30:21 to the two hundred **m** who had been too H408
1Sa 30:21 out to meet David and the **m** with him. H6639
1Sa 30:21 As David and his **m** approached, he H6639
1Sa 30:22 But all the evil **m** and troublemakers among H408
1Sa 30:31 places where he and his **m** had roamed. H408
1Sa 31: 6 all his **m** died together that same H408
1Sa 31:12 all their valiant **m** marched through the H408
2Sa 1: 4 "The **m** fled from the battle, H6639
2Sa 1:11 David and all the **m** with him took hold of H408
2Sa 1:15 Then David called one of his **m** and said H5853
2Sa 2: 3 David also took the **m** who were with him H408
2Sa 2: 4 Then the **m** *of* Judah came to Hebron, and H408
2Sa 2: 4 that it was the **m** *from* Jabesh Gilead who H408
2Sa 2:12 together with the **m** *of* Ish-Bosheth son of H6269
2Sa 2:13 Zeruiah and David's **m** went out and met H6269
2Sa 2:14 have *some* of the **young m** get up and H5853
2Sa 2:15 twelve **m** for Benjamin and Ish-Bosheth son NDT
2Sa 2:17 the Israelites were defeated by David's **m**. H6269
2Sa 2:21 on one of the **young m** and strip him of H5853
2Sa 2:25 Then the **m** *of* Benjamin rallied behind H1201
2Sa 2:26 before you order your **m** to stop pursuing H6639
2Sa 2:27 the **m** would have continued pursuing H6639
2Sa 2:29 Abner and his **m** marched through the H408
2Sa 2:30 of David's **m** were found missing. H6269
2Sa 2:31 But David's **m** had killed three hundred H6269
2Sa 2:32 Then Joab and his **m** marched all night H408
2Sa 3:20 who had twenty **m** with him, came to H408
2Sa 3:20 David prepared a feast for him and his **m**. H408
2Sa 3:22 Just then David's **m** and Joab returned H6269
2Sa 3:38 Then the king said to his **m**, "Do you not H6269
2Sa 4: 2 Saul's son had two **m** who were leaders of H408
2Sa 4:11 when wicked **m** have killed an innocent H408
2Sa 4:12 So David gave an order to his **m**, and they H5853
2Sa 5: 6 The king and his **m** marched to Jerusalem H408
2Sa 5:21 David and his **m** carried them off. H408
2Sa 6: 1 together all the **able young m** of Israel— AIT
2Sa 6: 2 He and all his **m** went to Baalah in Judah H6639
2Sa 6:19 crowd of Israelites, both **m** and women. H408
2Sa 7: 9 like the names of the **greatest** *m* on earth. AIT
2Sa 7:14 I will punish him with a rod wielded by **m** H408
2Sa 10: 2 When David's **m** came to the land of the H6269
2Sa 10: 5 he sent messengers to meet the **m**, for they H408
2Sa 10: 6 as the king of Maakah with a thousand **m**, H408
2Sa 10: 6 also twelve thousand **m** *from* Tob. H408
2Sa 10: 7 out with the entire army of **fighting m**. H1475
2Sa 10: 8 Rehob and the **m** *of* Tob and Maakah H408
2Sa 10:10 put the rest of the **m** under the command H6639
2Sa 11: 1 out with the king's **m** and the whole H6269
2Sa 11:11 Joab and my lord's **m** are camped in the H6269
2Sa 11:17 When the **m** *of* the city came out and H408
2Sa 11:17 some of the **m** *in* David's army fell H6269
2Sa 11:23 "The **m** overpowered us and came out H408
2Sa 11:24 the wall, and some of the king's **m** died. H6269
2Sa 12: 1 "There were two **m** in a certain town H408
2Sa 13:28 Absalom ordered his **m**, "Listen! When H5853
2Sa 13:29 So Absalom's **m** did to Amnon what H5853
2Sa 13:34 "I see **m** in the direction of Horonaim H408
2Sa 15: 1 with fifty **m** to run ahead of him. H408
2Sa 15:11 Two hundred **m** from Jerusalem had H408
2Sa 15:18 All his **m** marched past him, along with all H6269
2Sa 15:22 on with all his **m** and the families that H408
2Sa 16: 2 the bread and fruit are for the **m** to eat H5853
2Sa 16:13 So David and his **m** continued along the H408
2Sa 16:15 Absalom and all the **m** *of* Israel came to H6639
2Sa 16:18 by all the **m** *of* Israel—his I will be, H408
2Sa 17: 1 twelve thousand **m** and set out tonight in H408
2Sa 17: 8 You know your father and his **m**; they are H408
2Sa 17:12 he nor any of his **m** will be left alive. H408
2Sa 17:14 Absalom and all the **m** *of* Israel said, "The H408
2Sa 17:20 When Absalom's **m** came to the woman H6269
2Sa 17:20 The **m** searched but found no one, so they NDT
2Sa 17:24 crossed the Jordan with all the **m** *of* Israel. H408
2Sa 18: 1 David mustered the **m** who were with him H6639
2Sa 18: 3 But the **m** said, "You must not go out; if H6639
2Sa 18: 4 gate while all his **m** marched out in units H6639
2Sa 18: 7 Israel's troops were routed by David's **m**, H6269
2Sa 18: 7 that day were great—twenty thousand **m**. NDT
2Sa 18: 8 swallowed up more **m** that day than the H6639
2Sa 18: 9 Absalom happened to meet David's **m**. H6269
2Sa 18:10 When one of the **m** saw what had H408
2Sa 19: 3 The **m** stole into the city that day as men H6639
2Sa 19: 3 the city that day as **m** steal in who are H6639
2Sa 19: 5 "Today you have humiliated all your **m** H6269
2Sa 19: 6 their **m** mean nothing to you. H6269
2Sa 19: 7 Now go out and encourage your **m**. H6269
2Sa 19: 8 When the **m** were told, "The king is H6639
2Sa 19:14 the hearts of the **m** *of* Judah so that they H408
2Sa 19:14 to the king, "Return, you and all your **m**." H6269
2Sa 19:15 Now the **m** of Judah had come to Gilgal to NDT
2Sa 19:16 down with the **m** *of* Judah to meet King H408
2Sa 19:41 Soon all the **m** *of* Israel were coming to the H408
2Sa 19:41 did our brothers, the **m** *of* Judah, steal the H408
2Sa 19:41 across the Jordan, together with all his **m**?" H408
2Sa 19:42 All the **m** *of* Judah answered the men of H408
2Sa 19:42 men of Judah answered the **m** *of* Israel, H408
2Sa 19:43 Then the **m** *of* Israel answered the men of H408
2Sa 19:43 men of Israel answered the **m** *of* Judah, H408
2Sa 19:43 But the **m** *of* Judah pressed their claims H408
2Sa 19:43 even more forcefully than the **m** *of* Israel. H408
2Sa 20: 2 So all the **m** *of* Israel deserted David to H408
2Sa 20: 2 But the **m** *of* Judah stayed by their king all H408
2Sa 20: 4 "Summon the **m** *of* Judah to come to me H408
2Sa 20: 6 Take your master's **m** and pursue him, or H6269
2Sa 20: 7 So Joab's **m** and the Kerethites and H408
2Sa 20:11 One of Joab's **m** stood beside Amasa H5853
2Sa 20:22 trumpet, and his **m** dispersed from the city NDT
2Sa 21:15 went down with his **m** to fight against the H6269
2Sa 21:17 Then David's **m** swore to him, saying H408
2Sa 21:22 they fell at the hands of David and his **m**. H6269
2Sa 23: 6 But **evil m** are all to be cast aside like H1175
2Sa 23: 8 raised his spear against eight hundred **m**, NDT
2Sa 23:17 it not the blood of **m** who went at the risk H408
2Sa 23:18 raised his spear against three hundred **m**, NDT
2Sa 24: 2 to Beersheba and enroll the **fighting m**, H6639
2Sa 24: 4 the king to enroll the **fighting m** *of* Israel. H6639
2Sa 24: 9 the number of the **fighting m** to the king: H6639
2Sa 24: 9 able-bodied **m** who could handle a H408
2Sa 24:10 after he had counted the **fighting m**, H6639
1Ki 1: 5 with fifty **m** to run ahead of him. H408
1Ki 1:53 Then King Solomon sent **m**, and they NDT
1Ki 2:32 it he attacked two **m** and killed them with H408
1Ki 2:32 were **better** *m* and more upright than he. AIT
1Ki 5: 6 My **m** will work with yours, and I will pay H6269
1Ki 5: 6 pay you for your **m** whatever wages you H6269
1Ki 5: 9 My **m** will haul them down from Lebanon H6269
1Ki 5:13 laborers from all Israel—thirty thousand **m**. H408
1Ki 9:22 they were his fighting **m**, his government H408
1Ki 9:27 And Hiram sent his **m**—sailors who knew H6269
1Ki 9:27 to serve in the fleet with Solomon's **m**. H6269
1Ki 11:15 had struck down all the **m** in Edom. H2351
1Ki 11:16 they had destroyed all the **m** in Edom. H2351
1Ki 11:24 gathered a band of **m** around him and H408
1Ki 12: 8 consulted the **young m** who had grown up H3529
1Ki 12:10 The **young m** who had grown up with him H3529
1Ki 12:14 the advice of the **young m** and said, H3529
1Ki 12:21 eighty thousand **able young m**— H1033
1Ki 20:10 Samaria to give each of my **m** a handful." H6639
1Ki 20:12 in their tents, and he ordered his **m**: H6269
1Ki 20:17 reported, "**M** are advancing from Samaria." H408
1Ki 20:33 The **m** took this as a good sign and were H408
1Ki 22: 6 about four hundred **m**—and asked them, H408
1Ki 22:49 Jehoshaphat, "Let my **m** sail with yours," H6269
2Ki 1: 9 Elijah a captain with his *company of* **fifty** *m*. AIT
2Ki 1:10 heaven and consume you and your **fifty** *m*!" AIT
2Ki 1:10 consumed the captain and his **m**. H2822S
2Ki 1:11 sent to Elijah another captain with his **fifty** *m*. AIT
2Ki 1:12 heaven and consume you and your **fifty** *m*!" AIT
2Ki 1:12 heaven and consumed him and his **fifty** *m*. AIT
2Ki 1:13 the king sent a third captain with his **fifty** *m*. AIT
2Ki 1:13 my life and the lives of these **fifty** *m*, AIT
2Ki 1:14 the first two captains and *all* their **m**. H2822S
2Ki 2: 7 Fifty **m** from the company of the prophets H408
2Ki 2:16 "we your servants have fifty able **m**. H408
2Ki 2:17 And they sent fifty **m**, who searched for H408
2Ki 3:25 **m armed with slings** surrounded it H7847
2Ki 4:40 The stew was poured out for the **m**, but as H408
2Ki 4:43 "How can I set this before a hundred **m**?" H408
2Ki 5:22 'Two **young m** from the company of the H5853
2Ki 5:24 He sent the **m** away and they left. H408
2Ki 6:13 ordered, "so I can send **m** and capture him." NDT
2Ki 6:20 open the eyes of **these** *m* so they can see." AIT
2Ki 7: 3 Now there were four **m** with leprosy at the H408
2Ki 7: 8 The *m who* **had leprosy** reached the edge of AIT
2Ki 7:13 "*Have some m* **take** five of the horses that AIT
2Ki 8:12 kill their **young m** with the sword H1033
2Ki 10: 6 were with the **leading** *m of* the city, who AIT
2Ki 10: 7 **these m** took the princes and H2157S
2Ki 10:11 as well as all his **chief** *m*, his close friends AIT
2Ki 10:24 Jehu had posted eighty **m** outside with this H408
2Ki 10:24 you lets any of the **m** I am placing in your H408
2Ki 11: 9 Each one took his **m**—those who were H408
2Ki 12:11 the money to the *m* **appointed** to supervise AIT
2Ki 14:19 they sent **m** after him to Lachish and NDT
2Ki 15:25 Taking fifty **m** of Gilead with him, he H408
2Ki 20:14 "What did those **m** say, and where did H408
2Ki 22: 5 entrust it to the *m* **appointed** to supervise the AIT
2Ki 22: 5 And *have these m* **pay** the workers who AIT
2Ki 24:14 all the officers and **fighting m**, and H1475+2657
2Ki 24:16 entire force of seven thousand fighting **m**, H408
2Ki 25:19 took the officer in charge of the fighting **m**, H408
2Ki 25:23 officers and their **m** heard that the king of H408
2Ki 25:23 the son of the Maakathite, and their **m**. H408
2Ki 25:24 took an oath to reassure them and their **m**. H408
2Ki 25:25 came with ten **m** and assassinated H408
2Ki 25:25 also the **m of Judah** and the H3374
1Ch 4:12 These were the **m** *of* Rekah. H408
1Ch 4:22 the **m** *of* Kozeba, and Joash and H408
1Ch 4:38 The **m** listed above by name were leaders H465S
1Ch 4:41 **The m** whose names were listed came in H465S
1Ch 5:18 Manasseh had 44,760 **m** ready for military NDT
1Ch 5:18 able-bodied **m** who could handle shield H408
1Ch 5:24 warriors, famous **m**, and heads of their H408
1Ch 6:31 These are **the m** David put in charge of H889S
1Ch 6:33 Here are the *m who* **served**, together with AIT
1Ch 7: 2 of Tola listed as **fighting m** in their H1475+2657
1Ch 7: 4 36,000 **m ready for battle**, H1522+7372+4878
1Ch 7: 5 who were **fighting m** belonging to H1475+2657
1Ch 7: 7 record listed 22,034 **fighting m**. H1475+2657
1Ch 7: 9 of families and 20,200 **fighting m**. H1475+2657
1Ch 7:11 were 17,200 **fighting m** ready to go H1475+2657
1Ch 7:21 were killed by the native-born **m** *of* Gath, H408
1Ch 7:40 heads of families, **choice** *m*, brave warriors AIT
1Ch 7:40 The number of **m** ready for battle, as listed H408
1Ch 9: 9 All these **m** were heads of their families H408
1Ch 9:13 They were **able m**, responsible for H1475+2657
1Ch 10:12 all their valiant **m** went and took the bodies H408
1Ch 11:11 three hundred *m*, whom he **killed** in one AIT
1Ch 11:19 the blood of these **m** who went at the risk H408
1Ch 11:20 against three hundred *m*, *whom* **he killed**, AIT
1Ch 12: 1 These were the *m who* **came** to David at AIT
1Ch 12:16 and *some m* from Judah also **came** to David AIT
1Ch 12:19 *He and his m did* not **help** the Philistines AIT
1Ch 12:20 were *the m* of Manasseh *who* **defected** to AIT
1Ch 12:22 Day after day *m* **came** to help David, until he AIT
1Ch 12:23 the numbers of the **m** armed for battle H8031
1Ch 12:27 leader of the family of Aaron, with 3,700 **m**, NDT
1Ch 12:32 **m** who understood the times and knew H1201
1Ch 12:34 together with 37,000 **m** carrying shields NDT
1Ch 12:38 these were fighting **m** who volunteered to H408
1Ch 12:39 *The m* **spent** three days there with David AIT
1Ch 14:11 So David and *his m* **went up** to Baal Perazim AIT
1Ch 17: 8 like the names of the **greatest** *m* on earth. AIT
1Ch 17:17 as though I were the most exalted of **m**. H132
1Ch 19: 5 came and told David about the **m**, H408
1Ch 19: 8 out with the entire army of **fighting m**. H1475
1Ch 19:11 put the rest of the **m** under the command H6639
1Ch 20: 8 they fell at the hands of David and his **m**. H6269
1Ch 21: 5 the number of the **fighting m** to David: H6639
1Ch 21: 5 hundred thousand **m** who could handle a H408
1Ch 21:14 seventy thousand **m** of Israel fell dead. H408
1Ch 21:17 ordered the **fighting m** to be counted? H6639
1Ch 23: 3 the total number of **m** was thirty-eight H1505
1Ch 25: 1 Here is the list of the **m** who performed this H408
1Ch 25: 6 All **these** *m* were under the supervision of AIT
1Ch 26: 6 because they were **very capable m**. H1475+2657
1Ch 26: 7 and Semakiah were also **able m**. H1201+2657
1Ch 26: 8 were capable **m** with the strength to H408
1Ch 26: 9 who were **able m**—18 in all. H1201+2657
1Ch 26:30 seventeen hundred **able m**—were H1201+2657
1Ch 26:31 and **capable m** among the H1475+2657
1Ch 26:32 who were **able m** and heads of H1201+2657
1Ch 27: 1 Each division consisted of 24,000 **m**. NDT
1Ch 27: 2 There were 24,000 **m** in his division. NDT
1Ch 27: 4 There were 24,000 **m** in his division. NDT
1Ch 27: 5 there were 24,000 **m** in his division. NDT
1Ch 27: 7 There were 24,000 **m** in his division. NDT
1Ch 27: 8 There were 24,000 **m** in his division. NDT
1Ch 27: 9 There were 24,000 **m** in his division. NDT
1Ch 27:10 There were 24,000 **m** in his division. NDT
1Ch 27:11 There were 24,000 **m** in his division. NDT
1Ch 27:12 There were 24,000 **m** in his division. NDT
1Ch 27:13 There were 24,000 **m** in his division. NDT
1Ch 27:14 There were 24,000 **m** in his division. NDT
1Ch 27:15 There were 24,000 **m** in his division. NDT
1Ch 27:23 the number of the **m** twenty years old or NDT
1Ch 27:24 began to count the **m** but did not finish. NDT
1Ch 28: 1 the warriors and all the brave **fighting m**. H1475
2Ch 2: 2 He conscripted 70,000 **m** as carriers and H408
2Ch 8: 9 they were his fighting **m**, commanders of H408
2Ch 8:10 fifty officials supervising the **m**. H6639
2Ch 8:18 sent him ships commanded by his own **m**, H6269
2Ch 8:18 with Solomon's **m**, sailed to Ophir and H6269
2Ch 10: 8 consulted the **young m** who had grown up H3529
2Ch 10:10 The **young m** who had grown up with him H3529
2Ch 10:14 the advice of the **young m** and said, H3529
2Ch 11: 1 eighty thousand **able young m**— H1033
2Ch 13: 3 of four hundred thousand able fighting **m**, H1475
2Ch 13:15 the **m** *of* Judah raised the battle cry. H408
2Ch 13:17 casualties among Israel's able **m**. H408
2Ch 14: 8 of three hundred thousand **m** from Judah, NDT
2Ch 14: 8 All these were **brave fighting m**. H1475+2657
2Ch 14:13 The **m** of Judah carried off a large amount NDT
2Ch 16: 6 Then King Asa brought all the **m** of Judah NDT
2Ch 17:13 **experienced fighting m** H408+4878+1475+2657
2Ch 17:14 with 300,000 **fighting m**; H1475+2657
2Ch 17:17 with 200,000 *m* **armed** *with* bows and AIT
2Ch 17:18 Jehozabad, with 180,000 *m* **armed** *for* battle. AIT
2Ch 17:19 These were the *m who* **served** the king AIT
2Ch 18: 5 four hundred **m**—and asked them, H408
2Ch 20:10 "But now here are **m** *from* Ammon, Moab H1201
2Ch 20:13 All the **m** of Judah, with their wives and NDT
2Ch 20:21 appointed *m to* **sing** to the LORD and to AIT
2Ch 20:22 against the **m** *of* Ammon and Moab and H1201
2Ch 20:23 rose up against the **m** *from* Mount Seir to H3782
2Ch 20:23 finished slaughtering the **m** *from* Seir, H3782
2Ch 20:24 When the **m** of Judah came to the place NDT
2Ch 20:25 Jehoshaphat and his **m** went to carry off H6639
2Ch 20:27 all the **m** *of* Judah and Jerusalem returned H408
2Ch 21:13 own family, **m** who were better than you. H2021S
2Ch 22: 9 and *his m* **captured** him while he was hiding AIT
2Ch 23: 8 Levites and all the **m** of Judah did just as NDT
2Ch 23: 8 Each one took his **m**—those who were H408
2Ch 23:10 He stationed all the **m**, each with his H6639
2Ch 24:13 The *m* **in charge** *of* the work were diligent AIT
2Ch 24:24 army had come with only a few **m**, H408
2Ch 25: 5 three hundred thousand **m** fit for military H1033
2Ch 25: 6 thousand **fighting m** from Israel H1475+2657
2Ch 25:11 where he killed ten thousand **m** *of* Seir. H1201
2Ch 25:12 of Judah also captured ten thousand *m* **alive**, AIT
2Ch 25:27 they sent **m** after him to Lachish and NDT
2Ch 26:12 over the **fighting m** was 2,600. H1475+2657
2Ch 26:13 was an army of 307,500 *m* **trained** *for* war, AIT
2Ch 28: 8 The **m** *of* Israel took captive from their H1201
2Ch 28:10 **make** the **m** and women of Judah and
Jerusalem your **slaves** H3899+6269
2Ch 28:15 The **m** designated by name took the H408

2Ch 31:19 **m** were designated by name to distribute H408
2Ch 32:21 all the **fighting m** and the H1475+2657
2Ch 34:10 it to the *m* **appointed** to supervise the AIT
2Ch 34:10 **These m** paid the workers H6913+2021+4856S
2Ch 36:17 who killed their **young m** with the sword H1033
2Ch 36:17 did not spare **young m** or young women, H1033
Ezr 2: 2 The list of the **m** *of* the people of Israel: H408
Ezr 2:21 the **m** *of* Bethlehem 123 H1201
Ezr 4:21 issue an order to these **m** to stop work, A10131
Ezr 8: 3 with him were registered 150 **m**; H2351
Ezr 8: 4 son of Zerahiah, and with him 200 **m**; H2351
Ezr 8: 5 son of Jahaziel, and with him 300 **m**; H2351
Ezr 8: 6 son of Jonathan, and with him 50 **m**; H2351
Ezr 8: 7 son of Athaliah, and with him 70 **m**; H2351
Ezr 8: 8 son of Michael, and with him 80 **m**; H2351
Ezr 8: 9 son of Jehiel, and with him 218 **m**; H2351
Ezr 8:10 son of Josiphiah, and with him 160 **m**; H2351
Ezr 8:11 son of Bebai, and with him 28 **m**; H2351
Ezr 8:12 son of Hakkatan, and with him 110 **m**; H2351
Ezr 8:13 Shemaiah, and with them 60 **m**; H2351
Ezr 8:14 Uthai and Zakkur, and with them 70 **m**. H2351
Ezr 8:16 Elnathan, *who were m of* **learning**, AIT
Ezr 10: 1 of Israelites—**m**, women and children H408
Ezr 10: 9 all the **m** *of* Judah and Benjamin had H408
Ezr 10:16 the priest selected **m** who were family H408
Ezr 10:17 dealing with all the **m** who had married H408
Ne 1: 2 came from Judah with *some other* **m**, and I H408
Ne 3: 2 The **m** *of* Jericho built the adjoining section, H408
Ne 3: 5 section was repaired by the **m of Tekoa**, H9542
Ne 3: 7 were made by **m** *from* Gibeon and Mizpah H408
Ne 3:27 the **m of Tekoa** repaired another section H9542
Ne 4:16 half of my **m** did the work, while H5853
Ne 4:21 the work with half **the m** holding spears, H4392S
Ne 4:23 my brothers nor my **m** nor the guards with H5853
Ne 5: 1 Now the **m** and their wives raised a great H6639
Ne 5:10 my brothers and my **m** are also lending H5853
Ne 5:16 All my **m** were assembled there for the H5853
Ne 6:10 because *m are* **coming** to kill you—by AIT
Ne 7: 7 Baanah): The list of the **m** *of* Israel: H408
Ne 7:26 the **m** *of* Bethlehem and Netophah 188 H408
Ne 8: 2 was made up of **m** and women and all H408
Ne 8: 3 the Water Gate in the presence of the **m**, H408
Ne 11: 6 in Jerusalem totaled 468 **m** *of* standing. H408
Ne 11: 8 his followers, Gabbai and Sallai—928 **m**. NDT
Ne 11:12 the temple—822 **m**; Adaiah son of NDT
Ne 11:13 heads of families—242 **m**; Amashsai son of NDT
Ne 11:14 who were **m of standing**—128. H1475+2657
Ne 11:19 who kept watch at the gates—172 **m**. NDT
Ne 12:44 At that time **m** were appointed to be in H408
Ne 13:19 some of my own **m** at the gates so that no H5853
Ne 13:23 days I saw **m of Judah** who had married H3374
Ne 13:25 I beat some of the **m** and pulled out their H408
Est 1:13 he spoke with the **wise** *m* who understood AIT
Est 8:11 annihilate the **armed** *m of* any nationality AIT
Est 9: 6 Jews killed and destroyed five hundred **m**. H408
Est 9:12 five hundred **m** and the ten sons of H408
Est 9:15 they put to death in Susa three hundred **m**, H408
Job 15:10 on our side, *m even* **older** than your father. AIT
Job 29: 8 the **young m** saw me and stepped aside H5853
Job 29: 8 aside and the **old m** rose to their feet; H3813
Job 29: 9 the **chief m** refrained from speaking and H8569
Job 30: 1 now they mock me, *m* **younger** than I, whose AIT
Job 30: 9 "And now *those* **young m** mock me in H4392S
Job 31:10 and may **other** *m* sleep with her. AIT
Job 32: 1 So these three **m** stopped answering Job H408
Job 32: 5 saw that the three **m** had nothing more to H408
Job 34: 2 my words, you **wise** *m*; listen to me, you AIT
Job 34: 2 wise men; listen to me, you *m of* **learning**. AIT
Job 34:10 listen to me, you *m of* understanding. H408
Job 34:34 "**M** *of* understanding declare, wise men H408
Job 34:34 declare, wise **m** who hear me say to me, H1505
Ps 45: 2 most excellent of **m** and your lips H1201+132
Ps 57: 4 **m** whose teeth are spears and H1201+132
Ps 59: T When Saul had sent **m** to watch David's NDT
Ps 59: 3 **Fierce** *m* conspire against me for no offense AIT
Ps 74: 5 They behaved like *m* **wielding** axes to cut AIT
Ps 78: 9 The **m** *of* Ephraim, though armed with H1201
Ps 78:31 cutting down the **young m** *of* Israel. H1033
Ps 78:63 Fire consumed their **young m**, and their H1033
Ps 110: 3 your **young** *m* will come to you like dew from AIT
Ps 148:12 **young m** and women, old men and H1033
Ps 148:12 young men and women, **old** *m* and children. AIT
Pr 1:10 if **sinful** *m* entice you, do not give in AIT
Pr 1:18 **These** *m* lie in wait for their own blood; they AIT
Pr 2:12 will save you from the ways of **wicked** *m*, AIT
Pr 2:12 from **m** whose words are perverse H408
Pr 7: 7 I noticed among the **young m**, a youth H1201
Pr 11:16 gains honor, but **ruthless** *m* gain only wealth. AIT
Pr 20:29 The glory of **young m** is their strength H1033
Pr 23:28 multiplies the unfaithful among **m**. H132
Pr 25: 1 compiled by the **m** *of* Hezekiah king of H408
Pr 25: 6 do not claim a place among his **great** *m* AIT
Ecc 12: 3 tremble, and the strong **m** stoop, when the H408
SS 2: 3 forest is my beloved among the **young m**. H1201
Isa 3:25 Your **m** will fall by the sword, your H5493
Isa 9:17 Lord will take no pleasure in the **young m**, H1033
Isa 13:18 Their bows will strike down the **young m** H5853
Isa 15: 4 Therefore the **armed** *m of* Moab cry out, and AIT
Isa 19:11 "I am one of the **wise** *m*, a disciple of the AIT
Isa 19:12 Where are your **wise** *m* now? Let them show AIT
Isa 31: 8 sword and their **young m** will be put to H1033
Isa 33: 7 their **brave m** cry aloud in the streets H737
Isa 39: 3 "What did those **m** say, and where did H408
Isa 40:30 and **young m** stumble and fall; H1033
Jer 2:16 the **m** *of* Memphis and Tahpanhes have H1201
Jer 4:17 They surround her like *m* **guarding** a field AIT
Jer 5:26 in wait like **m who snare birds** and like H3687
Jer 6:11 street and on the **young m** gathered H1033
Jer 6:23 they come like **m** in battle formation to H408
Jer 8:10 give their wives to **other** *m* and their fields to AIT
Jer 9:21 streets and the **young m** from the public H1033
Jer 11:22 Their **young m** will die by the sword, their H1033
Jer 12: 5 you have raced with **m** on foot and they NDT
Jer 15: 8 against the mothers of their **young m**; H1033
Jer 16: 3 mothers and the **m** who are their fathers H3528S
Jer 17:25 accompanied by the **m** *of* Judah and those H408
Jer 18:21 widows; let their **m** be put to death H408
Jer 18:21 their **young m** slain by the sword in battle. H1033
Jer 26:22 Akbor to Egypt, along with *some* other **m**. H408
Jer 31:13 be glad, **young m** and old as well. H1033
Jer 37:10 you and only wounded **m** were left in their H408
Jer 38: 9 these **m** have acted wickedly in all they H408
Jer 38:10 "Take thirty **m** from here with you and lift H408
Jer 38:11 Ebed-Melek took the **m** with him and went H408
Jer 40: 7 officers and their **m** who were still in the H408
Jer 40: 7 land and had put him in charge of the **m**, H408
Jer 40: 8 the son of the Maakathite, and their **m**. H408
Jer 40: 9 took an oath to reassure them and their **m**. H408
Jer 41: 1 came with ten **m** to Gedaliah son of H408
Jer 41: 2 the ten **m** who were with him got H408
Jer 41: 3 killed all the **m of Judah** who were with H3374
Jer 41: 5 eighty **m** who had shaved off their beards H408
Jer 41: 7 Nethaniah and the **m** who were with him H408
Jer 41: 9 all the bodies of the **m** he had killed along H408
Jer 41:12 they took all their **m** and went to fight H408
Jer 41:15 eight of his **m** escaped from Johanan H408
Jer 43: 2 all the arrogant **m** said to Jeremiah, H408
Jer 43: 6 son of Shaphan—the **m**, the women, the H1505
Jer 44: 7 cutting off from Judah the **m** and women, H408
Jer 44:15 Then all the **m** who knew that their wives H408
Jer 44:20 the people, both **m** and women, who H1505
Jer 46: 9 **m** of Cush and Put who carry shields NDT
Jer 46: 9 shields, **m of Lydia** who draw the bow. H4276
Jer 46:22 her with axes, like *m who* **cut down** trees. AIT
Jer 48:12 "when I will send *m who* **pour** from pitchers AIT
Jer 48:14 'We are warriors, **m** valiant in battle'? H408
Jer 48:15 her finest **young m** will go down in the H1033
Jer 49:10 His **armed m** are destroyed, also his allies H2446
Jer 49:26 her **young m** will fall in the streets H1033
Jer 50:30 her **young m** will fall in the streets H1033
Jer 50:35 against her officials and **wise** *m*! AIT
Jer 50:42 they come like **m** in battle formation to H408
Jer 51: 3 Do not spare her **young m**; completely H1033
Jer 51:57 I will make her officials and **wise** *m* drunk AIT
Jer 52:25 took the officer in charge of the fighting **m**, H408
La 1:15 an army against me to crush my **young m**. H1033
La 1:18 My **young m** and young women have H1033
La 2:21 my **young m** and young women have H1033
La 5:13 **Young m** toil at the millstones; boys H1033
La 5:14 the **young m** have stopped their music. H1033
Eze 8:16 the altar, were about twenty-five **m**. H408
Eze 9: 2 And I saw six **m** coming from the direction H408
Eze 9: 6 Slaughter the **old** *m*, the young men and AIT
Eze 9: 6 old men, the **young m** and women, the H1033
Eze 9: 6 they began with the **old** *m* who were in front AIT
Eze 11: 1 entrance of the gate were twenty-five **m**, H408
Eze 11: 2 these are the **m** who are plotting evil and H408
Eze 14: 3 these **m** have set up idols in their hearts H408
Eze 14:14 even if these three **m**—Noah, Daniel and H408
Eze 14:16 even if these three **m** were in it, they could H408
Eze 14:18 even if these three **m** were in it, they could H408
Eze 14:21 plague—to kill its **m** and their animals! H132
Eze 17:13 carried away the **leading m** *of* the land, H380
Eze 21:31 I will deliver you into the hands of brutal **m**, H408
Eze 21:31 hands of brutal men, *m* **skilled** *in* destruction. AIT
Eze 23: 6 all of them handsome **young m**, and H1033
Eze 23: 8 when during her youth *m* **slept with** her AIT
Eze 23:12 horsemen, all handsome **young m**. H1033
Eze 23:14 She saw **m** portrayed on a wall, figures of H408
Eze 23:23 the **m** of Pekod and Shoa and Koa NDT
Eze 23:23 handsome **young m**, all of them H1033
Eze 23:23 chariot officers and **m of high rank**, all H7924
Eze 23:40 sent messengers for **m** who came from far H408
Eze 23:42 the desert along with **m** from the rabble, H408
Eze 23:44 As *m* **sleep with** a prostitute, so they slept AIT
Eze 26:10 your gates as *m* **enter** a city whose walls AIT
Eze 26:17 city of renown, **peopled** *by m of* the sea! AIT
Eze 27: 8 **M** *of* Sidon and Arvad were your oarsmen H3782
Eze 27: 8 were your oarsmen; your **skilled** *m*, Tyre, AIT
Eze 27:10 " '**M** of Persia, Lydia and Put served as NDT
Eze 27:11 **M** *of* Arvad and Helek guarded your walls H1201
Eze 27:11 **m of Gammad** were in your towers. H1689
Eze 27:14 " '**M** of Beth Togarmah exchanged chariot NDT
Eze 27:15 " 'The **m** *of* Rhodes traded with you, and H1201
Eze 30:17 The **young m** *of* Heliopolis and Bubastis H1033
Eze 31:17 along with the **armed** *m* who lived in its AIT
Eze 32:12 hordes to fall by the swords of **mighty m** H1475
Eze 33: 2 choose one of their **m** and make him their H408
Eze 39:18 eat the flesh of **mighty m** and drink the H1475
Eze 39:20 **mighty m** and soldiers of every kind H1475
Da 1: 4 **young m** without any physical defect H3529
Da 1:10 worse than the other **young m** your age? H3529
Da 1:13 with that of the **young m** who eat the H3529
Da 1:15 than any of the **young m** who ate the H3529
Da 1:17 To these four **young m** God gave H3529
Da 2:12 the execution of all the **wise** *m of* Babylon. AIT
Da 2:13 was issued to put the **wise** *m* to death, AIT
Da 2:13 and *m were sent to* **look for** Daniel and his AIT
Da 2:14 out to put to death the **wise** *m of* Babylon, AIT
Da 2:18 with the rest of the **wise** *m of* Babylon. AIT
Da 2:24 appointed to execute the **wise** *m of* Babylon, AIT
Da 2:24 "Do not execute the **wise** *m of* Babylon. AIT
Da 2:48 placed him in charge of all its **wise** *m*. AIT
Da 3:13 So these **m** were brought before the king A10131
Da 3:21 So these **m**, wearing their robes, trousers A10131
Da 3:23 these three **m**, firmly tied, fell into A10131
Da 3:24 there three **m** that we tied up and A10131
Da 3:25 I see four **m** walking around in the fire A10131
Da 4: 6 that all the **wise** *m of* Babylon be brought AIT
Da 4:18 none of the **wise** *m in* my kingdom can AIT
Da 5: 7 Then he said to these **wise** *m of* Babylon AIT
Da 5: 8 Then all the king's **wise** *m* came in, but they AIT
Da 5:15 The **wise** *m* and enchanters were brought AIT
Da 6: 5 Finally these **m** said, "We will never find A10131
Da 6:11 Then these **m** went as a group and found A10131
Da 6:15 Then the **m** went as a group to King A10131
Da 6:24 the **m** who had falsely accused Daniel A10131
Hos 4:14 because the *m* **themselves** consort with AIT
Joel 2:28 will prophesy, your **old** *m* will dream dreams AIT
Joel 2:28 dreams, your **young m** will see visions. H1033
Joel 2:29 Even on my **servants**, both **m** and women H6269
Joel 3: 9 Let all the fighting **m** draw near and attack H408
Am 4:10 I killed your **young m** with the sword H1033
Am 6: 1 *you* **notable** *m of* the foremost nation AIT
Am 8:13 women and **strong young m** will faint H1033
Ob 8 "will I not destroy the **wise** *m* of Edom, those AIT
Jnh 1:13 the **m** did their best to row back to land. H408
Jnh 1:16 At this the **m** greatly feared the LORD, and H408
Mic 2: 8 without a care, like *m* **returning** *from* battle. AIT
Na 3:10 all her **great** *m* were put in chains. AIT
Zec 3: 8 who are **m** symbolic of things to come: H408
Zec 7: 2 together with their **m**, to entreat the LORD H408
Zec 8: 4 again *m* and women of **ripe old age** will sit AIT
Zec 9:17 Grain will make the **young m** thrive, and H1033
Mal 3: 3 LORD will have *m who will* **bring** offerings in AIT
Mt 8:27 The **m** were amazed and asked, "What *G476*
Mt 8:28 two **demon-possessed** *m* coming from the AIT
Mt 8:33 had happened to the **demon-possessed** *m*. AIT
Mt 9: 2 *Some m* **brought** to him a paralyzed man AIT
Mt 9:27 on from there, two **blind** *m* followed him AIT
Mt 9:28 gone indoors, the **blind** *m* came to him, and AIT
Mt 12:41 The **m** of Nineveh will stand up at the *G467*
Mt 14:21 those who ate was about five thousand **m**, *G467*
Mt 14:35 And when the **m** of that place recognized *G467*
Mt 15:38 of those who ate was four thousand **m**, *G467*
Mt 17:22 going to be delivered into the hands *of* **m**. *G476*
Mt 20:30 Two **blind** *m* were sitting by the roadside, AIT
Mt 23:19 *You* **blind** *m*! Which is greater: the gift, or the AIT
Mt 24:40 **Two** *m* will be in the field; one will be taken AIT
Mt 26:40 "**Couldn't** *you m* keep watch with me for one AIT
Mt 26:50 Then *the m* **stepped forward**, seized Jesus AIT
Mt 26:62 this testimony that **these** *m* are bringing AIT
Mt 28: 4 that they shook and became like **dead** *m*. AIT
Mk 1:20 boat with the **hired m** and followed him *G3638*
Mk 2: 3 *Some m* **came**, bringing to him a paralyzed AIT
Mk 6:21 commanders and the **leading** *m* of Galilee. AIT
Mk 6:44 The number of the **m** who had eaten was *G467*
Mk 9:31 going to be delivered into the hands *of* **m**. *G476*
Mk 12:40 **These** *m* will be punished most severely." AIT
Mk 14:46 **The** *m* seized Jesus and arrested him. AIT
Mk 14:60 this testimony that **these** *m* are bringing AIT
Lk 5:18 *Some* **m** came carrying a paralyzed man on *G467*
Lk 7:10 Then the *m who had been* **sent** returned to AIT
Lk 7:20 When the **m** came to Jesus, they said *G467*
Lk 9:14 About five thousand **m** were there.) But he *G467*
Lk 9:30 Two **m**, Moses and Elijah, appeared in *G467*
Lk 9:32 his glory and the two **m** standing with him. *G467*
Lk 9:33 **As the m** were leaving Jesus, Peter said to *G899S*
Lk 9:44 going to be delivered into the hands *of* **m**." *G476*
Lk 11:32 The **m** of Nineveh will stand up at the *G467*
Lk 12:45 the other **servants**, both **m** and women, *G4090*
Lk 14:31 is able with ten **thousand** *m* to oppose the AIT
Lk 17:12 a village, ten **m** who had leprosy met him. *G467*
Lk 18:10 "Two **m** went up to the temple to pray, one *G476*
Lk 20:47 **These** *m* will be punished most severely." AIT
Lk 22:63 The **m** who were guarding Jesus began *G467*
Lk 23:32 Two **other** *m*, both criminals, were also led AIT
Lk 24: 4 suddenly two **m** in clothes that gleamed *G467*
Lk 24: 5 the ground, but the **m** said to them, "Why NDT
Jn 6:10 about five thousand **m** were there). *G467*
Jn 18: 8 you are looking for me, then let **these** *m* go." AIT
Ac 1:10 when suddenly two **m** dressed in white *G467*
Ac 1:11 "**M** of Galilee," they said, "why do you *G467*
Ac 1:21 to choose one *of* the **m** who have been *G467*
Ac 1:23 So they nominated **two** *m*: Joseph called AIT
Ac 2:17 prophesy, your **young m** will see visions *G3734*
Ac 2:17 see visions, your **old** *m* will dream dreams. AIT
Ac 2:18 Even on my **servants**, both **m** and women *G1528*
Ac 2:23 with the help *of* **wicked** *m*, put him to death AIT
Ac 4: 4 so the number *of* **m** who believed grew to *G467*
Ac 4:13 unschooled, ordinary **m**, they were *G476*
Ac 4:13 they took note that **these** *m* had been with AIT
Ac 4:16 "What are we going to do *with* these **m**?" *G476*
Ac 5: 6 Then some **young** *m* came forward, wrapped AIT
Ac 5: 9 The feet of **the** *m* who buried your husband AIT
Ac 5:10 Then the **young m** came in and, finding *G3734*

Ac 5:14 more and more **m** and women believed in G467
Ac 5:25 The **m** you put in jail are standing in the G467
Ac 5:34 ordered that the **m** be put outside for a G476
Ac 5:35 "**M** of Israel, consider carefully what you G467
Ac 5:35 carefully what you intend to do to these **m**. G476
Ac 5:36 about four hundred **m** rallied to him. G467
Ac 5:38 Leave these **m** alone! Let them go! G476
Ac 5:39 you will not be able to stop **these m**; you G899S
Ac 6:3 choose seven **m** from among you who are G467
Ac 6:6 They presented **these** *m* to the apostles, who AIT
Ac 6:11 they secretly persuaded *some* **m** to say, G467
Ac 7:26 them by saying, '**M**, you are brothers; G467
Ac 8:2 Godly **m** buried Stephen and mourned G467
Ac 8:3 he dragged off both **m** and women and put G467
Ac 8:12 they were baptized, both **m** and women. G467
Ac 9:2 the Way, whether **m** or women, he might G467
Ac 9:7 The **m** traveling with Saul stood there G467
Ac 9:38 they sent two **m** to him and urged him G467
Ac 10:5 Now send **m** to Joppa to bring back a man G467
Ac 10:17 the **m** sent by Cornelius found out where G467
Ac 10:19 "Simon, three **m** are looking for you. G467
Ac 10:21 Peter went down and said to the **m**, "I'm G467
Ac 10:22 The *m* **replied**, "We have come from AIT
Ac 10:23 Then Peter invited **the m** into the house to G899S
Ac 11:3 the house *of* uncircumcised **m** and ate with G467
Ac 11:11 "Right then three **m** who had been sent to G467
Ac 11:20 however, **m** from Cyprus and Cyrene, went G467
Ac 13:50 high standing and the **leading** *m* of the city. AIT
Ac 15:22 some of their own **m** and send them to G467
Ac 15:22 **m** who were leaders among the believers. G467
Ac 15:25 agreed to choose *some* **m** and send them G467
Ac 15:26 **m** who have risked their lives for the name G476
Ac 15:30 So **the** *m* were sent off and went down to AIT
Ac 16:17 "These **m** are servants of the Most High G476
Ac 16:20 said, "These **m** are Jews, and are G476
Ac 16:35 jailer with the order: "Release those **m**." G476
Ac 17:6 "**These** *m* who have caused trouble all over AIT
Ac 17:12 Greek women and many Greek **m**. G467
Ac 19:7 There were about twelve **m** in all. G467
Ac 19:37 You have brought these **m** here, though G467
Ac 20:5 **These** *m* went on ahead and waited for us at AIT
Ac 20:30 from your own number **m** will arise and G467
Ac 21:23 There are four **m** with us who have made a G467
Ac 21:24 Take **these** *m*, join in their purification rites AIT
Ac 21:26 day Paul took the **m** and purified himself G467
Ac 22:4 arresting both **m** and women and throwing G467
Ac 23:13 More *than* **forty** *m* were involved in this plot. AIT
Ac 24:15 hope in God as **these** *m* themselves have, AIT
Ac 25:23 officers and the prominent **m** of the city. G467
Ac 27:10 "**M**, I can see that our voyage is going to be G467
Ac 27:17 so the **m** hoisted it aboard. Then they NDT
Ac 27:21 "**M**, you should have taken my advice not G467
Ac 27:25 keep up your courage, **m**, for I have faith in G467
Ac 27:31 soldiers, "Unless **these** *m* stay with the ship AIT
Ro 1:27 In the same way the **m** also abandoned G781
Ro 1:27 **M** committed shameful acts with other men G781
Ro 1:27 committed shameful acts with *other* **m**, G781
1Co 6:9 **m who have sex with men** G3434+780
1Co 6:9 **men who have sex with m** G3434+780
1Co 13:1 If I speak in the tongues *of* **m** or of angels G476
1Co 16:3 introduction *to* **the m** you approve G4005+1569S
1Co 16:18 yours also. **Such** *m* deserve recognition. AIT
2Co 8:24 show **these** *m* the proof of your love AIT
2Co 12:17 you through any *of the* **m** I sent to you? G4005S
Gal 1:1 sent not from **m** nor by a man, but by G476
Gal 2:12 For before **certain** *m* came from James, he AIT
1Ti 2:8 Therefore I want the **m** everywhere to pray G467
1Ti 5:1 Treat **younger** *m* as brothers, AIT
2Ti 3:8 They are **m** of depraved minds, who, as far G476
2Ti 3:9 as in the case of **those** *m*, their folly will be AIT
Titus 2:2 Teach the **older** *m* to be temperate, worthy of AIT
Titus 2:6 encourage the **young** *m* to be self-controlled. AIT
Heb 7:28 as high priests **m** in all their weakness; G476
1Jn 2:13 writing to you, **young m**, because you G3734
1Jn 2:14 I write to you, **young m**, because you are G3734

MEN'S (3) [MAN]
Ge 44:1 "Fill the **m** sacks with as much food as they H408
Dt 22:5 A woman must not wear **m** clothing, nor a H1505
1Sa 21:5 The **m** bodies are holy even on missions H5853

MENAHEM (7) [MENAHEM'S]
2Ki 15:14 Then **M** son of Gadi went from Tirzah up H4968
2Ki 15:16 At that time **M**, starting out from Tirzah H4968
2Ki 15:17 **M** son of Gadi became king of Israel H4968
2Ki 15:19 **M** gave him a thousand talents of H4968
2Ki 15:20 **M** exacted this money from Israel. Every H4968
2Ki 15:22 **M** rested with his ancestors. And Pekahiah H4968
2Ki 15:23 Pekahiah son of **M** became king of Israel H4968

MENAHEM'S (1) [MENAHEM]
2Ki 15:21 As for the other events of **M** reign, and all H4968

MEND (2) [MENDED]
Ps 60:2 land and torn it open; **m** its fractures, for it H8324
Ecc 3:7 a time to tear and a time to **m**, a time to H9529

MENDED (1) [MEND]
Jos 9:4 sacks and old wineskins, cracked and **m**. H7674

MENE (3)
Da 5:25 that was written: **M**, MENE, TEKEL, PARSIN A10428
Da 5:25 that was written: MENE, **M**, TEKEL, PARSIN A10428
Da 5:26 **M**: God has numbered A10428

MENNA (1)
Lk 3:31 of Melea, the son *of* **M**, the son of G3527

MENPLEASERS (KJV) CURRY FAVOR, WIN FAVOR

MENSERVANTS (NIV84) (MALE) SERVANTS, SLAVES

MENSTRUAL (1)
Isa 30:22 them away like a **m cloth** and say to them H1865

MENTION (11) [MENTIONED]
Ge 40:14 **m** me to Pharaoh and get me out of this H2349
Job 28:18 Coral and jasper *are* not **worthy of m**; the H2349
Jer 19:5 something I did not command or **m**, nor H1819
Jer 20:9 "*I will* not **m** his word or speak anymore in H2349
Jer 23:36 But *you must* not **m** 'a message from the H2349
Eze 16:56 would not even **m** your sister H9019+928+7023
Am 6:10 *We must* not **m** the name of the LORD." H2349
Jn 5:34 but *I* **m** it that you may be saved. G3306
Eph 5:12 It is shameful even *to* **m** what the G3306
1Th 1:2 and continually **m** you in our G3644+4472
Phm 19 not to **m** that you owe me your very self. G3306

MENTIONED (4) [MENTION]
Ru 4:1 *he had* **m** came along. H1819
1Sa 4:18 When he **m** the ark of God, Eli fell H2349
Isa 14:20 *Let* the offspring of the wicked never **be m** H7924
Isa 19:17 to whom Judah *is* **m** will be terrified, H2349

MEON See BAAL MEON, BETH BAAL MEON, BETH MEON

MEONOTHAI (2)
1Ch 4:13 The sons of Othniel: Hathath and **M**. H5065
1Ch 4:14 **M** was the father of Ophrah. Seraiah was H5065

MEPHAATH (4)
Jos 13:18 Kedemoth, **M**, H4789
Jos 21:37 Kedemoth and **M**, together with their H4789
1Ch 6:79 Kedemoth and **M**, together with their H4789
Jer 48:21 the plateau—to Holon, Jahzah and **M**, H4789

MEPHIBOSHETH (16)
2Sa 4:4 became disabled. His name was **M**.) H5136
2Sa 9:6 When **M** son of Jonathan, the son of Saul, H5136
2Sa 9:6 David said, "**M**!" "At your service, H5136
2Sa 9:8 **M** bowed down and said, "What is your NDT
2Sa 9:10 And **M**, grandson of your master, will H5136
2Sa 9:11 So **M** ate at David's table like one of the H5136
2Sa 9:12 **M** had a young son named Mika, and all H5136
2Sa 9:12 of Ziba's household were servants of **M**. H5136
2Sa 9:13 And **M** lived in Jerusalem, because he H5136
2Sa 16:1 the steward of **M**, waiting to meet H5136
2Sa 16:4 "All that belonged to **M** is now yours." H5136
2Sa 19:24 **M**, Saul's grandson, also went down to H5136
2Sa 19:25 "Why didn't you go with me, **M**? H5136
2Sa 19:30 **M** said to the king, "Let him take H5136
2Sa 21:7 The king spared **M** son of Jonathan, the H5136
2Sa 21:8 But the king took Armoni and **M**, the two H5136

MERAB (4)
1Sa 14:49 The name of his older daughter was **M** H5266
1Sa 18:17 to David, "Here is my older daughter **M**. H5266
1Sa 18:19 So when the time came for **M**, Saul's H5266
2Sa 21:8 with the five sons of Saul's daughter **M**, H5266

MERAIAH (1)
Ne 12:12 of Seraiah's family, **M**; of Jeremiah's H5316

MERAIOTH (6)
1Ch 6:6 of Zerahiah, Zerahiah the father of **M**, H5318
1Ch 6:7 **M** the father of Amariah, Amariah the H5318
1Ch 6:52 **M** his son, Amariah his son, Ahitub his H5318
1Ch 9:11 of Zadok, the son of **M**, the son of Ahitub, H5318
Ezr 7:3 the son of Azariah, the son of **M**, H5318
Ne 11:11 of Zadok, the son of **M**, the son of Ahitub, H5318

MERARI (21) [MERARITE, MERARITES]
Ge 46:11 The sons of Levi: Gershon, Kohath and **M**. H5356
Ex 6:16 Gershon, Kohath and **M**. Levi lived 137 H5356
Ex 6:19 The sons of **M** were Mahli and Mushi H5356
Nu 3:17 the sons of Levi: Gershon, Kohath and **M**. H5356
Nu 3:33 To **M** belonged the clans of the Mahlites H5356
Nu 26:57 through **M**, the Merarite clan. H5356
Jos 21:7 The descendants of **M**, according to their H5356
1Ch 6:1 The sons of Levi: Gershon, Kohath and **M**. H5356
1Ch 6:16 The sons of Levi: Gershon, Kohath and **M**. H5356
1Ch 6:19 The sons of **M**: Mahli and Mushi. These H5356
1Ch 6:29 The descendants of **M**: Mahli, Libni his H5356
1Ch 6:47 of Mushi, the son of **M**, the son of Levi. H5356
1Ch 6:63 The descendants of **M**, clan by clan, were H5356
1Ch 15:6 from the descendants of **M**, Asaiah the H5356
1Ch 23:6 the sons of Levi: Gershon, Kohath and **M**. H5356
1Ch 23:21 The sons of **M**: Mahli and Mushi. H5356
1Ch 24:26 The sons of **M**: Mahli and Mushi. The son H5356
1Ch 24:27 The sons of **M**: from Jaaziah: Beno H5356
1Ch 26:19 who were descendants of Korah and **M**. H5356
2Ch 34:12 Levites descended from **M**, and Zechariah H5356
Ezr 8:19 with Jeshaiah from the descendants of **M**, H5356

MERARITE (10) [MERARI]
Nu 3:20 The **M** clans: Mahli and Mushi H1201+5356
Nu 3:33 the Mushites; these were the **M** clans. H5356
Nu 3:35 the families of the **M** clans was Zuriel son H5356
Nu 4:33 service of the **M** clans as they work H1201+5356
Nu 4:45 the total of those in the **M** clans. H1201+5356
Nu 26:57 through Merari, the **M** clan. H5357
Jos 21:34 The **M** clans (the rest of the Levites H1201+5356
Jos 21:40 of towns allotted to the **M** clans, H1201+5356
1Ch 9:14 the son of Hashabiah, a **M**; H1201+5356
1Ch 26:10 Hosah the **M** had sons: Shimri the H1201+5356

MERARITES (9) [MERARI]
Nu 3:36 The **M** were appointed to take care H1201+5356
Nu 4:29 "Count the **M** by their clans and H1201+5356
Nu 4:42 The **M** were counted by their clans H1201+5356
Nu 7:8 four carts and eight oxen to the **M**, H1201+5356
Nu 10:17 and the Gershonites and **M**, who H1201+5356
1Ch 6:44 associates, the **M**, at his left hand: H1201+5356
1Ch 6:77 The **M** (the rest of the Levites H1201+5356
1Ch 15:17 and from their relatives the **M** H1201+5356
2Ch 29:12 from the **M**, Kish son of Abdi H1201+5356

MERATHAIM (1)
Jer 50:21 "Attack the land of **M** and those who live H5361

MERCENARIES (1)
Jer 46:21 The **m** in her ranks are like fattened H8502

MERCHANDISE (11)
Ne 10:31 peoples bring **m** or grain to sell on the H5229
Ne 13:16 all kinds of **m** and selling them in H4836
Isa 45:14 "The products of Egypt and the **m** *of* Cush H6087
Eze 26:12 will plunder your wealth and loot your **m**; H8219
Eze 27:12 iron, tin and lead for your **m**. H6442
Eze 27:14 cavalry horses and mules for your **m**. H6442
Eze 27:16 fine linen, coral and rubies for your **m**. H6442
Eze 27:22 your **m** they exchanged the finest of all H6442
Eze 27:27 Your wealth, **m** and wares, your mariners H6442
Eze 27:33 When your **m** went out on the seas, you H6442
Mk 11:16 anyone to carry **m** through the temple G5007

MERCHANT (5) [MERCHANTS]
Pr 31:14 She is like the **m** ships, bringing her food H6086
SS 3:6 made from all the spices of the **m**? H8217
Eze 27:3 to the sea, **m** *of* peoples on many coasts H8217
Hos 12:7 The **m** uses dishonest scales and loves to H4047
Mt 13:45 of heaven is like a **m** looking for fine G476+1867

MERCHANTS (28) [MERCHANT]
Ge 23:16 to the weight current among the **m**. H6086
Ge 37:28 So when the Midianite **m** came by, his H6086
1Ki 10:15 revenues from **m** and traders and H408+9365
1Ki 10:28 the royal **m** purchased them from Kue at H6086
2Ch 1:16 the royal **m** purchased them from Kue at H6086
2Ch 9:14 brought in by **m** and traders. H408+9365
Ne 3:31 house of the temple servants and the **m**, H8217
Ne 3:32 Gate the goldsmiths and **m** made repairs. H8217
Ne 13:20 Once or twice the **m** and sellers of all H8217
Job 6:19 the **traveling m** *of* Sheba look in hope. H2142
Job 41:6 Will they divide it up among the **m**? H4051
Ps 107:23 *they were* **m** on the mighty waters. H6913+4856
Pr 31:24 and supplies the **m** with sashes. H4051
Isa 23:2 people of the island and you **m** *of* Sidon, H6086
Isa 23:8 of crowns, whose **m** are princes, whose H6086
Eze 16:29 Babylonia, a land of **m**, but even with this H4047
Eze 17:4 shoot and carried it away to a land of **m**, H4047
Eze 27:22 " 'The **m** *of* Sheba and Raamah traded H8217
Eze 27:23 Kanneh and Eden and **m** *of* Sheba, Ashur H8217
Eze 27:27 your **m** and all your soldiers H6842+5114
Eze 27:36 The **m** among the nations scoff at you H6086
Eze 38:13 Dedan and the **m** *of* Tarshish and all H6086
Na 3:16 the number of your **m** till they are more H8217
Zep 1:11 all your **m** will be wiped out H6639+4047
Rev 18:3 the **m** of the earth grew rich from her G1867
Rev 18:11 "The **m** of the earth will weep and mourn G1867
Rev 18:15 The **m who sold** these things and gained G1867
Rev 18:23 Your **m** were the world's important people G1867

MERCIFUL (19) [MERCY]
Ge 19:16 out of the city, for the LORD was **m** to them. H2799
Dt 4:31 For the LORD your God is a **m** God; he will H8157
1Ki 20:31 have heard that the kings of Israel are **m**. H2876
Ne 9:31 for you are a gracious and **m** God. H8157
Ps 26:11 deliver me and *be* **m** *to* me. H2858
Ps 27:7 LORD; *be* **m** *to* me and answer me. H2858
Ps 30:10 LORD, and *be* **m** *to* me; LORD, be my H2858
Ps 31:9 *Be* **m** *to* me, LORD, for I am in distress; my H2858
Ps 56:1 *Be* **m** *to* me, my God, for my enemies are H2858
Ps 77:9 Has God forgotten *to be* **m**? Has he in H2858
Ps 78:38 Yet he was **m**; he forgave their iniquities H8157
Da 9:9 The Lord our God is **m** and forgiving, even H8171
Mt 5:7 Blessed are the **m**, for they will be shown G1798
Lk 1:54 his servant Israel, remembering to be **m** G1799
Lk 6:36 Be **m**, just as your Father is merciful. G3881
Lk 6:36 Be merciful, just as your Father is **m**. G3881
Heb 2:17 he might become a **m** and faithful high G1798
Jas 2:13 be shown to anyone who has not been **m**. G1799
Jude 22 *Be* **m** to those who doubt; G1790

MERCILESSLY (1) [MERCY]
Isa 30:14 shattered *so* **m** that among its H4202+2798

MERCURIUS (KJV) HERMES

M

MERCY (131) [MERCIFUL, MERCILESSLY]
Ge 43:14 Almighty grant you **m** before the man so H8171
Ex 33:19 *I will* **have m** *on* whom I will have mercy H2858
Ex 33:19 I will have mercy on whom *I will* **have m** H2858
Dt 7: 2 treaty with them, and **show** them no **m**. H2858
Dt 13:17 will show you **m**, and will have H8171
Jos 11:20 exterminating them without **m**, as the H9382
2Sa 24:14 of the LORD, for his **m** is great; but do not H8171
1Ki 8:28 your servant's prayer and his **plea for m**, H9382
1Ki 8:50 cause their captors *to* **show** them **m**; H8163
1Ch 21:13 of the LORD, for his **m** is very great; but do H8171
2Ch 6:19 your servant's prayer and his **plea for m**. H9382
Ne 9:31 But in your great **m** you did not put an H8171
Ne 13:22 and **show m** to me according to your great H2571
Est 4: 8 presence to **beg for m** and plead with H2858
Job 9:15 *I could* only **plead** with my Judge **for m**. H2858
Job 27:22 against him without **m** as he flees H2798
Job 41: 3 Will it keep **begging** you **for m**? Will it H9384
Ps 4: 1 **have m** *on* me and hear my prayer. H2858
Ps 6: 2 **Have m** *on* me, LORD, for I am faint; heal H2858
Ps 6: 9 The LORD has heard my **cry for m**; H9382
Ps 9:13 **Have m** and lift me up from the gates of H2858
Ps 25: 6 your **great m** and love, for they are H8171
Ps 28: 2 Hear my **cry for m** as I call to you H7754+9384
Ps 28: 6 for he has heard my **cry for m**. H7754+9384
Ps 30: 8 I called; to the Lord *I* **cried for m**: H2858
Ps 31:22 you heard my **cry for m** when I H7754+9384
Ps 40:11 Do not withhold your **m** from me, LORD H8171
Ps 41: 4 "**Have m** *on* me, LORD; heal me, for H2858
Ps 41:10 But *may* you **have m** *on* me, LORD; raise H2858
Ps 51: 1 **Have m** *on* me, O God, according to your H2858
Ps 57: 1 **Have m** *on* me, my God, have mercy on H2858
Ps 57: 1 my God, **have m** *on* me, for in you I take H2858
Ps 59: 5 the nations; **show** no **m** *to* wicked traitors. H2858
Ps 69:16 of your love; in your great **m** turn to me. H8171
Ps 79: 8 may your **m** come quickly to meet us H8171
Ps 86: 3 **have m** *on* me, Lord, for I call to you all H2858
Ps 86: 6 LORD; listen to my **cry for m**. H7754+9384
Ps 86:16 Turn to me and **have m** *on* me; show your H2858
Ps 106:46 who held them captive to show them **m**. H8171
Ps 116: 1 he heard my voice; he heard my **cry for m**. H9384
Ps 119:132 Turn to me and **have m** *on* me, as you H2858
Ps 123: 2 the LORD our God, till *he* **shows** us *his* **m**. H2858
Ps 123: 3 **Have m** *on* us, LORD, have mercy on us, for H2858
Ps 123: 3 **have m** *on* us, for we have endured H2858
Ps 130: 2 ears be attentive to my **cry for m**. H7754+9384
Ps 140: 6 Hear, LORD, my **cry for m**. H7754+9384
Ps 142: 1 *I* **lift up** my voice to the LORD **for m**. H2858
Ps 143: 1 listen to my **cry for m**; in your H9384
Pr 6:34 and *he will* **show** no **m** when he takes H2798
Pr 18:23 The poor plead for **m**, but the rich answer H9384
Pr 21:10 their neighbors **get** no **m** from them. H2858
Pr 28:13 confesses and renounces them **finds m**. H8163
Isa 13:18 *they will* **have** no **m** *on* infants H8163
Isa 47: 6 your hand, and you showed them no **m**. H8171
Isa 55: 7 and *he will* **have m** on them, and to H8163
Isa 63: 9 In his love and **m** he redeemed them; he H2799
Jer 6:23 spear; they are cruel and **show** no **m**. H8163
Jer 13:14 allow no pity or **m** or compassion to keep H2571
Jer 21: 7 *he will* **show** them no **m** or pity or H2571
Jer 50:42 spears; they are cruel and without **m**. H8163
Da 2:18 them to plead for **m** from the God of A10664
Da 9:18 righteous, but because of your great **m**. H8171
Hos 6: 6 For I desire **m**, not sacrifice, and H2876
Am 5:15 God Almighty *will* **have m** *on* the remnant H2858
Mic 6: 8 justly and to love **m** and to walk humbly H2876
Mic 7:18 stay angry forever but delight to show **m**. H2876
Hab 1:17 destroying nations without **m**? H2798
Hab 3: 2 make them known; in wrath remember **m**. H8163
Zec 1:12 *will* you withhold **m** *from* Jerusalem and *from* H8163
Zec 1:16 'I will return to Jerusalem with **m**, and H8171
Zec 7: 9 show **m** and compassion to one another. H2876
Mt 5: 7 are the merciful, for they *will be* **shown m**. G1796
Mt 9:13 'I desire **m**, not sacrifice.' For I G1799
Mt 9:27 calling out, "**Have m** on us, Son of G1796
Mt 12: 7 words mean, 'I desire **m**, not sacrifice, G1799
Mt 15:22 "Lord, Son of David, **have m** on me! G1796
Mt 17:15 **have m** on my son," he said. "He G1796
Mt 18:33 Shouldn't you *have* **had m** on your fellow G1796
Mt 20:30 Son of David, **have m** on us! G1796
Mt 20:31 Son of David, **have m** on us! G1796
Mt 23:23 of the law—justice, **m** and faithfulness. G1799
Mk 5:19 you, and how *he has* **had m** on you." G1796
Mk 10:47 Son of David, **have m** on me! G1796
Mk 10:48 the more, "Son of David, **have m** on me!" G1796
Lk 1:50 His **m** extends to those who fear him G1799
Lk 1:58 that the Lord had shown her great **m**, G1799
Lk 1:72 to show **m** to our ancestors and to G1799
Lk 1:78 of the **tender m** of our God, G5073+1799
Lk 10:37 law replied, "The one who had **m** on him." G1799
Lk 18:13 said, 'God, **have m** on me, a sinner. G2661
Lk 18:38 "Jesus, Son of David, **have m** on me!" G1796
Lk 18:39 the more, "Son of David, **have m** on me!" G1796
Ro 1:31 understanding, no fidelity, no love, **no m**. G446
Ro 9:15 "*I will* **have m** on whom I have mercy G1796
Ro 9:15 "I will have mercy on whom *I* **have m**, and G1796
Ro 9:16 human desire or effort, but *on* God's **m**. G1790
Ro 9:18 Therefore God **has m** on whom he wants G1796
Ro 9:18 has mercy on whom he wants to have **m**, NDT
Ro 9:23 of his glory known to the objects *of* his **m**, G1799
Ro 11:30 to God *have* now **received m** as a result of G1796
Ro 11:31 they too *may* now **receive m** as a result G1796
Ro 11:31 mercy *as a result of* God's **m** to you. G1799
Ro 11:32 so that *he may* **have m** on them all. G1796
Ro 12: 1 in view of God's **m**, to offer your bodies as G3880
Ro 12: 8 if it is *to* **show m**, do it cheerfully. G1796
Ro 15: 9 the Gentiles might glorify God for his **m**. G1799
1Co 7:25 as one who by the Lord's **m** is trustworthy. G1796
2Co 4: 1 since *through* God's **m** we have this G1796
Gal 6:16 Peace and **m** to all who follow this rule G1799
Eph 2: 4 great love for us, God, who is rich in **m**, G1799
Php 2:27 But God **had m** on him, and not on him G1796
1Ti 1: 2 **m** and peace from God the Father and G1799
1Ti 1:13 *I was* **shown m** because I acted in G1796
1Ti 1:16 very reason *I was* **shown m** so that in me, G1796
2Ti 1: 2 **m** and peace from God the Father and G1799
2Ti 1:16 May the Lord show **m** to the household of G1799
2Ti 1:18 that he will find **m** from the Lord on that G1799
Titus 3: 5 we had done, but because of his **m**. G1799
Heb 4:16 that we may receive **m** and find grace to G1799
Heb 10:28 Moses died without **m** on the testimony of G3880
Jas 2:13 because judgment **without m** will be shown G447
Jas 2:13 been merciful. **M** triumphs over judgment G1799
Jas 3:17 submissive, full *of* **m** and good fruit G1799
Jas 5:11 The Lord is full of compassion and **m**. G3881
1Pe 1: 3 In his great **m** he has given us new birth G1799
1Pe 2:10 once you *had* not **received m**, but now G1796
1Pe 2:10 but now *you have* **received m**. G1796
2Jn 3 **m** and peace from God the Father and G1799
Jude 2 **M**, peace and love be yours in abundance G1799
Jude 21 as you wait for the **m** of our Lord Jesus G1799
Jude 23 to others **show m**, mixed with fear— G1790

MERCY SEAT (KJV) ATONEMENT COVER, COVER

MERE (37) [MERELY]
2Sa 7:19 Sovereign LORD, is for a *m* **human**! AIT
2Ki 8:13 your servant, a *m* **dog**, accomplish such a AIT
2Ch 14:11 do not let *m* **mortals** prevail against you." AIT
2Ch 19: 6 not judging for *m* **mortals** but for the LORD, AIT
Job 9: 2 But how can *m* **mortals** prove their innocence AIT
Job 9:32 "He is not a *m* **mortal** like me that I might AIT
Job 12: 4 he answered—a **m** laughingstock NDT
Job 41: 9 is false; the **m** sight of it is overpowering. H1685
Ps 10:18 so that *m* earthly **mortals** will never again AIT
Ps 39: 5 You have made my days a **m** handbreadth NDT
Ps 39: 6 everyone goes around like a *m* **phantom**; AIT
Ps 56: 4 What can *m* **mortals do** to me? AIT
Ps 82: 7 But you will die like *m* **mortals**; you will fall AIT
Ps 118: 6 What *can m* mortals **do** to me? AIT
Ps 144: 3 them, *m* **mortals** that you think of them? AIT
Pr 14:23 but **m talk** leads only to poverty. H1821+8557
Pr 29:19 Servants cannot be corrected by **m** words NDT
Isa 2:22 Stop trusting in *m* **humans**, who have but a AIT
Isa 3: 4 "I will make *m* **youths** their officials; children AIT
Isa 31: 3 But the Egyptians are *m* **mortals** and not God; AIT
Isa 50: 2 By a **m** rebuke I dry up the sea, I turn rivers NDT
Isa 51: 7 the reproach of *m* **mortals** or be terrified by AIT
Isa 51:12 Who are you that you fear *m* **mortals**, human AIT
Isa 57:13 a **m breath** will blow them away. H2039
Isa 65:20 dies at a hundred will be thought a *m* **child**; AIT
Jer 17: 5 draws strength from *m* **flesh** and whose heart AIT
Eze 28: 2 But you are a *m* **mortal** and not a god AIT
Mal 3: 8 "Will a *m* **mortal** rob God? Yet you rob me AIT
Jn 7:24 Stop judging by *m* **appearances**, but instead AIT
Jn 10:33 because you, a *m* **man**, claim to be God." AIT
Ro 2: 3 So when you, a *m* **human being**, pass AIT
1Co 3: 1 who are still worldly—*m* **infants** in Christ. AIT
1Co 3: 3 Are you not acting like *m* **humans**? AIT
1Co 3: 4 Apollos," are you not *m* **human beings**? AIT
Heb 8: 2 set up by the Lord, not by a *m* **human being**. AIT
Heb 13: 6 What can *m* **mortals** do to me?" AIT
Jude 19 who **follow m natural instincts** and do not G6035

MERED (2) [MERED'S]
1Ch 4:17 Jether, **M**, Epher and Jalon. H5279
1Ch 4:18 daughter Bithiah, whom **M** had married. H5279

MERED'S (1) [MERED]
1Ch 4:17 One of **M** wives gave birth to Miriam NDT

MERELY (14) [MERE]
Jdg 15:11 "I **m** did to them what they did to me." NDT
Est 7: 4 If we had **m** been sold as male and female NDT
Job 30:20 not answer; I stand up, but *you m* **look** at me. AIT
Isa 29:13 of me is based on *m* **human** rules they have AIT
Mt 15: 9 their teachings are *m* **human** rules. AIT
Mt 16:23 the concerns of God, but *m* **human** concerns." AIT
Mk 7: 7 their teachings are *m* **human** rules. AIT
Mk 8:33 the concerns of God, but *m* **human** concerns." AIT
Ro 2:28 is circumcision **m outward** and physical. AIT
1Co 2:15 person *is* not **subject to** *m human* **judgments**, AIT
1Co 9: 8 Do I say this *m* on **human** authority? Doesn't AIT
Col 2:22 are based on *m* **human** commands and AIT
Titus 1:14 myths or to the *m* **human** commands of those AIT
Jas 1:22 Do not **m** listen to the word, and so G3667

MEREMOTH (6) [MEREMOTH'S]
Ezr 8:33 articles into the hands of **M** son of Uriah, H5329
Ezr 10:36 Vaniah, **M**, Eliashib, H5329
Ne 3: 4 **M** son of Uriah, the son of Hakkoz H5329
Ne 3:21 Next to him, **M** son of Uriah, the son of H5329
Ne 10: 5 **M**, Obadiah, H5329
Ne 12: 3 Shekaniah, Rehum, **M**, H5329

MEREMOTH'S (1) [MEREMOTH]
Ne 12:15 of Harim's, Adna; of **M**, Helkai; H5329

MERES (1)
Est 1:14 Admatha, Tarshish, **M**, Marsena and H5332

MERIB-BAAL (2)
1Ch 8:34 son of Jonathan: **M**, who was the father H5311
1Ch 9:40 son of Jonathan: **M**, who was the father H5311

MERIBAH (7) [MERIBAH KADESH]
Ex 17: 7 the place Massah and **M** because the H5313
Nu 20:13 These were the waters of **M**, where the H5313
Nu 20:24 against my command at the waters of **M**. H5313
Dt 33: 8 contended with him at the waters of **M**. H5313
Ps 81: 7 I tested you at the waters of **M**. H5313
Ps 95: 8 not harden your hearts as you did at **M**, H5313
Ps 106:32 By the waters of **M** they angered the LORD H5313

MERIBAH KADESH (4) [MERIBAH]
Nu 27:14 These were the waters of **M**, in the H5315
Dt 32:51 at the waters of **M** *in* the Desert of H5315
Eze 47:19 Tamar as far as the waters of **M**, H5315
Eze 48:28 from Tamar to the waters of **M**, H5315

MERODACH (KJV) MARDUK

MERODACH-BALADAN (NIV84) MARDUK-BALADAN

MEROM (2)
Jos 11: 5 at the Waters of **M** to fight against Israel. H5295
Jos 11: 7 at the Waters of **M** and attacked them, H5295

MERON See SHIMRON MERON

MERONOTH (1) [MERONOTHITE]
Ne 3: 7 Melatiah of Gibeon and Jadon **of M** H5331

MERONOTHITE (1) [MERONOTH]
1Ch 27:30 Jehdeiah the **M** was in charge of the H5331

MEROZ (1)
Jdg 5:23 'Curse **M**,' said the angel of the LORD H5292

MERRIMENT (1) [MERRY]
Isa 32:13 all houses of **m** and for this city of H5375

MERRY (4) [MERRIMENT, MERRYMAKERS]
Job 21:12 *they* **make m** to the sound of the pipe. H8523
Ecc 10:19 wine **makes** life **m**, and money is H8523
Jer 15:17 revelers, never **made m** with them; I sat H6600
Lk 12:19 Take life easy; eat, drink and *be* **m**." G2370

MERRYMAKERS (1) [MERRY]
Isa 24: 7 the vine withers; all the **m** groan. H8524+4213

MESH (1)
Job 18: 8 him into a net; he wanders into its **m**. H8422

MESHA (4)
Ge 10:30 lived stretched from **M** toward Sephar, H5392
2Ki 3: 4 Now **M** king of Moab raised sheep, and H4795
1Ch 2:42 **M** his firstborn, who was the father of Ziph H4796
1Ch 8: 9 he had Jobab, Zibia, **M**, Malkam, H4791

MESHACH (14)
Da 1: 7 Shadrach; to Mishael, **M**; and to Azariah H4794
Da 2:49 **M** and Abednego administrators over A10415
Da 3:12 Shadrach, **M** and Abednego—who pay A10415
Da 3:13 summoned Shadrach, **M** and Abednego. A10415
Da 3:14 Shadrach, **M** and Abednego, that you do A10415
Da 3:16 **M** and Abednego replied to him A10415
Da 3:19 with Shadrach, **M** and Abednego, and A10415
Da 3:20 **M** and Abednego and throw them into A10415
Da 3:22 took up Shadrach, **M** and Abednego, A10415
Da 3:26 "Shadrach, **M** and Abednego, servants A10415
Da 3:26 **M** and Abednego came out of the fire A10415
Da 3:28 God of Shadrach, **M** and Abednego A10415
Da 3:29 **M** and Abednego be cut into pieces A10415
Da 3:30 **M** and Abednego in the province of A10415

MESHEK (10)
Ge 10: 2 Javan, Tubal, **M** and Tiras. H5434
Ge 10:23 The sons of Aram: Uz, Hul, Gether and **M**. H5434
1Ch 1: 5 Javan, Tubal, **M** and Tiras. H5434
1Ch 1:17 sons of Aram: Uz, Hul, Gether and **M**. H5434
Ps 120: 5 Woe to me that I dwell in **M**, that I live H5434
Eze 27:13 Tubal and **M** did business with you H5434
Eze 32:26 "**M** and Tubal are there, with all their H5434
Eze 38: 2 the chief prince of **M** and Tubal; prophesy H5434
Eze 38: 3 Gog, chief prince of **M** and Tubal. H5434
Eze 39: 1 Gog, chief prince of **M** and Tubal. H5434

MESHELEMIAH (4)
1Ch 9:21 Zechariah son of **M** was the gatekeeper at H5452
1Ch 26: 1 From the Korahites: **M** son of Kore, one of H5453
1Ch 26: 2 **M** had sons: Zechariah the firstborn H5453
1Ch 26: 9 **M** had sons and relatives, who were able H5453

MESHEZABEL (3)
Ne 3: 4 of Berekiah, the son of **M**, made repairs, H5430
Ne 10:21 **M**, Zadok, Jaddua, H5430
Ne 11:24 Pethahiah son of **M**, one of the H5430

MESHILLEMITH (1)

1Ch 9:12 the son of **M**, the son of Immer. H5454

MESHILLEMOTH (2)

2Ch 28:12 Berekiah son of **M**, Jehizkiah son of H5451
Ne 11:13 of Ahzai, the son of **M**, the son of Immer, H5451

MESHOBAB (1)

1Ch 4:34 **M**, Jamlech, Joshah son of Amaziah, H5411

MESHULLAM (25)

2Ki 22: 3 Azaliah, the son of **M**, to the temple of H5450
1Ch 3:19 sons of Zerubbabel: **M** and Hananiah H5450
1Ch 5:13 Michael, **M**, Sheba, Jorai, Jakan, Zia and H5450
1Ch 8:17 Zebadiah, **M**, Hizki, Heber, H5450
1Ch 9: 7 Sallu son of **M**, the son of Hodaviah, the H5450
1Ch 9: 8 the son of Mikri; and **M** son of Shephatiah H5450
1Ch 9:11 of Hilkiah, the son of **M**, the son of Zadok, H5450
1Ch 9:12 of Jahzerah, the son of **M**, the son of H5450
2Ch 34:12 Zechariah and **M**, descended from H5450
Ezr 8:16 Zechariah and **M**, who were leaders, H5450
Ezr 10:15 supported by **M** and Shabbethai the H5450
Ezr 10:29 **M**, Malluk, Adaiah, Jashub, Sheal and H5450
Ne 3: 4 Next to him **M** son of Berekiah, the son of H5450
Ne 3: 6 son of Paseah and **M** son of Besodeiah. H5450
Ne 3:30 **M** son of Berekiah made repairs opposite H5450
Ne 6:18 the daughter of **M** son of Berekiah. H5450
Ne 8: 4 Hashbaddanah, Zechariah and **M**. H5450
Ne 10: 7 **M**, Abijah, Mijamin, H5450
Ne 10:20 Magpiash, **M**, Hezir, H5450
Ne 11: 7 Sallu son of **M**, the son of Joed, the son H5450
Ne 11:11 of Hilkiah, the son of **M**, the son of Zadok, H5450
Ne 12:13 of Ezra's, **M**; of Amariah's, Jehohanan; H5450
Ne 12:16 of Iddo's, Zechariah; of Ginnethon's, **M**; H5450
Ne 12:25 Obadiah, **M**, Talmon and Akkub were H5450
Ne 12:33 along with Azariah, Ezra, **M**, H5450

MESHULLEMETH (1)

2Ki 21:19 mother's name was **M** daughter of Haruz; H5455

MESOPOTAMIA (2)

Ac 2: 9 Elamites; residents *of* **M**, Judea and *G3544*
Ac 7: 2 father Abraham while he was still in **M**, *G3544*

MESS (KJV) GIFT, PORTION

MESSAGE (131) [MESSENGER, MESSENGER'S, MESSENGERS]

Ge 32: 5 Now I am sending *this* **m** to my lord, that I H5583
Ge 38:25 she **sent a m** to her father-in-law. H8938
Ge 50:17 When their **m came** to him, Joseph wept. H1819
Nu 22:10 of Zippor, king of Moab, **sent me** *this* **m**: H8938
Nu 23: 7 Then Balaam spoke his **m**: "Balak brought H5442
Nu 23:18 Then he spoke his **m**: "Arise, Balak, and H5442
Nu 24: 3 he spoke his **m**: "The prophecy of H5442
Nu 24:15 Then he spoke his **m**: "The prophecy of H5442
Nu 24:20 Balaam saw Amalek and spoke his **m**: H5442
Nu 24:21 Then he saw the Kenites and spoke his **m**: H5442
Nu 24:23 Then he spoke his **m**: "Alas! Who can live H5442
Dt 18:21 can we know when a **m** has not been H1821
Dt 18:22 that is a **m** the LORD has not spoken. H1821
Jos 2: 3 the king of Jericho **sent** *this* **m** to Rahab: H8938
Jos 5:14 "What **m** *does* my Lord *have* for his H1819
Jdg 3:19 "Your Majesty, I have a secret **m** for you." H1821
Jdg 3:20 said, "I have a **m** *from* God for you." H1821
Jdg 11:28 no attention to the **m** Jephthah sent him. H1821
1Sa 9:27 so that I may give you a **m** *from* God." H1821
1Sa 15: 1 so listen now to the **m** *from* the LORD. H1821
1Sa 25: 9 they gave Nabal this **m** in David's name. H1821
2Sa 17:16 Now **send a m** at once and tell David, 'Do H8938
2Sa 19:11 King David sent this **m** to Zadok and H606
1Ki 5: 2 Solomon sent back this **m** to Hiram: H606
1Ki 5: 7 When Hiram heard Solomon's **m**, he was H1821
1Ki 5: 8 *"I have* **received** *the* **m** you sent me and H9048
1Ki 13:32 For the **m** he declared by the word of the H1821
1Ki 20:10 Then Ben-Hadad sent another **m** to Ahab H606
1Ki 20:12 heard this **m** while he and the H1821
2Ki 3: 7 He also sent this **m** to Jehoshaphat king of H606
2Ki 5: 8 had torn his robes, he sent him *this* **m**: H606
2Ki 9: 5 "I have a **m** for you, commander," he said. H1821
2Ki 10: 5 the guardians sent this **m** to Jehu: H606
2Ki 14: 9 in Lebanon sent a **m** to a cedar in Lebanon H606
2Ki 18:14 of Judah sent this **m** to the king of Assyria H606
2Ki 19:20 Isaiah son of Amoz sent a **m** to Hezekiah: H606
2Ch 2: 3 Solomon sent this **m** to Hiram king of Tyre H606
2Ch 25:18 in Lebanon sent a **m** to a cedar in Lebanon H606
2Ch 32: 9 to Jerusalem with *this* **m** for Hezekiah king H606
Ezr 4:14 *we are* **sending** *this* **m** to inform the king, A10714
Ne 6: 2 Sanballat and Geshem sent me *this* **m** H606
Ne 6: 4 Four times they sent me the same **m**, and H1821
Ne 6: 5 sent his aide to me with the same **m**, H1821
Ps 36: 1 a **m from God** in my heart *concerning* the H5536
Pr 26: 6 Sending a **m** by the hands of a fool is like H1821
Isa 9: 8 The Lord has sent a **m** against Jacob; it H1821
Isa 28: 9 To whom is he explaining his **m**? To H9019
Isa 28:19 understanding of this **m** will bring sheer H9019
Isa 30:12 "Because you have rejected this **m**, relied H1821
Isa 37:21 Isaiah son of Amoz sent a **m** to Hezekiah: H606
Isa 53: 1 has believed our **m** and to whom has the H9019
Jer 3:12 proclaim this **m** toward the north: H1821
Jer 7: 2 LORD's house and there proclaim this **m**: H1821
Jer 18: 2 and there I will give you my **m**. H1821
Jer 22: 1 king of Judah and proclaim this **m** there: H1821
Jer 23:21 they have run with their **m**; I did not NDT
Jer 23:33 ask you, 'What is the **m** *from* the LORD? H5363
Jer 23:33 say to them, 'What **m**? I will forsake you, H5363
Jer 23:34 'This is a **m** *from* the LORD,' I will H5363
Jer 23:36 not mention 'a **m** *from* the LORD' again, H5363
Jer 23:36 each one's word becomes their own **m**. H5363
Jer 23:38 'This is a **m** *from* the LORD,' this is H5363
Jer 23:38 'This is a **m** *from* the LORD,' even H5363
Jer 23:38 must not claim, 'This is a **m** *from* the LORD. H5363
Jer 27: 4 **Give** them a **m** for their masters and say H7422
Jer 27:12 *I* **gave the** same **m** to Zedekiah H1819+3972+2021+2021+465+1821
Jer 29:28 He has sent this **m** to us in Babylon: It will H606
Jer 29:31 "Send this **m** to all the exiles: 'This is what H606
Jer 37: 3 to Jeremiah the prophet with *this* **m**: H606
Jer 44:16 not listen to the **m** you have spoken to us H1821
Jer 46: 2 This is the **m** against the army of Pharaoh NDT
Jer 46:13 This is the **m** the LORD spoke to Jeremiah H1821
Jer 49:14 I have heard a **m** from the LORD; an envoy H9019
Jer 51:59 This is the **m** Jeremiah the prophet gave H1821
Eze 33:30 hear the **m** that has come from H1821
Da 10: 1 Its **m** was true and it concerned a great H1821
Da 10: 1 understanding of the **m** came to him in a H1821
Am 7:10 of Bethel sent a **m** to Jeroboam king of H606
Ob 1 We have heard a **m** from the LORD: H9019
Jnh 3: 2 proclaim to it the **m** I give you. H7952
Hag 1:12 their God and the **m** *of* the prophet H1821
Hag 1:13 gave this **m** *of* the LORD to the people: H4857
Mt 10: 7 As you go, **proclaim** *this* **m**: 'The kingdom *G3062*
Mt 13:19 anyone hears the **m** about the kingdom *G3364*
Mt 27:19 the judge's seat, his wife sent him *this* **m**: *G3306*
Mk 1: 7 And *this was his* **m**: "After me comes the *G3062*
Jn 12:38 has believed our **m** and to whom has the *G198*
Jn 17:20 who will believe in me through their **m**, *G3364*
Ac 2:41 Those who accepted his **m** were baptized *G3364*
Ac 4: 4 But many who heard the **m** believed; so *G3364*
Ac 10:36 You know the **m** God sent to the people of *G3364*
Ac 10:44 Holy Spirit came on all who heard the **m**. *G3364*
Ac 11:14 He will bring you a **m** through which you *G4839*
Ac 13:26 is to us that this **m** of salvation has been *G3364*
Ac 14: 3 who confirmed the **m** of his grace by *G3364*
Ac 15: 7 hear from my lips the **m** of the gospel *G3364*
Ac 15:31 it and were glad for its **encouraging m**. *G4155*
Ac 16:14 opened her heart to respond *to* Paul's **m**. *G3281*
Ac 17:11 they received the **m** with great eagerness *G3364*
Ac 19:31 **sent** him *a* **m** begging him not to venture AIT
Ac 26:23 would **bring** *the* **m** of light to his own *G2859*
Ro 10: 8 the **m** concerning faith that we proclaim: *G4839*
Ro 10:16 "Lord, who has believed our **m**? *G198*
Ro 10:17 faith comes from **hearing** the **m**, and the *G198*
Ro 10:17 the **m** is **heard** through the word about *G198*
Ro 16:25 the **m** I **proclaim** about Jesus Christ *G3060*
1Co 1:18 For the **m** of the cross is foolishness to *G3364*
1Co 2: 4 My **m** and my preaching were not with *G3364*
1Co 2: 6 speak a **m** of wisdom among the mature NDT
1Co 12: 8 is given through the Spirit a **m** of wisdom, *G3364*
1Co 12: 8 to another a **m** of knowledge by means of *G3364*
2Co 1:18 God is faithful, our **m** to you is not "Yes *G3364*
2Co 5:19 committed to us the **m** of reconciliation. *G3364*
Gal 2: 6 favoritism—they added nothing *to* **my m**. AIT
Eph 1:13 in Christ when you heard the **m** of truth, *G3364*
Col 1: 5 already heard in the true **m** of the gospel *G3364*
Col 3:16 Let the **m** of Christ dwell among you richly *G3364*
Col 4: 3 that God may open a door for our **m**, so *G3364*
1Th 1: 6 you welcomed the **m** in the midst of *G3364*
1Th 1: 8 The Lord's **m** rang out from you not only *G3364*
2Th 3: 1 pray for us that the **m** of the Lord may *G3364*
2Ti 4:15 because he strongly opposed our **m**. *G3364*
2Ti 4:17 so that through me the **m** might be fully *G3060*
Titus 1: 9 hold firmly *to* the trustworthy **m** as it has *G3364*
Heb 2: 2 For since the **m** spoken through angels *G3364*
Heb 4: 2 the **m** they heard was of no value to *G3364*
1Pe 2: 8 stumble because they disobey the **m**— *G3364*
2Pe 1:19 have the prophetic **m** as something *G3364*
1Jn 1: 5 This is the **m** we have heard from him and *G32*
1Jn 2: 7 old command is the **m** you have heard. *G3364*
1Jn 3:11 For this is the **m** you heard from the *G32*

MESSENGER (41) [MESSAGE]

1Sa 23:27 a **m** came to Saul, saying, "Come quickly H4855
2Sa 11:19 He instructed the **m**: "When you have H4855
2Sa 11:22 The **m** set out, and when he arrived he H4855
2Sa 11:23 The **m** said to David, "The men H4855
2Sa 11:25 David told the **m**, "Say this to Joab: 'Don't H4855
2Sa 15:13 A **m** came and told David, "The hearts of H5583
1Ki 19: 2 So Jezebel sent a **m** to Elijah to say, "May H4855
1Ki 22:13 The **m** who had gone to summon Micaiah H4855
2Ki 5:10 Elisha sent a **m** to say to him, "Go, wash H4855
2Ki 6:32 The king sent a **m** ahead, but before he H4855
2Ki 6:32 when the **m** comes, shut the door H4855
2Ki 6:33 talking to them, the **m** came down to him. H4855
2Ki 9:18 reported, "The **m** has reached them, but H4855
2Ki 10: 8 When the **m** arrived, he told Jehu, "They H4855
2Ch 18:12 The **m** who had gone to summon Micaiah H4855
Job 1:14 a **m** came to Job and said, "The oxen H4855
Job 1:16 still speaking, **another m** came and said H2296S
Job 1:17 still speaking, **another m** came and said H2296
Job 1:18 speaking, yet **another m** came and said H2296S
Job 33:23 at their side, a **m**, one out of a thousand H4885
Pr 13:17 A wicked **m** falls into trouble, but a H4855
Pr 16:14 A king's wrath is a **m** *of* death, but the H4855
Pr 17:11 the **m** *of* death will be sent against them. H4855
Pr 25:13 is a trustworthy **m** to the one who sends H7495
Ecc 5: 6 And do not protest to the *temple* **m**, "My H4855
Isa 41:27 I gave to Jerusalem a **m of good news**. H1413
Isa 42:19 my servant, and deaf like the **m** I send? H4855
Jer 51:31 follows another and **m** follows messenger H5583
Jer 51:31 messenger follows **m** to announce to the H5583S
Da 4:13 was a holy one, a **m**, coming down from A10541
Da 4:23 saw a holy one, a **m**, coming down from A10541
Hag 1:13 Haggai, the LORD's **m**, gave this message H4855
Mal 2: 7 because he is the **m** *of* the LORD Almighty H4855
Mal 3: 1 "I will send my **m**, who will prepare the H4855
Mal 3: 1 to his temple; the **m** *of* the covenant H4855
Mt 11:10 " 'I will send my **m** ahead of you, who will *G34*
Mk 1: 2 "I will send my **m** ahead of you, who will *G34*
Lk 7:27 " 'I will send my **m** ahead of you, who will *G34*
Jn 13:16 is a **m** greater than the one who sent *G693*
2Co 12: 7 a thorn in my flesh, a **m** of Satan, to torment *G34*
Php 2:25 who is also your **m**, whom you sent to take *G693*

MESSENGER'S (1) [MESSAGE]

Pr 15:30 Light in a **m** eyes brings joy to the heart NDT

MESSENGERS (72) [MESSAGE]

Ge 32: 3 Jacob sent **m** ahead of him to his brother H4855
Ge 32: 6 When the **m** returned to Jacob, they said H4855
Nu 20:14 Moses sent **m** from Kadesh to the king of H4855
Nu 21:21 Israel sent **m** to say to Sihon king of the H4855
Nu 22: 5 sent **m** to summon Balaam son of Beor H4855
Nu 24:12 "Did I not tell the **m** you sent me, H4855
Dt 2:26 of Kedemoth I sent **m** to Sihon king of H4855
Jos 7:22 So Joshua sent **m**, and they ran to the H4855
Jdg 6:35 He sent **m** throughout Manasseh, calling H4855
Jdg 7:24 Gideon sent **m** throughout the hill country H4855
Jdg 9:31 Under cover he sent **m** to Abimelek H4855
Jdg 11:12 Then Jephthah sent **m** to the Ammonite H4855
Jdg 11:13 the Ammonites answered Jephthah's **m**, H4855
Jdg 11:14 Jephthah sent back **m** to the Ammonite H4855
Jdg 11:17 Then Israel sent **m** to the king of Edom H4855
Jdg 11:19 "Then Israel sent **m** to Sihon king of the H4855
Jdg 20:12 tribes of Israel sent **m** throughout the tribe H408
1Sa 6:21 Then they sent **m** to the people of Kiriath H4855
1Sa 11: 3 days so we can send **m** throughout Israel; H4855
1Sa 11: 4 When the **m** came to Gibeah of Saul and H4855
1Sa 11: 7 sent the pieces by **m** throughout Israel, H4855
1Sa 11: 9 They told the **m** who had come, "Say to H4855
1Sa 11: 9 When the **m** went and reported this to the H4855
1Sa 16:19 Then Saul sent **m** to Jesse and said H4855
1Sa 25:14 "David sent **m** from the wilderness to give H4855
1Sa 25:42 went with David's **m** and became his wife. H4855
1Sa 31: 9 they sent **m** throughout the land of the NDT
2Sa 2: 5 he sent **m** to them to say to them, "The H4855
2Sa 3:12 Then Abner sent **m** on his behalf to say to H4855
2Sa 3:14 Then David sent **m** to Ish-Bosheth son of H4855
2Sa 3:26 then left David and sent **m** after Abner, H4855
2Sa 10: 5 about this, he sent **m** to meet the men, for NDT
2Sa 11: 4 Then David sent **m** to get her. She came H4855
2Sa 12:27 Joab then sent **m** to David, saying, "I have H4855
2Sa 15:10 Absalom sent **secret m** throughout the H8078
1Ki 20: 2 He sent **m** into the city to Ahab king of H4855
1Ki 20: 5 The **m** came again and said, "This is H4855
1Ki 20: 9 So he replied to Ben-Hadad's **m**, "Tell my H4855
2Ki 1: 2 So he sent **m**, saying to them, "Go and H4855
2Ki 1: 3 "Go up and meet the **m** *of* the king of H4855
2Ki 1: 5 When the **m** returned to the king, he H4855
2Ki 1: 6 that you are sending **m** to consult NDT
2Ki 1:16 that you have sent **m** to consult H4855
2Ki 7:15 So the **m** returned and reported to the H4855
2Ki 14: 8 Then Amaziah sent **m** to Jehoash son of H4855
2Ki 16: 7 Ahaz sent **m** to say to Tiglath-Pileser king H4855
2Ki 19: 9 So he again sent **m** to Hezekiah with this H4855
2Ki 19:14 received the letter from the **m** and read it. H4855
2Ki 19:23 By your **m** you have ridiculed the Lord H4855
1Ch 10: 9 and **sent m** throughout the land of the H8938
1Ch 14: 1 Now Hiram king of Tyre sent **m** to David H4855
1Ch 19: 5 the men, he sent **m** to meet them, for they NDT
1Ch 19:16 they sent **m** and had Arameans brought H4855
2Ch 35:21 But Necho sent **m** to him, saying, "What H4855
2Ch 36:15 to them through his **m** again and again, H4855
2Ch 36:16 But they mocked God's **m**, despised his H4855
Ne 6: 3 so I sent **m** to them with this reply: "I am H4855
Job 33:22 to the pit, and their life to the **m of death**. H4637
Ps 104: 4 He makes winds his **m**, flames of fire his H4855
Isa 18: 2 swift **m**, to a people tall and H4855
Isa 37: 9 he sent **m** to Hezekiah with this word: H4855
Isa 37:14 received the letter from the **m** and read it. H4855
Isa 37:24 By your **m** you have ridiculed the Lord H6269
Isa 44:26 fulfills the predictions of his **m**, H4855
Eze 23:16 them and sent **m** to them in Chaldea. H4855
Eze 23:40 "They even sent **m** for men who came H4855
Eze 30: 9 " 'On that day **m** will go out from me in H4855
Da 4:17 " 'The decision is announced by **m**, the A10541
Na 2:13 The voices of your **m** will no longer be H4855
Lk 7:22 So he replied *to* **the m**, "Go back and *G899S*
Lk 7:24 After John's **m** left, Jesus began to speak to *G34*
Lk 9:52 And he sent **m** on ahead, who went into a *G34*

MESSIAH (68) [CHRIST]

Mt 1: 1 of Jesus the **M** the son of David, *G5986*
Mt 1:16 the mother of Jesus who is called the **M**. *G5986*
Mt 1:17 fourteen from the exile to the **M**. *G5986*
Mt 1:18 how the birth of Jesus the **M** came about: *G5986*
Mt 2: 4 asked them where the **M** was to be born. *G5986*

M

Mt 11: 2 heard about the deeds *of* the **M**, he sent G5986
Mt 16:16 "You are the **M**, the Son of the living G5986
Mt 16:20 not to tell anyone that he was the **M**. G5986
Mt 22:42 "What do you think about the **M**? Whose G5986
Mt 23:10 you have one Instructor, the **M**. G5986
Mt 24: 5 claiming, 'I am the **M**,' and will deceive G5986
Mt 24:23 anyone says to you, 'Look, here is the **M**! G5986
Mt 26:63 Tell us if you are the **M**, the Son of God." G5986
Mt 26:68 said, "Prophesy to us, **M**. Who hit you?" G5986
Mt 27:17 Barabbas, or Jesus who is called the **M**?" G5986
Mt 27:22 then, with Jesus who is called the **M**?" G5986
Mk 1: 1 of the good news about Jesus the **M**, G5986
Mk 8:29 Peter answered, "You are the **M**." G5986
Mk 9:41 you belong to the **M** will certainly not lose G5986
Mk 12:35 law say that the **M** is the son of David? G5986
Mk 13:21 anyone says to you, 'Look, here is the **M**! G5986
Mk 14:61 "Are you the **M**, the Son of the G5986
Mk 15:32 Let this **M**, this king of Israel, come down G5986
Lk 2:11 been born to you; he is the **M**, the Lord. G5986
Lk 2:26 not die before he had seen the Lord's **M**. G5986
Lk 3:15 hearts if John might possibly be the **M**. G5986
Lk 4:41 because they knew he was the **M**. G5986
Lk 9:20 Peter answered, "God's **M**." G5986
Lk 20:41 is it said that the **M** is the son of David? G5986
Lk 22:67 "If you are the **M**," they said, "tell us." G5986
Lk 23: 2 of taxes to Caesar and claims to be **M**, G5986
Lk 23:35 let him save himself if he is God's **M**, the G5986
Lk 23:39 "Aren't you the **M**? Save yourself and G5986
Lk 24:26 Did not the **M** have to suffer these things G5986
Lk 24:46 The **M** will suffer and rise from the dead G5986
Jn 1:20 confessed freely, "I am not the **M**. G5986
Jn 1:25 then do you baptize if you are not the **M**, G5986
Jn 1:41 tell him, "We have found the **M**" G3549
Jn 3:28 'I am not the **M** but am sent ahead of him G5986
Jn 4:25 "I know that **M**" (called Christ) G3549
Jn 4:29 Could this be the **M**?" G5986
Jn 7:26 really concluded that he is the **M**? G5986
Jn 7:27 when the **M** comes, no one will G5986
Jn 7:31 They said, "When the **M** comes, will he G5986
Jn 7:41 "He is the **M**." Still others asked, G5986
Jn 7:41 "How can the **M** come from Galilee? G5986
Jn 7:42 say that the **M** will come from David's G5986
Jn 9:22 that Jesus was the **M** would be put out of G5986
Jn 10:24 If you are the **M**, tell us plainly." G5986
Jn 11:27 "I believe that you are the **M**, the Son of G5986
Jn 12:34 the Law that the **M** will remain forever, G5986
Jn 20:31 that you may believe that Jesus is the **M**, G5986
Ac 2:31 he spoke of the resurrection *of* the **M**, that G5986
Ac 2:36 whom you crucified, both Lord and **M**." G5986
Ac 3:18 prophets, saying that his **M** would suffer. G5986
Ac 3:20 that he may send the **M**, who has G5986
Ac 5:42 the good news that Jesus is the **M**. G5986
Ac 8: 5 in Samaria and proclaimed the **M** there. G5986
Ac 9:22 Damascus by proving that Jesus is the **M**. G5986
Ac 17: 3 proving that the **M** had to suffer and G5986
Ac 17: 3 Jesus I am proclaiming to you is the **M**," G5986
Ac 18: 5 to the Jews that Jesus was the **M**. G5986
Ac 18:28 from the Scriptures that Jesus was the **M**. G5986
Ac 26:23 that the **M** would suffer and, as the first to G5986
Ro 9: 5 is traced the human ancestry of the **M**, G5986
1Pe 1:11 sufferings of the **M** and the glories that G5986
Rev 11:15 the kingdom of our Lord and *of* his **M**, G5986
Rev 12:10 of our God, and the authority *of* his **M**. G5986

MESSIAHS (2) [CHRIST]

Mt 24:24 For **false m** and false prophets will appear G6023
Mk 13:22 For **false m** and false prophets will appear G6023

MET (56) [MEET]

Ge 32: 1 on his way, and the angels of God **m** him. H7003
Ge 33: 8 of all these flocks and herds *I* **m**? H7008
Ge 38: 2 There Judah **m** the daughter of a H8011
Ex 3:18 the God of the Hebrews, *has* **m** with us. H7936
Ex 4:24 the LORD **m** Moses and was about to kill H7008
Ex 4:27 So *he* **m** Moses at the mountain of God H7008
Ex 5: 3 "The God of the Hebrews *has* **m** with us. H7925
Ex 5:14 "Why haven't *you* **m** your quota of bricks H3983
Ex 18: 8 hardships they *had* **m** along the way and H5162
Nu 23: 4 God **m** with him, and Balaam said, "I H7936
Nu 23:16 The LORD **m** with Balaam and put a word H7936
Dt 25:18 *they* **m** you on your journey and attacked H7936
1Sa 9:11 they **m** some young women coming out to H5162
1Sa 10:10 a procession of prophets **m** him; the Spirit H7925
1Sa 16: 4 of the town trembled when *they* **m** him. H7925
1Sa 18:30 David **m with** more **success** than the rest H8505
1Sa 21: 1 Ahimelek trembled when *he* **m** him, and H7925
1Sa 25:20 descending toward her, and *she* **m** them. H7008
2Sa 2:13 men went out and **m** them at the pool of H7008
1Ki 11:29 the prophet of Shiloh **m** him on the way, H5162
1Ki 13:24 a lion **m** him on the road and killed him H5162
1Ki 18: 7 was walking along, Elijah **m** him. H7925
2Ki 9:21 *They* **m** him at the plot of ground that had H5162
2Ki 10:13 he **m** some relatives of Ahaziah king of H5162
2Ki 12:12 and **m** all *the other* **expenses** of restoring H3655
Ne 13: 2 because *they had* not **m** the Israelites with H7709
Job 2:11 and **m** together **by agreement** to go H3585
Ps 74: 4 roared in the **place where** you **m** with us; H4595
Jer 41: 6 When he **m** them, he said, "Come to H7008
Mt 8:28 men coming from the tombs **m** him. G5636
Mt 27:32 going out, *they* **m** a man from Cyrene G2351
Mt 28: 9 Suddenly Jesus **m** them. "Greetings," G5636
Mt 28:12 *When* the chief priests *had* **m** with the G5251
Lk 8:27 *he was* **m** *by* a demon-possessed man G5636
Lk 9:37 from the mountain, a large crowd **m** him. G5267
Lk 17:12 a village, ten men who had leprosy **m** him. G560
Lk 22:66 of the law, **m together**, and Jesus was led G5251
Jn 4:51 his servants **m** him with the news that his G5636
Jn 11:30 at the place where Martha *had* **m** him. G5636
Jn 18: 2 because Jesus *had* often **m** there with his G5251
Ac 4: 5 the teachers of the law **m** in Jerusalem. G5251
Ac 4:27 Pontius Pilate **m together** with the G5251
Ac 8:27 on his way **he m** an Ethiopian G2627
Ac 10:25 Cornelius **m** him and fell at his feet in G5267
Ac 11:26 Barnabas and Saul **m** with the church G5251
Ac 12: 3 he saw that *this* **m with** approval among G1639
Ac 13: 6 There *they* **m** a Jewish sorcerer and false G2351
Ac 15: 6 apostles and elders **m** to consider this G5251
Ac 16:16 we *were* **m** by a female slave who had a G5636
Ac 16:40 where *they* **m with** the brothers and sisters G3972
Ac 18: 2 There *he* **m** a Jew named Aquila, a native G2351
Ac 20:14 When *he* **m** us at Assos, we took him G5202
Ro 8: 4 of the law *might be* **fully m** in us, G4444
Col 2: 1 all *who have* not **m** me G3972+3836+4725
Heb 7: 1 He **m** Abraham returning from the defeat G5267
Heb 7:10 because when Melchizedek **m** Abraham G5267

METAL (12) [METALS, METALWORKER]

Lev 19: 4 to idols or make **m** gods for yourselves. H5011
1Ki 7:23 He made the Sea of **cast m**, circular in H4607
1Ki 7:33 spokes and hubs were all of **cast m**. H4607
1Ki 14: 9 other gods, **idols made of m**; you have H5011
2Ch 4: 2 He made the Sea of **cast m**, circular in H4607
Ps 106:19 a calf and worshiped an **idol cast from m**. H5011
Isa 48: 5 image and **m god** ordained them. H5822
Eze 1: 4 center of the fire looked like **glowing m**, H3133
Eze 1:27 be his waist up he looked like **glowing m**, H3133
Eze 8: 2 appearance was as bright as **glowing m**. H3133
Da 11: 8 their **m images** and their valuable articles H5816
Na 2: 3 The **m** *on* the chariots flashes on the day H7110

METALS (1) [METAL]

Jer 6:27 made you a **tester of m** and my people H1031

METALWORKER (4) [METAL, WORK]

Isa 40:19 As for an idol, a **m** casts it, and a H3093
Isa 41: 7 The **m** encourages the goldsmith, and the H3093
Hos 8: 6 This calf—a **m** has made it; it is H3093
2Ti 4:14 Alexander the **m** did me a great deal of G5906

METE (1)

Ps 58: 2 your hands **m out** violence on the H7142

METHEG AMMAH (1)

2Sa 8: 1 he took **M** from the control of H5497

METHOD (1) [METHODS]

Ru 4: 7 was the **m of legalizing transactions** in H9496

METHODS (1) [METHOD]

Isa 32: 7 Scoundrels use wicked **m**, they make up H3998

METHUSELAH (7)

Ge 5:21 65 years, he became the father of **M**. H5500
Ge 5:22 After he became the father of **M**, Enoch H5500
Ge 5:25 When **M** had lived 187 years, he became H5500
Ge 5:26 **M** lived 782 years and had other sons H5500
Ge 5:27 Altogether, **M** lived a total of 969 years H5500
1Ch 1: 3 **M**, Lamech, Noah. H5500
Lk 3:37 the son *of* **M**, the son of Enoch, the son of G3417

METHUSHAEL (2)

Ge 4:18 Mehujael was the father of **M**, and H5499
Ge 4:18 **M** was the father of Lamech. H5499

MEUNIM (2)

Ezr 2:50 Asnah, **M**, Nephusim, H5064
Ne 7:52 Besai, **M**, Nephusim, H5064

MEUNITES (3)

1Ch 4:41 also the **M** who were there and H5064
2Ch 20: 1 with some of the **M** came to wage war H5064
2Ch 26: 7 who lived in Gur Baal and against the **M**. H5064

MEZOBAITE (1)

1Ch 11:47 Obed and Jaasiel the **M**. H5168

MIBHAR (1)

1Ch 11:38 the brother of Nathan, **M** son of Hagri, H4437

MIBSAM (3)

Ge 25:13 firstborn of Ishmael, Kedar, Adbeel, **M**, H4452
1Ch 1:29 firstborn of Ishmael, Kedar, Adbeel, **M**, H4452
1Ch 4:25 **M** his son and Mishma his son. H4452

MIBZAR (2)

Ge 36:42 Kenaz, Teman, **M**, H4449
1Ch 1:53 Kenaz, Teman, **M**, H4449

MICA (NIV84) MIKA

MICAH (25) [MICAH'S]

Jdg 17: 1 Now a man named **M** from the hill H4781
Jdg 17: 5 Now this man **M** had a shrine, and he H4777
Jdg 17: 9 **M** asked him, "Where are you from?" H4777
Jdg 17:10 Then **M** said to him, "Live with me and be H4777
Jdg 17:12 Then **M** installed the Levite, and the H4777
Jdg 17:13 And **M** said, "Now I know that the LORD H4777
Jdg 18: 2 of Ephraim and came to the house of **M**, H4777
Jdg 18: 4 He told them what **M** had done for him H4777
Jdg 18:22 men who lived near **M** were called H4777
Jdg 18:23 the Danites turned and said to **M** H4777
Jdg 18:26 went their way, and **M**, seeing that they H4777
Jdg 18:27 Then they took what **M** had made, and H4777
Jdg 18:31 continued to use the idol **M** had made, H4777
1Ch 5: 5 **M** his son, Reaiah his son, Baal his son, H4777
1Ch 8:34 Merib-Baal, who was the father of **M**. H4777
1Ch 8:35 The sons of **M**: Pithon, Melek, Tarea and H4777
1Ch 9:40 Merib-Baal, who was the father of **M**. H4777
1Ch 9:41 The sons of **M**: Pithon, Melek, Tahrea H4777
1Ch 23:20 **M** the first and Ishiah the second H4777
1Ch 24:24 The son of Uzziel: **M**; from the sons of H4777
1Ch 24:24 from the sons of **M**: Shamir. H4777
1Ch 24:25 The brother of **M**: Ishiah; from the sons of H4777
2Ch 34:20 Shaphan, Abdon son of **M**, Shaphan the H4777
Jer 26:18 "**M** of Moresheth prophesied in the days of H4777
Mic 1: 1 LORD that came to **M** of Moresheth during H4777

MICAH'S (7) [MICAH]

Jdg 17: 4 And it was put in **M** house. H4781
Jdg 17: 8 his way he came to **M** house in the hill H4777
Jdg 18: 3 When they were near **M** house, they H4777
Jdg 18:13 country of Ephraim and came to **M** house. H4777
Jdg 18:15 the young Levite at **M** place and greeted H4777
Jdg 18:18 five men went into **M** house and took the H4777
Jdg 18:22 had gone some distance from **M** house, H4777

MICAIAH (28)

1Ki 22: 8 He is **M** son of Imlah." "The H4781
1Ki 22: 9 said, "Bring **M** son of Imlah at once." H4781
1Ki 22:13 who had gone to summon **M** said to him, H4781
1Ki 22:14 But **M** said, "As surely as the LORD lives, H4781
1Ki 22:15 king asked him, "**M**, shall we go to war H4781
1Ki 22:17 Then **M** answered, "I saw all Israel scattered NDT
1Ki 22:19 **M** continued, "Therefore hear the word of NDT
1Ki 22:24 went up and slapped **M** in the face. H4781
1Ki 22:25 **M** replied, "You will find out on the day H4781
1Ki 22:26 "Take **M** and send him back to Amon the H4781
1Ki 22:28 **M** declared, "If you ever return safely, the H4781
2Ki 22:12 Shaphan, Akbor son of **M**, Shaphan the H4779
2Ch 17: 7 Nethanel and **M** to teach in the towns of H4780
2Ch 18: 7 He is **M** son of Imlah." "The H4781
2Ch 18: 8 said, "Bring **M** son of Imlah at once." H4781
2Ch 18:12 who had gone to summon **M** said to him, H4781
2Ch 18:13 But **M** said, "As surely as the LORD lives, H4781
2Ch 18:14 king asked him, "**M**, shall we go to war H4777
2Ch 18:16 Then **M** answered, "I saw all Israel scattered NDT
2Ch 18:18 **M** continued, "Therefore hear the word of NDT
2Ch 18:23 went up and slapped **M** in the face. H4781
2Ch 18:24 **M** replied, "You will find out on the day H4781
2Ch 18:25 "Take **M** and send him back to Amon the H4781
2Ch 18:27 **M** declared, "If you ever return safely, the H4781
Ne 12:35 the son of **M**, the son of Zakkur, H4779
Ne 12:41 Maaseiah, Miniamin, **M**, Elioenai H4779
Jer 36:11 When **M** son of Gemariah, the son of H4781
Jer 36:13 After **M** told them everything he had heard H4781

MICE (KJV) RATS

MICHA (KJV) MIKA

MICHAEL (15)

Nu 13:13 from the tribe of Asher, Sethur son of **M**; H4776
1Ch 5:13 **M**, Meshullam, Sheba, Jorai, Jakan, Zia H4776
1Ch 5:14 the son of **M**, the son of Jeshishai H4776
1Ch 6:40 the son of **M**, the son of Baaseiah, the H4776
1Ch 7: 3 sons of Izrahiah: **M**, Obadiah, Joel and H4776
1Ch 8:16 **M**, Ishpah and Joha were the sons of H4776
1Ch 12:20 Jozabad, Jediael, **M**, Jozabad, Elihu and H4776
1Ch 27:18 of David; over Issachar: Omri son of **M**; H4776
2Ch 21: 2 Zechariah, Azariahu, **M** and Shephatiah. H4776
Ezr 8: 8 Zebadiah son of **M**, and with him 80 men H4776
Da 10:13 Then **M**, one of the chief princes, came to H4776
Da 10:21 one supports me against them except **M**, H4776
Da 12: 1 "At that time **M**, the great prince who H4776
Jude 9 But even the archangel **M**, when he was G3640
Rev 12: 7 **M** and his angels fought against the G3640

MICHAIAH (KJV) MICAIAH, MAAKAH

MICHAL (18)

1Sa 14:49 and that of the younger was **M**. H4783
1Sa 18:20 Now Saul's daughter **M** was in love with H4783
1Sa 18:27 gave him his daughter **M** in marriage. H4783
1Sa 18:28 that his daughter **M** loved David, H4783
1Sa 19:11 But **M**, David's wife, warned him, "If you H4783
1Sa 19:12 So **M** let David down through a window H4783
1Sa 19:13 Then **M** took an idol and laid it on the bed H4783
1Sa 19:14 men to capture David, **M** said, "He is ill." NDT
1Sa 19:17 Saul said to **M**, "Why did you deceive me H4783
1Sa 19:17 **M** told him, "He said to me, 'Let me get H4783
1Sa 25:44 But Saul had given his daughter **M** H4783
2Sa 3:13 unless you bring **M** daughter of Saul H4783
2Sa 3:14 "Give me my wife **M**, whom I betrothed to H4783
2Sa 6:16 **M** daughter of Saul watched from a H4783
2Sa 6:20 **M** daughter of Saul came out to meet him H4783
2Sa 6:21 David said to **M**, "It was before the LORD H4783
2Sa 6:23 And **M** daughter of Saul had no children H4783
1Ch 15:29 **M** daughter of Saul watched from a H4783

MICHMAS, MICHMASH (KJV) MIKMASH

MICMASH (NIV84) MIKMASH

MICMETHATH (NIV84) MIKMETHAH

MICRI (NIV84) MIKRI

MIDAIR (4) [AIR]

2Sa 18: 9 He was left hanging **in m**, H1068+2021+9028+2256+1068+2021+824
Rev 8:13 that was flying in **m** call out in a loud *G3547*
Rev 14: 6 Then I saw another angel flying in **m**, and *G3547*
Rev 19:17 in a loud voice to all the birds flying in **m**, *G3547*

MIDDAY (7) [DAY]

Dt 28:29 At **m** you will grope about like a blind H7416
1Ki 18:29 **M** passed, and they continued their frantic H7416
Ps 91: 6 the plague that destroys *at* **m**. H7416
SS 1: 7 flock and where you rest your sheep at **m**. H7416
Isa 59:10 At **m** we stumble as if it were twilight H7416
Jer 15: 8 At **m** I will bring a destroyer against the H7416
Zep 2: 4 At **m** Ashdod will be emptied and Ekron H7416

MIDDIN (1)

Jos 15:61 Beth Arabah, **M**, Sekakah, H4516

MIDDLE (48) [AMID, MIDST]

Ge 2: 9 In the **m** *of* the garden were the tree of H9348
Ge 3: 3 the tree that is in the **m** *of* the garden, H9348
Ge 6:16 ark and make lower, **m** and upper decks. H9108
Ex 26:28 from end to end at the **m** *of* the frames. H9348
Ex 36:33 from end to end at the **m** *of* the frames. H9348
Nu 2:17 Levites will set out in the **m** *of* the camps. H9348
Dt 3:16 the **m** *of* the gorge being the border H9348
Dt 11: 6 its mouth right in the **m** *of* all Israel and H7931
Dt 13:16 the town into the **m** *of* the public square H9348
Jos 3:17 LORD stopped in the **m** *of* the Jordan and H9348
Jos 4: 3 twelve stones from the **m** *of* the Jordan, H9348
Jos 4: 5 LORD your God into the **m** *of* the Jordan. H9348
Jos 4: 8 twelve stones from the **m** *of* the Jordan, H9348
Jos 4: 9 had been in the **m** *of* the Jordan at the H9348
Jos 4:10 standing in the **m** *of* the Jordan until H9348
Jos 8:22 so that they were caught in the **m**, with H9348
Jos 10:13 sun stopped in the **m** *of* the sky and H2942
Jos 12: 2 Gorge—from the **m** *of* the gorge—to the H9348
Jos 13: 9 from the town in the **m** *of* the gorge H9348
Jos 13:16 from the town in the **m** *of* the gorge H9348
Jdg 7:19 camp at the beginning of the **m** watch, H9399
Jdg 16: 3 lay there only until the **m** *of* the night. H2942
Ru 3: 8 In the **m** *of* the night something startled H2942
2Sa 20:12 in his blood in the **m** *of* the road, H9348
2Sa 23:12 took his stand in the **m** *of* the field. H9348
1Ki 3:20 she got up in the **m** *of* the night and took H9348
1Ki 6: 6 the **m** floor six cubits and the third floor H9399
1Ki 6: 8 led up to the **m** *level* and from there to H9399
1Ki 6:27 touched each other in the **m** *of* the room. H9348
1Ki 8:64 consecrated the **m** *part of* the courtyard in H9348
2Ki 20: 4 Before Isaiah had left the **m** court, the H9399
1Ch 11:14 they took their stand in the **m** *of* the field. H9348
2Ch 7: 7 consecrated the **m** *part of* the courtyard in H9348
Job 34:20 in an instant, in the **m** *of* the night; the H2940
Jer 39: 3 came and took seats in the **M** Gate: H9348
Eze 15: 4 the fire burns both ends and chars the **m**, H9348
Eze 37: 1 the LORD and set me in the **m** *of* a valley; H9348
Eze 41: 7 floor to the top floor through the **m** *floor*. H9399
Eze 42: 5 on the lower and **m** *floors* of the building. H9399
Eze 42: 6 than those on the lower and **m** *floors*. H9399
Da 4:10 me stood a tree in the **m** *of* the land. A10135
Da 9:27 *In* the **m** *of* the 'seven' he will put an end H2942
Mk 6:47 the boat was in the **m** of the lake, and he *G3545*
Lk 5:19 through the tiles into the **m** of the crowd, *G3545*
Lk 12:38 in the **m of the night** or toward *G1311+5871*
Lk 22:55 a fire in the **m** of the courtyard and *G3545*
Jn 19:18 one on each side and Jesus *in the* **m**. *G3545*
Rev 22: 2 down the **m** of the great street of the city *G3545*

MIDIAN (35) [MIDIAN'S, MIDIANITE, MIDIANITES]

Ge 25: 2 Jokshan, Medan, **M**, Ishbak and Shuah. H4518
Ge 25: 4 The sons of **M** were Ephah, Epher, Hanok H4518
Ge 36:35 who defeated **M** in the country of Moab H4518
Ex 2:15 from Pharaoh and went to live in **M**, H824+4518
Ex 2:16 Now a priest of **M** had seven daughters H4518
Ex 3: 1 the priest of **M**, and he led the flock to the H4518
Ex 4:19 Now the LORD had said to Moses in **M** H4518
Ex 18: 1 the priest of **M** and father-in-law of H4518
Nu 22: 4 The Moabites said to the elders of **M** H4518
Nu 22: 7 The elders of Moab and **M** left, taking H4518
Nu 31: 7 They fought against **M**, as the LORD H4518
Nu 31: 8 Hur and Reba—the five kings of **M**. H4518
Jdg 6: 2 the power of **M** was so oppressive, H4518
Jdg 6: 6 **M** so impoverished the Israelites that they H4518
Jdg 6: 7 cried out to the LORD because of **M**, H4518
Jdg 6:13 us and given us into the hand of **M**." H4518
Jdg 7: 1 The camp of **M** was north of them in the H4518
Jdg 7: 2 I cannot deliver **M** into their hands, or H4518
Jdg 7: 8 Now the camp of **M** lay below him in the H4518
Jdg 8: 1 you call us when you went to fight **M**?" H4518
Jdg 8: 5 Zebah and Zalmunna, the kings of **M**." H4518
Jdg 8:12 Zalmunna, the two kings of **M**, fled, H4518
Jdg 8:22 you have saved us from the hand of **M**." H4518
Jdg 8:26 worn by the kings of **M** or the chains that H4518
Jdg 8:28 Thus **M** was subdued before the Israelites H4518
Jdg 9:17 his life to rescue you from the hand of **M**. H4518
1Ki 11:18 They set out from **M** and went to Paran H4518
1Ch 1:32 Jokshan, Medan, **M**, Ishbak and Shuah. H4518
1Ch 1:33 The sons of **M**: Ephah, Epher, Hanok H4518
1Ch 1:46 who defeated **M** in the country of Moab H4518
Ps 83: 9 Do to them as you did to **M**, as you did to H4518
Isa 10:26 he struck down **M** at the rock of Oreb H4518
Isa 60: 6 your land, young camels of **M** and Ephah. H4518
Hab 3: 7 the dwellings of **M** in anguish. H824+4518
Ac 7:29 he fled to **M**, where he settled *G1178+3409*

MIDIAN'S (2) [MIDIAN]

Jdg 6:14 you have and save Israel out of **M** hand. H4518
Isa 9: 4 For as in the day of **M** defeat, you have H4518

MIDIANITE (14) [MIDIAN]

Ge 37:28 So when the **M** merchants came by, his H4520
Nu 10:29 Moses said to Hobab son of Reuel the **M**, H4520
Nu 25: 6 into the camp a **M** *woman* right before H4520
Nu 25:14 killed with the **M** *woman* was Zimri son of H4520
Nu 25:15 the name of the **M** woman who was put H4520
Nu 25:15 a tribal chief of a **M** family. H4518
Nu 25:18 the daughter of a **M** leader, the woman H4518
Nu 31: 9 captured the **M** women and children and H4518
Nu 31: 9 children and took all **the M** herds, H4392S
Jos 13:21 had defeated him and the **M** chiefs, H4518
Jdg 7:13 bread came tumbling into the **M** camp. H4518
Jdg 7:15 LORD has given the **M** camp into your H4518
Jdg 7:25 They also captured two of the **M** leaders H4518
Jdg 8: 3 Oreb and Zeeb, the **M** leaders, into your H4518

MIDIANITES (17) [MIDIAN]

Ge 37:36 the **M** sold Joseph in Egypt to Potiphar H4520
Nu 25:17 "Treat the **M** as enemies and kill them. H4520
Nu 31: 2 vengeance on the **M** for the Israelites. H4520
Nu 31: 3 go to war against the **M** so that they may H4518
Nu 31:10 all the towns where **the M** had settled, H4392S
Jdg 6: 1 he gave them into the hands of the **M**. H4518
Jdg 6: 3 their crops, the **M**, Amalekites and other H4518
Jdg 6:11 in a winepress to keep it from the **M**. H4518
Jdg 6:16 you will strike down *all* the **M** H4518
Jdg 6:33 Now all the **M**, Amalekites and other H4518
Jdg 7: 7 save you and give the **M** into your hands. H4518
Jdg 7:12 The **M**, the Amalekites and all the other H4518
Jdg 7:14 God has given the **M** and the whole camp H4518
Jdg 7:21 the camp, all the **M** ran, crying out as H4722S
Jdg 7:23 were called out, and they pursued the **M**. H4518
Jdg 7:24 down against the **M** and seize the waters H4518
Jdg 7:25 They pursued the **M** and brought the H4518

MIDNIGHT (11) [NIGHT]

Ex 11: 4 'About **m** I will go throughout H2940+4326
Ex 12:29 At **m** the LORD struck down H2942+2021+4326
Job 24:17 For all of them, **m** is their morning; they H7516
Ps 119:62 *At* **m** I rise to give you thanks for H2940+4326
Am 5: 8 who turns **m** into dawn and darkens day H7516
Mt 25: 6 "**At m** the cry rang out: 'Here's the *G3545+3816*
Mk 13:35 in the evening, or at **m**, or when the *G3543*
Lk 11: 5 you go to him *at* **m** and say, 'Friend, *G3543*
Ac 16:25 About **m** Paul and Silas were praying *G3543*
Ac 20: 7 the next day, kept on talking until **m**. *G3543*
Ac 27:27 when about **m** the sailors *G3545+3836+3816*

MIDST (26) [MIDDLE]

Lev 16:16 among them in the **m** *of* their H9348
Nu 16:47 and ran into the **m** *of* the assembly. H9348
Job 20:22 In the **m** *of* his plenty, distress will H4848
Ps 57: 4 I am in the **m** *of* lions; I am forced to H9348
Ps 102:24 my God, in the **m** *of* my days; your years H2942
Ps 110: 2 "Rule in the **m** *of* your enemies! H7931
Ps 116:19 house of the LORD—in your **m**, Jerusalem. H9348
Ps 135: 9 sent his signs and wonders into your **m**, H9348
Ps 136:14 brought Israel through the **m** *of* it, His H9348
Ps 138: 7 Though I walk in the **m** *of* trouble, you H7931
Jer 9: 6 You live in the **m** *of* deception; in their H9348
Jer 48:45 a blaze from the **m** *of* Sihon; it burns the H1068
La 1: 3 overtaken her **in the m of** her distress. H1068
La 1:15 Lord has rejected all the warriors in my **m**; H7931
Eze 5:10 Therefore in your **m** parents will eat their H9348
Eze 22: 3 blood in her **m** and defiles herself H9348
Eze 22:13 at the blood you have shed in your **m**. H9348
Eze 24: 7 " 'For the blood she shed is in her **m**: She H9348
Am 5:17 I will pass through your **m**," says the H7931
Mic 5: 7 will be in the **m** *of* many peoples like H7931
Mic 5: 8 nations, in the **m** *of* many peoples, like H7931
Lk 17:21 because the kingdom of God is **in your m**." *G1955*
Ac 20:19 with tears and **in the m of** severe testing *G5201*
1Co 3:16 that God's Spirit dwells **in** your **m**? *G1877*
2Co 8: 2 **In the m of** a very severe trial, their *G1877*
1Th 1: 6 the message **in the m of** severe suffering *G1877*

MIDWIFE (2) [MIDWIVES]

Ge 35:17 in childbirth, the **m** said to her, "Don't H3528
Ge 38:28 so the **m** took a scarlet thread and tied it H3528

MIDWIVES (7) [MIDWIFE]

Ex 1:15 The king of Egypt said to the Hebrew **m** H3528
Ex 1:17 The **m**, however, feared God and did not H3528
Ex 1:18 Egypt summoned the **m** and asked them, H3528
Ex 1:19 The **m** answered Pharaoh, "Hebrew H3528
Ex 1:19 give birth before the **m** arrive. H3528
Ex 1:20 So God was kind to the **m** and the people H3528
Ex 1:21 And because the **m** feared God, he gave H3528

MIGDAL EDER (1) [EDER]

Ge 35:21 pitched his tent beyond **M**. H4468

MIGDAL EL (1)

Jos 19:38 **M**, Horem, Beth Anath and Beth H4466

MIGDAL GAD (1) [GAD]

Jos 15:37 Hadashah, **M**, H4467

MIGDOL (6)

Ex 14: 2 near Pi Hahiroth, between **M** and the sea. H4465
Nu 33: 7 of Baal Zephon, and camped near **M**. H4465
Jer 44: 1 in Lower Egypt—in **M**, Tahpanhes and H4465
Jer 46:14 proclaim it in **M**; proclaim it also in H4465
Eze 29:10 a desolate waste from **M** to Aswan, H4465
Eze 30: 6 From **M** to Aswan they will fall by the H4465

MIGHT (200) [ALMIGHTY, MIGHTIER, MIGHTIEST, MIGHTILY, MIGHTY]

Ge 17:18 "If only Ishmael **m live** under your blessing!" AIT
Ge 26: 7 men of this place **m** kill me on account of H7153
Ge 26: 9 "Because I thought I **m** lose my life on H7153
Ge 26:10 of the men **m well have** slept with H3869+5071
Ge 42: 4 he was afraid that harm *m* **come** to him. AIT
Ge 49: 3 are my firstborn, my **m**, the first sign of my H3946
Ex 9:16 that *I m* **show** you my power and that my AIT
Ex 9:16 that my name *m be* **proclaimed** in all the AIT
Ex 13:17 they **m** change their minds and return to H7153
Ex 16:34 the covenant law, so that it **m** be preserved. NDT
Ex 29:46 out of Egypt so that I *m* **dwell** among them. AIT
Ex 33: 3 people and *I m* **destroy** you on the way." AIT
Ex 33: 5 with you even for a moment, *I m* **destroy** you. AIT
Lev 5: 4 in any matter one *m* **carelessly** swear about AIT
Dt 4:35 things so that *you m* **know** that the LORD is AIT
Dt 5:29 so that *it m* **go well** with them and their AIT
Dt 6:24 so that we **m** always prosper and be kept NDT
Dt 8:16 you so that in the end *it m* **go well** *with* you. AIT
Dt 19: 6 the avenger of blood *m* **pursue** him in a rage, AIT
Dt 29: 6 I did this so that *you m* **know** that I am the AIT
Jos 4:24 peoples of the earth *m* **know** that the hand of AIT
Jos 4:24 so that *you m* always **fear** the LORD your AIT
Jos 11:20 so that *he m* **destroy** them **totally** AIT
Jos 22:24 some day your descendants *m* **say** to ours, AIT
Jos 22:25 descendants *m* **cause** ours **to stop** fearing the AIT
Jdg 9:24 *m be* **avenged** on their brother Abimelek AIT
Jdg 14: 6 bare hands as *he m have* **torn** a young goat. AIT
Jdg 16:30 Then he pushed with all his **m**, and down H3946
Jdg 18: 1 a place of their own where they *m* **settle**, AIT
Ru 2:22 in someone else's field you *m be* **harmed**." AIT
Ru 4: 6 it because *I m* **endanger** my own estate. AIT
1Sa 18:27 that David *m become* the king's **son-in-law**. AIT
1Sa 27:11 he thought, "They **m** inform on us and say H7153
2Sa 6: 5 celebrating with **all** their *m* before the LORD, AIT
2Sa 6:14 dancing before the LORD with all his **m**, H6437
1Ki 2:22 *You m as well* **request** the kingdom for him AIT
1Ki 8:16 a temple built so that my Name *m* **be** there, AIT
1Ki 19: 4 sat down under it and prayed that he *m* **die**. AIT
2Ki 18:20 you have the counsel and the **m** for war— H1476
2Ki 23:33 Hamath so that he *m* not **reign** in Jerusalem, AIT
1Ch 13: 8 celebrating with all their **m** before God, H6437
2Ch 6: 5 a temple built so that my Name *m* **be** there, AIT
2Ch 6:41 resting place, you and the ark of your **m**. H6437
2Ch 20: 6 Power and **m** are in your hand, and no H1476
2Ch 23:19 no one who was in any way unclean *m* **enter**. AIT
2Ch 25:20 so worked that *he m* **deliver** them into the AIT
Ezr 8:17 so that they *m* **bring** attendants to us for the AIT
Ezr 8:21 so that we *m* **humble ourselves** before our AIT
Est 8:11 province who *m* **attack** them and their AIT
Est 10: 2 And all his acts of power and **m**, together H1476
Job 3:12 receive me and breasts that *I m be* **nursed**? AIT
Job 6: 8 that I *m* **have** my request, that God AIT
Job 9:32 a mere mortal like me that *I m* **answer** him, AIT
Job 9:32 that *we m* **confront** each other in court. AIT
Job 13: 9 you deceive him as you *m* **deceive** a mortal? AIT
Job 30:21 with the **m** *of* your hand you attack me. H6797
Job 34:36 that Job *m* **be tested** to the utmost for AIT
Job 38:13 that *it m* **take** the earth by the edges and AIT
Ps 21:13 we will sing and praise your **m**. H1476
Ps 54: 1 by your name; vindicate me by your **m**. H1476
Ps 59:11 In your **m** uproot them and bring them H2657
Ps 68:18 that you, LORD God, *m* **dwell** there. AIT
Ps 78:61 He sent the *ark of* his **m** into captivity, his H6437
Ps 80: 2 Awaken your **m**; come and save us. H1476
Ps 105:45 that *they m* **keep** his precepts and observe AIT
Ps 119:11 word in my heart that *I m* **not sin** against you. AIT
Ps 119:71 to be afflicted so that *I m* **learn** your decrees. AIT
Ps 119:101 every evil path so that *I m* **obey** your word. AIT
Ps 125: 3 the righteous *m* **use** their hands to **do** evil. AIT
Ps 132: 8 resting place, you and the ark of your **m**. H6437
Ps 145:11 of your kingdom and speak of your **m**, H1476
Ecc 9:10 do it with all your **m**, for in the realm of H3946
Isa 6:10 Otherwise *they m* **see** with their eyes, hear AIT
Isa 11: 2 the Spirit of counsel and of **m**, the Spirit H1476
Isa 36: 5 You say you have counsel and **m** for war— H1476
Isa 44:12 he forges it with the **m** *of* his arm. H3946
Isa 47: 7 these things or reflect on **what m happen**. H344
Isa 51:10 the sea so that the redeemed *m* **cross over**? AIT
Isa 63:15 Where are your zeal and your **m**? Your H1476
Jer 9: 2 so that *I m* **leave** my people and go away AIT
Jer 16:21 time I will teach them my power and **m**. H1476
Jer 49:35 the bow of Elam, the mainstay of their **m**. H1476
Eze 20:26 that *I m* **fill** them **with horror** so they would AIT

M

Eze 36: 5 so that they **m** plunder its pastureland NDT
Da 2:16 so that he *m* **interpret** the dream for him. AIT
Da 2:18 his friends *m* not *be* **executed** with the rest AIT
Da 2:37 dominion and power and **m** and glory; A10773
Da 5: 2 wives and his concubines *m* **drink** from them. AIT
Da 6: 2 to them so that the king *m* not **suffer loss**. AIT
Da 6:17 so that Daniel's situation *m* not *be* **changed**. AIT
Da 11:17 to come with the **m** *of* his entire kingdom H9549
Joel 3: 6 that *you m* **send** them **far** from their AIT
Am 6:10 them asks anyone who **m** be hiding there, NDT
Mic 3: 8 with justice and **m**, to declare to H1476
Zec 4: 6 'Not by **m** nor by power, but by my Spirit,' H2657
Mt 12:14 went out and plotted how *they m* **kill** Jesus. AIT
Mt 13:15 Otherwise *they m* **see** with their eyes, hear AIT
Mt 15: 5 that what **m have been** used to help G1569
Mt 26:56 the writings of the prophets *m be* **fulfilled**." AIT
Mk 3: 6 with the Herodians how *they m* **kill** Jesus. AIT
Mk 3:14 twelve that *they m* **be** with him and that he AIT
Mk 3:14 him and that *he m* **send** them **out** to preach AIT
Mk 4:12 otherwise they *m* **turn** and be forgiven! AIT
Mk 7:11 that what *m have been used to* **help** their AIT
Mk 14:35 that if possible the hour *m* **pass** from him. AIT
Mk 16: 1 spices so that *they m* **go** to anoint Jesus' AIT
Lk 1:29 wondered what kind of greeting this *m* **be**. AIT
Lk 3:15 hearts if John *m possibly* **be** the Messiah. AIT
Lk 6:11 with one another what they **m** do to Jesus. G323
Lk 11:54 waiting to catch him in something he **m** say. NDT
Lk 20:20 so that *they m* **hand** him **over** to the power AIT
Lk 22: 4 discussed with them how *he m* **betray** Jesus. AIT
Lk 22:23 which of them *it m* **be** who would do this. AIT
Jn 1: 7 that light, so that through him all *m* **believe**. AIT
Jn 1:31 water was that *he m be* **revealed** to Israel." AIT
Jn 9: 3 that the works of God *m be* **displayed** in him. AIT
Jn 11:57 should report it so that *they m* **arrest** him. AIT
Jn 15:16 you so that you *m* **go** and bear fruit— AIT
Jn 17: 2 all people that *he m* **give** eternal life to all AIT
Jn 19:24 that the scripture *m be* **fulfilled** that said, AIT
Ac 5:15 Peter's shadow *m* **fall on** some of them as he AIT
Ac 5:24 at a loss, wondering what this **m** lead to. G323
Ac 5:31 Savior that *he m* **bring** Israel to AIT
Ac 7:46 favor and asked *that he m* **provide** a dwelling AIT
Ac 8:15 there that *they m* **receive** the Holy Spirit, AIT
Ac 9: 2 *he m* **take** them as prisoners to Jerusalem. AIT
Ac 15:17 among you *that* the Gentiles *m* **hear** from my AIT
Ac 27: 3 to his friends *so they m* **provide for** his needs. AIT
Ac 28:27 Otherwise *they m* **see** with their eyes, hear AIT
Ro 1:13 in order that *I m* **have** a harvest among you AIT
Ro 3: 7 Someone **m** argue, "If my falsehood NDT
Ro 4:11 that righteousness *m be* **credited** to them. AIT
Ro 5: 7 person someone *m* possibly **dare** to die. AIT
Ro 5:20 brought in so that the trespass *m* **increase**. AIT
Ro 5:21 so also grace *m* **reign** through righteousness AIT
Ro 6: 6 the body ruled by sin *m be* **done away with**, AIT
Ro 7: 4 that you *m* **belong** to another, to him AIT
Ro 7: 4 in order that *we m* **bear fruit** for God. AIT
Ro 7:13 in order that sin *m be* **recognized** as sin, it AIT
Ro 7:13 commandment sin *m* **become** utterly sinful. AIT
Ro 8: 4 requirement of the law *m be* **fully met** in us, AIT
Ro 8:29 that he *m* **be** the firstborn among many AIT
Ro 9:11 order that God's purpose in election *m* **stand**: AIT
Ro 9:17 that *I m* **display** my power in you and that my AIT
Ro 9:17 that my name *m be* **proclaimed** in all the AIT
Ro 14: 9 to life so that *he m be* the **Lord** of both the AIT
Ro 15: 4 they provide *we m* **have** hope. AIT
Ro 15: 8 made to the patriarchs *m be* **confirmed** AIT
Ro 15: 9 *that* the Gentiles *m* **glorify** God for his mercy. AIT
Ro 15:16 so that the Gentiles *m* **become** an offering AIT
Ro 16:26 all the Gentiles *m come* **to** the obedience AIT
1Co 2: 5 that your faith *m* not **rest** on human wisdom, AIT
1Co 4: 8 to reign so that we also *m* **reign with** you! AIT
1Co 7:36 *that he m* **not be acting honorably** toward AIT
1Co 9:22 so that by all possible means *I m* **save** some. AIT
1Co 11: 6 *she m as well* **have** *her* **hair cut off**; but AIT
2Co 1: 9 happened that *we m* not **rely** on ourselves AIT
2Co 1:15 to visit you first so that *you m* **benefit** twice. AIT
2Co 2:11 in order that Satan *m* not **outwit** *us*. For we AIT
2Co 5:21 so that in him we *m* **become** the AIT
2Co 8: 9 that you through his poverty *m become* **rich**. AIT
2Co 8:13 is not that others **m** be relieved while you NDT
2Co 8:13 hard pressed, but that there **m** be equality. NDT
2Co 11: 2 *so that I m* **present** you as a pure virgin to AIT
Gal 1:16 Son in me so that *I m* **preach** him among the AIT
Gal 2: 5 truth of the gospel *m be* **preserved** for you. AIT
Gal 2:19 law I died to the law so that *I m* **live** for God. AIT
Gal 3:14 given to Abraham *m* **come** to the Gentiles AIT
Gal 3:14 so that by faith *we m* **receive** the promise of AIT
Gal 3:22 *m be* **given** to those who believe. AIT
Gal 3:24 Christ came that *we m be* **justified** by faith. AIT
Gal 4: 5 that *we m* **receive** adoption to sonship. AIT
Eph 1:12 in Christ, *m* **be** for the praise of his glory. AIT
Eph 2: 7 the coming ages *he m* **show** the AIT
Col 1:11 to his glorious **m** so that you may have G3197
Col 1:18 that in everything *he m* **have** the supremacy. AIT
1Th 3: 5 you and that our labors *m have* **been** in vain. AIT
2Th 1: 9 of the Lord and from the glory *of* his **m** G2709
2Th 2:14 that you **m** share in the glory of our Lord NDT
1Ti 1:16 Christ Jesus *m* **display** his immense patience AIT
1Ti 6:16 To him be honor and **m** forever. Amen. G3197
2Ti 4:17 the message *m be* **fully** *proclaimed* and all AIT
2Ti 4:17 proclaimed and all the Gentiles *m* **hear** it. AIT
Titus 1: 5 was that *you m* **put in order** what was left AIT
Titus 3: 7 *we m* **become** heirs having the hope of AIT
Phm 15 was that *you m* **have** him **back** forever— AIT
Heb 2: 9 the grace of God *he m* **taste** death for AIT
Heb 2:14 his death *he m* **break the power** of him who AIT
Heb 2:17 in order that *he m* **become** a merciful and AIT
Heb 2:17 that *he m* **make atonement** for the sins AIT
Heb 7: 9 **One m even say** that Levi G6055+2229+3306
Heb 11:35 released so that *they m* **gain** an even better AIT
Jas 1:18 that we *m* **be** a kind of firstfruits of all he AIT
1Pe 2:24 so that *we m* **die** to sins and live for AIT
1Pe 4: 6 so that they *m be* **judged** according to AIT
1Jn 3: 5 appeared so that *he m* **take away** our sins. AIT
1Jn 4: 9 into the world that *we m* **live** through him. AIT
Rev 12: 4 so that *it m* **devour** her child the moment he AIT
Rev 12: 6 where she *m be* **taken care of** for 1,260 days. AIT
Rev 12:14 so that *she m* **fly** to the place prepared for AIT

MIGHTIER (2) [MIGHT]

Ps 93: 4 **M** than the thunder of the great waters NDT
Ps 93: 4 **m** than the breakers of the sea H129

MIGHTIEST (3) [MIGHT]

2Sa 23:20 He struck down Moab's two **m warriors**. H738
1Ch 11:22 He struck down Moab's two **m warriors**. H738
Da 11:39 attack the **m fortresses** with the H4448+5057

MIGHTILY (1) [MIGHT]

Jer 25:30 dwelling and **roar m** against his H8613+8613

MIGHTY (189) [MIGHT]

Ge 10: 8 who became a **m warrior** on the earth. H1475
Ge 10: 9 He was a **m** hunter before the LORD; that is H1475
Ge 10: 9 Like Nimrod, a **m** hunter before the LORD. H1475
Ge 23: 6 You are a **m** prince among us. H466
Ge 49:24 because of the hand of the **M One** *of* Jacob H51
Ex 3:19 let you go unless a **m** hand compels him. H2617
Ex 6: 1 Because of my **m** hand he will let them H2617
Ex 6: 1 because of my **m** hand he will drive them H2617
Ex 6: 6 arm and with **m** acts of judgment. H1524
Ex 7: 4 on Egypt and with **m** acts of judgment I H1524
Ex 13: 3 LORD brought you out of it with a **m** hand. H2620
Ex 13: 9 brought you out of Egypt with his **m** hand. H2617
Ex 13:14 'With a **m** hand the LORD brought us out of H2620
Ex 13:16 brought us out of Egypt with his **m** hand." H2620
Ex 14:31 the Israelites saw the **m** hand of the LORD H1524
Ex 15:10 They sank like lead in the **m** waters. H129
Ex 32:11 of Egypt with great power and a **m** hand? H2617
Dt 3:24 can do the deeds and **m works** you do? H1476
Dt 4:34 by a **m** hand and an outstretched arm H2617
Dt 5:15 you out of there with a **m** hand and an H2617
Dt 6:21 brought us out of Egypt with a **m** hand. H2617
Dt 7: 8 you out with a **m** hand and redeemed you H2617
Dt 7:19 the **m** hand and outstretched arm H2617
Dt 9:26 brought out of Egypt with a **m** hand. H2617
Dt 10:17 the great God, **m** and awesome, who H1475
Dt 11: 2 his majesty, his **m** hand, his outstretched H2617
Dt 26: 8 us out of Egypt with a **m** hand and an H2617
Dt 34:12 has ever shown the **m** power or performed H2617
Jos 22:22 "The **M One**, God, the LORD! The Mighty H446
Jos 22:22 The **M One**, God, the LORD! He H446
Jdg 5:13 the LORD came down to me against the **m**. H1475
Jdg 5:22 galloping, galloping go his **m** steeds. H52
Jdg 5:23 the LORD, to help the LORD against the **m**. H1475
Jdg 6:12 said, "The LORD is with you, **m** warrior." H2657
Jdg 11: 1 the Gileadite was a **m warrior**. H2657+1475
1Sa 4: 8 deliver us from the hand of these **m** gods? H129
1Sa 14:52 whenever Saul saw a **m** or brave man, H1475
2Sa 1:19 heights, Israel. How the **m** have fallen! H1475
2Sa 1:21 there the shield of the **m** was despised, H1475
2Sa 1:22 from the flesh of the **m**, the bow of H1475
2Sa 1:25 "How the **m** have fallen in battle H1475
2Sa 1:27 "How the **m** have fallen! The weapons of H1475
2Sa 20: 7 all the **m warriors** went out under the H1475
2Sa 23: 8 are the names of David's **m warriors**: H1475
2Sa 23: 9 As one of the three **m warriors**, he was H1475
2Sa 23:16 So the three **m warriors** broke through the H1475
2Sa 23:17 were the exploits of the three **m warriors**. H1475
2Sa 23:22 was as famous as the three **m warriors**. H1475
1Ki 8:42 great name and your **m** hand and your H2617
2Ki 17:36 up out of Egypt with **m** power and H1524
1Ch 1:10 who became a **m warrior** on earth. H1475
1Ch 11:10 were the chiefs of David's **m warriors**— H1475
1Ch 11:11 this is the list of David's **m warriors** H1475
1Ch 11:12 the Ahohite, one of the three **m warriors**. H1475
1Ch 11:19 were the exploits of the three **m warriors**. H1475
1Ch 11:24 was as famous as the three **m warriors**. H1475
1Ch 11:26 The **m warriors** were: Asahel the H1475+2657
1Ch 12: 4 Gibeonite, a **m warrior** among the Thirty H1475
1Ch 27: 6 who was a **m warrior** *among* the Thirty H1475
2Ch 6:32 great name and your **m** hand and your H2617
2Ch 14:11 you to help the powerless against the **m**. H8041
2Ch 16: 8 and Libyans a **m** army with great H4200+8044
Ne 1:10 by your great strength and your **m** hand. H2617
Ne 9:11 the depths, like a stone into **m** waters. H6434
Ne 9:32 the great God, **m** and awesome, who H1475
Job 1:19 when suddenly a **m** wind swept in from H1524
Job 9:19 of strength, he is **m**! And if it is a matter of H579
Job 12:21 contempt on nobles and disarms the **m**. H693
Job 24:22 But God drags away the **m** by his power H52
Job 34:17 Will you condemn the just and **m** *One*? H3888
Job 34:20 the **m** are removed without human hand. H52
Job 34:24 he shatters the **m** and sets up others in H3888
Job 36: 5 "God is **m**, but despises no one; he is H3888
Job 36: 5 despises no one; he is **m**, and firm in his H3888
Job 36:19 even all your **m** efforts sustain you so H3946
Job 37: 6 to the rain shower, 'Be a **m** downpour. H6437
Job 41:25 When it rises up, the **m** are terrified; they H446
Ps 24: 8 The LORD strong and **m**, the LORD mighty H1475
Ps 24: 8 strong and mighty, the LORD **m** *in* battle. H1475
Ps 29: 3 the LORD thunders over the **m** waters. H8041
Ps 32: 6 the rising of the **m** waters will not reach H8041
Ps 42: 4 protection of the **M One** with shouts of joy H129
Ps 45: 3 on your side, you **m** *one*; clothe yourself H1475
Ps 50: 1 The **M One**, God, the LORD, speaks and H446
Ps 52: 1 you **m hero**? Why do you boast H1475
Ps 62: 7 on God; he is my **m** rock, my refuge. H6437
Ps 68:11 women who proclaim it are a **m** throng: H8041
Ps 68:33 heavens, who thunders with **m** voice. H6437
Ps 71:16 I will come and proclaim your **m acts** H1476
Ps 71:18 your **m acts** to all who are to come. H1476
Ps 77:12 works and meditate on all your **m deeds**." H6613
Ps 77:15 With your **m** arm you redeemed your people NDT
Ps 77:19 your way through the **m** waters, though H8041
Ps 80:10 its shade, the **m** cedars with its branches. H446
Ps 89: 8 are **m**, and your faithfulness H2886
Ps 93: 4 of the sea—the LORD on high is **m**. H129
Ps 99: 4 The King is **m**, he loves justice—you H6437
Ps 103:20 you **m** *ones* who do his bidding H1475+3946
Ps 106: 2 can proclaim the **m acts** *of* the LORD or H1476
Ps 106: 8 to make his **m power** known. H1476
Ps 107:23 they were merchants on the **m** waters. H8041
Ps 110: 2 will extend your **m** scepter from Zion, H6437
Ps 112: 2 Their children will be **m** in the land; the H1475
Ps 118:15 The LORD's right hand has done **m things**! H2657
Ps 118:16 the LORD's right hand has done **m things**!" H2657
Ps 132: 2 he made a vow to the **M One** *of* Jacob: H51
Ps 132: 5 LORD, a dwelling for the **M One** *of* Jacob." H51
Ps 135:10 down many nations and killed **m** kings— H6786
Ps 136:12 with a **m** hand and outstretched arm; His H2617
Ps 136:18 killed **m** kings—His love endures H129
Ps 144: 7 me and rescue me from the **m** waters, H8041
Ps 145: 4 works to another; they tell of your **m acts**. H1476
Ps 145:12 may know of your **m acts** and the glorious H1476
Ps 147: 5 Great is our Lord and **m** *in* power; his H8041
Ps 150: 1 sanctuary; praise him in his **m** heavens. H6437
Pr 7:26 brought down; her slain are a **m** throng. H6786
Pr 21:22 the city of the **m** and pull down the H1475
Pr 30:30 **m** among beasts, who retreats H1475
SS 8: 6 It burns like blazing fire, like a **m flame**. H8928
Isa 1:24 LORD Almighty, the **M One** *of* Israel, H51
Isa 1:31 The **m** *man* will become tinder and his H2891
Isa 8: 7 against them the **m** floodwaters of the H6786
Isa 9: 6 Wonderful Counselor, **M** God, Everlasting H1475
Isa 10:13 like a **m** *one* I subdued their kings. H52
Isa 10:21 of Jacob will return to the **M** God. H1475
Isa 10:34 Lebanon will fall before the **M One**. H129
Isa 22:17 of you and hurl you away, you **m man**. H1505
Isa 33:21 There the LORD will be our **M One**. It will H129
Isa 33:21 will ride them, no **m** ship will sail them. H129
Isa 40:10 with power, and he rules with a *m* **arm**. AIT
Isa 40:26 Because of his great power and **m** strength H579
Isa 43:16 the sea, a path through the **m** waters, H6434
Isa 49:26 your Redeemer, the **M One** *of* Jacob." H51
Isa 56:11 They are dogs with **m** appetites; they H6434
Isa 60:16 your Redeemer, the **M One** *of* Jacob. H51
Isa 60:22 a thousand, the smallest a **m** nation. H6786
Isa 62: 8 sworn by his right hand and by his **m** arm: H6437
Isa 63: 1 proclaiming victory, **m** to save." H8041
Jer 5:16 an open grave; all of them are **m warriors**. H1475
Jer 10: 6 are great, and your name is **m** in power. H1524
Jer 11:16 with the roar of a **m** storm he will set it H1524
Jer 20:11 But the LORD is with me like a **m** warrior H6883
Jer 21: 5 hand and a **m** arm in furious anger H2617
Jer 25:32 a **m** storm is rising from the ends of the H1524
Jer 32:18 Great and **m** God, whose name is the H1475
Jer 32:19 are your purposes and **m** are your deeds. H8041
Jer 32:21 by a **m** hand and an outstretched arm H2617
Jer 48:17 'How broken is the **m** scepter, how broken H6437
Eze 7:24 I will put an end to the pride of the **m** H6434
Eze 17:17 Pharaoh with his **m** army and great horde H1524
Eze 20:33 reign over you with a **m** hand and an H2617
Eze 20:34 with a **m** hand and an outstretched arm H2617
Eze 32:12 hordes to fall by the swords of **m men**— H1475
Eze 32:18 both her and the daughters of **m** nations, H129
Eze 32:21 realm of the dead the **m** leaders will say of H446
Eze 38:15 riding on horses, a great horde, a **m** army. H8041
Eze 39:18 eat the flesh of **m men** and drink the H1475
Eze 39:20 **m men** and soldiers of every kind H1475
Da 2:10 however great and **m**, has ever asked A10718
Da 4: 3 great are his signs, how **m** his wonders! A10768
Da 4:30 by my **m** power and for the glory of my A10278
Da 8:24 He will destroy *those who* are **m**, the holy H6786
Da 9:15 of Egypt with a **m** hand and who made H2617
Da 11: 3 Then a **m** king will arise, who will rule H1475
Hos 8:10 away under the oppression of the **m** king. H8569
Joel 1: 6 my land, a **m** *army* without number H6786
Joel 2: 2 mountains a large and **m** army comes, H6786
Joel 2: 5 like a **m** army drawn up for battle. H6786
Joel 2:11 **m** is the army that obeys his H6786
Zep 1:14 the **M** Warrior shouts his battle cry. NDT
Zep 3:17 God is with you, the **M Warrior** who saves. H1475
Zec 4: 7 "What are you, **m** mountain? Before H1524
Mt 26:64 right hand *of* the **M One** and coming on G1539
Mk 14:62 right hand *of* the **M One** and coming on G1539
Lk 1:49 the **M** *One* has done great things for G1543
Lk 1:51 He has performed **m deeds** with his arm G3197

Lk 22:69 be seated at the right hand *of* the **m** God." *G1539*
Ac 13:17 with **m** power he led them out of that *G5734*
Eph 1:19 That power is the same as the **m** strength *G3197*
Eph 6:10 be strong in the Lord and in his **m** power. *G3197*
1Pe 5: 6 under God's **m** hand, that he may lift *G3193*
Rev 5: 2 And I saw a **m** angel proclaiming in a *G2708*
Rev 6:15 the rich, the **m**, and everyone else *G2708*
Rev 10: 1 I saw another **m** angel coming down *G2708*
Rev 18: 2 With a **m** voice he shouted: " 'Fallen *G2708*
Rev 18: 8 for **m** is the Lord God who judges her. *G2708*
Rev 18:10 great city, you **m** city of Babylon! *G2708*
Rev 18:21 Then a **m** angel picked up a boulder the *G2708*
Rev 19:18 generals, and the **m**, of horses and their *G2708*

MIGRATION (1)

Jer 8: 7 the thrush observe the time of their **m**. H995

MIGRON (2)

1Sa 14: 2 Gibeah under a pomegranate tree in **M**. H4491
Isa 10:28 they pass through **M**; they store supplies H4491

MIJAMIN (4)

1Ch 24: 9 the fifth to Malkijah, the sixth to **M**, H4785
Ezr 10:25 Malkijah, **M**, Eleazar, Malkijah and H4785
Ne 10: 7 Meshullam, Abijah, **M**, H4785
Ne 12: 5 **M**, Moadiah, Bilgah, H4785

MIKA (5)

2Sa 9:12 had a young son named **M**, H4775
1Ch 9:15 Galal and Mattaniah son of **M**, the son of H4775
Ne 10:11 **M**, Rehob, Hashabiah, H4775
Ne 11:17 Mattaniah son of **M**, the son of Zabdi, the H4777
Ne 11:22 the son of Mattaniah, the son of **M**. H4775

MIKLOTH (4)

1Ch 8:32 **M**, who was the father of Shimeah H5235
1Ch 9:37 Ahio, Zechariah and **M**. H5235
1Ch 9:38 **M** was the father of Shimeam. They too H5235
1Ch 27: 4 Ahohite; **M** was the leader of his division. H5235

MIKMASH (11)

1Sa 13: 2 were with him at **M** and in the hill country H4825
1Sa 13: 5 They went up and camped at **M**, east of H4825
1Sa 13:11 that the Philistines were assembling at **M**, H4825
1Sa 13:16 while the Philistines camped at **M**. H4825
1Sa 13:23 Philistines had gone out to the pass at **M**. H4825
1Sa 14: 5 One cliff stood to the north toward **M**, the H4825
1Sa 14:31 down the Philistines from **M** to Aijalon, H4825
Ezr 2:27 of **M** 122 H4820
Ne 7:31 of **M** 122 H4820
Ne 11:31 of the Benjamites from Geba lived in **M**, H4825
Isa 10:28 through Migron; they store supplies at **M**. H4825

MIKMETHATH (2)

Jos 16: 6 From **M** on the north it curved eastward to H4826
Jos 17: 7 from Asher to **M** east of Shechem. H4826

MIKNEIAH (2)

1Ch 15:18 Eliphelehu, **M**, Obed-Edom and Jeiel H5240
1Ch 15:21 Eliphelehu, **M**, Obed-Edom, Jeiel and H5240

MIKRI (1)

1Ch 9: 8 the son of **M**; and Meshullam son H4840

MIKTAM (6)

Ps 16: T A **m** of David. H4846
Ps 56: T A **m**. When the Philistines had H4846
Ps 57: T A **m**. When he had fled from H4846
Ps 58: T tune of "Do Not Destroy." Of David. A **m**. H4846
Ps 59: T A **m**. When Saul had sent men H4846
Ps 60: T of the Covenant." A **m** of David. H4846

MILALAI (1)

Ne 12:36 Shemaiah, Azarel, **M**, Gilalai, Maai H4912

MILCAH (NIV84) MILKAH

MILCH (KJV) CALVED, FEMALE

MILDEW (5)

Dt 28:22 with blight and **m**, which will plague you H3766
1Ki 8:37 the land, or blight or **m**, locusts or H3766
2Ch 6:28 the land, or blight or **m**, locusts or H3766
Am 4: 9 destroying them with blight and **m**. H3766
Hag 2:17 hands with blight, **m** and hail, yet you did H3766

MILE (1) [MILES]

Mt 5:41 If anyone forces you to go one **m**, go with *G3627*

MILES (4) [MILE]

Mt 5:41 you to go one mile, go with them two **m**. NDT
Lk 24:13 **about seven m** from *G600+5084+2008*
Jn 6:19 rowed about **three** or four **m**, *G5084+1633+4297*
[Jn 6:19 rowed about three or **four m**, *G5084+5558*]
Jn 11:18 was **less than two m** from *G6055+5084+1278*

MILETUS (3)

Ac 20:15 on the following day arrived at **M**. *G3626*
Ac 20:17 From **M**, Paul sent to Ephesus for the *G3626*
2Ti 4:20 in Corinth, and I left Trophimus sick in **M**. *G3626*

MILITARY (16)

Jos 5: 4 Egypt—all the men of **m age**—died in the H4878
Jos 5: 6 men who were of **m age** when they left H4878
2Sa 5: 2 *one who* **led** Israel **on** their **m campaigns** H3655+2256+995
2Sa 11:10 you just come from a **m campaign**? H2006
2Sa 20: 8 Joab was wearing his **m tunic**, and H4496+4230
1Ki 22:45 the things he achieved and his **m exploits**, H4309
2Ki 14:28 all he did, and his **m** achievements H4309
1Ch 5:18 44,760 men **ready for m service**— H3655+7372
1Ch 11: 2 *one who* **led** Israel **on** their **m campaigns** H3655+2256+995
2Ch 25: 5 thousand men **fit for m service**, H3655+7372
2Ch 32: 3 his officials and **m staff** about blocking off H1475
2Ch 32: 6 He appointed **m** officers over the people H4878
2Ch 33:14 He stationed **m** commanders in all the H2657
Est 1: 3 The **m leaders** *of* Persia and Media, the H2657
Mk 6:21 officials and **m commanders** and the *G5941*
Ac 25:23 with the **high-ranking m officers** and the *G5941*

MILK (47)

Ge 18: 8 some curds and **m** and the calf that had H2692
Ge 49:12 darker than wine, his teeth whiter than **m**. H2692
Ex 3: 8 a land flowing with **m** and honey—the H2692
Ex 3:17 a land flowing with **m** and honey. H2692
Ex 13: 5 a land flowing with **m** and honey—you H2692
Ex 23:19 not cook a young goat in its mother's **m**. H2692
Ex 33: 3 up to the land flowing with **m** and honey. H2692
Ex 34:26 not cook a young goat in its mother's **m**." H2692
Lev 20:24 a land flowing with **m** and honey. H2692
Nu 13:27 and it does flow with **m** and honey! H2692
Nu 14: 8 a land flowing with **m** and honey, and H2692
Nu 16:13 a land flowing with **m** and honey to kill us H2692
Nu 16:14 a land flowing with **m** and honey or given H2692
Dt 6: 3 in a land flowing with **m** and honey, H2692
Dt 11: 9 a land flowing with **m** and honey. H2692
Dt 14:21 not cook a young goat in its mother's **m**. H2692
Dt 26: 9 a land flowing with **m** and honey; H2692
Dt 26:15 a land flowing with **m** and honey. H2692
Dt 27: 3 a land flowing with **m** and honey, just as H2692
Dt 31:20 into the land flowing with **m** and honey, H2692
Dt 32:14 with curds and **m** *from* herd and flock and H2692
Jos 5: 6 give us, a land flowing with **m** and honey. H2692
Jdg 4:19 She opened a skin of **m**, gave him a drink H2692
Jdg 5:25 she gave him **m**; in a bowl fit for H2692
Jdg 5:25 fit for nobles she brought him **curdled m**. H2772
2Sa 17:29 cheese from cows' **m** for David and his NDT
Job 10:10 not pour me out like **m** and curdle me like H2692
Pr 27:27 plenty of goats' **m** to feed your family H2692
SS 4:11 **m** and honey are under your tongue. H2692
SS 5: 1 I have drunk my wine and my **m**. H2692
SS 5:12 streams, washed in **m**, mounted like H2692
Isa 7:22 of the abundance of the **m** they give, H2692
Isa 28: 9 To children weaned from their **m**, to those H2692
Isa 55: 1 buy wine and **m** without money and H2692
Isa 60:16 You will drink the **m** *of* nations and be H2692
Jer 11: 5 them a land flowing with **m** and honey'— H2692
Jer 32:22 a land flowing with **m** and honey. H2692
La 4: 7 brighter than snow and whiter than **m**, H2692
Eze 20: 6 a land flowing with **m** and honey, the H2692
Eze 20:15 a land flowing with **m** and honey, the H2692
Eze 25: 4 they will eat your fruit and drink your **m**. H2692
Joel 3:18 the hills will flow with **m**; all the H2692
1Co 3: 2 I gave you **m**, not solid food, for you were *G1128*
1Co 9: 7 tends a flock and does not drink the **m**? *G1128*
Heb 5:12 You need **m**, not solid food! *G1128*
Heb 5:13 Anyone who lives on **m**, being still an *G1128*
1Pe 2: 2 crave pure spiritual **m**, so that by it you *G1128*

MILKAH (11)

Ge 11:29 the name of Nahor's wife was **M**; she H4894
Ge 11:29 of Haran, the father of both **M** and Iskah. H4894
Ge 22:20 Abraham was told, "**M** is also a mother H4894
Ge 22:23 **M** bore these eight sons to Abraham's H4894
Ge 24:15 was the daughter of Bethuel son of **M**, H4894
Ge 24:24 of Bethuel, the son that **M** bore to Nahor." H4894
Ge 24:47 son of Nahor, whom **M** bore to him. H4894
Nu 26:33 Mahlah, Noah, Hoglah, **M** and Tirzah.) H4894
Nu 27: 1 Mahlah, Noah, Hoglah, **M** and Tirzah. H4894
Nu 36:11 Hoglah, **M** and Noah—married their H4894
Jos 17: 3 Mahlah, Noah, Hoglah, **M** and Tirzah. H4894

MILL (4)

Ex 11: 5 who is at her **hand m**, and all the H8160
Nu 11: 8 ground it in a **hand m** or crushed it in a H8160
Joel 1:18 The herds **m about** because they have no H1003
Mt 24:41 women will be grinding with a **hand m**; *G3685*

MILLET (1)

Eze 4: 9 beans and lentils, **m** and spelt; put them H1893

MILLION (2)

1Ch 21: 5 Israel there were *one* **m** one hundred H547+547
1Ch 22:14 talents of gold, a **m** talents of silver H547+547

MILLO See BETH MILLO

MILLSTONE (8) [STONE]

Jdg 9:53 dropped an upper **m** on his head and H7115
2Sa 11:21 woman drop an upper **m** on him from the H7115
Job 41:24 chest is hard as rock, hard as a lower **m**. H7115
Mt 18: 6 to have a **large m** hung around *G3685+3948*
Mk 9:42 them if a **large m** were hung *G3685+3948*
Lk 17: 2 the sea with a **m** tied around their *G3345+3683*
Rev 18:21 the size of a large **m** and threw it into the *G3684*
Rev 18:22 The sound *of* a **m** will never be heard in *G3685*

MILLSTONES (4) [STONE]

Dt 24: 6 Do not take a **pair of m**—not even the H8160
Isa 47: 2 Take **m** and grind flour; take off your veil H8160
Jer 25:10 the sound of **m** and the light of the lamp. H8160
La 5:13 Young men toil at the **m**; boys stagger H3218

MINA (5) [MINAS]

Eze 45:12 shekels plus fifteen shekels equal one **m**. H4949
Lk 19:16 'Sir, your **m** has earned ten more. *G3641*
Lk 19:18 'Sir, your **m** has earned five more. *G3641*
Lk 19:20 here is your **m**; I have kept it laid *G3641*
Lk 19:24 'Take his **m** away from him and give it to *G3641*

MINAS (6) [MINA]

1Ki 10:17 with three **m** of gold in each shield. H4949
Ezr 2:69 5,000 **m** of silver and 100 priestly H4949
Ne 7:71 darics of gold and 2,200 **m** of silver. H4949
Ne 7:72 2,000 **m** of silver and 67 garments for H4949
Lk 19:13 ten of his servants and gave them ten **m**. *G3641*
Lk 19:24 him and give it to the one who has ten **m**. *G3641*

MIND (126) [DOUBLE-MINDED, LIKE-MINDED, MINDFUL, MINDS, MINDSET]

Ge 37:11 but his father **kept** the matter **in m**. H9068
Ge 41: 8 In the morning his **m** was troubled, so he H8120
Ge 45:20 Never **m** about your belongings, because H2571
Ex 16:29 **Bear in m** that the LORD has given you the H8011
Nu 23:19 that *he should* **change** *his* **m**. H5714
Dt 28:28 madness, blindness and confusion of **m**. H4222
Dt 28:65 the LORD will give you an anxious **m**, H4213
Dt 29: 4 has not given you a **m** that understands H4213
1Sa 2:35 according to what is in my heart and **m**. H5883
1Sa 14: 7 "Do all that you have in **m**," his H4222
1Sa 15:29 of Israel does not lie or **change** *his* **m**; H5714
1Sa 15:29 that *he should* **change** *his* **m**. H5714
2Sa 7: 3 "Whatever you have in **m**, go ahead and H4222
2Sa 19:14 so that they were all **of one m**. H3869+285+408
2Sa 19:19 May the king put it out of his **m**. H4213
1Ki 10: 2 with him about all that she had on her **m**. H4222
2Ki 10:30 to the house of Ahab all I had in **m** to do, H4222
1Ch 12:38 were also of one **m** to make David king. H4213
1Ch 17: 2 to David, "Whatever you have in **m**, do it, H4222
1Ch 28: 9 devotion and with a willing **m**, H5883
1Ch 28:12 Spirit had put in his **m** for the courts of the NDT
2Ch 7:11 out all he had in **m** to do in the temple of H4213
2Ch 9: 1 with him about all she had on her **m**. H4222
2Ch 30:12 give them unity of **m** to carry out what the H4213
Ne 5: 7 them in my **m** and then accused H4213
Job 10:13 and I know that this was **in** your **m**: H6640
Job 12: 3 But I have a **m** as well as you; I am not H4222
Ps 15: 4 and *does* not **change** *their* **m**; H4614
Ps 26: 2 try me, examine my heart and my **m**; H4213
Ps 64: 6 Surely the human **m** and heart are H7931
Ps 83: 5 *With one* **m** they plot together; they form H4213
Ps 110: 4 LORD has sworn and *will* not **change** *his* **m**: H5714
Pr 12: 8 one with a warped **m** is despised. H4213
Pr 23:33 your **m** will imagine confusing things. H4213
Ecc 1:13 I applied my **m** to study and to explore by H4213
Ecc 2: 3 my **m** still guiding me with wisdom. H4213
Ecc 7:25 So I turned my **m** to understand, to H4213
Ecc 8: 9 as I applied my **m** to everything done H4213
Ecc 8:16 When I applied my **m** to know wisdom H4213
Isa 10: 7 this is not what he **has in m**; his H3108+4222
Isa 16: 3 "**Make up** *your* **m**," Moab says H995+6783
Isa 46: 8 "Remember this, **keep** it **in m**, take it to H899
Isa 65:17 be remembered, nor will they come to **m**. H4213
Jer 7:31 I did not command, nor did it enter my **m**. H4213
Jer 11:20 righteously and test the heart and **m**, H4000
Jer 17:10 LORD search the heart and examine the **m**, H4000
Jer 19: 5 mention, nor did it enter my **m**. H4213
Jer 20:12 the righteous and probe the heart and **m**, H4000
Jer 32:35 did it enter my **m**—that they should do H4213
Jer 44:21 call to **m** the incense burned H4213
Jer 51:50 a distant land, and call to **m** Jerusalem." H4222
La 3:21 Yet this I **call to m** and H8740+448+4213
Eze 11: 5 I know what is going through your **m**. H8120
Eze 20:32 what you have in **m** will never happen. H8120
Eze 21:24 you people *have* **brought to m** your guilt H2349
Eze 38:10 will come into your **m** and you will devise H4222
Da 2: 1 his **m** was troubled and he could not H8120
Da 2:28 passed through your **m** as you were lying A10646
Da 2:29 your **m** turned to things to come A10669
Da 2:30 what went through your **m**. A10669+10381
Da 4: 5 that passed through my **m** terrified me. A10646
Da 4:16 Let his **m** be changed from that of a man A10381
Da 4:16 let him be given the **m** *of* an animal, A10381
Da 5:12 to have a keen **m** and knowledge and A10658
Da 5:21 people and given the **m** of an animal; A10381
Da 7: 1 passed through his **m** as he was lying in A10646
Da 7: 4 the **m** *of* a human was given to it. A10381
Da 7:15 that passed through my **m** disturbed me. A10646
Da 10:12 that you set your **m** to gain understanding H4213
Mt 1:19 *he* **had in m** to divorce her quietly. *G1089*
Mt 16:23 *you do* not **have in m** the concerns of God, *G5858*
Mt 21:29 later *he* **changed** *his* **m** and went. *G3564*
Mt 22:37 with all your soul and with all your **m**. *G1379*
Mk 3:21 for they said, "*He is* **out of** *his* **m**. *G2014*
Mk 5:15 dressed and **in** *his* **right m**; and they were *G5404*
Mk 8:33 "*You do* not **have in m** the concerns of *G5858*
Mk 12:30 soul and with all your **m** and with all your *G1379*
Lk 1: 3 With this in **m**, since I myself have carefully NDT
Lk 8:35 dressed and **in** *his* **right m**; and they were *G5404*

Lk 10:27 with all your strength and with all your m'; G1379
Lk 21:14 But make up your m not to worry G5502+1877+3836+2840
Jn 6:6 he already had in m what he was G3857
Jn 15:18 you, keep in m that it hated me first. G1182
Ac 4:32 All the believers were one in heart and m. G6034
Ac 12:15 "You're out of your m," they told her G3419
Ac 26:24 "You are out of your m, Paul! G3419
Ro 1:28 so God gave them over to a depraved m G3808
Ro 7:23 the law of my m and making me a G3808
Ro 7:25 I myself in my m am a slave to God's law G3808
Ro 8:6 The m governed by the flesh is death, but G5859
Ro 8:6 the m governed by the Spirit is life G5859
Ro 8:7 The m governed by the flesh is hostile to G5859
Ro 8:27 our hearts knows the m of the Spirit, G5859
Ro 11:34 "Who has known the m of the Lord? Or G3808
Ro 12:2 transformed by the renewing of your m. G3808
Ro 14:5 should be fully convinced in their own m. G3808
Ro 14:13 make up your m not to put any stumbling G3212
Ro 15:5 you the same attitude of m toward each G5858
Ro 15:6 so that with one m and one voice you may G3924
1Co 1:10 you be perfectly united in m and thought. G3808
1Co 2:9 what no human m has conceived"— G2840
1Co 2:16 "Who has known the m of the Lord so as G3808
1Co 2:16 But we have the m of Christ. G3808
1Co 7:37 who has settled the matter in his own m, G2840
1Co 7:37 who has made up his m not to marry the G2840
1Co 14:14 my spirit prays, but my m is unfruitful. G3808
1Co 14:23 they not say that you are out of your m? G3419
2Co 2:1 So I made up my m that I would not make G3212
2Co 2:13 I still had no peace of m, because I did G4460
2Co 5:13 If we are "out of our m," as some say, it is G2014
2Co 5:13 is for God; if we are in our right m, it is G5404
2Co 11:23 (I am out of my m to talk like this. G4196
2Co 13:11 one another, be of one m, live in peace. G5858
Eph 6:18 With this in m, be alert and always G1650+899
Php 2:2 being one in spirit and of one m. G5858
Php 3:19 Their m is set on earthly things. G5858
Php 4:2 Syntyche to be of the same m in the Lord. G5858
Col 2:18 with idle notions by their unspiritual m. G3808
1Th 4:11 You should m your own business and G4556
2Th 1:11 With this in m, we constantly pray for you AIT
1Ti 6:5 friction between people of corrupt m, G3808
Heb 7:21 Lord has sworn and will not change his m: G3564
1Pe 4:7 be alert and of sober m so that you may G3768
1Pe 5:8 Be alert and of sober m. Your enemy the G1213
2Pe 3:15 Bear in m that our Lord's patience means G2451
Rev 17:9 "This calls for a m with wisdom. G3808

MINDFUL (4) [MIND]

Ps 8:4 what is mankind that you are m of them H2349
Ps 26:3 always been m of your H4200+5584+6524
Lk 1:48 for he has been m of the humble state of G2098
Heb 2:6 "What is mankind that you are m of them G3630

MINDS (35) [MIND]

Ex 13:17 they might change their m and return to H5714
Ex 14:5 changed their m about them and said, H4222
Dt 11:18 these words of mine in your hearts and m; H5883
Job 17:4 You have closed their m to understanding; H4213
Ps 7:9 righteous God who probes m and hearts. H4000
Ecc 2:23 even at night their m do not rest. H4213
Isa 26:3 peace those whose m are steadfast, H3671
Isa 44:18 their m closed so they cannot H4213
Jer 3:16 never enter their m or be remembered; H4213
Jer 14:14 the delusions of their own m. H4213
Jer 23:16 They speak visions from their own m, not H4213
Jer 23:26 prophesy the delusions of their own m? H4213
Jer 31:33 put my law in their m and write it on their H7931
Jer 34:11 afterward they changed their m and took H8740
Lk 24:38 why do doubts rise in your m? G2840
Lk 24:45 Then he opened their m so they could G3808
Ac 14:2 poisoned their m against the brothers G6034
Ac 15:24 troubling your m by what they said. G6034
Ac 28:6 they changed their m and said he was a G3554
Ro 8:5 to the flesh have their m set on what the G5858
Ro 8:5 the Spirit have their m set on what the Spirit NDT
Ro 16:18 they deceive the m of naive people. G2840
2Co 3:14 But their m were made dull, for to this day G3784
2Co 4:4 age has blinded the m of unbelievers, G3784
2Co 11:3 your m may somehow be led astray from G3784
Eph 4:23 to be made new in the attitude of your m; G3808
Php 4:7 your hearts and your m in Christ Jesus. G3784
Col 1:21 were enemies in your m because of your G1379
Col 3:2 Set your m on things above, not on earthly G5858
2Ti 3:8 They are men of depraved m, who, as far G3808
Titus 1:15 both their m and consciences are G3808
Heb 8:10 put my laws in their m and write them on G1379
Heb 10:16 and I will write them on their m. G1379
1Pe 1:13 with m that are alert and fully sober G1379
Rev 2:23 that I am he who searches hearts and m, G3752

MINDSET (1) [MIND]

Php 2:5 another, have the same m as Christ Jesus: G5858

MINE (72) [I]

Ge 13:8 between your herders and m, for we H3276
Ge 24:8 you will be released from this oath of m. H3276
Ge 29:15 "Just because you are a relative of m H3276
Ge 31:37 Put it here in front of your relatives and m H3276
Ge 31:43 All you see is m. Yet what can I do H4200+3276
Ge 31:43 I do today about these daughters of m, H3276
Ge 37:7 gathered around m and bowed down to it H3276
Ge 48:5 to you here will be reckoned as m; H4200+3276
Ge 48:5 Ephraim and Manasseh will be m H4200+3276
Ge 48:5 be mine, just as Reuben and Simeon are m. NDT
Ex 10:1 perform these signs of m among them H3276
Ex 19:5 Although the whole earth is m, H4200+3276
Ex 22:9 'This is m,' both parties are to H2085
Lev 25:23 the land is m and you reside in H4200+3276
Nu 3:12 The Levites are m, H4200+3276
Nu 3:13 all the firstborn are m. When I H4200+3276
Nu 3:13 They are to be m. I am the LORD." H4200+3276
Nu 3:45 The Levites are to be m. I am the H4200+3276
Nu 8:14 and the Levites will be m. H4200+3276
Nu 8:17 whether human or animal, is m. H4200+3276
Dt 11:18 Fix these words of m in your hearts and H3276
Dt 32:35 It is m to avenge; I will repay. H4200+3276
2Sa 14:30 Joab's field is next to m, and he has H3276
1Ki 2:15 he said, "the kingdom was m. H4200+3276
1Ki 3:22 dead one is yours; the living one is m." H3276
1Ki 3:23 Your son is dead and m is alive.'" H3276
1Ki 8:59 And may these words of m, which I have H3276
1Ki 20:3 'Your silver and gold are m, and the H4200+3276
1Ki 20:3 of your wives and children are m. H4200+3276
Job 7:15 death, rather than this body of m. H3276
Job 15:6 condemns you, not m; your own lips testify H638
Job 28:1 There is a m for silver and a place where H4604
Ps 50:10 every animal of the forest is m H4200+3276
Ps 50:11 and the insects in the fields are m. H6643+3276
Ps 50:12 the world is m, and all that is in H4200+3276
Ps 59:3 against me for no offense or sin of m, H3276
Ps 60:7 Gilead is m, and Manasseh is H4200+3276
Ps 60:7 and Manasseh is m; Ephraim is my H4200+3276
Ps 108:8 Gilead is m, Manasseh is mine H4200+3276
Ps 108:8 Manasseh is m; Ephraim is my H4200+3276
Pr 8:14 and sound judgment are m; H4200+3276
Ecc 7:15 meaningless life of m I have seen both of H3276
SS 2:16 My beloved is m and I am his; he H4200+3276
SS 6:3 my beloved's and my beloved is m; H4200+3276
SS 8:12 own vineyard is m to give; H8611+4200+3276
Isa 30:1 who carry out plans that are not m, H4946+5761
Isa 43:1 you by name; you are m. H4200+3276
Jer 44:28 word will stand—m or theirs. H4946+5761
Eze 16:8 and you became m. H4200+3276
Eze 23:4 They were m and gave birth to H4200+3276
Eze 23:5 prostitution while she was still m; H9393+3276
Eze 29:9 you said, "The Nile is m; I made it," H4200+3276
Mic 7:1 What misery is m! I am like one H4200+3276
Hag 2:8 'The silver is m and the gold is H4200+3276
Hag 2:8 silver is mine and the gold is m, H4200+3276
Mt 7:24 hears these words of m and puts them G1609
Mt 7:26 hears these words of m and does not put G1609
Mt 20:21 one of these two sons of m may sit at your G1609
Mt 25:40 least of these brothers and sisters of m, G1609
Lk 11:6 a friend of m on a journey has come to me G1609
Lk 15:24 For this son of m was dead and is alive G1609
Lk 19:27 But those enemies of m who did not want G1609
Lk 22:21 going to betray me is with m on the table. G1609
Jn 3:29 That joy is m, and it is now G1847
Jn 12:30 "This voice was for your benefit, not m. G1609
Jn 16:15 All that belongs to the Father is m. That is G1847
Jn 17:10 all you have is m. And glory has G1847
Ac 20:34 that these hands of m have supplied my G3836
Ro 12:19 "It is m to avenge; I will repay," G1609+1847
1Co 5:12 What business is it of m to judge those G1609
2Co 11:10 of Achaia will stop this boasting of m. G1609
Heb 10:30 who said, "It is m to avenge; I will G1609+1847

MINGLE (1) [MINGLED]

Ps 102:9 as my food and m my drink with tears H5007

MINGLED (2) [MINGLE]

Ezr 9:2 and have m the holy race with the H6843
Ps 106:35 but they m with the nations and adopted H6843

MINIAMIN (2) [MINIAMIN'S]

2Ch 31:15 M, Jeshua, Shemaiah, Amariah and H4975
Ne 12:41 Maaseiah, M, Micaiah, Elioenai H4975

MINIAMIN'S (1) [MINIAMIN]

Ne 12:17 of Abijah's, Zikri; of M and of Moadiah's H4975

MINISH, MINISHED (KJV) DECREASED, REDUCED

MINISTER (41) [MINISTERED, MINISTERING, MINISTERS, MINISTRY]

Ex 28:43 approach the altar to m in the Holy Place, H9250
Ex 29:30 tent of meeting to m in the Holy Place is H9250
Ex 30:20 the altar to m by presenting a food H9250
Nu 16:9 before the community and m to them? H9250
Nu 18:2 you and your sons m before the tent of the NDT
Dt 10:8 before the LORD to m and to pronounce H9250
Dt 18:5 tribes to stand and m in the LORD's name H9250
Dt 18:7 he may m in the name of the LORD his God H9250
Dt 21:5 has chosen them to m and to pronounce H9250
1Sa 2:30 of your family would m before me forever. H2143
1Sa 2:35 and they will m before my anointed one H2143
1Ch 15:2 of the LORD and to m before him forever." H9250
1Ch 16:4 some of the Levites to m before the ark of H9250
1Ch 16:37 covenant of the LORD to m there regularly, H9250
1Ch 16:38 his sixty-eight associates to m with them. NDT
1Ch 23:13 to m before him and to pronounce H9250
2Ch 29:11 to m before him and to burn incense." H9250
2Ch 31:2 offerings, to m, to give thanks and to H9250
Ps 101:6 whose walk is blameless will m to me. H9250
Ps 134:1 of the LORD who m by night in the house H6641
Ps 135:2 you who m in the house of the LORD, in H6641
Isa 56:6 bind themselves to the LORD to m to him, H9250
Jer 33:22 the Levites who m before me as H9250
Eze 40:46 draw near to the LORD to m before him." H9250
Eze 42:14 behind the garments in which they m, H9250
Eze 43:19 who come near to m before me, declares H9250
Eze 44:15 are to come near to m before me; they H9250
Eze 44:16 my table to m before me and serve me H9250
Eze 44:27 of the sanctuary to m in the sanctuary, H9250
Eze 45:4 who m in the sanctuary and who draw H9250
Eze 45:4 who draw near to m before the LORD. H9250
Eze 46:24 where those who m at the temple H9250
Joel 1:9 mourning, those who m before the LORD. H9250
Joel 1:13 wail, you who m before the altar. H9250
Joel 1:13 sackcloth, you who m before my God; for H9250
Joel 2:17 the priests, who m before the LORD, weep H9250
Ro 15:16 to be a m of Christ Jesus to the Gentiles G3313
Col 1:7 who is a faithful m of Christ on our behalf G1356
Col 4:7 a faithful m and fellow servant in the Lord. G1356
1Ti 4:6 you will be a good m of Christ Jesus G1356
Heb 13:10 from which those who m at the tabernacle G3302

MINISTERED (3) [MINISTER]

1Sa 2:11 the boy m before the LORD under Eli H9250
1Sa 3:1 The boy Samuel m before the LORD under H9250
1Ch 6:32 They m with music before the tabernacle H9250

MINISTERING (23) [MINISTER]

Ex 35:19 garments worn for m in the sanctuary— H9250
Ex 39:1 woven garments for m in the sanctuary. H9250
Ex 39:26 the hem of the robe to be worn for m, H9250
Ex 39:41 garments worn for m in the sanctuary, H9250
Nu 3:31 the articles of the sanctuary used in m H9250
Nu 4:12 articles used for m in the sanctuary, H9251+9250
Nu 4:14 it all the utensils used for m at the altar, H9250
Dt 17:12 who stands m there to the LORD your God H9250
Jdg 20:28 of Eleazar, the son of Aaron, m before it.) H6641
1Sa 2:18 Samuel was m before the LORD—a boy H9250
1Ch 9:13 responsible for m in the house of God. H6275
1Ch 24:3 divisions for their appointed order of m. H6275
1Ch 24:19 appointed order of m when they entered H6275
1Ch 26:12 had duties for m in the temple of the LORD, H9250
Ezr 2:63 food until there was a priest m with the H6641
Ne 7:65 should be a priest m with the Urim and H6641
Ne 10:36 house of our God, to the priests m there. H9250
Ne 10:39 the sanctuary and for the m priests, H9250
Ne 12:44 pleased with the m priests and Levites. H6641
Jer 33:21 the Levites who are priests m before me— H9250
Eze 44:17 garment while m at the gates of the H9250
Eze 44:19 clothes they have been m in and are to H9250
Heb 1:14 Are not all angels m spirits sent to serve G3312

MINISTERS (3) [MINISTER]

Ex 28:35 Aaron must wear it when he m. The sound H9250
Isa 61:6 you will be named m of our God. H9250
2Co 3:6 made us competent as m of a new G1356

MINISTRATION (KJV) DISTRIBUTION, MINISTRY, SERVICE

MINISTRY (23) [MINISTER]

1Ch 25:1 Jeduthun for the m of prophesying, H6275
1Ch 25:6 harps, for the m at the house of God. H6275
Lk 3:23 thirty years old when he began his m. G806
Ac 1:17 one of our number and shared in our m." G1355
Ac 1:25 to take over this apostolic m, which Judas G1355
Ac 6:2 us to neglect the m of the word of God in NDT
Ac 6:4 attention to prayer and the m of the word." G1355
Ac 8:21 You have no part or share in this m G3364
Ac 21:19 done among the Gentiles through his m. G1355
Ro 11:13 to the Gentiles, I take pride in my m G1355
2Co 3:3 the result of our m, written not with ink G1354
2Co 3:7 Now if the m that brought death, which G1355
2Co 3:8 will not the m of the Spirit be even more G1355
2Co 3:9 If the m that brought condemnation was G1355
2Co 3:9 more glorious is the m that brings G1355
2Co 4:1 through God's mercy we have this m, G1355
2Co 5:18 Christ and gave us the m of reconciliation: G1355
2Co 6:3 so that our m will not be discredited. G1355
Col 4:17 you complete the m you have received in G1355
2Ti 4:5 discharge all the duties of your m. G1355
2Ti 4:11 because he is helpful to me in my m. G1355
Heb 8:6 But in fact the m Jesus has received is as G3311
Heb 9:6 into the outer room to carry on their m. G3301

MINNI (1)

Jer 51:27 Ararat, M and Ashkenaz H4973

MINNITH (2)

Jdg 11:33 towns from Aroer to the vicinity of M, H4976
Eze 27:17 wheat from M and confections, H4976

MINSTREL, MINSTRELS (KJV) HARPIST, PEOPLE PLAYING PIPES

MINT (2)

Mt 23:23 a tenth of your spices—m, dill and cumin. G2455
Lk 11:42 because you give God a tenth of your m G2455

MINUS (1)

2Co 11:24 from the Jews the forty lashes m one. G4123

MIRACLE (3) [MIRACLES, MIRACULOUS, MIRACULOUSLY]

Ex 7: 9 'Perform a **m**,' then say to Aaron, H4603
Mk 9:39 no one who does a **m** in my name can in G1539
Jn 7:21 to them, "I did one **m**, and you are all G2240

MIRACLES (27) [MIRACLE]

1Ch 16:12 he has done, his **m**, and the judgments H4603
Ne 9:17 to remember the **m** you performed among H7098
Job 5: 9 be fathomed, **m** that cannot be counted. H7098
Job 9:10 be fathomed, **m** that cannot be counted. H7098
Ps 77:11 I will remember your **m** of long ago. H7099
Ps 77:14 You are the God who performs **m**; you H7099
Ps 78:12 He did **m** in the sight of their ancestors in H7099
Ps 105: 5 he has done, his **m**, and the judgments H4603
Ps 106: 7 they gave no thought to your **m**; they did H7098
Ps 106:22 **m** in the land of Ham and awesome H7098
Mt 7:22 in your name perform many **m**? G1539
Mt 11:20 in which most *of* his **m** had been G1539
Mt 11:21 For if the **m** that were performed in you G1539
Mt 11:23 For if the **m** that were performed in you G1539
Mt 13:58 he did not do many **m** there because of G1539
Mk 6: 2 What are these **remarkable m** he is G1539
Mk 6: 5 He could not do any **m** there, except lay G1539
Lk 10:13 For if the **m** that were performed in you G1539
Lk 19:37 in loud voices for all the **m** they had seen: G1539
Ac 2:22 a man accredited by God to you *by* **m**, G1539
Ac 8:13 by the great signs and **m** he saw. G1539
Ac 19:11 God did extraordinary **m** through Paul, G1539
1Co 12:28 third teachers, then **m**, then gifts of G1539
1Co 12:29 Are all teachers? Do all **work m**? G1539
2Co 12:12 apostle, including signs, wonders and **m**. G1539
Gal 3: 5 his Spirit and work **m** among you by the G1539
Heb 2: 4 wonders and various **m**, and by gifts of G1539

MIRACULOUS (7) [MIRACLE]

2Ch 32:24 answered him and gave him a **m sign**. H4603
2Ch 32:31 ask him about the **m sign** that had H4603
Da 4: 2 you about the **m signs** and wonders that A10084
Mt 13:54 get this wisdom and these **m powers**?" G1539
Mt 14: 2 That is why **m powers** are at work in him." G1539
Mk 6:14 that is why **m powers** are at work in G1539
1Co 12:10 to another **m powers**, to another G1920+1539

MIRACULOUSLY (1) [MIRACLE]

Ac 4:22 For the man who was **m** healed was over G4956

MIRE (4) [MIRY]

Ps 40: 2 out of the mud and **m**; he set my feet on H3431
Ps 69:14 Rescue me from the **m**, do not let me sink; H3226
Isa 57:20 whose waves cast up **m** and mud. H8347
Mic 7:10 trampled underfoot like **m** *in* the streets. H3226

MIRIAM (12) [MIRIAM'S]

Ex 15:20 Then **M** the prophet, Aaron's sister, took a H5319
Ex 15:21 **M** sang to them: "Sing to the LORD, for he H5319
Nu 12: 1 **M** and Aaron began to talk against Moses H5319
Nu 12: 4 to Moses, Aaron and **M**, "Come out to the H5319
Nu 12: 5 to the tent and summoned Aaron and **M**. H5319
Nu 12:15 So **M** was confined outside the camp for H5319
Nu 20: 1 There **M** died and was buried. H5319
Nu 26:59 she bore Aaron, Moses and their sister **M**. H5319
Dt 24: 9 your God did to **M** along the way after H5319
1Ch 4:17 One of Mered's wives gave birth to **M** H5319
1Ch 6: 3 Moses and **M**. The sons of Aaron: H5319
Mic 6: 4 Moses to lead you, also Aaron and **M**. H5319

MIRIAM'S (1) [MIRIAM]

Nu 12:10 above the tent, **M** *skin* was leprous—it H5319

MIRMAH (1)

1Ch 8:10 Sakia and **M**. These were his sons H5328

MIRROR (3) [MIRRORS]

Job 37:18 out the skies, hard as a **m** *of* cast bronze? H8023
1Co 13:12 For now we see only a reflection as in a **m** G2269
Jas 1:23 like someone who looks at his face in a **m** G2269

MIRRORS (2) [MIRROR]

Ex 38: 8 stand from the **m** *of* the women who H5262
Isa 3:23 **m**, and the linen garments and tiaras H1663

MIRTH (1)

Job 20: 5 that the **m** *of* the wicked is brief, the joy of H8265

MIRY (2) [MIRE]

Ps 69: 2 I sink in the **m** depths, where there is no H3431
Ps 140:10 into the fire, into **m pits**, never to rise. H4549

MISCARRIED (1) [MISCARRY]

Ge 31:38 Your sheep and goats *have* not **m**, nor H8897

MISCARRIES (1) [MISCARRY]

Nu 5:22 your abdomen swells or your womb **m**." H5877

MISCARRY (5) [MISCARRIED, MISCARRIES]

Ex 23:26 none will **m** or be barren in your land H8897
Nu 5:21 makes your womb **m** and your abdomen H5877
Nu 5:27 abdomen will swell and her womb *will* **m**, H5877
Job 21:10 to breed; their cows calve and *do* not **m**. H8897
Hos 9:14 Give them wombs *that* **m** and breasts that H8897

MISCHIEF, MISCHIEFS (KJV) ASSAULT, CALAMITIES, DESTRUCTION, EVIL (INTENT), HARM, INJURY, MALICE, MISERY, PUNISHMENT, RUIN, SCHEMES, TROUBLE, WICKED

MISCHIEF (1)

Ps 140: 9 may the **m** *of* their lips engulf them. H6662

MISDEEDS (2)

Ps 99: 8 though you punished their **m**. H6613
Ro 8:13 Spirit you put to death the **m** of the body, G4552

MISDEMEANOR (1)

Ac 18:14 a complaint about some **m** or serious crime, G93

MISERABLE (4) [MISERY]

Nu 21: 5 And we detest this **m** food!" H7848
Job 16: 2 like these; you are **m** comforters, all of H6662
Ecc 4: 8 This too is meaningless—a **m** business! H8273
Gal 4: 9 turning back to those weak and **m** forces? G4777

MISERY (26) [MISERABLE]

Ge 16:11 Ishmael, for the LORD has heard of your **m**. H6715
Ge 29:32 "It is because the LORD has seen my **m**. H6715
Ge 44:29 my gray head down to the grave in **m**. H8288
Ge 44:34 not let me see the **m** that would come on H8273
Ex 3: 7 indeed seen the **m** *of* my people in Egypt. H6715
Ex 3:17 you up out of your **m** *in* Egypt into the H6715
Ex 4:31 about them and had seen their **m**, H6715
Nu 23:21 is seen in Jacob, no **m** observed in Israel. H6662
Dt 26: 7 the LORD heard our voice and saw our **m**, H6715
Jdg 10:16 And he could bear Israel's **m** no longer. H6662
1Sa 1:11 on your servant's **m** and remember me, H6715
2Sa 16:12 will look upon my **m** and restore to me his H6715
Job 3:20 "Why is light given to *those in* **m**, and life H6664
Job 6: 2 weighed and all my **m** be placed on the H2095
Job 7: 3 nights of **m** have been assigned to H6662
Job 9:18 breath but would overwhelm me with **m**. H4936
Job 20:22 the full force of **m** will come upon him. H6664
Ps 44:24 face and forget our **m** and oppression? H6715
Ps 56: 8 Record my **m**; list my tears on your scroll H5654
Ps 94:20 a throne that brings on **m** by its decrees? H6662
Pr 31: 7 poverty and remember their **m** no more. H6662
Ecc 8: 6 a person may be weighed down *by* **m**. H8288
Hos 5:15 in their **m** they will earnestly seek me." H7639
Mic 7: 1 **What m** is mine! I am like one who gathers H518
Ro 3:16 ruin and **m** mark their ways, G5416
Jas 5: 1 wail because of the **m** that is coming on G5416

MISFORTUNE (9)

Nu 23:21 "No **m** is seen in Jacob, no misery H224
Ru 1:21 the Almighty *has* **brought m** upon me." H8317
1Ch 7:23 because there had been **m** in his family. H8288
Job 12: 5 have contempt for **m** as the fate of those H7085
Job 31:29 at my enemy's **m** or gloated over the H7085
Ecc 2:21 This too is meaningless and a great **m**. H8288
Ecc 5:14 wealth lost through *some* **m**, so H6721+8273
Isa 65:23 will they bear children doomed to **m** H988
Ob 12 over your brother in the day of his **m**, H5798

MISHAEL (8)

Ex 6:22 The sons of Uzziel were **M**, Elzaphan and H4792
Lev 10: 4 Moses summoned **M** and Elzaphan, sons H4792
Ne 8: 4 on his left were Pedaiah, **M**, Malkijah, H4792
Da 1: 6 Daniel, Hananiah, **M** and Azariah. H4792
Da 1: 7 Shadrach; to **M**, Meshach; and to H4792
Da 1:11 over Daniel, Hananiah, **M** and Azariah, H4792
Da 1:19 Hananiah, **M** and Azariah; so they H4792
Da 2:17 to his friends Hananiah, **M** and Azariah. A10414

MISHAL (2)

Jos 19:26 Amad and **M**. On the west the H5398
Jos 21:30 from the tribe of Asher, **M**, Abdon, H5398

MISHAM (1)

1Ch 8:12 **M**, Shemed (who built Ono and Lod H5471

MISHMA (4)

Ge 25:14 **M**, Dumah, Massa, H5462
1Ch 1:30 **M**, Dumah, Massa, Hadad, Tema, H5462
1Ch 4:25 Mibsam his son and **M** his son. H5462
1Ch 4:26 The descendants of **M**: Hammuel his son H5462

MISHMANNAH (1)

1Ch 12:10 **M** the fourth, Jeremiah the fifth, H5459

MISHPAT See EN MISHPAT

MISHRAITES (1)

1Ch 2:53 Shumathites and **M**. From these H5490

MISLEAD (6) [MISLEADING, MISLEADS, MISLED]

2Ki 4:16 man of God, don't **m** your servant! H3941
2Ch 32:15 Hezekiah deceive you and **m** you like this. H6077
Pr 24:28 cause—*would you* use your lips to **m**? H7331
Isa 9:16 Those who guide this people **m** them H9494
Isa 36:18 "*Do* not **let** Hezekiah **m** you when he says, H6077
Isa 47:10 knowledge **m** you when you say to H8740

MISLEADING (4) [MISLEAD]

2Ki 18:32 to Hezekiah, for *he is* **m** you when he says H6077
2Ch 32:11 king of Assyria,' *he is* **m** you, to let you H6077
La 2:14 they gave you were false and **m**. H4505
Da 2: 9 to tell me **m** and wicked things, A10343

MISLEADS (2) [MISLEAD]

Isa 44:20 a deluded heart **m** him; he cannot save H5742
Rev 2:20 By her teaching *she* **m** my servants into G4414

MISLED (2) [MISLEAD]

Jer 38:22 " '*They* **m** you and overcame you—those H6077
1Co 15:33 *Do* not *be* **m**: "Bad company corrupts G4414

MISPAR (1)

Ezr 2: 2 Mordecai, Bilshan, **M**, Bigvai, Rehum and H5032

MISPERETH (1)

Ne 7: 7 Mordecai, Bilshan, **M**, Bigvai, Nehum H5033

MISREPHOTH MAIM (2)

Jos 11: 8 Greater Sidon, to **M**, and to the H5387
Jos 13: 6 regions from Lebanon to **M**, H5387

MISS (2) [MISSED, MISSES, MISSING]

Jdg 20:16 could sling a stone at a hair and not **m**. H2627
Pr 19: 2 how much more *will* hasty feet **m the way**! H2627

MISSED (3) [MISS]

1Sa 20:18 *You will* **be m**, because your seat will be H7212
Jer 3:16 be remembered; *it will* not *be* **m**, nor will H7212
Jer 46:17 a loud noise; *he has* **m** his opportunity. H6296

MISSES (1) [MISS]

1Sa 20: 6 If your father **m** me **at all**, tell him H7212+7212

MISSING (14) [MISS]

Nu 31:49 under our command, and not one *is* **m**. H7212
Jdg 21: 3 Why *should* one tribe *be* **m** from Israel H7212
1Sa 25: 7 were at Carmel nothing of theirs *was* **m**. H7212
1Sa 25:15 in the fields near them nothing *was* **m**. H7212
1Sa 25:21 wilderness so that nothing of his *was* **m**. H7212
1Sa 30:19 Nothing *was* **m**: young or old, boy or girl H6372
2Sa 2:30 nineteen of David's men **were found m**. H7212
1Ki 20:39 If *he is* **m**, it will be your life for his H7212+7212
2Ki 10:19 See that no one *is* **m**, because I am going H7212
Job 5:24 stock of your property and **find** nothing **m**. H2627
SS 6: 6 Each has its twin, not one of them is **m**. H8891
Isa 34:16 None of these *will be* **m**, not one will lack H6372
Isa 40:26 mighty strength, not one of them *is* **m**. H6372
Jer 23: 4 terrified, nor *will any* **be m**," declares the H7212

MISSION (9) [MISSIONS]

Jos 22: 3 have carried out the **m** the LORD your God H5466
1Sa 15:18 And he sent you on a **m**, saying, 'Go and H2006
1Sa 15:20 "I went on the **m** the LORD assigned me H2006
1Sa 18: 5 **Whatever** *m* Saul sent him on, David was so AIT
1Sa 21: 2 "The king sent me *on a* **m** and said to me, H1821
1Sa 21: 2 anything about the **m** I am sending you H1821
1Sa 21: 8 because the king's **m** was urgent. H1821
Isa 48:15 bring him, and he will succeed in his **m**. H2006
Ac 12:25 Barnabas and Saul had finished their **m**, G1355

MISSIONS (1) [MISSION]

1Sa 21: 5 are holy even on **m** that are not holy. H2006

MIST (5) [MISTS]

Isa 44:22 like a cloud, your sins like the **morning m**. H6727
Hos 6: 4 Your love is like the morning **m**, like the H6727
Hos 13: 3 Therefore they will be like the morning **m** H6727
Ac 13:11 Immediately **m** and darkness came over G944
Jas 4:14 You are a **m** that appears for a little while G874

MISTAKE (5) [MISTAKEN]

Ge 43:12 mouths of your sacks. Perhaps it was a **m**. H5405
Lev 22:14 a sacred offering by **m** must make H8705
Jdg 9:36 **m** the shadows of the mountains **for** H8011+3869
Ecc 5: 6 the temple messenger, "My vow was a **m**." H8705
Jer 42:20 that *you* **made a fatal m** when H9494+928+5883

MISTAKEN (1) [MISTAKE]

Mk 12:27 but of the living. *You are* badly **m**!" G4414

MISTREAT (9) [MISTREATED, MISTREATING]

Ge 31:50 If *you* **m** my daughters or if you take any H6700
Ex 22:21 "*Do* not **m** or oppress a foreigner, for you H3561
Lev 19:33 among you in your land, *do* not **m** them. H3561
1Sa 25: 7 were with us, *we did* not **m** them, and the H4007
1Sa 25:15 They *did* not **m** *us*, and the whole time H4007
Jer 38:19 me over to them and *they will* **m** me." H6618
Eze 22:29 the poor and needy and **m** the foreigner, H6943
Lk 6:28 who curse you, pray for those *who* **m** you. G2092
Ac 14: 5 their leaders, *to* **m** them and stone them. G5614

MISTREATED (12) [MISTREAT]

Ge 15:13 that they will be enslaved and **m** there. H6700
Ge 16: 6 Then Sarai **m** Hagar; so she fled from H6700
Nu 20:15 The Egyptians **m** us and our ancestors H8317
Dt 26: 6 But the Egyptians **m** us and made us suffer H8317
Jer 13:22 skirts have been torn off and your body **m**. H2803
Eze 22: 7 the foreigner and **m** the fatherless and H3561
Mt 22: 6 his servants, **m** them and killed them. G5614
Ac 7: 6 and they will be enslaved and **m**. G2808
Ac 7:24 He saw one of them *being* **m** by an Egyptian G92
Heb 11:25 He chose *to be* **m along with** the people G5156
Heb 11:37 goatskins, destitute, persecuted and **m**— G2807
Heb 13: 3 those *who are* **m** as if you yourselves G2807

MISTREATING (2) [MISTREAT]

Eze 18:17 withholds his hand **from** *m* the poor and AIT

Ac 7:27 "But the *man who was* **m** the other pushed G92

MISTRESS (8)

Ge 16: 4 pregnant, she began to despise her **m**. H1485
Ge 16: 8 "I'm running away from my **m** Sarai," H1485
Ge 16: 9 "Go back to your **m** and submit to her." H1485
2Ki 5: 3 She said to her **m**, "If only my master H1485
Ps 123: 2 a female slave look to the hand of her **m**, H1485
Pr 30:23 a servant who displaces her **m**. H1485
Isa 24: 2 his servant, for the **m** as for her servant H1485
Na 3: 4 alluring, the **m** *of* sorceries, who enslaved H1266

MISTS (1) [MIST]

2Pe 2:17 without water and **m** driven by a storm. G3920

MISUNDERSTAND (1)

Dt 32:27 lest the adversary **m** and say, 'Our hand H5795

MISUSE (3) [MISUSES]

Ex 20: 7 "*You shall* not **m** the H5951+4200+2021+8736
Dt 5:11 "*You shall* not **m** the H5951+4200+2021+8736
Ps 139:20 **m** your name. H5951+4200+2021+8736

MISUSES (2) [MISUSE]

Ex 20: 7 who **m** his name. H5951+4200+2021+8736
Dt 5:11 *who* **m** his name. H5951+4200+2021+8736

MITE, MITES (KJV) PENNY, SMALL COPPER COINS

MITHKAH (2)

Nu 33:28 They left Terah and camped at **M**. H5520
Nu 33:29 They left **M** and camped at Hashmonah. H5520

MITHNITE (1)

1Ch 11:43 Hanan son of Maakah, Joshaphat the **M**, H5512

MITHREDATH (2)

Ezr 1: 8 had them brought by **M** the treasurer, H5521
Ezr 4: 7 Bishlam, **M**, Tabeel and the rest of his H5521

MITRE (KJV) TURBAN

MITYLENE (1)

Ac 20:14 we took him aboard and went on to **M**. G3639

MIXED (54) [MIXTURE]

Ex 29: 2 without yeast and with olive oil **m in**, H1176
Ex 29:23 one **thick loaf** *with* olive oil *m in*, and one AIT
Ex 29:40 of the finest flour **m** with a quarter of a H1176
Lev 2: 4 with olive oil **m in** or thin loaves H1176
Lev 2: 5 to be made of the finest flour **m** with oil, H1176
Lev 7:10 offering, whether **m** with olive oil or dry H1176
Lev 7:12 without yeast and with olive oil **m in**, H1176
Lev 7:12 flour well-kneaded and with oil **m in**. H1176
Lev 8:26 one **thick loaf** *with* olive oil *m in*, and one AIT
Lev 9: 4 with a grain offering **m** with olive oil. H1176
Lev 14:10 the finest flour **m** with olive oil *for* a grain H1176
Lev 14:21 of the finest flour **m** with olive oil for a H1176
Lev 23:13 of the finest flour **m** with olive oil— H1176
Nu 6:15 thick loaves with olive oil **m in**, and thin H1176
Nu 7:13 with the finest flour **m** with olive oil as a H1176
Nu 7:19 with the finest flour **m** with olive oil as a H1176
Nu 7:25 with the finest flour **m** with olive oil as a H1176
Nu 7:31 with the finest flour **m** with olive oil as a H1176
Nu 7:37 with the finest flour **m** with olive oil as a H1176
Nu 7:43 with the finest flour **m** with olive oil as a H1176
Nu 7:49 with the finest flour **m** with olive oil as a H1176
Nu 7:55 with the finest flour **m** with olive oil as a H1176
Nu 7:61 with the finest flour **m** with olive oil as a H1176
Nu 7:67 with the finest flour **m** with olive oil as a H1176
Nu 7:73 with the finest flour **m** with olive oil as a H1176
Nu 7:79 with the finest flour **m** with olive oil as a H1176
Nu 8: 8 offering of the finest flour **m** with olive oil; H1176
Nu 15: 4 of the finest flour **m** with a quarter of a H1176
Nu 15: 6 of the finest flour **m** with a third of a hin H1176
Nu 15: 9 of the finest flour **m** with half a hin of H1176
Nu 28: 5 of the finest flour **m** with a quarter of a H1176
Nu 28: 9 ephah of the finest flour **m** with olive oil. H1176
Nu 28:12 of an ephah of the finest flour **m** with oil; H1176
Nu 28:12 of an ephah of the finest flour **m** with oil; H1176
Nu 28:13 of an ephah of the finest flour **m** with oil. H1176
Nu 28:20 of an ephah of the finest flour **m** with oil; H1176
Nu 28:28 of an ephah of the finest flour **m** with oil; H1176
Nu 29: 3 ephah of the finest flour **m** with olive oil; H1176
Nu 29: 9 of an ephah of the finest flour **m** with oil; H1176
Nu 29:14 of an ephah of the finest flour **m** with oil; H1176
Ps 75: 8 a cup full of foaming wine **m with spices**; H5008
Pr 9: 2 has prepared her meat and **m** her wine; H5007
Pr 9: 5 eat my food and drink the wine *I have* **m**. H5007
Pr 23:30 who go to sample **bowls of m wine**. H4932
Isa 65:11 fill **bowls of m wine** for Destiny, H4932
Da 2:41 even as you saw iron **m** with clay. A10569
Da 2:43 as you saw the iron **m** with baked clay, A10569
Mt 13:33 that a woman took and **m** into about sixty G1606
Mt 27:34 Jesus wine to drink, **m** with gall; but after G3502
Mk 15:23 Then they offered him wine **m with myrrh** G5046
Lk 13: 1 whose blood Pilate *had* **m** with their G3502
Lk 13:21 a woman took and **m into** about sixty G1606
Jude 23 show mercy, **m with** fear—hating even G1877
Rev 8: 7 there came hail and fire **m** with blood, G3502

MIXES (2) [MIXTURE]

Da 2:43 any more than iron **m** with clay. A10569
Hos 7: 8 "Ephraim **m** with the nations; Ephraim is H1176

MIXING (4) [MIXTURE]

1Ch 9:30 priests **took care of m** the spices H8379+5351
1Ch 23:29 the baking and the **m**, and all H8057
Isa 5:22 drinking wine and champions at **m** drinks, H5007
Eze 24:10 the meat well, **m in** the spices; and let H8379

MIXTURE (2) [MIXED, MIXES, MIXING, WELL-MIXED]

Da 2:43 people will be a **m** and will not remain A10569
Jn 19:39 brought a **m** of myrrh and aloes, G3623

MIZAR (1)

Ps 42: 6 the heights of Hermon—from Mount **M**. H5204

MIZPAH (43) [RAMATH MIZPAH]

Ge 31:49 It was also called **M**, because he said H5207
Jos 11: 3 Hivites below Hermon in the region of **M**. H5207
Jos 11: 8 to the Valley of **M** on the east, until H5207
Jos 15:38 **M**, Joktheel, H5206
Jos 18:26 **M**, Kephirah, Mozah, H5206
Jdg 10:17 Israelites assembled and camped at **M**. H5207
Jdg 11:11 all his words before the LORD in **M**. H5207
Jdg 11:29 passed through **M** *of* Gilead, and from H5206
Jdg 11:34 Jephthah returned to his home in **M**, H5207
Jdg 20: 1 one and assembled before the LORD in **M**. H5207
Jdg 20: 3 that the Israelites had gone up to **M**.) H5207
Jdg 21: 1 The men of Israel had taken an oath at **M**: H5207
Jdg 21: 5 before the LORD at **M** was to be put to H5207
Jdg 21: 8 failed to assemble before the LORD at **M**?" H5207
1Sa 7: 5 "Assemble all Israel at **M**, and I will H5207
1Sa 7: 6 When they had assembled at **M**, they H5207
1Sa 7: 6 was serving as leader of Israel at **M**. H5207
1Sa 7: 7 heard that Israel had assembled at **M**, H5207
1Sa 7:11 of Israel rushed out of **M** and pursued the H5207
1Sa 7:12 stone and set it up between **M** and Shen. H5207
1Sa 7:16 on a circuit from Bethel to Gilgal to **M**, H5207
1Sa 10:17 the people of Israel to the LORD at **M** H5207
1Sa 22: 3 David went to **M** *in* Moab and said to H5206
1Ki 15:22 built up Geba in Benjamin, and also **M**. H5207
2Ki 25:23 they came to Gedaliah at **M**—Ishmael H5207
2Ki 25:25 the Babylonians who were with him at **M**. H5207
2Ch 16: 6 With them he built up Geba and **M**. H5207
Ne 3: 7 were made by men from Gibeon and **M**— H5207
Ne 3:15 of Kol-Hozeh, ruler of the district of **M**. H5207
Ne 3:19 of Jeshua, ruler of **M**, repaired another H5207
Jer 40: 6 son of Ahikam at **M** and stayed with him H5207
Jer 40: 8 they came to Gedaliah at **M**—Ishmael son H5207
Jer 40:10 I myself will stay at **M** to represent you H5207
Jer 40:12 to Gedaliah at **M**, from all the H5207
Jer 40:13 the open country came to Gedaliah at **M** H5207
Jer 40:15 of Kareah said privately to Gedaliah in **M**, H5207
Jer 41: 1 ten men to Gedaliah son of Ahikam at **M**. H5207
Jer 41: 3 of Judah who were with Gedaliah at **M**, H5207
Jer 41: 6 went out from **M** to meet them, H5207
Jer 41:10 the rest of the people who were in **M**— H5207
Jer 41:14 taken captive at **M** turned and went over H5207
Jer 41:16 all the people of **M** who had survived, H5207
Hos 5: 1 You have been a snare at **M**, a net spread H5207

MIZRAIM See ABEL MIZRAIM

MIZZAH (3)

Ge 36:13 Shammah and **M**. These were H4645
Ge 36:17 Shammah and **M**. These were the H4645
1Ch 1:37 Nahath, Zerah, Shammah and **M**. H4645

MNASON (1)

Ac 21:16 us and brought us *to* the home of **M**, G3643

MOAB (149) [MOAB'S, MOABITE, MOABITES]

Ge 19:37 she named him **M**; he is the father of H4565
Ge 36:35 who defeated Midian in the country of **M** H4565
Ex 15:15 the leaders of **M** will be seized with H4566
Nu 21:11 that faces **M** toward the sunrise. H4566
Nu 21:13 The Arnon is the border of **M**, between H4566
Nu 21:13 of Moab, between **M** and the Amorites. H4566
Nu 21:15 of Ar and lie along the border of **M**." H4566
Nu 21:20 to the valley in **M** where the top of H8441+4566
Nu 21:26 the former king of **M** and had taken from H4566
Nu 21:28 It consumed Ar of **M**, the citizens of H4566
Nu 21:29 Woe to you, **M**! You are destroyed H4566
Nu 22: 1 to the plains of **M** and camped along the H4566
Nu 22: 3 **M** was terrified because there were so H4566
Nu 22: 3 **M** was filled with dread because of the H4566
Nu 22: 4 who was king of **M** at that time, H4566
Nu 22: 7 The elders of **M** and Midian left, taking H4566
Nu 22:10 of Zippor, king of **M**, sent me this H4566
Nu 23: 7 the king of **M** from the eastern mountains. H4566
Nu 24:17 He will crush the foreheads of **M**, the H4566
Nu 26: 3 So on the plains of **M** by the Jordan across H4566
Nu 26:63 on the plains of **M** by the Jordan across H4566
Nu 31:12 at their camp on the plains of **M**, H4566
Nu 33:44 at Iye Abarim, on the border of **M**. H4566
Nu 33:48 on the plains of **M** by the Jordan across H4566
Nu 33:49 on the plains of **M** they camped along the H4566
Nu 33:50 On the plains of **M** by the Jordan across H4566
Nu 35: 1 On the plains of **M** by the Jordan across H4566
Nu 36:13 on the plains of **M** by the Jordan across H4566
Dt 1: 5 East of the Jordan in the territory of **M** H4566
Dt 2: 8 traveled along the desert road of **M**. H4566
Dt 2:18 you are to pass by the region of **M** at Ar. H4566
Dt 29: 1 to make with the Israelites in **M**, H824+4566
Dt 32:49 Abarim Range to Mount Nebo in **M**, H824+4566
Dt 34: 1 from the plains of **M** to the top of Pisgah, H4566
Dt 34: 5 servant of the LORD died there in **M**, H824+4566
Dt 34: 6 He buried him in **M**, in the valley H824+4566
Dt 34: 8 Moses in the plains of **M** thirty days, H4566
Jos 13:32 was in the plains of **M** across the Jordan H4566
Jos 24: 9 of Zippor, the king of **M**, prepared to fight H4566
Jdg 3:12 gave Eglon king of **M** power over Israel. H4566
Jdg 3:14 to Eglon king of **M** for eighteen years. H4566
Jdg 3:15 sent him with tribute to Eglon king of **M**. H4566
Jdg 3:17 presented the tribute to Eglon king of **M**, H4566
Jdg 3:28 "for the LORD has given **M**, your enemy, H4566
Jdg 3:28 of the fords of the Jordan that led to **M**; H4566
Jdg 3:30 That day **M** was made subject to Israel H4566
Jdg 10: 6 of Sidon, the gods of **M**, the gods of the H4566
Jdg 11:15 not take the land of **M** or the land of the H4566
Jdg 11:17 They sent also to the king of **M**, and he H4566
Jdg 11:18 skirted the lands of Edom and **M**, passed H4566
Jdg 11:18 the eastern side of the country of **M**, H4566
Jdg 11:18 They did not enter the territory of **M**, for H4566
Jdg 11:25 than Balak son of Zippor, king of **M**? H4566
Ru 1: 1 to live for a while in the country of **M**. H4566
Ru 1: 2 they went to **M** and lived there. H8441+4566
Ru 1: 6 Naomi heard in **M** that the LORD H8441+4566
Ru 1:22 returned from **M** accompanied by H8441+4566
Ru 2: 6 came back from **M** with Naomi. H8441+4566
Ru 4: 3 who has come back from **M**, is H8441+4566
1Sa 12: 9 of the Philistines and the king of **M**, H4566
1Sa 14:47 **M**, the Ammonites, Edom, the kings of H4566
1Sa 22: 3 went to Mizpah in **M** and said to the king H4566
1Sa 22: 3 in Moab and said to the king of **M**, H4566
1Sa 22: 4 So he left them with the king of **M**, and H4566
2Sa 8:12 Edom and **M**, the Ammonites and the H4566
1Ki 11: 7 Chemosh the detestable god of **M**, H4566
2Ki 1: 1 Ahab's death, **M** rebelled against Israel. H4566
2Ki 3: 4 Now Mesha king of **M** raised sheep, and H4566
2Ki 3: 5 the king of **M** rebelled against the king of H4566
2Ki 3: 7 "The king of **M** has rebelled against me H4566
2Ki 3: 7 Will you go with me to fight against **M**?" H4566
2Ki 3:10 only to deliver us into the hands of **M**?" H4566
2Ki 3:13 together to deliver us into the hands of **M**." H4566
2Ki 3:18 he will also deliver **M** into your hands. H4566
2Ki 3:23 Now to the plunder, **M**!" H4566
2Ki 3:26 When the king of **M** saw that the battle H4566
2Ki 23:13 Chemosh the vile god of **M**, and for H4566
1Ch 1:46 who defeated Midian in the country of **M** H4566
1Ch 4:22 who ruled in **M** and Jashubi Lehem. H4566
1Ch 8: 8 to Shaharaim in **M** after he had H8441+4566
1Ch 18:11 Edom and **M**, the Ammonites and the H4566
2Ch 20:10 are men from Ammon, **M** and Mount Seir H4566
2Ch 20:22 men of Ammon and **M** and Mount Seir H4566
Ne 13:23 women from Ashdod, Ammon and **M**. H4567
Ps 60: 8 **M** is my washbasin, on Edom I toss my H4566
Ps 83: 6 the Ishmaelites, of **M** and the Hagrites, H4566
Ps 108: 9 **M** is my washbasin, on Edom I toss my H4566
Isa 11:14 They will subdue Edom and **M**, and the H4566
Isa 15: 1 A prophecy against **M**: Ar in Moab is H4566
Isa 15: 1 against Moab: Ar in **M** is ruined H4566
Isa 15: 1 Kir in **M** is ruined, destroyed in H4566
Isa 15: 2 to weep; **M** wails over Nebo and Medeba. H4566
Isa 15: 4 Therefore the armed men of **M** cry out H4566
Isa 15: 5 My heart cries out over **M**; her fugitives H4566
Isa 15: 8 Their outcry echoes along the border of **M**; H4566
Isa 15: 9 the fugitives of **M** and upon those who H4566
Isa 16: 2 so are the women of **M** at the fords of the H4566
Isa 16: 3 "Make up your mind," **M** says. "Render a NDT
Isa 16: 7 Moabites wail, they wail together for **M**. H4566
Isa 16:11 My heart laments for **M** like a harp, my H4566
Isa 16:12 When **M** appears at her high place, she H4566
Isa 16:13 LORD has already spoken concerning **M**. H4566
Isa 25:10 **M** will be trampled in their land as H4566
Jer 9:26 **M** and all who live in the wilderness in H4566
Jer 25:21 **M** and Ammon; H4566
Jer 27: 3 word to the kings of Edom, **M**, Ammon, H4566
Jer 40:11 When all the Jews in **M**, Ammon, Edom H4566
Jer 48: 1 Concerning **M**: This is what the LORD H4566
Jer 48: 2 **M** will be praised no more; in Heshbon H4566
Jer 48: 4 **M** will be broken; her little ones will cry H4566
Jer 48: 9 Put salt on **M**, for she will be laid waste H4566
Jer 48:11 "**M** has been at rest from youth, like wine H4566
Jer 48:13 Then **M** will be ashamed of Chemosh, as H4566
Jer 48:15 **M** will be destroyed and her towns H4566
Jer 48:16 "The fall of **M** is at hand; her calamity will H4566
Jer 48:18 one who destroys **M** will come up against H4566
Jer 48:20 **M** is disgraced, for she is shattered. H4566
Jer 48:20 by the Arnon that **M** is destroyed. H4566
Jer 48:24 to all the towns of **M**, far and near. H824+4566
Jer 48:26 Let **M** wallow in her vomit; let her be an H4566
Jer 48:28 dwell among the rocks, you who live in **M**. H4566
Jer 48:31 Therefore I wail over **M**, for all Moab I cry H4566
Jer 48:31 over Moab, for all **M** I cry out, I moan for H4566
Jer 48:33 gone from the orchards and fields of **M**. H4566
Jer 48:35 In **M** I will put an end to those who make H4566
Jer 48:36 my heart laments for **M** like the music of a H4566
Jer 48:38 On all the roofs in **M** and in the public H4566
Jer 48:38 I have broken **M** like a jar that no one H4566
Jer 48:39 How **M** turns her back in shame H4566
Jer 48:39 **M** has become an object of ridicule, an H4566
Jer 48:40 spreading its wings over **M**. H4566
Jer 48:42 **M** will be destroyed as a nation because H4566
Jer 48:43 you people of **M**," declares the LORD. H4566
Jer 48:44 I will bring on **M** the year of her H4566
Jer 48:45 it burns the foreheads of **M**, the skulls of H4566
Jer 48:46 Woe to you, **M**! The people of Chemosh H4566

Jer 48:47 restore the fortunes of **M** in days to come," H4566
Jer 48:47 Here ends the judgment on **M**. H4566
Eze 25: 8 'Because **M** and Seir said, "Look, Judah H4566
Eze 25: 9 therefore I will expose the flank of **M** H4566
Eze 25:10 I will give **M** along with the Ammonites H2023S
Eze 25:11 I will inflict punishment on **M**. H4566
Da 11:41 **M** and the leaders of Ammon will be H4566
Am 2: 1 "For three sins of **M**, even for four, I will H4566
Am 2: 2 I will send fire on **M** that will consume the H4566
Am 2: 2 **M** will go down in great tumult amid war H4566
Mic 6: 5 what Balak king of **M** plotted and what H4566
Zep 2: 8 heard the insults of **M** and the taunts of H4566
Zep 2: 9 "surely **M** will become like Sodom H4566

MOAB'S (7) [MOAB]

2Sa 23:20 He struck down **M** two mightiest warriors H4566
1Ch 11:22 He struck down **M** two mightiest warriors H4566
Isa 16: 6 We have heard of **M** pride—how great is H4566
Isa 16:14 **M** splendor and all her many people will H4566
Jer 48:25 **M** horn is cut off; her arm is broken," H4566
Jer 48:29 "We have heard of **M** pride—how great H4566
Jer 48:41 day the hearts of **M** warriors will be like H4566

MOABITE (21) [MOAB]

Nu 22: 8 So the **M** officials stayed with him H4566
Nu 22:14 So the **M** officials returned to Balak and H4566
Nu 22:21 his donkey and went with the **M** officials. H4566
Nu 22:36 to meet him at the **M** town on the Arnon H4566
Nu 23: 6 his offering, with all the **M** officials. H4566
Nu 23:17 beside his offering, with the **M** officials. H4566
Nu 25: 1 in sexual immorality with **M** women, H4566
Dt 23: 3 No Ammonite or **M** or any of their H4567
Ru 1: 4 They married **M** *women*, one named H4567
Ru 1:22 from Moab accompanied by Ruth the **M**, H4567
Ru 2: 2 And Ruth the **M** said to Naomi, "Let me H4567
Ru 2: 6 "She is the **M** who came back from Moab H4567
Ru 2:21 Then Ruth the **M** said, "He even said to H4567
Ru 4: 5 you also acquire Ruth the **M**, the dead H4567
Ru 4:10 I have also acquired Ruth the **M**, Mahlon's H4567
2Ki 13:20 Now **M** raiders used to enter the country H4566
2Ki 24: 2 **M** and Ammonite raiders against him to H4566
1Ch 11:46 the sons of Elnaam, Ithmah the **M**, H4567
2Ch 24:26 Jehozabad, son of Shimrith a **M** *woman*. H4567
Ne 13: 1 that no Ammonite or **M** should ever be H4567
Isa 16: 4 Let the **M** fugitives stay with you; be their H4566

MOABITES (19) [MOAB]

Ge 19:37 he is the father of the **M** of today. H4566
Nu 22: 4 The **M** said to the elders of Midian, "This H4566
Dt 2: 9 "Do not harass the **M** or provoke them to H4566
Dt 2:11 Rephaites, but the **M** called them Emites. H4567
Dt 2:29 live in Seir, and the **M**, who live in Ar, H4567
Jdg 3:29 struck down about ten thousand **M**, H408+4566
2Sa 8: 2 David also defeated the **M**. He made H4566
2Sa 8: 2 So the **M** became subject to David and H4566
1Ki 11: 1 Pharaoh's daughter—**M**, Ammonites, H4567
1Ki 11:33 Chemosh the god of the **M**, and Molek H4566
2Ki 3:21 Now all the **M** had heard that the kings H4566
2Ki 3:22 To the **M** across the way, the water looked H4566
2Ki 3:24 But when the **M** came to the camp of H4566
2Ki 3:24 invaded the land and slaughtered the **M**. H4566
1Ch 18: 2 David also defeated the **M**, and they H4566
2Ch 20: 1 the **M** and Ammonites with some H1201+4566
2Ch 20:23 The Ammonites and **M** rose up against H4566
Ezr 9: 1 Jebusites, Ammonites, **M**, Egyptians and H4567
Isa 16: 7 Therefore the **M** wail, they wail together H4566

MOADIAH (1) [MOADIAH'S]

Ne 12: 5 Mijamin, **M**, Bilgah, H5050

MOADIAH'S (1) [MOADIAH]

Ne 12:17 of Miniamin's and of **M**, Piltai; H4598

MOAN (7) [MOANED, MOANING]

Ps 90: 9 your wrath; we finish our years with a **m**. H2049
Isa 59:11 *we* **m** **mournfully** like doves. H2047+2047
Jer 48:31 *I* **m** for the people of Kir Hareseth. H2047
Eze 7:16 the valleys, they *will* all **m**, each for their H2159
Joel 1:18 How the cattle **m**! The herds mill about H634
Mic 1: 8 I will howl like a jackal and **m** like an owl. H65
Na 2: 7 Her female slaves **m** like doves and beat H5628

MOANED (1) [MOAN]

Isa 38:14 swift or thrush, *I* **m** like a mourning dove. H2047

MOANING (1) [MOAN]

Jer 31:18 "I have surely heard Ephraim's **m**: 'You H5653

MOB (6)

Eze 16:40 They will bring a **m** against you, who will H7736
Eze 23:46 Bring a **m** against them and give them H7736
Eze 23:47 The **m** will stone them and cut them down H7736
Jn 7:49 But this **m** that knows nothing of the law— *G4063*
Ac 17: 5 **formed a m** and started a riot in the city. *G4062*
Ac 21:35 the violence *of* the **m** was so great he had *G4063*

MOBILIZED (3)

Jdg 20:15 the Benjamites **m** twenty-six thousand H7212
2Ki 3: 6 set out from Samaria and **m** all Israel. H7212
2Ki 6:24 king of Aram **m** his entire army and H7695

MOCK (20) [MOCKED, MOCKER, MOCKERS, MOCKERY, MOCKING, MOCKS]

Job 11: 3 Will no one rebuke you when *you* **m**? H4352
Job 21: 3 I speak, and after I have spoken, **m** *on*. H4352
Job 22:19 rejoice; the innocent **m** them, saying, H4352
Job 30: 1 "But now *they* **m** me, men younger than I H8471
Job 30: 9 now those young men **m** me **in song**; H5593
Ps 22: 7 All who see me **m** me; they hurl insults H4352
Ps 69:12 Those who sit at the gate **m** me, and I am H8488
Ps 74:10 How long *will* the enemy **m** you, God H3070
Ps 74:22 remember how fools **m** you all day long. H3075
Ps 80: 6 to our neighbors, and our enemies **m** us. H4352
Ps 119:51 The arrogant **m** me unmercifully, but I do H4329
Pr 1:26 *I will* **m** when calamity overtakes you H4352
Pr 14: 9 Fools **m** *at* making amends for sin, but H4329
Isa 52: 5 those who rule them **m**," declares the H2147
La 3:14 people; they **m** me **in song** all day long. H5593
La 3:63 standing, they **m** me **in** their **songs**. H4947
Eze 22: 5 those who are far away *will* **m** you, H7840
Hab 1:10 They **m** kings and scoff at rulers. H7840
Mk 10:34 *who will* **m** him and spit on him, flog him *G1850*
Lk 18:32 *They will* **m** him, insult him and spit on *G1850*

MOCKED (16) [MOCK]

2Ch 36:16 But *they* **m** God's messengers, despised H4351
Ne 2:19 heard about it, *they* **m** and ridiculed us. H4352
Ps 35:16 the ungodly *they* **maliciously m**; H4352+4352
Ps 74:18 Remember how the enemy *has* **m** you H3070
Ps 89:50 how your servant has been **m**, how I bear H3075
Ps 89:51 *have* **m**, with which they have H3070
Ps 89:51 with which *they have* **m** every step of your H3070
Mt 20:19 to the Gentiles to *be* **m** and flogged and *G1850*
Mt 27:29 Then they knelt in front of him and **m** him. *G1850*
Mt 27:31 After *they had* **m** him, they took off the *G1850*
Mt 27:41 teachers of the law and the elders **m** him. *G1850*
Mk 15:20 And when *they had* **m** him, they took off *G1850*
Mk 15:31 teachers of the law **m** him among *G1850*
Lk 23:11 his soldiers ridiculed and **m** him. *G1850*
Lk 23:36 The soldiers also came up and **m** him *G1850*
Gal 6: 7 God cannot *be* **m**. A man reaps what *G3682*

MOCKER (10) [MOCK]

Pr 9: 7 Whoever corrects a **m** invites insults H4370
Pr 9:12 reward you; if *you are a* **m**, you alone will H4329
Pr 13: 1 a **m** does not respond to rebukes. H4370
Pr 14: 6 The **m** seeks wisdom and finds none, but H4370
Pr 19:25 Flog a **m**, and the simple will learn H4370
Pr 20: 1 Wine is a **m** and beer a brawler; whoever H4370
Pr 21:11 When a **m** is punished, the simple gain H4370
Pr 21:24 arrogant person—"**M**" is his name— H4370
Pr 22:10 Drive out the **m**, and out goes strife H4370
Pr 24: 9 of folly are sin, and people detest a **m**. H4370

MOCKERS (10) [MOCK]

Job 17: 2 Surely **m** surround me; my eyes must H2253
Ps 1: 1 sinners take or sit in the company of **m**, H4370
Pr 1:22 How long will **m** delight in mockery and H4370
Pr 3:34 He mocks **proud m** but shows favor to the H4370
Pr 9: 8 Do not rebuke **m** or they will hate you H4370
Pr 15:12 **M** resent correction, so they avoid the H4370
Pr 19:29 Penalties are prepared for **m**, and H4370
Pr 29: 8 **M** stir up a city, but the wise turn H408+4371
Isa 29:20 will vanish, the **m** will disappear, and all H4370
Hos 7: 5 with wine, and he joins hands with the **m**. H4372

MOCKERY (3) [MOCK]

Pr 1:22 will mockers delight in **m** and fools hate H4371
Jer 10:15 the objects of **m**; when their judgment H9511
Jer 51:18 the objects of **m**; when their judgment H9511

MOCKING (6) [MOCK]

Ge 21: 9 Egyptian had borne to Abraham *was* **m**, H7464
Isa 28:22 Now stop *your* **m**, or your chains will H4329
Isa 50: 6 did not hide my face from **m** and spitting. H4009
Isa 57: 4 Who *are you* **m**? At whom do you sneer H6695
Zep 2:10 insulting and **m** the people of the LORD H1540
Lk 22:63 guarding Jesus *began* **m** and beating him *G1850*

MOCKS (8) [MOCK]

2Ki 19:21 Daughter Zion despises you and **m** you. H4352
Job 9:23 *he* **m** the despair of the innocent. H4352
Pr 3:34 He **m** proud mockers but shows favor to H4329
Pr 17: 5 *Whoever* **m** the poor shows contempt H4352
Pr 19:28 A corrupt witness **m** *at* justice, and the H4329
Pr 30:17 "The eye *that* **m** a father, that scorns an H4352
Isa 37:22 Daughter Zion despises and **m** you. H4352
Jer 20: 7 ridiculed all day long; everyone **m** me. H4352

MODEL (3) [MODELS]

Php 3:17 just as you have us *as* a **m**, keep your *G5596*
1Th 1: 7 And so you became a **m** to all the *G5596*
2Th 3: 9 to offer ourselves *as* a **m** for you to imitate *G5596*

MODELS (2) [MODEL]

1Sa 6: 5 Make **m** *of* the tumors and of the rats that H7512
1Sa 6:11 the gold rats and the **m** *of* the tumors. H7512

MODERATION (KJV) GENTLENESS

MODESTLY (1) [MODESTY]

1Ti 2: 9 I also want the women to dress **m**, with *G3177*

MODESTY (1) [MODESTLY]

1Co 12:23 unpresentable are treated with special **m**, *G2362*

MOISTEN (1) [MOISTURE]

Eze 46:14 with a third of a hin of oil to **m** the flour. H8272

MOISTURE (3) [MOISTEN]

Job 36:28 the clouds **pour down** *their* **m** and H5688
Job 37:11 He loads the clouds with **m**; he scatters H8188
Lk 8: 6 plants withered because they had no **m**. *G2657*

MOLADAH (4)

Jos 15:26 Shema, **M**, H4579
Jos 19: 2 Beersheba (or Sheba), **M**, H4579
1Ch 4:28 They lived in Beersheba, **M**, Hazar Shual, H4579
Ne 11:26 in Jeshua, in **M**, in Beth Pelet, H4579

MOLD (21) [MOLDS]

Lev 13:47 fabric that is spoiled with a **defiling m**— H7669
Lev 13:49 it is a **defiling m** and must be shown to H7669
Lev 13:51 and if the **m** has spread in the fabric H5596
Lev 13:51 it is a persistent **defiling m**; the article is H7669
Lev 13:52 because the **defiling m** is persistent, the H7669
Lev 13:53 the **m** has not spread in the fabric H5596
Lev 13:55 if the **m** has not changed its H5596
Lev 13:56 the **m** has faded after the article has been H5596
Lev 13:57 it is a spreading **m**; whatever has the mold NDT
Lev 13:57 whatever has the **m** must be burned. H5596
Lev 13:58 that has been washed and is rid of the **m**, H5596
Lev 14:34 and I put a **spreading m** in a house H5596+7669
Lev 14:35 that looks like a **defiling m** in my house. H5596
Lev 14:36 before he goes in to examine the **m**, H5596
Lev 14:37 He is to examine the **m** on the walls, and H5596
Lev 14:39 If the **m** has spread on the walls, H5596
Lev 14:43 "If the **defiling m** reappears in the house H5596
Lev 14:44 if the **m** has spread in the house H5596
Lev 14:44 it is a persistent **defiling m**; the house is H7669
Lev 14:48 examine it and the **m** has not spread after H5596
Lev 14:48 because the **defiling m** is gone. H5596

MOLDED (1) [MOLDS]

Job 10: 9 Remember that *you* **m** me like clay. H6913

MOLDING (10) [MOLDS]

Ex 25:11 out, and make a gold **m** around it. H2425
Ex 25:24 pure gold and make a gold **m** around it. H2425
Ex 25:25 wide and put a gold **m** on the rim. H2425
Ex 30: 3 pure gold, and make a gold **m** around it. H2425
Ex 30: 4 two gold rings for the altar below the **m**— H2425
Ex 37: 2 out, and made a gold **m** around it. H2425
Ex 37:11 pure gold and made a gold **m** around it. H2425
Ex 37:12 wide and put a gold **m** on the rim. H2425
Ex 37:26 pure gold, and made a gold **m** around it. H2425
Ex 37:27 They made two gold rings below the **m** H2425

MOLDS (6) [MOLD, MOLDED, MOLDING, MOLDY]

Lev 13:59 concerning defiling **m** in woolen or linen H7669
Lev 14:55 for **defiling m** *in* fabric or in a house, H7669
Lev 14:57 **defiling skin diseases and defiling m.** H7669
1Ki 7:37 were all **cast** in the same **m** and were H4607
1Ki 7:46 them cast in clay **m** in the plain of the H5043
2Ch 4:17 them cast in clay **m** in the plain of the H6295

MOLDY (2) [MOLDS]

Jos 9: 5 bread of their food supply was dry and **m**. H5926
Jos 9:12 But now see how dry and **m** it is. H5926

MOLE (KJV) CHAMELEON

MOLEK (16)

Lev 18:21 any of your children to be sacrificed to **M**, H4891
Lev 20: 2 of his children to **M** is to be put to death. H4891
Lev 20: 3 by sacrificing his children to **M**, he has H4891
Lev 20: 4 one of his children to **M** and if they fail to H4891
Lev 20: 5 him in prostituting themselves to **M**. H4891
1Ki 11: 5 **M** the detestable god of the H4904
1Ki 11: 7 for **M** the detestable god of the H4891
1Ki 11:33 **M** the god of the Ammonites H4904
2Ki 23:10 their son or daughter in the fire to **M**. H4891
2Ki 23:13 for **M** the detestable god of the H4904
Isa 57: 9 You went to **M** with olive oil and H4891
Jer 32:35 to sacrifice their sons and daughters to **M**, H4891
Jer 49: 1 Why then has **M** taken possession of Gad? H4903
Jer 49: 3 inside the walls, for **M** will go into exile H4903
Zep 1: 5 by the LORD and who also swear by **M**, H4903
Ac 7:43 up the tabernacle *of* **M** and the star of *G3661*

MOLES (1)

Isa 2:20 throw away to the **m** and bats their idols H2923

MOLEST (1)

Est 7: 8 "*Will* he even **m** the queen while she is H3899

MOLID (1)

1Ch 2:29 Abihail, who bore him Ahban and **M**. H4582

MOLTEN (KJV) CAST, IDOL, IDOLS, METAL, OVERLAID

MOMENT (35) [MOMENT'S, MOMENTARY]

Ex 33: 5 If I were to go with you even for a **m**, H8092
Nu 4:20 holy things, even for a **m**, or they will die." H1180
2Ki 19: 3 come to the **m of birth** and there is no H5402
Ezr 9: 8 for a brief **m**, the LORD our God has H8092
Job 7:18 every morning and test them every **m**? H8092

Job 20: 5 the joy of the godless lasts but a m. H8092
Ps 2:12 his wrath can flare up in a m. H3869+5071
Ps 30: 5 For his anger lasts only a m, but his favor H8092
Pr 12:19 but a lying tongue lasts only a m. H8088
Isa 37: 3 come to the m of birth and there is no H5402
Isa 47: 9 Both of these will overtake you in a m, on H8092
Isa 54: 7 "For a brief m I abandoned you, but with H8092
Isa 54: 8 of anger I hid my face from you for a m, H8092
Isa 66: 8 a day or a nation be brought forth in a m? H7193
Isa 66: 9 Do I bring to the m of birth and not give H8689
Jer 4:20 my tents are destroyed, my shelter in a m. H8092
La 4: 6 was overthrown in a m without a H4017+8092
Eze 26:16 trembling every m, appalled at you. H8092
Eze 32:10 of them will tremble every m for his life. H8092
Mt 3:16 At that m heaven was opened, and G2779+2627
Mt 8:13 And his servant was healed at that m. G6052
Mt 9:22 And the woman was healed at that m. G6052
Mt 15:28 And her daughter was healed at that m. G6052
Mt 17:18 of the boy, and he was healed at that m. G6052
Mt 27:51 At that m the curtain of the temple G2779+2627
Mk 9:39 my name can in the next m say anything G5444
Lk 2:38 Coming up to them at that very m, she G6052
Lk 6:49 The m the torrent struck that house, it G2317
Jn 18:27 and at that m a rooster began to crow. G2311
Ac 5:10 At that m she fell down at his feet and G4202
Ac 16:18 At that m the spirit left her. G6052
Ac 22:13 And at that very m I was able to see him G6052
1Co 4:13 garbage of the world—right up to this m. G785
Gal 2: 5 We did not give in to them for a m, so that G6052
Rev 12: 4 devour her child the m he was born. G4020

MOMENT'S (1) [MOMENT]

Job 10:20 Turn away from me so I can have a m joy H5071

MOMENTARY (1) [MOMENT]

2Co 4:17 For our light and m troubles are achieving G4194

MONEY (121)

Ge 17:12 bought with m from a foreigner— H4084
Ge 17:13 in your household or bought with your m, H4084
Ge 17:23 in his household or bought with his m, H4084
Ge 42:35 they and their father saw the m pouches, H4084
Ge 47:14 collected all the m that was to be found H4084
Ge 47:15 When the m of the people of Egypt and H4084
Ge 47:15 die before your eyes? Our m is all gone." H4084
Ge 47:16 your livestock, since your m is gone." H4084
Ge 47:18 the fact that since our m is gone and our H4084
Ex 21:11 is to go free, without any payment of m. H4084
Ex 21:35 divide both the m and the dead animal H4084
Ex 22:15 the m paid for the hire covers the loss. H8510
Ex 22:25 "If you lend m to one of my people H4084
Ex 30:16 the atonement m from the Israelites H4084
Lev 22:11 But if a priest buys a slave with m, or if H4084
Lev 25:37 must not lend them m at interest or sell H4084
Nu 3:48 Give the m for the redemption of the H4084
Nu 3:49 the redemption m from those who H4084
Nu 3:51 gave the redemption m to Aaron and his H4084
Dt 18: 8 he has received m from the sale of family H4928
Dt 23:19 whether on m or food or anything else H4084
2Ki 5:26 the time to take m or to accept clothes— H4084
2Ki 12: 4 "Collect all the m that is brought as H4084
2Ki 12: 4 the LORD—the m collected in the census H4084
2Ki 12: 4 the m received from personal vows and H4084
2Ki 12: 4 vows and the m brought voluntarily H4084
2Ki 12: 5 every priest receive the m from one of the NDT
2Ki 12: 7 Take no more m from your treasurers, but H4084
2Ki 12: 8 collect any more m from the people and H4084
2Ki 12: 9 the chest all the m that was brought to H4084
2Ki 12:10 was a large amount of m in the chest, H4084
2Ki 12:10 counted the m that had been brought into H4084
2Ki 12:11 they gave the m to the men appointed to H4084
2Ki 12:13 The m brought into the temple was not H4084
2Ki 12:15 whom they gave the m to pay the workers, H4084
2Ki 12:16 The m from the guilt offerings and sin H4084
2Ki 15:20 Menahem exacted this m from Israel H4084
2Ki 22: 4 him get ready the m that has been H4084
2Ki 22: 7 not account for the m entrusted to them, H4084
2Ki 22: 9 have paid out the m that was in the H4084
2Ch 24: 5 collect the m due annually from all H4084
2Ch 24:11 saw that there was a large amount of m, H4084
2Ch 24:11 collected a great amount of m. H4084
2Ch 24:14 brought the rest of the m to the king and H4084
2Ch 34: 9 gave him the m that had been H4084
2Ch 34:11 They also gave m to the carpenters and NDT
2Ch 34:14 bringing out the m that had been taken H4084
2Ch 34:17 They have paid out the m that was in the H4084
Ezr 3: 7 Then they gave m to the masons and H4084
Ezr 7:17 With this m be sure to buy bulls, rams A10362
Ne 5: 4 have had to borrow m to pay the king's H4084
Ne 5:10 are also lending the people m and grain. H4084
Ne 5:11 one percent of the m, grain, H4084
Est 3:11 "Keep the m," the king said to Haman H4084
Est 4: 7 exact amount of m Haman had promised H4084
Ps 15: 5 who lends m to the poor without interest H4084
Pr 7:20 purse filled with m and will not be home H4084
Pr 13:11 Dishonest m dwindles away, but whoever H2104
Pr 13:11 whoever gathers m little by little makes NDT
Pr 17:16 should fools have m in hand to buy H4697
Ecc 5:10 Whoever loves m never has enough H4084
Ecc 7:12 Wisdom is a shelter as m is a shelter, but H4084
Ecc 10:19 and m is the answer for everything. H4084
Isa 52: 3 without m you will be redeemed. H4084
Isa 55: 1 and you who have no m, come, H4084
Isa 55: 1 milk without m and without cost. H4084
Isa 55: 2 Why spend m on what is not bread, and H4084
Mic 3:11 and her prophets tell fortunes for m. H4084
Mt 6:24 You cannot serve both God and m. G3440
Mt 20:15 the right to do what I want with my own m? AIT
Mt 21:12 the tables of the m changers and the G3142
Mt 25:16 at once and put his m to work and gained G899S
Mt 25:18 hole in the ground and hid his master's m. G736
Mt 25:27 should have put my m on deposit with the G736
Mt 26: 9 at a high price and the m given to the poor." NDT
Mt 27: 5 So Judas threw the m into the temple and G736
Mt 27: 6 this into the treasury, since it is blood m." G5507
Mt 27: 7 decided to use the m to buy the potter's G899S
Mt 28:12 they gave the soldiers a large sum of m, G736
Mt 28:15 soldiers took the m and did as they were G736
Mk 6: 8 no bread, no bag, no m in your belts. G5910
Mk 11:15 the tables of the m changers and the G3142
Mk 12:41 the crowd putting their m into the temple G5910
Mk 14: 5 a year's wages and the m given to the poor." NDT
Mk 14:11 to hear this and promised to give him m. G736
Lk 3:14 "Don't extort m and don't accuse people G1398
Lk 7:41 "Two people owed m to a certain G5971+1639
Lk 7:42 Neither of them had the m to pay him back NDT
Lk 9: 3 no bread, no m, no extra shirt. G736
Lk 14:28 to see if you have enough m to complete it? NDT
Lk 16:13 You cannot serve both God and m." G3440
Lk 16:14 Pharisees, who loved m, heard all G5795+5639
Lk 19:13 'Put this m to work,' he said, 'until I come NDT
Lk 19:15 the servants to whom he had given the m, G736
Lk 19:23 Why then didn't you put my m on deposit G736
Lk 22: 5 were delighted and agreed to give him m. G736
Jn 2:14 others sitting at tables exchanging m. G3048
Jn 2:15 the coins of the m changers and G3142
Jn 12: 5 m given to the poor? It was worth a year's wages G5559+1324
Jn 12: 6 as keeper of the m bag, he used to G1186
Jn 13:29 Since Judas had charge of the m, some G1186
Ac 3: 3 John about to enter, he asked them for m. G1797
Ac 4:34 sold them, brought the m from the sales G5507
Ac 4:37 brought the m and put it at the G5975
Ac 5: 2 he kept back part of the m for himself, G5507
Ac 5: 3 some of the m you received for the G5507
Ac 5: 4 it was sold, wasn't the m at your disposal? NDT
Ac 7:16 Hamor at Shechem for a certain sum of m. G736
Ac 8:18 of the apostles' hands, he offered them m G5975
Ac 8:20 "May your m perish with you, because you G736
Ac 8:20 you could buy the gift of God with m! G5975
Ac 16:16 a great deal of m for her owners by G2238
Ac 16:19 that their hope of making m was gone, G2238
Ac 22:28 I had to pay a lot of m for my citizenship." G3049
1Co 16: 2 set aside a sum of m in keeping G4123+1571S
1Ti 3: 3 not quarrelsome, not a lover of m. G921
1Ti 6:10 For the love of m is a root of all kinds of G5794
1Ti 6:10 eager for m, have wandered from NDT
2Ti 3: 2 of themselves, lovers of m, boastful, G5795
Heb 13: 5 your lives free from the love of m and be G921
Jas 4:13 year there, carry on business and make m." G3045

MONEYLENDER (1) [LEND]

Lk 7:41 "Two people owed money to a certain m G1250

MONGREL (1)

Zec 9: 6 A m people will occupy Ashdod, and I H4927

MONITOR (1)

Lev 11:30 the gecko, the m lizard, the wall lizard, H3947

MONOPOLY (1)

Job 15: 8 Do you have a m on wisdom? H1757

MONSTER (6)

Job 7:12 or the m of the deep, that you put H9490
Ps 74:13 broke the heads of the m in the waters. H9490
Isa 27: 1 serpent; he will slay the m of the sea. H9490
Isa 51: 9 to pieces, who pierced that m through? H9490
Eze 29: 3 you great m lying among your streams. H9490
Eze 32: 2 you are like a m in the seas thrashing H9490

(SEA) MONSTERS (KJV) JACKALS

MONTH (211) [MONTHLY, MONTHS]

Ge 7:11 on the seventeenth day of the second m— H2544
Ge 8: 4 day of the seventh m the ark came to rest H2544
Ge 8: 5 continued to recede until the tenth m, H2544
Ge 8: 5 first day of the tenth m the tops of the H2544
Ge 8:13 day of the first m of Noah's six hundred H2544
Ge 8:14 day of the second m the earth was H2544
Ge 29:14 had stayed with him for a whole m, H2544+3427
Ex 12: 2 "This m is to be for you the first month, H2544
Ex 12: 2 "This month is to be for you the first m, H2544
Ex 12: 2 the first month, the first m of your year. H2544
Ex 12: 3 tenth day of this m each man is to take a H2544
Ex 12: 6 of them until the fourteenth day of the m, H2544
Ex 12:18 In the first m you are to eat bread made H2544
Ex 13: 4 in the m of Aviv, you are leaving. H2544
Ex 13: 5 you are to observe this ceremony in this m: H2544
Ex 16: 1 day of the second m after they had come H2544
Ex 19: 1 first day of the third m after the Israelites H2544
Ex 23:15 at the appointed time in the m of Aviv, H2544
Ex 23:15 in that m you came out of Egypt. H2257S
Ex 34:18 at the appointed time in the m of Aviv, H2544
Ex 34:18 for in that m you came out of Egypt. H2544
Ex 40: 2 of meeting, on the first day of the first m. H2544
Ex 40:17 first day of the first m in the second year. H2544
Lev 16:29 day of the seventh m you must deny H2544
Lev 23: 5 on the fourteenth day of the first m. H2544
Lev 23: 6 fifteenth day of that m the LORD's Festival H2544
Lev 23:24 day of the seventh m you are to have a H2544
Lev 23:27 day of this seventh m is the Day of H2544
Lev 23:32 the ninth day of the m until the following H2544
Lev 23:34 day of the seventh m the LORD's Festival H2544
Lev 23:39 with the fifteenth day of the seventh m, H2544
Lev 23:41 to come; celebrate it in the seventh m. H2544
Lev 25: 9 on the tenth day of the seventh m; H2544
Lev 27: 6 a person between one m and five years, H2544
Nu 1: 1 day of the second m of the second year H2544
Nu 1:18 together on the first day of the second m. H2544
Nu 3:15 Count every male a m old or more." H2544
Nu 3:22 of all the males a m old or more who H2544
Nu 3:28 of all the males a m old or more was H2544
Nu 3:34 of all the males a m old or more who H2544
Nu 3:39 including every male a m old or more H2544
Nu 3:40 males who are a m old or more and make H2544
Nu 3:43 of firstborn males a m old or more, H2544
Nu 9: 1 of Sinai in the first m of the second year H2544
Nu 9: 3 at twilight on the fourteenth day of this m H2544
Nu 9: 5 on the fourteenth day of the first m. H2544
Nu 9:11 day of the second m at twilight. H2544
Nu 9:22 tabernacle for two days or a m or a year, H2544
Nu 10:11 day of the second m of the second year, H2544
Nu 11:20 but for a whole m—until it comes out of H2544
Nu 11:21 will give them meat to eat for a whole m! H2544
Nu 18:16 When they are a m old, you must redeem H2544
Nu 20: 1 In the first m the whole Israelite H2544
Nu 26:62 the male Levites a m old or more H2544
Nu 28:11 " 'On the first of every m, present to the H2544
Nu 28:16 day of the first m the LORD's Passover is to H2544
Nu 28:17 fifteenth day of this m there is to be a H2544
Nu 29: 1 day of the seventh m hold a sacred H2544
Nu 29: 7 day of this seventh m hold a sacred H2544
Nu 29:12 " 'On the fifteenth day of the seventh m H2544
Nu 33: 3 on the fifteenth day of the first m, H2544
Nu 33:38 first day of the fifth m of the fortieth year H2544
Dt 1: 3 on the first day of the eleventh m, Moses H2544
Dt 16: 1 Observe the m of Aviv and celebrate the H2544
Dt 16: 1 because in the m of Aviv he brought you H2544
Dt 21:13 her father and mother for a full m, H3732
Jos 4:19 day of the first m the people went up H2544
Jos 5:10 evening of the fourteenth day of the m, H2544
1Sa 20:27 the second day of the m, David's place H2544
1Ki 4: 7 to provide supplies for one m in the year. H2544
1Ki 4:27 each in his m, supplied provisions H2544
1Ki 5:14 to Lebanon in shifts of ten thousand a m, H2544
1Ki 5:14 they spent one m in Lebanon and two H2544
1Ki 6: 1 over Israel, in the m of Ziv, the second H2544
1Ki 6: 1 the second m, he began to build H2544
1Ki 6:37 laid in the fourth year, in the m of Ziv. H3732
1Ki 6:38 In the eleventh year in the m of Bul, the H3732
1Ki 6:38 the eighth m, the temple was H2544
1Ki 8: 2 time of the festival in the m of Ethanim, H3732
1Ki 8: 2 in the month of Ethanim, the seventh m. H2544
1Ki 12:32 on the fifteenth day of the eighth m, H2544
1Ki 12:33 On the fifteenth day of the eighth m, H2544
1Ki 12:33 eighth month, a m of his own choosing H2544
2Ki 15:13 and he reigned in Samaria one m. H3732+3427
2Ki 25: 1 on the tenth day of the tenth m H2544
2Ki 25: 3 day of the fourth m the famine in the city H2544
2Ki 25: 8 On the seventh day of the fifth m, in the H2544
2Ki 25:25 In the seventh m, however, Ishmael son H2544
2Ki 25:27 the twenty-seventh day of the twelfth m. H2544
1Ch 12:15 Jordan in the first m when it was H2544
1Ch 27: 1 that were on duty m by month throughout H2544
1Ch 27: 1 on duty month by m throughout the year. H2544
1Ch 27: 2 the first m, was Jashobeam son of H2544
1Ch 27: 3 chief of all the army officers for the first m. H2544
1Ch 27: 4 the second m was Dodai the Ahohite; H2544
1Ch 27: 5 the third m, was Benaiah son of H2544
1Ch 27: 7 for the fourth m, was Asahel the H2544
1Ch 27: 8 for the fifth m, was the commander H2544
1Ch 27: 9 for the sixth m, was Ira the son of H2544
1Ch 27:10 the seventh m, was Helez the Pelonite H2544
1Ch 27:11 for the eighth m, was Sibbekai the H2544
1Ch 27:12 for the ninth m, was Abiezer the H2544
1Ch 27:13 for the tenth m, was Maharai the H2544
1Ch 27:14 the eleventh m, was Benaiah the H2544
1Ch 27:15 for the twelfth m, was Heldai the H2544
2Ch 3: 2 day of the second m in the fourth year of H2544
2Ch 5: 3 the time of the festival in the seventh m. H2544
2Ch 7:10 day of the seventh m he sent the people H2544
2Ch 15:10 in the third m of the fifteenth year H2544
2Ch 29: 3 In the first m of the first year of his reign H2544
2Ch 29:17 consecration on the first day of the first m, H2544
2Ch 29:17 the eighth day of the m they reached the H2544
2Ch 29:17 on the sixteenth day of the first m. H2544
2Ch 30: 2 celebrate the Passover in the second m. H2544
2Ch 30:13 of Unleavened Bread in the second m. H2544
2Ch 30:15 on the fourteenth day of the second m. H2544
2Ch 31: 7 this in the third m and finished in the H2544
2Ch 31: 7 month and finished in the seventh m. H2544
2Ch 35: 1 on the fourteenth day of the first m. H2544
Ezr 3: 1 When the seventh m came and the H2544
Ezr 3: 6 day of the seventh m they began to offer H2544
Ezr 3: 8 In the second m of the second year after H2544
Ezr 6:15 on the third day of the m Adar, A10333

Ezr 6:19 On the fourteenth day of the first **m**, the H2544
Ezr 7: 8 in the fifth **m** of the seventh year of H2544
Ezr 7: 9 Babylon on the first day of the first **m**, H2544
Ezr 7: 9 Jerusalem on the first day of the fifth **m**, H2544
Ezr 8:31 day of the first **m** we set out from the H2544
Ezr 10: 9 And on the twentieth day of the ninth **m** H2544
Ezr 10:16 first day of the tenth **m** they sat down to H2544
Ezr 10:17 day of the first **m** they finished dealing H2544
Ne 1: 1 In the **m** *of* Kislev in the twentieth year H2544
Ne 2: 1 In the **m** *of* Nisan in the twentieth year of H2544
Ne 7:73 When the seventh **m** came and the H2544
Ne 8: 2 day of the seventh **m** Ezra the priest H2544
Ne 8:13 On the second day of the **m**, the heads of NDT
Ne 8:14 during the festival of the seventh **m** H2544
Ne 9: 1 On the twenty-fourth day of the same **m** H2544
Est 2:16 in the royal residence in the tenth **m**, H2544
Est 2:16 the tenth month, the **m** *of* Tebeth, in the H2544
Est 3: 7 in the first **m**, the month of Nisan, H2544
Est 3: 7 the first month, the **m** *of* Nisan, the pur H2544
Est 3: 7 to select a day and **m**. H4946+2544+4200+2544
Est 3: 7 And the lot fell on the twelfth **m**, the H2544
Est 3: 7 fell on the twelfth month, the **m** *of* Adar. H2544
Est 3:12 day of the first **m** the royal secretaries H2544
Est 3:13 the thirteenth day of the twelfth **m**, the H2544
Est 3:13 twelfth month, the **m** *of* Adar, and to H2544
Est 8: 9 on the twenty-third day of the third **m**, the H2544
Est 8: 9 day of the third month, the **m** *of* Sivan. H2544
Est 8:12 was the thirteenth day of the twelfth **m**, H2544
Est 8:12 day of the twelfth month, the **m** *of* Adar. H2544
Est 9: 1 On the thirteenth day of the twelfth **m**, the H2544
Est 9: 1 twelfth month, the **m** *of* Adar, the edict H2544
Est 9:15 on the fourteenth day of the **m** *of* Adar, H2544
Est 9:17 on the thirteenth day of the **m** *of* Adar, H2544
Est 9:19 fourteenth of the **m** *of* Adar as a day of H2544
Est 9:21 fifteenth days of the **m** *of* Adar H2544
Est 9:22 as the **m** when their sorrow was H2544
Isa 47:13 who make predictions **m** by month, NDT
Isa 47:13 who make predictions month by **m**, H2544
Jer 1: 3 down to the fifth **m** of the eleventh year of H2544
Jer 28: 1 In the fifth **m** of that same year, the fourth H2544
Jer 28:17 In the seventh **m** of that same year H2544
Jer 36: 9 In the ninth **m** of the fifth year of H2544
Jer 36:22 It was the ninth **m** and the king was sitting H2544
Jer 39: 1 in the tenth **m**, Nebuchadnezzar H2544
Jer 39: 2 day of the fourth **m** of Zedekiah's H2544
Jer 41: 1 In the seventh **m** Ishmael son of H2544
Jer 52: 4 on the tenth day of the tenth **m** H2544
Jer 52: 6 day of the fourth **m** the famine in the city H2544
Jer 52:12 On the tenth day of the fifth **m**, in the H2544
Jer 52:31 on the twenty-fifth day of the twelfth **m** H2544
Eze 1: 1 in the fourth **m** on the fifth day H2544
Eze 1: 2 On the fifth of the **m**—it was the fifth year H2544
Eze 8: 1 in the sixth **m** on the fifth day, while H2544
Eze 20: 1 in the fifth **m** on the tenth day, some H2544
Eze 24: 1 in the tenth **m** on the tenth day, the H2544
Eze 26: 1 In the eleventh **m** of the twelfth year, on H2544
Eze 26: 1 on the first day of the **m**, the word of the H2544
Eze 29: 1 in the tenth **m** on the twelfth day H2544
Eze 29:17 in the first **m** on the first day, the H2544
Eze 30:20 in the first **m** on the seventh day, the H2544
Eze 31: 1 in the third **m** on the first day, the H2544
Eze 32: 1 in the twelfth **m** on the first day, the H2544
Eze 32:17 on the fifteenth day of the **m**, the word of H2544
Eze 33:21 in the tenth **m** on the fifth day, H2544
Eze 40: 1 on the tenth of the **m**, in the fourteenth H2544
Eze 45:18 In the first **m** on the first day you are to H2544
Eze 45:20 seventh day of the **m** for anyone who sins H2544
Eze 45:21 " 'In the first **m** on the fourteenth day you H2544
Eze 45:25 in the seventh **m** on the fifteenth day, H2544
Eze 47:12 Every **m** they will bear fruit, because the H2544
Da 10: 4 On the twenty-fourth day of the first **m**, as H2544
Hag 1: 1 on the first day of the sixth **m**, the word of H2544
Hag 1:15 on the twenty-fourth day of the sixth **m**. H2544
Hag 2: 1 on the twenty-first day of the seventh **m** H2544
Hag 2:10 On the twenty-fourth day of the ninth **m**, in NDT
Hag 2:18 from this twenty-fourth day of the ninth **m** NDT
Hag 2:20 time on the twenty-fourth day of the **m**: H2544
Zec 1: 1 In the eighth **m** of the second year of H2544
Zec 1: 7 the twenty-fourth day of the eleventh **m**, H2544
Zec 1: 7 eleventh month, the **m** *of* Shebat, in the H2544
Zec 7: 1 on the fourth day of the ninth **m**, H2544
Zec 7: 1 day of the ninth month, the **m** of Kislev. NDT
Zec 7: 3 "Should I mourn and fast in the fifth **m**, as H2544
Zec 11: 8 In one **m** I got rid of the three shepherds H3732
Lk 1:26 In the sixth **m** of Elizabeth's pregnancy *G3604*
Lk 1:36 to be unable to conceive is in her sixth **m**. *G3604*
Rev 9:15 very hour and day and **m** and year were *G3604*
Rev 22: 2 crops of fruit, yielding its fruit every **m**. *G3604*

MONTHLY (12) [MONTH]

Lev 12: 2 is unclean during her **m period**. H5614+1864
Lev 15:19 the **impurity of** her **m period** will last H5614
Lev 15:24 with her and her **m flow** touches him, H5614
Lev 15:25 other than her **m period** or has a H5614
Lev 15:26 as is her bed during her **m period**, and H5614
Lev 15:33 a *woman* in her **m period**, for a H5614+1865
Lev 18:19 during the uncleanness of her **m period**. H5614
Lev 20:18 with a woman during her **m period**, H1865
Nu 28:14 This is the **m** burnt offering to H2544+928+2544
Nu 29: 6 are in addition to the **m** and daily burnt H2544
2Sa 11: 4 purifying herself from her *m* **uncleanness**.) AIT
Eze 36:17 a **woman's m uncleanness** H3240+2021+5614

MONTHS (51) [MONTH]

Ge 38:24 About three **m** later Judah was told, "Your H2544
Ex 2: 2 was a fine child, she hid him *for* three **m**. H3732
Jdg 11:37 "Give me two **m** to roam the hills and H2544
Jdg 11:38 And he let her go *for* two **m**. She and her H2544
Jdg 11:39 After the two **m**, she returned to her father H2544
Jdg 19: 2 After she had been there four **m**, H2544
Jdg 20:47 of Rimmon, where they stayed four **m**. H2544
1Sa 6: 1 had been in Philistine territory seven **m**, H2544
1Sa 27: 7 in Philistine territory a year and four **m**. H2544
2Sa 2:11 over Judah was seven years and six **m**. H2544
2Sa 5: 5 over Judah seven years and six **m**, H2544
2Sa 6:11 of Obed-Edom the Gittite *for* three **m**, H2544
2Sa 24: 8 at the end of nine **m** and twenty days. H2544
2Sa 24:13 Or three **m** of fleeing from your enemies H2544
1Ki 5:14 month in Lebanon and two **m** at home. H2544
1Ki 11:16 all the Israelites stayed there *for* six **m**, H2544
2Ki 15: 8 Israel in Samaria, and he reigned six **m**. H2544
2Ki 23:31 he reigned in Jerusalem three **m**. H2544
2Ki 24: 8 he reigned in Jerusalem three **m**. H2544
1Ch 3: 4 where he reigned seven years and six **m**. H2544
1Ch 13:14 of Obed-Edom in his house *for* three **m**, H2544
1Ch 21:12 three **m** of being swept away before your H2544
2Ch 36: 2 he reigned in Jerusalem three **m**. H2544
2Ch 36: 9 in Jerusalem three **m** and ten days. H2544
Est 2:12 to complete twelve **m** of beauty H2544
Est 2:12 six **m** with oil of myrrh and six with H2544
Job 3: 6 the year nor be entered in any of the **m**. H3732
Job 7: 3 so I have been allotted **m** *of* futility, and H3732
Job 14: 5 the number of his **m** and have set limits H2544
Job 21:21 when their allotted **m** come to an end? H2544
Job 29: 2 "How I long for the **m** gone by, for the H3732
Job 39: 2 Do you count the **m** till they bear? Do you H3732
Eze 39:12 " '*For* seven **m** the Israelites will be H2544
Eze 39:14 " 'After the seven **m** they will carry out a H2544
Da 4:29 Twelve **m** later, as the king was walking A10333
Am 4: 7 when the harvest was still three **m** away. H2544
Zec 7: 5 the fifth and seventh **m** for the past seventy NDT
Zec 8:19 seventh and tenth **m** will become joyful NDT
Lk 1:24 pregnant and *for* five **m** remained in *G3604*
Lk 1:56 with Elizabeth *for* about three **m** and then *G3604*
Jn 4:35 a saying, 'It's still **four m** until harvest'? *G5485*
Ac 7:20 *For* three **m** he was cared for by his family. *G3604*
Ac 19: 8 spoke boldly there for three **m**, *G3604*
Ac 20: 3 where he stayed three **m**. Because some *G3604*
Ac 28:11 After three **m** we put out to sea in a ship *G3604*
Gal 4:10 special days and **m** and seasons and *G3604*
Heb 11:23 parents hid him **for three m** after he was *G5564*
Rev 9: 5 them but only to torture them *for* five **m**. *G3604*
Rev 9:10 had power to torment people *for* five **m**. *G3604*
Rev 11: 2 will trample on the holy city *for* 42 **m**. *G3604*
Rev 13: 5 to exercise its authority *for* forty-two **m**. *G3604*

MONUMENT (6)

1Sa 15:12 he has set up a **m** in his own honor and H3338
2Sa 8: 3 went to restore his **m** at the Euphrates H3338
2Sa 18:18 **erected** it in the King's Valley **as a m** to H5893
2Sa 18:18 it is called Absalom's **M** to this day. H3338
1Ch 18: 3 he went to set up his **m** at the Euphrates H3338
Isa 19:19 Egypt, and a **m** to the LORD at its border. H5167

MOON (62) [MOONS]

Ge 37: 9 time the sun and **m** and eleven stars were H3734
Nu 10:10 festivals and **New M feasts**— H8031+2544
Nu 28:14 be made at each **new m** *during* the year. H2544
Dt 4:19 see the sun, the **m** and the stars—all H3734
Dt 17: 3 to the sun or the **m** or the stars in the H3734
Dt 33:14 forth and the finest the **m** can yield; H3732
Jos 10:12 Gibeon, and you, **m**, over the Valley of H3734
Jos 10:13 stood still, and the **m** stopped, till the H3734
1Sa 20: 5 tomorrow is the **New M feast**, and I am H2544
1Sa 20:18 to David, "Tomorrow is the **New M feast**. H2544
1Sa 20:24 when the **New M feast** came, the H2544
2Ki 4:23 "It's not the **New M** or the Sabbath." H2544
2Ki 23: 5 to the sun and **m**, to the H3734
1Ch 23:31 at the **New M feasts** and at the appointed H2544
Ezr 3: 5 the **New M** sacrifices and the sacrifices H2544
Ne 10:33 at the **New M feasts** and at the appointed H2544
Job 25: 5 If even the **m** is not bright and the stars H3734
Job 26: 9 He covers the face of the **full m** H4057
Job 31:26 its radiance or the **m** moving in splendor, H3734
Ps 8: 3 of your fingers, the **m** and the stars, which H3734
Ps 72: 5 the sun, as long as the **m**, through all H3734
Ps 72: 7 prosperity abound till the **m** is no more. H3734
Ps 74:16 the night; you established the sun and **m**. H4401
Ps 81: 3 Sound the ram's horn at the **New M**, and H2544
Ps 81: 3 when the **m** is **full**, on the day of H4057
Ps 89:37 it will be established forever like the **m** H3734
Ps 104:19 He made the **m** to mark the seasons, and H3734
Ps 121: 6 not harm you by day, nor the **m** by night. H3734
Ps 136: 9 the **m** and stars to govern the night; His H3734
Ps 148: 3 Praise him, sun and **m**; praise him, all H3734
Pr 7:20 and will not be home till **full m**." H3427+4057
Ecc 12: 2 the light and the **m** and the stars grow H3734
SS 6:10 the dawn, fair as the **m**, bright as the sun, H4244
Isa 1:14 Your **New M feasts** and your appointed H2544
Isa 13:10 be darkened and the **m** will not give its H3734
Isa 24:23 The **m** will be dismayed, the sun H4244
Isa 30:26 The **m** will shine like the sun, and the H4244
Isa 60:19 will the brightness of the **m** shine on you, H3734
Isa 60:20 set again, and your **m** will wane no more H3734
Isa 66:23 From *one* **New M** to another and from one H2544
Jer 8: 2 to the sun and the **m** and all the stars of H3734
Jer 31:35 who decrees the **m** and stars to shine by H3734
Eze 32: 7 a cloud, and the **m** will not give its light. H3734
Eze 46: 1 on the day of the **New M** it is to be H2544
Eze 46: 6 On the day of the **New M** he is to offer a H2544
Hos 5: 7 When they celebrate their **New M feasts** H2544
Joel 2:10 the sun and **m** are darkened, and H3734
Joel 2:31 to darkness and the **m** to blood before the H3734
Joel 3:15 The sun and **m** will be darkened, and the H3734
Am 8: 5 "When will the **New M** be over that we H2544
Hab 3:11 Sun and **m** stood still in the heavens at H3734
Mt 24:29 darkened, and the **m** will not give its light *G4943*
Mk 13:24 the **m** will not give its light; *G4943*
Lk 21:25 will be signs in the sun, **m** and stars. *G4943*
Ac 2:20 to darkness and the **m** to blood before the *G4943*
Ac 7:42 *of* the **sun, m and stars**. *G5131+3836+4041*
1Co 15:41 the **m** another and the stars another *G4943*
Col 2:16 a **New M celebration** or a Sabbath day. *G3741*
Rev 6:12 goat hair, the whole **m** turned blood red, *G4943*
Rev 8:12 was struck, a third *of* the **m**, and a third of *G4943*
Rev 12: 1 with the **m** under her feet and a crown of *G4943*
Rev 21:23 not need the sun or the **m** to shine on it, *G4943*

MOONS (7) [MOON]

2Ch 2: 4 at the **New M** and at the appointed H2544
2Ch 8:13 the **New M** and the three annual festivals H2544
2Ch 31: 3 at the **New M** and at the appointed H2544
Isa 1:13 **New M**, Sabbaths and convocations—I H2544
Eze 45:17 festivals, the **New M** and the Sabbaths H2544
Eze 46: 3 the Sabbaths and **New M** the people of H2544
Hos 2:11 festivals, her **New M**, her Sabbath days— H2544

MORAL (1)

Jas 1:21 get rid of all **m filth** and the evil that is so *G4864*

MORASTHITE (KJV) MORESHETH

MORDECAI (53) [MORDECAI'S]

Ezr 2: 2 Seraiah, Reelaiah, **M**, Bilshan, Mispar H5283
Ne 7: 7 Raamiah, Nahamani, **M**, Bilshan H5283
Est 2: 5 of Benjamin, named **M** son of Jair, the H5283
Est 2: 7 **M** had a cousin named Hadassah, whom he NDT
Est 2: 7 **M** had taken her as his own daughter H5283
Est 2:10 because **M** had forbidden her to do so. H5283
Est 2:15 the young woman **M** had adopted, the H5283
Est 2:19 **M** was sitting at the king's gate. H5283
Est 2:20 nationality just as **M** had told her to do, H5283
Est 2:21 During the time **M** was sitting at the H5283
Est 2:22 But **M** found out about the plot and told H5283
Est 2:22 reported it to the king, giving credit to **M**. H5283
Est 3: 2 But **M** would not kneel down or pay him H5283
Est 3: 3 royal officials at the king's gate asked **M**, H5283
Est 3: 5 Haman saw that **M** would not kneel H5283
Est 3: 6 he scorned the idea of killing only **M**. H5283
Est 4: 1 When **M** learned of all that had been H5283
Est 4: 4 attendants came and told her about **M**, NDT
Est 4: 5 to find out what was troubling **M** and why. H5283
Est 4: 6 Hathak went out to **M** in the open square H5283
Est 4: 7 **M** told him everything that had happened H5283
Est 4: 9 reported to Esther what **M** had said. H5283
Est 4:10 Then she instructed him to say to **M**, H5283
Est 4:12 When Esther's words were reported to **M**, H5283
Est 4:15 Then Esther sent this reply to **M**: H5283
Est 4:17 So **M** went away and carried out all of H5283
Est 5: 9 But when he saw **M** at the king's gate H5283
Est 5: 9 he was filled with rage against **M**. H5283
Est 5:13 as I see that Jew **M** sitting at the king's H5283
Est 5:14 in the morning to have **M** impaled on it. H5283
Est 6: 2 recorded there that **M** had exposed H5283
Est 6: 3 recognition has **M** received for this?" H5283
Est 6: 4 about impaling **M** on the pole he had H5283
Est 6:10 just as you have suggested for **M** the Jew, H5283
Est 6:11 He robed **M**, and led him on horseback H5283
Est 6:12 Afterward **M** returned to the king's gate H5283
Est 6:13 said to him, "Since **M**, before whom your H5283
Est 7: 9 He had it set up for **M**, who spoke up to H5283
Est 7:10 Haman on the pole he had set up for **M**. H5283
Est 8: 1 And **M** came into the presence of the king H5283
Est 8: 2 from Haman, and presented it to **M**. H5283
Est 8: 7 to Queen Esther and to **M** the Jew, H5283
Est 8:10 **M** wrote in the name of King Xerxes, sealed NDT
Est 8:15 When **M** left the king's presence, he was H5283
Est 9: 3 because fear of **M** had seized them. H5283
Est 9: 4 **M** was prominent in the palace; his H5283
Est 9:20 **M** recorded these events, and he sent H5283
Est 9:23 doing what **M** had written to them. H5283
Est 9:29 Abihail, along with **M** the Jew, wrote with H5283
Est 9:30 And **M** sent letters to all the Jews in the 127 NDT
Est 9:31 as **M** the Jew and Queen Esther had H5283
Est 10: 2 with a full account of the greatness of **M**, H5283
Est 10: 3 **M** the Jew was second in rank to King H5283

MORDECAI'S (5) [MORDECAI]

Est 2:20 continued to follow **M** instructions as she H5283
Est 3: 4 it to see whether **M** behavior would be H5283
Est 3: 6 Yet having learned who **M** people were H5283
Est 3: 6 looked for a way to destroy all **M** people, H5283
Est 8: 9 They wrote out all **M** orders to the Jews H5283

MORE (587)

Ge 3: 1 the serpent was **m** crafty **than** any of the H4946
Ge 4:13 "My punishment is **m** than I can bear. H1524
Ge 5:24 with God; then he **was no m**, because God H401

Ge 7:20 to a depth of **m than** fifteen cubits. H4946
Ge 8:10 He waited seven **m** days and again H6388+337
Ge 8:12 He waited seven **m** days and sent H6388+337
Ge 18:32 be angry, but let me speak just **once m**. H7193
Ge 24:20 ran back to the well to **draw** *m* **water**, and AIT
Ge 37:3 loved Joseph **m than** any of his other H4946
Ge 37:4 father loved him **m than** any of them, H4946
Ge 37:5 brothers, they hated him **all the m**. H3578+6388
Ge 37:8 hated him **all the m** because of H3578+6388
Ge 38:26 "She is **m** righteous **than** I, since I H4946
Ge 42:13 is now with our father, and one **is no m**." H401
Ge 42:32 One **is no m**, and the youngest is now with H401
Ge 42:36 Joseph **is no m** and Simeon is no more H401
Ge 42:36 Joseph is no more and Simeon **is no m** H401
Ge 43:2 "Go back and buy us a little **m** food. NDT
Ge 44:25 'Go back and buy a **little m** food. H5071
Ge 48:22 I give one **m** ridge of land **than** to your H6584
Ex 1:10 or *they will become even m* **numerous** and, AIT
Ex 1:12 But the **m** they were oppressed, the H3869+889
Ex 1:12 the **m** they multiplied and spread H4027
Ex 1:20 increased and became **even m** numerous. H4394
Ex 5:10 'I will not give you any **m** straw. NDT
Ex 9:29 will stop and there will be no **m** hail, H6388
Ex 10:17 my sin **once m** and pray to H421+2021+7193
Ex 11:1 "I will bring one **m** plague on Pharaoh H6388
Ex 28:27 Make two **m** gold rings and attach them to NDT
Ex 30:14 those twenty years old or **m**, are to H5087+2025
Ex 30:15 The rich *are* not *to* **give m** than a half H8049
Ex 36:5 people are bringing **m** than enough for H8049
Ex 36:6 the people were restrained from bringing **m**, NDT
Ex 36:7 already had *was m than* enough to do all H3855
Ex 38:26 twenty years old or **m**, a total of H5087+2025
Ex 39:20 Then they made two **m** gold rings and NDT
Lev 13:3 the sore appears to be **m than** skin deep, H4946
Lev 13:4 not appear to be **m than** skin deep and H4946
Lev 13:20 it appears to be **m than** skin deep and the H4946
Lev 13:21 it and it is not **m than** skin deep and has H4946
Lev 13:25 it appears to be **m than** skin deep, it H4946
Lev 13:26 if it is not **m than** skin deep and has H4946
Lev 13:30 it appears to be **m than** skin deep and the H4946
Lev 13:31 not seem to be **m than** skin deep and H4946
Lev 13:32 does not appear to be **m than** skin deep, H4946
Lev 13:34 appears to be no **m than** skin deep, H4946
Lev 27:7 a person sixty years old or **m**, set H5087+2025
Nu 1:3 years old or **m** and able to serve H5087+2025
Nu 1:18 years old or **m** were listed by name H5087+2025
Nu 1:20 years old or **m** who were able to H5087+2025
Nu 1:22 years old or **m** who were able to H5087+2025
Nu 1:24 years old or **m** who were able to H5087+2025
Nu 1:26 years old or **m** who were able to H5087+2025
Nu 1:28 years old or **m** who were able to H5087+2025
Nu 1:30 years old or **m** who were able to H5087+2025
Nu 1:32 years old or **m** who were able to H5087+2025
Nu 1:34 years old or **m** who were able to H5087+2025
Nu 1:36 years old or **m** who were able to H5087+2025
Nu 1:38 years old or **m** who were able to H5087+2025
Nu 1:40 years old or **m** who were able to H5087+2025
Nu 1:42 years old or **m** who were able to H5087+2025
Nu 1:45 years old or **m** who were able to H5087+2025
Nu 3:15 every male a month old or **m**." H5087+2025
Nu 3:22 a month old or **m** who were H5087+2025
Nu 3:28 a month old or **m** was 8,600. H5087+2025
Nu 3:34 a month old or **m** who were H5087+2025
Nu 3:39 every male a month old or **m**, H5087+2025
Nu 3:40 a month old or **m** and make a list H5087+2025
Nu 3:43 firstborn males a month old or **m**, H5087+2025
Nu 8:24 years old or **m** shall come to take H5087+2025
Nu 12:3 **m** humble **than** anyone else on the face H4946
Nu 14:29 years old or **m** who was counted in H5087+2025
Nu 22:15 **m** numerous and more distinguished than NDT
Nu 22:15 and **m** distinguished **than** the first. H4946
Nu 26:2 years old or **m** who are able to H5087+2025
Nu 26:4 of the men twenty years old or **m**, H5087+2025
Nu 26:62 a month old or **m** numbered H5087+2025
Nu 32:11 years old or **m** when they came up H5087+2025
Nu 32:14 **making** the LORD even **m** angry with H3578
Dt 3:11 iron and was *m than* **nine** cubits long and AIT
Dt 5:22 the deep darkness; and he added **nothing** *m*. AIT
Dt 7:7 you were **m** numerous **than** other peoples H4946
Dt 7:14 will be blessed **m than** any other people; H4946
Dt 9:14 stronger and **m** numerous **than** they." H4946
Dt 17:16 people return to Egypt to **get m** *of* them, H8049
Dt 19:9 you are to set aside three **m** cities. H3578+6388
Dt 25:3 must not impose **m** *than* forty lashes. H3578
Dt 25:3 guilty party is flogged **m** than that, H3578+8041
Dt 30:5 *He will* **make** you **m prosperous** and H3512
Dt 31:27 **how much m** will you rebel H2256+677+3954
Dt 33:11 against him, his foes **till** they rise **no m**." H4946
Jos 10:11 **m** of them died from the hail than H8041
Jos 19:9 Judah's portion was **m** than they needed. H8041
Jos 22:33 And they talked **no** *m* about going to war AIT
Jdg 2:19 to ways **even m** corrupt **than** those of their H4946
Jdg 6:39 Let me make just **one m** request. Allow H7193
Jdg 6:39 Allow me **one m** test with the fleece, but H7193
Jdg 7:12 camels could no **m** be counted than the NDT
Jdg 15:2 Isn't her younger sister **m** attractive? Take H4946
Jdg 16:18 "Come back **once m**; he has told me H7193
Jdg 16:28 strengthen me just **once m**, and let me H7193
Jdg 16:30 many **m** when he died **than** while he H4946
Jdg 20:45 Gidom and struck down two thousand **m**. H4408
Ru 1:11 Am I going to have **any m** sons, who H6388
Ru 1:13 It is **m** bitter for me than for you, because H4394
Ru 3:12 is another who is **m** closely related **than** I. H4946
1Sa 1:8 Don't I **mean m** to you than ten sons?" H3202
1Sa 2:5 those who were hungry are hungry **no m**. H2532
1Sa 2:29 honor your sons **m than** me by fattening H4946
1Sa 14:19 **increased m and more.** H2143+2256+8041+2143
1Sa 14:19 **increased more and m.** H2143+2256+8041+2143
1Sa 17:42 saw that he was little **m** than a boy, NDT
1Sa 18:8 What **m** can he get but the kingdom?" H6388
1Sa 18:29 Saul *became* still **m** afraid of him, and he H3578
1Sa 18:30 David met with **m** success **than** the rest of H4946
1Sa 19:8 **Once m** war broke out, and David went H3578
1Sa 19:21 about it, and he sent **m** men, and they H337
1Sa 21:5 **How much m so** today!" H677+3954
1Sa 23:3 **How much m**, then, if we go to Keilah H677
1Sa 23:22 Go and get **m** information. Find out where H6388
1Sa 24:17 "You are **m** righteous **than I**," he said H4946
2Sa 1:26 **m** wonderful **than** that of women. H4946
2Sa 4:11 **How much m**—when wicked men have H677
2Sa 5:10 **became m and more powerful** H2143+2143+2256+1524
2Sa 5:10 **became more and m powerful** H2143+2143+2256+1524
2Sa 5:13 David took **m** concubines and wives in H6388
2Sa 5:13 **m** sons and daughters were born to H6388
2Sa 5:22 **Once m** the Philistines came up H3578+6388
2Sa 6:22 become even **m** undignified **than** this, H4946
2Sa 7:20 "What **m** can David say to you? For H3578+6388
2Sa 11:12 "Stay here one **m** day, and tomorrow I H1685
2Sa 12:8 *I would have* **given** you **even m** H3578+3869+2179+2256+3869+2179
2Sa 13:15 he hated her **m** than he had loved her. H1524
2Sa 16:11 **How much m**, then, this H677+3954
2Sa 16:21 of everyone with you *will be* **m resolute**." H2616
2Sa 18:8 forest swallowed up **m** men that day than H8049
2Sa 19:28 do I have to make **any m** appeals to the H6388
2Sa 19:29 "Why say **m**? I order you and Ziba H6388
2Sa 19:34 "**How many m** years will I live H3869+4537
2Sa 19:43 claims **even m** forcefully **than** the men of H4946
2Sa 20:6 Bikri will do us **m** harm **than** Absalom did. H4946
1Ki 1:47 name **m** famous **than** yours and his H4946
1Ki 2:32 were better men and **m** upright **than** he. H4946
1Ki 8:65 our God for seven days and seven days **m**, NDT
1Ki 13:33 but **once m** appointed priests for the high H8740
1Ki 14:9 You have done **m** evil **than** all who lived H4946
1Ki 14:22 his jealous anger **m than** those who were H4946
1Ki 16:25 LORD and sinned **m than** all those before H4946
1Ki 16:30 did **m** evil in the eyes of the LORD **than** any H4946
1Ki 16:33 pole and did **m** to arouse the anger H3578
2Ki 2:12 And Elisha saw him no **m**. Then he took H6388
2Ki 3:9 the army had **no** *m* water for themselves AIT
2Ki 4:35 the bed and stretched out on him once **m**. NDT
2Ki 5:13 **How much m**, then, when he tells you H677
2Ki 6:16 who are with us are **m** than those who are H8041
2Ki 12:7 Take **no** *m* money from your treasurers, but AIT
2Ki 12:8 not collect any **m** money from the people NDT
2Ki 19:30 **Once m** a remnant of the kingdom of H3578
2Ki 21:9 that they did **m** evil **than** the nations the H4946
2Ki 21:11 He has done **m** evil than the Amorites H3972
2Ki 25:16 the LORD, was **m than** could be weighed. H4202
1Ch 4:9 Jabez was **m** honorable **than** his brothers H4946
1Ch 11:9 **became m and more powerful** H2143+2143+2256+1524
1Ch 11:9 **became more and m powerful** H2143+2143+2256+1524
1Ch 14:3 David took **m** wives and became the H6388
1Ch 14:3 the father of **m** sons and daughters. H6388
1Ch 14:13 **Once m** the Philistines raided the H3578+6388
1Ch 17:18 "What **m** can David say to you for H3578+6388
1Ch 22:3 and **m** bronze than could be H4200+8044
1Ch 22:4 provided **m** cedar logs **than** could be H4200+401
1Ch 23:3 thirty years old or **m** were counted, H5087+2025
1Ch 23:24 years old or **m** who served in the H5087+2025
1Ch 23:27 those twenty years old or **m**. H4200+5087+2025
2Ch 7:9 days and the festival for seven days **m**. NDT
2Ch 9:12 he gave her **m** than she had H4946+4200+963
2Ch 11:21 of Absalom **m than** any of his other H4946
2Ch 15:19 There was **no** *m* war until the thirty-fifth year AIT
2Ch 17:12 became **m and more powerful**; H2143+2256+1541+6330+4200+5087+2025
2Ch 17:12 became **more and m powerful**; H2143+2256+1541+6330+4200+5087+2025
2Ch 20:25 **m** *than* they could take away. H4200+401
2Ch 25:5 years old or **m** and found that H5087+2025
2Ch 25:9 The LORD can give you much **m than** that. H4946
2Ch 28:22 King Ahaz *became* even **m** unfaithful to H3578
2Ch 29:17 For eight **m** days they consecrated the NDT
2Ch 29:34 **m** conscientious in consecrating themselves **than** H4946
2Ch 30:23 to celebrate the festival seven **m** days; H337
2Ch 31:16 years old or **m** whose names were H5087+2025
2Ch 31:17 the Levites twenty years old or **m**, H5087+2025
2Ch 33:9 that they did **m** evil **than** the nations the H4946
2Ch 36:14 *became* **m and more unfaithful** H8049+5085+5086
2Ch 36:14 *became* **more and m unfaithful** H8049+5085+5086
Ezr 4:13 walls are restored, **no** *m* taxes, tribute or duty AIT
Ne 5:12 we will not demand anything **m** from them. NDT
Ne 7:2 feared God **m than** most people do. H4946
Ne 13:18 Now you *are* **stirring up m** wrath against H3578
Est 2:17 attracted to Esther **m than** to any of the H4946
Est 2:17 approval **m than** any of the other H4946
Est 9:4 **became m and more powerful** H2143+2256+1524
Est 9:4 **became more and m powerful** H2143+2256+1524
Job 3:5 gloom and utter darkness claim it once **m**; NDT
Job 3:21 who search for it **m than** for hidden H4946
Job 4:9 at the blast of his anger *they are* **no m**. H3983
Job 4:17 'Can a mortal be **m** righteous **than** God H4946
Job 4:17 a strong man be **m** pure **than** his Maker? H4946
Job 4:19 **how much m** those who live in houses of H677
Job 4:19 are crushed **m readily than** a moth! H4200+7156
Job 7:8 you will look for me, but I will **be no m**. H401
Job 7:10 his place will know him no **m**. H6388
Job 7:21 you will search for me, but I will **be no m**." H401
Job 8:12 they wither **m quickly than** grass. H4200+7156
Job 8:22 the tents of the wicked will **be no m**." H401
Job 9:34 so that his terror would frighten me **no** *m*. AIT
Job 11:12 can **no m** become wise **than** a wild H2256
Job 14:10 laid low; he breathes his last and is **no m**. H361
Job 14:12 till the heavens are **no m**, people will not H1194
Job 20:8 dream he flies away, **no** *m* to be found AIT
Job 20:9 his place will look on him no **m**. H6388
Job 23:12 of his mouth **m than** my daily bread. H4946
Job 27:19 wealthy, but *will* **do so** no **m**; when he H665
Job 29:22 I had spoken, *they* spoke no **m**; my words H9101
Job 32:5 that the three men had **nothing** *m* to say, AIT
Job 32:15 are dismayed and have no **m** to say; H6388
Job 34:31 'I am guilty but will offend **no m**. AIT
Job 35:11 who teaches us **m than** he teaches the H4946
Job 36:2 you that there is **m** to be said in God's H6388
Job 40:5 no answer—twice, but *I will* say no **m**." H3578
Job 42:12 part of Job's life **m than** the former part. H4946
Ps 16:4 after other gods *will* suffer **m and more**. H8049
Ps 16:4 after other gods *will* suffer **more and m**. H8049
Ps 19:10 They are **m** precious **than** gold, than H4946
Ps 37:10 the wicked will **be no m**; though you H401
Ps 37:36 he soon passed away and **was no m** H401
Ps 39:13 life again before I depart and **am no m**." H401
Ps 40:12 *They are* **m** than the hairs of my head H6793
Ps 55:21 his words are **m** soothing **than** oil, yet H4946
Ps 59:13 consume them till they **are no m**. H401
Ps 69:31 This will please the LORD **m than** an ox H4946
Ps 69:31 **m** than a bull with its horns and hooves. NDT
Ps 71:14 *I will* praise you **m and more** H3578+6584+3972
Ps 71:14 *I will* praise you **more and m** H3578+6584+3972
Ps 71:21 my honor and comfort me **once m**. H6015
Ps 72:7 prosperity abound till the moon is **no m**. H1172
Ps 75:4 'Boast **no** *m*,' and to the wicked, AIT
Ps 76:4 **m** majestic **than** mountains rich with H4946
Ps 83:4 that Israel's name is remembered **no m**." H6388
Ps 87:2 the gates of Zion **m than** all the other H4946
Ps 88:5 whom you remember no **m**, who are cut H6388
Ps 89:7 *he is* **m awesome** than all who surround H3707
Ps 103:16 is gone, and its place remembers it no **m**. H6388
Ps 104:35 from the earth and the wicked be no **m**. H6388
Ps 119:72 mouth is **m** precious to me **than** H4946
Ps 119:99 I have **m** insight **than** all my teachers, for I H4946
Ps 119:100 I have **m** understanding **than** the elders H4946
Ps 119:127 I love your commands **m than** gold, H4946
Ps 119:127 more than gold, **m than** pure gold, H4946
Ps 120:3 and what **m besides**, you deceitful H3578
Ps 130:6 the Lord **m than** watchmen wait for H4946
Ps 130:6 **m** than watchmen wait for the morning. NDT
Pr 3:14 she is **m** profitable **than** silver and H4946
Pr 3:15 She is **m** precious **than** rubies; nothing H4946
Pr 8:11 wisdom is **m** precious **than** rubies, and H4946
Pr 11:24 yet gains **even m**; another H6388
Pr 11:31 **how much m** the ungodly and the H677+3954
Pr 12:7 The wicked are overthrown and **are no m** H401
Pr 15:11 **how much m** do human hearts! H677+3954
Pr 17:10 person **m than** a hundred lashes H4946
Pr 18:19 wronged is **m** unyielding **than** a fortified H4946
Pr 19:2 **how much m** will hasty feet miss the way! H2256
Pr 19:7 **how much m** do their friends avoid H677+3954
Pr 21:3 just is **m** acceptable to the LORD **than** H4946
Pr 21:26 All day long *he* **craves for m**, but the H203+9294
Pr 21:27 **how much m so** when brought with H677+3954
Pr 22:1 good name is **m** desirable **than** great H4946
Pr 25:1 These are **m** proverbs of Solomon H1685
Pr 26:12 There is **m** hope for a fool **than** for them. H4946
Pr 29:20 There is **m** hope **for** a fool than for them. H4200
Pr 31:7 poverty and remember their misery no **m**. H6388
Pr 31:10 She is worth far **m than** rubies. H4946
Ecc 1:8 are wearisome, **m than** one can say. H4202
Ecc 1:16 in wisdom **m than** anyone who has H6584
Ecc 1:18 much sorrow; the **m** knowledge, the more H3578
Ecc 1:18 the more knowledge, the **m** grief. H3578
Ecc 2:7 I also owned **m** herds and flocks than H2221
Ecc 2:12 **What m** can the king's successor H3954+4537
Ecc 6:5 it has **m** rest **than** does that man— H4946
Ecc 6:11 The **m** the words, the less the meaning H2221
Ecc 7:19 wise person **m** powerful **than** ten rulers in H4946
Ecc 7:26 I find **m** bitter **than** death the woman who H4946
Ecc 9:17 wise are **m** to be heeded **than** the shouts H4946
Ecc 10:10 unsharpened, *m* **strength** is needed, but AIT
SS 1:2 your love is **m** delightful **than** wine. H4946
SS 1:4 we will praise your love **m than** wine. H4946
SS 4:10 How **much m** pleasing is your love **than** H4946
SS 4:10 of your perfume **m than** any spice! H4946
Isa 1:11 "*I have* **m than enough** *of* burnt offerings H8425
Isa 5:4 What **m** could have been done for my H6388
Isa 9:1 there will be **no** *m* gloom for those who were AIT

Isa 13:12 pure gold, **m** rare **than** the gold of Ophir. H4946
Isa 15: 9 I will bring **still m** upon Dimon—a H3578
Isa 19: 7 parched, will blow away and **be no m**. H401
Isa 23:12 He said, "No **m** *of* your reveling H3578+6388
Isa 25: 2 the foreigners' stronghold a city **no m**; it H4946
Isa 26:14 now dead, they live **no** *m*; their spirits do not AIT
Isa 29:14 Therefore **once m** I will astound these H3578
Isa 29:19 **Once m** the humble will rejoice in the H3578
Isa 30:10 to the seers, "**See** no *m* **visions**!" and to the AIT
Isa 30:10 "**Give** us no *m* **visions** *of* what is right! AIT
Isa 30:19 who live in Jerusalem, *you will* **weep** no *m*. AIT
Isa 30:20 your teachers will be hidden **no m**; with H6388
Isa 32:10 **In little m than** a year you who feel H3427+6584
Isa 33:19 You will see those arrogant people **no** *m* AIT
Isa 37:31 **Once m** a remnant of the kingdom of H3578
Isa 43:25 own sake, and remembers your sins **no** *m*. AIT
Isa 47: 1 No **m** will you be called tender or delicate H3578
Isa 47: 5 no **m** will you be called queen of H3578
Isa 49:20 small for us; **give** us **m space** to live in. H5602
Isa 54: 1 because **m** are the children of the H8041
Isa 54: 4 remember **no m** the reproach of your H6388
Isa 60:19 The sun will no **m** be your light by day H6388
Isa 60:20 your moon will wane **no m**; the LORD will AIT
Isa 65:19 of crying will be heard in it no **m**. H6388
Jer 2:31 free to roam; we will come to you no **m**'? H6388
Jer 3:11 Israel is **m** righteous **than** unfaithful H4946
Jer 7:26 did **m** evil **than** their ancestors. H4946
Jer 7:32 dead in Topheth until **there is no** *m* room. AIT
Jer 10:20 children are gone from me and **are no m**; H401
Jer 11:19 that his name be remembered no **m**." H6388
Jer 15: 8 widows **m** numerous **than** the sand of H4946
Jer 16:12 have behaved **m** wickedly **than** your H4946
Jer 19:11 dead in Topheth until **there is no** *m* room. AIT
Jer 22:15 you a king *to* **have m and more** cedar? H3013
Jer 22:15 you a king *to* **have more and m** cedar? H3013
Jer 25:27 fall to rise **no** *m* because of the sword I AIT
Jer 31:12 garden, and *they will* sorrow no **m**. H3578+6388
Jer 31:15 to be comforted, because they **are no m**." H401
Jer 31:34 will remember their sins **no m**. H6388
Jer 32:43 **Once m** fields will be bought in this land H2256
Jer 33:10 animals, there will be heard **once m** H6388
Jer 38:27 So *they* **said no m** to him, for no one had H3087
Jer 46:23 They are **m** numerous **than** locusts, they H4946
Jer 48: 2 Moab will be praised no **m**; in Heshbon H6388
Jer 51:64 Babylon sink to rise **no** *m* because of the AIT
Jer 52:20 the LORD, was **m than** could be weighed. H4202
La 2: 9 nations, the law **is no m**, and her prophets H401
La 4: 7 their bodies **m** ruddy **than** rubies, their H4946
La 5: 7 Our ancestors sinned and **are no m**, and H401
Eze 5: 6 laws and decrees **m than** the nations and H4946
Eze 5: 7 You have been **m** unruly **than** the nations H4946
Eze 5:16 *I will* **bring m and more** famine upon you H3578
Eze 5:16 *I will* **bring more and m** famine upon you H3578
Eze 8: 6 see things that are **even m** detestable." H1524
Eze 8:13 doing things that are **even m** detestable." H1524
Eze 8:15 things that are **even m** detestable than H1524
Eze 12:24 For there will be no **m** false visions or H6388
Eze 16:47 you soon became **m** depraved **than** they. H4946
Eze 16:51 *You have* **done m** detestable things than H8049
Eze 16:52 Because your sins were **m** vile **than** theirs H4946
Eze 16:52 they appear **m** righteous **than you**. H4946
Eze 21:32 you will be remembered **no** *m*; for I the LORD AIT
Eze 23:11 she was **m** depraved **than** her sister. H4946
Eze 23:19 Yet *she became* **m and more** promiscuous H8049
Eze 23:19 Yet *she became* **more and m** promiscuous H8049
Eze 26:13 music of your harps will be heard no **m**. H6388
Eze 26:21 you to a horrible end and you *will* **be no m**. H401
Eze 27:36 to a horrible end and will be **no m**. H6330+6409
Eze 28:19 to a horrible end and will be no **m**. H6330+6409
Eze 32:19 to them, '*Are you* **m favored** than others? H5838
Eze 33:32 them you are **nothing m than** one who H3869
Eze 36:11 will make you prosper **m than** before. H4946
Eze 39:14 *they will* **carry out a m detailed search**. H2983
Eze 42: 5 took **m** space from them **than** from the H4946
Da 2: 7 **Once m** they replied, "Let the king tell A10766
Da 2:43 **any m than** iron mixes A10195+10341+10168
Da 5: 9 Belshazzar became **even m** terrified and A10678
Da 5: 9 more terrified and his face grew **m** pale. NDT
Da 7:20 that looked **m** imposing **than** the others A10427
Da 11: 2 Three **m** kings will arise in Persia, and H6388
Da 11:19 will stumble and fall, to be seen **no** *m*. AIT
Hos 4: 7 *The* **m** priests *there were*, the more H3869+8045
Hos 4: 7 there were, *the* **m** they sinned against me H4027
Hos 10: 1 fruit increased, *he* **built m** altars; as his H8049
Hos 11: 2 But the **m** they were called, the more they NDT
Hos 11: 2 the **m** they went away from me. H4027
Hos 13: 2 Now they sin **m and more**; they make H3578
Hos 13: 2 Now they sin **more and m**; they make H3578
Hos 14: 8 Ephraim, what **m** have I to do with idols? H6388
Am 4: 4 go to Gilgal and sin **yet m**. H8049
Jnh 3: 4 "Forty **m** days and Nineveh will be H6388
Jnh 4:11 in which there are **m** than a hundred and H2221
Na 1:12 Judah, I will afflict you no **m**. H6388
Na 1:15 No **m** will the wicked invade you H3578+6388
Na 3:16 till they are **m numerous than** the stars in H4946
Hab 1:13 up those **m** righteous **than** themselves? H4946
Hag 2: 6 while I will once **m** shake the heavens H6388
Zec 13: 2 they will be remembered **no m**, H6388
Mt 2:18 to be comforted, because they are **no m**." *G4024*
Mt 3:11 me comes one who is **m powerful** *than* I, *G2708*
Mt 5:47 what are you doing **m** than others? *G4356*
Mt 6:25 Is not life **m** *than* food, and the body *G4498*
Mt 6:25 than food, and the body **m** than clothes? NDT
Mt 6:26 *Are* you not much **m valuable** than they? *G1422*
Mt 6:30 will he not much **m** clothe you—you of *G3437*
Mt 7:11 how much **m** will your Father in heaven *G3437*
Mt 10:15 it will be **m bearable** for Sodom and *G445*
Mt 10:25 how much **m** the members of his *G3437*
Mt 10:31 you *are* **worth m** than many sparrows. *G1422*
Mt 10:37 father or mother **m than** me is not worthy *G5642*
Mt 10:37 son or daughter **m than** me is not worthy *G5642*
Mt 11: 9 I tell you, and **m than** a prophet. *G4358*
Mt 11:22 it will be **m bearable** for Tyre and Sidon on *G445*
Mt 11:24 that it will be **m bearable** for Sodom on the *G445*
Mt 12:12 How much **m valuable** *is* a person than a *G1422*
Mt 12:45 it seven other spirits **m wicked** than itself, *G4505*
Mt 13:12 Whoever has *will be* **given** *m*, and they will AIT
Mt 20:10 hired first, they expected to receive **m**. *G4498*
Mt 21:36 servants to them, **m** than the first time *G4498*
Mt 22: 4 "Then he sent **some m** servants and said *G257*
Mt 22:46 no one dared to ask him **any m** questions. *G4033*
Mt 23:23 the **m important matters** of the law— *G987*
Mt 25:16 his money to work and gained five bags **m**. *G257*
Mt 25:17 one with two bags of gold gained two **m**. *G257*
Mt 25:20 See, I have gained five **m**.' *G257*
Mt 25:22 bags of gold; see, I have gained two **m**. *G257*
Mt 25:29 For whoever has *will be* **given** *m*, and they AIT
Mt 26:44 went away **once m** and prayed the *G4099*
Mt 26:53 put at my disposal **m** than twelve legions *G4498*
Mt 26:65 Why do we need **any m** witnesses? Look, *G2285*
Mk 1: 7 me comes the *one* **m powerful** than I, *G2708*
Mk 4:24 it will be measured to you—and **even m**. *G4707*
Mk 4:25 Whoever has will be given **m**; whoever does NDT
Mk 6:37 take **m than half a year's wages**! *G1324+1357*
Mk 7:36 But the **m** he did so, the more they kept *G4012*
Mk 7:36 the **m** they kept talking about it. *G3437+4358*
Mk 8:25 **Once m** Jesus put his hands on the man's *G4099*
Mk 10:26 The disciples were **even m** amazed, and *G4360*
Mk 10:48 he shouted **all the m**, "Son of *G4498+3437*
Mk 12:33 as yourself is **m important** than all burnt *G4358*
Mk 12:34 on no one dared **ask** him *any m* **questions**. AIT
Mk 12:43 poor widow has put **m** into the treasury *G4498*
Mk 14: 5 have been sold *for* **m than** a year's wages *G2062*
Mk 14:39 **Once m** he went away and prayed the *G4099*
Mk 14:63 "Why do we need **any m** witnesses?" *G2285*
Lk 3:13 "Don't collect any **m** than you are *G4498*
Lk 3:16 But one who is **m powerful** than I will *G2708*
Lk 5:15 Yet the news about him spread **all the m** *G3437*
Lk 7:26 I tell you, and **m than** a prophet. *G4358*
Lk 7:42 Now which of them will love him **m**?" *G4498*
Lk 8: 8 a **hundred times** *m* than was sown. AIT
Lk 8:18 Whoever has *will be* **given** *m*; whoever does AIT
Lk 10:12 it will be **m bearable** on that day for *G445*
Lk 10:14 it will be **m bearable** for Tyre and Sidon *G445*
Lk 11:13 how much **m** will your Father in heaven *G3437*
Lk 11:26 seven other spirits **m wicked** than itself, *G4505*
Lk 12: 4 kill the body and after that can do no **m**. *G4358*
Lk 12: 7 *you are* **worth m than** many sparrows. *G1422*
Lk 12:23 For life is **m** than food, and the body more *G4498*
Lk 12:23 than food, and the body **m** than clothes. NDT
Lk 12:24 And how much **m** valuable you are than *G3437*
Lk 12:28 the fire, how much **m** will he clothe you *G3437*
Lk 12:48 with much, **much m** will be asked. *G4358*
Lk 13: 4 think they were **m** guilty **than** all the others AIT
Lk 13: 8 'leave it alone for **one m** year, and I'll *G4047S*
Lk 14: 8 **a person m distinguished** than you *G1952*
Lk 15: 7 **m** rejoicing in heaven over one sinner who repents **than** *G2445*
Lk 16: 8 **m** shrewd in dealing with their own kind **than** *G5642*
Lk 18:39 he shouted **all the m**, "Son of *G4498+3437*
Lk 19:16 'Sir, your mina *has* **earned** ten **m**. *G4664*
Lk 19:18 'Sir, your mina has earned five **m**. *G3641S*
Lk 19:26 who has, *m will be* **given**, but as for the AIT
Lk 20:40 no one dared to ask him **any m** questions. *G4033*
Lk 21: 3 widow has put in **m** than all the others. *G4498*
Lk 22:44 he prayed **m earnestly**, and his sweat *G1757*
Lk 22:51 answered, "**No m** of this!" And he *G1572+2401*
Lk 22:71 "Why do we need **any m** testimony? *G2285*
Lk 24:21 And **what is m**, it is the third *G5250+4246+4047*
Jn 2: 3 said to him, "They have no **m** wine." *G4024*
Jn 4: 1 baptizing **m** disciples than John— *G4498*
Jn 4: 3 Judea and went back **once m** to Galilee. *G4099*
Jn 4:41 of his words many **m** became believers. *G4498*
Jn 4:46 **Once m** he visited Cana in Galilee, where *G4099*
Jn 5:18 this reason they tried **all the m** to kill him; *G3437*
Jn 6: 7 take **m than half a year's wages** to *G1357+1324*
Jn 7:31 will he perform **m** signs than this man?" *G4498*
Jn 8:21 **Once m** Jesus said to them, "I am going *G4099*
Jn 11: 6 he stayed where he was **two** *m* days, AIT
Jn 11:38 **once m** deeply moved, came to the *G4099*
Jn 12:43 loved human praise **m** than praise from *G3437*
Jn 14:30 will **not** say much **m** to you, for the prince *G4033*
Jn 15: 2 prunes so that it will be *even* **m** fruitful. *G4498*
Jn 16:12 "I have much **m** to say to you, more than *G4498*
Jn 16:12 to you, **m than** you can now bear. *G247+4024*
Jn 16:16 "In a little while you will see me **no m** *G4033*
Jn 16:17 'In a little while you will see me **no** *m*, and AIT
Jn 16:19 'In a little while you will see me **no** *m*, and AIT
Jn 17:14 of the world **any m than** I am of the *G2777+4024*
Jn 19: 4 **Once m** Pilate came out and said to the *G4099*
Jn 19: 8 Pilate heard this, he was **even m** afraid, *G3437*
Jn 21:15 of John, do you love me **m** than these?" *G4498*
Ac 5:14 **m and more** men and women believed in *G3437*
Ac 5:14 **more and m** men and women believed in *G3437*
Ac 9:22 Yet Saul grew **m and more** powerful and *G3437*
Ac 9:22 Yet Saul grew **more and m** powerful and *G3437*
Ac 17:11 Jews were of *m* noble character *than* **those** in AIT
Ac 18:20 asked him to spend **m** time with them, *G4498*
Ac 18:26 to him the way of God **m adequately**. *G209*
Ac 20:35 'It is **m** blessed to give than to receive *G3437*
Ac 23:13 **M** than forty men were involved in this plot *G4498*
Ac 23:15 of wanting **m accurate** information about *G209*
Ac 23:20 of wanting **m accurate** information about *G209*
Ac 23:21 because **m** than forty of them are waiting *G4498*
Ac 24:11 verify that no **m** than twelve days ago *G4498*
Ro 3: 5 **brings out** God's righteousness **m clearly**, *G5319*
Ro 5: 9 how much **m** shall we be saved from *G3437*
Ro 5:10 of his Son, how much **m**, having been *G3437*
Ro 5:15 how much **m** did God's grace and the gift *G3437*
Ro 5:17 how much **m** will those who receive God's *G3437*
Ro 5:20 sin increased, grace **increased all the m**, *G5668*
Ro 8:34 Jesus who died—**m than that**, who was *G3437*
Ro 8:37 things *we are* **m than conquerors** through *G5664*
Ro 11:24 how much **m** *readily* will these, the *G3437*
Ro 12: 3 *Do* not **think of yourself m highly** than *G5672*
Ro 14: 5 considers one day **m** *sacred* **than** another; *G4123*
Ro 15:23 now that there is **no m** place for me to *G3600*
1Co 3:21 **no m** boasting about human leaders! *G3594*
1Co 6: 3 **How much m** the things of this life *G3615+3615*
1Co 9:12 from you, shouldn't we have it **all the m**? *G3437*
1Co 11:17 meetings do **m** harm **than** good. *G4024+247*
1Co 11:31 But if *we were m* **discerning** with regard to AIT
1Co 14:18 that I speak in tongues **m** than all of you. *G3437*
1Co 15: 6 he appeared to **m than** five hundred of *G2062*
1Co 15:15 **M than that**, we are then found to be false *G2779*
1Co 15:32 in Ephesus with *no m than* **human** hopes, AIT
2Co 3: 8 ministry of the Spirit be even **m** glorious? *G3437*
2Co 3: 9 how much **m** glorious *is* the *G3437+4355*
2Co 4:15 *that is* **reaching m and more** *people* *G4429+1328+3836+4498*
2Co 4:15 *that is* **reaching more and m** *people* *G4429+1328+3836+4498*
2Co 8:19 **What is m**, he was chosen *G4024+3667+1254+247+2779*
2Co 8:22 now *even* **m** so because of his great *G4498*
2Co 11:23 I am **m**. I have worked much *G5642*
2Co 11:23 been in prison **m frequently**, been *G4359*
2Co 11:23 been flogged **m severely**, and been *G5649*
2Co 12: 6 think **m** of me **than is warranted** by what I *G5642*
2Co 12: 9 I will boast **all the m** gladly about my *G3437*
2Co 12:15 If I love you **m**, will you love me less *G4359*
Gal 3:20 however, implies **m than** one party; but *G4024*
Gal 4:27 because **m** are the children of the *G4498*
Eph 3:20 is able to do **immeasurably m** than all we *G5655*
Php 1: 9 your love may abound **m** and more in *G3437*
Php 1: 9 abound more and **m** in knowledge and *G3437*
Php 1:14 Lord and dare **all the m** to proclaim the *G4359*
Php 1:24 it is **m necessary** for you that I remain in *G338*
Php 2:12 now much **m** in my absence *G3437*
Php 2:28 Therefore *I am* **all the m eager** to send *G5081*
Php 3: 4 to put confidence in the flesh, I have **m**: *G3437*
Php 3: 8 **What is m**, I consider *G247+3529+2779*
Php 4:16 me aid **m than once** when I *G562+2779+1489*
Php 4:17 I desire is that **m** be credited to *G3836+2843S*
Php 4:18 full payment and **have m than enough**. *G4355*
1Th 4: 1 in the Lord Jesus to **do** *this* **m** and more. *G4355*
1Th 4: 1 in the Lord Jesus to do this more and **m**. *G3437*
1Th 4:10 sisters, *to* **do** *so* **m** and more, *G4355*
1Th 4:10 sisters, to do so more and **m**, *G3437*
2Th 1: 3 your faith *is* **growing m and more**, *G5647*
2Th 1: 3 your faith *is* **growing more and m**, *G5647*
2Ti 2:16 it *will* **become m and more** *G2093+4498+4621*
2Ti 2:16 it *will* **become more and m** *G2093+4498+4621*
Phm 21 that you will do even **m than** I ask. *G5642*
Phm 22 And **one thing m**: Prepare a guest room *G275*
Heb 7:15 we have said is even **m** clear if another *G4358*
Heb 8:12 will remember their sins no **m**. *G2285*
Heb 9:11 the greater and *m* **perfect** tabernacle that is AIT
Heb 9:14 How much **m**, then, will the blood of Christ *G3437*
Heb 10:17 lawless acts I will remember no **m**." *G2285*
Heb 10:25 and **all the m** as you see the Day *G5537+3437*
Heb 10:29 How much **m severely** do you think *G5937*
Heb 11:32 And what **m** shall I say? I do not have *G2285*
Heb 12: 9 How much **m** should we submit to the *G3437*
Heb 12:26 "Once **m** I will shake not only the earth *G2285*
Heb 12:27 The words "once **m**" indicate the removing *G2285*
Jas 3: 1 we who teach will be judged **m** *strictly*. *G3505*
Jas 4: 6 But he gives us **m** grace. That is why *G3505*
2Pe 2:11 they are stronger and **m** powerful, *G3505*
Rev 2:19 you are now doing **m** than you did at first. *G4498*
Rev 10: 6 and said, "There will be **no m** delay! *G4033*
Rev 10: 8 heard from heaven spoke to me **once m**: *G4099*
Rev 21: 4 There will be no **m** death' or mourning *G2285*
Rev 22: 5 There will be no **m** night. They will not *G2285*

MOREH (3)

Ge 12: 6 site of the great tree of **M** at Shechem. H4622
Dt 11:30 near the great trees of **M**, in the territory H4622
Jdg 7: 1 of them in the valley near the hill of **M**. H4622

MOREOVER (35)

Ge 31:20 **M**, Jacob deceived Laban the Aramean by H2256
Ex 6: 5 **M**, I have heard the groaning of the H2256+1685
Ex 31: 6 **M**, I have appointed Oholiab son of H2256
Nu 16:14 **M**, you haven't brought us into a land H677

Dt 7:20 **M,** the LORD your God will send the H2256+1685
Dt 17:16 The king, **m,** must not acquire great H8370
2Sa 8: 3 **M,** David defeated Hadadezer son of H2256
2Sa 11:17 army fell; **m,** Uriah the Hittite H2256+1685
2Sa 11:21 then say to him, '**M,** your servant Uriah H1685
2Sa 11:24 **M,** your servant Uriah the Hittite is H2256+1685
1Ki 1:46 **M,** Solomon has taken his seat on H2256+1685
1Ki 3:13 **M,** I will give you what you have not H2256+1685
1Ki 16: 7 **M,** the word of the LORD came H2256+1685
2Ki 21:16 **M,** Manasseh also shed so much innocent H1685
1Ch 18: 3 **M,** David defeated Hadadezer king of H2256
Ezr 1: 7 **M,** King Cyrus brought out the articles H2256
Ezr 6: 8 **M,** I hereby decree what you are to do A10221
Ezr 7:15 **M,** you are to take with you the silver A10221
Ne 5:14 **M,** from the twentieth year of King H1685
Ne 6: 6 **M,** according to these reports you are H2256
Ne 6:19 **M,** they kept reporting to me his good H1685
Ne 10:37 "**M,** we will bring to the storerooms of the H2256
Ne 13:23 **M,** in those days I saw men of Judah who H1685
Ecc 5:19 **M,** when God gives someone wealth and H1685
Ecc 9: 3 hearts of people, **m,** are full of evil H2256+1685
Ecc 9:12 **M,** no one knows when their hour H3954+1685
Jer 12: 4 **M,** the people are saying, "He will not H3954
Jer 21:11 "**M,** say to the royal house of Judah, 'Hear H2256
La 4:17 **M,** our eyes failed, looking in vain for H6388
Da 2:49 **M,** at Daniel's request the king A10221
Lk 4:41 **M,** demons came out of many *G1254+2779*
Jn 5:22 **M,** the Father judges no one, but has *G1142*
Ro 15: 9 **and, m,** that the Gentiles might glorify *G1254*
Php 4:15 **M,** as you Philippians know, in the early *G1254*
Heb 12: 9 **M,** we have all had human fathers *G1663+3525*

MORESHETH (2) [MORESHETH GATH]

Jer 26:18 "Micah of **M** prophesied in the days of H4629
Mic 1: 1 that came to Micah of **M** during the reigns H4629

MORESHETH GATH (1) [GATH, MORESHETH]

Mic 1:14 you will give parting gifts to **M.** H4628

MORIAH (2)

Ge 22: 2 Isaac—and go to the region of **M.** H5317
2Ch 3: 1 of the LORD in Jerusalem on Mount **M,** H5317

MORNING (222) [MORNING'S, MORNINGS]

Ge 1: 5 evening, and there was **m**—the first day. H1332
Ge 1: 8 there was **m**—the second day. H1332
Ge 1:13 evening, and there was **m**—the third day. H1332
Ge 1:19 there was **m**—the fourth day. H1332
Ge 1:23 evening, and there was **m**—the fifth day. H1332
Ge 1:31 evening, and there was **m**—the sixth day. H1332
Ge 19: 2 then go on your way **early in the m.**" H8899
Ge 19:27 Early the next **m** Abraham got up and H1332
Ge 20: 8 Early the next **m** Abimelek summoned all H1332
Ge 21:14 Early the next **m** Abraham took some food H1332
Ge 22: 3 Early the next **m** Abraham got up and H1332
Ge 24:54 When they got up the next **m,** he said H1332
Ge 26:31 Early the next **m** the men swore an oath to H1332
Ge 28:18 Early the next **m** Jacob took the stone he H1332
Ge 29:25 When **m** came, there was Leah! So Jacob H1332
Ge 31:55 Early the next **m** Laban kissed his H1332
Ge 40: 6 When Joseph came to them the next **m** H1332
Ge 41: 8 In the **m** his mind was troubled, so he H1332
Ge 44: 3 As **m** dawned, the men were sent on their H1332
Ge 49:27 in the **m** he devours the prey H1332
Ex 7:15 Go to Pharaoh in the **m** as he goes out to H1332
Ex 8:20 up early in the **m** and confront Pharaoh H1332
Ex 9:13 "Get up early in the **m,** confront Pharaoh H1332
Ex 10:13 *By* **m** the wind had brought the locusts; H1332
Ex 12:10 Do not leave any of it till **m;** if some is left H1332
Ex 12:10 if some is left till **m,** you must burn it. H1332
Ex 12:22 go out of the door of your house until **m.** H1332
Ex 16: 7 and *in* the **m** you will see the glory of the H1332
Ex 16: 8 all the bread you want in the **m,** H1332
Ex 16:12 in the **m** you will be filled with bread. H1332
Ex 16:13 in the **m** there was a layer of dew H1332
Ex 16:19 "No one is to keep any of it until **m.**" H1332
Ex 16:20 they kept part of it until **m,** but it was full H1332
Ex 16:21 **Each m** everyone gathered
H928+2021+1332+928+2021+1332
Ex 16:23 Save whatever is left and keep it until **m.**' H1332
Ex 16:24 So they saved it until **m,** as Moses H1332
Ex 18:13 stood around him from **m** till evening. H1332
Ex 18:14 stand around you from **m** till evening?" H1332
Ex 19:16 On the **m** of the third day there was H1332
Ex 23:18 festival offerings must not be kept until **m.** H1332
Ex 24: 4 up early the next **m** and built an altar at H1332
Ex 27:21 before the LORD from evening till **m.** H1332
Ex 29:34 ram or any bread is left over till **m,** H1332
Ex 29:39 Offer one in the **m** and the other at H1332
Ex 29:41 its drink offering as in the **m**— H1332
Ex 30: 7 altar **every m** when he tends
H928+2021+1332+928+2021+1332
Ex 34: 2 Be ready in the **m,** and then come up on H1332
Ex 34: 4 went up Mount Sinai early in the **m,** H1332
Ex 34:25 from the Passover Festival remain until **m.** H1332
Ex 36: 3 bring freewill offerings **m** after morning. H1332
Ex 36: 3 bring freewill offerings morning after **m.** H1332
Lev 6: 9 the night, till **m,** and the fire must be kept H1332
Lev 6:12 **Every m** the priest is to add
H928+2021+1332+928+2021+1332
Lev 6:20 half of it in the **m** and half in the evening. H1332
Lev 7:15 offered; they must leave none of it till **m.** H1332
Lev 22:30 that same day; leave none of it till **m.** H1332
Lev 24: 3 lamps before the LORD from evening till **m,** H1332
Nu 9:12 not leave any of it till **m** or break any of its H1332
Nu 9:15 From evening till **m** the cloud above the H1332
Nu 9:21 the cloud stayed only from evening till **m,** H1332
Nu 9:21 when it lifted in the **m,** they set out. H1332
Nu 14:40 Early the next **m** they set out for the H1332
Nu 16: 5 "In the **m** the LORD will show who belongs H1332
Nu 22:13 The next **m** Balaam got up and said to H1332
Nu 22:21 Balaam got up in the **m,** saddled his H1332
Nu 22:41 The next **m** Balak took Balaam up to H1332
Nu 28: 4 Offer one lamb in the **m** and the other at H1332
Nu 28: 8 drink offering that you offer in the **m.** H1332
Nu 28:23 addition to the regular **m** burnt offering. H1332
Dt 16: 4 evening of the first day remain until **m.** H1332
Dt 16: 7 Then in the **m** return to your tents H1332
Dt 28:67 In the **m** you will say, "If only it were H1332
Dt 28:67 and in the evening, "If only it were **m!**" H1332
Jos 3: 1 Early in the **m** Joshua and all the H1332
Jos 6:12 up early the next **m** and the priests took H1332
Jos 7:14 " 'In the **m,** present yourselves tribe by H1332
Jos 7:16 Early the next **m** Joshua had Israel come H1332
Jos 8:10 Early the next **m** Joshua mustered his H1332
Jos 8:14 hurried out **early in the m** to meet Israel H8899
Jdg 6:28 In the **m** when the people of the town got H1332
Jdg 6:31 fights for him shall be put to death by **m!** H1332
Jdg 7: 1 **Early in the m,** Jerub-Baal (that is, Gideon H8899
Jdg 9:33 In the **m** at sunrise, advance against the H1332
Jdg 19: 8 On the **m** of the fifth day, when he rose to H1332
Jdg 19: 9 **Early** tomorrow **m** *you can* **get up** and be H8899
Jdg 19:27 got up in the **m** and opened the door H1332
Jdg 20:19 The next **m** the Israelites got up and H1332
Ru 2: 7 has remained here from **m** till now, H1332
Ru 3:13 in the **m** if he wants to do his duty as H1332
Ru 3:13 LORD lives I will do it. Lie here until **m.**" H1332
Ru 3:14 So she lay at his feet until **m,** but got up H1332
1Sa 1:19 Early the next **m** they arose and H1332
1Sa 3:15 lay down until **m** and then opened the H1332
1Sa 5: 4 But the following **m** when they rose, there H1332
1Sa 9:19 in the **m** I will send you on your way H1332
1Sa 15:12 Early in the **m** Samuel got up and went to H1332
1Sa 17:16 came forward *every* **m** and evening and H8899
1Sa 17:20 Early in the **m** David left the flock in the H1332
1Sa 19: 2 Be on your guard tomorrow **m;** go into H1332
1Sa 19:11 house to watch it and to kill him in the **m.** H1332
1Sa 20:35 In the **m** Jonathan went out to the field H1332
1Sa 25:22 if by **m** I leave alive one male of all who H1332
1Sa 25:37 Then in the **m,** when Nabal was sober, his H1332
1Sa 29:10 leave in the **m** as soon as it is light." H1332
1Sa 29:11 got up early in the **m** to go back to the H1332
2Sa 2:27 have continued pursuing them until **m.**" H1332
2Sa 2:29 through the **m hours** and came to H1443
2Sa 11:14 In the **m** David wrote a letter to Joab and H1332
2Sa 13: 4 look so haggard **m** after morning? H1332
2Sa 13: 4 look so haggard morning after **m?** H1332
2Sa 23: 4 he is like the light of **m** at sunrise on a H1332
2Sa 23: 4 of morning at sunrise on a cloudless **m,** H1332
2Sa 24:11 Before David got up the next **m,** the word H1332
2Sa 24:15 on Israel from that **m** until the end of the H1332
1Ki 3:21 The next **m,** I got up to nurse my son—and H1332
1Ki 3:21 I looked at him closely in the **m light,** H1332
1Ki 17: 6 meat in the **m** and bread and meat H1332
1Ki 18:26 on the name of Baal from **m** till noon. H1332
2Ki 3:20 The next **m,** about the time for offering H1332
2Ki 3:22 When they got up early in the **m,** the sun H1332
2Ki 6:15 got up and went out **early the next m,** H8899
2Ki 10: 8 at the entrance of the city gate until **m.**" H1332
2Ki 10: 9 The next **m** Jehu went out. He stood H1332
2Ki 16:15 offer the **m** burnt offering and the evening H1332
2Ki 19:35 When the people got up the next **m** H1332
1Ch 9:27 for opening it **each m.**
H4200+2021+1332+4200+2021+1332
1Ch 16:40 offering regularly, **m** and evening, in H1332
1Ch 23:30 to stand **every m** to thank
H928+2021+1332+928+2021+1332
2Ch 2: 4 offerings every **m** and evening and on H1332
2Ch 13:11 **Every m** and evening they present
H928+2021+1332+928+2021+1332
2Ch 20:20 Early in the **m** they left for the Desert of H1332
2Ch 29:20 **Early the next m** King Hezekiah gathered H8899
2Ch 31: 3 possessions for the **m** and evening burnt H1332
Ezr 3: 3 both the **m** and evening sacrifices. H1332
Est 2:14 go there and in the **m** return to another H1332
Est 5:14 ask the king in the **m** to have Mordecai H1332
Job 1: 5 Early in the **m** he would sacrifice a burnt H1332
Job 3: 9 May its **m** stars become dark; may it wait H5974
Job 7:18 examine them every **m** and test them H1332
Job 11:17 darkness will become like **m.** H1332
Job 24:17 midnight is their **m;** they make friends H1332
Job 38: 7 while the **m** stars sang together and all H1332
Job 38:12 "Have you ever given orders to the **m,** or H1332
Ps 5: 3 *In* the **m,** LORD, you hear my voice; in the H1332
Ps 5: 3 *in* the **m** I lay my requests before you and H1332
Ps 22: T To the tune of "The Doe of the **M.**" A H8840
Ps 30: 5 the night, but rejoicing comes in the **m.** H1332
Ps 49:14 upright will prevail over them in the **m).** H1332
Ps 55:17 Evening, **m** and noon I cry out in distress H1332
Ps 59:16 strength, in the **m** I will sing of your love H1332
Ps 65: 8 your wonders; where **m** dawns, where H1332
Ps 73:14 every **m** brings new punishments. H1332
Ps 88:13 in the **m** my prayer comes before you. H1332
Ps 90: 5 they are like the new grass of the **m:** H1332
Ps 90: 6 In the **m** it springs up new, but by evening H1332
Ps 90:14 Satisfy us in the **m** with your unfailing H1332
Ps 92: 2 your love in the **m** and your faithfulness at H1332
Ps 101: 8 Every **m** I will put to silence all the wicked H1332
Ps 130: 6 Lord more than watchmen wait for the **m,** H1332
Ps 130: 6 more than watchmen wait for the **m.** H1332
Ps 143: 8 Let the **m** bring me word of your unfailing H1332
Pr 4:18 path of the righteous is like the **m** sun, H5586
Pr 7:18 let's drink deeply of love till **m;** let's enjoy H1332
Pr 27:14 blesses their neighbor early in the **m,** H1332
Ecc 10:16 servant and whose princes feast in the **m.** H1332
Ecc 11: 6 Sow your seed in the **m,** and at evening H1332
Isa 5:11 who rise early in the **m** to run after their H1332
Isa 14:12 from heaven, **m star,** son of the dawn! H2122
Isa 17:11 and on the **m** when you plant them H1332
Isa 17:14 Before the **m,** they are gone! This is H1332
Isa 21:12 watchman replies, "**M** is coming, but also H1332
Isa 26: 9 the night; in the **m** my spirit longs for you. H1332
Isa 26:19 your dew is like the dew of the **m;** the earth H245
Isa 28:19 will carry you away; **m** after morning, by H1332
Isa 28:19 morning after **m,** by day and by H1332
Isa 33: 2 Be our strength every **m,** our salvation in H1332
Isa 37:36 When the people got up the next **m** H1332
Isa 44:22 like a cloud, your sins like the **m mist.** H6727
Isa 50: 4 He wakens me **m** by morning, wakens my H1332
Isa 50: 4 He wakens me morning by **m,** wakens my H1332
Jer 20:16 May he hear wailing in the **m,** a battle cry H1332
Jer 21:12 " 'Administer justice every **m;** rescue from H1332
La 3:23 They are new every **m;** great is your H1332
Eze 12: 8 In the **m** the word of the LORD came to me: H1332
Eze 24:18 So I spoke to the people in the **m,** and in H1332
Eze 24:18 The next **m** I did as I had been H1332
Eze 33:22 before the man came to me in the **m.** H1332
Eze 46:13 **m** by morning you shall provide it. H1332
Eze 46:13 morning by **m** you shall provide it. H1332
Eze 46:14 to provide with it **m** by morning a grain H1332
Eze 46:14 with it morning by **m** a grain offering, H1332
Eze 46:15 oil shall be provided **m** by morning for a H1332
Eze 46:15 provided morning by **m** for a regular burnt H1332
Hos 6: 4 Your love is like the **m** mist, like the early H1332
Hos 7: 6 in the **m** it blazes like a flaming fire. H1332
Hos 13: 3 Therefore they will be like the **m** mist, like H1332
Am 4: 4 Bring your sacrifices every **m,** your tithes H1332
Zep 3: 3 who leave nothing for the **m.** H1332
Zep 3: 5 **M** by morning he dispenses his justice H1332
Zep 3: 5 Morning by **m** he dispenses his justice H1332
Mt 16: 3 and **in the m,** 'Today it will be stormy, for *G4745*
Mt 20: 1 who went out **early in the m** to hire *G275+4745*
Mt 20: 3 "About **nine in the m** he went out *G5569+6052*
Mt 21:18 **Early in the m,** as Jesus was on his way *G4745*
Mt 27: 1 **Early in the m,** all the chief priests and *G4746*
Mk 1:35 Very **early in the m,** while it was still dark *G4745*
Mk 11:20 **In the m,** as they went along, they saw *G4745*
Mk 15: 1 **Very early in the m,** the chief *G2317+4745*
Mk 15:25 It was **nine in the m** when they *G6052+5569*
Lk 6:13 When **m** came, he called his disciples to *G2465*
Lk 21:38 the people **came early in the m** to hear *G3983*
Lk 24: 1 the week, very **early in the m,** the women *G3986*
Lk 24:22 They went to the tomb **early** *this* **m** *G3984*
Jn 18:28 By now it was **early m,** and to avoid *G4745*
Jn 21: 4 **Early in the m,** Jesus stood on the shore *G4746*
Ac 2:15 It's *only* **nine in the m!** *G6052+5569+3836+2465*
Ac 12:18 **In the m,** there was no small *G1181+2465*
Ac 23:12 The next **m** some Jews formed a *G2465*
Ac 28:23 He witnessed to them from **m** till evening *G4745*
2Pe 1:19 day dawns and the **m star** rises in your *G5892*
Rev 2:28 I will also give that one the **m** star. *G4748*
Rev 22:16 Offspring of David, and the bright **M** Star." *G4748*

MORNING'S (3) [MORNING]

Lev 9:17 altar in addition to the **m** burnt offering. H1332
Ps 110: 3 come to you like dew from the **m** womb. H5423
Mic 2: 1 At **m** light they carry it out because it is in H1332

MORNINGS (2) [MORNING]

Da 8:14 "It will take 2,300 evenings and **m;** then H1332
Da 8:26 the evenings and **m** that has been given H1332

MORROW (KJV) DAY AFTER, FOLLOWING, MORNING, NEXT DAY, TOMORROW

MORSELS (2)

Pr 18: 8 The words of a gossip are like **choice m** H4269
Pr 26:22 The words of a gossip are like **choice m** H4269

MORTAL (25) [MORTALLY, MORTALS]

Ge 6: 3 for they are **m;** their days will be a H1414
Dt 5:26 For what **m** has ever heard the voice of the H1414
Job 4:17 'Can a **m** be more righteous than God? Can H632
Job 9:32 "He is not a *mere* **m** like me that I might H408
Job 10: 4 Do you see as a **m** sees? H632
Job 10: 5 days like those of a **m** or your years like H632
Job 13: 9 deceive him as you might deceive a **m?** H632
Job 25: 4 How then can a **m** be righteous before God H632
Job 25: 6 how much less a **m,** who is but a maggot H632
Job 28:13 No **m** comprehends its worth; it cannot be H632
Job 33:12 are not right, for God is greater than *any* **m.** H632
Ps 9:20 let the nations know they are *only* **m.** H632
Ps 17: 9 from my **m** enemies who surround H928+5883
Ps 42:10 My bones suffer **m agony** as my foes taunt H8358
Eze 28: 2 But you are a *mere* **m** and not a god H132
Eze 28: 9 You will be *but* a **m,** not a god, in the H132
Mic 6: 8 He has shown you, O **m,** what is good. H132
Mal 3: 8 "Will a *mere* **m** rob God? Yet you rob me H132

M

Ro 1:23 made to look like a **m** human being and *G5778*
Ro 6:12 sin reign in your **m** body so that you obey *G2570*
Ro 8:11 give life to your **m** bodies because of his *G2570*
1Co 15:53 imperishable, and the **m** with immortality. *G2570*
1Co 15:54 imperishable, and the **m** with immortality *G2570*
2Co 4:11 life may also be revealed in our **m** body. *G2570*
2Co 5: 4 so that what is **m** may be swallowed up *G2570*

MORTALLY (1) [MORTAL]

Eze 30:24 groan before him like a **m wounded man**. H2728

MORTALS (25) [MORTAL]

2Ch 14:11 do not let *mere* **m** prevail against you." H632
2Ch 19: 6 are not judging for *mere* **m** but for the LORD, H132
Job 7: 1 "Do not **m** have hard service on earth? Are H632
Job 9: 2 But how can *mere* **m** prove their innocence H632
Job 14: 1 "**M**, born of woman, are of few days and H132
Job 15:14 "What are **m**, that they could be pure, or H632
Job 15:16 how much less **m**, who are vile and corrupt H408
Job 28: 3 *M* **put** an end to the darkness; they search AIT
Job 34:21 "His eyes are on the ways of **m**; he sees H408
Job 36:25 has seen it; **m** gaze on it from afar. H632
Ps 9:19 do not let **m** triumph; let the nations H632
Ps 10:18 so that *mere* earthly **m** will never again H632
Ps 56: 4 What can *mere* **m** do to me? H1414
Ps 82: 7 But you will die like *mere* **m**; you will fall H132
Ps 90: 3 saying, "Return to dust, you **m**." H1201+132
Ps 103:15 The life of **m** is like grass, they flourish like H632
Ps 118: 6 What can mere **m** do to me? H132
Ps 144: 3 *mere* **m** that you think of them? H1201+632
Pr 11: 7 Hopes placed in **m** die with them; all the H132
Isa 31: 3 But the Egyptians are *mere* **m** and not God H132
Isa 31: 8 a sword, not *of* **m**, will devour them. H132
Isa 51: 7 the reproach of *mere* **m** or be terrified by H632
Isa 51:12 Who are you that you fear *mere* **m** H4637+632
Eze 31:14 among **m** who go down to the realm H1201+132
Heb 13: 6 What can *mere* **m** do to me?" *G476*

MORTAR (6)

Ge 11: 3 used brick instead of stone, and tar for **m**. H2817
Ex 1:14 labor in brick and **m** and with all kinds of H2817
Nu 11: 8 it in a hand mill or crushed it in a **m**. H4521
Pr 27:22 Though you grind a fool in a **m**, grinding H4847
Isa 41:25 He treads on rulers as if they were **m**, as if H2817
Na 3:14 the clay, tread the **m**, repair the brickwork! H2817

MORTER (KJV) CLAY, MORTAR, PLASTER, WHITEWASH

MORTGAGING (1)

Ne 5: 3 were saying, "We *are* **m** our fields, our H6842

MORTIFY (KJV) PUT TO DEATH

MOSAIC (1)

Est 1: 6 silver on a **m pavement** *of* porphyry, H8367

MOSERAH (1)

Dt 10: 6 from the wells of Bene Jaakan to **M**. H4594

MOSEROTH (2)

Nu 33:30 They left Hashmonah and camped at **M**. H5035
Nu 33:31 They left **M** and camped at Bene Jaakan. H5035

MOSES (829) [MOSES']

Ex 2:10 She named him **M**, saying, "I drew him H5407
Ex 2:11 One day, after **M** had grown up, he went H5407
Ex 2:14 Then **M** was afraid and thought, "What I H5407
Ex 2:15 he tried to kill **M**, but Moses fled from H5407
Ex 2:15 **M** fled from Pharaoh and went to live H5407
Ex 2:17 **M** got up and came to their rescue H5407
Ex 2:21 **M** agreed to stay with the man, who gave H5407
Ex 2:21 his daughter Zipporah to **M** in marriage. H5407
Ex 2:22 birth to a son, and **M** named him Gershom NDT
Ex 3: 1 Now **M** was tending the flock of Jethro his H5407
Ex 3: 2 **M** saw that though the bush was on fire it NDT
Ex 3: 3 So **M** thought, "I will go over and see this H5407
Ex 3: 4 called to him from within the bush, "**M**! H5407
Ex 3: 4 the bush, "Moses! **M**!" And Moses said H5407
Ex 3: 4 Moses!" And **M** said, "Here I am." NDT
Ex 3: 6 **M** hid his face, because he was H5407
Ex 3:11 But **M** said to God, "Who am I that I H5407
Ex 3:13 **M** said to God, "Suppose I go to the H5407
Ex 3:14 God said to **M**, "I AM WHO I AM. This is H5407
Ex 3:15 God also said to **M**, "Say to the Israelites H5407
Ex 4: 1 **M** answered, "What if they do not believe H5407
Ex 4: 3 **M** threw it on the ground and it became a H5407
Ex 4: 4 So **M** reached out and took hold of the H5407
Ex 4: 6 So **M** put his hand into his cloak, and when NDT
Ex 4: 7 So **M** put his hand back into his cloak, and NDT
Ex 4:10 **M** said to the LORD, "Pardon your servant H5407
Ex 4:13 But **M** said, "Pardon your servant, Lord NDT
Ex 4:14 anger burned against **M** and he said, H5407
Ex 4:18 Then **M** went back to Jethro his H5407
Ex 4:19 Now the LORD had said to **M** in Midian H5407
Ex 4:20 So **M** took his wife and sons, put them on H5407
Ex 4:21 The LORD said to **M**, "When you return to H5407
Ex 4:24 the LORD met **M** and was about to kill H2084S
Ex 4:27 "Go into the wilderness to meet **M**." H5407
Ex 4:27 So he met **M** at the mountain of God H2084S
Ex 4:28 Then **M** told Aaron everything the LORD H5407
Ex 4:29 **M** and Aaron brought together all the H5407
Ex 4:30 them everything the LORD had said to **M**. H5407
Ex 5: 1 Afterward **M** and Aaron went to Pharaoh H5407
Ex 5: 4 king of Egypt said, "**M** and Aaron, why are H5407
Ex 5:20 they found **M** and Aaron waiting to meet H5407
Ex 5:22 **M** returned to the LORD and said, "Why H5407
Ex 6: 1 Then the LORD said to **M**, "Now you will H5407
Ex 6: 2 God also said to **M**, "I am the LORD. H5407
Ex 6: 9 **M** reported this to the Israelites, but they H5407
Ex 6:10 Then the LORD said to **M**, H5407
Ex 6:12 But **M** said to the LORD, "If the Israelites H5407
Ex 6:13 the LORD spoke to **M** and Aaron about the H5407
Ex 6:20 Jochebed, who bore him Aaron and **M**. H5407
Ex 6:26 was this Aaron and **M** to whom the LORD H5407
Ex 6:27 out of Egypt—this same **M** and Aaron. H5407
Ex 6:28 Now when the LORD spoke to **M** in Egypt, H5407
Ex 6:30 But **M** said to the LORD, "Since I speak H5407
Ex 7: 1 Then the LORD said to **M**, "See, I have H5407
Ex 7: 6 **M** and Aaron did just as the LORD H5407
Ex 7: 7 **M** was eighty years old and Aaron H5407
Ex 7: 8 The LORD said to **M** and Aaron, H5407
Ex 7:10 So **M** and Aaron went to Pharaoh and did H5407
Ex 7:14 Then the LORD said to **M**, "Pharaoh's heart H5407
Ex 7:19 The LORD said to **M**, "Tell Aaron, 'Take H5407
Ex 7:20 **M** and Aaron did just as the LORD had H5407
Ex 7:22 he would not listen to **M and Aaron**, just H2157S
Ex 8: 1 Then the LORD said to **M**, "Go to Pharaoh H5407
Ex 8: 5 Then the LORD said to **M**, "Tell Aaron H5407
Ex 8: 8 Pharaoh summoned **M** and Aaron and H5407
Ex 8: 9 **M** said to Pharaoh, "I leave to you the H5407
Ex 8:10 **M** replied, "It will be as you say, so that you NDT
Ex 8:12 After **M** and Aaron left Pharaoh, Moses H5407
Ex 8:12 **M** cried out to the LORD about the frogs he H5407
Ex 8:13 the LORD did what **M** asked. The frogs H5407
Ex 8:15 would not listen to **M and Aaron**, H2157S
Ex 8:16 Then the LORD said to **M**, "Tell Aaron H5407
Ex 8:20 Then the LORD said to **M**, "Get up early in H5407
Ex 8:25 Pharaoh summoned **M** and Aaron and H5407
Ex 8:26 But **M** said, "That would not be right. H5407
Ex 8:29 **M** answered, "As soon as I leave you, H5407
Ex 8:30 Then **M** left Pharaoh and prayed to the H5407
Ex 8:31 the LORD did what **M** asked. The flies H5407
Ex 9: 1 Then the LORD said to **M**, "Go to Pharaoh H5407
Ex 9: 8 Then the LORD said to **M** and Aaron, "Take H5407
Ex 9: 8 a furnace and have **M** toss it into the air H5407
Ex 9:10 **M** tossed it into the air, and festering H5407
Ex 9:11 not stand before **M** because of the boils H5407
Ex 9:12 he would not listen to **M and Aaron**, H2157S
Ex 9:12 Aaron, just as the LORD had said to **M**. H5407
Ex 9:13 Then the LORD said to **M**, "Get up early in H5407
Ex 9:22 Then the LORD said to **M**, "Stretch out your H5407
Ex 9:23 When **M** stretched out his staff toward the H5407
Ex 9:27 Then Pharaoh summoned **M** and Aaron H5407
Ex 9:29 **M** replied, "When I have gone out of the H5407
Ex 9:33 Then **M** left Pharaoh and went out of the H5407
Ex 9:35 just as the LORD had said through **M**. H5407
Ex 10: 1 Then the LORD said to **M**, "Go to Pharaoh H5407
Ex 10: 3 So **M** and Aaron went to Pharaoh and H5407
Ex 10: 6 Then **M** turned and left Pharaoh NDT
Ex 10: 8 Then **M** and Aaron were brought back to H5407
Ex 10: 9 **M** answered, "We will go with our young H5407
Ex 10:11 Then **M and Aaron** were driven out of H4392S
Ex 10:12 And the LORD said to **M**, "Stretch out your H5407
Ex 10:13 So **M** stretched out his staff over Egypt H5407
Ex 10:16 quickly summoned **M** and Aaron and said H5407
Ex 10:18 **M** then left Pharaoh and prayed to the LORD. NDT
Ex 10:21 the LORD said to **M**, "Stretch out your H5407
Ex 10:22 So **M** stretched out his hand toward the sky H5407
Ex 10:24 Then Pharaoh summoned **M** and said H5407
Ex 10:25 But **M** said, "You must allow us to have H5407
Ex 10:28 Pharaoh said to **M**, "Get out of my sight H2257S
Ex 10:29 "Just as you say," **M** replied. "I will never H5407
Ex 11: 1 Now the LORD had said to **M**, "I will bring H5407
Ex 11: 3 **M** himself was highly regarded in H5407
Ex 11: 4 So **M** said, "This is what the LORD says H5407
Ex 11: 8 Then **M**, hot with anger, left NDT
Ex 11: 9 The LORD had said to **M**, "Pharaoh will H5407
Ex 11:10 **M** and Aaron performed all these wonders H5407
Ex 12: 1 The LORD said to **M** and Aaron in Egypt, H5407
Ex 12:21 Then **M** summoned all the elders of Israel H5407
Ex 12:28 what the LORD commanded **M** and Aaron. H5407
Ex 12:31 Pharaoh summoned **M** and Aaron and H5407
Ex 12:35 Israelites did as **M** instructed and asked H5407
Ex 12:43 The LORD said to **M** and Aaron, "These are H5407
Ex 12:50 the LORD had commanded **M** and Aaron. H5407
Ex 13: 1 The LORD said to **M**, H5407
Ex 13: 3 Then **M** said to the people H5407
Ex 13:19 **M** took the bones of Joseph with him H5407
Ex 14: 1 Then the LORD said to **M**, H5407
Ex 14:11 They said to **M**, "Was it because there H5407
Ex 14:13 **M** answered the people, "Do not be H5407
Ex 14:15 Then the LORD said to **M**, "Why are you H5407
Ex 14:21 Then **M** stretched out his hand over the H5407
Ex 14:26 Then the LORD said to **M**, "Stretch out your H5407
Ex 14:27 **M** stretched out his hand over the sea, and H5407
Ex 14:31 put their trust in him and in **M** his servant. H5407
Ex 15: 1 Then **M** and the Israelites sang this song H5407
Ex 15:22 Then **M** led Israel from the Red Sea and H5407
Ex 15:24 So the people grumbled against **M**, saying H5407
Ex 15:25 Then **M** cried out to the LORD, and the LORD NDT
Ex 16: 2 grumbled against **M** and Aaron. H5407
Ex 16: 4 Then the LORD said to **M**, "I will rain down H5407
Ex 16: 6 So **M** and Aaron said to all the Israelites H5407
Ex 16: 8 **M** also said, "You will know that it was the H5407
Ex 16: 9 Then **M** told Aaron, "Say to the entire H5407
Ex 16:11 The LORD said to **M**, H5407
Ex 16:15 **M** said to them, "It is the bread the LORD H5407
Ex 16:19 Then **M** said to them, "No one is to keep H5407
Ex 16:20 some of them paid no attention to **M** H5407
Ex 16:20 So **M** was angry with them H5407
Ex 16:22 community came and reported this to **M**. H5407
Ex 16:24 it until morning, as **M** commanded, and it H5407
Ex 16:25 **M** said, "because today is a sabbath to H5407
Ex 16:28 Then the LORD said to **M**, "How long will H5407
Ex 16:32 **M** said, "This is what the LORD has H5407
Ex 16:33 So **M** said to Aaron, "Take a jar and put H5407
Ex 16:34 As the LORD commanded **M**, Aaron put the H5407
Ex 17: 2 So they quarreled with **M** and said, "Give H5407
Ex 17: 2 us water to drink." **M** replied, "Why do H5407
Ex 17: 3 and they grumbled against **M**. H5407
Ex 17: 4 Then **M** cried out to the LORD, "What am I H5407
Ex 17: 5 The LORD answered **M**, "Go out in front of H5407
Ex 17: 6 So **M** did this in the sight of the elders of H5407
Ex 17: 9 **M** said to Joshua, "Choose some of our H5407
Ex 17:10 fought the Amalekites as **M** had ordered, H5407
Ex 17:10 had ordered, and **M**, Aaron and Hur went H5407
Ex 17:11 As long as **M** held up his hands, the H5407
Ex 17:14 Then the LORD said to **M**, "Write this on a H5407
Ex 17:15 **M** built an altar and called it The LORD is H5407
Ex 18: 1 priest of Midian and father-in-law of **M**, H5407
Ex 18: 1 God had done for **M** and for his people H5407
Ex 18: 2 After **M** had sent away his wife Zipporah H5407
Ex 18: 3 named Gershom, for **M** said, "I have NDT
Ex 18: 7 So **M** went out to meet his father-in-law H5407
Ex 18: 8 **M** told his father-in-law about everything H5407
Ex 18:13 The next day **M** took his seat to serve as H5407
Ex 18:14 saw all that **M** was doing for the people, H5407
Ex 18:15 **M** answered him, "Because the people H5407
Ex 18:24 **M** listened to his father-in-law and did H5407
Ex 18:26 The difficult cases they brought to **M**, but H5407
Ex 18:27 Then **M** sent his father-in-law on his way H5407
Ex 19: 3 Then **M** went up to God, and the LORD H5407
Ex 19: 7 So **M** went back and summoned the H5407
Ex 19: 8 So **M** brought their answer back to the H5407
Ex 19: 9 The LORD said to **M**, "I am going to come H5407
Ex 19: 9 Then **M** told the LORD what the people H5407
Ex 19:10 And the LORD said to **M**, "Go to the people H5407
Ex 19:14 After **M** had gone down the mountain to H5407
Ex 19:17 Then **M** led the people out of the camp to H5407
Ex 19:19 **M** spoke and the voice of God answered H5407
Ex 19:20 Sinai and called **M** to the top of the H5407
Ex 19:20 to the top of the mountain. So **M** went up H5407
Ex 19:23 **M** said to the LORD, "The people cannot H5407
Ex 19:25 So **M** went down to the people and told H5407
Ex 20:19 said to **M**, "Speak to us yourself and H5407
Ex 20:20 **M** said to the people, "Do not be afraid H5407
Ex 20:21 while **M** approached the thick darkness H5407
Ex 20:22 Then the LORD said to **M**, "Tell the H5407
Ex 24: 1 Then the LORD said to **M**, "Come up to the H5407
Ex 24: 2 **M** alone is to approach the LORD; the H5407
Ex 24: 3 When **M** went and told the people all the H5407
Ex 24: 4 **M** then wrote down everything the LORD H5407
Ex 24: 6 **M** took half of the blood and put it in H5407
Ex 24: 8 **M** then took the blood, sprinkled it on the H5407
Ex 24: 9 **M** and Aaron, Nadab and Abihu, and the H5407
Ex 24:12 The LORD said to **M**, "Come up to me on H5407
Ex 24:13 Then **M** set out with Joshua his aide, and H5407
Ex 24:13 **M** went up on the mountain of God. H5407
Ex 24:15 When **M** went up on the mountain, the H5407
Ex 24:16 LORD called to **M** from within the cloud H5407
Ex 24:18 Then **M** entered the cloud as he went on H5407
Ex 25: 1 The LORD said to **M**, H5407
Ex 30:11 Then the LORD said to **M**, H5407
Ex 30:17 Then the LORD said to **M**, H5407
Ex 30:22 Then the LORD said to **M**, H5407
Ex 30:34 Then the LORD said to **M**, "Take fragrant H5407
Ex 31: 1 Then the LORD said to **M**, H5407
Ex 31:12 Then the LORD said to **M**, H5407
Ex 31:18 finished speaking to **M** on Mount Sinai, H5407
Ex 32: 1 the people saw that **M** was so long in H5407
Ex 32: 1 As for this fellow **M** who brought us up H5407
Ex 32: 7 Then the LORD said to **M**, "Go down H5407
Ex 32: 9 the LORD said to **M**, "and they are a H5407
Ex 32:11 **M** sought the favor of the LORD his God H5407
Ex 32:15 **M** turned and went down the mountain H5407
Ex 32:17 he said to **M**, "There is the sound H5407
Ex 32:18 **M** replied: "It is not the sound of victory, NDT
Ex 32:19 When **M** approached the camp and saw H5407
Ex 32:23 As for this fellow **M** who brought us up H5407
Ex 32:25 **M** saw that the people were running wild H5407
Ex 32:28 The Levites did as **M** commanded, and H5407
Ex 32:29 Then **M** said, "You have been set apart to H5407
Ex 32:30 The next day **M** said to the people, "You H5407
Ex 32:31 So **M** went back to the LORD and said, "Oh H5407
Ex 32:33 The LORD replied to **M**, "Whoever has H5407
Ex 33: 1 the LORD said to **M**, "Leave this place H5407
Ex 33: 5 For the LORD had said to **M**, "Tell the H5407
Ex 33: 7 Now **M** used to take a tent and pitch it H5407
Ex 33: 8 And whenever **M** went out to the tent, all H5407
Ex 33: 8 watching **M** until he entered the tent. H5407
Ex 33: 9 As **M** went into the tent, the pillar of cloud H5407
Ex 33: 9 entrance, while the LORD spoke with **M**. H5407
Ex 33:11 The LORD would speak to **M** face to face, H5407
Ex 33:11 Then **M** would return to the camp, but his NDT
Ex 33:12 **M** said to the LORD, "You have been H5407
Ex 33:15 Then **M** said to him, "If your Presence does NDT
Ex 33:17 the LORD said to **M**, "I will do the very H5407

M

Ex 33:18 Then **M** said, "Now show me your glory." NDT
Ex 34: 1 The LORD said to **M**, "Chisel out two stone H5407
Ex 34: 4 So **M** chiseled out two stone tablets like H5407
Ex 34: 6 And he passed in front of **M**, proclaiming, H2257S
Ex 34: 8 **M** bowed to the ground at once and H5407
Ex 34:27 Then the LORD said to **M**, "Write down H5407
Ex 34:28 **M** was there with the LORD forty days and NDT
Ex 34:29 When **M** came down from Mount Sinai H5407
Ex 34:30 When Aaron and all the Israelites saw **M** H5407
Ex 34:31 But **M** called to them; so Aaron and all the H5407
Ex 34:33 When **M** finished speaking to them, he H5407
Ex 34:35 Then **M** would put the veil back over his H5407
Ex 35: 1 **M** assembled the whole Israelite H5407
Ex 35: 4 **M** said to the whole Israelite community H5407
Ex 35:29 the LORD through **M** had commanded H5407
Ex 35:30 Then **M** said to the Israelites, "See, the H5407
Ex 36: 2 Then **M** summoned Bezalel and Oholiab H5407
Ex 36: 3 They received from **M** all the offerings the H5407
Ex 36: 5 said to **M**, "The people are bringing H5407
Ex 36: 6 Then **M** gave an order and they sent this H5407
Ex 38:22 made everything the LORD commanded **M** H5407
Ex 39: 1 Aaron, as the LORD commanded **M**. H5407
Ex 39: 5 twisted linen, as the LORD commanded **M**. H5407
Ex 39: 7 sons of Israel, as the LORD commanded **M**. H5407
Ex 39:21 the ephod—as the LORD commanded **M**. H5407
Ex 39:26 ministering, as the LORD commanded **M**. H5407
Ex 39:29 embroiderer—as the LORD commanded **M**. H5407
Ex 39:31 to the turban, as the LORD commanded **M**. H5407
Ex 39:32 just as the LORD commanded **M**. H5407
Ex 39:33 Then they brought the tabernacle to **M** H5407
Ex 39:42 work just as the LORD had commanded **M**. H5407
Ex 39:43 **M** inspected the work and saw that they H5407
Ex 39:43 had commanded. So **M** blessed them. H5407
Ex 40: 1 Then the LORD said to **M**: H5407
Ex 40:16 **M** did everything just as the LORD H5407
Ex 40:18 When **M** set up the tabernacle, he put the H5407
Ex 40:22 **M** placed the table in the tent of meeting NDT
Ex 40:26 **M** placed the gold altar in the tent of NDT
Ex 40:31 **M** and Aaron and his sons used it to H5407
Ex 40:32 the altar, as the LORD commanded **M**. H5407
Ex 40:33 Then **M** set up the courtyard around the NDT
Ex 40:33 And so **M** finished the work. H5407
Ex 40:35 **M** could not enter the tent of meeting H5407
Lev 1: 1 The LORD called to **M** and spoke to him H5407
Lev 4: 1 The LORD said to **M**, H5407
Lev 5:14 The LORD said to **M**: H5407
Lev 6: 1 The LORD said to **M**: H5407
Lev 6: 8 The LORD said to **M**: H5407
Lev 6:19 The LORD also said to **M**, H5407
Lev 6:24 The LORD said to **M**, H5407
Lev 7:22 The LORD said to **M**, H5407
Lev 7:28 The LORD said to **M**, H5407
Lev 7:38 which the LORD gave **M** at Mount Sinai in H5407
Lev 8: 1 The LORD said to **M**, H5407
Lev 8: 4 **M** did as the LORD commanded him, and H5407
Lev 8: 5 **M** said to the assembly, "This is what the H5407
Lev 8: 6 Then **M** brought Aaron and his sons H5407
Lev 8: 9 the front of it, as the LORD commanded **M**. H5407
Lev 8:10 Then **M** took the anointing oil and H5407
Lev 8:13 caps on them, as the LORD commanded **M**. H5407
Lev 8:15 **M** slaughtered the bull and took some of H5407
Lev 8:16 **M** also took all the fat around the internal H5407
Lev 8:17 the camp, as the LORD commanded **M**. H5407
Lev 8:19 Then **M** slaughtered the ram and splashed H5407
Lev 8:21 to the LORD, as the LORD commanded **M**. H5407
Lev 8:23 **M** slaughtered the ram and took some of H5407
Lev 8:24 **M** also brought Aaron's sons forward and H5407
Lev 8:28 Then **M** took them from their hands and H5407
Lev 8:29 **M** also took the breast, which was his H5407
Lev 8:29 wave offering, as the LORD commanded **M**. H5407
Lev 8:30 Then **M** took some of the anointing oil H5407
Lev 8:31 **M** then said to Aaron and his sons, "Cook H5407
Lev 8:36 the LORD commanded through **M**. H5407
Lev 9: 1 On the eighth day **M** summoned Aaron H5407
Lev 9: 5 took the things **M** commanded to the H5407
Lev 9: 6 Then **M** said, "This is what the LORD has H5407
Lev 9: 7 **M** said to Aaron, "Come to the altar and H5407
Lev 9:10 sin offering, as the LORD commanded **M**; H5407
Lev 9:21 as a wave offering, as **M** commanded. H5407
Lev 9:23 **M** and Aaron then went into the tent of H5407
Lev 10: 3 **M** then said to Aaron, "This is what the H5407
Lev 10: 4 **M** summoned Mishael and Elzaphan H5407
Lev 10: 5 outside the camp, as **M** ordered. H5407
Lev 10: 6 Then **M** said to Aaron and his sons H5407
Lev 10: 7 So they did as **M** said. H5407
Lev 10:11 the LORD has given them through **M**." H5407
Lev 10:12 **M** said to Aaron and his remaining sons H5407
Lev 10:16 When **M** inquired about the goat of the H5407
Lev 10:19 Aaron replied to **M**, "Today they sacrificed H5407
Lev 10:20 When **M** heard this, he was satisfied. H5407
Lev 11: 1 The LORD said to **M** and Aaron, H5407
Lev 12: 1 The LORD said to **M**, H5407
Lev 13: 1 The LORD said to **M** and Aaron, H5407
Lev 14: 1 The LORD said to **M**, H5407
Lev 14:33 The LORD said to **M** and Aaron, H5407
*Lev 15: 1 The LORD said to **M** and Aaron, H5407*
Lev 16: 1 The LORD spoke to **M** after the death of the H5407
Lev 16: 2 The LORD said to **M**: "Tell your brother H5407
Lev 16:34 it was done, as the LORD commanded **M**. H5407
Lev 17: 1 The LORD said to **M**, H5407
Lev 18: 1 The LORD said to **M**, H5407
Lev 19: 1 The LORD said to **M**, H5407
Lev 20: 1 The LORD said to **M**, H5407
Lev 21: 1 The LORD said to **M**, "Speak to the priests H5407
Lev 21:16 The LORD said to **M**, H5407
Lev 21:24 So **M** told this to Aaron and his sons and H5407
Lev 22: 1 The LORD said to **M**, H5407
Lev 22:17 The LORD said to **M**, H5407
Lev 22:26 The LORD said to **M**, H5407
Lev 23: 1 The LORD said to **M**, H5407
Lev 23: 9 The LORD said to **M**, H5407
Lev 23:23 The LORD said to **M**, H5407
Lev 23:26 The LORD said to **M**, H5407
Lev 23:33 The LORD said to **M**, H5407
Lev 23:44 So **M** announced to the Israelites the H5407
Lev 24: 1 The LORD said to **M**, H5407
Lev 24:11 with a curse; so they brought him to **M**. H5407
Lev 24:13 Then the LORD said to **M**: H5407
Lev 24:23 Then **M** spoke to the Israelites, and they H5407
Lev 24:23 Israelites did as the LORD commanded **M**. H5407
Lev 25: 1 The LORD said to **M** at Mount Sinai, H5407
Lev 26:46 himself and the Israelites through **M**. H5407
Lev 27: 1 The LORD said to **M**, H5407
Lev 27:34 the LORD gave **M** at Mount Sinai for the H5407
Nu 1: 1 The LORD spoke to **M** in the tent of H5407
Nu 1:17 **M** and Aaron took these men whose H5407
Nu 1:19 as the LORD commanded **M**. And so he H5407
Nu 1:44 the men counted by **M** and Aaron and the H5407
Nu 1:48 The LORD had said to **M**: H5407
Nu 1:54 all this just as the LORD commanded **M**. H5407
Nu 2: 1 The LORD said to **M** and Aaron: H5407
Nu 2:33 Israelites, as the LORD commanded **M**. H5407
Nu 2:34 did everything the LORD commanded **M**; H5407
Nu 3: 1 family of Aaron and **M** at the time the H5407
Nu 3: 1 time the LORD spoke to **M** at Mount Sinai. H5407
Nu 3: 5 The LORD said to **M**, H5407
Nu 3:11 The LORD also said to **M**, H5407
Nu 3:14 The LORD said to **M** in the Desert of Sinai, H5407
Nu 3:16 So **M** counted them, as he was H5407
Nu 3:38 **M** and Aaron and his sons were to camp H5407
Nu 3:39 LORD's command by **M** and Aaron H5407
Nu 3:40 The LORD said to **M**, "Count all the H5407
Nu 3:42 So **M** counted all the firstborn of the H5407
Nu 3:44 The LORD also said to **M**, H5407
Nu 3:49 So **M** collected the redemption money H5407
Nu 3:51 **M** gave the redemption money to Aaron H5407
Nu 4: 1 The LORD said to **M** and Aaron: H5407
Nu 4:17 The LORD said to **M** and Aaron, H5407
Nu 4:21 The LORD said to **M**, H5407
Nu 4:34 **M**, Aaron and the leaders of the H5407
Nu 4:37 **M** and Aaron counted them according to H5407
Nu 4:37 to the LORD's command through **M**. H5407
Nu 4:41 **M** and Aaron counted them according to H5407
Nu 4:45 **M** and Aaron counted them according to H5407
Nu 4:45 to the LORD's command through **M**. H5407
Nu 4:46 So **M**, Aaron and the leaders of Israel H5407
Nu 4:49 At the LORD's command through **M**, each H5407
Nu 4:49 were counted, as the LORD commanded **M**. H5407
Nu 5: 1 The LORD said to **M**, H5407
Nu 5: 4 did just as the LORD had instructed **M**. H5407
Nu 5: 5 The LORD said to **M**, H5407
Nu 5:11 Then the LORD said to **M**, H5407
Nu 6: 1 The LORD said to **M**, H5407
Nu 6:22 The LORD said to **M**, H5407
Nu 7: 1 When **M** finished setting up the H5407
Nu 7: 4 The LORD said to **M**, H5407
Nu 7: 6 So **M** took the carts and oxen and gave H5407
Nu 7: 9 But **M** did not give any to the Kohathites NDT
Nu 7:11 For the LORD had said to **M**, "Each day H5407
Nu 7:89 When **M** entered the tent of meeting to H5407
Nu 8: 1 The LORD said to **M**, H5407
Nu 8: 3 just as the LORD commanded **M**. H5407
Nu 8: 4 like the pattern the LORD had shown **M**. H5407
Nu 8: 5 The LORD said to **M**: H5407
Nu 8:20 **M**, Aaron and the whole Israelite H5407
Nu 8:20 Levites just as the LORD commanded **M**. H5407
Nu 8:22 Levites just as the LORD commanded **M**. H5407
Nu 8:23 The LORD said to **M**, H5407
Nu 9: 1 LORD spoke to **M** in the Desert of Sinai H5407
Nu 9: 4 So **M** told the Israelites to celebrate the H5407
Nu 9: 5 just as the LORD commanded **M**. H5407
Nu 9: 6 So they came to **M** and Aaron that same H5407
Nu 9: 7 said to **M**, "We have become H2257S
Nu 9: 8 **M** answered them, "Wait until I find out H5407
Nu 9: 9 Then the LORD said to **M**, H5407
Nu 9:23 accordance with his command through **M**. H5407
Nu 10: 1 The LORD said to **M**: H5407
Nu 10:13 at the LORD's command through **M**. H5407
Nu 10:29 Now **M** said to Hobab son of Reuel the H5407
Nu 10:31 But **M** said, "Please do not leave us. NDT
Nu 10:35 the ark set out, **M** said, "Rise up, H5407
Nu 11: 2 When the people cried out to **M**, he H5407
Nu 11:10 **M** heard the people of every family H5407
Nu 11:10 exceedingly angry, and **M** was troubled. H5407
Nu 11:16 The LORD said to **M**: "Bring me seventy H5407
Nu 11:21 But **M** said, "Here I am among six H5407
Nu 11:23 The LORD answered **M**, "Is the LORD's H5407
*Nu 11:24 So **M** went out and told the people what H5407*
Nu 11:27 A young man ran and told **M**, "Eldad and H5407
Nu 11:28 up and said, "**M**, my lord, stop them H5407
Nu 11:29 But **M** replied, "Are you jealous for my H5407
Nu 11:30 Then **M** and the elders of Israel returned H5407
Nu 12: 1 began to talk against **M** because of his H5407
Nu 12: 2 "Has the LORD spoken only through **M**?" H5407
Nu 12: 3 Now **M** was a very humble man, more H5407
Nu 12: 4 At once the LORD said to **M**, Aaron and H5407
Nu 12: 7 But this is not true of my servant **M**; he is H5407
Nu 12: 8 not afraid to speak against my servant **M**?" H5407
Nu 12:11 he said to **M**, "Please, my lord, I ask H5407
Nu 12:13 So **M** cried out to the LORD, "Please, God H5407
Nu 12:14 The LORD replied to **M**, "If her father had H5407
Nu 13: 1 The LORD said to **M**, H5407
Nu 13: 3 LORD's command **M** sent them out from H5407
Nu 13:16 names of the men **M** sent to explore the H5407
Nu 13:16 **M** gave Hoshea son of Nun the name H5407
Nu 13:17 When **M** sent them to explore Canaan, he H5407
Nu 13:26 They came back to **M** and Aaron and the H5407
Nu 13:27 They gave **M** this account: "We went into H2257S
Nu 13:30 silenced the people before **M** and said, H5407
Nu 14: 2 Israelites grumbled against **M** and Aaron, H5407
Nu 14: 5 Then **M** and Aaron fell facedown in front H5407
Nu 14:11 The LORD said to **M**, "How long will these H5407
Nu 14:13 **M** said to the LORD, "Then the Egyptians H5407
Nu 14:26 The LORD said to **M** and Aaron: H5407
Nu 14:36 So the men **M** had sent to explore the H5407
Nu 14:39 When **M** reported this to all the Israelites H5407
Nu 14:41 But **M** said, "Why are you disobeying the H5407
Nu 14:44 though neither **M** nor the ark of the LORD's H5407
Nu 15: 1 The LORD said to **M**, H5407
Nu 15:17 The LORD said to **M**, H5407
Nu 15:22 of these commands the LORD gave **M**— H5407
Nu 15:33 brought him to **M** and Aaron and the H5407
Nu 15:35 Then the LORD said to **M**, "The man must H5407
Nu 15:36 him to death, as the LORD commanded **M**. H5407
Nu 15:37 The LORD said to **M**, H5407
Nu 16: 2 rose up against **M**. With them were H5407
Nu 16: 3 a group to oppose **M** and Aaron and said H5407
Nu 16: 4 When **M** heard this, he fell facedown. H5407
Nu 16: 8 **M** also said to Korah, "Now listen, you H5407
Nu 16:12 Then **M** summoned Dathan and Abiram H5407
Nu 16:15 Then **M** became very angry and said to H5407
Nu 16:16 **M** said to Korah, "You and all your H5407
Nu 16:18 stood with **M** and Aaron at the H5407
Nu 16:20 The LORD said to **M** and Aaron, H5407
Nu 16:22 But **M** and Aaron fell facedown and cried NDT
Nu 16:23 Then the LORD said to **M**, H5407
Nu 16:25 **M** got up and went to Dathan and Abiram H5407
Nu 16:28 Then **M** said, "This is how you will know H5407
Nu 16:36 The LORD said to **M**, H5407
Nu 16:40 as the LORD directed him through **M**. H5407
Nu 16:41 grumbled against **M** and Aaron. H5407
Nu 16:42 in opposition to **M** and Aaron and turned H5407
Nu 16:43 Then **M** and Aaron went to the front of the H5407
Nu 16:44 the LORD said to **M**, H5407
Nu 16:46 Then **M** said to Aaron, "Take your censer H5407
Nu 16:47 So Aaron did as **M** said, and ran into the H5407
Nu 16:50 Aaron returned to **M** at the entrance to H5407
Nu 17: 1 The LORD said to **M**, H5407
Nu 17: 6 So **M** spoke to the Israelites, and their H5407
Nu 17: 7 **M** placed the staffs before the LORD in the H5407
Nu 17: 8 The next day **M** entered the tent and saw H5407
Nu 17: 9 Then **M** brought out all the staffs from the H5407
Nu 17:10 The LORD said to **M**, "Put back Aaron's H5407
Nu 17:11 **M** did just as the LORD commanded him. H5407
Nu 17:12 The Israelites said to **M**, "We will die! We H5407
Nu 18:25 The LORD said to **M**, H5407
Nu 19: 1 The LORD said to **M** and Aaron: H5407
Nu 20: 2 gathered in opposition to **M** and Aaron. H5407
Nu 20: 3 They quarreled with **M** and said, "If only H5407
Nu 20: 6 **M** and Aaron went from the assembly to H5407
Nu 20: 7 The LORD said to **M**, H5407
Nu 20: 9 So **M** took the staff from the LORD's H5407
Nu 20:10 in front of the rock and **M** said to them, NDT
Nu 20:11 Then **M** raised his arm and struck the rock H5407
Nu 20:12 But the LORD said to **M** and Aaron H5407
Nu 20:14 **M** sent messengers from Kadesh to the H5407
Nu 20:23 of Edom, the LORD said to **M** and Aaron, H5407
Nu 20:27 **M** did as the LORD commanded: They H5407
Nu 20:28 **M** removed Aaron's garments and put H5407
Nu 20:28 Then **M** and Eleazar came down from the H5407
Nu 21: 5 they spoke against God and against **M** H5407
Nu 21: 7 The people came to **M** and said, "We H5407
Nu 21: 7 So **M** prayed for the people H5407
Nu 21: 8 The LORD said to **M**, "Make a snake and H5407
Nu 21: 9 So **M** made a bronze snake and put it up H5407
Nu 21:16 the well where the LORD said to **M** H5407
Nu 21:32 After **M** had sent spies to Jazer, the H5407
Nu 21:34 The LORD said to **M**, "Do not be afraid of H5407
Nu 25: 4 The LORD said to **M**, "Take all the leaders H5407
Nu 25: 5 So **M** said to Israel's judges, "Each of you H5407
Nu 25: 6 before the eyes of **M** and the whole H5407
Nu 25:10 The LORD said to **M**, H5407
Nu 25:16 The LORD said to **M**, H5407
Nu 26: 1 the LORD said to **M** and Eleazar son of H5407
Nu 26: 3 **M** and Eleazar the priest spoke with them H5407
Nu 26: 4 old or more, as the LORD commanded **M**." H5407
Nu 26: 9 rebelled against **M** and Aaron and were H5407
Nu 26:52 The LORD said to **M**, H5407
Nu 26:59 bore Aaron, **M** and their sister Miriam. H5407
Nu 26:63 the ones counted by **M** and Eleazar the H5407
Nu 26:64 those counted by **M** and Aaron the priest H5407
Nu 27: 2 stood before **M**, Eleazar the priest, the H5407
Nu 27: 5 So **M** brought their case before the LORD, H5407
Nu 27:11 the Israelites, as the LORD commanded **M**. H5407
Nu 27:12 Then the LORD said to **M**, "Go up this H5407
Nu 27:15 **M** said to the LORD, H5407

M

Nu 27:18 So the LORD said to **M**, "Take Joshua son H5407
Nu 27:22 **M** did as the LORD commanded him. H5407
Nu 27:23 as the LORD instructed through **M**. H5407
Nu 28: 1 The LORD said to **M**, H5407
Nu 29:40 **M** told the Israelites all that the LORD H5407
Nu 30: 1 **M** said to the heads of the tribes of Israel H5407
Nu 30:16 the LORD gave **M** concerning relationships H5407
Nu 31: 1 The LORD said to **M**, H5407
Nu 31: 3 So **M** said to the people, "Arm some of H5407
Nu 31: 6 **M** sent them into battle, a thousand from H5407
Nu 31: 7 as the LORD commanded **M**, and killed H5407
Nu 31:12 spoils and plunder to **M** and Eleazar the H5407
Nu 31:13 **M**, Eleazar the priest and all the leaders H5407
Nu 31:14 **M** was angry with the officers of the army H5407
Nu 31:21 required by the law that the LORD gave **M**: H5407
Nu 31:25 The LORD said to **M**, H5407
Nu 31:31 So **M** and Eleazar the priest did as the H5407
Nu 31:31 the priest did as the LORD commanded **M**. H5407
Nu 31:41 **M** gave the tribute to Eleazar the priest as H5407
Nu 31:41 LORD's part, as the LORD commanded **M**. H5407
Nu 31:42 which **M** set apart from that of the fighting H5407
Nu 31:47 **M** selected one out of every fifty people H5407
Nu 31:48 commanders of hundreds—went to **M** H5407
Nu 31:51 **M** and Eleazar the priest accepted from H5407
Nu 31:52 of hundreds that **M** and Eleazar presented NDT
Nu 31:54 **M** and Eleazar the priest accepted the H5407
Nu 32: 2 So they came to **M** and Eleazar the priest H5407
Nu 32: 6 **M** said to the Gadites and Reubenites H5407
Nu 32:20 Then **M** said to them, "If you will do this H5407
Nu 32:25 The Gadites and Reubenites said to **M** H5407
Nu 32:28 Then **M** gave orders about them to H5407
Nu 32:33 Then **M** gave to the Gadites, the H5407
Nu 32:40 So **M** gave Gilead to the Makirites, the H5407
Nu 33: 1 under the leadership of **M** and Aaron. H5407
Nu 33: 2 the LORD's command **M** recorded the H5407
Nu 33:50 across from Jericho the LORD said to **M**, H5407
Nu 34: 1 The LORD said to **M**, H5407
Nu 34:13 **M** commanded the Israelites: "Assign this H5407
Nu 34:16 The LORD said to **M**, H5407
Nu 35: 1 across from Jericho, the LORD said to **M**, H5407
Nu 35: 9 Then the LORD said to **M**: H5407
Nu 36: 1 spoke before **M** and the leaders, H5407
Nu 36: 5 the LORD's command **M** gave this order to H5407
Nu 36:10 daughters did as the LORD commanded **M**. H5407
Nu 36:13 LORD gave through **M** to the Israelites on H5407
Dt 1: 1 These are the words **M** spoke to all Israel H5407
Dt 1: 3 **M** proclaimed to the Israelites all that the H5407
Dt 1: 5 of Moab, **M** began to expound this law H5407
Dt 4:41 Then **M** set aside three cities east of the H5407
Dt 4:44 This is the law **M** set before the Israelites. H5407
Dt 4:45 decrees and laws **M** gave them when they H5407
Dt 4:46 was defeated by **M** and the Israelites H5407
Dt 5: 1 **M** summoned all Israel and said: Hear H5407
Dt 27: 1 **M** and the elders of Israel commanded H5407
Dt 27: 9 Then **M** and the Levitical priests said to H5407
Dt 27:11 On the same day **M** commanded the H5407
Dt 29: 1 the LORD commanded **M** to make with the H5407
Dt 29: 2 **M** summoned all the Israelites and said H5407
Dt 31: 1 Then **M** went out and spoke these words H5407
Dt 31: 7 Then **M** summoned Joshua and said to H5407
Dt 31: 9 So **M** wrote down this law and gave it to H5407
Dt 31:10 Then **M** commanded them: "At the end of H5407
Dt 31:14 The LORD said to **M**, "Now the day of your H5407
Dt 31:14 So **M** and Joshua came and presented H5407
Dt 31:16 And the LORD said to **M**: "You are going to H5407
Dt 31:22 So **M** wrote down this song that day and H5407
Dt 31:24 After **M** finished writing in a book the H5407
Dt 31:30 And **M** recited the words of this song from H5407
Dt 32:44 **M** came with Joshua son of Nun and H5407
Dt 32:45 When **M** finished reciting all these words H5407
Dt 32:48 On that same day the LORD told **M**, H5407
Dt 33: 1 is the blessing that **M** the man of God H5407
Dt 33: 4 the law that **M** gave us, the possession of H5407
Dt 34: 1 Then **M** climbed Mount Nebo from the H5407
Dt 34: 5 And **M** the servant of the LORD died there H5407
Dt 34: 7 **M** was a hundred and twenty years old H5407
Dt 34: 8 grieved for **M** in the plains of Moab H5407
Dt 34: 9 of wisdom because **M** had laid his hands H5407
Dt 34: 9 did what the LORD had commanded **M**. H5407
Dt 34:10 no prophet has risen in Israel like **M** H5407
Dt 34:12 awesome deeds that **M** did in the sight of H5407
Jos 1: 1 After the death of **M** the servant of the H5407
Jos 1: 2 "**M** my servant is dead. Now then, you H5407
Jos 1: 3 where you set your foot, as I promised **M**. H5407
Jos 1: 5 As I was with **M**, so I will be with you; H5407
Jos 1: 7 obey all the law my servant **M** gave you; H5407
Jos 1:13 the command that **M** the servant of the H5407
Jos 1:14 in the land that **M** gave you east of the H5407
Jos 1:15 which **M** the servant of the LORD gave you H5407
Jos 1:17 Just as we fully obeyed **M**, so we will obey H5407
Jos 1:17 your God be with you as he was with **M**. H5407
Jos 3: 7 know that I am with you as I was with **M**. H5407
Jos 4:10 people, just as **M** had directed Joshua. H5407
Jos 4:12 of the Israelites, as **M** had directed them. H5407
Jos 4:14 just as they had stood in awe of **M**. H5407
Jos 8:31 as **M** the servant of the LORD had H5407
Jos 8:31 is written in the Book of the Law of **M**— H5407
Jos 8:32 wrote on stones a copy of the law of **M**. H5407
Jos 8:33 as **M** the servant of the LORD had formerly H5407
Jos 8:35 a word of all that **M** had commanded that H5407
Jos 9:24 his servant **M** to give you the whole H5407
Jos 11:12 as **M** the servant of the LORD had H5407
Jos 11:15 As the LORD commanded his servant **M**, H5407
Jos 11:15 servant Moses, so **M** commanded Joshua H5407
Jos 11:15 of all that the LORD commanded **M**. H5407
Jos 11:20 as the LORD had commanded **M**. H5407
Jos 11:23 just as the LORD had directed **M**, and he H5407
Jos 12: 6 **M**, the servant of the LORD, and the H5407
Jos 12: 6 And **M** the servant of the LORD gave their H5407
Jos 13: 8 inheritance that **M** had given them east H5407
Jos 13:12 **M** had defeated them and taken over H5407
Jos 13:15 This is what **M** had given to the tribe of H5407
Jos 13:21 **M** had defeated him and the Midianite H5407
Jos 13:24 This is what **M** had given to the tribe of H5407
Jos 13:29 This is what **M** had given to the half-tribe H5407
Jos 13:32 is the inheritance **M** had given when he H5407
Jos 13:33 tribe of Levi, **M** had given no inheritance H5407
Jos 14: 2 as the LORD had commanded through **M**. H5407
Jos 14: 3 **M** had granted the two and a half tribes H5407
Jos 14: 5 just as the LORD had commanded **M**. H5407
Jos 14: 6 the LORD said to **M** the man of God at H5407
Jos 14: 7 forty years old when **M** the servant of the H5407
Jos 14: 9 So on that day **M** swore to me, 'The land H5407
Jos 14:10 years since the time he said this to **M**, H5407
Jos 14:11 as strong today as the day **M** sent me out; H5407
Jos 17: 4 "The LORD commanded **M** to give us an H5407
Jos 18: 7 **M** the servant of the LORD gave it to them." H5407
Jos 20: 2 of refuge, as I instructed you through **M**, H5407
Jos 21: 2 commanded through **M** that you give us H5407
Jos 21: 8 as the LORD had commanded through **M**. H5407
Jos 22: 2 have done all that **M** the servant of the H5407
Jos 22: 4 in the land that **M** the servant of the H5407
Jos 22: 5 the law that **M** the servant of the LORD H5407
Jos 22: 7 of Manasseh **M** had given land in H5407
Jos 22: 9 with the command of the LORD through **M**. H5407
Jos 23: 6 that is written in the Book of the Law of **M**, H5407
Jos 24: 5 " 'Then I sent **M** and Aaron, and I H5407
Jdg 1:20 As **M** had promised, Hebron was given to H5407
Jdg 3: 4 he had given their ancestors through **M**. H5407
Jdg 18:30 Gershom, the son of **M**, and his sons were H5407
1Sa 12: 6 LORD who appointed **M** and Aaron and H5407
1Sa 12: 8 the LORD sent **M** and Aaron, who H5407
1Ki 2: 3 regulations, as written in the Law of **M**. H5407
1Ki 8: 9 stone tablets that **M** had placed in it at H5407
1Ki 8:53 through your servant **M** when you, H5407
1Ki 8:56 promises he gave through his servant **M**. H5407
2Ki 14: 6 the Book of the Law of **M** where the LORD H5407
2Ki 18: 4 pieces the bronze snake **M** had made, H5407
2Ki 18: 6 kept the commands the LORD had given **M**. H5407
2Ki 18:12 all that **M** the servant of the LORD H5407
2Ki 21: 8 whole Law that my servant **M** gave them." H5407
2Ki 23:25 in accordance with all the Law of **M**. H5407
1Ch 6: 3 Aaron, **M** and Miriam. H5407
1Ch 6:49 with all that **M** the servant of God had H5407
1Ch 15:15 as **M** had commanded in accordance with H5407
1Ch 21:29 which **M** had made in the wilderness H5407
1Ch 22:13 laws that the LORD gave **M** for Israel. H5407
1Ch 23:13 Aaron and **M**. Aaron was set H5407
1Ch 23:14 The sons of **M** the man of God were H5407
1Ch 23:15 The sons of **M**: Gershom and Eliezer. H5407
1Ch 26:24 a descendant of Gershom son of **M**, was H5407
2Ch 1: 3 which **M** the LORD's servant had made in H5407
2Ch 5:10 the two tablets that **M** had placed in it at H5407
2Ch 8:13 commanded by **M** for the Sabbaths, H5407
2Ch 23:18 of the LORD as written in the Law of **M**, H5407
2Ch 24: 6 the tax imposed by **M** the servant of the H5407
2Ch 24: 9 the LORD the tax that **M** the servant of God H5407
2Ch 25: 4 Law, in the Book of **M**, where the LORD H5407
2Ch 30:16 in the Law of **M** the man of God. H5407
2Ch 33: 8 decrees and regulations given through **M**." H5407
2Ch 34:14 the LORD that had been given through **M**. H5407
2Ch 35: 6 what the LORD commanded through **M**." H5407
2Ch 35:12 the LORD, as it is written in the Book of **M**. H5407
Ezr 3: 2 is written in the Law of **M** the man of God. H5407
Ezr 6:18 to what is written in the Book of **M**. A10441
Ezr 7: 6 a teacher well versed in the Law of **M**, H5407
Ne 1: 7 laws you gave your servant **M**. H5407
Ne 1: 8 the instruction you gave your servant **M**, H5407
Ne 8: 1 to bring out the Book of the Law of **M**, H5407
Ne 8:14 the LORD had commanded through **M**, H5407
Ne 9:14 decrees and laws through your servant **M**. H5407
Ne 10:29 God given through **M** the servant of God H5407
Ne 13: 1 that day the Book of **M** was read aloud in H5407
Ps 77:20 like a flock by the hand of **M** and Aaron. H5407
Ps 90: T A prayer of **M** the man of God. H5407
Ps 99: 6 **M** and Aaron were among his priests H5407
Ps 103: 7 He made known his ways to **M**, his deeds H5407
Ps 105:26 He sent **M** his servant, and Aaron, whom H5407
Ps 106:16 they grew envious of **M** and of Aaron, H5407
Ps 106:23 had not **M**, his chosen one, H5407
Ps 106:32 trouble came to **M** because of them; H5407
Isa 63:11 the days of **M** and his people H5407
Jer 15: 1 "Even if **M** and Samuel were to stand H5407
Da 9:11 sworn judgments written in the Law of **M**, H5407
Da 9:13 Just as it is written in the Law of **M**, all H5407
Mic 6: 4 I sent **M** to lead you, also Aaron and H5407
Mal 4: 4 "Remember the law of my servant **M**, the H5407
Mt 8: 4 priest and offer the gift **M** commanded, *G3707*
Mt 17: 3 appeared before them **M** and Elijah, *G3707*
Mt 17: 4 one for you, one *for* **M** and one for Elijah." *G3707*
Mt 19: 7 "did **M** command that a man give his wife *G3707*
Mt 19: 8 "**M** permitted you to divorce your wives *G3707*
Mt 22:24 "**M** told us that if a man dies without *G3707*
Mk 1:44 the sacrifices that **M** commanded for your *G3707*
Mk 7:10 For **M** said, 'Honor your father and mother *G3707*
Mk 9: 4 appeared before them Elijah and **M**, *G3707*
Mk 9: 5 one for you, one *for* **M** and one for Elijah." *G3707*
Mk 10: 3 "What did **M** command you?" he replied. *G3707*
Mk 10: 4 "**M** permitted a man to write a certificate *G3707*
Mk 10: 5 hearts were hard that **M** wrote you this law," NDT
Mk 12:19 "**M** wrote for us that if a man's brother *G3707*
Mk 12:26 have you not read in the Book *of* **M**, in the *G3707*
Lk 2:22 purification rites required by the Law *of* **M**, *G3707*
Lk 5:14 the sacrifices that **M** commanded for your *G3707*
Lk 9:30 Two men, **M** and Elijah, appeared in *G3707*
Lk 9:33 one for you, one *for* **M** and one for Elijah." *G3707*
Lk 16:29 replied, 'They have **M** and the Prophets *G3707*
Lk 16:31 they do not listen to **M** and the Prophets, *G3707*
Lk 20:28 "**M** wrote for us that if a man's brother *G3707*
Lk 20:37 even **M** showed that the dead rise *G3707*
Lk 24:27 And beginning with **M** and all the *G3707*
Lk 24:44 that is written about me in the Law *of* **M**, *G3707*
Jn 1:17 For the law was given through **M**; grace *G3707*
Jn 1:45 have found the one **M** wrote about in the *G3707*
Jn 3:14 Just as **M** lifted up the snake in the *G3707*
Jn 5:45 Your accuser is **M**, on whom your hopes *G3707*
Jn 5:46 If you believed **M**, you would believe me *G3707*
Jn 6:32 it is not **M** who has given you the bread *G3707*
Jn 7:19 Has not **M** given you the law? Yet not one *G3707*
Jn 7:22 because **M** gave you circumcision *G3707*
Jn 7:22 though actually it did not come from **M** *G3707*
Jn 7:23 so that the law *of* **M** may not be broken, *G3707*
Jn 8: 5 In the Law **M** commanded us to stone such *G3707*
Jn 9:28 fellow's disciple! We are disciples *of* **M**! *G3707*
Jn 9:29 We know that God spoke *to* **M**, but as for *G3707*
Ac 3:22 For **M** said, 'The Lord your God will raise *G3707*
Ac 6:11 words against **M** and against God. *G3707*
Ac 6:14 the customs **M** handed down to us." *G3707*
Ac 7:20 "At that time **M** was born, and he was no *G3707*
Ac 7:22 **M** was educated in all the wisdom of the *G3707*
Ac 7:23 "When **M** was forty years old, he decided *G899S*
Ac 7:25 **M** thought that his own people would realize NDT
Ac 7:26 The next day **M** came upon two Israelites NDT
Ac 7:27 the other pushed **M** aside and said, *G899S*
Ac 7:29 When **M** heard this, he fled to Midian *G3707*
Ac 7:30 an angel appeared *to* **M** in the flames of *G899S*
Ac 7:32 **M** trembled with fear and did not dare to *G3707*
Ac 7:35 "This is the same **M** they had rejected *G3707*
Ac 7:37 "This is the **M** who told the Israelites *G3707*
Ac 7:40 As for this fellow **M** who led us out of *G3707*
Ac 7:44 It had been made as God directed **M** *G3707*
Ac 13:39 not able to obtain under the law *of* **M**. *G3707*
Ac 15: 1 according to the custom *taught by* **M**, you *G3707*
Ac 15: 5 required to keep the law *of* **M**. *G3707*
Ac 15:21 For *the law of* **M** has been preached in *G3707*
Ac 21:21 among the Gentiles to turn away from **M**, *G3707*
Ac 26:22 the prophets and **M** said would happen— *G3707*
Ac 28:23 from the Law *of* **M** and from the *G3707*
Ro 5:14 from the time of Adam to the time of **M**, *G3707*
Ro 9:15 For he says *to* **M**, "I will have mercy on *G3707*
Ro 10: 5 **M** writes this about the righteousness that *G3707*
Ro 10:19 **M** says, "I will make you envious by *G3707*
1Co 9: 9 For it is written in the Law *of* **M**: "Do not *G3707*
1Co 10: 2 all baptized into **M** in the cloud and in *G3707*
2Co 3: 7 steadily at the face *of* **M** because of its *G3707*
2Co 3:13 We are not like **M**, who would put a veil *G3707*
2Co 3:15 Even to this day when **M** is read, a veil *G3707*
2Ti 3: 8 Just as Jannes and Jambres opposed **M** *G3707*
Heb 3: 2 just as **M** was faithful in all God's house. *G3707*
Heb 3: 3 found worthy of greater honor than **M**, *G3707*
Heb 3: 5 "**M** was faithful as a servant in all God's *G3707*
Heb 3:16 they not all those **M** led out of Egypt? *G3707*
Heb 7:14 regard to that tribe **M** said nothing about *G3707*
Heb 8: 5 This is why **M** was warned when he was *G3707*
Heb 9:19 When **M** had proclaimed every command *G3707*
Heb 10:28 rejected the law *of* **M** died without mercy *G3707*
Heb 11:24 By faith **M**, when he had grown up *G3707*
Heb 12:21 The sight was so terrifying that **M** said, "I *G3707*
Jude 9 with the devil about the body *of* **M**, *G3707*
Rev 15: 3 song of God's servant **M** and of the Lamb: *G3707*

MOSES' (18) [MOSES]

Ex 4:25 foreskin and touched **M** feet with it. H2257S
Ex 17:12 When **M** hands grew tired, they took a H5407
Ex 18: 5 **M** father-in-law, together with H5407
Ex 18: 5 together with **M** sons and wife, came to H2257S
Ex 18:12 Then Jethro, **M** father-in-law, brought a H5407
Ex 18:12 to eat a meal with **M** father-in-law in the H5407
Ex 18:17 **M** father-in-law replied, "What you are H5407
Ex 35:20 community withdrew from **M** presence, H5407
Ex 38:21 were recorded at **M** command by the H5407
Nu 10:29 the Midianite, **M** father-in-law, "We H5407
Nu 11:28 who had been **M** aide since youth H5407
Jos 1: 1 LORD said to Joshua son of Nun, **M** aide: H5407
Jdg 1:16 The descendants of **M** father-in-law, the H5407
Jdg 4:11 of Hobab, **M** brother-in-law, and H5407
Ps 106:33 and rash words came from **M** lips. H2257S
Isa 63:12 arm of power to be at **M** right hand, H5407
Mt 23: 2 of the law and the Pharisees sit in **M** seat. *G3707*
Heb 11:23 By faith **M** parents hid him for three *G3707*

MOST (188) [FOREMOST, INMOST, INNERMOST, SOUTHERNMOST, TOPMOST]

Ge 14:18 He was priest of God **M High**, H6610
Ge 14:19 "Blessed be Abram by God **M High** H6610
Ge 14:20 And praise be to God **M High**, who H6610

M

Ge 14:22 to the LORD, God M High, Creator of H6610
Ge 34:19 who was the m honored of all his father's H4946
Ex 26:33 Holy Place from the M Holy Place. H7731+7731
Ex 26:34 covenant law in the M Holy Place. H7731+7731
Ex 29:37 Then the altar will be m holy, and H7731+7731
Ex 30:10 It is m holy to the LORD." H7731+7731
Ex 30:29 them so they will be m holy, H7731+7731
Ex 30:36 It shall be m holy to you. H7731+7731
Ex 40:10 the altar, and it will be m holy. H7731+7731
Lev 2: 3 it is a m holy part of the food H7731+7731
Lev 2:10 it is a m holy part of the food H7731+7731
Lev 6:17 and the guilt offering, it is m holy. H7731+7731
Lev 6:25 offering is slaughtered; it is m holy. H7731+7731
Lev 6:29 family may eat it; it is m holy. H7731+7731
Lev 7: 1 the guilt offering, which is m holy: H7731+7731
Lev 7: 6 in the sanctuary area; it is m holy. H7731+7731
Lev 10:12 it beside the altar, for it is m holy. H7731+7731
Lev 10:17 It is m holy; it was given to you to H7731+7731
Lev 14:13 belongs to the priest; it is m holy. H7731+7731
Lev 16: 2 chooses into the M Holy Place behind the H7731
Lev 16: 3 is how Aaron is to enter the M Holy Place: H7731
Lev 16:16 the M Holy Place because of the H7731
Lev 16:17 in the M Holy Place until he comes H7731
Lev 16:20 making atonement for the M Holy Place, H7731
Lev 16:23 on before he entered the M Holy Place, H7731
Lev 16:27 brought into the M Holy Place to make H7731
Lev 16:33 atonement for the M Holy Place, H7731+5219
Lev 21:22 He may eat the m holy food of his H7731+7731
Lev 24: 9 because it is a m holy part of their H7731+7731
Lev 27:28 so devoted is m holy to the LORD. H7731+7731
Nu 4: 4 the care of the m holy things. H7731+7731
Nu 4:19 they come near the m holy things, H7731+7731
Nu 18: 9 part of the m holy offerings that is H7731+7731
Nu 18: 9 they bring me as m holy offerings, H7731+7731
Nu 18:10 Eat it as something m holy; every H7731+7731
Nu 24:16 who has knowledge from the M High H6610
Dt 28:54 Even the m gentle and sensitive man H4394
Dt 28:56 The m gentle and sensitive woman among NDT
Dt 30: 4 to the m distant land under the heavens, H7895
Dt 30: 9 your God will make you m prosperous H3855
Dt 32: 8 When the M High gave the nations their H6610
Dt 33:24 "M blessed of sons is Asher; let him be AIT
Jdg 5:24 "M blessed of women be Jael, the wife of H4946
Jdg 5:24 m blessed of tent-dwelling women. H4946
1Sa 2:10 The M High will thunder from heaven; the H6583
1Sa 20:41 wept together—but David wept the m. H1540
2Sa 22:14 the voice of the M High resounded. H6610
2Sa 23: 1 of the man exalted by the M High, H6583
1Ki 3: 4 that was the m important high place H1524
1Ki 6:16 inner sanctuary, the M Holy Place. H7731+7731
1Ki 7:50 the M Holy Place, and also H7731+7731
1Ki 8: 6 the M Holy Place, and put it H7731+7731
1Ki 11:11 I will m certainly tear the kingdom away H7973+7973
2Ki 10: 3 the best and m worthy of your master's H4946
1Ch 6:49 that was done in the M Holy Place, H7731+7731
1Ch 12:29 m of whom had remained loyal to Saul's H5270
1Ch 16:25 great is the LORD and m worthy of praise; H4394
1Ch 17:17 I were the m exalted of men. H9366+5092
1Ch 23:13 to consecrate the m holy things, to H7731+7731
2Ch 3: 8 He built the M Holy Place, its H7731+7731
2Ch 3:10 For the M Holy Place he made a H7731+7731
2Ch 4:22 doors to the M Holy Place and the H7731+7731
2Ch 5: 7 temple, the M Holy Place, and put H7731+7731
2Ch 28:19 and had been m unfaithful to the H5085+5086
2Ch 30:18 Although m of the many people who H5270
Ezr 2:63 any of the m sacred food until H7731+7731
Ne 7: 2 feared God more than m people do. H8041
Ne 7:65 any of the m sacred food until H7731+7731
Est 6: 9 to one of the king's m noble princes. H7312
Ps 7: 8 according to my integrity, O M High. H6604
Ps 7:10 My shield is God M High, who saves the H6583
Ps 7:17 praises of the name of the LORD M High. H6610
Ps 9: 2 sing the praises of your name, O M High. H6610
Ps 18:13 the voice of the M High resounded. H6610
Ps 21: 7 love of the M High he will not be H6610
Ps 28: 2 hands toward your M Holy Place. H7731+1808
Ps 45: 2 You are the m excellent of men and your H3636
Ps 46: 4 the holy place where the M High dwells. H6610
Ps 47: 2 For the LORD M High is awesome, the H6610
Ps 48: 1 is the LORD, and m worthy of praise, in H4394
Ps 50:14 fulfill your vows to the M High, H6610
Ps 57: 2 I cry out to God M High, to God, who H6610
Ps 73:11 Does the M High know anything?" H6610
Ps 77:10 years when the M High stretched out his H6610
Ps 78:17 in the wilderness against the M High. H6610
Ps 78:35 that God M High was their Redeemer. H6610
Ps 78:56 the test and rebelled against the M High; H6610
Ps 82: 6 you are all sons of the M High. H6610
Ps 83:18 you alone are the M High over all the H6610
Ps 87: 5 the M High himself will establish her." H6610
Ps 89:27 the m exalted of the kings of the earth. H6609
Ps 91: 1 the shelter of the M High will rest in the H6610
Ps 91: 9 and you make the M High your dwelling, H6610
Ps 92: 1 make music to your name, O M High, H6610
Ps 96: 4 great is the LORD and m worthy of praise; H4394
Ps 97: 9 are the M High over all the earth H6610
Ps 107:11 despised the plans of the M High. H6610
Ps 145: 3 Great is the LORD and m worthy of praise H4394
Ecc 7:24 exists is far off and m profound— H6678+6678
SS 1: 8 do not know, m beautiful of women, follow AIT
SS 5: 9 better than others, m beautiful of women? AIT
SS 6: 1 your beloved gone, m beautiful of women? AIT
Isa 14:14 I will make myself like the M High." H6610
Jer 3:19 the m beautiful inheritance of any H7382+7382
Jer 9:17 to come; send for the m skillful of them. AIT
Jer 18:13 A m horrible thing has been done by H4394
La 1:20 for I have been m rebellious. H5286+5286
La 3:35 people their rights before the M High, H6610
La 3:38 the mouth of the M High that both H6610
Eze 7:24 I will bring the m wicked of nations to take AIT
Eze 20: 6 honey, the m beautiful of all lands. H7382
Eze 20:15 honey, the m beautiful of all lands— H7382
Eze 28: 7 against you, the m ruthless of nations; they AIT
Eze 30:11 his army—the m ruthless of nations—will AIT
Eze 31:12 the m ruthless of foreign nations cut it AIT
Eze 32:12 mighty men—the m ruthless of all nations. AIT
Eze 41: 4 to me, "This is the M Holy Place." H7731+7731
Eze 41:21 the front of the M Holy Place was similar. H7731
Eze 41:23 hall and the M Holy Place had double H7731
Eze 42:13 LORD will eat the m holy offerings. H7731+7731
Eze 42:13 they will put the m holy offerings— H7731+7731
Eze 43:12 top of the mountain will be m holy. H7731+7731
Eze 44:13 holy things or my m holy offerings; H7731+7731
Eze 45: 3 be the sanctuary, the M Holy Place. H7731+7731
Eze 48:12 of the land, a m holy portion H7731+7731
Da 3:26 servants of the M High God, come out! A10546
Da 4: 2 wonders that the M High God has A10546
Da 4:17 may know that the M High is sovereign A10546
Da 4:24 is the decree the M High has issued A10546
Da 4:25 that the M High is sovereign over A10546
Da 4:32 that the M High is sovereign over A10546
Da 4:34 Then I praised the M High; I honored A10546
Da 5:18 the M High God gave your father A10546
Da 5:21 that the M High God is sovereign A10546
Da 7:18 people of the M High will receive the A10548
Da 7:19 from all the others and m terrifying, A10339
Da 7:22 favor of the holy people of the M High, A10548
Da 7:25 against the M High and oppress his A10546
Da 7:27 over to the holy people of the M High. A10548
Da 9:24 and to anoint the M Holy Place. H7731+7731
Hos 7:16 They do not turn to the M High; they are H6583
Hos 11: 7 Even though they call me God M High, H6583
Mic 7: 4 the m upright worse than a thorn hedge. NDT
Mt 11:20 the towns in which m of his miracles had G4498
Mt 23: 6 the m important seats in the G4751
Mt 24:12 wickedness, the love of m will grow cold, G4498
Mk 5: 7 with me, Jesus, Son of the M High God? G5736
Mk 12:28 which is the m important? G4755
Mk 12:29 "The m important one," answered Jesus G4755
Mk 12:39 have the m important seats in the G4751
Mk 12:40 These men will be punished m severely." G4358
Lk 1: 3 account for you, m excellent Theophilus, G3196
Lk 1:32 will be called the Son of the M High. G5736
Lk 1:35 the power of the M High will G5736
Lk 1:76 will be called a prophet of the M High; for G5736
Lk 6:35 you will be children of the M High G5736
Lk 8:28 with me, Jesus, Son of the M High God? G5736
Lk 11:43 you love the m important seats in the G4751
Lk 20:46 have the m important seats in the G4751
Lk 20:47 These men will be punished m severely." G4358
Ac 7:48 the M High does not live in houses made G5736
Ac 16:17 men are servants of the M High God, G5736
Ac 19:32 M of the people did not even know why G4498
Ac 20:38 What grieved them m was his statement G3436
Ac 24: 3 in every way, m excellent Felix, we G3196
Ac 26:25 am not insane, m excellent Festus," G3196
1Co 10: 5 God was not pleased with m of them G4498
1Co 12:31 will show you the m excellent way. G2848+5651
1Co 14:27 a tongue, two—or at the m three—should G4498
1Co 15: 6 the same time, m of whom are still living G4498
1Co 15:19 we are of all people m to be pitied. G1795
2Co 9: 2 has stirred m of them to action. G4498
Eph 5:16 making the m of every opportunity G1973
Php 1:14 m of the brothers and sisters have G4498
Col 4: 5 make the m of every opportunity. G1973
1Th 3:10 day we pray m earnestly that we may G5655
Heb 2: 1 We must pay the m careful attention G4359
Heb 7: 1 king of Salem and priest of God M High. G5736
Heb 9: 3 was a room called the M Holy Place, G41+41
Heb 9: 8 the way into the M Holy Place had not yet G41
Heb 9:12 he entered the M Holy Place once for all by G41
Heb 9:25 enters the M Holy Place every year with G41
Heb 10:19 to enter the M Holy Place by the blood of G41
Heb 13:11 animals into the M Holy Place as a sin G41
Jude 20 up in your m holy faith and praying in AIT

MOTE (KJV) SPECK (OF SAWDUST)

MOTH (5)

Job 4:19 who are crushed more readily than a m! H6931
Ps 39:11 you consume their wealth like a m H6931
Isa 51: 8 For the m will eat them up like a garment H6931
Hos 5:12 I am like a m to Ephraim, like rot to the H6931
Lk 12:33 no thief comes near and no m destroys. G4962

MOTH'S (1) [MOTHS]

Job 27:18 The house he builds is like a m cocoon H6931

MOTHER (241) [GRANDMOTHER, GRANDMOTHER'S, MOTHER-IN-LAW, MOTHER'S, MOTHERS, MOTHERS']

Ge 2:24 leaves his father and m and is united to his H562
Ge 3:20 she would become the m of all the living. H562
Ge 17:16 her so that she will be the m of nations; NDT
Ge 20:12 daughter of my father though not of my m; H562
Ge 21:21 his m got a wife for him from Egypt. H562
Ge 22:20 "Milkah is also a m; she has borne sons to NDT
Ge 24:53 costly gifts to her brother and to her m. H562
Ge 24:55 But her brother and her m replied, "Let the H562
Ge 24:67 brought her into the tent of his m Sarah, H562
Ge 27:11 Jacob said to Rebekah his m, "But my H562
Ge 27:13 His m said to him, "My son, let the curse H562
Ge 27:14 got them and brought them to his m, H562
Ge 27:29 may the sons of your m bow down to you. H562
Ge 28: 5 who was the m of Jacob and Esau. H562
Ge 28: 7 obeyed his father and m and had gone to H562
Ge 30:14 which he brought to his m Leah. H562
Ge 37:10 Will your m and I and your brothers H562
Ex 2: 8 So the girl went and got the baby's m. H562
Ex 20:12 "Honor your father and your m, so that you H562
Ex 21:15 their father or m is to be put to death. H562
Ex 21:17 their father or m is to be put to death. H562
Lev 18: 7 by having sexual relations with your m. H562
Lev 18: 7 She is your m; do not have relations with H562
Lev 19: 3 of you must respect your m and father, H562
Lev 20: 9 their father or m is to be put to death. H562
Lev 20: 9 Because they have cursed their father or m H562
Lev 20:14 a man marries both a woman and her m, H562
Lev 20:17 the daughter of either his father or his m H562
Lev 20:19 the sister of either your m or your father, H562
Lev 21: 2 relative, such as his m or father, his son H562
Lev 21:11 himself unclean, even for his father or m, H562
Lev 22:27 it is to remain with its m for seven days. H562
Lev 24:10 son of an Israelite m and an Egyptian H851
Nu 6: 7 if their own father or m or brother or sister H562
Dt 5:16 Honor your father and your m, as the LORD H562
Dt 21:13 mourned her father and m for a full month, H562
Dt 21:18 obey his father and m and will not listen to H562
Dt 21:19 his father and m shall take hold of him H562
Dt 22: 6 the m is sitting on the young or on the H562
Dt 22: 6 do not take the m with the young. H562
Dt 22: 7 be sure to let the m go, so that it may H562
Dt 22:15 woman's father and m shall bring to the H562
Dt 27:16 is anyone who dishonors their father or m." H562
Dt 27:22 of his father or the daughter of his m." H562
Dt 33: 9 He said of his father and m, 'I have no H562
Jos 2:13 you will spare the lives of my father and m, H562
Jos 2:18 unless you have brought your father and m, H562
Jos 6:23 her father and m, her brothers and H562
Jdg 5: 7 Deborah, arose, until I arose, a m in Israel. H562
Jdg 5:28 "Through the window peered Sisera's m H562
Jdg 8:19 were my brothers, the sons of my own m. H562
Jdg 11: 1 father was Gilead; his m was a prostitute. H851
Jdg 14: 2 he said to his father and m, "I have seen a H562
Jdg 14: 3 His father and m replied, "Isn't there an H562
Jdg 14: 5 to Timnah together with his father and m. H562
Jdg 14: 6 his father nor his m what he had done. H562
Jdg 14:16 even explained it to my father or m," H562
Jdg 17: 2 said to his m, "The eleven hundred shekels H562
Jdg 17: 2 Then his m said, "The LORD bless you, my H562
Jdg 17: 3 eleven hundred shekels of silver to his m, H562
Jdg 17: 4 So after he returned the silver to his m, she H562
Ru 2:11 left your father and m and your homeland H562
1Sa 2:19 Each year his m made him a little robe H562
1Sa 15:33 so will your m be childless among women." H562
1Sa 20:30 to the shame of the m who bore you? H562
1Sa 22: 3 let my father and m come and stay with H562
2Sa 17:25 sister of Zeruiah the m of Joab. H562
2Sa 19:37 town near the tomb of my father and m. H562
2Sa 20:19 trying to destroy a city that is a m in Israel. H562
1Ki 1: 5 Now Adonijah, whose m was Haggith, put NDT
1Ki 1:11 Solomon's m, "Have you not heard H562
1Ki 2:13 Haggith, went to Bathsheba, Solomon's m. H562
1Ki 2:19 He had a throne brought for the king's m H562
1Ki 2:20 "Make it, my m; I will not refuse H562
1Ki 2:22 King Solomon answered his m, "Why do H562
1Ki 3:27 Do not kill him; she is his m." H562
1Ki 7:14 whose m was a widow from the tribe of H851
1Ki 11:26 his m was a widow named Zeruah. H562
1Ki 15:13 Maakah from her position as queen m, H1485
1Ki 17:23 He gave him to his m and said, "Look, your H562
1Ki 19:20 "Let me kiss my father and m goodbye," H562
1Ki 22:52 of his father and m and of Jeroboam son of H562
2Ki 3: 2 but not as his father and m had done. H562
2Ki 3:13 of your father and the prophets of your m." H562
2Ki 4:19 father told a servant, "Carry him to his m." H562
2Ki 4:20 had lifted him up and carried him to his m, H562
2Ki 4:30 But the child's m said, "As surely as the H562
2Ki 9:22 witchcraft of your m Jezebel abound?" H562
2Ki 10:13 families of the king and of the queen m." H1485
2Ki 11: 1 When Athaliah the m of Ahaziah saw that H562
2Ki 24:12 king of Judah, his m, his attendants, H562
2Ki 24:15 from Jerusalem to Babylon the king's m, H562
1Ch 2:17 Abigail was the m of Amasa, whose H3528
1Ch 2:26 name was Atarah; she was the m of Onam. H562
1Ch 2:46 concubine Ephah was the m of Haran, H3528
1Ch 2:48 Maakah was the m of Sheber and H3528
1Ch 4: 9 His m had named him Jabez, saying, "I H562
2Ch 2:14 whose m was from Dan and whose father H851
2Ch 15:16 Maakah from her position as queen m, H1485
2Ch 22: 3 his m encouraged him to act wickedly. H562
2Ch 22:10 When Athaliah the m of Ahaziah saw that H562
Est 2: 7 up because she had neither father nor m. H562
Est 2: 7 own daughter when her father and m died. H562
Job 17:14 to the worm, 'My m' or 'My sister,' H562

Ps 27:10 Though my father and **m** forsake me, the H562
Ps 35:14 head in grief as though weeping for my **m**. H562
Ps 51: 5 sinful from the time my **m** conceived me. H562
Ps 86:16 because I **serve** you **just as** my **m** did. H563
Ps 109:14 may the sin of his **m** never be blotted out. H562
Ps 113: 9 in her home as a happy **m** *of* children. H562
Ps 116:16 I serve you **just as** my **m did**; you have H563S
Ps 131: 2 I am like a weaned child with its **m**; like a H562
Pr 4: 3 still tender, and cherished by my **m**. H562
Pr 10: 1 a foolish son brings grief to his **m**. H562
Pr 15:20 but a foolish man despises his **m**. H562
Pr 17:25 bitterness to the **m** *who* **bore** him. H3528
Pr 19:26 drives out their **m** is a child who brings H562
Pr 20:20 If someone curses their father or **m**, their H562
Pr 23:22 do not despise your **m** when she is old. H562
Pr 23:25 May your father and **m** rejoice; may she H562
Pr 28:24 Whoever robs their father or **m** and says H562
Pr 29:15 a child left undisciplined disgraces its **m**. H562
Pr 30:17 that scorns an aged **m**, will be pecked out H562
Pr 31: 1 an inspired utterance his **m** taught him. H562
SS 3:11 with which his **m** crowned him on the H562
SS 6: 9 the only daughter of her **m**, the favorite of H562
SS 8: 5 there your **m** conceived you, there H562
Isa 8: 4 knows how to say 'My father' or 'My **m**, H562
Isa 45:10 to a **m**, 'What have you brought to birth? H851
Isa 49:15 "Can a **m** forget the baby at her breast H851
Isa 50: 1 your transgressions your **m** was sent away. H562
Isa 66:13 As a **m** comforts her child, so will I comfort H562
Jer 13:18 Say to the king and to the **queen m** H1485
Jer 15: 9 The **m** *of* seven will grow faint and H3528
Jer 15:10 my **m**, that you gave me birth, a man H562
Jer 16: 7 not even for a father or a **m**—nor will H562
Jer 20:14 May the day my **m** bore me not be blessed H562
Jer 20:17 in the womb, with my **m** as my grave, her H562
Jer 22:26 will hurl you and the **m** who gave you birth H562
Jer 29: 2 after King Jehoiachin and the **queen m**, H1485
Jer 50:12 your **m** will be greatly ashamed; she who H562
Eze 16: 3 father was an Amorite and your **m** a Hittite. H562
Eze 16:44 "Like **m**, like daughter." H562
Eze 16:45 You are a true daughter of your **m**, who H562
Eze 16:45 Your **m** was a Hittite and your father an H562
Eze 19: 2 a lioness was your **m** among the lions! H562
Eze 19:10 " 'Your **m** was like a vine in your vineyard H562
Eze 22: 7 have treated father and **m** with contempt; H562
Eze 23: 2 two women, daughters of the same **m**. H562
Eze 44:25 if the dead person was his father or **m**, son H562
Hos 2: 2 "Rebuke your **m**, rebuke her, for she is not H562
Hos 2: 5 Their **m** has been unfaithful and has H562
Hos 4: 5 So I will destroy your **m**— H562
Mic 7: 6 a daughter rises up against her **m**, H562
Zec 13: 3 their father and **m**, to whom they were born H562
Mt 1: 3 Zerah, whose **m** was Tamar, Perez *G1666*
Mt 1: 5 of Boaz, whose **m** was Rahab, Boaz the *G1666*
Mt 1: 5 of Obed, whose **m** was Ruth, Obed the *G1666*
Mt 1: 6 whose **m** had been Uriah's wife, *G1666*
Mt 1:16 Mary *was the* **m** *of* Jesus who is *G1164*
Mt 1:18 His **m** Mary was pledged to be married to *G3613*
Mt 2:11 they saw the child with his **m** Mary, and *G3613*
Mt 2:13 the child and his **m** and escape to Egypt. *G3613*
Mt 2:14 the child and his **m** during the night and *G3613*
Mt 2:20 the child and his **m** and go to the land of *G3613*
Mt 2:21 the child and his **m** and went to the land *G3613*
Mt 10:35 a daughter against her **m**, *G3613*
Mt 10:37 their father or **m** more than me is not *G3613*
Mt 12:46 his **m** and brothers stood outside *G3613*
Mt 12:47 "Your **m** and brothers are standing *G3613*
Mt 12:48 "Who is my **m**, and who are my *G3613*
Mt 12:49 he said, "Here are my **m** and my brothers. *G3613*
Mt 12:50 in heaven is my brother and sister and **m**." *G3613*
Mt 14: 8 Prompted by her **m**, she said, "Give me *G3613*
Mt 14:11 given to the girl, who carried it *to* her **m**. *G3613*
Mt 15: 4 your father and **m**' and 'Anyone who *G3613*
Mt 15: 4 their father or **m** is to be put to death. *G3613*
Mt 15: 5 help their father or **m** is 'devoted to God, *G3613*
Mt 15: 6 are not to 'honor their father or **m**' with it. *G3613*
Mt 19: 5 his father and **m** and be united to his *G3613*
Mt 19:19 honor your father and **m**,' and 'love your *G3613*
Mt 19:29 sisters or father or **m** or wife or children *G3613*
Mt 20:20 Then the **m** of Zebedee's sons came to *G3613*
Mt 27:56 Mary the **m** of James and Joseph *G3613*
Mt 27:56 Joseph, and the **m** of Zebedee's sons. *G3613*
Mk 3:31 Then Jesus' **m** and brothers arrived *G3613*
Mk 3:32 "Your **m** and brothers are outside looking *G3613*
Mk 3:33 "Who are my **m** and my brothers?" he *G3613*
Mk 3:34 "Here are my **m** and my brothers! *G3613*
Mk 3:35 God's will is my brother and sister and **m**." *G3613*
Mk 5:40 child's father and **m** and the disciples *G3613*
Mk 6:24 She went out and said *to* her **m**, "What *G3613*
Mk 6:28 it to the girl, and she gave it *to* her **m**. *G3613*
Mk 7:10 'Honor your father and **m**,' and, *G3613*
Mk 7:10 their father or **m** is to be put to death.' *G3613*
Mk 7:11 used to help their father or **m** is Corban *G3613*
Mk 7:12 let them do anything for their father or **m**. *G3613*
Mk 10: 7 his father and **m** and be united to his *G3613*
Mk 10:19 not defraud, honor your father and **m**.' *G3613*
Mk 10:29 sisters or **m** or father or children *G3613*
Mk 15:40 Mary the **m** of James the younger and of *G3613*
Mk 15:47 Mary **the m** of Joseph saw *G3836S*
Mk 16: 1 Magdalene, Mary **the m** of James, and *G3836S*
Lk 1:43 that the **m** of my Lord should come to me? *G3613*
Lk 1:60 his **m** spoke up and said, "No! He is to *G3613*
Lk 2:33 child's father and **m** marveled at what *G3613*
Lk 2:34 blessed them and said to Mary, his **m**: *G3613*
Lk 2:48 His **m** said to him, "Son, why have you *G3613*
Lk 2:51 But his **m** treasured all these things in her *G3613*
Lk 7:12 the only son *of* his **m**, and she was a *G3613*
Lk 7:15 and Jesus gave him back *to* his **m**. *G3613*
Lk 8:19 Now Jesus' **m** and brothers came to see *G3613*
Lk 8:20 "Your **m** and brothers are standing *G3613*
Lk 8:21 "My **m** and brothers are those who hear *G3613*
Lk 8:51 James, and the child's father and **m**. *G3613*
Lk 11:27 "Blessed is the **m** who gave you birth *G3120S*
Lk 12:53 **m** against daughter and daughter against *G3613*
Lk 12:53 daughter and daughter against **m**, *G3613*
Lk 14:26 to me and does not hate father and **m**, *G3613*
Lk 18:20 false testimony, honor your father and **m**.' *G3613*
Lk 24:10 Joanna, Mary **the m** of James, and the *G3836*
Jn 2: 1 at Cana in Galilee. Jesus' **m** was there, *G3613*
Jn 2: 3 was gone, Jesus' **m** said to him, "They *G3613*
Jn 2: 5 His **m** said to the servants, "Do whatever *G3613*
Jn 2:12 Capernaum with his **m** and brothers and *G3613*
Jn 6:42 of Joseph, whose father and **m** we know? *G3613*
Jn 19:25 Near the cross of Jesus stood his **m**, his *G3613*
Jn 19:26 When Jesus saw his **m** there, and the *G3613*
Jn 19:27 "Here is your **m**." From that time on, *G3613*
Ac 1:14 with the women and Mary the **m** of Jesus, *G3613*
Ac 12:12 went to the house of Mary the **m** of John, *G3613*
Ac 16: 1 whose **m** was Jewish and a believer but *G1222*
Ro 16:13 in the Lord, and his **m**, who has been a *G3613*
Ro 16:13 his mother, who has been a **m** to me, too. NDT
Gal 4:26 that is above is free, and she is our **m**. *G3613*
Eph 5:31 his father and **m** and be united to his *G3613*
Eph 6: 2 "Honor your father and **m**"—which is the *G3613*
1Th 2: 7 Just as a **nursing m** cares for her children, *G5577*
2Ti 1: 5 Lois and *in* your **m** Eunice and, *G3613*
Heb 7: 3 **Without** father or **m**, without genealogy *G298*
Rev 17: 5 the great THE **M** OF PROSTITUTES AND OF *G3613*

MOTHER'S (66) [MOTHER]

Ge 24:28 ran and told her **m** household about these H562
Ge 24:67 Isaac was comforted after his **m** death. H562
Ge 28: 2 to the house of your **m** father Bethuel. H562
Ge 28: 2 the daughters of Laban, your **m** brother. H562
Ge 43:29 Benjamin, his own **m** son, he asked, H562
Ge 44:20 he is the only one of his **m** sons left H562
Ex 23:19 "Do not cook a young goat in its **m** milk. H562
Ex 34:26 "Do not cook a young goat in its **m** milk." H562
Lev 18: 9 your father's daughter or your **m** daughter, H562
Lev 18:13 have sexual relations with your **m** sister, H562
Lev 18:13 because she is your **m** close relative. H562
Lev 24:11 His **m** name was Shelomith, the daughter H562
Nu 12:12 coming from its **m** womb with its flesh H562
Dt 14:21 Do not cook a young goat in its **m** milk. H562
Jdg 9: 1 went to his **m** brothers in Shechem H562
Jdg 9: 1 said to them and to all his **m** clan, H562
Jdg 16:17 dedicated to God from my **m** womb. H562
Ru 1: 8 "Go back, each of you, to your **m** home. H562
1Ki 14:21 His **m** name was Naamah; she was an H562
1Ki 14:31 His **m** name was Naamah; she was an H562
1Ki 15: 2 His **m** name was Maakah daughter of H562
1Ki 22:42 His **m** name was Azubah daughter of H562
2Ki 8:26 His **m** name was Athaliah, H562
2Ki 12: 1 His **m** name was Zibiah; she was from H562
2Ki 14: 2 His **m** name was Jehoaddan; she was from H562
2Ki 15: 2 His **m** name was Jekoliah; she was from H562
2Ki 15:33 His **m** name was Jerusha daughter of H562
2Ki 18: 2 His **m** name was Abijah daughter of H562
2Ki 21: 1 His **m** name was Hephzibah. H562
2Ki 21:19 His **m** name was Meshullemeth daughter H562
2Ki 22: 1 His **m** name was Jedidah daughter of H562
2Ki 23:31 His **m** name was Hamutal daughter of H562
2Ki 23:36 His **m** name was Zebidah daughter of H562
2Ki 24: 8 His **m** name was Nehushta daughter of H562
2Ki 24:18 His **m** name was Hamutal daughter of H562
2Ch 12:13 His **m** name was Naamah; she was an H562
2Ch 13: 2 His **m** name was Maakah, a daughter of H562
2Ch 20:31 His **m** name was Azubah daughter of H562
2Ch 22: 2 His **m** name was Athaliah, H562
2Ch 24: 1 His **m** name was Zibiah; she was from H562
2Ch 25: 1 His **m** name was Jehoaddan; she was from H562
2Ch 26: 3 His **m** name was Jekoliah; she was from H562
2Ch 27: 1 His **m** name was Jerusha daughter of H562
2Ch 29: 1 His **m** name was Abijah daughter of H562
Job 1:21 "Naked I came from my **m** womb, and H562
Ps 22: 9 made me trust in you, even at my **m** breast. H562
Ps 22:10 from my **m** womb you have been my God. H562
Ps 50:20 your brother and slander your own **m** son. H562
Ps 69: 8 a stranger to my own **m** children; H562
Ps 71: 6 you brought me forth from my **m** womb. H562
Ps 139:13 you knit me together in my **m** womb. H562
Pr 1: 8 do not forsake your **m** teaching. H562
Pr 6:20 do not forsake your **m** teaching. H562
Ecc 5:15 Everyone comes naked from their **m** womb H562
Ecc 11: 5 how the body is formed in a **m** womb H4849S
SS 1: 6 My **m** sons were angry with me and made H562
SS 3: 4 go till I had brought him to my **m** house, H562
SS 8: 1 a brother, who was nursed at my **m** breasts! H562
SS 8: 2 lead you and bring you to my **m** house— H562
Isa 49: 1 from my **m** womb he has spoken my name. H562
Isa 50: 1 "Where is your **m** certificate of divorce with H562
Jer 52: 1 His **m** name was Hamutal daughter of H562
Mt 13:55 Isn't his **m** name Mary, and aren't his *G3613*
Jn 3: 4 time into their **m** womb to be born!" *G3613*
Jn 19:25 his mother, his **m** sister, Mary the wife *G3613*
Gal 1:15 me apart from my **m** womb and called me *G3613*

MOTHER-IN-LAW (18) [MOTHER]

Dt 27:23 "Cursed is anyone who sleeps with his **m**." H3165
Ru 1:14 Then Orpah kissed her **m** goodbye, but H2792
Ru 2:11 have done for your **m** since the death of H2792
Ru 2:18 her **m** saw how much she had H2792
Ru 2:19 Her **m** asked her, "Where did you glean H2792
Ru 2:19 Then Ruth told her **m** about the one at H2792
Ru 2:23 were finished. And she lived with her **m**. H2792
Ru 3: 1 One day Ruth's **m** Naomi said to her, "My H2792
Ru 3: 6 did everything her **m** told her to do. H2792
Ru 3:16 When Ruth came to her **m**, Naomi asked H2792
Ru 3:17 'Don't go back to your **m** empty-handed.' H2792
Mic 7: 6 a daughter-in-law against her **m**—a H2792
Mt 8:14 he saw Peter's **m** lying in bed with a fever. *G4289*
Mt 10:35 a daughter-in-law against her **m**— *G4289*
Mk 1:30 Simon's **m** was in bed with a fever, and *G4289*
Lk 4:38 Now Simon's **m** was suffering from a high *G4289*
Lk 12:53 **m** against daughter-in-law and *G4289*
Lk 12:53 daughter-in-law against **m**. *G4289*

MOTHER-OF-PEARL (1) [PEARL]

Est 1: 6 marble, **m** and other costly stones. H1993

MOTHERS (18) [MOTHER]

Ge 32:11 and also the **m** with their children. H562
Ex 22:30 Let them stay with their **m** for seven days H562
Job 31:15 the same one form us both within our **m**? H8167
Pr 30:11 curse their fathers and do not bless their **m**; H562
Isa 49:23 and their queens your **nursing m**. H4787
Jer 15: 8 against the **m** *of* their young men; H562
Jer 16: 3 who are their **m** and the men who are H562
Jer 31: 8 **expectant m** and women in labor H2226
La 2:12 They say to their **m**, "Where is bread and H562
La 5: 3 have become fatherless, our **m** are widows. H562
Eze 9: 6 men and women, the **m** and children, but H851
Hos 10:14 when **m** were dashed to the ground with H562
Mt 24:19 days for pregnant women and **nursing m**! *G2558*
Mk 10:30 brothers, sisters, **m**, children and fields *G3613*
Mk 13:17 days for pregnant women and **nursing m**! *G2558*
Lk 21:23 days for pregnant women and **nursing m**! *G2558*
1Ti 1: 9 those who **kill** their fathers or **m**, for *G3618*
1Ti 5: 2 older women as **m**, and younger women *G3613*

MOTHERS' (1) [MOTHER]

La 2:12 as their lives ebb away in their **m** arms. H562

MOTHS (5) [MOTH'S]

Job 13:28 like a garment eaten by **m**. H6931
Isa 50: 9 like a garment; the **m** will eat them up. H6931
Mt 6:19 on earth, where **m** and vermin destroy *G4962*
Mt 6:20 where **m** and vermin do not destroy *G4962*
Jas 5: 2 and **m** *have* **eaten** your clothes. *G4963+1181*

MOTIONED (7) [MOTIONS]

Jn 13:24 Simon Peter **m** to this disciple and said *G3748*
Ac 12:17 Peter **m** with his hand for them to be quiet *G2939*
Ac 13:16 Paul **m** with his hand and said: *G2939*
Ac 19:33 He **m for silence** in order to *G2939+3836+5931*
Ac 21:40 steps and **m** to the crowd. *G2939+3836+5931*
Ac 24:10 *When* the governor **m** for him to speak *G3748*
Ac 26: 1 So Paul **m** with his hand and began his *G1753*

MOTIONS (1) [MOTIONED]

Pr 6:13 with his feet and **m** with his fingers, H3723

MOTIVES (5)

Pr 16: 2 to them, but **m** are weighed by the LORD. H8120
1Co 4: 5 will expose the **m** of the heart. *G1087*
Php 1:18 whether *from* **false m** or true, Christ *G4733*
1Th 2: 3 make does not spring from error or **impure** *m*, AIT
Jas 4: 3 because you ask **with wrong m**, that you *G2809*

MOUND (5) [MOUNDS]

SS 7: 2 Your waist is a **m** *of* wheat encircled by H6894
Jer 26:18 temple hill a **m** *overgrown with* thickets. H1195
Jer 49: 2 it will become a **m** *of* ruins, and its H9424
Eze 16:24 you built a **m** for yourself and made a lofty H1461
Mic 3:12 the temple hill a **m** overgrown with H1195

MOUNDS (3) [MOUND]

Jos 11:13 burn any of the cities built on their **m**— H9424
Eze 16:31 When you built your **m** at every street H1461
Eze 16:39 will tear down your **m** and destroy your H1461

MOUNT (151) [MOUNTAIN, MOUNTAINS, MOUNTAINSIDE, MOUNTAINTOP, MOUNTAINTOPS, MOUNTED, MOUNTINGS, MOUNTS]

Ex 19:11 will come down on **M** Sinai in the sight of H2215
Ex 19:18 **M** Sinai was covered with smoke, because H2215
Ex 19:20 to the top of **M** Sinai and called Moses H2215
Ex 19:23 "The people cannot come up **M** Sinai H2215
Ex 24:16 the glory of the LORD settled on **M** Sinai. H2215
Ex 28:11 Then **m** the stones in gold filigree settings H6913
Ex 28:17 Then **m** four rows of precious stones H4848+4853
Ex 28:20 **M** them in gold filigree settings H2118+4853
Ex 31:18 finished speaking to Moses on **M** Sinai, H2215
Ex 33: 6 stripped off their ornaments at **M** Horeb. H2215
Ex 34: 2 morning, and then come up on **M** Sinai. H2215
Ex 34: 4 ones and went up **M** Sinai early in the H2215
Ex 34:29 came down from **M** Sinai with the two H2215
Ex 34:32 the LORD had given him on **M** Sinai. H2215

M

Lev 7:38 LORD gave Moses at **M** Sinai in the Desert H2215
Lev 25: 1 The LORD said to Moses at **M** Sinai, H2215
Lev 26:46 LORD established at **M** Sinai between H2215
Lev 27:34 the LORD gave Moses at **M** Sinai for the H2215
Nu 3: 1 time the LORD spoke to Moses at **M** Sinai. H2215
Nu 20:22 set out from Kadesh and came to **M** Hor. H2215
Nu 20:23 At **M** Hor, near the border of Edom, the H2215
Nu 20:25 his son Eleazar and take them up **M** Hor. H2215
Nu 20:27 They went up **M** Hor in the sight of the H2215
Nu 21: 4 They traveled from **M** Hor along the route H2215
Nu 28: 6 instituted at **M** Sinai as a pleasing H2215
Nu 33:23 Kehelathah and camped at **M** Shepher. H2215
Nu 33:24 They left **M** Shepher and camped at H2215
Nu 33:37 They left Kadesh and camped at **M** Hor H2215
Nu 33:38 Aaron the priest went up **M** Hor, H2215
Nu 33:39 years old when he died on **M** Hor. H2215
Nu 33:41 They left **M** Hor and camped at Zalmonah H2215
Nu 34: 7 line from the Mediterranean Sea to **M** Hor H2215
Nu 34: 8 from **M** Hor to Lebo Hamath. Then the H2215
Dt 1: 2 to Kadesh Barnea by the **M** Seir road.) H2215
Dt 3: 8 the Arnon Gorge as far as **M** Hermon. H2215
Dt 4:48 the rim of the Arnon Gorge to **M** Sirion H2215
Dt 11:29 are to proclaim on **M** Gerizim the H2215
Dt 11:29 the blessings, and on **M** Ebal the curses. H2215
Dt 27: 4 set up these stones on **M** Ebal, as I H2215
Dt 27:12 shall stand on **M** Gerizim to bless the H2215
Dt 27:13 tribes shall stand on **M** Ebal to pronounce H2215
Dt 32:49 the Abarim Range to **M** Nebo in Moab, H2215
Dt 32:50 Aaron died on **M** Hor and was gathered H2215
Dt 33: 2 from Seir; he shone forth from **M** Paran. H2215
Dt 34: 1 Then Moses climbed **M** Nebo from the H2215
Jos 8:30 Joshua built on **M** Ebal an altar to the H2215
Jos 8:33 stood in front of **M** Gerizim and half of H2215
Jos 8:33 half of them in front of **M** Ebal, H2215
Jos 11:17 from **M** Halak, which rises toward Seir, to H2215
Jos 11:17 the Valley of Lebanon below **M** Hermon. H2215
Jos 12: 1 from the Arnon Gorge to **M** Hermon H2215
Jos 12: 5 He ruled over **M** Hermon, Salekah, all of H2215
Jos 12: 7 Gad in the Valley of Lebanon to **M** Halak, H2215
Jos 13: 5 from Baal Gad below **M** Hermon to Lebo H2215
Jos 13:11 all of **M** Hermon and all Bashan as far as H2215
Jos 15: 9 out at the towns of **M** Ephron and went H2215
Jos 15:10 it curved westward from Baalah to **M** Seir, H2215
Jos 15:10 ran along the northern slope of **M** Jearim H2215
Jos 15:11 passed along to **M** Baalah and reached H2215
Jos 24:30 hill country of Ephraim, north of **M** Gaash. H2215
Jdg 1:35 determined also to hold out in **M** Heres, H2215
Jdg 2: 9 hill country of Ephraim, north of **M** Gaash. H2215
Jdg 3: 3 mountains from **M** Baal Hermon to Lebo H2215
Jdg 4: 6 Zebulun and lead them up to **M** Tabor. H2215
Jdg 4:12 son of Abinoam had gone up to **M** Tabor, H2215
Jdg 4:14 So Barak went down **M** Tabor, with ten H2215
Jdg 7: 3 fear may turn back and leave **M** Gilead. H2215
Jdg 9: 7 up on the top of **M** Gerizim and shouted H2215
Jdg 9:48 he and all his men went up **M** Zalmon. H2215
1Sa 31: 1 and many fell dead on **M** Gilboa. H2215
1Sa 31: 8 his three sons fallen on **M** Gilboa. H2215
2Sa 1: 6 "I happened to be on **M** Gilboa," the H2215
2Sa 15:30 But David continued up the **M** *of* Olives H5090
1Ki 1:33 and **have** Solomon my son **m** my H8206+6584
1Ki 1:38 down and **had** Solomon **m** King H8206+6584
1Ki 18:19 all over Israel to meet me on **M** Carmel. H2215
1Ki 18:20 assembled the prophets on **M** Carmel. H2215
2Ki 2:25 And he went on to **M** Carmel and from H2215
2Ki 4:25 came to the man of God at **M** Carmel. H2215
2Ki 19:31 out of **M** Zion a band of survivors. H2215
1Ch 5:23 Hermon, that is, to Senir (**M** Hermon). H2215
1Ch 10: 1 and many fell dead on **M** Gilboa. H2215
1Ch 10: 8 Saul and his sons fallen on **M** Gilboa. H2215
2Ch 3: 1 of the LORD in Jerusalem on **M** Moriah, H2215
2Ch 13: 4 Abijah stood on **M** Zemaraim, in the hill H2215
2Ch 20:10 from Ammon, Moab and **M** Seir, whose H2215
2Ch 20:22 Ammon and Moab and **M** Seir who were H2215
2Ch 20:23 the men from **M** Seir to destroy and H2215
Ne 2:14 not enough room for my **m** to get through; H989
Ne 9:13 "You came down on **M** Sinai; you spoke H2215
Ps 42: 6 the heights of Hermon—from **M** Mizar. H2215
Ps 48: 2 like the heights of Zaphon is **M** Zion, the H2215
Ps 48:11 **M** Zion rejoices, the villages of Judah are H2215
Ps 68:14 it was like snow fallen on ***M* Zalmon**. AIT
Ps 68:15 **M** Bashan, majestic mountain, Mount H2215
Ps 68:15 majestic mountain, **M** Bashan, rugged H2215
Ps 74: 2 you redeemed—**M** Zion, where you H2215
Ps 78:68 the tribe of Judah, **M** Zion, which he H2215
Ps 89: 9 when its waves **m up**, you still them. H5951
Ps 125: 1 who trust in the LORD are like **M** Zion, H2215
Ps 133: 3 dew of Hermon were falling on **M** Zion. H2215
SS 7: 5 Your head crowns you like **M** Carmel. NDT
Isa 4: 5 create over all of **M** Zion and over those H2215
Isa 8:18 the LORD Almighty, who dwells on **M** Zion. H2215
Isa 10:12 his work against **M** Zion and Jerusalem, H2215
Isa 10:32 shake their fist at the **m** *of* Daughter Zion, H2215
Isa 14:13 I will sit enthroned on the **m** *of* assembly H2215
Isa 14:13 on the utmost heights of **M** Zaphon. NDT
Isa 16: 1 the desert, to the **m** *of* Daughter Zion. H2215
Isa 18: 7 the gifts will be brought to **M** Zion, the H2215
Isa 24:23 will reign on **M** Zion and in Jerusalem, H2215
Isa 28:21 LORD will rise up as he did at **M** Perazim, H2215
Isa 29: 8 all the nations that fight against **M** Zion. H2215
Isa 31: 4 down to do battle on **M** Zion and on its H2215
Isa 37:32 out of **M** Zion a band of survivors. H2215
Jer 46: 4 Harness the horses, **m** the steeds! Take H6590
La 5:18 **M** Zion, which lies desolate, with H2215
Eze 28:14 You were on the holy **m** *of* God; you H2215
Eze 28:16 I drove you in disgrace from the **m** *of* God, H2215
Eze 35: 2 set your face against **M** Seir; prophesy H2215
Eze 35: 3 I am against you, **M** Seir, and I will stretch H2215
Eze 35: 7 I will make **M** Seir a desolate waste and H2215
Eze 35:15 will be desolate, **M** Seir, you and all of H2215
Hos 14: 3 cannot save us; *we will* not **m** warhorses. H8206
Joel 2:32 on **M** Zion and in Jerusalem there will H2215
Am 4: 1 you cows of Bashan on **M** Samaria, you H2215
Am 6: 1 to you who feel secure on **M** Samaria, H2215
Ob 17 But on **M** Zion will be deliverance; it will H2215
Ob 21 will go up on **M** Zion to govern the H2215
Mic 4: 7 rule over them in **M** Zion from that day H2215
Hab 3: 3 from Teman, the Holy One from **M** Paran. H2215
Zec 14: 4 day his feet will stand on the **M** *of* Olives, H2215
Zec 14: 4 the **M** *of* Olives will be split in two H2215
Mt 21: 1 came to Bethphage on the **M** of Olives, *G4001*
Mt 24: 3 As Jesus was sitting on the **M** of Olives *G4001*
Mt 26:30 a hymn, they went out to the **M** of Olives. *G4001*
Mk 11: 1 Bethany at the **M** of Olives, *G4001*
Mk 13: 3 was sitting on the **M** of Olives opposite *G4001*
Mk 14:26 a hymn, they went out to the **M** of Olives. *G4001*
Lk 19:29 Bethany at the hill called the **M of Olives**, *G1779*
Lk 19:37 the road goes down the **M** of Olives, *G4001*
Lk 21:37 night on the hill called the **M of Olives**, *G1779*
Lk 22:39 went out as usual to the **M** of Olives, *G4001*
Jn 8: 1 Jesus went to the **M** of Olives. *G4001*
Ac 1:12 from the hill called the **M of Olives**, *G1779*
Ac 7:30 burning bush in the desert *near* **M** Sinai. *G4001*
Ac 7:38 the angel who spoke to him on **M** Sinai, *G4001*
Gal 4:24 One covenant is from **M** Sinai and bears *G4001*
Gal 4:25 Hagar stands for **M** Sinai in Arabia and *G4001*
Heb 12:22 But you have come to **M** Zion, to the city *G4001*
Rev 14: 1 standing on **M** Zion, and with him *G4001*

MOUNTAIN (161) [MOUNT]

Ge 22: 2 as a burnt offering on a **m** I will show you. H2215
Ge 22:14 On the **m** *of* the LORD it will be provided. H2215
Ex 3: 1 came to Horeb, the **m** *of* God. H2215
Ex 3:12 of Egypt, you will worship God on this **m**." H2215
Ex 4:27 met Moses at the **m** *of* God and kissed H2215
Ex 15:17 plant them on the **m** *of* your inheritance— H2215
Ex 18: 5 where he was camped near the **m** *of* God. H2215
Ex 19: 2 there in the desert in front of the **m**. H2215
Ex 19: 3 LORD called to him from the **m** and said, H2215
Ex 19:12 the people around the **m** and tell them, NDT
Ex 19:12 do not approach the **m** or touch the foot H2215
Ex 19:12 Whoever touches the **m** is to be put to H2215
Ex 19:13 a long blast may they approach the **m**." H2215
Ex 19:14 had gone down the **m** to the people, H2215
Ex 19:16 with a thick cloud over the **m**, and a very H2215
Ex 19:17 and they stood at the foot of the **m**. H2215
Ex 19:18 the whole **m** trembled violently. H2215
Ex 19:20 called Moses to the top of the **m**. H2215
Ex 19:23 limits around the **m** and set it apart as H2215
Ex 20:18 the trumpet and saw the **m** in smoke, H2215
Ex 24: 4 at the foot of the **m** and set up twelve H2215
Ex 24:12 "Come up to me on the **m** and stay here H2215
Ex 24:13 Moses went up on the **m** *of* God. H2215
Ex 24:15 When Moses went up on the **m**, the cloud H2215
Ex 24:16 For six days the cloud covered **the m** H2084S
Ex 24:17 like a consuming fire on top of the **m**. H2215
Ex 24:18 the cloud as he went on up the **m**. H2215
Ex 24:18 he stayed on the **m** forty days and forty H2215
Ex 25:40 to the pattern shown you on the **m**. H2215
Ex 26:30 to the plan shown you on the **m**. H2215
Ex 27: 8 made just as you were shown on the **m**. H2215
Ex 32: 1 was so long in coming down from the **m**, H2215
Ex 32:15 went down the **m** with the two tablets H2215
Ex 32:19 them to pieces at the foot of the **m**. H2215
Ex 34: 2 yourself to me there on top of the **m**. H2215
Ex 34: 3 with you or be seen anywhere on the **m**; H2215
Ex 34: 3 herds may graze in front of the **m**. H2215
Nu 10:33 they set out from the **m** *of* the LORD and H2215
Nu 20:28 And Aaron died there on top of the **m** H2215
Nu 20:28 Eleazar came down from the **m**, H2215
Nu 27:12 "Go up this **m** *in* the Abarim Range and H2215
Dt 1: 6 "You have stayed long enough at this **m**. H2215
Dt 4:11 at the foot of the **m** while it blazed with H2215
Dt 5: 4 you face to face out of the fire on the **m**. H2215
Dt 5: 5 afraid of the fire and did not go up the **m**.) H2215
Dt 5:22 there on the **m** from out of the fire, H2215
Dt 5:23 while the **m** was ablaze with fire H2215
Dt 9: 9 When I went up on the **m** to receive the H2215
Dt 9: 9 I stayed on the **m** forty days and forty H2215
Dt 9:10 to you on the **m** out of the fire, H2215
Dt 9:15 went down from the **m** while it was H2215
Dt 9:21 into a stream that flowed down the **m**. H2215
Dt 10: 1 first ones and come up to me on the **m**. H2215
Dt 10: 3 I went up on the **m** with the two tablets H2215
Dt 10: 4 he had proclaimed to you on the **m**, H2215
Dt 10: 5 came back down the **m** and put the H2215
Dt 10:10 I had stayed on the **m** forty days and forty H2215
Dt 14: 5 the ibex, the antelope and the **m sheep**. H2378
Dt 32:50 There on the **m** that you have climbed you H2215
Dt 33: 2 ones from the south, from his **m slopes**. H850
Dt 33:19 peoples to the **m** and there offer the H2215
Jos 10:40 the western foothills and the **m slopes** H844
Jos 12: 8 the Arabah, the **m slopes**, the wilderness H844
Jos 13: 6 of the **m regions** from Lebanon to H2215
Jdg 6: 2 shelters for themselves in **m clefts**, H2215
1Sa 23:26 Saul was going along one side of the **m** H2215
1Sa 25:20 came riding her donkey into a **m** ravine, H2215
1Ki 19: 8 until he reached Horeb, the **m** *of* God. H2215
1Ki 19:11 out and stand on the **m** in the presence of H2215
2Ki 2:16 him down on some **m** or in some valley." H2215
2Ki 4:27 she reached the man of God at the **m**, H2215
Job 14:18 "But as a **m** erodes and crumbles and as H2215
Job 24: 8 are drenched by **m** rains and hug the H2215
Job 39: 1 you know when the **m** goats give birth? H6152
Ps 2: 6 installed my king on Zion, my holy **m**." H2215
Ps 3: 4 and he answers me from his holy **m**. H2215
Ps 11: 1 you say to me: "Flee like a bird to your **m**. H2215
Ps 15: 1 Who may live on your holy **m**? H2215
Ps 24: 3 Who may ascend the **m** *of* the LORD? Who H2215
Ps 30: 7 *you* **made** my royal **m** stand firm H2215
Ps 43: 3 let them bring me to your holy **m**, to the H2215
Ps 48: 1 in the city of our God, his holy **m**. H2215
Ps 68:15 Bashan, majestic **m**, Mount Bashan, H2215
Ps 68:15 mountain, Mount Bashan, rugged **m**, H2215
Ps 68:16 in envy, you rugged **m**, at the mountain H2215
Ps 68:16 at the **m** where God chooses to reign H2215
Ps 87: 1 He has founded his city on the holy **m**. H2215
Ps 95: 4 and the **m** peaks belong to him. H2215
Ps 99: 9 LORD our God and worship at his holy **m**, H2215
SS 4: 6 I will go to the **m** *of* myrrh and to the hill H2215
SS 4: 8 lions' dens and the **m haunts** *of* leopards. H2215
Isa 2: 2 In the last days the **m** *of* the LORD's temple H2215
Isa 2: 3 let us go up to the **m** *of* the LORD, to the H2215
Isa 11: 9 harm nor destroy on all my holy **m**, H2215
Isa 18: 6 all be left to the **m** birds of prey and to H2215
Isa 25: 6 On this **m** the LORD Almighty will prepare H2215
Isa 25: 7 On this **m** he will destroy the shroud that H2215
Isa 25:10 The hand of the LORD will rest on this **m** H2215
Isa 27:13 the LORD on the holy **m** in Jerusalem. H2215
Isa 30:25 flow on every high **m** and every lofty hill. H2215
Isa 30:29 playing pipes go up to the **m** *of* the LORD, H2215
Isa 33:16 whose refuge will be the **m** fortress. H6152
Isa 40: 4 be raised up, every **m** and hill made low H2215
Isa 40: 9 good news to Zion, go up on a high **m**. H2215
Isa 56: 7 bring to my holy **m** and give them joy in H2215
Isa 57:13 inherit the land and possess my holy **m**." H2215
Isa 65:11 forsake the LORD and forget my holy **m**, H2215
Isa 65:25 harm nor destroy on all my holy **m**," H2215
Isa 66:20 to my holy **m** in Jerusalem as an offering H2215
Jer 16:16 them down on every **m** and hill and from H2215
Jer 17: 3 My **m** in the land and your wealth and all H2215
Jer 31:23 you prosperous city, you sacred **m**. H2215
Jer 50: 6 They wandered over **m** and hill and forgot H2215
Jer 51:25 you destroying **m**, you who destroy H2215
Jer 51:25 the cliffs, and make you a burned-out **m**. H2215
Eze 11:23 city and stopped above the **m** east of it. H2215
Eze 17:22 shoots and plant it on a high and lofty **m**. H2215
Eze 17:23 On the **m** heights of Israel I will plant it; it H2215
Eze 18: 6 not eat at the **m shrines** or look to the H2215
Eze 18:11 "He eats at the **m shrines**. He defiles his H2215
Eze 18:15 not eat at the **m shrines** or look to the H2215
Eze 20:40 For on my holy **m**, the high mountain of H2215
Eze 20:40 mountain, the high **m** *of* Israel, declares H2215
Eze 22: 9 who eat at the **m shrines** and commit H2215
Eze 34:14 the **m** heights of Israel will be their H2215
Eze 40: 2 of Israel and set me on a very high **m**, H2215
Eze 43:12 area on top of the **m** will be most holy. H2215
Da 2:35 became a huge **m** and filled the whole A10296
Da 2:45 of the vision of the rock cut out of a **m**, A10296
Da 11:45 between the seas at the beautiful holy **m**. H2215
Mic 4: 1 In the last days the **m** *of* the LORD's temple H2215
Mic 4: 2 let us go up to the **m** *of* the LORD, to the H2215
Mic 7:12 from sea to sea and from **m** to mountain. H2215
Mic 7:12 from sea to sea and from mountain to **m**. H2215
Zec 4: 7 are you, mighty **m**? Before Zerubbabel H2215
Zec 8: 3 the **m** *of* the LORD Almighty will be H2215
Zec 8: 3 LORD Almighty will be called the Holy **M**." H2215
Zec 14: 4 with half of the **m** moving north and half H2215
Zec 14: 5 You will flee by my **m** valley, for it will H2215
Mt 4: 8 him to a very high **m** and showed him all *G4001*
Mt 17: 1 led them up a high **m** by themselves. *G4001*
Mt 17: 9 As they were coming down the **m**, Jesus *G4001*
Mt 17:20 you can say *to* this **m**, 'Move from here *G4001*
Mt 21:21 but also you can say *to* this **m**, 'Go, *G4001*
Mt 28:16 to the **m** where Jesus had told them to go. *G4001*
Mk 9: 2 John with him and led them up a high **m**, *G4001*
Mk 9: 9 As they were coming down the **m**, Jesus *G4001*
Mk 11:23 I tell you, if anyone says *to* this **m**, 'Go, *G4001*
Lk 3: 5 be filled in, every **m** and hill made low. *G4001*
Lk 9:28 with him and went up onto a **m** to pray. *G4001*
Lk 9:37 when they came down from the **m**, *G4001*
Jn 4:20 Our ancestors worshiped on this **m**, but *G4001*
Jn 4:21 Father neither on this **m** nor in Jerusalem. *G4001*
Jn 6:15 withdrew again to a **m** by himself. *G4001*
Heb 8: 5 to the pattern shown you on the **m**." *G4001*
Heb 12:18 have not come to a **m** that can be *G4001*
Heb 12:20 "If even an animal touches the **m**, it must *G4001*
2Pe 1:18 when we were with him on the sacred **m**. *G4001*
Rev 6:14 every **m** and island was removed *G4001*
Rev 8: 8 something like a huge **m**, all ablaze, *G4001*
Rev 21:10 away in the Spirit to a **m** great and high, *G4001*

MOUNTAINS (149) [MOUNT]

Ge 7:19 all the high **m** under the entire H2215
Ge 7:20 covered the **m** to a depth of more H2215
Ge 8: 4 the ark came to rest on the **m** *of* Ararat. H2215
Ge 8: 5 month the tops of the **m** became visible. H2215

Ge 19:17 Flee to the **m** or you will be swept away!" H2215
Ge 19:19 But I can't flee to the **m**; this disaster will H2215
Ge 19:30 daughters left Zoar and settled in the **m**, H2215
Ge 49:26 than the blessings of the ancient **m**, H2215
Ex 32:12 to kill them in the **m** and to wipe them off H2215
Nu 23: 7 the king of Moab from the eastern **m**. H2215
Nu 33:47 camped in the **m** *of* Abarim, H2215
Nu 33:48 They left the **m** *of* Abarim and camped on H2215
Dt 1: 7 in the Arabah, in the **m**, in the western H2215
Dt 11:11 of is a land of **m** and valleys that drinks H2215
Dt 11:30 As you know, these **m** are across the Jordan NDT
Dt 12: 2 completely all the places on the high **m**, H2215
Dt 32:22 set afire the foundations of the **m**. H2215
Dt 33:15 gifts of the ancient **m** and the fruitfulness H2215
Jos 11: 2 to the northern kings who were in the **m**, H2215
Jos 11:16 the Arabah and the **m** *of* Israel with their H2215
Jdg 3: 3 living in the Lebanon **m** from Mount Baal H2215
Jdg 5: 5 The **m** quaked before the LORD, the One of H2215
Jdg 9:36 are coming down from the tops of the **m**!" H2215
Jdg 9:36 mistake the shadows of the **m** for men." H2215
1Sa 26:20 a flea—as one hunts a partridge in the **m**." H2215
2Sa 1:21 "**M** of Gilboa, may you have neither dew H2215
1Ki 19:11 wind tore the **m** apart and shattered H2215
2Ki 19:23 I have ascended the heights of the **m**, H2215
1Ch 12: 8 they were as swift as gazelles in the **m**. H2215
Job 9: 5 He moves **m** without their knowing it and H2215
Job 28: 9 hands and lay bare the roots of the **m**. H2215
Ps 18: 7 the foundations of the **m** shook; they H2215
Ps 36: 6 Your righteousness is like the highest **m** H2215
Ps 46: 2 give way and the **m** fall into the heart of H2215
Ps 46: 3 roar and foam and the **m** quake with their H2215
Ps 50:11 I know every bird in the **m**, and the insects H2215
Ps 65: 6 who formed the **m** by your power, having H2215
Ps 72: 3 May the **m** bring prosperity to the people H2215
Ps 76: 4 more majestic than **m** *rich with* game. H2215
Ps 80:10 The **m** were covered with its shade, the H2215
Ps 83:14 the forest or a flame sets the **m** ablaze, H2215
Ps 90: 2 Before the **m** were born or you brought H2215
Ps 97: 5 The **m** melt like wax before the LORD H2215
Ps 98: 8 their hands, let the **m** sing together for joy H2215
Ps 104: 6 a garment; the waters stood above the **m**. H2215
Ps 104: 8 they flowed over the **m**, they went down H2215
Ps 104:10 into the ravines; it flows between the **m**. H2215
Ps 104:13 He waters the **m** from his upper chambers; H2215
Ps 104:18 The high **m** belong to the wild goats; the H2215
Ps 104:32 who touches the **m**, and they smoke. H2215
Ps 114: 4 the **m** leaped like rams, the hills like H2215
Ps 114: 6 **m**, did you leap like rams, you hills H2215
Ps 121: 1 I lift up my eyes to the **m**—where does H2215
Ps 125: 2 As the **m** surround Jerusalem, so the LORD H2215
Ps 144: 5 touch the **m**, so that they smoke. H2215
Ps 148: 9 you **m** and all hills, fruit trees and all H2215
Pr 8:25 before the **m** were settled in place, before H2215
SS 2: 8 leaping across the **m**, bounding over the H2215
SS 8:14 like a young stag on the spice-laden **m**. H2215
Isa 2: 2 be established as the highest of the **m**; H2215
Isa 2:14 all the towering **m** and all the high H2215
Isa 5:25 The **m** shake, and the dead bodies are H2215
Isa 13: 4 a noise on the **m**, like that of a great H2215
Isa 14:25 on my **m** I will trample him down. H2215
Isa 18: 3 when a banner is raised on the **m**, you H2215
Isa 22: 5 down walls and of crying out to the **m**. H2215
Isa 34: 3 the **m** will be soaked with their blood. H2215
Isa 37:24 I have ascended the heights of the **m**, H2215
Isa 40:12 weighed the **m** on the scales and the H2215
Isa 41:15 You will thresh the **m** and crush them H2215
Isa 42:15 I will lay waste the **m** and hills and dry up H2215
Isa 44:23 Burst into song, you **m**, you forests and all H2215
Isa 45: 2 I will go before you and will level the **m**; H2215
Isa 49:11 I will turn all my **m** into roads, and my H2215
Isa 49:13 you earth; burst into song, you **m**! H2215
Isa 52: 7 How beautiful on the **m** are the feet of H2215
Isa 54:10 Though the **m** be shaken and the hills be H2215
Isa 55:12 the **m** and hills will burst into song before H2215
Isa 64: 1 that the **m** would tremble before you! H2215
Isa 64: 3 and the **m** trembled before you. H2215
Isa 65: 7 sacrifices on the **m** and defied me on the H2215
Isa 65: 9 from Judah those who will possess my **m**; H2215
Jer 3:23 on the hills and **m** is a deception; H2215
Jer 4:24 I looked at the **m**, and they were quaking H2215
Jer 9:10 wail for the **m** and take up a lament H2215
Jer 46:18 will come who is like Tabor among the **m**, H2215
Jer 50: 6 caused them to roam on the **m**. H2215
La 4:19 chased us over the **m** and lay in wait for H2215
Eze 6: 2 set your face against the **m** *of* Israel H2215
Eze 6: 3 'You **m** *of* Israel, hear the word of the H2215
Eze 6: 3 Sovereign LORD says to the **m** and hills, H2215
Eze 7: 7 There is panic, not joy, on the **m**. H2215
Eze 7:16 fugitives who escape will flee to the **m**. H2215
Eze 19: 9 was heard no longer on the **m** *of* Israel. H2215
Eze 31:12 boughs fell on the **m** and in all the H2215
Eze 32: 5 your flesh on the **m** and fill the valleys H2215
Eze 32: 6 your flowing blood all the way to the **m**, H2215
Eze 33:28 the **m** *of* Israel will become desolate H2215
Eze 34: 6 over all the **m** and on every high H2215
Eze 34:13 I will pasture them on the **m** *of* Israel, in H2215
Eze 34:14 feed in a rich pasture on the **m** *of* Israel. H2215
Eze 35: 8 I will fill your **m** with the slain; those H2215
Eze 35:12 you have said against the **m** *of* Israel. H2215
Eze 36: 1 prophesy to the **m** *of* Israel and say H2215
Eze 36: 1 of Israel and say, '**M** *of* Israel, hear the H2215
Eze 36: 4 therefore, **m** *of* Israel, hear the word of the H2215
Eze 36: 4 Sovereign LORD says to the **m** and hills, H2215
Eze 36: 6 land of Israel and say to the **m** and hills, H2215
Eze 36: 8 " 'But you, **m** *of* Israel, will produce H2215
Eze 37:22 one nation in the land, on the **m** *of* Israel. H2215
Eze 38: 8 from many nations to the **m** *of* Israel, H2215
Eze 38:20 The **m** will be overturned, the cliffs will H2215
Eze 38:21 a sword against Gog on all my **m**, H2215
Eze 39: 2 send you against the **m** *of* Israel. H2215
Eze 39: 4 On the **m** *of* Israel you will fall, you and all H2215
Eze 39:17 the great sacrifice on the **m** *of* Israel. H2215
Hos 10: 8 Then they will say to the **m**, "Cover us!" H2215
Joel 2: 2 across the **m** a large and mighty H2215
Joel 3:18 "In that day the **m** will drip new wine, and H2215
Am 3: 9 yourselves on the **m** *of* Samaria; H2215
Am 4:13 He who forms the **m**, who creates the H2215
Am 9:13 will drip from the **m** and flow from all the H2215
Ob 8 those of understanding in the **m** *of* Esau? H2215
Ob 9 everyone in Esau's **m** will be cut down in H2215
Ob 19 from the Negev will occupy the **m** *of* Esau, H2215
Ob 21 on Mount Zion to govern the **m** *of* Esau. H2215
Jnh 2: 6 To the roots of the **m** I sank down; the H2215
Mic 1: 4 The **m** melt beneath him and the valleys H2215
Mic 4: 1 be established as the highest of the **m**; H2215
Mic 6: 1 plead my case before the **m**; let the hills H2215
Mic 6: 2 you **m**, the LORD's accusation; listen H2215
Na 1: 5 The **m** quake before him and the hills H2215
Na 1:15 there on the **m**, the feet of one who H2215
Na 3:18 are scattered on the **m** with no one to H2215
Hab 3: 6 The ancient **m** crumbled and the age-old H2215
Hab 3:10 the **m** saw you and writhed. Torrents of H2215
Hag 1: 8 Go up into the **m** and bring down timber H2215
Hag 1:11 a drought on the fields and the **m**, H2215
Zec 6: 1 coming out from between two **m**— H2215
Zec 6: 1 between two mountains—**m** *of* bronze. H2215
Mt 24:16 let those who are in Judea flee to the **m**. *G4001*
Mk 13:14 let those who are in Judea flee to the **m**. *G4001*
Lk 21:21 let those who are in Judea flee to the **m**, *G4001*
Lk 23:30 " 'they will say *to* the **m**, "Fall on us!" *G4001*
1Co 13: 2 if I have a faith that can move **m**, but *G4001*
Heb 11:38 They wandered in deserts and **m**, living in *G4001*
Rev 6:15 in caves and among the rocks *of* the **m**. *G4001*
Rev 6:16 They called *to* the **m** and the rocks, "Fall *G4001*
Rev 16:20 fled away and the **m** could not be found. *G4001*

MOUNTAINSIDE (9) [MOUNT]

SS 2:14 in the hiding places on the **m**, show me H4533
Mt 5: 1 he went up on a **m** and sat down. *G4001*
Mt 8: 1 When Jesus came down from the **m** *G4001*
Mt 14:23 he went up on a **m** by himself to pray. *G4001*
Mt 15:29 Then he went up on a **m** and sat down. *G4001*
Mk 3:13 Jesus went up on a **m** and called to him *G4001*
Mk 6:46 leaving them, he went up on a **m** to pray. *G4001*
Lk 6:12 those days Jesus went out to a **m** to pray, *G4001*
Jn 6: 3 Jesus went up on a **m** and sat down with *G4001*

MOUNTAINTOP (1) [MOUNT]

Isa 30:17 you are left like a flagstaff on a **m**, H8031+2215

MOUNTAINTOPS (4) [MOUNT]

Isa 42:11 joy; let them shout from the **m**. H8031+2215
Eze 6:13 on every high hill and on all the **m** H8031+2215
Hos 4:13 sacrifice on the **m** and burn H2215+8031
Joel 2: 5 of chariots they leap over the **m**, H2215+8031

MOUNTED (19) [MOUNT]

Ge 24:61 got ready and **m** the camels and went H8206
Ex 25: 7 other gems to be **m** on the ephod and H4854
Ex 35: 9 other gems to be **m** on the ephod and H4854
Ex 35:27 other gems to be **m** on the ephod and H4854
Ex 39: 6 *They* **m** the onyx stones *in* gold filigree H6913
Ex 39:10 Then *they* **m** four rows of precious stones H4848
Ex 39:13 *They* **were m** in gold filigree settings. H6015
2Sa 13:29 sons got up, **m** their mules and fled. H8206
2Sa 22:11 *He* **m** the cherubim and flew; he soared H8206
1Ki 13:13 had saddled the donkey for him, *he* **m** it H8206
Est 8:10 and sent them by **m** couriers H928+2021+6061
Ps 18:10 *He* **m** the cherubim and flew; he soared H8206
Ps 107:26 *They* **m up** *to* the heavens and went down H6590
SS 5:12 in milk, **m like jewels**. H3782+6584+4859
Eze 23: 6 young men, and **m** horsemen. H8206+6061
Eze 23:12 in full dress, **m** horsemen, all H8206+6061
Eze 23:23 men of high rank, all **m** *on* horses. H8206
Zec 1: 8 before me was a man **m** on a red horse. H8206
Rev 9:16 The number of the **m** troops was twice ten *G2690*

MOUNTINGS (1) [MOUNT]

Eze 28:13 Your settings and **m** were made of gold H5920

MOUNTS (1) [MOUNT]

Ne 2:12 There were no **m** with me except the one I H989

MOURN (59) [MOURNED, MOURNERS, MOURNFUL, MOURNFULLY, MOURNING, MOURNS]

Ge 23: 2 Abraham went to **m** for Sarah and to H6199
Ge 37:35 "I will continue to **m** until I join my son in H63
Ex 33: 4 *they began to* **m** and no one put on any H61
Lev 10: 6 *may* **m** *for* those the LORD has destroyed by H1134
1Sa 16: 1 "How long *will* you **m** for Saul, since H61
1Ki 13:29 to his own city to **m** *for* him and bury him. H6199
1Ki 14:13 All Israel *will* **m** for him and bury him. H6199
Ezr 10: 6 because *he continued to* **m** over the H61
Ne 8: 9 LORD your God. *Do* not **m** or weep." For all H61
Job 5:11 and *those who* **m** are lifted to safety. H7722
Job 14:22 their own bodies and **m** only for themselves." H61
Ecc 3: 4 to laugh, a time *to* **m** and a time to dance H6199
Isa 3:26 The gates of Zion will lament and **m** H61
Isa 29: 2 she will **m** and lament, she will be H9302
Isa 32:13 **m** for all houses of merriment and for this NDT
Isa 61: 2 vengeance of our God, to comfort all *who* **m**, H63
Isa 66:10 greatly with her, all you who **m** over her. H61
Jer 4:28 Therefore the earth *will* **m** and the heavens H61
Jer 6:26 **m** with bitter wailing *as for* an only H6913+65
Jer 8:21 I am crushed; *I* **m**, and horror grips me. H7722
Jer 15: 5 Who *will* **m** for you? Who will H5653
Jer 16: 5 do not go to **m** or show sympathy H6199
Jer 16: 7 food to comfort those who **m** for the dead— H65
Jer 22:10 not weep for the dead king or **m** his **loss**; H5653
Jer 22:18 "*They will* not **m** for him: 'Alas, H6199
Jer 22:18 *They will* not **m** for him: 'Alas H6199
Jer 48:17 **M** for her, all who live around her, all who H5653
Jer 49: 3 Put on sackcloth and **m**; rush here and H6199
La 1: 4 The roads to Zion **m**, for no one comes to H63
Eze 7:27 The king *will* **m**, the prince will be clothed H61
Eze 24:17 Groan quietly; do not **m** for the dead. H65
Eze 24:23 *You will* not **m** or weep but will waste H6199
Eze 27:32 As they wail and **m** over you, they H5951+7806
Hos 10: 5 Its people *will* **m** over it, and so will its H61
Joel 1: 8 **M** like a virgin in sackcloth grieving for the H458
Joel 1:13 you priests, and **m**; wail, you who minister H6199
Am 8: 8 tremble for this, and all who live in it **m**? H61
Am 9: 5 all who live in it **m**; the whole land rises H61
Na 3: 7 'Nineveh is in ruins—who *will* **m** for her? H5653
Zep 3:18 from you *all who* **m** *over* the loss of H5652
Zec 7: 3 "*Should I* **m** and fast in the fifth month H1134
Zec 12:10 and *they will* **m** for him as one mourns H6199
Zec 12:12 The land *will* **m**, each clan by itself, with H6199
Mt 5: 4 Blessed are those *who* **m**, for they will be *G4291*
Mt 9:15 of the bridegroom **m** while he is with *G4291*
Mt 11:17 we sang a dirge, and *you did* not **m**. *G3164*
Mt 24:30 of the earth *will* **m** when they see the *G3164*
Lk 6:25 who laugh now, for *you will* **m** and weep. *G4291*
Jn 11:31 she was going to the tomb to **m** there. *G3081*
Jn 16:20 you will weep and **m** while the world *G2577*
Ro 12:15 who rejoice; **m** with those who mourn. *G3081*
Ro 12:15 who rejoice; mourn with *those who* **m**. *G3081*
1Co 7:30 those *who* **m**, as if they did not; those who *G3081*
Jas 4: 9 **m** and wail. Change your laughter *G4291*
Rev 1: 7 peoples on earth "*will* **m** because of him." *G3164*
Rev 18: 7 I am not a widow; *I will* never **m**.' *G4292+3972*
Rev 18: 9 burning, they will weep and **m** over her. *G3164*
Rev 18:11 will weep and **m** over her because no *G4291*
Rev 18:15 at her torment. They will weep and **m** *G4291*

MOURNED (24) [MOURN]

Ge 37:34 put on sackcloth and **m** for his son many H61
Ge 50: 3 And the Egyptians **m** *for* him seventy days. H1134
Nu 14:39 this to all the Israelites, they **m** bitterly. H61
Nu 20:29 all the Israelites **m** *for* him thirty days. H1134
Dt 21:13 in your house and **m** her father and H1134
1Sa 6:19 The people **m** because of the heavy blow H61
1Sa 15:35 see Saul again, though Samuel **m** for him. H61
1Sa 25: 1 all Israel assembled and **m** for him H6199
1Sa 28: 3 all Israel *had* **m** for him and buried H6199
2Sa 1:12 *They* **m** and wept and fasted till evening H6199
2Sa 11:26 her husband was dead, *she* **m** for him. H6199
2Sa 13:37 But King David **m** many days for his son H61
1Ki 13:30 own tomb, and *they* **m** over him and said H6199
1Ki 14:18 and all Israel **m** for him, as the LORD H6199
1Ch 7:22 Their father Ephraim **m** for them many days H61
2Ch 35:24 all Judah and Jerusalem **m** for him. H61
Ne 1: 4 For some days *I* **m** and fasted and prayed H61
Jer 16: 4 *They will* not **be m** or buried but will be H6199
Jer 16: 6 They will not be buried or **m**, and no one H6199
Jer 25:33 *They will* not **be m** or gathered up or H6199
Da 10: 2 At that time I, Daniel, **m** for three weeks. H61
Zec 7: 5 'When you fasted and **m** in the fifth and H6199
Lk 23:27 women who **m** and wailed for him. *G3164*
Ac 8: 2 Stephen and **m** deeply for him. *G4472+3157*

MOURNERS (8) [MOURN]

Job 29:25 his troops; I was like one who comforts **m**. H63
Ecc 12: 5 eternal home and **m** go about the streets. H6199
Isa 57:18 them and restore comfort to Israel's **m**, H63
Eze 24:17 beard or eat the *customary* food *of* **m**." H408[s]
Eze 24:22 beard or eat the *customary* food *of* **m**. H408[s]
Hos 9: 4 will be to them like the bread of **m**; H230
Am 5:16 to weep and the **m** to wail. H3359+5631
Mal 3:14 going about like **m** before the LORD H7726

MOURNFUL (1) [MOURN]

Mic 2: 4 they will taunt you with this **m song**: H5631

MOURNFULLY (1) [MOURN]

Isa 59:11 like bears; *we* **moan m** like doves. H2047+2047

MOURNING (48) [MOURN]

Ge 27:41 "The days of **m** *for* my father are near H65
Ge 50: 4 When the days of **m** had passed, Joseph H1143
Ge 50:10 a seven-day **period of m** for his father. H65
Ge 50:11 lived there saw the **m** at the threshing floor H65
Ge 50:11 are holding a solemn **ceremony of m**." H65
Dt 26:14 any of the sacred portion while I *was in* **m**, H627
Dt 34: 8 the time of weeping and **m** was over. H65
2Sa 3:31 on sackcloth and **walk in m** in front of H6199
2Sa 11:27 After the **time of m** was over, David had her H65
2Sa 14: 2 said to her, "**Pretend** *you are* **in m**. Dress in H61

2Sa 14: 2 Dress in **m** clothes, and don't use any H65
2Sa 19: 1 "The king is weeping and **m** for Absalom." H61
2Sa 19: 2 army the victory that day was turned into **m**, H65
Est 4: 3 there was great **m** among the Jews, with H65
Est 9:22 into joy and their **m** into a day of celebration H65
Job 30:31 My lyre is tuned to **m**, and my pipe to the H65
Ps 35:14 I went about **m** as though for my friend or NDT
Ps 38: 6 very low; all day long I go about **m**. H7722
Ps 42: 9 Why must I go about **m**, oppressed by the H7722
Ps 43: 2 Why must I go about **m**, oppressed by the H7722
Ecc 7: 2 to go to a house of **m** than to go to a house H65
Ecc 7: 4 The heart of the wise is in the house of **m** H65
Isa 38:14 a swift or thrush, I moaned like a **m** dove. NDT
Isa 61: 3 the oil of joy instead of **m**, and a garment of H65
Jer 31:13 I will turn their **m** into gladness; I will give H65
Jer 31:15 is heard in Ramah, **m** and great weeping H5631
Jer 47: 5 Gaza *will* **shave** *her* **head in m** H995+7947
Jer 48:38 the public squares there is nothing but **m**, H5027
La 2: 5 He has multiplied **m** and lamentation H9302
La 5:15 our hearts; our dancing has turned to **m**. H65
Eze 2:10 written words of lament and **m** and woe. H2049
Eze 8:14 women sitting there, **m** the god Tammuz. H1134
Eze 27:31 with anguish of soul and with bitter **m**. H5027
Eze 31:15 I covered the deep springs *with* **m** for it; H61
Joel 1: 9 The priests *are* **in m**, those who minister H61
Joel 2:12 with fasting and weeping and **m**. H5027
Am 8:10 festivals into **m** and all your singing H65
Am 8:10 make that time like **m** *for* an only son and H65
Mic 1:11 Beth Ezel is in **m**; it no longer protects you H5027
Mic 1:16 Shave your head in **m** for the children in NDT
Mt 2:18 weeping and great **m**, Rachel weeping *G3851*
Mk 16:10 with him and *who were* **m** and weeping. *G4291*
Lk 8:52 all the people were wailing and **m** for her. *G3164*
1Co 5: 2 *you* rather *have* **gone into m** and have *G4291*
Jas 4: 9 your laughter to **m** and your joy to gloom. *G4292*
Rev 18: 8 death, **m** and famine. She will *G4292*
Rev 18:19 and with weeping and **m** cry out: *G4291*
Rev 21: 4 be no more death' or **m** or crying or pain, *G4292*

MOURNS (2) [MOURN]

Jer 14: 2 "Judah **m**, her cities languish; they wail H61
Zec 12:10 mourn for him as one **m** for an only child, H5027

MOUSE (KJV) RAT, RATS

MOUTH (256) [MOUTHS]

Ge 4:11 which opened its **m** to receive your H7023
Ge 29: 2 The stone over the **m** *of* the well was H7023
Ge 29: 3 from the well's **m** and water the sheep. H7023
Ge 29: 3 stone to its place over the **m** *of* the well. H7023
Ge 29: 8 been rolled away from the **m** *of* the well. H7023
Ge 29:10 stone away from the **m** *of* the well and H7023
Ge 42:27 he saw his silver in the **m** *of* his sack. H7023
Ge 43:21 the exact weight—in the **m** *of* his sack. H7023
Ge 44: 1 put each man's silver in the **m** *of* his sack. H7023
Ge 44: 2 in the **m** *of* the youngest one's sack H7023
Ex 4:15 speak to him and put words in his **m**; H7023
Ex 4:16 as if he were your **m** and as if you were H7023
Nu 16:30 the earth opens its **m** and swallows them, H7023
Nu 16:32 earth opened its **m** and swallowed them H7023
Nu 22:28 Then the LORD opened the donkey's **m** H7023
Nu 22:38 I must speak only what God puts in my **m**. H7023
Nu 23: 5 LORD put a word in Balaam's **m** and said, H7023
Nu 23:12 I not speak what the LORD puts in my **m**?" H7023
Nu 23:16 Balaam and put a word in his **m** and said, H7023
Nu 26:10 earth opened its **m** and swallowed them H7023
Dt 8: 3 word that comes from the **m** *of* the LORD. H7023
Dt 11: 6 the earth opened its **m** right in the middle H7023
Dt 18:18 I will put my words in his **m**. H7023
Dt 23:23 to the LORD your God with your own **m**. H7023
Dt 30:14 it is in your **m** and in your heart so you H7023
Dt 32: 1 you earth, the words of my **m**. H7023
Jos 10:18 "Roll large rocks up to the **m** *of* the cave H7023
Jos 10:22 "Open the **m** *of* the cave and bring those H7023
Jos 10:27 At the **m** *of* the cave they placed large H7023
Jos 15: 5 Dead Sea as far as the **m** *of* the Jordan. H7895
Jos 15: 5 the bay of the sea at the **m** *of* the Jordan, H7895
Jos 18:19 at the **m** *of* the Jordan in the south. H7895
1Sa 1:12 praying to the LORD, Eli observed her **m**. H7023
1Sa 2: 1 My **m** boasts over my enemies, for I H7023
1Sa 2: 3 proudly or let your **m** speak such H7023
1Sa 14:26 no one put his hand to his **m**, because H7023
1Sa 14:27 He raised his hand to his **m**, and his eyes H7023
1Sa 17:35 struck it and rescued the sheep from its **m**. H7023
2Sa 1:16 Your own **m** testified against you when H7023
2Sa 14: 3 And Joab put the words in her **m**. H7023
2Sa 14:19 all these words into the **m** *of* your servant. H7023
2Sa 22: 9 consuming fire came from his **m**, burning H7023
1Ki 8:15 with his own **m** to my father David. H7023
1Ki 8:24 with your **m** you have promised and with H7023
1Ki 17:24 word of the LORD from your **m** is the truth. H7023
1Ki 19:13 went out and stood at the **m** *of* the cave. H7339
2Ki 4:34 lay on the boy, **m** to mouth, eyes to H7023
2Ki 4:34 lay on the boy, mouth to **m**, eyes to eyes, H7023
2Ki 19:28 hook in your nose and my bit in your **m**, H8557
2Ch 6: 4 promised with his **m** to my father David. H7023
2Ch 6:15 with your **m** you have promised and with H7023
Est 7: 8 As soon as the word left the king's **m** H7023
Job 3: 1 Job opened his **m** and cursed the day of H7023
Job 5:15 the needy from the sword in their **m**; H7023
Job 5:16 poor have hope, and injustice shuts its **m**. H7023
Job 6:30 Can my **m** not discern malice H2674
Job 8:21 He will yet fill your **m** with laughter and H7023
Job 9:20 were innocent, my **m** would condemn me H7023
Job 15: 5 Your sin prompts your **m**; you adopt the H7023
Job 15: 6 Your own **m** condemns you, not mine H7023
Job 15:13 pour out such words from your **m**? H7023
Job 15:30 the breath of God's **m** will carry him away. H7023
Job 16: 5 But my **m** would encourage you; comfort H7023
Job 19:16 answer, though I beg him with my own **m**. H7023
Job 20:12 evil is sweet in his **m** and he hides it H7023
Job 20:13 bear to let it go and lets it linger in his **m**, H2674
Job 21: 5 be appalled; clap your hand over your **m**. H7023
Job 22:22 from his **m** and lay up his words H7023
Job 23: 4 before him and fill my **m** with arguments. H7023
Job 23:12 the words of his **m** more than my daily H7023
Job 26: 4 And whose spirit spoke from your **m**? NDT
Job 31:30 have not allowed my **m** to sin by invoking H2674
Job 33: 2 I am about to open my **m**; my words are H7023
Job 35:16 So Job opens his **m** with empty talk H7023
Job 37: 2 to the rumbling that comes from his **m**. H7023
Job 40: 4 I reply to you? I put my hand over my **m**. H7023
Job 40:23 the Jordan should surge against its **m**. H7023
Job 41:14 Who dares open the doors of its **m** H7156
Job 41:19 Flames stream from its **m**; sparks of fire H7023
Job 41:21 coals ablaze, and flames dart from its **m**. H7023
Ps 5: 9 Not a word from their **m** can be trusted H7023
Ps 10: 7 His **m** is full of lies and threats; trouble H7023
Ps 17: 3 my **m** has not transgressed. H7023
Ps 18: 8 consuming fire came from his **m**, burning H7023
Ps 19:14 these words of my **m** and this meditation H7023
Ps 22:15 My **m** is dried up like a potsherd, and my H2674
Ps 22:15 my tongue sticks to the **roof of** my **m** H4918
Ps 22:21 Rescue me from the **m** *of* the lions; save H7023
Ps 33: 6 their starry host by the breath of his **m**. H7023
Ps 38:14 not hear, whose **m** can offer no reply. H7023
Ps 39: 1 put a muzzle on my **m** while in the H7023
Ps 39: 9 I would not open my **m**, for you are the H7023
Ps 40: 3 He put a new song in my **m**, a hymn of H7023
Ps 49: 3 My **m** will speak words of wisdom; the H7023
Ps 50:19 You use your **m** for evil and harness your H7023
Ps 51:15 and my **m** will declare your praise. H7023
Ps 54: 2 listen to the words of my **m**. H7023
Ps 63: 5 with singing lips my **m** will praise you. H7023
Ps 66:14 promised and my **m** spoke when I was in H7023
Ps 66:17 I cried out to him with my **m**; his praise H7023
Ps 69:15 me up or the pit close its **m** over me. H7023
Ps 71: 8 My **m** is filled with your praise, declaring H7023
Ps 71:15 My **m** will tell of your righteous deeds, of H7023
Ps 78: 1 my teaching; listen to the words of my **m**. H7023
Ps 78: 2 I will open my **m** with a parable; I will H7023
Ps 81:10 Open wide your **m** and I will fill it. H7023
Ps 89: 1 with my **m** I will make your faithfulness H7023
Ps 109:30 With my **m** I will greatly extol the LORD; H7023
Ps 119:13 all the laws that come from your **m**. H7023
Ps 119:43 Never take your word of truth from my **m** H7023
Ps 119:72 The law from your **m** is more precious to H7023
Ps 119:88 that I may obey the statutes of your **m**. H7023
Ps 119:103 to my taste, sweeter than honey to my **m**! H7023
Ps 119:108 the willing praise of my **m**, and teach me H7023
Ps 119:131 I open my **m** and pant, longing for your H7023
Ps 137: 6 cling to the **roof of** my **m** if I do not H2674
Ps 141: 3 Set a guard over my **m**, LORD; keep watch H7023
Ps 141: 7 been scattered at the **m** *of* the grave." H7023
Ps 145:21 My **m** will speak in praise of the LORD. H7023
Pr 2: 6 from his **m** come knowledge and H7023
Pr 4:24 Keep your **m** free of perversity; keep H7023
Pr 6: 2 ensnared by the words of your **m**. H7023
Pr 6:12 who goes about with a corrupt **m**, H7023
Pr 8: 7 My **m** speaks what is true, for my lips H2674
Pr 8: 8 All the words of my **m** are just; none of H7023
Pr 10: 6 violence overwhelms the **m** *of* the wicked. H7023
Pr 10:11 The **m** *of* the righteous is a fountain of H7023
Pr 10:11 the **m** *of* the wicked conceals violence. H7023
Pr 10:14 the **m** *of* a fool invites ruin. H7023
Pr 10:31 From the **m** *of* the righteous comes the H7023
Pr 10:32 the **m** *of* the wicked only what is H7023
Pr 11:11 by the **m** *of* the wicked it is destroyed. H7023
Pr 14: 3 A fool's **m** lashes out with pride, but the H7023
Pr 15: 2 the **m** *of* the fool gushes folly. H7023
Pr 15:14 the **m** *of* a fool feeds on folly. H7023
Pr 15:28 the **m** *of* the wicked gushes evil. H7023
Pr 16:10 and his **m** does not betray justice. H7023
Pr 18: 4 The words of the **m** are deep waters, but H7023
Pr 18:20 the fruit of their **m** a person's stomach is H7023
Pr 19:24 he will not even bring it back to his **m**! H7023
Pr 19:28 the **m** *of* the wicked gulps down evil. H7023
Pr 20:17 one ends up with a **m** full of gravel. H7023
Pr 22:14 The **m** *of* an adulterous woman is a deep H7023
Pr 26: 7 is lame is a proverb in the **m** *of* a fool. H7023
Pr 26: 9 hand is a proverb in the **m** *of* a fool. H7023
Pr 26:15 he is too lazy to bring it back to his **m**. H7023
Pr 26:28 and a flattering **m** works ruin. H7023
Pr 27: 2 and not your own **m**; an outsider, H7023
Pr 30:20 She eats and wipes her **m** and says, 'I've H7023
Pr 30:32 you plan evil, clap your hand over your **m**! H7023
Ecc 5: 2 Do not be quick with your **m**, do not be H7023
Ecc 5: 6 Do not let your **m** lead you into sin. H7023
Ecc 6: 7 Everyone's toil is for their **m**, yet their H7023
Ecc 10:12 Words from the **m** *of* the wise are H7023
SS 1: 2 Let him kiss me with the kisses of his **m** H7023
SS 4: 3 are like a scarlet ribbon; your **m** is lovely. H4498
SS 5:16 His **m** is sweetness itself; he is altogether H2674
SS 7: 9 your **m** like the best wine. May the H2674
Isa 1:20 For the **m** *of* the LORD has spoken. H7023
Isa 5:14 opening wide its **m**; into it will descend H7023
Isa 6: 7 With it he touched my **m** and said, "See H7023
Isa 9:12 west have devoured Israel with open **m**. H7023
Isa 9:17 ungodly and wicked, every **m** speaks folly. H7023
Isa 10:14 flapped a wing, or opened its **m** to chirp. H7023
Isa 11: 4 will strike the earth with the rod of his **m**; H7023
Isa 19: 7 along the Nile, at the **m** *of* the river. H7023
Isa 29:13 to me with their **m** and honor me with H7023
Isa 34:16 For it is his **m** that has given the order H7023
Isa 37:29 hook in your nose and my bit in your **m**, H8557
Isa 40: 5 For the **m** *of* the LORD has spoken. H7023
Isa 45:23 my **m** has uttered in all integrity a word H7023
Isa 48: 3 my **m** announced them and I made them H7023
Isa 49: 2 He made my **m** like a sharpened sword H7023
Isa 51:16 my words in your **m** and covered you with H7023
Isa 53: 7 he did not open his **m**; he was led like H7023
Isa 53: 7 is silent, so he did not open his **m**. H7023
Isa 53: 9 no violence, nor was any deceit in his **m**. H7023
Isa 55:11 so is my word that goes out from my **m**: It H7023
Isa 58:14 For the **m** *of* the LORD has spoken. H7023
Isa 59:21 I have put in your **m** will always be on H7023
Isa 62: 2 a new name that the **m** *of* the LORD will H7023
Jer 1: 9 hand and touched my **m** and said to me, H7023
Jer 1: 9 "I have put my words in your **m**. H7023
Jer 5:14 make my words in your **m** a fire and these H7023
Jer 9:20 open your ears to the words of his **m**. H7023
Jer 23:16 own minds, not from the **m** *of* the LORD. H7023
Jer 48:28 that makes its nest at the **m** *of* a cave. H7023
La 3:38 Is it not from the **m** *of* the Most High that H7023
La 4: 4 infant's tongue sticks to the **roof of** its **m**; H2674
Eze 2: 8 open your **m** and eat what I give you." H7023
Eze 3: 2 So I opened my **m**, and he gave me the H7023
Eze 3: 3 it tasted as sweet as honey in my **m**. H7023
Eze 3:26 stick to the **roof of** your **m** so that you will H2674
Eze 3:27 I will open your **m** and you shall say to H7023
Eze 4:14 No impure meat has ever entered my **m**." H7023
Eze 16:63 never again open your **m** because of your H7023
Eze 24:27 At that time your **m** will be opened; you H7023
Eze 29:21 I will open your **m** among them. H7023
Eze 33:22 he opened my **m** before the man H7023
Eze 33:22 So my **m** was opened and I was no longer H7023
Da 6:17 placed over the **m** *of* the den, A10588
Da 7: 5 had three ribs in its **m** between its teeth. A10588
Da 7: 8 a human being and a **m** that spoke A10588
Da 7:20 that had eyes and a **m** that spoke A10588
Da 10:16 I opened my **m** and began to speak. H7023
Hos 6: 5 I killed you with the words of my **m**—then H7023
Am 3:12 from the lion's **m** only two leg bones or a H7023
Na 3:12 the figs fall into the **m** *of* the eater. H7023
Mal 2: 6 was in his **m** and nothing false was H7023
Mal 2: 7 people seek instruction from his **m**. H7023
Mt 4: 4 every word that comes from the **m** of God. *G5125*
Mt 12:34 For the **m** speaks what the heart is full of. *G5125*
Mt 13:35 "I will open my **m** in parables, I will utter *G5125*
Mt 15:11 goes into someone's **m** does not defile *G5125*
Mt 15:11 what comes out of their **m**, that is *G5125*
Mt 15:17 whatever enters the **m** goes into the *G5125*
Mt 15:18 out of a person's **m** come from the heart, *G5125*
Mt 17:27 open its **m** and you will find a *G5125*
Mk 9:18 *He* **foams at the m**, gnashes his teeth and *G930*
Mk 9:20 rolled around, **foaming at the m**. *G930*
Lk 1:64 Immediately his **m** was opened and his *G5125*
Lk 6:45 For the **m** speaks what the heart is full of. *G5125*
Lk 9:39 so that he **foams at the m**. *G3552+931*
Ac 4:25 the Holy Spirit *through* the **m** of your *G5125*
Ac 8:32 is silent, so he did not open his **m**. *G5125*
Ac 11: 8 unclean has ever entered my **m**. *G5125*
Ac 15:27 Silas to confirm by **word of m** what we are *G3364*
Ac 22:14 One and to hear words from his **m**. *G5125*
Ac 23: 2 standing near Paul to strike him *on* the **m**. *G5125*
Ro 3:19 so that every **m** may be silenced and the *G5125*
Ro 10: 8 near you; it is in your **m** and in your heart, *G5125*
Ro 10: 9 you declare with your **m**, "Jesus is Lord," *G5125*
Ro 10:10 it is *with* your **m** that you profess your *G5125*
2Th 2: 2 a prophecy or by **word of m** or by letter— *G3364*
2Th 2: 8 with the breath *of* his **m** and destroy by *G5125*
2Th 2:15 whether by **word of m** or by letter. *G3364*
2Ti 4:17 And I was delivered from the lion's **m**. *G5125*
Jas 3:10 Out of the same **m** come praise and *G5125*
1Pe 2:22 and no deceit was found in his **m**. *G5125*
2Pe 2:18 For *they* **m** empty, boastful **words** and, by *G5779*
Rev 1:16 coming out of his **m** was a sharp *G5125*
Rev 2:16 against them with the sword *of* my **m**. *G5125*
Rev 3:16 I am about to spit you out of my **m**. *G5125*
Rev 10: 9 'in your **m** it will be as sweet as honey *G5125*
Rev 10:10 It tasted as sweet as honey in my **m**, but *G5125*
Rev 12:15 Then from his **m** the serpent spewed water *G5125*
Rev 12:16 by opening its **m** and swallowing the *G5125*
Rev 12:16 that the dragon had spewed out of his **m**. *G5125*
Rev 13: 2 of a bear and a **m** like that of a lion. *G5125*
Rev 13: 5 beast was given a **m** to utter proud words *G5125*
Rev 13: 6 It opened its **m** to blaspheme God, and to *G5125*
Rev 16:13 they came out of the **m** of the dragon, out *G5125*
Rev 16:13 out of the **m** of the beast and out of the *G5125*
Rev 16:13 out of the **m** of the false prophet *G5125*
Rev 19:15 Coming out of his **m** is a sharp sword with *G5125*
Rev 19:21 coming out of the **m** of the rider on the *G5125*

MOUTHS (59) [MOUTH]

Ge 43:12 that was put back into the **m** *of* your sacks. H7023
Ge 44: 8 silver we found inside the **m** *of* our sacks. H7023
Ex 4:11 "Who gave human beings their **m**? H7023

1Ki 19:18 to Baal and whose **m** have not kissed him H7023
1Ki 22:22 spirit in the **m** *of* all his prophets, H7023
1Ki 22:23 spirit in the **m** *of* all these prophets of H7023
2Ch 18:21 spirit in the **m** *of* all his prophets, H7023
2Ch 18:22 spirit in the **m** *of* these prophets of H7023
Ne 9:20 not withhold your manna from their **m**, H7023
Job 16:10 People open their **m** to jeer at me; they H7023
Job 29: 9 covered their **m** with their hands; H7023
Job 29:10 their tongues stuck to the **roof** of their **m**. H2674
Ps 17:10 and their **m** speak with arrogance. H7023
Ps 22:13 their prey open their **m** wide against me. H7023
Ps 36: 3 The words of their **m** are wicked and H7023
Ps 37:30 The **m** *of* the righteous utter wisdom, and H7023
Ps 58: 6 Break the teeth in their **m**, O God; LORD H7023
Ps 59: 7 See what they spew from their **m**—the H7023
Ps 59:12 For the sins of their **m**, for the words of H7023
Ps 62: 4 With their **m** they bless, but in their hearts H7023
Ps 63:11 while the **m** *of* liars will be silenced. H7023
Ps 73: 9 Their **m** lay claim to heaven, and their H7023
Ps 78:30 even while the food was still in their **m**, H7023
Ps 78:36 then they would flatter him with their **m**, H7023
Ps 107:42 but all the wicked shut their **m**. H7023
Ps 109: 2 have opened their **m** against me; H7023
Ps 115: 5 They have **m**, but cannot speak, eyes, but H7023
Ps 126: 2 Our **m** were filled with laughter, our H7023
Ps 135:16 They have **m**, but cannot speak, eyes, but H7023
Ps 135:17 nor is there breath in their **m**. H7023
Ps 144: 8 whose **m** are full of lies, whose right H7023
Ps 144:11 of foreigners whose **m** are full of lies, H7023
Ps 149: 6 of God be in their **m** and a double-edged H1744
Pr 11: 9 With their **m** the godless destroy their H7023
Pr 16:23 hearts of the wise make their **m** prudent, H7023
Pr 18: 6 them strife, and their **m** invite a beating. H7023
Pr 18: 7 The **m** *of* fools are their undoing, and H7023
Pr 21:23 who guard their **m** and their tongues H7023
Pr 24: 7 at the gate they must not open their **m**. H7023
Isa 52:15 kings will shut their **m** because of him. H7023
Jer 9: 8 With their **m** they all speak cordially to H7023
La 2:16 enemies open their **m** wide against you; H7023
La 3:46 have opened their **m** wide against us. H7023
Eze 33:31 Their **m** speak of love, but their hearts are H7023
Eze 34:10 I will rescue my flock from their **m**, and it H7023
Da 6:22 and he shut the **m** *of* the lions. A10588
Mic 7:16 hands over their **m** and their ears will H7023
Zep 3:13 tongue will not be found in their **m**. H7023
Zec 9: 7 I will take the blood from their **m**, the H7023
Zec 14:12 their tongues will rot in their **m**. H7023
Ro 3:14 "Their **m** are full of cursing and bitterness." *G5125*
Eph 4:29 unwholesome talk come out of your **m**, *G5125*
Heb 11:33 was promised; who shut the **m** of lions, *G5125*
Jas 3: 3 we put bits into the **m** of horses to make *G5125*
Rev 9:17 out of their **m** came fire, smoke and *G5125*
Rev 9:18 smoke and sulfur that came out of their **m**. *G5125*
Rev 9:19 horses was in their **m** and in their tails; *G5125*
Rev 11: 5 fire comes from their **m** and devours their *G5125*
Rev 14: 5 No lie was found in their **m**; they are *G5125*

MOVABLE (7) [MOVE]

1Ki 7:27 He also made ten **m stands** of bronze H4807
2Ki 16:17 removed the basins from the **m stands**. H4807
2Ki 25:13 the **m stands** and the bronze Sea that H4807
2Ki 25:16 the Sea and the **m stands**, which H4807
Jer 27:19 the **m stands** and the other articles that H4807
Jer 52:17 the **m stands** and the bronze Sea that H4807
Jer 52:20 under it, and the **m stands**, which King H4807

MOVE (52) [MOVABLE, MOVED, MOVEMENTS, MOVES, MOVING]

Ge 1:24 the **creatures that m** along the ground H8254
Ge 1:25 all the **creatures that m** *along* the ground H8254
Ge 1:26 all the creatures that **m** along the ground." H8253
Ge 1:30 sky and all the **creatures that m** along the H8253
Ge 6: 7 the **creatures that m along the ground**— H8254
Ge 7: 8 of all creatures *that* **m** along the ground, H8253
Ge 7:23 the **creatures that m** along the H8254
Ge 8:17 the creatures that **m** along the ground— H8253
Ge 8:19 all the **creatures that m** along the H8254
Ge 26:16 said to Isaac, "**M** away from us; you have H2143
Ge 33:14 while I **m along** slowly at the pace of the H5633
Ge 48:17 his father's hand to **m** it from Ephraim's H6073
Ex 10:23 else or **m about** for three H7756+4946+9393
Ex 14:15 Tell the Israelites *to* **m on**. H5825
Lev 11:29 'Of the animals that **m** along the ground, H9237
Lev 11:31 Of all those *that* **m along** the ground H9238
Lev 26:10 when *you will have to* **m** it **out** to make H3655
Nu 1:51 Whenever the tabernacle *is to* **m**, the H5825
Nu 4: 5 When the camp *is to* **m**, Aaron and his H5825
Nu 4:15 when the camp *is ready to* **m**, only H5825
Nu 12:15 the people *did* not **m on** till she was H5825
Nu 16:24 '**M away** from the tents of Korah H6590
Nu 16:26 "**M back** from the tents of these wicked H6073
Dt 19:14 *Do* not **m** your neighbor's boundary stone H6047
Jos 3: 3 you *are to* **m out** from your positions and H5825
Jdg 16: 2 *They* **made no m** during the night, saying H3087
2Sa 5:24 the poplar trees, **m quickly**, because that H3077
2Sa 15:14 or *he will* **m quickly** to overtake us and H4554
1Ch 14:15 the poplar trees, **m out** to battle, because H3655
Job 24: 2 *There are those who* **m** boundary stones H5952
Ps 69:34 the seas and all *that* **m** in them, H8253
Pr 22:28 *Do* not **m** an ancient boundary stone set H6047
Pr 23:10 *Do* not **m** an ancient boundary stone or H6047
Pr 30:29 four *that* **m** with stately bearing: H2143
Isa 46: 7 From that spot *it* cannot **m**. Even though H4631
Jer 31:24 farmers and *those who* **m about** with their H5825
Eze 36:27 my Spirit in you and **m** you to follow my H6913
Hos 2:18 the **creatures that m** *along* the H8254
Hos 5:10 are like *those who* **m** boundary stones H6047
Zec 12: 3 All *who try to* **m** it will injure themselves H6673
Mt 17:20 to this mountain, '**M** from here to there,' *G3553*
Mt 17:20 'Move from here to there,' and *it will* **m**. *G3553*
Mt 23: 4 are not willing *to lift* a finger *to* **m** them. *G3075*
Lk 10: 7 *Do* not **m around** from house to house *G3553*
Lk 14:10 say to you, 'Friend, **m up** to a better place. *G4646*
Ac 17:28 in him we live and **m** and have our being. *G3075*
Ac 27:41 The bow stuck fast and *would* **not m** *G3531+810*
1Co 13: 2 if I have a faith that *can* **m** mountains, *G3496*
1Co 15:58 Let **nothing m** you. Always give *G293*
2Co 11:26 I have been constantly **on the m**. I have *G3845*
Col 1:23 and *do* not **m** from the hope held out in *G3560*
Heb 6: 1 Therefore *let us* **m beyond** the elementary *G918*

MOVED (78) [MOVE]

Ge 7:21 living thing that **m** on land perished— H8253
Ge 11: 2 As people **m** eastward, they found a plain H5825
Ge 19: 9 on Lot and **m forward** to break down the H5602
Ge 20: 1 Now Abraham **m on** from there into the H5825
Ge 26:17 So Isaac **m** away from there and H2143
Ge 26:22 *He* **m on** from there and dug another well H6980
Ge 35:16 Then *they* **m on** from Bethel. While they H5825
Ge 35:21 Israel **m on** again and pitched his tent H5825
Ge 36: 6 **m** to a land some distance from his H2143
Ge 37:17 "*They have* **m on** from here," the man H5825
Ge 43:30 **Deeply m** at the sight of his brother H4023+8171
Ex 14:19 pillar of cloud also **m** from in front and H5825
Ex 35:21 whose heart **m** them came and H5951
Nu 14:44 of the LORD's covenant **m** from the camp. H4631
Nu 16:27 So *they* **m away** from the tents of Korah H6590
Nu 21:10 The Israelites **m on** and camped at Oboth. H5825
Nu 21:12 From there *they* **m on** and camped in the H5825
Nu 22:26 of the LORD **m on ahead** and stood in a H6296
Jos 5: 6 The Israelites *had* **m about** in the H2143
Jos 8: 3 the whole army **m out** to attack Ai. H7756
Jos 10: 5 They **m up** with all their troops and took H6590
Jos 10:29 Israel with him **m on** from Makkedah to H6296
Jos 10:31 all Israel with him **m on** from Libnah to H6296
Jos 10:34 all Israel with him **m on** from Lachish to H6296
Jos 14:10 while Israel **m about** in the wilderness. H2143
Jdg 9:26 Now Gaal son of Ebed **m** with his clan into H995
Jdg 20:33 the men of Israel **m** from their places and H7756
1Sa 5: 8 "*Have* the ark of the god of Israel **m** *to* H6015
1Sa 5: 8 So *they* **m** the ark of the God of Israel H6015
1Sa 5: 9 But after *they had* **m** it, the LORD's hand H6015
1Sa 14:23 the battle **m on beyond** Beth Aven. H6296
1Sa 15: 6 So the Kenites **m away** from the H6073
1Sa 17:48 As the Philistine **m** closer to attack him H2143
1Sa 25: 1 Then David **m down** into the Desert of H3718
2Sa 7: 7 Wherever *I have* **m** with all the Israelites H2143
2Sa 15:23 all the people **m on** toward the H6296
1Ki 3:26 was alive *was* **deeply m** *out of* love for her H4023
2Ki 16: 6 Edomites then **m into** Elath and have lived H995
1Ch 13: 7 *They* **m** the ark of God from Abinadab's H8206
1Ch 16:30 is firmly established; *it* cannot **be m**. H4572
1Ch 17: 5 *I have* **m** from one tent site to another H2118
1Ch 17: 6 Wherever *I have* **m** with all the Israelites H2143
1Ch 19: 7 from their towns and **m out** for battle. H995
2Ch 33:13 the LORD **was m by** his **entreaty** and H6983
2Ch 33:19 how God **was m by** his **entreaty**, H6983
2Ch 36:22 the LORD **m** the heart of Cyrus king of H6424
Ezr 1: 1 the LORD **m** the heart of Cyrus king of H6424
Ezr 1: 5 everyone whose heart God *had* **m** H6424
Ne 2:14 Then *I* **m on** toward the Fountain Gate H6296
Est 2: 9 the king's palace and **m** her and her H9101
Job 14:18 as a rock *is* **m** from its place, H6980
Job 15:19 given when no foreigners **m** among them): H6296
Job 18: 4 Or *must* the rocks *be* **m** from their place? H6980
Ps 96:10 established, *it* cannot **be m**; he will judge H4572
Ps 104: 5 on its foundations; *it can* never **be m**. H4572
Isa 33:20 a tent *that will* not *be* **m**; its stakes H7585
Eze 1: 9 they did not turn as they **m**. H2143
Eze 1:13 Fire **m back and forth** among the creatures H2143
Eze 1:17 As they **m**, they would go in any one of H2143
Eze 1:19 When the living creatures **m**, the wheels H2143
Eze 1:19 the wheels beside them **m**; and when the H2143
Eze 1:21 When the creatures **m**, they also moved H2143
Eze 1:21 creatures moved, *they* also **m**; when the H2143
Eze 1:24 When the creatures **m**, I heard the sound H2143
Eze 9: 3 and **m** to the threshold of the temple. NDT
Eze 10: 4 the cherubim and **m** to the threshold of NDT
Eze 10:11 As they **m**, they would go in any one of H2143
Eze 10:16 When the cherubim **m**, the wheels beside H2143
Eze 10:16 the wheels beside them **m**; and when the H2143
Mt 13:53 these parables, *he* **m on** from there. *G3558*
Mt 21:33 to some farmers and **m to another place.** *G623*
Mk 12: 1 to some farmers and **m to another place.** *G623*
Lk 2:27 *M* **by** the Spirit, he went into the temple AIT
Jn 11:33 he *was* **deeply m** in spirit and troubled. *G1839*
Jn 11:38 once more **deeply m**, came to the *G1839*
Jn 11:54 Jesus no longer **m about** publicly among *G4344*
Ac 9:28 them and **m about freely** in *G1660+2779+1744*
Ac 27: 8 *We* **m along** the coast with difficulty and *G4162*

MOVEMENTS (1) [MOVE]

2Sa 3:25 observe your **m** and find out H4604+2256+4569

MOVES (25) [MOVE]

Ge 1:21 the water teems and that **m about** in it, H8253
Ge 1:28 living creature that **m** on the ground." H8253
Ge 6:20 kind of **creature that m** *along* the ground H8254
Ge 7:14 every creature that **m** along the ground H8253
Ge 8:19 everything *that* **m** on land—came H8253
Ge 9: 2 every creature *that* **m along** the ground, H8253
Ge 9: 3 that lives and **m about** will be food for H8254
Lev 5: 2 **creature that m along the ground**) H9238
Lev 7:21 **creature that m along the ground**— H9238
Lev 11:41 'Every creature that **m** along the ground is H9237
Lev 11:42 eat any creature that **m** along the ground, H9237
Lev 11:42 whether *it* **m** on its belly or walks on all H2143
Lev 11:44 by any creature that **m** along the ground. H8253
Lev 11:46 living thing that **m about** in the water H8253
Lev 11:46 every creature that **m** along the ground. H9237
Lev 20:25 anything that **m along** the ground— H8253
Dt 4:18 like any **creature that m** along the H8253
Dt 18: 6 If a Levite **m** from one of your towns H995
Dt 23:14 LORD your God **m about** in your camp to H2143
Dt 27:17 "Cursed is *anyone who* **m** their neighbor's H6047
Job 9: 5 He **m** mountains without their knowing it H6980
Ps 58: 8 like a slug that melts away *as it* **m along**, H2143
Ps 102:14 servants; her very dust **m** *them* **to pity**. H2858
Isa 41: 3 He pursues them and **m on** unscathed, by H6296
Eze 38:20 every creature that **m** along the ground H8253

MOVING (8) [MOVE]

Ge 13: 5 Now Lot, who *was* **m about** with Abram H2143
1Sa 1:13 her lips *were* **m** but her voice was not H5675
1Sa 12:12 king of the Ammonites *was* **m** against you, H995
1Sa 23:13 and *kept* **m from place to place** H2143+928+889+2143
2Sa 7: 6 I have been **m from place to place** with a H2143
Job 31:26 in its radiance or the moon **m** in splendor, H2143
Zec 14: 4 half of the mountain **m** north and half H4631
Zec 14: 4 mountain moving north and half **m** south. NDT

MOWED (1) [MOWN]

Jas 5: 4 pay the workers who **m** your fields are *G286*

MOWN (1) [MOWED]

Ps 72: 6 May he be like rain falling on a **m field** H1600

MOZA (5)

1Ch 2:46 was the mother of Haran, **M** and Gazez. H4605
1Ch 8:36 Zimri, and Zimri was the father of **M**. H4605
1Ch 8:37 **M** was the father of Binea; Raphah was H4605
1Ch 9:42 Zimri, and Zimri was the father of **M**. H4605
1Ch 9:43 **M** was the father of Binea; Rephaiah was H4605

MOZAH (1)

Jos 18:26 Mizpah, Kephirah, **M**, H5173

MUCH (188)

Ge 16:10 *I will* **increase** your descendants **so m** H8049+8049
Ge 20: 8 had happened, they were **very m** afraid. H4394
Ge 30:26 You know **how m** work I've done for you." H889
Ge 41:49 it was **so m** that he stopped keeping H6330
Ge 43:34 *was* five times **as m as** anyone H8049+4946
Ge 44: 1 sacks with **as m** food **as** they can H3869+889
Ex 16: 5 that is to be **twice as m** as they gather H5467
Ex 16:16 is to gather **as m as** they need. H4200+7023
Ex 16:17 were told; some gathered **m**, some little. H8049
Ex 16:18 the *one who* **gathered m** did not have too H8049
Ex 16:18 who gathered much *did* not **have too m**, H6369
Ex 16:18 gathered **just as m as** they needed H4200+7023
Ex 16:21 gathered **as m as** they needed, H3869+7023
Ex 16:22 they gathered **twice as m**—two omers H5467
Ex 30:23 shekels of liquid myrrh, **half as m** (that is, H4734
Nu 16:15 I have not taken so **m** as a donkey from NDT
Dt 3:19 I know you have **m** livestock) may stay in H8041
Dt 12:15 towns and eat as **m** *of* the meat as you H3972
Dt 12:20 then you may eat as **m** *of* it as you want. H3972
Dt 12:21 you may eat as **m** *of* them as you want. H3972
Dt 15:18 has been worth **twice as m** *as* that of a H5467
Dt 28:38 You will sow **m** seed in the field but you H8041
Dt 31:27 **how m more** will you rebel H2256+677+3954
Jos 10: 2 his people were **very m** alarmed at this, H4394
Jdg 5:15 Reuben there was **m** searching of heart. H1524
Jdg 5:16 Reuben there was **m** searching of heart. H1524
Ru 2:18 saw **how m** she had gathered. H889
1Sa 14:30 **How m better** it would have been if H677+3954
1Sa 15:22 sacrifices **as m as** in obeying the LORD H3869
1Sa 16:21 Saul liked him **very m**, and David became H4394
1Sa 21: 5 **How m more so** today!" H677+3954
1Sa 21:12 to heart and was **very m** afraid of Achish H4394
1Sa 23: 3 **How m more**, then, if we go to Keilah H677
2Sa 4:11 **How m more**—when wicked men have H677
2Sa 16:11 **How m more**, then, this H677+3954
2Sa 17:13 valley until not **so m as** a pebble is left." H1685
1Ki 8:27 **How m less** this temple I have built H677+3954
1Ki 10:12 **So m** almugwood has never been H4027
1Ki 12:28 "It is too **m** for you to go up to Jerusalem. H8041
1Ki 19: 7 for the journey is too **m** for you. H8041
2Ki 5:13 **How m more**, then, when he tells you H677
2Ki 5:17 be given as **m** earth as a pair of mules can NDT
2Ki 10:18 Baal a little; Jehu will serve him **m**. H2221
2Ki 21: 6 *He* did **m** evil in the eyes of the LORD H8049
2Ki 21:16 also shed so **m** innocent blood that H2221
1Ch 22: 8 'You have shed **m** blood and have H4200+8044
1Ch 22: 8 you have shed **m** blood on the earth in H8041

2Ch 4:18 amounted to so m that the weight H4200+8044
2Ch 6:18 How m less this temple I have built H677+3954
2Ch 14:14 villages, since there was m plunder there. H8041
2Ch 20:25 There was so m plunder that it took three H8041
2Ch 24:24 into their hands a m larger army. H4394
2Ch 25: 9 "The LORD can give you m more than that." H2221
2Ch 26:10 because he had m livestock in the H8041
2Ch 32:15 How m less will your god H677+3954+4202
2Ch 33: 6 He did m evil in the eyes of the LORD H8049
2Ch 33:14 hill of Ophel; he also made it m higher. H4394
Ezr 3:13 because the people made so m noise. H1524
Ne 2: 2 sadness of heart." I was very m afraid, H2221
Ne 2:10 they were very m disturbed that someone H1524
Ne 4:10 there is so m rubble that we cannot H2221
Job 4:19 how m more those who live in houses of H677
Job 7:17 is mankind that you make so m of them, H1540
Job 7:17 of them, that you give them so m attention, NDT
Job 15:16 how m less mortals, who are vile H677+3954
Job 25: 6 how m less a mortal, who is but a H677+3954
Job 35:14 How m less, then, will he listen H677+3954
Job 42:10 gave him twice as m as he had before. H3972
Ps 19:10 than gold, than m pure gold; they are H8041
Ps 36: 2 own eyes they flatter themselves too m to AIT
Ps 119:107 I have suffered m; preserve my life H6330+4394
Pr 11:31 how m more the ungodly and the H677+3954
Pr 15:11 how m more do human hearts! H677+3954
Pr 16: 8 righteousness than m gain with injustice. H8044
Pr 16:16 How m better to get wisdom than gold, to H4537
Pr 17: 7 how m worse lying lips to a ruler! H677+3954
Pr 19: 2 how m more will hasty feet miss the way! H2256
Pr 19: 7 how m more do their friends avoid H677+3954
Pr 19:10 how m worse for a slave to rule over H677+3954
Pr 20:19 so avoid anyone who talks too m. H7331+8557
Pr 21:27 how m more so when brought with H677+3954
Pr 23:20 Do not join those who drink too m wine H6010
Pr 25:16 just enough—too m of it, and you will H8425
Pr 25:17 house—too m of you, and they H8425
Pr 25:27 It is not good to eat too m honey, nor is it H8049
Pr 30: 9 I may have too m and disown you and say H8425
Ecc 1:16 I have experienced m of wisdom and H2221
Ecc 1:18 For with m wisdom comes much sorrow H8044
Ecc 1:18 For with much wisdom comes m sorrow H8044
Ecc 5: 7 M dreaming and many words are H8044
Ecc 5:12 whether they eat little or m, but as for the H2221
Ecc 9:18 but one sinner destroys m good. H2221
Ecc 12:12 is no end, and m study wearies the body. H2221
SS 4:10 How m more pleasing is your love than H4946
Jer 2:36 Why do you go about so m, changing H4394
Jer 49: 9 they not steal only as m as they wanted? H1896
Eze 14:21 How m worse will it be when I send H677+3954
Eze 15: 5 how m less can it be made into H677+3954
Eze 23:32 bring scorn and derision, for it holds so m. H5268
Eze 38:13 goods and to seize m plunder? H1524
Eze 46: 5 lambs is to be as m as he pleases, H5522+3338
Eze 46: 7 with the lambs as m as he wants to H3869+889
Eze 46:11 with the lambs as m as he pleases, H5522+3338
Ob 5 they not steal only as m as they wanted? H1896
Ob 12 nor boast so m in the day of H1540+7023+3870
Hag 1: 6 You have planted m, but harvested little H2221
Hag 1: 9 "You expected m, but see, it turned out to H2221
Zec 9:12 that I will restore twice as m to you. H5467
Mal 3:10 pour out so m blessing that there will H6330
Mt 6:26 Are you not m more valuable than they? G3437
Mt 6:30 will he not m more clothe you—you G4498
Mt 7:11 how m more will your Father in heaven G4531
Mt 10:25 how m more the members of his G4531
Mt 12:12 How m more valuable is a person than a G4531
Mt 13: 5 rocky places, where it did not have m soil. G4498
Mt 14: 6 the guests and pleased Herod so m AIT
Mt 19:29 will receive a hundred times as m and will AIT
Mt 23:15 you make them twice as m a child of hell G1487
Mk 4: 5 rocky places, where it did not have m soil. G4498
Mk 4:33 to them, as m as they could understand. G2777
Mk 5:19 tell them how m the Lord has done G4012
Mk 5:20 in the Decapolis how m Jesus had done G4012
Mk 6:37 to go and spend that m on bread and give it NDT
Mk 9:12 of Man must suffer m and be rejected? G4498
Mk 9:26 The boy looked so m like a corpse G1181+6059
Mk 10:30 to receive a hundred times as m in this AIT
Lk 8:39 home and tell how m God has done for G4012
Lk 8:39 told all over town how m Jesus had done G4012
Lk 11: 8 get up and give you as m as you need. G4012
Lk 11:13 how m more will your Father in heaven G4531
Lk 12:24 And how m more valuable you are than G4531
Lk 12:28 the fire, how m more will he clothe you G4531
Lk 12:48 From everyone who has been given m G4498
Lk 12:48 been given much, m will be demanded G4498
Lk 12:48 the one who has been entrusted with m, G4498
Lk 12:48 with much, m more will be asked. G4358
Lk 16: 5 the first, 'How m do you owe my master? G4531
Lk 16: 7 the second, 'And how m do you owe?' G4531
Lk 16:10 with very little can also be trusted with m, G4498
Lk 16:10 very little will also be dishonest with m. G4498
Lk 18:30 to receive many times as m in this age, G4491
Jn 2:10 after the guests have had too m to drink; G3499
Jn 6:11 who were seated as m as they wanted. G4012
Jn 8:26 "I have m to say in judgment of you. G4498
Jn 14:30 I will not say m more to you, for the prince G4498
Jn 15: 5 you will bear m fruit; apart from me G4498
Jn 15: 8 that you bear m fruit, showing G4498
Jn 16:12 "I have m more to say to you, more than G2285
Ac 2:13 said, "They have had too m wine. G3551
Ac 9:16 I will show him how m he must suffer for G4012
Ac 15: 7 After m discussion, Peter got up and G4498
Ac 15:32 said m to encourage and strengthen the G4498
Ac 27: 9 M time had been lost, and sailing had G2653
Ac 27:38 When they had eaten as m as they wanted G3170+5575
Ro 3: 2 M in every way! First of all, the Jews have G4498
Ro 5: 9 how m more shall we be saved from G4498
Ro 5:10 of his Son, how m more, having been G4498
Ro 5:15 how m more did God's grace and the gift G4498
Ro 5:17 how m more will those who receive God's G4498
Ro 11:12 how m greater riches will their full G4531
Ro 11:24 olive tree, how m more readily will these G4531
1Co 6: 3 How m more the things of this life G3615+3615
1Co 9:11 is it too m if we reap a material harvest G3489
2Co 2: 5 he has not so m grieved me as he has G247
2Co 3: 9 how m more glorious is the ministry that G4498
2Co 3:11 how m greater is the glory of that which G4498
2Co 8: 3 that they gave as m as they were able, G2848
2Co 8:15 one who gathered m did not have too G4498
2Co 8:15 who gathered much did not have too m, G4429
2Co 8:17 coming to you with m enthusiasm and on his AIT
2Co 10: 7 we belong to Christ just as m as they do. G2777
2Co 11:23 I have worked m harder, been in prison more AIT
Gal 3: 4 Have you experienced so m in vain—if it G5537
Php 2:12 presence, but now m more in my absence G4498
1Th 2: 8 Because we loved you so m, we were G28+1181
1Ti 3: 8 not indulging in m wine, and not G4498
Titus 2: 3 to be slanderers or addicted to m wine, G4498
Heb 1: 4 So he became as m superior to the angels G5537
Heb 5:11 We have m to say about this, but it is G4498
Heb 9:14 How m more, then, will the blood of Christ, G4531
Heb 10:29 How m more severely do you think G4531
Heb 12: 9 How m more should we submit to the G4498
Heb 12:25 them on earth, how m less will we, if we G4498
2Jn 12 I have m to write to you, but I do not want G4498
3Jn 13 I have m to write you, but I do not want to G4498
Rev 8: 3 He was given m incense to offer, with the G4498
Rev 12:11 their lives so m as to shrink from death. G948
Rev 18: 7 Give her as m torment and grief as the G5537

MUD (16) [MUDDIED, MUDDY, MUDDYING]

2Sa 22:43 trampled them like m in the streets. H3226
Job 30:19 He throws me into the m, and I am H2817
Job 41:30 leaving a trail in the m like a threshing H3226
Ps 18:42 I trampled them like m in the streets. H3226
Ps 40: 2 out of the m and mire; he set my H3226
Isa 10: 6 trample them down like m in the streets. H2817
Isa 57:20 whose waves cast up mire and m. H3226
Jer 38: 6 no water in it, only m, and Jeremiah sank H3226
Jer 38: 6 Jeremiah sank down into the m. H3226
Jer 38:22 Your feet are sunk in the m; your friends H1288
Zec 10: 5 their enemy into the m of the streets. H3226
Jn 9: 6 the ground, made some m with the saliva G4384
Jn 9:11 call Jesus made some m and put it on my G4384
Jn 9:14 Jesus had made the m and opened the G4384
Jn 9:15 "He put m on my eyes," the man replied G4384
2Pe 2:22 washed returns to her wallowing in the m." G1079

MUDDIED (3) [MUD]

Pr 25:26 Like a m spring or a polluted well are the H8346
Eze 32:13 the foot of man or m by the hooves of H1931
Eze 34:19 drink what you have m with your feet? H5343

MUDDY (1) [MUD]

Eze 34:18 Must you also m the rest with your feet H8346

MUDDYING (1) [MUD]

Eze 32: 2 water with your feet and m the streams. H8346

MUFFLERS (KJV) VEILS

MULBERRY (1)

Lk 17: 6 you can say to this m tree, 'Be uprooted G5189

MULE (7) [MULES]

2Sa 18: 9 He was riding his m, and as the mule H7234
2Sa 18: 9 as the m went under the thick H7234
2Sa 18: 9 while the m he was riding kept on going. H7234
1Ki 1:33 son mount my own m and take him down H7235
1Ki 1:38 had Solomon mount King David's m, H7235
1Ki 1:44 they have put him on the king's m, H7235
Ps 32: 9 Do not be like the horse or the m, which H7234

MULES (11) [MULE]

2Sa 13:29 sons got up, mounted their m and fled. H7234
1Ki 10:25 weapons and spices, and horses and m. H7234
1Ki 18: 5 keep the horses and m alive so we will H7234
2Ki 5:17 as much earth as a pair of m can carry, H7234
1Ch 12:40 food on donkeys, camels, m and oxen. H7234
2Ch 9:24 weapons and spices, and horses and m. H7234
Ezr 2:66 They had 736 horses, 245 m, H7234
Ne 7:68 There were 736 horses, 245 m, H7234
Isa 66:20 wagons, and on m and camels," says H7234
Eze 27:14 cavalry horses and m for your H7234
Zec 14:15 plague will strike the horses and m, H7234

MULTICOLORED (1) [COLORED]

Eze 27:24 embroidered work and m rugs with cords H1394

MULTIPLIED (6) [MULTIPLY]

Ex 1: 7 they m greatly, increased in H9237
Ex 1:12 the more they m and spread; so the H8049
Ex 11: 9 so that my wonders may be m in Egypt." H8049
Dt 8:13 gold increase and all you have is m, H8049
Jdg 16:24 who laid waste our land and m our slain." H8049
La 2: 5 He has m mourning and lamentation H8049

MULTIPLIES (5) [MULTIPLY]

Job 34:37 hands among us and m his words against H8049
Job 35:16 without knowledge he m words. H3892
Pr 23:28 lies in wait and m the unfaithful among H3578
Pr 27: 6 can be trusted, but an enemy m kisses. H6984
Hos 12: 1 wind all day and m lies and violence. H8049

MULTIPLY (11) [MULTIPLIED, MULTIPLIES, MULTIPLYING]

Ge 8:17 so they can m on the earth and be fruitful H9237
Ge 9: 7 m on the earth and increase upon it." H9237
Ex 7: 3 though I m my signs and wonders in H8049
Lev 26:21 I will m your afflictions seven times over H3578
Dt 7:22 the wild animals will m around you. H8049
2Sa 24: 3 "May the LORD your God m the troops a H3578
1Ch 21: 3 "May the LORD m his troops a hundred H3578
Job 9:17 me with a storm and m my wounds for no H8049
Ecc 10:14 fools m words. No one knows what is H8049
Na 3:15 a swarm of locusts. M like grasshoppers H3877
Na 3:15 Multiply like grasshoppers, m like locusts! H3877

MULTIPLYING (2) [MULTIPLY]

Pr 10:19 Sin is not ended by m words, but the H8044
Mk 4: 8 some m thirty, some sixty, G5770

MULTITUDE (9) [MULTITUDES]

Isa 1:11 "The m of your sacrifices—what are they H8044
Isa 13: 4 on the mountains, like that of a great m! H6639
Isa 31: 1 who trust in the m of their chariots and in H8041
Da 10: 6 his voice like the sound of a m. H2162
Jas 5:20 from death and cover over a m of sins. G4436
1Pe 4: 8 because love covers over a m of sins. G4436
Rev 7: 9 me was a great m that no one could G4063
Rev 19: 1 like the roar of a great m in heaven G4063
Rev 19: 6 I heard what sounded like a great m, G4063

MULTITUDES (7) [MULTITUDE]

1Ki 22:19 throne with all the m of heaven standing H7372
2Ch 18:18 with all the m of heaven standing on H7372
Ne 9: 6 the m of heaven worship you. H7372
Da 12: 2 M who sleep in the dust of the earth will H8041
Joel 3:14 M, multitudes in the valley of decision H2162
Joel 3:14 Multitudes, m in the valley of decision H2162
Rev 17:15 are peoples, m, nations and G4063

MUMBLE (1)

Isa 29: 4 your speech will m out of the dust. H8820

MUNITION, MUNITIONS (KJV) FORTRESS

MUPPIM (1)

Ge 46:21 Naaman, Ehi, Rosh, M, Huppim and Ard. H5137

MURDER (32) [MURDERED, MURDERER, MURDERERS, MURDERING, MURDEROUS, MURDERS]

Ex 20:13 "You shall not m. H8357
Nu 35:12 so that anyone accused of m may not die H8357
Nu 35:25 protect the one accused of m from the H8357
Nu 35:27 kill the accused without being guilty of m. H1947
Dt 5:17 "You shall not m. H8357
Jos 21:13 a city of refuge for one accused of m), H8357
Jos 21:21 a city of refuge for one accused of m) and H8357
Jos 21:27 a city of refuge for one accused of m) and H8357
Jos 21:32 a city of refuge for one accused of m), H8357
Jos 21:38 a city of refuge for one accused of m), H8357
Jdg 9:24 who had helped him m his brothers. H2222
2Sa 3:37 had no part in the m of Abner son of Ner. H4637
Ps 94: 6 the foreigner; they m the fatherless. H8357
Pr 28:17 by the guilt of m will seek H1947+5883
Isa 33:15 against plots of m and shut their eyes H1947
Jer 7: 9 " 'Will you steal and m, commit adultery H8357
Hos 4: 2 cursing, lying and m, stealing and H8357
Hos 6: 9 of priests; they m on the road to Shechem H8357
Mt 5:21 long ago, 'You shall not m, and anyone G5839
Mt 15:19 heart come evil thoughts—m, adultery, G5840
Mt 19:18 replied, " 'You shall not m, you shall not G5839
Mk 7:21 come—sexual immorality, theft, m, G5840
Mk 10:19 'You shall not m, you shall not commit G5839
Mk 15: 7 who had committed m in the uprising. G5840
Lk 18:20 adultery, you shall not m, you shall not G5839
Lk 23:19 an insurrection in the city, and for m.) G5840
Lk 23:25 thrown into prison for insurrection and m, G5840
Ro 1:29 They are full of envy, m, strife, deceit and G5840
Ro 13: 9 adultery," "You shall not m," "You shall G5839
Jas 2:11 adultery," also said, "You shall not m." G5839
Jas 2:11 do not commit adultery but do commit m, G5839
1Jn 3:12 And why did he m him? Because G5377

MURDERED (17) [MURDER]

Jdg 9: 5 on one stone m his seventy brothers, H2222
Jdg 9:18 You have m his seventy sons on a single H2222
Jdg 20: 4 the husband of the m woman, said, H8357
2Sa 3:30 his brother Abishai m Abner because he H2222
1Ki 16:16 had plotted against the king and m him, H5782
1Ki 21:19 Have you not m a man and seized his H8357
2Ki 11: 2 royal princes, who were about to be m. H4637
2Ki 12:21 The officials who m him were Jozabad son H5782
2Ki 14: 5 the officials who had m his father the king H5782

2Ch 21:13 *You have* also **m** your own brothers H2222
2Ch 22:11 princes who *were about to* **be m** and put H4637
2Ch 25: 3 the officials who *had* **m** his father the king H5782
Mt 23:31 of those *who* **m** the prophets. *G5839*
Mt 23:35 whom *you* **m** between the temple and the *G5839*
Ac 7:52 you *have* betrayed and **m** him— *G5838+1181*
Jas 5: 6 condemned and **m** the innocent one, *G5839*
1Jn 3:12 to the evil one and **m** his brother. *G5377*

MURDERER (24) [MURDER]

Nu 35:16 that person *is a* **m**; the murderer is H8357
Nu 35:16 is a murderer; the **m** is to be put to death. H8357
Nu 35:17 that person *is a* **m**; the murderer is to H8357
Nu 35:17 is a murderer; the **m** is to be put to death. H8357
Nu 35:18 that person *is a* **m**; the murderer is to H8357
Nu 35:18 is a murderer; the **m** is to be put to death. H8357
Nu 35:19 of blood shall put the **m** to death; H8357
Nu 35:19 when the avenger comes upon **the m** H2257S
Nu 35:19 the avenger shall put **the m** to death. H5647S
Nu 35:21 is to be put to death; that person *is a* **m**. H8357
Nu 35:21 blood shall put the **m** to death when they H8357
Nu 35:30 be put to death as a **m** only on the H8357
Nu 35:31 not accept a ransom for the life of a **m**, H8357
2Sa 16: 7 get out, you **m**, you scoundrel! H408+2021+1947
2Sa 16: 8 come to ruin because you are a **m**!" H408+1947
2Ki 6:32 you see how this **m** is sending H1201+8357
2Ki 9:31 you Zimri, you **m** *of* your master? H2222
Job 24:14 daylight is gone, the **m** rises up, kills the H8357
Jn 8:44 He was a **m** from the beginning, not *G475*
Ac 3:14 and asked that a **m** be released to *G467+5838*
Ac 28: 4 "This man must be a **m**; for though he *G5838*
1Pe 4:15 should not be as a **m** or thief or any other *G5838*
1Jn 3:15 Anyone who hates a brother or sister is a **m** *G475*
1Jn 3:15 you know that no **m** has eternal life *G475*

MURDERERS (6) [MURDER]

Isa 1:21 used to dwell in her—but now **m**! H8357
Jer 4:31 I am fainting; my life is given over to **m**." H2222
Mt 22: 7 destroyed those **m** and burned their *G5838*
1Ti 1: 9 who kill their fathers or mothers, *for* **m**, *G439*
Rev 21: 8 the vile, the **m**, the sexually immoral *G5838*
Rev 22:15 immoral, the **m**, the idolaters and *G5838*

MURDERING (2) [MURDER]

Jdg 9:56 to his father by **m** his seventy brothers. H2222
2Ch 24:25 against him for **m** the son of Jehoiada the H1947

MURDEROUS (1) [MURDER]

Ac 9: 1 still breathing out **m** threats against the *G5840*

MURDERS (4) [MURDER]

Dt 22:26 who attacks and **m** a neighbor, H8357+5883
Ps 10: 8 villages; from ambush *he* **m** the innocent. H2222
Mt 5:21 anyone *who* **m** will be subject to *G5839*
Rev 9:21 Nor did they repent of their **m**, their magic *G5840*

MURMUR, MURMURED, MURMURERS, MURMURING, MURMURINGS (KJV)

COMPLAIN, COMPLAINED, GRUMBLE, GRUMBLED, GRUMBLERS, GRUMBLING, MUTTER, MUTTERED, REBUKED, WHISPERING

MUSCLES (2)

Job 40:16 its loins, what power in the **m** *of* its belly! H9235
Isa 48: 4 you were; your neck **m** were iron, your H1630

MUSHI (8) [MUSHITE, MUSHITES]

Ex 6:19 The sons of Merari were Mahli and **M** H4633
Nu 3:20 Mahli and **M**. These were the H4633
1Ch 6:19 Mahli and **M**. These are the clans H4633
1Ch 6:47 of Mahli, the son of **M**, the son of Merari, H4633
1Ch 23:21 Mahli and **M**. The sons of Mahli: H4633
1Ch 23:23 The sons of **M**: Mahli, Eder and Jerimoth H4633
1Ch 24:26 Mahli and **M**. The son of Jaaziah: H4633
1Ch 24:30 And the sons of **M**: Mahli, Eder and H4633

MUSHITE (1) [MUSHI]

Nu 26:58 the Mahlite clan, the **M** clan, the Korahite H4634

MUSHITES (1) [MUSHI]

Nu 3:33 the clans of the Mahlites and the **M**; H4634

MUSIC (90) [MUSICAL, MUSICIAN, MUSICIANS]

Ge 31:27 singing to the **m of timbrels** and harps? H9512
1Ch 6:31 put in charge of the **m** *in* the house of the H8877
1Ch 6:32 They ministered with **m** before the H8877
1Ch 25: 6 their father for the **m** of the temple of the H8877
1Ch 25: 7 trained and skilled in **m** for the LORD— H8877
Ne 12:27 thanksgiving and with the **m** *of* cymbals, H8877
Job 21:12 They sing to the **m of timbrel** and lyre H9512
Ps 4: T For the **director of m**. With stringed H5904
Ps 5: T For the **director of m**. For pipes. A psalm H5904
Ps 6: T For the **director of m**. With stringed H5904
Ps 8: T For the **director of m**. According to gittith H5904
Ps 9: T For the **director** *of* **m**. To the tune of "The H5904
Ps 11: T For the **director of m**. Of David. H5904
Ps 12: T For the **director of m**. According to H5904
Ps 13: T For the **director of m**. A psalm of David. H5904
Ps 14: T For the **director of m**. Of David. H5904
Ps 18: T For the **director of m**. Of David the H5904
Ps 19: T For the **director of m**. A psalm of David. H5904
Ps 20: T For the **director of m**. A psalm of David. H5904
Ps 21: T For the **director of m**. A psalm of David. H5904
Ps 22: T For the **director of m**. To the tune of "The H5904
Ps 27: 6 I will sing and **make m** to the LORD. H2376
Ps 31: T For the **director of m**. A psalm of David. H5904
Ps 33: 2 **make m** to him on the ten-stringed lyre. H2376
Ps 36: T For the **director of m**. Of David the H5904
Ps 39: T For the **director of m**. For Jeduthun. H5904
Ps 40: T For the **director of m**. Of David. A psalm. H5904
Ps 41: T For the **director of m**. A psalm of David. H5904
Ps 42: T For the **director of m**. A maskil of the H5904
Ps 44: T For the **director of m**. Of the Sons of H5904
Ps 45: T For the **director of m**. To the tune of H5904
Ps 45: 8 with ivory the **m of the strings** makes you H4944
Ps 46: T For the **director of m**. Of the Sons of H5904
Ps 47: T For the **director of m**. Of the Sons of H5904
Ps 49: T For the **director of m**. Of the Sons of H5904
Ps 51: T For the **director of m**. A psalm of David H5904
Ps 52: T For the **director of m**. A maskil of David H5904
Ps 53: T For the **director of m**. According to H5904
Ps 54: T For the **director of m**. With stringed H5904
Ps 55: T For the **director of m**. With stringed H5904
Ps 56: T For the **director of m**. To the tune of "A H5904
Ps 57: T For the **director of m**. To the tune of "Do H5904
Ps 57: 7 heart is steadfast; I will sing and **make m**. H2376
Ps 58: T For the **director of m**. To the tune of "Do H5904
Ps 59: T For the **director of m**. To the tune of "Do H5904
Ps 60: T For the **director of m**. To the tune of "The H5904
Ps 61: T For the **director of m**. With stringed H5904
Ps 62: T For the **director of m**. For Jeduthun. H5904
Ps 64: T For the **director of m**. A psalm of David. H5904
Ps 65: T For the **director of m**. A psalm of David. H5904
Ps 66: T For the **director of m**. A song. A psalm. H5904
Ps 67: T For the **director of m**. With stringed H5904
Ps 68: T For the **director of m**. Of David. A psalm H5904
Ps 69: T For the **director of m**. To the tune of H5904
Ps 70: T For the **director of m**. Of David. A petition. H5904
Ps 75: T For the **director of m**. To the tune of "Do H5904
Ps 76: T For the **director of m**. With stringed H5904
Ps 77: T For the **director of m**. For Jeduthun. H5904
Ps 80: T For the **director of m**. To the tune of "The H5904
Ps 81: T For the **director of m**. According to gittith H5904
Ps 81: 2 Begin the **m**, strike the timbrel, play the H2379
Ps 84: T For the **director of m**. According to gittith H5904
Ps 85: T For the **director of m**. Of the Sons of H5904
Ps 87: 7 As *they* **make m** they will sing, "All my H2727
Ps 88: T For the **director of m**. According to H5904
Ps 92: 1 the LORD and **make m** to your name, H2376
Ps 92: 3 to the **m** of the ten-stringed lyre and the NDT
Ps 95: 2 extol him with **m and song**. H2369
Ps 98: 4 the earth, burst into jubilant song with **m**; H2376
Ps 98: 5 **make m** to the LORD with the harp, with H2376
Ps 108: 1 I will sing and **make m** *with* all my soul. H2376
Ps 109: T For the **director of m**. Of David. A psalm. H5904
Ps 139: T For the **director of m**. Of David. A psalm. H5904
Ps 140: T For the **director of m**. A psalm of David. H5904
Ps 144: 9 the ten-stringed lyre *I will* **make m** to you, H2376
Ps 147: 7 **make m** to our God on the harp. H2376
Ps 149: 3 with dancing and **make m** to him with H2376
Isa 30:32 will be to the **m of timbrels** and harps, H9512
Jer 48:36 heart laments for Moab like the *m of* a **pipe**; AIT
La 5:14 the young men have stopped their **m**. H5593
Eze 26:13 the **m** *of* your harps will be heard no H7754
Da 3: 5 pipe and all kinds of **m**, you must fall A10233
Da 3: 7 harp and all kinds of **m**, all the nations A10233
Da 3:10 all kinds of **m** must fall down and A10233
Da 3:15 pipe and all kinds of **m**, if you are ready A10233
Am 5:23 I will not listen to the **m** *of* your harps. H2379
Hab 3:19 For the **director of m**. On my stringed H5904
Lk 15:25 near the house, he heard **m** and dancing. *G5246*
Eph 5:19 Sing and **make m** from your heart to the *G6010*
Rev 18:22 The **m** of harpists and musicians, pipers *G5889*

MUSICAL (6) [MUSIC]

1Ch 15:16 make a joyful sound with **m** instruments: H8877
1Ch 23: 5 with the *m* **instruments** I have provided AIT
2Ch 7: 6 the Levites with the LORD's **m** instruments, H8877
2Ch 34:12 were skilled in playing **m** instruments— H8877
Ne 12:36 with **m** instruments *prescribed by* David H8877
Am 6: 5 David and improvise on **m** instruments. H8877

MUSICIAN (1) [MUSIC]

1Ch 6:33 Heman, the **m**, the son of Joel, the son of H8876

MUSICIANS (32) [MUSIC]

1Ki 10:12 to make harps and lyres for the **m**. H8876
1Ch 9:33 Those who *were* **m**, heads of Levite H8876
1Ch 15:16 fellow Levites as **m** to make a joyful H8876
1Ch 15:19 The **m** Heman, Asaph and Ethan were to H8876
1Ch 15:27 and as were the **m**, and Kenaniah, H8876
2Ch 5:12 All the Levites who *were* **m**—Asaph H8876
2Ch 5:13 The trumpeters and **m** joined in unison to H8876
2Ch 9:11 to make harps and lyres for the **m**. H8876
2Ch 23:13 **m** with their instruments were H8876
2Ch 29:28 while the **m** played and the trumpets H8877
2Ch 35:15 The **m**, the descendants of Asaph, were H8876
Ezr 2:41 The **m**: the descendants of Asaph 128 H8876
Ezr 2:70 the Levites, the **m**, the gatekeepers and H8876
Ezr 7: 7 **m**, gatekeepers and temple H8876
Ezr 7:24 Levites, **m**, gatekeepers, temple A10234
Ezr 10:24 From the **m**: Eliashib. From the H8876
Ne 7: 1 the **m** and the Levites were appointed. H8876
Ne 7:44 The **m**: the descendants of Asaph 148 H8876
Ne 7:73 the **m** and the temple servants H8876
Ne 10:28 gatekeepers, **m**, temple servants and all H8876
Ne 10:39 the gatekeepers and the **m** are also kept. H8876
Ne 11:22 who *were* the **m** responsible for the H8876
Ne 11:23 The **m** were under the king's orders, which H8876
Ne 12:28 The **m** also were brought together H1201+8876
Ne 12:29 the **m** had built villages for themselves H8876
Ne 12:45 as did also the **m** and gatekeepers H8876
Ne 12:46 directors for the **m** and for the songs of H8876
Ne 12:47 portions for the **m** and the gatekeepers. H8876
Ne 13: 5 the Levites, **m** and gatekeepers, as H8876
Ne 13:10 all the Levites and **m** responsible for the H8876
Ps 68:25 after them the **m**; with them are the H5594
Rev 18:22 The music of harpists and **m**, pipers and *G3676*

MUST (753)

Ge 2:17 but *you m* not **eat** from the tree of the AIT
Ge 3: 1 '*You m* not **eat** from any tree in the garden'?" AIT
Ge 3: 3 '*You m* not **eat** fruit from the tree that is in AIT
Ge 3: 3 the garden, and *you m* not **touch** it, or you AIT
Ge 3:17 commanded you, '*You m* not **eat** from it,' AIT
Ge 3:22 *He m* not be allowed *to* **reach out** his hand AIT
Ge 4: 7 it desires to have you, but you *m* **rule** over it." AIT
Ge 9: 4 "But *you m* not **eat** meat that has its AIT
Ge 17: 9 "As for you, *you m* **keep** my covenant, you AIT
Ge 17:12 you who is eight days old *m* **be circumcised**, AIT
Ge 17:13 money, *they* **m be circumcised**. H4576+4576
Ge 24:37 '*You m* not **get** a wife for my son from the AIT
Ge 30:16 "*You m* **sleep with** me," she said AIT
Ge 33:13 tender and that I **m** care for the ewes and NDT
Ge 42:20 But *you m* **bring** your youngest brother to me AIT
Ge 42:22 Now *we m* **give an accounting** *for* his blood." AIT
Ge 43:11 said to them, "If **it m be**, then do this: H4027
Ge 43:12 for *you m* **return** the silver that was put back AIT
Ge 50:25 then *you m* **carry** my bones **up** from this AIT
Ex 1:10 *we m* **deal shrewdly** with them or they will AIT
Ex 1:22 boy that is born *you m* **throw** into the Nile, AIT
Ex 2:14 thought, "What I did *m have* **become known**." AIT
Ex 5:18 yet *you m* **produce** your full quota of bricks." AIT
Ex 8:27 *We m* **take** a three-day journey into the AIT
Ex 8:28 but *you* **m** not go **very far**. H8178+8178
Ex 10:25 "You *m* **allow** us to have sacrifices and burnt AIT
Ex 10:26 Our livestock too *m* **go** with us; not a hoof is AIT
Ex 12: 4 they *m* **share** one with their nearest neighbor, AIT
Ex 12: 5 The animals you choose *m* **be** year-old males AIT
Ex 12: 6 of Israel *m* **slaughter** them at twilight. AIT
Ex 12:10 if some is left till morning, *you m* **burn** it. AIT
Ex 12:15 through the seventh *m* **be cut off** from Israel. AIT
Ex 12:19 with yeast in it *m* **be cut off** from the AIT
Ex 12:20 you live, *you m* **eat** unleavened bread." AIT
Ex 12:46 "*It m* **be eaten** inside the house; take none AIT
Ex 12:47 The whole community of Israel *m* **celebrate** it. AIT
Ex 12:48 *m have* all the males in his household **circumcised** AIT
Ex 13:10 *You m* **keep** this ordinance at the appointed AIT
Ex 13:19 then *you m* **carry** my bones **up** with you AIT
Ex 18:19 You *m* **be** the people's representative before AIT
Ex 19:22 the LORD, *m* **consecrate themselves**, or the AIT
Ex 19:24 people *m* not **force** *their* **way through** to AIT
Ex 21: 6 then his master *m* **take** him before the judges. AIT
Ex 21: 8 her for himself, *he m* **let** her **be redeemed**. AIT
Ex 21: 9 *he m* **grant** her the rights of a daughter. AIT
Ex 21:10 *he m* not **deprive** the first one *of* her food AIT
Ex 21:19 party *m* **pay** the injured person *for* any loss of AIT
Ex 21:20 with a rod **m be punished** if the H5933+5933
Ex 21:22 the offender **m be fined** whatever H6740+6740
Ex 21:26 destroys it *m* **let** the slave **go** free to AIT
Ex 21:27 female slave *m* **let** the slave **go** free to AIT
Ex 21:28 to death, and its meat *m* not **be eaten**. AIT
Ex 21:32 the owner *m* **pay** thirty shekels of silver to the AIT
Ex 21:34 the pit *m* **pay** the owner **for the loss** and take AIT
Ex 21:36 the owner **m pay**, animal for H8966+8966
Ex 22: 1 sells it *m* **pay back** five head of cattle for AIT
Ex 22: 3 steals **m certainly make restitution**, H8966+8966
Ex 22: 3 nothing, *they m* **be sold** to pay for their theft. AIT
Ex 22: 4 donkey or sheep—*they m* **pay back** double. AIT
Ex 22: 5 offender *m* **make restitution** *from* the best of AIT
Ex 22: 6 started the fire **m make restitution**. H8966+8966
Ex 22: 7 the thief, if caught, *m* **pay back** double. AIT
Ex 22: 8 of the house *m* **appear** before the judges AIT
Ex 22: 8 they **m** determine whether the owner of NDT
Ex 22: 9 declare guilty *m* **pay back** double to the other AIT
Ex 22:12 **restitution** *m be* **made** to the owner. AIT
Ex 22:14 present, *they* **m make restitution**. H8966+8966
Ex 22:16 *he* **m pay the bride-price**, and H4555+4555
Ex 22:17 *he m still* **pay** the bride-price for virgins. AIT
Ex 22:20 any god other than the LORD *m* **be destroyed**. AIT
Ex 22:29 "*You m* **give** me the firstborn of your sons. AIT
Ex 23:18 offerings *m* not *be* **kept** until morning. AIT
Ex 23:24 *You* **m demolish** them and break H2238+2238
Ex 24: 2 the LORD; the others *m* not **come near**. AIT
Ex 26:24 these two corners *they m* **be** double from the AIT
Ex 28:35 Aaron *m* **wear** *it* when he ministers. AIT
Ex 28:43 his sons *m* **wear** *them* whenever they AIT
Ex 29:34 *It m* not **be eaten**, because it is AIT
Ex 30: 7 "Aaron *m* **burn** fragrant incense on the altar AIT
Ex 30: 8 *He m* **burn** incense again when he lights the AIT
Ex 30:10 This annual **atonement** *m be* **made** with the AIT
Ex 30:12 each one *m* **pay** the LORD a ransom for his life AIT
Ex 30:33 than a priest *m* **be cut off** from their people. AIT
Ex 30:38 its fragrance *m* **be cut off** from their people." AIT
Ex 31:13 the Israelites, '*You m* **observe** my Sabbaths. AIT
Ex 31:14 work on that day *m* **be cut off** from their AIT

M

Ex 33:23 will see my back; but my face *m* not **be seen**.” AIT
Ex 34:21 the plowing season and harvest *you m* **rest**. AIT
Lev 1: 3 *You m* **present** it at the entrance to the tent AIT
Lev 2:11 bring to the LORD *m* **be made** without yeast, AIT
Lev 3:17 you live: *You m* not **eat** any fat or any blood AIT
Lev 4: 3 *he m* **bring** to the LORD a young bull without AIT
Lev 4:12 *he m* **take** outside the camp to a place AIT
Lev 4:14 the assembly *m* **bring** a young bull as a sin AIT
Lev 4:23 *he m* **bring** as his offering a male goat AIT
Lev 4:28 *they m* **bring** as their offering for the sin they AIT
Lev 5: 5 *they m* **confess** in what way they have sinned. AIT
Lev 5: 6 *they m* **bring** to the LORD a female lamb or AIT
Lev 5: 9 of the blood *m* **be drained out** at the base of AIT
Lev 5:11 *They m* not **put** olive oil or incense on it AIT
Lev 5:16 *They m* **make restitution** *for* what they have AIT
Lev 6: 4 *they m* **return** what they have stolen or taken AIT
Lev 6: 5 *They m* **make restitution** in full, add a fifth of AIT
Lev 6: 6 And as a penalty *they m* **bring** to the priest AIT
Lev 6: 9 the fire *m* **be kept burning** on the altar. AIT
Lev 6:12 The fire on the altar *m* **be kept burning**; it AIT
Lev 6:12 altar must be kept burning; *it m* not **go out**. AIT
Lev 6:13 The fire *m* **be kept burning** on the altar AIT
Lev 6:13 on the altar continuously; *it m* not **go out**. AIT
Lev 6:17 *It m* not **be baked** with yeast; I have given it AIT
Lev 6:21 *It m* **be prepared** with oil on a griddle; bring AIT
Lev 6:23 be burned completely; *it m* not **be eaten**.” AIT
Lev 6:27 *you m* **wash** it in the sanctuary area. AIT
Lev 6:28 clay pot the meat is cooked in *m* **be broken**; AIT
Lev 6:30 atonement in the Holy Place *m* not **be eaten**; AIT
Lev 6:30 Place must not be eaten; *it m* **be burned up**. AIT
Lev 7: 6 but *it m* **be eaten** in the sanctuary area AIT
Lev 7:15 of thanksgiving *m* **be eaten** on the day it is AIT
Lev 7:15 *they m* **leave** none of it till morning. AIT
Lev 7:17 left over till the third day *m* **be burned up**. AIT
Lev 7:19 ceremonially unclean *m* not **be eaten**; AIT
Lev 7:19 must not be eaten; *it m* **be burned up**. AIT
Lev 7:20 the LORD, they *m* **be cut off** from their people. AIT
Lev 7:21 to the LORD *m* **be cut off** from their people. AIT
Lev 7:24 other purpose, but *you* **m** not **eat it**. H430+430
Lev 7:25 to the LORD *m* **be cut off** from their people. AIT
Lev 7:26 *you m* not **eat** the blood of any bird or AIT
Lev 7:27 who eats blood *m* **be cut off** from their AIT
Lev 8:35 *You m* **stay** at the entrance to the tent of AIT
Lev 10:15 that was waved *m be* **brought** with the fat AIT
Lev 11: 4 have a divided hoof, but *you m* not **eat** them. AIT
Lev 11: 8 *You m* not **eat** their meat or touch their AIT
Lev 11:11 as unclean, *you m* not **eat** their meat; you AIT
Lev 11:11 *you m* **regard** their carcasses **as unclean**. AIT
Lev 11:25 one of their carcasses *m* **wash** their clothes, AIT
Lev 11:28 picks up their carcasses *m* **wash** their clothes, AIT
Lev 11:33 it will be unclean, and *you m* **break** the pot. AIT
Lev 11:35 an oven or cooking pot *m* **be broken up**. AIT
Lev 11:40 eats some of its carcass *m* **wash** their clothes, AIT
Lev 11:40 picks up the carcass *m* **wash** their clothes. AIT
Lev 11:47 You *m* **distinguish** between the unclean and AIT
Lev 12: 4 Then the woman *m* **wait** thirty-three days to AIT
Lev 12: 4 *She m* not **touch** anything sacred or go to the AIT
Lev 12: 5 Then *she m* **wait** sixty-six days to be purified AIT
Lev 13: 2 *they m* **be brought** to Aaron the priest or to AIT
Lev 13: 6 *They m* **wash** their clothes, and they will be AIT
Lev 13: 7 *they m* **appear** before the priest again. AIT
Lev 13: 9 skin disease, *they m* **be brought** to the priest. AIT
Lev 13:16 turns white, *they m* **go** to the priest. AIT
Lev 13:19 *they m* **present themselves** to the priest. AIT
Lev 13:33 then *the man or woman m* **shave themselves** AIT
Lev 13:34 *They m* **wash** their clothes, and they will be AIT
Lev 13:45 such a defiling disease *m* **wear** torn clothes, AIT
Lev 13:46 *They m* **live** alone; they must live outside the AIT
Lev 13:46 live alone; they **m** live outside the camp. NDT
Lev 13:49 defiling mold and *m* **be shown** *to* the priest. AIT
Lev 13:52 *He m* **burn** the fabric, the woven or knitted AIT
Lev 13:52 mold is persistent, the article *m* **be burned**. AIT
Lev 13:57 whatever has the mold *m be* **burned**. AIT
Lev 13:58 is rid of the mold, *m* **be washed** again. AIT
Lev 14: 8 person to be cleansed *m* **wash** their clothes, AIT
Lev 14: 8 but *they m* **stay** outside their tent for seven AIT
Lev 14: 9 seventh day *they m* **shave off** all their hair AIT
Lev 14: 9 all their hair; *they m* **shave** their head, their AIT
Lev 14: 9 *They m* **wash** their clothes and bathe AIT
Lev 14:10 the eighth day *they m* **bring** two male lambs AIT
Lev 14:21 *they m* **take** one male lamb as a guilt AIT
Lev 14:23 the eighth day *they m* **bring** them for their AIT
Lev 14:35 owner of the house *m* **go** and tell the priest, AIT
Lev 14:41 He *m* **have** all the inside walls of the house **scraped** AIT
Lev 14:45 It *m be* **torn down**—its stones, timbers and AIT
Lev 14:47 eats in the house *m* **wash** their clothes. AIT
Lev 15: 5 touches his bed *m* **wash** their clothes and AIT
Lev 15: 6 a discharge sat on *m* **wash** their clothes and AIT
Lev 15: 7 has a discharge *m* **wash** their clothes and AIT
Lev 15: 8 *they m* **wash** their clothes and bathe with AIT
Lev 15:10 up those things *m* **wash** their clothes and AIT
Lev 15:11 hands with water *m* **wash** their clothes and AIT
Lev 15:12 clay pot that the man touches *m* **be broken**, AIT
Lev 15:13 *he m* **wash** his clothes and bathe himself AIT
Lev 15:14 On the eighth day *he m* **take** two doves or AIT
Lev 15:16 *he m* **bathe** his whole body with water AIT
Lev 15:17 has semen on it *m* **be washed** with water, AIT
Lev 15:18 of semen, *both of them m* **bathe** with water AIT
Lev 15:21 *they m* **wash** their clothes and bathe with AIT
Lev 15:22 *they m* **wash** their clothes and bathe with AIT
Lev 15:27 *they m* **wash** their clothes and bathe with AIT
Lev 15:28 her discharge, *she m* **count off** seven days AIT
Lev 15:29 On the eighth day *she m* **take** two doves or AIT
Lev 15:31 “ ‘*You m* **keep** the Israelites **separate** from AIT
Lev 16: 3 He **m** first bring a young bull for a sin NDT
Lev 16: 4 so *he m* **bathe** himself with water before he AIT
Lev 16:26 goat as a scapegoat *m* **wash** his clothes AIT
Lev 16:27 atonement, *m be* **taken** outside the camp AIT
Lev 16:28 man who burns them *m* **wash** his clothes AIT
Lev 16:29 seventh month *you m* **deny** yourselves and AIT
Lev 16:31 sabbath rest, and *you m* **deny** yourselves; it is AIT
Lev 17: 4 shed blood and *m* **be cut off** from their AIT
Lev 17: 5 *They m* **bring** them to the priest, that is, to AIT
Lev 17: 7 *They m* no longer **offer** any of their sacrifices AIT
Lev 17: 9 to the LORD *m* **be cut off** from the people of AIT
Lev 17:13 that may be eaten *m* **drain out** the blood AIT
Lev 17:14 “*You m* not **eat** the blood of any creature AIT
Lev 17:14 is its blood; anyone who eats it *m* **be cut off**.” AIT
Lev 17:15 by wild animals *m* **wash** their clothes and AIT
Lev 18: 3 *You m* not **do** as they do in Egypt, where you AIT
Lev 18: 3 and *you m* not **do** as they do in the land of AIT
Lev 18: 4 *You m* **obey** my laws and be careful to follow AIT
Lev 18:21 for *you m* not **profane** the name of your God. AIT
Lev 18:23 A woman *m* not **present** *herself* to an animal AIT
Lev 18:26 But you *m* **keep** my decrees and my laws. AIT
Lev 18:26 residing among you *m* not **do** any of these AIT
Lev 18:29 such persons *m* **be cut off** from their people. AIT
Lev 19: 3 “ ‘Each of *you m* **respect** your mother and AIT
Lev 19: 3 father, and *you m* **observe** my Sabbaths. AIT
Lev 19: 6 left over until the third day *m* **be burned up**. AIT
Lev 19: 8 the LORD; they *m* **be cut off** from their people. AIT
Lev 19:20 her freedom, *there m* **be** due punishment. AIT
Lev 19:21 *m* **bring** a ram to the entrance to the tent of AIT
Lev 19:23 to consider it forbidden; *it m* not **be eaten**. AIT
Lev 19:34 residing among you *m be* **treated** as your AIT
Lev 20:14 Both he and they *m be* **burned** in the fire, so AIT
Lev 20:15 be put to death, and *you m* **kill** the animal. AIT
Lev 20:23 *You m* not **live** according to the customs of AIT
Lev 20:25 “ ‘*You m* therefore **make a distinction** AIT
Lev 20:27 among you **m be put to death**. H4637+4637
Lev 21: 1 *m* not **make himself ceremonially unclean** AIT
Lev 21: 4 *He m* not **make himself unclean** for people AIT
Lev 21: 5 “ ‘Priests **m** not **shave** their heads H7942+7947
Lev 21: 6 *They m* **be** holy to their God and must not AIT
Lev 21: 6 to their God and *m* not **profane** the name of AIT
Lev 21: 7 “ ‘*They m* not **marry** women defiled by AIT
Lev 21: 9 her father; *she m* **be burnt** in the fire. AIT
Lev 21:10 *m* not *let* his hair *become* **unkempt** or tear AIT
Lev 21:11 *He m* not **enter** a place where there is a dead AIT
Lev 21:11 *He m* not **make himself unclean**, even for his AIT
Lev 21:13 “ ‘The woman he marries **m** be a virgin. NDT
Lev 21:14 *He m* not **marry** a widow, a divorced woman AIT
Lev 21:21 *he m* not **come near** to offer the food of his AIT
Lev 21:23 *he m* not **go** near the curtain or approach the AIT
Lev 22: 3 that person *m* **be cut off** from my presence. AIT
Lev 22: 6 *He m* not **eat** any of the sacred offerings AIT
Lev 22: 8 *He m* not **eat** anything found dead or torn by AIT
Lev 22:14 *m* **make restitution** to the priest *for* the AIT
Lev 22:15 The priests *m* not **desecrate** the sacred AIT
Lev 22:19 you **m** present a male without defect from NDT
Lev 22:21 *it m* **be** without defect or blemish to be AIT
Lev 22:24 *You m* not **offer** to the LORD an animal whose AIT
Lev 22:24 *You m* not **do** this in your own land AIT
Lev 22:25 you **m** not accept such animals from the NDT
Lev 22:30 *It m* **be eaten** that same day; leave none of it AIT
Lev 22:32 for *I m* **be acknowledged as holy** by the AIT
Lev 23: 6 seven days *you m* **eat** bread made AIT
Lev 23:12 *you m* **sacrifice** as a burnt offering to the AIT
Lev 23:14 *You m* not **eat** any bread, or roasted or new AIT
Lev 23:29 on that day *m* **be cut off** from their people. AIT
Lev 23:32 rest for you, and *you m* **deny** yourselves. AIT
Lev 24: 4 before the LORD *m be* **tended** continually. AIT
Lev 24:16 The entire assembly **m stone** him H8083+8083
Lev 24:18 of someone’s animal *m* **make restitution**— AIT
Lev 24:20 inflicted the injury *m* **suffer** the same injury. AIT
Lev 24:21 Whoever kills an animal *m* **make restitution** AIT
Lev 25: 2 itself **m observe a sabbath** to the H8697+8701
Lev 25:23 “ ‘The land *m* not **be sold** permanently AIT
Lev 25:24 *you m* **provide** *for* the redemption of the land. AIT
Lev 25:34 belonging to their towns *m* not **be sold**; AIT
Lev 25:37 *You m* not **lend** them money at interest or sell AIT
Lev 25:42 *they* **m** not **be sold** as slaves. H4835+4929
Lev 25:46 but *you m* not **rule** over your fellow Israelites AIT
Lev 25:51 *they m* **pay** *for* their redemption a larger AIT
Lev 25:53 you **m** see to it that those to whom they owe NDT
Lev 27:10 *They m* not **exchange** it or substitute a good AIT
Lev 27:11 the animal *m be* **presented** to the priest AIT
Lev 27:13 the animal, a fifth *m be* **added** to its value. AIT
Lev 27:15 to redeem it, *they m* **add** a fifth to its value AIT
Lev 27:19 to redeem it, *they m* **add** a fifth to its value AIT
Lev 27:23 the owner *m* **pay** its value on that day as AIT
Lev 27:31 any of their tithe *m* **add** a fifth of the value to AIT
Nu 1:49 “*You m* not **count** the tribe of Levi or include AIT
Nu 4:15 But *they m* not **touch** the holy things or they AIT
Nu 4:20 But the Kohathites *m* not **go in** to look at the AIT
Nu 5: 7 and *m* **confess** the sin they have committed AIT
Nu 5: 7 *They m* **make full restitution** *for* the wrong AIT
Nu 5: 8 to the LORD and **m** be given to the priest, NDT
Nu 5:15 *He m* also **take** an offering of a tenth of an AIT
Nu 5:15 *He m* not **pour** olive oil on it or put incense AIT
Nu 6: 3 *they m* **abstain** from wine and other AIT
Nu 6: 3 drink and *m* not **drink** vinegar made from AIT
Nu 6: 3 *They m* not **drink** grape juice or eat grapes AIT
Nu 6: 4 *they m* not **eat** anything that comes from the AIT
Nu 6: 5 *They m* **be** holy until the period of their AIT
Nu 6: 5 LORD is over; *they m let* their hair **grow long**. AIT
Nu 6: 6 the Nazirite *m* not **go** near a dead body. AIT
Nu 6: 7 *they m* not **make themselves ceremonially unclean** AIT
Nu 6: 9 *they m* **shave** their head on the seventh day AIT
Nu 6:10 the eighth day *they m* **bring** two doves or two AIT
Nu 6:12 *They m* **rededicate** *themselves* to the LORD AIT
Nu 6:12 of dedication and *m* **bring** a year-old male AIT
Nu 6:18 the Nazirite *m* **shave off** the hair that AIT
Nu 6:21 *They m* **fulfill** the vows they have made AIT
Nu 8:25 *they m* **retire** from their regular service and AIT
Nu 8:26 but *they themselves m* not **do** the work. AIT
Nu 9:12 *They m* not **leave** any of it till morning or AIT
Nu 9:12 Passover, they **m** follow all the regulations. NDT
Nu 9:13 they *m* **be cut off** from their people for not AIT
Nu 9:14 You *m* **have** the same regulations for both AIT
Nu 15:13 who is native-born *m* **do** these things in this AIT
Nu 15:14 to the LORD, *they m* **do** exactly as you do. AIT
Nu 15:27 *that person m* **bring** a year-old female goat AIT
Nu 15:30 the LORD and *m* **be cut off** from the people of AIT
Nu 15:31 they **m surely be cut off**; their guilt H4162+4162
Nu 15:35 said to Moses, “The man **m die**. H4637+4637
Nu 15:35 whole assembly *m* **stone** him outside the AIT
Nu 17: 3 there **m** be one staff for the head of each NDT
Nu 18: 3 but *they m* not **go near** the furnishings of the AIT
Nu 18:10 male shall eat it. You *m* **regard** it **as** holy. AIT
Nu 18:15 But *you* **m redeem** every firstborn H7009+7009
Nu 18:16 *you m* **redeem** them at the redemption price AIT
Nu 18:17 “But *you m* not **redeem** the firstborn of a cow AIT
Nu 18:22 on the Israelites *m* not **go near** the tent of AIT
Nu 18:26 *you m* **present** a tenth of that tithe as the AIT
Nu 18:28 From these tithes *you m* **give** the LORD’s AIT
Nu 18:29 *You m* **present** as the LORD’s portion the best AIT
Nu 19: 7 the priest *m* **wash** his clothes and bathe AIT
Nu 19: 8 who burns it *m* also **wash** his clothes and AIT
Nu 19:10 ashes of the heifer *m* also **wash** his clothes, AIT
Nu 19:12 They *m* **purify** themselves with the water on AIT
Nu 19:13 They *m* **be cut off** from Israel AIT
Nu 19:18 He **m** also sprinkle anyone who has touched NDT
Nu 19:19 are being cleansed *m* **wash** their clothes AIT
Nu 19:20 they *m* **be cut off** from the community AIT
Nu 19:21 water of cleansing *m* also **wash** his clothes, AIT
Nu 20:10 *m we* **bring** you water **out** of this rock?” AIT
Nu 22:12 *You m* not **put a curse on** those people AIT
Nu 22:38 *I m* **speak** only what God puts in my mouth.” AIT
Nu 23:12 “**M** *I* not speak what the LORD puts in my H9068
Nu 23:26 “Did I not tell you *I m* **do** whatever the LORD AIT
Nu 24:13 and *I m* **say** only what the LORD says”? AIT
Nu 25: 5 “Each of *you m* **put to death** those of your AIT
Nu 27: 7 *You* **m certainly give** them property H5989+5989
Nu 29: 7 *You m* **deny** yourselves and do no work. AIT
Nu 30: 2 *he m* not **break** his word but must do AIT
Nu 30: 2 break his word but *m* **do** everything he said. AIT
Nu 30:15 then *he m* **bear the consequences** *of* her AIT
Nu 31:19 who was killed *m* **stay** outside the camp AIT
Nu 31:19 days you *m* **purify yourselves** and your AIT
Nu 31:23 can withstand fire *m be* **put** through the fire, AIT
Nu 31:23 But *it m* also **be purified** with the water of AIT
Nu 31:23 withstand fire *m be* **put** through that water. AIT
Nu 32:29 *you m* **give** them the land of Gilead as their AIT
Nu 32:30 *they m* **accept** *their* **possession** with you in AIT
Nu 35: 7 In all *you m* **give** the Levites forty-eight towns AIT
Nu 35:24 the assembly *m* **judge** between the accused AIT
Nu 35:25 The assembly *m* **protect** the one accused of AIT
Nu 35:25 The accused *m* **stay** there until the death of AIT
Nu 35:28 The accused *m* **stay** in the city of refuge until AIT
Nu 36: 8 in any Israelite tribe *m* **marry** someone in her AIT
Dt 3:18 *m* **cross over** ahead of the other Israelites. AIT
Dt 7: 2 then *you* **m destroy** them **totally**. H3049+3049
Dt 7:16 *You m* **destroy** all the peoples the LORD your AIT
Dt 12: 1 laws *you m be* **careful** to follow in the AIT
Dt 12: 4 *You m* not **worship** the LORD your God in AIT
Dt 12: 5 his dwelling. To that place *you m* **go**; AIT
Dt 12:16 But *you m* not **eat** the blood; pour it out on AIT
Dt 12:17 *You* **m** not eat in your own towns the tithe H3523
Dt 12:23 and *you m* not **eat** the life with the meat. AIT
Dt 12:24 *You m* not **eat** the blood; pour it out on the AIT
Dt 12:27 your sacrifices *m* **be poured** beside the altar AIT
Dt 12:31 *You m* not **worship** the LORD your God in AIT
Dt 13: 3 *you m* not **listen** to the words of that prophet AIT
Dt 13: 4 It is the LORD your God *you m* **follow**, and AIT
Dt 13: 4 God you must follow, and him *you m* **revere**. AIT
Dt 13: 5 dreamer *m* **be put to death** for inciting AIT
Dt 13: 5 *You m* **purge** the evil from among you AIT
Dt 13: 9 *You* **m certainly put** them **to death** H2222+2222
Dt 13: 9 Your hand *m* **be** the first in putting them to AIT
Dt 13:14 then *you m* **inquire**, probe and investigate it AIT
Dt 13:15 *you* **m certainly put** to the sword all H5782+5782
Dt 13:15 *You m* **destroy** it **completely**, both its people AIT
Dt 15: 1 end of every seven years *you m* **cancel debts**. AIT
Dt 15: 3 you *m* **cancel** *any* **debt** your fellow AIT
Dt 15:12 in the seventh year *you m* **let** them **go** free. AIT
Dt 15:21 *you m* not **sacrifice** it to the LORD your God. AIT
Dt 15:23 But *you m* not **eat** the blood; pour it out on AIT
Dt 16: 5 *You* **m** not sacrifice the Passover in any H3523
Dt 16: 6 There *you m* **sacrifice** the Passover in the AIT
Dt 16:16 year all your men *m* **appear** before the LORD AIT
Dt 16:17 Each of you **m** bring a gift in proportion to NDT
Dt 17: 4 then *you m* **investigate** it thoroughly. AIT
Dt 17: 7 of the witnesses *m* **be** the first in putting AIT

Dt 17: 7 *You m* **purge** the evil from among you AIT
Dt 17:10 *You m* **act** according to the decisions they AIT
Dt 17:12 *You m* **purge** the evil from Israel. AIT
Dt 17:15 He **m** be from among your fellow Israelites NDT
Dt 17:16 *m* not **acquire great numbers** *of* horses for AIT
Dt 17:17 *He m* not **take many** wives, or his heart will AIT
Dt 17:17 *He m* not **accumulate large amounts** *of* silver AIT
Dt 18:13 *You m* **be** blameless before the LORD your AIT
Dt 18:15 your fellow Israelites. *You m* **listen** to him. AIT
Dt 19:13 *You m* **purge** from Israel the guilt of AIT
Dt 19:15 A matter *m be* **established** by the testimony AIT
Dt 19:17 in the dispute *m* **stand** in the presence of the AIT
Dt 19:18 The judges *m* **make** *a* thorough **investigation** AIT
Dt 19:19 *You m* **purge** the evil from among you AIT
Dt 21:14 *You* **m** not **sell** her or
H4835+928+2021+4084+4835
Dt 21:16 *he* **m** not give the rights of the firstborn to H3523
Dt 21:17 *He m* **acknowledge** the son of his unloved AIT
Dt 21:21 *You m* **purge** the evil from among you AIT
Dt 21:23 *you m* not **leave** the body hanging on the **pole** AIT
Dt 21:23 *You m* not **desecrate** the land the LORD your AIT
Dt 22: 5 A woman *m* not **wear** men's clothing, nor a AIT
Dt 22:19 *he* **m** not divorce her as long as he lives. H3523
Dt 22:21 *You m* **purge** the evil from among you AIT
Dt 22:22 who slept with her and the woman *m* **die**. AIT
Dt 22:22 *You m* **purge** the evil from Israel AIT
Dt 22:24 *You m* **purge** the evil from among you. AIT
Dt 22:29 He *m* **marry** the young woman, for he has AIT
Dt 22:30 *he m* not **dishonor** his father's **bed**. AIT
Dt 23:14 Your camp *m* **be** holy, so that he will not see AIT
Dt 23:18 *You m* not **bring** the earnings of a female AIT
Dt 23:23 Whatever your lips utter *you m* **be sure** to do AIT
Dt 23:25 but *you m* not **put** a sickle to their standing AIT
Dt 24: 5 *he m* not *be* **sent** to war or have any other AIT
Dt 24: 7 selling them as a slave, the kidnapper *m* **die**. AIT
Dt 24: 7 *You m* **purge** the evil from among you. AIT
Dt 24: 8 You *m* **follow** carefully what I have AIT
Dt 25: 3 judge *m* not **impose** more than forty **lashes**. AIT
Dt 25: 5 his widow *m* not **marry** outside the family. AIT
Dt 25:15 You *m* **have** accurate and honest weights AIT
Dt 31: 5 and *you m* **do** to them all that I have AIT
Dt 31: 7 you *m* **go** with this people into the land AIT
Dt 31: 7 *m* **divide** it *among* them **as** their **inheritance**. AIT
Dt 31:13 *m* **hear** it and learn to fear the LORD your God AIT
Jos 1:14 *m* **cross over** ahead of your fellow Israelites. AIT
Jos 6:19 to the LORD and *m* **go into** his treasury." AIT
Jos 20: 5 the elders *m* not **surrender** the fugitive AIT
Jos 23: 7 *You m* not **serve** them or bow down to them AIT
Jdg 3:24 "He *m be* **relieving himself** in the inner room AIT
Jdg 6:30 *He m* **die**, because he has broken down AIT
Jdg 13:13 "Your wife *m* **do** all that I have told her. AIT
Jdg 13:14 *She m* not **eat** anything that comes from the AIT
Jdg 13:14 *She m* **do** everything I have commanded her." AIT
Jdg 14: 3 *M* you **go** to the uncircumcised Philistines to AIT
Jdg 14:13 you *m* **give** me thirty linen garments and AIT
Jdg 15:18 *M I* now **die** of thirst and fall into the hands AIT
Jdg 19:30 *We* **m do something**! So speak H6418
Jdg 21:17 The Benjamite survivors **m have** heirs," NDT
Ru 3: 1 "My daughter, I **m** find a home for you H4202S
Ru 3:14 "No *one m* **know** that a woman came to the AIT
1Sa 5: 7 of the god of Israel *m* not **stay** here with us, AIT
1Sa 9:13 he comes, because he *m* **bless** the sacrifice AIT
1Sa 10: 8 but *you m* **wait** seven days until I come to AIT
1Sa 14:39 with my son Jonathan, *he* **m die**." H4637+4637
1Sa 14:43 with the end of my staff. And now I *m* **die**!" AIT
1Sa 20: 3 'Jonathan *m* not **know** this or he will be AIT
1Sa 20:22 beyond you,' then *you m* **go**, because the AIT
1Sa 20:26 "Something **m** have happened to David to NDT
1Sa 20:31 to bring him to me, for he **m die**!" H1201+4638
1Sa 21:15 *M* this man **come** into my house? AIT
1Sa 26:16 you and your men **m** die, because you H1201S
1Sa 28: 1 "*You* **m understand** that you and H3359+3359
1Sa 29: 4 He *m* not **go** with us into battle, or he will AIT
1Sa 29: 9 '*He m* not **go up** with us into battle. AIT
1Sa 30:23 *you m* not **do** that with what the LORD has AIT
2Sa 2:26 out to Joab, "*M* the sword **devour** forever? AIT
2Sa 12: 5 LORD lives, the man who did this **m** die! H1201S
2Sa 12: 6 *He m* **pay** *for* that lamb four times over AIT
2Sa 14:14 cannot be recovered, so *we* **m die**. H4637+4637
2Sa 14:24 But the king said, "*He m* **go** to his own house AIT
2Sa 14:24 go to his own house; *he m* not **see** my face." AIT
2Sa 15:14 *We m* **flee**, or none of us will escape from AIT
2Sa 15:14 *We m* leave **immediately**, or he will move AIT
2Sa 18: 3 the men said, "*You m* not **go out**; if we are AIT
2Sa 18:20 but *you m* not **do so** today, because AIT
2Sa 18:25 "If he is alone, he **m** have good news." NDT
2Sa 18:26 "He *m be* **bringing good news**, too. AIT
1Ki 1:42 man like you *m be* **bringing** good **news**." AIT
1Ki 10: 8 How happy your people **m** be! How happy NDT
1Ki 11: 2 Israelites, "*You m* not **intermarry** with them AIT
1Ki 13: 9 '*You m* not **eat** bread or drink water or return AIT
1Ki 13:17 '*You m* not **eat** bread or drink water there AIT
1Ki 18:27 Maybe he is sleeping and *m be* **awakened**." AIT
1Ki 20:22 your position and see what *m be* **done**, AIT
1Ki 20:25 You *m* also **raise** an army like the one you AIT
1Ki 20:39 life for his life, or *you m* **pay** a talent of silver. AIT
1Ki 22:16 many times *m* I **make** you **swear** to tell me AIT
2Ki 3:23 "Those kings **m have fought** and H2991+2991
2Ki 11:15 "*She m* not **be put to death** in the temple of AIT
2Ki 17:36 outstretched arm, is the one *you m* **worship**. AIT
2Ki 17:37 *You m* always *be* **careful** to keep the decrees AIT
2Ki 18:22 "*You m* **worship** before this altar in AIT
2Ch 2: 9 temple I build *m be* large and **magnificent**. AIT
2Ch 8:11 "My wife *m* not **live** in the palace of David AIT
2Ch 9: 7 How happy your people *m* be! How happy NDT
2Ch 18:15 many times *m* I **make** you **swear** to tell me AIT
2Ch 19: 9 "*You m* **serve** faithfully and wholeheartedly AIT
2Ch 25: 7 troops from Israel *m* not **march** with you, AIT
2Ch 28:13 "*You m* not **bring** those prisoners here," AIT
2Ch 32:12 '*You m* **worship** before one altar and burn AIT
Ezr 6: 9 *m be* given them daily without fail AIT
Ezr 7:26 law of the king *m* surely **be** punished by AIT
Ezr 10:12 "You are right! We *m* **do** as you say. AIT
Ne 5: 2 us to eat and stay alive, *we m* **get** grain." AIT
Ne 13:27 *M we* **hear** now that you too are doing all this AIT
Est 1:15 what *m be* **done** to Queen Vashti? AIT
Job 2: 6 he is in your hands; but *you m* **spare** his life." AIT
Job 10: 6 that *you m* **search out** my faults and probe AIT
Job 17: 2 my eyes *m* **dwell** *on* their hostility. AIT
Job 18: 4 Or *m* the rocks *be* **moved** from their place? AIT
Job 20:10 His children *m* **make amends** *to* the poor; his AIT
Job 20:10 his own hands *m* **give back** his wealth. AIT
Job 20:18 What he toiled for *he m* **give back** uneaten AIT
Job 24: 1 Why *m* those who know him **look** in vain *for* AIT
Job 32:16 *M I* **wait**, now that they are silent, now that AIT
Job 32:20 *I m* **speak** and find relief; I must open my lips AIT
Job 32:20 find relief; *I m* **open** my lips and reply. AIT
Job 34:33 You *m* **decide**, not I; so tell me what you AIT
Job 35:14 case is before him and *you m* **wait** for him, AIT
Job 41:11 Who has a claim against me that *I m* **pay** AIT
Ps 13: 2 How long *m I* **wrestle** *with* my thoughts and AIT
Ps 32: 9 *m be* **controlled** by bit and bridle AIT
Ps 42: 9 Why *m I* **go about** mourning, oppressed by AIT
Ps 43: 2 Why *m I* **go about** mourning, oppressed by AIT
Ps 69:10 When I weep and fast, I *m* **endure** scorn; AIT
Ps 119:84 **How long m** your servant **wait** H3869+4537+3427
Pr 6:31 if he is caught, *he m* **pay** sevenfold, though it AIT
Pr 19:19 A hot-tempered person *m* **pay** the penalty AIT
Pr 24: 7 at the gate *they m* not **open** their mouths. AIT
Ecc 2:16 Like the fool, the wise too *m* **die**! AIT
Ecc 2:18 because *I m* **leave** them to the one who AIT
Ecc 2:21 then *they m* **leave** all they own to AIT
SS 5: 3 have taken off my robe—*m I* **put** it **on** again? AIT
SS 5: 3 have washed my feet—*m I* **soil** them again? AIT
Isa 24: 6 the earth; its people *m* **bear** *their* **guilt**. AIT
Isa 28:28 Grain *m* **be ground** to make bread; so one AIT
Isa 36: 7 Jerusalem, "*You m* **worship** before this altar"? AIT
Isa 38:10 prime of my life *m I* **go** through the gates of AIT
Jer 1: 7 *You m* **go** to everyone I send you to and say AIT
Jer 2:25 I love foreign gods, and *I m* **go** after them.' AIT
Jer 4:21 How long *m I* **see** the battle standard and AIT
Jer 6: 6 This city *m* **be punished**; it is filled with AIT
Jer 9:19 *We m* **leave** our land because our houses AIT
Jer 10: 5 *they* **m be carried** because they H5951+5951
Jer 10:19 "This is my sickness, and *I m* **endure** it." AIT
Jer 15:19 turn to you, but you *m* not **turn** to them. AIT
Jer 16: 2 "*You m* not **marry** and have sons or daughters AIT
Jer 23:36 But *you m* not **mention** 'a message from the AIT
Jer 23:38 even though I told you that *you m* not **claim** AIT
Jer 25:28 Almighty says: *You* **m drink** it! H9272+9272
Jer 26: 8 seized him and said, "*You* **m die**! H4637+4637
Jer 32:31 wrath that I *m* **remove** it from my sight. AIT
Jer 34:14 year each of *you m* **free** any fellow Hebrews AIT
Jer 34:14 served you six years, *you m* **let** them **go** free. AIT
Jer 35: 6 you nor your descendants *m* ever **drink** wine. AIT
Jer 35: 7 Also *you m* never **build** houses, sow seed AIT
Jer 35: 7 you *m* never **have** any of these things AIT
Jer 35: 7 of these things, but *m* always **live** in tents. AIT
Jer 35:11 *we m* **go** *to* Jerusalem to escape the AIT
Jer 35:15 "Each of *you m* **turn** from your wicked ways AIT
Jer 36:16 "*We* **m report** all these words to H5583+5583
Jer 43: 2 '*You m* not **go** *to* Egypt to settle there. AIT
Jer 49:12 deserve to drink the cup **m drink** it, H9272+9272
Jer 49:12 not go unpunished, but **m drink** it. H9272+9272
Jer 51:49 "Babylon *m* **fall** because of Israel's slain, just AIT
La 5: 4 We **m** buy the water we drink; our wood can NDT
Eze 2: 7 *You m* **speak** my words to them, whether they AIT
Eze 8:17 *M they* also **fill** the land *with* violence and AIT
Eze 23:35 you *m* **bear** the consequences of your AIT
Eze 34:18 *M* you also **trample** the rest of your pasture AIT
Eze 34:18 *M* you also **muddy** the rest with your feet AIT
Eze 34:19 *M* my flock **feed** on what you have trampled AIT
Eze 44: 2 *It m* not **be opened**; no one may enter AIT
Eze 44:10 after their idols *m* **bear** the consequences of AIT
Eze 44:12 hand that *they m* **bear** the consequences AIT
Eze 44:13 *they m* **bear** the shame of their detestable AIT
Eze 44:17 they *m* not **wear** any woolen garment while AIT
Eze 44:18 *They m* not **wear** anything that makes them AIT
Eze 44:20 " '*They m* not **shave** their heads or let their AIT
Eze 44:22 They *m* not **marry** widows or divorced AIT
Eze 44:25 " 'A priest *m* not **defile** *himself* by going near AIT
Eze 44:26 After he is cleansed, *he m* **wait** seven days. AIT
Eze 44:31 The priests *m* not **eat** anything, whether bird AIT
Eze 46:18 The prince *m* not **take** any of the inheritance AIT
Eze 48:14 *They m* not **sell** or exchange any of it. This is AIT
Eze 48:14 of the land and *m* not **pass into other hands**, AIT
Da 3: 5 *you m* **fall down** and worship the image of AIT
Da 3:10 kinds of music *m* **fall down** and worship the AIT
Da 6:26 part of my kingdom *people* **m** fear and A10201
Da 11:36 what has been determined *m* **take place**. AIT
Hos 3: 3 you *m* not **be a prostitute** or be intimate with AIT
Hos 10: 2 is deceitful, and now *they m* **bear** *their* **guilt**. AIT
Hos 10:11 Ephraim, Judah *m* **plow**, and Jacob must AIT
Hos 10:11 and Jacob *m* **break up the ground**. AIT
Hos 12: 6 But you *m* **return** to your God; maintain love AIT
Hos 13:16 The people of Samaria *m* **bear** *their* **guilt** AIT
Am 6:10 *We m* not **mention** the name of the LORD." AIT
Mic 4:10 now *you m* **leave** the city to camp in the AIT
Hab 1: 2 LORD, *m I* **call for help**, but you do not AIT
Hab 2: 6 How long **m** this go on?' NDT
Zec 13: 3 say to them, '*You m* **die**, because you have AIT
Mt 5:31 divorces his wife *m* **give** her a certificate of AIT
Mt 16:21 disciples that he **m** go to Jerusalem and G1256
Mt 16:21 that he **m** be killed and on the third day NDT
Mt 16:24 to be my disciple *m* **deny** themselves and AIT
Mt 17:10 of the law say that Elijah **m** come first?" G1256
Mt 18: 7 Such things **m** come, but woe to the person G340
Mt 19:16 what good thing *m I* **do** to get eternal life?" AIT
Mt 20:26 become great among you *m* **be** your servant, AIT
Mt 20:27 whoever wants to be first *m* **be** your slave— AIT
Mt 22:24 his brother *m* **marry** the widow and raise up AIT
Mt 23: 3 So *you m be* **careful** to do everything they tell AIT
Mt 24: 6 Such things **m** happen, but the end is still G1256
Mt 24:44 So you also *m* **be** ready, because the Son of AIT
Mt 26:54 fulfilled that say it **m** happen in this way?" G1256
Mk 8:31 that the Son of Man **m** suffer many things G1256
Mk 8:31 and *that* he *m be* **killed** and after three days AIT
Mk 8:34 to be my disciple *m* **deny** themselves and AIT
Mk 9:11 of the law say that Elijah **m** come first?" G1256
Mk 9:12 that the Son of Man *m* **suffer** much and be AIT
Mk 9:35 who wants to be first *m* **be** the very last, AIT
Mk 10:17 he asked, "what *m I* **do** to inherit eternal life?" AIT
Mk 10:43 become great among you *m* **be** your servant, AIT
Mk 10:44 whoever wants to be first *m* **be** slave of all. AIT
Mk 12:19 the man *m* **marry** the widow and raise up AIT
Mk 13: 7 Such things **m** happen, but the end is still G1256
Mk 13: 9 "You *m* **be on** your **guard**. You will be AIT
Mk 13:10 And the gospel **m** first be preached to all G1256
Mk 14:49 But the Scriptures **m** be fulfilled." G2671
Lk 4:43 "I **m** proclaim the good news of the G1256
Lk 5:38 new wine **m be poured** into new G1064
Lk 9:22 "The Son of Man **m** suffer many things G1256
Lk 9:22 and he *m be* **killed** and on the third day be AIT
Lk 9:23 to be my disciple *m* **deny** themselves and AIT
Lk 10:25 he asked, "what *m I* **do** to inherit eternal life?" AIT
Lk 12:40 You also *m* **be** ready, because the Son of AIT
Lk 13:33 I **m** press on today and tomorrow and the G1256
Lk 14:18 a field, and I **m** go and see it. G2400+340
Lk 17: 4 to you saying 'I repent,' *you m* **forgive** them." AIT
Lk 17:25 But first he **m** suffer many things and be G1256
Lk 18:18 what *m I* **do** to inherit eternal life? AIT
Lk 19: 5 I **m** stay at your house today. G1256
Lk 20:28 the man *m* **marry** the widow and raise up AIT
Lk 21: 9 These things **m** happen first, but the end G1256
Lk 22:37 I tell you that *this* **m** be fulfilled in me G1256
Lk 24: 7 'The Son of Man **m** be delivered over to G1256
Lk 24:44 Everything **m** be fulfilled that is written G1256
Jn 3: 7 at my saying, 'You **m** be born again. G1256
Jn 3:14 so the Son of Man **m** be lifted up, G1256
Jn 3:30 He **m** become greater; I must become less." G1256
Jn 3:30 He must become greater; I *m become* **less**." AIT
Jn 4:20 that the place where *we* **m** worship is in G1256
Jn 4:24 his worshipers **m** worship in the Spirit G1256
Jn 6:28 "What *m we* **do** to do the works God requires AIT
Jn 9: 4 we **m** do the works of him who sent me. G1256
Jn 10:16 of this sheep pen. I **m** bring them also G1256
Jn 12:26 Whoever serves me *m* **follow** me; and where I AIT
Jn 12:34 you say, 'The Son of Man **m** be lifted up'? G1256
Jn 13:34 I have loved you, so you *m* **love** one another. AIT
Jn 15: 4 by itself; it **m** remain in the vine. G1569+3590
Jn 15:27 And you also *m* **testify**, for you have been AIT
Jn 19: 7 according to that law *he* **m** die G4053
Jn 21:22 what is that to you? You *m* **follow** me." AIT
Ac 1:22 For one of these *m* **become** a witness with us AIT
Ac 3:21 Heaven **m** receive him until the time G1256
Ac 3:22 *you m* **listen** to everything he tells you. AIT
Ac 4:12 to mankind by which we **m** be saved." G1256
Ac 4:17 *we m* **warn** them to speak no longer to AIT
Ac 5:29 "*We* **m** obey God rather than human G1256
Ac 9: 6 and you will be told what you **m** do." G1256
Ac 9:16 him how much he **m** suffer for my name." G1256
Ac 12:15 that it was so, they said, "*It m* **be** his angel." AIT
Ac 14:22 "We **m** go through many hardships to G1256
Ac 15: 5 "The Gentiles **m** be circumcised and G1256
Ac 16:30 "Sirs, what **m** I do to be saved?" G1256
Ac 19:21 he said, "I **m** visit Rome also. G1256
Ac 19:39 bring up, *it m be* **settled** in a legal assembly. AIT
Ac 20:21 Greeks that they **m** turn to God in NDT
Ac 20:35 kind of hard work *we* **m** help the weak, G1256
Ac 23:11 Jerusalem, so you **m** also testify in Rome." G1256
Ac 27:24 You **m** stand trial before Caesar; and God G1256
Ac 27:26 we **m** run aground on some island." G1256
Ac 28: 4 "This man **m** be a murderer; for G4122
Ro 12: 9 Love **m** be sincere. Hate what is evil; cling NDT
Ro 14: 3 *m* not **treat with contempt** the one AIT
Ro 14: 3 eat everything *m* not **judge** the one who AIT
1Co 4: 2 who have been given a trust *m* **prove** faithful. AIT
1Co 5:11 to you *that you m* not **associate with** anyone AIT
1Co 7:10 A wife *m* not **separate** from her husband. AIT
1Co 7:11 *she m* **remain** unmarried or else be AIT
1Co 7:11 And a husband *m* not **divorce** his wife. AIT
1Co 7:12 willing to live with him, *he m* not **divorce** her. AIT
1Co 7:13 to live with her, *she m* not **divorce** him. AIT
1Co 7:39 she wishes, but he **m** belong to the Lord. NDT
1Co 14:26 Everything *m be* **done** so that the church may AIT
1Co 14:27 one at a time, and someone *m* **interpret**. AIT

1Co 14:34 to speak, but m be in submission, as the law AIT
1Co 15:25 For he m reign until he has put all his G1256
1Co 15:53 For the perishable m clothe itself with the G1256
2Co 5:10 For we m all appear before the judgment G1256
2Co 11:30 If I m boast, I will boast of the things that G1256
2Co 12: 1 I m go on boasting. Although there is G1256
2Co 13: 1 "Every matter m be established by the AIT
Eph 4:17 that you m no longer live as the Gentiles do AIT
Eph 4:25 each of you m put off falsehood and speak AIT
Eph 4:28 who has been stealing m steal no longer, AIT
Eph 4:28 no longer, but m work, doing something AIT
Eph 5: 3 you there m not be even a hint of sexual AIT
Eph 5:33 each one of you also m love his wife as he AIT
Eph 5:33 the wife m respect her husband. G2671
Col 3: 8 But now you m also rid yourselves of all such AIT
1Ti 2:12 authority over a man; she m be quiet. AIT
1Ti 3: 4 He m manage his own family well and see AIT
1Ti 3: 4 he m do so in a manner worthy of full NDT
1Ti 3: 6 He m not be a recent convert, or he may NDT
1Ti 3: 7 He m also have a good reputation with G1256
1Ti 3: 9 They m keep hold of the deep truths of the AIT
1Ti 3:10 They m first be tested; and then if there is AIT
1Ti 3:12 A deacon m be faithful to his wife and must AIT
1Ti 3:12 to his wife and m manage his children and AIT
2Ti 2:19 of the Lord m turn away from wickedness AIT
2Ti 2:24 the Lord's servant m not be quarrelsome G1256
2Ti 2:24 be quarrelsome but m be kind to everyone, NDT
2Ti 2:25 Opponents m be gently instructed, in the AIT
Titus 1: 6 An elder m be blameless, faithful to his wife AIT
Titus 1: 7 God's household, he m be blameless G1256
Titus 1: 8 he m be hospitable, one who loves NDT
Titus 1: 9 He m hold firmly to the trustworthy message AIT
Titus 1:11 They m be silenced, because they are G1256
Titus 2: 1 m teach what is appropriate to sound AIT
Titus 3:14 Our people m learn to devote themselves to AIT
Heb 2: 1 We m pay the most careful attention G1256
Heb 4:13 eyes of him to whom we m give account. NDT
Heb 7:12 the law m be changed also. G1666+340
Heb 11: 6 who comes to him m believe that he G1256
Heb 12:20 the mountain, it m be stoned to death." AIT
Heb 13:17 over you as those who m give an account. AIT
Jas 1: 6 when you ask, you m believe and not doubt NDT
Jas 2: 1 Lord Jesus Christ m not show favoritism. AIT
1Pe 3:10 good days m keep their tongue from evil AIT
1Pe 3:11 They m turn from evil and do good; they AIT
1Pe 3:11 do good; they m seek peace and pursue it. AIT
1Pe 5: 2 not because you m, but because you are G339
2Pe 1:20 you m understand that no prophecy of AIT
2Pe 3: 3 you m understand that in the last days AIT
1Jn 2: 6 claims to live in him m live as Jesus did. G4053
1Jn 4:21 who loves God m also love their brother AIT
Rev 1: 1 his servants what m soon take place. G1256
Rev 4: 1 I will show you what m take place after G1256
Rev 10:11 "You m prophesy again about many G1256
Rev 11: 5 anyone who wants to harm them m die. G1256
Rev 17:10 he m remain for only a little while. G1256
Rev 20: 3 he m be set free for a short time. G1256
Rev 22: 6 the things that m soon take place. G1256

MUSTACHE (3)
2Sa 19:24 feet or trimmed his m or washed his H8559
Eze 24:17 do not cover your m and beard or eat the H8559
Eze 24:22 will not cover your m and beard or eat the H8559

MUSTARD (5)
Mt 13:31 "The kingdom of heaven is like a m seed G4983
Mt 17:20 if you have faith as small as a m seed G4983
Mk 4:31 It is like a m seed, which is the smallest of G4983
Lk 13:19 It is like a m seed, which a man took and G4983
Lk 17: 6 "If you have faith as small as a m seed G4983

MUSTER (5) [MUSTERED, MUSTERING]
1Sa 14:17 "M the forces and see who has left us." H7212
2Sa 12:28 Now m the rest of the troops and besiege H665
Pr 24: 5 who have knowledge m their strength. H599
Da 11:13 the king of the North will m another army, H6641
Am 2:14 the strong will not m their strength H599

MUSTERED (16) [MUSTER]
Nu 21:23 He m his entire army and marched out into H665
Jos 8:10 Early the next morning Joshua m his army, H7212
Jdg 11:20 He m all his troops and encamped at H665
Jdg 20:17 m four hundred thousand swordsmen H7212
1Sa 11: 8 When Saul m them at Bezek, the men of H7212
1Sa 15: 4 the men and m them at Telaim— H7212
2Sa 12:29 So David m the entire army and went to H665
2Sa 18: 1 David m the men who were with him and H7212
1Ki 12:21 he m all Judah and the tribe of Benjamin H7735
1Ki 20: 1 king of Aram m his entire army. H7695
1Ki 20:26 spring Ben-Hadad m the Arameans and H7212
1Ki 20:27 the Israelites were also m and given H7212
1Ch 19: 7 the Ammonites were m from their towns H665
2Ch 11: 1 in Jerusalem, he m Judah and Benjamin H7735
2Ch 25: 5 He then m those twenty years old or more H7212
2Ch 26:11 to their numbers as m by Jeiel the H7213

MUSTERING (1) [MUSTER]
Isa 13: 4 The LORD Almighty is m an army for war. H7212

MUTE (13)
Ex 4:11 Who makes them deaf or m? Who gives H522
Ps 38:13 cannot hear, like the m, who cannot speak; H522
Isa 35: 6 like a deer, and the m tongue shout for joy. H522
Isa 56:10 they are all m dogs, they cannot bark; H522
Mt 9:33 the man who had been m spoke. G3273
Mt 12:22 man who was blind and m, G3273
Mt 15:30 the crippled, the m and many others, and G3273
Mt 15:31 amazed when they saw the m speaking, G3273
Mk 7:37 makes the deaf hear and the m speak." G228
Mk 9:25 "You deaf and m spirit," he said, "I G228
Lk 11:14 was driving out a demon that was m. G3273
Lk 11:14 the man who had been m spoke, and G3273
1Co 12: 2 were influenced and led astray to m idols. G936

MUTILATORS (1)
Php 3: 2 those evildoers, those m of the flesh. G2961

MUTTER (3) [MUTTERED, MUTTERS]
Isa 8:19 who whisper and m, should not a people H2047
La 3:62 whisper and m against me all day H2053
Lk 19: 7 All the people saw this and began to m G1339

MUTTERED (1) [MUTTER]
Lk 15: 2 Pharisees and the teachers of the law m, G1339

MUTTERS (1) [MUTTER]
Isa 59: 3 and your tongue m wicked things. H2047

MUTUAL (4) [MUTUALLY]
Ro 14:19 leads to peace and to m edification. G1650+253
1Co 7: 5 perhaps by m consent and for a time, G5247
2Pe 1: 7 to godliness, m affection; and to mutual G5789
2Pe 1: 7 mutual affection; and to m affection, love. G5789

MUTUALLY (1) [MUTUAL]
Ro 1:12 that you and I may be m encouraged by G5220

MUZZLE (4)
Dt 25: 4 Do not m an ox while it is treading out H2888
Ps 39: 1 I will put a m on my mouth while in the H4727
1Co 9: 9 "Do not m an ox while it is treading out G3055
1Ti 5:18 "Do not m an ox while it is treading out G5821

MY (4637) [I] See Index of Articles Etc.

MYRA (1)
Ac 27: 5 Pamphylia, we landed at M in Lycia. G3688

MYRIADS (1)
Dt 33: 2 He came with m of holy ones from the H8047

MYRRH (18)
Ge 37:25 balm and m, and they were on H4320
Ge 43:11 some spices and m, some pistachio nuts H4320
Ex 30:23 500 shekels of liquid m, half as much H5255
Est 2:12 months with oil of m and six with H5255
Ps 45: 8 are fragrant with m and aloes and cassia; H5255
Pr 7:17 I have perfumed my bed with m, aloes H5255
SS 1:13 to me a sachet of m resting between my H5255
SS 3: 6 perfumed with m and incense made from H5255
SS 4: 6 go to the mountain of m and to the hill of H5255
SS 4:14 with m and aloes and all the finest spices. H5255
SS 5: 1 I have gathered my m with my spice. H5255
SS 5: 5 my hands dripped with m, my fingers H5255
SS 5: 5 my fingers with flowing m, on the handles H5255
SS 5:13 His lips are like lilies dripping with m. H5255
Mt 2:11 with gifts of gold, frankincense and m. G5043
Mk 15:23 Then they offered him wine mixed with m G5046
Jn 19:39 brought a mixture of m and aloes, G5043
Rev 18:13 of incense, m and frankincense, of wine G3693

MYRTLE (5) [MYRTLES]
Isa 41:19 the acacia, the m and the olive. H2072
Isa 55:13 instead of briers the m will grow. H2072
Zec 1: 8 standing among the m trees in a ravine. H2072
Zec 1:10 standing among the m trees explained, H2072
Zec 1:11 who was standing among the m trees, H2072

MYRTLES (1) [MYRTLE]
Ne 8:15 olive trees, and from m, palms and shade H2072

MYSELF (155) [I, SELF] See Index of Articles Etc.

MYSIA (2)
Ac 16: 7 When they came to the border of M, they G3695
Ac 16: 8 So they passed by M and went down to G3695

MYSTERIES (7) [MYSTERY]
Job 11: 7 "Can you fathom the m of God? Can you H2984
Da 2:28 there is a God in heaven who reveals m. A10661
Da 2:29 the revealer of m showed you what is A10661
Da 2:47 the Lord of kings and a revealer of m, A10661
1Co 4: 1 entrusted with the m God has revealed. G3696
1Co 13: 2 can fathom all m and all knowledge, G3696
1Co 14: 2 they utter m by the Spirit. G3696

MYSTERY (26) [MYSTERIES]
Da 2:18 the God of heaven concerning this m, A10661
Da 2:19 During the night the m was revealed to A10661
Da 2:27 to the king the m he has asked about, A10661
Da 2:30 this m has been revealed to me A10661
Da 2:47 you were able to reveal this m. A10661
Da 4: 9 and no m is too difficult for you. A10661
Ro 11:25 I do not want you to be ignorant of this m G3696
Ro 16:25 the revelation of the m hidden for long G3696
1Co 2: 7 a m that has been hidden and that God G3696
1Co 15:51 I tell you a m: We will not all sleep, G3696
Eph 1: 9 made known to us the m of his will G3696
Eph 3: 3 the m made known to me by revelation G3696
Eph 3: 4 my insight into the m of Christ, G3696
Eph 3: 6 This m is that through the gospel the NDT
Eph 3: 9 to everyone the administration of this m, G3696
Eph 5:32 This is a profound m—but I am talking G3696
Eph 6:19 make known the m of the gospel, G3696
Col 1:26 the m that has been kept hidden for ages G3696
Col 1:27 the Gentiles the glorious riches of this m, G3696
Col 2: 2 in order that they may know the m of God G3696
Col 4: 3 so that we may proclaim the m of Christ G3696
1Ti 3:16 the m from which true godliness springs is G3696
Rev 1:20 The m of the seven stars that you saw in G3696
Rev 10: 7 the m of God will be accomplished G3696
Rev 17: 5 name written on her forehead was a m: G3696
Rev 17: 7 explain to you the m of the woman and of G3696

MYTHS (4)
1Ti 1: 4 to devote themselves to m and endless G3680
1Ti 4: 7 to do with godless m and old wives' tales; G3680
2Ti 4: 4 away from the truth and turn aside to m. G3680
Titus 1:14 attention to Jewish m or to the merely G3680

N

NAAM (1)
1Ch 4:15 Elah and N. The son of Elah: H5839

NAAMAH (5)
Ge 4:22 Tubal-Cain's sister was N. H5841
Jos 15:41 Beth Dagon, N and Makkedah—sixteen H5842
1Ki 14:21 His mother's name was N; she was an H5841
1Ki 14:31 His mother's name was N; she was an H5841
2Ch 12:13 His mother's name was N; she was an H5841

NAAMAN (20) [NAAMAN'S, NAAMITE]
Ge 46:21 Ashbel, Gera, N, Ehi, Rosh, Muppim, H5845
Nu 26:40 of Bela through Ard and N were: H5845
Nu 26:40 Ardite clan; through N, the Naamite clan. H5845
2Ki 5: 1 Now N was commander of the army of the H5845
2Ki 5: 4 N went to his master and told him what the NDT
2Ki 5: 5 So N left, taking with him ten talents of NDT
2Ki 5: 6 sending my servant N to you so that you H5845
2Ki 5: 9 So N went with his horses and chariots H5845
2Ki 5:11 But N went away angry and said, "I H5845
2Ki 5:15 Then N and all his attendants went back H2085S
2Ki 5:16 And even though N urged him, he refused. NDT
2Ki 5:17 you will not," said N, "please let me, your H5845
2Ki 5:19 After N had traveled some distance NDT
2Ki 5:20 "My master was too easy on N, this H5845
2Ki 5:21 So Gehazi hurried after N. When Naaman H5845
2Ki 5:21 When N saw him running toward him, he H5845
2Ki 5:23 two talents," said N. He urged Gehazi to H5845
1Ch 8: 4 Abishua, N, Ahoah, H5845
1Ch 8: 7 N, Ahijah, and Gera, who deported them H5845
Lk 4:27 of them was cleansed—only N the Syrian." G3722

NAAMAN'S (3) [NAAMAN]
2Ki 5: 2 girl from Israel, and she served N wife. H5845
2Ki 5:13 N servants went to him and said, "My H2257S
2Ki 5:27 N leprosy will cling to you and to your H5845

NAAMATHITE (4)
Job 2:11 Bildad the Shuhite and Zophar the N H5847
Job 11: 1 Then Zophar the N replied: H5847
Job 20: 1 Then Zophar the N replied: H5847
Job 42: 9 Zophar the N did what the LORD told H5847

NAAMITE (1) [NAAMAN]
Nu 26:40 Ardite clan; through Naaman, the N clan. H5844

NAARAH (4)
Jos 16: 7 went down from Janoah to Ataroth and N, H5857
1Ch 4: 5 of Tekoa had two wives, Helah and N. H5856
1Ch 4: 6 N bore him Ahuzzam, Hepher, Temeni H5856
1Ch 4: 6 These were the descendants of N. H5856

NAARAI (1)
1Ch 11:37 Hezro the Carmelite, N son of Ezbai, H5858

NAARAN (1)
1Ch 7:28 surrounding villages, N to the east, Gezer H5860

NAASHON, NAASSON (KJV) NAHSHON

NABAL (18) [NABAL'S]
1Sa 25: 3 His name was N and his wife's name was H5573
1Sa 25: 4 he heard that N was shearing sheep. H5573
1Sa 25: 5 "Go up to N at Carmel and greet him in H5573
1Sa 25: 9 they gave N this message in David's H5573
1Sa 25:10 N answered David's servants, "Who is this H5573
1Sa 25:19 But she did not tell her husband N. H5573
1Sa 25:25 attention, my lord, to that wicked man N. H5573
1Sa 25:26 are intent on harming my lord be like N. H5573
1Sa 25:34 male belonging to N would have been H5573
1Sa 25:36 When Abigail went to N, he was in the H5573
1Sa 25:37 the morning, when N was sober, his wife H5573
1Sa 25:38 days later, the LORD struck N and he died. H5573
1Sa 25:39 When David heard that N was dead, he H5573
1Sa 25:39 my cause against N for treating me with H5573
1Sa 27: 3 Abigail of Carmel, the widow of N. H5573

1Sa 30: 5 Abigail, the widow of **N** of Carmel. H5573
2Sa 2: 2 Abigail, the widow of **N** of Carmel. H5573
2Sa 3: 3 son of Abigail the widow of **N** of Carmel; H5573

NABAL'S (2) [NABAL]
1Sa 25:14 servants told Abigail, **N** wife, "David sent H5573
1Sa 25:39 has brought **N** wrongdoing down on H5573

NABOTH (17) [NABOTH'S]
1Ki 21: 1 a vineyard belonging to **N** the Jezreelite. H5559
1Ki 21: 2 Ahab said to **N**, "Let me have your H5559
1Ki 21: 3 But **N** replied, "The LORD forbid that I H5559
1Ki 21: 4 angry because **N** the Jezreelite had H5559
1Ki 21: 6 "Because I said to **N** the Jezreelite, 'Sell H5559
1Ki 21: 7 get you the vineyard of **N** the Jezreelite." H5559
1Ki 21: 9 of fasting and seat **N** in a prominent H5559
1Ki 21:12 a fast and seated **N** in a prominent place H5559
1Ki 21:13 charges against **N** before the people, H5559
1Ki 21:13 "**N** has cursed both God and the king." H5559
1Ki 21:14 "**N** has been stoned to death." H5559
1Ki 21:15 Jezebel heard that **N** had been stoned to H5559
1Ki 21:15 of the vineyard of **N** the Jezreelite that he H5559
1Ki 21:16 When Ahab heard that **N** was dead, he H5559
2Ki 9:21 that had belonged to **N** the Jezreelite. H5559
2Ki 9:25 field that belonged to **N** the Jezreelite. H5559
2Ki 9:26 I saw the blood of **N** and the blood of his H5559

NABOTH'S (5) [NABOTH]
1Ki 21: 8 nobles who lived in **N** city with him. H5559
1Ki 21:11 nobles who lived in **N** city did as Jezebel H2257S
1Ki 21:16 down to take possession of **N** vineyard. H5559
1Ki 21:18 He is now in **N** vineyard, where he has H5559
1Ki 21:19 the place where dogs licked up **N** blood, H5559

NACHOR (KJV) NAHOR

NACON (NIV84) NAKON

NADAB (20) [NADAB'S]
Ex 6:23 she bore him **N** and Abihu, Eleazar H5606
Ex 24: 1 you and Aaron, **N** and Abihu, and seventy H5606
Ex 24: 9 Moses and Aaron, **N** and Abihu, and the H5606
Ex 28: 1 along with his sons **N** and Abihu, Eleazar H5606
Lev 10: 1 Aaron's sons **N** and Abihu took their H5606
Nu 3: 2 sons of Aaron were **N** the firstborn and H5606
Nu 3: 4 **N** and Abihu, however, died before the H5606
Nu 26:60 Aaron was the father of **N** and Abihu H5606
Nu 26:61 But **N** and Abihu died when they made H5606
1Ki 14:20 And **N** his son succeeded him as king H5606
1Ki 15:25 **N** son of Jeroboam became king of Israel H5606
1Ki 15:27 while **N** and all Israel were besieging it. H5606
1Ki 15:28 Baasha killed **N** in the third year of Asa H2084S
1Ch 2:28 The sons of Shammai: **N** and Abishur. H5606
1Ch 2:30 The sons of **N**: Seled and Appaim. Seled H5606
1Ch 6: 3 The sons of Aaron: **N**, Abihu, Eleazar H5606
1Ch 8:30 followed by Zur, Kish, Baal, Ner, **N**, H5606
1Ch 9:36 followed by Zur, Kish, Baal, Ner, **N**, H5606
1Ch 24: 1 The sons of Aaron were **N**, Abihu, Eleazar H5606
1Ch 24: 2 But **N** and Abihu died before their father H5606

NADAB'S (1) [NADAB]
1Ki 15:31 As for the other events of **N** reign, and all H5606

NAGGAI (1)
Lk 3:25 of Nahum, the son of Esli, the son *of* **N**, *G3710*

NAGGING (2)
Jdg 16:16 With such **n** she prodded him day after H7439
Pr 21:19 than with a quarrelsome and **n** wife. H4088

NAHALAL (2)
Jos 19:15 were Kattath, **N**, Shimron, Idalah and H5634
Jos 21:35 Dimnah and **N**, together with their H5634

NAHALIEL (2)
Nu 21:19 from Mattanah to **N**, from Nahaliel to H5712
Nu 21:19 Mattanah to Nahaliel, from **N** to Bamoth, H5712

NAHALOL (1)
Jdg 1:30 out the Canaanites living in Kitron or **N**, H5636

NAHAM (1)
1Ch 4:19 the sister of **N**: the father of Keilah H5715

NAHAMANI (1)
Ne 7: 7 Azariah, Raamiah, **N**, Mordecai, Bilshan H5720

NAHARAI (2)
2Sa 23:37 the Ammonite, **N** the Beerothite, the H5726
1Ch 11:39 Zelek the Ammonite, **N** the Berothite, the H5726

NAHARAIM See ARAM NAHARAIM

NAHASH (8) [IR NAHASH]
1Sa 11: 1 **N** the Ammonite went up and besieged H5731
1Sa 11: 2 But **N** the Ammonite replied, "I will make H5731
1Sa 12:12 when you saw that **N** king of the H5731
2Sa 10: 2 "I will show kindness to Hanun son of **N** H5731
2Sa 17:25 the daughter of **N** and sister of Zeruiah H5731
2Sa 17:27 Shobi son of **N** from Rabbah of the H5731
1Ch 19: 1 of time, **N** king of the Ammonites died H5731
1Ch 19: 2 "I will show kindness to Hanun son of **N** H5731

NAHATH (5)
Ge 36:13 The sons of Reuel: **N**, Zerah, Shammah H5740
Ge 36:17 Chiefs **N**, Zerah, Shammah H5740
1Ch 1:37 The sons of Reuel: **N**, Zerah, Shammah H5740
1Ch 6:26 his son, Zophai his son, **N** his son, H5740
2Ch 31:13 Azaziah, **N**, Asahel, Jerimoth H5740

NAHBI (1)
Nu 13:14 the tribe of Naphtali, **N** son of Vophsi; H5696

NAHOR (17) [NAHOR'S]
Ge 11:22 lived 30 years, he became the father of **N**. H5701
Ge 11:23 And after he became the father of **N** H5701
Ge 11:24 When **N** had lived 29 years, he became H5701
Ge 11:25 **N** lived 119 years and had other sons H5701
Ge 11:26 the father of Abram, **N** and Haran. H5701
Ge 11:27 the father of Abram, **N** and Haran. H5701
Ge 11:29 Abram and **N** both married. The name of H5701
Ge 22:20 she has borne sons to your brother **N**: H5701
Ge 22:23 these eight sons to Abraham's brother **N**. H5701
Ge 24:10 made his way to the town of **N**. H5701
Ge 24:15 who was the wife of Abraham's brother **N**. H5701
Ge 24:24 of Bethuel, the son that Milkah bore to **N**." H5701
Ge 24:47 'The daughter of Bethuel son of **N**, whom H5701
Ge 31:53 the God of Abraham and the God of **N**, H5701
Jos 24: 2 Terah the father of Abraham and **N**, H5701
1Ch 1:26 **N**, Terah H5701
Lk 3:34 Abraham, the son of Terah, the son *of* **N**, *G3732*

NAHOR'S (2) [NAHOR]
Ge 11:29 the name of **N** wife was Milkah; she H5701
Ge 29: 5 "Do you know Laban, **N** grandson? H5701

NAHSHON (13)
Ex 6:23 daughter of Amminadab and sister of **N** H5732
Nu 1: 7 from Judah, **N** son of Amminadab; H5732
Nu 2: 3 people of Judah is **N** son of Amminadab. H5732
Nu 7:12 the first day was **N** son of Amminadab of H5732
Nu 7:17 was the offering of **N** son of Amminadab. H5732
Nu 10:14 **N** son of Amminadab was in command. H5732
Ru 4:20 Amminadab the father of **N**, Nahshon the H5732
Ru 4:20 of Nahshon, **N** the father of Salmon, H5732
1Ch 2:10 Amminadab the father of **N**, the H5732
1Ch 2:11 **N** was the father of Salmon, Salmon the H5732
Mt 1: 4 Amminadab the father of **N**, Nahshon the *G3709*
Mt 1: 4 father of Nahshon, **N** the father of Salmon *G3709*
Lk 3:32 of Boaz, the son of Salmon, the son *of* **N**, *G3709*

NAHUM (2)
Na 1: 1 The book of the vision of **N** the Elkoshite. H5699
Lk 3:25 son of Amos, the son *of* **N**, the son of Esli, *G3725*

NAIL (1) [NAILING, NAILS]
Jn 20:25 "Unless I see the **n** marks in his hands *G2464*

NAILING (2) [NAIL]
Ac 2:23 put him to death *by* **n** him **to** *the* **cross**. *G4699*
Col 2:14 he has taken it away, **n** it **to** the cross. *G4669*

NAILS (8) [NAIL]
Dt 21:12 have her shave her head, trim her **n** H7632
1Ch 22: 3 of iron to make **n** for the doors of the H5021
2Ch 3: 9 The gold **n** weighed fifty shekels. He also H5021
Ecc 12:11 sayings like firmly embedded **n**— H5383
Isa 41: 7 The *other* **n down** the idol so H2616+928+5021
Jer 10: 4 it with hammer and **n** so it will not totter. H5021
Da 4:33 of an eagle and his **n** like the claws of a A10303
Jn 20:25 put my finger where the **n** were, *G2464*

NAIN (1)
Lk 7:11 Jesus went to a town called **N**, and his *G3723*

NAIOTH (6)
1Sa 19:18 Samuel went to **N** and stayed there. H5766
1Sa 19:19 came to Saul: "David is in **N** at Ramah"; H5766
1Sa 19:22 "Over in **N** at Ramah," they said H5766
1Sa 19:23 So Saul went to **N** at Ramah. But the H5766
1Sa 19:23 along prophesying until he came to **N**. H5766
1Sa 20: 1 David fled from **N** at Ramah and went to H5766

NAIVE (1)
Ro 16:18 flattery they deceive the minds *of* **n** *people*. *G179*

NAKED (44) [HALF-NAKED, NAKEDNESS]
Ge 2:25 Adam and his wife were both **n**, and they H6873
Ge 3: 7 they realized they were **n**; so they H6567
Ge 3:10 I was afraid because I was **n**; so I hid." H6567
Ge 3:11 he said, "Who told you that you were **n**? H6567
Ge 9:22 saw his father **n** and told his two brothers H6872
Ge 9:23 covered their father's **n body**. H6872
Ge 9:23 so that they would not see their father **n**. H6872
1Sa 19:24 He lay **n** all that day and all that night H6873
2Ch 28:15 the plunder they clothed all who were **n**. H5122
Job 1:21 "**N** I came from my mother's womb, and H6873
Job 1:21 my mother's womb, and **n** I will depart. H6873
Job 22: 6 people of their clothing, leaving them **n**. H6873
Job 24: 7 they spend the night **n**; they have nothing H6873
Job 24:10 clothes, they go about **n**; they carry the H6873
Job 26: 6 The realm of the dead is **n** before God H6873
Ecc 5:15 Everyone comes **n** from their mother's H6873
Isa 57: 8 you looked with lust on their **n bodies**. H3338
Isa 58: 7 when you see the **n**, to clothe them, H6873
La 1: 8 they have all seen her **n**; she herself H6872
La 4:21 passed; you will be drunk and **stripped n**. H6867
Eze 16: 7 grown, yet you were **stark n**. H6567+2256+6880
Eze 16: 8 over you and covered your **n body**. H6872
Eze 16:22 when you were **n** and bare, kicking H6567
Eze 16:36 exposed your **n body** in your H6872
Eze 16:37 and they will see you **stark n**. H3972+6872
Eze 16:39 and leave you **stark n**. H6567+2256+6880
Eze 18: 7 hungry and provides clothing for the **n**. H6567
Eze 18:16 hungry and provides clothing for the **n**. H6567
Eze 23:10 They stripped her **n**, took away her sons H6872
Eze 23:18 openly and exposed her **n body**, H6872
Eze 23:29 They will leave you **stark n** H6567+2256+6880
Hos 2: 3 I will strip her **n** and make her as bare as H6873
Hos 2: 9 my linen, intended to cover her **n body**. H6872
Am 2:16 bravest warriors will flee **n** on that day," H6873
Mic 1: 8 wail; I will go about barefoot and **n**. H6873
Mic 1:11 Pass by **n** and in shame, you who live in H6880
Hab 2:15 so that he can gaze on their **n bodies**! H5067
Mk 14:52 he fled **n**, leaving his garment behind. *G1218*
Ac 19:16 they ran out of the house **n** and bleeding. *G1218*
2Co 5: 3 we are clothed, we will not be found **n**. *G1218*
2Co 11:27 without food; I have been cold and **n**. *G1219*
Rev 3:17 are wretched, pitiful, poor, blind and **n**. *G1218*
Rev 16:15 so as not to go **n** and be shamefully *G1218*
Rev 17:16 will bring her to ruin and leave her **n**; *G1218*

NAKEDNESS (6) [NAKED]
Dt 28:48 thirst, in **n** and dire poverty, you H6567
Isa 47: 3 Your **n** will be exposed and your shame H6872
Na 3: 5 the nations your **n** and the kingdoms your H5113
Hab 2:16 Drink and *let your* **n be exposed**! The cup H6887
Ro 8:35 famine or **n** or danger or sword? *G1219*
Rev 3:18 so you can cover your shameful **n**; and *G1219*

NAKON (1)
2Sa 6: 6 they came to the threshing floor of **N**, H5789

NAME (773) [NAME'S, NAMED, NAMELESS, NAMELY, NAMES]
Ge 2:11 The **n** *of* the first is the Pishon; it winds H9005
Ge 2:13 The **n** *of* the second river is the Gihon; it H9005
Ge 2:14 The **n** *of* the third river is the Tigris; it runs H9005
Ge 2:19 to the man to see what *he would* **n** them; H7924
Ge 2:19 called each living creature, that was its **n**. H9005
Ge 4:21 His brother's **n** was Jubal; he was the H9005
Ge 4:26 people began to call on the **n** *of* the LORD. H9005
Ge 11: 4 so that we may make a **n** for ourselves H9005
Ge 11:29 The **n** *of* Abram's wife was Sarai, and the H9005
Ge 11:29 the **n** *of* Nahor's wife was Milkah H9005
Ge 12: 2 I will make your **n** great, and you will H9005
Ge 12: 8 the LORD and called on the **n** *of* the LORD. H9005
Ge 13: 4 There Abram called on the **n** *of* the LORD. H9005
Ge 16:11 *You shall* **n** him Ishmael, for the H9005+7924
Ge 16:13 She gave this **n** to the LORD who spoke to H9005
Ge 16:15 Abram gave the **n** Ishmael *to* the son she H9005
Ge 17: 5 called Abram; your **n** will be Abraham, for H9005
Ge 17:15 to call her Sarai; her **n** will be Sarah. H9005
Ge 21: 3 Abraham gave the **n** Isaac to the son H9005
Ge 21:33 there he called on the **n** *of* the LORD H9005
Ge 22:24 His concubine, whose **n** was Reumah, also H9005
Ge 25: 1 taken another wife, whose **n** was Keturah. H9005
Ge 26:25 there and called on the **n** *of* the LORD. H9005
Ge 26:33 to this day the **n** *of* the town has been H9005
Ge 29:16 daughters; the **n** *of* the older was Leah H9005
Ge 29:16 the **n** *of* the younger was Rachel. H9005
Ge 30:28 He added, "**N** your wages, and I will pay H5918
Ge 31:53 took an oath **in the n** of the Fear of his H928
Ge 32:27 man asked him, "What is your **n**?" "Jacob," H9005
Ge 32:28 man said, "Your **n** will no longer be Jacob H9005
Ge 32:29 "Please tell me your **n**." But he replied, H9005
Ge 32:29 "Why do you ask my **n**?" Then he blessed H9005
Ge 35:10 God said to him, "Your **n** is Jacob, but you H9005
Ge 35:10 be called Jacob; your **n** will be Israel." H9005
Ge 36:39 his wife's **n** was Mehetabel daughter H9005
Ge 36:40 from Esau, by **n**, according to their H9005
Ge 38: 6 his firstborn, and her **n** was Tamar. H9005
Ge 41:45 gave Joseph the **n** Zaphenath-Paneah H9005
Ge 48:16 be called by my **n** and the names of my H9005
Ge 48:20 "In your **n** will Israel pronounce this blessing NDT
Ex 3:13 and they ask me, 'What is his **n**? H9005
Ex 3:15 "This is my **n** forever, the name you shall H9005
Ex 3:15 the **n** you shall **call** me from generation to H2352
Ex 5:23 I went to Pharaoh to speak in your **n**, H9005
Ex 6: 3 but *by* my **n** the LORD I did not make H9005
Ex 9:16 power and that my **n** might be proclaimed H9005
Ex 15: 3 The LORD is a warrior; the LORD is his **n**. H9005
Ex 17:14 blot out the **n** *of* Amalek from under H2352
Ex 20: 7 not misuse the **n** *of* the LORD your God, H9005
Ex 20: 7 hold anyone guiltless who misuses his **n**. H9005
Ex 20:24 Wherever I cause my **n** to be honored, H9005
Ex 23:21 your rebellion, since my **N** is in him. H9005
Ex 28:21 like a seal with the **n** *of* one of the twelve H9005
Ex 33:12 'I know you by **n** and you have found favor H9005
Ex 33:17 am pleased with you and I know you by **n**." H9005
Ex 33:19 and I will proclaim my **n**, the LORD, H9005
Ex 34: 5 there with him and proclaimed his **n**, H9005
Ex 34:14 the LORD, whose **n** is Jealous, is a H9005
Ex 39:14 like a seal with the **n** of one of the twelve H9005
Lev 18:21 you must not profane the **n** *of* your God. H9005
Lev 19:12 swear falsely by my **n** and so profane the H9005
Lev 19:12 name and so profane the **n** *of* your God. H9005
Lev 20: 3 my sanctuary and profaned my holy **n**. H9005
Lev 21: 6 must not profane the **n** *of* their God. H9005
Lev 22: 2 so they will not profane my holy **n**. H9005
Lev 22:32 Do not profane my holy **n**, for I must be H9005

Lev 24:11 woman blasphemed the **N** with a curse; H9005
Lev 24:11 His mother's **n** was Shelomith, the H9005
Lev 24:16 who blasphemes the **n** *of* the LORD is to be H9005
Lev 24:16 they blaspheme the **N** they are to be put H9005
Nu 1: 2 listing every man by **n**, one by one. H9005
Nu 1:18 twenty years old or more were listed by **n**, H9005
Nu 1:20 able to serve in the army were listed by **n**, H9005
Nu 1:22 in the army were counted and listed by **n**, H9005
Nu 1:24 able to serve in the army were listed by **n**, H9005
Nu 1:26 able to serve in the army were listed by **n**, H9005
Nu 1:28 able to serve in the army were listed by **n**, H9005
Nu 1:30 able to serve in the army were listed by **n**, H9005
Nu 1:32 able to serve in the army were listed by **n**, H9005
Nu 1:34 able to serve in the army were listed by **n**, H9005
Nu 1:36 able to serve in the army were listed by **n**, H9005
Nu 1:38 able to serve in the army were listed by **n**, H9005
Nu 1:40 able to serve in the army were listed by **n**, H9005
Nu 1:42 able to serve in the army were listed by **n**, H9005
Nu 3:43 old or more, listed by **n**, was 22,273. H9005
Nu 6:27 "So they will put my **n** on the Israelites H9005
Nu 13:16 Moses **gave** Hoshea son of Nun *the* **n** H7924
Nu 17: 2 Write the **n** *of* each man on his staff H9005
Nu 17: 3 On the staff of Levi write Aaron's **n**, for H9005
Nu 25:14 The **n** *of* the Israelite who was killed with H9005
Nu 25:15 And the **n** *of* the Midianite woman who H9005
Nu 26:59 the **n** *of* Amram's wife was Jochebed, H9005
Nu 27: 4 should our father's **n** disappear from his H9005
Dt 5:11 not misuse the **n** *of* the LORD your God, H9005
Dt 5:11 hold anyone guiltless who misuses his **n**. H9005
Dt 6:13 him only and take your oaths in his **n**. H9005
Dt 9:14 blot out their **n** from under heaven. H9005
Dt 10: 8 to pronounce blessings in his **n**, H9005
Dt 10:20 fast to him and take your oaths in his **n**. H9005
Dt 12: 5 tribes to put his **N** there for his dwelling H9005
Dt 12:11 God will choose as a dwelling for his **N**— H9005
Dt 12:21 chooses to put his **N** is too far away from H9005
Dt 14:23 he will choose as a dwelling for his **N**, H9005
Dt 14:24 will choose to put his **N** is so far away), H9005
Dt 16: 2 LORD will choose as a dwelling for his **N**. H9005
Dt 16: 6 he will choose as a dwelling for his **N**. H9005
Dt 16:11 he will choose as a dwelling for his **N**— H9005
Dt 18: 5 stand and minister in the LORD's **n** always. H9005
Dt 18: 7 may minister in the **n** *of* the LORD his God H9005
Dt 18:19 my words that the prophet speaks in my **n**. H9005
Dt 18:20 to speak in my **n** anything I have not H9005
Dt 18:20 who speaks in the **n** *of* other gods, H9005
Dt 18:22 proclaims in the **n** *of* the LORD does not H9005
Dt 21: 5 blessings in the **n** *of* the LORD and to H9005
Dt 22:14 slanders her and gives her a bad **n** H9005
Dt 22:19 man has given an Israelite virgin a bad **n**. H9005
Dt 25: 6 shall carry on the **n** *of* the dead brother so H9005
Dt 25: 6 brother so that his **n** will not be blotted H9005
Dt 25: 7 refuses to carry on his brother's **n** in Israel. H9005
Dt 25:19 shall blot out the **n** *of* Amalek from under H2352
Dt 26: 2 God will choose as a dwelling for his **N** H9005
Dt 28:10 that you are called by the **n** *of* the LORD, H9005
Dt 28:58 not revere this glorious and awesome **n**— H9005
Dt 32: 3 I will proclaim the **n** *of* the LORD. H9005
Dt 32:26 erase their **n** from human **memory**, H2352
Jos 7: 9 us and wipe out our **n** from the earth. H9005
Jos 7: 9 then will you do for your own great **n**?" H9005
Jos 21: 9 they allotted the following towns by **n** H9005
Jos 22:34 the Gadites **gave** the altar *this* **n**: H7924
Jdg 1:26 called it Luz, which is its **n** to this day. H9005
Jdg 6:32 *they* **gave** him **the n** Jerub-Baal that day H7924
Jdg 13: 6 came from, and he didn't tell me his **n**. H9005
Jdg 13:17 "What is your **n**, so that we may H9005
Jdg 13:18 "Why do you ask my **n**? It is beyond H9005
Jdg 16: 4 the Valley of Sorek whose **n** was Delilah. H9005
Ru 1: 2 The man's **n** was Elimelek, his wife's H9005
Ru 1: 2 Elimelek, his wife's **n** was Naomi, and the H9005
Ru 2: 1 the clan of Elimelek, whose **n** was Boaz. H9005
Ru 2:19 "The **n** *of* the man I worked with today is H9005
Ru 4: 5 to maintain the **n** *of* the dead with his H9005
Ru 4:10 to maintain the **n** *of* the dead with his H9005
Ru 4:10 so that his **n** will not disappear from H9005
1Sa 1: 1 whose **n** was Elkanah son of Jeroham H9005
1Sa 8: 2 The **n** *of* his firstborn was Joel and the H9005
1Sa 8: 2 was Joel and the **n** *of* his second was H9005
1Sa 9: 1 standing, whose **n** was Kish son of Abiel H9005
1Sa 12:22 the sake of his great **n** the LORD will not H9005
1Sa 14:49 The **n** *of* his older daughter was Merab H9005
1Sa 14:50 His wife's **n** was Ahinoam daughter of H9005
1Sa 14:50 The **n** *of* the commander of Saul's army H9005
1Sa 17:45 against you in the **n** *of* the LORD Almighty, H9005
1Sa 18:30 officers, and his **n** became well known. H9005
1Sa 20:42 with each other in the **n** *of* the LORD, H9005
1Sa 24:21 wipe out my **n** from my father's family." H9005
1Sa 25: 3 His **n** was Nabal and his wife's name was H9005
1Sa 25: 3 was Nabal and his wife's **n** was Abigail. H9005
1Sa 25: 5 Nabal at Carmel and greet him in my **n**. H9005
1Sa 25: 9 gave Nabal this message in David's **n**. H9005
1Sa 25:25 He is just like his **n**—his name means H9005
1Sa 25:25 like his name—his **n** means Fool, and H9005
1Sa 28: 8 he said, "and bring up for me the one *I* **n**." H606
2Sa 4: 4 His **n** was Mephibosheth.) H9005
2Sa 6: 2 which is called by the **N**, the name of the H9005
2Sa 6: 2 by the Name, the **n** *of* the LORD Almighty H9005
2Sa 6:18 the people in the **n** *of* the LORD Almighty. H9005
2Sa 7: 9 Now I will make your **n** great, like the H9005
2Sa 7:13 the one who will build a house for my **N**, H9005
2Sa 7:23 to make a **n** for himself, and to H9005
2Sa 7:26 so that your **n** will be great forever. H9005
2Sa 12:25 the prophet *to* **n** him Jedidiah. H7924+9005
2Sa 14: 7 my husband neither **n** nor descendant on H9005
2Sa 14:27 His daughter's **n** was Tamar, and she H9005
2Sa 16: 5 His **n** was Shimei son of Gera, and he H9005
2Sa 18:18 no son to carry on the memory of my **n**." H9005
2Sa 22:50 nations; I will sing the praises of your **n**. H9005
1Ki 1:47 make Solomon's **n** more famous than H9005
1Ki 3: 2 not yet been built for the **N** *of* the LORD. H9005
1Ki 5: 3 a temple for the **N** *of* the LORD his God H9005
1Ki 5: 5 a temple for the **N** *of* the LORD my God, H9005
1Ki 5: 5 your place will build the temple for my **N**. H9005
1Ki 8:16 temple built so that my **N** might be there, H9005
1Ki 8:17 to build a temple for the **N** *of* the LORD, H9005
1Ki 8:18 it in your heart to build a temple for my **N**. H9005
1Ki 8:19 one who will build the temple for my **N**. H9005
1Ki 8:20 built the temple for the **N** *of* the LORD, H9005
1Ki 8:29 which you said, 'My **N** shall be there,' so H9005
1Ki 8:33 turn back to you and give praise to your **n**, H9005
1Ki 8:35 give praise to your **n** and turn from their H9005
1Ki 8:41 from a distant land because of your **n**— H9005
1Ki 8:42 hear of your great **n** and your mighty hand H9005
1Ki 8:43 the earth may know your **n** and fear you, H9005
1Ki 8:43 that this house I have built bears your **N**. H9005
1Ki 8:44 the temple I have built for your **N**, H9005
1Ki 8:48 the temple I have built for your **N**; H9005
1Ki 9: 3 have built, by putting my **N** there forever. H9005
1Ki 9: 7 this temple I have consecrated for my **N**. H9005
1Ki 9:13 the Land of Kabul, a **n** they have to this day. NDT
1Ki 11:36 the city where I chose to put my **N**. H9005
1Ki 14:21 the tribes of Israel in which to put his **N**. H9005
1Ki 14:21 His mother's **n** was Naamah; she was an H9005
1Ki 14:31 His mother's **n** was Naamah; she was an H9005
1Ki 15: 2 His mother's **n** was Maakah daughter of H9005
1Ki 15:10 His grandmother's **n** was Maakah H9005
1Ki 16:24 the **n** *of* the former owner of the hill. H9005
1Ki 18:24 Then you call on the **n** *of* your god, and I H9005
1Ki 18:24 and I will call on the **n** *of* the LORD. H9005
1Ki 18:25 Call on the **n** *of* your god, but do not light H9005
1Ki 18:26 they called on the **n** *of* Baal from morning H9005
1Ki 18:31 had come, saying, "Your **n** shall be Israel." H9005
1Ki 18:32 he built an altar in the **n** *of* the LORD, H9005
1Ki 21: 8 So she wrote letters in Ahab's **n**, placed H9005
1Ki 22:16 nothing but the truth in the **n** *of* the LORD?" H9005
1Ki 22:42 His mother's **n** was Azubah daughter of H9005
2Ki 2:24 a curse on them in the **n** *of* the LORD. H9005
2Ki 5:11 call on the **n** *of* the LORD his God, H9005
2Ki 8:26 His mother's **n** was Athaliah, H9005
2Ki 12: 1 His mother's **n** was Zibiah; she was from H9005
2Ki 14: 2 His mother's **n** was Jehoaddan; she was H9005
2Ki 14: 7 calling it Joktheel, the **n** it has to this day. H9005
2Ki 14:27 would blot out the **n** *of* Israel from under H9005
2Ki 15: 2 His mother's **n** was Jekoliah; she was H9005
2Ki 15:33 His mother's **n** was Jerusha daughter of H9005
2Ki 18: 2 His mother's **n** was Abijah daughter of H9005
2Ki 21: 1 His mother's **n** was Hephzibah. H9005
2Ki 21: 4 had said, "In Jerusalem I will put my **N**." H9005
2Ki 21: 7 the tribes of Israel, I will put my **N** forever. H9005
2Ki 21:19 His mother's **n** was Meshullemeth H9005
2Ki 22: 1 His mother's **n** was Jedidah daughter of H9005
2Ki 23:27 about which I said, 'My **N** shall be there.' H9005
2Ki 23:31 His mother's **n** was Hamutal daughter of H9005
2Ki 23:34 changed Eliakim's **n** to Jehoiakim. H9005
2Ki 23:36 His mother's **n** was Zebidah daughter of H9005
2Ki 24: 8 His mother's **n** was Nehushta daughter of H9005
2Ki 24:17 his place and changed his **n** to Zedekiah. H9005
2Ki 24:18 His mother's **n** was Hamutal daughter of H9005
1Ch 1:50 his wife's **n** was Mehetabel daughter H9005
1Ch 2:26 whose **n** was Atarah; she was H9005
1Ch 4:38 men listed above by **n** were leaders of H9005
1Ch 7:15 His sister's **n** was Maakah. Another H9005
1Ch 8:29 His wife's **n** was Maakah, H9005
1Ch 9:35 His wife's **n** was Maakah, H9005
1Ch 12:31 designated by **n** to come and make David H9005
1Ch 13: 6 cherubim—the ark that is called by the **N**. H9005
1Ch 16: 2 blessed the people in the **n** *of* the LORD. H9005
1Ch 16: 8 proclaim his **n**; make known among H9005
1Ch 16:10 Glory in his holy **n**; let the hearts of those H9005
1Ch 16:29 Ascribe to the LORD the glory due his **n** H9005
1Ch 16:35 that we may give thanks to your holy **n** H9005
1Ch 16:41 designated by **n** to give thanks to the H9005
1Ch 17: 8 Now I will make your **n** like the names of H9005
1Ch 17:21 to make a **n** for yourself, and to H9005
1Ch 17:24 that your **n** will be great forever. H9005
1Ch 21:19 that Gad had spoken in the **n** *of* the LORD. H9005
1Ch 22: 7 a house for the **N** *of* the LORD my God. H9005
1Ch 22: 8 You are not to build a house for my **N** H9005
1Ch 22: 9 His **n** will be Solomon, and I will grant H9005
1Ch 22:10 the one who will build a house for my **N**. H9005
1Ch 22:19 that will be built for the **N** *of* the LORD." H9005
1Ch 23:13 to pronounce blessings in his **n** forever. H9005
1Ch 28: 3 'You are not to build a house for my **N** H9005
1Ch 29:13 you thanks, and praise your glorious **n**. H9005
1Ch 29:16 your Holy **N** comes from your hand H9005
2Ch 2: 1 a temple for the **N** *of* the LORD and a royal H9005
2Ch 2: 4 a temple for the **N** *of* the LORD my God H9005
2Ch 6: 5 temple built so that my **N** might be there, H9005
2Ch 6: 6 chosen Jerusalem for my **N** to be there, H9005
2Ch 6: 7 to build a temple for the **N** *of* the LORD, H9005
2Ch 6: 8 it in your heart to build a temple for my **N**. H9005
2Ch 6: 9 one who will build the temple for my **N**. H9005
2Ch 6:10 built the temple for the **N** *of* the LORD, H9005
2Ch 6:20 you said you would put your **N** there. H9005
2Ch 6:24 they turn back and give praise to your **n**, H9005
2Ch 6:26 give praise to your **n** and turn from their H9005
2Ch 6:32 of your great **n** and your mighty hand H9005
2Ch 6:33 the earth may know your **n** and fear you, H9005
2Ch 6:33 that this house I have built bears your **N**. H9005
2Ch 6:34 the temple I have built for your **N**, H9005
2Ch 6:38 toward the temple I have built for your **N**; H9005
2Ch 7:14 who are called by my **n**, will humble H9005
2Ch 7:16 temple so that my **N** may be there forever. H9005
2Ch 7:20 this temple I have consecrated for my **N**. H9005
2Ch 12:13 the tribes of Israel in which to put his **N**. H9005
2Ch 12:13 His mother's **n** was Naamah; she was an H9005
2Ch 13: 2 His mother's **n** was Maakah, a daughter H9005
2Ch 14:11 in your **n** we have come against this H9005
2Ch 18:15 nothing but the truth in the **n** *of* the LORD?" H9005
2Ch 20: 8 have built in it a sanctuary for your **N**, H9005
2Ch 20: 9 that bears your **N** and will cry out to H9005
2Ch 20:31 His mother's **n** was Azubah daughter of H9005
2Ch 22: 2 His mother's **n** was Athaliah, H9005
2Ch 24: 1 His mother's **n** was Zibiah; she was from H9005
2Ch 25: 1 His mother's **n** was Jehoaddan; she was H9005
2Ch 26: 3 His mother's **n** was Jekoliah; she was H9005
2Ch 27: 1 His mother's **n** was Jerusha daughter of H9005
2Ch 28:15 men designated by **n** took the prisoners, H9005
2Ch 29: 1 His mother's **n** was Abijah daughter of H9005
2Ch 31:19 were designated by **n** to distribute H9005
2Ch 33: 4 "My **N** will remain in Jerusalem forever." H9005
2Ch 33: 7 the tribes of Israel, I will put my **N** forever. H9005
2Ch 33:18 seers spoke to him in the **n** *of* the LORD, H9005
2Ch 36: 4 changed Eliakim's **n** to Jehoiakim. H9005
2Ch 36:13 who had made him take an oath in God's **n**. NDT
Ezr 2:61 the Gileadite and was called by that **n**). H9005
Ezr 5: 1 Jerusalem in the **n** *of* the God of Israel, A10721
Ezr 6:12 who has caused his **N** to dwell there A10721
Ezr 8:20 All were registered by **n**. H9005
Ezr 10:16 division, and all of them designated by **n**. H9005
Ne 1: 9 I have chosen as a dwelling for my **N**. H9005
Ne 1:11 servants who delight in revering your **n**. H9005
Ne 6:13 would give me a bad **n** to discredit me. H9005
Ne 7:63 the Gileadite and was called by that **n**). H9005
Ne 9: 5 "Blessed be your glorious **n**, and may it H9005
Ne 9:10 You made a **n** for yourself, which remains H9005
Ne 13:25 them take an oath in God's **n** and said: NDT
Est 2:14 with her and summoned her by **n**. H9005
Est 3:12 were written in the **n** *of* King Xerxes H9005
Est 8: 8 decree in the king's **n** in behalf of the H9005
Est 8: 8 written in the king's **n** and sealed with his H9005
Est 8:10 Mordecai wrote in the **n** *of* King Xerxes H9005
Job 1: 1 of Uz there lived a man whose **n** was Job. H9005
Job 1:21 may the **n** *of* the LORD be praised. H9005
Job 18:17 from the earth; he has no **n** in the land. H9005
Ps 5:11 those who love your **n** may rejoice in you. H9005
Ps 6: 5 Among the dead no one **proclaims** your **n**. H2352
Ps 7:17 the praises of the **n** *of* the LORD Most High. H9005
Ps 8: 1 how majestic is your **n** in all the earth! H9005
Ps 8: 9 how majestic is your **n** in all the earth! H9005
Ps 9: 2 I will sing the praises of your **n**, O Most H9005
Ps 9: 5 have blotted out their **n** for ever and ever. H9005
Ps 9:10 Those who know your **n** trust in you, for H9005
Ps 18:49 nations; I will sing the praises of your **n**. H9005
Ps 20: 1 may the **n** *of* the God of Jacob protect you. H9005
Ps 20: 5 lift up our banners in the **n** *of* our God. H9005
Ps 20: 7 we trust in the **n** *of* the LORD our God. H9005
Ps 22:22 I will declare your **n** to my people; in the H9005
Ps 25:11 For the sake of your **n**, LORD, forgive my H9005
Ps 29: 2 Ascribe to the LORD the glory due his **n** H9005
Ps 30: 4 you his faithful people; praise his holy **n**. H2352
Ps 31: 3 the sake of your **n** lead and guide me. H9005
Ps 33:21 hearts rejoice, for we trust in his holy **n**. H9005
Ps 34: 3 LORD with me; let us exalt his **n** together. H9005
Ps 34:16 to blot out their **n** from the earth. H2352
Ps 41: 5 "When will he die and his **n** perish?" H9005
Ps 44: 5 through your **n** we trample our foes. H9005
Ps 44: 8 and we will praise your **n** forever. H9005
Ps 44:20 had forgotten the **n** *of* our God or spread H9005
Ps 48:10 Like your **n**, O God, your praise reaches to H9005
Ps 52: 9 And I will hope in your **n**, for your name is H9005
Ps 52: 9 I will hope in your name, for your **n** is good. NDT
Ps 54: 1 by your **n**; vindicate me by your H9005
Ps 54: 6 offering to you; I will praise your **n**, LORD, H9005
Ps 61: 5 me the heritage of those who fear your **n**. H9005
Ps 61: 8 sing in praise of your **n** and fulfill my vows H9005
Ps 63: 4 and in your **n** I will lift up my hands. H9005
Ps 66: 2 Sing the glory of his **n**; make his praise H9005
Ps 66: 4 they sing the praises of your **n**. H9005
Ps 68: 4 sing in praise of his **n**, extol him who H9005
Ps 68: 4 rejoice before him—his **n** is the LORD. H9005
Ps 69:30 I will praise God's **n** in song and glorify H9005
Ps 69:36 those who love his **n** will dwell there. H9005
Ps 72:17 May his **n** endure forever; may it continue H9005
Ps 72:19 Praise be to his glorious **n** forever; may H9005
Ps 74: 7 they defiled the dwelling place of your **N**. H9005
Ps 74:10 Will the foe revile your **n** forever? H9005
Ps 74:18 how foolish people have reviled your **n**. H9005
Ps 74:21 may the poor and needy praise your **n**. H9005
Ps 75: 1 praise you, for your **N** is near; people tell H9005
Ps 76: 1 in Judah; in Israel his **n** is great. H9005
Ps 79: 6 the kingdoms that do not call on your **n**; H9005
Ps 79: 9 the glory of your **n**; deliver us and H9005
Ps 80:18 revive us, and we will call on your **n**. H9005
Ps 83: 4 so that Israel's **n** is remembered no more." H9005

Ps 83:16 LORD, so that they will seek your **n**. H9005
Ps 83:18 know that you, whose **n** is the LORD—that H9005
Ps 86: 9 Lord; they will bring glory to your **n**. H9005
Ps 86:11 an undivided heart, that I may fear your **n**. H9005
Ps 86:12 all my heart; I will glorify your **n** forever. H9005
Ps 89:12 Tabor and Hermon sing for joy at your **n**. H9005
Ps 89:16 They rejoice in your **n** all day long; they H9005
Ps 89:24 through my **n** his horn will be exalted. H9005
Ps 91:14 protect him, for he acknowledges my **n**. H9005
Ps 92: 1 praise the LORD and make music to your **n**, H9005
Ps 96: 2 the LORD, praise his **n**; proclaim his H9005
Ps 96: 8 Ascribe to the LORD the glory due his **n** H9005
Ps 97:12 who are righteous, and praise his holy **n**. H2352
Ps 99: 3 them praise your great and awesome **n**— H9005
Ps 99: 6 was among those who called on his **n**; H9005
Ps 100: 4 give thanks to him and praise his **n**. H9005
Ps 102: 8 rail against me **use** my **n as a curse**. H8678+928
Ps 102:15 The nations will fear the **n** *of* the LORD, all H9005
Ps 102:21 So the **n** *of* the LORD will be declared in H9005
Ps 103: 1 all my inmost being, praise his holy **n**. H9005
Ps 105: 1 proclaim his **n**; make known among H9005
Ps 105: 3 Glory in his holy **n**; let the hearts of those H9005
Ps 106:47 thanks to your holy **n** and glory in your H9005
Ps 109:15 he may blot out their **n** from the earth. H2352
Ps 111: 9 forever—holy and awesome is his **n**. H9005
Ps 113: 1 you his servants; praise the **n** *of* the LORD. H9005
Ps 113: 2 Let the **n** *of* the LORD be praised, both now H9005
Ps 113: 3 the **n** *of* the LORD is to be praised. H9005
Ps 115: 1 not to us but to your **n** be the glory H9005
Ps 116: 4 Then I called on the **n** *of* the LORD: "LORD H9005
Ps 116:13 of salvation and call on the **n** *of* the LORD. H9005
Ps 116:17 to you and call on the **n** *of* the LORD. H9005
Ps 118:10 in the **n** *of* the LORD I cut them down. H9005
Ps 118:11 in the **n** *of* the LORD I cut them down. H9005
Ps 118:12 in the **n** *of* the LORD I cut them down. H9005
Ps 118:26 is he who comes in the **n** *of* the LORD. H9005
Ps 119:55 I remember your **n**, that I may keep your H9005
Ps 119:132 you always do to those who love your **n**. H9005
Ps 122: 4 to praise the **n** *of* the LORD according to H9005
Ps 124: 8 Our help is in the **n** *of* the LORD, the Maker H9005
Ps 129: 8 we bless you in the **n** *of* the LORD. H9005
Ps 135: 1 Praise the **n** *of* the LORD; praise him, you H9005
Ps 135: 3 sing praise to his **n**, for that is pleasant. H9005
Ps 135:13 Your **n**, LORD, endures forever, your H9005
Ps 138: 2 will praise your **n** for your unfailing H9005
Ps 139:20 evil intent; your adversaries misuse your **n**. NDT
Ps 140:13 Surely the righteous will praise your **n** H9005
Ps 142: 7 from my prison, that I may praise your **n**. H9005
Ps 145: 1 I will praise your **n** for ever and ever. H9005
Ps 145: 2 you and extol your **n** for ever and ever. H9005
Ps 145:21 praise his holy **n** for ever and ever. H9005
Ps 147: 4 of the stars and calls them each *by* **n**. H9005
Ps 148: 5 Let them praise the **n** *of* the LORD, for at H9005
Ps 148:13 Let them praise the **n** *of* the LORD, for his H9005
Ps 148:13 of the LORD, for his **n** alone is exalted; his H9005
Ps 149: 3 Let them praise his **n** with dancing and H9005
Pr 3: 4 favor and a good **n** in the sight of God H8507
Pr 10: 7 The **n** *of* the righteous is used in H2352
Pr 10: 7 blessings, but the **n** *of* the wicked will rot. H9005
Pr 18:10 The **n** *of* the LORD is a fortified tower; the H9005
Pr 21:24 "Mocker" is his **n**—behaves with insolent H9005
Pr 22: 1 A good **n** is more desirable than great H9005
Pr 30: 4 What is his **n**, and what is the name of H9005
Pr 30: 4 is his name, and what is the **n** *of* his son? H9005
Pr 30: 9 and so dishonor the **n** *of* my God. H9005
Ecc 6: 4 in darkness its **n** is shrouded. H9005
Ecc 7: 1 A good **n** is better than fine perfume, and H9005
Ecc 9: 5 and even their **n** is forgotten. H2352
SS 1: 3 your **n** is like perfume poured out. H9005
Isa 4: 1 clothes; only let us be called by your **n**. H9005
Isa 8: 3 "**N** him Maher-Shalal-Hash-Baz. H7924+9005
Isa 12: 4 proclaim his **n**; make known among H9005
Isa 12: 4 and proclaim that his **n** is exalted. H9005
Isa 14:22 "I will wipe out Babylon's **n** and survivors H9005
Isa 18: 7 the place of the **N** *of* the LORD Almighty. H9005
Isa 24:15 the LORD; exalt the **n** *of* the LORD, the God H9005
Isa 25: 1 I will exalt you and praise your **n**, for in H9005
Isa 26: 8 your **n** and renown are the desire of our H9005
Isa 26:13 over us, but your **n** alone do we honor. H9005
Isa 29:23 they will keep my **n** holy; they will H9005
Isa 30:27 the **N** *of* the LORD comes from afar H9005
Isa 40:26 by one and calls forth each of them by **n**. H9005
Isa 41:25 one from the rising sun who calls on my **n**. H9005
Isa 42: 8 the LORD; that is my **n**! I will not yield my H9005
Isa 43: 1 I have summoned you by **n**; you are mine. H9005
Isa 43: 7 everyone who is called by my **n**, whom I H9005
Isa 44: 5 will call themselves by the **n** *of* Jacob; H9005
Isa 44: 5 'The LORD's,' and will take the **n** Israel. H9005
Isa 45: 3 the God of Israel, who summons you by **n**. H9005
Isa 45: 4 I summon you by **n** and bestow on you a H9005
Isa 47: 4 the LORD Almighty is his **n**—is the Holy H9005
Isa 48: 1 are called by the **n** *of* Israel and come H9005
Isa 48: 1 take oaths in the **n** *of* the LORD and invoke H9005
Isa 48: 2 God of Israel—the LORD Almighty is his **n**: H9005
Isa 48:19 their **n** would never be blotted out nor H9005
Isa 49: 1 my mother's womb he has spoken my **n**. H9005
Isa 50:10 trust in the **n** *of* the LORD and rely on their H9005
Isa 51:15 waves roar—the LORD Almighty is his **n**. H9005
Isa 52: 5 "And all day long my **n** is constantly H9005
Isa 52: 6 Therefore my people will know my **n** H9005
Isa 54: 5 the LORD Almighty is his **n**—the Holy One H9005
Isa 56: 5 a memorial and a **n** better than sons and H9005
Isa 56: 5 them an everlasting **n** that will endure H9005
Isa 56: 6 to love the **n** *of* the LORD, and to H9005
Isa 57:15 he who lives forever, whose **n** is holy: H9005
Isa 59:19 people will fear the **n** *of* the LORD, and H9005
Isa 62: 2 be called by a new **n** that the mouth of H9005
Isa 62: 4 call you Deserted, or **n** your land Desolate. H606
Isa 63:14 people to make for yourself a glorious **n**. H9005
Isa 63:16 our Redeemer from of old is your **n**. H9005
Isa 63:19 they have not been called by your **n**. H9005
Isa 64: 2 down to make your **n** known to your H9005
Isa 64: 7 No one calls on your **n** or strives to lay H9005
Isa 65: 1 To a nation that did not call on my **n**, H9005
Isa 65:15 You will leave your **n** for my chosen ones H9005
Isa 65:15 to his servants he will give another **n**. H9005
Isa 66: 5 exclude you because of my **n**, have H9005
Isa 66:22 "so will your **n** and descendants endure. H9005
Jer 3:17 in Jerusalem to honor the **n** *of* the LORD. H9005
Jer 7:10 in this house, which bears my **N**, and say, H9005
Jer 7:11 which bears my **N**, become a den of H9005
Jer 7:12 where I first made a dwelling for my **N**, H9005
Jer 7:14 will now do to the house that bears my **N**, H9005
Jer 7:30 house that bears my **N** and have defiled it H9005
Jer 10: 6 are great, and your **n** is mighty in power. H9005
Jer 10:16 inheritance—the LORD Almighty is his **n**. H9005
Jer 10:25 on the peoples who do not call on your **n**. H9005
Jer 11:19 that his **n** be remembered no more." H9005
Jer 11:21 not prophesy in the **n** *of* the LORD or you H9005
Jer 12:16 ways of my people and swear by my **n**, H9005
Jer 14: 7 do something, LORD, for the sake of your **n**. H9005
Jer 14: 9 we bear your **n**; do not forsake us! H9005
Jer 14:14 prophets are prophesying lies in my **n**. H9005
Jer 14:15 prophets who are prophesying in my **n**: H9005
Jer 14:21 For the sake of your **n** do not despise us H9005
Jer 15:16 I bear your **n**, LORD God Almighty. H9005
Jer 16:21 Then they will know that my **n** is the LORD. H9005
Jer 20: 3 The LORD's **n** *for* you is not Pashhur H7924+9005
Jer 20: 9 his word or speak anymore in his **n**," H9005
Jer 23: 6 This is the **n** by which he will be called H9005
Jer 23:25 prophets say who prophesy lies in my **n**. H9005
Jer 23:27 another will make my people forget my **n**, H9005
Jer 23:27 ancestors forgot my **n** through Baal H9005
Jer 25:29 bring disaster on the city that bears my **N**, H9005
Jer 26: 9 in the LORD's **n** that this house will H9005
Jer 26:16 spoken to us in the **n** *of* the LORD our God." H9005
Jer 26:20 man who prophesied in the **n** *of* the LORD; H9005
Jer 27:15 'They are prophesying lies in my **n**. H9005
Jer 29: 9 They are prophesying lies to you in my **n**. H9005
Jer 29:21 who are prophesying lies to you in my **n**: H9005
Jer 29:23 and in my **n** they have uttered lies H9005
Jer 29:25 letters in your own **n** to all the people in H9005
Jer 31:35 waves roar—the LORD Almighty is his **n**: H9005
Jer 32:18 whose **n** is the LORD Almighty, H9005
Jer 32:34 the house that bears my **N** and defiled it. H9005
Jer 33: 2 it and established it—the LORD is his **n**: H9005
Jer 33:16 This is **the n** *by which* it will be called H889s
Jer 34:15 before me in the house that bears my **N**. H9005
Jer 34:16 have turned around and profaned my **n**; H9005
Jer 37:13 whose **n** was Irijah son of Shelemiah H9005
Jer 44:16 have spoken to us in the **n** *of* the LORD! H9005
Jer 44:26 'I swear by my great **n**,' says the LORD H9005
Jer 44:26 will ever again invoke my **n** or swear, H9005
Jer 46:18 the King, whose **n** is the LORD Almighty H9005
Jer 48:15 the King, whose **n** is the LORD Almighty. H9005
Jer 50:34 is strong; the LORD Almighty is his **n**. H9005
Jer 51:19 inheritance—the LORD Almighty is his **n**. H9005
Jer 51:57 the King, whose **n** is the LORD Almighty. H9005
Jer 52: 1 His mother's **n** was Hamutal daughter of H9005
La 3:55 I called on your **n**, LORD, from the depths H9005
Eze 20: 9 But for the sake of my **n**, I brought them H9005
Eze 20: 9 I did it to keep my **n** from being profaned in NDT
Eze 20:14 the sake of my **n** I did what would H9005
Eze 20:22 the sake of my **n** I did what would H9005
Eze 20:39 profane my holy **n** with your gifts and H9005
Eze 36:20 the nations they profaned my holy **n**, H9005
Eze 36:21 I had concern for my holy **n**, which the H9005
Eze 36:22 for the sake of my holy **n**, which you H9005
Eze 36:23 I will show the holiness of my great **n** H9005
Eze 36:23 **the n** you have profaned among them. H889s
Eze 39: 7 make known my holy **n** among my people H9005
Eze 39: 7 I will no longer let my holy **n** be profaned H9005
Eze 39:25 and I will be zealous for my holy **n**. H9005
Eze 43: 7 Israel will never again defile my holy **n**— H9005
Eze 43: 8 they defiled my holy **n** by their detestable H9005
Eze 48: 1 the tribes, listed by **n**: At the northern H9005
Eze 48:35 "And the **n** *of* the city from that time on H9005
Da 1: 7 to Daniel, the **n** Belteshazzar; to Hananiah NDT
Da 2:20 "Praise be to the **n** of God for ever and A10721
Da 4: 8 after the **n** *of* my god, and the spirit A10721
Da 9: 6 who spoke in your **n** to our kings, our H9005
Da 9:15 made for yourself a **n** that endures to this H9005
Da 9:18 desolation of the city that bears your **N**. H9005
Da 9:19 your city and your people bear your **N**." H9005
Da 12: 1 everyone whose **n** is found written in the NDT
Hos 12: 5 the LORD God Almighty, the LORD is his **n**! H2352
Joel 2:26 you will praise the **n** *of* the LORD your God, H9005
Joel 2:32 who calls on the **n** *of* the LORD will be H9005
Am 2: 7 the same girl and so profane my holy **n**. H9005
Am 4:13 the LORD God Almighty is his **n**. H9005
Am 5: 8 the face of the land—the LORD is his **n**. H9005
Am 5:27 says the LORD, whose **n** is God Almighty. H9005
Am 6:10 We must not mention the **n** *of* the LORD." H9005
Am 9: 6 the face of the land—the LORD is his **n**. H9005
Am 9:12 Edom and all the nations that bear my **n**," H9005
Mic 4: 5 nations may walk in the **n** *of* their gods, H9005
Mic 4: 5 we will walk in the **n** *of* the LORD our God H9005
Mic 5: 4 the majesty of the **n** *of* the LORD his God. H9005
Mic 6: 9 to fear your **n** is wisdom—"Heed the H9005
Na 1:14 will have no descendants to bear your **n**. H9005
Zep 3: 9 may call on the **n** *of* the LORD and serve H9005
Zep 3:12 of Israel will trust in the **n** *of* the LORD. H9005
Zec 5: 4 of anyone who swears falsely by my **n**. H9005
Zec 6:12 'Here is the man whose **n** is the Branch H9005
Zec 10:12 in the LORD and in his **n** they will live H9005
Zec 13: 3 because you have told lies in the LORD's **n**. H9005
Zec 13: 9 They will call on my **n** and I will answer H9005
Zec 14: 9 be one LORD, and his **n** the only name. H9005
Zec 14: 9 will be one LORD, and his name the only **n**. NDT
Mal 1: 6 you priests who show contempt for my **n**. H9005
Mal 1: 6 'How have we shown contempt for your **n**? H9005
Mal 1:11 My **n** will be great among the nations H9005
Mal 1:11 because my **n** will be great among the H9005
Mal 1:14 "and my **n** is to be feared among the H9005
Mal 2: 2 if you do not resolve to honor my **n**," H9005
Mal 2: 5 he revered me and stood in awe of my **n**. H9005
Mal 3:16 who feared the LORD and honored his **n**. H9005
Mal 4: 2 But for you who revere my **n**, the sun of H9005
Mt 1:21 you are to give him the **n** Jesus *G3950*
Mt 1:25 And he gave him the **n** Jesus. *G3950*
Mt 6: 9 Father in heaven, hallowed be your **n**, *G3950*
Mt 7:22 we not prophesy in your **n** and in your *G3950*
Mt 7:22 your name and *in* your **n** drive out *G3950*
Mt 7:22 out demons and *in* your **n** perform many *G3950*
Mt 12:21 *In* his **n** the nations will put their hope." *G3950*
Mt 13:55 Isn't his mother's **n** Mary, and aren't his *G3306*
Mt 18: 5 one such child in my **n** welcomes me. *G3950*
Mt 18:20 For where two or three gather in my **n** *G3950*
Mt 21: 9 is he who comes in the **n** of the Lord!" *G3950*
Mt 23:39 is he who comes in the **n** of the Lord. *G3950*
Mt 24: 5 For many will come in my **n**, claiming, 'I *G3950*
Mt 26: 3 of the high priest, whose **n** *was* Caiaphas, *G3306*
Mt 27:16 prisoner *whose* **n** *was* Jesus Barabbas. *G3306*
Mt 28:19 them in the **n** of the Father and of *G3950*
Mk 3:16 Simon (to whom he gave the **n** Peter), *G3950*
Mk 3:17 to them he gave the **n** Boanerges, which *G3950*
Mk 5: 7 **In God's n** don't torture me!" *G3991+3836+2536*
Mk 5: 9 "What is your **n**?" "My name is *G3950*
Mk 5: 9 "My **n** is Legion," he replied, "for we are *G3950*
Mk 6:14 for Jesus' **n** had become well known. *G3950*
Mk 9:37 little children in my **n** welcomes me; *G3950*
Mk 9:38 out demons in your **n** and we told him to *G3950*
Mk 9:39 does a miracle in my **n** can in the next *G3950*
Mk 9:41 cup of water in my **n** because you belong *G3950*
Mk 11: 9 is he who comes in the **n** of the Lord!" *G3950*
Mk 13: 6 Many will come in my **n**, claiming, 'I am *G3950*
Mk 16:17 In my **n** they will drive out demons; they *G3950*
Lk 1:27 The virgin's **n** was Mary. *G3950*
Lk 1:49 done great things for me—holy is his **n**. *G3950*
Lk 1:59 and *they were going to* **n** *G2813+3836+3950*
Lk 1:61 one among your relatives who has that **n**." *G3950*
Lk 1:62 find out what he would like *to* **n** the child. *G2813*
Lk 1:63 astonishment he wrote, "His **n** is John." *G3950*
Lk 2:21 the **n** the angel *had* **given** him before he *G2813*
Lk 5:27 a tax collector *by the* **n** *of* Levi sitting at *G3950*
Lk 6:22 insult you and reject your **n** as evil, *G3950*
Lk 8:30 asked him, "What is your **n**?" "Legion," *G3950*
Lk 9:48 this little child in my **n** welcomes me; *G3950*
Lk 9:49 out demons in your **n** and we tried to stop *G3950*
Lk 10:17 even the demons submit to us in your **n**." *G3950*
Lk 11: 2 hallowed be your **n**, your kingdom come. *G3950*
Lk 13:35 is he who comes in the **n** of the Lord. *G3950*
Lk 19: 2 was there *by the* **n** *of* Zacchaeus; *G3950+2813*
Lk 19:38 the king who comes in the **n** of the Lord!" *G3950*
Lk 21: 8 For many will come in my **n**, claiming, 'I *G3950*
Lk 21:12 governors, and all on account of my **n**. *G3950*
Lk 24:47 will be preached in his **n** to all nations, *G3950*
Jn 1: 6 a man sent from God whose **n** was John. *G3950*
Jn 1:12 to those who believed in his **n**, he gave *G3950*
Jn 2:23 he was performing and believed in his **n**. *G3950*
Jn 3:18 not believed in the **n** of God's one and *G3950*
Jn 5:43 I have come in my Father's **n**, and you do *G3950*
Jn 5:43 if someone else comes in his own **n** *G3950*
Jn 10: 3 his own sheep by **n** and leads them out. *G3950*
Jn 10:25 I do in my Father's **n** testify about me, *G3950*
Jn 12:13 is he who comes in the **n** of the Lord!" *G3950*
Jn 12:28 glorify your **n**!" Then a voice came *G3950*
Jn 14:13 And I will do whatever you ask in my **n**, so *G3950*
Jn 14:14 You may ask me for anything in my **n**, and *G3950*
Jn 14:26 whom the Father will send in my **n**, will *G3950*
Jn 15:16 you ask in my **n** the Father will give *G3950*
Jn 15:21 will treat you this way because of my **n**, *G3950*
Jn 16:23 will give you whatever you ask in my **n**. *G3950*
Jn 16:24 you have not asked for anything in my **n**. *G3950*
Jn 16:26 In that day you will ask in my **n**. I am not *G3950*
Jn 17:11 protect them by the power of your **n**, the *G3950*
Jn 17:11 of your name, **the n** you gave me, so *G4005s*
Jn 17:12 kept them safe by that **n** you gave me. *G3950*
Jn 18:10 (The servant's **n** was Malchus.) *G3950*
Jn 20:31 by believing you may have life in his **n**. *G3950*
Ac 2:21 who calls on the **n** of the Lord will be *G3950*
Ac 2:38 in the **n** of Jesus Christ for the forgiveness *G3950*
Ac 3: 6 In the **n** of Jesus Christ of Nazareth *G3950*
Ac 3:16 By faith *in* the **n** of Jesus, this man whom *G3950*
Ac 3:16 It is Jesus' **n** and the faith that comes *G3950*
Ac 4: 7 By what power or what **n** did you do this? *G3950*

Ac 4:10 It is by the **n** of Jesus Christ of Nazareth *G3950*
Ac 4:12 there is no other **n** under heaven given to *G3950*
Ac 4:17 to speak no longer to anyone in this **n**." *G3950*
Ac 4:18 to speak or teach at all in the **n** of Jesus. *G3950*
Ac 4:30 wonders through the **n** of your holy *G3950*
Ac 5:28 you strict orders not to teach in this **n**," *G3950*
Ac 5:40 them not to speak in the **n** of Jesus, *G3950*
Ac 5:41 worthy of suffering disgrace for the **N**. *G3950*
Ac 8:12 kingdom of God and the **n** of Jesus Christ, *G3950*
Ac 8:16 been baptized in the **n** of the Lord Jesus. *G3950*
Ac 9:14 priests to arrest all who call on your **n**." *G3950*
Ac 9:15 to proclaim my **n** to the Gentiles and their *G3950*
Ac 9:16 him how much he must suffer for my **n**." *G3950*
Ac 9:21 among those who call on this **n**? *G3950*
Ac 9:27 had preached fearlessly in the **n** of Jesus. *G3950*
Ac 9:28 speaking boldly in the **n** of the Lord. *G3950*
Ac 9:36 Tabitha (in Greek **her n** is Dorcas); *G4005S*
Ac 10:43 receives forgiveness of sins through his **n**." *G3950*
Ac 10:48 they be baptized in the **n** of Jesus Christ. *G3950*
Ac 13: 8 that is what his **n** means) opposed *G3950*
Ac 15:14 choose a people *for* his **n** from the *G3950*
Ac 15:17 even all the Gentiles who bear my **n**, says *G3950*
Ac 15:26 lives for the **n** of our Lord Jesus Christ *G3950*
Ac 16:18 "In the **n** of Jesus Christ I command you to *G3950*
Ac 19: 5 were baptized in the **n** of the Lord Jesus. *G3950*
Ac 19:13 tried to invoke the **n** of the Lord Jesus over *G3950*
Ac 19:13 "In the **n** of the Jesus whom Paul preaches NDT
Ac 19:17 the **n** of the Lord Jesus was held in *G3950*
Ac 19:27 *that* our trade *will* **lose** *its* **good n** *G1650+591+2262*
Ac 21:13 in Jerusalem for the **n** of the Lord Jesus." *G3950*
Ac 22:16 wash your sins away, calling on his **n**. *G3950*
Ac 26: 9 to oppose the **n** of Jesus of Nazareth. *G3950*
Ro 2:24 "God's **n** is blasphemed among the *G3950*
Ro 9:17 in you and that my **n** might be proclaimed *G3950*
Ro 10:13 who calls on the **n** of the Lord will be *G3950*
Ro 15: 9 Gentiles; I will sing the praises *of* your **n**." *G3950*
1Co 1: 2 who call on the **n** of our Lord Jesus Christ *G3950*
1Co 1:10 in the **n** of our Lord Jesus Christ *G3950*
1Co 1:13 Were you baptized in the **n** of Paul? *G3950*
1Co 1:15 can say that you were baptized in my **n**. *G3950*
1Co 5: 3 judgment in the **n** of our Lord Jesus on *G3950*
1Co 6:11 were justified in the **n** of the Lord Jesus *G3950*
Eph 1:21 dominion, and every **n** that is invoked, not *G3950*
Eph 3:15 in heaven and on earth **derives** *its* **n**. *G3951*
Eph 5:20 in the **n** of our Lord Jesus Christ. *G3950*
Php 2: 9 gave him the **n** that is above every *G3950*
Php 2: 9 gave him the name that is above every **n**, *G3950*
Php 2:10 that at the **n** of Jesus every knee should *G3950*
Col 3:17 do it all in the **n** of the Lord Jesus *G3950*
2Th 1:12 this so that the **n** of our Lord Jesus may *G3950*
2Th 3: 6 In the **n** of the Lord Jesus Christ, we *G3950*
1Ti 6: 1 so that God's **n** and our teaching may not *G3950*
2Ti 2:19 who confesses the **n** of the Lord must turn *G3950*
Heb 1: 4 to the angels as the **n** he has inherited is *G3950*
Heb 2:12 "I will declare your **n** to my brothers and *G3950*
Heb 7: 2 the **n** Melchizedek means "king of NDT
Heb 13:15 the fruit of lips that openly profess his **n**. *G3950*
Jas 2: 7 the noble **n** of him to whom you *G3950*
Jas 5:10 prophets who spoke in the **n** of the Lord. *G3950*
Jas 5:14 anoint them with oil in the **n** of the Lord. *G3950*
1Pe 4:14 are insulted because of the **n** of Christ, *G3950*
1Pe 4:16 praise God that you bear that **n**. *G3950*
1Jn 2:12 have been forgiven on account of his **n**. *G3950*
1Jn 3:23 to believe *in* the **n** of his Son, Jesus Christ, *G3950*
1Jn 5:13 who believe in the **n** of the Son of God so *G3950*
3Jn 7 the sake of the **N** that they went out, *G3950*
3Jn 14 Greet the friends there by **n**. *G3950*
Rev 2: 3 have endured hardships for my **n**, *G3950*
Rev 2:13 Yet you remain true *to* my **n**. You did not *G3950*
Rev 2:17 a white stone with a new **n** written on it, *G3950*
Rev 3: 5 never blot out the **n** of that person from *G3950*
Rev 3: 5 acknowledge that **n** before my Father and *G3950*
Rev 3: 8 kept my word and have not denied my **n**. *G3950*
Rev 3:12 write on them the **n** of my God and the *G3950*
Rev 3:12 of my God and the **n** of the city of my God *G3950*
Rev 3:12 I will also write on them my new **n**. *G3950*
Rev 8:11 the **n** of the star is Wormwood. A third of *G3950*
Rev 9:11 whose **n** in Hebrew is Abaddon and in *G3950*
Rev 11:18 your people who revere your **n**, *G3950*
Rev 13: 1 on each head a blasphemous **n**. *G3950*
Rev 13: 6 to slander his **n** and his dwelling *G3950*
Rev 13:17 which is the **n** of the beast or the number *G3950*
Rev 13:17 name of the beast or the number *of* its **n**. *G3950*
Rev 14: 1 144,000 who had his **n** and his Father's *G3950*
Rev 14: 1 name and his Father's **n** written on their *G3950*
Rev 14:11 anyone who receives the mark *of* its **n**." *G3950*
Rev 15: 2 its image and over the number *of* its **n**. *G3950*
Rev 15: 4 fear you, Lord, and bring glory *to* your **n**? *G3950*
Rev 16: 9 heat and they cursed the **n** of God, *G3950*
Rev 17: 5 The **n** written on her forehead was a *G3950*
Rev 19:12 He has a **n** written on him that no one *G3950*
Rev 19:13 in blood, and his **n** is the Word of God. *G3950*
Rev 19:16 on his thigh he has this **n** written: *G3950*
Rev 20:15 Anyone whose **n** was not found written in NDT
Rev 22: 4 and his **n** will be on their foreheads. *G3950*

NAME'S (8) [NAME]

Ps 23: 3 me along the right paths for his **n** sake. H9005
Ps 79: 9 us and forgive our sins for your **n** sake. H9005
Ps 106: 8 Yet he saved them for his **n** sake, to make H9005
Ps 109:21 help me for your **n** sake; out of the H9005
Ps 143:11 For your **n** sake, LORD, preserve my life; H9005
Isa 48: 9 For my own **n** sake I delay my wrath; for H9005
Eze 20:44 deal with you for my **n** sake and not H9005
Ro 1: 5 that comes from faith for his **n** sake. *G3950*

NAMED (164) [NAME]

Ge 3:20 Adam **n** his wife Eve, because she H7924+9005
Ge 4:17 and *he* **n** it after his son Enoch. H9005+7924
Ge 4:19 women, one **n** Adah and the other Zillah. H9005
Ge 4:25 gave birth to a son and **n** him Seth, H7924+9005
Ge 4:26 had a son, and *he* **n** him Enosh. H9005+7924
Ge 5: 2 And *he* **n** them "Mankind" when H7924+9005
Ge 5: 3 his own image; and *he* **n** him Seth. H9005+7924
Ge 5:29 *He* **n** him Noah and said, "He will H9005+7924
Ge 10:25 One was **n** Peleg, because in his time the H9005
Ge 10:25 was divided; his brother was **n** Joktan. H9005
Ge 16: 1 But she had an Egyptian slave **n** Hagar; H9005
Ge 19:37 and *she* **n** him Moab; he H9005+7924
Ge 19:38 and *she* **n** him Ben-Ammi H9005+7924
Ge 23:16 him the price *he had* **n** in the hearing of H1819
Ge 24:29 Now Rebekah had a brother **n** Laban, and H9005
Ge 25:25 hairy garment; so *they* **n** him Esau. H9005+7924
Ge 25:26 Esau's heel; so he *was* **n** Jacob. H9005+7924
Ge 26:20 So *he* **n** the well Esek, because H9005+7924
Ge 26:21 that one also; so *he* **n** it Sitnah. H9005+7924
Ge 26:22 *He* **n** it Rehoboth, saying, "Now the H9005+7924
Ge 27:36 "*Isn't* he rightly **n** Jacob? This H9005+7924
Ge 29:32 *She* **n** him Reuben, for she said, "It H9005+7924
Ge 29:33 So *she* **n** him Simeon. H9005+7924
Ge 29:34 him three sons." So he *was* **n** Levi. H9005+7924
Ge 29:35 So *she* **n** him Judah H9005+7924
Ge 30: 6 Because of this *she* **n** him Dan. H9005+7924
Ge 30: 8 So *she* **n** him Naphtali. H9005+7924
Ge 30:11 good fortune!" So *she* **n** him Gad. H9005+7924
Ge 30:13 So *she* **n** him Asher. H9005+7924
Ge 30:18 So *she* **n** him Issachar. H9005+7924
Ge 30:20 So *she* **n** him Zebulun. H9005+7924
Ge 30:21 to a daughter and **n** her Dinah. H9005+7924
Ge 30:24 *She* **n** him Joseph, and said, "May H9005+7924
Ge 32: 2 So *he* **n** that place Mahanaim. H9005+7924
Ge 35: 8 So it *was* **n** Allon Bakuth. H9005+7924
Ge 35:10 will be Israel." So *he* **n** him Israel. H9005+7924
Ge 35:18 was dying—*she* **n** her son Ben-Oni. H9005+7924
Ge 35:18 But his father **n** him Benjamin. H7924
Ge 36:12 son Eliphaz also had a concubine **n** Timna, NDT
Ge 36:32 king of Edom. His city was **n** Dinhabah. H9005
Ge 36:35 His city was **n** Avith. H9005
Ge 36:39 His city was **n** Pau, and his wife's name H9005
Ge 38: 1 to stay with a man of Adullam **n** Hirah. H9005
Ge 38: 2 the daughter of a Canaanite man **n** Shua. H9005
Ge 38: 3 gave birth to a son, who *was* **n** Er. H9005+7924
Ge 38: 4 birth to a son and **n** him Onan. H9005+7924
Ge 38: 5 still another son and **n** him Shelah. H9005+7924
Ge 38:29 broken out!" And he *was* **n** Perez. H9005+7924
Ge 38:30 And he *was* **n** Zerah. H7924+9005
Ge 41:51 Joseph **n** his firstborn Manasseh H9005+7924
Ge 41:52 The second son *he* **n** Ephraim and H9005+7924
Ex 2:10 *She* **n** him Moses, saying, "I drew H9005+7924
Ex 2:22 and Moses **n** him Gershom H9005+7924
Ex 18: 3 One son was **n** Gershom, for Moses said H9005
Ex 18: 4 the other was **n** Eliezer, for he said H9005
Nu 11:34 the place *was* **n** Kibroth Hattaavah H7924+9005
Nu 21: 3 towns; so the place *was* **n** Hormah. H9005+7924
Nu 26:46 Asher had a daughter **n** Serah.) H9005
Dt 3:14 Maakathites; it *was* **n** after him, so H9005+7924
Jos 2: 1 house of a prostitute **n** Rahab and stayed H9005
Jos 19:47 settled in Leshem and **n** it Dan after their H7924
Jdg 8:31 him a son, whom *he* **n** Abimelek. H9005+8492
Jdg 10: 1 a man of Issachar **n** Tola son of Puah, the NDT
Jdg 13: 2 man of Zorah, **n** Manoah, from the clan H9005
Jdg 13:24 birth to a boy and **n** him Samson. H7924+9005
Jdg 17: 1 Now a man **n** Micah from the hill country H9005
Jdg 18:29 *They* **n** it Dan after their ancestor H7924+9005
Ru 1: 4 women, one **n** Orpah and the other Ruth. H9005
Ru 4:17 And *they* **n** him Obed. H7924+9005
1Sa 1:20 *She* **n** him Samuel, saying H7924+9005
1Sa 4:21 *She* **n** the boy Ichabod, saying, "The Glory H7924
1Sa 7:12 *He* **n** it Ebenezer, saying, "Thus far H7924+9005
1Sa 9: 2 Kish had a son **n** Saul, as handsome a H9005
1Sa 17: 4 A champion **n** Goliath, who was from H9005
1Sa 17:12 was the son of an Ephrathite **n** Jesse, H9005
1Sa 22:20 son of Ahitub, **n** Abiathar, escaped and H9005
2Sa 3: 7 had a concubine **n** Rizpah daughter of H9005
2Sa 4: 2 One was **n** Baanah and the other Rekab H9005
2Sa 9: 2 was a servant of Saul's household **n** Ziba. H9005
2Sa 9:12 Mephibosheth had a young son **n** Mika H9005
2Sa 12:24 to a son, and *they* **n** him Solomon. H9005+7924
2Sa 12:28 the city, and it *will* **be n** after me." H7924+9005
2Sa 13: 3 Amnon had an adviser **n** Jonadab son of H9005
2Sa 18:18 *He* **n** the pillar after himself, and H7924+9005
2Sa 20: 1 Now a troublemaker **n** Sheba son of Bikri H9005
2Sa 20:21 A man **n** Sheba son of Bikri, from the hill H9005
1Ki 7:21 to the south *he* **n** Jakin and the H7924+9005
1Ki 11:20 of Tahpenes bore him a son **n** Genubath, NDT
1Ki 11:26 his mother was a widow **n** Zeruah. H9005
1Ki 13: 2 'A son **n** Josiah will be born to the house H9005
2Ki 17:34 of Jacob, whom *he* **n** Israel. H8492+9005
2Ki 23:11 the room of an official **n** Nathan-Melek. NDT
1Ch 1:19 One was **n** Peleg, because in his time the H9005
1Ch 1:19 was divided; his brother was **n** Joktan. H9005
1Ch 1:43 son of Beor, whose city was **n** Dinhabah. H9005
1Ch 1:46 His city was **n** Avith. H9005
1Ch 1:50 His city was **n** Pau, and his wife's name H9005
1Ch 2:29 Abishur's wife was **n** Abihail, who bore H9005
1Ch 2:34 He had an Egyptian servant **n** Jarha. H9005
1Ch 4: 3 Their sister was **n** Hazzelelponi. H9005
1Ch 4: 9 His mother *had* **n** him Jabez H7924+9005
1Ch 6:65 the *previously* **n** towns. H7924+928+9005
1Ch 7:15 Another descendant was **n** Zelophehad H9005
1Ch 7:16 birth to a son and **n** him Peresh. H7924+9005
1Ch 7:16 His brother was **n** Sheresh, and his sons H9005
1Ch 7:23 *He* **n** him Beriah, because there H7924+9005
1Ch 9:31 A Levite **n** Mattithiah, the firstborn son of NDT
2Ch 3:17 to the south *he* **n** Jakin and the H7924+9005
2Ch 28: 9 a prophet of the LORD **n** Oded was there, H9005
Ezr 5:14 gave them to a man **n** Sheshbazzar, A10721
Ne 9: 7 Chaldeans and **n** him Abraham. H8492+9005
Ne 13:13 a Levite **n** Pedaiah in charge of the NDT
Est 2: 5 tribe of Benjamin, **n** Mordecai son of Jair H9005
Est 2: 7 Mordecai had a cousin **n** Hadassah, whom NDT
Job 42:14 The first daughter *he* **n** Jemimah H7924+9005
Ps 49:11 though *they had* **n** lands after H7924+9005
Ecc 6:10 exists *has* already **been n**, H9005+7924
Isa 61: 6 you *will* **be n** ministers of our God. H606
Eze 23: 4 The older was **n** Oholah, and her sister H9005
Eze 48:31 of the city will be **n** after the tribes of H9005
Mt 9: 9 he saw a man **n** Matthew sitting at the tax *G3306*
Mt 27:32 a man from Cyrene, **n** Simon, and they *G3950*
Mt 27:57 man from Arimathea, **n** Joseph, who had *G5540*
Mk 5:22 of the synagogue leaders, **n** Jairus, came, *G3950*
Lk 1: 5 of Judea there was a priest **n** Zechariah, *G3950*
Lk 1:27 to be married to a man **n** Joseph, *G3950*
Lk 2:21 child, he *was* **n** Jesus, the *G2813+3836+3950*
Lk 6:14 whom *he* **n** Peter), his brother *G3951*
Lk 8:41 Then a man **n** Jairus, a synagogue leader *G3950*
Lk 10:38 where a woman **n** Martha opened her *G3950*
Lk 16:20 At his gate was laid a beggar **n** Lazarus *G3950*
Lk 23:50 Now there was a man **n** Joseph, *G3950*
Lk 24:18 One of them, **n** Cleopas, asked him, "Are *G3950*
Jn 3: 1 a man **n** Nicodemus who was a member *G3950*
Jn 11: 1 Now a man **n** Lazarus was sick. He was from NDT
Jn 11:49 Then one of them, **n** Caiaphas, who was NDT
Ac 5: 1 Now a man **n** Ananias, together with his *G3950*
Ac 5:34 But a Pharisee **n** Gamaliel, a teacher of *G3950*
Ac 7:58 coats at the feet of a young man **n** Saul. *G2813*
Ac 8: 9 some time a man **n** Simon had practiced *G3950*
Ac 9:10 there was a disciple **n** Ananias. *G3950*
Ac 9:11 ask for a man from Tarsus **n** Saul, *G3950*
Ac 9:12 he has seen a man **n** Ananias come and *G3950*
Ac 9:33 There he found a man **n** Aeneas, who was *G3950*
Ac 9:36 In Joppa there was a disciple **n** Tabitha *G3950*
Ac 9:43 Joppa for some time with a tanner **n** Simon. NDT
Ac 10: 1 At Caesarea there was a man **n** Cornelius *G3950*
Ac 10: 5 to bring back a man **n** Simon who is called NDT
Ac 11:28 One of them, **n** Agabus, stood up and *G3950*
Ac 12:13 a servant **n** Rhoda came to answer *G3950*
Ac 13: 6 sorcerer and false prophet **n** Bar-Jesus, *G3950*
Ac 16: 1 where a disciple **n** Timothy lived, whose *G3950*
Ac 16:14 a woman from the city of Thyatira **n** Lydia, *G3950*
Ac 17:34 also a woman **n** Damaris, and a number *G3950*
Ac 18: 2 There he met a Jew **n** Aquila, a native of *G3950*
Ac 18:24 Meanwhile a Jew **n** Apollos, a native of *G3950*
Ac 19:24 A silversmith **n** Demetrius, who made *G3950*
Ac 20: 9 a window was a young man **n** Eutychus, *G3950*
Ac 21:10 a prophet **n** Agabus came down from *G3950*
Ac 22:12 "A man **n** Ananias came to see me. He was NDT
Ac 24: 1 some of the elders and a lawyer **n** Tertullus, NDT
Ac 25:19 about a dead man **n** Jesus who Paul NDT
Ac 27: 1 were handed over to a centurion **n** Julius, *G3950*
Rev 6: 8 Its rider was **n** Death, and Hades was *G3950*

NAMELESS (1) [NAME]

Job 30: 8 A base and **n** brood, they were H1172+9005

NAMELY (2) [NAME]

Ezr 8:24 of the leading priests, **n**, Sherebiah, H4200
Col 2: 2 may know the mystery of God, *n*, **Christ**, AIT

NAMES (80) [NAME]

Ge 2:20 So the man gave **n** to all the livestock, the H9005
Ge 25:13 These are the **n** *of* the sons of Ishmael H9005
Ge 25:16 these are the **n** of the twelve tribal H9005
Ge 26:18 gave them the same **n** his father had H9005
Ge 36:10 These are the **n** *of* Esau's sons: Eliphaz H9005
Ge 46: 8 These are the **n** *of* the sons of Israel H9005
Ge 48: 6 be reckoned under the **n** *of* their brothers. H9005
Ge 48:16 by my name and the **n** *of* my fathers H9005
Ex 1: 1 These are the **n** *of* the sons of Israel who H9005
Ex 1:15 whose **n** were Shiphrah and Puah H9005
Ex 6:16 These were the **n** *of* the sons of Levi H9005
Ex 23:13 Do not invoke the **n** *of* other gods; do not H9005
Ex 28: 9 on them the **n** *of* the sons of Israel H9005
Ex 28:10 six **n** on one stone and the remaining six H9005
Ex 28:11 Engrave the **n** *of* the sons of Israel on the H9005
Ex 28:12 Aaron is to bear the **n** on his shoulders as H9005
Ex 28:21 one for each of the **n** *of* the sons of Israel H9005
Ex 28:29 he will bear the **n** *of* the sons of Israel H9005
Ex 39: 6 like a seal with the **n** *of* the sons of Israel. H9005
Ex 39:14 one for each of the **n** *of* the sons of Israel H9005
Nu 1: 5 These are the **n** *of* the men who are to H9005
Nu 1:17 these men whose **n** had been specified, H9005
Nu 3: 2 The **n** *of* the sons of Aaron were Nadab H9005
Nu 3: 3 Those were the **n** *of* Aaron's sons, the H9005
Nu 3:17 These were the **n** *of* the sons of Levi H9005

Nu 3:18 These were the n *of* the Gershonite clans H9005
Nu 3:40 old or more and make a list of their n. H9005
Nu 11:26 whose n were Eldad and Medad H9005
Nu 13: 4 These are their n: from the tribe of Reuben H9005
Nu 13:16 These are the n *of* the men Moses sent to H9005
Nu 26:33 daughters, whose n were Mahlah, Noah, H9005
Nu 26:53 an inheritance based on the number of n. H9005
Nu 26:55 be according to the n *for* its ancestral tribe H9005
Nu 27: 1 The n *of* the daughters were Mahlah H9005
Nu 32:38 Baal Meon (these n were changed) and H9005
Nu 32:38 They gave n to the cities they rebuilt H9005
Nu 34:17 "These are the n *of* the men who are to H9005
Nu 34:19 These are their n: Caleb son of Jephunneh H9005
Dt 7:24 will wipe out their n from under heaven. H9005
Dt 12: 3 wipe out their n from those places. H9005
Dt 29:20 will blot out their n from under heaven. H9005
Jos 17: 3 daughters, whose n were Mahlah, Noah, H9005
Jos 23: 7 do not invoke the n *of* their gods or swear H9005
Jdg 8:14 down for him the n of the seventy-seven NDT
Ru 1: 2 the n *of* his two sons were Mahlon H9005
2Sa 5:14 These are the n *of* the children born to H9005
2Sa 7: 9 like the n *of* the greatest men on earth. H9005
2Sa 23: 8 These are the n *of* David's mighty warriors H9005
1Ki 4: 8 These are their n: Ben-Hur—in the hill H9005
1Ch 4:41 The men whose n were listed came in the H9005
1Ch 6:17 These are the n *of* the sons of Gershon H9005
1Ch 8:38 six sons, and these were their n: Azrikam, H9005
1Ch 9:44 six sons, and these were their n: Azrikam, H9005
1Ch 14: 4 These are the n *of* the children born to H9005
1Ch 17: 8 your name like the n *of* the greatest men H9005
1Ch 23:24 registered under their n and counted H9005
1Ch 24: 6 recorded their n in the presence of the king NDT
2Ch 31:16 n *were* **in the genealogical records**— H3509
Ezr 5: 4 "What are the n *of* those who are A10721
Ezr 5:10 We also asked them their n, so that we A10721
Ezr 5:10 write down the n *of* their leaders for A10721
Ezr 8:13 the last ones, whose n were Eliphelet H9005
Ps 16: 4 to such gods or take up their n on my lips. H9005
Ps 109:13 their n blotted out from the next H9005
Da 1: 7 The chief official gave them new n: to H9005
Hos 2:17 I will remove the n *of* the Baals from her H9005
Hos 2:17 her lips; no longer will their n be invoked. H9005
Zep 1: 4 the *very* n *of* the idolatrous priests H9005
Zec 13: 2 I will banish the n *of* the idols from the H9005
Mt 10: 2 These are the n of the twelve apostles *G3950*
Lk 10:20 rejoice that your n are written in heaven *G3950*
Ac 18:15 about words and n and your own law— *G3950*
Php 4: 3 whose n are in the book of life. *G3950*
Heb 12:23 the firstborn, *whose n are* **written** in heaven. AIT
Rev 13: 8 all whose n have not been written in the *G3950*
Rev 17: 3 with blasphemous n and had seven *G3950*
Rev 17: 8 of the earth whose n have not been *G3950*
Rev 21:12 were written the n of the twelve tribes *G3950*
Rev 21:14 on them were the n of the twelve *G3950*
Rev 21:27 only those whose n are written in the NDT

NAOMI (26) [NAOMI'S]

Ru 1: 2 his wife's name was N, and the names of H5843
Ru 1: 5 and N was left without her two H2021+851S
Ru 1: 6 When N heard in Moab that the LORD had NDT
Ru 1: 8 Then N said to her two daughters-in-law H5843
Ru 1:11 But N said, "Return home, my daughters H5843
Ru 1:15 said N, "your sister-in-law is going back to NDT
Ru 1:18 When N realized that Ruth was determined NDT
Ru 1:19 the women exclaimed, "Can this be N?" H5843
Ru 1:20 "Don't call me N," she told them. "Call H5843
Ru 1:21 Why call me N? The LORD has H5843
Ru 1:22 So N returned from Moab accompanied H5843
Ru 2: 1 Now N had a relative on her husband's H5843
Ru 2: 2 And Ruth the Moabite said to N, "Let me H5843
Ru 2: 2 eyes I find favor." N said to her, "Go ahead NDT
Ru 2: 6 who came back from Moab with N. H5843
Ru 2:20 N said to her daughter-in-law H5843
Ru 2:22 N said to Ruth her daughter-in-law, "It H5843
Ru 3: 1 day Ruth's mother-in-law N said to her, H5843
Ru 3:16 her mother-in-law, N asked, "How did it go NDT
Ru 3:18 Then N said, "Wait, my daughter, until you NDT
Ru 4: 3 "N, who has come back H5843
Ru 4: 5 "On the day you buy the land from N, you H5843
Ru 4: 9 I have bought from N all the property of H5843
Ru 4:14 The women said to N: "Praise be to the H5843
Ru 4:16 Then N took the child in her arms and H5843
Ru 4:17 women living there said, "N has a son!" H5843

NAOMI'S (1) [NAOMI]

Ru 1: 3 Now Elimelek, N husband, died, and she H5843

NAPHISH (3)

Ge 25:15 Tema, Jetur, N and Kedemah. H5874
1Ch 1:31 N and Kedemah. These were the H5874
1Ch 5:19 against the Hagrites, Jetur, N and Nodab. H5874

NAPHOTH (1) [NAPHOTH DOR]

Jos 17:11 settlements (the third in the list is N). H5868

NAPHOTH DOR (3) [NAPHOTH]

Jos 11: 2 foothills and in N on the west; H5869
Jos 12:23 the king of Dor (in N) one the king of H5869
1Ki 4:11 Ben-Abinadab—in N (he was married H5869

NAPHTALI (53) [NAPHTALITES]

Ge 30: 8 I have won." So she named him N. H5889
Ge 35:25 of Rachel's servant Bilhah: Dan and N. H5889
Ge 46:24 The sons of N: Jahziel, Guni, Jezer and H5889
Ge 49:21 "N is a doe set free that bears beautiful H5889
Ex 1: 4 Dan and N; Gad and Asher. H5889
Nu 1:15 from N, Ahira son of Enan." H5889
Nu 1:42 From the descendants of N: All the men H5889
Nu 1:43 number from the tribe of N was 53,400. H5889
Nu 2:29 The tribe of N will be next. The leader of H5889
Nu 2:29 of the people of N is Ahira son of Enan. H5889
Nu 7:78 the leader of the people of N, brought his H5889
Nu 10:27 over the division of the tribe of N. H1201+5889
Nu 13:14 from the tribe of N, Nahbi son of Vophsi; H5889
Nu 26:48 The descendants of N by their clans were H5889
Nu 26:50 These were the clans of N; those H5889
Nu 34:28 the leader from the tribe of N." H1201+5889
Dt 27:13 Asher, Zebulun, Dan and N. H5889
Dt 33:23 About N he said: "Naphtali is abounding H5889
Dt 33:23 "N is abounding with the favor of the LORD H5889
Dt 34: 2 all of N, the territory of Ephraim and H5889
Jos 19:32 lot came out for N according to its H1201+5889
Jos 19:39 the inheritance of the tribe of N, H1201+5889
Jos 20: 7 Kedesh in Galilee in the hill country of N, H5889
Jos 21: 6 N and the half-tribe of Manasseh in H5889
Jos 21:32 from the tribe of N, Kedesh in Galilee (a H5889
Jdg 1:33 Neither did N drive out those living in Beth H5889
Jdg 4: 6 from Kedesh in N and said to him, H5889
Jdg 4: 6 men of N and Zebulun and H1201+5889
Jdg 4:10 There Barak summoned Zebulun and N H5889
Jdg 5:18 very lives; so did N on the terraced fields. H5889
Jdg 6:35 Zebulun and N, so that they too H5889
Jdg 7:23 Israelites from N, Asher and all Manasseh H5889
1Ki 4:15 Ahimaaz—in N (he had married H5889
1Ki 7:14 from the tribe of N and whose father was H5889
1Ki 15:20 and all Kinnereth in addition to N. H824+5889
2Ki 15:29 including all the land of N, and deported H5889
1Ch 2: 2 Joseph, Benjamin, N, Gad and Asher. H5889
1Ch 6:62 Issachar, Asher and N, and from the part H5889
1Ch 6:76 from the tribe of N they received Kedesh H5889
1Ch 7:13 The sons of N: Jahziel, Guni, Jezer and H5889
1Ch 12:34 from N—1,000 officers, together with H5889
1Ch 12:40 Zebulun and N came bringing food on H5889
1Ch 27:19 son of Obadiah; over N: Jerimoth son of H5889
2Ch 16: 4 Abel Maim and all the store cities of N. H5889
2Ch 34: 6 Simeon, as far as N, and in the ruins H5889
Ps 68:27 there the princes of Zebulun and of N. H5889
Isa 9: 1 the land of Zebulun and the land of N, H5889
Eze 48: 3 "N will have one portion; it will border the H5889
Eze 48: 4 border the territory of N from east to west. H5889
Eze 48:34 the gate of Asher and the gate of N. H5889
Mt 4:13 the lake in the area of Zebulun and N— *G3750*
Mt 4:15 "Land of Zebulun and land *of* N, the Way *G3750*
Rev 7: 6 from the tribe *of* N 12,000, from the *G3750*

NAPHTALITES (1) [NAPHTALI]

Jdg 1:33 the N too lived among the Canaanite NDT

NAPHTUHITES (2)

Ge 10:13 of the Ludites, Anamites, Lehabites, N, H5888
1Ch 1:11 of the Ludites, Anamites, Lehabites, N, H5888

NAPKIN (KJV) (PIECE OF) CLOTH

NARCISSUS (1)

Ro 16:11 in the household of N who are in the Lord *G3727*

NARD (4)

SS 4:13 with choice fruits, with henna and n, H5948
SS 4:14 n and saffron, calamus and cinnamon H5948
Mk 14: 3 very expensive perfume, *made of* pure n. *G3726*
Jn 12: 3 Then Mary took about a pint *of* pure n, an *G3726*

NARROW (12) [NARROWER]

Nu 22:24 stood in a n **path** *through* the vineyards, H5469
Nu 22:26 ahead and stood in a n place where there H7639
1Ki 6: 4 He made n windows high up in the temple H7639
Pr 23:27 deep pit, and a wayward wife is a n well. H7639
Isa 28:20 the blanket *too* n to wrap around you. H7639
Eze 40:16 were surmounted by n parapet openings H357
Eze 40:25 its portico had n openings all around, NDT
Eze 41:16 thresholds and the n windows and H357
Eze 41:26 of the portico were n windows with palm H357
Mt 7:13 "Enter through the n gate. For wide is the *G5101*
Mt 7:14 is the gate and n the road that leads *G2567*
Lk 13:24 every effort to enter through the n door, *G5101*

NARROWER (1) [NARROW]

Eze 42: 5 Now the upper rooms were n, for the H7900

NATHAN (43)

2Sa 5:14 Shammua, Shobab, N, Solomon, H5990
2Sa 7: 2 he said to N the prophet, "Here I am H5990
2Sa 7: 3 N replied to the king, "Whatever you have H5990
2Sa 7: 4 that night the word of the LORD came to N, H5990
2Sa 7:17 N reported to David all the words of this H5990
2Sa 12: 1 The LORD sent N to David. When he came H5990
2Sa 12: 5 anger against the man and said to N, H5990
2Sa 12: 7 Then N said to David, "You are the man H5990
2Sa 12:13 Then David said to N, "I have sinned H5990
2Sa 12:13 N replied, "The LORD has taken away your H5990
2Sa 12:15 After N had gone home, the LORD struck H5990
2Sa 12:25 sent word through N the prophet to name H5990
2Sa 23:36 Igal son of N from Zobah, the son of H5990
1Ki 1: 8 son of Jehoiada, N the prophet, Shimei H5990
1Ki 1:10 he did not invite N the prophet or H5990
1Ki 1:11 Then N asked Bathsheba, Solomon's H5990
1Ki 1:22 with the king, N the prophet arrived. H5990
1Ki 1:23 the king was told, "N the prophet is here." H5990
1Ki 1:24 N said, "Have you, my lord the king H5990
1Ki 1:32 N the prophet and Benaiah son of H5990
1Ki 1:34 Zadok the priest and N the prophet anoint H5990
1Ki 1:38 Zadok the priest, N the prophet, Benaiah H5990
1Ki 1:44 Zadok the priest, N the prophet, Benaiah H5990
1Ki 1:45 Zadok the priest and N the prophet have H5990
1Ki 4: 5 Azariah son of N—in charge of the district H5990
1Ki 4: 5 Zabud son of N—a priest and adviser to H5990
1Ch 2:36 Attai was the father of N, Nathan the H5990
1Ch 2:36 father of Nathan, N the father of Zabad, H5990
1Ch 3: 5 Shammua, Shobab, N and Solomon H5990
1Ch 11:38 Joel the brother of N, Mibhar son of Hagri, H5990
1Ch 14: 4 Shammua, Shobab, N, Solomon, H5990
1Ch 17: 1 he said to N the prophet, "Here I H5990
1Ch 17: 2 N replied to David, "Whatever you have H5990
1Ch 17: 3 But that night the word of God came to N H5990
1Ch 17:15 N reported to David all the words of this H5990
1Ch 29:29 the records of N the prophet and the H5990
2Ch 9:29 written in the records of N the prophet, H5990
2Ch 29:25 Gad the king's seer and N the prophet; H5990
Ezr 8:16 Elnathan, N, Zechariah and H5990
Ezr 10:39 Shelemiah, N, Adaiah, H5990
Ps 51: T When the prophet N came to him after H5990
Zec 12:12 the clan of the house of N and their wives, H5990
Lk 3:31 Mattatha, the son *of* N, the son of David, *G3718*

NATHAN-MELEK (1)

2Ki 23:11 near the room of an official named N. H5994

NATHANAEL (6)

Jn 1:45 Philip found N and told him, "We have *G3720*
Jn 1:46 come from there?" N asked. "Come and *G3720*
Jn 1:47 When Jesus saw N approaching, he said *G3720*
Jn 1:48 do you know me?" N asked. Jesus *G3720*
Jn 1:49 Then N declared, "Rabbi, you are the Son *G3720*
Jn 21: 2 N from Cana in Galilee, the sons of *G3720*

NATION (158) [NATIONAL, NATIONALITIES, NATIONALITY, NATIONS, NATIONS']

Ge 12: 2 "I will make you into a great n, and I will H1580
Ge 15:14 But I will punish the n they serve as slaves H1580
Ge 17:20 and I will make him into a great n. H1580
Ge 18:18 surely become a great and powerful n, H1580
Ge 20: 4 will you destroy an innocent n? H1580
Ge 21:13 make the son of the slave into a n also, H1580
Ge 21:18 for I will make him into a great n. H1580
Ge 35:11 A n and a community of nations will H1580
Ge 46: 3 I will make you into a great n there. H1580
Ex 9:24 land of Egypt since it had become a n. H1580
Ex 19: 6 me a kingdom of priests and a holy n. H1580
Ex 23:27 into confusion every n you encounter. H6639
Ex 32:10 Then I will make you into a great n." H1580
Ex 33:13 Remember that this n is your people." H1580
Ex 34:10 before done in any n in all the world. H1580
Nu 14:12 make you into a n greater and stronger H1580
Dt 4: 6 "Surely this great n is a wise and H1580
Dt 4: 7 What other n is so great as to have their H1580
Dt 4: 8 And what other n is so great as to have H1580
Dt 4:34 take for himself one n out of another H1580
Dt 4:34 himself one nation out of another n, H1580
Dt 9:14 will make you into a n stronger and more H1580
Dt 26: 5 lived there and became a great n, H1580
Dt 28:32 daughters will be given to another n, H6639
Dt 28:36 you set over you to a n unknown to you H1580
Dt 28:49 LORD will bring a n against you from far H1580
Dt 28:49 a n whose language you will not H1580
Dt 28:50 a fierce-looking n without respect for the H1580
Dt 32:21 make them angry by a n that has no H1580
Dt 32:28 They are a n without sense, there is no H1580
Jos 3:17 by until the whole n had completed the H1580
Jos 4: 1 When the whole n had finished crossing H1580
Jos 5: 8 And after the whole n had been H1580
Jos 10:13 till the n avenged itself on its enemies H1580
Jdg 2:20 "Because this n has violated the covenant H1580
2Sa 1:12 army of the LORD and for the n *of* Israel, H1074
2Sa 7:23 the one n on earth that God went out to H1580
1Ki 5: 7 David a wise son to rule over this great n." H6639
1Ki 18:10 there is not a n or kingdom where my H1580
1Ki 18:10 And whenever a n or kingdom claimed H1580
2Ki 18:33 Has the god of any n ever delivered his H1580
1Ch 16:20 they wandered from n to nation, from one H1580
1Ch 16:20 they wandered from nation to n, from one H1580
1Ch 17:21 the one n on earth whose God went out to H1580
2Ch 15: 6 *One* n was being crushed by another and H1580
2Ch 32:15 no god of any n or kingdom has been H1580
Job 34:29 Yet he is over individual and n alike, H1580
Ps 33:12 Blessed is the n whose God is the LORD H1580
Ps 43: 1 plead my cause against an unfaithful n. H1580
Ps 74: 2 Remember the n you purchased long ago H6337
Ps 83: 4 "let us destroy them as a n, so that H1580
Ps 105:13 they wandered from n to nation, from one H1580
Ps 105:13 they wandered from nation to n, from one H1580
Ps 106: 5 share in the joy of your n and join your H1580
Ps 147:20 He has done this for no other n; they do H1580
Pr 11:14 For lack of guidance a n falls, but victory H6639
Pr 14:34 Righteousness exalts a n, but sin H1580
Isa 1: 4 Woe to the sinful n, a people whose guilt H1580
Isa 2: 4 N will not take up sword against nation H1580
Isa 2: 4 Nation will not take up sword against n H1580

N

Isa 5: 7 of the LORD Almighty is the n *of* Israel, H1074
Isa 9: 3 have enlarged the n and increased their H1580
Isa 10: 6 I send him against a godless n, I dispatch H1580
Isa 14:32 shall be given to the envoys of that n? H1580
Isa 18: 2 an aggressive n *of* strange speech H1580
Isa 18: 7 an aggressive n *of* strange speech H1580
Isa 26: 2 the gates that the righteous n may enter, H1580
Isa 26: 2 nation may enter, the n that keeps faith. NDT
Isa 26:15 You have enlarged the n, LORD; you have H1580
Isa 26:15 the nation, LORD; you have enlarged the n. H1580
Isa 30: 6 humps of camels, to that unprofitable n, H6639
Isa 31: 2 He will rise up against that wicked n H1074
Isa 49: 7 who was despised and abhorred by the n, H1580
Isa 51: 4 people; hear me, my n: Instruction will go H4211
Isa 58: 2 as if they were a n that does what is right H1580
Isa 60:12 For the n or kingdom that will not serve H1580
Isa 60:22 a thousand, the smallest a mighty n. H1580
Isa 65: 1 To a n that did not call on my name, H1580
Isa 66: 8 born in a day or a n be brought forth in a H1580
Jer 2:11 Has a n ever changed its gods? (Yet they H1580
Jer 3:19 the most beautiful inheritance of *any* n. H1580
Jer 5: 9 I not avenge myself on such a n as this? H1580
Jer 5:15 "I am bringing a distant n against you H1580
Jer 5:15 an ancient and enduring n, a people H1580
Jer 5:29 I not avenge myself on such a n as this? H1580
Jer 6:22 a great n is being stirred up from the ends H1580
Jer 7:28 'This is the n that has not obeyed the LORD H1580
Jer 8: 3 survivors of this evil n will prefer death to H5476
Jer 9: 9 I not avenge myself on such a n as this?" H1580
Jer 12:17 But if any n does not listen, I will H1580
Jer 18: 7 I announce that a n or kingdom is to be H1580
Jer 18: 8 if that n I warned repents of its evil H1580
Jer 18: 9 I announce that a n or kingdom is to be H1580
Jer 19:11 I will smash this n and this city just as this H6639
Jer 25:12 will punish the king of Babylon and his n, H1580
Jer 25:32 Disaster is spreading from n to nation; H1580
Jer 25:32 Disaster is spreading from nation to n; H1580
Jer 27: 8 any n or kingdom will not serve H1580
Jer 27: 8 I will punish that n with the sword, famine H1580
Jer 27:11 But if any n will bow its neck under the H1580
Jer 27:11 I will let **that** n remain in its own land to H2257S
Jer 27:13 has threatened any n that will not serve H1580
Jer 28:15 you have persuaded this n to trust in lies. H6639
Jer 31:36 Israel ever cease being a n before me." H1580
Jer 33:24 people and no longer regard them as a n. H1580
Jer 48: 2 let us put an end to that n.' You, H1580
Jer 48:42 be destroyed as a n because she defied H6639
Jer 49:31 "Arise and attack a n at ease, which lives H1580
Jer 49:31 "a n that has neither gates nor bars NDT
Jer 49:36 there will not be a n where Elam's exiles H1580
Jer 50: 3 A n from the north will attack her and lay H1580
Jer 50:41 a great n and many kings are being H1580
La 4:17 we watched for a n that could not save us. H1580
Eze 2: 3 to a rebellious n that has rebelled against H1580
Eze 30:12 of the Nile and sell the land to an **evil** *n*; AIT
Eze 36:13 people and deprive your n of its children," H1580
Eze 36:14 devour people or make your n childless, H1580
Eze 36:15 of the peoples or cause your n to fall, H1580
Eze 37:22 I will make them one n in the land, on the H1580
Da 3:29 the people of any n or language who A10040
Da 8:22 will emerge from his n but will not have H1580
Joel 1: 6 A n has invaded my land, a mighty army H1580
Joel 3: 8 sell them to the Sabeans, a n far away." H1580
Am 6: 1 you notable men of the foremost n, to H1580
Am 6:14 "I will stir up a n against you, Israel, H1580
Mic 4: 3 N will not take up sword against nation H1580
Mic 4: 3 Nation will not take up sword against n H1580
Mic 4: 7 remnant, those driven away a strong n. H1580
Hab 3:16 of calamity to come on the n invading us. H6639
Zep 2: 1 yourselves together, you shameful n, H1580
Zep 2: 9 survivors of my n will inherit their land." H1580
Hag 2:14 is with this people and this n in my sight, H1580
Mal 3: 9 a curse—your whole n—because you are H1580
Mt 24: 7 N will rise against nation, and kingdom *G1620*
Mt 24: 7 Nation will rise against n, and kingdom *G1620*
Mk 13: 8 N will rise against nation, and kingdom *G1620*
Mk 13: 8 Nation will rise against n, and kingdom *G1620*
Lk 7: 5 because he loves our n and has built our *G1620*
Lk 21:10 "N will rise against nation, and kingdom *G1620*
Lk 21:10 "Nation will rise against n, and kingdom *G1620*
Lk 23: 2 have found this man subverting our n. *G1620*
Jn 11:48 take away both our temple and our n." *G1620*
Jn 11:50 the people than that the whole n perish." *G1620*
Jn 11:51 that Jesus would die for the Jewish n, *G1620*
Jn 11:52 not only for that n but also for the *G1620*
Ac 2: 5 Jews from every n under heaven. *G1620*
Ac 7: 7 But I will punish the n they serve as slaves *G1620*
Ac 10:35 accepts from every n the one who fears *G1620*
Ac 24: 2 has brought about reforms *in* this n. *G1620*
Ac 24:10 years you have been a judge *over* this n; *G1620*
Ro 10:19 you envious by those who are not a n; *G1620*
Ro 10:19 will make you angry by a n that has no *G1620*
1Pe 2: 9 royal priesthood, a holy n, God's special *G1620*
Rev 5: 9 tribe and language and people and n. *G1620*
Rev 7: 9 no one could count, from every n, tribe, *G1620*
Rev 11: 9 language and n will gaze on their bodies *G1620*
Rev 13: 7 over every tribe, people, language and n. *G1620*
Rev 14: 6 who live on the earth—to every n, tribe, *G1620*

NATIONAL (1) [NATION]

2Ki 17:29 **each** n **group** made its own gods in H1580+1580

NATIONALITIES (2) [NATION]

Est 8:17 people of **other** n became H6639+2021+824
Est 9: 2 of all the other n were afraid of them. H6639

NATIONALITY (5) [NATION]

Est 2:10 had not revealed her n and family H6639
Est 2:20 background and n just as Mordecai had H6639
Est 3:14 the people of every n so they would be NDT
Est 8:11 the armed men of any n or province who H6639
Est 8:13 the people of every n so that the Jews H6639

NATIONS (563) [NATION]

Ge 10: 5 territories by their clans within their n, H1580
Ge 10:20 languages, in their territories and n. H1580
Ge 10:31 languages, in their territories and n. H1580
Ge 10:32 to their lines of descent, within their n. H1580
Ge 10:32 From these the n spread out over the H1580
Ge 17: 4 You will be the father of many n. H1580
Ge 17: 5 I have made you a father of many n. H1580
Ge 17: 6 I will make n of you, and kings H1580
Ge 17:16 her so that she will be the mother of n; H1580
Ge 18:18 all n *on* earth will be blessed through H1580
Ge 22:18 your offspring all n *on* earth will be H1580
Ge 25:23 said to her, "Two n are in your womb, and H1580
Ge 26: 4 your offspring all n *on* earth will be H1580
Ge 27:29 May n serve you and peoples bow down H6639
Ge 35:11 a community of n will come from you, H1580
Ge 48:19 descendants will become a group of n." H1580
Ge 49:10 the obedience of the n shall be his. H6639
Ex 15:14 The n will hear and tremble; anguish will H6639
Ex 19: 5 then out of all n you will be my treasured H6639
Ex 34:24 I will drive out n before you and enlarge H1580
Lev 18:24 this is how the n that I am going to H1580
Lev 18:28 it vomited out the n that were before you. H1580
Lev 20:23 the customs of the n I am going to drive H1580
Lev 20:24 who has set you apart from the n. H6639
Lev 20:26 set you apart from the n to be my own. H6639
Lev 25:44 slaves are to come from the n around you; H1580
Lev 26:33 you among the n and will draw out my H1580
Lev 26:38 You will perish among the n; the land of H1580
Lev 26:45 Egypt in the sight of the n to be their God. H1580
Nu 14:15 the n who have heard this report about H1580
Nu 23: 9 do not consider themselves one of the n. H1580
Nu 24: 8 They devour hostile n and break their H1580
Nu 24:20 "Amalek was first among the n, but their H1580
Dt 2:25 fear of you on all the n under heaven. H6639
Dt 4: 6 your wisdom and understanding to the n, H6639
Dt 4:19 apportioned to all the n under heaven. H6639
Dt 4:27 survive among the n to which the LORD H1580
Dt 4:38 out before you n greater and stronger H1580
Dt 7: 1 drives out before you many n— H1580
Dt 7: 1 seven n larger and stronger than you H1580
Dt 7:17 "These n are stronger than we are. H1580
Dt 7:22 God will drive out those n before you, H1580
Dt 8:20 Like the n the LORD destroyed before you H1580
Dt 9: 1 in and dispossess n greater and stronger H1580
Dt 9: 4 wickedness of these n that the LORD is H1580
Dt 9: 5 on account of the wickedness of these n, H1580
Dt 10:15 above all the n—as it is today. H6639
Dt 11:23 LORD will drive out all these n before you, H1580
Dt 11:23 you will dispossess n larger and stronger H1580
Dt 12: 2 where the n you are dispossessing H1580
Dt 12:29 cut off before you the n you are about to H1580
Dt 12:30 "How do these n serve their gods? H1580
Dt 15: 6 will lend to many n but will borrow from H1580
Dt 15: 6 will rule over many n but none will rule H1580
Dt 17:14 set a king over us like all the n around us," H1580
Dt 18: 9 the detestable ways of the n there. H1580
Dt 18:12 God will drive out **those** n before you. H4392S
Dt 18:14 The n you will dispossess listen to those H1580
Dt 19: 1 God has destroyed the n whose land he is H1580
Dt 20:15 you and do not belong to the n nearby. H1580
Dt 20:16 in the cities of the n the LORD your God is H6639
Dt 26:19 high above all the n he has made and H1580
Dt 28: 1 will set you high above all the n *on* earth. H1580
Dt 28:12 will lend to many n but will borrow from H1580
Dt 28:64 the LORD will scatter you among all n, H6639
Dt 28:65 Among those n you will find no repose, H1580
Dt 29:18 to go and worship the gods of those n; H1580
Dt 29:24 All the n will ask: "Why has the LORD H1580
Dt 30: 1 LORD your God disperses you among the n, H1580
Dt 30: 3 again from all the n where he scattered H6639
Dt 31: 3 He will destroy these n before you, and H1580
Dt 32: 8 Most High gave the n their inheritance, H1580
Dt 32:43 Rejoice, you n, with his people, for he will H1580
Dt 33:17 With them he will gore the n, even those H6639
Jos 23: 3 God has done to all these n for your sake; H1580
Jos 23: 4 tribes all the land of the n that remain— H1580
Jos 23: 4 that remain—the n I conquered H1580
Jos 23: 7 associate with these n that remain among H1580
Jos 23: 9 out before you great and powerful n; H1580
Jos 23:12 survivors of these n that remain among H1580
Jos 23:13 no longer drive out these n before you. H1580
Jos 24:17 among all the n through which we H6639
Jos 24:18 And the LORD drove out before us all the n H6639
Jdg 2:21 them any of the n Joshua left when he H1580
Jdg 2:23 The LORD had allowed those n to remain H1580
Jdg 3: 1 These are the n the LORD left to test all H1580
1Sa 8: 5 to lead us, such as all the other n have." H1580
1Sa 8:20 Then we will be like all the other n, with a H1580
2Sa 7:23 by driving out n and their gods from H1580
2Sa 8:11 gold from all the n he had subdued: H1580
2Sa 22:44 you have preserved me as the head of n. H1580
2Sa 22:48 avenges me, who puts the n under me, H6639
2Sa 22:50 among the n; I will sing the praises H1580
1Ki 4:31 his fame spread to all the surrounding n. H1580
1Ki 4:34 From all n people came to listen to H6639
1Ki 8:53 out from all the n *of* the world to be your H6639
1Ki 11: 2 They were from n about which the LORD H1580
1Ki 14:24 practices of the n the LORD had driven out H1580
2Ki 16: 3 practices of the n the LORD had driven out H1580
2Ki 17: 8 the practices of the n the LORD had driven H1580
2Ki 17:11 as the n whom the LORD had driven out H1580
2Ki 17:15 They imitated the n around them H1580
2Ki 17:33 the customs of the n from which they had H1580
2Ki 19:12 Did the gods of the n that were destroyed H1580
2Ki 19:17 have laid waste these n and their lands. H1580
2Ki 21: 2 practices of the n the LORD had driven out H1580
2Ki 21: 9 more evil than the n the LORD had H1580
1Ch 14:17 the LORD made all the n fear him. H1580
1Ch 16: 8 known among the n what he has done. H6639
1Ch 16:24 Declare his glory among the n, his H1580
1Ch 16:26 For all the gods of the n are idols, but the H6639
1Ch 16:28 all you families of n, ascribe to the LORD H6639
1Ch 16:31 let them say among the n, "The LORD H1580
1Ch 16:35 gather us and deliver us from the n, that H1580
1Ch 17:21 wonders by driving out n from before your H1580
1Ch 18:11 gold he had taken from all these n: H1580
1Ch 22: 5 fame and splendor in the sight of all the n. H824
2Ch 20: 6 You rule over all the kingdoms of the n H1580
2Ch 28: 3 practices of the n the LORD had driven out H1580
2Ch 32:13 the gods of those n ever able to H824+1580
2Ch 32:14 the gods of these n that my predecessors H1580
2Ch 32:23 on he was highly regarded by all the n. H1580
2Ch 33: 2 practices of the n the LORD had driven out H1580
2Ch 33: 9 more evil than the n the LORD had H1580
2Ch 36:14 practices of the n and defiling the temple H1580
Ne 1: 8 unfaithful, I will scatter you among the n, H6639
Ne 5:17 who came to us from the surrounding n. H1580
Ne 6: 6 "It is reported among the n—and Geshem H1580
Ne 6:16 all the surrounding n were afraid and lost H1580
Ne 9:22 "You gave them kingdoms and n H6639
Ne 13:26 Among the many n there was no king like H1580
Job 12:23 He makes n great, and destroys them; he H1580
Job 12:23 he enlarges n, and disperses them. H1580
Job 36:31 way he governs the n and provides food H6639
Ps 2: 1 Why do the n conspire and the peoples H1580
Ps 2: 8 I will make the n your inheritance H1580
Ps 9: 5 have rebuked the n and destroyed the H1580
Ps 9:11 proclaim among the n what he has done. H6639
Ps 9:15 The n have fallen into the pit they have H1580
Ps 9:17 of the dead, all the n that forget God. H1580
Ps 9:19 let the n be judged in your presence. H1580
Ps 9:20 let the n know they are only mortal. H1580
Ps 10:16 ever; the n will perish from his land. H1580
Ps 18:43 you have made me the head of n. H1580
Ps 18:47 avenges me, who subdues n under me, H6639
Ps 18:49 among the n; I will sing the praises H1580
Ps 22:27 the families of the n will bow down H1580
Ps 22:28 to the LORD and he rules over the n. H1580
Ps 33:10 The LORD foils the plans of the n; he H1580
Ps 44: 2 hand you drove out the n and planted our H1580
Ps 44:11 have scattered us among the n. H1580
Ps 44:14 You have made us a byword among the n; H1580
Ps 45: 5 enemies; let the n fall beneath your feet. H6639
Ps 45:17 therefore the n will praise you for ever H6639
Ps 46: 6 N are in uproar, kingdoms fall; he lifts his H1580
Ps 46:10 I will be exalted among the n, I will be H1580
Ps 47: 1 your hands, all you n; shout to God with H6639
Ps 47: 3 He subdued n under us, peoples under H6639
Ps 47: 8 God reigns over the n; God is seated on H1580
Ps 47: 9 The nobles of the n assemble as the H6639
Ps 56: 7 in your anger, God, bring the n down. H6639
Ps 57: 9 among the n; I will sing of you H6639
Ps 59: 5 rouse yourself to punish all the n; show H1580
Ps 59: 8 at them, LORD; you scoff at all those n. H1580
Ps 65: 7 of their waves, and the turmoil of the n. H4211
Ps 66: 7 his eyes watch the n—let not the H1580
Ps 67: 2 on earth, your salvation among all n. H1580
Ps 67: 4 May the n be glad and sing for joy, for H4211
Ps 67: 4 with equity and guide the n of the earth. H4211
Ps 68:30 herd of bulls among the calves of the n. H6639
Ps 68:30 Scatter the n who delight in war. H6639
Ps 72:11 bow down to him and all n serve him. H1580
Ps 72:17 Then all n will be blessed through him H1580
Ps 78:55 He drove out n before them and allotted H1580
Ps 79: 1 the n have invaded your inheritance H1580
Ps 79: 6 out your wrath on the n that do not H1580
Ps 79:10 Why should the n say, "Where is their H1580
Ps 79:10 known among the n that you avenge the H1580
Ps 80: 8 you drove out the n and planted it. H1580
Ps 82: 8 for all the n are your inheritance. H1580
Ps 86: 9 All the n you have made will come and H1580
Ps 89:50 I bear in my heart the taunts of all the n, H6639
Ps 94:10 Does he who disciplines n not punish H1580
Ps 96: 3 Declare his glory among the n, his H1580
Ps 96: 5 For all the gods of the n are idols, but the H6639
Ps 96: 7 all you families of n, ascribe to the LORD H6639
Ps 96:10 Say among the n, "The LORD reigns." H1580
Ps 98: 2 revealed his righteousness to the n. H1580
Ps 99: 1 The LORD reigns, let the n tremble; he sits H6639
Ps 99: 2 LORD in Zion; he is exalted over all the n. H6639
Ps 102:15 The n will fear the name of the LORD, all H1580
Ps 105: 1 known among the n what he has done. H6639

Ps 105:44 he gave them the lands of the **n**, and they H1580
Ps 106:27 fall among the **n** and scatter them H1580
Ps 106:35 mingled with the **n** and adopted their H1580
Ps 106:41 He gave them into the hands of the **n** H1580
Ps 106:47 gather us from the **n**, that we may H1580
Ps 108: 3 among the **n**; I will sing of you H6639
Ps 110: 6 He will judge the **n**, heaping up the dead H1580
Ps 111: 6 giving them the lands of other **n**. H1580
Ps 113: 4 The LORD is exalted over all the **n**, his H1580
Ps 115: 2 Why do the **n** say, "Where is their God?" H1580
Ps 117: 1 the LORD, all you **n**; extol him, all you H1580
Ps 118:10 All the **n** surrounded me, but in the name H1580
Ps 126: 2 Then it was said among the **n**, "The LORD H1580
Ps 135:10 He struck down many **n** and killed mighty H1580
Ps 135:15 The idols of the **n** are silver and gold H1580
Ps 148:11 kings of the earth and all **n**, you princes H4211
Ps 149: 7 vengeance on the **n** and punishment on H1580
Pr 24:24 cursed by peoples and denounced by **n**. H4211
Isa 2: 2 above the hills, and all **n** will stream to it. H1580
Isa 2: 4 will judge between the **n** and will settle H1580
Isa 5:26 He lifts up a banner for the distant **n**, he H1580
Isa 8: 9 Raise the war cry, you **n**, and be shattered! H6639
Isa 9: 1 the future he will honor Galilee of the **n**, H1580
Isa 10: 7 is to destroy, to put an end to many **n**. H1580
Isa 10:13 I removed the boundaries of **n**, H6639
Isa 10:14 my hand reached for the wealth of the **n**; H6639
Isa 11:10 the peoples; the **n** will rally to him H1580
Isa 11:12 a banner for the **n** and gather the exiles H1580
Isa 12: 4 known among the **n** what he has done, H6639
Isa 13: 4 the kingdoms, like **n** massing together! H1580
Isa 14: 2 **N** will take them and bring them to their H6639
Isa 14: 2 take possession of **the n** and make them H4392S
Isa 14: 6 in fury subdued **n** with relentless H1580
Isa 14: 9 all those who were kings over the **n**. H1580
Isa 14:12 to the earth, you who once laid low the **n**! H1580
Isa 14:18 All the kings of the **n** lie in state, each in H1580
Isa 14:26 this is the hand stretched out over all **n**. H1580
Isa 16: 8 The rulers of the **n** have trampled down H1580
Isa 17:12 Woe to the many **n** that rage—they rage H6639
Isa 23: 3 she became the marketplace of the **n**. H1580
Isa 24:13 will it be on the earth and among the **n**, H6639
Isa 25: 3 cities of ruthless **n** will revere you. H1580
Isa 25: 7 all peoples, the sheet that covers all **n**; H1580
Isa 29: 7 the hordes of all the **n** that fight against H1580
Isa 29: 8 the hordes of all the **n** that fight against H1580
Isa 30:28 He shakes the **n** in the sieve of H1580
Isa 33: 3 when you rise up, the **n** scatter. H1580
Isa 33: 4 Your plunder, O **n**, is harvested as by young NDT
Isa 34: 1 Come near, you **n**, and listen; pay H1580
Isa 34: 2 The LORD is angry with all **n**; his wrath is H1580
Isa 36:18 the gods of any **n** ever delivered their H1580
Isa 37:12 Did the gods of the **n** that were destroyed H1580
Isa 40:15 Surely the **n** are like a drop in a bucket H1580
Isa 40:17 Before him all the **n** are as nothing; they H1580
Isa 41: 1 Let the **n** renew their strength H4211
Isa 41: 2 He hands **n** over to him and subdues H1580
Isa 42: 1 on him, and he will bring justice to the **n**. H1580
Isa 43: 4 **n** in exchange for your life. H4211
Isa 43: 9 All the **n** gather together and the peoples H1580
Isa 45: 1 hold of to subdue **n** before him and to H1580
Isa 45:20 assemble, you fugitives from the **n**. H1580
Isa 49: 1 you islands; hear this, you distant **n**: H4211
Isa 49:22 I will beckon to the **n**, I will lift up my H1580
Isa 51: 4 my justice will become a light to the **n**. H6639
Isa 51: 5 my arm will bring justice to the **n**. H6639
Isa 52:10 bare his holy arm in the sight of all the **n**, H1580
Isa 52:15 so he will sprinkle many **n**, and kings will H1580
Isa 54: 3 will dispossess **n** and settle in their H1580
Isa 55: 5 Surely you will summon **n** you know not H1580
Isa 55: 5 **n** you do not know will come running H1580
Isa 56: 7 will be called a house of prayer for all **n**." H6639
Isa 60: 3 **N** will come to your light, and kings to the H1580
Isa 60: 5 to you the riches of the **n** will come. H1580
Isa 60:11 may bring you the wealth of the **n**— H1580
Isa 60:16 drink the milk of **n** and be nursed at royal H1580
Isa 61: 6 You will feed on the wealth of **n**, and in H1580
Isa 61: 9 be known among the **n** and their offspring H1580
Isa 61:11 praise spring up before all **n**. H1580
Isa 62: 2 The **n** will see your vindication, and all H1580
Isa 62:10 Raise a banner for the **n**. H6639
Isa 63: 3 from the **n** no one was with me. H6639
Isa 63: 6 I trampled the **n** in my anger; in my wrath H6639
Isa 64: 2 cause the **n** to quake before you! H1580
Isa 66:12 the wealth of **n** like a flooding stream H1580
Isa 66:18 gather the **people of** all **n** and languages H1580
Isa 66:19 some of those who survive to the **n**— H1580
Isa 66:19 They will proclaim my glory among the **n**. H1580
Isa 66:20 from all the **n**, to my holy mountain H1580
Jer 1: 5 I appointed you as a prophet to the **n**." H1580
Jer 1:10 I appoint you over **n** and kingdoms to H1580
Jer 3:17 all **n** will gather in Jerusalem to H1580
Jer 4: 2 then the **n** will invoke blessings by him H1580
Jer 4: 7 out of his lair; a destroyer of **n** has set out. H1580
Jer 4:16 "Tell this to the **n**, proclaim concerning H1580
Jer 6:18 Therefore hear, you **n**; you who are H1580
Jer 9:16 scatter them among **n** that neither they H1580
Jer 9:26 For all these **n** are really uncircumcised H1580
Jer 10: 2 learn the ways of the **n** or be terrified by H1580
Jer 10: 2 though the **n** are terrified by them. H1580
Jer 10: 7 fear you, King of the **n**? This is your due. H1580
Jer 10: 7 the wise leaders of the **n** and in all their H1580
Jer 10:10 trembles; the **n** cannot endure his wrath. H1580
Jer 10:25 out your wrath on the **n** that do not H1580
Jer 14:22 of the worthless idols of the **n** bring rain? H1580
Jer 16:19 to you the **n** will come from the ends of H1580
Jer 18:13 "Inquire among the **n**: Who has ever H1580
Jer 22: 8 "People from many **n** will pass by this city H1580
Jer 25: 9 against all the surrounding **n**. H1580
Jer 25:11 these **n** will serve the king of Babylon H1580
Jer 25:13 prophesied by Jeremiah against all the **n**. H1580
Jer 25:14 be enslaved by many **n** and great kings; H1580
Jer 25:15 make all the **n** to whom I send you H1580
Jer 25:17 made all the **n** to whom he sent me H1580
Jer 25:31 the LORD will bring charges against the **n**; H1580
Jer 26: 6 city a curse among all the **n** *of* the earth. H1580
Jer 27: 7 All **n** will serve him and his son and his H1580
Jer 27: 7 then many **n** and great kings will H1580
Jer 28:11 off the neck of all the **n** within two years. H1580
Jer 28:14 necks of all these **n** to make them serve H1580
Jer 29:14 you from all the **n** and places where I H1580
Jer 29:18 among all the **n** where I drive them. H1580
Jer 30:11 destroy all the **n** among which I scatter H1580
Jer 31: 7 Jacob; shout for the foremost of the **n**. H1580
Jer 31:10 word of the LORD, you **n**; proclaim it in H1580
Jer 33: 9 honor before all **n** *on* earth that hear of H1580
Jer 36: 2 all the other **n** from the time I began H1580
Jer 43: 5 Judah from all the **n** where they had been H1580
Jer 44: 8 of reproach among all the **n** *on* earth. H1580
Jer 46: 1 to Jeremiah the prophet concerning the **n**: H1580
Jer 46:12 The **n** will hear of your shame; your cries H1580
Jer 46:28 destroy all the **n** among which I scatter H1580
Jer 49:14 an envoy was sent to the **n** to say H1580
Jer 49:15 "Now I will make you small among the **n** H1580
Jer 50: 2 "Announce and proclaim among the **n** H1580
Jer 50: 9 an alliance of great **n** from the land of the H1580
Jer 50:12 She will be the least of the **n**—a H1580
Jer 50:23 How desolate is Babylon among the **n**! H1580
Jer 50:46 tremble; its cry will resound among the **n**. H1580
Jer 51: 7 The **n** drank her wine; therefore they have H1580
Jer 51:20 with you I shatter **n**, with you I destroy H1580
Jer 51:27 Blow the trumpet among the **n**! Prepare H1580
Jer 51:27 Prepare the **n** for battle against her H1580
Jer 51:28 Prepare the **n** for battle against her—the H1580
Jer 51:41 desolate Babylon will be among the **n**! H1580
Jer 51:44 The **n** will no longer stream to him H1580
La 1: 1 who once was great among the **n**! H1580
La 1: 3 She dwells among the **n**; she finds no H1580
La 1:10 she saw **pagan n** enter her sanctuary H1580
La 2: 9 her princes are exiled among the **n**, H1580
La 3:45 made us scum and refuse among the **n**. H6639
La 4:15 people among the **n** say, "They can stay H1580
La 4:20 his shadow we would live among the **n**. H1580
Eze 4:13 food among the **n** where I will drive H1580
Eze 5: 5 which I have set in the center of the **n** H1580
Eze 5: 6 more than the **n** and countries around H1580
Eze 5: 7 unruly than the **n** around you and have H1580
Eze 5: 7 to the standards of the **n** around you. H1580
Eze 5: 8 punishment on you in the sight of the **n**. H1580
Eze 5:14 a reproach among the **n** around you, H1580
Eze 5:15 of horror to the **n** around you when I H1580
Eze 6: 8 you are scattered among the lands and **n**. H1580
Eze 6: 9 Then in the **n** where they have been H1580
Eze 7:24 the most wicked of **n** to take possession of H1580
Eze 11:12 to the standards of the **n** around you." H1580
Eze 11:16 far away among the **n** and scattered them H1580
Eze 11:17 gather you from the **n** and bring you back H6639
Eze 12:15 them among the **n** and scatter them H1580
Eze 12:16 so that in the **n** where they go they may H1580
Eze 16:14 spread among the **n** on account of your H1580
Eze 19: 4 The **n** heard about him, and he was H1580
Eze 19: 8 Then the **n** came against him, those from H1580
Eze 20: 9 in the eyes of the **n** among whom they H1580
Eze 20:14 in the eyes of the **n** in whose sight I had H1580
Eze 20:22 in the eyes of the **n** in whose sight I had H1580
Eze 20:23 them among the **n** and scatter them H1580
Eze 20:32 "We want to be like the **n**, like the H1580
Eze 20:34 bring you from the **n** and gather you from H6639
Eze 20:35 into the wilderness of the **n** and there, H6639
Eze 20:41 you out from the **n** and gather you from H6639
Eze 20:41 holy through you in the sight of the **n**. H1580
Eze 22: 4 of scorn to the **n** and a laughingstock to H1580
Eze 22:15 disperse you among the **n** and scatter you H1580
Eze 22:16 have been defiled in the eyes of the **n**, H1580
Eze 23:30 you lusted after the **n** and defiled yourself H1580
Eze 25: 7 you and give you as plunder to the **n**. H1580
Eze 25: 7 out from among the **n** and exterminate H6639
Eze 25: 8 Judah has become like all the other **n**," H1580
Eze 25:10 will not be remembered among the **n**; H1580
Eze 26: 2 The gate to the **n** is broken, and its doors H6639
Eze 26: 3 I will bring many **n** against you, like H1580
Eze 26: 5 She will become plunder for the **n**, H1580
Eze 27:33 you satisfied many **n**; with your great H6639
Eze 27:36 The merchants among the **n** scoff at you H6639
Eze 28: 7 the most ruthless of **n**; they will draw their H1580
Eze 28:19 All the **n** who knew you are appalled at H6639
Eze 28:25 of Israel from the **n** where they have been H6639
Eze 28:25 holy through them in the sight of the **n**. H1580
Eze 29:12 Egyptians among the **n** and scatter them H1580
Eze 29:13 the Egyptians from the **n** where they were H6639
Eze 29:15 never again exalt itself above the other **n**. H1580
Eze 29:15 that it will never again rule over the **n**. H1580
Eze 30: 3 a day of clouds, a time of doom for the **n**. H1580
Eze 30:11 the most ruthless of **n**—will be brought in H1580
Eze 30:23 Egyptians among the **n** and scatter them H1580
Eze 30:26 Egyptians among the **n** and scatter them H1580
Eze 31: 6 all the great **n** lived in its shade. H1580
Eze 31:11 it into the hands of the ruler of the **n**, H1580
Eze 31:12 ruthless of foreign **n** cut it down and left it H1580
Eze 31:12 All the **n** *of* the earth came out from H6639
Eze 31:16 I made the **n** tremble at the sound of its H1580
Eze 31:17 men who lived in its shade among the **n**. H1580
Eze 32: 2 " 'You are like a lion among the **n**; you H1580
Eze 32: 9 bring about your destruction among the **n**, H1580
Eze 32:12 mighty men—the most ruthless of all **n**. H1580
Eze 32:16 The daughters of the **n** will chant it; for H1580
Eze 32:18 both her and the daughters of mighty **n**, H1580
Eze 34:13 them out from the **n** and gather them H6639
Eze 34:28 They will no longer be plundered by the **n** H1580
Eze 34:29 in the land or bear the scorn of the **n**. H1580
Eze 35:10 "These two **n** and countries will be ours H1580
Eze 36: 3 of the rest of the **n** and the object of H1580
Eze 36: 4 ridiculed by the rest of the **n** around you— H1580
Eze 36: 5 I have spoken against the rest of the **n**, H1580
Eze 36: 6 you have suffered the scorn of the **n**. H1580
Eze 36: 7 hand that the **n** around you will also H1580
Eze 36:15 will I make you hear the taunts of the **n**, H1580
Eze 36:19 I dispersed them among the **n**, and they H1580
Eze 36:20 they went among the **n** they profaned my H1580
Eze 36:21 profaned among the **n** where they had H1580
Eze 36:22 profaned among the **n** where you have H1580
Eze 36:23 which has been profaned among the **n** H1580
Eze 36:23 Then the **n** will know that I am the LORD H1580
Eze 36:24 " 'For I will take you out of the **n**; I will H1580
Eze 36:30 disgrace among the **n** because of famine. H1580
Eze 36:36 Then the **n** around you that remain will H1580
Eze 37:21 out of the **n** where they have gone. H1580
Eze 37:22 never again be two **n** or be divided into H1580
Eze 37:28 Then the **n** will know that I the LORD make H1580
Eze 38: 6 with all its troops—the many **n** with you. H6639
Eze 38: 8 gathered from many **n** to the mountains H6639
Eze 38: 8 They had been brought out from the **n** H6639
Eze 38: 9 troops and the many **n** with you will go up H6639
Eze 38:12 ruins and the people gathered from the **n**, H1580
Eze 38:15 you and many **n** with you, all of H6639
Eze 38:16 so that the **n** may know me when I am H1580
Eze 38:22 his troops and on the many **n** with him. H6639
Eze 38:23 myself known in the sight of many **n**. H1580
Eze 39: 4 all your troops and the **n** with you. H6639
Eze 39: 7 the **n** will know that I the LORD am the H1580
Eze 39:21 "I will display my glory among the **n**, and H1580
Eze 39:21 all the **n** will see the punishment I H1580
Eze 39:23 And the **n** will know that the people of H1580
Eze 39:27 them back from the **n** and have gathered H6639
Eze 39:27 holy through them in the sight of many **n**. H1580
Eze 39:28 I sent them into exile among the **n**, H1580
Da 3: 4 "**N** and peoples of every language A10553
Da 3: 7 all the **n** and peoples of every language A10553
Da 4: 1 To the **n** and peoples of every language A10553
Da 5:19 all the **n** and peoples of every language A10553
Da 6:25 wrote to all the **n** and peoples of every A10553
Da 7:14 all **n** and peoples of every language A10553
Da 12: 1 from the beginning of **n** until then. H1580
Hos 7: 8 "Ephraim mixes with the **n**; Ephraim is a H6639
Hos 8: 8 she is among the **n** like something no H1580
Hos 8:10 they have sold themselves among the **n**, H1580
Hos 9: 1 do not be jubilant like the other **n**. H6639
Hos 9:17 they will be wanderers among the **n**. H1580
Hos 10:10 **n** will be gathered against them to put H6639
Joel 2: 6 the sight of them, **n** are in anguish; every H6639
Joel 2:17 an object of scorn, a byword among the **n**. H1580
Joel 2:19 I make you an object of scorn to the **n**. H1580
Joel 3: 2 I will gather all **n** and bring them down to H1580
Joel 3: 2 people among the **n** and divided up my H1580
Joel 3: 9 Proclaim this among the **n**: Prepare for H1580
Joel 3:11 all you **n** from every side, and H1580
Joel 3:12 "Let the **n** be roused; let them advance H1580
Joel 3:12 I will sit to judge all the **n** on every side. H1580
Am 9: 9 Israel among all the **n** as grain is shaken H1580
Am 9:12 of Edom and all the **n** that bear my name," H1580
Ob 1 An envoy was sent to the **n** to say, "Rise H1580
Ob 2 I will make you small among the **n**; you H1580
Ob 15 "The day of the LORD is near for all **n**. H1580
Ob 16 holy hill, so all the **n** will drink continually H1580
Mic 4: 2 Many **n** will come and say, "Come, let us H1580
Mic 4: 3 settle disputes for strong **n** far and wide. H1580
Mic 4: 5 All the **n** may walk in the name of their H6639
Mic 4:11 But now many **n** are gathered against you. H1580
Mic 4:13 you will break to pieces many **n**. H6639
Mic 5: 8 remnant of Jacob will be among the **n**, H1580
Mic 5:15 wrath on the **n** that have not obeyed H1580
Mic 6:16 derision; you will bear the scorn of the **n**." H6639
Mic 7:16 **N** will see and be ashamed, deprived of H1580
Na 3: 4 who enslaved **n** by her prostitution and H1580
Na 3: 5 I will show the **n** your nakedness and the H1580
Hab 1: 5 "Look at the **n** and watch—and be utterly H1580
Hab 1:17 destroying **n** without mercy? H1580
Hab 2: 5 to himself all the **n** and takes captive all H1580
Hab 2: 8 Because you have plundered many **n**, the H1580
Hab 2:13 that the **n** exhaust themselves for nothing? H4211
Hab 3: 6 he looked, and made the **n** tremble. H1580
Hab 3:12 earth and in anger you threshed the **n**. H1580
Zep 2:11 Distant **n** will bow down to him, all of H1580
Zep 3: 6 "I have destroyed **n**; their strongholds are H1580
Zep 3: 8 I have decided to assemble the **n**, to H1580
Hag 2: 7 I will shake all **n**, and what is desired by H1580
Hag 2: 7 what is desired by all **n** will come H1580

Zec 1:15 am very angry with the **n** that feel secure. H1580
Zec 1:21 these horns of the **n** who lifted up their H1580
Zec 2: 8 me against the **n** that have plundered H1580
Zec 2:11 "Many **n** will be joined with the LORD in H1580
Zec 7:14 them with a whirlwind among all the **n**, H1580
Zec 8:13 have been a curse among the **n**, so I will H1580
Zec 8:22 peoples and powerful **n** will come to H1580
Zec 8:23 all languages and **n** will take firm hold of H1580
Zec 9:10 He will proclaim peace to the **n**. His rule H1580
Zec 11:10 the covenant I had made with all the **n**. H6639
Zec 12: 3 when all the **n** *of* the earth are gathered H1580
Zec 12: 3 an immovable rock for all the **n**. H6639
Zec 12: 4 I will blind all the horses of the **n**. H6639
Zec 12: 9 to destroy all the **n** that attack Jerusalem. H1580
Zec 14: 2 I will gather all the **n** to Jerusalem to fight H1580
Zec 14: 3 LORD will go out and fight against those **n**, H1580
Zec 14:12 will strike all the **n** that fought against H6639
Zec 14:14 all the surrounding **n** will be collected— H1580
Zec 14:16 survivors from all the **n** that have attacked H1580
Zec 14:18 he inflicts on the **n** that do not go up to H1580
Zec 14:19 of all the **n** that do not go up to H1580
Mal 1:11 My name will be great among the **n**, from H1580
Mal 1:11 my name will be great among the **n**," H1580
Mal 1:14 my name is to be feared among the **n**. H1580
Mal 3:12 "Then all the **n** will call you blessed, for H1580
Mt 12:18 and he will proclaim justice *to* the **n**. *G1620*
Mt 12:21 In his name the **n** will put their hope." *G1620*
Mt 24: 9 you will be hated by all **n** because of me. *G1620*
Mt 24:14 in the whole world as a testimony to all **n**, *G1620*
Mt 25:32 All the **n** will be gathered before him, and *G1620*
Mt 28:19 Therefore go and make disciples of all **n** *G1620*
Mk 11:17 will be called a house of prayer *for* all **n**'? *G1620*
Mk 13:10 the gospel must first be preached to all **n**. *G1620*
Lk 2:31 you have prepared in the sight of all **n**: *G3295*
Lk 21:24 will be taken as prisoners to all the **n**. *G1620*
Lk 21:25 **n** will be in anguish and perplexity at the *G1620*
Lk 24:47 sins will be preached in his name to all **n**, *G1620*
Ac 4:25 " 'Why do the **n** rage and the peoples *G1620*
Ac 7:45 took the land *from* the **n** God drove out *G1620*
Ac 13:19 he overthrew seven **n** in Canaan *G1620*
Ac 14:16 In the past, he let all **n** go their own way. *G1620*
Ac 17:26 From one man he made all the **n** *G1620+476*
Ro 4:17 "I have made you a father of many **n**." *G1620*
Ro 4:18 so became the father of many **n**, *G1620*
Ro 15:12 one who will arise to rule *over* the **n**; in *G1620*
Gal 3: 8 "All **n** will be blessed through you." *G1620*
1Ti 3:16 was preached among the **n**, was believed *G1620*
Jas 1: 1 the twelve tribes **scattered among the n**: *G1402*
Rev 2:26 the end, I will give authority over the **n**— *G1620*
Rev 10:11 about many peoples, **n**, languages and *G1620*
Rev 11:18 The **n** were angry, and your wrath has *G1620*
Rev 12: 5 "will rule all the **n** with an iron scepter." *G1620*
Rev 14: 8 which made all the **n** drink the *G1620*
Rev 15: 3 Just and true are your ways, King *of* the **n**. *G1620*
Rev 15: 4 All **n** will come and worship before you *G1620*
Rev 16:19 and the cities *of* the **n** collapsed. *G1620*
Rev 17:15 peoples, multitudes, **n** and languages. *G1620*
Rev 18: 3 For all the **n** have drunk the maddening *G1620*
Rev 18:23 your magic spell all the **n** were led astray. *G1620*
Rev 19:15 sword with which to strike down the **n**. *G1620*
Rev 20: 3 from deceiving the **n** anymore until the *G1620*
Rev 20: 8 go out to deceive the **n** in the four corners *G1620*
Rev 21:24 The **n** will walk by its light, and the kings *G1620*
Rev 21:26 glory and honor *of* the **n** will be brought *G1620*
Rev 22: 2 of the tree are for the healing *of* the **n**. *G1620*

NATIONS' (1) [NATION]
Jer 51:58 the **n** labor is only fuel for the flames." H4211

NATIVE (14) [NATIVES]
Ge 24: 7 household and my **n** land and who spoke H4580
Ge 31:13 land at once and go back to your **n** land. H4580
Nu 22: 5 the Euphrates River, in his **n** land. H1201+6639
Est 1:22 his own household, using his **n** tongue. H6639
Ps 37:35 man flourishing like a luxuriant **n** tree, H275
Isa 13:14 own people, they will flee to their **n land**. H824
Jer 22:10 will never return nor see his **n** land again. H4580
Jer 46:16 back to our own people and our **n** lands, H4580
Am 7:11 surely go into exile, away from their **n land**. H141
Am 7:17 surely go into exile, away from their **n land**. H141
Jn 8:44 he speaks **his n language** *G1666+3836+2625*
Ac 2: 8 them in our **n** language? *G1877+4005+1164*
Ac 18: 2 named Aquila, a **n** of Pontus, who had *G1169*
Ac 18:24 named Apollos, a **n** of Alexandria, came *G1169*

NATIVE-BORN (16) [BEAR]
Ex 12:19 whether foreigner or **n**, who H275+2021+824
Ex 12:49 applies both to the **n** and to the foreigner H275
Lev 16:29 whether **n** or a foreigner residing among H275
Lev 17:15 " 'Anyone, whether **n** or foreigner, who H275
Lev 18:26 The **n** and the foreigners residing among H275
Lev 19:34 among you must be treated as your **n**. H275
Lev 23:42 All **n** Israelites are to live in such shelters H275
Lev 24:16 Whether foreigner or **n**, when they H275
Lev 24:22 the same law for the foreigner and the **n**. H275
Nu 9:14 both the foreigner and the **n**. H275+824
Nu 15:13 " 'Everyone who is **n** must do these things H275
Nu 15:29 whether a **n** Israelite or a foreigner residing H275
Nu 15:30 sins defiantly, whether **n** or foreigner H275
Jos 8:33 living among them and the **n** were there. H275
1Ch 7:21 by the **n** men of Gath, H3528+928+2021+824
Eze 47:22 You are to consider them as **n** Israelites H275

NATIVES (1) [NATIVE]
Eze 23:15 Babylonian chariot officers, **n** *of* Chaldea. H4580

NATIVITY (KJV) ANCESTRY, BIRTH, BORN, HOMELAND, NATIVE, NATIVES

NATURAL (13) [NATURE]
Nu 16:29 men die a **n** death and H3869+3972+2021+132
Nu 19:16 *someone who has* **died a n death**, H4637
Nu 19:18 killed or anyone *who has* **died a n death**. H4637
Jn 1:13 children born not of **n descent**, nor of *G135*
Jn 11:13 thought he meant **n sleep**. *G3122+5678*
Ro 1:26 women exchanged **n** sexual relations *G5879*
Ro 1:27 men also abandoned **n** relations with *G5879*
Ro 11:21 God did not spare the **n** branches, *G2848+5882*
Ro 11:24 will these, the **n** branches, be *G2848+5882*
1Co 15:44 it is sown a **n** body, it is raised a spiritual *G6035*
1Co 15:44 If there is a **n** body, there is also a *G6035*
1Co 15:46 come first, but the **n**, and after that the *G6035*
Jude 19 who **follow mere n instincts** and do not *G6035*

NATURE (14) [NATURAL]
Ro 1:20 his eternal power and **divine n**—have *G2522*
Ro 2:14 do *by* **n** things required by the law *G5882*
Ro 7:18 not dwell in me, that is, in my **sinful n**. *G4922*
Ro 7:25 but *in* my **sinful n** a slave to the law of sin. *G4922*
Ro 11:24 cut out of an olive tree that is wild by **n**, *G5882*
Ro 11:24 contrary to **n** were grafted into a *G5882*
1Co 11:14 not the very **n of things** teach you that *G5882*
Gal 4: 8 slaves to those who *by* **n** are not gods. *G5882*
Eph 2: 3 the rest, we were *by* **n** deserving of wrath. *G5882*
Php 2: 6 being in **very n** God, did not *G3671*
Php 2: 7 nothing by taking the **very n** of a servant, *G3671*
Col 3: 5 whatever *belongs to* your earthly **n**: *G3517*
Heb 6:17 to make the **unchanging** *n* of his purpose AIT
2Pe 1: 4 them you may participate in the divine **n**, *G5882*

(SINFUL) NATURE (NIV84) FLESH

NAUGHT (1)
Isa 40:23 He brings princes to **n** and reduces the H401

NAUGHTINESS, NAUGHTY (KJV) BAD, DECEITFUL, EVIL, TROUBLEMAKER, WICKED

NAVEL (1)
SS 7: 2 Your **n** is a rounded goblet that never H9219

NAVY (KJV) FLEET, SHIPS

NAY (KJV) NO, NOT

NAZARENE (4) [NAZARETH]
Mt 2:23 prophets, that he would be called a **N**. *G3717*
Mk 14:67 "You also were with that **N**, Jesus," she *G3716*
Mk 16: 6 "You are looking for Jesus the **N**, who was *G3716*
Ac 24: 5 He is a ringleader of the **N** sect *G3717*

NAZARETH (27) [NAZARETH]
Mt 2:23 he went and lived in a town called **N** *G3714*
Mt 4:13 Leaving **N**, he went and lived in *G3714*
Mt 21:11 is Jesus, the prophet from **N** in Galilee." *G3714*
Mt 26:71 "This fellow was with Jesus **of N**." *G3717*
Mk 1: 9 Jesus came from **N** in Galilee and was *G3714*
Mk 1:24 with us, Jesus **of N**? Have you come to *G3716*
Mk 10:47 When he heard that it was Jesus **of N**, he *G3716*
Lk 1:26 God sent the angel Gabriel to **N**, a town *G3714*
Lk 2: 4 up from the town *of* **N** in Galilee to Judea *G3714*
Lk 2:39 to Galilee to their own town *of* **N**. *G3714*
Lk 2:51 he went down to **N** with them and was *G3714*
Lk 4:16 He went to **N**, where he had been *G3714*
Lk 4:34 with us, Jesus **of N**? Have you come to *G3716*
Lk 18:37 They told him, "Jesus **of N** is passing by." *G3717*
Lk 24:19 "About Jesus **of N**," they replied. "He *G3716*
Jn 1:45 wrote—Jesus of **N**, the son of Joseph." *G3714*
Jn 1:46 "**N**! Can anything good come from there?" *G3714*
Jn 18: 5 "Jesus **of N**," they replied. "I am he," *G3717*
Jn 18: 7 is it you want?" "Jesus **of N**," they said. *G3717*
Jn 19:19 JESUS OF **N**, THE KING OF THE JEWS *G3717*
Ac 2:22 Jesus **of N** was a man accredited by God *G3717*
Ac 3: 6 In the name of Jesus Christ **of N**, walk." *G3717*
Ac 4:10 It is by the name of Jesus Christ **of N** *G3717*
Ac 6:14 say that this Jesus **of N** will destroy this *G3717*
Ac 10:38 anointed Jesus of **N** with the Holy Spirit *G3714*
Ac 22: 8 " 'I am Jesus **of N**, whom you are *G3717*
Ac 26: 9 to oppose the name of Jesus **of N**. *G3717*

NAZIRITE (14) [NAZIRITE'S, NAZIRITES]
Nu 6: 2 a vow of dedication to the LORD as a **N**, H5693
Nu 6: 4 As long as they remain **under** their **N vow** H5694
Nu 6: 5 the entire period of their **N vow**, H5624+5694
Nu 6: 6 the **N** must not go near a dead body. NDT
Nu 6:11 make atonement for **the N** because they H2257S
Nu 6:13 this is the law of the **N** when the period of H5687
Nu 6:18 the **N** must shave off the hair that H5687
Nu 6:19 " 'After the **N** has shaved off the hair that H5687
Nu 6:20 After that, the **N** may drink wine. H5687
Nu 6:21 is the law of the **N** who vows offerings to H5687
Nu 6:21 have made, according to the law of the **N**. H5694
Jdg 13: 5 is to be a **N**, *dedicated to* God from the H5687
Jdg 13: 7 the boy will be a **N** *of* God from the womb H5687
Jdg 16:17 have been a **N** *dedicated to* God from my H5687

NAZIRITE'S (1) [NAZIRITE]
Nu 6: 9 dies suddenly in the **N** presence, H2257S

NAZIRITES (2) [NAZIRITE]
Am 2:11 your children and **N** from among your H5687
Am 2:12 "But you made the **N** drink wine and H5687

NEAH (1)
Jos 19:13 out at Rimmon and turned toward **N**. H5828

NEAPOLIS (1)
Ac 16:11 the next day we went on to **N**. *G3735*

NEAR (299) [NEARBY, NEARED, NEARER, NEAREST, NEARLY, NEARSIGHTED]
Ge 13:12 the plain and pitched his tents **n** Sodom. H6330
Ge 13:18 So Abram went to live **n** the great trees of H928
Ge 14: 6 as far as El Paran **n** the desert. H6584
Ge 14:13 Now Abram was living **n** the great trees of H928
Ge 16: 7 the LORD found Hagar **n** a spring in the H6584
Ge 18: 1 appeared to Abraham **n** the great trees of H928
Ge 18: 8 they ate, he stood **n** them under a tree. H6584
Ge 19:20 here is a town **n** *enough* to run to, and it H7940
Ge 20: 4 Now Abimelek *had* not **gone n** her, so he H7928
Ge 23:17 field in Machpelah **n** Mamre— H7156+4200
Ge 23:19 the field of Machpelah **n** Mamre H6584+7156
Ge 24:11 camels kneel down **n** the well outside the H448
Ge 24:30 him standing by the camels **n** the spring. H6584
Ge 25: 9 the cave of Machpelah **n** Mamre, H6584+7156
Ge 25:11 who then lived **n** Beer Lahai Roi. H6640
Ge 25:18 to Shur, **n** the eastern border of Egypt H6584
Ge 27:21 said to Jacob, "**Come n** so I can touch you H5602
Ge 27:41 "The days of mourning for my father *are* **n**; H7928
Ge 29: 2 of sheep lying **n** it because the flocks H6584
Ge 30:41 so they would mate **n** the branches, H928
Ge 32:32 of Jacob's hip was touched **n** the tendon. H928
Ge 35:27 Isaac in Mamre, **n** Kiriath Arba (that is, NDT
Ge 37:12 to graze their father's flocks **n** Shechem, H928
Ge 37:13 brothers are grazing the flocks **n** Shechem. H928
Ge 37:17 his brothers and found them **n** Dothan. H928
Ge 45:10 in the region of Goshen and be **n** me— H7940
Ge 47:29 When the time **drew n** for Israel to die, he H7928
Ge 49:22 a fruitful vine **n** a spring, whose H6584
Ge 49:30 of Machpelah, **n** Mamre in Canaan H6584+7156
Ge 50:10 floor of Atad, **n** the Jordan, they H928+6298
Ge 50:11 is why that place **n** the Jordan is H928+6298
Ge 50:13 of Machpelah, **n** Mamre, which H6584+7156
Ex 14: 2 back and encamp **n** Pi Hahiroth, H7156+4200
Ex 14: 9 as they camped by the sea **n** Pi Hahiroth, H6584
Ex 14:20 so neither **went n** the other all night long. H7928
Ex 15:27 and they camped there **n** the water. H6584
Ex 18: 5 he was camped **n** the mountain of God NDT
Ex 24: 2 the LORD; the others *must* not **come n**. H5602
Ex 33:21 "There is a place **n** me where you may H907
Ex 34:30 they were afraid *to* **come n** him. H5602
Ex 34:32 Afterward all the Israelites **came n** him H5602
Ex 40:29 altar of burnt offering **n** the entrance to the NDT
Lev 3: 4 kidneys with the fat on them **n** the loins, H6584
Lev 3:10 kidneys with the fat on them **n** the loins, H6584
Lev 3:15 kidneys with the fat on them **n** the loins, H6584
Lev 4: 9 kidneys with the fat on them **n** the loins, H6584
Lev 7: 4 kidneys with the fat on them **n** the loins, H6584
Lev 9: 5 entire assembly **came n** and stood before H7928
Lev 21:17 who has a defect *may* **come n** to offer the H7928
Lev 21:18 No man who has any defect *may* **come n** H7928
Lev 21:21 has any defect *is to* **come n** to present the H5602
Lev 21:21 *he must* not **come n** to offer the food of H5602
Lev 21:23 he must not go **n** the curtain or approach H448
Lev 22: 3 unclean and yet **comes n** the sacred H7928
Nu 4:19 not die when they **come n** the most holy H5602
Nu 6: 6 the Nazirite must not go **n** a dead body. H6584
Nu 8:19 Israelites when they **go n** the sanctuary." H5602
Nu 13:29 the Canaanites live **n** the sea and along H6584
Nu 16: 5 and *he will* **have** that person **come n** him. H7928
Nu 16: 5 he chooses *he will* **cause to come n** him. H7928
Nu 16: 9 **brought** you **n** himself to do H7928
Nu 16:10 *He has* **brought** you and all your fellow Levites **n** H7928
Nu 17:13 Anyone who **even comes n** the H7929+7929
Nu 18: 3 but *they must* not **go n** the furnishings of H7928
Nu 18: 4 no *one* else *may* **come n** where you H7928
Nu 18: 7 Anyone else who **comes n** the sanctuary H7929
Nu 18:22 on the Israelites *must* not **go n** the tent of H7928
Nu 20:23 At Mount Hor, **n** the border of Edom, the H6584
Nu 22: 5 who was at Pethor, **n** the Euphrates River H6584
Nu 24:17 but not now; I behold him, but not **n**. H7940
Nu 33: 7 Zephon, and camped **n** Migdol. H4200+7156
Nu 33:47 the mountains of Abarim, **n** Nebo. H4200+7156
Dt 3:29 So we stayed in the valley **n** Beth Peor. H4578
Dt 4: 7 to have their gods **n** them the way the H7940
Dt 4: 7 the LORD our God is **n** us whenever we pray NDT
Dt 4:11 *You* **came n** and stood at the foot of the H7928
Dt 4:46 were in the valley **n** Beth Peor east of the H4578
Dt 5:27 **Go n** and listen to all that the LORD our H7928
Dt 11:30 the setting sun, **n** the great trees of Moreh H725
Dt 13: 7 around you, whether **n** or far, from one H7940
Dt 15: 9 canceling debts, *is* **n**," so that you do H7928
Dt 22: 2 If they do not live **n** you or if you do not H7940
Dt 30:14 the word is very **n** you; it is in your H7940
Dt 31:14 "Now the day of your death *is* **n**. H7928
Dt 32:35 day of disaster is **n** and their doom rushes H7940
Jos 3: 4 between you and the ark; *do* not **go n** it." H7928

Jos 5:13 Now when Joshua was n Jericho, he H928
Jos 7: 2 which is n Beth Aven to the east of Bethel, H6640
Jos 9: 7 "But perhaps you live n us, so how H928+7931
Jos 9:16 they were neighbors, living n them. H928+7931
Jos 9:22 while actually you live n us? H928+7931
Jos 12: 9 one the king of Ai (n Bethel) one H4946+7396
Jos 13:25 country as far as Aroer, n Rabbah; H6584+7156
Jos 19:11 extended to the ravine n Jokneam. H6584+7156
Jos 22:10 When they came to Geliloth *n* the Jordan in AIT
Jos 22:11 of Canaan at Geliloth *n* the Jordan on the AIT
Jos 24:26 there under the oak n the holy place of the H928
Jdg 1:16 of the Desert of Judah in the Negev *n* Arad. AIT
Jdg 3:19 the stone images n Gilgal he himself went H907
Jdg 4:11 by the great tree in Zaanannim n Kedesh. H907
Jdg 7: 1 of them in the valley n the hill of Moreh. H4946
Jdg 7:22 the border of Abel Meholah n Tabbath. H6584
Jdg 9:34 up concealed positions n Shechem in four H6584
Jdg 15: 9 camped in Judah, spreading out n Lehi. H928
Jdg 18: 3 When they were n Micah's house, they H6640
Jdg 18:12 way they set up camp n Kiriath Jearim in H928
Jdg 18:22 the men who lived n Micah were called H6640
Jdg 18:28 The city was in a valley n Beth Rehob H4200
Jdg 19:11 When they were n Jebus and the day was H6640
Jdg 20:19 got up and pitched camp n Gibeah. H6584
Jdg 20:24 the Israelites drew n to Benjamin the H7928
Jdg 20:34 did not realize how n disaster *was*. H5595
Jdg 20:36 on the ambush they had set n Gibeah. H448
1Sa 4:19 was pregnant and n the time of delivery. H3528
1Sa 7:10 the Philistines drew n to engage Israel in H5602
1Sa 10: 2 you will meet two men n Rachel's tomb H6640
1Sa 15: 7 to Shur, n the eastern border of Egypt. H6584
1Sa 17:26 David asked the men standing n him H6640
1Sa 24: 2 and his men n the Crags of the H6584+7156
1Sa 25:15 out in the fields n them nothing was H2143+907
1Sa 25:16 time we were herding our sheep n them. H6640
1Sa 26: 7 his spear stuck in the ground n his head. H5265
1Sa 26:11 spear and water jug that are n his head, H5265
1Sa 26:12 the spear and water jug n Saul's head, H5265
1Sa 26:16 spear and water jug that were n his head?" H5265
2Sa 2:24 n Giah on the way to the H6584+7156
2Sa 13:23 were at Baal Hazor n the border of H6640
2Sa 19:37 die in my own town n the tomb of my H6640
2Sa 23:15 water from the well n the gate of H928
2Sa 23:16 water from the well n the gate of H928
2Sa 24: 5 they camped n Aroer, south of the H928
1Ki 1: 9 calves at the Stone of Zoheleth n En Rogel. H725
1Ki 2: 1 When the time drew n for David to die H7928
1Ki 8:46 captive to their own lands, far away or n; H7940
1Ki 8:59 be n to the LORD our God day and night H7940
1Ki 9:26 which is n Elath in Edom, on the H907
1Ki 16:15 The army was encamped n Gibbethon, H6584
2Ki 9:27 his chariot on the way up to Gur n Ibleam, H907
2Ki 11:11 the king—n the altar and the temple H4200
2Ki 15: 7 was buried n them in the City of H6640
2Ki 23:11 They were in the court n the room of an H448
2Ki 23:12 had erected on the roof *n* the upper room of AIT
2Ki 25: 4 the two walls n the king's garden, H6584
1Ch 8:32 They too lived n their relatives in H5584
1Ch 9:38 They too lived n their relatives in H5584
1Ch 11:17 water from the well n the gate of H928
1Ch 11:18 water from the well n the gate of H928
1Ch 19: 7 who came and camped n Medeba H4200+7156
2Ch 6:36 them captive to a land far away or n; H7940
2Ch 14:10 in the Valley of Zephathah n Mareshah. H4200
2Ch 21:16 the Arabs who lived n the Cushites. H6584+3338
2Ch 23:10 the king—n the altar and the temple H4200
2Ch 26: 6 then rebuilt towns n Ashdod and H928
2Ch 26:23 was buried n them in a cemetery that H6640
Ne 3:25 from the upper palace n the court of the H4200
Ne 4:12 the Jews who lived n them came and told H725
Ne 7: 3 their posts and some n their own houses." H5584
Est 2:11 back and forth n the courtyard of H4200+7156
Est 9:20 the provinces of King Xerxes, n and far, H7940
Job 17:12 in the face of the darkness light is n. H7940
Job 33:22 They draw n to the pit, and their life to H7928
Ps 10: 8 He lies in wait *n* the villages; from ambush AIT
Ps 22:11 trouble is n and there is no one to H7940
Ps 65: 4 you choose and bring n to live in your H7928
Ps 69:18 Come n and rescue me; deliver me H7928
Ps 73:28 it is good to be n God. I have made the H7932
Ps 75: 1 your Name is n; people tell of your H7940
Ps 84: 3 have her young—a place n your altar, LORD H907
Ps 85: 9 his salvation is n those who fear him, H7940
Ps 88: 3 troubles and my life draws n to death. H5595
Ps 91: 7 right hand, but *it will* not come n you. H5602
Ps 91:10 no disaster *will* come n your tent. H7928
Ps 107:18 all food and drew n the gates of death. H5595
Ps 119:150 Those who devise wicked schemes *are* n H7928
Ps 119:151 Yet you are n, LORD, and all your H7940
Ps 145:18 The LORD is n to all who call on him, to all H7940
Pr 3:29 your neighbor, who lives trustfully n you. H907
Pr 5: 8 *do* not go n the door of her house H7928
Pr 7: 8 He was going down the street n her corner H725
Pr 24:15 Do not lurk like a thief n the house of the H4200
Ecc 5: 1 Go n to listen rather than to offer the H7928
Isa 11: 8 The infant will play n the cobra's den H6584
Isa 13: 6 the day of the LORD is n; it will come H7940
Isa 29:13 "These people come n to me with their H5602
Isa 33:13 have done; you *who* are n, acknowledge H7940
Isa 34: 1 Come n, you nations, and listen; pay H7928
Isa 46:13 *I am* bringing my righteousness n, it is not H7928
Isa 48:16 "Come n me and listen to this: "From the H7928
Isa 50: 8 He who vindicates me is n. Who then will H7940
Isa 51: 5 My righteousness *draws* n speedily, my H7940
Isa 54:14 be far removed; *it will* not come n you. H7928
Isa 55: 6 may be found; call on him while he is n. H7940
Isa 57:19 to those far and n," says the LORD. H7940
Isa 58: 2 seem eager for God to come n them. H7932
Isa 65: 5 don't come n me, for I am too H5602
Jer 5: 6 will lie in wait n their towns to tear to H6584
Jer 19: 2 n the entrance of the Potsherd Gate. NDT
Jer 25:26 kings of the north, n and far, one after the H7940
Jer 30:21 *I will* bring him n and he will come close H7928
Jer 41:12 caught up with him n the great pool in H448
Jer 41:17 at Geruth Kimham n Bethlehem on their H725
Jer 48:24 to all the towns of Moab, far and n. H7940
Jer 52: 7 the two walls n the king's garden, H6584
La 1:16 No *one is* n to comfort me, no one to H8178
La 3:57 *You* came n when I called you, and you H7928
La 4:18 Our end *was* n, our days were numbered H7928
Eze 3:15 who lived at Tel Aviv n the Kebar River. H448
Eze 6:12 one *who* is n will fall by the sword H7940
Eze 7: 7 The day is n! There is panic, H7940
Eze 9: 1 "Bring n those who are appointed to H7928
Eze 12:23 'The days *are* n when every vision will be H7928
Eze 22: 5 Those who are n and those who are far H7940
Eze 30: 3 For the day is n, the day of the LORD is H7940
Eze 30: 3 the day of the LORD is n—a day of clouds, H7940
Eze 39:16 n a town called Hamonah. And so H2256+1685
Eze 40:40 n the steps at the entrance of the north H4200
Eze 40:46 Levites who may draw n to the LORD to H7929
Eze 42:14 clothes before *they* go n the places that H7928
Eze 43:19 who come n to minister before me H7940
Eze 44:13 *They are* not *to* come n to serve me as H5602
Eze 44:13 me as priests or come n any of my holy H5602
Eze 44:15 *are to* come n to minister before me H7928
Eze 44:16 they alone *are to* come n my table to H7928
Eze 44:25 defile himself by going n a dead person; H448
Eze 45: 4 sanctuary and who draw n to minister H7929
Da 5: 5 n the lampstand in the royal A10378+10619
Da 6:20 When he came n the den, he called to A10638
Da 8:17 As he came n the place where I was H725
Da 9: 7 all Israel, both n and far, in all the H7940
Joel 1:15 For the day of the LORD is n; it will come H7940
Joel 3: 9 *Let* all the fighting men draw n and attack. H5602
Joel 3:14 the day of the LORD is n in the valley of H7940
Am 6: 3 of disaster and bring n a reign of terror. H5602
Ob 15 "The day of the LORD is n for all nations H7940
Zep 1: 7 for the day of the LORD is n. H7940
Zep 1:14 The great day of the LORD is n—near and H7940
Zep 1:14 the LORD is near—n and coming quickly. H7940
Zep 3: 2 the LORD, *she does* not draw n to her God. H7928
Mt 3: 2 the kingdom of heaven *has* come n." *G1581*
Mt 4:17 the kingdom of heaven *has* come n." *G1581*
Mt 10: 7 'The kingdom of heaven *has* come n.' *G1581*
Mt 24:32 come out, you know that summer is n. *G1584*
Mt 24:33 you know that it is n, right at the door. *G1584*
Mt 26:18 My appointed time is n. I am going to *G1584*
Mk 1:15 "The kingdom of God *has* come n. Repent *G1581*
Mk 13:28 come out, you know that summer is n. *G1584*
Mk 13:29 you know that it is n, right at the door. *G1584*
Mk 14:47 Then one *of* those standing n drew his *G4225*
Mk 14:70 little while, those standing n said to Peter *G4225*
Mk 15:35 When some *of* those standing n heard *G4225*
Lk 8:19 were not able *to* get n him because of *G5344*
Lk 10: 9 'The kingdom of God *has* come n to you. *G1581*
Lk 10:11 The kingdom of God *has* come n.' *G1581*
Lk 12:33 where no thief comes n and no moth *G1581*
Lk 15:25 When he came n the house, he heard *G1581*
Lk 18:40 *When* he came n, Jesus asked *G1581*
Lk 19:11 because he was n Jerusalem and the *G1584*
Lk 19:37 *When* he came n the place where the *G1581*
Lk 21: 8 claiming, 'I am he,' and, 'The time *is* n. *G1581*
Lk 21:20 you will know that its desolation *is* n. *G1581*
Lk 21:28 because your redemption *is* drawing n." *G1581*
Lk 21:30 yourselves and know that summer is n. *G1584*
Lk 21:31 you know that the kingdom of God is n. *G1584*
Jn 3:23 also was baptizing at Aenon n Salim, *G1584*
Jn 4: 5 n the plot of ground Jacob had given to *G4446*
Jn 5: 2 is in Jerusalem n the Sheep Gate a pool *G2093*
Jn 6: 4 The Jewish Passover Festival was n. *G1584*
Jn 6:23 Tiberias landed n the place where the *G1584*
Jn 7: 2 the Jewish Festival of Tabernacles was n, *G1584*
Jn 8:20 the temple courts n the place where the *G1877*
Jn 11:54 he withdrew to a region n the wilderness, *G1584*
Jn 19:20 where Jesus was crucified was n the city, *G1584*
Jn 19:25 N the cross of Jesus stood his mother, his *G4123*
Ac 2:10 Egypt and the parts of Libya n Cyrene *G2848*
Ac 7:17 "As the time drew n for God to fulfill his *G1581*
Ac 7:30 a burning bush in the desert *n* Mount Sinai. AIT
Ac 8:29 "Go to that chariot and stay n it. *G3140*
Ac 9:38 Lydda was n Joppa; so when the disciples *G1584*
Ac 22: 6 "About noon as I came n Damascus *G1581*
Ac 23: 2 ordered those standing n Paul to strike *G4225*
Ac 23: 4 Those *who were* standing n Paul said *G4225*
Ac 23:11 night the Lord stood n Paul and said, *G2392*
Ac 27: 8 called Fair Havens, n the town of Lasea. *G1584*
Ro 10: 8 "The word is n you; it is in your mouth *G1584*
1Co 8: 8 But food *does* not bring us n to God; we *G4225*
Eph 2:13 have been brought n by the blood of *G1584*
Eph 2:17 far away and peace to those who were n. *G1584*
Php 4: 5 be evident to all. The Lord is n. *G1584*
2Ti 4: 6 the time for my departure *is* n. *G2392*
Heb 7:19 is introduced, by which *we* draw n to God. *G1581*
Heb 10: 1 perfect those *who* draw n to worship. *G4665*
Heb 10:22 *let us* draw n to God with a sincere heart *G4665*
Heb 11:22 Joseph, *when his* end was n, spoke about *G5462*
Jas 4: 8 Come n to God and he will come near to *G1581*
Jas 4: 8 near to God and *he will* come n to you. *G1581*
Jas 5: 8 because the Lord's coming *is* n. *G1581*
1Pe 4: 7 The end of all things *is* n. Therefore be *G1581*
Rev 1: 3 is written in it, because the time is n. *G1584*
Rev 22:10 of this scroll, because the time is n. *G1584*

NEARBY (14) [NEAR]

Ge 18: 2 looked up and saw three men standing n. H6584
Dt 20:15 you and do not belong to the nations n. H2178
Job 1:14 and the donkeys were grazing n, H6584+3338
Job 40:20 produce, and all the wild animals play n. H9004
Pr 27:10 better a neighbor n than a relative far H7940
Jer 23:23 "Am I only a God n," declares the H4946+7940
Mk 1:38 to the n villages—so I can *G2400*
Mk 5:11 of pigs was feeding on the n hillside. *G1695*
Lk 2: 8 shepherds living out in the fields n, *G3836+899*
Jn 2: 6 N stood six stone water jars, the kind used *G1695*
Jn 18:22 one of the officials n slapped him in the *G4225*
Jn 19:26 the disciple whom he loved standing n, *G4225*
Jn 19:42 of Preparation and since the tomb was n, *G1584*
Ac 28: 7 an estate n that *G4309+3836+5536+1697*

NEARED (2) [NEAR]

Jdg 19:14 and the sun set as *they* n Gibeah in H2143+725
Ac 9: 3 *As* he n Damascus on his journey *G1181+1581*

NEARER (1) [NEAR]

Ro 13:11 our salvation is n now than when we first *G1584*

NEAREST (7) [NEAR]

Ex 12: 4 they must share one with their n neighbor, H7940
Lev 25:25 their n relative is to come and redeem H7940
Nu 27:11 inheritance to the n relative in his clan, H7940
Dt 21: 3 elders of the town n the body shall take a H7940
Dt 21: 6 elders of the town n the body shall wash H7940
Jer 32: 7 as n relative it is your right and duty to H1460
Eze 42: 8 row on the side n the sanctuary H6584+7156

NEARIAH (3)

1Ch 3:22 Bariah, N and Shaphat—six in all H5859
1Ch 3:23 The sons of N: Elioenai, Hizkiah and H5859
1Ch 4:42 led by Pelatiah, N, Rephaiah and Uzziel H5859

NEARLY (7) [NEAR]

Jdg 19: 9 the day *is* n over. Stay and enjoy H2837
Ps 73: 2 slipped; I had n lost my foothold. H3869+401
Mk 4:37 over the boat, so that it was n swamped. *G2453*
Lk 24:29 with us, for it is n evening; the day is *G4639*
Ac 21:27 When the seven days *were* n over, some *G3516*
Ro 13:12 The night *is* n over; the day is almost here *G4621*
Heb 9:22 the law requires that n everything be *G5385*

NEARSIGHTED (1) [NEAR, SEE]

2Pe 1: 9 does not have them is n and blind, *G3697*

NEBAI (1)

Ne 10:19 Hariph, Anathoth, N, H5763

NEBAIOTH (5)

Ge 25:13 N the firstborn of Ishmael, Kedar, Adbeel H5568
Ge 28: 9 the sister of N and daughter of Ishmael H5568
Ge 36: 3 daughter of Ishmael and sister of N. H5568
1Ch 1:29 N the firstborn of Ishmael, Kedar, Adbeel H5568
Isa 60: 7 the rams of N will serve you; they H5568

NEBALLAT (1)

Ne 11:34 in Hadid, Zeboim and N, H5579

NEBAT (25)

1Ki 11:26 Jeroboam son of N rebelled against the H5565
1Ki 12: 2 When Jeroboam son of N heard this (he H5565
1Ki 12:15 to Jeroboam son of N through Ahijah the H5565
1Ki 15: 1 year of the reign of Jeroboam son of N, H5565
1Ki 16: 3 house like that of Jeroboam son of N. H5565
1Ki 16:26 the ways of Jeroboam son of N, H5565
1Ki 16:31 to commit the sins of Jeroboam son of N, H5565
1Ki 21:22 of Jeroboam son of N and that of Baasha H5565
1Ki 22:52 mother and of Jeroboam son of N, H5565
2Ki 3: 3 clung to the sins of Jeroboam son of N, H5565
2Ki 9: 9 of Jeroboam son of N and like the house H5565
2Ki 10:29 away from the sins of Jeroboam son of N, H5565
2Ki 13: 2 following the sins of Jeroboam son of N, H5565
2Ki 13:11 any of the sins of Jeroboam son of N, H5565
2Ki 14:24 any of the sins of Jeroboam son of N, H5565
2Ki 15: 9 away from the sins of Jeroboam son of N, H5565
2Ki 15:18 away from the sins of Jeroboam son of N, H5565
2Ki 15:24 away from the sins of Jeroboam son of N, H5565
2Ki 15:28 away from the sins of Jeroboam son of N, H5565
2Ki 17:21 they made Jeroboam son of N their king. H5565
2Ki 23:15 high place made by Jeroboam son of N, H5565
2Ch 9:29 the seer concerning Jeroboam son of N? H5565
2Ch 10: 2 When Jeroboam son of N heard this (he H5565
2Ch 10:15 to Jeroboam son of N through Ahijah the H5565
2Ch 13: 6 Yet Jeroboam son of N, an official of H5565

NEBO (13) [NEBO-SARSEKIM]

Nu 32: 3 Heshbon, Elealeh, Sebam, N and Beon— H5549
Nu 32:38 as well as N and Baal Meon (these names H5549
Nu 33:47 in the mountains of Abarim, near N. H5549
Dt 32:49 the Abarim Range to Mount N in Moab, H5549

N

Dt 34: 1 climbed Mount N from the plains of H5549
1Ch 5: 8 the area from Aroer to N and Baal Meon. H5549
Ezr 2:29 of N 52 H5549
Ezr 10:43 From the descendants of N: Jeiel H5551
Ne 7:33 of the other N 52 H5549
Isa 15: 2 to weep; Moab wails over N and Medeba. H5549
Isa 46: 1 Bel bows down, N stoops low; their idols H5550
Jer 48: 1 "Woe to N, for it will be ruined H5549
Jer 48:22 to Dibon, N and Beth Diblathaim, H5549

NEBO-SARSEKIM (1) [NEBO]

Jer 39: 3 of Samgar, N a chief officer H5552

NEBUCHADNEZZAR (89) [NEBUCHADNEZZAR'S]

2Ki 24: 1 N king of Babylon invaded the land H5556
2Ki 24: 1 then he turned against N and rebelled. H2257S
2Ki 24:10 time the officers of N king of Babylon H5556
2Ki 24:11 N himself came up to the city while H5556
2Ki 24:13 N removed the treasures from the temple of NDT
2Ki 24:15 N took Jehoiachin captive to Babylon. NDT
2Ki 25: 1 N king of Babylon marched against H5556
2Ki 25: 8 the nineteenth year of N king of Babylon, H5556
2Ki 25:22 N king of Babylon appointed Gedaliah H5556
1Ch 6:15 Jerusalem into exile by the hand of N. H5556
2Ch 36: 6 N king of Babylon attacked him and bound H5556
2Ch 36: 7 N also took to Babylon articles from the H5556
2Ch 36:10 King N sent for him and brought him to H5556
2Ch 36:13 He also rebelled against King N, who had H5556
2Ch 36:17 God gave them all into the hands of N. H2257S
Ezr 1: 7 which N had carried away from Jerusalem H5556
Ezr 2: 1 whom N king of Babylon had taken H5556
Ezr 5:12 them into the hands of N the Chaldean, A10453
Ezr 5:14 which N had taken from the temple in A10453
Ezr 6: 5 which N took from the temple in A10453
Ne 7: 6 of the exiles whom N king of Babylon had H5556
Est 2: 6 from Jerusalem by N king of Babylon, H5556
Jer 21: 2 LORD for us because N king of Babylon is H5557
Jer 21: 7 into the hands of N king of Babylon and H5557
Jer 22:25 N king of Babylon and the Babylonians. H5557
Jer 24: 1 to Babylon by N king of Babylon, H5557
Jer 25: 1 was the first year of N king of Babylon. H5557
Jer 25: 9 north and my servant N king of Babylon," H5557
Jer 27: 6 hands of my servant N king of Babylon; H5556
Jer 27: 8 will not serve N king of Babylon or bow H5556
Jer 27:20 which N king of Babylon did not take away H5556
Jer 28: 3 the LORD's house that N king of Babylon H5556
Jer 28:11 break the yoke of N king of Babylon off H5556
Jer 28:14 to make them serve N king of Babylon, H5556
Jer 29: 1 all the other people N had carried into H5556
Jer 29: 3 king of Judah sent to King N in Babylon. H5556
Jer 29:21 them into the hands of N king of Babylon, H5557
Jer 32: 1 which was the eighteenth year of N. H5557
Jer 32:28 the Babylonians and to N king of Babylon, H5557
Jer 34: 1 While N king of Babylon and all his army H5557
Jer 35:11 But when N king of Babylon invaded this H5557
Jer 37: 1 made king of Judah by N king of Babylon; H5557
Jer 39: 1 N king of Babylon marched against H5557
Jer 39: 5 him and took him to N king of Babylon at H5557
Jer 39:11 Now N king of Babylon had given these H5557
Jer 43:10 send for my servant N king of Babylon, H5557
Jer 44:30 into the hands of N king of Babylon, H5557
Jer 46: 2 Euphrates River by N king of Babylon in H5557
Jer 46:13 about the coming of N king of Babylon to H5557
Jer 46:26 them—N king of Babylon and his officers. H5557
Jer 49:28 which N king of Babylon attacked: H5557
Jer 49:30 "N king of Babylon has plotted against H5557
Jer 50:17 crush their bones was N king of Babylon." H5557
Jer 51:34 "N king of Babylon has devoured us, he H5557
Jer 52: 4 N king of Babylon marched against H5557
Jer 52:12 the nineteenth year of N king of Babylon, H5557
Jer 52:28 number of the people N carried into exile: H5557
Eze 26: 7 to bring against Tyre N king of Babylon, H5557
Eze 29:18 N king of Babylon drove his army in a H5557
Eze 29:19 going to give Egypt to N king of Babylon, H5557
Eze 30:10 of Egypt by the hand of N king of Babylon. H5557
Da 1: 1 N king of Babylon came to Jerusalem H5556
Da 1:18 the chief official presented them to N. H5556
Da 2: 1 year of his reign, N had dreams; his mind H5556
Da 2:28 He has shown King N what will happen A10453
Da 2:46 Then King N fell prostrate before Daniel A10453
Da 3: 1 King N made an image of gold, sixty A10453
Da 3: 3 of the image that King N had set up, A10453
Da 3: 5 image of gold that King N has set up. A10453
Da 3: 7 image of gold that King N had set up. A10453
Da 3: 9 They said to King N, "May the king live A10453
Da 3:13 with rage, N summoned Shadrach A10453
Da 3:14 N said to them, "Is it true, Shadrach A10453
Da 3:16 "King N, we do not need to A10453
Da 3:19 Then N was furious with Shadrach A10453
Da 3:24 Then King N leaped to his feet in A10453
Da 3:26 N then approached the opening of the A10453
Da 3:28 Then N said, "Praise be to the God of A10453
Da 4: 1 King N, To the nations and peoples of A10453
Da 4: 4 N, was at home in my palace A10453
Da 4:18 is the dream that I, King N, had. A10453
Da 4:28 All this happened to King N. A10453
Da 4:31 "This is what is decreed for you, King N: A10453
Da 4:33 had been said about N was fulfilled. A10453
Da 4:34 end of that time, I, N, raised my eyes A10453
Da 4:37 N, praise and exalt and glorify A10453
Da 5: 2 silver goblets that N his father had taken A10453
Da 5:11 Your father, King N, appointed him chief A10453
Da 5:18 God gave your father N sovereignty and A10453

NEBUCHADNEZZAR'S (1) [NEBUCHADNEZZAR]

Jer 52:29 in N eighteenth year, 832 people H4200+5557

NEBUSHAZBAN (1)

Jer 39:13 commander of the guard, N a chief officer H5558

NEBUZARADAN (16)

2Ki 25: 8 N commander of the imperial guard H5555
2Ki 25:11 N the commander of the guard carried into H5555
2Ki 25:20 N the commander took them all and H5555
Jer 39: 9 N commander of the imperial guard H5555
Jer 39:10 But N the commander of the guard left H5555
Jer 39:11 Jeremiah through N commander of the H5555
Jer 39:13 So N the commander of the guard H5555
Jer 40: 1 from the LORD after N commander of the H5555
Jer 40: 5 turned to go, N added, "Go back to NDT
Jer 41:10 over whom N commander of the imperial H5555
Jer 43: 6 all those whom N commander of the H5555
Jer 52:12 N commander of the imperial guard H5555
Jer 52:15 N the commander of the guard carried into H5555
Jer 52:16 But N left behind the rest of the poorest H5555
Jer 52:26 N the commander took them all and H5555
Jer 52:30 taken into exile by N the commander of H5555

NECESSARY (9)

Ac 1:21 Therefore *it is* n to choose one of the men G1256
Ro 13: 5 Therefore, it is n to submit to the authorities G340
2Co 9: 5 So I thought it n to urge the brothers to visit G338
Php 1:24 it is **more** n for you that I remain in the G338
Php 2:25 But I think it is n to send back to you G338
Heb 8: 3 so it was n for this one also to have G338
Heb 9:16 it is n to prove the death of the one who G340
Heb 9:23 It was n, then, for the copies of the G340
Heb 10:18 been forgiven, sacrifice for sin is **no longer** *n.* AIT

NECHO (10)

2Ki 23:29 Pharaoh N king of Egypt went up to the H5785
2Ki 23:29 N faced him and killed him at H2257S
2Ki 23:33 Pharaoh N put him in chains at Riblah in H5785
2Ki 23:34 Pharaoh N made Eliakim son of Josiah H5785
2Ki 23:35 paid Pharaoh N the silver and gold NDT
2Ch 35:20 N king of Egypt went up to fight at H5786
2Ch 35:21 But N sent messengers to him, saying NDT
2Ch 35:22 not listen to what N had said at God's H5786
2Ch 36: 4 But N took Eliakim's brother Jehoahaz H5786
Jer 46: 2 the army of Pharaoh N king of Egypt, H5786

NECK (49) [NECKS, STIFF-NECKED]

Ge 27:16 smooth part of his n with the goatskins. H7418
Ge 27:40 you will throw his yoke from off your n." H7418
Ge 33: 4 his arms around his n and kissed him. H7418
Ge 41:42 linen and put a gold chain around his n. H7418
Ge 49: 8 hand will be on the n *of* your enemies; H6902
Ex 13:13 if you do not redeem it, **break** its n. H6904
Ex 34:20 if you do not redeem it, **break** its n. H6904
Lev 5: 8 He is to wring its head from its n, not H6902
Dt 21: 4 the valley *they are to* **break** the heifer's n. H6904
Dt 21: 6 heifer whose n **was broken** in the valley, H6904
Dt 28:48 an iron yoke on your n until he has H7418
Jdg 5:30 highly embroidered garments for my n H7418
1Sa 4:18 His n was broken and he died, for he was H5154
Job 16:12 he seized me by the n and crushed me. H6902
Job 30:18 he binds me like the n *of* my garment. H7023
Job 39:19 clothe its n with a flowing mane? H7418
Job 41:22 Strength resides in its n; dismay goes H7418
Ps 69: 1 the waters have come up to my n. H5883
Ps 105:18 feet with shackles, his n was put in irons, H5883
Pr 1: 9 your head and a chain to adorn your n. H1738
Pr 3: 3 bind them around your n, write them on H1738
Pr 3:22 life for you, an ornament to grace your n. H1738
Pr 6:21 on your heart; fasten them around your n. H1738
SS 1:10 earrings, your n with strings of jewels. H7418
SS 4: 4 Your n is like the tower of David, built H7418
SS 7: 4 Your n is like an ivory tower. Your eyes are H7418
Isa 8: 8 through it and reaching up to the n. H7418
Isa 10:27 their yoke from your n; the yoke will be H7418
Isa 30:28 is like a rushing torrent, rising up to the n. H7418
Isa 48: 4 you were; your n muscles were iron, your H6902
Isa 52: 2 Free yourself from the chains on your n H7418
Isa 66: 3 a lamb is like *one who* **breaks** a dog's n; H6904
Jer 27: 2 straps and crossbars and put it on your n. H7418
Jer 27: 8 of Babylon or bow its n under his yoke, H7418
Jer 27:11 nation will bow its n under the yoke of the H7418
Jer 27:12 "Bow your n under the yoke of the king of H7418
Jer 28:10 the yoke off the n *of* the prophet Jeremiah H7418
Jer 28:11 of Babylon off the n *of* all the nations H7418
Jer 28:12 the yoke off the n *of* the prophet Jeremiah H7418
La 1:14 They have been hung on my n, and the H7418
Eze 16:11 your arms and a necklace around your n, H1744
Da 5: 7 have a gold chain placed around his n, A10611
Da 5:16 have a gold chain placed around your n, A10611
Da 5:29 a gold chain was placed around his n A10611
Hos 10:11 to thresh; so I will put a yoke on her fair n. H7418
Na 1:13 their yoke from your n and tear your shackles NDT
Mt 18: 6 hung around their n and to be drowned in G5549
Mk 9:42 hung around their n and they were thrown G5549
Lk 17: 2 tied around their n than to cause one of G5549

NECK-IRONS (1) [IRON]

Jer 29:26 acts like a prophet into the stocks and n. H7485

NECKLACE (3) [NECKLACES]

Ps 73: 6 Therefore pride is their n; they clothe H6735
SS 4: 9 of your eyes, with one jewel of your n. H7454
Eze 16:11 on your arms and a n around your neck, H8054

NECKLACES (2) [NECKLACE]

Nu 31:50 earrings and n—to make atonement H3921
Isa 3:18 bangles and headbands and **crescent** n, H8448

NECKS (9) [NECK]

Jos 10:24 put your feet on the n *of* these kings." H7418
Jos 10:24 forward and placed their feet on their n. H7418
Jdg 8:21 took the ornaments off their camels' n. H7418
Jdg 8:26 the chains that were on their camels' n. H7418
Isa 3:16 walking along with outstretched n, flirting H1744
Jer 28:14 an iron yoke on the n *of* all these nations H7418
Jer 30: 8 the yoke off their n and will tear off their H7418
Eze 21:29 be laid on the n *of* the wicked who are H7418
Ac 15:10 by putting on the n of Gentiles a yoke G5549

NECO (NIV84) NECHO

NECROMANCER (KJV) CONSULTS THE DEAD

NECTAR (1)

SS 8: 2 wine to drink, the n *of* my pomegranates. H6747

NEDABIAH (1)

1Ch 3:18 Shenazzar, Jekamiah, Hoshama and N. H5608

NEED (84) [NEEDED, NEEDING, NEEDLESS, NEEDS, NEEDY]

Ge 33:11 has been gracious to me and I have **all** I *n.*" AIT
Ex 14:14 will fight for you; you *n only to be* **still.**" AIT
Ex 16:16 'Everyone is to gather as much as they n H430
Lev 13:36 the skin, he *does* not *n to* **look** for yellow hair AIT
Dt 15: 4 *there n* **be** no poor people among you AIT
Dt 15: 8 freely lend them whatever they n. H2893+4728
Dt 28:57 For in her dire n she intends to eat them H2896
Jdg 19:19 We don't n anything." H4728
Jdg 19:20 "Let me supply whatever you n. Only H4728
1Ki 8:59 people Israel according to each day's n, H1821
2Ki 22: 7 But they *n* not **account for** the money AIT
1Ch 23:26 Levites no *longer n* to **carry** the tabernacle AIT
2Ch 2:16 Lebanon that you n and will float them H7664
2Ch 35:15 at each gate *did* not *n to* **leave** their posts, AIT
Job 5:21 and *n* not **fear** when destruction comes. AIT
Job 5:22 famine, and *n* not **fear** the wild animals. AIT
Job 34:23 God *has* no *n to* **examine** people further, that AIT
Ps 50: 9 *I have* no *n of* a bull from your stall or of H4374
Ps 79: 8 to meet us, for *we are* **in** desperate n. H1937
Ps 142: 6 for *I am* **in** desperate n; rescue me H1937
Pr 24: 6 Surely you n guidance to wage war, and NDT
Jer 2:24 males that pursue her *n* not **tire** *themselves*; AIT
Eze 39:10 *They will* not *n to* **gather** wood from the fields AIT
Da 3:16 we *do* not n to defend ourselves before A10287
Hos 7: 4 whose fire the baker n **not** stir from the H8697
Mt 3:14 saying, "I n to be baptized by you G5970+2400
Mt 5:37 All you *n to* say **is** simply 'Yes' or 'No' AIT
Mt 6: 8 knows what *you* n before you ask G5970+2400
Mt 6:32 heavenly Father knows that *you* n them. G5974
Mt 9:12 is not the healthy *who* n a doctor, G5970+2400
Mt 14:16 replied, "*They do* not n to go away. G5970+2400
Mt 26:65 Why *do we* n any more witnesses G5970+2400
Mk 2:17 is not the healthy *who* n a doctor, G5970+2400
Mk 2:25 companions were hungry and **in** n? G5970+2400
Mk 14:63 "Why *do we* n any more witnesses?" G5970+2400
Lk 5:31 is not the healthy *who* n a doctor, G5970+2400
Lk 11: 8 get up and give you as much as *you* n. G5974
Lk 12:30 your Father knows that *you* n them. G5974
Lk 15: 7 persons who *do* not n to repent. G5970+2400
Lk 15:14 whole country, and he began *to be* **in** n. G5728
Lk 22:71 "Why *do we* n any more testimony? G2400+5970
Jn 2:25 *He did* not n any testimony about G5970+2400
Jn 13:10 have had a bath n only to wash G2400+5970
Jn 16:30 and that *you do* not even n to have G5970+2400
Ac 2:45 possessions to give to anyone who had n. G5970
Ac 4:35 it was distributed to anyone who had n. G5970
Ac 10: 2 *he* **gave** generously to those **in** n G4472+1797
Ac 27:34 take some food. You n it to survive. G5639
Ro 12:13 Share with the Lord's people who are *in* n G5970
Ro 16: 2 to give her any help *she may* n from you, G5974
1Co 12:21 say to the hand, "*I* don't n you!" G5970+2400
1Co 12:21 say to the feet, "*I* don't n you!" G5970+2400
1Co 12:24 *while* our presentable parts n no G5970+2400
2Co 3: 1 Or *do we* n, like some people, letters of G5974
2Co 8:14 time your plenty will supply what they n, G5729
2Co 8:14 in turn their plenty will supply what you n. G5729
2Co 9: 1 There is **no** n for me to write to you about G4356
2Co 9: 8 having all that you n, you will abound in G894
Eph 4:28 something to share *with those* **in** n. G5970+2400
Php 4:11 I am not saying this because I am in n, for G5730
Php 4:12 I know what it is *to be* **in** n, and I know G5427
Php 4:16 me aid more than once when I was in n. G5970
1Th 1: 8 Therefore we *do* not n to say G5970+2400
1Th 4: 9 one another *we do* not n to write to G5790+2400
1Th 5: 1 and dates *we do* not n to write to G5970+2400
1Ti 5: 3 to those widows who are **really** *in n.* AIT
1Ti 5: 5 The widow who is **really** *in n* and left all AIT
1Ti 5:16 can help those widows who are **really** *in n.* AIT
2Ti 2:15 worker *who does* **not** *n to be* **ashamed** and AIT
Titus 3:13 that they **have everything** they n. G3594+3309
Heb 4:16 find grace to help us in our **time of** n. G2322

N

Heb 5:12 *you* **n** someone to teach you the G5970+2400
Heb 5:12 over again. *You* **n** milk, not G1181+5970+2400
Heb 7:11 why was there still **n** for another priest to G5970
Heb 7:26 Such a high priest truly **meets** our **n**—one G4560
Heb 7:27 he *does* not **n** to offer sacrifices day G2400+340
Heb 10:36 *You* **n** to persevere so that when G2400+5970
Jas 5:12 *All* you *n to* **say** is a simple "Yes AIT
2Pe 1:3 given us everything we **n** for a godly life NDT
1Jn 2:27 and *you do* not **n** anyone to teach G5970+2400
1Jn 3:17 brother or sister **in n** but has no pity G5970+2400
Rev 3:17 wealth and *do* not **n** a thing. G5970+2400
Rev 21:23 The city *does* not **n** the sun or the G5970+2400
Rev 22:5 *They will* not **n** the light of a lamp G2400+5970

NEEDED (16) [NEED]
Ex 12:4 *You are to* **determine** the **amount** *of* lamb **n** H4082
Ex 16:18 had gathered just as much as they **n**. H430
Ex 16:21 everyone gathered as much as they **n**, H430
Jos 19:9 Judah's portion was more than they **n**. NDT
Ezr 6:9 Whatever is **n**—young bulls, rams, male A10288
Ezr 7:20 And anything else **n** *for* the temple of A10289
Ecc 10:10 more strength *is* **n**, but skill will bring H1504
Mt 25:36 I **n clothes** and you clothed me, I was sick G1218
Mt 25:43 I **n clothes** and you did not clothe me G1218
Lk 9:11 and healed those *who* **n** healing. G5970+2400
Lk 10:42 few things are **n**—or indeed only one G5970
Jn 13:29 him to buy what *was* **n** for the G5970+2400
Ac 17:25 by human hands, *as if he* **n** anything. G4656
Ac 28:10 they furnished us with the supplies we **n**. G5970
2Co 11:9 when I was with you and **n** *something*, G5728
2Co 11:9 came from Macedonia supplied what I **n**. G5729

NEEDING (2) [NEED]
Mt 25:38 invite you in, or **n clothes** and clothe you? G1218
Mt 25:44 a stranger or **n clothes** or sick or in G1218

NEEDLE (3)
Mt 19:24 through the eye *of* a **n** than for someone G4827
Mk 10:25 through the eye *of* a **n** than for someone G4827
Lk 18:25 through the eye *of* a **n** than for someone G1017

NEEDLESS (2) [NEED]
1Sa 25:31 staggering burden of **n** bloodshed or of H2855
Pr 23:29 Who has **n** bruises? Who has H2855

NEEDS (22) [NEED]
Nu 4:26 to do all that *n to* **be done** with these things AIT
Jos 9:27 **to provide for the n** of the altar of the H4200
Pr 12:10 righteous care for the **n** *of* their animals, H5883
Isa 58:10 hungry and satisfy the **n** *of* the oppressed, H5883
Isa 58:11 he will satisfy your **n** in a sun-scorched H5883
Jer 5:7 *I* **supplied all** their **n**, yet they committed H8425
Mt 21:3 say that the Lord **n** them, and he G5970+2400
Mt 27:55 Jesus from Galilee *to* **care for** his **n**. G1354
Mk 11:3 'The Lord **n** it and will send it back G5970+2400
Mk 15:41 had followed him and **cared for** his **n**. G1354
Lk 19:31 say, 'The Lord **n** it.'" G5970+2400
Lk 19:34 They replied, "The Lord **n** it." G5970+2400
Ac 20:34 supplied my own **n** and the needs of my G5970
Ac 20:34 my own needs and the **n** of my companions. NDT
Ac 24:23 permit his friends *to* **take care of** his **n**. G5676
Ac 27:3 his friends so they might provide for his **n**. G2149
2Co 9:12 only supplying the **n** of the Lord's people G5729
Eph 4:29 building others up *according to* their **n**, G5970
Php 2:25 whom you sent to take care of my **n**. G5970
Php 4:19 God will meet all your **n** according to the G5970
Titus 3:14 to provide for urgent **n** and not live G5970
Jas 2:16 does nothing *about* their physical **n** G2201

NEEDY (56) [NEED]
Ex 22:25 to one of my people among you who is **n**, H6714
Dt 15:9 ill will toward the **n** *among* your fellow H36
Dt 15:11 Israelites who are poor and **n** in your land. H36
Dt 24:14 of a hired worker who is poor and **n**, H36
1Sa 2:8 the dust and lifts the **n** from the ash heap; H36
Job 5:15 He saves the **n** from the sword in their H36
Job 24:4 They thrust the **n** from the path and force all H36
Job 24:14 kills the poor and **n**, and in the night H36
Job 29:16 I was a father to the **n**; I took up the case of H36
Job 31:19 lack of clothing, or the **n** without garments, H36
Job 34:28 so that he heard the cry of the **n**. H6714
Ps 9:18 But God will never forget the **n**; the hope of H36
Ps 12:5 the poor are plundered and the **n** groan, H36
Ps 12:7 will keep **the n** safe and will protect us H4392S
Ps 35:10 the poor and **n** from those who rob them." H36
Ps 37:14 bend the bow to bring down the poor and **n**, H36
Ps 40:17 I am poor and **n**; may the Lord think H36
Ps 69:33 The LORD hears the **n** and does not despise H36
Ps 70:5 I am poor and **n**; come quickly to me, H36
Ps 72:4 the people and save the children of the **n**; H36
Ps 72:12 For he will deliver the **n** who cry out, the H36
Ps 72:13 on the weak and the **n** and save the needy H36
Ps 72:13 the needy and save the **n** from death. H36
Ps 74:21 may the poor and **n** praise your name. H36
Ps 82:4 Rescue the weak and the **n**; deliver them H36
Ps 86:1 and answer me, for I am poor and **n**. H36
Ps 107:41 But he lifted the **n** out of their affliction and H36
Ps 109:16 the poor and the **n** and the brokenhearted. H36
Ps 109:22 For I am poor and **n**, and my heart is H36
Ps 109:31 For he stands at the right hand of the **n**, to H36
Ps 113:7 the dust and lifts the **n** from the ash heap; H36
Ps 140:12 the poor and upholds the cause of the **n**. H36
Pr 14:21 blessed is the one who is kind to the **n**. H6705
Pr 14:31 whoever is kind to the **n** honors God. H36
Pr 22:22 are poor and do not crush the **n** in court, H6714
Pr 30:14 the earth and the **n** from among mankind. H36
Pr 31:9 defend the rights of the poor and **n**. H36
Pr 31:20 to the poor and extends her hands to the **n**. H36
Isa 11:4 with righteousness he will judge the **n**, H1924
Isa 14:30 and the **n** will lie down in safety. H36
Isa 25:4 a refuge for the **n** in their distress, H36
Isa 29:19 the **n** will rejoice in the Holy One of H36+132
Isa 32:7 even when the plea of the **n** is just. H36
Isa 41:17 "The poor and **n** search for water, but there H36
Jer 20:13 the life of the **n** from the hands of the H36
Jer 22:16 He defended the cause of the poor and **n** H36
Eze 16:49 they did not help the poor and **n**. H36
Eze 18:12 He oppresses the poor and **n**. He commits H36
Eze 22:29 oppress the poor and **n** and mistreat the H36
Am 2:6 silver, and the **n** for a pair of sandals. H36
Am 4:1 the poor and crush the **n** and say to your H36
Am 8:4 you who trample the **n** and do away with the H36
Am 8:6 with silver and the **n** for a pair of sandals, H36
Mt 6:2 "So when *you* **give to the n**, do not G4472+1797
Mt 6:3 But *when* you **give to the n**, do not G4472+1797
Ac 4:34 that there were no **n** persons among them G1890

NEGEV (38) [RAMOTH NEGEV]
Ge 12:9 set out and continued toward the **N**. H5582
Ge 13:1 So Abram went up from Egypt to the **N** H5582
Ge 13:3 From the **N** he went from place to place H5582
Ge 20:1 the region of the **N** and lived between H5582
Ge 24:62 Lahai Roi, for he was living in the **N**. H824+5582
Nu 13:17 "Go up through the **N** and on into the hill H5582
Nu 13:22 up through the **N** and came to Hebron, H5582
Nu 13:29 The Amalekites live in the **N**; the H824+5582
Nu 21:1 who lived in the **N**, heard that Israel was H5582
Nu 33:40 who lived in the **N** of Canaan, heard that H5582
Dt 1:7 foothills, in the **N** and along the coast, to H5582
Dt 34:3 the **N** and the whole region from the H5582
Jos 10:40 the hill country, the **N**, the western H5582
Jos 11:16 hill country, all the **N**, the whole region of H5582
Jos 12:8 the wilderness and the **N**. H5582
Jos 15:19 Since you have given me land in the **N** H5582
Jos 15:21 of Judah in the **N** toward the boundary H5582
Jos 19:8 Ramah in the **N**). This was the H5582
Jdg 1:9 country, the **N** and the western foothills. H5582
Jdg 1:15 Since you have given me land in the **N** H5582
Jdg 1:16 of the Desert of Judah in the **N** *near* Arad. H5582
1Sa 27:10 "Against the **N** *of* Judah" or "Against H5582
1Sa 27:10 "Against the **N** *of* Jerahmeel" or H5582
1Sa 27:10 "Against the **N** *of* the Kenites. H5582
1Sa 30:1 Amalekites had raided the **N** and Ziklag. H5582
1Sa 30:14 We raided the **N** *of* the Kerethites, some H5582
1Sa 30:14 belonging to Judah and the **N** *of* Caleb. H5582
2Sa 24:7 went on to Beersheba in the **N** *of* Judah. H5582
2Ch 28:18 in the foothills and in the **N** of Judah. H5582
Ps 126:4 our fortunes, LORD, like streams in the **N**. H5582
Isa 30:6 concerning the animals of the **N**: H5582
Jer 13:19 The cities in the **N** will be shut up, and H5582
Jer 17:26 from the hill country and the **N**, bringing H5582
Jer 32:44 of the western foothills and of the **N** H5582
Jer 33:13 of the western foothills and of the **N**, in H5582
Ob 19 People from the **N** will occupy the H5582
Ob 20 Sepharad will possess the towns of the **N**. H5582
Zec 7:7 the **N** and the western foothills were H5582

NEGLECT (10) [NEGLECTED, NEGLECTING, NEGLIGENT]
Dt 12:19 Be careful not *to* **n** the Levites as long as H6440
Dt 14:27 And *do* not **n** the Levites living in your H6440
Ezr 4:22 Be careful not *to* **n** this matter A10522+10712
Ne 10:39 "*We will* not **n** the house of our God." H6440
Est 6:10 *Do* not **n** anything you have H5877
Ps 119:16 in your decrees; *I will* not **n** your word. H8894
SS 1:6 my own vineyard *I had to* **n**. H4202+5757
Lk 11:42 but *you* **n** justice and the love of God. G4216
Ac 6:2 not be right for us *to* **n** the ministry of the G2901
1Ti 4:14 *Do* not **n** your gift, which was given you G288

NEGLECTED (2) [NEGLECT]
Ne 13:11 asked them, "Why is the house of God **n**?" H6440
Mt 23:23 But *you have* **n** the more important matters G918

NEGLECTING (1) [NEGLECT]
Mt 23:23 practiced the latter, without **n** the former. G918

NEGLIGENT (2) [NEGLECT]
2Ch 29:11 My sons, *do* not *be* **n** now, for the LORD H8922
Da 6:4 trustworthy and neither corrupt nor **n**. A10712

NEHELAMITE (3)
Jer 29:24 Tell Shemaiah the **N**, H5713
Jer 29:31 the LORD says about Shemaiah the **N**: H5713
Jer 29:32 Shemaiah the **N** and his descendants H5713

NEHEMIAH (9)
Ezr 2:2 Joshua, **N**, Seraiah, Reelaiah, H5718
Ne 1:1 The words of **N** son of Hakaliah: In the H5718
Ne 3:16 Beyond him, **N** son of Azbuk, ruler of a H5718
Ne 7:7 Joshua, **N**, Azariah, Raamiah, H5718
Ne 8:9 Then **N** the governor, Ezra the priest and H5718
Ne 8:10 **N** said, "Go and enjoy choice food and NDT
Ne 10:1 who sealed it were: **N** the governor, the H5718
Ne 12:26 in the days of **N** the governor and of H5718
Ne 12:47 So in the days of Zerubbabel and of **N**, all H5718

NEHUM (1)
Ne 7:7 **N** and Baanah): The list of the H5700

NEHUSHTA (1)
2Ki 24:8 mother's name was **N** daughter of H5735

NEHUSHTAN (1)
2Ki 18:4 burning incense to it. (It was called **N**.) H5736

NEIEL (1)
Jos 19:27 went north to Beth Emek and **N** H5832

NEIGH (1) [NEIGHING, NEIGHINGS]
Jer 50:11 heifer threshing grain and **n** like stallions, H7412

NEIGHBOR (79) [NEIGHBOR'S, NEIGHBORING, NEIGHBORS, NEIGHBORS']
Ex 3:22 woman is to ask her **n** and any woman H8907
Ex 12:4 they must share one with their nearest **n** H8907
Ex 20:16 not give false testimony against your **n**. H8276
Ex 20:17 anything that belongs to your **n**. H8276
Ex 22:7 "If anyone gives a **n** silver or goods for H8276
Ex 22:10 animal to their **n** for safekeeping and H8276
Ex 22:11 the LORD that **the n** did not lay hands H2257S
Ex 22:12 But if the animal was stolen from **the n** H2257S
Ex 22:13 the **n** shall bring in the remains as evidence NDT
Ex 22:14 an animal from their **n** and it is injured H8276
Ex 22:27 cloak is the only covering **your n** has. H2257S
Ex 32:27 each killing his brother and friend and **n**. H7940
Lev 6:2 LORD by deceiving a **n** about something H6660
Lev 6:2 something stolen, or if they cheat their **n**, H6660
Lev 19:13 " 'Do not defraud or rob your **n**. " 'Do not H8276
Lev 19:15 to the great, but judge your **n** fairly. H6660
Lev 19:17 Rebuke your **n** frankly so you will not H6660
Lev 19:18 your people, but love your **n** as yourself. H8276
Lev 20:10 with the wife of his **n**—both the adulterer H8276
Lev 24:19 who injures their **n** is to be injured in the H6660
Dt 4:42 unintentionally killed a **n** without malice H8276
Dt 5:20 not give false testimony against your **n**. H8276
Dt 5:21 anything that belongs to your **n**. H8276
Dt 19:4 anyone who kills a **n** unintentionally H8276
Dt 19:5 go into the forest with his **n** to cut wood, H8276
Dt 19:5 may fly off and hit his **n** and kill him. H8276
Dt 19:6 since he did it to **his n** without malice H2257S
Dt 19:11 assaults and kills a **n**, and then flees to H8276
Dt 22:26 of someone who attacks and murders a **n**, H8276
Dt 24:10 you make a loan of any kind to your **n**, H8276
Dt 24:11 outside and let the **n** to whom you are H408
Dt 24:12 If the **n** is poor, do not go to sleep with their H408
Dt 24:13 by sunset so that your **n** may sleep in it. NDT
Dt 27:24 is anyone who kills their **n** secretly." H8276
Jos 20:5 fugitive killed their **n** unintentionally and H8276
1Ki 8:31 anyone wrongs their **n** and is required to H8276
2Ch 6:22 anyone wrongs their **n** and is required to H8276
Ps 12:2 Everyone lies to their **n**; they flatter with H8276
Ps 15:3 who does no wrong to a **n**, and casts no H8276
Ps 88:18 You have taken from me friend and **n** H8276
Ps 101:5 Whoever slanders their **n** in secret, I will H8276
Pr 3:28 Do not say to your **n**, "Come back H8276
Pr 3:29 Do not plot harm against your **n**, who H8276
Pr 6:1 if you have put up security for your **n**, if H8276
Pr 6:3 of exhaustion—and give your **n** no rest! H8276
Pr 11:12 Whoever derides their **n** has no sense H8276
Pr 14:21 It is a sin to despise one's **n**, but blessed H8276
Pr 16:29 entices their **n** and leads them down H8276
Pr 17:18 in pledge and puts up security for a **n**. H8276
Pr 24:28 not testify against your **n** without cause— H8276
Pr 25:8 do in the end if your **n** puts you to shame? H8276
Pr 25:9 If you take your **n** to court, do not betray H8276
Pr 25:18 who gives false testimony against a **n**. H8276
Pr 26:19 is one who deceives their **n** and says, "I H8276
Pr 27:10 better a **n** nearby than a relative far away. H8907
Pr 27:14 loudly blesses their **n** early in the morning H8276
Isa 3:5 man against man, **n** against neighbor. H408
Isa 3:5 man against man, neighbor against **n**. H8276
Isa 19:2 against brother, **n** against neighbor, city H408
Isa 19:2 neighbor against **n**, city against city, H8276
Jer 31:34 No longer will they teach their **n**, or say to H8276
Mic 7:5 Do not trust a **n**; put no confidence in a H8276
Zec 3:10 you will invite your **n** to sit under your vine H8276
Zec 8:10 I had turned everyone against their **n**. H8276
Mt 5:43 'Love your **n** and hate your enemy. G4446
Mt 19:19 mother,' and 'love your **n** as yourself.' G4446
Mt 22:39 second is like it: 'Love your **n** as yourself.' G4446
Mk 12:31 'Love your **n** as yourself.' There is G4446
Mk 12:33 to love your **n** as yourself is more G4446
Lk 10:27 your mind'; and, 'Love your **n** as yourself.' G4446
Lk 10:29 so he asked Jesus, "And who is my **n**?" G4446
Lk 10:36 do you think was a **n** to the man who fell G4446
Ro 13:9 one command: "Love your **n** as yourself." G4446
Ro 13:10 Love does no harm *to* a **n**. Therefore love G4446
Gal 5:14 one command: "Love your **n** as yourself." G4446
Eph 4:25 falsehood and speak truthfully to your **n**, G4446
Heb 8:11 No longer will they teach their **n**, or say to G4489
Jas 2:8 "Love your **n** as yourself," you are G4446
Jas 4:12 But you—who are you to judge your **n**? G4446

NEIGHBOR'S (21) [NEIGHBOR]
Ex 20:17 "You shall not covet your **n** house. H8276
Ex 20:17 You shall not covet your **n** wife, or his H8276
Ex 22:7 they are stolen from the **n** house, H408
Ex 22:26 If you take your **n** cloak as a pledge, return H8276

Lev 18:20 relations with your **n** wife and defile H6660
Lev 19:16 do anything that endangers your **n** life. H8276
Dt 5:21 "You shall not covet your **n** wife. You shall H8276
Dt 5:21 set your desire on your **n** house or land, H8276
Dt 19:14 Do not move your **n** boundary stone set H8276
Dt 23:24 If you enter your **n** vineyard, you may eat H8276
Dt 23:25 If you enter your **n** grainfield, you may pick H8276
Dt 27:17 who moves their **n** boundary stone." H8276
Job 31: 9 woman, or if I have lurked at my **n** door, H8276
Pr 6: 3 since you have fallen into your **n** hands: H8276
Pr 6:24 keeping you from your **n** wife, from the H8276
Pr 25:17 Seldom set foot in your **n** house—too H8276
Eze 18: 6 does not defile his **n** wife or have sexual H8276
Eze 18:11 mountain shrines. He defiles his **n** wife. H8276
Eze 18:15 He does not defile his **n** wife. H8276
Eze 22:11 a detestable offense with his **n** wife, H8276
Eze 33:26 and each of you defiles his **n** wife. H8276

NEIGHBORING (10) [NEIGHBOR]

Dt 1: 7 go to all the **n peoples** in the Arabah, in H8907
Dt 21: 2 the distance from the body to the **n** towns. H6017
1Sa 7:14 delivered the **n territory** from the hands of H1473
Ezr 9: 1 separate from the **n** peoples with their H824
Ne 9:30 gave them into the hands of the **n** peoples. H824
Ne 10:28 themselves from the **n** peoples for the sake H824
Ne 10:31 "When the **n** peoples bring merchandise H824
Ps 76:11 let all the **n** *lands* bring gifts to the One to H6017
Jer 49:18 along with their **n** towns," says the LORD, H8907
Jer 50:40 Gomorrah along with their **n** towns," H8907

NEIGHBORS (39) [NEIGHBOR]

Ex 11: 2 alike are to ask their **n** for articles of silver H8276
Jos 9:16 the Israelites heard that they were **n** H7940
1Sa 15:28 today and has given it to one of your **n**— H8276
1Sa 28:17 your hands and given it to one of your **n**— H8276
2Ki 4: 3 around and ask all your **n** for empty jars. H8907
1Ch 12:40 their **n** from as far away as Issachar H7940
Ezr 1: 6 All their **n** assisted them with articles of H6017
Ezr 6:21 of their Gentile **n** in order to seek the LORD, H824
Ps 28: 3 cordially with their **n** but harbor malice in H8276
Ps 31:11 utter contempt of my **n** and an object of H8907
Ps 38:11 of my wounds; my **n** stay far away. H7940
Ps 44:13 You have made us a reproach to our **n** H8907
Ps 79: 4 We are objects of contempt to our **n**, of H8907
Ps 79:12 into the laps of our **n** seven times the H8907
Ps 80: 6 made us an object of derision to our **n**, H8907
Ps 89:41 he has become the scorn of his **n**. H8907
Pr 11: 9 their mouths the godless destroy their **n**, H8276
Pr 14:20 The poor are shunned even by their **n**, but H8276
Pr 21:10 crave evil; their **n** get no mercy from them. H8276
Pr 29: 5 who flatter their **n** are spreading nets for H8276
Jer 6:21 over them; **n** and friends will perish." H8907
Jer 9: 8 mouths they all speak cordially to their **n**, H8276
Jer 12:14 "As for all my wicked **n** who seize the H8907
Jer 49:10 also his allies and **n**, so there is no one to H8907
La 1:17 Jacob that his **n** become his foes; H6017
Eze 16:26 the Egyptians, your **n** with large genitals H8907
Eze 16:57 of Edom and all her **n** and the daughters H6017
Eze 22:12 You extort unjust gain from your **n**. H8276
Eze 28:24 Israel have malicious **n** who are painful H6017
Eze 28:26 on all their **n** who maligned them. H6017
Hab 2:15 "Woe to him who gives drink to his **n** H8276
Zec 11: 6 into the hands of their **n** and their king. H8276
Lk 1:58 Her **n** and relatives heard that the Lord *G4341*
Lk 1:65 All the **n** were filled with awe, and *G4340*
Lk 14:12 your rich **n**; if you do, they may *G1150*
Lk 15: 6 calls his friends and **n** together and says, *G1150*
Lk 15: 9 calls her friends and **n** together and says, *G1150*
Jn 9: 8 His **n** and those who had formerly seen *G1150*
Ro 15: 2 of us should please our **n** for their good, *G4446*

NEIGHBORS' (1) [NEIGHBOR]

Jer 29:23 committed adultery with their **n** wives, H8276

NEIGHING (2) [NEIGH]

Jer 5: 8 stallions, each **n** for another man's wife. H7412
Jer 8:16 at the **n** *of* their stallions the whole H7754+5177

NEIGHINGS (1) [NEIGH]

Jer 13:27 your adulteries and **lustful n**, your H5177

NEITHER (121) [NOR]

Ex 4:10 **n** in the past nor since you have spoken to H1685
Ex 10: 6 something **n** your parents nor your H4202
Ex 13:22 **N** the pillar of cloud by day nor the pillar H4202
Ex 14:20 so **n** went near the other all night H4202+2296
Ex 20:10 shall not do any work, **n** you, nor your son NDT
Nu 14:44 though **n** Moses nor the ark of the LORD's H4202
Nu 23:25 "**N** curse them at all nor bless them H1685+4202
Dt 2:37 **n** the land along the course of the Jabbok NDT
Dt 5:14 shall not do any work, **n** you, nor your son NDT
Dt 8: 3 which **n** you nor your ancestors had known H4202
Dt 13: 6 gods that **n** you nor your ancestors have H4202
Dt 28:64 which **n** you nor your ancestors have H4202
Jos 5:14 "**N**," he replied, "but as commander of H4202
Jos 8:22 leaving them **n** survivors nor fugitives. H1194
Jdg 1:30 **N** did Zebulun drive out the Canaanites H4202
Jdg 1:33 **N** did Naphtali drive out those living in H4202
Jdg 2:10 grew up who knew **n** the LORD nor what he H4202
Jdg 6: 4 Israel, **n** sheep nor cattle nor donkeys. H2256
Jdg 11:34 Except for her he had **n** son nor daughter. H401
Jdg 14: 6 But he told **n** his father nor his mother H4202
1Sa 5: 5 is why to this day **n** the priests of Dagon H4202
1Sa 20:31 **n** you nor your kingdom will be H4202
2Sa 1:21 may you have **n** dew nor rain, may no H440
2Sa 2:19 turning **n** to the right nor to the left as he H4202
2Sa 14: 7 leaving my husband **n** name nor H1194
2Sa 17:12 **N** he nor any of his men will be left alive. H4202
1Ki 3:26 "**N** I nor you shall have him. H1685+4202
1Ki 13:28 The lion had **n** eaten the body nor H4202
1Ki 17: 1 there will be **n** dew nor rain in the next few H561
2Ki 3:17 You will see **n** wind nor rain, yet this H4202
2Ki 17:34 They **n** worship the LORD nor adhere to the H401
2Ki 18:12 They **n** listened to the commands nor H4202
2Ki 23:22 **N** in the days of the judges who led Israel H4202
2Ki 23:25 **N** before nor after Josiah was there H2256+4202
Ne 4:23 **N** I nor my brothers nor my men nor the H401
Ne 5:14 **n** I nor my brothers ate the food allotted to H4202
Est 2: 7 up because she had **n** father nor mother. H401
Est 5: 9 observed that he **n** rose nor showed fear H4202
Job 28:17 **N** gold nor crystal can compare with it, nor H4202
Ps 121: 4 over Israel will **n** slumber nor sleep. H4202
Pr 27:20 never satisfied, and **n** are human eyes. H4202
Pr 30: 8 far from me; give me **n** poverty nor riches H440
Ecc 4: 8 a man all alone; he had **n** son nor brother. H401
Ecc 7:16 overrighteous, **n** be overwise—why H2256+440
Ecc 9:10 **there is n** working nor planning nor H401
Isa 5: 6 it a wasteland, **n** pruned nor cultivated H4202
Isa 11: 9 They will **n** harm nor destroy on all my H4202
Isa 23: 4 "I have **n** been in labor nor given birth; H4202
Isa 23: 4 I have **n** reared sons nor brought up H2256
Isa 30: 5 to them, who bring **n** help nor advantage H4202
Isa 48: 8 You have **n** heard nor understood H1685+4202
Isa 49:10 They will **n** hunger nor thirst, nor will the H4202
Isa 55: 8 thoughts, **n** are your ways my ways," H2256+4202
Isa 57:11 have **n** remembered me nor taken H4202
Isa 65:25 They will **n** harm nor destroy on all my H4202
Jer 9:16 them among nations that **n** they nor their H4202
Jer 13:23 **N** can you do good who are accustomed H1685
Jer 15:10 I have **n** lent nor borrowed, yet everyone H4202
Jer 16:13 this land into a land **n** you nor your H4202
Jer 19: 4 in it to gods that **n** they nor their ancestors H4202
Jer 22:26 country, where **n** of you was born, and H4202
Jer 33:10 inhabited by **n** people nor animals H4946+401
Jer 35: 6 '**N** you nor your descendants must ever H4202
Jer 35: 8 **N** we nor our wives nor our sons and H1194
Jer 37: 2 **N** he nor his attendants nor the H2256+4202
Jer 38:16 I will **n** kill you nor hand you over to those H561
Jer 44: 3 other gods that **n** they nor you nor your H4202
Jer 49:31 "a nation that has **n** gates nor bars; its H4202
Jer 51:62 so that **n** people nor animals will live in it; H1194
Eze 14:20 they could save **n** son nor daughter. H561
Eze 29:11 The foot of **n** man nor beast will pass H4202
Eze 43: 7 defile my holy name—**n** they nor their kings NDT
Da 3:12 They **n** serve your gods nor worship the A10379
Da 6: 4 was trustworthy and **n** corrupt nor negligent. NDT
Da 11:24 will achieve what **n** his fathers nor his H4202
Am 7:14 "I was **n** a prophet nor the son of a H4202
Zep 1: 6 following the LORD and **n** seek the LORD H4202
Zep 1:18 **N** their silver nor their gold will be H1685+4202
Zec 14: 6 that day there will be **n** sunlight nor cold, H4202
Mt 5:15 **N** do people light a lamp and put it under *G4028*
Mt 9:17 **N** do people pour new wine into old *G4028*
Mt 11:18 For John came **n** eating nor drinking, and *G3612*
Mt 21:27 "**N** will I tell you by what authority I am *G4028*
Mt 22:30 people will **n** marry nor be given in *G4046*
Mk 11:33 "**N** will I tell you by what authority I am *G4028*
Mk 12:25 they will **n** marry nor be given in marriage; *G4046*
Lk 7:33 John the Baptist came **n** eating bread *G3590*
Lk 7:42 **N** of them had the money to pay him back *G3590*
Lk 14:35 It is fit **n** for the soil nor for the manure *G4046*
Lk 18: 2 was a judge who **n** feared God nor cared *G3590*
Lk 20: 8 "**N** will I tell you by what authority I am *G4028*
Lk 20:35 from the dead will **n** marry nor be given in *G4046*
Lk 23:15 **N** has Herod, for he sent him back to us *G4028*
Jn 4:21 worship the Father **n** on this mountain *G4046*
Jn 6:24 crowd realized that **n** Jesus nor his *G4024*
Jn 8:11 "Then **n** do I condemn you," Jesus *G4028*
Jn 9: 3 "**N** this man nor his parents sinned," *G4046*
Jn 12:40 so they can **n** see with their eyes *G3590*
Jn 14:17 because it **n** sees him nor knows him. *G4024*
Jn 15: 4 **N** can you bear fruit unless you remain in *G4028*
Ac 15:10 a yoke that **n** we nor our ancestors *G4046*
Ac 19:37 though they have **n** robbed temples nor *G4046*
Ac 23: 8 **and** that there are **n** angels nor spirits *G3612*
Ac 27:20 When **n** sun nor stars appeared for many *G3612*
Ro 1:21 they **n** glorified him as God nor gave *G4024*
Ro 8:38 For I am convinced that **n** death nor life *G4046*
Ro 8:38 death nor life, **n** angels nor demons *G4046*
Ro 8:38 demons, **n** the present nor the future *G4046*
Ro 8:39 **n** height nor depth, nor anything else in *G4046*
1Co 3: 7 So **n** the one who plants nor the one who *G4046*
1Co 6: 9 **N** the sexually immoral nor idolaters nor *G4046*
1Co 11: 9 **n** was man created for woman, but *G2779+4024*
2Co 7:12 it was **n** on account of the one who did *G4024*
2Co 10:15 **N** do we go beyond our limits by boasting *G4024*
Gal 3:28 There is **n** Jew nor Gentile, neither slave *G4024*
Gal 3:28 Jew nor Gentile, **n** slave nor free, nor is *G4024*
Gal 5: 6 For in Christ Jesus **n** circumcision nor *G4046*
Gal 6:15 **N** circumcision nor uncircumcision means *G4046*
Jas 3:12 **N** can a salt spring produce fresh water *G4046*
Rev 3:15 your deeds, that you are **n** cold nor hot. *G4046*
Rev 3:16 you are lukewarm—**n** hot nor cold—I am *G4046*

NEKEB See ADAMI NEKEB

NEKODA (4)

Ezr 2:48 Rezin, N, Gazzam, H5928
Ezr 2:60 of Delaiah, Tobiah and **N** 652 H5928
Ne 7:50 Reaiah, Rezin, N, H5928
Ne 7:62 of Delaiah, Tobiah and **N** 642 H5928

NEMUEL (3) [NEMUELITE]

Nu 26: 9 the sons of Eliab were N, Dathan and H5803
Nu 26:12 through N, the Nemuelite clan; through H5803
1Ch 4:24 N, Jamin, Jarib, Zerah H5803

NEMUELITE (1) [NEMUEL]

Nu 26:12 Nemuel, the **N** clan; through Jamin H5804

NEPHEG (4)

Ex 6:21 The sons of Izhar were Korah, **N** and Zikri. H5863
2Sa 5:15 Elishua, N, Japhia, H5863
1Ch 3: 7 Nogah, N, Japhia, H5863
1Ch 14: 6 Nogah, N, Japhia, H5863

NEPHEW (2) [NEPHEWS]

Ge 12: 5 his wife Sarai, his **n** Lot, all the H1201+278
Ge 14:12 carried off Abram's **n** Lot and his H1201+278

NEPHEWS (1) [NEPHEW]

Ezr 8:19 and his brothers and **n**, 20 in all. H1201+2157

NEPHILIM (3)

Ge 6: 4 The **N** were on the earth in those days H5872
Nu 13:33 We saw the **N** there (the descendants of H5872
Nu 13:33 the descendants of Anak come from the **N**). H5872

NEPHTHALIM (KJV) NAPHTALI

NEPHTOAH (2)

Jos 15: 9 toward the spring of the waters of **N**, H5886
Jos 18:15 came out at the spring of the waters of **N**. H5886

NEPHUSIM (2)

Ezr 2:50 Asnah, Meunim, N, H5866
Ne 7:52 Besai, Meunim, N, H5867

NER (18)

1Sa 14:50 of Saul's army was Abner son of **N**, H5945
1Sa 14:50 Abner son of Ner, and **N** was Saul's uncle. NDT
1Sa 14:51 Abner's father **N** were sons of Abiel. H5945
1Sa 26: 5 He saw where Saul and Abner son of **N** H5945
1Sa 26:14 out to the army and to Abner son of **N**, H5945
2Sa 2: 8 Abner son of **N**, the commander of H5945
2Sa 2:12 Abner son of **N**, together with the men of H5945
2Sa 3:23 that Abner son of **N** had come to the king H5945
2Sa 3:25 You know Abner son of **N**; he came to H5945
2Sa 3:28 concerning the blood of Abner son of **N**. H5945
2Sa 3:37 no part in the murder of Abner son of **N**. H5945
1Ki 2: 5 Abner son of **N** and Amasa son of Jether. H5945
1Ki 2:32 of them—Abner son of **N**, commander of H5945
1Ch 8:30 followed by Zur, Kish, Baal, **N**, Nadab, H5945
1Ch 8:33 **N** was the father of Kish, Kish the father of H5945
1Ch 9:36 followed by Zur, Kish, Baal, **N**, Nadab, H5945
1Ch 9:39 **N** was the father of Kish, Kish the father of H5945
1Ch 26:28 Abner son of **N** and Joab son of Zeruiah H5945

NEREUS (1)

Ro 16:15 **N** and his sister, and Olympas and *G3759*

NERGAL (1)

2Ki 17:30 those from Kuthah made **N**, and those H5946

NERGAL-SHAREZER (3)

Jer 39: 3 **N** *of* Samgar, Nebo-Sarsekim a chief H5947
Jer 39: 3 **N** a high official and all the other officials H5947
Jer 39:13 **N** a high official and all the other officers H5947

NERI (1)

Lk 3:27 the son of Shealtiel, the son *of* **N**, *G3760*

NERIAH (10)

Jer 32:12 I gave this deed to Baruch son of **N** H5949
Jer 32:16 the deed of purchase to Baruch son of **N**, H5949
Jer 36: 4 So Jeremiah called Baruch son of **N**, and H5949
Jer 36: 8 Baruch son of **N** did everything Jeremiah H5949
Jer 36:14 So Baruch son of **N** went to them with the H5950
Jer 36:32 gave it to the scribe Baruch son of **N**, H5950
Jer 43: 3 But Baruch son of **N** is inciting you against H5949
Jer 43: 6 Baruch son of **N** along with them. H5950
Jer 45: 1 When Baruch son of **N** wrote on a scroll H5949
Jer 51:59 gave to the staff officer Seraiah son of **N**, H5949

NEST (17) [NESTED, NESTING, NESTS]

Nu 24:21 place is secure, your **n** is set in a rock; H7860
Dt 22: 6 come across a bird's **n** beside the road, H7860
Dt 32:11 eagle that stirs up its **n** and hovers over its H7860
Job 39:27 at your command and build its **n** on high? H7860
Ps 84: 3 the swallow a **n** for herself, where H7860
Ps 104:12 The birds of the sky **n** by the waters; they H8905
Pr 27: 8 a bird that flees its **n** is anyone who flees H7860
Isa 10:14 As one reaches into a **n**, so my hand H7860
Isa 11: 8 child will put its hand into the viper's **n**. H4402
Isa 16: 2 Like fluttering birds pushed from the **n**, so H7860
Isa 34:11 the great owl and the raven *will* **n** there. H8905
Isa 34:15 The owl *will* **n** there and lay eggs, she H7873
Jer 48:28 like a dove *that* **makes** *its* **n** at the mouth H7873
Jer 49:16 Though you build your **n** as high as the H7860
Eze 17:23 Birds of every kind *will* **n** in it; they will H8905

Ob 4 eagle and make your **n** among the stars, H7860
Hab 2: 9 setting his **n** on high to escape the H7860

NESTED (1) [NEST]
Eze 31: 6 All the birds of the sky **n** in its boughs, all H7873

NESTING (1) [NEST]
Da 4:21 and *having* **n places** in its branches for A10709

NESTLED (1)
Jer 22:23 'Lebanon,' *who are* **n** in cedar buildings H7873

NESTS (4) [NEST]
Ps 104:17 There the birds **make** *their* **n**; the stork has H7873
Isa 60: 8 fly along like clouds, like doves to their **n**? H748
Mt 8:20 "Foxes have dens and birds have **n**, but *G2943*
Lk 9:58 "Foxes have dens and birds have **n**, but *G2943*

NET (31) [DRAGNET, FISHNETS, NETS]
Job 18: 8 His feet thrust him into a **n**; he wanders H8407
Job 19: 6 wronged me and drawn his **n** around me. H5178
Ps 9:15 feet are caught in the **n** they have hidden. H8407
Ps 10: 9 the helpless and drags them off in his **n**. H8407
Ps 35: 7 they hid their **n** for me without cause H8407
Ps 35: 8 may the **n** they hid entangle them H8407
Ps 57: 6 They spread a **n** for my feet—I was H8407
Ps 140: 5 the cords of their **n** and have set traps H8407
Pr 1:17 useless to spread a **n** where every bird H8407
Ecc 9:12 As fish are caught in a cruel **n**, or birds H5182
Isa 51:20 street corner, like antelope caught in a **n**. H4821
La 1:13 He spread a **n** for my feet and turned me H8407
Eze 12:13 I will spread my **n** for him, and he will be H8407
Eze 17:20 I will spread my **n** for him, and he will be H8407
Eze 19: 8 They spread their **n** for him, and he was H8407
Eze 32: 3 throng of people I will cast my **n** over you, H8407
Eze 32: 3 and they will haul you up in my **n**. H3052
Hos 5: 1 snare at Mizpah, a **n** spread out on Tabor. H8407
Hos 7:12 I will throw my **n** over them; I will pull H8407
Hab 1:15 he catches them in his **n**, he gathers them H3052
Hab 1:16 he sacrifices to his **n** and burns incense to H3052
Hab 1:16 for by **his n** he lives in luxury and enjoys H2156s
Hab 1:17 Is he to keep on emptying his **n** H3052
Mt 4:18 They were casting a **n** into the lake, for *G312*
Mt 13:47 of heaven is like a **n** that was let down *G4880*
Mk 1:16 brother Andrew **casting a n** into the lake, *G311*
Jn 21: 6 "Throw your **n** on the right side of the *G1473*
Jn 21: 6 unable to haul **the n** in because of the *G8998*
Jn 21: 8 the boat, towing the **n** full of fish, for they *G1473*
Jn 21:11 into the boat and dragged the **n** ashore. *G1473*
Jn 21:11 even with so many the **n** was not torn. *G1473*

NETAIM (1)
1Ch 4:23 the potters who lived at **N** and Gederah; H5751

NETHANEL (14)
Nu 1: 8 from Issachar, **N** son of Zuar; H5991
Nu 2: 5 of the people of Issachar is **N** son of Zuar. H5991
Nu 7:18 On the second day **N** son of Zuar, the H5991
Nu 7:23 This was the offering of **N** son of Zuar. H5991
Nu 10:15 **N** son of Zuar was over the division of the H5991
1Ch 2:14 the fourth **N**, the fifth Raddai, H5991
1Ch 15:24 Joshaphat, **N**, Amasai, Zechariah, H5991
1Ch 24: 6 The scribe Shemaiah son of **N**, a Levite H5991
1Ch 26: 4 the third, Sakar the fourth, **N** the fifth, H5991
2Ch 17: 7 **N** and Micaiah to teach in the towns of H5991
2Ch 35: 9 Konaniah along with Shemaiah and **N**, H5991
Ezr 10:22 Maaseiah, Ishmael, **N**, Jozabad and H5991
Ne 12:21 of Hilkiah's, Hashabiah; of Jedaiah's, **N**. H5991
Ne 12:36 Maai, **N**, Judah and Hanani H5991

NETHANIAH (20)
2Ki 25:23 Ishmael son of **N**, Johanan son of H5992
2Ki 25:25 Ishmael son of **N**, the son of Elishama, H5992
1Ch 25: 2 Joseph, **N** and Asarelah. The sons H5992
1Ch 25:12 the fifth to **N**, his sons and relatives 12 H5993
2Ch 17: 8 Levites—Shemaiah, **N**, Zebadiah, Asahel, H5993
Jer 36:14 all the officials sent Jehudi son of **N**, the H5993
Jer 40: 8 Ishmael son of **N**, Johanan and Jonathan H5993
Jer 40:14 sent Ishmael son of **N** to take your life?" H5992
Jer 40:15 "Let me go and kill Ishmael son of **N**, and H5992
Jer 41: 1 In the seventh month Ishmael son of **N** H5992
Jer 41: 2 Ishmael son of **N** and the ten men who H5992
Jer 41: 6 Ishmael son of **N** went out from Mizpah to H5992
Jer 41: 7 Ishmael son of **N** and the men who were H5992
Jer 41: 9 Ishmael son of **N** filled it with the dead H5993
Jer 41:10 Ishmael son of **N** took them captive and H5992
Jer 41:11 crimes Ishmael son of **N** had committed, H5992
Jer 41:12 men and went to fight Ishmael son of **N**. H5992
Jer 41:15 But Ishmael son of **N** and eight of his men H5992
Jer 41:16 from Ishmael son of **N** after Ishmael had H5992
Jer 41:18 Ishmael son of **N** had killed Gedaliah H5992

NETHER, NETHERMOST (KJV) BELOW, FOOT, LOWER, LOWEST

NETHINIMS (KJV) TEMPLE SERVANTS

NETOPHAH (2)
Ezr 2:22 of **N** 56 H5756
Ne 7:26 the men of Bethlehem and **N** 188 H5756

NETOPHATHITE (8) [NETOPHATHITES]
2Sa 23:28 Zalmon the Ahohite, Maharai the **N**, H5743
2Sa 23:29 Heled son of Baanah the **N**, Ithai son of H5743
2Ki 25:23 Seraiah son of Tanhumeth the **N** H5743
1Ch 11:30 Maharai the **N**, Heled son of Baanah the H5743
1Ch 11:30 Heled son of Baanah the **N**, H5743
1Ch 27:13 was Maharai the **N**, a Zerahite. H5743
1Ch 27:15 was Heldai the **N**, from the family of H5743
Jer 40: 8 the sons of Ephai the **N**, and Jaazaniah H5743

NETOPHATHITES (3) [NETOPHATHITE]
1Ch 2:54 Bethlehem, the **N**, Atroth Beth Joab, half H5743
1Ch 9:16 who lived in the villages of the **N**. H5743
Ne 12:28 Jerusalem—from the villages of the **N**, H5743

NETS (13) [NET]
Ps 141:10 Let the wicked fall into their own **n**, while H4821
Pr 29: 5 neighbors are spreading **n** for their feet. H8407
Isa 19: 8 those who throw **n** on the water will pine H4823
Eze 47:10 there will be places for spreading **n**. H3052
Mic 7: 2 shed blood; they hunt each other with **n**. H3052
Mt 4:20 At once they left their **n** and followed him. *G1473*
Mt 4:21 their father Zebedee, preparing their **n**. *G1473*
Mk 1:18 At once they left their **n** and followed him. *G1473*
Mk 1:19 brother John in a boat, preparing their **n**. *G1473*
Lk 5: 2 the fishermen, who were washing their **n**. *G1473*
Lk 5: 4 and let down the **n** for a catch. *G1473*
Lk 5: 5 because you say so, I will let down the **n**." *G1473*
Lk 5: 6 of fish that their **n** began to break. *G1473*

NETTLES (1)
Isa 34:13 citadels, **n** and brambles her strongholds. H7853

NETWORK (16)
Ex 27: 4 a bronze **n**, and make a H5126+8407
Ex 27: 4 ring at each of the four corners of the **n**. H8407
Ex 38: 4 a bronze **n**, to be under its H5126+8407
1Ki 7:17 A **n** of interwoven chains H8422+5126+8422
1Ki 7:18 rows encircling each **n** to decorate the H8422
1Ki 7:20 above the bowl-shaped part next to the **n** H8422
1Ki 7:41 the two sets of **n** decorating the two H8422
1Ki 7:42 pomegranates for the two sets of **n** H8422
1Ki 7:42 pomegranates for each **n** decorating the H8422
2Ki 25:17 decorated with a **n** and pomegranates of H8422
2Ki 25:17 The other pillar, with its **n**, was similar. H8422
2Ch 4:12 the two sets of **n** decorating the two H8422
2Ch 4:13 pomegranates for the two sets of **n** H8422
2Ch 4:13 two rows of pomegranates for each **n** H8422
Jer 52:22 decorated with a **n** and pomegranates of H8422
Jer 52:23 above the surrounding **n** was a hundred. H8422

NEVER (353)
Ge 8:21 "**N** again will I curse the ground because H4202
Ge 8:21 And **n** again will I destroy all living H4202
Ge 8:22 winter, day and night will **n** cease. H4202
Ge 9:11 **N** again will all life be destroyed by the H4202
Ge 9:11 **n** again will there be a flood to destroy H4202
Ge 9:15 **N** again will the waters become a flood to H4202
Ge 14:23 so that you will **n** be able to say, 'I made H4202
Ge 19: 8 daughters who have **n** slept with a man. H4202
Ge 20: 9 done things to me that should **n** be done." H4202
Ge 21:10 that woman's son will **n** share in the H4202
Ge 41:19 I had **n** seen such ugly cows in all the H4202
Ge 45:20 **N** mind about your belongings H440+6524
Ge 48:11 "I **n** expected to see your face again H4202
Ex 4:10 I have **n** been eloquent, neither in the H4202
Ex 10:14 **N** before had there been such a plague of H4202
Ex 10:29 "I will **n** appear before you again. H4202
Ex 14:13 today you will **n** see again. H4202+6330+6409
Ex 34:10 I will do wonders **n** before done in any H4202
Lev 27:20 it can **n** be redeemed. H4202+6388
Nu 11: 6 we **n** see anything but this manna! H401
Nu 19: 2 that has **n** been under a yoke. H4202
Nu 31:18 every girl who has **n** slept with a man. H4202
Nu 31:35 women who had **n** slept with a man. H4202
Dt 8:16 something your ancestors had **n** known, to H4202
Dt 9: 7 Remember this and **n** forget how you H440
Dt 13:16 a ruin forever, **n** to be rebuilt, H4202+6388
Dt 19:20 **n** again will such an evil thing be H4202
Dt 21: 3 a heifer that has **n** been worked and has H4202
Dt 21: 3 never been worked and has **n** worn a yoke H4202
Dt 22:29 He can **n** divorce her as long as he lives H4202
Dt 28:13 will always be at the top, **n** at the bottom. H4202
Dt 28:66 both night and day, **n** sure of your life. H4202
Dt 28:68 a journey I said you should **n** make again. H4202
Dt 29:20 The LORD will **n** be willing to forgive them H4202
Dt 31: 6 he will **n** leave you nor forsake you." H4202
Dt 31: 8 he will **n** leave you nor forsake you. H4202
Jos 1: 5 I will **n** leave you nor forsake you. H4202
Jos 3: 4 since you have **n** been this way before. H4202
Jos 9:23 You will **n** be released from service as H4202
Jos 10:14 There has **n** been a day like it before or H4202
Jdg 1:28 into forced labor but **n** drove them out H4202
Jdg 2: 1 'I will **n** break my covenant H4202+4200+6409
Jdg 11:37 with my friends, because I will **n marry**." H1436
Jdg 11:38 wept because she would **n marry**. H1436
Jdg 13: 5 a son whose head is **n** to be touched by a H4202
Jdg 16:11 with new ropes that have **n** been used, H4202
Jdg 19:30 "Such a thing has **n** been seen or done H4202
Jdg 21:12 women who had **n** slept with a man, H4202
1Sa 3:14 house will **n** be atoned for by H561+6330+6409
1Sa 6: 7 that have calved and have **n** been yoked. H4202
1Sa 14:45 **N**! As surely as the LORD H2721
1Sa 20: 2 "**N**!" Jonathan replied. "You are not going H2721
1Sa 20: 9 "**N**!" Jonathan said. "If I had the least H2721
2Sa 3:29 May Joab's family **n** be without someone H440
2Sa 7:15 But my love will **n** be taken away from H4202
2Sa 12:10 the sword will **n** depart from H4202+6330+6409
2Sa 13:22 And Absalom **n** said a word to Amnon H4202
2Sa 21:17 "**N** again will you go out with us to battle H4202
1Ki 1: 6 His father had **n** rebuked him H4202+4946+3427
1Ki 2: 4 you will **n** fail to have a successor on the H4202
1Ki 3:12 that there will **n** have been H4202+4200+7156
1Ki 8:25 'You shall **n** fail to have a successor to sit H4202
1Ki 8:57 may he **n** leave us nor forsake us. H440
1Ki 9: 5 'You shall **n** fail to have a successor on H4202
1Ki 10:10 **N** again were so many spices brought in H4202
1Ki 10:12 much almugwood has **n** been imported H4202
1Ki 21:25 There was **n** anyone like Ahab, who sold H4202
1Ki 22: 8 him because he **n** prophesies anything H4202
1Ki 22:18 I tell you that he **n** prophesies anything H4202
1Ki 22:48 gold, but they **n** set sail—they were H4202
2Ki 1:16 you will **n** leave the bed you are lying on. H4202
2Ki 2:21 **N** again will it cause death or make the H4202
2Ki 5:17 your servant will **n** again make burnt H4202
1Ch 17:13 I will **n** take my love away from him, as I H4202
2Ch 6:16 'You shall **n** fail to have a successor to sit H4202
2Ch 7:18 'You shall **n** fail to have a successor to H4202
2Ch 9: 9 There had **n** been such spices as those H4202
2Ch 18: 7 him because he **n** prophesies anything H401
2Ch 18:17 I tell you that he **n** prophesies anything H4202
Ne 5:18 I **n** demanded the food allotted to the H4202
Est 1:19 that Vashti is **n** *again* to enter the H4202
Est 9:28 days of Purim should **n** fail to be H4202
Job 3:16 like an infant who **n** saw the light of day? H4202
Job 7: 7 my eyes will **n** see happiness again. H4202
Job 7:10 He will **n** come to his house again; his H4202
Job 7:19 Will you **n** look away from me, or let me H4202
Job 8:18 place disowns it and says, 'I **n** saw you. H4202
Job 10:19 If only I had **n** come into being, or had H4202
Job 16: 3 Will your long-winded speeches **n** end NDT
Job 16:18 my blood; may my cry **n** be laid to rest! H440
Job 19:22 Will you **n** get enough of my flesh? H4202
Job 21:10 Their bulls **n** fail to breed; their cows H4202
Job 21:25 **n** having enjoyed anything good. H4202
Job 21:29 Have you **n** questioned those who travel H4202
Job 27: 5 I will **n** admit you are in the right; till H2721+561
Job 27: 6 maintain my innocence and **n** let go of it; H4202
Job 27:14 his offspring will **n** have enough to eat. H4202
Job 30:17 my bones; my gnawing pains **n** rest. H4202
Job 30:27 The churning inside me **n** stops; days of H4202
Job 31:31 if those of my household have **n** said H4202
Job 35:15 that his anger **n** punishes and he does not H401
Job 41: 8 remember the struggle and **n** do it again! H440
Ps 9:10 have **n** forsaken those who seek you. H4202
Ps 9:18 But God will **n** forget the H4202+4200+5905
Ps 9:18 hope of the afflicted will **n** perish. H4200+6329
Ps 10:11 himself, "God *will* **n notice**; he covers his H8894
Ps 10:11 covers his face and **n** sees." H4200+5905+1153
Ps 10:18 mortals will **n** again strike terror. H1153+6388
Ps 14: 4 eating bread; they **n** call on the LORD. H4202
Ps 15: 5 things will **n** be shaken. H4202+4200+6409
Ps 28: 5 tear them down and **n** build them up H4202
Ps 30: 6 I said, "I will **n** be shaken." H1153+4200+6409
Ps 31: 1 let me **n** be put to shame H440+4200+6409
Ps 34: 5 their faces are **n** covered with shame. H440
Ps 37:25 I have **n** seen the righteous forsaken H4202
Ps 41: 8 he will **n** get up from the place H4202+3578
Ps 49:19 who will **n again** see the H6330+5905+4202
Ps 53: 4 though eating bread; they **n** call on God. H4202
Ps 55:11 threats and lies **n** leave its streets. H4202
Ps 55:22 he will **n** let the righteous H4202+4200+6409
Ps 58: 8 like a stillborn child that **n** sees the sun. H1153
Ps 62: 2 he is my fortress, I will **n** be shaken. H4202+8041
Ps 71: 1 let me **n** be put to shame. H440+4200+6409
Ps 77: 7 Will he **n** show his favor again? H4202
Ps 89:28 my covenant with him *will* **n fail**. H586
Ps 94:14 people; he will **n** forsake his inheritance. H4202
Ps 95:11 in my anger, 'They shall **n** enter my rest. H561
Ps 102:27 the same, and your years will **n** end. H4202
Ps 104: 5 it can **n** be moved. H1153+6409+2256+6329
Ps 104: 9 **n** again will they cover the earth. H1153
Ps 109:14 may the sin of his mother **n** be blotted out. H440
Ps 109:16 For he **n** thought of doing a kindness, but H4202
Ps 112: 6 righteous will **n** be shaken; H4202+4200+6409
Ps 119:43 **N** take your word of truth from my mouth H440
Ps 119:93 I will **n** forget your precepts H4202+4200+6409
Ps 140:10 into the fire, into miry pits, **n** to rise. H1153
Ps 148: 6 he issued a decree that will **n** pass away. H4202
Pr 3: 3 Let love and faithfulness **n** leave you; bind H440
Pr 5:17 yours alone, **n** to be shared with strangers. H401
Pr 6:33 and his shame will **n** be wiped away. H4202
Pr 7:11 defiant, her feet **n** stay at home; H4202
Pr 10:30 will **n** be uprooted, H4200+6409+1153
Pr 13: 4 A sluggard's appetite *is* **n** *filled*, but the H401
Pr 17:13 Evil will **n** leave the house of one who H4202
Pr 21:17 loves wine and olive oil will **n** be rich. H4202
Pr 25:14 is one who boasts of **gifts n given**. H5522+9214
Pr 27:20 Death and Destruction are **n** satisfied H4202
Pr 30:15 are three things that are **n** satisfied, H4202
Pr 30:15 never satisfied, four that **n** say, 'Enough! H4202
Pr 30:16 which is **n** satisfied with water, and H4202
Pr 30:16 and fire, which **n** says, 'Enough! H4202
Ecc 1: 7 flow into the sea, yet the sea **is n** full. H401
Ecc 1: 8 The eye **n** has enough of seeing, nor the H4202
Ecc 4: 3 is the one who has **n** been born, H4202+6362
Ecc 5:10 Whoever loves money **n** has enough H4202
Ecc 5:10 loves wealth is **n** satisfied with their H4202

Ecc 6: 5 Though it **n** saw the sun or knew anything H4202
Ecc 6: 7 yet their appetite is **n** satisfied. H4202
Ecc 7:20 no one who does what is right and **n** sins. H4202
Ecc 9: 6 **n** again will they have a part H401+4200+6409
SS 7: 2 rounded goblet that **n** lacks blended wine. H440
Isa 6: 9 'Be ever hearing, but **n** understanding; be H440
Isa 6: 9 be ever seeing, but **n** perceiving.' H440
Isa 13:20 She will **n** be inhabited or H4202+4200+5905
Isa 14:20 of the wicked will **n** be mentioned again. H4202
Isa 24:20 its rebellion that it falls—**n** to rise again. H4202
Isa 25: 2 no more; it will **n** be rebuilt. H4202+4200+6409
Isa 28:16 who relies on it will **n** be stricken with H4202
Isa 33:20 stakes will **n** be pulled up, H1153+4200+5905
Isa 43:17 they lay there, **n** to rise again H1153
Isa 45:17 you will **n** be put to shame or disgraced H4202
Isa 47: 8 I will **n** be a widow or suffer the loss of H4202
Isa 48:19 their name would **n** be blotted out nor H4202
Isa 51: 6 last forever, my righteousness will **n** fail. H4202
Isa 51:22 of my wrath, you will **n** drink again. H4202+3578
Isa 54: 1 woman, you who **n** bore a child; burst H4202
Isa 54: 1 joy, you who were **n** in labor; because H4202
Isa 54: 9 waters of Noah would **n** again cover the H4946
Isa 54: 9 be angry with you, **n** to rebuke you again. H4946
Isa 56:11 mighty appetites; they **n** have enough. H4202
Isa 58:11 garden, like a spring whose waters **n** fail. H4202
Isa 60:11 they will **n** be shut, day or night H4202
Isa 60:20 Your sun will **n** set again, and your moon H4202
Isa 62: 6 they will **n** be silent day or night. H9458+4202
Isa 62: 8 "**N** again will I give your grain as food for H561
Isa 62: 8 **n** again will foreigners drink the new H561
Isa 65:20 "**N** again will there be in it an infant who H4202
Jer 3:16 It will **n** enter their minds or be H4202
Jer 5:12 we will **n** see sword or famine. H4202
Jer 15:17 I **n** sat in the company of revelers, never H4202
Jer 15:17 of revelers, **n** made merry with them NDT
Jer 17: 8 a year of drought and **n** fails to bear fruit." H4202
Jer 20:11 their dishonor will **n** be forgotten. H4202+6409
Jer 22:10 because he will **n** return nor see H4202+6388
Jer 22:11 from this place: "He will **n** return. H4202+6388
Jer 22:27 You will **n** come back to the land you long H4202
Jer 31:40 The city will **n** again be H4202+4200+6409
Jer 32:35 though I **n** commanded—nor did H4202
Jer 32:40 I will **n** stop doing good to them, and I H4202
Jer 32:40 so that they will **n** turn away from me. H1194
Jer 33:17 'David will **n** fail to have a man to sit on H4202
Jer 35: 7 Also you must **n** build houses, sow seed H4202
Jer 35: 7 you must **n** have any of these things H4202
Jer 35:19 Rekab will **n** fail to have H4202+3972+2021+3427
Jer 42:18 reproach; you will **n** see this place again. H4202
Jer 50:39 It will **n** again be inhabited H4202+4200+5905
La 3:22 not consumed, for his compassions **n** fail. H4202
Eze 4:14 I have **n** defiled myself. H4202
Eze 4:14 until now I have **n** eaten anything found H4202
Eze 5: 9 to you what I have **n** done before and will H4202
Eze 5: 9 never done before and **n** do again. H4202
Eze 16:48 her daughters **n** did what you and your H561
Eze 16:63 be ashamed and **n** again open your H4202
Eze 20:32 But what you have in mind will **n** happen. H4202
Eze 26:14 You will **n** be rebuilt, for I the LORD H4202+6388
Eze 26:21 but you will **n** again be H4202+4200+6409
Eze 29:15 of kingdoms and will **n** again exalt itself H4202
Eze 29:15 so weak that it will **n** *again* rule over the H1194
Eze 36:12 you will **n** again deprive them of their H4202
Eze 37:22 them and they will **n** again be two H4202
Eze 43: 7 of Israel will **n** again defile my holy H4202
Da 2:44 that will **n** be destroyed, A10379+10378+10550
Da 6: 5 "We will **n** find any basis for charges A10379
Da 6:26 his dominion will **n end**. A10527+10509+10002
Da 7:14 kingdom is one that will **n** be destroyed. A10379
Hos 14: 3 We will **n** again say 'Our gods' to what H4202
Joel 2: 2 such as **n** was in ancient times nor ever H4202
Joel 2:19 **n** again will I make you an object of scorn H4202
Joel 2:26 **n again** will my people be H4202+4200+6409
Joel 2:27 **n again** will my people be H4202+4200+6409
Joel 3:17 **n** again will foreigners invade her. H4202
Am 5: 2 is Virgin Israel, **n** to rise again, deserted H4202
Am 8: 7 "I will **n** forget anything they H561+4200+5905
Am 8:14 they will fall, **n** to rise again. H4202
Am 9:15 **n** again to be uprooted from the land I H4202
Ob 16 drink and be as if they had **n** been. H4202
Na 3: 1 full of plunder, **n** without victims! H4202
Hab 1: 4 and justice **n** prevails. H4202+4200+5905
Hab 1:12 my Holy One, you will **n** die. H4202
Hab 2: 5 betrays him; he is arrogant and **n** at rest. H4202
Hab 2: 5 as the grave and like death is **n** satisfied, H4202
Zep 3:11 **N** again will you be haughty on my holy H4202
Zep 3:15 with you; **n** again will you fear any harm. H4202
Hag 1: 6 You eat, but **n** have enough. H401
Hag 1: 6 You drink, but **n** have your fill. H401
Zec 9: 8 **N** again will an oppressor overrun my H4202
Zec 14:11 be inhabited; **n** again will it be destroyed. H4202
Mt 7:23 them plainly, 'I **n** knew you. Away from G4030
Mt 13:14 ever hearing but **n** understanding; G4024+3590
Mt 13:14 be ever seeing but **n** perceiving. G4024+3590
Mt 16:22 began to rebuke him. "**N**, Lord!" he said. G2664
Mt 16:22 "This shall **n** happen to you!" G4024+3590
Mt 18: 3 you will **n** enter the kingdom of G4024+3590
Mt 21:16 "have you **n** read, " 'From the lips G4030
Mt 21:19 he said to it, "May you **n** bear fruit again!" G3600
Mt 21:42 "Have you **n** read in the Scriptures: G4030
Mt 24:21 now—and **n** to be equaled **again**. G4024+3590
Mt 24:35 my words will **n** pass away. G4024+3590
Mt 26:33 if all fall away on account of you, I **n** will." G4030
Mt 26:35 to die with you, I will **n** disown you." G4024+3590
Mk 2:12 "We have **n** seen **anything** like this!" G4030
Mk 2:25 "Have you **n** read what David did when G4030
Mk 3:29 Spirit will **n** be forgiven; G4024+1650+3836+172
Mk 4:12 may be ever seeing but **n** perceiving, G3590
Mk 4:12 ever hearing but **n** understanding G3590
Mk 9:25 come out of him and **n** enter him **again**." G3600
Mk 9:43 to go into hell, where the fire **n goes out**. G812
Mk 10:15 God like a little child will **n** enter it." G4024+3590
Mk 13:19 now—and **n** to be equaled **again**. G4024+3590
Mk 13:31 my words will **n** pass away. G4024+3590
Mk 14:31 to die with you, I will **n** disown you." G4024+3590
Lk 1:15 He is **n** to take wine or other G4024+3590
Lk 1:33 his kingdom will **n** end. G4024
Lk 2:37 She **n** left the temple but worshiped night G4024
Lk 6: 3 "Have you **n** read what David did when G4028
Lk 12:33 a treasure in heaven *that will* **n fail**, where G444
Lk 15:29 slaving for you and **n** disobeyed your G4030
Lk 15:29 Yet you **n** gave me even a young goat so I G4030
Lk 18:17 God like a little child will **n** enter it." G4024+3590
Lk 21:33 my words will **n** pass away. G4024+3590
Lk 23:29 the wombs that **n** bore and the breasts G4024
Lk 23:29 never bore and the breasts that **n** nursed! G4024
Jn 4:14 I give them will **n** thirst.
G4024+3590+1650+3836+172
Jn 4:48 Jesus told him, "you will **n** believe." G4024+3590
Jn 5:37 You have **n** heard his voice nor G4046+4799
Jn 6:35 comes to me will **n** go hungry, G4024+3590
Jn 6:35 in me will **n** be thirsty. G4024+3590+4799
Jn 6:37 comes to me I will **n** drive away. G4024+3590
Jn 8:12 follows me will **n** walk in darkness, G4024+3590
Jn 8:33 descendants and have **n** been slaves of G4799
Jn 8:51 word will **n** see death."
G4024+3590+1650+3836+172
Jn 8:52 word will **n** taste death.
G4024+3590+1650+3836+172
Jn 10: 5 But they will **n** follow a stranger; in G4024+3590
Jn 10:28 and they shall **n** perish
G4024+3590+1650+3836+172
Jn 10:41 "Though John **n** performed a sign G4029
Jn 11:26 in me will **n** die. G4024+3590+1650+3836+172
Jn 13: 8 **No**," said Peter, "you shall **n**
G4024+3590+1650+3836+172
Ac 5:42 they **n** stopped teaching and proclaiming G4024
Ac 6:13 "This fellow **n** stops speaking against this G4024
Ac 10:14 "I have **n** eaten anything impure or G4030
Ac 13:10 Will you **n** stop perverting the right ways G4024
Ac 13:34 so that he will **n** be subject to G3600+3516
Ac 13:41 your days that you would **n** believe, G4024+3590
Ac 14: 8 that way from birth and had **n** walked. G4030
Ac 20:31 three years I **n** stopped warning each G4024
Ac 20:38 that they would **n** see his face **again**. G4033
Ac 28:26 ever hearing but **n** understanding; G4024+3590
Ac 28:26 be ever seeing but **n** perceiving." G4024+3590
Ro 4: 8 sin the Lord will **n** count against G4024+3590
Ro 9:33 believes in him will **n** be put to shame." G4024
Ro 10:11 believes in him will **n** be put to shame." G4024
Ro 12:11 **N** be lacking in zeal, but keep your G3590
1Co 6:15 unite them with a prostitute? **N**! G3590+1181
1Co 8:13 I will **n** eat meat **again**
G4024+3590+1650+3836+172
1Co 13: 8 Love **n** fails. But where there are G4030
2Co 12:13 except that I was **n** a burden to you? G4024
Gal 4:27 woman, you who **n** bore a child; shout G4024
Gal 4:27 you who were **n** in labor; because G4024
Gal 4:30 woman's son will **n** share in the G4024+3590
Gal 6:14 May I **n** boast except in the cross of G3590+1181
1Th 2: 5 You know we **n** used flattery, nor G4046+4537
2Th 3:13 sisters, **n** tire of doing what is good. G3590
2Ti 3: 7 always learning but **n** able to come to a G3595
Heb 1:12 the same, and your years will **n** end." G4024
Heb 3:11 in my anger, 'They shall **n** enter my rest. G1623
Heb 3:18 that they would **n** enter his rest if not G3590
Heb 4: 3 in my anger, 'They shall **n** enter my rest. G1623
Heb 4: 5 he says, "They shall **n** enter my rest." G1623
Heb 9: 7 once a year, and **n** without blood, which G4024
Heb 9:17 it **n** takes effect while the one who made G3607
Heb 10: 1 For this reason it can **n**, by the same G4030
Heb 10:11 sacrifices, which can **n** take away sins. G4030
Heb 13: 5 God has said, "**N** will I leave you G4024+3590
Heb 13: 5 I leave you; **n** will I forsake you." G4024+3590
Jas 3: 2 Anyone who is **n** at fault in what they say G4024
1Pe 1: 4 into an inheritance that can **n perish** G915
[1Pe 1: 4 an inheritance that can **n** perish, **spoil** G299]
[1Pe 1: 4 inheritance that can **n** perish, spoil or **fade**. G278]
1Pe 2: 6 in him will **n** be put to shame." G4024+3590
1Pe 5: 4 the crown of glory that will **n fade away**. G277
2Pe 1:10 things, you will **n** stumble, G4024+3590+4537
2Pe 1:21 For prophecy **n** had its origin in the G4024+4537
2Pe 2:14 of adultery, they **n stop** sinning; they G188
Rev 3: 5 I will **n** blot out the name of that G4024+3590
Rev 3:12 **N** again will they leave it G4024+3590
Rev 4: 8 Day and night they **n** stop saying: " 'Holy, G4024
Rev 7:16 '**N** again will they hunger; never again G4024
Rev 7:16 will they hunger; **n** again will they thirst. G4028
Rev 18: 7 I am not a widow; I will **n** mourn.' G4024+3590
Rev 18:14 vanished, **n** to be recovered. G4033+4024+3590
Rev 18:21 thrown down, **n** to be found again. G4024+3590
Rev 18:22 will **n** be heard in you again. G4024+3590
Rev 18:22 a millstone will **n** be heard in you G4024+3590
Rev 18:23 of a lamp will **n** shine in you again G4024+3590
Rev 18:23 and bride will **n** be heard in you G4024+3590

NEVER-FAILING (1)

Am 5:24 like a river, righteousness like a **n** stream! H419

NEVERTHELESS (40)

Ge 48:19 **N**, his younger brother will be H2256+219
Ex 16:27 **N**, some of the people went out on the H2256
Nu 14:21 **N**, as surely as I live and as surely as the H219
Nu 14:44 **N**, in their presumption they went up H2256
Dt 12:15 **N**, you may slaughter your animals in any H8370
Jdg 11: 8 said to him, "**N**, we are turning to H4200+4027
1Sa 29: 9 eyes as an angel of God; **n**, the Philistine H421
2Sa 5: 7 **N**, David captured the fortress of Zion H2256
1Ki 8:19 **N**, you are not the one to build the H8370
1Ki 11: 2 after their gods." **N**, Solomon held fast to NDT
1Ki 11:12 **N**, for the sake of David your father, I will H421
1Ki 15: 4 **N**, for David's sake the LORD his God gave H3954
2Ki 3: 3 **N** he clung to the sins of Jeroboam son of H8370
2Ki 8:10 **N**, the LORD has revealed to me that he H2256
2Ki 8:19 **N**, for the sake of his servant David, the H2256
2Ki 17:29 **N**, each national group made its own H2256
2Ki 23:26 **N**, the LORD did not turn away from the heat H421
1Ch 11: 5 **N**, David captured the fortress of Zion H2256
2Ch 6: 9 **N**, you are not the one to build the H8370
2Ch 21: 7 **N**, because of the covenant the LORD had H2256
2Ch 30:11 **N**, some from Asher, Manasseh and H421
Est 5:10 **N**, Haman restrained himself and went H2256
Job 17: 9 **N**, the righteous will hold to their ways H2256
Isa 9: 1 **N**, there will be no more gloom for those H3954
Jer 28: 7 **N**, listen to what I have to say in your H421
Jer 33: 6 " '**N**, I will bring health and healing to it; H2180
Da 5:17 **N**, I will read the writing for the king A10124
Ac 5:14 **N**, more and more men and women G1254
Ac 27:26 **N**, we must run aground on some island." G1254
Ro 5:14 **N**, death reigned from the time of Adam to G247
Ro 7: 7 **N**, I would not have known what sin was G247
Ro 7:13 **N**, in order that sin might be recognized as G247
1Co 7:17 **N**, each person should live as a G1623+3590
1Co 10: 5 **N**, God was not pleased with most of them G247
1Co 11:11 **N**, in the Lord woman is not independent G4440
1Co 11:32 **N**, when we are judged in this way by the G1254
Gal 6: 6 **N**, the one who receives instruction in the G1254
2Ti 2:19 **N**, God's solid foundation stands firm G3530
Rev 2:14 **N**, I have a few things against you: There G247
Rev 2:20 **N**, I have this against you: You tolerate that G247

NEW (201) [NEWLY]

Ge 27:28 an abundance of grain and **n wine**. H9408
Ge 27:37 sustained him with grain and **n wine**. H9408
Ge 45:22 To each of them he gave **n** clothing, but to H2722
Ex 1: 8 Then a **n** king, to whom Joseph meant H2543
Lev 2:14 crushed heads of **n grain** roasted in the H4152
Lev 14:42 these and take **n** clay and plaster the H337
Lev 23:14 roasted or **n grain**, until the very day H4152
Lev 23:16 present an offering of **n** grain to the LORD. H2543
Lev 26:10 to move it out to make room for the **n**. H2543
Nu 10:10 festivals and **N Moon feasts**— H8031+2544
Nu 16:30 the LORD brings about **something totally n**, H1375
Nu 18:12 all the finest **n wine** and grain they H9408
Nu 28:14 be made at each **n moon** *during* the year. H2544
Nu 28:26 the LORD an offering of **n** grain during the H2543
Dt 7:13 your grain, **n wine** and olive oil—the H9408
Dt 11:14 gather in your grain, **n wine** and olive oil. H9408
Dt 12:17 of your grain and **n wine** and olive oil, H9408
Dt 14:23 of your grain, **n wine** and olive oil, and H9408
Dt 18: 4 of your grain, **n wine** and olive oil, and H9408
Dt 20: 5 "Has anyone built a **n** house and not yet H2543
Dt 22: 8 When you build a **n** house, make a H2543
Dt 28:51 you no grain, **n wine** or olive oil, nor H9408
Dt 32: 2 like showers on **n grass**, like abundant H2013
Dt 33:28 secure in a land of grain and **n wine**, H9408
Jos 9:13 And these wineskins that we filled were **n** H2543
Jdg 5: 8 God chose **n** leaders when war came to H2543
Jdg 15:13 bound him with two **n** ropes and led him H2543
Jdg 16:11 me securely with **n** ropes that have never H2543
Jdg 16:12 So Delilah took **n** ropes and tied him with H2543
1Sa 6: 7 "Now then, get a **n** cart ready, with two H2543
1Sa 20: 5 tomorrow is the **N Moon feast**, and I am H2544
1Sa 20:18 to David, "Tomorrow is the **N Moon feast**. H2544
1Sa 20:24 when the **N Moon feast** came, the H2544
2Sa 6: 3 the ark of God on a **n** cart and brought it H2543
2Sa 6: 3 sons of Abinadab, were guiding the **n** cart H2543
2Sa 21:16 who was armed with a **n** sword, H2543
1Ki 11:29 met him on the way, wearing a **n** cloak. H2543
1Ki 11:30 took hold of the **n** cloak he was wearing H2543
2Ki 2:20 "Bring me a **n** bowl," he said, "and put H2543
2Ki 4:23 "It's not the **N Moon** or the Sabbath." H2544
2Ki 4:42 along with *some* **heads of n grain**. H4152
2Ki 16:14 from between the **n** altar and the temple of NDT
2Ki 16:14 put it on the north side of the **n** altar. NDT
2Ki 16:15 "On the large **n** altar, offer the morning NDT
2Ki 18:32 a land of grain and **n wine**, a land of H9408
2Ki 22:14 She lived in Jerusalem, in the **N Quarter**. H5467
1Ch 13: 7 God from Abinadab's house on a **n** cart, H2543
1Ch 23:31 at the **N Moon feasts** and at the H2544
2Ch 2: 4 at the **N Moons** and at the appointed H2544
2Ch 8:13 the **N Moons** and the three annual H2544
2Ch 20: 5 of the LORD in the front of the **n** courtyard H2543
2Ch 31: 3 at the **N Moons** and at the appointed H2544
2Ch 31: 5 of their grain, **n wine**, olive oil and honey H9408
2Ch 32:28 harvest of grain, **n wine** and olive oil; and H9408

2Ch 34:22 She lived in Jerusalem, in the **N Quarter**. H5467
Ezr 3: 5 the **N Moon** sacrifices and the sacrifices H2544
Ezr 9: 9 He has granted us **n life** to rebuild the H4695
Ne 5:11 of the money, grain, **n wine** and olive oil." H9408
Ne 10:33 at the **N Moon feasts** and at the H2544
Ne 10:37 our trees and of our **n wine** and olive oil. H9408
Ne 10:39 **n wine** and olive oil to the storerooms H9408
Ne 11: 9 was over the **N Quarter** of the city. H5467
Ne 13: 5 **n wine** and olive oil prescribed for the H9408
Ne 13:12 **n wine** and olive oil into the storerooms. H9408
Job 10:17 *You* **bring n** witnesses against me and H2542
Job 14: 7 sprout again, and its **n shoots** will not fail. H3438
Job 29:20 the bow *will be ever* **n** in my hand. H2736
Job 32:19 like **n** wineskins ready to burst. H2543
Ps 4: 7 joy when their grain and **n wine** abound. H9408
Ps 33: 3 Sing to him a **n** song; play skillfully, and H2543
Ps 40: 3 He put a **n** song in my mouth, a hymn of H2543
Ps 73:14 every morning brings **n** punishments. NDT
Ps 81: 3 Sound the ram's horn at the **N Moon**, and H2544
Ps 90: 5 they are like the **n** grass of the morning: H2736
Ps 90: 6 In the morning it springs up **n**, but by H2736
Ps 96: 1 Sing to the LORD a **n** song; sing to the H2543
Ps 98: 1 Sing to the LORD a **n** song, for he has done H2543
Ps 144: 9 I will sing a **n** song to you, my God; on H2543
Ps 149: 1 Sing to the LORD a **n** song, his praise in H2543
Pr 3:10 your vats will brim over with **n wine**. H9408
Pr 27:25 is removed and **n growth** appears and the H2013
Ecc 1: 9 there is nothing **n** under the sun. H2543
Ecc 1:10 This is something **n**"? It was here already H2543
SS 6:11 nut trees to look at the **n growth** *in* the valley, H4
SS 7:13 every delicacy, both **n** and old, that I have H2543
Isa 1:13 **N Moons**, Sabbaths and convocations—I H2544
Isa 1:14 Your **N Moon feasts** and your appointed H2544
Isa 24: 7 The **n wine** dries up and the vine withers H9408
Isa 36:17 a land of grain and **n wine**, a land of H9408
Isa 41:15 a threshing sledge, **n** and sharp, with H2543
Isa 42: 9 taken place, and **n** *things* I declare H2543
Isa 42:10 Sing to the LORD a **n** song, his praise from H2543
Isa 43:19 I am doing a **n** *thing*! Now it springs H2543
Isa 48: 6 "From now on I will tell you of **n** *things*, H2543
Isa 62: 2 will be called by a **n** name that the mouth H2543
Isa 62: 8 drink the **n wine** for which you have H9408
Isa 65:17 I will create **n** heavens and a new earth. H2543
Isa 65:17 I will create new heavens and a **n** earth. H2543
Isa 66:22 "As the **n** heavens and the new earth that H2543
Isa 66:22 new heavens and the **n** earth that I make H2543
Isa 66:23 From *one* **N Moon** to another and from H2544
Jer 8:10 to other men and their fields to **n owners**. H3769
Jer 26:10 at the entrance of the **N** Gate of the LORD's H2543
Jer 31:12 the grain, the **n wine** and the olive oil H9408
Jer 31:22 The LORD will create a **n** *thing* on earth H2543
Jer 31:31 "when I will make a **n** covenant with the H2543
Jer 36:10 the entrance of the **N** Gate of the temple, H2543
La 3:23 *They* are **n** every morning; great is your H2543
Eze 11:19 heart and put a **n** spirit in them; H2543
Eze 17: 9 All its **n** growth will wither. H3273
Eze 18:31 get a **n** heart and a new spirit. H2543
Eze 18:31 get a new heart and a **n** spirit. H2543
Eze 36:26 I will give you a **n** heart and put a new H2543
Eze 36:26 you a new heart and put a **n** spirit in you; H2543
Eze 45:17 festivals, the **N Moons** and the Sabbaths H2544
Eze 46: 1 on the day of the **N Moon** it is to be H2544
Eze 46: 3 the Sabbaths and **N Moons** the people of H2544
Eze 46: 6 On the day of the **N Moon** he is to offer a H2544
Da 1: 7 The chief official gave them **n** names: to NDT
Hos 2: 8 her the grain, the **n wine** and oil, who H9408
Hos 2: 9 it ripens, and my **n wine** when it is ready. H9408
Hos 2:11 festivals, her **N Moons**, her Sabbath days H2544
Hos 2:22 to the grain, the **n wine** and the olive oil H9408
Hos 4:11 old wine and **n wine** take away their H9408
Hos 5: 7 When they celebrate their **N Moon feasts** H2544
Hos 7:14 to their gods for grain and **n wine**, H9408
Hos 9: 2 the people; the **n wine** will fail them. H9408
Joel 1: 5 wail because of the **n wine**, for it has H6747
Joel 1:10 is destroyed, the **n wine** is dried up, the H9408
Joel 2:19 sending you grain, **n wine** and olive oil H9408
Joel 2:24 the vats will overflow with **n wine** and oil. H9408
Joel 3:18 that day the mountains will drip **n wine**, H6747
Am 8: 5 "When will the **N Moon** be over that we H2544
Am 9:13 **N wine** will drip from the mountains and H6747
Zep 1:10 wailing from the **N Quarter**, and a loud H5467
Zep 3: 5 and every **n day** he does not fail H240
Hag 1:11 on the grain, the **n wine**, the olive oil H9408
Zec 9:17 and **n wine** the young women. H9408
Mt 9:17 Neither do people pour **n** wine into old G3742
Mt 9:17 they pour **n** wine into new wineskins G3742
Mt 9:17 they pour new wine into **n** wineskins, and G2785
Mt 13:52 his storeroom **n** *treasures* as well as old." G2785
Mt 26:29 day when I drink it **n** with you in my G2785
Mt 27:60 it in his own **n** tomb that he had cut G2785
Mk 1:27 "What is this? A **n** teaching—and with G2785
Mk 2:21 the **n** piece will pull away from the old G2785
Mk 2:22 And no one pours **n** wine into old G3742
Mk 2:22 they pour **n** wine into new wineskins." G3742
Mk 2:22 they pour new wine into **n** wineskins." G2785
Mk 14:25 day when I drink it **n** in the kingdom of G2785
Mk 16:17 out demons; they will speak in **n** tongues; G2785
Lk 5:36 a piece out of a **n** garment to patch an G2785
Lk 5:36 they will have torn the **n** *garment*, and the G2785
Lk 5:36 the patch from the **n** will not match the G2785
Lk 5:37 And no one pours **n** wine into old G3742
Lk 5:37 Otherwise, the **n** wine will burst the skins G3742
Lk 5:38 **n** wine must be poured into new G3742
Lk 5:38 wine must be poured into **n** wineskins. G2785
Lk 5:39 one after drinking old wine wants the **n**, G3742
Lk 22:20 "This cup is the **n** covenant in my blood G2785
Jn 13:34 "A **n** command I give you: Love one G2785
Jn 19:41 in the garden a **n** tomb, in which no G2785
Ac 5:20 "and tell the people all about this *n* **life**." AIT
Ac 7:18 Then 'a **n** king, to whom Joseph meant G2283
Ac 8:15 they prayed for the **n believers** there that G899S
Ac 17:19 we know what this **n** teaching is that you G2785
Ro 6: 4 of the Father, we too may live a **n** life. G2786
Ro 7: 6 so that we serve in the **n way** of the Spirit, G2786
1Co 5: 7 that you may be a **n** unleavened batch— G3742
1Co 11:25 "This cup is the **n** covenant in my blood G2785
2Co 3: 6 competent as ministers of a **n** covenant— G2785
2Co 5:17 is in Christ, the **n** creation has come: G2785
2Co 5:17 The old has gone, the **n** is here! G2785
Gal 6:15 anything; what counts is the **n** creation. G2785
Eph 2:15 in himself one **n** humanity out of the G2785
Eph 4:23 *to be* **made n** in the attitude of your minds; G391
Eph 4:24 to put on the **n** self, created to be like G2785
Col 2:16 a **N Moon celebration** or a Sabbath day. G3741
Col 3:10 have put on the **n** self, which is being G3742
Heb 8: 6 since **the n covenant** is established on G4015S
Heb 8: 8 when I will make a **n** covenant with the G2785
Heb 8:13 By calling this covenant "**n**," he has made G2785
Heb 9:10 applying until the time *of* the **n order**. G1481
Heb 9:15 Christ is the mediator of a **n** covenant, G2785
Heb 10:20 by a **n** and living way opened for us G4710
Heb 12:24 to Jesus the mediator of a **n** covenant, and G3742
1Pe 1: 3 great mercy *he has* **given** us **n birth** into a G335
2Pe 3:13 looking forward to a **n** heaven and a new G2785
2Pe 3:13 forward to a new heaven and a **n** earth, G2785
1Jn 2: 7 not writing you a **n** command but an old G2785
1Jn 2: 8 Yet I am writing you a **n** command; its G2785
2Jn 5 not writing you a **n** command but one we G2785
Rev 2:17 a white stone with a **n** name written on it, G2785
Rev 3:12 city of my God, the **n** Jerusalem, which is G2785
Rev 3:12 I will also write on them my **n** name. G2785
Rev 5: 9 And they sang a **n** song, saying: "You are G2785
Rev 14: 3 And they sang a **n** song before the throne G2785
Rev 21: 1 Then I saw "a **n** heaven and a new earth," G2785
Rev 21: 1 Then I saw "a new heaven and a **n** earth," G2785
Rev 21: 2 the Holy City, the **n** Jerusalem, coming G2785
Rev 21: 5 throne said, "I am making everything **n**!" G2785

NEWBORN (3) [BEAR]

Jer 14: 5 field deserts *her* **n** *fawn* because there is H3528
Ac 7:19 throw out their **n babies** so that they G1100
1Pe 2: 2 Like **n** babies, crave pure spiritual milk, so G786

NEWLY (1) [NEW]

Jdg 6:28 second bull sacrificed on the **n built** altar! H1215

NEWS (84)

Ge 29:13 soon as Laban heard the **n** *about* Jacob, H9051
Ge 45:16 When the **n** reached Pharaoh's palace H7754
1Sa 4:17 The *man who* **brought the n** replied H1413
1Sa 4:19 When she heard the **n** that the ark of God H9019
1Sa 13: 4 So all Israel heard the **n**: "Saul has attacked H606
1Sa 31: 9 to **proclaim the n** *in* the temple of H1413
2Sa 4: 4 old when the **n** *about* Saul and Jonathan H9019
2Sa 4:10 and thought he was **bringing good n**, H1413
2Sa 4:10 That was the **reward** I gave him **for** his **n**! H1415
2Sa 18:19 me run and **take the n** *to* the king that H1413
2Sa 18:20 "You are not the one to take the **n** today," H1415
2Sa 18:20 "*You may* **take the n** another time, but H1413
2Sa 18:22 You don't have any **n** that will bring you a H1415
2Sa 18:25 "If he is alone, he must have **good n**." H1415
2Sa 18:26 "He *must be* **bringing good n**, too. H1413
2Sa 18:27 the king said. "He comes with good **n**." H1415
2Sa 18:31 "My lord the king, **hear** *the* **good n**! H1413
1Ki 1:42 man like you *must be* **bringing** good **n**." H1413
1Ki 2:28 When the **n** reached Joab, who had H9019
1Ki 14: 6 I have been sent to you with **bad n**. H7997
2Ki 7: 9 This is a day of **good n** and we are H1415
2Ki 7:11 The gatekeepers **shouted the n**, and it was H7924
2Ki 9:15 of the city to go and **tell the n** in Jezreel." H5583
1Ch 10: 9 to **proclaim the n** *among* their idols H1413
Ps 112: 7 They will have no fear of bad **n**; their H9019
Pr 15:30 good **n** gives health to the bones. H9019
Pr 25:25 weary soul is good **n** from a distant land. H9019
Isa 40: 9 You *who* **bring good n** *to* Zion, go up on a H1413
Isa 40: 9 You *who* **bring good n** *to* Jerusalem, lift H1413
Isa 41:27 to Jerusalem a **messenger of good n**. H1413
Isa 52: 7 are the feet of *those who* **bring good n**, H1413
Isa 61: 1 me to **proclaim good n** *to* the poor. H1413
Jer 20:15 be the man who **brought** my father **the n**, H1413
Jer 49:23 are dismayed, for they have heard bad **n**. H9019
Eze 21: 7 'Because of the **n** that is coming. H9019
Eze 24:26 a fugitive will come to tell you the **n**. H2245+265
Na 1:15 the feet of *one who* **brings good n**, who H1413
Na 3:19 All who hear the **n** *about* you clap their H9051
Mt 4:23 proclaiming the **good n** of the kingdom G2295
Mt 4:24 **N** about him spread all over Syria, and G198
Mt 9:26 **N** of this spread through all that region. G5773
Mt 9:31 went out and **spread the n** about him all G1424
Mt 9:35 proclaiming the **good n** of the kingdom G2295
Mt 11: 5 and **the good n is proclaimed** to the poor. G2294
Mk 1: 1 The beginning *of* the **good n** about Jesus G2295
Mk 1:14 Galilee, proclaiming the **good n** of God. G2295
Mk 1:15 Repent and believe the **good n**!" G2295
Mk 1:28 **N** about him spread quickly over the whole G198
Mk 1:45 began to talk freely, spreading the **n**. G3364
Lk 1:19 speak to you and *to* **tell** you this **good n**. G2294
Lk 2:10 *I* **bring** you **good n** that will cause great G2294
Lk 3:18 and **proclaimed the good n** to them. G2294
Lk 4:14 **n** about him spread through the G5773
Lk 4:18 anointed me *to* **proclaim good n** to the G2294
Lk 4:37 And the **n** about him spread throughout G2491
Lk 4:43 "I must **proclaim the good n** of the G2294
Lk 5:15 Yet the **n** about him spread all the more G3364
Lk 7:17 This **n** about Jesus spread throughout G3364
Lk 7:22 and **the good n** *is* **proclaimed** to the poor. G2294
Lk 8: 1 proclaiming **the good n** of the kingdom of G2294
Lk 9: 6 **proclaiming the good n** and healing G2294
Lk 16:16 **the good n** of the kingdom of God *is being* **preached** G2294
Lk 20: 1 courts and **proclaiming the good n**, G2294
Jn 4:51 servants met him **with the n** that his boy G3306
Jn 20:18 Magdalene went to the disciples **with the n**: G33
Ac 5:42 and **proclaiming the good n** *that* Jesus is G2294
Ac 8:12 Philip *as he* **proclaimed the good n** of the G2294
Ac 8:35 and **told** him **the good n** about Jesus. G2294
Ac 10:36 **announcing the good n** of peace through G2294
Ac 11:20 **telling** them **the good n** about the Lord G2294
Ac 11:22 **N** of this reached the church in Jerusalem G3364
Ac 13:32 "We **tell** you **the good n**: What God G2294
Ac 14:15 *We are* **bringing** you **good n**, telling you G2294
Ac 15: 3 This **n** made all the believers very glad NDT
Ac 17:18 Paul *was* **preaching the good n** about G2294
Ac 20:24 of testifying *to* the **good n** of God's grace. G2295
Ac 21:31 **n** reached the commander of the Roman G5762
Ro 10:15 are the feet *of* those *who* **bring** good **n**!" G2294
Ro 10:16 not all the Israelites accepted the **good n**. G2295
Php 2:19 be cheered *when I* **receive n** about you. G1182
Col 4: 7 Tychicus will tell you all **the n** about me. AIT
1Th 3: 6 you and *has* **brought good n** about your G2294
Heb 4: 2 have had **the good n proclaimed** *to* us, G2294
Heb 4: 6 *who* formerly *had* **the good n proclaimed** *to them* G2294

NEXT (188)

Ge 17:21 Sarah will bear to you by this time **n** year." H337
Ge 18:10 surely return to you about this time **n year**, H2645
Ge 18:14 to you at the appointed time **n year**, H2645
Ge 19:27 Early the **n** morning Abraham got up and NDT
Ge 19:34 The **n day** the older daughter said to the H4740
Ge 20: 8 Early the **n** morning Abimelek summoned NDT
Ge 21:14 Early the **n** morning Abraham took some NDT
Ge 22: 3 Early the **n** morning Abraham got up and NDT
Ge 24:54 When they got up the **n** morning, he said NDT
Ge 26:31 Early the **n** morning the men swore an oath NDT
Ge 28:18 Early the **n** morning Jacob took the stone he NDT
Ge 31:55 Early the **n** morning Laban kissed his NDT
Ge 33: 2 Leah and her children **n**, and Rachel and H340
Ge 33: 7 **N**, Leah and her children came and bowed H1685
Ge 40: 6 When Joseph came to them the **n** morning NDT
Ge 45: 6 for the **n** five years there will be no H6388
Ex 2:13 The **n** day he went out and saw two H9108
Ex 9: 6 And the **n day** the LORD did it: All the H4740
Ex 18:13 The **n day** Moses took his seat to serve as H4740
Ex 24: 4 He got up early the **n** morning and built an NDT
Ex 25:33 three on the **n** branch, and the same H285
Ex 28:26 on the inside edge **n to** the ephod. H448+6298
Ex 32: 6 So the **n day** the people rose early and H4740
Ex 32:30 The **n day** Moses said to the people, "You H4740
Ex 37:19 three on the **n** branch and the same for all H285
Ex 38: 9 **N** they made the courtyard. The south H2256
Ex 39:19 on the inside edge **n to** the ephod. H448+6298
Lev 6:10 with linen undergarments **n to** his body H6584
Lev 7:16 left over may be eaten on the **n day**. H4740
Lev 16: 4 with linen undergarments **n to** his body H6584
Lev 19: 6 on the day you sacrifice it or on the **n day**; H4740
Lev 27:18 that remain until the **n** Year of Jubilee, NDT
Nu 2: 5 The tribe of Issachar will camp **n to** them H6584
Nu 2: 7 The tribe of Zebulun will be **n**. The leader NDT
Nu 2:12 The tribe of Simeon will camp **n to** them H6584
Nu 2:14 The tribe of Gad will be **n**. The leader of H2256
Nu 2:20 The tribe of Manasseh will be **n to** them H6584
Nu 2:22 The tribe of Benjamin will be **n**. H2256
Nu 2:27 The tribe of Asher will camp **n to** them H6584
Nu 2:29 The tribe of Naphtali will be **n**. H2256
Nu 10:18 divisions of the camp of Reuben went **n**, H2256
Nu 10:22 divisions of the camp of Ephraim went **n**, H2256
Nu 11:32 night and all the **n day** the people went H4740
Nu 14:40 Early the **n** morning they set out for the NDT
Nu 16:41 The **n day** the whole Israelite community H4740
Nu 17: 8 The **n day** Moses entered the tent and H4740
Nu 22: 5 the land and have settled **n to** me. H4946+4578
Nu 22:13 The **n** morning Balaam got up and said to NDT
Nu 22:41 The **n** morning Balak took Balaam up to NDT
Dt 3: 1 **N** we turned and went up along the road H2256
Jos 6:12 got up early the **n** morning and the priests NDT
Jos 7:16 Early the **n** morning Joshua had Israel come NDT
Jos 8:10 Early the **n** morning Joshua mustered his NDT
Jdg 6:38 Gideon rose early the **n day**; he squeezed H4740
Jdg 9:10 "**N**, the trees said to the fig tree, 'Come H2256
Jdg 9:42 The **n day** the people of Shechem went H4740
Jdg 9:50 **N** Abimelek went to Thebez and H2256
Jdg 11:18 "**N** they traveled through the wilderness H2256
Jdg 20:19 The **n** morning the Israelites got up and NDT
Jdg 21: 4 Early the **n day** the people built an altar H4740
Ru 4: 4 right to do it except you, and I am **n in line**." H339

N

1Sa 1:19 Early the n morning they arose and NDT
1Sa 5: 3 people of Ashdod rose early the n day, H4740
1Sa 11:11 The n day Saul separated his men into H4740
1Sa 18:10 The n day an evil spirit from God came H4740
1Sa 20:25 and Abner sat n to Saul, but H4946+7396
1Sa 20:27 But the n day, the second day of the H4740
1Sa 30:17 from dusk until the evening of the n day, H4740
1Sa 31: 8 The n day, when the Philistines came to H4740
2Sa 11:12 in Jerusalem that day and the n. H4740
2Sa 14:30 Joab's field is n to mine, and he has H448+3338
2Sa 23: 9 N to him was Eleazar son of Dodai the H339
2Sa 23:11 N to him was Shammah son of Agee the H339
2Sa 24:11 Before David got up the n morning, the NDT
1Ki 1: 6 handsome and was born n after Absalom.) H339
1Ki 3:21 The n morning, I got up to nurse my son NDT
1Ki 4:12 in all of Beth Shan n to Zarethan below H725
1Ki 7:20 bowl-shaped part n to the network, H4200+6298
1Ki 17: 1 rain in the n *few* years except at my H465S
1Ki 20:22 because n spring the king of Aram will NDT
1Ki 20:26 The n spring Ben-Hadad mustered the NDT
2Ki 3:20 The n morning, about the time for offering NDT
2Ki 4:16 "About this time n year," Elisha H6961+2645
2Ki 4:17 and the n year about that same H6961+2645
2Ki 6:15 got up and went out early the n morning, H8899
2Ki 6:29 The n day I said to her, 'Give up your son H337
2Ki 8:15 But the n day he took a thick cloth, soaked H4740
2Ki 10: 9 The n morning Jehu went out. He stood NDT
2Ki 19:35 When the people got up the n morning NDT
2Ki 23: 4 the priests n in rank and the doorkeepers H5467
2Ki 25:18 the priest n in rank and the three H5467
1Ch 5:11 Gadites lived n to them in Bashan, H4200+5584
1Ch 10: 8 The n day, when the Philistines came to H4740
1Ch 11:12 N to him was Eleazar son of Dodai the H339
1Ch 15:18 with them their relatives n in rank H5467
1Ch 16: 5 and n to him in rank were Zechariah H5467
1Ch 29:21 The n day they made sacrifices to the LORD H4740
2Ch 17:15 n, Jehohanan the commander H6584+3338
2Ch 17:16 n, Amasiah son of Zikri, who H6584+3338
2Ch 17:18 n, Jehozabad, with 180,000 men H6584+3338
2Ch 29:20 Early the n morning King Hezekiah H8899
2Ch 29:22 n they slaughtered the rams and splashed H2256
2Ch 31:12 his brother Shimei was n in rank. H5467
Ne 3: 2 Zakkur son of Imri built n to them. H6584+3338
Ne 3: 4 of Hakkoz, repaired the n section. H6584+3338
Ne 3: 4 N to him Meshullam son of H6584+3338
Ne 3: 4 and n to him Zadok son of Baana H6584+3338
Ne 3: 5 The n section was repaired by the H6584+3338
Ne 3: 7 N to them, repairs were made by H6584+3338
Ne 3: 8 repaired the n section; and H6584+3338
Ne 3: 8 made repairs n to that. H6584+3338
Ne 3: 9 Jerusalem, repaired the n section. H6584+3338
Ne 3:10 made repairs n to him. H6584+3338
Ne 3:12 repaired the n section with the H6584+3338
Ne 3:17 N to him, the repairs were made by the H339
Ne 3:18 N to him, the repairs were made by their H339
Ne 3:19 N to him, Ezer son of Jeshua, ruler H6584+3338
Ne 3:20 N to him, Baruch son of Zabbai zealously H339
Ne 3:21 N to him, Meremoth son of Uriah, the son H339
Ne 3:22 The repairs n to him were made by the H339
Ne 3:23 of their house; and n to them, Azariah son H339
Ne 3:24 N to him, Binnui son of Henadad repaired H339
Ne 3:25 court of the guard. N to him, Pedaiah son H339
Ne 3:27 N to them, the men of Tekoa repaired H339
Ne 3:29 N to them, Zadok son of Immer made H339
Ne 3:29 N to him, Shemaiah son of Shekaniah, the H339
Ne 3:30 N to him, Hananiah son of Shelemiah, and H339
Ne 3:30 N to them, Meshullam son of Berekiah H339
Ne 3:31 N to him, Malkijah, one of the goldsmiths H339
Job 41:16 is so close to the n that no air can pass H285
Ps 48:13 you may tell of them to the n generation. H340
Ps 71:18 till I declare your power to the n generation NDT
Ps 78: 4 we will tell the n generation the H340
Ps 78: 6 so the n generation would know them H340
Ps 109:13 names blotted out from the n generation. H337
Isa 37:36 When the people got up the n morning NDT
Jer 20: 3 The n day, when Pashhur released him H4740
Jer 35: 4 It was n to the room of the officials, which H725
Jer 51:46 another the n, rumors of violence in H339
Jer 52:24 the priest n in rank and the three H5467
Eze 24:18 The n morning I did as I had been NDT
Eze 40: 7 of the gate n to the portico facing H4946+725
Eze 42: 8 rooms on the side n to the outer court was H4200
Eze 43: 8 their threshold n to my threshold and H907
Eze 48: 1 of Damascus n to Hamath will be H448+3338
Da 2:39 N, a third kingdom, one of bronze, will A10221
Da 6: 7 human being during the n thirty days, NDT
Da 6:12 that during the n thirty days anyone who NDT
Joel 1: 3 their children to the n generation. H337
Jnh 4: 7 But at dawn the n day God provided a H4740
Mt 27:62 The n day, the one after Preparation Day *G2069*
Mk 9:39 my name can in the n moment say *G5444*
Mk 11:12 The n day as they were leaving Bethany *G2069*
Lk 9:37 The n day, when they came down from *G2009*
Lk 10:35 The n day he took out two denarii and gave *G892*
Lk 13: 9 If it bears fruit n *year*, fine! *G1650+3836+3516*
Lk 13:33 on today and tomorrow and the n day— *G2400*
Jn 1:29 The n day John saw Jesus coming toward *G2069*
Jn 1:35 The n day John was there again with two *G2069*
Jn 1:43 The n day Jesus decided to leave for *G2069*
Jn 6:22 The n day the crowd that had stayed on *G2069*
Jn 12:12 The n day the great crowd that had come *G2069*
Jn 13:23 was reclining n to him. *G1877+3836+3146*
Jn 19:31 the n day was to be a special *G1697*
Ac 4: 3 they put them in jail until the n day. *G892*
Ac 4: 5 The n day the rulers, the elders and the *G892*
Ac 7:26 The n day Moses came upon two Israelites *G2079*
Ac 10:23 The n day Peter started out with them *G2069*
Ac 13:42 about these things on the n Sabbath. *G3568*
Ac 13:44 *On* the n Sabbath almost the whole city *G2262*
Ac 14:20 The n day he and Barnabas left for Derbe *G2069*
Ac 16:11 the n day we went on to Neapolis. *G2079*
Ac 18: 7 went n door to the house of *G5327*
Ac 20: 7 because he intended to leave the n day *G2069*
Ac 20:15 The n day we set sail from there and *G2079*
Ac 21: 1 The n *day* we went to Rhodes and from *G2009*
Ac 21: 8 Leaving the n day, we reached Caesarea *G2069*
Ac 21:18 The n day Paul and the rest of us went to *G2079*
Ac 21:26 The n day Paul took the men and purified *G2400*
Ac 22:30 So the n day he released him and *G2069*
Ac 23:12 The n morning some Jews formed a *G1181*
Ac 23:32 The n day they let the cavalry go on with *G2069*
Ac 25: 6 The n day he convened the court and *G2069*
Ac 25:17 the court the n *day* and ordered the man *G2009*
Ac 25:23 The n day Agrippa and Bernice came with *G2069*
Ac 27: 3 The n *day* we landed at Sidon; and Julius, *G2283*
Ac 27:18 the storm that the n *day* they began to *G2009*
Ac 28:13 The n day the south wind came up *G3552+1651*

NEZIAH (2)

Ezr 2:54 N and Hatipha H5909
Ne 7:56 N and Hatipha H5909

NEZIB (1)

Jos 15:43 Ashnah, N, H5908

NIBHAZ (1)

2Ki 17:31 the Avvites made N and Tartak, and the H5563

NIBSHAN (1)

Jos 15:62 N, the City of Salt and En Gedi—six towns H5581

NICANOR (1)

Ac 6: 5 Procorus, N, Timon, Parmenas, *G3770*

NICODEMUS (6)

Jn 3: 1 a man named N who was a member of *G3773*
Jn 3: 4 when they are old?" N asked. "Surely they *G3773*
Jn 3: 9 "How can this be?" N asked. *G3773*
Jn 7:50 N, who had gone to Jesus earlier and *G3773*
Jn 19:39 He was accompanied by N, the man who *G3773*
Jn 19:39 N brought a mixture of myrrh and aloes NDT

NICOLAITANS (2)

Rev 2: 6 You hate the practices *of* the N, which I *G3774*
Rev 2:15 those who hold to the teaching *of* the N. *G3774*

NICOLAS (1)

Ac 6: 5 Parmenas, and N from Antioch, a convert *G3775*

NICOPOLIS (1)

Titus 3:12 do your best to come to me at N, because *G3776*

NIGER (1)

Ac 13: 1 Simeon called N, Lucius of Cyrene, *G3769*

NIGH (KJV) ALMOST, APPROACH, APPROACHED, APPROACHED, CLOSER, DEPENDENT, NEAR, RELATIVE

NIGHT (319) [ALL-NIGHT, MIDNIGHT, NIGHTFALL, NIGHTS, OVERNIGHT]

Ge 1: 5 and the darkness he called "n. H4326
Ge 1:14 of the sky to separate the day from the n, H4326
Ge 1:16 day and the lesser light to govern the n. H4326
Ge 1:18 to govern the day and the n, and to H4326
Ge 8:22 winter, day and n will never cease." H4326
Ge 14:15 *During the* n Abram divided his men to H4326
Ge 19: 2 your feet and spend the n and then go on H4328
Ge 19: 2 "*we will* spend the n in the square." H4328
Ge 19:33 That n they got their father to drink wine H4326
Ge 19:34 the younger, "Last n I slept with my father. H621
Ge 19:35 got their father to drink wine that n also, H4326
Ge 20: 3 in a dream one n and said to him, H4326
Ge 24:23 your father's house for us to spend the n?" H4328
Ge 24:25 as well as room for you to spend the n." H4328
Ge 24:54 him ate and drank and spent the n there. H4328
Ge 26:24 That n the LORD appeared to him and said H4326
Ge 28:11 *he* stopped for the n because the sun had H4328
Ge 30:16 So he slept with her that n. H4326
Ge 31:24 in a dream at n and said to him, H4326
Ge 31:29 but last n the God of your father said to me, H621
Ge 31:39 me for whatever was stolen by day or n. H4326
Ge 31:40 me in the daytime and the cold at n, H4326
Ge 31:42 of my hands, and last n he rebuked you." H621
Ge 31:54 they had eaten, *they* spent the n there. H4328
Ge 32:13 He spent the n there, and from what he H4326
Ge 32:21 he himself spent the n in the camp. H4326
Ge 32:22 That n Jacob got up and took his two H4326
Ge 40: 5 had a dream the same n, and each dream H4326
Ge 41:11 Each of us had a dream the same n, and H4326
Ge 42:27 the place where they stopped for the n H4869
Ge 43:21 the place where we stopped for the n we H4869
Ge 46: 2 spoke to Israel in a vision at n and said, H4326
Ex 10:13 across the land all that day and all that n. H4326
Ex 12: 8 That same n they are to eat the meat H4326
Ex 12:12 "On that same n I will pass through Egypt H4326
Ex 12:30 all the Egyptians got up *during* the n, H4326
Ex 12:31 *During* the n Pharaoh summoned Moses H4326
Ex 12:42 LORD kept vigil that n to bring them out of H4325
Ex 12:42 on this n all the Israelites are to keep vigil H4326
Ex 13:21 on their way and *by* n in a pillar of fire H4326
Ex 13:21 so that they could travel by day or n. H4326
Ex 13:22 the pillar of fire *by* n left its place in H4326
Ex 14:20 *Throughout* the n the cloud brought H4326
Ex 14:20 so neither went near the other all n long. H4326
Ex 14:21 all that n the LORD drove the sea back H4326
Ex 14:24 the last watch of the n the LORD H874+1332
Ex 22: 2 caught breaking in at n and is struck a fatal NDT
Ex 40:38 fire was in the cloud *by* n, in the sight H4326
Lev 6: 9 on the altar hearth throughout the n, H4326
Lev 8:35 of meeting day and n for seven days and H4326
Nu 9:16 covered it, and *at* n it looked like fire. H4326
Nu 9:21 Whether by day or *by* n, whenever the H4326
Nu 11: 9 When the dew settled on the camp *at* n H4326
Nu 11:32 All that day and n and all the next day the H4326
Nu 14: 1 That n all the members of the community H4326
Nu 14:14 of cloud by day and a pillar of fire *by* n. H4326
Nu 22: 8 "Spend the n here," Balaam said to them H4326
Nu 22:19 Now spend the n here so that I can find H4326
Nu 22:20 That n God came to Balaam and said H4326
Dt 1:33 journey, in fire *by* n and in a cloud by day H4326
Dt 16: 1 of Aviv he brought you out of Egypt *by* n. H4326
Dt 28:66 filled with dread both n and day, never H4326
Jos 1: 8 meditate on it day and n, so that you may H4326
Jos 2: 8 Before the spies lay down for the n, she NDT
Jos 6:11 returned to camp and spent the n there. H4328
Jos 8: 3 best fighting men and sent them out *at* n H4326
Jos 8: 9 Joshua spent that n with the people. H4326
Jos 8:13 That n Joshua went into the valley H4326
Jdg 6:25 That same n the LORD said to him, "Take H4326
Jdg 6:27 he did it *at* n rather than in the daytime. H4326
Jdg 6:40 That n God did so. Only the fleece was dry; H4326
Jdg 7: 9 During that n the LORD said to Gideon H4326
Jdg 9:32 *during* the n you and your men should H4326
Jdg 9:34 his troops set out *by* n and took up H4326
Jdg 16: 1 *He* went in to spend the n with her. H995+448
Jdg 16: 2 lay in wait for him all n at the city gate. H4326
Jdg 16: 2 They made no move during the n, saying H4326
Jdg 16: 3 lay there only until the middle of the n. H4326
Jdg 18: 2 house of Micah, where *they* spent the n. H4328
Jdg 19: 7 so *he* stayed there *that* n. H3782+2256+4328
Jdg 19: 9 Spend the n here; the day H4328
Jdg 19:10 unwilling to stay another n, the man left H4328
Jdg 19:11 this city of the Jebusites and spend the n." H4328
Jdg 19:13 Ramah and spend the n in one of H4328
Jdg 19:15 There they stopped to spend the n. H4328
Jdg 19:15 but no one took them in for the n. H4328
Jdg 19:18 No one has taken me in for the n. NDT
Jdg 19:20 Only don't spend the n in the square." H4328
Jdg 19:25 her and abused her throughout the n, H4326
Jdg 20: 4 to Gibeah in Benjamin to spend the n. H4328
Jdg 20: 5 *During* the n the men of Gibeah came H4326
Ru 3: 8 In the middle of the n something startled H4326
Ru 3:13 Stay here *for* the n, and in the morning if H4326
1Sa 3: 2 One n Eli, whose eyes were becoming so H3427
1Sa 11:11 the last watch of the n they H874+2021+1332
1Sa 14:34 brought his ox that n and slaughtered it H4326
1Sa 14:36 the Philistines *by* n and plunder them till H4326
1Sa 15:11 he cried out to the LORD all that n. H4326
1Sa 15:16 what the LORD said to me last n." H2021+4326
1Sa 19:10 That n David made good his escape H4326
1Sa 19:24 He lay naked all that day and all that n H4326
1Sa 25:16 N and day they were a wall around us the H4326
1Sa 26: 7 David and Abishai went to the army *by* n, H4326
1Sa 28: 8 and *at* n he and two men went to the H4326
1Sa 28:20 eaten nothing all that day and all that n. H4326
1Sa 28:25 That same n they got up and left H4326
1Sa 31:12 men marched through the n to Beth Shan. H4326
2Sa 2:29 All that n Abner and his men marched H4326
2Sa 2:32 his men marched all n and arrived at H4326
2Sa 4: 7 they traveled all n by way of the Arabah. H4326
2Sa 7: 4 But that n the word of the LORD came to H4326
2Sa 17: 8 *he will* not spend the n with the troops. H4328
2Sa 17:16 'Do not spend the n at the fords in the H4328
2Sa 21:10 them by day or the wild animals *by* n. H4326
1Ki 3: 5 to Solomon *during* the n in a dream, H4326
1Ki 3:19 "*During* the n this woman's son died H4326
1Ki 3:20 the middle of the n and took my son from H4326
1Ki 8:29 be open toward this temple n and day, H4326
1Ki 8:59 be near to the LORD our God day and n H4326
1Ki 19: 9 There he went into a cave and spent the n. H4328
2Ki 6:14 They went *by* n and surrounded the city H4326
2Ki 7:12 The king got up *in* the n and said to his H4326
2Ki 8:21 he rose up and broke through *by* n H4326
2Ki 19:35 That n the angel of the LORD went out H4326
2Ki 25: 4 the whole army fled *at* n through the gate H4326
1Ch 9:27 *They would* spend the n stationed around H4328
1Ch 9:33 were responsible for the work day and n. H4326
1Ch 17: 3 But that n the word of God came to H4326
2Ch 1: 7 That n God appeared to Solomon and H4326
2Ch 6:20 be open toward this temple day and n, H4326
2Ch 7:12 the LORD appeared to him at n and said: "I H4326
2Ch 21: 9 he rose up and broke through *by* n. H4326
Ne 1: 6 before you day and n for your servants, H4326
Ne 2:12 I set out *during* the n with a few others. H4326
Ne 2:13 *By* n I went out through the Valley Gate H4326
Ne 2:15 so I went up the valley *by* n, examining H4326

Ne 4: 9 a guard day and n to meet this threat. H4326
Ne 4:22 *Have* every man and his helper **stay** inside Jerusalem **at n** H4328
Ne 4:22 serve us as guards *by* n and as workers by H4326
Ne 6:10 kill you—*by* n they are coming to kill you." H4326
Ne 9:12 and *by* n with a pillar of fire to give them H4326
Ne 9:19 the pillar of fire by n to shine on the way H4326
Ne 13:20 kinds of goods **spent the n** outside H4328
Ne 13:21 "Why *do* you **spend the n** by the wall? H4328
Est 4:16 not eat or drink for three days, n or day. H4326
Est 6: 1 That n the king could not sleep; so he H4326
Job 3: 3 birth perish, and the n that said, 'A boy is H4326
Job 3: 6 That n—may thick darkness seize it; may H4326
Job 3: 7 May that n be barren; may no shout of joy H4326
Job 4:13 Amid disquieting dreams in the n, when H4326
Job 5:14 daytime; at noon they grope as *in* the n. H4326
Job 7: 4 The n drags on, and I toss and turn until H6847
Job 10:22 to the land of **deepest n**, of H6547+4017+694
Job 17:12 turn n into day; in the face of the darkness H4326
Job 20: 8 be found, banished like a vision of the n. H4326
Job 24: 7 clothes, *they* **spend the n** naked; they H4328
Job 24:14 in the n steals forth like a thief. H4326
Job 27:20 a tempest snatches him away *in* the n. H4326
Job 29:19 the dew *will* **lie all n** on my branches. H4328
Job 30: 3 parched land in desolate wastelands *at* n. H621
Job 30:17 N pierces my bones; my gnawing pains H4326
Job 31:32 no stranger *had to* **spend the n** in the H4328
Job 33:15 in a vision of the n, when deep sleep falls H4326
Job 34:20 in the middle of the n; the people are H4326
Job 34:25 he overthrows them *in* the n and they are H4326
Job 35:10 God my Maker, who gives songs in the n, H4326
Job 36:20 Do not long for the n, to drag people H4326
Job 39: 9 *Will it* **stay** by your manger **at n**? H4328
Job 39:28 It dwells on a cliff and **stays** there **at n**; H4328
Ps 1: 2 who meditates on his law day and n. H4326
Ps 6: 6 All n long I flood my bed with weeping H4326
Ps 16: 7 even *at* n my heart instructs me. H4326
Ps 17: 3 though you examine me *at* n and test me H4326
Ps 19: 2 n after night they reveal knowledge. H4326
Ps 19: 2 night after n they reveal knowledge. H4326
Ps 22: 2 you do not answer, *by* n, but I find no rest. H4326
Ps 30: 5 weeping may stay for the n, but rejoicing H6847
Ps 32: 4 For day and n your hand was heavy on me H4326
Ps 42: 3 My tears have been my food day and n H4326
Ps 42: 8 directs his love, at n his song is with me H4326
Ps 55:10 Day and n they prowl about on its walls H4326
Ps 63: 6 I think of you through the **watches of the n**. H874
Ps 74:16 yours also the n; you established the H4326
Ps 77: 2 *at* n I stretched out untiring hands H4326
Ps 77: 6 I remembered my songs in the n. H4326
Ps 78:14 by day and with light from the fire all n. H4326
Ps 88: 1 who saves me; day and n I cry out to you. H4326
Ps 90: 4 has just gone by, or like a watch in the n. H4326
Ps 91: 5 You will not fear the terror of n, nor the H4326
Ps 92: 2 in the morning and your faithfulness at n, H4326
Ps 104:20 darkness, it becomes n, and all the beasts H4326
Ps 105:39 as a covering, and a fire to give light at n. H4326
Ps 119:55 In the n, LORD, I remember your name H4326
Ps 119:148 stay open through the **watches of the n**, H874
Ps 121: 6 not harm you by day, nor the moon by n. H4326
Ps 134: 1 LORD who minister by n in the house of the H4326
Ps 136: 9 the moon and stars to govern the n; His H4326
Ps 139:11 me and the light become n around me," H4326
Ps 139:12 dark to you; the n will shine like the day H4326
Pr 7: 9 day was fading, as the dark of n set in. H4326
Pr 31:15 She gets up while it is still n; she provides H4326
Pr 31:18 her lamp does not go out at n. H4326
Ecc 2:23 even at n their minds do not rest. H4326
Ecc 8:16 people getting no sleep day or n— H4326
SS 3: 1 **All n long** on my bed I looked H928+2021+4326
SS 3: 8 his side, prepared for the terrors of the n. H4326
SS 5: 2 my hair with the dampness of the n." H4326
SS 7:11 *let us* **spend the n** in the villages. H4328
Isa 4: 5 by day and a glow of flaming fire *by* n; H4326
Isa 5:11 who stay up late at n till they are H5974
Isa 15: 1 destroyed in a n! Kir in Moab is ruined H4325
Isa 15: 1 Kir in Moab is ruined, destroyed in a n! H4325
Isa 16: 3 Make your shadow like n—at high noon H4325
Isa 21: 8 the watchtower; every n I stay at my post. H4326
Isa 21:11 "Watchman, what is left of the n? H4326
Isa 21:11 Watchman, what is left of the n?" H4325
Isa 21:12 "Morning is coming, but also the n. H4326
Isa 26: 9 My soul yearns for you in the n; in the H4326
Isa 27: 3 I guard it day and n so that no one may H4326
Isa 28:19 by day and by n, it will sweep through H4326
Isa 29: 7 is with a dream, with a vision in the n— H4326
Isa 30:29 will sing as on the n you celebrate a holy H4325
Isa 34:10 It will not be quenched n or day; its H4326
Isa 34:14 there the **n creatures** will also lie down H4327
Isa 38:12 day and n you made an end of me. H4326
Isa 38:13 day and n you made an end of me. H4326
Isa 58:10 your n will become like the noonday. H696
Isa 60:11 be shut, day or n, so that people may H4326
Isa 62: 6 they will never be silent day or n. H4326
Jer 6: 5 let us attack at n and destroy her H4326
Jer 9: 1 would weep day and n for the slain of my H4326
Jer 14: 8 like a traveler *who* **stays only a n**? H5742+4328
Jer 14:17 overflow with tears n and day without H4326
Jer 16:13 there you will serve other gods day and n, H4326
Jer 31:35 decrees the moon and stars to shine *by* n, H4326
Jer 33:20 with the day and my covenant with the n, H4326
Jer 33:20 so that day and n no longer come at their H4326
Jer 33:25 with day and n and established the H4326
Jer 36:30 to the heat by day and the frost by n. H4326
Jer 39: 4 they left the city *at* n by way of the king's H4326
Jer 49: 9 If thieves came during the n, would they H4326
Jer 52: 7 They left the city *at* n through the gate H4326
La 1: 2 Bitterly she weeps at n, tears are on her H4326
La 2:18 let your tears flow like a river day and n H4326
La 2:19 cry out in the n, as the watches of H4326
La 2:19 as the **watches of the n** begin; pour H874
Da 2:19 During the n the mystery was revealed to A10391
Da 5:30 That very n Belshazzar, king of the A10391
Da 6:18 his palace and **spent the n** without A10102
Da 7: 2 "In my vision at n I looked, and there A10391
Da 7: 7 in my vision at n I looked, and there A10391
Da 7:13 "In my vision at n I looked, and there A10391
Hos 4: 5 You stumble day and n, and the prophets H4326
Hos 7: 6 Their passion smolders all n; in the H4326
Joel 1:13 **spend the n** in sackcloth, you who H4328
Am 5: 8 into dawn and darkens day into n, H4326
Ob 5 came to you, if robbers in the n—oh, H4326
Mic 3: 6 Therefore n will come over you, without H4326
Zec 1: 8 During the n I had a vision, and there H4326
Zec 14: 7 with no distinction between day and n. H4326
Mt 2:14 his mother *during* the n and left for G3816
Mt 14:23 Later that n, he was there alone, G4068
Mt 21:17 the city to Bethany, where *he* **spent the n**. G887
Mt 24:43 had known at what **time of n** the thief was G5871
Mt 26:31 "This very n you will all fall away on G3816
Mt 26:34 answered, "this very n, before the rooster G3816
Mt 28:13 disciples came *during* the n and stole him G3816
Mk 4:27 N and day, whether he sleeps or gets up G3816
Mk 5: 5 N and day among the tombs and in the G3816
Mk 6:47 Later that n, the boat was in the middle of G4068
Lk 2: 8 keeping watch over their flocks *at* n. G3816
Lk 2:37 left the temple but worshiped n and day, G3816
Lk 5: 5 worked hard all n and haven't caught G3816
Lk 6:12 and **spent the n** praying to God. G1639+1381
Lk 12:20 This very n your life will be demanded G3816
Lk 12:38 in the **middle of the n** or toward G1311+5871
Lk 17:34 *on* that n two people will be in one bed G3816
Lk 18: 7 who cry out to him day and n? G3816
Lk 21:37 he went out *to* **spend the n** on the hill G887
Jn 3: 2 He came to Jesus *at* n and said, "Rabbi G3816
Jn 9: 4 him who sent me. N is coming, when no G3816
Jn 11:10 a person walks at n that they stumble, G3816
Jn 13:30 the bread, he went out. And it was n. G3816
Jn 19:39 man who earlier had visited Jesus *at* n. G3816
Jn 21: 3 the boat, but that n they caught nothing. G3816
Ac 5:19 But during the n an angel of the Lord G3816
Ac 9:24 Day and n they kept close watch on the G3816
Ac 9:25 followers took him *by* n and lowered him G3816
Ac 12: 6 The n before Herod was to bring him to G3816
Ac 16: 9 During the n Paul had a vision of a man of G3816
Ac 16:33 At that hour *of* the n the jailer took them G3816
Ac 17:10 As soon as it was n, the believers sent G3816
Ac 18: 9 *One* n the Lord spoke to Paul in a vision G3816
Ac 20:31 warning each of you n and day with tears. G3816
Ac 23:11 The following n the Lord stood near Paul G3816
Ac 23:31 them during the n and brought him as G3816
Ac 26: 7 as they earnestly serve God day and n. G3816
Ac 27:23 Last n an angel of the God to whom I G3816
Ac 27:27 On the fourteenth n we were still being G3816
Ro 13:12 The n is nearly over; the day is almost G3816
1Co 11:23 Lord Jesus, on the n he was betrayed G3816
2Co 11:25 I spent **a n and a day** in the open sea, G3819
1Th 2: 9 we worked n and day in order not to be a G3816
1Th 3:10 N and day we pray most earnestly that we G3816
1Th 5: 2 of the Lord will come like a thief in the n. G3816
1Th 5: 5 do not belong to the n or to the darkness. G3816
1Th 5: 7 who sleep, sleep *at* n, and those who get G3816
1Th 5: 7 those who get drunk, get drunk *at* n. G3816
2Th 3: 8 contrary, we worked n and day, laboring G3816
1Ti 5: 5 God and continues n and day to pray and G3816
2Ti 1: 3 as n and day I constantly remember you G3816
Rev 4: 8 Day and n they never stop saying G3816
Rev 7:15 serve him day and n in his temple; G3816
Rev 8:12 without light, and also a third of the n. G3816
Rev 12:10 accuses them before our God day and n, G3816
Rev 14:11 be no rest day or n for those who worship G3816
Rev 20:10 be tormented day and n for ever and ever. G3816
Rev 21:25 ever be shut, for there will be no n there. G3816
Rev 22: 5 There will be no more n. They will not G3816

NIGHTFALL (2) [NIGHT]

2Sa 19: 7 a man will be left with you *by* n. H2021+4326
2Ch 35:14 offerings and the fat portions until n. H4326

NIGHTS (20) [NIGHT]

Ge 7: 4 rain on the earth for forty days and forty n, H4326
Ge 7:12 fell on the earth forty days and forty n. H4326
Ex 24:18 on the mountain forty days and forty n. H4326
Dt 34:28 forty days and forty n without eating bread H4326
Dt 9: 9 on the mountain forty days and forty n; H4326
Dt 9:11 At the end of the forty days and forty n H4326
Dt 9:18 before the LORD for forty days and forty n; H4326
Dt 9:25 days and forty n because the LORD had H4326
Dt 10:10 on the mountain forty days and forty n, H4326
1Sa 30:12 any water for three days and three n. H4326
2Sa 12:16 He fasted and **spent the n** lying in H4328
1Ki 19: 8 forty days and forty n until he reached H4326
Job 2:13 with him for seven days and seven n. H4326
Job 7: 3 and n *of* misery have been assigned to H4326
Isa 65: 4 the graves and **spend** *their* **n** keeping H4328
Jnh 1:17 belly of the fish three days and three n. H4326
Mt 4: 2 After fasting forty days and forty n, he was G3816
Mt 12:40 three days and three n in the belly of a G3816
Mt 12:40 three days and three n in the heart of the G3816
2Co 6: 5 in hard work, **sleepless n** and hunger; G71

NILE (34)

Ge 41: 1 had a dream: He was standing by the N, H3284
Ge 41: 3 came up out of the N and stood beside H3284
Ge 41:17 I was standing on the bank of the N, H3284
Ex 1:22 that is born you must throw into the N, H3284
Ex 2: 3 among the reeds along the bank of the N. H3284
Ex 2: 5 daughter went down to the N to bathe, H3284
Ex 4: 9 some water from the N and pour it on the H3284
Ex 7:15 Confront him on the bank of the N, and H3284
Ex 7:17 in my hand I will strike the water of the N, H3284
Ex 7:18 The fish in the N will die, and the river will H3284
Ex 7:20 his officials and struck the water of the N, H3284
Ex 7:21 The fish in the N died, and the river H3284
Ex 7:24 dug along the N to get drinking water, H3284
Ex 7:25 days passed after the LORD struck the N. H3284
Ex 8: 3 The N will teem with frogs. They will H3284
Ex 8: 9 except for those that remain in the N." H3284
Ex 8:11 people; they will remain only in the N." H3284
Ex 17: 5 hand the staff with which you struck the N, H3284
Isa 7:18 flies from the N delta *in* Egypt and for H3284
Isa 19: 7 also the plants along the N, at the mouth H3284
Isa 19: 7 field along the N will become parched, H3284
Isa 19: 8 all who cast hooks into the N; those who H3284
Isa 23: 3 the harvest of the N was the revenue of H3284
Isa 23:10 Till your land as they do along the N H3284
Jer 2:18 why go to Egypt to drink water from the N? H8865
Jer 46: 7 "Who is this that rises like the N, like H3284
Jer 46: 8 Egypt rises like the N, like rivers of surging H3284
Eze 29: 3 You say, "The N belongs to me; I made it H3284
Eze 29: 9 you said, "The N is mine; I made it," H3284
Eze 30:12 dry up the **waters of the N** and sell the H3284
Am 8: 8 The whole land will rise like the N; it will H3284
Am 9: 5 the whole land rises like the N, then sinks H3284
Na 3: 8 situated on the N, with water around her? H3284
Zec 10:11 all the depths of the N will dry up. H3284

NIMRAH (1) [BETH NIMRAH]

Nu 32: 3 Jazer, N, Heshbon, Elealeh H5809

NIMRIM (2)

Isa 15: 6 The waters of N are dried up and the H5810
Jer 48:34 even the waters of N are dried up. H5810

NIMROD (4)

Ge 10: 8 Cush was the father of N, who became a H5808
Ge 10: 9 why it is said, "Like N, a mighty hunter H5808
1Ch 1:10 Cush was the father of N, who became a H5808
Mic 5: 6 the land of N with drawn sword. H5808

NIMSHI (5)

1Ki 19:16 anoint Jehu son of N king over Israel, and H5811
2Ki 9: 2 Jehu son of Jehoshaphat, the son of N. H5811
2Ki 9:14 the son of N, conspired against H5811
2Ki 9:20 The driving is like that of Jehu son of N H5811
2Ch 22: 7 out with Joram to meet Jehu son of N, H5811

NINE (20) [NINTH]

Nu 29:26 " 'On the fifth day offer n bulls, two rams H9596
Nu 34:13 that it be given to the n and a half tribes, H9596
Dt 3:11 iron and was *more than* n cubits long H9596
Jos 13: 7 among the n tribes and half of H9596
Jos 14: 2 assigned by lot to the n and a half tribes, H9596
Jos 15:44 Mareshah—n towns and their villages. H9596
Jos 15:54 Zior—n towns and their villages. H9596
Jos 21:16 n towns from these two tribes. H9596
Jdg 4: 3 Because he had n hundred chariots fitted H9596
Jdg 4:13 all his men and his n hundred chariots H9596
2Sa 24: 8 at the end of n months and twenty days. H9596
2Ki 17: 1 Israel in Samaria, and he reigned n years. H9596
1Ch 3: 8 Elishama, Eliada and Eliphelet—n in all. H9596
Ne 11: 1 while the remaining n were to stay in H9596
Mt 20: 3 "About **n in the morning** he went G5569+6052
Mk 15:25 It was **n in the morning** when they G6052+5569
Lk 16: 6 " '**N hundred gallons** of olive oil,' G1669+1004
Lk 17:17 all ten cleansed? Where are the other n? G1933
Ac 2:15 *only* **n in the morning**! G6052+5569+3836+2465
Ac 23:23 to go to Caesarea at **n tonight**. G5569+6052

NINETEEN (2) [NINETEENTH]

Jos 19:38 There were n towns and their H9596+6926
2Sa 2:30 n of David's men were found H9596+6925

NINETEENTH (4) [NINETEEN]

2Ki 25: 8 in the n year of Nebuchadnezzar H9596+6926
1Ch 24:16 the n to Pethahiah, the twentieth H9596+6925
1Ch 25:26 the n to Mallothi, his sons and H9596+6925
Jer 52:12 in the n year of Nebuchadnezzar H9596+6926

NINETY (3) [90]

Ge 17:17 Will Sarah bear a child at the age of n?" H9596
Eze 41:12 all around, and its length was n cubits. H9596
Ac 27:28 and found it was **n feet deep**. G3976+1278

NINETY-EIGHT (1) [98]

1Sa 4:15 who was n years old and H9596+2256+9046

NINETY-NINE (6)
Ge 17: 1 Abram was **n** years old, H9596+2256+9596
Ge 17:24 Abraham was **n** years old H9596+2256+9596
Mt 18:12 he not leave the **n** on the hills and *G1916+1933*
Mt 18:13 than about the **n** that did not *G1916+1933*
Lk 15: 4 he leave the **n** in the open country *G1916+1933*
Lk 15: 7 than over **n** righteous persons *G1916+1933*

NINETY-SIX (2)
Ezr 8:35 all Israel, **n** rams H9596+2256+9252
Jer 52:23 There were **n** pomegranates H9596+2256+9252

NINEVEH (24) [NINEVITES]
Ge 10:11 to Assyria, where he built **N**, Rehoboth Ir, H5770
Ge 10:12 which is between **N** and Calah—which is H5770
2Ki 19:36 He returned to **N** and stayed there. H5770
Isa 37:37 He returned to **N** and stayed there. H5770
Jnh 1: 2 to the great city of **N** and preach against it H5770
Jnh 3: 2 to the great city of **N** and proclaim to it H5770
Jnh 3: 3 the word of the LORD and went to **N**. H5770
Jnh 3: 3 Now **N** was a very large city; it took three H5770
Jnh 3: 4 more days and **N** will be overthrown." H5770
Jnh 3: 6 Jonah's warning reached the king of **N**, H5770
Jnh 3: 7 This is the proclamation he issued in **N** H5770
Jnh 4:11 I not have concern for the great city of **N**, H5770
Na 1: 1 A prophecy concerning **N**. The book of the H5770
Na 1: 8 flood he will make an end of **N**; H5226+2023S
Na 1:11 From you, **N**, has one come forth who plots NDT
Na 1:14 has given a command concerning you, **N**: NDT
Na 2: 1 advances against you, **N**. Guard the fortress, NDT
Na 2: 5 **N** summons her picked troops, yet they NDT
Na 2: 7 It is decreed that **N** be exiled and carried NDT
Na 2: 8 **N** is like a pool whose water is draining H5770
Na 3: 7 from you and say, '**N** is in ruins—who will H5770
Zep 2:13 leaving **N** utterly desolate and dry as the H5770
Mt 12:41 The men *of* **N** will stand up at the *G3780*
Lk 11:32 The men *of* **N** will stand up at the *G3780*

NINEVITES (2) [NINEVEH]
Jnh 3: 5 The **N** believed God. A fast was H408+5770
Lk 11:30 For as Jonah was a sign *to* the **N**, so also *G3780*

NINTH (24) [NINE]
Lev 23:32 the evening of the **n** day of the month H9596
Lev 25:22 it until the harvest of the **n** year comes in. H9595
Nu 7:60 On the **n** day Abidan son of Gideoni, the H9595
2Ki 17: 6 In the **n** year of Hoshea, the king of H9595
2Ki 18:10 which was the **n** year of Hoshea king of H9596
2Ki 25: 1 So in the **n** year of Zedekiah's reign, on H9595
2Ki 25: 3 By the **n** day of the fourth month the H9596
1Ch 12:12 Johanan the eighth, Elzabad the **n**, H9595
1Ch 24:11 the **n** to Jeshua, the tenth to Shekaniah, H9595
1Ch 25:16 the **n** to Mattaniah, his sons and relatives H9595
1Ch 27:12 The **n**, for the ninth month, was Abiezer H9595
1Ch 27:12 The ninth, for the **n** month, was Abiezer H9595
Ezr 10: 9 And on the twentieth day of the **n** month H9595
Jer 36: 9 In the **n** month of the fifth year of H9595
Jer 36:22 It was the **n** month and the king was H9595
Jer 39: 1 In the **n** year of Zedekiah king of Judah H9595
Jer 39: 2 And on the **n** day of the fourth month of H9596
Jer 52: 4 So in the **n** year of Zedekiah's reign, on H9595
Jer 52: 6 By the **n** day of the fourth month the H9596
Eze 24: 1 In the **n** year, in the tenth month on the H9595
Hag 2:10 On the twenty-fourth day of the **n** month H9595
Hag 2:18 this twenty-fourth day of the **n** month, H9595
Zec 7: 1 on the fourth day of the **n** month, H9595
Rev 21:20 the eighth beryl, the **n** topaz, the tenth *G1888*

NISAN (2)
Ne 2: 1 In the month of **N** in the twentieth year of H5772
Est 3: 7 the first month, the month of **N**, the pur H5772

NISROK (2)
2Ki 19:37 worshiping in the temple of his god **N**, H5827
Isa 37:38 worshiping in the temple of his god **N**, H5827

NITRE (KJV) SOAP, WOUND

NO (1778) [NAUGHT, NONE, NOR, NOT, NOTHING]
Ge 2: 5 Now **n** shrub had **yet** appeared on the H3270
Ge 2: 5 earth and **n** plant had **yet** sprung H3972+3270
Ge 2: 5 the earth and **there was n** one to work the H401
Ge 2:20 But for Adam **n** suitable helper was found. H4202
Ge 2:25 were both naked, and they felt **n** shame. H4202
Ge 4:12 it will **n** longer yield its crops for you. H4202
Ge 4:15 on Cain so that **n** one who found him H1194
Ge 5:24 then he **was n more**, because God H401
Ge 15: 3 "You have given me **n** children; so a H4202
Ge 16: 1 Abram's wife, had borne him **n** children. H4202
Ge 17: 5 **N** longer will you be called Abram; your H4202
Ge 17:15 you are **n** *longer* to call her Sarai H4202
Ge 19: 2 "**N**," they answered, "we will spend the H4202
Ge 19: 7 "**N**, my friends. Don't do this NDT
Ge 19:18 But Lot said to them, "**N**, my lords, please! H440
Ge 19:31 and **there is n** man around here to give us H401
Ge 20:11 '**There** is surely **n** fear of God in this place H401
Ge 23:11 "**N**, my lord," he said. "Listen to me; I give H4202
Ge 24:16 a virgin; **n** man had ever slept with her. H4202
Ge 26:22 another well, and **n** one quarreled over it. H4202
Ge 26:29 that you will do us **n** harm, just as we did H561
Ge 27: 1 were so weak *that* he could **n** *longer* see, H4946
Ge 27:45 your brother *is* **n longer** angry with you H8740
Ge 31:50 daughters, even though **n** one is with us H401
Ge 32:28 "Your name will **n** longer be Jacob, but H4202
Ge 33:10 "**N**, please!" said Jacob. "If I have found H440
Ge 34:19 lost **n** time in doing what they said H4202
Ge 35: 5 around them so that **n** one pursued them. H4202
Ge 35:10 you will **n** longer be called Jacob H4202
Ge 37:24 cistern was empty; **there was n** water in it. H401
Ge 37:35 "**N**," he said, "I will continue to mourn H3954
Ge 39: 9 **N** one is greater in this house than I am. H401
Ge 39:23 The warden paid **n** attention to anything H401
Ge 40: 8 "but **there is n** one to interpret them." H401
Ge 41: 8 **n** one could interpret them for him. H401
Ge 41:15 "I had a dream, and **n** one can interpret it. H401
Ge 41:21 **n** one could tell that they had done so H4202
Ge 41:39 **there is n** one so discerning and wise as H401
Ge 41:44 without your word **n** one will lift hand H4202
Ge 42:10 "**N**, my lord," they answered. "Your H4202
Ge 42:12 "**N**!" he said to them. "You have come to H4202
Ge 42:13 is now with our father, and one **is n more**." H401
Ge 42:32 One **is n more**, and the youngest is now H401
Ge 42:36 Joseph **is n more** and Simeon is no more H401
Ge 42:36 Joseph is no more and Simeon **is n more** H401
Ge 44:34 boy is not with me? **N**! Do not let me see NDT
Ge 45: 1 Joseph could **n** *longer* control himself H4202
Ge 45: 1 So there was **n** one with Joseph when he H4202
Ge 45: 6 next five years **there will be n** plowing and H401
Ge 47: 4 your servants' flocks have **n** pasture. H401
Ge 47:13 **There was n** food, however, in the whole H401
Ge 48:18 said to him, "**N**, my father, this H4202+4027
Ge 49: 4 you will **n** *longer* excel, for you H440
Ex 2: 3 But when she could hide him **n** longer H4202
Ex 2:12 Looking this way and that and seeing **n** one, H401
Ex 5: 7 "You are **n** longer to supply the people H4202
Ex 5: 9 keep working and pay **n** attention to lies." H440
Ex 5:16 Your servants are given **n** straw, yet we are H401
Ex 8:10 you may know **there is n** *one* like the LORD H401
Ex 8:22 **n** swarms of flies will be there H1194
Ex 9: 4 so that **n** animal belonging H4202+4946+3972
Ex 9:14 may know that **there is n** *one* like me in all H401
Ex 9:29 will stop and there will be **n** more hail, H4202
Ex 9:33 the rain **n** longer poured down on the H4202
Ex 10:11 **N**! Have only the men go and H4202+4027
Ex 10:23 **N** one could see anyone else or move H4202
Ex 12:13 **N** destructive plague will touch you when H4202
Ex 12:16 Do **n** work at all on these days, except to H4202
Ex 12:19 For seven days **n** yeast is to be found in H4202
Ex 12:43 "**N** foreigner may eat it H3972+4202
Ex 12:48 **N** uncircumcised male may eat it H3972+4202
Ex 14:11 it because **there were n** graves in H1172+401
Ex 16:19 "**N** one is to keep any of it until morning." H440
Ex 16:20 some of them paid **n** attention to Moses H4202
Ex 16:29 are on the seventh day; **n** one is to go out." H440
Ex 17: 1 but **there was n** water for the people to H401
Ex 19:13 **N** person or animal shall be permitted to H4202
Ex 20: 3 "You shall have **n** other gods before me. H4202
Ex 21: 8 He has **n** right to sell her to foreigners H4202
Ex 21:22 prematurely but there is **n** serious injury, H4202
Ex 22:10 is taken away while **n** one is looking, H401
Ex 22:11 accept this, and **n** restitution is required. H4202
Ex 22:25 it like a business deal; charge **n** interest. H4202
Ex 23:15 "**N** one is to appear before me H4202
Ex 29:33 But **n** one else may eat them, because H4202
Ex 30:12 Then **n** plague will come on them when H4202
Ex 33: 4 began to mourn and **n** one put on any H4202
Ex 33:20 my face, for **n** one may see me and live." H4202
Ex 34: 3 **N** one is to come with you or be seen H4202
Ex 34:20 "**N** one is to appear before me H4202
Ex 34:24 **n** one will covet your land when you H4202
Ex 36: 6 "**N** man or woman is to make anything else H440
Lev 13:21 **there is n** white hair in it and it is not more H401
Lev 13:26 examines it and **there is n** white hair in the H401
Lev 13:31 skin deep and **there is n** black hair in it, H401
Lev 13:32 spread and there is **n** yellow hair in it H4202
Lev 13:34 skin and appears to **be n** more than skin H401
Lev 13:55 **n matter** which side of the fabric has been H196
Lev 16:17 **N** one is to be in the tent of H4202+3972
Lev 17: 7 They must **n** longer offer any of their H4202
Lev 18: 6 " '**N** one is to approach any close relative H4202
Lev 20:14 so that **n** wickedness will be among you. H4202
Lev 21: 3 on him since she has **n** husband— H4202
Lev 21:18 **N** man who has any defect may H4202+3972
Lev 21:18 **n** man who is blind or lame, disfigured or NDT
Lev 21:19 **n** man with a crippled foot or hand, NDT
Lev 21:21 **N** descendant of Aaron the priest H4202+3972
Lev 22:10 " '**N** one outside a priest's family may eat H4202
Lev 22:13 is divorced, yet has **n** children, and she H401
Lev 22:13 **N** unauthorized person, however H4202+3972
Lev 23: 7 assembly and do **n** regular work. H4202+3972
Lev 23: 8 assembly and do **n** regular work. H4202+3972
Lev 23:21 assembly and do **n** regular work. H4202+3972
Lev 23:25 Do **n** regular work, but present a H4202+3972
Lev 23:31 You shall do **n** work at all. This is to be a H4202
Lev 23:35 assembly; do **n** regular work. H4202+3972
Lev 23:36 assembly; do **n** regular work. H4202+3972
Lev 25:26 there is **n** one to redeem it for them but H4202
Lev 26: 6 you will lie down and **n** one will make you H401
Lev 26:13 of Egypt **so that** you would **n** *longer* be H4946
Lev 26:17 will flee even when **n** one is pursuing you. H401
Lev 26:31 I will take **n** delight in the pleasing H4202
Lev 26:36 even though **n** one is pursuing them. H401
Lev 26:37 even though **n** one is pursuing them. H401
Lev 27:26 " '**N** one, however, may dedicate the H4202
Lev 27:29 " '**N** person devoted to destruction H3972+4202
Lev 27:33 **N** one may pick out the good from the bad H4202
Nu 3: 4 They had **n** sons, so Eleazar and Ithamar H4202
Nu 5: 8 But if that person has **n** close relative to H401
Nu 5:13 since **there is n** witness against her and she H401
Nu 5:19 "If **n** other man has had sexual relations H4202
Nu 6: 5 **n** razor may be used on their head. H4202
Nu 8:19 them so that **n** plague will strike the H4202
Nu 8:25 their regular service and work **n** longer. H4202
Nu 10:30 He answered, "**N**, I will not go; I am H4202
Nu 11: 5 the fish we ate in Egypt **at n cost**— H2855
Nu 11:32 **N** one gathered **less than** ten homers H5070
Nu 14:23 **N** one who has treated me with contempt H4202
Nu 16:14 men like slaves? **N**, we will not come!" H4202
Nu 16:40 the Israelites that **n** one except a H4202
Nu 18: 4 **n** one else may come near where you H4202
Nu 18:20 "You will have **n** inheritance in their land H4202
Nu 18:23 They will receive **n** inheritance among the H4202
Nu 18:24 'They will have **n** inheritance among the H4202
Nu 20: 2 Now there was **n** water for the community H4202
Nu 20: 5 It has **n** grain or figs, grapevines or H4202
Nu 20: 5 And **there is n** water to drink! H401
Nu 21: 5 the wilderness? **There is n** bread! There is H401
Nu 21: 5 **There is n** water! And we H401
Nu 21:35 his whole army, leaving them **n** survivors. H1194
Nu 22:26 place where **there was n** room to turn, H401
Nu 22:30 habit of doing this to you?" "**N**," he said. H4202
Nu 23:21 "**N** misfortune is seen in Jacob, no misery H4202
Nu 23:21 in Jacob, **n** misery observed in Israel. H4202
Nu 23:23 There is **n** divination against Jacob, no H4202
Nu 23:23 **n** evil omens against Israel. H4202
Nu 26:33 Zelophehad son of Hepher had **n** sons; he H4202
Nu 26:62 they received **n** inheritance among H4202
Nu 27: 3 he died for his own sin and left **n** sons. H4202
Nu 27: 4 from his clan because he had **n** son? H401
Nu 27: 8 'If a man dies and leaves **n** son, give his H401
Nu 27: 9 If he has **n** daughter, give his inheritance to H401
Nu 27:10 If he has **n** brothers, give his inheritance to H401
Nu 27:11 If his father had **n** brothers, give his H401
Nu 28:18 assembly and do **n** regular work. H4202+3972
Nu 28:25 assembly and do **n** regular work. H4202+3972
Nu 28:26 assembly and do **n** regular work. H4202+3972
Nu 29: 1 assembly and do **n** regular work. H4202+3972
Nu 29: 7 deny yourselves and do **n** work. H4202+3972
Nu 29:12 assembly and do **n** regular work. H4202+3972
Nu 29:35 assembly and do **n** regular work. H4202+3972
Nu 33:14 where there was **n** water for the people to H4202
Nu 35:23 not an enemy and **n** harm was intended, H4202
Nu 35:30 But **n** one is to be put to death on the H4202
Nu 36: 7 **N** inheritance in Israel is to pass from one H4202
Nu 36: 9 **N** inheritance may pass from one tribe to H4202
Dt 1:35 "**N** one from this evil generation shall see H561
Dt 1:45 he paid **n** attention to your weeping H4202
Dt 2:34 women and children. We left **n** survivors. H4202
Dt 3: 3 We struck them down, leaving **n** survivors. H1194
Dt 4:12 heard the sound of words but saw **n** form; H401
Dt 4:15 You saw **n** form of any kind the day the H4202
Dt 4:35 LORD is God; besides him **there is n** other. H401
Dt 4:39 on the earth below. **There is n** other. H401
Dt 5: 7 "You shall have **n** other gods before me. H4202
Dt 7: 2 Make **n** treaty with them, and show them H4202
Dt 7: 2 treaty with them, and show them **n** mercy. H4202
Dt 7:24 **N** one will be able to stand up against H4202
Dt 9: 4 **N**, it is on account of the wickedness of NDT
Dt 9: 9 I ate **n** bread and drank no water. H4202
Dt 9: 9 I ate no bread and drank **n** water. H4202
Dt 9:18 I ate **n** bread and drank no water H4202
Dt 9:18 I ate no bread and drank **n** water H4202
Dt 10: 9 the Levites have **n** share or inheritance H4202
Dt 10:17 who shows **n** partiality and accepts no H4202
Dt 10:17 shows no partiality and accepts **n** bribes. H4202
Dt 11:17 rain and the ground will yield **n** produce, H4202
Dt 11:25 **N** one will be able to stand against you H4202
Dt 12:12 your towns who have **n** allotment or H401
Dt 13: 8 Show them **n** pity. Do not spare H4202
Dt 13:11 and **n** *one* among you will do such an evil H4202
Dt 14:27 they have **n** allotment or inheritance of H401
Dt 14:29 who have **n** allotment or inheritance of their H401
Dt 15: 4 there need be **n** poor people among you H4202
Dt 16: 4 Let **n** yeast be found in your possession in H4202
Dt 16: 8 to the LORD your God and do **n** work. H4202
Dt 16:16 **N** one should appear before the LORD H4202
Dt 17: 6 **n** one is to be put to death on the H4202
Dt 18: 1 are to have **n** allotment or inheritance with H4202
Dt 18: 2 They shall have **n** inheritance among their H4202
Dt 18:10 Let **n** one be found among you who H4202
Dt 19:13 Show **n** pity. You must purge from Israel H4202
Dt 19:21 Show **n** pity: life for life, eye for eye, tooth H4202
Dt 22:20 charge is true and **n** proof of the young H4202
Dt 22:26 she has committed **n** sin deserving death. H401
Dt 22:27 screamed, **there was n** one to rescue her. H401
Dt 23: 1 **N** one who has been emasculated by H4202
Dt 23: 2 **N** one born of a forbidden marriage nor H4202
Dt 23: 3 **N** Ammonite or Moabite or any of their H4202
Dt 23:17 **N** Israelite man or woman is to become a H4202
Dt 25:12 you shall cut off her hand. Show her **n** pity. H4202
Dt 25:18 lagging behind; they had **n** fear of God. H4202
Dt 28:26 and **there will be n** one to frighten them H401
Dt 28:29 robbed, with **n** one to rescue you. H401
Dt 28:31 your enemies, and **n** one will rescue them. H401
Dt 28:51 They will leave you **n** grain, new wine H4202
Dt 28:54 you *will* **have n compassion** on his H8317+6524
Dt 28:65 those nations you will find **n** repose, H4202

Dt 28:65 **n** resting place for the sole of your foot. H4202
Dt 28:68 female slaves, but **n** one will buy you. H401
Dt 29: 6 You ate **n** bread and drank no wine or H4202
Dt 29: 6 ate no bread and drank **n** wine or other H4202
Dt 29:18 Make sure there is **n** man or woman, clan H7153
Dt 29:18 make sure there is **n** root among you that H7153
Dt 29:23 **n** vegetation growing on it. H4202+3972
Dt 30:14 **N**, the word is very near you; it is in your H3954
Dt 31: 2 years old and I am **n** longer able to lead H4202
Dt 32: 4 A faithful God who does **n** wrong, upright H401
Dt 32:12 alone led him; **n** foreign god was with him. H401
Dt 32:21 jealous by what is **n** god and angered me H4202
Dt 32:21 by a nation that has **n understanding**. H5572
Dt 32:28 **there is n** discernment in them. H401
Dt 32:36 their strength is gone and **n** one is left, H700
Dt 32:39 I myself am he! **There is n** god besides me H401
Dt 32:39 **n** one can deliver out of my hand. H401
Dt 33: 9 mother, 'I have **n** regard for them. H4202
Dt 33:11 against him, his foes **till** they rise **n more**." H4946
Dt 33:26 "**There is n** *one* like the God of Jeshurun H401
Dt 34: 6 to this day **n** one knows where his H4202
Dt 34:10 **n** prophet has risen in Israel like Moses H4202
Dt 34:12 For **n** one has ever shown the mighty power NDT
Jos 1: 5 **N** one will be able to stand against you all H4202
Jos 4:18 **N sooner** had they set their feet on the dry ground **than** H3869
Jos 5: 1 in fear and they **n** longer had the courage H4202
Jos 5:12 there was **n** longer any manna for the H4202
Jos 6: 1 **N** one went out and no one came in. H401
Jos 6: 1 No one went out and **n** one came in. H401
Jos 8:20 they had **n** chance to escape in any H4202
Jos 8:31 on which **n** iron tool had been used. H4202
Jos 10:21 **n** one uttered a word against the H4202
Jos 10:28 He left **n** survivors. And he did H4202
Jos 10:30 He left **n** survivors there. H4202
Jos 10:33 his army—until **n** survivors were left. H1194
Jos 10:37 They left **n** survivors. Just as at H4202
Jos 10:39 They left **n** survivors. They did H4202
Jos 10:40 He left **n** survivors. He totally H4202
Jos 11: 8 on the east, until **n** survivors were left. H1194
Jos 11:22 **N** Anakites were left in Israelite territory H4202
Jos 13:14 to the tribe of Levi he gave **n** inheritance, H4202
Jos 13:33 Moses had given **n** inheritance; the LORD H4202
Jos 14: 4 The Levites received **n** share of the land H4202
Jos 17: 3 Manasseh, had **n** sons but only daughters H4202
Jos 22:24 "**N**! We did it for fear that some day your H4202
Jos 22:25 You have **n** share in the LORD.' H401
Jos 22:27 say to ours, 'You have **n** share in the LORD. H401
Jos 22:33 And they talked **n** *more* about going to H4202
Jos 23: 9 to this day **n** one has been able to H4202
Jos 23:13 LORD your God will **n** longer drive out H4202
Jos 24:21 said to Joshua, "**N**! We will serve the LORD. H4202
Jdg 2:14 whom they were **n** longer able to resist. H4202
Jdg 2:21 I will **n** longer drive out before them any H4202
Jdg 3:28 they allowed **n** one to cross over. H4202
Jdg 4:20 asks you, 'Is anyone in there?' say '**N**.'" H401
Jdg 5:19 of Megiddo, they took **n** plunder of silver. H4202
Jdg 7:12 Their camels could **n** more be counted H401
Jdg 8:33 **N sooner** had Gideon died **than** the H3869+889
Jdg 10: 6 forsook the LORD and **n** *longer* served him, H4202
Jdg 10:13 other gods, so I will **n** longer save you. H4202
Jdg 10:16 he *could* **bear** Israel's misery **n longer**. H7918
Jdg 11:28 paid **n** attention to the message Jephthah H4202
Jdg 11:35 his clothes and cried, "**Oh n**, my daughter! H177
Jdg 12: 5 you an Ephraimite?" If he replied, "**N**," H4202
Jdg 13: 4 to it that you drink **n** wine or other H440
Jdg 13: 7 drink **n** wine or other fermented drink and H440
Jdg 16: 2 *They* **made n move** during the night H3087
Jdg 16:17 "**N** razor has ever been used on my head," H4202
Jdg 17: 6 In those days Israel had **n** king; everyone H401
Jdg 18: 1 In those days Israel had **n** king. And in H401
Jdg 18: 7 the Sidonians and had **n** relationship with H401
Jdg 18:28 **There was n** one to rescue them because H401
Jdg 18:28 from Sidon and had **n** relationship with H401
Jdg 19: 1 In those days Israel had **n** king. Now a H401
Jdg 19:12 His master replied, "**N**. We won't go into NDT
Jdg 19:15 **n** one took them in for the night. H401
Jdg 19:18 **N** one has taken me in for the night H401
Jdg 19:23 outside and said to them, "**N**, my friends, H440
Jdg 19:28 But **there was n** answer. Then the H401
Jdg 20: 8 of us will go home. **N**, not one of us will NDT
Jdg 21: 8 They discovered that **n** one from Jabesh H4202
Jdg 21:25 In those days Israel had **n** king; everyone H401
Ru 1:13 unmarried for them? **N**, my daughters. It is H440
Ru 3:14 "**N** one must know that a woman came to H440
Ru 4: 4 For **n** one has the right to do it except you H401
1Sa 1:11 **n** razor will ever be used on his head." H4202
1Sa 1:18 her face was **n** longer downcast. H4202
1Sa 2: 2 "**There is n** one holy like the LORD; there is H401
1Sa 2: 2 like the LORD; **there is n** *one* besides you H401
1Sa 2: 2 besides you; **there is n** Rock like our God. H401
1Sa 2: 5 who were hungry are hungry **n more**. H2532
1Sa 2:12 scoundrels; they had **n** regard for the LORD. H4202
1Sa 2:16 would answer, "**N**, hand it over now; H4202
1Sa 2:24 **N**, my sons; the report I hear spreading H440
1Sa 2:31 so that **n** one in it will reach old age, H4946
1Sa 2:32 **n** one in your family line will ever reach H4202
1Sa 4: 7 "**Oh n**! Nothing like this has H208
1Sa 8:19 to listen to Samuel. "**N**!" they said. H4202
1Sa 9: 7 We have **n** gift to take to the man of God H401
1Sa 10:19 And you have said, '**N**, appoint a king H4202
1Sa 10:24 **There is n** *one* like him among all the H401
1Sa 10:27 despised him and brought him **n** gifts. H4202
1Sa 11: 3 if **n** one comes to rescue us H401
1Sa 11:11 so that **n** two of them were left together. H4202
1Sa 11:13 "**N** one will be put to death today H4202
1Sa 12:12 you said to me, '**N**, we want a king to rule H4202
1Sa 12:21 They can do you **n** good, nor can they H4202
1Sa 14: 3 **N** one was aware that Jonathan had left H4202
1Sa 14:26 yet **n** one put his hand to his mouth H401
1Sa 17:32 "Let **n** one lose heart on account of this H440
1Sa 18:25 'The king wants **n** other price for the bride H401
1Sa 19: 5 like David by killing him **for n reason**?" H2855
1Sa 20:21 LORD lives, you are safe; **there is n** danger. H401
1Sa 21: 1 are you alone? Why is **n** one with you?" H401
1Sa 21: 2 '**N** one is to know anything about the H440
1Sa 21: 6 since there was **n** bread there except the H4202
1Sa 21: 9 **there is n** sword here but that one. H401
1Sa 22: 8 **N** one tells me when my son makes a H401
1Sa 25:17 a wicked man that **n** one can talk to him." H4946
1Sa 25:25 Please pay **n** attention, my lord, to that H440
1Sa 25:28 **n** wrongdoing will be found in you as H4202
1Sa 26:12 **N** one saw or knew about it, nor did H401
1Sa 27: 4 to Gath, he **n** longer searched for him. H4202
1Sa 28:15 He **n** longer answers me, either by H4202
1Sa 29: 3 until now, I have found **n** fault in him." H4202
1Sa 29: 6 I have found **n** fault in you, but the H4202
1Sa 30: 4 aloud until they had **n** strength left to weep H401
1Sa 30:23 David replied, "**N**, my brothers, you must H4202
2Sa 1:21 may **n** showers fall on your terraced fields. NDT
2Sa 1:21 shield of Saul—**n longer** rubbed with oil. H1172
2Sa 2:28 to a halt; they **n** longer pursued Israel H4202
2Sa 3:22 But Abner **was n** *longer* with David in H401
2Sa 3:37 that the king had **n** part in the murder of H4202
2Sa 6:23 of Saul had **n** children to the day H4202
2Sa 7:10 of their own and **n** longer be disturbed. H4202
2Sa 7:22 **There is n** *one* like you, and there is no H401
2Sa 7:22 like you, and **there is n** God but you, as H401
2Sa 9: 3 "Is there **n** one still alive from the house of H700
2Sa 12: 6 he did such a thing and had **n** pity." H4202
2Sa 13:12 "**N**, my brother!" she said to him. "Don't H440
2Sa 13:16 "**N**!" she said to him. "Sending me away H440
2Sa 13:25 "**N**, my son," the king replied. "All of us H440
2Sa 14: 6 **n** one was there to separate them. H401
2Sa 14:19 **n** one can turn to the right or to the left H561
2Sa 14:25 of his foot there was **n** blemish in him. H4202
2Sa 15: 3 but **there is n** representative of the king to H401
2Sa 16:18 said to Absalom, "**N**, the one chosen by H4202
2Sa 17:19 **N** one knew anything about it. H4202
2Sa 17:20 The men searched but found **n** *one*, so H4202
2Sa 17:22 **n** one was left who had not crossed the H4202
2Sa 18:18 "I have **n** son to carry on the memory of my H401
2Sa 20: 1 shouted, "We have **n** share in David, no H401
2Sa 20: 1 no share in David, **n** part in Jesse's son! H4202
2Sa 20: 3 them but had **n** sexual relations with H4202
2Sa 21: 4 "We have **n** right to demand silver or gold H401
2Sa 21: 5 decimated and have **n** place anywhere in H4946
2Sa 22:42 help, but **there was n** one to save them H401
2Sa 24:24 replied to Araunah, "**N**, I insist on paying H4202
1Ki 1: 4 the king had **n** sexual relations with H4202
1Ki 2:30 But he answered, "**N**, I will die here." H4202
1Ki 3:13 you will have **n** equal among kings. H4202
1Ki 3:18 **there was n** one in the house but the two H401
1Ki 3:22 other woman said, "**N**! The living one is H4202
1Ki 3:22 first one insisted, "**N**! The dead one is H4202
1Ki 3:23 your son is dead,' while that one says, '**N**! H4202
1Ki 5: 4 and **there is n** adversary or disaster. H401
1Ki 5: 6 You know that we have **n** one so skilled in H401
1Ki 6: 7 were used, and **n** hammer, chisel or any H4202
1Ki 6:18 was cedar; **n** stone was to be seen. H401
1Ki 8:23 **there is n** God like you in heaven above H401
1Ki 8:35 shut up and there is **n** rain because your H4202
1Ki 8:46 for **there is n** one who does not sin H401
1Ki 8:60 the LORD is God and that **there is n** other. H401
1Ki 15:22 to all Judah—**n** *one* was exempt—and H401
1Ki 17: 7 there had been **n** rain in the land. H4202
1Ki 18:26 But **there was n** response; no one H401
1Ki 18:26 there was no response; **n** one answered. H401
1Ki 18:29 But **there was n** response, no one H401
1Ki 18:29 was no response, **n** one answered, no one H401
1Ki 18:29 no one answered, **n** *one* paid attention. H401
1Ki 19: 4 I am **n** better than my ancestors. H4202
1Ki 21:15 He **is n** *longer* alive, but dead. H401
1Ki 22: 1 For three years **there was n** war between H401
1Ki 22: 7 "**Is there n longer** a prophet of the LORD H401
1Ki 22:17 LORD said, 'These people have **n** master. H4202
1Ki 22:47 **There was** then **n** king in Edom; a provincial H401
2Ki 1: 3 'Is it because **there is n** God in Israel H1172+401
2Ki 1: 6 Is it because **there is n** God in Israel H1172+401
2Ki 1:16 Is it because **there is n** God in Israel H1172+401
2Ki 1:17 Because Ahaziah had **n** son, Joram H4202
2Ki 2:12 And Elisha saw him **n** more. Then he took H4202
2Ki 2:16 in some valley." "**N**," Elisha replied, "do NDT
2Ki 3: 9 the army had **n** *more* water for themselves H4202
2Ki 3:11 "**Is there n** prophet of the LORD here H401
2Ki 3:13 "**N**," the king of Israel answered, "because H440
2Ki 4:14 "She has **n** son, and her husband H401
2Ki 4:16 a son in your arms." "**N**, my lord!" she H440
2Ki 4:31 but **there was n** sound or response. H401
2Ki 4:39 though **n** one knew what they were. H4202
2Ki 5:15 "Now I know that **there is n** God in all the H401
2Ki 6: 5 into the water. "**Oh n**, my lord!" he cried H177
2Ki 6:15 "**Oh n**, my lord! What shall H177
2Ki 7: 5 the edge of the camp, **n** one was there, H401
2Ki 7:10 the Aramean camp and **n** one was there— H401
2Ki 9:10 ground at Jezreel, and **n** one will bury her. H401
2Ki 9:37 Jezreel, so that **n** one will be able to say H4202
2Ki 10:11 his priests, leaving him **n** survivor. H1194
2Ki 10:14 forty-two of them. He left **n** survivor. H4202
2Ki 10:19 See that **n** one is missing, because I am H440
2Ki 10:19 who fails to come will **n** longer live." H4202
2Ki 10:23 around and see **that n** one who serves the H7153
2Ki 10:25 in and kill them; let **n** one escape." So they H440
2Ki 12: 7 Take **n** *more* money from your treasurers H440
2Ki 14:26 suffering; **there was n** one to help them. H401
2Ki 15:20 withdrew and stayed in the land **n** longer. H4202
2Ki 17: 4 he **n** longer paid tribute to the king of H4202
2Ki 18: 5 There was **n** one like him among all the H4202
2Ki 19: 3 moment of birth and **there is n** strength to H401
2Ki 23:10 so **n** one could use it to sacrifice their son H1194
2Ki 25: 3 that there was **n** food for the people H4202
1Ch 2:34 Sheshan had **n** sons—only daughters. H4202
1Ch 15: 2 "**N** *one* but the Levites may carry the ark of H4202
1Ch 16:21 He allowed **n** one to oppress them; for H4202
1Ch 16:22 my anointed ones; do my prophets **n** harm." H440
1Ch 17: 9 of their own and **n** longer be disturbed. H4202
1Ch 17:20 "**There is n** *one* like you, LORD, and there is H401
1Ch 17:20 and **there is n** God but you, as we H401
1Ch 21:24 replied to Araunah, "**N**, I insist on paying H4202
1Ch 23:17 Eliezer had **n** other sons, but the sons of H4202
1Ch 23:26 the Levites **n** longer need to carry the H401
1Ch 24: 2 and they had **n** sons; so Eleazar and H4202
1Ch 24:28 Eleazar, who had **n** sons. H4202
1Ch 29:25 splendor such as **n** king over Israel ever H4202
2Ch 1:12 such as **n** king who was before you ever H4202
2Ch 6:14 **there is n** God like you in heaven or on H401
2Ch 6:26 shut up and there is **n** rain because your H4202
2Ch 6:36 for **there is n** one who does not sin H401
2Ch 7:13 up the heavens so that there is **n** rain, H4202
2Ch 14: 6 **N** *one* was at war with him during those H401
2Ch 14:11 **there is n** *one* like you to help the H401
2Ch 15:19 There was **n** *more* war until the thirty-fifth H4202
2Ch 18: 6 "**Is there n longer** a prophet of the LORD H401
2Ch 18:16 LORD said, 'These people have **n** master. H4202
2Ch 19: 7 with the LORD our God **there is n** injustice H401
2Ch 20: 6 in your hand, and **n** *one* can withstand you. H401
2Ch 20:12 For we have **n** power to face this vast army H401
2Ch 20:24 lying on the ground; **n** *one* had escaped. H401
2Ch 21:19 His people made **n** funeral fire in his H4202
2Ch 21:20 passed away, to **n** *one's* regret, and was H4202
2Ch 22: 9 So **there was n** *one* in the house of H401
2Ch 23: 6 **N** one is to enter the temple of the LORD H440
2Ch 23:19 temple so that **n** one who was in any H4202
2Ch 32:15 **n** god of any nation or kingdom H4202+3972
2Ch 33:10 his people, but they paid **n** attention. H4202
2Ch 36:16 his people and **there was n** remedy. H401
Ezr 3:13 **N** one could distinguish the sound of the H401
Ezr 4: 3 "You have **n** part with us in building a H4202
Ezr 4:13 are restored, **n** *more* taxes, tribute or A10379
Ezr 7:24 know that you have **n** authority to A10379
Ezr 8:15 the priests, I found **n** Levites there. H4202
Ezr 9:14 leaving us **n** remnant or survivor? H401
Ezr 10: 6 he ate **n** food and drank no water H4202
Ezr 10: 6 he ate no food and drank **n** water H4202
Ne 2:12 **There were n** mounts with me except the H401
Ne 2:17 we will **n** longer be in disgrace. H4202
Ne 2:20 you have **n** share in Jerusalem or any claim H401
Ne 9:30 Yet they paid **n** attention, so you gave H4202
Ne 13: 1 found written that **n** Ammonite or H4202
Ne 13:19 at the gates so that **n** load could be H4202
Ne 13:21 that time on they **n** *longer* came on the H4202
Ne 13:26 many nations there was **n** king like him. H4202
Est 1: 8 was allowed to **drink with n restrictions**, H9276
Est 1:18 There will be **n end** *of* disrespect H3869+1896
Est 4: 2 because **n** one clothed in sackcloth was H401
Est 5:13 But all this gives me **n** satisfaction as long H401
Est 7: 4 because **n** such distress would justify H401
Est 8: 8 **n** document written in the king's name H401
Est 9: 2 **N** one could stand against them, because H4202
Job 1: 8 **There is n** one on earth like him; he is H401
Job 2: 3 **There is n** one on earth like him; he is H401
Job 2:13 **N** one said a word to him, because they H401
Job 3: 4 not care about it; may **n** light shine on it. H440
Job 3: 7 may **n** shout of joy be heard in it. H440
Job 3:18 they **n** *longer* hear the slave driver's shout. H4202
Job 3:26 I have **n** peace, no quietness; I have no H4202
Job 3:26 I have no peace, **n** quietness; I have no H4202
Job 3:26 no quietness; I have **n** rest, but only H4202
Job 4: 9 at the blast of his anger *they are* **n more**. H3983
Job 4:18 If God places **n** trust in his servants, if he H4202
Job 5:12 so that their hands achieve **n** success. H4202
Job 5:19 in seven **n** harm will touch you. H4202
Job 6: 3 **n wonder** my words have been H6584+4027
Job 6:21 Now you too have proved to be of **n** help H4202
Job 7: 8 that now sees me will see me **n** *longer*; H4202
Job 7: 8 you will look for me, but I will **be n more**. H401
Job 7:10 his place will know him **n** more. H4202
Job 7:16 Let me alone; my days have **n meaning**. H2039
Job 7:21 will search for me, but I will **be n more**." H401
Job 8:11 papyrus grow tall where there is **n** marsh? H4202
Job 8:22 the tents of the wicked will **be n more**." H401
Job 9:17 multiply my wounds **for n reason**. H2855
Job 9:21 am blameless, I have **n** concern for myself H4202
Job 9:34 so that his terror would frighten me **n** *more*. H440
Job 10: 7 not guilty and that **n** one can rescue me H401
Job 10:21 before I go to the place of **n** return, to the H4202

N

Job 11: 3 Will **n** one rebuke you when you mock? H401
Job 11:12 can **n more** become wise **than** a wild H2256
Job 11:14 your hand and allow **n** evil to dwell in your H440
Job 11:19 lie down, with **n** one to make you afraid H401
Job 12:25 They grope in darkness with **n** light; he H4202
Job 13:16 **n** godless person would dare come H4202
Job 14: 4 what is pure from the impure? **N** one! H4202
Job 14:10 he breathes his last and is **n more**. H361
Job 14:12 till the heavens are **n more**, people will H1194
Job 15: 3 with speeches that have **n** value? H4202
Job 15:15 If God places **n** trust in his holy ones, if H4202
Job 15:19 land was given when **n** foreigners moved H4202
Job 15:28 towns and houses where **n** one lives, H4202
Job 15:29 He will **n** *longer* be rich and his wealth H4202
Job 16:22 pass before I take the path of **n** return. H4202
Job 18:17 the earth; he has **n** name in the land. H4202
Job 18:19 He has **n** offspring or descendants among H4202
Job 18:19 his people, **n** survivor where once he lived. H401
Job 19: 7 I get **n** response; though I call for help H4202
Job 19: 7 though I call for help, **there is n** justice. H401
Job 20: 8 dream he flies away, **n** *more* to be found H4202
Job 20: 9 his place will look on him **n** more. H4202
Job 20:20 "Surely he will have **n** respite from his H4202
Job 21:14 We have **n** desire to know your ways. H4202
Job 21:29 Have you paid **n** regard to their accounts H4202
Job 22: 6 security from your relatives **for n reason**; H2855
Job 22: 7 You gave **n** water to the weary and you H4202
Job 23: 6 **N**, he would not press charges against me H4202
Job 23: 9 to the south, I catch **n** glimpse of him. H4202
Job 24:12 But God charges **n** one with wrongdoing. H4202
Job 24:15 he thinks, '**N** eye will see me,' and he H4202
Job 24:18 so that **n** one goes to the vineyards. H4202
Job 24:20 the wicked are **n** longer remembered but H4202
Job 24:21 to the widow they show **n** kindness. H4202
Job 24:22 established, they have **n** assurance of life. H4202
Job 27:19 will do so **n** more; when he opens his H4202
Job 28: 7 **N** bird of prey knows that hidden path, no H4202
Job 28: 7 hidden path, **n** falcon's eye has seen it. H4202
Job 28: 8 not set foot on it, and **n** lion prowls there. H4202
Job 28:13 **N** mortal comprehends its worth; it cannot H4202
Job 29:22 spoken, they spoke **n** more; my words fell H4202
Job 30:13 in destroying me. '**N** one can help him,' H4202
Job 30:24 "Surely **n** one lays a hand on a broken H4202
Job 31:32 **n** stranger had to spend the night in H4202
Job 32: 3 they had found **n** way to refute Job, H4202
Job 32:15 are dismayed and have **n** more to say; H4202
Job 32:16 now that they stand there with **n** reply? H4202
Job 32:21 I will show **n** partiality, nor will I flatter H440
Job 33: 7 **N** fear of me should alarm you, nor H4202
Job 33: 9 am pure, I have done **n** wrong; I am clean H1172
Job 33:13 to him that he responds to **n** one's words? H4202
Job 33:14 now another—though **n** one perceives it. H4202
Job 34: 9 'There is **n** profit in trying to please God. H4202
Job 34:19 who shows **n** partiality to princes and H4202
Job 34:22 **There is n** deep shadow, no utter darkness H401
Job 34:22 is no deep shadow, **n** utter darkness, where H401
Job 34:23 God has **n** need to examine people H4202
Job 34:27 him and had **n** regard for any of his H4202
Job 34:31 'I am guilty but will offend **n** *more*. H4202
Job 35:10 But **n** one says, 'Where is God my Maker H4202
Job 35:13 the Almighty pays **n** attention to it. H4202
Job 36: 5 but despises **n** one; he is mighty, H4202
Job 36:18 Be careful **that n** one entices you by riches H7153
Job 37:21 Now **n** one can look at the sun, bright as H4202
Job 38:11 'This far you may come and **n** farther H4202
Job 38:26 to water a land where **n** one lives, an H4202
Job 40: 5 but I have **n** answer—twice, but I H4202
Job 40: 5 no answer—twice, but I will say **n** more." H4202
Job 41:10 **N** one is fierce enough to rouse it. H4202
Job 41:16 to the next that **n** air can pass between. H4202
Job 41:26 The sword that reaches it has **n** effect, nor H1172
Job 42: 2 **n** purpose of yours can be thwarted. H4202
Ps 6: 5 Among the dead **n** *one* proclaims your H401
Ps 7: 2 rip me to pieces with **n** one to rescue me. H401
Ps 10: 4 in all his thoughts **there is n** room for God. H401
Ps 10: 6 He swears, "**N** one will ever do me harm." H4202
Ps 12: 1 for **n** one is faithful **anymore**; those H1698
Ps 14: 1 in his heart, "**There is n** God." They are H401
Ps 14: 1 are vile; **there is n** one who does good. H401
Ps 14: 3 **there is n** one who does good H401
Ps 15: 3 whose tongue utters **n** slander, who does H4202
Ps 15: 3 slander, who does **n** wrong to a neighbor H4202
Ps 15: 3 to a neighbor, and casts **n** slur on others; H4202
Ps 16: 2 apart from you I have **n** good thing." H1153
Ps 17: 3 you will find that I have planned **n** evil H1153
Ps 18:41 help, but **there was n** one to save them H401
Ps 19: 3 They **have n** speech, they use no words; no H401
Ps 19: 3 no speech, they **use n** words; no sound is H401
Ps 19: 3 no words; **n** sound is heard from them. H1172
Ps 22: 2 do not answer, by night, but I find **n** rest. H4202
Ps 22:11 trouble is near and **there is n** one to help. H401
Ps 23: 4 I will fear **n** evil, for you are with H4202
Ps 25: 3 **N** one who hopes in you will ever be put H4202
Ps 28: 5 Because they have **n** regard for the deeds H4202
Ps 32: 2 them and in whose spirit **is n** deceit. H401
Ps 32: 9 which have **n** understanding but must be H401
Ps 33:16 **N** king is saved by the size of his army; no H401
Ps 33:16 **n** warrior escapes by his great strength. H4202
Ps 34:10 seek the LORD lack **n** good thing. H4202+3972
Ps 34:22 **n** one who takes refuge in him will be H4202
Ps 36: 1 **There is n** fear of God before their eyes. H401
Ps 37:10 the wicked will **be n more**; though you H401
Ps 37:36 he soon passed away and **was n more** H401
Ps 37:38 *there will be* **n** future for the wicked. H4162
Ps 38: 3 of your wrath **there is n** health in my body; H401
Ps 38: 3 **there is n** soundness in my bones because H401
Ps 38: 7 searing pain; **there is n** health in my body. H401
Ps 38:14 not hear, whose mouth can offer **n** reply. H401
Ps 39:13 life again before I depart and **am n more**." H401
Ps 44: 6 I put **n** trust in my bow, my sword does not H4202
Ps 44: 9 you **n** longer go out with our armies. H4202
Ps 49: 7 **N** one can redeem the life of another H4202
Ps 49: 8 life is costly, **n** payment *is* ever **enough**— H2532
Ps 50: 8 I bring **n** charges against you concerning H4202
Ps 50: 9 I have **n** need of a bull from your stall H4202
Ps 50:22 you to pieces, with **n** one to rescue you: H401
Ps 53: 1 in his heart, "**There is n** God." They are H401
Ps 53: 1 are vile; **there is n** one who does good. H401
Ps 53: 3 **there is n** one who does good H401
Ps 55:19 because they have **n** fear of God. H4202
Ps 58: 2 **N**, in your heart you devise injustice, and H677
Ps 59: 3 against me for **n** offense or sin of mine, H4202
Ps 59: 4 I have done **n** wrong, yet they are ready to H1172
Ps 59: 5 nations; show **n** mercy to wicked traitors. H440
Ps 59:13 consume them till they **are n more**. H401
Ps 60:10 rejected us and **n** *longer* go out with our H4202
Ps 63: 1 parched land where there is **n** water. H1172
Ps 69: 2 the miry depths, where **there is n** foothold. H401
Ps 69:25 let there be **n** one to dwell in their tents. H440
Ps 71:11 seize him, for **n** one will rescue him." H401
Ps 72: 7 prosperity abound till the moon is **n more**. H1172
Ps 72:12 the afflicted who have **n** one to help. H401
Ps 73: 4 They have **n** struggles; their bodies are H401
Ps 73: 7 their evil imaginations **have n limits**. H6296
Ps 74: 9 We are given **n** signs from God; no H4202
Ps 74: 9 no signs from God; **n** prophets are left, and H401
Ps 75: 4 'Boast **n** *more*,' and to the wicked, H440
Ps 75: 6 **N** *one* from the east or the west or from H4202
Ps 78:63 their young women had **n** wedding songs; H4202
Ps 79: 3 and **there is n** one to bury the dead. H401
Ps 81: 9 You shall have **n** foreign god among you H4202
Ps 83: 4 that Israel's name is remembered **n** more." H4202
Ps 84:11 **n** good thing does he withhold from those H4202
Ps 86: 8 Lord; **n** deeds can compare with yours. H401
Ps 86:14 to kill me—they have **n** regard for you. H4202
Ps 88: 5 whom you remember **n** more, who are cut H4202
Ps 91:10 **n** harm will overtake you, no disaster will H4202
Ps 91:10 **n** disaster will come near your tent. H4202
Ps 92:15 and there is **n** wickedness in him. H4202
Ps 94: 7 not see; the God of Jacob takes **n** notice." H4202
Ps 101: 3 people do; I *will* have **n** part in it. H4202
Ps 101: 7 **N** one who practices deceit will dwell in H4202
Ps 101: 7 **n** one who speaks falsely will stand in my H4202
Ps 103:16 and its place remembers it **n** more. H4202
Ps 104:35 from the earth and the wicked **be n** more. H401
Ps 105:14 He allowed **n** one to oppress them; for H4202
Ps 105:15 my anointed ones; do my prophets **n** harm." H440
Ps 105:37 from among their tribes **n** one faltered. H401
Ps 106: 7 they gave **n** thought to your miracles H4202
Ps 107: 4 finding **n** way to a city where they could H4202
Ps 107:12 stumbled, and **there was n** one to help. H401
Ps 108:11 rejected us and **n** *longer* go out with our H4202
Ps 109:12 May **n** one extend kindness to him or take H440
Ps 109:17 He found **n** pleasure in blessing—may it H4202
Ps 112: 7 They will have **n** fear of bad news; their H4202
Ps 112: 8 they will have **n** fear; in the end they H4202
Ps 119: 3 they do **n** wrong but follow his ways. H4202
Ps 119:133 to your word; let **n** sin rule over me. H440
Ps 123: 3 we have endured **n end** *of* contempt. H8041
Ps 123: 4 We have endured **n end** *of* ridicule from H8041
Ps 132: 4 I will allow **n** sleep to my eyes or slumber H561
Ps 142: 4 see, **there is n** *one* at my right hand H401
Ps 142: 4 at my right hand; **n** one is concerned for me. NDT
Ps 142: 4 I **have n** refuge; no one cares for my H6+4946
Ps 142: 4 I have no refuge; **n** one cares for my life H401
Ps 143: 2 **n** one living is righteous before you. H4202
Ps 144:14 **There will be n** breaching of walls, no H401
Ps 144:14 breaching of walls, **n** going into captivity H401
Ps 144:14 into captivity, **n** cry of distress in our streets. H401
Ps 145: 3 of praise; his greatness **n** *one* can fathom. H401
Ps 147: 5 in power; his understanding has **n** limit. H401
Ps 147:20 He has done this for **n** other nation; they H4202
Pr 1:24 listen when I call and **n** one pays attention H401
Pr 3:25 Have **n** fear of sudden disaster or of the H440
Pr 3:30 Do not accuse anyone **for n reason** H2855
Pr 3:30 when they have done you **n** harm. H4202
Pr 5: 6 She gives **n** thought to the way of life; her H7153
Pr 6: 3 and **give** your neighbor **n rest**! H8104
Pr 6: 4 Allow **n** sleep to your eyes, no slumber to H440
Pr 6: 4 to your eyes, **n** slumber to your eyelids. NDT
Pr 6: 7 It has **n** commander, no overseer or ruler, H401
Pr 6: 7 It has no commander, **n** overseer or ruler, NDT
Pr 6:29 **n** one who touches her will go H4202
Pr 6:32 a man who commits adultery **has n** sense; H2894
Pr 6:34 he will show **n** mercy when he takes H4202
Pr 7: 7 the young men, a youth who **had n** sense. H2894
Pr 8:24 When **there were n** watery depths, I was H401
Pr 8:24 when **there were n** springs overflowing with H401
Pr 9: 4 To those who **have n** sense she says, H2894
Pr 9:16 To those who have **n** sense she says, H2894
Pr 10: 2 Ill-gotten treasures have **n** lasting value H4202
Pr 10:13 is for the back of one who **has n** sense. H2894
Pr 11:12 derides their neighbor **has n** sense, H2894
Pr 11:22 beautiful woman *who* **shows n** discretion. H6073
Pr 12: 3 **N** one can be established through H4202
Pr 12: 7 The wicked are overthrown and **are n more** H401
Pr 12: 9 pretend to be somebody and **have n** food. H2894
Pr 12:11 those who chase fantasies **have n** sense. H2894
Pr 12:21 **N** harm overtakes the righteous H4202+3972
Pr 14: 4 Where **there are n** oxen, the manger is H401
Pr 14:10 **n** one else can share its joy. H4202
Pr 15:21 Folly brings joy to *one who* **has n** sense H2894
Pr 17:18 One who **has n** sense shakes hands in H2894
Pr 17:21 there is **n** joy for the parent of a godless H4202
Pr 18: 2 Fools find **n** pleasure in understanding H4202
Pr 20:14 "It's **n good**, it's no good!" says the buyer H8273
Pr 20:14 no good, it's **n good**!" says the buyer— H8273
Pr 21:10 their neighbors get **n** mercy from them. H4202
Pr 21:30 **There is n** wisdom, no insight, no plan that H401
Pr 21:30 There is no wisdom, **n** insight, no plan that H401
Pr 21:30 **n** plan that can succeed against the LORD. H401
Pr 24:20 the evildoer has **n** future hope, and H4202
Pr 24:30 vineyard of someone who **has n** sense; H2894
Pr 28: 1 The wicked flee though **n** one pursues, but H401
Pr 28: 3 is like a driving rain that leaves **n** crops. H401
Pr 28:17 in the grave; let **n** one hold them back. H440
Pr 29: 7 but the wicked have **n** such concern. H4202
Pr 29: 9 fool rages and scoffs, and **there is n** peace. H401
Pr 29:18 Where **there is n** revelation, people cast off H401
Pr 30:27 locusts have **n** king, yet they advance H401
Pr 31: 7 remember their misery **n** more. H4202
Pr 31:21 it snows, she has **n** fear for her household H4202
Ecc 1:11 **N one** remembers the former generations H401
Ecc 2:10 refused my heart **n** pleasure. H4202+4946+3972
Ecc 3:11 **n** one can fathom what God H2021+4202
Ecc 3:19 humans have **n** advantage over animals. H401
Ecc 4: 1 they have **n** comforter; power was on H401
Ecc 4: 1 oppressors—and they have **n** comforter. H401
Ecc 4: 8 **There was n** end to his toil, yet his eyes H401
Ecc 4:10 who falls and has **n** one to help them up. H401
Ecc 4:13 foolish king who **n** longer knows how to H4202
Ecc 4:16 **There was n** end to all the people who H401
Ecc 5: 4 He has **n** pleasure in fools H401
Ecc 5:12 their abundance permits them **n** sleep. H401
Ecc 6: 3 many years; yet **n** matter how long he lives NDT
Ecc 6:10 **n** one can contend with someone who is H4202
Ecc 7:14 **n** one can discover anything about their H4202
Ecc 7:20 **there is n** one on earth who is righteous H401
Ecc 7:20 **n** one who does what is right and never sins. NDT
Ecc 8: 5 obeys his command will come to **n** harm, H4202
Ecc 8: 7 Since **n** one knows the future, who can tell H401
Ecc 8: 8 As **n** one has power over the wind to H401
Ecc 8: 8 so **n** *one* has power over the time of their H401
Ecc 8: 8 As **n** *one* is discharged in time of war, so H401
Ecc 8:16 people getting **n** sleep day or night— H401
Ecc 8:17 **N** one can comprehend what goes on H4202
Ecc 8:17 **n** one can discover its meaning. H4202
Ecc 9: 1 **n** one knows whether love or hate H401
Ecc 9: 5 nothing; they have **n** further reward, and H401
Ecc 9:12 **n** one knows when their hour will come: H4202
Ecc 9:16 his words are **n** *longer* heeded. H401
Ecc 10:11 it is charmed, the charmer receives **n** fee. H401
Ecc 10:14 **N** one knows what is coming—who can H4202
Ecc 12: 1 you will say, "I find **n** pleasure in them"— H401
Ecc 12: 5 itself along and desire **n longer** *is* **stirred**. H7296
Ecc 12:12 Of making many books **there is n** end, and H401
SS 1: 3 **N wonder** the young women love H6584+4027
SS 4: 7 my darling; **there is n** flaw in you. H401
SS 8: 1 kiss you, and **n** one would despise me. H4202
Isa 1: 6 top of your head **there is n** soundness— H401
Isa 1:11 I have **n** pleasure in the blood of bulls H4202
Isa 1:31 together, with **n** one to quench the fire." H401
Isa 2: 7 gold; **there is n** end to their treasures. H401
Isa 2: 7 of horses; **there is n** end to their chariots. H401
Isa 3: 7 that day he will cry out, "I have **n** remedy. H4202
Isa 3: 7 I have **n** food or clothing in my house; do H401
Isa 5: 8 join field to field till **n** space is left and you H700
Isa 5:12 they have **n** regard for the deeds of H4202
Isa 5:12 **n** respect for the work of his hands. H4202
Isa 5:29 prey and carry it off with **n** one to rescue. H401
Isa 7:25 you will **n** *longer* go there for fear of the H4202
Isa 8:20 to this word, they have **n** light of dawn. H401
Isa 9: 1 there will be **n** *more* gloom for those who H4202
Isa 9: 7 government and peace **there will be n** end. H401
Isa 9:17 the Lord will take **n** pleasure in the young H4202
Isa 10:20 will **n** longer rely on him who struck them H4202
Isa 13:17 care for silver and have **n** delight in gold. H4202
Isa 13:18 they will have **n** mercy on infants H4202
Isa 13:20 there **n** nomads will pitch their tents H4202
Isa 13:20 there **n** shepherds will rest their flocks. H4202
Isa 14: 8 laid low, **n** one comes to cut us down." H4202
Isa 16:10 **n** one sings or shouts in the vineyards H4202
Isa 16:10 **n** one treads out wine at the presses H4202
Isa 16:12 goes to her shrine to pray, it is to **n** avail. H4202
Isa 17: 1 Damascus *will* **n longer be** a city H6073+4946
Isa 17: 2 lie down, with **n** one to make them afraid. H401
Isa 17: 8 they will have **n** regard for the H4202
Isa 19: 7 parched, will blow away and **be n more**. H401
Isa 22:22 what he opens **n** one can shut, and H401
Isa 22:22 and what he shuts **n** one can open. H401
Isa 23:10 Tarshish, for you **n** longer have a harbor. H401
Isa 23:12 He said, "**N** more of your reveling, Virgin H4202
Isa 23:12 to Cyprus; even there you will find **n** rest." H4202
Isa 23:13 this people that is now **of n account**! H4202
Isa 24: 9 **N** *longer* do they drink wine with a song H4202
Isa 25: 2 the foreigners' stronghold a city **n more**; it H4946

Book	Ref	Context	Code
Isa	26:14	they live **n** *more*; their spirits do	H1153
Isa	26:21	the earth will conceal its slain **n** longer.	H4202
Isa	27: 3	day and night **so that n** one may harm it.	H7153
Isa	27: 9	**n** Asherah poles or incense altars will be	H4202
Isa	27:11	so their Maker has **n** compassion on them,	H4202
Isa	27:11	their Creator shows them **n** favor.	H4202
Isa	29:22	"**N** longer will Jacob be ashamed; no	H4202
Isa	29:22	**n** longer will their faces grow pale.	H4202
Isa	30:10	say to the seers, "See **n** more visions!"	H4202
Isa	30:10	"Give us **n** more visions of what is right!	H4202
Isa	30:16	You said, '**N**, we will flee on horses.'	H4202
Isa	30:19	live in Jerusalem, you will weep **n** more.	H4202
Isa	30:20	your teachers will be hidden **n** more; with	H4202
Isa	31: 8	"Assyria will fall by **n** human sword;	H4202
Isa	32: 3	of those who see will **n** longer be closed,	H4202
Isa	32: 5	**N** longer will the fool be called noble	H4202
Isa	33: 8	are deserted, **n** travelers *are* on the roads.	H8697
Isa	33: 8	are despised, **n** one is respected.	H4202
Isa	33:19	will see those arrogant people **n** *more*,	H4202
Isa	33:21	**N** galley with oars will ride them, no	H1153
Isa	33:21	ride them, **n** mighty ship will sail them.	H4202
Isa	33:24	**N** one living in Zion will say, "I am ill";	H1153
Isa	34:10	**n** one will ever pass through it again.	H401
Isa	35: 9	**N** lion will be there, nor any ravenous	H4202
Isa	37: 3	moment of birth and **there is n** strength to	H401
Isa	38:11	**n** longer will I look on my fellow man	H4202
Isa	40:24	**N sooner** are they planted, no	H677+1153
Isa	40:24	planted, **n sooner** are they sown	H677+1153
Isa	40:24	**n sooner** do they take root in the	H677+1153
Isa	40:28	his understanding **n** one can fathom.	H401
Isa	41:26	**N** one told of this, no one foretold it, no	H401
Isa	41:26	No one told of this, **n** one foretold it, no	H401
Isa	41:26	**n** one heard any words from you.	H401
Isa	41:28	I look but **there is n** one—no one among	H401
Isa	41:28	**n** one among the gods to give counsel	H401
Isa	41:28	**n** one to give answer when I ask them.	NDT
Isa	42:20	but you pay **n** attention; your ears	H4202
Isa	42:22	plunder, with **n** one to rescue them	H401
Isa	42:22	been made loot, with **n** one to say, "Send	H401
Isa	43:10	Before me **n** god was formed, nor will	H4202
Isa	43:11	and apart from me **there is n** savior.	H401
Isa	43:13	**N** one can deliver out of my hand	H401
Isa	43:25	and remembers your sins **n** *more*.	H4202
Isa	44: 6	I am the last; apart from me **there is n** God.	H401
Isa	44: 8	any God besides me? **N**, there is no other	NDT
Isa	44: 8	No, **there is n** other Rock;	H401
Isa	44:12	he drinks **n** water and grows faint.	H4202
Isa	44:19	**N** one stops to think, no one has the	H4202
Isa	44:19	**n** one has the knowledge or	H4202
Isa	45: 5	am the LORD, and **there is n** other; apart	H401
Isa	45: 5	is no other; apart from me **there is n** God.	H401
Isa	45: 6	I am the LORD, and **there is n** other.	H401
Isa	45: 9	your work say, 'The potter has **n** hands'?	H401
Isa	45:14	is with you, and **there is n** other; there is no	H401
Isa	45:14	there is no other; there is **n** other god.	H700
Isa	45:18	"I am the LORD, and **there is n** other.	H401
Isa	45:21	And **there is n** God apart from me,	H401
Isa	45:22	for I am God, and **there is n** other.	H401
Isa	46: 9	I am God, and **there is n** other; I am God	H401
Isa	47: 1	**N** more will you be called tender or	H4202
Isa	47: 3	I will take vengeance; I will spare **n** one."	H4202
Isa	47: 5	**n** more will you be called queen of	H4202
Isa	47: 6	and you showed them **n** mercy.	H4202
Isa	47:10	have said, '**N** one sees me.	H401
Isa	48:22	"**There is n** peace," says the LORD, "for the	H401
Isa	49:15	her breast and have **n** compassion on the	H4946
Isa	50: 2	why **was there n** one? When I	H401
Isa	50: 2	I called, why **was there n** one to answer?	H401
Isa	50:10	in the dark, who has **n** light, trust in the	H401
Isa	52:11	Touch **n** unclean thing! Come	H440
Isa	53: 2	He had **n** beauty or majesty to attract us	H4202
Isa	53: 9	though he had done **n** violence, nor was	H4202
Isa	54: 4	youth and remember **n** more the reproach	H4202
Isa	54:17	**n** weapon forged against you will	H4202+3972
Isa	55: 1	and you who have **n** money, come,	H401
Isa	56: 3	Let **n** foreigner who is bound to the LORD	H440
Isa	56: 3	And let **n** eunuch complain, "I am only a	H440
Isa	57: 1	and **n** one takes it to heart	H401
Isa	57: 1	**n** one understands that the righteous	H401
Isa	57:21	"**There is n** peace," says my God, "for the	H401
Isa	59: 4	**N** one calls for justice; no one pleads a	H401
Isa	59: 4	**n** one pleads a case with integrity.	H401
Isa	59: 8	not know; **there is n** justice in their paths.	H401
Isa	59: 8	**n** one who walks along them will know	H4202
Isa	59:15	was displeased that **there was n** justice.	H401
Isa	59:16	He saw that **there was n** one, he was	H401
Isa	59:16	appalled that **there was n** one to intervene	H401
Isa	60:15	hated, with **n** one traveling through,	H401
Isa	60:18	**N** longer will violence be heard in your	H4202
Isa	60:19	The sun will **n** more be your light by day	H4202
Isa	60:20	your moon will wane **n** *more*; the	H4202
Isa	62: 4	**N** longer will they call you Deserted, or	H4202
Isa	62: 6	call on the LORD, give yourselves **n** rest,	H440
Isa	62: 7	give him **n** rest till he establishes	H440
Isa	62:12	Sought After, the City **N** Longer Deserted.	H4202
Isa	63: 3	from the nations **n** one was with me.	H401
Isa	63: 5	I looked, but **there was n** one to help, I was	H401
Isa	63: 5	I was appalled that **n** one gave support; so	H401
Isa	64: 4	Since ancient times **n** one has heard, no	H4202
Isa	64: 4	no one has heard, **n** ear has perceived	H4202
Isa	64: 4	**n** eye has seen any God besides you	H4202
Isa	64: 7	**N** one calls on your name or strives to lay	H401
Isa	65:19	of crying will be heard in it **n** more.	H4202
Isa	65:22	**N** *longer* will they build houses and	H4202
Isa	66: 4	For when I called, **n** one answered, when I	H401
Isa	66: 4	answered, when I spoke, **n** one listened.	H4202
Isa	66: 8	Yet **n sooner** is Zion in labor **than** she	H1685
Jer	2: 6	a land where **n** one travels and no one	H4202
Jer	2: 6	where no one travels and **n** one lives?	H4202
Jer	2:19	the LORD your God and have **n** awe of me,"	H4202
Jer	2:25	But you said, 'It's **n** use! I love foreign	H4202
Jer	2:31	to roam; we will come to you **n** more'?	H4202
Jer	3: 3	withheld, and **n** spring rains have fallen.	H4202
Jer	3: 8	that her unfaithful sister Judah had **n** fear;	H4202
Jer	3:12	'I will frown on you **n** *longer*, for I am	H4202
Jer	3:16	"people will **n** longer say, 'The ark	H4202
Jer	3:17	**N** longer will they follow the stubbornness	H4202
Jer	4: 1	out of my sight and **n** *longer* go astray,	H4202
Jer	4: 4	have done—burn with **n** one to quench it.	H401
Jer	4:22	children; they have **n** understanding.	H4202
Jer	4:25	I looked, and **there were n** people; every	H401
Jer	4:29	towns are deserted; **n** one lives in them.	H401
Jer	5: 3	but they felt **n** pain; you crushed	H4202
Jer	5:12	**N** harm will come to us; we will never see	H4202
Jer	5:28	Their evil deeds **have n limit**; they do not	H6296
Jer	6: 8	your land desolate so **n** one can live in it."	H4202
Jer	6:10	to them; they find **n** pleasure in it.	H4202
Jer	6:14	they say, when **there is n** peace.	H401
Jer	6:15	**N**, they have no shame at all; they do not	H1685
Jer	6:15	they have **n** shame at all; they do not	H4202
Jer	6:23	they are cruel and show **n** mercy.	H4202
Jer	7:32	when people will **n** longer call it Topheth	H4202
Jer	7:32	in Topheth until **there is n** *more* room.	H401
Jer	7:33	and **there will be n** one to frighten them	H401
Jer	8:11	they say, when **there is n** peace.	H401
Jer	8:12	**N**, they have no shame at all; they do not	H1685
Jer	8:12	they have **n** shame at all; they do not	H4202
Jer	8:13	**There will be n** grapes on the vine	H401
Jer	8:13	**There will be n** figs on the tree, and their	H401
Jer	8:15	We hoped for peace but **n** good has come	H401
Jer	8:19	**Is** her King **n** *longer* there?" "Why	H401
Jer	8:22	**Is there n** balm in Gilead? Is there no	H401
Jer	8:22	balm in Gilead? **Is there n** physician there	H401
Jer	8:22	Why then is there **n** healing for the	H4202
Jer	9: 5	and **n** one speaks the truth.	H4202
Jer	9:11	towns of Judah so **n** one can live there."	H1172
Jer	9:12	like a desert that **n** one can cross?	H4946+1172
Jer	9:22	the reaper, with **n** one to gather them.	H401
Jer	10: 5	they can do **n** harm nor can they do any	H4202
Jer	10: 6	**N** *one* is like you, LORD; you are great	H4946+401
Jer	10: 7	kingdoms, **there is n** *one* like you.	H4946+401
Jer	10:14	are a fraud; they have **n** breath in them.	H4202
Jer	10:20	children are gone from me and **are n more**;	H401
Jer	10:20	**n** *one* is left now to pitch my tent or to set	H401
Jer	11:19	that his name be remembered **n** more."	H4202
Jer	12:11	waste because **there is n** one who cares.	H401
Jer	12:12	of the land to the other; **n** one will be safe.	H401
Jer	13:14	I will allow **n** pity or mercy or compassion	H4202
Jer	13:19	and **there will be n** one to open them.	H401
Jer	14: 3	they go to the cisterns but find **n** water.	H4202
Jer	14: 4	because there is **n** rain in the land;	H4202
Jer	14: 5	newborn fawn because there is **n** grass.	H4202
Jer	14:15	'**N** sword or famine will touch this land.	H4202
Jer	14:16	**There will be n** one to bury them, their	H401
Jer	14:19	We hoped for peace but **n** good has come	H401
Jer	14:22	send down showers? **N**, it is you, LORD our	H4202
Jer	16: 6	**n** one will cut themselves or shave	H4202
Jer	16: 7	**N** one will offer food to comfort those who	H4202
Jer	16:13	day and night, for I will show you **n** favor.	H4202
Jer	16:14	"when it will **n** longer be said, 'As	H4202
Jer	16:19	worthless idols that did them **n** good.	H401
Jer	17: 6	in a salt land where **n** one lives.	H4202
Jer	17: 8	It has **n** worries in a year of drought and	H4202
Jer	17:24	bring **n** load through the gates of this	H1194
Jer	18:12	will reply, '*It's* **n use**. We will continue	H3286
Jer	18:18	our tongues and pay **n** attention to	H440
Jer	19: 6	when people will **n** longer call this place	H4202
Jer	19:11	in Topheth until **there is n** *more* room.	H401
Jer	21: 7	he will show them **n** mercy or pity or	H4202
Jer	21:12	have done—burn with **n** one to quench it.	H401
Jer	22: 3	Do **n** wrong or violence to the foreigner	H440
Jer	22:28	broken pot, an object **n** *one* wants?	H401
Jer	23: 4	they will **n** longer be afraid or	H4202
Jer	23: 7	"when people will **n** longer say, 'As surely	H4202
Jer	23:17	hearts they say, '**N** harm will come to you.	H4202
Jer	25:27	fall to rise **n** *more* because of the	H4202
Jer	25:35	the leaders of the flock **n** place to escape.	H4946
Jer	29:32	He will have **n** one left among this	H4202
Jer	30: 7	**N other will be** like it.	H4946+401
Jer	30: 8	**n** longer will foreigners enslave them.	H4202
Jer	30:10	security, and **n** one will make him afraid.	H401
Jer	30:13	**There is n** one to plead your cause, no	H401
Jer	30:13	to plead your cause, **n** remedy for your sore	NDT
Jer	30:13	no remedy for your sore, **n** healing for you.	H401
Jer	30:15	over your wound, your pain that has **n cure**?	H631
Jer	30:17	an outcast, Zion for whom **n** one cares.	H401
Jer	31:12	garden, and they will sorrow **n** more.	H4202
Jer	31:15	to be comforted, because they **are n more**."	H401
Jer	31:29	"In those days people will **n** longer say	H4202
Jer	31:34	**N** longer will they teach their neighbor, or	H4202
Jer	31:34	will remember their sins **n** more.	H4202
Jer	33:20	that day and night **n** longer come at their	H1194
Jer	33:21	David will **n** *longer* have a	H4946
Jer	33:24	my people and **n** longer regard them as	H4946
Jer	34: 9	**n** one was to hold a fellow Hebrew in	H1194
Jer	34:10	female slaves and **n** longer hold them in	H1194
Jer	34:22	the towns of Judah so **n** one can live there."	H401
Jer	36:24	who heard all these words showed **n** fear,	H4202
Jer	36:30	He will have **n** one to sit on the throne of	H4202
Jer	38: 6	the cistern; it had **n** water in it, only mud,	H401
Jer	38: 9	to death when **there is n** longer any bread	H401
Jer	38:27	So *they* **said n more** to him, for no one	H3087
Jer	38:27	**n** one had heard his conversation with	H4202
Jer	40:15	son of Nethaniah, and **n** one will know it.	H4202
Jer	42:14	if you say, '**N**, we will go and live in	H4202
Jer	44:17	were well off and suffered **n** harm.	H4202
Jer	44:22	When the LORD could **n** longer endure your	H4202
Jer	44:26	'that **n** one from Judah living anywhere in	H561
Jer	45: 3	worn out with groaning and find **n** rest.	H4202
Jer	46:11	**there is n** healing for you.	H401
Jer	46:27	security, and **n** one will make him afraid.	H401
Jer	48: 2	Moab will be praised **n** more; in Heshbon	H401
Jer	48: 9	desolate, with **n** one to live in them.	H4946+401
Jer	48:33	**n** one treads them with shouts of joy.	H4202
Jer	48:38	broken Moab like a jar that **n** *one* wants,"	H401
Jer	49: 1	"Has Israel **n** sons? Has Israel no	H401
Jer	49: 1	Has Israel **n** heir? Why then has	H401
Jer	49: 5	and **n** one will gather the fugitives.	H401
Jer	49: 7	"**Is there** n longer wisdom in Teman	H401
Jer	49:10	neighbors, so **there is n** one to say,	H401
Jer	49:18	says the LORD, "so **n** one will live there; no	H4202
Jer	49:18	will live there; **n** people will dwell in it.	H4202
Jer	49:33	**N** one will live there; no people will dwell	H4202
Jer	49:33	will live there; **n** people will dwell in it."	H4202
Jer	50: 3	**N** one will live in it; both people and	H4202
Jer	50:14	Spare **n** arrows, for she has sinned against	H440
Jer	50:26	destroy her and leave her **n** remnant.	H440
Jer	50:29	all around her; let **n** one escape. Repay her	H440
Jer	50:32	fall and **n** one will help her up	H401
Jer	50:40	declares the LORD, "so **n** one will live there	H4202
Jer	50:40	will live there; **n** people will dwell in it.	H4202
Jer	51:17	are a fraud; they have **n** breath in them.	H4202
Jer	51:26	**N** rock will be taken from you for a	H4202
Jer	51:29	of Babylon so that **n** one will live there.	H401
Jer	51:37	a place where **n** one lives.	H4946+401
Jer	51:43	a land where **n** one lives, through	H4202+3972
Jer	51:43	no one lives, through which **n** one travels.	H4202
Jer	51:44	The nations will **n** longer stream to him	H4202
Jer	51:64	sink to rise **n** *more* because of the	H4202
Jer	52: 6	that there was **n** food for the people	H4202
La	1: 2	all her lovers **there is n** one to comfort her.	H401
La	1: 3	the nations; she finds **n** resting place.	H4202
La	1: 4	**n** one comes to her appointed festivals	H1172
La	1: 6	princes are like deer that find **n** pasture;	H4202
La	1: 7	enemy hands, **there was n** one to help her.	H401
La	1:16	**N** *one is* **near** to comfort me, no one to	H8178
La	1:16	to comfort me, **n** one to restore my spirit.	NDT
La	1:17	but **there is n** one to comfort her.	H401
La	1:21	groaning, but **there is n** one to comfort me.	H401
La	2: 9	nations, the law **is n more**, and her	H401
La	2: 9	her prophets **n** *longer* find visions	H4202
La	2:18	give yourself **n** relief, your eyes no	H440
La	2:18	give yourself no relief, your eyes **n** rest.	H440
La	2:22	the LORD's anger **n** *one* escaped or	H4202
La	3:31	For **n** one is cast off by the Lord forever.	H4202
La	3:44	with a cloud so that **n** prayer can get	H4946
La	4: 4	beg for bread, but **n** one gives it to them.	H401
La	4:14	with blood that **n** one dares to touch	H4202
La	4:15	nations say, "They can stay here **n** longer."	H4202
La	4:16	he **n** longer watches over them.	H4202
La	4:16	The priests are shown **n** honor, the elders	H4202
La	4:16	are shown no honor, the elders **n** favor.	H4202
La	5: 5	at our heels; we are weary and find **n** rest.	H4202
La	5: 7	Our ancestors sinned and **are n more**, and	H401
La	5: 8	and **there is n** one to free us from their	H401
La	5:12	their hands; elders are shown **n** respect.	H4202
Eze	4:14	**N** impure meat has ever entered my	H4202
Eze	7:14	things ready, but **n** one will go into battle	H401
Eze	12:23	they will **n** longer quote it in Israel.	H4202
Eze	12:24	For there will be **n** more false visions or	H4202
Eze	13:10	when **there is n** peace, and	H401
Eze	13:16	of peace for her when **there was n** peace,	H401
Eze	13:21	they will **n** longer fall prey to your	H4202
Eze	13:22	when I had brought them **n** grief, and	H4202
Eze	13:23	therefore you will **n** longer see false	H4202
Eze	14:11	of Israel will **n** longer stray from me,	H4202
Eze	14:15	desolate so that **n** one can pass through it	H1172
Eze	16: 5	**N** one looked on you with pity or had	H4202
Eze	16:34	**n** one runs after you for your favors.	H4202
Eze	16:41	you will **n** longer pay your lovers.	H4202
Eze	16:42	I will be calm and **n** longer angry.	H4202
Eze	17:17	horde will be of **n** help to him in war,	H4202
Eze	18: 3	you will **n** longer quote this proverb in	H561
Eze	18:17	the poor and takes **n** interest or profit from	H4202
Eze	18:32	For I take **n** pleasure in the death of	H4202
Eze	19: 9	so his roar was heard **n** longer on the	H4202
Eze	19:14	**N** strong branch is left on it fit for a ruler's	H4202
Eze	20:39	listen to me and **n** longer profane my holy	H4202
Eze	21:32	you will be remembered **n** *more*; for I the	H4202
Eze	22:26	teach that there is **n** difference between	H4202
Eze	22:30	not have to destroy it, but I found **n** *one*.	H4202
Eze	24:27	with him and will **n** longer be silent.	H4202
Eze	26:13	music of your harps will be heard **n** more.	H4202
Eze	26:19	like cities **n** *longer* inhabited, and	H4202
Eze	26:21	to a horrible end and you *will* **be n more**.	H401
Eze	27:36	come to a horrible end and *will* **be n** more.	H401

N

Eze 28: 3 Is **n** secret hidden from you H4202
Eze 28:19 come to a horrible end and *will* **be n** more. H401
Eze 28:24 " '**N** longer will the people of Israel have H4202
Eze 29:11 **n** one will live there for forty years. H4202
Eze 29:16 Egypt will **n** longer be a source of H4202
Eze 29:18 Yet he and his army got **n** reward from the H4202
Eze 30:13 **N** longer will there be a prince in Egypt H4202
Eze 31: 8 **n** tree in the garden of God could H4202+3972
Eze 31:14 Therefore **n** other trees by the waters are H4202
Eze 31:14 **N** other trees so well-watered are ever to H4202
Eze 32:13 abundant waters **n** longer to be stirred H4202
Eze 33:11 I take **n** pleasure in the death of the wicked H561
Eze 33:15 give life, and do **n** evil—that person will H1194
Eze 33:22 was opened and I was **n** longer silent. H4202
Eze 33:28 desolate so that **n** one will cross them. H401
Eze 34: 5 scattered because there was **n** shepherd, H1172
Eze 34: 6 **n** one searched or looked for them. H401
Eze 34:10 the shepherds can **n** longer feed H4202
Eze 34:10 it will **n** *longer* be food for them. H4202
Eze 34:22 they will **n** longer be plundered. H4202
Eze 34:28 They will **n** longer be plundered by the H4202
Eze 34:28 in safety, and **n** one will make them afraid. H401
Eze 34:29 they will **n** longer be victims of H4202
Eze 36:14 therefore you will **n** longer devour people H4202
Eze 36:15 **N** longer will I make you hear the taunts of H4202
Eze 36:15 **n** longer will you suffer the scorn of H4202
Eze 36:30 so that you will **n** longer suffer disgrace H4202
Eze 37: 8 but **there was n** breath in them. H401
Eze 37:23 They will **n** longer defile themselves with H4202
Eze 39: 7 I will **n** longer let my holy name be H4202
Eze 39:26 in their land with **n** one to make them H401
Eze 39:29 I will **n** longer hide my face from them, for H4202
Eze 42: 6 The rooms on the top floor had **n** pillars, as H401
Eze 44: 2 be opened; **n** one may enter through it. H4202
Eze 44: 9 **N** foreigner uncircumcised in heart H3972+4202
Eze 44:21 **N** priest is to drink wine when he H4202+3972
Eze 44:28 are to give them **n** possession in Israel H4202
Eze 45: 8 And my princes will **n** longer oppress my H4202
Eze 46: 9 **N** one is to return through the gate by H4202
Eze 47: 5 to swim in—a river that **n** one could cross. H4202
Da 2:10 "There is **n** one on earth who can do A10379
Da 2:10 **N** king, however great and A10379+10353
Da 2:11 **N** one can reveal it to the king except A10379
Da 2:27 Daniel replied, "**N** wise man, enchanter A10379
Da 3:12 Abednego—who pay **n** attention to you A10379
Da 3:27 there was **n** smell of fire on them. A10379
Da 3:29 **n** other god can save in this way. A10379
Da 4: 9 and **n** mystery is too difficult for A10353+10379
Da 4:35 **N** one can hold back his hand or say to A10379
Da 6: 4 They could find **n** corruption in him A10379
Da 6:13 from Judah, pays **n** attention to you A10379
Da 6:15 and Persians **n** decree or edict A10379+10353
Da 6:23 **n** wound was found on him A10353+10379
Da 8: 4 **N** animal could stand against it H3972+4202
Da 10: 3 I ate **n** choice food; no meat or wine H4202
Da 10: 3 **n** meat or wine touched my lips H4202
Da 10: 3 I used **n** lotions at all until the three H4202
Da 10: 8 great vision; I had **n** strength left, my face H4202
Da 10:21 **N** one supports me against them except H401
Da 11:16 **n** one will be able to stand against him. H401
Da 11:19 will stumble and fall, to be seen **n** *more*. H4202
Da 11:27 each other, but to **n** avail, because an H4202
Da 11:37 He will show **n** regard for the gods of his H4202
Da 11:45 come to his end, and **n** one will help him. H401
Hos 1: 6 I will **n** longer show love to Israel, that H4202
Hos 2:10 **n** one will take her out of my hands. H4202
Hos 2:16 you will **n** longer call me 'my master.' H4202
Hos 2:17 **n** longer will their names be invoked. H4202
Hos 4: 1 "**There is n** faithfulness, no love, no H401
Hos 4: 1 is no faithfulness, **n** love, no H401
Hos 4: 1 **n** acknowledgment of God in the land. H401
Hos 4: 4 "But let **n** one bring a charge, let no one H440
Hos 4: 4 bring a charge, let **n** one accuse another H440
Hos 5:14 carry them off, with **n** one to rescue them. H401
Hos 8: 7 The stalk has **n** head; it will produce no H401
Hos 8: 7 stalk has no head; it will produce **n** flour. H1172
Hos 8: 8 the nations like something **n** *one* wants. H401
Hos 9:11 away like a bird—**n** birth, no pregnancy, H4946
Hos 9:11 like a bird—no birth, **n** pregnancy, no H4946
Hos 9:11 no birth, no pregnancy, **n** conception. H4946
Hos 9:15 I will **n** longer love them; all their leaders H4202
Hos 9:16 their root is withered, they yield **n** fruit. H1153
Hos 10: 3 "We have **n** king because we did not H401
Hos 11: 7 I will **by n means** exalt them. H4202+3480
Hos 13: 4 You shall acknowledge **n** God but me, no H4202
Hos 13: 4 no God but me, **n** Savior except me. H401
Hos 13:14 "I *will* **have n** compassion, H6259+4946+6524
Joel 1:18 mill about because they have **n** pasture; H401
Joel 2:10 and the stars **n longer shine**. H665+5586
Joel 2:27 your God, and that **there is n** other; never H401
Joel 3:15 and the stars **n longer shine**. H665+5586
Joel 3:21 blood unavenged? **N**, I will not." The LORD H4202
Am 3: 4 lion roar in the thicket when it has **n** prey? H401
Am 3: 5 a trap on the ground when **n** bait is there? H401
Am 5: 2 in her own land, with **n** one to lift her up." H401
Am 5: 6 Bethel will have **n** one to quench it. H401
Am 5:22 offerings, I will have **n** regard for them. H4202
Am 6:10 he says, "**N**," then he will go on to H700
Am 7: 8 people Israel; I will spare them **n** longer. H4202
Am 8: 2 people Israel; I will spare them **n** longer. H4202
Ob 18 There will be **n** survivors from Esau." H4202
Mic 1:11 mourning; it **n** longer protects you. H4374+4946
Mic 2: 3 You will **n** *longer* walk proudly, for it will H4202
Mic 2: 5 you will have **n** one in the assembly of H4202
Mic 3: 7 faces because **there is n** answer from God." H401
Mic 3:11 **N** disaster will come upon us. H4202
Mic 4: 4 and **n** one will make them afraid H401
Mic 4: 9 do you now cry aloud—have you **n** king? H401
Mic 5: 8 mangles as it goes, and **n** one can rescue. H401
Mic 5:12 you will **n** longer cast spells. H4202
Mic 5:13 you will **n** longer bow down to the work of H4202
Mic 7: 1 vineyard; **there is n** cluster of grapes to eat H401
Mic 7: 5 a neighbor; put **n** confidence in a friend. H440
Na 1:12 Judah, I will afflict you **n** more. H4202
Na 1:14 "You will have **n** descendants to bear your H4202
Na 1:15 **N** more will the wicked invade you; they H4202
Na 2: 8 they cry, but **n** one turns back. H401
Na 2:13 *I will* **leave** you **n** prey on the earth H4162
Na 2:13 your messengers will **n** longer be heard." H4202
Na 3:17 they fly away, and **n** one knows where. H4202
Na 3:18 the mountains with **n** one to gather them. H401
Hab 1:14 like the sea creatures that have **n** ruler. H4202
Hab 2:19 and silver; **there is n** breath in it." H401+3972
Hab 3:17 not bud and **there are n** grapes on the H401
Hab 3:17 crop fails and the fields produce **n** food, H4202
Hab 3:17 though **there are n** sheep in the pen and H1615
Hab 3:17 sheep in the pen and **n** cattle in the stalls, H401
Zep 3: 2 She obeys **n** one, she accepts no H4202
Zep 3: 2 obeys no one, she accepts **n** correction. H4202
Zep 3: 5 within her is righteous; he does **n** wrong. H4202
Zep 3: 5 yet the unrighteous know **n** shame. H4202
Zep 3: 6 deserted, with **n** one passing through. H1172
Zep 3:13 They will do **n** wrong; they will tell no lies. H4202
Zep 3:13 They will do no wrong; they will tell **n** lies. H4202
Zep 3:13 lie down and **n** one will make them H401
Zep 3:17 in his love *he will* **n longer rebuke** you H3087
Hag 2:12 The priests answered, "**N**." H4202
Zec 1:21 Judah so that **n** one could raise their H4202
Zec 4: 5 what these are?" "**N**, my lord," I replied. H4202
Zec 4:13 what these are?" "**N**, my lord," I said. H4202
Zec 7:14 so desolate that **n** one traveled through H4946
Zec 8:10 time there were **n** wages for people or H4202
Zec 8:10 **N** one could go about their business safely H401
Zec 8:14 on you and showed **n** pity when your H4202
Zec 11: 6 For I will **n** longer have pity on the people H4202
Zec 13: 2 they will be remembered **n** more, H4202
Zec 14: 7 *with* **n** *distinction between* day and night. H4202
Zec 14:17 the LORD Almighty, they will have **n** rain. H4202
Zec 14:18 go up and take part, they will have **n** rain. H4202
Zec 14:21 that day there will **n** longer be a H4202
Mal 1:10 "and I will accept **n** offering from your H4202
Mal 2:13 wail because he **n** longer looks with H401
Mt 2: 6 are **by n means** least among the rulers of *G4027*
Mt 2:18 be comforted, because they are **n more**." *G4024*
Mt 5:13 It is **n** longer good for **anything**, except to *G4029*
Mt 5:37 need to say is simply 'Yes' or '**N**'; *G4024+4024*
Mt 6: 1 you will have **n** reward from your Father in *G4024*
Mt 6:24 "**N one** can serve two masters. Either you *G4029*
Mt 7: 3 brother's eye and pay **n** attention to the *G4024*
Mt 8:20 the Son of Man has **n** place to lay his *G4024*
Mt 8:28 were so violent that **n** one could pass that *G3590*
Mt 9:16 "**N one** sews a patch of unshrunk cloth on *G4029*
Mt 9:17 **N**, they pour new wine into new wineskins *G247*
Mt 9:30 "See that **n** one knows about this. *G3594*
Mt 10:10 **n** bag for the journey or extra shirt or *G3590*
Mt 11: 8 **N**, those who wear fine clothes are in *G2627*
Mt 11:23 to the heavens? **N**, you will go down to *G3590*
Mt 11:27 **N** one knows the Son except the Father *G4029*
Mt 11:27 **and n** one knows the Father except the *G4028*
Mt 12:19 **n** one will hear his voice in the streets. *G4028*
Mt 13: 6 they withered because they had **n** root. *G3590*
Mt 13:21 But since they have **n** root, they last only a *G4024*
Mt 13:29 " '**N**,' he answered, 'because while *G4024+3607*
Mt 16: 8 among yourselves about having **n** bread? *G4024*
Mt 17: 8 looked up, they saw **n one** except Jesus. *G4029*
Mt 19: 6 So they are **n longer** two, but one flesh *G4033*
Mt 19: 6 has joined together, let **n** one separate." *G3590*
Mt 20: 7 " 'Because **n one** has hired us,' they *G4029*
Mt 22: 5 "But they **paid n attention** and went off *G288*
Mt 22:16 because you pay **n** attention to who they *G4024*
Mt 22:23 who say there is **n** resurrection, came to *G3590*
Mt 22:25 since he had **n** children, he left his *G3590*
Mt 22:46 **N one** could say a word in reply, and from *G4029*
Mt 22:46 **and** from that day on **n** one dared to ask *G4028*
Mt 24: 4 "Watch out that **n** one deceives you. *G3590*
Mt 24:17 Let **n** one on the housetop go down to *G3590*
Mt 24:18 Let **n** one in the field go back to get their *G3590*
Mt 24:22 been cut short, **n** one would survive *G4024+4246*
Mt 24:36 "But about that day or hour **n one** knows *G4029*
Mt 25: 9 " '**N**,' they replied, 'there may not be *G3607*
Mt 27:12 priests and the elders, he gave **n** answer. *G4029*
Mt 27:14 But Jesus made **n** reply, not even to a *G4024*
Mk 1:45 Jesus could **n longer** enter a town openly *G3600*
Mk 2: 2 large numbers that there was **n** room left, *G3600*
Mk 2:21 "**N one** sews a patch of unshrunk cloth on *G4029*
Mk 2:22 And **n one** pours new wine into old *G4029*
Mk 2:22 will be ruined. **N**, they pour new wine into *G247*
Mk 3:27 **n one** can enter a strong man's house *G4029*
Mk 4: 6 they withered because they had **n** root. *G3590*
Mk 4:17 But since they have **n** root, they last only a *G4024*
Mk 4:40 you so afraid? Do you **still** have **n** faith?" *G4037*
Mk 5: 3 and **n** one could bind him anymore *G4029*
Mk 5: 4 **N one** was strong enough to subdue him *G4029*
Mk 6: 8 journey except a staff—**n** bread, no bag, *G3590*
Mk 6: 8 a staff—no bread, **n** bag, no money in *G3590*
Mk 6: 8 no bread, no bag, **n** money in your belts. *G3590*
Mk 7:12 then you **n longer** let them do anything *G4033*
Mk 8:12 Truly I tell you, **n** sign will be given to it." *G1623*
Mk 8:16 said, "It is because we have **n** bread." *G4024*
Mk 8:17 are you talking about having **n** bread? *G4024*
Mk 9: 8 they **n longer** saw anyone with them *G4033*
Mk 9:39 "For **n one** who does a miracle in my *G4029*
Mk 10: 8 So they are **n longer** two, but one flesh *G4033*
Mk 10: 9 has joined together, let **n** one separate." *G3590*
Mk 10:18 Jesus answered. "**N one** is good—except *G4029*
Mk 10:29 "**n one** who has left home or brothers *G4029*
Mk 11: 2 tied there, which **n** one has ever ridden. *G4029*
Mk 11:14 "May **n one** ever eat fruit from you again." *G3594*
Mk 12:14 because you pay **n** attention to who they *G4024*
Mk 12:18 who say there is **n** resurrection, came to *G3590*
Mk 12:19 dies and leaves a wife but **n** children, *G3590*
Mk 12:21 but he also died, leaving **n** child. *G3590*
Mk 12:31 There is **n** commandment greater than *G4024*
Mk 12:32 God is one and there is **n** other but him. *G4024*
Mk 12:34 And from then on **n one** dared ask him *G4029*
Mk 13: 5 "Watch out that **n** one deceives you. *G3590*
Mk 13:15 Let **n** one on the housetop go down or *G3590*
Mk 13:16 Let **n** one in the field go back to get their *G3590*
Mk 13:20 cut short those days, **n** one would survive. *G4024*
Mk 13:32 "But about that day or hour **n one** knows *G4029*
Mk 14:61 Jesus remained silent and gave **n** answer. *G4024*
Mk 15: 5 But Jesus still made **n** reply, and Pilate *G4029*
Lk 1:37 For **n** word from God will ever fail." *G4024+4246*
Lk 1:60 spoke up and said, "**N**! He is to be called *G4049*
Lk 1:61 "There is **n one** among your relatives who *G4029*
Lk 2: 7 because there was **n** guest room *G4024*
Lk 4:24 "**n** prophet is accepted in his hometown. *G4029*
Lk 5:36 "**N one** tears a piece out of a new *G4029*
Lk 5:37 And **n** one pours new wine into old *G4029*
Lk 5:38 **N**, new wine must be poured into new *G247*
Lk 5:39 And **n one** after drinking old wine wants *G4029*
Lk 6:41 brother's eye and pay **n** attention to the *G4024*
Lk 6:43 "**N** good tree bears bad fruit, nor does a *G4024*
Lk 7:25 **N**, those who wear expensive clothes and *G2627*
Lk 7:28 of women there is **n one** greater than *G4029*
Lk 8: 6 withered because they had **n** moisture. *G3590*
Lk 8:13 when they hear it, but they have **n** root. *G4024*
Lk 8:16 "**N one** lights a lamp and hides it in a *G4029*
Lk 8:43 twelve years, but **n one** could heal her. *G4029*
Lk 9: 3 nothing for the journey—**n** staff, no bag, *G3612*
Lk 9: 3 the journey—no staff, **n** bag, no bread, no *G3612*
Lk 9: 3 no bag, **n** bread, no money, no *G3612*
Lk 9: 3 no bag, no bread, **n** money, no extra shirt. *G3612*
Lk 9: 3 no bag, no bread, no money, **n** extra shirt. *G3612*
Lk 9:58 the Son of Man has **n** place to lay his *G4024*
Lk 9:62 "**N one** who puts a hand to the plow and *G4029*
Lk 10:15 to the heavens? **N**, you will go down to *G3590*
Lk 10:22 **N one** knows who the Son is except the *G4029*
Lk 10:22 **n** one knows who the Father is except NDT
Lk 11: 6 and I have **n** food to offer him. *G4024*
Lk 11:33 "**N one** lights a lamp and puts it in a *G4029*
Lk 11:36 is full of light, and **n** part of it dark, it will *G3590*
Lk 12: 4 kill the body and after that can do **n** more. *G3590*
Lk 12:17 I have **n** place to store my crops *G4024*
Lk 12:24 reap, they have **n** storeroom or barn *G4024*
Lk 12:33 where **n** thief comes near and no moth *G4024*
Lk 12:33 no thief comes near **and n** moth destroys. *G4028*
Lk 12:51 to bring peace on earth? **N**, I tell you, but *G4049*
Lk 13: 3 I tell you, **n**! But unless you repent, you too *G4049*
Lk 13: 5 I tell you, **n**! But unless you repent, you too *G4049*
Lk 13:33 surely **n** prophet can die outside *G4024*
Lk 15:16 but **n one** gave him anything. *G4029*
Lk 15:19 I am **n longer** worthy to be called your son *G4033*
Lk 15:21 I am **n longer** worthy to be called your son *G4033*
Lk 16:13 "**N** one can serve two masters. Either you *G4029*
Lk 16:30 " '**N**, father Abraham,' he said, 'but if *G4049*
Lk 17:18 Has **n** one returned to give praise to God *G4024*
Lk 17:31 On that day **n** one who is on the housetop *G3590*
Lk 17:31 **n** one in the field should go back for *G3590*
Lk 18:19 Jesus answered. "**N one** is good—except *G4029*
Lk 18:29 "**n one** who has left home or wife or *G4029*
Lk 19:30 tied there, which **n** one has ever ridden. *G4029*
Lk 20:27 who say there is **n** resurrection, came to *G3590*
Lk 20:28 dies and leaves a wife but **n children**, *G866*
Lk 20:31 way the seven died, leaving **n** children. *G4024*
Lk 20:36 **and** they can **n** longer die; for they are like *G4028*
Lk 20:40 And **n** one dared to ask him any more *G4029*
Lk 22: 6 over to them **when n** crowd **was present**. *G868*
Lk 22:51 Jesus answered, "**N more** of this!" *G1572+2401*
Lk 23: 4 "I find **n** basis for a charge against this *G4029*
Lk 23: 9 questions, but Jesus gave him **n** answer. *G4029*
Lk 23:14 have found **n** basis for your charges *G4029*
Lk 23:22 I have found in him **n** grounds for the *G4029*
Lk 23:53 one in which **n one** had yet been laid. *G4029*
Jn 1:18 **N one** has ever seen God, but the one *G4029*
Jn 1:21 you the Prophet?" He answered, "**N**." *G4024*
Jn 1:47 is an Israelite in whom there is **n** deceit." *G4024*
Jn 2: 3 said to him, "They have **n more** wine." *G4024*
Jn 3: 2 For **n one** could perform the signs you are *G4029*
Jn 3: 3 **n** one can see the kingdom of God unless *G4024*
Jn 3: 5 **n** one can enter the kingdom of God *G4024*
Jn 3:13 **N one** has ever gone into heaven except *G4029*
Jn 3:32 but **n one** accepts his testimony. *G4029*
Jn 4:17 "I have **n** husband," she replied. Jesus *G4024*
Jn 4:17 right when you say you have **n** husband. *G4024*
Jn 4:27 But **n one** asked, "What do *G4029*

Book	Ref	Context	Number
Jn	4:42	“We **n longer** believe just because of	G4033
Jn	4:44	out that a prophet has **n** honor in his own	G4024
Jn	5:7	“I have **n** one to help me into the pool	G4024
Jn	5:13	who was healed had **n** idea who it was,	G4024
Jn	5:22	the Father judges **n one**, but has	G4029
Jn	6:44	“**N one** can come to me unless the Father	G4029
Jn	6:46	**N** one has seen the Father except the one	G4024
Jn	6:53	drink his blood, you have **n** life in you.	G4024
Jn	6:65	why I told you that **n one** can come to me	G4029
Jn	6:66	turned back and **n longer** followed him.	G4033
Jn	7:4	**N one** who wants to become a public	G4029
Jn	7:12	Others replied, “**N**, he deceives the	G4024
Jn	7:13	But **n one** would say anything publicly	G4029
Jn	7:27	**n one** will know where he is from.	G4029
Jn	7:30	seize him, but **n one** laid a hand on him	G4029
Jn	7:44	seize him, but **n one** laid a hand on him.	G4029
Jn	7:46	“**N** one **ever** spoke the way this man does,”	G4030
Jn	7:49	**N**! But this mob that knows nothing of the	NDT
Jn	8:10	Has **n one** condemned you?”	G4029
Jn	8:11	“**N one**, sir,” she said. “Then neither do I	G4029
Jn	8:14	But you have **n** idea where I come from	G4024
Jn	8:15	standards; I pass judgment *on* **n one**.	G4029
Jn	8:20	Yet **n one** seized him, because his hour	G4029
Jn	8:35	Now a slave has **n** permanent place in the	G4024
Jn	8:37	because you have **n** room for my word.	G4024
Jn	8:44	to the truth, for there is **n** truth in him.	G4024
Jn	9:4	Night is coming, when **n one** can work.	G4029
Jn	9:9	Others said, “**N**, he only looks like	G4049
Jn	10:18	**N one** takes it from me, but I lay it down of	G4029
Jn	10:28	**n** one will snatch them out of my hand.	G4024
Jn	10:29	**n one** can snatch them out of my Father's	G4029
Jn	11:4	**N**, it is for God's glory so that God's Son	G247
Jn	11:10	that they stumble, for they have **n** light.”	G4024
Jn	11:54	Therefore Jesus **n longer** moved about	G4033
Jn	12:27	**N**, it was for this very reason I came to this	G247
Jn	12:46	so that **n** one who believes in me should	G3590
Jn	13:8	**N**,” said Peter, “you shall **never**	G4024+3590+1650+3836+172
Jn	13:8	I wash you, you have **n** part with me.”	G4024
Jn	13:16	**n** servant is greater than his master	G4024
Jn	13:28	But **n one** at the meal understood why	G4029
Jn	14:6	**N one** comes to the Father except through	G4029
Jn	14:30	He has **n hold** over me,	G4024+4029
Jn	15:2	off every branch in me that bears **n** fruit,	G3590
Jn	15:4	**N** branch can bear fruit by itself; it must	G4024
Jn	15:13	Greater love has **n one** than this: to lay	G4029
Jn	15:15	I **n longer** call you servants, because a	G4033
Jn	15:22	now they have **n** excuse for their sin.	G4024
Jn	15:24	among them the works **n one** else did,	G4029
Jn	16:10	where you can see me **n longer**;	G4033
Jn	16:16	“In a little while you will see me **n more**	G4033
Jn	16:17	‘In a little while you will see me **n** *more*	G4024
Jn	16:19	‘In a little while you will see me **n** *more*	G4024
Jn	16:22	and **n one** will take away your joy.	G4029
Jn	16:23	day you will **n** *longer* ask me anything.	G4024
Jn	16:25	when I will **n longer** use this kind of	G4033
Jn	16:27	**N**, the Father himself loves you because you	NDT
Jn	17:11	I will remain in the world **n longer**, but	G4033
Jn	18:31	“But we have **n** right to execute anyone,”	G4024
Jn	18:38	“I find **n** basis for a charge against him.	G4029
Jn	18:40	They shouted back, “*N*, **not** him! Give us	AIT
Jn	19:4	you know that I find **n** basis for a charge	G4029
Jn	19:6	I find **n** basis for a charge against him.”	G4024
Jn	19:9	but Jesus gave him **n** answer.	G4024
Jn	19:11	“You would have **n** power over me	G4024+4029
Jn	19:12	this man go, you are **n** friend of Caesar.	G4024
Jn	19:15	“We have **n** king but Caesar,” the chief	G4024
Jn	19:41	in which **n one** had ever been laid.	G4029
Jn	21:5	haven't you any fish?” “**N**,” they answered.	G4024
Ac	1:20	let there be **n** one to dwell in it,’	G3590
Ac	2:16	**N**, this is what was spoken by the prophet	G247
Ac	4:12	Salvation is found in **n one** else, for there	G4029
Ac	4:12	there is **n** other name under heaven	G4028
Ac	4:17	them to speak **n longer** to anyone in this	G3600
Ac	4:32	**N** one claimed that any of their	G4028
Ac	4:34	that there were **n** needy persons among	G4028
Ac	5:13	**N one** else dared join them, even though	G4029
Ac	5:23	we opened them, we found **n one** inside.”	G4029
Ac	7:5	He gave him **n** inheritance here, not even	G4024
Ac	7:5	though at that time Abraham had **n** child.	G4024
Ac	7:20	and he was **n ordinary** *child.*	G842+3836+2536
Ac	8:21	You have **n** part or share in this ministry	G4024
Ac	10:47	“**Surely n** one can stand in the way of their	G3614
Ac	11:12	told me to have **n** hesitation about going	G3594
Ac	11:18	*they* **had n further objections** and praised	G2483
Ac	12:9	he had **n** idea that what the angel	G4024
Ac	12:18	there was **n** small commotion among the	G4024
Ac	13:28	Though they found **n** proper ground for a	G3594
Ac	15:11	**N**! We believe it is through the grace of our	G247
Ac	16:37	get rid of us quietly? **N**! Let them come	G4024
Ac	18:10	and **n one** is going to attack and harm	G4029
Ac	18:17	Gallio showed **n** concern **whatever**.	G4029
Ac	19:2	They answered, “**N**, we have not even	G247
Ac	19:26	made by human hands are **n** gods **at all**.	G4024
Ac	19:40	commotion, since there is **n** reason for it.”	G3594
Ac	21:24	will know there is **n** *truth* in these reports	G4029
Ac	21:39	in Cilicia, a citizen of **n** ordinary city.	G4024
Ac	23:8	Sadducees say that there is **n** resurrection,	G3590
Ac	23:29	there was **n** charge against him that	G3594
Ac	24:11	easily verify that **n** more than twelve days	G4024
Ac	24:18	There was **n** crowd with me, nor was I	G4024
Ac	25:11	**n one** has the right to hand me over to	G4029
Ac	28:5	off into the fire and suffered **n** ill effects.	G4029
Ro	1:31	they have **n understanding**, no fidelity, no	G852
Ro	1:31	have no understanding, **n fidelity**, no love,	G853
Ro	1:31	no fidelity, **n love**, no mercy.	G845
Ro	1:31	no fidelity, no love, **n mercy**.	G446
Ro	2:1	therefore, have **n excuse**, you who pass	G406
Ro	2:29	**N**, a person is a Jew who is one inwardly	G247
Ro	3:10	“There is **n** one righteous, not	G4024
Ro	3:11	there is **n** one who understands; there is	G4024
Ro	3:11	there is **n** one who seeks God.	G4024
Ro	3:12	worthless; there is **n** one who does good	G4024
Ro	3:18	“There is **n** fear of God before their eyes.”	G4024
Ro	3:20	Therefore **n** one will be declared righteous	G4024
Ro	3:22	There is **n** difference between Jew and	G4024
Ro	3:27	that requires works? **N**, because of the law	G4049
Ro	4:15	And where there is **n** law there is no	G4024
Ro	4:15	there is no law there is **n** transgression.	G4028
Ro	5:13	anyone's account where there is **n** law.	G3590
Ro	6:2	**By n means**! We are those who	G3590+1181
Ro	6:6	that we should **n longer** be slaves to sin	G3600
Ro	6:9	death **n longer** has mastery over him.	G4033
Ro	6:14	For sin shall **n** longer be your master	G4024
Ro	6:15	law but under grace? **By n means**!	G3590+1181
Ro	7:13	death to me? **By n means**	G3590+1181
Ro	7:17	it is **n longer** I myself who do it	G4033
Ro	7:20	want to do, it is **n longer** I who do it, but it	G4033
Ro	8:1	there is now **n** condemnation for those	G4029
Ro	8:24	But hope that is seen is **n** hope *at all*	G4024
Ro	8:34	one who condemns? **N** one. Christ Jesus	NDT
Ro	8:37	**N**, in all these things we are more than	G247
Ro	10:12	For there is **n** difference between Jew and	G4024
Ro	10:19	by a nation that has **n understanding**.”	G852
Ro	11:1	his people? **By n means**! I am an	G3590+1181
Ro	11:6	if it were, grace would **n longer** be grace.	G4033
Ro	13:1	there is **n** authority except that which	G4024
Ro	13:3	For rulers hold **n** terror for those who do	G4024
Ro	13:4	rulers do not bear the sword **for n reason**.	G1632
Ro	13:8	Let **n** debt remain outstanding, except the	G3594
Ro	13:10	Love does **n** harm to a neighbor. Therefore	G4024
Ro	14:15	you eat, you are **n longer** acting in love.	G4033
Ro	15:23	now that there is **n more** place for me to	G3600
1Co	1:10	that there be **n** divisions among you,	G3590
1Co	1:15	so **n** one can say that you were baptized in	G3590
1Co	1:29	so that **n** one may boast before him.	G3590
1Co	2:7	**N**, we declare God's wisdom, a mystery that	G247
1Co	2:9	“What **n** eye has seen, what no ear has	G4024
1Co	2:9	eye has seen, what **n** ear has heard, and	G4024
1Co	2:9	what **n** human mind has conceived	G4024
1Co	2:11	In the same way **n one** knows the	G4029
1Co	3:11	For **n one** can lay any foundation other	G4029
1Co	3:21	**n more** boasting about human leaders!	G3594
1Co	7:25	I have **n** command from the Lord, but I	G4024
1Co	7:37	who is under **n** compulsion but has	G3590
1Co	8:4	and that “There is **n** God but one.	G4029
1Co	8:8	we are **n** worse if we do not eat	G4046
1Co	8:8	if we do not eat, **and n** better if we do.	G4046
1Co	9:19	**free and belong to n one,**	G1801+1666+4246
1Co	9:27	**N**, I strike a blow to my body and make it	G247
1Co	10:13	**N** temptation has overtaken you except	G4024
1Co	10:20	**N, but** the sacrifices of pagans are offered	G247
1Co	10:24	**N one** should seek their own good, but the	G3594
1Co	11:16	about this, we have **n** other practice—nor	G4024
1Co	11:17	directives I have **n** praise for you,	G4024
1Co	11:19	**N doubt** there have to be differences	G1142
1Co	12:3	you to know that **n one** who is speaking	G4029
1Co	12:3	be cursed,” and **n one** can say, “Jesus is	G4029
1Co	12:24	parts need **n** special treatment.	G4024
1Co	12:25	there should be **n** division in the body	G3590
1Co	13:5	angered, it keeps **n** record of wrongs.	G4024
1Co	14:2	Indeed, **n one** understands them; they	G4029
1Co	14:17	well enough, but **n** one else is edified.	G4024
1Co	14:28	If there is **n** interpreter, the speaker should	G3590
1Co	15:10	**N**, I worked harder than all of them—yet	G247
1Co	15:12	you say that there is **n** resurrection of the	G4024
1Co	15:13	If there is **n** resurrection of the dead, then	G4024
1Co	15:29	Now if there is **n** resurrection, what will	NDT
1Co	15:32	in Ephesus with *n more than* **human** hopes,	AIT
1Co	16:2	so that when I come **n** collections will	G3590
1Co	16:11	**N** one, then, should treat him with	G3590
2Co	1:17	breath I say both “Yes, yes” and “**N**, no”?	G4024
2Co	1:17	breath I say both “Yes, yes” and “No, **n**”?	G4024
2Co	1:18	our message to you is not “Yes” and “**N**.”	G4024
2Co	1:19	was not “Yes” and “**N**,” but in him it has	G4024
2Co	1:20	For **n matter how many** promises God has	G4012
2Co	2:13	I still had **n** peace of mind, because I did	G4024
2Co	3:10	what was glorious has **n** glory now in	G4024
2Co	5:15	who live should **n longer** live for	G3600
2Co	5:16	now on we regard **n one** from a worldly	G4029
2Co	5:16	Christ in this way, we do so **n longer**.	G4033
2Co	5:21	God made him who had **n** sin to be sin	G3590
2Co	6:3	We put **n** stumbling block in anyone's	G3594
2Co	6:17	Touch **n** unclean thing, and I will receive	G3590
2Co	7:2	We have wronged **n one**, we have	G4029
2Co	7:2	we have corrupted **n one**, we have	G4029
2Co	7:2	no one, we have exploited **n one**.	G4029
2Co	7:4	in all our troubles my joy **knows n bounds**.	G5668
2Co	7:5	Macedonia, we had **n** rest, but we were	G4024
2Co	7:10	that leads to salvation and leaves **n regret**,	G294
2Co	9:1	There is **n need** for me to write to you	G4356
2Co	11:14	And **n** wonder, for Satan himself	G4024
2Co	11:16	Let **n** one take me for a fool.	G3590
2Co	12:4	things that **n** one is permitted to tell.	G4024
2Co	12:6	so **n** one will think more of me than is	G3590
Gal	1:7	which is really **n** gospel **at all**. Evidently	G4024
Gal	1:20	God that what I am writing you is **n** lie.	G4024
Gal	2:6	they were makes **n** difference to me;	G4029
Gal	2:16	the works of the law **n** one will be	G4024
Gal	2:20	crucified with Christ and I **n longer** live,	G4033
Gal	3:11	Clearly **n one** *who* relies on the law is	G4029
Gal	3:15	Just as **n one** can set aside or add to a	G4029
Gal	3:18	then it **n longer** depends on the promise	G4033
Gal	3:25	we are **n longer** under a guardian.	G4033
Gal	4:1	is underage, he is **n** different from a slave	G4029
Gal	4:7	So you are **n longer** a slave, but God's	G4033
Gal	4:12	I became like you. You did me **n** wrong.	G4029
Gal	4:17	zealous to win you over, but for **n** good.	G4024
Gal	5:2	Christ will be of **n** value to you **at all**.	G4029
Gal	5:10	in the Lord that you will take **n** other view.	G4029
Gal	5:23	Against such things there is **n** law.	G4024
Gal	6:17	From now on, let **n one** cause me trouble	G3594
Eph	2:9	not by works, so that **n** one can boast.	G3590
Eph	2:19	you are **n longer** foreigners and strangers	G4033
Eph	4:14	Then we will **n longer** be infants, tossed	G3600
Eph	4:17	that you must **n longer** live as the	G3600
Eph	4:28	has been stealing must steal **n longer**,	G3600
Eph	5:5	**N** immoral, impure or greedy	G4246+4024
Eph	5:6	Let **n** one deceive you with empty words	G3594
Eph	5:29	After all, **n one** ever hated their own body	G4029
Eph	6:9	there is **n** favoritism with him.	G4024
Php	1:20	hope that I will in **n way** be ashamed,	G4029
Php	2:20	I have **n one** *else* like him, who will show	G4029
Php	3:1	It is **n** trouble for me to write the same	G4024
Php	3:3	who put **n** confidence in the flesh	G4024
Php	4:10	but *you* **had n opportunity** *to show* it.	G177
Col	2:4	you this so that **n** one may deceive you by	G3594
Col	2:8	See to it that **n** one takes you captive	G3590
Col	3:11	Here there is **n** Gentile or Jew, circumcised	G4024
Col	3:25	their wrongs, and there is **n** favoritism.	G4024
1Th	3:1	So when we could stand it **n longer**, we	G3600
1Th	3:3	so that **n one** would be unsettled by these	G3594
1Th	3:5	when I could stand it **n longer**, I sent to	G3600
1Th	4:6	that in this matter **n** one should wrong	G3590
1Th	4:13	the rest of mankind, who have **n** hope.	G3590
1Ti	5:7	so that **n** one may be **open to blame**.	G455
1Ti	5:9	**N** widow may be put on the list of widows	G3590
1Ti	5:14	to give the enemy **n** opportunity for	G3594
1Ti	6:16	whom **n** one has seen or can see.	G4029
2Ti	1:12	Yet this is **n** cause for shame, because I	G4024
2Ti	2:4	**N one** serving as a soldier gets entangled	G4029
2Ti	2:14	it is of **n** value, and only ruins	G4029
2Ti	4:16	first defense, **n one** came to my support	G4029
Titus	1:14	will pay **n** attention to Jewish myths or	G3590
Titus	2:5	so that **n** one will malign the word of God.	G3590
Titus	2:12	It teaches us to **say** “**N**” **to** ungodliness and	G766
Titus	3:2	to slander **n one**, to be peaceable and	G3594
Phm	16	**n longer** as a slave, but better than a slave	G4033
Heb	4:2	they heard was of **n** value to them,	G4024
Heb	4:11	so that **n** one will perish by following their	G3590
Heb	5:4	And **n** one takes this honor on himself, but	G4024
Heb	5:11	you because *you* **n longer try** to	G3821+1181
Heb	6:13	since there was **n one** greater for him to	G4029
Heb	7:13	and **n one** from that tribe has ever served	G4029
Heb	8:7	**n** place would have been sought for	G4024
Heb	8:11	**N longer** will they teach their	G4024+3590
Heb	8:12	will remember their sins **n** more.”	G4024+3590
Heb	9:22	shedding of blood there is **n** forgiveness.	G4024
Heb	10:2	would **n** longer have felt guilty for	G3594
Heb	10:17	acts I will remember **n** more.	G4024+3590
Heb	10:18	sacrifice for sin is **n longer** *necessary*.	G4033
Heb	10:26	of the truth, **n** sacrifice for sins is left	G4033
Heb	10:38	And I take **n** pleasure in the one who	G4024
Heb	11:23	because they saw he was **n ordinary** child	G842
Heb	12:11	**N** discipline seems pleasant at the	G4246+4024
Heb	12:14	without holiness **n one** will see the Lord.	G4029
Heb	12:15	See to it that **n** one falls short of the grace	G3590
Heb	12:15	of God and that **n** bitter root grows up	G3590
Heb	12:16	See that **n** one is sexually immoral, or is	G3590
Heb	12:19	heard it begged that **n** further word be	G3590
Heb	13:9	which is of **n** benefit to those who do so.	G4024
Heb	13:10	at the tabernacle have **n** right to eat.	G4024
Heb	13:17	that would be **of n benefit** to you.	G269
Jas	1:13	When tempted, **n one** should say, “God is	G3594
Jas	2:14	claims to have faith but has **n** deeds?	G3590
Jas	3:8	**n** human being can tame the tongue	G4029
Jas	5:12	you need to say is a simple “Yes” or “**N**.”	G4024
1Pe	2:22	“He committed **n** sin, and no deceit was	G4024
1Pe	2:22	**and n** deceit was found in his mouth.”	G4028
1Pe	2:23	when he suffered, he made **n** threats.	G4024
2Pe	1:20	must understand that **n** prophecy of	G4246+4024
1Jn	1:5	in him there is **n** darkness **at all**.	G4024+4029
1Jn	2:21	it and because **n** lie comes from	G4246+4024
1Jn	2:23	**N** one who denies the Son has the Father	G4028
1Jn	3:5	take away our sins. And in him is **n** sin.	G4024
1Jn	3:6	**N** one who lives in him keeps on sinning	G4024
1Jn	3:6	**N** one who continues to sin has either	G4024
1Jn	3:9	**N** one who is born of God will continue to	G4024
1Jn	3:15	and you know that **n** murderer has	G4246+4024
1Jn	3:17	brother but **has n pity** on them	G3091+3836+5073
1Jn	4:12	**N one** has ever seen God; but if we love	G4029
1Jn	4:18	There is **n** fear in love. But perfect love	G4024
3Jn	4	I have **n** greater joy to hear that my	G4024
3Jn	7	receiving **n** *help* from the pagans.	G3594
Rev	3:7	What he opens **n one** can shut, and what	G4029
Rev	3:7	and what he shuts **n one** can open.	G4029

Rev 3: 8 you an open door that **n one** can shut. G4029
Rev 3:11 so that **n one** will take your crown. G3594
Rev 5: 3 But **n one** in heaven or on earth or under G4029
Rev 5: 4 wept because **n one** was found who G4029
Rev 7: 9 a great multitude that **n one** could count, G4029
Rev 10: 6 and said, "There will be **n more** delay! G4033
Rev 14: 3 **N one** could learn the song except the G4029
Rev 14: 5 **N** lie was found in their mouths; they are G4024
Rev 14:11 There will be **n** rest day or night for those G4024
Rev 15: 8 and **n one** could enter the temple until G4029
Rev 16:18 **N** earthquake like it has ever occurred G4024
Rev 18:11 over her because **n one** buys their cargoes G4029
Rev 18:22 **N** worker of any trade will **ever** G4246+4024+3590
Rev 19:12 written on him that **n one** knows but he G4029
Rev 20: 6 The second death has **n** power over them G4024
Rev 20:11 presence, and there was **n** place for them. G4024
Rev 21: 1 and there was **n** longer any sea. G4024
Rev 21: 4 There will be **n** more death' or mourning G4024
Rev 21:25 On **n** day will its gates **ever** be shut G4024+3590
Rev 21:25 be shut, for there will be **n** night there. G4024
Rev 22: 3 **N** longer will there be any curse. G4024
Rev 22: 5 There will be **n** more night. They will not G4024

NO (THE CITY) (KJV) THEBES

NOADIAH (2)

Ezr 8:33 son of Jeshua and **N** son of Binnui. H5676
Ne 6:14 also the prophet **N** and how she and the H5676

NOAH (54) [NOAH'S]

Ge 5:29 He named him **N** and said, "He will H5695
Ge 5:30 After **N** was born, Lamech lived 595 years H5695
Ge 5:32 After **N** was 500 years old, he became the H5695
Ge 6: 8 But **N** found favor in the eyes of the LORD. H5695
Ge 6: 9 This is the account of **N** and his family H5695
Ge 6: 9 **N** was a righteous man, blameless H5695
Ge 6:10 **N** had three sons: Shem, Ham and H5695
Ge 6:13 So God said to **N**, "I am going to put an H5695
Ge 6:22 **N** did everything just as God commanded H5695
Ge 7: 1 The LORD then said to **N**, "Go into the ark H5695
Ge 7: 5 And **N** did all that the LORD commanded H5695
Ge 7: 6 **N** was six hundred years old when the H5695
Ge 7: 7 And **N** and his sons and his wife and his H5695
Ge 7: 9 female, came to **N** and entered the ark H5695
Ge 7: 9 as God had commanded **N**. H5695
Ge 7:13 On that very day **N** and his sons, Shem H5695
Ge 7:15 in them came to **N** and entered the ark. H5695
Ge 7:16 living thing, as God had commanded **N**. H2257S
Ge 7:23 Only **N** was left, and those with him in the H5695
Ge 8: 1 But God remembered **N** and all the wild H5695
Ge 8: 6 After forty days **N** opened a window he H5695
Ge 8: 9 the earth; so it returned to **N** in the ark. H2257S
Ge 8:11 Then **N** knew that the water had receded H5695
Ge 8:13 **N** then removed the covering from the ark H5695
Ge 8:15 Then God said to **N**, H5695
Ge 8:18 So **N** came out, together with his sons H5695
Ge 8:20 Then **N** built an altar to the LORD and H5695
Ge 9: 1 Then God blessed **N** and his sons, saying H5695
Ge 9: 8 Then God said to **N** and to his sons with H5695
Ge 9:17 So God said to **N**, "This is the sign of the H5695
Ge 9:18 The sons of **N** who came out of the ark H5695
Ge 9:19 These were the three sons of **N**, and from H5695
Ge 9:20 **N**, a man of the soil, proceeded to plant a H5695
Ge 9:24 When **N** awoke from his wine and found H5695
Ge 9:28 After the flood **N** lived 350 years. H5695
Ge 9:29 **N** lived a total of 950 years, and then he H5695
Nu 26:33 names were Mahlah, **N**, Hoglah, Milkah H5829
Nu 27: 1 the daughters were Mahlah, **N**, Hoglah, H5829
Nu 36:11 Hoglah, Milkah and **N**—married their H5829
Jos 17: 3 names were Mahlah, **N**, Hoglah, Milkah H5829
1Ch 1: 3 Methuselah, Lamech, **N**. H5695
1Ch 1: 4 The sons of **N**: Shem, Ham and Japheth. H5695
Isa 54: 9 "To me this is like the days of **N**, when I H5695
Isa 54: 9 that the waters of **N** would never again H5695
Eze 14:14 if these three men—**N**, Daniel and Job— H5695
Eze 14:20 even if **N**, Daniel and Job were in H5695
Mt 24:37 As it was in the days *of* **N**, so it will be at G3820
Mt 24:38 marriage, up to the day **N** entered the ark; G3820
Lk 3:36 of Shem, the son *of* **N**, the son of Lamech, G3820
Lk 17:26 "Just as it was in the days *of* **N**, so also G3820
Lk 17:27 marriage up to the day **N** entered the ark. G3820
Heb 11: 7 By faith **N**, when warned about things not G3820
1Pe 3:20 in the days *of* **N** while the ark was G3820
2Pe 2: 5 people, but protected **N**, a preacher of G3820

NOAH'S (4) [NOAH]

Ge 7:11 In the six hundredth year of **N** life, on the H5695
Ge 8:13 of the first month of **N** six hundred and first NDT
Ge 10: 1 Ham and Japheth, **N** sons, who H5695
Ge 10:32 These are the clans of **N** sons, according H5695

NOB (6)

1Sa 21: 1 David went to **N**, to Ahimelek the priest H5546
1Sa 22: 9 come to Ahimelek son of Ahitub at **N**. H5546
1Sa 22:11 who were the priests at **N**, and they all H5546
1Sa 22:19 He also put to the sword **N**, the town of H5546
Ne 11:32 in Anathoth, **N** and Ananiah, H5546
Isa 10:32 This day they will halt at **N**; they will H5546

NOBAH (3)

Nu 32:42 And **N** captured Kenath and its H5561
Nu 32:42 settlements and called it **N** after himself. H5562
Jdg 8:11 the nomads east of **N** and Jogbehah and H5562

NOBILITY (2) [NOBLE]

Est 1:18 Median **women of** the **n** who have H8576
Da 1: 3 from the royal family and the **n**— H7312

NOBLE (19) [NOBILITY, NOBLES, NOBLEST]

Ru 3:11 that you are a woman of **n character**. H2657
Est 6: 9 to one of the king's **most n** princes. H7312
Ps 16: 3 "They are the **n** *ones* in whom is all my H129
Ps 45: 1 heart is stirred by a **n** theme as I recite my H3202
Pr 12: 4 A wife of **n character** is her husband's H2657
Pr 31:10 A wife of **n character** who can find? She H2657
Pr 31:29 "Many women do **n** *things*, but you H2657
Ecc 10:17 land whose king is of **n** birth and whose H2985
Isa 32: 5 the fool be called **n** nor the scoundrel be H5618
Isa 32: 8 But the **n** make noble plans, and by noble H5618
Isa 32: 8 But the noble make **n** plans, and by noble H5619
Isa 32: 8 noble plans, and by **n** *deeds* they stand. H5619
Lk 8:15 stands for those with a **n** and good heart, G2819
Lk 19:12 "A man of **n birth** went to a distant G2302
Ac 17:11 Jews were **of** more **n character** than those G2302
1Co 1:26 were influential; not many were **of n birth**. G2302
Php 4: 8 whatever is **n**, whatever is right, G4948
1Ti 3: 1 aspires to be an overseer desires a **n** task. G2819
Jas 2: 7 blaspheming the **n** name of him to whom G2819

NOBLES (60) [NOBLE]

Nu 21:18 that the **n** *of* the people sank—the H5618
Nu 21:18 the **n** with scepters and staffs. NDT
Jdg 5:13 "The remnant of the **n** came down; the H129
Jdg 5:25 in a bowl fit for **n** she brought him curdled H129
1Ki 21: 8 to the elders and **n** who lived in Naboth's H2985
1Ki 21:11 So the elders and **n** who lived in Naboth's H2985
2Ki 12:14 his **n** and his officials all surrendered to H8569
2Ch 23:20 of hundreds, the **n**, the rulers of the people H129
Ne 2:16 Jews or the priests or **n** or officials or any H2985
Ne 3: 5 their **n** would not put their shoulders to H129
Ne 4:14 I stood up and said to the **n**, the officials H2985
Ne 4:19 Then I said to the **n**, the officials and the H2985
Ne 5: 7 then accused the **n** and officials. H2985
Ne 5:12 made **the n and officials** take an H4392S
Ne 6:17 in those days the **n** *of* Judah were H2985
Ne 7: 5 put it into my heart to assemble the **n**, H2985
Ne 10:29 these now join their fellow Israelites the **n**, H129
Ne 13:17 I rebuked the **n** *of* Judah and said to them H2985
Est 1: 3 gave a banquet for all his **n** and officials. H8569
Est 1: 3 the **n** *of* the provinces were present. H8569
Est 1:11 to display her beauty to the people and **n**, H8569
Est 1:14 the seven **n** *of* Persia and Media who had H8569
Est 1:16 in the presence of the king and the **n**, H8569
Est 1:16 also against all the **n** and the peoples of H8569
Est 1:18 to all the king's **n** in the same way. H8569
Est 1:21 The king and his **n** were pleased with this H8569
Est 2:18 banquet, for all his **n** and officials. H8569
Est 3: 1 honor higher than that of all the other **n**. H8569
Est 3:12 provinces and the **n** *of* the various H8569
Est 5:11 him above the other **n** and officials. H8569
Est 8: 9 governors and **n** *of* the 127 provinces H8569
Est 9: 3 And all the **n** *of* the provinces, the satraps H8569
Job 12:21 He pours contempt on **n** and disarms the H5618
Job 29:10 the voices of the **n** were hushed, and their H5592
Job 34:18 are worthless,' and to **n**, 'You are wicked, H5618
Ps 47: 9 The **n** *of* the nations assemble as the H5618
Ps 83:11 Make their **n** like Oreb and Zeeb, all their H5618
Ps 107:40 pours contempt on **n** made them wander H5618
Ps 149: 8 with fetters, their **n** with shackles of iron, H3877
Pr 8:16 princes govern, and **n**—all who rule on H5618
Pr 25: 7 than for him to humiliate you before his **n**. H5618
Isa 5:14 it will descend their **n** and masses with all H2077
Isa 13: 2 to them to enter the gates of the **n**. H5618
Isa 34:12 Her **n** will have nothing there to be called H2985
Jer 14: 3 The **n** send their servants for water; they go H129
Jer 27:20 along with all the **n** *of* Judah and H2985
Jer 39: 6 eyes and also killed all the **n** *of* Judah. H2985
Eze 17:12 carried off her king and her **n**, H8569
Da 4:36 My advisers and **n** sought me out, and I A10652
Da 5: 1 a thousand of his **n** and drank wine with A10652
Da 5: 2 so that the king and his **n**, his wives and A10652
Da 5: 3 the king and his **n**, his wives and his A10652
Da 5: 9 grew more pale. His **n** were baffled. A10652
Da 5:10 hearing the voices of the king and his **n** A10652
Da 5:23 you and your **n**, your wives and your A10652
Da 6:17 signet ring and with the rings of his **n**, A10652
Jnh 3: 7 "By the decree of the king and his **n**: Do H1524
Mic 1:15 The **n** *of* Israel will flee to Adullam. H3883
Na 3:10 Lots were cast for her **n**, and all her great H3877
Na 3:18 shepherds slumber; your **n** lie down to rest. H129

NOBLEST (1) [NOBLE]

SS 3: 7 by sixty warriors, the **n** *of* Israel, H4946+1475

NOBODY (7)

Pr 12: 9 Better *to* **be a n** and yet have a servant H7829
Ecc 9:15 But **n** remembered that poor man. H4202+132
Isa 3: 5 the old, the **n** against the honored. H7829
Jn 9:32 **N** has ever heard of opening the G4024+5516
1Co 6: 5 that there is **n** among you wise enough G4029
2Co 11:10 **n** in the regions of Achaia will stop this G4024
1Th 5:15 Make sure that **n** pays back wrong G3590+5516

NOCTURNAL (1)

Dt 23:10 men is unclean because of a **n** emission, H4326

NOD (1)

Ge 4:16 presence and lived in the land of **N**, H5655

NODAB (1)

1Ch 5:19 the Hagrites, Jetur, Naphish and **N**. H5656

NOE (KJV) NOAH

NOGAH (2)

1Ch 3: 7 **N**, Nepheg, Japhia, H5587
1Ch 14: 6 **N**, Nepheg, Japhia, H5587

NOHAH (1)

1Ch 8: 2 **N** the fourth and Rapha the fifth. H5666

NOISE (20) [NOISY]

Ex 32:17 Joshua heard the **n** *of* the people H7754
1Ki 1:41 meaning of all the **n** *in* the city?" H7754+2159
1Ki 1:45 resounds with it. That's the **n** you hear. H7754
2Ki 11:13 heard the **n** *made by* the guards and H7754
2Ch 23:12 Athaliah heard the **n** *of* the people H7754
Ezr 3:13 the people **made** so much **n**. H8131+9558
Isa 13: 4 a **n** on the mountains, like that of H2162
Isa 14:11 along with the **n** *of* your harps; maggots H2166
Isa 24: 8 the **n** *of* the revelers has stopped H8623
Isa 29: 6 with thunder and earthquake and great **n**, H7754
Isa 66: 6 from the city, hear that **n** from the temple! H7754
Jer 46:17 'Pharaoh king of Egypt is only a **loud n** H8623
Jer 47: 3 at the **n** of enemy chariots and the rumble H8323
Jer 50:22 The **n** *of* battle is in the land, the noise of H7754
Jer 50:22 is in the land, the **n** of great destruction! NDT
Eze 23:42 "The **n** *of* a carefree crowd was around H7754
Eze 26:10 will tremble at the **n** *of* the warhorses, H7754
Eze 37: 7 there was a **n**, a rattling sound, H7754
Joel 2: 5 With a **n** like that of chariots they leap H7754
Am 5:23 Away with the **n** *of* your songs! I will not H2162

NOISOME (KJV) DEADLY, UGLY, WILD

NOISY (5) [NOISE]

Isa 32:14 be abandoned, the **n** city deserted H2162
Jer 48:45 Moab, the skulls of the **n boasters**. H1201+8623
Jer 51:55 Babylon; he will silence her **n din**. H7754+1524
Eze 26:13 I will put an end to your **n** songs, and the H2162
Mt 9:23 house and saw the **n** crowd and people G2572

NOMAD (1) [NOMADS]

Jer 3: 2 lovers, sat like a **n** in the desert. H6862

NOMADS (3) [NOMAD]

Jdg 8:11 route of the **n** east of Nobah H8905+928+185
Isa 13:20 there no **n** will pitch their tents H6862
Jer 35: 7 a long time in the land where you *are* **n**. H1591

NOMINATED (1)

Ac 1:23 So *they* **n** two men: Joseph called G2705

NON-GREEKS (1)

Ro 1:14 I am obligated both to Greeks and **N**, both G975

NONE (109) [NO]

Ge 23: 6 **N** of us will refuse you his tomb for H4202+408
Ge 28:17 This *is* **n** other than the house of God; this H401
Ge 39:11 **n** of the household servants was H401+408
Ge 41:24 **n** of them could explain it to me. H401
Ex 12:22 **N** *of* you shall go out of the door of H4202+408
Ex 12:46 take **n** of the meat outside the house. H4202
Ex 16:27 seventh day to gather it, but they found **n**. H4202
Ex 23:26 **n** will miscarry or be barren in your H4202
Lev 7:15 they must leave **n** of it till morning. H4202
Lev 17:12 "**N** of you may eat blood H3972+4202+5883
Lev 21:17 to come **n** of your descendants H4202+408
Lev 22:30 that same day; leave **n** of it till morning. H4202
Nu 14:15 to death, **leaving n alive**, the H3869+408+285
Nu 30: 5 **n** *of* her vows or the pledges by H4202+3972
Nu 30:12 then **n** of the vows or pledges that H3972+4202
Dt 7:14 **n** of your men or women will be childless H4202
Dt 13:17 **n** of the condemned things are H4202+4399
Dt 15: 6 to many nations but will borrow from **n**. H4202
Dt 15: 6 many nations but **n** will rule over you. H4202
Dt 28:12 to many nations but will borrow from **n**. H4202
Dt 28:31 before your eyes, but you will eat **n** of it. H4202
Jdg 6:16 the Midianites, **leaving n alive**." H3869+408+285
Jdg 20: 8 saying, "**N** *of* us will go home. H4202+408
Jdg 21: 9 they found that **n** of the people of H401+408
1Sa 1: 2 Peninnah had children, but Hannah had **n**. H401
1Sa 3:19 and he let **n** of Samuel's words fall H4202+3972
1Sa 14:24 So **n** *of* the troops tasted food H4202+3972
1Sa 21: 9 David said, "**There is n** like it; give it to H401
1Sa 22: 8 **N** of you is concerned about me or tells me H401
1Sa 30: 2 They killed **n** of them, but carried them off H4202
1Sa 30:17 next day, and **n** of them got away H4202+408
2Sa 15:14 or **n** of us will escape from Absalom. H4202
2Ki 6:12 "**N** of us, my lord the king," said one of H4202
2Ch 1:12 you ever had and **n** after you will have." H4202
2Ch 35:18 and **n** *of* the kings of Israel had H3972+4202
Job 29:12 the fatherless who had **n** to assist them. H4202
Job 32:12 **n** of you has answered his arguments. NDT
Ps 40: 5 **N** can compare with you; were I to speak H401
Ps 69:20 sympathy, but **there was n**, for comforters, H401
Ps 69:20 was none, for comforters, but I found **n**. H4202
Ps 74: 9 **n** of us knows how long this will be. H4202
Ps 86: 8 Among the gods **there is n** like you, Lord H401
Pr 2:19 **N** who go to her return or attain the H4202+3972

Pr 8: 8 are just; **n** of them is crooked or perverse. H401
Pr 14: 6 The mocker seeks wisdom and *finds* **n**, but H401
Isa 30:15 your strength, but you would have **n** of it. H4202
Isa 34:16 **N** of these will be missing, not one H4202+285
Isa 41:17 water, but **there is n**; their tongues are H401
Isa 45: 6 people may know there is **n** besides me. H700
Isa 45:21 God and a Savior; **there is n** but me. H401
Isa 46: 9 no other; I am God, and there is **n** like me. H700
Isa 47: 8 yourself, 'I am, and there is **n** besides me. H700
Isa 47:10 yourself, 'I am, and there is **n** besides me. H700
Isa 51:18 children she bore **there was n** to guide her; H401
Isa 51:18 she reared **there was n** to take her by the H401
Isa 59:11 look for justice, but find **n**; for deliverance, H401
Jer 8: 6 **N** *of* them repent of their wickedness H401
Jer 22:30 lifetime, for **n** of his offspring will prosper H4202
Jer 22:30 **n** will sit on the throne of David or rule H408S
Jer 44:14 **N** of the remnant of Judah who have gone H4202
Jer 44:14 **n** will return except a few fugitives." H4202
Jer 50:20 but **there will be n**, and for the sins H401
Jer 50:20 sins of Judah, but **n** will be found, for I H4202
La 1: 9 astounding; **there was n** to comfort her. H401
Eze 7:11 **N** of the people will be left, none of that H4202
Eze 7:11 will be left, **n** of that crowd—none H4202
Eze 7:11 none of that crowd—**n** of their wealth H4202
Eze 12:28 **N** *of* my words will be delayed any H4202+3972
Eze 16:34 you give payment and **n** is given to you. H4202
Eze 18:11 the father has done **n** *of* them): H4202+3972
Eze 18:22 **N** *of* the offenses they have H4202+3972
Eze 18:24 **N** *of* the righteous things that H4202+3972
Eze 33:13 **n** *of* the righteous things that H4202+3972
Eze 33:16 **N** *of* the sins that person has H4202+3972
Da 1:19 and he found **n** equal to H4202+4946+3972
Da 4:18 for **n** *of* the wise men in my A10353+10379
Da 8: 4 and **n** could rescue from its power. H401
Da 8: 7 **n** could rescue the ram from its power H4202
Da 12:10 **N** *of* the wicked will understand H4202+3972
Hos 7: 7 their kings fall, and **n** of them calls on me. H401
Am 4: 7 had rain; another had **n** and dried up. H4202
Am 9: 1 Not one will get away, **n** will escape. H4202
Mic 7: 1 grapes to eat, **n** of the early figs that I crave. NDT
Zep 2: 5 I will destroy you, and **n** will be left. H4946+401
Zep 2:15 And there is **n** besides me." What a H700
Mt 12:39 But **n** will be given it except the sign of *G4024*
Mt 16: 4 **n** will be given it except the sign of *G4024*
Mk 12:22 **n** of the seven left any children *G4024*
Lk 3:11 should share with the one who has **n**, *G3590*
Lk 11:29 **n** will be given it except the sign of *G4024*
Lk 21:15 and wisdom that **n** of your *G4024+570*
Jn 6:39 that I shall lose **n** of all those he has *G3590*
Jn 16: 5 to him who sent me. **N** of you asks me *G4029*
Jn 17:12 **N** has been lost except the one doomed *G4029*
Jn 21:12 **N** of the disciples dared ask him, "Who *G4029*
Ac 20:25 **n** of you ... will **ever** see me **again** *G4033+4246*
Ac 26:26 I am convinced that **n** of this has escaped *G4024*
Ac 28:21 **and n** of our people who have *G4046+5516*
Ro 14: 7 For **n** of us lives for ourselves alone, and *G4029*
Ro 14: 7 **n** of us dies for ourselves alone. *G4029*
1Co 2: 8 **N** of the rulers of this age understood it *G4029*
1Co 14:10 yet **n** of them is without meaning. *G4029*
Gal 1:19 I saw **n** of the other apostles—only James *G4024*
Phm 9 It is as **n other than** Paul—an old man *G5525*
Heb 3:12 sisters, that **n** of you has a sinful *G3607+5516*
Heb 3:13 so that **n** of you may be hardened *G3590+5516*
Heb 4: 1 us be careful **that n** of you be *G3607+5516*
Heb 11:39 **n** of them received what had been *G4024*
1Jn 2:19 showed that **n** *of them* belonged to *G4024+4246*

NONSENSE (5)

Job 21:34 "So how can you console me with your **n** H2039
Isa 44:25 learning of the wise and **turns** it **into n**, H6118
Lk 24:11 their words seemed to them like **n**. *G3333*
1Ti 5:13 also busybodies *who* **talk n**, saying *G4319*
3Jn 10 is doing, spreading malicious **n** about us. *G5826*

NOON (22) [AFTERNOON, NOONDAY]

Ge 43:16 a meal; they are to eat with me at **n**." H7416
Ge 43:25 their gifts for Joseph's arrival at **n**, H7416
1Ki 18:26 on the name of Baal from morning till **n**. H7416
1Ki 18:27 At **n** Elijah began to taunt them. "Shout H7416
1Ki 20:16 They set out at **n** while Ben-Hadad and H7416
2Ki 4:20 the boy sat on her lap until **n**, and then H7416
Ne 8: 3 daybreak till **n** as he faced H4734+2021+3427
Job 5:14 daytime; at **n** they grope as in the night. H7416
Ps 55:17 morning and **n** I cry out in distress H7416
Isa 16: 3 like night—at **high n**. Hide the fugitives, H7416
Jer 6: 4 Arise, let us attack at **n**! But, H7416
Jer 20:16 wailing in the morning, a battle cry at **n**. H7416
Am 8: 9 the sun go down at **n** and darken the H7416
Mt 20: 5 out again about **n** and about three *G1761+6052*
Mt 27:45 From **n** until three in the afternoon *G1761+6052*
Mk 15:33 **At n**, darkness came over the *G6052+1761*
Lk 23:44 It was now about **n**, and darkness *G6052+1761*
Jn 4: 6 down by the well. It was about **n**. *G6052+1761*
Jn 19:14 of the Passover; it was about **n**. *G6052+1761*
Ac 10: 9 About **n** the following day as they *G6052+1761*
Ac 22: 6 "About **n** as I came near Damascus *G3540*
Ac 26:13 **About n**, King Agrippa, as I was on *G2465+3545*

NOONDAY (4) [NOON]

2Sa 4: 5 of the day while he was taking his **n** rest. H7416
Job 11:17 Life will be brighter than **n**, and darkness H7416
Ps 37: 6 the dawn, your vindication like the **n sun**. H7416
Isa 58:10 your night will become like the **n**. H7416

NOOSE (2)

Job 18:10 A **n** is hidden *for* him on the ground; H2475
Pr 7:22 slaughter, like a deer stepping into a **n** H4591

NOPHAH (1)

Nu 21:30 We have demolished them as far as **N** H5871

NOR (320) [NEITHER, NO]

Ge 31:38 **n** have I eaten rams from your H2256+4202
Ge 49:10 **n** the ruler's staff from between his feet H2256
Ex 4:10 neither in the past **n** since you have H1685
Ex 10: 6 neither your parents **n** your ancestors have H2256
Ex 10:14 locusts, **n** will there ever be again. H2256+4202
Ex 13: 7 **n** shall any yeast be seen H2256+4202
Ex 13:22 pillar of cloud by day **n** the pillar of fire by H2256
Ex 20:10 neither you, **n** your son or daughter, nor H2256
Ex 20:10 daughter, **n** your male or female servant NDT
Ex 20:10 female servant, **n** your animals, nor any H2256
Ex 20:10 **n** any foreigner residing in your towns. H2256
Lev 17:12 **n** may any foreigner residing H2256+4202
Lev 21:12 **n** leave the sanctuary of his God H2256+4202
Lev 22:10 **n** may the guest of a priest or his hired H4202
Lev 26:20 **n** will the trees of your land yield H2256+4202
Nu 14:44 though neither Moses **n** the ark of the H2256
Nu 16:15 **n** have I wronged any of them." H2256+4202
Nu 18:20 **n** will you have any share among H2256+4202
Nu 23:25 them at all **n** bless them at all H1685+4202
Dt 2:37 course of the Jabbok **n** that around the H2256
Dt 5:14 neither you, **n** your son or daughter, nor H2256
Dt 5:14 daughter, **n** your male or female servant H2256
Dt 5:14 female servant, **n** your ox, your donkey H2256
Dt 5:14 **n** any foreigner residing in your towns H2256
Dt 7:14 **n** will any of your livestock be without H2256
Dt 8: 3 which neither you **n** your ancestors H2256+4202
Dt 13: 6 that neither you **n** your ancestors have H2256
Dt 18:16 the LORD our God **n** see this great H2256+4202
Dt 21: 7 blood, **n** did our eyes see it done. H2256+4202
Dt 22: 5 **n** a man wear women's clothing H2256+4202
Dt 23: 2 of a forbidden marriage **n** any of their H4202
Dt 24:16 **n** children put to death for their H2256+4202
Dt 26:13 your commands **n** have I forgotten H2256+4202
Dt 26:14 **n** have I removed any of it while I H2256+4202
Dt 26:14 **n** have I offered any of it to the H2256+4202
Dt 28:51 **n** any calves of your herds or lambs of your NDT
Dt 28:64 which neither you **n** your ancestors have H2256
Dt 29: 5 **n** did the sandals on your feet. H2256+4202
Dt 30:13 **N** is it beyond the sea, so that you H2256+4202
Dt 31: 6 will never leave you **n** forsake you." H2256+4202
Dt 31: 8 will never leave you **n** forsake you. H2256+4202
Dt 33: 6 live and not die, **n** his people be few." H2256
Dt 34: 7 were not weak **n** his strength gone. H2256+4202
Jos 1: 5 I will never leave you **n** forsake you. H2256+4202
Jos 8:22 leaving them neither survivors **n** fugitives. H2256
Jdg 1:29 **N** did Ephraim drive out the H2256+4202
Jdg 1:31 **N** did Asher drive out those living in Akko H4202
Jdg 2:10 the LORD **n** what he had done H2256+1685
Jdg 6: 4 neither sheep **n** cattle nor donkeys. H2256
Jdg 6: 4 neither sheep nor cattle **n** donkeys. H2256
Jdg 8:23 **n** will my son rule over you. H2256+4202
Jdg 11:34 her he had neither son **n** daughter. H196
Jdg 13:14 **n** drink any wine or other fermented H2256+440
Jdg 13:14 fermented drink **n** eat anything H2256+440
Jdg 13:23 **n** shown us all these things or now H2256+4202
Jdg 14: 6 neither his father **n** his mother what he H2256
1Sa 5: 5 priests of Dagon **n** any others who enter H2256
1Sa 12:21 you no good, **n** can they rescue you H2256+4202
1Sa 16: 9 "**N** has the LORD chosen this one." H1685+4202
1Sa 20:31 neither you **n** your kingdom will be H2256
1Sa 26:12 about it, **n** did anyone wake up. H2256+401
2Sa 1:21 may you have neither dew **n** rain H2256+440
2Sa 2:19 neither to the right **n** to the left as he H2256
2Sa 2:28 **n** did they fight anymore. H2256+4202
2Sa 14: 7 neither name **n** descendant on the H2256
2Sa 17:12 Neither he **n** any of his men will be left H2256
2Sa 21: 4 **n** do we have the right to put H2256+401
1Ki 3:11 **n** have asked for the death of your H2256+4202
1Ki 3:12 like you, **n** will there ever be. H2256+4202
1Ki 3:26 "Neither I **n** you shall have him. H1685
1Ki 8:57 may he never leave us **n** forsake us. H2256+440
1Ki 11:33 **n** done what is right in my eyes NDT
1Ki 11:33 **n** kept my decrees and laws as David H2256
1Ki 13: 8 **n** would I eat bread or drink water H2256+4202
1Ki 13:16 **n** can I eat bread or drink water H2256+4202
1Ki 13:28 eaten the body **n** mauled the H2256+4202
1Ki 17: 1 will be neither dew **n** rain in the next few H2256
2Ki 3:17 You will see neither wind **n** rain H2256+4202
2Ki 14: 6 **n** children put to death for their H2256+4202
2Ki 17:34 worship the LORD **n** adhere to the H2256+401
2Ki 18:12 to the commands **n** carried them H2256+4202
2Ki 23:22 judges who led Israel **n** in the days of the H2256
2Ki 23:25 Neither before **n** after Josiah was H2256+4202
2Ch 1:11 honor, **n** for the death of your enemies H2256
2Ch 6: 5 **n** have I chosen anyone to be ruler H2256+4202
2Ch 25: 4 **n** children be put to death for their H2256+4202
Ne 4:23 Neither I **n** my brothers nor my men nor H2256
Ne 4:23 I nor my brothers **n** my men nor the H2256
Ne 4:23 my men **n** the guards with me H2256
Ne 5:14 neither I **n** my brothers ate the food H2256
Ne 9:19 **n** the pillar of fire by night to shine on the H2256
Ne 9:21 did not wear out **n** did their feet H2256+4202
Ne 13:25 **n** are you to take their daughters in H561
Est 2: 7 because she had neither father **n** mother. H2256
Est 5: 9 he neither rose **n** showed fear in H2256+4202
Est 9:28 **n** should the memory of these days H2256+4202
Job 3: 6 the days of the year **n** be entered in any of H440
Job 5: 6 **n** does trouble sprout from the H2256+4202
Job 15:29 **n** will his possessions spread over H2256+4202
Job 28:15 **n** can its price be weighed out in H2256+4202
Job 28:17 Neither gold **n** crystal can compare with it H2256
Job 28:17 **n** can it be had for jewels of gold. H2256
Job 32:21 no partiality, **n** will I flatter anyone; H2256+4202
Job 33: 7 **n** should my hand be heavy on you. H2256+4202
Job 41:26 **n** does the spear or the dart or the javelin. NDT
Ps 1: 5 **n** sinners in the assembly of the righteous. H2256
Ps 16:10 **n** will you let your faithful one see decay. H4202
Ps 25: 2 **n** let my enemies triumph over me. H440
Ps 26: 4 **n** do I associate with hypocrites. H2256+4202
Ps 36:11 **n** the hand of the wicked drive me H2256+440
Ps 44: 3 **n** did their arm bring them victory H2256+4202
Ps 89:33 **n** will I ever betray my faithfulness. H2256+4202
Ps 91: 5 terror of night, **n** the arrow that flies by day NDT
Ps 91: 6 **n** the pestilence that stalks in the darkness NDT
Ps 91: 6 **n** the plague that destroys at midday. NDT
Ps 103: 9 **n** will he harbor his anger forever; H2256+4202
Ps 115: 7 **n** can they utter a sound with their throats. H4202
Ps 121: 4 Israel will neither slumber **n** sleep. H2256+4202
Ps 121: 6 harm you by day, **n** the moon by night. H2256
Ps 129: 7 **n** one who gathers fill his arms. H2256
Ps 135:17 **n** is there breath in their mouths. H677+401
Ps 147:10 **n** his delight in the legs of the warrior H4202
Pr 25:27 **n** is it honorable to search out matters H2256
Pr 30: 3 **n** have I attained to the knowledge of the H2256
Pr 30: 8 give me neither poverty **n** riches, but give H2256
Ecc 1: 8 seeing, **n** the ear its fill of hearing. H2256+4202
Ecc 4: 8 all alone; he had neither son **n** brother. H2256
Ecc 9:10 is neither working **n** planning nor H2256
Ecc 9:10 planning **n** knowledge nor wisdom H2256
Ecc 9:10 planning nor knowledge **n** wisdom. H2256
Ecc 9:11 **n** does food come to the H2256+1685+4202
Isa 2: 4 **n** will they train for war anymore. H2256+4202
Isa 5: 6 neither pruned **n** cultivated, and H2256+4202
Isa 9:13 **n** have they sought the LORD H2256+4202
Isa 9:17 **n** will he pity the fatherless and H2256+4202
Isa 11: 9 neither harm **n** destroy on all my H2256+4202
Isa 11:13 **n** Judah hostile toward Ephraim. H2256+4202
Isa 13:18 **n** will they look with compassion on H4202
Isa 22: 2 the sword, **n** did they die in battle. H2256+4202
Isa 23: 4 neither been in labor **n** given birth; H2256+4202
Isa 23: 4 neither reared sons **n** brought up H4202
Isa 28:27 **n** is the wheel of a cart rolled over cumin H2256
Isa 30: 5 bring neither help **n** advantage, H2256+4202
Isa 32: 5 be called noble **n** the scoundrel be H2256+4202
Isa 33:20 **n** any of its ropes broken. H2256+1153
Isa 35: 9 will be there, **n** any ravenous beast H2256+1153
Isa 40:16 **n** its animals enough for burnt H2256+401
Isa 43:10 **n** will there be one after me. H2256+4202
Isa 43:23 **n** honored me with your sacrifices. H2256+4202
Isa 43:23 grain offerings **n** wearied you with H2256+4202
Isa 48: 8 have neither heard **n** understood; H1685+4202
Isa 48:19 be blotted out **n** destroyed from H2256+4202
Isa 49:10 They will neither hunger **n** thirst H2256+4202
Isa 49:10 **n** will the desert heat or the sun H2256+4202
Isa 51:14 dungeon, **n** will they lack bread. H2256+4202
Isa 53: 9 **n** was any deceit in his mouth. H2256+4202
Isa 54:10 not be shaken **n** my covenant of H2256+4202
Isa 57:11 remembered me **n** taken this to heart? H4202
Isa 57:16 forever, **n** will I always be angry H2256+4202
Isa 59: 1 to save, **n** his ear too dull to hear. H2256+4202
Isa 60:18 **n** ruin or destruction within your borders NDT
Isa 60:19 **n** will the brightness of the moon H2256+4202
Isa 65:17 **n** will they come to mind. H2256+4202
Isa 65:23 **n** will they bear children doomed H2256+4202
Isa 65:25 neither harm **n** destroy on all my H2256+4202
Jer 3:16 **n** will another one be made. H2256+4202
Jer 7:16 this people **n** offer any plea or H2256+440
Jer 7:31 command, **n** did it enter my mind. H2256+4202
Jer 9:16 that neither they **n** their ancestors have H2256
Jer 10: 5 can do no harm **n** can they do H2256+1685+401
Jer 15:10 I have neither lent **n** borrowed, yet H2256+4202
Jer 16: 7 **n** will anyone give them a drink to console NDT
Jer 16:13 a land neither you **n** your ancestors have H2256
Jer 16:17 **n** is their sin concealed from my H2256+4202
Jer 18:18 not cease, **n** will counsel from the wise H2256
Jer 18:18 the wise, **n** the word from the prophets. H2256
Jer 19: 4 that neither they **n** their ancestors nor H2256
Jer 19: 4 their ancestors **n** the kings of Judah H2256
Jer 19: 5 mention, **n** did it enter my mind. H2256+4202
Jer 22:10 he will never return **n** see his native land H2256
Jer 23: 4 terrified, **n** will any be missing," H2256+4202
Jer 29:32 **n** will he see the good things I will H2256+4202
Jer 32:35 **n** did it enter my mind H2256+4202
Jer 33:10 by neither people **n** animals, H2256+4946+401
Jer 33:18 **n** will the Levitical priests ever fail H2256+4202
Jer 35: 6 'Neither you **n** your descendants must H2256
Jer 35: 8 Neither we **n** our wives nor our sons and NDT
Jer 35: 8 we nor our wives **n** our sons and daughters NDT
Jer 36:24 **n** did they tear their clothes. H2256+4202
Jer 37: 2 Neither he **n** his attendants nor the people H2256
Jer 37: 2 he nor his attendants **n** the people of the H2256
Jer 38:16 neither kill you **n** hand you over to H2256+561
Jer 44: 3 that neither they **n** you nor your ancestors NDT
Jer 44: 3 neither they nor you **n** your ancestors ever H2256

Jer 44:10 **n** have they followed my law and H2256+4202
Jer 46: 6 swift cannot flee **n** the strong escape H2256+440
Jer 49:31 that has neither gates **n** bars; H2256+4202
Jer 51: 3 his bow, **n** let him put on his armor. H2256+440
Jer 51:26 cornerstone, **n** any stone for a foundation H2256
Jer 51:62 that neither people **n** animals will live in H2256
La 4:12 **n** did any of the peoples of the world H2256
Eze 7:12 the buyer rejoice **n** the seller grieve, H2256+440
Eze 11:11 a pot for you, **n** will you be the meat in it H2256
Eze 13: 9 **n** will they enter the land of Israel. H2256+4202
Eze 14:11 **n** will they defile themselves H2256+4202
Eze 14:20 they could save neither son **n** daughter. H561
Eze 16: 4 **n** were you washed with water to H2256+4202
Eze 16: 4 **n** were you rubbed with salt or H2256+4202
Eze 18:20 **n** will the parent share the guilt of H2256+4202
Eze 20: 8 **n** did they forsake the idols of H2256+4202
Eze 24:14 I will not have pity, **n** will I relent. H2256+4202
Eze 29:11 The foot of neither man **n** beast will pass H2256
Eze 31: 8 **n** could the junipers equal its boughs H4202
Eze 31: 8 **n** could the plane trees compare H2256+4202
Eze 34:28 **n** will wild animals devour them. H2256+4202
Eze 43: 7 name—neither they **n** their kings—by H2256
Eze 47:12 will not wither, **n** will their fruit fail. H2256+4202
Da 2:44 **n** will it be left to another A10221+10379
Da 3:12 serve your gods **n** worship the A10221+10379
Da 3:27 **n** was a hair of their heads A10221+10379
Da 6: 4 neither corrupt **n** negligent. A10221
Da 6:22 **N** have I ever done any A10221+10059+10379
Da 11: 4 **n** will it have the power he H2256+4202
Da 11:24 neither his fathers **n** his forefathers did. H2256
Da 11:37 women, **n** will he regard any god H2256+4202
Hos 4:14 **n** your daughters-in-law when they H2256
Hos 9: 4 **n** will their sacrifices please him. H2256+4202
Hos 11: 9 **n** will I devastate Ephraim again. H4202
Joel 2: 2 in ancient times **n** ever will be in H4202+2256
Am 7:14 neither a prophet **n** the son of a H2256+4202
Ob 12 **n** rejoice over the people of Judah H2256+440
Ob 12 **n** boast so much in the day of their H2256+440
Ob 13 **n** gloat over them in their calamity in the H440
Ob 13 **n** seize their wealth in the day of H2256+440
Ob 14 **n** hand over their survivors in the day H2256+440
Mic 4: 3 **n** will they train for war anymore. H2256+4202
Zep 1: 6 seek the LORD **n** inquire of him." H2256+4202
Zep 1:18 Neither their silver **n** their gold will be H1685
Zep 3: 7 **n** all my punishments come upon her. NDT
Zec 4: 6 'Not by might **n** by power, but by H2256+4202
Zec 14: 6 day there will be neither sunlight **n** cold, H2256
Mt 10:24 the teacher, **n** a servant above his master. G4028
Mt 11:18 For John came neither eating **n** drinking G3612
Mt 22:30 will neither marry **n** be given in marriage; G4046
Mt 23:10 **N** are you to be called instructors, for you G3593
Mt 23:13 **n** will you let those enter who are trying to G4028
Mt 24:36 angels in heaven, **n** the Son, but only the G4028
Mk 12:25 will neither marry **n** be given in marriage; G4046
Mk 13:32 angels in heaven, **n** the Son, but only the G4028
Lk 6:43 **n** does a bad tree bear good fruit. G4028+4099
Lk 7:33 neither eating bread **n** drinking wine, G3612
Lk 14:35 neither for the soil **n** for the manure pile; G4046
Lk 16:26 **n** can anyone cross over from there to us. G3593
Lk 17:21 **n** will people say, 'Here it is,' or 'There it G4028
Lk 18: 2 feared God **n** cared what people G2779+3590
Lk 20:35 will neither marry **n** be given in marriage, G4046
Jn 1:13 **n** of human decision or a husband's will G4028
Jn 1:25 are not the Messiah, **n** Elijah, nor the G4028
Jn 1:25 the Messiah, nor Elijah, **n** the Prophet?" G4028
Jn 4:21 neither on this mountain **n** in Jerusalem. G4046
Jn 5:37 never heard his voice **n** seen his form, G4046
Jn 5:38 **n** does his word dwell in you, for G2779+4024
Jn 6:24 that neither Jesus **n** his disciples were G4028
Jn 9: 3 "Neither this man **n** his parents sinned," G4046
Jn 12:40 their eyes, **n** understand with their hearts G2779
Jn 12:40 with their hearts, **n** turn—and I would G2779
Jn 13:16 **n** is a messenger greater than the one G4028
Jn 14:17 because it neither sees him **n** knows him. G4028
Ac 2:31 of the dead, **n** did his body see decay. G4046
Ac 15:10 yoke that neither we **n** our ancestors have G4046
Ac 19:37 robbed temples **n** blasphemed our G4046
Ac 23: 8 that there are neither angels **n** spirits G3612
Ac 24:18 **n** was I involved in any disturbance. G4028
Ac 27:20 When neither sun **n** stars appeared for G3612
Ro 1:21 him as God **n** gave thanks to him, G2445
Ro 2:28 **n** is circumcision merely outward and G4028
Ro 5:16 **N** can the gift of God be compared G2779+4024
Ro 8: 7 not submit to God's law, **n** can it do so. G4028
Ro 8:38 I am convinced that neither death **n** life, G4046
Ro 8:38 neither angels **n** demons, neither the G4046
Ro 8:38 neither the present **n** the future, nor any G4046
Ro 8:38 the present nor the future, **n** any powers, G4046
Ro 8:39 neither height **n** depth, nor anything else G4046
Ro 8:39 depth, **n** anything else in all creation G4046
Ro 9: 7 **N** because they are his descendants are G4028
1Co 3: 7 the one who plants **n** the one who waters G4046
1Co 6: 9 the sexually immoral **n** idolaters nor G4046
1Co 6: 9 idolaters **n** adulterers nor men G4046
1Co 6: 9 adulterers **n** men who have sex with G4046
1Co 6:10 **n** thieves nor the greedy nor drunkards G4046
1Co 6:10 thieves **n** the greedy nor drunkards nor G4046
1Co 6:10 thieves nor the greedy **n** drunkards nor G4024
1Co 6:10 greedy nor drunkards **n** slanderers nor G4024
1Co 6:10 slanderers **n** swindlers will inherit G4024
1Co 11:11 of man, **n** is man independent of woman. G4046
1Co 11:16 other practice—**n** do the churches of God. G4028
1Co 15:50 **n** does the perishable inherit the G4028
2Co 4: 2 **n** do we distort the word of God. G3593
2Co 7:12 who did the wrong **n** on account of the G4028
Gal 1: 1 sent not from men **n** by a man, but by G4028
Gal 1:12 it from any man, **n** was I taught it; rather, G4046
Gal 3:28 There is neither Jew **n** Gentile, neither G4028
Gal 3:28 Gentile, neither slave **n** free, nor is there G4028
Gal 3:28 slave nor free, **n** is there male and female G4024
Gal 5: 6 neither circumcision **n** uncircumcision has G4046
Gal 6:15 Neither circumcision **n** uncircumcision G4046
Eph 5: 4 **N** should there be obscenity, foolish talk G2779
1Th 2: 3 motives, **n** are we trying to trick you. G4028
1Th 2: 5 **n** did we put on a mask to cover up greed G4046
2Th 3: 8 **n** did we eat anyone's food without paying G4028
1Ti 6:17 not to be arrogant **n** to put their hope in G3593
Heb 9:25 **N** did he enter heaven to offer himself G4028
Heb 10: 8 **n** were you pleased with them" G4028
Jas 1:13 **n** does he tempt **anyone**; G4029
1Jn 3:10 **n** is anyone who does not love their G2779
Rev 3:15 that you are neither cold **n** hot. G4046
Rev 3:16 neither hot **n** cold—I am about to G4046
Rev 7:16 down on them,' **n** any scorching heat. G4028
Rev 9:21 **N** did they repent of their murders G2779+4024
Rev 21:27 **n** will anyone who does what is shameful G2779

NORMALLY (1) [ABNORMAL]

2Ki 11: 7 two companies that **n** go off Sabbath duty NDT

NORTH (149) [NORTHERN, NORTHWARD]

Ge 13:14 where you are, to the **n** and south, to the H7600
Ge 14:15 as far as Hobah, **n** of Damascus. H4946+8520
Ge 28:14 to the east, to the **n** and to the south. H7600
Ex 26:20 other side, the **n** side of the tabernacle H7600
Ex 26:35 the curtain on the **n** side of the tabernacle H7600
Ex 27:11 The **n** side shall also be a hundred cubits H7600
Ex 36:25 other side, the **n** side of the tabernacle H7600
Ex 38:11 The **n** side was also a hundred cubits long H7600
Ex 40:22 of meeting on the **n** side of the H7600+2025
Lev 1:11 it at the **n** side of the altar H7600+2025
Nu 2:25 On the **n** will be the divisions of the camp H7600
Nu 3:35 were to camp on the **n** side of the H7600+2025
Nu 34: 9 This will be your boundary on the **n**. H7600
Nu 35: 5 on the west and two thousand on the **n**, H7600
Dt 2: 3 country long enough; now turn **n**. H7600+2025
Dt 3:12 Gadites the territory **n** of Aroer by the Arnon NDT
Dt 3:27 and look west and **n** and south and H7600+2025
Jos 8:11 They set up camp **n** of Ai, with the valley H7600
Jos 8:13 the main camp to the **n** of the city and the H7600
Jos 13: 3 of Egypt to the territory of Ekron on the **n**, H7600
Jos 15: 6 and continued **n** of Beth Arabah to H4946+7600
Jos 15: 7 of Achor and turned **n** to Gilgal, H7600+2025
Jos 16: 6 Mikmethath on the **n** it curved eastward to H7600
Jos 17:10 to Ephraim, on the **n** to Manasseh. H7600
Jos 17:10 Asher on the **n** and Issachar on the H7600
Jos 18: 5 tribes of Joseph in their territory on the **n**. H7600
Jos 18:12 On the **n** side their boundary began at the H7600
Jos 18:16 **n** of the Valley of Rephaim. H7600+2025
Jos 18:17 It then curved **n**, went to En H4946+7600
Jos 19:14 went around on the **n** to Hannathon and H7600
Jos 19:27 and went **n** to Beth Emek and H7600+2025
Jos 24:30 of Ephraim, **n** of Mount Gaash. H4946+7600
Jdg 2: 9 of Ephraim, **n** of Mount Gaash. H4946+7600
Jdg 7: 1 of Midian was **n** of them in the H4946+7600
Jdg 21:19 which lies **n** of Bethel, east H4946+7600+2025
1Sa 14: 5 One cliff stood to the **n** toward Mikmash H7600
1Ki 7:21 named Jakin and the one to the **n** Boaz. H8522
1Ki 7:25 three facing **n**, three facing west, H7600+2025
1Ki 7:39 of the temple and five on the **n**. H4946+8520
2Ki 11:11 the south side to the **n** side of the temple. H8522
2Ki 16:14 put it on the **n** side of the new H7600+2025
1Ch 9:24 east, west, **n** and south. H7600+2025
1Ch 26:14 the lot for the **N** Gate fell to him. H7600
1Ch 26:17 four a day on the **n**, four a day on H7600+2025
2Ch 3:17 one to the south and one to the **n**. H8520
2Ch 3:17 named Jakin and the *one to the* **n** Boaz. H8522
2Ch 4: 4 three facing **n**, three facing west, H7600+2025
2Ch 4: 6 five on the south side and five on the **n**. H8520
2Ch 4: 7 five on the south side and five on the **n**. H8520
2Ch 4: 8 five on the south side and five on the **n**. H8520
2Ch 23:10 the south side to the **n** side of the temple. H8522
Job 23: 9 When he is at work in the **n**, I do not see H8520
Job 37:22 Out of the **n** he comes in golden splendor; H7600
Ps 89:12 You created the **n** and the south; Tabor H7600
Ps 107: 3 from east and west, from **n** and south. H7600
Pr 25:23 Like a **n** wind that brings unexpected rain H7600
Ecc 1: 6 blows to the south and turns to the **n**; H7600
Ecc 11: 3 a tree falls to the south or to the **n**, H7600
SS 4:16 **n** wind, and come, south wind H7600
Isa 14:31 A cloud of smoke comes from the **n**, and H7600
Isa 41:25 "I have stirred up one from the **n**, and he H7600
Isa 43: 6 I will say to the **n**, 'Give them up!' and to H7600
Isa 49:12 some from the **n**, some from the west H7600
Jer 1:13 "It is tilting toward us from the **n**." H7600+2025
Jer 1:14 "From the **n** disaster will be poured out on H7600
Jer 3:12 proclaim this message toward the **n**: H7600
Jer 4: 6 For I am bringing disaster from the **n** H7600
Jer 6: 1 For disaster looms out of the **n**, even H7600
Jer 6:22 an army is coming from the land of the **n** H7600
Jer 10:22 a great commotion from the land of the **n**! H7600
Jer 13:20 see those who are coming from the **n**. H7600
Jer 15:12 break iron—iron from the **n**—or bronze? H7600
Jer 16:15 out of the land of the **n** and out of all the H7600
Jer 23: 8 the land of the **n** and out of all the H7600+2025
Jer 25: 9 all the peoples of the **n** and my servant H7600
Jer 25:26 all the kings of the **n**, near and far H7600
Jer 31: 8 the land of the **n** and gather them from H7600
Jer 46: 6 In the **n** by the River Euphrates they H7600
Jer 46:10 in the land of the **n** by the River Euphrates H7600
Jer 46:20 a gadfly is coming against her from the **n**. H7600
Jer 46:24 into the hands of the people of the **n**." H7600
Jer 47: 2 "See how the waters are rising in the **n** H7600
Jer 50: 3 A nation from the **n** will attack her and lay H7600
Jer 50: 9 of great nations from the land of the **n**. H7600
Jer 50: 9 and from **the n** she will be captured. H9004s
Jer 50:41 An army is coming from the **n**; a great H7600
Jer 51:48 out of the **n** destroyers will attack her," H7600
Eze 1: 4 I saw a windstorm coming out of the **n**— H7600
Eze 8: 3 entrance of the **n** gate of the inner H7600+2025
Eze 8: 5 "Son of man, look toward the **n**." H7600+2025
Eze 8: 5 in the entrance **n** of the gate of the H4946+7600
Eze 8:14 entrance of the **n** gate of the house H7600+2025
Eze 9: 2 which faces **n**, each with a H7600+2025
Eze 16:46 who lived to the **n** *of* you with her H8520
Eze 20:47 face from south to **n** will be scorched by it. H7600
Eze 21: 4 against everyone from south to **n**. H7600
Eze 26: 7 From the **n** I am going to bring against H7600
Eze 32:30 the princes of the **n** and all the Sidonians H7600
Eze 38: 6 from the far **n** with all its troops— H7600
Eze 38:15 You will come from your place in the far **n** H7600
Eze 39: 2 you from the far **n** and send you against H7600
Eze 40:19 on the east side as well as on the **n**. H7600
Eze 40:20 and width of the **n** gate, H7156+2006+2021+7600
Eze 40:23 gate to the inner court facing the **n** gate, H7600
Eze 40:35 brought me to the **n** gate and measured it H7600
Eze 40:40 entrance of the **n** gateway were H7600+2025
Eze 40:44 at the side of the **n** gate and facing south, H7600
Eze 40:44 the south gate and facing **n**. H2006+2021+7600
Eze 40:46 the room facing **n** is for the H2006+2021+7600
Eze 41:11 one on the **n** and another on the south H7600
Eze 42: 1 opposite the outer wall on the **n** *side*. H7600
Eze 42: 2 whose door faced **n** was a hundred cubits H7600
Eze 42: 4 Their doors were on the **n**. H7600
Eze 42:11 These were like the rooms on the **n**; they H7600
Eze 42:11 Similar to the doorways on the **n** NDT
Eze 42:13 "The **n** and south rooms facing the H7600
Eze 42:17 He measured the **n** side; it was five H7600
Eze 44: 4 me by way of the **n** gate to the front of the H7600
Eze 46: 9 enters by the **n** gate to worship is to H7600
Eze 46: 9 south gate is to go out the **n** gate. H7600+2025
Eze 46:19 gate to the sacred rooms facing **n**, H7600+2025
Eze 47: 2 out through the **n** gate and led me H7600+2025
Eze 47:15 "On the **n** side it will run from the H7600+2025
Eze 47:17 with the border of Hamath to the **n**. H7600
Eze 48:10 It will be 25,000 cubits long on the **n** *side*, H7600
Eze 48:16 the **n** side 4,500 cubits, the south side H7600
Eze 48:17 the city will be 250 cubits on the **n**, H7600
Eze 48:30 Beginning on the **n** side, which is 4,500 H7600
Eze 48:31 three gates on the **n** *side* will be the gate H7600
Da 8: 4 toward the west and the **n** and the south. H7600
Da 11: 6 to the king of the **N** to make an alliance, H7600
Da 11: 7 of the king of the **N** and enter his fortress; H7600
Da 11: 8 he will leave the king of the **N** alone. H7600
Da 11: 9 Then the king of the **N** will invade the realm NDT
Da 11:11 a rage and fight against the king of the **N**, H7600
Da 11:13 For the king of the **N** will muster another H7600
Da 11:15 the king of the **N** will come and build H7600
Da 11:28 The king of the **N** will return to his own NDT
Da 11:40 the king of the **N** will storm out H7600
Da 11:44 from the east and the **n** will alarm him, H7600
Am 8:12 sea to sea and wander from **n** to east, H7600
Zep 2:13 hand against the **n** and destroy Assyria, H7600
Zec 2: 6 Flee from the land of the **n**," declares the H7600
Zec 6: 6 horses is going toward the **n** country, H7600
Zec 6: 8 going toward the **n** country have given my H7600
Zec 6: 8 given my Spirit rest in the land of the **n**." H7600
Zec 14: 4 moving **n** and half moving H7600+2025
Lk 13:29 from east and west and **n** and south, G1080
Rev 21:13 three on the **n**, three on the south G1080

NORTHEASTER (1) [EAST]

Ac 27:14 called the **N**, swept down from the G2350

NORTHERN (19) [NORTH]

Nu 34: 7 " 'For your **n** boundary, run a line from the H7600
Jos 11: 2 to the **n** kings who were in the H4946+7600
Jos 15: 5 The **n** boundary started from the H7600+2025
Jos 15: 8 Valley at the **n** end of the Valley of H7600+2025
Jos 15:10 ran along the **n** slope of H4946+7600+2025
Jos 15:11 It went to the **n** slope of Ekron H7600+2025
Jos 17: 9 was the **n** *side* of the ravine H4946+7600
Jos 18:12 passed the **n** slope of Jericho and H4946+7600
Jos 18:18 It continued to the **n** slope of Beth H7600+2025
Jos 18:19 It then went to the **n** slope of Beth H7600+2025
Jos 18:19 came out at the **n** bay of the Dead H7600+2025
Job 26: 7 spreads out the **n** *skies* over empty space; H7600
Jer 1:15 all the peoples of the **n** kingdoms," H7600+2025
Jer 3:18 they will come from a **n** land to the land I H7600
Eze 47:17 along the **n** border of Damascus H7600
Eze 47:17 This will be the **n** boundary. H7600
Eze 48: 1 At the **n** frontier, Dan will have one H7600+2025
Eze 48: 1 Enan and the **n** border of H7600+2025
Joel 2:20 "I will drive the **n** *horde* far from you H7603

N

NORTHWARD (1) [NORTH]
Eze 42: 1 man led me **n** into the outer H2006+2021+7600

NORTHWEST (1) [WEST]
Ac 27:12 in Crete, facing both southwest and **n**. *G6008*

NOSE (13) [NOSES]
Ge 24:22 took out a gold **n ring** weighing a beka H5690
Ge 24:30 As soon as he had seen the **n ring**, and H5690
Ge 24:47 I put the ring in her **n** and the bracelets on H678
2Ki 19:28 put my hook in your **n** and my bit in your H678
2Ch 33:11 put a hook in his **n**, bound him with bronze NDT
Job 40:24 it by the eyes, or trap it and pierce its **n**? H678
Job 41: 2 a cord through its **n** or pierce its jaw with H678
Pr 30:33 as twisting the **n** produces blood, so H678
SS 7: 4 Your **n** is like the tower of Lebanon looking H678
Isa 3:21 the signet rings and **n** rings, H678
Isa 37:29 put my hook in your **n** and my bit in your H678
Eze 8:17 Look at them putting the branch to their **n**! H678
Eze 16:12 I put a ring on your **n**, earrings on your H678

NOSES (2) [NOSE]
Ps 115: 6 but cannot hear, **n**, but cannot smell. H678
Eze 23:25 They will cut off your **n** and your ears, and H678

NOSTRILS (13)
Ge 2: 7 breathed into his **n** the breath of life, H678
Ge 7:22 that had the breath of life in its **n** died. H678
Ex 15: 8 By the blast of your **n** the waters piled up H678
Nu 11:20 it comes out of your **n** and you loathe it— H678
2Sa 22: 9 Smoke rose from his **n**; consuming fire H678
2Sa 22:16 the LORD, at the blast of breath from his **n**. H678
Job 27: 3 life within me, the breath of God in my **n**, H678
Job 41:20 Smoke pours from its **n** as from a boiling H5705
Ps 18: 8 Smoke rose from his **n**; consuming fire H678
Ps 18:15 at the blast of breath from your **n**. H678
Isa 2:22 humans, who have but a breath in their **n**. H678
Isa 65: 5 Such people are smoke in my **n**, a fire that H678
Am 4:10 I filled your **n** with the stench of your camps H678

NOT (5859) [AREN'T, CAN'T, COULDN'T, DIDN'T, DOESN'T, DON'T, HASN'T, HAVEN'T, ISN'T, NO, SHOULDN'T, WASN'T, WEREN'T, WON'T, WOULDN'T] See Index of Articles Etc.

NOTABLE (2) [NOTE]
Am 6: 1 *you* **n** *men of* the foremost nation H5918
Ac 4:16 knows they have performed a **n** sign, *G1196*

NOTE (12) [ANNOTATIONS, NOTABLE, NOTES]
Ru 3: 4 lies down, **n** the place where he is lying. H3359
2Sa 3:36 All the people **took n** and were pleased H5795
Job 11:11 when he sees evil, *does he* not **take n**? H1067
Job 34:25 Because *he* **takes n of** their deeds, he H5795
Ps 106:44 Yet *he* **took n** of their distress when he H8011
Pr 21:12 Righteous One **takes n** of the house of H8505
Pr 23: 1 a ruler, **n well** what is before you H1067+1067
Jer 31:21 **Take n** of the highway, the road H8883+4213
Eze 20:37 *I will* **take n** *of* you **as** you **pass** under my H6296
Ac 4:13 astonished and *they* **took n** that these *G2105*
2Th 3:14 **Take special n** *of* anyone who does not *G4957*
Jas 1:19 dear brothers and sisters, **take n** of this: *G3857*

NOTES (1) [NOTE]
1Co 14: 7 unless there is a distinction *in* the **n**? *G5782*

NOTHING (337) [NO, THING]
Ge 11: 6 then **n** they plan to do will be H4202+3972
Ge 14:23 I will accept **n** belonging to H561+4946+3972
Ge 14:24 I will accept **n** but what my men have H1187
Ge 18:27 the Lord, though I am **n** but dust and ashes, NDT
Ge 24:50 we can say **n** to you one way or the other. H4202
Ge 29:15 of mine, should you work for me **for n**? H2855
Ge 31:33 the two female servants, but he found **n**. H4202
Ge 31:34 everything in the tent but found **n**. H4202
Ge 34: 5 so he **did n** *about* it until they came home H3087
Ge 39: 9 has withheld **n** from me except you H4202+4399
Ge 40:15 I have done **n** to deserve being H4202+4399
Ge 47:18 there is **n** left for our lord except our H4202
Ex 1: 8 to whom Joseph meant **n**, came to power H4202
Ex 10:15 **N** green remained on tree or plant H4202+3972
Ex 12:20 Eat **n** made with yeast. Wherever H4202+3972
Ex 13: 3 a mighty hand. Eat **n** containing yeast. H4202
Ex 13: 7 **n** with yeast in it is to be seen among you, H4202
Ex 22: 3 if they have **n**, they must be sold to pay H401
Ex 23: 7 **Have n to do** with a false charge and do H8178
Lev 14:36 so that **n** in the house will be H4202+3972
Lev 27:28 " 'But **n** that a person owns and H3972+4202
Nu 20:19 only want to pass through on foot—**n** else." H401
Nu 23:11 *you have* **done n but bless** H1385+1385
Nu 30: 4 about her vow or pledge but **says n** to her, H3087
Nu 30: 7 husband hears about it but **says n** to her, H3087
Nu 30:11 hears about it but **says n** to her and does H3087
Nu 30:14 husband **says n** to her *about* it from H3087+3087
Nu 30:14 confirms them by **saying n** to her when he H3087
Dt 5:22 the deep darkness; and he added **n** *more*. H4202
Dt 8: 9 not be scarce and you will lack **n**; H4202+3972
Dt 15: 9 your fellow Israelites and give them **n**. H4202
Dt 22:26 Do **n** to the woman; she has H4202+1821
Dt 28:33 you will have **n but** cruel oppression H8370
Dt 29:23 of salt and sulfur—**n** planted, nothing H4202
Dt 29:23 nothing planted, **n** sprouting, no H4202
Jos 11:15 he left **n** undone of all that the H4202+1821
Jdg 7:14 "This can **be n** other than the sword H401+1194
Jdg 18: 7 And since their land lacked **n**, they H401+1821
Jdg 18:10 a land that lacks **n whatever**." H401+3972+1821
1Sa 3:18 told him everything, hiding **n** from him. H4202
1Sa 4: 7 **N** like this has happened before H4202
1Sa 14: 6 **N** can hinder the LORD from saving, whether H401
1Sa 20:26 Saul said **n** that day, for he thought H4202+4399
1Sa 20:39 The boy knew **n** about all this; only H4202
1Sa 22:15 your servant knows **n** at all about this H4202
1Sa 24:11 See that **there is n** in my hand to indicate H401
1Sa 25: 7 they were at Carmel **n** of theirs was H4202+4399
1Sa 25:15 fields near them **n** was missing. H4202+4399
1Sa 25:21 so that **n** of his was missing H4202+4399
1Sa 25:36 So she told him **n** at all until H4202+1821
1Sa 28:20 he had eaten **n** all that day and H4312+4202
1Sa 29: 7 do **n** to displease the Philistine rulers." H4202
1Sa 30:19 **N** was missing: young or old, boy or girl H4202
2Sa 12: 3 the poor man had **n** except one little H401+3972
2Sa 15:11 knowing **n** about the matter. H4202+3972
2Sa 18:13 and **n** is hidden from the H4202+3972+1821
2Sa 19: 6 commanders and their men mean **n** to you. H401
2Sa 19:10 So why *do* you **say n** *about* bringing the H3087
2Sa 19:28 deserved **n** but death from my H4202
2Sa 24:24 my God burnt offerings that **cost** me **n**." H2855
1Ki 1:11 and our lord David knows **n** about it? H4202
1Ki 4:27 They saw to it that **n** was lacking. H4202+1821
1Ki 6: 6 of the temple so that **n** would be inserted H1194
1Ki 8: 9 **There was n** in the ark except the two stone H401
1Ki 10: 3 **n** was too hard for the king to H4202+1821
1Ki 10:20 **N** like it had ever been made for any H4202
1Ki 10:21 **N** was made of silver, because silver was H401
1Ki 11:22 Pharaoh asked. "**N**," Hadad replied, "but H4202
1Ki 18:21 But the people said **n**. H4202+1821
1Ki 18:43 and looked. "**There is n** there," he H401+4399
1Ki 22: 3 to us and yet we *are* **doing n** to retake it H3120
1Ki 22:16 you swear to tell me **n** but the truth in the H4202
1Ki 22:27 give him **n but** bread and water H4316
2Ki 4: 2 "Your servant has **n** there at all," she said H401
2Ki 4:41 And there was **n** harmful in the pot. H4202+1821
2Ki 9:35 bury her, they found **n** except her skull H4202
2Ki 13: 7 **N** had been left of the army of Jehoahaz H4202
2Ki 18:36 silent and said **n** in reply, H4202+1821
2Ki 20:13 There was **n** in his palace or in all H4202+1821
2Ki 20:15 "There is **n** among my treasures H4202+1821
2Ki 20:17 off to Babylon. **N** will be left, says H4202+1821
1Ch 21:24 sacrifice a burnt offering that **costs** me **n**." H2855
2Ch 5:10 **There was n** in the ark except the two H401
2Ch 9: 2 **n** was too hard for him to explain H4202+1821
2Ch 9:11 **N** like them had ever been seen in Judah.) H4202
2Ch 9:19 **N** like it had ever been made for any H4202
2Ch 9:20 **N** was made of silver, because silver was H401
2Ch 18:15 you swear to tell me **n** but the truth in the H4202
2Ch 18:26 give him **n but** bread and water H4316
2Ch 30:26 Israel there had been **n** like this in H4202
Ezr 4:16 will be left with **n** in A10379+10269
Ne 2: 2 This can be **n** but sadness of heart. H401
Ne 2:16 as yet I had said **n** to the Jews or the H4202
Ne 5: 8 because they could find **n** to say. H4202
Ne 6: 8 "**N** like what you are saying is happening H4202
Ne 8:10 send some to those who have **n** prepared. H401
Ne 9:21 they lacked **n**, their clothes did not H4202
Est 2:15 she asked for **n** other than what H4202+1821
Est 6: 3 "**N** has been done for him," his H4202+1821
Job 1: 9 "Does Job fear God **for n**?" Satan replied. H2855
Job 5:24 stock of your property and find **n** missing. H4202
Job 8: 9 we were born only yesterday and know **n**, H4202
Job 15:18 hiding **n** received from their ancestors H4202
Job 15:31 is worthless, for he will get **n** in return. H8736
Job 19:20 I am **n but skin** and bones; H6425+2256+1414
Job 20:21 **N** is left for him to devour; his prosperity H401
Job 21:34 **N** is left of your answers but falsehood!" NDT
Job 24: 7 they have **n** to cover themselves in the cold. H401
Job 24:16 they want **n** to do with the light. H4202
Job 24:25 prove me false and reduce my words to **n**?" H440
Job 26: 7 he suspends the earth over **n**. H1172+4537
Job 32: 5 saw that the three men had **n** *more* to say, H401
Job 33:21 Their flesh wastes away **to n**, and H4946+8024
Job 37: 4 his voice resounds, he holds **n** back. H4202
Job 39:22 afraid of **n**; it does not shy away H4202
Job 41:33 **N** on earth is its equal—a creature without H401
Ps 10: 6 says to himself, "**N** will ever shake me." H1153
Ps 14: 4 Do all these evildoers know **n**? They H4202
Ps 19: 6 to the other; **n** is deprived of its warmth. H401
Ps 23: 1 The LORD is my shepherd, I lack **n**. H4202
Ps 34: 9 holy people, for those who fear him lack **n**. H401
Ps 35:11 question me on things I know **n** about. H4202
Ps 39: 5 the span of my years **is** as **n** before you. H401
Ps 44:12 a pittance, gaining **n** from their sale. H4202
Ps 49:17 will take **n** with them when H4202+2021+3972
Ps 53: 4 Do all these evildoers know **n**? They H4202
Ps 53: 5 with dread, where there was **n** to dread. H4202
Ps 62: 9 on a balance, they are **n**; together they are NDT
Ps 73:25 And earth has **n** I desire besides you. H4202
Ps 82: 5 "The 'gods' know **n**, they understand H4202
Ps 82: 5 'gods' know nothing, they understand **n**. H4202
Ps 101: 4 I will have **n** to do with what is evil. H4202
Ps 112:10 the longings of the wicked *will* **come to n**. H6
Ps 119:118 decrees, for their delusions **come to n**. H9214
Ps 119:165 your law, and **n** can make them stumble. H401
Ps 139:22 I have **n but** hatred for them; I count them H9417
Ps 146: 4 on that very day their plans **come to n**. H6
Pr 3:15 **n** you desire can compare with her. H4202+3972
Pr 8:11 and **n** you desire can compare with H3972+4202
Pr 9:13 she is simple and knows **n**. H1153+4537
Pr 10:28 but the hopes of the wicked **come to n**. H6
Pr 11: 7 all the promise of their power **comes to n**. H6
Pr 13: 7 to be rich, yet *has* **n**; another H401+3972
Pr 20: 4 so at harvest time they look but find **n**. H401
Pr 24:12 "But we knew **n** about this," does not H4202
Pr 28:27 Those who give to the poor will lack **n**, but H401
Pr 30:20 her mouth and says, 'I've done **n** wrong. H4202
Pr 30:30 beasts, who retreats before **n**; H4202+3972
Pr 31:11 confidence in her and lacks **n** of value. H4202
Ecc 1: 9 **there is n** new under the sun. H401+3972
Ecc 2:10 I denied myself **n** my eyes desired H4202+3972
Ecc 2:11 the wind; **n** was gained under the sun. H401
Ecc 2:24 A person can do **n** better than to eat and H401
Ecc 3:12 I know that **there is n** better for people than H401
Ecc 3:14 **n** can be added to it and nothing taken H401
Ecc 3:14 can be added to it and **n** taken from it. H401
Ecc 3:22 So I saw that **there is n** better for a person H401
Ecc 5:14 have children **there is n** left for them H401+4399
Ecc 5:15 They take **n** from their toil that they H4202+4399
Ecc 6: 2 so that they lack **n** their hearts desire H401+3972
Ecc 8:15 because **there is n** better for a person H401
Ecc 9: 5 the dead know **n**; they have no H401+4399
Isa 10: 4 **N** will remain but to cringe among the H1194
Isa 15: 6 the vegetation is gone and **n** green is left. H4202
Isa 17:11 the harvest *will be as* **n** in the day of H5610
Isa 19: 3 and *I will* **bring** their plans **to n**; they H1182
Isa 19:11 The officials of Zoan are **n but** fools; the H421
Isa 19:15 There is **n** Egypt can do—head H4202+5126
Isa 29:11 whole vision is **n but** words sealed in a H3869
Isa 29:16 the pot say to the potter, "You know **n**"? H4202
Isa 34:12 Her nobles will have **n** there to be called a H401
Isa 36:21 silent and said **n** in reply, H4202+1821
Isa 39: 2 There was **n** in his palace or in all H4202+1821
Isa 39: 4 "There is **n** among my treasures H4202+1821
Isa 39: 6 off to Babylon. **N** will be left, says H4202+1821
Isa 40:17 Before him all the nations are as **n**; they H401
Isa 40:17 by him as worthless and less than **n**. H700
Isa 40:23 reduces the rulers of this world to **n**. H9332
Isa 41:11 who oppose you will be as **n** and perish. H401
Isa 41:12 against you will be as **n at all**. H401+2256+700
Isa 41:24 But you are less than **n** and your works are H401
Isa 41:29 Their deeds **amount to n**; their images are H700
Isa 44: 9 All who make idols are **n**, and the things H9332
Isa 44:10 god and casts an idol, which can profit **n**? H1194
Isa 44:18 They know **n**, they understand nothing H4202
Isa 44:18 nothing, they understand **n**; their eyes are H4202
Isa 45: 9 those who are **n** but potsherds among the NDT
Isa 49: 4 my strength for **n at all**. H9332+2256+2039
Isa 52: 3 "You were sold **for n**, and without money H2855
Isa 52: 5 my people have been taken away **for n**, H2855
Isa 53: 2 **n** in his appearance that we should desire H4202
Isa 54:14 be far from you; you will have **n** to fear. H4202
Jer 5:12 about the LORD; they said, "He will do **n**! H4202
Jer 10:24 in your anger, or *you will* **reduce** me **to n**. H5070
Jer 12:13 they will wear themselves out but gain **n**. H4202
Jer 16:19 "Our ancestors possessed **n but** false gods H421
Jer 22:13 making his own people work **for n**, not H2855
Jer 30:14 have forgotten you; they care **n** for you. H4202
Jer 32:17 **N** is too hard for you H4202+3972+1821
Jer 32:30 Judah have done **n but** evil in my sight H421
Jer 32:30 of Israel have done **n but** arouse my anger H421
Jer 38: 5 "The king can do **n** to oppose you." H401+1821
Jer 39:10 who owned **n**; and at that time H401+4399
Jer 42: 4 says and will keep **n** back from you." H4202+1821
Jer 44:18 *we have* **had n** and have been H2893+3972
Jer 48:30 "and her boasts accomplish **n**. H4202+4027
Jer 48:38 public squares there is **n but** mourning, H3972
Jer 50: 2 proclaim it; keep **n** back, but say, H440
Jer 51:58 exhaust themselves **for n**, H928+1896+8198
La 1:12 "Is it **n** to you, all you who pass by? Look H4202
Eze 7:11 crowd—none of their wealth, **n** of value. H4202
Eze 12:22 'The days go by and every vision **comes to n**'? H6
Eze 13: 3 follow their own spirit and have seen **n**! H1194
Eze 14:23 I have done **n** in it without H4202+3972+889
Eze 33:12 former righteousness will count for **n**. H4202
Eze 33:32 them you are **n more than** one who sings H3869
Da 1:12 Give us **n but** vegetables to eat and water H4946
Da 4:35 peoples of the earth are regarded as **n**. A10379
Da 9:12 the whole heaven **n** has ever been done H4202
Da 9:26 One will be put to death and will have **n**. H401
Joel 2: 3 a desert waste—**n** escapes them. H4202
Am 3: 4 it growl in its den when it has caught **n**? H1194
Am 3: 7 LORD does **n** without revealing H4202+1821
Am 5: 5 into exile, and Bethel will be reduced to **n**." H224
Mic 6:14 You will store up but save **n**, because H4202
Na 2:11 lioness went, and the cubs, with **n** to fear? H401
Na 3:19 **N** can heal you; your wound is fatal. H401
Hab 2:13 exhaust themselves **for n**? H928+1896+8198
Zep 1:12 'The LORD will do **n**, either good or bad. H4202
Zep 3: 3 who leave **n** for the morning. H4202
Hag 2: 3 Does it not seem to you like **n**? H401
Mal 2: 6 in his mouth and **n** false was found on H4202
Mt 9:33 "**N** like this has **ever** been seen in Israel." *G4030*
Mt 10:26 there is **n** concealed that will not be *G4029*
Mt 15:32 me three days and have **n** to eat. *G4024+5515*
Mt 17:20 **N** will be impossible for you. *G4029*
Mt 20: 3 standing in the marketplace **doing n**. *G734*
Mt 20: 6 been standing here all day long **doing n**? *G734*
Mt 21:19 up to it but found **n** on it except leaves. *G4029*
Mt 23:16 the temple, it means **n**; but anyone who *G4029*

N

Mt 23:18 the altar, it means **n**; but anyone who G4029
Mt 24:39 they knew **n** about what would G4024
Mt 25:42 For I was hungry and you gave me **n** to eat, G4024
Mt 25:42 I was thirsty and you gave me **n** to drink, G4024
Mk 6: 8 "Take **n** for the journey except a staff—no G3594
Mk 7:15 **N** outside a person can defile them by G4029
Mk 7:18 "Don't you see that **n** that enters a G4246+4024
Mk 8: 1 Since they had **n** to eat, Jesus G3590+5515
Mk 8: 2 me three days and have **n** to eat. G4024+5515
Mk 11:13 he found **n** but leaves, because G4029
Mk 14:51 **wearing n** but a linen G4314+2093+1218
Mk 16: 8 They said **n** to anyone, because they were G4029
Lk 4: 2 He ate **n** during those days, and at the G4029
Lk 8:17 For there is **n** hidden that will not be G4024
Lk 8:17 **and n** concealed that will not be known G4028
Lk 9: 3 "Take **n** for the journey—no staff, no bag G3594
Lk 10:19 the power of the enemy; **n** will harm you. G4029
Lk 12: 2 There is **n** concealed that will not be G4029
Lk 14: 6 And they had **n** to say. G4024
Lk 19:26 as for the one who has **n**, even what G3590
Lk 22:35 you lack anything?" "**N**," they answered. G4029
Lk 23:15 can see, he has done **n** to deserve death. G4029
Lk 23:41 But this man has done **n** wrong." G4029
Jn 1: 3 without him **n** was made that has G4028+1651
Jn 4:11 "you have **n** to draw with and the well is G4046
Jn 4:32 "I have food to eat that you know **n** about." G4024
Jn 5:19 the Son can do **n** by himself; he can G4029
Jn 5:30 By myself I can do **n**; I judge only as I hear G4029
Jn 6:12 are left over. Let **n** be wasted." G3590+5516
Jn 6:63 the flesh counts for **n**. The words I have G4029
Jn 7:18 a man of truth; there is **n** false about him. G4024
Jn 7:49 But this mob that knows **n** of the law G3590
Jn 8:28 he and that I do **n** on my own but speak G4029
Jn 8:54 "If I glorify myself, my glory means **n**. G4029
Jn 9:33 man were not from God, he could do **n**." G4029
Jn 10:13 is a hired hand and cares **n** for the sheep. G4024
Jn 11:49 spoke up, "You know **n at all**! G4024+4029
Jn 15: 5 apart from me you can do **n**. G4024+4029
Jn 18:20 the Jews come together. I said **n** in secret. G4029
Jn 21: 3 the boat, but that night they caught **n**. G4029
Ac 4:14 with them, there was **n** they could say. G4029
Ac 5:36 were dispersed, and it all came to **n**. G4029
Ac 7:18 to whom Joseph meant **n**, came to power G4024
Ac 8:24 Lord for me so that **n** you have said may G3594
Ac 9: 8 when he opened his eyes he could see **n**. G4029
Ac 11: 8 **N** impure or unclean has **ever** entered my G4030
Ac 17:21 their time doing **n** but talking about and G4029
Ac 20:24 I consider my life worth **n** to me G4029+3364
Ac 23: 9 "We find **n** wrong with this man," they G4029
Ac 25: 8 "I have done **n** wrong against the G4046+5516
Ac 25:25 I found he had done **n** deserving of death G3594
Ac 25:26 But I have **n** definite to write to His G5516+4024
Ac 26:22 I am saying **n** beyond what the prophets G4029
Ac 28: 6 time and seeing **n** unusual happen to G3594
Ac 28:17 I have done **n** against our people G4029
Ro 4:14 faith **means n** and the promise is G3033
Ro 14:14 the Lord Jesus, that **n** is unclean in itself. G4029
1Co 2: 2 resolved to know **n** while I was with G4024+5516
1Co 2: 6 rulers of this age, who *are* **coming to n**. G2934
1Co 4: 5 Therefore judge **n** before the G3590+5516
1Co 7:19 Circumcision is **n** and uncircumcision is G4029
1Co 7:19 is nothing and uncircumcision is **n**. G4029
1Co 8: 4 know that "An idol is **n at all** in the world" G4029
1Co 11:22 of God by humiliating those who have **n**? G3590
1Co 13: 2 mountains, but do not have love, I am **n**. G4029
1Co 13: 3 may boast, but do not have love, I gain **n**. G4029
1Co 15:58 Let **n move** you. Always give G293
1Co 16:10 to it that he has **n to fear** while he is with G925
2Co 6:10 many rich; having **n**, and yet possessing G3594
2Co 10:10 his speaking **amounts to n**. G2024
2Co 12: 1 Although there is **n** to be gained, I will go G4024
2Co 12:11 the "super-apostles," even though I am **n**. G4029
Gal 2: 6 favoritism—they added **n** to my message. G4029
Gal 2:21 gained through the law, Christ died **for n**!" G1562
Eph 5:11 Have **n** to do with the fruitless deeds of G3590
Php 2: 3 Do **n** out of selfish ambition or vain G3594
Php 2: 7 *he* **made** himself **n** by taking the very G3033
1Ti 3:10 then if there is **n against** them, let G441
1Ti 4: 4 **n** is to be rejected if it is received G4029
1Ti 4: 7 **Have n to do with** godless myths and old G4148
1Ti 5:21 partiality, and to do **n** out of favoritism. G3594
1Ti 6: 4 they are conceited and understand **n**. G3594
1Ti 6: 7 For we brought **n** into the world, and we G4029
1Ti 6: 7 **and** we can take **n** out of it. G4028+5516
2Ti 3: 5 **Have n to do with** such people. G706
Titus 1:15 corrupted and do not believe, **n** is pure. G4029
Titus 2: 8 because they have **n** bad to say about us. G3594
Titus 3:10 After that, **have n to do with** them. G4148
Heb 2: 8 God left **n** that is not subject to them. G4029
Heb 4:13 **N** in all creation is hidden from God's G4024
Heb 7:14 to that tribe Moses said **n** about priests. G4029
Heb 7:19 the law made **n** perfect), and a better G4029
Heb 8: 7 if there had been **n wrong** *with* that first G289
Jas 2:16 does **n** about their physical needs G3590
1Pe 3: 7 so that **n** will hinder your prayers. G3590
1Jn 2:10 there is **n** in them to make them G4024
Rev 21:27 **N** impure will ever enter it G4024+3590+4246

NOTICE (17) [NOTICED, NOTICING]

Ge 39: 7 master's wife **took n** of Joseph and H5951+6524
Dt 21:11 if *you* **n** among the captives a beautiful H8011
Ru 2:10 such favor in your eyes that you **n** me— H5795
Ru 2:19 Blessed be the *man who* **took n** *of* you!" H5795
2Sa 9: 8 that *you should* **n** a dead dog like me?" H7155
Job 35:15 and *he does* not **take** the least **n** of H3359
Ps 10:11 himself, "God *will* **never n**; he covers his H8894
Ps 94: 7 not see; the God of Jacob **takes** no **n**." H1067
Ps 94: 8 **Take n**, *you* senseless ones among the H1067
Eze 38:14 living in safety, *will you* not **take n** *of* it? H3359
Hos 7: 9 is sprinkled with gray, but he *does* not **n**. H3359
Jnh 1: 6 Maybe he *will* **take n** of us so that we will H6951
Mk 15:26 The **written n** of the charge against him G2107
Lk 23:38 There was a **written n** above him, which G2107
Jn 19:19 Pilate had a **n** prepared and fastened to G5518
Ac 21:26 to the temple *to* **give n** of the date when G1334
Ac 26:26 that none of this *has* **escaped** his **n**, G3291

NOTICED (10) [NOTICE]

Ge 31: 2 And Jacob **n** *that* Laban's attitude toward H8011
2Sa 12:19 David **n** that his attendants were H8011
1Ki 21:29 "*Have you* **n** how Ahab has humbled H8011
Pr 7: 7 the simple, *I* **n** among the young men H1067
Isa 58: 3 humbled ourselves, and *you have* not **n**? H3359
Jer 33:24 "*Have you* not **n** that these people are H8011
Mt 22:11 *he* **n** a man there who was not wearing G3972
Lk 11:38 was surprised *when he* **n** that Jesus did G3972
Lk 14: 7 *When he* **n** how the guests picked the G2091
Jn 11:31 *When* the Jews who had been with Mary in the house, comforting her, **n** G3972

NOTICING (1) [NOTICE]

Mk 12:28 **N** that Jesus had given them a good G3972

NOTIONS (2)

Job 15: 2 answer with empty **n** or fill their belly with H1981
Col 2:18 they are puffed up *with* **idle n** by their G1632

NOURISH (2) [NOURISHED, NOURISHING, NOURISHMENT, WELL-NOURISHED]

Pr 10:21 The lips of the righteous **n** many, but H8286
Pr 27:27 your family and to **n** your female servants. H2644

NOURISHED (5) [NOURISH]

Dt 32:13 *He* **n** him *with* honey from the rock, and H3567
Job 21:24 **well n** in body, bones rich with H4848+2692
Eze 31: 4 The waters **n** it, deep springs made it H1540
Da 1:15 and better **n** than any of the H1374+1414
1Ti 4: 6 **n** on the truths of the faith and of the G1957

NOURISHING (1) [NOURISH]

Ro 11:17 now share in the **n sap** from the olive root G4404

NOURISHMENT (1) [NOURISH]

Pr 3: 8 health to your body and **n** to your bones. H9198

NOVICE (KJV) RECENT CONVERT

NOW (1219)

Ge 1: 2 **N** the earth was formless and empty H2256
Ge 2: 5 **N** no shrub had yet appeared on the earth H2256
Ge 2: 8 **N** the LORD God had planted a garden in H2256
Ge 2:19 **N** the LORD God had formed out of the H2256
Ge 2:23 "This is **n** bone of my bones and flesh of H7193
Ge 3: 1 **N** the serpent was more crafty than any of H2256
Ge 3:22 "The man has **n** become like one of us H6964
Ge 4: 2 **N** Abel kept flocks, and Cain worked the H2256
Ge 4: 8 **N** Cain said to his brother Abel, "Let's go H2256
Ge 4:11 **N** you are under a curse and driven from H6964
Ge 6:11 **N** the earth was corrupt in God's sight H2256
Ge 7: 4 Seven days from **n** I will send rain on the H6388
Ge 8: 2 **N** the springs of the deep and the H2256
Ge 9: 3 the green plants, I **n** give you everything. NDT
Ge 9: 9 "I **n** establish my covenant with you and H2180
Ge 11: 1 **N** the whole world had one language H2256
Ge 11:30 **N** Sarai was childless because she was not H2256
Ge 12:10 **N** there was a famine in the land, and H2256
Ge 12:19 her to be my wife? **N** then, here is your H6964
Ge 13: 5 **N** Lot, who was moving about with Abram, H2256
Ge 13:13 **N** the people of Sodom were wicked and H2256
Ge 14:10 **N** the Valley of Siddim was full of tar pits H2256
Ge 14:13 **N** Abram was living near the great trees H2256
Ge 16: 1 **N** Sarai, Abram's wife, had borne him no H2256
Ge 16: 5 **and n** that she knows she is pregnant H2256
Ge 16:11 "You are **n** pregnant and you will give H2180
Ge 16:13 "I have **n** seen the One who sees me." H2151
Ge 17: 8 Canaan, where you **n** reside as a foreigner NDT
Ge 18: 5 **n** that you have come to your servant." H3954
Ge 18:10 **N** Sarah was listening at the entrance to H2256
Ge 18:12 my lord is old, *will* I **n have** this pleasure?" AIT
Ge 18:13 'Will I really have a child, **n that** I am old? H2256
Ge 18:27 "**N** that I have been so bold as to speak to H2180
Ge 18:31 "**N** that I have been so bold as to speak to H2180
Ge 19: 9 **n** he wants to play the judge! H6964
Ge 20: 1 **N** Abraham moved on from there into the H2256
Ge 20: 4 **N** Abimelek had not gone near her, so he H2256
Ge 20: 7 **N** return the man's wife, for he is a H6964
Ge 21: 1 **N** the LORD was gracious to Sarah as he H2256
Ge 21:23 **N** swear to me here before God that you H6964
Ge 21:23 where *you n* **reside as a foreigner** the same AIT
Ge 22:12 **N** I know that you fear God, because you H6964
Ge 24: 1 Abraham was **n** very old, and the LORD H2256
Ge 24:29 **N** Rebekah had a brother named Laban H2256
Ge 24:49 **N** if you will show kindness and H6964
Ge 24:56 **n that** the LORD has granted success to my H2256
Ge 24:62 **N** Isaac had come from Beer Lahai Roi, H2256
Ge 26: 1 **N** there was a famine in the land H2256
Ge 26:22 "**N** the LORD has given us room and we H6964
Ge 26:29 And **n** you are blessed by the LORD." H6964
Ge 27: 2 "I am **n** an old man and don't know the H2180
Ge 27: 3 **N** then, get your equipment—your quiver H6964
Ge 27: 5 **N** Rebekah was listening as Isaac spoke H2256
Ge 27: 8 **N**, my son, listen carefully and do what I H6964
Ge 27:36 birthright, and **n** he's taken my blessing!" H6964
Ge 27:43 **N** then, my son, do what I say: Flee at H6964
Ge 28: 4 the land where you **n** reside as a foreigner NDT
Ge 28: 6 **N** Esau learned that Isaac had blessed H2256
Ge 29:16 **N** Laban had two daughters; the name of H2256
Ge 29:32 Surely my husband will love me **n**." H6964
Ge 29:34 "**N** at last my husband will become H6964
Ge 30:30 But **n**, when may I do something for my H6964
Ge 31:13 **N** leave this land at once and go back to H6964
Ge 31:30 **N** you have gone off because you longed H6964
Ge 31:32 **N** Jacob did not know that Rachel had H2256
Ge 31:34 **N** Rachel had taken the household gods H2256
Ge 31:37 **N that** you have searched through all my H3954
Ge 31:38 "I have been with you for twenty years **n** H2296
Ge 31:44 Come **n**, let's make a covenant, you and I H6964
Ge 32: 4 Laban and have remained there till **n**. H6964
Ge 32: 5 **N** I am sending this message to my lord H2256
Ge 32: 6 and **n** he is coming to meet you H1685
Ge 32:10 but **n** I have become two camps. H6964
Ge 33:10 **n that** you have received me favorably. H2256
Ge 34: 1 **N** Dinah, the daughter Leah had borne to H2256
Ge 35: 8 **N** Deborah, Rebekah's nurse, died and H2256
Ge 37: 3 **N** Israel loved Joseph more than any of H2256
Ge 37:12 **N** his brothers had gone to graze their H2256
Ge 37:20 "Come **n**, let's kill him and throw him into H6964
Ge 37:30 "The boy isn't there! Where *can* I **turn** *n*?" AIT
Ge 38:14 though Shelah had **n** grown up, she had H2256
Ge 38:16 said, "Come **n**, let me sleep with you." H5528
Ge 38:24 as a result she is **n** pregnant. H2180
Ge 39: 1 **N** Joseph had been taken down to Egypt H2256
Ge 39: 6 **N** Joseph was well-built and handsome, H2256
Ge 40:20 **N** the third day was Pharaoh's birthday H2256
Ge 41:12 **N** a young Hebrew was there with us, H2256
Ge 41:33 "And **n** let Pharaoh look for a discerning H6964
Ge 42: 6 **N** Joseph was the governor of the land H2256
Ge 42:13 The youngest is **n** with our father H2021+3427
Ge 42:22 **N** we must give an accounting for his H2180
Ge 42:32 the youngest is **n** with our father in H2021+3427
Ge 42:36 **and n** you want to take Benjamin. H2256
Ge 43: 1 **N** the famine was still severe in the land. H2256
Ge 43:18 **N** the men were frightened when they H2256
Ge 44: 1 **N** Joseph gave these instructions to the H2256
Ge 44:16 We are **n** my lord's slaves—we ourselves H2180
Ge 44:30 "So **n**, if the boy is not with us when I go H6964
Ge 44:33 "**N** then, please let your servant remain H6964
Ge 45: 5 And **n**, do not be distressed and do not be H6964
Ge 45: 6 For two years **n** there has been H3954+2296
Ge 45: 9 **N** hurry back to my father and say to him H2256
Ge 46:28 **N** Jacob sent Judah ahead of him to H2256
Ge 46:30 to Joseph, "**N** I am ready to die H2021+7193
Ge 47: 1 the land of Canaan and are **n** in Goshen." H2180
Ge 47: 4 So **n**, please let your servants settle in H6964
Ge 47:23 "**N** *that* I have bought you and your land H2176
Ge 47:27 **N** the Israelites settled in Egypt in the H2256
Ge 48: 5 "**N** then, your two sons born to you in H6964
Ge 48:10 **N** Israel's eyes were failing because of H2256
Ge 48:11 **n** God has allowed me to see your H2180
Ge 50: 5 **N** let me go up and bury my father; then H6964
Ge 50:17 **N** please forgive the sins of the servants H6964
Ge 50:20 what is **n** being done, H2021+2021+3427+2296
Ex 1: 6 **N** Joseph and all his brothers and all that H2256
Ex 2: 1 **N** a man of the tribe of Levi married a H2256
Ex 2:16 **N** a priest of Midian had seven daughters H2256
Ex 3: 1 **N** Moses was tending the flock of Jethro H2256
Ex 3: 9 And **n** the cry of the Israelites has reached H6964
Ex 3:10 So **n**, go. I am sending you to Pharaoh to H6964
Ex 4: 7 "**N** put it back into your cloak," he said. H2256
Ex 4:12 **N** go; I will help you speak and will teach H6964
Ex 4:19 **N** the LORD had said to Moses in Midian H2256
Ex 5: 3 **N** let us take a three-day journey into the H5528
Ex 5: 5 the people of the land are **n** numerous H6964
Ex 5:18 **N** get to work. You will not be given any H6964
Ex 6: 1 "**N** you will see what I will do to Pharaoh: H6964
Ex 6:13 **N** the LORD spoke to Moses and Aaron H2256
Ex 6:28 **N** when the LORD spoke to Moses in Egypt, H2256
Ex 7:16 But until **n** you have not listened. H3907
Ex 8:28 you must not go very far. **N** pray for me." NDT
Ex 9:15 For *by* **n** I could have stretched out my H6964
Ex 9:18 from the day it was founded till **n**. H6964
Ex 9:19 Give an order **n** to bring your livestock and H6964
Ex 10: 6 settled in this land till **n**. H2021+3427+2021+2296
Ex 10:17 **N** forgive my sin once more and pray to H6964
Ex 11: 1 **N** the LORD had said to Moses, "I will bring H2256
Ex 12:40 **N** the length of time the Israelite people H2256
Ex 18: 1 **N** Jethro, the priest of Midian and H2256
Ex 18:11 **N** I know that the LORD is greater than all H6964
Ex 18:19 Listen **n** to me and I will give you some H6964
Ex 19: 5 **N** if you obey me fully and keep my H6964
Ex 32:10 **N** leave me alone so that my anger may H6964
Ex 32:30 But **n** I will go up to the LORD; perhaps I H6964
Ex 32:32 But **n**, please forgive their sin—but if not H6964
Ex 32:34 **N** go, lead the people to the place I spoke H6964
Ex 33: 5 **N** take off your ornaments and I will H6964
Ex 33: 7 **N** Moses used to take a tent and pitch it H2256
Ex 33:18 Then Moses said, "**N** show me your glory." H5528

N

Lev 17: 5 sacrifices they *are* n making in the open AIT
Lev 24:10 N the son of an Israelite mother and an H2256
Nu 6:13 " 'N this is the law of the Nazirite when H2256
Nu 10:29 N Moses said to Hobab son of Reuel the H2256
Nu 11: 1 N the people complained about their H2256
Nu 11: 6 But n we have lost our appetite; we never H6964
Nu 11:18 N the LORD will give you meat, and you H2256
Nu 11:23 N you will see whether or not what I say H6964
Nu 11:31 N a wind went out from the LORD and H2256
Nu 12: 3 (N Moses was a very humble man, more H2256
Nu 14:17 "N may the Lord's strength be H2256+6964
Nu 14:19 them from the time they left Egypt until n." H2178
Nu 14:40 "N we are ready to go up to the land the H2180
Nu 15:22 " 'N if you as a community unintentionally H2256
Nu 16: 8 also said to Korah, "N listen, you Levites! H5528
Nu 16:10 but n you are trying to get the priesthood H2256
Nu 16:13 And n you also want to lord it over us! H3954
Nu 18:22 From n on the Israelites must not go near H6388
Nu 20: 2 N there was no water for the community H2256
Nu 20:16 "N we are here at Kadesh, a town on the H2180
Nu 22: 2 N Balak son of Zippor saw all that Israel H2256
Nu 22: 6 N come and put a curse on these people H6964
Nu 22:11 N come and put a curse on them for me H6964
Nu 22:19 N spend the night here so that I can find H6964
Nu 22:29 sword in my hand, I would kill you right n. H6964
Nu 22:33 I would certainly have killed you by n, but H6964
Nu 22:34 to oppose me. N if you are displeased H6964
Nu 22:38 I have come to you n," Balaam replied. H6964
Nu 23:23 It will n be said of Jacob H3869+2021+6961
Nu 24: 1 N when Balaam saw that it pleased the H2256
Nu 24:11 N leave at once and go home! I said I H6964
Nu 24:14 N I am going back to my people, but come H6964
Nu 24:17 "I see him, but not n; I behold him, but H6964
Nu 31:17 N kill all the boys. And kill every woman H6964
Nu 36: 3 N suppose they marry men from other H2256
Dt 2: 3 this hill country long enough; n turn north. NDT
Dt 2:13 "N get up and cross the Zered Valley." H6964
Dt 2:16 N when the last of these fighting men H2256
Dt 2:24 "Set out n and cross the Arnon Gorge H7756
Dt 2:30 as he has n done. H2021+3427+2021+2296
Dt 2:31 N begin to conquer and possess his land." NDT
Dt 4: 1 N, Israel, hear the decrees and laws I am H6964
Dt 4:20 as you n are. H2021+3427+2021+2296
Dt 4:32 Ask n about the former days, long before H5528
Dt 5:25 But n, why should we die? This great fire H6964
Dt 7:19 do the same to all the peoples you n fear. NDT
Dt 9: 1 You are n about to cross the Jordan H2021+3427
Dt 10: 5 LORD commanded me, and they are there n. NDT
Dt 10:10 N I had stayed on the mountain forty days H2256
Dt 10:12 And n, Israel, what does the LORD your H6964
Dt 10:22 n the LORD your God has made you as H6964
Dt 22:17 N he has slandered her and said, 'I did H2180
Dt 26:10 n I bring the firstfruits of the soil that H6964
Dt 27: 9 You have n become the H2021+3427+2021+2296
Dt 29:28 another land, as it is n." H2021+3427+2021+2296
Dt 30:11 N what I am commanding you today is H3954
Dt 30:19 N choose life, so that you and your H2256
Dt 31: 2 "I am n a hundred and twenty years H2021+3427
Dt 31:14 "N the day of your death is near. H2176
Dt 31:19 "N write down this song and teach it to H6964
Dt 32:37 "N where are their gods, the rock they took NDT
Dt 32:39 "See n that I myself am he! There is no H6964
Dt 34: 9 N Joshua son of Nun was filled with the H2256
Jos 1: 2 N then, you and all these people, get H6964
Jos 1:11 Three days from n you will cross the H928+6388
Jos 2:12 "N then, please swear to me by the LORD H6964
Jos 2:17 N the men had said to her, "This oath you H2256
Jos 3:12 N then, choose twelve men from the tribes H6964
Jos 3:15 N the Jordan is at flood stage all during H2256
Jos 4:10 N the priests who carried the ark H2256
Jos 5: 1 N when all the Amorite kings west of the H2256
Jos 5: 4 N this is why he did so: All those who H2256
Jos 5:13 N when Joshua was near Jericho, he H2256
Jos 5:14 of the army of the LORD I have n come." H6964
Jos 6: 1 N the gates of Jericho were securely H2256
Jos 7: 2 N Joshua sent men from Jericho to Ai H2256
Jos 7: 8 n that Israel has been routed by its H339
Jos 9: 1 N when all the kings west of the Jordan H2256
Jos 9:12 But n see how dry and moldy it is H6964
Jos 9:19 of Israel, and we cannot touch them n. H6964
Jos 9:23 You are n under a curse: You will never be H6964
Jos 9:25 We are n in your hands. Do to us whatever H6964
Jos 10: 1 N Adoni-Zedek king of Jerusalem heard H2256
Jos 10:16 N the five kings had fled and hidden in H2256
Jos 13: 1 "You *are* n very old, and there are AIT
Jos 14: 1 N these are the areas the Israelites H2256
Jos 14: 6 N the people of Judah approached H2256
Jos 14:10 "N then, just as the LORD promised, he has H6964
Jos 14:11 to go out to battle n as I was then. H6964
Jos 14:12 N give me this hill country that the LORD H6964
Jos 17: 3 N Zelophehad son of Hepher, the son of H2256
Jos 21: 1 N the family heads of the Levites H2256
Jos 22: 3 For a long time n—to this very day—you H2296
Jos 22: 4 N that the LORD your God has given them H6964
Jos 22:16 an altar in rebellion against him n? H2021+3427
Jos 22:18 And are you n turning away from H2021+3427
Jos 22:31 N you have rescued the Israelites from the H255
Jos 23: 8 as you have until n. H2021+3427+2021+2296
Jos 23:14 "N I am about to go the way of all H2021+3427
Jos 24:14 "N fear the LORD and serve him with all H6964
Jos 24:23 "N then," said Joshua, "throw away the H6964
Jdg 1: 7 N God has paid me back for what I did to NDT
Jdg 1:22 N the tribes of Joseph attacked Bethel H2256
Jdg 3:16 N Ehud had made a double-edged sword H2256
Jdg 4: 1 eyes of the LORD, n that Ehud was dead. H2256
Jdg 4: 4 N Deborah, a prophet, the wife of H2256
Jdg 4:11 N Heber the Kenite had left the other H2256
Jdg 6:13 But n the LORD has abandoned us and H6964
Jdg 6:17 "If n I have found favor in your eyes H5528
Jdg 6:33 N all the Midianites, Amalekites and H2256
Jdg 7: 3 N announce to the army, 'Anyone who H6964
Jdg 7: 8 N the camp of Midian lay below him in H2256
Jdg 8: 1 N the Ephraimites asked Gideon, "Why H2256
Jdg 8:10 N Zebah and Zalmunna were in Karkor H2256
Jdg 9:26 N Gaal son of Ebed moved with his clan H2256
Jdg 9:32 N then, during the night you and your men H6964
Jdg 9:35 N Gaal son of Ebed had gone out and was H2256
Jdg 9:38 "Where is your big talk n, you who said, H686
Jdg 10:15 but please rescue us n." H2021+3427+2021+2296
Jdg 11: 7 Why do you come to me n, when you're H6964
Jdg 11: 8 we are turning to you n; come with us to H6964
Jdg 11:13 to the Jordan. N give it back peaceably." H6964
Jdg 11:23 "N since the LORD, the God of Israel, has H6964
Jdg 11:36 n that the LORD has avenged you of your H339
Jdg 12: 3 N why have you come up today to fight H2256
Jdg 13: 4 N see to it that you drink no wine or other H6964
Jdg 13: 7 N then, drink no wine or other fermented H6964
Jdg 13:23 things or n told us this. H3869+2021+6961
Jdg 14: 2 in Timnah; n get her for me as my wife." H6964
Jdg 14:10 N his father went down to see the woman. H2256
Jdg 15:18 Must I n die of thirst and fall into the H6964
Jdg 16:10 Come n, tell me how you can be H6964+5528
Jdg 16:23 N the rulers of the Philistines assembled H2256
Jdg 16:27 N the temple was crowded with men and H2256
Jdg 17: 1 N a man named Micah from the hill H2256
Jdg 17: 5 N this man Micah had a shrine, and he H2256
Jdg 17:13 "N I know that the LORD will be good to H6964
Jdg 18:14 N you know what to do. H6964
Jdg 19: 1 N a Levite who lived in a remote area in H2256
Jdg 19: 9 woman's father, said, "N look, it's almost H5528
Jdg 19:18 in Judah and n I am going to the H2256
Jdg 19:24 I will bring them out to you n, and you H5528
Jdg 20: 7 N, all you Israelites, speak up and tell me H2180
Jdg 20: 9 But n this is what we'll do to Gibeah H6964
Jdg 20:13 N turn those wicked men of Gibeah over to H6964
Jdg 20:36 N the men of Israel had given way before H2256
Jdg 21: 6 N the Israelites grieved for the tribe of H2256
Ru 1: 3 N Elimelek, Naomi's husband, died, and H2256
Ru 2: 1 N Naomi had a relative on her husband's H2256
Ru 2: 7 has remained here from morning till n, H6964
Ru 3: 2 N Boaz, with whose women you have H6964
Ru 3:11 And n, my daughter, don't be afraid. I will H6964
Ru 4: 7 (N in earlier times in Israel, for the H2256
1Sa 1: 9 N Eli the priest was sitting on his chair by H2256
1Sa 1:28 So n I give him to the LORD. For his whole H1685
1Sa 2:13 N it was the practice of the priests that H2256
1Sa 2:16 hand it over n; if you don't, I'll take H6964
1Sa 2:22 N Eli, who was very old, heard about H2256
1Sa 2:27 N a man of God came to Eli and said to H2256
1Sa 2:30 But n the LORD declares: 'Far H6964
1Sa 3: 7 N Samuel did not yet know the LORD: The H2256
1Sa 4: 1 N the Israelites went out to fight against H2256
1Sa 6: 7 "N then, get a new cart ready, with two H6964
1Sa 6:13 N the people of Beth Shemesh were H2256
1Sa 7: 6 N Samuel was serving as leader of Israel H2256
1Sa 8: 5 your ways; n appoint a king to lead us H6964
1Sa 8: 9 N listen to them; but warn them solemnly H6964
1Sa 9: 3 N the donkeys belonging to Saul's father H2256
1Sa 9: 6 Let's go there n. Perhaps he will tell H6964
1Sa 9:12 Hurry n; he has just come to our town H6964
1Sa 9:13 Go up n; you should find him about this H6964
1Sa 9:15 N the day before Saul came, the LORD had H2256
1Sa 10: 2 And n your father has stopped thinking H2180
1Sa 10:14 N Saul's uncle asked him and his servant H2256
1Sa 10:19 But you have n rejected your God H2021+3427
1Sa 10:19 So n present yourselves before the LORD H6964
1Sa 12: 2 N you have a king as your leader. As for H6964
1Sa 12: 7 N then, stand here, because I am going to H6964
1Sa 12:10 But n deliver us from the hands of our H6964
1Sa 12:13 N here is the king you have chosen, the H6964
1Sa 12:16 "N then, stand still and see this great H6964
1Sa 12:17 Is it not wheat harvest n? I will call H2021+3427
1Sa 13: 4 n Israel has become obnoxious to the H1685
1Sa 13:12 'N the Philistines will come down against H6964
1Sa 13:14 But n your kingdom will not endure; the H6964
1Sa 13:23 N a detachment of Philistines had gone H2256
1Sa 14:24 N the Israelites were in distress that day H2256
1Sa 14:43 the end of my staff. And n I must die!" H2180
1Sa 15: 1 so listen n to the message from the LORD. H6964
1Sa 15: 3 N go, attack the Amalekites and totally H6964
1Sa 15:25 N I beg you, forgive my sin and come back H6964
1Sa 16:14 N the Spirit of the LORD had departed from H2256
1Sa 17: 1 N the Philistines gathered their forces H2256
1Sa 17:12 N David was the son of an Ephrathite H2256
1Sa 17:17 N Jesse said to his son David, "Take this H2256
1Sa 17:25 N the Israelites had been saying, "Do you H2256
1Sa 17:29 "N what have I done?" said David. "Can't H6964
1Sa 18:20 N Saul's daughter Michal was in love with H2256
1Sa 18:21 "N you have a second opportunity H2021+3427
1Sa 18:22 all love you; n become his son-in-law. H6964
1Sa 20:31 N send someone to bring him to me, for H6964
1Sa 21: 3 N then, what do you have on hand? Give H6964
1Sa 21: 7 N one of Saul's servants was there that H2256
1Sa 22: 6 N Saul heard that David and his men had H2256
1Sa 22:12 Saul said, "Listen n, son of Ahitub." "Yes H5528
1Sa 23: 6 N Abiathar son of Ahimelek had brought H2256
1Sa 23:20 N, Your Majesty, come down whenever it H6964
1Sa 23:24 N David and his men were in the Desert H2256
1Sa 24:18 You have just n told me about the H2021+3427
1Sa 24:21 N swear to me by the LORD that you will H6964
1Sa 25: 1 N Samuel died, and all Israel assembled H2256
1Sa 25: 7 " 'N I hear that it is sheep-shearing time H6964
1Sa 25:17 N think it over and see what you can do H6964
1Sa 25:26 And n, my lord, as surely as the LORD your H6964
1Sa 26: 8 N let me pin him to the ground with one H6964
1Sa 26:11 N get the spear and water jug that are H6964
1Sa 26:19 N let my lord the king listen to his H6964
1Sa 26:20 N do not let my blood fall to the ground H6964
1Sa 27: 8 N David and his men went up and raided H2256
1Sa 28: 3 N Samuel was dead, and all Israel had H2256
1Sa 28:16 n that the LORD has departed from you H2256
1Sa 28:22 N please listen to your servant and let me H6964
1Sa 29: 3 day he left Saul until n, H2021+3427+2021+2296
1Sa 29: 7 N turn back and go in peace; do nothing H6964
1Sa 29: 8 I came to you until n? H2021+3427+2021+2296
1Sa 29:10 N get up early, along with your master's H6964
1Sa 30: 1 N the Amalekites had raided the Negev H2256
1Sa 31: 1 N the Philistines fought against Israel; the H2256
2Sa 2: 6 May the LORD n show you kindness and H6964
2Sa 2: 7 N then, be strong and brave, for Saul your H6964
2Sa 2:18 N Asahel was as fleet-footed as a wild H2256
2Sa 3: 7 N Saul had had a concubine named H2256
2Sa 3: 8 Yet n you accuse me of an offense H2021+3427
2Sa 3:18 N do it! For the LORD promised David, 'By H6964
2Sa 3:24 Why did you let him go? N he is gone! H2256
2Sa 3:27 N when Abner returned to Hebron, Joab H2256
2Sa 4: 2 N Saul's son had two men who were H2256
2Sa 4: 5 N Rekab and Baanah, the sons of H2256
2Sa 4:11 should I not n demand his blood from your H6964
2Sa 5:11 N Hiram king of Tyre sent envoys to David, H2256
2Sa 5:18 N the Philistines had come and spread out H2256
2Sa 6:12 N King David was told, "The LORD has H2256
2Sa 7: 8 "N then, tell my servant David, 'This is H6964
2Sa 7: 9 N I will make your name great, like the H2256
2Sa 7:25 "And n, LORD God, keep forever the H6964
2Sa 7:29 N be pleased to bless the house of your H6964
2Sa 9: 2 N there was a servant of Saul's household H2256
2Sa 9:10 N Ziba had fifteen sons and twenty H2256
2Sa 11: 4 N she was purifying herself from her H2256
2Sa 12: 4 "N a traveler came to the rich man, but H2256
2Sa 12:10 N, therefore, the sword will never depart H6964
2Sa 12:18 How can we n tell him the child is dead H2256
2Sa 12:21 but n that the child is dead H3869+889
2Sa 12:23 But n that he is dead, why should I go on H6964
2Sa 12:28 N muster the rest of the troops and H6964
2Sa 13: 3 N Amnon had an adviser named Jonadab H2256
2Sa 13:20 Be quiet *for* n, my sister; he is your brother H6964
2Sa 13:34 N the man standing watch looked up and H2256
2Sa 14: 7 N the whole clan has risen up against your H2180
2Sa 14:15 "And n I have come to say this to my lord H6964
2Sa 14:17 "And n your servant says, 'May the word H2256
2Sa 14:32 N then, I want to see the king's face H6964
2Sa 15:31 N David had been told, "Ahithophel is H2256
2Sa 15:34 in the past, but n I will be your servant,' H6964
2Sa 16: 4 belonged to Mephibosheth is n yours." H2180
2Sa 16:23 N in those days the advice Ahithophel H2256
2Sa 17: 9 Even n, he is hidden in a cave or some H6964
2Sa 17:16 N send a message at once and tell David H6964
2Sa 18: 3 It would be better n for you to give us H6964
2Sa 18: 9 N Absalom happened to meet David's H2256
2Sa 18:19 N Ahimaaz son of Zadok said, "Let me H2256
2Sa 19: 7 N go out and encourage your men. I swear H6964
2Sa 19: 7 have come on you from your youth till n." H6964
2Sa 19: 9 But n he has fled the country to escape H6964
2Sa 19:15 N the men of Judah had come to Gilgal H2256
2Sa 19:30 n that my lord the king has returned home H339
2Sa 19:32 N Barzillai was very old, eighty years of H2256
2Sa 19:35 I am n eighty years old. Can I tell H2021+3427
2Sa 20: 1 N a troublemaker named Sheba son of H2256
2Sa 20: 6 "N Sheba son of Bikri will do us more H6964
2Sa 21: 2 N the Gibeonites were not a part of Israel H2256
2Sa 22:44 People I did not know *n* serve me, AIT
2Sa 24:10 N, LORD, I beg you, take away the guilt of H6964
2Sa 24:13 N then, think it over and decide how I H6964
1Ki 1: 5 N Adonijah, whose mother was Haggith H2256
1Ki 1:12 N then, let me advise you how you can H6964
1Ki 1:18 But n Adonijah has become king, and you H6964
1Ki 1:25 Right n they are eating and drinking with H2180
1Ki 2: 5 "N you yourself know what Joab H2256+1685
1Ki 2: 9 But n, do not consider him innocent. H6964
1Ki 2:13 N Adonijah, the son of Haggith, went to H2256
1Ki 2:16 N I have one request to make of you. H6964
1Ki 2:24 And n, as surely as the LORD lives—he who H6964
1Ki 2:26 not put you to death n, H2021+3427+2021+2296
1Ki 2:44 N the LORD will repay you for your H2256
1Ki 2:46 The kingdom was n established in H2256
1Ki 3: 7 "N, LORD my God, you have made your H6964
1Ki 3:16 N two prostitutes came to the king and H255
1Ki 5: 4 But n the LORD my God has given me rest H6964
1Ki 8:20 David my father and n I sit on the throne H2256
1Ki 8:25 "N LORD, the God of Israel, keep for your H6964
1Ki 8:26 And n, O God of Israel, let your word that H6964
1Ki 9:14 N Hiram had sent to the king 120 talents H2256
1Ki 11:28 N Jeroboam was a man of standing, and H2256
1Ki 12: 4 n lighten the harsh labor and the H6964
1Ki 12:10 N tell them, 'My little finger is thicker H3907

N

1Ki 12:26 "The kingdom will **n** likely revert to the H6964
1Ki 13:11 **N** there was a certain old prophet living in H2256
1Ki 14: 4 **N** Ahijah could not see; his sight was H2256
1Ki 14:14 Even **n** this is beginning to happen. H6964
1Ki 15:19 **N** break your treaty with Baasha king of NDT
1Ki 17: 1 **N** Elijah the Tishbite, from Tishbe in H2256
1Ki 17:24 "**N** I know that you are a man of H6964+2296
1Ki 18: 2 **N** the famine was severe in Samaria H2256
1Ki 18:11 But **n** you tell me to go to my master and H6964
1Ki 18:14 And **n** you tell me to go to my master and H6964
1Ki 18:19 **N** summon the people from all over Israel H6964
1Ki 19: 1 **N** Ahab told Jezebel everything Elijah H2256
1Ki 19:10 **and n** they are trying to kill me too." H2256
1Ki 19:14 left, **and n** they are trying to kill me too." H2256
1Ki 20: 1 **N** Ben-Hadad king of Aram mustered his H2256
1Ki 20:17 **N** Ben-Hadad had dispatched scouts, who H2256
1Ki 21:18 He is **n** in Naboth's vineyard, where he H2180
1Ki 22:11 **N** Zedekiah son of Kenaanah had made H2256
1Ki 22:23 "So **n** the LORD has put a deceiving spirit H6964
1Ki 22:31 **N** the king of Aram had ordered his H2256
1Ki 22:48 **N** Jehoshaphat built a fleet of trading ships NDT
2Ki 1: 2 **N** Ahaziah had fallen through the lattice H2256
2Ki 1:14 But **n** have respect for my life! H6964
2Ki 2:14 "Where **n** is the LORD, the God H677
2Ki 3: 4 **N** Mesha king of Moab raised sheep, and H2256
2Ki 3:15 But **n** bring me a harpist." While the H6964
2Ki 3:21 **N** all the Moabites had heard that the H2256
2Ki 3:23 **N** to the plunder, Moab!" H6964
2Ki 4: 1 **But n** his creditor is coming to take my two H6964
2Ki 4:13 trouble for us. **N** what can be done for you NDT
2Ki 5: 1 **N** Naaman was commander of the army H2256
2Ki 5: 2 **N** bands of raiders from Aram had gone H2256
2Ki 5:15 "**N** I know that there is no God in all the H2180
2Ki 6: 8 **N** the king of Aram was at war with Israel H2256
2Ki 6:32 **N** Elisha was sitting in his house, and the H2256
2Ki 7: 3 **N** there were four men with leprosy at the H2256
2Ki 7:17 **N** the king had put the officer on whose H2256
2Ki 8: 1 **N** Elisha had said to the woman whose H2256
2Ki 8: 6 from the day she left the country until **n**." H6964
2Ki 9:14 **N** Joram and all Israel had been H2256
2Ki 9:26 **N** then, pick him up and throw him on H6964
2Ki 10: 1 **N** there were in Samaria seventy sons of H2256
2Ki 10: 2 **N** as soon as this letter reaches you H6964
2Ki 10: 6 **N** the royal princes, seventy of them H2256
2Ki 10:19 **N** summon all the prophets of Baal, all his H6964
2Ki 10:24 **N** Jehu had posted eighty men outside H2256
2Ki 13:14 **N** Elisha had been suffering from the H2256
2Ki 13:19 But **n** you will defeat it only three times." H6964
2Ki 13:20 **N** Moabite raiders used to enter the H2256
2Ki 14:10 defeated Edom **and n** you are arrogant. H2256
2Ki 18:23 " '**Come n**, make a bargain with my H6964+5528
2Ki 19: 9 **N** Sennacherib received a report that H2256
2Ki 19:19 **N**, LORD our God, deliver us from his hand H6964
2Ki 19:25 I planned it; **n** I have brought it to pass H6964
2Ki 20: 5 On the third day from **n** you will go up to the NDT
2Ki 20: 8 temple of the LORD on the third day from **n**? NDT
2Ki 24:20 **N** Zedekiah rebelled against the king of H2256
1Ch 9: 2 **N** the first to resettle on their own property H2256
1Ch 10: 1 **N** the Philistines fought against Israel; the H2256
1Ch 14: 1 **N** Hiram king of Tyre sent messengers to H2256
1Ch 14: 9 **N** the Philistines had come and raided the H2256
1Ch 15:27 **N** David was clothed in a robe of fine H2256
1Ch 17: 7 "**N** then, tell my servant David, 'This is H6964
1Ch 17: 8 **N** I will make your name like the names H2256
1Ch 17:23 "And **n**, LORD, let the promise you have H6964
1Ch 17:27 **N** you have been pleased to bless the H6964
1Ch 21: 8 **N**, I beg you, take away the guilt of your H6964
1Ch 21:12 **N** then, decide how I should answer the H6964
1Ch 22:11 "**N**, my son, the LORD be with you, and H6964
1Ch 22:16 beyond number. **N** begin the work, and the NDT
1Ch 22:19 **N** devote your heart and soul to seeking H6964
1Ch 28: 8 "So **n** I charge you in the sight of all Israel H6964
1Ch 28:10 Consider **n**, for the LORD has chosen you to H6964
1Ch 29: 3 the temple of my God *I n* **give** my personal AIT
1Ch 29: 5 **N**, who is willing to consecrate H2256
1Ch 29:13 **N**, our God, we give you thanks, and H6964
1Ch 29:17 And **n** I have seen with joy how willingly H6964
2Ch 1: 4 **N** David had brought up the ark of God from H66
2Ch 1: 9 **N**, LORD God, let your promise to my father H6964
2Ch 2: 4 **N** I am about to build a temple for the H2180
2Ch 2:15 "**N** let my lord send his servants the wheat H6964
2Ch 6: 6 **But n** I have chosen Jerusalem for my H2256
2Ch 6:10 David my father **and n** I sit on the throne H2256
2Ch 6:13 **N** he had made a bronze platform, five H3954
2Ch 6:16 "**N**, LORD, the God of Israel, keep for your H6964
2Ch 6:17 And **n**, LORD, the God of Israel, let your H6964
2Ch 6:40 "**N**, my God, may your eyes be open and H6964
2Ch 6:41 "**N** arise, LORD God, and come to your H6964
2Ch 7:15 **N** my eyes will be open and my ears H6964
2Ch 10: 4 **n** lighten the harsh labor and the H6964
2Ch 10:10 **N** tell them, 'My little finger is thicker H3907
2Ch 12: 5 therefore, I **n** abandon you to Shishak. H677
2Ch 13: 8 "And **n** you plan to resist the kingdom of H6964
2Ch 13:13 **N** Jeroboam had sent troops around to H2256
2Ch 16: 3 **N** break your treaty with Baasha king of NDT
2Ch 16: 9 and from **n** on you will be at war. H6964
2Ch 18: 1 **N** Jehoshaphat had great wealth and H2256
2Ch 18:10 **N** Zedekiah son of Kenaanah had made H2256
2Ch 18:22 "So **n** the LORD has put a deceiving spirit H6964
2Ch 18:30 **N** the king of Aram had ordered his H2256
2Ch 19: 7 **N** let the fear of the LORD be on you. Judge H6964
2Ch 20:10 "But **n** here are men from Ammon, Moab H6964
2Ch 21:14 So **n** the LORD is about to strike your H2180
2Ch 23: 4 **N** this is what you are to do: A third of you NDT
2Ch 24: 5 **Do** it **n**." But the Levites H4554
2Ch 24: 7 **N** the sons of that wicked woman H3954
2Ch 24:15 **N** Jehoiada was old and full of years, and H2256
2Ch 25:19 and **n** you are arrogant and proud. H6964
2Ch 28:10 And **n** you intend to make the men and H6964
2Ch 28:11 **N** listen to me! Send back your fellow H6964
2Ch 29: 5 yourselves **n** and consecrate the H6964
2Ch 29:10 **N** I intend to make a covenant with the H6964
2Ch 29:11 do not be negligent **n**, for the LORD has H6964
2Ch 29:19 They are **n** in front of the LORD's altar." H2180
2Ch 29:31 "You have **n** dedicated yourselves to the H6964
2Ch 32:15 **N** do not let Hezekiah deceive you and H6964
2Ch 34:28 **N** I will gather you to your ancestors, and H2180
2Ch 35: 3 **N** serve the LORD your God and his people H6964
Ezr 1: 4 any locality where survivors *may n be* **living**, AIT
Ezr 2: 1 **N** these are the people of the province H2256
Ezr 4:14 **N** since we are under obligation to the A10363
Ezr 4:21 **N** issue an order to these men to stop A10363
Ezr 5: 1 **N** Haggai the prophet and Zechariah the A10221
Ezr 5:17 **N** if it pleases the king, let a search be A10363
Ezr 6: 6 **N then**, Tattenai, governor of A10363
Ezr 7:13 **N** I decree that any of the Israelites in A10364
Ezr 7:21 **N** I, King Artaxerxes, decree that all the A10221
Ezr 9: 7 of our ancestors until **n**, H2021+3427+2021+2296
Ezr 9: 8 "But **n**, for a brief moment, the LORD our H6964
Ezr 9:10 "But **n**, our God, what can we say after H6964
Ezr 10: 3 **N** let us make a covenant before our God H6964
Ezr 10:11 **N** honor the LORD, the God of your H6964
Ne 5: 1 **N** the men and their wives raised a great H2256
Ne 5: 8 **N** you are selling your own people H2256+1685
Ne 6: 7 **N** this report will get back to the king; so H6964
Ne 6: 9 But I prayed, "**N** strengthen my hands." H6964
Ne 7: 4 **N** the city was large and spacious, but H2256
Ne 8:12 because they **n** understood the words that NDT
Ne 9:32 "**N** therefore, our God, the great God H6964
Ne 10:29 all these **n** join their fellow Israelites the NDT
Ne 11: 1 **N** the leaders of the people settled in H2256
Ne 11: 3 settled in Jerusalem (**n** some Israelites H2256
Ne 13:18 **N** you are stirring up more wrath against H2256
Ne 13:27 Must we hear **n** that you too are doing all NDT
Est 2: 5 **N** there was in the citadel of Susa a Jew of NDT
Est 2:17 **N** the king was attracted to Esther more H2256
Est 5: 6 asked Esther, "**N** what is your petition? NDT
Est 6: 4 **N** Haman had just entered the outer court H2256
Est 6: 6 **N** Haman thought to himself, "Who is H2256
Est 8: 8 **N** write another decree in the king's name H2256
Est 9: 1 **but n** the tables were turned and the Jews H2256
Est 9:12 king's provinces? **N** what is your petition H2256
Job 1:11 But **n** stretch out your hand and strike H219
Job 2: 5 **But n** stretch out your hand and strike his H219
Job 3:13 For **n** I would be lying down in peace; H6964
Job 3:14 built for themselves places **n** lying in ruins, NDT
Job 4: 5 But **n** trouble comes to you, and you are H6964
Job 4: 7 "Consider **n**: Who, being innocent, has H5528
Job 6:13 **n** that success has been driven from me? NDT
Job 6:21 **N** you too have proved to be of no help H6964
Job 6:28 "But **n** be so kind as to look at me. Would H2256
Job 7: 8 The eye *that n* **sees** me will see me no AIT
Job 8: 6 even **n** he will rouse himself on your H6964
Job 9:35 fear of him, but as it **n** stands with me, NDT
Job 10: 8 Will you **n** turn and destroy me? H339
Job 10: 9 Will you **n** turn me to dust again? H2256
Job 13: 6 Hear **n** my argument; listen to the pleas H5528
Job 13:18 **N** that I have prepared my case, I know I H2180
Job 16:19 Even **n** my witness is in heaven; my H6964
Job 19: 3 Ten times **n** you have reproached me H2296
Job 21:28 You say, 'Where **n** is the house of the great NDT
Job 30: 1 "But **n** they mock me, men younger than I H6964
Job 30: 9 "And **n** those young men mock me in H6964
Job 30:11 **N** that God has unstrung my bow and H3954
Job 30:16 "And **n** my life ebbs away; days of H6964
Job 31:35 I sign **n** my defense—let the Almighty H2176
Job 32: 4 **N** Elihu had waited before speaking to Job H2256
Job 32:16 Must I wait, **n that** they are silent, now H3954
Job 32:16 **n that** they stand there with no reply? H3954
Job 33: 1 "But **n**, Job, listen to my words; pay H5528
Job 33:14 For God does speak—**n** one way, now NDT
Job 33:14 now one way, **n** another—though no one H2256
Job 33:21 their bones, once hidden, **n** stick out. NDT
Job 36:17 **But n** you are laden with the judgment H2256
Job 37:21 **N** no one can look at the sun, bright as it H6964
Job 42: 4 "You said, 'Listen **n**, and I will speak; H5528
Job 42: 5 heard of you but **n** my eyes have seen H6964
Job 42: 8 So **n** take seven bulls and seven rams and H6964
Ps 12: 5 needy groan, I will **n** arise," says the LORD. H6964
Ps 17:11 me down, they **n** surround me, with H6964
Ps 18:43 People I did not know *n* **serve** me, AIT
Ps 20: 6 **N** this I know: The LORD gives victory to H6964
Ps 37:25 I was young **and n** I am old, yet I have H1685
Ps 39: 7 "But **n**, Lord, what do I look for? My hope H6964
Ps 44: 9 **But n** you have rejected and humbled us H677
Ps 50:21 But *I n* **arraign** you and set my accusations AIT
Ps 52: 7 "**Here n** is the man who did not make H2180
Ps 60: 1 you have been angry—**n** restore us! NDT
Ps 60:10 *you who have n* **rejected** us and no longer go AIT
Ps 113: 2 LORD be praised, both **n** and forevermore. H6964
Ps 115:18 extol the LORD, both **n** and forevermore. H6964
Ps 119:67 I went astray, but **n** I obey your word. H6964
Ps 121: 8 going both **n** and forevermore. H6964
Ps 125: 2 his people both **n** and forevermore. H6964
Ps 131: 3 hope in the LORD both **n** and forevermore. H6964
Pr 5: 7 **N** then, my sons, listen to me; do not turn H6964
Pr 7:12 **n** in the street, now in the squares, at H7193
Pr 7:12 now in the street, **n** in the squares, at H7193
Pr 7:24 **N** then, my sons, listen to me; pay H6964
Pr 8:32 "**N** then, my children, listen to me H6964
Ecc 2: 1 to myself, "Come **n**, I will test you with H5528
Ecc 9:15 **N** there lived in that city a man poor but H2256
Ecc 12:13 **N** all has been heard; here is the conclusion NDT
SS 3: 2 I will get up **n** and go about the city H5528
Isa 1:18 "Come **n**, let us settle the matter," says H5528
Isa 1:21 used to dwell in her—but **n** murderers! H6964
Isa 3: 1 See **n**, the Lord, the LORD Almighty, is H3954
Isa 5: 3 "**N** you dwellers in Jerusalem and people H6964
Isa 5: 5 **N** I will tell you what I am going to do to H6964
Isa 7: 2 **N** the house of David was told, "Aram has H2256
Isa 7:13 Isaiah said, "Hear **n**, you house of David! H5528
Isa 14: 8 "**N** that you have been laid low H4946+255
Isa 16:14 But **n** the LORD says: "Within three years, H6964
Isa 19:12 Where are your wise men **n**? Let them H686
Isa 22: 1 What troubles you **n**, that you have all H686
Isa 23:12 reveling, Virgin Daughter Sidon, *n* **crushed**! AIT
Isa 23:13 this people *that* **is** *n* of no account! AIT
Isa 26:14 *They are n* **dead**, they live no more; their AIT
Isa 28:22 **N** stop your mocking, or your chains will H6964
Isa 30: 8 Go **n**, write it on a tablet for them H6964
Isa 33:10 "**N** will I arise," says the LORD. "Now will I H6964
Isa 33:10 "**N** will I be exalted; now will I be lifted H6964
Isa 33:10 will I be exalted; **n** will I be lifted up. H6964
Isa 36: 8 " '**Come n**, make a bargain with my H6964+5528
Isa 37: 9 **N** Sennacherib received a report that H2256
Isa 37:20 **N**, LORD our God, deliver us from his hand H6964
Isa 37:26 I planned it; **n** I have brought it to pass H6964
Isa 38:11 be with *those who n* **dwell in** this world. AIT
Isa 42:14 But **n**, like a woman in childbirth, I cry out, NDT
Isa 43: 1 But **n**, this is what the LORD says—he who H6964
Isa 43:19 doing a new thing! **N** it springs up; do you H6964
Isa 44: 1 "But **n** listen, Jacob, my servant, Israel H6964
Isa 46:12 you who are **n** far from my righteousness. NDT
Isa 47: 8 "**N** then, listen, you lover of pleasure H6964
Isa 48: 6 "From **n** on I will tell you of new things, of H6964
Isa 48: 7 They are created **n**, and not long ago; you H6964
Isa 48:16 And **n** the Sovereign LORD has sent me H6964
Isa 49: 5 And **n** the LORD says—he who formed me H6964
Isa 49:19 **n** you will be too small for your people H6964
Isa 50:11 But **n**, all you who light fires and provide H2176
Isa 52: 2 on your neck, Daughter Zion, **n** a captive. NDT
Isa 52: 5 "And **n** what do I have here?" declares H6964
Isa 54: 9 So **n** I have sworn not to be angry with you NDT
Isa 63:18 **n** our enemies have trampled down your NDT
Jer 2:18 **N** why go to Egypt to drink water from the H6964
Jer 3: 1 many lovers—would you **n** return to me?" H2256
Jer 4:12 **N** I pronounce my judgments against H6964
Jer 5:19 so **n** you will serve foreigners in a land not NDT
Jer 7:12 " 'Go **n** to the place in Shiloh where I first H5528
Jer 7:14 I did to Shiloh *I will n* **do** to the house that AIT
Jer 7:25 left Egypt until **n**, H2021+3427+2021+2296
Jer 9:17 "Consider **n**! Call for the wailing H2256
Jer 9:20 **N**, you women, hear the word of the LORD H3954
Jer 10:20 no one is **left n** to pitch my tent or to set H6388
Jer 13: 4 go **n** to Perath and hide it there in a H7756
Jer 13: 6 "Go **n** to Perath and get the belt I told you H7756
Jer 13: 7 **n** it was ruined and completely H2180
Jer 14:10 he will **n** remember their wickedness and H6964
Jer 16:16 "But **n** I will send for many fishermen," H2180
Jer 17:15 word of the LORD? Let it **n** be fulfilled!" H5528
Jer 18:11 "**N** therefore say to the people of Judah H6964
Jer 21: 2 "Inquire **n** of the LORD for us because H5528
Jer 25: 5 They said, "Turn **n**, each of you, from your H5528
Jer 25:30 "**N** prophesy all these words against them H2256
Jer 26:13 **N** reform your ways and your actions and H6964
Jer 26:20 **N** Uriah son of Shemaiah from Kiriath H2256
Jer 27: 6 **N** I will give all your countries into the H6964
Jer 27:16 'Very soon **n** the articles from the LORD's H6964
Jer 32: 3 **N** Zedekiah king of Judah had imprisoned NDT
Jer 32:24 you said has happened, as you **n** see. H2180
Jer 32:31 day it was built until **n**, H2021+3427+2021+2296
Jer 34:16 **But n** you have turned around and H2256
Jer 34:17 So I **n** proclaim 'freedom' for you H2180
Jer 36: 2 the reign of Josiah till **n**. H2021+3427+2021+2296
Jer 37: 4 **N** Jeremiah was free to come and go H2256
Jer 37:20 But **n**, my lord the king, please listen. H6964
Jer 39:11 **N** Nebuchadnezzar king of Babylon had H2256
Jer 40: 3 **And n** the LORD has brought it about; he H2256
Jer 41: 9 **N** the cistern where he threw all the H2256
Jer 42: 2 For as you **n** see, though we were once NDT
Jer 42: 2 we were once many, **n** only a few are left. NDT
Jer 42:11 of the king of Babylon, whom you **n** fear. NDT
Jer 42:22 So **n**, be sure of this: You will die by the H6964
Jer 44: 7 "**N** this is what the LORD God Almighty, H6964
Jer 44:23 upon you, as you **n** see." H2021+3427+2021+2296
Jer 49:15 "**N** I will make you small among the H2180
Jer 51: 7 her wine; therefore they *have n* **gone mad**. AIT
Jer 52: 3 **N** Zedekiah rebelled against the king of H2256
La 1: 1 among the provinces *has n* **become** a slave. AIT
La 4: 2 are **n** considered as pots of clay NDT
La 4: 5 up in royal purple **n** lie on ash heaps. NDT
La 4: 8 But **n** they are blacker than soot; they are NDT
La 4:14 **N** they grope through the streets as if they NDT
Eze 3: 4 **go n** to the people of Israel and H2143+995
Eze 3:11 **Go n** to your people in exile and H2143+995
Eze 4: 1 "**N**, son of man, take a block of clay, put it H2256

N

Eze 4:14 From my youth until n I have never eaten H6964
Eze 5: 1 "N, son of man, take a sharp sword and H2256
Eze 7: 3 The end is n upon you, and I will unleash H6964
Eze 8: 8 "Son of man, n dig into the wall. H5528
Eze 9: 3 N the glory of the God of Israel went up H2256
Eze 10: 3 N the cherubim were standing on the H2256
Eze 11:13 N as I was prophesying, Pelatiah son of H2256
Eze 12:27 'The vision he sees is for many years *from n* AIT
Eze 13: 2 the prophets of Israel who *are n* prophesying. AIT
Eze 13:17 "N, son of man, set your face against the H2256
Eze 16:49 " 'N this was the sin of your sister Sodom H2180
Eze 16:57 you are n scorned by the daughters of H6961
Eze 17: 7 The vine n sent out its roots toward him H2180
Eze 19: 6 among the lions, for he was n a strong lion. NDT
Eze 19:13 N it is planted in the desert, in a dry and H6964
Eze 23:43 'N let them use her as a prostitute H6964
Eze 24: 6 bloodshed, to the pot n encrusted, whose NDT
Eze 24:13 " 'N your impurity is lewdness. Because I H928
Eze 26: 2 n that she lies in ruins I will prosper NDT
Eze 26:18 N the coastlands tremble on the day of H6964
Eze 27:34 N you are shattered by the sea in the H6961
Eze 33:22 N the evening before the man arrived, the H2256
Eze 36:35 destroyed, *are n* fortified and inhabited." AIT
Eze 38: 8 nations, and n all of them live in safety. H2256
Eze 39:25 I will n restore the fortunes of Jacob and H6964
Eze 42: 5 N the upper rooms were narrower, for the H2256
Eze 43: 9 N let them put away from me their H6964
Eze 47: 5 n it was a river that I could not cross NDT
Da 1: 9 N God had caused the official to show H2256
Da 2:36 and n we will interpret it to the king. A10221
Da 3:15 N when you hear the sound of the horn A10363
Da 4:18 N, Belteshazzar, tell me what it means A10221
Da 4:37 N I, Nebuchadnezzar, praise and exalt A10363
Da 5:16 N I have heard that you are able to give A10221
Da 6: 3 N Daniel so distinguished himself A10008
Da 6: 8 N, Your Majesty, issue the decree and A10363
Da 6:10 N when Daniel learned that the decree A10221
Da 9:15 "N, Lord our God, who brought your H6964
Da 9:17 "N, our God, hear the prayers and H6964
Da 9:22 I have n come to give you insight and H6964
Da 10:11 stand up, for I have n been sent to you." H6964
Da 10:14 N I have come to explain to you what will H2256
Da 10:19 Be strong n; be strong." When he H2256
Da 11: 2 "N then, I tell you the truth: Three more H6964
Hos 2: 7 as at first, for then I was better off than n. H6964
Hos 2:10 So n I will expose her lewdness before H6964
Hos 2:14 "Therefore I am n going to allure her; H2180
Hos 5: 3 Ephraim, you have n turned to prostitution H6964
Hos 7:11 senseless—n calling to Egypt, now NDT
Hos 7:11 now calling to Egypt, n turning to Assyria. NDT
Hos 8: 8 n she is among the nations like H6964
Hos 8:10 the nations, I will n gather them together. H6964
Hos 8:13 N he will remember their wickedness and H6964
Hos 10: 2 deceitful, and n they must bear their guilt. H6964
Hos 13: 2 N they sin more and more; they make H6964
Joel 2:12 "Even n," declares the LORD, "return to me H6964
Joel 3: 4 "N what have you against me, Tyre H2256+1685
Am 2:13 "N then, I will crush you as a cart crushes H2180
Am 7:16 N then, hear the word of the LORD. You say H6964
Jnh 1:17 N the LORD provided a huge fish to H2256
Jnh 3: 3 N Nineveh was a very large city; it took H2256
Jnh 4: 3 N, LORD, take away my life, for it is better H6964
Mic 4: 9 Why do you n cry aloud—have you no H6964
Mic 4:10 n you must leave the city to camp in H6964
Mic 4:11 But n many nations are gathered against H6964
Mic 5: 1 Marshal your troops n, city of troops, for a H6964
Mic 7: 4 N is the time of your confusion. H6964
Mic 7:10 even n she will be trampled underfoot H6964
Na 1:13 N I will break their yoke from your neck H6964
Na 2:11 Where n is the lions' den, the place where NDT
Hab 2:16 instead of glory. N it is your turn! Drink H1685
Hag 1: 5 N this is what the LORD Almighty says H6964
Hag 2: 3 How does it look to you n? Does it not H6964
Hag 2: 4 But n be strong, Zerubbabel,' declares the H6964
Hag 2:15 " 'N give careful thought to this from this H6964
Hag 2:19 Until n, the vine and the fig tree, the NDT
Zec 1: 5 Where are your ancestors n? And the NDT
Zec 3: 3 N Joshua was dressed in filthy clothes as H2256
Zec 8: 9 "N hear these words H928+2021+3427+2021+465
Zec 8:11 But n I will not deal with the remnant of H6964
Zec 8:15 "so n I have determined
H928+2021+3427+2021+465
Zec 9: 8 my people, for n I am keeping watch. H6964
Zec 9:12 even n I announce that I will H2021+3427
Mal 1: 9 "N plead with God to be gracious to us H6964
Mal 2: 1 "And n, you priests, this warning is for you H6964
Mal 3:15 But n we call the arrogant blessed H6964
Mt 3:15 "Let it be so n; it is proper for us to G785
Mt 5: 1 N when Jesus saw the crowds, he went up G1254
Mt 11:12 From the days of John the Baptist until n G785
Mt 12:41 n something greater than Jonah is G2627
Mt 12:42 n something greater than Solomon is G2627
Mt 14: 3 N Herod had arrested John and bound G1142
Mt 20:17 N Jesus was going up to Jerusalem. G2779
Mt 22:25 N there were seven brothers among us G1254
Mt 22:28 N then, at the resurrection, whose wife G4036
Mt 24:21 beginning of the world until n— G3836+3814
Mt 24:32 "N learn this lesson from the fig tree: As G1254
Mt 26:29 of the vine from n on until that day when I G785
Mt 26:48 N the betrayer had arranged a signal with G1254
Mt 26:64 From n on you will see the Son of Man G785
Mt 26:65 n you have heard the blasphemy G3814
Mt 26:69 N Peter was sitting out in the courtyard G1254
Mt 27:15 N it was the governor's custom at the G1254
Mt 27:42 Let him come down n from the cross, and G3814
Mt 27:43 Let God rescue him n if he wants him, for G3814
Mt 27:49 The rest said, "*N* leave him alone. Let's see if AIT
Mt 28: 7 you will see him.' N I have told you." G2627
Mk 2: 6 N some teachers of the law were sitting G1254
Mk 2:18 N John's disciples and the Pharisees were G2779
Mk 6:25 you to give me right n the head of John G1994
Mk 12:20 *N there* were seven brothers. The first one AIT
Mk 12:26 N about the dead rising—have you not G1254
Mk 13:19 the world, until n—and never to be G3814
Mk 13:28 "N learn this lesson from the fig tree: As G1254
Mk 14: 1 N the Passover and the Festival of G1254
Mk 14:44 N the betrayer had arranged a signal with G1254
Mk 15: 6 N it was the custom at the festival to G1254
Mk 15:32 come down n from the cross, that G3814
Mk 15:36 to Jesus to drink. "N leave him alone. Let's NDT
Lk 1:20 And n you will be silent and not able to G2627
Lk 1:48 From n on all generations will call G3836+3814
Lk 2:25 N there was a man in Jerusalem G2779+2627
Lk 2:29 you may n dismiss your servant in peace. G3814
Lk 3:23 N Jesus himself was about thirty years old G2779
Lk 4:38 N Simon's mother-in-law was suffering G1254
Lk 5:10 from n on you will fish for people." G3836+3814
Lk 6:21 Blessed are you who hunger n, for you G3814
Lk 6:21 Blessed are you who weep n, for you will G3814
Lk 6:25 Woe to you who are well fed n, for you G3814
Lk 6:25 Woe to you who laugh n, for you will G3814
Lk 7:42 N which of them will love him more?" G4036
Lk 8:19 N Jesus' mother and brothers came to see G1254
Lk 8:40 N when Jesus returned, a crowd G1254
Lk 9: 7 N Herod the tetrarch heard about all that G1254
Lk 11:19 N if I drive out demons by Beelzebul, by G1254
Lk 11:31 n something greater than Solomon is G2627
Lk 11:32 n something greater than Jonah is G2627
Lk 11:39 Lord said to him, "N then, you Pharisees G3814
Lk 11:41 But n as for what is inside you—be G4440
Lk 12:52 From n on there will be five in one G3836+3814
Lk 13: 1 N there were some present at that time G1254
Lk 13: 7 'For three years n I've been coming G608+4005
Lk 14:17 'Come, for everything is n ready. G2453
Lk 15: 1 N the tax collectors and sinners were all G1254
Lk 16: 3 manager said to himself, 'What *shall I* do *n*? AIT
Lk 16:25 n he is comforted here and you are in G3814
Lk 17: 7 'Come along n and sit down to eat'? G2311
Lk 17:11 N on his way to Jerusalem, Jesus G2779+1181
Lk 19: 8 *Here and n I* give half of my possessions to AIT
Lk 19:42 peace—but n it is hidden from your eyes. G3814
Lk 20:29 N there were seven brothers. The first one G4036
Lk 20:33 N then, at the resurrection whose wife will G4036
Lk 22: 1 N the Festival of Unleavened Bread G1254
Lk 22:36 said to them, "But n if you have a purse G3814
Lk 22:69 But from n on, the Son of Man will G3836+3814
Lk 23:44 It was n about noon, and darkness came G2453
Lk 23:50 N there was a man named Joseph G2779+2627
Lk 24:13 N that same day two of them were G2779+2627
Jn 1:19 N this was John's testimony when the G2779
Jn 1:24 N the Pharisees who had been sent G2779
Jn 2: 8 "N draw some out and take it to the G3814
Jn 2:10 to drink; but you have saved the best till n." G785
Jn 2:23 N while he was in Jerusalem at the G1254
Jn 3: 1 N there was a Pharisee, a man named G1254
Jn 3:23 N John also was baptizing at Aenon near G1254
Jn 3:29 That joy is mine, and *it is n* complete. AIT
Jn 4: 1 N Jesus learned that the Pharisees G6055+4036
Jn 4: 4 N he had to go through Samaria. G1254
Jn 4:18 the man you n have is not your G3814
Jn 4:23 is coming and has n come when the true G3814
Jn 4:36 Even n the one who reaps draws a wage G2453
Jn 4:42 you said; n we have heard for ourselves G1142
Jn 4:44 N Jesus himself had pointed out that a G1142
Jn 5: 2 N there is in Jerusalem near the Sheep G1254
Jn 5:25 is coming and has n come when the dead G3814
Jn 6:17 By n it was dark, and Jesus had not yet G2453
Jn 6:42 How can he n say, 'I came down from G3814
Jn 7:11 N at the festival the Jewish leaders were G4036
Jn 7:23 *N* if a boy can be circumcised on the Sabbath AIT
Jn 8: 5 stone such women. N what do you say?" G4036
Jn 8:11 "Go n and leave your life of G608+3836+3814
Jn 8:35 N a slave has no permanent place in the G1254
Jn 8:52 "N we know that you are G3814
Jn 9:14 N the day on which Jesus had made the G1254
Jn 9:15 the man replied, "and I washed, and *n I* see." AIT
Jn 9:19 How is it that n he can see?" G785
Jn 9:21 But how he can see n, or who opened his G3814
Jn 9:25 thing I do know. I was blind but n I see!" G785
Jn 9:30 The man answered, "N that is remarkable! G1142
Jn 9:37 "You have n seen him; in fact, he G2779
Jn 9:41 but n that you claim you can see G3814
Jn 11: 1 N a man named Lazarus was sick. He was G1254
Jn 11: 2 whose brother Lazarus *n lay* sick, was the AIT
Jn 11: 5 N Jesus loved Martha and her sister and G1254
Jn 11:18 N Bethany was less than two miles from G1254
Jn 11:22 But I know that even n God will give you G3814
Jn 11:30 N Jesus had not yet entered the village G1254
Jn 12:17 N the crowd that was with him when he G4036
Jn 12:20 N there were some Greeks among those G1254
Jn 12:27 "N my soul is troubled, and what shall I G3814
Jn 12:31 N is *the time for* judgment on this world G3814
Jn 12:31 n the prince of this world will be driven G3814
Jn 13: 7 "You do not realize n what I am doing, but G785
Jn 13:14 N that I, your Lord and Teacher, have G4036
Jn 13:17 *N* that *you* know these things, you will be AIT
Jn 13:19 "I am telling you n before it happens G608+785
Jn 13:31 "N the Son of Man is glorified and God is G3814
Jn 13:33 just as I told the Jews, so I tell you n: G785
Jn 13:36 you cannot follow n, but you will follow G3814
Jn 13:37 asked, "Lord, why can't I follow you n? G785
Jn 14: 7 From n on, you do know him and have G785
Jn 14:29 I have told you n before it happens, so G3814
Jn 14:31 has commanded me. "Come *n*; let us leave. AIT
Jn 15: 9 so have I loved you. *N* remain in my love. AIT
Jn 15:22 n they have no excuse for their sin. G3814
Jn 16: 5 n I am going to him who sent me G3814
Jn 16:11 the prince of this world *n* stands condemned. AIT
Jn 16:12 to say to you, more than you can n bear. G785
Jn 16:22 N is your time of grief, but I will see you G3814
Jn 16:24 Until n you have not asked for anything in G785
Jn 16:28 n I am leaving the world and going back G4099
Jn 16:29 "N you are speaking clearly and without G3814
Jn 16:30 N we can see that you know all things G3814
Jn 16:31 "Do you n believe?" Jesus replied. G785
Jn 17: 3 N this is eternal life: that they know you G1254
Jn 17: 5 And n, Father, glorify me in your presence G3814
Jn 17: 7 N they know that everything you have G3814
Jn 17:13 "I am coming to you n, but I say these G3814
Jn 18: 2 N Judas, who betrayed him, knew the G1254
Jn 18:28 By n it was early morning, and to avoid G1254
Jn 18:36 But n my kingdom is from another place." G3814
Jn 18:40 N Barabbas had taken part in an uprising. G1254
Jn 19:28 that everything had n been finished, G2453
Jn 19:31 N it was the day of Preparation, and the G2075
Jn 19:38 N Joseph was a disciple of Jesus, but NDT
Jn 20:11 N Mary stood outside the tomb crying. G1254
Jn 20:24 N Thomas (also known as Didymus), G1254
Jn 21:14 This was n the third time Jesus appeared G2453
Ac 2: 5 N there were staying in Jerusalem G1254
Ac 2:33 has poured out what you n see and hear. G2779
Ac 3: 2 N a man who was lame from birth was G2779
Ac 3:17 "N, fellow Israelites, I know that you acted G3814
Ac 4:29 N, Lord, consider their threats and enable G3814
Ac 5: 1 N a man named Ananias, together with G1254
Ac 6: 8 N Stephen, a man full of God's grace G1254
Ac 7: 4 him to this land where you are n living. G3814
Ac 7:34 to set them free. N come, I will send you G3814
Ac 7:52 And n you have betrayed and murdered G3814
Ac 8: 9 N for some time a man named Simon G1254
Ac 8:26 N an angel of the Lord said to Philip, "Go G1254
Ac 9: 6 "N get up and go into the city, and you will G247
Ac 10: 5 N send men to Joppa to bring back a man G3814
Ac 10:33 N we are all here in the presence of God G3814
Ac 10:34 "*I n* realize how true it is that God does not AIT
Ac 11:19 N those who had been scattered by the G4036
Ac 12:11 "N I know without a doubt that the Lord G3814
Ac 12:20 they n joined together and sought an G1254
Ac 13: 1 N in the church at Antioch there were G1254
Ac 13:11 N the hand of the Lord is against you. G3814
Ac 13:31 They are n his witnesses to our people G3814
Ac 13:36 "N when David had served God's purpose G1142
Ac 13:46 of eternal life, we n turn to the Gentiles. G2627
Ac 14:26 of God for the work *they had n* completed. AIT
Ac 15:10 N then, why do you try to test God by G3814
Ac 16:36 Silas be released. N you can leave. Go in G3814
Ac 16:37 And n do they want to get rid of us quietly G3814
Ac 17: 6 all over the world have n come here, G2779
Ac 17:11 N the Berean Jews were of more noble G1254
Ac 17:30 n he commands all people G3836+3814
Ac 18: 6 From n on I will go to the Gentiles." G3836+3814
Ac 19:18 those who believed *n* came and openly AIT
Ac 20:22 "And n, compelled by the Spirit, I am G3814
Ac 20:25 "N I know that none of you among whom G3814
Ac 20:32 "N I commit you to God and to the G3836+3814
Ac 22: 1 fathers, listen n to my defense. G3815
Ac 22:16 And n what are you waiting for? Get up G3814
Ac 23:15 N then, you and the Sanhedrin petition G3814
Ac 23:21 They are ready n, waiting for your consent G3814
Ac 24:13 charges they are n making against me. G3815
Ac 24:25 and said, "That's enough *for* n! G3836+3814
Ac 25:10 "I am *n* standing before Caesar's court AIT
Ac 26: 6 And n it is because of my hope in what G3814
Ac 26:16 'N get up and stand on your feet. I have G247
Ac 27: 9 dangerous because by n it was after the G2453
Ac 27:22 But n I urge you to keep up your G3836+3814
Ac 27:34 N I urge you to take some food. You need G1475
Ro 1:10 I pray that n at last by God's will G2453+4537
Ro 1:13 prevented from doing so until n) G3836+1306
Ro 2: 2 N we know that God's judgment against G1254
Ro 2:17 N you, if you call yourself a Jew; if you G1254
Ro 3:19 N we know that whatever the law says, it G1254
Ro 3:21 But n apart from the law the G3815
Ro 4: 4 N to the one who works, wages are not G1254
Ro 5: 2 by faith into this grace in which *we n* stand. AIT
Ro 5: 9 Since we have n been justified by his G3814
Ro 5:11 through whom we have n received G3814
Ro 6: 8 N if we died with Christ, we believe that G1254
Ro 6:17 teaching that *has n* claimed *your* allegiance. AIT
Ro 6:19 so n offer yourselves as slaves to G3814
Ro 6:21 from the things you are n ashamed of? G3814
Ro 6:22 But n that you have been set free from sin G3815
Ro 7: 6 But n, by dying to what once bound us, we G3815
Ro 7:20 N if I do what I do not want to do, it is no G1254
Ro 8: 1 there is n no condemnation for those who G3814
Ro 8:17 N if we are children, then we are heirs G1254

N

Ro 11:17 the others and *n* **share in** the nourishing sap AIT
Ro 11:30 to God have **n** received mercy as a G3814
Ro 11:31 so they too have **n** become disobedient in G3814
Ro 11:31 that they too may **n** receive mercy as a G3814
Ro 13:11 salvation is nearer **n** than when we first G3814
Ro 15:23 But **n** that there is no more place for me G3815
Ro 15:25 **N**, however, I am on my way to Jerusalem G3815
Ro 16:25 **N** to him who is able to establish you in G1254
Ro 16:26 **n** revealed and made known through G3814
1Co 4: 2 **N** it is required that those who have G6045+3370
1Co 4: 6 **N**, brothers and sisters, I have applied G1254
1Co 5:11 But **n** I am writing to you that you must not G3814
1Co 7: 1 **N** for the matters you wrote about: "It is G1254
1Co 7: 8 **N** to the unmarried and the widows I say G1254
1Co 7:25 **N** about virgins: I have no command from G1254
1Co 7:29 **From n on** those who have wives G3836+3370
1Co 8: 1 **N** about food sacrificed to idols: We know G1254
1Co 10: 6 **N** these things occurred as examples to G1254
1Co 12: 1 **N** about the gifts of the Spirit, brothers G1254
1Co 12: 7 **N** to each one the manifestation of the G1254
1Co 12:15 **N** if the foot should say, "Because I am not NDT
1Co 12:27 **N** you are the body of Christ, and each G1254
1Co 12:31 **N** eagerly desire the greater gifts. G1254
1Co 13:12 For **n** we see only a reflection as in a mirror G785
1Co 13:12 **N** I know in part; then I shall know fully G785
1Co 13:13 And **n** these three remain: faith, hope G3815
1Co 14: 6 **N**, brothers and sisters, if I come to you G3814
1Co 14:16 who *is n* **put in** the position of an inquirer AIT
1Co 15: 1 **N**, brothers and sisters, I want to remind G1254
1Co 15:27 **N** when it says that "everything" has G1254
1Co 15:29 **N if** there is no resurrection, what will G2075
1Co 16: 1 **N** about the collection for the Lord's G1254
1Co 16: 7 do not want to see you **n** and make only a G785
1Co 16:12 **N** about our brother Apollos: I strongly G1254
1Co 16:12 He was quite unwilling to go **n**, but he G3814
2Co 1:12 **N** this is our boast: Our conscience G1142
2Co 1:21 **N** it is God who makes both us and you G1254
2Co 2: 7 **N** instead, you ought to forgive and G6063
2Co 2:12 **N** when I went to Troas to preach the G1254
2Co 3: 7 **N** if the ministry that brought death, which G1254
2Co 3:10 was glorious **has** no **glory** *n* in comparison AIT
2Co 3:17 **N** the Lord is the Spirit, and where the G1254
2Co 5: 5 **N** the one who has fashioned us for this G1254
2Co 5:16 So from **n on** we regard no one G3836+3814
2Co 6: 2 **n** is the time of God's favor G2627+3814
2Co 6: 2 **n** is the day of salvation. G2627+3814
2Co 7: 9 **n** I am happy, not because you were G3814
2Co 8: 1 **And n**, brothers and sisters, we want you G1254
2Co 8:11 **N** finish the work, so that your eager G3815
2Co 8:22 **n** even more so because of his great G3815
2Co 9:10 **N** he who supplies seed to the sower and G1254
2Co 12:14 **N** I am ready to visit you for the third time G2627
2Co 13: 2 I **n** repeat it while absent G3814
2Co 13: 7 **N** we pray to God that you will not do G1254
Gal 1: 9 have already said, so **n** I say again: If G785
Gal 1:10 Am I **n** trying to win the approval of human G785
Gal 1:23 persecuted us is **n** preaching the faith he G3814
Gal 2:20 The life I **n** live in the body, I live by faith G3814
Gal 3: 3 are you **n** trying to finish by means of the G3814
Gal 3:25 **N that** this faith has come, we are no G1254
Gal 4: 9 But **n** that you know God—or rather are G3814
Gal 4:15 is your blessing of me **n**? I can testify that, NDT
Gal 4:16 Have I **n** become your enemy by telling G6063
Gal 4:20 I could be with you **n** and change my tone, G785
Gal 4:25 **N** Hagar stands for Mount Sinai in Arabia G1254
Gal 4:28 **N** you, brothers and sisters, like Isaac, are G1254
Gal 4:29 the power of the Spirit. It is the same **n**. G3814
Gal 6:17 **From n on**, let no one cause me G3836+3370
Eph 2: 2 the spirit who is **n** at work in those who G3814
Eph 2:13 But **n** in Christ Jesus you who once were G3815
Eph 3: 5 as it has **n** been revealed by the G3814
Eph 3:10 His intent was that **n**, through the church G3814
Eph 3:20 **N** to him who is able to do immeasurably G1254
Eph 5: 8 darkness, but **n** you are light in the Lord. G3814
Eph 5:24 **N** as the church submits to Christ, so also G247
Php 1: 5 gospel from the first day until **n**, G3836+3814
Php 1:12 **N** I want you to know, brothers and sisters G1254
Php 1:20 courage so that **n** as always Christ will be G3814
Php 1:30 you saw I had, and **n** hear that I still have. G3814
Php 2:12 **n** much more in my absence G3814
Php 3: 7 were gains to me *I n* **consider** loss for the AIT
Php 3:18 you before and **n** tell you *again* even with G3814
Php 4:18 *n that I have* **received** from Epaphroditus the AIT
Col 1:22 But **n** he has reconciled you by Christ's G3815
Col 1:24 **N** I rejoice in what I am suffering for you G3814
Col 1:26 is **n** disclosed to the Lord's people. G3814
Col 3: 3 your life *is n* **hidden** with Christ in God. AIT
Col 3: 8 But **n** you must also rid yourselves of all G3815
1Th 3: 6 But Timothy has **just n** come to us from you G785
1Th 3: 8 For **n** we really live, since you are standing G3814
1Th 3:11 **N** may our God and Father himself and G1254
1Th 4: 1 *N we* **ask** you and urge you in the Lord Jesus AIT
1Th 4: 9 **N** about your love for one another we do G1254
1Th 5: 1 **N**, brothers and sisters, about times and G1254
1Th 5:12 **N** we ask you, brothers and sisters, to G1254
2Th 2: 6 And **n** you know what is holding him back G3814
2Th 2: 7 the one who **n** holds it back will G785
2Th 3:16 **N** may the Lord of peace himself give you G1254
1Ti 1:17 **N** to the King eternal, immortal, invisible G1254
1Ti 2: 6 This has **n** been witnessed to at the proper NDT
1Ti 3: 2 **N** the overseer is to be above reproach G4036
2Ti 1: 5 I am persuaded, **n** lives in you also. NDT
2Ti 1:10 it has **n** been revealed through the G3814
2Ti 4: 8 **N** there is in store for me the crown of G3370
Titus 1: 3 *n* at his appointed season *he has* **brought to light** AIT
Phm 9 an old man and **n** also a prisoner of Christ G3815
Phm 11 **n** he has become useful both to you G3815
Heb 2: 9 *n* **crowned** with glory and honor because he AIT
Heb 4: 3 **N** we who have believed enter that rest G1142
Heb 7: 5 **N** the law requires the descendants of Levi G2779
Heb 7:23 **N** there have been many of those priests G2779
Heb 8: 1 **N** the main point of what we are saying is G1254
Heb 9: 1 **N** the first covenant had regulations for G4036
Heb 9: 5 cannot discuss these things in detail **n**. G3814
Heb 9:11 of the good things *that* **are** *n already here*, AIT
Heb 9:15 *n that he has* **died** as a ransom to set them AIT
Heb 9:24 **n** to appear for us in God's presence. G3814
Heb 11: 1 **N** faith is confidence in what we hope G1254
Heb 12:26 shook the earth, but **n** he has promised G3814
Heb 13:20 **N** may the God of peace, who through the G1254
Jas 4:13 **N** listen, you who say, "Today or tomorrow G3814
Jas 5: 1 **N** listen, you rich people, weep and wail G3814
1Pe 1: 6 though **n** for a little while you may have G785
1Pe 1: 8 even though you do not see him **n** G785
1Pe 1:12 the things that have **n** been told you by G3814
1Pe 1:22 *N that you have* **purified** yourselves by AIT
1Pe 2: 3 **n** that you have tasted that the Lord is G1623
1Pe 2: 7 **N** to you who believe, this stone is G4036
1Pe 2:10 people, but **n** you are the people of God G3814
1Pe 2:10 but **n** you have received mercy. G3814
1Pe 2:25 **n** you have returned to the Shepherd G3814
1Pe 3:21 baptism that **n** saves you also— G3814
1Pe 4: 6 was preached even *to those who are n* **dead**, AIT
2Pe 1:12 firmly established in the truth *you* **n have**. G4205
2Pe 3: 1 this is **n** my second letter to you. G2453
2Pe 3:18 To him be glory both **n** and forever! Amen G3814
1Jn 2:18 even **n** many antichrists have come. G3814
1Jn 2:28 And **n**, dear children, continue in him, so G3814
1Jn 3: 2 Dear friends, **n** we are children of God G3814
1Jn 4: 3 is coming and *even* **n** is already in the G3814
2Jn 5 And **n**, dear lady, I am not writing you a G3814
Jude 25 before all ages, **n** and forevermore! G3814
Rev 1:18 I was dead, **and n** look, I am alive for ever G2779
Rev 1:19 what **is** *n* and what will take place later. AIT
Rev 2:19 that you are **n** doing more than you G2274
Rev 2:24 **N** I say to the rest of you in Thyatira, to G1254
Rev 11: 7 **N** when they have finished their testimony G2779
Rev 12:10 "**N** have come the salvation and the power G785
Rev 14:13 the dead who die in the Lord from **n on**." G785
Rev 17: 8 once was, *n* **is** not, and yet will come up out AIT
Rev 17: 8 because it once was, *n* **is** not, and yet will AIT
Rev 17:11 who once was, and *n* **is** not, is an eighth king AIT
Rev 21: 3 dwelling place is **n** among the people, NDT

NOWHERE (7)

Ge 8: 9 dove could find **n** to perch because H4202+4955
Job 42:15 **N** in all the land were there found women H4202
Pr 19: 7 with pleading, they are **n** *to be found*. H4202
Isa 59:15 Truth is **n to be found**, and whoever shuns H6372
Jer 25:35 The shepherds *will* **have n** to flee, the H6+4946
Mt 27:24 When Pilate saw that he was getting **n** G4029
Jn 12:19 "See, *this is* **getting** us **n**. G4024+6067+4029

NUBIANS (NIV84) CUSHITES

NUGGETS (2)

Job 22:24 assign your **n** to the dust, your gold of H1309
Job 28: 6 its rocks, and its dust contains **n of gold**. H2298

NULLIFIED (1) [ANNULLED, NULLIFY]

Nu 30:12 Her husband *has* **n** them, and the LORD H7296

NULLIFIES (3) [NULLIFY]

Nu 30: 8 *he* **n** the vow that obligates her or the H7296
Nu 30:12 But if her husband **n** them when he H7296+7296
Nu 30:15 *he* **n** them some time after he H7296+7296

NULLIFY (6) [NULLIFIED, NULLIFIES]

Nu 30:13 may confirm or **n** any vow she makes or H7296
Mt 15: 6 Thus *you* **n** the word of God for the sake of G218
Mk 7:13 Thus *you* **n** the word of God by your G218
Ro 3: 3 *Will* their unfaithfulness **n** God's G2934
Ro 3:31 *Do we*, then, **n** the law by this faith? Not at G2934
1Co 1:28 that are not—to **n** the things that are, G2934

NUMBER (166) [NUMBERED, NUMBERING, NUMBERLESS, NUMBERS, NUMEROUS]

Ge 1:22 "Be fruitful and **increase in n** and fill the H8049
Ge 1:28 "Be fruitful and **increase in n**; fill the earth H8049
Ge 6: 1 began to **increase in n** on the earth H8045
Ge 8:17 be fruitful and **increase in n** on it. H8049
Ge 9: 1 "Be fruitful and **increase in n** and fill the H8049
Ge 9: 7 be fruitful and **increase in n**; multiply on H8049
Ge 18:28 the **n** of the righteous is five **less than** fifty H2893
Ge 26:24 bless you and *will* **increase the n** *of* your H8049
Ge 34:30 We are few in **n**, and if they join forces H5031
Ge 35:11 Almighty; be fruitful and **increase in n**. H8049
Ge 42:16 Send one of **your** *n* to get your brother; the AIT
Ge 47:12 according to the **n** *of* their children. H7023
Ge 47:27 were fruitful and **increased** greatly in **n**. H8049
Ex 5: 8 to make the same **n** *of* bricks as before; H5504
Ex 5:19 "*You are* not *to* **reduce the n** *of* bricks H1757
Ex 12: 4 into account the **n** *of* people there are. H4831
Ex 30:12 will come on them when *you* **n** them. H7212
Lev 25:15 on the basis of the **n** *of* years since the H5031
Lev 25:15 you on the basis of the **n** *of* years left for H5031
Lev 25:16 really being sold to you is the **n** *of* crops. H5031
Lev 25:50 paid to a hired worker for that **n** *of* years. H5031
Lev 26:22 cattle and **make** you *so* **few in n** that your H5070
Lev 27:18 according to the **n** *of* years that remain H7023
Nu 1:21 The **n** from the tribe of Reuben was H7212
Nu 1:23 The **n** from the tribe of Simeon was H7212
Nu 1:25 The **n** from the tribe of Gad was 45,650. H7212
Nu 1:27 The **n** from the tribe of Judah was 74,600. H7212
Nu 1:29 The **n** from the tribe of Issachar was H7212
Nu 1:31 The **n** from the tribe of Zebulun was H7212
Nu 1:33 The **n** from the tribe of Ephraim was H7212
Nu 1:35 The **n** from the tribe of Manasseh was H7212
Nu 1:37 The **n** from the tribe of Benjamin was H7212
Nu 1:39 The **n** from the tribe of Dan was 62,700. H7212
Nu 1:41 The **n** from the tribe of Asher was 41,500. H7212
Nu 1:43 The **n** from the tribe of Naphtali was H7212
Nu 1:46 The total **n** was 603,550. H7212
Nu 2: 9 according to their divisions, **n** 186,400. NDT
Nu 2:16 according to their divisions, **n** 151,450. NDT
Nu 2:24 according to their divisions, **n** 108,100. NDT
Nu 2:31 assigned to the camp of Dan **n** 157,600. NDT
Nu 2:32 the camps, by their divisions, **n** 603,550. H7212
Nu 3:22 The **n** *of* all the males a month old or H5031
Nu 3:28 The **n** *of* all the males a month old or H5031
Nu 3:34 The **n** *of* all the males a month old or H5031
Nu 3:39 The total **n** *of* Levites counted at the H7212
Nu 3:43 The total **n** *of* firstborn males a month old H7212
Nu 3:46 Israelites who **exceed** the **n** *of* the Levites, H6369
Nu 3:49 those *who* **exceeded** the **n** redeemed H6369
Nu 7:87 The **total** *n of* animals for the burnt offering AIT
Nu 7:88 The **total** *n of* animals for the sacrifice of the AIT
Nu 23:10 the dust of Jacob or **n** even a fourth of H5031
Nu 26:51 The total **n** *of* the men of Israel was H7212
Nu 26:53 an inheritance based on the **n** *of* names. H5031
Nu 26:54 according to the **n** *of* those listed. H7023
Nu 29:18 offerings according to the **n** specified. H5031
Nu 29:21 offerings according to the **n** specified. H5031
Nu 29:24 offerings according to the **n** specified. H5031
Nu 29:27 offerings according to the **n** specified. H5031
Nu 29:30 offerings according to the **n** specified. H5031
Nu 29:33 offerings according to the **n** specified. H5031
Nu 29:37 offerings according to the **n** specified. H5031
Dt 25: 2 presence with the **n** of lashes the crime H5031
Dt 28:62 in the sky will be left but **few in n**. H5493+5071
Dt 28:63 to make you prosper and **increase in n**. H8049
Dt 32: 8 according to the **n** *of* the sons of Israel. H5031
Jos 4: 5 according to the **n** *of* the tribes of the H5031
Jos 4: 8 according to the **n** *of* the tribes of the H5031
Jos 11: 4 troops and a large **n** of horses and H8041
Jos 21:19 The **total** *n of* towns for the priests, the AIT
Jos 21:33 The **total** *n of* towns of the Gershonite clans AIT
Jos 21:40 The **total** *n of* towns allotted to the Merarite AIT
1Sa 6: 4 according to the **n** *of* the Philistine rulers H5031
1Sa 6:18 And the **n** *of* the gold rats was according H5031
1Sa 6:18 was according to the **n** of Philistine towns NDT
1Sa 9:22 of those who were invited—about thirty in **n**. NDT
1Sa 18:27 *They* **counted out the full n** to the king so H4848
1Sa 23:13 about six hundred in **n**, left Keilah and kept NDT
2Sa 12: 2 man had a very **large n** *of* sheep and H2221
2Sa 24: 9 reported the **n** *of* the fighting men H5031+5152
1Ki 3: 8 great people, too numerous to count or **n**. H4948
1Ch 6:60 The **total** *n of* towns distributed among the AIT
1Ch 7:40 The **n** *of* men ready for battle, as listed in H5031
1Ch 16:19 When they were but few in **n**, few indeed H5031
1Ch 21: 5 Joab reported the **n** *of* the fighting H5031+5152
1Ch 22:16 bronze and iron—craftsmen beyond **n**. H5031
1Ch 23: 3 the total **n** of men was thirty-eight H5031
1Ch 23:31 regularly in the *proper* **n** and in the way H5031
1Ch 24: 4 A **larger n** of leaders were found among H8041
1Ch 27:23 did not take the **n** *of* the men twenty years H5031
1Ch 27:24 the **n** was not entered in the book of H5031
2Ch 14:13 Such a great **n** of Cushites fell that they NDT
2Ch 26:12 The total **n** *of* family leaders over the H5031
2Ch 29:32 The **n** *of* burnt offerings the assembly H5031
2Ch 30:24 A **great n** of priests consecrated H4200+8044
Ezr 3: 4 with the required **n** of burnt offerings H5031
Ezr 8:34 was accounted for by **n** and weight, H5031
Est 9:11 The **n** *of* those killed in the citadel of H5031
Job 1: 3 donkeys, and had a large **n** of servants. H8041
Job 14: 5 have decreed the **n** *of* his months and H5031
Job 36:26 The **n** *of* his years is past finding out H5031
Ps 39: 4 my life's end and the **n** *of* my days; let me H4500
Ps 40:12 For troubles without **n** surround me; my H5031
Ps 90:12 Teach us to **n** our days, that we may gain H4948
Ps 104:25 teeming with creatures beyond **n**—living H5031
Ps 105:12 When they were but few in **n**, few indeed H5031
Ps 105:34 the locusts came, grasshoppers without **n**; H5031
Ps 147: 4 He determines the **n** of the stars and calls H5031
SS 6: 8 eighty concubines, and virgins beyond **n**; H5031
Jer 2:32 have forgotten me, days without **n**. H5031
Jer 23: 3 they will be fruitful and **increase in n**. H8049
Jer 29: 6 daughters. **Increase in n** there; do not H8049
Jer 52:23 the total **n** of pomegranates above the AIT
Jer 52:28 This is the **n** of the people Nebuchadnezzar NDT
Eze 4: 4 their sin for the **n** *of* days you lie on your H5031
Eze 4: 5 you the same **n** *of* days as the years of H5031
Eze 36:11 *I will* **increase the n** *of* people and H8049
Eze 47: 7 I saw a great **n** of trees on each side of H8041
Joel 1: 6 a mighty army without **n**; it has the teeth H5031
Joel 2:11 his forces are **beyond n**, and H4394+8041

Na 3: 3 bodies without **n**, people stumbling H7897
Na 3:16 *You have* **increased** *the* **n** *of* your H8049
Zec 2: 4 because of the **great n** *of* people and H8044
Mt 14:21 The **n** of those who ate was about five NDT
Mt 15:38 The **n** of those who ate was four thousand NDT
Mk 5:13 about **two thousand in n**, rushed *G1493*
Mk 6:44 The **n** of the men who had eaten was five NDT
Lk 5: 6 caught such a large **n** of fish that their *G4436*
Lk 6:17 there and a great **n** of people from all *G4436*
Lk 23:27 A large **n** of people followed him *G4436*
Jn 5: 3 Here a **great n** of disabled people used to *G4436*
Jn 7:50 earlier and who was one of **their** *own n*, AIT
Jn 21: 6 the net in because of the **large n** of fish. *G4436*
Ac 1:17 He was *one* of our **n** and shared in our *G2935*
Ac 2:41 thousand *were* **added to** *their* **n** that day. *G4707*
Ac 2:47 Lord added **to their n** daily *G2093+3836+899*
Ac 4: 4 so the **n** of men who believed grew to *G750*
Ac 5:14 in the Lord and were added to their **n**. *G4436*
Ac 6: 1 *when the* **n** of disciples *was* **increasing**, *G4437*
Ac 6: 7 The **n** of disciples in Jerusalem increased *G750*
Ac 6: 7 a large **n** of priests became obedient *G4063*
Ac 7:17 *the* **n** of our people in Egypt
had **greatly increased** *G889+2779+4437*
Ac 11:21 a great **n** of people believed and *G750*
Ac 11:24 a great **n of people** were brought to *G4063*
Ac 14: 1 that a great **n** of Jews and Greeks *G4436*
Ac 14:21 in that city and won a **large n** of disciples. *G2653*
Ac 17: 4 as did a large **n** of God-fearing Greeks *G4436*
Ac 17:12 as did also a **n** of prominent Greek women NDT
Ac 17:34 a woman named Damaris, and a *n of* **others**. AIT
Ac 19:19 A **n** who had practiced sorcery brought *G2653*
Ac 20:30 Even from your **own** *n* men will arise and AIT
Ac 21:10 After we had been there a **n** of days, *G4498*
Ac 24:10 "I know that for a **n** of years you have *G4498*
Ro 9:27 "Though the **n** of the Israelites be like the *G750*
Ro 11:25 in part until the **full n** of the Gentiles has *G4445*
1Co 11:30 and a **n** of you have fallen asleep. *G2653*
2Ti 4: 3 *they will* **gather around** them **a great n** of *G2197*
Rev 6:11 until the **full n** *of* their fellow servants *G4444*
Rev 7: 4 Then I heard the **n** of those who were *G750*
Rev 9:16 The **n** of the mounted troops was twice ten *G750*
Rev 9:16 times ten thousand. I heard their **n**. *G750*
Rev 13:17 the name of the beast or the **n** of its name. *G750*
Rev 13:18 has insight calculate the **n** of the beast, *G750*
Rev 13:18 of the beast, for it is the **n** of a man. *G750*
Rev 13:18 it is the number of a man. That **n** is 666. *G750*
Rev 15: 2 its image and over the **n** of its name. *G750*
Rev 20: 8 *In* **n** they are like the sand on the seashore. *G750*

NUMBERED (35) [NUMBER]

Ge 46:26 his sons' wives—**n** sixty-six persons. H3972
Ex 1: 5 The descendants of Jacob **n** seventy in all H2118
Nu 4:48 **n** 8,580. H7212
Nu 25: 9 those who died in the plague **n** 24,000. H2118
Nu 26: 7 clans of Reuben; those **n** were 43,730. H7212
Nu 26:14 the clans of Simeon; those **n** were 22,200. NDT
Nu 26:18 the clans of Gad; those **n** were 40,500. H7212
Nu 26:22 the clans of Judah; those **n** were 76,500. H7212
Nu 26:25 clans of Issachar; those **n** were 64,300. H7212
Nu 26:27 clans of Zebulun; those **n** were 60,500. H7212
Nu 26:34 clans of Manasseh; those **n** were 52,700. H7212
Nu 26:37 clans of Ephraim; those **n** were 32,500. H7212
Nu 26:41 clans of Benjamin; those **n** were 45,600. H7212
Nu 26:43 and those **n** were 64,400. H7212
Nu 26:47 the clans of Asher; those **n** were 53,400. H7212
Nu 26:50 clans of Naphtali; those **n** were 45,400. H7212
Nu 26:62 Levites a month old or more **n** 23,000. H7212
1Sa 11: 8 the men of Israel **n** three hundred H2118
1Sa 13:15 were with him. They **n** about six hundred. NDT
1Ki 4:32 his songs **n** a thousand and five. H2118
1Ch 7: 2 fighting men in their genealogy **n** 22,600. NDT
1Ch 9: 6 The people from Judah **n** 690. NDT
1Ch 9: 9 as listed in their genealogy, **n** 956. NDT
1Ch 9:13 who were heads of families, **n** 1,760. NDT
1Ch 9:22 to be gatekeepers at the thresholds **n** 212. NDT
1Ch 25: 7 skilled in music for the LORD—they **n** 288. H5031
Ezr 2:64 The whole company **n** 42,360, H3869+285
Ne 7:66 The whole company **n** 42,360, H3869+285
Job 25: 3 Can his forces be **n**? On whom does his H5031
Isa 53:12 and **was n** with the transgressors. H4948
La 4:18 our days *were* **n**, for our end had H4848
Da 5:26 God *has* **n** the days of your reign and A10431
Mt 10:30 even the very hairs of your head are all **n**. *G749*
Lk 12: 7 the very hairs of your head *are* all **n**. *G749*
Lk 22:37 'And *he was* **n** with the transgressors' *G3357*

NUMBERING (4) [NUMBER]

1Ch 21: 6 *did* not include Levi and Benjamin *in the* **n** H7212
1Ch 27:24 wrath came on Israel on account of this **n**, NDT
Ac 1:15 a group **n** about a hundred and twenty *G1639S*
Rev 5:11 **n** thousands upon thousands *G1639+3836+750*

NUMBERLESS (1) [NUMBER]

Isa 48:19 your children like its **n grains**; their name H5054

NUMBERS (45) [NUMBER]

Ge 17: 2 you and *will* greatly **increase** your **n**." H8049
Ge 17:20 him fruitful and *will* greatly **increase** his **n**. H8049
Ge 28: 3 you fruitful and **increase** your **n** until you H8049
Ge 48: 4 to make you fruitful and **increase** your **n**. H8049
Ex 1: 7 **increased in n** and became so numerous H8049
Ex 10:14 every area of the country *in* **great n**. H3878+4394
Lev 26: 9 make you fruitful and **increase** your **n**, H8049
Nu 2: 4 His division **n** 74,600. H7212
Nu 2: 6 His division **n** 54,400. H7212
Nu 2: 8 His division **n** 57,400. H7212
Nu 2:11 His division **n** 46,500. H7212
Nu 2:13 His division **n** 59,300. H7212
Nu 2:15 His division **n** 45,650. H7212
Nu 2:19 His division **n** 40,500. H7212
Nu 2:21 His division **n** 32,200. H7212
Nu 2:23 His division **n** 35,400. H7212
Nu 2:26 His division **n** 62,700. H7212
Nu 2:28 His division **n** 41,500. H7212
Nu 2:30 His division **n** 53,400. H7212
Dt 1:10 your God *has* **increased** your **n** so that H8049
Dt 7:13 you and bless you and **increase** your **n**. H8049
Dt 13:17 *He will* **increase** your **n**, as he promised H8049
Dt 17:16 *must* not **acquire great n** *of* horses for H8049
1Ki 1:19 He has sacrificed **great n** of cattle H8044
1Ki 1:25 down and sacrificed **great n** of cattle, H8044
1Ch 12:23 These are the **n** *of* the men armed for H5031
1Ch 22: 4 had brought **large n** of them to H4200+8044
2Ch 15: 9 for **large n** had come over to him H4200+8044
2Ch 16: 8 army with **great n** of chariots and H2221+4394
2Ch 26:11 according to their **n** as mustered by Jeiel H5031
2Ch 30: 5 celebrated **in large n** according to H4200+8044
2Ch 32: 5 He also made **large n** of weapons H4200+8044
2Ch 32:29 and acquired **great n** of flocks and H4200+8044
Ps 107:38 and *their* **n** greatly **increased**, and he H8049
Ps 107:39 Then *their* **n decreased**, and they were H5070
Jer 3:16 *your* **n** *have* **increased greatly** H8049+2256+7238
Jer 30:19 *I will* **add to** their **n**, and they will not be H8049
Eze 37:26 I will establish them and **increase** their **n** H8049
Eze 47: 9 There will be large **n** *of* fish, because this H8041
Mk 2: 2 They gathered *in* such **large** *n* that there was AIT
Ac 9:31 by the Holy Spirit, *it* **increased in n**. *G4437*
Ac 11:26 the church and taught great **n of people**. *G4063*
Ac 16: 5 in the faith and grew daily *in* **n**. *G750*
Ac 19:26 astray large **n of people** here in Ephesus *G4063*
Ac 28:23 came *in even* **larger** *n* to the place AIT

NUMEROUS (48) [NUMBER]

Ge 16:10 so much that they will be too **n** to count." H8044
Ge 22:17 **make** your descendants as **n** as H8049+8049
Ge 26: 4 *I will* **make** your descendants as **n** as the H8049
Ex 1: 7 numbers and *became* so **n** that the land H6793
Ex 1: 9 become **far too n** for us. H8041+2256+6786
Ex 1:10 or *they will become even more* **n** and, H8049
Ex 1:20 increased and *became* even more **n**. H6793
Ex 5: 5 the people of the land are now **n**, and H8041
Ex 23:29 the wild animals too **n** for you. H8045
Ex 32:13 '*I will* **make** your descendants as **n** as the H8049
Nu 22:15 more **n** and more distinguished than the H8041
Dt 1:10 that today you are as **n** as the stars in the H8044
Dt 2:10 a people strong and **n**, and as tall as the H8041
Dt 2:21 They were a people strong and **n**, and as H8041
Dt 7: 7 you because you *were* more **n** than other H8045
Dt 9:14 a nation stronger and more **n** than they." H8041
Dt 10:22 God has made you as **n** as the stars in the H8044
Dt 26: 5 became a great nation, powerful and **n**. H8041
Dt 28:62 You who were as **n** as the stars in H4200+8044
Dt 30: 5 prosperous and **n** than your ancestors H8049
Jos 11: 4 as **n** as the sand on the seashore. H8044
Jos 17:14 We are a **n** people, and the LORD has H8041
Jos 17:15 "If you are so **n**," Joshua answered, "and H8041
Jos 17:17 Manasseh—"You are **n** and very powerful. H8041
1Sa 13: 5 soldiers as **n** as the sand on the H8044
2Sa 17:11 as **n** as the sand on the seashore H8044
1Ki 3: 8 a great people, too **n** to count or number. H8044
1Ki 4:20 Israel were as **n** as the sand on the H8041
1Ch 4:27 entire clan *did* not *become* as **n** as the H8049
1Ch 5:23 of the half-tribe of Manasseh *were* **n**; H8049
1Ch 23:17 the sons of Rehabiah *were* very **n**. H8049
1Ch 27:23 promised to **make** Israel as **n** as the stars H8049
2Ch 1: 9 a people who are as **n** as the dust of the H8041
Ne 5: 2 "We and our sons and daughters are **n**; in H8041
Ne 9:23 *You* **made** their children as **n** as the stars H8049
Job 29:18 my days as **n** as the grains of sand. H8049
Ps 25:19 See how **n** *are* my enemies and how H8045
Ps 38:19 those who hate me without reason *are* **n**. H8045
Ps 105:24 *he* **made** them too **n** for their foes H6793
Jer 15: 8 I *will make* their widows more **n** than the H6793
Jer 46:23 *They are* more **n** than locusts, they cannot H8045
Eze 36:11 they will be fruitful and *become* **n**. H8049
Eze 36:37 *I will* **make** their people as **n** as sheep, H8049
Eze 36:38 as **n** as the flocks for offerings at Jerusalem NDT
Na 1:12 "Although they have allies and are **n** H8041
Na 3:16 till they are **more n than** the stars in the H4946
Zec 10: 8 redeem them; *they will be* as **n** as before. H8049
Heb 11:12 came descendants as **n** as the stars in the *G4436*

NUN (30)

Ex 33:11 aide Joshua son of **N** did not leave the H5673
Nu 11:28 Joshua son of **N**, who had been Moses' H5673
Nu 13: 8 the tribe of Ephraim, Hoshea son of **N**; H5673
Nu 13:16 gave Hoshea son of **N** the name Joshua.) H5673
Nu 14: 6 Joshua son of **N** and Caleb son of H5673
Nu 14:30 son of Jephunneh and Joshua son of **N**. H5673
Nu 14:38 only Joshua son of **N** and Caleb son of H5673
Nu 26:65 son of Jephunneh and Joshua son of **N**. H5673
Nu 27:18 "Take Joshua son of **N**, a man in whom is H5673
Nu 32:12 the Kenizzite and Joshua son of **N**, H5673
Nu 32:28 Joshua son of **N** and to the family H5673
Nu 34:17 Eleazar the priest and Joshua son of **N**. H5673
Dt 1:38 assistant, Joshua son of **N**, will enter it. H5673
Dt 31:23 gave this command to Joshua son of **N**: H5673
Dt 32:44 with Joshua son of **N** and spoke all the H5673
Dt 34: 9 Now Joshua son of **N** was filled with the H5673
Jos 1: 1 the LORD said to Joshua son of **N**, Moses' H5673
Jos 2: 1 Then Joshua son of **N** secretly sent two H5673
Jos 2:23 came to Joshua son of **N** and told him H5673
Jos 6: 6 So Joshua son of **N** called the priests and H5673
Jos 14: 1 Joshua son of **N** and the heads of the H5673
Jos 17: 4 Joshua son of **N**, and the leaders and H5673
Jos 19:49 gave Joshua son of **N** an inheritance H5673
Jos 19:51 Joshua son of **N** and the heads of the H5673
Jos 21: 1 Joshua son of **N**, and the heads of the H5673
Jos 24:29 Joshua son of **N**, the servant of the H5673
Jdg 2: 8 Joshua son of **N**, the servant of the LORD H5673
1Ki 16:34 of the LORD spoken by Joshua son of **N**. H5673
1Ch 7:27 **N** his son and Joshua his son. H5673
Ne 8:17 the days of Joshua son of **N** until that day, H5673

NURSE (14) [NURSED, NURSING]

Ge 21: 7 to Abraham that Sarah *would* **n** children? H3567
Ge 24:59 along with her **n** and Abraham's servant H4787
Ge 35: 8 Deborah, Rebekah's **n**, died and was H4787
Ex 2: 7 the Hebrew women *to* **n** the baby for you?" H3567
Ex 2: 9 "Take this baby and **n** him for me, and I H3567
Nu 11:12 in my arms, as a **n** carries an infant, to H587
2Sa 4: 4 His **n** picked him up and fled, but as she H587
1Ki 3:21 I got up to **n** my son—and he was H3567
2Ki 11: 2 She put him and his **n** in a bedroom to H4787
2Ki 11: 3 hidden with **his n** at the temple of H2023S
2Ch 22:11 put him and his **n** in a bedroom. H4787
Isa 66:11 For *you will* **n** and be satisfied at her H3567
Isa 66:12 *you will* **n** and be carried on her arm and H3567
La 4: 3 jackals offer their breasts *to* **n** their young, H3567

NURSED (8) [NURSE]

Ex 2: 9 So the woman took the baby and **n** him. H3567
1Sa 1:23 stayed at home and **n** her son until she H3567
Job 3:12 receive me and breasts that *I might be* **n**? H3567
SS 8: 1 *who* was **n** *at* my mother's breasts! H3437
Isa 60:16 milk of nations and *be* **n** *at* royal breasts. H3567
Mk 6:19 So Herodias **n a grudge against** John and *G1923*
Lk 11:27 who gave you birth and **n** *you*." *G3466+2558*
Lk 23:29 never bore and the breasts that never **n**! *G5555*

NURSING (7) [NURSE]

Ge 33:13 the ewes and cows *that are* **n** *their* **young**. H6402
Isa 49:23 and their queens your **n mothers**. H4787
Joel 2:16 gather the children, *those* **n** *at* the breast. H3437
Mt 24:19 days for pregnant women and **n mothers**! *G2558*
Mk 13:17 days for pregnant women and **n mothers**! *G2558*
Lk 21:23 days for pregnant women and **n mothers**! *G2558*
1Th 2: 7 Just as a **n mother** cares for her children, *G5577*

NUT (1) [NUTS]

SS 6:11 to the grove of **n trees** to look at the new H100

NUTS (1) [NUT]

Ge 43:11 myrrh, *some* **pistachio n** and almonds. H1063

NYMPHA (1)

Col 4:15 and *to* **N** and the church in her house. *G3809*

O

O (67) [OH] See Index of Articles Etc.

OAK (14) [OAKS]

Ge 35: 4 buried them under the **o** at Shechem. H461
Ge 35: 8 was buried under the **o** outside Bethel. H473
Jos 24:26 it up there under the **o** near the holy place H464
Jdg 6:11 sat down under the **o** in Ophrah that H461
Jdg 6:19 out and offered them to him under the **o**. H461
2Sa 18: 9 went under the thick branches of a large **o**, H461
2Sa 18:10 "I just saw Absalom hanging in an **o tree**." H461
2Sa 18:14 while Absalom was still alive in the **o tree**. H461
1Ki 13:14 him sitting under an **o tree** and asked, H461
Isa 1:30 You will be like an **o** with fading leaves H461
Isa 6:13 as the terebinth and **o** leave stumps when H473
Isa 44:14 or perhaps took a cypress or **o**. H473
Eze 6:13 every spreading tree and every leafy **o**— H461
Hos 4:13 on the hills, under **o**, poplar and terebinth, H473

OAKS (9) [OAK]

Ps 29: 9 the LORD twists the **o** and strips the forests H381
Ps 56: T To the tune of "A Dove on Distant **O**." H381
Isa 1:29 because of the **sacred o** in which you have H381
Isa 2:13 tall and lofty, and all the **o** *of* Bashan, H473
Isa 57: 5 with lust among the **o** and under every H381
Isa 61: 3 They will be called **o** *of* righteousness, H381
Eze 27: 6 Of **o** from Bashan they made your oars; of H473
Am 2: 9 were tall as the cedars and strong as the **o**. H473
Zec 11: 2 **o** *of* Bashan; the dense forest has H473

OARS (4) [OARSMEN]

Isa 33:21 No galley with **o** will ride them, no mighty H8868
Eze 27: 6 Of oaks from Bashan they made your **o**; of H5415
Eze 27:29 All who handle the **o** will abandon their H5414
Mk 6:48 He saw the disciples straining at **the o** *G1785S*

OARSMEN (2) [OARS]
Eze 27: 8 Men of Sidon and Arvad were your o; your H8763
Eze 27:26 Your o take you out to the high seas. H8763

OATH (129) [OATHS]
Ge 14:22 "*With* **raised** hand *I have* **sworn an o** to H8123
Ge 21:31 because the two men **swore an o** there. H8678
Ge 24: 7 who spoke to me and **promised** me **on o**, H8678
Ge 24: 8 you will be released from this **o** *of* mine. H8652
Ge 24: 9 Abraham and **swore an o** to him H8678
Ge 24:37 And my master **made** me **swear an o**, and H8678
Ge 24:41 You will be released from my **o** if, when you H460
Ge 24:41 then you will be released from my **o**. H460
Ge 25:33 So *he* **swore an o** to him, selling his H8678
Ge 26: 3 will confirm the **o** I swore to your H8652
Ge 26:31 next morning *the men* **swore an o** to each H8678
Ge 31:53 So Jacob **took an o** in the name of the H8678
Ge 50: 5 'My father **made** me **swear an o** and said H8678
Ge 50:24 the land *he* **promised on o** to Abraham, H8678
Ge 50:25 **made** the Israelites **swear an o** and H8678
Ex 13:11 as *he* **promised on o** to you and your H8678
Ex 13:19 *had* **made** the Israelites **swear an o** H8678+8678
Ex 22:11 the taking of an **o** *before* the LORD that the H8652
Ex 33: 1 to the land *I* **promised on o** to Abraham, H8678
Lev 5: 4 thoughtlessly **takes an o** to do anything, H8678
Nu 5:19 priest *shall* **put** the woman **under o** and H8678
Nu 11:12 to the land *you* **promised on o** to their H8678
Nu 14:16 into the land *he* **promised** them **on o**, H8678
Nu 14:23 ever see the land *I* **promised on o** to their H8678
Nu 30: 2 the LORD or **takes an o** to obligate H8678+8652
Nu 30:10 obligates herself by a pledge under **o** H8652
Nu 32:10 was aroused that day and *he* **swore** *this* **o**: H8678
Nu 32:11 see the land *I* **promised on o** to Abraham, H8678
Dt 4:31 which *he* **confirmed** to them **by o**. H8678
Dt 6:18 land the LORD **promised on o** to your H8678
Dt 6:23 us the land *he* **promised on o** to our H8678
Dt 7: 8 loved you and kept the **o** he swore to your H8652
Dt 8: 1 the land the LORD **promised on o** to your H8678
Dt 13:17 as *he* **promised on o** to your ancestors H8678
Dt 19: 8 as *he* **promised on o** to your ancestors H8678
Dt 26:15 given us as *you* **promised on o** to our H8678
Dt 28: 9 people, as *he* **promised** you **on o**, if you H8678
Dt 29:12 with you this day and sealing with an **o**, H460
Dt 29:14 this covenant, with its **o**, not only with you H460
Dt 29:19 hears the words of this **o** and they invoke a H460
Dt 31:20 the land *I* **promised on o** to their H8678
Dt 31:21 them into the land *I* **promised** them **on o**." H8678
Dt 31:23 into the land *I* **promised** them **on o**, H8678
Dt 34: 4 is the land *I* **promised on o** to Abraham, H8678
Jos 2:17 "This **o** you made us swear will not be H8652
Jos 2:20 released from the **o** you made us swear." H8652
Jos 6:22 in accordance with *your* **o** to her. H8678
Jos 6:26 time Joshua **pronounced** *this* **solemn o**: H8678
Jos 9:15 leaders of the assembly **ratified** it **by o**. H8678
Jos 9:18 the assembly *had* **sworn an o** to them by H8678
Jos 9:19 "We *have* **given** them *our* **o** by the LORD H8678
Jos 9:20 us for breaking the **o** we swore to them." H8652
Jdg 21: 1 men of Israel *had* **taken an o** at Mizpah: H8678
Jdg 21: 5 had taken a solemn **o** that anyone who H8652
Jdg 21: 7 since we *have* **taken an o** by the LORD not H8678
Jdg 21:18 since *we* Israelites *have* **taken** *this* **o**: H8678
Jdg 21:22 of breaking your **o** because you did not NDT
1Sa 14:24 Saul *had* **bound** the people **under an o**, H457
1Sa 14:26 to his mouth, because they feared the **o**. H8652
1Sa 14:27 father *had* **bound** the people **with the o**, H8678
1Sa 14:28 **bound** the army **under a strict o**, H8678+8678
1Sa 19: 6 Saul listened to Jonathan and **took** *this* **o** H8678
1Sa 20: 3 But David **took an o** and said, "Your father H8678
1Sa 20:17 David reaffirm his **o** out of love for him, H8678
1Sa 24:22 So David **gave** *his* **o** to Saul. Then Saul H8678
2Sa 3: 9 David what the LORD **promised** him **on o** H8678
2Sa 3:35 was still day; but David **took an o**, saying, H8678
2Sa 19:23 And the king **promised** him **on o**. H8678
2Sa 21: 7 because of the **o** *before* the LORD between H8652
1Ki 1:29 The king then **took an o**: "As surely as the H8678
1Ki 2:43 you not keep your **o** *to* the LORD and obey H8652
1Ki 8:31 is required to **take an o** and they come H457
1Ki 8:31 they come and **swear the o** before your H457
2Ki 11: 4 with them and **put** them **under o** at the H8678
2Ki 25:24 Gedaliah **took an o** to reassure them and H8678
1Ch 16:16 with Abraham, the **o** he **swore** to Isaac. H8652
2Ch 6:22 is required to **take an o** and they come H457
2Ch 6:22 they come and **swear the o** before your H457
2Ch 15:14 *They* **took an o** to the LORD with loud H8678
2Ch 15:15 rejoiced about the **o** because they had H8652
2Ch 36:13 who *had* **made** him **take an o** in God's H8678
Ezr 10: 5 **put** the leading priests and Levites and
all Israel **under o** H8678
Ezr 10: 5 been suggested. And *they* **took the o**. H8678
Ne 5:12 **made** the nobles and officials **take an o** H8678
Ne 6:18 in Judah were **under o** to him, H1251+8652
Ne 10:29 with a curse and an **o** to follow the Law of H8652
Ne 13:25 *I* **made** them **take an o** in God's name H8678
Ps 15: 4 *who* **keeps an o** even when it hurts H8678
Ps 95:11 So *I* **declared on o** in my anger, 'They H8678
Ps 105: 9 with Abraham, the **o** he swore to Isaac. H8652
Ps 119:106 *I have* **taken an o** and confirmed it, that I H8678
Ps 132: 2 He **swore an o** to the LORD, he made a H8678
Ps 132:11 The LORD **swore an o** to David, a sure oath H8678
Ps 132:11 to David, a sure **o** he will not revoke: H5626S
Pr 29:24 *they are* **put under o** and dare not H460+9048
Ecc 8: 2 because you took an **o** *before* God. H8652
Isa 65:16 whoever **takes an o** in the land will swear H8678
Jer 11: 5 Then I will fulfill the **o** I swore to your H8652
Jer 38:16 But King Zedekiah **swore** *this* **o** secretly to H8678
Jer 40: 9 **took an o** to reassure them and their men. H8678
Eze 16: 8 *I* **gave** you *my* **solemn o** and entered into H8678
Eze 16:59 you have despised my **o** by breaking the H460
Eze 17:13 a treaty with him, putting him under **o**. H460
Eze 17:16 whose **o** he despised and whose treaty he H460
Eze 17:18 He despised the **o** by breaking the covenant H460
Eze 17:19 him for despising my **o** and breaking my H460
Mic 7:20 as *you* **pledged on o** to our ancestors in H8678
Mt 5:33 long ago, '*Do* not **break** *your* **o**, but fulfill *G2155*
Mt 5:34 I tell you, *do* not **swear an o** at all: either *G3923*
Mt 14: 7 he promised with an **o** to give her *G3992*
Mt 23:16 the gold of the temple *is* **bound by** *that* **o**. *G4053*
Mt 23:18 by the gift on the altar *is* **bound by** *that* **o**. *G4053*
Mt 26:63 "*I* **charge** you **under o** by the living God: *G2019*
Mt 26:72 it again, with an **o**: "I don't know the man *G3992*
Mk 6:23 And *he* **promised** her **with an o** *G3923*
Lk 1:73 the **o** he swore to our father Abraham: *G3992*
Ac 2:30 had promised him *on* **o** that he would *G3992*
Ac 23:12 and **bound** themselves **with an o** not to eat *G354*
Ac 23:14 "We *have* **taken a solemn o** not to *G353+354*
Ac 23:21 They *have* **taken an o** not to eat or drink *G354*
Heb 3:11 So *I* **declared on o** in my anger, 'They *G3923*
Heb 4: 3 has said, "So *I* **declared on o** in my anger *G3923*
Heb 6:16 the **o** confirms what is said and puts *G3992*
Heb 6:17 was promised, he confirmed it *with* an **o**. *G3992*
Heb 7:20 And it was not without an **o**! Others *G3993*
Heb 7:20 Others became priests without any **o**, *G3993*
Heb 7:21 a priest with an **o** when God said to him: *G3993*
Heb 7:22 Because of this **o**, Jesus has become the NDT
Heb 7:28 weakness; but the **o**, which came after the *G3993*

OATHS (7) [OATH]
Dt 6:13 him only and **take** *your* **o** in his name. H8678
Dt 10:20 fast to him and **take** *your* **o** in his name. H8678
Ecc 9: 2 as it is with those *who* **take o**, so with H8678
Isa 48: 1 you who **take o** in the name of the LORD H8678
Hos 10: 4 **take** false **o** and make agreements H457
Mt 14: 9 because of his **o** and his dinner *G3992*
Mk 6:26 because of his **o** and his dinner *G3992*

OBADIAH (22)
1Ki 18: 3 Ahab had summoned **O**, his palace H6282
1Ki 18: 3 (**O** was a devout believer in the LORD H6282
1Ki 18: 4 **O** had taken a hundred prophets and H6282
1Ki 18: 5 Ahab had said to **O**, "Go through the land H6282
1Ki 18: 6 going in one direction and **O** in another. H6282
1Ki 18: 7 As **O** was walking along, Elijah met him H6282
1Ki 18: 7 **O** recognized him, bowed down to the NDT
1Ki 18: 9 asked **O**, "that you are handing your NDT
1Ki 18:16 So **O** went to meet Ahab and told him H6282
1Ch 3:21 of Arnan, of **O** and of Shekaniah. H6281
1Ch 7: 3 Michael, **O**, Joel and Ishiah. H6281
1Ch 8:38 Ishmael, Sheariah, **O** and Hanan. H6281
1Ch 9:16 **O** son of Shemaiah, the son of Galal, the H6281
1Ch 9:44 Ishmael, Sheariah, **O** and Hanan. H6281
1Ch 12: 9 was the chief, **O** the second in command H6281
1Ch 27:19 Ishmaiah son of **O**; over Naphtali H6282
2Ch 17: 7 sent his officials Ben-Hail, **O**, Zechariah, H6281
2Ch 34:12 them to direct them were Jahath and **O**, H6282
Ezr 8: 9 descendants of Joab, **O** son of Jehiel, and H6281
Ne 10: 5 Meremoth, **O**, H6281
Ne 12:25 Bakbukiah, **O**, Meshullam, Talmon H6281
Ob 1 The vision of **O**. This is what the H6281

OBAL (2)
Ge 10:28 **O**, Abimael, Sheba, H6382
1Ch 1:22 **O**, Abimael, Sheba, H6382

OBED (13)
Ru 4:17 And they named him **O**. He was the H6381
Ru 4:21 the father of Boaz, Boaz the father of **O**, H6381
Ru 4:22 **O** the father of Jesse, and Jesse the father H6381
1Ch 2:12 Boaz the father of **O** and Obed the father H6381
1Ch 2:12 father of Obed and **O** the father of Jesse. H6381
1Ch 2:37 father of Ephlal, Ephlal the father of **O**, H6381
1Ch 2:38 **O** the father of Jehu, Jehu the father of H6381
1Ch 11:47 **O** and Jaasiel the Mezobaite. H6381
1Ch 26: 7 Rephael, **O** and Elzabad; his relatives H6381
2Ch 23: 1 Azariah son of **O**, Maaseiah son of H6381
Mt 1: 5 Boaz the father of **O**, whose mother was *G2725*
Mt 1: 5 mother was Ruth, **O** the father of Jesse, *G2725*
Lk 3:32 of Jesse, the son *of* **O**, the son of Boaz, *G2725*

OBED-EDOM (19) [OBED-EDOM'S]
2Sa 6:10 he took it to the house of **O** the Gittite. H6273
2Sa 6:11 in the house of **O** the Gittite for three H6273
2Sa 6:12 the household of **O** and everything he has H6273
2Sa 6:12 from the house of **O** to the City of David H6273
1Ch 13:13 he took it to the house of **O** the Gittite. H6273
1Ch 13:14 with the family of **O** in his house for three H6273
1Ch 15:18 Eliphelehu, Mikneiah, **O** and Jeiel, the H6273
1Ch 15:21 Mikneiah, **O**, Jeiel and Azaziah were to H6273
1Ch 15:24 **O** and Jehiah were also to be H6273
1Ch 15:25 covenant of the LORD from the house of **O**, H6273
1Ch 16: 5 Mattithiah, Eliab, Benaiah, **O** and Jeiel. H6273
1Ch 16:38 He also left **O** and his sixty-eight H6273
1Ch 16:38 **O** son of Jeduthun, and also Hosah, were H6273
1Ch 26: 4 **O** also had sons: Shemaiah the firstborn H6273
1Ch 26: 5 (For God had blessed **O**.) H2257S
1Ch 26: 8 All these were descendants of **O**; they H6273
1Ch 26: 8 do the work—descendants of **O**, 62 in all. H6273
1Ch 26:15 The lot for the South Gate fell to **O**, and H6273
2Ch 25:24 of God that had been in the care of **O**, H6273

OBED-EDOM'S (1) [OBED-EDOM]
1Ch 26: 6 **O** son Shemaiah also had sons, who H2257S

OBEDIENCE (34) [OBEY]
Ge 49:10 shall come and the **o** *of* the nations shall H3682
Dt 5:33 Walk in **o** *to* all that the LORD your God has H2006
Dt 8: 6 walking in **o** *to* him and revering him. H2006
Dt 10:12 to walk in **o** *to* him, to love H3972+2006
Dt 11:22 to walk in **o** *to* him and to hold fast H3972+2006
Dt 19: 9 God and to walk always in **o** *to* him— H2006
Dt 26:17 God and that you will walk in **o** *to* him, H2006
Dt 28: 9 of the LORD your God and walk in **o** *to* him. H2006
Dt 30:16 your God, to walk in **o** *to* him, and to keep H2006
Jos 22: 5 to walk in **o** *to* him, to keep H3972+2006
1Ki 2: 3 Walk in **o** *to* him, and keep his decrees H2006
1Ki 3:14 And if you walk in **o** *to* me and keep my H2006
1Ki 8:58 to walk in **o** *to* him and keep the H3972+2006
1Ki 11:33 have not walked in **o** *to* me, nor done H2006
1Ki 11:38 you and walk in **o** *to* me and do what is H2006
2Ki 21:22 ancestors, and did not walk in **o** *to* him. H2006
1Ch 21:19 So David went up **in o to** the word that Gad H928
2Ch 6:31 fear you and walk in **o** *to* you all the time H2006
2Ch 31:21 God's temple and **in o to** the law and the H928
Ps 128: 1 who fear the LORD, who walk in **o** *to* him. H2006
Jer 7:23 Walk in **o** *to* all I command you, that it H2006
Zec 3: 7 'If you will walk in **o** *to* me and keep my H2006
Lk 23:56 on the Sabbath **in o to** the commandment *G2848*
Ac 21:24 that you yourself are living **in o to** the law. *G5875*
Ro 1: 5 the Gentiles to the **o** that comes from *G5633*
Ro 5:19 so also through the **o** of the one man the *G5633*
Ro 6:16 leads to death, or *to* **o**, which leads to *G5633*
Ro 16:19 Everyone has heard about your **o**, so I *G5633*
Ro 16:26 might come to the **o** that comes from faith *G5633*
2Co 9:13 praise God for the **o** that accompanies *G5717*
2Co 10: 6 of disobedience, once your **o** is complete. *G5633*
Phm 21 Confident *of* your **o**, I write to you, *G5633*
Heb 5: 8 he learned **o** from what he suffered *G5633*
2Jn 6 that we walk **in o to** his commands. *G2848*

OBEDIENT (13) [OBEY]
Dt 30:17 if your heart turns away and *you are* not **o**, H9048
Jdg 2:17 *who had been* **o** *to* the LORD's commands. H9048
Isa 1:19 If you are willing and **o**, you will eat the H9048
Lk 2:51 to Nazareth with them and was **o** to them. *G5718*
Ac 6: 7 number of priests *became* **o** to the faith. *G5634*
Ro 6:16 offer yourselves to someone as **o** slaves, *G5633*
2Co 2: 9 stand the test and be **o** in everything. *G5675*
2Co 7:15 when he remembers that you were all **o**, *G5633*
2Co 10: 5 every thought to make it **o** to Christ. *G5633*
Php 2: 8 himself by becoming **o** to death— *G5675*
Titus 3: 1 authorities, *to be* **o**, to be ready to do *G4272*
1Pe 1: 2 to be **o** to Jesus Christ and sprinkled with *G5633*
1Pe 1:14 As **o** children, do not conform to the evil *G5633*

OBEISANCE (KJV) BOW, BOWED, BOWING, HOMAGE, PAY HONOR

OBEY (143) [OBEDIENCE, OBEDIENT, OBEYED, OBEYING, OBEYS]
Ex 5: 2 that *I should* **o** him and let H9048+928+7754
Ex 12:24 "**O** these instructions as a lasting H9068
Ex 19: 5 if *you* **o** me **fully** and H9048+928+7754+9048
Ex 24: 7 do everything the LORD has said; *we will* **o**." H9048
Ex 34:11 **O** what I command you today. I will drive H9068
Lev 18: 4 *You must* **o** my laws and be careful to H6913
Lev 25:18 my decrees and be careful *to* **o** my laws, H6913
Lev 26: 3 are careful *to* **o** my commands, H6913
Nu 15:39 that *you may* **o** them and not prostitute H6913
Nu 15:40 you will remember *to* **o** all my commands H6913
Nu 27:20 the whole Israelite community *will* **o** him. H9048
Dt 4:30 the LORD your God and **o** him. H9048+928+7754
Dt 5:27 our God tells you. We will listen and **o**." H6913
Dt 6: 3 be careful to **o** so that it may go well H6913
Dt 6:24 commanded us to **o** all these decrees H6913
Dt 6:25 if we are careful to **o** all this law before H6913
Dt 9:23 did not trust him or **o** him. H9048+928+7754
Dt 11:13 So if *you* **faithfully o** the commands H9048+9048
Dt 11:27 the blessing if *you* **o** the commands of the H9048
Dt 11:32 be sure that *you* **o** all the decrees and H6913
Dt 12:28 Be careful *to* **o** all these regulations I am H9048
Dt 13: 4 his commands and **o** him; H9048+928+7754
Dt 13:18 because *you* **o** the LORD your H9048+928+7754
Dt 15: 5 if only *you* **fully o** the H9048+928+7754+9048
Dt 21:18 son who *does* not **o** his father H9048+928+7754
Dt 21:20 He *will* not **o** us. He is a H9048+928+7754
Dt 27:10 **O** the LORD your God and H9048+928+7754
Dt 28: 1 If *you* **fully o** the LORD H9048+928+7754+9048
Dt 28: 2 you if *you* **o** the LORD your H9048+928+7754
Dt 28:15 if *you do* not **o** the LORD your H9048+928+7754
Dt 28:45 because *you did* not **o** the H9048+928+7754
Dt 28:62 because *you did* not **o** the H9048+928+7754
Dt 30: 2 your God and **o** him with all H9048+928+7754
Dt 30: 8 You *will* again **o** the LORD and H9048+928+7754
Dt 30:10 if *you* **o** the LORD your God H9048+928+7754
Dt 30:12 it and proclaim it to us so *we may* **o** it?" H6913
Dt 30:13 it and proclaim it to us so *we may* **o** it?" H6913
Dt 30:14 mouth and in your heart so you *may* **o** it. H6913
Dt 32:46 your children to **o** carefully all the words H6913
Jos 1: 7 Be careful to **o** all the law my servant H6913

Jos 1:17 we fully obeyed Moses, so *we will* o you. H9048
Jos 1:18 against your word and *does* not o it, H9048
Jos 23: 6 be careful to o all that is written in the H6913
Jos 24:24 the LORD our God and o him." H9048+928+7754
Jdg 3: 4 to see whether *they would* o the LORD's H9048
1Sa 12:14 and serve and o him and do H9048+928+7754
1Sa 12:15 But if *you do* not o the LORD H9048+928+7754
1Sa 15:19 Why *did you* not o the LORD H9048+928+7754
1Sa 15:20 "But *I did* o the LORD," Saul H9048+928+7754
1Sa 15:22 *To* o is better than sacrifice, and to heed H9048
1Sa 28:18 Because *you did* not o the H9048+928+7754
2Sa 22:45 as soon as they hear of me, *they* o me. H9048
1Ki 2:42 'What you say is good. *I will* o.' H9048
1Ki 2:43 oath to the LORD and o the command I gave NDT
1Ki 6:12 keep all my commands and o them, H2143+928
1Ki 8:61 live by his decrees and o his commands, H9068
2Ki 10: 6 on my side and *will* o me, H9048+4200+7754
2Ki 17:13 your ancestors to o and that I delivered to NDT
1Ch 28:21 all the people will o your every command." H4200
2Ch 14: 4 to o his laws and commands. H6913
2Ch 34:31 to o the words of the covenant written H6913
Ezr 7:26 Whoever *does* not o the law of your God A10522
Ne 1: 9 to me and o my commands, H9068+2256+6913
Ne 9:16 and *they did* not o your commands. H9048
Ne 10:29 servant of God and to o carefully all the H6913
Est 3: 8 people, and they *do* not o the king's laws H6913
Job 36:11 If *they* o and serve him, they will spend H9048
Ps 18:44 as soon as they hear of me, *they* o me. H9048
Ps 103:18 covenant and remember to o his precepts. H6913
Ps 103:20 his bidding, *who* o his word. H9048+928+7754
Ps 106:25 tents and *did* not o the LORD. H9048+928+7754
Ps 119: 8 *I will* o your decrees; do not utterly forsake H9068
Ps 119:17 while I live, that *I may* o your word. H9068
Ps 119:34 keep your law and o it with all my heart. H9068
Ps 119:44 *I will* always o your law, for ever and ever. H9068
Ps 119:56 has been my practice: *I* o your precepts. H5915
Ps 119:57 I have promised to o your words. H9068
Ps 119:60 not delay to o your commands. H9068
Ps 119:67 I went astray, but now *I* o your word. H9068
Ps 119:88 that *I may* o the statutes of your mouth. H9068
Ps 119:100 than the elders, for *I* o your precepts. H5915
Ps 119:101 evil path so that *I might* o your word. H9068
Ps 119:129 statutes are wonderful; therefore I o them. H5915
Ps 119:134 oppression, that *I may* o your precepts. H9068
Ps 119:145 LORD, and *I will* o your decrees. H5915
Ps 119:158 loathing, for *they do* not o your word. H9068
Ps 119:167 I o your statutes, for I love them greatly. H9068
Ps 119:168 *I* o your precepts and your statutes, for all H9068
Pr 5:13 *I would* not o my teachers or H9048+928+7754
Ecc 8: 2 **O** the king's command, I say, because you H9068
Isa 42:24 follow his ways; *they did* not o his law. H9048
Jer 7:23 **O** me, and I will be your God H9048+928+7754
Jer 11: 3 is the one who *does* not o the terms of H9048
Jer 11: 4 '**O** me and do everything I H9048+928+7754
Jer 11: 7 and again, saying, "**O** me." H9048+928+7754
Jer 17:24 But if *you are* **careful to** o me H9048+9048
Jer 17:27 But if *you do* not o me to keep the H9048
Jer 18:10 my sight and *does* not o me, H9048+928+7754
Jer 22: 5 But if *you do* not o these commands H9048
Jer 26:13 actions and o the LORD your H9048+928+7754
Jer 32:23 but *they did* not o you or H9048+928+7754
Jer 35:13 you not learn a lesson and o my words? H9048
Jer 35:14 because *they* o their forefather's H9048
Jer 38:20 "**O** the LORD by doing what I H9048+928+7754
Jer 40: 3 the LORD and *did* not o him. H9048+928+7754
Jer 42: 6 *we will* o the LORD our God H9048+928+7754
Jer 42: 6 for *we will* o the LORD our God. H9048+928+7754
Da 7:27 all rulers will worship and o him. A10725
Da 9:11 away, refusing *to* o you. H9048+928+7754
Zec 6:15 if *you* **diligently** o the H9048+928+7754+9048
Mt 8:27 Even the winds and the waves o him!" *G5634*
Mt 28:20 teaching them *to* o everything I have *G5498*
Mk 1:27 orders to impure spirits and *they* o him." *G5634*
Mk 4:41 Even the wind and the waves o him!" *G5634*
Lk 8:25 the winds and the water, and *they* o him." *G5634*
Lk 11:28 those who hear the word of God and o it." *G5875*
Lk 17: 6 planted in the sea,' and *it will* o you. *G5634*
Jn 8:55 but I do know him and o his word. *G5498*
Jn 14:23 who loves me *will* o my teaching. *G5498*
Jn 14:24 does not love me *will* not o my teaching. *G5498*
Jn 15:20 my teaching, *they will* o yours also. *G5498*
Ac 5:29 "We must o God rather than human *G4272*
Ac 5:32 whom God has given *to* those *who* o him." *G4272*
Ac 7:39 "But our ancestors refused *to* o him. *G5675+1181*
Ac 16: 4 elders in Jerusalem for the people *to* o. *G5875*
Ro 2:13 it is those *who* o the law who will be *G4475*
Ro 6:12 mortal body so that *you* o its evil desires. *G5634*
Ro 6:16 you are slaves of the one *you* o—whether *G5634*
Ro 6:17 *you have come to* o from your heart the *G5634*
Ro 15:18 the Gentiles to o God by what I have said *G5633*
Gal 5: 3 that he is obligated *to* o the whole law. *G4472*
Eph 6: 1 Children, o your parents in the Lord, for *G5634*
Eph 6: 5 o your earthly masters with respect and *G5634*
Eph 6: 5 sincerity of heart, just as you would o Christ. NDT
Eph 6: 6 **O** them not only to win their favor when NDT
Col 3:20 Children, o your parents in everything, for *G5634*
Col 3:22 o your earthly masters in everything *G5634*
2Th 1: 8 not know God and *do* not o the gospel of *G5634*
2Th 3:14 note of anyone *who does* not o our *G5634*
1Ti 3: 4 and see that his children o him, *G1877+5717*
Heb 5: 9 of eternal salvation for all who o him *G5634*
Jas 3: 3 the mouths of horses to **make** them o us, *G4275*
1Pe 4:17 outcome be *for* those *who do* not o the *G578*

OBEYED (48) [OBEY]

Ge 22:18 because *you have* o me. H9048+928+7754
Ge 26: 5 Abraham o me and did H9048+928+7754
Ge 28: 7 that Jacob *had* o his father and H9048
Nu 9:19 the Israelites o the LORD's order and did H9068
Nu 9:23 *They* o the LORD's order, in accordance H9068
Dt 26:14 *I have* o the LORD my God; H9048+928+7754
Jos 1:17 Just as we fully o Moses, so we will obey H9048
Jos 5: 6 since *they had* not o the LORD. H9048+928+7754
Jos 22: 2 and *you have* o me in H9048+928+7754
1Sa 28:21 "Look, your servant *has* o you. H9048+928+7754
1Ki 11:34 I chose and who o my commands and H9068
1Ki 12:24 So *they* o the word of the LORD and went H9048
1Ki 20:36 "Because *you have* not o the H9048+928+7754
2Ki 18:12 because *they had* not o the H9048+928+7754
2Ki 22:13 gone before us *have* not o the words of H9048
1Ch 29:23 He prospered and all Israel o him. H9048
2Ch 11: 4 So *they* o the words of the LORD and H9048
Ne 1: 7 *We have* not o the commands, decrees H9068
Est 1:15 "*She has* not o the command of King H6913
Ps 119: 4 laid down precepts that *are to be* fully **o.** H9068
Ps 119:136 flow from my eyes, for your law *is* not o. H9068
Jer 3:13 and *have* not o me,'" H9048+928+7754
Jer 3:25 day *we have* not o the LORD H9048+928+7754
Jer 7:28 nation that *has* not o the LORD H9048+928+7754
Jer 9:13 *they have* not o me or H9048+928+7754
Jer 22:21 youth; *you have* not o me. H9048+928+7754
Jer 34:17 You *have* not o me; you have not H9048
Jer 35: 8 *We have* o everything our H9048+928+7754
Jer 35:10 tents and *have* **fully** o H9048+2256+6913
Jer 35:14 again and again, yet *you have* not o me. H9048
Jer 35:16 but these people *have* not o me. H9048
Jer 35:18 '*You have* o the command of your H9048
Jer 42:21 but *you still have* not o the H9048+928+7754
Jer 44:23 LORD and *have* not o him or H9048+928+7754
Eze 20:24 because *they had* not o my laws but had H6913
Da 9:10 *we have* not o the LORD our H9048+928+7754
Da 9:14 does; yet *we have* not o him. H9048+928+7754
Hos 9:17 reject them because *they have* not o him; H9048
Jnh 3: 3 Jonah o the word of the LORD and H3869+7756
Mic 5:15 wrath on the nations that *have* not o me." H9048
Hag 1:12 of the people o the voice of the LORD H9048
Jn 15:20 If *they* o my teaching, they will obey yours *G5498*
Jn 17: 6 them to me and *they have* o your word. *G5498*
Ac 7:53 given through angels but *have* not o it." *G5875*
Php 2:12 as *you have* always o—not only in *G5634*
Heb 4: 2 they did not share the faith *of* those *who* o. *G201*
Heb 11: 8 as his inheritance, o and went, even *G5634*
1Pe 3: 6 *who* o Abraham and called him her lord. *G5634*

OBEYING (7) [OBEY]

Dt 8:20 not o the LORD your God H9048+928+7754
1Sa 15:22 as much as *in* o the LORD? H9048+928+7754
1Ki 11:38 is right in my eyes by o my decrees and H9068
Ps 119: 5 my ways were steadfast *in* o your decrees! H9068
Jer 16:12 of your evil hearts instead of o me. H9048
Gal 5: 7 cut in on you to keep you from o the truth? *G4275*
1Pe 1:22 yourselves by o the truth so that you *G5633*

OBEYS (13) [OBEY]

Lev 18: 5 the person who o them will live by H6913
Ne 9:29 'The person *who* o them will live by them. H6913
Ecc 8: 5 *Whoever* o his command will come to no H9068
Isa 50:10 you fears the LORD and o the word of his H9048
Eze 20:11 by which the person *who* o them will live. H6913
Eze 20:13 by which the person who o them will live H6913
Eze 20:21 "The person who o them will live by them, H6913
Joel 2:11 mighty is the army *that* o his command. H6913
Zep 3: 2 *She* o no one, she accepts no H9048+928+7754
Jn 8:51 whoever o my word will never see death." *G5498*
Jn 8:52 say that whoever o your word will never *G5498*
Ro 2:27 physically and *yet* o the law will condemn *G5464*
1Jn 2: 5 But if anyone o his word, love for God is *G5498*

OBIL (1)

1Ch 27:30 **O** the Ishmaelite was in charge of the H201

OBJECT (36) [OBJECTED, OBJECTION, OBJECTIONS, OBJECTS]

Nu 35:16 someone a fatal blow with an iron **o,** H3998
Nu 35:18 holding a wooden o and strikes someone H3998
Dt 28:37 byword and an **o of ridicule** among all the H9110
1Ki 9: 7 a byword and an **o of ridicule** among all H9110
2Ch 7:20 a byword and an **o of ridicule** among all H9110
2Ch 29: 8 made them an **o of dread** and horror and H2317
2Ch 30: 7 so that he made them an **o of horror,** as H9014
Ps 31:11 neighbors and an **o of dread** to my closest H7065
Ps 80: 6 have made us an **o of derision** to our H4954
Ps 109:25 I am an **o of scorn** to my accusers; when H3075
Jer 18:16 land will be an **o of horror** and of lasting H9014
Jer 19: 8 city and make it an **o of horror** and scorn; H9014
Jer 22:28 despised, broken pot, an o no one wants? H3998
Jer 24: 9 a curse and an **o of ridicule,** wherever I H9110
Jer 25: 9 make them an **o of horror** and scorn, H9014
Jer 25:18 them a ruin and an **o of horror** and scorn, H9014
Jer 29:18 a curse and an **o of horror,** of scorn and H9014
Jer 42:18 You will be a curse and an **o of horror,** H9014
Jer 42:18 a curse and an **o of reproach;** you will H3075
Jer 44: 8 curse and an **o of reproach** among all the H3075
Jer 44:12 will become a curse and an **o of horror,** H9014
Jer 44:12 of horror, a curse and an **o of reproach.** H3075
Jer 48:26 in her vomit; let her be an **o of ridicule.** H8468
Jer 48:27 Was not Israel the **o of** your **ridicule?** Was H8468
Jer 48:39 Moab has become an **o of ridicule,** an H8468
Jer 48:39 an **o of horror** to all those around her." H4745
Jer 49:13 a curse, an **o of horror** and reproach H2997
Jer 49:17 "Edom will become an **o of horror;** all H9014
Jer 51:37 of jackals, an **o of horror** and scorn, H9014
Eze 5:15 warning and an **o of horror** to the nations H5457
Eze 22: 4 will make you an **o of scorn** to the nations H3075
Eze 24:21 of your eyes, the o *of* your affection. H4720
Eze 36: 3 *the* **o of** people's **malicious talk** H6590+6584+8557+4383
Da 9:16 your people an **o of scorn** to all those H3075
Joel 2:17 not make your inheritance an **o of scorn,** H3075
Joel 2:19 I make you an **o of scorn** to the nations. H3075

OBJECTED (4) [OBJECT]

2Ki 4:16 *she* **o.** "Please, man of God H606
Jn 12: 4 Iscariot, who was later to betray him, **o,** *G3306*
Jn 18:31 have no right to execute anyone," they **o.** *G3306*
Ac 28:19 The Jews **o,** so I was compelled to make an *G515*

OBJECTION (1) [OBJECT]

Ac 10:29 I was sent for, I came **without raising any o.** *G395*

OBJECTIONS (1) [OBJECT]

Ac 11:18 *they* **had no further** o and praised God *G2483*

OBJECTS (13) [OBJECT]

1Sa 6: 8 it put the gold o you are sending back H3998
1Sa 6:15 with the chest containing the gold o, H3998
1Ki 7:45 All these o that Huram made for King H3998
2Ki 12:18 took all the **sacred** o dedicated by his H7731
2Ch 4:16 All the o that Huram-Abi made for King NDT
2Ch 24: 7 had used even its **sacred** o for the Baals. H7731
2Ch 24:14 also dishes and other o *of* gold and silver. H3998
Ps 79: 4 We are **o of contempt** to our neighbors, of H3075
Jer 10:15 are worthless, the o *of* mockery; when H5126
Jer 51:18 are worthless, the o *of* mockery; when H5126
Ac 17:23 looked carefully at your **o of worship,** *G4934*
Ro 9:22 with great patience the o of his wrath— *G5007*
Ro 9:23 of his glory known to the o of his mercy, *G5007*

OBLATION, OBLATIONS (KJV) GIFT, GIFTS, OFFERING, OFFERINGS, PORTION, SACRIFICE

OBLIGATE (1) [OBLIGATED, OBLIGATES, OBLIGATION, OBLIGATIONS]

Nu 30: 2 takes an oath to o himself by a pledge, H673

OBLIGATED (6) [OBLIGATE]

Nu 30: 4 pledge by which *she* o herself will stand. H673
Nu 30: 5 pledges by which *she* o herself will stand; H673
Nu 30: 7 pledges by which *she* o herself will stand. H673
Nu 30:11 pledges by which *she* o herself will stand. H673
Ro 1:14 I am o both to Greeks and non-Greeks *G4050*
Gal 5: 3 that he is o to obey the whole law. *G4050*

OBLIGATES (5) [OBLIGATE]

Nu 30: 3 a vow to the LORD or o *herself* by a pledge H673
Nu 30: 6 utter a rash promise by which *she* o herself H673
Nu 30: 8 nullifies the vow that o her or the rash H6584
Nu 30: 8 the rash promise by which *she* o herself, H673
Nu 30:10 makes a vow or o herself by a pledge H673

OBLIGATION (5) [OBLIGATE]

Nu 30: 9 Any vow or **o taken** by a widow or divorced H673
Nu 32:22 return and be **free from** your o to the LORD H5929
Ezr 4:14 Now since *we are* **under** o *to* the A10419+10420
Ro 4: 4 are not credited as a gift but as an **o.** *G4052*
Ro 8:12 we have an o—but it is not to the *G4050*

OBLIGATIONS (2) [OBLIGATE]

Nu 3: 8 fulfilling the o *of* the Israelites by doing H5466
1Ki 9:25 with them, and so **fulfilled** the temple **o.** H8966

OBLIVION (1)

Ps 88:12 your righteous deeds in the land of **o?** H5964

OBNOXIOUS (7)

Ge 34:30 trouble on me by **making** me o to the H944
Ex 5:21 *You have* **made** us o to Pharaoh and H944+8194
1Sa 13: 4 now Israel *has become* o to the H944
1Sa 27:12 "*He has become* **so** o to his people H944+944
2Sa 10: 6 realized that they had become o to David, H944
2Sa 16:21 hear that *you have* **made yourself** o to your H944
1Ch 19: 6 realized that *they had become* o to David, H944

OBOTH (4)

Nu 21:10 The Israelites moved on and camped at **O.** H95
Nu 21:11 Then they set out from **O** and camped in Iye H95
Nu 33:43 They left Punon and camped at **O.** H95
Nu 33:44 They left **O** and camped at Iye Abarim, on H95

OBSCENITY (1)

Eph 5: 4 Nor should there be **o,** foolish talk or coarse *G157*

OBSCURE (3) [OBSCURES]

Isa 33:19 people whose speech is **o** H6680+4946+9048
Eze 3: 5 sent to a people of o speech and strange H6680
Eze 3: 6 to many peoples of o speech and strange H6680

OBSCURES (2) [OBSCURE]

Job 38: 2 "Who is this *that* o my plans with words H3124

Job 42: 3 'Who is this *that* **o** my plans without H6623

OBSERVANCE (2) [OBSERVE]

Ex 13: 9 This **o** will be for you like a sign on your NDT
Ezr 7:10 to the study and **o** *of* the Law of the LORD, H6913

OBSERVE (47) [OBSERVANCE, OBSERVED, OBSERVER, OBSERVES, OBSERVING]

Ex 12:25 give you as he promised, **o** this ceremony. H9068
Ex 13: 5 *you are to* **o** this ceremony in this month: H6268
Ex 31:13 the Israelites, '*You must* **o** my Sabbaths. H9068
Ex 31:14 " '**O** the Sabbath, because it is holy to you H9068
Ex 31:16 The Israelites *are to* **o** the Sabbath H9068
Lev 19: 3 father, and *you must* **o** my Sabbaths. H9068
Lev 19:30 " '**O** my Sabbaths and have reverence H9068
Lev 23:32 evening *you are to* **o** your **sabbath**." H8697+8701
Lev 25: 2 land itself **must o a sabbath** to the H8697+8701
Lev 26: 2 " '**O** my Sabbaths and have reverence H9068
Dt 4: 6 **O** them carefully, for this will show your H6913
Dt 5:12 "**O** the Sabbath day by keeping it holy, as H9068
Dt 5:15 commanded you to **o** the Sabbath day. H6913
Dt 6: 1 me to teach you to **o** in the land that you H6913
Dt 8: 6 **O** the commands of the LORD your God H9068
Dt 8:11 your God, failing *to* **o** his commands, his H9068
Dt 10:13 to **o** the LORD's commands and H9068
Dt 11: 8 **O** therefore all the commands I am giving H9068
Dt 11:22 If *you* **carefully o** all these H9068+9068
Dt 12:14 there **o** everything I command you. H6913
Dt 16: 1 **O** the month of Aviv and celebrate the H9068
Dt 26:16 carefully **o** them with all your heart and H6913
Dt 28:45 LORD your God and **o** the commands and H9068
2Sa 3:25 deceive you and **o** your movements and H3359
1Ki 2: 3 **o** what the LORD your God requires H9068
1Ki 6:12 **o** my laws and keep all my commands H6913
1Ki 9: 4 all I command and **o** my decrees and H9068
1Ki 9: 6 from me and *do* not **o** the commands H9068
2Ki 17:13 **O** my commands and decrees, in H9068
1Ch 22:13 you are careful to **o** the decrees and laws H6913
2Ch 7:17 I command, and **o** my decrees and laws, H9068
2Ch 23: 6 all the others *are to* **o** the LORD's H9068
Est 9:19 **o** the fourteenth of the month of Adar as a H6913
Est 9:22 He wrote them to **o** the days as days of H6913
Est 9:27 should without fail **o** these two days every H6913
Ps 37:37 the blameless, **o** the upright; a future H8011
Ps 91: 8 *You will* only **o** with your eyes and see the H5564
Ps 105:45 might keep his precepts and **o** his laws. H5915
Ecc 8:16 to know wisdom and to **o** the labor that is H8011
Jer 2:10 send to Kedar and **o** closely; see if there H1067
Jer 6:18 *you* who are witnesses, **o** what will H3359
Jer 6:27 that *you may* **o** and test their ways. H3359
Jer 8: 7 the swift and the thrush **o** the time of their H9068
Eze 45:21 fourteenth day *you are to* **o** the Passover, H2118
Mk 7: 4 And *they* **o** many other traditions, such as G3195
Mk 7: 9 of God in order to **o** your own traditions! G5498
Ro 2:25 Circumcision has value if *you* **o** the law G4556

OBSERVED (15) [OBSERVE]

Ge 50:10 there Joseph **o** a seven-day period of H6913
Nu 23:21 is seen in Jacob, no misery **o** in Israel. H8011
1Sa 1:12 on praying to the LORD, Eli **o** her mouth. H9068
1Ki 8:65 So Solomon **o** the festival at that time H6913
2Ki 23:22 of Judah *had* any such Passover **been o**. H6913
2Ch 7: 8 So Solomon **o** the festival at that time H6913
2Ch 35:17 Passover at that time and **o** the Festival of NDT
2Ch 35:18 The Passover *had* not **been o** like this in H6913
Est 5: 9 at the king's gate and **o** that he neither rose NDT
Est 9:28 be remembered and **o** in every H6913
Job 4: 8 As *I have* **o**, those who plow evil and H8011
Pr 24:32 my heart to what *I* **o** and learned a lesson H2600
Ecc 5:18 This is what I *have* **o** to be good: that it is H8011
Mic 6:16 *You have* **o** the statutes of Omri and all H9068
Lk 17:20 of God is not **something that can be o**, G4191

OBSERVER (1) [OBSERVE]

Ac 22:12 He was a devout **o of** the law and highly G2848

OBSERVES (1) [OBSERVE]

Ps 11: 4 He **o** everyone on earth; his eyes examine H2600

OBSERVING (4) [OBSERVE]

1Sa 20:29 because our family is **o** a sacrifice in the NDT
2Ch 13:11 We *are* **o** the requirements of the LORD our H9068
Lk 1: 6 **o** all the Lord's commands and G4513+1877
Gal 4:10 *You are* **o** special days and months and G4190

OBSESSED (2)

2Sa 13: 2 Amnon *became so* **o** with his sister Tamar H7674
Ac 26:11 *I was* so **o** with persecuting them that I G1841

OBSOLETE (2)

Heb 8:13 " *he has* **made** the first one **o**; and what is G4096
Heb 8:13 what *is* **o** and outdated will soon G4096

OBSTACLE (1) [OBSTACLES]

Ro 14:13 any stumbling block or **o** in the way of a G4998

OBSTACLES (3) [OBSTACLE]

Isa 57:14 Remove the **o** out of the way of my H4842
Jer 6:21 "I will put **o** before this people H4842
Ro 16:17 put **o in** your **way** that are contrary G4998

OBSTINATE (7)

Dt 2:30 his heart **o** in order to give him H599
Isa 30: 1 "Woe to the **o** children," declares the LORD H6253
Isa 65: 2 I have held out my hands to an **o** people, H6253
Eze 2: 4 sending you are **o** and stubborn. H7997+7156
Eze 3: 7 the Israelites are hardened and **o**. H7997+4213
Ac 19: 9 But some of them *became* **o**; they refused G5020
Ro 10:21 my hands to a disobedient and **o** people." G515

OBTAIN (7) [OBTAINED, OBTAINING]

Nu 27:21 *who will* **o decisions** for him by inquiring H8626
Ezr 7:16 silver and gold *you may* **o** from the A10708
Pr 12: 2 Good people **o** favor from the LORD, but H7049
Pr 20:18 so if you wage war, **o** guidance. NDT
Ac 13:39 a **justification** you were not able *to* **o** G1467
Ro 11: 7 Israel sought so earnestly *they did* not **o**. G2209
2Ti 2:10 that they too *may* **o** the salvation that is in G5593

OBTAINED (4) [OBTAIN]

Ex 38:25 The **silver** *o from* those of the community AIT
Ac 22: 5 *I* even **o** letters from them to their G1312
Ro 9:30 righteousness, *have* **o** it, a righteousness G2898
Php 3:12 Not that *I have* already **o** all this, or have G3284

OBTAINING (1) [OBTAIN]

Heb 9:12 his own blood, *thus* **o** eternal redemption. G2351

OBVIOUS (5)

Mt 6:18 so that *it will* not *be* **o** to others that you G5743
Gal 5:19 The acts of the flesh are **o**: sexual G5745
1Ti 5:24 The sins of some are **o**, reaching the G4593
1Ti 5:25 good deeds are **o**, and even those G4593
1Ti 5:25 even those that are **not o** cannot remain G261S

OCCASION (8) [OCCASIONS]

Jdg 14: 4 who was seeking an **o** to confront the H9301
1Sa 9:24 you for this **o** from the time I said, H4595
2Ch 13:18 The Israelites were subdued on that **o** H6961
Ezr 10: 9 distressed by the **o** and because of the H1821
Ne 8: 4 on a high wooden platform built for the **o**. H1821
Lk 10:25 **On one o** an expert in the law G2779+2627
Ac 1: 4 **On one o**, while he was eating with them G2779
2Co 9:11 way so that you can be generous on **every o**, AIT

OCCASIONS (2) [OCCASION]

Zec 8:19 become joyful and **glad o** and happy H8525
Eph 6:18 in the Spirit on all **o** with all kinds of G2789

OCCUPANTS (1) [OCCUPY]

Isa 5: 9 the fine mansions left without **o**. H3782

OCCUPATION (2)

Ge 46:33 calls you in and asks, 'What is your **o**? H5126
Ge 47: 3 asked the brothers, "What is your **o**?" H5126

OCCUPIED (12) [OCCUPY]

Ge 36:43 to their settlements in the land they **o**. H299
Nu 21:25 all the cities of the Amorites and **o** them, H3782
Jos 19:47 put it to the sword and **o** it. H3769
Jdg 11:26 For three hundred years Israel **o** Heshbon H3782
1Sa 17: 3 The Philistines **o** one hill and the H6641+448
1Sa 31: 7 And the Philistines came and **o** them. H3782
1Ch 5: 9 To the east *they* **o** the land up to the H3782
1Ch 5:10 *they* **o** the dwellings of the Hagrites H3782
1Ch 5:22 And *they* **o** the land until the exile. H3782
1Ch 10: 7 And the Philistines came and **o** them. H3782
2Ch 28:18 They captured and **o** Beth Shemesh H3782
Ecc 5:20 because God **keeps** them **o** with gladness H6701

OCCUPY (8) [OCCUPANTS, OCCUPIED]

Jos 1:15 you may go back and **o** your own land H3769
Jos 17:12 were not able to **o** these towns, H3769
Ne 2: 8 wall and for the residence *I will* **o**?" H995+448
Ecc 10: 6 positions, while the rich **o** the low ones. H3782
Jer 49:16 of the rocks, *who* **o** the heights of the hill. H9530
Ob 19 from the Negev *will* **o** the mountains of H3769
Ob 19 *They will* **o** the fields of Ephraim and H3769
Zec 9: 6 A mongrel people *will* **o** Ashdod, and I H3782

OCCUR (1) [OCCURRED, OCCURRING, OCCURS]

Ex 8:23 This sign *will* **o** tomorrow.' " H2118

OCCURRED (3) [OCCUR]

2Ch 32:31 miraculous sign that *had* **o** in the land, H2118
1Co 10: 6 Now these things **o** as examples to keep G1181
Rev 16:18 like it *has ever* **o** since mankind has G1181

OCCURRING (1) [OCCUR]

1Co 7: 2 But since sexual immorality is **o**, each man NDT

OCCURS (2) [OCCUR]

Ecc 8:14 else meaningless that **o** on earth: H6913
2Th 2: 3 come until the rebellion **o** and the man of G2262

OCEAN (2)

Ps 148: 7 you great sea creatures and all **o depths**, H9333
Eze 26:19 when I bring the **o depths** over you and its H9333

OCRAN (NIV84) OKRAN

ODED (3)

2Ch 15: 1 Spirit of God came on Azariah son of **O**. H6389
2Ch 15: 8 prophecy of Azariah son of **O** the prophet, H6389
2Ch 28: 9 a prophet of the LORD named **O** was there, H6389

ODOR (1)

Jn 11:39 "by this time *there is a* **bad o**, for he has G3853

ODOUR, ODOURS (KJV) AROMA, FRAGRANCE, INCENSE, PERFUMES, SPICES

OF (24887) See Index of Articles Etc.

OFF (400) [OFFSET, OFFSHOOTS, OFFSPRING]

Ge 14:12 They also carried **o** Abram's nephew Lot H2143
Ge 17:14 in the flesh, *will* **be cut o** from his people H4162
Ge 21:14 then **sent** her **o** with the boy. H8938
Ge 21:16 Then *she* **went o** and sat down about a H2143
Ge 22:19 *they* **set o** together for Beersheba. H2143
Ge 27:40 *you will* **throw** his yoke from **o** your neck." H7293
Ge 31:26 and *you've* **carried o** my daughters like H5627
Ge 31:27 Why *did you* **run o** secretly and deceive H1368
Ge 31:30 Now *you have* **gone o** because you H2143+2143
Ge 34:29 *They* **carried o** all their wealth and all their H8647
Ge 37:14 Then *he* **sent** him **o** from the Valley of H8938
Ge 38:14 *she* **took o** her widow's clothes, covered H6073
Ge 38:19 *she* **took o** her veil and put on her H6073
Ge 40:15 *I* **was forcibly carried o** from the H1704+1704
Ge 40:19 Pharaoh will lift **o** your head and H4946+6584
Ex 3: 5 "**Take o** your sandals, for the place where H5970
Ex 4:25 **cut o** her son's foreskin and touched H4162
Ex 9:15 that would have wiped you **o** the earth. H4946
Ex 12:15 the seventh *must* **be cut o** from Israel. H4162
Ex 12:19 with yeast in it *must* **be cut o** from the H4162
Ex 23: 4 your enemy's ox or donkey **wandering o**, H9494
Ex 30:33 than a priest *must* **be cut o** from their H4162
Ex 30:38 its fragrance *must* **be cut o** from their H4162
Ex 31:14 work on that day *must* **be cut o** from their H4162
Ex 32: 2 "**Take o** the gold earrings that your wives H7293
Ex 32: 3 So all the people **took o** their earrings H7293
Ex 32:12 and to wipe them **o** the face of the H4946+6584
Ex 32:24 'Whoever has any gold jewelry, **take** it **o**. H7293
Ex 33: 5 Now **take o** your ornaments H3718+4946+6584
Ex 33: 6 the Israelites **stripped o** their ornaments H5911
Lev 1:15 **wring o** the head and burn it on the altar H4916
Lev 3: 9 the entire fat tail **cut o** close to the H6073
Lev 6:11 Then *he is to* **take o** these clothes and put H7320
Lev 7:20 they *must* **be cut o** from their people. H4162
Lev 7:21 to the LORD *must* **be cut o** from their H4162
Lev 7:25 to the LORD *must* **be cut o** from their H4162
Lev 7:27 who eats blood *must* **be cut o** from their H4162
Lev 14: 8 **shave o** all their hair and bathe with H1662
Lev 14: 9 seventh day *they must* **shave o** all their H1662
Lev 14:41 material that *is* **scraped o** dumped into an H7894
Lev 15:13 *he is to* **count o** seven days for his H6218
Lev 15:28 discharge, *she must* **count o** seven days H6218
Lev 16:23 of meeting and **take o** the linen garments H7320
Lev 17: 4 shed blood and *must* **be cut o** from their H4162
Lev 17: 9 it to the LORD *must* **be cut o** from the H4162
Lev 17:10 and *I will* **cut** them **o** from the people. H4162
Lev 17:14 anyone who eats it *must* **be cut o**. H4162
Lev 18:29 such persons *must* **be cut o** from their H4162
Lev 19: 8 they *must* **be cut o** from their people. H4162
Lev 19:27 of your head or **clip o** the edges of your H8845
Lev 20: 3 against him and *will* **cut** him **o** from his H4162
Lev 20: 5 his family and *will* **cut** them **o** from their H4162
Lev 20: 6 and *I will* **cut** them **o** from their people. H4162
Lev 20:18 Both of them *are to* **be cut o** from their H4162
Lev 21: 5 their heads or **shave o** the edges of their H1662
Lev 22: 3 that person *must* **be cut o** from my H4162
Lev 23:15 wave offering, **count o** seven full weeks. H6218
Lev 23:16 **Count o** fifty days up to the day after the H6218
Lev 23:29 on that day *must* **be cut o** from their H4162
Lev 25: 8 " '**Count o** seven sabbath years—seven H6218
Lev 26:26 When I **cut o** your supply of bread, ten H8689
Nu 5:23 scroll and then **wash** them **o** into the H4681
Nu 6:18 the Nazirite *must* **shave o** the hair that H1662
Nu 6:19 the Nazirite *has* **shaved o** the hair that H1662
Nu 9:13 they *must* **be cut o** from their people for H4162
Nu 11:18 We were **better o** in Egypt!" Now H3202
Nu 13:23 *they* **cut o** a branch bearing a single H4162
Nu 13:24 cluster of grapes the Israelites **cut o** there. H4162
Nu 15:30 the LORD and *must* **be cut o** from the H4162
Nu 15:31 they **must surely be cut o**; their H4162+4162
Nu 19:13 They *must* **be cut o** from Israel H4162
Nu 19:20 they *must* **be cut o** from the community H4162
Nu 22:23 his hand, it turned **o** the road into a field. H4946
Nu 23: 3 Then *he* **went o** *to* a barren height H2143
Dt 2:35 had captured *we* **carried o** for ourselves. H1024
Dt 3: 7 from their cities *we* **carried o** for ourselves. H1024
Dt 12:29 LORD your God *will* **cut o** before you the H4162
Dt 15:16 your family and *is* **well o** with you, H3201
Dt 16: 9 **Count o** seven weeks from the time you H6218
Dt 19: 5 the head *may* **fly o** and hit his neighbor H5970
Dt 25: 9 of the elders, **take o** one of his sandals H2740
Dt 25:12 *you shall* **cut o** her hand. Show her no pity. H7915
Dt 28:40 because the olives *will* **drop o**. H5970
Dt 29:26 *They* **went o** and worshiped other gods H2143
Jos 3:13 downstream *will* **be cut o** and stand up in H4162
Jos 3:16 the Dead Sea) **was** completely **cut o**. H4162
Jos 4: 7 of the Jordan **was cut o** before the ark of H4162
Jos 4: 7 the waters of the Jordan **were cut o**. H4162
Jos 5:15 army replied, "**Take o** your sandals, for H5970
Jos 8: 2 except that *you may* **carry o** their plunder H1024
Jos 8: 9 Then Joshua **sent** them **o**, and they went H8938
Jos 8:27 But Israel *did* **carry o** for themselves the H1024
Jos 11:14 The Israelites **carried o** for themselves all H1024
Jos 15:18 When *she* **got o** her donkey H7563+4946+6584
Jdg 1: 6 and **cut o** his thumbs and big toes. H7915
Jdg 1: 7 thumbs and big toes **cut o** have picked up H7915

Jdg 1:14 When *she* **got o** her donkey H7563+4946+6584
Jdg 8:21 took the ornaments **o** their camels' necks. H928
Jdg 9:48 He took an ax and **cut o** some branches H4162
Jdg 16:12 snapped the ropes **o** his arms as if H4946+6584
Jdg 16:19 someone *to* **shave o** the seven braids H1662
Jdg 21:6 "Today one tribe *is* **cut o** from Israel," H1548
Jdg 21:23 caught one and **carried** her **o** to be his H5951
Ru 4:7 one party **took o** his sandal and gave it to H8990
1Sa 2:33 one of you that *I do* not **cut o** from serving H4162
1Sa 4:18 Eli fell backward **o** his chair by the H4946+6584
1Sa 5:4 hands *had* **been broken o** and were H4162
1Sa 17:34 a bear came and **carried o** a sheep from H5951
1Sa 17:39 am not used to them." So he **took** them **o**. H6073
1Sa 17:46 I'll strike you down and **cut o** your head. H6073
1Sa 17:51 *he* **cut o** his head with the sword. H4162
1Sa 18:4 Jonathan **took o** the robe he was wearing H7320
1Sa 19:24 He **stripped o** his garments, and he too H7320
1Sa 20:15 and *do* not ever **cut o** your kindness from H4162
1Sa 20:15 even when the LORD *has* **cut o** every one of H4162
1Sa 23:5 Philistines and **carried o** their livestock. H5627
1Sa 23:28 Then Saul **broke o** his pursuit of H8740+4946
1Sa 24:4 up unnoticed and **cut o** a corner of Saul's H4162
1Sa 24:5 *having* **cut o** a corner of his robe. H4162
1Sa 24:11 I **cut o** the corner of your robe but did not H4162
1Sa 24:21 the LORD that *you will* not **kill o** my H4162
1Sa 25:23 she quickly **got o** her donkey H3718+4946+6584
1Sa 28:9 *He has* **cut o** the mediums and spiritists H4162
1Sa 30:2 but **carried** them **o** as they went on their H5627
1Sa 30:17 young men who **rode o** on camels and H8206
1Sa 31:9 *They* **cut o** his head and stripped off his H4162
1Sa 31:9 cut off his head and **stripped o** his armor, H7320
2Sa 2:15 up and *were* **counted o**— H6296+928+5031
2Sa 4:7 killed him, *they* **cut o** his head. H6073
2Sa 4:12 *They* **cut o** their hands and feet and hung H7915
2Sa 5:6 the blind and the lame *can* **ward** you **o**." H6073
2Sa 5:21 David and his men **carried** them **o**. H5951
2Sa 7:9 and *I have* **cut o** all your enemies from H4162
2Sa 8:2 ground and **measured** them **o** with a H4499
2Sa 10:4 **shaved o** half of each man's beard H1662
2Sa 10:4 **cut o** their garments at the buttocks H4162
2Sa 11:1 at the time when kings **go o to war**, David H3655
2Sa 14:16 of the man *who is trying to* **cut o** both me H9012
2Sa 16:9 Let me go over and **cut o** his head." H6073
2Sa 18:21 bowed down before Joab and **ran o**. H8132
2Sa 20:22 and *they* **cut o** the head of Sheba son of H4162
1Ki 2:39 of Shimei's slaves **ran o** to Achish son of H1368
1Ki 5:14 *He* **sent** them **o** to Lebanon in shifts of ten H8938
1Ki 6:16 *He* **partitioned o** twenty cubits at the rear H1215
1Ki 9:6 have given you and **go o** to serve other H2143
1Ki 9:7 then *I will* **cut o** Israel from the land I H4162
1Ki 14:10 *I will* **cut o** from Jeroboam every last male H4162
1Ki 14:14 over Israel who *will* **cut o** the family of H4162
1Ki 14:26 *He* **carried o** the treasures of the temple of H4374
1Ki 16:11 *he* **killed o** Baasha's whole family. H5782
1Ki 18:4 While Jezebel *was* **killing o** the LORD's H4162
1Ki 18:42 So Ahab **went o** to eat and drink, but H6590
1Ki 18:45 falling and Ahab **rode o** to Jezreel. H8206
1Ki 20:11 should not boast like *one who* **takes** *it* **o**. H7337
1Ki 21:21 descendants and **cut o** from Ahab every H4162
2Ki 1:3 in Israel that you *are* **going o** to consult H2143
2Ki 5:12 So he turned and **went o** in a rage. H2143
2Ki 6:32 is sending someone to **cut o** my head? H6073
2Ki 7:8 clothes, and **went o** and hid them. H2143
2Ki 9:8 *I will* **cut o** from Ahab every last male in H4162
2Ki 9:18 The horseman **rode o** to meet Jehu and H2143
2Ki 11:7 *that* normally **go o** Sabbath **duty** are all H3655
2Ki 11:9 and *those who were* **going o duty**— H3655
2Ki 16:17 King Ahaz **cut o** the side panels and H7915
2Ki 17:26 which *are* **killing** them **o**, because H4637
2Ki 18:16 king of Judah **stripped o** the gold with H7915
2Ki 20:17 until this day, *will* **be carried o** to Babylon. H5951
2Ki 23:34 took Jehoahaz and **carried** him **o** *to* Egypt, H995
1Ch 17:8 and *I have* **cut o** all your enemies from H4162
1Ch 19:4 **cut o** their garments at the buttocks H4162
1Ch 20:1 at the time when kings **go o** to war, Joab H3655
2Ch 7:19 have given you and **go o** to serve other H2143
2Ch 12:9 *he* **carried o** the treasures of the temple of H4374
2Ch 14:13 men of Judah **carried o** a large amount H5951
2Ch 14:15 the herders and **carried o** droves of sheep H8647
2Ch 20:25 his men went to **carry o** their plunder, H1024
2Ch 21:17 invaded it and **carried o** all the goods H8647
2Ch 23:8 and *those who were* **going o duty**— H3655
2Ch 25:13 people and **carried o** great quantities H1024
2Ch 32:3 staff about **blocking o** the water from the H6258
2Ch 36:4 Jehoahaz and **carried** him **o** to Egypt. H995
Ne 4:23 the guards with me **took o** our clothes; H7320
Est 8:2 The king **took o** his signet ring, which he H6073
Job 1:15 Sabeans attacked and **made o with** them. H4374
Job 1:17 on your camels and **made o with** them. H4374
Job 6:9 to let loose his hand and **cut o** my life! H1298
Job 6:18 *they* **go o** into the wasteland and perish. H6590
Job 9:7 *he* **seals o** the light of the stars. H3159+1237
Job 12:18 He **takes o** the shackles put on by kings H7337
Job 18:14 of his tent and **marched o** to the king of H7575
Job 20:28 A flood *will* **carry o** his house, rushing H1655
Job 22:16 They **were carried o** before their time H7855
Job 24:24 *they* **are cut o** like heads of grain. H4909
Job 27:8 have the godless when *they are* **cut o**, H1298
Job 27:21 The east wind **carries** him **o**, and he is H5951
Job 30:11 *they* **throw o** restraint in my presence. H8938
Job 31:22 shoulder, *let* it **be broken o** at the joint. H8689
Job 36:7 He does not take his eyes **o** the righteous H4946
Job 38:5 Who **marked o** its dimensions? Surely you H8492
Job 41:13 Who *can* **strip o** its outer coat? Who can H1655
Ps 2:3 their chains and **throw o** their shackles." H8959
Ps 10:1 do you stand **far o**? Why do you hide H928+8158
Ps 10:9 the helpless and **drags** them **o** in his net. H5432
Ps 31:22 alarm I said, "*I* **am cut o** from your sight!" H1746
Ps 60:6 out Shechem and **measure o** the Valley of H4499
Ps 75:10 "*I will* **cut o** the horns of all the wicked H1548
Ps 88:5 no more, who **are cut o** from your care. H1615
Ps 101:8 I *will* **cut o** every evildoer from the city of H4162
Ps 108:7 out Shechem and **measure o** the Valley of H4499
Ps 109:13 May his descendants be **cut o**, their H4162
Ps 109:23 shadow; *I* **am shaken o** like a locust. H5850
Pr 2:22 the wicked *will* **be cut o** from the land H4162
Pr 20:14 then **goes o** and boasts about the purchase H261
Pr 22:6 **Start** children **o** on the way they should go H2852
Pr 23:5 sprout wings and **fly o** *to* the sky like an H6414
Pr 23:18 you, and your hope *will* not **be cut o**. H4162
Pr 24:14 you, and your hope *will* not **be cut o**. H4162
Pr 26:6 of a fool is like **cutting o** one's feet or H7894
Pr 29:18 people **cast o restraint**; but blessed is H7277
Ecc 6:3 that a stillborn child is **better o** than he. H3202
Ecc 7:24 exists is **far o** and most profound H8158
Ecc 9:4 a live dog is **better o** than a dead lion H3202
Ecc 11:10 from your heart and **cast o** the troubles of H6296
SS 5:3 *I have* **taken o** my robe—must I put it on H7320
Isa 5:29 their prey and **carry** it **o** with no one to H7117
Isa 7:20 private parts, and *to* **cut o** your beard also. H6200
Isa 8:4 of Samaria *will* **be carried o** by the king H5951
Isa 9:14 So the LORD *will* **cut o** from Israel both H4162
Isa 10:33 *will* **lop o** the boughs with great power. H6188
Isa 15:2 head is shaved and every beard **cut o**. H1757
Isa 18:5 *he will* **cut o** the shoots with pruning H4162
Isa 20:2 "**Take o** the sackcloth from your body and H7337
Isa 22:25 give way; *it will* **be sheared o** and will fall H1548
Isa 27:11 *they* **are broken o** and women come and H8689
Isa 30:11 Leave this way, **get o** this path, and stop H5742
Isa 30:16 You said, '*We will* **ride o** on swift horses H8206
Isa 32:11 **Strip o** *your* **fine clothes** and H7320+2256+6910
Isa 33:23 even the lame *will* **carry o** plunder. H1024
Isa 38:12 and *he has* **cut** me **o** from the loom H1298
Isa 39:6 until this day, *will* **be carried o** to Babylon. H5951
Isa 40:12 of his hand **marked o** the heavens? H9419
Isa 45:16 *they will* **go o** into disgrace together. H2143
Isa 46:2 *they* themselves **go o** into captivity. H2143
Isa 47:2 grind flour; **take o** your veil. H1655
Isa 47:11 that you cannot **ward o with a ransom**; H4105
Isa 52:2 **Shake o** your dust; rise up, sit enthroned H5850
Isa 53:8 For *he* **was cut o** from the land of the H1615
Isa 57:13 The wind *will* **carry** all of them **o**, a mere H5951
Jer 2:20 "Long ago *you* **broke o** your yoke and tore H8689
Jer 2:20 broke off your yoke and **tore o** your bonds; H5998
Jer 5:5 they too *had* **broken o** the yoke and H8689
Jer 5:5 broken off the yoke and **torn o** the bonds. H5998
Jer 5:10 **Strip o** her branches, for these people do H6073
Jer 7:29 " '**Cut o** your hair and throw it away; take H1605
Jer 11:19 *let us* **cut** him **o** from the land of the living H4162
Jer 12:3 **Drag** them **o** like sheep to be butchered H5998
Jer 13:22 your skirts *have* **been torn o** and your body H1655
Jer 20:5 away as plunder and **carry** it **o** to Babylon. H995
Jer 22:24 on my right hand, *I would* still **pull** you **o**. H5998
Jer 28:10 took the yoke **o** the neck of the H4946+6584
Jer 28:11 king of Babylon **o** the neck of all H4946+6584
Jer 28:12 broken the yoke **o** the neck of the H4946+6584
Jer 30:8 break the yoke **o** their necks and H4946+6584
Jer 30:8 off their necks and *will* **tear o** their bonds; H5998
Jer 36:23 the king **cut** them **o** with a scribe's knife H7973
Jer 41:5 eighty men *who had* **shaved o** their beards H1662
Jer 44:7 on yourselves by **cutting o** from Judah the H4162
Jer 44:17 of food and were **well o** and suffered no H3202
Jer 48:25 Moab's horn **is cut o**; her arm is broken," H1548
Jer 48:37 head is shaved and every beard **cut o**; H1757
Jer 49:29 their shelters *will* **be carried o** with all H5951
Jer 50:16 **Cut o** from Babylon the sower, and the H4162
Jer 51:25 roll you **o** the cliffs, and make H4946
La 2:3 In fierce anger *he has* **cut o** every horn of H1548
La 2:14 expose your sin to **ward o** your captivity. H8740
La 3:31 For no *one is* **cast o** *by* the Lord forever. H2396
La 4:9 by the sword are **better o** than those who H3202
Eze 4:16 I *am about to* **cut o** the food supply in H8689
Eze 5:16 famine upon you and **cut o** your supply of H8689
Eze 13:21 *I will* **tear o** your veils and save my people H7973
Eze 14:13 my hand against it *to* **cut o** its food supply H8689
Eze 17:4 *he* **broke o** its topmost shoot and carried it H7786
Eze 17:12 to Jerusalem and **carried o** her king and H4374
Eze 17:22 *I will* **break o** a tender sprig from its H7786
Eze 21:3 its sheath and **cut o** from you both the H4162
Eze 21:4 Because *I am going to* **cut o** the righteous H4162
Eze 21:19 where the road **branches o** *to* the city. H8031
Eze 21:26 **Take o** the turban, remove H6073
Eze 23:25 *They will* **cut o** your noses and your ears H6073
Eze 26:16 their robes and **take o** their embroidered H7320
Eze 29:19 of Babylon, and *he will* **carry o** its wealth. H5951
Eze 32:20 *let* her *be* **dragged o** with all her hordes. H5432
Eze 35:7 a desolate waste and **cut o** from it all who H4162
Eze 37:11 up and our hope is gone; we **are cut o**. H1615
Eze 38:13 hordes to loot, to **carry o** silver and gold H5951
Eze 44:19 *they are to* **take o** the clothes they have H7320
Eze 45:3 **measure o** a section 25,000 cubits long H4499
Eze 46:18 the people, driving them **o** their property. H4946
Eze 47:3 *he* **measured o** a thousand cubits and H4499
Eze 47:4 *He* **measured o** another thousand cubits H4499
Eze 47:4 *He* **measured o** another thousand and led H4499
Eze 47:5 *He* **measured o** another thousand, but H4499
Da 1:2 These *he* **carried o** *to* the temple of his god H995
Da 4:14 down the tree and **trim o** its branches; A10635
Da 4:14 **strip o** its leaves and scatter its fruit. A10499
Da 7:4 until its wings **were torn o** and it was A10440
Da 8:8 of its power the large horn **was broken o**, H8689
Da 8:22 the *one that* **was broken o** represent H8689
Da 11:8 and **carry** them **o** *to* H995+928+2021+8660
Da 11:12 When the army **is carried o**, the king of the H5951
Hos 2:7 for then I was **better o** than now. H3202
Hos 5:14 go away; *I will* **carry** them **o**, with no one H5951
Joel 1:7 *It has* **stripped o** their **bark** and H3106+3106
Joel 1:9 drink offerings *are* **cut o** from the house of H4162
Joel 1:16 *Has* not the food **been cut o** before our H4162
Joel 3:5 my gold and **carried o** my finest H995
Am 3:14 of the altar *will* **be cut o** and fall to the H1548
Am 6:2 Are *they* **better o** than your two kingdoms H3202
Am 6:3 *You* **put o** the day of disaster and bring H5612
Ob 11 while strangers **carried o** his wealth and H8647
Jnh 3:6 from his throne, **took o** his royal robes H6296
Mic 2:8 You strip **o** the rich robe from those H4946+4578
Mic 3:3 **strip o** their skin and break their bones in H7320
Zec 3:4 before him, "**Take o** his filthy clothes." H6073
Zec 11:16 the choice sheep, **tearing o** their hooves. H7293
Mal 2:3 you *will be* **carried o** with it. H5951
Mt 5:30 you to stumble, **cut it o** and throw it away. *G1716*
Mt 8:33 Those tending the pigs **ran o**, went into *G5771*
Mt 10:14 town and **shake** the dust **o** your feet. *G1759*
Mt 12:29 man's house and **carry o** his possessions *G773*
Mt 18:8 you to stumble, **cut it o** and throw it away. *G1716*
Mt 18:12 go to look for the *one that* **wandered o**? *G4414*
Mt 18:13 the ninety-nine that *did* not **wander o**. *G4414*
Mt 18:30 *he* **went o** and had the man thrown into *G599*
Mt 22:5 "But they paid no attention and **went o** *G599*
Mt 25:18 man who had received one bag **went o**, *G599*
Mt 26:51 servant of the high priest, **cutting o** his ear. *G904*
Mt 27:31 *they* **took o** the robe and put his own *G1694*
Mk 1:35 left the house and **went o** to a solitary *G599*
Mk 5:14 tending the pigs **ran o** and reported this *G5771*
Mk 6:11 place and **shake** the dust **o** your feet as *G1759*
Mk 9:43 you to stumble, **cut it o**. It is better for you *G644*
Mk 9:45 if your foot causes you to stumble, **cut it o**. *G644*
Mk 14:47 servant of the high priest, **cutting o** his ear. *G904*
Mk 15:20 *they* **took o** the purple robe and put his *G1694*
Lk 2:16 So *they* **hurried o** and found Mary *G2262+5067*
Lk 4:29 was built, in order to **throw** him **o the cliff**. *G2889*
Lk 8:34 *they* **ran o** and reported this in the town *G5771*
Lk 9:5 town and **shake** the dust **o** your feet as *G701*
Lk 12:58 adversary *may* **drag** you **o** to the judge, *G2955*
Lk 14:32 other is still **a long way o** and will ask *G4522*
Lk 15:13 **set o** for a distant country and there *G623*
Lk 15:20 "But *while* he *was* still **a long way o**, his *G600*
Lk 17:23 Do not go **running o after** them. *G1503*
Lk 18:7 *Will he keep* **putting** them **o**? *G3428*
Lk 22:50 of the high priest, **cutting o** his right ear. *G904*
Lk 23:1 assembly rose and **led** him **o** to Pilate. *G72*
Jn 6:17 got into a boat and **set o** across the lake *G2262*
Jn 11:44 "**Take o** the grave clothes and let him go." *G3395*
Jn 13:4 from the meal, **took o** his outer clothing *G5502*
Jn 15:2 *He* **cuts o** every branch in me that bears no *G149*
Jn 18:10 high priest's servant, **cutting o** his right ear. *G644*
Jn 18:26 of the man whose ear Peter *had* **cut o**, *G644*
Jn 21:7 for he had **taken it o**) and jumped *G1218*
Ac 2:39 children and for all who are **far o**— *G1650+3426*
Ac 3:23 to him *will be* **completely cut o** from their *G2017*
Ac 7:33 Lord said to him, '**Take o** your sandals, for *G3395*
Ac 8:3 *he* **dragged o** both men and women and *G5359*
Ac 9:30 to Caesarea and **sent** him **o** to Tarsus. *G1990*
Ac 12:7 and the chains **fell o** Peter's wrists. *G1738*
Ac 13:3 their hands on them and **sent** them **o**. *G668*
Ac 13:51 **shook** the dust **o** their feet **as a warning** to *G1759*
Ac 15:30 So the men *were* **sent o** and went down to *G668*
Ac 15:33 *they were* **sent o** by the believers with the *G668*
Ac 18:16 So *he* **drove** them **o**. *G590*
Ac 18:18 *he had* his hair **cut o** at Cenchreae *G3025*
Ac 20:15 we set sail from there and arrived **o** Chios. *G513*
Ac 22:23 shouting and **throwing o** their cloaks and *G4848*
Ac 27:5 the open sea **o the coast of** Cilicia and *G2848*
Ac 27:7 days and had difficulty arriving **o** Cnidus. *G2848*
Ac 28:5 But Paul **shook** the snake **o** into the fire *G701*
Ro 9:3 were cursed and **cut o from** Christ for the *G608*
Ro 11:17 of the branches *have been* **broken o**, *G1709*
Ro 11:19 "Branches *were* **broken o** so that I could *G1709*
Ro 11:20 But *they were* **broken o** because of *G1709*
Ro 11:22 Otherwise, you also *will be* **cut o**. *G1716*
1Co 11:6 *she might as well* **have** *her* **hair cut o**; but *G3025*
1Co 11:6 a woman to **have** her **hair cut o** or her *G3025*
Eph 4:22 former way of life, *to* **put o** your old self *G700*
Eph 4:25 each of you *must* **put o** falsehood and *G700*
Col 2:11 ruled by the flesh was **put o** when you were *G589*
Col 3:9 *since you have* **taken o** your old self with its *G588*
Heb 12:1 *let us* **throw o** everything that hinders and *G700*
Jas 2:25 to the spies and **sent** them **o** in a different *G1675*
2Pe 2:15 straight way and **wandered o** to follow the *G4414*
2Pe 2:20 they are **worse o** at the end than they *G5937*
Rev 12:17 at the woman and **went o** to wage war *G599*
Rev 18:10 they will stand **far o** and cry: *G608+3427*
Rev 18:15 wealth from her will stand **far o**, *G608+3427*
Rev 18:17 living from the sea, will stand **far o**. *G608+3427*

OFFAL (NIV84) DUNG, INTESTINES

O

OFFEND (2) [OFFENDED, OFFENDER, OFFENSE, OFFENSES, OFFENSIVE]

Job 34:31 'I am guilty but *will* **o** no more. H2472
Jn 6:61 Jesus said to them, "*Does* this **o** you? G4997

OFFENDED (2) [OFFEND]

Ge 40: 1 baker of the king of Egypt **o** their master, H2627
Mt 15:12 the Pharisees *were* **o** when they heard G4997

OFFENDER (3) [OFFEND]

Ex 21:22 **the o** must be fined whatever the H2257S
Ex 22: 5 the **o** must make restitution from the best of NDT
1Sa 2:25 God may mediate for **the o**; but if H2257S

OFFENSE (15) [OFFEND]

Ge 20:16 This is to **cover the o** against you H4064+6524
Dt 19:15 of any crime or **o** they may have H2633
Dt 21:22 guilty of a **capital o** is put to death H5477+4638
2Sa 3: 8 accuse me of an **o** *involving* this woman! H6411
Job 10:14 would not let my **o** go unpunished. H6411
Job 13:23 Show me my **o** and my sin. H7322
Ps 59: 3 against me *for* no **o** or sin of mine, H7322
Pr 17: 9 would foster love covers over an **o**, H7322
Pr 19:11 it is to one's glory to overlook an **o**. H7322
Jer 24: 9 abhorrent and an **o** to all the kingdoms H8288
Eze 22:11 one man commits a **detestable o** with his H9359
Mt 13:57 And *they* **took o** at him. But Jesus said to G4997
Mt 17:27 "But so that *we may* not **cause o**, go to the G4997
Mk 6: 3 And *they* **took o** at him. G4997
Gal 5:11 In that case the **o** of the cross has been G4998

OFFENSES (19) [OFFEND]

Nu 18: 1 the **responsibility for o** *connected with* the H6411
Nu 18: 1 the **responsibility for o** *connected with* the H6411
Nu 18:23 the **responsibility for** *any* **o** they *commit* H6411
1Ki 8:50 forgive all the **o** they have committed H7322
Job 7:21 you not pardon my **o** and forgive my sins? H7322
Job 14:17 My **o** will be sealed up in a bag; you will H7322
Ecc 10: 4 calmness can lay great **o** to rest. H2628
Isa 43:24 your sins and wearied me with your **o**. H6411
Isa 44:22 I have swept away your **o** like a cloud H7322
Isa 59:12 For our **o** are many in your sight, and our H7322
Isa 59:12 Our **o** are ever with us, and we H7322
Eze 18:22 None of the **o** they have committed will be H7322
Eze 18:28 consider all the **o** they have committed H7322
Eze 18:30 Turn away from all your **o**; then sin will H7322
Eze 18:31 of all the **o** you have committed, H7322
Eze 33:10 "Our **o** and sins weigh us down, and we H7322
Eze 37:23 vile images or with any of their **o**, H7322
Eze 39:24 to their uncleanness and their **o**, H7322
Am 5:12 how many are your **o** and how great your H7322

OFFENSIVE (3) [OFFEND]

Job 19:17 My breath *is* **o** to my wife; I am loathsome H2320
Ps 139:24 See if there is any **o** way in me, and lead H6778
Jer 6:10 The word of the LORD is **o** to them; they H3075

OFFER (159) [OFFERED, OFFERING, OFFERINGS, OFFERS, REMINDER-OFFERING]

Ex 3:18 the wilderness *to* **o sacrifices** to the LORD H2284
Ex 5: 3 the wilderness *to* **o sacrifices** to the LORD H2284
Ex 8: 8 people go *to* **o sacrifices** to the LORD." H2284
Ex 8:26 *The* **sacrifices** *we* **o** the LORD our God H2284
Ex 8:26 And if *we* **o sacrifices** that are detestable H2284
Ex 8:27 the wilderness *to* **o sacrifices** to the LORD H2284
Ex 8:28 will let you go *to* **o sacrifices** to the LORD H2284
Ex 8:29 the people go *to* **o sacrifices** to the LORD." H2284
Ex 23:18 "*Do* not **o** the blood of a sacrifice to me H2284
Ex 29:38 "This is what *you are to* **o** on the altar H6913
Ex 29:39 **O** one in the morning and the other at H6913
Ex 29:40 With the first lamb **o** a tenth of an ephah of NDT
Ex 30: 9 *Do* not **o** on this altar any other incense H6590
Ex 34:25 "*Do* not **o** the blood of a sacrifice to me H8821
Lev 1: 3 herd, *you are to* **o** a male without defect. H7928
Lev 1:10 goats, *you are to* **o** a male without defect. H7928
Lev 1:14 *you are to* **o** a dove or a young pigeon. H7928
Lev 2:14 **o** crushed heads of new grain roasted in H7928
Lev 3: 1 you **o** an animal from the herd H7928
Lev 3: 6 " 'If you **o** an animal from the flock as a H7933
Lev 3: 6 *you are to* **o** a male or female without H7928
Lev 3: 7 If you **o** a lamb, you are to present it H7928
Lev 3:14 From what you **o** you are to present this H7933
Lev 5: 8 who *shall* first **o** the one for the sin H7928
Lev 5:10 The priest *shall* then **o** the other as a burnt H6913
Lev 7:12 " 'If *they* **o** it as an expression of H7928
Lev 7:12 thank offering *they are to* **o** thick loaves H7928
Lev 7:16 shall be eaten on the day *they* **o** it, H7928
Lev 12: 7 *He shall* **o** them before the LORD to make H7928
Lev 14:12 of the male lambs and **o** it as a guilt H7928
Lev 14:20 **o** it on the altar, together with the H6590
Lev 16: 6 "Aaron *is to* **o** the bull for his own sin H7928
Lev 17: 7 *They must* no longer **o** any of their H2284
Lev 21: 8 because they **o up** the food of your God. H7928
Lev 21:17 may come near to **o** the food of his God. H7928
Lev 21:21 not come near to **o** the food of his God. H7928
Lev 22:22 *Do* not **o** to the LORD the blind, the injured H7928
Lev 22:24 *You must* not **o** to the LORD an animal H7928
Lev 22:25 of a foreigner and **o** them as the food of H7928
Nu 6:11 The priest *is to* **o** one as a sin offering H6913
Nu 15: 7 **O** it as an aroma pleasing to the LORD. H7928
Nu 15:24 whole community *is to* **o** a young bull H6913
Nu 28: 4 **O** one lamb in the morning and the other H6913
Nu 28: 8 **O** the second lamb at twilight, along with H6913
Nu 28: 8 drink offering that *you* **o** in the morning. H6913
Nu 28:20 With each bull **o** a grain offering of H6913
Nu 28:23 **O** these in addition to the regular morning H6913
Nu 28:31 **O** these together with their drink offerings H6913
Nu 29: 2 **o** a burnt offering of one young bull H6913
Nu 29: 3 With the bull **o** a grain offering of NDT
Nu 29: 9 With the bull **o** a grain offering of NDT
Nu 29:14 of the thirteen bulls **o** a grain offering of NDT
Nu 29:17 " 'On the second day **o** twelve young bulls NDT
Nu 29:18 **o** their grain offerings and drink offerings NDT
Nu 29:20 " 'On the third day **o** eleven bulls, two rams NDT
Nu 29:21 **o** their grain offerings and drink offerings NDT
Nu 29:23 " 'On the fourth day **o** ten bulls, two rams NDT
Nu 29:24 **o** their grain offerings and drink offerings NDT
Nu 29:26 " 'On the fifth day **o** nine bulls, two rams NDT
Nu 29:27 **o** their grain offerings and drink offerings NDT
Nu 29:29 " 'On the sixth day **o** eight bulls, two rams NDT
Nu 29:30 **o** their grain offerings and drink offerings NDT
Nu 29:32 " 'On the seventh day **o** seven bulls, two NDT
Nu 29:33 **o** their grain offerings and drink offerings NDT
Nu 29:37 **o** their grain offerings and drink offerings NDT
Nu 29:39 **o** these to the LORD at your appointed H6913
Dt 12:14 **O** them only at the place the LORD will H6590
Dt 20:10 **make** its people **an o** of peace. H7924
Dt 27: 6 with fieldstones and **o** burnt offerings on H6590
Dt 28:68 There *you will* **o yourselves for sale** to H4835
Dt 33:19 mountain and there **o** the sacrifices of the H2284
Jos 22:23 from the LORD and to **o** burnt offerings H6590
Jdg 5: 2 when the people **willingly o themselves** H5605
Jdg 6:26 **o** the second bull as a burnt offering." H6590
Jdg 13:16 prepare a burnt offering, **o** it to the LORD." H6590
Jdg 16:23 assembled to **o** a great sacrifice to H2284
Jdg 21:13 whole assembly sent an **o** *of* peace to the H7924
1Sa 1:21 all his family to **o** the annual sacrifice H2284
1Sa 2:19 with her husband to **o** the annual sacrifice H2284
1Sa 10: 4 will greet you and **o** you two loaves of H5989
1Sa 13:12 So I felt compelled *to* **o** the burnt offering." H6590
2Sa 24:22 king take whatever he wishes and **o it up**. H6590
1Ki 3: 4 The king went to Gibeon to **o sacrifices** H2284
1Ki 12:27 If these people go up to **o** sacrifices at the H6913
1Ki 22:43 people continued *to* **o sacrifices** and burn H2284
2Ki 12: 3 people continued *to* **o sacrifices** and burn H2284
2Ki 14: 4 people continued *to* **o sacrifices** and burn H2284
2Ki 15: 4 people continued *to* **o sacrifices** and burn H2284
2Ki 15:35 people continued *to* **o sacrifices** and burn H2284
2Ki 16:15 **o** the morning burnt offering and the H7787
2Ki 17:36 shall bow down and to him **o sacrifices**. H2284
1Ch 23:13 holy things, to **o sacrifices** before the LORD H7787
2Ch 11:16 to Jerusalem to **o sacrifices** to the LORD, H2284
2Ch 29:21 to **o** these on the altar of the LORD. H6590
2Ch 31: 2 to **o** burnt offerings and fellowship offerings NDT
2Ch 35:12 families of the people to **o** to the LORD, H7928
Ezr 3: 6 month they began to **o** burnt offerings to H6590
Ezr 6:10 so that *they may* **o sacrifices** pleasing to A10638
Ne 4: 2 *Will they* **o sacrifices**? Will they H2284
Ps 4: 5 **O** the sacrifices of the righteous and trust H2284
Ps 38:14 not hear, whose mouth can **o** no reply. H928
Ps 66:15 offering of rams; *I will* **o** bulls and goats. H6913
Ecc 5: 1 to listen rather than *to* **o** the sacrifice of H5989
Ecc 9: 2 those *who* **o sacrifices** and those who do H2284
Isa 1:15 even when *you* **o many** prayers, I am H8049
Isa 57: 7 there you went up to **o** your sacrifices. H2284
Jer 7:16 this people nor **o** any plea or petition H5951
Jer 7:18 make cakes *to* **o** *to* the Queen of Heaven AIT
Jer 11:14 this people or **o** any plea or petition H5951
Jer 14:12 though *they* **o** burnt offerings and grain H6590
Jer 16: 7 No *one will* **o food** to comfort those who H7271
Jer 33:18 before me continually *to* **o** burnt offerings, H6590
Jer 46:10 will **o** sacrifice in the land of the north by NDT
La 3:30 *Let him* **o** his cheek to one who would H5989
La 4: 3 Even jackals **o** their breasts to nurse their H2740
Eze 20:31 When you **o** your gifts—the sacrifice of H5951
Eze 43:22 the second day *you are to* **o** a male goat H7928
Eze 43:23 *you are to* **o** a young bull and a ram from H7928
Eze 43:24 *You are to* **o** them before the LORD, and the H7928
Eze 44:15 before me to **o sacrifices** *of* fat and blood, H7928
Eze 44:27 *he is to* **o** a sin offering *for* himself H7928
Eze 45:13 " 'This is the special gift *you are to* **o**: H8123
Eze 46: 6 of the New Moon he is to **o** a young bull, NDT
Eze 46:12 *He shall* **o** his burnt offering or his H6913
Eze 48: 9 special portion *you are to* **o** to the LORD H8123
Hos 8:13 *Though they* **o** sacrifices as gifts to me H2284
Hos 13: 2 these people, "*They* **o** human **sacrifices**! H2284
Hos 14: 2 that *we may* **o** the fruit of our lips. H8966
Mic 6: 7 *Shall I* **o** my firstborn for my transgression H5989
Hag 2:14 do and whatever *they* **o** there is defiled. H7928
Mal 1: 8 When *you* **o** blind animals for sacrifice, is H5602
Mal 1:13 diseased animals and **o** them as sacrifices, H995
Mt 5:24 to them; then come and **o** your gift. G4712
Mt 8: 4 to the priest and **o** the gift Moses G4712
Mk 1:44 the priest and **o** *the* **sacrifices** that Moses G4712
Lk 2:24 *to* **o** a sacrifice in keeping with what is G1443
Lk 5:14 the priest and **o** *the* **sacrifices** that Moses G4712
Lk 11: 6 come to me, and I have no food *to* **o** him. G4192
Ac 14:13 the crowd wanted *to* **o sacrifices** to them. G2604
Ac 24:26 hoping that Paul *would* **o** him a bribe, G1443
Ro 6:13 *Do* not **o** any part of yourself to sin as an G4225
Ro 6:13 rather **o** yourselves to God as those G4225
Ro 6:13 **o** every part of yourself to him as an NDT
Ro 6:16 you know that *when you* **o** yourselves to G4225
Ro 6:19 Just as *you used to* **o** yourselves as slaves G4225
Ro 6:19 so now **o** yourselves as slaves to G4225
Ro 12: 1 *to* **o** your bodies as a living sacrifice G4225
1Co 9:18 the gospel *I may* **o** it free of charge, G5502
2Th 3: 9 in order to **o** ourselves as a model for G1443
Heb 5: 1 to **o** gifts and sacrifices for sins. G4712
Heb 5: 3 is why he has to **o sacrifices** for his own G4712
Heb 7:27 he does not need *to* **o** sacrifices day after G429
Heb 8: 3 priest is appointed to **o** both gifts and G4712
Heb 8: 3 this one also to have something *to* **o**. G4712
Heb 8: 4 already priests who **o** the gifts prescribed G4712
Heb 9:25 he enter heaven to **o** himself again and G4712
Heb 13:15 *let us* continually **o** to God a sacrifice of G429
1Pe 4: 9 **O hospitality** to one another without G5811
Rev 8: 3 He was given much incense to **o**, with the G1443

OFFERED (90) [OFFER]

Ge 31:54 He **o** a sacrifice there in the hill country H2284
Ge 46: 1 *he* **o** sacrifices to the God of his father H2284
Ex 24: 5 and *they* **o** burnt offerings and sacrificed H6590
Ex 40:29 **o** on it burnt offerings and grain H6590
Lev 2:12 but *they are* not *to be* **o** on the altar as a H6590
Lev 7: 3 All its fat *shall be* **o**: the fat tail and the fat H7928
Lev 7:15 must be eaten on the day it is **o**; H7933
Lev 7:18 the *one who* **o** it will not be accepted. H7928
Lev 9:15 it and **o** it **for a sin offering** as he did with H2627
Lev 9:16 burnt offering and **o** it in the prescribed H6913
Lev 10: 1 and *they* **o** unauthorized fire before the H7928
Nu 16:47 Aaron **o** the incense and made H5989
Nu 18:15 animal, that *is* **o** to the LORD is yours. H7928
Nu 23: 2 the two of them **o** a bull and a ram on H6590
Nu 23: 4 on each altar *I have* **o** a bull and a ram H6590
Nu 23:14 seven altars and **o** a bull and a ram on H6590
Nu 23:30 **o** a bull and a ram on each altar. H6590
Nu 28:24 *it is to* **be o** in addition to the regular H6913
Dt 24:10 house to get *what is* **o** *to* you **as a pledge**. H6287
Dt 26:14 nor *have I* **o** any of it to the dead. H5989
Jos 8:31 On it *they* **o** to the LORD burnt offerings H6590
Jdg 2: 5 There *they* **o sacrifices** to the LORD. H2284
Jdg 6:19 them out and **o** them *to* him under the H5602
Ru 2:14 harvesters, *he* **o** her some roasted grain. H7381
1Sa 2:13 whenever any of the people **o** a sacrifice H2284
1Sa 6:15 of Beth Shemesh **o** burnt offerings and H6590
1Sa 13: 9 And Saul **o up** the burnt offering H6590
2Sa 15:24 Abiathar **o sacrifices** until all the H6590
1Ki 3: 3 except that he **o sacrifices** and burned H2284
1Ki 3: 4 Solomon **o** a thousand burnt H6590
1Ki 8:62 all Israel with him **o** sacrifices before the H2284
1Ki 8:63 Solomon **o a sacrifice** of fellowship H2284
1Ki 8:64 of the LORD, and there *he* **o** burnt offerings H6913
1Ki 11: 8 incense and **o sacrifices** to their gods. H2284
1Ki 12:32 in Judah, and **o sacrifices** on the altar. H6590
1Ki 12:33 *he* **o sacrifices** on the altar he had built at H6590
1Ki 20:34 father took from your father," Ben-Hadad **o**. H606
2Ki 3:27 **o** him as a sacrifice on the city wall. H6590
2Ki 16: 4 *He* **o sacrifices** and burned incense at the H2284
2Ki 16:13 *He* **o up** his burnt offering and grain H7787
1Ch 21:28 the Jebusite, *he* **o sacrifices** there. H2284
2Ch 1: 6 tent of meeting and **o** a thousand burnt H6590
2Ch 6:40 ears attentive to the **prayers** *o in* this place. AIT
2Ch 7: 4 all the people **o** sacrifices before the H2284
2Ch 7: 5 And King Solomon **o** a sacrifice of H2284
2Ch 7: 7 there *he* **o** burnt offerings and the fat H6913
2Ch 7:15 ears attentive to the **prayers** *o in* this place. AIT
2Ch 28: 4 *He* **o sacrifices** and burned incense at the H2284
2Ch 28:23 *He* **o sacrifices** to the gods of Damascus H2284
2Ch 30:22 portion and **o** fellowship offerings H2284
2Ch 33:22 worshiped and **o sacrifices** to all the idols H2284
Ezr 6:17 house of God *they* **o** a hundred bulls, A10638
Ne 12:43 And on that day *they* **o** great sacrifices H2284
Job 26: 3 What **advice** *you have* **o** to one without H3619
Job 31:27 **o** them **a kiss of homage**, H5975+4200+7023
Ps 51:19 in burnt offerings **o whole**; then bulls will H4003
Ps 51:19 then bulls *will be* **o** on your altar. H6590
Ps 106:28 of Peor and ate **sacrifices** *o to* lifeless gods; AIT
Isa 50: 6 *I* **o** my back to those who beat me, my H5989
Isa 57: 6 out drink offerings and **o** grain offerings. H6590
Eze 6:13 places where *they* **o** fragrant incense to all H5989
Eze 16:18 and *you* **o** my oil and incense before H5989
Eze 16:19 *you* **o** as fragrant incense before them. H5989
Eze 20:28 any leafy tree, there *they* **o** their sacrifices H2284
Eze 27:18 wealth of goods. They **o** wine from Helbon H928
Eze 44: 7 my temple while you **o** me food, H7928
Jnh 1:16 and *they* **o** a sacrifice to the LORD and H2284
Mt 27:34 There *they* **o** Jesus wine to drink, mixed G1443
Mt 27:48 put it on a staff, and **o** it to Jesus *to* **drink**. G4540
Mk 15:23 Then *they* **o** him wine mixed with myrrh G1443
Mk 15:36 put it on a staff, and **o** it to Jesus **to drink**. G4540
Lk 10: 8 are welcomed, eat what *is* **o** *to* you. G4192
Lk 23:36 mocked him. *They* **o** him wine vinegar G4712
Ac 8:18 of the apostles' hands, *he* **o** them money G4712
Ro 11:16 the **part** *of the dough* **o as firstfruits** is holy G569
1Co 9:13 at the altar share in what is **o** on the altar? NDT
1Co 10:20 the sacrifices of pagans *are* **o** to demons, G2604
1Co 10:28 "This has been **o in sacrifice**," then do not G2638
Heb 5: 7 he **o up** prayers and petitions with fervent G4712
Heb 7:27 their sins once for all *when he* **o** himself. G429
Heb 9: 7 which *he* **o** for himself and for the sins the G4712
Heb 9: 9 sacrifices *being* **o** were not able to G4712
Heb 9:14 the eternal Spirit **o** himself unblemished G4712
Heb 10: 2 would they not have stopped *being* **o**? G4712
Heb 10: 8 *though* they *were* **o** in accordance with the G4712
Heb 10:12 But *when* this priest *had* **o** for all time one G4712

Heb 11:17 God tested him, **o** Isaac **as a sacrifice**. *G4712*
Jas 2:21 what he did *when he* **o** his son Isaac on *G429*
Jas 5:15 And the prayer *o in* **faith** will make the sick AIT
Rev 14: 4 mankind and *o as* **firstfruits** to God and the AIT

OFFERING (692) [OFFER]

Ge 4: 3 of the fruits of the soil as an **o** to the LORD. H4966
Ge 4: 4 And Abel also brought an **o**—fat portions NDT
Ge 4: 4 LORD looked with favor on Abel and his **o**, H4966
Ge 4: 5 on Cain and his **o** he did not look with H4966
Ge 22: 2 him there as a **burnt o** on a mountain I H6592
Ge 22: 3 he had cut enough wood for the **burnt o**, H6592
Ge 22: 6 the wood for the **burnt o** and placed it on H6592
Ge 22: 7 "but where is the lamb for the **burnt o**?" H6592
Ge 22: 8 will provide the lamb for the **burnt o**, H6592
Ge 22:13 sacrificed it as a **burnt o** instead of his son H6592
Ge 35:14 he poured out a **drink o** on it; he also H5821
Ex 18:12 brought a **burnt o** and other sacrifices to H6592
Ex 25: 2 "Tell the Israelites to bring me an **o**. H9556
Ex 25: 2 are to receive the **o** *for* me from everyone H9556
Ex 29:14 intestines outside the camp. It is a **sin o**. H2633
Ex 29:18 It is a **burnt o** to the LORD, a pleasing H6592
Ex 29:18 a **food o** presented to the LORD. H852
Ex 29:24 wave them before the LORD as a **wave o**. H9485
Ex 29:25 altar along with the **burnt o** for a pleasing H6592
Ex 29:25 to the LORD, a **food o** presented to the LORD. H852
Ex 29:26 wave it before the LORD as a **wave o**, and H9485
Ex 29:36 each day as a **sin o** to make atonement H2633
Ex 29:40 a quarter of a hin of wine as a **drink o**. H5821
Ex 29:41 with the same **grain o** and its drink H4966
Ex 29:41 offering and its **drink o** as in the morning H5821
Ex 29:41 a **food o** presented to the LORD. H852
Ex 29:42 to come this **burnt o** is to be made H6592
Ex 30: 9 incense or any **burnt o** or grain offering, H6592
Ex 30: 9 incense or any burnt offering or **grain o**, H4966
Ex 30: 9 offering, and do not pour a **drink o** on it. H5821
Ex 30:10 of the atoning **sin o** for the generations H2633
Ex 30:13 This half shekel is an **o** to the LORD. H9556
Ex 30:14 old or more, are to give an **o** *to* the LORD. H9556
Ex 30:15 when you make the **o** *to* the LORD to atone H9556
Ex 30:20 minister by presenting a **food o** to the LORD, H852
Ex 30:28 the altar of **burnt o** and all its utensils, and H6592
Ex 31: 9 the altar of **burnt o** and all its utensils, the H6592
Ex 35: 5 what you have, take an **o** for the LORD. H9556
Ex 35: 5 willing is to bring *to* the LORD an **o** *of* gold, H9556
Ex 35:16 the altar of **burnt o** with its bronze grating H6592
Ex 35:21 came and brought an **o** *to* the LORD for the H9556
Ex 35:22 their gold as a **wave o** to the LORD. H9485
Ex 35:24 Those presenting an **o** *of* silver or bronze H9556
Ex 35:24 bronze brought it as an **o** *to* the LORD, H9556
Ex 36: 6 anything else as an **o** *for* the sanctuary." H9556
Ex 38: 1 built the altar of **burnt o** *of* acacia wood, H6592
Ex 38:24 the gold from the **wave o** used for all the H9485
Ex 38:29 bronze from the **wave o** was 70 talents H9485
Ex 40: 6 "Place the altar of **burnt o** in front of the H6592
Ex 40:10 anoint the altar of **burnt o** and all its H6592
Ex 40:29 set the altar of **burnt o** near the entrance H6592
Lev 1: 2 among you brings an **o** to the LORD, H7933
Lev 1: 2 bring as your **o** an animal from either the H7933
Lev 1: 3 'If the **o** is a burnt offering from the herd, H7933
Lev 1: 3 'If the offering is a **burnt o** from the herd, H6592
Lev 1: 4 lay your hand on the head of the **burnt o**, H6592
Lev 1: 6 You are to skin the **burnt o** and cut it into H6592
Lev 1: 9 It is a **burnt o**, a food offering, an aroma H6592
Lev 1: 9 burnt offering, a **food o**, an aroma pleasing H852
Lev 1:10 'If the **o** is a burnt offering from the flock, H7933
Lev 1:10 'If the offering is a **burnt o** from the flock, H6592
Lev 1:13 It is a **burnt o**, a food offering, an aroma H6592
Lev 1:13 burnt offering, a **food o**, an aroma pleasing H852
Lev 1:14 " 'If the **o** to the LORD is a burnt offering H7933
Lev 1:14 offering to the LORD is a **burnt o** of birds, H6592
Lev 1:17 It is a **burnt o**, a food offering, an aroma H6592
Lev 1:17 burnt offering, a **food o**, an aroma pleasing H852
Lev 2: 1 anyone brings a **grain o** to the LORD, H4966
Lev 2: 1 the LORD, their **o** is to be of the finest flour. H7933
Lev 2: 2 on the altar, a **food o**, an aroma pleasing H852
Lev 2: 3 The rest of the **grain o** belongs to Aaron H4966
Lev 2: 4 " 'If you bring a **grain o** baked in an oven H4966
Lev 2: 5 If your **grain o** is prepared on a griddle, it H4966
Lev 2: 6 it and pour oil on it; it is a **grain o**. H4966
Lev 2: 7 If your **grain o** is cooked in a pan, it is to H4966
Lev 2: 8 Bring the **grain o** made of these things to H4966
Lev 2: 9 portion from the **grain o** and burn it on H4966
Lev 2: 9 burn it on the altar as a **food o**, H852
Lev 2:10 The rest of the **grain o** belongs to Aaron H4966
Lev 2:11 " 'Every **grain o** you bring to the LORD H4966
Lev 2:11 yeast or honey in a **food o** presented to the H852
Lev 2:12 them to the LORD as an **o** *of* the firstfruits, H7933
Lev 2:14 " 'If you bring a **grain o** *of* firstfruits to the H4966
Lev 2:15 Put oil and incense on it; it is a **grain o**. H4966
Lev 2:16 incense, as a **food o** presented to the LORD. H852
Lev 3: 1 " 'If your **o** is a fellowship offering, and H7933
Lev 3: 1 " 'If your offering is a fellowship **o**, and H2285
Lev 3: 2 on the head of your **o** and slaughter it at H7933
Lev 3: 3 From the fellowship **o** you are to bring a H2285
Lev 3: 3 you are to bring a **food o** to the LORD: H852
Lev 3: 5 altar on top of the **burnt o** that is lying on H6592
Lev 3: 5 it is a **food o**, an aroma pleasing H852
Lev 3: 6 the flock as a fellowship **o** to the LORD, H2285
Lev 3: 9 From the fellowship **o** you are to bring a H2285
Lev 3: 9 you are to bring a **food o** to the LORD: H852
Lev 3:11 the altar as a **food o** presented to H4312+852
Lev 3:12 " 'If your **o** is a goat, you are to present it H7933
Lev 3:14 you are to present this **food o** to the LORD: H852
Lev 3:16 burn them on the altar as a **food o**, H4312+852
Lev 4: 3 defect as a **sin o** for the sin he has H2633
Lev 4: 7 of the altar of **burnt o** at the entrance to H6592
Lev 4: 8 all the fat from the bull of the **sin o**— H2633
Lev 4:10 from the ox sacrificed as a **fellowship o**. H8968
Lev 4:10 shall burn them on the altar of **burnt o**. H6592
Lev 4:14 a young bull as a **sin o** and present it H2633
Lev 4:18 of the altar of **burnt o** at the entrance to H6592
Lev 4:20 just as he did with the bull for the **sin o**. H2633
Lev 4:21 This is the **sin o** *for* the community. H2633
Lev 4:23 must bring as his **o** a male goat without H7933
Lev 4:24 place where the **burnt o** is slaughtered H6592
Lev 4:24 slaughtered before the LORD. It is a **sin o**. H2633
Lev 4:25 of the blood of the **sin o** with his finger H2633
Lev 4:25 of the altar of **burnt o** and pour out the H6592
Lev 4:26 as he burned the fat of the fellowship **o**. H2285
Lev 4:28 they must bring as their **o** for the sin they H7933
Lev 4:29 on the head of the **sin o** and slaughter it H2633
Lev 4:29 slaughter it at the place of the **burnt o**. H6592
Lev 4:30 of the altar of **burnt o** and pour out the H6592
Lev 4:31 the fat is removed from the fellowship **o**, H2285
Lev 4:32 " 'If someone brings a lamb as their sin **o** H7933
Lev 4:33 slaughter it for a **sin o** at the place where H2633
Lev 4:33 place where the **burnt o** is slaughtered. H6592
Lev 4:34 of the blood of the **sin o** with his finger H2633
Lev 4:34 of the altar of **burnt o** and pour out the H6592
Lev 4:35 from the lamb of the fellowship **o**, H2285
Lev 5: 6 lamb or goat from the flock as a **sin o**; H2633
Lev 5: 7 one for a **sin o** and the other for a burnt H2633
Lev 5: 7 a sin offering and the other for a **burnt o**. H6592
Lev 5: 8 who shall first offer the one for the **sin o**. H2633
Lev 5: 9 of the blood of the **sin o** against the side H2633
Lev 5: 9 out at the base of the altar. It is a **sin o**. H2633
Lev 5:10 the other as a **burnt o** in the prescribed H6592
Lev 5:11 are to bring as an **o** for their sin a tenth H7933
Lev 5:11 of an ephah of the finest flour for a **sin o**. H2633
Lev 5:11 oil or incense on it, because it is a **sin o**. H2633
Lev 5:12 presented to the LORD. It is a **sin o**. H2633
Lev 5:13 The rest of the **o** will belong to the priest, as NDT
Lev 5:13 to the priest, as in the case of the **grain o**. H4966
Lev 5:15 to the sanctuary shekel. It is a **guilt o**. H871
Lev 5:16 them with the ram as a **guilt o**, H871
Lev 5:18 to the priest as a **guilt o** a ram from the H871
Lev 5:19 It is a **guilt o**; they have been guilty of H871
Lev 6: 5 owner on the day they present their **guilt o**. H873
Lev 6: 6 to the LORD, their **guilt o**, a ram from the H871
Lev 6: 9 'These are the regulations for the **burnt o** H6592
Lev 6: 9 The **burnt o** is to remain on the altar H6592
Lev 6:10 the ashes of the **burnt o** that the fire has H6592
Lev 6:12 arrange the **burnt o** on the fire and H6592
Lev 6:14 'These are the regulations for the **grain o**: H4966
Lev 6:15 with all the incense on the **grain o**, H4966
Lev 6:17 Like the **sin o** and the guilt offering, it is H2633
Lev 6:17 Like the sin offering and the **guilt o**, it is H871
Lev 6:20 "This is the **o** to Aaron and his sons are to H7933
Lev 6:20 of the finest flour as a regular **grain o**, H4966
Lev 6:21 present the **grain o** broken in pieces H4966
Lev 6:23 Every **grain o** *of* a priest shall be burned H4966
Lev 6:25 'These are the regulations for the **sin o** H2633
Lev 6:25 The **sin o** is to be slaughtered before the H2633
Lev 6:25 in the place the **burnt o** is slaughtered; H6592
Lev 6:30 But any **sin o** whose blood is brought into H2633
Lev 7: 1 " 'These are the regulations for the **guilt o** H871
Lev 7: 2 The **guilt o** is to be slaughtered in the place H871
Lev 7: 2 place where the **burnt o** is slaughtered, H6592
Lev 7: 5 on the altar as a **food o** presented to the H852
Lev 7: 5 presented to the LORD. It is a **guilt o**. H871
Lev 7: 7 applies to both the **sin o** and the guilt H2633
Lev 7: 7 to both the sin offering and the **guilt o**: H871
Lev 7: 8 who offers a **burnt o** *for* anyone may keep H6592
Lev 7: 9 Every **grain o** baked in an oven or cooked H4966
Lev 7:10 every **grain o**, whether mixed with H4966
Lev 7:11 the fellowship **o** anyone may present H2285
Lev 7:12 along with this thank **o** they are to offer H2285
Lev 7:13 their fellowship **o** *of* thanksgiving they H2285
Lev 7:13 are to present an **o** with thick loaves of H7933
Lev 7:14 They are to bring one of each kind as an **o**, H7933
Lev 7:14 the blood of the **fellowship o** against the H8968
Lev 7:15 of their fellowship **o** *of* thanksgiving must H2285
Lev 7:16 their **o** is the result of a vow or is a H7933
Lev 7:16 is the result of a vow or is a freewill **o**, H2285
Lev 7:18 of the fellowship **o** is eaten on the third H2285
Lev 7:20 of the fellowship **o** belonging to the LORD, H2285
Lev 7:21 of the fellowship **o** belonging to the LORD H2285
Lev 7:25 from which a **food o** may be presented H852
Lev 7:29 brings a fellowship **o** to the LORD is to H2285
Lev 7:30 they are to present the **food o** *to* the LORD; H852
Lev 7:30 the breast before the LORD as a **wave o**. H9485
Lev 7:33 the fat of the **fellowship o** shall have the H8968
Lev 7:37 are the regulations for the **burnt o**, the H6592
Lev 7:37 offering, the **grain o**, the sin offering, H4966
Lev 7:37 grain offering, the **sin o**, the guilt offering, H2633
Lev 7:37 the sin offering, the **guilt o**, the ordination H871
Lev 7:37 the **ordination o** and the fellowship H4854
Lev 7:37 ordination offering and the fellowship **o**, H2285
Lev 8: 2 the bull for the **sin o**, the two rams and H2633
Lev 8:14 He then presented the bull for the **sin o** H2633
Lev 8:18 He then presented the ram for the **burnt** *o* AIT
Lev 8:21 It was a **burnt o**, a pleasing aroma, a food H6592
Lev 8:21 a **food o** presented to the LORD H852
Lev 8:27 waved them before the LORD as a **wave o**. H9485
Lev 8:28 on top of the **burnt o** as an ordination H6592
Lev 8:28 of the burnt offering as an **ordination o**, H4854
Lev 8:28 a **food o** presented to the LORD. H852
Lev 8:29 waved it before the LORD as a **wave o** H9485
Lev 9: 2 bull calf for your **sin o** and a ram for your H2633
Lev 9: 2 sin offering and a ram for your **burnt o**, H6592
Lev 9: 3 'Take a male goat for a **sin o**, a calf and a H2633
Lev 9: 3 old and without defect—for a **burnt o**, H6592
Lev 9: 4 a ram for a **fellowship o** to sacrifice H8968
Lev 9: 4 together with a **grain o** mixed with olive H4966
Lev 9: 7 sacrifice your **sin o** and your burnt H2633
Lev 9: 7 offering and your **burnt o** and make H6592
Lev 9: 7 sacrifice the **o** that is *for* the people and H7933
Lev 9: 8 slaughtered the calf as a **sin o** for himself. H2633
Lev 9:10 the long lobe of the liver from the **sin o**, H2633
Lev 9:12 Then he slaughtered the **burnt o**. His sons H6592
Lev 9:13 handed him the **burnt o** piece by piece, H6592
Lev 9:14 them on top of the **burnt o** on the altar. H6592
Lev 9:15 brought the **o** that was *for* the people. H7933
Lev 9:15 the people's **sin o** and slaughtered it H2633
Lev 9:15 it and **offered** it **for a sin o** as he did with H2627
Lev 9:16 He brought the **burnt o** and offered it in H6592
Lev 9:17 He also brought the **grain o**, took a H4966
Lev 9:17 altar in addition to the morning's **burnt o**. H6592
Lev 9:18 ram as the fellowship **o** for the people. H2285
Lev 9:21 right thigh before the LORD as a **wave o**, H9485
Lev 9:22 And having sacrificed the **sin o**, the burnt H2633
Lev 9:22 the **burnt o** and the fellowship offering H6592
Lev 9:22 the burnt offering and the **fellowship o** H8968
Lev 9:24 consumed the **burnt o** and the fat H6592
Lev 10:12 "Take the **grain o** left over from the food H4966
Lev 10:15 to be waved before the LORD as a **wave o**. H9485
Lev 10:16 the goat of the **sin o** and found that it H2633
Lev 10:17 didn't you eat the **sin o** in the sanctuary H2633
Lev 10:19 they sacrificed their **sin o** and their burnt H2633
Lev 10:19 offering and their **burnt o** before the LORD, H6592
Lev 10:19 pleased if I had eaten the **sin o** today?" H2633
Lev 12: 6 lamb for a **burnt o** and a young pigeon H6592
Lev 12: 6 a young pigeon or a dove for a **sin o**. H2633
Lev 12: 8 one for a **burnt o** and the other for a sin H6592
Lev 12: 8 a burnt offering and the other for a **sin o**. H2633
Lev 14:10 flour mixed with olive oil for a **grain o**, H4966
Lev 14:12 of the male lambs and offer it as a **guilt o**, H871
Lev 14:12 wave them before the LORD as a **wave o**. H9485
Lev 14:13 area where the **sin o** and the burnt H2633
Lev 14:13 offering and the **burnt o** are slaughtered. H6592
Lev 14:13 Like the **sin o**, the guilt offering belongs H2633
Lev 14:13 offering, the **guilt o** belongs to the priest H871
Lev 14:14 of the blood of the **guilt o** and put it on the H871
Lev 14:17 on top of the blood of the **guilt o**. H871
Lev 14:19 to sacrifice the **sin o** and make atonement H2633
Lev 14:19 the priest shall slaughter the **burnt o** H6592
Lev 14:20 together with the **grain o**, and make H4966
Lev 14:21 one male lamb as a **guilt o** to be waved to H871
Lev 14:21 flour mixed with olive oil for a **grain o**, H4966
Lev 14:22 one for a **sin o** and the other for a burnt H2633
Lev 14:22 a sin offering and the other for a **burnt o**. H6592
Lev 14:24 The priest is to take the lamb for the **guilt o** H871
Lev 14:24 wave them before the LORD as a **wave o**. H9485
Lev 14:25 the lamb for the **guilt o** and take some of H871
Lev 14:28 places he put the blood of the **guilt o**— H871
Lev 14:31 one as a **sin o** and the other as a burnt H2633
Lev 14:31 a sin offering and the other as a **burnt o**, H6592
Lev 14:31 a burnt offering, together with the **grain o**. H4966
Lev 15:15 the one for a **sin o** and the other for a H2633
Lev 15:15 a sin offering and the other for a **burnt o**. H6592
Lev 15:30 sacrifice one for a **sin o** and the other H2633
Lev 15:30 a sin offering and the other for a **burnt o**. H6592
Lev 16: 3 a young bull for a **sin o** and a ram for a H2633
Lev 16: 3 a sin offering and a ram for a **burnt o**. H6592
Lev 16: 5 two male goats for a **sin o** and a ram for a H2633
Lev 16: 5 a sin offering and a ram for a **burnt o**. H6592
Lev 16: 6 bull for his own **sin o** to make atonement H2633
Lev 16: 9 falls to the LORD and sacrifice it for a **sin o**. H2633
Lev 16:11 bull for his own **sin o** to make atonement H2633
Lev 16:11 is to slaughter the bull for his own **sin o**. H2633
Lev 16:15 the goat for the **sin o** for the people and H2633
Lev 16:24 sacrifice the **burnt o** *for* himself and the H6592
Lev 16:24 himself and the **burnt o** *for* the people, H6592
Lev 16:25 also burn the fat of the **sin o** on the altar. H2633
Lev 17: 4 to present it as an **o** to the LORD in front of H7933
Lev 17: 8 them who offers a **burnt o** or sacrifice H6592
Lev 19: 5 you sacrifice a fellowship **o** to the LORD, H2285
Lev 19:21 the tent of meeting for a **guilt o** to the LORD. H871
Lev 19:22 With the ram of the **guilt o** the priest is to H871
Lev 19:24 will be holy, an **o of praise** to the LORD. H2136
Lev 22:10 a priest's family may eat the **sacred o**, H7731
Lev 22:14 who eats a **sacred o** by mistake must H7731
Lev 22:14 to the priest for the **o** and add a fifth of H7731
Lev 22:18 presents a gift for a **burnt o** to the LORD H6592
Lev 22:18 either to fulfill a vow or as a **freewill o**, H5607
Lev 22:21 flock a fellowship **o** to the LORD to fulfill H2285
Lev 22:21 to fulfill a special vow or as a **freewill o**, H5607
Lev 22:22 on the altar as a **food o** presented to the H852
Lev 22:23 present as a **freewill o** an ox or a sheep H5607
Lev 22:27 acceptable as a **food o** presented to H7933+852
Lev 22:29 "When you sacrifice a thank **o** to the LORD H2285
Lev 23: 8 For seven days present a **food o** to the LORD H852
Lev 23:12 sacrifice as a **burnt o** to the LORD a lamb H6592
Lev 23:13 together with its **grain o** *of* two-tenths of H4966
Lev 23:13 olive oil—a **food o** presented to the LORD H852

Lev 23:13 its **drink o** *of* a quarter of a hin of wine H5821
Lev 23:14 the very day you bring this **o** *to* your God. H7933
Lev 23:15 day you brought the sheaf of the **wave o**, H9485
Lev 23:16 present an **o of** new **grain** to the LORD. H4966
Lev 23:17 as a **wave o** of firstfruits to the LORD. H9485
Lev 23:18 They will be a **burnt o** to the LORD H6592
Lev 23:18 drink offerings—a **food o**, an aroma H852
Lev 23:19 one male goat for a **sin o** and two lambs, H2633
Lev 23:19 each a year old, for a fellowship **o**. H2285
Lev 23:20 two lambs before the LORD as a **wave o**, H9485
Lev 23:20 They are a **sacred o** to the LORD for the H7731
Lev 23:25 but present a **food o** to the LORD. H852
Lev 23:27 present a **food o** to the LORD. H852
Lev 23:36 assembly and present a **food o** to the LORD. H852
Lev 24: 7 bread and to be a **food o** presented to the H852
Lev 27: 9 that is acceptable as an **o** to the LORD, H7933
Lev 27:11 is not acceptable as an **o** to the LORD— H7933
Nu 3: 4 when they **made an o** *with* unauthorized H7928
Nu 4:16 the regular **grain o** and the anointing oil. H4966
Nu 5:15 must also take an **o** *of* a tenth of an H7933
Nu 5:15 because it is a **grain o** *for* jealousy, H4966
Nu 5:18 the **grain o** *for* jealousy, while he H4966
Nu 5:25 from her hands the **grain o** *for* jealousy, H4966
Nu 5:26 a handful of the **grain o** as a memorial H4966
Nu 5:26 offering as a **memorial o** and burn it on the H260
Nu 6:11 to offer one as a **sin o** and the other as a H2633
Nu 6:11 the other as a **burnt o** to make atonement H6592
Nu 6:12 bring a year-old male lamb as a **guilt o**. H871
Nu 6:14 male lamb without defect for a **burnt o**, H6592
Nu 6:14 ewe lamb without defect for a **sin o**, H2633
Nu 6:14 a ram without defect for a **fellowship o**, H8968
Nu 6:16 the LORD and make the **sin o** and the burnt H2633
Nu 6:16 make the sin offering and the **burnt o**. H6592
Nu 6:17 the ram as a fellowship **o** to the LORD, H2285
Nu 6:17 together with its **grain o** and drink offering H4966
Nu 6:17 with its grain offering and **drink o**. H5821
Nu 6:18 is under the sacrifice of the **fellowship o**. H8968
Nu 6:20 wave these before the LORD as a **wave o**; H9485
Nu 7:11 is to bring his **o** for the dedication of H7933
Nu 7:12 one who brought his **o** on the first day H7933
Nu 7:13 His **o** was one silver plate weighing a H7933
Nu 7:13 flour mixed with olive oil as a **grain o**; H4966
Nu 7:15 one male lamb a year old for a **burnt o**; H6592
Nu 7:16 one male goat for a **sin o**; H2633
Nu 7:17 year old to be sacrificed as a **fellowship o**. H8968
Nu 7:17 This was the **o** *of* Nahshon son of H7933
Nu 7:18 the leader of Issachar, **brought** his **o**. H7928
Nu 7:19 The **o** he brought was one silver plate H7933
Nu 7:19 flour mixed with olive oil as a **grain o**; H4966
Nu 7:21 one male lamb a year old for a **burnt o**; H6592
Nu 7:22 one male goat for a **sin o**; H2633
Nu 7:23 year old to be sacrificed as a **fellowship o**. H8968
Nu 7:23 This was the **o** *of* Nethanel son of Zuar H7933
Nu 7:24 of the people of Zebulun, brought his **o**. NDT
Nu 7:25 His **o** was one silver plate weighing a H7933
Nu 7:25 flour mixed with olive oil as a **grain o**; H4966
Nu 7:27 one male lamb a year old for a **burnt o**; H6592
Nu 7:28 one male goat for a **sin o**; H2633
Nu 7:29 year old to be sacrificed as a **fellowship o**. H8968
Nu 7:29 This was the **o** *of* Eliab son of Helon. H7933
Nu 7:30 of the people of Reuben, brought his **o**. NDT
Nu 7:31 His **o** was one silver plate weighing a H7933
Nu 7:31 flour mixed with olive oil as a **grain o**; H4966
Nu 7:33 one male lamb a year old for a **burnt o**; H6592
Nu 7:34 one male goat for a **sin o**; H2633
Nu 7:35 year old to be sacrificed as a **fellowship o**. H8968
Nu 7:35 This was the **o** *of* Elizur son of Shedeur H7933
Nu 7:36 of the people of Simeon, brought his **o**. NDT
Nu 7:37 His **o** was one silver plate weighing a H7933
Nu 7:37 flour mixed with olive oil as a **grain o**; H4966
Nu 7:39 one male lamb a year old for a **burnt o**; H6592
Nu 7:40 one male goat for a **sin o**; H2633
Nu 7:41 year old to be sacrificed as a **fellowship o**. H8968
Nu 7:41 This was the **o** *of* Shelumiel son of H7933
Nu 7:42 leader of the people of Gad, brought his **o**. NDT
Nu 7:43 His **o** was one silver plate weighing a H7933
Nu 7:43 flour mixed with olive oil as a **grain o**; H4966
Nu 7:45 one male lamb a year old for a **burnt o**; H6592
Nu 7:46 one male goat for a **sin o**; H2633
Nu 7:47 year old to be sacrificed as a **fellowship o**. H8968
Nu 7:47 This was the **o** *of* Eliasaph son of Deuel H7933
Nu 7:48 of the people of Ephraim, brought his **o**. NDT
Nu 7:49 His **o** was one silver plate weighing a H7933
Nu 7:49 flour mixed with olive oil as a **grain o**; H4966
Nu 7:51 one male lamb a year old for a **burnt o**; H6592
Nu 7:52 one male goat for a **sin o**; H2633
Nu 7:53 year old to be sacrificed as a **fellowship o**. H8968
Nu 7:53 This was the **o** *of* Elishama son of H7933
Nu 7:54 of the people of Manasseh, brought his **o**. NDT
Nu 7:55 His **o** was one silver plate weighing a H7933
Nu 7:55 flour mixed with olive oil as a **grain o**; H4966
Nu 7:57 one male lamb a year old for a **burnt o**; H6592
Nu 7:58 one male goat for a **sin o**; H2633
Nu 7:59 year old to be sacrificed as a **fellowship o**. H8968
Nu 7:59 This was the **o** *of* Gamaliel son of H7933
Nu 7:60 of the people of Benjamin, brought his **o**. NDT
Nu 7:61 His **o** was one silver plate weighing a H7933
Nu 7:61 flour mixed with olive oil as a **grain o**; H4966
Nu 7:63 one male lamb a year old for a **burnt o**; H6592
Nu 7:64 one male goat for a **sin o**; H2633
Nu 7:65 year old to be sacrificed as a **fellowship o**. H8968
Nu 7:65 This was the **o** *of* Abidan son of Gideoni H7933
Nu 7:66 leader of the people of Dan, brought his **o**. NDT
Nu 7:67 His **o** was one silver plate weighing a H7933
Nu 7:67 flour mixed with olive oil as a **grain o**; H4966
Nu 7:69 one male lamb a year old for a **burnt o**; H6592
Nu 7:70 one male goat for a **sin o**; H2633
Nu 7:71 year old to be sacrificed as a **fellowship o**. H8968
Nu 7:71 This was the **o** *of* Ahiezer son of H7933
Nu 7:72 of the people of Asher, brought his **o**. NDT
Nu 7:73 His **o** was one silver plate weighing a H7933
Nu 7:73 flour mixed with olive oil as a **grain o**; H4966
Nu 7:75 one male lamb a year old for a **burnt o**; H6592
Nu 7:76 one male goat for a **sin o**; H2633
Nu 7:77 year old to be sacrificed as a **fellowship o**. H8968
Nu 7:77 This was the **o** *of* Pagiel son of Okran. H7933
Nu 7:78 of the people of Naphtali, brought his **o**. NDT
Nu 7:79 His **o** was one silver plate weighing a H7933
Nu 7:79 flour mixed with olive oil as a **grain o**; H4966
Nu 7:81 one male lamb a year old for a **burnt o**; H6592
Nu 7:82 one male goat for a **sin o**; H2633
Nu 7:83 year old to be sacrificed as a **fellowship o**. H8968
Nu 7:83 This was the **o** *of* Ahira son of Enan. H7933
Nu 7:87 of animals for the **burnt o** came to twelve H6592
Nu 7:87 a year old, together with their **grain o**. H4966
Nu 7:87 male goats were used for the **sin o**. H2633
Nu 7:88 sacrifice of the **fellowship o** came to H8968
Nu 8: 8 bull with its **grain o** *of* the finest flour H4966
Nu 8: 8 to take a second young bull for a **sin o**. H2633
Nu 8:11 the LORD as a **wave o** from the Israelites H9485
Nu 8:12 using one for a **sin o** to the LORD and the H2633
Nu 8:12 to the LORD and the other for a **burnt o**, H6592
Nu 8:13 present them as a **wave o** to the LORD. H9485
Nu 8:15 Levites and presented them as a **wave o**, H9485
Nu 8:21 them as a **wave o** before the LORD H9485
Nu 9: 7 presenting the LORD's **o** with the other H7933
Nu 9:13 the LORD's **o** at the appointed time H7933
Nu 15: 4 who brings an **o** shall present to the H7933
Nu 15: 4 to the LORD a **grain o** *of* a tenth of an H4966
Nu 15: 5 each lamb for the **burnt o** or the sacrifice, H6592
Nu 15: 5 a quarter of a hin of wine as a **drink o**. H5821
Nu 15: 6 a ram prepare a **grain o** *of* two-tenths of H4966
Nu 15: 7 a third of a hin of wine as a **drink o** H5821
Nu 15: 8 a young bull as a **burnt o** or sacrifice, H6592
Nu 15: 8 special vow or a **fellowship o** to the LORD, H8968
Nu 15: 9 with the bull a **grain o** *of* three-tenths of H4966
Nu 15:10 also bring half a hin of wine as a **drink o**. H5821
Nu 15:10 This will be a **food o**, an aroma pleasing to H852
Nu 15:13 when they present a **food o** as an aroma H852
Nu 15:14 among you presents a **food o** as an aroma H852
Nu 15:19 present a portion as an **o** to the LORD. H9556
Nu 15:20 present it as an **o** *from* the threshing floor H9556
Nu 15:21 you are to give this **o** to the LORD from the H9556
Nu 15:24 a young bull for a **burnt o** as an aroma H6592
Nu 15:24 its prescribed **grain o** and drink offering H4966
Nu 15:24 its prescribed grain offering and **drink o**, H5821
Nu 15:24 offering, and a male goat for a **sin o**. H2633
Nu 15:25 their wrong a food **o** and a sin offering. H7933
Nu 15:25 their wrong a food offering and a **sin o**. H2633
Nu 15:27 bring a year-old female goat for a **sin o**. H2633
Nu 16:15 said to the LORD, "Do not accept their **o**. H4966
Nu 16:35 the 250 men *who were* **o** the incense. H7928
Nu 18:17 as a food **o**, an aroma **pleasing** to the H5767
Nu 18:18 the breast of the **wave o** and the right H9485
Nu 18:24 the Israelites present as an **o** to the LORD. H9556
Nu 18:26 a tenth of that tithe as the LORD's **o**. H9556
Nu 18:27 Your **o** will be reckoned to you as grain H9556
Nu 18:28 also will present an **o** *to* the LORD from all H9556
Nu 19:17 the burned **purification o** into a jar and H2633
Nu 23: 3 "Stay here beside your **o** while I go aside. H6592
Nu 23: 6 him and found him standing beside his **o**, H6592
Nu 23:15 here beside your **o** while I meet with him H6592
Nu 23:17 him and found him standing beside his **o**, H6592
Nu 26:61 they **made an o** before the LORD *with* H7928
Nu 28: 3 'This is the **food o** you are to present to the H852
Nu 28: 3 as a regular **burnt o** each day. H6592
Nu 28: 5 together with a **grain o** of a tenth of an H4966
Nu 28: 6 This is the regular **burnt o** instituted at H6592
Nu 28: 6 a **food o** presented to the LORD. H852
Nu 28: 7 The accompanying **drink o** is to be a H5821
Nu 28: 7 Pour out the **drink o** to the LORD at the H5821
Nu 28: 8 the same kind of **grain o** and drink H4966
Nu 28: 8 grain offering and **drink o** that you offer in H5821
Nu 28: 8 This is a **food o**, an aroma pleasing to the H852
Nu 28: 9 make an **o** of two lambs a year old without NDT
Nu 28: 9 together with its **drink o** and a grain H5821
Nu 28: 9 offering and a **grain o** of two-tenths of an H4966
Nu 28:10 This is the **burnt o** *for* every Sabbath, in H6592
Nu 28:10 to the regular **burnt o** and its drink H6592
Nu 28:10 the regular burnt offering and its **drink o**. H5821
Nu 28:11 to the LORD a **burnt o** of two young bulls, H6592
Nu 28:12 there is to be a **grain o** of three-tenths of H4966
Nu 28:12 a **grain o** of two-tenths of an ephah of the H4966
Nu 28:13 a **grain o** of a tenth of an ephah of the H4966
Nu 28:13 This is for a **burnt o**, a pleasing aroma, H6592
Nu 28:13 a **food o** presented to the LORD. H852
Nu 28:14 there is to be a **drink o** of half a hin of H5821
Nu 28:14 is the monthly **burnt o** to be made at each H6592
Nu 28:15 Besides the regular **burnt o** with its drink H6592
Nu 28:15 the regular burnt offering with its **drink o**, H5821
Nu 28:15 is to be presented to the LORD as a **sin o**. H2633
Nu 28:19 Present to the LORD a **food o** consisting of a H852
Nu 28:19 consisting of a **burnt o** of two young bulls, H6592
Nu 28:20 each bull offer a **grain o** of three-tenths of H4966
Nu 28:22 male goat as a **sin o** to make atonement H2633
Nu 28:23 addition to the regular morning **burnt o**. H6592
Nu 28:24 way present the **food o** every day for seven H852
Nu 28:24 to the regular **burnt o** and its drink H6592
Nu 28:24 the regular burnt offering and its **drink o**. H5821
Nu 28:26 to the LORD an **o of** new **grain** during the H4966
Nu 28:27 Present a **burnt o** of two young bulls, one H6592
Nu 28:28 there is to be a **grain o** of three-tenths of H4966
Nu 28:31 to the regular **burnt o** and its grain H6592
Nu 28:31 the regular burnt offering and its **grain o**. H4966
Nu 29: 2 LORD, offer a **burnt o** of one young bull H6592
Nu 29: 3 the bull offer a **grain o** of three-tenths of H4966
Nu 29: 5 male goat as a **sin o** to make atonement H2633
Nu 29: 8 to the LORD a **burnt o** of one young bull, H6592
Nu 29: 9 the bull offer a **grain o** of three-tenths of H4966
Nu 29:11 Include one male goat as a **sin o**, in H2633
Nu 29:11 addition to the **sin o** *for* atonement and H2633
Nu 29:11 the regular **burnt o** with its grain H6592
Nu 29:11 the regular burnt offering with its **grain o**, H4966
Nu 29:13 to the LORD a **food o** consisting of a burnt H852
Nu 29:13 consisting of a **burnt o** of thirteen young H6592
Nu 29:14 bulls offer a **grain o** of three-tenths of an H4966
Nu 29:16 Include one male goat as a **sin o**, in H2633
Nu 29:16 to the regular **burnt o** with its grain H6592
Nu 29:16 offering with its **grain o** and drink offering. H4966
Nu 29:16 offering with its grain offering and **drink o**. H5821
Nu 29:19 Include one male goat as a **sin o**, in H2633
Nu 29:19 to the regular **burnt o** with its grain H6592
Nu 29:19 the regular burnt offering with its **grain o**, H4966
Nu 29:22 Include one male goat as a **sin o**, in H2633
Nu 29:22 to the regular **burnt o** with its grain H6592
Nu 29:22 offering with its **grain o** and drink offering. H4966
Nu 29:22 offering with its grain offering and **drink o**. H5821
Nu 29:25 Include one male goat as a **sin o**, in H2633
Nu 29:25 to the regular **burnt o** with its grain H6592
Nu 29:25 offering with its **grain o** and drink offering. H4966
Nu 29:25 offering with its grain offering and **drink o**. H5821
Nu 29:28 Include one male goat as a **sin o**, in H2633
Nu 29:28 to the regular **burnt o** with its grain H6592
Nu 29:28 offering with its **grain o** and drink offering. H4966
Nu 29:28 offering with its grain offering and **drink o**. H5821
Nu 29:31 Include one male goat as a **sin o**, in H2633
Nu 29:31 to the regular **burnt o** with its grain H6592
Nu 29:31 offering with its **grain o** and drink offering. H4966
Nu 29:31 offering with its grain offering and **drink o**. H5821
Nu 29:34 Include one male goat as a **sin o**, in H2633
Nu 29:34 to the regular **burnt o** with its grain H6592
Nu 29:34 offering with its **grain o** and drink offering. H4966
Nu 29:34 offering with its grain offering and **drink o**. H5821
Nu 29:36 to the LORD a **food o** consisting of a burnt H852
Nu 29:36 consisting of a **burnt o** of one bull, H6592
Nu 29:38 Include one male goat as a **sin o**, in H2633
Nu 29:38 to the regular **burnt o** with its grain H6592
Nu 29:38 offering with its **grain o** and drink offering. H4966
Nu 29:38 offering with its grain offering and **drink o**. H5821
Nu 31:50 have brought as an **o** *to* the LORD the gold H7933
Dt 2:26 king of Heshbon **o** peace and saying, H1821
Dt 13:16 its plunder as a **whole burnt o** to the LORD H4003
Dt 16:10 God by giving a **freewill o** in proportion to H5607
Jdg 6:18 and bring my **o** and set it before you." H4966
Jdg 6:26 offer the second bull as a **burnt o**. H6592
Jdg 11:31 and I will sacrifice it as a **burnt o**. H6592
Jdg 13:16 But if you prepare a **burnt o**, offer it to the H6592
Jdg 13:19 together with the **grain o**, and sacrificed it H4966
Jdg 13:23 have accepted a **burnt o** and grain H6592
Jdg 13:23 burnt offering and **grain o** from our hands, H4966
1Sa 2:17 were treating the LORD's **o** with contempt. H4966
1Sa 2:29 **o** that I prescribed *for* my dwelling? H4966
1Sa 2:29 parts of every **o** *made* by my people Israel H4966
1Sa 3:14 will never be atoned for by sacrifice or **o**. H4966
1Sa 6: 3 by all means send a **guilt o** to him. H871
1Sa 6: 4 "What **guilt o** should we send to him?" H871
1Sa 6: 8 you are sending back to him as a **guilt o**. H871
1Sa 6:14 the cows as a **burnt o** to the LORD. H6592
1Sa 6:17 Philistines sent as a **guilt o** to the LORD— H871
1Sa 7: 9 it *as* a whole **burnt o** to the LORD. H6592
1Sa 7:10 While Samuel was sacrificing the **burnt o** H6592
1Sa 13: 9 "Bring me the **burnt o** and the fellowship H6592
1Sa 13: 9 And Saul offered up the **burnt o**. H6592
1Sa 13:10 Just as he finished making the **o**, Samuel H6592
1Sa 13:12 So I felt compelled to offer the **burnt o**." H6592
1Sa 26:19 you against me, then may he accept an **o**. H4966
2Sa 15:12 While Absalom *was* **o** sacrifices, he also H2284
2Sa 24:22 Here are oxen for the **burnt o**, and here H6592
1Ki 13: 1 was standing by the altar to **make** *an* **o**. H7787
1Ki 18:33 pour it on the **o** and on the wood. H6592
2Ki 3:20 about the time for **o** the sacrifice, there it H6590
2Ki 10:25 as Jehu had finished making the **burnt o**, H6592
2Ki 16:13 He offered up his **burnt o** and grain H6592
2Ki 16:13 offered up his burnt offering and **grain o**, H4966
2Ki 16:13 poured out his **drink o**, and splashed the H5821
2Ki 16:15 offer the morning **burnt o** and the evening H6592
2Ki 16:15 burnt offering and the evening **grain o**, H4966
2Ki 16:15 the king's **burnt o** and his grain offering H6592
2Ki 16:15 the king's burnt offering and his **grain o** H4966
2Ki 16:15 the **burnt o** *of* all the people of the H6592
2Ki 16:15 their **grain o** and their drink offering. H4966
2Ki 16:15 their grain offering and their **drink o**. H5821
1Ch 6:49 on the altar of **burnt o** and on the altar of H6592
1Ch 9:31 the responsibility for baking the **o bread**. H2503
1Ch 16:29 bring an **o** and come before him. H4966
1Ch 16:40 the LORD on the altar of **burnt o** regularly, H6592

1Ch 21:23 the wood, and the wheat for the **grain o**. H4966
1Ch 21:24 sacrifice a **burnt o** that costs me H6592
1Ch 21:26 fire from heaven on the altar of **burnt o**. H6592
1Ch 21:29 the altar of **burnt o** were at that time H6592
1Ch 22: 1 also the altar of **burnt o** for Israel. H6592
2Ch 7: 1 consumed the **burnt o** and the H6592
2Ch 29:18 the altar of **burnt o** with all its utensils H6592
2Ch 29:21 male goats as a **sin o** for the kingdom, H2633
2Ch 29:23 The goats for the **sin o** were brought H2633
2Ch 29:24 **presented** their blood on the altar **for a sin o** H2627
2Ch 29:24 king had ordered the **burnt o** and the sin H6592
2Ch 29:24 burnt offering and the **sin o** for all Israel. H2633
2Ch 29:27 order to sacrifice the **burnt o** on the altar. H6592
2Ch 29:27 As the **o** began, singing to the LORD H6592
2Ch 29:28 sacrifice of the **burnt o** was completed. H6592
2Ch 35:16 Passover and the **o** *of* burnt offerings on H6590
Ezr 6:17 male lambs and, as a **sin o** for all Israel A10260
Ezr 8:25 out to them the **o** *of* silver and gold and H9556
Ezr 8:28 gold are a **freewill o** to the LORD, H5607
Ezr 8:35 lambs and, as a **sin o**, twelve male goats. H2633
Ezr 8:35 All this was a **burnt o** to the LORD. H6592
Ezr 10:19 presented a ram from the flock as a **guilt o**.) H871
Job 1: 5 would sacrifice a **burnt o** for each of them, H6592
Job 42: 8 Job and sacrifice a **burnt o** for yourselves. H6592
Ps 40: 6 Sacrifice and **o** you did not desire—but H4966
Ps 54: 6 I will sacrifice a **freewill o** to you; I will H5607
Ps 66:15 fat animals to you and an **o** *of* rams; H7792
Ps 96: 8 bring an **o** and come into his courts. H4966
Ps 116:17 sacrifice a thank **o** to you and call on the H2285
Pr 7:14 I have **food from** my fellowship **o** at home H2285
Isa 40:20 too poor to **present** *such* **an o** selects H9556
Isa 53:10 though the LORD makes his life an **o for sin**, H871
Isa 65: 3 **o sacrifices** in gardens and burning H2284
Isa 66: 3 *whoever* **makes** a grain **o** is like one who H6590
Isa 66:20 in Jerusalem as an **o** to the LORD— H4966
Eze 43:19 a young bull as a **sin o** to the Levitical H2633
Eze 43:21 the bull for the **sin o** and burn it in the H2633
Eze 43:22 a male goat without defect for a **sin o**, H2633
Eze 43:24 sacrifice them as a **burnt o** to the LORD. H6592
Eze 43:25 to provide a male goat daily for a **sin o**; H2633
Eze 44:27 he is to offer a **sin o** for himself, declares H2633
Eze 45:16 to give this **special o** to the prince in H9556
Eze 45:19 of the blood of the **sin o** and put it on the H2633
Eze 45:22 provide a bull as a **sin o** for himself and H2633
Eze 45:23 without defect as a **burnt o** to the LORD, H6592
Eze 45:23 to the LORD, and a male goat for a **sin o**. H2633
Eze 45:24 to provide as a **grain o** an ephah for each H4966
Eze 46: 2 to sacrifice his **burnt o** and his fellowship H6592
Eze 46: 4 The **burnt o** the prince brings to the LORD H6592
Eze 46: 5 The **grain o** given with the ram is to be an H4966
Eze 46: 5 the **grain o** with the lambs is to be as H4966
Eze 46: 7 is to provide as a **grain o** one ephah with H4966
Eze 46:11 the **grain o** is to be an ephah with a bull H4966
Eze 46:12 prince provides a **freewill o** to the LORD— H5607
Eze 46:12 whether a **burnt o** or fellowship offerings H6592
Eze 46:12 He shall offer his **burnt o** or his fellowship H6592
Eze 46:13 without defect for a **burnt o** to the LORD; H6592
Eze 46:14 with it morning by morning a **grain o**, H4966
Eze 46:14 presenting of this **grain o** to the LORD is a H4966
Eze 46:15 the lamb and the **grain o** and the oil shall H4966
Eze 46:15 morning by morning for a regular **burnt o**. H6592
Eze 46:20 are to cook the **guilt o** and the sin offering H871
Eze 46:20 offering and the **sin o** and bake the grain H2633
Eze 46:20 the sin offering and bake the **grain o**, H4966
Da 2:46 ordered that an **o** and incense be A10432
Da 9:27 he will put an end to sacrifice and **o**. H4966
Am 4: 5 bread as a **thank o** and brag about H9343
Mal 1: 7 "*By* **o** defiled food on my altar. "But you H5602
Mal 1: 8 *Try* **o** them to your governor H7928
Mal 1:10 "and I will accept no **o** from your hands. H4966
Mal 2:12 though he brings an **o** to the LORD H4966
Mt 5:23 if *you are* **o** your gift at the altar and there *G4712*
Jn 16: 2 you will think *they are* **o** a service to God. *G4712*
Ac 10: 4 come up as a **memorial o** before God. *G3649*
Ac 21:26 would end and the **o** would be made *G4714*
Ro 8: 3 in the likeness of sinful flesh to be a **sin o**. *G281*
Ro 15:16 might become an **o** acceptable to God, *G4714*
2Co 8:19 to accompany us as we carry the **o**, *G5921*
Eph 5: 2 us as a fragrant **o** and sacrifice to God. *G4714*
Php 2:17 if *I am being* **poured out like a drink o** on *G5064*
Php 4:18 They are a **fragrant o**, an *G4011+2380*
2Ti 4: 6 *am* already *being* **poured out like a drink o** *G5064*
Heb 10: 5 "Sacrifice and **o** you did not desire, but a *G4714*
Heb 11: 4 brought God a better **o** than Cain did. *G2602*
Heb 13:11 into the Most Holy Place *as* a **sin o**, *G4309+281*
1Pe 2: 5 **o** spiritual sacrifices acceptable to God *G429*

OFFERINGS (376) [OFFER]

Ge 8:20 clean birds, he sacrificed **burnt o** on it. H6592
Ex 10:25 sacrifices and **burnt o** to present to the H6592
Ex 20:24 sacrifice on it your **burnt o** and fellowship H6592
Ex 20:24 it your burnt offerings and **fellowship o**, H8968
Ex 22:29 "Do not hold back **o** from your granaries NDT
Ex 23:18 "The fat of my **festival o** must not be kept H2504
Ex 24: 5 they offered **burnt o** and sacrificed H6592
Ex 24: 5 young bulls as fellowship **o** to the LORD. H2285
Ex 25: 3 These are the **o** you are to receive from H9556
Ex 25:29 bowls *for the* **pouring out of o**. H5818
Ex 29:28 make to the LORD from their fellowship **o**. H2285
Ex 29:33 They are to eat **these o** by which H4392S
Ex 32: 6 early and sacrificed **burnt o** and presented H6592
Ex 32: 6 offerings and presented **fellowship o**. H8968
Ex 35:29 to the LORD **freewill o** for all the work H5607
Ex 36: 3 from Moses all the **o** the Israelites had H9556
Ex 36: 3 to bring **freewill o** morning after H5607
Ex 37:16 its pitchers for the **pouring out of drink o**. H5818
Ex 40:29 offered on it **burnt o** and grain H6592
Ex 40:29 offered on it burnt offerings and **grain o**, H4966
Lev 2: 3 part of the **food o** *presented to* the LORD. H852
Lev 2:10 part of the **food o** *presented to* the LORD. H852
Lev 2:13 Season all your **grain o** with salt. Do not H4966
Lev 2:13 covenant of your God out of your **grain o**; H4966
Lev 2:13 your grain offerings; add salt to all your **o**. H7933
Lev 4:35 on top of the **food o** *presented to* the LORD. H852
Lev 5:12 on top of the **food o** *presented to* the LORD. H852
Lev 6:12 burn the fat of the **fellowship o** on it. H8968
Lev 6:17 their share of the **food o** *presented to* me. H852
Lev 6:18 share of the **food o** *presented to* the LORD. H852
Lev 7:32 of your fellowship **o** to the priest as a H2285
Lev 7:34 From the fellowship **o** of the Israelites, H2285
Lev 7:35 of the **food o** *presented to* the LORD that H852
Lev 7:38 the Israelites to bring their **o** to the LORD. H7933
Lev 8:31 the bread from the basket of **ordination o**, H4854
Lev 10:12 **food o** prepared without yeast and *presented to* H852
Lev 10:13 share of the **food o** *presented to* the LORD; H852
Lev 10:14 your share of the Israelites' fellowship **o**. H2285
Lev 10:15 brought with the fat portions of the **food o**, H852
Lev 14:11 be cleansed and **their o** before the LORD H4392S
Lev 14:32 afford the regular **o** for their cleansing. NDT
Lev 16:27 The bull and the goat for the **sin o**, whose H2633
Lev 17: 5 sacrifice them as fellowship **o**. H2285
Lev 21: 6 they present the **food o** to the LORD, H852
Lev 21:21 near to present the **food o** to the LORD. H852
Lev 22: 2 with respect the **sacred o** the Israelites H7731
Lev 22: 3 comes near the **sacred o** that the H7731
Lev 22: 4 he may not eat the **sacred o** until he is H7731
Lev 22: 6 not eat any of the **sacred o** unless he has H7731
Lev 22: 7 after that he may eat the **sacred o**, for H7731
Lev 22:15 not desecrate the **sacred o** the Israelites H7731
Lev 22:16 them to eat the **sacred o** and so bring H7731
Lev 23:18 together with their **grain o** and drink H4966
Lev 23:18 with their grain offerings and **drink o**— H5821
Lev 23:36 For seven days present **food o** to the LORD H852
Lev 23:37 bringing **food o** to the LORD— H852
Lev 23:37 the LORD—the **burnt o** and grain offerings H6592
Lev 23:37 the burnt offerings and **grain o**, sacrifices H4966
Lev 23:37 sacrifices and **drink o** required for each H5821
Lev 23:38 These **o** are in addition to those for the NDT
Lev 23:38 all the **freewill o** you give to the H5607
Lev 24: 9 share of the **food o** *presented to* the LORD." H852
Lev 26:31 no delight in the pleasing aroma of your **o**. NDT
Nu 4: 7 the jars for **drink o**; the bread that is H5821
Nu 6:14 they are to present their **o** to the LORD: H7933
Nu 6:15 together with their **grain o** and drink H4966
Nu 6:15 with their grain offerings and **drink o**, H5821
Nu 6:21 of the Nazirite who vows **o** to the LORD in H7933
Nu 7: 2 of those who were counted, **made o**. H7928
Nu 7:10 brought their **o** *for* its dedication and H7933
Nu 7:84 **o** of the Israelite leaders **for the dedication** *of* H2853
Nu 7:88 were the **o for** the **dedication** *of* the altar H2853
Nu 10:10 trumpets over your **burnt o** and fellowship H6592
Nu 10:10 over your burnt offerings and fellowship **o**, H2285
Nu 15: 3 present to the LORD **food o** from the herd H852
Nu 15: 3 the LORD—whether **burnt o** or sacrifices, H6592
Nu 15: 3 special vows or **freewill o** or festival H5607
Nu 15: 3 vows or freewill offerings or **festival o**— H4595
Nu 18: 8 you in charge of the **o** *presented to* me; H9556
Nu 18: 8 all the **holy o** the Israelites give me I give H7731
Nu 18: 9 part of the **most holy o** that is kept H7731+7731
Nu 18: 9 gifts they bring me as **most holy o**, H7731+7731
Nu 18: 9 whether grain or sin or **guilt o**, that part H871
Nu 18:11 the gifts of all the **wave o** *of* the Israelites. H9485
Nu 18:19 is set aside from the **holy o** the Israelites H7731
Nu 18:32 will not defile the **holy o** *of* the Israelites, H7731
Nu 28: 2 at the appointed time my **food o**, H7933+852
Nu 28:31 Offer these together with their **drink o**, in H5821
Nu 29: 6 monthly and daily **burnt o** with their grain H6592
Nu 29: 6 with their **grain o** and drink offerings H4966
Nu 29: 6 grain offerings and **drink o** as specified. H5821
Nu 29: 6 They are **food o** presented to the LORD, H852
Nu 29:11 with its grain offering, and their **drink o**. H5821
Nu 29:18 offer their **grain o** and drink offerings H4966
Nu 29:18 offerings and **drink o** according to the H5821
Nu 29:19 with its grain offering, and their **drink o**. H5821
Nu 29:21 offer their **grain o** and drink offerings H4966
Nu 29:21 offerings and **drink o** according to the H5821
Nu 29:24 offer their **grain o** and drink offerings H4966
Nu 29:24 offerings and **drink o** according to the H5821
Nu 29:27 offer their **grain o** and drink offerings H4966
Nu 29:27 offerings and **drink o** according to the H5821
Nu 29:30 offer their **grain o** and drink offerings H4966
Nu 29:30 offerings and **drink o** according to the H5821
Nu 29:33 offer their **grain o** and drink offerings H4966
Nu 29:33 offerings and **drink o** according to the H5821
Nu 29:37 offer their **grain o** and drink offerings H4966
Nu 29:37 offerings and **drink o** according to the H5821
Nu 29:39 to what you vow and your **freewill o**, H5607
Nu 29:39 your **burnt o**, grain offerings, drink H6592
Nu 29:39 burnt offerings, **grain o**, drink offerings H4966
Nu 29:39 offerings, **drink o** and fellowship offerings. H5821
Nu 29:39 offerings, drink offerings and **fellowship o**. H8968
Dt 12: 6 there bring your **burnt o** and sacrifices H6592
Dt 12: 6 have vowed to give and your **freewill o**, H5607
Dt 12:11 your **burnt o** and sacrifices, your tithes H6592
Dt 12:13 to sacrifice your **burnt o** anywhere you H6592
Dt 12:17 or your **freewill o** or special gifts. H5607
Dt 12:27 Present your **burnt o** on the altar of the H6592
Dt 18: 1 live on the **food o** *presented to* the LORD, H852
Dt 27: 6 offer **burnt o** on it to the LORD H6592
Dt 27: 7 Sacrifice **fellowship o** there, eating them H8968
Dt 32:38 drank the wine of their **drink o**? H5816
Dt 33:10 you and **whole burnt o** on your altar H4003
Jos 8:31 offered to the LORD **burnt o** and sacrificed H6592
Jos 8:31 offerings and sacrificed **fellowship o**. H8968
Jos 13:14 since the **food o** *presented to* the LORD, the H852
Jos 22:23 LORD and to offer **burnt o** and grain H6592
Jos 22:23 to offer burnt offerings and **grain o**, H4966
Jos 22:23 to sacrifice fellowship **o** on it, may the H2285
Jos 22:26 an altar—but not for **burnt o** or sacrifices. H6592
Jos 22:27 the LORD at his sanctuary with our **burnt o**, H6592
Jos 22:27 offerings, sacrifices and **fellowship o**. H8968
Jos 22:28 not for **burnt o** and sacrifices, but as H6592
Jos 22:29 him today by building an altar for **burnt o**, H6592
Jos 22:29 burnt offerings, **grain o** and sacrifices H4966
Jdg 20:26 presented **burnt o** and fellowship H6592
Jdg 20:26 offerings and **fellowship o** to the LORD. H8968
Jdg 21: 4 presented **burnt o** and fellowship H6592
Jdg 21: 4 burnt offerings and **fellowship o**. H8968
1Sa 2:28 family all the **food o** *presented by* the H852
1Sa 6:15 Shemesh offered **burnt o** and made H6592
1Sa 10: 8 to you to sacrifice **burnt o** and fellowship H6592
1Sa 10: 8 sacrifice burnt offerings and fellowship **o**, H2285
1Sa 11:15 sacrificed fellowship **o** before the LORD, H2285
1Sa 13: 9 the burnt offering and the **fellowship o**." H8968
1Sa 15:22 LORD delight in **burnt o** and sacrifices as H6592
2Sa 6:17 David sacrificed **burnt o** and fellowship H6592
2Sa 6:17 offerings and **fellowship o** before the LORD H8968
2Sa 6:18 sacrificing the **burnt o** and fellowship H6592
2Sa 6:18 the burnt offerings and **fellowship o**, H8968
2Sa 24:24 to the LORD my God **burnt o** that cost me H6592
2Sa 24:25 sacrificed **burnt o** and fellowship H6592
2Sa 24:25 burnt offerings and **fellowship o**. H8968
1Ki 3: 4 offered a thousand **burnt o** on that altar. H6592
1Ki 3:15 sacrificed **burnt o** and fellowship H6592
1Ki 3:15 burnt offerings and **fellowship o**. H8968
1Ki 8:63 a sacrifice of fellowship **o** to the LORD: H2285
1Ki 8:64 there he offered **burnt o**, grain H6592
1Ki 8:64 **grain o** and the fat of the fellowship H4966
1Ki 8:64 offerings and the fat of the **fellowship o**, H8968
1Ki 8:64 LORD was too small to hold the **burnt o**, H6592
1Ki 8:64 the **grain o** and the fat of the fellowship H4966
1Ki 8:64 offerings and the fat of the **fellowship o**. H8968
1Ki 9:25 Solomon sacrificed **burnt o** and fellowship H6592
1Ki 9:25 offerings and **fellowship o** on the altar he H8968
1Ki 10: 5 the **burnt o** he made at the temple of H6592
1Ki 12:33 went up to the altar to **make o**. H7787
1Ki 13: 2 of the high places who **make o** here, H7787
2Ki 5:17 never again make **burnt o** and sacrifices H6592
2Ki 10:24 went in to make sacrifices and **burnt o**. H6592
2Ki 12: 4 is brought as **sacred o** to the temple of H7731
2Ki 12:16 The money from the **guilt o** and sin H871
2Ki 12:16 guilt offerings and **sin o** was not brought H2633
2Ki 16:12 he approached it and **presented o** on it. H6590
2Ki 16:13 the blood of his **fellowship o** against the H8968
2Ki 16:15 the blood of all the **burnt o** and sacrifices. H6592
1Ch 6:49 were the *ones who* **presented o** on the H7787
1Ch 16: 1 they presented **burnt o** and fellowship H6592
1Ch 16: 1 offerings and **fellowship o** before God. H8968
1Ch 16: 2 sacrificing the **burnt o** and fellowship H6592
1Ch 16: 2 the burnt offerings and **fellowship o**, H8968
1Ch 16:40 to present **burnt o** to the LORD on the altar H6592
1Ch 21:23 I will give the oxen for the **burnt o**, the H6592
1Ch 21:26 sacrificed **burnt o** and fellowship H6592
1Ch 21:26 burnt offerings and **fellowship o**. H8968
1Ch 23:29 the special flour for the **grain o**, the thin H4966
1Ch 23:31 whenever **burnt o** were presented to H6592
1Ch 29:21 to the LORD and presented **burnt o** to him: H6592
1Ch 29:21 together with their **drink o**, and other H5821
2Ch 1: 6 offered a thousand **burnt o** on it. H6592
2Ch 2: 4 for making **burnt o** every morning and H6592
2Ch 4: 6 to be used for the **burnt o** were rinsed, H6592
2Ch 7: 7 there he offered **burnt o** and the fat of the H6592
2Ch 7: 7 offerings and the fat of the **fellowship o**, H8968
2Ch 7: 7 he had made could not hold the **burnt o**, H6592
2Ch 7: 7 offerings, the **grain o** and the fat portions. H4966
2Ch 8:12 Solomon sacrificed **burnt o** to the LORD, H6592
2Ch 8:13 requirement for **o** commanded by Moses H6590
2Ch 9: 4 robes and the **burnt o** he made at the H6592
2Ch 13:11 evening they present **burnt o** and fragrant H6592
2Ch 23:18 to present the **burnt o** *of* the LORD as H6592
2Ch 24:14 articles for the service and for the **burnt o** H6590
2Ch 24:14 **burnt o** were presented continually in the H6592
2Ch 29: 7 present any **burnt o** at the sanctuary to H6592
2Ch 29:29 When the **o** were finished, the king and H6590
2Ch 29:31 sacrifices and **thank o** to the temple of H9343
2Ch 29:31 assembly brought sacrifices and **thank o**, H9343
2Ch 29:31 hearts were willing brought **burnt o**. H6592
2Ch 29:32 The number of **burnt o** the assembly H6592
2Ch 29:32 all of them for **burnt o** to the LORD. H6592
2Ch 29:34 were too few to skin all the **burnt o**; so H6592
2Ch 29:35 There were **burnt o** in abundance H6592
2Ch 29:35 the fat of the **fellowship o** and the drink H8968
2Ch 29:35 the **drink o** that accompanied H5821

2Ch 29:35 offerings that accompanied the **burnt o**. H6592
2Ch 30:15 brought **burnt o** to the temple of the H6592
2Ch 30:22 offered fellowship **o** and praised the LORD, H2285
2Ch 31: 2 to offer **burnt o** and fellowship offerings H6592
2Ch 31: 2 to offer burnt offerings and **fellowship o**, H8968
2Ch 31: 3 evening **burnt o** and for the burnt H6592
2Ch 31: 3 for the **burnt o** on the Sabbaths, H6592
2Ch 31:14 in charge of the **freewill o** *given to* God, H5607
2Ch 32:23 Many brought **o** to Jerusalem for the LORD H4966
2Ch 33:16 sacrificed fellowship **o** and thank offerings H2285
2Ch 33:16 fellowship offerings and **thank o** on it, H9343
2Ch 35: 7 lambs and goats for the **Passover o**, H7175
2Ch 35: 8 hundred **Passover o** and three hundred H7175
2Ch 35: 9 five thousand **Passover o** and five H7175
2Ch 35:12 They set aside the **burnt o** to give them to H6592
2Ch 35:13 boiled the **holy o** in pots, caldrons H7731
2Ch 35:14 were sacrificing the **burnt o** and the fat H6592
2Ch 35:16 the offering of **burnt o** on the altar of H6592
Ezr 1: 4 with **freewill o** for the temple of God H5607
Ezr 1: 6 in addition to all the **freewill o**. H5605
Ezr 2:68 of the families **gave freewill o** toward the H5605
Ezr 3: 2 the God of Israel to sacrifice **burnt o** on it, H6592
Ezr 3: 3 sacrificed **burnt o** on it to the LORD, H6592
Ezr 3: 4 required number of **burnt o** prescribed H6592
Ezr 3: 5 they presented the regular **burnt o**, the H6592
Ezr 3: 5 those **brought as freewill o** to the H5605+5607
Ezr 3: 6 they began to offer **burnt o** to the LORD, H6592
Ezr 6: 9 male lambs for **burnt o** to the God of A10545
Ezr 7:16 as well as the **freewill o** *of* the people A10461
Ezr 7:17 together with their **grain o** and drink A10432
Ezr 7:17 with their grain offerings and **drink o**, A10483
Ezr 8:35 captivity sacrificed **burnt o** to the God of H6592
Ne 10:33 the regular **grain o** and burnt offerings H4966
Ne 10:33 the regular grain offerings and **burnt o** H6592
Ne 10:33 offerings; for the **o** on the Sabbaths, at the NDT
Ne 10:33 festivals; for the **holy o**; for sin offerings to H7731
Ne 10:33 **sin o** to make atonement for Israel H2633
Ne 10:37 ground meal, of our *grain* **o**, of the fruit of H9556
Ne 13: 5 used to store the **grain o** and incense H4966
Ne 13: 9 with the **grain o** and the incense. H4966
Ps 20: 3 all your sacrifices and accept your **burnt o**. H6592
Ps 40: 6 **burnt o** and sin offerings you did not H6592
Ps 40: 6 burnt offerings and **sin o** you did not H2631
Ps 50: 8 your sacrifices or concerning your **burnt o**, H6592
Ps 50:14 "Sacrifice **thank o** to God, fulfill your vows H9343
Ps 50:23 Those who sacrifice **thank o** honor me H9343
Ps 51:16 you do not take pleasure in **burnt o**. H6592
Ps 51:19 the righteous, in **burnt o** offered whole H6592
Ps 56:12 my God; I will present my **thank o** to you. H9343
Ps 66:13 to your temple with **burnt o** and fulfill my H6592
Ps 107:22 them sacrifice thank **o** and tell of his H2285
Isa 1:11 "I have more than enough of **burnt o**, of H6592
Isa 1:13 Stop bringing meaningless **o**! Your H4966
Isa 19:21 will worship with sacrifices and **grain o**; H4966
Isa 40:16 nor its animals enough for **burnt o**. H6592
Isa 43:23 have not brought me sheep for **burnt o**, H6592
Isa 43:23 you with **grain o** nor wearied you H4966
Isa 56: 7 Their **burnt o** and sacrifices will be H6592
Isa 57: 6 have poured out **drink o** and offered grain H5821
Isa 57: 6 out drink offerings and offered **grain o**. H4966
Isa 60: 7 *they will be* accepted *as* **o** *on* my altar H6590
Isa 66:20 as the Israelites bring their **grain o**, to the H4966
Jer 6:20 Your **burnt o** are not acceptable; your H6592
Jer 7:18 They pour out **drink o** to other gods to H5821
Jer 7:21 add your **burnt o** to your other sacrifices H6592
Jer 7:22 commands about **burnt o** and sacrifices, H6592
Jer 14:12 though they offer **burnt o** and grain H6592
Jer 14:12 they offer burnt offerings and **grain o**, H4966
Jer 17:26 the Negev, bringing **burnt o** and sacrifices H6592
Jer 17:26 sacrifices, **grain o** and incense, and H4966
Jer 17:26 bringing **thank o** to the house of the H9343
Jer 19: 5 their children in the fire as **o** to Baal— H6592
Jer 19:13 poured out **drink o** to other gods. H5821
Jer 32:29 by pouring out **drink o** to other gods. H5821
Jer 33:11 those who bring **thank o** to the house of H9343
Jer 33:18 before me continually to offer **burnt o**, H6592
Jer 33:18 to burn **grain o** and to present sacrifices. H4966
Jer 41: 5 bringing **grain o** and incense with them to H4966
Jer 44:17 will pour out **drink o** to her just as we H5821
Jer 44:18 of Heaven and pouring out **drink o** to her, H5821
Jer 44:19 of Heaven and poured out **drink o** to her, H5821
Jer 44:19 her image and pouring out **drink o** to her?" H5821
Jer 44:25 pour out **drink o** to the Queen of H5821
Jer 48:35 an end to *those who* **make o** *on* the high H6590
Jer 52:19 dishes and **bowls used for drink o**—all H4984
Eze 20:28 sacrifices, made **o** that aroused my anger H7933
Eze 20:28 incense and poured out their **drink o**. H5821
Eze 20:40 I will require your **o** and your choice gifts, H9556
Eze 36:38 as the flocks for **o** at Jerusalem during her H7731
Eze 40:38 where the **burnt o** were washed. H6592
Eze 40:39 on which the **burnt o**, sin offerings H6592
Eze 40:39 **sin o** and guilt offerings were slaughtered. H2633
Eze 40:39 sin offerings and **guilt o** were slaughtered. H871
Eze 40:42 tables of dressed stone for the **burnt o**, H6592
Eze 40:42 slaughtering the **burnt o** and the other H6592
Eze 40:43 The tables were for the flesh of the **o**. H7933
Eze 42:13 the LORD will eat the **most holy o**. H7731+7731
Eze 42:13 they will put the **most holy o**— H7731+7731
Eze 42:13 holy offerings—the **grain o**, the sin H4966
Eze 42:13 offerings, the **sin o** and the guilt offerings H2633
Eze 42:13 the sin offerings and the **guilt o**—for the H871
Eze 43: 7 the **funeral o** *for* their kings at H7007
Eze 43: 9 the **funeral o** *for* their kings, H7007
Eze 43:18 sacrificing **burnt o** and splashing blood H6592
Eze 43:27 are to present your **burnt o** and fellowship H6592
Eze 43:27 offerings and **fellowship o** on the altar. H8968
Eze 44:11 may slaughter the **burnt o** and sacrifices H6592
Eze 44:13 my holy things or my **most holy o**; H7731+7731
Eze 44:29 They will eat the **grain o**, the sin offerings H4966
Eze 44:29 offerings, the **sin o** and the guilt offerings H2633
Eze 44:29 the sin offerings and the **guilt o**; and H871
Eze 45:15 These will be used for the **grain o**, burnt H4966
Eze 45:15 **burnt o** and fellowship offerings to make H6592
Eze 45:15 offerings and **fellowship o** to make H8968
Eze 45:17 duty of the prince to provide the **burnt o**, H6592
Eze 45:17 **grain o** and drink offerings at the festivals H4966
Eze 45:17 grain offerings and **drink o** at the festivals H5821
Eze 45:17 He will provide the **sin o**, grain offerings H2633
Eze 45:17 the sin offerings, **grain o**, burnt offerings H4966
Eze 45:17 **burnt o** and fellowship offerings to make H6592
Eze 45:17 offerings and **fellowship o** to make H8968
Eze 45:25 he is to make the same provision for **sin o**, H2633
Eze 45:25 sin offerings, **burnt o**, grain offerings H6592
Eze 45:25 offerings, burnt offerings, **grain o** and oil. H4966
Eze 46: 2 his burnt offering and his **fellowship o**. H8968
Eze 46:12 whether a burnt offering or **fellowship o** H8968
Eze 46:12 offering or his **fellowship o** as he does on H8968
Hos 4:13 the mountaintops and **burn o** on the hills, H7787
Hos 6: 6 of God rather than **burnt o**. H6592
Hos 8:11 Ephraim built many altars for **sin o**, H2627
Hos 9: 4 They will not pour out **wine o** to the LORD H3516
Joel 1: 9 **Grain o** and drink offerings are cut off H4966
Joel 1: 9 offerings and **drink o** are cut off from H5821
Joel 1:13 the **grain o** and drink offerings are H4966
Joel 1:13 offerings and **drink o** are withheld from H5821
Joel 2:14 **grain o** and drink offerings for the LORD H4966
Joel 2:14 offerings and **drink o** for the LORD your H5821
Am 4: 5 offering and brag about your **freewill o**— H5607
Am 5:22 though you bring me **burnt o** and grain H6592
Am 5:22 you bring me burnt offerings and **grain o**, H4966
Am 5:22 Though you bring choice **fellowship o**, H8968
Am 5:25 bring me sacrifices and **o** forty years in the H4966
Mic 6: 6 Shall I come before him with **burnt o**, with H6592
Zep 3:10 my scattered people, will bring me **o**. H4966
Mal 1: 9 With **such o** from your hands, will he H2296S
Mal 1:11 incense and pure **o** will be brought to me, H4966
Mal 2:13 with favor on your **o** or accepts them with H4966
Mal 3: 3 men who will bring **o** in righteousness, H4966
Mal 3: 4 the **o** *of* Judah and Jerusalem will be H4966
Mal 3: 8 are we robbing you?' "In tithes and **o**. H9556
Mk 12:33 important than all **burnt o** and sacrifices." *G3906*
Mk 12:41 the **place where the o were put** and *G1126*
Jn 8:20 near the **place where the o were put**. *G1126*
Ac 7:42 bring me sacrifices and **o** forty years in the *G2602*
Ac 24:17 people gifts for the poor and to present **o**. *G4714*
Heb 10: 6 *with* **burnt o** and sin offerings you were *G3906*
Heb 10: 6 offerings and **sin o** you were not *G4309+281*
Heb 10: 8 "Sacrifices and **o**, burnt offerings and *G4714*
Heb 10: 8 **burnt o** and sin offerings you did not *G3906*
Heb 10: 8 offerings and **sin o** you did not *G4309+281*
Heb 11: 4 righteous, when God spoke well of his **o**. *G1565*

OFFERS (9) [OFFER]

Lev 6:26 The priest who **o** it shall eat it; it is to be H2627
Lev 7: 8 The priest who **o** a burnt offering for H7928
Lev 7: 9 a griddle belongs to the priest who **o** it, H7928
Lev 7:33 The son of Aaron who **o** the blood and the H7928
Lev 17: 8 among them who **o** a burnt offering or H6590
Dt 33:10 *He* **o** incense before you and whole burnt H8492
Isa 66: 3 and *whoever* **o** a lamb is like one who H2284
Titus 2:11 has appeared *that* **o salvation** to all *G5403*
Heb 10:11 again and again *he* **o** the same sacrifices *G4712*

OFFICE (7) [OFFICER, OFFICERS, OFFICIAL, OFFICIALS, OFFICIATE]

Dt 17: 9 to the **judge** who is **in o** at that time. H9149
Dt 19:17 the **judges** who are **in o** at the time. H9149
Dt 26: 3 say to the priest **in o** at the time, "I H2118
1Sa 2:36 me to some **priestly o** so I can have food H3914
Ne 13:29 they defiled the **priestly o** and the H3914
Isa 22:19 I will depose you from your **o**, and you H5163
Heb 7:23 prevented them from **continuing in o**; *G4169*

OFFICER (32) [OFFICE]

1Sa 29: 3 who was an **o** *of* Saul king of Israel? H6269
2Ki 3:11 An **o** *of* the king of Israel answered H6269
2Ki 7: 2 The **o** on whose arm the king was leaning H8957
2Ki 7:17 the king had put the **o** on whose arm he H8957
2Ki 7:19 The **o** had said to the man of God, "Look H8957
2Ki 9:25 to Bidkar, his **chariot o**, "Pick him up and H8957
2Ki 18:17 his chief **o** and his field commander with H6247
2Ki 18:24 can you repulse one **o** *of* the least of my H7068
2Ki 25:19 he took the **o** in charge of the fighting H6247
2Ki 25:19 who was **chief o** in charge of H8569+2021+7372
2Ch 24:11 secretary and the **o** *of* the chief priest H7224
2Ch 26:11 Maaseiah the **o** under the direction H8853
2Ch 28: 7 Azrikam the **o in charge** *of* the palace H5592
Ezr 4: 8 Rehum the **commanding o** and A10116+10302
Ezr 4: 9 Rehum the **commanding o** and A10116+10302
Ezr 4:17 To Rehum the **commanding o** A10116+10302
Ne 11: 9 Joel son of Zikri was their **chief o**, and H7224
Ne 11:14 Their **chief o** was Zabdiel son of H7224
Ne 11:22 The **chief o** *of* the Levites in Jerusalem H7224
Isa 33:18 "Where is that **chief o**? Where is the one H6221
Isa 33:18 Where is the **o in charge** *of* the towers?" H6221
Isa 36: 9 repulse one **o** *of* the least *of* my master's H7068
Jer 39: 3 Nebo-Sarsekim a chief **o** H6247
Jer 39:13 Nebushazban a chief **o**, Nergal-Sharezer H6247
Jer 51:59 gave to the staff **o** Seraiah son of Neriah, H8569
Jer 52:25 he took the **o** in charge of the fighting H6247
Jer 52:25 who was **chief o** in charge of H8569+2021+7372
Da 2:15 He asked the king's **o**, "Why did the king A10718
Mt 5:25 the judge may hand you over *to* the **o**, *G5677*
Lk 12:58 the judge turn you over *to* the **o**, and *G4551*
Lk 12:58 and the **o** throw you into prison. *G4551*
2Ti 2: 4 rather tries to please his **commanding o**. *G5133*

OFFICERS (83) [OFFICE]

Ex 14: 7 chariots of Egypt, with **o** over all of them. H8957
Ex 15: 4 best of Pharaoh's **o** are drowned in the H8957
Nu 31:14 Moses was angry with the **o** *of* the army H7212
Nu 31:48 Then the **o** who were over the units of the H7212
Dt 20: 5 The **o** shall say to the army: "Has anyone H8853
Dt 20: 8 Then the **o** shall add, "Is anyone afraid H8853
Dt 20: 9 When the **o** have finished speaking to the H8853
Jos 1:10 So Joshua ordered the **o** *of* the people: H8853
Jos 3: 2 After three days the **o** went throughout the H8853
1Sa 18: 5 all the troops, and Saul's **o** as well. H6269
1Sa 18:30 more success than the rest of Saul's **o**, H6269
2Sa 8: 7 that belonged to the **o** *of* Hadadezer and H6269
1Ki 9:22 government officials, his **o**, his captains, H8569
1Ki 20:14 'The **junior o** *under* the provincial H5853
1Ki 20:15 the 232 **junior o** *under* the provincial H5853
1Ki 20:17 The **junior o** *under* the provincial H5853
1Ki 20:19 The **junior o** *under* the provincial H5853
1Ki 20:24 replace them with *other* **o**. H7068
2Ki 6: 8 After conferring with his **o**, he said, "I will H6269
2Ki 6:11 He summoned his **o** and demanded of H6269
2Ki 6:12 said one of his **o**, "but Elisha, the H6269
2Ki 7:12 king got up in the night and said to his **o**, H6269
2Ki 7:13 One of his **o** answered, "Have some men H6269
2Ki 9: 5 he found the army **o** sitting together. H8569
2Ki 9:11 When Jehu went out to his **fellow o** H6269+123
2Ki 10:25 offering, he ordered the guards and **o**: H8957
2Ki 10:25 The guards and **o** threw the bodies out H8957
2Ki 11:14 The **o** and the trumpeters were beside the H8569
2Ki 15:25 One of his **chief o**, Pekah son of Remaliah H8957
2Ki 24:10 At that time the **o** *of* Nebuchadnezzar H6269
2Ki 24:11 to the city while his **o** were besieging it. H6269
2Ki 24:14 all the **o** and fighting men, and all the H8569
2Ki 25:23 When all the army **o** and their men heard H8569
2Ki 25:26 together with the army **o**, fled to Egypt H8569
1Ch 11:11 was chief of the **o**; he raised his spear H8957
1Ch 12:28 young warrior, with 22 **o** from his family; H8569
1Ch 12:34 from Naphtali—1,000 **o**, together with H8569
1Ch 13: 1 David conferred with each of his **o**, the H5592
1Ch 18: 7 carried by the **o** *of* Hadadezer and H6269
1Ch 27: 1 hundreds, and their **o**, who served the H8853
1Ch 27: 3 chief of all the army **o** for the first month. H8569
1Ch 28: 1 the **o** *over* the tribes, the commanders of H8569
1Ch 29: 6 of families, the **o** *of* the tribes of Israel H8569
1Ch 29:24 All the **o** and warriors, as well as all of H8569
2Ch 21: 9 went there with his **o** and all his chariots. H8569
2Ch 23:13 The **o** and the trumpeters were beside the H8569
2Ch 32: 6 appointed military **o** over the people and H8569
2Ch 32: 9 he sent his **o** to Jerusalem with this H6269
2Ch 32:16 Sennacherib's **o** spoke further against the H6269
2Ch 32:21 the commanders and **o** in the camp of the H8569
2Ch 35:23 and he told his **o**, "Take me away; H6269
Ne 2: 9 had also sent army **o** and cavalry with me. H8569
Ne 4:16 The **o** posted themselves behind all the H8569
Est 2:21 two of the king's **o** who guarded the H6247
Est 6: 2 two of the king's **o** who guarded the H6247
Isa 21: 5 Get up, you **o**, oil the shields! H8569
Jer 26:21 all his **o** and officials heard H1475
Jer 38:17 surrender to the **o** *of* the king of Babylon H8569
Jer 38:18 surrender to the **o** *of* the king of Babylon H8569
Jer 39:13 all the other **o** *of* the king of Babylon H8042
Jer 40: 7 When all the army **o** and their men who H8569
Jer 40:13 all the army **o** still in the open H8569
Jer 41: 1 blood and had been one of the king's **o**, H8042
Jer 41:11 all the army **o** who were with him H8569
Jer 41:13 the army **o** who were with him, H8569
Jer 41:16 all the army **o** who were with him led H8569
Jer 42: 1 Then all the army **o**, including Johanan H8569
Jer 42: 8 all the army **o** who were with him H8569
Jer 43: 4 all the army **o** and all the people H8569
Jer 43: 5 all the army **o** led away all the H8569
Jer 46:26 king of Babylon and his **o**. H6269
Jer 51:57 her governors, **o** and warriors as well; they H6036
Eze 23:15 of them looked like Babylonian **chariot o**, H8957
Eze 23:23 **chariot o** and men of high rank H8957
Lk 22: 4 the **o of the temple guard** and *G5130*
Lk 22:52 the **o of the temple guard**, and the *G5130*
Ac 5:22 at the jail, the **o** did not find them there. *G5677*
Ac 5:26 captain went with his **o** and brought the *G5677*
Ac 16:35 sent their **o** to the jailer with the *G4812*
Ac 16:37 But Paul said to **the o**: "They beat us *G899S*
Ac 16:38 The **o** reported this to the magistrates *G4812*
Ac 21:32 He at once took *some* **o** and soldiers and *G1672*
Ac 25:23 with the **high-ranking military o** and the *G5941*

OFFICIAL (26) [OFFICE]

2Ki 8: 6 Then he assigned an **o** to her case and H6247
2Ki 23:11 the room of an **o** named Nathan-Melek. H6247
2Ki 25: 8 an **o** *of* the king of Babylon H6269

1Ch 9:11 the o in charge of the house of God H5592
1Ch 9:20 of Eleazar was the o in charge of the H5592
1Ch 26:24 was the o in charge of the treasuries. H5592
2Ch 13: 6 of Nebat, an o of Solomon son of David H6269
2Ch 31:13 Azariah the o in charge of the temple of H5592
Ne 2:10 Tobiah the Ammonite o heard about this, H6269
Ne 2:19 the Ammonite o and Geshem the Arab H6269
Ne 11:11 the o in charge of the house of God H5592
Ecc 5: 8 for one o is eyed by a higher one H1469
Jer 20: 1 the o in charge of the temple of the LORD H7224
Jer 38: 7 a Cushite, an o in the royal palace, heard H6247
Jer 39: 3 a high o and all the other H4454
Jer 39:13 a high o and all the other H4454
Da 1: 7 The chief o gave them new names: to H6247
Da 1: 8 he asked the chief o for permission not to H6247
Da 1: 9 God had caused the o to show favor and H6247
Da 1:10 the o told Daniel, "I am afraid of my H6247
Da 1:11 whom the chief o had appointed over H6247
Da 1:18 the chief o presented them to H6247
Jn 4:46 was a certain royal o whose son lay sick G997
Jn 4:49 The royal o said, "Sir, come down before G997
Ac 8:27 an important o in charge of all the G1541
Ac 28: 7 to Publius, the chief o of the island. AIT

OFFICIALS (244) [OFFICE]

Ge 12:15 And when Pharaoh's o saw her, they H8569
Ge 20: 8 morning Abimelek summoned all his o, H6269
Ge 37:36 Potiphar, one of Pharaoh's o, the captain H6247
Ge 39: 1 an Egyptian who was one of Pharaoh's o H6247
Ge 40: 2 Pharaoh was angry with his two o, the H6247
Ge 40: 7 he asked Pharaoh's o who were in H6247
Ge 40:20 birthday, and he gave a feast for all his o. H6269
Ge 40:20 the chief baker in the presence of his o: H6269
Ge 41:37 seemed good to Pharaoh and to all his o. H6269
Ge 45:16 Pharaoh and all his o were pleased. H6269
Ge 50: 7 All Pharaoh's o accompanied him—the H6269
Ex 5:21 to Pharaoh and his o and have put a H6269
Ex 7:10 staff down in front of Pharaoh and his o, H6269
Ex 7:20 of Pharaoh and his o and struck the water H6269
Ex 8: 3 the houses of your o and on your people, H6269
Ex 8: 4 up on you and your people and all your o. H6269
Ex 8: 9 you and your o and your people that H6269
Ex 8:11 your houses, your o and your people; they H6269
Ex 8:21 send swarms of flies on you and your o, H6269
Ex 8:24 palace and into the houses of his o; H6269
Ex 8:29 leave Pharaoh and his o and his people. H6269
Ex 8:31 left Pharaoh and his o and his people; H6269
Ex 9:14 you and against your o and your people, H6269
Ex 9:20 Those o of Pharaoh who feared the word H6269
Ex 9:30 that you and your o still do not fear the H6269
Ex 9:34 He and his o hardened their hearts H6269
Ex 10: 1 the hearts of his o so that I may perform H6269
Ex 10: 6 those of all your o and all the Egyptians H6269
Ex 10: 7 Pharaoh's o said to him, "How long will H6269
Ex 11: 3 Egypt by Pharaoh's o and by the people.) H6269
Ex 11: 8 All these o of yours will come to me H6269
Ex 12:30 Pharaoh and all his o and all the H6269
Ex 14: 5 Pharaoh and his o changed their minds H6269
Ex 18:21 appoint them as o over thousands H8569
Ex 18:25 of the people, o over thousands H8569
Nu 11:16 you as leaders and o among the people. H8853
Nu 22: 8 So the Moabite o stayed with him. H8569
Nu 22:13 Balaam got up and said to Balak's o, H8569
Nu 22:14 So the Moabite o returned to Balak and H8569
Nu 22:15 Then Balak sent other o, more numerous H8569
Nu 22:21 his donkey and went with the Moabite o. H8569
Nu 22:35 So Balaam went with Balak's o. H8569
Nu 22:40 to Balaam and the o who were with him. H8569
Nu 23: 6 his offering, with all the Moabite o. H8569
Nu 23:17 beside his offering, with the Moabite o. H8569
Nu 26: 9 were the community o who rebelled H7951
Dt 1:15 of fifties and of tens and as tribal o. H8853
Dt 16:18 Appoint judges and o for each of your H8853
Dt 29: 2 Pharaoh, to all his o and to all his land. H6269
Dt 29:10 your elders and o, and all the other H8853
Dt 31:28 all the elders of your tribes and all your o, H8853
Dt 34:11 to all his o and to his whole land. H6269
Jos 8:33 with their elders, o and judges, were H8853
Jos 23: 2 leaders, judges and o—and said to them: H8853
Jos 24: 1 leaders, judges and o of Israel, and they H8853
Jdg 8: 6 But the o of Sukkoth said, "Do you already H8569
Jdg 8:14 names of the seventy-seven o of Sukkoth, H8569
1Sa 8:15 give it to his o and attendants. H6247
1Sa 22: 6 with all his o standing at his side. H6269
1Sa 22: 9 who was standing with Saul's o, said, H6269
1Sa 22:17 But the king's o were unwilling to raise a H6269
2Sa 15:14 said to all his o who were with him in H6269
2Sa 15:15 The king's o answered him, "Your H6269
2Sa 16: 6 David and all the king's o with stones, H6269
2Sa 16:11 David then said to Abishai and all his o H6269
2Sa 24:20 the king and his o coming toward him, H6269
1Ki 1: 9 and all the royal o of Judah, H6269+408
1Ki 1:47 the royal o have come to congratulate our H6269
1Ki 4: 2 And these were his chief o: Azariah son of H8569
1Ki 9:22 his government o, his officers, H6269
1Ki 9:23 were also the chief o in charge of H5893
1Ki 9:23 550 o supervising those who did the work. H8097
1Ki 10: 5 the seating of his o, the attending H6269
1Ki 10: 8 How happy your o, who continually stand H6269
1Ki 11:17 with some Edomite o who had served his H408
1Ki 11:26 He was one of Solomon's o, an H6269
1Ki 15:18 He entrusted it to his o and sent them to H6269
1Ki 16: 9 one of his o, who had command of H6269
1Ki 20: 6 am going to send my o to search your H6269
1Ki 20: 6 your palace and the houses of your o. H6269
1Ki 20:23 the o of the king of Aram advised him H6269
1Ki 20:31 His o said to him, "Look, we have heard H6269
1Ki 22: 3 The king of Israel had said to his o, "Don't H6269
1Ki 22: 9 king of Israel called one of his o and said, H6247
2Ki 10: 1 to the o of Jezreel, to the elders and to H8569
2Ki 12:20 His o conspired against him and H6269
2Ki 12:21 The o who murdered him were Jozabad H6269
2Ki 14: 5 he executed the o who had murdered his H6269
2Ki 18:24 one officer of the least of my master's o, H6269
2Ki 19: 5 When King Hezekiah's o came to Isaiah, H6269
2Ki 21:23 Amon's o conspired against him and H6269
2Ki 22: 9 "Your o have paid out the money that was H6269
2Ki 24:12 his nobles and his o all surrendered to H6247
2Ki 24:15 his o and the prominent people of the H6247
2Ki 25:24 "Do not be afraid of the Babylonian o," H6269
1Ch 18:17 David's sons were chief o at the king's H8037
1Ch 23: 4 six thousand are to be o and judges. H8853
1Ch 24: 5 there were o of the sanctuary and H8569
1Ch 24: 5 of the sanctuary and o of God among the H8569
1Ch 24: 6 in the presence of the king and of the o: H8569
1Ch 26:29 the temple, as o and judges over Israel. H8853
1Ch 27:31 were the o in charge of King David's H8569
1Ch 28: 1 summoned all the o of Israel to assemble H8569
1Ch 28: 1 the o in charge of all the property H8569
1Ch 28: 1 together with the palace o, the warriors H6247
1Ch 28:21 The o and all the people will obey your H8569
1Ch 29: 6 the o in charge of the king's work H8569
2Ch 8:10 They were also King Solomon's chief o H5893
2Ch 8:10 hundred and fifty o supervising the men. H8097
2Ch 9: 4 the seating of his o, the attending H6269
2Ch 9: 7 How happy your o, who continually stand H6269
2Ch 17: 7 year of his reign he sent his o Ben-Hail, H8569
2Ch 18: 8 king of Israel called one of his o and said, H6247
2Ch 19:11 the Levites will serve as o before you. H8853
2Ch 21: 4 sword along with some of the o of Israel. H8569
2Ch 22: 8 he found the o of Judah and the sons of H8569
2Ch 24:10 All the o and all the people brought their H8569
2Ch 24:11 Levites to the king's o and they saw that H7213
2Ch 24:17 the o of Judah came and paid homage to H8569
2Ch 24:25 His o conspired against him for murdering H6269
2Ch 25: 3 he executed the o who had murdered his H6269
2Ch 26:11 direction of Hananiah, one of the royal o. H8569
2Ch 28:14 the presence of the o and all the H8569
2Ch 28:21 from the o and presented them H8569
2Ch 29:20 gathered the city o together and went up H8569
2Ch 29:30 Hezekiah and his o ordered the Levites H8569
2Ch 30: 2 The king and his o and the whole H8569
2Ch 30: 6 with letters from the king and from his o, H8569
2Ch 30:12 out what the king and his o had ordered, H8569
2Ch 30:24 the o provided them with a thousand H8569
2Ch 31: 8 Hezekiah and his o came and saw the H8569
2Ch 32: 3 he consulted with his o and military staff H8569
2Ch 33:24 Amon's o conspired against him and H6269
2Ch 34:16 "Your o are doing everything that has H6269
2Ch 35: 8 His o also contributed voluntarily to the H8569
2Ch 35: 8 the o in charge of God's temple H5592
2Ch 36:18 the treasures of the king and his o. H8569
Ezr 4: 5 They bribed o to work against them and H3446
Ezr 4: 9 o and administrators over the people A10062
Ezr 5: 6 associates, the o of Trans-Euphrates A10061
Ezr 6: 6 you other o of that province, A10061
Ezr 7:28 his advisers and all the king's powerful o. H8569
Ezr 8:20 that David and the o had established to H8569
Ezr 8:25 his o and all Israel present there had H8569
Ezr 9: 2 the leaders and o have led the way in H6036
Ezr 10: 8 with the decision of the o and elders, H8569
Ezr 10:14 Let our o act for the whole assembly. H8569
Ne 2:16 The o did not know where I had gone or H6036
Ne 2:16 priests or nobles or o or any others who H6036
Ne 4:14 the o and the rest of the people H6036
Ne 4:19 the o and the rest of the people H6036
Ne 5: 7 mind and then accused the nobles and o. H6036
Ne 5:12 made the nobles and o take an H4392S
Ne 5:17 fifty Jews and o ate at my table, H6036
Ne 7: 5 the o and the common people for H6036
Ne 9:10 against all his o and all the people of his H6269
Ne 12:40 so did I, together with half the o, H6036
Ne 13:11 So I rebuked the o and asked them, "Why H6036
Est 1: 3 gave a banquet for all his nobles and o. H6269
Est 2:18 Esther's banquet, for all his nobles and o. H6269
Est 2:23 the two o were impaled on poles. H2157S
Est 3: 2 All the royal o at the king's gate knelt H6269
Est 3: 3 Then the royal o at the king's gate asked H6269
Est 4:11 "All the king's o and the people of the H6269
Est 5:11 him above the other nobles and o. H6269
Job 12:19 stripped and overthrows o long established. AIT
Pr 17:26 surely to flog honest o is not right. H5618
Pr 22:29 they will not serve before o of low rank. H3126
Pr 24:21 and do not join with rebellious o, AIT
Pr 25: 5 remove wicked o from the king's presence AIT
Pr 29:12 listens to lies, all his o become wicked. H9250
Isa 3: 4 "I will make mere youths their o; children H8569
Isa 19:11 The o of Zoan are nothing but fools; the H8569
Isa 19:13 The o of Zoan have become fools, the H8569
Isa 30: 4 Though they have o in Zoan and their H8569
Isa 36: 9 one officer of the least of my master's o, H6269
Isa 37: 5 When King Hezekiah's o came to Isaiah, H6269
Jer 1:18 kings of Judah, its o, its priests and the H8569
Jer 2:26 their kings and their o, their priests and H8569
Jer 4: 9 "the king and the o will lose heart, the H8569
Jer 8: 1 the bones of the kings and o of Judah H8569
Jer 17:25 through the gates of this city with their o. H8569
Jer 17:25 They and their o will come riding in H8569
Jer 21: 7 his o and the people in this city who H6269
Jer 22: 2 your o and your people who come H6269
Jer 22: 4 accompanied by their o and their people. H6269
Jer 24: 1 son of Jehoiakim king of Judah and the o, H8569
Jer 24: 8 his o and the survivors from Jerusalem H8569
Jer 25:18 its kings and o, to make them a ruin H8569
Jer 25:19 his attendants, his o and all his people, H8569
Jer 26:10 When the o of Judah heard about these H8569
Jer 26:11 prophets said to the o and all the people, H8569
Jer 26:12 said to all the o and all the people: H8569
Jer 26:16 Then the o and all the people said to the H8569
Jer 26:21 all his officers and o heard his words, H8569
Jer 29: 2 the court o and the leaders of Judah and H6247
Jer 32:32 their kings and o, their priests and H8569
Jer 34:10 So all the o and people who entered into H8569
Jer 34:19 Jerusalem, the court o, the priests and H6247
Jer 34:21 king of Judah and his o into the hands of H8569
Jer 35: 4 It was next to the room of the o, which H8569
Jer 36:12 royal palace, where all the o were sitting: H8569
Jer 36:12 son of Hananiah, and all the other o. H8569
Jer 36:14 all the o sent Jehudi son of Nethaniah H8569
Jer 36:19 Then the o said to Baruch, "You and H8569
Jer 36:21 king and all the o standing beside him. H8569
Jer 37:14 Jeremiah and brought him to the o. H8569
Jer 38: 4 Then the o said to the king, "This man H8569
Jer 38:22 brought out to the o of the king of H8569
Jer 38:25 If the o hear that I talked with you, and H8569
Jer 38:27 All the o did come to Jeremiah and H8569
Jer 39: 3 Then all the o of the king of Babylon came H8569
Jer 39: 3 all the other o of the king of Babylon. H8569
Jer 41:16 children and court o he had recovered H6247
Jer 44:17 our kings and our o did in the towns of H8569
Jer 44:21 your kings and your o and the people of H8569
Jer 48: 7 into exile, together with his priests and o. H8569
Jer 49: 3 into exile, together with his priests and o. H8569
Jer 49:38 in Elam and destroy her king and o," H8569
Jer 50:35 Babylon and against her o and wise men! H8569
Jer 51:23 with you I shatter governors and o. H6036
Jer 51:28 their governors and all their o, and all the H6036
Jer 51:57 I will make her o and wise men drunk, her H8569
Jer 52:10 his eyes; he also killed all the o of Judah. H8569
Eze 22:27 Her o within her are like wolves tearing H8569
Da 1: 3 chief of his court o, to bring into the H6247
Da 3: 2 all the other provincial o to come to the A10716
Da 3: 3 the other provincial o assembled for the A10716
Am 1:15 he and his o together," says the H8569
Am 2: 3 her ruler and kill all her o with him," H8569
Na 3:17 your o like swarms of locusts that settle in H3261
Zep 1: 8 I will punish the o and the king's sons H8569
Zep 3: 3 Her o within her are roaring lions; her H8569
Mt 20:25 their high o exercise authority over G3489
Mk 6:21 gave a banquet for his high o and military G3491
Mk 10:42 their high o exercise authority over G3489
Jn 18: 3 of soldiers and some o from the chief G5677
Jn 18:12 the Jewish o arrested Jesus. G5677
Jn 18:18 the servants and o stood around a fire G5677
Jn 18:22 one of the o nearby slapped him in the G5677
Jn 19: 6 as the chief priests and their o saw him, G5677
Ac 17: 6 some other believers before the city o, G4485
Ac 17: 8 the crowd and the city o were thrown into G4485
Ac 19:31 Even some of the o of the province, friends G825

OFFICIATE (1) [OFFICE]

2Ki 17:32 own people to o for them as priests in the H6913

OFFSCOURING (KJV) SCUM

OFFSET (1) [OFF]

1Ki 6: 6 He made o ledges around the outside of H4492

OFFSHOOTS (1) [OFF, SHOOT]

Isa 22:24 its offspring and o—all its lesser vessels H7617

OFFSPRING (65) [OFF]

Ge 3:15 between your o and hers; he will H2446
Ge 12: 7 said, "To your o I will give this land." H2446
Ge 13:15 see I will give to you and your o forever. H2446
Ge 13:16 I will make your o like the dust of the earth H2446
Ge 13:16 the dust, then your o could be counted. H2446
Ge 15: 5 he said to him, "So shall your o be." H2446
Ge 17:12 a foreigner—those who are not your o. H2446
Ge 21:12 Isaac that your o will be reckoned. H2446
Ge 21:13 into a nation also, because he is your o." H2446
Ge 22:18 through your o all nations on earth H2446
Ge 24: 7 'To your o I will give this land' H2446
Ge 24:60 may your o possess the cities of their H2446
Ge 26: 4 through your o all nations on earth H2446
Ge 28:14 will be blessed through you and your o. H2446
Ge 38: 8 to raise up o for your brother. H2446
Ge 38: 9 to keep from providing o for his brother. H2446
Ge 46: 6 So Jacob and all his o went to Egypt H2446
Ge 46: 7 daughters and granddaughters—all his o. H2446
Ex 13: 2 The first o of every womb among the H7081
Ex 13:12 over to the LORD the first o of every womb. H7081
Ex 13:15 the LORD the first male o of every womb H7081
Ex 34:19 "The first o of every womb belongs to me H7081
Lev 21:15 he will not defile his o among his people. H2446
Nu 3:12 of the first male o of every H1147+7081+8167
Nu 8:16 the first male o from every Israelite H1147

Nu 18:15 The first o of every womb, both human H7081
Nu 18:19 before the LORD for both you and your o." H2446
Ru 4:12 Through the o the LORD gives you by this H2446
2Sa 4: 8 my lord the king against Saul and his o." H2446
2Sa 7:12 I will raise up your o to succeed you, your H2446
1Ch 17:11 I will raise up your o to succeed you, one H2446
Job 14:21 not know it; if their o are brought low, they NDT
Job 18:19 He has no o or descendants among his H5769
Job 21: 8 around them, their o before their eyes. H7368
Job 27:14 his o will never have enough to eat. H7368
Ps 37:28 destroyed; the o of the wicked will perish. H2446
Ps 127: 3 o a reward from him. H7262+2021+1061
Isa 9:20 Each will feed on the flesh of their own o H2446
Isa 14:20 Let the o of the wicked never be H2446
Isa 14:22 survivors, her o and descendants, H5769
Isa 22:24 its o and offshoots—all its lesser vessels H7368
Isa 44: 3 I will pour out my Spirit on your o, and my H2446
Isa 53:10 he will see his o and prolong his days H2446
Isa 57: 3 you o of adulterers and prostitutes! H2446
Isa 57: 4 you not a brood of rebels, the o of liars? H2446
Isa 61: 9 nations and their o among the peoples. H7368
Jer 22:30 none of his o will prosper, none will H2446
Jer 31:27 Judah with the o of people and of H2446
La 2:20 Should women eat their o, the children H7262
Hos 9:16 bear children, I will slay their cherished o." H1061
Mal 2:15 one God seek? Godly o. So be on your H2446
Mt 22:24 marry the widow and raise up o for him. G5065
Mk 12:19 the widow and raise up o for his brother. G5065
Lk 20:28 the widow and raise up o for his brother. G5065
Ac 3:25 'Through your o all peoples on earth will G5065
Ac 17:28 your own poets have said, 'We are his o. G1169
Ac 17:29 "Therefore since we are God's o, we G1169
Ro 4:13 Abraham and his o received the promise G5065
Ro 4:16 may be guaranteed to all Abraham's o— G5065
Ro 4:18 been said to him, "So shall your o be." G5065
Ro 9: 7 Isaac that your o will be reckoned. G5065
Ro 9: 8 who are regarded as Abraham's o. G5065
Heb 11:18 Isaac that your o will be reckoned. G5065
Rev 12:17 off to wage war against the rest of her o— G5065
Rev 22:16 I am the Root and the O of David, and the G1169

OFTEN (26)

1Sa 18:30 to battle, and as o as they did H4946+1896
2Ki 4: 9 that this man who o comes our way is a H9458
Job 21:17 "Yet how o is the lamp of the H3869+4537
Job 21:17 How o does calamity come upon them, the NDT
Job 21:18 How o are they like straw before the wind NDT
Ps 78:40 How o they rebelled against him in H3869+4537
Isa 28:19 As o as it comes it will carry you H4946+1896
Jer 14: 7 For we have o rebelled; we have sinned H8045
Jer 31:20 Though I o speak against him, H4946+1896
Mt 9:14 is it that we and the Pharisees fast o, G4498
Mt 17:15 He o falls into the fire or into the water G4490
Mt 23:37 how o I have longed to gather your G4529
Mk 5: 4 For he had o been chained hand and foot G4490
Mk 9:22 "It has o thrown him into fire or water to G4490
Lk 5:16 But Jesus o withdrew to lonely places and AIT
Lk 5:33 "John's disciples o fast and pray, and so G4781
Lk 13:34 how o I have longed to gather your G4529
Jn 18: 2 because Jesus had o met there with his G4490
Ro 15:22 is why I have o been hindered from G3836+4498
2Co 8:22 our brother who has o proved to us in G4490
2Co 11:27 toiled and have o gone without sleep; G4490
2Co 11:27 thirst and have o gone without food; G4490
Php 3:18 as I have o told you before and now tell G4490
2Ti 1:16 because he o refreshed me and was not G4490
Heb 6: 7 drinks in the rain o falling on it and that G4490
Rev 11: 6 kind of plague as o as they want. G4006+1569

OG (20) [OG'S]

Nu 21:33 O king of Bashan and his whole army H6384
Nu 32:33 the kingdom of O king of Bashan— H6384
Dt 1: 4 at Edrei had defeated O king of Bashan, H6384
Dt 3: 1 O king of Bashan with his whole army H6384
Dt 3: 3 gave into our hands O king of Bashan H6384
Dt 3:11 O king of Bashan was the last of the H6384
Dt 3:13 Bashan, the kingdom of O, I gave to the H6384
Dt 4:47 land and the land of O king of Bashan, H6384
Dt 29: 7 of Heshbon and O king of Bashan came H6384
Dt 31: 4 do to them what he did to Sihon and O, H6384
Jos 2:10 what you did to Sihon and O, the two H6384
Jos 9:10 of Heshbon, and O king of Bashan, who H6384
Jos 12: 4 And the territory of O king of Bashan, one H6384
Jos 13:12 the whole kingdom of O in Bashan, who H6384
Jos 13:30 the entire realm of O king of Bashan—all H6384
Jos 13:31 the royal cities of O in Bashan). H6384
1Ki 4:19 the country of O king of Bashan). H6384
Ne 9:22 the country of O king of Bashan. H6384
Ps 135:11 of the Amorites, O king of Bashan, and H6384
Ps 136:20 O king of Bashan—His love endures H6384

OG'S (2) [OG]

Dt 3: 4 region of Argob, O kingdom in Bashan. H6384
Dt 3:10 Edrei, towns of O kingdom in Bashan. H6384

OH (34) [O] See Index of Articles Etc.

OHAD (2)

Ge 46:10 Jemuel, Jamin, O, Jakin, Zohar and Shaul H176
Ex 6:15 were Jemuel, Jamin, O, Jakin, Zohar and H176

OHEL (1)

1Ch 3:20 Hashubah, O, Berekiah, Hasadiah and H186

OHOLAH (5)

Eze 23: 4 The older was named O, and her sister was H188
Eze 23: 4 to sons and daughters. O is Samaria, and H188
Eze 23: 5 "O engaged in prostitution while she was H188
Eze 23:36 will you judge O and Oholibah? H188
Eze 23:44 with those lewd women, O and Oholibah. H188

OHOLIAB (5)

Ex 31: 6 I have appointed O son of Ahisamak, of H190
Ex 35:34 given both him and O son of Ahisamak, H190
Ex 36: 1 O and every skilled person to whom the H190
Ex 36: 2 summoned Bezalel and O and every skilled H190
Ex 38:23 with him was O son of Ahisamak, of the H190

OHOLIBAH (6)

Eze 23: 4 was named Oholah, and her sister was O. H191
Eze 23: 4 Oholah is Samaria, and O is Jerusalem. H191
Eze 23:11 "Her sister O saw this, yet in her lust and H191
Eze 23:22 "Therefore, O, this is what the Sovereign H191
Eze 23:36 "Son of man, will you judge Oholah and O? H191
Eze 23:44 with those lewd women, Oholah and O. H191

OHOLIBAMAH (8)

Ge 36: 2 O daughter of Anah and H192
Ge 36: 5 O bore Jeush, Jalam and Korah. These H192
Ge 36:14 sons of Esau's wife O daughter of Anah H192
Ge 36:18 The sons of Esau's wife O: Chiefs Jeush H192
Ge 36:18 from Esau's wife O daughter of Anah. H192
Ge 36:25 Dishon and O daughter of Anah. H192
Ge 36:41 O, Elah, Pinon, H192
1Ch 1:52 O, Elah, Pinon, H192

OIL (211) [OILS]

Ge 28:18 it up as a pillar and poured o on top of it. H9043
Ge 35:14 offering on it; he also poured o on it. H9043
Ex 25: 6 olive o for the light; spices for the H9043
Ex 25: 6 the anointing o and for the fragrant H9043
Ex 27:20 to bring you clear o of pressed olives for H9043
Ex 29: 2 without yeast and with olive o mixed in, H9043
Ex 29: 2 without yeast and brushed with olive o. H9043
Ex 29: 7 Take the anointing o and anoint him by H9043
Ex 29:21 some of the anointing o and sprinkle it on H9043
Ex 29:23 one thick loaf with olive o mixed in, and H9043
Ex 29:40 quarter of a hin of o from pressed olives, H9043
Ex 30:24 sanctuary shekel—and a hin of olive o. H9043
Ex 30:25 Make these into a sacred anointing o, H9043
Ex 30:25 It will be the sacred anointing o. H9043
Ex 30:31 my sacred anointing o for the generations H9043
Ex 30:32 do not make any other o using the same NDT
Ex 31:11 the anointing o and fragrant incense H9043
Ex 35: 8 olive o for the light; spices for the H9043
Ex 35: 8 the anointing o and for the fragrant H9043
Ex 35:14 its accessories, lamps and o for the light; H9043
Ex 35:15 the anointing o and the fragrant incense H9043
Ex 35:28 spices and olive o for the light and H9043
Ex 35:28 the anointing o and for the fragrant H9043
Ex 37:29 the sacred anointing o and the pure, H9043
Ex 39:37 accessories, and the olive o for the light; H9043
Ex 39:38 the anointing o, the fragrant H9043
Ex 40: 9 "Take the anointing o and anoint the H9043
Lev 2: 1 They are to pour olive o on it, put incense H9043
Lev 2: 2 shall take a handful of the flour and o, H9043
Lev 2: 4 yeast and with olive o mixed in or thin H9043
Lev 2: 4 without yeast and brushed with olive o. H9043
Lev 2: 5 be made of the finest flour mixed with o, H9043
Lev 2: 6 Crumble it and pour o on it; it is a grain H9043
Lev 2: 7 made of the finest flour and some olive o. H9043
Lev 2:15 Put o and incense on it; it is a grain H9043
Lev 2:16 portion of the crushed grain and the o, H9043
Lev 5:11 They must not put olive o or incense on it H9043
Lev 6:15 of the finest flour and some olive o, H9043
Lev 6:21 It must be prepared with o on a griddle H9043
Lev 7:10 whether mixed with olive o or dry H9043
Lev 7:12 without yeast and with olive o mixed in, H9043
Lev 7:12 made without yeast and brushed with o, H9043
Lev 7:12 flour well-kneaded and with o mixed in. H9043
Lev 8: 2 the anointing o, the bull for the sin H9043
Lev 8:10 took the anointing o and anointed the H9043
Lev 8:11 sprinkled some of the o on the altar H5647S
Lev 8:12 of the anointing o on Aaron's head and H9043
Lev 8:26 one thick loaf with olive o mixed in, and H9043
Lev 8:30 of the anointing o and some of the blood H9043
Lev 9: 4 with a grain offering mixed with olive o. H9043
Lev 10: 7 because the LORD's anointing o is on you." H9043
Lev 14:10 flour mixed with olive o for a grain H9043
Lev 14:10 oil for a grain offering, and one log of o. H9043
Lev 14:12 along with the log of o; he shall wave H9043
Lev 14:15 shall then take some of the log of o, H9043
Lev 14:16 his right forefinger into the o in his palm, H9043
Lev 14:17 to put some of the o remaining in his H9043
Lev 14:18 The rest of the o in his palm the priest H9043
Lev 14:21 flour mixed with olive o for a grain H9043
Lev 14:21 olive oil for a grain offering, a log of o, H9043
Lev 14:24 together with the log of o, and wave them H9043
Lev 14:26 to pour some of the o into the palm of his H9043
Lev 14:27 some of the o from his palm seven H9043
Lev 14:28 Some of the o in his palm he is to put on H9043
Lev 14:29 The rest of the o in his palm the priest H9043
Lev 21:10 had the anointing o poured on his head H9043
Lev 21:12 dedicated by the anointing o of his God. H9043
Lev 23:13 of the finest flour mixed with olive o— H9043
Lev 24: 2 to bring you clear o of pressed olives for H9043
Nu 4: 9 all its jars for the olive o used to supply it. H9043
Nu 4:16 is to have charge of the o for the light, the H9043
Nu 4:16 grain offering and the anointing o. H9043
Nu 5:15 He must not pour olive o on it or put H9043
Nu 6:15 thick loaves with olive o mixed in, and thin H9043
Nu 6:15 and thin loaves brushed with olive o. H9043
Nu 7:13 flour mixed with olive o as a grain H9043
Nu 7:19 flour mixed with olive o as a grain H9043
Nu 7:25 flour mixed with olive o as a grain H9043
Nu 7:31 flour mixed with olive o as a grain H9043
Nu 7:37 flour mixed with olive o as a grain H9043
Nu 7:43 flour mixed with olive o as a grain H9043
Nu 7:49 flour mixed with olive o as a grain H9043
Nu 7:55 flour mixed with olive o as a grain H9043
Nu 7:61 flour mixed with olive o as a grain H9043
Nu 7:67 flour mixed with olive o as a grain H9043
Nu 7:73 flour mixed with olive o as a grain H9043
Nu 7:79 flour mixed with olive o as a grain H9043
Nu 8: 8 of the finest flour mixed with olive o; H9043
Nu 11: 8 tasted like something made with olive o. H9043
Nu 15: 4 mixed with a quarter of a hin of olive o. H9043
Nu 15: 6 flour mixed with a third of a hin of olive o, H9043
Nu 15: 9 flour mixed with half a hin of olive o, H9043
Nu 18:12 you all the finest olive o and all the finest H3658
Nu 28: 5 quarter of a hin of o from pressed olives. H9043
Nu 28: 9 of the finest flour mixed with olive o. H9043
Nu 28:12 an ephah of the finest flour mixed with o; H9043
Nu 28:12 an ephah of the finest flour mixed with o; H9043
Nu 28:13 an ephah of the finest flour mixed with o. H9043
Nu 28:20 an ephah of the finest flour mixed with o; H9043
Nu 28:28 an ephah of the finest flour mixed with o; H9043
Nu 29: 3 of the finest flour mixed with olive o; H9043
Nu 29: 9 an ephah of the finest flour mixed with o; H9043
Nu 29:14 an ephah of the finest flour mixed with o; H9043
Nu 35:25 who was anointed with the holy o. H9043
Dt 7:13 new wine and olive o—the calves of your H3658
Dt 8: 8 pomegranates, olive o and honey; H9043
Dt 11:14 in your grain, new wine and olive o. H3658
Dt 12:17 of your grain and new wine and olive o, H3658
Dt 14:23 new wine and olive o, and the firstborn H3658
Dt 18: 4 new wine and olive o, and the first H3658
Dt 28:40 your country but you will not use the o, H9043
Dt 28:51 new wine or olive o, nor any calves H3658
Dt 32:13 the rock, and with o from the flinty crag, H9043
Dt 33:24 brothers, and let him bathe his feet in o. H9043
Jdg 9: 9 'Should I give up my o, by which both H2016
1Sa 10: 1 took a flask of olive o and poured it on H9043
1Sa 16: 1 Fill your horn with o and be on your way; H9043
1Sa 16:13 took the horn of o and anointed him in H9043
2Sa 1:21 shield of Saul—no longer rubbed with o. H9043
1Ki 1:39 took the horn of o from the sacred tent H9043
1Ki 5:11 twenty thousand baths of pressed olive o. H9043
1Ki 17:12 flour in a jar and a little olive o in a jug. H9043
1Ki 17:14 up and the jug of o will not run dry until H9043
1Ki 17:16 used up and the jug of o did not run dry, H9043
2Ki 4: 2 she said, "except a small jar of olive o." H9043
2Ki 4: 4 Pour o into all the jars, and as each is filled NDT
2Ki 4: 6 Then the o stopped flowing. H9043
2Ki 4: 7 "Go, sell the o and pay your debts. H9043
2Ki 9: 1 this flask of olive o with you and go to H9043
2Ki 9: 3 the flask and pour the o on his head and H9043
2Ki 9: 6 prophet poured the o on Jehu's head H9043
2Ki 20:13 the spices and the fine olive o—his H9043
1Ch 9:29 wine, and the olive o, incense and H9043
1Ch 12:40 wine, olive o, cattle and sheep H9043
1Ch 27:28 was in charge of the supplies of olive o. H9043
2Ch 2:10 twenty thousand baths of olive o. H9043
2Ch 2:15 barley and the olive o and wine he H9043
2Ch 11:11 with supplies of food, olive o and wine. H9043
2Ch 31: 5 olive o and honey and all that the fields H3658
2Ch 32:28 new wine and olive o; and he made H3658
Ezr 3: 7 drink and olive o to the people of H9043
Ezr 6: 9 wine and olive o, as requested by A10442
Ezr 7:22 a hundred baths of olive o, and salt A10442
Ne 5:11 the money, grain, new wine and olive o." H3658
Ne 10:37 trees and of our new wine and olive o. H3658
Ne 10:39 new wine and olive o to the storerooms H3658
Ne 13: 5 new wine and olive o prescribed for the H3658
Ne 13:12 new wine and olive o into the storerooms. H3658
Est 2:12 six months with o of myrrh and six with H9043
Job 29: 6 rock poured out for me streams of olive o. H9043
Ps 23: 5 You anoint my head with o; my cup H9043
Ps 45: 7 by anointing you with the o of joy. H9043
Ps 55:21 his words are more soothing than o, yet H9043
Ps 89:20 with my sacred o I have anointed him. H9043
Ps 104:15 human hearts, o to make their faces shine H9043
Ps 109:18 his body like water, into his bones like o. H9043
Ps 133: 2 It is like precious o poured on the head H9043
Ps 141: 5 let him rebuke me—that is o on my head. H9043
Pr 5: 3 her speech is smoother than o; H9043
Pr 21:17 loves wine and olive o will never be rich. H9043
Pr 21:20 The wise store up choice food and olive o, H9043
Pr 27:16 the wind or grasping o with the hand. H9043
Ecc 9: 8 always anoint your head with o. H9043
Isa 1: 6 bandaged or soothed with olive o. H9043
Isa 21: 5 Get up, you officers, o the shields! H5417
Isa 39: 2 the fine olive o—his entire armory H9043
Isa 57: 9 to Molek with olive o and increased your H9043
Isa 61: 3 of ashes, the o of joy instead of mourning H9043
Jer 31:12 the new wine and the olive o, the young H3658
Jer 40:10 summer fruit and olive o, and put them in H9043
Jer 41: 8 barley, olive o and honey, hidden H9043

Eze 16:13 was honey, **olive o** and the finest flour. H9043
Eze 16:18 you offered my **o** and incense before H9043
Eze 16:19 **olive o** and honey I gave you to eat H9043
Eze 23:41 incense and **olive o** *that belonged to* me. H9043
Eze 27:17 **olive o** and balm for your wares. H9043
Eze 32:14 settle and make her streams flow like **o**, H9043
Eze 45:14 The prescribed portion of **olive o** H9043
Eze 45:24 with a hin of **olive o** for each ephah. H9043
Eze 45:25 burnt offerings, grain offerings and **o**. H9043
Eze 46:5 with a hin of **olive o** for each ephah. H9043
Eze 46:7 along with a hin of **o** for each ephah. H9043
Eze 46:11 along with a hin of **o** for each ephah. H9043
Eze 46:14 a third of a hin of **o** to moisten the flour. H9043
Eze 46:15 grain offering and the **o** shall be provided H9043
Hos 2:5 my linen, my **olive o** and my drink. H9043
Hos 2:8 the new wine and **o**, who lavished on her H3658
Hos 2:22 the new wine and the **olive o**, and they H3658
Hos 12:1 with Assyria and sends **olive o** to Egypt. H9043
Joel 1:10 the new wine is dried up, the **olive o** fails. H3658
Joel 2:19 new wine and **olive o**, enough to satisfy H3658
Joel 2:24 vats will overflow with new wine and **o**. H3658
Mic 6:7 with ten thousand rivers of **olive o**? H9043
Mic 6:15 you will press olives but not use the **o** H9043
Hag 1:11 the **olive o** and everything else the H3658
Hag 2:12 some wine, **olive o** or other food, does it H9043
Zec 4:12 the two gold pipes that pour out **golden** *o*?" AIT
Mt 6:17 **put o on** your head and wash your face, G230
Mt 25:3 lamps but did not take *any* **o** with them. G1778
Mt 25:4 took **o** in jars along with their lamps. G1778
Mt 25:8 'Give us some of your **o**; our lamps are G1778
Mt 25:9 go to those who sell **o** and buy some for NDT
Mt 25:10 while they were on their way to buy the **o**, NDT
Mk 6:13 many sick people *with* **o** and healed them G1778
Lk 7:46 You did not put **o** on my head, but she has G1778
Lk 10:34 his wounds, pouring on **o** and wine. G1778
Lk 16:6 " 'Nine hundred gallons *of* **olive o**,' he G1778
Heb 1:9 by anointing you *with* the **o** of joy. G1778
Jas 5:14 anoint them *with* **o** in the name of G1778
Rev 6:6 do not damage the **o** and the wine!" G1778
Rev 18:13 of wine and **olive o**, of fine flour and G1778

OILS (1) [OIL]

Ps 92:10 wild ox; fine **o** have been poured on me. H9043

OINTMENT (1) [OINTMENTS]

Job 41:31 stirs up the sea like a **pot of o**. H5350

OINTMENTS (1) [OINTMENT]

Eze 16:9 the blood from you and put **o** on you. H9043

OKRAN (5)

Nu 1:13 from Asher, Pagiel son of **O**; H6581
Nu 2:27 of the people of Asher is Pagiel son of **O**. H6581
Nu 7:72 On the eleventh day Pagiel son of **O**, the H6581
Nu 7:77 This was the offering of Pagiel son of **O**. H6581
Nu 10:26 Pagiel son of **O** was over the division of H6581

OLD (326) [OLDER, OLDEST]

Ge 5:32 After Noah was 500 years **o**, he became H1201
Ge 6:4 They were the heroes of **o**, men of H6409
Ge 7:6 six hundred years **o** when the floodwaters H1201
Ge 11:10 when Shem was 100 years **o**, he became H1201
Ge 12:4 seventy-five years **o** when he set out from H1201
Ge 15:9 each **three years o**, along with a H8992
Ge 15:15 in peace and be buried at a good **o age**. H8484
Ge 16:16 eighty-six years **o** when Hagar bore him H1201
Ge 17:1 When Abram was ninety-nine years **o** H1201
Ge 17:12 who is eight days **o** must be circumcised, H1201
Ge 17:17 son be born to a *man* a hundred years **o**? H1201
Ge 17:24 was ninety-nine years **o** when he was H1201
Ge 18:11 were already **very o**, H2418+995+928+2021+3427
Ge 18:12 "After I am worn out and my lord *is* **o**, will H2416
Ge 18:13 I really have a child, now that I *am* **o**? H2416
Ge 19:4 both young and **o**—surrounded the house H2418
Ge 19:11 young and **o**, with blindness so H1524
Ge 19:31 younger, "Our father *is* **o**, and there is no H2416
Ge 21:2 bore a son to Abraham in his **o age**, H2421
Ge 21:4 When his son Isaac was eight days **o** H1201
Ge 21:5 was a hundred years **o** when his son Isaac H1201
Ge 21:7 Yet I have borne him a son in his **o age**." H2421
Ge 23:1 to be a hundred and twenty-seven **years** *o*. AIT
Ge 24:1 *was* now **very o**, H2416+995+928+2021+3427
Ge 24:36 Sarah has borne him a son in her **o age**, H2420
Ge 25:8 his last and died at a good **o age**, H8484
Ge 25:8 good old age, an **o** *man* and full of years H2418
Ge 25:20 Isaac was forty years **o** when he married H1201
Ge 25:26 was sixty years **o** when Rebekah gave H1201
Ge 26:34 When Esau was forty years **o**, he married H1201
Ge 27:1 When Isaac *was* **o** and his eyes were so H2416
Ge 27:2 "*I am* now *an* **o** *man* and don't know the H2416
Ge 35:29 to his people, **o** and full of years. H2418
Ge 37:3 he had been born to him in his **o age**; H2421
Ge 41:46 was thirty years **o** when he entered the H1201
Ge 44:20 is a young son born to him in his **o age**. H2421
Ge 47:8 asked him, "How **o** are you?" H3427+9102+2644
Ge 48:10 eyes were failing because of **o age**, H2419
Ex 7:7 Moses was eighty years **o** and Aaron H1201
Ex 10:9 "We will go with our young and our **o** H2418
Ex 29:38 regularly each day: two lambs a year **o**. H1201
Ex 30:14 those twenty years **o** or more, are to give H1201
Ex 38:26 counted, twenty years **o** or more, a total of H1201
Lev 9:3 a lamb—*both* a year **o** and without defect H1201
Lev 14:10 male lambs and one ewe lamb a year **o**, H1426
Lev 23:12 the LORD a lamb a year **o** without defect, H1201
Lev 23:18 each a year **o** and without defect H1201
Lev 23:19 two lambs, each a year **o**, for a fellowship H1201
Lev 25:22 you will eat from the **o** crop and will H3824
Lev 27:7 a person sixty years **o** or more, set the H1201
Nu 1:3 are twenty years **o** or more and able to H1201
Nu 1:18 men twenty years **o** or more were listed H1201
Nu 1:20 the men twenty years **o** or more who were H1201
Nu 1:22 the men twenty years **o** or more who were H1201
Nu 1:24 the men twenty years **o** or more who were H1201
Nu 1:26 the men twenty years **o** or more who were H1201
Nu 1:28 the men twenty years **o** or more who were H1201
Nu 1:30 the men twenty years **o** or more who were H1201
Nu 1:32 the men twenty years **o** or more who were H1201
Nu 1:34 the men twenty years **o** or more who were H1201
Nu 1:36 the men twenty years **o** or more who were H1201
Nu 1:38 the men twenty years **o** or more who were H1201
Nu 1:40 the men twenty years **o** or more who were H1201
Nu 1:42 the men twenty years **o** or more who were H1201
Nu 1:45 twenty years **o** or more who were able H1201
Nu 3:15 Count every male a month **o** or more." H1201
Nu 3:22 the males a month **o** or more who were H1201
Nu 3:28 the males a month **o** or more was 8,600. H1201
Nu 3:34 the males a month **o** or more who were H1201
Nu 3:39 including every male a month **o** or more H1201
Nu 3:40 who are a month **o** or more and make a H1201
Nu 3:43 of firstborn males a month **o** or more, H1201
Nu 7:15 male lamb a year **o** for a burnt offering H1201
Nu 7:17 male lambs a year **o** to be sacrificed as a H1201
Nu 7:21 male lamb a year **o** for a burnt offering H1201
Nu 7:23 male lambs a year **o** to be sacrificed as a H1201
Nu 7:27 male lamb a year **o** for a burnt offering H1201
Nu 7:29 male lambs a year **o** to be sacrificed as a H1201
Nu 7:33 male lamb a year **o** for a burnt offering H1201
Nu 7:35 male lambs a year **o** to be sacrificed as a H1201
Nu 7:39 male lamb a year **o** for a burnt offering H1201
Nu 7:41 male lambs a year **o** to be sacrificed as a H1201
Nu 7:45 male lamb a year **o** for a burnt offering H1201
Nu 7:47 male lambs a year **o** to be sacrificed as a H1201
Nu 7:51 male lamb a year **o** for a burnt offering H1201
Nu 7:53 male lambs a year **o** to be sacrificed as a H1201
Nu 7:57 male lamb a year **o** for a burnt offering H1201
Nu 7:59 male lambs a year **o** to be sacrificed as a H1201
Nu 7:63 male lamb a year **o** for a burnt offering H1201
Nu 7:65 male lambs a year **o** to be sacrificed as a H1201
Nu 7:69 male lamb a year **o** for a burnt offering H1201
Nu 7:71 male lambs a year **o** to be sacrificed as a H1201
Nu 7:75 male lamb a year **o** for a burnt offering H1201
Nu 7:77 male lambs a year **o** to be sacrificed as a H1201
Nu 7:81 male lamb a year **o** for a burnt offering H1201
Nu 7:83 male lambs a year **o** to be sacrificed as a H1201
Nu 7:87 rams and twelve male lambs a year **o**, H1201
Nu 7:88 goats and sixty male lambs a year **o**. H1201
Nu 8:24 twenty-five years **o** or more shall come to H1201
Nu 14:29 of you twenty years **o** or more who was H1201
Nu 18:16 When they are a month **o**, you must H1201
Nu 26:2 those twenty years **o** or more who are H1201
Nu 26:4 census of the *men* twenty years **o** or more, H1201
Nu 26:62 Levites a month **o** or more numbered H1201
Nu 28:3 two lambs a year **o** without defect, as a H1201
Nu 28:9 of two lambs a year **o** without defect, H1201
Nu 28:11 one ram and seven male lambs a year **o** H1201
Nu 28:19 one ram and seven male lambs a year **o** H1201
Nu 28:27 male lambs a year **o** as an aroma H1201
Nu 29:2 one ram and seven male lambs a year **o** H1201
Nu 29:8 one ram and seven male lambs a year **o** H1201
Nu 29:13 rams and fourteen male lambs a year **o**, H1201
Nu 29:17 rams and fourteen male lambs a year **o**, H1201
Nu 29:20 rams and fourteen male lambs a year **o**, H1201
Nu 29:23 rams and fourteen male lambs a year **o**, H1201
Nu 29:26 rams and fourteen male lambs a year **o**, H1201
Nu 29:29 rams and fourteen male lambs a year **o**, H1201
Nu 29:32 rams and fourteen male lambs a year **o**, H1201
Nu 29:36 one ram and seven male lambs a year **o** H1201
Nu 32:11 were twenty years **o** or more when they H1201
Nu 33:39 twenty-three years **o** when he died on H1201
Dt 28:50 respect for the **o** or pity for the young. H2418
Dt 31:2 twenty years **o** and I am no longer H1201
Dt 32:7 Remember the days **of o**; consider the H6409
Dt 34:7 twenty years **o** when he died, H1201
Jos 6:21 women, young and **o**, cattle, sheep and H2418
Jos 9:4 with worn-out sacks and **o** wineskins, H1165
Jos 9:5 sandals on their feet and wore **o** clothes. H1165
Jos 13:1 Joshua *had* **grown o**, H2416+995+928+2021+3427
Jos 13:1 "You *are now* **very o** H2416+995+928+2021+3427
Jos 14:7 I was forty years **o** when Moses the servant H1201
Jos 14:10 So here I am today, eighty-five years **o**! H1201
Jos 23:1 by then a **very o** *man*, H2416+995+928+2021+3427
Jos 23:2 to them: "I *am* **very o**. H2416+995+928+2021+3427
Jdg 6:25 your father's herd, the one seven years **o**. NDT
Jdg 8:32 died at a good **o age** and was buried in H8484
Jdg 19:16 That evening an **o** man from the hill H2418
Jdg 19:17 the city square, the **o** man asked, "Where H2418
Jdg 19:20 welcome at my house," the **o** man said. H2418
Jdg 19:22 shouted to the **o** man who owned the H2418
Ru 1:12 *I am* too **o** to have another husband. H2416
Ru 4:15 your life and sustain you in your **o age**. H8484
1Sa 2:22 Now Eli, *who was* very **o**, heard about H2416
1Sa 2:31 so that no one in it will reach **o age**, H2418
1Sa 2:32 in your family line will ever reach **o age**. H2418
1Sa 4:15 ninety-eight years **o** and whose eyes had H1201
1Sa 4:18 for he was an **o** man, and he was H2418
1Sa 5:9 both young and **o**, with an outbreak of H1524
1Sa 8:1 When Samuel **grew o**, he appointed his H2416
1Sa 8:5 said to him, "You *are* **o**, and your sons do H2416
1Sa 12:2 As for me, *I am* **o** and gray, and my sons H2416
1Sa 13:1 was thirty years **o** when he became king, H1201
1Sa 17:12 time he *was* **very o**. H2416+995+928+2021+408
1Sa 24:13 As the **o** saying goes, 'From evildoers H7719
1Sa 28:14 "An **o** man wearing a robe is coming up," H2418
1Sa 30:2 everyone else in it, both young and **o**. H1524
1Sa 30:19 young or **o**, boy or girl, plunder or H1524
2Sa 2:10 was forty years **o** when he became king H1201
2Sa 4:4 He was five years **o** when the news about H1201
2Sa 5:4 was thirty years **o** when he became king, H1201
2Sa 19:32 Now Barzillai was very **o**, eighty years of H2416
2Sa 19:35 I am now eighty years **o**. Can I tell the H1201
1Ki 1:1 King David *was* **very o**, H2416+995+928+2021+3427
1Ki 11:4 As Solomon **grew o**, his wives turned his H2420
1Ki 13:11 there was a certain **o** prophet living in H2418
1Ki 13:18 The **o** prophet answered, "I too am a NDT
1Ki 13:20 the LORD came to the **o** prophet who had NDT
1Ki 13:25 it in the city where the **o** prophet lived. H2418
1Ki 14:21 forty-one years **o** when he became king H1201
1Ki 15:23 In his **o age**, however, his feet became H2420
1Ki 22:42 thirty-five years **o** when he became king, H1201
2Ki 3:21 man, **young and o**, who H2256+5087+2025
2Ki 4:14 "She has no son, and her husband *is* **o**." H2416
2Ki 8:17 thirty-two years **o** when he became king, H1201
2Ki 8:26 twenty-two years **o** when he became king, H1201
2Ki 11:21 was seven years **o** when he began to H1201
2Ki 14:2 twenty-five years **o** when he became king, H1201
2Ki 14:21 who was sixteen years **o**, and made him H1201
2Ki 15:2 was sixteen years **o** when he became king H1201
2Ki 15:33 twenty-five years **o** when he became king, H1201
2Ki 16:2 was twenty years **o** when he became king, H1201
2Ki 18:2 twenty-five years **o** when he became king, H1201
2Ki 19:25 In days **of o** I planned it; now I have H7710
2Ki 21:1 was twelve years **o** when he became king, H1201
2Ki 21:19 twenty-two years **o** when he became king, H1201
2Ki 22:1 was eight years **o** when he became king, H1201
2Ki 23:31 twenty-three years **o** when he became H1201
2Ki 23:36 twenty-five years **o** when he became king, H1201
2Ki 24:8 was eighteen years **o** when he became H1201
2Ki 24:18 twenty-one years **o** when he became king H1201
1Ch 2:21 when he was sixty years **o**, married the H1201
1Ch 23:1 When David *was* **o** and full of years, he H2416
1Ch 23:3 thirty years **o** or more were counted H1201
1Ch 23:24 twenty years **o** or more who served H1201
1Ch 23:27 from *those* twenty years **o** or more. H1201
1Ch 25:8 Young and **o** alike, teacher as well as H1524
1Ch 26:13 to their families, young and **o** alike. H1524
1Ch 27:23 number of the men twenty years **o** or less, H1201
1Ch 29:28 He died at a good **o age**, having enjoyed H8484
2Ch 3:3 using the cubit of the **o** standard). H8037
2Ch 12:13 forty-one years **o** when he became king H1201
2Ch 20:31 thirty-five years **o** when he became king H1201
2Ch 21:5 thirty-two years **o** when he became king, H1201
2Ch 21:20 thirty-two years **o** when he became king, H1201
2Ch 22:2 twenty-two years **o** when he became king, H1201
2Ch 24:1 was seven years **o** when he became king, H1201
2Ch 24:15 Now Jehoiada *was* **o** and full of years H2416
2Ch 25:1 twenty-five years **o** when he became king, H1201
2Ch 25:5 those twenty years **o** or more and found H1201
2Ch 26:1 who was sixteen years **o**, and made him H1201
2Ch 26:3 was sixteen years **o** when he became king H1201
2Ch 27:1 twenty-five years **o** when he became king, H1201
2Ch 27:8 twenty-five years **o** when he became king, H1201
2Ch 28:1 was twenty years **o** when he became king, H1201
2Ch 29:1 twenty-five years **o** when he became king, H1201
2Ch 31:15 to their divisions, **o** and young alike. H1524
2Ch 31:16 males three years **o** or more whose H1201
2Ch 31:17 to the Levites twenty years **o** or more, H1201
2Ch 33:1 was twelve years **o** when he became king, H1201
2Ch 33:21 twenty-two years **o** when he became king, H1201
2Ch 34:1 was eight years **o** when he became king, H1201
2Ch 36:2 twenty-three years **o** when he became H1201
2Ch 36:5 twenty-five years **o** when he became king, H1201
2Ch 36:9 was eighteen years **o** when he became H1201
2Ch 36:11 twenty-one years **o** when he became king, H1201
Ezr 3:8 Levites twenty years **o** and older to H1201
Est 3:13 the Jews—young and **o**, women and H2418
Job 14:8 Its roots *may* **grow o** in the ground and its H2416
Job 20:4 you know how it has been from **of o**, H6329
Job 21:7 **growing o** and increasing in power? H6980
Job 22:15 you keep to the **o** path that the wicked H6409
Job 29:8 aside and the **o men** rose to their feet; H3813
Job 32:6 in years, and you are **o**; that is why I was H3813
Job 32:9 It is not only the **o** who are wise, not only H8041
Job 42:17 so Job died, an **o** *man* and full of years. H2418
Ps 25:6 mercy and love, for they are from **of o**. H6409
Ps 37:25 I was young and now *I am* **o**, yet I have H2416
Ps 55:19 who is enthroned **from of o**, who does not H7710
Ps 71:9 Do not cast me away when I am **o**; do not H2420
Ps 71:18 Even when I am **o** and gray, do not H2420
Ps 78:2 utter hidden things, things from **of o**— H7710
Ps 92:14 They will still bear fruit in **o age**, they will H8484
Ps 148:12 men and women, **o** *men* and children. H2418
Pr 8:22 the first of his works, before his deeds of **o**; H255
Pr 20:29 strength, gray hair the splendor of the **o**. H2418
Pr 22:6 even when *they are* **o** they will not H2416

Pr 23:22 not despise your mother when *she is* **o**. H2416
Ecc 4:13 wise youth than an **o** but foolish king who H2418
Ecc 7:10 "Why were the **o** days better than these?" H8037
SS 7:13 both new and **o**, that I have stored up H3824
Isa 1:26 I will restore your leaders as in **days of o** H8037
Isa 3: 5 The young will rise up against the **o**, the H2418
Isa 20: 4 young and **o**, with buttocks bared H2418
Isa 22:11 the two walls for the water of the **O** Pool, H3824
Isa 23: 7 city of revelry, the **o**, old city, H4946+3427+7710
Isa 23: 7 the old, **o** city, whose feet have taken her H7712
Isa 37:26 In days **of o** I planned it; now I have H7710
Isa 46: 4 Even to your **o age** and gray hairs I am he, H2420
Isa 48: 8 from **of o** your ears have not been open. H255
Isa 51: 9 as in days gone by, as in generations **of o**. H6409
Isa 63: 9 up and carried them all the days **of o**. H6409
Isa 63:11 Then his people recalled the days **of o** H6409
Isa 63:16 our Redeemer from **of o** is your name. H6409
Isa 63:19 We are yours from **of o**; but you have not H6409
Isa 65:20 an **o** *man* who does not live out his H2418
Jer 6:11 and the **o**, those weighed down H2418
Jer 30:20 Their children will be as in **days of o**, and H7710
Jer 31:13 be glad, young men and **o** as well. H2418
Jer 38:11 He took some **o** rags and worn-out H1170
Jer 38:12 "Put these **o** rags and worn-out clothes H1170
Jer 51:22 with you I shatter **o** *man* and youth, with H2418
Jer 52: 1 twenty-one years **o** when he became king H1201
La 1: 7 the treasures that were hers in days **of o**. H7710
La 2:21 "Young and **o** lie together in the dust of H2418
La 3: 4 *He has* **made** my skin and my flesh **grow o** H1162
La 5:21 that we may return; renew our days as **of o** H7710
Eze 9: 6 Slaughter the **o** *men*, the young men and H2418
Eze 9: 6 began with the **o** *men* who were in front H2418
Eze 16: 8 saw that you were **o** *enough for* love, H6961
Eze 32:27 not lie with the fallen warriors **of o**, H4946+6409
Hos 4:11 **o wine** and new wine take away their H3516
Joel 2:28 prophesy, your **o** *men* will dream dreams H2418
Mic 5: 2 whose origins are from **of o**, from ancient H7710
Mic 6: 6 with burnt offerings, with calves a year **o**? H1201
Zec 8: 4 again *men* and women **of ripe o age** will H2418
[Zec 8: 4 again men and *women* **of ripe o age** will H2418]
Mt 2:16 vicinity who were **two years o** and under, *G1453*
Mt 9:16 patch of unshrunk cloth on an **o** garment, *G4094*
Mt 9:17 people pour new wine into **o** wineskins. *G4094*
Mt 13:52 his storeroom new treasures as well as **o**." *G4094*
Mk 2:21 patch of unshrunk cloth on an **o** garment. *G4094*
Mk 2:21 the new piece will pull away from the **o** *G4094*
Mk 2:22 no one pours new wine into **o** wineskins. *G4094*
Mk 5:42 she was twelve **years** *o*). At this they were AIT
Lk 1: 7 they were both **very o**. *G4581+1877+3836+2465*
Lk 1:18 I am an **o man** and my wife is well along *G4566*
Lk 1:36 is going to have a child in her **o age**, *G1179*
Lk 2:36 She *was* very **o**; she had *G4581+1877+2465*
Lk 2:42 When he was twelve **years** *o*, they went up to AIT
Lk 3:23 was about thirty **years** *o* when he began his AIT
Lk 5:36 out of a new garment to patch an **o** one. *G4094*
Lk 5:36 patch from the new will not match the **o**. *G4094*
Lk 5:37 no one pours new wine into **o** wineskins. *G4094*
Lk 5:39 one after drinking **o** *wine* wants the new, *G4094*
Lk 5:39 the new, for they say, 'The **o** is better. *G4094*
Jn 3: 4 can someone be born when they are **o**?" *G1173*
Jn 8:57 "You are not yet fifty **years** *o*," they said to AIT
Jn 21:18 when *you are* **o** you will stretch out *G1180*
Ac 2:17 your **o** *men* will dream dreams. *G4565*
Ac 4:22 miraculously healed was over forty **years** *o*. AIT
Ac 7:23 "When Moses was forty years **o**, he *G5989*
Ro 4:19 since he was about **a hundred years o** *G1670*
Ro 6: 6 For we know that our **o** self was crucified *G4094*
Ro 7: 6 not *in* the **o way** of the written code. *G4095*
1Co 5: 7 Get rid of the **o** yeast, so that you may be *G4094*
1Co 5: 8 not with the **o** bread leavened with *G4094*
2Co 3:14 veil remains when the **o** covenant is read. *G4094*
2Co 5:17 The **o** has gone, the new is *G792*
Eph 4:22 to put off your **o** self, which is being *G4094*
Col 3: 9 have taken off your **o** self with its practices *G4094*
1Ti 4: 7 do with godless myths and **o** wives' tales; *G1212*
Phm 9 an **o man** and now also a prisoner of *G4566*
Heb 8: 6 he is mediator is superior to the **o** one, NDT
Jas 2: 2 a poor man in **filthy** *o* clothes also AIT
1Jn 2: 7 you a new command but an **o** one, *G4094*
1Jn 2: 7 This **o** command is the message you have *G4094*
Rev 21: 4 the **o order of things** has passed away." *G4755*

OLDER (31) [OLD]

Ge 10:21 to Shem, whose **o** brother was Japheth H1524
Ge 19:31 One day the **o** *daughter* said to the H1142
Ge 19:33 the **o** *daughter* went in and slept with H1142
Ge 19:34 The next day the **o** *daughter* said to the H1142
Ge 19:37 The **o** *daughter* had a son, and she H1142
Ge 25:23 and the **o** will serve the younger. H8041
Ge 27: 1 called for Esau his **o** son and said to him, H1524
Ge 27:15 took the best clothes of Esau her **o** son, H1524
Ge 27:42 was told what her **o** son Esau had said, H1524
Ge 29:16 the name of the **o** was Leah, and the H1524
Ge 29:26 daughter in marriage before the **o** *one*. H1142
Ex 2:10 When the child **grew o**, she took him to H1540
1Sa 14:49 The name of his **o** daughter was Merab H1142
1Sa 18:17 to David, "Here is my **o** daughter Merab. H1524
1Ki 2:22 he is my **o** brother—yes, for H1524+4946
2Ch 22: 1 into the camp, had killed all the **o** sons. H8037
Ezr 3: 8 years old and **o** to supervise the H5087+2025
Ezr 3:12 But many of the **o** priests and Levites and H2418
Job 15:10 *men even* **o** than your father. H3888+3427
Job 32: 4 they were **o** than he. H2418+4200+3427
Eze 16:46 Your **o** sister was Samaria, who lived to H1524
Eze 16:61 both those *who* are **o** than you and those H1524
Eze 23: 4 The **o** was named Oholah, and her sister H1524
Lk 15:25 "Meanwhile, the **o** son was in the field *G4565*
Lk 15:28 "The **o** brother became angry and refused to NDT
Jn 8: 9 one at a time, the **o** *ones* first, until only *G4565*
Ro 9:12 was told, "The **o** will serve the younger." *G3505*
1Ti 5: 1 Do not rebuke an **o** *man* harshly, but *G4565*
1Ti 5: 2 **o** *women* as mothers, and younger women *G4565*
Titus 2: 2 Teach the **o** *men* to be temperate, worthy *G4566*
Titus 2: 3 teach the **o** *women* to be reverent in the *G4567*

OLDEST (9) [OLD]

Ge 44:12 beginning with the **o** and ending with the H1524
Jdg 8:20 to Jether, his **o** *son*, he said, "Kill them H1147
1Sa 17:13 Jesse's three **o** sons had followed Saul to H1524
1Sa 17:14 the youngest. The three **o** followed Saul, H1524
1Sa 17:28 When Eliab, David's **o** brother, heard him H1524
1Ch 24:31 The families of the **o** brother were treated H8031
Job 1:13 drinking wine at the **o** brother's house, H1147
Job 1:18 drinking wine at the **o** brother's house, H1147
Heb 12:16 sold his **inheritance rights as the o son**. *G4757*

OLIVE (139) [OLIVE-WOOD, OLIVES]

Ge 8:11 in its beak was a freshly plucked **o** leaf! H2339
Ex 23:11 same with your vineyard and your **o grove**. H2339
Ex 25: 6 **o oil** for the light; spices for the anointing H9043
Ex 29: 2 without yeast and with **o oil** mixed in, H9043
Ex 29: 2 without yeast and brushed with **o oil**. H9043
Ex 29:23 one thick loaf with **o oil** mixed in, and H9043
Ex 30:24 the sanctuary shekel—and a hin of **o** oil. H2339
Ex 35: 8 **o oil** for the light; spices for the anointing H9043
Ex 35:28 brought spices and **o oil** for the light and H9043
Ex 39:37 its accessories, and the **o oil** *for* the light; H9043
Lev 2: 1 They are to pour **o oil** on it, put incense H9043
Lev 2: 4 yeast and with **o oil** mixed in or thin H9043
Lev 2: 4 without yeast and brushed with **o oil**. H9043
Lev 2: 7 made of the finest flour and some **o oil**. H9043
Lev 5:11 They must not put **o oil** or incense on it H9043
Lev 6:15 handful of the finest flour and some **o oil**, H9043
Lev 7:10 whether mixed with **o oil** or dry, belongs H9043
Lev 7:12 without yeast and with **o oil** mixed in, H9043
Lev 8:26 one thick loaf with **o oil** mixed in, and H9043
Lev 9: 4 with a grain offering mixed with **o oil**. H9043
Lev 14:10 flour mixed with **o oil** for a grain offering, H9043
Lev 14:21 flour mixed with **o oil** for a grain offering, H9043
Lev 23:13 of the finest flour mixed with **o oil**— H9043
Nu 4: 9 all its jars for the **o oil** used to supply it. H9043
Nu 5:15 He must not pour **o oil** on it or put H9043
Nu 6:15 thick loaves with **o oil** mixed in, and thin H9043
Nu 6:15 and thin loaves brushed with **o oil**. H9043
Nu 7:13 flour mixed with **o oil** as a grain offering; H9043
Nu 7:19 flour mixed with **o oil** as a grain offering; H9043
Nu 7:25 flour mixed with **o oil** as a grain offering; H9043
Nu 7:31 flour mixed with **o oil** as a grain offering; H9043
Nu 7:37 flour mixed with **o oil** as a grain offering; H9043
Nu 7:43 flour mixed with **o oil** as a grain offering; H9043
Nu 7:49 flour mixed with **o oil** as a grain offering; H9043
Nu 7:55 flour mixed with **o oil** as a grain offering; H9043
Nu 7:61 flour mixed with **o oil** as a grain offering; H9043
Nu 7:67 flour mixed with **o oil** as a grain offering; H9043
Nu 7:73 flour mixed with **o oil** as a grain offering; H9043
Nu 7:79 flour mixed with **o oil** as a grain offering; H9043
Nu 8: 8 of the finest flour mixed with **o oil**; H9043
Nu 11: 8 it tasted like something made with **o oil**. H9043
Nu 15: 4 mixed with a quarter of a hin of **o oil**. H9043
Nu 15: 6 flour mixed with a third of a hin of **o oil**, H9043
Nu 15: 9 finest flour mixed with half a hin of **o oil**, H9043
Nu 18:12 you all the finest **o oil** and all the finest H3658
Nu 28: 9 ephah of the finest flour mixed with **o oil**. H9043
Nu 29: 3 ephah of the finest flour mixed with **o oil**; H9043
Dt 6:11 vineyards and **o groves** you did not H2339
Dt 7:13 new wine and **o oil**—the calves of your H3658
Dt 8: 8 fig trees, pomegranates, **o** oil and honey; H2339
Dt 11:14 gather in your grain, new wine and **o oil**. H3658
Dt 12:17 of your grain and new wine and **o oil**, H3658
Dt 14:23 new wine and **o oil**, and the firstborn H3658
Dt 18: 4 new wine and **o oil**, and the first H3658
Dt 28:40 You will have **o trees** throughout your H2339
Dt 28:51 new wine or **o oil**, nor any calves of H3658
Jos 24:13 vineyards and **o groves** that you did not H2339
Jdg 9: 8 They said to the **o tree**, 'Be our king.' H2339
Jdg 9: 9 "But the **o tree** answered, 'Should I give H2339
Jdg 15: 5 together with the vineyards and **o groves**. H2339
1Sa 8:14 vineyards and **o groves** and give them to H2339
1Sa 10: 1 took a flask of **o oil** and poured it on H9043
1Ki 5:11 to twenty thousand baths of **pressed o** oil. H4184
1Ki 6:23 made a pair of cherubim out of **o** wood, H9043
1Ki 6:31 made doors out of **o** wood that were one H9043
1Ki 6:33 doorframes out of **o** wood that were one H9043
1Ki 17:12 of flour in a jar and a little **o oil** in a jug. H9043
2Ki 4: 2 she said, "except a small jar of **o oil**." H9043
2Ki 5:26 accept clothes—or **o groves** and vineyards H2339
2Ki 9: 1 take this flask of **o oil** with you and go to H9043
2Ki 18:32 a land of **o trees** and honey. H2339+3658
2Ki 20:13 the spices and the fine **o oil**—his armory H9043
1Ch 9:29 wine, and the **o oil**, incense and H9043
1Ch 12:40 raisin cakes, wine, **o oil**, cattle and sheep H9043
1Ch 27:28 was in charge of the **o** and sycamore-fig H2339
1Ch 27:28 was in charge of the supplies of **o oil**. H9043
2Ch 2:10 wine and twenty thousand baths of **o oil**." H9043
2Ch 2:15 barley and the **o oil** and wine he H9043
2Ch 11:11 with supplies of food, **o oil** and wine. H9043
2Ch 31: 5 **o oil** and honey and all that the fields H3658
2Ch 32:28 new wine and **o oil**; and he made H3658
Ezr 3: 7 food and drink and **o oil** to the people of H9043
Ezr 6: 9 wine and **o oil**, as requested by the A10442
Ezr 7:22 a hundred baths of **o oil**, and salt A10442
Ne 5:11 vineyards, **o groves** and houses, and also H2339
Ne 5:11 of the money, grain, new wine and **o oil**." H3658
Ne 8:15 back branches from **o** and wild olive trees, H2339
Ne 8:15 back branches from olive and **wild o** trees, H9043
Ne 9:25 **o groves** and fruit trees in abundance. H2339
Ne 10:37 our trees and of our new wine and **o oil**. H3658
Ne 10:39 new wine and **o oil** to the storerooms H3658
Ne 13: 5 new wine and **o oil** prescribed for the H3658
Ne 13:12 new wine and **o oil** into the storerooms. H3658
Job 15:33 like an **o tree** shedding its blossoms. H2339
Job 29: 6 rock poured out for me streams of **o oil**. H9043
Ps 52: 8 But I am like an **o tree** flourishing in the H2339
Ps 128: 3 children will be like **o** shoots around your H2339
Pr 21:17 loves wine and **o oil** will never be rich. H9043
Pr 21:20 The wise store up choice food and **o oil** H9043
Isa 1: 6 bandaged or soothed with **o oil**. H9043
Isa 17: 6 remain, as when an **o tree** is beaten H2339
Isa 24:13 as when an **o tree** is beaten, or as H2339
Isa 39: 2 the fine **o oil**—his entire armory H9043
Isa 41:19 the acacia, the myrtle and the **o**. H6770+9043
Isa 57: 9 to Molek with **o oil** and increased your H9043
Jer 11:16 you a thriving **o tree** with fruit beautiful H2339
Jer 31:12 the new wine and the **o oil**, the young of H3658
Jer 40:10 summer fruit and **o oil**, and put them in H9043
Jer 41: 8 barley, **o oil** and honey, hidden H9043
Eze 16:13 food was honey, **o oil** and the finest flour. H9043
Eze 16:19 the flour, **o oil** and honey I gave you to eat H9043
Eze 23:41 incense and **o oil** *that belonged to* me. H9043
Eze 27:17 **o oil** and balm for your wares. H9043
Eze 45:14 The prescribed portion of **o oil**, measured H9043
Eze 45:24 along with a hin of **o oil** for each ephah. H9043
Eze 46: 5 along with a hin of **o oil** for each ephah. H9043
Hos 2: 5 wool and my linen, my **o oil** and my drink. H9043
Hos 2:22 the new wine and the **o oil**, and they will H3658
Hos 12: 1 with Assyria and sends **o oil** to Egypt. H9043
Hos 14: 6 His splendor will be like an **o tree**, his H2339
Joel 1:10 the new wine is dried up, the **o oil** fails. H3658
Joel 2:19 new wine and **o oil**, enough to satisfy H3658
Am 4: 9 Locusts devoured your fig and **o trees**, yet H2339
Mic 6: 7 of rams, with ten thousand rivers of **o oil**? H9043
Hab 3:17 though the **o** crop fails and the fields H2339
Hag 1:11 the **o oil** and everything else the ground H3658
Hag 2:12 some wine, **o oil** or other food, does it H9043
Hag 2:19 the **o** tree have not borne H2339
Zec 4: 3 Also there are two **o trees** by it, one on the H2339
Zec 4:11 are these two **o trees** on the right and H2339
Zec 4:12 are these two **o** branches beside the H2339
Lk 16: 6 " 'Nine hundred gallons *of* **o** oil,' he *G1778*
Ro 11:17 though a **wild o shoot**, have been *G66*
Ro 11:17 in the nourishing sap from the **o** root, *G1777*
Ro 11:24 cut out of an **o tree that is wild** by nature, *G66*
Ro 11:24 were grafted into a **cultivated o tree**, *G2814*
Ro 11:24 branches, be grafted into their own **o tree**! *G1777*
Rev 11: 4 They are "the two **o trees**" and the two *G1777*
Rev 18:13 of wine and **o oil**, of fine flour and wheat *G1778*

OLIVE-WOOD (1) [OLIVE, WOOD]

1Ki 6:32 And on the two **o** doors he carved H9043+6770

OLIVES (25) [OLIVE]

Ex 27:20 clear oil of pressed **o** for the light so that H2339
Ex 29:40 a quarter of a hin of oil from **pressed o**, H4184
Lev 24: 2 clear oil of pressed **o** for the light so that H2339
Nu 28: 5 a quarter of a hin of oil from **pressed o**. H4184
Dt 24:20 When you beat the **o from** your **trees**, do H2339
Dt 28:40 use the oil, because the **o** will drop off. H2339
2Sa 15:30 But David continued up the Mount of **O** H2339
Job 24:11 *They* **crush o** among the terraces; they H7414
Isa 17: 6 leaving two or three **o** on the topmost H1737
Mic 6:15 you will press **o** but not use the oil H2339
Zec 14: 4 day his feet will stand on the Mount of **O**, H2339
Zec 14: 4 the Mount of **O** will be split in two H2339
Mt 21: 1 to Bethphage on the Mount *of* **O**, *G1777+1779*
Mt 24: 3 was sitting on the Mount *of* **O**, *G1777+1779*
Mt 26:30 they went out to the Mount *of* **O**. *G1777+1779*
Mk 11: 1 and Bethany at the Mount *of* **O**, *G1777+1779*
Mk 13: 3 on the Mount *of* **O** opposite the *G1777+1779*
Mk 14:26 they went out to the Mount *of* **O**. *G1777+1779*
Lk 19:29 Bethany at the hill called the **Mount of O**, *G1779*
Lk 19:37 road goes down the Mount *of* **O**, *G1777+1779*
Lk 21:37 night on the hill called the **Mount of O**, *G1779*
Lk 22:39 out as usual to the Mount *of* **O**, *G1777+1779*
Jn 8: 1 Jesus went to the Mount *of* **O**. *G1777+1779*
Ac 1:12 from the hill called the **Mount of O**, *G1779*
Jas 3:12 can a fig tree bear **o**, or a grapevine bear *G1777*

OLIVET (KJV) OLIVES

OLYMPAS (1)

Ro 16:15 **O** and all the Lord's people who are *G3912*

OMAR (3)

Ge 36:11 Teman, **O**, Zepho, Gatam and H223
Ge 36:15 Chiefs Teman, **O**, Zepho, Kenaz, H223
1Ch 1:36 **O**, Zepho, Gatam and Kenaz; by H223

OMEGA (3)

Rev 1: 8 "I am the Alpha and the O," G6043+1639+6042
Rev 21: 6 I am the Alpha and the O G6043+1639+6042
Rev 22:13 I am the Alpha and the O G6043+1639+6042

OMEN (2) [OMENS]

Eze 21:21 of the two roads, to **seek an o**: H7876+7877
Eze 21:23 will seem like a false o to those who have H7876

OMENS (6) [OMEN]

Lev 19:26 " 'Do not practice divination or **seek o**. H6726
Nu 23:23 against Jacob, no **evil o** against Israel. H7877
Dt 18:10 sorcery, **interprets o**, engages in H5727
2Ki 17:17 divination and **sought o** and sold H5727
2Ki 21: 6 divination, **sought o**, and consulted H5727
2Ch 33: 6 witchcraft, **sought o**, and consulted H4175

OMER (5) [OMERS]

Ex 16:16 Take an o for each person you have in H6685
Ex 16:18 And when they measured it by the o, the H6685
Ex 16:32 'Take an o of manna and keep it for the H6685
Ex 16:33 "Take a jar and put an o *of* manna in it. H6685
Ex 16:36 An o is one-tenth of an ephah. H6685

OMERS (1) [OMER]

Ex 16:22 twice as much—two o for each person H6685

OMIT (1)

Jer 26: 2 I command you; *do* not o a word. H1757

OMNIPOTENT (KJV) ALMIGHTY

OMRI (15) [OMRI'S]

1Ki 16:16 they proclaimed O, the commander of H6687
1Ki 16:17 Then O and all the Israelites with him H6687
1Ki 16:21 king, and the other half supported O. H6687
1Ki 16:22 So Tibni died and O became king. H6687
1Ki 16:23 king of Judah, O became king of Israel H6687
1Ki 16:25 But O did evil in the eyes of the LORD and H6687
1Ki 16:28 O rested with his ancestors and was buried H6687
1Ki 16:29 Ahab son of O became king of Israel H6687
1Ki 16:30 Ahab son of O did more evil in the eyes of H6687
2Ki 8:26 a granddaughter of O king of Israel. H6687
1Ch 7: 8 Elioenai, O, Jeremoth, Abijah H6687
1Ch 9: 4 Ammihud, the son of O, the son of Imri, H6687
1Ch 27:18 of David; over Issachar: O son of Michael; H6687
2Ch 22: 2 was Athaliah, a granddaughter of O. H6687
Mic 6:16 the statutes of O and all the practices of H6687

OMRI'S (2) [OMRI]

1Ki 16:22 But O followers proved stronger than those H6687
1Ki 16:27 As for the other events of O reign, what H6687

ON (4 of 4894) [ONTO] For ON as a Preposition, see Index of Articles Etc.

Ge 41:45 of Potiphera, priest of O, to be his wife. H228
Ge 41:50 Asenath daughter of Potiphera, priest of O. H228
Ge 46:20 Asenath daughter of Potiphera, priest of O. H228
Nu 16: 1 sons of Eliab, and O son of Peleth— H227

ONAM (4)

Ge 36:23 Manahath, Ebal, Shepho and O. H231
1Ch 1:40 Shepho and O. The sons of Zibeon: H231
1Ch 2:26 was Atarah; she was the mother of O. H231
1Ch 2:28 The sons of O: Shammai and Jada. H231

ONAN (7)

Ge 38: 4 gave birth to a son and named him O. H232
Ge 38: 8 Then Judah said to O, "Sleep with your H232
Ge 38: 9 But O knew that the child would not be his H232
Ge 46:12 O, Shelah, Perez and Zerah (but Er and H232
Ge 46:12 Er and O had died in the land of H232
Nu 26:19 Er and O were sons of Judah, but they died H232
1Ch 2: 3 sons of Judah: Er, O and Shelah. These H232

ONCE (180) [ONE]

Ge 18:29 **O again** he spoke to him, "What if H3578+6388
Ge 18:32 be angry, but let me speak just **o more**. H7193
Ge 25:29 O when Jacob was cooking some stew, Esau NDT
Ge 27:43 Flee **at o** to my brother Laban in Harran. H7756
Ge 28: 2 Go **at o** to Paddan Aram, to the house of H7756
Ge 31:10 breeding season *I o* **had** a dream in which I AIT
Ge 31:13 Now leave this land **at o** and go back to H7756
Ge 40:21 so that *he o again* **put** the cup into Pharaoh's AIT
Ge 41:10 Pharaoh *was o* **angry** with his servants, and AIT
Ge 43: 8 boy along with me and we will go **at o**, H7756
Ge 43:13 brother also and go back to the man **at o**. H7756
Ge 44: 4 "Go after those men **at o**, and when you H7756
Ex 10:17 my sin **o more** and pray to H421+2021+7193
Ex 12:21 "**Go at o** and select the animals for your H5432
Ex 30:10 **O** a year Aaron shall make atonement on H285
Ex 34: 8 bowed to the ground **at o** and worshiped. H4554
Lev 16:34 is to be made **o** a year for all the sins H285
Nu 12: 4 **At o** the LORD said to Moses, Aaron and H7328
Nu 16:21 so I can put an end to them **at o**." H3869+8092
Nu 16:45 so I can put an end to them **at o**." H3869+8092
Nu 24:11 Now **leave at o** and go home! I said I H1368
Dt 7:22 not be allowed to eliminate them **all at o**, H4554
Dt 9:12 "Go down from here **at o**, because your H4554
Dt 9:18 Then **o again** I fell prostrate H3869+2021+8037
Jos 6: 3 around the city **o** with all the armed H285+7193
Jos 6:11 carried around the city, circling it **o**. H285+7193
Jos 6:14 around the city **o** and returned to the H7193+285
Jdg 2:23 not drive them out **at o** by giving them H4554
Jdg 16:18 "Come back **o more**; he has told me H7193
Jdg 16:28 strengthen me just **o more**, and let me H7193
Jdg 20:15 **At o** the Benjamites H928+2021+3427+2021+2085
1Sa 1: 9 **O** when they had finished eating and NDT
1Sa 10: 7 **O** these signs are fulfilled, do whatever H3954
1Sa 14:33 "Roll a large stone over here **at o**." H2021+3427
1Sa 15:17 "Although you were **o** small in your own NDT
1Sa 19: 8 **O more** war broke out, and David went H3578
1Sa 23: 4 **O again** David inquired of the LORD H3578+6388
1Sa 28:24 at the house, which she butchered **at o**. H4554
2Sa 3:21 "Let me go **at o** and assemble all Israel H7756
2Sa 5:22 **O more** the Philistines came up H3578+6388
2Sa 14:26 cut his hair **o a year** because H4946+7891+3427+4200+2021+3427
2Sa 17:16 Now send a message **at o** and tell David H4559
2Sa 17:18 the two of them left **at o** and went to the H4559
2Sa 17:21 "Set out and cross the river **at o** H4559
2Sa 21:15 **O again** there was a battle between the H6388
1Ki 10:22 **O** every three years it returned, carrying H285
1Ki 13:33 but **o more** appointed priests for the high H8740
1Ki 17: 9 "Go **at o** to Zarephath in the region of H7756
1Ki 19: 5 **All at o** an angel touched him and H2180+2296
1Ki 22: 9 "**Bring** Micaiah son of Imlah **at o**." H4554
2Ki 1:11 is what the king says, 'Come down **at o**!" H4559
2Ki 4:35 the bed and stretched out on him **o** more. NDT
2Ki 7: 9 *Let's* **go at o** and report this to H2143+2256+995
2Ki 13:21 **O** while some Israelites were burying a H2118
2Ki 19:30 **O more** a remnant of the kingdom of H3578
1Ch 14:13 **O more** the Philistines raided the H3578+6388
2Ch 9:21 **O** every three years it returned, carrying H285
2Ch 18: 8 "**Bring** Micaiah son of Imlah **at o**." H4554
2Ch 24: 5 But the Levites *did* not **act at o**. H4554
Ne 13:20 **O** or twice the merchants and sellers of all H7193
Est 5: 5 "**Bring** Haman **at o**," the king said, "so H4554
Est 6:10 "**Go at o**," the king commanded Haman H4554
Est 8: 9 **At o** the royal secretaries H928+2021+6961+2021+2085
Job 3: 5 gloom and utter darkness claim it **o** more; NDT
Job 14:20 You overpower them **o for all**, and H4200+5905
Job 18:19 his people, no survivor where **o** he lived. NDT
Job 33:21 their bones, *o* **hidden**, now stick out. AIT
Job 40: 5 I spoke **o**, but I have no answer—twice H285
Ps 55:14 with whom *I o* **enjoyed sweet** fellowship at AIT
Ps 71:21 my honor and comfort me **o more**. H6015
Ps 89:19 **O** you spoke in a vision, to your faithful H255
Ps 89:35 **O for all**, I have sworn by my holiness H285
Pr 7:22 **All at o** he followed her like an ox going H7328
Pr 12:16 show their annoyance **at o**, H928+2021+3427
Ecc 9:14 There was **o** a small city with only a few NDT
Isa 1:21 She **o** was full of justice; righteousness used NDT
Isa 7:25 As for all the hills *o* **cultivated** by the hoe, AIT
Isa 14: 1 **o again** he will choose Israel and will H6388
Isa 14:12 to the earth, *you who o* **laid low** the nations! AIT
Isa 16: 8 *which o* **reached** Jazer and spread toward the AIT
Isa 29:14 Therefore **o more** I will astound these H3578
Isa 29:19 **O more** the humble will rejoice in the H3578
Isa 35: 7 In the haunts where jackals **o** lay, grass NDT
Isa 37:31 **O more** a remnant of the kingdom of H3578
Jer 12:16 even as *they o* **taught** my people to swear by AIT
Jer 31:23 in its towns will **o again** use these words: H6388
Jer 32:43 **O more** fields will be bought in this land H2256
Jer 33:10 animals, there will be heard **o more** H6388
Jer 42: 2 though we were **o** many, now only a H4946
La 1: 1 deserted lies the city, **o** so full of people! NDT
La 1: 1 who **o** was great among the nations! NDT
La 4: 2 **o** worth their weight in gold NDT
La 4: 5 Those *who o* **ate** delicacies are destitute in AIT
Eze 31: 3 Consider Assyria, **o** a cedar in Lebanon, with NDT
Eze 36:37 **O** again I will yield to Israel's plea and do H2296
Eze 42:14 **O** the priests enter the holy precincts, they H928
Da 2: 7 **O more** they replied, "Let the king tell A10766
Da 2:25 took Daniel to the king **at o** and said, A10097
Hag 2: 6 a little while I will **o** more shake the H285
Zec 8: 4 "**O again** men and women of ripe old age H6388
Zec 8:21 '*Let us* **go at o** to entreat the LORD H2143+2143
Mt 4:20 **At o** they left their nets and followed him. G2311
Mt 13:20 hears the word and **at o** receives it with G2317
Mt 13:47 "**O again**, the kingdom of heaven is like a G4099
Mt 21: 2 and **at o** you will find a donkey tied there G2311
Mt 25:16 bags of gold went **at o** and put his money G2311
Mt 26:44 went away **o more** and prayed the G4099
Mt 26:49 Going **at o** to Jesus, Judas said G2311
Mt 26:53 he will **at o** put at my disposal more G785
Mk 1:12 **At o** the Spirit sent him out into the G2317
Mk 1:18 **At o** they left their nets and followed him. G2317
Mk 1:43 Jesus sent him away **at o** with a strong G2317
Mk 2:13 **O** again Jesus went out beside the lake G2779
Mk 4:16 hear the word and **at o** receive it with joy. G2317
Mk 5:30 **At o** Jesus realized that power had gone G2317
Mk 6:25 **At o** the girl hurried in to the king with the G2317
Mk 8:25 **O more** Jesus put his hands on the man's G4099
Mk 14:39 **O more** he went away and prayed the G4099
Mk 14:45 Going **at o** to Jesus, Judas said, "Rabbi!" G2317
Lk 1: 8 **O** when Zechariah's division was G1181+1254
Lk 4:39 She got up **at o** and began to wait on G4202
Lk 8:55 returned, and **at o** she stood up. G4202
Lk 9:18 **O** when Jesus was praying in G2779+1181
Lk 13:25 **O** the owner of the house gets G608+4005+323
Lk 17:20 **O**, on being asked by the Pharisees when G1254
Lk 19: 6 So he came down **at o** and welcomed him G5067
Lk 19:11 of God was going to appear **at o**. G4202
Lk 24:33 and returned **at o** to G899+3836+6052
Jn 4: 3 Judea and went back **o more** to Galilee. G4099
Jn 4:46 **O more** he visited Cana in Galilee, where G4099
Jn 5: 9 **At o** the man was cured; he picked up his G2311
Jn 6:24 **O** the crowd realized that neither Jesus G4021
Jn 8:21 **O more** Jesus said to them, "I am going G4099
Jn 11:38 **o more** deeply moved, came to the G4099
Jn 13:32 Son in himself, and will glorify him **at o**. G2317
Jn 19: 4 **O more** Pilate came out and said to the G4099
Ac 9:20 **At o** he began to preach in the G2311
Ac 9:38 and urged him, "*Please* **come at o**!" G3590+3890
Ac 16:10 we got ready **at o** to leave for Macedonia G2311
Ac 16:16 **O** when we were going to the G1181+1254
Ac 16:26 **At o** all the prison doors flew open, and G4202
Ac 21:32 He **at o** took some officers and soldiers G1994
Ac 23:30 against the man, I sent him to you **at o**. G1994
Ac 28: 1 **O** safely on shore, we found out that the G5538
Ro 6:10 he died to sin **o for all**; but the life he G2384
Ro 7: 6 by dying to what *o* **bound** *us*, we have been AIT
Ro 7: 9 **O** I was alive apart from the law; but when G1254
2Co 5:16 Though *we o* **regarded** Christ in this way, AIT
2Co 10: 6 **o** your obedience is complete. G4020
2Co 11:25 with rods, **o** I was pelted with stones G562
Gal 1:23 preaching the faith he **o** tried to destroy." G4537
Eph 2:13 Jesus you who **o** were far away have G4537
Eph 5: 8 For you were **o** darkness, but now you are G4537
Php 4:16 me aid **more than o** when I G562+2779+1489
Col 1:21 **O** you were alienated from God and were G4537
Col 3: 7 walk in these ways, in the life you **o** lived. G4021
1Ti 1:13 though I was **o** a blasphemer and G3836+4728
1Ti 1:18 with the prophecies **o made** about you, G4575
Titus 3:10 Warn a divisive person **o**, and then warn G1651
Heb 5: 9 *o* **made perfect**, he became the source AIT
Heb 6: 4 those who have **o** been enlightened, G562
Heb 7:27 their sins **o for all** when he offered G2384
Heb 9: 7 and that *only* **o** a year, and never G562
Heb 9:12 Most Holy Place **o for all** by his own blood G2384
Heb 9:26 he has appeared **o for all** at the G562
Heb 9:27 Just as people are destined to die **o**, and G562
Heb 9:28 Christ was sacrificed **o** to take away the sins G562
Heb 10: 2 would have been cleansed **o for all**, G562
Heb 10:10 of the body of Jesus Christ **o for all**. G2384
Heb 12:26 "**O** more I will shake not only the earth G562
Heb 12:27 The words "**o** more" indicate the removing G562
1Pe 2:10 **O** you were not a people, but now you are G4537
1Pe 2:10 **o** you had not received mercy NDT
1Pe 3:18 For Christ also suffered **o** for sins, the G562
Jude 3 the faith that was **o for all** entrusted to G562
Rev 4: 2 **At o** I was in the Spirit, and there before G2311
Rev 10: 8 heard from heaven spoke to me **o more**: G4099
Rev 17: 8 which you saw, *o* **was**, now is not, and yet AIT
Rev 17: 8 see the beast, because *it o* **was**, now is not, AIT
Rev 17:11 The beast who *o* **was**, and now is not, is an AIT

ONE (2697) [ONCE, ONE'S, ONE-TENTH, ONE-THIRD, ONES, ONESELF]

Ge 1: 9 water under the sky be gathered to **o** place, H285
Ge 2: 5 there was no **o** to work the ground, H132
Ge 2:21 he took **o** of the man's ribs and then closed H285
Ge 2:24 to his wife, and they become **o** flesh. H285
Ge 3:22 "The man has now become like **o** of us H285
Ge 4:15 on Cain so that no **o** who found him H3972
Ge 4:19 **o** named Adah and the other Zillah. H285
Ge 6:16 the roof an opening *o* **cubit** high all around. AIT
Ge 7: 2 and **o** and **pair** of every kind of unclean H9109
Ge 8:19 the ark, **o kind after another**. H4200+5476+2157
Ge 10:25 **O** was named Peleg, because in his time H285
Ge 11: 1 the whole world had **o** language and a H285
Ge 11: 6 "If as **o** people speaking the same H285
Ge 15: 2 and the **o who will inherit** my H1201+5479
Ge 16:13 "I have now seen the *O* **who sees** me." AIT
Ge 18:10 Then *o of them* **said**, "I will surely return to AIT
Ge 19:17 them out, *o of them* **said**, "Flee for your AIT
Ge 19:31 **O day** the older daughter said to the H2256
Ge 20: 3 Abimelek in a dream **o** night and said to H2021
Ge 21:15 she put the boy under **o** *of* the bushes. H285
Ge 24: 2 household, the *o* **in charge** of all that he had AIT
Ge 24:14 let her be the **o** you have chosen for your NDT
Ge 24:44 let her be the **o** the LORD has chosen for my H851
Ge 24:50 say nothing to you **o way** or the other. H8273S
Ge 24:63 went out to the field **o** evening to meditate, NDT
Ge 25:23 *o* **people** will be stronger than the other AIT
Ge 26:10 **O** *of* the men might well have slept with H285
Ge 26:21 they quarreled over *that* **o** also; so he H2023
Ge 26:22 dug another well, and no *o* **quarreled** over it. AIT
Ge 27:38 "Do you have only **o** blessing, my father? H285
Ge 27:45 Why should I lose both of you in **o** day?" H285
Ge 28:11 Taking *o of* the stones there, he put it H4946
Ge 29:26 daughter in marriage before the **older** *o*. AIT
Ge 29:27 then we will give you **the younger** *o* also, H2296S
Ge 29:33 that I am not loved, he gave me **this** *o* too." AIT
Ge 30:31 "But if you will do this *o* **thing** for me, I will AIT
Ge 31:50 even though no **o** is with us, remember H408
Ge 32: 8 "If Esau comes and attacks **o** group, the H285
Ge 32:17 He instructed the **o in the lead**: "When H8037
Ge 33:13 If they are driven hard just **o** day, all the H285
Ge 34:15 agreement with you on **o condition** only: H2296S
Ge 34:16 you and become **o** people with you. H285
Ge 34:22 to live with us as **o** people only on the H285
Ge 35: 5 all around them so that no *o* **pursued** them. AIT
Ge 37:20 throw him into **o** *of* these cisterns and H285
Ge 37:36 Potiphar, *o of* Pharaoh's **officials**, the captain AIT

Ge 38:28 giving birth, *o of them* **put out** his hand; so AIT
Ge 38:28 on his wrist and said, "**This** *o* came out first." AIT
Ge 39: 1 an Egyptian who was **o** of Pharaoh's NDT
Ge 39: 9 No **o** is greater in this house than I am. H5647
Ge 39:11 **O** day he went into the house to attend to H2296
Ge 40: 8 "but there is no *o to* **interpret** them. AIT
Ge 41: 8 no *o could* **interpret** them for him. AIT
Ge 41:15 "I had a dream, and no *o can* **interpret** it. AIT
Ge 41:21 no *o could* **tell** that they had done so AIT
Ge 41:25 dreams of Pharaoh are **o and the same**. H285
Ge 41:26 seven years; it is **o and the same** dream. H285
Ge 41:38 this man, **o** in whom is the spirit of God?" H2257
Ge 41:39 there is no *o so* **discerning** and wise as you. AIT
Ge 41:44 without your word no **o** will lift hand or foot H408
Ge 42:11 We are all the sons of **o** man. Your servants H285
Ge 42:13 the sons of **o** man, who lives in the H285
Ge 42:13 is now with our father, and **o** is no more." H285
Ge 42:16 Send **o** of your number to get your brother H285
Ge 42:19 let **o** *of* your brothers stay here in prison H285
Ge 42:21 They said to **o** another, "Surely we are H408
Ge 42:27 stopped for the night **o** of them opened his H285
Ge 42:32 brothers, sons of **o** father. One is no more, H5646
Ge 42:32 **O** is no more, and the youngest is now with H285
Ge 42:33 Leave **o** *of* your brothers here with me, and H285
Ge 42:38 and he is the **only o** left. H4200+963+2257
Ge 43:29 youngest brother, the **o** you told me about?" H889
Ge 44: 2 my cup, the silver **o**, in the mouth of the H1483S
Ge 44:16 we ourselves and the **o** who was found to H2257
Ge 44:20 he is the only **o** of his mother's sons H2257
Ge 44:28 **O** *of them* went away from me, and I said H285
Ge 44:29 If you take **this** *o* from me too and harm AIT
Ge 45: 1 So there was no **o** with Joseph when he H408
Ge 45: 4 brother Joseph, **the o** you sold into Egypt! H889S
Ge 47:20 The Egyptians, **o and all**, sold their fields H408
Ge 47:21 to servitude, from *o* **end** *of* Egypt to the other. AIT
Ge 48:18 my father, **this** *o* is the firstborn; put your right AIT
Ge 48:22 And to you I give **o** more ridge of land than H285
Ge 49:16 his people as **o** *of* the tribes of Israel. H285
Ge 49:24 of the hand of the **Mighty O** *of* Jacob, H51
Ex 2: 6 "This is **o** *of* the Hebrew babies," she said H4946
Ex 2: 7 I go and get **o** *of* the Hebrew women to H4946
Ex 2:11 **O** day, after Moses had grown up, he H2021
Ex 2:11 beating a Hebrew, **o** *of* his own people. H4946
Ex 2:12 Looking this way and that and seeing no **o** H408
Ex 2:13 He asked the **o in the wrong**, "Why are H8401
Ex 6:25 of Aaron married **o** *of* the daughters of H4946
Ex 7:12 **Each** *o* threw down his staff and it became a AIT
Ex 8:10 you may know **there is no o** like the LORD our AIT
Ex 9: 6 not **o** animal belonging to the H285
Ex 9: 7 found that not even **o** of the animals of the H285
Ex 9:14 may know that **there is no o** like me in all AIT
Ex 10:23 No **o** could see anyone else or move about H408
Ex 11: 1 "I will bring **o** more plague on Pharaoh H285
Ex 12: 3 his family, **o** for each household. H8445S
Ex 12: 4 they must share **o** with their nearest NDT
Ex 12:16 assembly, and **another** *o* on the seventh day. AIT
Ex 12:48 then he may take part like *o* **born** *in* the land. AIT
Ex 14:20 darkness to the **o** side and light to the NDT
Ex 14:28 Not **o** of them survived. H285
Ex 16:18 the *o who* **gathered much** did not have too AIT
Ex 16:18 the *o who* **gathered little** did not have AIT
Ex 16:19 "No **o** is to keep any of it until morning." H408
Ex 16:29 are on the seventh day; no **o** is to go out." H408
Ex 17:12 held his hands up—**o** on one side, one on H285
Ex 17:12 hands up—one on *o* **side**, one on the other AIT
Ex 17:12 one on one side, **o** on the other—so that H285
Ex 18: 3 **O** son was named Gershom, for Moses said H285
Ex 21:10 he must not deprive the first **o** of her food NDT
Ex 21:18 quarrel and *o* **person** hits another with AIT
Ex 21:19 the *o who* **struck the blow** will not be held AIT
Ex 21:33 a pit or digs **o** and fails to cover it H1014S
Ex 21:34 the *o who* **opened** the pit must pay the owner AIT
Ex 21:35 are to sell the live **o** and divide both the H8802S
Ex 22: 6 the *o who* **started** the fire must make AIT
Ex 22: 9 *The o* **whom** the judges declare guilty must AIT
Ex 22:10 is taken away *while* no *o is* **looking**, AIT
Ex 22:25 you lend money to **o** of my people among NDT
Ex 23:15 "No *o is to* **appear** before me empty-handed. AIT
Ex 24: 3 they responded with **o** voice, "Everything H285
Ex 25:12 with two rings on **o** side and two rings on H285
Ex 25:19 Make **o** cherub on one end and the second H285
Ex 25:19 Make one cherub on **o** end and the H2296
Ex 25:19 the cherubim **of o piece with** the cover, H4946
Ex 25:31 buds and blossoms **of o piece with** them. H4946
Ex 25:32 three on **o** side and three on the other. H285
Ex 25:33 buds and blossoms are to be on **o** branch, H285
Ex 25:35 **O** bud shall be under the first pair of NDT
Ex 25:36 shall all be of *o piece* with the lampstand, H285
Ex 26: 4 along the edge of the end curtain in **o** set, H285
Ex 26: 5 Make fifty loops on **o** curtain and fifty loops H285
Ex 26: 9 together **into o set** and the other H4200+963
Ex 26:10 of the end curtain in **o** set and also along H285
Ex 26:19 each frame, **o** under each projection. NDT
Ex 26:26 the frames on **o** side of the tabernacle H285
Ex 27: 2 the horns and the altar are **of o piece**, H4946
Ex 27:14 long are to be on **o** side of the entrance, H2021
Ex 28: 8 **of o piece with** the ephod and made with H4946
Ex 28:10 six names on **o** stone and the remaining six H285
Ex 28:21 **o** for each of the names of the sons of Israel, NDT
Ex 28:21 seal with the name of **o** of the twelve tribes. NDT
Ex 29:15 "Take **o** of the rams, and Aaron and his H285
Ex 29:23 the LORD, take **o** round loaf, one thick H285
Ex 29:23 **o** thick loaf with olive oil mixed in H285
Ex 29:23 loaf with olive oil mixed in, and **o** thin loaf. H285
Ex 29:33 But no *o* else *may* **eat** them, because they AIT
Ex 29:39 Offer **o** in the morning and the other at H285
Ex 30: 2 cubits high—its horns **of o piece with** it. H4946
Ex 30:12 **each** *o* must pay the LORD a ransom for his AIT
Ex 30:13 Each *o* who **crosses over** to those already AIT
Ex 32:27 through the camp from *o* **end** to the other, AIT
Ex 33: 4 to mourn and no **o** put on any ornaments. H408
Ex 33:11 Moses face to face, as **o** speaks to a friend. H408
Ex 33:20 see my face, for no **o** may see me and live." H132
Ex 34: 3 No **o** is to come with you or be seen H408
Ex 34:20 "No *o is to* **appear** before me empty-handed. AIT
Ex 34:24 no **o** will covet your land when you go H408
Ex 36:11 along the edge of the end curtain in **o** set, H285
Ex 36:12 made fifty loops on **o** curtain and fifty loops H285
Ex 36:16 of the curtains into **o set** and the other six AIT
Ex 36:17 of the end curtain in **o** set and also along H2021
Ex 36:24 each frame, **o** under each projection. NDT
Ex 36:31 the frames on **o** side of the tabernacle H285
Ex 37: 3 with two rings on **o** side and two rings on H285
Ex 37: 8 He made **o** cherub on one end and the H285
Ex 37: 8 one cherub on **o** end and the second H2296
Ex 37: 8 he made them **of o piece with** the cover. H4946
Ex 37:17 buds and blossoms **of o piece with** them. H4946
Ex 37:18 three on **o** side and three on the other. H285
Ex 37:19 with buds and blossoms were on **o** branch, H285
Ex 37:21 **O** bud was under the first pair of branches NDT
Ex 37:22 were all **of o piece with** the lampstand, H4946
Ex 37:24 all its accessories from *o* **talent** *of* pure gold. AIT
Ex 37:25 cubits high—its horns **of o piece with** it. H4946
Ex 38: 2 the horns and the altar were **of o piece**, H4946
Ex 38:14 cubits long were on **o** side of the entrance H2021
Ex 38:26 *o* **beka** per person, that is, half a shekel AIT
Ex 38:27 from the 100 talents, **o** talent for each base. NDT
Ex 39: 5 **of o piece with** the ephod and made with H4946
Ex 39:14 **o** for each of the names of the sons of Israel, NDT
Ex 39:14 seal with the name of **o** of the twelve tribes. NDT
Lev 5: 4 in any matter **o** might carelessly swear H132
Lev 5: 7 **o** for a sin offering and the other for a burnt H285
Lev 5: 8 shall first offer **the o** for the sin offering. H889S
Lev 5:15 **o** without defect and of the proper value in NDT
Lev 5:18 **o** without defect and of the proper value. NDT
Lev 6: 6 **o** without defect and of the proper value. NDT
Lev 7:14 They are to bring **o** of each kind as an H285
Lev 7:18 the *o who* **offered** it will not be accepted. AIT
Lev 8:26 the LORD, he took **o** thick loaf, one thick H285
Lev 8:26 **o** thick loaf with olive oil mixed in H285
Lev 8:26 oil mixed in, and **o** thin loaf, and he put H285
Lev 9:15 a sin offering as he did with the **first** *o*. AIT
Lev 11:25 Whoever picks up **o** *of* their carcasses must H4946
Lev 11:32 When **o** of them dies and falls on H3972
Lev 11:33 If **o** *of* them falls into a clay pot, everything H4946
Lev 11:35 Anything that **o** *of* their carcasses falls on H4946
Lev 11:36 anyone who touches **o** of these carcasses is NDT
Lev 12: 8 **o** for a burnt offering and the other for a sin H285
Lev 13: 2 Aaron the priest or to **o** of his sons who is a H285
Lev 14: 5 shall order that **o** of the birds be killed H285
Lev 14: 7 sprinkle the *o to* **be cleansed** of the defiling AIT
Lev 14:10 two male lambs and **o** ewe lamb a year H285
Lev 14:10 oil for a grain offering, and **o** log of oil. H285
Lev 14:11 present both the **o** to be cleansed and H408
Lev 14:12 priest is to take **o** of the male lambs and H285
Lev 14:14 lobe of the right ear of the *o to* **be cleansed,** AIT
Lev 14:17 lobe of the right ear of the *o to* **be cleansed,** AIT
Lev 14:18 the head of the *o to* **be cleansed** and make AIT
Lev 14:19 the *o to* **be cleansed** from their AIT
Lev 14:21 they must take **o** male lamb as a guilt H285
Lev 14:22 **o** for a sin offering and the other for a burnt H285
Lev 14:25 lobe of the right ear of the *o to* **be cleansed,** AIT
Lev 14:28 lobe of the right ear of the *o to* **be cleansed,** AIT
Lev 14:29 put on the head of the *o to* **be cleansed,** AIT
Lev 14:31 **o** as a sin offering and the other as a burnt H285
Lev 14:31 the LORD on behalf of the *o to* **be cleansed**." AIT
Lev 14:50 He shall kill **o** of the birds over fresh water H285
Lev 15:15 the **o** for a sin offering and the other for a H285
Lev 15:30 priest is to sacrifice **o** for a sin offering and H285
Lev 16: 8 **o** lot for the LORD and the other for the H285
Lev 16:17 No **o** is to be in the tent of meeting from H132
Lev 18: 6 " 'No **o** is to approach any close relative to H408
Lev 18:22 with a man as **o** does with a woman; NDT
Lev 19:11 " 'Do not deceive **o** another. H408
Lev 20: 4 that man sacrifices **o** *of* his children to H4946
Lev 20:13 with a man as **o** does with a woman, NDT
Lev 21:10 the **o** among his brothers who has had the NDT
Lev 22: 6 The **o** who touches any such thing will be H5883
Lev 22:10 " 'No **o** outside a priest's family may eat H3972
Lev 23:18 without defect, **o** young bull and two rams. H285
Lev 23:19 Then sacrifice **o** male goat for a sin offering H285
Lev 24:20 *The o who has* **inflicted** the injury must suffer AIT
Lev 25:25 " 'If **o** of your fellow Israelites becomes poor NDT
Lev 25:26 there is no *o to* **redeem** it for them but later AIT
Lev 25:27 the balance to the **o** to whom they sold it; H408
Lev 25:48 **O** of their relatives may redeem them H285
Lev 26: 6 will lie down and no *o will* **make** you **afraid**. AIT
Lev 26:17 you will flee even when no *o is* **pursuing** you. AIT
Lev 26:26 will be able to bake your bread in **o** oven, H285
Lev 26:36 even though no *o is* **pursuing** them. AIT
Lev 26:37 They will stumble over **o** another as though H408
Lev 26:37 even though no *o is* **pursuing** them. AIT
Lev 27: 6 a person between *o* **month** and five years AIT
Lev 27: 8 to what the *o* **making** *the* **vow** can afford. AIT
Lev 27:10 substitute a good **o** for a bad one, H2257
Lev 27:10 substitute a good one for a **bad** *o*, AIT
Lev 27:10 a bad one, or a **bad** *o* for a good one; if AIT
Lev 27:10 a bad one for a **good** *o*; if they should AIT
Lev 27:10 if they should substitute *o* **animal** for another, AIT
Lev 27:11 **o** that is not acceptable as an offering to H5626
Lev 27:15 If the *o who* **dedicates** their house wishes to AIT
Lev 27:19 If the *o who* **dedicates** the field wishes to AIT
Lev 27:24 it was bought, **the o** whose land it was. H2257
Lev 27:26 " 'No **o**, however, may dedicate the H408
Lev 27:27 If it is **o** of the unclean animals, it may be H928S
Lev 27:33 No *o may* **pick out** the good from the bad AIT
Nu 1: 2 man by name, **o by one.** H4200+1653+4392
Nu 1: 2 man by name, **one by o.** H4200+1653+4392
Nu 1: 4 **O** man from each tribe, each of them the H408
Nu 1:18 listed by name, **o by one,** H4200+1653+4392
Nu 1:18 listed by name, **one by o,** H4200+1653+4392
Nu 1:20 listed by name, **o by one** H4200+1653+4392
Nu 1:20 listed by name, **one by o** H4200+1653+4392
Nu 1:22 listed by name, **o by one** H4200+1653+4392
Nu 1:22 listed by name, **one by o** H4200+1653+4392
Nu 1:44 of Israel, each **o** representing his family. H285
Nu 3:47 collect five shekels for **each o**, according to H1653
Nu 6:11 The priest is to offer **o** as a sin offering and H285
Nu 6:19 **o** thick loaf and one thin loaf from the H285
Nu 6:19 one thick loaf and **o** thin loaf from the H285
Nu 7:11 "Each day **o** leader is to bring his offering H285
Nu 7:12 The *o who* **brought** his offering on the first AIT
Nu 7:13 His offering was **o** silver plate weighing a H285
Nu 7:13 thirty shekels and **o** silver sprinkling bowl H285
Nu 7:14 **o** gold dish weighing ten shekels, filled H285
Nu 7:15 **o** young bull, one ram and one male lamb H285
Nu 7:15 **o** ram and one male lamb a year old for a H285
Nu 7:15 one ram and **o** male lamb a year old for a H285
Nu 7:16 **o** male goat for a sin offering; H285
Nu 7:19 he brought was **o** silver plate weighing a H285
Nu 7:19 thirty shekels and **o** silver sprinkling bowl H285
Nu 7:20 **o** gold dish weighing ten shekels, filled H285
Nu 7:21 **o** young bull, one ram and one male lamb H285
Nu 7:21 **o** ram and one male lamb a year old for a H285
Nu 7:21 one ram and **o** male lamb a year old for a H285
Nu 7:22 **o** male goat for a sin offering; H285
Nu 7:25 His offering was **o** silver plate weighing a H285
Nu 7:25 thirty shekels and **o** silver sprinkling bowl H285
Nu 7:26 **o** gold dish weighing ten shekels, filled H285
Nu 7:27 **o** young bull, one ram and one male lamb H285
Nu 7:27 **o** ram and one male lamb a year old for a H285
Nu 7:27 one ram and **o** male lamb a year old for a H285
Nu 7:28 **o** male goat for a sin offering; H285
Nu 7:31 His offering was **o** silver plate weighing a H285
Nu 7:31 thirty shekels and **o** silver sprinkling bowl H285
Nu 7:32 **o** gold dish weighing ten shekels, filled H285
Nu 7:33 **o** young bull, one ram and one male lamb H285
Nu 7:33 **o** ram and one male lamb a year old for a H285
Nu 7:33 one ram and **o** male lamb a year old for a H285
Nu 7:34 **o** male goat for a sin offering; H285
Nu 7:37 His offering was **o** silver plate weighing a H285
Nu 7:37 thirty shekels and **o** silver sprinkling bowl H285
Nu 7:38 **o** gold dish weighing ten shekels, filled H285
Nu 7:39 **o** young bull, one ram and one male lamb H285
Nu 7:39 **o** ram and one male lamb a year old for a H285
Nu 7:39 one ram and **o** male lamb a year old for a H285
Nu 7:40 **o** male goat for a sin offering; H285
Nu 7:43 His offering was **o** silver plate weighing a H285
Nu 7:43 thirty shekels and **o** silver sprinkling bowl H285
Nu 7:44 **o** gold dish weighing ten shekels, filled H285
Nu 7:45 **o** young bull, one ram and one male lamb H285
Nu 7:45 **o** ram and one male lamb a year old for a H285
Nu 7:45 one ram and **o** male lamb a year old for a H285
Nu 7:46 **o** male goat for a sin offering; H285
Nu 7:49 His offering was **o** silver plate weighing a H285
Nu 7:49 thirty shekels and **o** silver sprinkling bowl H285
Nu 7:50 **o** gold dish weighing ten shekels, filled H285
Nu 7:51 **o** young bull, one ram and one male lamb H285
Nu 7:51 **o** ram and one male lamb a year old for a H285
Nu 7:51 one ram and **o** male lamb a year old for a H285
Nu 7:52 **o** male goat for a sin offering; H285
Nu 7:55 His offering was **o** silver plate weighing a H285
Nu 7:55 thirty shekels and **o** silver sprinkling bowl H285
Nu 7:56 **o** gold dish weighing ten shekels, filled H285
Nu 7:57 **o** young bull, one ram and one male lamb H285
Nu 7:57 **o** ram and one male lamb a year old for a H285
Nu 7:57 one ram and **o** male lamb a year old for a H285
Nu 7:58 **o** male goat for a sin offering; H285
Nu 7:61 His offering was **o** silver plate weighing a H285
Nu 7:61 thirty shekels and **o** silver sprinkling bowl H285
Nu 7:62 **o** gold dish weighing ten shekels, filled H285
Nu 7:63 **o** young bull, one ram and one male lamb H285
Nu 7:63 **o** ram and one male lamb a year old for a H285
Nu 7:63 one ram and **o** male lamb a year old for a H285
Nu 7:64 **o** male goat for a sin offering; H285
Nu 7:67 His offering was **o** silver plate weighing a H285
Nu 7:67 thirty shekels and **o** silver sprinkling bowl H285
Nu 7:68 **o** gold dish weighing ten shekels, filled H285
Nu 7:69 **o** young bull, one ram and one male lamb H285
Nu 7:69 **o** ram and one male lamb a year old for a H285
Nu 7:69 one ram and **o** male lamb a year old for a H285
Nu 7:70 **o** male goat for a sin offering; H285
Nu 7:73 His offering was **o** silver plate weighing a H285
Nu 7:73 thirty shekels and **o** silver sprinkling bowl H285
Nu 7:74 **o** gold dish weighing ten shekels, filled H285
Nu 7:75 **o** young bull, one ram and one male lamb H285

Nu 7:75 **o** ram and one male lamb a year old for a H285
Nu 7:75 one ram and **o** male lamb a year old for a H285
Nu 7:76 **o** male goat for a sin offering; H285
Nu 7:79 His offering was **o** silver plate weighing a H285
Nu 7:79 thirty shekels and **o** silver sprinkling bowl H285
Nu 7:80 **o** gold dish weighing ten shekels, filled H285
Nu 7:81 **o** young bull, one ram and one male lamb H285
Nu 7:81 **o** ram and one male lamb a year old for a H285
Nu 7:81 one ram and **o** male lamb a year old for a H285
Nu 7:82 **o** male goat for a sin offering; H285
Nu 8:12 using **o** for a sin offering to the LORD and H285
Nu 10: 4 If only **o** is sounded, the leaders—the H285
Nu 11:19 You will not eat it for just **o** day, or two days, H285
Nu 11:32 No **o** gathered less than ten homers H2021
Nu 13: 2 each ancestral tribe send **o** of its leaders." H285
Nu 14:22 not **o** *of* those who saw my glory and the H3972
Nu 14:23 not *o* of them *will ever* **see** the land I AIT
Nu 14:23 No **o** who has treated me with contempt H3972
Nu 14:29 **every** *o of* you twenty years old or more who AIT
Nu 14:30 Not **o** of you will enter the land I swore with NDT
Nu 14:34 **o** year for each of the forty days you H2021
Nu 15:12 Do this for **each o**, for as many as you H285
Nu 15:27 " 'But if just **o** person sins unintentionally H285
Nu 15:28 the LORD for the **o** who erred by sinning H5883
Nu 15:29 **O and the same** law applies to everyone H285
Nu 16: 3 community is holy, **every** *o of* them, and the AIT
Nu 16: 7 LORD chooses will be the **o** who is holy. H2085
Nu 16:22 the entire assembly when only **o** man sins?" H285
Nu 16:40 Israelites that no **o** except a H408+2424
Nu 17: 2 **o** from the leader of each of their H4751[S]
Nu 17: 3 there must be **o** staff for the head of H285
Nu 17: 6 **o** for the leader of each of their ancestral H285
Nu 18: 4 no *o* else *may* **come near** where you are. AIT
Nu 22:32 because your path *is a* **reckless** *o* before me. AIT
Nu 23: 9 do not consider themselves **o of** the nations. AIT
Nu 24: 3 the prophecy of **o** whose eye sees clearly, H1505
Nu 24: 4 the prophecy of *o who* **hears** the words of AIT
Nu 24:15 the prophecy of **o** whose eye sees clearly H1505
Nu 24:16 the prophecy of *o who* **hears** the words of AIT
Nu 26:54 to a smaller group a smaller **o**; each H5709[S]
Nu 26:64 Not **o** of them was among those counted by H408
Nu 26:65 not **o** of them was left except Caleb H408
Nu 27:17 *o* who *will* **lead** them **out** and bring them in AIT
Nu 28: 4 Offer **o** lamb in the morning and the other H285
Nu 28:11 **o** ram and seven male lambs a year old H285
Nu 28:15 **o** male goat is to be presented to the LORD H285
Nu 28:19 **o** ram and seven male lambs a year old H285
Nu 28:22 Include **o** male goat as a sin offering to H285
Nu 28:27 **o** ram and seven male lambs a year old as H285
Nu 28:30 Include **o** male goat to make atonement H285
Nu 29: 2 offer a burnt offering of **o** young bull, one H285
Nu 29: 2 **o** ram and seven male lambs a year old H285
Nu 29: 5 Include **o** male goat as a sin offering to H285
Nu 29: 8 to the LORD a burnt offering of **o** young bull, H285
Nu 29: 8 **o** ram and seven male lambs a year old H285
Nu 29:11 Include **o** male goat as a sin offering, in H285
Nu 29:16 Include **o** male goat as a sin offering, in H285
Nu 29:19 Include **o** male goat as a sin offering, in H285
Nu 29:22 Include **o** male goat as a sin offering, in H285
Nu 29:25 Include **o** male goat as a sin offering, in H285
Nu 29:28 Include **o** male goat as a sin offering, in H285
Nu 29:31 Include **o** male goat as a sin offering, in H285
Nu 29:34 Include **o** male goat as a sin offering, in H285
Nu 29:36 consisting of a burnt offering of **o** bull, H285
Nu 29:36 **o** ram and seven male lambs a year old H285
Nu 29:38 Include **o** male goat as a sin offering, in H285
Nu 31:28 as tribute for the LORD **o** out of every five H285
Nu 31:30 Israelites' half, select **o** out of every fifty H285
Nu 31:47 Moses selected **o** out of every fifty people H285
Nu 31:49 under our command, and not **o** is missing. H408
Nu 32:11 **not o** of those who were twenty years old H561
Nu 32:12 not **o** except Caleb son of Jephunneh the NDT
Nu 33:54 to a smaller group a smaller **o**. H5709[S]
Nu 34:18 And appoint **o** leader from each tribe to H285
Nu 35: 8 has many, but few from **o** that has few." H2021
Nu 35:21 if out of enmity *o person* **hits** another with AIT
Nu 35:25 protect the *o* **accused of murder** from the AIT
Nu 35:30 But no **o** is to be put to death on the H5883
Nu 35:30 death on the testimony of only **o** witness. H285
Nu 35:33 except by the blood of the *o who* **shed** it. AIT
Nu 36: 7 in Israel is to pass from *o* **tribe** to another, AIT
Nu 36: 9 inheritance may pass from *o* **tribe** to another, AIT
Dt 1:23 twelve of you, **o** man from each tribe. H285
Dt 1:35 "No **o** from this evil generation shall see H408
Dt 1:41 So **every** *o* of you put on his weapons AIT
Dt 2:36 as Gilead, not **o** town was too strong for us. NDT
Dt 3: 4 There was not **o** of the sixty cities that H7953[S]
Dt 4:32 ask from *o* **end** *of* the heavens to the other. AIT
Dt 4:34 to take for himself **o** nation out of another NDT
Dt 4:42 They could flee into **o** of these cities and H285
Dt 6: 4 The LORD our God, the LORD is **o**. H285
Dt 7:24 No **o** will be able to stand up against you H408
Dt 9: 3 God is the *o who* **goes across** ahead of you AIT
Dt 10:21 He is the **o** you praise; he is your God, who NDT
Dt 11:25 No **o** will be able to stand against you. H408
Dt 12:14 the LORD will choose in **o** *of* your tribes, H285
Dt 13: 1 or *o who* **foretells by dreams**, appears AIT
Dt 13: 7 from **o** end of the land to the other) NDT
Dt 13:11 and **no** *o* among you will do such an evil AIT
Dt 13:12 hear it said about **o** *of* the towns the LORD H285
Dt 16:16 No *o should* **appear** before the LORD AIT
Dt 17: 2 living among you in **o** *of* the towns the LORD H285
Dt 17: 6 no *o is to* **be put to death** on the AIT
Dt 17: 6 death on the testimony of only **o** witness. H285
Dt 17:15 over you, **o** who is not an Israelite. H408
Dt 18: 6 a Levite moves from **o** *of* your towns H285
Dt 18:10 *Let* no *o* **be found** among you who sacrifices AIT
Dt 19: 3 may flee for refuge to **o of these cities**. H9004[S]
Dt 19: 5 That man may flee to **o** *of* these cities and H285
Dt 19:11 then flees to **o** *of* these cities, H285
Dt 19:15 **O** witness is not enough to convict anyone H285
Dt 20: 4 LORD your God *is* the *o who* **goes** with you to AIT
Dt 21:15 and he loves **o** but not the other H285
Dt 22:27 screamed, there was no *o to* **rescue** her. AIT
Dt 23: 1 No *o who has* **been emasculated** *by* crushing AIT
Dt 23: 2 No **o born of a forbidden marriage** nor H4927
Dt 23:10 If *o* of your men **is** unclean because of a AIT
Dt 24: 5 For **o** year he is to be free to stay at home H285
Dt 24: 6 not even the **upper o**—as security for a H8207
Dt 24:14 a foreigner residing in **o** of your towns. NDT
Dt 25: 5 living together and **o** of them dies without H285
Dt 25: 9 the elders, take off **o** of his sandals, spit in NDT
Dt 25:11 the wife of **o** of them comes to rescue H285
Dt 25:13 weights in your bag—**o** heavy, one light. NDT
Dt 25:13 weights in your bag—one heavy, **o** light. NDT
Dt 25:14 in your house—**o** large, one small. NDT
Dt 25:14 in your house—one large, **o** small. NDT
Dt 28: 7 will come at you from **o** direction but flee H285
Dt 28:25 will come at them from **o** direction but flee H285
Dt 28:26 there will be no *o to* **frighten** them **away**. AIT
Dt 28:29 robbed, with no *o to* **rescue** you. AIT
Dt 28:31 to your enemies, and no *o will* **rescue** them. AIT
Dt 28:55 he will not give to **o** of them any of the H285
Dt 28:64 from **o** end of the earth to the other. NDT
Dt 28:68 female slaves, but no *o will* **buy** you. AIT
Dt 32:22 *o that* **burns** down to the realm of the dead AIT
Dt 32:30 How could **o** *man* chase a thousand, or two H285
Dt 32:36 sees their strength is gone and no **o** is left, NDT
Dt 32:39 and no *o can* **deliver** out of my hand. AIT
Dt 33:12 the *o* the LORD loves **rests** between his AIT
Dt 33:26 "**There is no** *o* like the God of Jeshurun, who AIT
Dt 34: 6 to this day no **o** knows where his grave H408
Dt 34:12 For no **o** has ever shown the mighty power NDT
Jos 1: 5 No **o** will be able to stand against you all H408
Jos 3:12 from the tribes of Israel, **o** from each tribe. H285
Jos 4: 2 from among the people, **o** from each tribe, H285
Jos 4: 4 from the Israelites, **o** from each tribe, H285
Jos 6: 1 No **o went out** and no one came in. AIT
Jos 6: 1 No one went out and no *o* **came in**. AIT
Jos 6:26 before the LORD is the **o** who undertakes to H408
Jos 8:24 when **every** *o of* them had been put to AIT
Jos 10: 2 important city, like **o** *of* the royal cities; it H285
Jos 10: 8 Not **o** of them will be able to withstand you H408
Jos 10:21 no **o** uttered a word against the H408
Jos 10:42 lands Joshua conquered in **o** campaign, H285
Jos 11:19 not **o** city made a treaty of peace with the NDT
Jos 12: 4 of Bashan, **o** *of* the last of the Rephaites H4946
Jos 12: 9 the king of Jericho **o** the king of Ai (near H285
Jos 12: 9 Jericho one the king of Ai (near Bethel) **o** H285
Jos 12:10 the king of Jerusalem **o** the king of Hebron H285
Jos 12:10 king of Jerusalem one the king of Hebron **o** H285
Jos 12:11 the king of Jarmuth **o** the king of Lachish H285
Jos 12:11 king of Jarmuth one the king of Lachish **o** H285
Jos 12:12 the king of Eglon **o** the king of Gezer one H285
Jos 12:12 the king of Eglon one the king of Gezer **o** H285
Jos 12:13 the king of Debir **o** the king of Geder one H285
Jos 12:13 the king of Debir one the king of Geder **o** H285
Jos 12:14 the king of Hormah **o** the king of Arad one H285
Jos 12:14 the king of Hormah one the king of Arad **o** H285
Jos 12:15 the king of Libnah **o** the king of Adullam H285
Jos 12:15 king of Libnah one the king of Adullam **o** H285
Jos 12:16 the king of Makkedah **o** the king of Bethel H285
Jos 12:16 king of Makkedah one the king of Bethel **o** H285
Jos 12:17 the king of Tappuah **o** the king of Hepher H285
Jos 12:17 king of Tappuah one the king of Hepher **o** H285
Jos 12:18 the king of Aphek **o** the king of Lasharon H285
Jos 12:18 king of Aphek one the king of Lasharon **o** H285
Jos 12:19 the king of Madon **o** the king of Hazor one H285
Jos 12:19 the king of Madon one the king of Hazor **o** H285
Jos 12:20 of Shimron Meron **o** the king of Akshaph H285
Jos 12:20 Shimron Meron one the king of Akshaph **o** H285
Jos 12:21 the king of Taanach **o** the king of Megiddo H285
Jos 12:21 king of Taanach one the king of Megiddo **o** H285
Jos 12:22 the king of Kedesh **o** the king of Jokneam H285
Jos 12:22 one the king of Jokneam in Carmel **o** H285
Jos 12:23 **o** the king of Goyim in Gilgal one H285
Jos 12:23 one the king of Goyim in Gilgal **o** H285
Jos 12:24 the king of Tirzah **o** thirty-one kings in all. H285
Jos 15:18 **O day** when she came to Othniel H2256+2118
Jos 17:14 you given us only **o** allotment and one H285
Jos 17:14 us only one allotment and **o** portion for an H285
Jos 17:17 You will have not only **o** allotment H285
Jos 20: 4 When they flee to **o** of these cities, they are H285
Jos 21:13 a city of refuge for *o* **accused of murder**), AIT
Jos 21:21 a city of refuge for *o* **accused of murder**) AIT
Jos 21:27 a city of refuge for *o* **accused of murder**), AIT
Jos 21:32 a city of refuge for *o* **accused of murder**), AIT
Jos 21:38 a city of refuge for *o* **accused of murder**), AIT
Jos 21:44 Not **o** of their enemies withstood them; the H408
Jos 21:45 Not **o** of all the LORD's good promises to H1821[S]
Jos 21:45 to Israel failed; **every** *o* was fulfilled. AIT
Jos 22:14 **o** from each of the tribes of Israel H285
Jos 22:20 He was not the only **o** who died for his sin.' H408
Jos 22:22 "The **Mighty O**, God, the LORD! The Mighty H446
Jos 22:22 The **Mighty O**, God, the LORD! He H446
Jos 23: 9 to this day no **o** has been able to withstand H408
Jos 23:10 **O** of you routs a thousand, because the LORD H285
Jos 23:14 heart and soul that not **o** of all the good H285
Jos 23:14 has been fulfilled; not **o** has failed. H285
Jdg 1:14 **O day** when she came to Othniel H2256+2118
Jdg 3:28 to Moab; they allowed no **o** to cross over. H408
Jdg 3:29 all vigorous and strong; not **o** escaped. H408
Jdg 5: 5 before the LORD, the **O** of Sinai, before the H2296
Jdg 6:25 your father's herd, the **o** seven years old. H7228[S]
Jdg 6:39 Let me make just **o more** request. Allow H7193
Jdg 6:39 Allow me **o more** test with the fleece, but H7193
Jdg 7: 4 '**This** *o* shall go with you,' he shall go AIT
Jdg 7: 4 if I say, '**This** *o* shall not go with you,' he AIT
Jdg 8:18 "*each* **o** with the bearing of a prince." H285
Jdg 8:24 And he said, "*I do* **have** *o* **request**, that each AIT
Jdg 9: 2 sons rule over you, or just **o** man? H285
Jdg 9: 5 in Ophrah and on **o** stone murdered his H285
Jdg 9: 8 **O** day the trees went out to anoint a king NDT
Jdg 11:37 But grant me **this** *o* request," she said. "Give AIT
Jdg 14: 3 "Get her for me. She's the **right** *o* for me." AIT
Jdg 14:20 was given to *o of* his **companions** who had AIT
Jdg 16: 1 **O day** Samson went to Gaza, where he H2256
Jdg 16: 5 **Each** *o* of us will give you eleven hundred AIT
Jdg 16:24 the *o who* **laid waste** our land and multiplied AIT
Jdg 16:28 let me with *o* **blow** get revenge on the H285
Jdg 16:29 right hand on the **o** and his left hand on H285
Jdg 17: 5 gods and installed **o** of his sons as his H285
Jdg 17:11 man became like **o** of his sons to him. H285
Jdg 18:14 "Do you know that **o** of these houses has an NDT
Jdg 18:19 priest rather than just **o** man's household?" H285
Jdg 18:28 There was no *o to* **rescue** them because they AIT
Jdg 19:13 spend the night in **o** *of* those places." H285
Jdg 19:15 but no **o** took them in for the night. H408
Jdg 19:18 No **o** has taken me in for the night H408
Jdg 19:30 Everyone who saw it was saying to **o** another, NDT
Jdg 20: 1 came together as **o** and assembled H285+408
Jdg 20: 6 pieces and sent *o* **piece** to each region of AIT
Jdg 20: 8 All the men rose up together as **o** H285+408
Jdg 20: 8 not **o** of us will return to his house H408
Jdg 20:11 united as **o** against the city. H285+408
Jdg 20:22 encouraged **o another** and again H2021+6639
Jdg 20:31 the **o** leading to Bethel and the other to H285
Jdg 21: 1 "Not **o** of us will give his daughter in H408
Jdg 21: 3 Why should **o** tribe be missing from Israel H285
Jdg 21: 6 "Today **o** tribe is cut off from Israel," they H285
Jdg 21: 8 "Which **o** of the tribes of Israel failed to H285
Jdg 21: 8 discovered that no **o** from Jabesh Gilead H408
Jdg 21:21 each of you seize **o of** them to be your H4946
Jdg 21:23 each man caught **o** and carried her off to H889[S]
Ru 1: 4 **o** named Orpah and the other Ruth. H285
Ru 2:13 not have the standing of **o** *of* your servants." H285
Ru 2:19 about the **o** at whose place she had H2257
Ru 2:20 he is **o** *of* our guardian-redeemers." H4946
Ru 3: 1 **O day** Ruth's mother-in-law Naomi said H2256
Ru 3:14 "No *o* **must know** that a woman came to the AIT
Ru 4: 4 For no **o has the right to do it** except you, AIT
Ru 4: 7 **o party** took off his sandal and gave it to H408[S]
1Sa 1: 2 **o** was called Hannah and the other H285
1Sa 2: 2 "There is no *o* **holy** like the LORD; there is no AIT
1Sa 2: 2 like the LORD; **there is no** *o* besides you; there AIT
1Sa 2: 9 "It is not by strength that **o** prevails; H408
1Sa 2:20 place of the *o* she **prayed for** and gave to the AIT
1Sa 2:25 If *o* **person** sins against another, God may AIT
1Sa 2:31 so that no *o* in it *will* **reach** old age, AIT
1Sa 2:32 no *o* in your family line *will* ever **reach** old AIT
1Sa 2:33 **Every** *o* of you that I do not cut off from AIT
1Sa 2:35 will minister before my **anointed** *o* always. AIT
1Sa 3: 2 **O** night Eli, whose eyes were becoming H2085
1Sa 6:17 to the LORD—**o** *each* for Ashdod, Gaza, H285
1Sa 9: 3 "Take **o** of the servants with you and go H285
1Sa 9:23 I gave you, **the o** I told you to lay aside." H889[S]
1Sa 10: 3 **O** will be carrying three young goats H285
1Sa 10:24 **There is no** *o* like him among all the people." AIT
1Sa 11: 2 the right eye of **every** *o of* you and so bring AIT
1Sa 11: 3 if no *o* comes *to* **rescue** us, we will AIT
1Sa 11: 7 they came out together as **o**. H285+408
1Sa 11:13 Saul said, "No **o** will be put to death today H408
1Sa 12:13 you have chosen, **the o** you asked for; see H889[S]
1Sa 13:17 **O** turned toward Ophrah in the vicinity of H285
1Sa 14: 1 **O** day Jonathan son of Saul said to his H2021
1Sa 14: 3 No **o** was aware that Jonathan H2021+6639[S]
1Sa 14: 4 **o** was called Bozez and the other Seneh. H285
1Sa 14: 5 **O** cliff stood to the north toward Mikmash H285
1Sa 14:26 yet no *o* **put** his hand to his mouth AIT
1Sa 14:28 Then **o** of the soldiers told him, "Your father H408
1Sa 14:36 and let us not leave **o** of them alive." H408
1Sa 14:39 But not **o** of them said a word. H3972
1Sa 15: 1 "I am the **o** the LORD sent to anoint you king NDT
1Sa 15:28 has given it to **o** of your neighbors— NDT
1Sa 15:28 of your neighbors—to **o** better than you. H2021
1Sa 16: 1 I have chosen **o** *of* his sons to be king." H928
1Sa 16: 3 You are to anoint for me **the o** I indicate." H889[S]
1Sa 16: 8 "The LORD has not chosen **this** *o* either." AIT
1Sa 16: 9 "Nor has the LORD chosen **this** *o*." AIT
1Sa 16:12 "Rise and anoint him; this is the **o**." H2085
1Sa 16:18 **O** of the servants answered, "I have seen a H285
1Sa 16:21 David became **o** of his armor-bearers. NDT
1Sa 17: 3 Philistines occupied **o** hill and the H2296
1Sa 17:32 "Let no **o** lose heart on account of this H132
1Sa 17:36 Philistine will be like **o** of them, H285
1Sa 18: 1 Jonathan **became o** in spirit **with** David H8003

1Sa 20:15 LORD has cut off every o of David's enemies AIT
1Sa 21: 1 are you alone? Why is no o with you?" H408
1Sa 21: 2 'No o is to know anything about the H408
1Sa 21: 7 Now o of Saul's servants was there that day H408
1Sa 21: 9 there is no sword here but that o. H2023
1Sa 21:11 Isn't he the o they sing about in their NDT
1Sa 22: 8 No o tells me when my son makes a AIT
1Sa 22:20 But o son of Ahimelek son of Ahitub H285
1Sa 23:26 was going along o side of the mountain H2296
1Sa 25:14 O of the servants told Abigail, Nabal's wife, H285
1Sa 25:17 such a wicked man that no o can talk to him." AIT
1Sa 25:22 I leave alive o male of all who belong to AIT
1Sa 25:34 not o male belonging to Nabal would have AIT
1Sa 26: 8 to the ground with o thrust of the spear; H285
1Sa 26:12 No o saw or knew about it, nor did anyone AIT
1Sa 26:20 as o hunts a partridge in the mountains." AIT
1Sa 26:22 "Let o of your young men come over and H285
1Sa 27: 1 "O of these days I will be destroyed by the H285
1Sa 27: 5 assigned to me in o of the country towns, H285
1Sa 28: 7 "There is o in Endor," they H1266+200S
1Sa 28: 8 "and bring up for me the o I name." H889S
1Sa 28:17 hands and given it to o of your neighbors— NDT
1Sa 30: 6 each o was bitter in spirit because of his H408
2Sa 1:15 Then David called o of his men and said H285
2Sa 2: 1 "Shall I go up to o of the towns of Judah?" H285
2Sa 2:13 O group sat down on one side of the pool H465S
2Sa 2:13 group sat down on o side of the pool and AIT
2Sa 2:13 of the pool and o group on the other side. H465S
2Sa 2:21 take on o of the young men and strip him H285
2Sa 3:13 But I demand o thing of you: Do not H285
2Sa 3:34 You fell as o falls before the wicked. AIT
2Sa 4: 2 O was named Baanah and the other Rekab; H285
2Sa 5: 2 o who led Israel on their military campaigns. AIT
2Sa 7: 5 Are you the o to build me a house to dwell NDT
2Sa 7:13 He is the o who will build a house for my NDT
2Sa 7:22 There is no o like you, and there is no God AIT
2Sa 7:23 the o nation on earth that God went out to H285
2Sa 9: 3 "Is there no o still alive from the house of H408
2Sa 9:11 at David's table like o of the king's sons. H285
2Sa 11: 2 O evening David got up from his bed and H2021
2Sa 11:12 "Stay here o more day, and H2021
2Sa 11:25 the sword devours o as well as another. H2297
2Sa 12: 1 in a certain town, o rich and the other poor. H285
2Sa 12: 3 had nothing except o little ewe lamb he H285
2Sa 12: 4 from taking o of his own sheep or H4946
2Sa 12: 4 prepared it for the o who had come to him." H408
2Sa 12:11 give them to o who is close to you, H8291
2Sa 13:13 You would be like o of the wicked fools in H285
2Sa 13:30 all the king's sons; not o of them is left." H285
2Sa 14: 6 and no o was there to separate them. AIT
2Sa 14: 6 O struck the other and killed him H285
2Sa 14: 7 over the o who struck his brother down, AIT
2Sa 14:11 "not o hair of your son's head will fall to H4946
2Sa 14:19 no o can turn to the right or to the left from H838
2Sa 15: 2 servant is from o of the tribes of Israel H285
2Sa 16:18 the o chosen by the LORD, by these H889S
2Sa 16:23 was like that of o who inquires of God. H408
2Sa 17:19 No o knew anything about it. AIT
2Sa 17:20 The men searched but found no o, so they AIT
2Sa 17:22 no o was left who had not crossed the H285
2Sa 18:10 When o of the men saw what had H285
2Sa 18:20 "You are not the o to take the news today," H408
2Sa 18:27 to me that the first o runs like Ahimaaz AIT
2Sa 19: 9 he is the o who rescued us from the hand of AIT
2Sa 19:14 so that they were all of o mind. H3869+285+408
2Sa 20:11 O of Joab's men stood beside Amasa and H408
2Sa 20:21 Hand over this o man, and I'll H4200+963
2Sa 21: 6 at Gibeah of Saul—the LORD's chosen o." AIT
2Sa 21:16 Ishbi-Benob, o of the descendants of Rapha NDT
2Sa 21:18 killed Saph, o of the descendants of Rapha. NDT
2Sa 22:42 there was no o to save them—to the AIT
2Sa 23: 3 'When o rules over people in righteousness AIT
2Sa 23: 8 whom he killed in o encounter. H285
2Sa 23: 9 As o of the three mighty warriors, he was NDT
2Sa 24:12 Choose o of them for me to carry out H285
2Sa 24:13 how I should answer the o who sent me." AIT
1Ki 2:16 Now I have o request to make of you. H285
1Ki 2:20 "I have o small request to make of you," H285
1Ki 3:17 O of them said, "Pardon me, my lord. H285
1Ki 3:18 there was no o in the house but the two H2424S
1Ki 3:22 The living o is my son; the dead one is AIT
1Ki 3:22 one is my son; the dead o is yours." But the AIT
1Ki 3:22 But the first o insisted, "No H2296S
1Ki 3:22 The dead o is yours; the living one is AIT
1Ki 3:22 one is yours; the living o is mine." And so AIT
1Ki 3:23 The king said, "This o says, 'My son is alive AIT
1Ki 3:23 your son is dead,' while that o says, 'No! AIT
1Ki 3:25 two and give half to o and half to the other H285
1Ki 4: 7 Each o had to provide supplies for one H285
1Ki 4: 7 to provide supplies for o month in the year. NDT
1Ki 5: 6 know that we have no o so skilled in felling H408
1Ki 5:14 so that they spent o month in Lebanon and NDT
1Ki 6:24 O wing of the first cherub was five cubits NDT
1Ki 6:27 The wing of o cherub touched one wall H285
1Ki 6:27 The wing of one cherub touched o wall H2021
1Ki 6:31 wood that were o fifth of the width of the H2797
1Ki 6:33 that were o fourth of the width of the hall. H8055
1Ki 6:36 of dressed stone and o course of trimmed NDT
1Ki 7:12 of dressed stone and o course of trimmed NDT
1Ki 7:21 Jakin and the o to the north Boaz. H6647S
1Ki 7:24 cast in two rows in o piece with the Sea. H3669
1Ki 7:31 that had a circular frame o cubit deep. NDT
1Ki 7:34 had four handles, o on each corner H4190S
1Ki 7:38 o basin to go on each of the ten stands. H285
1Ki 8:19 you are not the o to build the temple, but AIT
1Ki 8:19 he is the o who will build the temple for my AIT
1Ki 8:46 for there is no o who does not sin H132
1Ki 8:56 Not o word has failed of all the good H285
1Ki 10:20 the six steps, o at either end of each step. NDT
1Ki 11:11 you and give it to o of your subordinates. NDT
1Ki 11:13 will give him o tribe for the sake of H285
1Ki 11:26 He was o of Solomon's officials, an NDT
1Ki 11:32 all the tribes of Israel, he will have o tribe. H285
1Ki 11:36 I will give o tribe to his son so that David H285
1Ki 11:38 as enduring as the o I built for David and NDT
1Ki 12:24 Go home, every o of you, for this is AIT
1Ki 12:29 O he set up in Bethel, and the other in Dan. H285
1Ki 12:30 to worship the o at Bethel and went as H285
1Ki 14: 2 the o who told me I would be king over H2085
1Ki 14:10 up the house of Jeroboam as o burns dung, AIT
1Ki 14:13 He is the only o belonging to Jeroboam H2296
1Ki 14:13 because he is the only o in the house of NDT
1Ki 15:22 order to all Judah—no o was exempt—and AIT
1Ki 16: 9 o of his officials, who had command NDT
1Ki 18: 6 Ahab going in o direction and Obadiah in H285
1Ki 18:22 "I am the only o of the LORD's H4200+963
1Ki 18:23 Baal's prophets choose o for themselves, H285
1Ki 18:25 "Choose o of the bulls and prepare it first H285
1Ki 18:26 no response; no o answered. And they AIT
1Ki 18:29 no response, no o answered, no one paid AIT
1Ki 18:29 no one answered, no o paid attention. AIT
1Ki 18:31 o for each of the tribes descended H3869+5031
1Ki 19: 2 do not make your life like that of o of them." H285
1Ki 19:10 I am the only o left, and now they H4200+963
1Ki 19:14 I am the only o left, and now they H4200+963
1Ki 20:11 'O who puts on his armor should not boast AIT
1Ki 20:11 should not boast like o who takes it off. AIT
1Ki 20:20 and each o struck down his opponent. At that AIT
1Ki 20:25 also raise an army like the o you lost— H2657S
1Ki 20:29 on the Aramean foot soldiers in o day. H285
1Ki 20:35 the word of the LORD o of the company of H285
1Ki 20:41 recognized him as o of the prophets. H4946
1Ki 22: 8 "There is still o prophet through whom we H285
1Ki 22: 9 king of Israel called o of his officials and H285
1Ki 22:17 Let each o go home in peace.' AIT
1Ki 22:20 his death there?' "O suggested this, and H2296
2Ki 4: 4 and as each is filled, put it to o side." H5825
2Ki 4: 6 she said to her son, "Bring me another o." H3998S
2Ki 4: 8 O day Elisha went to Shunem. And a H2021
2Ki 4:11 O day when Elisha came, he went up to H2021
2Ki 4:18 and o day he went out to his father H2021
2Ki 4:22 "Please send me o of the servants and a H285
2Ki 4:39 O of them went out into the fields to gather H285
2Ki 4:39 though no o knew what they were. AIT
2Ki 5:18 the LORD forgive your servant for this o thing: AIT
2Ki 6: 3 Then o of them said, "Won't you please H285
2Ki 6: 5 As o of them was cutting down a tree, the H285
2Ki 6:12 lord the king," said o of his officers, "but H285
2Ki 7: 5 the edge of the camp, no o was there, H408
2Ki 7: 6 so that they said to o another, "Look, H408
2Ki 7: 8 entered o of the tents and ate and drank. H285
2Ki 7:10 the Aramean camp and no o was there— H408
2Ki 7:13 O of his officers answered, "Have some H285
2Ki 8:26 and he reigned in Jerusalem o year. H285
2Ki 9:10 of ground at Jezreel, and no o will bury her. AIT
2Ki 9:11 fellow officers, o of them asked him, "Is AIT
2Ki 9:37 so that no o will be able to say, 'This is AIT
2Ki 10:19 See that no o is missing, because I am H408
2Ki 10:21 servants of Baal came; not o stayed away. H408
2Ki 10:21 Baal until it was full from o end to the other. AIT
2Ki 10:23 see that no o who serves the LORD is here AIT
2Ki 10:24 "If o of you lets any of the men I am placing NDT
2Ki 10:25 kill them; let no o escape." So they cut H408
2Ki 11: 9 Each o took his men—those who were going AIT
2Ki 12: 5 receive the money from o of the treasurers, NDT
2Ki 12: 9 on the right side as o enters the temple of H408
2Ki 14: 7 He was the o who defeated ten thousand AIT
2Ki 14:22 He was the o who rebuilt Elath and restored it AIT
2Ki 14:25 He was the o who restored the boundaries of AIT
2Ki 14:26 was suffering; there was no o to help them. AIT
2Ki 15:13 he reigned in Samaria o month. H3732+3427
2Ki 15:25 O of his chief officers, Pekah son of NDT
2Ki 17:27 "Have o of the priests you took captive from H285
2Ki 17:28 So o of the priests who had been exiled H285
2Ki 17:36 is the o you must worship. H2257
2Ki 18: 5 There was no o like him among all the kings AIT
2Ki 18:22 isn't he the o whose high places and H889S
2Ki 18:24 How can you repulse o officer of the least H285
2Ki 19:22 Against the Holy O of Israel! AIT
2Ki 19:37 O day, while he was worshiping in H2118+2256
2Ki 21:13 I will wipe out Jerusalem as o wipes a dish AIT
2Ki 23:10 so no o could use it to sacrifice their son H408
2Ki 25:17 capital on top of o pillar was three cubits NDT
1Ch 1:19 O was named Peleg, because in his time H285
1Ch 4:17 O of Mered's wives gave birth to Miriam NDT
1Ch 5:21 They also took o hundred thousand people AIT
1Ch 11: 2 o who led Israel on their military campaigns. AIT
1Ch 11:11 whom he killed in o encounter. H285
1Ch 11:12 Ahohite, o of the three mighty warriors. H2085
1Ch 12:38 were also of o mind to make David king H285
1Ch 15: 2 "No o but the Levites may carry the ark of AIT
1Ch 16:20 to nation, from o kingdom to another. NDT
1Ch 16:21 He allowed no o to oppress them; for their H408
1Ch 17: 4 You are not the o to build me a house to NDT
1Ch 17: 5 I have moved from o tent site to another NDT
1Ch 17: 5 another, from o dwelling place to another. NDT
1Ch 17:11 to succeed you, o of your own sons, and I H4946
1Ch 17:12 He is the o who will build a house for me AIT
1Ch 17:20 "There is no o like you, LORD, and there is no AIT
1Ch 17:21 the o nation on earth whose God went out H285
1Ch 20: 4 o of the descendants of the Rephaites H4946
1Ch 21: 5 Israel there were o million one hundred AIT
1Ch 21: 5 one million o hundred thousand men who AIT
1Ch 21:10 Choose o of them for me to carry out H285
1Ch 21:12 how I should answer the o who sent me." AIT
1Ch 22:10 He is the o who will build a house for my AIT
1Ch 23:11 so they were counted as o family with one NDT
1Ch 23:11 counted as one family with o assignment. H285
1Ch 24: 6 o family being taken from Eleazar and then H285
1Ch 24: 6 from Eleazar and then o from Ithamar. H285
1Ch 26: 1 son of Kore, o of the sons of Asaph. H4946
1Ch 28: 6 your son is the o who will build my house H2085
1Ch 29: 1 son Solomon, the o whom God has chosen H285
2Ch 3:11 O wing of the first cherub was five cubits H285
2Ch 3:12 Similarly o wing of the second cherub was NDT
2Ch 3:17 o to the south and one to the north. H285
2Ch 3:17 one to the south and o to the north. H285
2Ch 3:17 The o to the south he named Jakin and the AIT
2Ch 3:17 he named Jakin and the o to the north Boaz. AIT
2Ch 4: 3 cast in two rows in o piece with the Sea. H4609
2Ch 6: 9 you are not the o to build the temple, but AIT
2Ch 6: 9 he is the o who will build the temple for my AIT
2Ch 6:36 for there is no o who does not sin H132
2Ch 6:42 do not reject your anointed o. Remember the AIT
2Ch 9:19 the six steps, o at either end of each step. NDT
2Ch 11: 4 Go home, every o of you, for this is AIT
2Ch 14: 6 No o was at war with him during those years AIT
2Ch 14:11 there is no o like you to help the powerless AIT
2Ch 15: 6 O nation was being crushed by another and AIT
2Ch 15: 6 crushed by another and o city by another, AIT
2Ch 18: 7 "There is still o prophet through whom we H285
2Ch 18: 8 king of Israel called o of his officials and H285
2Ch 18:16 Let each o go home in peace.' AIT
2Ch 18:19 his death there?' "O suggested this, and H2296
2Ch 20: 6 in your hand, and no o can withstand you. AIT
2Ch 20:23 from Seir, they helped to destroy o another. H408
2Ch 20:24 lying on the ground; no o had escaped. AIT
2Ch 22: 2 and he reigned in Jerusalem o year. H285
2Ch 22: 9 So there was no o in the house of Ahaziah AIT
2Ch 23: 6 No o is to enter the temple of the LORD except AIT
2Ch 23: 8 Each o took his men—those who were going AIT
2Ch 23:19 that no o who was in any way unclean might AIT
2Ch 26: 2 He was the o who rebuilt Elath and restored NDT
2Ch 26:11 of Hananiah, o of the royal officials. H4946
2Ch 28: 6 In o day Pekah son of Remaliah killed a H285
2Ch 32: 5 wall outside that o and reinforced the NDT
2Ch 32:12 'You must worship before o altar and burn H285
Ezr 3: 1 together as o in Jerusalem. H285+408
Ezr 3:13 No o could distinguish the sound H2021+6639S
Ezr 5:11 o that a great king of Israel built and A10204
Ezr 6: 4 courses of large stones and o of timbers. A10248
Ezr 6:17 male goats, o for each of the tribes of Israel. NDT
Ezr 9:11 it with their impurity from o end to the other. AIT
Ezr 9:15 though because of it not o of us can stand in AIT
Ezr 10: 2 of Jehiel, o of the descendants of Elam H4946
Ezr 10:16 family heads, o from each family division NDT
Ne 1: 2 o of my brothers, came from Judah H285
Ne 2:12 with me except the o I was riding on. H989S
Ne 3: 8 Uzziel son of Harhaiah, o of the goldsmiths NDT
Ne 3: 8 Hananiah, o of the perfume-makers H1201S
Ne 3:31 Malkijah, o of the goldsmiths, made H1201S
Ne 4:17 did their work with o hand and held a H285
Ne 5:11 charging them—o percent of the money H4395
Ne 5:18 Each day o ox, six choice sheep and some H285
Ne 6: 2 us meet together in o of the villages on the NDT
Ne 6:10 O day I went to the house of Shemaiah H2256
Ne 8: 1 came together as o in the square H285+408
Ne 8:16 Water Gate and the o by the Gate of H8148S
Ne 11: 1 cast lots to bring o out of every ten of them H285
Ne 11:22 Uzzi was o of Asaph's descendants, who H4946
Ne 11:24 o of the descendants of Zerah son of H4946
Ne 12:24 o section responding to the other AIT
Ne 12:31 O was to proceed on top of the wall to the H285
Ne 13:24 of o of the other peoples, H6639+2256+6639
Ne 13:28 O of the sons of Joiada son of Eliashib H4946
Est 1: 7 of gold, each o different from the other H3998S
Est 4: 2 because no o clothed in sackcloth was AIT
Est 4: 5 o of the king's eunuchs assigned to H4946
Est 4:11 being summoned the king has but o law: H285
Est 6: 8 o with a royal crest placed on its head. H889S
Est 6: 9 horse be entrusted to o of the king's most H408
Est 7: 9 o of the eunuchs attending the king H285
Est 9: 2 No o could stand against them, because H408
Est 9:22 presents of food to o another and gifts to H408
Job 1: 6 O day the angels came to present H2021
Job 1: 8 There is no o on earth like him; he is NDT
Job 1:13 O day when Job's sons and daughters H2021
Job 1:15 and I am the only o who has H4200+963
Job 1:16 and I am the only o who has H4200+963
Job 1:17 and I am the only o who has H4200+963
Job 1:19 and I am the only o who has H4200+963
Job 2: 3 There is no o on earth like him; he is NDT
Job 2:13 No o said a word to him, because they saw AIT
Job 5:17 "Blessed is the o whom God corrects; so do H632
Job 6:10 I had not denied the words of the Holy O. H7705
Job 7: 9 so o who goes down to the grave does not AIT

Job 8:20 not reject *o who is* **blameless** or strengthen AIT
Job 9: 3 not answer him **o** *time* out of a thousand. H285
Job 10: 7 that no *o can* **rescue** me from your hand AIT
Job 11: 3 *Will* no *o* **rebuke** you when you mock? AIT
Job 11:19 with no *o to* **make** you **afraid**, and many AIT
Job 14: 4 bring what is pure from the impure? No **o**! H285
Job 15:28 ruined towns and houses where no *o* **lives**, AIT
Job 16:21 pleads with God as **o** pleads for a H1201+132
Job 18:21 is the place of *o who does* not **know** God." AIT
Job 21:23 **O** *person* dies in full vigor, completely H2296S
Job 22:30 He will deliver even *o who* is not **innocent** AIT
Job 24:12 But God charges no **o** with wrongdoing. NDT
Job 24:18 is cursed, so that no *o* **goes** to the vineyards. AIT
Job 25: 4 How can *o* **born** *of* woman be pure? AIT
Job 26: 3 you have offered to **o** without wisdom! NDT
Job 29:13 The *o who was* **dying** blessed me; I made AIT
Job 29:25 I was like *o who* **comforts** mourners. AIT
Job 30:13 'No *o can* **help** him,' they say. AIT
Job 30:24 "Surely no *o* **lays** a hand on a broken man AIT
Job 31:15 Did not the **same** *o* form us both within our H285
Job 32:12 But not **o** of you *has* **proved** Job **wrong**; none AIT
Job 33:14 speak—now **o** **way**, now another— H928+285
Job 33:14 now another—though no *o* **perceives** it. AIT
Job 33:23 a messenger, **o** out of a thousand, sent to H285
Job 34:17 Will you condemn the just and **mighty** *O*? AIT
Job 34:18 Is he not the *O who* **says** to kings, 'You are AIT
Job 35:10 But no *o* **says**, 'Where is God my Maker, who AIT
Job 36: 4 *o who has* perfect **knowledge** is with you. AIT
Job 36: 5 is mighty, but despises no **o**; he is mighty, NDT
Job 36:18 Be careful that no *o* **entices** you by riches; do AIT
Job 37:21 Now no *o can* **look** *at* the sun, bright as it is AIT
Job 38:26 to water a land where no **o** lives, an H408
Job 40: 2 "*Will* the *o who* **contends** with the Almighty AIT
Job 41:10 No *o* is **fierce** *enough* to rouse it. Who then AIT
Job 41:17 They are joined fast to **o** another; they H408
Job 41:32 *o would* **think** the deep had white hair. AIT
Job 42:11 and **each** *o* gave him a piece of silver and a AIT
Ps 1: 1 Blessed is the **o** who does not walk in step H408
Ps 2: 4 The *O* **enthroned** in heaven laughs; the Lord AIT
Ps 3: 3 my glory, the *O who* **lifts** my head **high**. AIT
Ps 6: 5 Among the dead **no** *o* proclaims your name AIT
Ps 7: 2 rip me to pieces with no *o to* **rescue** me. AIT
Ps 10: 6 He swears, "No **o** will ever do me harm." H889
Ps 12: 1 for no *o* is **faithful** anymore; those who AIT
Ps 14: 1 deeds are vile; there is no *o who* **does** good. AIT
Ps 14: 3 there is no *o who* **does** good, not even one. AIT
Ps 14: 3 there is no one who does good, not even **o**. H285
Ps 15: 2 The *o whose* **walk** *is* blameless, who does AIT
Ps 16:10 will you let your **faithful** *o* see decay. AIT
Ps 18:41 there was no *o to* **save** them—to the AIT
Ps 19: 6 It rises at *o* **end** *of* the heavens and makes its AIT
Ps 22: 3 Yet you are enthroned as the **Holy O**; you H7705
Ps 22: 3 the Holy One; you are the **o** Israel praises. NDT
Ps 22:11 trouble is near and there is no *o to* **help**. AIT
Ps 22:24 scorned the suffering of the **afflicted** *o*; AIT
Ps 24: 4 The *o who* has **clean** hands and a pure heart, AIT
Ps 25: 3 No **o** who hopes in you will ever be put to H3972
Ps 27: 4 **O** *thing* I ask from the LORD, this only do I H285
Ps 28: 8 a fortress of salvation for his **anointed** *o*. AIT
Ps 32: 1 is the *o whose* transgressions **are forgiven**, AIT
Ps 32: 2 Blessed is the **o** whose sin the LORD does H132
Ps 32:10 love surrounds the *o who* **trusts** in him. AIT
Ps 34: 8 blessed is the **o** who takes refuge in him. H1505
Ps 34:20 all his bones, not **o** of them will be broken. H285
Ps 34:22 no **o** who takes refuge in him will be H3972
Ps 35:12 evil for good and leave me like *o* **bereaved**. AIT
Ps 37:23 the steps of the **o** who delights in him; H1505
Ps 38:14 I have become like **o** who does not hear H408
Ps 39: 9 for you are the *o who has* **done** this. AIT
Ps 40: 4 Blessed is the **o** who trusts in the LORD H1505
Ps 41: 6 When *o of them* **comes** to see me, he speaks AIT
Ps 41: 9 I trusted, *o who* **shared** my bread, has AIT
Ps 42: 4 protection of the **Mighty O** with shouts of H129
Ps 45: 3 on your side, you **mighty** *o*; clothe yourself AIT
Ps 49: 7 No **o** can redeem the life of another or give H408
Ps 50: 1 The **Mighty O**, God, the LORD, speaks and H446
Ps 50:22 tear you to pieces, with no *o to* **rescue** you: AIT
Ps 53: 1 ways are vile; there is no *o who* **does** good. AIT
Ps 53: 3 there is no *o who* **does** good, not even one. AIT
Ps 53: 3 there is no one who does good, not even **o**. H285
Ps 54: 4 my help; the Lord is the *o who* **sustains** me. AIT
Ps 62:11 **O** *thing* God has spoken, two things I have H285
Ps 68: 8 before God, the **O** *of* Sinai, before God H2296
Ps 69:25 let there be no *o to* **dwell** in their tents. AIT
Ps 71:11 him and seize him, for no *o will* **rescue** him." AIT
Ps 71:22 to you with the lyre, **Holy O** *of* Israel. H7705
Ps 72:12 the afflicted who have no *o to* **help**. AIT
Ps 73:20 They are like a dream when *o* **awakes**; when AIT
Ps 75: 6 **No** *o* from the east or the west or from the AIT
Ps 75: 7 He brings **o** down, he exalts H2296
Ps 76: 5 not **o** *of* the warriors can lift his hands. H3972
Ps 76:11 lands bring gifts to the *O* to be **feared**. AIT
Ps 78:41 the test; they vexed the **Holy O** *of* Israel. H7705
Ps 79: 3 there is no *o to* **bury** the dead. AIT
Ps 83: 5 *With o* **mind** they plot together; they form an AIT
Ps 84: 9 look with favor on your **anointed** *o*. AIT
Ps 84:10 Better is *o* **day** in your courts than a thousand AIT
Ps 84:12 blessed is the **o** who trusts in you. H132
Ps 87: 4 and will say, '**This** *o* was born in Zion.' AIT
Ps 87: 5 "*This* **o** and that one were born in her H408
Ps 87: 5 "This one and *that* **o** were born in her H408
Ps 87: 6 of the peoples: "**This** *o* was born in Zion." AIT
Ps 88: 4 to the pit; I am like **o** without strength. H1505
Ps 89: 3 "I have made a covenant with my **chosen** *o*, AIT
Ps 89:10 You crushed Rahab like *o of* the **slain**; with AIT
Ps 89:18 the LORD, our king to the **Holy O** *of* Israel. H7705
Ps 89:38 have been very angry with your **anointed** *o*. AIT
Ps 89:51 have mocked every step of your **anointed** *o*. AIT
Ps 94:12 Blessed is the **o** you discipline, LORD, the H1505
Ps 94:12 **the o** you teach from your law H5647S
Ps 101: 6 the *o whose* **walk** *is* blameless will minister AIT
Ps 101: 7 No *o who* **practices** deceit will dwell in my AIT
Ps 101: 7 no *o who* **speaks** falsely will stand in my AIT
Ps 105:13 nation to nation, from *o* **kingdom** to another. AIT
Ps 105:14 He allowed no **o** to oppress them; for their H132
Ps 105:37 from among their tribes no *o* **faltered**. AIT
Ps 106:11 their adversaries; not **o** of them survived. H285
Ps 106:23 had not Moses, his **chosen** *o*, stood in the AIT
Ps 107:12 they stumbled, and there was no *o to* **help**. AIT
Ps 107:43 Let the *o* **who** is wise heed these things and AIT
Ps 109:12 *May* no *o* **extend** kindness to him or take pity AIT
Ps 113: 5 our God, the *O who* sits enthroned *on* **high**, AIT
Ps 119:14 your statutes as **o** rejoices in great riches. NDT
Ps 119:162 in your promise like *o who* **finds** great spoil. AIT
Ps 129: 7 hands with it, nor *o who* **gathers** fill his arms. AIT
Ps 132: 2 he made a vow to the **Mighty O** *of* Jacob: H51
Ps 132: 5 a dwelling for the **Mighty O** *of* Jacob." H51
Ps 132:10 servant David, do not reject your **anointed** *o*. AIT
Ps 132:11 "**O** *of* your own descendants I will place H4946
Ps 132:17 David and set up a lamp for my **anointed** *o*. AIT
Ps 137: 3 they said, "Sing us **o** *of* the songs of Zion!" H4946
Ps 137: 8 happy is the *o who* **repays** you according to AIT
Ps 137: 9 Happy is the *o who* **seizes** your infants and AIT
Ps 139:16 in your book before **o** of them came to be. H285
Ps 141: 7 "As *o* **plows** and breaks up the earth AIT
Ps 142: 4 Look and see, **there is no** *o* at my right hand AIT
Ps 142: 4 at my right hand; no *o is* **concerned** for me. AIT
Ps 142: 4 I have no refuge; no *o* **cares for** my life. AIT
Ps 143: 2 no **o** living is righteous before you. H3972
Ps 144:10 to the *O who* **gives** victory to kings, who AIT
Ps 145: 3 of praise; his greatness **no** *o* can fathom. AIT
Ps 145: 4 *O* **generation** commends your works to AIT
Pr 1:24 I call and no *o* **pays attention** when I stretch AIT
Pr 5: 9 to others and your dignity to *o who is* **cruel**, AIT
Pr 6:29 no **o** who touches her will go unpunished. H3972
Pr 9:10 knowledge of the **Holy O** is understanding H7705
Pr 10:13 a rod is for the back of **o** who has no sense. NDT
Pr 11:12 the *o who has* understanding holds H408
Pr 11:18 the *o who* **sows** righteousness reaps a AIT
Pr 11:24 *O person* **gives freely**, yet gains even more AIT
Pr 11:26 People curse the *o who* **hoards** grain, but AIT
Pr 11:26 blessing on the *o who is willing to* **sell**. AIT
Pr 11:27 evil comes to **o** who searches for it. H5647
Pr 11:30 tree of life, and the *o who* is **wise** saves lives. AIT
Pr 12: 3 No **o** can be established through H132
Pr 12: 8 and *o with* a **warped** mind is despised. AIT
Pr 13: 7 *O person* **pretends to be rich**, yet has nothing; AIT
Pr 13:24 the *o who* **loves** their children is careful AIT
Pr 14: 1 her own hands the **foolish** *o* tears hers down. AIT
Pr 14:10 bitterness, and no *o* **else** can share its joy. AIT
Pr 14:17 the *o who devises* evil schemes is H408
Pr 14:21 blessed is the **o** who is kind to the H2257
Pr 14:29 but *o who* is **quick-tempered** displays folly. AIT
Pr 15:10 the path; the *o who* **hates** correction will die. AIT
Pr 15:18 the *o who* is **patient** calms a quarrel. AIT
Pr 15:21 Folly brings joy to *o who* **has no** sense, but AIT
Pr 15:27 the *o who* **hates** bribes will live. AIT
Pr 15:32 the *o who* **heeds** correction gains AIT
Pr 16:13 they value the *o who* **speaks** what is right. AIT
Pr 16:20 blessed is the **o** who trusts in the LORD H2257
Pr 16:32 *o with* **self-control** than one who takes a city. AIT
Pr 16:32 one with self-control than *o who* **takes** a city. AIT
Pr 17: 2 the inheritance **as** *o of* the family. H928+9348
Pr 17: 8 is seen as a charm by the **o who gives** it; H1251
Pr 17:13 the house of *o who* **pays back** evil for good. AIT
Pr 17:18 **O** who has no sense shakes hands in H132
Pr 17:20 *O whose* heart is **corrupt** does not prosper AIT
Pr 17:20 *o whose* tongue *is* **perverse** falls into trouble. AIT
Pr 17:27 The *o who* **has knowledge** uses words with AIT
Pr 18: 9 *O who is* **slack** in his work is brother to one AIT
Pr 18: 9 work is brother to *o* **who destroys**. H1251+5422
Pr 18:24 **O** *who has* unreliable friends soon comes H408
Pr 19: 6 everyone is the friend of **o** *who gives* gifts. H408
Pr 19: 8 The *o who* **gets** wisdom loves life; the one AIT
Pr 19: 8 the *o who* **cherishes** understanding will soon AIT
Pr 19:23 leads to life; then *o* **rests** content, untouched AIT
Pr 20: 5 but **o** *who has* insight draws them out. H408
Pr 20:16 of *o who* **puts up security** *for* a stranger AIT
Pr 20:17 **o** ends up with a mouth full of gravel. H408
Pr 21:12 The **Righteous O** takes note of the house H7404
Pr 21:22 *O who* is **wise** can go up against the city of AIT
Pr 22:11 *O who* **loves** a pure heart and who speaks AIT
Pr 22:16 *O who* **oppresses** the poor to increase his AIT
Pr 22:16 his wealth and *o who* **gives gifts** to the rich— AIT
Pr 22:24 do not associate with **o** easily angered, H408
Pr 22:26 not be *o who* **shakes** hands **in pledge** or puts AIT
Pr 23:34 You will be like *o* **sleeping** on the high seas AIT
Pr 25:10 the *o who* **hears** it may shame you and the AIT
Pr 25:13 messenger to the *o who* **sends** him; AIT
Pr 25:14 wind without rain is **o** who boasts of gifts H408
Pr 25:18 a sharp arrow is **o** who gives false H408
Pr 25:20 Like *o who* **takes away** a garment on a cold AIT
Pr 25:20 is *o who* **sings** songs to a heavy heart. AIT
Pr 26: 7 useless legs of *o who* is **lame** is a proverb in AIT
Pr 26:10 at random is *o who* **hires** a fool or any AIT
Pr 26:17 Like *o who* **grabs** a stray dog by the ears is AIT
Pr 26:19 is **o** who deceives their neighbor and says H408
Pr 27: 7 **O** who is full loathes honey from the H5883
Pr 27:13 Take the garment of **o** who puts up H2257
Pr 27:17 sharpens iron, so *o* **person** sharpens another. AIT
Pr 27:18 The *o who* **guards** a fig tree will eat its fruit AIT
Pr 28: 1 The wicked flee though no *o* **pursues**, but the AIT
Pr 28:11 *o who is* **poor** and discerning sees how AIT
Pr 28:13 the *o who* **confesses** and renounces them AIT
Pr 28:14 Blessed is the **o** who always trembles H132
Pr 28:16 but *o who* **hates** ill-gotten gain will enjoy a AIT
Pr 28:17 refuge in the grave; *let* no *o* **hold** them **back**. AIT
Pr 28:18 The *o whose* **walk** is blameless is kept safe AIT
Pr 28:18 the *o* whose ways are perverse *will* **fall** into AIT
Pr 28:20 but *o* **eager** to get rich will not go AIT
Pr 28:23 rather than *o who has a* **flattering** tongue. AIT
Pr 28:24 not wrong," is partner to **o** who destroys. H408S
Pr 29:18 blessed is the **o** who heeds wisdom's H2084
Pr 29:26 it is from the LORD that **o** gets justice. H408
Pr 30: 3 I attained to the knowledge of the **Holy O**. H7705
Ecc 1: 8 are wearisome, more than **o** can say. H408
Ecc 1:10 Is there anything of which *o can* say, "Look AIT
Ecc 1:11 **No o** remembers the former generations H401
Ecc 2:18 leave them to the **o** who comes after me. H132
Ecc 2:26 to hand it over to the *o who* **pleases** God. AIT
Ecc 3:11 no **o** can fathom what God has done H132
Ecc 3:19 awaits them both: As **o** dies, so dies the H2296
Ecc 4: 3 than both is the *o* who *has* never **been** *born*, AIT
Ecc 4: 4 spring from *o* **person's** envy of another. AIT
Ecc 4: 6 Better *o* **handful** with tranquillity than two AIT
Ecc 4: 9 Two are better than **o**, because they have a H285
Ecc 4:10 falls down, **o** can help the other up. H2492S
Ecc 4:10 who falls and has no **o** to help them up. H9108
Ecc 4:11 But how can **o** keep warm *alone*? H285
Ecc 4:12 Though **o** may be overpowered, two can H285
Ecc 5: 5 a vow than *to* **make** **o** and not fulfill H5623S
Ecc 5: 8 for *o* **official** is eyed by a higher one AIT
Ecc 5: 8 one official is eyed by a higher **o** H1469S
Ecc 6:10 no *o* **can** contend with someone who is AIT
Ecc 7:14 God has made the **o** as well as the other H2296
Ecc 7:14 no **o** can discover anything about their H132
Ecc 7:18 is good to grasp the **o** and not let go of H2296
Ecc 7:19 Wisdom makes **o** wise person more H2021
Ecc 7:20 there is no **o** on earth who is righteous H132
Ecc 7:20 no *o who* **does** what is right and never sins. AIT
Ecc 7:27 "Adding *o thing* to another to discover the H285
Ecc 7:28 I found **o** upright man among a thousand H285
Ecc 7:28 not **o** upright woman among them all. NDT
Ecc 8: 7 Since no **o** knows the future, who can tell H5647
Ecc 8: 8 As no **o** has power over the wind to contain H132
Ecc 8: 8 so **no** *o* has power over the time of their AIT
Ecc 8: 8 As no *o* is discharged in time of war, so AIT
Ecc 8:17 No **o** can comprehend what goes on under H132
Ecc 8:17 no **o** can discover its meaning. H132
Ecc 9: 1 no **o** knows whether love or hate awaits H132
Ecc 9:12 no **o** knows when their hour will come: H132
Ecc 9:18 but **o** sinner destroys much good. H285
Ecc 10:14 No **o** knows what is coming—who can tell H132
Ecc 12:11 embedded nails—given by **o** shepherd. H285
SS 2:10 my darling, my **beautiful** *o*, come with me. AIT
SS 2:13 my darling; my **beautiful** *o*, come with me." AIT
SS 3: 1 my bed I looked for **the o** my heart loves; H8611S
SS 3: 2 I will search for **the o** my heart loves. H8611S
SS 3: 3 "Have you seen **the o** my heart loves?" H8611S
SS 3: 4 them when I found **the o** my heart loves. H8611S
SS 3: 4 to the room of the *o who* **conceived** me. AIT
SS 4: 2 Each has its twin; not **o** of them is alone. NDT
SS 4: 9 stolen my heart with **o** glance of your eyes, H285
SS 4: 9 of your eyes, with **o** jewel of your necklace. H285
SS 5: 2 my sister, my darling, my dove, my **flawless** *o*. AIT
SS 6: 6 Each has its twin, not **o** of them is missing. AIT
SS 6: 9 my dove, my **perfect** *o*, is unique, the AIT
SS 6: 9 the favorite of the *o who* **bore** her. AIT
SS 8: 1 I would kiss you, and no *o would* **despise** me. AIT
SS 8: 7 If **o** were to give all the wealth of one's H408
SS 8:10 in his eyes like *o* **bringing** contentment. AIT
Isa 1: 4 have spurned the **Holy O** *of* Israel and H7705
Isa 1:24 Almighty, the **Mighty O** *of* Israel, declares: H51
Isa 1:31 burn together, with no *o to* **quench** *the* **fire**." AIT
Isa 3: 6 man will seize *o of* his **brothers** in his father's AIT
Isa 4: 1 women will take hold of **o** man and say, H285
Isa 5: 1 I will sing for the *o* I **love** a song about his AIT
Isa 5: 1 My **loved o** had a vineyard on a fertile H3351
Isa 5:19 The plan of the **Holy O** *of* Israel—let it H7705
Isa 5:24 spurned the word of the **Holy O** *of* Israel. H7705
Isa 5:27 Not *o* of them grows **tired** or stumbles, not AIT
Isa 5:27 stumbles, not *o* **slumbers** or sleeps; not a AIT
Isa 5:29 their prey and carry it off with no *o to* **rescue**. AIT
Isa 5:30 And if *o* **looks** at the land, there is only AIT
Isa 6: 3 And they were calling to **o** another: "Holy H2296
Isa 6: 6 Then **o** of the seraphim flew to me with a H285
Isa 8:13 Almighty is the **o** you are to regard as H2257
Isa 8:13 he is the **o** you are to fear, he is NDT
Isa 8:13 you are to fear, he is the *o* you are to **dread**. AIT
Isa 9:19 the fire; they will not spare **o** another. H408
Isa 10:13 like a **mighty** *o* I subdued their kings. AIT
Isa 10:14 As *o* **reaches** into a nest, so my hand AIT
Isa 10:14 countries; not *o* **flapped** a wing, or opened AIT
Isa 10:15 the saw boast against the *o who* **uses** it? AIT
Isa 10:15 a club brandish the **o** who is not wood! NDT
Isa 10:17 become a fire, their **Holy O** a flame; in a H7705

Isa 10:20 truly rely on the LORD, the **Holy O** *of* Israel. H7705
Isa 10:34 Lebanon will fall before the **Mighty O**. H129
Isa 12: 6 great is the **Holy O** *of* Israel among H7705
Isa 14: 8 been laid low, no *o* **comes** to cut us down." AIT
Isa 16: 5 will sit on it—**o** from the house of David NDT
Isa 16: 5 *o who in* **judging** seeks justice and speeds AIT
Isa 16:10 no *o* **sings** or shouts in the vineyards AIT
Isa 16:10 no *o* **treads out** wine at the presses AIT
Isa 17: 2 will lie down, with no *o to* **make** them **afraid**. AIT
Isa 17: 7 turn their eyes to the **Holy O** *of* Israel. H7705
Isa 19:11 to Pharaoh, "I am **o** *of* the wise men, H1201
Isa 19:18 **O** of them will be called the City of the Sun. H285
Isa 21:16 "Within *o* **year**, as a servant bound by AIT
Isa 22:11 you did not look to the *O who* **made** it, or AIT
Isa 22:11 regard for the *O who* **planned** it long ago. AIT
Isa 22:22 what he opens no *o can* **shut**, and what he AIT
Isa 22:22 can shut, and what he shuts no *o can* **open**. AIT
Isa 24:16 "Glory to the **Righteous O**." But I said, H7404
Isa 26: 7 the **Upright** *O*, make the way of the AIT
Isa 27: 3 it day and night so that no *o may* **harm** it. AIT
Isa 27:12 Israel, will be gathered up **o** by one. H285
Isa 27:12 Israel, will be gathered up one by **o**. H285
Isa 28: 2 the Lord has *o who* is **powerful** and strong. AIT
Isa 28: 6 spirit of justice to the *o who* **sits** in judgment, AIT
Isa 28:16 the *o who* **relies on** it will never be stricken AIT
Isa 28:28 so *o does* not **go on threshing** it forever. AIT
Isa 28:28 **o** does not use horses to grind grain. H2257
Isa 29:16 what is formed say to the *o who* **formed** it, AIT
Isa 29:19 needy will rejoice in the **Holy O** *of* Israel. H7705
Isa 29:23 the holiness of the **Holy O** *of* Jacob, H7705
Isa 30:11 confronting us with the **Holy O** *of* Israel!" H7705
Isa 30:12 this is what the **Holy O** *of* Israel says: H7705
Isa 30:15 Sovereign LORD, the **Holy O** *of* Israel, says: H7705
Isa 30:17 A thousand will flee at the threat of **o**; at H285
Isa 31: 1 do not look to the **Holy O** *of* Israel, or H7705
Isa 31: 6 to the **O** you have so greatly revolted H889
Isa 31: 7 For in that day **every** *o* of you will reject the AIT
Isa 32: 2 *Each* **o** will be like a shelter from the wind H408
Isa 33: 8 witnesses are despised, no **o** is respected. H632
Isa 33:18 Where is the *o who* **took** *the* **revenue**? Where AIT
Isa 33:21 There the LORD will be our **Mighty O**. H129
Isa 33:24 No **o living** in Zion will say, "I am ill"; H8907
Isa 34:10 no *o will* ever **pass** through it again. AIT
Isa 34:16 will be missing, not **o** will lack her mate. H851
Isa 36: 7 isn't he **the o** whose high places and H889S
Isa 36: 9 then can you repulse **o** officer of the least H285
Isa 37:23 Against the **Holy O** *of* Israel! H7705
Isa 37:38 **O day**, while he was worshiping in H2256+2118
Isa 40: 3 A voice of *o* **calling**: "In the wilderness AIT
Isa 40:25 Or who is my equal?" says the **Holy O**. H7705
Isa 40:26 the starry host **o by one** and calls H928+5031
Isa 40:26 the starry host **one by o** and calls H928+5031
Isa 40:26 mighty strength, not **o** of them is missing. H408
Isa 40:28 his understanding no **o** can fathom. NDT
Isa 41: 2 "Who has stirred up **o** from the east, calling NDT
Isa 41: 7 the *o who* **smooths** *with* the hammer AIT
Isa 41: 7 hammer spurs on the *o who* **strikes** the anvil. AIT
Isa 41: 7 strikes the anvil. *O* **says** of the welding, "It is AIT
Isa 41:14 your Redeemer, the **Holy O** *of* Israel. H7705
Isa 41:16 the LORD and glory in the **Holy O** *of* Israel. H7705
Isa 41:20 that the **Holy O** *of* Israel has created it. H7705
Isa 41:25 "I have stirred up **o** from the north, and he NDT
Isa 41:25 **o** from the rising sun who calls on my name. NDT
Isa 41:26 No *o* **told** *of* this, no one foretold it, no one AIT
Isa 41:26 told of this, no *o* **foretold** it, no one heard AIT
Isa 41:26 foretold it, no *o* **heard** any words from you. AIT
Isa 41:28 I look but there is no **o**—no one among H408
Isa 41:28 no *o* among the gods *to* **give counsel**, no AIT
Isa 41:28 no *o to* **give** answer when I ask them. AIT
Isa 42: 1 I uphold, my **chosen** *o* in whom I delight AIT
Isa 42:19 Who is blind like the *o* **in covenant with** me AIT
Isa 42:22 plunder, with no *o to* **rescue** them; they have AIT
Isa 42:22 with no *o to* **say**, "Send them back. AIT
Isa 43: 3 LORD your God, the **Holy O** *of* Israel, your H7705
Isa 43:10 god was formed, nor *will there* **be** *o* after me. AIT
Isa 43:13 No *o can* **deliver** out of my hand AIT
Isa 43:14 your Redeemer, the **Holy O** *of* Israel: H7705
Isa 43:15 am the LORD, your **Holy O**, Israel's Creator, H7705
Isa 44: 8 there is no other Rock; I know not **o**." NDT
Isa 44:19 No **o** stops to think, no one has the H2257
Isa 44:19 no **o** has the knowledge or understanding to NDT
Isa 45:10 Woe to the *o who* **says** to a father, 'What AIT
Isa 45:11 LORD says—the **Holy O** *of* Israel, and its H7705
Isa 47: 3 I will take vengeance; I will spare no **o**." H132
Isa 47: 4 is his name—is the **Holy O** *of* Israel. H7705
Isa 47:10 wickedness and have said, 'No *o* **sees** me. AIT
Isa 47:15 in their error; there is not *o that can* **save** you. AIT
Isa 48:17 your Redeemer, the **Holy O** *of* Israel: H7705
Isa 49: 7 the Redeemer and **Holy O** *of* Israel—to H7705
Isa 49: 7 is faithful, the **Holy O** *of* Israel, who has H7731
Isa 49:26 your Redeemer, the **Mighty O** *of* Jacob." H51
Isa 50: 2 why was there no **o**? When I called, H408
Isa 50: 2 why was there no *o to* **answer**? AIT
Isa 50: 4 my ear to listen like **o** being **instructed**. H4341
Isa 50:10 Let the *o* who **walks** *in* the dark, who has no AIT
Isa 51: 2 When I called him he was *only* **o** *man*, and H285
Isa 51:21 hear this, you **afflicted** *o*, made drunk, AIT
Isa 53: 3 Like *o* from whom people **hide** their faces he AIT
Isa 54: 5 the **Holy O** *of* Israel is your Redeemer H7705
Isa 55: 5 LORD your God, the **Holy O** *of* Israel, for H7705
Isa 56: 2 Blessed is the **o** who does this—the H632
Isa 56:12 each **o** cries, "let me get wine! Let NDT
Isa 57: 1 and no **o** takes it to heart; the H408
Isa 57: 1 no *o* **understands** that the righteous are AIT
Isa 57:15 For this is what the high and exalted *O* **says**— AIT
Isa 57:15 also with the *o who* is **contrite** and lowly in AIT
Isa 59: 4 No *o* **calls** for justice; no one pleads a case AIT
Isa 59: 4 justice; no *o* **pleads a case** with integrity. AIT
Isa 59: 5 will die, and when **o** is broken, an adder H2021
Isa 59: 8 no **o** who walks along them will know H3972
Isa 59:16 He saw that there was no **o**, he was H408
Isa 59:16 appalled that there was no *o to* **intervene**; AIT
Isa 60: 9 LORD your God, the **Holy O** *of* Israel, for H7705
Isa 60:14 of the LORD, Zion of the **Holy O** *of* Israel. H7705
Isa 60:15 with no *o* **traveling through**, I will make AIT
Isa 60:16 your Redeemer, the **Mighty O** *of* Jacob. H51
Isa 63: 2 like those of *o* **treading** the winepress? AIT
Isa 63: 3 from the nations no **o** was with me. H408
Isa 63: 5 there was no *o to* **help**, I was appalled AIT
Isa 63: 5 I was appalled that no *o* **gave support**; so my AIT
Isa 64: 4 Since ancient times no *o has* **heard**, no ear AIT
Isa 64: 6 of us have become like **o** who is unclean, H2021
Isa 64: 7 No *o* **calls** on your name or strives to lay hold AIT
Isa 65:16 in the land will do so by the **o** true God; NDT
Isa 65:16 in the land will swear by the **o** true God. NDT
Isa 65:20 the *o who* **dies** at a hundred will be thought AIT
Isa 65:20 the *o who* **fails to reach** a hundred will be AIT
Isa 66: 3 sacrifices a bull is like *o who* **kills** a person, AIT
Isa 66: 3 a lamb is like *o who* **breaks** a dog's **neck**; AIT
Isa 66: 3 grain offering is like **o** who presents pig's NDT
Isa 66: 3 incense is like *o who* **worships** an idol. AIT
Isa 66: 4 when I called, no *o* **answered**, when I spoke, AIT
Isa 66: 4 one answered, when I spoke, no *o* **listened**. AIT
Isa 66:17 following **o** who is among those who eat H285
Isa 66:17 their end together with the **o** they follow," NDT
Isa 66:23 From *o* **New Moon** to another and from one AIT
Isa 66:23 to another and from *o* **Sabbath** to another, AIT
Jer 1: 1 **o** *of* the priests at Anathoth in the territory H4946
Jer 2: 6 a land where no **o** travels and no one lives? H408
Jer 2: 6 a land where no one travels and no **o** lives? H132
Jer 3:14 you—**o** from a town and two from a clan H285
Jer 3:16 not be missed, nor *will* another *o* **be made**. AIT
Jer 4: 4 you have done—burn with no *o to* **quench** it. AIT
Jer 4:29 the towns are deserted; no **o** lives in them. H408
Jer 4:30 are you doing, you **devastated** *o*? Why dress AIT
Jer 4:31 a groan as of *o* **bearing** *her* **first child**—the AIT
Jer 5: 1 you can find but *o* **person** who deals honestly AIT
Jer 5: 5 But **with o accord** they too had broken off H3481
Jer 6: 8 your land desolate so no *o can* **live in** *it*." AIT
Jer 6: 9 the branches again, like *o* **gathering grapes**." AIT
Jer 7:19 But am I the **o** they are provoking? declares NDT
Jer 7:33 there will be no *o to* **frighten** them **away**. AIT
Jer 9: 3 They go from *o* **sin** to another; they do not AIT
Jer 9: 4 For **every** *o of* them is a deceiver, and every AIT
Jer 9: 5 deceives friend, and no *o* **speaks** the truth. AIT
Jer 9:11 the towns of Judah so no *o can* **live** there." AIT
Jer 9:12 laid waste like a desert that no *o can* **cross**? AIT
Jer 9:20 how to wail; teach **o** another a lament. H851
Jer 9:22 behind the reaper, with no *o to* **gather** them. AIT
Jer 9:24 but *let* the *o who* **boasts** boast about this AIT
Jer 10: 6 **No** *o* is like you, LORD; you are great, and AIT
Jer 10: 7 in all their kingdoms, **there is no** *o* like you. AIT
Jer 10:20 **no** *o* is left now to pitch my tent or to set up AIT
Jer 11: 3 'Cursed is the **o** who does not obey the H408
Jer 12: 7 I will give the *o* I **love** into the hands of her AIT
Jer 12:11 waste because there is no **o** who cares. H408
Jer 12:12 LORD will devour from *o* **end** *of* the land to AIT
Jer 12:12 to the other; no **o** will be safe. H3972+1414S
Jer 13:14 I will smash them **o** against the other H408
Jer 13:19 and there will be no *o to* **open** them. AIT
Jer 14:16 There will be no *o to* **bury** them, their wives AIT
Jer 14:22 is in you, for you are the *o who* **does** all this. AIT
Jer 16: 6 no *o will* **cut themselves** or shave their AIT
Jer 16: 7 No *o will* **offer food** to comfort those who AIT
Jer 17: 5 "Cursed is the **o** who trusts in man, who H1505
Jer 17: 6 of the desert, in a salt land where no *o* **lives**. AIT
Jer 17: 7 "But blessed is the **o** who trusts in the H1505
Jer 17:14 I will be saved, for you are the *o* I **praise**. AIT
Jer 18:11 your evil ways, **each** *o* of you, and reform AIT
Jer 19: 9 they will eat **o** another's flesh because H408
Jer 21:12 of the oppressor the *o who has* **been robbed**, AIT
Jer 21:12 you have done—burn with no *o to* **quench** it. AIT
Jer 22: 3 of the oppressor the *o who has* **been robbed**. AIT
Jer 22: 8 will pass by this city and will ask **o** another, H408
Jer 22:28 despised, broken pot, an object **no** *o* wants? AIT
Jer 23:14 so that not *o of* them turns from their H408
Jer 23:27 dreams they tell **o** another will make my H408
Jer 23:28 let the **o** who has my word speak it H2257
Jer 23:30 prophets who steal from **o** another words H408
Jer 24: 2 **O** basket had very good figs, like those that H285
Jer 25:26 near and far, **o** after the other—all the H408
Jer 25:33 from *o* **end** *of* the earth to the other. AIT
Jer 28: 9 be recognized as **o** truly sent by H2021+5566S
Jer 29:32 He will have no **o** left among this people H408
Jer 30:10 security, and no *o will* **make** him **afraid**. AIT
Jer 30:13 There is no *o to* **plead** your cause, no remedy AIT
Jer 30:17 called an outcast, Zion for whom no *o* **cares**. AIT
Jer 30:21 Their leader will be **o** *of* their own; their H4946
Jer 31:34 neighbor, or say to **o** another, 'Know the H408
Jer 33:13 under the hand of the *o who* **counts** them, AIT
Jer 33:26 will not choose **o** *of* his sons to rule H4946
Jer 34: 9 no **o** was to hold a fellow Hebrew in H408
Jer 34:22 the towns of Judah so no *o can* **live** there." AIT
Jer 35: 2 them to come to **o** *of* the side rooms of the H285
Jer 36:30 He will have no *o to* **sit** on the throne of AIT
Jer 38:27 no *o had* **heard** his conversation with the AIT
Jer 40:15 son of Nethaniah, and no **o** will know it. H408
Jer 41: 1 blood and had been **o** of the king's officers, NDT
Jer 41: 2 killing the **o** whom the king of Babylon H2257
Jer 41: 9 Gedaliah was the **o** King Asa had made H2085
Jer 42:17 not *o* of them **will** survive or escape the AIT
Jer 44:26 'that no *o from* Judah living anywhere in H408
Jer 46:12 *O* **warrior** will stumble over another; both AIT
Jer 46:18 "*o will* **come** who is like Tabor among the AIT
Jer 46:27 security, and no *o will* **make** him **afraid**. AIT
Jer 48: 9 become desolate, with no *o to* **live** in them. AIT
Jer 48:11 not poured from *o* **jar** to another—she has AIT
Jer 48:18 the *o who* **destroys** Moab will come up AIT
Jer 48:33 no *o* **treads** them with shouts of joy. AIT
Jer 48:38 have broken Moab like a jar that **no** *o* wants," AIT
Jer 49: 5 "**Every** *o* of you will be driven away, and no AIT
Jer 49: 5 and no *o will* **gather** the fugitives. AIT
Jer 49:10 neighbors, so there is no **o** to say, H5647
Jer 49:18 says the LORD, "so no **o** will live there; no H408
Jer 49:19 Who *is the* **chosen** *o* I will appoint for this AIT
Jer 49:33 No **o** will live there; no people will dwell in H408
Jer 50: 3 No *o will* **live** in it; both people and animals AIT
Jer 50:29 around her; let no *o* **escape**. Repay her for AIT
Jer 50:29 has defied the LORD, the **Holy O** *of* Israel. H7705
Jer 50:31 against you, you **arrogant** *o*," declares the AIT
Jer 50:32 The **arrogant** *o* will stumble and fall and no AIT
Jer 50:32 stumble and fall and no *o will* **help her up**; AIT
Jer 50:40 the LORD, "so no **o** will live there; no H408
Jer 50:44 Who *is* the **chosen** *o* I will appoint for this AIT
Jer 51: 5 is full of guilt before the **Holy O** *of* Israel. H7705
Jer 51:29 land of Babylon so that no *o will* **live** there. AIT
Jer 51:31 *O* **courier** follows another and messenger AIT
Jer 51:37 of horror and scorn, a place where no *o* **lives**. AIT
Jer 51:43 a land where no **o** lives, through which H408
Jer 51:43 through which no **o** travels. H1201+132
Jer 51:46 heard in the land; *o* **rumor** comes this year AIT
Jer 52:22 capital on top of **o** pillar was five cubits NDT
La 1: 2 all her lovers there is no *o to* **comfort** her. AIT
La 1: 4 no *o* **comes** *to* her appointed festivals. AIT
La 1: 7 enemy hands, there was no *o to* **help** her. AIT
La 1:16 **No** *o is* **near** to comfort me, no one to restore AIT
La 1:16 near to comfort me, no *o to* **restore** my spirit. AIT
La 1:17 her hands, but there is no *o to* **comfort** her. AIT
La 1:21 my groaning, but there is no *o to* **comfort** me. AIT
La 2:22 of the LORD's anger **no** *o* escaped or survived; AIT
La 3:25 hope is in him, to the **o** who seeks him; H5883
La 3:30 offer his cheek to *o who would* **strike** him, AIT
La 3:31 For no *o is* **cast off** *by* the Lord forever. AIT
La 4: 4 beg for bread, but no *o* **gives** it to them. AIT
La 4:14 with blood that no *o* **dares** to touch their AIT
La 5: 8 there is no *o to* **free** us from their hands. AIT
Eze 1: 9 the wings of **o** touched the wings of H851
Eze 1: 9 **Each** *o* went straight ahead; they did not turn AIT
Eze 1:12 **Each** *o* went straight ahead. Wherever the AIT
Eze 1:17 they would go in any **o** of the four directions NDT
Eze 1:23 were stretched out **o** toward the other, H851
Eze 1:28 I heard the voice of *o* **speaking**. AIT
Eze 4: 8 you cannot turn from **o** side to the other H3870S
Eze 6:12 **O** who is far away will die of the plague H2021S
Eze 6:12 **o** who is near will fall by the sword H2021S
Eze 7:13 not **o** of them will preserve their life. H408
Eze 7:14 but no *o will* **go** into battle, for my AIT
Eze 10: 7 Then **o** of the cherubim reached H2021+4131S
Eze 10: 9 four wheels, **o** beside each of the cherubim H285
Eze 10:11 they would go in any **o** of the four directions NDT
Eze 10:14 **O** face was that of a cherub, the second the H285
Eze 10:22 the Kebar River. **Each** *o* went straight ahead. AIT
Eze 14:10 will be as guilty as the *o who* **consults** him. AIT
Eze 14:15 so that no *o can* **pass through** it because of AIT
Eze 16: 5 No *o* **looked** on you **with pity** or had AIT
Eze 16:34 of others; no *o* **runs after** you **for** your **favors**. AIT
Eze 17: 5 " 'He took *o of* the seedlings of the land H4946
Eze 18: 4 The **o** who sins is the one who will die. H5883
Eze 18: 4 The one who sins is the **o** who will die. H2085
Eze 18:20 The **o** who sins is the one who will die H5883
Eze 18:20 The one who sins is the **o** who will die H2085
Eze 19: 3 She brought up **o** of her cubs, and he H285
Eze 19:14 Fire spread **from** *o of* its main branches and AIT
Eze 20:39 serve your idols, **every** *o* of you! But AIT
Eze 21:20 Mark out *o* **road** for the sword to come AIT
Eze 22:11 In you *o* **man** commits a detestable offense AIT
Eze 22:30 not have to destroy it, but I found **no** *o*. AIT
Eze 23:43 Then I said about the *o* **worn out** *by* adultery AIT
Eze 24:16 with *o* **blow** I am about to take away from AIT
Eze 29:11 through it; no *o will* **live** there for forty years. AIT
Eze 30:22 the good arm as well as the **broken** *o*, and AIT
Eze 33: 2 of the land choose **o** of their men and H285
Eze 33:24 'Abraham was only **o** *man*, yet he H285
Eze 33:28 desolate so that no *o will* **cross** them. AIT
Eze 33:32 nothing more than **o** who sings love songs NDT
Eze 34: 6 and no *o* **searched** or looked for them. AIT
Eze 34:17 I will judge between *o* **sheep** and another AIT
Eze 34:22 I will judge between *o* **sheep** and another. AIT
Eze 34:23 I will place over them **o** shepherd, my H285
Eze 34:28 in safety, and no *o will* **make** them **afraid**. AIT
Eze 37:17 Join them together into **o** stick so that they H285
Eze 37:17 so that they will become **o** in your hand. H285
Eze 37:19 and they will become **o** in my hand. H285
Eze 37:22 I will make them **o** nation in the land, on H285
Eze 37:22 There will be **o** king over all of them and H285
Eze 37:24 and they will all have **o** shepherd. H285

Eze 38:17 You are the **o** I spoke of in former days by H2085
Eze 39: 7 that I the LORD am the **Holy O** in Israel. H7705
Eze 39:26 in their land with no *o to* **make** them **afraid**. AIT
Eze 40: 5 it was **o** measuring rod thick and one rod H285
Eze 40: 5 one measuring rod thick and **o** rod high. H285
Eze 40: 6 threshold of the gate; it was **o** rod deep. H285
Eze 40: 7 the guards were **o** rod long and one rod H285
Eze 40: 7 guards were one rod long and **o** rod wide, H285
Eze 40: 7 portico facing the temple was **o** rod deep. H285
Eze 40:12 of each alcove was a wall **o** cubit high, H285
Eze 40:13 of the rear wall of **o** alcove to the top of H2021
Eze 40:13 of one alcove to the top of the **opposite** *o*; AIT
Eze 40:13 cubits from *o* **parapet opening** to the AIT
Eze 40:13 one parapet opening to the opposite **o**. H7339S
Eze 40:23 He measured from **o** gate to the opposite NDT
Eze 40:23 measured from one gate to the **opposite** *o*; AIT
Eze 40:41 four tables on *o* **side** of the gateway and AIT
Eze 40:44 **o** at the side of the north gate and facing H285
Eze 41: 6 on three levels, **o** above another, thirty H7521S
Eze 41: 7 that the rooms widened as **o** went upward. NDT
Eze 41:11 **o** on the north and another on the south H285
Eze 41:19 the palm tree on **o** side and the face of a NDT
Eze 41:21 the **o** at the front of the Most Holy Place NDT
Eze 42: 9 on the east side as **o** enters them from H2257
Eze 42:12 eastward, by which *o* **enters** the rooms. AIT
Eze 43:13 with a rim of **o** span around the edge. H285
Eze 43:17 altar is a gutter of *o* **cubit** with a rim of half a AIT
Eze 44: 1 of the sanctuary, the *o* **facing** east, and it was AIT
Eze 44: 2 not be opened; no **o** may enter through it. H408
Eze 44: 3 himself is the *only* **o** who may sit inside H2085
Eze 45: 7 border parallel to **o** *of* the tribal portions. H285
Eze 45:12 shekels plus fifteen shekels equal **o** mina. H2021
Eze 45:14 which consists of ten baths or **o** homer, for NDT
Eze 45:15 Also **o** sheep is to be taken from every flock H285
Eze 46: 7 as a grain offering *o* **ephah** with the bull, AIT
Eze 46: 7 with the bull, *o* **ephah** with the ram, and AIT
Eze 46: 9 No *o is to* **return** through the gate by which AIT
Eze 46:16 a gift from his inheritance to **o** of his sons, H408
Eze 46:17 from his inheritance to **o** of his servants, H285
Eze 46:18 so that not **o** of my people will be H408
Eze 47: 5 to swim in—a river that no *o could* **cross**. AIT
Eze 48: 1 Dan will have **o** *portion*; it will follow the H285
Eze 48: 2 "Asher will have **o** *portion*; it will border H285
Eze 48: 3 "Naphtali will have **o** *portion*; it will border H285
Eze 48: 4 "Manasseh will have **o** *portion*; it will H285
Eze 48: 5 "Ephraim will have **o** *portion*; it will border H285
Eze 48: 6 "Reuben will have **o** *portion*; it will border H285
Eze 48: 7 "Judah will have **o** *portion*; it will border H285
Eze 48: 8 to west will equal **o** *of* the tribal portions; H285
Eze 48:23 Benjamin will have **o** *portion*; it will extend H285
Eze 48:24 "Simeon will have **o** *portion*; it will border H285
Eze 48:25 "Issachar will have **o** *portion*; it will border H285
Eze 48:26 "Zebulun will have **o** *portion*; it will border H285
Eze 48:27 "Gad will have **o** *portion*; it will border the H285
Da 2: 9 there is *only* **o** penalty for you. A10248
Da 2:10 "There is no **o** on earth who can do what A10050
Da 2:11 No **o** can reveal it to the king except the A10025
Da 2:39 a third kingdom, **o** of bronze, will rule A10023
Da 4:13 there before me was a **holy** *o*, AIT
Da 4:23 "Your Majesty saw a **holy** *o*, a messenger AIT
Da 4:35 No **o** can hold back his hand or say to A10168
Da 5:13 **o** *of* the exiles my father the king A10427
Da 6: 2 over them, **o** of whom was Daniel. A10248
Da 6:13 who is **o** *of* the exiles from Judah A10427
Da 7: 5 It was raised up on **o** of its sides, and it A10248
Da 7: 6 another beast, **o** that looked like a leopard. NDT
Da 7: 8 was another horn, a **little** *o*, which came up AIT
Da 7:13 there before me was **o** like a son of man, NDT
Da 7:14 his kingdom is **o that** will never be AIT
Da 7:16 I approached **o** of those standing there A10248
Da 8: 1 after the *o that had* already **appeared** to me. AIT
Da 8: 3 **O** of the horns was longer than the other H285
Da 8: 9 Out of **o** of them came another horn, which H285
Da 8:13 Then I heard a **holy** *o* speaking, and another AIT
Da 8:13 another **holy** *o* said to him, "How AIT
Da 8:15 before me stood **o** who looked like a man NDT
Da 8:22 replaced the *o that* **was broken off** represent AIT
Da 9:25 rebuild Jerusalem until the **Anointed** *O*, AIT
Da 9:26 the **Anointed** *O* will be put to death and will AIT
Da 9:27 confirm a covenant with many for **o** 'seven. H285
Da 10: 7 was the **only o** who saw the vision H4200+963
Da 10:13 Then Michael, **o** *of* the chief princes, came H285
Da 10:16 Then *o* who looked like a man **touched** my AIT
Da 10:16 I said to the *o* **standing** before me, "I am AIT
Da 10:18 *the o* who looked like a man **touched** me AIT
Da 10:21 No **o** supports me against them except H285
Da 11: 5 but **o** *of* his commanders will become H4946
Da 11: 6 her father and the *o who* **supported** her. AIT
Da 11: 7 "*O* from her family line *will* **arise** to take her AIT
Da 11:16 no *o will be able to* **stand** against him. AIT
Da 11:37 his ancestors nor for the **o desired** *by* women, AIT
Da 11:45 will come to his end, and no *o will* **help** him. AIT
Da 12: 5 **o** on this bank of the river and one on the H285
Da 12: 5 of the river and **o** on the opposite bank. H285
Da 12: 6 *O of them* **said** to the man clothed in linen AIT
Da 12:12 Blessed is the *o who* **waits for** and reaches AIT
Hos 1:11 they will appoint **o** leader and will come H285
Hos 2: 1 'My people,' and of your sisters, 'My **loved** *o*. AIT
Hos 2: 8 that I was the *o who* **gave** her the grain, AIT
Hos 2:10 no **o** will take her out of my hands. H408
Hos 2:23 show my love to the **o** I called 'Not my loved NDT
Hos 2:23 my love to the one I called 'Not my **loved** *o*. AIT

Hos 4: 4 "But let no **o** bring a charge, let no one H408
Hos 4: 4 bring a charge, let no **o** accuse another, for H408
Hos 5:14 I will carry them off, with no *o to* **rescue** them. AIT
Hos 8: 8 the nations like something **no** *o* wants. AIT
Hos 9:12 rear children, I will bereave them of **every** *o*. AIT
Hos 11: 4 To them I was like *o who* **lifts** a little child to AIT
Hos 11: 9 not a man—the **Holy O** among you. H7705
Hos 11:12 even against the faithful **Holy O**. H7705
Am 1: 1 words of Amos, **o** of the shepherds of Tekoa NDT
Am 1: 5 of Aven and the *o who* **holds** the scepter in AIT
Am 1: 8 Ashdod and the *o who* **holds** the scepter in AIT
Am 4: 7 I sent rain on **o** town, but withheld it from H285
Am 4: 7 **O** field had rain; another had none and H285
Am 5: 2 in her own land, with no *o to* **lift** her **up**." AIT
Am 5: 6 and Bethel will have no *o to* **quench** it. AIT
Am 5:10 who hate the *o who* **upholds justice** in court AIT
Am 5:10 in court and detest the *o who* **tells** the truth. AIT
Am 6: 9 If ten people are left in **o** house, they too H285
Am 6:12 *Does o* **plow** the sea with oxen AIT
Am 9: 1 Not **o** will get away, none will H4200+2157S
Am 9:13 the planter by the *o* **treading** grapes. AIT
Ob 11 lots for Jerusalem, you were like **o** of them. H285
Mic 2: 5 no *o* in the assembly of the LORD *to* **divide** the AIT
Mic 2: 7 do good to the *o whose* **ways** are upright? AIT
Mic 2:13 The *O who* **breaks open** the way will go up AIT
Mic 4: 4 and no *o will* **make** them **afraid**, for the AIT
Mic 5: 2 will come for me *o who will* **be** ruler over AIT
Mic 5: 8 mangles as it goes, and no *o can* **rescue**. AIT
Mic 6: 9 "Heed the rod and the *O* **who** appointed it. AIT
Mic 7: 1 I am like *o who* **gathers** summer fruit at the AIT
Mic 7: 2 from the land; not **o** upright person remains. NDT
Na 1:11 *has o* **come forth** who plots evil against the AIT
Na 1:15 the feet of *o who* **brings good news**, who AIT
Na 2: 8 they cry, but no *o* **turns back**. AIT
Na 3:17 they fly away, and no *o* **knows** where. AIT
Na 3:18 on the mountains with no *o to* **gather** them. AIT
Hab 1:12 My God, my **Holy O**, you will never die H7705
Hab 2:18 For the *o who* **makes** it trusts in his own AIT
Hab 3: 3 Teman, the **Holy O** from Mount Paran. H7705
Hab 3:13 deliver your people, to save your **anointed** *o*. AIT
Zep 2:15 said to herself, "**I** am *the o*! And there is AIT
Zep 3: 2 She obeys no **o**, she accepts no correction NDT
Zep 3: 6 streets deserted, with no *o* **passing through**. AIT
Zep 3:13 lie down and no *o will* **make** them **afraid**." AIT
Hag 2:13 a dead body touches **o** *of* these things, H3972
Hag 2:15 how things were before **o** stone was laid on NDT
Zec 1:21 Judah so that no **o** could raise their head, H408
Zec 2: 8 "After the **Glorious O** has sent me against H3883
Zec 3: 9 There are seven eyes on that **o** stone, and I H285
Zec 4: 3 **o** on the right of the bowl and the other on H285
Zec 5: 3 according to what it says on *o* **side**, every AIT
Zec 6: 6 The **o** with the black horses is going H2023
Zec 6: 6 the **o** with the white horses toward the west NDT
Zec 6: 6 the **o** with the dappled horses toward NDT
Zec 7: 9 show mercy and compassion to **o** another. H408
Zec 7:14 was so desolate that no *o* **traveled through** it. AIT
Zec 8:10 No **o** could go about their business safely H2021
Zec 8:21 the inhabitants of **o** city will go to H285
Zec 8:23 take firm hold of **o** Jew by the hem of his H408
Zec 11: 7 two staffs and called **o** Favor and the other H285
Zec 11: 8 In **o** month I got rid of the three shepherds H285
Zec 11: 9 Let those who are left eat **o** another's flesh." H851
Zec 12:10 will look on me, **the o** they have pierced H889S
Zec 12:10 will mourn for him as **o** mourns for an only NDT
Zec 12:10 bitterly for him as *o* **grieves** for a firstborn son AIT
Zec 13: 3 parents will stab the **o** who prophesies. H2257
Zec 14: 9 On that day there will be **o** LORD, and his H285
Zec 14:13 other by the hand and attack **o** another. H2084
Mal 1:10 that **o** of you would shut the temple doors, H4769
Mal 2:10 Do we not all have **o** Father? Did not one H285
Mal 2:10 Did not **o** God create us? Why H285
Mal 2:10 ancestors by being unfaithful to **o** another? H408
Mal 2:15 Has not the **o** God made you? You belong H285
Mal 2:15 And what does the **o** God seek? Godly H285
Mal 2:16 "does violence to the **o** he should protect," NDT
Mt 2: 2 is the *o who has been* **born** king of the AIT
Mt 3: 3 "A voice *of o* **calling** in the wilderness AIT
Mt 3:11 But after me comes **o** who is more *G3836*
Mt 5:19 who sets aside **o** of the least of these *G1651*
Mt 5:29 you to lose **o** part of your body than *G1651*
Mt 5:30 you to lose **o** part of your body than *G1651*
Mt 5:36 you cannot make *even* **o** hair white or *G1651*
Mt 5:37 anything beyond this comes from the **evil** *o*. AIT
Mt 5:41 If anyone forces you to go **o** mile, go with *G1651*
Mt 5:42 Give *to* the *o who* **asks** you, and do not turn AIT
Mt 5:42 away from the *o who* **wants** to borrow from AIT
Mt 6:13 temptation, but deliver us from the **evil** *o*. AIT
Mt 6:24 "**No o** can serve two masters. Either you *G4029*
Mt 6:24 you will hate the **o** and love the other, *G1651*
Mt 6:24 be devoted to the **o** and despise the other *G1651*
Mt 6:27 Can **any o** of you by worrying add a single *G5515*
Mt 6:29 his splendor was dressed like **o** of these. *G1651*
Mt 7: 8 receives; the *o who* **seeks** finds; and to the AIT
Mt 7: 8 and *to* the *o who* **knocks**, the door will AIT
Mt 7:21 only the *o who* **does** the will of my Father AIT
Mt 7:29 because he taught as *o who* **had** authority AIT
Mt 8: 9 I tell **this** *o*, 'Go,' and he goes; and that one AIT
Mt 8: 9 he goes; and **that** *o*, 'Come,' and he AIT
Mt 8:28 so violent that no **o** could pass that way. *G5516*
Mt 9:16 "**No o** sews a patch of unshrunk cloth on *G4029*
Mt 9:30 "See that **no o** knows about this. *G3594*
Mt 10:22 the *o who* **stands firm** to the end will be AIT

Mt 10:23 When you are persecuted in **o** place, flee *G4047*
Mt 10:28 be afraid *of* the *O who* **can** destroy both soul AIT
Mt 10:29 Yet not **o** of them will fall to the ground *G1651*
Mt 10:40 welcomes me welcomes the *o who* **sent** me. AIT
Mt 10:42 cup of cold water to **o** of these little ones *G1651*
Mt 11: 3 "Are you the *o who is to* **come**, or should we AIT
Mt 11:10 This **is** *the o* about whom it is written: " 'I will AIT
Mt 11:27 No **o** knows the Son except the Father *G5516*
Mt 11:27 no *o* **knows** the Father except the Son AIT
Mt 12:18 I have chosen, the *o* I **love**, in whom I delight AIT
Mt 12:19 no **o** will hear his voice in the streets. *G5516*
Mt 13:19 the **evil** *o* comes and snatches away what AIT
Mt 13:23 This is *the* **o** who produces a crop *G4005*
Mt 13:37 "The *o who* **sowed** the good seed is the Son AIT
Mt 13:38 The weeds are the people *of* the **evil** *o*, AIT
Mt 13:46 When he found **o** of great value, he went *G1651*
Mt 16:14 still others, Jeremiah or **o** of the prophets." *G1651*
Mt 17: 4 put up three shelters—**o** for you, one for *G1651*
Mt 17: 4 **o** for Moses and one for Elijah. *G1651*
Mt 17: 4 you, one for Moses and **o** for Elijah." *G1651*
Mt 17: 8 looked up, they saw **no o** except Jesus. *G4029*
Mt 18: 5 And whoever welcomes **o** such child in my *G1651*
Mt 18: 6 "If anyone causes **o** of these little ones *G1651*
Mt 18: 9 to enter life **with o eye** than to have two *G3669*
Mt 18:10 you do not despise **o** of these little ones. *G1651*
Mt 18:12 and **o** of them wanders away *G1651*
Mt 18:12 go to look for the *o that* **wandered off**? AIT
Mt 18:13 happier about **that o sheep** than about *G899S*
Mt 18:16 will not listen, take **o** or two others along *G1651*
Mt 18:28 he found **o** of his fellow servants who *G1651*
Mt 19: 5 and the two will become **o** flesh'? *G1651*
Mt 19: 6 no longer two, but **o** flesh. Therefore what *G1651*
Mt 19: 6 God has joined together, let no **o** separate." *G476*
Mt 19:12 The *o who* **can** accept this should accept it." AIT
Mt 19:17 "There is *only* **O** who is good. *G1651*
Mt 20: 7 " 'Because **no o** has hired us,' they *G4029*
Mt 20:10 But **each** *o* of them also received a denarius. AIT
Mt 20:12 who were hired last worked *only* **o** hour, *G1651*
Mt 20:13 "But he answered **o** of them, 'I am not *G1651*
Mt 20:14 I want to give *the* **o** who was hired last *G4047*
Mt 20:21 "Grant that **o** of these two sons of mine *G1651*
Mt 21:24 replied, "I will also ask you **o** question. *G1651*
Mt 21:35 they beat **o**, killed another, *G4005+3525*
Mt 22: 5 and went off—**o** to his field *G4005+3525*
Mt 22:25 The **first** *o* married and died, and since he AIT
Mt 22:35 **O** of them, an expert in the law, tested *G1651*
Mt 22:46 **No o** could say a word in reply, and from *G4029*
Mt 22:46 from that day on no **o** dared to ask him *G5516*
Mt 23: 8 you have **o** Teacher, and you are *G1651*
Mt 23: 9 you have **o** Father, and he is in *G1651*
Mt 23:10 you have **o** Instructor, the Messiah. *G1651*
Mt 23:21 swears by it and by the *o who* **dwells** in it. AIT
Mt 23:22 by God's throne and by the *o who* **sits** on it. AIT
Mt 24: 2 **not o** stone here will be left on another AIT
Mt 24: 2 on another; *every* **o** will be thrown down." *G4005*
Mt 24: 4 "Watch out that no **o** deceives you. *G5516*
Mt 24:13 the *o who* **stands firm** to the end will be AIT
Mt 24:17 Let no **o** on the housetop go down to take *G3836*
Mt 24:18 Let no **o** in the field go back to get their *G3836*
Mt 24:22 been cut short, no **o** would survive, but *G4922*
Mt 24:31 from *o* **end** of the heavens to the other. AIT
Mt 24:36 "But about that day or hour **no o** knows *G4029*
Mt 24:40 **o** will be taken and the other left. *G1651*
Mt 24:41 **o** will be taken and the other left. *G1651*
Mt 25:15 *To o* he gave five bags of gold, to *G4005+3525*
Mt 25:15 to another **o** bag, each according *G1651*
Mt 25:17 **the** *o with* two bags of gold gained two more. AIT
Mt 25:18 man who had received **o** bag went off, *G1651*
Mt 25:24 who had received **o** bag of gold came. *G1651*
Mt 25:28 him and give it *to* the *o who* **has** ten bags. AIT
Mt 25:32 the people **o** from **another** as a shepherd *G253*
Mt 25:40 whatever you did *for* **o** of the least of *G1651*
Mt 25:45 you did not do *for* **o** of the least of these, *G1651*
Mt 26:14 Then **o** of the Twelve—the one called *G1651*
Mt 26:14 of the Twelve—the *o* **called** Judas Iscariot AIT
Mt 26:21 "Truly I tell you, **o** of you will betray me." *G1651*
Mt 26:22 began to say to him **o** after the other, *G1651*
Mt 26:23 "The *o who has* **dipped** his hand into the AIT
Mt 26:25 the *o who would* **betray** him, said, AIT
Mt 26:40 you men keep watch with me for **o** hour?" *G1651*
Mt 26:47 speaking, Judas, **o** of the Twelve, arrived *G1651*
Mt 26:48 "**The o** I kiss is the man *G4005+323*
Mt 26:51 **o** of Jesus' companions reached for his *G1651*
Mt 26:64 right hand *of* the **Mighty** *O* and coming on AIT
Mt 26:73 "Surely you are **o of** them; your accent *G1666*
Mt 27:17 "**Which** *o* do you want me to release to you: AIT
Mt 27:38 **o** on his right and one on his left. *G1651*
Mt 27:38 one on his right and **o** on his left. *G1651*
Mt 27:48 Immediately **o** of them ran and got a *G1651*
Mt 27:62 The next day, **the o** after Preparation Day *G4015*
Mk 1: 3 "a voice *of o* **calling** in the wilderness AIT
Mk 1: 7 "After me comes the *o* **more powerful** than I AIT
Mk 1:22 he taught them as *o who* **had** authority, AIT
Mk 1:24 I know who you are—the **Holy** *O* of God!" AIT
Mk 2:21 "**No o** sews a patch of unshrunk cloth on *G4029*
Mk 2:22 And **no o** pours new wine into old *G4029*
Mk 2:23 **O** Sabbath Jesus was going through the *G3836*
Mk 3:27 **no o** can enter a strong man's house *G4029*
Mk 5: 3 and **no o** could bind him anymore *G4029*
Mk 5: 4 **No o** was strong enough to subdue him *G4029*
Mk 5:22 Then **o** of the synagogue leaders, named *G1651*
Mk 6:15 like **o** of the prophets of long ago. *G1651*

Mk 8:14 except for **o** loaf they had with them in G1651
Mk 8:16 discussed this with **o another** and said, G253
Mk 8:28 and still others, **o** of the prophets. G1651
Mk 9: 5 put up three shelters—**o** for you, one for G1651
Mk 9: 5 **o** for Moses and one for Elijah. G1651
Mk 9: 5 you, one for Moses and **o** for Elijah." G1651
Mk 9:23 "Everything is possible for **o** who believes." G3836
Mk 9:37 "Whoever welcomes **o** of these little G1651
Mk 9:37 not welcome me but the *o who* **sent** me." AIT
Mk 9:38 him to stop, because *he* **was** not **o of** us." G199
Mk 9:39 "For **no o** who does a miracle in my name G4029
Mk 9:42 "If anyone causes **o** of these little ones G1651
Mk 9:47 kingdom of God *with* **o eye** than to have G3669
Mk 10: 8 the two will become **o** flesh.' So they G1651
Mk 10: 8 So they are no longer two, but **o** flesh. G1651
Mk 10: 9 God has joined together, let no **o** separate." G476
Mk 10:18 Jesus answered. "**No o** is good—except G4029
Mk 10:21 loved him. "**O** *thing* you lack," he G1651
Mk 10:29 "**no o** who has left home or brothers or G4029
Mk 10:37 "Let **o** of us sit at your right and the other G1651
Mk 11: 2 colt tied there, which no **o** has ever ridden. G476
Mk 11:14 "May **no o** ever eat fruit from you again." G3594
Mk 11:29 "I will ask you **o** question. Answer me, G1651
Mk 12: 5 sent still another, **and that** *o* they killed. AIT
Mk 12: 6 "He had **o** left to send, a son, whom he G1651
Mk 12: 7 "But the tenants said to **o another**, 'This is G1571
Mk 12:20 The **first** *o* married and died without leaving AIT
Mk 12:21 The **second** *o* married the widow, but he also AIT
Mk 12:28 **O** of the teachers of the law came and G1651
Mk 12:29 "The **most important** *o*," answered Jesus, "is AIT
Mk 12:29 The Lord our God, the Lord is **o**. G1651
Mk 12:32 saying that God is **o** and there is no other G1651
Mk 12:34 And from then on **no o** dared ask him any G4029
Mk 13: 1 the temple, **o** of his disciples said to him G1651
Mk 13: 2 "**Not o** stone here will be left on G4024+3590
Mk 13: 2 on another; *every* **o** will be thrown down." G4005
Mk 13: 5 "Watch out that no **o** deceives you. G5516
Mk 13:13 the *o who* **stands firm** to the end will be AIT
Mk 13:15 Let no **o** on the housetop go down or enter G3836
Mk 13:16 Let no **o** in the field go back to get their G3836
Mk 13:20 those days, no **o** would survive. G4246+4922
Mk 13:32 "But about that day or hour **no o** knows G4029
Mk 13:34 tells the **o at the door** to keep watch. G2601
Mk 14: 4 were saying indignantly to **o another**, G1571
Mk 14:10 Then Judas Iscariot, **o** of the Twelve, went G1651
Mk 14:18 "Truly I tell you, **o** of you will betray me G1651
Mk 14:18 will betray me—**o** who is eating with me." G3836
Mk 14:19 saddened, and **o** by one they said to him G1651
Mk 14:19 saddened, and one by **o** they said to him G1651
Mk 14:20 "It is **o** of the Twelve," he replied, "one G1651
Mk 14:20 "**o** who dips bread into the bowl with me. G3836
Mk 14:37 Couldn't you keep watch for **o** hour? G1651
Mk 14:43 was speaking, Judas, **o** of the Twelve G1651
Mk 14:44 "The **o** I kiss is the man; arrest him G4005+323
Mk 14:47 Then **o** of those standing near drew his G1651
Mk 14:61 you the Messiah, the Son *of* the **Blessed** *O*?" AIT
Mk 14:62 right hand *of* the **Mighty O** and coming on G1539
Mk 14:66 **o** of the servant girls of the high priest G1651
Mk 14:69 around, "This fellow is **o of** them. G1666
Mk 14:70 "Surely you are **o of** them, for you are a G1666
Mk 15:12 *with the* **o** you call the king of the Jews?" G4005
Mk 15:27 **o** on his right and one on his left. G1651
Mk 15:27 one on his right and **o** on his left. G1651
Lk 1:35 So the **holy** *o* to be born will be called the AIT
Lk 1:49 the **Mighty** *O* has done great things for AIT
Lk 1:61 "There is **no o** among your relatives who G4029
Lk 2:15 the shepherds said to **o another**, "Let's go G253
Lk 3: 4 "A voice *of o* **calling** in the wilderness AIT
Lk 3:11 shirts should share with the *o who* **has** none, AIT
Lk 3:16 But *o who* is more powerful than I will G3836
Lk 4:27 prophet, yet **not o** of them was cleansed G4029
Lk 4:34 I know who you are—the **Holy** *O* of God!" AIT
Lk 4:40 laying his hands on each **o**, he G1651
Lk 5: 1 **O day** as Jesus was standing by the G1181+1254
Lk 5: 3 He got into **o** of the boats, the one G1651
Lk 5: 3 of the boats, **the o** belonging to Simon G4005
Lk 5:12 While Jesus was in **o** of the towns, a man G1651
Lk 5:17 **O** day Jesus was teaching, and Pharisees G1651
Lk 5:36 "**No o** tears a piece out of a new garment G4029
Lk 5:36 out of a new garment to patch an old **o**. G2668S
Lk 5:37 And **no o** pours new wine into old G4029
Lk 5:39 And **no o** after drinking old wine wants the G4029
Lk 6: 1 *O* **Sabbath** Jesus was going through the AIT
Lk 6:11 to discuss with **o another** what they might G253
Lk 6:12 **O** of those days Jesus went out to a NDT
Lk 6:29 If someone slaps you on **o** cheek, turn to G3836
Lk 6:49 But the *o who* **hears** my words and does not AIT
Lk 7: 8 I tell **this** *o*, 'Go,' and he goes; and that one AIT
Lk 7: 8 he goes; and **that** *o*, 'Come,' and he AIT
Lk 7:19 "Are you the *o who is to* **come**, or should we AIT
Lk 7:20 'Are you the *o who is to* **come**, or should we AIT
Lk 7:27 This is *the o* about whom it is written: " 'I will AIT
Lk 7:28 of women there is **no o** greater than John; G4029
Lk 7:28 the *o who is* **least** in the kingdom of God AIT
Lk 7:36 When **o** of the Pharisees invited Jesus to G5516
Lk 7:41 **O** owed him five hundred denarii, and the G1651
Lk 7:43 "I suppose *the o* **who** had the bigger debt AIT
Lk 8: 1 about **from o** town and village **to another**, G2848
Lk 8:16 "No **o** lights a lamp and hides it in a clay G4029
Lk 8:22 **O** day Jesus said to his disciples, "Let us G1651
Lk 8:25 fear and amazement they asked **o another**, G253
Lk 8:43 twelve years, but **no o** could heal her. G4029
Lk 9: 8 still others that **o** of the prophets of G5516
Lk 9:19 that **o** of the prophets of long ago has G5516
Lk 9:33 put up three shelters—**o** for you, one for G1651
Lk 9:33 **o** for Moses and one for Elijah. G1651
Lk 9:33 you, one for Moses and **o** for Elijah." G1651
Lk 9:48 welcomes me welcomes the *o who* **sent** me. AIT
Lk 9:48 For it is the *o who* **is** least among you all who AIT
Lk 9:49 stop him, because *he* **is** not **o of** us." G199+3552
Lk 9:62 "**No o** who puts a hand to the plow and G4029
Lk 10:22 **No o** knows who the Son is except the G4029
Lk 10:22 no **o** knows who the Father is except the NDT
Lk 10:25 **On o occasion** an expert in the law G2779+2627
Lk 10:37 law replied, "The *o who* **had** mercy on him." AIT
Lk 10:42 few things are needed—or indeed *only* **o**. G1651
Lk 11: 1 **O day** Jesus was praying in a G2779+1181
Lk 11: 1 he finished, **o** of his disciples said to him G5516
Lk 11: 7 **And** suppose **the o** inside answers, 'Don't G2797
Lk 11:10 receives; the *o who* **seeks** finds; and to the AIT
Lk 11:10 and *to the o who* **knocks**, the door will AIT
Lk 11:33 "**No o** lights a lamp and puts it in a place G4029
Lk 11:40 Did not the *o who* **made** the outside make AIT
Lk 11:45 **O** of the experts in the law answered him G5516
Lk 11:46 will not lift **o** finger to help them. G1651
Lk 12: 1 so that they were trampling on **o another** G253
Lk 12: 6 Yet not **o** of them is forgotten by God. G1651
Lk 12:27 his splendor was dressed like **o** of these. G1651
Lk 12:48 But the *o who does* not **know** and does things AIT
Lk 12:48 and *from the* **o** who has been entrusted G4005
Lk 12:52 there will be five in **o** family divided G1651
Lk 13: 8 'leave it alone for **o more** year, and I'll G4047S
Lk 13:10 was teaching in **o** of the synagogues, G1651
Lk 14: 1 **O** Sabbath, when Jesus went to eat in the NDT
Lk 14: 5 "If **o** of you has a child or an ox that falls G5515
Lk 14:15 When **o** of those at the table with him G5516
Lk 14:15 "Blessed is *the* **o** who will eat at the feast G4015
Lk 14:24 **not o** of those who were invited will get a G4029
Lk 14:28 "Suppose **o** of you wants to build a G5515+5516
Lk 14:31 to oppose the *o* **coming** against him with AIT
Lk 15: 4 "Suppose **o** of you has a G5515+5516+476
Lk 15: 4 a hundred sheep and loses **o** of them. G1651
Lk 15: 7 in heaven over **o** sinner who repents than G1651
Lk 15: 8 a woman has ten silver coins and loses **o**. G1651
Lk 15:10 angels of God over **o** sinner who repents." G1651
Lk 15:12 The **younger** *o* said to his father, 'Father, AIT
Lk 15:16 were eating, but **no o** gave him anything. G4029
Lk 15:19 make me like **o** of your hired servants. G1651
Lk 15:26 So he called **o** of the servants and asked G1651
Lk 16: 5 "So he called in each **o** of his master's G1651
Lk 16:13 "No **o** can serve two masters. Either you G3860S
Lk 16:13 you will hate the **o** and love the other, G1651
Lk 16:13 be devoted to the **o** and despise the other G1651
Lk 17: 2 neck than to cause **o** of these little ones G1651
Lk 17: 7 "Suppose **o** of you has a servant plowing G5515
Lk 17:15 **O** of them, when he saw he was healed G1651
Lk 17:18 *Has* no *o* **returned** to give praise to God AIT
Lk 17:22 you will long to see **o** of the days of the G1651
Lk 17:24 lights up the sky from **o** end to the other. G3836
Lk 17:31 On that day no **o** who is on the housetop G4005
Lk 17:31 no **o** in the field should go back for G3836
Lk 17:34 on that night two people will be in **o** bed G1651
Lk 17:34 **o** will be taken and the other left. G1651
Lk 17:35 **o** will be taken and the other left. G1651
Lk 18:10 **o** a Pharisee and the other a tax collector. G1651
Lk 18:19 Jesus answered. "**No o** is good—except G4029
Lk 18:22 he said to him, "You still lack **o** *thing*. G1651
Lk 18:29 "**no o** who has left home or wife or G4029
Lk 19:16 "The **first** *o* came and said, 'Sir, your mina AIT
Lk 19:24 him and give it *to the o who* **has** ten minas. AIT
Lk 19:26 as for the *o who* **has** nothing, even what AIT
Lk 19:30 colt tied there, which no **o** has ever ridden. G476
Lk 19:44 They will not leave **o** stone on another NDT
Lk 20: 1 **O** day as Jesus was teaching the people G1651
Lk 20:11 **that** *o* also they beat and treated AIT
Lk 20:29 The **first** *o* married a woman and died AIT
Lk 20:40 And no *o* **dared** to ask him any more AIT
Lk 21: 6 will come when not *o* **stone** will be left on AIT
Lk 21: 6 *every o of* **them** will be thrown down. AIT
Lk 22: 3 Iscariot, **o of** the Twelve. G1666+3836+750
Lk 22:26 the *o who* **rules** like the one who serves. AIT
Lk 22:26 the one who rules like the *o who* **serves**. AIT
Lk 22:27 the *o who is* **at the table** or the one who AIT
Lk 22:27 one who is at the table or the *o who* **serves**? AIT
Lk 22:27 Is it not the *o who is* **at the table**? But I am AIT
Lk 22:27 But I am among you as **o** who serves. G3836
Lk 22:29 just as my Father conferred **o** on me, NDT
Lk 22:36 have a sword, sell your cloak and buy **o**. NDT
Lk 22:47 was called Judas, **o** of the Twelve, was G1651
Lk 22:50 And **o** of them struck the servant of G1651+5516
Lk 22:58 him and said, "You also are **o of** them." G1666
Lk 23:14 *o who was* **inciting** the people **to rebellion**. AIT
Lk 23:25 murder, the **o** they asked for, and G4005
Lk 23:33 the criminals—**o** on his right, the G4005+3525
Lk 23:35 if he is God's Messiah, the **Chosen** *O*." AIT
Lk 23:39 **O** of the criminals who hung there hurled G1651
Lk 23:53 *o in* **which** no one had yet been laid. AIT
Lk 23:53 one in which **no o** had yet been laid. G4029
Lk 24:18 **O** of them, named Cleopas, asked him G1651
Lk 24:18 "*Are* you the only *o* **visiting** Jerusalem who AIT
Lk 24:21 he was the *o who* **was going** to redeem AIT
Jn 1:14 the glory of the **o and only Son**, who G3666
Jn 1:15 "This is *the* **o** I spoke about when I said G4005
Jn 1:18 **No o** has ever seen God, but the one and G4029
Jn 1:18 but the **o and only Son**, who is G3666
Jn 1:23 "I am the voice *of o* **calling** in the wilderness AIT
Jn 1:26 among you stands **o** you do not know. G4005
Jn 1:27 He is the *o who* **comes** after me, the straps of AIT
Jn 1:30 This is **the o** I **meant** when I said G5642+4005
Jn 1:33 the *o who* **sent** me to baptize with water AIT
Jn 1:33 remain is the *o who will* **baptize** with the AIT
Jn 1:34 and I testify that this is God's **Chosen** *O*." AIT
Jn 1:40 was **o** of the two who heard what John G1651
Jn 1:45 "We have found *the* **o** Moses wrote about G4005
Jn 3: 2 For **no o** could perform the signs you are G4029
Jn 3: 3 no **o** can see the kingdom of God unless G5516
Jn 3: 5 no **o** can enter the kingdom of God unless G5516
Jn 3:13 **No o** has ever gone into heaven except G4029
Jn 3:13 except the *o who* **came** from heaven— AIT
Jn 3:16 world that he gave his **o and only** Son, G3666
Jn 3:18 in the name of God's **o and only** Son. G3666
Jn 3:26 Jordan—*the* **o** you testified *about*—look, G4005
Jn 3:31 The *o who* **comes** from above is above all AIT
Jn 3:31 the *o who* **is from** the earth belongs to the AIT
Jn 3:31 to the earth, and speaks *as o* **from** the earth. AIT
Jn 3:31 The *o who* **comes** from heaven is above all AIT
Jn 3:32 but **no o** accepts his testimony. G4029
Jn 3:34 For *the o* **whom** God has sent speaks the AIT
Jn 4:26 declared, "I, the *o* **speaking** to you—I am he." AIT
Jn 4:27 with a woman. But **no o** asked, "What do G4029
Jn 4:36 Even now the *o who* **reaps** draws a wage AIT
Jn 4:37 Thus the saying '**O** sows and another reaps' G257
Jn 4:52 *at* **o in the afternoon**, the fever G6052+1575
Jn 5: 1 up to Jerusalem for **o** of the Jewish festivals. NDT
Jn 5: 5 **O** who was there had been an G5516+476
Jn 5: 7 "I have no **o** to help me into the pool when G476
Jn 5:22 the Father judges **no o**, but has entrusted G4029
Jn 5:38 for you do not believe **the** *o* he sent. AIT
Jn 5:44 accept glory from **o another** but do not seek G253
Jn 6: 7 buy enough bread for **each** *o* to have a bite!" AIT
Jn 6:22 realized that only **o** boat had been there, G1651
Jn 6:29 to believe in the **o** he has sent." G1697
Jn 6:44 "**No o** can come to me unless the Father G4029
Jn 6:46 No **o** has seen the Father except the one G5516
Jn 6:46 the Father except the *o who* **is** from God; AIT
Jn 6:47 I tell you, the *o who* **believes** has eternal life. AIT
Jn 6:57 so the *o who* **feeds on** me will live because AIT
Jn 6:65 why I told you that **no o** can come to me G4029
Jn 6:69 to know that you are the **Holy** *O* of God." AIT
Jn 6:70 the Twelve? Yet **o** of you is a devil!" G1651
Jn 6:71 though **o** of the Twelve, was later to G1651
Jn 7: 4 **No o** who wants to become a public figure G4029
Jn 7:13 But **no o** would say anything publicly G4029
Jn 7:16 It comes *from* the *o who* **sent** me. AIT
Jn 7:18 the glory *of* the *o who* **sent** him is a man AIT
Jn 7:19 Yet **not o** of you keeps the law G4029
Jn 7:21 to them, "I did **o** miracle, and you are G1651
Jn 7:27 **no o** will know where he is from. G4029
Jn 7:30 to seize him, but **no o** laid a hand on him G4029
Jn 7:33 then I am going to the *o who* **sent** me. AIT
Jn 7:35 The Jews said to **o another**, "Where does G1571
Jn 7:44 seize him, but **no o** laid a hand on him. G4029
Jn 7:46 "No *o* ever **spoke** the way this man does," AIT
Jn 7:50 who was **o** of their own number G1651
Jn 8: 7 "Let *any o* of you **who** is without sin be the AIT
Jn 8: 9 to go away **o at a time**, G1651+2848+1651
Jn 8:10 Has **no o** condemned you?" G4029
Jn 8:11 "**No o**, sir," she said. "Then neither do I G4029
Jn 8:15 standards; I pass judgment *on* **no o**. G4029
Jn 8:18 I am **o** who testifies for myself; my other G3836
Jn 8:20 Yet **no o** seized him, because his hour G4029
Jn 8:29 The *o who* **sent** me is with me; he has not left AIT
Jn 8:50 but there is **o** who seeks it, and he G3836
Jn 8:54 claim as your God, is the *o who* **glorifies** me. AIT
Jn 9: 4 Night is coming, when **no o** can work. G4029
Jn 9:19 "Is **this** *the o* you say was born blind AIT
Jn 9:25 **O** *thing* I do know. I was G1651
Jn 9:37 in fact, he is the *o* **speaking** with you." AIT
Jn 10: 2 The *o who* **enters** by the gate is the shepherd AIT
Jn 10:16 there shall be **o** flock and one G1651
Jn 10:16 there shall be one flock and **o** shepherd. G1651
Jn 10:18 **No o** takes it from me, but I lay it down of G4029
Jn 10:28 no **o** will snatch them out of my hand. G5516
Jn 10:29 **no o** can snatch them out of my Father's G4029
Jn 10:30 I and the Father are **o**. G1651
Jn 10:36 what about *the o* **whom** the Father set apart AIT
Jn 11: 2 was **the** *same o* who poured perfume on the AIT
Jn 11: 3 to Jesus, "Lord, *the* **o** you love is sick." G4005
Jn 11:25 The *o who* **believes** in me will live, even AIT
Jn 11:49 Then **o** of them, named Caiaphas, who G1651
Jn 11:50 better for you that **o** man die for the G1651
Jn 11:52 to bring them together and make them **o**. G1651
Jn 11:56 in the temple courts they asked **o another**, G253
Jn 12: 4 But **o** of his disciples, Judas Iscariot, who G1651
Jn 12:19 So the Pharisees said to **o another**, "See G1571
Jn 12:26 will honor *the* **o** who serves me. G1569+5516
Jn 12:44 in me only, but in the *o who* **sent** me. AIT
Jn 12:45 The *o who* **looks at** me is seeing the one who AIT
Jn 12:45 looks at me is seeing the *o who* **sent** me. AIT
Jn 12:46 so that no **o** who believes in me should G4246
Jn 12:48 a judge for the *o who* **rejects** me and does AIT
Jn 13:10 you are clean, though not **every** *o* of you." AIT
Jn 13:11 that was why he said not **every** *o* was clean. AIT
Jn 13:14 you also should wash **o another's** feet. G253
Jn 13:16 messenger greater *than* the *o who* **sent** him. AIT
Jn 13:20 accepts me accepts the *o who* **sent** me." AIT

Jn 13:21 I tell you, **o** of you is going to betray me." *G1651*
Jn 13:22 His disciples stared at **o another**, at a loss *G253*
Jn 13:23 **O** of them, the disciple whom Jesus loved *G1651*
Jn 13:24 "Ask him **which o** he means. *G5515+323*
Jn 13:26 "It is *the* **o** to whom I will give this piece *G1697*
Jn 13:28 But **no o** at the meal understood why *G4029*
Jn 13:34 Love **o another**. As I have loved *G253*
Jn 13:34 loved you, so you must love **o another**. *G253*
Jn 13:35 you are my disciples, if you love **o another**." *G253*
Jn 14: 6 **No o** comes to the Father except through *G4029*
Jn 14:21 keeps them is the *o who* **loves** me. AIT
Jn 14:21 The *o who* **loves** me will be loved by my AIT
Jn 15:13 Greater love has **no o** than this: to lay *G4029*
Jn 15:21 they do not know the *o who* **sent** me. AIT
Jn 15:24 among them the works **no o** else did, *G4029*
Jn 16:17 some of his disciples said to **o another** *G253*
Jn 16:19 "Are you asking **o another** what I meant *G253*
Jn 16:22 and **no o** will take away your joy. *G4029*
Jn 17:11 so that they may be **o** as we are one. *G1651*
Jn 17:11 so that they may be one as we are **o**. NDT
Jn 17:12 except the **o doomed** to destruction so *G5626*
Jn 17:15 that you protect them from the **evil** *o*. AIT
Jn 17:21 that all of them may be **o**, Father, just as *G1651*
Jn 17:22 that they may be **o** as we are one— *G1651*
Jn 17:22 that they may be one as we are **o**— *G1651*
Jn 18: 9 "I have not lost **o** of those you gave me." *G4029*
Jn 18:14 was the *o who had* **advised** the Jewish AIT
Jn 18:14 it would be good if **o** man died for the *G1651*
Jn 18:17 "You aren't **o of** this man's disciples too *G1666*
Jn 18:22 **o** of the officials nearby slapped him in *G1651*
Jn 18:25 "You aren't **o of** his disciples too *G1666*
Jn 18:26 **O** of the high priest's servants, a relative *G1651*
Jn 18:39 to release to you **o** *prisoner* at the time of *G1651*
Jn 19:11 the *o who* **handed** me **over** to you is AIT
Jn 19:18 **o on each side** and Jesus in *G1949+2779+1949*
Jn 19:23 into four shares, **o** for each of them, with *G3538S*
Jn 19:23 **woven** *in o piece* from top to bottom. AIT
Jn 19:24 they said to **o another**. "Let's decide by *G253*
Jn 19:34 **o** of the soldiers pierced Jesus' side with *G1651*
Jn 19:36 "Not *o* of his bones *will be* **broken**," AIT
Jn 19:37 "They will look on *the* **o** they have pierced *G4005*
Jn 19:41 in which **no o** had ever been laid. *G4029*
Jn 20: 2 the other disciple, **the o** Jesus loved, and AIT
Jn 20:12 **o** at the head and the other at the foot. *G1651*
Jn 20:24 **o** of the Twelve, was not with the *G1651*
Jn 21:20 This was *the o* **who** had leaned back against AIT
Jn 21:25 If every **o** of them were written down, *G1651*
Ac 1: 4 **On o occasion**, while he was eating with *G2779*
Ac 1:17 He was *o* of our **number** and shared in our AIT
Ac 1:20 let there be no **o** to dwell in it,' and, *G3836*
Ac 1:21 necessary to choose **o** of the men who have NDT
Ac 1:22 For **o** of these must become a witness *G1651*
Ac 2: 1 they were all together in **o place**. *G3836+899*
Ac 2: 6 because each **o** heard their own *G1651*
Ac 2:12 they asked **o another**, "What *G257+4639+257*
Ac 2:27 you will not let your **holy** *o* see decay. AIT
Ac 2:30 he would place **o of** his descendants on *G1666*
Ac 2:38 be baptized, **every** *o* of you, in the name AIT
Ac 3: 1 **O day** Peter and John were going up to *G1254*
Ac 3:14 the Holy and **Righteous** *O* and asked that a AIT
Ac 4:12 Salvation is found in **no o** else, for there *G4029*
Ac 4:26 against the Lord and against his **anointed** *o*. AIT
Ac 4:32 the believers were **o** in heart and mind. *G1651*
Ac 4:32 No **o** claimed that any of their *G1651*
Ac 5:13 **No o** else dared join them, even though *G4029*
Ac 5:23 we opened them, we found **no o** inside." *G4029*
Ac 7:24 He saw **o** of them being mistreated by an *G5516*
Ac 7:52 predicted the coming *of* the **Righteous** *O*. AIT
Ac 10: 3 **O** day at about three in the afternoon he had NDT
Ac 10: 7 a devout soldier who *was o of* his **attendants**. AIT
Ac 10:21 to the men, "I'm **the o** you're looking for. *G4005*
Ac 10:35 every nation the *o who* **fears** him and does AIT
Ac 10:42 he is the *o whom* God **appointed** as judge of AIT
Ac 10:47 "Surely no **o** can stand in the way of their *G5516*
Ac 11:28 **O** of them, named Agabus, stood up and *G1651*
Ac 11:29 disciples, as each **o** was able, decided to *G5516*
Ac 12:10 they had walked the length of **o** street, *G1651*
Ac 13:25 I am not the **o** you are looking for. NDT
Ac 13:25 But there is *o* **coming** after me whose AIT
Ac 13:35 " 'You will not let your **holy** *o* see decay.' AIT
Ac 13:37 But *the* **o whom** God raised from the dead did AIT
Ac 16:14 **O** of those listening was a woman from *G5516*
Ac 17: 7 that there is another king, **o** called Jesus." NDT
Ac 17:26 From **o** *man* he made all the nations, that *G1651*
Ac 17:27 though he is not far from any **o** of us. *G1651*
Ac 18: 9 *O* **night** the Lord spoke to Paul in a vision AIT
Ac 18:10 and **no o** is going to attack and harm you *G4029*
Ac 19: 4 people to believe in the *o* **coming** after him, AIT
Ac 19:15 **O** day the evil spirit answered them, "Jesus I NDT
Ac 19:32 Some were shouting *o* **thing**, some another AIT
Ac 21: 8 of Philip the evangelist, **o** of the Seven. *G1639*
Ac 21:16 a man from Cyprus and **o** of the early NDT
Ac 21:34 crowd shouted *o thing* and some another *G5516*
Ac 22:14 to see the **Righteous** *O* and to hear AIT
Ac 22:19 I went **from o** synagogue **to another** to *G2848*
Ac 23:17 Then Paul called **o** of the centurions and *G1651*
Ac 24:21 unless it was this **o** thing I shouted as I *G1651*
Ac 25:11 **no o** has the right to hand me over to *G4029*
Ac 26:11 **from o** synagogue **to another** to *G2848+4246*
Ac 26:12 "On **o of these journeys** I was going to *G4005S*
Ac 26:31 they began saying to **o another**, "This man *G253*
Ac 27:22 because **not o** of you will be lost *G6034+4029*
Ac 27:34 **Not o** of you will lose a single hair from *G4029*
Ro 1:24 degrading of their bodies with **o another**. *G899*
Ro 1:27 were inflamed with lust for **o another**. *G253*
Ro 2:27 **The** *o* who is not circumcised physically and AIT
Ro 2:28 person is not a Jew who is **o** only outwardly, NDT
Ro 2:29 a person is a Jew who is **o** inwardly; and NDT
Ro 3:10 "*There* is no *o* righteous, not AIT
Ro 3:10 "There is no one righteous, not even **o**; *G1651*
Ro 3:11 there is no **o** who understands; there is no *G3836*
Ro 3:11 there is no **o** who seeks God. *G3836*
Ro 3:12 there is no **o** who does good, not *G3836*
Ro 3:12 is no one who does good, not even **o**." *G1651*
Ro 3:20 Therefore no **o** will be declared *G4246+4922*
Ro 3:26 just and the *o who* **justifies** those who have AIT
Ro 3:30 since there is *only* **o** God, who will justify *G1651*
Ro 4: 4 Now *to* the *o who* **works**, wages are not AIT
Ro 4: 5 *to* the *o who does* not **work** but trusts God AIT
Ro 4: 6 of the blessedness *of* the **o** to whom God *G476*
Ro 4: 8 Blessed is the **o** whose sin the Lord will *G467*
Ro 5:12 as sin entered the world through **o** man, *G1651*
Ro 5:14 did Adam, who is a pattern *of* the *o to* **come**. AIT
Ro 5:15 many died by the trespass *of* the **o** *man*, *G1651*
Ro 5:15 gift that came by the grace *of* the **o** man, *G1651*
Ro 5:16 compared with the result *of* **o** *man's* sin: *G1651*
Ro 5:16 The judgment followed **o** sin and brought *G1651*
Ro 5:17 by the trespass *of* the **o** *man*, death *G1651*
Ro 5:17 death reigned through that **o** *man*, how *G1651*
Ro 5:17 reign in life through the **o** *man*, *G1651*
Ro 5:18 just as **o** trespass resulted in *G1651*
Ro 5:18 so also **o** righteous act resulted in *G1651*
Ro 5:19 the disobedience *of* the **o** man the many *G1651*
Ro 5:19 the obedience *of* the **o** *man* the many will *G1651*
Ro 6:16 you are slaves *of the* **o** you obey *G4005*
Ro 8:20 by the will of the *o who* **subjected** it, in AIT
Ro 8:34 Who then *is* the *o who* **condemns**? No one AIT
Ro 8:34 one who condemns? No **o**. Christ Jesus who NDT
Ro 9:19 *O of you will* **say** to me: "Then why does God AIT
Ro 9:20 what is formed say *to* the *o who* **formed** it, AIT
Ro 9:25 I will call her 'my **loved** *o*' who is not my AIT
Ro 9:25 her 'my loved one' who is not my **loved** *o*," AIT
Ro 9:33 the *o who* **believes** in him will never be AIT
Ro 10:14 can they call on *the* **o** they have not *G4005*
Ro 10:14 they believe in the **o** of whom they have not NDT
Ro 11: 3 your altars; I am the **only** *o* left, and they are AIT
Ro 11:30 as you who were **at o time** disobedient to *G4537*
Ro 12: 3 by the grace given me I say *to* **every** *o* of you: AIT
Ro 12: 4 as each of us has **o** body with many *G1651*
Ro 12: 5 though many, form **o** body, and each *G1651*
Ro 12:10 Be devoted to **o another** in love. Honor one *G253*
Ro 12:10 Honor **o another** above yourselves. *G253*
Ro 12:16 Live in harmony with **o another**. Do not be *G253*
Ro 13: 3 to be free from fear *of* **the** *o* in authority? AIT
Ro 13: 4 For the **o** in authority is God's servant for NDT
Ro 13: 8 the continuing debt to love **o another**, *G253*
Ro 13: 9 are summed up in this **o** command: *G3836*
Ro 14: 1 Accept the *o* whose faith *is* **weak**, without AIT
Ro 14: 2 **O person's** faith allows them to eat *G4005*
Ro 14: 3 The *o who* **eats** everything must not treat with AIT
Ro 14: 3 not treat with contempt the *o who* **does** not, AIT
Ro 14: 3 the *o who does* not **eat** everything must AIT
Ro 14: 3 everything must not judge the *o who* **does**, AIT
Ro 14: 5 **O person** considers one day more *G4005+3525*
Ro 14: 5 person considers *o* **day** more sacred than AIT
Ro 14: 6 Whoever regards **o** day as special does so *G3836*
Ro 14:13 let us stop passing judgment *on* **o another**. *G253*
Ro 14:22 is the *o who does* not **condemn** himself by AIT
Ro 15: 6 so that **with o mind** and one voice you *G3924*
Ro 15: 6 with one mind and **o** voice you may *G1651*
Ro 15: 7 Accept **o another**, then, just as Christ *G253*
Ro 15:12 **o** who will arise to rule over the nations *G3836*
Ro 15:14 competent to instruct **o another**. *G253*
Ro 16:16 Greet **o another** with a holy kiss. All the *G253*
1Co 1:10 *of you* **agree** *with o another* **in what** *you* **say** AIT
1Co 1:12 **O** of you says, "I follow Paul"; another, "I *G1667*
1Co 1:15 so no **o** can say that you were baptized in *G5516*
1Co 1:29 so that no **o** may boast before him. *G4246+4922*
1Co 1:31 "Let the *o who* **boasts** boast in the Lord." AIT
1Co 2:11 In the same way **no o** knows the thoughts *G4029*
1Co 3: 4 For when **o** says, "I follow Paul," and *G5516*
1Co 3: 7 So neither the *o who* **plants** nor the one who AIT
1Co 3: 7 who plants nor the *o who* **waters** is anything, AIT
1Co 3: 8 The *o who* **plants** and the one who waters AIT
1Co 3: 8 plants and the *o who* **waters** have one AIT
1Co 3: 8 the one who waters have **o** *purpose*, *G1651*
1Co 3:10 But **each o** should build with care *G1667*
1Co 3:11 For **no o** can lay any foundation other than *G4029*
1Co 3:11 any foundation other than the *o already* **laid**, AIT
1Co 3:15 even though only as **o** escaping through the NDT
1Co 4: 6 in being a follower *of* **o** of us over against *G1651*
1Co 5: 3 As *o who is* **present** with you in this way, AIT
1Co 5: 3 Lord Jesus *on* the *o who has been* **doing** this. AIT
1Co 6: 6 **o** brother **takes** another **to court**—and this AIT
1Co 6:16 with a prostitute is **o** with her in body? *G1651*
1Co 6:16 it is said, "The two will become **o** flesh." *G1651*
1Co 6:17 united with the Lord is **o** with him in spirit. *G1651*
1Co 7: 7 own gift from God; **o** has this gift *G3836+3525*
1Co 7:22 For **the** *o who* was a slave when called to AIT
1Co 7:22 **the** *o who* was free when called is Christ's AIT
1Co 7:25 judgment as *o who* by the Lord's mercy **is** AIT
1Co 8: 4 and that "There is no God but **o**. *G1651*
1Co 8: 6 for us there is *but* **o** God, the Father *G1651*
1Co 8: 6 and there is *but* **o** Lord, Jesus Christ, *G1651*
1Co 9:19 am **free and belong to no o**, *G1801+1666+4246*
1Co 9:20 the law I became like **o** under the law NDT
1Co 9:21 the law I became like *o* **not having the law** AIT
1Co 9:24 the runners run, but *only* **o** gets the prize? *G1651*
1Co 10: 8 in **o** day twenty-three thousand of *G1651*
1Co 10:17 Because there is **o** loaf, we, who are many, *G1651*
1Co 10:17 who are many, are **o** body, for we all *G1651*
1Co 10:17 are one body, for we all share the **o** loaf. *G1651*
1Co 10:24 **No o** should seek their own good, but the *G3594*
1Co 10:28 the sake of the **o** who told you and for *G1697*
1Co 11:21 **o** *person* remains hungry and another *G4005*
1Co 12: 3 you to know that **no o** who is speaking by *G4029*
1Co 12: 3 be cursed," and **no o** can say, "Jesus is *G4029*
1Co 12: 7 Now *to* **each** *o* the manifestation of the Spirit AIT
1Co 12: 8 *To* **o** there is given through the Spirit a *G4005*
1Co 12: 9 to another gifts of healing by that **o** Spirit *G1651*
1Co 12:11 are the work of **o** and the same Spirit, *G1651*
1Co 12:11 he distributes them *to* **each** *o*, just as he AIT
1Co 12:12 as a body, though **o**, has many parts, but *G1651*
1Co 12:12 all its many parts form **o** body, so it is *G1651*
1Co 12:13 were all baptized by **o** Spirit so as to form *G1651*
1Co 12:13 by one Spirit so as to form **o** body— *G1651*
1Co 12:13 we were all given the **o** Spirit to drink. *G1651*
1Co 12:14 is not made up of **o** part but of many. *G1651*
1Co 12:18 in the body, every **o** of them, just as he *G1651*
1Co 12:19 If they were all **o** part, where would the *G1651*
1Co 12:20 there are many parts, but **o** body. *G1651*
1Co 12:26 If **o** part suffers, every part suffers with it; *G1651*
1Co 12:26 suffers with it; if **o** part is honored, every *G1651*
1Co 12:27 and **each o** of you is a part of it. *G3517S*
1Co 14: 2 Indeed, **no o** understands them; they utter *G4029*
1Co 14: 3 But the *o who* **prophesies** speaks to people AIT
1Co 14: 4 the *o who* **prophesies** edifies the church. AIT
1Co 14: 5 I would like **every** *o* of you to speak in AIT
1Co 14: 5 The *o who* **prophesies** is greater than the AIT
1Co 14: 5 is greater than the *o who* **speaks** in tongues, AIT
1Co 14:13 this reason the *o who* **speaks** in a tongue AIT
1Co 14:17 thanks well enough, but no *o* **else** is edified. AIT
1Co 14:27 **o at a time**, and someone *G324+3538*
1Co 15: 8 to me also, as to **o** abnormally born. *G3836*
1Co 15:39 People have **o kind** *of* flesh, animals have *G257*
1Co 15:40 splendor of the heavenly bodies is **o kind**, *G2283*
1Co 15:41 The sun has **o kind** *of* splendor, the moon *G257*
1Co 16: 2 **each o** of you should set aside a sum of *G1667*
1Co 16:11 No **o**, then, should treat him with *G5516*
1Co 16:20 Greet **o another** with a holy kiss. *G253*
2Co 2:16 *To the* **o** we are an aroma that *G4005+3525*
2Co 4:14 *o who* **raised** the Lord Jesus **from the dead** AIT
2Co 5: 5 Now the *o who has* **fashioned** us for this very AIT
2Co 5:14 we are convinced that **o** died for all, *G1651*
2Co 5:16 now on we regard **no o** from a worldly *G4029*
2Co 7: 2 We have wronged **no o**, we have *G4029*
2Co 7: 2 we have corrupted **no o**, we have *G4029*
2Co 7: 2 no one, we have exploited **no o**. *G4029*
2Co 7:12 account of the *o who* **did** the **wrong** nor on AIT
2Co 8:12 gift is acceptable according to what *o* **has**, AIT
2Co 8:12 not according to what *o* **does** not **have**. AIT
2Co 8:15 "**The** *o who* gathered much did not have too AIT
2Co 8:15 and **the** *o who* gathered little did not have AIT
2Co 9: 5 generous gift, not as **o grudgingly given**. *G4432*
2Co 10:17 "Let the *o who* **boasts** boast in the Lord." AIT
2Co 10:18 it is not the *o who* **commends** himself who is AIT
2Co 10:18 but *the o* **whom** the Lord commends. AIT
2Co 11: 2 I promised you *to* **o** husband, to Christ, so *G1651*
2Co 11: 4 a different gospel from **the** *o* you accepted, AIT
2Co 11:16 Let no **o** take me for a fool. But if *G5516*
2Co 11:24 from the Jews the forty lashes minus **o**. *G1651*
2Co 12: 4 things that no **o** is permitted to tell. *G476*
2Co 12: 6 so no **o** will think more of me than is *G5516*
2Co 13:11 restoration, **encourage** *o another*, be of one AIT
2Co 13:11 one another, be of **o** mind, live in *G3836+899*
2Co 13:12 Greet **o another** with a holy kiss. *G253*
Gal 1: 6 deserting the *o who* **called** you to live in the AIT
Gal 1: 8 gospel other than **the** *o* we preached to you AIT
Gal 2:16 of the law no **o** will be justified. *G4246+4922*
Gal 3: 2 I would like to learn just **o** *thing* from you *G3667*
Gal 3:11 Clearly **no o** *who* relies on the law is *G4029*
Gal 3:15 Just as **no o** can set aside or add to a *G4029*
Gal 3:16 meaning **o** *person*, who is Christ. *G1651*
Gal 3:20 implies more than **o** *party*; but God is one *G1651*
Gal 3:20 implies more than one party; but God is **o**. *G1651*
Gal 3:28 female, for you are all **o** in Christ Jesus. *G1651*
Gal 4:22 **o** by the slave woman and the other by *G1651*
Gal 4:24 **O** covenant is from Mount Sinai and bears *G1651*
Gal 5: 8 does not come from the *o who* **calls** you. AIT
Gal 5:10 The *o who is* **throwing** you **into confusion** AIT
Gal 5:13 serve **o another** humbly in love. *G253*
Gal 5:14 is fulfilled in keeping this **o** command: *G1651*
Gal 6: 4 **Each** *o* should test their own actions. AIT
Gal 6: 5 for **each** *o* should carry their own load. AIT
Gal 6: 6 the *o who* **receives instruction** in the word AIT
Gal 6:17 From now on, let **no o** cause me trouble *G3594*
Eph 1: 6 he has freely given us in **the** *O* he loves. AIT
Eph 1:21 in the present age but also in the *o* **to come**. AIT
Eph 2: 3 All of us also lived among them **at o time** *G4537*
Eph 2: 9 not by works, so that no **o** can boast. *G5516*
Eph 2:14 made the two groups **o** and has destroyed *G1651*
Eph 2:15 create in himself **o** new humanity out of *G1651*
Eph 2:16 in **o** body to reconcile both of them to *G1651*
Eph 2:18 both have access to the Father by **o** Spirit. *G1651*
Eph 3: 6 **members together of o body**, and *G5362*
Eph 4: 2 be patient, bearing with **o another** in love. *G253*

Eph 4: 4 There is o body and one Spirit, just as you G1651
Eph 4: 4 There is one body and o Spirit, just as you G1651
Eph 4: 4 you were called to o hope when you were G1651
Eph 4: 5 o Lord, one faith, one baptism; G1651
Eph 4: 5 one Lord, o faith, one baptism; G1651
Eph 4: 5 one Lord, one faith, o baptism; G1651
Eph 4: 6 o God and Father of all, who is over all G1651
Eph 4: 7 But to each o of us grace has been given G1651
Eph 4:10 who descended is the very o who ascended G899
Eph 4:25 we are all members *of* o body. G253
Eph 4:32 Be kind and compassionate to o another G253
Eph 5: 6 Let no o deceive you with empty words, G3594
Eph 5:19 speaking *to* o another with psalms, hymns G1571
Eph 5:21 Submit *to* o another out of reverence for G253
Eph 5:29 After all, no o ever hated their own body G4029
Eph 5:31 his wife, and the two will become o flesh." G1651
Eph 5:33 each o of you also must love his wife as G1651
Eph 6: 8 Lord will reward each *o* for whatever good AIT
Eph 6:16 all the flaming arrows *of* the evil *o*. AIT
Php 1:27 know that you stand firm in the o Spirit, G1651
Php 1:27 together *as* o for the faith of G1651+6034
Php 2: 2 being o in spirit and of one mind. G5249
Php 2: 2 being one in spirit and of o mind. G1651
Php 2: 5 In your relationships with o another G1877+5148
Php 2:20 I have no o *else* like him, who will show G4029
Php 3:13 But o *thing* I do: Forgetting G1651
Php 4:15 not o church shared with me in the matter G4029
Col 1:28 *He is the* o we proclaim, admonishing G4005
Col 2: 4 you this so that no o may deceive you by G3594
Col 2: 8 See to it that no o takes you captive G5516
Col 3:13 other and forgive o another if any of you G1571
Col 3:15 since as members of o body you were G1651
Col 3:16 admonish o another with all wisdom G1571
Col 4: 9 faithful and dear brother, who is o of you. G1666
Col 4:12 who is o of you and a servant of Christ G1666
1Th 3: 3 so that no o would be unsettled by these G3594
1Th 4: 6 this matter no *o should* wrong or take AIT
1Th 4: 9 about your love for o another we do not G5789
1Th 4:18 encourage o another with these words. G253
1Th 5:11 encourage o another and build each G253
1Th 5:24 The *o who* calls you is faithful, and he will do AIT
2Th 1: 3 all of you have for o another is increasing. G253
2Th 2: 7 the *o who* now holds it back will continue AIT
2Th 2: 8 And then the lawless *o* will be revealed AIT
2Th 2: 9 The coming *of* the lawless o will be in G4005S
2Th 3: 3 you and protect you from the evil *o*. AIT
2Th 3:10 "*The* o who is unwilling to work shall not G5516
1Ti 1: 8 that the law is good if o uses it properly. G5516
1Ti 2: 5 For there is o God and one mediator G1651
1Ti 2: 5 is one God and o mediator between God G1651
1Ti 2:14 And Adam *was* not *the o* deceived; it was the AIT
1Ti 5: 7 so that no *o may* be open to blame. AIT
1Ti 6:16 whom no o has seen or can see. G476
2Ti 2: 4 No o serving as a soldier gets entangled G4029
2Ti 2:15 to present yourself to God *as o* approved, AIT
2Ti 4:16 my first defense, no o came to my support G4029
Titus 1: 8 be hospitable, o who loves what is good NDT
Titus 1:12 O of Crete's own prophets has said it G5516
Titus 2: 5 so that no *o will* malign the word of God. AIT
Titus 3: 2 to slander no o, to be peaceable and G3594
Titus 3: 3 At o time we too were foolish G4537
Titus 3: 3 being hated and hating o another. G253
Phm 22 And o thing more: Prepare a guest room G275
Heb 2:11 Both the *o who* makes people holy and those AIT
Heb 3: 2 He was faithful *to* the *o who* appointed him AIT
Heb 3:13 But encourage o another daily, as long as G1571
Heb 4:11 so that no o will perish by following their G5516
Heb 4:15 we have *o who has been* tempted in every AIT
Heb 5: 4 And no o takes this honor on himself, but G5516
Heb 5: 7 tears to the *o who* could save him from AIT
Heb 6:13 since there was no o greater for him to G4029
Heb 7: 8 In the o case, the tenth is collected G6045+3525
Heb 7: 9 O might even say that Levi G6055+2229+3306
Heb 7:11 to come, o in the order of Melchizedek NDT
Heb 7:13 and no o from that tribe has ever served G4029
Heb 7:16 *o* who has become a priest not on the basis AIT
Heb 7:26 meets our need—*o who* is holy, blameless, AIT
Heb 8: 3 so it was necessary *for* this *o* also to have AIT
Heb 8: 6 he is mediator is superior to the old o, NDT
Heb 8:11 say *to* o another, 'Know the Lord, G81
Heb 8:13 he has made the first *o* obsolete; and what AIT
Heb 9:16 to prove the death *of* the *o who* made it, AIT
Heb 9:17 takes effect while the *o who* made it is living. AIT
Heb 9:24 hands that was only a copy *of* the true *o*; AIT
Heb 10:12 had offered for all time o sacrifice for sins, G1651
Heb 10:14 For by o sacrifice he has made perfect G1651
Heb 10:24 how we may spur o another on toward love G253
Heb 10:25 encouraging o another—and all the NDT
Heb 10:38 "But my righteous *o* will live by faith AIT
Heb 10:38 take no pleasure in the o who shrinks back." G899
Heb 11: 5 he was commended *as o who* pleased God. AIT
Heb 11:12 And so from this o *man*, and he as good G1651
Heb 11:16 longing for a better country—a heavenly *o*. AIT
Heb 11:17 was about to sacrifice his o and only son, G3666
Heb 12: 6 the Lord disciplines *the* o he loves, G4005
Heb 12:14 without holiness no o will see the Lord. G4029
Heb 12:15 See to it that no o falls short of the grace G5516
Heb 12:16 See that no o is sexually immoral, or is G5516
Heb 13: 1 loving o another as brothers and sisters. G5789
Jas 1: 6 because the *o who* doubts is like a wave of AIT
Jas 1:12 Blessed is the o who perseveres under trial G467
Jas 1:13 When tempted, no o should say, "God is G3594
Jas 2:10 stumbles at *just* o *point* is guilty of G1651
Jas 2:16 If o of you says to them, "Go in peace G5516
Jas 2:19 You believe that there is o God. G1651
Jas 4:11 sisters, do not slander o another. G253
Jas 4:12 There is *only* o Lawgiver and Judge, the G1651
Jas 4:12 the *o who is* able to save and destroy. AIT
Jas 5: 6 condemned and murdered the innocent *o*, AIT
Jas 5: 9 Don't grumble against o another, brothers G253
Jas 5:19 if o of you should wander from the truth G5516
1Pe 1:22 each other, love o another deeply, from the G253
1Pe 2: 6 the *o who* trusts in him will never be put AIT
1Pe 3: 8 be sympathetic, love o another, be G5790
1Pe 4: 9 hospitality to o another without grumbling. G253
1Pe 4:11 they should do so as o who speaks the very NDT
1Pe 5: 5 yourselves with humility *toward* o another, G253
1Pe 5:14 Greet o another with a kiss of love. Peace G253
2Pe 3: 8 But do not forget this o *thing*, dear friends: G1651
1Jn 1: 7 we have fellowship with o another, and the G253
1Jn 2: 1 the Father—Jesus Christ, the Righteous *O*. AIT
1Jn 2: 7 you a new command but an old o, G1953S
1Jn 2:13 because you have overcome the evil *o*. AIT
1Jn 2:14 and you have overcome the evil *o*. AIT
1Jn 2:20 But you have an anointing from the Holy *O* AIT
1Jn 2:23 No o who denies the Son has the Father G4246
1Jn 3: 6 No o who lives in him keeps on sinning G4246
1Jn 3: 6 No o who continues to sin has either seen G4246
1Jn 3: 7 The *o who* does what is right is righteous AIT
1Jn 3: 8 The *o who* does what is sinful is of the devil AIT
1Jn 3: 9 No o who is born of God will continue to G4246
1Jn 3:11 the beginning: We should love o another. G253
1Jn 3:12 who belonged to the evil *o* and murdered his AIT
1Jn 3:23 to love o another as he commanded G253
1Jn 3:24 The *o who* keeps God's commands lives in AIT
1Jn 4: 4 because the *o who* is in you is greater than AIT
1Jn 4: 4 you is greater than the *o who* is in the world. AIT
1Jn 4: 7 let us love o another, for love comes G253
1Jn 4: 9 He sent his o and only Son into the world G3666
1Jn 4:11 loved us, we also ought to love o another. G253
1Jn 4:12 No o has ever seen God; but if we love G4029
1Jn 4:12 if we love o another, God lives in us G253
1Jn 4:18 The *o who* fears is not made perfect in love AIT
1Jn 5: 5 Only the *o who* believes that Jesus is the Son AIT
1Jn 5: 6 This is the *o who* came by water and blood AIT
1Jn 5:18 the *O who was* born of God keeps them safe AIT
1Jn 5:18 them safe, and the evil *o* cannot harm them. AIT
1Jn 5:19 whole world is under the control of the evil *o*. AIT
2Jn 5 a new command but o we have had from G4005
2Jn 5 I ask that we love o another. G253
Jude 5 you that the Lord at o time delivered his G562
Rev 1: 3 Blessed is the *o who* reads aloud the words of AIT
Rev 1:18 I am the Living *O*; I was dead, and now look, AIT
Rev 2: 7 *To* the *o who is* victorious, I will give the right AIT
Rev 2:11 The *o who is* victorious will not be hurt at all AIT
Rev 2:17 *To* the *o who is* victorious, I will give some of AIT
Rev 2:17 known only *to* the *o who* receives it. AIT
Rev 2:26 *To* the *o who is* victorious and does my will AIT
Rev 2:27 *that o* '*will* rule them with an iron scepter AIT
Rev 2:28 I will also give that o the morning star. G899
Rev 3: 5 The *o who is* victorious will, like them, be AIT
Rev 3: 7 What he opens no o can shut, and what G4029
Rev 3: 7 and what he shuts no o can open. G4029
Rev 3: 8 you an open door that no o can shut. G4029
Rev 3:11 so that no o will take your crown. G3594
Rev 3:12 The *o who is* victorious I will make a pillar in AIT
Rev 3:15 I wish you were either o or the other! G6037S
Rev 3:21 *To* the *o who is* victorious, I will give the right AIT
Rev 4: 3 And the *o who* sat there had the appearance AIT
Rev 5: 3 But no o in heaven or on earth or under G4029
Rev 5: 4 wept because no o was found who G4029
Rev 5: 5 Then o of the elders said to me, "Do not G1651
Rev 5: 8 Each *o* had a harp and they were holding AIT
Rev 6: 1 Then I heard o of the four living creatures G1651
Rev 6: 4 horse came out, a fiery red *o*. Its rider was AIT
Rev 7: 9 a great multitude that no o could count, G4029
Rev 7:13 Then o of the elders asked me, "These in G1651
Rev 11:17 God Almighty, the *O who* is and who was AIT
Rev 13: 3 O of the heads of the beast seemed to G1651
Rev 14: 3 No o could learn the song except the G4029
Rev 14:14 and seated on the cloud *was o* like a son of AIT
Rev 15: 7 Then o of the four living creatures gave to G1651
Rev 15: 8 and no o could enter the temple until the G4029
Rev 16: 5 these judgments, O Holy *O*, you who are AIT
Rev 16:15 is the *o who* stays awake and remains AIT
Rev 17: 1 O of the seven angels who had the seven G1651
Rev 17:10 Five have fallen, o is, the other has not G1651
Rev 17:12 who for o hour will receive authority G1651
Rev 17:13 They have o purpose and will give their G1651
Rev 18: 8 Therefore in o day her plagues will G1651
Rev 18:10 In o hour your doom has come G1651
Rev 18:11 over her because no o buys their cargoes G4029
Rev 18:17 In o hour such great wealth has been G1651
Rev 18:19 In o hour she has been brought to ruin G1651
Rev 19:12 written on him that no o knows but he G4029
Rev 21: 9 O of the seven angels who had the seven G1651
Rev 22: 7 Blessed is the *o who* keeps the words of the AIT
Rev 22: 8 am the *o who* heard and saw these things. AIT
Rev 22:11 Let the *o who* does wrong continue to do AIT
Rev 22:11 let the *o who* does right continue to do right AIT
Rev 22:17 And let the *o who* hears say, "Come!" Let AIT
Rev 22:17 Let the *o who is* thirsty come; and let the AIT
Rev 22:17 let the *o who* wishes take the free gift of AIT

ONE'S (19) [ONE]

Ge 44: 2 in the mouth of the youngest *o* sack, along AIT
Lev 17:11 blood that makes atonement for o life. H2021
2Ch 21:20 He passed away, to no *o* regret, and was AIT
Job 33:13 to him that he responds to no o words? H2257S
Ps 127: 4 of a warrior are children born in o youth. H2021
Pr 4:22 find them and health to o whole body. H2257
Pr 14:21 It is a sin to despise o neighbor, but H2084
Pr 19:11 it is to o glory to overlook an offense. H2257
Pr 20: 3 It is to o honor to avoid strife, but every fool H408
Pr 20:25 rashly and only later to consider o vows. NDT
Pr 20:27 the LORD that sheds light on o inmost being. NDT
Pr 26: 6 is like cutting off o feet or drinking poison. NDT
Pr 27:19 the face, so o life reflects the heart. H2021S
SS 8: 7 to give all the wealth of o house for love, H2257
Isa 58: 5 it only for bowing o head like a reed and H2257
Jer 23:36 because *each* o word becomes their own H408
Jn 15:13 to lay down o life for one's friends. G899
Jn 15:13 to lay down one's life for o friends. G899
Jas 3: 6 sets the whole course of o life on fire, and G3836

ONE-TENTH (6) [ONE, TEN]

Ex 16:36 An omer is o *of* an ephah. H6920
Nu 28:21 with each of the seven lambs, o. H6928
Nu 28:29 with each of the seven lambs, o. H6928
Nu 29: 4 with each of the seven lambs, o. H6928+285
Nu 29:10 with each of the seven lambs, o. H6928
Nu 29:15 with each of the fourteen lambs, o. H6928

ONE-THIRD (1) [ONE, THREE]

Zec 13: 8 down and perish; yet o will be left in it. H8958

ONES (82) [ONE]

Ge 30:42 went to Laban and the strong *o* to Jacob. AIT
Ge 31: 8 If he said, 'The speckled *o* will be your wages AIT
Ge 31: 8 if he said, 'The streaked *o* will be your wages AIT
Ex 6:27 *were* the *o who* spoke to Pharaoh king of Egypt *about* AIT
Ex 18:26 the simple o they decided H1821S
Ex 34: 1 "Chisel out two stone tablets like the first *o* AIT
Ex 34: 4 tablets like the first *o* and went up Mount AIT
Lev 11: 2 on land, these are the o you may eat: H2651S
Nu 16:27 children and little o at the entrances to H3251
Nu 26:63 These are the o counted *by* Moses and AIT
Nu 31:16 "They were *the o who* followed Balaam's AIT
Dt 1:39 And the little o that you said would be H3251
Dt 10: 1 tablets like the first *o* and come up to me on AIT
Dt 10: 3 chiseled out two stone tablets like the first *o*, AIT
Dt 11: 2 your children *were* not *the o* who saw and AIT
Dt 33: 2 with myriads of holy o from the south, H7731
Dt 33: 3 the people; all the holy *o* are in your hand. AIT
Jos 5: 7 these were the o Joshua circumcised. NDT
2Ki 23:13 the o Solomon king of Israel had built H889S
1Ch 6:49 were the *o who* presented offerings on the AIT
1Ch 16:13 of Israel, his chosen *o*, the children of Jacob. AIT
1Ch 16:22 "Do not touch my anointed *o*; do my AIT
2Ch 20:13 with their wives and children and little o H3251
2Ch 31:18 They included all the little o, the wives H3251
Ezr 8:13 of Adonikam, the last *o*, whose names were AIT
Job 5: 1 To which of the holy *o* will you turn? AIT
Job 15:15 If God places no trust in his holy *o*, if even AIT
Job 21:11 as a flock; their little o dance about. H3529
Job 39:30 Its young o feast on blood, and where the H711
Ps 16: 3 "They are the noble *o* in whom is all my AIT
Ps 17:14 may there be leftovers for their little o. H6407
Ps 37:28 the just and will not forsake his faithful *o*. AIT
Ps 72: 2 in righteousness, your afflicted *o* with justice. AIT
Ps 89: 5 in the assembly of the holy *o*. AIT
Ps 89: 7 In the council of the holy *o* God is greatly AIT
Ps 94: 8 you senseless *o* among the people AIT
Ps 97:10 the lives of his faithful *o* and delivers them AIT
Ps 103:20 his angels, you mighty *o* who do his bidding AIT
Ps 105: 6 of Abraham, his chosen *o*, the children of AIT
Ps 105:15 "Do not touch my anointed *o*; do my AIT
Ps 105:43 with rejoicing, his chosen *o* with shouts of joy AIT
Ps 106: 5 I may enjoy the prosperity of your chosen *o*, AIT
Pr 2: 8 the just and protects the way of his faithful *o*. AIT
Ecc 10: 6 positions, while the rich occupy the low *o*. AIT
Isa 1:27 her penitent *o* with righteousness. AIT
Isa 10:33 will be felled, the tall *o* will be brought low. AIT
Isa 33:16 they are the *o who will* dwell on the heights AIT
Isa 49:13 will have compassion on his afflicted *o*. AIT
Isa 65:15 your name for my chosen *o* to use in their AIT
Isa 65:22 my chosen *o* will long enjoy the work of their AIT
Isa 66: 2 "These are *the o* I look on with favor AIT
Jer 24: 3 "The good o are very good, but the bad H9300S
Jer 24: 3 the bad *o* are so bad they cannot be AIT
Jer 48: 4 Moab will be broken; her little *o* will cry out. AIT
Da 4:17 by messengers, the holy *o* declare the verdict AIT
Da 7:24 different from the earlier *o*; he will subdue AIT
Hos 13:16 their little o will be dashed to the ground H6407
Zec 1:10 "They are the o the LORD has sent to go H889S
Zec 13: 7 I will turn my hand against the little o. H7592
Zec 14: 5 God will come, and all the holy *o* with him. AIT
Mt 10:42 cold water to one *of* these little *o* who is my AIT
Mt 18: 6 "If anyone causes one *of* these little *o* AIT
Mt 18:10 that you do not despise one *of* these little *o*. AIT
Mt 18:14 that any *of* these little *o* should perish. AIT
Mt 19:18 "Which *o*?" he inquired. Jesus replied, " 'You AIT
Mt 20: 8 beginning with the last *o* hired and going on AIT
Mt 25: 3 The foolish *o* took their lamps but did not AIT
Mt 25: 4 The wise *o*, however, took oil in jars along AIT

Mt 25: 8 The **foolish** *o* said to the wise, 'Give us some AIT
Mk 9:42 "If anyone causes one of these **little o** *G3625*
Lk 8:12 Those along the path are the *o who* **hear** AIT
Lk 8:13 rocky ground are the *o* **who** receive the word AIT
Lk 12:18 I will tear down my barns and build **bigger** *o* AIT
Lk 16:15 "You are the *o who* **justify** yourselves in the AIT
Lk 17: 2 to cause one *of* these **little** *o* to stumble. AIT
Lk 18: 7 not God bring about justice *for* his **chosen** *o*, AIT
Jn 8: 9 one at a time, the **older** *o* first, until only AIT
Ro 1:26 natural sexual relations for **unnatural** *o*. AIT
1Th 3:13 our Lord Jesus comes with all his **holy** *o*. AIT
Jas 2: 6 they not the *o who are* **dragging** you into AIT
Jas 2: 7 not the *o who are* **blaspheming** the noble AIT
Jude 14 with thousands upon thousands *of* his **holy** *o* AIT

ONESELF (1) [ONE, SELF]

Jas 1:27 to keep **o** from being polluted *G1571*

ONESIMUS (2)

Col 4: 9 He is coming with **O**, our faithful and dear *G3946*
Phm 10 that I appeal to you for my son **O**, who *G3946*

ONESIPHORUS (2)

2Ti 1:16 Lord show mercy to the household *of* **O**, *G3947*
2Ti 4:19 Aquila and the household *of* **O**. *G3947*

ONIONS (1)

Nu 11: 5 cucumbers, melons, leeks, **o** and garlic. H1294

ONLY (500)

Ge 6: 5 the human heart was **o** evil all the time. H8370
Ge 7:23 **O** Noah was left, and those with him in the H421
Ge 17:18 "**If o** Ishmael might live under your H4273
Ge 18:29 "What if **o** forty are found there? NDT
Ge 18:30 What if **o** thirty can be found there? NDT
Ge 18:31 what if **o** twenty can be found there? NDT
Ge 18:32 What if **o** ten can be found there? NDT
Ge 21:26 and I heard about it **o** today. H4202+1194
Ge 22: 2 your son, your **o son**, whom you love— H3495
Ge 22:12 withheld from me your son, your **o son**." H3495
Ge 22:16 have not withheld your son, your **o son**, H3495
Ge 24: 8 **O** do not take my son back there. H8370
Ge 27:38 "Do you have **o** one blessing, my H2085S
Ge 29:20 they seemed like **o a few** days to him H285
Ge 31:15 **Not o** has he sold us, but he has used up H3954
Ge 32:10 I had **o** my staff when I crossed this H3954
Ge 34:12 **O** give me the young woman as my wife." H2256
Ge 34:15 an agreement with you on one condition **o**: H421
Ge 34:22 **But** the men will agree to live with us as one people **o** H421
Ge 41:40 **O** with respect to the throne will I be H8370
Ge 42:38 dead and he is the **o one** left. H4200+963+2257
Ge 44:17 **O** the man who was found to have the H2085
Ge 44:20 and he is the **o** one of his mother's H4200+963
Ge 44:26 **O if** our youngest brother is with us will we H561
Ge 47:26 It was **o** the land of the priests that did H8370
Ge 50: 8 **O** their children and their flocks and herds H8370
Ex 8:11 people; they will remain **o** in the Nile." H8370
Ex 8:29 **O** let Pharaoh be sure that he does not H8370
Ex 9:26 The **o** place it did not hail was the land of H8370
Ex 10:11 Have **o** the men go and worship the LORD NDT
Ex 10:24 **o** leave your flocks and herds behind." H8370
Ex 14:14 will fight for you; you *need o to be* **still**." AIT
Ex 16: 3 "**If o** we had died by the LORD's H4769+5989
Ex 18:18 to you *will* **o wear** *yourselves* **out**. H5570+5570
Ex 19:13 **O** when the ram's horn sounds a long blast NDT
Ex 21: 4 and **o** the man shall go free. H928+1727+2257
Ex 22:27 that cloak is the **o** covering your H4200+963
Lev 11: 4 'There are some that **o** chew the cud or only NDT
Lev 11: 4 only chew the cud or **o** have a divided hoof, NDT
Lev 13: 6 shall pronounce them clean; it is **o** a rash. NDT
Lev 13:23 has not spread, it is **o** a scar from the boil NDT
Lev 13:28 them clean; it is **o** a scar from the burn. H3954
Lev 21:14 **but o** a virgin from his own people, H3954+561
Lev 25:12 eat **o** what is taken directly from the fields. NDT
Lev 25:52 If **o a few** years remain until the Year of H5071
Nu 4:15 **o then** are the Kohathites to come H339+4027
Nu 9:20 was over the tabernacle **o a few** days; H5031
Nu 9:21 the cloud stayed **o** from evening till morning NDT
Nu 10: 4 If **o** one is sounded, the leaders—the heads NDT
Nu 11: 4 said, "**If o** we had meat to eat! H4769
Nu 11:18 you wailed, "**If o** we had meat to eat! H4769
Nu 12: 2 the LORD spoken **o** through Moses?" H8370+421
Nu 14: 2 said to them, "**If o** we had died in Egypt! H4273
Nu 14: 3 bringing us to this land **o** to let us fall by the NDT
Nu 14: 9 **O** do not rebel against the LORD. And do not H421
Nu 14:38 **o** Joshua son of Nun and Caleb son of H2256
Nu 16:22 the entire assembly when **o** one man sins?" NDT
Nu 17: 8 had not **o** sprouted but had budded NDT
Nu 18: 7 But **o** you and your sons may serve as priests NDT
Nu 20: 3 "**If o** we had died when our brothers fell H4273
Nu 20:19 We **o** want to pass through on foot H8370
Nu 21:24 the Jabbok, but **o** as far as the Ammonites NDT
Nu 22:20 go with them, but do **o** what I tell you." H421
Nu 22:29 **If o** I had a sword in my hand, I would kill H4273
Nu 22:35 with the men, but speak **o** what I tell you." H700
Nu 22:38 I must speak **o** what God puts in my mouth." NDT
Nu 23:13 not see them all but **o** the outskirts of their H700
Nu 24:13 and I must say **o** what the LORD says'? NDT
Nu 26:33 no sons; he had **o** daughters, whose H3954+561
Nu 35:28 **o** after the death of the high priest may H2256
Nu 35:30 death as a murderer **o** on the testimony of NDT
Nu 35:30 to death on the testimony of **o** one witness. NDT

Dt 2:28 **O** let us pass through on foot— H8370
Dt 4: 9 **O** be careful, and watch yourselves closely H8370
Dt 4:12 saw no form; there was **o** a voice. H2314
Dt 4:27 and **o a few** *of* you will survive H5493+5031
Dt 6:13 serve him **o** and take your oaths in his name NDT
Dt 12:14 Offer them **o** at the place the LORD H3954+561
Dt 15: 5 if **o** you fully obey the LORD your God and H8370
Dt 17: 6 to death on the testimony of **o** one witness. NDT
Dt 22: 9 not **o** the crops you plant but also the fruit of NDT
Dt 22:25 **o** the man who has done this shall H4200+963
Dt 28:67 you will say, "**If o** it were evening!" H4769+5989
Dt 28:67 the evening, "**If o** it were morning!" H4769+5989
Dt 29:14 with its oath, not **o** with you H4200+963
Dt 32:29 **If o** they were wise and would understand H4273
Dt 32:52 you will see the land **o** from a distance; you NDT
Jos 1:17 **O** may the LORD your God be with you as H8370
Jos 1:18 **O** be strong and courageous! H8370
Jos 6:17 **O** Rahab the prostitute and all who are H8370
Jos 7: 3 whole army, for **o a few** people live there." H5071
Jos 7: 7 **If o** we had been content to stay on the H4273
Jos 11:22 in Israelite territory; **o** in Gaza, Gath and H8370
Jos 14: 4 no share of the land but **o** towns to live in, H561
Jos 17: 3 had no sons but **o** daughters, whose H561
Jos 17:14 have you given us **o** one allotment and one NDT
Jos 17:17 You will have not **o** one allotment NDT
Jos 22:20 He was not the **o** one who died for his sin H285
Jdg 3: 2 he did this **o** to teach warfare to the H8370
Jdg 6:37 If there is dew **o** on the fleece and H4200+963
Jdg 6:40 **O** the fleece was dry; all the ground H4200+963
Jdg 8:20 because he was **o** a boy and was afraid. H6388
Jdg 9:29 **If o** this people were under my H4769+5989
Jdg 11:34 She was an **o child**. Except for her he H3495
Jdg 15:13 "We will **o** tie you up and hand you over H3954
Jdg 16: 3 But Samson lay there **o** until the middle of NDT
Jdg 19:20 **O** don't spend the night in the square." H8370
1Sa 1:11 if *you will* **o look** on your servant's H8011+8011
1Sa 1:23 **o** may the LORD make good his word." H421
1Sa 2:15 accept boiled meat from you, but **o** raw." H561
1Sa 2:33 my altar I will spare **o** to destroy your sight NDT
1Sa 5: 4 on the threshold; **o** his body remained. H8370
1Sa 7: 3 to the LORD and serve him **o**, H4200+963
1Sa 7: 4 Ashtoreths, and served the LORD **o**. H4200+963
1Sa 11: 2 a treaty with you **o** on the condition that NDT
1Sa 13:22 **o** Saul and his son Jonathan had them. H2256
1Sa 17:28 you came down **o** to watch the battle." H3954
1Sa 17:33 fight him; you are **o** a young man, and he H3954
1Sa 18: 8 he thought, "but me with **o** thousands. NDT
1Sa 18:17 **o** serve me bravely and fight the battles of H421
1Sa 18:23 I'm **o** a poor man and little known. NDT
1Sa 20: 3 there is **o** a step between me and death." H3954
1Sa 20:39 about all this; **o** Jonathan and David knew.) H421
2Sa 10: 3 sent them to you **o to** explore the H928+6288
2Sa 13:25 we would **o** be a burden to you. H4202S
2Sa 13:32 all the princes; **o** Amnon is dead. H4200+963
2Sa 13:33 sons are dead. **O** Amnon is dead." H4200+963
2Sa 14: 7 would put out the **o** burning coal I have NDT
2Sa 15: 4 "**If o** I were appointed judge in the land! H4769
2Sa 15:20 You came **o** yesterday. And today shall I NDT
2Sa 17: 2 I would strike down **o** the king H4200+963
2Sa 18:33 **If o** I had died instead of you— H4769+5989
2Sa 23:10 returned to Eleazar, **but o** to strip the dead. H421
1Ki 3: 7 But I am **o** a little child and do not know NDT
1Ki 4:19 He was the **o** governor over the district H285
1Ki 6: 7 **o** blocks dressed at the quarry were used NDT
1Ki 8:25 if **o** your descendants are careful in all H8370
1Ki 11:17 But Hadad, still **o** a boy, fled to Egypt with NDT
1Ki 12:20 **O** the tribe of Judah H2314+4200+963
1Ki 14: 8 doing **o** what was right in my eyes. H8370
1Ki 14:13 He is the **o** one belonging to H4200+963
1Ki 14:13 because he is the **o** one in the house of NDT
1Ki 16:31 He **not o** considered it trivial to commit the H2022
1Ki 17:12 **o** a handful of flour in a jar and a H3954+561
1Ki 18:22 "I am the **o one** of the LORD's H4200+963
1Ki 19:10 I am the **o one** left, and now they H4200+963
1Ki 19:14 I am the **o one** left, and now they H4200+963
1Ki 22:14 I can tell him **o** what the LORD tells me." H3954
1Ki 22:18 anything good about me, **but o** bad?" H3954+561
2Ki 3:10 three kings together *o* **to** deliver us into the AIT
2Ki 3:25 **O** Kir Hareseth was left with its stones in H6330
2Ki 5: 3 "**If o** my master would see the prophet who H332
2Ki 7:10 **o** tethered horses and donkeys H3954+561
2Ki 7:13 they will **o** be like all these Israelites who NDT
2Ki 10:23 is here with you—**o** servants of Baal." H3954+561
2Ki 13:19 But now you will defeat it **o** three times." NDT
2Ki 17:18 **O** the tribe of Judah was left, H4202+8370
2Ki 18:20 war—**but** you speak **o** empty words. H421
2Ki 18:27 "Was it **o** to your master and you that my NDT
2Ki 19:18 they were not gods but **o** wood and stone, H561
2Ki 21: 8 if **o** they will be careful to do everything I H8370
2Ki 24:14 **O** the poorest people of the land H4202+2314
1Ch 2:34 had no sons—**o** daughters. He had H3954+561
1Ch 7:15 named Zelophehad, who had **o** daughters. NDT
1Ch 19: 3 envoys come to you **o to** explore and spy out AIT
1Ch 23:22 he had **o** daughters. Their H3954+561
1Ch 29:14 we have given you **o** what comes from your NDT
2Ch 6:16 if **o** your descendants are careful in all H8370
2Ch 16:12 from the LORD, **but o** from the physicians. H3954
2Ch 18:13 I can tell him **o** what my God says. H3954
2Ch 18:17 anything good about me, but **o** bad?" H561
2Ch 20:24 they saw **o** dead bodies lying on the H2256
2Ch 24:24 army had come with **o a few** men, H5203
2Ch 32: 8 With him is **o** the arm of flesh, but with us is NDT

2Ch 33: 8 if **o** they will be careful to do everything I H8370
2Ch 33:17 high places, **but o** to the LORD their God. H8370
Ezr 10:15 **O** Jonathan son of Asahel and Jahzeiah H421
Ne 5: 8 people, **o** for them to be sold back to us!" H2256
Est 1:16 not **o** against the king but also H4200+963
Est 3: 6 the idea of killing **o** Mordecai. H4200+963
Est 4: 2 But he went **o** as far as the king's gate NDT
Est 5:12 "I'm the **o** person Queen Esther H3954+561
Job 1:15 and I am the **o one** who has H4200+963
Job 1:16 and I am the **o one** who has H4200+963
Job 1:17 and I am the **o one** who has H4200+963
Job 1:19 and I am the **o one** who has H4200+963
Job 3:26 no quietness; I have no rest, but **o** turmoil." NDT
Job 6: 2 "**If o** my anguish could be weighed and H4273
Job 6:20 they arrive there, **o** to be disappointed. H2256
Job 8: 9 we were born **o** yesterday and know NDT
Job 9:15 I could **o** plead with my Judge for mercy. NDT
Job 9:33 **If o** there were someone to mediate H4273
Job 10:19 **If o** I had never come into being, or H3869+889
Job 11:16 recalling it **o** as waters gone by. NDT
Job 12: 2 you are the **o** people who matter, NDT
Job 13: 5 **If o** you would be altogether silent H4769+5989
Job 13:20 "**O** grant me these two things, God, and H421
Job 14:13 "**If o** you would hide me in the H4769+5989
Job 14:13 If **o** you would set me a time and then NDT
Job 14:22 own bodies and mourn **o** for themselves." NDT
Job 16:22 "**O** a few years will pass before I take the H3954
Job 17:13 If the **o** home I hope for is the grave, if I NDT
Job 19:20 I have escaped *o* **by** the skin of my teeth. AIT
Job 23: 3 **If o** I knew where to find him; if H4769+5989
Job 23: 3 to find him; if **o** I could go to his dwelling! NDT
Job 25: 6 maggot—a human being, who is **o** a worm!" NDT
Job 28:22 "**O** a rumor of it has reached our ears." NDT
Job 32: 9 It is not **o** the old who are wise, not only the NDT
Job 32: 9 not **o** the aged who understand what is right NDT
Job 35: 8 wickedness *o* affects **humans** like yourself, AIT
Job 35: 8 your righteousness **o** other people. NDT
Ps 9:20 let the nations know they are *o* **mortal**. AIT
Ps 25:15 **o** he will release my feet from the snare. NDT
Ps 27: 4 thing I ask from the LORD, this **o** do I seek: NDT
Ps 30: 5 For his anger lasts **o** a moment, but his favor NDT
Ps 37: 8 from wrath; do not fret—it leads **o** to evil. H421
Ps 38:20 though I **seek** *o* **to do** what is good. AIT
Ps 51: 4 Against you, you **o**, have I sinned H4200+963
Ps 62: 9 are nothing; together they are **o** a breath. H4946
Ps 81: 8 warn you—*if you would o* **listen** to me, Israel AIT
Ps 81:13 "If my people *would o* **listen** to me, if Israel AIT
Ps 81:13 if Israel *would o* **follow** my ways, AIT
Ps 90:11 **If o** we knew the power of your anger H4769
Ps 91: 8 You will **o** observe with your eyes and see H8370
Ps 95: 7 Today, **if o** you would hear his voice H561
Ps 139:19 **If o** you, God, would slay the wicked! Away H561
Pr 1:18 their own blood; they ambush **o** themselves! NDT
Pr 3:35 wise inherit honor, but fools get *o* **shame**. AIT
Pr 10:32 the mouth of the wicked **o** what is perverse. NDT
Pr 11:16 but ruthless men gain **o** wealth. NDT
Pr 11:23 The desire of the righteous ends **o** in good H421
Pr 11:23 but the hope of the wicked **o** in wrath. NDT
Pr 11:29 brings ruin on their family will inherit *o* **wind**, AIT
Pr 12:19 but a lying tongue lasts *o a* **moment**. AIT
Pr 14:23 but mere talk leads **o** to poverty. H421
Pr 20:25 something rashly **and** *o* later to consider AIT
Pr 26:19 neighbor and says, "I was **o** joking!" H2022+4202
Pr 30: 2 Surely I am *o a* **brute**, not a man; I do not AIT
Pr 30: 8 riches, but give me **o** my daily bread. NDT
Ecc 7:29 This **o** have I found: God created H4200+963
Ecc 9:14 a small city with **o a few** people in it. H5071
Ecc 12: 9 **Not o** was the Teacher wise, but he also H3463
SS 6: 9 is unique, the **o** daughter of her mother H285
SS 8: 1 **If o** you were to me like a brother H4769+5989
Isa 1: 6 **o** wounds and welts and open sores NDT
Isa 4: 1 clothes; **o** let us be called by your name. H8370
Isa 5: 2 of good grapes, but it yielded **o** bad fruit. NDT
Isa 5: 4 good grapes, why did it yield **o** bad? NDT
Isa 5:10 vineyard will produce **o** a bath of wine; NDT
Isa 5:10 of seed will yield **o** an ephah of grain." NDT
Isa 5:30 at the land, there is **o** darkness and distress NDT
Isa 7: 8 the head of Damascus is **o** Rezin. NDT
Isa 7: 9 the head of Samaria is **o** Remaliah's son. NDT
Isa 7:23 there will be **o** briers and thorns. NDT
Isa 8:22 the earth and see **o** distress and darkness NDT
Isa 10:22 by the sea, Israel, **o** a remnant will return. NDT
Isa 16:12 at her high place, she **o** wears herself out H3954
Isa 27: 4 **If o** there were briers and thorns H4769+5989
Isa 30: 5 advantage, **but o** shame and disgrace." H3954
Isa 35: 9 But **o** the redeemed will walk there NDT
Isa 36: 5 war—but you speak **o** empty words. NDT
Isa 36:12 "Was it **o** to your master and you that my NDT
Isa 37:19 they were not gods but **o** wood and stone, H561
Isa 37:20 know that you, LORD, are the **o** God." H4200+963
Isa 44:11 such craftsmen are *o* **human beings**. AIT
Isa 47:13 you have received *has o* **worn** *you* **out**! AIT
Isa 48:18 **If o** you had paid attention to my H4273
Isa 51: 2 When I called him he was *o* **one** *man*, and I AIT
Isa 54: 6 who married young, **o** to be rejected," H3954
Isa 56: 3 no eunuch complain, "I am **o** a dry tree." H2176
Isa 58: 5 **o** a day for people to humble themselves? NDT
Isa 58: 5 Is it **o** for bowing one's head like a reed NDT
Jer 3:10 all her heart, but **o** in pretense," declares H561
Jer 3:13 **O** acknowledge your guilt—you have H421
Jer 5: 4 I thought, "These are **o** the poor; they are H421
Jer 6:26 mourn with bitter wailing as for an **o son** H3495

O

Jer 8:15 a time of healing but there is o terror. NDT
Jer 9:25 all who are circumcised o in the flesh— NDT
Jer 10:24 but o in due measure—not in your H421
Jer 14: 8 like a traveler *who* stays o a night? H5742+4328
Jer 14:19 a time of healing but there is o terror. NDT
Jer 22:17 heart are set o on dishonest gain, H3954+561
Jer 23:23 "Am I o a God nearby," declares the LORD NDT
Jer 27:10 you that *will o serve to* remove you far from AIT
Jer 28: 9 sent by the LORD o if his prediction comes H928
Jer 30:11 I will discipline you but o in due measure; NDT
Jer 31:36 "O if these decrees vanish from my sight," H561
Jer 31:37 "O if the heavens above can be measured H561
Jer 34: 7 These were the o fortified cities left in NDT
Jer 37:10 is attacking you and o wounded men were NDT
Jer 38: 6 no water in it, o mud, and Jeremiah H3954+561
Jer 42: 2 we were once many, now o a few are left. H5071
Jer 46:17 'Pharaoh king of Egypt is o a loud noise; he NDT
Jer 46:28 I will discipline you but o in due measure; NDT
Jer 49: 9 would they not steal o as much as they NDT
Jer 51:58 the nations' labor is o fuel for the flames." NDT
La 1:20 sword bereaves; inside, there is o death. H3869
La 5: 4 we drink; our wood can be had o at a price. NDT
Eze 14:14 they could save o themselves by their NDT
Eze 14:20 They would save o themselves by their NDT
Eze 16:47 You not o followed their ways and copied H2256
Eze 17:14 rise again, surviving o by keeping his treaty. NDT
Eze 33:24 'Abraham was o one man, yet he NDT
Eze 34: 2 of Israel who *o* take care of yourselves! AIT
Eze 40:46 who are the o Levites who may draw near H4946
Eze 43: 8 with o a wall between me and them NDT
Eze 44: 3 himself is the *o* one who may sit inside AIT
Eze 44:22 they may marry o virgins of Israelite H3954+561
Eze 44:28 " 'I am to be the o inheritance the priests NDT
Eze 46:17 His inheritance belongs to his sons o; it is H421
Da 2: 9 me the dream, there is *o* one penalty for you. AIT
Da 4:19 if o the dream applied to your enemies NDT
Da 10: 7 was the o one who saw the vision H4200+963
Da 11:23 with o a few people he will rise to H5071
Da 11:24 the overthrow of fortresses—but o for a time. NDT
Hos 4: 2 There is o cursing, lying and murder NDT
Am 3: 2 "You o have I chosen of all the families of H8370
Am 3:12 from the lion's mouth o two leg bones or a NDT
Am 3:12 with o the head of a bed and a piece of NDT
Am 5: 3 thousand strong will have o a hundred left; NDT
Am 5: 3 out a hundred strong will have o ten left." NDT
Am 5:19 a man fled from a lion o to meet a bear, H2256
Am 5:19 hand on the wall o to have a snake bite H2256
Am 8:10 mourning for an o son and the end of it H3495
Ob 5 would they not steal o as much as they NDT
Hab 2:13 that the people's labor is o fuel for the fire, NDT
Hag 1: 6 o to put them in a purse with holes in it." NDT
Hag 2:16 heap of twenty measures, there were o ten. NDT
Hag 2:16 to draw fifty measures, there were o twenty. NDT
Zec 1:15 I was o a little angry, but they went too far H5071
Zec 12:10 him as one mourns for an o child, H3495
Zec 14: 7 a day known *o* to the LORD—with no AIT
Zec 14: 9 be one LORD, and his name the o name. H285
Mt 4:10 the Lord your God, and serve him o. G3668
Mt 5:47 And if you greet o your own people, what G3667
Mt 6:18 you are fasting, but o to your Father, who is NDT
Mt 7:14 road that leads to life, and *o* a few find it. AIT
Mt 7:21 but o the one who does the will of my G247
Mt 9:21 said to herself, "If I o touch his cloak, G3667
Mt 12: 4 lawful for them to do, but o for the priests. G3668
Mt 12:24 they said, "It is o by Beelzebul, the G1623+3590
Mt 13:21 they have no root, they last o a short time. G247
Mt 14:17 "We have here o five loaves G4024+1623+3590
Mt 15:24 "I was sent o to the lost G4024+1623+3590
Mt 19:11 but o those to whom it has been given. G247
Mt 19:17 "There is *o* One who is good. If you AIT
Mt 20:12 who were hired last worked *o* one hour, AIT
Mt 21:21 not o can you do what was done to the fig G3667
Mt 24:36 in heaven, nor the Son, but o the Father. G3668
Mk 2:26 which is lawful o for priests to eat. G1623+3590
Mk 4:17 they have no root, they last o a short time. G247
Mk 9:29 kind can come out o by prayer." G1623+3590
Mk 12:42 small copper coins, worth o a few cents. G3119
Mk 13:32 the Son, but o the Father. G1623+3590
Mk 14: 1 of Unleavened Bread were *o* two days away, AIT
Lk 4: 8 the Lord your God and serve him o.' G3668
Lk 4:27 cleansed—o Naaman the Syrian." G1623+3590
Lk 6: 4 what is lawful o for priests to G1623+3590+3668
Lk 7:12 carried out—the o son of his mother G3666
Lk 8:42 because his o daughter, a girl of about G3666
Lk 9:13 "We have o five loaves of G4024+4498+2445
Lk 9:38 you to look at my son, for he is my o child. G3666
Lk 10:42 needed—or indeed *o* one. Mary has chosen AIT
Lk 13:23 are o a few people going to be saved?" G1623
Lk 17:10 unworthy servants; *we have o* done our duty. AIT
Lk 19:42 "If you, even you, had o known on this G1623
Lk 24:18 "Are you the o one visiting Jerusalem G3668
Jn 1: 8 he came o as a witness to the light. G247
Jn 1:14 the glory of the one and o Son, who came G3666
Jn 1:18 but the one and o Son, who is G3666
Jn 3:16 the world that he gave his one and o Son, G3666
Jn 3:18 in the name of God's one and o Son. G3666
Jn 3:27 can receive o what is G4028+1651+1569+3590
Jn 5:18 not o was he breaking the Sabbath G3667
Jn 5:19 he can do o what he sees his G1569+3590
Jn 5:30 do nothing; I judge o as I hear, and my G2777
Jn 5:44 seek the glory that comes from the o God? G3668
Jn 6: 6 He asked this o to test him, for he already G1254
Jn 6:22 realized that o one boat had been G1623+3590
Jn 6:46 who is from God; o he has seen the Father. NDT
Jn 7:33 "I am with you *for* o a short time, and G2285
Jn 8: 9 ones first, until o Jesus was left, with G3668
Jn 8:41 "The o Father we have is God himself." G1651
Jn 9: 9 Others said, "No, he o looks like him." G247
Jn 10:10 The thief comes o to steal and kill G1623+3590
Jn 10:17 that I lay down my life—*o* to take it up again. AIT
Jn 11:52 not o for that nation but also for the G3667
Jn 12: 9 not o because of him but also to see G3667
Jn 12:16 O after Jesus was glorified did they realize G247
Jn 12:24 it remains o a single seed. G3668
Jn 12:44 believes in me does not believe in me *o*, AIT
Jn 13:10 a bath need o to wash their G4024+1623+3590
Jn 13:33 children, I will be with you *o a* little longer. AIT
Jn 16:13 he will speak o what he hears, and G247
Jn 17: 3 they know you, the o true God, and Jesus G3668
Jn 21:23 he would not die; he o said, "If I want him G247
Ac 2:15 as you suppose. It's *o* nine in the morning! AIT
Ac 5:39 *you will o* find *yourselves* fighting against AIT
Ac 10:26 "Stand up," he said, "I am *o a* man myself." AIT
Ac 11:19 the word o among Jews. G1623+3590+3667
Ac 14:15 We too are *o* human, like you. We are AIT
Ac 18:25 though he knew o the baptism of John. G3667
Ac 19:27 There is danger not o that our trade will G3667
Ac 20:23 I o know that in every city the Holy Spirit G4440
Ac 20:24 my o aim is to finish the race and complete NDT
Ac 21:13 I am ready not o to be bound, but also to G3667
Ac 26:29 pray to God that not o you but all who are G3667
Ac 27:22 will be lost; o the ship will be destroyed. G4440
Ro 1:32 they not o continue to do these very G3667
Ro 2:28 person is not a Jew who is one *o* outwardly, AIT
Ro 3:29 Or is God the God of Jews o? Is he G3667+3668
Ro 3:30 since there is *o* one God, who will justify the AIT
Ro 4: 9 Is this blessedness *o* for the circumcised, or AIT
Ro 4:12 circumcised who not o are circumcised G3667
Ro 4:16 not o to those who are of the law but also G3667
Ro 5: 3 Not o so, but we also glory in our G3667
Ro 5:11 Not o is this so, but we also boast in God G3667
Ro 7: 1 someone o as long as that G2093+4012+5989
Ro 8:23 Not o so, but we ourselves, who have the G3667
Ro 9:10 Not o that, but Rebekah's children were G3667
Ro 9:24 not o from the Jews but also from the G3667
Ro 9:27 by the sea, *o* the remnant will be saved. AIT
Ro 11: 3 I am the *o one* left, and they are G3668
Ro 13: 5 not o because of possible punishment G3667
Ro 14: 2 whose faith is weak, eats *o* vegetables. AIT
Ro 16: 4 Not o I but all the churches of the G3668
Ro 16:27 to the o wise God be glory forever through G3668
1Co 2:14 they are discerned o through the Spirit. NDT
1Co 3: 5 O servants, through whom you came to NDT
1Co 3: 7 is anything, but o God, who makes things NDT
1Co 3:15 even though o as one escaping through G4048
1Co 4:19 then I will find out not *o* how these arrogant AIT
1Co 9: 6 Or is it o I and Barnabas who lack the right G3668
1Co 9:24 all the runners run, but *o* one gets the prize? AIT
1Co 13: 1 *I* am *o* a resounding gong or a clanging AIT
1Co 13:12 For now we see *o* a reflection as in a mirror AIT
1Co 14:36 Or are you the o *people* it has reached? G3668
1Co 15:19 If o for this life we have hope in Christ, we G3667
1Co 16: 7 to see you now and make *o* a passing visit; AIT
2Co 3:14 because *o* in Christ is it taken away. AIT
2Co 7: 7 not o by his coming but also by the G3667
2Co 7: 8 letter hurt you, but o for a little while— G2779
2Co 8:10 you were the first not o to give but also to G3667
2Co 8:17 For Titus not o welcomed our appeal, but G3525
2Co 8:21 not o in the eyes of the Lord but also in G3667
2Co 9:12 you perform is not o supplying the needs G3667
2Co 13: 8 anything against the truth, but *o* for the truth. AIT
Gal 1:19 other apostles—o James, the G1623+3590
Gal 1:23 They o heard the report: "The man who G3667
Gal 5: 6 The o thing that counts is faith expressing G247
Gal 6:12 The o *reason* they do this is to avoid G3667
Eph 1:21 not o in the present age but also in the G3667
Eph 4:29 o what is helpful for building others G1623
Eph 6: 6 Obey them not o to win their favor when G3590
Php 1:27 come and see you or *o* hear about you in my AIT
Php 1:29 behalf of Christ not o to believe in him, G3667
Php 2:12 always obeyed—not o in my presence G3667
Php 2:27 and not on him o but also on me, to G3667
Php 3:16 O let us live up to what we have already G4440
Php 4:15 of giving and receiving, except you o; G3668
Col 3:22 not *o* when their eye is on you and to curry AIT
Col 4:11 These are the o Jews among my G3668
1Th 1: 8 out from you not o in Macedonia and G3667
1Th 2: 8 share with you not o the gospel of God G3667
1Ti 1:17 invisible, the o God, be honor and glory G3668
1Ti 5:13 And not o do they become idlers, but also G3667
1Ti 5:23 Stop drinking o water, and use a little G5621
1Ti 6:15 the blessed and o Ruler, the King of G3668
2Ti 2:14 it is of no value, and *o* ruins those who listen. AIT
2Ti 2:20 there are articles not o of gold and silver, G3667
2Ti 4: 8 on that day—and not o to me, but also to G3667
2Ti 4:11 O Luke is with me. Get Mark and bring G3668
Heb 9: 7 But o the high priest entered the inner G3668
Heb 9: 7 and that *o* once a year, and never AIT
Heb 9:10 They are o a matter of food and drink and G3667
Heb 9:17 a will is in force o when somebody has died NDT
Heb 9:24 hands that was *o a* copy of the true one; AIT
Heb 10: 1 The law is *o a* shadow of the good things AIT
Heb 10:27 but *o a* fearful expectation of judgment and AIT
Heb 11:13 they o saw them and welcomed them from G247
Heb 11:17 was about to sacrifice his one and o son, G3666
Heb 11:40 us so that *o* together with us would they AIT
Heb 12:26 more I will shake not o the earth but also G3667
Jas 4:12 There is *o* one Lawgiver and Judge, the one AIT
1Pe 2:18 not o to those who are good and G3667
1Pe 3:20 In it *o a* few people, eight in all, were saved AIT
2Pe 2:12 born o to be caught and destroyed NDT
1Jn 2: 2 not o for ours but also for the sins of G3667
1Jn 4: 9 He sent his one and o Son into the world G3666
1Jn 5: 5 O the one who believes that Jesus G1623+3590
1Jn 5: 6 He did not come by water o, but by water G3667
2Jn 1 the truth—and not I o, but also all who G3668
Jude 4 Jesus Christ our o Sovereign and Lord. G3668
Jude 12 qualm—shepherds who feed *o* themselves. AIT
Jude 25 to the o God our Savior be glory, majesty G3668
Rev 2:17 known o to the one who G4029+1623+3590
Rev 9: 4 but o those people who did not G1623+3590
Rev 9: 5 allowed to kill them but *o* to torture them AIT
Rev 17:10 he must remain *for o a* little *while*. AIT
Rev 21:27 but o those whose names are G1623+3590

ONO (5)

1Ch 8:12 who built O and Lod with its surrounding H229
Ezr 2:33 Hadid and O 725 H229
Ne 6: 2 in one of the villages on the plain of O." H229
Ne 7:37 Hadid and O 721 H229
Ne 11:35 in Lod and O, and in Ge Harashim. H229

ONTO (9) [ON]

Ge 49: 4 for *you* went up *o* your father's bed AIT
Ge 49: 4 your father's bed, o my couch and defiled it. NDT
Ex 8: 3 palace and your bedroom and o your bed, H6584
Nu 19: 6 and throw them o the burning heifer H448+9348
Jdg 8:25 of them threw a ring from his plunder o it. H2025
1Ki 22:35 from his wound ran o the floor of the H448
Est 9:25 Jews should come back o his own head, H6584
Jnh 2:10 the fish, and it vomited Jonah o dry land. H448
Lk 9:28 him and went up o a mountain to pray. G1650

ONYCHA (1)

Ex 30:34 gum resin, o and galbanum—and pure H8829

ONYX (12)

Ge 2:12 aromatic resin and o are also there.) H74+8732
Ex 25: 7 o stones and other gems to be H8732
Ex 28: 9 "Take two o stones and engrave on them H8732
Ex 28:20 the fourth row shall be topaz, o and jasper. H8732
Ex 35: 9 o stones and other gems to be H8732
Ex 35:27 The leaders brought o stones and other H8732
Ex 39: 6 They mounted the o stones in gold H8732
Ex 39:13 row was topaz, o and jasper. They were H8732
1Ch 29: 2 the wood, as well as o for the settings H74+8732
Job 28:16 of Ophir, with precious o or lapis lazuli. H8732
Eze 28:13 emerald, topaz, o and jasper, lapis H8732
Rev 21:20 the fifth o, the sixth ruby, the seventh G4918

OOZING (1)

1Sa 14:26 they saw the honey o out; yet no one put H2144

OPEN (162) [OPENED, OPENHANDED, OPENING, OPENINGS, OPENLY, OPENS]

Ge 25:27 a man of the o country, while Jacob was H8441
Ge 25:29 Esau came in from the o country H8441
Ge 27: 3 go out to the o country to hunt some H8441
Ge 27: 5 left for the o country to hunt game and H8441
Ge 29: 2 There he saw a well in the o country, with H8441
Ge 34:10 among us; the land is *o to* you. H7156+4200
Lev 1:17 *He shall* tear it o by the wings, not H9117
Lev 14: 7 is to release the live bird in the o fields. H7156
Lev 14:53 the live bird in the o fields outside the H7156
Lev 17: 5 they are now making in the o fields. H7156
Lev 25:31 considered as belonging to the o country. H8441
Nu 19:15 every o container without a lid H7337
Nu 19:16 "Anyone out in the o who touches H8441
Dt 20:11 If they accept and o their gates, all the H7337
Dt 28:12 The LORD *will* o the heavens, the H7337
Jos 8:17 They left the city o and went in pursuit of H7337
Jos 10:22 "O the mouth of the cave and bring those H7337
Jdg 3:25 when he *did* not o the doors of the H7337
Jdg 20:31 men fell in the o field and on the roads— H8441
2Sa 10: 8 were by themselves in the o country. H8441
2Sa 11:11 lord's men are camped in the o country. H7156
2Sa 11:23 us and came out against us in the o, H8441
1Ki 6:18 carved with gourds and o flowers. H7080
1Ki 6:29 cherubim, palm trees and o flowers. H7080
1Ki 6:32 palm trees and o flowers, and overlaid H7080
1Ki 6:35 palm trees and o flowers on them and H7080
1Ki 8:29 May your eyes be o toward this temple H7337
1Ki 8:52 "May your eyes be o to your servant's plea H7337
2Ki 6:17 And Elisha prayed, "O his eyes, LORD, so H7337
2Ki 6:20 o the eyes of these men so they can see." H7219
2Ki 7: 2 *even if* the LORD *should* o the floodgates H6913
2Ki 7:19 *even if* the LORD *should* o the floodgates H6913
2Ki 8:12 ground, and rip o their pregnant women." H1324
2Ki 9: 3 Then o the door and run H7337
2Ki 13:17 "O the east window," he said, and he H7337
2Ki 15:16 because *they* refused *to* o their gates. H7337
2Ki 15:16 Tiphsah and ripped o all the pregnant H1324
2Ki 19:16 and hear; o your eyes, LORD, and see; H7219
1Ch 19: 9 were by themselves in the o country. H8441
2Ch 6:20 May your eyes be o toward this temple H7337
2Ch 6:40 may your eyes be o and your ears H7337
2Ch 7:15 Now my eyes will be o and my ears H7337

Ne 1: 6 your eyes **o** to hear the prayer your H7337
Est 4: 6 Mordecai in the **o square** *of* the city in H8148
Job 11: 5 that *he would* **o** his lips against you H7337
Job 16:10 *People* **o** their mouths to jeer at me; they H7196
Job 31:32 my door *was always* **o** to the traveler H7337
Job 32:20 find relief; *I must* **o** my lips and reply. H7337
Job 33: 2 *I am about to* **o** my mouth; my words are H7337
Job 41:14 Who *dares* **o** the doors of its mouth H7337
Ps 5: 9 Their throat is an **o** grave; with their H7337
Ps 22:13 their prey **o** their mouths **wide** against me H7198
Ps 38: 9 All my longings lie **o** before you, Lord; my NDT
Ps 39: 9 I was silent; *I would* not **o** my mouth, for H7337
Ps 51:15 **O** my lips, Lord, and my mouth will H7337
Ps 60: 2 You have shaken the land and **torn** it **o** H7204
Ps 74:13 It was you *who* **split o** the sea by your H7297
Ps 78: 2 *I will* **o** my mouth with a parable; I will H7337
Ps 81:10 **O wide** your mouth and I will fill it H8143
Ps 104:28 gather it up; *when you* **o** your hand, they H7337
Ps 118:19 **O** for me the gates of the righteous; I will H7337
Ps 119:18 **O** my eyes that I may see wonderful H1655
Ps 119:131 *I* **o** my mouth and pant, longing for your H7196
Ps 119:148 My eyes **stay o** *through* the watches of H7709
Ps 145:16 You **o** your hand and satisfy the desires of H7337
Pr 1:20 Out in the **o** wisdom calls aloud, she H2575
Pr 8: 6 I **o** my lips to speak what is right. H5157
Pr 15:11 Destruction lie **o** before the LORD— NDT
Pr 24: 7 at the gate *they must* not **o** their mouths. H7337
Pr 27: 5 Better is **o** rebuke than hidden love. H1655
SS 5: 2 "**O** to me, my sister, my darling, my dove H7337
SS 5: 5 I arose to **o** for my beloved, and my hands H7337
Isa 1: 6 only wounds and welts and **o** sores, not H3269
Isa 9:12 west have devoured Israel with **o** mouth. H3972
Isa 22:22 and what he shuts no *one can* **o**. H7337
Isa 26: 2 **O** the gates that the righteous nation may H7337
Isa 37:17 and hear; **o** your eyes, LORD, and see; H7219
Isa 42: 7 to **o** eyes that are blind, to free captives H7219
Isa 42:20 attention; your ears *are* **o**, but you do not H7219
Isa 45: 1 to **o** doors before him so that gates will H7337
Isa 45: 8 *Let* the earth **o wide**, let salvation spring H7337
Isa 48: 8 from of old your ears *have* not *been* **o**. H7337
Isa 53: 7 afflicted, yet *he did* not **o** his mouth; he H7337
Isa 53: 7 is silent, so *he did* not **o** his mouth. H7337
Isa 60:11 Your gates *will* always *stand* **o**, they will H7337
Isa 63:13 Like a horse in **o country**, they did not H4497
Jer 5:16 Their quivers are like an **o** grave; all of H7337
Jer 9:20 **o** your ears to the words of his mouth. H4374
Jer 9:22 bodies will lie like dung on the **o** field, H7156
Jer 13:19 and there will be no *one to* **o** them. H7337
Jer 17:16 passes my lips is **o before** you. H5790+7156
Jer 32:19 Your eyes *are* **o** to the ways of all H7219
Jer 40: 7 were still in the **o country** heard that the H8441
Jer 40:13 still in the **o country** came to Gedaliah at H8441
Jer 50:26 **Break o** her granaries; pile her up like H7337
La 2:16 enemies **o** their mouths **wide** against you H7198
Eze 2: 8 **o** your mouth and eat what I give you." H7198
Eze 3:27 *I will* **o** your mouth and you shall say to H7337
Eze 16: 5 you were thrown out into the **o** field, for H7156
Eze 16:63 never again **o** your mouth because of H7341
Eze 21:24 to mind your guilt by your **o** rebellion, H1655
Eze 26: 2 its doors *have* **swung o** to me; now H6015
Eze 29: 5 You will fall on the **o** field and not be H7156
Eze 29: 7 splintered and *you* **tore o** their shoulders; H1324
Eze 29:21 and *I will* **o** your mouth among H5989+7341
Eze 32: 4 on the land and hurl you on the **o** field. H7156
Eze 37:12 *I am going to* **o** your graves and bring you H7337
Eze 37:13 when **I o** your graves and bring you up H7337
Eze 39: 5 You will fall in the **o** field, for I have H8441
Eze 41: 9 The **o area** between the side rooms of the H4965
Eze 41:11 to the side rooms from the **o area**, H4965
Eze 41:11 base adjoining the **o area** was five cubits H4965
Eze 45: 2 with 50 cubits around it for **o land**. H4494
Da 9:18 **o** your eyes and see the desolation of the H7219
Hos 13: 8 attack them and **rip** them **o**; H7973+6033+4213
Hos 13:16 ground, their pregnant women **ripped o**." H1324
Am 1:13 Because he **ripped o** the pregnant women H1324
Mic 2:13 The *One who* **breaks o** the way will go up H7287
Mic 4:10 must leave the city to camp in the **o field**. H8441
Na 2: 6 river gates *are* **thrown o** and the palace H7337
Na 3:13 of your land *are* **wide o** to your H7337+7337
Zec 11: 1 **O** your doors, Lebanon, so that fire may H7337
Mal 3:10 "and see if *I will* not **throw o** the H7337
Mt 13:35 "*I will* **o** my mouth in parables, I will utter *G487*
Mt 17:27 **o** its mouth and you will find a *G487*
Mt 25:11 Lord,' they said, '**o** the door for us!' *G487*
Mt 27:52 the tombs **broke o**. The bodies of many *G487*
Mk 1:10 he saw heaven *being* **torn o** and the Spirit *G5387*
Mk 4:22 is meant to be brought out into the **o**. *G5745*
Lk 8:17 not be known or brought out into the **o**. *G5745*
Lk 12:36 knocks *they can* immediately **o** *the door* *G487*
Lk 13:25 pleading, 'Sir, **o** the door for us.' *G487*
Lk 15: 4 in the **o country** and go after the *G2245*
Jn 1:51 you will see 'heaven **o**, and the angels of *G487*
Jn 4:35 **o** your eyes and look at the fields! *G2048*
Jn 9:26 How *did he* **o** your eyes?" *G487*
Jn 10:21 Can a demon **o** the eyes of the blind?" *G487*
Ac 1:18 *his body* **burst o** and all his *G3279+3545*
Ac 7:56 "I see heaven **o** and the Son of Man *G1380*
Ac 8:32 shearer is silent, so *he did* not **o** his mouth. *G487*
Ac 16:26 At once all the prison doors **flew o**, and *G487*
Ac 16:27 when he saw the prison doors **o**, he *G487*
Ac 19:38 the courts *are* **o** and there are proconsuls. *G72*
Ac 26:18 *to* **o** their eyes and turn them from darkness *G487*
Ac 27: 5 sailed across the **o sea** off the coast of *G4283*
Ro 3:13 "Their throats *are* **o** graves; their tongues *G487*
2Co 6:13 to my children—**o wide** your hearts also. *G4425*
2Co 11:25 I spent a night and a day in the **o sea**, *G1113*
Col 4: 3 that God *may* **o** a door for our message *G487*
1Ti 5: 7 so that no one may be **o to blame**. *G455*
Titus 1: 6 believe and are not **o to** the charge of *G1877*
Rev 3: 7 can shut, and what he shuts no one *can* **o**. *G487*
Rev 3: 8 before you an **o** door that no one can *G487*
Rev 4: 1 before me *was* a door **standing o** in *G487*
Rev 5: 2 worthy to break the seals and **o** the scroll?" *G487*
Rev 5: 3 under the earth could **o** the scroll or even *G487*
Rev 5: 4 who was worthy *to* **o** the scroll or look *G487*
Rev 5: 5 *He is able to* **o** the scroll and its seven *G487*
Rev 5: 9 worthy to take the scroll and *to* **o** its seals, *G487*
Rev 10: 2 a little scroll, *which lay* **o** in his hand. *G487*
Rev 10: 8 take the scroll that *lies* **o** in the hand of the *G487*
Rev 19:11 I saw heaven **standing o** and there before *G487*

OPENED (109) [OPEN]

Ge 3: 5 when you eat from it your eyes *will* **be o**, H7219
Ge 3: 7 Then the eyes of both of them **were o**, and H7219
Ge 4:11 which **o** its mouth to receive your brother's H7198
Ge 7:11 the floodgates of the heavens **were o**. H7337
Ge 8: 6 forty days Noah **o** a window he had made H7337
Ge 21:19 Then God **o** her eyes and she saw a well H7219
Ge 41:56 Joseph **o** all the storehouses and sold H7337
Ge 42:27 night one of them **o** his sack to get feed H7337
Ge 43:21 the night *we* **o** our sacks and each of H7337
Ge 44:11 lowered his sack to the ground and **o** it. H7337
Ex 2: 6 *She* **o** it and saw the baby. He was crying H7337
Ex 21:34 the *one who* **o** the pit must pay the H1251S
Nu 16:32 the earth **o** its mouth and swallowed H7337
Nu 22:28 Then the LORD **o** the donkey's mouth, and H7337
Nu 22:31 Then the LORD **o** Balaam's eyes, and he H1655
Nu 24: 4 who falls prostrate, and whose eyes *are* **o**: H1655
Nu 24:16 who falls prostrate, and whose eyes *are* **o**: H1655
Nu 26:10 The earth **o** its mouth and swallowed H7337
Dt 11: 6 when the earth **o** its mouth right in the H7198
Jdg 4:19 *She* **o** a skin of milk, gave him a drink H7337
Jdg 15:19 Then God **o up** the hollow place in Lehi H1324
Jdg 19:27 in the morning and **o** the door of the H7337
1Sa 3:15 morning and then **o** the doors of the H7337
2Ki 4:35 boy sneezed seven times and **o** his eyes. H7219
2Ki 6:17 Then the LORD **o** the servant's eyes, and H7219
2Ki 6:20 Then the LORD **o** their eyes and they H7219
2Ki 9:10 Then *he* **o** the door and ran. H7337
2Ki 13:17 the east window," he said, and *he* **o** it. H7337
2Ch 29: 3 he **o** the doors of the temple of the LORD H7337
Ne 7: 3 of Jerusalem *are* not *to* **be o** until the sun H7337
Ne 8: 5 Ezra **o** the book. All the people could see H7337
Ne 8: 5 above them; and as *he* **o** it, the people H7337
Ne 13:19 to be shut and not **o** until the Sabbath H7337
Job 3: 1 Job **o** his mouth and cursed the day of his H7337
Ps 40: 6 my ears *you have* **o**—burnt offerings H4125
Ps 74:15 It was you *who* **o up** springs and streams H1324
Ps 78:23 to the skies above and **o** the doors of the H7337
Ps 105:41 *He* **o** the rock, and water gushed out; it H7337
Ps 106:17 The earth **o up** and swallowed Dathan; it H7337
Ps 109: 2 deceitful *have* **o** their mouths against H7337
SS 5: 6 I **o** for my beloved, but my beloved had H7337
SS 7:12 if their blossoms *have* **o**, and if the H7337
Isa 10:14 flapped a wing, or **o** its mouth to chirp. H7198
Isa 24:18 The floodgates of the heavens **are o**, the H7337
Isa 35: 5 Then *will* the eyes of the blind **be o** and H7219
Isa 50: 5 The Sovereign LORD *has* **o** my ears; I have H7337
Isa 57: 8 you climbed into it and **o** it **wide**; you H8143
Jer 50:25 The LORD *has* **o** his arsenal and brought H7337
La 3:46 enemies *have* **o** their mouths **wide** H7198
Eze 1: 1 the heavens **were o** and I saw visions of H7337
Eze 3: 2 So *I* **o** my mouth, and he gave me the H7337
Eze 24:27 At that time your mouth *will* **be o**; you will H7337
Eze 33:22 and *he'd* **o** my mouth before the man came H7337
Eze 33:22 So my mouth **was o** and I was no longer H7337
Eze 44: 2 *It must* not **be o**; no one may enter H7337
Eze 46: 1 on the day of the New Moon *it is to* **be o**. H7337
Eze 46:12 the gate facing east *is to be* **o** for him. H7337
Da 6:10 where the windows **o** toward Jerusalem. A10602
Da 7:10 court was seated, and the books **were o**. A10602
Da 10:16 and *I* **o** my mouth and began to speak. H7337
Zec 13: 1 a fountain will be **o** to the house of David H7337
Mt 2:11 Then *they* **o** their treasures and presented *G487*
Mt 3:16 At that moment heaven *was* **o**, and he saw *G487*
Mt 7: 7 knock and *the door will* **be o** to you. *G487*
Mt 7: 8 to the one who knocks, *the door will* **be o**. *G487*
Mk 7:34 (which means "*Be* **o**!"). *G1380*
Mk 7:35 the man's ears *were* **o**, his tongue was *G487*
Mk 8:25 Then *his* **eyes** *were* **o**, his sight was *G1332*
Lk 1:64 his mouth *was* **o** and his tongue set *G487*
Lk 3:21 And as he was praying, heaven *was* **o** *G487*
Lk 10:38 named Martha **o** *her* **home to** him. *G5685*
Lk 11: 9 knock and *the door will* **be o** to you. *G487*
Lk 11:10 to the one who knocks, *the door will* **be o**. *G487*
Lk 24:31 Then their eyes *were* **o** and they *G1380*
Lk 24:32 us on the road and **o** the Scriptures to us?" *G1380*
Lk 24:45 Then *he* **o** their minds so they could *G1380*
Jn 9:10 "How then *were* your eyes **o**?" they asked. *G487*
Jn 9:14 made the mud and **o** the man's eyes was a *G487*
Jn 9:17 It was your eyes *he* **o**." The man replied, *G487*
Jn 9:21 can see now, or who **o** his eyes, we don't *G487*
Jn 9:30 where he comes from, yet *he* **o** my eyes. *G487*
Jn 11:37 "Could not he who **o** the eyes of the blind *G487*
Ac 5:19 an angel of the Lord **o** the doors of the jail *G487*
Ac 5:23 the doors; but *when we* **o** them, we found *G487*
Ac 9: 8 but *when he* **o** his eyes he could see *G487*
Ac 9:40 She **o** her eyes, and seeing Peter she sat *G487*
Ac 10:11 He saw heaven **o** and something like a *G487*
Ac 12:10 It **o** for them by itself, and they went *G487*
Ac 12:16 and *when they* **o** the door and saw him *G487*
Ac 14:27 them and how *he had* **o** a door of faith to *G487*
Ac 16:14 The Lord **o** her heart to respond to Paul's *G1380*
Ro 1:10 will *the* **way** *may be* **o** *for me* to come *G2338*
1Co 16: 9 a great door for effective work *has* **o** to me, *G487*
2Co 2:12 found *that* the Lord *had* **o** a door for *G487*
2Co 6:11 Corinthians, and **o wide** our hearts to you. *G4425*
Heb 10:20 a new and living way **o** for us through the *G1590*
Rev 6: 1 I watched as the Lamb **o** the first of the *G487*
Rev 6: 3 When the Lamb **o** the second seal, I heard *G487*
Rev 6: 5 When the Lamb **o** the third seal, I heard *G487*
Rev 6: 7 When the Lamb **o** the fourth seal, I heard *G487*
Rev 6: 9 When *he* **o** the fifth seal, I saw under the *G487*
Rev 6:12 I watched as *he* **o** the sixth seal. There was *G487*
Rev 8: 1 When *he* **o** the seventh seal, there was *G487*
Rev 9: 2 *When he* **o** the Abyss, smoke rose from it *G487*
Rev 11:19 Then God's temple in heaven *was* **o**, and *G487*
Rev 13: 6 *It* **o** its mouth to blaspheme God, and to *G487*
Rev 15: 5 of the covenant law—and *it was* **o**. *G487*
Rev 20:12 before the throne, and books *were* **o**. *G487*
Rev 20:12 Another book *was* **o**, which is the book of *G487*

OPENHANDED (2) [OPEN, HAND]

Dt 15: 8 *be* **o** and freely lend H7337+906+3338+7337
Dt 15:11 you *to be* **o** toward your H7337+3338+906+7337

OPENING (19) [OPEN]

Ge 6:16 **leaving** *below* the roof *an o* one cubit high AIT
Ex 28:32 with an **o** *for* the head in its center. There H7023
Ex 28:32 a woven edge like a collar around this **o**, H7023
Ex 39:23 with an **o** in the center of the robe like the H7023
Ex 39:23 center of the robe like the **o** *of* a collar, H7023
Ex 39:23 a band around this **o**, so that it would H7023
2Sa 17:19 spread it out over the **o** *of* the well and H7156
1Ki 7:31 stand there was an **o** that had a circular H7023
1Ki 7:31 This **o** was round, and with its basework it H7023
1Ki 7:31 Around its **o** there was engraving H7023
1Ch 9:27 charge of the **key for o** it each morning. H5158
Isa 5:14 expands its jaws, **o** wide its mouth; into it H7196
Eze 40:13 cubits from *one* **parapet o** to the opposite H7339
Da 3:26 then approached the **o** *of* the blazing A10776
Mk 2: 4 *they* **made an o** in the roof above Jesus by *G689*
Jn 9:32 has ever heard of **o** the eyes of a man born *G487*
Ac 9:25 him in a basket **through** *an o* in the wall. AIT
Ac 12:14 she ran back without **o** it and exclaimed, *G487*
Rev 12:16 helped the woman *by* **o** its mouth and *G487*

OPENINGS (8) [OPEN]

Eze 40:16 by narrow **parapet o** all around, H2707
Eze 40:16 the portico; the **o** all around faced inward. H2707
Eze 40:22 Its **o**, its portico and its palm tree H2707
Eze 40:25 its portico had narrow **o** all around, H2707
Eze 40:25 all around, like the **o** of the others. H2707
Eze 40:29 gateway and its portico had **o** all around. H2707
Eze 40:33 gateway and its portico had **o** all around. H2707
Eze 40:36 its portico, and it had **o** all around. H2707

OPENLY (6) [OPEN]

Eze 23:18 When *she* **carried on** her prostitution **o** H1655
Mk 1:45 longer enter a town **o** but stayed outside *G5747*
Jn 12:42 *they would* not **o acknowledge** *their* **faith** *G3933*
Jn 18:20 "I have spoken **o** to the world," Jesus *G4244*
Ac 19:18 came and **o confessed** what *G2018+2779+334*
Heb 13:15 the fruit of lips *that* **o profess** his name. *G3933*

OPENS (9) [OPEN]

Nu 16:30 the earth **o** its mouth and swallows H7198
Job 27:19 do so no more; *when he* **o** his eyes, all is H7219
Job 35:16 So Job **o** his mouth *with* empty talk H7198
Pr 18:16 A gift **o the way** and ushers the giver into H8143
Pr 31:20 *She* **o** her arms to the poor and extends H7298
Isa 22:22 of David; what *he* **o** no one can shut H7337
Jn 10: 3 The gatekeeper **o** the gate for him, and the *G487*
Rev 3: 7 What he **o** no one can shut, and what he *G487*
Rev 3:20 If anyone hears my voice and **o** the door, *G487*

OPERATION, OPERATIONS (KJV) DEEDS, DONE, WORK, WORKINGS

OPHEL (5)

2Ch 27: 3 extensive work on the wall at the **hill of O**. H6755
2Ch 33:14 the Fish Gate and encircling the **hill of O**; H6755
Ne 3:26 living on the **hill of O** made repairs up to H6755
Ne 3:27 great projecting tower to the wall of **O**. H6755
Ne 11:21 The temple servants lived on the **hill of O** H6755

OPHIR (12)

Ge 10:29 **O**, Havilah and Jobab. All these were sons H234
1Ki 9:28 They sailed to **O** and brought back 420 H234
1Ki 10:11 Hiram's ships brought gold from **O**; and H234
1Ki 22:48 a fleet of trading ships to go to **O** for gold, H234
1Ch 1:23 **O**, Havilah and Jobab. All these were sons H235
1Ch 29: 4 of gold (gold of **O**) and seven thousand H234
2Ch 8:18 sailed to **O** and brought back four hundred H234
2Ch 9:10 servants of Solomon brought gold from **O**; H234
Job 22:24 your **gold of O** to the rocks in the ravines, H234
Job 28:16 It cannot be bought with the gold of **O** H234

Ps 45: 9 right hand is the royal bride in gold of O. H234
Isa 13:12 pure gold, more rare than the gold of O. H234

OPHNI (1)
Jos 18:24 Kephar Ammoni, O and Geba—twelve H6756

OPHRAH (8) [BETH OPHRAH]
Jos 18:23 Parah, O, H6764
Jdg 6:11 down under the oak in O that belonged to H6764
Jdg 6:24 To this day it stands in O of the Abiezrites. H6764
Jdg 8:27 which he placed in O, his town. H6764
Jdg 8:32 of his father Joash in O of the Abiezrites. H6764
Jdg 9: 5 his father's home in O and on one stone H6764
1Sa 13:17 One turned toward O in the vicinity of H6764
1Ch 4:14 Meonothai was the father of O. Seraiah H6763

OPINION (2) [OPINIONS]
2Sa 17: 6 do what he says? If not, give us your o." H1819
Mt 22:17 Tell us then, what is your o? Is it right to G1506

OPINIONS (2) [OPINION]
1Ki 18:21 "How long will you waver between two o? H6191
Pr 18: 2 delight in airing their own o. H4213

OPPONENT (3) [OPPOSE]
2Sa 2:16 each man grabbed his o by the head and H8276
1Ki 20:20 each one struck down his o. At that, the H408
Job 16: 9 my o fastens on me his piercing eyes. H7640

OPPONENT'S (1) [OPPOSE]
2Sa 2:16 thrust his dagger into his o side, H8276

OPPONENTS (7) [OPPOSE]
Ps 127: 5 when they contend with their o in court. H367
Pr 18:18 lot settles disputes and keeps strong o apart. AIT
Lk 13:17 he said this, all his o were humiliated, but G512
Jn 10:31 Again his Jewish o picked up stones to G2681
Ac 18:28 refuted his Jewish o in public debate, G2681
Ac 20:19 severe testing by the plots of my Jewish o. G2681
2Ti 2:25 O must be gently instructed, in the hope G507

OPPORTUNE (2) [OPPORTUNITY]
Mk 6:21 Finally the o time came. On his birthday G2322
Lk 4:13 this tempting, he left him until an o time. G2789

OPPORTUNITY (19) [OPPORTUNE]
Jdg 9:33 seize the o to attack them. H5162+3338
1Sa 18:21 "Now you have a second o to become my AIT
Jer 46:17 is only a loud noise; he has missed his o. H4595
Mt 26:16 Judas watched for an o to hand him over. G2321
Mk 14:11 So he watched for an o to hand him over. G2323
Lk 22: 6 watched for an o to hand Jesus over G2321
Ac 25:16 have had an o to defend themselves G5536
Ac 27:13 they saw their o; so they weighed G4606+3195
Ro 7: 8 seizing the o afforded by the G929
Ro 7:11 seizing the o afforded by the G929
1Co 16:12 but he will go when he has the o. G2320
2Co 5:12 are giving you an o to take pride in us G929
2Co 11:12 those who want an o to be considered G929
Gal 6:10 Therefore, as we have o, let us do good to G2789
Eph 5:16 making the most of every o, because the G2789
Php 4:10 concerned, but you had no o to show it. G177
Col 4: 5 outsiders; make the most of every o. G2789
1Ti 5:14 to give the enemy no o for slander. G929
Heb 11:15 had left, they would have had o to return. G2789

OPPOSE (26) [OPPONENT, OPPONENT'S, OPPONENTS, OPPOSED, OPPOSES, OPPOSING, OPPOSITE, OPPOSITION]
Ex 23:22 your enemies and will o those who H7444
Ex 23:22 will oppose those who o you. H7675
Nu 16: 3 came as a group to o Moses and Aaron H6584
Nu 22:22 of the LORD stood in the road to o him. H8477
Nu 22:32 I have come here to o you because your H8477
Nu 22:34 you were standing in the road to o me. H7925
Jdg 20:25 came out from Gibeah to o them, H7925
1Sa 2:10 those who o the LORD will be broken. H8189
Job 11:10 convenes a court, who can o him? H8740
Job 23: 6 Would he vigorously o me? No, he H8189+6643
Job 23:13 "But he stands alone, and who can o him? H8740
Ps 55:18 against me, even though many o me. H6643
Ps 109: 6 Appoint someone evil to o my enemy; let H6584
Isa 41:11 those who o you will be as nothing and H8190
Jer 38: 5 "The king can do nothing to o you." H907
Jer 51: 2 they will o her on every side in the day of H6584
Da 11:30 of the western coastlands will o him, H995+928
Lk 11:53 of the law began to o him fiercely and to G1923
Lk 14:31 ten thousand men to o the one coming G5636
Ac 26: 9 was possible to o the name of Jesus of G1885
1Co 16: 9 and there are many who o me. G512
Php 1:28 frightened in any way by those who o you. G512
2Th 2: 4 He will o and will exalt himself over G512
2Ti 3: 8 so also these teachers o the truth. G468
Titus 1: 9 sound doctrine and refute those who o it. G515
Titus 2: 8 so that those who o you may be ashamed G1885

OPPOSED (10) [OPPOSE]
Ex 15: 7 majesty you threw down those who o you. H7756
2Ch 13: 7 around him and o Rehoboam son of H599+6584
Ezr 10:15 and Shabbethai the Levite, o this. H6641+6584
Jer 50:24 captured because you o the LORD. H1741
Ac 13: 8 o them and tried to turn the proconsul from G468
Ac 18: 6 But when they o Paul and became abusive G530
Gal 2:11 came to Antioch, I o him to his face G468
Gal 3:21 therefore, o to the promises of God? G2848
2Ti 3: 8 Just as Jannes and Jambres o Moses, so G468
2Ti 4:15 because he strongly o our message. G468

OPPOSES (5) [OPPOSE]
Mk 3:26 And if Satan o himself and is divided G482+2093
Lk 23: 2 He o payment of taxes to Caesar and G3266
Jn 19:12 Anyone who claims to be a king o Caesar." G515
Jas 4: 6 "God o the proud but shows favor to the G530
1Pe 5: 5 "God o the proud but shows favor to the G530

OPPOSING (3) [OPPOSE]
2Ch 35:21 to hurry; so stop o God, who is with me, H4946
1Ti 6:20 chatter and the o ideas of what is falsely G509
Jas 5: 6 the innocent one, who was not o you. G530

OPPOSITE (49) [OPPOSE]
Ge 15:10 arranged the halves o each other; H7925
Ex 14: 2 directly o Baal Zephon. H5790+4200+7156
Ex 14: 9 near Pi Hahiroth, o Baal Zephon. H4200+7156
Ex 26: 5 the other set, with the loops o each other. H7691
Ex 26:35 put the lampstand o it on the south side. H5790
Ex 30: 4 two on each of the o sides—to hold H7521+7396
Ex 36:12 the other set, with the loops o each other. H7691
Ex 37:27 two on each of the o sides—to hold H7521+7396
Ex 40:24 the tent of meeting o the table on the H5790
Dt 1: 1 in the Arabah—o Suph, between Paran H4578
Dt 34: 6 in the valley o Beth Peor, but to H4578
Jos 3:16 So the people crossed over o Jericho. H5584
1Sa 20:25 place by the wall, o Jonathan, and Abner H7709
2Sa 16:13 going along the hillside o him, H4200+6645
1Ki 20:27 Israelites camped o them like two small H5584
1Ki 20:29 For seven days they camped o each other H5790
1Ki 21:10 seat two scoundrels o him and have them H5584
1Ki 21:13 came and sat o him and brought charges H5584
1Ch 19:17 them and formed his battle lines o them. H448
2Ch 7: 6 O the Levites, the priests blew their H5584
Ne 3:10 of Harumaph made repairs o his house, H5584
Ne 3:16 up to a point o the tombs of David, H5584
Ne 3:25 of Uzai worked o the angle and the H4946+5584
Ne 3:26 up to a point o the Water Gate toward H5584
Ne 3:29 son of Immer made repairs o his house. H5584
Ne 3:30 made repairs o his living quarters. H5584
Ne 3:31 the merchants, o the Inspection Gate H5584
Ne 12: 9 stood o them in the services. H4200+5584
Ne 12:24 who stood o them to give praise H4200+5584
Ne 12:38 second choir proceeded in the o direction. H4578
Eze 16:34 your prostitution you are the o of others; H2201
Eze 16:34 You are the very o, for you give payment H2201
Eze 40:13 of one alcove to the top of the o one; H2257S
Eze 40:13 from one parapet opening to the o one. H5584
Eze 40:22 led up to it, with its portico o them. H4200+7156
Eze 40:23 measured from one gate to the o one; H9133S
Eze 40:26 with its portico o them; it had palm H4200+7156
Eze 42: 1 me to the rooms o the temple courtyard H5584
Eze 42: 1 temple courtyard and o the outer wall on H5584
Eze 42: 3 in the section o the pavement of the H5584
Eze 42:10 courtyard and o the outer wall, H448+7156
Eze 46: 9 entered, but each is to go out the o gate. H5790
Eze 47:20 the boundary to a point o Lebo Hamath. H5790
Da 12: 5 bank of the river and one on the o bank. H2178
Mt 27:61 other Mary were sitting there o the tomb. G595
Mk 12:41 Jesus sat down o the place where the G2978
Mk 13: 3 on the Mount of Olives o the temple, G2978
Jn 6:22 that had stayed on the o shore of the lake G4305
Ac 27: 7 we sailed to the lee of Crete, o Salmone. G2848

OPPOSITION (7) [OPPOSE]
Nu 16:19 all his followers in o to them at the H6584
Nu 16:42 gathered in o to Moses and Aaron H6584
Nu 20: 2 people gathered in o to Moses and Aaron H6584
Jdg 9:25 In o to him these citizens of Shechem set H4200
Ac 6: 9 O arose, however, from members of the G482
1Th 2: 2 to tell you his gospel in the face of strong o. G74
Heb 12: 3 him who endured such o from sinners, G517

OPPRESS (27) [OPPRESSED, OPPRESSES, OPPRESSING, OPPRESSION, OPPRESSIVE, OPPRESSOR, OPPRESSORS]
Ex 1:11 masters over them to o them with forced H6700
Ex 22:21 "Do not mistreat or o a foreigner, for you H4315
Ex 23: 9 "Do not o a foreigner; you yourselves H4315
Dt 23:16 town they choose. Do not o them. H3561
2Sa 7:10 Wicked people will not o them anymore H6700
1Ch 16:21 He allowed no one to o them; for their H6943
1Ch 17: 9 Wicked people will not o them anymore H1162
Job 10: 3 Does it please you to o me, to spurn the H6943
Job 37:23 great righteousness, he does not o. H6700
Ps 89:22 better of him; the wicked will not o him. H6700
Ps 94: 5 your people, LORD; they o your inheritance. H6700
Ps 105:14 He allowed no one to o them; for their H6943
Ps 119:122 well-being; do not let the arrogant o me. H6943
Isa 3: 5 People will o each other—man against H5601
Isa 3:12 Youths o my people, women rule over H5601
Jer 7: 6 if you do not o the foreigner, the fatherless H6943
Jer 30:20 before me; I will punish all who o them. H4315
Eze 18: 7 He does not o anyone, but returns what H3561
Eze 18:16 He does not o anyone or require a pledge H3561
Eze 22:29 they o the poor and needy and mistreat H3561
Eze 45: 8 my princes will no longer o my people H3561
Da 7:25 the Most High and o his holy people A10106
Am 4: 1 you women who o the poor and crush the H6943
Am 5:12 There are those who o the innocent and H7674
Am 6:14 that will o you all the way from Lebo H4315
Zec 7:10 Do not o the widow or the fatherless, the H6943
Mal 3: 5 who o the widows and the fatherless NDT

OPPRESSED (49) [OPPRESS]
Ex 1:12 But the more they were o, the more they H6700
Dt 28:29 day after day you will be o and robbed H6943
Jdg 2:18 groaning under those who o and afflicted H4315
Jdg 4: 3 with iron and had cruelly o the Israelites H4315
Jdg 10: 8 eighteen years they o all the Israelites on NDT
Jdg 10:12 the Maonites o you and you cried to H4315
1Sa 10:18 of Egypt and all the kingdoms that o you. H4315
1Sa 12: 3 Whom have I o? From whose H8368
1Sa 12: 4 "You have not cheated or o us," they H8368
2Ki 13:22 Hazael king of Aram o Israel throughout H4315
2Ch 16:10 the same time Asa brutally o some of the H8368
Ne 9:27 the hands of their enemies, who o them. H7674
Ne 9:27 But when they were o they cried out to H7650
Job 20:19 For he has o the poor and left them H8368
Ps 9: 9 The LORD is a refuge for the o, H1916
Ps 10:18 defending the fatherless and the o, so H1916
Ps 42: 9 I go about mourning, o by the enemy?" H4316
Ps 43: 2 I go about mourning, o by the enemy? H4316
Ps 74:21 Do not let the o retreat in disgrace; may H1916
Ps 82: 3 uphold the cause of the poor and the o. H8133
Ps 103: 6 righteousness and justice for all the o. H6943
Ps 106:42 Their enemies o them and subjected H4315
Ps 129: 1 "They have greatly o me from my youth," H7675
Ps 129: 2 "they have greatly o me from my youth H7675
Ps 146: 7 the cause of the o and gives food to the H6943
Pr 3:34 shows favor to the humble and o. H6705
Pr 15:15 All the days of the o are wretched, but the H6714
Pr 16:19 along with the o than to share plunder H6705
Pr 31: 5 and deprive all the o of their rights. H1201+6715
Ecc 4: 1 I saw the tears of the o—and they have H6943
Ecc 5: 8 If you see the poor o in a district, and H6945
Isa 1:17 Defend the o. Take up the cause H2787
Isa 10: 2 withhold justice from the o of my people, H6714
Isa 26: 6 the feet of the o, the footsteps of the H6714
Isa 52: 4 Egypt to live; lately, Assyria has o them. H6943
Isa 53: 7 He was o and afflicted, yet he did not H5601
Isa 58: 6 to set the o free and break every yoke? H8368
Isa 58:10 the hungry and satisfy the needs of the o, H6700
Jer 50:33 "The people of Israel are o, and the H6943
Eze 22: 7 in you they have o the H6913+928+2021+6945
Da 4:27 your wickedness by being kind to the o. A10559
Hos 5:11 Ephraim is o, trampled in judgment H6943
Am 2: 7 of the ground and deny justice to the o. H6705
Zep 3:19 At that time I will deal with all who o you H6700
Zec 10: 2 wander like sheep o for lack of a H6700
Zec 11: 7 slaughter, particularly the o of the flock. H6714
Zec 11:11 so the o of the flock who were H6714
Lk 4:18 of sight for the blind, to set the o free, G2575
Ac 7:19 with our people and o our ancestors by G2808

OPPRESSES (4) [OPPRESS]
Pr 14:31 Whoever o the poor shows contempt for H6943
Pr 22:16 One who o the poor to increase his H6943
Pr 28: 3 A ruler who o the poor is like a driving H6943
Eze 18:12 He o the poor and needy. He commits H3561

OPPRESSING (3) [OPPRESS]
Ex 3: 9 seen the way the Egyptians are o them. H4315
Nu 10: 9 own land against an enemy who is o you, H7675
2Ki 13: 4 severely the king of Aram was o H4315+4316

OPPRESSION (19) [OPPRESS]
Dt 26: 7 our voice and saw our misery, toil and o. H4316
Dt 28:33 have nothing but cruel o all your days. H6943
Job 35: 9 "People cry out under a load of o; they H6935
Ps 44:24 your face and forget our misery and o? H4316
Ps 72:14 He will rescue them from o and violence H9412
Ps 73: 8 with arrogance they threaten o. H6945
Ps 107:39 they were humbled by o, calamity H6808
Ps 119:134 Redeem me from human o, that I may H6945
Ecc 4: 1 saw all the o that was taking place H6935
Isa 30:12 relied on o and depended on deceit H6945
Isa 53: 8 By o and judgment he was taken away H6808
Isa 58: 9 "If you do away with the yoke of o, with the NDT
Isa 59:13 inciting revolt and o, uttering lies our H6945
Jer 6: 6 city must be punished; it is filled with o. H6945
Jer 22:17 innocent blood and on o and extortion." H6945
Eze 45: 9 your violence and o and do what is just H8719
Hos 8:10 away under the o of the mighty king. H5362
Am 3: 9 within her and the o among her people." H6935
Ac 7:34 have indeed seen the o of my people in G2810

OPPRESSIVE (2) [OPPRESS]
Jdg 6: 2 Because the power of Midian was so o H6451
Isa 10: 1 unjust laws, to those who issue o decrees, H6662

OPPRESSOR (14) [OPPRESS]
Ps 72: 4 children of the needy; may he crush the o. H6943
Ps 78:42 the day he redeemed them from the o, H7640
Pr 29:13 The poor and the o have this in H408+9412
Isa 9: 4 across their shoulders, the rod of their o. H5601
Isa 14: 4 How the o has come to an end H5601
Isa 16: 4 The o will come to an end, and H5160
Isa 51:13 every day because of the wrath of the o, H7439
Isa 51:13 For where is the wrath of the o? H7439
Jer 21:12 the hand of the o the one who has been H6943

O

Jer 22: 3 the hand of the o the one who has been H6934
Jer 25:38 of the sword of the o and because of the H3561
Jer 46:16 away from the sword of the o. H3561
Jer 50:16 of the sword of the o let everyone return H3561
Zec 9: 8 Never again will an o overrun my people H5601

OPPRESSORS (9) [OPPRESS]

Jdg 6: 9 delivered you from the hand of all your o; H4315
Ps 27:11 me in a straight path because of my o. H8806
Ps 119:121 just; do not leave me to my o. H6943
Ecc 4: 1 power was on the side of their o—and H6943
Isa 14: 2 of their captors and rule over their o. H5601
Isa 19:20 they cry out to the LORD because of their o, H4315
Isa 49:26 I will make your o eat their own flesh H3561
Isa 60:14 The children of your o will come bowing H6700
Zep 3: 1 Woe to the city of o, rebellious and H3561

OPTIONS (2)

2Sa 24:12 I am giving you **three** *o*. Choose one of them AIT
1Ch 21:10 I am giving you **three** *o*. Choose one of them AIT

OR (1979)

Ge 3: 3 you must not touch it, o you will die. H7153
Ge 13: 8 o between your herders and mine H2256
Ge 14:23 not even a thread o the strap of a sandal H2256
Ge 17:12 in your household o bought with money H2256
Ge 17:13 *Whether* born in your household o bought H2256
Ge 17:23 in his household o bought with his money H2256
Ge 17:27 born in his household o bought from a H2256
Ge 19:12 sons-in-law, sons o daughters, or anyone H2256
Ge 19:12 o anyone else in the city who belongs to H2256
Ge 19:15 o you will be swept away when the city is H7153
Ge 19:17 Flee to the mountains o you will be swept H7153
Ge 19:33 it when she lay down o when she got up. H2256
Ge 19:35 it when she lay down o when she got up. H2256
Ge 21:23 deal falsely with me o my children or my H2256
Ge 21:23 with me or my children o my descendants. H2256
Ge 24:21 to learn whether o not the LORD had made H561
Ge 24:50 say nothing to you one way o the other. H196
Ge 24:55 woman remain with us ten days o so; H196
Ge 26:11 who harms this man o his wife shall H2256
Ge 27:21 whether you really are my son Esau o not." H561
Ge 30: 1 "Give me children, o I'll die!" H2256+561+401
Ge 30:32 them every speckled o spotted sheep, H2256
Ge 30:32 lamb and every spotted o speckled goat. H2256
Ge 30:33 possession that is not speckled o spotted, H2256
Ge 30:33 o any lamb that is not dark-colored H2256
Ge 30:35 male goats that were streaked o spotted, H2256
Ge 30:35 all the speckled o spotted female goats H2256
Ge 30:39 that were streaked o speckled or spotted. NDT
Ge 30:39 that were streaked or speckled o spotted. H2256
Ge 31:10 flock were streaked, speckled o spotted. H2256
Ge 31:12 streaked, speckled o spotted, for I have H2256
Ge 31:24 say anything to Jacob, either good o bad." H6330
Ge 31:29 say anything to Jacob, either good o bad. H6330
Ge 31:39 whatever was stolen by day o night. H2256
Ge 31:43 o about the children they have borne? H196
Ge 31:50 my daughters o if you take any wives H2256
Ge 38:23 o we will become a laughingstock. H7153
Ge 39:10 to go to bed with her o even be with her. NDT
Ge 41:44 no one will lift hand o foot in all Egypt." H2256
Ge 44: 8 would we steal silver o gold from your H196
Ge 44:19 servants, 'Do you have a father o a brother? H196
Ex 1:10 shrewdly with them o they will become H7153
Ex 4: 1 do not believe me o listen to me and say, H2256
Ex 4: 8 do not believe you o pay attention to the H2256
Ex 4: 9 believe these two signs o listen to you, H2256
Ex 4:11 Who makes them deaf o mute? Who gives H196
Ex 4:11 Who gives them sight o makes them blind H196
Ex 5: 3 o he may strike us with plagues or with H7153
Ex 5: 3 strike us with plagues o with the sword." H196
Ex 5:14 your quota of bricks yesterday o today, H1685
Ex 9:14 o this time I will send the full force of my H3954
Ex 10:15 remained on tree o plant in all the land H2256
Ex 10:23 see anyone else o move about for three H2256
Ex 11: 6 there has ever been o ever will be again. H2256
Ex 11: 7 a dog will bark at any person o animal. H2256
Ex 12: 5 take them from the sheep o the goats. H2256
Ex 12: 9 Do not eat the meat raw o boiled in water H2256
Ex 12:19 whether foreigner o native-born, who eats H2256
Ex 12:45 a temporary resident o a hired worker may H2256
Ex 13: 2 belongs to me, whether human o animal." H2256
Ex 13:21 so that they could travel by day o night. H2256
Ex 16:24 it did not stink o get maggots in it. H2256
Ex 17: 7 saying, "Is the LORD among us o not?" H561
Ex 19:12 the mountain o touch the foot of it. H2256
Ex 19:13 They are to be stoned o shot with arrows H196
Ex 19:13 No person o animal shall be permitted to H561
Ex 19:22 o the LORD will break out against them." H7153
Ex 19:24 o he will break out against them. H7153
Ex 20: 4 in heaven above o on the earth beneath H2256
Ex 20: 4 the earth beneath o in the waters below. H2256
Ex 20: 5 not bow down to them o worship them; H2256
Ex 20:10 nor your son o daughter, nor your H2256
Ex 20:10 your male o female servant, nor H2256
Ex 20:17 o his male or female servant H2256
Ex 20:17 or his male o female servant, his ox H2256
Ex 20:17 servant, his ox o donkey, or anything H2256
Ex 20:17 o anything that belongs to your neighbor." H2256
Ex 20:19 not have God speak to us o we will die." H7153
Ex 20:23 yourselves gods of silver o gods of gold. H2256
Ex 20:26 o your private parts may be exposed. H889+4202
Ex 21: 4 wife and she bears him sons o daughters, H196
Ex 21: 6 take him to the door o the doorpost and H196
Ex 21:15 attacks their father o mother is to be put H2256
Ex 21:16 the victim has been sold o is still in the H2256
Ex 21:17 curses their father o mother is to be put to H2256
Ex 21:18 another with a stone o with their fist and H196
Ex 21:20 who beats their male o female slave with a H196
Ex 21:21 if the slave recovers after a day o two, H196
Ex 21:26 who hits a male o female slave in the H196
Ex 21:27 the tooth of a male o female slave must let H196
Ex 21:28 "If a bull gores a man o woman to death H196
Ex 21:29 it penned up and it kills a man o woman, H196
Ex 21:31 applies if the bull gores a son o daughter. H196
Ex 21:32 If the bull gores a male o female slave, the H196
Ex 21:33 uncovers a pit o digs one and fails to H196
Ex 21:33 to cover it and an ox o a donkey falls into it H196
Ex 22: 1 "Whoever steals an ox o a sheep and H196
Ex 22: 1 slaughters it o sells it must pay back H196
Ex 22: 4 whether ox o donkey or sheep—they H6330
Ex 22: 4 whether ox or donkey o sheep—they must H6330
Ex 22: 5 livestock in a field o vineyard and lets them H196
Ex 22: 5 the best of their own field o vineyard. H2256
Ex 22: 6 shocks of grain o standing grain or the H196
Ex 22: 6 grain or standing grain o the whole field, H196
Ex 22: 7 a neighbor silver o goods for safekeeping H196
Ex 22: 9 o any other lost property about which NDT
Ex 22:10 a sheep o any other animal to their H2256
Ex 22:10 it dies o is injured or is taken H196
Ex 22:10 it dies or is injured o is taken away while H196
Ex 22:14 it is injured o dies while the owner is H196
Ex 22:21 "Do not mistreat o oppress a foreigner, for H2256
Ex 22:22 advantage of the widow o the fatherless. H2256
Ex 22:28 not blaspheme God o curse the ruler of H2256
Ex 22:29 offerings from your granaries o your vats. H2256
Ex 23: 4 your enemy's ox o donkey wandering off, H196
Ex 23: 7 not put an innocent o honest person to H2256
Ex 23:24 before their gods o worship them or H2256
Ex 23:24 gods or worship them o follow their H2256
Ex 23:26 none will miscarry o be barren in your H2256
Ex 23:32 a covenant with them o with their gods. H2256
Ex 23:33 live in your land o they will cause you to H7153
Ex 28:43 the tent of meeting o approach the altar to H196
Ex 29:34 of the ordination ram o any bread is left H2256
Ex 30: 9 any other incense o any burnt offering H2256
Ex 30: 9 any burnt offering o grain offering, H2256
Ex 30:14 those twenty years old o more, are to give H2256
Ex 34: 3 come with you o be seen anywhere H2256+1685
Ex 34:12 o they will be a snare among you. H7153
Ex 34:19 your livestock, whether from herd o flock. H2256
Ex 34:28 without eating bread o drinking water. H2256
Ex 35:23 purple o scarlet yarn or fine linen H2256
Ex 35:23 purple or scarlet yarn o fine linen, or goat H2256
Ex 35:23 yarn or fine linen, o goat hair, ram skins H2256
Ex 35:23 ram skins dyed red o the other durable H2256
Ex 35:24 an offering of silver o bronze brought it as H2256
Ex 35:25 purple o scarlet yarn or fine linen. NDT
Ex 35:25 purple or scarlet yarn o fine linen. H2256
Ex 36: 6 "No man o woman is to make anything H2256
Ex 38:26 twenty years old o more, a total of H2256
Ex 40:32 the tent of meeting o approached the H2256
Lev 1: 2 animal from **either** the herd o the flock. H2256
Lev 1:10 from **either** the sheep o the goats H196
Lev 1:14 you are to offer a dove o a young pigeon. H196
Lev 2: 4 **either** thick loaves made without yeast
and with olive oil mixed in o H2256
Lev 2:11 not to burn any yeast o honey in a food H2256
Lev 3: 1 whether male o female, you are to H561
Lev 3: 6 are to offer a male o female without defect H196
Lev 3:17 You must not eat any fat o any blood.'" H2256
Lev 5: 1 they have seen o learned about, H196
Lev 5: 2 unclean animal, wild o domestic, or of any H196
Lev 5: 2 o of any unclean creature that moves along H196
Lev 5: 3 o if they touch human uncleanness H196
Lev 5: 4 o if anyone thoughtlessly takes an oath to H196
Lev 5: 4 to do anything, **whether** good o evil (in any H196
Lev 5: 6 LORD a female lamb o goat from the flock H196
Lev 5: 7 to bring two doves o two young pigeons to H196
Lev 5:11 afford two doves o two young pigeons, H196
Lev 5:11 must not put olive oil o incense on it, H2256
Lev 6: 2 entrusted to them o left in their care or H196
Lev 6: 2 left in their care o about something H196
Lev 6: 2 o if they cheat their neighbor H196
Lev 6: 3 o if they find lost property and lie about it H196
Lev 6: 3 o if they swear falsely about any such sin H2256
Lev 6: 4 what they have stolen o taken by extortion, H196
Lev 6: 4 by extortion, o what was entrusted to them H196
Lev 6: 4 to them, o the lost property they found H196
Lev 6: 5 o whatever it was they swore falsely about H196
Lev 7: 9 baked in an oven o cooked in a pan or on H2256
Lev 7: 9 cooked in a pan o on a griddle belongs H2256
Lev 7:10 **whether** mixed with olive oil o dry H2256
Lev 7:16 is the result of a vow o is a freewill offering H196
Lev 7:21 **whether** human uncleanness o an unclean H196
Lev 7:21 an unclean animal o any unclean creature H196
Lev 7:23 eat any of the fat of cattle, sheep o goats. H2256
Lev 7:24 animal found dead o torn by wild animals H2256
Lev 7:26 not eat the blood of any bird o animal. H2256
Lev 10: 6 o you will die and the LORD will be H2256+4202
Lev 10: 7 to the tent of meeting o you will die, H7153
Lev 10: 9 not to drink wine o other fermented drink H2256
Lev 10: 9 the tent of meeting, o you will die. H2256+4202
Lev 11: 4 only chew the cud o only have a divided H2256
Lev 11: 8 not eat their meat o touch their carcasses; H2256
Lev 11:10 in the seas o streams that do not H2256
Lev 11:10 **whether** among all the swarming things o H2256
Lev 11:22 of locust, katydid, cricket o grasshopper. H2256
Lev 11:26 have a divided hoof o that does not chew H2256
Lev 11:32 **whether** it is made of wood, cloth, hide o H196
Lev 11:35 an oven o cooking pot must be broken up. H2256
Lev 11:36 o a cistern for collecting water remains H2256
Lev 11:42 **whether** it moves on its belly o walks on H2256
Lev 11:42 belly or walks on all fours o on many feet; H6330
Lev 11:43 by means of them o be made unclean by H2256
Lev 12: 4 anything sacred o go to the sanctuary H2256
Lev 12: 6 purification for a son o daughter are over, H196
Lev 12: 6 a young pigeon o a dove for a sin H196
Lev 12: 7 woman who gives birth to a boy o a girl. H196
Lev 12: 8 is to bring two doves o two young pigeons, H196
Lev 13: 2 anyone has a swelling o a rash or a shiny H196
Lev 13: 2 a swelling or a rash o a shiny spot on their H196
Lev 13: 2 to Aaron the priest o to one of his sons H196
Lev 13:19 a white swelling o reddish-white spot H196
Lev 13:24 a reddish-white o white spot appears H196
Lev 13:29 "If a man o woman has a sore on their H196
Lev 13:29 woman has a sore on their head o chin, H196
Lev 13:30 a defiling skin disease on the head o chin. H196
Lev 13:33 *the man o woman must* **shave themselves**, AIT
Lev 13:38 "When a man o woman has white spots on H196
Lev 13:42 sore on his bald head o forehead, H196
Lev 13:42 breaking out on his head o forehead. H196
Lev 13:43 swollen sore on his head o forehead is H196
Lev 13:47 any woolen o linen clothing, H196
Lev 13:48 any woven o knitted material of linen or H196
Lev 13:48 woven or knitted material of linen o wool, H2256
Lev 13:48 any leather o anything made of leather H196
Lev 13:49 the woven o knitted material, or H196
Lev 13:49 knitted material, o any leather article, is H196
Lev 13:49 is greenish o reddish, it is a defiling H196
Lev 13:51 the fabric, the woven o knitted material, or H196
Lev 13:51 knitted material, o the leather, whatever H196
Lev 13:52 the woven o knitted material of wool or H196
Lev 13:52 woven or knitted material of wool o linen, H196
Lev 13:52 o any leather article that has been spoiled H196
Lev 13:53 the fabric, the woven o knitted material, or H196
Lev 13:53 knitted material, o the leather article, H196
Lev 13:56 o the woven or knitted material. H196
Lev 13:56 or the woven o knitted material. H196
Lev 13:57 in the woven o knitted material, or H196
Lev 13:57 knitted material, o in the leather article H196
Lev 13:58 Any fabric, woven o knitted material, or any H196
Lev 13:58 o any leather article that has been washed H196
Lev 13:59 defiling molds in woolen o linen clothing, H196
Lev 13:59 linen clothing, woven o knitted material, or H196
Lev 13:59 knitted material, o any leather article, for H196
Lev 13:59 pronouncing them clean o unclean. H196
Lev 14:22 two doves o two young pigeons, such H196
Lev 14:30 sacrifice the doves o the young pigeons, H196
Lev 14:37 if it has greenish o reddish depressions H196
Lev 14:47 Anyone who sleeps o eats in the house H2256
Lev 14:55 defiling molds in fabric o in a house, H2256
Lev 14:56 for a swelling, a rash o a shiny spot, H2256
Lev 14:57 when something is clean o unclean. H2256
Lev 15: 3 **Whether** it continues flowing from
his body o H196
Lev 15:14 must take two doves o two young pigeons H196
Lev 15:17 Any clothing o leather that has semen on H2256
Lev 15:23 Whether it is the bed o anything she was H196
Lev 15:25 her monthly period o has a discharge that H196
Lev 15:29 must take two doves o two young pigeons H196
Lev 15:33 a man o a woman with a discharge H2256
Lev 16: 2 cover on the ark, o else he will die. H2256
Lev 16:29 **whether** native-born o a foreigner residing H2256
Lev 17: 3 a lamb o a goat in the camp or outside of it H196
Lev 17: 3 a lamb or a goat in the camp o outside of it H196
Lev 17: 8 'Any Israelite o any foreigner residing H2256
Lev 17: 8 them who offers a burnt offering o sacrifice H196
Lev 17:10 against any Israelite o any foreigner H2256
Lev 17:13 " 'Any Israelite o any foreigner residing H2256
Lev 17:13 who hunts any animal o bird that may be H196
Lev 17:15 whether native-born o foreigner, who eats H2256
Lev 17:15 anything found dead o torn by wild H2256
Lev 18: 9 **either** your father's daughter o your H196
Lev 18: 9 **whether** she was born in the same home o H196
Lev 18:10 your son's daughter o your daughter's H196
Lev 18:17 with **either** her son's daughter o her H2256
Lev 19: 4 not turn to idols o make metal gods for H2256
Lev 19: 6 the day you sacrifice it o on the next day; H2256
Lev 19: 9 edges of your field o gather the gleanings H2256
Lev 19:10 a second time o pick up the grapes H2256
Lev 19:13 " 'Do not defraud o rob your neighbor. H2256
Lev 19:14 not curse the deaf o put a stumbling block H2256
Lev 19:15 partiality to the poor o favoritism to the H2256
Lev 19:18 'Do not seek revenge o bear a grudge H2256
Lev 19:20 not been ransomed o given her freedom, H196
Lev 19:26 'Do not practice divination o seek omens. H2256
Lev 19:27 sides of your head o clip off the edges of H2256
Lev 19:28 bodies for the dead o put tattoo marks on H2256
Lev 19:29 o the land will turn to prostitution H2256+4202
Lev 19:31 not turn to mediums o seek out spiritists, H2256
Lev 19:35 measuring length, weight o quantity. H2256
Lev 20: 2 'Any Israelite o any foreigner residing in H2256
Lev 20: 9 curses their father o mother is to be put to H2256
Lev 20: 9 they have cursed their father o mother, H2256
Lev 20:17 daughter of **either** his father o his mother, H196

Lev 20:19 sister of **either** your mother **o** your father, H2256
Lev 20:25 by any animal **o** bird or anything that H2256
Lev 20:25 any animal or bird **o** anything that moves H2256
Lev 20:27 " 'A man **o** woman who is a medium or H196
Lev 20:27 who is a medium **o** spiritist among you H196
Lev 21: 2 such as his mother **o** father, his son or H2256
Lev 21: 2 father, his son **o** daughter, his brother, H2256
Lev 21: 3 **o** an unmarried sister who is dependent H2256
Lev 21: 5 shave their heads **o** shave off the edges H2256
Lev 21: 5 edges of their beards **o** cut their bodies. H2256
Lev 21: 7 by prostitution **o** divorced from their H2256
Lev 21:10 hair become unkempt **o** tear his clothes. H2256
Lev 21:11 unclean, even for his father **o** mother, H2256
Lev 21:12 the sanctuary of his God **o** desecrate it, H2256
Lev 21:14 **o** a woman defiled by prostitution H2256
Lev 21:18 no man who is blind **o** lame, disfigured H196
Lev 21:18 is blind or lame, disfigured **o** deformed; H196
Lev 21:19 no man with a crippled foot **o** hand, H196
Lev 21:20 **o** who is a hunchback or a dwarf, or who H196
Lev 21:20 who is a hunchback **o** a dwarf, or who H196
Lev 21:20 a dwarf, **o** who has any eye defect H196
Lev 21:20 **o** who has festering or running sores or H196
Lev 21:20 who has festering **o** running sores or H196
Lev 21:20 running sores **o** damaged testicles. H196
Lev 21:23 go near the curtain **o** approach the altar, H2256
Lev 22: 4 defiling skin disease **o** a bodily discharge, H196
Lev 22: 4 defiled by a corpse **o** by anyone who has H196
Lev 22: 5 **o** if he touches any crawling thing that H196
Lev 22: 5 **o** any person who makes him unclean H196
Lev 22: 8 anything found dead **o** torn by wild H2256
Lev 22:10 the guest of a priest **o** his hired worker eat H2256
Lev 22:11 **o** if slaves are born in his household H2256
Lev 22:13 daughter becomes a widow **o** is divorced, H2256
Lev 22:18 **whether** an Israelite **o** a foreigner residing H2256
Lev 22:18 **either** to fulfill a vow **o** as a freewill H2256
Lev 22:19 sheep **o** goats in order that it may be H2256
Lev 22:21 brings from the herd **o** flock a fellowship H196
Lev 22:21 fulfill a special vow **o** as a freewill offering, H196
Lev 22:21 must be without defect **o** blemish to be H4202
Lev 22:22 the blind, the injured **o** the maimed, or H196
Lev 22:22 **o** anything with warts or festering or H196
Lev 22:22 anything with warts **o** festering or running H196
Lev 22:22 with warts or festering **o** running sores. H196
Lev 22:23 freewill offering an ox **o** a sheep that is H2256
Lev 22:23 ox or a sheep that is deformed **o** stunted, H2256
Lev 22:24 testicles are bruised, crushed, torn **o** cut. H2256
Lev 22:27 "When a calf, a lamb **o** a goat is born, it is H196
Lev 22:28 not slaughter a cow **o** a sheep and its H196
Lev 23:14 not eat any bread, **o** roasted or new grain H2256
Lev 23:14 or roasted **o** new grain, until the H2256
Lev 23:22 edges of your field **o** gather the gleanings H2256
Lev 24:16 Whether foreigner **o** native-born, when H3869
Lev 25: 4 not sow your fields **o** prune your vineyards H2256
Lev 25: 5 what grows of itself **o** harvest the grapes H2256
Lev 25:11 grows of itself **o** harvest the untended H2256
Lev 25:14 of your own people **o** buy land from them, H196
Lev 25:20 if we do not plant **o** harvest our crops?" H2256
Lev 25:36 Do not take interest **o** any profit from them, H2256
Lev 25:37 money at interest **o** sell them food at a H2256
Lev 25:40 as hired workers **o** temporary residents NDT
Lev 25:47 to the foreigner **o** to a member of the H196
Lev 25:49 An uncle **o** a cousin or any blood relative in H196
Lev 25:49 An uncle or a cousin **o** any blood relative in H196
Lev 25:49 **O** if they prosper, they may redeem H196
Lev 26: 1 'Do not make idols **o** set up an image H2256
Lev 26: 1 set up an image **o** a sacred stone for H2256
Lev 26:44 will not reject them **o** abhor them so as to H2256
Lev 27: 7 a person sixty years old **o** more, set the H2256
Lev 27:10 must not exchange it **o** substitute a good H2256
Lev 27:10 a bad one, **o** a bad one for a good one H196
Lev 27:12 who will judge its quality as good **o** bad H2256
Lev 27:14 priest will judge its quality as good **o** bad. H2256
Lev 27:20 **o** if they have sold it to someone else H2256
Lev 27:26 the LORD; whether an ox **o** a sheep, it is the H561
Lev 27:28 a human being **o** an animal or family H2256
Lev 27:28 being or an animal **o** family land— H2256
Lev 27:28 may be sold **o** redeemed H2256
Lev 27:30 grain from the soil **o** fruit from the trees, H4946
Lev 27:33 good from the bad **o** make any H2256
Nu 1: 3 are twenty years old **o** more and able to H2256
Nu 1:18 twenty years old **o** more were listed by H2256
Nu 1:20 twenty years old **o** more who were able H2256
Nu 1:22 twenty years old **o** more who were able H2256
Nu 1:24 twenty years old **o** more who were able H2256
Nu 1:26 twenty years old **o** more who were able H2256
Nu 1:28 twenty years old **o** more who were able H2256
Nu 1:30 twenty years old **o** more who were able H2256
Nu 1:32 twenty years old **o** more who were able H2256
Nu 1:34 twenty years old **o** more who were able H2256
Nu 1:36 twenty years old **o** more who were able H2256
Nu 1:38 twenty years old **o** more who were able H2256
Nu 1:40 twenty years old **o** more who were able H2256
Nu 1:42 twenty years old **o** more who were able H2256
Nu 1:45 twenty years old **o** more who were able to H2256
Nu 1:49 the tribe of Levi **o** include them in the H2256
Nu 3:13 in Israel, whether human **o** animal. H6330
Nu 3:15 Count every male a month old **o** more." H2256
Nu 3:22 males a month old **o** more who were H2256
Nu 3:28 the males a month old **o** more was 8,600. H2256
Nu 3:34 males a month old **o** more who were H2256
Nu 3:39 including every male a month old **o** more H2256
Nu 3:40 who are a month old **o** more and make a H2256
Nu 3:43 of firstborn males a month old **o** more, H2256
Nu 4:15 not touch the holy things **o** they will die. H2256
Nu 4:20 even for a moment, **o** they will die." H2256
Nu 4:27 whether carrying **o** doing other work, is to H2256
Nu 5: 2 defiling skin disease **o** a discharge of any H2256
Nu 5: 2 **o** who is ceremonially unclean because of H2256
Nu 5: 6 'Any man **o** woman who wrongs another in H196
Nu 5:14 **o** if he is jealous and suspects her even H196
Nu 5:15 not pour olive oil on it **o** put incense on it, H2256
Nu 5:22 your abdomen swells **o** your womb H2256
Nu 5:30 **o** when feelings of jealousy come over a H196
Nu 6: 2 'If a man **o** woman wants to make a H196
Nu 6: 3 made from wine **o** other fermented drink. H2256
Nu 6: 3 drink grape juice **o** eat grapes or raisins H2256
Nu 6: 3 eat **grapes o raisins**. H6694+4300+2256+3313
Nu 6: 4 the grapevine, not even the seeds **o** skins. H2256
Nu 6: 7 if their own father **o** mother or brother H2256
Nu 6: 7 own father or mother **o** brother or sister dies, NDT
Nu 6: 7 father or mother or brother **o** sister dies, H2256
Nu 6:10 bring two doves **o** two young pigeons to H196
Nu 8:17 whether human **o** animal, is mine. H2256
Nu 8:24 years old **o** more shall come to H2256
Nu 9:10 'When any of you **o** your descendants are H196
Nu 9:10 of a dead body **o** are away on a journey, H196
Nu 9:12 of it till morning **o** break any of its bones H2256
Nu 9:21 Whether by day **o** by night, whenever the H2256
Nu 9:22 two days **o** a month or a year, H196
Nu 9:22 two days or a month **o** a year, H196
Nu 11: 8 it in a hand mill **o** crushed it in a mortar. H196
Nu 11: 8 cooked it in a pot **o** made it into loaves. H2256
Nu 11:19 eat it for just one day, **o** two days, or five, H2256
Nu 11:19 one day, or two days, **o** five, ten or twenty H2256
Nu 11:19 two days, or five, ten **o** twenty days, H2256
Nu 11:23 you will see whether **o** not what I say will H561
Nu 13:18 people who live there are strong **o** weak, H2022
Nu 13:18 live there are strong or weak, few **o** many. H561
Nu 13:19 Is it good **o** bad? What kind of H561
Nu 13:19 Are they unwalled **o** fortified? H561
Nu 13:20 Is it fertile **o** poor? Are there trees H561
Nu 13:20 Are there trees in it **o** not? Do your best to H561
Nu 14: 2 we had died in Egypt! **O** in this wilderness! H196
Nu 14:29 twenty years old **o** more who was counted H2256
Nu 15: 3 food offerings from the herd **o** the flock, H196
Nu 15: 3 LORD—**whether** burnt offerings **o** sacrifices H196
Nu 15: 3 special vows **o** freewill offerings or H196
Nu 15: 3 freewill offerings **o** festival offerings— H196
Nu 15: 5 lamb for the burnt offering **o** the sacrifice, H196
Nu 15: 8 a young bull as a burnt offering **o** sacrifice, H196
Nu 15: 8 a special vow **o** a fellowship offering to H196
Nu 15:11 Each bull **o** ram, each lamb or young goat H196
Nu 15:11 each lamb **o** young goat, is to be H196
Nu 15:14 whenever a foreigner **o** anyone else living H196
Nu 15:29 Israelite **o** a foreigner residing H2256
Nu 15:30 defiantly, **whether** native-born **o** foreigner H2256
Nu 16:14 with milk and honey **o** given us an H2256
Nu 16:26 **o** you will be swept away because of all H7153
Nu 16:40 **o** he would become like Korah and H2256+4202
Nu 18: 3 furnishings of the sanctuary **o** the altar. H2256
Nu 18: 9 **whether** grain **o** sin or guilt offerings H2256
Nu 18: 9 whether grain or sin **o** guilt offerings, that H2256
Nu 18:17 of a cow, a sheep **o** a goat; they are holy. H196
Nu 18:22 **o** they will bear the consequences of their NDT
Nu 18:27 the threshing floor **o** juice from the H2256
Nu 18:30 of the threshing floor **o** the winepress. H2256
Nu 19: 2 without defect **o** blemish and that has H401
Nu 19:16 killed with a sword **o** someone who has H196
Nu 19:16 **o** anyone who touches a human bone or a H196
Nu 19:16 who touches a human bone **o** a grave, H196
Nu 19:18 a human bone **o** a grave or anyone H196
Nu 19:18 bone or a grave **o** anyone who has been H196
Nu 19:18 has been killed **o** anyone who has died H196
Nu 20: 5 It has no grain **o** figs, grapevines or H2256
Nu 20: 5 grain or figs, grapevines **o** pomegranates. H2256
Nu 20:17 will not go through any field **o** vineyard, H2256
Nu 20:17 vineyard, **o** drink water from any well. H2256
Nu 20:17 not turn to the right **o** to the left until we H2256
Nu 20:19 if we **o** our livestock drink any of your H2256
Nu 21:22 not turn aside into any field **o** vineyard, H2256
Nu 21:22 vineyard, **o** drink water from any well. H4202
Nu 22:18 not do anything great **o** small to go beyond H196
Nu 22:26 **either** to the right **o** to the left. H2256
Nu 23:10 the dust of Jacob **o** number even a fourth H2256
Nu 24:13 my own accord, good **o** bad, to go beyond H196
Nu 26: 2 twenty years old **o** more who are able to H2256
Nu 26: 4 of the men twenty years old **o** more, H2256
Nu 26:62 Levites a month old **o** more numbered H2256
Nu 30: 2 makes a vow to the LORD **o** takes an oath to H196
Nu 30: 3 a vow to the LORD **o** obligates herself by a H2256
Nu 30: 4 hears about her vow **o** pledge but says H2256
Nu 30: 5 none of her vows **o** the pledges by which H2256
Nu 30: 6 after she makes a vow **o** after her lips utter H196
Nu 30: 7 then her vows **o** the pledges by which she H2256
Nu 30: 8 that obligates her **o** the rash promise by H2256
Nu 30: 9 "Any vow **o** obligation taken by a widow NDT
Nu 30: 9 taken by a widow **o** divorced woman will H2256
Nu 30:10 husband makes a vow **o** obligates herself H196
Nu 30:11 then all her vows **o** the pledges by which H2256
Nu 30:12 none of the vows **o** pledges that came H2256
Nu 30:13 may confirm **o** nullify any vow she H2256
Nu 30:13 any vow she makes **o** any sworn pledge to H2256
Nu 30:14 all her vows **o** the pledges binding H196
Nu 31:19 has killed someone **o** touched someone H2256
Nu 31:20 made of leather, goat hair **o** wood." H2256
Nu 31:28 whether people, cattle, donkeys **o** sheep. H2256
Nu 31:30 donkeys, sheep **o** other animals. H2256
Nu 32:11 twenty years old **o** more when they came H2256
Nu 35:17 **O** if anyone is holding a stone and strikes H2256
Nu 35:18 **O** if anyone is holding a wooden object H196
Nu 35:20 shoves another **o** throws something at H196
Nu 35:21 **o** if out of enmity one person hits another H196
Nu 35:22 pushes another **o** throws something at H196
Nu 35:23 **o**, without seeing them, drops on them a H196
Dt 1:16 **whether** the case is between two Israelites **o** H2256
Dt 2: 9 the Moabites **o** provoke them to war H2256
Dt 2:19 do not harass them **o** provoke them to war H2256
Dt 2:27 not turn aside to the right **o** to the left. H2256
Dt 3:24 is there in heaven **o** on earth who can do H2256
Dt 4: 9 your eyes have seen **o** let them fade from H2256
Dt 4:16 **whether** formed like a man **o** a woman H196
Dt 4:17 **o** like any animal on earth or any bird that NDT
Dt 4:17 any animal on earth **o** any bird that flies in NDT
Dt 4:18 **o** like any creature that moves along the NDT
Dt 4:18 along the ground **o** any fish in the waters NDT
Dt 4:28 which cannot see **o** hear or eat or smell. H2256
Dt 4:28 which cannot see or hear **o** eat or smell. H2256
Dt 4:28 which cannot see or hear or eat **o** smell. H2256
Dt 4:31 he will not abandon **o** destroy you or H2256
Dt 4:31 destroy you **o** forget the covenant H2256
Dt 4:32 **o** has anything like it ever been heard of? H196
Dt 4:34 **o** by great and awesome deeds H2256
Dt 5: 8 in heaven above **o** on the earth beneath H2256
Dt 5: 8 the earth beneath **o** in the waters below. H2256
Dt 5: 9 not bow down to them **o** worship them; H2256
Dt 5:14 nor your son **o** daughter, nor your H2256
Dt 5:14 your male **o** female servant, nor H2256
Dt 5:14 your donkey **o** any of your animals H2256
Dt 5:21 desire on your neighbor's house **o** land, NDT
Dt 5:21 land, his male **o** female servant, his ox H2256
Dt 5:21 servant, his ox **o** donkey, or anything H2256
Dt 5:21 **o** anything that belongs to your neighbor." H2256
Dt 5:32 do not turn aside to the right **o** to the left. H2256
Dt 7: 3 to their sons **o** take their daughters H2256
Dt 7:14 none of your men **o** women will be H2256
Dt 7:22 **o** the wild animals will multiply around H7153
Dt 7:25 yourselves, **o** you will be ensnared by it H7153
Dt 7:26 a detestable thing into your house **o** you, H2256
Dt 8: 2 whether **o** not you would keep his H561
Dt 9: 5 of your righteousness **o** your integrity that H2256
Dt 9:23 You did not trust him **o** obey him. H2256
Dt 10: 9 have no share **o** inheritance among H2256
Dt 11:16 **o** you will be enticed to turn away and H7153
Dt 12:12 have no allotment **o** inheritance of their H2256
Dt 12:15 as if it were gazelle **o** deer, according to H2256
Dt 12:17 **o** the firstborn of your herds and flocks H2256
Dt 12:17 **o** whatever you have vowed to give H2256
Dt 12:17 **o** your freewill offerings or special gifts. H2256
Dt 12:17 your freewill offerings **o** special gifts. H2256
Dt 12:22 Eat them as you would gazelle **o** deer H2256
Dt 12:32 do not add to it **o** take away from it. H2256
Dt 13: 1 If a prophet, **o** one who foretells by dreams H196
Dt 13: 1 announces to you a sign **o** wonder, H196
Dt 13: 2 if the sign **o** wonder spoken of takes H2256
Dt 13: 3 to the words of that prophet **o** dreamer. H196
Dt 13: 5 That prophet **o** dreamer must be put to H196
Dt 13: 5 That prophet **o** dreamer tried to turn you NDT
Dt 13: 6 very own brother, **o** your son or daughter H196
Dt 13: 6 or your son **o** daughter, or the wife H196
Dt 13: 6 son or daughter, **o** the wife you love, or H196
Dt 13: 6 **o** your closest friend secretly entices you H196
Dt 13: 7 around you, **whether** near **o** far, from one H196
Dt 13: 8 do not yield to them **o** listen to them H2256
Dt 13: 8 Do not spare them **o** shield them. H2256
Dt 14: 1 Do not cut yourselves **o** shave the front of H2256
Dt 14: 7 that chew the cud **o** that have a divided H2256
Dt 14: 7 not eat the camel, the rabbit **o** the hyrax. H2256
Dt 14: 8 to eat their meat **o** touch their carcasses H2256
Dt 14:21 **o** you may sell it to any other foreigner. H196
Dt 14:26 wine **o** other fermented drink, or H2256
Dt 14:26 fermented drink, **o** anything you wish. H2256
Dt 14:27 have no allotment **o** inheritance of their H2256
Dt 14:29 have no allotment **o** inheritance of their H2256
Dt 15: 7 not be hardhearted **o** tightfisted toward H2256
Dt 15:12 people—Hebrew men **o** women—sell H196
Dt 15:21 has a defect, is lame **o** blind, or has any H196
Dt 15:21 is lame or blind, **o** has any serious flaw, you NDT
Dt 15:22 may eat it, as if it were gazelle **o** deer. H2256
Dt 16: 2 from your flock **o** herd at the place the H2256
Dt 16:19 Do not pervert justice **o** show partiality. H4202
Dt 17: 1 LORD your God an ox **o** a sheep that has H2256
Dt 17: 1 a sheep that has any defect **o** flaw in it, NDT
Dt 17: 2 If a man **o** woman living among you in one H196
Dt 17: 3 bowing down to them **o** to the sun or the H2256
Dt 17: 3 them or to the sun **o** the moon or the stars H196
Dt 17: 3 the sun or the moon **o** the stars in the sky, H196
Dt 17: 5 take the man **o** woman who has done this H196
Dt 17: 6 On the testimony of two **o** three witnesses a H196
Dt 17: 8 lawsuits **o** assaults—take them H1068
Dt 17:11 they tell you, to the right **o** to the left. H2256
Dt 17:12 contempt for the judge **o** for the priest who H196
Dt 17:16 of horses for himself **o** make the people H2256
Dt 17:17 **o** his heart will be led astray. H2256+4202
Dt 17:20 turn from the law to the right **o** to the left. H2256
Dt 18: 1 to have no allotment **o** inheritance with H2256
Dt 18: 3 the people who sacrifice a bull **o** a sheep: H561

Dt 18:10 sacrifices their son **o** daughter in the fire, H2256
Dt 18:10 who practices divination **o** sorcery H2256
Dt 18:11 **o** casts spells, or who is a medium or H2256
Dt 18:11 **o** who is a medium or spiritist or who H2256
Dt 18:11 who is a medium **o** spiritist or who H2256
Dt 18:11 medium or spiritist **o** who consults the H2256
Dt 18:14 to those who practice sorcery **o** divination. H2256
Dt 18:16 great fire anymore, **o** we will die." H2256+4202
Dt 18:20 **o** a prophet who speaks in the name of H2256
Dt 18:22 the LORD does not take place **o** come true, H2256
Dt 19:15 accused of any crime **o** offense they may H2256
Dt 19:15 by the testimony of two **o** three witnesses. H196
Dt 20: 3 Do not be fainthearted **o** afraid; do not H2256
Dt 20: 3 *do* not panic **o** be terrified by them. H2256
Dt 20: 5 **o** he may die in battle and someone else H7153
Dt 20: 6 **o** he may die in battle and someone else H7153
Dt 20: 7 **o** he may die in battle and someone else H7153
Dt 20: 8 "Is anyone afraid **o** fainthearted? H2256
Dt 21: 4 not been plowed **o** planted and where H2256
Dt 21:14 must not sell her **o** treat her as a slave, H4202
Dt 22: 1 your fellow Israelite's ox **o** sheep straying, H196
Dt 22: 2 do not live near you **o** if you do not know H2256
Dt 22: 3 you find their donkey **o** cloak or anything H2256
Dt 22: 3 their donkey or cloak **o** anything else they H2256
Dt 22: 4 Israelite's donkey **o** ox fallen on the road, H196
Dt 22: 6 the road, **either** in a tree **o** on the ground H196
Dt 22: 6 is sitting on the young **o** on the eggs, H196
Dt 23: 1 by crushing **o** cutting may enter the H2256
Dt 23: 3 No Ammonite **o** Moabite or any of their H2256
Dt 23: 3 No Ammonite or Moabite **o** any of their NDT
Dt 23:17 No Israelite man **o** woman is to become a H2256
Dt 23:18 a female prostitute **o** of a male prostitute H2256
Dt 23:19 whether on money **o** food or anything else NDT
Dt 23:19 on money or food **o** anything else that may NDT
Dt 24: 3 sends her from his house, **o** if he dies, H196
Dt 24: 5 not be sent to war **o** have any other duty H2256
Dt 24: 7 Israelite and treating **o** selling them as a H2256
Dt 24:14 **whether** that worker is a fellow Israelite **o** a H196
Dt 24:17 deprive the foreigner **o** the fatherless of NDT
Dt 24:17 **o** take the cloak of the widow as a pledge. H2256
Dt 27:16 who dishonors their father **o** mother." H2256
Dt 27:19 the foreigner, the fatherless **o** the widow." H2256
Dt 27:22 daughter of his father **o** the daughter of his H196
Dt 28:14 to the right **o** to the left, following H2256
Dt 28:36 a nation unknown to you **o** your ancestors. H2256
Dt 28:39 not drink the wine **o** gather the grapes, H2256
Dt 28:50 respect for the old **o** pity for the young. H2256
Dt 28:51 no grain, new wine **o** olive oil, nor any H2256
Dt 28:51 calves of your herds **o** lambs of your flocks H2256
Dt 28:54 on his own brother **o** the wife he loves H2256
Dt 28:54 the wife he loves **o** his surviving H2256
Dt 28:56 she loves and her own son **o** daughter H2256
Dt 29: 4 that understands **o** eyes that see or ears H2256
Dt 29: 4 eyes that see **o** ears that hear. H2256
Dt 29: 6 drank no wine **o** other fermented H2256
Dt 29:18 Make sure there is no man **o** woman, clan H196
Dt 29:18 clan **o** tribe among you today whose heart H196
Dt 30:11 too difficult for you **o** beyond your reach. H2256
Dt 31: 6 Do not be afraid **o** terrified because of H2256
Dt 32:30 thousand, **o** two put ten thousand to flight H2256
Dt 32:36 is gone and no one is left, slave **o** free. H2256
Dt 33: 9 his brothers **o** acknowledge his own H2256
Dt 33:20 there like a lion, tearing at arm **o** head. H677
Dt 34:12 the mighty power **o** performed the H2256
Jos 1: 7 do not turn from it to the right **o** to the left, H2256
Jos 5:13 "Are you for us **o** for our enemies? H561
Jos 7: 3 Send two **o** three thousand men to take it H196
Jos 8:17 man remained in Ai **o** Bethel who did not H2256
Jos 10:14 never been a day like it before **o** since, H2256
Jos 15:36 Gederah (**o** Gederothaim)— H2256
Jos 19: 2 Beersheba (**o** Sheba), Moladah, H2256
Jos 20: 9 Any of the Israelites **o** any foreigner H2256
Jos 22:19 against the LORD **o** against us by building H2256
Jos 22:22 been in rebellion **o** disobedience to the H2256
Jos 22:23 **o** to sacrifice fellowship offerings on it H2256
Jos 22:26 not for burnt offerings **o** sacrifices. H2256
Jos 22:28 ever say this to us, **o** to our descendants H2256
Jos 23: 6 turning aside to the right **o** to the left. H2256
Jos 23: 7 the names of their gods **o** swear by them. H2256
Jos 23: 7 must not serve them **o** bow down to them. H2256
Jos 24:15 the Euphrates, **o** the gods of the Amorites H561
Jdg 1:27 people of Beth Shan **o** Taanach or Dor H2256
Jdg 1:27 Beth Shan or Taanach **o** Dor or Ibleam H2256
Jdg 1:27 Taanach or Dor **o** Ibleam or Megiddo H2256
Jdg 1:27 Dor or Ibleam **o** Megiddo and their H2256
Jdg 1:30 the Canaanites living in Kitron **o** Nahalol, H2256
Jdg 1:31 those living in Akko **o** Sidon or Ahlab H2256
Jdg 1:31 in Akko or Sidon **o** Ahlab or Akzib or H2256
Jdg 1:31 Sidon or Ahlab **o** Akzib or Helbah or H2256
Jdg 1:31 Ahlab or Akzib **o** Helbah or Aphek or H2256
Jdg 1:31 Akzib or Helbah **o** Aphek or Rehob. H2256
Jdg 1:31 Akzib or Helbah or Aphek **o** Rehob. H2256
Jdg 1:33 living in Beth Shemesh **o** Beth Anath; H2256
Jdg 5: 8 not a shield **o** spear was seen among H2256
Jdg 5:30 a woman **o** two for each man, colorful NDT
Jdg 6: 5 impossible to count them **o** their camels; H2256
Jdg 7: 2 **o** Israel would boast against me H7153
Jdg 8:26 the kings of Midian **o** the chains that were H2256
Jdg 9: 2 sons rule over you, **o** just one man? H561
Jdg 11:15 take the land of Moab **o** the land of the H2256
Jdg 11:25 ever quarrel with Israel **o** fight with them? H561
Jdg 13: 4 you drink no wine **o** other fermented drink H2256
Jdg 13: 7 drink no wine **o** other fermented drink H2256
Jdg 13:14 drink any wine **o** other fermented H2256
Jdg 13:23 us all these things **o** now told us this." H2256
Jdg 14: 3 your relatives **o** among all our people H2256
Jdg 14:15 **o** we will burn you and your father's H7153
Jdg 14:16 even explained it to my father **o** mother," H2256
Jdg 18:25 **o** some of the men may get angry and H7153
Jdg 19:13 to reach Gibeah **o** Ramah and spend the H196
Jdg 19:30 a thing has never been seen **o** done, H2256
Jdg 20:28 the Benjamites, our fellow Israelites, **o** not?" H561
Jdg 21:22 When their fathers **o** brothers complain to H196
Ru 1:16 urge me to leave you **o** to turn back from NDT
Ru 3:10 younger men, whether rich **o** poor. H561+2256
Ru 4:10 among his family **o** from his hometown. H2256
1Sa 1:15 I have not been drinking wine **o** beer; H2256
1Sa 2: 3 talking so proudly **o** let your mouth speak NDT
1Sa 2:14 the fork into the pan **o** kettle or caldron H196
1Sa 2:14 fork into the pan or kettle **o** caldron or pot. H196
1Sa 2:14 fork into the pan or kettle or caldron **o** pot. H196
1Sa 3:14 never be atoned for by sacrifice **o** offering. H2256
1Sa 4: 9 **o** you will be subject to the Hebrews H7153
1Sa 4:20 she did not respond **o** pay any attention. H2256
1Sa 5:11 **o** it will kill us and our people." H2256+4202
1Sa 6:12 they did not turn to the right **o** to the left. H2256
1Sa 9: 5 **o** my father will stop thinking about the H7153
1Sa 12: 4 "You have not cheated **o** oppressed us," H2256
1Sa 13:19 the Hebrews will make swords **o** spears!" H196
1Sa 13:22 had a sword **o** spear in his hand; H2256
1Sa 14: 6 from saving, **whether** by many **o** by few." H196
1Sa 14:41 If the fault is in me **o** my son Jonathan H196
1Sa 14:52 Saul saw a mighty **o** brave man, H2256
1Sa 15:29 of Israel does not lie **o** change his mind; H2256
1Sa 16: 7 not consider his appearance **o** his height, H2256
1Sa 17:34 When a lion **o** a bear came and carried H2256
1Sa 17:47 it is not by sword **o** spear that the LORD H2256
1Sa 18:18 what is my family **o** my clan in Israel NDT
1Sa 20: 2 do anything, great **o** small, without letting H196
1Sa 20: 3 must not know this **o** he will be grieved. H7153
1Sa 20:27 to the meal, either yesterday **o** today?" H1685
1Sa 21: 3 loaves of bread, **o** whatever you can find." H196
1Sa 21: 8 "Don't you have a spear **o** a sword here? H196
1Sa 21: 8 my sword **o** any other weapon H2256+1685
1Sa 22: 2 who were in distress **o** in debt or H2256
1Sa 22: 2 distress or in debt **o** discontented H2256
1Sa 22: 8 concerned about me **o** tells me that my H2256
1Sa 22:15 king accuse your servant **o** any of his father's NDT
1Sa 24: 6 the LORD's anointed, **o** lay my hand on him NDT
1Sa 24:11 I am guilty of wrongdoing **o** rebellion. H2256
1Sa 24:21 off my descendants **o** wipe out my name H561
1Sa 25:31 needless bloodshed **o** of having avenged H2256
1Sa 26:10 **o** his time will come and he will die H196
1Sa 26:10 will die, **o** he will go into battle and perish. H196
1Sa 26:12 No one saw **o** knew about it, nor did H2256
1Sa 27: 9 he did not leave a man **o** woman alive H2256
1Sa 27:10 **o** "Against the Negev of Jerahmeel H2256
1Sa 27:10 **o** "Against the Negev of the Kenites." H2256
1Sa 27:11 did not leave a man **o** woman alive to be H2256
1Sa 28: 6 him by dreams **o** Urim or prophets. H1685
1Sa 28: 6 him by dreams or Urim **o** prophets. H1685
1Sa 28:15 either by prophets **o** by dreams. H1685
1Sa 28:18 did not obey the LORD **o** carry out his H2256
1Sa 29: 4 **o** he will turn against us during the H2256+4202
1Sa 30:12 not eaten any food **o** drunk any water H2256
1Sa 30:15 you will not kill me **o** hand me over to my H2256
1Sa 30:19 young **o** old, boy or girl, plunder or H2256
1Sa 30:19 young or old, boy **o** girl, plunder or H2256
1Sa 30:19 plunder **o** anything else they had taken. H2256
1Sa 31: 4 **o** these uncircumcised fellows will come H7153
2Sa 2:21 "Turn aside to the right **o** to the left; take H196
2Sa 3:29 has a running sore **o** leprosy or who leans H2256
2Sa 3:29 sore or leprosy **o** who leans on a crutch H2256
2Sa 3:29 who leans on a crutch **o** who falls by the H2256
2Sa 3:29 who falls by the sword **o** who lacks food." H2256
2Sa 3:35 if I taste bread **o** anything else before the H196
2Sa 6:21 than your father **o** anyone from his house H2256
2Sa 12: 4 of his own sheep **o** cattle to prepare a H2256
2Sa 13:22 Amnon, either good **o** bad; he hated H2256
2Sa 14:19 can turn to the right **o** to the left from H2256
2Sa 15: 4 has a complaint **o** case could come to H2256
2Sa 15:14 **o** none of us will escape from Absalom. H3954
2Sa 15:14 **o** he will move quickly to overtake us and H7153
2Sa 15:21 whether it means life **o** death, there will H561
2Sa 17: 9 he is hidden in a cave **o** some other place. H196
2Sa 17:16 **o** the king and all the people with him H7153
2Sa 19:24 care of his feet **o** trimmed his mustache H2256
2Sa 19:24 his mustache **o** washed his clothes H2256
2Sa 20: 6 **o** he will find fortified cities and escape H7153
2Sa 20:20 it from me to swallow up **o** destroy! H2256+561
2Sa 21: 4 to demand silver **o** gold from Saul or his H2256
2Sa 21: 4 silver or gold from Saul **o** his family, H2256
2Sa 21:10 touch them by day **o** the wild animals by H2256
2Sa 23: 7 uses a tool of iron **o** the shaft of a spear; H2256
2Sa 24:13 **O** three months of fleeing from your H561
2Sa 24:13 **O** three days of plague in your land H561
1Ki 1:10 Nathan the prophet **o** Benaiah or the H2256
1Ki 1:10 prophet or Benaiah **o** the special guard H2256
1Ki 1:10 the special guard **o** his brother Solomon. H2256
1Ki 3: 8 people, too numerous to count **o** number. H2256
1Ki 3:11 not for long life **o** wealth for yourself, H2256
1Ki 5: 4 and there is no adversary **o** disaster. H2256
1Ki 6: 7 chisel **o** any other iron tool was heard at the NDT
1Ki 8: 5 they could not be recorded **o** counted. H2256
1Ki 8:23 you in heaven above **o** on earth below— H2256
1Ki 8:37 "When famine **o** plague comes to the land NDT
1Ki 8:37 comes to the land, **o** blight or mildew NDT
1Ki 8:37 to the land, or blight **o** mildew, locusts or NDT
1Ki 8:37 mildew, locusts **o** grasshoppers, or when NDT
1Ki 8:37 **o** when an enemy besieges them in any of NDT
1Ki 8:37 whatever disaster **o** disease may come, NDT
1Ki 8:38 when a prayer **o** plea is made by NDT
1Ki 8:46 to their own lands, far away **o** near; H196
1Ki 9: 6 "But if you **o** your descendants turn away H2256
1Ki 10:12 been imported **o** seen since that day H2256
1Ki 13: 8 would I eat bread **o** drink water here. H2256
1Ki 13: 9 must not eat bread **o** drink water or return H2256
1Ki 13: 9 bread or drink water **o** return by the way H2256
1Ki 13:16 can I eat bread **o** drink water with you H2256
1Ki 13:17 must not eat bread **o** drink water there H2256
1Ki 13:17 drink water there **o** return by the way H4202
1Ki 13:22 where he told you not to eat **o** drink. H2256
1Ki 14:10 every last male in Israel—slave **o** free. H2256
1Ki 15:17 anyone from leaving **o** entering the H2256
1Ki 16:11 a single male, whether relative **o** friend. H2256
1Ki 18:10 there is not a nation **o** kingdom where my H2256
1Ki 18:10 whenever a nation **o** kingdom claimed H2256
1Ki 18:27 deep in thought, **o** busy, or H2256+3954
1Ki 18:27 in thought, or busy, **o** traveling. H2256+3954
1Ki 20: 8 listen to him **o** agree to his demands H2256
1Ki 20:39 **o** you must pay a talent of silver. H196
1Ki 21: 2 exchange I will give you a better vineyard **o**, NDT
1Ki 21: 6 'Sell me your vineyard; **o** if you prefer, I will H196
1Ki 21:21 every last male in Israel—slave **o** free. H2256
1Ki 22: 6 against Ramoth Gilead, **o** shall I refrain?" H561
1Ki 22:15 go to war against Ramoth Gilead, **o** not?" H561
1Ki 22:31 with anyone, small **o** great, except the H2256
2Ki 2:16 down on some mountain **o** in some valley." H196
2Ki 2:21 again will it cause death **o** make the land H2256
2Ki 3: 9 themselves **o** for the animals with H2256
2Ki 4:13 behalf to the king **o** the commander of the H196
2Ki 4:23 "It's not the New Moon **o** the Sabbath." H2256
2Ki 4:31 but there was no sound **o** response. H2256
2Ki 5:26 time to take money **o** to accept clothes— H2256
2Ki 5:26 clothes—**o** olive groves and vineyards H2256
2Ki 5:26 vineyards, **o** flocks and herds, or H2256
2Ki 5:26 herds, **o** male and female slaves? H2256
2Ki 6:22 captured with your own sword **o** bow? H2256
2Ki 9: 8 every last male in Israel—slave **o** free. H2256
2Ki 9:32 Two **o** three eunuchs looked down at him NDT
2Ki 12:13 trumpets **o** any other articles of gold or silver NDT
2Ki 12:13 articles of gold **o** silver for the temple H2256
2Ki 13:19 have struck the ground five **o** six times; H196
2Ki 13:23 to destroy them **o** banish them from his H2256
2Ki 14:26 whether slave **o** free, was suffering; H2256+700
2Ki 17:35 any other gods **o** bow down to them, H2256
2Ki 17:35 to them, serve them **o** sacrifice to them. H2256
2Ki 18: 5 of Judah, **either** before him **o** after him. H2256
2Ki 19:13 the king of Hamath **o** the king of Arpad? H2256
2Ki 19:32 not enter this city **o** shoot an arrow here. H2256
2Ki 19:32 before it with shield **o** build a siege ramp H2256
2Ki 20: 9 ten steps, **o** shall it go back ten steps?" H561
2Ki 20:13 nothing in his palace **o** in all his kingdom H2256
2Ki 22: 2 not turning aside to the right **o** to the left. H2256
2Ki 23:10 to sacrifice their son **o** daughter in the fire H2256
2Ki 25:15 all that were made of pure gold **o** silver. H2256
1Ch 10: 4 **o** these uncircumcised fellows will come H7153
1Ch 12: 2 able to shoot arrows **o** to sling stones H2256
1Ch 12: 2 sling stones right-handed **o** left-handed; H2256
1Ch 21:12 **o** three days of the sword of the LORD H2256+561
1Ch 21:24 **o** sacrifice a burnt offering that costs me H2256
1Ch 22:13 Do not be afraid **o** discouraged. H2256
1Ch 23: 3 thirty years old **o** more were counted, H2256
1Ch 23:24 twenty years old **o** more who served in the H2256
1Ch 23:26 carry the tabernacle **o** any of the articles H2256
1Ch 23:27 from those twenty years old **o** more. H2256
1Ch 27:23 of the men twenty years old **o** less, H2256
1Ch 28:20 Do not be afraid **o** discouraged, for the H2256
1Ch 28:20 He will not fail you **o** forsake you until all H2256
2Ch 1:11 possessions **o** honor, nor for the H2256
2Ch 5: 6 they could not be recorded **o** counted. H2256
2Ch 6:14 is no God like you in heaven **o** on earth— H2256
2Ch 6:28 "When famine **o** plague comes to the land NDT
2Ch 6:28 comes to the land, **o** blight or mildew NDT
2Ch 6:28 to the land, or blight **o** mildew, locusts H2256
2Ch 6:28 mildew, locusts **o** grasshoppers, or H2256
2Ch 6:28 **o** when enemies besiege them in any of NDT
2Ch 6:28 whatever disaster **o** disease may come, H2256
2Ch 6:29 when a prayer **o** plea is made by NDT
2Ch 6:36 them captive to a land far away **o** near; H196
2Ch 7:13 **o** command locusts to devour the land H2256
2Ch 7:13 to devour the land **o** send a plague H2256
2Ch 8:15 to the priests **o** to the Levites in any H2256
2Ch 15:13 whether small **o** great, man or woman. H6330
2Ch 15:13 whether small or great, man **o** woman. H6330
2Ch 16: 1 anyone from leaving **o** entering the H2256
2Ch 18: 5 war against Ramoth Gilead, **o** shall I not?" H561
2Ch 18:14 war against Ramoth Gilead, **o** shall I not?" H561
2Ch 18:30 with anyone, small **o** great, except the king NDT
2Ch 19: 7 there is no injustice **o** partiality or bribery." H2256
2Ch 19: 7 there is no injustice or partiality **o** bribery." H2256
2Ch 19:10 whether bloodshed **o** other concerns of the H1068
2Ch 19:10 commands, decrees **o** regulations—you H2256
2Ch 20: 9 **whether** the sword of judgment, **o** plague H2256
2Ch 20: 9 judgment, or plague **o** famine, we will H2256
2Ch 20:15 'Do not be afraid **o** discouraged because H2256

2Ch 21:12 father Jehoshaphat **o** of Asa king of H2256
2Ch 25: 5 twenty years old **o** more and found that H2256
2Ch 25: 8 God has the power to help **o** to overthrow." H2256
2Ch 28:13 "**o** we will be guilty before the LORD. H3954
2Ch 29: 7 did not burn incense **o** present any burnt H2256
2Ch 31: 2 to their duties as priests **o** Levites— H2256
2Ch 31:16 three years old **o** more whose names H2256
2Ch 31:17 to the Levites twenty years old **o** more, H2256
2Ch 31:19 around their towns **o** in any other towns, NDT
2Ch 32: 7 Do not be afraid **o** discouraged because H2256
2Ch 32:15 no god of any nation **o** kingdom has been H2256
2Ch 32:15 people from my hand **o** the hand of my H2256
2Ch 34: 2 not turning aside to the right **o** to the left. H2256
2Ch 35:21 is with me, **o** he will destroy you." H2256+440
2Ch 36:17 not spare young men **o** young women, H2256
2Ch 36:17 young women, the elderly **o** the infirm. H2256
Ezr 4:13 more taxes, tribute **o** duty will be paid A10221
Ezr 6:12 overthrow any king **o** people who lifts a A10221
Ezr 6:12 to change this decree **o** to destroy this NDT
Ezr 7:24 tribute **o** duty on any of the priests A10221
Ezr 7:24 temple servants **o** other workers at this A10221
Ezr 7:26 confiscation of property, **o** imprisonment. A10221
Ezr 9:12 to their sons **o** take their daughters H2256
Ezr 9:14 leaving us no remnant **o** survivor? H2256
Ezr 10:13 cannot be taken care of in a day **o** two, H2256
Ne 2:16 where I had gone **o** what I was doing, H2256
Ne 2:16 nothing to the Jews **o** the priests or H2256
Ne 2:16 Jews or the priests **o** nobles or officials H2256
Ne 2:16 the priests or nobles **o** officials or any H2256
Ne 2:16 nobles or officials **o** any others who would H2256
Ne 2:20 share in Jerusalem **o** any claim or historic H2256
Ne 2:20 any claim **o** historic right to it. H2256
Ne 4: 5 cover up their guilt **o** blot out their sins H2256
Ne 4:11 "Before they know it **o** see us, we will be H2256
Ne 6:11 **O** should someone like me go into the H2256
Ne 8: 9 Do not mourn **o** weep." For all the H2256
Ne 9:18 **o** when they committed awful H2256
Ne 9:31 not put an end to them **o** abandon them, H2256
Ne 9:34 to your commands **o** the statutes you H2256
Ne 9:35 did not serve you **o** turn from their evil H2256
Ne 10:30 peoples around us **o** take their daughters H2256
Ne 10:31 bring merchandise **o** grain to sell on the H2256
Ne 10:31 them on the Sabbath **o** on any holy day. H2256
Ne 13: 1 that no Ammonite **o** Moabite should ever H2256
Ne 13:20 Once **o** twice the merchants and sellers of H2256
Ne 13:24 language of Ashdod **o** the language of H2256
Ne 13:25 in marriage for your sons **o** for yourselves. H2256
Est 3: 2 would not kneel down **o** pay him honor. H2256
Est 3: 5 would not kneel down **o** pay him honor, H2256
Est 4:11 that for any man **o** woman who H2256
Est 4:16 Do not eat **o** drink for three days, night H2256
Est 4:16 eat or drink for three days, night **o** day. H2256
Est 8:11 of any nationality **o** province who might H2256
Job 3:16 **O** why was I not hidden away in the ground H196
Job 6: 5 **o** an ox bellow when it has fodder? H561
Job 6: 6 **o** is there flavor in the sap of the mallow? H561
Job 7: 2 **o** a hired laborer waiting to be paid, H2256
Job 7:12 Am I the sea, **o** the monster of the deep H561
Job 7:19 **o** let me alone even for an instant? H4202
Job 8:20 who is blameless **o** strengthen the hands H2256
Job 10: 5 those of a mortal **o** your years like those H561
Job 10:19 **o** had been carried straight from the womb NDT
Job 12: 7 they will teach you, **o** the birds in the sky H2256
Job 12: 8 **o** speak to the earth, and it will teach you H196
Job 12: 8 **o** let the fish in the sea inform you. H2256
Job 13:22 I will answer, **o** let me speak, and you H196
Job 14:11 of a lake dries up **o** a riverbed becomes H2256
Job 14:12 will not awake **o** be roused from their H2256
Job 15: 2 with empty notions **o** fill their belly with H2256
Job 15:14 could be pure, **o** those born of woman H2256
Job 17:14 to the worm, 'My mother' **o** 'My sister,' H2256
Job 18: 4 **O** must the rocks be moved from their H2256
Job 18:19 has no offspring **o** descendants among H2256
Job 19:24 iron tool on lead, **o** engraved in rock forever! NDT
Job 24:13 do not know its ways **o** stay in its paths. H2256
Job 28:16 of Ophir, with precious onyx **o** lapis lazuli. H2256
Job 31: 5 with falsehood **o** my foot has hurried H2256
Job 31: 7 **o** if my hands have been defiled, H2256
Job 31: 9 **o** if I have lurked at my neighbor's door H2256
Job 31:13 servants, **whether** male **o** female, when H2256
Job 31:16 desires of the poor **o** let the eyes of the H2256
Job 31:19 clothing, **o** the needy without garments, H2256
Job 31:24 put my trust in gold **o** said to pure gold, H2256
Job 31:26 sun in its radiance **o** the moon moving in H2256
Job 31:29 my enemy's misfortune **o** gloated over the H2256
Job 31:39 without payment **o** broken the spirit of H2256
Job 33:19 "**O** someone may be chastened on a bed H2256
Job 35: 7 **o** what does he receive from your hand? H196
Job 36:19 Would your wealth **o** *even* all your mighty H2256
Job 36:23 his ways for him, **o** said to him, 'You have H2256
Job 37:13 **o** to water his earth and show his love. H561
Job 38: 6 its footings set, **o** who laid its cornerstone H196
Job 38:12 to the morning, **o** shown the dawn its place, NDT
Job 38:16 springs of the sea **o** walked in the H2256
Job 38:22 of the snow **o** seen the storehouses of H2256
Job 38:24 **o** the place where the east winds are NDT
Job 38:32 in their seasons **o** lead out the Bear with H2256
Job 38:36 gives the ibis wisdom **o** gives the rooster H196
Job 38:40 crouch in their dens **o** lie in wait in a thicket NDT
Job 39:17 her with wisdom **o** give her a share H2256+4202
Job 39:19 horse its strength **o** clothe its neck with a H2022
Job 40:24 it by the eyes, **o** trap it and pierce its nose? NDT
Job 41: 1 with a fishhook **o** tie down its tongue with H2256
Job 41: 2 through its nose **o** pierce its jaw with a H2256
Job 41: 5 pet of it like a bird **o** put it on a leash H2256
Job 41: 7 hide with harpoons **o** its head with fishing H2256
Job 41:26 does the spear **o** the dart or the javelin. NDT
Job 41:26 does the spear or the dart **o** the javelin. H2256
Ps 1: 1 step with the wicked **o** stand in the way H2256
Ps 1: 1 that sinners take **o** sit in the company of H2256
Ps 2:12 **o** he will be angry and your way will lead H7153
Ps 6: 1 me in your anger **o** discipline me in your H2256
Ps 7: 2 **o** they will tear me apart like a lion and H7153
Ps 7: 4 my ally with evil **o** without cause have H2256
Ps 13: 3 light to my eyes, **o** I will sleep in death, H7153
Ps 16: 4 blood to such gods **o** take up their names H2256
Ps 22:24 he has not despised **o** scorned the H2256
Ps 24: 4 not trust in an idol **o** swear by a false god. H2256
Ps 27: 9 Do not reject me **o** forsake me, God my H2256
Ps 32: 9 Do not be like the horse **o** the mule, which NDT
Ps 32: 9 by bit and bridle **o** they will not come to you NDT
Ps 35:14 mourning as though for my friend **o** brother. NDT
Ps 35:25 just what we wanted!" **o** say, "We have H440
Ps 36: 2 too much to detect **o** hate their sin. NDT
Ps 36: 3 deceitful; they fail to act wisely **o** do good. NDT
Ps 37: 1 of those who are evil **o** be envious of those H440
Ps 37:25 righteous forsaken **o** their children H2256
Ps 37:33 power of the wicked **o** let them be H2256
Ps 38: 1 me in your anger **o** discipline me in your H2256
Ps 38:16 not let them gloat **o** exalt themselves over NDT
Ps 44:20 the name of our God **o** spread out our H2256
Ps 49: 7 the life of another **o** give to God a ransom H4202
Ps 50: 8 your sacrifices **o** concerning your burnt H2256
Ps 50: 9 a bull from your stall **o** of goats from your NDT
Ps 50:13 eat the flesh of bulls **o** drink the blood of H2256
Ps 50:16 to recite my laws **o** take my covenant on H2256
Ps 50:22 who forget God, **o** I will tear you to pieces H7153
Ps 51:11 from your presence **o** take your Holy Spirit H2256
Ps 51:16 delight in sacrifice, **o** I would bring it; you H2256
Ps 58: 9 whether they be green **o** dry—the wicked H4017
Ps 59: 3 against me for no offense **o** sin of mine, H2256
Ps 59:11 Lord our shield, **o** my people will forget. H7153
Ps 62:10 not trust in extortion **o** put vain hope in H2256
Ps 66:20 rejected my prayer **o** withheld his love H2256
Ps 69:15 engulf me **o** the depths swallow me H2256
Ps 69:15 depths swallow me up **o** the pit close its H2256
Ps 75: 6 one from the east **o** the west or from the H2256
Ps 75: 6 the east or the west **o** from the desert can H2256
Ps 78:22 did not believe in God **o** trust in his H2256
Ps 83:14 consumes the forest **o** a flame sets the H2256
Ps 88:12 **o** your righteous deeds in the land of H2256
Ps 89:34 violate my covenant **o** alter what my lips H2256
Ps 89:48 **o** who can escape the power of the grave? NDT
Ps 90: 2 mountains were born **o** you brought forth H2256
Ps 90: 4 just gone by, **o** like a watch in the night. H2256
Ps 90:10 come to seventy years, **o** eighty, if our H2256
Ps 103:10 as our sins deserve **o** repay us according H2256
Ps 106: 2 mighty acts of the LORD **o** fully declare his NDT
Ps 109:12 extend kindness to him **o** take pity on his H2256
Ps 131: 1 with great matters **o** things too wonderful H2256
Ps 132: 3 "I will not enter my house **o** go to my bed, H561
Ps 132: 4 no sleep to my eyes **o** slumber to my eyelids NDT
Ps 143: 7 your face from me **o** I will be like those H2256
Pr 2:19 who go to her return **o** attain the paths of H2256
Pr 3:25 fear of sudden disaster **o** of the ruin that H2256
Pr 3:31 not envy the violent **o** choose any of their H2256
Pr 4: 5 forget my words **o** turn away from them H2256
Pr 4:14 path of the wicked **o** walk in the way of H2256
Pr 4:27 Do not turn to the right **o** the left; keep H2256
Pr 5:13 not obey my teachers **o** turn my ear to my H2256
Pr 6: 7 It has no commander, no overseer **o** ruler, H2256
Pr 6:25 after her beauty **o** let her captivate you H2256
Pr 7:25 heart turn to her ways **o** stray into her paths. NDT
Pr 8: 8 none of them is crooked **o** perverse. H2256
Pr 8:26 he made the world **o** its fields or any of H2256
Pr 8:26 world or its fields **o** any of the dust of the H2256
Pr 9: 8 not rebuke mockers **o** they will hate you; H7153
Pr 20:13 Do not love sleep **o** you will grow poor H7153
Pr 20:20 If someone curses their father **o** mother H2256
Pr 22: 1 be esteemed is better than silver **o** gold. H2256
Pr 22:25 **o** you may learn their ways and get H7153
Pr 22:26 hands in pledge **o** puts up security for NDT
Pr 23:10 boundary stone **o** encroach on the fields H2256
Pr 23:20 drink too much wine **o** gorge themselves on NDT
Pr 24:18 **o** the LORD will see and disapprove and H7153
Pr 24:19 because of evildoers **o** be envious of the H440
Pr 25:10 **o** the one who hears it may shame you H7153
Pr 25:12 an earring of gold **o** an ornament of fine H2256
Pr 25:18 Like a club **o** a sword or a sharp arrow is H2256
Pr 25:18 a club or a sword **o** a sharp arrow is one H2256
Pr 25:19 Like a broken tooth **o** a lame foot is H2256
Pr 25:20 cold day, **o** like vinegar poured on a wound NDT
Pr 25:26 a muddied spring **o** a polluted well are H2256
Pr 26: 1 Like snow in summer **o** rain in harvest H2256
Pr 26: 2 Like a fluttering sparrow **o** a darting swallow, NDT
Pr 26: 4 **o** you yourself will be just like him. H7153
Pr 26: 5 **o** he will be wise in his own eyes. H7153
Pr 26: 6 like cutting off one's feet **o** drinking poison. NDT
Pr 26:10 is one who hires a fool **o** any passer-by. H2256
Pr 27:10 forsake your friend **o** a friend of your H2256
Pr 27:16 restraining the wind **o** grasping oil with H2256
Pr 28: 8 by taking interest **o** profit from the poor H2256
Pr 28:15 Like a roaring lion **o** a charging bear is a H2256
Pr 28:24 robs their father **o** mother and says, H2256
Pr 30: 6 **o** he will rebuke you and prove you a liar. H7153
Pr 30: 9 **O** I may become poor and steal, and so H7153
Pr 30:10 to their master, **o** they will curse you, and H7153
Pr 30:32 exalt yourself, **o** if you plan evil, clap H2256
Ecc 2:19 whether that person will be wise **o** foolish? H196
Ecc 2:25 who can eat **o** find enjoyment? H2256
Ecc 4:14 **o** he may have been born in H3954+1685
Ecc 5:12 whether they eat little **o** much, but as H2256
Ecc 5:14 **o** wealth lost through some misfortune, so H2256
Ecc 6: 5 it never saw the sun **o** knew anything, H2256
Ecc 7:21 **o** you may hear your servant cursing H889+4202
Ecc 8:16 people getting no sleep day **o** night— H2256
Ecc 9: 1 knows whether love **o** hate awaits them. H1685
Ecc 9:11 is not to the swift **o** the battle to the H2256
Ecc 9:11 come to the wise **o** wealth to the H2256+1685
Ecc 9:11 to the brilliant **o** favor to the H2256+1685
Ecc 9:12 in a cruel net, **o** birds are taken in a snare H2256
Ecc 10:20 thoughts, **o** curse the rich in your bedroom H2256
Ecc 11: 3 a tree falls to the south **o** to the north, H561
Ecc 11: 5 **o** how the body is formed in a mother's NDT
Ecc 11: 6 whether this **o** that, or whether both H196
Ecc 11: 6 **o** whether both will do equally well. H2256
Ecc 12:14 hidden thing, whether it is good **o** evil. H2256
SS 2: 7 Do not arouse **o** awaken love until it so H2256
SS 2: 9 beloved is like a gazelle **o** a young stag. H196
SS 2:17 be like a gazelle **o** like a young stag on H196
SS 3: 5 Do not arouse **o** awaken love until it so H2256
SS 6:11 the vines had budded **o** the pomegranates NDT
SS 8: 4 Do not arouse **o** awaken love until it so H2256
SS 8:14 be like a gazelle **o** like a young stag on H196
Isa 1: 6 not cleansed **o** bandaged or soothed with H2256
Isa 1: 6 bandaged **o** soothed with olive H2256
Isa 3: 7 I have no food **o** clothing in my house; do H2256
Isa 5:27 Not one of them grows tired **o** stumbles H2256
Isa 5:27 not one slumbers **o** sleeps; not a belt is H2256
Isa 7:11 **whether** in the deepest depths **o** in the H196
Isa 8: 4 how to say 'My father' **o** 'My mother, H2256
Isa 10: 4 among the captives **o** fall among the H2256
Isa 10:14 **o** opened its mouth to chirp. H2256
Isa 10:15 **o** the saw boast against the one who uses H561
Isa 10:15 **o** a club brandish the one who is not wood! NDT
Isa 11: 3 **o** decide by what he hears with his ears; H2256
Isa 13:20 never be inhabited **o** lived in through all H2256
Isa 16:10 no one sings **o** shouts in the vineyards H4202
Isa 17: 6 leaving two **o** three olives on the topmost NDT
Isa 17: 6 branches, four **o** five on the fruitful boughs," NDT
Isa 19:15 Egypt can do—head **o** tail, palm branch H2256
Isa 19:15 head or tail, palm branch **o** reed. H2256
Isa 21: 7 riders on donkeys **o** riders on camels, let NDT
Isa 22:11 **o** have regard for the One who planned it H2256
Isa 23: 1 destroyed and left without house **o** harbor. NDT
Isa 23:18 they will not be stored up **o** hoarded. H2256
Isa 24:13 **o** as when gleanings are left after the grape NDT
Isa 27: 5 **O else** let them come to me for refuge; let H196
Isa 27: 9 no Asherah poles **o** incense altars will be H2256
Isa 28:22 **o** your chains will become heavier H7153
Isa 29:12 **O** if you give the scroll to someone who H2256
Isa 30:14 coals from a hearth **o** scooping water out H2256
Isa 30:21 Whether you turn to the right **o** to the left H2256
Isa 31: 1 One of Israel, **o** seek help from the LORD. H2256
Isa 31: 4 by their shouts **o** disturbed by their clamor H2256
Isa 34:10 It will not be quenched night **o** day; its H2256
Isa 37:13 the king of Hamath **o** the king of Arpad? H2256
Isa 37:33 not enter this city **o** shoot an arrow here. H2256
Isa 37:33 before it with shield **o** build a siege ramp H2256
Isa 38:11 **o** be with those who now dwell in this world. NDT
Isa 38:14 I cried like a swift **o** thrush, I moaned like a NDT
Isa 39: 2 nothing in his palace **o** in all his kingdom H2256
Isa 40:12 **o** with the breadth of his hand marked off H2256
Isa 40:12 **o** weighed the mountains on the scales H2256
Isa 40:13 **o** instruct the LORD as his counselor? H2256
Isa 40:14 **o** showed him the path of understanding? H2256
Isa 40:25 will you compare me? **O** who is my equal?" H2256
Isa 40:28 He will not grow tired **o** weary, and his H2256
Isa 41:22 **O** declare to us the things to come, H196
Isa 41:23 whether good **o** bad, so that we will be H2256
Isa 41:26 so we could know, **o** beforehand, so we H2256
Isa 42: 2 He will not shout **o** cry out, or raise his H2256
Isa 42: 2 cry out, **o** raise his voice in the streets. H2256
Isa 42: 4 he will not falter **o** be discouraged till he H2256
Isa 42: 8 my glory to another **o** my praise to idols. H2256
Isa 42:22 them trapped in pits **o** hidden away in H2256
Isa 42:23 will listen to this **o** pay close attention in NDT
Isa 43:24 **o** lavished on me the fat of your sacrifices. H2256
Isa 44:14 **o** perhaps took a cypress or oak. H2256
Isa 44:14 or perhaps took a cypress **o** oak. H2256
Isa 44:14 trees of the forest, **o** planted a pine, and the NDT
Isa 44:19 has the knowledge **o** understanding to H2256
Isa 44:20 cannot save himself, **o** say, "Is not this H2256
Isa 45:10 **o** to a mother, 'What have you brought to H2256
Isa 45:11 **o** give me orders about the work of my H2256
Isa 45:13 not for a price **o** reward, says the LORD H2256
Isa 45:17 will never be put to shame **o** disgraced, H2256
Isa 46: 5 will you compare me **o** count me equal? H2256
Isa 47: 1 more will you be called tender **o** delicate. H2256
Isa 47: 7 these things **o** reflect on what might H4202
Isa 47: 8 I will never be a widow **o** suffer the loss of H2256
Isa 48: 1 not in truth **o** righteousness— H2256
Isa 49:10 the desert heat **o** the sun beat down on H2256
Isa 49:24 **o** captives be rescued from the fierce? H2256
Isa 50: 1 **O** to which of my creditors did I sell you H196
Isa 51: 7 of mere mortals **o** be terrified by their H2256

Book	Ref	Context	Number
Isa	52:12	you will not leave in haste **o** go in flight;	H2256
Isa	53: 2	He had no beauty **o** majesty to attract us	H2256
Isa	56:12	will be like today, **o** even far better.	NDT
Isa	58:13	as you please **o** speaking idle words	H2256
Isa	60:11	never be shut, day **o** night, so that people	H2256
Isa	60:12	For the nation **o** kingdom that will not	H2256
Isa	60:18	ruin **o** destruction within your borders	H2256
Isa	62: 4	Deserted, **o** name your land Desolate.	H2256
Isa	62: 6	they will never be silent day **o** night.	H2256
Isa	63:16	does not know us **o** Israel acknowledge us	H2256
Isa	64: 7	calls on your name **o** strives to lay hold of	NDT
Isa	65:20	**o** an old man who does not live out his	H2256
Isa	65:22	live in them, **o** plant and others eat.	H4202
Isa	66: 8	be born in a day **o** a nation be brought	H561
Isa	66:19	not heard of my fame **o** seen my glory.	H2256
Jer	1:17	by them, **o** I will terrify you before them.	H7153
Jer	2:31	been a desert to Israel **o** a land of great	H561
Jer	3:16	enter their minds **o** be remembered;	H2256
Jer	4: 4	**o** my wrath will flare up and burn like fire	H7153
Jer	4:11	my people, but not to winnow **o** cleanse;	H2256
Jer	5:12	we will never see sword **o** famine.	H2256
Jer	6: 8	**o** I will turn away from you and make your	H7153
Jer	6:20	from Sheba **o** sweet calamus from	H2256
Jer	6:25	go out to the fields **o** walk on the roads,	H2256
Jer	7: 6	the fatherless **o** the widow and do not	H2256
Jer	7:16	offer any plea **o** petition for them;	H2256
Jer	7:24	But they did not listen **o** pay attention	H2256
Jer	7:26	they did not listen to me **o** pay attention.	H2256
Jer	7:28	the LORD its God **o** responded to correction	H2256
Jer	7:32	longer call it Topheth **o** the Valley of Ben	H2256
Jer	8: 2	They will not be gathered up **o** buried	H2256
Jer	9:13	have not obeyed me **o** followed my law.	H2256
Jer	9:23	of their wisdom **o** the strong boast of their	H2256
Jer	9:23	of their strength **o** the rich boast of their	H440
Jer	10: 2	ways of the nations **o** be terrified by signs	H2256
Jer	10:20	to pitch my tent **o** to set up my shelter	H2256
Jer	10:24	**o** you will reduce me to nothing.	H7153
Jer	11: 8	But they did not listen **o** pay attention	H2256
Jer	11:14	this people **o** offer any plea or	H2256+440
Jer	11:14	offer any plea **o** petition for them,	H2256
Jer	11:21	name of the LORD **o** you will die by	H2256+4202
Jer	13:14	I will allow no pity **o** mercy or compassion	H2256
Jer	13:14	no pity or mercy **o** compassion to keep me	H2256
Jer	13:23	change his skin **o** a leopard its spots?	H2256
Jer	14:13	will not see the sword **o** suffer famine.	H2256
Jer	14:14	I have not sent them **o** appointed them	H2256
Jer	14:14	appointed them **o** spoken to them.	H2256
Jer	14:15	'No sword **o** famine will touch this land.	H2256
Jer	15:12	iron from the north—**o** bronze?	H2256
Jer	16: 2	marry and have sons **o** daughters in this	H2256
Jer	16: 4	will not be mourned **o** buried but will be	H2256
Jer	16: 5	do not go to mourn **o** show sympathy	H2256
Jer	16: 6	They will not be buried **o** mourned, and	H2256
Jer	16: 6	will cut themselves **o** shave their head	H2256
Jer	16: 7	not even for a father **o** a mother—nor will	H2256
Jer	17:21	on the Sabbath day **o** bring it through the	H2256
Jer	17:22	out of your houses **o** do any work on the	H2256
Jer	17:23	Yet they did not listen **o** pay attention	H2256
Jer	17:23	would not listen **o** respond to	H2256
Jer	18: 7	that a nation **o** kingdom is to be	H2256
Jer	18: 9	that a nation **o** kingdom is to be built	H2256
Jer	18:23	forgive their crimes **o** blot out their sins	H2256
Jer	19: 5	something I did not command **o** mention	H2256
Jer	19: 6	this place Topheth **o** the Valley of Ben	H2256
Jer	20: 4	them away to Babylon **o** put them to the	H2256
Jer	20: 9	mention his word **o** speak anymore in his	H2256
Jer	21: 7	show them no mercy **o** pity or compassion	H2256
Jer	21: 7	them no mercy or pity **o** compassion.	H2256
Jer	21: 9	will die by the sword, famine **o** plague.	H2256
Jer	21:12	**o** my wrath will break out and burn like	H7153
Jer	22: 3	Do no wrong **o** violence to the foreigner	H440
Jer	22: 3	the fatherless **o** the widow, and do not	H2256
Jer	22:10	weep for the dead king **o** mourn his loss;	H2256
Jer	22:30	the throne of David **o** rule anymore in	H2256
Jer	23: 4	they will no longer be afraid **o** terrified,	H2256
Jer	23:18	of the LORD to see **o** to hear his word?	H2256
Jer	23:32	yet I did not send **o** appoint them.	H2256
Jer	23:33	these people, **o** a prophet or a priest	H196
Jer	23:33	or a prophet **o** a priest, ask you,	H196
Jer	23:34	If a prophet **o** a priest or anyone else	H2256
Jer	23:34	prophet or a priest **o** anyone else claims,	H2256
Jer	23:35	**o** 'What has the LORD spoken	H2256
Jer	23:37	**o** 'What has the LORD spoken	H2256
Jer	24: 8	**whether** they remain in this land **o** live in	H2256
Jer	25: 4	have not listened **o** paid any attention.	H2256
Jer	25:33	will not be mourned **o** gathered up or	H2256
Jer	25:33	not be mourned or gathered up **o** buried,	H2256
Jer	26:19	king of Judah **o** anyone else in Judah	H2256
Jer	27: 8	any nation **o** kingdom will not serve	H2256
Jer	27: 8	king of Babylon **o** bow its neck under his	H2256
Jer	27: 9	your mediums **o** your sorcerers who tell	H2256
Jer	31:34	teach their neighbor, **o** say to one another	H2256
Jer	31:40	never again be uprooted **o** demolished."	H2256
Jer	32:23	they did not obey you **o** follow your law;	H2256
Jer	32:33	they would not listen **o** respond to discipline	NDT
Jer	32:43	without people **o** animals, for it has	H2256
Jer	33:10	without people **o** animals.	H2256
Jer	33:12	desolate and without people **o** animals	H2256
Jer	34:14	did not listen to me **o** pay attention to me.	H2256
Jer	35: 7	houses, sow seed **o** plant vineyards; you	H2256
Jer	35: 9	**o** built houses to live in or had vineyards	H2256
Jer	35: 9	built houses to live in **o** had vineyards	H2256
Jer	35: 9	to live in or had vineyards, fields **o** crops.	H2256
Jer	35:15	have not paid attention **o** listened to me.	H2256
Jer	36:23	had read three **o** four columns of the	H2256
Jer	37:18	against you **o** your attendants or	H2256
Jer	37:18	you or your attendants **o** this people,	H2256
Jer	37:19	of Babylon will not attack you **o** this land'?	H2256
Jer	37:20	the secretary, **o** I will die there."	H2256+4202
Jer	38: 2	the sword, famine **o** plague, but whoever	H2256
Jer	38:24	this conversation, **o** you may die.	H2256+4202
Jer	38:25	hide it from us **o** we will kill you,	H2256+4202
Jer	40: 5	**o** go anywhere else you please.	H196
Jer	42: 6	it is favorable **o** unfavorable,	H2256+561
Jer	42:14	we will not see war **o** hear the trumpet	H2256
Jer	42:14	hear the trumpet **o** be hungry for bread,	H2256
Jer	42:17	of them will survive **o** escape the disaster	H2256
Jer	43: 3	so they may kill us **o** carry us into exile to	H2256
Jer	44: 5	But they did not listen **o** pay attention	H2256
Jer	44: 5	their wickedness **o** stop burning incense	NDT
Jer	44:10	humbled themselves **o** shown reverence,	H2256
Jer	44:12	will fall by the sword **o** die from famine.	NDT
Jer	44:12	greatest, they will die by sword **o** famine.	H2256
Jer	44:14	in Egypt will escape **o** survive to return to	H2256
Jer	44:23	not obeyed him **o** followed his law or	H2256
Jer	44:23	followed his law **o** his decrees or his	H2256
Jer	44:23	his law or his decrees **o** his stipulations,	H2256
Jer	44:26	will ever again invoke my name **o** swear,	NDT
Jer	44:28	whose word will stand—mine **o** theirs.	H2256
Jer	50:39	again be inhabited **o** lived in from	H2256
Jer	51:46	Do not lose heart **o** be afraid when	H2256
Jer	52:19	all that were made of pure gold **o** silver.	H2256
La	2:22	LORD's anger no one escaped **o** survived;	H2256
La	3: 8	Even when I call out **o** cry for help, he	H2256
La	3:33	willingly bring affliction **o** grief to anyone.	H2256
La	3:63	Sitting **o** standing, they mock me in their	H2256
Eze	1:13	was like burning coals of fire **o** like torches.	NDT
Eze	2: 5	And whether they listen **o** fail to listen	H2256
Eze	2: 6	do not be afraid of them **o** their words.	H2256
Eze	2: 6	of what they say **o** be terrified by them,	H2256
Eze	2: 7	whether they listen **o** fail to listen, for they	H2256
Eze	3: 9	not be afraid of them **o** terrified by them,	H2256
Eze	3:11	whether they listen **o** fail to listen."	H2256
Eze	3:18	you do not warn them **o** speak out to	H2256
Eze	3:19	their wickedness **o** from their evil ways,	H2256
Eze	4:14	anything found dead **o** torn by wild	H2256
Eze	5: 7	not followed my decrees **o** kept my laws.	H2256
Eze	5:11	will not look on you with pity **o** spare you.	H2256
Eze	5:12	will die of the plague **o** perish by famine	H2256
Eze	7:19	satisfy their hunger **o** fill their stomachs,	H2256
Eze	8:18	not look on them with pity **o** spare them.	H2256
Eze	9: 5	without showing pity **o** compassion.	H2256
Eze	9:10	not look on them with pity **o** spare them,	H2256
Eze	11:12	followed my decrees **o** kept my laws but	H2256
Eze	12:24	no more false visions **o** flattering	H2256
Eze	13: 9	council of my people **o** be listed in the	H2256
Eze	13:23	see false visions **o** practice divination.	H2256
Eze	14: 7	any of the Israelites **o** any foreigner	H2256
Eze	14:15	"**O** if I send wild beasts through that country	NDT
Eze	14:16	not save their own sons **o** daughters.	H2256
Eze	14:17	"**O** if I bring a sword against that country	H196
Eze	14:18	not save their own sons **o** daughters.	H2256
Eze	14:19	"**O** if I send a plague into that land and	H196
Eze	16: 4	you rubbed with salt **o** wrapped in cloths.	H2256
Eze	16: 5	on you with pity **o** had compassion enough	NDT
Eze	17: 9	take a strong arm **o** many people to pull	H2256
Eze	18: 6	mountain shrines **o** look to the idols of	H2256
Eze	18: 6	his neighbor's wife **o** have sexual	H2256
Eze	18: 8	to them at interest **o** take a profit from	H2256
Eze	18:10	who sheds blood **o** does any of these	H2256
Eze	18:15	mountain shrines **o** look to the idols of	H2256
Eze	18:16	not oppress anyone **o** require a pledge	H4202
Eze	18:17	takes no interest **o** profit from them.	H2256
Eze	20:17	not destroy them **o** put an end to them	H2256
Eze	20:18	of your parents **o** keep their laws or	H2256
Eze	20:18	keep their laws **o** defile yourselves with	H2256
Eze	20:28	they saw any high hill **o** any leafy tree,	H2256
Eze	22:14	your courage endure **o** your hands be	H561
Eze	22:24	not been cleansed **o** rained on in the day	H4202
Eze	23:27	things with longing **o** remember Egypt	H2256
Eze	24:16	Yet do not lament **o** weep or shed any	H2256
Eze	24:16	do not lament or weep **o** shed any tears.	H2256
Eze	24:17	mustache and beard **o** eat the customary	H2256
Eze	24:22	mustache and beard **o** eat the customary	H2256
Eze	24:23	You will not mourn **o** weep but will waste	H2256
Eze	26:20	you will not return **o** take your place in the	H2256
Eze	29: 5	field and not be gathered **o** picked up.	H2256
Eze	30:21	bound up to be healed **o** put in a splint so	NDT
Eze	32:13	by the foot of man **o** muddied by the	H2256
Eze	34: 4	the weak **o** healed the sick or	H2256
Eze	34: 4	healed the sick **o** bound up the injured.	H2256
Eze	34: 4	back the strays **o** searched for the lost.	H2256
Eze	34: 6	no one searched **o** looked for them.	H2256
Eze	34:29	famine in the land **o** bear the scorn of the	H2256
Eze	36:14	longer devour people **o** make your nation	H2256
Eze	36:15	of the peoples **o** cause your nation to	H2256
Eze	37:22	be two nations **o** be divided into two	H2256
Eze	37:23	idols and vile images **o** with any of their	H2256
Eze	39:10	wood from the fields **o** cut it from the	H2256
Eze	44:13	me as priests **o** come near any of my	H2256
Eze	44:13	any of my holy things **o** my most holy	NDT
Eze	44:17	of the inner court **o** inside the temple.	H2256
Eze	44:20	not shave their heads **o** let their hair grow	H2256
Eze	44:22	not marry widows **o** divorced women;	H2256
Eze	44:22	of Israelite descent **o** widows of priests.	H2256
Eze	44:25	the dead person was his father **o** mother,	H2256
Eze	44:25	mother, son **o** daughter, brother or	H2256
Eze	44:25	daughter, brother **o** unmarried sister	H2256
Eze	44:31	whether bird **o** animal, found dead or	H2256
Eze	44:31	found dead **o** torn by wild animals.	H2256
Eze	45:14	which consists of ten baths **o** one homer, for	NDT
Eze	45:20	sins unintentionally **o** through ignorance;	H2256
Eze	46:12	**whether** a burnt offering **o** fellowship	H196
Eze	46:12	his burnt offering **o** his fellowship	H2256
Eze	48:14	They must not sell **o** exchange any of it	H2256
Da	2:10	thing of any magician **o** enchanter or	A10221
Da	2:10	any magician or enchanter **o** astrologer.	A10221
Da	2:27	magician **o** diviner can explain to the king	NDT
Da	3:14	not serve my gods **o** worship the image	A10221
Da	3:18	not serve your gods **o** worship the image	A10221
Da	3:28	rather than serve **o** worship any god	A10221
Da	3:29	of any nation **o** language who say	A10221
Da	4:19	not let the dream **o** its meaning alarm	A10221
Da	4:35	can hold back his hand **o** say to him:	A10221
Da	5: 8	not read the writing **o** tell the king what	A10221
Da	5:23	which cannot see **o** hear or understand.	A10221
Da	5:23	which cannot see or hear **o** understand.	A10221
Da	6: 7	prays to any god **o** human being during	A10221
Da	6:12	prays to any god **o** human being except	A10221
Da	6:13	**o** to the decree you put in writing.	A10221
Da	6:15	Persians no decree **o** edict that the king	A10221
Da	9:10	the LORD our God **o** kept the laws he gave	NDT
Da	10: 3	no meat **o** wine touched my lips	H2256
Da	11:17	his plans will not succeed **o** help him.	H2256
Da	11:20	be destroyed, yet not in anger **o** in battle.	H2256
Da	11:33	fall by the sword **o** be burned or captured	H2256
Da	11:33	sword or be burned **o** captured or plundered	NDT
Da	11:33	be burned or captured **o** plundered.	H2256
Da	11:37	of his ancestors **o** for the one desired	H2256
Hos	1: 7	not by bow, sword **o** battle, or by horses	H2256
Hos	1: 7	sword or battle, **o** by horses and horsemen	NDT
Hos	1:10	which cannot be measured **o** counted.	H2256
Hos	3: 3	not be a prostitute **o** be intimate with any	H2256
Hos	3: 4	will live many days without king **o** prince,	H2256
Hos	3: 4	without sacrifice **o** sacred stones, without	H2256
Hos	3: 4	without ephod **o** household gods.	H2256
Hos	7:10	to the LORD his God **o** search for him.	H2256
Hos	12: 8	they will not find in me any iniquity **o** sin."	H889
Joel	1: 2	in your days **o** in the days of your	H2256+561
Am	3:12	only two leg bones **o** a piece of an ear,	H196
Am	5: 6	**o** he will sweep through the tribes of	H7153
Am	8:11	not a famine of food **o** a thirst for water	H2256
Am	8:14	**o**, 'As surely as the god of	H2256
Am	9:10	'Disaster will not overtake **o** meet us.	H2256
Jnh	3: 7	Do not let people **o** animals, herds or	H2256
Jnh	3: 7	animals, herds **o** flocks, taste anything;	H2256
Jnh	3: 7	anything; do not let them eat **o** drink.	H2256
Jnh	4:10	though you did not tend it **o** make it grow.	H2256
Mic	5: 7	do not wait for anyone **o** depend on man.	H2256
Hab	1: 2	you do not listen? **O** cry out to you	NDT
Hab	2:18	**O** an image that teaches lies	H2256
Hab	2:19	**O** to lifeless stone, 'Wake up	NDT
Zep	1:12	LORD will do nothing, either good **o** bad.	H2256
Hag	2:12	that fold touches some bread **o** stew	H2256
Hag	2:12	some wine, olive oil **o** other food, does it	H2256
Zec	1: 4	would not listen **o** pay attention to me,	H2256
Zec	7:10	Do not oppress the widow **o** the fatherless	H2256
Zec	7:10	the fatherless, the foreigner **o** the poor.	H2256
Zec	7:12	listen to the law **o** to the words that the	H2256
Zec	8:10	wages for people **o** hire for animals.	H2256+401
Zec	11:16	not care for the lost, **o** seek the young, or	H4202
Zec	11:16	seek the young, **o** heal the injured, or	H2256
Zec	11:16	heal the injured, **o** feed the healthy	H4202
Mal	1: 8	you sacrifice lame **o** diseased animals,	H2256
Mal	1:13	lame **o** diseased animals and offer them	H2256
Mal	2:13	on your offerings **o** accepts them with	H2256
Mal	2:17	with them" **o** "Where is the God of justice?"	H196
Mal	3: 2	like a refiner's fire **o** a launderer's soap.	H2256
Mal	4: 1	"Not a root **o** a branch will be left to them.	H2256
Mal	4: 6	**o else** I will come and strike the land with	H7153
Mt	5:17	come to abolish the Law **o** the Prophets;	*G2445*
Mt	5:22	who is angry *with* a **brother o sister** will be	*G81*
Mt	5:22	anyone who says *to* a **brother o sister**, 'Raca,	*G81*
Mt	5:23	that your **brother o sister** has something	*G81*
Mt	5:25	**o** your adversary may hand you over to the	*G3607*
Mt	5:35	**o** by the earth, for it is his footstool; or by	*G3612*
Mt	5:35	it is his footstool; **o** by Jerusalem, for it is	*G3612*
Mt	5:36	cannot make even one hair white **o** black.	*G2445*
Mt	5:37	All you need to say is simply 'Yes' **o** 'No'	NDT
Mt	6:24	**o** you will be devoted to the one and	*G2445*
Mt	6:25	what you will eat **o** drink; or about your	*G2445*
Mt	6:25	will eat or drink; **o** about your body, what	*G3593*
Mt	6:26	they do not sow **o** reap or store away in	*G4028*
Mt	6:26	do not sow or reap **o** store away in barns,	*G4028*
Mt	6:28	the field grow. They do not labor **o** spin.	*G4028*
Mt	6:31	**o** 'What shall we drink	*G2445*
Mt	6:31	shall we drink?' **o** 'What shall we wear?'	*G2445*
Mt	7: 1	judge, **o** you too will be judged.	*G2671+3590*
Mt	7:10	**O** if he asks for a fish, will give him a	*G2445*
Mt	7:16	from thornbushes, **o** figs from thistles?	*G2445*
Mt	9: 5	sins are forgiven,' **o** to say, 'Get up and	*G2445*
Mt	10: 5	the Gentiles **o** enter any town of	*G2779+3590*
Mt	10: 9	"Do not get any gold **o** silver or copper to	*G3593*
Mt	10: 9	any gold or silver **o** copper to take with	*G3593*
Mt	10:10	no bag for the journey **o** extra shirt or	*G3593*
Mt	10:10	journey or extra shirt **o** sandals or a staff,	*G3593*

Mt 10:10 journey or extra shirt or sandals o a staff, G3593
Mt 10:11 Whatever town o village you enter, search G2445
Mt 10:14 not welcome you o listen to your words G3593
Mt 10:14 leave that home o town and shake the G2445
Mt 10:19 worry about what to say o how to say it. G2445
Mt 10:26 o hidden that will not be made known. G2779
Mt 10:37 loves their father o mother more than me G2445
Mt 10:37 who loves their son o daughter more than G2445
Mt 11: 3 o should we expect someone else?" G2445
Mt 12: 5 O haven't you read in the Law that the G2445
Mt 12:19 He will not quarrel o cry out; no one will G4028
Mt 12:25 every city o household divided G2445
Mt 12:29 "O again, how can anyone enter a strong G2445
Mt 12:32 either in this age o in the age to come. G4046
Mt 12:33 o make a tree bad and its fruit will be bad G2445
Mt 13: 8 sixty o thirty times what was sown. G1254
Mt 13:13 hearing, they do not hear o understand. G4028
Mt 13:21 When trouble o persecution comes G2445
Mt 13:23 sixty o thirty times what was sown. G1254
Mt 15: 4 curses their father o mother is to be put to G2445
Mt 15: 5 to help their father o mother is 'devoted G2445
Mt 15: 6 not to 'honor their father o mother' with it. G2445
Mt 15:32 o they may collapse on the way. G3607
Mt 16:10 O the seven loaves for the four thousand G4028
Mt 16:14 Jeremiah o one of the prophets. G2445
Mt 16:26 O what can anyone give in exchange for G2445
Mt 17:15 often falls into the fire o into the water. G2779
Mt 17:25 from their own children o from others?" G2445
Mt 18: 8 If your hand o your foot causes you to G2445
Mt 18: 8 to enter life maimed o crippled than to G2445
Mt 18: 8 to have two hands o two feet and be G2445
Mt 18:15 "If your brother o sister sins, go and point G81
Mt 18:16 not listen, take one o two others along, so G2445
Mt 18:16 by the testimony of two o three witnesses. G2445
Mt 18:17 as you would a pagan o a tax collector. G2779
Mt 18:20 For where two o three gather in my name G2445
Mt 18:21 I forgive my brother o sister who sins against G81
Mt 18:35 forgive your brother o sister from your heart G81
Mt 19:29 who has left houses o brothers or sisters G2445
Mt 19:29 houses or brothers o sisters or father or G2445
Mt 19:29 brothers or sisters o father or mother or G2445
Mt 19:29 sisters or father o mother or wife or G2445
Mt 19:29 father or mother o wife or children or G2445
Mt 19:29 mother or wife o children or fields for G2445
Mt 19:29 wife or children o fields for my sake will G2445
Mt 20:15 O are you envious because I am generous G2445
Mt 20:23 to sit at my right o left is not for me to G2779
Mt 21:25 Was it from heaven, o of human origin?" G2445
Mt 22:17 to pay the imperial tax to Caesar o not?" G2445
Mt 22:29 know the Scriptures o the power of God. G3593
Mt 23:17 o the temple that makes the gold sacred? G2445
Mt 23:19 o the altar that makes the gift sacred? G2445
Mt 24:20 not take place in winter o on the Sabbath. G3593
Mt 24:23 here is the Messiah!' o, 'There he is!' do G2445
Mt 24:26 do not go out; o, 'Here he is, in the inner NDT
Mt 24:36 "But about that day o hour no one knows G2779
Mt 25:13 you do not know the day o the hour. G4028
Mt 25:37 o thirsty and give you something to drink? G2445
Mt 25:38 o needing clothes and clothe you? G2445
Mt 25:39 did we see you sick o in prison and go to G2445
Mt 25:44 we see you hungry o thirsty or a stranger G2445
Mt 25:44 hungry or thirsty o a stranger or needing G2445
Mt 25:44 thirsty or a stranger o needing clothes G2445
Mt 25:44 needing clothes o sick or in prison, G2445
Mt 25:44 needing clothes or sick o in prison, G2445
Mt 26: 5 "o there may be a riot among the G2671+3590
Mt 27:17 o Jesus who is called the Messiah?" G2445
Mk 2: 9 sins are forgiven,' o to say, 'Get up, take G2445
Mk 3: 4 to do good o to do evil, to save life or to G2445
Mk 3: 4 do good or to do evil, to save life o to kill?" G2445
Mk 4:17 When trouble o persecution comes G2445
Mk 4:21 in a lamp to put it under a bowl o a bed? G2445
Mk 4:27 day, whether he sleeps o gets up, the G2779
Mk 4:30 o what parable shall we use to describe it G2445
Mk 6:11 will not welcome you o listen to you, G3593
Mk 6:56 into villages, towns o countryside—they G2445
Mk 7:10 curses their father o mother is to be put to G2445
Mk 7:11 to help their father o mother is Corban G2445
Mk 7:12 do anything for their father o mother. G2445
Mk 8:17 Do you still not see o understand? Are G4028
Mk 8:37 O what can anyone give in exchange for G1142
Mk 9:22 thrown him into fire o water to kill him. G2779
Mk 10:29 who has left home o brothers or sisters G2445
Mk 10:29 home or brothers o sisters or mother or G2445
Mk 10:29 brothers or sisters o mother or father or G2445
Mk 10:29 sisters or mother o father or children or G2445
Mk 10:29 mother or father o children or fields for G2445
Mk 10:29 father or children o fields for me and the G2445
Mk 10:38 the cup I drink o be baptized with the G2445
Mk 10:40 to sit at my right o left is not for me to G2445
Mk 11:30 was it from heaven, o of human origin? G2445
Mk 12:14 to pay the imperial tax to Caesar o not? G2445
Mk 12:15 Should we pay o shouldn't we?" But Jesus G2445
Mk 12:24 know the Scriptures o the power of God? G3593
Mk 13:15 housetop go down o enter the house to G3593
Mk 13:21 here is the Messiah!' o, 'Look, there he is!' NDT
Mk 13:32 "But about that day o hour no one knows G2445
Mk 13:35 in the evening, o at midnight, or when G2445
Mk 13:35 at midnight, o when the rooster crows G2445
Mk 13:35 when the rooster crows, o at dawn. G2445
Mk 14: 2 they said, "o the people may riot. G3607
Mk 14:68 "I don't know o understand what you're G4046

Lk 1:15 never to take wine o other fermented G2779
Lk 2:24 "a pair of doves o two young pigeons." G2445
Lk 5:23 sins are forgiven,' o to say, 'Get up and G2445
Lk 6: 9 to do good o to do evil, to save life or to G2445
Lk 6: 9 to do evil, to save life o to destroy it?" G2445
Lk 6:44 from thornbushes, o grapes from briers. G4028
Lk 7:19 o should we expect someone else?" G2445
Lk 7:20 o should we expect someone else? G2445
Lk 8:16 hides it in a clay jar o puts it under a bed. G2445
Lk 8:17 will not be known o brought out into the G2779
Lk 8:27 had not worn clothes o lived in a house, G2779
Lk 9:25 and yet lose o forfeit their very self? G2445
Lk 10: 4 Do not take a purse o bag or sandals; and G3590
Lk 10: 4 Do not take a purse or bag o sandals; and G3590
Lk 10:42 things are needed—o *indeed* only one. G2445
Lk 11:12 O if he asks for an egg, will give him a G2445
Lk 11:33 where it will be hidden, o under a bowl. G4028
Lk 12: 2 o hidden that will not be made known. G2779
Lk 12:11 defend yourselves o what you will say, G2445
Lk 12:14 me a judge o an arbiter between G2445
Lk 12:22 what you will eat; o about your body G3593
Lk 12:24 They do not sow o reap, they have no G4028
Lk 12:24 they have no storeroom o barn; yet God G4028
Lk 12:27 They do not labor o spin. Yet I tell you, G4028
Lk 12:29 your heart on what you will eat o drink; G2779
Lk 12:38 middle of the night o toward daybreak. G2829
Lk 12:41 telling this parable to us, o to everyone?" G2445
Lk 12:47 does not get ready o does not do what G2445
Lk 12:58 o your adversary may drag you off to the G3607
Lk 13: 4 O those eighteen who died when the G2445
Lk 13:15 untie your ox o donkey from the stall G2445
Lk 13:25 'I don't know you o where you come from. NDT
Lk 13:27 'I don't know you o where you come from. NDT
Lk 14: 3 "Is it lawful to heal on the Sabbath o not?" G2445
Lk 14: 5 of you has a child o an ox that falls into G2445
Lk 14:12 "When you give a luncheon o dinner, do G2445
Lk 14:12 your brothers o sisters, your relatives, G81
Lk 14:12 your relatives, o your rich neighbors; if you G3593
Lk 14:31 "O suppose a king is about to go to war G2445
Lk 15: 8 "O suppose a woman has ten silver coins G2445
Lk 16:13 o you will be devoted to the one and G2445
Lk 17: 3 "If your brother o sister sins against you G81
Lk 17: 7 has a servant plowing o looking after the G2445
Lk 17:21 'Here it is,' o 'There it is,' because the G2445
Lk 17:23 o 'Here he is!' Do not go G2445
Lk 18: 4 I don't fear God o care what people think, G4028
Lk 18:11 adulterers—o even like this tax collector. G2445
Lk 18:29 who has left home o wife or brothers or G2445
Lk 18:29 has left home or wife o brothers or sisters G2445
Lk 18:29 wife or brothers o sisters or parents or G81
Lk 18:29 brothers or sisters o parents or children G2445
Lk 18:29 sisters or parents o children for the sake G2445
Lk 20: 4 was it from heaven, o of human origin?" G2445
Lk 20:22 it right for us to pay taxes to Caesar o not?" G2445
Lk 21:15 will be able to resist o contradict. G2445
Lk 21:34 o your hearts will be weighed down with G3607
Lk 22:27 who is at the table o the one who serves? G2445
Lk 22:35 without purse, bag o sandals, did you lack G2779
Jn 1:13 of human decision o a husband's will G4028
Jn 3: 8 where it comes from o where it is going. G2779
Jn 4:27 o "Why are you talking with her? G2445
Jn 5:14 Stop sinning o something worse G2671+3590
Jn 6:19 they had rowed about three o four miles, G2445
Jn 7:17 comes from God o whether I speak on my G2445
Jn 7:48 "Have any of the rulers o of the Pharisees G2445
Jn 8:14 where I come from o where I am going. G2445
Jn 8:19 "You do not know me o my Father," Jesus G4046
Jn 9: 2 this man o his parents, that he G2445
Jn 9:21 he can see now, o who opened his eyes G2445
Jn 9:25 "Whether he is a sinner o not, I don't G1623
Jn 13:29 festival, o to give something to the poor. G2445
Jn 14:11 o at least believe on the evidence of the G1254
Jn 16: 3 they have not known the Father o me. G4028
Jn 18:20 taught in synagogues o at the temple, G2779
Jn 18:34 "o did others talk to you about me?" G2445
Jn 19:10 I have power either to free you o to crucify G2779
Ac 1: 7 to know the times o dates the Father has G2445
Ac 3: 6 Peter said, "Silver o gold I do not have G2779
Ac 3:12 if by our own power o godliness we had G2445
Ac 4: 7 "By what power o what name did you do G2445
Ac 4:18 them not to speak o teach at all in the G3593
Ac 4:19 to listen to you, o to him? You be G3437+2445
Ac 4:34 who owned land o houses sold them, G2445
Ac 5:38 For if their purpose o activity is of human G2445
Ac 7:49 O where will my resting place be G2445
Ac 8: 7 who were paralyzed o lame were healed. G2779
Ac 8:21 You have no part o share in this ministry G4028
Ac 8:34 talking about, himself o someone else?" G2445
Ac 9: 2 whether men o women, he might G2779
Ac 9: 9 and did not eat o drink anything. G4028
Ac 10:14 never eaten anything impure o unclean." G2779
Ac 10:28 a Jew to associate with o visit a Gentile. G2445
Ac 10:28 should not call anyone impure o unclean. G2445
Ac 11: 8 Nothing impure o unclean has ever G2445
Ac 16:21 us Romans to accept o practice. G4028
Ac 17:29 being is like gold o silver or stone— G2445
Ac 17:29 being is like gold or silver o stone— G2445
Ac 18:14 some misdemeanor o serious crime, G2445
Ac 20:33 coveted anyone's silver o gold or clothing. G2445
Ac 20:33 coveted anyone's silver or gold o clothing. G2445
Ac 21:21 their children o live according to our G3593
Ac 23: 9 "What if a spirit o an angel has spoken to G2445

Ac 23:12 an oath not to eat o drink until they had G3612
Ac 23:21 an oath not to eat o drink until they have G3612
Ac 23:29 him that deserved death o imprisonment. G2445
Ac 24:12 o stirring up a crowd in the synagogues G2445
Ac 24:12 in the synagogues o anywhere else in the G4046
Ac 24:20 O these who are here should state what G2445
Ac 25: 6 spending eight o ten days with them, G2445
Ac 25: 8 the Jewish law o against the temple or G4046
Ac 25: 8 against the temple o against Caesar." G4046
Ac 26:29 replied, "Short time o long—I pray to God G2779
Ac 26:31 that deserves death o imprisonment." G2445
Ac 27:44 get there on planks o on other pieces of G1254
Ac 28: 6 him to swell up o suddenly fall dead; G2445
Ac 28:17 against our people o against the customs G2445
Ac 28:21 there has reported o said anything bad G2445
Ro 2: 4 O do you show contempt for the riches of G2445
Ro 3: 1 o what value is there in circumcision? G2445
Ro 3:29 O is God the God of Jews only? Is he not G2445
Ro 4: 9 circumcised, o also for the uncircumcised? G2445
Ro 4:10 he was circumcised, o before? It was not G2445
Ro 6: 3 O don't you know that all of us who were G2445
Ro 6:16 leads to death, o to obedience, which G2445
Ro 8:35 Shall trouble o hardship or persecution G2445
Ro 8:35 trouble or hardship o persecution or G2445
Ro 8:35 persecution o famine or nakedness or G2445
Ro 8:35 famine o nakedness or danger G2445
Ro 8:35 famine or nakedness o danger or sword? G2445
Ro 8:35 famine or nakedness or danger o sword? G2445
Ro 9:11 the twins were born o had done anything G3593
Ro 9:11 born or had done anything good o bad— G2445
Ro 9:16 depend on human desire o effort, but on G4028
Ro 10: 7 "o 'Who will descend into the deep?'" G2445
Ro 11:34 O who has been his counselor? G2445
Ro 14: 4 servants stand o fall. And they will G2445
Ro 14: 8 whether we live o die, we belong G1569+5445
Ro 14:10 why do you judge your brother o sister? G81
Ro 14:10 O why do you treat them with contempt G2445
Ro 14:13 any stumbling block o obstacle in the way G2445
Ro 14:13 obstacle in the way *of* a brother o sister. G81
Ro 14:15 If your brother o sister is distressed because G81
Ro 14:21 not to eat meat o drink wine or to do G3593
Ro 14:21 meat or drink wine o to do anything else G3593
Ro 14:21 that will cause your brother o sister to fall. G81
1Co 2: 1 with eloquence o human wisdom as I G2445
1Co 2: 6 wisdom of this age o of the rulers of this G4028
1Co 3:12 costly stones, wood, hay o straw, NDT
1Co 3:22 whether Paul o Apollos or Cephas or the G1664
1Co 3:22 Paul or Apollos o Cephas or the world G1664
1Co 3:22 Apollos or Cephas o the world or life or G1664
1Co 3:22 Cephas or the world o life or death or the G1664
1Co 3:22 the world or life o death or the present G1664
1Co 3:22 world or life or death o the present or the G1664
1Co 3:22 life or death or the present o the future— G1664
1Co 4: 3 I am judged by you o by any human court; G2445
1Co 4:21 o shall I come in love and with a gentle G2445
1Co 5:10 are immoral, o the greedy and swindlers G2445
1Co 5:10 the greedy and swindlers, o idolaters. G2445
1Co 5:11 claims to be a brother o sister but is sexually G81
1Co 5:11 sister but is sexually immoral o greedy, G2445
1Co 5:11 an idolater o slanderer, G2445
1Co 5:11 slanderer, a drunkard o swindler. G2445
1Co 6: 2 O do you not know that the Lord's people G2445
1Co 6: 9 O do you not know that wrongdoers will G2445
1Co 7:11 remain unmarried o else be reconciled to G2445
1Co 7:15 The brother o the sister is not bound in G2445
1Co 7:16 O, how do you know, husband, whether G2445
1Co 7:34 An unmarried woman o virgin is G2779
1Co 8: 5 whether in heaven o on earth (as indeed G1664
1Co 8:11 So this weak brother o sister, for whom G81
1Co 8:13 I eat causes my brother o sister to fall into G81
1Co 9: 6 O is it only I and Barnabas who lack the G2445
1Co 10:19 is anything, o that an idol is anything? G2445
1Co 10:31 So whether you eat o drink or whatever G1664
1Co 10:31 you eat or drink o whatever you do, G1664
1Co 10:32 Greeks o the church of God— G2779
1Co 11: 4 Every man who prays o prophesies with his G2445
1Co 11: 5 woman who prays o prophesies with her G2445
1Co 11: 6 have her hair cut off o her head shaved, G2445
1Co 11:22 O do you despise the church of God by G2445
1Co 11:27 eats the bread o drinks the cup of the G2445
1Co 12: 2 somehow o other you were G6055+323
1Co 12:13 whether Jews o Gentiles, slave or G1664
1Co 12:13 Gentiles, slave o free—and we were all G1664
1Co 13: 1 speak in the tongues of men o of angels, G2779
1Co 13: 1 a resounding gong o a clanging cymbal. G2445
1Co 14: 6 you some revelation o knowledge or G2445
1Co 14: 6 knowledge o prophecy or word of G2445
1Co 14: 6 prophecy o word of instruction? G2445
1Co 14: 7 such as the pipe o harp, how will anyone G1664
1Co 14:23 inquirers o unbelievers come in G2445
1Co 14:24 But if an unbeliever o an inquirer comes in G2445
1Co 14:26 of you has a hymn, o a word of instruction NDT
1Co 14:26 a revelation, a tongue o an interpretation. NDT
1Co 14:27 in a tongue, two—o at the most three G2445
1Co 14:29 Two o three prophets should speak, and G2445
1Co 14:36 O did the word of God originate with you G2445
1Co 14:36 O are you the only people it has reached G2445
1Co 14:37 are a prophet o otherwise gifted by the G2445
1Co 15:11 it is I o they, this is what we G1664
1Co 15:37 perhaps of wheat o of something else. G2445
1Co 16: 6 you for a while, o even spend the winter G2445
2Co 1:13 anything you cannot read o understand. G2445

2Co 1:17 **O** do I make my plans in a worldly G2445
2Co 3: 1 **O** do we need, like some people, letters G2445
2Co 3: 1 of recommendation to you **o** from you? G2445
2Co 5: 9 are at home in the body **o** away from it. G1664
2Co 5:10 while in the body, whether good **o** bad. G1664
2Co 6:14 **O** what fellowship can light have with G2445
2Co 6:15 **O** what does a believer have in common G2445
2Co 7: 3 hearts that we would live **o** die with you. G2779
2Co 9: 7 not reluctantly **o** under compulsion, for G2445
2Co 10:12 not dare to classify **o** compare ourselves G2445
2Co 11: 4 **o** if you receive a different spirit from the G2445
2Co 11: 4 **o** a different gospel from the one you G2445
2Co 11:20 who enslaves you **o** exploits you or takes G1623
2Co 11:20 you or exploits you **o** takes advantage of G1623
2Co 11:20 advantage of you **o** puts on airs or slaps G1623
2Co 11:20 you or puts on airs **o** slaps you in the face. G1623
2Co 12: 2 it was in the body **o** out of the body I do G1664
2Co 12: 3 whether in the body **o** apart from the body G1664
2Co 12: 6 me than is warranted by what I do **o** say, G2445
2Co 12: 7 **o** because of these surpassingly great G2779
2Co 13: 1 by the testimony of two **o** three witnesses." G2779
2Co 13: 2 who sinned earlier **o** any of the others, G2779
Gal 1: 8 But even if we **o** an angel from heaven G2445
Gal 1:10 the approval of human beings, **o** of God? G2445
Gal 1:10 **O** am I trying to please people G2445
Gal 3: 2 the law, **o** by believing what you heard? G2445
Gal 3: 5 **o** by your believing what you heard? G2445
Gal 3:15 no one can set aside **o** add to a human G2445
Gal 4: 9 know God—**o** rather are known by God G1254
Gal 4:14 did not treat me with contempt **o** scorn. G4028
Gal 5:15 watch out **o** you will be destroyed by each G3590
Gal 6: 1 yourselves, **o** you also may be tempted. G3590
Eph 3:20 more than all we ask **o** imagine, G2445
Eph 5: 3 immorality, **o** of any kind of impurity G2779
Eph 5: 3 any kind of impurity, **o** of greed, because G2445
Eph 5: 4 foolish talk **o** coarse joking, which G2445
Eph 5: 5 immoral, impure **o** greedy person—such G2445
Eph 5:27 without stain **o** wrinkle or any other G2445
Eph 5:27 stain or wrinkle **o** any other blemish, G2445
Eph 6: 8 they do, whether they are slave **o** free. G1664
Php 1: 7 **whether** I am in chains **o** defending and G2779
Php 1:18 whether from false motives **o** true, Christ G1664
Php 1:20 in my body, whether by life **o** by death. G1664
Php 1:27 I come and see you **o** only hear about you G1664
Php 2: 3 out of selfish ambition **o** vain conceit. G3593
Php 2:14 everything without grumbling **o** arguing, G2779
Php 2:16 of Christ that I did not run **o** labor in vain. G4028
Php 3:12 **o** have already arrived at my goal G2445
Php 4: 8 if anything is excellent **o** praiseworthy G2779
Php 4: 9 you have learned **o** received or heard G2779
Php 4: 9 learned or received **o** heard from me, G2779
Php 4: 9 heard from me, **o** seen in me—put it G2779
Php 4:12 whether well fed **o** hungry, whether living G2779
Php 4:12 whether living in plenty **o** in want. G2779
Col 1:16 whether thrones **o** powers or rulers or G1664
Col 1:16 thrones or powers **o** rulers or authorities; G1664
Col 1:16 thrones or powers or rulers **o** authorities; G1664
Col 1:20 things on earth **o** things in heaven, G1664
Col 2:16 judge you by what you eat **o** drink, G2779
Col 2:16 **o** with regard to a religious festival G2445
Col 2:16 a New Moon celebration **o** a Sabbath day. G2445
Col 3:11 Here there is no Gentile **o** Jew G2779
Col 3:11 circumcised **o** uncircumcised G2779
Col 3:11 Scythian, slave **o** free, but Christ is all NDT
Col 3:17 you do, *whether* in word **o** deed, do it all G2445
Col 3:21 **o** they will become discouraged. G2671+3590
1Th 2: 3 not spring from error **o** impure motives, G4028
1Th 2: 6 people, not from you **o** anyone else, even G4046
1Th 2:19 **o** the crown in which we will glory in the G2445
1Th 4: 6 one should wrong **o** take advantage of a G2779
1Th 4: 6 take advantage of a **brother o sister**. G81
1Th 5: 5 not belong to the night **o** to the darkness. G4028
1Th 5:10 whether we are awake **o** asleep, we may G1664
2Th 2: 2 easily unsettled **o** alarmed by the G3593
2Th 2: 2 by a prophecy **o** by word of mouth or G3612
2Th 2: 2 by word of mouth **o** by letter— G3612
2Th 2: 4 that is called God **o** is worshiped, G2445
2Th 2:15 whether by word of mouth **o** by letter. G1664
1Ti 1: 4 **o** to devote themselves to myths and G3593
1Ti 1: 7 they are talking about **o** what they so G3612
1Ti 1: 9 those who kill their fathers **o** mothers G2779
1Ti 2: 8 up holy hands without anger **o** disputing. G2779
1Ti 2: 9 elaborate hairstyles **o** gold or pearls or G2779
1Ti 2: 9 hairstyles or gold **o** pearls or expensive G2445
1Ti 2: 9 gold or pearls **o** expensive clothes, G2445
1Ti 2:12 a woman to teach **o** to assume authority G4028
1Ti 3: 6 **o** he may become conceited and G2671+3590
1Ti 5: 4 if a widow has children **o** grandchildren, G2445
1Ti 5:19 it is brought by two **o** three witnesses. G2445
1Ti 6:14 command without spot **o** blame until the NDT
1Ti 6:16 whom no one has seen **o** can see. G4028
2Ti 1: 8 about our Lord **o** of me his prisoner. G3593
Titus 1:14 to Jewish myths **o** to the merely human G2779
Titus 2: 3 not to be slanderers **o** addicted to much G3590
Titus 3:12 soon as I send Artemas **o** Tychicus to you, G2445
Phm 18 done you any wrong **o** owes you anything, G2445
Heb 1: 5 **O** again, "I will be his Father, and he will G2779
Heb 7: 3 Without father **o** mother, without genealogy NDT
Heb 7: 3 without beginning of days **o** end of life G3612
Heb 8:11 teach their neighbor, **o** say to one another G2779
Heb 10:28 on the testimony of two **o** three witnesses. G2445
Heb 12:16 is sexually immoral, **o** is godless like Esau G2445
Heb 12:19 to a trumpet blast **o** to such a voice G2779
Jas 2: 3 stand there" **o** "Sit on the floor by my feet," G2445
Jas 2:15 Suppose a brother **o** a sister is without G2445
Jas 3: 4 **O** take ships as an example. Although G2779
Jas 3:12 tree bear olives, **o** a grapevine bear figs? G2445
Jas 3:14 do not boast about it **o** deny the truth. G2779
Jas 4: 5 **O** do you think Scripture says without G2445
Jas 4:11 against a **brother o sister** or judges them G81
Jas 4:11 a brother or sister **o** judges them speaks G2445
Jas 4:13 "Today **o** tomorrow we will go to this or G2445
Jas 4:13 tomorrow we will go to **this o that** city, G3840
Jas 4:15 Lord's will, we will live and do this **o** that." G2445
Jas 5: 9 and sisters, **o** you will be judged. G2671+3590
Jas 5:12 not by heaven **o** by earth or by anything G3612
Jas 5:12 by heaven or by earth **o** by anything else. G3612
Jas 5:12 you need to say is a simple "Yes" **o** "No." G2779
1Pe 1: 4 that can never perish, spoil **o** fade. G2779
1Pe 1:18 things such as silver **o** gold that you were G2445
1Pe 1:19 a lamb without blemish **o** defect. G2779
1Pe 2:14 **o** to governors, who are sent by him to G1664
1Pe 3: 3 the wearing of gold jewelry **o** fine clothes. G2445
1Pe 3: 9 not repay evil with evil **o** insult with insult. G2445
1Pe 4:15 not be as a murderer **o** thief or any other G2445
1Pe 4:15 as a murderer or thief **o** any other kind of G2445
1Pe 4:15 kind of criminal, **o** *even* as a meddler. G2445
1Jn 2: 9 light but hates a **brother o sister** is still in the G81
1Jn 2:11 anyone who hates a **brother o sister** is in the G81
1Jn 2:15 not love the world **o** anything in the world G3593
1Jn 3: 6 to sin has **either** seen him **o** known him. G4028
1Jn 3:15 who hates a **brother o sister** is a murderer, G81
1Jn 3:17 sees a **brother o sister** in need but has G81
1Jn 3:18 us not love with words **o** speech but with G3593
1Jn 4:20 love God yet hates a **brother o sister** is a liar. G81
1Jn 5:16 If you see any **brother o sister** commit a sin G81
2Jn 10 into your house **o** welcome them. G2779+3590
Rev 3:15 I wish you were **either** one **o** the other! G2445
Rev 5: 3 But no one in heaven **o** on earth or under G4028
Rev 5: 3 heaven or on earth **o** under the earth G4028
Rev 5: 3 open the scroll **o even** look inside it. G4046
Rev 5: 4 worthy to open the scroll **o** look inside. G4046
Rev 7: 1 blowing on the land **o** on the sea or on G3612
Rev 7: 1 on the land or on the sea **o** on any tree. G3612
Rev 7: 3 not harm the land **o** the sea or the trees G3612
Rev 7: 3 the land or the sea **o** the trees until we G3612
Rev 9: 4 the grass of the earth **o** any plant or tree, G4028
Rev 9: 4 the grass of the earth or any plant **o** tree, G4028
Rev 9:20 idols that cannot see **o** hear or walk. G4046
Rev 9:20 idols that cannot see or hear **o** walk. G4046
Rev 9:21 their sexual immorality **o** their thefts. G4046
Rev 12: 9 called the devil, **o** Satan, who leads the G2779
Rev 13:16 on their right hands **o** on their foreheads, G2445
Rev 13:17 they could not buy **o** sell unless they had G2445
Rev 13:17 the name of the beast **o** the number of its G2445
Rev 14: 9 mark on their forehead **o** on their hand, G2445
Rev 14:11 will be no rest day **o** night for those who G2779
Rev 14:11 **o** for anyone who receives the mark of its G2779
Rev 20: 2 who is the devil, **o** Satan, and bound him G2779
Rev 20: 4 worshiped the beast **o** its image and had G4028
Rev 20: 4 its mark on their foreheads **o** their hands. G2779
Rev 21: 4 be no more death' **o** mourning or crying G4046
Rev 21: 4 more death' or mourning **o** crying or pain, G4046
Rev 21: 4 more death' or mourning or crying **o** pain, G4046
Rev 21:23 not need the sun **o** the moon to shine on G4028
Rev 21:27 who does what is shameful **o** deceitful, G2779
Rev 22: 5 the light of a lamp **o** the light of the sun, G2779

ORACLE (1)

Pr 16:10 The lips of a king speak as an **o**, and his H7877

ORCHARD (1) [ORCHARDS]

SS 4:13 plants are an **o** *of* pomegranates with H7236

ORCHARDS (2) [ORCHARD]

Isa 16:10 gladness are taken away from the **o**; H4149
Jer 48:33 are gone from the **o** and fields of Moab. H4149

ORDAIN (3) [ORDAINED, ORDINATION]

Ex 28:41 his sons, anoint and **o** them. H4848+906+3338
Ex 29: 9 "Then *you shall* **o** Aaron and his H4848+3338
Ex 29:35 taking seven days *to* **o** them. H4848+3338

ORDAINED (13) [ORDAIN]

Ex 29:29 be anointed and **o** in them. H4848+906+3338
Lev 16:32 anointed and **o** to succeed H4848+906+3338
Lev 21:10 and *who has been* **o** to wear H4848+906+3338
Nu 3: 3 who *were* **o** to serve as priests. H4848+906+3338
Jdg 2:20 the covenant *I* **o** *for* their ancestors and H7422
2Ki 19:25 Long ago *I* **o** it. In days of old I H6913
Ps 65: 9 people with grain, for so *you have* **o** it. H3922
Ps 111: 9 his people; *he* **o** his covenant forever H7422
Ps 139:16 all the days **o** for me were written in your H3670
Isa 37:26 Long ago *I* **o** it. In days of old I H6913
Isa 48: 5 my wooden image and metal god **o** them. H7422
Eze 28:14 as a guardian cherub, for so *I* **o** you. H5989
Hab 1:12 *you*, my Rock, *have* **o** them to punish. H3569

ORDEAL (1)

1Pe 4:12 not be surprised *at* the **fiery** *o* that has come AIT

ORDER (150) [ORDERED, ORDERLY, ORDERS]

Ge 25:13 of Ishmael, listed in the **o of** their **birth**: H9352
Ge 38:20 the Adullamite **in o to** get his pledge H4200
Ge 43:33 seated before him **in the o of** their ages, H3869
Ex 1:22 Then Pharaoh **gave** *this* **o** to all his H7422
Ex 5: 6 day Pharaoh **gave** *this* **o** to the slave H7422
Ex 9:19 **Give an o** now to bring your livestock and H8938
Ex 28:10 **in the o of** their birth—six names on one H3869
Ex 36: 6 Then Moses **gave an o** and they sent this H7422
Lev 13:54 he *shall* **o** that the spoiled article be H7422
Lev 14: 4 the priest *shall* **o** that two live clean birds H7422
Lev 14: 5 Then the priest *shall* **o** that one of the H7422
Lev 14:36 The priest *is to* **o** the house to be emptied H7422
Lev 14:40 he *is to* **o** that the contaminated stones be H7422
Lev 22:19 sheep or goats **in o that** it may be H4200
Nu 2:17 will set out **in the same o** as they encamp H4027
Nu 9:19 obeyed the LORD's **o** and did not set out. H5466
Nu 9:23 They obeyed the LORD's **o**, in accordance H5466
Nu 10:28 This was the **o of march** for the Israelite H5023
Nu 36: 5 command Moses **gave** *this* **o** *to* the H7422
Dt 2:30 obstinate **in o to** give him into H4200+5100
Dt 8: 2 test you **in o to** know what was in H4200
Dt 29:12 You are standing here **in o to** enter into a H4200
Jos 10:27 sunset Joshua **gave** *the* **o** and they took H7422
Jdg 9:24 God did this **in o that** the crime against H4200
Jdg 20: 9 go up against it **in the o** decided by casting H928
Ru 4: 5 **in o to** maintain the name of the dead H4200
Ru 4:10 **in o to** maintain the name of the dead H4200
1Sa 1: 6 provoking her **in o to** irritate her. H928+6288
1Sa 15:21 **in o to** sacrifice them to the LORD your God H4200
2Sa 2:26 How long before *you* **o** your men to stop H606
2Sa 4:12 So David **gave** *an* **o** *to* his men, and they H7422
2Sa 13:28 Haven't I **given** you *this* **o**? Be strong and H7422
2Sa 14: 8 I *will* **issue an o** in your behalf. H7422
2Sa 14:29 sent for Joab **in o to** send him to the king H4200
2Sa 17:14 of Ahithophel **in o to** bring disaster H928+6288
2Sa 17:23 *He* **put** his house **in o** and then hanged H7422
2Sa 19:29 *I* **o** you and Ziba to divide the land. H606
1Ki 2:46 Then the king **gave the o** *to* Benaiah son H7422
1Ki 3:25 He then **gave an o**: "Cut the living child in H606
1Ki 15:22 Then King Asa **issued an o** *to* all Judah H9048
2Ki 10:19 deceptively **in o to** destroy the H4200+5100
2Ki 17:27 Then the king of Assyria **gave** *this* **o** H7422
2Ki 20: 1 **Put** your house **in o**, because you are H7422
2Ki 23:21 The king **gave** *this* **o** *to* all the people H7422
2Ki 23:35 **In o to** do so, he taxed the land and H4200
2Ki 24: 3 **in o to** remove them from his presence H4200
1Ch 15:14 themselves **in o to** bring up the ark of H4200
1Ch 24: 3 their **appointed o** of ministering. H7213
1Ch 24:19 This was their **appointed o** of ministering H7213
2Ch 11:22 his brothers, **in o to** make him king. H3954
2Ch 24:21 by **o** *of* the king they stoned him to H5184
2Ch 29:27 Hezekiah **gave the o** to sacrifice the burnt H606
2Ch 31: 5 As soon as the **o** went out, the Israelites H1821
2Ch 32:18 them afraid **in o to** capture the H4200+5100
2Ch 35:20 when Josiah *had* **set** the temple **in o** H3922
2Ch 36:22 **in o to** fulfill the word of the LORD spoken H4200
Ezr 1: 1 **in o to** fulfill the word of the LORD spoken H4200
Ezr 4:19 I issued an **o** and a search was made A10302
Ezr 4:21 Now issue an **o** to these men to stop A10302
Ezr 4:21 be rebuilt until I so **o**. A10682+10302+10002
Ezr 6: 1 King Darius then issued an **o**, and they A10302
Ezr 6:21 Gentile neighbors **in o to** seek the LORD, H4200
Ne 5: 2 numerous; **in o for** us to eat and stay alive H2256
Ne 9:17 appointed a leader **in o to** return to their H4200
Ne 9:26 had warned them **in o to** turn them back H4200
Ne 9:29 "You warned them **in o to** turn them back H4200
Ne 13:22 guard the gates **in o to** keep the Sabbath H4200
Est 1:11 **in o to** display her beauty to the people H4200
Est 2: 8 When the king's **o** and edict had been H1821
Est 3:13 all the king's provinces with the **o** to destroy, NDT
Est 4: 3 to which the edict and **o** *of* the king came, H2017
Est 8: 5 *let an* **o be written** overruling the H4180
Job 25: 2 he establishes **o** in the heights of heaven. H8934
Ps 59: T to watch David's house **in o to** kill him. H4200
Ps 110: 4 a priest forever, in the **o** *of* Melchizedek." H1826
Pr 24:27 **Put** your outdoor work **in o** and get your H3922
Pr 28: 2 discernment and knowledge maintains **o**. H4026
Ecc 12: 9 searched out and **set in o** many proverbs. H9545
Isa 23:11 *He has* **given an o** concerning Phoenicia H7422
Isa 34:16 For it is his mouth *that has* **given the o** H7422
Isa 38: 1 **Put** your house **in o**, because you are H7422
Jer 34:22 I *am going to* **give the o**, declares the LORD, H7422
Eze 3:18 from their evil ways **in o to** save their life, H4200
Eze 13:18 their heads **in o to** ensnare people. H4200
Eze 24: 6 piece **in whatever o** it H4202+5877+1598+6584
Eze 39:12 burying them **in o to** cleanse the H4200+5100
Da 6:16 So the king **gave the o**, and they brought A10042
Da 11:17 in marriage **in o to** overthrow the H4200
Am 1:13 women of Gilead **in o to** extend his H4200+5100
Zec 13: 4 garment of hair **in o to** deceive. H4200+5100
Mt 12:44 unoccupied, swept clean and **put in o**. G3175
Mt 27:64 So **give the o** *for* the tomb to be made G3027
Mk 7: 9 commands of God **in o to** observe your G2671
Lk 4:29 was built, **in o to** throw him off the cliff. G6063
Lk 8:31 repeatedly not to **o** them to go into the G2199
Lk 11:25 finds the house swept clean and **put in o**. G3175
Lk 19:15 **in o to** find out what they had gained with G2671
Jn 8: 6 **in o to** have a basis for accusing him. G2671
Jn 17:26 to make you known **in o that** the love you G2671
Ac 6: 2 of the word of God *in o to* **wait on** tables. AIT
Ac 9:24 watch on the city gates **in o to** kill him. G3968
Ac 16:35 sent their officers to the jailer *with the* **o**: G3306
Ac 17: 5 Silas *in o to* **bring** them **out** to the crowd. AIT
Ac 19:33 silence **in o to** make a defense G2527
Ac 20:30 the truth *in o to* **draw away** disciples after AIT

Ac 22:24 interrogated **in o to** find out why the G2671
Ac 24: 4 But **in o** not to weary you further, I would G2671
Ro 1:13 **in o that** I might have a harvest among G2671
Ro 4:11 **in o that** righteousness might be G1650+3836
Ro 6: 4 him through baptism into death **in o that,** G2671
Ro 7: 4 **in o that** we might bear fruit for God. G2671
Ro 7:13 **in o that** sin might be recognized as sin G2671
Ro 8: 4 **in o that** the righteous requirement of the G2671
Ro 8:17 in his sufferings **in o that** we may also G2671
Ro 9:11 **in o that** God's purpose in election might G2671
Ro 11:31 disobedient **in o that** they too may now G2671
Ro 15: 7 accepted you, **in o to bring** praise to God. G1650
2Co 1:23 that *it was in o to* **spare** you that I did not AIT
2Co 2:11 **in o that** Satan might not outwit us. For G2671
2Co 8:19 we administer **in o to** honor the Lord G4639
2Co 9: 3 the brothers **in o that** our boasting about G2671
2Co 11: 7 me to lower myself **in o to** elevate you by G2671
2Co 11:12 what I am doing **in o to** cut the ground G2671
2Co 11:32 the Damascenes guarded *in o to* **arrest** me. AIT
2Co 12: 7 **in o to** keep me from becoming conceited, G2671
Gal 3:14 He redeemed us **in o that** the blessing G2671
Eph 1:12 **in o that** we, who were the first to G1650+3836
Eph 1:18 enlightened **in o that** you may G1650+3836
Eph 2: 7 **in o that** in the coming ages he might G2671
Eph 4:10 heavens, **in o to** fill the whole universe.) G2671
Php 2:13 will and to act **in o to fulfill** his good G5642
Col 2: 2 **in o that** they may know the mystery of G1650
1Th 2: 9 and day **in o** not to be a burden G4639+3836
1Th 4: 1 you how to live **in o to** please God, G2671
2Th 3: 9 but **in o to** offer ourselves as a model G2671
2Th 3:14 them, **in o that** they may feel ashamed. G2671
1Ti 4: 3 to marry and **o** them **to abstain** from certain G600
Titus 1: 5 was that *you might* **put in o** what was left G2114
Titus 3:14 **in o to** provide for urgent needs and not G2671
Phm 8 I could be bold and **o** you to do what you G2199
Heb 2:17 **in o that** he might become a merciful G2671
Heb 5: 6 a priest forever, in the **o** of Melchizedek." G5423
Heb 5:10 to be high priest in the **o** of Melchizedek. G5423
Heb 6:20 priest forever, in the **o** of Melchizedek. G5423
Heb 7:11 to come, one in the **o** of Melchizedek, not G5423
Heb 7:11 of Melchizedek, not in the **o** of Aaron? G5423
Heb 7:17 a priest forever, in the **o** of Melchizedek." G5423
Heb 9:10 applying until the time *of* the **new o.** G1481
Heb 12:10 **in o that** we may share in his G1650+3836
Rev 21: 4 the **old o of things** has passed away." G4755

ORDERED (95) [ORDER]

Ex 17:10 fought the Amalekites as Moses *had* **o,** H606
Lev 10: 5 outside the camp, as Moses **o.** H1819
Nu 34:13 The LORD *has* **o** that it be given to the nine H7422
Nu 36: 2 he **o** you to give the inheritance of our H7422
Jos 1:10 So Joshua **o** the officers of the people: H7422
Jos 6: 7 And *he* **o** the army, "Advance! March H606
Jos 8:29 Joshua **o** them to take the body from the H7422
Jdg 3:28 "Follow me," *he* **o,** "for the LORD has given H606
Jdg 9:48 to his shoulders. *He* **o** the men with him H606
1Sa 18:22 Then Saul **o** his attendants: "Speak to H7422
1Sa 20:29 my brother *has* **o** me to be there. H7422
1Sa 22:17 Then the king **o** the guards at his side H606
1Sa 22:18 The king then **o** Doeg, "You turn and strike H606
2Sa 1:18 and *he* **o** that the people of Judah be H606
2Sa 13:28 Absalom **o** his men, "Listen! When H7422
2Sa 13:29 men did to Amnon what Absalom *had* **o.** H7422
1Ki 2:29 Then Solomon **o** Benaiah son of H8938
1Ki 12:24 went home again, as the LORD had **o.** H1821
1Ki 18:34 it a third time," *he* **o,** and they did it the H606
1Ki 20:12 drinking in their tents, and *he* **o** his men: H606
1Ki 22:26 The king of Israel then **o,** "Take Micaiah H606
1Ki 22:31 Now the king of Aram *had* **o** his thirty-two H7422
2Ki 6:13 the king **o,** "so I can send men and H606
2Ki 9:17 a horseman," Joram **o.** "Send him to meet H606
2Ki 9:21 up my chariot," Joram **o.** And when it was H606
2Ki 10: 8 Then Jehu **o,** "Put them in two piles at the H606
2Ki 10:14 "Take them alive!" *he* **o.** So they took them H606
2Ki 10:25 burnt offering, he **o** the guards and officers: H606
2Ki 11: 9 hundred did just as Jehoiada the priest **o.** H7422
2Ki 11:15 Jehoiada the priest **o** the commanders of H7422
2Ki 16:16 the priest did just as King Ahaz *had* **o.** H7422
2Ki 17:15 them although the LORD *had* **o** them, H7422
2Ki 23: 4 The king **o** Hilkiah the high priest, the H7422
1Ch 21:17 "Was it not I *who* **o** the fighting men to be H606
1Ch 21:18 the angel of the LORD **o** Gad to tell David to H606
1Ch 22:17 Then David **o** all the leaders of Israel to H7422
2Ch 8:14 was what David the man of God had **o.** H5184
2Ch 18:25 The king of Israel then **o,** "Take Micaiah H606
2Ch 18:30 Now the king of Aram *had* **o** his chariot H7422
2Ch 23: 8 of Judah did just as Jehoiada the priest **o.** H7422
2Ch 23:18 rejoicing and singing, as David had **o.** H3338
2Ch 29:15 as the king had **o,** following the word H5184
2Ch 29:24 because the king *had* **o** the burnt offering H606
2Ch 29:30 his officials **o** the Levites to praise the H606
2Ch 30:12 out **what** the king and his officials had **o,** H5184
2Ch 31: 4 *He* **o** the people living in Jerusalem to give H606
2Ch 35:10 in their divisions as the king had **o.** H5184
2Ch 35:16 altar of the LORD, as King Josiah had **o.** H5184
Ezr 2:63 The governor **o** them not to eat any of the H606
Ezr 8:17 and *I* **o** them to go to Iddo, the leader in H7422
Ne 7:65 **o** them not to eat any of the most sacred H606
Ne 13:19 *I* **o** the doors to be shut and not opened H606
Est 4: 5 **o** him to find out what was troubling H7422
Est 6: 1 so *he* **o** the book of the chronicles H606
Est 6: 5 "Bring him in," the king **o.** H606
Jer 35:14 son of Rekab **o** his descendants not to H7422
Jer 35:18 have done everything *he* **o.** H7422
Jer 38:27 everything the king *had* **o** him to say. H7422
Jer 47: 7 when *he has* **o** it to attack Ashkelon and H3585
Da 1: 3 Then the king **o** Ashpenaz, chief of his H606
Da 2:12 furious that *he* **o** the execution of all A10042
Da 2:46 paid him honor and **o** that an offering A10042
Da 3:19 *He* **o** the furnace heated seven times A10558
Mt 14: 9 *he* **o** that her request be granted G3027
Mt 16:20 Then *he* **o** his disciples not to tell anyone G1403
Mt 18:25 the master **o** *that* he and his wife and his G3027
Mt 27:58 and Pilate **o** that it be given to him. G3027
Lk 5:14 Then Jesus **o** him, "Don't tell anyone, but G4133
Lk 8:56 he **o** them not to tell anyone what G4133
Lk 14:21 house became angry and **o** his servant, G3306
Lk 14:22 'what *you* **o** has been done, but G2199
Lk 18:40 Jesus stopped and **o** the man to be G3027
Ac 4:15 So *they* **o** them to withdraw from the G3027
Ac 5:34 the Sanhedrin and **o** *that* the men be put G3027
Ac 5:40 Then *they* **o** them not to speak in the G4133
Ac 10:48 So *he* **o** *that* they be baptized in the name G4705
Ac 12:19 the guards and **o** that they be executed. G3027
Ac 16:22 the magistrates **o** them to be stripped G3027
Ac 16:36 "The magistrates *have* **o** that you and Silas G690
Ac 18: 2 because Claudius *had* **o** all Jews to leave G1411
Ac 21:33 arrested him and **o** him to be bound with G3027
Ac 21:34 *he* **o** that Paul be taken into the barracks. G3027
Ac 22:24 the commander **o** that Paul be taken into G3027
Ac 22:30 he released him and **o** the chief priests G3027
Ac 23: 2 high priest Ananias **o** those standing near G2199
Ac 23:10 *He* **o** the troops to go down and take him G3027
Ac 23:23 called two of his centurions and **o** them, G3306
Ac 23:30 *I* also **o** his accusers to present to you G4133
Ac 23:35 Then *he* **o** that Paul be kept under guard G3027
Ac 24:23 *He* **o** the centurion to keep Paul under G1411
Ac 25: 6 the court and **o** that Paul be brought G3027
Ac 25:17 the next day and **o** the man to be brought G3027
Ac 25:21 *I* **o** him held until I could send him to G3027
Ac 27:43 *He* **o** those who could swim to jump G3027
Rev 13:14 *It* **o** them to set up an image in honor of G3306

ORDERLY (2) [ORDER]

Lk 1: 3 too decided to write an **o** account for you, G2759
1Co 14:40 be done in a fitting and **o way.** G2848+5423

ORDERS (50) [ORDER]

Ge 12:20 Pharaoh **gave o** about Abram *to* his men, H7422
Ge 26:11 So Abimelek **gave o** *to* all the people H7422
Ge 41:40 all my people are to submit to your **o.** H7023
Ge 42:25 Joseph **gave o** to fill their bags with grain H7422
Nu 32:28 Moses **gave o** about them to Eleazar H7422
Dt 2: 4 **Give** the people *these* **o**: 'You are about to H7422
Jos 3: 3 **giving o** *to* the people: "When you see the H7422
Jos 8: 4 with these **o**: "Listen carefully. You are to H7422
Jos 8: 8 See to it; you *have my* **o.**" H7422
Ru 2:15 up to glean, Boaz **gave o** *to* his men, "Let H7422
2Sa 3:15 So Ish-Bosheth **gave o** and had her taken H8938
2Sa 18: 5 king **giving o** concerning Absalom *to* each H7422
1Ki 2:25 So King Solomon **gave o** to Benaiah son H8938
1Ki 5: 6 "So **give o** that cedars of Lebanon be cut H7422
2Ki 16:15 King Ahaz then **gave** *these* **o** *to* Uriah the H7422
2Ki 22:12 He **gave** *these* **o** *to* Hilkiah the priest H7422
1Ch 14:12 David **gave o** to burn them in the fire. H606
1Ch 22: 2 So David **gave o** to assemble the H606
2Ch 2: 1 Solomon **gave o** to build a temple for the H606
2Ch 19: 9 *He* **gave** them *these* **o**: "You must serve H7422
2Ch 31:11 Hezekiah **gave o** to prepare storerooms in H606
2Ch 34:20 He **gave** *these* **o** *to* Hilkiah, Ahikam son of H7422
Ezr 8:36 delivered the king's **o** to the royal satraps H2017
Ne 11:23 The musicians were under the king's **o** H5184
Ne 13: 9 *I* **gave o** to purify the rooms, and then I put H606
Est 3:12 people all Haman's **o** to the king's H7422
Est 8: 9 wrote out all Mordecai's **o** to the Jews, H7422
Est 8: 9 These **o** were written in the script of each NDT
Est 9:25 *he* **issued** written **o** that the evil scheme H606
Job 38:12 "*Have you* ever **given o** *to* the morning, or H7422
Isa 45:11 or **give** me **o** about the work of my hands? H7422
Jer 37:21 Zedekiah then **gave o** *for* Jeremiah to be H7422
Jer 39:11 of Babylon *had* **given** *these* **o** about H7422
Da 5: 2 *he* **gave o** to bring in the gold and silver A10042
Da 6:23 was overjoyed and **gave o** to lift Daniel A10042
Mt 2:16 and *he* **gave o** to kill all the boys in G690
Mt 8:18 *he* **gave o** to cross to the other side of the G3027
Mk 1:27 *He* even **gives o** to impure spirits and they G2199
Mk 3:12 But *he* **gave** them strict **o** not to tell others G2203
Mk 5:43 *He* **gave** strict **o** not to let anyone know G1403
Mk 6:17 Herod himself *had* **given o** to have John G690
Mk 6:27 sent an executioner *with* **o** to bring John's G2199
Mk 9: 9 Jesus **gave** them **o** not to tell anyone G1403
Lk 4:36 power *he* **gives o** to impure spirits G2199
Lk 15:29 you and never disobeyed your **o.** G1953
Jn 11:57 Pharisees had given **o** that anyone who G1953
Ac 5:28 "*We* **gave** you **strict o** not to teach G4132+4133
Ac 8:38 And *he* **gave o** to stop the chariot. G3027
Ac 16:24 When he received these **o,** he put them in G4132
Ac 23:31 carrying out their **o,** took Paul with them G1411

ORDINANCE (29) [ORDINANCES]

Ex 12:14 it as a festival to the LORD—a lasting **o.** H2978
Ex 12:17 this day as a lasting **o** for the generations H2978
Ex 12:24 instructions as a lasting **o** for you and your H2976
Ex 13:10 You must keep this **o** at the appointed H2978
Ex 27:21 is to be a lasting **o** among the Israelites H2978
Ex 28:43 is to be a lasting **o** for Aaron and his H2978
Ex 29: 9 The priesthood is theirs by a lasting **o** H2978
Ex 30:21 This is to be a lasting **o** for Aaron and his H2976
Lev 3:17 " 'This is a lasting **o** for the generations to H2978
Lev 10: 9 This is a lasting **o** for the generations to H2978
Lev 16:29 "This is to be a lasting **o** for you: On the H2978
Lev 16:31 you must deny yourselves; it is a lasting **o.** H2978
Lev 16:34 "This is to be a lasting **o** for you H2978
Lev 17: 7 is to be a lasting **o** for them and for the H2978
Lev 23:14 is to be a lasting **o** for the generations to H2978
Lev 23:21 is to be a lasting **o** for the generations to H2978
Lev 23:31 is to be a lasting **o** for the generations to H2978
Lev 23:41 is to be a lasting **o** for the generations to H2978
Lev 24: 3 is to be a lasting **o** for the generations to H2978
Nu 10: 8 This is to be a lasting **o** for you and the H2978
Nu 15:15 this is a lasting **o** for the generations to H2978
Nu 18:23 This is a lasting **o** for the generations to H2978
Nu 19:10 This will be a lasting **o** both for the H2978
Nu 19:21 This is a lasting **o** for them. "The man who H2978
1Sa 30:25 this a statute and **o** for Israel from that H5477
2Ch 2: 4 This is a lasting **o** for Israel. NDT
2Ch 8:14 In keeping with the **o** *of* his father David H5477
Ps 81: 4 Israel, an **o** of the God of Jacob. H5477
Eze 46:14 grain offering to the LORD is a lasting **o.** H2978

ORDINANCES (2) [ORDINANCE]

Ne 9:29 They sinned against your **o,** of which you H5477
Eze 44:24 judges and decide it according to my **o.** H5477

ORDINARY (6)

1Sa 21: 4 "I don't have any **o** bread on hand H2687
Isa 8: 1 a large scroll and write on it with an **o** pen: H632
Ac 4:13 they were unschooled, **o** men, they were G2626
Ac 7:20 and he was **no o** *child.* G842+3836+2536
Ac 21:39 from Tarsus in Cilicia, a citizen of no **o** city. G817
Heb 11:23 because they saw he was **no o** child, and G842

ORDINATION (13) [ORDAIN]

Ex 29:22 the right thigh. (This is the ram for the **o.**) H4854
Ex 29:26 take the breast of the ram for Aaron's **o,** H4854
Ex 29:27 those parts of the **o** ram that belong to H4854
Ex 29:31 the ram for the **o** and cook the meat in H4854
Ex 29:33 made for their **o** and H4848+906+3338
Ex 29:34 of the meat of the **o ram** or any bread is H4854
Lev 7:37 the **o offering** and the fellowship offering H4854
Lev 8:22 the ram for the **o,** and Aaron and his H4854
Lev 8:28 top of the burnt offering as an **o offering,** H4854
Lev 8:29 which was his share of the **o** ram, and H4854
Lev 8:31 the bread from the basket of **o offerings,** H4854
Lev 8:33 until the days of your **o** are completed, for H4854
Lev 8:33 your **o** will last seven days. H4848+906+3338

ORE (3)

Job 28: 2 the earth, and copper is smelted from **o.** H74
Job 28: 3 farthest recesses for **o** in the blackest H74
Jer 6:27 a tester of metals and my people the **o,** H4450

OREB (7)

Jdg 7:25 two of the Midianite leaders, **O** and Zeeb. H6855
Jdg 7:25 They killed **O** at the rock of Oreb, and H6855
Jdg 7:25 They killed Oreb at the rock of **O,** and H6855
Jdg 7:25 the heads of **O** and Zeeb to Gideon, H6855
Jdg 8: 3 God gave **O** and Zeeb, the Midianite H6855
Ps 83:11 Make their nobles like **O** and Zeeb, all H6855
Isa 10:26 he struck down Midian at the rock of **O**; H6855

OREN (1)

1Ch 2:25 his firstborn, Bunah, **O,** Ozem and Ahijah. H816

ORGAN, ORGANS (KJV) PIPE, PIPES

ORGANS (17)

Ex 12: 9 with the head, legs and **internal o.** H7931
Ex 29:13 Then take all the fat on the **internal o,** the H7931
Ex 29:17 wash the **internal o** and the legs, H7931
Ex 29:22 the fat on the **internal o,** the long lobe of H7931
Lev 1: 9 are to wash the **internal o** and the legs H7931
Lev 1:13 are to wash the **internal o** and the legs H7931
Lev 3: 3 the **internal o** and all the fat that is H7931
Lev 3: 9 the **internal o** and all the fat that is H7931
Lev 3:14 the **internal o** and all the fat that is H7931
Lev 4: 8 the fat that is connected to the **internal o,** H7931
Lev 4:11 legs, the **internal o** and the intestines H7931
Lev 7: 3 tail and the fat that covers the **internal o,** H7931
Lev 8:16 also took all the fat around the **internal o,** H7931
Lev 8:21 He washed the **internal o** and the legs H7931
Lev 8:25 all the fat around the **internal o,** the long H7931
Lev 9:14 He washed the **internal o** and the legs H7931
Dt 18: 3 the **internal o** and the meat from the H7687

ORGIES (2)

Gal 5:21 drunkenness, **o,** and the like. I warn G3269
1Pe 4: 3 drunkenness, **o,** carousing and detestable G3269

ORIGIN (10) [ORIGINAL, ORIGINATE, ORIGINS]

Est 6:13 is of Jewish **o,** you cannot stand H2446
Mt 21:25 from heaven, or of human **o?**" They G1666
Mt 21:26 But if we say, '**Of** human **o**'—we are afraid G1666
Mk 11:30 was it from heaven, or of human **o?** G1666
Mk 11:32 But if we say, '**Of** human **o**' ..." (They G1666
Lk 20: 4 was it from heaven, or of human **o?** G1666
Lk 20: 6 But if we say, '**Of** human **o,**' all the people G1666
Ac 5:38 if their purpose or activity is **of** human **o,** G1666

Gal 1:11 the gospel I preached is not **of** human **o**. *G2848*
2Pe 1:21 For prophecy never **had** *its* **o** in the human *G5770*

ORIGINAL (2) [ORIGIN]

2Ch 24:13 according to its **o design** and reinforced it. H5504
Heb 3:14 if indeed we hold our **o** conviction firmly to *G794*

ORIGINATE (1) [ORIGIN]

1Co 14:36 Or *did* the word of God **o** with you? Or are *G2002*

ORIGINS (1) [ORIGIN]

Mic 5: 2 over Israel, whose **o** are from of old, from H4606

ORION (2) [ORION'S]

Job 9: 9 He is the Maker of the Bear and **O**, the H4068
Am 5: 8 He who made the Pleiades and **O**, who H4068

ORION'S (1) [ORION]

Job 38:31 of the Pleiades? Can you loosen **O** belt? H4068

ORNAMENT (2) [ORNAMENTS, ORNATE]

Pr 3:22 be life for you, an **o to grace** your neck. H2834
Pr 25:12 earring of gold or an **o** *of* fine gold is the H2717

ORNAMENTS (10) [ORNAMENT]

Ex 33: 4 began to mourn and no one put on any **o**. H6344
Ex 33: 5 Now take off your **o** and I will decide what H6344
Ex 33: 6 stripped off their **o** at Mount Horeb. H6344
Ex 35:22 earrings, rings and **o**. They all presented H3921
Jdg 8:21 took the **o** off their camels' necks. H8448
Jdg 8:26 not counting the **o**, the pendants and the H8448
2Sa 1:24 adorned your garments with **o** *of* gold. H6344
Isa 3:16 with **o jingling** on their ankles. H6576
Isa 49:18 "you will wear them all as **o**; you will put H6344
Jer 2:32 forget her jewelry, a bride her **wedding o**? H8005

ORNATE (5) [ORNAMENT]

Ge 37: 3 old age; and he made an **o** robe for him. H7168
Ge 37:23 of his robe—the **o** robe he was wearing H7168
Ge 37:32 They took the **o** robe back to their father H7168
2Sa 13:18 She was wearing an **o** robe, for this was H7168
2Sa 13:19 head and tore the **o** robe she was H7168

ORPAH (2)

Ru 1: 4 one named **O** and the other Ruth. H6905
Ru 1:14 Then **O** kissed her mother-in-law H6905

ORPHAN'S (1) [ORPHANED]

Job 24: 3 drive away the **o** donkey and take the H3846

ORPHANED (1) [ORPHAN'S, ORPHANS]

1Th 2:17 *when* we *were* **o** by being separated from *G682*

ORPHANS (2) [ORPHANED]

Jn 14:18 I will not leave you as **o**; I will come to you *G4003*
Jas 1:27 to look after **o** and widows in their distress *G4003*

OSEE (KJV) HOSEA

OSHEA (KJV) HOSHEA

OSPRAY (KJV) BLACK VULTURE

OSPREY (2)

Lev 11:18 the white owl, the desert owl, the **o**, H8164
Dt 14:17 the desert owl, the **o**, the cormorant, H8168

OSSIFRAGE (KJV) VULTURE

OSTRICH (1) [OSTRICHES]

Job 39:13 "The wings of the **o** flap joyfully, though H8266

OSTRICHES (1) [OSTRICH]

La 4: 3 become heartless like **o** in the desert. H3612

OTHER (757) [OTHER'S, OTHERS, OTHERWISE]

Ge 4:19 one named Adah and the **o** Zillah. H9108
Ge 5: 4 800 years and had **o** sons and daughters. NDT
Ge 5: 7 807 years and had **o** sons and daughters. NDT
Ge 5:10 815 years and had **o** sons and daughters. NDT
Ge 5:13 840 years and had **o** sons and daughters. NDT
Ge 5:16 830 years and had **o** sons and daughters. NDT
Ge 5:19 800 years and had **o** sons and daughters. NDT
Ge 5:22 300 years and had **o** sons and daughters. NDT
Ge 5:26 782 years and had **o** sons and daughters. NDT
Ge 5:30 595 years and had **o** sons and daughters. NDT
Ge 9:23 faces were **turned the o way** so that they H345
Ge 11: 3 They said to each **o**, "Come, let's make H8276S
Ge 11: 7 so they will not understand each **o**." H8276S
Ge 11:11 500 years and had **o** sons and daughters. NDT
Ge 11:13 403 years and had **o** sons and daughters. NDT
Ge 11:15 403 years and had **o** sons and daughters. NDT
Ge 11:17 430 years and had **o** sons and daughters. NDT
Ge 11:19 209 years and had **o** sons and daughters. NDT
Ge 11:21 207 years and had **o** sons and daughters. NDT
Ge 11:23 200 years and had **o** sons and daughters. NDT
Ge 11:25 119 years and had **o** sons and daughters. NDT
Ge 14:16 together with the women and the **o** people. NDT
Ge 15:10 arranged the halves opposite each **o**; H8276S
Ge 24:50 can say nothing to you one way or **the o**. H3202S
Ge 25:22 The babies **jostled each o** within her, and H8368
Ge 25:23 one people will be stronger than the **o** H4211S
Ge 26:31 the men swore an oath to each **o**. H278S
Ge 28:17 This is none **o than** the house of H3954+561
Ge 29:19 that I give her to you than to *some* **o** man. H337
Ge 31:49 me when we are away from each **o**. H8276S
Ge 34:23 all their *o* **animals** become ours? AIT
Ge 36: 6 all his *o* **animals** and all the goods he AIT
Ge 37: 3 loved Joseph more than any of his *o* **sons**, AIT
Ge 37:19 comes that dreamer!" they said to each **o**. H278S
Ge 41: 3 After them, seven **o** cows, ugly and gaunt H337
Ge 41: 6 After them, seven **o** heads of grain sprouted NDT
Ge 41:13 position, and **the o man** was impaled." H2257S
Ge 41:19 After them, seven **o** cows came up H337
Ge 41:23 After them, seven **o** heads sprouted NDT
Ge 41:54 There was famine in all the **o** lands, but in NDT
Ge 42: 1 "Why *do you just keep* **looking at each o**?" H8011
Ge 42:28 they turned to each **o** trembling and said, H278S
Ge 43:14 he will let your **o** brother and Benjamin H337
Ge 43:33 they looked at each **o** in astonishment. H8276S
Ge 45:23 bread and *o* **provisions** for his journey. AIT
Ge 47:21 from one end of Egypt to the **o**. H7895S
Ge 47:24 The *o* **four-fifths** you may keep as seed for AIT
Ex 12:38 Many **o people** went up with them, and H6850
Ex 14: 7 along with all the **o** chariots of Egypt, with NDT
Ex 14:20 to the one side and light to the **o** side; NDT
Ex 14:20 so neither went near the **o** all night long. H2296S
Ex 16: 5 much as they gather *on* the **o days**." H3427+3427
Ex 16:15 they said to each **o**, "What is it? H278S
Ex 17:12 one on the **o**—so that his hands H2296S
Ex 18: 4 the **o** was named Eliezer, for he said H285S
Ex 18: 7 They greeted each **o** and then went into H8276S
Ex 18:11 that the LORD is greater than all **o** gods, H2021S
Ex 18:12 a burnt offering and **o** sacrifices to God, NDT
Ex 20: 3 "You shall have no **o** gods before me. H337
Ex 21:19 be held liable if the **o** can get up and walk NDT
Ex 22: 8 has laid hands on the **o person's** property. H8276
Ex 22: 9 **any** *o* lost property about which somebody AIT
Ex 22: 9 guilty must pay back double to the **o**. H8276
Ex 22:10 a sheep or **any** *o* animal to their neighbor AIT
Ex 22:11 not lay hands on the **o person's** property. H8276
Ex 22:20 to any god **o than** the LORD H1194+4200+963
Ex 23:13 Do not invoke the names of **o** gods; do not H337
Ex 24: 6 the **o** half he splashed against the H1947S
Ex 25: 7 onyx stones and *o* **gems** to be mounted on AIT
Ex 25:12 rings on one side and two rings on the **o**. H9108
Ex 25:19 end and the second cherub on the **o**; H7896S
Ex 25:20 The cherubim are to face each **o**, looking H278S
Ex 25:32 three on one side and three on the **o**. H9108
Ex 26: 3 do the same with the **o** five. H3749S
Ex 26: 4 same with the end curtain in the **o** set. H9108
Ex 26: 5 fifty loops on the end curtain of the **o** set, H9108
Ex 26: 5 other set, with the loops opposite each **o**. H295S
Ex 26: 9 one set and the **o** six into another set H3749S
Ex 26:10 the edge of the end curtain in the **o** set. H9108
Ex 26:14 that a covering of the **o** durable leather. H9391S
Ex 26:17 with two projections set parallel to each **o** H295S
Ex 26:20 For the **o** side, the north side of the H9108
Ex 26:27 five for those on the **o** side, and five for H9108
Ex 27:15 fifteen cubits long are to be on the **o** side, H9108
Ex 27:19 All the **o** articles used in the service of the NDT
Ex 28:10 one stone and the remaining six on the **o**. H9108
Ex 28:25 the **o** ends of the chains to the two H9109S
Ex 28:26 attach them to the **o** two corners of the NDT
Ex 29:17 putting them with the head and the *o* **pieces**. AIT
Ex 29:19 "Take the **o** ram, and Aaron and his sons H9108
Ex 29:39 one in the morning and the **o** at twilight. H9108
Ex 29:41 Sacrifice the **o** lamb at twilight with the H9108
Ex 30: 9 on this altar any **o** incense or any burnt H2424
Ex 30:32 do not make any **o** oil using the same NDT
Ex 30:33 puts it on **anyone o than a priest** must be H2424
Ex 31: 7 and all the **o** furnishings of the tent NDT
Ex 32:27 through the camp from one end to the **o**, H9133S
Ex 33:16 people from all the **o** people on the face of NDT
Ex 34:14 Do not worship *any* **o** god, for the LORD H337
Ex 35: 9 onyx stones and **o** gems to be mounted NDT
Ex 35:23 skins dyed red or the **o** durable leather H9391S
Ex 35:27 onyx stones and **o** gems to be mounted on NDT
Ex 36:10 did the same with the **o** five. H3749S
Ex 36:11 done with the end curtain in the **o** set. H9108
Ex 36:12 fifty loops on the end curtain of the **o** set, H9108
Ex 36:12 other set, with the loops opposite each **o**. H285S
Ex 36:16 one set and the **o** six into another set H3749S
Ex 36:17 the edge of the end curtain in the **o** set. H9108
Ex 36:19 that a covering of the **o** durable leather. H9391S
Ex 36:22 with two projections set parallel to each **o** H285S
Ex 36:25 For the **o** side, the north side of the H9108
Ex 36:32 five for those on the **o** side, and five for H9108
Ex 37: 3 rings on one side and two rings on the **o**. H9108
Ex 37: 8 end and the second cherub on the **o**; H2296S
Ex 37: 9 The cherubim faced each **o**, looking H278S
Ex 37:18 three on one side and three on the **o**. H9108
Ex 38:15 long were on the **o** side of the entrance to H9108
Ex 39:18 the **o** ends of the chains to the two H9109
Ex 39:19 attached them to the **o** two corners of the NDT
Lev 5: 7 sin offering and the **o** for a burnt offering. H285S
Lev 5:10 shall then offer the **o** as a burnt offering H9108
Lev 7:19 As for **o** meat, anyone ceremonially H2021S
Lev 7:24 animals may be used for any **o** purpose, NDT
Lev 8:22 He then presented the **o** ram, the ram H9108
Lev 10: 9 not to drink wine or **o** fermented drink NDT
Lev 11:10 among all the **o** living creatures in the NDT
Lev 11:23 But all **o** flying insects that have four legs NDT
Lev 12: 8 burnt offering and the **o** for a sin offering. H285S
Lev 14:22 sin offering and the **o** for a burnt offering. H285S
Lev 14:31 sin offering and the **o** as a burnt offering, H285S
Lev 14:42 Then they are to take **o** stones to replace H337
Lev 15:15 sin offering and the **o** for a burnt offering. H285S
Lev 15:25 days at a time **o than** her monthly period H4202
Lev 15:30 sin offering and the **o** for a burnt offering. H285S
Lev 16: 8 the LORD and the **o** for the scapegoat. H285S
Lev 22:12 daughter marries **anyone o than a priest**, H2424
Lev 23:40 willows and *o* leafy **trees**—and rejoice AIT
Lev 25:14 do not take advantage of each **o**. H278S
Lev 25:17 Do not take advantage of each **o**, but H6660S
Nu 1:49 them in the census of the **o** Israelites. NDT
Nu 2:33 were not counted along with the **o** Israelites, NDT
Nu 4:24 clans in their carrying and their *o* **work**: AIT
Nu 4:27 whether carrying or doing **o** work, is to H3972S
Nu 5:19 "If no **o** man has had sexual relations with NDT
Nu 5:20 with a man **o than** your husband"— H4946+1187
Nu 6: 3 from wine and **o** fermented drink and NDT
Nu 6: 3 made from wine or **o** fermented drink. NDT
Nu 6:11 sin offering and the **o** as a burnt offering H285S
Nu 8:12 to the LORD and the **o** for a burnt offering, H285S
Nu 8:14 to set the Levites apart from the **o** Israelites, NDT
Nu 9: 7 LORD's offering with the **o** Israelites at the NDT
Nu 11: 4 with them *began to* **crave o food**, H203+9294
Nu 11:34 buried the people who *had* **craved o food**. H203
Nu 14: 4 And they said to each **o**, "We should H278S
Nu 22:15 Then Balak sent **o** officials, more H6388
Nu 24: 1 to divination as **at o times**, H7193+928+7193
Nu 26:62 counted along with the **o** Israelites because NDT
Nu 28: 4 lamb in the morning and the **o** at twilight, H9108
Nu 31:30 donkeys, sheep or **o** animals. H3972S
Nu 32:19 **on the o side of** the H4946+6298+2256+2134
Nu 35: 3 the cattle they own and all their *o* **animals**. AIT
Nu 35: 6 In addition, give them forty-two **o** towns. NDT
Nu 35:21 hits another with their fist so that *the o* **dies**, AIT
Nu 35:23 then since **that o person** was not an H2085S
Nu 36: 3 they marry men from **o** Israelite tribes; H285S
Dt 3:18 must cross over ahead of the **o** Israelites. H278S
Dt 4: 7 What **o** nation is so great as to have their NDT
Dt 4: 8 And what **o** nation is so great as to have NDT
Dt 4:32 one end of the heavens to the **o**. H7895+9028S
Dt 4:33 Has any **o** people heard the voice of God NDT
Dt 4:35 LORD is God; besides him there is no **o**. H6388
Dt 4:39 on the earth below. There is no **o**. H6388
Dt 5: 7 "You shall have no **o** gods before me. H337
Dt 6:14 Do not follow **o** gods, the gods of the H337
Dt 7: 4 away from following me to serve **o** gods, H337
Dt 7: 7 were more numerous than **o** peoples, H3972S
Dt 7:14 will be blessed more than any **o** people; H2021S
Dt 8:19 your God and follow **o** gods and worship H337
Dt 11:16 away and worship **o** gods and bow down to H337
Dt 11:28 I command you today by following **o** gods, H337
Dt 13: 2 the prophet says, "Let us follow **o** gods" H337
Dt 13: 6 "Let us go and worship **o** gods" (gods that H337
Dt 13: 7 end of the land to **the o**), H7895+2021+824S
Dt 13:13 "Let us go and worship **o** gods" (gods you H337
Dt 14:21 or you may sell it to any **o** foreigner. NDT
Dt 14:26 wine or **o** fermented drink, or H2021S
Dt 17: 3 to my command has worshiped **o** gods, H337
Dt 18:20 prophet who speaks in the name of **o** gods, H337
Dt 19:19 that witness intended to do to the **o party**. H278S
Dt 21:15 he loves one but not the **o**, and both H285S
Dt 24: 5 sent to war or have any **o** duty laid on him. NDT
Dt 28:14 following **o** gods and serving them. H337
Dt 28:36 There you will worship **o** gods, gods of H337
Dt 28:64 from one end of the earth to the **o**. H7895S
Dt 28:64 There you will worship **o** gods—gods of H337
Dt 29: 6 drank no wine or **o** fermented drink. NDT
Dt 29:10 officials, and all the **o** men of Israel, NDT
Dt 29:26 off and worshiped **o** gods and bowed down H337
Dt 30:17 away to bow down to **o** gods and worship H337
Dt 31:18 of all their wickedness in turning to **o** gods. H337
Dt 31:20 they will turn to **o** gods and worship them H337
Jos 4:11 the priests **came to the o side** while the H6296
Jos 7: 7 to stay on the **o side** *of* the Jordan! H6298
Jos 7: 9 Canaanites and the **o** people of the H3972S
Jos 13: 8 **The o half of Manasseh**, the Reubenites H2257S
Jos 17: 2 These are the **o** male descendants of NDT
Jos 20: 8 of the Jordan (*on the o* **side** from Jericho AIT
Jos 21: 1 the heads of the **o** tribal families of NDT
Jos 22: 4 LORD gave you on the **o side** *of* the Jordan. H6298
Jos 22: 7 to the **o** half of the tribe Joshua gave NDT
Jos 22:19 **o than** the altar of the LORD our God H4946+1187
Jos 22:29 **o than** the altar of the LORD H4946+4200+963
Jos 23:16 go and serve **o** gods and bow down to H337
Jos 24: 2 the Euphrates River and worshiped **o** gods. H337
Jos 24:16 from us to forsake the LORD to serve **o** gods! H337
Jdg 2:17 themselves to **o** gods and worshiped them. H337
Jdg 2:19 following **o** gods and serving and H337
Jdg 4:11 Heber the Kenite had left the **o** Kenites, NDT
Jdg 6: 3 Amalekites and **o** eastern peoples invaded NDT
Jdg 6:29 They asked each **o**, "Who did this?" H8276S
Jdg 6:33 Amalekites and **o** eastern peoples joined NDT
Jdg 7:12 all the **o** eastern peoples had NDT
Jdg 7:14 can be nothing **o than** the sword of Gideon H561
Jdg 7:22 to turn on each **o** with their swords. H8276S
Jdg 10:13 you have forsaken me and served **o** gods, H337
Jdg 10:18 of the people of Gilead said to each **o**, H8276S
Jdg 11:18 camped on the **o side** *of* the Arnon. H6298
Jdg 13: 4 you drink no wine or **o** fermented drink and NDT
Jdg 13: 7 drink no wine or **o** fermented drink and do NDT
Jdg 13:10 The man who appeared to me the **o** day!" NDT
Jdg 13:14 drink any wine or **o** fermented drink nor NDT
Jdg 16: 7 I'll become as weak as any **o** man." H2021S
Jdg 16:11 I'll become as weak as any **o** man." H2021S

O

Jdg 16:13 I'll become as weak as any o man." H2021S
Jdg 16:17 I would become as weak as any o man." H2021S
Jdg 16:29 on the one and his left hand on the o, H285S
Jdg 17: 8 town in search of some o place to stay. H889S
Jdg 20:31 leading to Bethel and the o to Gibeah. H285S
Ru 1: 4 one named Orpah and the o Ruth. H9108
Ru 4: 7 took off his sandal and gave it to the o. H8276S
1Sa 1: 2 was called Hannah and the o Peninnah. H9108
1Sa 3:10 calling as at the o times, "Samuel! H7193S
1Sa 8: 5 to lead us, such as all the o nations have." NDT
1Sa 8: 8 forsaking me and serving o gods, so they H337
1Sa 8:20 Then we will be like all the o nations, with a NDT
1Sa 10:11 they asked each o, "What is this that has H8276S
1Sa 12:19 have added to all our o sins the evil of NDT
1Sa 14: 1 to the Philistine outpost on the o side." H6298
1Sa 14: 4 one was called Bozez and the o Seneh. H285S
1Sa 14: 5 Mikmash, the o to the south toward Geba. H285S
1Sa 14:20 striking each o with their swords. H8276S
1Sa 17:10 Give me a man and let us fight each o." H3480
1Sa 17:21 up their lines facing each o. H7925+5120
1Sa 18:25 wants no o price for the bride than a H3954
1Sa 20:41 they kissed each o and wept together— H8276S
1Sa 20:42 with each o in the name of H9109+5646
1Sa 21: 8 I haven't brought my sword or any o weapon AIT
1Sa 23:26 David and his men were on the o side, H2296S
1Sa 26:13 over to the o side and stood on top H6298
1Sa 26:19 have said, 'Go, serve o gods. H337
1Sa 28: 8 himself, putting on o clothes, and at night H337
1Sa 30:10 David and the o four hundred H408S
1Sa 30:20 drove them ahead of the o livestock, H2085S
1Sa 30:31 to those in all the o places where he and his AIT
2Sa 2:13 of the pool and one group on the o side. AIT
2Sa 4: 2 One was named Baanah and the o Rekab; H9108
2Sa 12: 1 in a certain town, one rich and the o poor. H285S
2Sa 14: 6 a fight with each o in the field, H9109+2157S
2Sa 14: 6 One struck the o and killed him. H285S
2Sa 17: 9 he is hidden in a cave or some o place. H285S
1Ki 3:22 The o woman said, "No! The living one is H337
1Ki 3:25 give half to one and half to the o. H285S
1Ki 3:26 But the o said, "Neither I nor you shall H2296S
1Ki 4:28 the chariot horses and the o horses. NDT
1Ki 6: 7 chisel or any o iron tool was heard at the NDT
1Ki 6:24 and the o wing five cubits—ten H9108
1Ki 6:27 while the wing of the o touched the other H9108
1Ki 6:27 the wing of the other touched the o wall, H9108
1Ki 6:27 wings touched each o in the middle of H4053S
1Ki 7: 4 sets of three, facing each o. H4691+448+4691
1Ki 7: 5 sets of three, facing each o. H4691+448+4691
1Ki 8:60 the LORD is God and that there is no o. H6388
1Ki 9: 6 go off to serve o gods and worship H337
1Ki 9: 9 have embraced o gods, worshiping H337
1Ki 10:20 it had ever been made for any o kingdom. NDT
1Ki 10:23 wisdom than all the o kings of the earth. NDT
1Ki 11: 4 his wives turned his heart after o gods, and H337
1Ki 11:10 had forbidden Solomon to follow o gods, H337
1Ki 11:41 As for the o events of Solomon's reign H3856
1Ki 12:29 One he set up in Bethel, and the o in Dan. H285S
1Ki 12:30 went as far as Dan to worship the o. H285
1Ki 14: 9 You have made for yourself o gods, idols H337
1Ki 14:19 The o events of Jeroboam's reign, his H3856
1Ki 14:29 As for the o events of Rehoboam's reign H3856
1Ki 15: 7 As for the o events of Abijah's reign, and H3856
1Ki 15:23 As for all the o events of Asa's reign, all H3856
1Ki 15:31 As for the o events of Nadab's reign, and H3856
1Ki 16: 5 As for the o events of Baasha's reign H3856
1Ki 16:14 As for the o events of Elah's reign, and all H3856
1Ki 16:20 As for the o events of Zimri's reign, and H3856
1Ki 16:21 king, and the o half supported Omri. NDT
1Ki 16:27 As for the o events of Omri's reign, what H3856
1Ki 18:23 I will prepare the o bull and put it on the H285S
1Ki 20:24 commands and replace them with o officers. AIT
1Ki 20:29 seven days they camped opposite each o, H465
1Ki 22:12 All the o prophets were prophesying the NDT
1Ki 22:13 the o prophets without exception are NDT
1Ki 22:39 As for the o events of Ahab's reign H3856
1Ki 22:45 As for the o events of Jehoshaphat's reign H3856
2Ki 1:18 As for all the o events of Ahaziah's reign H3856
2Ki 3:17 your cattle and your o animals will drink. NDT
2Ki 3:23 have fought and slaughtered each o. H8276S
2Ki 5:17 sacrifices to any o god but the LORD. H337
2Ki 7: 3 They said to each o, "Why stay here H8276S
2Ki 7: 9 Then they said to each o, "What we're H8276S
2Ki 8:23 As for the o events of Jehoram's reign H3856
2Ki 10:21 until it was full from one end to the o. H7023S
2Ki 10:34 As for the o events of Jehu's reign, all he H3856
2Ki 11: 7 you who are in the o two companies that NDT
2Ki 12: 7 the priest and the o priests and asked them, NDT
2Ki 12:12 and met all the o expenses of restoring the AIT
2Ki 12:13 trumpets or any o articles of gold or silver NDT
2Ki 12:19 As for the o events of the reign of Joash H3856
2Ki 13: 8 As for the o events of the reign of H3856
2Ki 13:12 As for the o events of the reign of H3856
2Ki 14: 8 let us face each o in battle." H8011+7156
2Ki 14:11 king of Judah faced each o at Beth H8011+7156
2Ki 14:15 As for the o events of the reign of H3856
2Ki 14:18 As for the o events of Amaziah's reign, are H3856
2Ki 14:28 As for the o events of Jeroboam's reign H3856
2Ki 15: 6 As for the o events of Azariah's reign, and H3856
2Ki 15:11 The o events of Zechariah's reign are H3856
2Ki 15:15 The o events of Shallum's reign, and the H3856
2Ki 15:21 As for the o events of Menahem's reign H3856
2Ki 15:26 The o events of Pekahiah's reign, and all H3856
2Ki 15:31 As for the o events of Pekah's reign, and H3856
2Ki 15:36 As for the o events of Jotham's reign, and H3856
2Ki 16:19 As for the o events of the reign of Ahaz H3856
2Ki 17: 7 They worshiped o gods H337
2Ki 17:35 "Do not worship any o gods or bow down H337
2Ki 17:37 he wrote for you. Do not worship o gods. H337
2Ki 17:38 made with you, and do not worship o gods. H337
2Ki 20:20 As for the o events of Hezekiah's reign H3856
2Ki 21:17 As for the o events of Manasseh's reign H3856
2Ki 21:25 As for the o events of Amon's reign, and H3856
2Ki 22:17 burned incense to o gods and aroused my H337
2Ki 23:24 the idols and all the o detestable things NDT
2Ki 23:28 As for the o events of Josiah's reign, and H3856
2Ki 24: 5 As for the o events of Jehoiakim's reign H3856
2Ki 25:17 bronze all around. The o pillar, with its H9108
2Ki 25:28 than those of the o kings who were with him NDT
1Ch 6:48 assigned to all the o duties of the NDT
1Ch 9:29 furnishings and all the o articles of the NDT
1Ch 9:33 and were exempt from o duties because AIT
1Ch 12:16 O Benjamites and some men from Judah NDT
1Ch 16:42 the playing of the o instruments for sacred NDT
1Ch 23:17 Eliezer had no o sons, but the sons of H337
1Ch 23:28 performance of o duties at the house of God. AIT
1Ch 26:26 hundreds, and by the o army commanders. NDT
1Ch 26:28 all the o dedicated things were in the NDT
1Ch 29:21 o sacrifices in abundance for all Israel. NDT
1Ch 29:30 Israel and the kingdoms of all the o lands. NDT
2Ch 2: 5 our God is greater than all o gods. H2021S
2Ch 3:11 while its o wing, also five cubits H337
2Ch 3:11 touched the wing of the o cherub. H337
2Ch 3:12 cubits long and touched the o temple wall, NDT
2Ch 3:12 temple wall, and its o wing, also five cubits H337
2Ch 5:13 trumpets, cymbals and o instruments, the NDT
2Ch 7:19 go off to serve o gods and worship H337
2Ch 7:22 have embraced o gods, worshiping H337
2Ch 9:19 it had ever been made for any o kingdom. NDT
2Ch 9:22 wisdom than all the o kings of the earth. NDT
2Ch 9:28 from Egypt and from all o countries. H2021S
2Ch 9:29 As for the o events of Solomon's reign H8637
2Ch 11:21 than any of his o wives and concubines NDT
2Ch 12: 8 me and serving the kings of o lands." H2021S
2Ch 13: 9 your own as the peoples of o lands do? H2021S
2Ch 13:22 The o events of Abijah's reign, what he H3856
2Ch 18:11 All the o prophets were prophesying the NDT
2Ch 18:12 the o prophets without exception are NDT
2Ch 19:10 whether bloodshed or o concerns of the law NDT
2Ch 20: 2 from the o side of the Dead Sea. H6298
2Ch 20:34 The o events of Jehoshaphat's reign, from H3856
2Ch 24:14 also dishes and o objects of gold and NDT
2Ch 25:17 let us face each o in battle." H8011+7156
2Ch 25:21 king of Judah faced each o at Beth H8011+7156
2Ch 25:26 As for the o events of Amaziah's reign H3856
2Ch 26:17 priest with eighty o courageous priests of NDT
2Ch 26:20 priest and all the o priests looked at him, NDT
2Ch 26:22 The o events of Uzziah's reign, from H3856
2Ch 27: 7 The o events in Jotham's reign, including H3856
2Ch 27: 7 all his wars and the o things he did, NDT
2Ch 28:25 burn sacrifices to o gods and aroused the H337
2Ch 28:26 The o events of his reign and all his ways H3856
2Ch 29:34 finished and until o priests had been H2021S
2Ch 31:19 around their towns or in any o towns, AIT
2Ch 32:13 have done to all the peoples of the o lands? NDT
2Ch 32:17 of the peoples of the o lands did not rescue NDT
2Ch 32:19 the gods of the o peoples of the world— NDT
2Ch 32:32 The o events of Hezekiah's reign and his H3856
2Ch 33:18 The o events of Manasseh's reign H3856
2Ch 34:25 burned incense to o gods and aroused my H337
2Ch 35:24 put him in his o chariot and brought him H5467
2Ch 35:26 The o events of Josiah's reign and his H3856
2Ch 36: 8 The o events of Jehoiakim's reign, the H3856
Ezr 1:10 matching silver bowls 410 o articles 1,000 H337
Ezr 2:31 of the o Elam 1,254 H337
Ezr 2:70 along with some of the o people, and the NDT
Ezr 4:10 the o people whom the great and A10692
Ezr 6: 6 you o officials of that A10360
Ezr 7:24 temple servants or o workers at this house NDT
Ezr 9:11 their impurity from one end to the o. H7023S
Ezr 10:25 And among the o Israelites: From the NDT
Ne 1: 2 came from Judah with some o men, and I AIT
Ne 3:18 ruler of the o half-district of Keilah. NDT
Ne 4:16 while the o half were equipped with spears NDT
Ne 4:17 one hand and held a weapon in the o, H285S
Ne 4:19 separated from each o along the wall. H278S
Ne 7:33 of the o Nebo 52 H337
Ne 7:34 of the o Elam 1,254 H337
Ne 9:36 eat its fruit and the o good things it NDT
Ne 11: 4 while o people from both Judah and NDT
Ne 12:24 one section responding to the o, as H5464S
Ne 12:47 also set aside the portion for the o Levites, NDT
Ne 13:15 grapes, figs and all o kinds of loads. AIT
Ne 13:24 of one of the o peoples, H6639+2256+6639
Est 1: 6 mother-of-pearl and o costly stones. NDT
Est 1: 7 each one different from the o, and the H3998S
Est 2:15 nothing o than what Hegai, H3954+561
Est 2:17 to Esther more than to any of the o women, NDT
Est 2:17 approval more than any of the o virgins. NDT
Est 3: 1 higher than that of all the o nobles. H889+907S
Est 3: 8 are different from those of all o people, NDT
Est 5:11 him above the o nobles and officials. NDT
Est 8:17 of o nationalities became H6639+2021+824
Est 9: 2 the people of all the o nationalities were NDT
Est 9:19 a day for giving presents to each o. H8276S
Job 8:19 and from the soil o plants grow. H337
Job 9:32 that we might confront each o in court. H3481
Job 28: 4 far from o people they dangle and sway. AIT
Job 31:10 and may o men sleep with her. H337
Job 35: 8 your righteousness only o people. AIT
Ps 16: 4 Those who run after o gods will suffer more H337
Ps 19: 6 the heavens and makes its circuit to the o; H7895
Ps 64: 5 They encourage each o in evil plans H4564S
Ps 81: 9 shall not worship any god o than me. H5797S
Ps 82: 7 mortals; you will fall like every o ruler." H285S
Ps 85:10 righteousness and peace kiss each o. AIT
Ps 87: 2 of Zion more than all the o dwellings of AIT
Ps 111: 6 giving them the lands of o nations. NDT
Ps 147:20 He has done this for no o nation; they H3972S
Ecc 2: 7 slaves and had o slaves who were born NDT
Ecc 3:19 one dies, so dies the o. All have the H2296S
Ecc 4:10 them falls down, one can help the o up. H2257S
Ecc 7:14 God has made the one as well as the o H2296S
Ecc 7:18 to grasp the one and not let go of the o. H2296S
Isa 3: 5 People will oppress each o—man H5601
Isa 13: 8 They will look aghast at each o, their H8276S
Isa 26:13 o lords besides you have ruled over us NDT
Isa 34:14 wild goats will bleat to each o H8276S
Isa 41: 6 they help each o and say to their H8276S
Isa 41: 7 The o nails down the idol so it will not AIT
Isa 44: 8 there is no o Rock; I know not one. NDT
Isa 45: 5 there is no o; apart from me there H6388
Isa 45: 6 I am the LORD, and there is no o. H6388
Isa 45:14 and there is no o; there is no other H6388
Isa 45:14 there is no other; there is no o god. NDT
Isa 45:18 "I am the LORD, and there is no o. H6388
Isa 45:22 the earth; for I am God, and there is no o. H6388
Isa 46: 9 there is no o; I am God, and there H6388
Isa 50: 8 Let us face each o! Who is my H3480
Isa 58: 4 and in striking each o with wicked fists. AIT
Isa 66:17 rats and o unclean things—they H2021S
Jer 1:16 in burning incense to o gods and in H337
Jer 7: 5 your actions and deal with each o justly, H8276S
Jer 7: 6 if you do not follow o gods to your own H337
Jer 7: 9 to Baal and follow o gods you have not H337
Jer 7:18 out drink offerings to o gods to arouse my H337
Jer 7:21 offerings to your o sacrifices and eat the NDT
Jer 8:10 give their wives to o men and their fields to H337
Jer 11:10 They have followed o gods to serve them H337
Jer 12: 9 bird of prey that o birds of prey surround H2021S
Jer 12:12 from one end of the land to the o; H7895S
Jer 13:10 hearts and go after o gods to serve and H337
Jer 13:14 I will smash them one against the o H278S
Jer 16:11 'and followed o gods and served and H337
Jer 16:13 there you will serve o gods day and night, H337
Jer 17:19 stand also at all the o gates of Jerusalem. NDT
Jer 19:13 poured out drink offerings to o gods. H337
Jer 22: 9 have worshiped and served o gods. H337
Jer 23:35 saying to your friends and o Israelites: H278
Jer 24: 2 ripen early; the o basket had very bad figs H285S
Jer 25: 6 Do not follow o gods to serve and worship H337
Jer 25:26 one after the o—all the kingdoms on H278S
Jer 25:33 end of the earth to the o. H7895+2021+824S
Jer 26:22 of Akbor to Egypt, along with some o men. NDT
Jer 27:19 stands and the o articles that are left H3856
Jer 28: 4 of Judah and all the o exiles from Judah NDT
Jer 29: 1 prophets and all the o people NDT
Jer 29:25 son of Maaseiah, and to all the o priests. NDT
Jer 30: 7 No o will be like it. H4946+401
Jer 32:29 by pouring out drink offerings to o gods. H337
Jer 34: 7 Jerusalem and the o cities of Judah that H3972S
Jer 35:15 do not follow o gods to serve them. H337
Jer 36: 2 Judah and all the o nations from the time I NDT
Jer 36:12 son of Hananiah, and all the o officials. NDT
Jer 36:16 they looked at each o in fear and said to H8276S
Jer 39: 3 official and all the o officials of the king H8642
Jer 39:13 official and all the o officers of the king of NDT
Jer 40:11 Edom and all the o countries heard that the NDT
Jer 44: 3 to and worshiping o gods that neither they H337
Jer 44: 5 stop burning incense to o gods. H337
Jer 44: 8 burning incense to o gods in Egypt, where H337
Jer 44:15 their wives were burning incense to o gods, H337
Jer 46:16 repeatedly; they will fall over each o. H8276S
Jer 52:22 The o pillar, with its pomegranates, was H9108
Jer 52:32 than those of the o kings who were with him NDT
Eze 1:11 each had two o wings covering its body. NDT
Eze 1:23 were stretched out one toward the o, H295S
Eze 3:13 against each o and the sound of the H295S
Eze 4: 8 from one side to the o until you have H7396S
Eze 4:17 at the sight of each o and will waste away H278S
Eze 11:15 of your fellow exiles and all the o Israelites, AIT
Eze 16:23 In addition to all your o wickedness, NDT
Eze 16:43 lewdness to all your o detestable practices? NDT
Eze 18:10 sheds blood or does any of these o things H278S
Eze 20:25 So I gave them o statutes that were not good NDT
Eze 25: 8 Judah has become like all the o nations," NDT
Eze 29:15 never again exalt itself above the o nations. NDT
Eze 31:14 Therefore no o trees by the waters are H3972S
Eze 31:14 No o trees so well-watered are ever to H3972S
Eze 33:30 saying to each o, 'Come and hear the H285S
Eze 40:40 on the o side of the steps were two H337
Eze 40:41 side of the gateway and four on the o— H7024S
Eze 40:42 the burnt offerings and the o sacrifices. NDT
Eze 41:19 of a lion toward the palm tree on the o. H7024S
Eze 42:14 They are to put on o clothes before they go H337
Eze 44: 7 In addition to all your o detestable practices NDT
Eze 44:19 and put on o clothes, so that the H337

Eze 48:14 the land and *must* not **pass into o hands**, H6296
Da 1:10 worse than the **o** young men your age? NDT
Da 3: 2 all the **o** provincial officials to NDT
Da 3: 3 magistrates and all the **o** provincial officials NDT
Da 3:21 trousers, turbans and **o** clothes, were bound NDT
Da 3:29 no **o** god can save in this way. A10025
Da 7:12 The **o** beasts had been stripped of their A10692
Da 7:20 about the **o** horn that came up, A10023
Da 7:23 different from all the **o** kingdoms and will NDT
Da 8: 3 was longer than the **o** but grew up later. H9108
Da 11:27 will sit at the same table and **lie** *to each o* AIT
Hos 3: 1 though they turn to **o** gods and love the H337
Hos 9: 1 do not be jubilant like the **o** nations. NDT
Joel 1: 4 locusts have left **o** locusts have eaten. H2021S
Joel 2: 8 They do not jostle each **o**; each marches H278S
Joel 2:25 the **o** locusts and the locust swarm NDT
Joel 2:27 that there is no **o**; never again will H6388
Jnh 1: 7 Then the sailors said to each **o**, "Come H8276S
Mic 7: 2 to shed blood; they hunt each **o** with nets. H278S
Hag 2:12 olive oil or **o** food, does it become H3972S
Zec 4: 3 the right of the bowl and **the o** on its left." H285S
Zec 5: 3 according to what it says on **the o** H2296S
Zec 7:10 Do not plot evil against each **o**.' H278S
Zec 8:16 Speak the truth to each **o**, and render H8276S
Zec 8:17 do not plot evil against each **o**, and do H8276S
Zec 11: 7 called one Favor and **the o** Union, H285S
Zec 14:13 They will seize each **o** by the hand and H8276S
Mal 3:16 who feared the LORD talked with each **o**, H8276S
Mt 4:21 he saw two **o** brothers, James son of G257
Mt 5:39 right cheek, turn to them the **o** cheek also. G257
Mt 6:14 For if you forgive **o people** when they sin G476
Mt 6:24 you will hate the one and love the **o**, G2283
Mt 6:24 be devoted to the one and despise the **o**. G2283
Mt 8:18 orders to cross to the **o side of the lake**. G4305
Mt 8:28 he arrived at the **o side** in the region of G4305
Mt 12:13 completely restored, just as sound as *the* **o**. G257
Mt 12:45 takes with it seven **o** spirits more wicked G2283
Mt 13: 7 **O** seed fell among thorns, which G257+1254
Mt 13: 8 Still **o** seed fell on good soil, where it G257
Mt 14:22 go on ahead of him to the **o side**, G4305
Mt 18:31 When the **o servants** saw what had G5281
Mt 19: 1 of Judea to the **o side** of the Jordan. G4305
Mt 20:21 at your right and **the o** at your left in your G1651S
Mt 21:30 father went to the **o** son and said the G2283
Mt 21:36 Then he sent **o** servants to them, more than G257
Mt 21:38 they said to **each o**, 'This is the heir. G1571
Mt 21:41 "and he will rent the vineyard to **o** tenants G257
Mt 23: 4 put them on **o** people's shoulders, G3836
Mt 24:10 the faith and will betray and hate **each o**, G253
Mt 24:31 from one end of the heavens to the **o**. G216S
Mt 24:40 one will be taken and **the o** left. G1651S
Mt 24:41 one will be taken and **the o** left. G1651
Mt 25:20 five bags of gold brought *the* **o** five. G257
Mt 26:22 began to say to him one *after the* **o**, G1667
Mt 26:35 And all **the** *o* disciples said the same AIT
Mt 27:61 Magdalene and the **o** Mary were sitting G257
Mt 28: 1 Magdalene and the **o** Mary went to look at G257
Mk 1:27 all so amazed that they asked **each o**, G1571
Mk 4: 7 **O** seed fell among thorns, which grew up G257
Mk 4: 8 Still **o** seed fell on good soil. It came up G257
Mk 4:19 the desires for **o** *things* come in and G3370
Mk 4:35 his disciples, "Let us go over to the **o side**." G4305
Mk 4:36 There were also **o** boats with him. G257
Mk 4:41 They were terrified and asked **each o** G253
Mk 5:21 over by boat to the **o side of the lake**, G4305
Mk 7: 4 And they observe many **o** traditions, such G257
Mk 8:13 into the boat and crossed to the **o side**. G4305
Mk 9:14 When they came to **the** *o* disciples, they saw AIT
Mk 9:50 yourselves, and be at peace with **each o**." G253
Mk 10:26 said to **each o**, "Who then can be G1571
Mk 10:37 at your right and **the o** at your left in your G1651S
Mk 12:32 that God is one and there is no **o** but him. G257
Mk 15:41 Many **o** *women* who had come up with him G257
Mk 16: 3 they asked **each o**, "Who will roll the G1571
Lk 1:15 is never to take wine or *o* **fermented drink**, AIT
Lk 3:18 And with many **o** *words* John exhorted the G2283
Lk 3:19 *all* the **o** evil things he had done G4246
Lk 4:36 people were amazed and said to **each o**, G253
Lk 4:43 the kingdom of God to the **o** towns also, G2283
Lk 5: 7 partners in the **o** boat to come and help G2283
Lk 6:29 you on one cheek, turn to them the **o** also. G257
Lk 7:32 the marketplace and calling out *to* **each o**: G253
Lk 7:41 him five hundred denarii, and the **o** fifty. G2283
Lk 7:49 The **o guests** began to say among G5263
Lk 8: 7 **O** *seed* fell among thorns, which grew up G2283
Lk 8: 8 Still **o** *seed* fell on good soil. It came up G2283
Lk 8:22 "Let us go over to the **o side** of the lake." G4305
Lk 10:31 saw the man, *he* **passed by on the o side**. G524
Lk 10:32 saw him, **passed by on the o side**. G524
Lk 11:26 takes seven **o** spirits more wicked G2283
Lk 11:42 rue and **all o** *kinds of* garden herbs, but AIT
Lk 12:45 he then begins to beat the **o** servants NDT
Lk 12:52 be five in one family **divided** *against each o*, AIT
Lk 13: 2 sinners than all **the** *o* Galileans because AIT
Lk 14:10 in the presence of all the **o guests**. G5263
Lk 14:32 a delegation while **the o** is still a long G899S
Lk 16:13 you will hate the one and love the **o**, G2283
Lk 16:13 be devoted to the one and despise the **o**. G2283
Lk 17:17 not all ten cleansed? Where are **the** *o* nine? AIT
Lk 17:24 up the sky from one end to the **o**. G5679+4041S
Lk 17:34 one bed; one will be taken and the **o** left. G2283
Lk 17:35 together; one will be taken and the **o** left." G2283
Lk 18:10 one a Pharisee and the **o** a tax collector. G2283
Lk 18:11 I thank you that I am not like **o** people G3370
Lk 18:14 rather than *the* **o**, went home G1697
Lk 22:65 they said many **o** insulting *things* to him. G2283
Lk 23:32 Two **o** *men*, both criminals, were also led G2283
Lk 23:33 one on his right, **the o** on his left. G4005+1254
Lk 23:40 But the **o** criminal rebuked him. "Don't G2283
Lk 24:14 were talking with **each o** about everything G253
Lk 24:15 discussed these things with each **o**, NDT
Lk 24:32 They asked **each o**, "Were not our hearts G253
Jn 1:28 at Bethany **on the o side of** the Jordan, G4305
Jn 3:26 with you **on the o side of** the Jordan— G4305
Jn 4:33 Then his disciples said to **each o**, "Could G253
Jn 6:25 they found him **on the o side** of the lake, G4305
Jn 8:18 myself; my *o* **witness** *is* the Father, who AIT
Jn 10: 1 climbs in **by some o way**, is a thief and G249
Jn 10:16 I have **o** sheep that are not of this sheep G257
Jn 15:12 Love **each o** as I have loved you. G253
Jn 15:17 This is my command: Love **each o**. G253
Jn 18: 1 **On the o side** there was a garden, and G3963S
Jn 18:16 The **o** disciple, who was known to the high G257
Jn 19:32 with Jesus, and then those *of* the **o**. G257
Jn 20: 2 running to Simon Peter and the **o** disciple, G257
Jn 20: 3 So Peter and the **o** disciple started for the G257
Jn 20: 4 the **o** disciple outran Peter and reached G257
Jn 20: 8 Finally the **o** disciple, who had reached the G257
Jn 20:12 one at the head and **the o** at the foot. G1651S
Jn 20:25 So the **o** disciples told him, "We have seen G257
Jn 20:30 Jesus performed many **o** signs in the G257
Jn 21: 2 two **o** disciples were together. G257
Jn 21: 8 The **o** disciples followed in the boat, towing G257
Jn 21:25 Jesus did many **o** *things* as well. If every G257
Ac 2: 4 began to speak in **o** tongues as the Spirit G2283
Ac 2:37 said to Peter and the **o** apostles, G3370
Ac 2:40 With many **o** words he warned them; and G2283
Ac 4:12 there is no **o** name under heaven G2283
Ac 5:29 Peter and **the** *o* apostles replied: "We must AIT
Ac 7:26 brothers; why do you want to hurt **each o**? G253
Ac 7:27 mistreating the **o** pushed Moses aside G4446
Ac 9:39 him the robes and **o clothing** that Dorcas had AIT
Ac 12:17 the *o* **brothers and sisters** about this, AIT
Ac 14: 2 stirred up the *o* **Gentiles** and poisoned their AIT
Ac 15: 2 along with some **o** believers, to go up to G257
Ac 16:25 and **the** *o* prisoners were listening to them. AIT
Ac 17: 5 But **o** Jews were jealous; so they rounded G3836
Ac 17: 6 dragged Jason and **some** *o* believers before AIT
Ac 21: 6 After saying goodbye *to* **each o**, we went G253
Ac 24: 9 **The** *o* Jews joined in the accusation AIT
Ac 27: 1 Paul and some **o** prisoners were handed G2283
Ac 27:44 there on planks or on **o** pieces of the ship. G5516
Ac 28: 4 they said to **each o**, "This man must G253
Ro 1:13 just as I have had among the **o** Gentiles. G3370
Ro 1:27 Men committed shameful acts with *o* **men** AIT
Ro 2:15 them **and** *at o times even* defending AIT
Ro 2:29 Such a person's praise is not from *o* **people** AIT
Ro 9: 8 **In o words**, it is not the children by G4047+1639
Ro 11:18 yourself to be superior to **those** *o* branches. AIT
Ro 13: 9 and whatever **o** command there may be G2283
Ro 15: 5 of mind toward **each o** that Christ Jesus G253
Ro 16:14 Hermas and **the** *o* brothers and sisters with AIT
1Co 3:11 one can lay **any** foundation **o** than the one G257
1Co 4: 6 a follower of one of us over against the **o**. G2283
1Co 6:18 **All** *o* sins a person commits are outside the AIT
1Co 7: 5 Do not deprive **each o** except perhaps by G253
1Co 9: 5 as do the **o** apostles and the Lord's G3370
1Co 10:29 I am referring to the **o** *person's* conscience, G2283
1Co 11:16 we have no **o** practice—nor do the G5525
1Co 12: 2 **somehow or o** you were influenced G6055+323
1Co 12:25 should have equal concern for **each o**. G253
1Co 14:21 "With **o tongues** and through the lips of G2280
2Co 2:16 brings death; *to the* **o**, an aroma G4005+1254
2Co 11: 4 preaches a Jesus **o than** the Jesus we G257
2Co 11: 8 I robbed **o** churches by receiving support G257
2Co 12:13 How were you inferior to the **o** churches G3370
Gal 1: 8 preach a gospel **o than** the one we G4123
Gal 1: 9 to you a gospel **o than** what you accepted G4123
Gal 1:19 I saw none of the **o** apostles—only James G2283
Gal 2:13 The **o** Jews joined him in his hypocrisy, so G3370
Gal 4:22 woman and the **o** by the free woman. G1651
Gal 5:10 in the Lord that you will take no **o** view. G257
Gal 5:15 If you bite and devour **each o**, watch out G253
Gal 5:15 out or you will be destroyed by **each o**. G253
Gal 5:17 They are in conflict *with* **each o**, so that you G253
Gal 5:26 conceited, provoking and envying **each o**. G253
Eph 3: 5 known to people in **o** generations as it G2283
Eph 4:32 another, forgiving **each o**, just as in Christ G1571
Eph 5:27 without stain or wrinkle or **any** *o* blemish, AIT
Col 3: 9 Do not lie to **each o**, since you have taken G253
Col 3:13 Bear with **each o** and forgive one another if G253
1Th 3:12 overflow for **each o** and for everyone G253
1Th 4: 1 As for **o** *matters*, brothers and sisters, we G3370
1Th 4: 9 have been taught by God to love **each o**. G253
1Th 5:11 one another and build each **o** up, G1651
1Th 5:13 Live in peace with **each o**. G1571
1Th 5:15 what is good for **each o** and for everyone G253
2Th 3: 1 As for **o** *matters*, brothers and sisters, pray G3370
Phm 9 It is as **none o than** Paul—an old man G5525
Heb 7: 8 who die; but **in the o case**, by him who is G1695
Heb 7:27 Unlike **the** *o* high priests, he does not need to AIT
Heb 10:33 **at o times** you stood side by side G4047+1254
Jas 5:16 confess your sins *to* **each o** and pray for G253
Jas 5:16 other and pray for **each o** so that you may G253
1Pe 1:22 so that you have sincere **love for each o**, G5789
1Pe 4: 8 Above all, love **each o** deeply, because G1571
1Pe 4:15 a murderer or thief or *any o kind of* **criminal**, AIT
2Pe 3:16 as they do the **o** Scriptures, to their G3370
1Jn 3:14 from death to life, because we love **each o**. G81
3Jn 10 he even refuses to welcome **o** believers. G3836
Rev 2:24 'I will not impose *any* **o** burden on you, G257
Rev 3:15 I wish you were either one or **the o**! G2412S
Rev 4: 4 the throne were twenty-four **o** thrones, NDT
Rev 6: 4 the earth and to make people kill **each o**. G253
Rev 8:13 to be sounded by the **o** three angels!" G3370
Rev 9:12 two **o** woes are yet to come. G3552+4047
Rev 11:10 will celebrate by sending **each o** gifts, G253
Rev 17:10 the **o** has not yet come; but when G257

OTHER'S (2) [OTHER]

Ro 1:12 encouraged by **each o** faith. G1877+253
Gal 6: 2 Carry **each o** burdens, and in this way you G253

OTHERS (203) [OTHER]

Ge 32:19 third and all the *o who* **followed** the herds: AIT
Ge 42: 4 brother, with the **o**, because he was afraid H278S
Ge 50:14 all the *o who had* **gone** with him to bury AIT
Ex 24: 2 the LORD; **the o** must not come near. H2156S
Ex 35:34 of the tribe of Dan, the ability to teach **o**. NDT
Lev 6:11 he is to take off these clothes and put on **o**, H337
Nu 1:47 was not counted along with the **o**. H4392S
Jdg 7: 7 into your hands. Let all the **o** go home." H6639S
Jdg 7: 8 the provisions and trumpets of the **o**. H6639S
1Sa 5: 5 Dagon nor any *o* who **enter** Dagon's temple AIT
1Sa 8:12 **o** to plow his ground and reap his NDT
1Sa 8:12 still **o** to make weapons of war and NDT
1Sa 10:23 he was a head taller than any of the **o**. H6639S
1Ch 3:20 There were also five **o**: Hashubah, Ohel NDT
1Ch 5:22 and **many** *o* fell slain, because the battle was AIT
1Ch 9:29 **O** were assigned to take care of H4946+2157S
2Ch 23: 5 all the **o** are to be in the courtyards of H6639
2Ch 23: 6 all the **o** are to observe the LORD's H6639
2Ch 32:22 king of Assyria and from the hand of all **o**. NDT
Ezr 3:12 being laid, while **many** *o* shouted for joy. AIT
Ne 2:12 I set out during the night with a few **o**. I had H408
Ne 2:16 officials or *any* **o** who would be doing H3856
Ne 5: 3 **O** were saying, "We are mortgaging our H889S
Ne 5: 4 Still **o** were saying, "We have had to H889S
Ne 5: 5 our fields and our vineyards belong to **o**." H337
Ne 8: 3 women and **o** who could understand. H2021S
Job 11: 3 Will your idle talk reduce **o** to silence H5493
Job 24:24 are brought low and gathered up like **all** *o*; AIT
Job 31: 8 then may **o** eat what I have sown, and may H337
Job 33:27 And they will go to **o** and say, 'I have H408
Job 34:24 the mighty and sets up **o** in their place. H337
Ps 15: 3 to a neighbor, and casts no slur on **o**; H7940
Ps 49:10 also perish, leaving their wealth to **o**. H337
Ps 49:16 Do not be overawed when **o** grow rich H408
Ps 52: 7 wealth and grew strong by destroying **o**!" H2257S
Ps 105:44 they fell heir to what **o** had toiled for— H4211S
Pr 5: 9 you lose your honor to **o** and your dignity to H337
Pr 10:17 whoever ignores correction leads **o** astray. NDT
Pr 11:25 whoever refreshes **o** will be refreshed. NDT
Ecc 5: 8 over them both are **o** higher still. H1469S
Ecc 6: 8 how to conduct themselves before **o**? H2645S
Ecc 7:22 many times you yourself have cursed **o**. H337
Ecc 8: 9 a man lords it over **o** to his own hurt. H132S
SS 5: 9 How is your beloved better than **o**, most H1856S
SS 5: 9 How is your beloved better than **o**, that H1856S
Isa 43: 9 were right, so that *o may* **hear** and say, "It is AIT
Isa 44: 5 **o** will call themselves by the name of H2296S
Isa 44: 5 of Jacob; still **o** will write on their hand H2296S
Isa 56: 8 "I will gather *still* **o** to them besides those H6388
Isa 65:22 will they build houses and **o** live in them, H337
Isa 65:22 others live in them, or plant and **o** eat. H337
Jer 6:12 Their houses will be turned over to **o** H337
Jer 11:15 with **many** *o*, works out her evil. AIT
Jer 41: 8 alone and did not kill them with the **o**. H278S
Jer 41:10 along with all the **o** who were left there, H6639S
Jer 50:15 do to her as she has done to **o**. NDT
Eze 9: 5 listened, he said to **the o**, "Follow him H465S
Eze 16:34 you are the opposite of **o**; H2021+851S
Eze 32:19 to them, 'Are you more favored than **o**? H4769S
Eze 39:14 along with **o**, they will bury H2021+6296S
Eze 40:24 they had the same measurements as the **o**. NDT
Eze 40:25 all around, like the openings of the **o**. H465S
Eze 40:28 it had the same measurements as the **o**. H465S
Eze 40:29 had the same measurements as the **o**. H465S
Eze 40:32 it had the same measurements as the **o**. H465S
Eze 40:33 had the same measurements as the **o**. H465S
Eze 40:35 It had the same measurements as the **o**. H465S
Eze 44: 8 you put **o in charge** of my sanctuary. AIT
Da 2:21 he deposes kings and raises up **o**. A10421S
Da 2:40 so it will crush and break all **the o**. A10036S
Da 7: 3 each different from the **o**, came up out A10154S
Da 7:19 different from all **the o** and most A10214S
Da 7:20 imposing than the **o** and that had eyes A10246
Da 11: 2 a fourth, who will be far richer than **all** *the o*. AIT
Da 11: 4 his empire will be uprooted and given to **o**. H337
Da 12: 2 **o** to shame and everlasting contempt. H465S
Da 12: 5 there before me stood two **o**, one on H337
Mt 5:16 let your light shine before **o**, that they may G476
Mt 5:19 teaches **o** accordingly will be G476
Mt 5:47 what are you doing more than **o**? NDT
Mt 6: 1 in front of **o** to be seen by them. G476
Mt 6: 2 on the streets, to be honored by **o**. G476

Mt 6: 5 on the street corners to be seen by o. G476
Mt 6:15 But if you do not forgive o their sins, your G476
Mt 6:16 their faces to show o they are fasting. G476
Mt 6:18 will not be obvious to o that you are fasting G476
Mt 7: 2 For in the same way you judge o, you will be NDT
Mt 7:12 do to o what you would have them do to G899
Mt 10:32 "Whoever acknowledges me before o, G476
Mt 10:33 But whoever disowns me before o, I will G476
Mt 11:16 in the marketplaces and calling out to o: G2283
Mt 12:16 He warned them not to tell o about him. NDT
Mt 15:30 the mute and many o, and laid them at G2283
Mt 16:14 say John the Baptist; and still o say Elijah; and still G257
Mt 16:14 say Elijah; and still o, Jeremiah or one of G2283
Mt 17:25 from their own children or from o? G259
Mt 17:26 "From o," Peter answered. "Then the G259
Mt 18:16 take one or two o along, so that 'every AIT
Mt 19:12 who have been made eunuchs by o— G476
Mt 20: 3 he went out and saw o standing in the G257
Mt 20: 6 went out and found still o standing around. G257
Mt 21: 8 while o cut branches from the trees and G257
Mt 22:16 You aren't swayed by o, because you pay G4029
Mt 23: 7 marketplaces and to be called 'Rabbi' by o. G476
Mt 23:34 o you will flog in your synagogues and G899
Mt 25:11 "Later the o also came. 'Lord, Lord,' they G3370
Mt 26:67 him with their fists. O slapped him G3836+1254
Mt 27:42 "He saved o," they said, "but he can't save G257
Mk 3:12 them strict orders not to tell o about him. NDT
Mk 4:10 the Twelve and the o around him asked him AIT
Mk 4:16 O, like seed sown on rocky places, hear G4047
Mk 4:18 Still o, like seed sown among thorns, hear G257
Mk 4:20 O, like seed sown on good soil, hear the G1697
Mk 6:15 O said, "He is Elijah." And still others G257
Mk 6:15 And still o claimed, "He is a prophet, like G257
Mk 8:28 say John the Baptist; o say Elijah; and still G257
Mk 8:28 say Elijah; and still o, one of the prophets." G257
Mk 11: 8 while o spread branches they had cut in G257
Mk 12: 5 He sent many o; some of them they beat G257
Mk 12: 5 of them they beat, o they killed. G4005+1254
Mk 12: 9 those tenants and give the vineyard to o. G257
Mk 12:14 You aren't swayed by o, because you pay G4029
Mk 12:43 put more into the treasury than all the o. G965S
Mk 14:31 And all the o said the same. AIT
Mk 15:31 "He saved o," they said, "but he can't save G257
Lk 5:29 tax collectors and o were eating with them G257
Lk 6:31 Do to o as you would have them do to you. G899
Lk 8: 3 household; Susanna; and many o. G2283
Lk 8:10 given to you, but to o I speak in parables G3370
Lk 9: 8 o that Elijah had appeared, and still G5516
Lk 9: 8 and still o that one of the prophets of long G257
Lk 9:19 say John the Baptist; o say Elijah; and still G257
Lk 9:19 say Elijah; and still o, that one of the G257
Lk 10: 1 seventy-two o and sent them two by G2283
Lk 11:16 O tested him by asking for a sign from G2283
Lk 11:49 they will kill and o they will persecute. NDT
Lk 12: 8 publicly acknowledges me before o, G476
Lk 12: 9 disowns me before o will be disowned G476
Lk 13: 4 guilty than all the o living in Jerusalem? G476
Lk 16:15 who justify yourselves in the eyes of o, G476
Lk 20:16 those tenants and give the vineyard to o." G257
Lk 21: 3 poor widow has put in more than all the o. AIT
Lk 23:35 They said, "He saved o; let him save G257
Lk 24: 9 things to the Eleven and to all the o. G3370
Lk 24:10 the o with them who told this to the G3370
Jn 2:14 o sitting at tables exchanging money. G3836
Jn 4:38 O have done the hard work, and you have G257
Jn 7:12 "He is a good man." O replied, "No, he G257
Jn 7:41 O said, "He is the Messiah." Still others G257
Jn 7:41 Still o asked, "How can the G3836+1254
Jn 9: 9 claimed that he was. O said, "No, he only G257
Jn 9:16 But o asked, "How can a sinner perform G257
Jn 10:21 But o said, "These are not the sayings of a G257
Jn 12:29 o said an angel had spoken to him. G257
Jn 18:34 "or did o talk to you about me? G257
Jn 19:18 with him two o—one on each side and G257
Ac 4: 6 Alexander and o of the high priest's G4012
Ac 14: 4 with the Jews, o with the apostles. G3836+1254
Ac 15:35 they and many o taught and preached G2283
Ac 16:32 the Lord to him and to all the o in his house. AIT
Ac 17: 9 made Jason and the o post bond and let G3370
Ac 17:18 O remarked, "He seems to be advocating G3836
Ac 17:32 of them sneered, but o said, "We want to G3836
Ac 17:34 named Damaris, and a number of o. G2283
Ac 20: 6 five days later joined the o at Troas G899
Ac 23: 6 were Sadducees and the o Pharisees, G2283
Ac 28:24 by what he said, but o would not believe. G3836
Ro 2:21 who teach o, do you not teach G2283
Ro 11: 7 them did, but the o were hardened, G3370
Ro 11:17 in among the o and now share in the G899
Ro 12: 5 each member belongs to all the o. G253
Ro 13: 8 whoever loves o has fulfilled the law. G2283
1Co 9: 2 Even though I may not be an apostle to o G257
1Co 9:12 If o have this right of support from you G257
1Co 9:27 my slave so that after I have preached to o, G257
1Co 10:24 seek their own good, but the good of o. G2283
1Co 13: 5 It does not dishonor o, it is not self-seeking NDT
1Co 14:19 words to instruct o than ten thousand words G257
1Co 14:29 the o should weigh carefully what is G257
2Co 5:11 it is to fear the Lord, we try to persuade o. G476
2Co 8: 8 by comparing it with the earnestness of o. G2283
2Co 8:13 Our desire is not that o might be relieved G257
2Co 9:13 o will praise God for the obedience that AIT
2Co 10:15 our limits by boasting of work done by o. G259
2Co 13: 2 those who sinned earlier or any of the o, G3370
Eph 4:29 helpful for building o up according to their NDT
Php 1:15 of envy and rivalry, but o out of goodwill. G5516
Php 2: 3 in humility value o above yourselves, G253
Php 2: 4 each of you to the interests of the o. G2283
1Th 5: 6 let us not be like o, who are asleep, G3370
1Ti 5:20 everyone, so that the o may take warning. G3370
1Ti 5:22 of hands, and do not share in the sins of o. G259
1Ti 5:24 of them; the sins of o trail behind them. G5516
2Ti 2: 2 who will also be qualified to teach o. G2283
Titus 1: 9 he can encourage o by sound doctrine and NDT
Heb 7:20 O became priests without any oath G3836+3525
Heb 11:35 There were o who were tortured, refusing G257
Heb 13:16 not forget to do good and to share with o, G3126
1Pe 4:10 gift you have received to serve o, G1571
2Pe 2: 5 preacher of righteousness, and seven o; G3838S
Jude 16 themselves and flatter o for their own NDT
Jude 23 save o by snatching them from the fire; to G4005
Jude 23 from the fire; to o show mercy, mixed G4005

OTHERWISE (38) [OTHER]

Ge 11: 4 o we will be scattered over the face of the H7153
Ge 45:11 O you and your household and all who H7153
Ex 12:33 leave the country. "For o," they said, "we H3954
Nu 18: 3 O both they and you will die. H2256+4202
Dt 8:12 O, when you eat and are satisfied, when H7153
Dt 9:28 O, the country from which you brought us H7153
Dt 19: 6 O, the avenger of blood might pursue him H7153
Dt 20:18 O, they will teach you to H4200+5100+889+4202
Dt 24:15 O they may cry to the LORD against H2256+4202
Jos 6:18 O you will make the camp of Israel liable H2256
1Sa 13:19 "O the Hebrews will make swords or H7153
1Sa 25:34 O, as surely as the LORD, the God of Israel H219
2Sa 12:28 O I will take the city, and it will be named H7153
1Ki 1:21 O, as soon as my lord the king is laid to H2256
2Ki 2:10 from you, it will be yours—o, it will not." H561
2Ch 19:10 o his wrath will come on you and your H2256
Ps 10:15 wickedness that would not o be found out. AIT
Pr 30: 9 O, I may have too much and disown you H7153
Isa 6:10 O they might see with their eyes, hear H7153
Hos 2: 3 O I will strip her naked and make her as H7153
Mt 13:15 O they might see with their eyes, hear G3607
Mt 27:64 O, his disciples may come and steal the G3607
Mk 2:21 O, the new piece will pull G1623+1254+3590
Mk 2:22 O, the wine will burst the G1623+1254+3590
Mk 4:12 o they might turn and be forgiven! G3607
Lk 5:36 O, they will have torn G1623+1254+3590+1145
Lk 5:37 O, the new wine will G1623+1254+3590+1145
Ac 28:27 O they might see with their eyes, hear G3607
Ro 11:22 in his kindness. O, you also will be cut off G2075
1Co 7:14 O your children would be unclean G2075+726
1Co 14:16 O when you are praising God in the Spirit G2075
1Co 14:37 they are a prophet or o gifted by the Spirit G2445
1Co 15: 2 O, you have believed in vain G1760+1623+3590
1Ti 6: 3 If anyone teaches o and does not agree to G2281
Heb 9:26 O Christ would have had to suffer many G2075
Heb 10: 2 O, would they not have stopped being G2075
Jas 5:12 O you will be condemned. G2671+3590
Rev 2:16 O, I will soon come to you G1623+1254+3590

OTHNI (1)

1Ch 26: 7 O, Rephael, Obed and Elzabad; his H6978

OTHNIEL (10)

Jos 15:17 O son of Kenaz, Caleb's brother, took it; H6979
Jos 15:18 One day when she came to O, she urged NDT
Jdg 1:13 O son of Kenaz, Caleb's younger brother H6979
Jdg 1:14 One day when she came to O, she urged NDT
Jdg 3: 9 them a deliverer, O son of Kenaz, Caleb's H6979
Jdg 3:10 king of Aram into the hands of O, H2257S
Jdg 3:11 forty years, until O son of Kenaz died. H6979
1Ch 4:13 The sons of Kenaz: O and Seraiah. H6979
1Ch 4:13 The sons of O: Hathath and H6979
1Ch 27:15 the Netophathite, from the family of O. H6979

OUCHES (KJV) (FILIGREE) SETTINGS

OUGHT (37)

Ge 26:28 'There o to be a sworn agreement between AIT
Mal 2: 7 the lips of a priest o to preserve knowledge, AIT
Ac 19:36 you o to calm down and not do anything G1256
Ac 24:19 who o to be here before you and bring G1256
Ac 25:10 Caesar's court, where I o to be tried. G1256
Ac 25:24 shouting that he o not to live any longer. G1256
Ac 26: 9 too was convinced that I o to do all that G1256
Ro 1:28 so that they do what o not to be done. G2763
Ro 8:26 We do not know what we o to pray for G1256
Ro 12: 3 think of yourself more highly than you o, G1256
Ro 15: 1 We who are strong o to bear with the G4053
1Co 4: 1 is how you o to regard us: as servants AIT
1Co 7:36 are too strong and he feels he o to marry, G4053
1Co 8: 2 do not yet know as they o to know. G1256
1Co 11: 7 A man o not to cover his head, since he is G4053
1Co 11:10 this reason that a woman o to have G4053
1Co 11:28 Everyone o to examine themselves before AIT
1Co 15:34 Come back to your senses as you o, and G1469
2Co 2: 7 you o to forgive and comfort him AIT
2Co 12:11 I o to have been commended by you, for I G4053
Eph 5:28 husbands o to love their wives as their G4053
2Th 1: 3 We o always to thank God for you G4053
2Th 2:13 But we o always to thank God for you G4053
2Th 3: 7 know how you o to follow our example G1256
1Ti 3:15 you will know how people o to conduct G1256
1Ti 5:13 talk nonsense, saying things they o not to. G1256
Titus 1:11 by teaching things they o not to teach— G1256
Phm 8 bold and order you to do what you o to do, G465
Heb 5:12 though by this time you o to be teachers G4053
Jas 1: 9 circumstances o to take pride in their high AIT
Jas 4:15 you o to say, "If it is the Lord's will AIT
Jas 4:17 knows the good they o to do and doesn't do AIT
2Pe 3:11 this way, what kind of people o you to be? G1256
2Pe 3:11 You o to live holy and godly lives NDT
1Jn 3:16 And we o to lay down our lives for our G4053
1Jn 4:11 loved us, we also o to love one another. G4053
3Jn 8 We o therefore to show hospitality to such G4053

OUR (1217) [WE] See Index of Articles Etc.

OURS (18) [WE] See Index of Articles Etc.

OURSELVES (48) [SELF, WE] See Index of Articles Etc.

OUSTED (1)

Isa 22:19 you will be o from your position. H2238

OUT (2440) [OUTER] See Index of Articles Etc.

OUTBREAK (1)

1Sa 5: 9 both young and old, with an o of tumors. H8609

OUTCAST (1) [CAST]

Jer 30:17 'because you are called an o, Zion for H5615

OUTCOME (6)

Isa 41:22 may consider them and know their final o. H344
Da 11:29 the o will be different from what it H4202+3869
Da 12: 8 "My lord, what will the o of all this be?" H344
Mt 26:58 sat down with the guards to see the o. G5465
Heb 13: 7 Consider the o of their way of life and G1676
1Pe 4:17 what will the o be for those who do not G5465

OUTCRY (8)

Ge 18:20 "The o against Sodom and Gomorrah is H2411
Ge 18:21 is as bad as the o that has reached me. H7591
Ge 19:13 The o to the LORD against its people is so H7591
1Sa 4:14 Eli heard the o and asked, "What H7754+7591
1Sa 5:12 the o of the city went up to heaven. H8784
Ne 5: 1 wives raised a great o against their fellow H7591
Ne 5: 6 When I heard their o and these charges, H2411
Isa 15: 8 Their o echoes along the border of Moab H2411

OUTDATED (1)

Heb 8:13 is obsolete and o will soon disappear. G1180

OUTDOOR (1)

Pr 24:27 Put your o work in order and H928+2021+2575

OUTER (41) [OUT]

Nu 4:25 and its o covering of H4946+4200+5087+2025
2Sa 18:24 sitting between the inner and o gates, H9109S
2Sa 20:15 it stood against the o fortifications. H2658
1Ki 6:29 in both the inner and o rooms, he carved H2667
1Ki 6:30 of both the inner and o rooms of the H2667
1Ki 7: 9 smoothed on their inner and o faces. H2575
2Ch 6:13 had placed it in the center of the o court. H6478
2Ch 33:14 he rebuilt the o wall of the City of H2667
Est 6: 4 had just entered the o court of the palace H2667
Job 26:14 these are but the o fringe of his works; H7896
Job 41:13 Who can strip off its o coat? Who can H7156
Eze 10: 5 could be heard as far away as the o court, H2667
Eze 40:17 Then he brought me into the o court H2667
Eze 40:20 of the north gate, leading into the o court. H2667
Eze 40:27 from this gate to the o gate on the south NDT
Eze 40:31 Its portico faced the o court; palm trees H2667
Eze 40:34 Its portico faced the o court; palm trees H2667
Eze 40:37 Its portico faced the o court; palm trees H2667
Eze 41: 9 The o wall of the side rooms was five H2575
Eze 41:17 all around the inner and o sanctuary H2667
Eze 42: 1 northward into the o court and brought H2667
Eze 42: 1 opposite the o wall on the north side. H1230
Eze 42: 3 opposite the pavement of the o court, H2667
Eze 42: 7 There was an o wall parallel H4200+2021+2575
Eze 42: 7 wall parallel to the rooms and the o court; H2667
Eze 42: 8 the side next to the o court was fifty cubits H2667
Eze 42: 9 side as one enters them from the o court. H2667
Eze 42:10 along the length of the wall of the o court, NDT
Eze 42:10 temple courtyard and opposite the o wall, H1230
Eze 42:14 not to go into the o court until they leave H2667
Eze 44: 1 me back to the o gate of the sanctuary, H2667
Eze 44:19 they go out into the o court where the H2667
Eze 46:20 them into the o court and consecrating H2667
Eze 46:21 brought me to the o court and led me H2667
Eze 46:22 the four corners of the o court were enclosed NDT
Eze 47: 2 the outside to the o gate facing east, H2575
Jn 13: 4 took off his o clothing, and wrapped a G2668
Jn 21: 7 he wrapped his o garment around him G2087
Ac 12:13 Peter knocked at the o entrance, and a G4784
Heb 9: 6 regularly into the o room to carry on their G4755
Rev 11: 2 But exclude the o court; do not measure it G2033

OUTLANDISH (KJV) FOREIGN

OUTLET (1)

2Ch 32:30 blocked the upper o of the Gihon spring H4604

OUTLINE (1)

Isa 44:13 with a line and makes an o with a marker; H9306

OUTLIVED (2) [LIVE]
Jos 24:31 the elders who **o** him and who H799+3427+339
Jdg 2: 7 the elders who **o** him and who H799+3427+339

OUTLYING (2)
1Ch 5:16 in Bashan and its **o villages**, and on all H1426
1Ch 27:25 of the storehouses in the **o districts**, H8441

OUTNUMBER (2) [NUMBER]
Ps 69: 4 without reason **o** the hairs of my H8045+4946
Ps 139:18 *they would* **o** the grains of sand H8049+4946

OUTPOST (8) [OUTPOSTS]
1Sa 10: 5 where there is a Philistine **o**. H5907
1Sa 13: 3 attacked the Philistine **o** at Geba, H5907
1Sa 13: 4 "Saul has attacked the Philistine **o**, and H5907
1Sa 14: 1 over to the Philistine **o** on the other side." H5163
1Sa 14: 4 cross to reach the Philistine **o** was a cliff; H5163
1Sa 14: 6 go over to the **o** *of* those uncircumcised H5163
1Sa 14:11 showed themselves to the Philistine **o**. H5163
1Sa 14:12 The men of the **o** shouted to Jonathan H5165

OUTPOSTS (2) [OUTPOST]
Jdg 7:11 went down to the **o** of the camp. H7895+2821
1Sa 14:15 those in the **o** and raiding parties H5163

OUTPOURED (3) [POUR]
Ps 79:10 that you avenge the **o** blood of your H9161
Eze 20:33 an outstretched arm and with **o** wrath. H9161
Eze 20:34 an outstretched arm and with **o** wrath. H9161

OUTPOURING (1) [POUR]
Eze 9: 8 of Israel in this **o** *of* your wrath on H9161

OUTRAGED (1) [RAGE]
Mt 18:31 *they were* **o** and went and told *G3382+5379*

OUTRAGEOUS (8) [RAGE]
Ge 34: 7 Shechem had done an **o thing** in Israel by H5576
Dt 22:21 She has done an **o thing** in Israel by H5576
Jos 7:15 LORD and has done an **o thing** in Israel! H5576
Jdg 19:23 man is my guest, don't do this **o thing**. H5576
Jdg 19:24 as for this man, don't do such an **o** thing." H5576
Jdg 20: 6 committed this lewd and **o** act in Israel. H5576
Jdg 20:10 they deserve for this **o act** done in Israel." H5576
Jer 29:23 For they have done **o things** in Israel; they H5576

OUTRAGEOUSLY (1) [RAGE]
1Th 2: 2 suffered and *been* **treated o** in Philippi, *G5614*

OUTRAN (2) [RUN]
2Sa 18:23 ran by way of the plain and **o** the Cushite. H6296
Jn 20: 4 other disciple **o** Peter and reached *G4731+5441*

OUTSIDE (133) [OUTSIDER, OUTSIDERS]
Ge 9:22 and told his two brothers **o**. H928+2021+2575
Ge 15: 5 He took him **o** and said, "Look up at H2575+2025
Ge 19: 6 Lot went **o** to meet them and shut H7339+2025
Ge 24:11 down near the well **o** the town; H4946+2575
Ge 35: 8 was buried under the oak **o** Bethel. H4946+9393
Ex 12:46 take none of the meat **o** the house. H2575+2025
Ex 21:19 walk around **o** with a staff; H928+2021+2575
Ex 26:35 Place the table **o** the curtain on the H4946+2575
Ex 27:21 **o** the curtain that shields the ark of H4946+2575
Ex 29:14 hide and its intestines **o** the camp. H4946+2575
Ex 33: 7 tent and pitch it **o** the camp some H4946+2575
Ex 33: 7 to the tent of meeting **o** the camp. H4946+2575
Ex 40:22 side of the tabernacle **o** the curtain H4946+2575
Lev 4:12 he must take **o** the camp to a place H4946+2575
Lev 4:21 take the bull **o** the camp and burn H4946+2575
Lev 6:11 carry the ashes **o** the camp to a H4946+2575
Lev 8:17 he burned up **o** the camp, H4946+2575
Lev 9:11 the hide he burned up **o** the camp. H4946+2575
Lev 10: 4 carry your cousins **o** the camp H4946+2575
Lev 10: 5 in their tunics, **o** the camp, as H4946+2575
Lev 13:46 alone; they must live **o** the camp. H4946+2575
Lev 14: 3 The priest is to go **o** the camp and H4946+2575
Lev 14: 8 they must stay **o** their tent for H4946+2575
Lev 14:40 into an unclean place **o** the town. H4946+2575
Lev 14:41 into an unclean place **o** the town. H4946+2575
Lev 14:53 bird in the open fields **o** the town. H4946+2575
Lev 16:27 must be taken **o** the camp; their H4946+2575
Lev 17: 3 a goat in the camp or **o** of it H4946+2575
Lev 22:10 " 'No one **o a priest's family** may eat the H2424
Lev 24: 3 **O** the curtain that shields the ark of H4946+2575
Lev 24:14 "Take the blasphemer **o** the camp H4946+2575
Lev 24:23 the blasphemer **o** the camp and H4946+2575
Nu 5: 3 send them **o** the camp so they will H4946+2575
Nu 5: 4 did so; they sent them **o** the camp. H4946+2575
Nu 12:14 Confine her **o** the camp for seven H4946+2575
Nu 12:15 was confined **o** the camp for seven H4946+2575
Nu 15:35 must stone him **o** the camp. H4946+2575
Nu 15:36 assembly took him **o** the camp and H4946+2575
Nu 19: 3 it is to be taken **o** the camp and H4946+2575
Nu 19: 9 clean place **o** the camp. H4946+2575
Nu 31:13 went to meet them **o** the camp. H4946+2575
Nu 31:19 killed must stay **o** the camp seven H4946+2575
Nu 35: 5 **O** the town, measure two thousand H4946+2575
Nu 35:26 the accused **ever goes o** the limits H3655+3655
Nu 35:27 of blood finds them **o** the city, H4946+2575
Dt 23:10 he is to go **o** the camp and stay H4946+2575
Dt 23:12 a place **o** the camp where H4946+2575
Dt 24:11 Stay **o** and let the neighbor to whom you H2575
Dt 25: 5 not marry **o the family**. H2021+2575+2025+2424
Jos 2:19 If any of them go **o** your house into H4946+1946
Jos 6:23 them in a place **o** the camp of H4946+2575
Jdg 12: 9 away in marriage to those **o** his *clan*, H2575
Jdg 12: 9 young women as wives from **o** his *clan*. H2575
Jdg 19:23 of the house **went o** and said to them, H3655
Jdg 19:25 his concubine and sent her **o** to them, H2575
1Sa 9:26 he and Samuel went **o** together. H2575+2025
1Ki 6: 6 around the **o** of the temple so H2575+2025
1Ki 7: 9 from the **o** to the great courtyard and from H2575
1Ki 8: 8 not from **o** the Holy Place; and H2575+2025
1Ki 21:13 So they took him **o** the city and H4946+2575
2Ki 10:24 eighty men **o** with this H928+2021+2575
2Ki 16:18 royal entryway **o** the temple of the H2667+2025
2Ki 23: 4 He burned them **o** Jerusalem in H4946+2575
2Ki 23: 6 the Kidron Valley **o** Jerusalem and H4946+2575
2Ki 25: 1 He encamped **o** the city and built siege H6584
2Ch 5: 9 not from **o** the Holy Place; and H2575+2025
2Ch 24: 8 a chest was made and placed **o**, at H2575+2025
2Ch 32: 3 water from the springs **o** the city, H4946+2575
2Ch 32: 5 built another wall **o** that one and H2575+2025
Ezr 10:13 so we cannot stand **o**. H928+2021+2575
Ne 11:16 had charge of the **o** work of the house of H2667
Ne 13:20 goods spent the night **o** Jerusalem. H4946+2575
Job 31:34 that I kept silent and would not go **o**— H7339
Pr 22:13 "There's a lion **o**! H928+2021+2575
SS 8: 1 if I found you **o**, I would kiss H928+2021+2575
Jer 21: 4 who are **o** the wall besieging H4946+2575
Jer 22:19 away and thrown **o** the gates of H4946+2134
Jer 52: 4 They encamped **o** the city and built siege H6584
La 1:20 **O**, the sword bereaves; inside H4946+2575
Eze 5:12 a third will fall by the sword **o** your **walls** H6017
Eze 7:15 **O** is the sword; inside are H928+2021+2575
Eze 40:19 gateway to the **o** of the inner court; H4946+2575
Eze 40:40 By the **o** wall of the portico of H4946+2575+2025
Eze 40:44 **O** the inner gate, within the H4946+2575+2025
Eze 41:17 the space above the **o** of the entrance to H2575
Eze 43:21 of the temple area **o** the sanctuary. H4946+2575
Eze 46: 2 is to enter from the **o** through the portico H2575
Eze 47: 2 led me around the **o** to the outer gate H2575
Mt 8:12 subjects of the kingdom will be thrown **o**, *G2035*
Mt 9:25 After the crowd *had been* **put o**, he went *G1675*
Mt 10:29 will fall to the ground **o** your Father's care. *G459*
Mt 12:46 his mother and brothers stood **o**, wanting *G2032*
Mt 12:47 "Your mother and brothers are standing **o** *G2032*
Mt 22:13 and throw him **o**, into the darkness, *G2035*
Mt 23:25 You clean the **o** of the cup and dish, but *G2033*
Mt 23:26 and then the **o** also will be clean. *G1760*
Mt 23:27 look beautiful **on the o** but on the inside *G2033*
Mt 23:28 **on the o** you appear to people as *G2033*
Mt 25:30 And throw that worthless servant **o**, into *G2035*
Mt 26:75 And he went **o** and wept bitterly. *G2032*
Mk 1:45 town openly but stayed **o** in lonely places. *G2032*
Mk 2: 2 no room left, not even **o** the door, and he *G4639*
Mk 3:31 Standing **o**, they sent someone in to call *G2032*
Mk 3:32 mother and brothers are **o** looking for you." *G2032*
Mk 4:11 But to those *on* the **o** everything is said in *G2032*
Mk 7:15 Nothing **o** a person can defile them by *G2033*
Mk 7:18 enters a person **from** the **o** can defile *G2033*
Mk 8:23 by the hand and led him **o** the village. *G2032*
Mk 11: 4 They went and found a colt **o** in the street, *G2032*
Lk 1:10 the assembled worshipers were praying **o**. *G2032*
Lk 8:20 "Your mother and brothers are standing **o**, *G2032*
Lk 11:39 Pharisees clean the **o** of the cup and dish, *G2033*
Lk 11:40 one who made the **o** make the inside *G2033*
Lk 11:53 *When* Jesus **went o**, the Pharisees and *G2002*
Lk 13:25 you will stand **o** knocking and pleading *G2032*
Lk 13:33 surely no prophet can die **o** Jerusalem! *G2032*
Lk 22:62 And he went **o** and wept bitterly. *G2032*
Jn 18:16 Peter had to wait **o** at the door. *G2032*
Jn 20:11 Now Mary stood **o** the tomb crying. As she *G2032*
Ac 5:34 that the men be put **o** for a little while. *G2032*
Ac 7:21 *When* he *was* **placed o**, Pharaoh's *G1758*
Ac 14:13 whose temple was **just o** the city, brought *G4574*
Ac 14:19 stoned Paul and dragged him **o** the city, *G2032*
Ac 16:13 the Sabbath we went **o** the city gate to *G2032*
1Co 5:12 is it of mine to judge those **o** the church? *G2032*
1Co 5:13 God will judge those **o**. "Expel the wicked *G2032*
1Co 6:18 sins a person commits are **o** the body, *G1760*
2Co 7: 5 conflicts **on the o**, fears within. *G2033*
Heb 13:11 the bodies are burned **o** the camp. *G2032*
Heb 13:12 Jesus also suffered **o** the city gate to *G2032*
Heb 13:13 go to him **o** the camp, bearing the *G2032*
Rev 14:20 were trampled in the winepress **o** the city, *G2033*
Rev 22:15 **O** are the dogs, those who practice magic *G2032*

OUTSIDER (3) [OUTSIDE]
Pr 20:16 hold it in pledge if it is done for an **o**. H5799
Pr 27: 2 your own mouth; an **o**, and not your own H5799
Pr 27:13 hold it in pledge if it is done for an **o**. H5799

OUTSIDERS (3) [OUTSIDE]
Col 4: 5 Be wise in the way you act toward **o**; *G3836+2032*
1Th 4:12 the respect of **o** and so that you *G3836+2032*
1Ti 3: 7 have a good reputation with **o**, *G3836+2033*

OUTSKIRTS (6)
Nu 11: 1 consumed some of the **o** *of* the camp. H7895
Nu 22:41 he could see the **o** *of* the Israelite *camp*. H7895
Nu 23:13 see them all but only the **o** *of* their *camp*. H7895
Jos 18:15 side began at the **o** *of* Kiriath Jearim on H7895
1Sa 14: 2 was staying on the **o** *of* Gibeah under a H7895
1Ch 4:39 they went to the **o** *of* Gedor to the east H4427

OUTSPREAD (1) [SPREAD]
Isa 8: 8 Its **o** wings will cover the breadth of your H5742

OUTSTANDING (5)
1Ch 7:40 choice men, brave warriors and **o** leaders. H8031
SS 5:10 ruddy, **o** among ten thousand. H1838
Da 5:14 have insight, intelligence and **o** wisdom. A10339
Ro 13: 8 *Let* no **debt remain o**, except the *G4053*
Ro 16: 7 They are **o** among the apostles, and they *G2168*

OUTSTRETCHED (18) [STRETCH]
Ex 6: 6 redeem you with an **o** arm and with H5742
Dt 4:34 by a mighty hand and an **o** arm, or by H5742
Dt 5:15 there with a mighty hand and an **o** arm. H5742
Dt 7:19 the mighty hand and **o** arm, with which H5742
Dt 9:29 out by your great power and your **o** arm." H5742
Dt 11: 2 his majesty, his mighty hand, his **o** arm; H5742
Dt 26: 8 Egypt with a mighty hand and an **o** arm, H5742
1Ki 8:42 your mighty hand and your **o** arm— H5742
2Ki 17:36 of Egypt with mighty power and **o** arm, H5742
2Ch 6:32 your mighty hand and your **o** arm— H5742
Ps 136:12 with a mighty hand and **o** arm; His love H5742
Isa 3:16 walking along with **o** necks, flirting with H5742
Jer 21: 5 against you with an **o** hand and a mighty H5742
Jer 27: 5 my great power and **o** arm I made the H5742
Jer 32:17 the earth by your great power and **o** arm. H5742
Jer 32:21 mighty hand and an **o** arm and with great H5742
Eze 20:33 a mighty hand and an **o** arm and with H5742
Eze 20:34 a mighty hand and an **o** arm and with H5742

OUTWARD (3) [OUTWARDLY]
1Sa 16: 7 People look at the **o appearance**, but the H6524
Ro 2:28 circumcision *merely* **o** and *G1877+3836+5745*
1Pe 3: 3 should not come *from* **o** adornment, *G2033*

OUTWARDLY (3) [OUTWARD]
Ro 2:28 not a Jew who is one *only* **o**, *G1877+3836+5745*
2Co 4:16 Though **o** we are wasting *G3836+2032+476*
Heb 9:13 sanctify them so that they are **o** clean. *G4922*

OUTWEIGH (1) [WEIGH]
Job 6: 3 *It would* surely **o** the sand of the H3877+4946

OUTWEIGHS (2) [WEIGH]
Ecc 10: 1 a little folly **o** wisdom and honor. H3701+4946
2Co 4:17 glory *that* **far o them all**.
G2848+5651+1650+5651+983

OUTWIT (1) [OUTWITTED]
2Co 2:11 in order that Satan *might* not **o** *us*. For we *G4430*

OUTWITTED (1) [OUTWIT]
Mt 2:16 realized that *he had been* **o** by the Magi, *G1850*

OVEN (8) [OVENS]
Lev 2: 4 you bring a grain offering baked in an **o**, H9486
Lev 7: 9 offering baked in an **o** or cooked in a pan H9486
Lev 11:35 an **o** or cooking pot must be broken up. H9486
Lev 26:26 will be able to bake your bread in one **o**, H9486
La 5:10 Our skin is hot as an **o**, feverish from H9486
Hos 7: 4 burning like an **o** whose fire the baker H9486
Hos 7: 6 Their hearts are like an **o**; they approach H9486
Hos 7: 7 All of them are hot as an **o**; they devour H9486

OVENS (3) [OVEN]
Ex 8: 3 into your **o** and kneading troughs. H9486
Ne 3:11 another section and the Tower of the **O**. H9486
Ne 12:38 past the Tower of the **O** to the Broad Wall, H9486

OVER (1103)
Ge 1: 2 darkness was **o** the surface of the deep H6584
Ge 1: 2 of God was hovering **o** the waters. H6584+7156
Ge 1:26 so that they may rule **o** the fish in the sea H928
Ge 1:26 **o** the livestock and all the wild animals H928
Ge 1:26 **o** all the creatures that move along the H928
Ge 1:28 Rule **o** the fish in the sea and the birds in H928
Ge 1:28 birds in the sky and **o** every living creature H928
Ge 3:16 your husband, and he will rule **o** you." H928
Ge 4: 7 desires to have you, but you must rule **o** it." H928
Ge 4:15 Cain will suffer vengeance **seven** *times o*." AIT
Ge 7:21 all the creatures that swarm **o** the earth H6584
Ge 8: 1 he sent a wind **o** the earth, and the H6584
Ge 8: 9 there was water **o** all the surface of the H6584
Ge 9:14 I bring clouds **o** the earth and the H6584
Ge 9:19 came *the people who were* **scattered o** the AIT
Ge 10:32 the nations spread out **o** the earth after the H928
Ge 11: 4 we will be scattered **o** the face of the H6584
Ge 11: 8 them from there **o** all the earth, H6584+7156
Ge 11: 9 LORD scattered them **o** the face of the H6584
Ge 15:12 thick and dreadful darkness came **o** him. H6584
Ge 19:23 the sun had risen **o** the land. H6584
Ge 19:31 us children—as is the custom **all** *o* the earth. AIT
Ge 22: 5 donkey while I and the boy go **o** there. H6330
Ge 22:13 He **went o** and took the ram and H2143
Ge 23: 2 went to mourn for Sarah and to **weep** *o* her. AIT
Ge 26:21 they quarreled **o** that one also; so he H6584
Ge 26:22 another well, and no one quarreled **o** it. H6584
Ge 27:29 Be lord **o** your brothers, and may the sons H4200
Ge 27:37 made him lord **o** you and have made H4200
Ge 28:15 with you and *will* **watch o** you wherever H9068
Ge 28:20 be with me and *will* **watch o** me on this H9068
Ge 29: 2 The stone **o** the mouth of the well was H6584

O

Ge 29: 3 stone to its place **o** the mouth of the well. H6584
Ge 29:10 he **went o** and rolled the stone away from H5602
Ge 30:31 tending your flocks and **watching o** them: H9068
Ge 32:23 the stream, *he* **sent o** all his possessions. H6296
Ge 35:20 **O** her tomb Jacob set up a pillar, and to H6584
Ge 37: 8 said to him, "Do you intend to reign **o** us? H6584
Ge 38:16 *he* **went o** to her by the roadside and said, H5742
Ge 41:34 commissioners **o** the land to take a H6584
Ge 41:56 had spread **o** the whole country H6584+7156
Ge 42:30 "The man who is **lord** *o* the land spoke AIT
Ge 42:33 the man who is **lord** *o* the land said to us AIT
Ge 45:15 kissed all his brothers and wept **o** them. H6584
Ge 47:18 When that year *was* **o**, they came to him H9462
Ge 49:22 a spring, whose branches climb **o** a wall. H6584
Ge 50: 1 his father and wept **o** him and kissed him. H6584
Ex 1:11 put slave masters **o** them to oppress them H6584
Ex 2:14 "Who made you ruler and judge **o** us? H6584
Ex 3: 3 "*I will* **go o** and see this strange sight H6073
Ex 3: 4 the LORD saw that *he had* **gone o** to look, H6073
Ex 3:16 *I have* **watched o** you and *have* **seen** H7212+7212
Ex 5:12 people scattered all **o** Egypt to gather H928
Ex 7:19 out your hand **o** the waters of Egypt— H6584
Ex 7:19 of Egypt—**o** the streams and canals H6584
Ex 7:19 **o** the ponds and all the reservoirs H6584
Ex 8: 5 hand with your staff **o** the streams and H6584
Ex 8: 6 out his hand **o** the waters of Egypt, H6584
Ex 9: 9 will become fine dust **o** the whole land of H6584
Ex 9:22 the sky so that hail will fall all **o** Egypt— H928
Ex 10:12 out your hand **o** Egypt so that locusts H6584
Ex 10:12 that locusts swarm **o** the land and devour H6584
Ex 10:13 So Moses stretched out his staff **o** Egypt H6584
Ex 10:21 the sky so that darkness spreads **o** Egypt— H6584
Ex 12: 8 they are to eat the meat **roasted** *o* the fire, AIT
Ex 12: 9 boiled in water, but **roast** it *o* a fire—with the AIT
Ex 12:13 when I see the blood, *I will* **pass o** you. H7173
Ex 12:23 doorframe and *will* **pass o** that doorway, H7173
Ex 12:27 who **passed o** the houses of the Israelites H7173
Ex 13:12 *you are to* **give o** to the LORD the first H6296
Ex 14: 7 of Egypt, with officers **o** all of them. H6584
Ex 14:16 out your hand **o** the sea to divide the H6584
Ex 14:21 Moses stretched out his hand **o** the sea, H6584
Ex 14:26 out your hand **o** the sea so that the H6584
Ex 14:26 waters may flow back **o** the Egyptians H6584
Ex 14:27 Moses stretched out his hand **o** the sea H6584
Ex 15:19 the waters of the sea back **o** them, H6584
Ex 18:21 appoint them as officials **o** thousands H6584
Ex 18:25 of the people, **officials** *o* thousands AIT
Ex 19:16 with a thick cloud **o** the mountain, and a H6584
Ex 25:22 two cherubim that are **o** the ark of the H6584
Ex 26: 7 goat hair for the tent **o** the tabernacle— H6584
Ex 26:12 half curtain that *is* **left o** is to hang down H6369
Ex 26:13 what is left will hang **o** the sides of the H6584
Ex 26:14 and **o** that a covering of H4946+4200+5087+2025
Ex 28:29 of the sons of Israel **o** his heart on the H6584
Ex 28:30 so they may be **o** Aaron's heart whenever H6584
Ex 28:30 the Israelites **o** his heart before the H6584
Ex 29:34 ram or any bread *is* **left o** till morning, H3855
Ex 30: 6 cover that is **o** the tablets of the H6584
Ex 30:13 Each *one* who **crosses o** to those already H6296
Ex 30:14 All who **cross o**, those twenty years old H6296
Ex 34:33 speaking to them, he put a veil **o** his face. H6584
Ex 34:35 put the veil back **o** his face until he went H6584
Ex 36:14 goat hair for the tent **o** the tabernacle— H6584
Ex 36:19 and **o** that a covering of H4946+4200+5087+2025
Ex 38:26 everyone who *had* **crossed o** to those H6296
Ex 40:19 he spread the tent **o** the tabernacle and H6584
Ex 40:19 put the covering **o** the tent, H6584
Ex 40:20 the ark and put the atonement cover **o** it. H6584
Ex 40:38 of the LORD was **o** the tabernacle by day H6584
Lev 7:16 anything **left o** may be eaten on the H3855
Lev 7:17 of the sacrifice **left o** till the third day H3855
Lev 10:12 the grain offering **left o** from the food H3855
Lev 12: 4 until the days of her purification *are* **o**. H4848
Lev 12: 6 purification for a son or daughter *are* **o**, H4848
Lev 13:12 disease **breaks out all o** their skin H7255+7255
Lev 14: 5 the birds be killed **o** fresh water in a clay H6584
Lev 14: 6 the bird that was killed **o** the fresh water. H6584
Lev 14:50 kill one of the birds **o** fresh water in a clay H6584
Lev 16: 2 in the cloud **o** the atonement cover H6584
Lev 16:21 goat and confess **o** it all the wickedness H6584
Lev 19: 6 anything **left o** until the third day must be H3855
Lev 19:10 *Do* not **go o** your vineyard **a second time** H6618
Lev 25:43 Do not rule **o** them ruthlessly, but fear your H928
Lev 25:46 you must not rule **o** your fellow H928
Lev 25:53 owe service *do* not **rule o** them ruthlessly H8097
Lev 26:17 those who hate you will rule **o** you, and H928
Lev 26:18 punish you for your sins seven times **o**. H3578
Lev 26:21 I will multiply your afflictions **seven** *times o* AIT
Lev 26:24 will afflict you for your sins **seven** *times o*. AIT
Lev 26:28 will punish you for your sins **seven** *times o*. AIT
Lev 26:37 They will stumble **o** one another as though H928
Nu 1:50 **o** all its furnishings and everything H6584
Nu 3:32 He was **appointed** *o* those who were AIT
Nu 4: 5 curtain and **put** it **o** the ark of the H4059
Nu 4: 6 solid blue **o** that and put H4946+5087+4200+2025
Nu 4: 7 "**O** the table of the Presence they are to H6584
Nu 4: 8 They are to spread a scarlet cloth **o** them H6584
Nu 4:11 "**O** the gold altar they are to spread a H6584
Nu 4:13 altar and spread a purple cloth **o** it. H6584
Nu 4:14 **O** it they are to spread a covering of the H6584
Nu 5:14 of jealousy come **o** her husband and he H6584
Nu 5:30 of jealousy come **o** a man because he H6584
Nu 6: 5 period of their dedication to the LORD *is* **o**; H4848
Nu 6:13 when the period of their dedication *is* **o**. H4848
Nu 9:18 long as the cloud stayed **o** the tabernacle, H6584
Nu 9:19 the cloud remained **o** the tabernacle a H6584
Nu 9:20 the cloud was **o** the tabernacle only a H6584
Nu 9:22 the cloud stayed **o** the tabernacle for two H6584
Nu 10:10 sound the trumpets **o** your burnt offerings H6584
Nu 10:15 son of Zuar was **o** the division of the H6584
Nu 10:16 son of Helon was **o** the division of the H6584
Nu 10:19 of Zurishaddai was **o** the division of the H6584
Nu 10:20 son of Deuel was **o** the division of the H6584
Nu 10:23 son of Pedahzur was **o** the division of the H6584
Nu 10:24 son of Gideoni was **o** the division of the H6584
Nu 10:26 son of Okran was **o** the division of the H6584
Nu 10:27 son of Enan was **o** the division of the H6584
Nu 10:34 of the LORD was **o** them by day when they H6584
Nu 14:14 that your cloud stays **o** them, and that you H6584
Nu 16:13 And now you also want to lord it **o** us! H6584
Nu 16:33 the earth closed **o** them, and they H6584
Nu 19:17 into a jar and pour fresh water **o** them. H6584
Nu 21: 3 plea and **gave** the Canaanites **o** to them. H5989
Nu 21:24 to the sword and **took o** his land from the H3769
Nu 23:15 offering while I meet with him **o there**." H3907
Nu 27:16 appoint someone **o** this community H6584
Nu 31:48 officers who were **o** the units of the army H4200
Nu 32: 7 Israelites from **crossing o** into the land the H6296
Nu 32: 8 from Kadesh Barnea to **look o** the land. H8011
Nu 32:21 you who are armed **cross o** the Jordan H6296
Nu 32:27 *will* **cross o** to fight before the LORD H6296
Nu 32:29 **cross o** the Jordan with you before the H6296
Nu 32:30 But if *they do* not **cross o** with you armed H6296
Nu 32:32 We *will* **cross o** before the LORD *into* H6296
Nu 34: 4 it will go to Hazar Addar and **o** to Azmon, H6296
Dt 1:13 and I will set them **o** you. H928+8031
Dt 1:15 appointed them to have authority **o** you— H6584
Dt 2: 7 *He has* **watched o** your journey through H3359
Dt 2:31 to **deliver** Sihon and his country **o** to H5989
Dt 2:33 LORD our God **delivered** him **o** to us and H5989
Dt 3:12 Of the land that *we* **took o** at that time, H3769
Dt 3:18 *must* **cross o** ahead of the other Israelites. H6296
Dt 3:20 they too *have* **taken o** the land that H3769
Dt 3:21 kingdoms **o** there where you *are* **going**. H6296
Dt 3:25 *Let me* **go o** and see the good land H6296
Dt 4:22 you *are about to* **cross o** and take H6296
Dt 6:18 you may go in and **take o** the good land H3769
Dt 7: 2 your God *has* **delivered** them **o** to you H5989
Dt 7:16 peoples the LORD your God **gives o** to you. H5989
Dt 7:23 LORD your God *will* **deliver** them **o** to you, H5989
Dt 11: 8 to go in and **take o** the land that you H3769
Dt 11:10 you are entering to **take o** is not like the H3769
Dt 11:31 When *you have* **taken** it **o** and are living H3769
Dt 15: 6 You will rule **o** many nations but none will H928
Dt 15: 6 over many nations but none will rule **o** you. H928
Dt 17:14 "Let us set a king **o** us like all the nations H6584
Dt 17:15 be sure to appoint **o** you a king the LORD H6584
Dt 17:15 Do not place a foreigner **o** you, one who H6584
Dt 17:20 will **reign** a long time **o** his kingdom in H6584
Dt 19:12 and *be* **handed o** *to* the H5989+928+3338
Dt 20: 9 they shall appoint commanders **o** it. H928+8031
Dt 21: 6 wash their hands **o** the heifer whose neck H6584
Dt 23:15 *do* not **hand** them **o** to their master. H6037
Dt 24:20 *do* not **go o the branches a second time** H6994+339
Dt 24:21 vineyard, *do* not **go o the vines again**. H6618
Dt 27: 3 law when you *have* **crossed o** to enter the H6296
Dt 28:23 The sky **o** your head will be bronze, the H6584
Dt 28:36 the king you set **o** you to a nation H6584
Dt 28:42 Swarms of locusts *will* **take o** all your trees H3769
Dt 31: 3 God himself *will* **cross o** ahead of you. H6296
Dt 31: 3 Joshua also *will* **cross o** ahead of you, as H6296
Dt 31:15 the cloud stood **o** the entrance to the H6584
Dt 32:11 stirs up its nest and hovers **o** its young, H6584
Dt 33: 2 from Sinai and dawned **o** them from Seir; H4200
Dt 33: 5 He was king **o** Jeshurun when the leaders H928
Dt 33: 9 but *he* **watched o** your word and guarded H9068
Dt 34: 4 your eyes, but *you will* not **cross o** into it." H6296
Dt 34: 8 the time of weeping and mourning *was* **o**. H9462
Jos 1:14 *must* **cross o** ahead of your fellow H6296
Jos 2: 1 **look o** the land," he said, "especially H8011
Jos 3: 1 where they camped before **crossing o**. H6296
Jos 3:16 So the people **crossed o** opposite Jericho. H6296
Jos 4: 3 and **carry** them **o** with you and put them H6296
Jos 4: 5 "**Go o** before the ark of the LORD your God H6296
Jos 4: 8 and *they* **carried** them **o** with them to their H6296
Jos 4:10 directed Joshua. The people hurried **o**, H6296
Jos 4:12 the half-tribe of Manasseh **crossed o**, H6296
Jos 4:13 armed for battle **crossed o** before the LORD H6296
Jos 4:23 before you until you *had* **crossed o**. H6296
Jos 4:23 it up before us until we *had* **crossed o**. H6296
Jos 5: 1 the Israelites until they *had* **crossed o**, H6296
Jos 7:26 **O** Achan they heaped up a large pile of H6584
Jos 8:29 And they raised a large pile of rocks **o** it H6584
Jos 10:12 the LORD **gave** the Amorites **o** to Israel, H5989
Jos 10:12 stand still **o** Gibeon, and you, moon H928
Jos 10:12 you, moon, **o** the Valley of Aijalon. H928
Jos 11: 6 I *will* **hand** all of them, slain, **o** to Israel H5989
Jos 12: 1 whose territory *they* **took o** east of the H3769
Jos 12: 3 He also ruled **o** the eastern Arabah from the NDT
Jos 12: 5 He ruled **o** Mount Hermon, Salekah, all of H928
Jos 13: 1 still very large areas of land to *be* **taken o**. H3769
Jos 13:12 defeated them and **taken o** their land. H3769
Jos 15: 3 on to Zin and **went o** to the south of H6590
Jos 16: 2 **crossed o** to the territory of the Arkites in H6296
Jos 22:19 is defiled, **come o** to the LORD's land H6296
Jos 24: 7 he brought the sea **o** them and covered H6584
Jdg 3:12 gave Eglon king of Moab power **o** Israel. H6584
Jdg 3:22 the sword out, and the fat closed in **o** it. H1237
Jdg 3:28 to Moab; they allowed no one to **cross o**. H6296
Jdg 6:33 forces and **crossed o** the Jordan and H6296
Jdg 7: 8 *who* **took o** the provisions and trumpets of H4374
Jdg 8:22 Israelites said to Gideon, "Rule **o** us—you, H928
Jdg 8:23 "I will not rule **o** you, nor will my son H928
Jdg 8:23 rule over you, nor will my son rule **o** you. H928
Jdg 8:23 The LORD will rule **o** you." H928
Jdg 9: 2 all seventy of Jerub-Baal's sons rule **o** you, H928
Jdg 9: 9 are honored, to hold sway **o** the trees? H6584
Jdg 9:11 good and sweet, to hold sway **o** the trees? H6584
Jdg 9:13 humans, to hold sway **o** the trees? H6584
Jdg 9:15 you really want to anoint me king **o** you, H6584
Jdg 9:18 king **o** the citizens of Shechem because H6584
Jdg 9:45 he destroyed the city and **scattered** salt *o* it. AIT
Jdg 10:18 will be head **o** all who live in Gilead H4200
Jdg 11: 8 you will be head **o** all of us who live H4200
Jdg 11:11 made him head and commander **o** them. H6584
Jdg 11:21 Israel **took o** all the land of the Amorites H3769
Jdg 11:23 what right have you *to* **take** it **o**? H3769
Jdg 11:32 Then Jephthah went **o** to fight the H448
Jdg 12: 1 called out, and *they* **crossed o** to Zaphon. H6296
Jdg 12: 1 to burn down your house **o** your head." H6584
Jdg 12: 3 my hands and crossed **o** to fight the H448
Jdg 12: 3 the LORD **gave** me the **victory** *o* them. AIT
Jdg 12: 5 "*Let me* **cross o**," the men of H6296
Jdg 14: 4 at that time they were ruling **o** Israel.) H928
Jdg 15:11 realize that the Philistines are rulers **o** us? H928
Jdg 15:12 you up and **hand** you **o** *to* the H928+5989+3338
Jdg 15:13 up and **hand** you **o** *to* them. H5989+3338+928
Jdg 18: 9 Don't hesitate to go there and **take** it **o**. H3769
Jdg 19: 9 the day is **nearly o**. Stay and enjoy H2837
Jdg 20:13 Now **turn** those wicked men of Gibeah **o** H5989
Ru 2:14 mealtime Boaz said to her, "Come **o here**. H2151
Ru 2:14 ate all she wanted and **had some left o**. H3855
Ru 2:18 gave her what *she* **had left o** after she H3855
Ru 3: 7 *he* **went o** to lie down at the far end of the H995
Ru 3: 9 "Spread the corner of your garment **o** me H6584
Ru 4: 1 Boaz said, "**Come o** here, my friend, and H6073
Ru 4: 1 So *he* **went o** and sat down. H6073
1Sa 1:28 whole life he *will* **be given o** to the LORD." H8626
1Sa 2: 1 My mouth boasts **o** my enemies, for I H6584
1Sa 2:16 answer, "No, **hand** it **o** now; if you don't H5989
1Sa 4:14 of this uproar?" The man hurried **o** to Eli, H995
1Sa 8: 9 king who will reign **o** them will claim as H6584
1Sa 8:11 king who will reign **o** you will claim as his H6584
1Sa 8:19 they said. "We want a king **o** us. H6584
1Sa 9:16 Anoint him ruler **o** my people Israel; he H6584
1Sa 10: 1 LORD anointed you ruler **o** his inheritance? H6584
1Sa 10:19 you have said, 'No, appoint a king **o** us. H6584
1Sa 11:12 was it that asked, 'Shall Saul reign **o** us? H6584
1Sa 11:12 **Turn** these men **o** to us so that we may H5989
1Sa 12: 1 you said to me and have set a king **o** you. H6584
1Sa 12:12 we want a king to rule **o** us'—even H6584
1Sa 12:13 see, the LORD has set a king **o** you. H6584
1Sa 12:14 the king who reigns **o** you follow the LORD H6584
1Sa 13: 1 he reigned **o** Israel forty- two years. H6584
1Sa 13:13 your kingdom **o** Israel for all time. H448
1Sa 14: 1 *let's* **go o** to the Philistine outpost on the H6296
1Sa 14: 6 *let's* **go o** to the outpost of those H6296
1Sa 14: 8 we *will* **cross o** toward them and let them H6296
1Sa 14:21 to their camp **went o** to the H2118+6017
1Sa 14:33 "Roll a large stone **o** here at once." H448
1Sa 14:40 "You stand **o there**; I and H4200+6298+285
1Sa 14:40 my son will stand **o here**." H4200+6298+285
1Sa 14:47 After Saul had assumed rule **o** Israel, he H6584
1Sa 15: 1 to anoint you king **o** his people Israel; H6584
1Sa 15:17 The LORD anointed you king **o** Israel. H6584
1Sa 15:26 the LORD has rejected you as king **o** Israel!" H6584
1Sa 15:35 that he had made Saul king **o** Israel. H6584
1Sa 16: 1 since I have rejected him as king **o** Israel? H6584
1Sa 17:39 on his sword **o** the tunic and tried H4946+6584
1Sa 17:42 He **looked** David **o** and saw that he was H5564
1Sa 17:50 So David triumphed **o** the Philistine with H4946
1Sa 17:51 David ran and stood **o** him. He took hold of H448
1Sa 18:13 gave him **command** *o* a thousand men, AIT
1Sa 19:22 "**O** in Naioth at Ramah, NDT
1Sa 20: 8 Why **hand** me **o** to your father? H995
1Sa 23:17 You will be king **o** Israel, and I will be H6584
1Sa 25:17 Now **think** it **o** and see what you can do H3359
1Sa 25:17 disaster is hanging **o** our master and his H448
1Sa 25:21 all *my* **watching o** this fellow's property in H9068
1Sa 25:30 him and has appointed him ruler **o** Israel, H6584
1Sa 26:13 Then David **crossed o** to the other side H6296
1Sa 26:22 "*Let* one of your young men **come o** and H6296
1Sa 27: 2 with him left and **went o** to Achish son of H6296
1Sa 29: 3 been with me for **o a year**, H2296+3427+196+2296+9102
1Sa 30:15 me or **hand** me **o** *to* my H6037+928+3338
1Sa 30:16 scattered **o** the countryside H6584+7156
2Sa 2: 4 anointed David king **o** the tribe of Judah. H6584
2Sa 2: 7 of Judah have anointed me king **o** them." H6584
2Sa 2: 8 of Saul and **brought** him **o** *to* Mahanaim. H6296
2Sa 2: 9 He made him king **o** Gilead, Ashuri and H448
2Sa 2: 9 Jezreel, and also **o** Ephraim, Benjamin H6584
2Sa 2:10 years old when he became king **o** Israel, H6584
2Sa 2:11 was king in Hebron **o** Judah was seven H6584
2Sa 3: 8 *I haven't* **handed** you **o** *to* H5162+928+3338

2Sa 3:10 David's throne **o** Israel and Judah from H6584
2Sa 3:12 I will help you **bring** all Israel **o** to you." H6015
2Sa 3:21 that you may rule **o** all that your heart H928
2Sa 3:34 And all the people wept **o** him again. H6584
2Sa 5: 2 while Saul was king **o** us, you were the H6584
2Sa 5: 3 they anointed David king **o** Israel. H6584
2Sa 5: 5 In Hebron he reigned **o** Judah seven years H6584
2Sa 5: 5 he reigned **o** all Israel and Judah H6584
2Sa 5:12 him as king **o** Israel and had exalted H6584
2Sa 5:17 David had been anointed king **o** Israel, H6584
2Sa 6:21 appointed me ruler **o** the LORD's people H6584
2Sa 7: 8 appointed you ruler **o** my people Israel. H6584
2Sa 7:11 I appointed leaders **o** my people Israel. H6584
2Sa 7:12 When your days *are* **o** and you rest with H4848
2Sa 7:26 'The LORD Almighty is God **o** Israel! H6584
2Sa 8:10 him on his victory in battle **o** Hadadezer, H928
2Sa 8:15 David reigned **o** all Israel, doing what H6584
2Sa 8:16 Joab son of Zeruiah was **o** the army H6584
2Sa 8:18 son of Jehoiada was **o** the Kerethites and NDT
2Sa 11:27 After the time of mourning *was* **o**, David H6296
2Sa 12: 6 He must pay for that lamb **four** *times o* AIT
2Sa 12: 7 'I anointed you king **o** Israel, and I H6584
2Sa 14: 7 '**Hand o** the one who struck his brother H5989
2Sa 16: 9 *Let me* **go o** and cut off his head. H6296
2Sa 17:16 **cross o without fail**, or the H6296+6296
2Sa 17:19 spread it out **o** the opening of the H6584
2Sa 17:19 of the well and scattered grain **o** it. H6584
2Sa 17:20 "*They* **crossed o** the brook. H6296
2Sa 17:25 appointed Amasa **o** the army in place H6584
2Sa 18: 1 him and appointed **o** them commanders H6584
2Sa 18: 8 The battle spread out **o** the whole H6584+7156
2Sa 18:17 piled up a large heap of rocks **o** him. H6584
2Sa 18:33 went up to the **room o** the gateway and H6608
2Sa 19:10 whom we anointed to **rule o** us, has died H6584
2Sa 19:14 *He* **won o** the hearts of the men of Judah H5742
2Sa 19:18 ford to **take** the king's household **o** and to H6296
2Sa 19:22 Don't I know that today I am king **o** Israel?" H6584
2Sa 19:33 "**Cross o** with me and stay with me in H6296
2Sa 19:36 Your servant *will* **cross o** the Jordan with H6296
2Sa 19:37 *Let him* **cross o** with my lord the king H6296
2Sa 19:38 "Kimham *shall* **cross o** with me, and H6296
2Sa 19:39 the Jordan, and then the king **crossed o**. H6296
2Sa 19:40 When the king **crossed o** to Gilgal H6296
2Sa 19:40 the troops of Israel *had* **taken** the king **o**. H6296
2Sa 20: 8 strapped **o** it at his waist was a belt H6584
2Sa 20:12 into a field and threw a garment **o** him. H6584
2Sa 20:21 **Hand o** this one man, and I'll withdraw H5989
2Sa 20:23 Joab was **o** Israel's entire army; Benaiah H448
2Sa 20:23 son of Jehoiada was **o** the Kerethites and H6584
2Sa 21: 9 *He* **handed** them **o** *to* the H5989+928+3338
2Sa 23: 3 'When one rules **o** people in righteousness H928
2Sa 24: 3 God multiply the troops a hundred **times** *o*, AIT
2Sa 24:13 **think** *it* **o** and decide how I should answer H3359
1Ki 1: 1 warm even when *they* **put** covers **o** him. H4059
1Ki 1:34 the prophet anoint him king **o** Israel. H6584
1Ki 1:35 appointed him ruler **o** Israel and Judah." H6584
1Ki 2:11 He had reigned forty years **o** Israel—seven H6584
1Ki 2:35 son of Jehoiada **o** the army in Joab's H6584
1Ki 4: 1 So King Solomon ruled **o** all Israel. H6584
1Ki 4: 7 had twelve district governors **o** all Israel, H6584
1Ki 4:19 He was the only governor **o** the district. H928
1Ki 4:21 And Solomon ruled **o** all the kingdoms from H928
1Ki 4:24 For he ruled **o** all the kingdoms west of the H928
1Ki 5: 7 a wise son to **rule o** this great nation." H6584
1Ki 6: 1 fourth year of Solomon's reign **o** Israel, H6584
1Ki 6:35 gold hammered evenly **o** the carvings. H6584
1Ki 8: 7 spread their wings **o** the place of the ark H448
1Ki 8:46 with them and **give** them **o** to their H5989
1Ki 9: 5 your royal throne **o** Israel forever, H6584
1Ki 11:37 you will rule **o** all that your heart H928
1Ki 11:37 heart desires; you will be king **o** Israel. H6584
1Ki 11:42 reigned in Jerusalem **o** all Israel forty H6584
1Ki 12:17 of Judah, Rehoboam still ruled **o** them. H6584
1Ki 12:20 assembly and made him king **o** all Israel. H6584
1Ki 13:26 The LORD *has* **given** him **o** to the lion H5989
1Ki 13:30 they mourned **o** him and said, "Alas, H6584
1Ki 14: 2 told me I would be king **o** this people. H6584
1Ki 14: 7 appointed you ruler **o** my people Israel. H6584
1Ki 14:14 up for himself a king **o** Israel who will cut H6584
1Ki 14:17 soon as she stepped **o** the threshold of the H928
1Ki 15:25 and he reigned **o** Israel two years. H6584
1Ki 16: 2 appointed you ruler **o** my people Israel, H6584
1Ki 16:16 king **o** Israel that very day there in the H6584
1Ki 16:29 he reigned in Samaria **o** Israel twenty-two H6584
1Ki 18: 9 *are* **handing** your servant **o** *to* H5989+928+3338
1Ki 18:19 the people from **all o** Israel to meet me H3972
1Ki 19: 6 head was some bread **baked o hot coals**, H8363
1Ki 19:13 *he* **pulled** his cloak **o** his face and went H4286
1Ki 19:15 you get there, anoint Hazael king **o** Aram. H6584
1Ki 19:16 anoint Jehu son of Nimshi king **o** Israel H6584
1Ki 20:38 with his headband down **o** his eyes. H6584
1Ki 21: 7 "Is this how you act as king **o** Israel? H6584
1Ki 22:51 and he reigned **o** Israel two years. H6584
2Ki 2: 8 the two of them **crossed o** on dry ground. H6296
2Ki 2:14 the right and to the left, and he **crossed o**. H6296
2Ki 4:27 Gehazi **came o** to push her away, but the H5602
2Ki 4:43 'They will eat and **have** *some* **left o**.'" H3855
2Ki 4:44 they ate and **had** *some* **left o** H3855
2Ki 5:11 wave his hand **o** the spot and cure me of H448
2Ki 7: 4 So *let's* **go o** to the camp of the H2143
2Ki 8:15 it in water and spread it **o** the king's face, H6584
2Ki 9: 3 I anoint you king **o** Israel.' Then open the H448
2Ki 9: 6 'I anoint you king **o** the LORD's people Israel H448
2Ki 9:12 I anoint you king **o** Israel.'" H448
2Ki 10:36 that Jehu reigned **o** Israel in Samaria was H6584
2Ki 12: 7 but **hand** it **o** for repairing the temple." H5989
2Ki 13:14 down to see him and wept **o** him. H6584+7156
2Ki 13:17 of victory, the arrow of victory **o** Aram!" H928
2Ki 17:24 *They* **took o** Samaria and lived in its H3769
2Ki 19:15 you alone are God **o** all the kingdoms of H4200
2Ki 21:13 I will stretch out **o** Jerusalem the H6584
2Ki 23: 6 scattered the dust **o** the graves of the H6584
2Ki 25:22 to be **o** the people he had left behind in H6584
1Ch 10:14 death and **turned** the kingdom **o** to David H6015
1Ch 11: 3 they anointed David king **o** Israel, as H6584
1Ch 11:10 support to extend it **o** the whole land, H6584
1Ch 12:23 Hebron to **turn** Saul's kingdom **o** to him, H6015
1Ch 12:38 to make David king **o** all Israel. H6584
1Ch 14: 2 him as king **o** Israel and that his H6584
1Ch 14: 8 had been anointed king **o** all Israel, H6584
1Ch 17: 7 appointed you ruler **o** my people Israel. H6584
1Ch 17:10 I appointed leaders **o** my people Israel. H6584
1Ch 17:11 When your days *are* **o** and you go to be H4848
1Ch 17:14 I will set him **o** my house and my kingdom H928
1Ch 17:24 LORD Almighty, the **God o** Israel, is Israel's AIT
1Ch 18:10 him on his victory in battle **o** Hadadezer, H928
1Ch 18:14 David reigned **o** all Israel, doing what H6584
1Ch 18:15 Joab son of Zeruiah was **o** the army H6584
1Ch 18:17 son of Jehoiada was **o** the Kerethites and H6584
1Ch 21: 3 LORD multiply his troops a hundred **times** *o*. AIT
1Ch 21:16 sword in his hand extended **o** Jerusalem. H6584
1Ch 22:10 the throne of his kingdom **o** Israel forever. H6584
1Ch 22:12 when he puts you in command **o** Israel, H6584
1Ch 23: 1 he made his son Solomon king **o** Israel. H6584
1Ch 26:29 temple, as officials and judges **o** Israel. H6584
1Ch 27: 6 among the Thirty and was **o** the Thirty. H6584
1Ch 27:16 the tribes of Israel: **o** the Reubenites H4200
1Ch 27:16 Eliezer son of Zikri; **o** the Simeonites H4200
1Ch 27:17 **o** Levi: Hashabiah son of Kemuel; over H4200
1Ch 27:17 son of Kemuel; **o** Aaron: Zadok; H4200
1Ch 27:18 **o** Judah: Elihu, a brother of David; over H4200
1Ch 27:18 a brother of David; **o** Issachar: Omri son of H4200
1Ch 27:19 **o** Zebulun: Ishmaiah son of Obadiah H4200
1Ch 27:19 son of Obadiah; **o** Naphtali: Jerimoth son H4200
1Ch 27:20 **o** the Ephraimites: Hoshea son of Azaziah H4200
1Ch 27:20 of Azaziah; **o** half the tribe of Manasseh: H4200
1Ch 27:21 **o** the half-tribe of Manasseh in Gilead H4200
1Ch 27:21 son of Zechariah; **o** Benjamin: Jaasiel son H4200
1Ch 27:22 **o** Dan: Azarel son of Jeroham. These H4200
1Ch 28: 1 the **officers** *o* the tribes, the commanders of AIT
1Ch 28: 4 whole family to be king **o** Israel forever. H6584
1Ch 28: 4 was pleased to make me king **o** all Israel. H6584
1Ch 28: 5 throne of the kingdom of the LORD **o** Israel. H6584
1Ch 29: 3 **o and above** everything I H4200+5087+2025
1Ch 29:11 kingdom; you are exalted as head **o** all. H4200
1Ch 29:25 such as no king **o** Israel ever had before. H6584
1Ch 29:26 David son of Jesse was king **o** all Israel. H6584
1Ch 29:27 He ruled **o** Israel forty years—seven in H6584
2Ch 1: 1 established himself firmly **o** his kingdom, H6584
2Ch 1: 9 have made me king **o** a people who are H6584
2Ch 1:11 govern my people **o** whom I have made H6584
2Ch 1:13 tent of meeting. And he reigned **o** Israel. H6584
2Ch 2: 2 in the hills and 3,600 as foremen **o** them. H6584
2Ch 2:18 with 3,600 foremen **o** them to keep the NDT
2Ch 5: 8 spread their wings **o** the place of the ark H6584
2Ch 6: 5 anyone to be ruler **o** my people Israel. H6584
2Ch 6:36 with them and **give** them **o** to the enemy, H5989
2Ch 7:18 fail to have a successor to rule **o** Israel. H928
2Ch 9: 8 he has made you king **o** them, to H6584
2Ch 9:26 He ruled **o** all the kings from the Euphrates H928
2Ch 9:30 reigned in Jerusalem **o** all Israel forty H6584
2Ch 10:17 of Judah, Rehoboam still ruled **o** them. H6584
2Ch 15: 9 large numbers *had* **come o** to him from H5877
2Ch 19:11 the chief priest will be **o** you in any matter H6584
2Ch 19:11 will be **o** you in any matter concerning the NDT
2Ch 20: 6 You rule **o** all the kingdoms of the nations H928
2Ch 20:27 them cause to rejoice **o** their enemies. H4946
2Ch 20:31 So Jehoshaphat reigned **o** Judah. He was H6584
2Ch 21: 4 himself firmly **o** his father's kingdom, H6584
2Ch 26:12 of family leaders **o** the fighting men was H4200
2Ch 31:10 people, and this great amount *is* **left o**." H3855
2Ch 32: 6 military officers **o** the people and H6584
2Ch 34: 4 and scattered **o** the graves of those H6584+7156
2Ch 34:12 **O** them to direct them were Jahath and H6584
2Ch 35:13 the Passover animals **o** the fire as H928
2Ch 36: 4 king **o** Judah and Jerusalem and changed H6584
2Ch 36:10 Zedekiah, king **o** Judah and Jerusalem. H6584
Ezr 4: 9 administrators **o** the people from Persia NDT
Ezr 4:20 had powerful kings ruling **o** the whole of A10089
Ezr 5: 1 of the God of Israel, who was **o** them. A10542
Ezr 5: 5 God was watching **o** the elders of the A10542
Ezr 10: 6 continued to mourn **o** the unfaithfulness H6584
Ne 3:15 **roofing** it **o** and putting its doors and bolts H3233
Ne 4: 4 **Give** them **o** as plunder in a land of H5989
Ne 4:12 near them came and told us ten **times** *o*, AIT
Ne 4:14 After *I* **looked things o**, I stood up and said H8011
Ne 5:15 assistants also **lorded it o** the people. H8948
Ne 9:22 *They* **took o** the country of Sihon king of H3769
Ne 9:28 of their enemies so that they ruled **o** them. H928
Ne 9:37 goes to the kings you have placed **o** us. H6584
Ne 9:37 They rule **o** our bodies and our cattle as H6584
Ne 11: 9 of Hassenuah was **o** the New Quarter of H6584
Ne 12:39 **o** the Gate of Ephraim, the H4946+6584
Ne 13:19 not opened until the Sabbath was **o**. H339
Ne 13:26 God made him king **o** all Israel, but H6584
Est 1: 1 the Xerxes who **ruled o** 127 provinces H4887
Est 1: 5 When these days *were* **o**, the king gave a H4848
Est 1:22 man should be ruler **o** his own household, H928
Est 8: 2 Esther appointed him **o** Haman's estate. H6584
Est 9: 1 got the upper hand **o** those who hated H928
Job 3: 5 may a cloud settle **o** it; may blackness H6584
Job 8: 4 *he* **gave** them **o** to the penalty of their sin. H8938
Job 8:16 spreading its shoots **o** the garden; H6584
Job 10:12 in your providence **watched o** my spirit. H9068
Job 10:20 *Are* not my few days *almost* **o**? Turn away H2532
Job 14:17 up in a bag; you will cover **o** my sin. H6584
Job 15:29 will his possessions spread **o** the land. H4200
Job 16:11 God *has* **turned** me **o** to the ungodly and H6037
Job 16:15 sewed sackcloth **o** my skin and buried H6584
Job 18:15 burning sulfur is scattered **o** his dwelling. H6584
Job 20:25 out of his liver. Terrors will come **o** him; H6584
Job 21: 5 appalled; clap your hand **o** your mouth. H6584
Job 21:32 and watch is kept **o** their tombs. H6584
Job 26: 7 out the northern skies **o** empty space; H6584
Job 26: 7 he suspends the earth **o** nothing. H6584
Job 26: 9 the full moon, spreading his clouds **o** it. H6584
Job 29: 2 for the days when God **watched o** me, H9068
Job 31:25 if *I have* **rejoiced** *o* my great wealth, the AIT
Job 31:29 misfortune or **gloated** *o* the trouble that AIT
Job 34:13 Who appointed him **o** the earth? Who put H2025
Job 34:19 does not favor the rich **o** the poor, H4200+7156
Job 34:29 Yet he is **o** individual and nation alike, H6584
Job 37:12 they swirl around **o** the face of the whole H6584
Job 38:24 the east winds are scattered **o** the earth? H6584
Job 38:33 you set up God's dominion **o** the earth? H928
Job 38:37 Who *can* **tip o** the water jars of the H8886
Job 40: 4 I reply to you? I put my hand **o** my mouth. H4344
Job 41:20 as from a boiling pot **o** burning reeds. NDT
Job 41:34 are haughty; it is king **o** all that are proud." H6584
Job 42:11 consoled him **o** all the trouble the H6584
Ps 1: 6 For the LORD **watches o** the way of the H3359
Ps 5:11 Spread your protection **o** them, that those H6584
Ps 7: 7 while you sit enthroned **o** them on high. H6584
Ps 8: 6 You made them rulers **o** the works of your H928
Ps 12: 4 own lips will defend us—who is lord **o** us?" H4200
Ps 13: 2 How long will my enemy triumph **o** me? H6584
Ps 19:13 from willful sins; may they not rule **o** me. H928
Ps 20: 5 May we shout for joy **o** your victory and lift H928
Ps 22:17 on display; people stare and gloat **o** me. H928
Ps 22:28 to the LORD and he rules **o** the nations. H928
Ps 25: 2 nor let my enemies triumph **o** me. H4200
Ps 27:12 *Do* not **turn** me **o** to the desire of my foes H5989
Ps 29: 3 The voice of the LORD is **o** the waters; the H6584
Ps 29: 3 the LORD thunders **o** the mighty waters. H6584
Ps 29:10 The LORD sits enthroned **o** the flood; the H4200
Ps 30: 1 did not let my enemies gloat **o** me. H4200
Ps 35:19 not let those gloat **o** me who are my H4200
Ps 35:24 LORD my God; do not let them gloat **o** me. H4200
Ps 35:26 May all *who* **gloat** *o* my distress be put to AIT
Ps 35:26 exalt themselves **o** me be clothed with H6584
Ps 38:16 exalt themselves **o** me when my feet H6584
Ps 41: 2 does not give them **o** to the desire of their H928
Ps 41:11 for my enemy does not triumph **o** me. H6584
Ps 42: 7 waves and breakers have swept **o** me. H6584
Ps 44: 7 you give us victory **o** our enemies, you H4946
Ps 44:19 you covered us **o** with deep darkness. H6584
Ps 47: 2 awesome, the great King **o** all the earth. H6584
Ps 47: 8 God reigns **o** the nations; God is seated H6584
Ps 49:14 upright will prevail **o** them in the morning). H928
Ps 57: 5 heavens; let your glory be **o** all the earth. H6584
Ps 57:11 heavens; let your glory be **o** all the earth. H6584
Ps 59:10 will let me gloat **o** those who slander me. H928
Ps 59:13 ends of the earth that God rules **o** Jacob. H928
Ps 60: 8 my sandal; **o** Philistia I shout in triumph." H6584
Ps 63:10 They *will be* **given o** *to* the H5599+6584+3338
Ps 66:12 You let people ride **o** our heads; we went H4200
Ps 68:34 whose majesty is **o** Israel, whose power H6584
Ps 69:15 me up or the pit close its mouth **o** me. H6584
Ps 74:19 *Do* not **hand o** the life of your dove to H5989
Ps 78:48 *He* **gave o** their cattle to the hail, their H6037
Ps 78:50 from death but **gave** them **o** to the plague H6037
Ps 78:62 *He* **gave** his people **o** to the sword; he H6037
Ps 80:14 from heaven and see! **Watch o** this vine, H7212
Ps 81:12 So *I* **gave** them **o** to their stubborn hearts H8938
Ps 83:18 alone are the Most High **o** all the earth. H6584
Ps 88:16 Your wrath has swept **o** me; your terrors H6584
Ps 89: 9 You rule **o** the surging sea; when its waves H928
Ps 89:25 I will set his hand **o** the sea, his right hand H928
Ps 89:25 over the sea, his right hand **o** the rivers. H928
Ps 97: 9 are the Most High **o** all the earth; you are H6584
Ps 99: 2 in Zion; he is exalted **o** all the nations. H6584
Ps 103:16 the wind blows **o** it and it is gone, and its H928
Ps 103:19 in heaven, and his kingdom rules **o** all. H928
Ps 104: 8 *they* **flowed o** the mountains, they went H6590
Ps 105:21 of his household, ruler **o** all he possessed, H928
Ps 106:41 of the nations, and their foes ruled **o** them. H928
Ps 108: 5 heavens; let your glory be **o** all the earth. H6584
Ps 108: 9 my sandal; **o** Philistia I shout in triumph." H6584
Ps 113: 4 The LORD is exalted **o** all the nations, his H6584
Ps 116: 3 the anguish of the grave **came o** me; H5162
Ps 118:18 but *he has* not **given** me **o** to death. H5989
Ps 119:133 to your word; let no sin rule **o** me. H928
Ps 121: 3 *he who* **watches o** you will not slumber H9068
Ps 121: 4 *he who* **watches o** Israel will neither H9068
Ps 121: 5 The LORD **watches o** you—the LORD is H9068
Ps 121: 7 from all harm—*he will* **watch o** your life; H9068

Ps 121: 8 the LORD *will* **watch** **o** your coming and H9068
Ps 124: 4 the torrent would have swept **o** us, H6584
Ps 125: 3 will not remain **o** the land allotted to H6584
Ps 127: 1 Unless the LORD **watches** **o** the city, the H9068
Ps 129: 2 they have not gained the victory **o** me. H4200
Ps 141: 3 Set a guard **o** my mouth, LORD; keep watch H4200
Ps 141: 3 keep watch **o** the door of my lips. H6584
Ps 141: 8 I take refuge—*do* not **give** me **o** **to death**. H6867
Ps 142: 3 within me, it is you *who* **watch** **o** my way. H3359
Ps 145:20 The LORD **watches** **o** all who love him, but H9068
Ps 146: 9 The LORD **watches** **o** the foreigner and H9068
Pr 1:27 when disaster **sweeps** **o** you like a H910
Pr 3:10 your vats *will* **brim** **o** *with* new wine. H7287
Pr 4: 6 love her, and *she will* **watch** **o** you. H5915
Pr 6:22 they will watch **o** you; when you awake, H6584
Pr 10:12 up conflict, but love covers **o** all wrongs. H6584
Pr 17: 2 servant will rule **o** a disgraceful son and H928
Pr 17: 5 whoever gloats **o** disaster will not go H4200
Pr 17: 9 would foster love **covers** **o** an offense, H4059
Pr 19:10 much worse for a slave to rule **o** princes! H928
Pr 20:26 he drives the threshing wheel **o** them. H6584
Pr 22: 7 The rich rule **o** the poor, and the borrower H928
Pr 22:12 eyes of the LORD **keep watch** **o** knowledge, H5915
Pr 23:30 Those who linger **o** wine, who go to H6584
Pr 28:15 is a wicked ruler **o** a helpless people. H6584
Pr 30:32 plan evil, clap your hand **o** your mouth! H4200
Pr 31:27 *She* **watches** **o** the affairs of her H7595
Ecc 1:12 Teacher, was king **o** Israel in Jerusalem. H6584
Ecc 1:16 anyone who has **ruled** **o** Jerusalem before H6584
Ecc 2:19 they will have control **o** all the fruit of my H928
Ecc 2:20 began to despair **o** all my toilsome labor H6584
Ecc 2:26 up wealth to **hand** it **o** to the one who H5989
Ecc 3:19 humans have no advantage **o** animals. H4946
Ecc 5: 8 and **o** them both are others **higher** still. H6584
Ecc 6: 6 a thousand years **twice** **o** but fails to enjoy H7193
Ecc 6: 8 What advantage have the wise **o** fools H4946
Ecc 8: 8 As no one has power **o** the wind to contain H928
Ecc 8: 8 so no one has power **o** the time of their H928
Ecc 8: 9 a time when a man **lords it** **o** others to his H8948
SS 2: 4 and let his banner **o** me be love. H6584
SS 2: 8 the mountains, bounding **o** the hills. H6584
SS 2:11 winter is past; the rains *are* **o** and gone. H2736
SS 7: 9 my beloved, **flowing gently** *o* lips and teeth. AIT
SS 8: 6 Place me like a seal **o** your heart, like a H6584
Isa 3: 4 their officials; children will rule **o** them." H928
Isa 3:12 oppress my people, women rule **o** them. H928
Isa 4: 5 the LORD will create **o** all of Mount Zion H6584
Isa 4: 5 of Mount Zion and **o** those who assemble H6584
Isa 4: 5 **o** everything the glory will be a canopy. H6584
Isa 5:30 day they will roar **o** it like the roaring of H6584
Isa 7: 6 make the son of Tabeel king **o** it." H928+9348
Isa 8: 6 rejoices **o** Rezin and the son of H907
Isa 8: 7 all its channels, run **o** all its banks H6584
Isa 8: 8 on into Judah, **swirling** **o** it, passing H8851
Isa 9: 7 on David's throne and **o** his kingdom, H6584
Isa 10:26 he will raise his staff **o** the waters, as H6584
Isa 10:29 *They* **go** **o** the pass, and say, "We will H6296
Isa 11:15 will sweep his hand **o** the Euphrates River H6584
Isa 11:15 so that *anyone can* **cross** **o** in sandals. H2005
Isa 14: 2 of their captors and rule **o** their oppressors. H928
Isa 14: 8 cedars of Lebanon gloat **o** you and say, H4200
Isa 14: 9 all *those who* were **kings** *o* the nations. AIT
Isa 14:26 is the hand stretched out **o** all nations. H6584
Isa 15: 2 Moab wails **o** Nebo and Medeba. H6584
Isa 15: 5 My heart cries out **o** Moab; her fugitives H4200
Isa 15: 7 up they carry away **o** the Ravine of the H6584
Isa 16: 9 The shouts of joy **o** your ripened fruit and H6584
Isa 16: 9 ripened fruit and **o** your harvests have H6584
Isa 18: 2 sea in papyrus boats **o** the water. H6584+7156
Isa 19: 4 *I will* **hand** the Egyptians **o** to the power H6127
Isa 19: 4 a fierce king will rule **o** them, H928
Isa 22: 4 try to console me **o** the destruction of my H6584
Isa 22:21 and **hand** your authority **o** *to* H5989+928+3338
Isa 23: 6 **Cross** **o** to Tarshish; wail, *you* people of H6296
Isa 23:11 out his hand **o** the sea and made its H6584
Isa 23:12 **cross** **o** *to* Cyprus; even there you will H6296
Isa 26:13 other lords besides you *have* **ruled** **o** us H1249
Isa 27: 3 the LORD, **watch** **o** it; I water it H5915
Isa 28:27 is the wheel of a cart rolled **o** cumin H6584
Isa 28:28 of a threshing cart *may be* **rolled** **o** it, H2169
Isa 29:10 The LORD has brought **o** you a deep sleep H6584
Isa 31: 4 a great lion **o** its prey—and though H6584
Isa 31: 5 *he will* '**pass** **o**' it and will rescue it." H7173
Isa 34: 2 *he will* **give** them **o** to slaughter. H5989
Isa 34:11 will stretch out **o** Edom the measuring H6584
Isa 37:16 you alone are God **o** all the kingdoms of H4200
Isa 41: 2 *He* **hands** nations **o** *to* him and subdues H5989
Isa 42:13 battle cry and will triumph **o** his enemies. H6584
Isa 42:24 Who **handed** Jacob **o** to become loot H5989
Isa 43: 2 the rivers, *they will* not **sweep** **o** you. H8851
Isa 44:16 burns in the fire; **o** it he prepares his meal H6584
Isa 44:18 their eyes *are* **plastered** **o** so they cannot H3220
Isa 44:19 I even baked bread **o** its coals, I roasted H6584
Isa 45:14 *they will* **come** **o** to you and will be yours H6296
Isa 45:14 behind you, **coming** **o** to you in chains. H6296
Isa 51:10 sea so that the redeemed *might* **cross** **o**? H6296
Isa 60: 2 earth and thick darkness is **o** the peoples, NDT
Isa 60: 2 upon you and his glory appears **o** you. H6584
Isa 62: 5 as a bridegroom rejoices **o** his bride, so H6584
Isa 62: 5 his bride, so will your God rejoice **o** you. H6584
Isa 63:19 you have not ruled **o** them, they have H928
Isa 64: 7 from us and *have* **given** us **o** to our sins. H4481
Isa 65:19 I will rejoice **o** Jerusalem and take delight H928
Isa 66:10 greatly with her, all you who mourn **o** her. H6584
Isa 66:13 you will be comforted **o** Jerusalem. H928
Jer 1:10 today I appoint you **o** nations and H6584
Jer 2:10 **Cross** **o** *to* the coasts of Cyprus and look H6296
Jer 4:31 fainting; my life is **given** **o** **to** murderers." H4200
Jer 6: 1 Raise the signal **o** Beth Hakkerem! For H6584
Jer 6: 9 pass your hand **o** the branches again H6584
Jer 6:12 Their houses *will* **be turned** **o** to others H6015
Jer 6:17 I appointed watchmen **o** you and said H6584
Jer 6:21 children alike will stumble **o** them; H928
Jer 9:18 come quickly and wail **o** us till our eyes H6584
Jer 12:12 **O** all the barren heights in the desert H6584
Jer 13:21 say when the LORD sets **o** you those you H6584
Jer 13:26 pull up your skirts **o** your face that your H6584
Jer 18:21 So **give** their children **o** to famine; hand H5989
Jer 18:21 **hand** them **o** to the power of the sword. H5599
Jer 20:10 then we will prevail **o** him and take our H4200
Jer 23: 4 place shepherds **o** them who will tend H6584
Jer 24: 6 My eyes *will* **watch** **o** them for their H8492+6584
Jer 26:24 he *was* not **handed** **o** *to the* H5989+928+3338
Jer 28:14 even give him control **o** the wild animals. NDT
Jer 30:15 Why do you cry out **o** your wound, your H6584
Jer 31:10 gather them and *will* **watch** **o** his flock like H9068
Jer 31:28 Just as I watched **o** them to uproot and H6584
Jer 31:28 so I will watch **o** them to build and to H6584
Jer 33:26 of his sons to rule **o** the descendants of H448
Jer 35: 4 which was **o** that of Maaseiah son H4946+5087
Jer 38: 2 whoever **goes** **o** to the Babylonians H3655
Jer 38:16 you nor **hand** you **o** *to* those H5989+928+3338
Jer 38:19 of the Jews who *have* **gone** **o** to the H5877
Jer 38:19 *may* **hand** me **o** *to* them and H5989+928+3338
Jer 38:20 "*They will* not **hand** you **o**," Jeremiah H5989
Jer 39: 9 along with those who *had* **gone** **o** to him H5877
Jer 39:14 *They* **turned** him **o** to Gedaliah son of H5989
Jer 40: 5 has appointed **o** the towns of Judah, H928
Jer 40: 7 Ahikam as governor **o** the land and had H928
Jer 40:10 live in the towns *you have* **taken** **o**." H9530
Jer 40:11 the son of Shaphan, as governor **o** them, H6584
Jer 41: 2 had appointed as governor **o** the land. H928
Jer 41:10 *o* whom Nebuzaradan ... *had* **appointed** AIT
Jer 41:10 set out to **cross** **o** to the Ammonites. H6296
Jer 41:14 turned and **went** **o** to Johanan son H2143
Jer 41:18 had appointed as governor **o** the land. H928
Jer 43: 3 against us to **hand** us **o** *to* the H5989+928+3338
Jer 43:10 set his throne **o** these stones I have H4946+5087
Jer 44:27 For I am watching **o** them for harm, not H6584
Jer 46:12 One warrior will stumble **o** another; both H928
Jer 46:16 repeatedly; they will fall **o** each other. H448
Jer 48: 5 Horonaim anguished **cries** *o* the destruction AIT
Jer 48:31 Therefore I wail **o** Moab, for all Moab I cry H6584
Jer 48:40 spreading its wings **o** Moab. H448
Jer 49:22 spreading its wings **o** Bozrah. H6584
Jer 50: 6 They wandered **o** mountain and hill and H4946
Jer 51: 8 be broken. Wail **o** her! Get balm for H6584
Jer 51:14 they will shout in triumph **o** you. H6584
Jer 51:42 The sea will rise **o** Babylon; its roaring H6584
Jer 51:48 is in them will shout for joy **o** Babylon, H6584
La 2:17 he has let the enemy gloat **o** you, he has H6584
La 3:54 the waters closed **o** my head, and I H6584
La 3:65 Put a **veil** *o* their hearts, and may your curse AIT
La 4:16 he no longer **watches** **o** them. H5564
La 4:19 they chased us **o** the mountains and lay H6584
La 5: 2 inheritance *has* **been turned** **o** to H2200
La 5: 8 Slaves rule **o** us, and there is no one to H928
La 5:18 lies desolate, with jackals prowling **o** it. H928
Eze 1:25 from above the vault **o** their heads as they H6584
Eze 1:26 Above the vault **o** their heads was what H6584
Eze 4:15 bake your bread **o** cow dung instead of H6584
Eze 8:10 saw portrayed **all** **o** the walls H6017+6017+6584
Eze 9: 4 grieve and lament **o** all the detestable H6584
Eze 10: 1 the vault that was **o** the heads of the H6584
Eze 10: 2 the cherubim and scatter them **o** the city." H6584
Eze 10:18 LORD departed from **o** the threshold of the H6584
Eze 16: 8 of my garment **o** you and covered your H6584
Eze 16:27 *I* **gave** you **o** to the greed of your enemies, H5989
Eze 20:33 I will reign **o** you with a mighty hand and H6584
Eze 23:24 *I will* **turn** you **o** to them for punishment H5989
Eze 23:46 them and **give** them **o** to terror and H5989
Eze 25: 3 **o** my sanctuary when it was desecrated H448
Eze 25: 3 it was desecrated and **o** the land of Israel H448
Eze 25: 3 was laid waste and **o** the people of Judah H448
Eze 26:19 bring the ocean depths **o** you and its vast H6584
Eze 27:30 will raise their voice and cry bitterly **o** you; H6584
Eze 27:31 They will weep **o** you with anguish of soul H448
Eze 27:32 As they wail and mourn **o** you, they will H448
Eze 29:15 that it will never again rule **o** the nations. H928
Eze 31:10 cedar towered **o** the thick foliage, H448+1068
Eze 32: 3 throng of people I will cast my net **o** you, H6584
Eze 32: 8 lights in the heavens I will darken **o** you; H6584
Eze 32: 8 I will bring darkness **o** your land, declares H6584
Eze 34: 6 My sheep wandered **o** all the mountains H928
Eze 34: 6 were scattered **o** the whole earth, H6584+7156
Eze 34:23 I will place **o** them one shepherd, my H6584
Eze 35: 5 and **delivered** the Israelites **o** to the sword H5599
Eze 35: 6 *I will* **give** you **o** to bloodshed and it will H6913
Eze 35:12 laid waste and *have been* **given** **o** to us to H5989
Eze 37:22 will be one king **o** all of them and they H4200
Eze 37:24 " 'My servant David will be king **o** them H6584
Eze 39:23 and **handed** them **o** *to* their H5989+928+3338
Da 1:11 the chief official had appointed **o** Daniel, H6584
Da 2:38 he has made you ruler **o** them all. A10089
Da 2:39 of bronze, will rule **o** the whole earth. A10089
Da 2:48 He made him ruler **o** the entire province A10542
Da 2:49 administrators **o** the province of Babylon A10168
Da 3:12 whom you have set **o** the affairs of the A10542
Da 4:17 High is sovereign **o** all kingdoms on A10089
Da 4:17 he wishes and sets **o** them the lowliest A10542
Da 4:25 High is sovereign **o** all kingdoms on A10089
Da 4:32 High is sovereign **o** all kingdoms on A10089
Da 5:21 God is sovereign **o** all kingdoms on A10089
Da 5:21 on earth and sets **o** them anyone he A10542
Da 5:31 Darius the Mede **took** **o** the kingdom, A10618
Da 6: 2 with three administrators **o** them A10543+10427
Da 6: 3 to set him **o** the whole kingdom. A10542
Da 6:17 brought and placed **o** the mouth of the A10542
Da 7:27 heaven *will* **be handed** **o** to the holy A10314
Da 8:12 the daily sacrifice **were given** **o** to it. H5989
Da 9: 1 who was made ruler **o** the Babylonian H6584
Da 10: 3 lotions at all until the three weeks *were* **o**. H4848
Da 11:39 make them rulers **o** many people and will H928
Da 11:42 He will extend his power **o** many countries H928
Hos 7: 8 Ephraim is a flat loaf not **turned** **o**. H2200
Hos 7:12 I will throw my net **o** them; I will pull H6584
Hos 8: 1 An eagle is **o** the house of the LORD H6584
Hos 9: 6 of silver *will* **be taken** **o** *by* briers, H3769
Hos 9: 8 with my God, *is* the **watchman** *o* Ephraim, AIT
Hos 10: 5 Its people will mourn **o** it, and so will its H6584
Hos 10: 5 those who had rejoiced **o** its splendor H6584
Hos 11: 5 will not Assyria **rule** **o** them because they H4889
Hos 11: 8 How *can I* **hand** you **o**, Israel H4481
Joel 2: 5 of chariots they leap **o** the mountaintops, H6584
Am 5: 8 pours them out **o** the face of the land H6584
Am 6: 6 you do not grieve **o** the ruin of Joseph. H6584
Am 8: 5 "When *will* the New Moon **be** **o** that we H6296
Am 9: 6 pours them out **o** the face of the land H6584
Ob 12 *You should* not **gloat** **o** your brother in the H8011
Ob 12 rejoice **o** the people of Judah in the H4200
Ob 13 nor **gloat** **o** them in their calamity in the H8011
Ob 14 nor **hand** **o** their survivors in the day of H6037
Jnh 2: 3 all your waves and breakers swept **o** me. H6584
Jnh 4: 6 it grow up **o** Jonah to give H4946+6584+4200
Mic 3: 6 Therefore night will come **o** you, without H4200
Mic 4: 7 The LORD will rule **o** them in Mount Zion H6584
Mic 4:11 her be defiled, let our eyes gloat **o** Zion!" H928
Mic 5: 2 come for me one who will be ruler **o** Israel, H928
Mic 5: 9 be lifted up in triumph **o** your enemies, H6584
Mic 6:16 Therefore I *will* **give** you **o** to ruin and H5989
Mic 7: 8 Do not gloat **o** me, my enemy! Though I H4200
Mic 7:16 will put their hands **o** their mouths and H6584
Na 3: 3 number, people stumbling **o** the corpses— H928
Na 3: 5 "I will lift your skirts **o** your face. I will H6584
Zep 3:17 but will rejoice **o** you with singing. H6584
Zep 3:18 remove from you *all who* **mourn** *o* the loss of AIT
Zec 1:16 line will be stretched out **o** Jerusalem, H6584
Zec 5: 3 that is going out **o** the whole land; H6584+7156
Zec 9:14 Then the LORD will appear **o** them; his H6584
Zec 11:16 raise up a shepherd **o** the land who will H928
Zec 12: 4 "I will keep a watchful eye **o** Judah, but I H6584
Zec 14: 9 The LORD will be king **o** the whole earth H6584
Mt 2: 9 until it stopped **o** the place where the *G2062*
Mt 4:24 News about him spread **all** **o** Syria *G1650+3910*
Mt 5:25 adversary *may* **hand** you **o** to the judge, *G4140*
Mt 5:25 the judge may hand you **o** to the officer, NDT
Mt 5:40 take your shirt, **hand** **o** your coat as well. *G918*
Mt 8:24 so that the waves **swept** **o** the boat. *G2821*
Mt 9: 1 **crossed** **o** and came to his own town. *G1385*
Mt 9:31 news about him **all** **o** that region. *G1877+3910*
Mt 10:17 you *will be* **handed** **o** to the local councils *G4140*
Mt 14:20 of broken pieces that *were* **left** **o**. *G4355*
Mt 14:34 *When they had* **crossed** **o**, they landed at *G1385*
Mt 15:37 of broken pieces that *were* **left** **o**. *G4355*
Mt 18:15 If they listen to you, *you have* **won** them **o**. *G3045*
Mt 18:34 his master **handed** him **o** to the jailers *G4140*
Mt 20:18 Son of Man *will be* **delivered** **o** to the *G4140*
Mt 20:19 and *will* **hand** him **o** to the Gentiles to be *G4140*
Mt 20:25 the rulers of the Gentiles **lord it** **o** them, *G2894*
Mt 20:25 high officials **exercise authority** **o** them. *G2980*
Mt 23:15 *You* **travel** **o** land and sea to win a single *G4310*
Mt 24: 9 "Then you *will be* **handed** **o** to be *G4140*
Mt 26: 2 the Son of Man *will be* **handed** **o** to be *G4140*
Mt 26:15 to give me if I **deliver** him **o** to you?" *G4140*
Mt 26:16 watched for an opportunity to **hand** him **o**. *G4140*
Mt 26:36 "Sit here while *I* **go** **o** there and pray." *G599*
Mt 27: 2 him away and **handed** him **o** to Pilate the *G4140*
Mt 27:18 *that they had* **handed** Jesus **o** to him. *G4140*
Mt 27:26 and **handed** him **o** to be crucified. *G4140*
Mt 27:36 sitting down, *they* **kept watch** **o** him there. *G5498*
Mt 27:45 afternoon darkness came **o** all the land. *G2093*
Mk 1:28 him spread quickly **o** the whole region of *G1650*
Mk 3:23 So Jesus **called** them **o** to him and began *G4673*
Mk 4:35 disciples, "*Let us* **go** **o** to the other side." *G1451*
Mk 4:37 and the waves **broke** **o** the boat, so *G2095*
Mk 5:21 *When* Jesus *had* again **crossed** **o** by boat *G1385*
Mk 6: 7 two and gave them authority *o* impure **spirits**. AIT
Mk 6:53 *When they had* **crossed** **o**, they landed at *G1385*
Mk 8: 8 of broken pieces *that were* **left** **o**. *G4354*
Mk 10:33 Son of Man *will be* **delivered** **o** to the *G4140*
Mk 10:33 to death and *will* **hand** him **o** to the *G4140*
Mk 10:42 as rulers of the Gentiles **lord it** **o** them, *G2894*
Mk 10:42 high officials **exercise authority** **o** them. *G2980*
Mk 11: 7 colt to Jesus and **threw** their cloaks **o** it, *G2095*
Mk 13: 9 You *will be* **handed** **o** to the local councils *G4140*
Mk 14:11 watched for an opportunity *to* **hand** him **o**. *G4140*

Mk 15: 1 led him away and **handed** him **o** to Pilate. G4140
Mk 15:10 chief priests *had* **handed** Jesus **o** to him. G4140
Mk 15:15 and **handed** him **o** to be crucified. G4140
Mk 15:33 darkness came **o** the whole land until G2093
Mk 16: 1 *When* the Sabbath *was* **o**, Mary G1335
Lk 1:33 he will reign **o** Jacob's descendants G2093
Lk 2: 8 keeping watch **o** their flocks at night. G2093
Lk 2:43 *After* the festival *was* **o**, while his parents G5457
Lk 4:39 So he bent **o** her and rebuked the fever G2062
Lk 6:17 great number of people from **all o** Judea, G4246
Lk 6:38 shaken together and **running o**, will be G5658
Lk 8:22 "*Let us* **go o** to the other side of the lake." G1451
Lk 8:39 away and told **all o** town how G2848+3910
Lk 9:17 of broken pieces that *were* **left o**. G4355
Lk 11:44 which people walk **o** without knowing it." G2062
Lk 12:58 the judge **turn** you **o** to the officer G4140
Lk 13:11 She was **bent o** and could not straighten G5174
Lk 15: 7 rejoicing in heaven **o** one sinner who G2093
Lk 15: 7 who repents than **o** ninety-nine righteous G2093
Lk 15:10 of the angels of God **o** one sinner who G2093
Lk 16:26 nor *can anyone* **cross o** from there to us. G1385
Lk 18:32 *He will be* **delivered o** to the Gentiles G4140
Lk 19: 3 he was short he could not see **o** the crowd. G608
Lk 19:27 who did not want me to be king **o** them— G2093
Lk 19:41 Jerusalem and saw the city, he wept **o** it G2093
Lk 20:14 *they* **talked the matter o**. G1368+4639+253
Lk 20:20 so that *they might* **hand** him **o** to the G4140
Lk 21:12 *They will* **hand** you **o** to synagogues and G4140
Lk 22: 6 opportunity *to* **hand** Jesus **o** to them when G4140
Lk 22:25 "The kings of the Gentiles **lord it o** them G3259
Lk 22:25 those *who* **exercise authority o** them G2027
Lk 23: 5 up the people **all o** Judea by his G2848+3910
Lk 23:44 darkness came **o** the whole land until G2093
Lk 24: 7 of Man must *be* **delivered o** to the hands G4140
Lk 24:12 **Bending o**, he saw the strips of linen lying G4160
Lk 24:20 our rulers **handed** him **o** to be G4140
Lk 24:29 it is nearly evening; the day *is* almost **o**." G3111
Jn 3:25 a certain Jew **o the matter of** ceremonial G4309
Jn 5:24 be judged but *has* **crossed o** from death G3553
Jn 6:12 "Gather the pieces *that are* **left o**. G4355
Jn 6:13 five barley loaves **left o** by those who had G4355
Jn 12:11 of the Jews *were* **going o** to Jesus and G5632
Jn 14:30 world is coming. He has no hold **o** me, G1877
Jn 17: 2 him authority *o* **all** people that he might AIT
Jn 18:30 "*we* would not have **handed** him **o** to you." G4140
Jn 18:35 chief priests **handed** you **o** to me. G4140
Jn 19:11 would have no power **o** me if it were not G2848
Jn 19:11 the *one who* **handed** me **o** to you is G4140
Jn 19:16 Finally Pilate **handed** him **o** to them to be G4140
Jn 20: 5 *He* **bent o** and looked in at the strips of G4160
Jn 20:11 *she* **bent o to look** into the tomb G4160
Ac 1: 3 appeared to them **o a period** of forty days G1328
Ac 1:25 *to* **take o** this apostolic G3284+3836+5536
Ac 2:23 This man was **handed o** to you by God's G1692
Ac 3:13 You **handed** him **o** *to be killed*, and you G4140
Ac 4:22 miraculously healed was **o** forty years old. G4498
Ac 6: 3 *We will* **turn** this responsibility **o** to them G2770
Ac 7:10 made him ruler **o** Egypt and all his G2093
Ac 7:27 'Who made you ruler and judge **o** us? G2093
Ac 7:31 *As* he **went o** to get a closer look, he G4665
Ac 7:42 from them and **gave** them **o** to the G4140
Ac 9:42 This became known **all o** Joppa G2848+3910
Ac 11:28 famine would spread **o** the entire Roman G2093
Ac 12: 4 **handing** him **o** to be guarded by four G4140
Ac 13:11 mist and darkness came **o** him, G2093
Ac 14:19 Iconium and **won** the crowd **o**. G4275
Ac 16: 9 "**Come o** to Macedonia and help us." G1329
Ac 17: 6 trouble **all o the world** have now come G3876
Ac 19:13 name of the Lord Jesus **o** those who were G2093
Ac 20:15 The day after that *we* **crossed o** to Samos G4125
Ac 20:28 **Keep watch o** yourselves and all the flock G4668
Ac 21: 2 We found a ship **crossing o** to Phoenicia G1385
Ac 21:11 Coming **o** to us, he took Paul's belt, tied G4639
Ac 21:11 and *will* **hand** him **o** to the G4140+1650+5931
Ac 21:27 When the seven days were nearly **o** G5334
Ac 23:33 the governor and **handed** Paul **o** to him. G4225
Ac 24: 5 up riots among the Jews all **o** the world. G2848
Ac 24:10 of years you have been a judge *o* this **nation**; AIT
Ac 25:11 one has the right *to* **hand** me **o** to them. G5919
Ac 25:16 Roman custom *to* **hand o** anyone before G5919
Ac 25:21 made his appeal *to be* **held o** for the G5498
Ac 27: 1 prisoners *were* **handed o** to a centurion G4140
Ac 28:17 *I was* arrested in Jerusalem and **handed o** G4140+3836+5931
Ro 1: 8 faith is being reported all **o** the world. G1877
Ro 1:24 Therefore God **gave** them **o** in the sinful G4140
Ro 1:26 God **gave** them **o** to shameful lusts. G4140
Ro 1:28 so God **gave** them **o** to a depraved mind G4140
Ro 4:25 He *was* **delivered o to death** for our sins G4140
Ro 5:14 even **o** those who did not sin by breaking G2093
Ro 6: 9 death no longer **has mastery o** him. G3259
Ro 7: 1 that the law **has authority o** someone only G3259
Ro 9: 5 Messiah, who is God **o** all, forever praised G2093
Ro 9:32 *They* **stumbled o** the stumbling stone. G4684
Ro 11:32 has bound everyone **o to** disobedience so G1650
Ro 13:12 The night *is* **nearly o**; the day is almost G4621
Ro 14: 1 without quarreling **o** disputable matters. G1650
Ro 15:12 one who will arise to rule *o* the **nations**; in AIT
1Co 4: 6 follower of one of us **o against** the other. G2848
1Co 5: 5 **hand** this man **o** to Satan for the G4140
1Co 7: 4 have authority *o* her own **body** but yields it to AIT
1Co 7: 4 have authority *o* his own **body** but yields it to AIT
1Co 7:37 compulsion but has control **o** his own will, G4309
1Co 11:10 ought to have authority **o** her own head, G2093
1Co 13: 3 **give o** my body *to hardship* that I G4140
1Co 15:24 when *he* **hands o** the kingdom to God the G4140
2Co 1:24 Not that *we* **lord it o** your faith, but we G3259
2Co 3:13 who would put a veil **o** his face to prevent G2093
2Co 4:11 alive *are* always *being* **given o** to death G4140
2Co 12:21 I will be grieved **o** many who have sinned AIT
Gal 4: 9 to be enslaved by them **all o again**? G4099+540
Gal 4:17 *Those people are* **zealous** *to win* you *o*, but AIT
Eph 1:22 him to be head **o** everything for the G5642
Eph 4: 6 who is **o** all and through all and in all. G2093
Eph 4:19 they *have* **given** themselves **o** to G4140
Col 1:15 the invisible God, the firstborn *o* all **creation**. AIT
Col 2:10 He is the head *o* every **power** and authority. AIT
Col 2:15 of them, triumphing *o* **them** by the cross. AIT
Col 3:14 And **o** all these virtues put on love, which G2093
2Th 2: 4 will exalt himself **o** everything that is G2093
1Ti 1:20 whom *I have* **handed o** to Satan to be G4140
1Ti 2:12 to teach or *to* **assume authority o** a man; G883
1Ti 5: 9 on the list of widows **unless** she is **o** sixty, G1781
2Ti 3: 6 into homes and **gain control o** gullible G170
Heb 3: 6 is faithful as the Son **o** God's house. G2093
Heb 5:12 truths of God's word **all o again**. G4099
Heb 6: 6 *they are* **crucifying** the Son of God **all o again** G416
Heb 10:21 have a great priest **o** the house of God, G2093
Heb 13:17 they keep watch **o** you as those who must G5642
Jas 2:13 Mercy **triumphs o** judgment. G2878
Jas 5:14 the church to pray **o** them and anoint G2093
Jas 5:20 from death and **cover o** a multitude of G2821
1Pe 3: 1 *they may be* **won o** without words by the G3045
1Pe 4: 8 because love **covers o** a multitude of sins. G2821
1Pe 5: 2 your care, **watching o** them—not because G2174
1Pe 5: 3 not **lording it o** those entrusted to you, but G2894
2Pe 2: 3 *has* long *been* **hanging o** them, G4024+733
Rev 2:26 I will give authority **o** the nations— G2093
Rev 6: 8 were given power **o** a fourth of the earth G2093
Rev 9:11 They had as king **o** them the angel of the G2093
Rev 11:10 the earth will gloat **o** them and will G2093
Rev 12:11 They **triumphed o** him by the blood of the G3771
Rev 13: 7 And it was given authority **o** every tribe G2093
Rev 14:16 on the cloud swung his sickle **o** the earth, G2093
Rev 15: 2 had been victorious **o** the beast and its G1666
Rev 15: 2 its image and **o** the number of its G1666
Rev 16: 9 who had control **o** these plagues, but G2093
Rev 17:14 the Lamb *will* **triumph o** them G3771
Rev 17:17 by agreeing *to* **hand o** to the beast their G1443
Rev 17:18 great city that rules **o** the kings of the G2093
Rev 18: 9 burning, they will weep and mourn **o** her. G2093
Rev 18:11 weep and mourn **o** her because no one G2093
Rev 18:20 "Rejoice **o** her, you heavens! Rejoice, you G2093
Rev 20: 3 locked and sealed it **o** him, to keep G2062
Rev 20: 6 The second death has no power **o** them G2093
Rev 20: 7 When the thousand years *are* **o**, Satan G5464

OVERAWED (1) [AWE]

Ps 49:16 *Do* not *be* **o** when others grow rich, when H3707

OVERBEARING (1)

Titus 1: 7 be blameless—not **o**, not quick-tempered, G881

OVERBOARD (4)

Jnh 1:15 took Jonah and threw him **o**, H448+2021+3542
Ac 27:18 next day they began to **throw the cargo o**. G1678
Ac 27:19 *they* **threw** the ship's tackle **o** with their G4849
Ac 27:43 who could swim *to* **jump o** first and get to G681

OVERCAME (3) [OVERCOME]

Ex 17:13 So Joshua **o** the Amalekite army with the H2765
Jer 38:22 " 'They misled you and **o** you—those H3523
Hos 12: 4 He struggled with the angel and **o** him H3523

OVERCAST (1)

Mt 16: 3 it will be stormy, for the sky is red and **o**. G5145

OVERCHARGE, OVERCHARGED (KJV) PUT IT TOO SEVERELY, WEIGHED DOWN

OVERCOME (25) [OVERCAME, OVERCOMES]

Ge 32:28 with God and with humans and *have* **o**." H3523
1Sa 4:19 gave birth, but **was o** *by* her labor pains. H2200
1Sa 17: 9 subjects; but if I **o** him and kill him, you H3523
Ps 13: 4 enemy will say, "*I have* **o** him," and my H3523
Ps 39:10 from me; *I am* **o** by the blow of your hand. H3983
Ps 116: 3 over me; *I was* **o** *by* distress and sorrow. H5162
Jer 1:19 will fight against you but *will* not **o** you, H3523
Jer 15:20 will fight against you but *will* not **o** you, H3523
Jer 23: 9 like a strong man **o** *by* wine, because of H6296
Da 10:16 "*I am* **o** *with* anguish because of the H2200
Zec 9:15 They will destroy and **o** *with* slingstones H3899
Mt 16:18 the gates of Hades *will* not **o** it. G2996
Mk 9:24 "I do believe; **help** me *o* my unbelief!" AIT
Lk 8:37 because *they were* **o** with fear. G3489+5309
Lk 10:19 scorpions and *to* **o** all the power of G2093
Jn 1: 5 darkness, and the darkness *has* not **o** it. G2898
Jn 16:33 But take heart! I *have* **o** the world." G3771
Ro 12:21 *Do* not *be* **o** by evil, but overcome evil G3771
Ro 12:21 be overcome by evil, but **o** evil with good. G3771
1Ti 5:11 *their* **sensual desires o** *their* **dedication** to G2952
2Pe 2:20 are again entangled in it and *are* **o**, G2487
1Jn 2:13 because *you have* **o** the evil one. G3771
1Jn 2:14 lives in you, and *you have* **o** the evil one. G3771
1Jn 4: 4 are from God and *have* **o** them, because G3771
1Jn 5: 4 This is the victory that *has* **o** the world G3771

OVERCOMES (2) [OVERCOME]

1Jn 5: 4 everyone born of God **o** the world. G3771
1Jn 5: 5 Who is it that **o** the world? Only the one G3771

OVERFED (1) [FEED]

Eze 16:49 were arrogant, **o** and unconcerned H8430+4312

OVERFLOW (18) [OVERFLOWING, OVERFLOWS]

Job 6:15 intermittent streams, as the streams *that* **o** H6296
Ps 65:11 and your carts **o** *with* abundance. H8319
Ps 65:12 The grasslands of the wilderness **o**; the H8319
Ps 119:171 *May* my lips **o** *with* praise, for you teach H5580
Pr 5:16 *Should* your springs **o** in the streets, your H7046
Isa 8: 7 *It will* **o** all its channels, run over H6590+6584
Isa 28:17 and water *will* **o** your hiding place. H8851
Jer 9:18 over us till our eyes **o** *with* tears and water H3718
Jer 14:17 " '*Let* my eyes **o** *with* tears night and day H3718
Jer 47: 2 *They will* **o** the land and everything in it H8851
La 1:16 is why I weep and my eyes **o** *with* tears. H3718
Joel 2:24 the vats *will* **o** *with* new wine and oil. H8796
Joel 3:13 the winepress is full and the vats **o** H8796
Zec 1:17 'My towns *will* again **o** with prosperity H7046
Ro 5:15 *did* God's grace and the gift that came by the grace of the one man, Jesus Christ, **o** G4355
Ro 15:13 so that you *may* **o** with hope by the power G4355
2Co 4:15 people *may cause* thanksgiving *to* **o** to G4355
1Th 3:12 love increase and **o** for each other and G4355

OVERFLOWING (9) [OVERFLOW]

1Ch 12:15 the first month when it *was* **o** all its banks, H4848
Pr 3:10 then your barns will be filled *to* **o**, and H8426
Pr 8:24 when there were no springs **o** *with* water; H3877
Isa 66:11 deeply and delight in her **o** abundance." H2329
Jer 13:17 weep bitterly, **o** *with* tears, because the H3718
Jer 47: 2 the north; they will become an **o** torrent. H8851
2Co 8: 2 their **o** joy and their extreme poverty G4353
2Co 9:12 Lord's people but is also **o** in many G4355
Col 2: 7 you were taught, and **o** with thankfulness. G4355

OVERFLOWS (1) [OVERFLOW]

Ps 23: 5 You anoint my head with oil; my cup **o**. H8122

OVERGROWN (3) [GROW]

Isa 32:13 people, a land **o** *with* thorns and briers H6590
Jer 26:18 the temple hill a **mound** *o with* thickets. AIT
Mic 3:12 the temple hill a mound **o** with thickets. NDT

OVERHANG (1) [HANG]

Eze 41:25 there was a wooden **o** on the front of the H6264

OVERHANGING (3) [HANG]

1Ki 7: 6 in front of that were pillars and an **o roof**. H6264
Isa 2:21 the rocks and to the **o** crags from the H6186
Isa 57: 5 in the ravines and under the **o** crags. H6186

OVERHANGS (1) [HANG]

Eze 41:26 The side rooms of the temple also had **o**. H6264

OVERHEAD (1)

Isa 31: 5 Like birds **hovering o**, the LORD Almighty H6414

OVERHEARD (2) [HEAR]

Ge 27: 6 *I* **o** your father say to your brother Esau, H9048
1Sa 17:31 What David said **was o** and reported to H9048

OVERHEARING (1) [HEAR]

Mk 5:36 **O** what they said, Jesus told him, "Don't G4159

OVERJOYED (5) [JOY]

Da 6:23 The king *was* **o** and gave orders A10293+10678
Mt 2:10 the star, *they were* **o**. G5897+5915+3489+5379
Jn 20:20 The disciples *were* **o** when they saw the G5897
Ac 12:14 she was **so o** she ran back G608+3836+5915
1Pe 4:13 so that *you may be* **o** when his glory G5897+22

OVERLAID (35) [OVERLAY]

Ex 26:32 of acacia wood **o** *with* gold and standing H7596
Ex 26:37 five posts of acacia wood **o** *with* gold. H7596
Ex 36:34 *They* **o** the frames *with* gold and made H7596
Ex 36:34 *They* also **o** the crossbars *with* gold. H7596
Ex 36:36 acacia wood for it and **o** them *with* gold. H7596
Ex 36:38 *They* **o** the tops of the posts and their bands *with* H7596
Ex 37: 2 *He* **o** it *with* pure gold, both inside and out H7596
Ex 37: 4 of acacia wood and **o** them *with* gold. H7596
Ex 37:11 Then *they* **o** it *with* pure gold and made a H7596
Ex 37:15 of acacia wood and *were* **o** *with* gold. H7596
Ex 37:26 *They* **o** the top and all the sides and the H7596
Ex 37:28 of acacia wood and **o** them *with* gold. H7596
Ex 38: 2 and *they* **o** the altar *with* bronze. H7596
Ex 38: 6 of acacia wood and **o** them *with* bronze. H7596
Ex 38:17 their tops were **o** *with* silver; so all H7599
Ex 38:19 and their tops were **o** *with* silver. H7599
Jdg 17: 3 my son to make an image **o** with silver. H5011
Jdg 18:14 gods and an image **o with silver**? H5011
1Ki 6:20 *He* **o** the inside with pure gold, and he H7596
1Ki 6:20 and he also **o** the altar of cedar. H7596
1Ki 6:21 inner sanctuary, which *was* **o** *with* gold. H7596
1Ki 6:22 So *he* **o** the whole interior *with* gold. H7596
1Ki 6:22 *He* also **o** *with* gold the altar that H7596
1Ki 6:28 *He* **o** the cherubim *with* gold. H7596

1Ki 6:32 and o the cherubim and palm trees with H7596
1Ki 6:35 on them and o them with gold hammered H7596
1Ki 10:18 covered with ivory and o with fine gold. H7596
2Ch 3: 4 He o the inside with pure gold. H7596
2Ch 3: 7 He o the ceiling beams, doorframes, walls and doors of the temple with H2902
2Ch 3: 8 He o the inside with six hundred talents H2902
2Ch 3: 9 He also o the upper parts with gold. H2902
2Ch 3:10 cherubim and o them with gold. H7596
2Ch 4: 9 the court, and o the doors with bronze. H7596
2Ch 9:17 covered with ivory and o with pure gold. H7596
Isa 30:22 desecrate your idols o with silver and your H7599

OVERLAY (13) [OVERLAID, OVERLAYING, OVERLAYS]
Ex 25:11 O it with pure gold, both inside and out H7596
Ex 25:13 of acacia wood and o them with gold. H7596
Ex 25:24 O it with pure gold and make a gold H7596
Ex 25:28 o them with gold and carry the table with H7596
Ex 26:29 O the frames with gold and make gold H7596
Ex 26:29 Also o the crossbars with gold. H7596
Ex 27: 2 of one piece, and o the altar with bronze. H7596
Ex 27: 6 the altar and o them with bronze. H7596
Ex 30: 3 O the top and all the sides and the horns H7596
Ex 30: 5 of acacia wood and o them with gold. H7596
Ex 38:28 the posts, to o the tops of the posts H7596
Nu 16:38 the censers into sheets to o the altar, H7599
Nu 16:39 had them hammered out to o the altar, H7599

OVERLAYING (1) [OVERLAY]
1Ch 29: 4 the o of the walls of the buildings H3212

OVERLAYS (1) [OVERLAY]
Isa 40:19 a goldsmith o it with gold and H8392

OVERLOOK (4) [OVERLOOKED, OVERLOOKING, OVERLOOKS]
Dt 9:27 O the stubbornness of this people H440+7155
Dt 24:19 harvesting in your field and you o a sheaf, H8894
Pr 12:16 at once, but the prudent o an insult. H4059
Pr 19:11 it is to one's glory to o an offense. H6296

OVERLOOKED (2) [OVERLOOK]
Ac 6: 1 their widows were being o in the daily G4145
Ac 17:30 In the past God o such ignorance, but now G5666

OVERLOOKING (3) [OVERLOOK]
Nu 23:28 to the top of Peor, o the wasteland. H9207
Jos 8:14 at a certain place o the Arabah. H4200+7156
1Sa 13:18 the borderland o the Valley of Zeboyim H9207

OVERLOOKS (2) [OVERLOOK]
Nu 21:20 where the top of Pisgah o the wasteland. H9207
2Ch 20:24 came to the place that o the desert and H5205

OVERNIGHT (5) [NIGHT]
Lev 19:13 Do not hold back the wages of a hired worker o H4328+6330+1332
Dt 21:23 leave the body hanging on the pole o. H4328
Isa 10:29 and say, "We will camp o at Geba." H4869
Jnh 4:10 It sprang up o and died overnight H1201+4326
Jnh 4:10 It sprang up overnight and died o. H1201+4326

OVERPOWER (9) [POWER]
Ge 32:25 the man saw that he could not o him, H3523
Ge 43:18 to attack us and o us and seize us as H5877
Jdg 16: 5 how we can o him so we may H3523
2Ki 16: 5 besieged Ahaz, but they could not o him. H4309
Est 9: 1 of the Jews had hoped to o them, H8948
Job 14:20 You o them once for all, and they are H9548
Isa 7: 1 Jerusalem, but they could not o it. H4309+6584
Ob 7 your friends will deceive and o you; those H3523
Rev 11: 7 will attack them, and o and kill them. G3771

OVERPOWERED (8) [POWER]
Jdg 3:10 of Othniel, who o him. H6451+3338+6584
2Sa 11:23 "The men o us and came out against us H1504
1Ki 20:21 of Israel advanced and o the horses and H5782
2Ki 10:32 Hazael o the Israelites throughout their H5782
Ecc 4:12 Though one may be o, two can defend H9548
Jer 20: 7 I was deceived; you o me and prevailed. H2616
Da 6:24 the lions o them and crushed all their A10715
Ac 19:16 spirit jumped on them and o them all. G2894

OVERPOWERING (1) [POWER]
Job 41: 9 it is false; the mere sight of it is o. H3214

OVERPOWERS (1) [POWER]
Lk 11:22 someone stronger attacks and o him, G3771

OVERRAN (1) [RUN]
Jdg 20:43 them and easily o them in the vicinity H2005

OVERRIGHTEOUS (1) [RIGHTEOUS]
Ecc 7:16 Do not be o, neither be overwise H7404+2221

OVERRULED (2) [OVERRULING]
2Sa 24: 4 o Joab and the army commanders H2616+448
1Ch 21: 4 however, o Joab; so Joab left and H2616+6584

OVERRULING (1) [OVERRULED]
Est 8: 5 an order be written o the dispatches that H8740

OVERRUN (4) [RUN]
Isa 34:13 Thorns will o her citadels, nettles and H6590
Hos 9: 6 over by briers, and thorns will o their tents. H928
Am 3:11 "An enemy will o your land, pull down H6017
Zec 9: 8 again will an oppressor o my people, H6296

OVERSEER (8) [OVERSEERS, OVERSIGHT]
Ru 2: 5 Boaz asked the o of his harvesters H5853+5893
Ru 2: 6 The o replied, "She is the Moabite H5853+5893
2Ch 31:12 was the o in charge of these things H5592
Pr 6: 7 It has no commander, no o or ruler, H8853
1Ti 3: 1 aspires to be an o desires a noble task. G2175
1Ti 3: 2 Now the o is to be above reproach, faithful G2176
Titus 1: 7 Since an o manages God's household, he G2176
1Pe 2:25 to the Shepherd and O of your souls. G2176

OVERSEERS (7) [OVERSEER]
Ex 5: 6 the slave drivers and o in charge of the H8853
Ex 5:10 drivers and the o went out and said to H8853
Ex 5:14 beat the Israelite o they had appointed, H8853
Ex 5:15 Then the Israelite o went and appealed H8853
Ex 5:19 The Israelite o realized they were in H8853
Ac 20:28 of which the Holy Spirit has made you o. G2176
Php 1: 1 Philippi, together with the o and deacons: G2176

OVERSHADOW (2) [OVERSHADOWED, OVERSHADOWING]
1Ch 28:18 spread their wings and o the ark of the H6114
Lk 1:35 the power of the Most High will o you. G2173

OVERSHADOWED (1) [OVERSHADOW]
1Ki 8: 7 place of the ark and o the ark and its H6114

OVERSHADOWING (4) [OVERSHADOW]
Ex 25:20 spread upward, o the cover with them. H6114
Ex 37: 9 spread upward, o the cover with them. H6114
Eze 31: 3 with beautiful branches o the forest; it H7511
Heb 9: 5 of the Glory, o the atonement cover. G2944

OVERSIGHT (1) [OVERSEER]
2Ch 23:18 placed the o of the temple of the H7213

OVERSTEP (1) [STEP]
Pr 8:29 so the waters would not o his command, H6296

OVERTAKE (28) [OVERTAKEN, OVERTAKES, OVERTAKING, OVERTOOK]
Ge 19:19 this disaster will o me, and I'll die. H1815
Ex 15: 9 boasted, 'I will pursue, I will o them. H5952
Dt 19: 6 o him if the distance is too great H5952
Dt 28:15 these curses will come on you and o you: H5952
Dt 28:45 will pursue you and o you until you are H5952
1Sa 30: 8 raiding party? Will I o them?" "Pursue H5952
1Sa 30: 8 "You will certainly o them and H5952+5952
2Sa 15:14 will move quickly to o us and bring ruin H5952
2Ki 7: 9 wait until daylight, punishment will o us. H5162
Job 20:22 distress will o him; the full force of H4200
Job 27:20 Terrors o him like a flood; a tempest H5952
Ps 7: 5 then let my enemy pursue and o me; let H5952
Ps 35: 8 may ruin o them by surprise—may the net H995
Ps 69:24 on them; let your fierce anger o them. H5952
Ps 91:10 no harm will o you, no disaster will H628+448
Pr 6:15 Therefore disaster will o him in an instant H995
Pr 10:24 What the wicked dread will o them; what H995
Ecc 2:15 "The fate of the fool will o me also. H7936
Isa 35:10 Gladness and joy will o them, and sorrow H5952
Isa 47: 9 Both of these will o you in a moment, on a H995
Isa 51:11 Gladness and joy will o them, and sorrow H5952
Jer 42:16 then the sword you fear will o you there H5952
Hos 10: 9 Will not war again o the evildoers in H5952
Am 9:10 who say, 'Disaster will not o or meet us.' H5602
Mic 2: 6 about these things; disgrace will not o us." H6047
Zec 1: 6 did not my words and my decrees, which I commanded my servants the prophets, o H5952
Rev 12:15 to o the woman and sweep her away with G3958
Rev 18: 8 in one day her plagues will o her: G2457

OVERTAKEN (5) [OVERTAKE]
Ps 9: 6 Endless ruin has o my enemies, you have H9462
Ps 40:12 my sins have o me, and I cannot H5952
La 1: 3 who pursue her have o her in the midst H5952
Am 9:13 the reaper will be o by the plowman H5602
1Co 10:13 No temptation has o you except what is G3284

OVERTAKES (7) [OVERTAKE]
Pr 1:26 I will mock when calamity o you— H995
Pr 1:27 when calamity o you like a storm, when H995
Pr 3:25 disaster or of the ruin that o the wicked, H995
Pr 12:21 No harm o the righteous, but the H628+4200
Ecc 2:14 to realize that the same fate o them both. H7936
Ecc 9: 3 The same destiny o all. The hearts of H4200
Jn 12:35 you have the light, before darkness o you. G2898

OVERTAKING (1) [OVERTAKE]
1Ch 21:12 with their swords o you, or three days of H5952

OVERTHREW (9) [OVERTHROW]
Ge 19:25 he o those cities and the entire plain, destroying H2200
Ge 19:29 the catastrophe that o the cities where Lot H2200
Dt 29:23 Zeboyim, which the LORD o in fierce anger. H2200
Isa 14:17 who o its cities and would not let his H2238
Jer 20:16 be like the towns the LORD o without pity. H2200
Jer 50:40 As I o Sodom and Gomorrah along with H4550
Am 4:11 "I o some of you as I overthrew Sodom H2200
Am 4:11 some of you as I o Sodom and Gomorrah. H4550
Ac 13:19 and he o seven nations in Canaan, giving G2747

OVERTHROW (14) [OVERTHREW, OVERTHROWN, OVERTHROWS]
Ge 19:21 I will not o the town you speak of. H2200
2Sa 10: 3 to explore the city and spy it out and o it?" H2200
2Ki 3:19 You will o every fortified city and every H5782
1Ch 19: 3 explore and spy out the country and o it?" H2200
2Ch 25: 8 God will o you before the enemy H4173
2Ch 25: 8 God has the power to help or to o. H4173
Ezr 6:12 May God, who has caused his Name to dwell there, o A10400
Jer 1:10 to destroy and o, to build and to H2238
Jer 31:28 tear down, and to o, destroy and bring H2238
Jer 45: 4 I will o what I have built and uproot what H2238
Da 11:17 in marriage in order to o the kingdom, H8845
Da 11:24 He will plot the o of fortresses—but only H4742
Hag 2:22 I will o chariots and their drivers; horses H2200
2Th 2: 8 the Lord Jesus will o with the breath of G359

OVERTHROWN (10) [OVERTHROW]
Nu 21:30 "But we have o them; Heshbon's H3721
Pr 12: 7 The wicked are o and are no more, but H2200
Isa 1: 7 laid waste as when o by strangers. H4550
Isa 13:19 will be o by God like Sodom and H4550
Jer 18:23 Let them be o before you; deal with them H4173
Jer 49:18 As Sodom and Gomorrah were o, along H4550
La 2:17 He has o you without pity, he has let the H2238
La 4: 6 which was o in a moment without a hand H2200
Eze 32:12 of Egypt, and all her hordes will be o. H9012
Jnh 3: 4 "Forty more days and Nineveh will be o." H2200

OVERTHROWS (4) [OVERTHROW]
Job 12:19 priests away stripped and o officials long H6156
Job 34:25 he o them in the night and they are H2200
Pr 13: 6 of integrity, but wickedness o the sinner. H6156
Isa 44:25 who o the learning of the wise and H8740+294

OVERTOOK (10) [OVERTAKE]
Ge 31:25 hill country of Gilead when Laban o him, H5952
Ex 14: 9 the Israelites and o them as they camped H5952
Jdg 18:22 were called together and o the Danites. H1815
1Sa 31: 3 when the archers o him, they H5162
2Ki 25: 5 the king and o him in the plains of H5952
1Ch 10: 3 when the archers o him, they H5162
Ps 18:37 I pursued my enemies and o them; I did H5952
Jer 2: 3 held guilty, and disaster o them,' " H995+448
Jer 39: 5 army pursued them and o Zedekiah in the H5952
Jer 52: 8 King Zedekiah and o him in the plains of H5952

OVERTURN (1) [OVERTURNED, OVERTURNS]
Hag 2:22 I will o royal thrones and shatter the power H2200

OVERTURNED (5) [OVERTURN]
Jdg 7:13 the tent o and collapsed H2200+4200+5087+2025
Eze 38:20 The mountains will be o, the cliffs will H2238
Mt 21:12 He o the tables of the money changers G2951
Mk 11:15 He o the tables of the money changers G2951
Jn 2:15 of the money changers and o their tables. G426

OVERTURNS (1) [OVERTURN]
Job 9: 5 their knowing it and o them in his anger. H2200

OVERWEENING (NIV84) INSOLENCE

OVERWHELM (7) [OVERWHELMED, OVERWHELMING, OVERWHELMS]
Job 3: 5 a cloud settle over it; may blackness o it. H1286
Job 9:18 my breath but would o me with misery. H8425
Job 15:24 with terror; troubles o him, like a king H9548
Job 30:15 Terrors o me; my dignity is driven away as H2200
Pr 1:27 when distress and trouble o you. H995+6584
SS 6: 5 eyes from me; they o me. Your hair is like H8104
Hab 2:17 you have done to Lebanon will o you, H4059

OVERWHELMED (19) [OVERWHELM]
Dt 11: 4 how he o them with the waters of the Red H7429
2Sa 22: 5 the torrents of destruction o me. H1286
1Ki 10: 5 temple of the LORD, she was o. H4202+2118+6388+8120+928
2Ch 9: 4 temple of the LORD, she was o. H4202+2118+6388+8120+928
Ps 6:10 my enemies will be o with shame and H1017
Ps 14: 5 they are, o with dread, for God is H7064+7065
Ps 18: 4 the torrents of destruction o me. H1286
Ps 38: 4 My guilt has o me like a burden H6296+8031
Ps 53: 5 they are, o with dread, where there H7064+7065
Ps 55: 5 have beset me; horror has o me. H4059
Ps 65: 3 When we were o by sins, you forgave our H1504
Ps 88: 3 I am o with troubles and my life draws H8425
Ps 88: 7 you have o me with all your waves. H6700
Da 10: 7 such terror o them that they H5877+6584
Mt 26:38 "My soul is o with sorrow to the point of G4337
Mk 7:37 People were o with amazement. "He has G5669
Mk 9:15 they were o with wonder and ran to greet G1701
Mk 14:34 "My soul is o with sorrow to the point of G4337
2Co 2: 7 so that he will not be o by excessive G2927

OVERWHELMING (6) [OVERWHELM]
Pr 27: 4 Anger is cruel and fury o, but who can H8852
Isa 10:22 has been decreed, o and righteous. H8851
Isa 28:15 When an o scourge sweeps by, it cannot H8851

Isa 28:18 When the **o** scourge sweeps by, you will H8851
Da 11:22 Then an **o** army will be swept away before H8852
Na 1: 8 with an **o** flood he will make an end H6296

OVERWHELMS (1) [OVERWHELM]

Pr 10: 6 violence **o** the mouth of the wicked. H4059

OVERWICKED (1) [WICKED]

Ecc 7:17 *Do* not *be* **o**, and do not be a fool H8399+2221

OVERWISE (1) [WISE]

Ecc 7:16 neither *be* **o**—why destroy yourself H2681+3463

OWE (9) [OWED, OWES]

Lev 25:53 those to whom they **o** service do not rule NDT
Mt 18:28 'Pay back what *you* **o** me!' he demanded. *G4053*
Lk 16: 5 the first, 'How much *do you* **o** my master? *G4053*
Lk 16: 7 the second, 'And how much *do* you **o**? *G4053*
Ro 13: 7 Give to everyone what you **o** them: If you *G4051*
Ro 13: 7 If you **o** taxes, pay taxes; if revenue, then NDT
Ro 15:27 and indeed *they* **o** it to them. *G4050+1639*
Ro 15:27 *they* **o** it to the Jews to share with them *G4053*
Phm 19 to mention that *you* **o** me your very self. *G4695*

OWED (5) [OWE]

Mt 18:24 a *man who* **o** him ten thousand bags of *G4050*
Mt 18:28 fellow servants who **o** him a hundred *G4053*
Mt 18:34 until he should pay back all *he* **o**. *G4053*
Lk 7:41 "Two people **o money** to a certain *G5971+1639*
Lk 7:41 One **o** him five hundred denarii, and the *G4053*

OWES (2) [OWE]

Dt 15: 3 any debt your fellow Israelite **o** you. H2118
Phm 18 done you any wrong or **o** you anything, *G4053*

OWL (22) [OWLS]

Lev 11:16 the **horned o**, the screech owl, the H1426+3613
Lev 11:16 horned owl, the **screech o**, the gull, any H9379
Lev 11:17 the **little o**, the cormorant, the great owl, H3927
Lev 11:17 the little owl, the cormorant, the **great o**, H3568
Lev 11:18 the **white o**, the desert owl, the osprey, H9492
Lev 11:18 the white owl, the **desert o**, the osprey, H7684
Dt 14:15 the **horned o**, the screech owl, the H1426+3613
Dt 14:15 horned owl, the **screech o**, the gull, any H9379
Dt 14:16 the **little o**, the great owl, the white owl, H3927
Dt 14:16 the little owl, the **great o**, the white owl, H3568
Dt 14:16 the little owl, the great owl, the **white o**, H9492
Dt 14:17 the **desert o**, the osprey, the cormorant, H7684
Ps 102: 6 I am like a desert **o**, like an owl among H7684
Ps 102: 6 a desert owl, like an **o** *among* the ruins. H3927
Isa 34:11 The **desert o** and screech owl will possess H7684
Isa 34:11 desert owl and **screech o** will possess it; H7887
Isa 34:11 the **great o** and the raven will nest there. H3568
Isa 34:15 The **o** will nest there and lay eggs, she H7889
Jer 50:39 and there the **o** will dwell. H1426+3613
Mic 1: 8 like a jackal and moan like an **o**. H1426+3613
Zep 2:14 The **desert o** and the screech owl will H7684
Zep 2:14 owl and the **screech o** will roost on her H7887

OWLS (5) [OWL]

Job 30:29 of jackals, a companion of **o**. H1426+3613
Isa 13:21 houses; there the **o** will dwell, and H1426+3613
Isa 14:23 into a place for **o** and into swampland; H7887
Isa 34:13 a haunt for jackals, a home for **o**. H1426+3613
Isa 43:20 the jackals and the **o**, because I H1426+3613

OWN (672) [OWNED, OWNER, OWNER'S, OWNERS, OWNERSHIP, OWNING, OWNS]

Ge 1:27 So God created mankind in **his o** image H2257
Ge 5: 3 he had a son in **his o** likeness, in his own H2257
Ge 5: 3 own likeness, in **his o** image; and he H2257
Ge 10: 5 their nations, each with **its o** language.) H2257
Ge 15: 4 a son who is **your o** flesh and blood H3870
Ge 15:13 a country not **their o** and that they H4200+2157
Ge 24: 4 to my country and **my o** relatives and get H3276
Ge 24:38 go to my father's family and to **my o** clan, H3276
Ge 24:40 my son from **my o** clan and from my H3276
Ge 29:14 "You are **my o** flesh and blood. H3276
Ge 30:25 way so I can go back to **my o** homeland. H3276
Ge 30:30 may I do something for **my o** household?" H3276
Ge 30:43 and *came to* **o** large flocks, H2118+4200
Ge 37:27 he is our brother, **our o** flesh and blood." H5646
Ge 40: 5 each dream had a meaning of **its o**. H2257
Ge 41:11 each dream had a meaning of **its o**. H2257
Ge 43:29 brother Benjamin, **his o** mother's son, he H2257
Ge 46: 4 And Joseph's **o** hand will close your eyes." H2257
Ge 46:32 flocks and herds and everything they **o**. H4200
Ge 47: 1 flocks and herds and everything they **o**, H4200
Ge 47: 6 them in charge of **my o** livestock." H4200+3276
Ex 1:21 he gave them families of their **o**. NDT
Ex 2:11 went out to where **his o** people were and H2257
Ex 2:11 beating a Hebrew, one of **his o** people. H2257
Ex 4:18 "Let me return to **my o** people in Egypt to H3276
Ex 5: 7 them go and gather **their o** straw. H4200+2157
Ex 5:11 Go and get **your o** straw wherever H4200+4013
Ex 5:16 the fault is with **your o** people. H3870
Ex 6: 7 I will take you as **my o** people, and H4200+3276
Ex 18:27 and Jethro returned to **his o** country. H2257
Ex 22: 5 from the best of **their o** field or vineyard. H2084
Ex 32:13 to whom you swore by **your o self**: H3870
Ex 32:29 you were against **your o** sons and brothers H2257
Lev 7:30 With **their o** hands they are to present the H2257
Lev 14:15 it in the palm of **his o** left hand, H2021+3913S
Lev 14:26 into the palm of **his o** left hand, H2021+3913S
Lev 16: 6 offer the bull for **his o** sin offering to make H2257
Lev 16:11 bring the bull for **his o** sin offering to H2257
Lev 16:11 to slaughter the bull for **his o** sin offering. H2257
Lev 20: 9 their blood will be on **their o** head. H2257
Lev 20:11 their blood will be on **their o** heads. H4392
Lev 20:12 their blood will be on **their o** heads. H4392
Lev 20:13 their blood will be on **their o** heads. H4392
Lev 20:16 their blood will be on **their o** heads. H4392
Lev 20:26 apart from the nations to be **my o**. H4200+3276
Lev 20:27 their blood will be on **their o** heads. H4392
Lev 21:14 only a virgin from **his o** people, H2257
Lev 22:24 You must not do this in **your o** land, H4013
Lev 25:10 to your family property and to **your o** clan. H2257
Lev 25:13 everyone is to return to **their o** property. H2257
Lev 25:14 land to any of **your o** people or buy land H3870
Lev 25:15 You are to buy from **your o** people on the H3870
Lev 25:27 they can then go back to **their o** property. H2257
Lev 25:41 will go back to **their o** clans and to the H2257
Nu 1:52 each of them in **their o** camp under their H2084
Nu 2:17 each in **their o** place under their standard. H2257
Nu 6: 7 Even if **their o** father or mother or brother H2257
Nu 8:16 I have taken them as **my o** in place of the H3276
Nu 10: 9 go into battle in **your o** land against an H4013
Nu 10:30 I am going back to **my o** land and my own H3276
Nu 10:30 back to my own land and **my o** people." H3276
Nu 11:15 and do not let me face **my o** ruin. H3276
Nu 13:33 seemed like grasshoppers in **our o** eyes, H5646
Nu 15:39 after the lusts of **your o** hearts and eyes. H4013
Nu 17: 9 each of the leaders took **his o** staff. H2084
Nu 22:13 "Go back to **your o** country, for the LORD H4013
Nu 22:30 Balaam, "Am I not **your o** donkey, which H3870
Nu 24:13 I could not do anything of **my o** accord H3276
Nu 24:25 returned home, and Balak went **his o** way. H2257
Nu 27: 3 he died for **his o** sin and left no sons. H2257
Nu 35: 3 the cattle they **o** and all their other H8214
Nu 35:28 priest may they return to **their o** property. H2257
Nu 35:32 back and live on **their o** land before the H2021S
Dt 2: 5 Esau the hill country of Seir as his **o**. H3772
Dt 3:21 have seen with **your o** eyes all that the H3870
Dt 3:27 Look at the land with **your o** eyes, since H3870
Dt 4: 3 You saw with **your o** eyes what the LORD H4013
Dt 7:19 You saw with **your o** eyes the great trials H3870
Dt 9:26 **your o** inheritance that you redeemed by H3870
Dt 10:13 giving you today for **your o** good? H4200+3870
Dt 10:21 wonders you saw with **your o** eyes. H3870
Dt 11: 7 But it was **your o** eyes that saw all these H4013
Dt 12:12 no allotment or inheritance of **their o**. H2257
Dt 12:17 You must not eat in **your o** towns the tithe H3870
Dt 12:21 in **your o** towns you may eat as much H3870
Dt 13: 6 If your **very o brother**, or H278+1201+562+3870
Dt 14:27 have no allotment or inheritance of their **o**. NDT
Dt 14:29 have no allotment or inheritance of their **o**) NDT
Dt 15: 2 from anyone among **their o** people, H2084
Dt 15:22 You are to eat it in **your o** towns. Both the H3870
Dt 23:23 to the LORD your God with **your o** mouth. H3870
Dt 24:16 their parents; each will die for **their o** sin. H2257
Dt 28:54 no compassion on **his o** brother or the H2257
Dt 28:56 she loves and **her o** son or daughter H2023
Dt 29: 3 With **your o** eyes you saw those great trials H3870
Dt 29:19 though I **persist in** going my **o way**," H9244+4213
Dt 32:49 giving the Israelites as their **o** possession. NDT
Dt 33: 7 With **his o** hands he defends his cause H2257
Dt 33: 9 brothers or acknowledge **his o** children, H2257
Jos 1:11 the LORD your God is giving you for your **o**.H3769
Jos 1:15 you may go back and occupy your **o** land H3772
Jos 2:19 their blood will be on **their o** heads; we H2257
Jos 6:18 *you will* not **bring about** *your o* **destruction** AIT
Jos 7: 9 then will you do for **your o** great name?" H3870
Jos 7:11 have put them with **their o** possessions. H2157
Jos 20: 6 may go back to **their o** home in the town H2257
Jos 21: 3 pasturelands out of **their o** inheritance: H4392
Jos 22: 9 return to Gilead, **their o** land, which they H4392
Jos 22:23 If we have built **our o** altar to turn away H5646
Jos 24: 7 You saw with **your o** eyes what I did to the H4013
Jos 24:12 did not do it with **your o** sword and bow. H3870
Jos 24:28 the people, each to **their o** inheritance. H2257
Jdg 2: 6 of the land, each to **their o** inheritance. H2257
Jdg 3: 6 marriage and gave **their o** daughters to H2157
Jdg 7: 2 against me, '**My o** strength has saved me. H3276
Jdg 8:19 my brothers, the sons of **my o** mother. H3276
Jdg 8:30 He had seventy sons of **his o** H3655+3751+2257
Jdg 11:19 pass through your country to **our o** place. H3276
Jdg 18: 1 a place of **their o** where they might H2257
Jdg 21:24 clans, each to **his o** inheritance. H2257
Ru 4: 6 it because I might endanger **my o** estate. H3276
1Sa 5:11 let it go back to **its o** place, or it will kill H2257
1Sa 6: 9 If it goes up to **its o** territory, toward Beth H2257
1Sa 8:16 donkeys he will take for **his o** use. H2257
1Sa 8:22 "Everyone go back to **your o** town. H2257
1Sa 10:25 the people to go to **their o** homes. H2257
1Sa 12:22 was pleased to make you **his o**. H4200+2257
1Sa 13:14 out a man after **his o** heart and appointed H2257
1Sa 14:46 they withdrew to **their o** land. H4392
1Sa 15:12 up a monument in **his o** honor and has H2257
1Sa 15:17 you were once small in **your o** eyes, H3870
1Sa 17:38 Then Saul dressed David in **his o** tunic H2257
1Sa 17:54 put the Philistine's weapons in **his o** tent. H2257
1Sa 20:30 son of Jesse to **your o** shame and to the H3870
1Sa 24:10 have seen with **your o** eyes how the LORD H3870
1Sa 25: 8 Ask **your o** servants and they will tell you H3870
1Sa 25:26 from avenging yourself with **your o** hands, H3870
1Sa 25:33 from avenging myself with **my o** hands. H3276
1Sa 25:39 Nabal's wrongdoing down on **his o** head." H2257
1Sa 28: 3 buried him in **his o** town of Ramah. H2257
1Sa 29: 4 than by taking the heads of **our o** men? H2156S
1Sa 31: 4 so Saul took **his o** sword and fell on it. H2021S
2Sa 1:16 "Your blood be on **your o** head. H3870
2Sa 1:16 **Your o** mouth testified against you when H3870
2Sa 3: 6 been **strengthening his o position** in the H2616
2Sa 4:11 innocent man in **his o** house and on his H2257
2Sa 4:11 man in his own house and on **his o** bed— H2257
2Sa 5: 1 said, "We are **your o** flesh and blood. H3870
2Sa 6:22 I will be humiliated in **my o** eyes. H3276
2Sa 7:10 have a home of **their o** and no longer be H2257
2Sa 7:12 to succeed you, **your o** flesh and blood H3870
2Sa 7:22 as we have heard with **our o** ears. H5646
2Sa 7:24 people Israel as **your very o** forever, H4200+3870
2Sa 12: 4 from taking one of **his o** sheep or cattle to H2257
2Sa 12: 9 the sword and took his wife to be **your o**. H3870
2Sa 12:10 of Uriah the Hittite to be **your o**. H4200+3870
2Sa 12:11 'Out of **your o** household I am going to H3870
2Sa 12:20 Then he went to **his o** house, and at his H2257
2Sa 12:30 and it was placed on **his o** head. H1858
2Sa 14:24 "He must go to **his o** house; he must not H2257
2Sa 14:24 Absalom went to **his o** house and did not H2257
2Sa 16:11 "My son, **my o** flesh and blood, is trying to H3276
2Sa 19:12 are my relatives, **my o** flesh and blood. H3276
2Sa 19:13 'Are you not **my o** flesh and blood? H3276
2Sa 19:37 that I may die in **my o** town near the tomb H3276
2Sa 23:21 hand and killed him with **his o** spear. H2257
1Ki 1:12 how you can save **your o** life and the life H3871
1Ki 1:33 my son mount **my o** mule and take H4200+3276
1Ki 2:37 your blood will be on **your o** head. H3870
1Ki 4:25 everyone under **their o** vine and under H2257
1Ki 4:25 their own vine and under **their o** fig tree. H2257
1Ki 8:15 who with **his o** hand has fulfilled what he H2257
1Ki 8:15 he promised with **his o** mouth to my H2257
1Ki 8:19 your son, **your o** flesh and blood—he H3870
1Ki 8:38 aware of the afflictions of **their o** hearts, H2257
1Ki 8:43 fear you, as do **your o** people Israel, and H3870
1Ki 8:46 take them captive to **their o** lands, H2021+367S
1Ki 8:53 the world to be **your o** inheritance, H4200+3870
1Ki 9:15 the LORD's temple, **his o** palace, the H2257
1Ki 10: 6 report I heard in **my o** country about your H3276
1Ki 10: 7 until I came and saw with **my o** eyes. H3276
1Ki 10:13 returned with her retinue to **her o** country. H2023
1Ki 11:19 that he gave him a sister of **his o** wife, H2257
1Ki 11:20 Genubath lived with **Pharaoh's** *o* children. AIT
1Ki 11:21 that I may return to **my o** country. H3276
1Ki 11:22 you want to go back to **your o** country?" H3870
1Ki 12:16 Look after **your o** house, David!" So H3870
1Ki 12:33 a month of **his o** choosing H4946+4213+2257
1Ki 13:29 it back to **his o** city to H2021+5566+2021+2418S
1Ki 13:30 Then he laid the body in **his o** tomb, and H2257
1Ki 15:18 LORD's temple and of **his o** palace. H2021+4889S
1Ki 20:34 may set up **your o** market areas H4200+3870
2Ki 3:27 withdrew and returned to **their o** land. H2021S
2Ki 4:13 "I have a home among **my o** people." H3276
2Ki 6:22 have captured with **your o** sword or bow? H3870
2Ki 7: 2 "You will see it with **your o** eyes, H3870
2Ki 7:19 "You will see it with **your o** eyes, but you H3870
2Ki 8:20 against Judah and set up **its o** king. H2157
2Ki 9:21 rode out, each in **his o** chariot, to meet H2257
2Ki 13: 5 lived in **their o** homes as they had H2157
2Ki 14: 6 their parents; each will die for **their o** sin." H2257
2Ki 14:10 trouble and cause **your o** downfall and that H911
2Ki 15:19 strengthen **his o** hold on the kingdom H2257
2Ki 17:29 national group made **its o** gods in the H2257
2Ki 17:32 all sorts of **their o** people to officiate H4392
2Ki 17:33 they also served **their o** gods in H2157
2Ki 18:27 will have to eat **their o** excrement and H2157
2Ki 18:27 own excrement and drink **their o** urine?" H2157
2Ki 18:31 will eat fruit from **your o** vine and fig tree H2257
2Ki 18:31 tree and drink water from **your o** cistern, H2257
2Ki 18:32 come and take you to a land like **your o**— H4013
2Ki 19: 7 make him want to return to **his o** country, H2257
2Ki 20:18 **your o flesh and blood** who H3655+4946+3870
2Ki 21: 6 He sacrificed **his o** son in the fire H2257
2Ki 23:30 Jerusalem and buried him in **his o** tomb. H2257
2Ki 24: 7 not march out from **his o** country again, H2257
1Ch 9: 2 first to resettle on **their o** property in their H4392
1Ch 9: 2 own property in **their o** towns were some H2157
1Ch 10: 4 so Saul took **his o** sword and fell on it. H2021S
1Ch 11: 1 said, "We are **your o** flesh and blood. H3870
1Ch 11:23 hand and killed him with **his o** spear. H2257
1Ch 12:30 warriors, famous in **their o** clans—20,800; H4392
1Ch 16:43 each for **their o** home, and David H2257
1Ch 17: 9 that *they can* **have a home** *of their o* and no AIT
1Ch 17:11 one of **your o** sons, and I will H3870
1Ch 17:20 as we have heard with **our o** ears. H5646
1Ch 17:22 people Israel **your very o** forever, H4200+3870
2Ch 6: 9 your son, **your o** flesh and blood—he H3870
2Ch 6:33 fear you, as do **your o** people Israel, and H3870
2Ch 7:11 temple of the LORD and in **his o** palace, H2257
2Ch 8: 1 the temple of the LORD and **his o** palace, H2257
2Ch 8:18 sent him ships commanded by **his o** men, H2257
2Ch 9: 5 report I heard in **my o** country about your H3276
2Ch 9: 6 said until I came and saw with **my o** eyes. H3276
2Ch 9:12 returned with her retinue to **her o** country. H2023
2Ch 10:16 Look after **your o** house, David!" So H3870
2Ch 11:15 he appointed **his o** priests for the H4200+2257
2Ch 13: 9 make priests of **your o** as the peoples of H4013
2Ch 16: 2 temple and of **his o** palace and H2021+4889S

2Ch 21: 8 against Judah and set up **its o** king. H2157
2Ch 21:13 You have also murdered **your o** brothers H3870
2Ch 21:13 members of **your o** family, men who H3870
2Ch 25: 4 their parents; each will die for **their o** sin." H2257
2Ch 25:14 He set them up as **his o** gods H4200+2257
2Ch 25:15 could not save **their o** people from your H4392
2Ch 25:19 trouble and cause **your o** downfall and that H911
2Ch 29: 8 as you can see with **your o** eyes. H4013
2Ch 31: 1 returned to **their o** towns and to their H2157
2Ch 31: 1 to their own towns and to **their o** property. H2257
2Ch 31: 3 contributed from **his o** possessions for the H2257
2Ch 32:21 So he withdrew to **his o** land in disgrace H2257
2Ch 32:21 some of his sons, **his o** flesh and blood H2257
2Ch 35: 7 all from the **king's** *o* possessions. AIT
Ezr 2: 1 Judah, each to **their o** town, H2257
Ezr 2:70 temple servants settled in **their o** towns, H2157
Ne 3:28 each in front of **his o** house. H2257
Ne 4: 4 Turn their insults back on **their o** heads H4392
Ne 4:15 returned to the wall, each to **our o** work. H2257
Ne 5: 7 "You are charging **your o** people interest!" H2257
Ne 5: 8 Now you are selling **your o** people, only H4013
Ne 7: 3 their posts and some near **their o** houses." H2257
Ne 7: 6 Judah, each to **his o** town, H2257
Ne 7:73 of the Israelites, settled in **their o** towns. H2157
Ne 8:16 temporary shelters on **their o** roofs, H2257
Ne 11: 1 nine were to stay in **their o** towns. H2021S
Ne 11: 3 each on **their o** property in the various H2257
Ne 13:10 service had gone back to **their o** fields. H2084
Ne 13:19 stationed some of **my o** men at the gates H3276
Ne 13:30 assigned them duties, each to **his o** task. H2257
Est 1:22 to each province in **its o** script and to each H2023
Est 1:22 to each people in **their o** language, H2257
Est 1:22 should be ruler over **his o** household, H2257
Est 2: 7 taken her as **his o** daughter when H4200+2257
Est 3:12 and sealed with **his o** ring. H2021+4889S
Est 8: 9 also to the Jews in **their o** script and H4392
Est 9:25 Jews should come back onto **his o** head, H2257
Job 2: 4 "A man will give all he has for **his o** life. H2257
Job 9:21 no concern for myself; I despise **my o** life. H3276
Job 14:22 the pain of **their o** bodies and mourn H2257
Job 15: 6 **Your o** mouth condemns you, not mine H3870
Job 15: 6 not mine; **your o** lips testify against you. H3870
Job 18: 7 **his o** schemes throw him down. H2257
Job 19:16 though I beg him with **my o** mouth. H3276
Job 19:17 my wife; I am loathsome to **my o** family. H3276
Job 19:27 I myself will see him with **my o** eyes—I H3276
Job 20: 7 perish forever, like **his o** dung; those who H2257
Job 20:10 **his o** hands must give back his wealth. H2257
Job 21:16 But their prosperity is not in **their o** hands H4392
Job 21:20 Let **their o** eyes see their destruction; let H2257
Job 29:18 'I will die in **my o** house, my days as H3276
Job 32: 1 because he was righteous in **his o** eyes. H2257
Job 40:14 admit to you that **your o** right hand can H3870
Ps 7:16 violence comes down on **their o** heads. H2257
Ps 12: 4 we will prevail; **our o** lips will defend us H5646
Ps 19:12 But who can discern their **o** errors? Forgive NDT
Ps 35:21 With **our o** eyes we have seen it. H5646
Ps 36: 2 In **their o** eyes they flatter themselves too H2257
Ps 37:15 But their swords will pierce **their o** hearts H4392
Ps 40:15 be appalled at **their o** shame. H4392
Ps 50:20 brother and slander **your o** mother's son. H3870
Ps 64: 8 He will turn **their o** tongues against them H4392
Ps 69: 8 I am a foreigner to **my o** family, a stranger H3276
Ps 69: 8 a stranger to **my o** mother's children; H3276
Ps 79: 2 the flesh of your **o people** for the animals H2883
Ps 81:12 stubborn hearts to follow **their o** devices. H2157
Ps 132:11 "One of **your o** descendants I will place H3870
Ps 135: 4 LORD has chosen Jacob to be **his o**, H4200+2257
Ps 141:10 Let the wicked fall into **their o** nets, while H2257
Pr 1:18 These men lie in wait for **their o** blood H4392
Pr 3: 5 lean not on **your o** understanding; H3870
Pr 3: 7 Do not be wise in **your o** eyes; fear the H3870
Pr 5:15 Drink water from **your o** cistern, running H3870
Pr 5:15 running water from **your o** well. H3870
Pr 5:23 will die, led astray by **their o** great folly. H2257
Pr 11: 5 are brought down by **their o** wickedness. H2257
Pr 14: 1 with **her o** hands the foolish one tears H2023
Pr 14:10 Each heart knows **its o** bitterness H5883+2257
Pr 18: 2 delight in airing **their o** opinions. H2257
Pr 19: 3 A **person's** *o* folly leads to their ruin, yet their AIT
Pr 20:24 then can anyone understand **their o** way? H2257
Pr 21: 2 A person may think **their o** ways are right H2257
Pr 23: 4 to get rich; do not trust **your o** cleverness. H3870
Pr 26: 5 his folly, or he will be wise in **his o** eyes. H2257
Pr 26:12 Do you see a person wise in **their o** eyes H2257
Pr 26:16 sluggard is wiser in **his o** eyes than seven H2257
Pr 26:17 rushes into a quarrel not **their o**. H4200+2257
Pr 27: 2 and not **your o** mouth; an outsider H3870
Pr 27: 2 an outsider, and not **your o** lips. H3870
Pr 28:10 an evil path will fall into **their o** trap, H2257
Pr 28:11 The rich are wise in **their o** eyes; one who H2257
Pr 29: 6 Evildoers are snared by their **o** sin, but the NDT
Pr 29:24 of thieves are **their o** enemies; H5883+2257
Pr 30:12 who are pure in **their o** eyes and yet are H2257
Ecc 2:21 they must leave *all* they **o** to another who H2750
Ecc 2:24 drink and find satisfaction in **their o** toil. H2257
Ecc 8: 9 lords it over others to **his o** hurt. H4200+2257
Ecc 10:12 fools are consumed by **their o** lips. H5647
SS 1: 6 **my o** vineyard I had to H8611+4200+3276
SS 8:12 But **my o** vineyard is mine to give; the H3276
Isa 4: 1 "We will eat **our o** food and provide our H5646
Isa 4: 1 our own food and provide **our o** clothes; H5646
Isa 5:17 sheep will graze as in **their o** pasture; H4392
Isa 5:21 who are wise in **their o** eyes and clever in H2157
Isa 5:21 their own eyes and clever in **their o** sight. H2157
Isa 9:20 will feed on the flesh of **their o** offspring: H2257
Isa 13:14 they will all return to **their o** people, they H2257
Isa 14: 1 Israel and will settle them in **their o** land. H4392
Isa 14: 2 them and bring them to **their o** place. H4392
Isa 14:18 nations lie in state, each in **his o** tomb. H2257
Isa 30:20 with **your o** eyes you will see them. H3870
Isa 36:12 will have to eat **their o** excrement and H2157
Isa 36:12 own excrement and drink **their o** urine?" H2157
Isa 36:16 will eat fruit from **your o** vine and fig tree H2257
Isa 36:16 tree and drink water from **your o** cistern, H2257
Isa 36:17 come and take you to a land like **your o**— H4013
Isa 37: 7 make him want to return to **his o** country, H2257
Isa 39: 7 **your o flesh and blood** who H3655+4946+3870
Isa 43:25 transgressions, for **my o** sake, and H3276
Isa 44: 9 they are ignorant, to *their o* **shame**. AIT
Isa 45:12 **My o** hands stretched out the heavens; H3276
Isa 48: 9 For **my o** name's sake I delay my wrath H3276
Isa 48:11 For **my o** sake, for my own sake, I do this H3276
Isa 48:11 For my own sake, for **my o** sake, I do this H3276
Isa 48:13 **My o** hand laid the foundations of the H3276
Isa 49:26 make your oppressors eat **their o** flesh; H4392
Isa 49:26 they will be drunk on **their o** blood, as H4392
Isa 52: 8 they will see it with their **o** eyes. NDT
Isa 53: 6 each of us has turned to **our o** way; and H2257
Isa 56:11 they all turn to **their o** way, they seek their H4392
Isa 56:11 to their own way, they seek **their o** gain. H2257
Isa 58: 7 to turn away from **your o** flesh and blood? H3870
Isa 58:13 it by not going **your o** way and not doing H3870
Isa 59:16 so **his o** arm achieved salvation for him H2257
Isa 59:16 and **his o** righteousness sustained him. H2257
Isa 63: 5 so **my o** arm achieved salvation for me H3276
Isa 63: 5 me, and **my o** wrath sustained me. H3276
Isa 65: 2 pursuing **their o** imaginations— H2157
Isa 66: 3 They have chosen **their o** ways, and they H2157
Isa 66: 5 "**Your o** people who hate you, and H4013
Jer 2:13 and have dug **their o** cisterns H4200+2157
Jer 3:15 I will give you shepherds after **my o** heart, H3276
Jer 4:18 "**Your o** conduct and actions have brought H3871
Jer 5:19 served foreign gods in **your o** land, H4013
Jer 5:19 foreigners in a land not **your o**. H4200+4013
Jer 5:31 the priests rule by **their o** authority, and H2157
Jer 6: 3 around her, each tending **his o** portion." H2257
Jer 7: 6 follow other gods to **your o** harm, H4200+4013
Jer 7:19 themselves, to **their o** shame? H7156+2157
Jer 8: 6 Each pursues **their o** course like a horse H4392
Jer 10:23 I know that people's lives are not **their o** H2257
Jer 12: 6 members of **your o** family—even they H3870
Jer 12:15 of them back to **their o** inheritance and H2257
Jer 12:15 their own inheritance and **their o** country. H2257
Jer 14:14 the delusions of **their o** minds. H4392
Jer 16:20 Do people make **their o** gods? Yes H4200+2257
Jer 17: 4 Through **your o** fault you will lose the H3870
Jer 18:12 We will continue with **our o** plans; we will H5646
Jer 20: 4 with **your o** eyes you will see them fall by H3870
Jer 22:13 **making** his **o people** work for nothing H8276
Jer 23: 8 Then they will live in **their o** land." H4392
Jer 23:16 They speak visions from **their o** minds, not H4392
Jer 23:26 prophesy the delusions of **their o** minds? H4392
Jer 23:31 prophets who wag **their o** tongues and H4392
Jer 23:36 one's word becomes **their o** message. H2257
Jer 26:11 You have heard it with **your o** ears!" H4013
Jer 27:11 nation remain in **its o** land to till it and H2257
Jer 29:25 You sent letters in **your o** name to all the H3870
Jer 30:21 Their leader will be one of **their o**; their H5647
Jer 31:17 "Your children will return to **their o** land. H4392
Jer 31:30 everyone will die for **their o** sin; whoever H2257
Jer 31:30 grapes—**their o** teeth will be set on edge. H2257
Jer 32: 4 face to face and see him with **his o** eyes. H2257
Jer 34: 3 see the king of Babylon with **your o** eyes, H3870
Jer 34:15 you proclaimed freedom to your **o people**. H8276
Jer 34:17 freedom to your **o people**. H278+8276
Jer 37: 7 will go back to **its o** land, to Egypt. H2257
Jer 39:14 So he remained among **his o** people. H2021S
Jer 46:16 let us go back to **our o** people and our H5646
Jer 50: 6 hill and forgot **their o** resting place. H4392
Jer 50:16 let everyone return to **their o** people, H2257
Jer 50:16 people, let everyone flee to **their o** land. H2257
Jer 50:19 I will bring Israel back to **their o** pasture, H2084
Jer 51: 9 us leave her and each go to **our o** land, H2257
La 4:10 With their **o** hands compassionate women NDT
La 4:10 women have cooked **their o** children, H2177
Eze 7:16 they will all moan, each for **their o** sins. H2257
Eze 7:27 by **their o** standards I will judge them. H2157
Eze 8:12 darkness, each at the shrine of **his o** idol? H2257
Eze 9:10 bring down on **their o** heads what they H4392
Eze 11:21 bring down on **their o** heads what they H4392
Eze 13: 2 who prophesy out of **their o** imagination: H4392
Eze 13: 3 who follow **their o** spirit and have H4392
Eze 13:17 who prophesy out of **their o** imagination. H2177
Eze 13:18 lives of my people but preserve **your o**? H4032
Eze 14:16 could not save their **o** sons or daughters. NDT
Eze 14:18 could not save their **o** sons or daughters. NDT
Eze 16:32 You prefer strangers to **your o** husband! H2023
Eze 18:13 to death; his blood will be on **his o** head. H2257
Eze 18:18 But his father will die for **his o** sin H2257
Eze 18:30 each of you according to **your o** ways, H2257
Eze 22:11 violates his sister, **his o** father's daughter. H2257
Eze 22:31 bringing down on **their o** heads all they H4392
Eze 28:25 Then they will live in **their o** land, which I H4392
Eze 33: 4 their blood will be on **their o** head. H2257
Eze 33: 5 their blood will be on **their o** head. H2257
Eze 33:20 each of you according to **your o** ways." H2257
Eze 34:13 I will bring them into **their o** land. H4392
Eze 36: 5 made my land **their o** possession H4200+2157
Eze 36:17 of Israel were living in **their o** land, H4392
Eze 36:24 bring you back into **your o** land. H4013
Eze 37:14 and I will settle you in **your o** land. H4013
Eze 37:21 bring them back into **their o** land. H4392
Eze 39:28 I will gather them to **their o** land, not H4392
Eze 46:18 their inheritance out of **his o** property, H2257
Da 3:28 worship any god except **their o** God. A10203
Da 6:17 king sealed it with **his o** signet ring and A10192
Da 8:24 very strong, but not by **his o** power. H2257
Da 11: 5 he and will rule **his o** kingdom with great H2257
Da 11: 9 the South but will retreat to **his o** country. H2257
Da 11:14 are violent among **your o** people will H3870
Da 11:19 the fortresses of **his o** country but will H2257
Da 11:28 will return to **his o** country with great H2257
Da 11:28 against it and then return to **his o** country. H2257
Hos 8: 4 idols for themselves to *their o* **destruction**. AIT
Hos 10:13 have depended on **your o** strength and on H3870
Hos 14: 3 gods' to what **our o** hands have made, H5646
Joel 3: 4 speedily return on **your o** heads what you H4013
Joel 3: 7 I will return on **your o** heads what you H4013
Am 5: 2 deserted in **her o** land, with no one H2023
Am 6:13 we not take Karnaim by **our o** strength?" H5646
Am 9:15 I will plant Israel in **their o** land, never H4392
Ob 15 your deeds will return upon **your o** head. H3870
Jnh 1: 5 afraid and each cried out to **his o** god. H2257
Mic 4: 4 will sit under **their** *o* vine and under their AIT
Mic 4: 4 their own vine and under **their** *o* fig tree, AIT
Mic 7: 6 are the members of **his** *o* household. AIT
Hab 1: 6 earth to seize dwellings not **their o**. H2257+4200
Hab 1: 7 to themselves and promote **their o** honor. H2257
Hab 1:11 people, whose **o** strength is their god." H2257
Hab 2:10 shaming **your o** house and forfeiting your H3870
Hab 2:18 one who makes it trusts in **his o** creation; H2257
Hab 3:14 With **his o** spear you pierced his head H2257
Zep 2:11 down to him, all of them in **their o** lands. H2257
Hag 1: 9 each of you is busy with **your o** house. H2257
Zec 11: 5 **Their o** shepherds do not spare them. H2157
Zec 13: 3 Then **their o** parents will stab the one H2084
Mal 1: 5 You will see it with **your o** eyes and say H4013
Mt 5:47 And if you greet only **your o** people, what *G5148*
Mt 6:34 Each day has enough trouble *of* **its o**. *G899*
Mt 7: 3 no attention to the plank in **your o** eye? *G5050*
Mt 7: 4 all the time there is a plank in **your o** eye? *G5148*
Mt 7: 5 first take the plank out of **your o** eye, and *G5148*
Mt 8:22 and let the dead bury **their o** dead." *G1571*
Mt 9: 1 crossed over and came to **his o** town. *G2625*
Mt 10:36 will be the members of **his o** household. *G899*
Mt 13:57 honor except in his **o town** and in his own *G4258*
Mt 13:57 except in his own town and in **his o** home." *G899*
Mt 17:25 from **their o** children or from others? *G899*
Mt 20:15 right to do what I want with **my o** *money*? *G1847*
Mt 27:31 off the robe and put **his o** clothes on him. *G899*
Mt 27:60 placed it in **his o** new tomb that he had *G899*
Mk 4:34 when he was alone with **his o** disciples, *G2625*
Mk 5:19 "Go home to **your o** *people* and tell them *G5050*
Mk 6: 4 is not without honor except in **his o** town, *G899*
Mk 6: 4 among his relatives and in **his o** home." *G899*
Mk 7: 9 God in order to observe **your o** traditions! *G5148*
Mk 15:20 purple robe and put **his o** clothes on him. *G899*
Lk 2: 3 everyone went to **their o** town to register. *G1571*
Lk 2:35 And a sword will pierce your **o** soul too." *G899*
Lk 2:39 to Galilee to **their o** town of Nazareth. *G1571*
Lk 6:41 no attention to the plank in **your o** eye? *G2625*
Lk 6:42 fail to see the plank in **your o** eye? *G5148*
Lk 6:44 Each tree is recognized by **its o** fruit *G2625*
Lk 8: 3 to support them out of **their o** means. *G899*
Lk 9:60 "Let the dead bury **their o** dead, but you *G1571*
Lk 10:34 Then he put the man on **his o** donkey *G2625*
Lk 11:21 fully armed, guards **his o** house, his *G1571*
Lk 14:26 even **their o** life—such a person *G1571*
Lk 16: 8 in dealing with **their o** kind than are the *G1571*
Lk 16:12 who will give you property *of* **your o**? *G5629*
Lk 18: 9 were confident of **their o** righteousness *G1571*
Lk 19:22 'I will judge you by **your o** words, you *G5148*
Lk 22:71 We have heard it from **his o** lips." *G899*
Jn 1:11 He came to that which was **his o**, but his *G2625*
Jn 1:11 his own, but **his o** did not receive him. *G2625*
Jn 4:44 a prophet has no honor in **his o** country.) *G2625*
Jn 5:18 he was even calling God **his o** Father *G2625*
Jn 5:43 if someone else comes in **his o** name *G2625*
Jn 7: 5 For even **his o** brothers did not believe in *G899*
Jn 7:16 Jesus answered, "My teaching is not **my o**. *G1847*
Jn 7:17 from God or whether I speak on **my o**. *G1831*
Jn 7:18 Whoever speaks on **their o** does so to gain *G1571*
Jn 7:28 I am not here on **my o** authority, but he *G1831*
Jn 7:50 earlier and who was one of **their** *o number*, AIT
Jn 8:13 you are, appearing as **your o** witness; your *G4932*
Jn 8:14 "Even if I testify on **my o** behalf, my *G1831*
Jn 8:17 In **your o** Law it is written that the *G5629*
Jn 8:28 I do nothing on **my o** but speak just what *G1831*
Jn 8:41 You are doing the works of **your o** father." *G5148*
Jn 8:42 I have not come on **my o**; God sent me. *G1831*
Jn 10: 3 He calls **his o** sheep by name and leads *G2625*
Jn 10: 4 When he has brought out all **his o**, he *G2625*
Jn 10:12 and *does* not **o** the sheep. *G1639+2625*
Jn 10:18 from me, but I lay it down of **my o** accord. *G1831*
Jn 10:36 the Father **set apart as** *his* **very o** and sent *G39*

Jn 11:51 He did not say this on **his o**, but as high *G1571*
Jn 12:49 For I did not speak on **my o**, but the Father *G1831*
Jn 13: 1 Having loved **his o** who were in the world *G2625*
Jn 14:10 I do not speak **on my o authority**. *G608+1831*
Jn 14:24 These words you hear are not **my o**; they *G1847*
Jn 15:19 to the world, it would love you as **its o**. *G2625*
Jn 16:13 He will not speak on **his o**; he will speak *G1571*
Jn 16:32 be scattered, each to **your o home**. *G3836+2625*
Jn 18:31 yourselves and judge him by **your o** law." *G5148*
Jn 18:34 "*Is* that **your o idea**," Jesus *G608+4932+3306*
Jn 18:35 "**Your o** people and chief priests handed *G5050*
Jn 19:17 Carrying **his o** cross, he went out to the *G1571*
Ac 1: 7 dates the Father has set by **his o** authority. *G2625*
Ac 2: 6 each one heard **their o** language being *G2625*
Ac 2:11 the wonders of God in **our o** tongues!" *G2466*
Ac 3:12 stare at us as if *by* **our o** power or *G2625*
Ac 3:22 like me from among **your o** people; *G5148*
Ac 4:23 went back to **their o** *people* and reported *G2625*
Ac 4:32 that any of their possessions was **their o**, *G2625*
Ac 5:31 God exalted him to **his o** right hand as *G899*
Ac 7: 6 will be strangers in a country **not their o**, *G259*
Ac 7:21 him and brought him up as **her o** son. *G1571*
Ac 7:23 he decided to visit **his o** people, the *G899*
Ac 7:25 Moses thought that **his o** people would *G3836*
Ac 7:37 you a prophet like me from **your o** people. *G5148*
Ac 7:41 reveled in what **their o** hands had made. *G899*
Ac 13:22 a man after **my o** heart; he will do *G1609*
Ac 13:36 served God's purpose in **his o** generation, *G2625*
Ac 14:16 In the past, he let all nations go **their o** way. *G899*
Ac 15:22 to choose some of **their o** men and send *G899*
Ac 17:28 As some of **your o** poets have said, *G2848+5148*
Ac 18: 6 to them, "Your blood be on **your o** heads! *G5148*
Ac 18:15 words and names and **your o** law— *G2848+5148*
Ac 20:28 which he bought with **his o** blood. *G2625*
Ac 20:30 Even from your o *number* men will arise *G899*
Ac 20:34 mine have supplied **my o** needs and the *G1609*
Ac 21:11 tied **his o** hands and feet with it and said *G1571*
Ac 25:19 with him about **their o** religion and about *G2625*
Ac 26: 4 the beginning of my life in **my o** country, *G1609*
Ac 26:17 rescue you from **your o** people and from *G3836*
Ac 26:23 of light to **his o** people and to the *G3836*
Ac 27:10 to ship and cargo, and to **our o** lives also." *G1609*
Ac 27:19 ship's tackle overboard **with their o hands**. *G901*
Ac 28:19 to bring any charge against **my o** people. *G1609*
Ac 28:30 stayed there in **his o** rented house and *G2625*
Ro 5: 8 God demonstrates **his o** love for us in this *G1571*
Ro 8: 3 God did by sending **his o** Son in the *G1571*
Ro 8:20 frustration, not **by its o choice**, but by the *G1776*
Ro 8:32 He who did not spare **his o** Son, but gave *G2625*
Ro 9: 3 people, those of my **o race**, *G5150+2848+4922*
Ro 10: 3 of God and sought to establish **their o**, *G2625*
Ro 11:14 somehow arouse **my o** people to envy *G1609*
Ro 11:24 be grafted into **their o** olive tree! *G2625*
Ro 14: 4 else's servant? *To* **their o** master, servants *G2625*
Ro 14: 5 should be fully convinced in **their o** mind. *G2625*
Ro 16:18 our Lord Christ, but **their o** appetites. *G1571*
1Co 2:11 thoughts except **their o** spirit within *G3836+476S*
1Co 3: 8 be rewarded according to **their o** labor. *G2625*
1Co 4:12 We work hard with **our o** hands. When we *G2625*
1Co 6:18 sins sexually, sins against **their o** body. *G2625*
1Co 6:19 received from God? You are not **your o**; *G1571*
1Co 7: 2 have sexual relations with **his o** wife, *G1571*
1Co 7: 2 each woman with **her o** husband. *G2625*
1Co 7: 4 authority over **her o** body but yields it *G2625*
1Co 7: 4 have authority over **his o** body but yields it *G2625*
1Co 7: 7 But each of you has **your o** gift from God *G2625*
1Co 7:35 I am saying this for your **o** good, not to *G899*
1Co 7:37 who has settled the matter in **his o** mind, *G899*
1Co 7:37 compulsion but has control over **his o** will, *G2625*
1Co 9: 7 Who serves as a soldier at **his o** expense *G2625*
1Co 10:24 No one should seek **their o** *good*, but the *G1571*
1Co 10:33 I am not seeking **my o** good but the good *G1831*
1Co 11:10 ought to have authority over **her o** head, *G3836*
1Co 11:21 ahead with **your o private** suppers. *G3836+2625*
1Co 14:35 they should ask **their o** husbands at home; *G2625*
1Co 15:38 to each kind of seed he gives **its o** body. *G2625*
1Co 16:21 Paul, write this greeting in **my o** hand. *G1847*
2Co 7:13 In addition to **our o** encouragement, we *G1609*
2Co 8: 3 beyond their ability. **Entirely on their o**, *G882*
2Co 8:17 much enthusiasm and **on his o initiative**. *G882*
Gal 1:14 beyond many of *my* **o age** among my *G5312*
Gal 6: 4 Each one should test **their o** actions. *G1571*
Gal 6: 5 each one should carry **their o** load. *G2625*
Gal 6:11 I use as I write to you with **my o** hand! *G1847*
Eph 4:28 something useful with **their o** hands, *G2625*
Eph 5:22 yourselves to **your o** husbands as you do *G2625*
Eph 5:28 to love their wives as **their o** bodies. *G1571*
Eph 5:29 no one ever hated **their o** body, but they *G1571*
Php 2: 4 not looking to **your o** interests but each of *G1571*
Php 2: 6 **something** to be **used to** his **o advantage**; *G772*
Php 2:21 For everyone looks out for **their o** interests *G1571*
Php 3: 9 a righteousness **of my o** that comes from *G1847*
Col 4:18 write this greeting in **my o** hand *G1847*
1Th 2:11 you as a father deals with **his o** children, *G1571*
1Th 2:14 from your **o people** the same *G2625+5241*
1Th 4: 4 learn to control **your o** body in a way that *G1571*
1Th 4:11 You should mind **your o** business and *G2625*
2Th 3:17 write this greeting in **my o** hand, which is *G1847*
1Ti 3: 4 He must manage **his o** family well and *G2625*
1Ti 3: 5 not know how to manage **his o** family, *G2625*
1Ti 5: 4 by caring for **their o** family and so *G2625*
1Ti 5: 8 especially for their **o** household, has NDT
1Ti 6:15 which God will bring about in **his o** time *G2625*
2Ti 1: 9 because of **his o** purpose and grace. *G2625*
2Ti 4: 3 Instead, to suit **their o** desires, they will *G2625*
Titus 1:12 One of Crete's **o** prophets has said it *G2625*
Titus 2:14 himself a people that are **his very o**, *G4342*
Phm 19 am writing this with **my o** hand. I will pay *G1847*
Heb 5: 3 why he has to offer sacrifices for **his o** sins, *G899*
Heb 7:27 after day, first for **his o** sins, and then for *G2625*
Heb 9:12 Holy Place once for all by **his o** blood, *G2625*
Heb 9:25 every year with blood that is **not his o**. *G259*
Heb 11:14 they are looking for a **country of their o**. *G4258*
Heb 13:12 the people holy through **his o** blood. *G2625*
Jas 1:14 dragged away by **their o** evil desire and *G2625*
1Pe 3: 1 yourselves to **your o** husbands so that, *G2625*
1Pe 3: 5 themselves to **their o** husbands, *G2625*
2Pe 1: 3 who called us by **his o** glory and *G2625*
2Pe 1:20 about by the prophet's **o** interpretation of *G2625*
2Pe 3: 3 scoffing and following their **o** evil desires. *G2625*
2Pe 3:16 the other Scriptures, to their **o** destruction. *G2625*
1Jn 3:12 Because **his o** actions were evil and his *G899*
Jude 8 ungodly people pollute their **o** bodies, NDT
Jude 16 they follow **their o** evil desires; they boast *G1571*
Jude 16 flatter others for their **o** advantage. NDT
Jude 18 who will follow **their o** ungodly desires." *G1571*
Rev 18: 6 Pour her a double portion from **her** *o* cup. AIT

OWNED (12) [OWN]

Ge 25: 5 Abraham left everything he **o** to Isaac. H4200
Ge 31: 1 everything our father **o** and has gained all H4200
Ge 39: 4 to his care everything he **o**. H4200+3780
Ge 39: 5 his household and of all that he **o**, H4200+3780
Nu 16:33 with everything they **o**; the earth closed H4200
Jdg 19:22 shouted to the old man who **o** the house, H1251
1Ki 17:17 of the woman who **o** the house became H1266
Job 1: 3 he **o** seven thousand sheep H2118+5238
Ecc 2: 7 I also **o** more herds and flocks than H2118+5238
Jer 39:10 poor people, who **o** nothing; and at that H4200
Ac 4:34 to time those *who* **o** land or houses *G3230+5639*
Ac 4:37 sold a field he **o** and brought the money *G5639*

OWNER (39) [OWN]

Ex 21:26 "An **o** who hits a male or female slave in H408S
Ex 21:27 And an **o** who knocks out the tooth of a male NDT
Ex 21:28 But the **o** *of* the bull will not be held H1251
Ex 21:29 of goring and the **o** has been warned H1251
Ex 21:29 to be stoned and its **o** also is to be put to H1251
Ex 21:30 the **o** may redeem his life by the payment of NDT
Ex 21:32 the **o** must pay thirty shekels of silver to the NDT
Ex 21:34 the pit must pay the **o** for the loss and H1251
Ex 21:36 the **o** did not keep it penned up H1251
Ex 21:36 it penned up, the **o** must pay, animal for NDT
Ex 22: 8 the **o** *of* the house must appear before H1251
Ex 22: 8 whether the **o** of the house has laid NDT
Ex 22:11 The **o** is to accept this, and no restitution H1251
Ex 22:12 restitution must be made to the **o**. H1251
Ex 22:14 injured or dies while the **o** is not present, H1251
Ex 22:15 But if the **o** is with the animal, the H1251
Lev 6: 5 give it all to the **o** on the day they H4200+2257
Lev 14:35 the **o** *of* the house must go and tell H4200+2257
Lev 27:13 If the **o** wishes to redeem the animal, a fifth NDT
Lev 27:23 the **o** must pay its value on that day as NDT
Dt 22: 1 it but be sure to take it back to **its o**. H278S
Dt 22: 4 Help **the o** get it to its feet. H2257S
Jdg 19:23 The **o** *of* the house went outside and said H1251
1Ki 16:24 the name of the former **o** *of* the hill. H123
Mt 13:52 is like the **o of a house** who brings *G476+3867*
Mt 20: 8 the **o** of the vineyard said to his foreman *G3261*
Mt 21:40 when the **o** of the vineyard comes *G3261*
Mt 24:43 If the **o of the house** had known at what *G3867*
Mk 12: 9 "What then will the **o** of the vineyard do *G3261*
Mk 13:35 do not know when the **o** of the house will *G3261*
Mk 14:14 Say *to* the **o of the house** he enters, 'The *G3867*
Lk 12:39 If the **o of the house** had known at what *G3867*
Lk 13:25 Once the **o of the house** gets up and *G3867*
Lk 14:21 Then the **o of the house** became angry *G3867*
Lk 20:13 "Then the **o** of the vineyard said, 'What *G3261*
Lk 20:15 "What then will the **o** of the vineyard do *G3261*
Lk 22:11 say *to* the **o** of the house, 'The *G3867*
Ac 21:11 will bind the **o of** this belt and will *G467+4005*
Ac 27:11 of the pilot and *of* the **o of the ship**. *G3729*

OWNER'S (2) [OWN]

Isa 1: 3 the donkey its **o** manger, but Israel H1251
Mt 13:27 "The **o** servants came to him and said *G3867*

OWNERS (8) [OWN]

Nu 5:10 Sacred things belong to *their* **o**, but what H2257
Job 3:19 and the slaves are freed from their **o**. H123
Ecc 5:11 are they to the **o** except to feast their H1251
Ecc 5:13 wealth hoarded to the harm of its **o**, H1251
Jer 8:10 to other men and their fields to **new o**. H3769
Lk 19:33 the colt, its **o** asked them, "Why are *G3261*
Ac 16:16 deal of money *for* her **o** by fortune-telling *G3261*
Ac 16:19 When her **o** realized that their hope of *G3261*

OWNERSHIP (1) [OWN]

2Co 1:22 **set** *his* **seal of o on** us, and put his Spirit in *G5381*

OWNING (1) [OWN]

Job 22: 8 a powerful man, **o** land—an honored H4200

OWNS (8) [OWN]

Ge 24:36 he has given him everything he **o**. H4200
Ge 32:17 who **o** all these animals in front of H4200
Ge 38:25 "I am pregnant by the man who **o** these," H4200
Ge 39: 8 everything he **o** he has entrusted to H4200+3780
Lev 27:28 that a person **o** and devotes to the H4200
Dt 22: 2 near you or if you do not know *who* **o** it, H2257S
Mt 18:12 If a man **o** a hundred sheep, and one of *G1181*
Gal 4: 1 *although he* **o** the whole estate. *G3261+1639*

OX (56) [OXEN]

Ex 20:17 female servant, his **o** or donkey, or H8802
Ex 21:33 to cover it and an **o** or a donkey falls into H8802
Ex 22: 1 "Whoever steals an **o** or a sheep and H8802
Ex 22: 1 of cattle for the **o** and four sheep for the H8802
Ex 22: 4 whether **o** or donkey or sheep H8802
Ex 22: 9 In all cases of illegal possession of an **o**, H8802
Ex 22:10 gives a donkey, an **o**, a sheep or any H8802
Ex 23: 4 your enemy's **o** or donkey wandering H8802
Ex 23:12 so that your **o** and your donkey may rest H8802
Lev 4:10 fat is removed from the **o** sacrificed as a H8802
Lev 9: 4 an **o** and a ram for a fellowship H8802
Lev 9:18 He slaughtered the **o** and the ram as the H8802
Lev 9:19 But the fat portions of the **o** and the ram H8802
Lev 17: 3 Any Israelite who sacrifices an **o**, a lamb H8802
Lev 22:23 a freewill offering an **o** or a sheep that is H8802
Lev 27:26 the LORD; whether an **o** or a sheep, it is H8802
Nu 7: 3 an **o** from each leader and a cart from H8802
Nu 22: 4 as an **o** licks up the grass of the field." H8802
Nu 23:22 they have the strength of a **wild o**. H8028
Nu 24: 8 they have the strength of a **wild o**. H8028
Dt 5:14 servant, nor your **o**, your donkey or any of H8802
Dt 5:21 female servant, his **o** or donkey, or H8802
Dt 14: 4 the **o**, the sheep, the goat, H8802
Dt 17: 1 LORD your God an **o** or a sheep that has H8802
Dt 22: 1 your fellow Israelite's **o** or sheep straying, H8802
Dt 22: 4 Israelite's donkey or **o** fallen on the road, H8802
Dt 22:10 not plow with an **o** and a donkey yoked H8802
Dt 25: 4 Do not muzzle an **o** while it is treading H8802
Dt 28:31 Your **o** will be slaughtered before your H8802
Dt 33:17 his horns are the horns of a **wild o**. H8028
1Sa 12: 3 Whose **o** have I taken? Whose H8802
1Sa 14:34 So everyone brought his **o** that night and H8802
2Sa 24:22 sledges and **o** yokes for the wood. H1330
Ne 5:18 Each day one **o**, six choice sheep and H8802
Job 6: 5 or an **o** bellow when it has fodder? H8802
Job 24: 3 donkey and take the widow's **o** in pledge. H8802
Job 39: 9 "Will the **wild o** consent to serve you H8028
Job 40:15 you and which feeds on grass like an **o**. H1330
Ps 29: 6 leap like a calf, Sirion like a young **wild o**. H8028
Ps 69:31 This will please the LORD more than an **o** H8802
Ps 92:10 have exalted my horn like that of a **wild o**; H8028
Pr 7:22 followed her like an **o** going to the H8802
Pr 14: 4 the strength of an **o** come abundant H8802
Isa 1: 3 The **o** knows its master, the donkey its H8802
Isa 11: 7 the lion will eat straw like the **o**. H1330
Isa 65:25 the lion will eat straw like the **o**, and H1330
Eze 1:10 on the left the face of an **o**; each also H8802
Da 4:25 eat grass like the **o** and be drenched A10756
Da 4:32 animals; you will eat grass like the **o**. A10756
Da 4:33 from people and ate grass like the **o**. A10756
Da 5:21 wild donkeys and ate grass like the **o**; A10756
Lk 13:15 Sabbath untie your **o** or donkey from the *G1091*
Lk 14: 5 you has a child or an **o** that falls into a *G1091*
1Co 9: 9 "Do not muzzle an **o** while it is treading *G1091*
1Ti 5:18 "Do not muzzle an **o** while it is treading *G1091*
Rev 4: 7 the second was like an **o**, the third had a *G3675*

OXEN (43) [OX]

Ge 49: 6 anger and hamstrung **o** as they pleased. H8802
Nu 7: 3 the LORD six covered carts and twelve **o**— H1330
Nu 7: 6 took the carts and **o** and gave them to the H1330
Nu 7: 7 two carts and four **o** to the Gershonites, H1330
Nu 7: 8 four carts and eight **o** to the Merarites, H1330
Nu 7:17 two **o**, five rams, five male goats and H1330
Nu 7:23 two **o**, five rams, five male goats and H1330
Nu 7:29 two **o**, five rams, five male goats and H1330
Nu 7:35 two **o**, five rams, five male goats and H1330
Nu 7:41 two **o**, five rams, five male goats and H1330
Nu 7:47 two **o**, five rams, five male goats and H1330
Nu 7:53 two **o**, five rams, five male goats and H1330
Nu 7:59 two **o**, five rams, five male goats and H1330
Nu 7:65 two **o**, five rams, five male goats and H1330
Nu 7:71 two **o**, five rams, five male goats and H1330
Nu 7:77 two **o**, five rams, five male goats and H1330
Nu 7:83 two **o**, five rams, five male goats and H1330
Nu 7:88 fellowship offering came to twenty-four **o**, H7228
1Sa 11: 5 the fields, behind his **o**, and he asked, H1330
1Sa 11: 7 He took a pair of **o**, cut them into pieces H1330
1Sa 11: 7 will be done to the **o** *of* anyone who does H1330
2Sa 6: 6 the ark of God, because the **o** stumbled. H1330
2Sa 24:22 Here are **o** for the burnt offering, and here H1330
2Sa 24:24 floor and the **o** and paid fifty shekels H1330
1Ki 19:19 He was plowing with twelve **yoke of o** H7538
1Ki 19:20 Elisha then left his **o** and ran after Elijah H1330
1Ki 19:21 He took his yoke of **o** and slaughtered H1330
1Ch 12:40 food on donkeys, camels, mules and **o**. H1330
1Ch 13: 9 steady the ark, because the **o** stumbled. H1330
1Ch 21:23 I will give the **o** for the burnt offerings H1330
Job 1: 3 five hundred yoke of **o** and five hundred H1330
Job 1:14 "The **o** were plowing and the donkeys H1330
Job 42:12 a thousand yoke of **o** and a thousand H1330
Ps 22:21 save me from the horns of the **wild o**. H8028
Ps 144:14 our **o** will draw heavy loads. There will be H476

Pr 14: 4 Where there are no **o**, the manger is empty H546
Isa 30:24 The **o** and donkeys that work the soil will H546
Isa 34: 7 And the **wild o** will fall with them, the H8028
Jer 51:23 with you I shatter farmer and **o**, with you I H7538
Am 6:12 Does one plow the sea with **o**? But you H1330
Mt 22: 4 My **o** and fattened cattle have been *G5436*
Lk 14:19 'I have just bought five yoke *of* **o**, and I'm *G1091*
1Co 9: 9 Is it about **o** that God is concerned? *G1091*

OXGOAD (1)

Jdg 3:31 six hundred Philistines with an **o**. H4913+1330

OZEM (2)

1Ch 2:15 the sixth **O** and the seventh David. H730
1Ch 2:25 his firstborn, Bunah, Oren, **O** and Ahijah. H730

OZIAS (KJV) UZZIAH

OZNI (1) [OZNITE]

Nu 26:16 through **O**, the Oznite clan; through Eri, the H269

OZNITE (1) [OZNI]

Nu 26:16 through Ozni, the **O** clan; through Eri, the H270

P

PAARAI (1)

2Sa 23:35 Hezro the Carmelite, **P** the Arbite, H7197

PACE (2)

Ge 33:14 along slowly at the **p** *of* the flocks and H8079
Ge 33:14 before me and the **p** *of* the children, H8079

PACIFIES (1) [PEACE]

Pr 21:14 bribe concealed in the cloak **p** great wrath. NDT

PACIFY (1) [PEACE]

Ge 32:20 "*I will* **p** him with these gifts I am H4105+7156

PACK (3) [PACKED]

Ps 22:16 surround me, a **p** *of* villains encircles me H6337
Jer 46:19 **P** your belongings for exile, you who live H6913
Eze 12: 3 **p** your belongings for exile and in the H6913

PACKED (3) [PACK]

Jos 9:12 ours was warm *when we* **p** it at home on H7472
Eze 12: 4 bring out your belongings **p** *for* exile. H3998
Eze 12: 7 day I brought out my things **p** *for* exile. H3998

PACT (1)

Isa 57: 8 *you* **made a p** with those whose beds you H4162

PAD (1)

Jer 38:12 under your arms to **p** the ropes." H4946+9393

PADDAN (1) [PADDAN ARAM]

Ge 48: 7 As I was returning from **P**, to my sorrow H7019

PADDAN ARAM (10) [ARAM, PADDAN]

Ge 25:20 the Aramean from **P** and sister of H7020
Ge 28: 2 Go at once to **P**, to the house of your H7020
Ge 28: 5 he went to **P**, to Laban son of H7020
Ge 28: 6 had sent him to **P** to take a wife H7020
Ge 28: 7 mother and had gone to **P**. H7020
Ge 31:18 goods he had accumulated in **P**, H7020
Ge 33:18 After Jacob came from **P**, he arrived H7020
Ge 35: 9 After Jacob returned from **P**, God H7020
Ge 35:26 who were born to him in **P**. H7020
Ge 46:15 the sons Leah bore to Jacob in **P**, H7020

PADON (2)

Ezr 2:44 Keros, Siaha, **P**, H7013
Ne 7:47 Keros, Sia, **P**, H7013

PAGAN (6) [PAGANS]

Isa 2: 6 Philistines and embrace **p** customs. H3529+5799
Isa 57: 8 doorposts you have put your **p symbols**. H2355
La 1:10 she saw **p nations** enter her sanctuary H1580
Am 7:17 you yourself will die in a **p** country. H3238
Mt 18:17 them as you would a **p** or a tax collector. *G1618*
Lk 12:30 For the **p** world runs after all such things *G1620*

PAGANS (10) [PAGAN]

Mt 5:47 more than others? Do not even **p** do that? *G1618*
Mt 6: 7 do not keep on babbling like **p**, for they *G1618*
Mt 6:32 For the **p** run after all these things, and *G1620*
1Co 5: 1 of a kind that even **p** do not tolerate: *G1620*
1Co 10:20 the sacrifices of **p** are offered to demons, NDT
1Co 12: 2 You know that when you were **p**, somehow *G1620*
1Th 4: 5 not in passionate lust like the **p**, who do *G1620*
1Pe 2:12 Live such good lives among the **p** that *G1620*
1Pe 4: 3 in the past doing what **p** choose to do— *G1620*
3Jn 7 went out, receiving no help from the **p**. *G1618*

PAGIEL (5)

Nu 1:13 from Asher, **P** son of Okran; H7005
Nu 2:27 of the people of Asher is **P** son of Okran. H7005
Nu 7:72 On the eleventh day **P** son of Okran, the H7005
Nu 7:77 This was the offering of **P** son of Okran. H7005
Nu 10:26 **P** son of Okran was over the division of the H7005

PAHATH-MOAB (6)

Ezr 2: 6 of **P** (through the line of Jeshua and Joab H7075
Ezr 8: 4 of the descendants of **P**, Eliehoenai son H7075
Ezr 10:30 From the descendants of **P**: Adna, Kelal H7075
Ne 3:11 Hasshub son of **P** repaired another H7075
Ne 7:11 of **P** (through the line of Jeshua and Joab H7075
Ne 10:14 Parosh, **P**, Elam, Zattu, Bani, H7075

PAID (50) [PAY]

Ge 30:33 you check on the **wages** you *have p* me. AIT
Ge 31:15 but he has used up **what** was **p** *for* us. H4084
Ge 39:23 The warden **p** no **attention** *to* anything H8011
Ex 16:20 some of them **p** no **attention** to Moses H9048
Ex 22:15 the **money p for** *the* **hire** covers the loss. H8510
Lev 25:50 to be **based on the rate p** *to a* H3869+3427
Lev 25:51 a larger share of the price **p** *for* them. H5239
Dt 1:45 he **p** no **attention** to your weeping H9048
Jdg 1: 7 Now God *has* **p** me **back** *for* what I did to H8966
Jdg 11:28 **p** no **attention** to the message Jephthah H9048
1Sa 25:21 *He has* **p** me **back** evil for good H8740
2Sa 24:24 floor and the oxen and **p** fifty shekels of H928
1Ki 18:29 no one answered, no one **p attention**. H7993
2Ki 12:11 *With* it *they* **p** those who worked on the H3655
2Ki 12:14 it *was* **p** to the workers, who used it to H5989
2Ki 17: 3 vassal and *had* **p** him tribute. H8740
2Ki 17: 4 and *he* no *longer* **p** tribute to the king of H6590
2Ki 22: 9 "Your officials *have* **p out** the money that H5988
2Ki 23:35 Jehoiakim **p** Pharaoh Necho the silver H5989
1Ch 21:25 So David **p** Araunah six hundred H5989+5486
2Ch 24:17 of Judah came and **p homage** to the king, H2556
2Ch 25: 9 the hundred talents *I* **p** for these Israelite H5989
2Ch 27: 5 year the Ammonites **p** him a hundred H5989
2Ch 33:10 his people, but *they* **p** no **attention**. H7992
2Ch 34:10 These men **p** the workers who repaired H5989
2Ch 34:17 *They have* **p out** the money that was in the H5988
Ezr 4:13 tribute or duty *will be* **p**, and eventually A10498
Ezr 4:20 tribute and duty **were p** to them. A10314
Ezr 6: 4 The costs *are to* **be p** by the royal A10314
Ezr 6: 8 are to be fully **p** out of the royal A10314
Ne 9:30 Yet *they* **p** no **attention**, so you gave them H263
Est 3: 2 gate knelt down and **p honor** to Haman, H2556
Job 7: 2 a hired laborer waiting to be **p**, H7189
Job 21:29 *Have you* **p** no **regard** *to* their accounts H5795
Isa 3:11 They *will* **be p back** *for* what their hands H6913
Isa 40: 2 that her sin *has* **been p for**, that she has H8355
Isa 48:18 If only *you had* **p attention** to my H7992
Jer 25: 4 **p any attention.** H5742+265+4200+9048
Jer 35:15 But *you have* not **p attention** or H5742+265
Jer 37: 2 of the land **p** *any* **attention** to the words H9048
Eze 27:15 *they* **p** you *with* ivory tusks and H8740+868
Da 2:46 Daniel and **p** him **honor** and ordered A10504
Zec 11:12 So *they* **p** me thirty pieces of silver. H9202+8510
Mt 5:26 not get out until *you have* **p** the last penny. *G625*
Mt 22: 5 "But they **p no attention** and went off—one *G288*
Mk 15:19 on their knees, *they* **p homage** to him. *G4686*
Lk 12:59 not get out until *you have* **p** the last penny." *G625*
Ac 8: 6 they all **p close attention** to what he said. *G4668*
Heb 7: 9 the tenth, **p the tenth** through Abraham, *G1282*
2Pe 2:13 They will be **p back** with harm for the *G3635*

PAIN (39) [PAINFUL, PAINS]

Ge 34:25 while all of them were *still* **in p**, two of H3872
1Ch 4: 9 saying, "I gave birth to him in **p**. H6778
1Ch 4:10 from harm so that I *will be* free from **p**." H6772
2Ch 21:19 of the disease, and he died in great **p**. H9377
Job 6:10 my joy in unrelenting **p**—that I had not H2660
Job 14:22 *They* **feel** but *the* **p** of their own bodies H3872
Job 16: 6 "Yet if I speak, my **p** is not relieved; and if H3873
Job 33:19 chastened on a bed of **p** with constant H4799
Ps 38: 7 My back is filled with **searing p**; there is H7828
Ps 38:17 about to fall, and my **p** is ever with me. H4799
Ps 48: 6 **p** like that of a woman in labor. H2659
Ps 69:26 talk about the **p** *of* those you hurt. H4799
Ps 69:29 afflicted and **in p**—may your H3872
Ecc 2:23 All their days their work is grief and **p** H4799
Isa 13: 8 seize them, **p** and anguish will grip them H7496
Isa 17:11 in the day of disease and incurable **p**. H3873
Isa 21: 3 At this my body is racked with **p**, pangs H2714
Isa 26:17 to give birth writhes and cries out in her **p**, H2477
Isa 53: 3 a man of suffering, and familiar with **p**. H2716
Isa 53: 4 Surely he took up our **p** and bore our H2716
Jer 4:19 *I* **writhe in p**. Oh, the agony H2655
Jer 5: 3 but *they* **felt** no **p**; you crushed H2655
Jer 6:24 **p** like that of a woman in labor. H2659
Jer 13:21 Will not **p** grip you like that of a woman H2477
Jer 15:18 Why is my **p** unending and my wound H3873
Jer 22:23 upon you, **p** like that of a woman in labor! H2659
Jer 30:15 over your wound, your **p** that has no cure? H4799
Jer 45: 3 The LORD has added sorrow to my **p**; I am H4799
Jer 49:24 anguish and **p** have seized her, pain H2477
Jer 49:24 seized her, **p** like that of a woman in labor. NDT
Jer 50:43 **p** like that of a woman in labor. H2659
Jer 51: 8 Get balm for her **p**; perhaps she can be H4799
Mic 1:12 Those who live in Maroth **writhe in p** H2655
Mic 4: 9 that **p** seizes you like that of a woman in H2659
Mt 4:24 those suffering **severe p**, the *G992*
Jn 16:21 to a child has **p** because her time has *G3383*
1Pe 2:19 if someone bears up *under* the **p** of unjust *G3383*
Rev 12: 2 and cried out *in* **p** as she was *G6048+2779+989*
Rev 21: 4 more death' or mourning or crying or **p**, *G4506*

PAINFUL (10) [PAIN]

Ge 3:16 with **p labor** you will give birth to children. H6776
Ge 3:17 through **p toil** you will eat food from it all H6779
Ge 5:29 the labor and **p toil** *of* our hands caused H6779
Dt 28:35 knees and legs with **p** boils that cannot H8273
Job 2: 7 afflicted Job with **p** sores from the soles H8273
Job 6:25 How **p** *are* honest words! But what do your H5344
Pr 10:22 LORD brings wealth, without **p toil** for it. H6776
Eze 28:24 neighbors *who are* **p** briers and sharp H4421
2Co 2: 1 not make another **p** visit to you. *G1877+3383*
Heb 12:11 seems pleasant at the time, but **p**. *G3383*

PAINS (15) [PAIN]

Ge 3:16 "I will make your **p** in childbearing very H6779
1Sa 4:19 but was overcome by her **labor p**. H7496
1Ch 22:14 "I have **taken great p** to provide for H928+6715
2Ch 6:29 being aware of their afflictions and **p**, and H4799
Job 30:17 my bones; my **gnawing p** never rest. H6908
Job 39: 3 forth their young; their **labor p** are ended. H2477
Isa 66: 7 before the **p** come upon her, she H2477
Hos 13:13 **P** *as of* a woman in childbirth come to H2477
Mt 24: 8 All these are the beginning *of* **birth p**. *G6047*
Mk 13: 8 These are the beginning *of* **birth p**. *G6047*
Ro 8:22 groaning *as* **in the p of childbirth** right up *G5349*
2Co 8:21 For we are **taking p** to do what is right, not *G4629*
Gal 4:19 whom *I am* again **in the p of childbirth** *G6048*
1Th 5: 3 as **labor p** on a pregnant woman *G6047*
Rev 16:11 heaven because of their **p** and their sores, *G4506*

PAINT, PAINTED (NIV84) MAKEUP

PAIR (18) [PAIRS]

Ge 7: 2 and **one p** of every kind of unclean H9109
Ex 25:35 be under the first **p** *of* branches extending H9109
Ex 25:35 a second bud under the second **p**, and a H9109
Ex 25:35 a third bud under the third **p**—six H9109
Ex 37:21 under the first **p** *of* branches extending H9109
Ex 37:21 a second bud under the second **p**, and a H9109
Ex 37:21 a third bud under the third **p**—six H9109
Dt 24: 6 Do not take a **p of millstones**—not even H8160
Jdg 15: 4 then fastened a torch to every **p** *of* tails, H9109
1Sa 11: 7 He took a **p** *of* oxen, cut them into pieces H7538
1Ki 6:23 sanctuary he made a **p** *of* cherubim out of H9109
1Ki 19:19 he himself was driving the twelfth **p**. NDT
2Ki 5:17 as much earth as a **p** *of* mules can carry, H7538
2Ch 3:10 Holy Place he made a **p** of sculptured H9109
Am 2: 6 silver, and the needy for a **p of sandals**. AIT
Am 8: 6 with silver and the needy for a *p of* **sandals**, AIT
Lk 2:24 "a **p** of doves or two young pigeons." *G2414*
Rev 6: 5 was holding a **p of scales** in his hand. *G2433*

PAIRS (5) [PAIR]

Ge 7: 2 Take with you **seven p** of every kind H8679+8679
Ge 7: 3 also **seven p** of every kind of H8679+8679
Ge 7: 8 **P** of clean and unclean animals, of H9109+9109
Ge 7:15 **P** of all creatures that have the H9109+9109
Jdg 15: 4 hundred foxes and tied them tail to tail in **p**. NDT

PALACE (166) [PALACES, PALATIAL]

Ge 12:15 to Pharaoh, and she was taken into his **p**. H1074
Ge 41:40 You shall be in charge of my **p**, and all my H1074
Ge 45:16 reached Pharaoh's **p** that Joseph's H1074
Ge 47:14 and he brought it to Pharaoh's **p**. H1074
Ex 7:23 he turned and went into his **p**, and did H1074
Ex 8: 3 come up into your **p** and your bedroom H1074
Ex 8:24 into Pharaoh's **p** and into the houses H1074
Nu 22:18 gave me all the silver and gold in his **p**, H1074
Nu 24:13 gave me all the silver and gold in his **p**, H1074
Jdg 3:20 in the upper room of his **p** and said, H5249
Jdg 3:24 himself in the inner room of the **p**. H5249
2Sa 5: 8 "The 'blind and lame' will not enter the **p**." H1074
2Sa 5:11 they built a **p** for David. H1074
2Sa 7: 1 was settled in his **p** and the LORD had H1074
2Sa 11: 2 walked around on the roof of the **p**. H1074+4889
2Sa 11: 8 So Uriah left the **p**, and a gift from H1074+4889
2Sa 11: 9 the entrance to the **p** with all his H1074+4889
2Sa 13: 7 David sent word to Tamar at the **p**: "Go to H1074
2Sa 15:16 left ten concubines to take care of the **p**. H1074
2Sa 15:35 them anything you hear in the king's **p**. H1074
2Sa 16:21 whom he left to take care of the **p**. H1074
2Sa 19:11 be the last to bring the king back to his **p**, H1074
2Sa 20: 3 David returned to his **p** in Jerusalem, H1074
2Sa 20: 3 to take care of the **p** and put them in a H1074
1Ki 3: 1 building his **p** and the temple of the H1074
1Ki 4: 6 Ahishar—**p** administrator; Adoniram son H1074
1Ki 7: 1 to complete the construction of his **p**. H1074
1Ki 7: 2 He built the **P** *of* the Forest of Lebanon a H1074
1Ki 7: 8 And the **p** in which he was to live, set H1074
1Ki 7: 8 Solomon also made a **p** like this hall for H1074
1Ki 9: 1 the temple of the LORD and the royal **p**, H1074
1Ki 9:10 the temple of the LORD and the royal **p**— H1074
1Ki 9:15 the LORD's temple, his own **p**, the terraces, H1074
1Ki 9:24 City of David to the **p** Solomon had built H1074
1Ki 10: 4 of Solomon and the **p** he had built, H1074
1Ki 10:12 the temple of the LORD and for the royal **p**, H1074
1Ki 10:17 king put them in the **P** *of* the Forest of H1074
1Ki 10:21 articles in the **P** *of* the Forest of Lebanon H1074
1Ki 11:20 Tahpenes brought up in the royal **p**. H1074
1Ki 14:26 the LORD and the treasures of the royal **p**. H1074
1Ki 14:27 on duty at the entrance to the royal **p**. H1074
1Ki 15:18 of the LORD's temple and of his own **p**. H1074
1Ki 16: 9 of Arza, the **p** administrator at Tirzah. H1074

1Ki 16:18 citadel of the royal **p** and set the palace H1074
1Ki 16:18 palace and set the **p** on fire around him. H1074
1Ki 18: 3 summoned Obadiah, his **p** administrator. H1074
1Ki 20: 6 to search your **p** and the houses of your H1074
1Ki 20:43 the king of Israel went to his **p** in Samaria. H1074
1Ki 21: 1 close to the **p** *of* Ahab king of Samaria. H2121
1Ki 21: 2 garden, since it is close to my **p**. H1074
1Ki 22:39 the **p** he built and adorned with ivory H1074
2Ki 7: 9 go at once and report this to the royal **p**." H1074
2Ki 7:11 and it was reported within the **p**. H1074+4889
2Ki 10: 5 So the **p** administrator, the city governor H1074
2Ki 11: 5 a third of you guarding the royal **p**, H1074
2Ki 11:16 the horses enter the **p grounds**, H1074+4889
2Ki 11:19 of the LORD and went into the **p**, H1074+4889
2Ki 11:20 been slain with the sword at the **p**. H1074+4889
2Ki 12:18 the temple of the LORD and of the royal **p**, H1074
2Ki 14:14 LORD and in the treasuries of the royal **p**. H1074
2Ki 15: 5 son had charge of the **p** and governed the H1074
2Ki 15:25 in the citadel of the royal **p** at Samaria. H1074
2Ki 16: 8 of the royal **p** and sent it as a gift H1074
2Ki 18:15 LORD and in the treasuries of the royal **p**. H1074
2Ki 18:18 Eliakim son of Hilkiah the **p** administrator, H1074
2Ki 18:37 Eliakim son of Hilkiah the **p** administrator, H1074
2Ki 19: 2 He sent Eliakim the **p** administrator H1074
2Ki 20:13 was nothing in his **p** or in all his kingdom H1074
2Ki 20:15 "What did they see in your **p**? H1074
2Ki 20:15 "They saw everything in my **p**," Hezekiah H1074
2Ki 20:17 surely come when everything in your **p**, H1074
2Ki 20:18 eunuchs in the **p** *of* the king of Babylon." H2121
2Ki 21:18 ancestors and was buried in his **p** garden, H1074
2Ki 21:23 him and assassinated the king in his **p**. H1074
2Ki 24:13 temple of the LORD and from the royal **p**, H1074
2Ki 25: 9 the royal **p** and all the houses of H1074
1Ch 14: 1 carpenters to build a **p** for him. H1074
1Ch 17: 1 After David was settled in his **p**, he said H1074
1Ch 28: 1 together with the **p officials**, the warriors H6247
2Ch 2: 1 of the LORD and a royal **p** for himself. H1074
2Ch 2: 3 you sent him cedar to build a **p** to live in. H1074
2Ch 2:12 the LORD and a **p** for himself. H1074+4895
2Ch 7:11 the temple of the LORD and the royal **p**, H1074
2Ch 7:11 the temple of the LORD and in his own **p**, H1074
2Ch 8: 1 the temple of the LORD and his own **p**, H1074
2Ch 8:11 City of David to the **p** he had built for her, H1074
2Ch 8:11 must not live in the **p** *of* David king of H1074
2Ch 9: 3 Solomon, as well as the **p** he had built, H1074
2Ch 9:11 the temple of the LORD and for the royal **p**, H1074
2Ch 9:16 king put them in the **P** *of* the Forest of H1074
2Ch 9:20 articles in the **P** *of* the Forest of Lebanon H1074
2Ch 12: 9 the LORD and the treasures of the royal **p**. H1074
2Ch 12:10 on duty at the entrance to the royal **p**. H1074
2Ch 16: 2 temple and of his own **p** and sent it to H1074
2Ch 19: 1 returned safely to his **p** in Jerusalem, H1074
2Ch 21:17 off all the goods found in the king's **p**, H1074
2Ch 23: 5 of you at the royal **p** and a third at the H1074
2Ch 23:15 the Horse Gate on the **p grounds**, H1074+4889
2Ch 23:20 went into the **p** through the Upper H1074+4889
2Ch 25:24 with the **p** treasures and the H1074+4889
2Ch 26:21 charge of the **p** and governed the H1074+4889
2Ch 28: 7 Azrikam the officer in charge of the **p**, and H1074
2Ch 28:21 from the royal **p** and from the officials H1074
2Ch 33:20 his ancestors and was buried in his **p**. H1074
2Ch 33:24 him and assassinated him in his **p**. H1074
Ezr 4:14 obligation to the **p** and it is not proper A10206
Ne 3:25 from the upper **p** near the court of H1074+4889
Ne 12:37 above the **site of** David's **p** to the Water H1074
Est 1: 5 in the enclosed garden of the king's **p**, for H1131
Est 1: 9 the women in the royal **p** of King Xerxes. H1074
Est 2: 8 taken to the king's **p** and entrusted to H1074
Est 2: 9 from the king's **p** and moved her and her H1074
Est 2:13 with her from the harem to the king's **p**. H1074
Est 5: 1 stood in the inner court of the **p**, H1074+4889
Est 6: 4 outer court of the **p** to speak to the H1074+4889
Est 7: 7 his wine and went out into the **p** garden. H1131
Est 7: 8 returned from the **p** garden to the H1131
Est 9: 4 Mordecai was prominent in the **p** H1074+4889
Ps 45:15 gladness, they enter the **p** *of* the king. H2121
Ps 144:12 will be like pillars carved to adorn a **p**. H2121
Isa 22: 8 day to the weapons in the **P** *of* the Forest. H1074
Isa 22:15 steward, to Shebna the **p** administrator: H1074
Isa 36: 3 Eliakim son of Hilkiah the **p** administrator H1074
Isa 36:22 Eliakim son of Hilkiah the **p** administrator, H1074
Isa 37: 2 He sent Eliakim the **p** administrator H1074
Isa 39: 2 was nothing in his **p** or in all his kingdom H1074
Isa 39: 4 "What did they see in your **p**? H1074
Isa 39: 4 "They saw everything in my **p**," Hezekiah H1074
Isa 39: 6 surely come when everything in your **p**, H1074
Isa 39: 7 eunuchs in the **p** *of* the king of Babylon." H2121
Jer 22: 1 "Go down to the **p** *of* the king of Judah H1074
Jer 22: 4 will come through the gates of this **p**, H1074
Jer 22: 5 by myself that this **p** will become a ruin. H1074
Jer 22: 6 says about the **p** *of* the king of Judah: H1074
Jer 22:13 him who builds his **p** by unrighteousness, H1074
Jer 22:14 myself a great **p** with spacious upper H1074
Jer 26:10 up from the royal **p** to the house of the H1074
Jer 27:18 the LORD and in the **p** *of* the king of Judah H1074
Jer 27:21 the LORD and in the **p** *of* the king of Judah H1074
Jer 30:18 the **p** will stand in its proper place. H810
Jer 32: 2 of the guard in the royal **p** *of* Judah. H1074
Jer 36:12 to the secretary's room in the royal **p**, H1074
Jer 37:17 him and had him brought to the **p**, H1074
Jer 38: 7 an official in the royal **p**, heard that they H1074
Jer 38: 8 went out of the **p** and said to him, H1074+4889
Jer 38:11 a room under the treasury in the **p**. H1074+4889
Jer 38:22 women left in the **p** *of* the king of Judah H1074
Jer 39: 8 fire to the royal **p** and the houses of the H1074
Jer 43: 9 entrance to Pharaoh's **p** in Tahpanhes. H1074
Jer 52:13 the royal **p** and all the houses of H1074
Da 1: 4 qualified to serve in the king's **p**. H2121
Da 4: 4 was at home in my **p**, contented and A10206
Da 4:29 on the roof of the royal **p** of Babylon, A10206
Da 5: 5 near the lampstand in the royal **p**. A10206
Da 6:18 returned to his **p** and spent the night A10206
Am 9: 6 he builds his **lofty p** in the heavens and H5092
Na 2: 6 are thrown open and the **p** collapses. H1074
Mt 26: 3 assembled in the **p** of the high priest, *G885*
Mk 15:16 The soldiers led Jesus away into the **p** (that *G885*
Jn 18:28 Caiaphas to the **p of the Roman governor**. *G4550*
Jn 18:28 uncleanness they did not enter the **p**, *G4550*
Jn 18:33 Pilate then went back inside the **p** *G4550*
Jn 19: 9 he went back inside the **p**. "Where do *G4550*
Ac 7:10 made him ruler over Egypt and all his **p**. *G3875*
Ac 23:35 Paul be kept under guard in Herod's **p**. *G4550*
Php 1:13 the whole **p guard** and to everyone *G4550*

PALACES (10) [PALACE]

2Ch 36:19 they burned all the **p** and destroyed H810
Ps 45: 8 from **p** *adorned with* ivory the music of the H2121
Pr 30:28 with the hand, yet it is found in kings' **p**. H2121
Isa 13:22 her strongholds, jackals her luxurious **p**. H2121
Jer 33: 4 city and the royal **p** *of* Judah that have H1074
La 2: 5 swallowed up all her **p** and destroyed her H810
La 2: 7 the walls of her **p** into the hands of the H810
Hos 8:14 has forgotten their Maker and built **p**; H2121
Mt 11: 8 who wear fine clothes are in kings' **p**. *G3875*
Lk 7:25 clothes and indulge in luxury are in **p**. *G994*

PALAL (1)

Ne 3:25 **P** son of Uzai worked opposite the H7138

PALATIAL (2) [PALACE]

1Ch 29: 1 because this **p structure** is not for man H1072
1Ch 29:19 to build the **p structure** for which I have H1072

PALE (10)

Isa 29:22 no longer *will* their faces **grow p**. H2578
Jer 30: 6 in labor, every face turned **deathly p**? H3766
Da 5: 6 His **face** turned **p** and he was so A10228
Da 5: 9 more terrified and his **face** grew more **p**. A10228
Da 5:10 be alarmed! Don't **look so p**! A10731+10228
Da 7:28 my **face** turned **p**, but I kept the A10228
Da 10: 8 my face turned **deathly p** and I was H5422
Joel 2: 6 are in anguish; every face **turns p**. H6999+7695
Na 2:10 bodies tremble, every face **grows p**. H6999+7695
Rev 6: 8 there before me was a **p** horse! *G5952*

PALESTINA, PALESTINE (KJV) PHILISTIA, PHILISTINES

PALLU (5) [PALLUITE]

Ge 46: 9 Hanok, **P**, Hezron and Karmi. H7112
Ex 6:14 firstborn son of Israel were Hanok and **P**, H7112
Nu 26: 5 through **P**, the Palluite clan; H7112
Nu 26: 8 The son of **P** was Eliab, H7112
1Ch 5: 3 Hanok, **P**, Hezron and Karmi. H7112

PALLUITE (1) [PALLU]

Nu 26: 5 Hanokite clan; through Pallu, the **P** clan; H7101

PALM (38) [PALMS]

Ex 15:27 were twelve springs and seventy **p trees**, H9469
Lev 14:15 pour it in the **p** of his own left **hand**, H4090
Lev 14:16 dip his right forefinger into the oil in his **p** H4090
Lev 14:17 oil remaining in his **p** on the lobe of the H4090
Lev 14:18 rest of the oil in his **p** the priest shall put H4090
Lev 14:26 of the oil into the **p of** his own left **hand**, H4090
Lev 14:27 of the oil from his **p** seven times before H4090
Lev 14:28 Some of the oil in his **p** he is to put on the H4090
Lev 14:29 rest of the oil in his **p** the priest shall put H4090
Nu 33: 9 were twelve springs and seventy **p trees**, H9469
Jdg 4: 5 court under the **P** *of* Deborah between H9472
1Ki 6:29 cherubim, **p trees** and open flowers. H9474
1Ki 6:32 cherubim, **p trees** and open flowers H9474
1Ki 6:32 the cherubim and **p trees** with hammered H9474
1Ki 6:35 **p trees** and open flowers on them and H9474
1Ki 7:36 lions and **p trees** on the surfaces of the H9474
2Ch 3: 5 it with **p tree** and chain **designs**. H9474
Ps 92:12 The righteous will flourish like a **p tree** H9469
SS 7: 7 Your stature is like that of the **p**, and your H9469
SS 7: 8 "I will climb the **p tree**; I will take hold of H9469
Isa 9:14 both **p branch** and reed in a single day; H4093
Isa 19:15 can do—head or tail, **p branch** or reed. H4093
Eze 40:16 walls were decorated with **p trees**. H9474
Eze 40:22 its **p tree decorations** had the same H9474
Eze 40:26 it had **p tree decorations** on the faces of H9474
Eze 40:31 outer court; **p trees** decorated its jambs H9474
Eze 40:34 **p trees** decorated the jambs on either H9474
Eze 40:37 **p trees** decorated the jambs on either H9474
Eze 41:18 were carved cherubim and **p trees**. H9474
Eze 41:18 **P trees** alternated with cherubim H9474
Eze 41:19 being toward the **p tree** on one side and H9474
Eze 41:19 of a lion toward the **p tree** on the other. H9474
Eze 41:20 cherubim and **p trees** were carved on the H9474
Eze 41:25 cherubim and **p trees** like those carved H9474
Eze 41:26 windows with **p trees** carved on each H9474
Joel 1:12 pomegranate, the **p** and the apple tree H9469
Jn 12:13 They took **p** branches and went out to *G5836*
Rev 7: 9 were holding **p branches** in their hands. *G5836*

PALMERWORM (KJV) LOCUST SWARM, LOCUSTS

PALMS (7) [PALM]

Lev 23:40 luxuriant trees—from **p**, willows and other H9469
Dt 34: 3 of Jericho, the City of **P**, as far as Zoar. H9469
Jdg 1:16 up from the City of **P** with the people of H9469
Jdg 3:13 they took possession of the City of **P**. H9469
2Ch 28:15 at Jericho, the City of **P**, and returned to H9469
Ne 8:15 from myrtles, **p** and shade trees, to H9469
Isa 49:16 have engraved you on the **p of** my **hands**; H4090

PALSIES, PALSY (KJV) PARALYZED

PALTI (1)

Nu 13: 9 the tribe of Benjamin, **P** son of Raphu; H7120

PALTIEL (3)

Nu 34:26 **P** son of Azzan, the leader from the tribe H7123
1Sa 25:44 David's wife, to **P** son of Laish, who was H7120
2Sa 3:15 away from her husband **P** son of Laish. H7123

PALTITE (1)

2Sa 23:26 Helez the **P**, Ira son of Ikkesh from Tekoa, H7121

PAMPERED (1)

Pr 29:21 A servant **p** from youth will turn out to be H7167

PAMPHYLIA (5)

Ac 2:10 Phrygia and **P**, Egypt and the parts of Libya *G4103*
Ac 13:13 his companions sailed to Perga *in* **P**, *G4103*
Ac 14:24 going through Pisidia, they came into **P**, *G4103*
Ac 15:38 had deserted them in **P** and had not *G4103*
Ac 27: 5 open sea off the coast of Cilicia and **P**, *G4103*

PAN (6) [PANS]

Lev 2: 7 If your grain offering is cooked in a **p**, it is H5306
Lev 7: 9 an oven or cooked in a **p** or on a griddle H5306
1Sa 2:14 the fork into the **p** or kettle or caldron or H3963
2Sa 13: 9 Then she took the **p** and served him the H5389
Eze 4: 3 Then take an iron **p**, place it as an iron H4679
Mic 3: 3 who chop them up like meat for the **p** H6105

PANELED (2) [PANELING, PANELS]

2Ch 3: 5 *He* **p** the main hall *with* juniper and H2902
Hag 1: 4 yourselves to be living in your **p** houses, H6211

PANELING (2) [PANELED]

1Ki 6:15 **p** them from the floor of the temple H7596+6770
Ps 74: 6 smashed all the **carved p** with their axes H7334

PANELS (9) [PANELED]

1Ki 7:28 They had **side p** attached to uprights H4995
1Ki 7:29 On the **p** between the uprights were lions H4995
1Ki 7:31 The **p** *of* the stands were square, not H4995
1Ki 7:32 The four wheels were under the **p**, and the H4995
1Ki 7:35 The supports and **p** were attached to the H4995
1Ki 7:36 the surfaces of the supports and on the **p**, H4995
2Ki 16:17 Ahaz cut off the **side p** and removed the H4995
SS 8: 9 we will enclose her with **p** *of* cedar. H4283
Jer 22:14 **p** it with cedar and decorates it in red. H6211

PANGS (2)

Isa 21: 3 is racked with pain, **p** seize me, like those H7496
Jer 22:23 you will groan when **p** come upon you, H2477

PANIC (12)

Dt 20: 3 afraid; do not **p** or be terrified by them. H2905
1Sa 5: 9 that city, throwing it into a great **p**. H4539
1Sa 5:11 For death had filled the city with **p**; God's H4539
1Sa 7:10 and **threw** them **into** *such* **a p** that they H2169
1Sa 14:15 Then **p** struck the whole army—those in H3010
1Sa 14:15 the ground shook. It was a **p** *sent by* God. H3010
Isa 28:16 relies on it *will* never *be* **stricken with p**. H2591
Isa 31: 9 battle standard their commanders *will* **p**," H3169
Jer 49:24 has turned to flee and **p** has gripped her; H8185
Eze 7: 7 There is **p**, not joy, on the H4539
Zec 12: 4 strike every horse with **p** and its rider with H9451
Zec 14:13 will be stricken by the LORD with great **p**. H4539

PANS (2) [PAN]

2Ch 35:13 caldrons and **p** and served them quickly to H7505
Ezr 1: 9 dishes 30 silver dishes 1,000 silver **p** 29 H4709

PANT (5) [PANTS]

Job 5: 5 and the thirsty **p** *after* his wealth. H8634
Ps 119:131 I open my mouth and **p**, longing for your H8634
Isa 42:14 in childbirth, I cry out, I gasp and **p**. H8634
Jer 14: 6 barren heights and **p** like jackals; H8634+8120
Joel 1:20 Even the wild animals **p** for you; the H6864

PANTED, PANTETH (KJV) FALTERS, PANT, PANTS, POUNDS, TRAMPLE

PANTS (2) [PANT]

Ps 42: 1 As the deer **p** for streams of water, so my H6864
Ps 42: 1 of water, so my soul **p** for you, my God. H6864

PAPER (1)

2Jn 12 but I do not want to use **p** and ink. *G5925*

PAPHOS (2)

Ac 13: 6 the whole island until they came to **P**. *G4265*

P

Ac 13:13 From P, Paul and his companions sailed G4265

PAPYRUS (5)
Ex 2: 3 she got a p basket for him and coated it H1687
Job 8:11 Can p grow tall where there is no marsh H1687
Job 9:26 They skim past like boats of p, like eagles H15
Isa 18: 2 envoys by sea in p boats over the water. H1687
Isa 35: 7 once lay, grass and reeds and p will grow. H1687

PARABLE (33) [PARABLES]
Ps 78: 2 I will open my mouth with a p; I will utter H5442
Eze 17: 2 allegory and tell it to the Israelites as a p. H5442
Eze 24: 3 rebellious people a p and say to them: H5442
Mt 13:18 then to what the p of the sower means: G4130
Mt 13:24 Jesus told them another p: "The kingdom G4130
Mt 13:31 He told them another p: "The kingdom of G4130
Mt 13:33 He told them still another p: "The G4130
Mt 13:34 say anything to them without using a p. G4130
Mt 13:36 "Explain to us the p of the weeds in the G4130
Mt 15:15 Peter said, "Explain the p to us. G4130
Mt 21:33 "Listen to another p: There was a G4130
Mk 4:13 to them, "Don't you understand this p? G4130
Mk 4:13 How then will you understand any p? G4130
Mk 4:30 or what p shall we use to describe it? G4130
Mk 4:34 say anything to them without using a p. G4130
Mk 7:17 his disciples asked him about this p. G4130
Mk 12:12 knew he had spoken the p against them. G4130
Lk 5:36 He told them this p: "No one tears a G4130
Lk 6:39 He also told them this p: "Can the blind G4130
Lk 8: 4 Jesus from town after town, he told this p: G4130
Lk 8: 9 disciples asked him what this p meant. G4130
Lk 8:11 "This is the meaning of the p: The seed is G4130
Lk 12:16 And he told them this p: "The ground of a G4130
Lk 12:41 are you telling this p to us, or to everyone G4130
Lk 13: 6 Then he told this p: "A man had a fig tree G4130
Lk 14: 7 of honor at the table, he told them this p: G4130
Lk 15: 3 Then Jesus told them this p: G4130
Lk 18: 1 told his disciples a p to show them that G4130
Lk 18: 9 down on everyone else, Jesus told this p: G4130
Lk 19:11 he went on to tell them a p, because he G4130
Lk 20: 9 He went on to tell the people this p: "A G4130
Lk 20:19 knew he had spoken this p against them. G4130
Lk 21:29 He told them this p: "Look at the fig tree G4130

PARABLES (18) [PARABLE]
Pr 1: 6 understanding proverbs and p, the H4886
Eze 20:49 are saying of me, 'Isn't he just telling p?' H5442
Hos 12:10 many visions and told p through them." H1948
Mt 13: 3 Then he told them many things in p G4130
Mt 13:10 "Why do you speak to the people in p?" G4130
Mt 13:13 This is why I speak to them in p: "Though G4130
Mt 13:34 spoke all these things to the crowd in p; G4130
Mt 13:35 "I will open my mouth in p, I will utter G4130
Mt 13:53 When Jesus had finished these p, he G4130
Mt 21:45 priests and the Pharisees heard Jesus' p, G4130
Mt 22: 1 Jesus spoke to them again in p, saying: G4130
Mk 3:23 to him and began to speak to them in p: G4130
Mk 4: 2 He taught them many things by p, and in G4130
Mk 4:10 others around him asked him *about* the p. G4130
Mk 4:11 on the outside everything is said in p G4130
Mk 4:33 *With* many similar p Jesus spoke the word G4130
Mk 12: 1 Jesus then began to speak to them in p G4130
Lk 8:10 but to others I speak in p, so that, G4130

PARADE (1)
Isa 3: 9 against them; *they* p their sin like Sodom H5583

PARADISE (3)
Lk 23:43 I tell you, today you will be with me in p." G4137
2Co 12: 4 was caught up to p and heard G4137
Rev 2: 7 the tree of life, which is in the p of God. G4137

PARAH (1)
Jos 18:23 Avvim, P, Ophrah, H7240

PARALLEL (5)
Ex 26:17 with two projections set p to each other H8917
Ex 36:22 with two projections set p to each other H8917
Eze 42: 7 an outer wall p to the rooms and H4200+6645
Eze 42:12 that was p *to* the corresponding H928+7156
Eze 45: 7 eastern border p to one of the H4200+6645

PARALYTIC (NIV84) PARALYZED (MAN)

PARALYZED (13)
Hab 1: 4 Therefore the law *is* p, and justice never H7028
Mt 4:24 seizures, and the p; and he healed them. G4166
Mt 8: 6 "my servant lies at home p, suffering G4166
Mt 9: 2 Some men brought to him a p *man*, lying G4166
Mt 9: 6 So he said *to* the p *man*, "Get up, take G4166
Mk 2: 3 bringing to him a p *man*, carried by four G4166
Mk 2: 5 their faith, he said *to* the p *man*, "Son, G4166
Mk 2: 9 to say *to* this p *man*, 'Your sins are G4166
Lk 5:18 men came carrying a p man on a mat G4168
Lk 5:24 So he said *to* the p *man*, "I tell you, get G4168
Jn 5: 3 used to lie—the blind, the lame, the p. G3831
Ac 8: 7 many *who were* p or lame were G4168
Ac 9:33 who was p and had been bedridden for G4168

PARAN (11)
Ge 21:21 While he was living in the Desert of P, his H7000
Nu 10:12 the cloud came to rest in the Desert of P. H7000
Nu 12:16 encamped in the Desert of P. H7000
Nu 13: 3 Moses sent them out from the Desert of P. H7000
Nu 13:26 community at Kadesh in the Desert of P. H7000
Dt 1: 1 between P and Tophel, Laban, H7000
Dt 33: 2 from Seir; he shone forth from Mount P. H7000
1Sa 25: 1 David moved down into the Desert of P. H7000
1Ki 11:18 They set out from Midian and went to P H7000
1Ki 11:18 Then taking people from P with them H7000
Hab 3: 3 from Teman, the Holy One from Mount P. H7000

PARAPET (3)
Dt 22: 8 make a p around your roof so that you H5111
Eze 40:13 cubits from *one* p opening to the opposite H7339
Eze 40:16 by narrow p openings all around, H2707

PARBAR (KJV) COURT

PARCEL (2) [PARCELED]
Ps 60: 6 "In triumph *I will* p out Shechem and H2745
Ps 108: 7 "In triumph *I will* p out Shechem and H2745

PARCELED (1) [PARCEL]
Da 11: 4 be broken up and p out toward the four H2936

PARCHED (19)
Job 14:11 dries up or a riverbed *becomes* p and dry, H2990
Job 30: 3 they roamed the p land in desolate H7480
Ps 63: 1 in a dry and p land where there is no H6546
Ps 69: 3 worn out calling for help; my throat *is* p. H3081
Ps 107:35 of water and the p ground into flowing H7480
Ps 143: 6 hands to you; I thirst for you like a p land. H6546
Isa 5:13 the common people will be p *with* thirst. H7457
Isa 19: 5 and the riverbed *will be* p and dry. H2990
Isa 19: 7 sown field along the Nile *will become* p, H3312
Isa 35: 1 The desert and the p land will be glad H7480
Isa 41:17 is none; their tongues *are* p with thirst. H5980
Isa 41:18 of water, and the p ground into springs. H7480
Jer 12: 4 How long *will* the land *lie* p and the grass in H62
Jer 12:11 a wasteland, p and desolate before me H62
Jer 17: 6 will dwell in the p places of the desert, H3083
Jer 23:10 the curse the land *lies* p and the pastures in H62
Jer 48:18 from your glory and sit on the p ground, H7533
Hos 2: 3 turn her into a p land, and slay her with H7480
Joel 2:20 pushing it into a p and barren land; its H7480

PARCHMENTS (1)
2Ti 4:13 at Troas, and my scrolls, especially the p. G3521

PARDON (15) [PARDONED, PARDONS]
Ge 43:20 "We beg your p, our lord," they said, "we H1065
Ge 44:18 "P your servant, my lord, let me speak a H1065
Ex 4:10 said to the LORD, "P your servant, Lord. H1065
Ex 4:13 But Moses said, "P your servant, Lord H1065
Jos 7: 8 P your servant, Lord. What can I say, now H1065
Jdg 6:13 "P me, my lord," Gideon replied, "but if H1065
Jdg 6:15 "P me, my lord," Gideon replied, "but H1065
Jdg 13: 8 "P your servant, Lord. I beg H1065
1Sa 1:26 she said to him, "P me, my lord. As surely H1065
1Sa 25:24 "P your servant, my lord, and H1065+2021+6411
2Sa 14: 9 lord the king p me and my H2021+6411+6584
1Ki 3:17 One of them said, "P me, my lord. H1065
2Ch 30:18 "*May* the LORD, who is good, p everyone H4105
Job 7:21 Why *do you* not p my offenses and forgive H5951
Isa 55: 7 and to our God, for he will freely p. H6142

PARDONED (1) [PARDON]
Nu 14:19 just as *you have* p them from the time H5951

PARDONS (1) [PARDON]
Mic 7:18 *who* p sin and forgives the transgression H5951

PARENT (4) [GRANDPARENT, PARENT'S, PARENTS, PARENTS']
Pr 17:21 there is no joy for the p *of* a godless fool. H3
Eze 18: 4 belongs to me, the p as well as the child H3
Eze 18:20 The child will not share the guilt of the p, nor H3
Eze 18:20 will the p share the guilt of the child. H3

PARENT'S (1) [PARENT]
Pr 15: 5 A fool spurns a p discipline, but whoever H3

PARENTS (57) [PARENT]
Ex 10: 6 something neither your p nor your ancestors H3
Ex 20: 5 the sin of the p to the third and fourth H3
Ex 34: 7 the sin of the p to the third and fourth H3
Nu 14:18 the sin of the p to the third and fourth H3
Dt 5: 9 the sin of the p to the third and fourth H3
Dt 22:17 Then her p shall display the cloth before the NDT
Dt 24:16 P are not to be put to death for their children H3
Dt 24:16 children put to death for their p; each will H3
Jos 4:21 the future when your descendants ask their p, H3
Jos 24:17 who brought us and our p up out of Egypt, H3
Jdg 14: 4 His p did not know that this was H3+2256+562
Jdg 14: 9 When he rejoined his p, he gave H3+2256+562
2Ki 14: 6 "P are not to be put to death for their children, H3
2Ki 14: 6 children put to death for their p; each will H3
2Ch 25: 4 "P shall not be put to death for their children H3
2Ch 25: 4 children be put to death for their p; each H3
2Ch 29: 6 Our p were unfaithful; they did evil in the eyes H3
2Ch 30: 7 Do not be like your p and your fellow H3
Ne 9:23 that you told their p to enter and possess. H3
Pr 17: 6 and p are the pride of their children. H3
Pr 19:14 Houses and wealth are inherited from p, but H3
Isa 38:19 p tell their children about your faithfulness. H3
Jer 6:21 P and children alike will stumble over them H3
Jer 13:14 one against the other, p and children alike H3
Jer 31:29 no longer say, 'The p have eaten sour grapes H3
Jer 47: 3 P will not turn to help their children; their H3
Eze 5:10 Therefore in your midst p will eat their H3
Eze 5:10 their children, and children will eat their p. H3
Eze 18: 2 " 'The p eat sour grapes, and the children's H3
Eze 20:18 the statutes of your p or keep their laws or H3
Zec 13: 3 Then their own p will stab the H3+2256+562
Mal 4: 6 will turn the hearts of the p to their children, H3
Mal 4: 6 the hearts of the children to their p; or H3
Mt 10:21 rebel against their p and have them put G1204
Mk 13:12 rebel against their p and have them put G1204
Lk 1:17 to turn the hearts *of the* p to their children G4252
Lk 2:27 When the p brought in the child Jesus to G1204
Lk 2:41 Every year Jesus' p went to Jerusalem G1204
Lk 2:43 while his p were returning home G1204
Lk 2:48 When his p saw him, they were astonished NDT
Lk 8:56 Her p were astonished, but he ordered G1204
Lk 18:29 brothers or sisters or p or children for the G1204
Lk 21:16 You will be betrayed even by p, brothers G1204
Jn 9: 2 this man or his p, that he was born blind G1204
Jn 9: 3 "Neither this man nor his p sinned," G1204
Jn 9:18 his sight until they sent for the man's p. G1204
Jn 9:20 the p answered, "and we know he was G1204
Jn 9:22 His p said this because they were afraid of G1204
Jn 9:23 That was why his p said, "He is of age; ask G1204
Ro 1:30 ways of doing evil; they disobey their p; G1204
2Co 12:14 should not have to save up *for* their p, G1204
2Co 12:14 their parents, but p for their children. G1204
Eph 6: 1 Children, obey your p in the Lord, for this G1204
Col 3:20 Children, obey your p in everything, for G1204
1Ti 5: 4 so repaying their p and grandparents, G4591
2Ti 3: 2 disobedient *to* their p, ungrateful, G1204
Heb 11:23 By faith Moses' p hid him for three G4252

PARENTS' (4) [PARENT]
Jdg 19: 2 went back to her p home in Bethlehem, H3
Jdg 19: 3 She took him into her p home, and when her H3
Jer 32:18 the punishment for the p sins into the laps of H3
Eze 20:24 their eyes lusted after their p idols. H3

PARK (1) [PARKS]
Ne 2: 8 keeper of the royal p, so he will give me H7236

PARKS (1) [PARK]
Ecc 2: 5 I made gardens and p and planted all H7236

PARMASHTA (1)
Est 9: 9 P, Arisai, Aridai and Vaizatha, H7269

PARMENAS (1)
Ac 6: 5 Nicanor, Timon, P, and Nicolas from G4226

PARNAK (1)
Nu 34:25 Elizaphan son of P, the leader from the H7270

PAROSH (6)
Ezr 2: 3 the descendants of P 2,172 H7283
Ezr 8: 3 of the descendants of P, Zechariah, H7283
Ezr 10:25 From the descendants of P: Ramiah, H7283
Ne 3:25 Next to him, Pedaiah son of P H7283
Ne 7: 8 the descendants of P 2,172 H7283
Ne 10:14 of the people: P, Pahath-Moab, Elam H7283

PARSHANDATHA (1)
Est 9: 7 They also killed P, Dalphon, Aspatha, H7309

PARSIN (1)
Da 5:25 that was written: MENE, MENE, TEKEL, P A10593

PART (97) [APART, PARTED, PARTING, PARTITIONED, PARTLY, PARTS]
Ge 13: 9 *Let's* p company. If you go to H7233
Ge 19: 4 all the men from every p of the city of H7895
Ge 27:16 his hands and the smooth *p of* his neck with AIT
Ge 47: 6 your brothers in the best *p of* the land. AIT
Ge 47:11 gave them property in the best *p of* the land, AIT
Ex 12:48 then *he may* take p like one born H6913+7928
Ex 16:20 to Moses; they kept p *of* it until morning H4946
Ex 35:24 acacia wood for any p *of* the work brought H4856
Lev 2: 3 it is a most holy *p* of the food offerings AIT
Lev 2:10 it is a most holy *p* of the food offerings AIT
Lev 7:29 the LORD is to bring p *of* it as their sacrifice H4946
Lev 13:45 cover the lower p of their face and cry out H8559
Lev 13:56 he is to tear the spoiled p out of the H2257S
Lev 24: 9 it is a most holy p *of* their perpetual share H4946
Lev 27:16 to the LORD p *of* their family land, H4946
Lev 27:22 which is not p *of* their family land, H4946
Nu 4:31 *As* p *of* all their service at the tent, they H5466S
Nu 8:24 shall come to take p in the work at H7371+7372
Nu 18: 9 You are to have the p *of* the most holy H4946
Nu 18: 9 that p belongs to you and your sons. H2085S
Nu 18:29 the best and holiest p of everything given H4946
Nu 18:30 'When you present the best p, it will be H4946
Nu 18:32 presenting the best p *of* it you will not be H4946
Nu 31:27 soldiers who took p in the battle H3655+4200
Nu 31:29 it to Eleazar the priest as the LORD's p. H9556
Nu 31:41 to Eleazar the priest as the LORD's p, H9556
Nu 36: 3 And so p *of* the inheritance allotted to us H4946
Dt 2: 9 I will not give you any p of their land. H3772
Dt 23:13 As p *of* your equipment have something to H6584
Jos 2:15 house she lived in was p of the city wall. H928
1Sa 30:12 p *of* a cake of pressed figs and two cakes H7115
2Sa 3:37 the king had no p in the murder H2118+4946

2Sa 4: 2 Beeroth is considered **p of** Benjamin, H6584
2Sa 4: 6 went into the **inner p** *of* the house as if H9348
2Sa 20: 1 no share in David, no **p** in Jesse's son! H5709
2Sa 21: 2 Gibeonites were not a **p** *of* Israel but were H4946
2Sa 23: 5 arranged and secured in **every** *p*; surely he AIT
1Ki 7: 5 they were **in the front p** in sets of three H4578
1Ki 7:20 above the **bowl-shaped p** next to the H1061
1Ki 8:64 consecrated the **middle** *p of* the courtyard in AIT
1Ki 12:16 we have in David, what **p** in Jesse's son? H5709
1Ch 6:62 from the **p** of the tribe of Manasseh that NDT
1Ch 21:12 of the LORD ravaging every **p** *of* Israel. H1473
1Ch 23:14 God were counted **as p** of the tribe of Levi H6584
2Ch 7: 7 consecrated the **middle** *p of* the courtyard in AIT
2Ch 10:16 we have in David, what **p** in Jesse's son? H5709
2Ch 25:13 and *had* not *allowed to* **take p** in H2143+6640
Ezr 4: 3 "You **have** no **p** with us in building a H4200
Est 2:14 return to **another p** *of* the harem to the H9108
Job 42:12 blessed the **latter p of** Job's **life** more than H344
Job 42:12 part of Job's life more than the **former p**. H8040
Ps 101: 3 faithless people do; I will **have** no **p** *in* it. H1815
Ps 141: 4 is evil so that I **take p** in wicked deeds H6618
Ps 144: 5 **P** your heavens, LORD, and come down H5742
Ecc 9: 6 again will they have a **p** in anything that H2750
Jer 41: 9 King Asa had made as **p** of his defense NDT
Eze 43:21 burn it in the **designated p** *of* the temple H5152
Eze 48: 1 to Hamath will be **p** of its border from the NDT
Da 6:26 that in every **p** *of* my kingdom people A10717
Da 8:23 "In the **latter p** *of* their reign, when rebels H344
Zec 14:18 Egyptian people do not go up and **take p**, H995
Mt 5:29 to lose one **p of** your **body** than for your G3517
Mt 5:30 to lose one **p of** your **body** than for your G3517
Mt 23:30 *we* would not have **taken p** with G1639+3128
Lk 11:36 full of light, and no **p** of it dark, it will be G3538
Lk 20:35 worthy *of* **taking p** in the age to G5593
Jn 13: 8 I wash you, you have no **p** with me." G3538
Jn 18:40 *had* **taken p in an uprising**. G1639+3334
Ac 5: 2 he kept back **p of** the money for himself G608
Ac 8:21 You have no **p** or share in this ministry G3535
Ro 6:13 Do not offer any **p** of yourself to sin as an G3517
Ro 6:13 offer every **p** of yourself to him as an G3517
Ro 11:16 If the **p** *of the dough* **offered as firstfruits** is G569
Ro 11:25 a hardening in **p** until the full number of G3538
1Co 5: 3 *For* **my** *p*, even though I am not physically AIT
1Co 10:21 you cannot **have a p in** both the Lord's G3576
1Co 10:30 If I **take p in** the meal with thankfulness G3576
1Co 12:14 is not made up of one **p** but of many. G3517
1Co 12:15 that reason stop being **p of** the body. G1666
1Co 12:16 that reason stop being **p of** the body. G1666
1Co 12:19 If they were all one **p**, where would the G3517
1Co 12:26 If one **p** suffers, every part suffers with it; G3517
1Co 12:26 part suffers, every **p** suffers with it; if one G3517
1Co 12:26 if one **p** is honored, every part G3517
1Co 12:26 part is honored, every **p** rejoices with it. G3517
1Co 12:27 of Christ, and each one of you is a **p** of it. G3538
1Co 13: 9 For we know in **p** and we prophesy in part, G3538
1Co 13: 9 For we know in part and we prophesy in **p**, G3538
1Co 13:10 what is in **p** disappears. G3538
1Co 13:12 Now I know in **p**; then I shall know fully G3538
2Co 1:14 as you have understood us in **p**, you will G3538
2Co 8: 6 to completion this act of grace **on** your **p**. G1650
Eph 4:16 itself up in love, as each **p** does its work. G3538
Heb 9:11 that is to say, is not a *p of* this **creation**. AIT
Jas 3: 5 the tongue is a small **p of the body**, but it G3517
Rev 13:10 faithfulness *on the p of* **God's people**. AIT
Rev 14:12 *on the p of* the **people of God** who keep AIT

PARTED (7) [PART]

Ge 13:11 toward the east. The two men **p company**: H7233
Ge 13:14 said to Abram after Lot *had* **p** from him, H7233
2Sa 1:23 admired, and in death they **were** not **p**. H7233
2Sa 22:10 *He* **p** the heavens and came down; dark H5742
Job 41:17 they cling together and cannot **be p**. H7233
Ps 18: 9 *He* **p** the heavens and came down; dark H5742
Ac 15:39 a sharp disagreement that they **p company**. G714

PARTHIANS (1)

Ac 2: 9 **P**, Medes and Elamites; residents of G4222

PARTIAL (1) [PARTIALITY]

Pr 18: 5 It is not good *to be* **p** *to* the wicked H5951+7156

PARTIALITY (15) [PARTIAL]

Lev 19:15 *do* not **show p** *to* the poor or H5951+7156
Dt 1:17 *Do* not **show p** in judging; hear H5795+7156
Dt 10:17 who **shows** no **p** and accepts no H5951+7156
Dt 16:19 Do not pervert justice or **show p**. H5795+7156
2Ch 19: 7 there is no injustice or **p** or bribery." H5365+7156
Job 13: 8 *Will you* **show** him **p**? Will you H5951+7156
Job 13:10 to account if *you* secretly **showed p**. H5951+7156
Job 32:21 *I will* **show** no **p**, nor will I flatter H5951+7156
Job 34:19 who **shows** no **p** *to* princes and H5951+7156
Ps 82: 2 unjust and **show p** *to* the wicked? H5951+7156
Pr 24:23 *To* **show p** in judging is not good: H5795+7156
Pr 28:21 *To* **show p** is not good—yet a H5795+7156
Mal 2: 9 ways but *have* **shown p** in matters H5951+7156
Lk 20:21 and that *you do* not **show p** but G3284+4725
1Ti 5:21 to keep these instructions without **p**, and G4622

PARTICIPANTS (1) [PARTICIPATE]

1Co 10:20 I do not want you to be **p with** demons. G3128

PARTICIPATE (3) [PARTICIPANTS, PARTICIPATION]

1Co 10:18 those who eat the sacrifices **p in** the altar? G3128
1Pe 4:13 inasmuch as *you* **p in** the sufferings of G3125
2Pe 1: 4 them *you may* **p in** the divine G1181+3128

PARTICIPATION (3) [PARTICIPATE]

1Co 10:16 we give thanks a **p** in the blood of Christ G3126
1Co 10:16 that we break a **p** in the body of Christ G3126
Php 3:10 of his resurrection and **p** in his sufferings, G3126

PARTICULARLY (2)

Zec 11: 7 **p** the oppressed of the flock. H4200+4027
Heb 13:19 I **p** urge you to pray so that I may be G4359

PARTIES (7) [PARTY]

Ex 18:16 decide between **the p** H408+2256+8276+2084
Ex 21:35 the two **p** are to sell the live one and divide NDT
Ex 22: 9 **both** *p* are to bring their cases before the AIT
1Sa 13:17 **Raiding p** went out from the Philistine H8845
1Sa 14:15 those in the outposts and **raiding p** H8845
Job 1:17 formed three **raiding p** and swept down H8031
Eze 18: 8 judges fairly between **two p**. H408+4200+408

PARTING (1) [PART]

Mic 1:14 you will give **p gifts** to Moresheth Gath. H8933

PARTITIONED (1) [PART]

1Ki 6:16 *He* **p off** twenty cubits at the rear of the H1215

PARTLY (8) [PART]

Da 2:33 its feet **p** of iron and partly of baked clay. A10427
Da 2:33 its feet partly of iron and **p** of baked clay. A10427
Da 2:41 feet and toes were **p** *of* baked clay and A10427
Da 2:41 were partly of baked clay and **p** *of* iron, A10427
Da 2:42 As the toes were **p** iron and partly clay A10427
Da 2:42 As the toes were partly iron and **p** clay A10427
Da 2:42 kingdom will be **p** strong and A10427+10636
Da 2:42 will be partly strong and **p** brittle. A10427

PARTNER (6) [PARTNERS, PARTNERSHIP]

Pr 2:17 who has left the **p** *of* her youth and ignored H476
Pr 28:24 "It's not wrong," is **p** to one who destroys. H2492
Mal 2:14 though she is your **p**, the wife of your H2500
2Co 8:23 he is my **p** and co-worker among you G3128
Phm 17 So if you consider me a **p**, welcome him G3128
1Pe 3: 7 as the weaker **p** and as heirs with you G5007

PARTNERS (4) [PARTNER]

Isa 1:23 rulers are rebels, **p** *with* thieves; they all H2492
Lk 5: 7 they signaled their **p** in the other boat to G3581
Lk 5:10 the sons of Zebedee, Simon's **p**. G3128
Eph 5: 7 Therefore do not be **p with** them. G5212

PARTNERSHIP (2) [PARTNER]

Php 1: 5 because of your **p** in the gospel from the G3126
Phm 6 I pray that your **p with** us in the faith may G3126

PARTRIDGE (2)

1Sa 26:20 as one hunts a **p** in the mountains. H7926
Jer 17:11 Like a **p** that hatches eggs it did not lay H7926

PARTS (31) [PART]

Ex 20:26 or your **private p** may be exposed. H6872
Ex 29:27 "Consecrate those **p** of the ordination ram NDT
Dt 19: 3 divide into three **p** the land the LORD H1473
Dt 25:11 out and seizes him by his **private p**, H4434
Jos 18: 5 You are to divide the land into seven **p** H2750
Jos 18: 6 descriptions of the seven **p** of the land, H2750
Jos 18: 9 town by town, in seven **p**, and returned to H2750
Jdg 19:29 into twelve **p** and sent them into all the H5984
1Sa 2:29 on the **choice p** *of* every offering H8040
2Ki 19:23 I have reached its remotest **p**, the finest of H4869
1Ch 28:11 its storerooms, its **upper p**, its inner rooms H6608
2Ch 3: 9 He also overlaid the **upper p** with gold. H6608
Est 1:22 He sent dispatches to all **p** *of* the kingdom, H4519
Job 18:13 It eats away **p** *of* his skin; death's firstborn H963
Pr 18: 8 they go down to the **inmost p**. H2540+1061
Pr 26:22 they go down to the **inmost p**. H2540+1061
Isa 7:20 to shave your head and **private p** H8552+8079
Da 4:22 extends to **distant p** *of* the earth. A10509
Ac 2:10 Egypt and the **p** of Libya near Cyrene G3538
1Co 12:12 though one, has many **p**, but all its many G3517
1Co 12:12 all its many **p** form one body, so it is G3517
1Co 12:18 in fact God has placed the **p** in the body, G3517
1Co 12:20 there are many **p**, but one body. G3517
1Co 12:22 those **p** of the body that seem to be G3517
1Co 12:23 and **the p** that we think are less G3836+5393S
1Co 12:23 And the **p** that are unpresentable are NDT
1Co 12:24 while our **presentable** *p* need no special AIT
1Co 12:24 giving greater honor to the **p** that lacked it, NDT
1Co 12:25 that its **p** should have equal concern G3517
Jas 3: 6 a world of evil among the **p of the body**. G3517
Rev 16:19 The great city split into three **p**, and the G3538

PARTY (12) [PARTIES]

Ex 21:19 the guilty **p** must pay the injured person NDT
Dt 19:19 that witness intended to do to the **other p**. H278S
Dt 25: 3 If **the guilty p** is flogged more than that H2257S
Ru 4: 7 **one p** took off his sandal and gave it to H408S
1Sa 30: 8 the LORD, "Shall I pursue this **raiding p**? H1522
1Sa 30:15 "Can you lead me down to this **raiding p**?" H1522
1Sa 30:23 our hands the **raiding p** that came against H1522
Pr 19:18 *do* not **be a willing p** to their death. H5951+5883
Ac 5:17 who were *members of* the **p** of the G146
Ac 15: 5 who belonged to the **p** of the Pharisees G146
2Co 7:12 the wrong nor on account of the **injured** *p*, AIT
Gal 3:20 implies more than **one** *p*; but God is one. AIT

PARUAH (1)

1Ki 4:17 Jehoshaphat son of **P**—in Issachar; H7245

PARVAIM (1)

2Ch 3: 6 And the gold he used was gold of **P**. H7246

PAS DAMMIM (2)

2Sa 23: 9 gathered **at P** for battle. H9004S
1Ch 11:13 was with David at **P** when the H7169

PASAK (1)

1Ch 7:33 sons of Japhlet: **P**, Bimhal and Ashvath H7179

PASEAH (4)

1Ch 4:12 **P** and Tehinnah the father of Ir Nahash. H7176
Ezr 2:49 Uzza, **P**, Besai, H7176
Ne 3: 6 by Joiada son of **P** and Meshullam son of H7176
Ne 7:51 Gazzam, Uzza, **P**, H7176

PASHHUR (13)

1Ch 9:12 Jeroham, the son of **P**, the son of H7319
Ezr 2:38 of **P** 1,247 H7319
Ezr 10:22 From the descendants of **P**: Elioenai H7319
Ne 7:41 of **P** 1,247 H7319
Ne 10: 3 **P**, Amariah, Malkijah, H7319
Ne 11:12 the son of **P**, the son of Malkijah, H7319
Jer 20: 1 When the priest **P** son of Immer, the H7319
Jer 20: 3 when **P** released him from the stocks H7319
Jer 20: 3 "The LORD's name for you is not **P**, but H7319
Jer 20: 6 And you, **P**, and all who live in your house H7319
Jer 21: 1 sent to him **P** son of Malkijah and H7319
Jer 38: 1 Mattan, Gedaliah son of **P**, Jehukal son of H7319
Jer 38: 1 **P** son of Malkijah heard what H7319

PASS (116) [PASSED, PASSER-BY, PASSES, PASSING]

Ge 18: 3 my lord, *do* not **p** your servant by. H6296
Ex 12:12 that same night *I will* **p** through Egypt H6296
Ex 12:13 when I see the blood, *I will* **p over** you. H7173
Ex 12:23 doorframe and *will* **p over** that doorway, H7173
Ex 15:16 as a stone—until your people **p by**, LORD, H6296
Ex 15:16 until the people you bought **p by**. H6296
Ex 33:19 "I *will* **cause** all my goodness **to p** in front H6296
Lev 26: 6 the sword *will* not **p** through your H6296
Nu 20:17 Please *let us* **p** through your country. H6296
Nu 20:18 "*You may* not **p** through here; if you try H6296
Nu 20:19 *We* only *want to* **p through** on foot H6296
Nu 20:20 "*You may* not **p through.**" Then H6296
Nu 21:22 "*Let us* **p** through your country. We will H6296
Nu 21:23 would not let Israel **p** through his territory. H6296
Nu 34: 4 cross south of Scorpion **P**, continue on to H5090
Nu 36: 7 in Israel *is to* **p** from one tribe to H6015
Nu 36: 9 No inheritance *may* **p** from one tribe to H6015
Dt 2: 4 'You *are about to* **p** through the territory of H6296
Dt 2:18 "Today you *are to* **p by** the region of Moab H6296
Dt 2:27 "*Let us* **p** through your country. We will H6296
Dt 2:28 Only *let us* **p through** on foot— H6296
Dt 2:30 of Heshbon refused *to* **let** us **p** through. H6296
Jos 3: 6 of the covenant and **p on** ahead of the H6296
Jos 15: 3 crossed south of Scorpion **P**, continued on H5090
Jos 15: 7 which faces the **P** *of* Adummim south of H5090
Jos 18:17 which faces the **P** *of* Adummim, and ran H5090
Jdg 1:36 was from Scorpion **P** to Sela and beyond. H5090
Jdg 8:13 returned from the battle by the **P** *of* Heres. H5090
Jdg 11:19 '*Let us* **p** through your country to our own H6296
Jdg 11:20 did not trust Israel *to* **p** through his H6296
1Sa 13:23 had gone out to the **p** *at* Mikmash. H5044
1Sa 14: 4 On each side of the **p** that Jonathan H5045
1Sa 16: 8 Abinadab and **had** him **p** in front of H6296
1Sa 16: 9 Jesse then **had** Shammah **p by**, but H6296
1Sa 16:10 Jesse **had** seven of his sons **p** before H6296
1Ki 9: 8 All *who* **p** by will be appalled and will H6296
1Ki 19:11 of the LORD, for the LORD *is about to* **p by**." H6296
2Ki 19:25 now *I have* **brought** it **to p**, that you have H995
1Ch 28: 8 land and **p** *it* **on as an inheritance** to your H5706
2Ch 7:21 All *who* **p** by will be appalled and say H6296
2Ch 20:16 They will be climbing up by the **P** *of* Ziz H5090
Job 16:22 "Only a few years *will* **p** before I take the H910
Job 19: 8 He has blocked my way so *I* cannot **p**; he H6296
Job 34:20 the people are shaken and *they* **p away** H6296
Job 41:16 close to the next that no air *can* **p** between. H995
Ps 80:12 so that all *who* **p by** pick its grapes? H6296+2006
Ps 84: 6 *As they* **p** through the Valley of Baka, they H6296
Ps 89:41 All *who* **p by** have plundered him H6296+2006
Ps 90: 9 All our days **p away** under your wrath; we H7155
Ps 90:10 sorrow, for *they* quickly **p**, and we fly H1577
Ps 105:19 till what he foretold **came to p**, till the word H995
Ps 129: 8 May those *who* **p by** not say to them, "The H6296
Ps 141:10 into their own nets, while I **p by** in safety. H6296
Ps 148: 6 he issued a decree *that will* never **p away**. H6296
Pr 9:15 calling out to *those who* **p by**, who H6296+2006
Ecc 6:12 days *they* **p through** like a shadow? H6913
Isa 10:28 They enter Aiath; *they* **p** through Migron H6296
Isa 10:29 They go over the **p**, and say, "We will H5045
Isa 31: 5 *he will* '**p over**' it and will rescue it." H7173
Isa 34:10 no *one will* ever **p** through it again. H6296
Isa 37:26 now *I have* **brought** it **to p**, that you have H995
Isa 43: 2 When *you* **p** through the waters, I will be H6296
Isa 43: 2 with you; and when you **p** through the rivers NDT
Isa 48: 3 then suddenly I acted, and *they* **came to p**. H995
Isa 62:10 **P through**, pass through the gates H6296
Isa 62:10 Pass through, **p through** the gates H6296

Jer 2:35 But I will p judgment on you because you H9149
Jer 6: 9 p your hand over the branches again, like H8740
Jer 18:16 all who p by will be appalled and will H6296
Jer 19: 8 all who p by will be appalled and will H6296
Jer 22: 8 from many nations will p by this city and H6296
Jer 33:13 flocks will again p under the hand of the H6296
Jer 49:17 all who p by will be appalled and will H6296
Jer 50:13 All who p Babylon will be appalled; they H6296
La 1:12 it nothing to you, all you who p by? H6296+2006
La 2:15 All who p your way clap their hands at H6296
Eze 5:14 around you, in the sight of all who p by. H6296
Eze 14:15 so that no one can p through it because H6296
Eze 14:17 'Let the sword p throughout the land H6296
Eze 20:37 I will take note of you as you p under my H6296
Eze 29:11 of neither man nor beast will p through it; H6296
Eze 36:34 in the sight of all who p through it. H6296
Eze 48:14 the land and must not p into other hands, H6296
Da 4:16 an animal, till seven times p by for him. A10268
Da 4:23 animals, until seven times p by for him. A10268
Da 4:25 Seven times will p by for you until you A10268
Da 4:32 Seven times will p by for you until you A10268
Da 7:14 dominion that will not p away, A10528
Am 5:17 vineyards, for I will p through your midst," H6296
Mic 1:11 P by naked and in shame, you who live in H6296
Mic 2: 8 rich robe from those who p by without a H6296
Mic 2:13 Their King will p through before them, the H6296
Na 1:12 they will be destroyed and p away. H6296
Zep 2:15 All who p by her scoff and shake their fists H6296
Zec 10:11 They will p through the sea of trouble; the H6296
Zec 10:11 down and Egypt's scepter will p away. H6073
Mt 8:28 so violent that no one could p that way. G4216
Mt 24:34 will certainly not p away until all G4216
Mt 24:35 Heaven and earth will p away, but my G4216
Mt 24:35 but my words will never p away. G4216
Mk 6:48 He was about to p by them, G4216
Mk 13:30 will certainly not p away until all G4216
Mk 13:31 Heaven and earth will p away, but my G4216
Mk 13:31 but my words will never p away. G4216
Mk 14:35 if possible the hour might p from him. G4216
Lk 21:32 will certainly not p away until all G4216
Lk 21:33 Heaven and earth will p away, but my G4216
Lk 21:33 but my words will never p away. G4216
Jn 8:15 standards; I p judgment on no one. G3212
Ac 7:38 he received living words to p on to us. G1443
Ro 2: 1 you who p judgment on someone else G3212
Ro 2: 1 because you who p judgment do the G3212
Ro 2: 3 when you, a mere human being, p judgment G3212
1Co 13: 8 where there is knowledge, it will p away. G2934
Jas 1:10 since they will p away like a wild flower. G4216
1Jn 2:17 The world and its desires p away, but G4135

PASSAGE (7) [PASSAGEWAY]

Mk 12:10 Haven't you read this p of Scripture: G1210
Jn 13:18 But this is to fulfill this p of Scripture: G1210
Ac 8:32 This is the p of Scripture the eunuch was G4343
Ac 8:35 with that very p of Scripture and told him G1210
Ro 11: 2 what Scripture says in the p about Elijah— AIT
Heb 4: 5 And again in the p above he says, "They AIT
Heb 4: 7 through David, as in the p already quoted: NDT

PASSAGEWAY (3) [PASSAGE]

Eze 42: 4 rooms was an inner p ten cubits wide H4544
Eze 42:11 with a p in front of them. These were like H2006
Eze 42:12 beginning of the p that was parallel to H2006

PASSED (77) [PASS]

Ge 15:17 torch appeared and p between the pieces H6296
Ge 32:31 The sun rose above him as he p Peniel H6296
Ge 41: 1 When two full years had p, Pharaoh had H7891
Ge 50: 4 When the days of mourning had p H6296
Ex 7:25 Seven days p after the LORD struck the Nile. H4848
Ex 12:27 who p over the houses of the Israelites in H7173
Ex 33:22 cover you with my hand until I have p by. H6296
Ex 34: 6 And he p in front of Moses, proclaiming H6296
Lev 25:30 is not redeemed before a full year has p, H4848
Nu 14: 7 "The land we p through and explored is H6296
Nu 20:17 the left until we have p through your H6296
Nu 21:22 Highway until we have p through your H6296
Nu 33: 8 Pi Hahiroth and p through the sea into H6296
Dt 2:14 Thirty-eight years p from the time we left NDT
Dt 29:16 in Egypt and how we p through the H6296
Jos 3:17 while all Israel p by until the whole H6296
Jos 15: 4 It then p along to Azmon and joined the H6296
Jos 15:11 p along to Mount Baalah and reached H6296
Jos 18:12 p the northern slope of Jericho and H6590
Jos 23: 1 After a long time had p and the LORD had H2118
Jdg 3:26 He p by the stone images and escaped to H6296
Jdg 9:25 to ambush and rob everyone who p by, H6296
Jdg 11:18 p along the eastern side of the country of H995
Jdg 11:29 Manasseh, p through Mizpah of Gilead H6296
1Sa 9: 4 So he p through the hill country of H6296
1Sa 9: 4 Then he p through the territory of H6296
2Sa 15:23 wept aloud as all the people p by. H6296
2Sa 20:14 Sheba p through all the tribes of Israel to H6296
1Ki 13:25 Some people who p by saw the body lying H6296
1Ki 18:29 Midday p, and they continued their frantic H6296
1Ki 20:39 As the king p by, the prophet called out to H6296
2Ch 21:20 He p away, to no one's regret, and was H2143
Ne 9:11 so that they p through it on dry ground H6296
Ne 12:37 ascent to the wall and p above the site of NDT
Est 4:11 But thirty days have p since I was called to NDT
Job 14:13 conceal me till your anger has p! H8740
Job 17:11 My days have p, my plans are shattered H6296
Ps 37:36 but he soon p away and was no more H6296
Ps 57: 1 of your wings until the disaster has p. H6296
Ps 66: 6 they p through the waters on foot H6296
SS 3: 4 Scarcely had I p them when I found the H6296
Isa 26:20 a little while until his wrath has p by. H6296
La 4:21 But to you also the cup will be p; you will H6296
Eze 16: 6 " 'Then I p by and saw you kicking about H6296
Eze 16: 8 " 'Later I p by, and when I looked at you H6296
Eze 16:15 on anyone who p by and your beauty H6296
Eze 16:25 promiscuity to anyone who p by. H6296
Da 2:28 the visions that p through your mind as AIT
Da 4: 5 images and visions that p through my mind AIT
Da 7: 1 and visions p through his mind as he was AIT
Da 7:15 the visions that p through my mind AIT
Mt 27:39 Those who p by hurled insults at him G4182
Mk 9:30 left that place and p through Galilee. G4182
Mk 15:29 Those who p by hurled insults at him G4182
Lk 10:31 he saw the man, he p by on the other side. G524
Lk 10:32 place and saw him, p by on the other side. G524
Ac 5:15 might fall on some of them as he p by. G2262
Ac 7:30 "After forty years had p, an angel G4444
Ac 12:10 They p the first and second guards and G1451
Ac 16: 8 So they p by Mysia and went down to G4216
Ac 17: 1 When Paul and his companions had p through G1476
Ac 24:27 When two years had p, Felix was G4444
Ac 27: 4 sea again and p to the lee of Cyprus G5709
Ac 27:16 As we p to the lee of a small island called G5720
Ac 27:17 Then they p ropes under the ship itself to G5968
1Co 5: 3 I have already p judgment in the name of G3212
1Co 10: 1 cloud and that they all p through the sea. G1451
1Co 11: 2 the traditions just as I p them on to you. G4140
1Co 11:23 from the Lord what I also p on to you: G4140
1Co 15: 3 For what I received I p on to you as of first G4140
2Th 2:15 hold fast to the teachings we p on to you, G1438
Heb 11:29 By faith the people p through the Red Sea G1329
2Pe 2:21 sacred command that was p on to them. G4140
1Jn 3:14 We know that we have p from death to life G3553
Rev 11:14 The second woe has p; the third woe is G599
Rev 21: 1 first heaven and the first earth had p away, G599
Rev 21: 4 the old order of things has p away. G599

PASSER-BY (1) [PASS]

Pr 26:10 random is one who hires a fool or any p. H6296

PASSES (5) [PASS]

Ex 33:22 When my glory p by, I will put you in a H6296
Lev 27:32 tenth animal that p under the shepherd's H6296
Job 9:11 When he p me, I cannot see him; when H6296
Jer 17:16 What p my lips is open before you H4604
Zep 2: 2 effect and that day p like windblown chaff H6296

PASSING (20) [PASS]

Jos 16: 6 p by it to Janoah on the east. H6296
Jos 19:27 Beth Emek and Neiel, p Kabul on the left. H3655
Jos 19:33 p Adami Nekeb and Jabneel to Lakkum NDT
2Ki 6: 9 "Beware of p that place, because the H6296
2Ki 6:26 As the king of Israel was p by on the wall H6296
Ps 78:39 flesh, a p breeze that does not return. H2143
Isa 8: 8 p through it and reaching up to the neck. H6296
Zep 3: 6 streets deserted, with no one p through. H6296
Mk 15:21 was p by on his way in from the country G4135
Lk 18:37 They told him, "Jesus of Nazareth is p by." G4216
Lk 19: 1 Jesus entered Jericho and was p through. G1451
Jn 1:36 When he saw Jesus p by, he said, "Look G4344
Ac 19:21 p through Macedonia and Achaia. G1451
Ac 21: 3 sighting Cyprus and p to the south of it, G2901
Ro 14:13 Therefore let us stop p judgment on one G3212
Ro 15:24 to see you while p through and to have G1388
1Co 7:31 For this world in its present form is p away. G4135
1Co 16: 7 to see you now and make only a p visit; G4227
2Co 3:13 from seeing the end of what was p away. G2934
1Jn 2: 8 the darkness is p and the true light G4135

PASSION (3) [PASSIONATE, PASSIONS]

Ps 11: 5 who love violence, he hates with a p. H5883
Hos 7: 6 Their p smolders all night; in the morning H678
1Co 7: 9 it is better to marry than to burn with p. G4792

PASSIONATE (1) [PASSION]

1Th 4: 5 not in p lust like the pagans, who do not G4079

PASSIONS (5) [PASSION]

Ro 7: 5 the sinful p aroused by the law were at G4077
1Co 7:36 if his p are too strong and he feels he G5644
Gal 5:24 crucified the flesh with its p and desires. G4077
Titus 2:12 to ungodliness and worldly p, and to live G2123
Titus 3: 3 enslaved by all kinds of p and pleasures. G2123

PASSOVER (77)

Ex 12:11 Eat it in haste; it is the LORD's P. H7175
Ex 12:21 your families and slaughter the P lamb. H7175
Ex 12:27 tell them, 'It is the P sacrifice to the LORD H7175
Ex 12:43 "These are the regulations for the P meal: H7175
Ex 12:48 celebrate the LORD's P must have all the H7175
Ex 34:25 sacrifice from the P Festival remain until H7175
Lev 23: 5 The LORD's P begins at twilight on the H7175
Nu 9: 2 celebrate the P at the appointed time. H7175
Nu 9: 4 told the Israelites to celebrate the P, H7175
Nu 9: 6 not celebrate the P on that day because H7175
Nu 9:10 they are still to celebrate the LORD's P, H7175
Nu 9:12 When they celebrate the P, they must H7175
Nu 9:13 not on a journey fails to celebrate the P, H7175
Nu 9:14 celebrate the LORD's P in accordance with H7175
Nu 28:16 the first month the LORD's P is to be held. H7175
Nu 33: 3 day of the first month, the day after the P. H7175
Dt 16: 1 celebrate the P of the LORD your God, H7175
Dt 16: 2 Sacrifice as the P to the LORD your God an H7175
Dt 16: 5 not sacrifice the P in any town the LORD H7175
Dt 16: 6 you must sacrifice the P in the evening, H7175
Jos 5:10 of Jericho, the Israelites celebrated the P. H7175
Jos 5:11 The day after the P, that very day, they ate H7175
2Ki 23:21 "Celebrate the P to the LORD your God, as H7175
2Ki 23:22 of Judah had any such P been observed. H7175
2Ki 23:23 this P was celebrated to the LORD in H7175
2Ch 30: 1 celebrate the P to the LORD, H7175
2Ch 30: 2 to celebrate the P in the second month. H7175
2Ch 30: 5 celebrate the P to the LORD, H7175
2Ch 30:15 slaughtered the P lamb on the fourteenth H7175
2Ch 30:17 had to kill the P lambs for all those who H7175
2Ch 30:18 they ate the P, contrary to what was H7175
2Ch 35: 1 Josiah celebrated the P to the LORD in H7175
2Ch 35: 1 the P lamb was slaughtered on the H7175
2Ch 35: 6 Slaughter the P lambs, consecrate H7175
2Ch 35: 7 lambs and goats for the P offerings, H7175
2Ch 35: 8 hundred P offerings and three hundred H7175
2Ch 35: 9 five thousand P offerings and five H7175
2Ch 35:11 The P lambs were slaughtered, and the H7175
2Ch 35:13 They roasted the P animals over the fire as H7175
2Ch 35:16 celebration of the P and the offering of H7175
2Ch 35:17 present celebrated the P at that time and H7175
2Ch 35:18 The P had not been observed like this in H7175
2Ch 35:18 ever celebrated such a P as did Josiah, H7175
2Ch 35:19 This P was celebrated in the eighteenth H7175
Ezr 6:19 first month, the exiles celebrated the P. H7175
Ezr 6:20 slaughtered the P lamb for all the exiles, H7175
Eze 45:21 fourteenth day you are to observe the P, H7175
Mt 26: 2 "As you know, the P is two days away G4247
Mt 26:17 to make preparations for you to eat the P?" G4247
Mt 26:18 to celebrate the P with my disciples at G4247
Mt 26:19 had directed them and prepared the P. G4247
Mk 14: 1 Now the P and the Festival of Unleavened G4247
Mk 14:12 it was customary to sacrifice the P lamb, G4247
Mk 14:12 make preparations for you to eat the P?" G4247
Mk 14:14 where I may eat the P with my disciples? G4247
Mk 14:16 had told them. So they prepared the P. G4247
Lk 2:41 to Jerusalem for the Festival of the P. G4247
Lk 22: 1 called the P, was approaching, G4247
Lk 22: 7 Bread on which the P lamb had to be G4247
Lk 22: 8 make preparations for us to eat the P." G4247
Lk 22:11 where I may eat the P with my disciples? G4247
Lk 22:13 had told them. So they prepared the P. G4247
Lk 22:15 desired to eat this P with you before I G4247
Jn 2:13 When it was almost time for the Jewish P G4247
Jn 2:23 he was in Jerusalem at the P Festival, G4247
Jn 4:45 had done in Jerusalem at the P Festival, G2038
Jn 6: 4 The Jewish P Festival was near. G4247
Jn 11:55 When it was almost time for the Jewish P G4247
Jn 11:55 their ceremonial cleansing before the P. G4247
Jn 12: 1 Six days before the P, Jesus came to G4247
Jn 13: 1 It was just before the P Festival. Jesus G4247
Jn 18:28 they wanted to be able to eat the P. G4247
Jn 18:39 to you one prisoner at the time of the P. G4247
Jn 19:14 It was the day of Preparation of the P; it G4247
Ac 12: 4 to bring him out for public trial after the P. G4247
1Co 5: 7 For Christ, our P lamb, has been sacrificed. G4247
Heb 11:28 By faith he kept the P and the application G4247

PAST (49)

Ge 18:11 Sarah was p the age of childbearing. H2532
Ge 31:52 that I will not go p this heap to your side H6296
Ge 31:52 that you will not go p this heap and H6296
Ex 4:10 neither in the p nor since you have H9453+8997
Dt 2: 8 So we went on p our relatives the H4946+907
Dt 32: 7 the generations long p. H9102+1887+2256+1887
Jos 13:16 and the whole plateau p Medeba H6584
Jos 15: 3 Then it ran p Hezron up to Addar and H6296
1Sa 15:32 "Surely the bitterness of death is p." H6073
2Sa 5: 2 In the p, while Saul was H1685+919+1685+8997
2Sa 15:18 All his men marched p him H6296+6584+3338
2Sa 15:34 I was your father's servant in the p, but now H255
1Ch 11: 2 In the p, even while Saul was king H9453+8997
Ne 12:38 p the Tower of the Ovens to the H4946+6584
Job 4:15 A spirit glided p my face, and the hair on H2736
Job 9:26 They skim p like boats of papyrus, like H2736
Job 36:26 The number of his years is p finding out. H4202
Ps 79: 8 hold against us the sins of p generations; H8037
Pr 24:30 I went p the field of a sluggard, past the H6584
Pr 24:30 p the vineyard of someone who has no H6584
Ecc 3:15 and God will call the p to account. H8103
SS 2:11 The winter is p; the rains are over and H6296
Isa 9: 1 In the p he humbled the land of H6961+8037
Isa 43:18 the former things; do not dwell on the p. H7719
Isa 43:26 Review the p for me, let us argue the H2349
Isa 45:21 who declared it from the distant p? H255
Isa 65:16 For the p troubles will be forgotten and H8037
Jer 8:20 "The harvest is p, the summer has ended H6296
Jer 21: 2 us as in times p so that he H3869+3972
Jer 31: 3 The LORD appeared to us in the p, saying H8158
Jer 46:26 Egypt will be inhabited as in times p," H7710
Eze 36:11 people on you as in the p and will make H7712
Eze 47:15 by the Hethlon road p Lebo Hamath to NDT
Hab 1:11 Then they sweep p like the wind and go H2736
Zec 7: 5 seventh months for the p seventy years, NDT

Zec 8:11 of this people as I did in the **p**," H8037+3427
Ac 14:16 In the **p**, he let all nations go their *G4233+1155*
Ac 17:30 *In* the **p** God overlooked such ignorance *G5989*
Ac 20:16 Paul had decided *to* **sail p** Ephesus to *G4179*
Ro 15: 4 that *was* **written in the p** was written to *G4592*
Ro 16:25 of the mystery hidden *for* long **ages p**, *G173*
Eph 3: 9 which for **ages p** was kept hidden in God *G172*
Heb 1: 1 **In the p** God spoke to our ancestors *G4093*
Heb 11:11 even Sarah, who was **p** childbearing age *G4123*
1Pe 3: 5 the holy women *of* the **p** who put their *G4537*
1Pe 4: 3 For *you have* **spent** enough time **in the p** *G4216*
2Pe 1: 9 have been cleansed from their **p** sins. *G4093*
2Pe 3: 2 the words **spoken in the p** by the holy *G4625*
Rev 9:12 The first woe *is* **p**; two other woes are yet to *G599*

PASTOR, PASTORS (KJV) LEADERS, SHEPHERD, SHEPHERDS

PASTORS (1)

Eph 4:11 the evangelists, the **p** and teachers, *G4478*

PASTURE (39) [PASTURE-FED, PASTURELAND, PASTURELANDS, PASTURES]

Ge 29: 7 Water the sheep and take them back to **p**." H8286
Ge 47: 4 your servants' flocks have no **p**. H5337
2Sa 7: 8 I took you from the **p**, from tending the H5659
1Ch 4:39 of the valley in search of **p** for their flocks. H5337
1Ch 4:40 They found rich, good **p**, and the land was H5337
1Ch 4:41 because there was **p** for their flocks. H5337
1Ch 17: 7 I took you from the **p**, from tending the H5659
Job 24: 2 *they* **p** flocks they have stolen. H8286
Job 39: 8 the hills for its **p** and searches for any H5337
Ps 37: 3 dwell in the land and **enjoy** safe **p**. H8286
Ps 74: 1 smolder against the sheep of your **p**? H5338
Ps 79:13 the sheep of your **p**, will praise you H5338
Ps 95: 7 our God and we are the people of his **p**, H5338
Ps 100: 3 we are his people, the sheep of his **p**. H5338
Isa 5:17 Then sheep will graze as in their own **p** H1824
Isa 14:30 The poorest of the poor *will* **find p**, and H8286
Isa 32:14 the delight of donkeys, a **p** *for* flocks, H5337
Isa 49: 9 the roads and find **p** on every barren hill. H5338
Isa 65:10 Sharon will become a **p** *for* flocks, and the H5659
Jer 23: 1 scattering the sheep of my **p**! H5338
Jer 23: 3 them and will bring them back to their **p**, H5659
Jer 25:36 the flock, for the LORD is destroying their **p**. H5338
Jer 49:20 their **p** will be appalled at their fate. H5659
Jer 50: 7 against the LORD, their verdant **p**, the LORD, H5659
Jer 50:19 But I will bring Israel back to their own **p** H5659
Jer 50:45 their **p** will be appalled at their fate. H5659
La 1: 6 Her princes are like deer that find no **p**; in H5337
Eze 25: 5 Rabbah into a **p** *for* camels and Ammon H5659
Eze 34:13 *I will* **p** them on the mountains of Israel H8286
Eze 34:14 I will tend them in a good **p**, and the H5337
Eze 34:14 will feed in a rich **p** on the mountains of H5337
Eze 34:18 enough for you to feed on the good **p**? H5337
Eze 34:18 trample the rest of your **p** with your feet? H5337
Eze 34:31 the sheep of my **p**, and I am your God, H5338
Hos 4:16 How then *can* the LORD **p** them like lambs H8286
Joel 1:18 herds mill about because they have no **p**; H5337
Mic 2:12 like a flock in its **p**; the place will throng H1824
Zep 2: 7 people of Judah; there *they will* **find p**. H8286
Jn 10: 9 They will come in and go out, and find **p**. *G3786*

PASTURE-FED (1) [FEED, PASTURE]

1Ki 4:23 twenty of **p** cattle and a hundred sheep H8297

PASTURELAND (8) [PASTURE]

Lev 25:34 But the **p** *belonging to* their towns H8441+4494
Nu 35: 5 will have this area as **p** *for* the towns. H4494
Jos 21:11 with its surrounding **p**, in the hill country H4494
Jer 49:19 up from Jordan's thickets to a rich **p**, H5659
Jer 50:44 up from Jordan's thickets to a rich **p**, H5659
Eze 36: 5 so that they might plunder its **p**. H4494
Eze 48:15 use of the city, for houses and for **p**. H4494
Eze 48:17 The **p** for the city will be 250 cubits on the H4494

PASTURELANDS (43) [PASTURE]

Nu 35: 2 And give them **p** around the towns. H4494
Nu 35: 3 towns to live in and **p** for the cattle they H4494
Nu 35: 4 "The **p** around the towns that you give the H4494
Nu 35: 7 forty-eight towns, together with their **p**. H4494
Jos 14: 4 to live in, with **p** for their flocks and herds. H4494
Jos 21: 2 towns to live in, with **p** for our livestock." H4494
Jos 21: 3 following towns and **p** out of their own H4494
Jos 21: 8 to the Levites these towns and their **p**, H4494
Jos 21:16 together with their **p**—nine towns from H4494
Jos 21:18 together with their **p**—four towns. H4494
Jos 21:19 came to thirteen, together with their **p**. H4494
Jos 21:22 together with their **p**—four towns. H4494
Jos 21:24 together with their **p**—four towns. H4494
Jos 21:25 together with their **p**—two towns. H4494
Jos 21:26 ten towns and their **p** were given to the H4494
Jos 21:27 together with their **p**—two towns; H4494
Jos 21:29 together with their **p**—four towns; H4494
Jos 21:31 together with their **p**—four towns; H4494
Jos 21:32 together with their **p**—three towns. H4494
Jos 21:33 came to thirteen, together with their **p**. H4494
Jos 21:35 together with their **p**—four towns; H4494
Jos 21:37 together with their **p**—four towns; H4494
Jos 21:39 together with their **p**—four towns in all. H4494
Jos 21:41 forty-eight in all, together with their **p**. H4494
Jos 21:42 Each of these towns had **p** surrounding it H4494
1Ch 5:16 on all the **p** *of* Sharon as far as they H4494
1Ch 6:55 Hebron in Judah with its surrounding **p**. H4494
1Ch 6:59 Beth Shemesh, together with their **p**. H4494
1Ch 6:60 Anathoth, together with their **p**. H4494
1Ch 6:64 gave the Levites these towns and their **p**. H4494
1Ch 6:69 Gath Rimmon, together with their **p**. H4494
1Ch 6:70 together with their **p**, to the rest of the H4494
1Ch 6:71 also Ashtaroth, together with their **p**; H4494
1Ch 6:73 Ramoth and Anem, together with their **p**; H4494
1Ch 6:75 Hukok and Rehob, together with their **p**; H4494
1Ch 6:76 Kiriathaim, together with their **p**. H4494
1Ch 6:77 Tabor, together with their **p**; H4494
1Ch 6:79 Mephaath, together with their **p**; H4494
1Ch 6:81 Heshbon and Jazer, together with their **p**. H4494
1Ch 13: 2 who are with them in their towns and **p**, H4494
2Ch 11:14 even abandoned their **p** and property H4494
Ps 83:12 "Let us take possession of the **p** *of* God." H5661
Mic 7:14 which lives by itself in a forest, in **fertile p**. H4149

PASTURES (10) [PASTURE]

Ps 23: 2 He makes me lie down in green **p**, he H5661
Jer 23:10 parched and the **p** *in* the wilderness are H5661
Jer 33:12 there will again be **p** *for* shepherds to rest H5659
Eze 45:15 hundred from the well-watered **p** of Israel. NDT
Joel 1:19 has devoured the **p** *in* the wilderness and H5661
Joel 1:20 fire has devoured the **p** *in* the wilderness. H5661
Joel 2:22 the **p** *in* the wilderness are becoming H5661
Am 1: 2 Jerusalem; the **p** *of* the shepherds dry up H5661
Zep 2: 6 by the sea will become **p** having wells H5661
Zec 11: 3 of the shepherds; their **rich p** are destroyed! H168

PATARA (1)

Ac 21: 1 we went to Rhodes and from there to **P**. *G4249*

PATCH (5) [PATCHED]

Mt 9:16 "No one sews a **p** of unshrunk cloth on an *G2099*
Mt 9:16 the **p** will pull away from the garment *G4445*
Mk 2:21 "No one sews a **p** of unshrunk cloth on an *G2099*
Lk 5:36 out of a new garment *to* **p** an old one. *G2095*
Lk 5:36 the **p** from the new will not match the *G2099*

PATCHED (1) [PATCH]

Jos 9: 5 They put worn and **p** sandals on their feet H3229

PATH (63) [PATHS]

Ge 49:17 a viper along the **p**, that bites the horse's H784
Nu 22:24 stood in a **narrow p** *through* the vineyards, H5469
Nu 22:32 you because your **p** is a reckless one H2006
2Sa 22:37 You provide a broad **p** for my feet, so that H7576
Ne 9:19 did not fail to guide them on their **p**, H2006
Job 16:22 will pass before I take the **p** of no return. H784
Job 18:10 him on the ground; a trap lies in his **p**. H5985
Job 22:15 you keep to the old **p** that the wicked have H784
Job 24: 4 the needy from the **p** and force all the H2006
Job 28: 7 No bird of prey knows that **hidden p**, no H5985
Job 28:26 the rain and a **p** for the thunderstorm, H2006
Job 29: 6 when my **p** was drenched with cream and H2141
Job 31: 7 if my steps have turned from the **p**, if my H2006
Job 38:25 and a **p** for the thunderstorm, H2006
Ps 16:11 You make known to me the **p** *of* life; you H784
Ps 18:36 You provide a broad **p** for my feet, so that H7576
Ps 27:11 lead me in a straight **p** because of my H784
Ps 35: 6 may their **p** be dark and slippery, with the H2006
Ps 44:18 our feet had not strayed from your **p**. H784
Ps 57: 6 They dug a pit **in** my **p**—but they H4200+7156
Ps 77:19 Your **p** led through the sea, your way H2006
Ps 78:50 He prepared a **p** for his anger; he did not H5985
Ps 119: 9 How *can* a young person **stay on the p** *of* H784
Ps 119:32 I run in the **p** *of* your commands, for you H2006
Ps 119:35 Direct me in the **p** *of* your commands, for H5985
Ps 119:101 feet from every evil **p** so that I might obey H784
Ps 119:104 precepts; therefore I hate every wrong **p**. H784
Ps 119:105 is a lamp for my feet, a light on my **p**. H5986
Ps 119:128 your precepts right, I hate every wrong **p**. H784
Ps 140: 5 net and have set traps for me along my **p**. H5047
Ps 142: 3 In the **p** where I walk people have hidden H784
Pr 2: 9 is right and just and fair—every good **p**. H5047
Pr 4:14 not set foot on the **p** *of* the wicked or walk H784
Pr 4:18 The **p** *of* the righteous is like the morning H784
Pr 5: 8 Keep to a **p** far from her, do not go near H2006
Pr 12:28 there is life; along that **p** is immortality. H5986
Pr 15:10 discipline awaits anyone who leaves the **p**; H784
Pr 15:19 the **p** *of* the upright is a highway. H784
Pr 15:24 The **p** *of* life leads upward for the prudent H784
Pr 16:29 leads them down a **p** that is not good. H2006
Pr 21:16 strays from the **p** *of* prudence comes to H2006
Pr 23:19 be wise, and set your heart on the right **p**: H2006
Pr 28:10 upright along an evil **p** will fall into their H2006
Ecc 11: 5 As you do not know the **p** *of* the wind, or H2006
Isa 3:12 you astray; they turn you from the **p**. H2006+784
Isa 26: 7 The **p** of the righteous is level; you, the H784
Isa 30:11 get off this **p**, and stop confronting H784
Isa 40:14 showed him the **p** *of* understanding? H2006
Isa 41: 3 by a **p** his feet have not traveled before. H784
Isa 43:16 the sea, a **p** through the mighty waters, H5986
Jer 23:12 "Therefore their **p** will become slippery H2006
Jer 31: 9 of water on a level **p** where they will not H2006
La 3:11 me from the **p** and mangled me and H2006
Hos 2: 6 I will block her **p** with thornbushes; H2006
Hos 13: 7 to them, like a leopard I will lurk by the **p**. H2006
Mt 13: 4 some fell along the **p**, and the birds came *G3847*
Mt 13:19 This is the seed sown along the **p**. *G3847*
Mk 4: 4 some fell along the **p**, and the birds came *G3847*
Mk 4:15 Some people are like seed along the **p** *G3847*
Lk 1:79 to guide our feet into the **p** of peace." *G3847*
Lk 8: 5 some fell along the **p**; it was trampled on, *G3847*
Lk 8:12 Those along the **p** are the ones who hear *G3847*
2Co 6: 3 We put no stumbling block **in** anyone's *p*, so AIT

PATHRUSITES (2)

Ge 10:14 **P**, Kasluhites (from whom the Philistines H7357
1Ch 1:12 **P**, Kasluhites (from whom the Philistines H7357

PATHS (43) [PATH]

Jdg 5: 6 abandoned; travelers took to winding **p**. H784
Job 13:27 watch on all my **p** by putting marks on H784
Job 19: 8 he has shrouded my **p** in darkness. H5986
Job 24:13 who do not know its ways or stay in its **p**. H5986
Job 33:11 shackles; he keeps close watch on all my **p**. H784
Job 38:20 Do you know the **p** *to* their dwellings? H5986
Ps 8: 8 in the sea, all that swim the **p** *of* the seas. H784
Ps 17: 5 My steps have held to your **p**; my feet H5047
Ps 23: 3 me along the right **p** for his name's sake. H5047
Ps 25: 4 me your ways, LORD, teach me your **p**. H2006
Pr 1:15 with them, do not set foot on their **p**; H5986
Pr 1:19 Such are the **p** *of* all who go after ill-gotten H784
Pr 2:13 left the straight **p** to walk in dark ways, H784
Pr 2:15 whose **p** are crooked and who are devious H784
Pr 2:18 to death and her **p** to the spirits of the H5047
Pr 2:19 who go to her return or attain the **p** *of* life. H784
Pr 2:20 good and keep to the **p** *of* the righteous. H784
Pr 3: 6 and he will make your **p** straight. H784
Pr 3:17 pleasant ways, and all her **p** are peace. H5986
Pr 4:11 of wisdom and lead you along straight **p**. H5047
Pr 4:26 thought to the **p** *for* your feet and be H5047
Pr 5: 6 the way of life; her **p** wander aimlessly H5047
Pr 5:21 of the LORD, and he examines all your **p**. H5047
Pr 7:25 heart turn to her ways or stray into her **p**. H5986
Pr 8: 2 the way, where the **p** meet, she takes her H5986
Pr 8:20 of righteousness, along the **p** *of* justice, H5986
Pr 10: 9 takes crooked **p** will be found out. H2006
Pr 11: 5 of the blameless makes their **p** straight, H2006
Pr 22: 5 In the **p** *of* the wicked are snares and H2006
Isa 2: 3 us his ways, so that we may walk in his **p**." H784
Isa 42:16 along unfamiliar **p** I will guide them; H5986
Isa 59: 8 do not know; there is no justice in their **p**. H5047
Jer 6:16 ask for the ancient **p**, ask where the good H5986
Jer 18:15 stumble in their ways, in the ancient **p**. H8666
La 3: 9 of stone; he has made my **p** crooked. H5986
Hos 9: 8 snares await him on all his **p**, and H2006
Mic 4: 2 us his ways, so that we may walk in his **p**." H784
Mt 3: 3 way for the Lord, make straight **p** for him. *G5561*
Mk 1: 3 way for the Lord, make straight **p** for him. *G5561*
Lk 3: 4 way for the Lord, make straight **p** for him. *G5561*
Ac 2:28 You have made known to me **the** *p* of life AIT
Ro 11:33 judgments, and his **p** beyond tracing out! *G3847*
Heb 12:13 "Make level **p** for your feet," so that the *G5579*

PATIENCE (16) [PATIENT]

Pr 19:11 A person's wisdom **yields p**; it is to H799+678
Pr 25:15 Through **p** a ruler can be persuaded H802+678
Ecc 7: 8 and **p** is better than pride. H800+8120
Isa 7:13 Is it not enough *to* **try** *the* **p** *of* humans H4206
Isa 7:13 *Will you* **try** *the* **p** *of* my God also H4206
Ro 2: 4 forbearance and **p**, not realizing that *G3429*
Ro 9:22 bore with great **p** the objects of his wrath *G3429*
2Co 6: 6 understanding, **p** and kindness; in the *G3429*
Col 1:11 you may have great endurance and **p**, *G3429*
Col 3:12 kindness, humility, gentleness and **p**. *G3429*
1Ti 1:16 display his immense **p** as an example *G3429*
2Ti 3:10 my purpose, faith, **p**, love, endurance, *G3429*
2Ti 4: 2 with great **p** and careful instruction. *G3429*
Heb 6:12 through faith and **p** inherit what has been *G3429*
Jas 5:10 as an example *of* **p** in the face of *G3429*
2Pe 3:15 in mind that our Lord's **p** means salvation, *G3429*

PATIENT (18) [PATIENCE, PATIENTLY]

Ne 9:30 For many years *you were* **p** with them. H5432
Job 6:11 What prospects, that I *should be* **p**? H799
Pr 14:29 *Whoever* is **p** has great H800+678
Pr 15:18 the *one who* is **p** calms a quarrel. H800+678
Pr 16:32 Better a **p** *person* than a warrior, one H800+678
Mt 18:26 '*Be* **p** with me,' he begged, 'and I will pay *G3428*
Mt 18:29 begged him, '*Be* **p** with me, and I *G3428*
Ro 12:12 Be joyful in hope, **p** in affliction, faithful in *G5702*
1Co 13: 4 Love *is* **p**, love is kind. It does not envy, it *G3428*
2Co 1: 6 produces in you **p endurance** of the same *G5705*
Eph 4: 2 gentle; be **p**, bearing with one *G3429*
1Th 5:14 help the weak, *be* **p** with everyone. *G3428*
Jas 5: 7 *Be* **p**, then, brothers and sisters, until the *G3428*
Jas 5: 8 You too, *be* **p** and stand firm, because the *G3428*
2Pe 3: 9 Instead *he is* **p** with you, not wanting *G3428*
Rev 1: 9 kingdom and **p endurance** that are ours *G5705*
Rev 13:10 This calls for **p endurance** and *G5705*
Rev 14:12 This calls for **p endurance** on the part of *G5705*

PATIENTLY (10) [PATIENT]

Ps 37: 7 Be still before the LORD and **wait p** for him H2565
Ps 40: 1 *I* **waited p for** the LORD; he turned to H7747+7747
Isa 38:13 *I* **waited p** till dawn, but like a lion he H8750
Hab 3:16 Yet *I will* **wait p** for the day of calamity to H5663
Ac 26: 3 Therefore, I beg you to listen to me **p**. *G3430*
Ro 8:25 do not yet have, we wait for it **p**. *G1328+5705*
Heb 6:15 And so *after* **waiting p**, Abraham received *G3428*
Jas 5: 7 **p waiting** for the autumn and spring rains. *G3428*
1Pe 3:20 when God waited **p** in the days of Noah *G3429*
Rev 3:10 you have kept my command to **endure p**, *G5705*

PATMOS (1)
Rev 1: 9 was on the island *of* **P** because of the G4253

PATRIARCH (2) [PATRIARCHS]
Ac 2:29 confidently that the **p** David died and was G4256
Heb 7: 4 Even the **p** Abraham gave him a tenth of G4256

PATRIARCHS (6) [PATRIARCH]
Jn 7:22 but from the **p**), you circumcise a G4252
Ac 7: 8 Jacob became the father of the twelve **p**. G4256
Ac 7: 9 "Because the **p** were jealous of Joseph G4256
Ro 9: 5 Theirs are the **p**, and from them is traced G4252
Ro 11:28 they are loved on account of the **p**, G4252
Ro 15: 8 that the promises *made to* the **p** might be G4252

PATROBAS (1)
Ro 16:14 Hermes, **P**, Hermas and the other brothers G4259

PATTERN (9)
Ex 25: 9 exactly like the **p** I will show you. H9322
Ex 25:40 them according to the **p** shown you on the H9322
Nu 8: 4 exactly like the **p** the LORD had shown H5260
Ac 7:44 according to the **p** he had seen. G5596
Ro 5:14 did Adam, who is a **p** of the one to come. G5596
Ro 6:17 from your heart the **p** of teaching that has G5596
Ro 12: 2 *Do* not **conform to the p** of this world, but G5372
2Ti 1:13 from me, keep *as* the **p** of sound teaching G5721
Heb 8: 5 according to the **p** shown you on the G5596

PAU (2)
Ge 36:39 His city was named **P**, and his wife's H7185
1Ch 1:50 His city was named **P**, and his wife's H7185

PAUL (206) [PAUL'S, SAUL]
Ac 13: 9 who was also called **P**, filled with the G4263
Ac 13:13 **P** and his companions sailed to Perga in G4263
Ac 13:16 **P** motioned with his hand and said: G4263
Ac 13:42 As **P and Barnabas** were leaving the G899S
Ac 13:43 to Judaism followed **P** and Barnabas, G4263
Ac 13:45 to contradict what **P** was saying and G4263
Ac 13:46 Then **P** and Barnabas answered them G4263
Ac 13:50 up persecution against **P** and Barnabas, G4263
Ac 14: 1 At Iconium **P and Barnabas** went as usual G899S
Ac 14: 3 So **P** and Barnabas spent considerable time NDT
Ac 14: 9 He listened *to* **P** as he was speaking. G4263
Ac 14: 9 **P** looked directly at him, saw that he had G4005S
Ac 14:11 When the crowd saw what **P** had done G4263
Ac 14:12 **P** they called Hermes because he G4263
Ac 14:14 apostles Barnabas and **P** heard of this, G4263
Ac 14:19 They stoned **P** and dragged him outside G4263
Ac 14:23 **P** and Barnabas appointed elders for them in NDT
Ac 15: 2 This brought **P** and Barnabas into sharp G4263
Ac 15: 2 So **P** and Barnabas were appointed G4263
Ac 15:12 to Barnabas and **P** telling about the signs G4263
Ac 15:22 them to Antioch with **P** and Barnabas. G4263
Ac 15:25 with our dear friends Barnabas and **P**— G4263
Ac 15:35 But **P** and Barnabas remained in Antioch G4263
Ac 15:36 Some time later **P** said to Barnabas, "Let G4263
Ac 15:38 **P** did not think it wise to take him G4263
Ac 15:40 **P** chose Silas and left, commended by G4263
Ac 16: 1 **P** came to Derbe and then to Lystra, where a NDT
Ac 16: 3 **P** wanted to take him along on the journey G4263
Ac 16: 6 **P** and his companions traveled throughout NDT
Ac 16: 9 During the night **P** had a vision of a man G4263
Ac 16:10 After **P** had seen the vision, we got ready at NDT
Ac 16:17 She followed **P** and the rest of us G4263
Ac 16:18 Finally **P** became so annoyed that he G4263
Ac 16:19 they seized **P** and Silas and dragged G4263
Ac 16:22 joined in the attack against **P and Silas**, G899S
Ac 16:25 About midnight **P** and Silas were praying G4263
Ac 16:28 But **P** shouted, "Don't harm yourself! We G4263
Ac 16:29 in and fell trembling before **P** and Silas. G4263
Ac 16:36 The jailer told **P**, "The magistrates have G4263
Ac 16:37 But **P** said to the officers: "They beat us G4263
Ac 16:38 they heard that **P** and Silas were Roman NDT
Ac 16:40 After **P** and Silas came out of the prison NDT
Ac 17: 1 When **P** and his companions had passed NDT
Ac 17: 2 his custom, **P** went into the synagogue G4263
Ac 17: 4 were persuaded and joined **P** and Silas, G4263
Ac 17: 5 in search of **P and Silas** in order to bring G899S
Ac 17:10 the believers sent **P** and Silas away to G4263
Ac 17:11 every day to see if **what P said** was true. G4047S
Ac 17:13 learned that **P** was preaching the word of G4263
Ac 17:14 believers immediately sent **P** to the coast, G4263
Ac 17:15 Those who escorted **P** brought him to G4263
Ac 17:16 While **P** was waiting for them in Athens G4263
Ac 17:18 said this because **P** was preaching the good NDT
Ac 17:22 **P** then stood up in the meeting of the G4263
Ac 17:33 **P** left the Council. G4263
Ac 17:34 became followers of **P** and believed. G899
Ac 18: 1 After this, **P** left Athens and went to Corinth. NDT
Ac 18: 2 Jews to leave Rome. **P** went to see them, NDT
Ac 18: 5 **P** devoted himself exclusively to G4263
Ac 18: 6 when they opposed **P** and became abusive, NDT
Ac 18: 7 Then **P** left the synagogue and went next NDT
Ac 18: 8 Corinthians who heard **P** believed and were NDT
Ac 18: 9 One night the Lord spoke *to* **P** in a vision G4263
Ac 18:11 So **P** stayed in Corinth for a year and a half NDT
Ac 18:12 a united attack *on* **P** and brought him to G4263
Ac 18:14 Just as **P** was about to speak, Gallio said G4263
Ac 18:18 **P** stayed on in Corinth for some time G4263
Ac 18:19 where **P** left Priscilla and Aquila. G899S
Ac 18:23 **P** set out from there and traveled from place NDT
Ac 19: 1 **P** took the road through the interior and G4263
Ac 19: 3 So **P** asked, "Then what baptism did you NDT
Ac 19: 4 **P** said, "John's baptism was a baptism of G4263
Ac 19: 6 When **P** placed his hands on them, the G4263
Ac 19: 8 **P** entered the synagogue and spoke boldly NDT
Ac 19: 9 maligned the Way. So **P** left them. He took NDT
Ac 19:11 God did extraordinary miracles through **P**, G4263
Ac 19:13 the name of the Jesus whom **P** preaches, G4263
Ac 19:15 "Jesus I know, and **P** I know about, but G4263
Ac 19:21 happened, **P** decided to go to Jerusalem G4263
Ac 19:26 hear how this fellow **P** has convinced and G4263
Ac 19:30 **P** wanted to appear before the crowd, but G4263
Ac 19:31 province, friends *of* **P**, sent him a G899S
Ac 20: 1 had ended, **P** sent for the disciples and G4263
Ac 20: 7 **P** spoke to the people and, because he G4263
Ac 20: 9 into a deep sleep as **P** talked on and on. G4263
Ac 20:10 **P** went down, threw himself on the young G4263
Ac 20:13 where we were going to take **P** aboard. G4263
Ac 20:16 **P** had decided to sail past Ephesus to G4263
Ac 20:17 **P** sent to Ephesus for the elders of the NDT
Ac 20:36 When **P** had finished speaking, he knelt NDT
Ac 21: 4 the Spirit they urged **P** not to go on to G4263
Ac 21:12 there pleaded with **P** not to go up to G899S
Ac 21:13 Then **P** answered, "Why are you weeping G4263
Ac 21:18 The next day **P** and the rest of us went to G4263
Ac 21:19 **P** greeted them and reported in detail what NDT
Ac 21:20 Then they said *to* **P**: "You see, G899S
Ac 21:26 The next day **P** took the men and purified G4263
Ac 21:27 the province of Asia saw **P** at the temple. G899S
Ac 21:29 in the city with **P** and assumed that Paul G4263
Ac 21:29 assumed that **P** had brought him into G4263
Ac 21:30 Seizing **P**, they dragged him from the G4263
Ac 21:32 his soldiers, they stopped beating **P**. G4263
Ac 21:34 he ordered that **P** be taken into the G899S
Ac 21:35 When **P** reached the steps, the violence of NDT
Ac 21:37 were about to take **P** into the barracks, G4263
Ac 21:39 **P** answered, "I am a Jew, from Tarsus in G4263
Ac 21:40 **P** stood on the steps and motioned to the G4263
Ac 22: 2 they became very quiet. Then **P** said: NDT
Ac 22:22 The crowd listened *to* **P** until he said this G899S
Ac 22:24 ordered that **P** be taken into the G899S
Ac 22:25 **P** said to the centurion standing there G4263
Ac 22:27 The commander went to **P** and asked G899S
Ac 22:28 "But I was born a citizen," **P** replied. G4263
Ac 22:29 when he realized that he had put **P**, G899S
Ac 22:30 find out exactly why **P** was being accused by NDT
Ac 22:30 Then he brought **P** and had him stand G4263
Ac 23: 1 **P** looked straight at the Sanhedrin and G4263
Ac 23: 2 those standing near **P** to strike him on the G899S
Ac 23: 3 Then **P** said to him, "God will strike you G4263
Ac 23: 4 Those who were standing near **P** said, "How NDT
Ac 23: 5 **P** replied, "Brothers, I did not realize that G4263
Ac 23: 6 Then **P**, knowing that some of them were G4263
Ac 23:10 commander was afraid **P** would be torn to G4263
Ac 23:11 night the Lord stood near **P** and said, G899S
Ac 23:12 not to eat or drink until they had killed **P**. G4263
Ac 23:14 not to eat anything until we have killed **P**. G4263
Ac 23:16 he went into the barracks and told **P**. G4263
Ac 23:17 Then **P** called one of the centurions and G4263
Ac 23:18 The centurion said, "**P**, the prisoner, sent G4263
Ac 23:20 to ask you to bring **P** before the Sanhedrin G4263
Ac 23:24 Provide horses *for* **P** so that he may be G4263
Ac 23:31 took **P** with them during the night and G4263
Ac 23:33 the governor and handed **P** over to him. G4263
Ac 23:35 he ordered that **P** be kept under guard G899S
Ac 24: 1 charges against **P** before the governor. G4263
Ac 24: 2 When **P** was called in, Tertullus presented G899S
Ac 24:10 motioned for him to speak, **P** replied: G4263
Ac 24:23 centurion to keep **P** under guard but to G899S
Ac 24:24 He sent for **P** and listened to him as he G4263
Ac 24:25 As **P** talked about righteousness G899S
Ac 24:26 he was hoping that **P** would offer him a G4263
Ac 24:27 a favor to the Jews, he left **P** in prison. G4263
Ac 25: 2 him and presented the charges against **P**. G4263
Ac 25: 3 to them, to have **P** transferred to Jerusalem G899
Ac 25: 4 answered, "**P** is being held at Caesarea G4263
Ac 25: 6 ordered that **P** be brought before him G4263
Ac 25: 7 When **P** came in, the Jews who had come G899S
Ac 25: 8 Then **P** made his defense: "I have done G4263
Ac 25: 9 Jews a favor, said *to* **P**, "Are you willing to G4263
Ac 25:10 **P** answered: "I am now standing before G4263
Ac 25:19 named Jesus who **P** claimed was alive. G4263
Ac 25:21 But when **P** made his appeal to be held G4263
Ac 25:23 the command of Festus, **P** was brought in. G4263
Ac 26: 1 Then Agrippa said to **P**, "You have G4263
Ac 26: 1 So **P** motioned with his hand and began G4263
Ac 26:24 are out of your mind, **P**!" he shouted. G4263
Ac 26:25 most excellent Festus," **P** replied. G4263
Ac 26:28 Then Agrippa said to **P**, "Do you think G4263
Ac 26:29 **P** replied, "Short time or long—I pray to G4263
Ac 27: 1 **P** and some other prisoners were handed G4263
Ac 27: 3 in kindness *to* **P**, allowed him to go G4263
Ac 27: 9 Day of Atonement. So **P** warned them, G4263
Ac 27:11 instead of listening to what **P** said G4263
Ac 27:21 **P** stood up before them and said: G4263
Ac 27:24 'Do not be afraid, **P**. You must stand trial G4263
Ac 27:31 Then **P** said to the centurion and the G4263
Ac 27:33 Just before dawn **P** urged them all to eat G4263
Ac 28: 3 **P** gathered a pile of brushwood and, as he G4263
Ac 28: 5 But **P** shook the snake off into the fire G3836S
Ac 28: 8 **P** went in to see him and, after prayer G4263
Ac 28:15 of these people **P** thanked God and was G4263
Ac 28:16 to Rome, **P** was allowed to live by himself G4263
Ac 28:17 they had assembled, **P** said to them: "My NDT
Ac 28:23 They arranged to meet **P** on a certain day G899S
Ac 28:25 to leave after **P** had made this final G4263
Ac 28:30 For two whole years **P** stayed there in his NDT
Ro 1: 1 **P**, a servant of Christ Jesus, called to be G4263
1Co 1: 1 **P**, called to be an apostle of Christ Jesus G4263
1Co 1:12 of you says, "I follow **P**"; another, "I follow G4263
1Co 1:13 Is Christ divided? Was **P** crucified for you G4263
1Co 1:13 Were you baptized in the name *of* **P**? G4263
1Co 3: 4 when one says, "I follow **P**," and another, G4263
1Co 3: 5 And what is **P**? Only servants G4263
1Co 3:22 whether **P** or Apollos or Cephas or the G4263
1Co 16:21 **P**, write this greeting in my own hand. G4263
2Co 1: 1 **P**, an apostle of Christ Jesus by the will of G4263
2Co 10: 1 I appeal to you—I, **P**, who am "timid G4263
Gal 1: 1 **P**, an apostle—sent not from men nor by G4263
Gal 5: 2 **P**, tell you that if you let yourselves be G4263
Eph 1: 1 **P**, an apostle of Christ Jesus by the will of G4263
Eph 3: 1 For this reason I, **P**, the prisoner of Christ G4263
Php 1: 1 **P** and Timothy, servants of Christ Jesus G4263
Col 1: 1 **P**, an apostle of Christ Jesus by the will of G4263
Col 1:23 of which I, **P**, have become a servant. G4263
Col 4:18 **P**, write this greeting in my own hand G4263
1Th 1: 1 **P**, Silas and Timothy, To the church of the G4263
1Th 2:18 to you—certainly I, **P**, did, again and G4263
2Th 1: 1 **P**, Silas and Timothy, To the church of the G4263
2Th 3:17 **P**, write this greeting in my own hand G4263
1Ti 1: 1 **P**, an apostle of Christ Jesus by the G4263
2Ti 1: 1 **P**, an apostle of Christ Jesus by the will of G4263
Titus 1: 1 **P**, a servant of God and an apostle of G4263
Phm 1 **P**, a prisoner of Christ Jesus, and Timothy G4263
Phm 9 It is as none other than **P**—an old man G4263
Phm 19 **P**, am writing this with my own hand. G4263
2Pe 3:15 as our dear brother **P** also wrote you with G4263

PAUL'S (7) [PAUL]
Ac 16:14 her heart to respond to **P** message. G4263
Ac 19:29 **P** traveling companions from Macedonia G4263
Ac 21:11 over to us, he took **P** belt, tied his own G4263
Ac 23:16 But when the son of **P** sister heard of this G4263
Ac 25:14 Festus discussed **P** case with the king. G4263
Ac 26:24 At this point Festus interrupted **P** defense G899S
Ac 27:43 wanted to spare **P** life and kept them from G4263

PAULUS (1) [SERGIUS]
Ac 13: 7 an attendant of the proconsul, Sergius **P**. G4263

PAVEMENT (9)
Ex 24:10 something like a **p** made of lapis lazuli H4246
2Ch 7: 3 they knelt on the **p** with their faces to the H8367
Est 1: 6 gold and silver on a **mosaic p** *of* porphyry, H8367
Jer 43: 9 in clay in the **brick p** at the entrance to H4861
Eze 40:17 I saw some rooms and a **p** that had been H8367
Eze 40:17 there were thirty rooms along the **p**. H8367
Eze 40:18 as they were long; this was the lower **p**. H8367
Eze 42: 3 section opposite the **p** of the outer court, H8367
Jn 19:13 seat at a place known as the **Stone P** G3346

PAVILION (1)
Job 36:29 the clouds, how he thunders from his **p**? H6109

PAW (2) [PAWS]
1Sa 17:37 rescued me from the **p** *of* the lion and the H3338
1Sa 17:37 of the lion and the **p** *of* the bear will H3338

PAWS (2) [PAW]
Lev 11:27 that walk on their **p** are unclean for you; H4090
Job 39:21 *It* **p** fiercely, rejoicing in its strength, and H2916

PAY (143) [PAID, PAYING, PAYMENT, PAYS, REPAID, REPAY, REPAYING, REPAYMENT, REPAYS]
Ge 23:13 *I will* **p** the price of the field H5989
Ge 30:28 "Name your wages, and *I will* **p** them." H5989
Ge 34:12 you like, and *I'll* **p** whatever you ask me. H5989
Ex 2: 9 nurse him for me, and I *will* **p** you." H5989+8510
Ex 4: 8 believe you or **p attention** to the first sign, H9048
Ex 5: 9 keep working and **p** no **attention** to lies." H9120
Ex 15:26 if *you* **p attention** to his commands and H263
Ex 21:19 party *must* **p** the injured person *for* any H5989
Ex 21:32 the owner *must* **p** thirty shekels of silver to H5989
Ex 21:34 pit *must* **p** the owner **for the loss** H8966+4084
Ex 21:36 the owner **must p**, animal for H8966+8966
Ex 22: 1 sells it *must* **p back** five head of cattle H8966
Ex 22: 3 they must be sold to **p** for their theft. NDT
Ex 22: 4 sheep—*they must* **p back** double. H8966
Ex 22: 7 the thief, if caught, *must* **p back** double. H8966
Ex 22: 9 declare guilty *must* **p back** double to the H8966
Ex 22:13 and *shall* not *be required to* **p** *for* the torn H8966
Ex 22:15 animal, the borrower *will* not *have to* **p**. H8966
Ex 22:16 *he* **must p** the **bride-price**, and H4555+4555
Ex 22:17 *he must still* **p** the bride-price for H9202+4084
Ex 23:21 **P attention** to him and listen to what he H9068
Ex 30:12 each one *must* **p** the LORD a ransom for his H5989
Lev 5:16 **p an additional** *penalty of* a fifth of its H3578
Lev 25:51 *they must* **p** *for* their redemption a larger H8740
Lev 25:52 compute that and **p** *for* their redemption H8740
Lev 26:41 are humbled and *they* **p for** their sin, H8355
Lev 26:43 They *will* **p for** their sins because they H8355
Lev 27: 8 the vow *is* too **poor to p** the specified H4575
Lev 27:23 the owner *must* **p** its value on that H5989
Nu 20:19 any of your water, *we will* **p** *for* it. H4836+5989

Dt 2: 6 You are to p them in silver for the food you H8690
Dt 7:12 If you p attention to these laws and are H9048
Dt 22:29 he shall p her father fifty shekels of silver H5989
Dt 23:18 house of the LORD your God to p any vow, NDT
Dt 23:21 do not be slow to p it, for the LORD your H8966
Dt 24:15 P them their wages each day before H5989
Dt 28:13 If you p attention to the commands of the H9048
Jdg 9:57 made the people of Shechem p for H8740+928+8031
1Sa 4:20 she did not respond or p any attention. H8883
1Sa 25:25 Please p no attention, my lord, to that H8492
2Sa 1: 2 he fell to the ground to p him honor. H2556
2Sa 9: 6 to David, he bowed down to p him honor. H2556
2Sa 12: 6 He must p for that lamb four times over H8966
2Sa 14: 4 her face to the ground to p him honor, H2556
2Sa 14:22 his face to the ground to p him honor, H2556
1Ki 2:23 if Adonijah does not p with his life for this H928
1Ki 5: 6 and I will p you for your men whatever H5989
1Ki 20:39 his life, or you must p a talent of silver. H9202
1Ki 21: 2 I will p you whatever it is worth." H5989+4084
2Ki 3: 4 he had to p the king of Israel a tribute of H8740
2Ki 3:14 I would not p any attention H5564+2256+8011
2Ki 4: 7 "Go, sell the oil and p your debts. H8966
2Ki 9:26 and I will surely make you p for it on this H8966
2Ki 12:15 they gave the money to p the workers, H5989
2Ki 18:14 and I will p whatever you demand of me." H5951
2Ki 22: 5 And have these men p the workers who H5989
Ne 5: 4 to borrow money to p the king's tax on our H4200
Ne 9:34 they did not p attention to your H7992
Est 3: 2 would not kneel down or p him honor. H2556
Est 3: 5 would not kneel down or p him honor, H2556
Est 4: 7 Haman had promised to p into the royal H9202
Job 6:22 p a ransom for me from your wealth, H8815
Job 33: 1 to my words; p attention to everything I say. H263
Job 33:31 "P attention, Job, and listen to me; be H7992
Job 41:11 has a claim against me that I must p? H8966
Ps 45:10 and p careful attention: H8011+2256+5742+265
Ps 79:12 P back into the laps of our neighbors H8740
Ps 94: 2 p back to the proud what they deserve. H8740
Pr 4: 1 p attention and gain understanding. H7992
Pr 4:20 My son, p attention to what I say; turn H7992
Pr 5: 1 My son, p attention to my wisdom, turn H7992
Pr 6:31 if he is caught, he must p sevenfold H8966
Pr 7:24 listen to me; p attention to what I say. H7992
Pr 13:13 Whoever scorns instruction will p for it H2472
Pr 19:19 hot-tempered person must p the penalty; H5951
Pr 20:22 not say, "I'll p you back for this wrong!" H8966
Pr 22: 3 the simple keep going and p the penalty. H6740
Pr 22:17 P attention and turn your ear to the H9048
Pr 22:27 if you lack the means to p, your very bed H8966
Pr 24:29 I'll p them back for what they did. H8740
Pr 27:12 the simple keep going and p the penalty. H6740
Pr 30:10 they will curse you, and you will p for it. H870
Ecc 7:21 Do not p attention to every word people H5989
Isa 28:23 my voice; p attention and hear what I say. H7992
Isa 34: 1 listen; p attention, you peoples! H7992
Isa 42:20 but you p no attention; your ears H9068
Isa 42:23 this or p close attention in H7992+2256+9048
Isa 65: 6 I will not keep silent but will p back in full; H8966
Isa 65: 6 back in full; I will p it back into their laps H8966
Jer 7:24 But they did not listen or p attention H5742+265
Jer 7:26 did not listen to me or p attention. H5742+265
Jer 11: 8 But they did not listen or p attention H5742+265
Jer 13:15 Hear and p attention, do not be arrogant H263
Jer 17:23 Yet they did not listen or p attention H5742+265
Jer 18:18 tongues and p no attention to anything H7992
Jer 34:14 listen to me or p attention to me. H5742+265
Jer 44: 5 But they did not listen or p attention H5742+265
La 3:64 P them back what they deserve, LORD, for H8740
Eze 16:41 and you will no longer p your lovers. H924+5989
Eze 29:19 plunder the land as p for his army. H8510
Eze 40: 4 listen closely and p attention to H8492
Da 3:12 Abednego—who p no attention to you A10682
Hos 2:12 which she said were her p from her lovers; H921
Hos 5: 1 P attention, you Israelites H7992
Hos 12:12 and to p for her he tended sheep. NDT
Zec 1: 4 they would not listen or p attention to me, H7992
Zec 7:11 "But they refused to p attention H7992
Zec 11:12 you think it best, give me my p; but if not, H8510
Mt 7: 3 eye and p no attention to the plank in G2917
Mt 17:24 "Doesn't your teacher p the temple tax?" G5464
Mt 18:25 Since he was not able to p, the master G625
Mt 18:26 he begged, 'and I will p back everything. G625
Mt 18:28 'P back what you owe me!' G625
Mt 18:29 'Be patient with me, and I will p it back. G625
Mt 18:30 into prison until he could p the debt. G625
Mt 18:34 until he should p back all he owed. G625
Mt 20: 2 He agreed to p them a denarius for the G1666
Mt 20: 4 and I will p you whatever is right. G1443
Mt 20: 8 'Call the workers and p them their wages G625
Mt 20:14 Take your p and go. I want to give the one AIT
Mt 22:16 you p no attention to who they are G1063+1650+4725+476
Mt 22:17 Is it right to p the imperial tax to Caesar G1443
Mk 12:14 because you p no attention to who they G1063
Mk 12:14 Is it right to p the imperial tax to Caesar G1443
Mk 12:15 Should we p or shouldn't we?" But Jesus G1443
Lk 3:14 people falsely—be content with your p." G4072
Lk 6:41 eye and p no attention to the plank in G2917
Lk 7:42 of them had the money to p him back, G625
Lk 19: 8 I will p back four times the amount. G625
Lk 20:22 Is it right for us to p taxes to Caesar or not?" G1443
Ac 21:24 purification rites and p their expenses, G1251
Ac 22:28 "I had to p a lot of money for my G3227
Ac 25:13 at Caesarea to p their respects to Festus. G832
Ro 13: 6 This is also why you p taxes, for the G5464
Ro 13: 7 If you owe taxes, p taxes; if revenue, then NDT
Gal 5:10 that may be, will have to p the penalty. G1002
2Th 1: 6 He will p back trouble to those who trouble G500
Titus 1:14 and will p no attention to Jewish myths G4668
Phm 19 I will p it back—not to mention that you G702
Heb 2: 1 We must p the most careful attention G4668
Jas 5: 4 The wages you failed to p the workers who G691
2Pe 1:19 you will do well to p attention to it G4668
Rev 18: 6 p her back double for what she has done. G1488

PAYING (9) [PAY]

Ex 21: 2 he shall go free, without p anything. H2855
2Sa 24:24 I insist on p you for it. H7864+928+4697+7864
1Ch 21:24 I insist on p the full price. H7864+7864
Pr 21:11 by p attention to the wise they get H8505
Jer 22:13 nothing, not p them for their labor. H5989
Joel 3: 4 If you are p me back, I will swiftly and H1694
Jnh 1: 3 After p the fare, he went aboard and H5989
Mt 22:19 Show me the coin used for p the tax." They AIT
2Th 3: 8 did we eat anyone's food without p for it. G1562

PAYMENT (17) [PAY]

Ge 31:39 And you demanded p from me for H1335
Ge 47:14 in Egypt and Canaan in p for the grain they H928
Ex 21:11 to go free, without any p of money. H2855+401
Ex 21:30 However, if p is demanded, the owner H4111
Ex 21:30 redeem his life by the p of whatever is H5989
Lev 22:16 so bring upon them guilt requiring p. H873
Dt 15: 2 They shall not require p from anyone H5601
Dt 15: 3 You may require p from a foreigner, but H5601
Job 31:39 its yield without p or broken the spirit of H4084
Ps 49: 8 a life is costly, no p is ever enough— NDT
Ps 109:20 the LORD's p to my accusers, to those who H7190
Isa 65: 7 I will measure into their laps the full p for H4499
Eze 16:31 unlike a prostitute, because you scorned p. H924
Eze 16:34 you give p and none is given to you. H924
Lk 23: 2 He opposes p of taxes to Caesar and G1443
Ac 1:18 With the p he received for his wickedness G3635
Php 4:18 I have received full p and have more than G600

PAYS (8) [PAY]

Ge 50:15 against us and p us back for all the H8740+8740
Job 35:13 the Almighty p no attention to it. H8800
Ps 31:23 but the proud he p back in full. H8966
Pr 1:24 I call and no one p attention when I H7992
Pr 17: 4 a liar p attention to a destructive tongue. H263
Pr 17:13 the house of one who p back evil for good H8740
Da 6:13 exiles from Judah, p no attention to you A10682
1Th 5:15 Make sure that nobody p back wrong for G625

PAZZEZ See BETH PAZZEZ

PEACE (251) [PACIFIES, PACIFY, PEACE-LOVING, PEACEABLE, PEACEABLY, PEACEFUL, PEACEFULLY, PEACEMAKERS, PEACETIME]

Ge 15:15 to your ancestors in p and be buried at a H8934
Ge 44:17 rest of you, go back to your father in p." H8934
Lev 26: 6 " 'I will grant p in the land, and you will H8934
Nu 6:26 turn his face toward you and give you p." H8934
Nu 25:12 I am making my covenant of p with him. H8934
Dt 2:26 king of Heshbon offering p and saying, H8934
Dt 20:10 make its people an offer of p. H8934
Dt 20:12 If they refuse to make p and they engage H8966
Jos 9:15 made a treaty of p with them to let them H8934
Jos 10: 1 of Gibeon had made a treaty of p with H8966
Jos 10: 4 "because it has made p with Joshua and H8966
Jos 11:19 not one city made a treaty of p with the H8966
Jdg 3:11 So the land had p for forty years, until H9200
Jdg 3:30 the land had p for eighty years. H9200
Jdg 5:31 Then the land had p forty years. H9200
Jdg 6:23 the LORD said to him, "P! Do not be afraid. H8934
Jdg 6:24 the LORD there and called it The LORD Is P. H8934
Jdg 8:28 lifetime, the land had p forty years. H9200
Jdg 18: 6 "Go in p. Your journey has the H8934
Jdg 18: 7 like the Sidonians, at p and secure. H9200
Jdg 18:27 against a people at p and secure. H9200
Jdg 21:13 sent an offer of p to the Benjamites at the H8934
1Sa 1:17 answered, "Go in p, and may the God of H8934
1Sa 7:14 And there was p between Israel and the H8934
1Sa 16: 4 They asked, "Do you come in p?" H8934
1Sa 16: 5 in p; I have come to sacrifice to the H8934
1Sa 20:13 not let you know and send you away in p. H8934
1Sa 20:42 said to David, "Go in p, for we have sworn H8934
1Sa 25:35 brought him and said, "Go home in p. H8934
1Sa 29: 7 Now turn back and go in p; do nothing to H8934
2Sa 3:21 David sent Abner away, and he went in p. H8934
2Sa 3:22 sent him away, and he had gone in p. H8934
2Sa 3:23 sent him away and that he had gone in p. H8934
2Sa 10:19 they made p with the Israelites and H8966
2Sa 15: 9 said to him, "Go in p." So he went to H8934
1Ki 2: 6 his gray head go down to the grave in p. H8934
1Ki 2:33 may there be the LORD's p forever. H8934
1Ki 4:24 Tiphsah to Gaza, and had p on all sides. H8934
1Ki 20:18 "If they have come out for p, take them H8934
1Ki 22:17 Let each one go home in p.'" H8934
1Ki 22:44 Jehoshaphat was also at p with the king of H8966
2Ki 5:19 "Go in p," Elisha said. After Naaman had H8934
2Ki 9:17 meet them and ask, 'Do you come in p? H8934
2Ki 9:18 what the king says: 'Do you come in p?'" H8934
2Ki 9:18 "What do you have to do with p?" Jehu H8934
2Ki 9:19 what the king says: 'Do you come in p?'" H8934
2Ki 9:19 replied, "What do you have to do with p? H8934
2Ki 9:22 he asked, "Have you come in p, Jehu?" H8934
2Ki 9:22 "How can there be p," Jehu replied, "as H8934
2Ki 9:31 "Have you come in a, you Zimri, H8934
2Ki 18:31 Make p with me and come out to me H1388
2Ki 20:19 "Will there not be p and security in my H8934
2Ki 22:20 ancestors, and you will be buried in p. H8934
1Ch 12:17 "If you have come to me in p to help me H8934
1Ch 19:19 they made p with David and became H8966
1Ch 22: 9 a son who will be a man of p and rest, H4957
1Ch 22: 9 I will grant Israel p and quiet during his H8934
2Ch 14: 1 his days the country was at p for ten years. H9200
2Ch 14: 5 the kingdom was at p under him. H9200
2Ch 14: 6 cities of Judah, since the land was at p. H9200
2Ch 18:16 Let each one go home in p.'" H8934
2Ch 20:30 And the kingdom of Jehoshaphat was at p, H9200
2Ch 34:28 ancestors, and you will be buried in p. H8934
Job 3:13 For now I would be lying down in p; H9200
Job 3:26 I have no p, no quietness; I have no rest H8922
Job 5:23 the wild animals will be at p with you. H8966
Job 21:13 prosperity and go down to the grave in p. H8092
Job 22:21 "Submit to God and be at p with him; in H8966
Ps 4: 8 In p I will lie down and sleep, for you H8934
Ps 29:11 the LORD blesses his people with p. H8934
Ps 34:14 evil and do good; seek p and pursue it. H8934
Ps 37:11 the land and enjoy p and prosperity. H8934
Ps 37:37 upright; a future awaits those who seek p. H8934
Ps 85: 8 he promises p to his people, his H8934
Ps 85:10 righteousness and p kiss each other. H8934
Ps 119:165 Great p have those who love your law H8934
Ps 120: 6 have I lived among those who hate p. H8934
Ps 120: 7 I am for p; but when I speak, they are H8934
Ps 122: 6 Pray for the p of Jerusalem: "May those H8934
Ps 122: 7 May there be p within your walls and H8934
Ps 122: 8 friends, I will say, "P be within you." H8934
Ps 125: 5 banish with the evildoers. P be on Israel. H8934
Ps 128: 6 your children's children—p be on Israel. H8934
Ps 147:14 He grants p to your borders and satisfies H8934
Pr 3: 2 years and bring you p and prosperity. H8934
Pr 3:17 pleasant ways, and all her paths are p. H8934
Pr 12:20 but those who promote p have joy. H8934
Pr 14:30 A heart at p gives life to the body, but H5341
Pr 16: 7 he causes their enemies to make p with H8966
Pr 17: 1 a dry crust with p and quiet than a house H8932
Pr 29: 9 fool rages and scoffs, and there is no p. H5739
Pr 29:17 and they will give you p; they will H5663
Ecc 3: 8 to hate, a time for war and a time for p. H8934
Isa 9: 6 Everlasting Father, Prince of P. H8934
Isa 9: 7 his government and p there will be no H8934
Isa 14: 7 All the lands are at rest and at p; they H9200
Isa 26: 3 will keep in perfect p those whose H8934+8934
Isa 26:12 you establish p for us; all that we H8934
Isa 27: 5 refuge; let them make p with me, yes, H8934
Isa 27: 5 with me, yes, let them make p with me." H8934
Isa 32:17 The fruit of that righteousness will be p H8934
Isa 33: 7 the streets; the envoys of p weep bitterly. H8934
Isa 36:16 Make p with me and come out to me H1388
Isa 39: 8 "There will be p and security in my H8934
Isa 48:18 your p would have been like a river H8934
Isa 48:22 "There is no p," says the LORD, "for the H8934
Isa 52: 7 who proclaim p, who bring good H8934
Isa 53: 5 that brought us p was on him, H8934
Isa 54:10 shaken nor my covenant of p be removed," H8934
Isa 54:13 by the LORD, and great will be their p. H8934
Isa 55:12 will go out in joy and be led forth in p; H8934
Isa 57: 2 Those who walk uprightly enter into p H8934
Isa 57:19 P, peace, to those far and near," says the H8934
Isa 57:19 p, to those far and near," says the H8934
Isa 57:21 "There is no p," says my God, "for the H8934
Isa 59: 8 The way of p they do not know; there is H8934
Isa 59: 8 one who walks along them will know p. H8934
Isa 60:17 I will make p your governor and H8934
Isa 66:12 "I will extend p to her like a river, and the H8934
Jer 4:10 'You will have p,' when the sword is at H8934
Jer 6:14 'P, peace,' they say, when there is no H8934
Jer 6:14 p,' they say, when there is no H8934
Jer 6:14 they say, when there is no p. H8934
Jer 8:11 "P, peace," they say, when there is no H8934
Jer 8:11 "Peace, p," they say, when there is no H8934
Jer 8:11 they say, when there is no p. H8934
Jer 8:15 We hoped for p but no good has come H8934
Jer 14:13 I will give you lasting p in this place. H8934
Jer 14:19 We hoped for p but no good has come H8934
Jer 23:17 You will have p.' And to all who H8934
Jer 28: 9 who prophesies p will be recognized as H8934
Jer 29: 7 seek the p and prosperity of the city to H8934
Jer 30: 5 " 'Cries of fear are heard—terror, not p. H8934
Jer 30:10 Jacob will again have p and security, and H9200
Jer 33: 6 let them enjoy abundant p and security. H8934
Jer 33: 9 abundant prosperity and p I provide for it. H8934
Jer 46:27 Jacob will again have p and security, and H9200
La 3:17 I have been deprived of p; I have H8934
Eze 7:25 terror comes, they will seek p in vain. H8934
Eze 13:10 saying, "P," when there is no H8934
Eze 13:10 when there is no p, and because, when H8934
Eze 13:16 saw visions of p for her when there H8934
Eze 13:16 of peace for her when there was no p, H8934
Eze 34:25 make a covenant of p with them and rid H8934
Eze 37:26 I will make a covenant of p with them; it H8934
Da 10:19 "P! Be strong now; be H8934

P

Mic 3: 5 they proclaim '**p**' if they have something H8934
Mic 5: 5 And he will be our **p** when the Assyrians H8934
Na 1:15 who brings good news, who proclaims **p**! H8934
Hag 2: 9 'And in this place I will grant **p**,' declares H8934
Zec 1:11 found the whole world at rest and **in p**." H9200
Zec 8:19 Therefore love truth and **p**." H8934
Zec 9:10 He will proclaim **p** to the nations. His rule H8934
Mal 2: 5 a covenant of life and **p**, and I gave them H8934
Mal 2: 6 He walked with me in **p** and uprightness H8934
Mt 10:13 is deserving, let your **p** rest on it; if it is *G1645*
Mt 10:13 if it is not, let your **p** return to you. *G1645*
Mt 10:34 that I have come to bring **p** to the earth. *G1645*
Mt 10:34 I did not come to bring **p**, but a sword. *G1645*
Mk 5:34 Go in **p** and be freed from your suffering." *G1645*
Mk 9:50 yourselves, and *be* **at p** with each other." *G1644*
Lk 1:79 to guide our feet into the path *of* **p**." *G1645*
Lk 2:14 on earth **p** to those on whom his *G1645*
Lk 2:29 you may now dismiss your servant in **p**. *G1645*
Lk 7:50 "Your faith has saved you; go in **p**. *G1645*
Lk 8:48 your faith has healed you. Go in **p**." *G1645*
Lk 10: 5 enter a house, first say, '**P** to this house. *G1645*
Lk 10: 6 If someone who promotes **p** is there, your *G1645*
Lk 10: 6 peace is there, your **p** will rest on them; if *G1645*
Lk 12:51 Do you think I came to bring **p** on earth *G1645*
Lk 14:32 a long way off and will ask for terms of **p**. *G1645*
Lk 19:38 "**P** in heaven and glory in the highest!" *G1645*
Lk 19:42 on this day what would bring you **p**— *G1645*
Lk 24:36 them and said to them, "**P** be with you." *G1645*
Jn 14:27 **P** I leave with you; my peace I give you. *G1645*
Jn 14:27 I leave with you; my **p** I give you. I do not *G1645*
Jn 16:33 so that in me you may have **p**. *G1645*
Jn 20:19 among them and said, "**P** be with you!" *G1645*
Jn 20:21 Again Jesus said, "**P** be with you! As the *G1645*
Jn 20:26 among them and said, "**P** be with you!" *G1645*
Ac 9:31 Samaria enjoyed a *time of* **p** and was *G1645*
Ac 10:36 the good news *of* **p** through Jesus Christ, *G1645*
Ac 12:20 the king, they asked *for* **p**, because they *G1645*
Ac 15:33 with the **blessing of p** to return to *G1645*
Ac 16:36 Now you can leave. Go in **p**." *G1645*
Ac 24: 2 enjoyed a long period *of* **p** under you, *G1645*
Ro 1: 7 Grace and **p** to you from God our Father *G1645*
Ro 2:10 honor and **p** for everyone who does good: *G1645*
Ro 3:17 the way *of* **p** they do not know. *G1645*
Ro 5: 1 we have **p** with God through our Lord *G1645*
Ro 8: 6 mind governed by the Spirit is life and **p**. *G1645*
Ro 12:18 depends on you, **live at p** with everyone. *G1644*
Ro 14:17 **p** and joy in the Holy Spirit, *G1645*
Ro 14:19 effort to do what *leads to* **p** and to mutual *G1645*
Ro 15:13 you with all joy and **p** as you trust in him, *G1645*
Ro 15:33 The God *of* **p** be with you all. Amen. *G1645*
Ro 16:20 The God *of* **p** will soon crush Satan under *G1645*
1Co 1: 3 Grace and **p** to you from God our Father *G1645*
1Co 7:15 God has called us to live in **p**. *G1645*
1Co 14:33 For God is not a God of disorder but *of* **p** *G1645*
1Co 16:11 him on his way in **p** so that he may return *G1645*
2Co 1: 2 Grace and **p** to you from God our Father *G1645*
2Co 2:13 I still had no **p** of mind, because I did not *G457*
2Co 13:11 one another, be of one mind, **live in p**. *G1644*
2Co 13:11 the God of love and **p** will be with you. *G1645*
Gal 1: 3 Grace and **p** to you from God our Father *G1645*
Gal 5:22 Spirit is love, joy, **p**, forbearance, kindness *G1645*
Gal 6:16 **P** and mercy to all who follow this rule— *G1645*
Eph 1: 2 Grace and **p** to you from God our Father *G1645*
Eph 2:14 For he himself is our **p**, who has made the *G1645*
Eph 2:15 humanity out of the two, thus making **p**, *G1645*
Eph 2:17 came and preached **p** to you who were far *G1645*
Eph 2:17 were far away and **p** to those who were *G1645*
Eph 4: 3 unity of the Spirit through the bond *of* **p**. *G1645*
Eph 6:15 that comes from the gospel *of* **p**. *G1645*
Eph 6:23 **P** to the brothers and sisters, and love *G1645*
Php 1: 2 Grace and **p** to you from God our Father *G1645*
Php 4: 7 And the **p** of God, which transcends all *G1645*
Php 4: 9 And the God *of* **p** will be with you. *G1645*
Col 1: 2 Grace and **p** to you from God our Father. *G1645*
Col 1:20 in heaven, *by* **making p** through his blood *G1647*
Col 3:15 Let the **p** of Christ rule in your hearts *G1645*
Col 3:15 of one body you were called to **p**. *G4005S*
1Th 1: 1 the Lord Jesus Christ: Grace and **p** to you. *G1645*
1Th 5: 3 people are saying, "**P** and safety, *G1645*
1Th 5:13 **Live in p** with each other. *G1644*
1Th 5:23 God himself, the God *of* **p**, sanctify you *G1645*
2Th 1: 2 Grace and **p** to you from God the Father *G1645*
2Th 3:16 Now may the Lord *of* **p** himself give you *G1645*
2Th 3:16 himself give you **p** at all times and in *G1645*
1Ti 1: 2 mercy and **p** from God the Father and *G1645*
2Ti 1: 2 mercy and **p** from God the Father and *G1645*
2Ti 2:22 love and **p**, along with those who *G1645*
Titus 1: 4 Grace and **p** from God the Father and *G1645*
Phm 3 Grace and **p** to you from God our Father *G1645*
Heb 7: 2 "king of Salem" means "king *of* **p**. *G1645*
Heb 12:11 righteousness and **p** for those who have *G1646*
Heb 12:14 every effort to live *in* **p** with everyone and *G1645*
Heb 13:20 Now may the God *of* **p**, who through the *G1645*
Jas 2:16 to them, "Go in **p**; keep warm and well *G1645*
Jas 3:18 who sow in **p** reap a harvest of *G1645*
1Pe 1: 2 Grace and **p** be yours in abundance. *G1645*
1Pe 3:11 do good; they must seek **p** and pursue it. *G1645*
1Pe 5:14 **P** to all of you who are in Christ *G1645*
2Pe 1: 2 Grace and **p** be yours in abundance *G1645*
2Pe 3:14 spotless, blameless and at **p** with him. *G1645*
2Jn 3 mercy and **p** from God the Father and *G1645*
3Jn 14 will talk face to face. **P** to you. The friends *G1645*
Jude 2 **p** and love be yours in abundance. *G1645*
Rev 1: 4 Grace and **p** to you from him who is, and *G1645*
Rev 6: 4 given power to take **p** from the earth and *G1645*

PEACE-LOVING (1) [PEACE, LOVE]
Jas 3:17 is first of all pure; then **p**, considerate, *G1646*

PEACEABLE (1) [PEACE]
Titus 3: 2 to be **p** and considerate, and *G285*

PEACEABLY (2) [PEACE]
Jdg 11:13 to the Jordan. Now give it back **p**." H928+8934
Ps 35:20 They do not speak **p**, but devise false H8934

PEACEFUL (8) [PEACE]
2Sa 20:19 We are the **p** and faithful in Israel. H8966
1Ki 5:12 There were **p relations** between Hiram H8934
1Ch 4:40 the land was spacious, **p** and quiet. H9200
Isa 32:18 My people will live in **p** dwelling places H8934
Isa 33:20 will see Jerusalem, a **p** abode, a tent that H8633
Jer 25:37 The **p** meadows will be laid waste H8934
Eze 38:11 I will attack a **p** and unsuspecting people H9200
1Ti 2: 2 that we may live **p** and quiet lives in all *G2475*

PEACEFULLY (5) [PEACE]
Ge 26:29 you well and sent you away **p**. H928+8934
Ge 26:31 on their way, and they went away **p**. H928+8934
1Ki 2:13 "Do you come **p**?" He answered, H8934
1Ki 2:13 He answered, "Yes, **p**." H8934
Jer 34: 5 you will die **p**. As people made a H928+8934

PEACEMAKERS (2) [PEACE]
Mt 5: 9 Blessed are the **p**, for they will be called *G1648*
Jas 3:18 **P** who sow in peace reap a harvest *G4472+1645*

PEACETIME (1) [PEACE]
1Ki 2: 5 shedding their blood in **p** as if in battle H8934

PEACOCKS (KJV) BABOONS, OSTRICH

PEAKS (2)
Nu 23: 9 From the rocky **p** I see them, from the H8031
Ps 95: 4 and the mountain **p** belong to him. H9361

PEAL (1) [PEALS]
Rev 14: 2 waters and like a loud **p** of thunder. *G5889*

PEALS (5) [PEAL]
Rev 4: 5 of lightning, rumblings and **p of thunder**. *G1103*
Rev 8: 5 there came **p of thunder**, rumblings, *G1103*
Rev 11:19 rumblings, **p of thunder**, an earthquake *G1103*
Rev 16:18 **p of thunder** and a severe earthquake. *G1103*
Rev 19: 6 rushing waters and like loud **p** of thunder, *G5889*

PEARL (1) [MOTHER-OF-PEARL, PEARLS]
Rev 21:21 each gate made of a single **p**. *G3449*

PEARLS (7) [PEARL]
Mt 7: 6 is sacred; do not throw your **p** to pigs. *G3449*
Mt 13:45 is like a merchant looking for fine **p**. *G3449*
1Ti 2: 9 gold or **p** or expensive clothes, *G3449*
Rev 17: 4 with gold, precious stones and **p**. *G3449*
Rev 18:12 precious stones and **p**; fine linen, purple, *G3449*
Rev 18:16 with gold, precious stones and **p**! *G3449*
Rev 21:21 The twelve gates were twelve **p**, each gate *G3449*

PEBBLE (2) [PEBBLES]
2Sa 17:13 the valley until not so much as a **p** is left." H7656
Am 9: 9 and not a **p** will reach the ground. H7656

PEBBLES (1) [PEBBLE]
Ps 147:17 He hurls down his hail like **p**. Who can H7326

PECKED (1)
Pr 30:17 *will be* **p out** *by* the ravens of the valley H5941

PEDAHEL (1)
Nu 34:28 **P** son of Ammihud, the leader from the H7010

PEDAHZUR (5)
Nu 1:10 from Manasseh, Gamaliel son of **P**; H7011
Nu 2:20 people of Manasseh is Gamaliel son of **P**. H7011
Nu 7:54 On the eighth day Gamaliel son of **P**, the H7011
Nu 7:59 was the offering of Gamaliel son of **P**. H7011
Nu 10:23 Gamaliel son of **P** was over the division of H7011

PEDAIAH (8)
2Ki 23:36 name was Zebidah daughter of **P**; H7015
1Ch 3:18 Malkiram, **P**, Shenazzar, Jekamiah H7015
1Ch 3:19 The sons of **P**: Zerubbabel and Shimei H7015
1Ch 27:20 half the tribe of Manasseh: Joel son of **P**; H7016
Ne 3:25 Next to him, **P** son of Parosh H7015
Ne 8: 4 on his left were **P**, Mishael, H7015
Ne 11: 7 of Joed, the son of **P**, the son of Kolaiah, H7015
Ne 13:13 a Levite named **P** in charge of the H7015

PEDDLE (1)
2Co 2:17 *we do* not **p** the word of God **for profit** *G1639+2836*

PEDESTAL (1)
Am 5:26 of your king, the **p** *of* your idols, the star of H3962

PEELED (1) [PEELING, PEELS]
Ge 30:38 Then he placed the **p** branches in all the H7202

PEELING (1) [PEELED]
Ge 30:37 *made* white stripes on them *by* **p** *the* bark H7202

PEELS (1) [PEELED]
Job 30:30 My skin grows black and **p**; my H4946+6584

PEERED (1) [PEERING]
Jdg 5:28 "Through the window **p** Sisera's mother H9207

PEERING (1) [PEERED]
SS 2: 9 the windows, **p** through the lattice. H7438

PEG (7) [PEGS]
Jdg 4:21 picked up a tent **p** and a hammer and H3845
Jdg 4:21 She drove the **p** through his temple into H3845
Jdg 4:22 Sisera with the **tent p** through his temple H3845
Jdg 5:26 Her hand reached for the **tent p**, her right H3845
Isa 22:23 I will drive him like a **p** into a firm place H3845
Isa 22:25 "the **p** driven into the firm place will give H3845
Zec 10: 4 from him the **tent p**, from him the battle H3845

PEGS (8) [PEG]
Ex 27:19 including all the **tent p** *for* it and those H3845
Ex 35:18 the **tent p** *for* the tabernacle and for the H3845
Ex 38:20 All the **tent p** of the tabernacle and of the H3845
Ex 38:31 all the **tent p** *for* the tabernacle and H3845
Ex 39:40 the ropes and **tent p** *for* the courtyard; all H3845
Nu 3:37 with their bases, **tent p** and ropes. H3845
Nu 4:32 courtyard with their bases, **tent p**, ropes, H3845
Eze 15: 3 Do they make **p** from it to hang things on? H3845

PEKAH (11) [PEKAH'S]
2Ki 15:25 of his chief officers, **P** son of Remaliah H7220
2Ki 15:25 So **P** killed Pekahiah and succeeded him as NDT
2Ki 15:27 **P** son of Remaliah became king of Israel H7220
2Ki 15:29 In the time of **P** king of Israel H7220
2Ki 15:30 conspired against **P** son of Remaliah. H7220
2Ki 15:32 the second year of **P** son of Remaliah king H7220
2Ki 15:37 king of Aram and **P** son of Remaliah H7220
2Ki 16: 1 seventeenth year of **P** son of Remaliah, H7220
2Ki 16: 5 king of Aram and **P** son of Remaliah king H7220
2Ch 28: 6 In one day **P** son of Remaliah killed a H7220
Isa 7: 1 Rezin of Aram and **P** son of Remaliah H7220

PEKAH'S (1) [PEKAH]
2Ki 15:31 As for the other events of **P** reign, and all H7220

PEKAHIAH (5) [PEKAHIAH'S]
2Ki 15:22 And **P** his son succeeded him as king H7222
2Ki 15:23 **P** son of Menahem became king of Israel H7222
2Ki 15:24 **P** did evil in the eyes of the LORD. He did NDT
2Ki 15:25 he assassinated **P**, along with Argob H2084S
2Ki 15:25 So Pekah killed **P** and succeeded him as H2084S

PEKAHIAH'S (1) [PEKAHIAH]
2Ki 15:26 The other events of **P** reign, and all he H7222

PEKOD (2)
Jer 50:21 of Merathaim and those who live in **P**. H7216
Eze 23:23 the men of **P** and Shoa and Koa, and H7216

PELAIAH (3)
1Ch 3:24 Hodaviah, Eliashib, **P**, Akkub, Johanan H7126
Ne 8: 7 Jozabad, Hanan and **P**—instructed the H7102
Ne 10:10 Shebaniah, Hodiah, Kelita, **P**, Hanan, H7102

PELALIAH (1)
Ne 11:12 of Jeroham, the son of **P**, the son of Amzi, H7139

PELATIAH (5)
1Ch 3:21 **P** and Jeshaiah, and the sons of H7124
1Ch 4:42 of these Simeonites, led by **P**, Neariah, H7124
Ne 10:22 **P**, Hanan, Anaiah, H7124
Eze 11: 1 son of Azzur and **P** son of Benaiah, H7125
Eze 11:13 I was prophesying, **P** son of Benaiah died. H7125

PELEG (8)
Ge 10:25 One was named **P**, because in his time H7105
Ge 11:16 lived 34 years, he became the father of **P**. H7105
Ge 11:17 And after he became the father of **P**, Eber H7105
Ge 11:18 When **P** had lived 30 years, he became H7105
Ge 11:19 **P** lived 209 years and had other sons and H7105
1Ch 1:19 One was named **P**, because in his time H7105
1Ch 1:25 **P**, Reu, H7105
Lk 3:35 son of Reu, the son *of* **P**, the son of Eber, *G5744*

PELET (2) [BETH PELET]
1Ch 2:47 Jotham, Geshan, **P**, Ephah and Shaaph. H7118
1Ch 12: 3 Jeziel and **P** the sons of Azmaveth H7118

PELETH (2) [PELETHITES]
Nu 16: 1 and On son of **P**—became insolent H7150
1Ch 2:33 sons of Jonathan: **P** and Zaza. These H7150

PELETHITES (7) [PELETH]
2Sa 8:18 Jehoiada was over the Kerethites and **P**; H7152
2Sa 15:18 along with all the Kerethites and **P**; and H7152
2Sa 20: 7 the Kerethites and **P** and all the mighty H7152
2Sa 20:23 Jehoiada was over the Kerethites and **P**; H7152
1Ki 1:38 Kerethites and the **P** went down and had H7152
1Ki 1:44 the Kerethites and the **P**, and they have H7152
1Ch 18:17 Jehoiada was over the Kerethites and **P**; H7152

PELICAN (KJV) DESERT OWL

PELONITE (3)

1Ch 11:27 Shammoth the Harorite, Helez the P, H7113
1Ch 11:36 Hepher the Mekerathite, Ahijah the P, H7113
1Ch 27:10 was Helez the P, an Ephraimite. H7113

PELT (1) [PELTED]

Na 3: 6 *I will* p you *with* filth, I will treat you with H8959

PELTED (2) [PELT]

2Sa 16: 6 *He* p David and all the king's officials with H6232
2Co 11:25 once *I was* p with stones, three G3342

PELUSIUM (2)

Eze 30:15 I will pour out my wrath on P, the H6096
Eze 30:16 set fire to Egypt; P will writhe in agony. H6096

PEN (11) [PENNED, PENS, PENT-UP]

1Sa 6: 7 their calves away and p them up. H1074+2025
Ps 45: 1 my tongue is the p *of* a skillful writer. H6485
Isa 8: 1 scroll and write on it with an ordinary p: H3032
Jer 8: 8 actually the lying p *of* the scribes has H6485
Mic 2:12 will bring them together like sheep in a p, H1312
Hab 3:17 are no sheep in the p and no cattle in the H4813
Mt 5:18 not the least stroke of a p, will by any G3037
Lk 16:17 than *for* the least stroke of a p to drop out G3037
Jn 10: 1 does not enter the sheep p by the gate, G885
Jn 10:16 other sheep that are not of this sheep p. G885
3Jn 13 I do not want to do so with p and ink. G2812

PENALTIES (1) [PENALTY]

Pr 19:29 P are prepared for mockers, and beatings H9150

PENALTY (14) [PENALTIES]

Lev 5: 6 As a p for the sin they have committed, they H871
Lev 5: 7 pigeons to the LORD as a p *for* their sin— H871
Lev 5:15 to the LORD as a p a ram from the flock, H871
Lev 5:16 pay an additional p *of* a fifth of its value AIT
Lev 6: 6 And as a p they must bring to the priest H871
Job 8: 4 he gave them over to the p of their sin. H7322
Pr 19:19 A hot-tempered person must pay the p H6741
Pr 22: 3 the simple keep going and pay the p. H6740
Pr 27:12 the simple keep going and pay the p. H6740
Eze 23:49 suffer the p for your lewdness and bear H2365
Da 2: 9 the dream, there is only one p *for* you. A10186
Lk 23:22 in him no grounds for the death p. G165+2505
Ro 1:27 in themselves the due p for their error. G521
Gal 5:10 that may be, will have to pay the p. G3210

PENCE (KJV) A YEAR'S WAGES, COINS, DENARII

PENDANTS (1)

Jdg 8:26 the p and the purple garments worn by H5755

PENETRATE (1) [PENETRATES]

Job 41:13 Who *can* p its double coat of armor? H995+928

PENETRATES (1) [PENETRATE]

Heb 4:12 *it* p even to dividing soul and spirit G1459

PENIEL (6) [PENUEL]

Ge 32:30 So Jacob called the place P, saying, "It is H7161
Ge 32:31 The sun rose above him as he passed P H7159
Jdg 8: 8 he went up to P and made the same H7159
Jdg 8: 9 So he said to the men of P, "When I return H7159
Jdg 8:17 down the tower of P and killed the men of H7159
1Ki 12:25 From there he went out and built up P. H7159

PENINNAH (3)

1Sa 1: 2 one was called Hannah and the other P. H7166
1Sa 1: 2 the other Peninnah. P had children, but H7166
1Sa 1: 4 the meat to his wife P and to all her sons H7166

PENITENT (1) [REPENT]

Isa 1:27 her p *ones* with righteousness. H8740

PENNED (3) [PEN]

Ex 21:29 warned but *has* not kept it p up and it kills H9068
Ex 21:36 the owner *did* not keep it p up, the H9068
1Sa 6:10 the cart and p up their H3973+1074+928+2021

PENNIES (1) [PENNY]

Lk 12: 6 Are not five sparrows sold *for* two p? Yet not G837

PENNY (3) [PENNIES]

Mt 5:26 not get out until you have paid the last p. G3119
Mt 10:29 Are not two sparrows sold *for* a p? Yet not G837
Lk 12:59 not get out until you have paid the last p." G3321

PENNYWORTH (KJV) HALF A YEAR'S WAGES

PENS (11) [PEN]

Ge 49:14 donkey lying down among the sheep p. H5478
Nu 32:16 would like to build p here for our H1556+7366
Nu 32:24 children, and p for your flocks, but do H1556
Nu 32:36 fortified cities, and built p *for* their flocks. H1556
Jdg 5:16 you stay among the sheep p to hear the H5478
1Sa 24: 3 He came to the sheep p along the way; H1556
2Ch 32:28 various kinds of cattle, and p for the flocks. H774
Ps 50: 9 from your stall or of goats from your p, H4813
Ps 68:13 Even while you sleep among the sheep p H9190
Ps 78:70 servant and took him from the sheep p; H4813
Zep 2: 6 wells for shepherds and p *for* flocks. H1556

PENT-UP (1) [PEN]

Isa 59:19 he will come like a p flood that the breath H7639

PENTECOST (3)

Ac 2: 1 When the day *of* P came, they were all G4300
Ac 20:16 Jerusalem, if possible, by the day *of* P. G4300
1Co 16: 8 But I will stay on at Ephesus until P, G4300

PENUEL (3) [PENIEL]

1Ch 4: 4 P was the father of Gedor, and Ezer the H7158
1Ch 8:25 Iphdeiah and P were the sons of Shashak. H7158
Lk 2:36 the daughter *of* P, of the tribe of G5750

PEOPLE (2699) [PEOPLE'S, PEOPLED, PEOPLES]

Ge 4:26 At that time *p* began to call on the name of AIT
Ge 6: 9 blameless among the p of his time, and H1887
Ge 6:12 all the p on earth had corrupted their H1414
Ge 6:13 "I am going to put an end to all p, for the H1414
Ge 7:23 p and animals and the creatures that move H132
Ge 9:19 came *the p who were* scattered *over* the AIT
Ge 11: 2 As p moved eastward, they found a plain H4392s
Ge 11: 5 and the tower the p were building. H1201+132
Ge 11: 6 "If as one p speaking the same language H6639
Ge 12: 1 your p and your father's household to the H4580
Ge 12: 5 accumulated and the p they had acquired H5883
Ge 13:13 Now the p *of* Sodom were wicked and were H408
Ge 14:16 together with the women and the other p. H6639
Ge 14:21 "Give me the p and keep the goods for H5883
Ge 17:14 will be cut off from his p; he has broken H6639
Ge 18:24 What if there are fifty righteous *p* in the city AIT
Ge 18:24 the sake of the fifty righteous *p* in it? AIT
Ge 18:26 "If I find fifty righteous *p* in the city of Sodom AIT
Ge 18:28 you destroy the whole city for lack of five *p*?" AIT
Ge 19:13 to the LORD against its p is so great that H4392s
Ge 23: 7 bowed down before the p *of* the land, H6639
Ge 23:10 sitting among his p and he H3147+1201s
Ge 23:11 it to you in the presence of my p. H1201+6639
Ge 23:12 bowed down before the p *of* the land H6639
Ge 25: 8 of years; and he was gathered to his p. H6639
Ge 25:17 died, and he was gathered to his p. H6639
Ge 25:23 *one* p will be stronger than the other H4211
Ge 26:11 So Abimelek gave orders to all the p H6639
Ge 29:22 together all the p *of* the place and gave a H408
Ge 32: 7 Jacob divided the p who were with him H6639
Ge 34:16 among you and become one p with you. H6639
Ge 34:22 live with us as one p only on the H6639
Ge 34:30 Perizzites, the *p* living in this land. AIT
Ge 35: 6 Jacob and all the p with him came to Luz H6639
Ge 35:29 last and died and was gathered to his p, H6639
Ge 41:40 all my p are to submit to your orders. H6639
Ge 41:43 and *p* shouted before him, "Make way AIT
Ge 41:55 famine, the p cried to Pharaoh for food. H6639
Ge 42: 6 the person who sold grain to all its p. H6639
Ge 47:15 the money of the p of Egypt and Canaan NDT
Ge 47:21 Joseph reduced the p to servitude H6639
Ge 47:23 Joseph said to the p, "Now that I have H6639
Ge 48:19 He too will become a p, and he too will H6639
Ge 49:16 justice for his p as one of the tribes of H6639
Ge 49:29 "I am about to be gathered to my p. H6639
Ge 49:33 his last and was gathered to his p. H6639
Ex 1: 9 he said to his p, "the Israelites have H6639
Ex 1:20 midwives and the p increased and H6639
Ex 1:22 Then Pharaoh gave this order to all his p H6639
Ex 2:11 out to where his own p were and watched H278
Ex 2:11 beating a Hebrew, one of his own p. H278
Ex 3: 7 indeed seen the misery of my p in Egypt. H6639
Ex 3:10 Pharaoh to bring my p the Israelites out of H6639
Ex 3:12 you have brought the p out of Egypt, H6639
Ex 3:21 favorably disposed toward this p, H6639
Ex 4:16 He will speak to the p for you, and it will H6639
Ex 4:18 me return to my own p in Egypt to see if H278
Ex 4:21 his heart so that he will not let the p go. H6639
Ex 4:30 He also performed the signs before the p, H6639
Ex 5: 1 'Let my p go, so that they may hold a H6639
Ex 5: 4 are you taking the p away from their labor H6639
Ex 5: 5 the p *of* the land are now numerous H6639
Ex 5: 6 drivers and overseers in charge of the p: H6639
Ex 5: 7 longer to supply the p with straw for H6639
Ex 5: 9 the work harder for the p so that they keep H408
Ex 5:10 the overseers went out and said to the p, H6639
Ex 5:12 So the p scattered all over Egypt to gather H6639
Ex 5:16 beaten, but the fault is with your own p." H6639
Ex 5:22 why have you brought trouble on this p? H6639
Ex 5:23 he has brought trouble on this p, and you H6639
Ex 5:23 you have not rescued your p at all. H6639
Ex 6: 7 I will take you as my own p, and I will be H6639
Ex 7: 4 bring out my divisions, my p the Israelites. H6639
Ex 7:14 is unyielding; he refuses to let the p go. H6639
Ex 7:16 Let my p go, so that they may worship me H6639
Ex 8: 1 Let my p go, so that they may H6639
Ex 8: 3 the houses of your officials and on your p, H6639
Ex 8: 4 up on you and your p and all your officials H6639
Ex 8: 8 to take the frogs away from me and my p, H6639
Ex 8: 8 I will let your p go to offer sacrifices H6639
Ex 8: 9 your officials and your p that you and your H6639
Ex 8:11 your officials and your p; they will remain H6639
Ex 8:17 the ground, gnats came on p and animals. H132
Ex 8:18 the gnats were on p and animals H132
Ex 8:20 Let my p go, so that they may H6639
Ex 8:21 If you do not let my p go, I will send H6639
Ex 8:21 officials, on your p and into your houses. H6639
Ex 8:22 of Goshen, where my p live; no swarms of H6639
Ex 8:23 between my p and your people. H6639
Ex 8:23 between my people and your p. H6639
Ex 8:29 leave Pharaoh and his officials and his p. H6639
Ex 8:29 by not letting the p go to offer sacrifices H6639
Ex 8:31 left Pharaoh and his officials and his p; H6639
Ex 8:32 his heart and would not let the p go. H6639
Ex 9: 1 "Let my p go, so that they may worship H6639
Ex 9: 7 unyielding and he would not let the p go. H6639
Ex 9: 9 will break out on p and animals throughout H132
Ex 9:10 festering boils broke out on p and animals. H132
Ex 9:13 Let my p go, so that they may worship me H6639
Ex 9:14 you and against your officials and your p, H6639
Ex 9:15 struck you and your p with a plague that H6639
Ex 9:17 yourself against my p and will not let H6639
Ex 9:22 on p and animals and on everything H132
Ex 9:25 in the fields—both p and animals; it beat H132
Ex 9:27 and I and my p are in the wrong. H6639
Ex 10: 3 Let my p go, so that they may H6639
Ex 10: 7 Let the p go, so that they may worship the H408
Ex 11: 2 Tell the p that men and women alike are H6639
Ex 11: 3 favorably disposed toward the p, H6639
Ex 11: 3 Egypt by Pharaoh's officials and by the p.) H6639
Ex 11: 8 you and all the p who follow you! H6639
Ex 12: 4 into account the number of p there are. H5883
Ex 12:12 down every firstborn of both p and animals, H132
Ex 12:27 Then the p bowed down and worshiped. H6639
Ex 12:31 Leave my p, you and the Israelites H6639
Ex 12:33 Egyptians urged the p to hurry and leave H6639
Ex 12:34 So the p took their dough before the yeast H6639
Ex 12:36 favorably disposed toward the p, H6639
Ex 12:38 Many other p went up with them, and also H6850
Ex 12:40 length of time the Israelite *p* lived in Egypt AIT
Ex 13: 3 Then Moses said to the p H6639
Ex 13:15 firstborn of both p and animals in Egypt. H132
Ex 13:17 When Pharaoh let the p go, God did not H6639
Ex 13:18 So God led the p around by the desert H6639
Ex 13:22 fire by night left its place in front of the p. H6639
Ex 14: 5 king of Egypt was told that the p had fled, H6639
Ex 14:13 Moses answered the p, "Do not be afraid H6639
Ex 14:31 the p feared the LORD and put their trust in H6639
Ex 15:13 you will lead the p you have redeemed. H6639
Ex 15:14 anguish will grip the p *of* Philistia. H3782
Ex 15:15 trembling, the p *of* Canaan will melt away H3782
Ex 15:16 as a stone—until your p pass by, LORD, H6639
Ex 15:16 LORD, until the p you bought pass by. H6639
Ex 15:24 So the p grumbled against Moses, saying H6639
Ex 16: 4 The p are to go out each day and gather H6639
Ex 16:27 some of the p went out on the seventh H6639
Ex 16:30 So the p rested on the seventh day. H6639
Ex 16:31 The p *of* Israel called the bread manna. H1074
Ex 17: 1 there was no water for the p to drink. H6639
Ex 17: 3 But the p were thirsty for water there, and H6639
Ex 17: 4 the LORD, "What am I to do with these p? H6639
Ex 17: 5 "Go out in front of the p. H6639
Ex 17: 6 water will come out of it for the p to drink." H6639
Ex 18: 1 had done for Moses and for his p Israel, H6639
Ex 18:10 who rescued the p from the hand of H6639
Ex 18:13 took his seat to serve as judge for the p, H6639
Ex 18:14 saw all that Moses was doing for the p, H6639
Ex 18:14 "What is this you are doing for the p? H6639
Ex 18:14 while all these p stand around you from H6639
Ex 18:15 "Because the p come to me to seek God's H6639
Ex 18:18 You and these p who come to you will H6639
Ex 18:21 But select capable men from all the p H6639
Ex 18:22 serve as judges for the p at all times, H6639
Ex 18:23 all these p will go home satisfied. H6639
Ex 18:25 Israel and made them leaders of the p, H6639
Ex 18:26 served as judges for the p at all times. H6639
Ex 19: 3 what you are to tell the p *of* Israel: H1201
Ex 19: 7 the elders of the p and set before them H6639
Ex 19: 8 The p all responded together, "We will do H6639
Ex 19: 9 so that the p will hear me speaking with H6639
Ex 19: 9 Moses told the LORD what the p had said. H6639
Ex 19:10 "Go to the p and consecrate them today H6639
Ex 19:11 on Mount Sinai in the sight of all the p. H6639
Ex 19:12 Put limits for the p around the mountain H6639
Ex 19:14 had gone down the mountain to the p, H6639
Ex 19:15 Then he said to the p, "Prepare yourselves H6639
Ex 19:17 Then Moses led the p out of the camp to H6639
Ex 19:21 down and warn the p so they do not force H6639
Ex 19:23 "The p cannot come up Mount Sinai H6639
Ex 19:24 the priests and the p must not force their H6639
Ex 19:25 Moses went down to the p and told them. H6639
Ex 20:18 When the p saw the thunder and H6639
Ex 20:20 Moses said to the p, "Do not be afraid H6639
Ex 20:21 The p remained at a distance, while H6639
Ex 21:18 "If p quarrel and one person hits another H408
Ex 21:22 "If p are fighting and hit a pregnant H408
Ex 22:25 money to one of my p among you who is H6639
Ex 22:28 God or curse the ruler of your p. H6639
Ex 22:31 "You are to be my holy p. So do not eat the H408
Ex 23: 6 deny justice to your poor *p* in their lawsuits. AIT
Ex 23:11 the poor among your p may get food from H6639
Ex 23:31 into your hands the *p who* live in the land, AIT
Ex 24: 2 And the p may not come up with him." H6639
Ex 24: 3 went and told the p all the LORD's words H6639
Ex 24: 7 Book of the Covenant and read it to the p. H6639
Ex 24: 8 sprinkled it on the p and said, "This is the H6639
Ex 30:33 than a priest must be cut off from their p. H6639
Ex 30:38 its fragrance must be cut off from their p." H6639
Ex 31:14 on that day must be cut off from their p. H6639
Ex 32: 1 When the p saw that Moses was so long H6639
Ex 32: 3 So all the p took off their earrings and H6639
Ex 32: 6 So the next day the p rose early and H6639
Ex 32: 7 because your p, whom you brought H6639

P

Ex 32: 9 "I have seen these **p**," the LORD said to H6639
Ex 32: 9 to Moses, "and they are a stiff-necked **p**. H6639
Ex 32:11 should your anger burn against your **p**, H6639
Ex 32:12 relent and do not bring disaster on your **p**. H6639
Ex 32:14 did not bring on his **p** the disaster he had H6639
Ex 32:17 Joshua heard the noise of the **p** shouting, H6639
Ex 32:20 he took the calf the **p** had made and burned NDT
Ex 32:21 "What did these **p** do to you, that you H6639
Ex 32:22 "You know how prone these **p** are to evil. H6639
Ex 32:25 Moses saw that the **p** were running wild H6639
Ex 32:28 day about three thousand of the **p** died. H6639
Ex 32:30 The next day Moses said to the **p**, "You H6639
Ex 32:31 what a great sin these **p** have committed! H6639
Ex 32:34 Now go, lead the **p** to the place I spoke of H6639
Ex 32:35 the LORD struck the **p** with a plague H6639
Ex 33: 1 you and the **p** you brought up out of Egypt H6639
Ex 33: 3 are a stiff-necked **p** and I might destroy H6639
Ex 33: 4 When the **p** heard these distressing words H6639
Ex 33: 5 the Israelites, 'You are a stiff-necked **p**. H6639
Ex 33: 8 all the **p** rose and stood at the entrances H6639
Ex 33:10 Whenever the **p** saw the pillar of cloud H6639
Ex 33:12 'Lead these **p**,' but you have not let H6639
Ex 33:13 Remember that this nation is your **p**." H6639
Ex 33:16 me and with your **p** unless you go with us H6639
Ex 33:16 me and your **p** from all the other H6639
Ex 33:16 from all the other **p** on the face of the H6639
Ex 34: 9 Although this is a stiff-necked **p**, forgive H6639
Ex 34:10 Before all your **p** I will do wonders never H6639
Ex 34:10 The **p** you live among will see how H6639
Ex 36: 3 And **the p** continued to bring freewill H2156S
Ex 36: 5 "The **p** are bringing more than enough H6639
Ex 36: 6 And so the **p** were restrained from H6639
Lev 4: 3 bringing guilt on the **p**, he must bring to H6639
Lev 6: 3 about any such sin that **p** may commit— H132
Lev 7:20 the LORD, they must be cut off from their **p**. H6639
Lev 7:21 to the LORD must be cut off from their **p**. H6639
Lev 7:25 to the LORD must be cut off from their **p**. H6639
Lev 7:27 eats blood must be cut off from their **p**. H6639
Lev 9: 7 make atonement for yourself and the **p**; H6639
Lev 9: 7 that is for the **p** and make atonement H6639
Lev 9:15 brought the offering that was for the **p**. H6639
Lev 9:18 ram as the fellowship offering for the **p**. H6639
Lev 9:22 his hands toward the **p** and blessed them. H6639
Lev 9:23 they blessed the **p**; and the glory of the H6639
Lev 9:23 glory of the LORD appeared to all the **p**. H6639
Lev 9:24 And when all the **p** saw it, they shouted H6639
Lev 10: 3 in the sight of all the **p** I will be honored. H6639
Lev 16:15 sin offering for the **p** and take its blood H6639
Lev 16:24 himself and the burnt offering for the **p**, H6639
Lev 16:24 atonement for himself and for the **p**. H6639
Lev 17: 4 blood and must be cut off from their **p**. H6639
Lev 17: 9 LORD must be cut off from the **p** of Israel. H6639
Lev 17:10 and I will cut them off from the **p**. H6639
Lev 18:27 done by the **p** who lived *in* the land before H408
Lev 18:29 such persons must be cut off from their **p**. H6639
Lev 19: 8 the LORD; they must be cut off from their **p**. H6639
Lev 19:16 about spreading slander among your **p**. H6639
Lev 19:18 a grudge against anyone among your **p**, H6639
Lev 20: 3 him and will cut him off from his **p**; H6639
Lev 20: 5 them off from their **p** together with all H6639
Lev 20: 6 and I will cut them off from their **p**. H6639
Lev 20:17 be publicly removed from their **p**. H1201+6639
Lev 20:18 Both of them are to be cut off from their **p**. H6639
Lev 21: 1 unclean for any of his **p** who die, H6639
Lev 21: 4 himself unclean for **p** related to him by H6639
Lev 21:14 only a virgin from his own **p**, H6639
Lev 21:15 will not defile his offspring among his **p**. H6639
Lev 23:29 on that day must be cut off from their **p**. H6639
Lev 23:30 from among their **p** anyone who does any H6639
Lev 25:14 to any of your own **p** or buy land from H6660
Lev 25:15 to buy from your own **p** on the basis of the H6660
Lev 26:12 be your God, and you will be my **p**. H6639
Nu 1:18 The **p** registered their ancestry by their clans NDT
Nu 2: 3 The leader of the **p** *of* Judah is Nahshon H1201
Nu 2: 5 The leader of the **p** *of* Issachar is H1201
Nu 2: 7 The leader of the **p** *of* Zebulun is Eliab H1201
Nu 2:10 The leader of the **p** *of* Reuben is Elizur H1201
Nu 2:12 The leader of the **p** *of* Simeon is H1201
Nu 2:14 The leader of the **p** *of* Gad is Eliasaph H1201
Nu 2:18 The leader of the **p** *of* Ephraim is H1201
Nu 2:20 The leader of the **p** *of* Manasseh is H1201
Nu 2:22 The leader of the **p** *of* Benjamin is H1201
Nu 2:25 The leader of the **p** *of* Dan is Ahiezer son H1201
Nu 2:27 The leader of the **p** *of* Asher is Pagiel son H1201
Nu 2:29 The leader of the **p** *of* Naphtali is Ahira H1201
Nu 5:21 curse among your **p** when he makes your H6639
Nu 7:24 the leader of the **p** *of* Zebulun, brought H1201
Nu 7:30 the leader of the **p** *of* Reuben, brought his H1201
Nu 7:36 the leader of the **p** *of* Simeon, brought his H1201
Nu 7:42 the leader of the **p** *of* Gad, brought his H1201
Nu 7:48 the leader of the **p** *of* Ephraim, brought H1201
Nu 7:54 the leader of the **p** *of* Manasseh, brought H1201
Nu 7:60 the leader of the **p** *of* Benjamin, brought H1201
Nu 7:66 the leader of the **p** *of* Dan, brought his H1201
Nu 7:72 the leader of the **p** *of* Asher, brought his H1201
Nu 7:78 the leader of the **p** *of* Naphtali, brought H1201
Nu 9:13 be cut off from their **p** for not presenting H6639
Nu 10:30 back to my own land and my own **p**." H4580
Nu 11: 1 Now the **p** complained about their H6639
Nu 11: 2 When the **p** cried out to Moses, he prayed H6639
Nu 11: 8 The **p** went around gathering it, and then H6639
Nu 11:10 Moses heard the **p** of every family wailing H6639
Nu 11:11 you put the burden of all these **p** on me? H6639
Nu 11:12 Did I conceive all these **p**? Did I give them H6639
Nu 11:13 Where can I get meat for all these **p**? They H6639
Nu 11:14 I cannot carry all these **p** by myself; the H6639
Nu 11:16 you as leaders and officials among the **p**. H6639
Nu 11:17 the burden of the **p** with you so that you H6639
Nu 11:18 "Tell the **p**: 'Consecrate yourselves in H6639
Nu 11:24 went out and told the **p** what the LORD had H6639
Nu 11:29 that all the LORD's **p** were prophets and H6639
Nu 11:32 all the next day the **p** went out and H6639
Nu 11:33 anger of the LORD burned against the **p**, H6639
Nu 11:34 they buried the **p** who had craved other H6639
Nu 11:35 Hattaavah the **p** traveled to Hazeroth H6639
Nu 12:15 the **p** did not move on till she was H6639
Nu 12:16 the **p** left Hazeroth and encamped in the H6639
Nu 13:18 like and whether the **p** who live there are H6639
Nu 13:28 But the **p** who live there are powerful, and H6639
Nu 13:30 Caleb silenced the **p** before Moses and H6639
Nu 13:31 "We can't attack those **p**; they are H6639
Nu 13:32 All the **p** we saw there are of great size. H6639
Nu 14: 9 And do not be afraid of the **p** *of* the land H6639
Nu 14:11 "How long will these **p** treat me with H6639
Nu 14:13 you brought these **p** up from among them H6639
Nu 14:14 are with these **p** and that you, LORD H6639
Nu 14:15 If you put all these **p** to death, leaving H6639
Nu 14:16 not able to bring these **p** into the land he H6639
Nu 14:19 forgive the sin of these **p**, just as you have H6639
Nu 15:26 because all the **p** were involved in the H6639
Nu 15:30 must be cut off from the **p** of Israel. H6639
Nu 16:41 "You have killed the LORD's **p**," they said. H6639
Nu 16:47 plague had already started among the **p**, H6639
Nu 16:49 But 14,700 *p* **died** from the plague, in AIT
Nu 19:18 the furnishings and the **p** who were there. H5883
Nu 20: 2 the **p** gathered in opposition to Moses NDT
Nu 20:24 "Aaron will be gathered to his **p**. He will H6639
Nu 20:26 Aaron will be gathered to his **p**; he will NDT
Nu 21: 2 "If you will deliver these **p** into our hands H6639
Nu 21: 4 But the **p** grew impatient on the way; H6639
Nu 21: 6 they bit the **p** and many Israelites died. H6639
Nu 21: 7 The **p** came to Moses and said, "We H6639
Nu 21: 7 So Moses prayed for the **p**. H6639
Nu 21:16 "Gather the **p** together and I will give H6639
Nu 21:18 that the nobles of the **p** sank—the nobles H6639
Nu 21:29 You are destroyed, **p** *of* Chemosh! He has H6639
Nu 22: 3 terrified because there were so many **p**. H6639
Nu 22: 5 "A **p** has come out of Egypt; they cover H6639
Nu 22: 6 Now come and put a curse on these **p** H6639
Nu 22:11 'A **p** that has come out of Egypt covers the H6639
Nu 22:12 You must not put a curse on those **p** H6639
Nu 22:17 Come and put a curse on these **p** for me." H6639
Nu 23: 9 I see a **p** who live apart and do not H6639
Nu 23:24 The **p** rise like a lioness; they rouse H6639
Nu 24:14 Now I am going back to my **p**, but come H6639
Nu 24:14 warn you of what this **p** will do to your H6639
Nu 24:14 people will do to your **p** in days to come." H6639
Nu 24:17 of Moab, the skulls of all the **p** *of* Sheth. H1201
Nu 25: 2 The **p** ate the sacrificial meal and bowed H6639
Nu 25: 4 "Take all the leaders of these **p**, kill them H6639
Nu 25: 5 to death those of your **p** who have yoked H408
Nu 27:13 you too will be gathered to your **p**, as your H6639
Nu 27:17 so the LORD's **p** will not be like sheep H6337
Nu 31: 2 you will be gathered to your **p**." H6639
Nu 31: 3 So Moses said to the **p**, "Arm some of H6639
Nu 31:11 spoils, including the **p** and animals, H132
Nu 31:16 so that a plague struck the LORD's **p**. H6337
Nu 31:26 are to count all the **p** and animals that H132
Nu 31:28 out of every five hundred, whether **p**, cattle, H132
Nu 31:30 one out of every fifty, whether **p**, cattle, H132
Nu 31:40 16,000 **p**, of whom the tribute for the LORD H132
Nu 31:46 16,000 **p**. H132
Nu 31:47 one out of every fifty **p** and animals, H132
Nu 32: 4 the LORD subdued before the **p** *of* Israel— H6337
Nu 32:15 again leave all this **p** in the wilderness, H6639
Nu 33:14 there was no water for the **p** to drink. H6639
Dt 1:16 disputes between your **p** and judge fairly, H278
Dt 1:28 'The **p** are stronger and taller than we are; H6639
Dt 2: 4 Give the **p** these orders: 'You are about to H6639
Dt 2:10 to live there—a **p** strong and numerous H6639
Dt 2:16 fighting men among the **p** had died, H6639
Dt 2:21 They were a **p** strong and numerous, and H6639
Dt 3:28 he will lead this **p** across and will cause H6639
Dt 4: 6 nation is a wise and understanding **p**." H6639
Dt 4:10 "Assemble the **p** before me to hear my H6639
Dt 4:20 of Egypt, to be the **p** *of* his inheritance, as H6639
Dt 4:33 Has any other **p** heard the voice of God H6639
Dt 5:28 "I have heard what this **p** said to you. H6639
Dt 7: 6 For you are a **p** holy to the LORD your God H6639
Dt 7: 6 on the face of the earth to be his **p**, H6639
Dt 7:14 You will be blessed more than any other **p**; H6639
Dt 9: 2 The **p** are strong and tall—Anakites! You H6639
Dt 9: 6 to possess, for you are a stiff-necked **p**. H6639
Dt 9:12 because your **p** whom you brought out of H6639
Dt 9:13 "I have seen this **p**, and they are a H6639
Dt 9:13 they are a stiff-necked **p** indeed! H6639
Dt 9:26 do not destroy your **p**, your own H6639
Dt 9:27 Overlook the stubbornness of this **p**, their H6639
Dt 9:29 But they are your **p**, your inheritance that H6639
Dt 10:11 "and lead the **p** on their way, so H6639
Dt 13: 9 to death, and then the hands of all the **p**. H6639
Dt 13:13 have led the **p** *of* their town astray, H3782
Dt 13:15 both its **p** and its livestock. H3972+889+928S
Dt 14: 2 you are a **p** holy to the LORD your God H6639
Dt 14:21 But you are a **p** holy to the LORD your God H6639
Dt 15: 2 **anyone among** their own **p**, H8276+2256+278
Dt 15: 4 there need be no **poor** *p* among you, for in AIT
Dt 15:11 There will always be **poor** *p* in the land AIT
Dt 15:12 If any of your **p**—Hebrew men or women H278
Dt 16:18 and they shall judge the **p** fairly. H6639
Dt 17: 7 to death, and then the hands of all the **p**. H6639
Dt 17:13 All the **p** will hear and be afraid, and will H6639
Dt 17:16 himself or make the **p** return to Egypt to H6639
Dt 18: 3 the priests from the **p** who sacrifice a bull H6639
Dt 19:17 the two **p** involved in the dispute must H408
Dt 19:20 The **rest** *of the p* will hear of this and be AIT
Dt 20:10 to attack a city, make its **p** an offer of peace. NDT
Dt 20:11 all the **p** in it shall be subject to forced H6639
Dt 20:19 Are the trees **p**, that you should besiege H132
Dt 21: 8 Accept this atonement for your **p** Israel H6639
Dt 21: 8 do not hold your **p** guilty of the blood H6639
Dt 25: 1 When **p** have a dispute, they are to take it H408
Dt 26: 5 Egypt with a few **p** and lived there and H5493
Dt 26:15 bless your **p** Israel and the land you H6639
Dt 26:18 has declared this day that you are his **p**, H6639
Dt 26:19 that you will be a **p** holy to the LORD your H6639
Dt 27: 1 the elders of Israel commanded the **p**: H6639
Dt 27: 9 have now become the **p** of the LORD your H6639
Dt 27:11 the same day Moses commanded the **p**: H6639
Dt 27:12 stand on Mount Gerizim to bless the **p**: H6639
Dt 27:14 recite to all the **p** *of* Israel in a loud voice H408
Dt 27:15 Then all the **p** shall say, "Amen!" H6639
Dt 27:16 Then all the **p** shall say, "Amen!" H6639
Dt 27:17 Then all the **p** shall say, "Amen!" H6639
Dt 27:18 Then all the **p** shall say, "Amen!" H6639
Dt 27:19 Then all the **p** shall say, "Amen!" H6639
Dt 27:20 Then all the **p** shall say, "Amen!" H6639
Dt 27:21 Then all the **p** shall say, "Amen!" H6639
Dt 27:22 Then all the **p** shall say, "Amen!" H6639
Dt 27:23 Then all the **p** shall say, "Amen!" H6639
Dt 27:24 Then all the **p** shall say, "Amen!" H6639
Dt 27:25 Then all the **p** shall say, "Amen!" H6639
Dt 27:26 Then all the **p** shall say, "Amen!" H6639
Dt 28: 9 The LORD will establish you as his holy **p** H6639
Dt 28:33 A **p** that you do not know will eat what H6639
Dt 29:13 to confirm you this day as his **p**, that he H6639
Dt 29:25 "It is because this **p** abandoned the NDT
Dt 31: 7 you must go with this **p** into the land that H6639
Dt 31:12 Assemble the **p**—men, women and H6639
Dt 31:16 these **p** will soon prostitute H6639
Dt 32: 6 repay the LORD, you foolish and unwise **p**? H6639
Dt 32: 9 For the LORD's portion is his **p**, Jacob his H6639
Dt 32:21 them envious by those who are not a **p**; H6639
Dt 32:36 will vindicate his **p** and relent concerning H6639
Dt 32:43 you nations, with his **p**, for he will avenge H6639
Dt 32:43 make atonement for his land and **p**. H6639
Dt 32:44 words of this song in the hearing of the **p**. H6639
Dt 32:50 you will die and be gathered to your **p**, H6639
Dt 32:50 on Mount Hor and was gathered to his **p**. H6639
Dt 32:52 the land I am giving to the **p** *of* Israel." H1201
Dt 33: 3 Surely it is you who love the **p**; all the H6639
Dt 33: 5 when the leaders of the **p** assembled, H6639
Dt 33: 6 Reuben live and not die, nor his **p** be few." H5493
Dt 33: 7 the cry of Judah; bring him to his **p**. H6639
Dt 33:21 When the heads of the **p** assembled, he H6639
Dt 33:29 Who is like you, a **p** saved by the LORD H6639
Jos 1: 2 you and all these **p**, get ready to cross the H6639
Jos 1: 6 you will lead these **p** to inherit the land I H6639
Jos 1:10 So Joshua ordered the officers of the **p**: H6639
Jos 1:11 "Go through the camp and tell the **p**, 'Get H6639
Jos 2:24 all the **p** are melting in fear because of us H3782
Jos 3: 3 giving orders to the **p**: "When you see the H6639
Jos 3: 5 Joshua told the **p**, "Consecrate yourselves H6639
Jos 3: 6 the covenant and pass on ahead of the **p**." H6639
Jos 3:14 So when the **p** broke camp to cross the H6639
Jos 3:16 So the **p** crossed over opposite Jericho. H6639
Jos 4: 2 "Choose twelve men from among the **p**, H6639
Jos 4: 7 be a memorial to the **p** *of* Israel forever." H1201
Jos 4:10 commanded Joshua was done by the **p**, H6639
Jos 4:10 had directed Joshua. The **p** hurried over, H6639
Jos 4:11 to the other side while the **p** watched. H6639
Jos 4:19 of the first month the **p** went up from the H6639
Jos 5: 5 All the **p** that came out had been H6639
Jos 5: 5 all the **p** born in the wilderness during H6639
Jos 6: 8 When Joshua had spoken to the **p**, the H6639
Jos 7: 3 whole army, for only a few **p** live there." H2156S
Jos 7: 5 this the hearts of the **p** melted in fear H6639
Jos 7: 7 you ever bring this **p** across the Jordan to H6639
Jos 7: 9 the other **p** *of* the country will hear H3782
Jos 7:13 consecrate the **p**. Tell them H6639
Jos 8: 1 the king of Ai, his **p**, his city and his land. H6639
Jos 8: 9 Joshua spent that night with the **p**. H6639
Jos 8:25 women fell that day—all the **p** *of* Ai. H408
Jos 8:33 Half of **the p** stood in front of Mount H2257S
Jos 8:33 gave instructions to bless the **p** *of* Israel. H6639
Jos 9: 3 when the **p** *of* Gibeon heard what Joshua H3782
Jos 10: 1 that the **p** *of* Gibeon had made a H3782
Jos 10: 2 *He and his p were* very much **alarmed** at this AIT
Jos 11:14 all the **p** they put to the sword until H132
Jos 12: 5 border of the **p of Geshur** and Maakah, H1771
Jos 13:11 territory of the **p of Geshur** and Maakah, H1771
Jos 13:13 drive out the **p of Geshur** and Maakah, H1771
Jos 14: 6 Now the **p** *of* Judah approached Joshua H1201
Jos 14: 8 me made the hearts of the **p** melt in fear. H6639
Jos 15:12 around the **p** *of* Judah by their clans H1201
Jos 15:15 he marched against the *p* **living in** Debir AIT

Jos 15:63 Jebusites live there with the **p** *of* Judah. H1201
Jos 16:10 live among the **p** of Ephraim but are NDT
Jos 17: 2 was for the rest of the **p** *of* Manasseh— H1201
Jos 17: 7 there to include the *p* **living at** En Tappuah. AIT
Jos 17:11 Ibleam and the **p** *of* Dor, Endor, H3782
Jos 17:14 The **p** *of* Joseph said to Joshua, "Why H1201
Jos 17:14 We are a numerous **p**, and the LORD has H6639
Jos 17:16 The **p** *of* Joseph replied, "The hill country H1201
Jos 18:14 Kiriath Jearim), a town of the **p** *of* Judah. H1201
Jos 24: 2 Joshua said to all the **p**, "This is what the H6639
Jos 24: 6 When I brought your **p** out of Egypt, you came H3
Jos 24:16 Then the **p** answered, "Far be it from us to H6639
Jos 24:19 Joshua said to the **p**, "You are not able to H6639
Jos 24:21 But the **p** said to Joshua, "No! We will H6639
Jos 24:24 And the **p** said to Joshua, "We will serve H6639
Jos 24:25 day Joshua made a covenant for the **p**, H6639
Jos 24:27 he said to all the **p**. "This stone will be a H6639
Jos 24:28 Then Joshua dismissed the **p**, each to H6639
Jdg 1:11 they advanced against the *p* **living in** Debir AIT
Jdg 1:16 of Palms with the **p** *of* Judah to live H1201
Jdg 1:19 unable to drive the **p** from the plains, H3782
Jdg 1:27 did not drive out *the* **p** *of* Beth Shan or H3782
Jdg 2: 2 make a covenant with the **p** *of* this land, H3782
Jdg 2: 4 to all the Israelites, the **p** wept aloud, H6639
Jdg 2: 7 The **p** served the LORD throughout the H6639
Jdg 2:19 *the p* **returned** *to* ways even more corrupt AIT
Jdg 5: 2 when the **p** willingly offer themselves H6639
Jdg 5: 9 with the willing volunteers among the **p**. H6639
Jdg 5:11 "Then the **p** *of* the LORD went down to the H6639
Jdg 5:13 the **p** *of* the LORD came down to me H6639
Jdg 5:14 was with the **p** who followed you. H6639
Jdg 5:18 The **p** of Zebulun risked their very lives; so H6639
Jdg 5:23 'Curse its **p** bitterly, because they did not H3782
Jdg 6:28 morning when the **p** *of* the town got up, H408
Jdg 6:30 The **p** *of* the town demanded of Joash H408
Jdg 9:29 If only this **p** were under my command H6639
Jdg 9:36 **p** are coming down from the tops of the H6639
Jdg 9:37 **p** are coming down from the central hill H6639
Jdg 9:42 The next day the **p** of Shechem went out H6639
Jdg 9:43 When he saw the **p** coming out of the city, H6639
Jdg 9:45 until he had captured it and killed its **p**. H6639
Jdg 9:49 set it on fire with **the p** still inside. H2157S
Jdg 9:49 So all the **p** *in* the tower of Shechem H408
Jdg 9:51 women—all the **p** *of* the city—had H1251
Jdg 9:57 God also made the **p** *of* Shechem pay for H408
Jdg 10:18 The leaders of the **p** of Gilead said to H6639
Jdg 11:11 the **p** made him head and H6639
Jdg 11:23 the Amorites out before his **p** Israel, H6639
Jdg 12: 2 "I and my **p** were engaged in a great H6639
Jdg 14: 3 among your relatives or among all our **p**? H6639
Jdg 14:11 When **the p** saw him, they chose thirty H4392S
Jdg 14:16 You've given my **p** a riddle, but you H1201+6639
Jdg 14:17 turn explained the riddle to her **p**. H1201+6639
Jdg 15:10 The **p** *of* Judah asked, "Why have you come H408
Jdg 16: 2 The **p of Gaza** were told, "Samson is here!" H6484
Jdg 16:24 When the **p** saw him, they praised their H6639
Jdg 16:30 temple on the rulers and all the **p** in it. H6639
Jdg 18: 7 they saw that the **p** were living in safety, H6639
Jdg 18:10 an unsuspecting **p** and a spacious land H6639
Jdg 18:20 the idol and went along with the **p**. H6639
Jdg 18:27 to Laish, against a **p** at peace and secure. H6639
Jdg 19:12 into any city whose **p** are not Israelites. H2179S
Jdg 20: 2 leaders of all the **p** *of* the tribes of Israel H6639
Jdg 20: 2 their places in the assembly of God's **p**, H6639
Jdg 21: 2 The **p** went to Bethel, where they sat H6639
Jdg 21: 4 Early the next day the **p** built an altar and H6639
Jdg 21: 9 For when they counted the **p**, they found H6639
Jdg 21: 9 that none of the **p** *of* Jabesh Gilead were H3782
Jdg 21:12 found among the *p* **living in** Jabesh Gilead AIT
Jdg 21:15 The **p** grieved for Benjamin, because the H6639
Ru 1: 6 to the aid of his **p** by providing food for H6639
Ru 1:10 "We will go back with you to your **p**." H6639
Ru 1:15 is going back to her **p** and her gods. H6639
Ru 1:16 Your **p** will be my people and your God H6639
Ru 1:16 people will be my **p** and your God my H6639
Ru 2:11 came to live with a **p** you did not know H6639
Ru 3:11 All the **p** *of* my town know that you are a H6639
Ru 4: 4 in the presence of the elders of my **p**. H6639
Ru 4: 9 announced to the elders and all the **p**, H6639
Ru 4:11 the elders and all the **p** at the gate said, H6639
1Sa 2:13 whenever any of the **p** offered a sacrifice H6639
1Sa 2:23 I hear from all the **p** about these wicked H6639
1Sa 2:24 among the LORD's **p** is not good. H6639
1Sa 2:26 in favor with the LORD and with **p**. H408
1Sa 2:29 of every offering made by my **p** Israel? H6639
1Sa 4: 4 So the **p** sent men to Shiloh, and they H6639
1Sa 5: 3 When the **p of Ashdod** rose early the next H847
1Sa 5: 6 was heavy on the **p of Ashdod** and its H847
1Sa 5: 7 When the **p** *of* Ashdod saw what was H408
1Sa 5: 9 He afflicted the **p** *of* the city, both young H408
1Sa 5:10 the **p of Ekron** cried out, "They H6834
1Sa 5:10 of Israel around to us to kill us and our **p**." H6639
1Sa 5:11 its own place, or it will kill us and our **p**." H6639
1Sa 6:13 Now the **p** of Beth Shemesh were harvesting NDT
1Sa 6:14 The **p** chopped up the wood of the cart and NDT
1Sa 6:15 On that day the **p** *of* Beth Shemesh offered H408
1Sa 6:19 The **p** mourned because of the heavy H6639
1Sa 6:20 And the **p** *of* Beth Shemesh asked, "Who H408
1Sa 6:21 messengers to the **p** *of* Kiriath Jearim, H3782
1Sa 7: 2 Then all the **p** *of* Israel turned back to the H1074
1Sa 8: 7 "Listen to all that the **p** are saying to you H6639
1Sa 8:10 of the LORD to the **p** who were asking him H6639
1Sa 8:19 But the **p** refused to listen to Samuel. "No!" H6639
1Sa 8:21 When Samuel heard all that the **p** said H6639
1Sa 9:12 the **p** have a sacrifice at the high place H6639
1Sa 9:13 The **p** will not begin eating until he H6639
1Sa 9:16 Anoint him ruler over my **p** Israel; he will H6639
1Sa 9:16 I have looked on my **p**, for their cry has H6639
1Sa 9:17 I spoke to you about; he will govern my **p**." H6639
1Sa 10:17 Samuel summoned the **p** of Israel to the H6639
1Sa 10:23 he stood among the **p** he was a head H6639
1Sa 10:24 Samuel said to all the **p**, "Do you see the H6639
1Sa 10:24 There is no one like him among all the **p**." H6639
1Sa 10:24 Then the **p** shouted, "Long live H6639
1Sa 10:25 explained to the **p** the rights and duties H6639
1Sa 10:25 dismissed the **p** to go to their own H6639
1Sa 11: 4 of Saul and reported these terms to the **p**, H6639
1Sa 11: 7 Then the terror of the LORD fell on the **p** H6639
1Sa 11:12 The **p** then said to Samuel, "Who was it H6639
1Sa 11:14 Then Samuel said to the **p**, "Come, let us H6639
1Sa 11:15 So all the **p** went to Gilgal and made Saul H6639
1Sa 12: 6 Then Samuel said to the **p**, "It is the LORD H6639
1Sa 12:18 So all the **p** stood in awe of the LORD and H6639
1Sa 12:19 The **p** all said to Samuel, "Pray to the H6639
1Sa 12:22 great name the LORD will not reject his **p**, H6639
1Sa 13: 4 And the **p** were summoned to join Saul at H6639
1Sa 13:14 heart and appointed him ruler of his **p**, H6639
1Sa 14:24 Saul had bound the **p** under an oath, H6639
1Sa 14:27 his father had bound the **p** with the oath, H6639
1Sa 15: 1 sent to anoint you king over his **p** Israel; H6639
1Sa 15: 8 all his **p** he totally destroyed with the H6639
1Sa 15:18 completely destroy those **wicked p**, H2629
1Sa 15:30 the elders of my **p** and before Israel; H6639
1Sa 16: 7 LORD does not look at the things **p** look at. H132
1Sa 16: 7 **P** look at the outward appearance, but the H132
1Sa 19:24 This is why *p* **say**, "Is Saul also among the AIT
1Sa 23: 5 the Philistines and saved the **p** *of* Keilah. H3782
1Sa 26:19 however, **p** have done it, may H1201+2021+132
1Sa 27:12 "He has become so obnoxious to his **p** H6639
1Sa 31: 9 temple of their idols and among their **p**. H6639
1Sa 31:11 When the **p** *of* Jabesh Gilead heard what H3782
2Sa 1:18 he ordered that the **p** *of* Judah be taught H1201
2Sa 2: 7 the **p** *of* Judah have anointed me H1074
2Sa 3:18 I will rescue my **p** Israel from the hand H6639
2Sa 3:31 David said to Joab and all the **p** with him, H6639
2Sa 3:32 at Abner's tomb. All the **p** wept also. H6639
2Sa 3:34 And all the **p** wept over him again H6639
2Sa 3:36 All the **p** took note and were pleased H6639
2Sa 3:37 on that day all the **p** there and all Israel H6639
2Sa 4: 3 because the **p of Beeroth** fled to Gittaim H943
2Sa 5: 2 'You will shepherd my **p** Israel, and you H6639
2Sa 5:12 his kingdom for the sake of his **p** Israel. H6639
2Sa 6:18 he blessed the **p** in the name of the LORD H6639
2Sa 6:19 And all the **p** went to their homes H6639
2Sa 6:21 me ruler over the LORD's **p** Israel— H6639
2Sa 7: 7 I commanded to shepherd my **p** Israel, H6639
2Sa 7: 8 appointed you ruler over my **p** Israel. H6639
2Sa 7:10 a place for my **p** Israel and will plant H6639
2Sa 7:10 Wicked **p** will not oppress them anymore H1201
2Sa 7:11 time I appointed leaders over my **p** Israel. H6639
2Sa 7:23 And who is like your **p** Israel—the one H6639
2Sa 7:23 went out to redeem as a **p** for himself, H6639
2Sa 7:23 nations and their gods from before your **p**, H6639
2Sa 7:24 have established your **p** Israel as your very H6639
2Sa 7:26 Then **p** will say, 'The LORD Almighty is God NDT
2Sa 8:15 doing what was just and right for all his **p**. H6639
2Sa 10:12 fight bravely for our **p** and the cities of our H6639
2Sa 12:31 brought out the **p** who were there H6639
2Sa 13:34 up and saw many **p** on the road west of H6639
2Sa 14:13 a thing like this against the **p** *of* God? H6639
2Sa 14:15 king because the **p** have made me afraid. H6639
2Sa 15: 6 so he stole the hearts of the **p** *of* Israel. H408
2Sa 15:13 "The hearts of the **p** *of* Israel are with H408
2Sa 15:17 with all the **p** following him, and H6639
2Sa 15:20 and take your **p** with you. May the H278
2Sa 15:23 wept aloud as all the **p** passed by. H6639
2Sa 15:23 all the **p** moved on toward the H6639
2Sa 15:24 until all the **p** had finished leaving the H6639
2Sa 15:30 All the **p** with him covered their heads too H6639
2Sa 15:32 where *p used to* **worship** God, Hushai AIT
2Sa 16:14 The king and all the **p** with him arrived at H6639
2Sa 16:18 the LORD, by these **p**, and by all the men H6639
2Sa 17: 2 then all the **p** with him will flee. H6639
2Sa 17: 3 bring all the **p** back to you. The death H6639
2Sa 17: 3 return of all; all the **p** will be unharmed." H6639
2Sa 17:16 the king and all the **p** with him will be H6639
2Sa 17:22 So David and all the **p** with him set out H6639
2Sa 17:29 from cows' milk for David and his **p** to eat. H6639
2Sa 17:29 "The **p** have become exhausted and H6639
2Sa 19: 9 all the **p** were arguing among themselves, H6639
2Sa 19:39 So all the **p** crossed the Jordan, and then H6639
2Sa 20:22 went to all the **p** with her wise advice, H6639
2Sa 22: 3 my savior—from **violent** *p* you save me. AIT
2Sa 22:44 **P** I did not know now serve me H6639
2Sa 23: 3 'When one rules over **p** in righteousness H132
2Sa 24:15 thousand of the **p** from Dan to Beersheba H6639
2Sa 24:16 said to the angel who was afflicting the **p**, H6639
2Sa 24:17 the angel who was striking down the **p**, H6639
2Sa 24:21 that the plague on the **p** may be stopped." H6639
1Ki 1:39 the trumpet and all the **p** shouted, H6639
1Ki 1:40 And all the **p** went up after him, playing H6639
1Ki 3: 2 The **p**, however, were still sacrificing at the H6639
1Ki 3: 8 is here among the **p** you have chosen, H6639
1Ki 3: 8 have chosen, a great **p**, too numerous to H6639
1Ki 3: 9 heart to govern your **p** and to distinguish H6639
1Ki 3: 9 is able to govern this great **p** *of* yours?" H6639
1Ki 4:20 The **p** of Judah and Israel were as NDT
1Ki 4:30 than the wisdom of all the **p** *of* the East, H1201
1Ki 4:34 all nations *p* came to **listen** *to* Solomon's AIT
1Ki 6:13 will not abandon my **p** Israel. H6639
1Ki 8:16 the day I brought my **p** Israel out of Egypt, H6639
1Ki 8:16 I have chosen David to rule my **p** Israel. H6639
1Ki 8:30 servant and of your **p** Israel when they H6639
1Ki 8:33 "When your **p** Israel have been defeated H6639
1Ki 8:34 the sin of your **p** Israel and bring them H6639
1Ki 8:35 no rain because your **p** have sinned against NDT
1Ki 8:36 the sin of your servants, your **p** Israel. H6639
1Ki 8:36 land you gave your **p** for an inheritance. H6639
1Ki 8:38 is made by anyone among your **p** Israel— H6639
1Ki 8:41 not belong to your **p** Israel but has come H6639
1Ki 8:43 as do your own **p** Israel, and may H6639
1Ki 8:44 "When your **p** go to war against their H6639
1Ki 8:50 And forgive your **p**, who have sinned H6639
1Ki 8:51 they are your **p** and your inheritance H6639
1Ki 8:52 plea and to the plea of your **p** Israel, H6639
1Ki 8:56 has given rest to his **p** Israel just as he H6639
1Ki 8:59 the cause of his **p** Israel according to H6639
1Ki 8:65 **p** from Lebo Hamath to the Wadi of Egypt. NDT
1Ki 8:66 On the following day he sent the **p** away H6639
1Ki 8:66 his servant David and his **p** Israel. H6639
1Ki 9: 9 *P will* **answer**, 'Because they have forsaken AIT
1Ki 9:20 There were still **p** left from the Amorites H6639
1Ki 10: 8 How happy your **p** must be! How happy H408
1Ki 11:18 Then taking **p** from Paran with them, they H408
1Ki 12: 5 come back to me." So the **p** went away. H6639
1Ki 12: 6 would you advise me to answer these **p**?" H6639
1Ki 12: 7 a servant to these **p** and serve them and H6639
1Ki 12: 9 should we answer these **p** who say to me, H6639
1Ki 12:10 him replied, "These **p** have said to you H6639
1Ki 12:12 all the **p** returned to Rehoboam H6639
1Ki 12:13 The king answered the **p** harshly H6639
1Ki 12:15 So the king did not listen to the **p**, for this H6639
1Ki 12:23 Benjamin, and to the rest of the **p**, H6639
1Ki 12:27 If these **p** go up to offer sacrifices at the H6639
1Ki 12:28 He said to **the p**, "It is too much for you H2157S
1Ki 12:30 the **p** came to worship the one at Bethel H6639
1Ki 12:31 appointed priests from all sorts of **p**, H6639
1Ki 13:25 *Some* **p** who passed by saw the body lying H408
1Ki 13:33 the high places from all sorts of **p**. H6639
1Ki 14: 2 who told me I would be king over this **p**. H6639
1Ki 14: 7 up from among the **p** and appointed you H6639
1Ki 14: 7 appointed you ruler over my **p** Israel. H6639
1Ki 14:24 the **p** engaged in all the detestable NDT
1Ki 16: 2 appointed you ruler over my **p** Israel, H6639
1Ki 16: 2 caused my **p** Israel to sin and to H6639
1Ki 16:21 Then the **p** *of* Israel were split into two H6639
1Ki 18:19 Now summon the **p** from all over Israel to NDT
1Ki 18:21 Elijah went before the **p** and said, "How H6639
1Ki 18:21 follow him." But the **p** said nothing. H6639
1Ki 18:24 Then all the **p** said, "What you say is H6639
1Ki 18:30 Then Elijah said to all the **p**, "Come here H6639
1Ki 18:37 answer me, so these **p** will know that you H6639
1Ki 18:39 When all the **p** saw this, they fell H6639
1Ki 19:21 to cook the meat and gave it to the **p**, H6639
1Ki 20: 8 The elders and the **p** all answered, "Don't H6639
1Ki 20:42 your life for his life, your **p** for his people. H6639
1Ki 20:42 your life for his life, your people for his **p**. H6639
1Ki 21: 9 in a prominent place among the **p**. H6639
1Ki 21:12 in a prominent place among the **p**. H6639
1Ki 21:13 charges against Naboth before the **p**, H6639
1Ki 22: 4 "I am as you are, my **p** as your people, my H6639
1Ki 22: 4 my people as your **p**, my horses as your H6639
1Ki 22:17 the LORD said, '**These** *p* have no master. AIT
1Ki 22:28 he added, "Mark my words, all you **p**!" H6639
1Ki 22:43 the **p** continued to offer sacrifices and H6639
2Ki 2:19 The **p** *of* the city said to Elisha, "Look, our H408
2Ki 3: 7 "I am as you are, my **p** as your people, my H6639
2Ki 3: 7 my people as your **p**, my horses as your H6639
2Ki 4:13 "I have a home among my own **p**. H6639
2Ki 4:41 the pot and said, "Serve it to the **p** to eat." H6639
2Ki 4:42 "Give it to the **p** to eat," Elisha said. H6639
2Ki 4:43 Elisha answered, "Give it to the **p** to eat. H6639
2Ki 6:30 along the wall, the **p** looked, and they H6639
2Ki 7:16 Then the **p** went out and plundered the H6639
2Ki 7:17 the **p** trampled him in the gateway H6639
2Ki 7:20 the **p** trampled him in the gateway H6639
2Ki 9: 6 'I anoint you king over the LORD's **p** Israel. H6639
2Ki 10: 9 He stood before all the **p** and said, "You H6639
2Ki 10:18 brought all the **p** together and said to H6639
2Ki 10:27 and *p have* **used** it for a latrine to this day. AIT
2Ki 11:12 the **p** clapped their hands and shouted NDT
2Ki 11:13 the noise made by the guards and the **p**, H6639
2Ki 11:13 she went to the **p** at the temple of the H6639
2Ki 11:14 all the **p** *of* the land were rejoicing H6639
2Ki 11:17 the king and **p** that they would be H6639
2Ki 11:17 people that they would be the LORD's **p**. H6639
2Ki 11:17 a covenant between the king and the **p**. H6639
2Ki 11:18 All the **p** *of* the land went to the temple of H6639
2Ki 11:19 the guards and all the **p** *of* the land, and H6639
2Ki 11:20 All the **p** *of* the land rejoiced, and the city H6639
2Ki 12: 3 the **p** continued to offer sacrifices and H6639
2Ki 12: 8 money from the **p** and that they would H6639
2Ki 14: 4 the **p** continued to offer sacrifices and H6639
2Ki 14:21 Then all the **p** *of* Judah took Azariah, who H6639
2Ki 15: 4 the **p** continued to offer sacrifices and H6639
2Ki 15: 5 palace and governed the **p** *of* the land. H6639

Book	Ref	Context	Number
2Ki	15:10	He attacked him in front of the **p**	H6639
2Ki	15:29	Naphtali, and deported **the p** to Assyria.	H4392S
2Ki	15:35	the **p** continued to offer sacrifices and	H6639
2Ki	16: 6	Aram by driving out the **p of Judah**.	H3374
2Ki	16:15	the burnt offering of all the **p** *of* the land,	H6639
2Ki	17:20	the LORD rejected all the **p** *of* Israel;	H2446
2Ki	17:23	So the **p** of Israel were taken from their	NDT
2Ki	17:24	The king of Assyria brought **p** from Babylon	NDT
2Ki	17:25	them and they killed some of **the p**.	H2157S
2Ki	17:26	"The **p** you deported and resettled in the	H1580
2Ki	17:26	because the **p** do not know what he	H4392S
2Ki	17:27	there and teach **the p** what the god of	H4392S
2Ki	17:29	the shrines the **p of Samaria** had made at	H9085
2Ki	17:30	The **p** *from* Babylon made Sukkoth Benoth	H408
2Ki	17:32	appointed **all sorts** *of* their own *p* to officiate	AIT
2Ki	17:41	Even while these **p** were worshiping the	H1580
2Ki	18:26	in the hearing of the **p** on the wall."	H6639
2Ki	18:27	and not to the **p** sitting on the wall	H408
2Ki	18:36	But the **p** remained silent and said	H6639
2Ki	19:12	Rezeph and the **p** *of* Eden who were in	H1201
2Ki	19:26	Their **p**, drained of power, are dismayed	H3782
2Ki	19:35	When *the p* **got up** the next morning—there	AIT
2Ki	20: 5	the ruler of my **p**, 'This is what the LORD,	H6639
2Ki	21: 9	But *the p did* not **listen**. Manasseh led them	AIT
2Ki	21:24	Then the **p** *of* the land killed all who had	H6639
2Ki	22: 4	doorkeepers have collected from the **p**.	H6639
2Ki	22:13	me and for the **p** and for all Judah	H6639
2Ki	22:16	to bring disaster on this place and its **p**,	H3782
2Ki	22:19	spoken against this place and its **p**—	H3782
2Ki	23: 2	the temple of the LORD with the **p** *of* Judah,	H408
2Ki	23: 2	all the **p** from the least to the greatest.	H6639
2Ki	23: 3	Then all the **p** pledged themselves to the	H6639
2Ki	23: 6	over the graves of the **common p**.	H1201+6639
2Ki	23:13	the detestable god of the **p** *of* Ammon.	H1201
2Ki	23:17	The **p** *of* the city said, "It marks the tomb	H408
2Ki	23:21	The king gave this order to all the **p**	H6639
2Ki	23:30	And the **p** *of* the land took Jehoahaz son	H6639
2Ki	23:35	gold from the **p** *of* the land according	H6639
2Ki	24:14	Only the poorest **p** *of* the land were left.	H6639
2Ki	24:15	officials and the **prominent p** *of* the land.	H380
2Ki	25: 3	that there was no food for the **p** to eat.	H6639
2Ki	25:11	into exile the **p** who remained in the	H6639
2Ki	25:12	some of the **poorest** *p* *of* the land to work	AIT
2Ki	25:19	of conscripting the **p** *of* the land and sixty	H6639
2Ki	25:22	to be over the **p** he had left behind in	H6639
2Ki	25:26	all the **p** from the least to the greatest	H6639
1Ch	2:10	of Nahshon, the leader of the **p** *of* Judah.	H1201
1Ch	4:14	called this because *its p* **were** skilled workers.	AIT
1Ch	4:27	become as numerous as the **p** *of* Judah.	H1201
1Ch	5:21	one hundred thousand **p** captive,	H5883+132
1Ch	5:23	The **p** *of* the half-tribe of Manasseh were	H1201
1Ch	9: 6	The **p from Judah** numbered 690	H278+2157
1Ch	9: 9	The **p from Benjamin**, as listed in	H278+2157
1Ch	10: 9	the news among their idols and their **p**.	H6639
1Ch	11: 2	'You will shepherd my **p** Israel, and you	H6639
1Ch	13: 2	wide to the rest of our **p** throughout the	H278
1Ch	13: 4	because it seemed right to all the **p**.	H6639
1Ch	14: 2	highly exalted for the sake of his **p** Israel.	H6639
1Ch	16: 2	he blessed the **p** in the name of the LORD.	H6639
1Ch	16:36	Then all the **p** said "Amen" and "Praise	H6639
1Ch	16:43	Then all the **p** left, each for their own	H6639
1Ch	17: 6	whom I commanded to shepherd my **p**,	H6639
1Ch	17: 7	appointed you ruler over my **p** Israel.	H6639
1Ch	17: 9	a place for my **p** Israel and will plant	H6639
1Ch	17: 9	Wicked **p** will not oppress them anymore	H1201
1Ch	17:10	time I appointed leaders over my **p** Israel.	H6639
1Ch	17:21	And who is like your **p** Israel—the one	H6639
1Ch	17:21	God went out to redeem a **p** for himself,	H6639
1Ch	17:21	by driving out nations from before your **p**,	H6639
1Ch	17:22	You made your **p** Israel your very own	H6639
1Ch	17:24	Then **p** will say, 'The LORD Almighty, the	NDT
1Ch	18:14	doing what was just and right for all his **p**.	H6639
1Ch	19:13	fight bravely for our **p** and the cities of our	H6639
1Ch	20: 3	brought out the **p** who were there	H6639
1Ch	21:15	said to the angel who was destroying the **p**,	NDT
1Ch	21:17	do not let this plague remain on your **p**."	H6639
1Ch	21:22	that the plague on the **p** may be stopped.	H6639
1Ch	22:18	land is subject to the LORD and to his **p**.	H6639
1Ch	23:25	granted rest to his **p** and has come to	H6639
1Ch	28: 2	fellow Israelites, my **p**. I had it in my heart	H6639
1Ch	28:21	officials and all the **p** will obey your every	H6639
1Ch	29: 9	The **p** rejoiced at the willing response of	H6639
1Ch	29:14	and who are my **p**, that we should be	H6639
1Ch	29:17	how willingly your **p** who are here have	H6639
1Ch	29:18	thoughts in the hearts of your **p** forever,	H6639
2Ch	1: 9	me king over a **p** who are as numerous	H6639
2Ch	1:10	that I may lead this **p**, for who is able to	H6639
2Ch	1:10	is able to govern this great **p** *of* yours?"	H6639
2Ch	1:11	to govern my **p** over whom I have made	H6639
2Ch	2:11	"Because the LORD loves his **p**, he has	H6639
2Ch	2:18	foremen over them to keep the **p** working.	H6639
2Ch	6: 5	'Since the day I brought my **p** out of Egypt,	H6639
2Ch	6: 5	anyone to be ruler over my **p** Israel.	H6639
2Ch	6: 6	I have chosen David to rule my **p** Israel.'	H6639
2Ch	6:11	the LORD that he made with the **p** *of* Israel."	H1201
2Ch	6:21	servant and of your **p** Israel when they	H6639
2Ch	6:24	"When your **p** Israel have been defeated	H6639
2Ch	6:25	the sin of your **p** Israel and bring them	H6639
2Ch	6:26	no rain because your **p** have sinned against	NDT
2Ch	6:27	the sin of your servants, your **p** Israel.	H6639
2Ch	6:27	land you gave your **p** for an inheritance.	H6639
2Ch	6:29	is made by anyone among your **p** Israel—	H6639
2Ch	6:32	not belong to your **p** Israel but has come	H6639
2Ch	6:33	as do your own **p** Israel, and may	H6639
2Ch	6:34	"When your **p** go to war against their	H6639
2Ch	6:39	And forgive your **p**, who have sinned	H6639
2Ch	6:41	may your **faithful p** rejoice in your	H2883
2Ch	7: 4	the king and all the **p** offered sacrifices	H6639
2Ch	7: 5	king and all the **p** dedicated the temple	H6639
2Ch	7: 8	**p** from Lebo Hamath to the Wadi of Egypt.	NDT
2Ch	7:10	month he sent the **p** to their homes,	H6639
2Ch	7:10	David and Solomon and for his **p** Israel.	H6639
2Ch	7:13	the land or send a plague among my **p**,	H6639
2Ch	7:14	if my **p**, who are called by my name, will	H6639
2Ch	7:22	*P will* **answer**, 'Because they have forsaken	AIT
2Ch	8: 7	There were still **p** left from the Hittites	H6639
2Ch	8: 7	Jebusites (these **p** were not Israelites).	H889S
2Ch	8: 8	descendants of *all* **these** *p* remaining in the	AIT
2Ch	9: 7	How happy your **p** must be! How happy	H408
2Ch	10: 5	me in three days." So the **p** went away.	H6639
2Ch	10: 6	would you advise me to answer these **p**?"	H6639
2Ch	10: 7	be kind to these **p** and please them and	H6639
2Ch	10: 9	should we answer these **p** who say to me,	H6639
2Ch	10:10	with him replied, "The **p** have said to you	H6639
2Ch	10:12	all the **p** returned to Rehoboam	H6639
2Ch	10:15	So the king did not listen to the **p**, for this	H6639
2Ch	13:12	**P** *of* Israel, do not fight against the LORD	H1201
2Ch	13:18	the **p** *of* Judah were victorious	H1201
2Ch	15: 9	*p* from Ephraim, Manasseh and Simeon *who had* **settled**	AIT
2Ch	16:10	Asa brutally oppressed some of the **p**.	H6639
2Ch	17: 9	all the towns of Judah and taught the **p**.	H6639
2Ch	18: 2	him and the **p** with him and urged him	H6639
2Ch	18: 3	as you are, and my **p** as your people; we	H6639
2Ch	18: 3	my people as your **p**; we will join you	H6639
2Ch	18:16	the LORD said, '**These** *p* have no master.	AIT
2Ch	18:27	he added, "Mark my words, all you **p**!"	H6639
2Ch	19: 4	out again among the **p** from Beersheba to	H6639
2Ch	19:10	before you from your **p** who live in the	H278
2Ch	19:10	his wrath will come on you and your **p**.	H278
2Ch	20: 2	*Some p* **came** and told Jehoshaphat, "A vast	AIT
2Ch	20: 4	The **p** of Judah came together to seek help	NDT
2Ch	20: 7	this land before your **p** Israel and give it	H6639
2Ch	20:18	all the **p** *of* Judah and Jerusalem fell	H3782
2Ch	20:20	"Listen to me, Judah and **p** *of* Jerusalem!	H3782
2Ch	20:21	After consulting the **p**, Jehoshaphat	H6639
2Ch	20:33	the **p** still had not set their hearts on	H6639
2Ch	21:11	had caused the **p** *of* Jerusalem to	H3782
2Ch	21:13	have led Judah and the **p** *of* Jerusalem to	H3782
2Ch	21:14	So now the LORD is about to strike your **p**	H6639
2Ch	21:19	His **p** made no funeral fire in his honor	H6639
2Ch	22: 1	The **p** *of* Jerusalem made Ahaziah	H3782
2Ch	23:12	the noise of the **p** running and cheering	H6639
2Ch	23:13	all the **p** *of* the land were rejoicing	H6639
2Ch	23:16	the **p** and the king would be the LORD's	H6639
2Ch	23:16	the king would be the LORD's **p**.	H6639
2Ch	23:17	All the **p** went to the temple of Baal and	H6639
2Ch	23:20	the rulers of the **p** and all the people of	H6639
2Ch	23:20	people and all the **p** *of* the land and	H6639
2Ch	23:21	All the **p** *of* the land rejoiced, and the city	H6639
2Ch	24:10	the officials and all the **p** brought their	H6639
2Ch	24:19	sent prophets to **the p** to bring them	H2157S
2Ch	24:20	He stood before the **p** and said, "This is	H6639
2Ch	24:23	killed all the leaders of the **p**.	H6639
2Ch	25: 5	Amaziah called the **p** of Judah together	NDT
2Ch	25: 7	Israel—not with any of the **p** *of* Ephraim.	H1201
2Ch	25:13	three thousand **p** and carried off great	H2157S
2Ch	25:14	he brought back the gods of the **p** *of* Seir.	H1201
2Ch	25:15	not save their own **p** from your hand?"	H6639
2Ch	26: 1	Then all the **p** *of* Judah took Uzziah, who	H6639
2Ch	26:10	He had **p** working his fields and vineyards	H438
2Ch	26:21	palace and governed the **p** *of* the land.	H6639
2Ch	26:23	to the kings, for *p* **said**, "He had leprosy."	AIT
2Ch	27: 2	The **p**, however, continued their corrupt	H6639
2Ch	28: 5	him and took **many** of his *p* as prisoners	AIT
2Ch	29:36	Hezekiah and all the **p** rejoiced at what	H6639
2Ch	29:36	at what God had brought about for his **p**,	H6639
2Ch	30: 3	themselves and the **p** had not assembled	H6639
2Ch	30: 5	calling the **p** to come to Jerusalem and	NDT
2Ch	30: 6	"**P** *of* Israel, return to the LORD, the God of	H1201
2Ch	30:10	Zebulun, but **p** scorned and ridiculed them.	NDT
2Ch	30:12	of God was on the **p** to give them unity of	NDT
2Ch	30:13	A very large crowd of **p** assembled in	H6639
2Ch	30:18	most of the many **p** who came from	H6639
2Ch	30:20	LORD heard Hezekiah and healed the **p**.	H6639
2Ch	30:27	the Levites stood to bless the **p**,	H6639
2Ch	31: 4	He ordered the **p** living in Jerusalem to	H6639
2Ch	31: 6	The **p** *of* Israel and Judah who lived in the	H1201
2Ch	31: 8	praised the LORD and blessed his **p** Israel.	H6639
2Ch	31:10	"Since the **p** began to bring their	NDT
2Ch	31:10	because the LORD has blessed his **p**, and	H6639
2Ch	32: 4	a large **group of p** who blocked all	H6639
2Ch	32: 6	officers over the **p** and assembled them	H6639
2Ch	32: 8	And the **p** gained confidence from what	H6639
2Ch	32: 9	Judah and for all the **p** of Judah who were	NDT
2Ch	32:14	has been able to save his **p** from me?	H6639
2Ch	32:15	able to deliver his **p** from my hand or the	H6639
2Ch	32:17	did not rescue their **p** from my hand,	H6639
2Ch	32:17	will not rescue his **p** from my hand."	H6639
2Ch	32:18	in Hebrew to the **p** *of* Jerusalem who	H6639
2Ch	32:22	Hezekiah and the **p** *of* Jerusalem from the	H3782
2Ch	32:26	as did the **p** *of* Jerusalem; therefore	H3782
2Ch	32:33	All Judah and the **p** *of* Jerusalem	H3782
2Ch	33: 9	led Judah and the **p** *of* Jerusalem astray,	H3782
2Ch	33:10	The LORD spoke to Manasseh and his **p**	H6639
2Ch	33:17	The **p**, however, continued to sacrifice at	H6639
2Ch	33:25	Then the **p** *of* the land killed all who had	H6639
2Ch	34: 9	had collected from the **p** of Manasseh,	NDT
2Ch	34: 9	from all the **p** of Judah and Benjamin	NDT
2Ch	34:24	to bring disaster on this place and its **p**—	H3782
2Ch	34:27	he spoke against this place and its **p**,	H3782
2Ch	34:30	the temple of the LORD with the **p** *of* Judah,	H408
2Ch	34:30	all the **p** from the least to the greatest.	H6639
2Ch	34:32	the **p** *of* Jerusalem did this in accordance	H3782
2Ch	35: 3	serve the LORD your God and his **p** Israel.	H6639
2Ch	35: 5	of your fellow Israelites, the **lay p**.	H1201+6639
2Ch	35: 7	all the **lay p** who were there a	H1201+6639
2Ch	35: 8	voluntarily to the **p** and the priests and	H6639
2Ch	35:12	the families of the **p** to offer to the	H1201+6639
2Ch	35:13	served them quickly to all the **p**.	H1201+6639
2Ch	35:18	who were there with the **p** *of* Jerusalem.	H3782
2Ch	36: 1	And the **p** *of* the land took Jehoahaz son	H6639
2Ch	36:14	the priests and the **p** became more and	H6639
2Ch	36:15	he had pity on his **p** and on his dwelling	H6639
2Ch	36:16	aroused against his **p** and there was no	H6639
2Ch	36:23	Any of his **p** among you may go up, and	H6639
Ezr	1: 3	Any of his **p** among you may go up to	H6639
Ezr	1: 4	the **p** are to provide them with silver and	H408
Ezr	2: 1	Now these are the **p** *of* the province who	H1201
Ezr	2: 2	The list of the men of the **p** *of* Israel:	H6639
Ezr	2:70	along with some of the other **p**, and the	H6639
Ezr	3: 1	the **p** assembled together as one in	H6639
Ezr	3: 7	olive oil to the **p of Sidon** and Tyre,	H7479
Ezr	3: 8	son of Jozadak and the rest of the **p**	H278
Ezr	3:11	And all the **p** gave a great shout of praise	H6639
Ezr	3:13	because the **p** made so much noise.	H6639
Ezr	4: 4	to discourage the **p** *of* Judah and make	H6639
Ezr	4: 6	against the **p** *of* Judah and Jerusalem.	H3782
Ezr	4: 9	administrators over the **p from Persia**,	A10060
Ezr	4:10	the other **p** whom the great and	A10040
Ezr	4:12	know that the **p** who came up to us	A10316S
Ezr	5: 8	The **p** are building it with large stones and	NDT
Ezr	5:12	temple and deported the **p** to Babylon.	A10553
Ezr	6:12	any king or **p** who lifts a hand to	A10553
Ezr	6:16	Then the **p** *of* Israel—the priests, the	A10120
Ezr	7:16	offerings of the **p** and priests for the	A10553
Ezr	7:25	justice to all the **p** of Trans-Euphrates—	A10553
Ezr	8:15	I checked among the **p** and the priests,	H6639
Ezr	8:36	assistance to the **p** and to the house of	H6639
Ezr	9: 1	me and said, "The **p** of Israel, including	H6639
Ezr	10: 9	all the **p** were sitting in the square before	H6639
Ezr	10:13	But there are many **p** here and it is the	H6639
Ne	1: 6	night for your servants, the **p** *of* Israel.	H1201
Ne	1: 9	then even if your **exiled** *p* are at the farthest	AIT
Ne	1:10	"They are your servants and your **p**, whom	H6639
Ne	4: 6	the **p** worked with all their heart.	H6639
Ne	4: 7	the **p of Ashdod** heard that the	H847
Ne	4:10	Meanwhile, the **p** in Judah said, "The	NDT
Ne	4:13	I stationed *some of* the **p** behind the	H6639
Ne	4:14	the officials and the rest of the **p**, "Don't	H6639
Ne	4:16	themselves behind all the **p** *of* Judah	H1074
Ne	4:19	the officials and the rest of the **p**, "The	H6639
Ne	4:22	At that time I also said to the **p**, "Have	H6639
Ne	5: 7	"You are charging your own **p** interest!"	H278
Ne	5: 8	Now you are selling your own **p**, only for	H278
Ne	5:10	are also lending **the p** money and grain.	H2157S
Ne	5:13	And the **p** did as they had promised.	H6639
Ne	5:15	a heavy burden on the **p** and took forty	H6639
Ne	5:15	Their assistants also lorded it over the **p**	H6639
Ne	5:18	the demands were heavy on these **p**.	H6639
Ne	5:19	my God, for all I have done for these **p**.	H6639
Ne	7: 2	feared God more than **most** *p* do.	AIT
Ne	7: 4	there were few **p** in it, and the houses	H6639
Ne	7: 5	the **common p** for registration	H6639
Ne	7: 6	These are the **p** *of* the province who came	H1201
Ne	7:72	by the rest of the **p** was 20,000 darics of	H6639
Ne	7:73	with certain of the **p** and the rest of the	H6639
Ne	8: 1	all the **p** came together as one in the	H6639
Ne	8: 3	And all the **p** listened attentively to the	H6639
Ne	8: 5	All the **p** could see him because he was	H6639
Ne	8: 5	as he opened it, the **p** all stood up.	H6639
Ne	8: 6	all the **p** lifted their hands and	H6639
Ne	8: 7	instructed the **p** in the Law while the	H6639
Ne	8: 7	the Law while the **p** were standing there.	H6639
Ne	8: 8	meaning so that the **p** understood what was	NDT
Ne	8: 9	were instructing the **p** said to them all,	H6639
Ne	8: 9	For all the **p** had been weeping as they	H6639
Ne	8:11	The Levites calmed all the **p**, saying, "Be	H6639
Ne	8:12	Then all the **p** went away to eat and drink,	H6639
Ne	8:16	So the **p** went out and brought back	H6639
Ne	9:10	all his officials and all the **p** *of* his land,	H6639
Ne	9:32	on our ancestors and all your **p**, from the	H6639
Ne	10:14	The leaders of the **p**: Parosh	H6639
Ne	10:28	"The rest of the **p**—priests, Levites	H6639
Ne	10:34	the Levites and the **p**—have cast lots to	H6639
Ne	10:39	The **p** *of* Israel, including the Levites, are	H1201
Ne	11: 1	the leaders of the **p** settled in Jerusalem.	H6639
Ne	11: 1	The rest of the **p** cast lots to bring one out	H6639
Ne	11: 2	The **p** commended all who volunteered to	H6639
Ne	11: 4	while other **p** from both Judah and	H1201
Ne	11:24	king's agent in all affairs relating to the **p**.	H6639
Ne	11:25	some of the **p** *of* Judah lived in Kiriath	H1201
Ne	12:30	they purified the **p**, the gates and the wall	H6639
Ne	12:38	together with half the **p**—past the Tower	H6639
Ne	13: 1	in the hearing of the **p** and there it was	H6639
Ne	13: 3	When **the p** heard this law, they	H4392S

Ne 13:15 days I saw *p* in Judah **treading** winepresses AIT
Ne 13:16 **P from Tyre** who lived in Jerusalem were H7660
Ne 13:16 on the Sabbath to the **p** *of* Judah. H1201
Est 1: 5 all the **p** from the least to the greatest H6639
Est 1:11 to display her beauty to the **p** and nobles, H6639
Est 1:22 and to **each p** in their own H6639+2256+6639
Est 3: 6 having learned who Mordecai's **p** were, H6639
Est 3: 6 a way to destroy all Mordecai's **p**, H6639
Est 3: 8 "There is a certain **p** dispersed among the H6639
Est 3: 8 are different from those of all other **p**, H6639
Est 3:11 "and do with the **p** as you please. H6639
Est 3:12 language of **each p** all H6639+2256+6639
Est 3:14 made known to the **p** of every nationality H6639
Est 4: 8 mercy and plead with him for her **p**. H6639
Est 4:11 officials and the **p** *of* the royal provinces H6639
Est 7: 3 And spare my **p**—this is my request. H6639
Est 7: 4 For I and my **p** have been sold to be H6639
Est 8: 6 can I bear to see disaster fall on my **p**? H6639
Est 8: 9 of **each p** and also H6639+2256+6639
Est 8:13 made known to the **p** of every nationality NDT
Est 8:17 And **many** *p* of other nationalities became AIT
Est 9: 2 because the **p** of all the other nationalities NDT
Est 10: 3 the good of his **p** and spoke up for the H6639
Job 1: 3 greatest man among all the **p** *of* the East. H1201
Job 4:13 in the night, when deep sleep falls on **p**, H408
Job 12: 2 "Doubtless you are the only **p** who matter H6639
Job 14:12 **p** will not awake or be roused from their NDT
Job 16:10 *P* **open** their mouths to jeer at me; they strike AIT
Job 17: 6 to everyone, a man in whose face **p** spit. NDT
Job 18:19 no offspring or descendants among his **p**, H6639
Job 18:20 *P of* the **west** are appalled at his fate; those AIT
Job 22: 6 no reason; you stripped **p** of their clothing NDT
Job 22:29 When *p are* **brought low** and you say, 'Lift AIT
Job 28: 4 far from *other* **p** they dangle and sway. H632
Job 28: 9 *P* **assault** the flinty rock *with* their hands and AIT
Job 29:21 "*P* **listened** to me expectantly, waiting in AIT
Job 31:33 if I have concealed my sin as **p** do, by H132
Job 33:15 deep sleep falls on **p** as they slumber in H408
Job 34:20 the **p** are shaken and they pass away H6639
Job 34:23 God has no need to examine **p** further, that H408
Job 34:30 from ruling, from laying snares for the **p**. H6639
Job 35: 8 and your righteousness only *other* **p**. H1201+132
Job 35: 9 "*P* **cry out** under a load of oppression; they AIT
Job 35:12 not answer when *p* **cry out** because of the AIT
Job 36: 8 But if *p* **are bound** in chains, held fast by AIT
Job 36:20 to drag **p** away from their homes. H6639
Job 36:24 his work, which **p** have praised in song. H408
Job 37: 7 his work, he stops all **p** from their labor. H132
Job 37:13 He brings the clouds to punish **p**, or to water NDT
Job 37:24 Therefore, **p** revere him, for does he not H408
Ps 3: 8 May your blessing be on your **p**. H6639
Ps 4: 2 How long will you **p** turn my glory H1201+408
Ps 5: 4 with you, **evil** *p* are not welcome. AIT
Ps 14: 4 They devour my **p** as though eating bread; H6639
Ps 14: 7 When the LORD restores his **p**, let Jacob H6639
Ps 16: 3 I say of the **holy p** who are in the land H7705
Ps 17: 4 Though **p** tried to bribe me, I have kept H132
Ps 17:14 By your hand save me from *such* **p**, LORD H5493
Ps 18:43 delivered me from the attacks of the **p**; H6639
Ps 18:43 **P** I did not know now serve me H6639
Ps 22: 6 scorned by everyone, despised by the **p**. H6639
Ps 22:17 on display; **p** stare and gloat over me. H2156S
Ps 22:22 I will declare your name to my **p**; in the H278
Ps 22:31 declaring to a **p** yet unborn: H6639
Ps 28: 8 The LORD is the strength of **his p**, H4564S
Ps 28: 9 Save your **p** and bless your inheritance H6639
Ps 29:11 The LORD gives strength to his **p**; the LORD H6639
Ps 29:11 people; the LORD blesses his **p** with peace. H6639
Ps 30: 4 the LORD, you his **faithful p**; praise his H2883
Ps 31:23 the LORD, all his **faithful p**! The LORD H2883
Ps 33: 8 let all the **p** *of* the world revere him. H3782
Ps 33:12 the **p** he chose for his inheritance. H6639
Ps 34: 9 the LORD, you his **holy p**, for those who H7705
Ps 36: 6 LORD, preserve both **p** and animals. H132
Ps 36: 7 **P** take refuge in the shadow of your H1201+132
Ps 37: 7 do not fret when **p** succeed in their ways H408
Ps 42: 3 day and night, while *p* **say** to me all day long AIT
Ps 44:12 You sold your **p** for a pittance, gaining H6639
Ps 45:10 Forget your **p** and your father's house H6639
Ps 45:12 **p** of wealth will seek your favor. H6639
Ps 47: 9 assemble as the **p** *of* the God of Abraham H6639
Ps 49:12 **P**, despite their wealth, do not endure; they H132
Ps 49:18 and *p* **praise** you when you prosper— AIT
Ps 49:20 **P** who have wealth but lack understanding H132
Ps 50: 4 the earth, that he may judge his **p**: H6639
Ps 50: 5 "Gather to me this **consecrated p**, who H2883
Ps 50: 7 my **p**, and I will speak; I will H6639
Ps 52: 9 you in the presence of your **faithful p**. H2883
Ps 53: 4 They devour my **p** as though eating bread; H6639
Ps 53: 6 When God restores his **p**, let Jacob H6639
Ps 54: 3 attacking me; **ruthless** *p* are trying to kill me AIT
Ps 54: 3 to kill me—**p** without regard for God. H4392S
Ps 58: 1 Do you judge **p** with equity? H1201+132
Ps 58:11 Then **p** will say, "Surely the righteous still H132
Ps 59:11 Lord our shield, or my **p** will forget. H6639
Ps 60: 3 You have shown your **p** desperate times H6639
Ps 62: 8 at all times, you **p**; pour out your hearts H6639
Ps 64: 9 All **p** will fear; they will proclaim the works H132
Ps 65: 2 who answer prayer, to you all **p** will come. H1414
Ps 65: 9 with water to provide **the p** with grain, H4392S
Ps 66:12 You let **p** ride over our heads; we went H632
Ps 68: 7 went out before your **p**, when you H6639
Ps 68:10 Your **p** settled in it, and from your bounty H2653
Ps 68:18 you received gifts from **p**, even from the H132
Ps 68:35 Israel gives power and strength to his **p**. H6639
Ps 69:11 I put on sackcloth, **p** make sport of me. H2157S
Ps 69:33 needy and does not despise his **captive** *p*. AIT
Ps 69:35 Then *p will* **settle** there and possess it AIT
Ps 72: 2 May he judge your **p** in righteousness H6639
Ps 72: 3 the mountains bring prosperity to the **p**, H6639
Ps 72: 4 afflicted among the **p** and save the H6639
Ps 72:15 *May p* ever **pray** for him and bless him all AIT
Ps 73:10 Therefore their **p** turn to them and drink H6639
Ps 74: 2 long ago, the **p** *of* your inheritance, whom H8657
Ps 74:18 how foolish **p** have reviled your name. H6639
Ps 74:19 not forget the lives of your **afflicted** *p* forever. AIT
Ps 75: 1 Name is near; *p* **tell** *of* your wonderful deeds. AIT
Ps 75: 3 When the earth and all its **p** quake, it is I H3782
Ps 77:15 your mighty arm you redeemed your **p**, H6639
Ps 77:20 You led your **p** like a flock by the hand of H6639
Ps 78: 1 My **p**, hear my teaching; listen to the H6639
Ps 78:20 Can he supply meat for his **p**?" H6639
Ps 78:24 he rained down manna for **the p** to eat H2157S
Ps 78:52 But he brought his **p** out like a flock; he H6639
Ps 78:62 He gave his **p** over to the sword; he was H6639
Ps 78:71 him to be the shepherd of his **p** Jacob, H6639
Ps 79: 2 the flesh of your **own p** for the animals of H2883
Ps 79:13 Then we your **p**, the sheep of your pasture H6639
Ps 80: 4 smolder against the prayers of your **p**? H6639
Ps 80:16 burned with fire; at your rebuke your *p* **perish**. AIT
Ps 81: 8 Hear me, my **p**, and I will warn you—if H6639
Ps 81:11 "But my **p** would not listen to me; Israel H6639
Ps 81:13 "If my **p** would only listen to me, if Israel H6639
Ps 83: 3 cunning they conspire against your **p**; H6639
Ps 83: 7 Amalek, Philistia, with the **p** *of* Tyre. H3782
Ps 85: 2 the iniquity of your **p** and covered all their H6639
Ps 85: 6 us again, that your **p** may rejoice in you? H6639
Ps 85: 8 he promises peace to his **p**, his faithful H6639
Ps 86:14 ruthless **p** *are* trying to kill me H6337
Ps 89:19 spoke in a vision, to your **faithful** *p* you said: AIT
Ps 89:19 up a young man from among the **p**. H6639
Ps 90: 3 You turn **p** back to dust, saying, "Return to H632
Ps 90: 5 Yet you sweep **p** away in the sleep of H4392S
Ps 92: 6 Senseless **p** do not know, fools do not H408
Ps 94: 5 They crush your **p**, LORD; they oppress H6639
Ps 94: 8 you senseless ones among the **p**; you H6639
Ps 94:14 For the LORD will not reject his **p**; he will H6639
Ps 95: 7 our God and we are the **p** *of* his pasture, H6639
Ps 95:10 'They are a **p** *whose* hearts go astray H6639
Ps 100: 3 we are his; we are his **p**, the sheep of his H6639
Ps 101: 3 I hate what **faithless** *p* do; I will have no part AIT
Ps 102:18 that a **p** not yet created may praise the H6639
Ps 103: 7 to Moses, his deeds to the **p** *of* Israel: H1201
Ps 104:14 plants for **p** to cultivate—bringing H132
Ps 104:23 Then **p** go out to their work, to their labor H132
Ps 105:24 The LORD made his **p** very fruitful; he H6639
Ps 105:25 whose hearts he turned to hate his **p**, to H6639
Ps 105:43 He brought out his **p** with rejoicing, his H6639
Ps 106: 4 when you show favor to your **p**, come to H6639
Ps 106:40 was angry with his **p** and abhorred his H6639
Ps 106:48 Let all the **p** say, "Amen!" Praise the H6639
Ps 107:32 the assembly of the **p** and praise him in H6639
Ps 109: 2 for *p who* are **wicked** and deceitful have AIT
Ps 111: 6 He has shown his **p** the power of his H6639
Ps 111: 9 He provided redemption for his **p**; he H6639
Ps 113: 8 with princes, with the princes of his **p**. H6639
Ps 114: 1 Jacob from a **p** *of* foreign tongue, H6639
Ps 115:12 He will bless his **p** Israel, he will bless the H1074
Ps 116:14 to the LORD in the presence of all his **p**. H6639
Ps 116:18 to the LORD in the presence of all his **p**, H6639
Ps 119:113 I hate **double-minded** *p*, but I love your law. AIT
Ps 124: 2 not been on our side when **p** attacked us, H132
Ps 125: 2 the LORD surrounds his **p** both now and H6639
Ps 132: 9 may your **faithful p** sing for joy. H2883
Ps 132:16 her **faithful p** will ever sing for joy. H2883
Ps 133: 1 pleasant it is when **God's p** live together in H278
Ps 135: 8 of Egypt, the firstborn of **p** and animals. H132
Ps 135:12 inheritance, an inheritance to his **p** Israel. H6639
Ps 135:14 will vindicate his **p** and have compassion H6639
Ps 136:16 to him who led his **p** through the H6639
Ps 142: 3 where I walk *p have* **hidden** a snare for me. AIT
Ps 144:15 Blessed is the **p** of whom this is true H6639
Ps 144:15 blessed is the **p** whose God is the LORD. H6639
Ps 145:10 praise you, LORD; your **faithful p** extol you. H2883
Ps 145:12 so that **all p** may know of your H1201+2021+132
Ps 147:13 your gates and blesses your **p** within you. H1201
Ps 148:14 And he has raised up for his **p** a horn, the H6639
Ps 148:14 servants, of Israel, the **p** close to his heart. H6639
Ps 149: 1 his praise in the assembly of his **faithful p**. H2883
Ps 149: 2 let the **p** *of* Zion be glad in their King. H1201
Ps 149: 4 For the LORD takes delight in his **p**; he H6639
Ps 149: 5 Let his **faithful p** rejoice in this honor and H2883
Ps 149: 9 this is the glory of all his **faithful p**. H2883
Pr 5:14 trouble in the assembly of **God's p**." H6337
Pr 6:30 *P do* not **despise** a thief if he steals to satisfy AIT
Pr 8: 4 "To you, O **p**, I call out; I raise my voice to H408
Pr 11:26 **P** curse the one who hoards grain, but H4211
Pr 12: 2 **Good** *p* obtain favor from the LORD, but he AIT
Pr 12:14 the fruit of their lips **p** are filled with good H408
Pr 12:22 but he delights in *p who* **are** trustworthy. AIT
Pr 13: 2 the fruit of their lips **p** enjoy good things, H408
Pr 14:34 exalts a nation, but sin condemns any **p**. H4211
Pr 24: 9 of folly are sin, and **p** detest a mocker. H132
Pr 26:16 eyes than seven *p who* **answer** discreetly. AIT
Pr 27:21 gold, but **p** are tested by their praise. H408
Pr 28:12 the wicked rise to power, **p** go into hiding. H132
Pr 28:15 bear is a wicked ruler over a helpless **p**. H6639
Pr 28:28 wicked rise to power, **p** go into hiding; but H132
Pr 29: 2 righteous thrive, the **p** rejoice; when the H6639
Pr 29: 2 when the wicked rule, the **p** groan. H6639
Pr 29:18 is no revelation, **p** cast off restraint; but H6639
Ecc 1: 3 What do **p** gain from all their labors at H132
Ecc 2: 3 was good for **p** to do under H1201+2021+132
Ecc 2:22 What do **p** get for all the toil and anxious H132
Ecc 3:12 nothing better for **p** than to be happy and H4392
Ecc 3:14 God does it so that *p will* **fear** him. AIT
Ecc 4:16 no end to all the **p** who were before them H6639
Ecc 6: 2 God gives *some* **p** wealth, possessions and H408
Ecc 7:21 Do not pay attention to every word *p* **say**, or AIT
Ecc 8:16 **p** getting no sleep day or night H2257+6524S
Ecc 9: 3 The hearts of **p**, moreover H1201+2021+132
Ecc 9:12 so **p** are trapped by evil times H1201+2021+132
Ecc 9:14 once a small city with only a few **p** in it. H408
Ecc 12: 4 when *p* **rise up** at the sound of birds AIT
Ecc 12: 5 when *p are* **afraid** of heights and of dangers AIT
Ecc 12: 5 Then **p** go to their eternal home and H132
Ecc 12: 9 he also imparted knowledge to the **p**. H6639
SS 6:12 set me among the royal chariots of my **p**. H6639
Isa 1: 3 does not know, my **p** do not understand." H6639
Isa 1: 4 the sinful nation, a **p** whose guilt is great H6639
Isa 1:10 instruction of our God, you **p** *of* Gomorrah! H6639
Isa 2: 6 have abandoned your **p**, the descendants H6639
Isa 2: 9 So **p** will be brought low and everyone H132
Isa 2:19 *P will* **flee** to caves in the rocks and to holes AIT
Isa 2:20 In that day **p** will throw away to the moles H132
Isa 3: 5 **P** will oppress each other—man against H6639
Isa 3: 7 do not make me the leader of the **p**." H6639
Isa 3:12 Youths oppress my **p**, women rule over H6639
Isa 3:12 My **p**, your guides lead you astray; they H6639
Isa 3:13 his place in court; he rises to judge the **p**. H6639
Isa 3:14 against the elders and leaders of his **p**: H6639
Isa 3:15 mean by crushing my **p** and grinding the H6639
Isa 5: 3 you dwellers in Jerusalem and **p** *of* Judah, H408
Isa 5: 7 the **p** *of* Judah are the vines he H408
Isa 5:13 Therefore my **p** will go into exile for lack H6639
Isa 5:13 hunger and the **common p** will be H2162
Isa 5:15 So **p** will be brought low and everyone H132
Isa 5:25 the LORD's anger burns against his **p**; H6639
Isa 6: 5 I live among a **p** *of* unclean lips, and H6639
Isa 6: 9 "Go and tell this **p**: " 'Be ever hearing, H6639
Isa 6:10 Make the heart of this **p** calloused; make H6639
Isa 7: 2 the hearts of Ahaz and his **p** were shaken, H6639
Isa 7: 8 Ephraim will be too shattered to be a **p**. H6639
Isa 7:17 on you and on your **p** and on the house of H6639
Isa 8: 6 "Because this **p** has rejected the gently H6639
Isa 8:11 me not to follow the way of this **p**: H6639
Isa 8:12 everything this **p** calls a conspiracy; H6639
Isa 8:14 a stone that causes **p** to stumble and a rock NDT
Isa 8:14 And for the **p** *of* Jerusalem he will be a H3782
Isa 8:19 should not a **p** inquire of their God? H6639
Isa 9: 2 The **p** walking in darkness have seen a H6639
Isa 9: 3 rejoice before you as **p** rejoice at the harvest NDT
Isa 9: 9 All the **p** will know it—Ephraim and the H6639
Isa 9:13 But the **p** have not returned to him who H6639
Isa 9:16 Those who guide this **p** mislead them H6639
Isa 9:19 be scorched and the **p** will be fuel for the H6639
Isa 10: 2 justice from the oppressed of my **p**, H6639
Isa 10: 6 I dispatch him against a **p** who anger me H6639
Isa 10:14 of the nations; as *p* **gather** abandoned eggs AIT
Isa 10:22 Though your **p** be like the sand by the sea H6639
Isa 10:24 "My **p** who live in Zion, do not be afraid H6639
Isa 10:31 is in flight; the **p** *of* Gebim take cover. H3782
Isa 11:11 surviving remnant of his **p** from Assyria, H6639
Isa 11:12 assemble the **scattered** *p of* Judah from the AIT
Isa 11:14 they will plunder the **p** *to* the east. H1201
Isa 11:16 the remnant of his **p** that is left from H6639
Isa 12: 6 sing for joy, **p** *of* Zion, for great is the H3782
Isa 13:12 I will make **p** scarcer than pure gold, more H632
Isa 13:14 they will all return to their own **p**, they will H6639
Isa 14:20 destroyed your land and killed your **p**. H6639
Isa 14:25 His yoke will be taken from **my p**, and H2157S
Isa 14:32 in her his afflicted **p** will find refuge." H6639
Isa 16:14 all her many **p** will be despised, H2162
Isa 17: 7 In that day **p** will look to their Maker and H132
Isa 18: 2 to a **p** tall and smooth-skinned H1580
Isa 18: 2 to a **p** feared far and wide H6639
Isa 18: 3 All you **p** *of* the world, you who live on H3782
Isa 18: 7 LORD Almighty from a **p** tall and H6639
Isa 18: 7 from a **p** feared far and wide H6639
Isa 19:25 "Blessed be Egypt my **p**, Assyria my H6639
Isa 20: 6 In that day the *p who* **live** *on* this coast will AIT
Isa 21:10 My **p** who are crushed on the threshing H1201
Isa 22: 4 me over the destruction of my **p**." H1426+6639
Isa 22:21 live in Jerusalem and to the **p** *of* Judah. H1074
Isa 23: 2 you **p** *of* the island and you merchants of H3782
Isa 23: 6 over to Tarshish; wail, you **p** *of* the island. H3782
Isa 23:13 this **p** that is now of no account! H6639
Isa 24: 2 it will be the same for priest as for **p**, for H6639
Isa 24: 5 The earth is defiled by its **p**; they have H3782
Isa 24: 6 the earth; its **p** must bear their guilt. H3782
Isa 24:17 pit and snare await you, **p** *of* the earth. H3782
Isa 26: 9 the **p** *of* the world learn righteousness. H3782
Isa 26:11 your zeal for your **p** and be put to shame; H6639
Isa 26:18 the **p** *of* the world have not come to H3782
Isa 26:20 my **p**, enter your rooms and shut the H6639
Isa 26:21 to punish the **p** *of* the earth for their H3782

Isa 27:11 For this is a **p** without understanding; so H6639
Isa 28: 4 as soon as **p** see them and take H2021+8011S
Isa 28: 5 beautiful wreath for the remnant of his **p.** H6639
Isa 28:11 strange tongues God will speak to this **p,** H6639
Isa 28:14 you scoffers who rule this **p** in Jerusalem. H6639
Isa 29:13 "These **p** come near to me with their H6639
Isa 29:14 I will astound these **p** with wonder upon H6639
Isa 30: 5 to shame because of a **p** useless to them, H6639
Isa 30: 9 For these are rebellious **p,** deceitful H6639
Isa 30:19 **P** of Zion, who live in Jerusalem, you will H6639
Isa 30:26 the bruises of his **p** and heals the wounds H6639
Isa 30:29 rejoice as when **p** playing pipes go up H2021S
Isa 30:30 The LORD will cause **p** to hear his majestic NDT
Isa 32:13 for the land of my **p,** a land H6639
Isa 32:18 My **p** will live in peaceful dwelling places H6639
Isa 33: 4 like a swarm of locusts *p* **pounce** on it. AIT
Isa 33:19 You will see those arrogant **p** no more H6639
Isa 33:19 no more, **p** whose speech is obscure H6639
Isa 34: 5 on Edom, the **p** I have totally destroyed. H6639
Isa 36:11 in the hearing of the **p** on the wall." H6639
Isa 36:12 and not to the **p** sitting on the wall H408
Isa 36:21 But *the p remained* **silent** and said nothing AIT
Isa 37:12 Rezeph and the **p** *of* Eden who were in H1201
Isa 37:27 Their **p,** drained of power, are dismayed H3782
Isa 37:36 When *the p* **got up** the next morning—there AIT
Isa 38:16 by such things *p* **live;** and my spirit finds AIT
Isa 40: 1 Comfort, comfort my **p,** says your God. H6639
Isa 40: 5 be revealed, and all **p** will see it together. H1414
Isa 40: 6 "All **p** are like grass, and all their H1414
Isa 40: 7 blows on them. Surely the **p** are grass. H6639
Isa 40:22 the earth, and its **p** are like grasshoppers. H3782
Isa 41:20 so that **p** may see and know, may H3481S
Isa 42: 5 who gives breath to its **p,** and life to those H6639
Isa 42: 6 be a covenant for the **p** and a light for the H6639
Isa 42:11 Let the **p** *of* Sela sing for joy; let them H3782
Isa 42:22 But this is a **p** plundered and looted, all H6639
Isa 43: 4 I love you, I will give **p** in exchange for you H132
Isa 43:20 to give drink to my **p,** my chosen, H6639
Isa 43:21 the **p** I formed for myself that they may H6639
Isa 44: 7 since I established my ancient **p,** H6639
Isa 44:11 **P** who do that will be put to shame; such H3972S
Isa 45: 6 place of its setting *p may* **know** there is none AIT
Isa 46: 3 all the remnant of the **p** *of* Israel, you H1074
Isa 47: 6 I was angry with my **p** and desecrated my H6639
Isa 49: 8 will make you to be a covenant for the **p,** H6639
Isa 49:13 the LORD comforts his **p** and will have H6639
Isa 49:19 now you will be too small for your **p,** and H3782
Isa 51: 4 "Listen to me, my **p;** hear me, my nation H6639
Isa 51: 7 you **p** who have taken my instruction to H6639
Isa 51:16 who say to Zion, 'You are my **p.** H6639
Isa 51:17 to its dregs the goblet that makes **p** stagger. NDT
Isa 51:22 LORD says, your God, who defends his **p:** H6639
Isa 52: 4 "At first my **p** went down to Egypt to live H6639
Isa 52: 5 "For my **p** have been taken away for H6639
Isa 52: 6 Therefore my **p** will know my name H6639
Isa 52: 9 the LORD has comforted his **p,** he has H6639
Isa 53: 3 Like one from whom **p** hide their faces he NDT
Isa 53: 8 transgression of my **p** he was punished. H6639
Isa 56: 3 LORD will surely exclude me from his **p."** H6639
Isa 57:14 the obstacles out of the way of my **p."** H6639
Isa 57:16 of me—the **very p** I have created. H5972S
Isa 58: 1 Declare to my **p** their rebellion and to the H6639
Isa 58: 5 only a day for **p** to humble themselves? H132
Isa 58:12 *Your p will* **rebuild** the ancient ruins and will AIT
Isa 59:10 feeling our way like **p** without eyes. NDT
Isa 59:19 the west, *p will* **fear** the name of the LORD AIT
Isa 60:11 so that **p** may bring you the wealth of the NDT
Isa 60:21 Then all your **p** will be righteous and they H6639
Isa 61: 8 I will reward **my p** and make an H4392S
Isa 61: 9 that they are a **p** the LORD has blessed." H2446
Isa 62:10 Prepare the way for the **p.** Build up, H6639
Isa 62:12 They will be called the Holy **P,** the H6639
Isa 63: 8 "Surely they are my **p,** children who will H6639
Isa 63:11 Then *his p* **recalled** the days of old, the days AIT
Isa 63:11 the days of Moses and his **p**—where is H6639
Isa 63:14 how you guided your **p** to make for H6639
Isa 63:18 a little while your **p** possessed your holy H6639
Isa 64: 9 look on us, we pray, for we are all your **p.** H6639
Isa 65: 2 held out my hands to an obstinate **p,** H6639
Isa 65: 3 a **p** who continually provoke me to my H6639
Isa 65: 5 **Such** *p* are smoke in my nostrils, a fire that AIT
Isa 65: 8 is still found in a cluster of grapes and *p* **say,** AIT
Isa 65: 9 my mountains; my **chosen** *p* will inherit them AIT
Isa 65:10 place for herds, for my **p** who seek me. H6639
Isa 65:18 Jerusalem to be a delight and its **p** a joy. H6639
Isa 65:19 over Jerusalem and take delight in my **p;** H6639
Isa 65:22 so will be the days of my **p;** my chosen H6639
Isa 65:23 they will be a **p** blessed by the LORD H2446
Isa 66: 5 "Your own **p** who hate you, and exclude H278
Isa 66:16 the LORD will execute judgment on all **p,** H1414
Isa 66:18 gather the **p** of all **nations** and languages H1580
Isa 66:20 And they will bring all your **p,** from all the H278
Jer 1: 3 when the **p** of Jerusalem went into exile. NDT
Jer 1:16 my judgments on **my p** because of their H4392S
Jer 1:18 officials, its priests and the **p** *of* the land. H6639
Jer 2:11 But my **p** have exchanged their glorious H6639
Jer 2:13 "My **p** have committed two sins: They H6639
Jer 2:26 is caught, so the **p** *of* Israel are disgraced H1074
Jer 2:30 "In vain I punished your **p;** they did not H1201
Jer 2:31 Why do my **p** say, 'We are free to roam H6639
Jer 2:32 Yet my **p** have forgotten me, days without H6639
Jer 3:14 "Return, faithless **p,"** declares the LORD H1201
Jer 3:16 the LORD, "*p will* no longer **say,** 'The ark of AIT
Jer 3:18 In those days the **p** *of* Judah will join the H1074
Jer 3:18 people of Judah will join the **p** *of* Israel, H1074
Jer 3:21 weeping and pleading of the **p** *of* Israel, H1201
Jer 3:22 "Return, faithless **p;** I will cure you of H1201
Jer 4: 3 the LORD says to the **p** *of* Judah and to H408
Jer 4: 4 you **p** *of* Judah and inhabitants of H408
Jer 4:10 have deceived this **p** and Jerusalem by H6639
Jer 4:11 At that time this **p** and Jerusalem will be H6639
Jer 4:11 in the desert blows toward my **p,** H1426+6639
Jer 4:22 "My **p** are fools; they do not know me H6639
Jer 4:25 there were no **p;** every bird in the sky H132
Jer 5:10 for **these** *p* do not belong to the LORD. AIT
Jer 5:11 The **p** *of* Israel and the people of Judah H1074
Jer 5:11 of Israel and the **p** *of* Judah have been H1074
Jer 5:14 "Because the **p** have spoken these words H4013S
Jer 5:14 a fire and these **p** the wood it consumes. H6639
Jer 5:15 **P** *of* Israel," declares the LORD, "I am H1074
Jer 5:15 a **p** whose language you do not know H1580
Jer 5:19 And when *the p* **ask,** 'Why has the LORD our AIT
Jer 5:21 you foolish and senseless **p,** who have H6639
Jer 5:23 But these **p** have stubborn and rebellious H6639
Jer 5:26 "Among my **p** are the wicked who lie in H6639
Jer 5:26 like those who set traps to catch **p.** H408
Jer 5:31 own authority, and my **p** love it this way. H6639
Jer 6: 1 "Flee for safety, **p** *of* Benjamin! Flee from H1201
Jer 6:14 the wound of my **p** as though it were not H6639
Jer 6:19 I am bringing disaster on this **p,** the fruit H6639
Jer 6:21 "I will put obstacles before this **p.** Parents H6639
Jer 6:26 on sackcloth, my **p,** and roll in H1426+6639
Jer 6:27 you a tester of metals and my **p** the ore, H6639
Jer 7: 2 all you **p** of Judah who come through these NDT
Jer 7:12 because of the wickedness of my **p** Israel. H6639
Jer 7:15 your fellow Israelites, the **p** *of* Ephraim. H2446
Jer 7:16 do not pray for this **p** nor offer any plea H6639
Jer 7:23 I will be your God and you will be my **p.** H6639
Jer 7:30 " 'The **p** *of* Judah have done evil in my H1201
Jer 7:32 when **p** will no longer call it Topheth or the NDT
Jer 7:33 carcasses of this **p** will become food for H6639
Jer 8: 1 the bones of the **p** *of* Jerusalem will be H3782
Jer 8: 4 " 'When *p* **fall down,** do they not get AIT
Jer 8: 5 Why then have these **p** turned away? Why H6639
Jer 8: 7 But my **p** do not know the requirements of H6639
Jer 8:11 the wound of my **p** as though it H1426+6639
Jer 8:19 to the cry of my **p** from a land far H1426+6639
Jer 8:21 Since my **p** are crushed, I am H1426+6639
Jer 8:22 no healing for the wound of my **p?** H1426+6639
Jer 9: 1 day and night for the slain of my **p.** H1426+6639
Jer 9: 2 I might leave my **p** and go away from H6639
Jer 9: 2 are all adulterers, a crowd of **unfaithful** *p.* AIT
Jer 9: 7 I do because of the sin of my **p?** H1426+6639
Jer 9:15 I will make this **p** eat bitter food and drink H6639
Jer 10: 1 Hear what the LORD says to you, **p** *of* Israel. H1074
Jer 10:16 the **p** *of* his inheritance—the H8657
Jer 11: 2 tell them to the **p** *of* Judah and to those H408
Jer 11: 4 you will be my **p,** and I will be your H6639
Jer 11: 9 among the **p** *of* Judah and those who H408
Jer 11:12 of Judah and the **p** *of* Jerusalem will go H3782
Jer 11:14 "Do not pray for this **p** or offer any plea H6639
Jer 11:17 because the **p** *of* both Israel and Judah H1074
Jer 11:21 LORD says about the **p** *of* Anathoth who are H408
Jer 11:23 disaster on the **p** *of* Anathoth in the year H408
Jer 12: 4 Moreover, *the p are* **saying,** "He will not see AIT
Jer 12:14 seize the inheritance I gave my **p** Israel, H6639
Jer 12:14 I will uproot the **p** *of* Judah from among H1074
Jer 12:16 well the ways of my **p** and swear by my H6639
Jer 12:16 they once taught my **p** to swear by Baal— H6639
Jer 12:16 then they will be established among my **p.** H6639
Jer 13:10 These wicked **p,** who refuse to listen to my H6639
Jer 13:11 so I bound all the **p** *of* Israel and all the H1074
Jer 13:11 of Israel and all the **p** *of* Judah to me, H1074
Jer 13:11 'to be my **p** for my renown and praise H6639
Jer 14:10 This is what the LORD says about this **p** H6639
Jer 14:11 "Do not pray for the well-being of this **p.** H6639
Jer 14:16 And the **p** they are prophesying to will be H6639
Jer 14:17 the Virgin Daughter, my **p,** has suffered a H6639
Jer 15: 1 my heart would not go out to this **p.** H6639
Jer 15: 7 bereavement and destruction on my **p,** H6639
Jer 15:19 Let **this** *p* turn to you, but you must not turn to AIT
Jer 15:20 I will make you a wall to this **p,** a fortified H6639
Jer 16: 5 my love and my pity from this **p,"** declares H6639
Jer 16:10 "When you tell these **p** all this and they H6639
Jer 16:20 Do **p** make their own gods? Yes, but they H132
Jer 17:19 "Go and stand at the Gate of the **P** H1201+6639
Jer 17:20 of Judah and all **p** of Judah and everyone NDT
Jer 17:26 *P will* **come** from the towns of Judah and the AIT
Jer 18:11 therefore say to the **p** *of* Judah and those H408
Jer 18:15 Yet my **p** have forgotten me; they burn H6639
Jer 19: 1 of the elders of the **p** and of the priests H6639
Jer 19: 3 you kings of Judah and **p** *of* Jerusalem. H3782
Jer 19: 6 when *p will* no longer **call** this place Topheth AIT
Jer 19:14 of the LORD's temple and said to all the **p,** H6639
Jer 21: 7 his officials and the **p** in this city who H6639
Jer 21: 8 "Furthermore, tell the **p,** 'This is what the H6639
Jer 22: 2 officials and your **p** who come through H6639
Jer 22: 4 accompanied by their officials and their **p.** H6639
Jer 22: 8 "**P** from many nations will pass by this city NDT
Jer 22:13 **making** his **own p** work for nothing H8276
Jer 23: 2 says to the shepherds who tend my **p:** H6639
Jer 23: 7 "when *p will* no longer **say,** 'As surely AIT
Jer 23:13 by Baal and led my **p** Israel astray. H6639
Jer 23:14 the **p** *of* Jerusalem are like Gomorrah." H3782
Jer 23:22 my words to my **p** and would have turned H6639
Jer 23:27 another will make my **p** forget my name, H6639
Jer 23:32 tell them and lead my **p** astray with their H6639
Jer 23:32 They do not benefit these **p** in the least," H6639
Jer 23:33 "When these **p,** or a prophet or a priest H6639
Jer 24: 7 They will be my **p,** and I will be their God H6639
Jer 25: 1 concerning all the **p** *of* Judah in the fourth H6639
Jer 25: 2 said to all the **p** *of* Judah and to all those H6639
Jer 25:19 his attendants, his officials and all his **p,** H6639
Jer 25:20 all the **foreign p** there; all the kings of H6850
Jer 25:20 Ekron, and the *p* **left** *at* Ashdod); AIT
Jer 25:24 the kings of the **foreign p** who live in the H6850
Jer 26: 2 speak to all the **p** of the towns of Judah NDT
Jer 26: 7 all the **p** heard Jeremiah speak H6639
Jer 26: 8 telling all the **p** everything the LORD had H6639
Jer 26: 8 all the **p** seized him and said, H6639
Jer 26: 9 And all the **p** crowded around Jeremiah H6639
Jer 26:11 said to the officials and all the **p,** H6639
Jer 26:12 said to all the officials and all the **p:** H6639
Jer 26:16 officials and all the **p** said to the priests H6639
Jer 26:17 said to the entire assembly of **p,** H6639
Jer 26:18 He told all the **p** *of* Judah, 'This is what H6639
Jer 26:23 the burial place of the **common p.)** H1201+6639
Jer 26:24 handed over to the **p** to be put to death. H6639
Jer 27: 5 the earth and its **p** and the animals that H132
Jer 27:12 serve him and his **p,** and you will live. H6639
Jer 27:13 Why will you and your **p** die by the sword H6639
Jer 27:16 Then I said to the priests and all these **p** H6639
Jer 28: 1 the presence of the priests and all the **p:** H6639
Jer 28: 5 priests and all the **p** who were standing in H6639
Jer 28: 7 hearing and in the hearing of all the **p:** H6639
Jer 28:11 he said before all the **p,** "This is what H6639
Jer 29: 1 all the other **p** Nebuchadnezzar had H6639
Jer 29:16 throne and all the **p** who remain in this H6639
Jer 29:25 your own name to all the **p** in Jerusalem, H6639
Jer 29:32 He will have no one left among this **p** H6639
Jer 29:32 he see the good things I will do for my **p,** H6639
Jer 30: 3 I will bring my **p** Israel and Judah back H6639
Jer 30:22 " 'So you will be my **p,** and I will be your H6639
Jer 31: 1 families of Israel, and they will be my **p."** H6639
Jer 31: 2 "The **p** who survive the sword will find H6639
Jer 31: 7 'LORD, save your **p,** the remnant of H6639
Jer 31:14 my **p** will be filled with my bounty, H6639
Jer 31:23 *the p* in the land of Judah and in its towns *will* once again **use** AIT
Jer 31:24 *P will* **live** together in Judah and all its towns AIT
Jer 31:27 with the offspring of **p** and of animals. H132
Jer 31:29 "In those days *p will* no longer **say,** 'The AIT
Jer 31:31 covenant with the **p** *of* Israel and with the H1074
Jer 31:31 people of Israel and with the **p** *of* Judah. H1074
Jer 31:33 I will make with the **p** *of* Israel after that H1074
Jer 31:33 I will be their God, and they will be my **p.** H6639
Jer 32:21 You brought your **p** Israel out of Egypt H6639
Jer 32:29 where *the p* **aroused** my **anger** by burning AIT
Jer 32:30 "The **p** *of* Israel and Judah have done H1201
Jer 32:30 the **p** *of* Israel have done nothing but H1201
Jer 32:32 The **p** *of* Israel and Judah have provoked H1201
Jer 32:32 the **p** *of* Judah and those living in H408
Jer 32:38 They will be my **p,** and I will be their God. H6639
Jer 32:42 brought all this great calamity on this **p,** H6639
Jer 32:43 without **p** or animals, for it has H132
Jer 33: 5 the dead bodies of the **p** I will slay in my H132
Jer 33: 6 I will heal **my p** and will let them enjoy H4392S
Jer 33:10 is a desolate waste, without **p** or animals." H132
Jer 33:10 inhabited by neither **p** nor animals, there H132
Jer 33:12 desolate and without **p** or animals—in all H132
Jer 33:14 I made to the **p** *of* Israel and Judah. H1074
Jer 33:24 you not noticed that these **p** are saying, H6639
Jer 33:24 So they despise my **p** and no longer H6639
Jer 34: 5 As **p** made a funeral fire in honor of your NDT
Jer 34: 8 a covenant with all the **p** in Jerusalem to H6639
Jer 34:10 the officials and **p** who entered into this H6639
Jer 34:15 of you proclaimed freedom to your **own p.** H8276
Jer 34:17 proclaimed freedom to your **own p.** H278+8276
Jer 34:19 priests and all the **p** *of* the land who H6639
Jer 35:13 Go and tell the **p** *of* Judah and those living H408
Jer 35:16 but these **p** have not obeyed me. H6639
Jer 36: 3 Perhaps when the **p** *of* Judah hear about H1074
Jer 36: 6 read to the **p** from the scroll the H6639
Jer 36: 6 Read them to **all** *the p of* Judah who come in AIT
Jer 36: 7 against this **p** by the LORD are great." H6639
Jer 36: 9 all the **p** in Jerusalem and those H6639
Jer 36:10 read to all the **p** at the LORD's temple H6639
Jer 36:13 heard Baruch read to the **p** from the scroll, H6639
Jer 36:14 which you have read to the **p** and come." H6639
Jer 36:31 in Jerusalem and the **p** *of* Judah every H408
Jer 37: 2 attendants nor the **p** *of* the land paid any H6639
Jer 37: 4 was free to come and go among the **p,** H6639
Jer 37:12 share of the property among the **p** there. H6639
Jer 37:18 against you or your attendants or this **p,** H6639
Jer 38: 1 was telling all the **p** when he said, H6639
Jer 38: 4 as well as all the **p,** by the things he is H6639
Jer 38: 4 seeking the good of these **p** but their ruin." H6639
Jer 39: 8 the houses of the **p** and broke down the H6639
Jer 39: 9 to Babylon the **p** who remained in the H6639
Jer 39: 9 gone over to him, and the rest of the **p.** H6639
Jer 39:10 in the land of Judah some of the poor **p,** H6639
Jer 39:14 So he remained among his own **p.** H6639
Jer 40: 3 happened because *you p* **sinned** against the AIT
Jer 40: 5 live with him among the **p,** or go H6639
Jer 40: 6 with him among the **p** who were left H6639
Jer 41:10 all the rest of the **p** who were in Mizpah— H6639

P

Jer 41:13 When all the p Ishmael had with him saw H6639
Jer 41:14 All the p Ishmael had taken captive at H6639
Jer 41:16 led away all the p of Mizpah who had H6639
Jer 42: 1 all the p from the least to the H6639
Jer 42: 8 with him and all the p from the least to H6639
Jer 43: 1 finished telling the p all the words of the H6639
Jer 43: 4 officers and all the p disobeyed the LORD's H6639
Jer 44:15 all the p living in Lower and Upper H6639
Jer 44:20 Then Jeremiah said to all the p, both H6639
Jer 44:21 your officials and the p of the land? H6639
Jer 44:24 Then Jeremiah said to all the p, including H6639
Jer 44:24 "**Hear** the word of the LORD, all *you p* of AIT
Jer 45: 5 For I will bring disaster on all p, declares H1414
Jer 46: 8 the earth; I will destroy cities and their p. H3782
Jer 46:16 go back to our own p and our native lands H6639
Jer 46:24 given into the hands of the p of the north." H6639
Jer 47: 2 The p will cry out; all who dwell in the land H132
Jer 48: 2 in Heshbon *p will* **plot** her downfall: AIT
Jer 48: 2 the p of Madmen, will also be NDT
Jer 48:31 I cry out, I moan for the p of Kir Hareseth. H408
Jer 48:36 like a pipe for the p of Kir Hareseth. H408
Jer 48:43 await you, you p of Moab," declares the H3782
Jer 48:46 The p of Chemosh are destroyed; your H6639
Jer 49: 1 Why do his p live in its towns? H6639
Jer 49:18 will live there; no p will dwell in it. H1201+132
Jer 49:28 attack Kedar and destroy the p of the East. H1201
Jer 49:29 *P will* **shout** to them, 'Terror AIT
Jer 49:31 gates nor bars; its *p* **live** far from danger. AIT
Jer 49:33 will live there; no p will dwell in it." H1201+132
Jer 50: 3 both p and animals will flee away. H132
Jer 50: 4 "the p of Israel and the people of Judah H1201
Jer 50: 4 of Israel and the p of Judah together will H1201
Jer 50: 6 "My p have been lost sheep; their H6639
Jer 50:16 let everyone return to their own p, H6639
Jer 50:33 "The p of Israel are oppressed, and the H1201
Jer 50:33 oppressed, and the p of Judah as well. H1201
Jer 50:40 will live there; no p will dwell in it. H1201+132
Jer 51: 1 against Babylon and the p of Leb Kamai. H3782
Jer 51:12 his decree against the p of Babylon. H3782
Jer 51:19 including the p of his inheritance—the H8657
Jer 51:38 Her *p* all **roar** like young lions, they growl like AIT
Jer 51:45 "Come out of her, my p! Run for your lives H6639
Jer 51:62 so that neither p nor animals will live in it H132
Jer 51:64 I will bring on her. And *her p will* **fall**.' " AIT
Jer 52: 6 that there was no food for the p to eat. H6639
Jer 52:15 some of the poorest p and those who H6639
Jer 52:16 the rest of the **poorest** *p* of the land to work AIT
Jer 52:25 charge of conscripting the p of the land, H6639
Jer 52:28 is the number of the p Nebuchadnezzar H6639
Jer 52:29 eighteenth year, 832 p from Jerusalem; H5883
Jer 52:30 imperial guard. There were 4,600 p in all. H5883
La 1: 1 deserted lies the city, once so full of p! H6639
La 1: 7 When her p fell into enemy hands, there H6639
La 1:11 All her p groan as they search for bread H6639
La 1:21 "*P have* **heard** my groaning, but there is no AIT
La 2:11 because my p are destroyed, H1426+6639
La 2:18 The hearts of **the** p cry out to the Lord H4392S
La 3:14 I became the laughingstock of all my p H6639
La 3:35 to deny p their rights before the Most H1505
La 3:48 eyes because my p are destroyed. H1426+6639
La 4: 3 my p have become heartless H1426+6639
La 4: 6 punishment of my p is greater than H1426+6639
La 4:10 food when my p were destroyed. H1426+6639
La 4:15 You are unclean!" *p* **cry** to them. "Away AIT
La 4:15 *p* among the nations **say**, "They can AIT
La 4:18 *P* **stalked** us *at* every step, so we could not AIT
Eze 2: 4 The p to whom I am sending you are H1201
Eze 2: 5 they are a rebellious p—they will know H1074
Eze 2: 6 by them, though they are a rebellious p. H1074
Eze 2: 8 Do not rebel like that rebellious p; open H1074
Eze 3: 1 then go and speak to the p of Israel." H1074
Eze 3: 4 go now to the p of Israel and speak my H1074
Eze 3: 5 being sent to a p of obscure speech and H6639
Eze 3: 5 strange language, but to the p of Israel— H1074
Eze 3: 7 But the p of Israel are not willing to listen H1074
Eze 3: 9 by them, though they are a rebellious p." H1074
Eze 3:11 Go now to your p in exile and speak H1201+6639
Eze 3:17 made you a watchman for the p of Israel; H1074
Eze 3:25 so that you cannot go out among **the** p. H4392S
Eze 3:26 rebuke them, for they are a rebellious p. H1074
Eze 3:27 them refuse; for they are a rebellious p. H1074
Eze 4: 3 This will be a sign to the p of Israel. H1074
Eze 4: 4 put the sin of the p of Israel upon yourself H1074
Eze 4: 5 you will bear the sin of the p of Israel. H1074
Eze 4: 6 and bear the sin of the p of Judah. H1074
Eze 4:12 bake it in the sight of **the** p, using H2157S
Eze 4:13 "In this way the p of Israel will eat defiled H1201
Eze 4:16 *The p will* **eat** rationed food in anxiety and AIT
Eze 5:12 A **third** *of* your *p* will die of the plague or AIT
Eze 6: 4 I will slay your p in front of your idols. H2728
Eze 6: 7 Your *p will* **fall** slain among you, and you will AIT
Eze 6:11 detestable practices of the p of Israel, H1074
Eze 6:13 when their *p* lie **slain** among their idols AIT
Eze 7:11 None of **the** p will be left, none of that H2157S
Eze 7:22 I will turn my face away from the p, and H2157S
Eze 7:27 the hands of the p of the land will H6639
Eze 8:17 trivial matter for the p of Judah to do the H1074
Eze 9: 9 "The sin of the p of Israel and Judah is H1074
Eze 11: 1 Pelatiah son of Benaiah, leaders of the p. H6639
Eze 11: 6 You have **killed** many *p* in this city and filled AIT
Eze 11:15 the p of Jerusalem have said of your H3782
Eze 11:20 They will be my p, and I will be their H6639
Eze 12: 2 you are living among a rebellious p. H1074
Eze 12: 2 do not hear, for they are a rebellious p. H1074
Eze 12: 3 though they are a rebellious p. H1074
Eze 12: 9 *did* not the Israelites, that rebellious p H1074
Eze 12:19 Say to the p of the land: 'This is what the H6639
Eze 12:24 divinations among the p of Israel. H1074
Eze 12:25 you rebellious p, I will fulfill H1074
Eze 13: 5 to repair it for the p of Israel so that it will H1074
Eze 13: 9 to the council of my p or be listed in the H6639
Eze 13:10 " 'Because they lead my p astray, saying H6639
Eze 13:12 wall collapses, will p not ask you, "Where is NDT
Eze 13:17 daughters of your p who prophesy out of H6639
Eze 13:18 their heads in order to ensnare p. H5883
Eze 13:18 the lives of my p but preserve your own? H6639
Eze 13:19 me among my p for a few handfuls H6639
Eze 13:19 By lying to my p, who listen to lies, you H6639
Eze 13:20 which you ensnare p like birds and I will H5883
Eze 13:20 I will set free the p that you ensnare like H5883
Eze 13:21 your veils and save my p from your hands, H6639
Eze 13:23 I will save my p from your hands. H6639
Eze 14: 5 to recapture the hearts of the p of Israel, H1074
Eze 14: 6 "Therefore say to the p of Israel, 'This is H1074
Eze 14: 8 I will remove them from my p. Then you H6639
Eze 14: 9 destroy him from among my p Israel. H6639
Eze 14:11 Then the p of Israel will no longer stray H1074
Eze 14:11 They will be my p, and I will be their God H6639
Eze 14:13 upon it and kill its p and their animals, H132
Eze 14:17 the land,' and I kill its p and their animals, H132
Eze 14:19 bloodshed, killing its p and their animals, H132
Eze 15: 6 so will I treat the *p* **living in** Jerusalem. AIT
Eze 17: 9 a strong arm or many p to pull it up by the H6639
Eze 17:12 "Say to this rebellious p, 'Do you not know H1074
Eze 18: 2 "What do you p mean by quoting this H917S
Eze 18:18 did what was wrong among his p. H6639
Eze 18:29 Are my ways unjust, p of Israel? Is it not H1074
Eze 18:31 Why will you die, p of Israel? H1074
Eze 20:13 " 'Yet the p of Israel rebelled against me H1074
Eze 20:27 speak to the p of Israel and say to them H1074
Eze 20:39 " 'As for you, p of Israel, this is what the H1074
Eze 20:40 in the land all the p of Israel will serve H1074
Eze 20:44 practices, you p of Israel, declares the H1074
Eze 21: 5 Then all p will know that I the LORD have H1414
Eze 21:12 it is against my p; it is against all the H6639
Eze 21:12 are thrown to the sword along with my p. H6639
Eze 21:24 'Because **you** *p* have brought to mind your AIT
Eze 22:12 In you *are p who* **accept** bribes to shed blood AIT
Eze 22:18 the p of Israel have become dross to me H1074
Eze 22:25 its prey; they devour p, take treasures and H5883
Eze 22:27 shed blood and kill p to make unjust gain H5883
Eze 22:29 The p of the land practice extortion and H6639
Eze 23:24 wagons and with a throng of p; H6639
Eze 24: 3 Tell this rebellious p a parable and say to H1074
Eze 24:18 So I spoke to the p in the morning, and in H6639
Eze 24:19 Then the p asked me, "Won't you tell us H6639
Eze 24:21 Say to the p of Israel, 'This is what the H1074
Eze 25: 3 waste and over the p of Judah when they H1074
Eze 25: 4 going to give you to the p of the East as a H1201
Eze 25:10 the Ammonites to the p of the East as a H1201
Eze 25:14 on Edom by the hand of my p Israel, H6639
Eze 26:11 he will kill your p with the sword, and your H6639
Eze 26:20 go down to the pit, to the p of long ago. H6639
Eze 28:24 " 'No longer will the p of Israel have H1074
Eze 28:25 When I gather the p of Israel from the H1074
Eze 29: 6 been a staff of reed for the p of Israel. H1074
Eze 29:16 confidence for the p of Israel but will be a H1074
Eze 30: 5 Kub and the p of the covenant land will H1201
Eze 32: 3 a great throng of p I will cast my net over H6639
Eze 33: 2 speak to your p and say to them: H1201+6639
Eze 33: 2 the p of the land choose one of their H6639
Eze 33: 3 land and blows the trumpet to warn the p, H6639
Eze 33: 6 to warn the p and the sword comes H6639
Eze 33: 7 made you a watchman for the p of Israel; H1074
Eze 33:11 Why will you die, p of Israel?' H1074
Eze 33:12 say to your p, 'If someone who H1201+6639
Eze 33:17 "Yet your p say, 'The way of the H1201+6639
Eze 33:24 the *p* **living in** those ruins in the land of AIT
Eze 33:30 your p are talking together about H1201+6639
Eze 33:31 My p come to you, as they usually do, and H6639
Eze 34:27 its crops; *the p will* **be** secure in their land. AIT
Eze 34:30 the Israelites, are my p, declares the H6639
Eze 36: 8 produce branches and fruit for my p Israel, H6639
Eze 36:10 I will cause many p to live on you—yes H132
Eze 36:11 the number of p and animals living on H132
Eze 36:11 *I will* **settle** *p* **on** you as in the past and will AIT
Eze 36:12 I will cause p, my people Israel, to live on H132
Eze 36:12 will cause people, my p Israel, to live on H6639
Eze 36:13 "You devour p and deprive your nation of H132
Eze 36:14 no longer devour p or make your nation H132
Eze 36:17 when the p of Israel were living in their H1074
Eze 36:20 'These are the LORD's p, and yet they had H6639
Eze 36:21 which the p of Israel profaned among the H1074
Eze 36:22 is not for your sake, p of Israel, that I am H1074
Eze 36:28 you will be my p, and I will be your God. H6639
Eze 36:32 disgraced for your conduct, p of Israel! H1074
Eze 36:37 I will make their p as numerous as sheep, H132
Eze 36:38 the ruined cities be filled with flocks of p. H132
Eze 37:11 of man, these bones are the p of Israel. H1074
Eze 37:12 My p, I am going to open your graves H6639
Eze 37:13 Then you, my p, will know that I am the H6639
Eze 37:18 "When your p ask you, 'Won't you H1201+6639
Eze 37:23 They will be my p, and I will be their H6639
Eze 37:27 I will be their God, and they will be my p. H6639
Eze 38: 8 whose *p* **were gathered** from many nations to AIT
Eze 38:11 attack a peaceful and unsuspecting p— H3782
Eze 38:12 ruins and the p gathered from the H6639
Eze 38:14 when my p Israel are living in safety H6639
Eze 38:16 advance against my p Israel like a cloud H6639
Eze 38:20 all the p on the face of the earth will H132
Eze 39: 7 known my holy name among my p Israel. H6639
Eze 39:13 All the p of the land will bury them, and H6639
Eze 39:14 P will be continually employed in cleansing H408
Eze 39:22 that day forward the p of Israel will know H1074
Eze 39:23 will know that the p of Israel went into H1074
Eze 39:25 have compassion on all the p of Israel, H1074
Eze 39:29 I will pour out my Spirit on the p of Israel, H1074
Eze 40: 4 Tell the p of Israel everything you see." H1074
Eze 42:14 they go near the places that are for the p." H6639
Eze 43: 7 The p of Israel will never again defile my H1074
Eze 43:10 describe the temple to the p of Israel, that H1074
Eze 44: 6 of your detestable practices, p of Israel! H1074
Eze 44:11 sacrifices for the p and stand before the H6639
Eze 44:11 stand before **the** p and serve them. H2157S
Eze 44:12 idols and made the p of Israel fall into sin H1074
Eze 44:19 out into the outer court where the p are, H6639
Eze 44:19 so that the p are not consecrated through H6639
Eze 44:23 They are to teach my p the difference H6639
Eze 45: 8 no longer oppress my p but will allow the H6639
Eze 45: 8 will allow the p of Israel to possess H1074
Eze 45: 9 Stop dispossessing my p, declares the H6639
Eze 45:15 offerings to make atonement for **the** p, H2157S
Eze 45:16 All the p of the land will be required to H6639
Eze 45:22 himself and for all the p of the land. H6639
Eze 46: 3 New Moons the p of the land are to H6639
Eze 46: 9 " 'When the p of the land come before H6639
Eze 46:18 not take any of the inheritance of the p, H6639
Eze 46:18 so that not one of my p will be separated H6639
Eze 46:20 the outer court and consecrating the p." H6639
Eze 46:24 temple are to cook the sacrifices of the p." H6639
Da 2:43 so the p will be a mixture and A10240+10050
Da 2:44 destroyed, nor will it be left to another p. A10553
Da 3:29 I decree that the p of any nation or A10553
Da 4:17 sets over them the lowliest of p. A10050
Da 4:25 be driven away from p and will live with A10050
Da 4:32 be driven away from p and will live with A10050
Da 4:33 driven away from p and ate grass like A10050
Da 5:21 away from p and given the A10120+10050
Da 6:26 part of my kingdom *p* **must** fear and AIT
Da 7:18 But the **holy** *p* of the Most High will A10620
Da 7:21 war against the **holy** p and defeating A10620
Da 7:22 in favor of the **holy** p of the Most High, A10620
Da 7:25 oppress his **holy** p and try to change A10620
Da 7:25 The holy p will be delivered into his hands NDT
Da 7:27 over to the holy p of the Most High. A10553
Da 8:12 **the** LORD's p and the daily sacrifice were H7372
Da 8:13 the trampling underfoot of **the** LORD's p?" H7372
Da 8:24 destroy those who are mighty, the holy p. H6639
Da 9: 6 our ancestors, and to all the p of the land. H6639
Da 9: 7 the p of Judah and the inhabitants of H408
Da 9:15 who brought your p out of Egypt with a H6639
Da 9:16 Jerusalem and your p an object of scorn H6639
Da 9:19 your city and your p bear your Name." H6639
Da 9:20 the sin of my p Israel and making my H6639
Da 9:24 are decreed for your p and your holy city H6639
Da 9:26 The p of the ruler who will come will H6639
Da 10:14 what will happen to your p in the future, H6639
Da 11:14 violent among your own p will rebel in H6639
Da 11:21 invade the kingdom when its p feel secure, NDT
Da 11:23 with only a few p he will rise to H1580
Da 11:32 the p who know their God will firmly H6639
Da 11:39 them rulers over **many** *p* and will distribute AIT
Da 12: 1 great prince who protects your p, H1201+6639
Da 12: 1 But at that time your p—everyone whose H6639
Da 12: 7 the power of the holy p has been finally H6639
Hos 1: 9 "Call him **Lo-Ammi** (*which means "not my p"*) AIT
Hos 1: 9 you are not my p, and I am not your H6639
Hos 1:10 'You are not my p,' they will be called H6639
Hos 1:11 The p of Judah and the people of Israel H1201
Hos 1:11 of Judah and the p of Israel will come H1201
Hos 2: 1 of your brothers, 'My p,' and of your sisters H6639
Hos 2:23 I will say to those called 'Not my p,' 'You H6639
Hos 2:23 'You are my p'; and they will say, H6639
Hos 4: 4 your p are like those who bring H6639
Hos 4: 6 my p are destroyed from lack of H6639
Hos 4: 8 feed on the sins of my p and relish their H6639
Hos 4: 9 And it will be: Like p, like priests. I will H6639
Hos 4:12 My p consult a wooden idol, and a H6639
Hos 4:14 a p without understanding will come to H6639
Hos 5:12 to Ephraim, like rot to the p of Judah. H1074
Hos 6:11 I would restore the fortunes of my p, H6639
Hos 8: 1 the LORD because the p have broken my NDT
Hos 9: 2 winepresses will not feed **the** p; H4392S
Hos 10: 5 The *p* **who live in** Samaria fear for the H8907
Hos 10: 5 Its p will mourn over it, and so will its H6639
Hos 10:14 the roar of battle will rise against your p H6639
Hos 11: 7 My p are determined to turn from me H6639
Hos 12:11 Is Gilead wicked? *Its p* **are** worthless! Do they AIT
Hos 13: 1 When Ephraim spoke, p trembled; he was NDT
Hos 13: 2 It is said of **these** *p*, "They offer human AIT
Hos 13:14 "I will deliver **this** p from the power of H4392S
Hos 13:16 The p of Samaria must bear their guilt NDT
Hos 14: 7 *P will* **dwell** again in his shade; they will AIT
Joel 2:16 Gather the p, consecrate the assembly H6639
Joel 2:17 "Spare your p, LORD. Do not make H6639
Joel 2:18 jealous for his land and took pity on his p. H6639

Joel 2:23 Be glad, **p** *of* Zion, rejoice in the LORD H1201
Joel 2:26 you; never again will my **p** be shamed. H6639
Joel 2:27 never again will my **p** be shamed. H6639
Joel 2:28 I will pour out my Spirit on all **p**. H1414
Joel 3: 2 my inheritance, my **p** Israel, because they H6639
Joel 3: 2 they scattered **my p** among the nations H889S
Joel 3: 3 They cast lots for my **p** and traded boys H6639
Joel 3: 6 You sold the **p** *of* Judah and Jerusalem to H1201
Joel 3: 8 sons and daughters to the **p** *of* Judah, H1201
Joel 3:16 But the LORD will be a refuge for his **p**, H6639
Joel 3:16 people, a stronghold for the **p** *of* Israel. H1201
Joel 3:19 of violence done to the **p** *of* Judah, H1201
Am 1: 5 The **p** *of* Aram will go into exile to Kir," H6639
Am 2:11 Is this not true, **p** *of* Israel?" declares the H1201
Am 3: 1 Hear this word, **p** *of* Israel, the word the H1201
Am 3: 6 sounds in a city, do not the **p** tremble? H6639
Am 3: 9 within her and the oppression among her **p**." NDT
Am 4: 8 **P** staggered from town to town H9109+8993S
Am 5:25 forty years in the wilderness, **p** *of* Israel? H1074
Am 6: 1 to whom the **p** *of* Israel come! H1074
Am 6: 9 If ten **p** are left in one house, they too will H408
Am 7: 8 setting a plumb line among my **p** Israel; H6639
Am 7:15 said to me, 'Go, prophesy to my **p** Israel. H6639
Am 8: 2 "The time is ripe for my **p** Israel; I will H6639
Am 8:12 *P will* **stagger** from sea to sea and wander AIT
Am 9: 1 them down on the heads of all **the p**; H4392S
Am 9: 9 I will shake the **p** *of* Israel among all H1074
Am 9:10 the sinners among my **p** will die by the H6639
Am 9:14 I will bring my **p** Israel back from H6639
Ob 12 rejoice over the **p** *of* Judah in the day of H1201
Ob 13 the gates of my **p** in the day of their H6639
Ob 19 **P** from the Negev will occupy the mountains NDT
Ob 19 **p** from the foothills will possess the NDT
Jnh 1: 8 is your country? From what **p** are you?" H6639
Jnh 3: 7 Do not let **p** or animals, herds or flocks H132
Jnh 3: 8 But let **p** and animals be covered with H132
Jnh 4:11 twenty thousand **p** who cannot tell H132
Mic 1: 5 because of the sins of the **p** *of* Israel. H1074
Mic 1: 9 It has reached the very gate of my **p**, even H6639
Mic 2: 2 They defraud **p** of their homes, they rob H1505
Mic 2: 3 "I am planning disaster against this **p** H5476
Mic 2: 4 In that day *p will* **ridicule** you; they will taunt AIT
Mic 2: 8 Lately my **p** have risen up like an enemy H6639
Mic 2: 9 the women of my **p** from their pleasant H6639
Mic 2:11 that would be just the prophet for this **p**! H6639
Mic 2:12 in its pasture; the place will throng with **p**. H132
Mic 3: 2 tear the skin from **my p** and the flesh H2157S
Mic 3: 5 "As for the prophets who lead my **p** astray, H6639
Mic 6: 2 For the LORD has a case against his **p**; he H6639
Mic 6: 3 "My **p**, what have I done to you? How H6639
Mic 6: 5 My **p**, remember what Balak king of Moab H6639
Mic 6:12 Your **rich** *p* are violent; your inhabitants are AIT
Mic 6:16 you over to ruin and your **p** to derision; H3782
Mic 7:12 In that day *p will* **come** to you from Assyria AIT
Mic 7:14 Shepherd your **p** with your staff, the flock H6639
Na 3: 3 number, *p* **stumbling** over the corpses AIT
Na 3:18 Your **p** are scattered on the mountains H6639
Hab 1: 6 that ruthless and impetuous **p**, who H1580
Hab 1: 7 They are a feared and **dreaded** *p*; they are a AIT
Hab 1:11 wind and go on—**guilty** *p*, whose own AIT
Hab 1:14 You have made **p** like the fish in the sea H132
Hab 3:13 You came out to deliver your **p**, to save H6639
Zep 1:17 such distress on all **p** that they will grope H132
Zep 2: 5 you Kerethite **p**; the word of the LORD H1580
Zep 2: 7 belong to the remnant of the **p** *of* Judah; H1074
Zep 2: 8 who insulted my **p** and made threats H6639
Zep 2: 9 The remnant of my **p** will plunder them H6639
Zep 2:10 mocking the **p** *of* the LORD Almighty. H6639
Zep 3: 4 are unprincipled; they are treacherous **p**. H408
Zep 3:10 my scattered **p**, will bring me offerings H1426
Hag 1: 2 "These **p** say, 'The time has not yet come H6639
Hag 1:11 ground produces, on **p** and livestock, and H132
Hag 1:12 remnant of the **p** obeyed the voice of H6639
Hag 1:12 had sent him. And the **p** feared the LORD. H6639
Hag 1:13 gave this message of the LORD to the **p**: H6639
Hag 1:14 the spirit of the whole remnant of the **p**. H6639
Hag 2: 2 high priest, and to the remnant of the **p**. H6639
Hag 2: 4 Be strong, all you **p** *of* the land,' declares H6639
Hag 2:14 " 'So it is with this **p** and this nation in my H6639
Zec 1: 3 Therefore tell **the p**: This is what the LORD H2157S
Zec 1:21 against the land of Judah to scatter **its p**." H2023S
Zec 2: 4 of the great number of **p** and animals in it. H132
Zec 2:11 LORD in that day and will become my **p**. H6639
Zec 5: 6 is the iniquity of **the p** throughout the H4392
Zec 7: 2 The **p** of Bethel had sent Sharezer and NDT
Zec 7: 5 "Ask all the **p** *of* the land and the priests H6639
Zec 8: 6 to the remnant of this **p** at that time, H6639
Zec 8: 7 "I will save my **p** from the countries of the H6639
Zec 8: 8 they will be my **p**, and I will be faithful H6639
Zec 8:10 were no wages for **p** or hire for animals. H132
Zec 8:11 the remnant of this **p** as I did in the past," H6639
Zec 8:12 as an inheritance to the remnant of this **p**. H6639
Zec 8:23 "In those days ten **p** from all languages H408
Zec 9: 1 the eyes of *all* **p** and all the tribes of H132
Zec 9: 6 A **mongrel p** will occupy Ashdod, and I H4927
Zec 9: 8 again will an oppressor overrun **my p**, H2157S
Zec 9:16 their God will save his **p** on that day as a H6639
Zec 10: 1 He gives showers of rain to *all* **p**, and H2157S
Zec 10: 2 Therefore *the p* **wander** like sheep oppressed AIT
Zec 10: 3 his flock, the **p** *of* Judah, and make H1074
Zec 11: 6 no longer have pity on the **p** *of* the land," H3782
Zec 12: 5 'The **p** *of* Jerusalem are strong H3782

Zec 13: 9 'They are my **p**,' and they will say, H6639
Zec 14: 2 the rest of the **p** will not be taken from H6639
Zec 14:13 On that day **p** will be stricken by the LORD H2157S
Zec 14:18 If the Egyptian **p** do not go up and take H5476
Mal 1: 4 a **p** always under the wrath of the LORD. H6639
Mal 2: 7 LORD Almighty and *p* **seek** instruction from AIT
Mal 2: 9 despised and humiliated before all the **p**, H6639
Mt 1:21 because he will save his **p** from their sins." G3295
Mt 2: 6 a ruler who will shepherd my **p** Israel.' G3295
Mt 3: 5 *P* **went out** to him from Jerusalem and all AIT
Mt 4:16 the **p** living in darkness have seen a great G3295
Mt 4:19 "and I will send you out to fish *for* **p**." G476
Mt 4:23 every disease and sickness among the **p**. G3295
Mt 4:24 and *p* **brought** to him all who were ill with AIT
Mt 5:11 "Blessed are you when *p* **insult** you AIT
Mt 5:15 Neither *do p* **light** a lamp and put it under a AIT
Mt 5:21 heard that it was said *to* the **p long ago**, G792
Mt 5:33 heard that it was said *to* the **p long ago**, G792
Mt 5:47 And if you greet only your own **p**, what are G81
Mt 6:14 For if you forgive **other p** when they sin G476
Mt 7:16 *Do p* **pick** grapes from thornbushes, or figs AIT
Mt 9:17 Neither *do p* **pour** new wine into old AIT
Mt 9:23 saw the noisy crowd and **p playing pipes**, G886
Mt 11:12 violence, and **violent** *p* have been raiding it. AIT
Mt 12:23 All the **p** were astonished and said G4063
Mt 12:27 by whom do your **p** drive them out? G5626
Mt 13: 2 while all the **p** stood on the shore. G4063
Mt 13:10 "Why do you speak *to the* **p** in parables?" G899S
Mt 13:17 prophets and **righteous** *p* longed to see AIT
Mt 13:38 seed stands for the **p** of the kingdom. G5626
Mt 13:38 The weeds are the **p** of the evil one, G5626
Mt 13:54 he began teaching **the p** in their G899S
Mt 14: 5 he was afraid *of* the **p**, because they G4063
Mt 14:19 And he directed the **p** to sit down on the G4063
Mt 14:19 the disciples gave them *to* the **p**. G4063
Mt 14:35 *P* **brought** all their sick to him AIT
Mt 15: 8 " 'These **p** honor me with their lips, but G3295
Mt 15:31 The **p** were amazed when they saw the G4063
Mt 15:32 "I have compassion for these **p**; they have G4063
Mt 15:36 to the disciples, and they in turn *to* the **p**. G4063
Mt 16:13 "Who do **p** say the Son of Man is? G476
Mt 18: 7 of the things that cause **p** to stumble! NDT
Mt 19:13 Then *p* **brought** little children **to** Jesus for AIT
Mt 21:23 the elders *of* the **p** came to him. G3295
Mt 21:26 we are afraid *of* the **p**, for they all hold G4063
Mt 21:43 you and given *to* a **p** who will produce G1620
Mt 21:46 the crowd because the **p** held that he was a NDT
Mt 22:10 gathered all **the p** they could find, G4005S
Mt 22:30 resurrection *p will* neither **marry** nor be given AIT
Mt 23: 5 "Everything they do is done for **p** to see G476
Mt 23:28 outside you appear *to* **p** as righteous but G476
Mt 24:11 prophets will appear and deceive **many** *p*. AIT
Mt 24:38 before the flood, *p* **were** eating and drinking AIT
Mt 25:32 he will separate **the p** one from another G899S
Mt 26: 3 the elders *of* the **p** assembled in the G3295
Mt 26: 5 "or there may be a riot among the **p**." G3295
Mt 26:47 the chief priests and the elders *of* the **p**. G3295
Mt 26:71 servant girl saw him and said *to* **the** *p* there, AIT
Mt 27: 1 the elders *of* the **p** made their plans G3295
Mt 27: 9 the price set on him by the **p** of Israel, G5626
Mt 27:25 All the **p** answered, "His blood is on us G3295
Mt 27:52 The bodies *of* many **holy** *p* who had died AIT
Mt 27:53 into the holy city and appeared *to* **many** *p*. AIT
Mt 27:64 the body and tell the **p** that he has been G3295
Mk 1: 5 all the **p of Jerusalem** went out to G2643
Mk 1:17 "and I will send you out to fish *for* **p**." G476
Mk 1:22 *The p* were **amazed** at his teaching, because AIT
Mk 1:27 *The p were* all so **amazed** that they asked AIT
Mk 1:32 after sunset *the p* **brought** to Jesus all the AIT
Mk 1:45 Yet *the p still* **came** to him from everywhere. AIT
Mk 2: 1 *the p* **heard** that he had come home. AIT
Mk 2:18 *Some p* **came** and asked Jesus, "How is it AIT
Mk 3: 8 many **p** came to him from Judea G4436
Mk 3: 9 to keep *the p* from **crowding** him. AIT
Mk 3:28 **p** can be forgiven all G3836+5626+3836+476
Mk 4: 1 while all the **p** were along the shore at G4063
Mk 4:15 **Some** *p* are like seed along the path, where AIT
Mk 5:14 and *the p* **went out** to see what had AIT
Mk 5:16 had seen it told **the p** what had G899S
Mk 5:17 Then *the p* **began** to plead with Jesus to AIT
Mk 5:19 "Go home to **your own** *p* and tell them how AIT
Mk 5:20 done for him. And **all** *the p* were amazed. AIT
Mk 5:31 "You see the **p** crowding against you," G4063
Mk 5:35 *some p* **came** from the house of Jairus AIT
Mk 5:38 commotion, with *p* **crying** and wailing loudly. AIT
Mk 6: 5 lay his hands on a few **sick** *p* and heal them. AIT
Mk 6:12 went out and preached that *p should* **repent**. AIT
Mk 6:13 anointed many **sick** *p* with oil and AIT
Mk 6:31 because so many *p* **were** coming and going AIT
Mk 6:36 Send **the p** away so that they can go to the G899S
Mk 6:39 them to have **all** *the p* sit down in groups AIT
Mk 6:41 them to his disciples to distribute to **the p**. G899S
Mk 6:54 they got out of the boat, *p* **recognized** Jesus. AIT
Mk 7: 6 " 'These **p** honor me with their lips, but G3295
Mk 7:32 There *some p* **brought** to him a man who was AIT
Mk 7:37 *P were* overwhelmed *with* **amazement**. "He AIT
Mk 8: 2 "I have compassion for these **p**; they have G4063
Mk 8: 6 them to his disciples to distribute to the **p**, G4063
Mk 8: 8 *The p* **ate** and were satisfied. Afterward the AIT
Mk 8:22 and *some p* **brought** a blind man and AIT
Mk 8:24 up and said, "I see **p**; they look like trees G476
Mk 8:27 way he asked them, "Who do **p** say I am?" G476

Mk 9:15 As soon as all the **p** saw Jesus, they were G4063
Mk 10: 1 Again **crowds of p** came to him, and as G4063
Mk 10:13 *P were* **bringing** little children **to** Jesus for AIT
Mk 11: 5 **some** *p* standing there asked, "What are you AIT
Mk 11: 6 had told them to, and *the p* **let** them **go**. AIT
Mk 11: 8 **Many** *p* spread their cloaks on the road, while AIT
Mk 11:32 They feared the **p**, for everyone held that G4063
Mk 12:41 Many **rich** *p* threw in large amounts AIT
Mk 13:26 "At that time *p will* **see** the Son of Man AIT
Mk 14: 2 the festival," they said, "or the **p** may riot." G3295
Mk 15: 6 release a prisoner whom **the p** requested. G899S
Mk 16:18 they will place their hands on **sick** *p*, and AIT
Lk 1:16 bring back many *of* the **p** of Israel to the G5626
Lk 1:17 to make ready a **p** prepared for the Lord." G3295
Lk 1:21 the **p** were waiting for Zechariah and G3295
Lk 1:25 taken away my disgrace among the **p**." G476
Lk 1:65 of Judea *p were* **talking about** all these AIT
Lk 1:68 he has come *to* his **p** and redeemed them G3295
Lk 1:77 to give his **p** the knowledge of salvation G3295
Lk 2:10 that will cause great joy for all the **p**. G3295
Lk 2:32 Gentiles, and the glory *of* your **p** Israel." G3295
Lk 3: 6 And all **p** will see God's salvation.' " G4922
Lk 3:14 extort money and don't **accuse** *p* **falsely**— AIT
Lk 3:15 The **p** were waiting expectantly and were G3295
Lk 3:18 John exhorted the **p** and proclaimed the G3295
Lk 3:21 When all the **p** were being baptized G3295
Lk 4:28 All *the p* in the synagogue *were* **furious** AIT
Lk 4:31 on the Sabbath he taught **the p**. G899S
Lk 4:36 **All** *the p* were amazed and said to each AIT
Lk 4:40 *the p* **brought** to Jesus all who had various AIT
Lk 4:41 demons came out of **many** *p*, shouting, AIT
Lk 4:42 The **p** were looking for him and when G4063
Lk 5: 1 the **p** were crowding around him and G4063
Lk 5: 3 sat down and taught the **p** from the boat. G4063
Lk 5:10 be afraid; from now on you will fish *for* **p**." G476
Lk 5:15 so that crowds of **p** came to hear him and G4063
Lk 6:17 a great number *of* **p** from all over G3295
Lk 6:19 the **p** all tried to touch him, because G4063
Lk 6:22 Blessed are you when **p** hate you, when G476
Lk 6:44 *P do* not **pick** figs from thornbushes, or AIT
Lk 7: 1 all this to the **p** who were listening, G3295
Lk 7:16 "God has come to help his **p**." G3295
Lk 7:29 All the **p**, even the tax collectors, when G3295
Lk 7:31 can I compare the **p** of this generation? G476
Lk 7:41 "**Two** *p* owed money to a certain AIT
Lk 8: 4 was gathering and **p** were coming to G3836
Lk 8:35 and *the p* **went out** to see what had AIT
Lk 8:36 who had seen it told **the p** how the G899S
Lk 8:37 Then all the **p** of the region of the G4436
Lk 8:45 the **p** are crowding and pressing against G4063
Lk 8:47 In the presence of all the **p**, she told why G3295
Lk 8:52 **all** *the p* were wailing and mourning for her. AIT
Lk 9: 5 If **p** do not welcome you, leave their town G4012
Lk 9: 6 the good news and healing **p** everywhere. NDT
Lk 9:16 to the disciples to distribute to the **p**. G4063
Lk 9:53 but *the p there did* not **welcome** him AIT
Lk 11:31 the judgment with the **p** of this generation G467
Lk 11:40 *You* **foolish** *p*! Did not the one who made the AIT
Lk 11:44 which **p** walk over without knowing it." G476
Lk 11:46 because you load **p** down with burdens G476
Lk 13:14 the synagogue leader said *to* the **p** G4063
Lk 13:17 the **p** were delighted with all the G4063
Lk 13:23 are only a **few** *p* going to be saved? AIT
Lk 13:29 *P will* **come** from east and west and north AIT
Lk 13:32 out demons and **healing** *p* today and AIT
Lk 16: 4 *p will* **welcome** me into their houses. AIT
Lk 16: 8 For the **p** of this world are more shrewd in G5626
Lk 16: 8 their own kind than are the **p** of the light. G5626
Lk 16:15 What **p** value highly is detestable in God's G476
Lk 17: 1 "**Things that cause p to stumble** are G4998
Lk 17:21 nor *will p* **say**, 'Here it is,' or 'There it is,' AIT
Lk 17:23 *P will* **tell** you, 'There he is!' or 'Here he is!' AIT
Lk 17:27 *P were* **eating**, drinking, marrying and being AIT
Lk 17:28 *P were* **eating** and drinking, buying and AIT
Lk 17:34 on that night two *p will* **be** in one bed; one AIT
Lk 18: 2 feared God nor cared what **p** thought. G476
Lk 18: 4 I don't fear God or care what **p** think, G476
Lk 18:11 I thank you that I am not like other **p** G476
Lk 18:15 *P were* also **bringing** babies **to** Jesus for him AIT
Lk 18:43 When all the **p** saw it, they also praised G3295
Lk 19: 7 **All** *the p* saw this and began to mutter, "He AIT
Lk 19:11 Jerusalem and **the p** thought that the G899S
Lk 19:36 *p* **spread** their cloaks on the road. AIT
Lk 19:47 the leaders *among* the **p** were trying to G3295
Lk 19:48 because all the **p** hung on his words. G3295
Lk 20: 1 was teaching the **p** in the temple courts G3295
Lk 20: 6 all the **p** will stone us, because G3295
Lk 20: 9 He went on to tell the **p** this parable: "A G3295
Lk 20:16 When the **p** heard this, they said, "God NDT
Lk 20:19 But they were afraid *of* the **p**. G3295
Lk 20:34 "The **p** of this age marry and are given in G5626
Lk 20:45 While all the **p** were listening, Jesus said G3295
Lk 21: 4 All **these** *p* gave their gifts out of their wealth AIT
Lk 21:23 in the land and wrath *against* this **p**. G3295
Lk 21:26 **P** will faint from terror, apprehensive of G476
Lk 21:38 all the **p** came early in the morning to G3295
Lk 22: 2 rid of Jesus, for they were afraid *of* the **p**. G3295
Lk 22:66 the council of the elders *of* the **p**, G3295
Lk 23: 5 "He stirs up the **p** all over Judea by his G3295
Lk 23:13 the chief priests, the rulers and the **p**, G3295
Lk 23:14 one who was inciting the **p** to rebellion. G3295
Lk 23:27 A large number *of* **p** followed him G3295

Lk 23:31 For if *p* **do** these things when the tree is AIT
Lk 23:35 The **p** stood watching, and the rulers even *G3295*
Lk 23:48 When all the **p** who had gathered to *G4063*
Lk 24:19 word and deed before God and all the **p**. *G3295*
Jn 2:14 temple courts he found **p** selling cattle, *G3836S*
Jn 2:23 **many** *p* saw the signs he was performing AIT
Jn 2:24 entrust himself to them, for he knew **all** *p*. AIT
Jn 3:11 but *still you p do* not **accept** our testimony. AIT
Jn 3:19 **p** loved darkness instead of light *G476*
Jn 3:23 and *p were* **coming** and being baptized. AIT
Jn 4:28 went back to the town and said *to* the **p**, *G476*
Jn 4:48 "Unless *you p* **see** signs and wonders," AIT
Jn 5: 3 a great number *of* **disabled p** used to lie— *G820*
Jn 6: 2 a great **crowd of p** followed him *G4063*
Jn 6: 5 shall we buy bread for **these** *p* to eat?" AIT
Jn 6:10 "Have the **p** sit down." There was *G476*
Jn 6:14 After the **p** saw the sign Jesus performed *G476*
Jn 6:23 the place where *the p had* **eaten** the bread AIT
Jn 7:12 Others replied, "No, he deceives the **p**." *G4063*
Jn 7:25 some of the **p of Jerusalem** began to ask, *G2643*
Jn 7:35 where **our p live scattered** among *G3836+1402*
Jn 7:40 some of the **p** said, "Surely this *G4063*
Jn 7:43 Thus the **p** were divided because of Jesus. *G4063*
Jn 8: 2 where all the **p** gathered around him *G3295*
Jn 8:12 When Jesus spoke again *to* **the p**, he said *G899S*
Jn 10:41 and **many** *p* came to him. They said, "Though AIT
Jn 11:42 this for the benefit of the **p** standing here, *G4063*
Jn 11:50 one man die for the **p** than that the whole *G3295*
Jn 11:54 about publicly among the **p of Judea**. *G2681*
Jn 12:18 **Many p**, because they had heard that he *G4063*
Jn 12:32 up from the earth, will draw **all** *p* to myself." AIT
Jn 16: 9 about sin, because *p do* not **believe** in me; AIT
Jn 17: 2 him authority over all **p** that he might give *G4922*
Jn 18:14 would be good if one man died for the **p**. *G3295*
Jn 18:35 "Your own **p** and chief priests handed you *G1620*
Ac 2:15 **These** *p* are not drunk, as you suppose. AIT
Ac 2:17 God says, I will pour out my Spirit on all **p**. *G4922*
Ac 2:37 *When the p* **heard** this, they were cut to the AIT
Ac 2:47 God and enjoying the favor of all the **p**. *G3295*
Ac 3: 9 When all the **p** saw him walking and *G3295*
Ac 3:11 all the **p** were astonished and came *G3295*
Ac 3:22 a prophet like me from among your own **p**; *G81*
Ac 3:23 will be completely cut off from their **p**. *G3295*
Ac 4: 1 John while they were speaking to the **p**. *G3295*
Ac 4: 2 the apostles were teaching the **p**, *G3295*
Ac 4: 8 "Rulers and elders *of* the **p**! *G3295*
Ac 4:10 you and all the **p** of Israel: It is by the *G3295*
Ac 4:17 from spreading any further among the **p**, *G3295*
Ac 4:21 because all the **p** were praising God for *G3295*
Ac 4:23 went back to **their own** *p* and reported all AIT
Ac 4:27 the Gentiles and the **p** of Israel in this city *G3295*
Ac 5:12 many signs and wonders among the **p**. *G3295*
Ac 5:13 they were highly regarded by the **p**. *G3295*
Ac 5:15 *p* **brought** the sick into the streets and laid AIT
Ac 5:20 "and tell the **p** all about this new life." *G3295*
Ac 5:21 had been told, and began to teach the **p**. NDT
Ac 5:25 in the temple courts teaching the **p**." *G3295*
Ac 5:26 they feared that the **p** would stone them. *G3295*
Ac 5:34 who was honored by all the **p**, stood up in *G3295*
Ac 5:37 the census and led a **band of p** in revolt. *G3295*
Ac 6: 8 great wonders and signs among the **p**. *G3295*
Ac 6:12 they stirred up the **p** and the elders and *G3295*
Ac 7: 3 'Leave your country and your **p**,' God said *G5149*
Ac 7:17 the number *of* our **p** in Egypt had greatly *G3295*
Ac 7:19 treacherously *with* our **p** and oppressed *G1169*
Ac 7:23 he decided to visit his own **p**, the Israelites. *G81*
Ac 7:25 thought that his own **p** would realize that *G81*
Ac 7:34 seen the oppression *of* my **p** in Egypt. *G3295*
Ac 7:37 you a prophet like me from your own **p**. *G81*
Ac 7:42 forty years in the wilderness, **p** of Israel? *G3875*
Ac 7:51 "*You* **stiff-necked** *p*! Your hearts and ears are AIT
Ac 8: 9 the city and amazed *all* the **p** of Samaria. *G1620*
Ac 8:10 all the **p**, both high and low, gave him NDT
Ac 9:13 he has done *to* your **holy p** in Jerusalem. *G41*
Ac 9:15 their kings and *to* the **p** of Israel. *G5626*
Ac 9:32 went to visit the **Lord's p** who lived in Lydda. *G41*
Ac 9:42 over Joppa, and **many** *p* believed in the Lord. AIT
Ac 10:22 who is respected by all the Jewish **p**. *G1620*
Ac 10:27 inside and found a large **gathering** *of p*. AIT
Ac 10:36 the message God sent *to* the **p** of Israel, *G5626*
Ac 10:41 He was not seen by all the **p**, but by *G3295*
Ac 10:42 us to preach *to* the **p** and to testify that *G3295*
Ac 11:21 a great number of **p** believed and turned *G3836S*
Ac 11:24 a great **number of p** were brought to *G4063*
Ac 11:26 the church and taught great **numbers of p**. *G4063*
Ac 12:11 the Jewish **p** were hoping would *G3295*
Ac 12:12 where **many** *p* had gathered and were AIT
Ac 12:20 quarreling *with the* **p of Tyre** and Sidon; *G5601*
[Ac 12:20 quarreling *with the* **p of** Tyre and **Sidon**; *G4973*]
Ac 12:21 delivered a public address *to* **the p**. *G899S*
Ac 13:15 if you have a word of exhortation for the **p**, *G3295*
Ac 13:17 The God *of* the **p** of Israel chose our *G3295*
Ac 13:17 he made the **p** prosper during their stay in *G3295*
Ac 13:19 their land to his **p** as their inheritance. NDT
Ac 13:21 Then the **p** asked for a king, and he gave NDT
Ac 13:24 baptism to all the **p** of Israel. *G3295*
Ac 13:27 The **p** of Jerusalem and their rulers did *G2997S*
Ac 13:31 They are now his witnesses to our **p**. *G3295*
Ac 13:42 *the p* **invited** them to speak further about AIT
Ac 14: 4 The **p** of the city were divided; some sided *G4436*
Ac 15: 1 **Certain** *p* came down from Judea to Antioch AIT
Ac 15:14 to choose a **p** for his name from the *G3295*
Ac 15:31 The **p** read it and were glad for its NDT
Ac 16: 4 elders in Jerusalem *for the* **p** to obey. *G899S*
Ac 17:22 Areopagus and said: "**P** of Athens! I see *G467*
Ac 17:30 now he commands all **p** everywhere to *G476*
Ac 17:34 Some *of* the **p** became followers of Paul *G467*
Ac 18:10 because I have many **p** in this city." *G3295*
Ac 18:13 "is persuading the **p** to worship God in ways NDT
Ac 19: 4 He told the **p** to believe in the one *G3295*
Ac 19:26 astray large **numbers of p** here in Ephesus *G4063*
Ac 19:29 *The p* **seized** Gaius and Aristarchus, Paul's AIT
Ac 19:32 Most of the **p** did not even know why they NDT
Ac 19:33 in order to make a defense *before* the **p**. *G1322*
Ac 20: 2 many words of encouragement *to* **the p**, *G899S*
Ac 20: 7 Paul spoke *to* **the p** and, because he *G899S*
Ac 20:12 *The p* **took** the young man **home** alive and AIT
Ac 21:12 we and the **p there** pleaded with Paul not *G1954*
Ac 21:28 against our **p** and our law and this *G3295*
Ac 21:30 the **p** came running from all *G3295*
Ac 21:39 Please let me speak to the **p**." *G3295*
Ac 22: 5 went there to bring **these** *p* as prisoners to AIT
Ac 22:15 his witness to all **p** of what you have seen *G476*
Ac 22:18 because *the p* here *will* not **accept** your AIT
Ac 22:19 '**these** *p* know that I went from one AIT
Ac 22:24 find out why *the p were* **shouting** at him like AIT
Ac 23: 5 not speak evil about the ruler *of* your **p**. *G3295*
Ac 24:17 Jerusalem to bring my **p** gifts for the poor *G1620*
Ac 26: 4 "The **Jewish p** all know the way I have *G2681*
Ac 26:10 priests I put many *of* the **Lord's p** in prison, *G41*
Ac 26:17 you from your own **p** and from the *G3295*
Ac 26:23 message of light *to* his own **p** and to the *G3295*
Ac 28: 6 The *p* **expected** him to swell up or suddenly AIT
Ac 28:15 At the sight *of* **these** *p* Paul thanked God AIT
Ac 28:17 nothing against our **p** or against the *G3295*
Ac 28:19 to bring any charge against my own **p**. *G1620*
Ac 28:21 none *of* **our p** who have come from *G81*
Ac 28:22 that *p* everywhere *are* **talking against** this AIT
Ac 28:26 " 'Go to this **p** and say, "You will be ever *G3295*
Ro 1: 7 are loved by God and called to be his **holy** *p*: AIT
Ro 1:18 all the godlessness and wickedness *of* **p**, *G476*
Ro 1:20 been made, so that **p** are without excuse. *G899S*
Ro 2:22 who say *that p should* not **commit adultery**, AIT
Ro 2:29 Such a person's praise is not from *other* **p** *G476*
Ro 5:12 in this way death came to all **p** *G476*
Ro 5:18 trespass resulted in condemnation for all **p**, *G476*
Ro 5:18 resulted in justification and life for all **p**. *G476*
Ro 8:27 intercedes for **God's p** in accordance with *G41*
Ro 9: 3 cut off from Christ for the sake of my **p**, *G81*
Ro 9: 4 the **p of Israel**. Theirs is the adoption to *G2703*
Ro 9:25 "I will call them 'my **p**' who are not my *G3295*
Ro 9:25 call them 'my people' who are not my **p**; *G3295*
Ro 9:26 'You are not my **p**,' there they will be *G3295*
Ro 9:31 the **p of Israel**, who pursued the law as *G2702*
Ro 9:33 a stone that causes **p** to stumble and a rock NDT
Ro 10:21 hands to a disobedient and obstinate **p**." *G3295*
Ro 11: 1 Did God reject his **p**? By no means! *G3295*
Ro 11: 2 God did not reject his **p**, whom he *G3295*
Ro 11: 7 What the **p of Israel** sought so earnestly *G2702*
Ro 11:14 arouse my own **p** to envy and save some *G4922*
Ro 12:13 Share *with* **the Lord's p** who are in need *G41*
Ro 12:16 to associate with **p** of low position. *G3836S*
Ro 15:10 "Rejoice, you Gentiles, with his **p**. *G3295*
Ro 15:25 in the service *of* **the Lord's p** there. *G41*
Ro 15:26 the poor *among* **the Lord's p** in Jerusalem *G41*
Ro 15:31 be favorably received *by* **the Lord's p** there, *G41*
Ro 16: 2 in a way worthy *of* **his p** and to give her any *G41*
Ro 16: 2 she has been the benefactor *of* **many** *p* AIT
Ro 16:15 Olympas and all **the Lord's p** who are with *G41*
Ro 16:18 For **such** *p* are not serving our Lord Christ, AIT
Ro 16:18 flattery they deceive the minds *of* **naive** *p*. AIT
1Co 1: 2 in Christ Jesus and called to be **his holy p**, *G41*
1Co 3: 1 you as **p who live by the Spirit** but as *G4461*
1Co 3: 1 the Spirit but as **p who are** *still* **worldly**— *G4921*
1Co 4:19 not only how these **arrogant** *p* are talking, AIT
1Co 5: 9 to associate with **sexually immoral p**— *G4521*
1Co 5:10 the **p** of this world who are **immoral**, *G4521*
1Co 5:11 Do not even eat with **such** *p*. AIT
1Co 6: 1 judgment instead of before **the Lord's p**? *G41*
1Co 6: 2 you not know that **the Lord's p** will judge the *G41*
1Co 8: 7 **Some** *p* are still so accustomed to idols that AIT
1Co 9:22 have become all things *to* **all** *p* so that by all AIT
1Co 10: 7 "The **p** sat down to eat and drink and got *G3295*
1Co 10:15 I speak *to* **sensible** *p*; judge for yourselves AIT
1Co 10:18 Consider the **p** of Israel: Do not *G2848+4922*
1Co 14: 2 a tongue does not speak *to* **p** but to God. *G476*
1Co 14: 3 who prophesies speaks *to* **p** for their *G476*
1Co 14:21 the lips of foreigners I will speak *to* this **p**, *G3295*
1Co 14:33 as in all the congregations *of* **the Lord's p**. *G41*
1Co 14:36 Or are you the **only** *p* it has reached? AIT
1Co 15:19 in Christ, we are of all **p** most to be pitied. *G476*
1Co 15:29 raised at all, why *are p* **baptized** for them? AIT
1Co 15:39 **P** have one kind of flesh, animals have *G476*
1Co 16: 1 Now about the collection for **the Lord's p**: *G41*
1Co 16:15 themselves to the service *of* **the Lord's p**. *G41*
1Co 16:16 to submit *to* **such** *p* and to everyone who joins AIT
2Co 1: 1 with all his **holy p** throughout Achaia: *G41*
2Co 3: 1 Or do we need, like **some** *p*, letters of AIT
2Co 4:15 grace *that is* **reaching more and more** *p* may AIT
2Co 6:16 I will be their God, and they will be my **p**." *G3295*
2Co 8: 4 of sharing in this service to **the Lord's p**. *G41*
2Co 9: 1 to you about this service to **the Lord's p**. *G41*
2Co 9:12 the needs *of* **the Lord's p** but is also *G41*
2Co 10: 2 to be toward **some** *p* who think that we AIT
2Co 10:11 **Such** *p* should realize that what we are in our AIT
2Co 11:13 For **such** *p* are false apostles, deceitful AIT
2Co 13: 7 not so that *p will* **see** *that* we have stood the AIT
2Co 13:13 All **God's p** here send their greetings. *G41*
Gal 1: 7 Evidently **some** *p* are throwing you into AIT
Gal 1:10 Or am I trying to please **p**? If I were still *G476*
Gal 1:10 If I were still trying to please **p**, I would not *G476*
Gal 1:14 own age among my **p** and was extremely *G1169*
Gal 3:16 to seeds," meaning **many** *p*, but "and to your AIT
Gal 4:17 *Those p are* **zealous** *to win* you *over*, but AIT
Gal 6:10 let us do good to **all** *p*, especially to those AIT
Gal 6:12 who want to impress **p** by means of the NDT
Eph 1: 1 will of God, *To* **God's holy p** in Ephesus, the *G41*
Eph 1:15 the Lord Jesus and your love for all **God's p**, *G41*
Eph 1:18 of his glorious inheritance in his **holy p**, *G41*
Eph 2:19 fellow citizens *with* **God's p** and also *G41*
Eph 3: 5 known *to* **p** in other *G3836+5626+3836+476*
Eph 3: 8 I am less than the least of all **the Lord's p**, *G41*
Eph 3:18 together with all **the Lord's holy p**, to grasp *G41*
Eph 4: 8 took many captives and gave gifts *to* his **p**." *G476*
Eph 4:12 to equip **his p** for works of service, so that the *G41*
Eph 4:14 craftiness *of* **p** in their deceitful *G476*
Eph 5: 3 because these are improper *for* **God's holy p**. *G41*
Eph 6: 7 as if you were serving the Lord, not **p**, *G476*
Eph 6:18 always keep on praying for all **the Lord's p**. *G41*
Php 1: 1 To all **God's holy p** in Christ Jesus at Philippi *G41*
Php 2:29 the Lord with great joy, and honor *p* **like him**, AIT
Php 3: 5 the eighth day, of the **p** of Israel, of the *G1169*
Php 4:21 Greet all **God's p** in Christ Jesus. *G41*
Php 4:22 All **God's p** here send you greetings *G41*
Col 1: 2 *To* **God's holy p** in Colossae, the faithful *G41*
Col 1: 4 of the love you have for all **God's p**— *G41*
Col 1:12 the inheritance *of* **his holy p** in the kingdom *G41*
Col 1:26 is now disclosed *to* **the Lord's p**. *G41*
Col 3:12 as God's **chosen** *p*, holy and dearly AIT
1Th 2: 4 We are not trying to please **p** but God, who *G476*
1Th 2: 6 We were not looking for praise from **p**, not *G476*
1Th 2:14 from your **own p** the same things *G2625+5241*
1Th 5: 3 While *p are* **saying**, "Peace and safety," AIT
1Th 5:26 Greet all **God's p** with a holy kiss. *G81*
2Th 1:10 be glorified in his **holy** *p* and to be marveled AIT
2Th 3: 2 may be delivered from wicked and evil **p**, *G476*
2Th 3:12 **Such** *p* we command and urge in the Lord AIT
1Ti 1: 3 you may command **certain** *p* not to teach AIT
1Ti 2: 1 thanksgiving be made for all **p**— *G476*
1Ti 2: 4 who wants all **p** to be saved and to come to *G476*
1Ti 2: 6 who gave himself as a ransom for **all** *p*. AIT
1Ti 3:15 you will know how *p* **ought to** conduct AIT
1Ti 4: 3 They forbid **p** to marry and order them to NDT
1Ti 4:10 who is the Savior *of* all **p**, and especially of *G476*
1Ti 5: 7 Give the **p** these instructions, so that no one NDT
1Ti 5:10 washing the feet *of* **the Lord's p**, helping *G41*
1Ti 6: 5 constant friction *between* **p** of corrupt mind, *G476*
1Ti 6: 9 desires that plunge **p** into ruin and *G476*
1Ti 6:10 **Some** *p*, eager for money, have wandered AIT
2Ti 2: 2 entrust *to* reliable **p** who will also be *G476*
2Ti 2:14 Keep reminding God's **p** of these things NDT
2Ti 3: 2 **P** will be lovers of themselves, lovers of *G476*
2Ti 3: 5 Have nothing to do with **such** *p*. AIT
2Ti 4: 3 will come when *p will* not **put up with** sound AIT
Titus 1:10 For there are many **rebellious** *p*, full of AIT
Titus 2:11 has appeared that offers salvation *to* all **p**. *G476*
Titus 2:14 purify for himself a **p** that are his very own *G3295*
Titus 3: 1 Remind **the p** to be subject to rulers and *G899S*
Titus 3:11 You may be sure that **such** *p* are warped and AIT
Titus 3:14 **Our** *p* must learn to devote themselves to AIT
Phm 5 your love for all **his holy p** and your faith in *G41*
Phm 7 have refreshed the hearts *of* **the Lord's p**. *G41*
Heb 2:11 the one who makes **p** holy and those who NDT
Heb 2:17 make atonement for the sins *of* the **p**. *G3295*
Heb 4: 9 a Sabbath-rest *for* the **p** of God; *G3295*
Heb 5: 1 from among the **p** and is appointed to *G476*
Heb 5: 1 to represent the **p** in matters related to God *G476*
Heb 5: 3 own sins, as well as for the sins *of* the **p**. *G3295*
Heb 6:10 as you have helped **his p** and continue to *G41*
Heb 6:16 **P** swear by someone greater than *G476*
Heb 7: 5 priests to collect a tenth *from* the **p**— *G3295*
Heb 7: 8 the tenth is collected by **p** who die; but in *G476*
Heb 7:11 the law given to the **p** established that *G3295*
Heb 7:27 own sins, and then for the sins *of* the **p**. *G3295*
Heb 8: 8 But God found fault with **the p** and said *G899S*
Heb 8: 8 covenant with the **p** of Israel and with *G3875*
Heb 8: 8 people of Israel and with the **p** of Judah. *G3875*
Heb 8:10 I will establish *with* the **p** of Israel after *G3875*
Heb 8:10 I will be their God, and they will be my **p**. *G3295*
Heb 9: 7 for the sins the **p** had committed in *G3295*
Heb 9:19 every command of the law *to* all the **p**, *G3295*
Heb 9:19 sprinkled the scroll and all the **p**. *G3295*
Heb 9:27 Just as **p** are destined to die once, and after *G476*
Heb 10:30 and again, "The Lord will judge his **p**." *G3295*
Heb 11:13 All **these** *p* were still living by faith when AIT
Heb 11:14 **P** who say such things show that they are *G3836S*
Heb 11:25 along with the **p** of God rather than to *G3295*
Heb 11:29 By faith *the p* **passed through** the Red Sea as AIT
Heb 13: 2 by so doing **some** *p* have shown AIT
Heb 13:12 gate to make the **p** holy through his own *G3295*
Heb 13:24 Greet all your leaders and all **the Lord's p** *G41*
Jas 4: 4 *You* **adulterous** *p*, don't you know that AIT
Jas 5: 1 Now listen, you **rich** *p*, weep and wail AIT
1Pe 1:24 "All **p** are like grass, and all their glory *G4922*
1Pe 2: 8 "A stone that causes **p** to stumble and a NDT
1Pe 2: 9 But you are a chosen **p**, a royal priesthood *G1169*

1Pe 2:10 Once you were not a **p**, but now you are *G3295*
1Pe 2:10 now you are the **p** of God; once you *G3295*
1Pe 2:15 silence the ignorant talk *of* foolish **p**. *G476*
1Pe 2:16 Live as **free** *p*, but do not use your freedom as AIT
1Pe 3:20 In it only a few **p**, eight in all, were saved *G6034*
2Pe 2: 1 were also false prophets among the **p**, *G3295*
2Pe 2: 5 when he brought the flood on its **ungodly** *p*, AIT
2Pe 2:12 But **these** *p* blaspheme in matters they do not AIT
2Pe 2:17 **These** *p* are springs without water and mists AIT
2Pe 2:18 they entice **p** who are just escaping from *G3836S*
2Pe 2:19 "**p** are slaves to whatever has mastered *G5516*
2Pe 3:11 in this way, **what kind of** *p* ought you to be? AIT
2Pe 3:16 which ignorant and **unstable** *p* distort, as AIT
3Jn 8 show hospitality *to* **such** *p* so that we may AIT
Jude 3 was once for all entrusted *to* **God's holy p**. *G41*
Jude 4 They are **ungodly** *p*, who pervert the grace of AIT
Jude 5 at one time delivered his **p** out of Egypt, *G3295*
Jude 8 dreams these ungodly **p** pollute their own NDT
Jude 10 Yet **these** *p* slander whatever they do not AIT
Jude 12 **These** *p* are blemishes at your love feasts AIT
Jude 16 **These** *p* are grumblers and faultfinders; they AIT
Jude 19 These are the *p* **who divide** you, who follow AIT
Rev 2: 2 I know that you cannot tolerate **wicked** *p*, that AIT
Rev 3: 4 Yet you have a few **p** in Sardis who have *G3950*
Rev 5: 8 of incense, which are the prayers *of* **God's p**. *G41*
Rev 5: 9 tribe and language and **p** and nation. *G3295*
Rev 6: 4 from the earth and to make *p* **kill** each other. AIT
Rev 7: 9 **p** and language, standing before *G3295*
Rev 8: 3 with the prayers *of* all **God's p**, on the *G41*
Rev 8: 4 together with the prayers *of* **God's p**, went *G41*
Rev 8:11 many **p** died from the waters that had *G476*
Rev 9: 4 only those **p** who did not have the seal *G476*
Rev 9: 6 During those days **p** will seek death but will *G476*
Rev 9:10 had power to torment **p** for five months. *G476*
Rev 11: 9 three and a half days some from every **p**, *G3295*
Rev 11:13 Seven thousand **p** were killed in the *G3950+476*
Rev 11:18 the prophets and **your p** who revere your *G41*
Rev 13: 4 *P* **worshiped** the dragon because he had AIT
Rev 13: 7 war against **God's holy p** and to conquer *G41*
Rev 13: 7 over every tribe, **p**, language and nation. *G3295*
Rev 13:10 faithfulness *on the part of* **God's p**. *G41*
Rev 13:13 heaven to the earth in full view of the **p**. *G476*
Rev 13:16 It also forced **all** *p*, great and small, rich and AIT
Rev 14: 6 to every nation, tribe, language and **p**. *G3295*
Rev 14:12 *on the part of* the **p of God** who keep *G41*
Rev 16: 2 broke out on the **p** who had the mark of *G476*
Rev 16: 6 shed the blood *of* **your holy p** and your *G41*
Rev 16: 8 the sun was allowed to scorch **p** with fire. *G476*
Rev 16:10 *P* **gnawed** their tongues in agony AIT
Rev 16:21 about a hundred pounds, fell on **p**. *G476*
Rev 17: 6 was drunk with the blood *of* **God's holy p**, *G41*
Rev 18: 4 'Come out of her, my **p**,' so that you will *G3295*
Rev 18:20 you **p of God**! Rejoice, apostles *G41*
Rev 18:23 merchants were the world's **important p**. *G3491*
Rev 18:24 the blood of prophets and *of* **God's holy p**, *G41*
Rev 19: 8 stands for the righteous acts *of* **God's holy p**.) *G41*
Rev 19:18 and the flesh *of* **all** *p*, free and slave, AIT
Rev 20: 9 earth and surrounded the camp *of* **God's p**, *G41*
Rev 21: 3 God's dwelling place is now among the **p** *G476*
Rev 21: 3 They will be his **p**, and God himself will *G3295*
Rev 22:21 The grace of the Lord Jesus be with **God's p** *G41*

PEOPLE'S (18) [PEOPLE]

Ex 18:19 You must be the **p** representative H4200+6639
Lev 9:15 He took the goat for the **p** sin offering H6639
2Ch 25:15 "Why do you consult this **p** gods, which H6639
Ecc 8:11 **p** hearts are filled with H1201+2021+132
Isa 25: 8 he will remove his **p** disgrace from all the H6639
Jer 10:23 I know that **p** lives are not their own H4200+132
Eze 36: 3 the object of **p** malicious talk and H6639
Joel 1:12 Surely the **p** joy is withered H4946+1201+132
Mic 2: 4 my **p** possession is divided up. H6639
Mic 3: 3 who eat my **p** flesh, strip off their skin H6639
Hab 2:13 determined that the **p** labor is only fuel H6639
Mt 2: 4 called together all the **p** chief priests and *G3295*
Mt 13:15 For this **p** heart has become calloused *G3295*
Mt 23: 4 loads and put them on other **p** shoulders, *G476*
Mt 23:13 door of the kingdom of heaven in **p** faces. *G476*
Ac 28:27 For this **p** heart has become calloused *G3295*
Ro 2:16 day when God judges **p** secrets through *G476*
2Co 5:19 not counting **p** sins against them. *G899S*

PEOPLED (1) [PEOPLE]

Eze 26:17 city of renown, **p** *by men of* the sea! H3782

PEOPLES (160) [PEOPLE]

Ge 10: 5 these the maritime **p** spread out into their H1580
Ge 12: 3 all **p** *on* earth will be blessed through H5476
Ge 17:16 of nations; kings of **p** will come from her." H6639
Ge 25:23 two **p** from within you will be H4211
Ge 27:29 nations serve you and **p** bow down to you. H4211
Ge 28: 3 until you become a community of **p**. H6639
Ge 28:14 All **p** *on* earth will be blessed through you H5476
Ge 29: 1 came to the land of the eastern **p**. H1201
Ge 48: 4 I will make you a community of **p**, and I H6639
Dt 1: 7 go to all the **neighboring p** in the Arabah H8907
Dt 4:27 The LORD will scatter you among the **p**, H6639
Dt 6:14 other gods, the gods of the **p** around you; H6639
Dt 7: 6 you out of all the **p** on the face of the H6639
Dt 7: 7 you were more numerous than other **p**, H6639
Dt 7: 7 peoples, for you were the fewest of all **p**. H6639
Dt 7:16 must destroy all the **p** the LORD your God H6639
Dt 7:19 do the same to all the **p** you now fear. H6639
Dt 13: 7 gods of the **p** around you, whether near H6639
Dt 14: 2 Out of all the **p** on the face of the earth H6639
Dt 28:10 Then all the **p** *on* earth will see that you H6639
Dt 28:37 among all the **p** where the LORD will H6639
Dt 32: 8 up boundaries for the **p** according to the H6639
Dt 33:19 They will summon **p** to the mountain and H6639
Jos 4:24 this so that all the **p** *of* the earth might H6639
Jdg 2:12 various gods of the **p** around them. H6639
Jdg 6: 3 other eastern **p** invaded the country. H1201
Jdg 6:33 other eastern **p** joined forces and H1201
Jdg 7:12 all the other eastern **p** had settled in the H1201
Jdg 8:10 were left of the armies of the eastern **p**; H1201
1Sa 27: 8 From ancient times **these** *p* had lived in the AIT
2Sa 22:44 delivered me from the attacks of the **p**; H6639
1Ki 8:43 so that all the **p** *of* the earth may know H6639
1Ki 8:60 so that all the **p** *of* the earth may know H6639
1Ki 9: 7 an object of ridicule among all **p**. H6639
1Ki 9:20 Jebusites (these **p** were not Israelites). H889S
1Ki 9:21 descendants of *all these* **p** remaining in H2157S
1Ch 5:25 to the gods of the **p** *of* the land, H6639
1Ch 16:24 his marvelous deeds among all **p**. H6639
2Ch 6:33 so that all the **p** *of* the earth may know H6639
2Ch 7:20 an object of ridicule among all **p**. H6639
2Ch 13: 9 of your own as the **p** *of* other lands do? H6639
2Ch 32:13 have done to all the **p** *of* the other lands? H6639
2Ch 32:17 as the gods of the **p** *of* the other lands did H1580
2Ch 32:19 the gods of the other **p** *of* the world— H6639
Ezr 3: 3 Despite their fear of the **p** around them H6639
Ezr 4: 4 Then the **p** around them set out to H6639
Ezr 9: 1 from the neighboring **p** with their H6639
Ezr 9: 2 the holy race with the **p** around them. H6639
Ezr 9:11 a land polluted by the corruption of its **p**. H6639
Ezr 9:14 with the **p** *who commit* such detestable H6639
Ezr 10: 2 foreign women from the **p** around us. H6639
Ezr 10:11 from the **p** around you and from H6639
Ne 9:24 with their kings and the **p** *of* the land, H6639
Ne 9:30 them into the hands of the neighboring **p**. H6639
Ne 10:28 from the neighboring **p** for the sake of the H6639
Ne 10:30 in marriage to the **p** around us or take H6639
Ne 10:31 the neighboring **p** bring merchandise H6639
Ne 13:24 of **one of the other p**, H6639+2256+6639
Est 1:16 the nobles and the **p** of all the provinces H6639
Est 3: 8 dispersed among the **p** in all the H6639
Est 3:12 the nobles of the **various p**. H6639+2256+6639
Ps 2: 1 nations conspire and the **p** plot in vain? H4211
Ps 7: 7 Let the assembled **p** gather around you H4211
Ps 7: 8 Let the LORD judge the **p**. Vindicate me H6639
Ps 9: 8 judges the **p** with equity. H4211
Ps 33:10 nations; he thwarts the purposes of the **p**. H6639
Ps 44: 2 you crushed the **p** and made our H4211
Ps 44:14 the nations; the **p** shake their heads at us. H4211
Ps 47: 3 nations under us, **p** under our feet. H4211
Ps 49: 1 Hear this, all you **p**; listen, all who live in H6639
Ps 57: 9 nations; I will sing of you among the **p**. H4211
Ps 66: 8 Praise our God, *all* **p**, let the sound of his H6639
Ps 67: 3 May the **p** praise you, God; may all the H6639
Ps 67: 3 praise you, God; may all the **p** praise you. H6639
Ps 67: 4 you rule the **p** with equity and guide H6639
Ps 67: 5 May the **p** praise you, God; may all the H6639
Ps 67: 5 praise you, God; may all the **p** praise you. H6639
Ps 77:14 you display your power among the **p**. H6639
Ps 87: 6 The LORD will write in the register of the **p** H6639
Ps 96: 3 his marvelous deeds among all **p**. H6639
Ps 96:10 he will judge the **p** with equity. H6639
Ps 96:13 the **p** in his faithfulness. H6639
Ps 97: 6 his righteousness, and all **p** see his glory. H6639
Ps 98: 9 in righteousness and the **p** with equity. H6639
Ps 102:22 when the **p** and the kingdoms assemble H6639
Ps 105:20 released him, the ruler of **p** set him free. H6639
Ps 106:34 They did not destroy the **p** as the LORD had H6639
Ps 108: 3 nations; I will sing of you among the **p**. H4211
Ps 117: 1 all you nations; extol him, all you **p**. H569
Ps 144: 2 I take refuge, who subdues **p** under me. H6639
Ps 149: 7 on the nations and punishment on the **p**, H4211
Pr 24:24 will be cursed by **p** and denounced by H6639
Isa 2: 3 Many **p** will come and say, "Come, let us H6639
Isa 2: 4 will settle disputes for many **p**. H6639
Isa 11:10 of Jesse will stand as a banner for the **p**; H6639
Isa 14: 6 anger struck down **p** with unceasing blows H6639
Isa 17:12 Woe to the **p** who roar—they roar like the H4211
Isa 17:13 Although the **p** roar like the roar of H4211
Isa 19:13 cornerstones of her **p** have led Egypt H8657
Isa 25: 3 Therefore strong **p** will honor you; cities of H6639
Isa 25: 6 will prepare a feast of rich food for all **p**, H6639
Isa 25: 7 will destroy the shroud that enfolds all **p**, H6639
Isa 30:28 in the jaws of the **p** a bit that leads them H6639
Isa 33: 3 of your army, the **p** flee; when you rise up, H6639
Isa 33:12 The **p** will be burned to ashes; like cut H6639
Isa 34: 1 nations, and listen; pay attention, you **p**! H4211
Isa 37:18 have laid waste all these **p** and their lands. H824
Isa 43: 9 gather together and the **p** assemble. H4211
Isa 49:22 I will lift up my banner to the **p**; they will H6639
Isa 55: 4 I have made him a witness to the **p**, H4211
Isa 55: 4 peoples, a ruler and commander of the **p**. H4211
Isa 60: 2 the earth and thick darkness is over the **p**, H4211
Isa 61: 9 nations and their offspring among the **p**. H6639
Jer 1:15 to summon all the **p** *of* the northern H5476
Jer 10: 3 For the practices of the **p** are worthless H6639
Jer 10:25 on the **p** who do not call on your name. H5476
Jer 25: 9 will summon all the **p** *of* the north and my H5476
Jer 34: 1 the kingdoms and **p** *in* the empire he H6639
Jer 51:58 the **p** exhaust themselves for nothing H6639
La 1:18 all you **p**; look on my suffering H6639
La 4:12 did any of the **p** *of* the world, that H3782
Eze 3: 6 not to many **p** *of* obscure speech and H6639
Eze 20:32 nations, like the **p** *of* the world, who serve H5476
Eze 27: 3 the sea, merchant of **p** on many coasts H6639
Eze 32: 9 the hearts of many **p** when I bring about H6639
Eze 32:10 I will cause many **p** to be appalled at you H6639
Eze 36:15 the scorn of the **p** or cause your nation to H6639
Da 3: 4 "Nations and **p** of every language, this A10040
Da 3: 7 all the nations and **p** of every language A10040
Da 4: 1 To the nations and **p** of every language A10040
Da 4:35 All the **p** *of* the earth are regarded as A10163
Da 4:35 powers of heaven and the **p** *of* the earth. A10163
Da 5:19 all the nations and **p** of every language A10040
Da 6:25 all the nations and **p** of every language A10040
Da 7:14 all nations and **p** of every language A10040
Joel 2:17 Why should they say among the **p** H6639
Mic 1: 2 you **p**, all of you, listen, earth and H6639
Mic 4: 1 above the hills, and **p** will stream to it. H6639
Mic 4: 3 will judge between many **p** and will settle H6639
Mic 5: 7 in the midst of many **p** like dew from the H6639
Mic 5: 8 in the midst of many **p**, like a lion among H6639
Na 3: 4 by her prostitution and **p** by her witchcraft. H5476
Hab 2: 5 all the nations and takes captive all the **p**. H6639
Hab 2: 8 the **p** who are left will plunder you. H6639
Hab 2:10 You have plotted the ruin of many **p** H6639
Zep 3: 9 "Then I will purify the lips of the **p**, that H6639
Zep 3:20 among all the **p** *of* the earth when I H6639
Zec 8:20 "Many **p** and the inhabitants of many H6639
Zec 8:22 And many **p** and powerful nations will H6639
Zec 10: 9 Though I scatter them among the **p**, yet in H6639
Zec 12: 2 that sends all the surrounding **p** reeling. H6639
Zec 12: 6 all the surrounding **p** right and left, H6639
Zec 14:17 If any of the **p** *of* the earth do not go up to H5476
Mt 24:30 And then all the **p** of the earth will mourn *G5876*
Ac 3:25 your offspring all **p** on earth will be *G4255*
Ac 4:25 the nations rage and the **p** plot in vain? *G3295*
Ro 15:11 all you Gentiles; let all the **p** extol him." *G3295*
Rev 1: 7 all **p** on earth "will mourn because of *G5876*
Rev 10:11 "You must prophesy again about many **p** *G3295*
Rev 17:15 the prostitute sits, are **p**, multitudes, *G3295*

PEOR (8) [BAAL PEOR, BETH PEOR]

Nu 23:28 And Balak took Balaam to the top of **P** H7186
Nu 25: 3 Israel yoked themselves to the Baal of **P**. H7186
Nu 25: 5 have yoked themselves to the Baal of **P**." H7186
Nu 25:18 deceived you in the **P** incident involving H7186
Nu 31:16 be unfaithful to the LORD in the **P** incident, H7186
Dt 4: 3 you everyone who followed the Baal of **P**, H7186
Jos 22:17 Was not the sin of **P** enough for us? Up to H7186
Ps 106:28 to the Baal of **P** and ate sacrifices H7186

PER (1)

Ex 38:26 one beka **p** person, that is, half a shekel H4200

PERATH (4)

Jer 13: 4 go now to **P** and hide it there in a H7310
Jer 13: 5 So I went and hid it at **P**, as the LORD told H7310
Jer 13: 6 "Go now to **P** and get the belt I told you H7310
Jer 13: 7 So I went to **P** and dug up the belt and H7310

PERAZIM (1) [BAAL PERAZIM]

Isa 28:21 The LORD will rise up as he did at Mount **P**, H7292

PERCEIVE (4) [PERCEIVED, PERCEIVES, PERCEIVING]

Job 9:11 when he goes by, *I* cannot **p** him. H1067
Ps 139: 2 when I rise; *you* **p** my thoughts from afar. H1067
Pr 24:12 *does* not he who weighs the heart **p** it? H1067
Isa 43:19 it springs up; *do you* not **p** it? I am making H3359

PERCEIVED (1) [PERCEIVE]

Isa 64: 4 has heard, no **ear** *has* **p**, no eye has seen H263

PERCEIVES (1) [PERCEIVE]

Job 33:14 now another—though no *one* **p** it. H8800

PERCEIVING (4) [PERCEIVE]

Isa 6: 9 be ever seeing, but never **p**. H3359
Mt 13:14 you will be ever seeing but never **p**. *G3972*
Mk 4:12 " 'they may be ever seeing but never **p** *G3972*
Ac 28:26 you will be ever seeing but never **p**." *G3972*

PERCENT (1)

Ne 5:11 charging them—**one p** *of* the money H4395

PERCH (3) [PERCHED]

Ge 8: 9 find nowhere *to* **p** because H4200+4090+8079
Mt 13:32 that the birds come and **p** in its branches." *G2942*
Mk 4:32 branches that the birds can **p** in its shade." *G2942*

PERCHED (1) [PERCH]

Lk 13:19 and the birds **p** in its branches. *G2942*

PERES (1)

Da 5:28 **P**: Your kingdom is divided and given to A10593

PERESH (1)

1Ch 7:16 gave birth to a son and named him **P**. H7303

PEREZ (18) [PEREZ UZZAH, PEREZITE, RIMMON PEREZ]

Ge 38:29 have broken out!" And he was named **P**. H7289
Ge 46:12 Shelah, **P** and Zerah (but Er and Onan H7289

Ge 46:12 The sons of **P**: Hezron and Hamul. H7289
Nu 26:20 through **P**, the Perezite clan; H7289
Nu 26:21 The descendants of **P** were: through H7289
Ru 4:12 may your family be like that of **P**, whom H7289
Ru 4:18 is the family line of **P**: Perez was the H7289
Ru 4:18 **P** was the father of Hezron, H7289
1Ch 2: 4 Tamar bore **P** and Zerah to Judah. H7289
1Ch 2: 5 The sons of **P**: Hezron and Hamul. H7289
1Ch 4: 1 **P**, Hezron, Karmi, Hur H7289
1Ch 9: 4 of Bani, a descendant of **P** son of Judah. H7289
1Ch 27: 3 was a descendant of **P** and chief of all the H7289
Ne 11: 4 the son of Mahalalel, a descendant of **P**; H7289
Ne 11: 6 The descendants of **P** who lived in H7289
Mt 1: 3 Judah the father of **P** and Zerah, whose *G5756*
Mt 1: 3 mother was Tamar, **P** the father of Hezron *G5756*
Lk 3:33 of Hezron, the son *of* **P**, the son of Judah, *G5756*

PEREZ UZZAH (2) [PEREZ]
2Sa 6: 8 to this day that place is called **P**. H7290
1Ch 13:11 to this day that place is called **P**. H7290

PEREZITE (1) [PEREZ]
Nu 26:20 through Perez, the **P** clan; through Zerah H7291

PERFECT (34) [PERFECTER, PERFECTING, PERFECTION, PERFECTLY]
Dt 32: 4 his works are **p**, and all his ways are H9459
2Sa 22:31 God, his way is **p**: The LORD's word is H9459
Job 36: 4 one who has **p** knowledge is with you. H9459
Job 37:16 wonders of him who has **p** knowledge? H9459
Ps 18:30 God, his way is **p**: The LORD's word is H9459
Ps 19: 7 The law of the LORD is **p**, refreshing the H9459
Ps 50: 2 From Zion, **p** *in* beauty, God shines forth. H4817
Ps 64: 6 say, "*We have* devised *a* **p** plan! H9462
SS 6: 9 my dove, my **p** *one*, is unique, the H9447
Isa 25: 1 in **p** faithfulness you have done H590
Isa 26: 3 will keep in **p peace** those whose H8934+8934
Eze 16:14 I had given you made your beauty **p**, H4003
Eze 27: 3 " 'You say, Tyre, "I am **p** *in* beauty." H4003
Eze 28:12 full of wisdom and **p** *in* beauty. H4003
Mt 5:48 Be **p**, therefore, as your heavenly Father is *G5455*
Mt 5:48 therefore, as your heavenly Father is **p**. *G5455*
Mt 19:21 "If you want to be **p**, go, sell your *G5455*
Ro 12: 2 will is—his good, pleasing and **p** will. *G5455*
2Co 12: 9 for my power is **made p** in weakness." *G5464*
Col 3:14 which binds them all together *in* **p unity**. *G5456*
Heb 2:10 *should* **make** the pioneer of their salvation **p** *G5457*
Heb 5: 9 *once* **made p**, he became the source *G5457*
Heb 7:19 the law **made** nothing **p**), and a better *G5457*
Heb 7:28 the Son, *who has been* **made p** forever. *G5457*
Heb 9:11 the greater and *more* **p** tabernacle that is *G5455*
Heb 10: 1 **make p** those who draw near to worship. *G5457*
Heb 10:14 one sacrifice *he has* **made p** forever those *G5457*
Heb 11:40 together with us *would they be* **made p**. *G5457*
Heb 12:23 to the spirits of the righteous **made p**, *G5457*
Jas 1:17 Every good and **p** gift is from above *G5455*
Jas 1:25 intently into the **p** law that gives freedom, *G5455*
Jas 3: 2 who is never at fault in what they say is **p**, *G5455*
1Jn 4:18 But **p** love drives out fear, because fear *G5455*
1Jn 4:18 The one who fears *is* not **made p** in love. *G5457*

PERFECTER (1) [PERFECT]
Heb 12: 2 eyes on Jesus, the pioneer and **p** of faith. *G5460*

PERFECTING (1) [PERFECT]
2Co 7: 1 **p** holiness out of reverence for God. *G2200*

PERFECTION (7) [PERFECT]
Ps 119:96 To all **p** I see a limit, but your commands H9416
La 2:15 the city that was called the **p** *of* beauty, H4003
Eze 27: 4 your builders **brought** your beauty **to p**. H4005
Eze 27:11 your walls; they **brought** your beauty **to p**. H4005
Eze 28:12 " 'You were the seal of **p**, full of wisdom H9422
Eze 43:10 Let them consider its **p**, H9422
Heb 7:11 If **p** could have been attained through the *G5459*

PERFECTLY (2) [PERFECT]
1Co 1:10 that you be **p** united in mind and *G2936*
2Co 11: 6 have made this **p** clear to you in *G1877+4246*

PERFORM (29) [PERFORMANCE, PERFORMED, PERFORMING, PERFORMS]
Ex 3:20 all the wonders that *I will* **p** among them. H6913
Ex 4:17 in your hand so *you can* **p** the signs with it H6913
Ex 4:21 see that *you* **p** before Pharaoh all the H6913
Ex 4:28 all the signs he had commanded him to **p**. NDT
Ex 7: 9 says to you, '**P** a miracle,' then say H5989
Ex 10: 1 officials so that I *may* **p** these signs of H8883
Lev 22: 9 " 'The priests *are to* **p** my service in such a H9068
Nu 3: 7 *They are to* **p** duties for him and for the H9068
Nu 18: 3 to you and are to **p** all the duties of the tent, NDT
Jdg 16:27 men and women watching Samson **p**. H8471
2Sa 7:23 to **p** great and awesome wonders by H6913
1Ki 8:11 priests could not **p** their service because H6641
1Ch 17:21 to **p** great and awesome wonders by NDT
2Ch 5:14 priests could not **p** their service because H6641
2Ch 31:16 temple of the LORD to **p** the daily duties of NDT
Isa 28:21 his strange work, and **p** his task, his alien H6268
Jer 21: 2 Perhaps the LORD *will* **p** wonders for us as H6913
Mt 7:22 in your name **p** many miracles? *G4472*
Mt 24:24 will appear and **p** great signs and *G1443*
Mk 13:22 will appear and **p** signs and wonders to *G1443*
Lk 23: 8 hoped to see him **p** a sign of some *G5679+1181*
Jn 3: 2 For no one could **p** the signs you are *G4472*
Jn 7:31 *will he* **p** more signs than this man?" *G4472*
Jn 9:16 "How can a sinner **p** such signs? *G4472*
Ac 4:30 hand to heal and **p** signs and wonders *G1181*
Ac 14: 3 them *to* **p** signs and *G1181+1328+3836+5931*
2Co 9:12 service that you **p** is not only supplying *G3311*
Rev 13:14 it was given power *to* **p** on behalf of the *G4472*
Rev 16:14 They are demonic spirits *that* **p** signs, and *G4472*

PERFORMANCE (1) [PERFORM]
1Ch 23:28 things and the **p** *of* other duties at the H5126

PERFORMED (45) [PERFORM]
Ex 4:30 *He* also **p** the signs before the people H6913
Ex 10: 2 Egyptians and how *I* **p** my signs among H8492
Ex 11:10 Moses and Aaron **p** all these wonders H6913
Nu 14:11 of all the signs *I have* **p** among them? H6913
Nu 14:22 glory and the signs *I* **p** in Egypt and in the H6913
Dt 10:21 who **p** for you those great and awesome H6913
Dt 11: 3 the signs *he* **p** and the things he did in the H6913
Dt 34:12 the mighty power or **p** the awesome deeds NDT
Jos 24:17 **p** those great signs before our eyes. H6913
Jdg 16:25 out of the prison, and *he* **p** for them. H7464
1Sa 12: 7 the righteous acts **p** *by* the LORD for you H6913
2Sa 23:20 fighter from Kabzeel, **p** great exploits. NDT
1Ch 6:32 *They* **p** their duties according to the H6641
1Ch 11:22 fighter from Kabzeel, **p** great **exploits**. H7189
1Ch 25: 1 is the list of the men who **p** this service: H4856
Ne 9:17 the miracles *you* **p** among them. H6913
Ne 12:45 *They* **p** the service of their God and the H9068
Ps 105:27 *They* **p** his signs among them, his H8492
Jer 32:20 *You* **p** signs and wonders in Egypt and H8492
Da 4: 2 that the Most High God *has* **p** for me. A10522
Mt 11:20 in which most of his miracles *had been* **p**, *G1181*
Mt 11:21 the miracles that *were* **p** in you had been *G1181*
Mt 11:21 performed in you *had been* **p** in Tyre and *G1181*
Mt 11:23 the miracles that *were* **p** in you had been *G1181*
Mt 11:23 performed in you *had been* **p** in Sodom, *G1181*
Lk 1:51 *He has* **p** mighty deeds with his arm; he *G4472*
Lk 10:13 the miracles that *were* **p** in you had been *G1181*
Lk 10:13 performed in you *had been* **p** in Tyre and *G1181*
Jn 4:54 the second sign Jesus **p** after coming from *G4472*
Jn 6: 2 saw the signs *he had* **p** by healing the *G4472*
Jn 6:14 After the people saw the sign Jesus **p** *G4472*
Jn 6:26 you saw the signs I **p** but because you ate NDT
Jn 10:41 "Though John never **p** a sign, all that *G4472*
Jn 12:18 they had heard *that* he *had* **p** this sign, *G4472*
Jn 12:37 Even *after* Jesus *had* **p** so many signs in *G4472*
Jn 20:30 Jesus **p** many other signs in the presence *G4472*
Ac 2:43 wonders and signs **p** by the apostles. *G1181*
Ac 4:16 knows they *have* **p** a notable sign, *G1181+1328*
Ac 5:12 apostles **p** many signs *G1328+3836+5931+1181*
Ac 6: 8 **p** great wonders and signs among the *G4472*
Ac 7:36 out of Egypt and **p** wonders and signs in *G4472*
Ac 8: 6 heard Philip and saw the signs *he* **p**, *G4472*
Col 2:11 with a circumcision **not p by human hands**. *G942*
Rev 13:13 And *it* **p** great signs, even causing fire to *G4472*
Rev 19:20 false prophet who *had* **p** the signs on its *G4472*

PERFORMING (4) [PERFORM]
Nu 8:26 their brothers in **p** their duties at the tent H9068
Mk 6: 2 are these remarkable miracles he *is* **p**? *G1181*
Jn 2:23 saw the signs he *was* **p** and believed in *G4472*
Jn 11:47 "Here *is* this man **p** many signs. *G4472*

PERFORMS (5) [PERFORM]
Job 5: 9 *He* **p** wonders that cannot be fathomed H6913
Job 9:10 *He* **p** wonders that cannot be fathomed H6913
Ps 77:14 You are the God *who* **p** miracles; you H6913
Da 6:27 *he* **p** signs and wonders in the heavens A10522
Heb 10:11 priest stands and **p** *his* **religious duties**; *G3310*

PERFUME (25) [PERFUME-MAKERS, PERFUMED, PERFUMER, PERFUMERS, PERFUMES]
Ex 30:33 Whoever **makes p** like it and puts it on H8379
Ru 3: 3 **put on p**, and get dressed in your H6057
Pr 27: 9 **P** and incense bring joy to the heart, and H9043
Ecc 7: 1 A good name is better than **fine p**, and H9043
Ecc 10: 1 As dead flies give **p** a bad smell H9043+8379
SS 1: 3 perfumes; your name is like **p** poured out. H9043
SS 1:12 at his table, my **p** spread its fragrance. H5948
SS 4:10 fragrance of your **p** more than any spice! H9043
SS 5:13 cheeks are like beds of spice yielding **p**. H5349
Isa 3:20 sashes, the **p** bottles and charms, H5883
Mt 26: 7 with an alabaster jar *of* very expensive **p**, *G3693*
Mt 26: 9 "This **p** could have been sold at a high price NDT
Mt 26:12 When she poured this **p** on my body, she *G3693*
Mk 14: 3 with an alabaster jar *of* very expensive **p**, *G3693*
Mk 14: 3 broke the jar and poured the **p** on his head. NDT
Mk 14: 4 to one another, "Why this waste *of* **p**? *G3693*
Mk 14: 8 *She* **poured p** on my body beforehand to *G3690*
Lk 7:37 she came there with an alabaster jar *of* **p**. *G3693*
Lk 7:38 kissed them and poured **p** on them. *G3693*
Lk 7:46 but she has poured **p** on my feet. *G3693*
Jn 11: 2 same one who poured **p** on the Lord and *G3693*
Jn 12: 3 an expensive **p**; she poured it on *G3693*
Jn 12: 3 was filled with the fragrance *of* the **p**. *G3693*
Jn 12: 5 "Why wasn't this **p** sold and the money *G3693*
Jn 12: 7 she should save **this p** for the day of my *G899S*

PERFUME-MAKERS (1) [PERFUME]
Ne 3: 8 one of the **p**, made repairs next H8382

PERFUMED (2) [PERFUME]
Pr 7:17 *I have* **p** my bed *with* myrrh, aloes and H5678
SS 3: 6 **p** *with* myrrh and incense made from all H7787

PERFUMER (3) [PERFUME]
Ex 30:25 a fragrant blend, the work of a **p**. H8379
Ex 30:35 fragrant blend of incense, the work of a **p**. H8379
Ex 37:29 fragrant incense—the work of a **p**. H8379

PERFUMERS (1) [PERFUME]
1Sa 8:13 daughters to be **p** and cooks and bakers H8384

PERFUMES (5) [PERFUME]
2Ch 16:14 with spices and various blended **p**, H5351+5126
Est 2:12 oil of myrrh and six with **p** and cosmetics. H1411
SS 1: 3 Pleasing is the fragrance of your **p**; your H9043
Isa 57: 9 Molek with olive oil and increased your **p**. H8383
Lk 23:56 went home and prepared spices and **p**. *G3693*

PERGA (3)
Ac 13:13 his companions sailed to **P** in Pamphylia, *G4308*
Ac 13:14 From **P** they went on to Pisidian Antioch *G4308*
Ac 14:25 when they had preached the word in **P**, *G4308*

PERGAMUM (2)
Rev 1:11 to Ephesus, Smyrna, **P**, Thyatira, Sardis *G4307*
Rev 2:12 "To the angel of the church in **P** write *G4307*

PERHAPS (36)
Ge 16: 2 **p** I can build a family through her. H218
Ge 32:20 when I see him, **p** he will receive me." H218
Ge 43:12 mouths of your sacks. **P** it was a mistake. H218
Ex 32:30 **p** I can make atonement for your sin." H218
Nu 22: 6 **P** then I will be able to defeat them and H218
Nu 22:11 **P** then I will be able to fight them and H218
Nu 23: 3 **P** the LORD will come to meet with me H218
Nu 23:27 **P** it will please God to let you curse them H218
Jos 9: 7 to the Hivites, "**But p** you live near us, so H218
1Sa 6: 5 **P** he will lift his hand from you and your H218
1Sa 9: 6 **P** he will tell us what way to take. H218
1Sa 14: 6 **P** the LORD will act in our behalf H218
2Sa 14:15 **p** he will grant his servant's request. H218
2Sa 14:16 **P** the king will agree to deliver his servant H3954
1Ki 18:27 **P** he is deep in thought, or busy, or H3954
1Ki 20:31 around our heads. **P** he will spare your life." H218
2Ki 2:16 **P** the Spirit of the LORD has picked him up H7153
Job 1: 5 "**P** my children have sinned and cursed H218
Isa 44:14 cut down cedars, or **p** took a cypress or oak. NDT
Isa 47:12 **P** you will succeed, perhaps you will cause H218
Isa 47:12 you will succeed, **p** you will cause terror. H218
Jer 20:10 "**P** he will be deceived; then we H218
Jer 21: 2 **P** the LORD will perform wonders for us as H218
Jer 26: 3 **P** they will listen and each will turn from H218
Jer 36: 3 **P** when the people of Judah hear about H218
Jer 36: 7 **P** they will bring their petition before the H218
Jer 51: 8 balm for her pain; **p** she can be healed. H218
Eze 12: 3 **P** they will understand, though they are a H218
Am 5:15 **P** the LORD God Almighty will have mercy H218
Zep 2: 3 **p** you will be sheltered on the day of the H218
Lk 20:13 whom I love; **p** they will respect him. *G2711*
Ac 17:27 seek him and **p** reach out for *G1623+726+1145*
1Co 7: 5 each other except **p** by mutual consent *G323*
1Co 15:37 **p** of wheat or of something else. *G1623+5593*
1Co 16: 6 **P** I will stay with you for a while, or even *G5593*
Phm 15 **P** the reason he was separated from you *G5440*

PERIDA (1)
Ne 7:57 the descendants of Sotai, Sophereth, **P**, H7263

PERIL (3)
Job 22:10 around you, why sudden **p** terrifies you, H7065
Ps 107:26 in their **p** their courage melted away. H8288
2Co 1:10 He has delivered us from such a **deadly p** *G2505*

PERIOD (29) [PERIODS]
Ge 31:35 in your presence; I'm having my **p**." H2006+851
Ge 50:10 a seven-day **p of mourning** for his father. H65
Ex 2:23 During that long **p**, the king of Egypt died H3427
Lev 12: 2 is unclean during her **monthly p**. H5614+1864
Lev 12: 5 woman will be unclean, as during her **p**. H5614
Lev 15:19 the **impurity** of her **monthly p** will last H5614
Lev 15:20 she lies on during her **p** will be unclean, H5614
Lev 15:25 other than her **monthly p** or has a H5614
Lev 15:25 a discharge that continues beyond her **p**, H5614
Lev 15:25 the discharge, just as in the days of her **p**. H5614
Lev 15:26 as is her bed during her **monthly p**, and H5614
Lev 15:26 sits on will be unclean, as during her **p**. H5614
Lev 15:33 a *woman* in her **monthly p**, for a H5614+1865
Lev 18:19 during the uncleanness of her **monthly p**. H5614
Lev 20:18 with a woman during her **monthly p**, H1865
Lev 25: 8 years amount to a **p** *of* forty-nine years. H3427
Nu 6: 5 " '*During* the entire **p** *of* their Nazirite vow, H3427
Nu 6: 5 be holy until the **p** of their dedication to H3427
Nu 6: 6 " 'Throughout the **p** *of* their dedication to H3427
Nu 6: 8 Throughout the **p** *of* their dedication, they H3427
Nu 6:12 LORD for the same **p** *of* dedication and H3427
Nu 6:12 defiled during their **p of dedication**. H5694
Nu 6:13 Nazirite when the **p** *of* their dedication is H3427
Job 1: 5 When a **p** *of* feasting had run its course H3427
Eze 18: 6 relations with a woman *during* her **p**. H5614
Eze 22:10 those who violate women during their **p**, H5614
Da 7:12 to live for a **p of time**.) A10232+10221+10530
Ac 1: 3 appeared to them **over a p** of forty days *G1328*

P

Ac 24: 2 have enjoyed a **long p** of peace under *G4498*

PERIODS (1) [PERIOD]
1Ch 9:25 their duties for **seven-day p**. H8679+2021+3427

PERISH (87) [PERISHABLE, PERISHED, PERISHES, PERISHING]
Ge 6:17 Everything on earth *will* **p**. H1588
Ge 47:19 Why *should we* **p** before your eyes—we H4637
Ex 19:21 to see the LORD and many of them **p**. H5877
Lev 26:38 *You will* **p** among the nations; the land of your H6
Dt 4:26 this day that *you will* quickly **p** from the H6+6
Dt 11:17 and *you will* soon **p** from the good land the H6
Dt 28:22 which will plague you until you **p**. H6
Dt 32:25 The young men and young women will **p** NDT
Jos 23:13 in your eyes, until you **p** from this good land H6
Jos 23:16 and *you will* quickly **p** from the good land he H6
Jdg 5:31 "So *may* all your enemies **p**, LORD! But may H6
1Sa 12:25 doing evil, both you and your king *will* **p**." H6200
1Sa 26:10 will die, or he will go into battle and **p**. H6200
2Ki 9: 8 The whole house of Ahab *will* **p**. I will cut off H6
Est 4:14 but you and your father's family *will* **p**. H6
Est 4:16 it is against the law. And if *I* **p**, I perish." H6
Est 4:16 it is against the law. And if I perish, *I* **p**." H6
Job 3: 3 "*May* the day of my birth **p**, and the night that H6
Job 3:11 "Why *did I* not **p** at birth, and die as I H4637
Job 4: 9 At the breath of God *they* **p**; at the blast of his H6
Job 4:20 broken to pieces; unnoticed, *they* **p** forever. H6
Job 6:18 they go off into the wasteland and **p**. H6
Job 20: 7 *he will* **p** forever, like his own dung; those H6
Job 34:15 all humanity *would* **p** together and H1588
Job 36:12 *they will* **p** by the sword and die without H6296
Ps 9: 3 turn back; they stumble and **p** before you. H6
Ps 9:18 the hope of the afflicted *will* never **p**. H6
Ps 10:16 ever; the nations *will* **p** from his land. H6
Ps 37:20 But the wicked *will* **p**: Though the LORD's H6
Ps 37:28 the offspring of the wicked *will* **p**. H4162
Ps 41: 5 "When will he die and his name **p**? H6
Ps 49:10 that the foolish and the senseless also **p** H6
Ps 49:12 endure; they are like the beasts *that* **p**. H1950
Ps 49:20 understanding are like the beasts *that* **p**. H1950
Ps 68: 2 before the fire, *may* the wicked **p** before God. H6
Ps 71:13 *May* my accusers **p** in shame; may those H3983
Ps 73:27 Those who are far from you *will* **p**; you destroy H6
Ps 80:16 with fire; at your rebuke your *people* **p**. H6
Ps 83:17 dismayed; *may they* **p** in disgrace. H6
Ps 92: 9 surely your enemies *will* **p**; all evildoers will H6
Ps 102:26 They *will* **p**, but you remain; they will all wear H6
Pr 11:10 when the wicked **p**, there are shouts of joy. H6
Pr 19: 9 whoever pours out lies *will* **p**. H6
Pr 21:28 A false witness *will* **p**, but a careful listener H6
Pr 28:28 when the wicked **p**, the righteous thrive. H6
Isa 1:28 those who forsake the LORD *will* **p**. H3983
Isa 29:14 the wisdom of the wise *will* **p**, the H6
Isa 31: 3 are helped will fall; all *will* **p** together. H3983
Isa 41:11 who oppose you will be as nothing and **p**. H6
Isa 57: 1 The righteous **p**, and no one takes it to heart H6
Isa 60:12 kingdom that will not serve you *will* **p**; H6
Jer 6:21 over them; neighbors and friends *will* **p**." H6
Jer 8:14 us flee to the fortified cities and **p** there! H1959
Jer 8:14 our God *has* **doomed** us **to p** and given H1959
Jer 10:11 *will* **p** from the earth and from under the A10005
Jer 10:15 when their judgment comes, *they will* **p**. H6
Jer 14:15 Those same prophets *will* **p** by sword and H9462
Jer 16: 4 *They will* **p** by sword and famine, and H3983
Jer 27:10 your lands; I will banish you and *you will* **p**. H6
Jer 27:15 I will banish you and *you will* **p**, both you H6
Jer 40:15 be scattered and the remnant of Judah *to* **p**?" H6
Jer 44:12 *They will* all **p** in Egypt; they will fall by H9462
Jer 44:27 the Jews in Egypt *will* **p** by sword and H9462
Jer 51:18 when their judgment comes, *they will* **p**. H6
La 3:54 my head, and I thought *I was about to* **p**. H1615
Eze 5:12 of the plague or **p** by famine inside you H3983
Jnh 1: 6 he will take notice of us so that *we will* not **p**." H6
Jnh 3: 9 from his fierce anger so that *we will* not **p**." H6
Zec 11: 9 the perishing **p**. Let those who are H3948
Zec 13: 8 "two-thirds will be struck down and **p**; yet H1588
Mt 18:14 that any of these little ones *should* **p**. *G660*
Lk 13: 3 But unless you repent, *you* too *will* all **p**. *G660*
Lk 13: 5 But unless you repent, *you* too *will* all **p**." *G660*
Lk 21:18 But not a hair of your head *will* **p**. *G660*
Jn 3:16 believes in him *shall* not **p** but have *G660*
Jn 10:28 and *they shall* never **p**; no one will *G660*
Jn 11:50 the people than that the whole nation **p**." *G660*
Ac 8:20 "*May* your money **p** with you *G1639+1650+724*
Ac 13:41 scoffers, wonder and **p**, for I am going to *G906*
Ro 2:12 from the law *will* also **p** apart from the *G660*
Col 2:22 things that are all destined to **p** with use, *G5785*
2Th 2:10 They **p** because they refused to love the NDT
Heb 1:11 They *will* **p**, but you remain; they will all *G660*
Heb 4:11 so that no one *will* **p** by following their *G4406*
1Pe 1: 4 into an inheritance that can **never p** *G915*
2Pe 2:12 and like animals *they* too *will* **p**. *G5785+5780*
2Pe 3: 9 not wanting anyone *to* **p**, but everyone to *G660*

PERISHABLE (6) [PERISH]
1Co 15:42 The body that is sown is **p**, it is *G1877+5785*
1Co 15:50 does the **p** inherit the imperishable. *G5785*
1Co 15:53 For the **p** must clothe itself with the *G5778*
1Co 15:54 When the **p** has been clothed with the *G5778*
1Pe 1:18 that it was not *with* **p** *things* such as silver *G5778*
1Pe 1:23 been born again, not of **p** seed, but of *G5778*

PERISHED (15) [PERISH]
Ge 7:21 Every living thing that moved on land **p** H1588
Nu 16:33 and *they* **p** and were gone from the H6
Dt 2:14 of fighting men *had* **p** from the camp, H9462
Dt 7:20 even the survivors who hide from you *have* **p**. H6
2Sa 1:27 The weapons of war *have* **p**!" H6
Job 4: 7 being innocent, *has ever* **p**? Where were the H6
Ps 9: 6 their cities; even the memory of them *has* **p**. H6
Ps 83:10 *who* **p** at Endor and became like dung on H9012
Ps 119:92 my delight, *I would have* **p** in my affliction. H6
Jer 7:28 Truth *has* **p**; it has vanished H6
Jer 12: 4 are wicked, the animals and birds *have* **p**. H6200
Jer 49: 7 *Has* counsel **p** from the prudent H6
La 1:19 priests and my elders **p** in the city while H1588
Mic 4: 9 *Has* your ruler **p**, that pain seizes you like that H6
Heb 3:17 whose bodies **p** in the wilderness? *G4406*

PERISHES (4) [PERISH]
Job 4:11 The lion **p** for lack of prey, and the cubs of the H6
Job 8:13 who forget God; so **p** the hope of the godless. H6
Job 18:17 The memory of him **p** from the earth; he has H6
1Pe 1: 7 which **p** even though refined by fire *G660*

PERISHING (11) [PERISH]
Job 31:19 if I have seen *anyone* **p** for lack of clothing, or H6
Job 33:18 their lives from **p** by the sword. H6296
Pr 31: 6 Let beer be for *those who are* **p**, wine for H6
Ecc 7:15 the righteous **p** in their righteousness, and H6
Isa 27:13 Those *who were* **p** in Assyria and those who H6
Jer 44:18 nothing and *have been* **p** by sword and H9462
Zec 11: 9 dying die, and the **p** perish. Let those who H3948
1Co 1:18 the cross is foolishness to those *who are* **p**, *G660*
2Co 2:15 who are being saved and those *who are* **p**. *G660*
2Co 4: 3 is veiled, it is veiled to those *who are* **p**. *G660*
2Th 2:10 that wickedness deceives those *who are* **p**. *G660*

PERIZZITES (23)
Ge 13: 7 The Canaanites and **P** were also living in H7254
Ge 15:20 **P**, Rephaites, H7254
Ge 34:30 me obnoxious to the Canaanites and **P**, H7254
Ex 3: 8 Hittites, Amorites, **P**, Hivites and H7254
Ex 3:17 Hittites, Amorites, **P**, Hivites and H7254
Ex 23:23 Amorites, Hittites, **P**, Canaanites, Hivites H7254
Ex 33: 2 Amorites, Hittites, **P**, Hivites and H7254
Ex 34:11 Canaanites, Hittites, **P**, Hivites and H7254
Dt 7: 1 Amorites, Canaanites, **P**, Hivites and H7254
Dt 20:17 Amorites, Canaanites, **P**, Hivites and H7254
Jos 3:10 Hittites, Hivites, **P**, Girgashites, Amorites H7254
Jos 9: 1 Amorites, Canaanites, **P**, Hivites and H7254
Jos 11: 3 Hittites, **P** and Jebusites in the hill country H7254
Jos 12: 8 Amorites, Canaanites, **P**, Hivites and H7254
Jos 17:15 there in the land of the **P** and Rephaites." H7254
Jos 24:11 also the Amorites, **P**, Canaanites, Hittites, H7254
Jdg 1: 4 the Canaanites and **P** into their hands, H7254
Jdg 1: 5 putting to rout the Canaanites and **P**. H7254
Jdg 3: 5 Hittites, Amorites, **P**, Hivites and H7254
1Ki 9:20 Amorites, Hittites, **P**, Hivites and H7254
2Ch 8: 7 Hittites, Amorites, **P**, Hivites and H7254
Ezr 9: 1 Hittites, **P**, Jebusites, Ammonites H7254
Ne 9: 8 Hittites, Amorites, **P**, Jebusites and H7254

PERJURERS (2) [PERJURY]
Mal 3: 5 adulterers and **p** H8678+4200+2021+9214
1Ti 1:10 slave traders and liars and **p**—and for *G2156*

PERJURY (1) [PERJURERS]
Jer 7: 9 commit adultery and **p** H8678+4200+2021+9214

PERMANENT (4) [PERMANENTLY]
Lev 25:34 must not be sold; it is their **p** possession. H6409
Jos 8:28 burned Ai and made it a **p** heap of ruins, H6409
Jn 8:35 a slave has no **p** place in the *G1650+3836+172*
Heb 7:24 Jesus lives forever, he has a **p** priesthood. *G563*

PERMANENTLY (2) [PERMANENT]
Lev 25:23 " 'The land must not be sold **p** H4200+7552
Lev 25:30 shall belong **p** to the buyer H4200+2021+7552

PERMISSION (12) [PERMIT]
Jdg 11:17 '*Give us* **p** *to* **go** through your country AIT
1Sa 20: 6 'David **earnestly asked** my **p** to H8626+8626
1Sa 20:28 **earnestly asked** me **for p** to go H8626+8626
Ne 13: 6 Some time later I asked his **p** H4946
Est 9:13 "**give** the Jews in Susa **p** to carry out this H5989
Isa 22:16 here and who **gave** you **p** to cut out a H4200
Da 1: 8 and *he* **asked** the chief official **for p** not to H1335
Mk 5:13 *He* **gave** them **p**, and the impure spirits *G2205*
Lk 8:32 go into the pigs, and *he* **gave** them **p**. *G2205*
Jn 19:38 *With* Pilate's **p**, he came and took the *G2205*
Ac 21:40 *After* **receiving** the commander's **p**, Paul *G2205*
Ac 26: 1 to Paul, "You **have p** to speak for yourself." *G2205*

PERMIT (4) [PERMISSION, PERMITS, PERMITTED, PERMITTING]
Ex 12:23 he *will* not **p** the destroyer to enter H5989
Hos 5: 4 "Their deeds *do* not **p** them to return to H5989
Ac 24:23 some freedom and **p** his friends to *G3594+3266*
1Ti 2:12 *I do* not **p** a woman to teach or to assume *G2205*

PERMITS (2) [PERMIT]
Ecc 5:12 their abundance **p** them no sleep. H5663
1Co 16: 7 spend some time with you, if the Lord **p**. *G2205*

PERMITTED (5) [PERMIT]
Ex 19:13 No person or animal *shall be* **p** *to* **live**.' Only AIT
Dt 18:14 the LORD your God *has* not **p** you **to do** so. H5989
Mt 19: 8 "Moses **p** you to divorce your wives *G2205*
Mk 10: 4 "Moses **p** a man to write a certificate of *G2205*
2Co 12: 4 things that no one *is* **p** to tell. *G2003*

PERMITTING (1) [PERMIT]
Heb 6: 3 And God **p**, we will do so. *G2205*

PERPETUAL (10) [PERPETUATE]
Ex 29:28 is always to be the **p share** from the H2976
Lev 6:18 to come it is his **p** share of the food H6409
Lev 6:22 It is the LORD's **p** share and is to be burned H6409
Lev 7:34 his sons as their **p** share from the H6409
Lev 7:36 this to them as their **p** share for the H6409
Lev 10:15 This will be the **p** share for you and your H6409
Lev 24: 9 most holy part of their **p** share of the food H6409
Nu 18: 8 your sons as your portion, your **p** share. H6409
Nu 18:11 your sons and daughters as your **p** share. H6409
Nu 18:19 your sons and daughters as your **p** share. H6409

PERPETUATE (1) [PERPETUAL]
Ps 45:17 *I will* **p** your **memory** through all H2349+9005

PERPLEXED (5) [PERPLEXITY]
Da 4:19 Belteshazzar) *was* **greatly p** for a time A10724
Lk 9: 7 And *he was* **p** because some were saying *G1389*
Ac 2:12 Amazed and **p**, they asked one another *G1389*
2Co 4: 8 not crushed; **p**, but not in despair; *G679*
Gal 4:20 my tone, because *I am* **p** about you! *G679*

PERPLEXITY (1) [PERPLEXED]
Lk 21:25 will be in anguish and **p** at the roaring *G680*

PERSECUTE (17) [PERSECUTED, PERSECUTING, PERSECUTION, PERSECUTIONS, PERSECUTOR, PERSECUTORS]
Dt 30: 7 on your enemies who hate and **p** you. H8103
Ps 9:13 see how my enemies **p** me! Have mercy H6715
Ps 69:26 For *they* **p** those you wound and talk H8103
Ps 119:157 Many are the foes *who* **p** me, but I have H8103
Ps 119:161 Rulers **p** me without cause, but my heart H8103
Mt 5:11 **p** you and falsely say all kinds of evil *G1503*
Mt 5:44 enemies and pray for those *who* **p** you, *G1503*
Lk 11:49 whom they will kill and others *they will* **p**. *G1503*
Lk 21:12 they will seize you and **p** you. *G1503*
Jn 5:16 the Jewish leaders *began to* **p** him. *G1503*
Jn 15:20 they persecuted me, *they will* **p** you also. *G1503*
Ac 7:52 ever a prophet your ancestors *did* not **p**? *G1503*
Ac 9: 4 say to him, "Saul, Saul, why *do you* **p** me?" *G1503*
Ac 12: 1 to the church, *intending to* **p** them. *G2808*
Ac 22: 7 Saul! Why *do you* **p** me?' *G1503*
Ac 26:14 Aramaic, 'Saul, Saul, why *do you* **p** me? *G1503*
Ro 12:14 Bless those *who* **p** you; bless and do not *G1503*

PERSECUTED (18) [PERSECUTE]
Ps 119:86 help me, for I am *being* **p** without cause. H8103
Mt 5:10 Blessed are those *who are* **p** because of *G1503*
Mt 5:12 in the same way *they* **p** the prophets who *G1503*
Mt 10:23 When you *are* **p** in one place, flee to *G1503*
Mt 24: 9 be handed over to be **p** and put to death, *G2568*
Jn 15:20 than his master.' If *they* **p** me, they will *G1503*
Ac 22: 4 I **p** the followers of this Way to their death *G1503*
1Co 4:12 we bless; *when we are* **p**, we endure it; *G1503*
1Co 15: 9 apostle, because *I* **p** the church of God. *G1503*
2Co 4: 9 **p**, but not abandoned; struck down, but *G1503*
Gal 1:13 how intensely *I* **p** the church of God and *G1503*
Gal 1:23 "The man *who* formerly **p** us is now *G1503*
Gal 4:29 to the flesh **p** the son born by the *G1503*
Gal 5:11 circumcision, why *am I* still *being* **p**? *G1503*
Gal 6:12 do this is to avoid *being* **p** for the cross of *G1503*
1Th 3: 4 we kept telling you that we would be **p**. *G2567*
2Ti 3:12 live a godly life in Christ Jesus *will be* **p**, *G1503*
Heb 11:37 goatskins, destitute, **p** and mistreated— *G2567*

PERSECUTING (5) [PERSECUTE]
Ac 9: 5 am Jesus, whom you *are* **p**," he replied. *G1503*
Ac 22: 8 of Nazareth, whom you *are* **p**,' he replied. *G1503*
Ac 26:11 I was so obsessed *with* **p** them that I even *G1503*
Ac 26:15 am Jesus, whom you *are* **p**,' the Lord *G1503*
Php 3: 6 as for zeal, **p** the church; as for *G1503*

PERSECUTION (9) [PERSECUTE]
Mt 13:21 When trouble or **p** comes because of the *G1501*
Mk 4:17 When trouble or **p** comes because of the *G1501*
Ac 8: 1 On that day a great **p** broke out against *G1501*
Ac 11:19 scattered by the **p** that broke out when *G2568*
Ac 13:50 They stirred up **p** against Paul and *G1501*
Ro 8:35 hardship or **p** or famine or nakedness *G1501*
1Th 3: 7 our distress and **p** we were encouraged *G2568*
Heb 10:33 you were publicly exposed to insult and **p**; *G2568*
Rev 2:10 test you, and you will suffer **p** for ten days. *G2568*

PERSECUTIONS (5) [PERSECUTE]
Mk 10:30 fields—along with **p**—and in the age to *G1501*
2Co 12:10 in insults, in hardships, in **p**, in difficulties. *G1501*
2Th 1: 4 faith in all the **p** and trials you are *G1501*
2Ti 3:11 **p**, sufferings—what kinds of things *G1501*
2Ti 3:11 Iconium and Lystra, the **p** I endured. *G1501*

PERSECUTOR (1) [PERSECUTE]
1Ti 1:13 a blasphemer and a **p** and a violent man, *G1502*

PERSECUTORS (4) [PERSECUTE]

Ps 119:84 When will you punish my **p**? H8103
Jer 15:15 Avenge me on my **p**. You are H8103
Jer 17:18 Let my **p** be put to shame, but keep me H8103
Jer 20:11 so my **p** will stumble and not prevail. H8103

PERSEVERANCE (12) [PERSEVERE]

Ro 5: 3 we know that suffering produces **p**; *G5705*
Ro 5: 4 **p**, character; and character, hope. *G5705*
2Th 1: 4 we boast about your **p** and faith in all the *G5705*
2Th 3: 5 your hearts into God's love and Christ's **p**. *G5705*
Heb 12: 1 And let us run with **p** the race marked out *G5705*
Jas 1: 3 that the testing of your faith produces **p**. *G5705*
Jas 1: 4 Let **p** finish its work so that you may be *G5705*
Jas 5:11 You have heard *of* Job's **p** and have seen *G5705*
2Pe 1: 6 to self-control, **p**; and to perseverance *G5705*
2Pe 1: 6 perseverance; and to **p**, godliness; *G5705*
Rev 2: 2 your deeds, your hard work and your **p**. *G5705*
Rev 2:19 your service and **p**, and that you are now *G5705*

PERSEVERE (2) [PERSEVERANCE, PERSEVERED, PERSEVERES, PERSEVERING]

1Ti 4:16 **P** in them, because if you do, you will *G2152*
Heb 10:36 You need to **p** so that when you have *G5705*

PERSEVERED (4) [PERSEVERE]

2Co 12:12 I **p** in demonstrating among *G1877+4246+5705*
Heb 11:27 *he* **p** because he saw him who is invisible. *G2846*
Jas 5:11 we count as blessed those *who have* **p**. *G5702*
Rev 2: 3 *You have* **p** and have endured *G5705+2400*

PERSEVERES (2) [PERSEVERE]

1Co 13: 7 always trusts, always hopes, always **p**. *G5702*
Jas 1:12 is the one who **p** under trial because, *G5702*

PERSEVERING (1) [PERSEVERE]

Lk 8:15 retain it, and by **p** produce a crop. *G5705*

PERSIA (29) [PERSIAN, PERSIANS]

2Ch 36:20 until the kingdom of **P** came to power. H7273
2Ch 36:22 In the first year of Cyrus king of **P**, in order H7273
2Ch 36:22 of Cyrus king of **P** to make a proclamation H7273
2Ch 36:23 "This is what Cyrus king of **P** says: " 'The H7273
Ezr 1: 1 In the first year of Cyrus king of **P**, in order H7273
Ezr 1: 1 of Cyrus king of **P** to make a proclamation H7273
Ezr 1: 2 "This is what Cyrus king of **P** says: " 'The H7273
Ezr 1: 8 Cyrus king of **P** had them brought by H7273
Ezr 3: 7 to Joppa, as authorized by Cyrus king of **P**. H7273
Ezr 4: 3 King Cyrus, the king of **P**, commanded us." H7273
Ezr 4: 5 of Cyrus king of **P** and down to the reign H7273
Ezr 4: 5 down to the reign of Darius king of **P**. H7273
Ezr 4: 7 And in the days of Artaxerxes king of **P** H7273
Ezr 4: 9 administrators over the **people from P**, A10060
Ezr 4:24 year of the reign of Darius king of **P**. A10594
Ezr 6:14 Darius and Artaxerxes, kings of **P**. A10594
Ezr 7: 1 during the reign of Artaxerxes king of **P** H7273
Ezr 9: 9 us kindness in the sight of the kings of **P**: H7273
Est 1: 3 The military leaders of **P** and Media, the H7273
Est 1:14 seven nobles of **P** and Media who had H7273
Est 1:19 it be written in the laws of **P** and Media, H7273
Est 10: 2 the annals of the kings of Media and **P**? H7273
Eze 27:10 " 'Men of **P**, Lydia and Put served as H7273
Eze 38: 5 **P**, Cush and Put will be with them, all with H7273
Da 8:20 saw represents the kings of Media and **P**. H7273
Da 10: 1 In the third year of Cyrus king of **P**, H7273
Da 10:13 I was detained there with the king of **P**. H7273
Da 10:20 will return to fight against the prince of **P**, H7273
Da 11: 2 Three more kings will arise in **P**, and then H7273

PERSIAN (4) [PERSIA]

Ne 12:22 were recorded in the reign of Darius the **P**. H7275
Est 1:18 This very day the **P** and Median women of H7273
Da 6:28 of Darius and the reign of Cyrus the **P**. A10595
Da 10:13 the prince of the **P** kingdom resisted me H7273

PERSIANS (4) [PERSIA]

Da 5:28 divided and given to the Medes and **P**." A10594
Da 6: 8 with the law of the Medes and **P**, A10594
Da 6:12 with the law of the Medes and **P**, A10594
Da 6:15 of the Medes and **P** no decree or edict A10594

PERSIS (1)

Ro 16:12 Greet my dear friend **P**, another woman *G4372*

PERSIST (5) [PERSISTED, PERSISTENCE, PERSISTENT, PERSISTS]

Dt 29:19 though I **p in** going my **own way**," H9244+4213
1Sa 12:25 Yet if *you* **p in doing evil**, both you H8317+8317
2Ki 17:34 To this day they **p** in their former practices. H6913
Isa 1: 5 Why *do you* **p** *in* rebellion H3578
Ro 11:23 And if they *do* not **p** in unbelief, they will *G2152*

PERSISTED (3) [PERSIST]

2Ki 2:17 But *they* **p** until he was too embarrassed H7210
2Ki 17:22 The Israelites **p** in all the sins of Jeroboam H2143
2Ki 17:40 but **p in** their former practices. H6913+3869

PERSISTENCE (1) [PERSIST]

Ro 2: 7 To those who by **p** in doing good seek *G5705*

PERSISTENT (3) [PERSIST]

Lev 13:51 it is a **p** defiling mold; the H4421
Lev 13:52 because the defiling mold *is* **p**, the article H4421
Lev 14:44 in the house, it *is* a **p** defiling mold; the H4421

PERSISTS (1) [PERSIST]

Dt 25: 8 If *he* **p** in saying, "I do not want to marry H6641

PERSON (298) [PERSON'S, PERSONAL, PERSONALLY, PERSONS]

Ge 31:32 who has your gods, *that p shall* not **live**. AIT
Ge 42: 6 the *p who* **sold grain** to all its people. AIT
Ex 9:19 will fall on every **p** and animal that has not H132
Ex 11: 7 not a dog will bark at any **p** or animal. H408
Ex 12: 4 in accordance with what **each** *p* will eat. AIT
Ex 16:16 an omer for each **p** you have in your tent H5883
Ex 16:22 two omers for **each** *p*—and the leaders of AIT
Ex 19:13 No **p** or animal shall be permitted to live H408
Ex 21:12 who strikes a **p** with a fatal blow is H408
Ex 21:14 *that* **p** is to be taken from my altar and put H5647
Ex 21:18 people quarrel and *one* **p** hits another with H408
Ex 21:19 party must pay **the injured p** for any loss H2257S
Ex 23: 1 Do not help a **guilty** *p* by being a malicious AIT
Ex 23: 3 not show favoritism to a **poor** *p* in a lawsuit. AIT
Ex 23: 7 do not put an innocent or **honest** *p* to death, AIT
Ex 36: 1 every skilled **p** to whom the LORD has H408
Ex 36: 2 every skilled **p** to whom the LORD had H408
Ex 38:26 one beka per **p**, that is, half a shekel H1653
Lev 7:18 the **p** who eats any of it will be held H5883
Lev 13: 3 When the priest examines **that p**, he H2084S
Lev 13: 4 is to isolate the **affected p** for seven days. H5596
Lev 13: 8 The priest is to examine **that p**, and if the NDT
Lev 13:12 the skin of the **affected p** from head to H5596
Lev 13:17 shall pronounce the **affected p** clean; H5596
Lev 13:20 priest shall pronounce **that p** unclean. H2257S
Lev 13:27 day the priest is to examine **that p**, H2084S
Lev 13:31 to isolate the **affected p** for seven H5596+5999
Lev 13:37 has grown in it, the **affected p** is healed. H5999
Lev 14: 2 regulations for any **diseased** *p* at the time of AIT
Lev 14: 4 hyssop be brought for the *p to* **be cleansed**. AIT
Lev 14: 8 "The *p to* **be cleansed** must wash their AIT
Lev 14:30 young pigeons, such as **the p** can afford, H2257S
Lev 17: 4 that **p** shall be considered guilty of H408
Lev 18: 5 the **p** who obeys them will live by them. H132
Lev 22: 3 that **p** must be cut off from my presence. H5883
Lev 22: 5 unclean, or *any* **p** who makes him unclean H132
Lev 22:13 No **unauthorized p**, however, may H2424
Lev 27: 2 vow to dedicate a **p** to the LORD by giving H5883
Lev 27: 5 a **p** between the ages of five and twenty NDT
Lev 27: 6 a **p** between one month and five years NDT
Lev 27: 7 a **p** sixty years old or more, set the value NDT
Lev 27: 8 **the p being dedicated** is to be presented H2257
Lev 27:24 will revert to **the p** from whom it was H2257S
Lev 27:28 " 'But nothing that a **p** owns and devotes to H408
Lev 27:29 " 'No **p** devoted to destruction may be H132
Nu 5: 7 give it all to **the p** they have wronged H889S
Nu 5: 8 But if that **p** has no close relative to whom H408
Nu 15: 4 then the *p who* **brings** an offering shall AIT
Nu 15:27 " 'But if just one **p** sins unintentionally H5883
Nu 15:27 *that p must* **bring** a year-old female goat AIT
Nu 15:28 has been made, **that p** will be forgiven. H2257S
Nu 16: 5 he will have that **p** come near him. NDT
Nu 19:14 law that applies when a **p** dies in a tent: H132
Nu 19:17 "For the **unclean** *p*, put some ashes from the AIT
Nu 19:22 Anything that an **unclean** *p* touches becomes AIT
Nu 35: 6 to which *a p who has* **killed** someone may AIT
Nu 35:11 to which *a p who has* **killed** someone AIT
Nu 35:16 an iron object, **that p** is a murderer; the H2085S
Nu 35:17 blow with it, **that p** is a murderer; the H2085S
Nu 35:18 blow with it, **that p** is a murderer; the H2085S
Nu 35:21 if out of enmity *one p* **hits** another with AIT
Nu 35:21 other dies, that **p** is to be put to death H5782S
Nu 35:21 to be put to death; **that p** is a murderer. H2085S
Nu 35:23 then since **that other p** was not an H2085S
Nu 35:30 'Anyone who kills a **p** is to be put to H5883
Dt 4:42 to which *anyone* who *had* **killed a p** could H8357
Dt 5:24 we have seen that a **p** can live even if God H132
Dt 17: 5 your city gate and stone **that p** to death. H4392S
Dt 17: 6 three witnesses a **p** is to be put to H4637S
Dt 17: 7 be the first in putting **that p** to death, H2257S
Dt 19: 3 so that a **p** who kills someone may flee H3972
Dt 19: 4 anyone *who* **kills a p** and flees there H8357
Dt 21: 8 people guilty of the blood of an **innocent** *p*." AIT
Dt 25: 2 If the **guilty** *p* deserves to be beaten, the AIT
Dt 27:25 accepts a bribe to kill an innocent **p**." H1947S
Dt 28:29 will grope about like a **blind** *p* in the dark. AIT
Dt 29:19 When such a **p** hears the words of this H2257S
Jos 20: 3 that anyone who kills a **p** accidentally H5883
1Sa 2:15 come and say to the **p** who was sacrificing, H408
1Sa 2:16 If the **p** said to him, "Let the fat be burned H408
1Sa 2:25 If *one* **p** sins against another, God may H408
1Sa 10: 6 you will be changed into a different **p**. H408
2Sa 3:19 also spoke to the Benjamites **in p**. H928+265
2Sa 6:19 of raisins to each **p** in the whole crowd of H6639
2Sa 14:14 ways so that a **banished** *p* does not remain AIT
2Ki 15:20 Every wealthy **p** had to contribute fifty H1475
1Ch 28:21 every **willing** *p* skilled in any craft will AIT
Ne 5:13 So *may such a p* **be** shaken out and emptied!" AIT
Ne 9:29 'The **p** who obeys them will live by them. H132
Est 5:12 "I'm the only **p** Queen Esther invited to NDT
Job 13:16 no **godless** *p* would dare come before AIT
Job 15: 2 "Would a **wise** *p* answer with empty notions AIT
Job 20: 6 the pride of the **godless** *p* reaches to the AIT
Job 21:23 **One** *p* dies in full vigor, completely secure AIT
Job 22: 2 Can even a **wise** *p* benefit him? AIT
Job 32: 8 But it is the spirit in a **p**, the breath of the H632
Job 33:24 he is gracious to **that p** and says to God, H5647S
Job 33:26 then *that p can* **pray** to God and find favor AIT
Job 33:29 "God does all these things to a **p**—twice H1505
Ps 1: 3 *That p* **is** like a tree planted by streams of AIT
Ps 15: 4 who despises a **vile** *p* but honors those who AIT
Ps 34:19 The **righteous** *p* may have many troubles, but AIT
Ps 50:16 But to the **wicked** *p*, God says: "What right AIT
Ps 102: T A prayer of an **afflicted** *p* who has grown AIT
Ps 119: 9 How can a **young p** stay on the path of H5853
Pr 6:19 out lies and *a p who* **stirs up** conflict in the AIT
Pr 10:23 a **p** *of* understanding delights in H408
Pr 11: 8 The **righteous** *p* is rescued from trouble, and AIT
Pr 11:13 a **trustworthy** *p* keeps a secret. AIT
Pr 11:18 A **wicked** *p* earns deceptive wages, but the AIT
Pr 11:24 *One p* **gives freely**, yet gains even more AIT
Pr 11:25 A generous **p** will prosper; whoever H5883
Pr 12: 8 A **p** is praised according to their prudence H408
Pr 13: 6 guards the **p of integrity**, H9448+2006
Pr 13: 7 *One p* **pretends to be rich**, yet has nothing AIT
Pr 13:14 turning a **p** from the snares of death. NDT
Pr 13:22 A **good** *p* leaves an inheritance for their AIT
Pr 14:17 A **quick-tempered** *p* does foolish things, and AIT
Pr 14:27 turning a **p** from the snares of death. NDT
Pr 15:18 A hot-tempered **p** stirs up conflict, but the H408
Pr 15:23 A **p** finds joy in giving an apt reply—and H408
Pr 16:28 A perverse **p** stirs up conflict, and a gossip H408
Pr 16:29 A violent **p** entices their neighbor and H408
Pr 16:32 Better a **patient** *p* than a warrior, one with AIT
Pr 17: 4 A **wicked** *p* listens to deceitful lips; a liar AIT
Pr 17:10 rebuke impresses a **discerning** *p* more than a AIT
Pr 17:24 A **discerning** *p* keeps wisdom in view, but a AIT
Pr 18: 1 An **unfriendly** *p* pursues selfish ends and AIT
Pr 19: 4 the closest friend of the **poor** *p* deserts them. AIT
Pr 19:19 A **hot-tempered** *p* must pay the penalty AIT
Pr 19:22 What a **p** desires is unfailing love; better to H132
Pr 20: 6 but a faithful **p** who can find? H408
Pr 21: 2 A **p** may think their own ways are right, but H408
Pr 21:24 The proud and **arrogant** *p*—"Mocker" is his AIT
Pr 22:24 not make friends with a hot-tempered **p**, H1251
Pr 23: 7 kind of *p who is always* **thinking** about the AIT
Pr 25:28 broken through is a **p** who lacks self-control H408
Pr 26:12 Do you see a **p** wise in their own eyes H408
Pr 26:21 so is a quarrelsome **p** for kindling strife. H408
Pr 27:17 sharpens iron, so *one* **p** sharpens another. H408
Pr 28:20 A faithful **p** will be richly blessed, but one H408
Pr 28:21 a **p** will do wrong for a piece of bread. H1505
Pr 28:23 Whoever rebukes a **p** will in the end gain H132
Pr 29: 9 If a wise **p** goes to court with a fool, the H408
Pr 29:10 hate a *p of* **integrity** and seek to kill AIT
Pr 29:22 An angry **p** stirs up conflict, and a H408
Pr 29:22 a **hot-tempered** *p* commits many sins. AIT
Pr 29:23 Pride brings a **p** low, but the lowly in spirit H132
Ecc 2:19 knows whether *that p will* **be** wise or foolish? AIT
Ecc 2:21 For a **p** may labor with wisdom, knowledge H132
Ecc 2:24 A **p** can do nothing better than to eat and H132
Ecc 2:26 To the **p** who pleases him, God gives H132
Ecc 3:22 is nothing better for a **p** than to enjoy their H132
Ecc 5:18 that it is appropriate for a **p** to eat, to drink NDT
Ecc 6:12 For who knows what is good for a **p** in life H132
Ecc 7: 5 heed the rebuke of a **wise** *p* than to listen to AIT
Ecc 7: 7 Extortion turns a **wise** *p* into a fool, and a AIT
Ecc 7:19 Wisdom makes one **wise** *p* more powerful AIT
Ecc 8: 6 though a **p** may be weighed down by H132
Ecc 8:12 Although a **wicked** *p* who commits a hundred AIT
Ecc 8:15 nothing better for a **p** under the sun than to H132
Isa 7:21 a **p** will keep alive a young cow and two H408
Isa 10:15 the ax raise itself above the *p who* **swings** it, AIT
Isa 10:15 As if a rod were to wield the *p who* **lifts it up** AIT
Isa 10:18 as when a **sick** *p* wastes away. AIT
Isa 29: 8 as when a **hungry** *p* dreams of eating, but AIT
Isa 29: 8 as when a **thirsty** *p* dreams of drinking AIT
Isa 40:20 A *p* **too poor** *to* present such an offering AIT
Isa 44:20 *Such a p* **feeds on** ashes; a deluded heart AIT
Isa 56: 2 does this—the **p** who holds it fast H1201+132
Isa 66: 3 sacrifices a bull is like one who kills a **p**, H408
Jer 5: 1 you can find but *one* **p** who deals honestly H408
Jer 17: 6 *That p will* **be** like a bush in the wastelands AIT
Jer 17:10 to reward *each* **p** according to their conduct, H408
Jer 32:19 you reward *each* **p** according to their H408
Eze 3:18 When I say to a **wicked** *p*, 'You will surely die AIT
Eze 3:18 their life, that **wicked** *p* will die for their sin AIT
Eze 3:19 if you do warn the **wicked** *p* and they do not AIT
Eze 3:20 when a **righteous** *p* turns from their AIT
Eze 3:20 The righteous things *that p* **did** will not be AIT
Eze 3:21 if you do warn the **righteous** *p* not to sin AIT
Eze 18:21 "But if a **wicked** *p* turns away from all the sins AIT
Eze 18:21 right, *that p will* **surely live**; they will not AIT
Eze 18:24 "But if a **righteous** *p* turns from their AIT
Eze 18:24 same detestable things the **wicked** *p* does, AIT
Eze 18:24 righteous things *that p has* **done** will be AIT
Eze 18:26 If a **righteous** *p* turns from their righteousness AIT
Eze 18:27 But if a **wicked** *p* turns away from the AIT
Eze 18:28 from them, *that p will* **surely live**; they will AIT
Eze 20:11 by which the **p** who obeys them will live. H132
Eze 20:13 by which the **p** who obeys them will live H132
Eze 20:21 "The **p** who obeys them will live by them," H132
Eze 33: 8 to the wicked, 'You **wicked** *p*, you will surely AIT
Eze 33: 8 their ways, that **wicked** *p* will die for their sin AIT
Eze 33: 9 if you do warn the **wicked** *p* to turn from their AIT
Eze 33:12 The **righteous** *p* who sins will not be allowed AIT
Eze 33:13 If I tell a **righteous** *p* that they will surely live AIT

Eze 33:13 the righteous things that p has done will be NDT
Eze 33:14 if I say to a wicked p, 'You will surely die AIT
Eze 33:15 do no evil—that p will surely live; they will AIT
Eze 33:16 None of the sins that p has committed will be AIT
Eze 33:18 If a righteous p turns from their righteousness AIT
Eze 33:19 And if a wicked p turns away from their AIT
Eze 44:25 not defile himself by going near a dead p; H132
Eze 44:25 if the dead p was his father or mother NDT
Da 11:21 succeeded by a contemptible p who has not AIT
Hos 9: 7 considered a fool, the inspired p a maniac. H408
Mic 7: 2 from the land; not one upright p remains. H132
Hab 2: 4 the righteous p will live by his AIT
Hag 2:13 "If a p defiled by contact with a dead body AIT
Zec 12: 1 who forms the human spirit within a p, H2257S
Mt 5:39 do not resist an evil p. If anyone slaps you AIT
Mt 10:11 there for some worthy p and stay at their AIT
Mt 10:41 welcomes a righteous p as a righteous AIT
Mt 10:41 person as a righteous p will receive a AIT
Mt 10:42 that p will certainly not lose their reward." AIT
Mt 12:12 much more valuable is a p than a sheep! G476
Mt 12:43 "When an impure spirit comes out of a p, it G476
Mt 12:45 final condition of that p is worse than the G476
Mt 15:20 These are what defile a p; but eating with G476
Mt 16:27 then he will reward each p according to what AIT
Mt 18: 7 woe to the p through whom they come! G476
Mk 7:15 Nothing outside a p can defile them by G476
Mk 7:15 is what comes out of a p that defiles them." G476
Mk 7:18 that enters a p from the outside can G476
Mk 7:20 comes out of a p is what defiles them G476
Mk 7:23 evils come from inside and defile a p." G476
Lk 7:12 town gate, a dead p was being carried out AIT
Lk 11:24 "When an impure spirit comes out of a p, it G476
Lk 11:26 final condition of that p is worse than the G476
Lk 14: 8 a p more distinguished than you may G1952
Lk 14: 9 come and say to you, 'Give this p your seat. AIT
Lk 14:26 own life—such a p cannot be my disciple. AIT
Lk 14:30 'This p began to build and wasn't able to G476
Jn 2:25 mankind, for he knew what was in each p. G476
Jn 3:27 "A p can receive only what is given them G476
Jn 9:31 He listens to the godly p who does his will. AIT
Jn 11:10 It is when a p walks at night that they G5516
Jn 12:47 does not keep them, I do not judge that p. G899
Ro 2: 6 God "will repay each p according to what G1667
Ro 2:28 A p is not a Jew who is one only outwardly NDT
Ro 2:29 a p is a Jew who is one inwardly; and NDT
Ro 3:28 For we maintain that a p is justified by faith G476
Ro 5: 7 Very rarely will anyone die for a righteous p AIT
Ro 5: 7 though for a good p someone might possibly AIT
Ro 7: 1 over someone only as long as that p lives? AIT
Ro 10: 5 "The p who does these things will live by G476
Ro 14: 5 One p considers one day more G4005+3525
Ro 14:14 as unclean, then for that p it is unclean. AIT
Ro 14:20 it is wrong for a p to eat anything that G476
1Co 1:20 Where is the wise p? Where is the teacher of AIT
1Co 2:14 The p without the Spirit does not accept the G476
1Co 2:15 The p with the Spirit makes judgments about AIT
1Co 2:15 but such a p is not subject to merely human AIT
1Co 3:17 God will destroy that p; for God's temple is AIT
1Co 5:13 "Expel the wicked p from among you." AIT
1Co 6:18 All other sins a p commits are outside the G476
1Co 7:17 each p should live as a believer in whatever AIT
1Co 7:20 Each p should remain in the situation they AIT
1Co 7:22 to faith in the Lord is the Lord's freed p; G592
1Co 7:24 Brothers and sisters, each p, as responsible to AIT
1Co 8:10 won't that p be emboldened to eat what is AIT
1Co 11:21 one p remains hungry and another gets AIT
1Co 16:22 does not love the Lord, let that p be cursed! AIT
2Co 10:10 in p he is unimpressive G3836+4242+3836+5393
Gal 2:16 know that a p is not justified by the works of G476
Gal 3:12 "The p who does these things will live by AIT
Gal 3:16 to your seed," meaning one p, who is Christ. AIT
Gal 6: 1 live by the Spirit should restore that p gently. AIT
Eph 5: 5 impure or greedy p—such a person is AIT
Eph 5: 5 greedy person—such a p is an idolater AIT
Col 2:18 Such a p also goes into great detail about AIT
1Th 2:17 you for a short time (in p, not in thought), G4725
Titus 3:10 Warn a divisive p once, and then warn G476
Jas 1: 7 That p should not expect to receive G476
Jas 1: 8 Such a p is double-minded and unstable in G467
Jas 1:12 that p will receive the crown of life that the AIT
Jas 1:14 but each p is tempted when they are dragged AIT
Jas 2:20 You foolish p, do you want evidence that G476
Jas 2:24 You see that a p is considered righteous by G476
Jas 5:15 offered in faith will make the sick p well; AIT
Jas 5:16 The prayer of a righteous p is powerful and AIT
Jas 5:19 someone should bring that p back, G899
1Jn 2: 4 and the truth is not in that p. AIT
1Jn 2:22 Such a p is the antichrist—denying the Father AIT
1Jn 3:17 how can the love of God be in that p? G899
2Jn 7 Any such p is the deceiver and the antichrist. AIT
Rev 2:17 I will also give that p a white stone with a G899
Rev 3: 5 out the name of that p from the book of G899
Rev 3:20 I will come in and eat with that p, and they G899
Rev 13:18 Let the p who has insight calculate the AIT
Rev 16: 3 it turned into blood like that of a dead p AIT
Rev 20:13 and each p was judged according to what AIT
Rev 22:11 to do wrong; let the vile p continue to be vile AIT
Rev 22:11 and let the holy p continue to be holy." AIT
Rev 22:12 I will give to each p according to what AIT
Rev 22:18 God will add to that p the plagues G899
Rev 22:19 will take away from that p any share in the G899

PERSON'S (27) [PERSON]

Ex 22: 8 has laid hands on the other p property. H8276
Ex 22:11 did not lay hands on the other p property. H8276
Dt 24: 6 would be taking a p livelihood as security NDT
Job 14: 5 A p days are determined; you have H2257S
Job 14:19 away the soil, so you destroy a p hope. H632
Pr 13: 8 A p riches may ransom their life, but the H408
Pr 16: 2 All a p ways seem pure to them, but H408
Pr 18:20 fruit of their mouth a p stomach is filled; H408
Pr 19: 3 A p own folly leads to their ruin, yet their H132
Pr 19:11 A p wisdom yields patience; it is to one's H132
Pr 19:21 Many are the plans in a p heart, but it is H408
Pr 20: 5 The purposes of a p heart are deep waters H408
Pr 20:24 A p steps are directed by the LORD. H1505
Ecc 4: 4 spring from one p envy of another. H408
Ecc 8: 1 A p wisdom brightens their face and H132
Eze 33: 6 that p life will be taken because of their H2085S
Eze 33:12 that p former righteousness will count for NDT
Eze 33:12 that p former wickedness will not bring NDT
Mt 10:41 person will receive a righteous p reward. AIT
Mt 15:18 that come out of a p mouth come from G3836S
Mk 7:21 is from within, out of a p heart, that evil G476
Ro 2:29 Such a p praise is not from other people, but AIT
Ro 14: 2 One p faith allows them to eat anything G4005
1Co 2:11 For who knows a p thoughts except their G476
1Co 3:13 the fire will test the quality of each p work. AIT
1Co 10:29 I am referring to the other p conscience, not AIT
1Pe 1:17 a Father who judges each p work impartially, AIT

PERSONAL (7) [PERSON]

Ge 26:26 Ahuzzath his p adviser and Phicol the H5335
2Sa 13:17 He called his p servant and said H5853+9250
2Ki 12: 4 received from p vows and the H5883+6886
1Ch 29: 3 I now give my p treasures of gold and H6035
Est 2: 2 the king's p attendants proposed, H5853+9250
Jn 7:18 on their own does so to gain p glory, G2625
Ac 12:20 a trusted p servant of the G2093+3836+3131

PERSONALLY (3) [PERSON]

Ge 43: 9 you can hold me p responsible for him. AIT
Gal 1:22 I was p unknown to the churches of Judea G4725
Col 2: 1 and for all who have not met me p. G1877+4922

PERSONS (5) [PERSON]

Ge 46:26 his sons' wives—numbered sixty-six p. H5883
Lev 18:29 such p must be cut off from their people. H5883
Lk 15: 7 ninety-nine righteous p who do not need AIT
Ac 4:34 that there were no needy p among them G5516
Rev 5: 9 you purchased for God p from every tribe AIT

PERSPIRE (1)

Eze 44:18 not wear anything that makes them p. H3472

PERSUADE (7) [PERSUADED, PERSUADING, PERSUASION, PERSUASIVE, PERSUASIVELY]

Jdg 19: 3 to her to p her to return. H1819+6584+4213
2Ki 18:30 Do not let Hezekiah p you to trust in the H1053
Isa 36:15 Do not let Hezekiah p you to trust in the H1053
Ac 18: 4 synagogue, trying to p Jews and Greeks. G4275
Ac 26:28 in such a short time you can p me to be a G4275
Ac 28:23 the Prophets he tried to p them about G4275
2Co 5:11 it is to fear the Lord, we try to p others. G4275

PERSUADED (13) [PERSUADE]

Jdg 19: 7 his father-in-law p him, so he stayed H7210
Pr 25:15 Through patience a ruler can be p, and a H7331
Jer 28:15 you have p this nation to trust in lies. H1053
Jer 29:31 send him, and has p you to trust in lies, H1053
Mt 27:20 the elders p the crowd to ask for G4275
Lk 20: 6 because they are p that John was a G4275
Ac 5:40 His speech p them. They called the G4275
Ac 6:11 Then they secretly p some men to say G5680
Ac 16:15 stay at my house." And she p us. G4128
Ac 17: 4 Some of the Jews were p and joined Paul G4275
Ro 4:21 being fully p that God had power to do G4442
Ro 14:14 convinced, being fully p in the Lord Jesus G4275
2Ti 1: 5 Eunice and, I am p, now lives in you G4275

PERSUADING (1) [PERSUADE]

Ac 18:13 "is p the people to worship God in ways G400

PERSUASION (1) [PERSUADE]

Gal 5: 8 That kind of p does not come from the one G4282

PERSUASIVE (2) [PERSUADE]

Pr 7:21 With p words she led him astray; she H4375
1Co 2: 4 were not with wise and p words, G4273

PERSUASIVELY (1) [PERSUADE]

Ac 19: 8 arguing p about the kingdom of God. G4275

PERTAINING (1)

1Ch 26:32 every matter p to God and for the AIT

PERUDA (1)

Ezr 2:55 descendants of Sotai, Hassophereth, P, H7243

PERVERSE (18) [PERVERT]

Dt 32:20 for they are a p generation, children H9337
1Sa 20:30 "You son of a p and rebellious woman! H6390
Ps 101: 4 The p of heart shall be far from me; I will H6836
Pr 2:12 from men whose words are p, H9337
Pr 3:32 the LORD detests the p but takes the H4279
Pr 8: 8 are just; none of them is crooked or p. H6836
Pr 8:13 arrogance, evil behavior and p speech. H9337
Pr 10:31 wisdom, but a p tongue will be silenced. H9337
Pr 10:32 the mouth of the wicked only what is p. H9337
Pr 11:20 LORD detests those whose hearts are p, H6836
Pr 15: 4 but a p tongue crushes the spirit. H6157
Pr 16:28 A p person stirs up conflict, and a gossip H9337
Pr 17:20 one whose tongue is p falls into trouble. H2200
Pr 19: 1 is blameless than a fool whose lips are p. H6836
Pr 28: 6 than the rich whose ways are p. H6836
Pr 28:18 the one whose ways are p will fall into H6835
Mt 17:17 "You unbelieving and p generation," G1406
Lk 9:41 "You unbelieving and p generation," G1406

PERVERSENESS (1) [PERVERT]

Pr 2:14 doing wrong and rejoice in the p of evil, H9337

PERVERSION (3) [PERVERT]

Lev 18:23 have sexual relations with it; that is a p. H9316
Lev 20:12 What they have done is a p; their blood H9316
Jude 7 sexual immorality and p. G599+3958+4922+2283

PERVERSITY (2) [PERVERT]

Pr 4:24 Keep your mouth free of p; keep corrupt H6838
Pr 16:30 Whoever winks with their eye is plotting p; H9337

PERVERT (9) [PERVERSE, PERVERSENESS, PERVERSION, PERVERSITY, PERVERTED, PERVERTING]

Ex 23: 2 do not p justice by siding with the crowd, H5742
Lev 19:15 " 'Do not p justice; do not show H6404+6913
Dt 16:19 Do not p justice or show partiality. Do not H5742
Job 8: 3 Does God p justice? Does the Almighty H6430
Job 8: 3 Does the Almighty p what is right? H6430
Job 34:12 that the Almighty would p justice. H6430
Pr 17:23 bribes in secret to p the course of justice. H5742
Gal 1: 7 are trying to p the gospel of Christ. G3570
Jude 4 who p the grace of our God into a license G3572

PERVERTED (4) [PERVERT]

1Sa 8: 3 gain and accepted bribes and p justice. H5742
Job 33:27 'I have sinned, I have p what is right, but I H6390
Jer 3:21 because they have p their ways and have H6390
Hab 1: 4 hem in the righteous, so that justice is p. H6823

PERVERTING (1) [PERVERT]

Ac 13:10 Will you never stop p the right ways of the G1406

PESTILENCE (4) [PESTILENCES]

Dt 32:24 consuming p and deadly plague; H8404
Ps 91: 3 the fowler's snare and from the deadly p. H1822
Ps 91: 6 the p that stalks in the darkness, nor H1822
Hab 3: 5 went before him; p followed his steps. H8404

PESTILENCES (1) [PESTILENCE]

Lk 21:11 famines and p in various places, and G3369

PESTLE (1)

Pr 27:22 grinding them like grain with a p, you will H6605

PESTS (1)

Mal 3:11 I will prevent p from devouring your crops H430

PET (1)

Job 41: 5 Can you make a p of it like a bird or put it H8471

PETER (171) [CEPHAS, PETER'S, SIMON]

Mt 4:18 Simon called P and his brother Andrew. G4377
Mt 10: 2 Simon (who is called P) and his brother G4377
Mt 14:28 P replied, "tell me to come to you on the G4377
Mt 14:29 Then P got down out of the boat, walked G4377
Mt 15:15 P said, "Explain the parable to us. G4377
Mt 16:16 Simon P answered, "You are the Messiah G4377
Mt 16:18 And I tell you that you are P, and on this G4377
Mt 16:22 P took him aside and began to rebuke G4377
Mt 16:23 Jesus turned and said to P, "Get behind G4377
Mt 17: 1 After six days Jesus took with him P G4377
Mt 17: 4 P said to Jesus, "Lord, it is good for us to G4377
Mt 17:24 temple tax came to P and asked, G4377
Mt 17:25 When P came into the house, Jesus was the NDT
Mt 17:26 "From others," P answered. "Then the NDT
Mt 18:21 Then P came to Jesus and asked, "Lord G4377
Mt 19:27 P answered him, "We have left everything G4377
Mt 26:33 P replied, "Even if all fall away on G4377
Mt 26:35 But P declared, "Even if I have to die with G4377
Mt 26:37 He took P and the two sons of Zebedee G4377
Mt 26:40 watch with me for one hour?" he asked P. G4377
Mt 26:58 But P followed him at a distance, right up G4377
Mt 26:69 Now P was sitting out in the courtyard G4377
Mt 26:73 standing there went up to P and said, G4377
Mt 26:75 Then P remembered the word Jesus had G4377
Mk 3:16 Simon (to whom he gave the name P), G4377
Mk 5:37 did not let anyone follow him except P, G4377
Mk 8:29 do you say I am?" P answered, "You are G4377
Mk 8:32 P took him aside and began to G4377
Mk 8:33 looked at his disciples, he rebuked P. G4377
Mk 9: 2 After six days Jesus took P, James and G4377
Mk 9: 5 P said to Jesus, "Rabbi, it is good for us to G4377
Mk 10:28 Then P spoke up, "We have left G4377
Mk 11:21 P remembered and said to Jesus, "Rabbi G4377
Mk 13: 3 of Olives opposite the temple, P, James, G4377
Mk 14:29 P declared, "Even if all fall away, I will G4377
Mk 14:31 But P insisted emphatically, "Even if I G3836S

Mk 14:33 He took **P**, James and John along with *G4377*
Mk 14:37 "Simon," he said *to* **P**, "are you asleep *G4377*
Mk 14:54 **P** followed him at a distance, right into the *G4377*
Mk 14:66 While **P** was below in the courtyard, one *G4377*
Mk 14:67 When she saw **P** warming himself, she *G4377*
Mk 14:70 those standing near said *to* **P**, "Surely you *G4377*
Mk 14:72 Then **P** remembered the word Jesus had *G4377*
Mk 16: 7 tell his disciples and **P**, 'He is going *G4377*
Lk 5: 8 When Simon **P** saw this, he fell at Jesus' *G4377*
Lk 6:14 whom he named **P**), his brother *G4377*
Lk 8:45 they all denied it, **P** said, "Master, the *G4377*
Lk 8:51 not let anyone go in with him except **P**, *G4377*
Lk 9:20 do you say I am?" **P** answered, "God's *G4377*
Lk 9:28 said this, he took **P**, John and James with *G4377*
Lk 9:32 **P** and his companions were very sleepy *G4377*
Lk 9:33 were leaving Jesus, **P** said to him *G4377*
Lk 12:41 **P** asked, "Lord, are you telling this *G4377*
Lk 18:28 **P** said to him, "We have left all we had to *G4377*
Lk 22: 8 Jesus sent **P** and John, saying, "Go and *G4377*
Lk 22:34 "I tell you, **P**, before the rooster crows *G4377*
Lk 22:54 the high priest. **P** followed at a distance. *G4377*
Lk 22:55 sat down together, **P** sat down with them. *G4377*
Lk 22:58 "Man, I am not!" **P** replied. *G4377*
Lk 22:60 **P** replied, "Man, I don't know what you're *G4377*
Lk 22:61 The Lord turned and looked straight at **P** *G4377*
Lk 22:61 Then **P** remembered the word the Lord *G4377*
Lk 24:12 **P**, however, got up and ran to the tomb *G4377*
Jn 1:42 Cephas" (which, when translated, is **P**). *G4377*
Jn 1:44 like Andrew and **P**, was from the town of *G4377*
Jn 6:68 Simon **P** answered him, "Lord, to whom *G4377*
Jn 13: 6 He came to Simon **P**, who said to him *G4377*
Jn 13: 8 said **P**, "you shall never wash my *G4377*
Jn 13: 9 Simon **P** replied, "not just my feet but my *G4377*
Jn 13:24 Simon **P** motioned to this disciple and *G4377*
Jn 13:36 Simon **P** asked him, "Lord, where are you *G4377*
Jn 13:37 **P** asked, "Lord, why can't I follow you now *G4377*
Jn 18:10 Then Simon **P**, who had a sword, drew it *G4377*
Jn 18:11 Jesus commanded **P**, "Put your sword *G4377*
Jn 18:15 Simon **P** and another disciple were *G4377*
Jn 18:16 **P** had to wait outside at the door. *G4377*
Jn 18:16 girl on duty there and brought **P** in. *G4377*
Jn 18:17 she asked **P**. He replied, "I am *G4377*
Jn 18:18 **P** also was standing with them, warming *G4377*
Jn 18:25 Simon **P** was still standing there warming *G4377*
Jn 18:26 of the man whose ear **P** had cut off, *G4377*
Jn 18:27 Again **P** denied it, and at that moment a *G4377*
Jn 20: 2 came running to Simon **P** and the other *G4377*
Jn 20: 3 So **P** and the other disciple started for the *G4377*
Jn 20: 4 disciple outran **P** and reached the tomb *G4377*
Jn 20: 6 Then Simon **P** came along behind him *G4377*
Jn 21: 2 Simon **P**, Thomas (also known as Didymus *G4377*
Jn 21: 3 out to fish," Simon **P** told them, and they *G4377*
Jn 21: 7 the disciple whom Jesus loved said *to* **P**, *G4377*
Jn 21: 7 As soon as Simon **P** heard him say, "It is *G4377*
Jn 21:11 So Simon **P** climbed back into the boat *G4377*
Jn 21:15 Jesus said to Simon **P**, "Simon son of *G4377*
Jn 21:17 **P** was hurt because Jesus asked him the *G4377*
Jn 21:19 kind of death by which **P** would glorify God. NDT
Jn 21:20 **P** turned and saw that the disciple whom *G4377*
Jn 21:21 When **P** saw him, he asked, "Lord, what *G4377*
Ac 1:13 Those present were **P**, John, James and *G4377*
Ac 1:15 In those days **P** stood up among the *G4377*
Ac 1:20 said **P**, "it is written in the Book of NDT
Ac 2:14 Then **P** stood up with the Eleven, raised *G4377*
Ac 2:37 the heart and said to **P** and the other *G4377*
Ac 2:38 **P** replied, "Repent and be baptized, every *G4377*
Ac 3: 1 One day **P** and John were going up to the *G4377*
Ac 3: 3 When he saw **P** and John about to enter *G4377*
Ac 3: 4 **P** looked straight at him, as did John *G4377*
Ac 3: 4 as did John. Then **P** said, "Look at us!" NDT
Ac 3: 6 Then **P** said, "Silver or gold I do not have *G4377*
Ac 3:11 While the man held on *to* **P** and John, all *G4377*
Ac 3:12 When **P** saw this, he said to them: "Fellow *G4377*
Ac 4: 1 came up to **P and John** while they were *G899S*
Ac 4: 3 They seized **P and John** and, because it *G899S*
Ac 4: 7 They had **P and John** brought before them *G899S*
Ac 4: 8 Then **P**, filled with the Holy Spirit, said to *G4377*
Ac 4:13 they saw the courage *of* **P** and John and *G4377*
Ac 4:19 But **P** and John replied, "Which is right in *G4377*
Ac 4:23 **P** and John went back to their own people NDT
Ac 5: 3 Then **P** said, "Ananias, how is it that *G4377*
Ac 5: 8 **P** asked her, "Tell me, is this the price you *G4377*
Ac 5: 9 **P** said to her, "How could you conspire to *G4377*
Ac 5:29 **P** and the other apostles replied: "We *G4377*
Ac 8:14 they sent **P** and John to Samaria. *G4377*
Ac 8:17 Then **P** and John placed their hands on NDT
Ac 8:20 **P** answered: "May your money perish with *G4377*
Ac 8:25 **P** and John returned to Jerusalem NDT
Ac 9:32 As **P** traveled about the country, he went *G4377*
Ac 9:34 "Aeneas," **P** said to him, "Jesus Christ *G4377*
Ac 9:38 the disciples heard that **P** was in Lydda, *G4377*
Ac 9:39 **P** went with them, and when he arrived *G4377*
Ac 9:40 **P** sent them all out of the room; then he *G4377*
Ac 9:40 her eyes, and seeing **P** she sat up. *G4377*
Ac 9:43 **P** stayed in Joppa for some time with a NDT
Ac 10: 5 a man named Simon who is called **P**. *G4377*
Ac 10: 9 the city, **P** went up on the roof to pray. *G4377*
Ac 10:13 a voice told him, "Get up, **P**. Kill and eat." *G4377*
Ac 10:14 **P** replied. "I have never eaten *G4377*
Ac 10:17 While **P** was wondering about the *G4377*
Ac 10:18 who was known as **P** was staying there. *G4377*
Ac 10:19 While **P** was still thinking about the vision *G4377*
Ac 10:21 **P** went down and said to the men, "I'm *G4377*
Ac 10:23 Then **P** invited the men into the house to be NDT
Ac 10:23 The next day **P** started out with them, and NDT
Ac 10:25 As **P** entered the house, Cornelius met *G4377*
Ac 10:26 But **P** made him get up. "Stand up," he *G4377*
Ac 10:27 **P** went inside and found a large gathering NDT
Ac 10:32 Send to Joppa for Simon who is called **P** *G4377*
Ac 10:34 Then **P** began to speak: "I now realize *G4377*
Ac 10:44 While **P** was still speaking these words *G4377*
Ac 10:45 who had come with **P** were astonished *G4377*
Ac 10:46 tongues and praising God. Then **P** said, *G4377*
Ac 10:48 Then they asked **P** to stay with them for a *G899S*
Ac 11: 2 So when **P** went up to Jerusalem, the *G4377*
Ac 11: 4 beginning, **P** told them the whole story: *G4377*
Ac 11: 7 I heard a voice telling me, 'Get up, **P**. *G4377*
Ac 11:13 'Send to Joppa for Simon who is called **P**. *G4377*
Ac 12: 3 the Jews, he proceeded to seize **P** also. *G4377*
Ac 12: 5 So **P** was kept in prison, but the church *G4377*
Ac 12: 6 **P** was sleeping between two soldiers *G4377*
Ac 12: 7 He struck **P** on the side and woke him up *G4377*
Ac 12: 8 And **P** did so. "Wrap your NDT
Ac 12: 9 **P** followed him out of the prison, but he had NDT
Ac 12:11 Then **P** came to himself and said, "Now I *G4377*
Ac 12:13 **P** knocked at the outer entrance, and a *G899S*
Ac 12:14 it and exclaimed, "**P** is at the door!" *G4377*
Ac 12:16 But **P** kept on knocking, and when they *G4377*
Ac 12:17 **P** motioned with his hand for them to be NDT
Ac 12:18 the soldiers as to what had become of **P**. *G4377*
Ac 15: 7 discussion, **P** got up and addressed them: *G4377*
Gal 2: 7 just as **P** had been to the circumcised. *G4377*
Gal 2: 8 who was at work *in* **P** as an apostle to the *G4377*
1Pe 1: 1 **P**, an apostle of Jesus Christ, To God's *G4377*
2Pe 1: 1 Simon **P**, a servant and apostle of Jesus *G4377*

PETER'S (7) [PETER]

Mt 8:14 When Jesus came into **P** house, he saw *G4377*
Mt 8:14 he saw **P** mother-in-law lying in bed with *G899S*
Jn 1:40 Andrew, Simon **P** brother, was one of the *G4377*
Jn 6: 8 Andrew, Simon **P** brother, spoke up, *G4377*
Ac 5:15 so that at least **P** shadow might fall on *G4377*
Ac 12: 7 he said, and the chains fell off **P** wrists. *G899S*
Ac 12:14 When she recognized **P** voice, she was so *G4377*

PETHAHIAH (4)

1Ch 24:16 the nineteenth to **P**, the twentieth to H7342
Ezr 10:23 that is, Kelita), **P**, Judah and Eliezer. H7342
Ne 9: 5 Hodiah, Shebaniah and **P**—said: H7342
Ne 11:24 **P** son of Meshezabel, one of the H7342

PETHOR (2)

Nu 22: 5 of Beor, who was at **P**, near the Euphrates H7335
Dt 23: 4 son of Beor from **P** *in* Aram Naharaim to H7335

PETHUEL (1)

Joel 1: 1 of the LORD that came to Joel son of **P**. H7333

PETITION (17) [PETITIONED, PETITIONS]

Est 5: 6 again asked Esther, "Now what is your **p**? H8629
Est 5: 7 replied, "My **p** and my request is this: H8629
Est 5: 8 the king to grant my **p** and fulfill my H8629
Est 7: 2 "Queen Esther, what is your **p**? H8629
Est 7: 3 grant me my life—this is my **p**. H8629
Est 9:12 Now what is your **p**? It will be given you. H8629
Ps 38: T A psalm of David. A **p**. H2349
Ps 70: T For the director of music. Of David. A **p**. H2349
Jer 7:16 people nor offer any plea or **p** for them; H9525
Jer 11:14 people or offer any plea or **p** for them, H9525
Jer 36: 7 they will bring their **p** before the LORD and H9382
Jer 37:20 Let me bring my **p** before you: Do not H9382
Jer 42: 2 "Please hear our **p** and pray to the LORD H9382
Jer 42: 9 to whom you sent me to present your **p** H9382
Da 9: 3 pleaded with him in prayer and **p**, H9384
Ac 23:15 the Sanhedrin **p** the commander to *G1872*
Php 4: 6 by prayer and **p**, with thanksgiving, *G1255*

PETITIONED (2) [PETITION]

Ezr 8:23 So we fasted and **p** our God about this H1335
Ac 25:24 Jewish community *has* **p** me about him in *G1961*

PETITIONS (3) [PETITION]

Da 9:17 hear the prayers and **p** *of* your servant. H9384
1Ti 2: 1 first of all, that **p**, prayers, intercession *G1255*
Heb 5: 7 up prayers and **p** with fervent cries and *G2656*

PEULLETHAI (1)

1Ch 26: 5 Issachar the seventh and **P** the eighth. H7191

PHALTI, PHALTIEL (KJV) PALTIEL

PHANTOM (1)

Ps 39: 6 everyone goes around like a *mere* **p**; H7513

PHANUEL (NIV84) PENUEL

PHARAOH (214) [PHARAOH'S]

Ge 12:15 they praised her to **P**, and she was taken H7281
Ge 12:17 serious diseases on **P** and his household H7281
Ge 12:18 So **P** summoned Abram. "What have you H7281
Ge 12:20 Then **P** gave orders about Abram to his H7281
Ge 40: 2 **P** was angry with his two officials, the chief H7281
Ge 40:13 Within three days **P** will lift up your head H7281
Ge 40:14 mention me to **P** and get me out of this H7281
Ge 40:17 were all kinds of baked goods for **P**, H7281
Ge 40:19 Within three days **P** will lift off your head H7281
Ge 41: 1 two full years had passed, **P** had a dream: H7281
Ge 41: 4 seven sleek, fat cows. Then **P** woke up. H7281
Ge 41: 7 Then **P** woke up; it had been a H7281
Ge 41: 8 **P** told them his dreams, but no one could H7281
Ge 41: 9 Then the chief cupbearer said to **P** H7281
Ge 41:10 **P** was once angry with his servants, and he H7281
Ge 41:14 So **P** sent for Joseph, and he was quickly H7281
Ge 41:14 changed his clothes, he came before **P**. H7281
Ge 41:15 **P** said to Joseph, "I had a dream, and no H7281
Ge 41:16 Joseph replied to **P**, "but God will give H7281
Ge 41:16 "but God will give **P** the answer he H7281
Ge 41:17 Then **P** said to Joseph, "In my dream I H7281
Ge 41:25 Then Joseph said to **P**, "The dreams of H7281
Ge 41:25 "The dreams of **P** are one and the same. H7281
Ge 41:25 God has revealed to **P** what he is about to H7281
Ge 41:28 "It is just as I said to **P**: God has shown H7281
Ge 41:28 God has shown **P** what he is about to do. H7281
Ge 41:32 dream was given to **P** in two forms is that H7281
Ge 41:33 "And now let **P** look for a discerning and H7281
Ge 41:34 Let **P** appoint commissioners over the land H7281
Ge 41:35 up the grain under the authority of **P**, H7281
Ge 41:37 The plan seemed good to **P** and to all his H7281
Ge 41:38 So **P** asked them, "Can we find anyone H7281
Ge 41:39 Then **P** said to Joseph, "Since God has H7281
Ge 41:41 So **P** said to Joseph, "I hereby put you in H7281
Ge 41:42 Then **P** took his signet ring from his finger H7281
Ge 41:44 Then **P** said to Joseph, "I am Pharaoh H7281
Ge 41:44 said to Joseph, "I am **P**, but without your H7281
Ge 41:45 **P** gave Joseph the name H7281
Ge 41:46 he entered the service of **P** king of Egypt. H7281
Ge 41:55 the famine, the people cried to **P** for food. H7281
Ge 41:55 Then **P** told all the Egyptians, "Go to H7281
Ge 42:15 As surely as **P** lives, you will not leave this H7281
Ge 42:16 then as surely as **P** lives, you are spies!" H7281
Ge 44:18 though you are equal to **P** *himself*. H7281
Ge 45: 8 He made me father to **P**, lord of his entire H7281
Ge 45:16 **P** and all his officials were pleased. H7281
Ge 45:17 **P** said to Joseph, "Tell your brothers, 'Do H7281
Ge 45:21 them carts, as **P** had commanded, and H7281
Ge 46: 5 in the carts that **P** had sent to transport H7281
Ge 46:31 go up and speak to **P** and will say to him, H7281
Ge 46:33 When **P** calls you in and asks, 'What is H7281
Ge 47: 1 Joseph went and told **P**, "My father and H7281
Ge 47: 2 his brothers and presented them before **P**. H7281
Ge 47: 3 **P** asked the brothers, "What is your H7281
Ge 47: 3 they replied to **P**, "just as our fathers H7281
Ge 47: 5 **P** said to Joseph, "Your father and your H7281
Ge 47: 7 Jacob in and presented him before **P**. H7281
Ge 47: 7 before Pharaoh. After Jacob blessed **P**, H7281
Ge 47: 8 **P** asked him, "How old are you?" H7281
Ge 47: 9 And Jacob said to **P**, "The years of my H7281
Ge 47:10 Then Jacob blessed **P** and went out from H7281
Ge 47:11 the district of Rameses, as **P** directed. H7281
Ge 47:19 we with our land will be in bondage to **P**. H7281
Ge 47:20 Joseph bought all the land in Egypt for **P**. H7281
Ge 47:22 allotment from **P** and had food enough H7281
Ge 47:22 enough from the allotment **P** gave them. H7281
Ge 47:23 bought you and your land today for **P**, H7281
Ge 47:24 the crop comes in, give a fifth of it to **P**. H7281
Ge 47:25 of our lord; we will be in bondage to **P**." H7281
Ge 47:26 that a fifth of the produce belongs to **P**. H7281
Ge 50: 4 favor in your eyes, speak to **P** for me. H7281
Ge 50: 6 **P** said, "Go up and bury your father, as he H7281
Ex 1:11 Pithom and Rameses as store cities for **P**. H7281
Ex 1:19 The midwives answered **P**, "Hebrew H7281
Ex 1:22 Then **P** gave this order to all his people H7281
Ex 2:15 When **P** heard of this, he tried to kill H7281
Ex 2:15 Moses fled from **P** and went to live in H7281
Ex 3:10 I am sending you to **P** to bring my people H7281
Ex 3:11 I that I should go to **P** and bring the H7281
Ex 4:21 you perform before **P** all the wonders I H7281
Ex 4:22 Then say to **P**, 'This is what the LORD says H7281
Ex 5: 1 Moses and Aaron went to **P** and said, H7281
Ex 5: 2 **P** said, "Who is the LORD, that I should H7281
Ex 5: 5 Then **P** said, "Look, the people of the land H7281
Ex 5: 6 That same day **P** gave this order to the H7281
Ex 5:10 said to the people, "This is what **P** says: H7281
Ex 5:15 overseers went and appealed to **P**: H7281
Ex 5:17 **P** said, "Lazy, that's what you are—lazy NDT
Ex 5:20 When they left **P**, they found Moses and H7281
Ex 5:21 made us obnoxious to **P** and his officials H7281
Ex 5:23 Ever since I went to **P** to speak in your H7281
Ex 6: 1 "Now you will see what I will do to **P**: H7281
Ex 6:11 tell **P** king of Egypt to let the Israelites go H7281
Ex 6:12 why would **P** listen to me, since I H7281
Ex 6:13 about the Israelites and **P** king of Egypt, H7281
Ex 6:27 ones who spoke to **P** king of Egypt about H7281
Ex 6:29 Tell **P** king of Egypt everything I tell you." H7281
Ex 6:30 faltering lips, why would **P** listen to me?" H7281
Ex 7: 1 I have made you like God to **P**, and your H7281
Ex 7: 2 Aaron is to tell **P** to let the Israelites go H7281
Ex 7: 7 Aaron eighty-three when they spoke to **P**. H7281
Ex 7: 9 "When **P** says to you, 'Perform a miracle,' H7281
Ex 7: 9 your staff and throw it down before **P**, H7281
Ex 7:10 Aaron went to **P** and did just as the H7281
Ex 7:10 staff down in front of **P** and his officials, H7281
Ex 7:11 **P** then summoned wise men and sorcerers, H7281
Ex 7:15 Go to **P** in the morning as he goes out to H7281
Ex 7:20 in the presence of **P** and his officials and H7281
Ex 8: 1 to Moses, "Go to **P** and say to him, 'This H7281
Ex 8: 8 **P** summoned Moses and Aaron and said H7281
Ex 8: 9 Moses said to **P**, "I leave to you the honor H7281

P

Ex 8:10 "Tomorrow," **P** said. Moses replied, "It will NDT
Ex 8:12 After Moses and Aaron left **P**, Moses cried H7281
Ex 8:12 LORD about the frogs he had brought on **P**. H7281
Ex 8:15 But when **P** saw that there was relief, he H7281
Ex 8:19 the magicians said to **P**, "This is the finger H7281
Ex 8:20 morning and confront **P** as he goes to the H7281
Ex 8:25 Then **P** summoned Moses and Aaron H7281
Ex 8:28 **P** said, "I will let you go to offer sacrifices H7281
Ex 8:29 the flies will leave **P** and his officials and H7281
Ex 8:29 Only let **P** be sure that he does not act H7281
Ex 8:30 Then Moses left **P** and prayed to the LORD, H7281
Ex 8:31 The flies left **P** and his officials and his H7281
Ex 8:32 But this time also **P** hardened his heart H7281
Ex 9: 1 to Moses, "Go to **P** and say to him, 'This H7281
Ex 9: 7 **P** investigated and found that not even H7281
Ex 9: 8 toss it into the air in the presence of **P**. H7281
Ex 9:10 soot from a furnace and stood before **P**. H7281
Ex 9:13 morning, confront **P** and say to him, 'This H7281
Ex 9:20 Those officials of **P** who feared the word H7281
Ex 9:27 Then **P** summoned Moses and Aaron H7281
Ex 9:33 Then Moses left **P** and went out of the city H7281
Ex 9:34 When **P** saw that the rain and hail and H7281
Ex 10: 1 to Moses, "Go to **P**, for I have hardened H7281
Ex 10: 3 Aaron went to **P** and said to him, H7281
Ex 10: 6 Then Moses turned and left **P**. H7281
Ex 10: 8 Moses and Aaron were brought back to **P**. H7281
Ex 10:10 **P** said, "The LORD be with you—if I let you NDT
Ex 10:16 **P** quickly summoned Moses and Aaron H7281
Ex 10:18 Moses then left **P** and prayed to the LORD. H7281
Ex 10:24 Then **P** summoned Moses and said, "Go H7281
Ex 10:28 **P** said to Moses, "Get out of my sight H7281
Ex 11: 1 one more plague on **P** and on Egypt. H7281
Ex 11: 5 from the firstborn son of **P**, who sits on the H7281
Ex 11: 8 Then Moses, hot with anger, left **P**. H7281
Ex 11: 9 to Moses, "**P** will refuse to listen to you H7281
Ex 11:10 performed all these wonders before **P**, H7281
Ex 12:29 from the firstborn of **P**, who sat on the H7281
Ex 12:30 **P** and all his officials and all the Egyptians H7281
Ex 12:31 During the night **P** summoned Moses and NDT
Ex 13:15 When **P** stubbornly refused to let us go H7281
Ex 13:17 When **P** let the people go, God did not H7281
Ex 14: 3 **P** will think, 'The Israelites are wandering H7281
Ex 14: 4 myself through **P** and all his army, H7281
Ex 14: 5 **P** and his officials changed their minds H7281
Ex 14: 8 hardened the heart of **P** king of Egypt, H7281
Ex 14:10 As **P** approached, the Israelites looked up, H7281
Ex 14:17 will gain glory through **P** and all his army, H7281
Ex 14:18 I am the LORD when I gain glory through **P**, H7281
Ex 14:28 the entire army of **P** that had followed the H7281
Ex 18: 4 he saved me from the sword of **P**. H7281
Ex 18: 8 the LORD had done to **P** and the Egyptians H7281
Ex 18:10 from the hand of the Egyptians and of **P**, H7281
Dt 6:21 "We were slaves of **P** in Egypt, but the H7281
Dt 6:22 on Egypt and **P** and his whole household. H7281
Dt 7: 8 from the power of **P** king of Egypt. H7281
Dt 7:18 LORD your God did to **P** and to all Egypt. H7281
Dt 11: 3 both to **P** king of Egypt and to his whole H7281
Dt 29: 2 seen all that the LORD did in Egypt to **P**, H7281
Dt 34:11 to **P** and to all his officials and to his H7281
1Sa 2:27 family when they were in Egypt under **P**? H7281
1Sa 6: 6 your hearts as the Egyptians and **P** did? H7281
1Ki 3: 1 an alliance with **P** king of Egypt and H7281
1Ki 9:16 **P** king of Egypt had attacked and captured H7281
1Ki 11:18 went to Egypt, to **P** king of Egypt, who H7281
1Ki 11:19 **P** was so pleased with Hadad that he H7281
1Ki 11:21 Then Hadad said to **P**, "Let me go, that I H7281
1Ki 11:22 to your own country?" **P** asked. "Nothing," H7281
2Ki 17: 7 from under the power of **P** king of Egypt. H7281
2Ki 18:21 Such is **P** king of Egypt to all who depend H7281
2Ki 23:29 **P** Necho king of Egypt went up to the H7281
2Ki 23:33 **P** Necho put him in chains at Riblah in the H7281
2Ki 23:34 **P** Necho made Eliakim son of Josiah king H7281
2Ki 23:35 Jehoiakim paid **P** Necho the silver and H7281
Ne 9:10 You sent signs and wonders against **P** H7281
Ps 135: 9 against **P** and all his servants. H7281
Ps 136:15 swept **P** and his army into the Red H7281
Isa 19:11 wise counselors of **P** give senseless H7281
Isa 19:11 How can you say to **P**, "I am one of the H7281
Isa 36: 6 Such is **P** king of Egypt to all who depend H7281
Jer 25:19 **P** king of Egypt, his attendants, his officials H7281
Jer 44:30 am going to deliver **P** Hophra king of H7281
Jer 46: 2 against the army of **P** Necho king of Egypt H7281
Jer 46:17 '**P** king of Egypt is only a loud noise H7281
Jer 46:25 god of Thebes, on **P**, on Egypt and her H7281
Jer 46:25 her kings, and on those who rely on **P**. H7281
Jer 47: 1 the Philistines before **P** attacked Gaza: H7281
Eze 17:17 **P** with his mighty army and great horde H7281
Eze 29: 2 set your face against **P** king of Egypt and H7281
Eze 29: 3 " 'I am against you, **P** king of Egypt, you H7281
Eze 30:21 I have broken the arm of **P** king of Egypt. H7281
Eze 30:22 I am against **P** king of Egypt. I will H7281
Eze 30:24 I will break the arms of **P**, and he will H7281
Eze 30:25 Babylon, but the arms of **P** will fall limp. H7281
Eze 31: 2 say to **P** king of Egypt and to his hordes: H7281
Eze 31:18 " 'This is **P** and all his hordes, declares H7281
Eze 32: 2 a lament concerning **P** king of Egypt and H7281
Eze 32:28 "You too, **P**, will be broken and will lie NDT
Eze 32:31 "**P**—he and all his army—will see them H7281
Eze 32:32 **P** and all his hordes will be laid among H7281
Ac 7:10 to gain the goodwill of **P** king of Egypt. G5755
Ac 7:10 So **P** made him ruler over Egypt and all his NDT
Ac 7:13 **P** learned about Joseph's family. G5755
Ro 9:17 For Scripture says *to* **P**: "I raised you up G5755

PHARAOH'S (57) [PHARAOH]

Ge 12:15 And when **P** officials saw her, they praised H7281
Ge 37:36 to Potiphar, one of **P** officials, the captain H7281
Ge 39: 1 an Egyptian who was one of **P** officials H7281
Ge 40: 7 So he asked **P** officials who were in H7281
Ge 40:11 **P** cup was in my hand, and I took the H7281
Ge 40:11 squeezed them into **P** cup and put the H7281
Ge 40:13 you will put **P** cup in his hand, just as H7281
Ge 40:20 Now the third day was **P** birthday, and he H7281
Ge 40:21 he once again put the cup into **P** hand— H7281
Ge 41:46 Joseph went out from **P** presence and H7281
Ge 45: 2 and **P** household heard about it. H7281
Ge 45:16 the news reached **P** palace that Joseph's H7281
Ge 47:14 and he brought it to **P** palace. H7281
Ge 47:20 The land became **P**, H4200+7281
Ge 47:26 the priests that did not become **P**. H4200+7281
Ge 50: 4 passed, Joseph said to **P** court, "If I have H7281
Ge 50: 7 All **P** officials accompanied him—the H7281
Ex 2: 5 Then **P** daughter went down to the Nile to H7281
Ex 2: 7 Then his sister asked **P** daughter, "Shall I H7281
Ex 2: 9 **P** daughter said to her, "Take this baby H7281
Ex 2:10 she took him to **P** daughter and he H7281
Ex 5:14 And **P** slave drivers beat the Israelite H7281
Ex 7: 3 But I will harden **P** heart, and though I H7281
Ex 7:13 Yet **P** heart became hard and he would H7281
Ex 7:14 LORD said to Moses, "**P** heart is unyielding H7281
Ex 7:22 secret arts, and **P** heart became hard; he H7281
Ex 8:19 But **P** heart was hard and he would not H7281
Ex 8:24 of flies poured into **P** palace and into the H7281
Ex 9:12 the LORD hardened **P** heart and he would H7281
Ex 9:35 So **P** heart was hard and he would not let H7281
Ex 10: 7 **P** officials said to him, "How long will this H7281
Ex 10:11 Aaron were driven out of **P** presence. H7281
Ex 10:20 But the LORD hardened **P** heart, and he H7281
Ex 10:27 But the LORD hardened **P** heart, and he H7281
Ex 11: 3 regarded in Egypt by **P** officials and by the H7281
Ex 11:10 the LORD hardened **P** heart, and he H7281
Ex 14: 4 And I will harden **P** heart, and he will H7281
Ex 14: 9 The Egyptians—all **P** horses and chariots H7281
Ex 14:23 all **P** horses and chariots and H7281
Ex 15: 4 **P** chariots and his army he has hurled into H7281
Ex 15: 4 The best of **P** officers are drowned in the H2257S
Ex 15:19 When **P** horses, chariots and horsemen H7281
1Ki 7: 8 a palace like this hall for **P** daughter, H7281
1Ki 9:24 After **P** daughter had come up from the H7281
1Ki 11: 1 foreign women besides **P** daughter— H7281
1Ki 11:20 Genubath lived with **P** *own* children. H7281
1Ch 4:18 were the children of **P** daughter Bithiah, H7281
2Ch 8:11 Solomon brought **P** daughter up from the H7281
SS 1: 9 to a mare among **P** chariot horses. H7281
Isa 30: 2 who look for help to **P** protection, to H7281
Isa 30: 3 But **P** protection will be to your shame H7281
Jer 37: 5 **P** army had marched out of Egypt, and H7281
Jer 37: 7 you to inquire of me, '**P** army, which has H7281
Jer 37:11 from Jerusalem because of **P** army, H7281
Jer 43: 9 at the entrance to **P** palace in Tahpanhes. H7281
Ac 7:21 **P** daughter took him and brought him up G5755
Heb 11:24 to be known as the son of **P** daughter. G5755

PHARES, PHAREZ (KJV) PEREZ

PHARISEE (12) [PHARISEE'S, PHARISEES]

Mt 23:26 Blind **P**! First clean the inside of the cup G5757
Lk 7:39 When the **P** who had invited him saw this, G5757
Lk 11:37 speaking, a **P** invited him to eat with him G5757
Lk 11:38 But the **P** was surprised when he noticed G5757
Lk 14: 1 to eat in the house of a prominent **P**, G5757
Lk 18:10 one a **P** and the other a tax collector. G5757
Lk 18:11 The **P** stood by himself and prayed: 'God, G5757
Jn 3: 1 Now there was a **P**, a man named G5757
Ac 5:34 But a **P** named Gamaliel, a teacher of the G5757
Ac 23: 6 "My brothers, I am a **P**, descended from G5757
Ac 26: 5 strictest sect of our religion, living *as* a **P**. G5757
Php 3: 5 of Hebrews; in regard to the law, a **P**; G5757

PHARISEE'S (2) [PHARISEE]

Lk 7:36 he went to the **P** house and reclined at G5757
Lk 7:37 that Jesus was eating at the **P** house, G5757

PHARISEES (87) [PHARISEE]

Mt 3: 7 he saw many *of* the **P** and Sadducees G5757
Mt 5:20 surpasses that *of* the **P** and the teachers G5757
Mt 9:11 When the **P** saw this, they asked his G5757
Mt 9:14 "How is it that we and the **P** fast often G5757
Mt 9:34 But the **P** said, "It is by the prince of G5757
Mt 12: 2 When the **P** saw this, they said to him G5757
Mt 12:14 But the **P** went out and plotted how they G5757
Mt 12:24 But when the **P** heard this, they said, "It is G5757
Mt 12:38 Then some *of* the **P** and teachers of the G5757
Mt 15: 1 Then *some* **P** and teachers of the law G5757
Mt 15:12 you *know* that the **P** were offended when G5757
Mt 16: 1 The **P** and Sadducees came to Jesus and G5757
Mt 16: 6 against the yeast *of* the **P** and Sadducees." G5757
Mt 16:11 against the yeast *of* the **P** and Sadducees." G5757
Mt 16:12 the teaching *of* the **P** and Sadducees. G5757
Mt 19: 3 *Some* **P** came to him to test him. G5757
Mt 21:45 priests and the **P** heard Jesus' parables G5757
Mt 22:15 Then the **P** went out and laid plans to G5757
Mt 22:34 the Sadducees, the **P** got together. G5757
Mt 22:41 While the **P** were gathered together G5757
Mt 23: 2 of the law and the **P** sit in Moses' seat. G5757
Mt 23:13 teachers of the law and **P**, you hypocrites! G5757
Mt 23:15 teachers of the law and **P**, you hypocrites! G5757
Mt 23:23 teachers of the law and **P**, you hypocrites! G5757
Mt 23:25 teachers of the law and **P**, you hypocrites! G5757
Mt 23:27 teachers of the law and **P**, you hypocrites! G5757
Mt 23:29 teachers of the law and **P**, you hypocrites! G5757
Mt 27:62 the chief priests and the **P** went to Pilate. G5757
Mk 2:16 the law who were **P** saw him eating with G5757
Mk 2:18 John's disciples and the **P** were fasting. G5757
Mk 2:18 the disciples *of* the **P** are fasting, G5757
Mk 2:24 The **P** said to him, "Look, why are they G5757
Mk 3: 6 Then the **P** went out and began to plot G5757
Mk 7: 1 The **P** and some of the teachers of the G5757
Mk 7: 3 The **P** and all the Jews do not eat unless G5757
Mk 7: 5 So the **P** and teachers of the law asked G5757
Mk 8:11 The **P** came and began to question Jesus G5757
Mk 8:15 out for the yeast *of* the **P** and that of G5757
Mk 10: 2 Some **P** came and tested him by asking G5757
Mk 12:13 they sent some *of* the **P** and Herodians to G5757
Lk 5:17 **P** and teachers of the law were sitting G5757
Lk 5:21 The **P** and the teachers of the law began G5757
Lk 5:30 But the **P** and the teachers of the law who G5757
Lk 5:33 so do the disciples *of* the **P**, but yours G5757
Lk 6: 2 Some *of* the **P** asked, "Why are you doing G5757
Lk 6: 7 The **P** and the teachers of the law were G5757
Lk 6:11 But **the P and the teachers of the law** were G899S
Lk 7:30 But the **P** and the experts in the law G5757
Lk 7:36 When one *of* the **P** invited Jesus to have G5757
Lk 11:39 you **P** clean the outside of the cup and G5757
Lk 11:42 "Woe to you **P**, because you give God a G5757
Lk 11:43 "Woe to you **P**, because you love the G5757
Lk 11:53 the **P** and the teachers of the law began G5757
Lk 12: 1 on your guard against the yeast *of* the **P**, G5757
Lk 13:31 At that time some **P** came to Jesus and G5757
Lk 14: 3 Jesus asked the **P** and experts in the law G5757
Lk 15: 2 But the **P** and the teachers of the law G5757
Lk 16:14 The **P**, who loved money, heard all this G5757
Lk 17:20 being asked by the **P** when the kingdom G5757
Lk 19:39 Some *of* the **P** in the crowd said to Jesus G5757
Jn 1:24 Now the **P** who had been sent G5757
Jn 4: 1 learned that the **P** had heard that he was G5757
Jn 7:32 The **P** heard the crowd whispering such G5757
Jn 7:32 priests and the **P** sent temple guards to G5757
Jn 7:45 went back to the chief priests and the **P**, G5757
Jn 7:47 he has deceived you also?" the **P** retorted. G5757
Jn 7:48 of the rulers or of the **P** believed in him? G5757
Jn 8: 3 of the law and the **P** brought in a woman G5757
Jn 8:13 The **P** challenged him, "Here you are G5757
Jn 9:13 They brought to the **P** the man who had G5757
Jn 9:15 Therefore the **P** also asked him how he G5757
Jn 9:16 Some of the **P** said, "This man is not from G5757
Jn 9:40 Some **P** who were with him heard him say G5757
Jn 10: 1 "Very truly I tell you **P**, anyone who does not NDT
Jn 10: 6 but **the P** did not understand what he G1697S
Jn 11:46 of them went to the **P** and told them what G5757
Jn 11:47 priests and the **P** called a meeting of G5757
Jn 11:57 priests and the **P** had given orders that G5757
Jn 12:19 So the **P** said to one another, "See, this is G5757
Jn 12:42 But because of the **P** they would not G5757
Jn 18: 3 officials from the chief priests and the **P**. G5757
Ac 15: 5 to the party *of* the **P** stood up and said, G5757
Ac 23: 6 them were Sadducees and the others **P**, G5757
Ac 23: 6 I am a Pharisee, descended from **P**. G5757
Ac 23: 7 dispute broke out *between* the **P** and the G5757
Ac 23: 8 but the **P** believe all these things. G5757
Ac 23: 9 the law who were **P** stood up and argued G5757

PHARPAR (1)

2Ki 5:12 Are not Abana and **P**, the rivers of H7286

PHENICE, PHENICIA (KJV) PHOENIX, PHOENICIA

PHICOL (3)

Ge 21:22 time Abimelek and **P** the commander of H7087
Ge 21:32 Abimelek and **P** the commander of his H7087
Ge 26:26 adviser and **P** the commander of his H7087

PHILADELPHIA (2)

Rev 1:11 Thyatira, Sardis, **P** and Laodicea. G5788
Rev 3: 7 "To the angel of the church in **P** write G5788

PHILEMON (1)

Phm 1 *To* **P** our dear friend and fellow worker G5800

PHILETUS (1)

2Ti 2:17 Among them are Hymenaeus and **P**, G5801

PHILIP (34) [PHILIP'S]

Mt 10: 3 **P** and Bartholomew; Thomas and Matthew G5805
Mk 3:18 Andrew, **P**, Bartholomew, Matthew G5805
Lk 3: 1 his brother **P** tetrarch of Iturea and G5805
Lk 6:14 Andrew, James, John, **P**, Bartholomew, G5805
Jn 1:43 Finding **P**, he said to him G5805
Jn 1:44 **P**, like Andrew and Peter, was from the G5805
Jn 1:45 **P** found Nathanael and told him, "We G5805
Jn 1:46 "Come and see," said **P**. G5805
Jn 1:48 still under the fig tree before **P** called you." G5805
Jn 6: 5 he said to **P**, "Where shall we buy G5805
Jn 6: 7 **P** answered him, "It would take more than G5805
Jn 12:21 They came to **P**, who was from Bethsaida G5805
Jn 12:22 **P** went to tell Andrew; Andrew and Philip G5805
Jn 12:22 Andrew; Andrew and **P** in turn told Jesus. G5805
Jn 14: 8 **P** said, "Lord, show us the Father and that G5805

Jn 14: 9 “Don't you know me, **P**, even after I have *G5805*
Ac 1:13 James and Andrew; **P** and Thomas *G5805*
Ac 6: 5 of the Holy Spirit; also **P**, Procorus, *G5805*
Ac 8: 5 **P** went down to a city in Samaria and *G5805*
Ac 8: 6 the crowds heard **P** and saw the signs he *G5805*
Ac 8:12 when they believed **P** as he proclaimed *G5805*
Ac 8:13 And he followed **P** everywhere *G5805*
Ac 8:26 Now an angel of the Lord said to **P**, “Go *G5805*
Ac 8:29 The Spirit told **P**, “Go to that chariot and *G5805*
Ac 8:30 Then **P** ran up to the chariot and heard *G5805*
Ac 8:30 what you are reading?” **P** asked. NDT
Ac 8:31 So he invited **P** to come up and sit with *G5805*
Ac 8:34 The eunuch asked **P**, “Tell me, please *G5805*
Ac 8:35 Then **P** began with that very passage of *G5805*
Ac 8:38 Then both **P** and the eunuch went down *G5805*
Ac 8:38 down into the water and **P** baptized him. NDT
Ac 8:39 Spirit of the Lord suddenly took **P** away, *G5805*
Ac 8:40 **P**, however, appeared at Azotus and *G5805*
Ac 21: 8 stayed at the house *of* **P** the evangelist, *G5805*

PHILIP'S (2) [PHILIP]

Mt 14: 3 because of Herodias, his brother **P** wife, *G5805*
Mk 6:17 his brother **P** wife, whom he had *G5805*

PHILIPPI (6) [PHILIPPIANS]

Mt 16:13 Jesus came to the region of Caesarea **P**, *G5805*
Mk 8:27 on to the villages around Caesarea **P**. *G5805*
Ac 16:12 From there we traveled to **P**, a Roman *G5804*
Ac 20: 6 But we sailed from **P** after the Festival of *G5804*
Php 1: 1 all God's holy people in Christ Jesus at **P**, *G5804*
1Th 2: 2 been treated outrageously in **P**, *G5804*

PHILIPPIANS (1) [PHILIPPI]

Php 4:15 Moreover, as you **P** know, in the early days *G5803*

PHILISTIA (8) [PHILISTINE]

Ex 15:14 anguish will grip the people of **P**. H7148
Ps 60: 8 toss my sandal; over **P** I shout in triumph.” H7148
Ps 83: 7 Ammon and Amalek, **P**, with the people H7148
Ps 87: 4 who acknowledge me—**P** too, and Tyre, H7148
Ps 108: 9 toss my sandal; over **P** I shout in triumph.” H7148
Isa 11:14 down on the slopes of **P** to the west; H7149
Joel 3: 4 Tyre and Sidon and all you regions of **P**? H7148
Am 6: 2 Hamath, and then go down to Gath in **P**. H7148

PHILISTINE (62) [PHILISTIA, PHILISTINE'S, PHILISTINES]

Ex 13:17 them on the road through the **P** country, H7149
Jos 13: 3 though held by the five **P** rulers in Gaza, H7149
Jdg 14: 1 Timnah and saw there a young **P** woman. H7149
Jdg 14: 2 “I have seen a **P** woman in Timnah; now H7149
1Sa 6: 1 the LORD had been in **P** territory seven H7149
1Sa 6: 4 according to the number of the **P** rulers H7149
1Sa 6:18 to the number of **P** towns belonging to H7149
1Sa 10: 5 where there is a **P** outpost. H7149
1Sa 13: 3 Jonathan attacked the **P** outpost at Geba H7149
1Sa 13: 4 “Saul has attacked the **P** outpost, and H7149
1Sa 13:17 went out from the **P** camp in three H7149
1Sa 14: 1 let's go over to the **P** outpost on the other H7149
1Sa 14: 4 to cross to reach the **P** outpost was a cliff; H7149
1Sa 14:11 showed themselves to the **P** outpost. H7149
1Sa 14:19 the tumult in the **P** camp increased more H7149
1Sa 17: 4 was from Gath, came out of the **P** camp. H7149
1Sa 17: 8 Am I not a **P**, and are you not the servants H7149
1Sa 17:10 Then the **P** said, “This day I defy the H7149
1Sa 17:16 For forty days the **P** came forward every H7149
1Sa 17:23 Goliath, the **P** champion from Gath H7149
1Sa 17:26 the man who kills this **P** and removes this H7149
1Sa 17:26 this uncircumcised **P** that he should defy H7149
1Sa 17:32 no one lose heart on account of this **P**; H7149
1Sa 17:33 to go out against this **P** and fight him; H7149
1Sa 17:36 this uncircumcised **P** will be like one of H7149
1Sa 17:37 will rescue me from the hand of this **P**.” H7149
1Sa 17:40 his sling in his hand, approached the **P**. H7149
1Sa 17:41 Meanwhile, the **P**, with his shield bearer H7149
1Sa 17:43 And the **P** cursed David by his gods H7149
1Sa 17:45 David said to the **P**, “You come against H7149
1Sa 17:46 the carcasses of the **P** army to the birds H7149
1Sa 17:48 As the **P** moved closer to attack him H7149
1Sa 17:49 slung it and struck the **P** on the forehead. H7149
1Sa 17:50 triumphed over the **P** with a sling and a H7149
1Sa 17:50 hand he struck down the **P** and killed him. H7149
1Sa 17:55 watched David going out to meet the **P**, H7149
1Sa 17:57 soon as David returned from killing the **P**, H7149
1Sa 18: 6 home after David had killed the **P**, H7149
1Sa 18:25 the bride than a hundred **P** foreskins, H7149
1Sa 18:30 The **P** commanders continued to go out to H7149
1Sa 19: 5 his life in his hands when he killed the **P**. H7149
1Sa 21: 9 “The sword of Goliath the **P**, whom you H7149
1Sa 22:10 provisions and the sword of Goliath the **P**.” H7149
1Sa 23: 3 if we go to Keilah against the **P** forces!” H7149
1Sa 27: 7 David lived in **P** territory a year and four H7149
1Sa 27:11 practice as long as he lived in **P** territory. H7149
1Sa 28: 5 When Saul saw the **P** army, he was afraid H7149
1Sa 29: 2 As the **P** rulers marched with their units of H7149
1Sa 29: 4 But the **P** commanders were angry with H7149
1Sa 29: 7 do nothing to displease the **P** rulers.” H7149
1Sa 29: 9 the **P** commanders have said H7149
2Sa 3:14 the price of a hundred **P** foreskins. H7149
2Sa 5:24 out in front of you to strike the **P** army.” H7149
2Sa 21:17 he struck the **P** down and killed him. H7149
2Sa 23:14 the **P** garrison was at Bethlehem. H7149
2Sa 23:16 mighty warriors broke through the **P** lines, H7149
1Ki 15:27 at Gibbethon, a **P** town, while Nadab H7149
1Ki 16:15 was encamped near Gibbethon, a **P** town. H7149
1Ch 11:16 the **P** garrison was at Bethlehem. H7149
1Ch 11:18 So the Three broke through the **P** lines H7149
1Ch 14:15 out in front of you to strike the **P** army.” H7149
1Ch 14:16 they struck down the **P** army, all the H7149

PHILISTINE'S (5) [PHILISTINE]

1Sa 17:11 On hearing the **P** words, Saul and all the H7149
1Sa 17:51 He took hold of the **P** sword and drew it H7149
1Sa 17:54 David took the **P** head and brought it to H7149
1Sa 17:54 he put **the P** weapons in his own tent. H2257S
1Sa 17:57 with David still holding the **P** head. H7149

PHILISTINES (209) [PHILISTINE]

Ge 10:14 from whom the **P** came) and Caphtorites. H7149
Ge 21:32 of his forces returned to the land of the **P**. H7149
Ge 21:34 in the land of the **P** for a long time. H7149
Ge 26: 1 went to Abimelek king of the **P** in Gerar. H7149
Ge 26: 8 king of the **P** looked down from a H7149
Ge 26:14 herds and servants that the **P** envied him. H7149
Ge 26:15 father Abraham, the **P** stopped up, filling H7149
Ge 26:18 which the **P** had stopped up after H7149
Jos 13: 2 all the regions of the **P** and Geshurites, H7149
Jdg 3: 3 the five rulers of the **P**, all the Canaanites H7149
Jdg 3:31 down six hundred **P** with an oxgoad. H7149
Jdg 10: 6 of the Ammonites and the gods of the **P**. H7149
Jdg 10: 7 the hands of the **P** and the Ammonites, H7149
Jdg 10:11 the Amorites, the Ammonites, the **P**, H7149
Jdg 13: 1 into the hands of the **P** for forty years. H7149
Jdg 13: 5 delivering Israel from the hands of the **P**.” H7149
Jdg 14: 3 go to the uncircumcised **P** to get a wife?” H7149
Jdg 14: 4 seeking an occasion to confront the **P**; H7149
Jdg 15: 3 time I have a right to get even with the **P**; H7149
Jdg 15: 5 foxes loose in the standing grain of the **P**. H7149
Jdg 15: 6 When the **P** asked, “Who did this?” they H7149
Jdg 15: 6 So the **P** went up and burned her and her H7149
Jdg 15: 9 The **P** went up and camped in Judah H7149
Jdg 15:11 you realize that the **P** are rulers over us? H7149
Jdg 15:12 to tie you up and hand you over to the **P**.” H7149
Jdg 15:14 the **P** came toward him shouting. H7149
Jdg 15:20 Israel for twenty years in the days of the **P**. H7149
Jdg 16: 5 The rulers of the **P** went to her and said H7149
Jdg 16: 8 Then the rulers of the **P** brought her seven H7149
Jdg 16: 9 “Samson, the **P** are upon you! H7149
Jdg 16:12 “Samson, the **P** are upon you! H7149
Jdg 16:14 “Samson, the **P** are upon you! H7149
Jdg 16:18 she sent word to the rulers of the **P** H7149
Jdg 16:18 So the rulers of the **P** returned with the H7149
Jdg 16:20 she called, “Samson, the **P** are upon you!” H7149
Jdg 16:21 Then the **P** seized him, gouged out his H7149
Jdg 16:23 the rulers of the **P** assembled to offer a H7149
Jdg 16:27 all the rulers of the **P** were there, and on H7149
Jdg 16:28 get revenge on the **P** for my two eyes.” H7149
Jdg 16:30 “Let me die with the **P**!” Then he pushed H7149
1Sa 4: 1 Israelites went out to fight against the **P**. H7149
1Sa 4: 1 camped at Ebenezer, and the **P** at Aphek. H7149
1Sa 4: 2 The **P** deployed their forces to meet Israel H7149
1Sa 4: 2 Israel was defeated by the **P**, who killed H7149
1Sa 4: 3 bring defeat on us today before the **P**? H7149
1Sa 4: 6 the uproar, the **P** asked, “What's all H7149
1Sa 4: 7 the **P** were afraid. “A god has come into H7149
1Sa 4: 9 Be strong, **P**! Be men, or you will be H7149
1Sa 4:10 So the **P** fought, and the Israelites were H7149
1Sa 4:17 “Israel fled before the **P**, and the army H7149
1Sa 5: 1 After the **P** had captured the ark of God H7149
1Sa 5: 8 all the rulers of the **P** and asked them, H7149
1Sa 5:11 together all the rulers of the **P** and said, H7149
1Sa 6: 2 the **P** called for the priests and the diviners H7149
1Sa 6: 4 The **P** asked, “What guilt offering should we NDT
1Sa 6:12 The rulers of the **P** followed them as far H7149
1Sa 6:16 five rulers of the **P** saw all this and then H7149
1Sa 6:17 are the gold tumors the **P** sent as a guilt H7149
1Sa 6:21 “The **P** have returned the ark of the LORD. H7149
1Sa 7: 3 will deliver you out of the hand of the **P**.” H7149
1Sa 7: 7 When the **P** heard that Israel had H7149
1Sa 7: 7 the rulers of the **P** came up to attack them. H7149
1Sa 7: 7 they were afraid because of the **P**. H7149
1Sa 7: 8 he may rescue us from the hand of the **P**.” H7149
1Sa 7:10 the **P** drew near to engage Israel in battle. H7149
1Sa 7:10 against the **P** and threw them into H7149
1Sa 7:11 rushed out of Mizpah and pursued the **P**, H7149
1Sa 7:13 So the **P** were subdued and they stopped H7149
1Sa 7:13 the hand of the LORD was against the **P**. H7149
1Sa 7:14 to Gath that the **P** had captured from H7149
1Sa 7:14 territory from the hands of the **P**. H7149
1Sa 9:16 will deliver them from the hand of the **P**. H7149
1Sa 12: 9 the hands of the **P** and the king of Moab, H7149
1Sa 13: 3 at Geba, and the **P** heard about it. H7149
1Sa 13: 4 Israel has become obnoxious to the **P**.” H7149
1Sa 13: 5 The **P** assembled to fight Israel, with H7149
1Sa 13:11 that the **P** were assembling at H7149
1Sa 13:12 ‘Now the **P** will come down against me at H7149
1Sa 13:16 while the **P** camped at Mikmash. H7149
1Sa 13:19 because the **P** had said H7149
1Sa 13:20 went down to the **P** to have their plow H7149
1Sa 13:23 a detachment of **P** had gone out to the H7149
1Sa 14:11 said the **P**. “The Hebrews are H7149
1Sa 14:13 The **P** fell before Jonathan, and his NDT
1Sa 14:20 They found the **P** in total confusion, striking NDT
1Sa 14:21 been with the **P** and had gone up with H7149
1Sa 14:22 Ephraim heard that the **P** were on the run, H7149
1Sa 14:30 the slaughter of the **P** have been even H7149
1Sa 14:31 had struck down the **P** from Mikmash to H7149
1Sa 14:36 down and pursue the **P** by night and H7149
1Sa 14:37 “Shall I go down and pursue the **P**? H7149
1Sa 14:46 Then Saul stopped pursuing the **P**, and H7149
1Sa 14:47 the kings of Zobah, and the **P**. H7149
1Sa 14:52 of Saul there was bitter war with the **P**, H7149
1Sa 17: 1 Now the **P** gathered their forces for war H7149
1Sa 17: 2 drew up their battle line to meet the **P**. H7149
1Sa 17: 3 The **P** occupied one hill and the Israelites H7149
1Sa 17:19 the Valley of Elah, fighting against the **P**.” H7149
1Sa 17:21 Israel and the **P** were drawing up their H7149
1Sa 17:51 When the **P** saw that their hero was dead H7149
1Sa 17:52 pursued the **P** to the entrance of H7149
1Sa 17:53 the Israelites returned from chasing the **P**, H7149
1Sa 18:17 a hand against him. Let the **P** do that!” H7149
1Sa 18:21 the hand of the **P** may be against him.” H7149
1Sa 18:25 to have David fall by the hands of the **P**. H7149
1Sa 18:27 killed two hundred **P** and brought back H7149
1Sa 19: 8 and David went out and fought the **P**. H7149
1Sa 23: 1 the **P** are fighting against Keilah and are H7149
1Sa 23: 2 “Shall I go and attack these **P**? H7149
1Sa 23: 2 “Go, attack the **P** and save Keilah. H7149
1Sa 23: 4 I am going to give the **P** into your hand.” H7149
1Sa 23: 5 fought the **P** and carried off their livestock. H7149
1Sa 23: 5 heavy losses on **the P** and saved the H2157S
1Sa 23:27 The **P** are raiding the land. H7149
1Sa 23:28 pursuit of David and went to meet the **P**. H7149
1Sa 24: 1 After Saul returned from pursuing the **P** H7149
1Sa 27: 1 I can do is to escape to the land of the **P**. H7149
1Sa 28: 1 In those days the **P** gathered their forces H7149
1Sa 28: 4 The **P** assembled and came and set up H7149
1Sa 28:15 “The **P** are fighting against me, and God H7149
1Sa 28:19 Israel and you into the hands of the **P**, H7149
1Sa 28:19 the army of Israel into the hands of the **P**.” H7149
1Sa 29: 1 The **P** gathered all their forces at Aphek H7149
1Sa 29: 3 The commanders of the **P** asked, “What H7149
1Sa 29:11 morning to go back to the land of the **P**, H7149
1Sa 29:11 Philistines, and the **P** went up to Jezreel. H7149
1Sa 30:16 from the land of the **P** and from Judah. H7149
1Sa 31: 1 Now the **P** fought against Israel; the H7149
1Sa 31: 2 The **P** were in hot pursuit of Saul and his H7149
1Sa 31: 7 And the **P** came and occupied them H7149
1Sa 31: 8 when the **P** came to strip the dead H7149
1Sa 31: 9 the land of the **P** to proclaim the news in H7149
1Sa 31:11 heard what the **P** had done to Saul, H7149
2Sa 1:20 lest the daughters of the **P** be glad, lest H7149
2Sa 3:18 the hand of the **P** and from the hand of H7149
2Sa 5:17 When the **P** heard that David had been H7149
2Sa 5:18 Now the **P** had come and spread out in H7149
2Sa 5:19 of the LORD, “Shall I go and attack the **P**? H7149
2Sa 5:19 I will surely deliver the **P** into your hands.” H7149
2Sa 5:21 The **P** abandoned their idols there, and NDT
2Sa 5:22 Once more the **P** came up and spread out H7149
2Sa 5:25 he struck down the **P** all the way from H7149
2Sa 8: 1 David defeated the **P** and subdued them H7149
2Sa 8: 1 Metheg Ammah from the control of the **P**. H7149
2Sa 8:12 the Ammonites and the **P**, and Amalek. H7149
2Sa 19: 9 who rescued us from the hand of the **P**. H7149
2Sa 21:12 where the **P** had hung them after they H7149
2Sa 21:15 was a battle between the **P** and Israel. H7149
2Sa 21:15 down with his men to fight against the **P**, H7149
2Sa 21:18 there was another battle with the **P**, at H7149
2Sa 21:19 In another battle with the **P** at Gob H7149
2Sa 23: 9 when they taunted the **P** gathered at Pas H7149
2Sa 23:10 struck down the **P** till his hand grew H7149
2Sa 23:11 When the **P** banded together at a place H7149
2Sa 23:12 He defended it and struck the **P** down H7149
2Sa 23:13 while a band of **P** was encamped in the H7149
1Ki 4:21 the Euphrates River to the land of the **P**, H7149
2Ki 8: 2 stayed in the land of the **P** seven years. H7149
2Ki 8: 3 from the land of the **P** and went to appeal H7149
2Ki 18: 8 he defeated the **P**, as far as Gaza and H7149
1Ch 1:12 from whom the **P** came) and Caphtorites. H7149
1Ch 10: 1 Now the **P** fought against Israel; the H7149
1Ch 10: 2 The **P** were in hot pursuit of Saul and his H7149
1Ch 10: 7 And the **P** came and occupied them H7149
1Ch 10: 8 when the **P** came to strip the dead H7149
1Ch 10: 9 the land of the **P** to proclaim the news H7149
1Ch 10:11 heard what the **P** had done to Saul, H7149
1Ch 11:13 Dammim when the **P** gathered there for H7149
1Ch 11:13 full of barley, the troops fled from the **P**. H7149
1Ch 11:14 They defended it and struck the **P** down H7149
1Ch 11:15 while a band of **P** was encamped in the H7149
1Ch 12:19 he went with the **P** to fight against Saul H7149
1Ch 12:19 his men did not help the **P** because, H7149
1Ch 14: 8 When the **P** heard that David had been H7149
1Ch 14: 9 Now the **P** had come and raided the H7149
1Ch 14:10 “Shall I go and attack the **P**? Will you H7149
1Ch 14:12 The **P** had abandoned their gods there, and NDT
1Ch 14:13 Once more the **P** raided the valley; H7149
1Ch 18: 1 David defeated the **P** and subdued them H7149
1Ch 18: 1 villages from the control of the **P**. H7149
1Ch 18:11 the Ammonites and the **P**, and Amalek. H7149
1Ch 20: 4 war broke out with the **P**, at Gezer. H7149
1Ch 20: 4 the Rephaites, and the **P** were subjugated. NDT
1Ch 20: 5 In another battle with the **P**, Elhanan son H7149
2Ch 9:26 the Euphrates River to the land of the **P**, H7149
2Ch 17:11 Some **P** brought Jehoshaphat gifts and H7149
2Ch 21:16 the hostility of the **P** and of the Arabs who H7149
2Ch 26: 6 to war against the **P** and broke down the H7149
2Ch 26: 6 Ashdod and elsewhere among the **P**. H7149

2Ch 26: 7 him against the P and against the Arabs H7149
2Ch 28:18 while the P had raided towns in the H7149
Ps 56: T When the P had seized him in Gath H7149
Isa 2: 6 divination like the P and embrace pagan H7149
Isa 9:12 from the east and P from the west have H7149
Isa 14:29 Do not rejoice, all you P, that the rod that H7148
Isa 14:31 Melt away, all you P! A cloud of smoke H7148
Jer 25:20 all the kings of the P (those of H824+7149
Jer 47: 1 prophet concerning the P before Pharaoh H7149
Jer 47: 4 to destroy all the P and to remove all H7149
Jer 47: 4 The LORD is about to destroy the P, the H7149
Eze 16:27 the daughters of the P, who were shocked H7149
Eze 16:57 neighbors and the daughters of the P— H7149
Eze 25:15 'Because the P acted in vengeance and H7149
Eze 25:16 to stretch out my hand against the P, H7149
Am 1: 8 till the last of the P are dead," says the H7149
Am 9: 7 the P from Caphtor and the Arameans H7149
Ob 19 foothills will possess the land of the P. H7149
Zep 2: 5 is against you, Canaan, land of the P. H7149
Zec 9: 6 I will put an end to the pride of the P. H7149

PHILOLOGUS (1)
Ro 16:15 Greet P, Julia, Nereus and his sister, and G5807

PHILOSOPHER (1) [PHILOSOPHY]
1Co 1:20 Where is the p of this age? Has not G5186

PHILOSOPHERS (1) [PHILOSOPHY]
Ac 17:18 Epicurean and Stoic p began to debate G5815

PHILOSOPHY (1) [PHILOSOPHER, PHILOSOPHERS]
Col 2: 8 captive through hollow and deceptive p, G5814

PHINEHAS (25)
Ex 6:25 daughters of Putiel, and she bore him P. H7090
Nu 25: 7 When P son of Eleazar, the son of Aaron H7090
Nu 25:11 "P son of Eleazar, the son of Aaron, the H7090
Nu 31: 6 along with P son of Eleazar, the H7090
Jos 22:13 So the Israelites sent P son of Eleazar, the H7090
Jos 22:30 When P the priest and the leaders of the H7090
Jos 22:31 And P son of Eleazar, the priest, said to H7090
Jos 22:32 Then P son of Eleazar, the priest, and the H7090
Jos 24:33 allotted to his son P in the hill country of H7090
Jdg 20:28 with P son of Eleazar, the son of Aaron H7090
1Sa 1: 3 where Hophni and P, the two sons of Eli, H7090
1Sa 2:34 two sons, Hophni and P, will be a sign to H7090
1Sa 4: 4 Hophni and P, were there with the H7090
1Sa 4:11 Eli's two sons, Hophni and P, died. H7090
1Sa 4:17 your two sons, Hophni and P, are dead, H7090
1Sa 4:19 the wife of P, was pregnant and near the H7090
1Sa 14: 3 son of Ichabod's brother Ahitub son of P, H7090
1Ch 6: 4 Eleazar was the father of P, Phinehas the H7090
1Ch 6: 4 of Phinehas, P the father of Abishua H7090
1Ch 6:50 Eleazar his son, P his son, Abishua his H7090
1Ch 9:20 In earlier times P son of Eleazar was the H7090
Ezr 7: 5 Abishua, the son of P, the son of Eleazar, H7090
Ezr 8: 2 of the descendants of P, Gershom; of the H7090
Ezr 8:33 Eleazar son of P was with him, and so H7090
Ps 106:30 But P stood up and intervened, and the H7090

PHLEGON (1)
Ro 16:14 Greet Asyncritus, P, Hermes, Patrobas G5823

PHOEBE (1)
Ro 16: 1 I commend to you our sister P, a deacon G5833

PHOENICIA (5) [SYRIAN PHOENICIA]
Isa 23:11 an order concerning P that her fortresses H4046
Mk 7:26 a Greek, born in Syrian P. She begged G5355
Ac 11:19 Stephen was killed traveled as far as P, G5834
Ac 15: 3 as they traveled through P and Samaria, G5834
Ac 21: 2 We found a ship crossing over to P, went G5834

PHOENIX (1)
Ac 27:12 hoping to reach P and winter there. G5837

PHRYGIA (3)
Ac 2:10 P and Pamphylia, Egypt and the parts of G5867
Ac 16: 6 throughout the region of P and Galatia, G5867
Ac 18:23 throughout the region of Galatia and P, G5867

PHUT (KJV) PUT

PHYGELUS (1)
2Ti 1:15 including P and Hermogenes. G5869

PHYLACTERIES (1)
Mt 23: 5 They make their p wide and the tassels G5873

PHYSICAL (6) [PHYSICALLY]
Da 1: 4 young men without any p defect H4583
Ro 2:28 circumcision merely outward and p. G1877+4922
Ro 9: 8 the children by p descent who are God's G4922
Col 1:22 you by Christ's p body through death to G4922
1Ti 4: 8 For p training is of some value, but G5394
Jas 2:16 does nothing about their p needs G5393

PHYSICALLY (2) [PHYSICAL]
Ro 2:27 not circumcised p and yet obeys G1666+5882
1Co 5: 3 even though I am not p present, I am with G5393

PHYSICIAN (2) [PHYSICIANS]
Jer 8:22 Is there no p there? Why then is H8324
Lk 4:23 this proverb to me: 'P, heal yourself!' And G2620

PHYSICIANS (4) [PHYSICIAN]
Ge 50: 2 Joseph directed the p in his service to H8324
Ge 50: 2 his father Israel. So the p embalmed him, H8324
2Ch 16:12 help from the LORD, but only from the p. H8324
Job 13: 4 with lies; you are worthless p, all of you! H8324

PI HAHIROTH (4)
Ex 14: 2 to turn back and encamp near P, H7084
Ex 14: 9 they camped by the sea near P, H7084
Nu 33: 7 turned back to P, to the east of H7084
Nu 33: 8 They left P and passed through H7084

PICK (25) [PICKED, PICKERS, PICKS]
Lev 19:10 a second time or p up the grapes that H4377
Lev 27:33 No one may p out the good from the bad H1329
Dt 23:25 you may p kernels with your hands H7786
Ru 2: 2 to the fields and p up the leftover grain H4377
Ru 2:16 bundles and leave them for her to p up, H4377
1Ki 20:33 sign and were quick to p up his word. H2715
2Ki 5: 7 how he is trying to p a quarrel with me!" H628
2Ki 9:25 "P him up and throw him on the field that H5951
2Ki 9:26 p him up and throw him on that plot H5951
Ps 80:12 walls so that all who pass by p its grapes? H768
Isa 41:16 the wind will p them up, and a gale H5951
Jer 43:12 so he will p Egypt clean and depart. H6487
Eze 24: 5 take the p of the flock. Pile wood beneath H4436
Jnh 1:12 "P me up and throw me into the sea," H5951
Mt 7:16 Do people p grapes from thornbushes, or G5198
Mt 12: 1 hungry and began to p some heads of G5504
Mk 2:23 they began to p some heads of grain. G5504
Mk 8:19 many basketfuls of pieces did you p up?" G149
Mk 8:20 many basketfuls of pieces did you p up?" G149
Mk 16:18 they will p up snakes with their hands; and G149
Lk 6: 1 his disciples began to p some heads of G5504
Lk 6:44 People do not p figs from thornbushes, or G5198
Jn 5: 8 "Get up! P up your mat and walk." G149
Jn 5:11 well said to me, 'P up your mat and walk. G149
Jn 5:12 fellow who told you to p it up and walk?" G149

PICKED (24) [PICK]
Jdg 1: 7 toes cut off have p up scraps under my H4377
Jdg 4:21 p up a tent peg and a hammer and went H4374
1Sa 20:38 The boy p up the arrow and returned to H4377
2Sa 4: 4 His nurse p him up and fled, but as she H5951
1Ki 13:29 So the prophet p up the body of the man H5951
1Ki 17:23 Elijah p up the child and carried him down H4374
2Ki 2:13 Elisha then p up Elijah's cloak that had H8123
2Ki 2:16 of the LORD has p him up and set him H5951
2Ki 4:39 a wild vine and p as many of its gourds H4377
Eze 29: 5 open field and not be gathered or p up. H7695
Na 2: 5 Nineveh summons her p troops, yet they H129
Mt 14:20 the disciples p up twelve basketfuls of G149
Mt 15:37 the disciples p up seven basketfuls of G149
Mt 27: 6 The chief priests p up the coins and said G3284
Mk 6:43 the disciples p up twelve basketfuls of G149
Mk 8: 8 the disciples p up seven basketfuls of G149
Lk 9:17 the disciples p up twelve basketfuls of G149
Lk 14: 7 how the guests p the places of honor at G1721
Jn 5: 9 was cured; he p up his mat and walked. G149
Jn 8:59 they p up stones to stone him, but G149
Jn 10:31 Jewish opponents p up stones to stone G1002
Jn 15: 6 such branches are p up, thrown into the G5251
Ac 20: 9 from the third story and was p up dead. G149
Rev 18:21 a mighty angel p up a boulder the size G149

PICKERS (2) [PICK]
Jer 49: 9 If grape p came to you, would they not H1305
Ob 5 If grape p came to you, would they not H1305

PICKS (7) [PICK]
Lev 11:25 Whoever p up one of their carcasses must H5951
Lev 11:28 Anyone who p up their carcasses must H5951
Lev 11:40 Anyone who p up the carcass must wash H5951
Lev 15:10 whoever p up those things must wash H5951
2Sa 12:31 labor with saws and with iron p and axes, H3044
1Ch 20: 3 labor with saws and with iron p and axes. H3044
Jer 43:12 As a shepherd p his garment clean of lice, H6487

PIECE (41) [PIECES]
Ex 15:25 the LORD showed him a p of wood. H6770
Ex 25:19 the cherubim of one p with the cover, H4946
Ex 25:31 buds and blossoms of one p with them. H4946
Ex 25:36 shall all be of one p with the lampstand, AIT
Ex 27: 2 that the horns and the altar are of one p, H4946
Ex 28: 8 of one p with the ephod and made with H4946
Ex 30: 2 cubits high—its horns of one p with it. H4946
Ex 37: 8 he made them of one p with the cover. H4946
Ex 37:17 buds and blossoms of one p with them. H4946
Ex 37:22 were all of one p with the lampstand, H4946
Ex 37:25 cubits high—its horns of one p with it. H4946
Ex 38: 2 the horns and the altar were of one p. H4946
Ex 39: 5 of one p with the ephod and made with H4946
Lev 9:13 him the burnt offering p by piece, H4200+5984
Lev 9:13 him the burnt offering piece by p, H4200+5984
Jdg 16: 9 easily as a p of string snaps when H7348+5861
Jdg 20: 6 pieces and sent one p to each region of H2023S
Ru 4: 3 is selling the p of land that belonged to H2754
1Sa 2:36 before him for a p of silver and a loaf of H102
1Sa 9:23 "Bring the p of meat I gave you, the H4950
1Sa 24:11 look at this p of your robe in my hand! H4053
1Ki 7:24 cast in two rows in one p with the Sea. H3669
1Ki 17:11 "And bring me, please, a p of bread." H7326
2Ch 4: 3 cast in two rows in one p with the Sea. H4609
Job 2: 8 Job took a p of broken pottery and H3084
Job 33: 6 as you in God's sight; I too am a p of clay. H7975
Job 41:29 A club seems to it but a p of straw; it H7990
Job 42:11 one gave him a p of silver and a gold ring H7988
Pr 28:21 a person will do wrong for a p of bread. H7326
Eze 24: 6 Take the meat out p by piece in whatever H5984
Eze 24: 6 meat out piece by p in whatever order it H5984
Am 3:12 mouth only two leg bones or a p of an ear, H977
Am 3:12 of a bed and a p of fabric from a couch." H1967
Mk 2:21 the new p will pull away from the old G4445
Lk 5:36 "No one tears a p out of a new garment G2099
Lk 19:20 I have kept it laid away in a p of cloth. G5051
Lk 24:42 They gave him a p of broiled fish, G3538
Jn 13:26 I will give this p of bread when I have G6040
Jn 13:26 dipping the p of bread, he gave it to G6040
Jn 19:23 woven in one p from top to bottom. AIT
Ac 5: 1 wife Sapphira, also sold a p of property. G3228

PIECES (101) [PIECE]
Ge 15:17 appeared and passed between the p. H1617
Ge 33:19 For a hundred p of silver, he bought from H7988
Ge 37:33 Joseph has surely been torn to p." H3271+3271
Ge 44:28 "He has surely been torn to p." H3271+3271
Ex 22:13 If it was torn to p by a wild animal H3271+3271
Ex 23:24 and break their sacred stones to p. H8689+8689
Ex 28: 7 is to have two shoulder p attached to two H4190
Ex 28:12 them on the shoulder p of the ephod as H4190
Ex 28:25 them to the shoulder p of the ephod at H4190
Ex 28:27 bottom of the shoulder p on the front of H4190
Ex 29:17 Cut the ram into p and wash the internal H5984
Ex 29:17 them with the head and the other p. H5984
Ex 32:19 breaking them to p at the foot of the H8689
Ex 39: 4 They made shoulder p for the ephod H4190
Ex 39: 7 them on the shoulder p of the ephod as H4190
Ex 39:18 them to the shoulder p of the ephod at H4190
Ex 39:20 bottom of the shoulder p on the front of H4190
Lev 1: 6 to skin the burnt offering and cut it into p. H5984
Lev 1: 8 sons the priests shall arrange the p, H5984
Lev 1:12 You are to cut it into p, and the priest shall H5984
Lev 6:21 offering broken in p as an aroma pleasing H7326
Lev 8:20 He cut the ram into p and burned the H5984
Lev 8:20 burned the head, the p and the fat. H5984
Nu 24: 8 nations and break their bones in p; H1751
Dt 9:17 breaking them to p before your eyes. H8689
Jos 24:32 a hundred p of silver from the sons of H7988
Jdg 20: 6 cut her into p and sent one piece to each H5983
1Sa 11: 7 pair of oxen, cut them into p, and sent the H5983
1Sa 11: 7 sent the p by messengers throughout NDT
1Ki 11:30 he was wearing and tore it into twelve p. H7974
1Ki 11:31 Jeroboam, "Take ten p for yourself, for H7974
1Ki 18:23 and let them cut it into p and put it on the H5983
1Ki 18:33 cut the bull into p and laid it on the wood. H5983
2Ki 11:18 the altars and idols to p and killed Mattan H3512
2Ki 18: 4 He broke into p the bronze snake Moses H4198
2Ki 23:12 smashed them to p and threw the rubble H8368
2Ch 25:12 them down so that all were dashed to p. H1324
2Ch 28:24 the temple of God and cut them in p. H7915
2Ch 34: 4 he cut to p the incense altars that were H1548
2Ch 34: 4 These he broke to p and scattered over H1990
2Ch 34: 7 to powder and cut to p all the incense H1548
Job 4:20 dawn and dusk they are broken to p; H4198
Job 18: 4 You who tear yourself to p in your anger H3271
Job 26:12 the sea; by his wisdom he cut Rahab to p. H4730
Ps 2: 9 you will dash them to p like pottery." H5879
Ps 7: 2 like a lion and rip me to p with no one to H7293
Ps 29: 5 the LORD breaks in p the cedars of H8689
Ps 50:22 or I will tear you to p, with no one H3271
Ps 119:72 to me than thousands of p of silver and gold. AIT
Isa 13:16 infants will be dashed to p before their H8187
Isa 24:12 in ruins, its gate is battered to p. H4198+8625
Isa 27: 9 stones to be like limestone crushed to p, H5879
Isa 30:14 It will break in p like pottery, shattered so H8691
Isa 30:14 that among its p not a fragment will be H4845
Isa 51: 9 Was it not you who cut Rahab to p, who H2933
Jer 5: 6 their towns to tear to p any who venture H3271
Jer 23:29 like a hammer that breaks a rock in p? H7207
Jer 34:18 cut in two and then walked between its p. H1440
Jer 34:19 who walked between the p of the calf, H1440
Eze 16:40 stone you and hack you to p with their H1438
Eze 23:34 it and drain it dry and chew on its p— H3084
Eze 24: 4 Put into it the p of meat, all the choice H5984
Eze 24: 4 of meat, all the choice p—the leg and the H5984
Eze 27:26 the east wind will break you to p far out at H8689
Da 2: 5 have you cut into p and your houses A10197
Da 2:35 the gold were all broken to p and A10182
Da 2:40 as iron breaks things to p, so it will A10671
Da 2:45 that broke the iron, the bronze, the clay, the silver and the gold to p A10182
Da 3:29 be cut into p and their houses be A10197
Hos 5:14 I will tear them to p and go away; I will H3271
Hos 6: 1 He has torn us to p but he will heal us; he H3271
Hos 6: 5 Therefore I cut you in p with my prophets H2933
Hos 8: 6 It will be broken in p, that calf of H8646
Am 6:11 great house into p and the small house H8269
Mic 1: 7 All her idols will be broken to p; all her H4198
Mic 3: 3 off their skin and break their bones in p; H7200
Mic 4:13 and you will break to p many nations." H1990
Na 3:10 Her infants were dashed to p at every H8187
Zec 11:12 So they paid me thirty p of silver. AIT
Zec 11:13 So I took the thirty p of silver and threw them AIT
Mt 7: 6 their feet, and turn and tear you to p. G4838

Mt 14:20 basketfuls of broken p that were left G3083
Mt 15:37 seven basketfuls of broken p that were left G3083
Mt 21:44 falls on this stone will be broken to p; G5314
Mt 24:51 He will cut him to p and assign him a G1497
Mt 26:15 they counted out for him thirty p of silver. G736
Mt 27: 3 returned the thirty p of silver to the chief G736
Mt 27: 9 "They took the thirty p of silver, the price G736
Mk 6:43 basketfuls of broken p of bread and G3083
Mk 8: 8 seven basketfuls of broken p that were left G3083
Mk 8:19 how many basketfuls of p did you pick up?" G3083
Mk 8:20 how many basketfuls of p did you pick up?" G3083
Lk 9:17 basketfuls of broken p that were left G3083
Lk 12:46 He will cut him to p and assign him a G1497
Lk 20:18 falls on that stone will be broken to p; G5314
Jn 6:12 disciples, "Gather the p that are left over. G3083
Jn 6:13 twelve baskets with the p of the five G3083
Ac 23:10 afraid Paul would be torn to p by them. G1400
Ac 27:41 the stern was broken to p by the G3395
Ac 27:44 there on planks or on other p of the ship. G3836S
Rev 2:27 scepter and will dash them to p like G5341

PIERCE (10) [PIERCED, PIERCES, PIERCING]

Ex 21: 6 the doorpost and p his ear with an awl. H8361
Nu 24: 8 in pieces; with their arrows they p them. H4730
Job 40:24 it by the eyes, or trap it and p its nose? H5918
Job 41: 2 through its nose or p its jaw with a hook? H5918
Ps 22:16 they p my hands and my feet. H4125
Ps 37:15 But their swords will p their own H995+928
Ps 45: 5 Let your sharp arrows p the hearts of the H928
Pr 12:18 The words of the reckless p like swords H4532
Eze 28: 7 wisdom and p your shining splendor H2726
Lk 2:35 And a sword will p your own soul too." G1451

PIERCED (14) [PIERCE]

Jdg 5:26 his head, she shattered and p his temple. H2737
2Ki 9:24 The arrow p his heart and he slumped H3655
Job 26:13 his hand p the gliding serpent. H2726
Ps 38: 2 Your arrows have p me, and your H5737+928
Isa 14:19 the slain, with those p by the sword, those H3249
Isa 51: 9 to pieces, who p that monster through? H2726
Isa 53: 5 But he was p for our transgressions, he H2726
La 3:13 He p my heart with arrows from his H995+928
Hab 3:14 his own spear you p his head when his H5918
Zec 12:10 the one they have p, and they will H1991
Jn 19:34 one of the soldiers p Jesus' side with a G3817
Jn 19:37 "They will look on the one they have p." G1708
1Ti 6:10 from the faith and p themselves with G4345
Rev 1: 7 see him, even those who p him"; and all G1708

PIERCES (7) [PIERCE]

2Ki 18:21 which p the hand of H5918+2256+995+928
Job 16:13 he p my kidneys and spills my gall on the H7114
Job 20:24 weapon, a bronze-tipped arrow p him. H2737
Job 30:17 Night p my bones; my gnawing pains H5941
Pr 7:23 till an arrow p his liver, like a bird darting H7114
Isa 36: 6 which p the hand of H5918+2256+995+928
Jer 4:18 How bitter it is! How it p to the heart!" H5595

PIERCING (1) [PIERCE]

Job 16: 9 my opponent fastens on me his p eyes. H4323

PIETY (3)

Job 4: 6 Should not your p be your confidence H3711
Job 15: 4 you even undermine p and hinder H3711
Job 22: 4 "Is it for your p that he rebukes you and H3711

PIG (2) [PIG'S, PIGS]

Lev 11: 7 And the p, though it has a divided hoof H2614
Dt 14: 8 The p is also unclean; although it has a H2614

PIG'S (2) [PIG]

Pr 11:22 Like a gold ring in a p snout is a beautiful H2614
Isa 66: 3 offering is like one who presents p blood, H2614

PIGEON (3) [PIGEONS]

Ge 15: 9 along with a dove and a young p. H1578
Lev 1:14 you are to offer a dove or a young p. H3433
Lev 12: 6 offering and a young p or a dove for a sin H3433

PIGEONS (9) [PIGEON]

Lev 5: 7 two doves or two young p to the LORD as a H3433
Lev 5:11 cannot afford two doves or two young p, H3433
Lev 12: 8 she is to bring two doves or two young p H3433
Lev 14:22 two doves or two young p, such as H3433
Lev 14:30 shall sacrifice the doves or the young p, H3433
Lev 15:14 doves or two young p and come before H3433
Lev 15:29 doves or two young p and bring them to H3433
Nu 6:10 doves or two young p to the priest at the H3433
Lk 2:24 "a pair of doves or two young p." G4361

PIGS (18) [PIG]

Isa 65: 4 who eat the flesh of p, and whose pots H2614
Isa 66:17 is among those who eat the flesh of p, H2614
Mt 7: 6 is sacred; do not throw your pearls to p. G5956
Mt 8:30 from them a large herd of p was feeding. G5956
Mt 8:31 drive us out, send us into the herd of p." G5956
Mt 8:32 So they came out and went into the p G5956
Mt 8:33 Those tending the p ran off, went into the NDT
Mk 5:11 A large herd of p was feeding on the G5956
Mk 5:12 "Send us among the p; allow us to go G5956
Mk 5:13 spirits came out and went into the p. G5956
Mk 5:14 Those tending the p ran off and reported G899S
Mk 5:16 and told about the p as well. G5956
Lk 8:32 A large herd of p was feeding there on G5956
Lk 8:32 begged Jesus to let them go into the p, G1697S
Lk 8:33 they went into the p, and the herd rushed G5956
Lk 8:34 those tending the p saw what had NDT
Lk 15:15 who sent him to his fields to feed p. G5956
Lk 15:16 with the pods that the p were eating, G5956

PILATE (61) [PILATE'S]

Mt 27: 2 handed him over to P the governor. G4397
Mt 27:13 Then P asked him, "Don't you hear the G4397
Mt 27:17 had gathered, P asked them, "Which G4397
Mt 27:19 While P was sitting on the judge's seat G899S
Mt 27:22 is called the Messiah?" P asked. They all G4397
Mt 27:23 asked P. But they shouted G3836S
Mt 27:24 When P saw that he was getting nowhere, G4397
Mt 27:58 Going to P, he asked for Jesus' body, and G4397
Mt 27:58 P ordered that it be given to him. G4397
Mt 27:62 chief priests and the Pharisees went to P. G4397
Mt 27:65 "Take a guard," P answered. "Go, make G4397
Mk 15: 1 led him away and handed him over to P. G4397
Mk 15: 2 asked P. "You have said so, G4397
Mk 15: 4 So again P asked him, "Aren't you going G4397
Mk 15: 5 still made no reply, and P was amazed. G4397
Mk 15: 8 came up and asked P to do for them what NDT
Mk 15: 9 to you the king of the Jews?" asked P, G4397
Mk 15:11 up the crowd to have P release Barabbas NDT
Mk 15:12 call the king of the Jews?" P asked them. G4397
Mk 15:14 he committed?" asked P. But they shouted G4397
Mk 15:15 the crowd, P released Barabbas to them. G4397
Mk 15:43 went boldly to P and asked for Jesus' G4397
Mk 15:44 P was surprised to hear that he was G4397
Lk 3: 1 when Pontius P was governor of Judea G4397
Lk 13: 1 whose blood P had mixed with their G4397
Lk 23: 1 whole assembly rose and led him off to P. G4397
Lk 23: 3 So P asked Jesus, "Are you the king of the G4397
Lk 23: 4 Then P announced to the chief priests G4397
Lk 23: 6 P asked if the man was a Galilean. G4397
Lk 23:11 an elegant robe, they sent him back to P. G4397
Lk 23:12 That day Herod and P became friends G4397
Lk 23:13 P called together the chief priests, the G4397
Lk 23:20 release Jesus, P appealed to them again. G4397
Lk 23:24 So P decided to grant their demand. G4397
Lk 23:52 Going to P, he asked for Jesus' body. G4397
Jn 18:29 So P came out to them and asked, "What G4397
Jn 18:31 P said, "Take him yourselves and judge G4397
Jn 18:33 P then went back inside the palace G4397
Jn 18:35 P replied. "Your own G4397
Jn 18:37 said P. Jesus answered G4397
Jn 18:38 retorted P. With this he went out G4397
Jn 19: 1 Then P took Jesus and had him flogged. G4397
Jn 19: 4 Once more P came out and said to the G4397
Jn 19: 5 the purple robe, P said to them, "Here NDT
Jn 19: 6 But P answered, "You take him and G4397
Jn 19: 8 When P heard this, he was even more G4397
Jn 19:10 refuse to speak to me?" P said. "Don't you G4397
Jn 19:12 From then on, P tried to set Jesus free, but G4397
Jn 19:13 When P heard this, he brought Jesus out G4397
Jn 19:14 "Here is your king," P said to the Jews. NDT
Jn 19:15 I crucify your king?" P asked. "We have no G4397
Jn 19:16 Finally P handed him over to them to be NDT
Jn 19:19 P had a notice prepared and fastened to G4397
Jn 19:21 chief priests of the Jews protested to P, G4397
Jn 19:22 P answered, "What I have written, I have G4397
Jn 19:31 they asked P to have the legs broken and G4397
Jn 19:38 of Arimathea asked P for the body of G4397
Ac 3:13 you disowned him before P, though G4397
Ac 4:27 Herod and Pontius P met together with G4397
Ac 13:28 they asked P to have him executed. G4397
1Ti 6:13 before Pontius P made the good G4397

PILATE'S (1) [PILATE]

Jn 19:38 With P permission, he came and took the G4397

PILDASH (1)

Ge 22:22 Hazo, P, Jidlaph and Bethuel." H7109

PILE (11) [PILED, PILES]

Lev 26:30 incense altars and p your dead bodies on H5989
Jos 7:26 Achan they heaped up a large p of rocks, H1643
Jos 8:29 And they raised a large p of rocks over it H1643
Ru 3: 7 to lie down at the far end of the grain p. H6894
Ezr 6:11 their house is to be made a p of rubble. A10470
Job 8:17 roots around a p of rocks and looks for a H1643
Jer 50:26 granaries; p her up like heaps of grain. H6148
Eze 24: 5 P wood beneath it for the bones; bring it H1883
Eze 24: 9 I, too, will p the wood high. H1540
Lk 14:35 neither for the soil nor for the manure p; G3161
Ac 28: 3 Paul gathered a p of brushwood and, as G4436

PILED (8) [PILE]

Ge 31:46 So they took stones and p them in a heap, H6913
Ex 8:14 They were p into heaps, and the land H7392
Ex 15: 8 the blast of your nostrils the waters p up. H6890
Jos 3:16 It p up in a heap a great distance away H7756
Jdg 9:49 They p them against the stronghold and H8492
2Sa 18:17 pit in the forest and p up a large heap of H5893
2Ch 31: 6 LORD their God, and they p them in heaps. H5989
Rev 18: 5 her sins are p up to heaven, and God G3140

PILES (9) [PILE]

2Ki 10: 8 "Put them in two p at the entrance of the H7393
2Ki 19:25 fortified cities into p of stone. H1643+5898
Job 27:16 silver like dust and clothes like p of clay, H3922
Isa 37:26 fortified cities into p of stone. H1643+5898
Da 2: 5 your houses turned into p of rubble. A10470
Da 3:29 their houses be turned into p of rubble, A10470
Hos 12:11 will be like p of stones on a plowed field. H1643
Na 3: 3 Many casualties, p of dead, bodies H3880
Hab 2: 6 " 'Woe to him who p up stolen goods H8049

PILGRIMAGE (3)

Ge 47: 9 "The years of my p are a hundred and H4472
Ge 47: 9 not equal the years of the p of my fathers." H4472
Ps 84: 5 is in you, whose hearts are set on p. H5019

PILGRIMS (KJV) EXILES, STRANGERS

PILHA (1)

Ne 10:24 Hallohesh, P, Shobek, H7116

PILLAGE (2) [PILLAGED]

Ezr 9: 7 to p and humiliation at the hand of H1023
Jer 50:11 are glad, you who p my inheritance H9115

PILLAGED (2) [PILLAGE]

Ob 6 will be ransacked, his hidden treasures p! H1239
Na 2:10 She is p, plundered, stripped! Hearts melt, H1011

PILLAR (45) [PILLARS]

Ge 19:26 looked back, and she became a p of salt. H5907
Ge 28:18 set it up as a p and poured oil on top H5167
Ge 28:22 I have set up as a p will be God's house, H5167
Ge 31:13 you anointed a p and where you made a H5167
Ge 31:45 So Jacob took a stone and set it up as a p. H5167
Ge 31:51 here is this p I have set up between H5167
Ge 31:52 is a witness, and this p is a witness, that I H5167
Ge 31:52 past this heap and p to my side to harm H5167
Ge 35:14 Jacob set up a stone p at the place where H5167
Ge 35:20 Over her tomb Jacob set up a p, and to H5167
Ge 35:20 to this day that p marks Rachel's tomb. H5167
Ex 13:21 ahead of them in a p of cloud to guide H6647
Ex 13:21 by night in a p of fire to give them H6647
Ex 13:22 Neither the p of cloud by day nor the pillar H6647
Ex 13:22 cloud by day nor the p of fire by night left H6647
Ex 14:19 The p of cloud also moved from in front H6647
Ex 14:24 down from the p of fire and cloud at H6647
Ex 33: 9 the p of cloud would come down and stay H6647
Ex 33:10 the people saw the p of cloud standing at H6647
Nu 12: 5 Then the LORD came down in a p of cloud H6647
Nu 14:14 before them in a p of cloud by day and a H6647
Nu 14:14 of cloud by day and a p of fire by night. H6647
Dt 31:15 LORD appeared at the tent in a p of cloud, H6647
Jdg 9: 6 great tree at the p in Shechem to crown H5164
2Sa 18:18 Absalom had taken a p and erected it in H5170
2Sa 18:18 He named the p after himself, and it is H5170
1Ki 7:21 The p to the south he named Jakin and H6647
2Ki 11:14 standing by the p, as the custom was. H6647
2Ki 23: 3 The king stood by the p and renewed the H6647
2Ki 25:17 Each p was eighteen cubits high. H6647
2Ki 25:17 on top of one p was three cubits high H2257S
2Ki 25:17 The other p, with its network H6647
2Ch 23:13 standing by his p at the entrance. H6647
2Ch 34:31 The king stood by his p and renewed the H6642
Ne 9:12 By day you led them with a p of cloud H6647
Ne 9:12 by night with a p of fire to give them H6647
Ne 9:19 By day the p of cloud did not fail to guide H6647
Ne 9:19 the p of fire by night to shine on the H6647
Ps 99: 7 He spoke to them from the p of cloud H6647
Jer 1:18 an iron p and a bronze wall to stand H6647
Jer 52:21 Each p was eighteen cubits high and H6647
Jer 52:22 on top of one p was five cubits high H2257S
Jer 52:22 The other p, with its pomegranates, was H6647
1Ti 3:15 the p and foundation of the truth. G5146
Rev 3:12 I will make a p in the temple of my God. G5146

PILLARS (44) [PILLAR]

Ex 24: 4 set up twelve stone p representing the H5167
Jdg 16:25 When they stood him among the p, H6647
Jdg 16:26 where I can feel the p that support the H6647
Jdg 16:29 the two central p on which the temple H6647
1Ki 7: 6 front of that were p and an overhanging H6647
1Ki 7:15 He cast two bronze p, each eighteen H6647
1Ki 7:16 of cast bronze to set on the tops of the p; H6647
1Ki 7:17 adorned the capitals on top of the p, H6647
1Ki 7:18 to decorate the capitals on top of the p. H6647
1Ki 7:19 on top of the p in the portico were in H6647
1Ki 7:20 On the capitals of both p, above the H6647
1Ki 7:21 He erected the p at the portico of the H6647
1Ki 7:22 And so the work on the p was completed. H6647
1Ki 7:41 the two p; the two bowl-shaped capitals H6647
1Ki 7:41 two bowl-shaped capitals on top of the p; H6647
1Ki 7:41 two bowl-shaped capitals on top of the p; H6647
1Ki 7:42 the bowl-shaped capitals on top of the p); H6647
2Ki 25:13 The Babylonians broke up the bronze p H6647
2Ki 25:16 The bronze from the two p, the Sea and H6647
1Ch 18: 8 the p and various bronze articles. H6647
2Ch 3:15 For the front of the temple he made two p, H6647
2Ch 3:16 chains and put them on top of the p. H6647
2Ch 3:17 He erected the p in the front of the temple, H6647
2Ch 4:12 the two p; the two bowl-shaped capitals H6647
2Ch 4:12 two bowl-shaped capitals on top of the p; H6647
2Ch 4:12 two bowl-shaped capitals on top of the p; H6647
2Ch 4:13 the bowl-shaped capitals on top of the p); H6647
Est 1: 6 material to silver rings on marble p. H6647
Job 9: 6 from its place and makes its p tremble. H6647
Job 26:11 The p of the heavens quake, aghast at his H6647

P

Ps 75: 3 people quake, it is I who hold its **p** firm. H6647
Ps 144:12 daughters will be like **p** carved to adorn a H2312
Pr 9: 1 her house; she has set up its seven **p**. H6647
SS 5:15 His legs are **p** *of* marble set on bases of H6647
Jer 27:19 what the LORD Almighty says about the **p**, H6647
Jer 43:13 will demolish the **sacred p** and will burn H5167
Jer 52:17 The Babylonians broke up the bronze **p** H6647
Jer 52:20 The bronze from the two **p**, the Sea and H6647
Eze 26:11 your strong **p** will fall to the ground. H5167
Eze 40:49 there were **p** on each side of the H6647
Eze 42: 6 The rooms on the top floor had no **p**, as H6647
Am 9: 1 "Strike the **tops of the p** so that the H4117
Gal 2: 9 those esteemed as **p**, gave me and *G5146*
Rev 10: 1 like the sun, and his legs were like fiery **p**. *G5146*

PILOT (2)
Ac 27:11 the advice *of* the **p** and of the owner *G3237*
Jas 3: 4 small rudder wherever the **p** wants to go. *G3995*

PILTAI (1)
Ne 12:17 of Miniamin's and of Moadiah's, **P**; H7122

PIN (6)
Jdg 16:13 on the loom and tighten it with the **p**, H3845
Jdg 16:14 tightened it with the **p**. Again she H3845
Jdg 16:14 sleep and pulled up the **p** and the loom, H3845
1Sa 18:11 saying to himself, "*I'll* **p** David to the wall." H5782
1Sa 19:10 Saul tried to **p** him to the wall with his H5782
1Sa 26: 8 Now *let me* **p** him to the ground with one H5782

PINE (2) [PINES]
Isa 19: 8 who throw nets on the water *will* **p away**. H581
Isa 44:14 or planted a **p**, and the rain made it H815

PINES (1) [PINE]
1Sa 2: 5 she who has had many sons **p away**. H581

PINON (2)
Ge 36:41 Oholibamah, Elah, **P**, H7091
1Ch 1:52 Oholibamah, Elah, **P**, H7091

PINS (KJV) TENT PEGS

PINT (1)
Jn 12: 3 Then Mary took **about a p** of pure nard, an *G3354*

PIONEER (2)
Heb 2:10 should make the **p** of their salvation perfect *G795*
Heb 12: 2 eyes on Jesus, the **p** and perfecter of faith. *G795*

PIPE (11) [PIPERS, PIPES]
Job 21:12 they make merry to the sound of the **p**. H6385
Job 30:31 my **p** to the sound of wailing. H6385
Ps 150: 4 praise him with the strings and **p**, H6385
Jer 48:36 laments for Moab like the *music of* a **p**; H2720
Jer 48:36 it laments like a **p** for the people of Kir H2720
Da 3: 5 **p** and all kinds of music, you must A10507
Da 3:10 **p** and all kinds of music must fall down A10507
Da 3:15 **p** and all kinds of music, if you are A10507
Mt 11:17 " '*We* **played the p** for you, and you did not *G884*
Lk 7:32 " '*We* **played the p** for you, and you did not *G884*
1Co 14: 7 such as the **p** or harp, how will *G888*

PIPERS (1) [PIPE]
Rev 18:22 musicians, **p** and trumpeters, will *G886*

PIPES (8) [PIPE]
Ge 4:21 all who play stringed instruments and **p**. H6385
1Sa 10: 5 **p** and harps being played before them H2720
1Ki 1:40 after him, playing **p** and rejoicing greatly H2720
Ps 5: T director of music. For **p**. A psalm of David. H5704
Isa 5:12 their banquets, **p** and timbrels and wine H2720
Isa 30:29 when people playing **p** go up to the H2720
Zec 4:12 beside the two gold **p** that pour out H7574
Mt 9:23 saw the noisy crowd and **people playing p**, *G886*

PIRAM (1)
Jos 10: 3 Hoham king of Hebron, **P** king of Jarmuth H7231

PIRATHON (2) [PIRATHONITE]
Jdg 12:13 Abdon son of Hillel, **from P**, led Israel. H7285
Jdg 12:15 died and was buried at **P** in Ephraim, H7284

PIRATHONITE (3) [PIRATHON]
2Sa 23:30 Benaiah the **P**, Hiddai from the ravines of H7285
1Ch 11:31 from Gibeah in Benjamin, Benaiah the **P**, H7285
1Ch 27:14 was Benaiah the **P**, an Ephraimite. H7285

PISGAH (8)
Nu 21:20 Moab where the top of **P** overlooks the H7171
Nu 23:14 to the field of Zophim on the top of **P**, H7171
Dt 3:17 the Dead Sea), below the slopes of **P**. H7171
Dt 3:27 Go up to the top of **P** and look west and H7171
Dt 4:49 as the Dead Sea, below the slopes of **P**. H7171
Dt 34: 1 from the plains of Moab to the top of **P**, H7171
Jos 12: 3 then southward below the slopes of **P**. H7171
Jos 13:20 the slopes of **P**, and Beth Jeshimoth H7171

PISHON (1)
Ge 2:11 The name of the first is the **P**; it winds H7093

PISIDIA (1)
Ac 14:24 After going through **P**, they came into *G4407*

PISIDIAN (1)
Ac 13:14 From Perga they went on to **P** Antioch. *G4408*

PISPAH (1)
1Ch 7:38 sons of Jether: Jephunneh, **P** and Ara. H7183

PISS (KJV) URINE

PISSETH (KJV) MALE

PISTACHIO (1)
Ge 43:11 myrrh, *some* **p nuts** and almonds. H1063

PIT (66) [PITS]
Ex 21:33 anyone uncovers a **p** or digs one and fails H1014
Ex 21:34 who opened the **p** must pay the owner H1014
2Sa 18:17 threw him into a big **p** in the forest and H7074
2Sa 23:20 went down into a **p** on a snowy day and H1014
1Ch 11:22 went down into a **p** on a snowy day and H1014
Job 9:31 plunge me into a **slime p** so that even my H8846
Job 33:18 to preserve them from the **p**, their lives H8846
Job 33:22 They draw near to the **p**, and their life to H8846
Job 33:24 'Spare them from going down to the **p**; H8846
Job 33:28 delivered me from going down to the **p**, H8846
Job 33:30 to turn them back from the **p**, that the H8846
Ps 7:15 it out falls into the **p** they have made. H8846
Ps 9:15 have fallen into the **p** they have dug; H8846
Ps 28: 1 I will be like those who go down to the **p**. H1014
Ps 30: 3 you spared me from going down to the **p**. H1014
Ps 30: 9 if I am silenced, if I go down to the **p**? H8846
Ps 35: 7 cause and without cause dug a **p** for me, H8846
Ps 35: 8 may they fall into **the p**, to their ruin. H2023S
Ps 40: 2 He lifted me out of the **slimy p**, out H1014+8622
Ps 55:23 bring down the wicked into the **p** *of* decay; H931
Ps 57: 6 They dug a **p** in my path—but they have H8864
Ps 69:15 me up or the **p** close its mouth over H931
Ps 88: 4 among those who go down to the **p**; H1014
Ps 88: 6 You have put me in the lowest **p**, in the H1014
Ps 94:13 of trouble, till a **p** is dug for the wicked. H8846
Ps 103: 4 your life from the **p** and crowns you with H8846
Ps 143: 7 I will be like those who go down to the **p**. H1014
Pr 1:12 like those who go down to the **p**; H1014
Pr 22:14 of an adulterous woman is a deep **p**; H8757
Pr 23:27 an adulterous woman is a deep **p**, and H8757
Pr 26:27 Whoever digs a **p** will fall into it; if H8846
Pr 28:18 ways are perverse will fall into the **p**. H8846
Ecc 10: 8 Whoever digs a **p** may fall into it H1585
Isa 14:15 realm of the dead, to the depths of the **p**. H1014
Isa 14:19 those who descend to the stones of the **p**. H1014
Isa 24:17 Terror and **p** and snare await you, people H7074
Isa 24:18 at the sound of terror will fall into a **p**; H7074
Isa 24:18 climbs out of the **p** will be caught in a H7074
Isa 30:33 Its **fire p** has been made deep and wide H4509
Isa 38:17 you kept me from the **p** *of* destruction; H8846
Isa 38:18 who go down to the **p** cannot hope for H1014
Jer 18:20 Yet they have dug a **p** for me. Remember H8757
Jer 18:22 they have dug a **p** to capture me and H8757
Jer 48:43 Terror and **p** and snare await you, you H7074
Jer 48:44 flees from the terror will fall into a **p**, H7074
Jer 48:44 climbs out of the **p** will be caught in a H7074
La 3:53 to end my life in a **p** and threw stones at H1014
La 3:55 your name, LORD, from the depths of the **p**. H1014
Eze 19: 4 about him, and he was trapped in their **p**. H8846
Eze 19: 8 him, and he was trapped in their **p**. H8846
Eze 26:20 down with those who go down to the **p**, H1014
Eze 26:20 with those who go down to the **p**, and you H1014
Eze 28: 8 They will bring you down to the **p**, and H8846
Eze 31:16 to be with those who go down to the **p**. H1014
Eze 32:18 along with those who go down to the **p**. H1014
Eze 32:23 in the depths of the **p** and her army lies H1014
Eze 32:24 shame with those who go down to the **p**. H1014
Eze 32:25 shame with those who go down to the **p**; H1014
Eze 32:29 with those who go down to the **p**. H1014
Eze 32:30 shame with those who go down to the **p**. H1014
Jnh 2: 6 my God, brought my life up from the **p**. H8846
Zec 9:11 free your prisoners from the waterless **p**. H1014
Mt 12:11 it falls into a **p** on the Sabbath, *G1073*
Mt 15:14 lead the blind, both will fall into a **p**." *G1073*
Mk 12: 1 dug a **p for the winepress** and built a *G5700*
Lk 6:39 Will they not both fall into a **p**? *G1073*

PITCH (11) [PITCHED]
Ge 6:14 in it and coat it with **p** inside and out. H4109
Ex 2: 3 him and coated it with tar and **p**. H2413
Ex 33: 7 to take a tent and **p** it outside the camp H5742
Pr 20:20 will be snuffed out in **p darkness**. H854+3125
Isa 13:20 there no nomads *will* **p** *their* **tents**, there no H182
Isa 34: 9 Edom's streams will be turned into **p**, her H2413
Isa 34: 9 her land will become blazing **p**! H2413
Jer 6: 3 *they will* **p** their tents around her H9546
Jer 10:20 no one is left now *to* **p** my tent or to set H5742
Eze 25: 4 up their camps and **p** their tents among H5989
Da 11:45 *He will* **p** his royal tents between the seas H5749

PITCH-DARK (1) [DARK]
Am 5:20 be darkness, not light—**p**, without a ray of H695

PITCHED (16) [PITCH]
Ge 12: 8 the hills east of Bethel and **p** his tent, H5742
Ge 13:12 of the plain and **p** *his* **tents** near Sodom. H182
Ge 13:18 of Mamre at Hebron, where *he* **p** *his* **tents**. H182
Ge 26:25 There *he* **p** his tent, and there his servants H5742
Ge 31:25 Jacob *had* **p** his tent in the hill country of H9546
Ge 33:19 the plot of ground where *he* **p** his tent. H5742
Ge 35:21 moved on again and **p** his tent beyond H5742
Jdg 4:11 **p** his tent by the great tree in H5742
Jdg 20:19 got up and **p camp** near Gibeah. H2837
1Sa 17: 1 *They* **p camp** at Ephes Dammim, between H2837
2Sa 6:17 inside the tent that David *had* **p** for it, H5742
2Sa 16:22 So *they* **p** a tent for Absalom on the roof H5742
1Ch 15: 1 place for the ark of God and **p** a tent for it. H5742
1Ch 16: 1 it inside the tent that David *had* **p** for it, H5742
2Ch 1: 4 because *he had* **p** a tent for it in H5742
Ps 19: 4 In the heavens God *has* **p** a tent for the H8492

PITCHER (1) [PITCHERS]
Ecc 12: 6 before the **p** is shattered at the spring H3902

PITCHERS (6) [PITCHER]
Ex 25:29 as well as its **p** and bowls for the pouring H7987
Ex 37:16 bowls and its **p** for the pouring out of H7987
1Ch 28:17 sprinkling bowls and **p**; the weight of gold H7987
Jer 48:12 "when I will send men who pour from **p** NDT
Jer 48:12 they will empty her **p** and smash her jars. H3998
Mk 7: 4 as the washing of cups, **p** and kettles. *G3829*

PITFALLS (2)
Pr 22: 5 the paths of the wicked are snares and **p**, H7062
La 3:47 We have suffered terror and **p**, ruin and H7074

PITHOM (1)
Ex 1:11 they built **P** and Rameses as store H7351

PITHON (2)
1Ch 8:35 The sons of Micah: **P**, Melek, Tarea and H7094
1Ch 9:41 The sons of Micah: **P**, Melek, Tahrea and H7094

PITIED (1) [PITY]
1Co 15:19 we are of all people **most to be p**. *G1795*

PITIFUL (1) [PITY]
Rev 3:17 not realize that you are wretched, **p**, poor, *G1795*

PITS (6) [PIT]
Ge 14:10 the Valley of Siddim was **full of** tar **p**, H931+931
1Sa 13: 6 among the rocks, and in **p** and cisterns. H7663
Ps 119:85 The arrogant dig **p** to trap me, contrary to H8864
Ps 140:10 into the fire, into **miry p**, never to rise. H4549
Isa 42:22 of them trapped in **p** or hidden away in H2987
Zep 2: 9 a place of weeds and salt **p**, a wasteland H4838

PITTANCE (1)
Ps 44:12 You sold your people for a **p** H4202+2104

PITY (43) [PITIED, PITIFUL]
Dt 7:16 *Do* not **look** on them **with p** and do H2571+6524
Dt 13: 8 **Show** them no **p**. Do not H2571+6524
Dt 19:13 **Show** no **p**. You must purge from H6524+2571
Dt 19:21 **Show** no **p**: life for life, eye for eye H6524+2571
Dt 25:12 cut off her hand. **Show** her no **p**. H2571+6524
Dt 28:50 respect for the old or **p** *for* the young. H2858
2Sa 12: 6 he did such a thing and **had** no **p**. H2798
2Ch 36:15 because *he* **had p** on his people and on H2798
Job 16:13 Without **p**, he pierces my kidneys and H2798
Job 19:21 "**Have p** *on* me, my friends, have pity, for H2858
Job 19:21 my friends, **have p**, for the hand of God H2858
Ps 72:13 *He will* **take p** on the weak and the needy H2571
Ps 102:14 servants; her very dust **moves** *them* **to p**. H2858
Ps 109:12 kindness to him or **take p** on his fatherless H2858
Ecc 4:10 But **p** anyone who falls and has no one to H365
Isa 9:17 nor *will he* **p** the fatherless and widows H8163
Jer 13:14 *I will* **allow** no **p** or mercy or compassion H2798
Jer 15: 5 "Who *will* **have p** on you, Jerusalem H2798
Jer 16: 5 my love and my **p** from this people," H8171
Jer 20:16 the towns the LORD overthrew without **p**. H5714
Jer 21: 7 show them no mercy or **p** or compassion. H2798
La 2: 2 Without **p** the Lord has swallowed up all H2798
La 2:17 He has overthrown you without **p**, he has H2798
La 2:21 you have slaughtered them without **p**. H2798
La 3:43 pursued us; you have slain without **p**. H2798
Eze 5:11 I *will* not **look** *on* you **with p** or H2571+6524
Eze 7: 4 I *will* not **look** *on* you **with p**; I will H2571+6524
Eze 7: 9 I *will* not **look** *on* you **with p**; I will H2571+6524
Eze 8:18 I *will* not **look** *on* them **with p** or H2571+6524
Eze 9: 5 without **showing p** or compassion. H2571+6524
Eze 9:10 So I *will* not **look** on them **with p** H2571+6524
Eze 16: 5 No *one* **looked** on you **with p** or had H2571+6524
Eze 20:17 Yet I **looked** on them **with p** and did H2571+6524
Eze 24:14 not hold back; *I will* not **have p**, nor will I H2571
Joel 2:18 his land and **took p** on his people. H2798
Zec 8:14 on you and **showed** no **p** when your H5714
Zec 11: 6 For *I will* no longer **have p** on the people H2798
Mt 18:27 The servant's master **took p** *on* him *G5072*
Mk 9:22 do anything, **take p** on us and help us." *G5072*
Lk 10:33 when he saw him, *he* **took p** *on* him. *G5072*
Lk 16:24 **have p** on me and send Lazarus to dip the *G1796*
Lk 17:13 loud voice, "Jesus, Master, **have p** on us!" *G1796*
1Jn 3:17 need but **has no p** on them, *G3091+3836+5073*

PLACE (782) [PLACED, PLACES, PLACING]
Ge 1: 9 water under the sky be gathered to one **p**, H5226
Ge 2:21 ribs and then closed up the **p** with flesh. H9393
Ge 4:25 granted me another child **in p of** Abel, H9393
Ge 13: 3 he went **from p to place** until he H4200+5023
Ge 13: 3 he went **from place to p** until he H4200+5023
Ge 13: 3 to the **p** between Bethel and Ai where his H5226
Ge 18:24 not spare the **p** for the sake of the H5226

Ge 18:26 I will spare the whole **p** for their sake." H5226
Ge 19:13 because we are going to destroy this **p** H5226
Ge 19:14 "Hurry and get out of this **p**, because the H5226
Ge 19:27 returned to the **p** where he had stood H5226
Ge 20:11 'There is surely no fear of God in this **p** H5226
Ge 21:31 So that **p** was called Beersheba, because H5226
Ge 22: 3 he set out for the **p** God had told him H5226
Ge 22: 4 looked up and saw the **p** in the distance. H5226
Ge 22: 9 they reached the **p** God had told him H5226
Ge 22:14 Abraham called that **p** The LORD Will H5226
Ge 24:31 the house and a **p** for the camels. H5226
Ge 26: 7 the men of that **p** asked him about his H5226
Ge 26: 7 "The men of this **p** might kill me on H5226
Ge 28:11 When he reached a certain **p**, he stopped H5226
Ge 28:16 "Surely the LORD is in this **p**, and I was not H5226
Ge 28:17 afraid and said, "How awesome is this **p**! H5226
Ge 28:19 He called that **p** Bethel, though the city H5226
Ge 29: 3 the stone to its **p** over the mouth of the H5226
Ge 29:22 all the people of the **p** and gave a feast. H5226
Ge 30: 2 said, "Am I **in the p of** God, who has H9393
Ge 30:41 Jacob *would* **p** the branches in the H8492
Ge 30:42 were weak, *he would* not **p** them there. H8492
Ge 32: 2 So he named that **p** Mahanaim. H5226
Ge 32:30 So Jacob called the **p** Peniel, saying, "It is H5226
Ge 33:17 where he built a **p** for himself and made H1074
Ge 33:17 That is why the **p** is called Sukkoth. H5226
Ge 35: 7 he called the **p** El Bethel, because it H5226
Ge 35:13 up from him at the **p** where he had talked H5226
Ge 35:14 stone pillar at the **p** where God had H5226
Ge 35:15 Jacob called the **p** where God had talked H5226
Ge 39:20 the **p** where the king's prisoners were H5226
Ge 42:15 you will not leave **this** *p* unless your youngest AIT
Ge 42:27 the **p where they stopped for the night** H4869
Ge 43:21 the **p where we stopped for the night** we H4869
Ge 43:30 hurried out and looked for a **p** to weep. NDT
Ge 44:33 here as my lord's slave **in p of** the boy, H9393
Ge 49:15 how good is his **resting p** and how H4957
Ge 49:30 the field as a burial **p** from Ephron the H299
Ge 50:11 That is why **that p** near the Jordan is H2023S
Ge 50:13 the field as a burial **p** from Ephron the H299
Ge 50:19 "Don't be afraid. Am I **in** *the* **p of** God? H9393
Ge 50:25 then you must carry my bones up from **this** *p*." AIT
Ex 3: 5 the **p** where you are standing is holy H5226
Ex 4:24 At a **lodging p** on the way, the LORD met H4869
Ex 9:19 *to* **bring** your livestock and everything
you have in the field **to a p of shelter** H6395
Ex 9:26 The only **p** it did not hail was the land of H9004
Ex 13:19 must carry my bones up with you from **this** *p*."AIT
Ex 13:22 of fire by night **left** *its* **p** in front of the H4631
Ex 14:27 at daybreak the sea went back to its **p**. H419
Ex 15:17 of your inheritance—the **p**, LORD, H4806
Ex 15:23 That is why **the p** is called Marah.) H2023S
Ex 16:33 Then **p** it before the LORD to be kept for H5663
Ex 17: 1 **traveling from p to place** as the LORD H5023
Ex 17: 1 **traveling from place to p** as the LORD H5023
Ex 17: 7 And he called the **p** Massah and Meribah H5226
Ex 21:13 they are to flee to a **p** I will designate. H5226
Ex 23:20 to bring you to the **p** I have prepared. H5226
Ex 25:21 **P** the cover on top of the ark and put in the H5989
Ex 26:33 from the clasps and **p** the ark of the H995
Ex 26:33 will separate the **Holy P** from the Most H7731
Ex 26:33 Holy Place from the **Most Holy P**. H7731+7731
Ex 26:34 covenant law in the **Most Holy P**. H7731+7731
Ex 26:35 **P** the table outside the curtain on the H8492
Ex 28:29 "Whenever Aaron enters the **Holy P**, he H7731
Ex 28:35 when he enters the **Holy P** before the LORD H7731
Ex 28:43 the altar to minister in the **Holy P**, H7731
Ex 29:30 to minister in the **Holy P** is to wear them H7731
Ex 29:31 cook the meat in a sacred **p**. H5226
Ex 29:43 the **p** will be consecrated by my glory. NDT
Ex 30:18 **P** it between the tent of meeting and the H5989
Ex 30:36 of it to powder and **p** it in front of the ark H5989
Ex 31:11 oil and fragrant incense for the **Holy P**. H7731
Ex 32:34 lead the people to **the p** I spoke of, and H889S
Ex 33: 1 to Moses, "Leave this **p**, you and the people NDT
Ex 33:21 "There is a **p** near me where you may H5226
Ex 40: 3 **P** the ark of the covenant law in it and H8492
Ex 40: 5 **P** the gold altar of incense in front of the H5989
Ex 40: 6 "**P** the altar of burnt offering in front of the H5989
Ex 40: 7 **p** the basin between the tent of meeting H5989
Ex 40:18 tabernacle, *he* **put** the bases **in p**, erected H5989
Lev 4:12 the camp to a **p** ceremonially clean, H5226
Lev 4:24 slaughter it at the **p** where the burnt H5226
Lev 4:29 slaughter it at the **p** *of* the burnt offering. H5226
Lev 4:33 a sin offering at the **p** where the burnt H5226
Lev 6:10 on the altar and **p** them beside the altar. H8492
Lev 6:11 the camp to a **p** that is ceremonially H5226
Lev 6:25 the LORD in the **p** the burnt offering is H5226
Lev 6:30 atonement in the **Holy P** must not be H7731
Lev 7: 2 be slaughtered in the **p** where the burnt H5226
Lev 10:14 Eat them in a ceremonially clean **p**; they H5226
Lev 10:18 its blood was not taken into the **Holy P**, H7731
Lev 13:19 in the **p** where the boil was, a white H5226
Lev 14:40 into an unclean **p** outside the town. H5226
Lev 14:41 into an unclean **p** outside the town. H5226
Lev 14:45 taken out of the town to an unclean **p**. H5226
Lev 15:31 uncleanness for defiling my **dwelling p**, H5438
Lev 16: 2 chooses into the **Most Holy P** behind the H7731
Lev 16: 3 is how Aaron is to enter the **Most Holy P**: H7731
Lev 16:16 the **Most Holy P** because of the H7731
Lev 16:17 in the **Most Holy P** until he comes H7731
Lev 16:20 making atonement for the **Most Holy P**, H7731
Lev 16:22 carry on itself all their sins to a remote **p**; H824
Lev 16:23 put on before he entered the **Most Holy P**, H7731
Lev 16:27 brought into the **Most Holy P** to make H7731
Lev 16:33 atonement for the **Most Holy P**, H7731+5219
Lev 21:11 He must not enter a **p** where there is a dead NDT
Lev 22:22 *Do* not **p** any of these on the altar as a H5989
Lev 26: 1 and *do* not **p** a carved stone in your land H5989
Lev 26:11 I will put my **dwelling p** among you, and I H5438
Nu 2:17 each in their own **p** under their standard. H3338
Nu 3:12 among the Israelites **in p of** the first male H9393
Nu 3:41 the Levites for me **in p of** all the firstborn H9393
Nu 3:41 of the Levites **in p of** all the firstborn of H9393
Nu 3:45 "Take the Levites **in p of** all the firstborn of H9393
Nu 3:45 of the Levites **in p of** their livestock. H9393
Nu 4: 6 blue over that and **put** the poles **in p**. H8492
Nu 4: 8 durable leather and **put** the poles **in p**. H8492
Nu 4:11 durable leather and **put** the poles **in p**. H8492
Nu 4:14 Then *they are to* **p** on it all the utensils H5989
Nu 4:14 durable leather and **put** the poles **in p**. H8492
Nu 5:18 loosen her hair and **p** in her hands the H5989
Nu 6:19 the priest *is to* **p** in their hands a boiled H5989
Nu 8:16 them as my own **in p of** the firstborn, H9393
Nu 8:18 taken the Levites **in p of** all the firstborn H9393
Nu 10:12 **traveled from p to place** until the H5023
Nu 10:12 **traveled from place to p** until the H5023
Nu 10:29 setting out for the **p** about which the LORD H5226
Nu 10:33 those three days to find them a **p to rest**. H4957
Nu 11: 3 So that **p** was called Taberah, because fire H5226
Nu 11:34 Therefore the **p** was named Kibroth H5226
Nu 13:24 That **p** was called the Valley of Eshkol H5226
Nu 17: 4 **P** them in the tent of meeting in front of H5663
Nu 19: 9 a ceremonially clean **p** outside the camp. H5226
Nu 20: 5 bring us up out of Egypt to this terrible **p**? H5226
Nu 21: 3 their towns; so the **p** was named Hormah. H5226
Nu 22:26 stood in a narrow **p** where there was no H5226
Nu 23:13 with me to another **p** where you can see H5226
Nu 23:27 let me take you to another **p**. H5226
Nu 24:21 "Your **dwelling p** is secure, your nest is set H4632
Nu 32:14 standing **in the p of** your fathers and H9393
Nu 32:17 until we have brought them to their **p**. H5226
Nu 35:15 towns will be a **p of refuge** for Israelites H5236
Dt 1:31 the way you went until you reached this **p**." H5226
Dt 2:12 from before them and settled **in** their **p**, H9393
Dt 2:21 who drove them out and settled **in** their **p**. H9393
Dt 2:22 out and have lived **in** their **p** to this day. H9393
Dt 2:23 destroyed them and settled **in** their **p**.) H9393
Dt 11: 5 the wilderness until you arrived at this **p**, H5226
Dt 11:24 Every **p** where you set your foot will be H5226
Dt 12: 5 you are to seek the **p** the LORD your God H5226
Dt 12: 5 his dwelling. To **that p** you must go; H9004S
Dt 12: 9 not yet reached the **resting p** and the H4957
Dt 12:11 Then to the **p** the LORD your God will H5226
Dt 12:14 them only at the **p** the LORD will choose H5226
Dt 12:18 LORD your God at the **p** the LORD your God H5226
Dt 12:21 If the **p** where the LORD your God chooses H5226
Dt 12:26 and go to the **p** the LORD will choose. H5226
Dt 13: 2 if the sign or wonder spoken of **takes p** H995
Dt 14:23 LORD your God at the **p** he will choose as a H5226
Dt 14:24 But if that **p** is too distant and you have been NDT
Dt 14:24 because the **p** where the LORD will choose H5226
Dt 14:25 you and go to the **p** the LORD your God will H5226
Dt 15:20 the LORD your God at the **p** he will choose. H5226
Dt 16: 2 flock or herd at the **p** the LORD will choose H5226
Dt 16: 6 except in the **p** he will choose as a H5226
Dt 16: 7 it and eat it at the **p** the LORD your God H5226
Dt 16:11 LORD your God at the **p** he will choose as a H5226
Dt 16:15 your God at the **p** the LORD will choose H5226
Dt 16:16 the LORD your God at the **p** he will choose: H5226
Dt 17: 8 take them to the **p** the LORD your God will H5226
Dt 17:10 they give you at the **p** the LORD will choose H5226
Dt 17:15 *Do* not **p** a foreigner over you, one who is H5989
Dt 18: 6 earnestness to the **p** the LORD will choose, H5226
Dt 18:22 of the LORD *does* not **take p** or come true, H2118
Dt 23:12 Designate a **p** outside the camp where H3338
Dt 26: 2 Then go to the **p** the LORD your God will H5226
Dt 26: 9 He brought us to this **p** and gave us this H5226
Dt 26:10 **P** the basket before the LORD your God H5663
Dt 26:15 your holy **dwelling p**, and bless your H5061
Dt 28:65 no **resting p** for the sole of your foot. H4955
Dt 29: 7 When you reached this **p**, Sihon king of H5226
Dt 31:11 the LORD your God at the **p** he will choose, H5226
Dt 31:26 Book of the Law and **p** it beside the ark of H8492
Jos 1: 3 I will give you every **p** where you set your H5226
Jos 4: 3 put them down at the **p** where you stay H4869
Jos 4:18 returned to their **p** and ran at flood stage H5226
Jos 5: 7 So he raised up their sons **in** their **p**, and H9393
Jos 5: 9 So the **p** has been called Gilgal to this H5226
Jos 5:15 the **p** where you are standing is holy." H5226
Jos 6:23 put them in a **p** outside the camp of NDT
Jos 7:26 Therefore that **p** has been called the H5226
Jos 8: 9 went to the **p of ambush** and lay in wait H4422
Jos 8:14 in battle at a **certain p** overlooking the H4595
Jos 8:28 heap of ruins, a **desolate p** to this day. H9039
Jos 9:27 the LORD at the **p** the LORD would choose H5226
Jos 20: 4 city and provide a **p** to live among them. H5226
Jos 24:26 under the oak near the **holy p** *of* the LORD. H5219
Jdg 2: 5 they called that **p** Bokim. There they H5226
Jdg 6:20 unleavened bread, **p** them on this rock H5663
Jdg 6:37 I *will* **p** a wool fleece on the threshing H3657
Jdg 9:35 his troops came out from their **hiding p**. H4422
Jdg 11:19 us pass through your country to our own **p**. H5226
Jdg 15:17 the **p** was called Ramath Lehi. H5226
Jdg 15:19 Then God opened up the **hollow p** in Lehi H4847
Jdg 16: 2 So they surrounded the **p** and lay in wait NDT
Jdg 17: 8 town in search of **some other p** to stay. H889S
Jdg 17: 9 he said, "and I'm looking for **a p** to stay." H889S
Jdg 18: 1 was seeking a **p** of their own where H5709
Jdg 18: 3 What are you doing in **this** *p*? Why are you AIT
Jdg 18:12 This is why the **p** west of Kiriath Jearim is H5226
Jdg 18:15 Levite at Micah's **p** and greeted him. H1074
Jdg 19:16 the inhabitants of the **p** were Benjamites), H5226
Jdg 20:33 charged out of its **p** on the west of Gibeah H5226
Jdg 21:24 Israelites left **that p** and went home to H9004S
Ru 1: 7 she left the **p** where she had been living H5226
Ru 2:19 the one at whose **p** she had been working. NDT
Ru 3: 4 lies down, note the **p** where he is lying. H5226
1Sa 2: 9 will be silenced in the **p of darkness**. H3125
1Sa 2:20 this woman to **take the p** of the one she H9393
1Sa 3: 2 barely see, was lying down in his usual **p**. H5226
1Sa 3: 9 So Samuel went and lay down in his **p**. H5226
1Sa 5: 3 took Dagon and put him back in his **p**. H5226
1Sa 5:11 let it go back to its own **p**, or it will kill us H5226
1Sa 6: 2 us how we should send it back to its **p**." H5226
1Sa 9:12 the people have a sacrifice at the **high p**. H1195
1Sa 9:13 before he goes up to the **high p** to eat. H1195
1Sa 9:14 toward them on his way up to the **high p**. H1195
1Sa 9:19 "Go up ahead of me to the **high p**, for H1195
1Sa 9:25 came down from the **high p** to the town, H1195
1Sa 10: 5 coming down from the **high p** with lyres, H1195
1Sa 10:13 prophesying, he went to the **high p**. H1195
1Sa 12: 8 out of Egypt and settled them in this **p**. H5226
1Sa 20:19 go to the **p** where you hid when this H5226
1Sa 20:25 He sat in his customary **p** by the wall H4632
1Sa 20:25 sat next to Saul, but David's **p** was empty. H5226
1Sa 20:27 of the month, David's **p** was empty again. H5226
1Sa 20:37 the boy came to the **p** where Jonathan's H5226
1Sa 21: 2 have told them to meet me at a certain **p**. H5226
1Sa 23:13 *kept* **moving from p to place**
H2143+928+889+2143
1Sa 23:13 *kept* **moving from place to p**
H2143+928+889+2143
1Sa 23:28 why they call this **p** Sela Hammahlekoth. H5226
1Sa 26: 5 out and went to the **p** where Saul had H5226
1Sa 27: 5 let a **p** be assigned to me in one of the H5226
1Sa 29: 4 he may return to the **p** you assigned him. H5226
2Sa 2:16 So that **p** in Gibeon was called Helkath H5226
2Sa 2:23 when he came to the **p** where Asahel had H5226
2Sa 5:20 So that **p** was called Baal Perazim. H5226
2Sa 6: 8 to this day that **p** is called Perez H5226
2Sa 6:17 LORD and set it in its **p** inside the tent that H5226
2Sa 7: 6 have been **moving from p to place** with a H2143
2Sa 7: 6 have been **moving from place to p** with a H2143
2Sa 7:10 And I will provide a **p** for my people Israel H5226
2Sa 11:16 he put Uriah at a **p** where he knew the H5226
2Sa 15:25 let me see it and his **dwelling p** again. H5659
2Sa 16: 8 of Saul, **in** whose **p** you have reigned. H9393
2Sa 17: 9 he is hidden in a cave or some other **p**. H5226
2Sa 17:25 Amasa over the army **in p of** Joab. H9393
2Sa 18: 6 the battle **took p** in the forest of H2118
2Sa 19:13 of my army for life **in p of** Joab. H9393
2Sa 19:28 but *you* **gave** your servant **a p** among H8883
2Sa 21: 5 decimated and *have* no **p** anywhere in H3656
2Sa 21:20 *which* **took p** at Gath, there H2118
2Sa 22:20 He brought me out into a **spacious p**; he H5303
2Sa 23:11 banded together at a **p** where there was a NDT
1Ki 1:30 and he will sit on my throne **in** my **p**." H9393
1Ki 1:35 sit on my throne and reign **in** my **p**. H9393
1Ki 3: 4 that was the most important **high p** H1195
1Ki 3: 7 your servant king **in p of** my father David. H9393
1Ki 4:28 to the **proper p** their H5226+889+2118+9004
1Ki 5: 5 put on the throne **in** your **p** will build the H9393
1Ki 5: 9 them as rafts by sea to the **p** you specify. H5226
1Ki 6:16 inner sanctuary, the **Most Holy P**. H7731+7731
1Ki 7:50 the **Most Holy P**, and also for H7731+7731
1Ki 8: 6 covenant to its **p** in the inner sanctuary H5226
1Ki 8: 6 temple, the **Most Holy P**, and put it H7731+7731
1Ki 8: 7 their wings over the **p** *of* the ark and H5226
1Ki 8: 8 be seen from the **Holy P** in front of the H7731
1Ki 8: 8 not from outside the Holy P; and they NDT
1Ki 8:10 the priests withdrew from the **Holy P**, H7731
1Ki 8:13 you, a **p** for you to dwell forever. H4806
1Ki 8:21 I have provided a **p** there for the ark, in H5226
1Ki 8:29 night and day, this **p** of which you said H5226
1Ki 8:29 prayer your servant prays toward this **p**. H5226
1Ki 8:30 Israel when they pray toward this **p**. H5226
1Ki 8:30 your dwelling **p**, and when you hear, H5226
1Ki 8:35 they pray toward this **p** and give praise to H5226
1Ki 8:39 heaven, your dwelling **p**. Forgive and act; H4806
1Ki 8:43 heaven, your dwelling **p**. Do whatever the H4806
1Ki 8:49 heaven, your dwelling **p**, hear their prayer H4806
1Ki 11: 7 Solomon built a **high p** for Chemosh the H1195
1Ki 13:16 eat bread or drink water with you in this **p**. H5226
1Ki 13:22 drank water in the **p** where he told you H5226
1Ki 21: 6 I will give you another vineyard **in** its **p**. H9393
1Ki 21: 9 in a **prominent p** *among* the people H8031
1Ki 21:12 in a **prominent p** *among* the people H8031
1Ki 21:19 In the **p** where dogs licked up Naboth's H5226
2Ki 2: 7 facing the **p** where Elijah and Elisha had NDT
2Ki 3:25 Kir Hareseth was left with its stones in **p**, NDT
2Ki 6: 1 the **p** where we meet with you is too H5226
2Ki 6: 2 let us build a **p** there for us to meet." H5226
2Ki 6: 6 When he showed him the **p**, Elisha cut a H5226
2Ki 6: 8 will set up my camp in such and such a **p**." H5226
2Ki 6: 9 "Beware of passing that **p**, because the H5226

2Ki 6:10 checked on the **p** indicated by the man H5226
2Ki 11:16 she reached the **p** *where* the horses enter H2006
2Ki 11:19 The king then **took** *his* **p** on the royal H3782
2Ki 14:21 made him king **in p of** his father H9393
2Ki 17:7 *All this* **took p** because the Israelites had H2118
2Ki 17:11 At every **high p** they burned incense, as H1195
2Ki 18:25 destroy this **p** without word from the H5226
2Ki 21:24 they made Josiah his son king **in his p**. H9393
2Ki 22:16 to bring disaster on this **p** and its people, H5226
2Ki 22:17 will burn against this **p** and will not be H5226
2Ki 22:19 spoken against this **p** and its people— H5226
2Ki 22:20 the disaster I am going to bring on this **p**. H5226
2Ki 23:15 the **high p** made by Jeroboam son of H1195
2Ki 23:15 even that altar and **high p** he demolished. H1195
2Ki 23:15 He burned the **high p** and ground it to H1195
2Ki 23:30 him and made him king **in p of** his father. H9393
2Ki 23:34 son of Josiah king **in p of** his father Josiah H9393
2Ki 24:17 king **in** his **p** and changed his name to H9393
1Ch 4:41 Then they settled **in** their **p**, because H9393
1Ch 6:49 that was done in the **Most Holy P**, H7731+7731
1Ch 11:13 At a **p** where there was a field full of barley NDT
1Ch 13:11 to this day that **p** is called Perez H5226
1Ch 14:11 So that **p** was called Baal Perazim. H5226
1Ch 15:1 he prepared a **p** for the ark of God and H5226
1Ch 15:3 of the LORD to the **p** he had prepared for it H5226
1Ch 15:12 God of Israel, to the **p** I have prepared for it. NDT
1Ch 16:27 strength and joy are in his **dwelling p**. H5226
1Ch 16:39 of the LORD at the **high p** in Gibeon H1195
1Ch 17:5 another, from one **dwelling p** to another. H5438
1Ch 17:9 And I will provide a **p** for my people Israel H5226
1Ch 20:6 *which* **took p** at Gath, there H2118
1Ch 21:29 at that time on the **high p** at Gibeon. H1195
1Ch 23:32 meeting, for the **Holy P** and, under their H7731
1Ch 28:2 build a house as a **p of rest** for the ark of H4957
1Ch 28:11 its inner rooms and the **p** *of* atonement. H1074
1Ch 29:23 the LORD as king **in p of** his father David. H9393
2Ch 1:3 assembly went to the **high p** at Gibeon, H1195
2Ch 1:4 Kiriath Jearim to **the p** he had prepared H2021S
2Ch 1:8 father and have made me king **in his p**. H9393
2Ch 1:13 to Jerusalem from the **high p** at Gibeon, H1195
2Ch 2:6 except as a **p** to burn sacrifices before him? NDT
2Ch 3:1 the Jebusite, the **p** provided by David. H5226
2Ch 3:8 He built the **Most Holy P**, its length H7731+7731
2Ch 3:10 For the Most Holy **P** he made a pair of H1074
2Ch 4:22 doors to the **Most Holy P** and the H7731+7731
2Ch 5:7 covenant to its **p** in the inner sanctuary H5226
2Ch 5:7 temple, the **Most Holy P**, and put it H7731+7731
2Ch 5:8 wings over the **p** *of* the ark and covered H5226
2Ch 5:9 not from outside the Holy **P**; and they NDT
2Ch 5:11 The priests then withdrew from the **Holy P**. H7731
2Ch 6:2 you, a **p** for you to dwell forever. H4806
2Ch 6:20 this **p** of which you said you would put H5226
2Ch 6:20 prayer your servant prays toward this **p**. H5226
2Ch 6:21 Israel when they pray toward this **p**. H5226
2Ch 6:21 your dwelling **p**; and when you hear, H5226
2Ch 6:26 they pray toward this **p** and give praise to H5226
2Ch 6:30 from heaven, your dwelling **p**. Forgive, H4806
2Ch 6:33 heaven, your dwelling **p**. Do whatever the H4806
2Ch 6:39 heaven, your dwelling **p**, hear their prayer H4806
2Ch 6:40 attentive to the prayers offered in this **p**. H5226
2Ch 6:41 come to your **resting p**, you and the H5665
2Ch 7:12 have chosen this **p** for myself as a H5226
2Ch 7:15 attentive to the prayers offered in this **p**. H5226
2Ch 20:24 came to the **p that overlooks** the desert H5205
2Ch 22:1 king **in his p**, since the raiders H9393
2Ch 24:11 empty the chest and carry it back to its **p**. H5226
2Ch 26:1 made him king **in p of** his father H9393
2Ch 29:6 from the LORD's **dwelling p** and turned H5438
2Ch 30:27 reached heaven, his holy **dwelling p**. H5061
2Ch 33:25 they made Josiah his son king **in his p**. H9393
2Ch 34:24 bring disaster on this **p** and its people— H5226
2Ch 34:25 be poured out on this **p** and will not be H5226
2Ch 34:27 he spoke against this **p** and its people, H5226
2Ch 34:28 to bring on this **p** and on those who live H5226
2Ch 35:5 "Stand in the **holy p** with a group of H7731
2Ch 36:1 him king in Jerusalem **in p of** his father. H9393
2Ch 36:15 pity on his people and on his **dwelling p**. H5061
Ezr 4:15 a **p** with a long history of A10089+10135+10193S
Ezr 4:19 and has been a **p** of rebellion A10089+10135+10193S
Ezr 6:3 be rebuilt as a **p** to present sacrifices, A10087
Ezr 9:8 giving us a **firm p** in his sanctuary, H3845
Ne 1:9 bring them to the **p** I have chosen as a H5226
Ne 3:1 They dedicated it and **set** its doors **in p** H6641
Ne 3:3 and **put** its doors and bolts and bars **in p**. H6641
Ne 3:6 **put** its doors with their bolts and bars **in p**. H6641
Ne 3:13 **put** its doors with their bolts and bars **in p**. H6641
Ne 3:14 **put** its doors with their bolts and bars **in p**. H6641
Ne 3:15 **putting** its doors and bolts and bars **in p**. H6641
Ne 7:1 been rebuilt and *I had* **set** the doors **in p**, H6641
Est 2:9 her attendants into the **best** *p in* the harem. AIT
Est 4:14 the Jews will arise from another **p**, H5226
Job 7:10 his **p** will know him no more. H5226
Job 8:17 of rocks and looks for a *p* **among** the stones. AIT
Job 8:18 from its spot, that **p** disowns it and says, 'I NDT
Job 9:6 the earth from its **p** and makes its pillars H5226
Job 10:21 before I go to the **p** of no return, to the land NDT
Job 14:18 as a rock is moved from its **p**, H5226
Job 16:4 if you were **in my p**; I could make H9393
Job 18:4 Or must the rocks be moved from their **p**? H5226
Job 18:21 such is the **p** *of* one who does not know H5226
Job 20:9 his **p** will look on him no more. H5226
Job 27:21 he is gone; it sweeps him out of his **p**. H5226
Job 27:23 in derision and hisses him out of his **p**." H5226
Job 28:1 silver and a **p** where gold is refined H5226
Job 30:23 to the **p** appointed for all the living. H1074
Job 34:24 the mighty and sets up others **in** their **p**. H9393
Job 36:16 jaws of distress to a **spacious p** free from H8144
Job 37:1 this my heart pounds and leaps from its **p**. H5226
Job 38:10 limits for it and **set** its doors and bars **in p**, H8492
Job 38:12 to the morning, or shown the dawn its **p**, H5226
Job 38:24 is the way to the **p** where the lightning is NDT
Job 38:24 the **p** where the east winds are scattered NDT
Ps 8:3 the stars, which *you have* **set in p**, H3922
Ps 18:19 He brought me out into a **spacious p**; he H5303
Ps 24:3 Who may stand in his holy **p**? H5226
Ps 26:8 you live, the **p** where your glory dwells. H5226
Ps 28:2 my hands toward your **Most Holy P**. H7731+1808
Ps 31:8 have set my feet in a **spacious p**. H5303
Ps 32:7 You are my **hiding p**; you will protect me H6260
Ps 33:14 from his dwelling **p** he watches all who H4806
Ps 40:2 on a rock and gave me a firm **p to stand**. H892
Ps 41:8 will never get up from the **p** where he lies." NDT
Ps 43:3 holy mountain, to the **p where** you **dwell**. H5438
Ps 45:16 Your sons *will* **take the p of** your H2118+9393
Ps 46:4 the **holy** *p* where the Most High dwells. AIT
Ps 51:6 you taught me wisdom in that **secret p**. H6258
Ps 55:8 I would hurry to my **p of shelter**, far from H5144
Ps 62:4 they intend to topple me from my **lofty p**; H8420
Ps 66:12 you brought us to a **p of abundance**. H8122
Ps 69:25 May their **p** be deserted; let there be no H3227
Ps 73:18 Surely *you* **p** them on slippery ground; you H8883
Ps 74:4 roared in the **p where** you **met** with us; H4595
Ps 74:7 they defiled the **dwelling p** *of* your Name. H5438
Ps 74:8 every **p where** God was **worshiped** in the H4595
Ps 76:2 tent is in Salem, his **dwelling p** in Zion. H5104
Ps 84:1 How lovely is your **dwelling p**, LORD H5438
Ps 84:3 have her young—a **p** near your altar, LORD NDT
Ps 84:6 they make it a **p** of springs; the NDT
Ps 88:12 Are your wonders known in the *p of* **darkness** AIT
Ps 90:1 have been our **dwelling p** throughout all H5061
Ps 103:16 is gone, and its **p** remembers it no more. H5226
Ps 104:8 to the **p** you assigned for them. H5226
Ps 109:8 may another take his **p of leadership**. H7213
Ps 113:3 the rising of the sun to the **p where** it **sets**, H4427
Ps 115:17 those who go down to the **p of silence**; H1872
Ps 118:5 he brought me into a **spacious p**. H5303
Ps 132:5 till I find a **p** for the LORD, a dwelling for H5226
Ps 132:7 "Let us go to his **dwelling p**, let us H5438
Ps 132:8 come to your **resting p**, you and the H4957
Ps 132:11 own descendants *I will* **p** on your throne. H8883
Ps 132:14 "This is my **resting p** for ever and ever H4957
Ps 139:15 you when I was made in the **secret p**, H6260
Pr 3:19 by understanding *he* **set** the heavens **in p** H3922
Pr 8:25 before the mountains **were settled in p** H3190
Pr 8:27 I was there when he **set** the heavens **in p** H3922
Pr 15:25 *he* **sets** the widow's boundary stones **in p**. H5893
Pr 24:15 do not plunder their **dwelling p**; H8070
Pr 25:6 do not claim a **p** among his great H5226
Ecc 1:7 To the **p** the streams come from, there H5226
Ecc 3:16 In the **p** *of* judgment—wickedness was H5226
Ecc 3:16 was there, in the **p** *of* justice—wickedness H5226
Ecc 3:20 All go to the same **p**; all come from dust H5226
Ecc 4:1 that *was* **taking p** under the sun: H6913
Ecc 6:6 Do not all go to the same **p**? H5226
Ecc 8:10 go from the holy **p** and receive praise H5226
Ecc 11:3 to the north, in the **p** where it falls, there H5226
SS 8:6 **P** me like a seal over your heart, like a H8492
Isa 3:13 The LORD **takes** *his* **p** in court; he rises to H5893
Isa 4:6 a refuge and **hiding p** from the storm H5039
Isa 7:7 " '*It will* **not take p**, it will not H7756
Isa 7:23 in every **p** where there were a thousand H5226
Isa 8:14 He will be a **holy p**; for both Israel and H5219
Isa 11:10 and his **resting p** will be glorious. H4957
Isa 13:13 will shake from its **p** at the wrath of the H5226
Isa 14:2 take them and bring them to their own **p**. H5226
Isa 14:21 Prepare a **p to slaughter** his children for H4749
Isa 14:23 "I will turn her into a **p** *for* owls and into H4625
Isa 16:12 When Moab appears at her **high p**, she H1195
Isa 18:4 will look on from my **dwelling p**, H4806
Isa 18:7 the **p** *of* the Name of the LORD Almighty. H5226
Isa 22:16 chiseling your **resting p** in the rock? H5438
Isa 22:22 *I will* **p** on his shoulder the key to the H5989
Isa 22:23 I will drive him like a peg into a firm **p**; he H5226
Isa 22:25 peg driven into the firm **p** will give way; H5226
Isa 23:13 The Assyrians *have* **made** it **a p** for desert H3569
Isa 28:12 "This is the **resting p**, let the weary H4957
Isa 28:12 "This is the **p of repose**"—but they would H5276
Isa 28:15 lie our refuge and falsehood *our* **hiding p**." H6259
Isa 28:17 and water will overflow your **hiding p**. H6260
Isa 28:25 Does he not plant wheat *in* its **p**, barley in H8463
Isa 33:21 It will be like a **p** *of* broad rivers and H5226
Isa 41:1 let us meet together at the **p of judgment**. H5477
Isa 42:9 the former things *have* **taken p**, and new H995
Isa 45:6 the sun to the **p of** its **setting** people may H5115
Isa 46:7 they set it up **in** its **p**, and there it H9393
Isa 49:20 in your hearing, 'This **p** is too small for us H5226
Isa 51:16 I *who* **set** the heavens **in p**, who H5749
Isa 54:2 "Enlarge the **p** *of* your tent, stretch your H5226
Isa 57:15 "I live in a high and **holy** *p*, but also with the AIT
Isa 60:13 I will glorify the **p** *for* my feet. H5226
Isa 60:17 will bring you gold, and silver **in p of** iron. H9393
Isa 60:17 bring you bronze, and iron **in p of** stones. H9393
Isa 63:18 while your people possessed your **holy p**, H7731
Isa 65:10 the Valley of Achor a **resting p** *for* herds, H8070
Isa 66:1 Where will my resting **p** be? H5226
Jer 2:37 You will also leave **that** *p* with your hands on AIT
Jer 3:2 Is there *any* **p where** you have not been AIT
Jer 4:7 He has left his **p** to lay waste your land H5226
Jer 7:3 actions, and I will let you live in this **p**. H5226
Jer 7:6 do not shed innocent blood in this **p**, H5226
Jer 7:7 then I will let you live in this **p**, in the land H5226
Jer 7:12 " 'Go now to the **p** in Shiloh where I first H5226
Jer 7:14 the **p** I gave to you and your ancestors. H5226
Jer 7:20 my wrath will be poured out on this **p**— H5226
Jer 9:2 had in the desert a **lodging p** *for* travelers, H4869
Jer 13:7 took it from the **p** where I had hidden H5226
Jer 14:13 I will give you lasting peace in this **p**. H5226
Jer 16:2 have sons or daughters in this **p**. H5226
Jer 16:9 voices of bride and bridegroom in this **p**. H5226
Jer 17:12 the beginning, is the **p** *of* our sanctuary. H5226
Jer 19:3 a disaster on this **p** that will make the H5226
Jer 19:4 me and made this a **p** of foreign gods; H5226
Jer 19:4 have filled this **p** with the blood of the H5226
Jer 19:6 no longer call this **p** Topheth or the Valley H5226
Jer 19:7 " 'In this **p** I will ruin the plans of Judah H5226
Jer 19:12 I will do to this **p** and to those who live H5226
Jer 19:13 kings of Judah will be defiled like this **p**, H5226
Jer 22:3 do not shed innocent blood in this **p**. H5226
Jer 22:11 as king of Judah but has gone from this **p**: H5226
Jer 22:12 He will die in the **p** where they have led H5226
Jer 23:4 *I will* **p** shepherds over them who will tend H7756
Jer 24:5 I sent away from this **p** to the land of the H5226
Jer 25:35 the leaders of the flock no **p to escape**. H7129
Jer 26:23 thrown into the **burial p** *of* the common H7700
Jer 27:22 them back and restore them to this **p**. H5226
Jer 28:3 bring back to this **p** all the articles of the H5226
Jer 28:4 also bring back to this **p** Jehoiachin son of H5226
Jer 28:6 all the exiles back to this **p** from Babylon. H5226
Jer 28:13 but **in** its **p** you will get a yoke of iron. H9393
Jer 29:10 good promise to bring you back to this **p**. H5226
Jer 29:14 you back to the **p** from which I carried H5226
Jer 29:26 you priest **in p of** Jehoiada to be in H9393
Jer 30:10 'I will surely save you out of a **distant p** H8158
Jer 30:18 the palace will stand in its **proper p**. H5477
Jer 32:37 them back to this **p** and let them live in H5226
Jer 33:10 'You say about this **p**, "It is a desolate H5226
Jer 33:12 'In this **p**, desolate and without people H5226
Jer 37:1 he reigned **in p of** Jehoiachin son of H9393
Jer 40:2 your God decreed this disaster for this **p**. H5226
Jer 42:18 reproach; you will never see this **p** again. H5226
Jer 42:22 plague in the **p** where you want to go H5226
Jer 44:29 sign to you that I will punish you in this **p**, H5226
Jer 46:27 I will surely save you out of a **distant p** H8158
Jer 49:33 a haunt of jackals, a **desolate p** forever. H9039
Jer 50:6 hill and forgot their own **resting p**. H8070
Jer 51:37 of horror and scorn, a **p** where no one lives. NDT
Jer 51:62 you have said you will destroy this **p**, so H5226
La 1:3 the nations; she finds no **resting p**. H4955
La 2:6 he has destroyed his **p of meeting**. H4595
Eze 3:12 rose from the **p where** it was **standing**. H5226
Eze 4:3 **p** it as an iron wall between you and the H5989
Eze 7:22 robbers will desecrate the *p* I **treasure**. AIT
Eze 12:3 go from where you are to another **p**. H5226
Eze 20:29 What is this **high p** you go to?' " H1195
Eze 21:7 *It will* **surely take p**, declares the H2118
Eze 21:30 In the **p** where you were created, in the H5226
Eze 25:5 Ammon into a **resting p** *for* sheep. H5271
Eze 26:5 she will become a **p to spread** fishnets, H5427
Eze 26:14 you will become a **p to spread** fishnets. H5427
Eze 26:15 and *the* **slaughter takes p** in you? H2222+2223
Eze 26:20 will not return or **take** *your* **p** in the land of H3656
Eze 34:23 *I will* **p** over them one shepherd, my H7756
Eze 37:27 My **dwelling p** will be with them; I will be H5438
Eze 38:15 You will come from your **p** in the far north H5226
Eze 39:8 *It will* surely **take p**, declares the H2118
Eze 39:11 day I will give Gog a burial **p** in Israel, H5226
Eze 41:4 to me, "This is the **Most Holy P**." H7731+7731
Eze 41:21 the front of the **Most Holy P** was similar. H7731
Eze 41:23 hall and the **Most Holy P** had double H7731
Eze 42:13 the guilt offerings—for the **p** is holy. H5226
Eze 43:7 this is the **p** *of* my throne and the place H5226
Eze 43:7 of my throne and the **p** *for* the soles of my H5226
Eze 45:3 be the sanctuary, the **Most Holy P**. H7731+7731
Eze 45:4 It will be a **p** for their houses as well as a H5226
Eze 45:4 as well as a **holy p** for the sanctuary. H5219
Eze 46:19 showed me a **p** at the western end. H5226
Eze 46:20 "This is the **p** where the priests are to H5226
Da 2:45 the king what *will* **take p** in the future. A10201
Da 7:9 "thrones **were set in p**, and the A10667
Da 8:8 and **in** its **p** four prominent horns grew up H9393
Da 8:17 he came near the **p where** I was **standing**, H6642
Da 9:24 and to anoint the **Most Holy P**. H7731+7731
Da 11:7 her family line will arise to take her **p**. H4030
Da 11:36 what has been determined *must* **take p**. H6913
Hos 1:10 In the **p** where it was said to them, 'You H5226
Hos 9:13 like Tyre, planted in a **pleasant p**. H5659
Jnh 4:5 out and sat down at a **p** east of the city. NDT
Mic 1:3 The LORD is coming from his **dwelling p** H5226
Mic 1:5 What is Judah's **high p**? Is it not H1195
Mic 1:6 heap of rubble, a **p** for planting vineyards. H8441
Mic 2:10 For this is not your **resting p**, because it is H4957
Mic 2:12 in its pasture; the **p** will throng with people. NDT
Na 2:5 city wall; the protective shield *is* **put in p**. H3922
Na 2:11 the **p where** they **fed** their young H5337
Zep 1:4 every remnant of Baal worship in this **p**, H5226
Zep 2:9 Gomorrah—a **p** *of* weeds and salt pits H4940

Zep 3: 7 Then her **p of refuge** would not be H5061
Hag 2: 9 'And in this **p** I will grant peace,' declares H5226
Zec 3: 7 I will give you a **p** among these standing H4544
Zec 5:11 the basket will be set there in its **p**." H4807
Zec 6:12 branch out from his **p** and build the H9393
Zec 12: 6 Jerusalem will remain intact **in** her **p**. H9393
Zec 14:10 winepresses, and will remain **in** its **p**. H9393
Mal 1:11 In every **p** incense and pure offerings will H5226
Mt 1:22 All this **took p** to fulfill what the Lord had G1181
Mt 2: 9 it stopped over **the p where** the child was. G4023
Mt 2:22 reigning in Judea **in p** of his father Herod, G505
Mt 8:20 the Son of Man has no **p** to lay his head." G4544
Mt 10:23 When you are persecuted in one **p**, flee to G4484
Mt 12: 9 Going on **from that p**, he went into their G1696
Mt 12:15 Jesus withdrew **from that p**. A large crowd G1696
Mt 14:13 withdrew by boat privately to a solitary **p**. G5536
Mt 14:15 "This is a remote **p**, and it's already G5536
Mt 14:35 And when the men *of* that **p** recognized G5536
Mt 15:21 Leaving **that p**, Jesus withdrew to the G1696
Mt 15:33 bread in this **remote p** to feed such a G2244
Mt 19:13 Jesus for him *to* **p** his hands **on** them and G2202
Mt 21: 4 This **took p** to fulfill what was spoken G1181
Mt 21:33 to some farmers and **moved to another p**. G623
Mt 23: 6 they love the **p of honor** at banquets and G4752
Mt 24:15 standing in the holy **p** 'the abomination G5536
Mt 24:20 your flight *will* not **take p** in winter or on G1181
Mt 24:51 assign him a **p** with the hypocrites, G3538
Mt 26:36 his disciples to a **p** called Gethsemane, G6005
Mt 26:52 "Put your sword back in its **p**," Jesus said G5536
Mt 26:56 But this *has* all **taken p** that the writings of G1181
Mt 27: 7 potter's field as a **burial p** for foreigners. G5438
Mt 27:33 They came to a **p** called Golgotha (which G5536
Mt 27:33 which means "the **p** of the skull"). G5536
Mt 28: 6 Come and see the **p** where he lay. G5536
Mk 1:35 left the house and went off to a solitary **p** G5536
Mk 6:11 And if any **p** will not welcome you or listen G5536
Mk 6:11 leave *that* **p** and shake the dust off your G1696
Mk 6:31 yourselves to a quiet **p** and get some rest." G5536
Mk 6:32 by themselves in a boat to a solitary **p**. G5536
Mk 6:35 "This is a remote **p**," they said, "and it's G5536
Mk 7:24 Jesus left **that p** and went to the vicinity of G1696
Mk 7:32 they begged Jesus to **p** his hand **on** him. G2202
Mk 8: 4 where in this **remote p** can anyone get G2244
Mk 9:30 They left **that p** and passed through G2796
Mk 10: 1 Jesus then left **that p** and went into the G1696
Mk 10:13 to Jesus for him *to* **p** *his* **hands on** them, G721
Mk 12: 1 to some farmers and **moved to another p**. G623
Mk 12:41 the **p where the offerings were put** and G1126
Mk 13:18 Pray that *this will* not **take p** in winter, G1181
Mk 14:32 They went to a **p** called Gethsemane, and G6005
Mk 15:22 brought Jesus to the **p** called Golgotha G5536
Mk 15:22 which means "the **p** of the skull"). G5536
Mk 16: 6 See the **p** where they laid him G5536
Mk 16:18 *they will* **p** their hands **on** sick people G2202
Lk 2: 2 the first census *that* **took p** while Quirinius G1181
Lk 4: 5 him up to a high **p** and showed him in an G4001
Lk 4:17 he found the **p** where it is written: G5536
Lk 4:42 daybreak, Jesus went out to a solitary **p**. G5536
Lk 6:17 down with them and stood on a level **p**. G5536
Lk 9:12 because we are in a remote **p** here." G5536
Lk 9:58 the Son of Man has no **p** to lay his head." G4544
Lk 10: 1 to every town and **p** where he was about G5536
Lk 10:32 when he came to the **p** and saw him G5536
Lk 11: 1 One day Jesus was praying in a certain **p** G5536
Lk 11:33 puts it in a **p** *where it will be* **hidden**, G3219
Lk 12:17 I have no **p** to store my crops.' G4544
Lk 12:46 assign him a **p** with the unbelievers. G3538
Lk 13:31 "Leave **this p** and go somewhere else. G1949
Lk 14: 8 do not take the **p of honor**, for a person G4752
Lk 14: 9 will have to take the least important **p**. G5536
Lk 14:10 take the lowest **p**, so that when your host G5536
Lk 14:10 say to you, 'Friend, move up *to a* **better** *p*. AIT
Lk 16:26 you a great chasm *has been* **set in p**, G5114
Lk 16:28 will not also come to this **p** of torment. G5536
Lk 18:15 to Jesus for *him to* **p** *his* **hands on** them. G721
Lk 19:37 near the **p where the road goes down the** G2853
Lk 21: 7 be the sign that they are about to **take p**?" G1181
Lk 21:28 When these things begin *to* **take p**, stand G1181
Lk 22:40 On reaching the **p**, he said to them, "Pray G5536
Lk 23:33 When they came to the **p** called the Skull G5536
Lk 23:48 to witness this sight saw what **took p**, G1181
Lk 24:21 it is the third day since all this **took p**. G1181
Jn 1:16 received grace **in p** of grace **already given**. G505
Jn 2: 1 day a wedding **took p** at Cana in Galilee G1181
Jn 4:20 Jews claim that the **p** where we must G5536
Jn 5: 9 The day on which this took **p** was a Sabbath, NDT
Jn 6:10 There was plenty of grass in that **p**, and G5536
Jn 6:23 landed near the **p** where the people had G5536
Jn 8:20 near the **p where the offerings were put**. G1126
Jn 8:35 Now a slave **has** no permanent **p** in the G3531
Jn 10:40 the Jordan to the **p** where John had been G5536
Jn 10:42 And **in that p** many believed in Jesus. G1695
Jn 11:30 was still at the **p** where Martha had met G5536
Jn 11:32 Mary reached **the p where** Jesus was and G3963
Jn 13:12 on his clothes and **returned to** *his* **p**. G404+4099
Jn 14: 2 I am going there to prepare a **p** for you? G5536
Jn 14: 3 And if I go and prepare a **p** for you, I will G5536
Jn 14: 4 You know the way *to the* **p where** I am going." AIT
Jn 18: 2 knew the **p**, because Jesus had G5536
Jn 18:32 This took **p** to fulfill what Jesus had said NDT
Jn 18:36 my kingdom is **from another p**." G4024+1949
Jn 19:13 judge's seat at a **p** known as the Stone G5536
Jn 19:17 he went out to the **p** of the Skull (which in G5536
Jn 19:20 the **p** where Jesus was crucified was G5536
Jn 19:41 At the **p** where Jesus was crucified, there G5536
Jn 20: 7 The cloth was still lying in its **p**, separate G5536
Ac 1:20 " 'May his **p** be deserted; let there be no G2068
Ac 1:20 " 'May another take his **p of leadership**. G2175
Ac 2: 1 they were all together in **one p**. G3836+899
Ac 2:30 him on oath *that he would* **p** one of his G2767
Ac 3:11 to them in the *p* **called** Solomon's AIT
Ac 4:31 the **p** where they were meeting was G5536
Ac 6:13 against this holy **p** and against the law. G5536
Ac 6:14 will destroy this **p** and change the G5536
Ac 7: 7 of that country and worship me in this **p**. G5536
Ac 7:33 the **p** where you are standing is holy G5536
Ac 7:46 might provide a **dwelling p** for the God of G5013
Ac 7:49 Or where will my resting **p** be? G5536
Ac 9:12 come and **p** his hands **on** him to restore G2202
Ac 12:17 he said, and then he left for another **p**. G5536
Ac 16:13 where we expected to find a **p of prayer**. G4666
Ac 16:16 when we were going to the **p of prayer**, G4666
Ac 18:12 brought him to the **p of judgment**. G1037
Ac 18:23 traveled **from p to place** throughout G2759
Ac 18:23 traveled **from place to p** throughout G2759
Ac 21:28 our people and our law and this **p**. G5536
Ac 21:28 into the temple and defiled this holy **p**." G5536
Ac 26:18 of sins and a **p** among those who are G3102
Ac 27: 8 came to a **p** called Fair Havens, G5536
Ac 28:23 numbers to the **p where** he was **staying**. G3825
Ro 2:16 This will take **p** on the day when God judges NDT
Ro 9:26 "In the very **p** where it was said to them G5536
Ro 15:23 that there is no more **p** for me to work in G5536
1Co 11:18 **In the first p**, I hear that when you come G4754
2Co 7: 3 before that *you* **have** such a **p** in our G1639
Eph 5: 4 joking, which *are* **out of p**, but rather G4024+465
Eph 6:14 *with* the breastplate of righteousness **in p**, G1907
Php 2: 9 God **exalted** him **to the highest p** and G5671
1Ti 5:24 reaching **the p of** judgment ahead of G1650
2Ti 2:18 *that* the resurrection *has* already **taken p**, G1181
Phm 13 that he could **take** your **p** in helping me G5642
Heb 2: 6 But there is a **p where** someone has G4543
Heb 5: 6 And he says in **another** *p*, "You are a priest AIT
Heb 8: 7 no **p** would have been sought for another. G5536
Heb 9: 2 this was called the **Holy P**. G41
Heb 9: 3 was a room called the **Most Holy P**, G41+41
Heb 9: 8 the way *into* the **Most Holy P** had not yet G41
Heb 9:12 he entered the **Most Holy P** once for all by G41
Heb 9:25 priest enters the **Most Holy P** every year with G41
Heb 10:19 to enter the **Most Holy P** by the blood of G41
Heb 11: 8 called to go to a **p** he would later receive G5536
Heb 13:11 animals into the **Most Holy P** as a sin G41
2Pe 1:19 as to a light shining in a dark **p**, until the G5536
Rev 1: 1 show his servants what must soon **take p**. G1181
Rev 1:19 what is now and what will **take p** later. G1181
Rev 2: 5 remove your lampstand from its **p**. G5536
Rev 4: 1 will show you what must **take p** after this." G1181
Rev 6:14 island was removed from its **p**. G5536
Rev 12: 6 into the wilderness *to* a **p** prepared for her G5536
Rev 12: 8 enough, and they lost their **p** in heaven. G5536
Rev 12:14 she might fly to the **p** prepared for her in G5536
Rev 13: 6 name and his **dwelling p** and those who G5008
Rev 16:16 kings together to the **p** that in Hebrew is G5536
Rev 20:11 presence, and there was no **p** for them. G5536
Rev 21: 3 God's **dwelling p** is now among the G5008
Rev 22: 6 servants the things that must soon **take p**." G1181

PLACED (94) [PLACE]

Ge 3:24 *he* **p** on the east side of the Garden of H8905
Ge 22: 6 burnt offering and **p** it on his son Isaac, H8492
Ge 28:18 took the stone *he had* **p** under his head H8492
Ge 30:35 and *he* **p** them in the care of his sons. H5989
Ge 30:38 Then *he* **p** the peeled branches in all the H3657
Ge 50:23 of Manasseh *were* **p at birth** on Joseph's H3528
Ge 50:26 *he* **was p** in a coffin in Egypt. H8492
Ex 2: 3 Then *she* **p** the child in it and put it H8492
Ex 40:20 the covenant law and **p** them in the ark, H5989
Ex 40:22 Moses **p** the table in the tent of meeting H5989
Ex 40:24 *He* **p** the lampstand in the tent of H8492
Ex 40:26 Moses **p** the gold altar in the tent of H8492
Ex 40:30 *He* **p** the basin between the tent of H8492
Lev 8: 8 *He* **p** the breastpiece on him and put the H8492
Lev 8: 9 Then *he* **p** the turban on Aaron's head H8492
Nu 17: 7 Moses **p** the staffs before the LORD in the H5663
Jos 10:24 came forward and **p** their feet on their H8492
Jos 10:27 the mouth of the cave *they* **p** large rocks, H8492
Jdg 7:16 *he* **p** trumpets and empty jars in the H5989
Jdg 8:27 an ephod, which *he* **p** in Ophrah, his town H3657
Ru 3:15 of barley and **p** the bundle on her. H8883
1Sa 6:11 *They* **p** the ark of the LORD on the cart and H8492
1Sa 6:15 objects, and **p** them on the large rock. H8492
2Sa 12:30 king's head, and it was *p* **on** his own head. AIT
2Sa 15: 2 with a complaint to *be* **p** before the king H995
1Ki 6:27 *He* **p** the cherubim inside the innermost H5989
1Ki 7: 4 Its **windows** were **p high** in sets of three H9209
1Ki 7:39 *He* **p** five of the stands on the south side H5989
1Ki 7:39 *He* **p** the Sea on the south side, at the H5989
1Ki 7:51 and *he* **p** them in the treasuries of the H5989
1Ki 8: 9 tablets that Moses *had* **p** *in* it at Horeb, H5663
1Ki 10: 9 in you and **p** you on the throne of H5989
1Ki 21: 8 name, **p** his **seal** *on* them H3159+928+2597
2Ki 12: 9 *He* **p** it beside the altar, on the right side H5989
1Ch 20: 2 stones—and it was **p on** David's head. H6584
2Ch 4: 6 washing and **p** five on the south side H5989
2Ch 4: 7 them and **p** them in the temple, H5989
2Ch 4: 8 ten tables and **p** them in the temple, H5663
2Ch 4:10 *He* **p** the Sea on the south side, at the H5989
2Ch 5: 1 and *he* **p** them in the treasuries of God's H5989
2Ch 5:10 tablets that Moses *had* **p** in it at Horeb, H5989
2Ch 6:11 There *I have* **p** the ark, in which is the H8492
2Ch 6:13 and *had* **p** it in the center of the outer H5989
2Ch 9: 8 in you and **p** you on his throne as H5989
2Ch 23:18 Then Jehoiada **p** the oversight of the H8492
2Ch 24: 8 a chest was made and **p** outside, at the H5989
2Ch 28:27 he *was* not **p** in the tombs of the kings H995
Ezr 1: 7 Jerusalem and *had* **p** in the temple of H5989
Ne 5:15 **p a heavy burden** on the people and took H3877
Ne 9:37 goes to the kings *you have* **p** over us. H5989
Est 2: 3 Let them be **p** under the care of Hegai, the NDT
Est 6: 8 one with a royal crest **p** on its head. H5989
Job 6: 2 all my misery *be* **p** on the scales! H5951
Job 20: 4 ever since mankind *was* **p** on the earth, H8492
Ps 21: 3 rich blessings and **p** a crown of pure gold H8883
Pr 11: 7 Hopes **p** in mortals die with them; all the NDT
Jer 24: 1 two baskets of figs **p** in front of the temple H3585
Jer 37:21 Jeremiah *to be* **p** in the courtyard H7212
Eze 23:41 it on which *you had* **p** the incense and H8492
Eze 32:27 their swords **p** under their heads and their H5989
Eze 40:42 On them *were* **p** the utensils for H5663
Eze 43: 8 When they **p** their threshold next to my H5989
Da 2:38 in your hands *he has* **p** all mankind and A10314
Da 2:48 the king **p** Daniel **in a high position** and A10648
Da 2:48 of Babylon and **p** him in charge of all NDT
Da 5: 7 have a gold chain **p** around his neck, NDT
Da 5:16 have a gold chain **p** around your neck, NDT
Da 5:29 a gold chain was **p** around his neck, and he NDT
Da 6:17 was brought and **p** over the mouth of the A10682
Mt 18: 2 and **p** the child among them. G2705
Mt 19:15 *When he had* **p** his hands **on** them, he G2202
Mt 21: 7 the colt and **p** their cloaks on them G2202
Mt 27:37 Above his head *they* **p** the written charge G2202
Mt 27:60 **p** it in his own new tomb that he had G5502
Mk 6:56 *they* **p** the sick in the marketplaces. G5502
Mk 9:36 a little child whom *he* **p** among them. G2705
Mk 10:16 **p** his hands on them and blessed them. G5502
Mk 15:46 and **p** it in a tomb cut out of rock. G5502
Lk 2: 7 him in cloths and **p** him in a manger, G369
Lk 23:53 it in linen cloth and **p** it in a tomb cut in G5502
Jn 3:35 loves the Son and *has* **p** everything in his G1443
Jn 6:27 God the Father *has* **p** *his* **seal of approval**." G5381
Ac 7:16 back to Shechem and **p** in the tomb that G5502
Ac 7:21 *When* he *was* **p outside**, Pharaoh's G1758
Ac 8:17 Peter and John **p** their hands **on** them, G2202
Ac 9:37 was washed and **p** in an upstairs room G5502
Ac 13: 3 *they* **p** their hands **on** them and sent them G2202
Ac 19: 6 *When* Paul **p** his hands **on** them, the Holy G2202
Ac 28: 8 **p** his hands **on** him and healed him. G2202
1Co 12:18 But in fact God *has* **p** the parts in the body G5502
1Co 12:28 And God *has* **p** in the church first of all G5502
Eph 1:22 And God **p** all things **under** his feet and G5718
Rev 1:17 Then *he* **p** his right hand on me and said G5502
Rev 3: 8 *I have* **p** before you an open door that no G1443

PLACES (137) [PLACE]

Ex 10:23 had light in the **p where** they **lived**. H4632
Lev 14:28 to put on the same **p** he put the blood of H5226
Lev 26:30 I will destroy your **high p**, cut down your H1195
Nu 24: 5 your tents, Jacob, your **dwelling p**, Israel! H5438
Nu 33:52 cast idols, and demolish all their **high p**. H1195
Nu 35:12 They will be **p** of refuge from the avenger H6551
Dt 1:33 to search out **p** for you to camp and to H5226
Dt 12: 2 completely all the **p** on the high H5226
Dt 12: 3 wipe out their names from those **p**. H5226
Jdg 5:11 the voice of the singers at the **watering p** H5393
Jdg 19:13 spend the night in one of those **p**. H5226
Jdg 20: 2 of Israel took *their* **p** in the assembly H3656
Jdg 20:33 moved from their **p** and took up positions H5226
1Sa 7:16 to Mizpah, judging Israel in all those **p**. H5226
1Sa 23:23 about all the **hiding p** he uses and come H4676
1Sa 30:31 those in all the *other* **p** where he and his H5226
1Ki 3: 2 were still sacrificing at the **high p** H1195
1Ki 3: 3 burned incense on the **high p**. H1195
1Ki 12:31 built shrines on **high p** and appointed H1195
1Ki 12:32 priests at the **high p** he had made. H1195
1Ki 13: 2 the priests of the **high p** who make H1195
1Ki 13:32 the shrines on the **high p** in the towns of H1195
1Ki 13:33 priests for the **high p** from all sorts of H1195
1Ki 13:33 a priest he consecrated for the **high p**. H1195
1Ki 14:23 They also set up for themselves **high p** H1195
1Ki 15:14 Although he did not remove the **high p** H1195
1Ki 22:43 The **high p**, however, were not removed H1195
2Ki 6:10 so that he was on his guard **in such p**. H9004S
2Ki 8:12 "You will set fire to their **fortified p**, kill H4448
2Ki 12: 3 The **high p**, however, were not removed H1195
2Ki 14: 4 The **high p**, however, were not removed H1195
2Ki 15: 4 The **high p**, however, were not removed H1195
2Ki 15:35 The **high p**, however, were not removed H1195
2Ki 16: 4 burned incense at the **high p**, H1195
2Ki 17: 9 built themselves **high p** in all their towns. H1195
2Ki 17:29 of Samaria had made at the **high p**. H1195
2Ki 17:32 as priests in the shrines at the **high p**. H1195
2Ki 18: 4 He removed the **high p**, smashed the H1195
2Ki 18:22 he the one whose **high p** and altars H1195
2Ki 21: 3 He rebuilt the **high p** his father Hezekiah H1195
2Ki 23: 5 incense on the **high p** of the towns of H1195
2Ki 23: 8 of Judah and desecrated the **high p**, H1195

2Ki 23: 9 the priests of the **high p** did not serve at H1195
2Ki 23:13 desecrated the **high p** that were east of H1195
2Ki 23:19 the shrines at the **high p** that the kings of H1195
2Ki 23:20 priests of those **high p** on the altars and H1195
2Ch 8:11 because **the p** the ark of the LORD has H2156S
2Ch 11:15 own priests for the **high p** and for the goat H1195
2Ch 14: 3 the foreign altars and the **high p**, H1195
2Ch 14: 5 He removed the **high p** and incense altars H1195
2Ch 15:17 he did not remove the **high p** from Israel, H1195
2Ch 17: 6 he removed the **high p** and the Asherah H1195
2Ch 20:33 The **high p**, however, were not removed H1195
2Ch 21:11 He had also built **high p** on the hills of H1195
2Ch 28: 4 burned incense at the **high p**, H1195
2Ch 28:25 in Judah he built **high p** to burn sacrifices H1195
2Ch 31: 1 They destroyed the **high p** and the altars H1195
2Ch 32:12 remove this god's **high p** and altars, H1195
2Ch 33: 3 He rebuilt the **high p** his father Hezekiah H1195
2Ch 33:17 continued to sacrifice at the **high p**, but H1195
2Ch 33:19 where he built **high p** and set up Asherah H1195
2Ch 34: 3 to purge Judah and Jerusalem of **high p**, H1195
2Ch 35:10 priests stood in their **p** with the Levites in H6642
2Ch 35:15 were in the **p** prescribed by David H5096
Ezr 3:10 cymbals, **took** *their* **p** to praise the LORD H6641
Ezr 6: 5 to be returned to their **p** in the temple in A10087
Ne 3: 7 **p** under the authority of the governor of NDT
Ne 4:13 points of the wall at the **exposed p**, H7460
Ne 9: 2 *They* **stood in** *their* **p** and confessed their H6641
Ne 12:40 thanks then **took** *their* **p** in the house of H6641
Job 3:14 built for themselves **p** now **lying in ruins**, H2999
Job 4:18 If God **p** no **trust** in his servants, if he H586
Job 15:15 If God **p** no **trust** in his holy ones, if even H586
Job 28: 4 in **p** untouched by human feet H2021S
Job 38:20 Can you take them to their **p**? Do you H1473
Ps 16: 6 lines have fallen for me in **pleasant** *p*; AIT
Ps 74:20 of violence fill the **dark p** *of* the land. H4743
Ps 78:58 They angered him with their **high p**; they H1195
SS 2:14 in the **hiding p** *on* the mountainside H6260
Isa 7:25 **p where** cattle are **turned loose** and H5448
Isa 15: 2 its temple, to its **high p** to weep; Moab H1195
Isa 17: 9 will be like **p abandoned** *to* thickets and AIT
Isa 22: 9 City of David were broken through *in* **many** *p*; AIT
Isa 30:28 he **p** in the jaws of the peoples a bit that NDT
Isa 32:18 people will live in peaceful **dwelling p**, H5659
Isa 32:18 in secure homes, in undisturbed **p of rest**. H4957
Isa 34:14 lie down and find for themselves **p of rest**. H4955
Isa 36: 7 he the one whose **high p** and altars H1195
Isa 40: 4 shall become level, the **rugged p** a plain. H8221
Isa 42:16 them and make the **rough p** smooth. H5112
Isa 45: 3 riches stored in **secret p**, so that you may H5041
Isa 61: 4 ruins and restore the *p* long **devastated**; AIT
Jer 7:31 have built the **high p** *of* Topheth in the H1195
Jer 9:26 live in the wilderness in **distant p**. H7916+6991
Jer 17: 3 together with your **high p**, because of sin H1195
Jer 17: 6 will dwell in the **parched p** *of* the desert, H3083
Jer 19: 5 They have built the **high p** *of* Baal to burn H1195
Jer 23:24 Who can hide in **secret p** so that I cannot H5041
Jer 25:23 Buz and all who are in **distant p**; H7916+6991
Jer 26:10 of the LORD and **took** *their* **p** at the H3782
Jer 29:14 all the nations and **p** where I have H5226
Jer 32:35 They built **high p** *for* Baal in the Valley of H1195
Jer 48:35 offerings on the **high p** and burn incense H1195
Jer 49:10 I will uncover his **hiding p**, so that he H5041
Jer 49:32 who are in **distant p** and will bring H7916+6991
Jer 51:51 have entered the **holy p** *of* the LORD's H5219
Eze 6: 3 and I will destroy your **high p**. H1195
Eze 6: 6 be laid waste and the **high p** demolished, H1195
Eze 6:13 **p** where they offered fragrant incense to H5226
Eze 16:16 of your garments to make gaudy **high p**, H1195
Eze 34:12 them from all the **p** where they were H5226
Eze 34:26 make them and the *p* **surrounding** my hill a AIT
Eze 42:14 they go near **the p** *that* are for the people." H889S
Eze 46:23 with **p for fire** built all around under the H4453
Eze 47:10 Eglaim there will be **p for spreading** nets. H5427
Da 4:21 and *having* **nesting p** in its branches A10709
Hos 10: 8 The **high p** *of* wickedness will be H1195
Joel 3: 7 rouse them out of the **p** to which you sold H5226
Am 7: 9 "The **high p** *of* Isaac will be destroyed H1195
Mt 8:11 and *will* **take** *their* **p at the feast** with *G369*
Mt 12:43 it goes through arid **p** seeking rest and *G5536*
Mt 13: 5 Some fell on **rocky p**, where it did not have *G4378*
Mt 20:23 These **p** belong to those for whom they NDT
Mt 24: 7 be famines and earthquakes in various **p**. *G5536*
Mk 1:45 openly but stayed outside in lonely **p**. *G5536*
Mk 4: 5 Some fell on **rocky p**, where it did not have *G4378*
Mk 4:16 like seed sown on **rocky p**, hear the word *G4378*
Mk 10:40 These **p** belong to those for whom they NDT
Mk 12:39 the **p of honor** at banquets. *G4752*
Mk 13: 8 There will be earthquakes in various **p** *G5536*
Lk 5:16 often withdrew to **lonely p** and prayed. *G2245*
Lk 8:29 been driven by the demon into **solitary p**. *G2245*
Lk 11:24 it goes through arid **p** seeking rest and *G5536*
Lk 13:29 and *will* **take** *their* **p at the feast** in the *G369*
Lk 14: 7 guests picked the **p of honor at the table**, *G4752*
Lk 20:46 the **p of honor** at banquets. *G4752*
Lk 21:11 famines and pestilences in various **p**, and *G5536*

PLACING (4) [PLACE]

Ge 48:17 Joseph saw his father **p** his right hand on H8883
2Ki 10:24 any of the men I *am* **p** in your hands H995
Ezr 5: 8 large stones and **p** the timbers in the A10682
Ac 9:17 **P** his hands **on** Saul, he said, "Brother *G2202*

PLAGUE (85) [PLAGUED, PLAGUES]

Ex 8: 2 I *will* **send a p** of frogs *on* your whole H5597
Ex 9: 3 will bring a terrible **p** on your livestock in H1822
Ex 9:15 your people with a **p** that would have H1822
Ex 10:14 before had there been such a **p** of locusts, NDT
Ex 10:17 God to take this **deadly p** away from me." H4638
Ex 11: 1 will bring one more **p** on Pharaoh and on H5596
Ex 12:13 No destructive **p** will touch you when I H5598
Ex 30:12 Then no **p** will come on them when you H5598
Ex 32:35 LORD **struck** the people **with a p** because H5597
Lev 26:25 I will send a **p** among you, and you H1822
Nu 8:19 them so that no **p** will strike the H5598
Nu 11:33 he struck them with a severe **p**. H4804
Nu 14:12 them down with a **p** and destroy them, H1822
Nu 14:37 down and died of a **p** before the LORD. H4487
Nu 16:46 come out from the LORD; the **p** has started." H5598
Nu 16:47 The **p** had already started among the H5598
Nu 16:48 living and the dead, and the **p** stopped. H4487
Nu 16:49 But 14,700 people died from the **p**, in H4487
Nu 16:50 tent of meeting, for the **p** had stopped. H4487
Nu 25: 8 Then the **p** against the Israelites was H4487
Nu 25: 9 who died in the **p** numbered 24,000. H4487
Nu 25:18 was killed when the **p** came as a result of H4487
Nu 26: 1 After the **p** the LORD said to Moses and H4487
Nu 31:16 so that a **p** struck the LORD's people. H4487
Dt 28:21 The LORD *will* **p** you *with* diseases until he H1815
Dt 28:22 mildew, *which will* **p** you until you perish. H8103
Dt 32:24 consuming pestilence and deadly **p**; I will H7776
Jos 22:17 even though a **p** fell on the community of H5598
1Sa 6: 4 because the same **p** has struck both you H4487
2Sa 24:13 Or three days of **p** in your land? Now H1822
2Sa 24:15 So the LORD sent a **p** on Israel from that H1822
2Sa 24:21 that the **p** on the people may be stopped." H4487
2Sa 24:25 and the **p** on Israel was stopped. H4487
1Ki 8:37 "When famine or **p** comes to the land, or H1822
1Ch 21:12 of the LORD—days of **p** in the land, with H1822
1Ch 21:14 So the LORD sent a **p** on Israel, and H1822
1Ch 21:17 do not let this **p** remain on your H4487
1Ch 21:22 that the **p** on the people may be stopped. H4487
2Ch 6:28 "When famine or **p** comes to the land, or H1822
2Ch 7:13 the land or send a **p** among my people, H1822
2Ch 20: 9 of judgment, or **p** or famine, we will H1822
Job 27:15 The **p** will bury those who survive him H4638
Ps 78:50 from death but gave them over to the **p**. H1822
Ps 91: 6 the **p** that destroys at midday. H7776
Ps 106:29 and a **p** broke out among them. H4487
Ps 106:30 intervened, and the **p** was checked. H4487
Isa 19:22 The LORD *will* **strike** Egypt **with a p**; H5597
Jer 14:12 them with the sword, famine and **p**." H1822
Jer 21: 6 beast—and they will die of a terrible **p**. H1822
Jer 21: 7 the people in this city who survive the **p**, H1822
Jer 21: 9 this city will die by the sword, famine or **p**. H1822
Jer 24:10 famine and **p** against them until they are H1822
Jer 27: 8 famine and **p**, declares the LORD, H1822
Jer 27:13 famine and **p** with which the LORD has H1822
Jer 28: 8 disaster and **p** against many countries H1822
Jer 29:17 famine and **p** against them and I will H1822
Jer 29:18 famine and **p** and will make them H1822
Jer 32:24 the sword, famine and **p**, the city will be H1822
Jer 32:36 famine and **p** it will be given into the H1822
Jer 34:17 to fall by the sword, **p** and famine. H1822
Jer 38: 2 the sword, famine or **p**, but whoever goes H1822
Jer 42:17 famine and **p**; not one of them will H1822
Jer 42:22 famine and **p** in the place where you H1822
Jer 44:13 the sword, famine and **p**, as I punished H1822
Eze 5:12 will die of the **p** or perish by famine H1822
Eze 5:17 **P** and bloodshed will sweep through you H1822
Eze 6:11 they will fall by the sword, famine and **p**. H1822
Eze 6:12 One who is far away will die of the **p**, and H1822
Eze 7:15 is the sword; inside are **p** and famine. H1822
Eze 7:15 the city will be devoured by famine and **p**. H1822
Eze 12:16 the sword, famine and **p**, so that in the H1822
Eze 14:19 "Or if I send a **p** into that land and pour H1822
Eze 14:21 sword and famine and wild beasts and **p**— H1822
Eze 28:23 I will send a **p** upon you and make blood H1822
Eze 33:27 in strongholds and caves will die of a **p**. H1822
Eze 38:22 judgment on him with **p** and bloodshed; H1822
Mic 1: 9 For Samaria's **p** is incurable; it has spread H4804
Hab 3: 5 **P** went before him; pestilence followed H1822
Zec 14:12 This is the **p** with which the LORD will strike H4487
Zec 14:15 A similar **p** will strike the horses and H4487
Zec 14:18 will bring on them the **p** he inflicts on the H4487
Rev 6: 8 by sword, famine and **p**, and by the wild *G2505*
Rev 11: 6 earth with every kind *of* **p** as often as they *G4435*
Rev 16:21 cursed God on account of the **p** of hail, *G4435*
Rev 16:21 because the **p** was so terrible. *G4435*

PLAGUED (1) [PLAGUE]

Ps 73: 5 burdens; *they* **are** not **p** by human ills. H5595

PLAGUES (16) [PLAGUE]

Ex 5: 3 he may strike us with **p** or with the sword." H1822
Ex 9:14 the full force of my **p** against you and H4487
Dt 28:59 LORD will send fearful **p** *on* you and your H4804
1Sa 4: 8 with all kinds of **p** in the wilderness. H4804
Hos 13:14 O death, are your **p**? Where, H1822
Am 4:10 "I sent **p** among you as I did to Egypt. H1822
Rev 9:18 mankind was killed by the three **p** of fire, *G4435*
Rev 9:20 not killed by these **p** still did not repent of *G4435*
Rev 15: 1 seven angels with the seven last **p**—last *G4435*
Rev 15: 6 came the seven angels with the seven **p**. *G4435*
Rev 15: 8 until the seven **p** of the seven angels *G4435*
Rev 16: 9 who had control over these **p**, but they *G4435*
Rev 18: 4 so that you will not receive any *of* her **p**; *G4435*
Rev 18: 8 in one day her **p** will overtake her: *G4435*
Rev 21: 9 of the seven last **p** came and said to me, *G4435*
Rev 22:18 add to that person the **p** described in this *G4435*

PLAIN (30) [PLAINLY, PLAINS]

Ge 11: 2 they found a **p** in Shinar and settled there. H1326
Ge 13:10 saw that the whole **p** *of* the Jordan toward H3971
Ge 13:11 himself the whole **p** *of* the Jordan and set H3971
Ge 13:12 the cities of the **p** and pitched his tents H3971
Ge 19:17 and don't stop anywhere in the **p**! H3971
Ge 19:25 he overthrew those cities and the entire **p**, H3971
Ge 19:28 toward all the land of the **p**, and he saw H3971
Ge 19:29 So when God destroyed the cities of the **p**, H3971
Jos 17:16 who live in the **p** have chariots fitted H824+6677
Jdg 1:34 allowing them to come down into the **p**. H6677
2Sa 18:23 ran by way of the **p** and outran the H3971
1Ki 7:46 clay molds in the **p** *of* the Jordan between H3971
2Ch 4:17 clay molds in the **p** *of* the Jordan between H3971
2Ch 26:10 livestock in the foothills and in the **p**. H4793
2Ch 35:22 went to fight him on the **p** *of* Megiddo. H1326
Ne 6: 2 in one of the villages on the **p** *of* Ono." H1326
Isa 40: 4 become level, the rugged places a **p**. H1326
Isa 63:14 like cattle that go down to the **p**, they H1326
Jer 47: 5 You remnant on the **p**, how long will you H6677
Eze 3:22 "Get up and go out to the **p**, and there I H1326
Eze 3:23 So I got up and went out to the **p**. And the H1326
Eze 8: 4 as in the vision I had seen in the **p**. H1326
Da 3: 1 set it up on the **p** *of* Dura in the A10117
Hab 2: 2 the revelation and **make** it **p** on tablets so H930
Zec 12:11 of Hadad Rimmon in the **p** *of* Megiddo. H1326
Ro 1:19 may be known about God is **p** to them, *G5745*
Ro 1:19 because God *has* **made** it **p** to them. *G5746*
2Co 5:11 *What we are is* **p** to God, and I hope it is *G5746*
2Co 5:11 I hope *it is* also **p** to your conscience. *G5746*
Eph 3: 9 and *to* **make p** to everyone the *G5894*

PLAINLY (8) [PLAIN]

Mt 7:23 Then *I will* **tell** them **p**, 'I never knew you *G3933*
Mk 7:35 was loosened and he began to speak **p**. *G3987*
Mk 8:32 He spoke **p** about this, and Peter took him *G4244*
Jn 3:21 so that *it may be* **seen p** that what they *G5746*
Jn 10:24 If you are the Messiah, tell us **p**." *G4244*
Jn 11:14 So then he told them **p**, "Lazarus is dead, *G4244*
Jn 16:25 will tell you **p** about my Father. *G4244*
2Co 4: 2 *by* **setting forth** the truth **p** we commend *G5748*

PLAINS (20) [PLAIN]

Nu 22: 1 traveled to the **p** *of* Moab and camped H6858
Nu 26: 3 So on the **p** *of* Moab by the Jordan across H6858
Nu 26:63 Israelites on the **p** *of* Moab by the Jordan H6858
Nu 31:12 assembly at their camp on the **p** *of* Moab, H6858
Nu 33:48 camped on the **p** *of* Moab by the H6858
Nu 33:49 There on the **p** *of* Moab they camped H6858
Nu 33:50 On the **p** *of* Moab by the Jordan across H6858
Nu 35: 1 On the **p** *of* Moab by the Jordan across H6858
Nu 36:13 Israelites on the **p** *of* Moab by the Jordan H6858
Dt 34: 1 Nebo from the **p** *of* Moab to the top of H6858
Dt 34: 8 Moses in the **p** *of* Moab thirty days, H6858
Jos 4:13 before the LORD to the **p** *of* Jericho for war. H6858
Jos 5:10 camped at Gilgal on the **p** *of* Jericho, H6858
Jos 13:32 when he was in the **p** *of* Moab across the H6858
Jdg 1:19 unable to drive the people from the **p**, H6677
1Ki 20:23 But if we fight them on the **p**, surely we H4793
1Ki 20:25 chariot—so we can fight Israel on the **p**. H4793
2Ki 25: 5 king and overtook him in the **p** *of* Jericho. H6858
Jer 39: 5 overtook Zedekiah in the **p** *of* Jericho. H6858
Jer 52: 8 overtook him in the **p** *of* Jericho. H6858

PLAN (33) [PLANNED, PLANNING, PLANS]

Ge 11: 6 then nothing *they* **p** to do will be H2372
Ge 41:37 The **p** seemed good to Pharaoh and to all H1821
Ex 26:30 according to the **p** shown you on the H5477
Nu 33:56 I will do to you what *I* **p** to do to them. H1948
1Sa 18:25 Saul's **p** *was* to have David fall by the H3108
2Sa 17: 4 This **p** seemed good to Absalom and to H1821
1Ch 28:18 He also gave him the **p** *for* the chariot H9322
1Ch 28:19 me to understand all the details of the **p**." H9322
2Ch 13: 8 "And now you **p** to resist the kingdom of H606
2Ch 30: 4 The **p** seemed right both to the king and H1821
Est 8: 3 end to the evil **p** *of* Haman the Agagite, H4742
Ps 64: 6 say, "We have devised a perfect **p**!" H2925
Ps 106:13 done and did not wait for his **p** to unfold. H6783
Pr 14:22 But *those who* **p** what is good find love H3086
Pr 16: 9 In their hearts humans **p** their course, but H3108
Pr 21:30 no **p** that can succeed against the LORD. H6783
Pr 30:32 yourself, or if *you* **p evil**, clap your hand H2372
Isa 5:19 The **p** *of* the Holy One of Israel—let it H6783
Isa 8:10 propose your **p**, but it will not stand H1821
Isa 14:26 This is the **p** determined for the whole H6783
Isa 28:29 Almighty, whose **p** is wonderful, whose H6783
Jer 18:11 you and devising a **p** against you. H4742
Jer 36: 3 about every disaster I **p** to inflict on them, H3108
Jer 49:30 he has devised a **p** against you. H4742
Am 3: 7 without revealing his **p** to his servants the H6051
Mic 2: 1 Woe to *those who* **p** iniquity, to those H3108
Mic 4:12 they do not understand his **p**, that he has H6783
Mt 28:12 had met with the elders and devised a **p**, *G5206*
Ac 2:23 over to you *by* God's deliberate **p** and *G1087*
Ac 9:24 Saul learned of their **p**. Day and night *G2101*
Ac 27:43 kept them from carrying out their **p**. *G1088*
Ro 15:24 I **p** to do so when I go to Spain. I hope to NDT

P

Eph 1:11 according to the **p** of him who works out *G4606*

PLANE (2)

Ge 30:37 almond and **p trees** and made white H6895
Eze 31: 8 could the **p trees** compare with its H6895

PLANK (6) [PLANKS]

Mt 7: 3 pay no attention to the **p** in your own eye? *G1512*
Mt 7: 4 all the time there is a **p** in your own eye? *G1512*
Mt 7: 5 first take the **p** out of your own eye, and *G1512*
Lk 6:41 pay no attention to the **p** in your own eye? *G1512*
Lk 6:42 yourself fail to see the **p** in your own eye? *G1512*
Lk 6:42 first take the **p** out of your eye, and then *G1512*

PLANKS (3) [PLANK]

1Ki 6: 9 roofing it with beams and cedar **p**. H8444
1Ki 6:15 the floor of the temple with **p** *of* juniper. H7521
Ac 27:44 were to get there on **p** or on other pieces *G4909*

PLANNED (20) [PLAN]

2Ki 19:25 In days of old *I* **p** it; now I have brought it H3670
Ps 17: 3 you will find that *I have* **p** no **evil**; my H2372
Ps 40: 5 you have done, the **things** you **p** for us. H4742
Isa 14:24 "Surely, as *I have* **p**, so it will be H1948
Isa 19:12 the LORD Almighty *has* **p** against Egypt. H3619
Isa 22:11 regard for the *One who* **p** it long ago. H3670
Isa 23: 8 Who **p** this against Tyre, the bestower of H3619
Isa 23: 9 The LORD Almighty **p** it, to bring down her H3619
Isa 25: 1 done wonderful things, *things* **p** long ago. H6783
Isa 37:26 In days of old *I* **p** it; now I have brought it H3670
Isa 46:11 bring about; what *I have* **p**, that I will do. H3670
Isa 66:18 because of **what** they have **p** and done H4742
Jer 18: 8 not inflict on it the disaster *I had* **p**. H3108
Jer 49:20 what the LORD *has* **p** against Edom, H3619+6783
Jer 50:45 what the LORD *has* **p** against H3619+6783
La 2:17 The LORD has done what *he* **p**; he has H2372
Da 6: 3 that the king **p** to set him over the A10575
Ac 27:42 The soldiers **p** to kill the prisoners *G1087+1181*
Ro 1:13 that *I* **p** many times to come to you *G4729*
Heb 11:40 *since* God *had* **p** something better for us *G4587*

PLANNING (5) [PLAN]

Ge 27:42 Esau *is* **p to avenge himself** by killing H5714
Ecc 9:10 neither working nor **p** nor knowledge nor H3113
Isa 19:17 LORD Almighty *is* **p** against them. H3619+6783
Jer 26: 3 them the disaster I *was* **p** because of the H3108
Mic 2: 3 "I *am* **p** disaster against this people, from H3108

PLANS (50) [PLAN]

1Sa 23:10 definitely that Saul **p** to come to Keilah H1335
2Ki 16:10 with detailed **p** for its construction. H9322
2Ki 16:11 with all **the p** that King Ahaz had H889S
1Ch 28: 2 of our God, and *I* **made p** to build it. H3922
1Ch 28:11 son Solomon the **p** *for* the portico of the H9322
1Ch 28:12 He gave him the **p** *of* all that the Spirit H9322
Ezr 4: 5 frustrate their **p** during the entire H6783
Job 5:12 He thwarts the **p** *of* the crafty, so that their H4742
Job 10: 3 while you smile on the **p** *of* the wicked? H6783
Job 17:11 days have passed, my **p** are shattered. H2365
Job 21:16 so I stand aloof from the **p** *of* the wicked. H6783
Job 22:18 so I stand aloof from the **p** *of* the wicked. H6783
Job 23:14 many such **p** he still has in store. H2179S
Job 38: 2 that obscures my **p** with words without H6783
Job 42: 3 that obscures my **p** without knowledge? H6783
Ps 14: 6 You evildoers frustrate the **p** *of* the poor H6783
Ps 20: 4 your heart and make all your **p** succeed. H6783
Ps 33:10 The LORD foils the **p** *of* the nations; he H6783
Ps 33:11 But the **p** *of* the LORD stand firm forever H6783
Ps 64: 5 They encourage each other in evil **p**, they H1821
Ps 94:11 The LORD knows *all* human **p**; he knows H4742
Ps 107:11 despised the **p** *of* the Most High. H6783
Ps 140: 2 who **devise** evil **p** in their hearts and stir H3108
Ps 140: 8 desires, LORD; do not let their **p** succeed. H2373
Ps 146: 4 on that very day their **p** come to nothing. H6955
Pr 12: 5 The **p** *of* the righteous are just, but the H4742
Pr 15:22 **P** fail for lack of counsel, but with many H4742
Pr 16: 1 To humans belong the **p** *of* the heart, but H5119
Pr 16: 3 and he will establish your **p**. H4742
Pr 19:21 Many are the **p** in a person's heart, but it H4742
Pr 20:18 **P** are established by seeking advice; so if H4742
Pr 21: 5 The **p** *of* the diligent lead to profit as H4742
Isa 19: 3 I will bring their **p** to nothing; they H6783
Isa 29:15 great depths to hide their **p** from the LORD, H6783
Isa 30: 1 those who carry out **p** that are not mine, H6783
Isa 32: 8 But the noble **make** noble **p**, and by H3619
Jer 18:12 We will continue with our own **p**; we will H4742
Jer 18:18 *let's* **make p** against Jeremiah H3108+4742
Jer 19: 7 I will ruin the **p** *of* Judah and Jerusalem. H1238
Jer 29:11 For I know the **p** I **have** for you," H3108+4742
Jer 29:11 "**p** to prosper you and not to harm you H4742
Jer 29:11 harm you, **p** to give you hope and a future. NDT
Da 11:17 his **p** will not succeed or help him. NDT
Hos 11: 6 false prophets and put an end to their **p**. H4600
Na 1:11 against the LORD and **devises** wicked **p**. H3619
Mt 22:15 went out and laid **p** to trap him in his *G5206*
Mt 27: 1 people made their **p** how to have Jesus *G5206*
Mk 15: 1 the whole Sanhedrin, made their **p**. *G5206*
Jn 12:10 the chief priests **made p** to kill Lazarus as *G1086*
2Co 1:17 Or *do I* **make** *my* **p** in a worldly manner so *G1086*

PLANT (63) [PLANTED, PLANTER, PLANTING, PLANTS, REPLANTED, TRANSPLANTED]

Ge 1:29 every seed-bearing **p** on the face of the H6912
Ge 1:30 of life in it—I give every green **p** for food." H6912
Ge 2: 5 earth and no **p** had yet H6912+2021+8441
Ge 9:20 of the soil, proceeded *to* **p** a vineyard. H5749
Ge 47:23 is seed for you so *you can* **p** the ground. H2445
Ex 10:15 remained on tree or **p** in all the land of H6912
Ex 15:17 bring them in and **p** them on the H5749
Lev 19:19 *Do* not **p** your field **with** two kinds of **seed**. H2445
Lev 19:23 enter the land and **p** any kind of fruit tree H5749
Lev 25:20 seventh year if *we do* not **p** or harvest our H2445
Lev 25:22 While *you* **p** during the eighth year, you H2445
Lev 26:16 *You will* **p** seed in vain, because your H2445
Dt 6:11 olive groves *you did* not **p**— H5749
Dt 22: 9 *Do* not **p** two kinds of **seed** in your H2445
Dt 22: 9 only the crops *you* **p** but also the H2445+2446
Dt 28:30 *You will* **p** a vineyard, but you will not H5749
Dt 28:39 *You will* **p** vineyards and cultivate them H5749
Jos 24:13 olive groves that you *did* not **p**. H5749
2Sa 7:10 people Israel and *will* **p** them so that they H5749
1Ki 4:33 He spoke about **p life**, from the cedar of H6770
2Ki 19:29 reap, **p** vineyards and eat their fruit. H5749
1Ch 17: 9 people Israel and *will* **p** them so that they H5749
Job 8:16 They are like a **well-watered p** in the H8183
Job 14: 9 it will bud and put forth shoots like a **p**. H5750
Ecc 3: 2 a time to **p** and a time to uproot, H5749
Ecc 11: 4 Whoever watches the wind *will* not **p** H2445
Isa 17:10 the finest plants and **p** imported vines, H2445
Isa 17:11 on the morning when you **p** them H2445
Isa 28:25 *Does he* not **p** wheat in its place, barley H8492
Isa 37:30 reap, **p** vineyards and eat their fruit. H5749
Isa 65:21 *they will* **p** vineyards and eat their fruit. H5749
Isa 65:22 others live in them, or **p** and others eat. H5749
Jer 1:10 destroy and overthrow, to build and to **p**." H5749
Jer 24: 6 *I will* **p** them and not uproot them. H5749
Jer 29: 5 **p** gardens and eat what they produce. H5749
Jer 29:28 **p** gardens and eat what they produce. H5749
Jer 31: 5 Again *you will* **p** vineyards on the hills of H5749
Jer 31: 5 the farmers *will* **p** them and enjoy their H5749
Jer 31:27 *I will* **p** the kingdoms of Israel and Judah *with* H2445
Jer 31:28 I will watch over them to build and to **p**," H5749
Jer 32:41 good and *will* assuredly **p** them in this H5749
Jer 35: 7 sow seed or **p** vineyards; you must H5749
Jer 42:10 you down; *I will* **p** you and not uproot you H5749
Eze 16: 7 I made you grow like a **p** *of* the field. H7542
Eze 17:22 from the very top of a cedar and **p** it; H5989
Eze 17:22 topmost shoots and **p** it on a high and H9278
Eze 17:23 the mountain heights of Israel *I will* **p** it; H9278
Eze 28:26 will build houses and **p** vineyards; H5749
Hos 2:23 *I will* **p** her for myself in the land; I will H2445
Am 9:14 They will **p** vineyards and drink their wine H5749
Am 9:15 *I will* **p** Israel in their own land, never H5749
Jnh 4: 6 God provided a **leafy p** and made it grow H7813
Jnh 4: 6 Jonah was very happy about the **p**. H7813
Jnh 4: 7 which chewed the **p** so that it withered. H7813
Jnh 4: 9 "Is it right for you to be angry about the **p**?" H7813
Jnh 4:10 "You have been concerned about this **p** H7813
Mic 6:15 You *will* **p** but not harvest; you will press H2445
Zep 1:13 in them; though *they* **p** vineyards, they H5749
Mt 15:13 "Every **p** that my heavenly Father has not *G5884*
Jn 19:29 put the sponge on a **stalk of the hyssop p** *G5727*
1Co 15:37 *you do* not **p** the body that will be *G5062*
Jas 1:11 with scorching heat and withers the **p**; *G5965*
Rev 9: 4 the grass of the earth or any **p** or tree, *G5952*

PLANTED (51) [PLANT]

Ge 2: 8 Now the LORD God *had* **p** a garden in the H5749
Ge 21:33 Abraham **p** a tamarisk tree in Beersheba H5749
Ge 26:12 Isaac **p crops** in that land and the same H2445
Lev 11:37 falls on any seeds that *are to* **be p**, H2445
Nu 24: 6 like aloes **p** *by* the LORD, like H5749
Dt 11:10 where *you* **p** your seed and irrigated it by H2445
Dt 20: 6 *Has* anyone **p** a vineyard and not begun to H5749
Dt 21: 4 not been plowed or **p** and where there is H2445
Dt 29:23 sulfur—nothing **p**, nothing sprouting, H2445
Jdg 6: 3 Whenever the Israelites **p** *their* **crops**, the H2445
Ps 1: 3 person is like a tree **p** by streams of water, H9278
Ps 44: 2 drove out the nations and **p** our ancestors; H5749
Ps 80: 8 you drove out the nations and **p** it. H5749
Ps 80:15 the root your right hand *has* **p**, the son H5749
Ps 92:13 **p** in the house of the LORD, they will H9278
Ps 104:16 watered, the cedars of Lebanon that *he* **p**. H5749
Ps 107:37 They sowed fields and **p** vineyards that H5749
Ecc 2: 4 I built houses for myself and **p** vineyards. H5749
Ecc 2: 5 gardens and parks and **p** all kinds of fruit H5749
Isa 5: 2 it of stones and **p** it with the choicest H5749
Isa 40:24 No sooner **are** *they* **p**, no sooner are they H5749
Isa 44:14 of the forest, or a **p** a pine, and the rain H5749
Isa 60:21 They are the shoot I have **p**, the work of H4760
Jer 2:21 *I had* **p** you like a choice vine of sound H5749
Jer 11:17 LORD Almighty, who **p** you, has decreed H5749
Jer 12: 2 *You have* **p** them, and they have taken H5749
Jer 17: 8 will be like a tree **p** by the water that H9278
Jer 18: 9 nation or kingdom is to be built up and **p**, H5749
Jer 45: 4 I have built and uproot what *I have* **p**, H5749
Eze 17: 4 where *he* **p** it in a city of traders. H8492
Eze 17: 5 *He* **p** it like a willow by abundant water, H8492
Eze 17: 7 plot where it was **p** and stretched out its H4760
Eze 17: 8 It *had* **been p** in good soil by abundant H9278
Eze 17:10 *It has* **been p**, but will it thrive? Will it not H9278
Eze 19:10 like a vine in your vineyard **p** by the water; H9278
Eze 19:13 Now *it* **is p** in the desert, in a dry and H9278
Hos 9:13 Ephraim, like Tyre, **p** in a pleasant place. H9278
Hos 10:13 But *you have* **p** wickedness, you have H3086
Am 5:11 though *you have* **p** lush vineyards H5749
Hag 1: 6 *You have* **p** much, but harvested little. H2445
Mt 13:31 which a man took and **p** in his field. *G5062*
Mt 15:13 heavenly Father *has* not **p** will be pulled *G5885*
Mt 21:33 There was a landowner who **p** a vineyard *G5885*
Mk 4:32 Yet when **p**, it grows and becomes the *G5062*
Mk 12: 1 "A man **p** a vineyard. He put *G5885*
Lk 13:19 which a man took and **p** in his garden. *G965*
Lk 17: 6 'Be uprooted and **p** in the sea,' and it *G5885*
Lk 20: 9 "A man **p** a vineyard, rented it to some *G5885*
1Co 3: 6 I **p** *the* **seed**, Apollos watered it, but God *G5885*
Jas 1:21 humbly accept the word **p in** you, *G1875*
Rev 10: 2 *He* **p** his right foot on the sea and his left *G5502*

PLANTER (1) [PLANT]

Am 9:13 plowman and the **p** by the one H5432+2446

PLANTING (5) [PLANT]

Lev 26: 5 the grape harvest will continue until **p**, H2446
Isa 28:24 When a farmer plows for **p**, does he plow H2445
Isa 61: 3 a **p** *of* the LORD for the display of his H4760
Mic 1: 6 a heap of rubble, a place for **p** vineyards. H4760
Lk 17:28 buying and selling, **p** and building. *G5885*

PLANTS (30) [PLANT]

Ge 1:11 seed-bearing **p** and trees on the land that H6912
Ge 1:12 **p** bearing seed according to their kinds H6912
Ge 3:18 you, and you will eat the **p** *of* the field. H6912
Ge 9: 3 Just as I gave you the green **p**, I now give H6912
Ge 30:14 the fields and found *some* **mandrake p**, H1859
Dt 32: 2 like abundant rain on **tender p**. H6912
2Ki 19:26 They are like **p** *in* the field, like tender H6912
Job 8:19 and from the soil other **p** grow. NDT
Job 40:21 Under the **lotus p** it lies, hidden among H7365
Ps 37: 2 like green **p** they will soon die away. H3764
Ps 104:14 the cattle, and **p** for people to cultivate H6912
Ps 144:12 in their youth will be like well-nurtured **p**, H5745
Pr 31:16 out of her earnings *she* **p** a vineyard. H5749
SS 4:13 Your **p** are an orchard of pomegranates H8945
Isa 17:10 set out the finest **p** and plant imported H5750
Isa 19: 7 also the **p** along the Nile, at the mouth of H6868
Isa 37:27 They are like **p** *in* the field, like tender H6912
Da 4:15 the animals among the **p** *of* the earth. A10572
Zec 10: 1 all people, and **p** of the field to everyone. H6912
Mt 13: 6 the sun came up, the **p** were scorched, and NDT
Mt 13: 7 which grew up and choked the **p**. *G899S*
Mt 13:32 is the largest *of* **garden p** and becomes a *G3303*
Mk 4: 6 sun came up, *the p were* **scorched**, and they AIT
Mk 4: 7 which grew up and choked **the p**, so that *G899S*
Mk 4:32 becomes the largest of all **garden p**, *G3303*
Lk 8: 6 the **p** withered because they had no NDT
Lk 8: 7 which grew up with it and choked **the p**. *G899S*
1Co 3: 7 So neither the *one who* **p** nor the one who *G5885*
1Co 3: 8 The *one who* **p** and the one who waters *G5885*
1Co 9: 7 Who **p** a vineyard and does not eat its *G5885*

PLASTER (5) [PLASTERED]

Lev 14:42 these and take new clay and **p** the house. H3212
Lev 14:45 timbers and all the **p**—and taken out of H6760
Dt 27: 2 some large stones and coat them with **p**. H8487
Dt 27: 4 you today, and coat them with **p**. H8487
Da 5: 5 wrote on the **p** of the wall, A10142

PLASTERED (3) [PLASTER]

Lev 14:43 torn out and the house scraped and **p**, H3212
Lev 14:48 not spread after the house *has* **been p**, H3212
Isa 44:18 their eyes *are* **p over** so they cannot see H3220

PLATE (16) [PLATES, PLATTER]

Ex 28:36 "Make a **p** *of* pure gold and engrave on it H7488
Ex 39:30 They made the **p**, the sacred emblem, out H7488
Lev 8: 9 on Aaron's head and set the gold **p**, H7488
Nu 7:13 was one silver **p** weighing a hundred and H7883
Nu 7:19 was one silver **p** weighing a hundred and H7883
Nu 7:25 was one silver **p** weighing a hundred and H7883
Nu 7:31 was one silver **p** weighing a hundred and H7883
Nu 7:37 was one silver **p** weighing a hundred and H7883
Nu 7:43 was one silver **p** weighing a hundred and H7883
Nu 7:49 was one silver **p** weighing a hundred and H7883
Nu 7:55 was one silver **p** weighing a hundred and H7883
Nu 7:61 was one silver **p** weighing a hundred and H7883
Nu 7:67 was one silver **p** weighing a hundred and H7883
Nu 7:73 was one silver **p** weighing a hundred and H7883
Nu 7:79 was one silver **p** weighing a hundred and H7883
Nu 7:85 Each silver **p** weighed a hundred and thirty H7883

PLATEAU (10)

Dt 3:10 We took all the towns on the **p**, and all H4793
Dt 4:43 Bezer in the wilderness **p**, for the H824+4793
Jos 13: 9 included the whole **p** *of* Medeba as far as H4793
Jos 13:16 the gorge, and the whole **p** past Medeba H4793
Jos 13:17 to Heshbon and all its towns on the **p** H4793
Jos 13:21 the towns on the **p** and the entire realm H4793
Jos 20: 8 the wilderness on the **p** in the tribe of H4793
Jer 21:13 who live above this valley on the rocky **p**, H4793
Jer 48: 8 valley will be ruined and the **p** destroyed, H4793
Jer 48:21 Judgment has come to the **p**—to Holon H4793

PLATES (4) [PLATE]

Ex 25:29 And make its **p** and dishes of pure gold H7883
Ex 37:16 its **p** and dishes and bowls and its pitchers H7883
Nu 4: 7 to spread a blue cloth and put on it the **p**, H7883

P

Nu 7:84 twelve silver p, twelve silver sprinkling H7883

PLATFORM (3)
2Ch 6:13 Now he had made a bronze p, five cubits H3963
2Ch 6:13 He stood on the p and then knelt down H2257S
Ne 8: 4 stood on a high wooden p built for the H4463

PLATTED (KJV) TWISTED

PLATTER (4) [PLATE]
Mt 14: 8 "Give me here on a p the head of John G4402
Mt 14:11 was brought in on a p and given to the G4402
Mk 6:25 now the head of John the Baptist on a p." G4402
Mk 6:28 brought back his head on a p. G4402

PLAY (15) [PLAYED, PLAYERS, PLAYING, PLAYS]
Ge 4:21 the father of all who p stringed H9530
Ge 19: 9 and now he wants to p the judge! H9149+9149
1Sa 16:16 to search for someone who can p the lyre. H5594
1Sa 16:16 He will p when the evil spirit H5594+928+3338
1Sa 16:18 Bethlehem who knows how to p the lyre. H5594
1Sa 16:23 would take up his lyre and p. H5594+928+3338
1Ch 15:20 Benaiah were to p the lyres according NDT
1Ch 15:21 Jeiel and Azaziah were to p the harps NDT
1Ch 16: 5 They were to p the lyres and harps, Asaph NDT
Job 40:20 all the wild animals p nearby. H8471
Ps 33: 3 to him a new song; p skillfully, and shout H5594
Ps 81: 2 the timbrel, p the melodious harp and lyre. NDT
Pr 30:32 "If you p the fool and exalt yourself, or if H5571
Isa 11: 8 The infant will p near the cobra's den H9130
Isa 23:16 prostitute; p the harp well, sing many a H5594

PLAYED (5) [PLAY]
1Sa 10: 5 pipes and harps being p before them, and NDT
2Ch 29:28 while the musicians p and the trumpets H8876
Mt 11:17 " 'We p the pipe for you, and you did not G884
Lk 7:32 " 'We p the pipe for you, and you did not G884
1Co 14: 7 what tune is being p unless G884+2445+3068

PLAYING (13) [PLAY]
1Sa 18:10 while David was p the lyre, as H5594+928+3338
1Sa 19: 9 While David was p the lyre, H5594+928+3338
1Ki 1:40 up after him, p pipes and rejoicing greatly H2727
2Ki 3:15 While the harpist was p, the hand of the H5594
1Ch 15:28 of cymbals, and the p of lyres and harps. H9048
1Ch 16:42 cymbals and for the p of the other NDT
2Ch 5:12 dressed in fine linen and p cymbals, harps NDT
2Ch 34:12 who were skilled in p musical instruments— NDT
Ps 68:25 are the young women p the timbrels. H9528
Isa 30:29 rejoice as when people p pipes go up to H928S
Zec 8: 5 will be filled with boys and girls p there." H8471
Mt 9:23 saw the noisy crowd and people p pipes, G886
Rev 14: 2 was like that of harpists p their harps. G3068

PLAYS (2) [PLAY]
1Sa 16:17 "Find someone who p well and bring him H5594
Eze 33:32 beautiful voice and p an instrument well, H5594

PLEA (23) [PLEAD, PLEADED, PLEADING, PLEADS, PLEAS]
Ge 30: 6 has listened to my p and given me a son." H7754
Nu 21: 3 listened to Israel's p and gave the H7754
1Ki 8:28 your servant's prayer and his p for mercy, H9382
1Ki 8:38 when a prayer or p is made by anyone H9382
1Ki 8:45 hear from heaven their prayer and their p, H9382
1Ki 8:49 hear their prayer and their p, and uphold H9382
1Ki 8:52 to your servant's p and to the plea of H9382
1Ki 8:52 plea and to the p of your people Israel, H9382
1Ki 9: 3 the prayer and p you have made before H9382
2Ch 6:19 your servant's prayer and his p for mercy. H9382
2Ch 6:29 when a prayer or p is made by anyone H9382
2Ch 6:35 hear from heaven their prayer and their p, H9382
2Ch 33:13 by his entreaty and listened to his p; H9382
Job 35:13 God does not listen to their empty p; the H8736
Ps 17: 1 Hear me, LORD, my p is just; listen to my cry NDT
Ps 55: 1 to my prayer, O God, do not ignore my p; H9382
Ps 102:17 the destitute; he will not despise their p. H9525
Isa 32: 7 even when the p of the needy is just. H1819
Jer 7:16 people nor offer any p or petition for them H8262
Jer 11:14 people or offer any p or petition for them, H8262
La 3:56 You heard my p: "Do not close your ears H7754
Eze 36:37 again I will yield to Israel's p and do H2011
Lk 18: 3 town who kept coming to him with the p, G3306

PLEAD (23) [PLEA]
Jdg 6:31 "Are you going to p Baal's cause? H8189
1Sa 2:36 a piece of silver and a loaf of bread and p, H606
1Ki 8:47 repent and p with you in the land of H2858
2Ch 6:37 repent and p with you in the land of H2858
Est 4: 8 beg for mercy and p with him for her H1335
Job 8: 5 God earnestly and p with the Almighty, H2858
Job 9:15 I could only p with my Judge for mercy. H2858
Job 35: 9 they p for relief from the arm of the H8775
Ps 43: 1 p my cause against an unfaithful H8189
Pr 18:23 The poor p for mercy, but the rich answer H1819
Isa 1:17 of the fatherless; p the case of the widow. H8189
Isa 45:14 will bow down before you and p with you, H7137
Jer 7:16 petition for them; do not p with me, for I H7003
Jer 15:11 surely I will make your enemies p with H7003
Jer 27:18 let them p with the LORD Almighty that the H7003
Jer 30:13 There is no one to p your cause, no H1906
Da 2:18 He urged them to p for mercy from the A10114
Mic 6: 1 p my case before the mountains H8189
Mal 1: 9 "Now p with God to be gracious to H2704+7156
Mk 5:17 the people began to p with Jesus to leave G4151
Gal 4:12 I p with you, brothers and sisters, become G1289
Php 4: 2 I p with Euodia and I plead with Syntyche G4151
Php 4: 2 with Euodia and I p with Syntyche to be of G4151

PLEADED (13) [PLEA]
Ge 42:21 he was when he p with us for his life, H2858
Dt 3:23 At that time I p with the LORD: H2858
2Sa 12:16 David p with God for the child. He fasted H1335
Est 8: 3 Esther again p with the king, falling at his H1819
Da 9: 3 the Lord God and p with him in prayer H1335
Mt 8:34 they p with him to leave their region. G4151
Mk 5:23 He p earnestly with him, "My little G4151
Lk 7: 4 to Jesus, they p earnestly with him, "This G4151
Lk 15:28 So his father went out and p with him. G4151
Ac 2:40 warned them; and he p with them, "Save G4151
Ac 21:12 the people there p with Paul not to go up G4151
2Co 8: 4 they urgently p with us for the privilege of G1289
2Co 12: 8 Three times I p with the Lord to take it G4151

PLEADING (5) [PLEA]
Pr 19: 7 Though the poor pursue them with p, they H609
Jer 3:21 the weeping and p of the people of Israel, H9384
Jer 38:26 'I was p with the king not to send H5877+9382
Lk 8:41 p with him to come to his house G4151
Lk 13:25 you will stand outside knocking and p, 'Sir G3306

PLEADS (4) [PLEA]
Job 16:21 on behalf of a man he p with God as one H3519
Job 16:21 he pleads with God as one p for a friend. NDT
Isa 59: 4 justice; no one p a case with integrity. H9149
Mic 7: 9 until he p my case and upholds my cause. H8189

PLEAS (3) [PLEA]
2Ch 6:39 hear their prayer and their p, and uphold H9382
Job 13: 6 my argument; listen to the p of my lips. H8191
Isa 19:22 and he will respond to their p and heal H6983

PLEASANT (19) [PLEASE]
Ge 49:15 is his resting place and how p is his land, H5838
Ps 16: 6 lines have fallen for me in p places; H5833
Ps 106:24 Then they despised the p land; they did H2775
Ps 133: 1 How good and p it is when God's people H5833
Ps 135: 3 sing praise to his name, for that is p. H5833
Ps 147: 1 our God, how p and fitting to praise him! H5833
Pr 2:10 knowledge will be p to your soul. H5838
Pr 3:17 Her ways are p ways, and all her paths H5840
Isa 30:10 Tell us p things, prophesy H2747
Isa 32:12 Beat your breasts for the p fields, for the H2774
Jer 3:19 like my children and give you a p land, H2775
Jer 12:10 they will turn my p field into a desolate H2775
Jer 31:26 My sleep had been p to me. H6844
Hos 4:13 terebinth, where the shade is p. H3202
Hos 9:13 Ephraim, like Tyre, planted in a p place. H5659
Mic 2: 9 women of my people from their p homes. H9503
Zec 7:14 is how they made the p land desolate. H2775
1Th 3: 6 that you always have p memories of us and G19
Heb 12:11 No discipline seems p at the time, but G5915

PLEASANTNESS (1) [PLEASE]
Pr 27: 9 the p of a friend springs from their H5518

PLEASE (121) [PLEASANT, PLEASANTNESS, PLEASED, PLEASES, PLEASING, PLEASURE, PLEASURES]
Ge 19: 2 "p turn aside to your servant's house. H5528
Ge 19:18 But Lot said to them, "No, my lords, p! H5528
Ge 24:14 'P let down your jar that I may have a H5528
Ge 24:17 "P give me a little water from your jar." H5528
Ge 24:23 P tell me, is there room in your father's H5528
Ge 24:42 p grant success to the journey on which I H5528
Ge 24:43 "P let me drink a little water from your jar," H5528
Ge 24:45 I said to her, 'P give me a drink.' H5528
Ge 27:19 P sit up and eat some of my game, so H5528
Ge 27:31 p sit up and eat some of my game AIT
Ge 30:14 "P give me some of your son's mandrakes." H5528
Ge 30:27 "If I have found favor in your eyes, p stay. H5528
Ge 32:29 Jacob said, "P tell me your name." But he H5528
Ge 33:10 p!" said Jacob. "If I have found favor H5528
Ge 33:11 P accept the present that was brought to H5528
Ge 34: 8 P give her to him as his wife. H5528
Ge 44:33 p let your servant remain here as my H5528
Ge 47: 4 p let your servants settle in Goshen." H5528
Ge 50:17 Now p forgive the sins of the servants of H5528
Ex 4:13 your servant, Lord. P send someone else." H5528
Ex 21: 8 If she does not p the master H8317+928+6524
Ex 32:32 But now, p forgive their sin—but if not, then H561
Nu 10:31 But Moses said, "P do not leave us. H5528
Nu 11:15 going to treat me, p go ahead and kill me H5528
Nu 12:11 he said to Moses, "P, my lord, I ask you H1065
Nu 12:13 cried out to the LORD, "P, God, heal her!" H5528
Nu 20:17 P let us pass through your country. H5528
Nu 22:38 "But I can't say whatever I p. I must speak AIT
Nu 23:27 Perhaps it will p God to let H3837+928+6524
Nu 36: 6 anyone they p as long as they H3202+928+6524
Dt 12:13 your burnt offerings anywhere you p. H8011
Dt 28:63 so it will p him to ruin and destroy you. H8464
Jos 2:12 p swear to me by the LORD that you will H5528
Jdg 4:19 "P give me some water." She H5528
Jdg 6:18 P do not go away until I come back and H5528
Jdg 10:15 you think best, but p rescue us now." H5528
Jdg 16:28 P, God, strengthen me just once more H5528
Jdg 18: 5 "P inquire of God to learn whether our H5528
Jdg 19: 6 "P stay tonight and enjoy yourself. H5528
Ru 2: 7 'P let me glean and gather among the H5528
1Sa 9:18 "Would you p tell me where the seer's H5528
1Sa 15:30 But p honor me before the elders of my H5528
1Sa 25: 8 P give your servants and your son David H5528
1Sa 25:25 P pay no attention, my lord, to that wicked H5528
1Sa 25:28 "P forgive your servant's presumption. H5528
1Sa 28:22 Now p listen to your servant and let me H5528
2Sa 13:13 P speak to the king; he will not keep me H5528
2Sa 13:24 the king and his attendants p join me?" H5528
2Sa 13:26 p let my brother Amnon come with us." H5528
2Sa 18:22 p let me run behind the Cushite. H5528
1Ki 2:17 So he continued, "P ask King Solomon H5528
1Ki 3:26 her son and said to the king, "P, my lord, H1065
1Ki 17:11 "And bring me, p, a piece of bread." H5528
1Ki 20:32 servant Ben-Hadad says: 'P let me live.' " H5528
1Ki 20:37 another man and said, "Strike me, p." H5528
2Ki 1:13 "p have respect for my life and the lives of H5528
2Ki 4:16 "P, man of God, don't mislead your servant!" AIT
2Ki 4:22 "P send me one of the servants and a H5528
2Ki 5:15 So p accept a gift from your servant." H5528
2Ki 5:17 said Naaman, "p let me, your servant, be H5528
2Ki 5:22 P give them a talent of silver and two sets H5528
2Ki 6: 3 "Won't you p come with your H3283+5528
2Ki 18:26 "P speak to your servants in Aramaic H5528
2Ch 10: 7 these people and p them and give them H8354
Ne 9:37 over our bodies and our cattle as they p. H8356
Est 3:11 do with the people as you p." H3202+928+6524
Job 10: 3 Does it p you to oppress me, to spurn the H3202
Job 34: 9 'There is no profit in trying to p God. H8354
Ps 51:18 May it p you to prosper Zion, to build up H8356
Ps 69:31 This will p the LORD more than an ox H3512
Pr 20:23 dishonest scales do not p him. H3202
Pr 21: 1 that he channels toward all who p him. H2911
Isa 29:11 say, "Read this, p," they will answer H5528
Isa 29:12 say, "Read this, p," they will answer H5528
Isa 36:11 "P speak to your servants in Aramaic H5528
Isa 44:28 shepherd and will accomplish all that I p; H2914
Isa 46:10 will stand, and I will do all that I p. H2914
Isa 58: 3 you do as you p and exploit all your H2914
Isa 58:13 from doing as you p on my holy day, H2914
Isa 58:13 not doing as you p or speaking idle H2914
Jer 6:20 acceptable; your sacrifices do not p me." H6844
Jer 27: 5 and I give it to anyone I p. H3837+928+6524
Jer 36:15 "Sit down, p, and read it to us." H5528
Jer 37: 3 "P pray to the LORD our God for us." H5528
Jer 37:20 my lord the king, p listen. Let me bring H5528
Jer 40: 4 go wherever you p. H3202+2256+3838+928+6524
Jer 40: 5 go anywhere else you p. H3838+928+6524
Jer 42: 2 "P hear our petition and pray to the LORD H5528
Da 1:12 "P test your servants for ten days: Give us H5528
Hos 9: 4 to the LORD, nor will their sacrifices p him. H6844
Hos 10:10 When I p, I will punish them; nations will H205
Jnh 1:14 out to the LORD, "P, LORD, do not let us H5528
Mk 5:23 P come and put your hands on her so that G2671
Lk 14:18 I must go and see it. P excuse me.' G2263+5148
Lk 14:19 way to try them out. P excuse me.' G2263+5148
Jn 5:30 I seek not to p myself but him who G2525
Ac 8:34 asked Philip, "Tell me, p, who is the G1289
Ac 9:38 men to him and urged him, "P come at once!" AIT
Ac 13:15 word of exhortation for the people, p speak." AIT
Ac 21:39 P let me speak to the people. G1289
Ro 8: 8 are in the realm of the flesh cannot p God. G743
Ro 15: 1 failings of the weak and not to p ourselves. G743
Ro 15: 2 Each of us should p our neighbors for their G743
Ro 15: 3 For even Christ did not p himself but, as it is G743
1Co 7:32 the Lord's affairs—how he can p the Lord. G743
1Co 7:33 of this world—how he can p his wife— G743
1Co 7:34 of this world—how she can p her husband. G743
1Co 10:33 even as I try to p everyone in every way. G743
2Co 5: 9 So we make it our goal to p him G2298+1639
2Co 11: 1 in a little foolishness. Yes, p put up with me! AIT
Gal 1:10 Or am I trying to p people? If I were G743
Gal 1:10 If I were still trying to p people, I would not G743
Gal 6: 8 Whoever sows to p their flesh, from the flesh AIT
Gal 6: 8 whoever sows to p the Spirit, from the AIT
Col 1:10 worthy of the Lord and p him in every way: G742
1Th 2: 4 We are not trying to p people but God G743
1Th 4: 1 you how to live in order to p God, G743
2Ti 2: 4 rather tries to p his commanding officer. G743
Titus 2: 9 everything, to try to p them, not to talk G2298
Heb 11: 6 And without faith it is impossible to p God, G2297
3Jn 6 P send them on their way in a manner G2822

PLEASED (79) [PLEASE]
Ge 45:16 and all his officials were p. H3512+928+6524
Ge 49: 6 anger and hamstrung oxen as they p. H8356
Ex 33:13 If you are p with me H5162+2834+928+6524
Ex 33:16 you are p with me and H5162+2834+928+6524
Ex 33:17 I am p with you and I H5162+2834+928+6524
Lev 10:19 Would the LORD have been p H3512+928+6524
Nu 14: 8 If the LORD is p with us, he will lead us into H2911
Nu 24: 1 saw that it p the LORD to H3201+928+6524
Dt 21:14 If you are not p with her, let her go H2911
Dt 28:63 Just as it p the LORD to make you prosper H8464
Dt 33:11 and be p with the work of his hands. H8354
Jos 22:30 had to say, they were p. H3512+928+6524
Jdg 18:20 The priest was very p. He took the H3512+4213
1Sa 12:22 because the LORD was p to make you his H3283
1Sa 16:22 for I am p with him. H5162+2834+928+6524
1Sa 18: 5 This p all the troops, and H3512+928+6524
1Sa 18:20 told Saul about it, he was p. H3837+928+6524

1Sa 18:26 he *was* **p** to become the H3837+928+6524
1Sa 29: 6 and I would be **p** to have you H3202+928+6524
2Sa 3:36 people took note and *were* **p**; H3512+928+6524
2Sa 3:36 the king did **p** them. H3202+928+6524
2Sa 7:29 Now *be* **p** to bless the house of your H3283
2Sa 15:26 But if he says, '*I am* not **p** with you,' then I H2911
2Sa 19: 6 you would be **p** if Absalom H3838+928+6524
1Ki 3:10 The Lord *was* **p** that Solomon H3512+928+6524
1Ki 5: 7 message, *he was* greatly **p** and said H8523
1Ki 9:12 he *was* not **p with** them. H3837+928+6524
1Ki 11:19 *was* so **p with** Hadad H5162+2834+928+6524
1Ch 17:27 Now *you have been* **p** to bless the house H3283
1Ch 28: 4 father's sons *he was* **p** to make me king H8354
1Ch 29:17 you test the heart and *are* **p with** integrity. H8354
Ne 2: 6 you get back?" *It* **p** the king to send me H3512
Ne 9:24 of the land, to deal with them as they **p**. H8356
Ne 12:44 Judah *was* **p** with the ministering H8525
Est 1:21 his nobles *were* **p with** this H3512+928+6524
Est 2: 9 She **p** him and won his favor H3512+928+6524
Est 2:14 to the king unless he *was* **p** with her and H2911
Est 5: 2 he *was* **p with** *her* and H5951+2834+928+6524
Est 8: 5 and if he is **p with** me, let an H3202+928+6524
Est 9: 5 they did what they **p** to those who hated H8356
Ps 5: 4 are not a God *who is* **p with** wickedness; H2913
Ps 40:13 *Be* **p** to save me, LORD; come quickly, LORD H8354
Ps 41:11 I know that *you are* **p** with me, for my H2911
Ps 105:22 his princes as he **p** and teach his elders H5883
Ecc 4:16 who came later *were* not **p** with the H8523
Isa 42:21 *It* **p** the LORD for the sake of his H2911
Eze 18:23 am I not **p** when they turn from their ways NDT
Da 4:27 Your Majesty, *be* **p** to accept my advice: A10739
Da 6: 1 *It* **p** Darius to appoint 120 satraps to rule A10739
Da 8: 4 It did as it **p** and became great. H8356
Hos 8:13 eat the meat, the LORD *is* not **p with** them. H8354
Jnh 1:14 for you, LORD, have done as *you* **p**. H2911
Mic 6: 7 *Will* the LORD *be* **p** with thousands of rams, H8354
Mal 1: 8 *Would he be* **p with** you H8354
Mal 1:10 I am not **p** with you," says the LORD H2914
Mal 2:17 of the LORD, and he *is* **p** with them" or H2911
Mt 3:17 whom I love; with him *I am* **well p**." *G2305*
Mt 11:26 for this is what you were **p** to do. *G2306*
Mt 14: 6 the guests and **p** Herod *so much* *G743*
Mt 17: 5 whom I love; with him *I am* **well p**. *G2305*
Mk 1:11 whom I love; with you *I am* **well p**. *G2305*
Mk 6:22 *she* **p** Herod and his dinner guests. *G743*
Lk 3:22 whom I love; with you *I am* **well p**. *G2305*
Lk 10:21 for this is what you were **p** to do. *G2306*
Lk 12:32 your Father *has been* **p** to give you the *G2305*
Lk 23: 8 saw Jesus, *he was* greatly **p**, because *G5897*
Jn 5:21 Son gives life to whom *he is* **p** to give it. *G2527*
Ac 6: 5 This proposal **p** the whole group. *G743*
Ro 15:26 Macedonia and Achaia *were* **p** to make a *G2305*
Ro 15:27 *They were* **p** to do it, and indeed they owe *G2305*
1Co 1:21 God *was* **p** through the foolishness of *G2305*
1Co 10: 5 God *was* not **p** with most of them *G2305*
Gal 1:15 womb and called me by his grace, *was* **p** *G2305*
Col 1:19 For God *was* **p** to have all his fullness *G2305*
Heb 10: 6 offerings and sin offerings *you were* not **p**. *G2305*
Heb 10: 8 not desire, nor *were you* **p** with them"— *G2305*
Heb 11: 5 he was commended *as one who* **p** God. *G2297*
Heb 13:16 for with such sacrifices God *is* **p**. *G2297*
2Pe 1:17 whom I love; with him *I am* **well p**." *G2305*

PLEASES (35) [PLEASE]

1Sa 23:20 come down whenever it **p** you to do so H205
1Ch 21:23 the king do whatever **p** him. H3202+928+6524
Ezr 5:17 Now if it **p** the king, let a search be A10294
Ne 2: 5 "If *it* **p** the king and if your servant has H3201
Ne 2: 7 said to him, "If *it* **p** the king, may I have H3201
Est 1:19 "Therefore, if *it* **p** the king, let him issue a H3201
Est 2: 4 woman who **p** the king be H3512+928+6524
Est 3: 9 If *it* **p** the king, let a decree be issued to H3201
Est 5: 4 "If *it* **p** the king," replied Esther, "let the H3201
Est 5: 8 me with favor and if *it* **p** the king to grant H3201
Est 7: 3 Your Majesty, and if *it* **p** you, grant me my H3201
Est 8: 5 "If *it* **p** the king," she said, "and if he H3202
Est 9:13 "If *it* **p** the king," Esther answered, "give H3202
Job 23:13 can oppose him? He does whatever he **p**. H203
Ps 115: 3 is in heaven; he does whatever **p** *him*. H2911
Ps 135: 6 The LORD does whatever **p** *him*, in the H2911
Pr 15: 8 the prayer of the upright **p** him. H8356
Ecc 2:26 To the person who **p** him, God gives H3202
Ecc 2:26 to hand it over to the *one who* **p** God. H3202
Ecc 7:26 The *man who* **p** God will escape her, but H3202
Ecc 8: 3 a bad cause, for he will do whatever *he* **p**. H2911
Ecc 11: 7 is sweet, and it **p** the eyes to see the sun. H3202
Isa 56: 4 who choose what **p** me and hold fast to H2911
Eze 46: 5 lambs is to be **as much as** he **p**, H5522+3338
Eze 46:11 with the lambs **as much as** he **p**, H5522+3338
Da 4:35 He does as he **p** with the powers of A10605
Da 11: 3 will rule with great power and do as he **p**. H8356
Da 11:16 The invader will do as he **p**; no one will H8356
Da 11:36 "The king will do as he **p**. He will exalt H8356
Jn 3: 8 The wind blows wherever *it* **p**. You hear its *G2527*
Jn 8:29 left me alone, for I always do what **p** him." *G744*
Eph 5:10 find out what **p** the Lord. *G1639+2298*
Col 3:20 in everything, for this **p** the Lord. *G2298+1639*
1Ti 2: 3 This is good, and **p** God our Savior, *G621*
1Jn 3:22 keep his commands and do what **p** him. *G744*

PLEASING (57) [PLEASE]

Ge 2: 9 trees *that were* **p** to the eye and good for H2773
Ge 3: 6 tree was good for food and **p** to the eye, H9294
Ge 8:21 The LORD smelled the **p** aroma and said in H5767
Ex 29:18 to the LORD, a **p** aroma, a food offering H5767
Ex 29:25 burnt offering for a **p** aroma to the LORD, H5767
Ex 29:41 as in the morning—a **p** aroma, a food H5767
Lev 1: 9 a food offering, an aroma **p** to the LORD. H5767
Lev 1:13 a food offering, an aroma **p** to the LORD. H5767
Lev 1:17 a food offering, an aroma **p** to the LORD. H5767
Lev 2: 2 a food offering, an aroma **p** to the LORD. H5767
Lev 2: 9 a food offering, an aroma **p** to the LORD. H5767
Lev 2:12 to be offered on the altar as a **p** aroma. H5767
Lev 3: 5 is a food offering, an aroma **p** to the LORD. H5767
Lev 3:16 on the altar as a food offering, a **p** aroma. H5767
Lev 4:31 it on the altar as an aroma **p** to the LORD. H5767
Lev 6:15 on the altar as an aroma **p** to the LORD. H5767
Lev 6:21 in pieces as an aroma **p** to the LORD. H5767
Lev 8:21 a burnt offering, a **p** aroma, a food H5767
Lev 8:28 offering, a **p** aroma, a food offering H5767
Lev 17: 6 burn the fat as an aroma **p** to the LORD. H5767
Lev 23:13 to the LORD, a **p** aroma—and its drink H5767
Lev 23:18 a food offering, an aroma **p** to the LORD. H5767
Lev 26:31 take no delight in the **p** aroma of your H5767
Nu 15: 3 as an aroma **p** to the LORD—whether H5767
Nu 15: 7 Offer it as an aroma **p** to the LORD. H5767
Nu 15:10 a food offering, an aroma **p** to the LORD. H5767
Nu 15:13 a food offering as an aroma **p** to the LORD. H5767
Nu 15:14 a food offering as an aroma **p** to the LORD, H5767
Nu 15:24 burnt offering as an aroma **p** to the LORD, H5767
Nu 18:17 as a food **offering**, an aroma **p** to the LORD H5767
Nu 28: 2 my food offerings, as an aroma **p** *to* me. H5767
Nu 28: 6 instituted at Mount Sinai as a **p** aroma, H5767
Nu 28: 8 is a food offering, an aroma **p** to the LORD. H5767
Nu 28:13 a burnt offering, a **p** aroma, a food H5767
Nu 28:24 seven days as an aroma **p** to the LORD; H5767
Nu 28:27 a year old as an aroma **p** to the LORD. H5767
Nu 29: 2 As an aroma **p** to the LORD, offer a burnt H5767
Nu 29: 6 presented to the LORD, a **p** aroma. H5767
Nu 29: 8 Present as an aroma **p** to the LORD a burnt H5767
Nu 29:13 Present as an aroma **p** to the LORD a food H5767
Nu 29:36 Present as an aroma **p** to the LORD a food H5767
1Sa 29: 9 that you have been as **p** in my eyes as an H3202
Ezr 6:10 offer sacrifices **p** to the God of heaven A10478
Ps 19:14 meditation of my heart be **p** in your sight, H8356
Ps 104:34 *May* my meditation *be* **p** to him, as I H6844
Pr 22:18 it is **p** when you keep them in your H5833
SS 1: 3 **P** is the fragrance of your perfumes; your H3202
SS 4:10 How much more **p** *is* your love than wine H3201
SS 7: 6 How beautiful you are and how **p**, my H5838
La 2: 4 he has slain all *who* were **p** *to* the eye; H4718
Ro 12: 1 sacrifice, holy and **p** to God—this is your *G2298*
Ro 12: 2 will is—his good, **p** and perfect will. *G2298*
Ro 14:18 Christ in this way is **p** to God and receives *G2298*
2Co 2:15 are to God the **p aroma** of Christ among *G2380*
Php 4:18 an acceptable sacrifice, **p** to God. *G2298*
1Ti 5: 4 grandparents, for this is **p** to God. *G621*
Heb 13:21 may he work in us what is **p** to him *G2298*

PLEASURE (33) [PLEASE]

Ge 18:12 my lord is old, will I now have this **p**?" H6366
Job 22: 3 What **p** would it give the Almighty if you H2914
Ps 51:16 *you do* not **take p in** burnt offerings. H8354
Ps 109:17 *He* **found** no **p** in blessing—may it be far H2911
Ps 147:10 *His* **p** *is* not in the strength of the horse H2911
Pr 10:23 A fool finds **p** in wicked schemes, but a H8468
Pr 16: 7 When the LORD **takes p** *in* anyone's way H8354
Pr 16:13 Kings take **p** in honest lips; they value the H8356
Pr 18: 2 Fools **find** no **p** in understanding but H2911
Pr 21:17 Whoever loves **p** will become poor H8525
Ecc 2: 1 I will test you with **p** to find out what is H8525
Ecc 2: 2 And what does **p** accomplish?" H8525
Ecc 2:10 my eyes desired; I refused my heart no **p**. H8525
Ecc 5: 4 He has no **p** in fools; fulfill your H2914
Ecc 7: 4 the heart of fools is in the house of **p**. H8525
Ecc 12: 1 you will say, "I find no **p** in them"— H2914
Isa 1:11 *I* **have** no **p** *in* the blood of bulls and H2911
Isa 9:17 the Lord *will* **take** no **p** in the young men, H8523
Isa 47: 8 you **lover of p**, lounging in your H6349
Jer 6:10 is offensive to them; *they* **find** no **p** in it. H2911
Eze 16:37 with whom *you* **found p**, those you loved H6844
Eze 18:23 *Do I* **take any p in** the death of the H2911+2911
Eze 18:32 For *I* **take** no **p** in the death of anyone H2911
Eze 33:11 *I* **take** no **p** in the death of the wicked H2911
Da 4: 2 *It is* my **p** to tell you about the A10739
Hag 1: 8 so that *I may* **take p** in it and be honored," H8354
Mal 2:13 accepts them *with* **p** from your hands. H8356
Eph 1: 5 in accordance with his **p** and will— *G2306*
Eph 1: 9 of his will according to his **good p**, *G2306*
1Ti 5: 6 But the widow who **lives for p** is dead even *G5059*
2Ti 3: 4 **lovers of p** rather than lovers of God *G5798*
Heb 10:38 And I **take** no **p** in the one who shrinks *G2305*
2Pe 2:13 Their idea of **p** is to carouse in broad *G2454*

PLEASURES (6) [PLEASE]

Ps 16:11 with eternal **p** at your right hand. H5833
Lk 8:14 worries, riches and **p**, and they do not *G2454*
Titus 3: 3 enslaved by all kinds of passions and **p**. *G2454*
Heb 11:25 rather than to enjoy the fleeting **p** of sin. *G656*
Jas 4: 3 you may spend what you get on your **p**. *G2454*
2Pe 2:13 reveling in their **p** while they feast with you. *G573*

PLEDGE (32) [PLEDGED, PLEDGES]

Ge 38:17 me something as a **p** until you send it?" H6860
Ge 38:18 He said, "What **p** should I give you?" H6860
Ge 38:20 in order to get his **p** back from the woman H6860
Ex 22:26 *you* **take** your neighbor's cloak **as a p** H2471+2471
Nu 30: 2 takes an oath to obligate himself by a **p**, H674
Nu 30: 3 vow to the LORD or obligates herself by a **p** H674
Nu 30: 4 about her vow or **p** but says nothing to H674
Nu 30: 4 her vows and every **p** by which she H674
Nu 30:10 vow or obligates herself by a **p** under oath H674
Nu 30:13 she makes or any sworn **p** to deny herself. H674
Dt 24:10 house to get *what* is **offered** *to* you **as a p**. H6287
Dt 24:11 making the loan bring the **p** out to you. H6287
Dt 24:12 to sleep with their **p** in your possession. H6287
Dt 24:17 **take** the cloak of the widow **as a p**. H2471
2Ch 34:32 *he* **had** everyone in Jerusalem and Benjamin **p** *themselves to* H6641
Ezr 10:19 *They all* **gave** their hands **in p** to put away H5989
Job 17: 3 O God, the **p** you demand. Who else H6842
Job 24: 3 donkey and **take** the widow's ox **in p**. H2471
Pr 6: 1 if *you have* **shaken** hands **in p** for a H9546
Pr 11:15 refuses to **shake hands in p** is safe. H9364
Pr 17:18 no sense **shakes** hands **in p** and puts up H9546
Pr 20:16 **hold it in p** if it is done for an outsider. H2471
Pr 22:26 not be *one who* **shakes** hands **in p** or puts H9546
Pr 27:13 **hold it in p** if it is done for an outsider. H2471
Eze 17:18 *he had* **given** his hand **in p** and yet H5989
Eze 18: 7 returns **what** he **took in p** *for* a loan. H2481
Eze 18:12 He does not return **what** he **took in p**. H2478
Eze 18:16 anyone or **require a p for a loan.** H2471+2478
Eze 33:15 give back **what** they **took in p for a loan,** H2478
Am 2: 8 beside every altar on garments **taken in p**. H2471
1Ti 5:12 because they have broken their first **p**. *G4411*
1Pe 3:21 the body but the **p** of a clear conscience *G2090*

PLEDGED (14) [PLEDGE]

Ge 19:14 *who were* **p to marry** his daughters. H4374
Ex 22:16 virgin who **is** not **p to be married** and H829
Dt 20: 7 *Has* anyone *become* **p** *to* a woman and not H829
Dt 22:23 a virgin **p to be married** and he sleeps H829
Dt 22:25 young woman **p to be married** and rapes H829
Dt 22:28 virgin who *is* not **p to be married** and rapes H829
Dt 28:30 *You will be* **p to be married** *to* a woman H829
2Ki 23: 3 all the people **p** *themselves* to the H6641
1Ch 29:24 **p** their submission to King H5989+3338
Mic 7:20 as *you* **p on oath** to our ancestors in days H8678
Mt 1:18 Mary *was* **p to be married** to Joseph, *G3650*
Lk 1:27 to a virgin **p to be married** to a man *G3650*
Lk 2: 5 who *was* **p to be married** to him and was *G3650*
1Co 7:27 *Are you* **p** to a woman? Do not seek to be *G1313*

PLEDGES (5) [PLEDGE]

Nu 30: 5 of her vows or the **p** by which she obligated H674
Nu 30: 7 then her vows or the **p** by which she H674
Nu 30:11 all her vows or the **p** by which she H674
Nu 30:12 none of the vows or **p** that came from her H674
Nu 30:14 all her vows or the **p** binding on her. H674

PLEIADES (3)

Job 9: 9 the **P** and the constellations of the south. H3966
Job 38:31 "Can you bind the chains of the **P**? Can H3966
Am 5: 8 He who made the **P** and Orion, who turns H3966

PLENTIFUL (8) [PLENTY]

1Ki 10:27 and cedar as **p** as sycamore-fig H4200+8044
1Ch 12:40 There were **p** supplies of flour, fig H4200+8044
2Ch 1:15 and cedar as **p** as sycamore-fig H4200+8044
2Ch 9:27 and cedar as **p** as sycamore-fig H4200+8044
Isa 30:23 comes from the land will be rich and **p**. H9045
Eze 36:29 the grain and **make** it **p** and will not H8049
Mt 9:37 "The harvest is **p** but the workers are few. *G4498*
Lk 10: 2 "The harvest is **p**, but the workers are *G4498*

PLENTIFULLY (1) [PLENTY]

Ge 41:47 of abundance the land produced **p**. H4200+7859

PLENTY (21) [PLENTIFUL, PLENTIFULLY]

Ge 24:25 "We have **p** *of* straw and fodder H8041
Ge 33: 9 Esau said, "I already have **p**, my brother. H8041
Ge 34:21 the land has **p of room** for them. H8146+3338
2Ch 2: 9 to provide me with **p** of lumber H4200+8044
2Ch 31:10 had enough to eat and **p** to spare, H4200+8044
2Ch 32: 4 kings of Assyria come and find **p** of water?" H8041
Job 20:22 In the midst of his **p**, distress will overtake H8565
Ps 37:19 in days of famine *they will* **enjoy p**. H8425
Pr 27:27 You will have **p** *of* goats' milk to feed your H1896
Pr 30:22 a godless fool *who* **gets p** to eat, H8425
Jer 44:17 At that time *we* **had p** *of* food and were H8425
Joel 2:26 *You will* **have p to eat**, until you are H430+430
Mic 2:11 'I will prophesy for you **p** of wine and beer,' NDT
Lk 12:19 "You have **p** of grain laid up for many *G4498*
Jn 3:23 because there was **p** of water, and people *G4498*
Jn 6:10 There was **p** of grass in that place, and *G4498*
Ac 14:17 *he* **provides** you **with p** of food and fills *G1855*
2Co 8:14 present time your **p** will supply what they *G4354*
2Co 8:14 so that in turn their **p** will supply what you *G4354*
Php 4:12 in need, and I know what it is *to* **have p**. *G4355*
Php 4:12 hungry, whether **living in p** or in want. *G4355*

PLIED (1) [PLY]

Lk 23: 9 *He* **p** him with many questions, but Jesus *G2089*

PLIGHT (2)

2Ki 7:13 Their **p** will be like that of all the Israelites NDT
Ps 59: 4 Arise to help me; look on my **p**! NDT

PLOT (41) [PLOTS, PLOTTED, PLOTTING]
Ge 33:19 the **p** *of* ground where he pitched his tent. H2754
2Ki 9:10 devour her on the **p of ground** *at* Jezreel, H2750
2Ki 9:21 at the **p of ground** *that had belonged to* H2754
2Ki 9:26 make you pay for it on this **p of ground**, H2754
2Ki 9:26 pick him up and throw him on that **p**, in H2754
2Ki 9:36 On the **p of ground** *at* Jezreel dogs will H2750
2Ki 9:37 dung on the ground in the **p** *at* Jezreel, H2750
Ne 4:15 were aware of their **p** and that God had H6783
Est 2:22 found out about the **p** and told Queen H1821
Est 9:25 But when the **p** came to the king's H2023S
Ps 2:1 conspire and the peoples **p** in vain? H2047
Ps 21:11 Though *they* **p** evil against you and H5742
Ps 31:13 conspire against me and **p** to take my life. H2372
Ps 35:4 may *those who* **p** my ruin be turned back H3108
Ps 36:4 Even on their beds *they* **p** evil; they H3108
Ps 37:12 The wicked **p** against the righteous and H2372
Ps 64:6 *They* **p** injustice and say, "We have H2924
Ps 83:3 people; *they* **p** against those you cherish. H3619
Ps 83:5 With one mind *they* **p** together; they form H3619
Pr 3:29 *Do* not **p** harm against your neighbor H3086
Pr 12:20 Deceit is in the hearts of *those who* **p** evil H3086
Pr 14:22 Do not *those who* **p** evil go astray? But H3086
Pr 24:2 their hearts **p** violence, and their lips H2047
Isa 28:25 in its place, barley *in its* **p**, and spelt in its H6168
Jer 11:18 Because the LORD revealed their **p** to me, NDT
Jer 48:2 in Heshbon *people will* **p** her downfall: H3108
Eze 17:7 him from the **p** *where* it was planted and H6870
Eze 17:10 wither away in the **p** *where* it grew? H6870
Da 11:24 *He will* **p** the overthrow of fortresses—but H3108
Hos 7:15 their arms, but *they* **p** evil against me. H3108
Mic 2:1 iniquity, to *those who* **p** evil on their beds! H7188
Na 1:9 Whatever *they* **p** against the LORD he will H3108
Zec 7:10 *Do* not **p** evil *against* each H3108+928+4222
Zec 8:17 *do* not **p** evil **against** each H3108+928+4222
Mk 3:6 went out and *began to* **p** with the G5206+1443
Jn 4:5 near the **p of ground** Jacob had given to G6005
Ac 4:25 nations rage and the peoples **p** in vain? G3509
Ac 14:5 There was a **p** afoot among both Gentiles G3995
Ac 23:13 than forty men were involved in this **p**. G5350
Ac 23:16 the son of Paul's sister heard *of* this **p**, G1909
Ac 23:30 I was informed of a **p** to be carried out G2101

PLOTS (12) [PLOT]
Ps 52:2 your tongue **p** destruction; it is like H3108
Ps 64:2 of the wicked, from the **p** *of* evildoers. H8095
Pr 6:14 *who* **p** evil with deceit in his heart—he H3086
Pr 16:27 A scoundrel **p** evil, and on their lips it is H4125
Pr 24:8 *Whoever* **p** evil will be known as a H3108
Isa 33:15 their ears against **p** *of* murder and shut H9048
Jer 18:23 know all their **p** to kill me. Do not H6783
La 3:60 of their vengeance, all their **p** against me. H4742
La 3:61 their insults, all their **p** against me— H4742
Da 11:25 because of the **p** devised against him. H4742
Na 1:11 has one come forth *who* **p** evil against the H3108
Ac 20:19 severe testing by the **p** of my Jewish G2101

PLOTTED (18) [PLOT]
Ge 37:18 he reached them, *they* **p** to kill him. H5792
2Sa 21:5 who destroyed us and **p** against us so that H1948
1Ki 15:27 from the tribe of Issachar **p** against him, H8003
1Ki 16:9 of half his chariots, **p** against him. H8003
1Ki 16:16 that Zimri *had* **p** *against* the king and H8003
2Ki 21:24 killed all who *had* **p** against King Amon, H8003
2Ch 24:21 But *they* **p** against him, and by order of H8003
2Ch 33:25 killed all who *had* **p** against King Amon, H8003
Ne 4:8 They all **p** together to come and fight H8003
Est 9:24 *had* **p** against the Jews to destroy them H3108
Isa 7:5 Remaliah's son *have* **p** your ruin, H3619
Jer 11:19 realize that *they had* **p** against me, H3108+4742
Jer 49:30 king of Babylon *has* **p** against you; H3619+6783
Mic 6:5 Balak king of Moab **p** and what Balaam H3619
Hab 2:10 *You have* **p** the ruin of many peoples H3619
Mt 12:14 went out and **p** how they might kill G5206+3284
Jn 11:53 So from that day on *they* **p** to take his life. G1086
Ac 20:3 *Because* some Jews *had* **p** against G1181+2101

PLOTTING (4) [PLOT]
1Sa 23:9 that Saul *was* **p** against him, H3086+2021+8288
Ne 6:6 that you and the Jews *are* **p** to revolt, and H3108
Pr 16:30 winks with their eye *is* **p** perversity; H3108
Eze 11:2 are the men who *are* **p** evil and giving H3108

PLOW (10) [PLOWED, PLOWING, PLOWMAN, PLOWMEN, PLOWS, PLOWSHARES]
Dt 22:10 *Do* not **p** with an ox and a donkey yoked H3086
1Sa 8:12 others to **p** his ground and reap his H3086
1Sa 13:20 to the Philistines to have their **p points**, H4739
1Sa 13:21 sharpening **p points** and mattocks, H4739
Job 4:8 *those who* **p** evil and those who sow H3086
Pr 20:4 Sluggards *do* not **p** in season; so at H3086
Isa 28:24 plows for planting, does he **p** continually? NDT
Hos 10:11 Ephraim, Judah *must* **p**, and Jacob must H3086
Am 6:12 *Does one* **p** the sea with oxen H3086
Lk 9:62 puts a hand to the **p** and looks back is fit G770

PLOWED (8) [PLOW]
Dt 21:4 a valley that *has* not **been p** or planted H6268
Jdg 14:18 to them, "If *you had* not **p** with my heifer H3086
Ps 129:3 Plowmen *have* **p** my back and made their H3086
Jer 26:18 " 'Zion *will* **be p** like a field, Jerusalem H3086
Eze 36:9 on you with favor; *you will* **be p** and sown, H6268
Hos 10:4 up like poisonous weeds in a **p** field. H9439
Hos 12:11 will be like piles of stones on a **p** field. H9439
Mic 3:12 because of you, Zion *will* **be p** like a field H3086

PLOWING (6) [PLOW]
Ge 45:6 five years there will be no **p** and reaping. H3045
Ex 34:21 even during the **p season** and harvest you H3045
1Ki 19:19 He *was* **p** *with* twelve yoke of oxen, and H3086
1Ki 19:21 He burned the **p** equipment to cook the H1330
Job 1:14 "The oxen were **p** and the donkeys were H3086
Lk 17:7 of you has a servant **p** or looking after the G769

PLOWMAN (1) [PLOW]
Am 9:13 be overtaken by the **p** and the planter by H3086

PLOWMEN (1) [PLOW]
Ps 129:3 **P** have plowed my back and made their H3086

PLOWS (3) [PLOW]
Ps 141:7 "As *one* **p** and breaks up the earth H7114
Isa 28:24 When a farmer **p** for planting, does he H3086
1Co 9:10 because whoever **p** and threshes should be G769

PLOWSHARES (3) [PLOW]
Isa 2:4 their swords into **p** and their spears into H908
Joel 3:10 Beat your **p** into swords and your pruning H908
Mic 4:3 their swords into **p** and their spears into H908

PLUCK (2) [PLUCKED]
Ps 52:5 snatch you up and **p** you from your tent; H5815
Mk 9:47 if your eye causes you to stumble, **p** it **out**. G1675

PLUCKED (1) [PLUCK]
Ge 8:11 there in its beak was a **freshly p** olive leaf! H3273

PLUMAGE (2)
Eze 17:3 feathers and full **p** of varied colors came H5681
Eze 17:7 eagle with powerful wings and full **p**. H5681

PLUMB (7)
2Ki 21:13 the **p line** *used against* the house of H5487
Isa 28:17 line and righteousness the **p line**; H5487
Isa 34:11 line of chaos and the **p line** *of* desolation. H74
Am 7:7 by a wall that had been built **true to p**, H643
Am 7:7 true to plumb, with a **p line** in his hand. H643
Am 7:8 "A **p line**," I replied. Then the Lord H643
Am 7:8 I am setting a **p line** among my people H643

PLUNDER (105) [PLUNDERED, PLUNDERERS]
Ge 34:29 **taking as p** everything in the houses. H1024
Ge 49:27 the prey, in the evening he divides the **p**." H8965
Ex 3:22 And so *you will* **p** the Egyptians." H5911
Nu 14:3 Our wives and children will be taken as **p** H1020
Nu 14:31 that you said would be taken as **p**, H1020
Nu 31:9 **took** all the Midianite herds, flocks and goods **as p** H1024
Nu 31:11 They took all the **p** and spoils, including H8965
Nu 31:12 spoils and **p** to Moses and Eleazar the H8965
Nu 31:32 The **p** remaining from the spoils that the H1020
Nu 31:53 Each soldier *had* **taken p** for himself. H1024
Dt 2:35 livestock and the **p** *from* the towns we had H8965
Dt 3:7 the livestock and the **p** *from* their cities we H8965
Dt 13:16 are to gather all the **p** *of* the town into the H8965
Dt 13:16 the town and all its **p** as a whole burnt H8965
Dt 20:14 you may take these as **p** for yourselves. H8965
Dt 20:14 the **p** the LORD your God gives you *from* H8965
Jos 7:21 When I saw in the **p** a beautiful robe from H8965
Jos 8:2 you may carry off their **p** and livestock H8965
Jos 8:27 themselves the livestock and **p** *of* this city, H8965
Jos 11:14 all the **p** and livestock *of* these cities, H8965
Jos 22:8 divide the **p** *from* your enemies with H8965
Jdg 5:19 of Megiddo, they took no **p** *of* silver. H1299
Jdg 5:30 colorful garments as **p** for Sisera, colorful H8965
Jdg 5:30 garments for my neck—all this as **p**? H8965
Jdg 8:24 me an earring from your **share of the p**." H8965
Jdg 8:25 of them threw a ring from his **p** onto it. H8965
1Sa 14:30 some of the **p** they took *from* their H8965
1Sa 14:32 They pounced on the **p** and, taking sheep H8965
1Sa 14:36 Philistines by night and **p** them till dawn, H1024
1Sa 15:19 you pounce on the **p** and do evil in the H8965
1Sa 15:21 soldiers took sheep and cattle from the **p**, H8965
1Sa 30:16 great amount of **p** they had taken from H8965
1Sa 30:19 **p** or anything else they had taken. H8965
1Sa 30:20 other livestock, saying, "This is David's **p**." H8965
1Sa 30:22 not share with them the **p** we recovered. H8965
1Sa 30:26 he sent some of the **p** to the elders of H8965
1Sa 30:26 you from the **p** *of* the LORD's enemies." H8965
2Sa 3:22 brought with them a great deal of **p**. H8965
2Sa 8:12 also dedicated the **p** taken from H8965
2Sa 12:30 took a great quantity of **p** from the city H8965
2Ki 3:23 Now to the **p**, Moab!" H8965
1Ch 20:2 He took a great quantity of **p** from the city H8965
1Ch 26:27 Some of the **p** taken in battle they H8965
2Ch 14:13 of Judah carried off a large amount of **p**. H8965
2Ch 14:14 villages, since there was much **p** there. H1023
2Ch 15:11 goats from the **p** they had brought H8965
2Ch 20:25 his men went to carry off their **p**, H8965
2Ch 20:25 There was so much **p** that it took three H8965
2Ch 24:23 They sent all the **p** to their king in H8965
2Ch 25:13 carried off great quantities of **p**. H1023
2Ch 28:8 They also took a great deal of **p**, which H8965
2Ch 28:14 up the prisoners and **p** in the presence of H1023
2Ch 28:15 from the **p** they clothed all who were H8965
Ne 4:4 Give them over as **p** in a land of captivity. H1023
Est 3:13 the month of Adar, and to **p** their goods. H1024
Est 8:11 to **p** the property of their enemies. H1024
Est 9:10 But they did not lay their hands on the **p**. H1023
Est 9:15 they did not lay their hands on the **p**. H1023
Est 9:16 them but did not lay their hands on the **p**. H1023
Ps 68:12 the women at home divide the **p**. H8965
Ps 109:11 *may* strangers **p** the fruits of his labor. H1024
Pr 1:13 valuable things and fill our houses with **p**; H8965
Pr 16:19 oppressed than to share **p** with the proud. H8965
Pr 24:15 righteous, *do* not **p** their dwelling place H8720
Isa 3:14 the **p** *from* the poor is in your houses. H1611
Isa 8:4 of Damascus and the **p** *of* Samaria will be H8965
Isa 9:3 as warriors rejoice when dividing the **p**. H8965
Isa 10:6 to seize loot and snatch **p**, and to trample H1020
Isa 11:14 together *they will* **p** the people to the east H1024
Isa 17:14 who loot us, the lot of *those who* **p** us. H1024
Isa 33:4 Your **p**, O nations, is harvested as by H8965
Isa 33:23 divided and even the lame will carry off **p**. H1020
Isa 42:22 They have become **p**, with no one to H1020
Isa 49:24 Can **p** be taken from warriors, or captives H4917
Isa 49:25 warriors, and **p** retrieved from the fierce H4917
Jer 2:14 Why then has he become **p**? H1020
Jer 15:13 wealth and your treasures I will give as **p**, H1020
Jer 17:3 all your treasures I will give away as **p**, H1020
Jer 20:5 will take it away *as* **p** and carry it off to H1024
Jer 30:16 *Those who* **p** you will be plundered; all H9116
Jer 49:32 Their camels will become **p**, and their H1020
Jer 50:10 all *who* **p** her will have their fill, H8964
Eze 7:21 give their wealth as **p** to foreigners and as H1020
Eze 23:46 them and give them over to terror and **p**. H1020
Eze 25:7 you and give you as **p** to the nations. H1020
Eze 26:5 She will become **p** for the nations, H1020
Eze 26:12 *They will* **p** your wealth and loot your H8964
Eze 29:19 He will loot and **p** the land as pay H1024+1020
Eze 36:5 so that they might **p** its pastureland. H1020
Eze 38:12 I *will* **p** and loot and turn my hand H8964+8965
Eze 38:13 say to you, "Have you come to **p**? H8964+8965
Eze 38:13 livestock and goods and to seize much **p**?" H8965
Eze 39:10 And *they will* **p** those who plundered H8964
Da 11:24 He will distribute **p**, loot and wealth H1023
Am 3:11 your strongholds and **p** your fortresses." H1024
Na 2:9 **P** the silver! Plunder the gold! The supply H1024
Na 2:9 Plunder the silver! **P** the gold! The supply H1024
Na 3:1 full of lies, full of **p**, never without victims! H7294
Hab 2:8 the peoples who are left *will* **p** you. H8964
Zep 2:9 The remnant of my people *will* **p** them H1024
Zec 2:9 them so that their slaves will **p** them. H8965
Mt 12:29 Then *he can* **p** his house. G1395
Mk 3:27 Then *he can* **p** the strong man's house. G1395
Lk 11:22 the man trusted and divides up his **p**. G5036
Heb 7:4 Abraham gave him a tenth of the **p**! G215

PLUNDERED (29) [PLUNDER]
Ex 12:36 they asked for; so *they* **p** the Egyptians. H5911
Jdg 2:14 into the hands of raiders *who* **p** them. H9116
1Sa 14:48 from the hands of *those who had* **p** them. H9115
1Sa 17:53 chasing the Philistines, *they* **p** their camp. H9116
2Ki 7:16 people went out and **p** the camp of the H1024
2Ki 21:14 will be looted and **p** by all their enemies; H5468
Ps 12:5 the poor are **p** and the needy groan, H8719
Ps 44:10 and our adversaries *have* **p** us. H9115
Ps 76:5 The valiant *lie* **p**, they sleep their last H8964
Ps 89:41 All who pass by *have* **p** him; he has H9116
Isa 10:13 of nations, *I* **p** their treasures; like H9115
Isa 24:3 laid waste and **totally p**. H1024+1024
Isa 42:22 But this is a people **p** and looted, all of H1024
Jer 30:16 Those who plunder you will be **p**; all who H5468
Jer 50:10 So Babylonia will be **p**; all who plunder H8965
Jer 50:37 against her treasures! *They will* **be p**. H1024
Eze 34:8 so has been **p** and has become food H1020
Eze 34:22 my flock, and they will no longer be **p**. H1020
Eze 34:28 They will no longer be **p** by the nations H1020
Eze 36:4 that have been **p** and ridiculed by the H1020
Eze 39:10 will plunder *those who* **p** them and loot H8964
Da 11:33 the sword or be burned or captured or **p**. H1023
Hos 13:15 His storehouse *will be* **p** *of* all its H9115
Am 3:10 fortresses *what* they have **p** and looted." H2805
Na 2:10 She is pillaged, **p**, stripped! Hearts melt H4433
Hab 2:8 Because you *have* **p** many nations, the H8964
Zep 1:13 Their wealth will be **p**, their houses H5468
Zec 2:8 me against the nations that *have* **p** you— H8964
Zec 14:1 when your **possessions** will be **p** and H8965

PLUNDERERS (2) [PLUNDER]
2Ki 17:20 them and gave them into the hands of **p**, H9115
Isa 42:24 over to become loot, and Israel to the **p**? H1024

PLUNGE (4) [PLUNGED]
1Sa 2:14 and *would* **p** the fork into the pan or kettle H5782
Job 9:31 *you would* **p** me into a slime pit so that H3188
Joel 2:8 *They* **p** through defenses without breaking H5877
1Ti 6:9 desires that **p** people into ruin and G1112

PLUNGED (4) [PLUNGE]
Jdg 3:21 his right thigh and **p** it into the king's H9546
2Sa 18:14 in his hand and **p** them into Absalom's H9546
2Sa 20:10 Joab's hand, and Joab **p** it into his belly H5782
Rev 16:10 its kingdom was **p into darkness**. G5031

PLUS (2)
Eze 45:12 Twenty shekels **p** twenty-five shekels plus NDT
Eze 45:12 twenty-five shekels **p** fifteen shekels equal NDT

PLY (1) [PLIED]
Isa 23:17 and *will* **p her trade** with all the H2388S

POCKET (1)
1Sa 25:29 he will hurl away as from the **p** *of* a sling. H4090

PODS (2)
2Ki 6:25 quarter of a cab of **seed p** for five shekels. H1807
Lk 15:16 his stomach with the **p** that the pigs were *G3044*

POETS (2)
Nu 21:27 That is why the **p** say: "Come to Heshbon H5439
Ac 17:28 As some *of* your own **p** have said, 'We *G4475*

POINT (35) [POINTED, POINTING, POINTS]
Nu 14:40 set out for the **highest p** *in* the hill country H8031
Nu 14:44 up toward the **highest p** *in* the hill country H8031
Jdg 3:25 They waited **to the p of** embarrassment H6330
1Sa 7:11 them along the way to a **p** below Beth Kar. NDT
1Sa 17:7 its iron **p** weighed six hundred H4259
2Ki 20:1 became ill and was **at the p of** death. H4200
2Ch 32:24 became ill and was **at the p of** death. H6330
Ne 3:16 made repairs up to a **p** opposite the tombs NDT
Ne 3:19 from a **p** facing the ascent to the armory as NDT
Ne 3:26 made repairs up to a **p** opposite the Water NDT
Job 20:25 his back, the **gleaming p** out of his liver. H1398
Pr 6:3 Go—**to the p of exhaustion**—and give H8332
Pr 8:2 At the **highest p** along the way H8031+5294
Pr 9:3 calls from the **highest p** *of* the city, H1726+5294
Pr 9:14 on a seat at the **highest p** *of* the city, H5294
Isa 38:1 became ill and was **at the p of** death. H4200
Jer 17:1 inscribed with a flint **p**, on the tablets of H7632
Eze 47:20 the boundary to a **p** opposite Lebo Hamath NDT
Mt 4:5 him stand on the **highest p** of the temple. *G4762*
Mt 18:15 go and **p out** their **fault**, just *G1794*
Mt 26:38 with sorrow **to the p of** death. *G2401*
Mk 14:34 with sorrow **to the p of** death, *G2401*
Lk 4:9 him stand on the **highest p** of the temple. *G4762*
Jn 7:25 **At that p** some of the people of *G4036*
Ac 26:24 **At this p** Festus interrupted Paul's *G4047+1254*
Ro 2:1 for at **whatever** *p* you judge another AIT
2Co 5:16 regard no one **from** a worldly **p of view**. *G2848*
2Co 7:11 At **every** *p* you have proved yourselves to be AIT
Php 3:15 And if *on* **some** *p* you think differently, that AIT
1Ti 4:6 *If you* **p** these things out to the brothers *G5719*
2Ti 2:9 am suffering **even to the p of** being *G3588*
Heb 8:1 Now the **main p** of what we are saying is *G3049*
Heb 12:4 not yet resisted **to the p of** shedding your *G3588*
Jas 2:10 yet stumbles at *just* **one** *p* is guilty of AIT
Rev 2:10 Be faithful, **even to the p of** death, and I *G948*

POINTED (1) [POINT]
Jn 4:44 Jesus himself *had* **p out** that a prophet *G3455*

POINTING (3) [POINT]
Isa 58:9 *with the* **p** finger and malicious talk, H8938
Mt 12:49 **P** to his disciples, he said, "Here *G1753+5931*
1Pe 1:11 of Christ in them *was* **p** when he predicted *G1317*

POINTS (5) [POINT]
1Sa 13:20 to the Philistines to have their **plow p**, H4739
1Sa 13:21 sharpening **plow p** and mattocks, H4739
Ne 4:13 behind the lowest **p** of the wall at the H5226
Ac 25:19 they had some **p of dispute** with him *G2427*
Ro 15:15 you quite boldly *on* some **p** to remind you *G3538*

POISED (2)
Job 15:24 overwhelm him, like a king **p** to attack, H6969
Job 37:16 Do you know how the clouds **hang p** H5146

POISON (11) [POISONED, POISONOUS, POISONS]
Dt 29:18 among you that produces such bitter **p**. H8032
Dt 32:32 Their grapes are filled with **p**, and their H8032
Dt 32:33 of serpents, the deadly **p** *of* cobras. H8032
Job 6:4 my spirit drinks in their **p**; God's terrors are H2779
Job 20:16 He will suck the **p** *of* serpents; the fangs H8032
Ps 140:3 a serpent's; the **p** *of* vipers is on their lips. H2779
Pr 26:6 is like cutting off one's feet or drinking **p**. H2805
Am 6:12 have turned justice into **p** and the fruit of H8032
Mk 16:18 when they drink **deadly p**, it will not *G2503*
Ro 3:13 "The **p** of vipers is on their lips." *G2675*
Jas 3:8 It is a restless evil, full *of* deadly **p**. *G2675*

POISONED (4) [POISON]
Jer 8:14 us to perish and given us **p** water to drink, H8032
Jer 9:15 people eat bitter food and drink **p** water. H8032
Jer 23:15 them eat bitter food and drink **p** water, H8032
Ac 14:2 other Gentiles and **p** their minds against *G2808*

POISONOUS (1) [POISON]
Hos 10:4 spring up like **p weeds** in a plowed field. H8032

POISONS (1) [POISON]
Pr 23:32 it bites like a snake and **p** like a viper. H7301

POKERETH-HAZZEBAIM (2)
Ezr 2:57 Shephatiah, Hattil, **P** and Ami H7097
Ne 7:59 Shephatiah, Hattil, **P** and Amon H7097

POLE (29) [POLES]
Ge 40:19 your head and impale your body on a **p**. H6770
Nu 13:23 of them carried it on a **p** between them, H4573
Nu 21:8 "Make a snake and put it up on a **p** H5812
Nu 21:9 a bronze snake and put it up on a **p**. H5812
Dt 16:21 up any wooden **Asherah p** beside the altar H895
Dt 21:22 death and their body is exposed on a **p**, H6770
Dt 21:23 *you must* not **leave** the body hanging on the **p** H6770
Dt 21:23 who is hung on a **p** is under God's curse. NDT
Jos 8:29 of the king of Ai on a **p** and left it there H6770
Jos 8:29 the body from the **p** and throw it down at H6770
Jdg 6:25 Baal and cut down the **Asherah p** beside it. H895
Jdg 6:26 the wood of the **Asherah p** that you cut H895
Jdg 6:28 with the **Asherah p** beside it cut down and H895
Jdg 6:30 altar and cut down the **Asherah p** beside it." H895
1Ki 16:33 also made an **Asherah p** and did more to H895
2Ki 6:2 where each of us can get a **p**; and let us H7771
2Ki 13:6 the **Asherah p** remained standing in H895
2Ki 17:16 in the shape of calves, and an **Asherah p**. H895
2Ki 21:3 altars to Baal and made an **Asherah p**, H895
2Ki 21:7 took the carved **Asherah p** he had made H895
2Ki 23:6 He took the **Asherah p** from the temple of H895
2Ki 23:15 to powder, and burned the **Asherah p** also. H895
Est 5:14 said to him, "Have a **p** set up, reaching to H6770
Est 5:14 Haman, and he had the **p** set up. H6770
Est 6:4 Mordecai on the **p** he had set up for him. H6770
Est 7:9 "A **p** reaching to a height of fifty cubits H6770
Est 7:10 Haman on the **p** he had set up for H6770
Est 8:7 have impaled him on the **p** he set up. H6770
Gal 3:13 "Cursed is everyone who is hung on a **p**." *G3833*

POLES (62) [POLE]
Ex 25:13 Then make **p** *of* acacia wood and overlay H964
Ex 25:14 Insert the **p** into the rings on the sides of H964
Ex 25:15 The **p** are to remain in the rings of this ark H964
Ex 25:27 to the rim to hold the **p** used in carrying the H964
Ex 25:28 Make the **p** of acacia wood, overlay them H964
Ex 27:6 Make **p** *of* acacia wood for the altar and H964
Ex 27:7 The **p** are to be inserted into the rings so H964
Ex 30:4 to hold the **p** used to carry it. H964
Ex 30:5 Make the **p** of acacia wood and overlay H964
Ex 34:13 stones and cut down their **Asherah p**. H895
Ex 35:12 the ark with its **p** and the atonement cover H964
Ex 35:13 the table with its **p** and all its articles and H964
Ex 35:15 the altar of incense with its **p**, the anointing H964
Ex 35:16 its bronze grating, its **p** and all its utensils H964
Ex 37:4 Then he made **p** *of* acacia wood and H964
Ex 37:5 And he inserted the **p** into the rings on the H964
Ex 37:14 to the rim to hold the **p** used in carrying the H964
Ex 37:15 The **p** for carrying the table were made of H964
Ex 37:27 to hold the **p** used to carry it. H964
Ex 37:28 They made the **p** *of* acacia wood and H964
Ex 38:5 rings to hold the **p** for the four corners of H964
Ex 38:6 They made the **p** of acacia wood and H964
Ex 38:7 They inserted the **p** into the rings so they H964
Ex 39:35 covenant law with its **p** and the atonement H964
Ex 39:39 its bronze grating, its **p** and all its utensils H964
Ex 40:20 attached the **p** to the ark and put the H964
Nu 4:6 solid blue over that and put the **p** in place. H964
Nu 4:8 the durable leather and put the **p** in place. H964
Nu 4:11 the durable leather and put the **p** in place. H964
Nu 4:14 the durable leather and put the **p** in place. H964
Dt 7:5 cut down their **Asherah p** and burn their H895
Dt 12:3 stones and burn their **Asherah p** in the fire; H895
Jos 10:26 death and exposed their bodies on five **p**, H6770
Jos 10:26 were left hanging on the **p** until evening. H6770
Jos 10:27 them down from the **p** and threw them H6770
1Ki 8:7 overshadowed the ark and its **carrying p**. H964
1Ki 8:8 These **p** were so long that their ends could H964
1Ki 14:15 the LORD's anger by making **Asherah p**. H895
1Ki 14:23 sacred stones and **Asherah p** on every high H895
2Ki 17:10 sacred stones and **Asherah p** on every high H895
2Ki 18:4 sacred stones and cut down the **Asherah p**. H895
2Ki 23:14 cut down the **Asherah p** and covered the H895
1Ch 15:15 ark of God with the **p** on their shoulders, H4574
2Ch 5:8 ark and covered the ark and its **carrying p**. H964
2Ch 5:9 These **p** were so long that their ends H964
2Ch 14:3 sacred stones and cut down the **Asherah p**. H895
2Ch 17:6 high places and the **Asherah p** from Judah. H895
2Ch 19:3 the land of the **Asherah p** and have set H895
2Ch 24:18 worshiped **Asherah p** and idols. H895
2Ch 31:1 sacred stones and cut down the **Asherah p**. H895
2Ch 33:3 altars to the Baals and made **Asherah p**. H895
2Ch 33:19 set up **Asherah p** and idols before H895
2Ch 34:3 of high places, **Asherah p** and idols. H895
2Ch 34:4 smashed the **Asherah p** and the idols. H895
2Ch 34:7 altars and the **Asherah p** and crushed the H895
Est 2:23 the two officials were impaled on **p**. H6770
Est 9:13 let Haman's ten sons be impaled on **p**." H6770
Est 9:25 he and his sons should be impaled on **p**. H6770
Isa 17:8 regard for the **Asherah p** and the incense H895
Isa 27:9 no **Asherah p** or incense altars will be left H895
Jer 17:2 their altars and **Asherah p** beside the H895
Mic 5:14 among you your **Asherah p** when I H895

POLISH (1) [POLISHED]
Jer 46:4 with helmets on! **P** your spears, put on H5347

POLISHED (9) [POLISH]
2Ch 4:16 the temple of the LORD were of **p** bronze. H5347
Ezr 8:27 two fine articles of **p** bronze, as H7410
SS 5:14 His body is like **p** ivory decorated with H6952
Isa 49:2 he made me into a **p** arrow and H1406
Eze 21:9 " 'A sword, a sword, sharpened and **p**— H5307
Eze 21:10 the slaughter, **p** to flash like lightning! H5307
Eze 21:11 " 'The sword is appointed to *be* **p**, to be H5307
Eze 21:11 it is sharpened and **p**, made ready for the H5307
Eze 21:28 **p** to consume and to flash like lightning! H5307

POLLUTE (2) [POLLUTED, POLLUTES]
Nu 35:33 " '*Do* not **p** the land where you are H2866
Jude 8 these ungodly people **p** their own bodies, *G3620*

POLLUTED (4) [POLLUTE]
Ezr 9:11 to possess is a land **p** by the corruption of H5614
Pr 25:26 a muddied spring or a **p** well are the H8845
Ac 15:20 them to abstain *from food* **p** by idols, *G246*
Jas 1:27 to keep oneself **from being p** by the world. *G834*

POLLUTES (1) [POLLUTE]
Nu 35:33 Bloodshed **p** the land, and atonement H2866

POLLUX (1)
Ac 28:11 figurehead *of* the **twin gods Castor and P**. *G1483*

POMEGRANATE (5) [POMEGRANATES]
1Sa 14:2 of Gibeah under a **p tree** in Migron. H8232
SS 4:3 behind your veil are like the halves of a **p**. H8232
SS 6:7 behind your veil are like the halves of a **p**. H8232
Joel 1:12 tree is withered; the **p**, the palm and the H8232
Hag 2:19 the **p** and the olive tree have not borne H8232

POMEGRANATES (24) [POMEGRANATE]
Ex 28:33 Make **p** *of* blue, purple and scarlet yarn H8232
Ex 28:34 The gold bells and the **p** are to alternate H8232
Ex 39:24 They made **p** *of* blue, purple and scarlet H8232
Ex 39:25 them around the hem between the **p**. H8232
Ex 39:26 The bells and **p** alternated around the H8232
Nu 13:23 along with some **p** and figs. H8232
Nu 20:5 grapevines or **p**. And there is no H8232
Dt 8:8 vines and fig trees, **p**, olive oil and honey; H8232
1Ki 7:18 He made **p** in two rows encircling each H8232
1Ki 7:20 the two hundred **p** in rows all around. H8232
1Ki 7:42 the four hundred **p** for the two sets of H8232
1Ki 7:42 two rows of **p** for each network decorating H8232
2Ki 25:17 with a network and **p** of bronze all around H8232
2Ch 3:16 made a hundred **p** and attached them H8232
2Ch 4:13 the four hundred **p** for the two sets of H8232
2Ch 4:13 of network (two rows of **p** for each network H8232
SS 4:13 are an orchard of **p** with choice fruits, H8232
SS 6:11 vines had budded or the **p** were in bloom. H8232
SS 7:12 opened, and if the **p** are in bloom—there H8232
SS 8:2 spiced wine to drink, the nectar of my **p**. H8232
Jer 52:22 with a network and **p** of bronze all around H8232
Jer 52:22 The other pillar, with its **p**, was similar. H8232
Jer 52:23 There were ninety-six **p** on the sides; the H8232
Jer 52:23 the total number of **p** above the H8232

POMP (4)
Isa 8:7 the king of Assyria with all his **p**. H3883
Isa 10:16 under his **p** a fire will be kindled like a H3883
Isa 14:11 All your **p** has been brought down to the H1454
Ac 25:23 came with great **p** and entered the *G5752*

PONDER (5) [PONDERED]
Ps 64:9 works of God and **p** what he has done. H8505
Ps 107:43 these things and **p** the loving deeds of H1067
Ps 119:95 to destroy me, but *I will* **p** your statutes. H1067
Isa 14:16 who see you stare at you, *they* **p** your fate: H1067
Isa 33:18 In your thoughts *you will* **p** the former H2047

PONDERED (4) [PONDER]
Ne 5:7 I **p** them in my mind and then accused the H4888
Ps 111:2 *they* **are p** by all who delight in them. H2011
Ecc 12:9 *He* **p** and searched out and set in order H264
Lk 2:19 all these things and **p** them in her heart. *G5202*

PONDS (2)
Ex 7:19 over the **p** and all the reservoirs H106
Ex 8:5 staff over the streams and canals and **p**, H106

PONTIUS (3)
Lk 3:1 when **P** Pilate was governor of Judea *G4508*
Ac 4:27 Indeed Herod and **P** Pilate met together *G4508*
1Ti 6:13 testifying before **P** Pilate made the good *G4508*

PONTUS (3)
Ac 2:9 Judea and Cappadocia, **P** and Asia, *G4510*
Ac 18:2 a native **of P**, who had recently *G4507*
1Pe 1:1 scattered throughout the provinces of **P**, *G4510*

POOL (20) [POOLS]
2Sa 2:13 out and met them at the **p** *of* Gibeon. H1391
2Sa 2:13 on one side of the **p** and one group on H1391
2Sa 4:12 hung the bodies by the **p** in Hebron. H1391
1Ki 22:38 washed the chariot at a **p** *in* Samaria H1391
2Ki 18:17 stopped at the aqueduct of the Upper **P**, H1391
2Ki 20:20 how he made the **p** and the tunnel by H1391
Ne 2:14 the Fountain Gate and the King's **P**, H1391
Ne 3:15 also repaired the wall of the **P** *of* Siloam, H1391
Ne 3:16 far as the artificial **p** and the House of the H1391
Ps 114:8 who turned the rock into a **p**, the H106+4784
Isa 7:3 the end of the aqueduct of the Upper **P**, H1391
Isa 22:9 you stored up water in the Lower **P**. H1391
Isa 22:11 the two walls for the water of the Old **P**, H1391
Isa 35:7 The burning sand will become a **p**, the H106
Isa 36:2 stopped at the aqueduct of the Upper **P**, H1391
Jer 41:12 up with him near the great **p** in Gibeon. H4784
Na 2:8 Nineveh is like a **p** whose water is H1391+4784
Jn 5:2 is in Jerusalem near the Sheep Gate a **p**, *G3148*

P

Jn 5: 7 to help me into the **p** when the water is G3148
Jn 9: 7 "wash in the **P** of Siloam" (this word G3148

POOLS (6) [POOL]

2Ki 3:16 I will fill this valley with **p of water**. H1463+1463
Ps 84: 6 the autumn rains also cover it with **p**. H1391
Ps 107:35 the desert into **p** *of* water and the parched H106
SS 7: 4 Your eyes are the **p** of Heshbon by the H1391
Isa 41:18 I will turn the desert into **p** *of* water, and H106
Isa 42:15 turn rivers into islands and dry up the **p**. H106

POOR (176) [IMPOVERISHED, POOREST, POVERTY]

Ex 23: 3 show favoritism to a **p** *person* in a lawsuit. H1924
Ex 23: 6 justice to your **p** *people* in their lawsuits. H36
Ex 23:11 Then the **p** *among* your people may get H36
Ex 30:15 half shekel and the **p** are not to give less H1924
Lev 14:21 they are **p** and cannot afford these H1924
Lev 19:10 Leave them for the **p** and the foreigner. H6714
Lev 19:15 show partiality to the **p** or favoritism to the H1924
Lev 23:22 Leave them for the **p** and for the foreigner H6714
Lev 25:25 Israelites *becomes* **p** and sells some H4575
Lev 25:35 Israelites *become* **p** and are unable H4575
Lev 25:39 fellow Israelites *become* **p** and sell H4575
Lev 25:47 fellow Israelites **become p** and sell H4575
Lev 27: 8 the vow *is* too **p to pay** the specified H4575
Nu 13:20 Is it fertile or **p**? Are there trees in it H8136
Dt 15: 4 there need be no **p** *people* among you, for H36
Dt 15: 7 If anyone is **p** among your fellow Israelites H36
Dt 15:11 There will always be **p** *people* in the land H36
Dt 15:11 Israelites who are **p** and needy in your H6714
Dt 24:12 If the neighbor is **p**, do not go to sleep H6714
Dt 24:14 of a hired worker who is **p** and needy, H6714
Dt 24:15 because they are **p** and are counting on it. H6714
Ru 3:10 after the younger men, whether rich or **p**. H1924
1Sa 2: 8 He raises the **p** from the dust and lifts the H1924
1Sa 18:23 I'm only a **p** man and little known. H8133
2Sa 12: 1 a certain town, one rich and the other **p**. H8133
2Sa 12: 3 the **p** *man* had nothing except one H8133
2Sa 12: 4 belonged to the **p** man and prepared it H8133
Est 9:22 of food to one another and gifts to the **p**. H36
Job 5:16 So the **p** have hope, and injustice shuts H1924
Job 20:10 His children must make amends to the **p** H1924
Job 20:19 he has oppressed the **p** and left them H1924
Job 24: 4 force all the **p** *of* the land into hiding. H6714
Job 24: 5 the **p** go about their labor of foraging food NDT
Job 24: 9 the infant of the **p** is seized for a debt. H6714
Job 24:14 rises up, kills the **p** and needy, and in the H6714
Job 29:12 I rescued the **p** who cried for help, H6714
Job 30:25 Has not my soul grieved for the **p**? H36
Job 31:16 the desires of the **p** or let the eyes of the H1924
Job 34:19 does not favor the rich over the **p**, H1924
Job 34:28 the cry of the **p** to come before him, H1924
Ps 12: 5 "Because the **p** are plundered and the H6714
Ps 14: 6 You evildoers frustrate the plans of the **p** H6714
Ps 15: 5 who lends money to the **p** without interest NDT
Ps 22:26 The **p** will eat and be satisfied; those who H6705
Ps 34: 6 This **p** *man* called, and the LORD heard H6714
Ps 35:10 You rescue the **p** from those too strong H6714
Ps 35:10 the **p** and needy from those who rob them H6714
Ps 37:14 the bow to bring down the **p** and needy, H6714
Ps 40:17 But as for me, I am **p** and needy; may the H6714
Ps 49: 2 both low and high, rich and **p** alike: H36
Ps 68:10 your bounty, God, you provided for the **p**. H6714
Ps 69:32 The **p** will see and be glad—you who H6705
Ps 70: 5 But as for me, I am **p** and needy; come H6714
Ps 74:21 may the **p** and needy praise your name. H6714
Ps 82: 3 the cause of the **p** and the oppressed. H6714
Ps 86: 1 answer me, for I am **p** and needy. H6714
Ps 109:16 to death the **p** and the needy and H6714
Ps 109:22 For I am **p** and needy, and my heart is H6714
Ps 112: 9 They have freely scattered their gifts to the **p**, H36
Ps 113: 7 He raises the **p** from the dust and lifts the H1924
Ps 132:15 provisions; her **p** I will satisfy with food. H36
Ps 140:12 justice for the **p** and upholds the cause H6714
Pr 10:15 but poverty is the ruin of the **p**. H1924
Pr 13: 7 nothing; *another* **pretends to be p**, yet has H8133
Pr 13: 8 the **p** cannot respond to threatening H8133
Pr 13:23 unplowed field produces food for the **p**, H8133
Pr 14:20 The **p** are shunned even by their H8133
Pr 14:31 oppresses the **p** shows contempt for H1924
Pr 17: 5 Whoever mocks the **p** shows contempt H8133
Pr 18:23 The **p** plead for mercy, but the rich answer H8133
Pr 19: 1 Better the **p** whose walk is blameless than H8133
Pr 19: 4 friend of the **p** *person* deserts them. H1924
Pr 19: 7 The **p** are shunned by all their relatives H8133
Pr 19: 7 Though the **p** pursue them with pleading NDT
Pr 19:17 Whoever is kind to the **p** lends to the LORD, H1924
Pr 19:22 unfailing love; better *to be* **p** than a liar. H8133
Pr 20:13 Do not love sleep or *you will* **grow p**; stay H3769
Pr 21:13 to the cry of the **p** will also cry out and H1924
Pr 21:17 Whoever loves pleasure will become **p** H4728
Pr 22: 2 Rich and **p** have this in common: The LORD H8133
Pr 22: 7 The rich rule over the **p**, and the borrower H8133
Pr 22: 9 they share their food with the **p**. H1924
Pr 22:16 One who oppresses the **p** to increase his H1924
Pr 22:22 Do not exploit the **p** because they are H1924
Pr 22:22 because they are **p** and do not crush the H1924
Pr 23:21 drunkards and gluttons *become* **p**, and H3769
Pr 28: 3 who oppresses the **p** is like a driving rain H1924
Pr 28: 6 Better the **p** whose walk is blameless than H8133
Pr 28: 8 profit from the **p** amasses it for another, NDT
Pr 28: 8 it for another, who will be kind to the **p**. H1924
Pr 28:11 *one who is* **p** and discerning sees how H1924
Pr 28:27 Those who give to the **p** will lack nothing H8133
Pr 29: 7 The righteous care about justice for the **p** H1924
Pr 29:13 The **p** and the oppressor have this in H8133
Pr 29:14 If a king judges the **p** with fairness, his H1924
Pr 30: 9 Or *I may* **become p** and steal, and so H3769
Pr 30:14 knives to devour the **p** from the earth and H6714
Pr 31: 9 defend the rights of the **p** and needy. H6714
Pr 31:20 her arms to the **p** and extends her hands H6714
Ecc 4:13 Better a **p** but wise youth than an old but H5014
Ecc 5: 8 If you see the **p** oppressed in a district H8133
Ecc 6: 8 What do the **p** gain by knowing how to H6714
Ecc 9:15 there lived in that city a man **p** but wise, H5014
Ecc 9:15 But nobody remembered that **p** man. H5014
Ecc 9:16 But the **p** *man's* wisdom is despised, and H5014
Isa 3:14 the plunder from the **p** is in your houses. H6714
Isa 3:15 people and grinding the faces of the **p**?" H6714
Isa 10: 2 to deprive the **p** of their rights and H1924
Isa 10:30 Listen, Laishah! **P** Anathoth! H6714
Isa 11: 4 will give decisions for the **p** *of* the earth. H6705
Isa 14:30 The **poorest of the p** will find H1147+1924
Isa 25: 4 You have been a refuge for the **p**, H1924
Isa 26: 6 of the oppressed, the footsteps of the **p**. H1924
Isa 32: 7 up evil schemes to destroy the **p** with lies, H6714
Isa 40:20 A *person* **too p** *to* present such an offering H6123
Isa 41:17 "The **p** and needy search for water, but H6714
Isa 58: 7 to provide the **p** wanderer with H6714
Isa 61: 1 me to proclaim good news to the **p**. H6705
Jer 2:34 is found the lifeblood of the innocent **p**, H36
Jer 5: 4 "These are only the **p**; they are foolish, H1924
Jer 5:28 they do not defend the just cause of the **p**. H36
Jer 22:16 defended the cause of the **p** and needy, H6714
Jer 39:10 the land of Judah some of the **p** people, H1924
Eze 16:49 they did not help the **p** and needy. H6714
Eze 18:12 He oppresses the **p** and needy. H6714
Eze 18:17 from mistreating the **p** and takes no H6714
Eze 22:12 take interest and make a profit from the **p**. NDT
Eze 22:29 they oppress the **p** and needy and H6714
Am 2: 7 on the heads of the **p** as on the dust of H1924
Am 4: 1 who oppress the **p** and crush the needy H1924
Am 5:11 a straw tax on the **p** and impose a tax on H1924
Am 5:12 bribes and deprive the **p** of justice in the H36
Am 8: 4 do away with the **p** *of* the land, H6714
Am 8: 6 buying the **p** with silver and the needy H1924
Zec 7:10 the fatherless, the foreigner or the **p**. H6714
Mt 5: 3 "Blessed are the **p** in spirit, for theirs is G4777
Mt 11: 5 the good news is proclaimed *to* the **p**. G4777
Mt 19:21 sell your possessions and give *to* the **p** G4777
Mt 26: 9 high price and the money given *to* the **p**." G4777
Mt 26:11 The **p** you will always have with you, but G4777
Mk 10:21 sell everything you have and give *to* the **p**, G4777
Mk 12:42 But a **p** widow came and put in two very G4777
Mk 12:43 this **p** widow has put more into the G4777
Mk 14: 5 wages and the money given *to* the **p**." G4777
Mk 14: 7 The **p** you will always have with you, and G4777
Lk 4:18 me to proclaim good news *to* the **p**. G4777
Lk 6:20 "Blessed are you who are **p**, for yours is G4777
Lk 7:22 the good news is proclaimed *to* the **p**. G4777
Lk 11:41 you—**be generous to the p**, and G1443+1797
Lk 12:33 your possessions and **give to the p**. G1443+1797
Lk 14:13 give a banquet, invite the **p**, the crippled, G4777
Lk 14:21 alleys of the town and bring in the **p**, G4777
Lk 18:22 everything you have and give *to* the **p**, G4777
Lk 19: 8 I give half of my possessions *to* the **p**, G4777
Lk 21: 2 He also saw a **p** widow put in two very G4293
Lk 21: 3 "this **p** widow has put in more than all the G4777
Jn 12: 5 sold and the money given *to* the **p**? G4777
Jn 12: 6 he cared about the **p** but because he was G4777
Jn 12: 8 You will always have the **p** among you G4777
Jn 13:29 the festival, or to give something *to* the **p**. G4777
Ac 9:36 doing good and **helping the p**. G1797+4472
Ac 10: 4 prayers and **gifts to the p** have come up G1797
Ac 10:31 remembered your **gifts to the p**. G1797
Ac 24:17 my people **gifts for the p** and to present G1797
Ro 15:26 a contribution for the **p** among the Lord's G4777
1Co 13: 3 If *I* **give** all I possess **to the p** and give over G6039
2Co 6:10 always rejoicing; **p**, yet making many rich G4777
2Co 8: 9 for your sake *he became* **p**, so that you G4776
2Co 9: 9 have freely scattered their gifts *to* the **p**; G4288
Gal 2:10 we should continue to remember the **p**, G4777
Jas 2: 2 a **p** *man* in filthy old clothes also G4777
Jas 2: 3 you," but say *to* the **p** *man*, "You stand G4777
Jas 2: 5 chosen those *who are* **p** in the eyes of G4777
Jas 2: 6 But you have dishonored the **p**. Is it not G4777
Rev 3:17 are wretched, pitiful, **p**, blind and naked. G4777
Rev 13:16 small, rich and **p**, free and slave, G4777

POOREST (6) [POOR]

2Ki 24:14 Only the **p** people of the land were left H1930
2Ki 25:12 some of the **p** *people of* the land to work H1930
Isa 14:30 The **p of the poor** will find pasture H1147+1924
Jer 40: 7 who were the **p** *in* the land and who had H1930
Jer 52:15 exile some of the **p** people and those H1930
Jer 52:16 the rest of the **p** *people of* the land to H1930

POPLAR (7) [POPLARS]

Ge 30:37 took fresh-cut branches from **p**, almond H4242
2Sa 5:23 attack them in front of the **p trees**. H1132
2Sa 5:24 of marching in the tops of the **p trees**, H1132
1Ch 14:14 attack them in front of the **p trees**. H1132
1Ch 14:15 of marching in the tops of the **p trees**, H1132
Isa 44: 4 meadow, like **p trees** by flowing streams. H6857
Hos 4:13 under oak, **p** and terebinth, where the H4242

POPLARS (3) [POPLAR]

Job 40:22 shadow; the **p** *by* the stream surround it. H6857
Ps 137: 2 There on the **p** we hung our harps, H6857
Isa 15: 7 they carry away over the Ravine of the **P**. H6857

POPULACE (1) [POPULATION]

2Ki 25:11 with the rest of the **p** and those who had H2162

POPULATION (1) [POPULACE]

Pr 14:28 A large **p** is a king's glory, but without H6639

PORATHA (1)

Est 9: 8 **P**, Adalia, Aridatha, H7054

PORCH (1) [PORTICO, PORTICOES]

Jdg 3:23 Then Ehud went out to the **p**; he shut the H4997

PORCIUS (1) [FESTUS]

Ac 24:27 Felix was succeeded by **P** Festus, but G4517

PORPHYRY (1)

Est 1: 6 gold and silver on a mosaic pavement of **p**, H985

PORT (1)

Jnh 1: 3 where he found a ship bound for **that p**. H9576S

PORTENT (1)

Isa 20: 3 as a sign and **p** against Egypt and Cush, H4603

PORTICO (45) [PORCH]

1Ki 6: 3 The **p** at the front of the main hall of the H395
1Ki 7: 6 In front of it was a **p**, and in front of that H395
1Ki 7:12 of the temple of the LORD with its **p**. H395
1Ki 7:19 of the pillars in the **p** were in the shape of H395
1Ki 7:21 erected the pillars at the **p** *of* the temple. H395
1Ch 28:11 Solomon the plans for the **p** of the temple, H395
2Ch 3: 4 The **p** at the front of the temple was twenty H395
2Ch 8:12 the LORD that he had built in front of the **p**, H395
2Ch 15: 8 was in front of the **p** *of* the LORD's temple. H395
2Ch 29: 7 the doors of the **p** and put out the lamps H395
2Ch 29:17 the month they reached the **p** *of* the LORD. H395
Eze 8:16 between the **p** and the altar, were H395
Eze 40: 7 the gate next to the **p** facing the temple H395
Eze 40: 8 Then he measured the **p** *of* the gateway; H395
Eze 40: 9 The **p** *of* the gateway faced the temple H395
Eze 40:14 was up to the **p** *facing* the courtyard. H395
Eze 40:15 to the far end of its **p** was fifty cubits. H395
Eze 40:16 all around, as was the **p**; the openings all H395
Eze 40:21 projecting walls and its **p** had the same H395
Eze 40:22 its **p** and its palm tree decorations had the H395
Eze 40:22 steps led up to it, with its **p** opposite them. H395
Eze 40:24 He measured its jambs and its **p**, and they H395
Eze 40:25 The gateway and its **p** had narrow openings H395
Eze 40:26 led up to it, with its **p** opposite them; it had H395
Eze 40:29 projecting walls and its **p** had the same H395
Eze 40:29 The gateway and its **p** had openings all H395
Eze 40:31 Its **p** faced the outer court; palm trees H395
Eze 40:33 projecting walls and its **p** had the same H395
Eze 40:33 The gateway and its **p** had openings all H395
Eze 40:34 Its **p** faced the outer court; palm trees H395
Eze 40:36 its projecting walls and its **p**, and it had H395
Eze 40:37 Its **p** faced the outer court; palm trees H395
Eze 40:38 doorway was by the **p** *in* each of the inner H395
Eze 40:39 In the **p** *of* the gateway were two tables on H395
Eze 40:40 By the outside wall of the **p** *of* the gateway H395
Eze 40:48 He brought me to the **p** *of* the temple and H395
Eze 40:48 temple and measured the jambs of the **p**; H395
Eze 40:49 The **p** was twenty cubits wide, and twelve H395
Eze 41:15 inner sanctuary and the **p** *facing* the court, H395
Eze 41:25 a wooden overhang on the front of the **p**. H395
Eze 41:26 sidewalls of the **p** were narrow windows H395
Eze 44: 3 by way of the **p** *of* the gateway and go H395
Eze 46: 2 outside through the **p** *of* the gateway and H395
Eze 46: 8 he is to go in through the **p** *of* the gateway H395
Joel 2:17 weep between the **p** and the altar. H395

PORTICOES (1) [PORCH]

Eze 40:30 The **p** of the gateways around the inner H395

PORTION (73) [APPORTIONED, PORTIONS]

Ge 43:34 Benjamin's **p** was five times as much as H5368
Lev 2: 2 burn this as a **memorial p** on the altar H260
Lev 2: 9 take out the **memorial p** from the grain H260
Lev 2:16 shall burn the **memorial p** of the crushed H260
Lev 5:12 of it as a **memorial p** and burn it on H260
Lev 6:15 burn the **memorial p** on the altar as an H260
Lev 7:35 **p** of the food offerings presented to the LORD that were *allotted to* H5419
Lev 24: 7 incense as a **memorial p** to represent the H260
Nu 15:19 **present a p** as an offering to the LORD. H8123
Nu 18: 8 me I give to you and your sons as your **p**, H5421
Nu 18:28 must give the LORD's **p** to Aaron the priest. H9556
Nu 18:29 as the LORD's **p** the best and holiest H9556
Dt 26:13 my house the **sacred p** and have given H7731
Dt 26:14 eaten any of the **sacred p** while I was in H5647S
Dt 32: 9 For the LORD's **p** is his people, Jacob his H2750
Dt 33:21 himself; the leader's **p** was kept for him. H2754
Jos 15:13 Caleb son of Jephunneh a **p** in Judah— H2750
Jos 17:14 allotment and one **p** for an inheritance? H2475
Jos 18: 7 do not get a **p** among you, because H2750
Jos 19: 9 because Judah's **p** was more than they H2750
1Sa 1: 5 he gave a double **p** because he loved her H4950

2Ki 2: 9 "Let me inherit a double **p** of your spirit," H7023
1Ch 16:18 land of Canaan as the **p** you will inherit." H2475
2Ch 30:22 days they ate their **assigned p** and offered H4595
2Ch 31: 4 to give the **p** *due* the priests and H4987
Ne 12:47 also set aside the **p** for the other Levites, NDT
Ne 12:47 Levites set aside the **p** for the descendants NDT
Job 24:18 of the water; their **p** of the land is cursed H2754
Ps 16: 5 you alone are my **p** and my cup H4987+2750
Ps 73:26 the strength of my heart and my **p** forever. H2750
Ps 105:11 land of Canaan as the **p** you will inherit." H2475
Ps 119:57 You are my **p**, LORD; I have promised to H2750
Ps 142: 5 my refuge, my **p** in the land of the living." H2750
Isa 17:14 This is the **p** *of* those who loot us, the lot H2750
Isa 53:12 Therefore *I will* **give** him **a p** among the H2745
Isa 57: 6 smooth stones of the ravines are your **p**; H2750
Isa 61: 7 your shame you will receive a **double p**, H5467
Isa 61: 7 you will inherit a **double p** in your land, H5467
Jer 6: 3 tents around her, each tending his own **p**." H3338
Jer 10:16 He who is the **P** *of* Jacob is not like these H2750
Jer 13:25 is your lot, the **p** I have decreed for you," H4987
Jer 51:19 He who is the **P** *of* Jacob is not like these H2750
La 3:24 "The LORD is my **p**; therefore I will wait H2750
Eze 44:30 to give them the **first** *p of* your ground meal AIT
Eze 45: 1 present to the LORD **a p** of the land as a H9556
Eze 45: 4 It will be the sacred **p** of the land for the NDT
Eze 45: 6 adjoining the sacred **p**; it will belong to H9556
Eze 45:14 The **prescribed p** *of* olive oil, measured by H2976
Eze 48: 1 Dan will have **one** *p*; it will follow the AIT
Eze 48: 2 "Asher will have **one** *p*; it will border the AIT
Eze 48: 3 "Naphtali will have **one** *p*; it will border the AIT
Eze 48: 4 "Manasseh will have **one** *p*; it will border the AIT
Eze 48: 5 "Ephraim will have **one** *p*; it will border the AIT
Eze 48: 6 "Reuben will have **one** *p*; it will border the AIT
Eze 48: 7 "Judah will have **one** *p*; it will border the AIT
Eze 48: 8 the **p** you are to present **as a special gift**. H9556
Eze 48: 9 "The **special p** you are to offer to the LORD H9556
Eze 48:10 This will be the sacred **p** for the priests. H9556
Eze 48:12 gift to them from the sacred **p** *of* the land, H9556
Eze 48:12 the land, a most holy **p**, bordering the NDT
Eze 48:18 on the sacred **p** and running the length H9556
Eze 48:20 The entire **p** will be a square, 25,000 H9556
Eze 48:20 gift you will set aside the sacred **p**, H9556
Eze 48:21 by the sacred **p** and the property of H9556
Eze 48:21 cubits of the sacred **p** to the eastern H9556
Eze 48:21 the sacred **p** with the temple H9556
Eze 48:23 Benjamin will have **one** *p*; it will extend from AIT
Eze 48:24 "Simeon will have **one** *p*; it will border the AIT
Eze 48:25 "Issachar will have **one** *p*; it will border the AIT
Eze 48:26 "Zebulun will have **one** *p*; it will border the AIT
Eze 48:27 "Gad will have **one** *p*; it will border the AIT
Zec 2:12 Judah as his **p** in the holy land and H2750
Rev 18: 6 Pour her a **double** *p* from her own cup. AIT

PORTIONS (22) [PORTION]

Ge 4: 4 **fat p** from some of the firstborn of his flock. H2693
Ge 43:34 When **p** were served to them from H5368
Lev 8:26 he put these on the **fat p** and on the right H2693
Lev 9:19 But the **fat p** of the ox and the ram—the H2693
Lev 9:24 burnt offering and the **fat p** on the altar. H2693
Lev 10:15 brought with the **fat p** *of* the food H2693
Jos 19:49 dividing the land into its **allotted p**, H1474
1Sa 1: 4 he would give **p of** the **meat** to his wife H4950
2Ch 7: 7 the grain offerings and the **fat p**. H2693
2Ch 31:19 name to distribute **p** to every male among H4950
2Ch 35:14 offerings and the **fat p** until nightfall. H2693
Ne 8:12 to send **p of food** and to celebrate with H4950
Ne 12:44 storerooms the **p** *required by* the Law for H4987
Ne 12:47 the daily **p** *for* the musicians and the H4987
Ne 13:10 that the **p** *assigned to* the Levites had H4987
Pr 31:15 her family and **p** for her female H2976
Isa 34:17 He allots their **p**; his hand distributes H1598
Eze 45: 7 border parallel to one of the tribal **p**. H2750
Eze 47:13 their inheritance, with *two* **p** for Joseph. H2475
Eze 48: 8 east to west will equal one of the tribal **p**; H2750
Eze 48:21 length of the tribal **p** will belong to the H2750
Eze 48:29 these will be their **p**," declares the H4713

PORTRAYED (4)

Eze 8:10 I saw **p** all over the walls all kinds of H2977
Eze 23:14 She saw men **p** on a wall, figures of H2977
Eze 23:14 on a wall, figures of Chaldeans **p** in red, H2980
Gal 3: 1 Jesus Christ *was* **clearly p** as crucified. *G4592*

PORTS (1)

Ac 27: 2 about to sail for **p** along the coast of the *G5536*

POSES (1)

Jer 29:27 who **p as a prophet** among you? H5547

POSITION (22) [POSITIONS]

Ge 40:13 up your head and restore you to your **p**, H4030
Ge 40:21 He restored the chief cupbearer to his **p** H5482
Ge 41:13 I was restored to my **p**, and the other man H4030
Jos 8:19 quickly from their **p** and rushed forward. H5226
Jdg 7:21 each man held his **p** around the camp, H9393
Jdg 9:44 rushed forward *to a* **p** at the entrance of H6641
2Sa 3: 6 had been **strengthening his own p** in the H2616
1Ki 2:35 over the army **in** Joab's **p** and replaced H9393
1Ki 15:13 Maakah from her **p as queen mother**, H1485
1Ki 20:22 "**Strengthen** *your* **p** and see what must be H2616
2Ch 12: 1 Rehoboam's **p as king** was established H4895
2Ch 15:16 Maakah from her **p as queen mother**, H1485
Est 1:19 the king give her **royal p** to someone else H4895
Est 4:14 have come to your **royal p** for such a time H4895
Isa 22:19 and you will be ousted from your **p**. H5096
Da 2:48 the king **placed** Daniel **in a high p** and A10648
Da 5:19 Because of the **high p** he gave him, all A10650
Mt 18: 4 whoever **takes the lowly p** of this child is *G5427*
Ro 12:16 willing to associate with people **of low p**. *G5424*
1Co 14:16 who is now put in the **p** of an inquirer, say *G5536*
Jas 1: 9 ought to take pride in their **high p**. *G5737*
2Pe 3:17 of the lawless and fall from your **secure p**. *G5113*

POSITIONS (23) [POSITION]

Jos 3: 3 are to move out from your **p** and follow it. H5226
Jos 8:13 So the soldiers **took up** *their* **p**—with the H8492
Jos 10: 5 their troops and **took up p** against Gibeon H2837
Jos 10:31 *he* **took up p** against it and attacked it. H2837
Jos 10:34 *they* **took up p** against it and attacked it. H2837
Jdg 9:34 by night and **took up concealed p** near H741
Jdg 20:20 **took up** battle **p** against them H6885
Jdg 20:22 again **took up** *their* **p** where they had H6885
Jdg 20:30 third day and **took up p** against Gibeah H6885
Jdg 20:33 their places and **took up p** at Baal Tamar, H6885
1Sa 17:20 as the army was going out to its **battle p**, H5120
1Ch 9:22 *had been* **assigned to** their **p** of trust *by* H3569
2Ch 7: 6 The priests took their **p**, as did the Levites H5466
2Ch 14:10 and *they* **took up** battle **p** in the Valley of H6885
2Ch 20:17 **Take up** *your* **p**; stand firm and see the H3656
2Ch 30:16 took up their *regular* **p** as prescribed in H6642
Ecc 10: 6 Fools are put in many **high p**, while the H5294
Jer 46: 4 **Take** *your* **p** with helmets on H3656
Jer 46:14 '**Take** *your* **p** and get ready, for the sword H3656
Jer 50: 9 *They* **will take up** *their* **p** against her, and H6885
Jer 50:14 "**Take up** *your* **p** around Babylon, all you H6885
Eze 23:24 *they will* **take up p** against you on every H8492
Jude 6 keep their **p of authority** but abandoned *G794*

POSSESS (65) [DEMON-POSSESSED, POSSESSED, POSSESSES, POSSESSING, POSSESSION, POSSESSIONS]

Ge 24:60 *may* your offspring **p** the cities of their H3769
Lev 20:24 I said to you, "You *will* **p** their land; I will H3769
Lev 25:32 houses in the Levitical towns, which they **p**. H299
Nu 27:11 relative in his clan, that *he may* **p** it. H3769
Nu 33:53 for I have given you the land to **p**. H3769
Nu 35: 2 in from the inheritance the Israelites will **p**. H299
Nu 35: 8 the land the Israelites **p** are to be given in H299
Nu 36: 8 every Israelite *will* **p** the inheritance of H3769
Dt 2:31 Now begin to conquer and **p** his land." H3769
Dt 4:14 land that you are crossing the Jordan to **p**. H3769
Dt 4:26 land that you are crossing the Jordan to **p**. H3769
Dt 5:31 follow in the land I am giving them to **p**." H3769
Dt 5:33 your days in the land that *you will* **p**. H3769
Dt 6: 1 land that you are crossing the Jordan to **p**, H3769
Dt 7: 1 you are entering to **p** and drives out H3769
Dt 8: 1 may enter and **p** the land the LORD H3769
Dt 9: 6 God is giving you this good land to **p**, H3769
Dt 10:11 they may enter and **p** the land I swore to H3769
Dt 11: 8 land that you are crossing the Jordan to **p**, H3769
Dt 11:29 you into the land you are entering to **p**, H3769
Dt 12: 1 has given you to **p**—as long as you live in H3769
Dt 15: 4 God is giving you to **p** as your inheritance, H3769
Dt 16:20 that you may live and **p** the land the LORD H3769
Dt 19: 2 land the LORD your God is giving you to **p**. H3769
Dt 19:14 land the LORD your God is giving you to **p**. H3769
Dt 21: 1 land the LORD your God is giving you to **p**, H3769
Dt 23:20 hand to in the land you are entering to **p**. H3769
Dt 25:19 he is giving you to **p** as an inheritance, H3769
Dt 28:21 you from the land you are entering to **p**. H3769
Dt 28:63 from the land you are entering to **p**. H3769
Dt 30:16 you in the land you are entering to **p**. H3769
Dt 30:18 are crossing the Jordan to enter and **p**. H3769
Dt 31:13 the land you are crossing the Jordan to **p**." H3769
Dt 32:47 the land you are crossing the Jordan to **p**." H3769
Jos 22:19 If the land you **p** is defiled, come over to H299
Jdg 11:24 the LORD our God has given us, *we will* **p**. H3769
1Ch 28: 8 that *you may* **p** this good land and pass it H3769
Ezr 7:25 your God, which you **p**, appoint A10089+10311
Ezr 9:11 you are entering to **p** is a land polluted by H3769
Ne 9:23 that you told their parents to enter and **p**. H3769
Ps 69:35 Then people will settle there and **p** it; H3769
Pr 8:12 prudence; *I* **p** knowledge and discretion. H5162
Isa 34:11 The desert owl and screech owl *will* **p** it H3769
Isa 34:17 *They will* **p** it forever and dwell there from H3769
Isa 57:13 inherit the land and **p** my holy mountain." H3769
Isa 60:21 be righteous and *they will* **p** the land H3769
Isa 65: 9 from Judah *those who will* **p** my H3769
Jer 11: 5 with milk and honey'—the land you **p** today." NDT
Jer 30: 3 to the land I gave their ancestors *to* **p**, H3769
Jer 32: 8 Since it is your right to redeem it and **p** it H3772
Eze 33:25 shed blood, *should you* then **p** the land? H3769
Eze 33:26 wife. *Should you* then **p** the land?' H3769
Eze 36:12 *They will* **p** you, and you will be their H3769
Eze 45: 8 but *will* **allow** the people of Israel **to p** the H5989
Da 7:18 the kingdom and *will* **p** it forever— A10277
Am 9:12 so that *they may* **p** the remnant of Edom H3769
Ob 17 be holy, and Jacob *will* **p** his inheritance. H3769
Ob 19 from the foothills will **p** the land of the NDT
Ob 19 Samaria, and Benjamin will **p** Gilead. NDT
Ob 20 who are in Canaan will **p** the land as far as NDT
Ob 20 are in Sepharad *will* **p** the towns of the H3769
Ac 7: 5 after him *would* **p** the land, *G1443+1650+2959*
1Co 8: 1 We know that "*We* all **p** knowledge." *G2400*
1Co 13: 3 If I give all I **p** to the poor and give over *G5639*
2Pe 1: 8 For *if* you **p** these qualities in increasing *G5639*

POSSESSED (14) [POSSESS]

Ps 105:21 of his household, ruler over all he **p**, H7871
Isa 63:18 little while your people **p** your holy place, H3769
Jer 16:19 "Our ancestors **p** nothing but false gods H5706
Eze 16:16 went to him, and he **p** your beauty. H2118+4200
Eze 33:24 was only one man, yet *he* **p** the land. H3769
Da 7:22 time came when they **p** the kingdom. A10277
Mk 1:23 synagogue who was **p by** an impure spirit *G1877*
Mk 3:22 Jerusalem said, "*He is* **p by** Beelzebul! *G2400*
Mk 5:15 who had been **p by** the legion of **demons**, *G1227*
Mk 7:25 little daughter *was* **p by** an impure spirit *G2400*
Mk 9:17 *who is* **p by** a spirit that has robbed him of *G2400*
Lk 4:33 there was a man **p by** a demon, *G2400*
Jn 8:49 "I *am* not **p by** a demon," said Jesus, "but *G2400*
Jn 10:21 not the sayings *of a man* **p by a demon**. *G1227*

POSSESSES (1) [POSSESS]

1Co 8: 7 But not everyone **p** this knowledge. *G1877*

POSSESSING (1) [POSSESS]

2Co 6:10 having nothing, and yet **p** everything. *G2988*

POSSESSION (99) [POSSESS]

Ge 15: 7 to give you this land to **take p** *of* it." H3769
Ge 15: 8 how can I know that *I will* **gain p** *of* it?" H3769
Ge 17: 8 give as an everlasting **p** to you and your H299
Ge 22:17 descendants *will* **take p** *of* the cities of H3769
Ge 28: 4 so that you *may* **take p** *of* the land where H3769
Ge 30:33 Any goat **in** my **p** that is not speckled or H907
Ge 48: 4 as an everlasting **p** to your descendants H299
Ex 6: 8 I will give it to you as a **p**. I am the LORD. H4627
Ex 19: 5 of all nations you will be my **treasured p**. H6035
Ex 21:16 been sold or is still in the kidnapper's **p**. H3338
Ex 22: 4 stolen animal is found alive in their **p**— H3338
Ex 22: 9 In all cases of **illegal p** of an ox, a donkey H7322
Ex 23:30 increased enough *to* **take p** *of* the land. H5706
Lev 14:34 which I am giving you as your **p**, and I put H299
Lev 25:24 Throughout the land that you **hold as a p** H299
Lev 25:28 will remain in the **p** *of* the buyer until the H3338
Lev 25:34 must not be sold; it is their permanent **p**. H299
Nu 13:30 "We should go up and **take p** *of* the land H3769
Nu 21:35 And *they* **took p** *of* his land. H3769
Nu 32: 5 this land be given to your servants as our **p**. H299
Nu 32:22 this land will be your **p** before the LORD. H299
Nu 32:29 give them the land of Gilead as their **p**. H299
Nu 32:30 *they must* **accept** *their* **p** with you in H296
Nu 33:53 **Take p** *of* the land and settle in it, for I H3769
Dt 1: 8 Go in and **take p** *of* the land the LORD H3769
Dt 1:21 Go up and **take p** *of* it as the LORD, the H3769
Dt 1:39 give it to them and they *will* **take p** *of* it. H3769
Dt 2: 9 given Ar to the descendants of Lot as a **p**." H3772
Dt 2:12 in the land the LORD gave them as their **p**.) H3772
Dt 2:19 I will not give you **p** of any land H3772
Dt 2:19 I have given it as a **p** to the descendants H3772
Dt 2:24 Begin *to* **take p** *of* it and engage him in H3769
Dt 3:18 has given you this land to **take p** *of* it. H3769
Dt 3:20 may go back to the **p** I have given you." H3772
Dt 4: 1 may go in and **take p** *of* the land the H3769
Dt 4: 5 the land you are entering to **take p** *of* it. H3769
Dt 4:22 to cross over and **take p** *of* that good land. H3769
Dt 4:47 *They* **took p** *of* his land and the land of Og H3769
Dt 7: 6 earth to be his people, his **treasured p**. H6035
Dt 9: 4 me here to **take p** *of* this land because H3769
Dt 9: 5 you are going in to **take p** *of* their land; H3769
Dt 9:23 "Go up and **take p** *of* the land I have H3769
Dt 11:11 the Jordan to **take p** *of* is a land of H3769
Dt 11:31 to enter and **take p** *of* the land the LORD H3769
Dt 14: 2 LORD has chosen you to be his **treasured p**. H6035
Dt 16: 4 yeast be found **in** your **p** in all your land H4200
Dt 17:14 giving you and *have* **taken p** *of* it and H3769
Dt 24:12 not go to sleep with their pledge **in** your **p**. H928
Dt 26: 1 and *have* **taken p** *of* it and settled H3769
Dt 26:18 people, his **treasured p** as he promised H6035
Dt 30: 5 to your ancestors, and *you will* **take p** *of* it. H3769
Dt 31: 3 and *you will* **take p** *of* their land. H3769
Dt 32:49 I am giving the Israelites as their own **p**. H299
Dt 33: 4 gave us, the **p** *of* the assembly of Jacob. H4627
Jos 1:11 here to go in and **take p** *of* the land the H3769
Jos 1:15 until they too *have* **taken p** *of* the land the H3769
Jos 12: 6 the half-tribe of Manasseh to be their **p**. H3772
Jos 18: 3 you begin to **take p** *of* the land that the H3769
Jos 21:12 given to Caleb son of Jephunneh as his **p**. H299
Jos 21:43 and *they* **took p** *of* it and settled there. H3769
Jos 23: 5 and *you will* **take p** *of* their land, as H3769
Jos 24: 8 before you, and *you* **took p** *of* their land. H3769
Jdg 1:19 *They* **took p** *of* the hill country, but they H3769
Jdg 2: 6 they went to **take p** *of* the land, each to H3769
Jdg 3:13 and *they* **took p** *of* the City of Palms. H3769
Jdg 3:28 him down and **took p** *of* the fords of the H4334
Jdg 8: 6 hands of Zebah and Zalmunna in your **p**? H3338
Jdg 8:15 hands of Zebah and Zalmunna in your **p**? H3338
1Ki 21:15 "Get up and **take p** *of* the vineyard of H3769
1Ki 21:16 went down to **take p** *of* Naboth's H3769
1Ki 21:18 where he has gone to **take p** *of* it. H3769
2Ch 20:11 to drive us out of the **p** you gave us as an H3772
Ne 9:15 to go in and **take p** *of* the land you had H3769
Ne 9:24 children went in and **took p** *of* the land. H3769
Ne 9:25 *they* **took p** *of* houses filled with all kinds H3769
Ps 2: 8 inheritance, the ends of the earth your **p**. H299
Ps 73: 9 their tongues **take p** of the earth. H2143
Ps 83:12 "*Let us* **take p** *of* the pasturelands of God." H3769

P

Ps 135: 4 to be his own, Israel to be his **treasured p**. H6035
Isa 14: 2 And Israel *will* **take p** *of* the nations and H5706
Jer 32:23 They came in and **took p** *of* it, but they H3769
Jer 49: 1 Why then *has* Molek **taken p** *of* Gad? Why H3769
Eze 7:24 of nations *to* **take p** *of* their houses. H3769
Eze 11:15 this land was given to us as our **p**. H4627
Eze 25: 4 give you to the people of the East as a **p**. H4627
Eze 25:10 to the people of the East as a **p**, H4627
Eze 33:24 the land has been given to us as our **p**. H4627
Eze 35:10 will be ours and *we will* **take p** *of* them," H3769
Eze 36: 2 The ancient heights have become our **p**." H4627
Eze 36: 3 that you became the **p** of the rest of the H4627
Eze 36: 5 my land their own **p** so that they might H4627
Eze 44:28 You are to give them no **p** in Israel; I will H299
Eze 44:28 no possession in Israel; I will be their **p**. H299
Eze 45: 5 the temple, as their **p** for towns to live in. H299
Eze 45: 8 This land will be his **p** in Israel. And my H299
Mic 2: 4 my people's **p** is divided up. H2750
Mal 3:17 Almighty, "they will be my **treasured p**. H6035
Eph 1:14 redemption of those who are God's **p**— *G4348*
1Pe 2: 9 holy nation, God's **special p**, that you may *G4348*

POSSESSIONS (40) [POSSESS]

Ge 12: 5 all the **p** they had accumulated and the H8214
Ge 13: 6 their **p** were so great that they were H8214
Ge 14:12 carried off Abram's nephew Lot and his **p**, H8214
Ge 14:16 brought back his relative Lot and his **p**, H8214
Ge 15:14 afterward they will come out with great **p**. H8214
Ge 32:23 across the stream, he sent over all his **p**. H889S
Ge 36: 7 Their **p** were too great for them to remain H8214
Ge 46: 6 livestock and the **p** they had acquired in H8214
Nu 16:32 with Korah, together with their **p**. H8214
Dt 12:11 all the **choice p** you have vowed to H4436
Dt 18: 8 received money from the sale of **family p**. H3
Jos 7:11 they have put them with their own **p**. H3998
Jdg 18:21 their livestock and their **p** in front of them H3885
1Ki 13: 8 "Even if you were to give me half your **p**, H1074
2Ch 1:11 asked for wealth, **p** or honor, nor for the H5794
2Ch 1:12 give you wealth, **p** and honor, such as no H5794
2Ch 31: 3 from his own **p** for the morning and H8214
2Ch 35: 7 cattle—all from the king's own **p**. H8214
Ezr 8:21 us and our children, with all our **p**. H8214
Ne 5:13 of their house and **p** anyone who does H3330
Job 15:29 will his **p** spread over the land. H4978
Ecc 5:19 when God gives someone wealth and **p** H5794
Ecc 6: 2 some people wealth, **p** and honor, so that H5794
Zec 9: 4 the Lord *will* **take away** her **p** and destroy H3769
Zec 14: 1 when your **p** will be **plundered** and H8965
Mt 12:29 carry off his **p** unless he first ties up *G5007*
Mt 19:21 sell your **p** and give to the poor, and *G5639*
Mt 24:47 he will put him in charge of all his **p**. *G5639*
Lk 11:21 guards his own house, his **p** are safe. *G5639*
Lk 12:15 does not consist in an abundance of **p**." *G5639*
Lk 12:33 Sell your **p** and give to the poor. Provide *G5639*
Lk 12:44 he will put him in charge of all his **p**. *G5639*
Lk 16: 1 manager was accused of wasting his **p**. *G5639*
Lk 17:31 on the housetop, with **p** inside, should go *G5007*
Lk 19: 8 now I give half of my **p** to the poor, *G5639*
Ac 2:45 sold property and **p** to give to anyone who *G5638*
Ac 4:32 claimed that any *of* their **p** was their own, *G5639*
2Co 12:14 because what I want is not your **p** but you. *G3836*
Heb 10:34 you yourselves had better and lasting **p**. *G5638*
1Jn 3:17 anyone has material **p** and sees a brother *G1050*

POSSIBLE (19) [POSSIBLY]

Ne 5: 8 "**As far as p**, we have bought back H3869+1896
Mt 19:26 impossible, but with God all things are **p**." *G1543*
Mt 24:24 wonders to deceive, if **p**, even the elect. *G1543*
Mt 26:39 "My Father, if it is **p**, may this cup be *G1543*
Mt 26:42 if *it is* not **p** for this cup to be taken away *G1538*
Mk 9:23 "Everything *is* **p** for one who believes." *G1543*
Mk 10:27 not with God; all things are **p** with God." *G1543*
Mk 13:22 wonders to deceive, if **p**, even the elect. *G1543*
Mk 14:35 prayed that if **p** the hour might pass *G1543*
Mk 14:36 Father," he said, "everything is **p** for you. *G1543*
Lk 18:27 is impossible with man is **p** with God." *G1543*
Ac 17:15 Timothy to join him **as soon as p**. *G6055+5441*
Ac 20:16 to reach Jerusalem, if **p**, by the day of *G1543*
Ac 26: 9 I ought to do **all** *that was p* to oppose the AIT
Ro 12:18 If it is **p**, as far as it depends on you, live *G1543*
Ro 13: 5 not only because of **p** punishment but also NDT
1Co 6: 5 **Is it p** that there is nobody among you *G4024*
1Co 9:19 a slave to everyone, to win *as* **many** *as p*. AIT
1Co 9:22 so that **by all p means** I might save *G4122*

POSSIBLY (3) [POSSIBLE]

Ge 27:37 So what *can I p* **do** for you, my son? AIT
Lk 3:15 their hearts if John *might p* **be** the Messiah. AIT
Ro 5: 7 person someone might **p** dare to die. *G5440*

POST (5) [POSTED, POSTING, POSTS]

Jos 10:18 and **p** some men there to guard it. H7212
Ecc 10: 4 do not leave your **p**; calmness can lay H5226
Isa 21: 6 **p** a lookout and have him report what he H6641
Isa 21: 8 the watchtower; every night I stay at my **p**. H5466
Ac 17: 9 *they* **made** Jason and the others **p bond** *G3284+3836+2653+4123*

POSTED (6) [POST]

2Ki 10:24 Now Jehu *had* **p** eighty men outside with H8492
2Ki 11:18 Jehoiada the priest **p** guards at the H8492
Ne 4: 9 to our God and **p** a guard day and night H6641
Ne 4:16 The officers **p** themselves behind all the NDT
Isa 22: 7 and horsemen *are* **p** at the city H8883+8883
Isa 62: 6 *I have* **p** watchmen on your walls H7212

POSTERITY (2)

Ps 21:10 from the earth, their **p** from mankind. H2446
Ps 22:30 **P** will serve him; future generations will H2446

POSTING (2) [POST]

Ne 4:13 the exposed places, **p** them by families H6641
Mt 27:66 a seal on the stone and **p** the guard. *G3552*

POSTS (42) [POST]

Ex 26:32 gold hooks on four **p** *of* acacia wood H6647
Ex 26:37 curtain and five **p** *of* acacia wood overlaid H6647
Ex 27:10 with twenty **p** and twenty bronze bases H6647
Ex 27:10 with silver hooks and bands on the **p**. H6647
Ex 27:11 with twenty **p** and twenty bronze bases H6647
Ex 27:11 with silver hooks and bands on the **p**. H6647
Ex 27:12 have curtains, with ten **p** and ten bases. H6647
Ex 27:14 entrance, with three **p** and three bases, H6647
Ex 27:15 other side, with three **p** and three bases. H6647
Ex 27:16 embroiderer—with four **p** and four bases. H6647
Ex 27:17 All the **p** around the courtyard are to have H6647
Ex 35:11 frames, crossbars, **p** and bases; H6647
Ex 35:17 of the courtyard with its **p** and bases, H6647
Ex 36:36 They made four **p** *of* acacia wood for it H6647
Ex 36:38 they made five **p** with hooks for them H6647
Ex 36:38 the tops of **the p** and their bands H2157S
Ex 38:10 with twenty **p** and twenty bronze bases H6647
Ex 38:10 with silver hooks and bands on the **p**. H6647
Ex 38:11 long and had twenty **p** and twenty bronze H6647
Ex 38:11 with silver hooks and bands on the **p**. H6647
Ex 38:12 curtains, with ten **p** and ten bases, with H6647
Ex 38:12 with silver hooks and bands on the **p**. H6647
Ex 38:14 entrance, with three **p** and three bases, H6647
Ex 38:15 courtyard, with three **p** and three bases. H6647
Ex 38:17 The bases for the **p** were bronze. H6647
Ex 38:17 The hooks and bands on the **p** were silver, H6647
Ex 38:17 so all the **p** *of* the courtyard had silver H6647
Ex 38:19 with four **p** and four bronze bases. Their H6647
Ex 38:28 shekels to make the hooks for the **p**, H6647
Ex 38:28 to overlay the tops of **the p**, and to make H2157S
Ex 39:33 its clasps, frames, crossbars, **p** and bases; H6647
Ex 39:40 of the courtyard with its **p** and bases, H6647
Ex 40:18 inserted the crossbars and set up the **p**. H6647
Nu 3:36 its crossbars, **p**, bases, all its equipment, H6647
Nu 3:37 as well as the **p** *of* the surrounding H6647
Nu 4:31 tabernacle, its crossbars, **p** and bases, H6647
Nu 4:32 as well as the **p** *of* the surrounding H6647
Jdg 16: 3 together with the two **p**, and tore them H4647
2Ch 35:15 each gate did not need to leave their **p**, H6275
Ne 7: 3 some at their **p** and some near their own H5464
Ne 13:11 together and stationed them at their **p**. H6642
SS 3:10 Its **p** he made of silver, its base of gold H6647

POT (35) [POTS, POTSHERD, POTSHERDS, POTTER, POTTER'S, POTTERS, POTTERY]

Lev 6:28 The clay **p** the meat is cooked in must be H3998
Lev 6:28 if it is cooked in a bronze **p**, the pot is H3998
Lev 6:28 the **p** is to be scoured and rinsed with water. NDT
Lev 11:33 If one of them falls into a clay **p** H3998
Lev 11:33 be unclean, and you must break **the p**. H2257S
Lev 11:34 with water from any such **p** is unclean, H3998
Lev 11:34 liquid that is drunk from such a **p** is unclean. NDT
Lev 11:35 an oven or **cooking p** must be broken up. H3968
Lev 14: 5 birds be killed over fresh water in a clay **p**. H3998
Lev 14:50 of the birds over fresh water in a clay **p**. H3998
Lev 15:12 " 'A clay **p** that the man touches must be H3998
Nu 11: 8 They cooked it in a **p** or made it into H7248
Jdg 6:19 the meat in a basket and its broth in a **p**, H7248
1Sa 2:14 fork into the pan or kettle or caldron or **p**. H7248
2Ki 4:38 "Put on the large **p** and cook some stew H6105
2Ki 4:39 he cut them up into the **p** *of* stew, though H6105
2Ki 4:40 "Man of God, there is death in the **p**!" H6105
2Ki 4:41 He put it into the **p** and said, "Serve it to H6105
2Ki 4:41 And there was nothing harmful in the **p**. H6105
Job 41:20 as from a boiling **p** over burning reeds. H1857
Job 41:31 stirs up the sea like a **p of ointment**. H5350
Ecc 7: 6 Like the crackling of thorns under the **p**, H6105
Isa 29:16 Can the **p** say to the potter, "You know H3671
Jer 1:13 "I see a **p** that is boiling," I H6105
Jer 18: 4 But the **p** he was shaping from the clay H3998
Jer 18: 4 so the potter formed it into another **p** H3998
Jer 22:28 a despised, broken **p**, an object no one H6775
Eze 11: 3 This city is a **p**, and we are the meat in H6105
Eze 11: 7 there are the meat and this city is the **p**, H6105
Eze 11:11 This city will not be a **p** for you, nor will H6105
Eze 24: 3 " 'Put on the **cooking p**; put it on and pour H6105
Eze 24: 6 bloodshed, to the **p** now encrusted H6105
Eze 24:11 Then set the empty **p** on the coals till it NDT
Mic 3: 3 like meat for the pan, like flesh for the **p**?" H7831
Zec 14:21 Every **p** in Jerusalem and Judah will be H6105

POTENT (1)

Isa 47: 9 your many sorceries and all your **p** spells. H6800

POTENTATE (KJV) RULER

POTIPHAR (5)

Ge 37:36 the Midianites sold Joseph in Egypt to **P** H7035
Ge 39: 1 **P**, an Egyptian who was one of Pharaoh's H7035
Ge 39: 4 **P** put him in charge of his household, and NDT
Ge 39: 5 of the LORD was on everything **P** had, H2257S
Ge 39: 6 So **P** left everything he had in Joseph's care NDT

POTIPHERA (3)

Ge 41:45 gave him Asenath daughter of **P**, H7036
Ge 41:50 born to Joseph by Asenath daughter of **P**, H7036
Ge 46:20 born to Joseph by Asenath daughter of **P**, H7036

POTS (16) [POT]

Ex 16: 3 we sat around **p** *of* meat and ate all H6105
Ex 27: 3 of bronze—its **p** to remove the ashes H6105
Ex 38: 3 all its utensils of bronze—its **p**, shovels, H6105
1Ki 7:40 He also made the **p** and shovels and H6105
1Ki 7:45 the **p**, shovels and sprinkling bowls. H6105
2Ki 25:14 They also took away the **p**, shovels, wick H6105
2Ch 4:11 Huram also made the **p** and shovels and H6105
2Ch 4:16 the **p**, shovels, meat forks and all related H6105
2Ch 35:13 boiled the holy offerings in **p** H6105
Ps 58: 9 Before your **p** can feel the heat of the H6105
Isa 65: 4 whose **p** hold broth of impure meat H3998
Jer 52:18 They also took away the **p**, shovels, wick H6105
Jer 52:19 sprinkling bowls, **p**, lampstands, dishes H6105
La 4: 2 are now considered as **p** *of* clay, the work H5574
Zec 14:20 the **cooking p** in the LORD's house will H6105
Zec 14:21 will take some of **the p** and cook in them H2157S

POTSHERD (2) [POT]

Ps 22:15 My mouth is dried up like a **p**, and my H3084
Jer 19: 2 Hinnom, near the entrance of the **P** Gate. H3068

POTSHERDS (3) [POT]

Job 41:30 Its undersides are jagged **p**, leaving a H3084
Isa 45: 9 are nothing but **p** among the potsherds H3084
Isa 45: 9 potsherds among the **p** *on* the ground. H3084

POTTAGE (KJV) STEW

POTTER (13) [POT]

Isa 29:16 as if the **p** were thought to be like the clay H3450
Isa 29:16 Can the pot say to the **p**, "You know H3450
Isa 41:25 as if he were a **p** treading the clay. H3450
Isa 45: 9 Does the clay say to the **p**, 'What are you H3450
Isa 45: 9 your work say, '**The p** has no hands'? H2257S
Isa 64: 8 you are the **p**; we are all the work H3450
Jer 18: 4 so the **p** formed it into another pot H3450
Jer 18: 6 I not do with you, Israel, as this **p** does?" H3450
Jer 18: 6 "Like clay in the hand of the **p**, so are you H3450
Jer 19: 1 "Go and buy a clay jar from a **p**. H3450
Zec 11:13 "Throw it to the **p**"—the handsome price H3450
Zec 11:13 threw them to the **p** *at* the house of the H3450
Ro 9:21 Does not the **p** have the right to make out *G3038*

POTTER'S (6) [POT]

Jer 18: 2 "Go down to the **p** house, and there I will H3450
Jer 18: 3 So I went down to the **p** house, and I saw H3450
Jer 19:11 this city just as this **p** jar is smashed and H3450
La 4: 2 as pots of clay, the work of a **p** hands! H3450
Mt 27: 7 the money to buy the **p** field as a burial *G3038*
Mt 27:10 they used them to buy the **p** field, as *G3038*

POTTERS (1) [POT]

1Ch 4:23 They were the **p** who lived at Netaim and H3450

POTTERY (7) [POT]

2Sa 17:28 bedding and bowls and articles of **p**. H3450
Job 2: 8 Job took a **piece of broken p** and scraped H3084
Ps 2: 9 you will dash them to pieces like **p**." H3998+3450
Ps 31:12 I were dead; I have become like broken **p**. H3998
Isa 30:14 It will break in pieces like **p** H5574+3450
Ro 9:21 lump of clay some **p** for special purposes *G5007*
Rev 2:27 them to pieces like **p**'— *G5007+3836+3039*

POUCH (2) [POUCHES]

Ge 42:35 in each man's sack was his **p** *of* silver! H7655
1Sa 17:40 put them in the **p** of his shepherd's bag H3541

POUCHES (1) [POUCH]

Ge 42:35 they and their father saw the money **p**, H7655

POULTICE (2)

2Ki 20: 7 "Prepare a **p** of figs." They did so H1811
Isa 38:21 "Prepare a **p** *of* figs and apply it to the H1811

POULTRY (1)

Ne 5:18 choice sheep and *some* **p** were prepared H7606

POUNCE (2) [POUNCED]

1Sa 15:19 Why *did you* **p** on the plunder and do evil H6513
Isa 33: 4 like a swarm of locusts *people* **p** on it. H9212

POUNCED (1) [POUNCE]

1Sa 14:32 They **p** on the plunder and, taking sheep H6513

POUND (1) [POUNDED, POUNDING, POUNDS]

SS 5: 4 my heart *began to* **p** for him. H2159

POUNDED (2) [POUND]

2Sa 22:43 *I* **p** and trampled them like mud in the H1990
Hab 3:16 I heard and my heart **p**, my lips quivered H8074

POUNDING (3) [POUND]

Jdg 19:22 **P** on the door, they shouted to the old H1985
Ps 93: 3 the seas have lifted up their **p waves**. H1922
Ac 27:41 was broken to pieces by the **p** of the surf. *G1040*

P

POUNDS (9) [POUND]

Job 37: 1 "At this my heart **p** and leaps from its H3006
Ps 38:10 My heart **p**, my strength fails me; even the H6086
Jer 4:19 My heart **p** within me, I cannot keep silent H2159
Mt 13:33 mixed into **about sixty p** of flour *G4929+5552*
Lk 13:21 mixed into **about sixty p** of flour *G4929+5552*
Jn 19:39 and aloes, about **seventy-five p**. *G3354+1669*
Rev 6: 6 "**Two p** of wheat for a day's wages *G5955*
Rev 6: 6 and **six p** of barley for a day's *G5552+5955*
Rev 16:21 each **weighing** about **a hundred p**, fell on *G5418*

POUR (83) [DOWNPOUR, OUTPOURED, OUTPOURING, POURED, POURING, POURS]

Ex 4: 9 from the Nile and **p** it *on* the dry ground. H9161
Ex 29:12 and **p out** the rest of it at the base of the H9161
Ex 30: 9 and *do* not **p** a drink offering on it. H5818
Ex 30:32 *Do* not **p** it on anyone else's body and do H6057
Lev 2: 1 *They are to* **p** olive oil on it, put incense H3668
Lev 2: 6 Crumble it and **p** oil on it; it is a grain H3668
Lev 4: 7 bull's blood *he shall* **p out** at the base of H9161
Lev 4:18 of the blood *he shall* **p out** at the base of H9161
Lev 4:25 of burnt offering and **p out** the rest of the H9161
Lev 4:30 of burnt offering and **p out** the rest of the H9161
Lev 4:34 of burnt offering and **p out** the rest of the H9161
Lev 14:15 **p** it in the palm of his own left hand, H3668
Lev 14:26 The priest *is to* **p** some of the oil into the H3668
Nu 5:15 *He must* not **p** olive oil on it or put H3668
Nu 19:17 into a jar and **p** fresh water over them. H5989
Nu 20: 8 their eyes and *it will* **p out** its water. H5989
Nu 28: 7 **P out** the drink offering to the LORD at the H5818
Dt 12:16 blood; **p** it **out** on the ground like water. H9161
Dt 12:24 **p** it **out** on the ground like water. H9161
Dt 15:23 **p** it **out** on the ground like water. H9161
Jdg 6:20 them on this rock, and **p out** the broth." H9161
1Ki 18:33 jars with water and **p** it on the offering H3668
2Ki 3:11 He *used to* **p** water on the hands of Elijah." H3668
2Ki 4: 4 **P** oil into all the jars, and as each is filled, H3668
2Ki 9: 3 take the flask and **p** the oil on his head H3668
Job 3:24 my daily food; my groans **p out** like water. H5988
Job 10:10 *Did you* not **p** me **out** like milk and curdle H5988
Job 15:13 against God and **p out** such words from H3655
Job 16:20 my friend *as* my eyes **p out tears** to God; H1940
Job 36:28 the clouds **p down** *their* **moisture** and H5688
Ps 16: 4 *I will* not **p out** libations of blood *to* such H5818
Ps 19: 2 Day after day *they* **p forth** speech; night H5580
Ps 42: 4 things I remember as *I* **p out** my soul: H9161
Ps 62: 8 you people; **p out** your hearts to him, for H9161
Ps 69:24 **P out** your wrath on them; let your fierce H9161
Ps 79: 6 **P out** your wrath on the nations that do H9161
Ps 94: 4 *They* **p out** arrogant words; all the H5580
Ps 104:10 He **makes** springs **p** water into the ravines; H8938
Ps 142: 2 *I* **p out** before him my complaint; before H9161
Pr 1:23 Then *I will* **p out** my thoughts to you, I will H5580
Ecc 11: 3 are full of water, *they* **p** rain on the earth. H8197
Isa 44: 3 For *I will* **p** water on the thirsty land, and H3668
Isa 44: 3 *I will* **p out** my Spirit on your offspring H3668
Isa 46: 6 Some **p out** gold from their bags and H2313
Jer 6:11 "**P** it **out** on the children in the street and H9161
Jer 7:18 *They* **p out** drink offerings to other gods to H5818
Jer 10:25 **P out** your wrath on the nations that do H9161
Jer 14:16 *I will* **p out** on them the calamity they H9161
Jer 44:17 of Heaven and *will* **p out** drink offerings to H5818
Jer 44:25 burn incense and **p out** drink offerings to H5818
Jer 48:12 I will send *men who* **p** from pitchers, H7579
Jer 48:12 pitchers, and *they will* **p** her **out**; they will H7579
La 2:19 **p out** your heart like water in the presence H9161
Eze 6:12 So *will I* **p out** my wrath on them. H3983
Eze 7: 8 *I am* about to **p out** my wrath on you and H9161
Eze 13:15 So *I will* **p out** my wrath against the wall H3983
Eze 14:19 into that land and **p out** my wrath on it H9161
Eze 20: 8 So I said I *would* **p out** my wrath on them H9161
Eze 20:13 So I said *I would* **p out** my wrath on them H9161
Eze 20:21 So I said I *would* **p out** my wrath on them H9161
Eze 21:31 *I will* **p out** my wrath on you and breathe H9161
Eze 22:31 So *I will* **p out** my wrath on them and H9161
Eze 24: 3 cooking pot; put it on and **p** water into it. H3668
Eze 24: 7 bare rock; *she did* not **p** it on the ground H9161
Eze 30:15 *I will* **p out** my wrath on Pelusium, the H9161
Eze 38:22 bloodshed; *I will* **p down** torrents of rain H4763
Eze 39:29 for *I will* **p out** my Spirit on the people of H9161
Hos 5:10 *I will* **p out** my wrath on them like a flood H9161
Hos 9: 4 *They will* not **p out** wine offerings to the H5818
Joel 2:28 *I will* **p out** my Spirit on all people. H9161
Joel 2:29 *I will* **p out** my Spirit in those days. H9161
Mic 1: 6 *I will* **p** her stones into the valley and lay H5599
Zep 3: 8 kingdoms and to **p out** my wrath on them H9161
Zec 4:12 the two gold pipes that **p out** golden oil?" H8197
Zec 12:10 "And *I will* **p out** on the house of David H9161
Mal 3:10 of heaven and **p out** so much blessing H8197
Mt 9:17 Neither *do people* **p** new wine into old *G965*
Mt 9:17 *they* **p** new wine into new wineskins *G965*
Mk 2:22 they **p** new wine into new wineskins." NDT
Ac 2:17 *I will* **p out** my Spirit on all people. *G1772*
Ac 2:18 *I will* **p out** my Spirit in those days *G1772*
Rev 16: 1 **p out** the seven bowls of God's wrath on *G1772*
Rev 18: 6 **P** her a double portion from her own cup. *G3042*

POURED (92) [POUR]

Ge 28:18 set it up as a pillar and **p** oil on top of it. H3668
Ge 35:14 and *he* **p out** a drink offering on it H5818
Ge 35:14 a drink offering on it; *he* also **p** oil on it. H3668
Ex 8:24 swarms of flies **p** into Pharaoh's palace H995
Ex 9:33 the rain no *longer* **p down** on the land. H5988
Lev 8:12 *He* **p** some of the anointing oil on Aaron's H3668
Lev 8:15 *He* **p out** the rest of the blood at the base H3668
Lev 9: 9 rest of the blood *he* **p out** at the base of H3668
Lev 21:10 who *has had* the anointing oil **p** on his H3668
Dt 12:27 your sacrifices *must* **be p** beside the altar H9161
Jdg 5: 4 the heavens **p**, the clouds poured H5752
Jdg 5: 4 poured, the clouds **p down** water. H5752
Ru 3:15 *he* **p into** it six **measures** of barley and H4499
1Sa 7: 6 drew water and **p** it out before the LORD. H9161
1Sa 10: 1 of olive oil and **p** it on Saul's head and H3668
2Sa 21:10 till the rain **p down** from the heavens on H5988
2Sa 23:16 instead, *he* **p** it **out** before the LORD. H5818
1Ki 13: 3 apart and the ashes on it *will* **be p out**." H9161
1Ki 13: 5 and its ashes **p out** according to H9161+4946
2Ki 4:40 The stew *was* **p out** for the men, but as H3668
2Ki 9: 6 Then the prophet **p** the oil on Jehu's H3668
2Ki 16:13 grain offering, **p out** his drink offering H5818
1Ch 11:18 to drink it; instead, *he* **p** it **out** to the LORD. H5818
2Ch 12: 7 My wrath *will* not *be* **p out** on Jerusalem H5988
2Ch 34:21 LORD's anger that **is p out** on us because H5988
2Ch 34:25 my anger *will be* **p out** on this place and H5988
Job 29: 6 the rock **p out** for me streams of H3668
Ps 22:14 *I* **am p out** like water, and all my bones H9161
Ps 68: 8 the heavens **p down rain**, before God, H5752
Ps 77:17 The clouds **p down** water, the heavens H2442
Ps 79: 3 *They have* **p out** blood like water all H9161
Ps 92:10 of a wild ox; fine oils *have been* **p** *on me*. H1176
Ps 133: 2 It is like precious oil **p** on the head, running NDT
Pr 25:20 or like vinegar **p** on a wound, is one NDT
Ecc 2:19 toil into which *I have* **p** *my* **effort** and skill H6661
SS 1: 3 your name is like perfume **p out**. H8197
Isa 19:14 The LORD *has* **p** into them a spirit of H5007
Isa 32:15 till the Spirit **is p** on us from on high, and H6867
Isa 42:25 So *he* **p out** on them his burning anger H9161
Isa 53:12 because *he* **p out** his life unto death H6867
Isa 57: 6 to them *you have* **p out** drink offerings H9161
Isa 63: 6 them drunk and **p** their blood on the H3718
Jer 1:14 north disaster *will* **be p out** on all who live H7337
Jer 7:20 my wrath *will* **be p out** on this place H5988
Jer 19:13 starry hosts and **p out** drink offerings to H5818
Jer 42:18 wrath *have* **been p out** on those who H5988
Jer 42:18 so *will* my wrath *be* **p out** on you when H5988
Jer 44: 6 my fierce anger *was* **p out**; it raged H5988
Jer 44:19 of Heaven and **p out** drink offerings to H5818
Jer 48:11 on its dregs, not **p** from one jar to another H8197
La 2: 4 *he has* **p out** his wrath like fire on the tent H9161
La 2:11 my heart *is* **p out** on the ground because H9161
La 4:11 to his wrath; *he has* **p out** his fierce anger. H9161
Eze 16:36 Because you **p out** your lust and exposed H9161
Eze 20:28 fragrant incense and **p out** their drink H5818
Eze 22:22 that I the LORD *have* **p out** my wrath on you H9161
Eze 23: 8 virgin bosom and **p out** their lust on her. H9161
Eze 24: 7 *She* **p** it on the bare rock; she did not pour H8492
Eze 36:18 So *I* **p out** my wrath on them because they H9161
Da 9:11 *have been* **p out** on us, because H5988
Da 9:27 the end that is decreed *is* **p out** on him." H5988
Na 1: 6 His wrath *is* **p out** like fire; the rocks are H5988
Zep 1:17 Their blood *will* **be p out** like dust and H9161
Mt 26: 7 which *she* **p** on his head as he was *G2972*
Mt 26:12 *When* she **p** this perfume on my body, she *G965*
Mt 26:28 which *is* **p out** for many for the forgiveness *G1773*
Mk 14: 3 broke the jar and **p** the perfume on his *G2972*
Mk 14: 8 *She* **p perfume on** my body beforehand to *G3690*
Mk 14:24 covenant, which *is* **p out** for many," he *G1773*
Lk 5:38 new wine **must be p** into new wineskins. *G1064*
Lk 6:38 running over, *will be* **p** into your lap. *G1443*
Lk 7:38 kissed them and **p** perfume **on** them. *G230*
Lk 7:46 but she *has* **p** perfume **on** my feet. *G230*
Lk 22:20 in my blood, which *is* **p out** for you. *G1773*
Jn 11: 2 the same one *who* **p** perfume **on** the Lord *G230*
Jn 12: 3 *she* **p** it **on** Jesus' feet and wiped his feet *G230*
Jn 13: 5 *he* **p** water into a basin and began to wash *G965*
Ac 2:33 Holy Spirit and *has* **p out** what you now *G1772*
Ac 10:45 the Holy Spirit *had been* **p out** even on *G1772*
Ro 5: 5 God's love *has been* **p out** into our hearts *G1772*
Php 2:17 if *I am being* **p out like a drink offering** on *G5064*
1Ti 1:14 of our Lord *was* **p out** on me **abundantly**, *G5670*
2Ti 4: 6 *am* already *being* **p out like a drink offering** *G5064*
Titus 3: 6 whom *he* **p out** on us generously through *G1772*
Rev 14:10 which *has been* **p** full strength into the *G3042*
Rev 16: 2 first angel went and **p out** his bowl on the *G1772*
Rev 16: 3 The second angel **p out** his bowl on the *G1772*
Rev 16: 4 The third angel **p out** his bowl on the *G1772*
Rev 16: 8 The fourth angel **p out** his bowl on the *G1772*
Rev 16:10 The fifth angel **p out** his bowl on the *G1772*
Rev 16:12 The sixth angel **p out** his bowl on the *G1772*
Rev 16:17 The seventh angel **p out** his bowl into the *G1772*

POURING (10) [POUR]

Ex 25:29 bowls *for the* **p out of offerings**. H5818
Ex 29: 7 oil and anoint him *by* **p** it on his head. H3668
Ex 37:16 its pitchers for the **p out of drink offerings**. H5818
1Sa 1:15 *I was* **p out** my soul to the LORD. H9161
2Ki 4: 5 brought the jars to her and she *kept* **p**. H3668
Jer 32:29 to Baal and by **p out** drink offerings to H5818
Jer 44:18 of Heaven and **p out** drink offerings to H5818
Jer 44:19 with her image and **p out** drink offerings H5818
Hab 2:15 **p** it *from* the wineskin till they are drunk H6203
Lk 10:34 bandaged his wounds, **p on** oil and wine. *G2219*

POURS (15) [POUR]

Job 12:21 *He* **p** contempt on nobles and disarms the H9161
Job 41:20 Smoke **p** from its nostrils as from a boiling H3655
Ps 75: 8 mixed with spices; *he* **p** it **out**, and all the H5599
Ps 102: T grown weak and **p out** a lament before H9161
Ps 107:40 *he who* **p** contempt on nobles made them H9161
Pr 6:19 a false witness *who* **p out** lies and a H7032
Pr 14: 5 not deceive, but a false witness **p out** lies. H7032
Pr 19: 5 and *whoever* **p out** lies will not go free. H7032
Pr 19: 9 and *whoever* **p out** lies will perish. H7032
Jer 6: 7 As a well **p out** its water, so she pours out H7981
Jer 6: 7 out its water, so *she* **p out** her wickedness. H7981
Am 5: 8 of the sea and **p** them **out** over the face of H9161
Am 9: 6 of the sea and **p** them **out** over the face of H9161
Mk 2:22 And no one **p** new wine into old wineskins *G965*
Lk 5:37 And no one **p** new wine into old wineskins *G965*

POVERTY (21) [POOR]

Dt 28:48 in nakedness and dire **p**, you will serve H2896
1Sa 2: 7 The LORD **sends p** and wealth; he humbles H3769
Pr 6:11 **p** will come on you like a thief and H8203
Pr 10: 4 Lazy hands make *for* **p**, but diligent hands H8133
Pr 10:15 fortified city, but **p** is the ruin of the poor. H8203
Pr 11:24 another withholds unduly, but comes to **p**. H4728
Pr 13:18 discipline comes to **p** and shame, H8203
Pr 14:23 a profit, but mere talk leads only to **p**. H4728
Pr 21: 5 to profit as surely as haste leads to **p**. H4728
Pr 22:16 gives gifts to the rich—both come to **p**. H4728
Pr 24:34 **p** will come on you like a thief and H8203
Pr 28:19 chase fantasies will have their fill of **p**. H8203
Pr 28:22 rich and are unaware that **p** awaits them. H2895
Pr 30: 8 give me neither **p** nor riches, but give H8203
Pr 31: 7 forget their **p** and remember their H8203
Ecc 4:14 have been born in **p** within his kingdom. H8133
Mk 12:44 she, out of her **p**, put in everything *G5730*
Lk 21: 4 she out of her **p** put in all she had to *G5729*
2Co 8: 2 joy and their extreme **p** welled up in rich *G4775*
2Co 8: 9 so that you *through* his **p** might become *G4775*
Rev 2: 9 I know your afflictions and your **p**—yet you *G4775*

POWDER (9)

Ex 30:36 Grind some of it to **p** and place it in front H1990
Ex 32:20 then he ground it to **p**, scattered it on the H1990
Dt 9:21 it and **ground** it **to p** as fine as H3221+3512
Dt 28:24 turn the rain of your country into dust and **p**; H85
2Ki 23: 6 He ground it to **p** and scattered the dust H6760
2Ki 23:15 burned the high place and ground it to **p**, H6760
2Ch 34: 7 crushed the idols to **p** and cut to pieces H1990
Job 9:30 with soap and my hands with **cleansing p**, H1342
Jer 2:22 use an abundance of **cleansing p**, H1383

POWER (263) [OVERPOWER, OVERPOWERED, OVERPOWERING, OVERPOWERS, POWERFUL, POWERFULLY, POWERLESS, POWERS]

Ge 31:29 I have the **p** to harm you; but last H445+3338
Ge 49: 3 excelling in honor, excelling in **p**. H6435
Ex 1: 8 meant nothing, **came to p** in Egypt. H7756
Ex 4:21 the wonders I have given you the **p** to do. H3338
Ex 9:16 I might show you my **p** and that my name H3946
Ex 15: 6 was majestic in **p**. Your right hand, H3946
Ex 15:16 By the **p** *of* your arm they will be as still as H1524
Ex 32:11 of Egypt with great **p** and a mighty hand? H3946
Nu 11:17 some of the **p of the Spirit** that is on you H8120
Nu 11:25 some of the **p of the Spirit** that was on H8120
Nu 14:13 By your **p** you brought these people up H3946
Dt 7: 8 from the **p** *of* Pharaoh king of Egypt. H3338
Dt 8:17 "My **p** and the strength of my hands have H3946
Dt 9:26 by your **great p** and brought out H1542
Dt 9:29 out by your great **p** and your outstretched H3946
Dt 34:12 ever shown the mighty **p** or performed the H3338
Jdg 1:35 when the **p** *of* the tribes of Joseph H3338
Jdg 3:12 the LORD **gave** Eglon king of Moab **p** over H2616
Jdg 6: 2 Because the **p** *of* Midian was so H3338
1Sa 10:18 you from the **p** *of* Egypt and all the H3338
1Ki 18:46 The **p** *of* the LORD came on Elijah and H3338
2Ki 13: 3 kept them under the **p** *of* Hazael king of H3338
2Ki 13: 5 they escaped from the **p** *of* Aram. H3338
2Ki 17: 7 Egypt from under the **p** *of* Pharaoh king of H3338
2Ki 17:36 Egypt with mighty **p** and outstretched arm H3946
2Ki 19:26 people, drained of **p**, are dismayed and H3338
1Ch 29:11 greatness and the **p** and the glory and the H1476
1Ch 29:12 are strength and **p** to exalt and give H1476
1Ch 29:30 with the details of his reign and **p**, H1476
2Ch 13:20 did not regain **p** during the time of H3946
2Ch 20: 6 **P** and might are in your hand, and no one H3946
2Ch 20:12 For we have no **p** to face this vast army H3946
2Ch 25: 8 God has the **p** to help or to overthrow." H3946
2Ch 32: 7 there is a **greater p** with us than with H8041
2Ch 36:20 until the kingdom of Persia **came to p**. H4887
Est 10: 2 And all his acts of **p** and might, together H9549
Job 1:12 everything he has is in your **p**, but on the H3338
Job 6:13 Do I have any **p** to help myself, now that NDT
Job 9: 4 is profound, his **p** is vast. Who has H3946
Job 10:16 again **display** *your* **awesome p** against H7098
Job 12:13 "To God belong wisdom and **p**; counsel H1476
Job 21: 7 growing old and increasing in **p**? H2657
Job 24:22 But God drags away the mighty by his **p** H3946
Job 26:12 By his **p** he churned up the sea; by his H3946
Job 26:14 then can understand the thunder of his **p**?" H1476
Job 27:11 "I will teach you about the **p** *of* God; the H3338
Job 27:22 mercy as he flees headlong from its **p**. H3338
Job 30:18 In his great **p** God becomes like clothing H3946

P

Job 36:22 "God is exalted in his **p**. Who is a teacher H3946
Job 37:23 is beyond our reach and exalted in **p**; H3946
Job 40:16 its loins, what **p** in the muscles of its belly! H226
Ps 20: 6 with the victorious **p** *of* his right hand. H1476
Ps 22:20 my precious life from the **p** *of* the dogs. H3338
Ps 37:17 the **p** *of* the wicked will be broken, but H2432
Ps 37:33 leave them in the **p** *of* the wicked or let H3338
Ps 62:11 "**P** belongs to you, God, H6437
Ps 63: 2 beheld your **p** and your glory. H6437
Ps 65: 6 who formed the mountains by your **p** H3946
Ps 66: 3 So great is your **p** that your enemies H6437
Ps 66: 7 He rules forever by his **p**, his eyes watch H1476
Ps 68:28 Summon your **p**, God; show us your H6437
Ps 68:34 Proclaim the **p** of God, whose majesty is H6437
Ps 68:34 is over Israel, whose **p** is in the heavens. H6437
Ps 68:35 God of Israel gives **p** and strength to his H6437
Ps 71:18 till I declare your **p** to the next generation H2432
Ps 74:13 was you who split open the sea by your **p**; H6437
Ps 77:14 you display your **p** among the peoples. H6437
Ps 78: 4 of the LORD, his **p**, and the wonders he H6449
Ps 78:26 heavens and by his **p** made the south H6437
Ps 78:42 They did not remember his **p**—the day H3338
Ps 89:13 Your arm is endowed with **p**; your hand is H1476
Ps 89:48 who can escape the **p** *of* the grave? H3338
Ps 90:11 If only we knew the **p** *of* your anger! Your H6437
Ps 106: 8 to make his **mighty p** known. H1476
Ps 106:42 them and subjected them to their **p**. H3338
Ps 111: 6 has shown his people the **p** *of* his works, H3946
Ps 145: 6 They tell of the **p** *of* your awesome works H6449
Ps 147: 5 Great is our Lord and mighty in **p**; his H3946
Ps 150: 2 Praise him for his **acts of p**; praise him H1476
Pr 3:27 it is due, when it is in your **p** to act. H445+3338
Pr 8:14 are mine; I have insight, I have **p**. H1476
Pr 11: 7 all the promise of their **p** comes to nothing. H226
Pr 18:21 The tongue has the **p** *of* life and death H3338
Pr 24: 5 The wise prevail through **great p**, and H6437
Pr 28:12 when the wicked **rise to p**, people go H7756
Pr 28:28 When the wicked **rise to p**, people go into H7756
Pr 30:26 hyraxes are creatures of little **p**, yet they H6786
Ecc 4: 1 **p** was on the side of their oppressors H3946
Ecc 8: 8 As no one has **p** over the wind to contain H8954
Ecc 8: 8 so no one has **p** over the time of their H8950
Isa 10:33 will lop off the boughs with **great p**. H5124
Isa 17: 3 from Ephraim, and **royal p** from Damascus H4930
Isa 19: 4 Egyptians over to the **p** *of* a cruel master, H3338
Isa 33:13 you who are near, acknowledge my **p**! H1476
Isa 37:27 people, drained of **p**, are dismayed and H3338
Isa 40:10 the Sovereign LORD comes with **p**, and he H2617
Isa 40:26 Because of his great **p** and mighty strength H226
Isa 40:29 weary and increases the **p** of the weak. H6800
Isa 47:14 save themselves from the **p** *of* the flame. H3338
Isa 63:12 sent his glorious **arm of p** to be at Moses' H2432
Jer 10: 6 are great, and your name is mighty in **p**. H1476
Jer 10:12 But God made the earth by his **p**; he H3946
Jer 16:21 time I will teach them my **p** and might. H3338
Jer 18:21 hand them over to the **p** *of* the sword. H3338
Jer 23:10 an evil course and use their **p** unjustly. H1476
Jer 27: 5 With my great **p** and outstretched arm I H3946
Jer 32:17 earth by your great **p** and outstretched H3946
Jer 51:15 "He made the earth by his **p**; he founded H3946
Eze 13:21 they will no longer fall prey to your **p**. H3338
Eze 22: 6 who are in you uses his **p** to shed blood. H2432
Eze 26:17 You were a **p** on the seas, you and your H2617
Eze 32:29 princes; despite their **p**, they are laid with H1476
Eze 32:30 despite the terror caused by their **p**. H1476
Da 2:20 ever and ever; wisdom and **p** are his. A10130
Da 2:23 You have given me wisdom and **p**, you A10130
Da 2:37 you dominion and **p** and might and A10278
Da 4:30 by my mighty **p** and for the glory of my A10774
Da 6:27 rescued Daniel from the **p** *of* the lions." A10311
Da 7:14 glory and **sovereign p**; all nations and A10424
Da 7:26 his **p** will be taken away and A10717
Da 7:27 **p** and greatness of all the kingdoms A10717
Da 8: 4 and none could rescue from its **p**. H3338
Da 8: 7 none could rescue the ram from its **p**. H3338
Da 8: 8 at the **height** of its **p** the large horn H6793
Da 8: 9 small but grew in **p** to the south and to H3856
Da 8:22 his nation but will not have the same **p**. H3946
Da 8:24 become very strong, but not by his own **p**. H3946
Da 8:25 he will be destroyed, but not by human **p**. H3338
Da 11: 2 When he has **gained p** by his wealth, he H2621
Da 11: 3 rule with great **p** and do as he pleases H4938
Da 11: 4 will it have the **p** he exercised H5445
Da 11: 5 will rule his own kingdom with great **p**. H4938
Da 11: 6 she will not retain her **p**, and H3946+2432
Da 11: 6 her power, and he and his **p** will not last. H2432
Da 11:16 Land and will have the **p to destroy** it. H3986
Da 11:23 with only a few people he will rise *to* **p**. H6793
Da 11:42 He will extend his **p** over many countries H3338
Da 12: 7 When the **p** *of* the holy people has been H3338
Hos 13:14 this people from the **p** *of* the grave; H3338
Mic 2: 1 it out because it is in their **p** to do it. H445+3338
Mic 3: 8 I am filled with **p**, with the Spirit of H3946
Mic 7:16 be ashamed, deprived of all their **p**. H1476
Na 1: 3 The LORD is slow to anger but great in **p** H3946
Hab 3: 4 from his hand, where his **p** was hidden. H6437
Hag 2:22 shatter the **p** *of* the foreign kingdoms. H2620
Zec 4: 6 'Not by might nor by **p**, but by my Spirit,' H3946
Zec 9: 4 possessions and destroy her **p** on the sea, H2657
Mt 22:29 not know the Scriptures or the **p** of God. *G1539*
Mt 24:30 clouds of heaven, with **p** and great glory. *G1539*
Mk 5:30 Jesus realized that **p** had gone out from *G1539*
Mk 9: 1 that the kingdom of God has come with **p**." *G1539*
Mk 12:24 not know the Scriptures or the **p** of God? *G1539*
Mk 13:26 coming in clouds with great **p** and glory. *G1539*
Lk 1:17 in the spirit and **p** of Elijah, to turn the *G1539*
Lk 1:35 the **p** of the Most High will *G1539*
Lk 4:14 returned to Galilee in the **p** of the Spirit, *G1539*
Lk 4:36 With authority and **p** he gives orders to *G1539*
Lk 5:17 And the **p** of the Lord was with Jesus to *G1539*
Lk 6:19 because **p** was coming from him and *G1539*
Lk 8:46 I know that **p** has gone out from me." *G1539*
Lk 9: 1 he gave them **p** and authority to drive out *G1539*
Lk 10:19 to overcome all the **p** of the enemy; *G1539*
Lk 20:20 hand him over to the **p** and authority of the *G794*
Lk 21:27 coming in a cloud with **p** and great glory. *G1539*
Lk 24:49 have been clothed with **p** from on high." *G1539*
Jn 13: 3 the Father had put all things under his **p**, *G5931*
Jn 17:11 protect them **by the p of** your name, the *G1877*
Jn 19:10 you realize I have **p** either to free you *G2026*
Jn 19:11 "You would have no **p** over me if it were *G2026*
Ac 1: 8 But you will receive **p** when the Holy Spirit *G1539*
Ac 3:12 us as if by our own **p** or godliness we had *G1539*
Ac 4: 7 "By what **p** or what name did you do this?" *G1539*
Ac 4:28 They did what your **p** and will had decided *G5931*
Ac 4:33 *With* great **p** the apostles continued to *G1539*
Ac 6: 8 a man full of God's grace and **p** *G1539*
Ac 7:18 Joseph meant nothing, **came to p** in Egypt. *G482*
Ac 8:10 man is rightly called the Great **P** of God." *G1539*
Ac 10:38 of Nazareth with the Holy Spirit and **p**, *G1539*
Ac 10:38 all who *were* **under the p** of the devil, *G2872*
Ac 13:17 with mighty **p** he led them out of that *G1098*
Ac 19:20 of the Lord spread widely and grew in **p**. *G3197*
Ac 26:18 to light, and *from* the **p** of Satan to God *G2026*
Ro 1: 4 the Son of God in **p** by his resurrection *G1539*
Ro 1:16 because it is the **p** of God that brings *G1539*
Ro 1:20 qualities—his eternal **p** and divine nature *G1539*
Ro 3: 9 Gentiles alike are all **under the p of** sin. *G5679*
Ro 4:21 that God had **p** to do what he had *G1543*
Ro 9:17 I might display my **p** in you and that my *G1539*
Ro 9:22 to show his wrath and make his **p** known, *G1543*
Ro 15:13 with hope by the **p** of the Holy Spirit. *G1539*
Ro 15:19 by the **p** of signs and wonders, through the *G1539*
Ro 15:19 through the **p** of the Spirit of God. *G1539*
1Co 1:17 lest the cross of Christ *be* **emptied of** its **p**. *G3033*
1Co 1:18 us who are being saved it is the **p** of God. *G1539*
1Co 1:24 Christ the **p** of God and the wisdom of *G1539*
1Co 2: 4 with a demonstration of the Spirit's **p**, *G1539*
1Co 2: 5 rest on human wisdom, but on God's **p**. *G1539*
1Co 4:19 people are talking, but what **p** they have. *G1539*
1Co 4:20 of God is not a matter of talk but of **p**. *G1539*
1Co 5: 4 the **p** of our Lord Jesus is present *G1539*
1Co 6:14 By his **p** God raised the Lord from the dead *G1539*
1Co 15:24 destroyed all dominion, authority and **p**. *G1539*
1Co 15:43 it is sown in weakness, it is raised in **p**; *G1539*
1Co 15:56 of death is sin, and the **p** of sin is the law. *G1539*
2Co 4: 7 this all-surpassing **p** is from God and not *G1539*
2Co 6: 7 in truthful speech and in the **p** of God *G1539*
2Co 10: 4 they have divine **p** to demolish *G1543*
2Co 12: 9 my **p** is made perfect in weakness. *G1539*
2Co 12: 9 so that Christ's **p** may rest on me. *G1539*
2Co 13: 4 in weakness, yet he lives by God's **p**. *G1539*
2Co 13: 4 by God's **p** we will live with him in our *G1539*
Gal 4:29 the son born **by the p of** the Spirit. *G2848*
Eph 1:19 incomparably great **p** for us who believe. *G1539*
Eph 1:19 That **p** is the same as the mighty strength *G1918*
Eph 1:21 rule and authority, **p** and dominion, and *G1539*
Eph 3: 7 given me through the working *of* his **p**. *G1539*
Eph 3:16 may strengthen you *with* **p** through his *G1539*
Eph 3:18 *may have* **p**, together with all the Lord's *G2015*
Eph 3:20 according to his **p** that is at work within us, *G1539*
Eph 6:10 be strong in the Lord and in his mighty **p**. *G2709*
Php 3:10 to know the **p** of his resurrection and *G1539*
Php 3:21 by the **p** that enables him to bring *G1918*
Col 1:11 strengthened with all **p** according to his *G1539*
Col 2:10 He is the head *over* every **p** and authority. *G794*
1Th 1: 5 you not simply with words but also with **p**, *G1539*
2Th 1:11 that by his **p** he may bring to fruition *G1539*
2Th 2: 7 For the **secret** *p* of lawlessness is already at AIT
2Th 2: 9 use all sorts of **displays of p** through signs *G1539*
2Ti 1: 7 us timid, but gives us **p**, love and *G1539*
2Ti 1: 8 suffering for the gospel, by the **p** of God. *G1539*
2Ti 3: 5 a form of godliness but denying its **p**. *G1539*
Heb 2:14 his death *he might* **break the p** of him *G2934*
Heb 2:14 power of him who holds the **p** of death— *G3197*
Heb 7:16 on the basis of the **p** of an indestructible *G1539*
1Pe 1: 5 shielded by God's **p** until the coming of *G1539*
1Pe 4:11 be the glory and the **p** for ever and ever. *G3197*
1Pe 5:11 To him be the **p** for ever and ever. Amen. *G3197*
2Pe 1: 3 His divine **p** has given us everything we *G1539*
2Pe 1:16 the coming of our Lord Jesus Christ *in* **p**, *G1539*
Jude 25 majesty, **p** and authority, through Jesus *G3197*
Rev 1: 6 to him be glory and **p** for ever and ever! *G3197*
Rev 4:11 to receive glory and honor and **p**, for you *G1539*
Rev 5:12 to receive **p** and wealth and wisdom and *G1539*
Rev 5:13 be praise and honor and glory and **p**, *G3197*
Rev 6: 4 Its rider was given *p to* **take** peace from the AIT
Rev 6: 8 They were given **p** over a fourth of the *G2026*
Rev 7: 2 angels who *had been* **given** *p* to harm the AIT
Rev 7:12 honor and **p** and strength be to *G1539*
Rev 9: 3 earth and were given **p** like that of *G2026*
Rev 9:10 their tails they had **p** to torment people *G2026*
Rev 9:19 The **p** of the horses was in their mouths *G2026*
Rev 11: 6 They have **p** to shut up the heavens so *G2026*
Rev 11: 6 they have **p** to turn the waters into *G2400*
Rev 11:17 taken your great **p** and have begun to *G1539*
Rev 12:10 salvation and the **p** and the kingdom of *G1539*
Rev 13: 2 gave the beast his **p** and his throne and *G1539*
Rev 13: 7 It was given **p** to wage war against God's NDT
Rev 13:14 signs it was given **p** to perform on behalf NDT
Rev 13:15 beast was given **p** to give breath to the NDT
Rev 15: 8 from the glory of God and from his **p**, *G1539*
Rev 17:13 will give their **p** and authority to the *G1539*
Rev 19: 1 glory and **p** belong to our God, *G1539*
Rev 20: 6 The second death has no **p** over them *G2026*

POWERFUL (54) [POWER]

Ge 18:18 will surely become a great and **p** nation, H6786
Ge 26:16 from us; *you have become* too **p** for us." H6793
Nu 13:28 But the people who live there are **p**, and H6434
Nu 20:20 out against them with a large and **p** army. H2617
Nu 22: 6 people, because they are too **p** for me. H6786
Dt 26: 5 became a great nation, **p** and numerous. H6786
Jos 4:24 hand of the LORD is **p** and so that you H2617
Jos 17:17 "You are numerous and very **p**. H3946
Jos 23: 9 driven out before you great and **p** nations; H6786
2Sa 5:10 **became more and more p** H2143+2143+2256+1524
2Sa 22:18 He rescued me from my **p** enemy, from H6434
1Ki 19:11 Then a great and **p** wind tore the H2617
1Ch 11: 9 **became more and more p** H2143+2143+2256+1524
2Ch 17:12 **more and more p**; H2143+2256+1541+6330+4200+5087+2025
2Ch 22: 9 house of Ahaziah **p** *enough* to retain the H3946
2Ch 26: 8 of Egypt, because *he had become* very **p**. H2616
2Ch 26:13 a **p** force to support the king against his H3946
2Ch 26:15 he was greatly helped until *he became* **p**. H2616
2Ch 26:16 But after Uzziah **became p**, his pride led H2621
2Ch 27: 6 Jotham *grew* **p** because he walked H2616
Ezr 4:20 Jerusalem has had **p** kings ruling over A10768
Ezr 7:28 his advisers and all the king's **p** officials. H1475
Est 9: 4 **became more and more p**. H2143+2256+1524
Job 5:15 he saves them from the clutches of the **p**. H2617
Job 22: 8 though you were a **p** man, owning land H2432
Job 35: 9 they plead for relief from the arm of the **p**. H8041
Ps 18:17 He rescued me from my **p** enemy, from H6434
Ps 29: 4 The voice of the LORD is **p**; the voice of the H3946
Ecc 7:19 **makes** one wise person more **p** than H6451
Ecc 9:14 And a **p** king came against it, surrounded H1524
Isa 27: 1 great and **p** sword—Leviathan the H2617
Isa 28: 2 the Lord has *one who is* **p** and strong. H2617
Jer 5:27 of deceit; they have become rich and **p** H1540
Eze 17: 3 A great eagle with **p** wings, long feathers H1524
Eze 17: 7 great eagle with **p** wings and full H1524
Da 7: 7 terrifying and frightening and very **p**. A10768
Da 11:25 wage war with a large and very **p** army, H6786
Mic 7: 3 the **p** dictate what they desire H1524
Zec 6: 3 the fourth dappled—*all of them* **p**. H600
Zec 6: 7 When the **p** horses went out, they were H600
Zec 8:22 many peoples and **p** nations will come H6786
Mt 3:11 after me comes one who is **more p** *than* I, *G2708*
Mk 1: 7 "After me comes the *one* **more p** than I *G2708*
Lk 3:16 But one who is **more p** than I will come *G2708*
Lk 24:19 **p** in word and deed before God and all *G1543*
Ac 7:22 Egyptians and was **p** in speech and action *G1543*
Ac 9:22 Yet Saul *grew* more and more **p** and *G1904*
2Co 13: 3 in dealing with you, but *is* **p** among you. *G1542*
2Th 1: 7 heaven in blazing fire with his **p** angels. *G1539*
2Th 2:11 God sends them a **p** delusion so that they *G1918*
Heb 1: 3 sustaining all things by his **p** word. *G1539*
Heb 11:34 who became **p** in battle and routed *G2708*
Jas 5:16 righteous person *is* **p** and effective. *G4498+2710*
2Pe 2:11 although they are stronger and more **p** *G1539*

POWERFULLY (9) [POWER]

Jdg 14: 6 Spirit of the LORD **came p** upon him so that H7502
Jdg 14:19 the Spirit of the LORD **came p** upon him. H7502
Jdg 15:14 The Spirit of the LORD **came p** upon him H7502
1Sa 10: 6 Spirit of the LORD *will* **come p** upon you, H7502
1Sa 10:10 the Spirit of God **came p** upon him, and H7502
1Sa 11: 6 the Spirit of God **came p** upon him, and H7502
1Sa 16:13 the Spirit of the LORD **came p** upon David. H7502
Ac 4:33 And God's grace was *so* **p** at work in them *G3489*
Col 1:29 the energy Christ **so p** works in me. *G1877+1539*

POWERLESS (9) [POWER]

Dt 28:32 day after day, **p** to lift a hand. H401+4200+445
2Ch 14:11 you to help the **p** against the mighty H401+3946
Ne 5: 5 but we are **p**, because H401+4200+445+3338
Job 26: 2 "How you have helped the **p**! How H4202+3946
Jer 14: 9 by surprise, like a warrior **p** to save? H4202+3523
Da 8: 7 The ram was **p** to stand against it H4202+3946
Da 11:15 The forces of the South will be **p** to resist H4202
Ro 5: 6 when we were still **p**, Christ died for the *G822*
Ro 8: 3 For what the law was **p** to do because it was *G105*

POWERS (12) [POWER]

Isa 24:21 will punish the **p** *in* the heavens above H7372
Da 4:35 he pleases with the **p** *of* heaven and the A10264
Mt 13:54 get this wisdom and these **miraculous p**?" *G1539*
Mt 14: 2 That is why **miraculous p** are at work in *G1539*
Mk 6:14 that is why **miraculous p** are at work in *G1539*
Ro 8:38 the present nor the future, nor any **p**, *G1539*
1Co 12:10 to another **miraculous p**, to another *G1920+1539*
Eph 6:12 against the **p of** this dark **world** and *G3179*
Col 1:16 whether thrones or **p** or rulers or *G3262*

Col 2:15 And having disarmed the **p** and authorities *G794*
Heb 6: 5 word of God and the **p** of the coming age *G1539*
1Pe 3:22 authorities and **p** in submission to him. *G1539*

PRACTICALLY (1)

Ac 19:26 in Ephesus and in **p** the whole province of *G5385*

PRACTICE (33) [PRACTICED, PRACTICES, PRACTICING]

Lev 19:26 " '*Do* not **p divination** or seek omens. H5727
Dt 18:14 listen to *those who* **p sorcery** or divination. H6726
1Sa 2:13 Now it was the **p** *of* the priests that H5477
1Sa 27:11 And such was his **p** as long as he lived in H5477
Ps 52: 2 You *who* **p** deceit, your tongue plots H6913
Ps 119:56 **This** has been my *p*: I obey your precepts. AIT
Ecc 8: 8 will not release *those who* **p** it. H1251
Isa 2: 6 *they* **p divination** like the Philistines and H6726
Isa 32: 6 They **p** ungodliness and spread error H6913
Jer 6:13 prophets and priests alike, all **p** deceit. H6913
Jer 8:10 prophets and priests alike, all **p** deceit. H6913
Eze 13:23 see false visions or **p divination**. H7876+7877
Eze 22:29 of the land **p extortion** and commit H6943+6945
Eze 33:31 but *they do* not **put** them **into p**. H6913
Eze 33:32 your words but *do* not **put** them **into p**. H6913
Hos 7: 1 *They* **p** deceit, thieves break into houses H7188
Mt 6: 1 "Be careful not *to* **p** your righteousness in *G4472*
Mt 7:24 of mine and **puts** them **into p** is like a *G4472*
Mt 7:26 mine and *does* not **put** them **into p** is like *G4472*
Mt 23: 3 for *they do* not **p** what they preach. *G4472*
Lk 6:47 hears my words and **puts** them **into p**, *G4472*
Lk 6:49 words and *does* not **put** them **into p** is like *G4472*
Lk 8:21 who hear God's word and **put** it **into p**." *G4472*
Ac 16:21 unlawful for us Romans to accept or **p**." *G4472*
Ro 1:32 also approve of those *who* **p** them. *G4556*
Ro 3:13 are open graves; their tongues **p deceit**." *G1514*
Ro 12:13 people who are in need. **P** hospitality. *G1503*
1Co 11:16 we have no other **p**—nor do the churches *G5311*
Php 4: 9 from me, or seen in me—**put** it **into p**. *G4556*
1Ti 5: 4 all *to* **put** *their* **religion into p by caring for** *G2355*
Jas 3:16 there you find disorder and every evil **p**. *G4547*
Rev 21: 8 immoral, **those who p magic arts**, the *G5761*
Rev 22:15 those **who p magic arts**, the *G5761*

PRACTICED (10) [PRACTICE]

Lev 18:30 customs that **were p** before you came H6913
Jos 13:22 Balaam son of Beor, who **p divination**. H7876
2Ki 17:17 *They* **p divination** and sought H7876+7877
2Ki 21: 6 in the fire, **p divination**, sought omens, H6726
2Ch 33: 6 Ben Hinnom, **p divination** and witchcraft H6726
Eze 18:18 because *he* **p extortion**, robbed his H6943+6945
Mt 23:23 You should have **p** the latter, without *G4472*
Lk 11:42 You should have **p** the latter without *G4472*
Ac 8: 9 named Simon *had* **p sorcery** in the city *G3405*
Ac 19:19 A number who *had* **p** sorcery brought their *G4556*

PRACTICES (56) [PRACTICE]

Ex 23:24 gods or worship them or follow their **p**. H5126
Lev 18: 3 I am bringing you. Do not follow their **p**. H2978
Dt 18:10 the fire, *who* **p divination** or sorcery H7876+7877
Dt 18:12 of these same **detestable p** the LORD your H9359
Jdg 2:19 to give up their **evil p** and stubborn ways. H5095
1Ki 14:24 in all the **detestable p** *of* the nations the H9359
2Ki 16: 3 in the **detestable p** *of* the nations H9359
2Ki 17: 8 followed the **p** *of* the nations the LORD H2978
2Ki 17: 8 as well as the **p** that the kings of Israel had NDT
2Ki 17:19 They followed the **p** Israel had introduced. H2978
2Ki 17:34 To this day they persist in their former **p** H5477
2Ki 17:40 however, but persisted in their former **p**. H5477
2Ki 21: 2 following the **detestable p** *of* the nations H9359
2Ch 17: 4 his commands rather than the **p** *of* Israel. H5126
2Ch 27: 2 however, continued *their* **corrupt p**. H8845
2Ch 28: 3 in the **detestable p** *of* the nations H9359
2Ch 33: 2 following the **detestable p** *of* the nations H9359
2Ch 36:14 all the **detestable p** *of* the nations and H9359
Ezr 6:21 from the **unclean p** *of* their Gentile H3240
Ezr 9: 1 peoples with their **detestable p**, H9359
Ezr 9:11 By their **detestable p** they have filled it H9359
Ezr 9:14 peoples who commit such **detestable p**? H9359
Ps 101: 7 No *one who* **p** deceit will dwell in my H6913
Pr 28:16 A tyrannical ruler **p** extortion, but one who H8041
Jer 10: 3 For the **p** *of* the peoples are worthless H2978
Jer 25: 5 from your evil ways and your evil **p**, and H5095
Eze 5:11 all your vile images and **detestable p**, H9359
Eze 6: 9 have done and for all their **detestable p**. H9359
Eze 6:11 wicked and **detestable p** *of* the people of H9359
Eze 7: 3 repay you for all your **detestable p**. H9359
Eze 7: 4 for the **detestable p** among you. H9359
Eze 7: 8 repay you for all your **detestable p**. H9359
Eze 7: 9 for the **detestable p** among you. H9359
Eze 12:16 may acknowledge all their **detestable p**. H9359
Eze 14: 6 idols and renounce all your **detestable p**! H9359
Eze 16: 2 confront Jerusalem with her **detestable p** H9359
Eze 16:22 In all your **detestable p** and your H9359
Eze 16:43 lewdness to all your other **detestable p**? H9359
Eze 16:47 their ways and copied their **detestable p**, H9359
Eze 16:58 of your lewdness and your **detestable p**, H9359
Eze 20: 4 them with the **detestable p** *of* their H9359
Eze 20:44 to your evil ways and your corrupt **p**, H6613
Eze 22: 2 confront her with all her **detestable p** H9359
Eze 23:36 confront them with their **detestable p**, H9359
Eze 36:31 yourselves for your sins and **detestable p**. H9359
Eze 43: 8 my holy name by their **detestable p**. H9359
Eze 44: 6 Enough of your **detestable p**, people of H9359
Eze 44: 7 In addition to all your other **detestable p** H9359
Eze 44:13 bear the shame of their **detestable p**. H9359
Mic 6:16 of Omri and all the **p** *of* Ahab's house; H5126
Zec 1: 4 'Turn from your evil ways and your evil **p**.' H5095
Zec 1: 6 done to us what our ways and **p** deserve, H5095
Mt 5:19 whoever **p** and teaches these *G4472*
Col 3: 9 you have taken off your old self with its **p** *G4552*
Rev 2: 6 You hate the **p** of the Nicolaitans, which I *G2240*
Rev 22:15 everyone who loves and **p** falsehood. *G4472*

PRACTICING (1) [PRACTICE]

1Ti 1:10 immoral, *for those* **p homosexuality**, for *G780*

PRAETORIUM (2)

Mt 27:27 took Jesus into the **P** and gathered the *G4550*
Mk 15:16 the **P**) and called together the *G4550*

PRAISE (347) [PRAISED, PRAISES, PRAISEWORTHY, PRAISING]

Ge 9:26 He also said, "**P** *be to* the LORD, the God H1385
Ge 14:20 And **p** *be to* God Most High, who H1385
Ge 24:27 "**P** *be to* the LORD, the God of my H1385
Ge 29:35 son she said, "This time *I will* **p** the LORD." H3344
Ge 49: 8 your brothers *will* **p** you; your hand will H3344
Ex 15: 2 is my God, and *I will* **p** him, my father's H5658
Ex 18:10 He said, "**P** *be to* the LORD, who rescued H1385
Lev 19:24 will be holy, an **offering of p** to the LORD. H2136
Dt 8:10 **p** the LORD your God for the good land he H1385
Dt 10:21 He is the one you **p**; he is your God, who H9335
Dt 26:19 He has declared that he will set you in **p** H9335
Dt 32: 3 Oh, **p** the greatness of our God H2035
Jdg 5: 2 willingly offer themselves—**p** the LORD! H1385
Jdg 5: 3 *I will* **p** the LORD, the God of Israel, **in song** H2376
Jdg 5: 9 volunteers among the people. **P** the LORD! H1385
Ru 4:14 "**P** *be to* the LORD, who this day has not H1385
1Sa 25:32 said to Abigail, "**P** *be to* the LORD, the God H1385
1Sa 25:39 he said, "**P** *be to* the LORD, who has H1385
2Sa 18:28 said, "**P** *be to* the LORD your God! H1385
2Sa 22: 4 to the LORD, *who is* **worthy of p**, and have H2146
2Sa 22:47 "The LORD lives! **P** *be to* my Rock! Exalted H1385
2Sa 22:50 Therefore *I will* **p** you, LORD, among the H3344
1Ki 1:48 '**P** *be to* the LORD, the God of H1385
1Ki 5: 7 pleased and said, "**P** *be to* the LORD today H1385
1Ki 8:15 "**P** *be to* the LORD, the God of Israel, who H1385
1Ki 8:33 turn back to you and **give p** *to* your name, H3344
1Ki 8:35 this place and **give p** *to* your name and H3344
1Ki 8:56 "**P** *be to* the LORD, who has given rest to H1385
1Ki 10: 9 **P** be *to* the LORD your God, who has H1385
1Ch 16: 4 to extol, thank, and **p** the LORD, the God of H2146
1Ch 16: 7 his associates to **give p** to the LORD in this H3344
1Ch 16: 8 **Give p** to the LORD, proclaim his name H3344
1Ch 16: 9 Sing to him, **sing p** to him; tell of all his H2376
1Ch 16:25 For great is the LORD and most **worthy of p** H2146
1Ch 16:35 to your holy name, and glory in your **p**." H9335
1Ch 16:36 **P** *be to* the LORD, the God of Israel, from H1385
1Ch 16:36 the people said "Amen" and "**P** the LORD." H2146
1Ch 23: 5 four thousand *are to* **p** the LORD with H2146
1Ch 23:30 every morning to thank and **p** the LORD. H2146
1Ch 29:10 "**P** *be to* you, LORD, the God H1385
1Ch 29:13 you thanks, and **p** your glorious name. H2146
1Ch 29:20 whole assembly, "**P** the LORD your God." H1385
2Ch 2:12 "**P** *be to* the LORD, the God of Israel, who H1385
2Ch 5:13 in unison to **give p** and thanks to the H2146
2Ch 5:13 their voices in **p** to the LORD and sang: H2146
2Ch 6: 4 "**P** *be to* the LORD, the God of Israel, who H1385
2Ch 6:24 they turn back and **give p to** your name, H3344
2Ch 6:26 this place and **give p to** your name and H3344
2Ch 8:14 the Levites to lead the **p** and to assist the H2146
2Ch 9: 8 **P** *be to* the LORD your God, who has H1385
2Ch 20:21 sing to the LORD and *to* **p** him for the H2146
2Ch 20:22 As they began to sing and **p**, the LORD set H9335
2Ch 29:30 ordered the Levites to **p** the LORD with the H2146
Ezr 3:10 took their places to **p** the LORD, as H2146
Ezr 3:11 With **p** and thanksgiving they sang to the H2146
Ezr 3:11 gave a great shout of **p** to the LORD, H2146
Ezr 7:27 **P** *be to* the LORD, the God of our ancestors H1385
Ne 9: 5 "Stand up and **p** the LORD your God, who H1385
Ne 9: 5 it be exalted above all blessing and **p**. H9335
Ne 12:24 opposite them to **give p** and thanksgiving, H2146
Ne 12:46 for the songs of **p** and thanksgiving to H9335
Ps 8: 2 Through the **p** *of* children and infants you H7023
Ps 13: 6 *I will* **sing** the LORD's **p**, for he has been H8876
Ps 16: 7 *I will* **p** the LORD, who counsels me; even H1385
Ps 18: 3 to the LORD, *who is* **worthy of p**, and I have H2146
Ps 18:46 The LORD lives! **P** *be to* my Rock! Exalted H1385
Ps 18:49 Therefore *I will* **p** you, LORD, among the H3344
Ps 21:13 we will sing and **p** your might. H2376
Ps 22:22 my people; in the assembly *I will* **p** you. H2146
Ps 22:23 *You* who fear the LORD, **p** him! All you H2146
Ps 22:25 you comes the **theme** of my **p** in the great H9335
Ps 22:26 those who seek the LORD *will* **p** him—may H2146
Ps 26: 7 aloud your **p** and telling of all H9343
Ps 26:12 in the great congregation *I will* **p** the LORD. H1385
Ps 28: 6 **P** *be to* the LORD, for he has heard my cry H1385
Ps 28: 7 leaps for joy, and with my song *I* **p** him. H3344
Ps 30: 4 you his faithful people; **p** his holy name. H3344
Ps 30: 9 *Will* the dust **p** you? Will it H3344
Ps 30:12 LORD my God, *I will* **p** you forever. H3344
Ps 31:21 **P** *be to* the LORD, for he showed me the H1385
Ps 33: 1 it is fitting for the upright to **p** him. H9335
Ps 33: 2 **P** the LORD with the harp; make music to H3344
Ps 34: 1 all times; his **p** will always be on my lips. H9335
Ps 35:18 assembly; among the throngs *I will* **p** you. H2146
Ps 40: 3 in my mouth, a **hymn of p** to our God. H9335
Ps 41:13 **P** *be to* the LORD, the God of Israel, from H1385
Ps 42: 4 shouts of joy and **p** among the festive H9343
Ps 42: 5 for *I will* yet **p** him, my Savior H3344
Ps 42:11 for *I will* yet **p** him, my Savior H3344
Ps 43: 4 my delight. *I will* **p** you with the lyre H3344
Ps 43: 5 for *I will* yet **p** him, my Savior H3344
Ps 44: 8 and *we will* **p** your name forever. H3344
Ps 45:17 the nations *will* **p** you for ever and H3344
Ps 47: 7 of all the earth; sing to him a **psalm of p**. H5380
Ps 48: 1 and most **worthy of p**, in the city of H2146
Ps 48:10 your **p** reaches to the ends of the earth H9335
Ps 49:18 and *people* **p** you when you prosper— H3344
Ps 51:15 and my mouth will declare your **p**. H9335
Ps 52: 9 you have done *I will* always **p** you in the H3344
Ps 54: 6 offering to you; *I will* **p** your name, LORD, H3344
Ps 56: 4 whose word *I* **p**—in God I trust H2146
Ps 56:10 whose word *I* **p**, in the LORD H2146
Ps 56:10 I praise, in the LORD, whose word *I* **p**— H2146
Ps 57: 9 *I will* **p** you, Lord, among the nations; H3344
Ps 59:17 are my strength, *I* **sing p** to you; you, God, H2376
Ps 61: 8 Then *I will* ever **sing in p** *of* your name H2376
Ps 63: 4 *I will* **p** you as long as I live, and in your H1385
Ps 63: 5 with singing lips my mouth *will* **p** you. H2146
Ps 65: 1 **P** awaits you, our God, in Zion; to you our H9335
Ps 66: 2 glory of his name; make his **p** glorious. H9335
Ps 66: 4 down to you; *they* **sing p** to you, they sing H2376
Ps 66: 8 **P** our God, all peoples, let the sound of H1385
Ps 66: 8 peoples, let the sound of his **p** be heard; H9335
Ps 66:17 with my mouth; his **p** was on my tongue. H8128
Ps 66:20 **P** *be to* God, who has not rejected my H1385
Ps 67: 3 *May* the peoples **p** you, God; may all the H3344
Ps 67: 3 God; *may* all the peoples **p** you. H3344
Ps 67: 5 *May* the peoples **p** you, God; may all the H3344
Ps 67: 5 God; *may* all the peoples **p** you. H3344
Ps 68: 4 Sing to God, **sing in p** *of* his name, extol H2376
Ps 68:19 **P** *be to* the Lord, to God our Savior, who H1385
Ps 68:26 **P** God in the great congregation; praise H1385
Ps 68:26 **p** the LORD in the assembly of Israel. NDT
Ps 68:32 kingdoms of the earth, **sing p** *to* the Lord, H2376
Ps 68:35 strength to his people. **P** *be to* God! H1385
Ps 69:30 *I will* **p** God's name in song and glorify H2146
Ps 69:34 *Let* heaven and earth **p** him, the seas H2146
Ps 71: 6 my mother's womb. I will ever **p** you. H9335
Ps 71: 8 My mouth is filled with your **p**, declaring H9335
Ps 71:14 have hope; I will **p** you more and more. H9335
Ps 71:22 I *will* **p** you with the harp *for* your H3344
Ps 71:22 my God; *I will* **sing p** to you with the lyre H2376
Ps 71:23 will shout for joy when *I* **sing p** to you— H2376
Ps 72:18 **P** *be to* the LORD God, the God of Israel H1385
Ps 72:19 **P** *be to* his glorious name forever; may H1385
Ps 74:21 *may* the poor and needy **p** your name. H2146
Ps 75: 1 *We* **p** you, God, we praise you, for your H3344
Ps 75: 1 praise you, God, *we* **p** you, for your Name H3344
Ps 75: 9 *I will* **sing p** to the God of Jacob, H2376
Ps 76:10 your wrath against mankind **brings** you **p**, H3344
Ps 79:13 of your pasture, *will* **p** you forever; from H3344
Ps 79:13 to generation we will proclaim your **p**. H9335
Ps 86:12 *I will* **p** you, Lord my God, with all my H3344
Ps 88:10 Do their spirits rise up and **p** you? H3344
Ps 89: 5 The heavens **p** your wonders, LORD, your H3344
Ps 89:52 **P** *be to* the LORD forever! Amen and Amen. H1385
Ps 92: 1 It is good to **p** the LORD and make music to H3344
Ps 96: 2 Sing to the LORD, **p** his name; proclaim his H1385
Ps 96: 4 For great is the LORD and most **worthy of p** H2146
Ps 97:12 who are righteous, and **p** his holy name. H3344
Ps 99: 3 *Let them* **p** your great and awesome H3344
Ps 100: T For **giving grateful p**. H9343
Ps 100: 4 with thanksgiving and his courts with **p**; H9335
Ps 100: 4 give thanks to him and **p** his name. H1385
Ps 101: 1 love and justice; to you, LORD, *I will* **sing p**. H2376
Ps 102:18 a people not yet created *may* **p** the LORD: H2146
Ps 102:21 declared in Zion and his **p** in Jerusalem H9335
Ps 103: 1 **P** the LORD, my soul; all my inmost being H1385
Ps 103: 1 all my inmost being, **p** his holy name. NDT
Ps 103: 2 **P** the LORD, my soul, and forget not all his H1385
Ps 103:20 **P** the LORD, you his angels, you mighty H1385
Ps 103:21 **P** the LORD, all his heavenly hosts, you his H1385
Ps 103:22 **P** the LORD, all his works everywhere in his H1385
Ps 103:22 in his dominion. **P** the LORD, my soul. H1385
Ps 104: 1 **P** the LORD, my soul. LORD my God, you H1385
Ps 104:33 *I will* **sing p** to my God as long as I live. H2376
Ps 104:35 wicked be no more. **P** the LORD, my soul H1385
Ps 104:35 Praise the LORD, my soul. **P** the LORD. H2146
Ps 105: 1 **Give p** to the LORD, proclaim his name H3344
Ps 105: 2 Sing to him, **sing p** to him; tell of all his H2376
Ps 105:45 precepts and observe his laws. **P** the LORD. H2146
Ps 106: 1 **P** the LORD. Give thanks to the LORD, for he H2146
Ps 106: 2 acts of the LORD or fully declare his **p**? H9335
Ps 106: 5 join your inheritance in **giving p**. H2146
Ps 106:12 believed his promises and sang his **p**. H9335
Ps 106:47 to your holy name and glory in your **p**. H9335
Ps 106:48 **P** *be to* the LORD, the God of Israel, from H1385
Ps 106:48 all the people say, "Amen!" **P** the LORD. H2146
Ps 107:32 of the people and **p** him in the council of H2146
Ps 108: 3 *I will* **p** you, LORD, among the nations; H3344
Ps 109: 1 My God, whom I **p**, do not remain silent, H9335
Ps 109:30 great throng of worshipers *I will* **p** him. H2146
Ps 111: 1 **P** the LORD. I will extol the LORD with all H2146
Ps 111:10 understanding. *To* him *belongs* eternal **p**. H9335

P

Ps 112: 1 **P** the LORD. Blessed are those who fear the H2146
Ps 113: 1 **P** the LORD. Praise the LORD, you his H2146
Ps 113: 1 **P** the LORD, *you* his servants; praise the H2146
Ps 113: 1 you his servants; **p** the name of the LORD. H2146
Ps 113: 9 a happy mother of children. **P** the LORD. H2146
Ps 115:17 It is not the dead *who* **p** the LORD, those H2146
Ps 115:18 both now and forevermore. **P** the LORD. H2146
Ps 116:19 in your midst, Jerusalem. **P** the LORD. H2146
Ps 117: 1 **P** the LORD, all *you* nations; extol him, all H2146
Ps 117: 2 of the LORD endures forever. **P** the LORD. H2146
Ps 118:28 are my God, and *I will* **p** you; you are my H3344
Ps 119: 7 *I will* **p** you with an upright heart as I H3344
Ps 119:12 **P** *be to* you, LORD; teach me your decrees. H1385
Ps 119:108 the willing **p** of my mouth, and teach NDT
Ps 119:164 Seven times a day *I* **p** you for your H2146
Ps 119:171 May my lips overflow with **p**, for you H9335
Ps 119:175 Let me live that I *may* **p** you, and may H2146
Ps 122: 4 to **p** the name of the LORD according to the H3344
Ps 124: 6 **P** *be to* the LORD, who has not let us be H1385
Ps 134: 1 **P** the LORD, all *you* servants of the LORD H1385
Ps 134: 2 hands in the sanctuary and **p** the LORD. H1385
Ps 135: 1 **P** the LORD. Praise the name of the LORD H2146
Ps 135: 1 **P** the name of the LORD; praise him, you H2146
Ps 135: 1 the LORD; **p** him, *you* servants of the LORD H2146
Ps 135: 3 **P** the LORD, for the LORD is good; sing H2146
Ps 135: 3 the LORD is good; **sing p** to his name, for H2376
Ps 135:19 *All you* Israelites, **p** the LORD; house of H1385
Ps 135:19 the LORD; house of Aaron, **p** the LORD; H1385
Ps 135:20 house of Levi, **p** the LORD; you who fear H1385
Ps 135:20 the LORD; *you* who fear him, **p** the LORD. H1385
Ps 135:21 **P** *be to* the LORD from Zion, *to* him who H1385
Ps 135:21 him who dwells in Jerusalem. **P** the LORD. H2146
Ps 138: 1 *I will* **p** you, LORD, with all my heart; H3344
Ps 138: 1 before the "gods" *I will* **sing** your **p**. H2376
Ps 138: 2 holy temple and *will* **p** your name for your H3344
Ps 138: 4 *May* all the kings of the earth **p** you, LORD H3344
Ps 139:14 *I* **p** you because I am fearfully and H3344
Ps 140:13 Surely the righteous *will* **p** your name H3344
Ps 142: 7 from my prison, that I *may* **p** your name. H3344
Ps 144: 1 **P** *be to* the LORD my Rock, who trains my H1385
Ps 145: T A **psalm of p**. Of David. H9335
Ps 145: 1 *I will* **p** your name for ever and ever. H1385
Ps 145: 2 Every day *I will* **p** you and extol your name H1385
Ps 145: 3 Great is the LORD and most **worthy of p**; H2146
Ps 145:10 All your works **p** you, LORD; your faithful H3344
Ps 145:21 My mouth will speak *in* **p** *of* the LORD. H9335
Ps 145:21 *Let* every creature **p** his holy name for ever H1385
Ps 146: 1 **P** the LORD. Praise the LORD, my soul. H2146
Ps 146: 1 Praise the LORD. **P** the LORD, my soul. H2146
Ps 146: 2 *I will* **p** the LORD all my life; I will sing H2146
Ps 146: 2 *I will* **sing p** to my God as long as I live. H2376
Ps 146:10 for all generations. **P** the LORD. H2146
Ps 147: 1 **P** the LORD. How good it is to sing praises H2146
Ps 147: 1 how pleasant and fitting to **p** him! H9335
Ps 147: 7 Sing to the LORD with **grateful p**; make H9343
Ps 147:12 the LORD, Jerusalem; **p** your God, Zion. H2146
Ps 147:20 they do not know his laws. **P** the LORD. H2146
Ps 148: 1 **P** the LORD. Praise the LORD from the H2146
Ps 148: 1 **P** the LORD from the heavens; praise him H2146
Ps 148: 1 the heavens; **p** him in the heights above. H2146
Ps 148: 2 **P** him, all his angels; praise him, all his H2146
Ps 148: 2 all his angels; **p** him, all his heavenly H2146
Ps 148: 3 **P** him, sun and moon; praise him, all you H2146
Ps 148: 3 sun and moon; **p** him, all you shining H2146
Ps 148: 4 **P** him, you highest heavens and you H2146
Ps 148: 5 *Let them* **p** the name of the LORD, for at his H2146
Ps 148: 7 **P** the LORD from the earth, *you* great sea H2146
Ps 148:13 *Let them* **p** the name of the LORD, for his H2146
Ps 148:14 the **p** of all his faithful servants H9335
Ps 148:14 the people close to his heart. **P** the LORD. H2146
Ps 149: 1 **P** the LORD. Sing to the LORD a new song H2146
Ps 149: 1 his **p** in the assembly of his faithful H9335
Ps 149: 3 *Let them* **p** his name with dancing and H2146
Ps 149: 6 May the **p** *of* God be in their mouths and H8128
Ps 149: 9 glory of all his faithful people. **P** the LORD. H2146
Ps 150: 1 **P** the LORD. Praise God in his sanctuary H2146
Ps 150: 1 **P** God in his sanctuary; praise him in his H2146
Ps 150: 1 sanctuary; **p** him in his mighty heavens. H2146
Ps 150: 2 **P** him for his acts of power; praise him H2146
Ps 150: 2 **p** him for his surpassing greatness. H2146
Ps 150: 3 **P** him with the sounding of the trumpet H2146
Ps 150: 3 the trumpet, **p** him with the harp and lyre, H2146
Ps 150: 4 **p** him with timbrel and dancing, praise H2146
Ps 150: 4 dancing, **p** him with the strings and pipe, H2146
Ps 150: 5 **p** him with the clash of cymbals, praise H2146
Ps 150: 5 cymbals, **p** him with resounding cymbals. H2146
Ps 150: 6 *Let* everything that has breath **p** the LORD H2146
Ps 150: 6 has breath praise the LORD. **P** the LORD. H2146
Pr 27: 2 *Let* someone else **p** you, and not your H2146
Pr 27:21 gold, but people are tested by their **p**. H4545
Pr 28: 4 who forsake instruction **p** the wicked, H2146
Pr 31:31 and *let* her works **bring** her **p** at the city H2146
Ecc 8:10 holy place and **receive p** in the city where H8655
SS 1: 4 *we will* **p** your love more than wine. H2349
Isa 12: 1 day you will say: "*I will* **p** you, LORD H3344
Isa 12: 4 "**Give p** to the LORD, proclaim his name H3344
Isa 25: 1 exalt you and **p** your name, for *in* perfect H3344
Isa 38:18 For the grave cannot **p** you, death cannot H3344
Isa 38:18 death cannot **sing** your **p**; those who go H2146
Isa 38:19 the living—they **p** you, as I am doing H3344
Isa 42: 8 yield my glory to another or my **p** to idols. H9335
Isa 42:10 his **p** from the ends of the earth H9335
Isa 42:12 the LORD and proclaim his **p** in the islands. H9335
Isa 43:21 myself that they may proclaim my **p**. H9335
Isa 48: 9 the sake of my **p** I hold it back from H9335
Isa 57:19 creating **p** *on* their lips. Peace, peace, to H5762
Isa 60: 6 proclaiming the **p** *of* the LORD. H9335
Isa 60:18 call your walls Salvation and your gates **P**. H9335
Isa 61: 3 a garment of **p** instead of a spirit of H9335
Isa 61:11 righteousness and **p** spring up before all H9335
Isa 62: 7 makes her the **p** of the earth. H9335
Isa 62: 9 who harvest it will eat it and **p** the LORD, H2146
Jer 13:11 people for my renown and **p** and honor. H9335
Jer 17:14 I will be saved, for you are the *one* I **p**. H9335
Jer 20:13 Sing to the LORD! **Give p** *to* the LORD! He H2146
Jer 33: 9 **p** and honor before all nations on earth H9335
Da 2:20 "**P** be to the name of God for ever and A10122
Da 2:23 I thank and **p** you, God of my ancestors A10693
Da 3:28 "**P** *be to* the God of Shadrach A10122
Da 4:37 **p** and exalt and glorify the King of A10693
Joel 2:26 and *you will* **p** the name of the LORD your H2146
Jnh 2: 9 with shouts of **grateful p**, will sacrifice to H9343
Hab 3: 3 the heavens and his **p** filled the earth. H9335
Zep 3:19 I will give them **p** and honor in every land H9335
Zep 3:20 give you honor and **p** among all the H9335
Zec 11: 5 who sell them say, '**P** the LORD, I am rich! H1385
Mt 11:25 time Jesus said, "*I* **p** you, Father, Lord of *G2018*
Mt 21:16 infants you, Lord, have called forth your **p**'?" *G142*
Lk 1:68 "**P** be to the Lord, the God of Israel *G2329*
Lk 5:26 Everyone was amazed and **gave p** to God *G1519*
Lk 10:21 Holy Spirit, said, "*I* **p** you, Father, Lord of *G2018*
Lk 17:18 one returned to give **p** to God except this *G1518*
Lk 19:37 began joyfully *to* **p** God in loud voices for *G140*
Jn 12:43 they loved human **p** more than praise *G1518*
Jn 12:43 human praise more than **p** from God. *G1518*
Ac 12:23 because Herod did not give **p** to God, an *G1518*
Ro 2:29 Such a person's **p** is not from other *G2047*
Ro 15: 7 accepted you, in order to bring **p** to God. *G1518*
Ro 15: 9 "Therefore *I will* **p** you among the *G2018*
Ro 15:11 And again, "**P** the Lord, all you Gentiles *G140*
1Co 4: 5 time each will receive their **p** from God. *G2047*
1Co 11: 2 *I* **p** you for remembering me in everything *G2046*
1Co 11:17 following directives *I* **have** no **p** for you, *G2046*
1Co 11:22 *Shall I* **p** you? Certainly not *G2046*
2Co 1: 3 **P** be to the God and Father of our Lord *G2329*
2Co 9:13 *others will* **p** God for the obedience that *G1519*
Eph 1: 3 **P** be to the God and Father of our Lord *G2329*
Eph 1: 6 to the **p** of his glorious grace, which he *G2047*
Eph 1:12 in Christ, might be for the **p** of his glory. *G2047*
Eph 1:14 God's possession—to the **p** of his glory. *G2047*
Php 1:11 Jesus Christ—to the glory and **p** of God. *G2047*
1Th 2: 6 We were not looking for **p** from people *G1518*
Heb 13:15 continually offer to God a sacrifice *of* **p**— *G139*
Jas 3: 9 With the tongue *we* **p** our Lord and Father, *G2328*
Jas 3:10 of the same mouth come **p** and cursing. *G2330*
Jas 5:13 anyone happy? *Let them* **sing songs of p**. *G6010*
1Pe 1: 3 **P** be to the God and Father of our Lord *G2329*
1Pe 1: 7 may result in **p**, glory and honor *G2047*
1Pe 4:16 **p** God that you bear that name. *G1519*
Rev 5:12 strength and honor and glory and **p**!" *G2330*
Rev 5:13 to the Lamb be **p** and honor and *G2330*
Rev 7:12 **P** and glory and wisdom and thanks and *G2330*
Rev 19: 5 "**P** our God, all you his servants, you who *G140*

PRAISED (45) [PRAISE]

Ge 12:15 officials saw her, *they* **p** her to Pharaoh H2146
Ge 24:48 *I* **p** the LORD, the God of my master H1385
Jos 22:33 were glad to hear the report and **p** God. H1385
Jdg 16:24 people saw him, *they* **p** their god, saying, H2146
2Sa 14:25 not a man so highly **p** *for* his handsome H2146
1Ch 29:10 David **p** the LORD in the presence of the H1385
1Ch 29:20 So they all **p** the LORD, the God of their H1385
2Ch 20:19 Korahites stood up and **p** the LORD, H2146
2Ch 20:26 Valley of Berakah, where *they* **p** the LORD. H1385
2Ch 30:21 Levites and priests **p** the LORD every day H2146
2Ch 30:22 fellowship offerings and **p** the LORD, H3344
2Ch 31: 8 they **p** the LORD and blessed his people NDT
Ne 5:13 assembly said, "Amen," and **p** the LORD. H2146
Ne 8: 6 Ezra **p** the LORD, the great God; and all the H1385
Job 1:21 may the name of the LORD be **p**. H1385
Job 36:24 his work, which people *have* **p in song**. H8876
Ps 113: 2 Let the name of the LORD be **p**, both now H1385
Ps 113: 3 the name of the LORD *is to* **be p**. H2146
Pr 12: 8 A person **is p** according to their prudence H2146
Pr 31:30 a woman who fears the LORD *is to* **be p**. H2146
SS 6: 9 the queens and concubines **p** her. H2146
Isa 63: 7 the *deeds for which* he is to be **p** H9335
Isa 64:11 where our ancestors **p** you, has been H2146
Jer 48: 2 Moab will be **p** no more; in Heshbon H9335
Da 2:19 Then Daniel **p** the God of heaven A10122
Da 4:34 Then *I* **p** the Most High; I honored and A10122
Da 5: 4 *they* **p** the gods of gold and silver A10693
Da 5:23 *You* **p** the gods of silver and gold, of A10693
Mt 9: 8 with awe; and *they* **p** God, who had given *G1519*
Mt 15:31 And *they* **p** the God of Israel. *G1519*
Mk 2:12 This amazed everyone and *they* **p** God *G1519*
Lk 2:28 Simeon took him in his arms and **p** God *G2328*
Lk 4:15 in their synagogues, and everyone **p** him. *G1519*
Lk 7:16 They were all filled with awe and **p** God *G1519*
Lk 13:13 she straightened up and **p** God. *G1519*
Lk 18:43 the people saw it, *they also* **p** God. *G1443+142*
Lk 23:47 what had happened, **p** God and said *G1519*
Ac 11:18 they had no further objections and **p** God *G1519*
Ac 21:20 they heard this, *they* **p** God. Then they *G1519*
Ro 1:25 rather than the Creator—who is forever **p**. *G2329*
Ro 9: 5 Messiah, who is God over all, forever **p**! *G2329*
2Co 8:18 the brother who is **p** by all the churches *G2047*
2Co 11:31 who is to be **p** forever, knows that I *G2329*
Gal 1:24 And *they* **p** God because of me. *G1519*
1Pe 4:11 in all things God *may be* **p** through Jesus *G1519*

PRAISES (25) [PRAISE]

2Sa 22:50 nations; *I will* **sing the p** of your name. H2376
2Ch 23:13 with their instruments were leading the **p**. H2146
2Ch 29:30 So *they* **sang p** with gladness and bowed H2146
2Ch 31: 2 give thanks and to **sing p** at the gates of H2146
Ps 6: 5 Who **p** you from the grave? H3344
Ps 7:17 *I will* **sing the p** *of* the name of the LORD H2376
Ps 9: 2 *I will* **sing the p** *of* your name, H2376
Ps 9:11 **Sing the p** of the LORD, enthroned in Zion H2376
Ps 9:14 that I may declare your **p** in the gates of H9335
Ps 18:49 nations; *I will* **sing the p** of your name. H2376
Ps 22: 3 as the Holy One; you are the one Israel **p**. H9335
Ps 30: 4 **Sing the p** of the LORD, you his faithful H2376
Ps 30:12 that my heart *may* **sing** your **p** and not be H2376
Ps 35:28 your righteousness, your **p** all day long. H9335
Ps 47: 6 **Sing p** *to* God, sing praises; sing praises H2376
Ps 47: 6 praises to God, **sing p**; sing praises to our H2376
Ps 47: 6 sing praises; **sing p** to our King, sing H2376
Ps 47: 6 praises; sing praises to our King, **sing p**. H2376
Ps 66: 4 *they* **sing the p** *of* your name. H2376
Ps 147: 1 How good it is *to* **sing p** *to* our God, how H2376
Pr 31:28 blessed; her husband also, and *he* **p** her: H2146
Jer 31: 7 Make *your* **p** heard, and say, 'LORD, save H2146
Ro 15: 9 Gentiles; *I will* **sing the p** of your name." *G6010*
Heb 2:12 in the assembly *I will* **sing** your **p**. *G5630*
1Pe 2: 9 you may declare the **p** of him who called *G746*

PRAISEWORTHY (2) [PRAISE]

Ps 78: 4 next generation the **p deeds** *of* the LORD, H9335
Php 4: 8 if anything is excellent or **p**—think about *G2047*

PRAISING (16) [PRAISE]

1Ch 25: 3 using the harp in thanking and **p** the LORD. H2146
2Ch 7: 6 David had made for **p** the LORD and which H3344
Ps 84: 4 dwell in your house; *they are* ever **p** you. H2146
Lk 1:64 set free, and he began to speak, **p** God. *G2328*
Lk 2:13 with the angel, **p** God and saying, *G140*
Lk 2:20 glorifying and **p** God for all the things they *G140*
Lk 5:25 had been lying on and went home **p** God. *G1519*
Lk 17:15 came back, **p** God in a loud voice. *G1519*
Lk 18:43 his sight and followed Jesus, **p** God. *G1519*
Lk 24:53 stayed continually at the temple, **p** God. *G2328*
Ac 2:47 **p** God and enjoying the favor of all the *G140*
Ac 3: 8 walking and jumping, and **p** God. *G140*
Ac 3: 9 all the people saw him walking and **p** God, *G140*
Ac 4:21 all the people *were* **p** God for what had *G1519*
Ac 10:46 them speaking in tongues and **p** God. *G3486*
1Co 14:16 Otherwise when *you are* **p** God in the *G2328*

PRAY (125) [PRAYED, PRAYER, PRAYERS, PRAYING, PRAYS]

Ge 20: 7 and *he will* **p** for you and you will live. H7137
Ge 32:11 Save me, **I p**, from the hand of my brother H5528
Ex 8: 8 "**P** to the LORD *to take* the frogs away from H6983
Ex 8: 9 setting the time *for me to* **p** for you and H6983
Ex 8:28 you must not go very far. Now **p** for me." H6983
Ex 8:29 as I leave you, *I will* **p** to the LORD, and H6983
Ex 9:28 **P** to the LORD, for we have had enough H6983
Ex 10:17 sin once more and **p** to the LORD your God H6983
Nu 21: 7 **P** that the LORD will take the snakes away H7137
Dt 4: 7 our God is near us whenever we **p** to him? H7924
1Sa 12:19 "**P** to the LORD your God for your servants H7137
1Sa 12:23 sin against the LORD by failing to **p** for you. H7137
2Sa 7:27 has found courage to **p** this prayer to you. H7137
1Ki 8:30 Israel when *they* **p** toward this place H7137
1Ki 8:35 when *they* **p** toward this place and H7137
1Ki 8:42 when they come and **p** toward this temple H7137
1Ki 8:44 when *they* **p** to the LORD toward the H7137
1Ki 8:48 **p** to you toward the land you gave H7137
1Ki 13: 6 LORD your God and **p** for me that my hand H7137
2Ki 19: 4 Therefore **p** for the remnant that H5951+9525
1Ch 17:25 servant has found courage to **p** to you. H7137
2Ch 6:21 Israel when *they* **p** toward this place H7137
2Ch 6:26 when *they* **p** toward this place and H7137
2Ch 6:32 when they come and **p** toward this temple H7137
2Ch 6:34 when *they* **p** to you toward this city H7137
2Ch 6:38 **p** toward the land you gave their H7137
2Ch 7:14 themselves and **p** and seek my face and H7137
Ezr 6:10 God of heaven and **p** for the well-being A10612
Job 22:27 *You will* **p** to him, and he will hear you H6983
Job 33:26 then *that person can* **p** to God and find H6983
Job 42: 8 My servant Job *will* **p** for you, and I will H7137
Ps 5: 2 my King and my God, for to you *I* **p**. H7137
Ps 32: 6 let all the faithful **p** to you while you may H7137
Ps 69:13 But I **p** to you, LORD, in the time of your H9525
Ps 72:15 *May people* ever **p** for him and bless him H7137
Ps 122: 6 **P** *for* the peace of Jerusalem: "May those H8626
Pr 11:26 they **p** God's blessing on the one who is NDT
Isa 16:12 when she goes to her shrine to **p**, it is to H7137
Isa 37: 4 Therefore **p** for the remnant that H5951+9525
Isa 45:20 of wood, *who* **p** to gods that cannot save. H7137
Isa 64: 9 look on us, **we p**, for we are all your H5528
Jer 7:16 "So *do* not **p** for this people nor offer any H7137
Jer 11:14 "*Do* not **p** for this people or offer any plea H7137
Jer 14:11 "*Do* not **p** for the well-being of this H7137

Jer 29: 7 **P** to the LORD for it, because if it prospers H7137
Jer 29:12 will call on me and come and **p** to me, H7137
Jer 31: 9 weeping; they will **p** as I bring them back. H9384
Jer 37: 3 "Please **p** to the LORD our God for us." H7137
Jer 42: 2 our petition and **p** to the LORD your God H7137
Jer 42: 3 **P** that the LORD your God will tell us where NDT
Jer 42: 4 "I *will* certainly **p** to the LORD your God as H7137
Jer 42:20 said, '**P** to the LORD our God for us H7137
Da 9:23 As soon as you began to **p**, a word went H9384
Mt 5:44 love your enemies and **p** for those who *G4667*
Mt 6: 5 "And when *you* **p**, do not be like the *G4667*
Mt 6: 5 they love *to* **p** standing in the *G4667*
Mt 6: 6 But when you **p**, go into your room, close *G4667*
Mt 6: 6 close the door and **p** to your Father, who *G4667*
Mt 6: 7 And *when you* **p**, do not keep on babbling *G4667*
Mt 6: 9 is how you *should* **p**: " 'Our Father in *G4667*
Mt 14:23 up on a mountainside by himself *to* **p**. *G4667*
Mt 19:13 place his hands on them and **p** for them. *G4667*
Mt 24:20 **P** that your flight will not take place in *G4667*
Mt 26:36 "Sit here while I go over there and **p**." *G4667*
Mt 26:41 "Watch and **p** so that you will not fall into *G4667*
Mk 6:46 he went up on a mountainside *to* **p**. *G4667*
Mk 13:18 **P** that this will not take place in winter, *G4667*
Mk 14:32 said to his disciples, "Sit here while *I* **p**." *G4667*
Mk 14:38 Watch and **p** so that you will not fall into *G4667*
Lk 5:33 "John's disciples often fast and **p** *G1255+4472*
Lk 6:12 Jesus went out to a mountainside *to* **p**, *G4667*
Lk 6:28 curse you, **p** for those who mistreat you. *G4667*
Lk 9:28 him and went up onto a mountain *to* **p**. *G4667*
Lk 11: 1 teach us *to* **p**, just as John taught *G4667*
Lk 11: 2 said to them, "When *you* **p**, say: " 'Father, *G4667*
Lk 18: 1 they should always **p** and not give up. *G4667*
Lk 18:10 "Two men went up to the temple *to* **p**, one *G4667*
Lk 21:36 **p** that you may be able to escape all *G1289*
Lk 22:40 "**P** that you will not fall into temptation." *G4667*
Lk 22:46 "Get up and **p** so that you will not fall into *G4667*
Jn 17: 9 I **p** for them. I am not praying for the *G2263*
Jn 17:20 I **p** also for those who will believe in me NDT
Ac 8:22 of this wickedness and **p** to the Lord in the *G1289*
Ac 8:24 "**P** to the Lord for me so that nothing you *G1289*
Ac 10: 9 the city, Peter went up on the roof *to* **p**. *G4667*
Ac 21: 5 and there on the beach we knelt *to* **p**. *G4667*
Ac 26:29 *I* **p** to God *that* not only you but all who *G2377*
Ro 1:10 and *I* **p** that now at last by God's will the *G1289*
Ro 8:26 We do not know what *we* ought to **p** for *G4667*
Ro 15:31 **P** that I may be kept safe from the NDT
1Co 11:13 proper for a woman *to* **p** to God with her *G4667*
1Co 14:13 in a tongue *should* **p** that they may *G4667*
1Co 14:14 For if *I* **p** in a tongue, my spirit prays, but *G4667*
1Co 14:15 *I will* **p** with my spirit, but I will also pray *G4667*
1Co 14:15 but *I will* also **p** with my understanding *G4667*
2Co 13: 7 Now *we* **p** to God that you will not do *G2377*
Eph 1:18 I **p** that the eyes of your heart may be NDT
Eph 3:16 I **p** that out of his glorious riches he may NDT
Eph 3:17 And I **p** that you, being rooted and NDT
Eph 6:18 And **p** in the Spirit on all occasions with *G4667*
Eph 6:19 **P** also for me, that whenever I speak, words NDT
Eph 6:20 **P** that I may declare it fearlessly, as I should. NDT
Php 1: 4 all of you, *I* always **p** with joy *G1255+4472*
Col 1: 3 our Lord Jesus Christ, *when we* **p** for you, *G4667*
Col 4: 3 And **p** for us, too, that God may open a *G4667*
Col 4: 4 **P** that I may proclaim it clearly, as I should. NDT
1Th 3:10 Night and day *we* **p** most earnestly that we *G1289*
1Th 5:17 **p** continually, *G4667*
1Th 5:25 Brothers and sisters, **p** for us. *G4667*
2Th 1:11 this in mind, *we* constantly **p** for you, that *G4667*
2Th 1:12 We **p** this so that the name of our Lord Jesus NDT
2Th 3: 1 **p** for us that the message of the Lord may *G4667*
2Th 3: 2 And **p** that we may be delivered from wicked NDT
1Ti 2: 8 Therefore I want the men everywhere *to* **p**, *G4667*
1Ti 5: 5 night and day to **p** and to ask God for *G4666*
Phm 6 I **p** that your partnership with us in the faith NDT
Heb 13:18 **P** for us. We are sure that we have a clear *G4667*
Heb 13:19 urge you *to* **p** so that I may be *G4047+4472S*
Jas 5:13 you in trouble? *Let them* **p**. Is anyone *G4667*
Jas 5:14 of the church *to* **p** over them and anoint *G4667*
Jas 5:16 to each other and **p** for each other so that *G2377*
1Pe 4: 7 of sober mind so that you may **p**. *G4666*
1Jn 5:16 *you should* **p** and God will give them life. *G160*
1Jn 5:16 not saying that *you should* **p** about that. *G2263*
3Jn 2 *I* **p** that you may enjoy good health and *G2377*

PRAYED (68) [PRAY]

Ge 20:17 Then Abraham **p** to God, and God healed H7137
Ge 24:12 Then *he* **p**, "LORD, God of my master H606
Ge 25:21 Isaac **p** to the LORD on behalf of his wife H6983
Ge 32: 9 Then Jacob **p**, "O God of my father H606
Ex 8:30 Moses left Pharaoh and **p** to the LORD, H6983
Ex 10:18 then left Pharaoh and **p** to the LORD. H6983
Nu 11: 2 he **p** to the LORD and the fire died down. H7137
Nu 21: 7 So Moses **p** for the people. H7137
Dt 9:20 but at that time *I* **p** for Aaron too. H7137
Dt 9:26 *I* **p** to the LORD and said, "Sovereign LORD H7137
Jdg 13: 8 Then Manoah **p** to the LORD: "Pardon your H6983
Jdg 16:28 Then Samson **p** to the LORD, "Sovereign H7924
1Sa 1:10 In her deep anguish Hannah **p** to the LORD H7137
1Sa 1:27 *I* **p** for this child, and the LORD has granted H7137
1Sa 2: 1 Then Hannah **p** and said: "My heart H7137
1Sa 2:20 place of the *one* she **p for** and gave to the H8629
1Sa 8: 6 displeased Samuel; so he **p** to the LORD. H7137
1Sa 14:41 Then Saul **p** to the LORD, the God of Israel H606
2Sa 15:31 So David **p**, "LORD, turn Ahithophel's H606
1Ki 8:59 of mine, which *I have* **p** before the LORD H2858
1Ki 18:36 the prophet Elijah stepped forward and **p**: H606
1Ki 19: 4 sat down under it and **p** that he might die. H8626
2Ki 4:33 on the two of them and **p** to the LORD. H7137
2Ki 6:17 And Elisha **p**, "Open his eyes, LORD, so H7137
2Ki 6:18 toward him, Elisha **p** to the LORD, "Strike H7137
2Ki 19:15 And Hezekiah **p** to the LORD: "LORD, the H7137
2Ki 20: 2 his face to the wall and **p** to the LORD, H7137
2Ch 30:18 But Hezekiah **p** for them, saying, "May the H7137
2Ch 32:24 *He* **p** to the LORD, who answered him and H7137
2Ch 33:13 And when *he* **p** to him, the LORD was H7137
Ezr 9: 6 **p**: "I am too ashamed and disgraced H606
Ne 1: 4 fasted and **p** before the God of H7137
Ne 2: 4 Then *I* **p** to the God of heaven H7137
Ne 4: 9 But *we* **p** to our God and posted a guard H7137
Ne 6: 9 be completed." But I **p**, "Now strengthen my NDT
Job 42:10 After Job *had* **p** for his friends, the LORD H7137
Isa 37:15 And Hezekiah **p** to the LORD: H7137
Isa 37:21 Because *you have* **p** to me concerning H7137
Isa 38: 2 his face to the wall and **p** to the LORD, H7137
Jer 32:16 to Baruch son of Neriah, *I* **p** to the LORD: H7137
Da 6:10 a day he got down on his knees and **p**, A10612
Da 9: 4 *I* **p** to the LORD my God and confessed H7137
Jnh 2: 1 the fish Jonah **p** to the LORD his God. H7137
Jnh 4: 2 *He* **p** to the LORD, "Isn't this what I said H7137
Mt 26:39 he fell with his face to the ground and **p** *G4667*
Mt 26:42 He went away a second time and **p**, "My *G4667*
Mt 26:44 away once more and **p** the third time, *G4667*
Mk 1:35 went off to a solitary place, where *he* **p**. *G4667*
Mk 14:35 to the ground and **p** that if possible the *G4667*
Mk 14:39 he went away and **p** the same thing. *G4667*
Lk 5:16 often withdrew to lonely places and **p**. *G4667*
Lk 18:11 The Pharisee stood by himself and **p**: 'God *G4667*
Lk 22:32 But I *have* **p** for you, Simon, that your faith *G1289*
Lk 22:41 throw beyond them, knelt down and **p**, *G4667*
Lk 22:44 being in anguish, *he* **p** more earnestly *G4667*
Jn 17: 1 said this, he looked toward heaven and **p**: *G3306*
Ac 1:24 Then *they* **p**, "Lord, you know everyone's *G4667*
Ac 4:31 *After* they **p**, the place where they were *G1289*
Ac 6: 6 *who* **p** and laid their hands on them. *G4667*
Ac 7:59 were stoning him, Stephen **p**, "Lord Jesus, *G2126*
Ac 8:15 *they* **p** for the new believers there that *G4667*
Ac 9:40 then he got down on his knees and **p**. *G4667*
Ac 10: 2 to those in need and **p** to God regularly. *G1289*
Ac 13: 3 So after they had fasted and **p**, they *G4667*
Ac 20:36 he knelt down with all of them and **p**. *G4667*
Ac 27:29 anchors from the stern and **p** for daylight. *G2377*
Jas 5:17 *He* **p earnestly** that it would not *G4666+4667*
Jas 5:18 Again *he* **p**, and the heavens gave rain *G4667*

PRAYER (105) [PRAY]

Ge 25:21 The LORD **answered** his **p**, and his wife H6983
Ex 9:29 I will spread out my hands in **p** to the LORD. NDT
2Sa 7:27 has found courage to pray this **p** to you. H9525
2Sa 21:14 God **answered p** in behalf of the land. H6983
2Sa 24:25 Then the LORD **answered** his **p** in behalf of H6983
1Ki 8:28 to your servant's **p** and his plea for mercy, H9525
1Ki 8:28 Hear the cry and the **p** that your servant is H9525
1Ki 8:29 that you will hear the **p** your servant prays H9525
1Ki 8:38 when a **p** or plea is made by anyone H9525
1Ki 8:45 hear from heaven their **p** and their plea, H9525
1Ki 8:49 hear their **p** and their plea, and H9525
1Ki 9: 3 "I have heard the **p** and plea you have H9525
2Ki 19:20 I have heard *your* **p** concerning H7137
2Ki 20: 5 I have heard your **p** and seen your tears; H9525
2Ch 6:19 to your servant's **p** and his plea for mercy. H9525
2Ch 6:19 Hear the cry and the **p** that your servant is H9525
2Ch 6:20 May you hear the **p** your servant prays H9525
2Ch 6:29 when a **p** or plea is made by anyone H9525
2Ch 6:35 hear from heaven their **p** and their plea, H9525
2Ch 6:39 hear their **p** and their pleas, and H9525
2Ch 7:12 "I have heard your **p** and have chosen this H9525
2Ch 30:27 for their **p** reached heaven, his H9525
2Ch 32:20 of Amoz cried out *in* **p** *to* heaven about H7137
2Ch 33:18 including his **p** to his God and the words H9525
2Ch 33:19 His **p** and how God was moved by his H9525
Ezr 8:23 God about this, and *he* **answered** our **p**. H6983
Ne 1: 6 eyes open to hear the **p** your servant is H9525
Ne 1:11 be attentive to the **p** *of* this your servant H9525
Ne 1:11 servant and to the **p** *of* your servants who H9525
Ne 11:17 director who led in thanksgiving and **p**; H9525
Job 16:17 been free of violence and my **p** is pure. H9525
Job 42: 8 I will accept his **p** and not deal with you NDT
Job 42: 9 told them; and the LORD accepted Job's **p**. NDT
Ps 4: 1 have mercy on me and hear my **p**. H9525
Ps 6: 9 my cry for mercy; the LORD accepts my **p**. H9525
Ps 17: T A **p** of David. H9525
Ps 17: 1 Hear my **p**—it does not rise from H9525
Ps 17: 6 turn your ear to me and hear my **p**. H614
Ps 39:12 "Hear my **p**, LORD, listen to my cry for help H9525
Ps 42: 8 is with me—a **p** to the God of my life. H9525
Ps 54: 2 Hear my **p**, O God; listen to the words of H9525
Ps 55: 1 Listen to my **p**, O God, do not ignore my H9525
Ps 61: 1 Hear my cry, O God; listen to my **p**. H9525
Ps 65: 2 You who answer **p**, to you all people will H9525
Ps 66:19 has surely listened and heard my **p**. H9525
Ps 66:20 has not rejected my **p** or withheld his love H9525
Ps 84: 8 Hear my **p**, LORD God Almighty; listen to H9525
Ps 86: T A **p** of David. H9525
Ps 86: 6 Hear my **p**, LORD; listen to my cry for mercy. H9525
Ps 88: 2 May my **p** come before you; turn your ear H9525
Ps 88:13 in the morning my **p** comes before you. H9525
Ps 90: T A **p** of Moses the man of God. H9525
Ps 102: T A **p** of an afflicted person who has grown H9525
Ps 102: 1 Hear my **p**, LORD; let my cry for help come H9525
Ps 102:17 He will respond to the **p** *of* the destitute H9525
Ps 109: 4 they accuse me, but I am a man of **p**. H9525
Ps 141: 2 May my **p** be set before you like incense H9525
Ps 141: 5 my **p** will still be against the deeds of H9525
Ps 142: T When he was in the cave. A **p**. H9525
Ps 143: 1 hear my **p**, listen to my cry for mercy H9525
Pr 15: 8 the **p** *of* the upright pleases him. H9525
Pr 15:29 he hears the **p** *of* the righteous. H9525
Isa 1:15 When you spread out your hands in **p**, NDT
Isa 26:16 *they could* **barely whisper a p**. H4318+7440
Isa 38: 5 I have heard your **p** and seen your tears; H9525
Isa 56: 7 give them joy in my house of **p**. H9525
Isa 56: 7 will be called a house of **p** for all nations." H9525
La 3: 8 call out or cry for help, he shuts out my **p**. H9525
La 3:44 with a cloud so that no **p** can get through. H9525
Da 9: 3 pleaded with him in **p** and petition, H9525
Da 9:21 while I was still in **p**, Gabriel, the man I H9525
Jnh 2: 7 and my **p** rose to you, to your holy H9525
Hab 3: 1 A **p** of Habakkuk the prophet. H9525
Mt 21:13 " 'My house will be called a house *of* **p**,' *G4666*
Mt 21:22 you will receive whatever you ask for in **p**." *G4666*
Mk 9:29 "This kind can come out only by **p**." *G4666*
Mk 11:17 be called a house *of* **p** for all nations'? *G4666*
Mk 11:24 whatever you ask for *in* **p**, believe that you *G4667*
Lk 1:13 Zechariah; your **p** has been heard. *G1255*
Lk 19:46 " 'My house will be a house *of* **p**'; but you *G4666*
Lk 22:45 When he rose from **p** and went back to *G4666*
Jn 17:15 *My* **p** *is* not that you take them out of the *G2263*
Jn 17:20 "*My* **p** *is* not for them alone. I pray also *G2263*
Ac 1:14 They all joined together constantly *in* **p** *G4666*
Ac 2:42 to the breaking of bread and *to* **p**. *G4666*
Ac 3: 1 going up to the temple at the time *of* **p**— *G4666*
Ac 4:24 *they* **raised** their voices together *in* **p** *to* God. AIT
Ac 6: 4 give our attention *to* **p** and the ministry of *G4666*
Ac 10:31 God has heard your **p** and remembered *G4666*
Ac 14:23 each church and, with **p** and fasting *G4667*
Ac 16:13 where we expected to find a **place of p**. *G4666*
Ac 16:16 when we were going to the **place of p**, *G4666*
Ac 28: 8 to see him and, *after* **p**, placed his hands *G4667*
Ro 10: 1 my heart's desire and **p** to God for the *G1255*
Ro 12:12 in hope, patient in affliction, faithful *in* **p**. *G4666*
1Co 7: 5 so that you may devote yourselves to **p**. *G4666*
2Co 13: 9 and *our* **p** *is* that you may be fully restored *G2377*
Php 1: 9 And this *is my* **p**: that your love may *G4667*
Php 4: 6 in every situation, *by* **p** and petition, with *G4666*
Col 4: 2 Devote yourselves *to* **p**, being watchful *G4666*
Col 4:12 He is always wrestling in **p** for you, that *G4666*
1Ti 4: 5 is consecrated by the word of God and **p**. *G1950*
Jas 5:15 And the **p** offered in faith will make the *G2376*
Jas 5:16 The **p** of a righteous person is powerful *G1255*
1Pe 3:12 his ears are attentive to their **p**, *G1255*

PRAYERS (33) [PRAY]

1Ki 8:54 finished all these **p** and supplications to H9525
1Ch 5:20 He **answered** their **p**, because they trusted H6983
2Ch 6:40 attentive to the **p** *offered in* this place. H9525
2Ch 7:15 attentive to the **p** *offered in* this place. H9525
Ps 35:13 When my **p** returned to me unanswered H9525
Ps 72:20 This concludes the **p** *of* David son of H9525
Ps 80: 4 smolder against the **p** *of* your people? H9525
Ps 109: 7 and may his **p** condemn him. H9525
Pr 28: 9 instruction, even their **p** are detestable. H9525
Pr 31: 2 my son, the **answer to** my **p**! H5624
Isa 1:15 even when you offer many **p**, I am not H9525
Da 9:17 hear the **p** and petitions of your servant. H9525
Mk 12:40 houses and for a show **make** lengthy **p**. *G4667*
Lk 20:47 houses and for a show **make** lengthy **p**. *G4667*
Ac 10: 4 "Your **p** and gifts to the poor have come *G4666*
Ro 1:10 in my **p** at all times; and I pray that now at *G4666*
2Co 1:11 as you help us *by* your **p**. Then many will *G1255*
2Co 1:11 favor granted us in answer to the **p** of many. NDT
2Co 9:14 And *in* their **p** for you their hearts will go *G1255*
Eph 1:16 thanks for you, remembering you in my **p**. *G4666*
Eph 6:18 occasions with all kinds of **p** and requests. *G4666*
Php 1: 4 In all my **p** for all of you, I always pray *G1255*
Php 1:19 that through your **p** and God's provision of *G1255*
1Th 1: 2 you and continually mention you in our **p**. *G4666*
1Ti 2: 1 that petitions, **p**, intercession and *G4666*
2Ti 1: 3 day I constantly remember you in my **p**. *G1255*
Phm 4 thank my God as I remember you in my **p**, *G4666*
Phm 22 to be restored to you in answer to your **p**. *G4666*
Heb 5: 7 he offered up **p** and petitions with fervent *G1255*
1Pe 3: 7 so that nothing will hinder your **p**. *G4666*
Rev 5: 8 incense, which are the **p** of God's people. *G4666*
Rev 8: 3 to offer, *with* the **p** of all God's people *G4666*
Rev 8: 4 *together with* the **p** of God's people *G4666*

PRAYING (37) [PRAY]

Ge 24:15 Before he had finished **p**, Rebekah came H1819
Ge 24:45 "Before I finished **p** in my heart, Rebekah H1819
1Sa 1:12 As she kept on **p** to the LORD, Eli observed H7137
1Sa 1:13 Hannah *was* **p** in her heart, and her lips H1819
1Sa 1:16 *I have been* **p** here out of my great H1819
1Sa 1:26 who stood here beside you **p** to the LORD. H7137
1Ki 8:28 that your servant *is* **p** in your presence this H7137
1Ki 8:33 **p** and making supplication to you in this H7137
2Ch 6:19 that your servant *is* **p** in your presence. H7137
2Ch 6:24 **p** and making supplication before you in H7137
2Ch 7: 1 When Solomon finished **p**, fire came H7137

P

Ezr 10: 1 While Ezra *was* **p** and confessing H7137
Ne 1: 6 your servant *is* **p** before you day and H7137
Job 21:15 What would we gain by **p** to him?' H7003
Da 6:11 found Daniel **p** and asking God for A10114
Da 9:20 While I was speaking and **p**, confessing H7137
Mk 11:25 And when you stand **p**, if you hold G4667
Lk 1:10 the assembled worshipers were **p** outside. G4667
Lk 2:37 worshiped night and day, fasting and **p**. G1255
Lk 3:21 And *as he was* **p**, heaven was G4667
Lk 6:12 and spent the night **p** to God. G4666
Lk 9:18 Once when Jesus was **p** in private and his G4667
Lk 9:29 As he *was* **p**, the appearance of his face G4667
Lk 11: 1 One day Jesus was **p** in a certain place G4667
Jn 17: 9 *I am* not **p** for the world, but for those you G2263
Jn 18: 1 *When he had finished* **p**, Jesus left with G3306
Ac 9:11 man from Tarsus named Saul, for *he is* **p**. G4667
Ac 10:30 days ago I was in my house **p** at this hour, G4667
Ac 11: 5 "I was in the city of Joppa **p**, and in a G4667
Ac 12: 5 was earnestly **p** to God for him. G4666+1181
Ac 12:12 many people had gathered and *were* **p**. G4667
Ac 16:25 Paul and Silas *were* **p** and singing hymns G4667
Ac 22:17 to Jerusalem and *was* **p** at the temple, G4667
Ro 15:30 me in my struggle by **p** to God for me. G4666
Eph 6:18 always keep on **p** for all the Lord's G1255
Col 1: 9 about you, we have not stopped **p** for you. G4667
Jude 20 most holy faith and **p** in the Holy Spirit, G4667

PRAYS (9) [PRAY]

1Ki 8:29 prayer your servant **p** toward this place. H7137
2Ch 6:20 prayer your servant **p** toward this place. H7137
Isa 44:17 to it and worships. *He* **p** to it and says H7137
Da 6: 7 that anyone who **p** to any god A10114+10115
Da 6:12 days anyone who **p** to any god or human A10114
Da 6:13 *He still* **p** three times a day." A10114+10115
1Co 11: 4 Every man *who* **p** or prophesies with his G4667
1Co 11: 5 But every woman *who* **p** or prophesies with G4667
1Co 14:14 in a tongue, my spirit **p**, but my mind is G4667

PREACH (36) [PREACHED, PREACHER, PREACHES, PREACHING]

Eze 20:46 **p** against the south and prophesy against H5752
Eze 21: 2 Jerusalem and **p** against the sanctuary H5752
Jnh 1: 2 the great city of Nineveh and **p** against it, H7924
Mt 4:17 From that time on Jesus began *to* **p** G3062
Mt 11: 1 there to teach and **p** in the towns of G3062
Mt 23: 3 for they do not practice what *they* **p**. G3306
Mk 1:38 the nearby villages—so *I can* **p** there also. G3062
Mk 3:14 him and that he might send them out *to* **p** G3062
Mk 16:15 into all the world and **p** the gospel to all G3062
Ac 9:20 At once *he began to* **p** in the synagogues G3062
Ac 10:42 He commanded us *to* **p** to the people and G3062
Ac 14: 7 where they continued *to* **p the gospel**. G2294
Ac 16:10 had called us *to* **p the gospel** to them. G2294
Ac 20:20 have not hesitated *to* **p** anything that G334
Ro 1:15 I am so eager *to* **p the gospel** also to you G2294
Ro 2:21 You *who* **p** against stealing G3062
Ro 10:15 And how *can anyone* **p** unless they are G3062
Ro 15:20 my ambition *to* **p the gospel** where Christ G2294
1Co 1:17 to baptize, but *to* **p the gospel**—not with G2294
1Co 1:23 we **p** Christ crucified: a stumbling block G3062
1Co 9:14 that those *who* **p** the gospel should G2859
1Co 9:16 For when *I* **p the gospel**, I cannot boast G2294
1Co 9:16 I cannot boast, since I am compelled to **p**. NDT
1Co 9:16 Woe to me if *I do* not **p the gospel**! G2294
1Co 9:17 If *I* **p** voluntarily, I have a reward; G4047+4556S
1Co 15:11 this is what *we* **p**, and this is what G3062
2Co 2:12 to Troas to **p the gospel** of Christ and G2295
2Co 4: 5 For what *we* **p** is not ourselves, but Jesus G3062
2Co 10:16 *so that we can* **p the gospel** in the regions G2294
Gal 1: 8 from heaven *should* **p a gospel** other than G2294
Gal 1:16 in me so that *I might* **p** him among the G2294
Gal 2: 2 the gospel that *I* **p** among the Gentiles. G3062
Eph 3: 8 *to* **p** to the Gentiles the boundless riches G2294
Php 1:15 It is true that some **p** Christ out of envy G3062
Php 1:17 The former **p** Christ out of selfish ambition G2859
2Ti 4: 2 **P** the word; be prepared in season and out G3062

PREACHED (38) [PREACH]

Jer 28:16 because *you have* **p** rebellion against the H1819
Jer 29:32 because *he has* **p** rebellion against me. H1819
Mt 24:14 of the kingdom *will be* **p** in the whole G3062
Mt 26:13 wherever this gospel *is* **p** throughout the G3062
Mk 2: 2 the door, and *he* **p** the word to them. G3281
Mk 6:12 They went out and **p** that people should G3062
Mk 13:10 the gospel must first *be* **p** to all nations. G3062
Mk 14: 9 wherever the gospel *is* **p** throughout the G3062
Mk 16:20 the disciples went out and **p** everywhere, G3062
Lk 16:16 **the good news** of the kingdom of God *is being* **p** G2294
Lk 24:47 of sins *will be* **p** in his name to all G3062
Ac 8: 4 had been scattered **p** the word wherever G2294
Ac 9:27 in Damascus *he had* **p fearlessly** in the G4245
Ac 10:37 in Galilee after the baptism that John **p**— G3062
Ac 13:24 John **p** repentance and baptism to all the G4619
Ac 14:21 *They* **p the gospel** in that city and won a G2294
Ac 14:25 and *when they had* **p** the word in Perga G3281
Ac 15:21 law of Moses *has been* **p** in every G3062+2400
Ac 15:35 others taught and **p** the word of the Lord. G2294
Ac 15:36 all the towns where *we* **p** the word of the G2859
Ac 26:20 *I* **p** that they should repent and turn to God G550
1Co 1:21 foolishness *of* what was **p** to save those G3060
1Co 9:27 it my slave so that *after I have* **p** to others, G3062
1Co 15: 1 to remind you of the gospel *I* **p** to you, G2294
1Co 15: 2 if you hold firmly to the word *I* **p** to you. G2294
1Co 15:12 But if *it is* **p** that Christ has been raised G3062
2Co 1:19 Jesus Christ, who *was* **p** among you by us G3062
2Co 11: 4 a Jesus other than the Jesus *we* **p**, G3062
Gal 1: 8 a gospel other than the one *we* **p** to you, G2294
Gal 1:11 that the gospel I **p** is not of human origin. G2294
Gal 4:13 an illness *that I* first **p the gospel** to you, G2294
Eph 2:17 He came and **p** peace to you who were far G2294
Php 1:18 from false motives or true, Christ *is* **p**. G2859
1Th 2: 9 to anyone *while we* **p** the gospel of G3062
1Ti 3:16 seen by angels, *was* **p** among the nations G3062
1Pe 1:12 by those *who have* **p the gospel** to you by G2294
1Pe 1:25 And this is the word that *was* **p** to you. G2294
1Pe 4: 6 is the reason **the gospel** *was* **p** even to G2294

PREACHER (2) [PREACH]

1Co 9:18 full use of my rights as a **p of the gospel**. G2295
2Pe 2: 5 protected Noah, a **p** of righteousness, and G3061

PREACHES (2) [PREACH]

Ac 19:13 "In the name of the Jesus whom Paul **p**, G3062
2Co 11: 4 comes to you and **p** a Jesus other than G3062

PREACHING (29) [PREACH]

Ezr 6:14 prosper under the **p** *of* Haggai the A10452
Am 7:16 stop **p** against the descendants of H5752
Mt 3: 1 **p** in the wilderness of Judea G3062
Mt 12:41 they repented at the **p** of Jonah, and G3060
Mk 1: 4 **p** a baptism of repentance for the G3062
Mk 1:39 **p** in their synagogues and driving out G3062
Lk 3: 3 **p** a baptism of repentance for the G3062
Lk 4:44 And he kept on **p** in the synagogues of G3062
Lk 11:32 they repented at the **p** of Jonah; and G3060
Ac 8:25 **p the gospel** in many Samaritan villages. G2294
Ac 8:40 **p the gospel** in all the towns until he G2294
Ac 16: 6 by the Holy Spirit from **p** the word in the G3281
Ac 17:13 learned that Paul *was* **p** the word of God G2859
Ac 17:18 Paul *was* **p the good news** about Jesus G2294
Ac 18: 5 Paul devoted himself exclusively *to* **p** G3364
Ac 20:25 I have gone about **p** the kingdom will G3062
Ro 1: 9 in my spirit in **p the gospel** of his Son, G2295
Ro 10:14 they hear without *someone* **p** to them? G3062
1Co 2: 4 My message and my **p** were not with wise G3060
1Co 9:18 that *in* **p the gospel** I may offer it free of G2294
1Co 15:14 our **p** is useless and so is your faith. G3060
2Co 11: 7 to elevate you by **p** the gospel of God to G2294
Gal 1: 9 If anybody *is* **p** to you **a gospel** other than G2294
Gal 1:23 persecuted us *is* now **p** the faith he once G2294
Gal 2: 7 with the task *of* **p the gospel** to the G2295
Gal 5:11 if I *am* still **p** circumcision, why G3062
1Ti 4:13 reading of Scripture, *to* **p** and to teaching. G4155
1Ti 5:17 those whose work is **p** and teaching. G3364
Titus 1: 3 to light through the **p** entrusted to me by G3060

PRECEDE (1) [PRECEDED, PRECEDING]

1Th 4:15 *will* certainly not **p** those who have fallen G5777

PRECEDED (3) [PRECEDE]

2Ki 17: 2 kings of Israel who **p** him. H2118+4200+7156
2Ki 21:11 Amorites who **p** him and has led H4200+7156
Jer 28: 8 prophets who **p** you and me have H4200+7156

PRECEDING (1) [PRECEDE]

Ne 5:15 governors—those **p** me—placed a H4200+7156

PRECEPTS (27)

Dt 33:10 He teaches your **p** to Jacob and your law H5477
Ps 19: 8 The **p** *of* the LORD are right, giving joy to H7218
Ps 103:18 his covenant and remember to obey his **p**. H7218
Ps 105:45 they might keep his **p** and observe his H2976
Ps 111: 7 faithful and just; all his **p** are trustworthy. H7218
Ps 111:10 all who follow **his p** have good H2157S
Ps 119: 4 You have laid down **p** that are to be fully H7218
Ps 119:15 I meditate on your **p** and consider your H7218
Ps 119:27 me to understand the way of your **p**, H7218
Ps 119:40 How I long for your **p**! In your H7218
Ps 119:45 in freedom, for I have sought out your **p**. H7218
Ps 119:56 This has been my practice: I obey your **p**. H7218
Ps 119:63 all who fear you, to all who follow your **p**. H7218
Ps 119:69 with lies, I keep your **p** with all my heart. H7218
Ps 119:78 but I will meditate on your **p**. H7218
Ps 119:87 the earth, but I have not forsaken your **p**. H7218
Ps 119:93 I will never forget your **p**, for by them you H7218
Ps 119:94 I am yours; I have sought out your **p**. H7218
Ps 119:100 than the elders, for I obey your **p**. H7218
Ps 119:104 I gain understanding from your **p** H7218
Ps 119:110 me, but I have not strayed from your **p**. H7218
Ps 119:128 because I consider all your **p** right, H7218
Ps 119:134 oppression, that I may obey your **p**. H7218
Ps 119:141 and despised, I do not forget your **p**. H7218
Ps 119:159 See how I love your **p**; preserve my life H7218
Ps 119:168 I obey your **p** and your statutes, for all H7218
Ps 119:173 to help me, for I have chosen your **p**. H7218

PRECINCTS (1)

Eze 42:14 Once the priests enter the **holy p**, they are H7731

PRECIOUS (48)

Ge 30:20 "God has presented me with a **p** gift. H3202
Ex 28:17 Then mount four rows of **p** stones on it. NDT
Ex 39:10 they mounted four rows of **p** stones on it. NDT
Dt 33:13 his land with the **p** dew from heaven H4458
1Sa 26:21 Because you considered my life **p** today, H3700
2Sa 12:30 of gold, and it was set with **p** stones. H3701
1Ki 10: 2 of gold, and **p** stones—she came to H3701
1Ki 10:10 large quantities of spices, and **p** stones. H3701
1Ki 10:11 cargoes of almugwood and **p** stones. H3701
1Ch 20: 2 it was set with **p** stones—and it was H3701
1Ch 29: 8 Anyone who had **p** stones gave them to the NDT
2Ch 3: 6 He adorned the temple with **p** stones. H3701
2Ch 9: 1 of gold, and **p** stones—she came to H3701
2Ch 9: 9 large quantities of spices, and **p** stones. H3701
2Ch 9:10 also brought algumwood and **p** stones. H3701
2Ch 32:27 his silver and gold and for his **p** stones, H3701
Ezr 8:27 articles of polished bronze, as **p** as gold. H2776
Job 28:16 gold of Ophir, with **p** onyx or lapis lazuli. H3701
Job 29:24 the light of my face *was* **p** *to them*. H4202+5877
Ps 19:10 They *are* more **p** than gold, than much H2773
Ps 22:20 my **p life** from the power of the dogs. H3495
Ps 35:17 their ravages, my **p life** from these lions. H3495
Ps 72:14 violence, for **p** *is* their blood in his sight. H3700
Ps 116:15 **P** in the sight of the LORD is the death of H3701
Ps 119:72 your mouth is more **p** to me than H3202
Ps 133: 2 It is like **p** oil poured on the head H3202
Ps 139:17 How **p** to me are your thoughts, God! H3700
Pr 3:15 She is more **p** than rubies; nothing you H3701
Pr 8:11 wisdom is more **p** than rubies, and H3202
Isa 28:16 a **p** cornerstone for a sure foundation H3701
Isa 43: 4 Since *you are* **p** and honored in my sight H3700
Isa 54:12 and all your walls of **p** stones. H2914
La 4: 2 How the **p** children of Zion, once worth H3701
Eze 22:25 treasures and **p things** and make many H3702
Eze 27:22 finest of all kinds of spices and **p** stones, H3701
Eze 28:13 every **p** stone adorned you: H3701
Da 11:38 silver, with **p** stones and costly gifts. H3701
1Pe 1:19 with the **p** blood of Christ, a lamb G5508
1Pe 2: 4 chosen by God and **p** to him— G1952
1Pe 2: 6 a chosen and **p** cornerstone, and G1952
1Pe 2: 7 this stone is **p**. But to those who do G5507
2Pe 1: 1 Christ have received a faith **as p as** ours: G2700
2Pe 1: 4 given us his very great and **p** promises, G5508
Rev 17: 4 glittering with gold, **p** stones and pearls. G5508
Rev 18:12 of gold, silver, **p** stones and pearls; fine G5508
Rev 18:16 glittering with gold, **p** stones and pearls! G5508
Rev 21:11 brilliance was like that of a **very p** jewel, G5508
Rev 21:19 were decorated with every kind of **p** stone. G5508

PREDECESSOR (1) [PREDECESSORS]

1Ch 17:13 took it away from your **p**. H889+2118+4200+7156

PREDECESSORS (15) [PREDECESSOR]

Dt 19:14 stone set up by your **p** in the inheritance H8037
2Ki 12:18 all the sacred objects dedicated by his **p**— H3
2Ki 15: 9 in the eyes of the LORD, as his **p** had done. H3
2Ki 19:12 that were destroyed by my **p** deliver them— H3
2Ki 20:17 all that your **p** have stored up until this H3
2Ki 23:32 the eyes of the LORD, just as his **p** had done. H3
2Ki 23:37 the eyes of the LORD, just as his **p** had done. H3
2Ch 21:19 funeral fire in his honor, as they had for his **p**. H3
2Ch 32:13 know what I and my **p** have done to all the H3
2Ch 32:14 these nations that my **p** destroyed has been H3
2Ch 32:15 his people from my hand or the hand of my **p**. H3
Ezr 4:15 may be made in the archives of your **p**. A10003
Isa 37:12 that were destroyed by my **p** deliver them— H3
Isa 39: 6 all that your **p** have stored up until this H3
Jer 34: 5 people made a funeral fire in honor of your **p**, H3

PREDESTINED (4) [DESTINE]

Ro 8:29 God foreknew *he* also **p** to be conformed G4633
Ro 8:30 And those *he* **p**, he also called; those he G4633
Eph 1: 5 *he* **p** us for adoption to sonship through G4633
Eph 1:11 *having been* **p** according to the plan of G4633

PREDICTED (5) [PREDICTION]

1Sa 28:17 The LORD has done what *he* **p** through me H1819
Ac 7:52 even killed those *who* **p** the coming of the G4615
Ac 11:28 through the Spirit **p** *that* a severe famine G4955
Ac 16:16 had a spirit by **which** she **p the future**. G4780
1Pe 1:11 was pointing *when he* **p** the sufferings G4626

PREDICTING (2) [PREDICTION]

1Ki 22:13 exception are **p** success for the king. H1821
2Ch 18:12 exception are **p** success for the king. H1821

PREDICTION (1) [PREDICTED, PREDICTING, PREDICTIONS]

Jer 28: 9 sent by the LORD only if his **p** comes true." H1821

PREDICTIONS (2) [PREDICTION]

Isa 44:26 fulfills the **p** *of* his messengers, H6783
Isa 47:13 stargazers *who* **make p** month by month, H3359

PREEMINENT (1)

Est 10: 3 to King Xerxes, **p** among the Jews, and H1524

PREFECTS (4)

Da 3: 2 summoned the satraps, **p**, governors, A10505
Da 3: 3 So the satraps, **p**, governors, advisers A10505
Da 3:27 the satraps, **p**, governors and royal A10505
Da 6: 7 royal administrators, **p**, satraps, advisers A10505

PREFER (9) [PREFERENCE]

1Ki 21: 2 if you **p**, I will pay you H3202+928+6524
1Ki 21: 6 vineyard; or if you **p**, I will give you H2913
Job 7:15 so that I **p** strangling and death, rather H1047

Job 36:21 which you seem to p to affliction. H1047
Jer 8: 3 of this evil nation will p death to life, H1047
Eze 16:32 You p strangers to your own husband H4374
1Co 4:21 What do you p? Shall I come to you with a G2527
2Co 5: 8 and would p to be away from the G2305+3437
Phm 9 I p to appeal to you on the basis of G3437

PREFERENCE (1) [PREFER]
Dt 21:16 the wife he loves in p to his actual H6584+7156

PREGNANCY (2) [PREGNANT]
Hos 9:11 a bird—no birth, no p, no conception. H1061
Lk 1:26 In the sixth month of Elizabeth's p, God sent NDT

PREGNANT (40) [PREGNANCY]
Ge 4: 1 and she became p and gave birth to Cain. H2225
Ge 4:17 and she became p and gave birth to H2225
Ge 16: 4 When she knew she was p, she began to H2225
Ge 16: 5 now that she knows she is p, she H2225
Ge 16:11 "You are now p and you will give birth to H2226
Ge 19:36 Lot's daughters became p by their father. H2225
Ge 21: 2 Sarah became p and bore a son to H2225
Ge 25:21 and his wife Rebekah became p. H2225
Ge 29:32 Leah became p and gave birth to a son H2225
Ge 30: 5 she became p and bore him a son. H2225
Ge 30:17 and she became p and bore Jacob a fifth H2225
Ge 30:23 She became p and gave birth to a son H2225
Ge 38: 3 she became p and gave birth to a son H2225
Ge 38:18 slept with her, and she became p by him. H2225
Ge 38:24 prostitution, and as a result she is now p." H2226
Ge 38:25 "I am p by the man who owns these," H2226
Ex 2: 2 she became p and gave birth to a son. H2225
Ex 21:22 fighting and hit a p woman and she gives H2226
Lev 12: 2 'A woman who becomes p and gives birth H2445
Jdg 13: 3 but you are going to become p and give H2225
Jdg 13: 5 You will become p and have a son whose H2225
Jdg 13: 7 'You will become p and have a son. H2225
1Sa 1:20 of time Hannah became p and gave birth H2225
1Sa 4:19 was p and near the time of delivery. H2226
2Sa 11: 5 sent word to David, saying, "I am p." H2226
2Ki 4:17 But the woman became p, and the next H2225
2Ki 8:12 the ground, and rip open their p women." H2226
2Ki 15:16 ripped open all the p women. H2226
1Ch 7:23 and she became p and gave birth to a H2225
Ps 7:14 Whoever is p with evil conceives trouble H2473
Isa 26:17 As a p woman about to give birth writhes H2225
Hos 13:16 the ground, their p women ripped open." H2230
Am 1:13 ripped open the p women of Gilead in H2226
Mt 1:18 was found to be p through G1877+1143+2400
Mt 24:19 those days for p women and G1877+1143+2400
Mk 13:17 those days for p women and G1877+1143+2400
Lk 1:24 his wife Elizabeth became p and for five G5197
Lk 21:23 those days for p women and G1877+1143+2400
1Th 5: 3 labor pains on a p woman, G1877+1143+2400
Rev 12: 2 She was p and cried out in G1877+1143+2400

PREMATURELY (1) [MATURE]
Ex 21:22 and she gives birth p but there is H3655+3529

PREPARATION (8) [PREPARE]
Nu 11:18 'Consecrate yourselves in p for tomorrow H4200
Jos 7:13 'Consecrate yourselves in p for tomorrow; NDT
Mt 27:62 the one after P Day, the chief priests G4187
Mk 15:42 It was P Day (that is, the day before the G4187
Lk 23:54 It was P Day, and the Sabbath was about G4187
Jn 19:14 It was the day of P of the Passover; it was G4187
Jn 19:31 Now it was the day of P, and the next day G4187
Jn 19:42 it was the Jewish day of P and since the G4187

PREPARATIONS (11) [PREPARE]
1Ch 22: 5 Therefore I will make p for it." So David H3922
1Ch 22: 5 So David made extensive p before his H3922
2Ch 35:14 they made p for themselves and for the H3922
2Ch 35:14 So the Levites made p for themselves H3922
2Ch 35:15 their fellow Levites made the p for them. H3922
Mt 26:17 do you want us to make p for you to eat G2286
Mk 14:12 want us to go and make p for you to eat G2286
Mk 14:15 Make p for us there." G2286
Lk 10:40 by all the p that had to be made. G1355
Lk 22: 8 "Go and make p for us to eat the Passover G2286
Lk 22:12 upstairs, all furnished. Make p there." G2286

PREPARE (66) [PREPARATION, PREPARATIONS, PREPARED, PREPARES, PREPARING]
Ge 18: 7 gave it to a servant, who hurried to p it. H6913
Ge 27: 4 P me the kind of tasty food I like and bring H6913
Ge 27: 7 me some game and p me some tasty H6913
Ge 27: 9 so I can p some tasty food for your father H6913
Ge 43:16 slaughter an animal and p a meal; they H3922
Ex 12:16 except to p food for everyone to eat; that is H430
Ex 12:39 did not have time to p food for H6913
Ex 16: 5 the sixth day they are to p what they bring H3922
Ex 19:15 "P yourselves for the third day. H2118+3922
Lev 6:22 succeed him as anointed priest shall p it. H6913
Nu 15: 5 p a quarter of a hin of wine as a drink H6913
Nu 15: 6 " 'With a ram p a grain offering of H6913
Nu 15: 8 " 'When you p a young bull as a burnt H6913
Nu 15:12 Do this for each one, for as many as you p. H6913
Nu 23: 1 p seven bulls and seven rams for me." H3922
Nu 23:29 p seven bulls and seven rams for me." H3922
Jdg 13:15 you to stay until we p a young goat for H6913
Jdg 13:16 But if you p a burnt offering, offer it to the H6913
2Sa 12: 4 own sheep or cattle to p a meal for the H6913
2Sa 13: 5 Let her p the food in my sight so I may H6913
2Sa 13: 7 brother Amnon and p some food for him." H6913
1Ki 18:23 I will p the other bull and put it on the H6913
1Ki 18:25 "Choose one of the bulls and p it first H6913
1Ki 20:12 he ordered his men: "P to attack." So they H8492
2Ki 20: 7 Then Isaiah said, "P a poultice of figs." H4374
1Ch 22: 2 stonecutters to p dressed stone for H2933
2Ch 31:11 gave orders to p storerooms in the H3922
2Ch 35: 4 P yourselves by families in your divisions H3922
2Ch 35: 6 yourselves and p the lambs for your fellow H3922
Est 5: 8 tomorrow to the banquet I will p for them. H6913
Ps 23: 5 You p a table before me in the presence H6885
Isa 8: 9 P for battle, and be shattered H273
Isa 8: 9 P for battle, and be shattered H273
Isa 14:21 P a place to slaughter his children for the H3922
Isa 25: 6 the LORD Almighty will p a feast of rich H6913
Isa 38:21 "P a poultice of figs and apply it to the H5951
Isa 40: 3 "In the wilderness p the way for the LORD H7155
Isa 57:14 build up, p the road! Remove the H7155
Isa 62:10 P the way for the people H7155
Jer 6: 4 "P for battle against her! Arise, let us H7727
Jer 46: 3 "P your shields, both large and small, and H6885
Jer 51:12 station the watchmen, p an ambush! H3922
Jer 51:27 P the nations for battle against her H7727
Jer 51:28 P the nations for battle against her—the H7727
Eze 7:23 " 'P chains! For the land is full of H6913
Da 11:10 His sons will p for war and assemble a H1741
Joel 3: 9 among the nations: P for war! Rouse the H7727
Am 4:12 do this to you, Israel, p to meet your God." H3922
Mic 3: 5 p to wage war against anyone who H7727
Na 1:14 I will p your grave, for you H8492
Mal 3: 1 who will p the way before me. H7155
Mt 3: 3 in the wilderness, 'P the way for the Lord G2286
Mt 11:10 who will p your way before you. G2941
Mt 26:12 on my body, she did it to p me for burial. G4472
Mk 1: 2 ahead of you, who will p your way"— G2941
Mk 1: 3 in the wilderness, 'P the way for the Lord G2286
Mk 14: 8 on my body beforehand to p for my burial. AIT
Lk 1:76 on before the Lord to p the way for him, G2286
Lk 3: 4 in the wilderness, 'P the way for the Lord G2286
Lk 7:27 who will p your way before you. G2941
Lk 17: 8 Won't he rather say, 'P my supper, get G2286
Lk 22: 9 "Where do you want us to p for it?" they G2286
Jn 14: 2 that I am going there to p a place for you? G2286
Jn 14: 3 And if I go and p a place for you, I will G2286
Phm 22 P a guest room for me, because I hope to G2286
Rev 16:12 was dried up to p the way for the kings G2286

PREPARED (79) [PREPARE]
Ge 18: 8 milk and the calf that had been p, H6913
Ge 19: 3 He p a meal for them, baking bread H6913
Ge 24:31 I have p the house and a place for the H7155
Ge 27:14 his mother, and she p some tasty food H6913
Ge 27:31 He too p some tasty food and brought it to H6913
Ge 43:25 They p their gifts for Joseph's arrival at H3922
Ex 23:20 to bring you to the place I have p. H3922
Lev 2: 5 If your grain offering is p on a griddle, it is NDT
Lev 6:21 It must be p with oil on a griddle; bring it H6913
Lev 10:12 offerings p without yeast and presented H5174
Nu 15:11 young goat, is to be p in this manner. H6913
Nu 23: 4 Balaam said, "I have p seven altars, and H6885
Jos 24: 9 the king of Moab, p to fight against Israel H7756
Jdg 6: 2 the Israelites p shelters for themselves in H6913
Jdg 6:19 Gideon went inside, p a young goat, and H6913
Jdg 19: 5 day they got up early and he p to leave, H7756
Ru 1: 6 daughters-in-law p to return home from H7756
2Sa 3:20 David p a feast for him and his men. H6913
2Sa 12: 4 to the poor man and p it for the one who H6913
2Sa 13:10 took the bread she had p and brought it H6913
1Ki 5:18 from Byblos cut and p the timber and H3922
1Ki 6:19 He p the inner sanctuary within the H3922
1Ki 18:26 So they took the bull given them and p it H6913
1Ki 20:12 So they p to attack the city. H8492
2Ki 6:23 So he p a great feast for them, and H4127+4130
1Ch 12:33 soldiers p for battle with every H6885
1Ch 12:36 experienced soldiers p for battle—40,000; H6885
1Ch 15: 1 he p a place for the ark of God and H3922
1Ch 15: 3 ark of the LORD to the place he had p for it. H3922
1Ch 15:12 God of Israel, to the place I have p for it. H3922
2Ch 1: 4 Kiriath Jearim to the place he had p for it, H3922
2Ch 29:19 We have p and consecrated all the articles H3922
Ezr 1: 5 p to go up and build the house of the LORD H7756
Ne 5:18 sheep and some poultry were p for me, H6913
Ne 8:10 send some to those who have nothing p. H3922
Est 5: 4 come today to a banquet I have p for him." H6913
Est 5: 5 Haman went to the banquet Esther had p. H6913
Est 6:14 away to the banquet Esther had p. H6913
Job 13:18 Now that I have p my case, I know I will H6885
Ps 7:13 He has p his deadly weapons; he makes H3922
Ps 78:50 He p a path for his anger; he did not H7142
Pr 9: 2 She has p her meat and mixed her wine H3180
Pr 19:29 Penalties are p for mockers, and beatings H3922
SS 3: 8 at his side, p for the terrors of the night. NDT
Isa 13: 3 I have commanded those I p for battle; H7727
Isa 30:33 Topheth has long been p; it has been H6885
Eze 28:13 on the day you were created they were p. H3922
Eze 38: 7 " 'Get ready; be p, you and all the hordes H3922
Zep 1: 7 The LORD has p a sacrifice; he has H3922
Mt 20:23 whom they have been p by my Father." G2286
Mt 22: 2 is like a king who p a wedding banquet G4472
Mt 22: 4 been invited that I have p my dinner: G2286
Mt 25:34 the kingdom p for you since the creation G2286
Mt 25:41 into the eternal fire p for the devil and his G2286
Mt 26:19 had directed them and p the Passover. G2286
Mk 10:40 to those for whom they have been p." G2286
Mk 14:16 had told them. So they p the Passover. G2286
Lk 1:17 to make ready a people p for the Lord." G2941
Lk 2:31 which you have p in the sight of all G2286
Lk 12:20 who will get what you have p for yourself? G2286
Lk 22:13 had told them. So they p the Passover. G2286
Lk 23:56 they went home and p spices and G2286
Lk 24: 1 the spices they had p and went to the G2286
Jn 19:19 Pilate had a notice p and fastened to G1211S
Ac 10:10 and while the meal was being p, he G4186
Ro 9:22 objects of his wrath—p for destruction? G2936
Ro 9:23 whom he p in advance for glory— G4602
1Co 2: 9 the things God has p for those who love G2286
Eph 2:10 which God p in advance for us to do. G4602
2Ti 2:21 to the Master and p to do any good work. G2286
2Ti 4: 2 word; be p in season and out of season G2392
Heb 10: 5 did not desire, but a body you p for me; G2936
Heb 11:16 their God, for he has p a city for them. G2286
1Pe 3:15 Always be p to give an answer to G2289
Rev 8: 6 had the seven trumpets p to sound them. G2286
Rev 9: 7 The locusts looked like horses p for battle G2286
Rev 12: 6 wilderness to a place p for her by God, G2286
Rev 12:14 fly to the place p for her in the wilderness, AIT
Rev 21: 2 p as a bride beautifully dressed for her G2286

PREPARES (2) [PREPARE]
Ps 85:13 goes before him and p the way for his H8492
Isa 44:16 in the fire; over it he p his meal, he roasts H430

PREPARING (9) [PREPARE]
1Ch 9:32 were in charge of p for every Sabbath the H3922
Jer 18:11 I am p a disaster for you and devising a H3670
Eze 39:17 all around to the sacrifice I am p for you, H2284
Eze 39:19 At the sacrifice I am p for you, you will eat H2284
Am 7: 1 He was p swarms of locusts after the H3670
Mt 4:21 with their father Zebedee, p their nets. G2936
Mk 1:19 his brother John in a boat, p their nets. G2936
Lk 14:16 "A certain man was p a great banquet G4472
Ac 25: 3 for they were p an ambush to kill him G4472

PRESBYTERY (KJV) BODY OF ELDERS

PRESCRIBED (23)
Lev 5:10 offering in the p way and make H5477
Lev 9:16 burnt offering and offered it in the p way. H5477
Nu 15:24 along with its p grain offering and drink H5477
1Sa 2:29 offering that I p for my dwelling? H7422
1Ch 15:13 of him about how to do it in the p way." H5477
1Ch 23:31 proper number and in the way p for them. H5477
1Ch 24:19 to the regulations p for them by their H5477
2Ch 4:20 to burn in front of the inner sanctuary as p; H5477
2Ch 29:25 lyres in the way p by David and Gad H5184
2Ch 30:16 regular positions as p in the Law of Moses H5477
2Ch 35:13 the Passover animals over the fire as p, H5477
2Ch 35:15 were in the places p by David, Asaph, H5184
Ezr 3: 4 of burnt offerings p for each day. H3869+5477
Ezr 3:10 as p by David king of Israel. H6584+3338
Ezr 7:23 the God of heaven has p, A10427+10302
Ne 12:24 the other, as p by David the man of God. H5184
Ne 12:36 with musical instruments p by David the man AIT
Ne 13: 5 new wine and olive oil p for the Levites H5184
Est 2:12 of beauty treatments p for the women, H2017
Est 9:27 in the way p and at the time appointed. H4181
Job 36:23 Who has p his ways for him, or said to H7212
Eze 45:14 The p portion of olive oil, measured by the H2976
Heb 8: 4 priests who offer the gifts p by the law. G2848

PRESENCE (204) [PRESENT]
Ge 4:14 I will be hidden from your p; I will be H7156
Ge 4:16 from the LORD's p and lived in the H4200+7156
Ge 23:11 I give it to you in the p of my people. H6524
Ge 23:18 as his property in the p of all the Hittites H6524
Ge 27: 7 my blessing in the p of the LORD before I H7156
Ge 27:30 Jacob had scarcely left his father's p H7156
Ge 31:32 In the p of our relatives, see for yourself H5584
Ge 31:35 that I cannot stand up in your p; I'm H7156
Ge 40:20 the chief baker in the p of his officials: H9348
Ge 41:46 out from Pharaoh's p and traveled H4200+7156
Ge 45: 1 "Have everyone leave my p! H4946+6584
Ge 45: 3 because they were terrified at his p. H7156
Ge 47:10 Pharaoh and went out from his p. H4200+7156
Ex 7:20 his staff in the p of Pharaoh and his H6524
Ex 9: 8 toss it into the air in the p of Pharaoh. H6524
Ex 10:11 Aaron were driven out of Pharaoh's p. H7156
Ex 18:12 with Moses' father-in-law in the p of God. H7156
Ex 25:30 Put the bread of the P on this table to be H7156
Ex 28:30 he enters the p of the LORD. H4200+7156
Ex 29:11 it in the LORD's p at the entrance to the H7156
Ex 33:14 LORD replied, "My P will go with you, and H7156
Ex 33:15 said to him, "If your P does not go with us H7156
Ex 33:19 proclaim my name, the LORD, in your p. H7156
Ex 34:34 the LORD's p to speak with him, H4200+7156
Ex 35:13 all its articles and the bread of the P; H7156
Ex 35:20 withdrew from Moses' p, H4200+7156
Ex 39:36 with all its articles and the bread of the P; H7156
Lev 9:24 out from the p of the LORD and H4200+7156
Lev 10: 2 out from the p of the LORD and H4200+7156
Lev 19:32 " 'Stand up in the p of the aged, show H7156
Lev 22: 3 person must be cut off from my p. H4200+7156
Nu 4: 7 the table of the P they are to spread a H7156
Nu 6: 9 dies suddenly in the Nazirite's p, H6584

Nu 6:11 by being **in the p of** the dead body. H6584
Nu 17: 9 from the LORD's **p** to all the H7156
Nu 19: 3 the camp and slaughtered in his **p**. H7156
Nu 20: 9 took the staff from the LORD's **p**, H4200+7156
Nu 27:19 assembly and commission him in their **p**. H6524
Dt 4:37 out of Egypt by his **P** and his great H7156
Dt 12: 7 in the **p** *of* the LORD your God, you H7156
Dt 12:18 to eat them in the **p** *of* the LORD your God H7156
Dt 14:23 flocks in the **p** *of* the LORD your God at H7156
Dt 14:26 eat there in the **p** *of* the LORD your God H7156
Dt 15:20 to eat them in the **p** *of* the LORD your God H7156
Dt 18: 7 who serve there in the **p** *of* the LORD. H7156
Dt 19:17 must stand in the **p** *of* the LORD before the H7156
Dt 25: 2 them flogged in his **p** with the number of H7156
Dt 25: 9 shall go up to him in the **p** *of* the elders, H6524
Dt 27: 7 rejoicing in the **p** *of* the LORD your God. H7156
Dt 29:10 today in the **p** *of* the LORD your God— H7156
Dt 29:15 with us today in the **p** *of* the LORD our God H7156
Dt 31: 7 said to him in the **p** *of* all Israel, H6524
Dt 32:51 faith with me in the **p** *of* the Israelites at H9348
Jos 8:32 in the **p** *of* the Israelites, Joshua H7156
Jos 10:12 Joshua said to the LORD in the **p** *of* Israel: H6524
Jos 18: 6 lots for you in the **p** *of* the LORD our God. H7156
Jos 18: 8 you here at Shiloh in the **p** *of* the LORD." H7156
Jos 18:10 them in Shiloh in the **p** *of* the LORD, H7156
Jos 19:51 by lot at Shiloh in the **p** *of* the LORD at the H7156
Ru 4: 4 that you buy it **in the p of** these seated H5584
Ru 4: 4 seated here and **in the p of** the elders of H5584
1Sa 2:21 boy Samuel grew up **in the p of** the LORD. H6640
1Sa 2:28 incense, and to wear an ephod in my **p**. H7156
1Sa 6:20 "Who can stand in the **p** *of* the LORD, this H7156
1Sa 11:15 made Saul king in the **p** *of* the LORD. H7156
1Sa 12: 3 against me **in the p of** the LORD and his H5584
1Sa 16:13 anointed him in the **p** *of* his brothers, H7931
1Sa 19:24 he too prophesied in Samuel's **p**. H7156
1Sa 21: 6 the bread of the **P** that had been removed H7156
1Sa 21:13 So he pretended to be insane in their **p** H6524
1Sa 26:20 to the ground far from the **p** *of* the LORD. H7156
2Sa 3:13 *Do* not **come into** my **p** unless H8011+906+7156
2Sa 22:13 the brightness of his **p** bolts of lightning H5584
2Sa 24: 4 so they left the **p** *of* the king to H4200+7156
1Ki 1:28 she came *into* the king's **p** and H4200+7156
1Ki 7:48 table on which was the bread of the **P**; H7156
1Ki 8: 1 summoned **into** his **p** at Jerusalem H448
1Ki 8:28 your servant is praying in your **p** this day. H7156
1Ki 19:11 on the mountain in the **p** *of* the LORD, H7156
2Ki 3:14 respect for the **p** *of* Jehoshaphat king of H7156
2Ki 5:27 from Elisha's **p** and his skin was H4200+7156
2Ki 13:23 destroy them or banish them from his **p**. H7156
2Ki 17:18 with Israel and removed them from his **p**. H7156
2Ki 17:20 until he thrust them from his **p**. H7156
2Ki 17:23 the LORD removed them from his **p**, as H7156
2Ki 22:10 Shaphan read from it in the **p** *of* the king. H7156
2Ki 22:19 you tore your robes and wept in my **p**, H7156
2Ki 23: 3 the covenant in the **p** *of* the LORD— H7156
2Ki 23:27 Judah also from my **p** as I removed Israel, H7156
2Ki 24: 3 them from his **p** because of the sins H7156
2Ki 24:20 in the end he thrust them from his **p**. H7156
1Ch 12: 1 banished from the **p** *of* Saul son of Kish H7156
1Ch 24: 6 their names in the **p** *of* the king and of H7156
1Ch 24:31 in the **p** *of* King David and of Zadok H7156
1Ch 29:10 the LORD in the **p** *of* the whole assembly, H6524
1Ch 29:22 great joy in the **p** *of* the LORD that day. H7156
2Ch 4:19 tables on which was the bread of the **P**; H7156
2Ch 6:19 that your servant is praying in your **p**. H7156
2Ch 20: 9 we will stand in your **p** before this temple H7156
2Ch 26:19 at the priests in their **p** before the incense H7156
2Ch 28:14 plunder in the **p** *of* the officials and H7156
2Ch 34:18 Shaphan read from it in the **p** *of* the king. H7156
2Ch 34:24 been read in the **p** *of* the king of Judah. H7156
2Ch 34:27 me and tore your robes and wept in my **p**, H7156
2Ch 34:31 the covenant in the **p** *of* the LORD— H7156
Ezr 4:18 has been read and translated **in** my **p**. A10621
Ezr 9:15 of it not one of us can stand in your **p**." H7156
Ne 1:11 by granting him favor in the **p** *of* this man." H7156
Ne 2: 1 I had not been sad in his **p** before, H7156
Ne 4: 2 in the **p** *of* his associates and the H7156
Ne 8: 3 the Water Gate **in the p of** the men, H5584
Est 1:16 replied in the **p** *of* the king and the H7156
Est 1:19 again to enter the **p** *of* King Xerxes. H4200+7156
Est 2:23 book of the annals in the **p** *of* the king. H7156
Est 3: 7 was cast in the **p** *of* Haman to select a H7156
Est 4: 8 her to go **into** the king's **p** to beg for mercy H448
Est 5: 9 he neither rose nor showed fear **in** his **p**, H4946
Est 8: 1 And Mordecai came into the **p** *of* the king, H7156
Est 8:15 When Mordecai left the king's **p** H4200+7156
Job 1:12 Satan went out from the **p** *of* the LORD. H7156
Job 2: 7 went out from the **p** *of* the LORD and H7156
Job 30:11 they throw off restraint in my **p**. H7156
Ps 5: 5 cannot stand **in** your **p**. H4200+5584+6524
Ps 9:19 let the nations be judged in your **p**. H7156
Ps 16:11 you will fill me with joy in your **p**, with H7156
Ps 18:12 the brightness of his **p** clouds advanced, H5584
Ps 21: 6 made him glad with the joy of your **p**. H7156
Ps 23: 5 table before me **in the p of** my enemies. H5584
Ps 31:20 the shelter of your **p** you hide them from H7156
Ps 39: 1 on my mouth while **in the p of** the wicked." H5584
Ps 41:12 uphold me and set me in your **p** forever. H7156
Ps 51:11 me from your **p** or take your Holy H4200+7156
Ps 52: 9 always praise you **in the p of** your faithful H5584
Ps 61: 7 May he be enthroned in God's **p** forever H7156
Ps 89:15 who walk in the light of your **p**, LORD. H7156
Ps 90: 8 our secret sins in the light of your **p**. H7156
Ps 101: 7 falsely will stand **in** my **p**. H4200+5584+6524
Ps 102:28 children of your servants will live in your **p**; NDT
Ps 114: 7 at the **p** *of* the Lord, at the H4200+7156
Ps 114: 7 at the **p** *of* the God of Jacob H4200+7156
Ps 116:14 to the LORD **in the p of** all his H5584+2025
Ps 116:18 to the LORD **in the p of** all his H5584+2025
Ps 139: 7 Where can I flee from your **p**? H7156
Ps 140:13 and the upright will live **in** your **p**. H907+7156
Pr 8:30 day after day, rejoicing always in his **p**, H7156
Pr 14:19 will bow down in the **p** *of* the good, H7156
Pr 18:16 ushers the giver into the **p** *of* the great. H7156
Pr 25: 5 remove wicked officials from the king's **p** H7156
Pr 25: 6 Do not exalt yourself in the king's **p**, and H7156
Ecc 8: 3 Do not be in a hurry to leave the king's **p** H7156
Isa 2:10 ground from the **fearful p** *of* the LORD and H7065
Isa 2:19 ground from the **fearful p** *of* the LORD and H7065
Isa 2:21 crags from the **fearful p** *of* the LORD and H7065
Isa 3: 8 against the LORD, defying his glorious **p**. H6524
Isa 26:17 in her pain, so were we in your **p**, LORD. H7156
Isa 63: 9 the angel of his **p** saved them. H7156
Jer 5:22 "Should you not tremble in my **p**? I made H7156
Jer 7:15 I will thrust you from my **p**, just as I did all H7156
Jer 15: 1 Send them away from my **p**! Let them go! H7156
Jer 23:39 cast you out of my **p** along with the city I H7156
Jer 28: 1 of the LORD in the **p** *of* the priests and all H6524
Jer 32:12 in the **p** *of* my cousin Hanamel and of the H6524
Jer 32:13 "In their **p** I gave Baruch these instructions H6524
Jer 52: 3 in the end he thrust them from his **p**. H7156
La 2:19 like water **in the p of** the Lord. H5790+7156
Eze 28: 9 am a god," in the **p** *of* those who kill you? H7156
Eze 38:20 the face of the earth will tremble at my **p**. H7156
Eze 44: 3 the gateway to eat in the **p** *of* the LORD. H7156
Eze 44:12 served them in the **p** *of* their idols and H7156
Eze 46: 3 are to worship in the **p** *of* the LORD at the H7156
Da 4: 8 came into my **p** and I told him the A10621
Da 7:13 Ancient of Days and was led **into** his **p**. A10621
Hos 6: 2 will restore us, that we may live in his **p**. H7156
Na 1: 5 The earth trembles at his **p**, the world H7156
Zec 6: 5 from standing **in the p of** the Lord of the H6584
Mal 3:16 was written in his **p** concerning those who H7156
Mk 7:24 yet he could not keep his **p** secret. NDT
Lk 1:19 I stand **in the p** of God, and I have been *G1967*
Lk 8:47 **In the p of** all the people, she told why *G1967*
Lk 14:10 will be honored **in the p of** all the other *G1967*
Lk 15:10 is rejoicing **in the p of** the angels of God *G1967*
Lk 23:14 examined him **in** your **p** and have found *G1967*
Lk 24:43 he took it and ate it **in** their **p**. *G1967*
Jn 8:38 you what I have seen **in** the Father's **p**, *G4123*
Jn 12:37 had performed so many signs **in** their **p**, *G1869*
Jn 17: 5 glorify me **in** your **p** with the glory I had *G4123*
Jn 20:30 many other signs **in the p of** his disciples, *G1967*
Ac 2:28 you will fill me with joy in your **p**. *G4725*
Ac 10:33 we are all here **in the p of** God to listen to *G1967*
Ac 24:21 one thing I shouted as I stood **in** their **p**: *G1877*
Php 2:12 not only in my **p**, but now much more in *G4242*
1Th 2:19 we will glory **in the p of** our Lord Jesus *G1869*
1Th 3: 9 the joy we have **in the p of** our God *G1869*
1Th 3:13 holy **in the p of** our God and *G1869*
2Th 1: 9 shut out from the **p** of the Lord and from *G4725*
1Ti 6:12 confession **in the p of** many witnesses *G1967*
2Ti 2: 2 heard me say **in the p of** many witnesses *G1328*
2Ti 4: 1 **In the p of** God and of Christ Jesus, who *G1967*
Heb 9:24 now to appear for us *in* God's **p**. *G4725*
1Jn 3:19 how we set our hearts at rest **in** his **p**: *G1869*
Jude 24 you before his **glorious** *p* without fault and AIT
Rev 7:15 throne *will* **shelter** them **with** *his* **p**. *G5012+2093*
Rev 14:10 burning sulfur **in the p of** the holy angels *G1967*
Rev 20:11 earth and the heavens fled from his **p**, *G4725*

PRESENT (154) [EVER-PRESENT, PRESENCE, PRESENTABLE, PRESENTED, PRESENTING, PRESENTS]

Ge 33:11 Please accept the **p** that was brought to H1388
Ex 10:25 burnt offerings *to* **p** to the LORD our God H6913
Ex 22:14 is injured or dies while the owner is not **p**, H6640
Ex 29: 3 in a basket and **p** them along with the H7928
Ex 34: 2 **P yourself** to me there on top of the H5893
Lev 1: 3 *You must* **p** it at the entrance to the tent H7928
Lev 2: 8 things to the LORD; **p** it to the priest, who H7928
Lev 3: 1 *you are to* **p** before the LORD an animal H7928
Lev 3: 7 a lamb, *you are to* **p** it before the LORD, H7928
Lev 3:12 is a goat, *you are to* **p** it before the LORD H7928
Lev 3:14 From what you offer *you are to* **p** this food H7928
Lev 4: 4 *He is to* **p** the bull at the entrance to the H995
Lev 4:14 as a sin offering and **p** it before the tent of H995
Lev 6: 5 owner on the day they **p** their guilt offering. NDT
Lev 6:21 it well-mixed and **p** the grain offering H7928
Lev 7:11 offering *anyone may* **p** to the LORD: H7928
Lev 7:13 of thanksgiving *they are to* **p** an offering H7928
Lev 7:30 their own hands *they are to* **p** the food H995
Lev 9: 2 and **p** them before the LORD. H7928
Lev 13:19 *they must* **p themselves** to the priest. H8011
Lev 14:11 them clean *shall* **p** both the one to be H6641
Lev 16: 7 the two goats and **p** them before the LORD H6641
Lev 17: 4 tent of meeting to **p** it as an offering to H7928
Lev 18:23 A woman *must* not **p** *herself* to an animal H6641
Lev 21: 6 they **p** the food offerings *to* the LORD, H7928
Lev 21:21 near to **p** the food offerings *to* the LORD. H7928
Lev 22:15 offerings the Israelites **p** to the LORD H8123
Lev 22:19 you must **p** a male without defect from the NDT
Lev 22:23 *You may*, however, **p** as a freewill offering H6913
Lev 23: 8 For seven days **p** a food offering to the H7928
Lev 23:16 then **p** an offering of new grain to the H7928
Lev 23:18 **P** with this bread seven male lambs, each H7928
Lev 23:25 but **p** a food offering to the LORD. H7928
Lev 23:27 **p** a food offering to the LORD. H7928
Lev 23:36 For seven days **p** food offerings to the LORD H7928
Lev 23:36 sacred assembly and **p** a food offering to H7928
Nu 3: 6 the tribe of Levi and **p** them to Aaron the H6641
Nu 6:14 There *they are to* **p** their offerings to the H7928
Nu 6:16 " 'The priest *is to* **p** all these before the H7928
Nu 6:17 He *is to* **p** the basket of unleavened bread H6913
Nu 8:11 Aaron *is to* **p** the Levites before the LORD as H5677
Nu 8:13 his sons and then **p** them as a wave H5677
Nu 15: 3 and *you* **p** to the LORD food offerings from H6913
Nu 15: 4 brings an offering *shall* **p** to the LORD a H7928
Nu 15:13 in this way when *they* **p** a food offering as H7928
Nu 15:19 **p a portion** as an offering to the LORD. H8123
Nu 15:20 **P** a loaf from the first of your ground H8123+9556
Nu 15:20 your ground meal and **p** it as an offering H8123
Nu 16:17 censers in all—and **p** it before the LORD. H7928
Nu 16:17 You and Aaron are to **p** your censers also." NDT
Nu 18:19 the Israelites **p** to the LORD I give to H8123
Nu 18:24 that the Israelites **p** as an offering to the H8123
Nu 18:26 *you must* **p** a tenth of that tithe as the H8123
Nu 18:28 this way you also *will* **p** an offering to the H8123
Nu 18:29 *You must* **p** as the LORD's portion the best H8123
Nu 18:30 'When you **p** the best part, it will be H8123
Nu 28: 2 'Make sure that *you* **p** to me at the H7928
Nu 28: 3 the food offering *you are to* **p** to the LORD: H7928
Nu 28:11 **p** to the LORD a burnt offering of two young H7928
Nu 28:19 **P** to the LORD a food offering consisting of H7928
Nu 28:24 In this way **p** the food offering every day H6913
Nu 28:26 when you **p** to the LORD an offering of new H7928
Nu 28:27 **P** a burnt offering of two young bulls, one H7928
Nu 29: 8 **P** as an aroma pleasing to the LORD a burnt H7928
Nu 29:13 **P** as an aroma pleasing to the LORD a food H7928
Nu 29:36 **P** as an aroma pleasing to the LORD a food H7928
Dt 12:27 **P** your burnt offerings on the altar of the H6913
Dt 31:14 Joshua and **p yourselves** at the tent of H3656
Jos 7:14 the morning, **p yourselves** tribe by tribe. H7928
1Sa 1:22 I will take him and **p** him before the LORD H8011
1Sa 10:19 So now **p yourselves** before the LORD by H3656
2Sa 14:20 Joab did this to change the **p** situation. H7156
1Ki 18: 1 "Go and **p yourself** to Ahab, and I will H8011
1Ki 18: 2 So Elijah went to **p himself** to Ahab. H8011
1Ki 18:15 *I will* surely **p myself** to Ahab today." H8011
1Ch 9:18 King's Gate on the east, up to **the p time**. H2178
1Ch 16:40 to **p** burnt offerings to the LORD on the altar H6590
2Ch 13:11 evening *they* **p** burnt offerings H7787
2Ch 23:18 to **p** the burnt offerings of the LORD as H6590
2Ch 29: 7 not burn incense or **p** any burnt offerings H6590
2Ch 29:29 king and everyone **p** with him knelt down H5162
2Ch 30:21 The Israelites who *were* **p** in Jerusalem H5162
2Ch 34:33 he had all who *were* **p** in Israel serve H5162
2Ch 35:17 The Israelites who *were* **p** celebrated the H5162
Ezr 5:16 From that day to **the p** it has been under A10363
Ezr 6: 3 be rebuilt as a place *to* **p** sacrifices, A10156
Ezr 8:25 all Israel **p** there had donated for H5162
Est 1: 3 the nobles of the provinces were **p**. H4200+7156
Job 1: 6 angels came to **p themselves** before the H3656
Job 2: 1 angels came to **p themselves** before the H3656
Job 2: 1 came with them to **p himself** before him. H3656
Job 31:37 *I would* **p** *it* to him as to a ruler. H7928
Ps 14: 5 God is **p in** the company of the H928
Ps 56:12 my God; *I will* **p** my thank offerings to you. H8966
Ps 72:10 *May* the kings of Sheba and Seba **p** him H7928
Pr 4: 9 your head and **p** you *with* a glorious H4481
Isa 40:20 too poor to **p** *such* **an offering** selects H9556
Isa 41:21 "**P** your case," says the LORD. "Set forth H7928
Isa 45:21 Declare what is to be, **p** it—let them take H5602
Jer 33:18 to burn grain offerings and *to* **p** sacrifices. H6913
Jer 40: 5 him provisions and a **p** and let him go. H5368
Jer 42: 9 sent me to **p** your petition, H5877+4200+7156
Jer 44:15 along with all the women who *were* **p**—a H6641
Eze 43:27 the priests *are to* **p** your burnt offerings H6913
Eze 45: 1 *you are to* **p** to the LORD a portion of the H8123
Eze 48: 8 be the portion *you are to* **p** as a special H8123
Hag 2: 9 'The glory of this **p** house will be greater H340
Zec 8: 9 said who were **p** when the foundation NDT
Mk 8: 9 About four thousand *were* **p**. After he had *G1639*
Mk 10:30 a hundred times as much in this **p** age: *G3814*
Mk 14: 4 Some *of those* **p** were saying indignantly *G1639*
Lk 2:22 him to Jerusalem *to* **p** him to the Lord *G4225*
Lk 12:56 don't know how to interpret this **p** time? *G2789*
Lk 13: 1 Now *there were* some **p** at that time who *G4205*
Lk 22: 6 Jesus over to them **when no** crowd **was p**. *G868*
Ac 1:13 Those **p** were Peter, John, James and NDT
Ac 5:38 **in the p case** I advise you: *G3836+3814*
Ac 21:18 to see James, and all the elders *were* **p**. *G4134*
Ac 23:30 ordered his accusers *to* **p** to you their case *G3306*
Ac 24:17 people gifts for the poor and to **p** offerings. NDT
Ac 25:24 all who *are* **p with** us, you see this *G5223*
Ro 3:26 his righteousness at the **p** time, *G3814*
Ro 8:18 that our **p** sufferings are *G3836+3814+2789*
Ro 8:22 pains of childbirth right up to the **p time**. *G3814*
Ro 8:38 demons, neither the **p** nor the future, nor *G1931*
Ro 11: 5 at the **p** time there is a remnant chosen *G3814*
Ro 13:11 understanding the *p* **time**: The hour has AIT
1Co 3:22 life or death or **the p** or the future— *G1931*
1Co 5: 3 even though I am not physically **p**, I am *G4205*
1Co 5: 3 As *one who is* **p** with you in this way, *G4205*
1Co 5: 4 the power of our Lord Jesus is **p**, *G5250*

1Co 7:26 Because of the **p** crisis, I think that it is *G1931*
1Co 7:31 For this world *in* its *p* **form** is passing away. AIT
2Co 4:14 us with Jesus and **p** us with you to himself *G4225*
2Co 8:14 At the **p** time your plenty will supply what *G3814*
2Co 10:11 we will be in our actions *when we are* **p**. *G4205*
2Co 11:2 *so that I might* **p** you as a pure virgin to *G4225*
Gal 1:4 our sins to rescue us from the **p** evil age, *G1931*
Gal 4:25 corresponds to the **p** city of Jerusalem, *G3814*
Eph 1:21 not only in the **p** age but also in the one *G4047*
Eph 5:27 to **p** her to himself as a radiant church, *G4225*
Php 4:6 with thanksgiving, **p** your requests to God. *G1192*
Col 1:22 body through death *to* **p** you holy in his *G4225*
Col 1:25 *to* **p** to you the word of God **in** its **fullness** *G4444*
Col 1:28 so that *we may* **p** everyone fully mature in *G4225*
Col 2:5 *I am* **p** with you in spirit and delight to *G1639*
1Ti 4:8 promise for both the **p** life and the life to *G3814*
1Ti 6:17 who are rich in this **p** world not to be *G3814*
2Ti 2:15 Do your best *to* **p** yourself to God as one *G4225*
Titus 2:12 upright and godly lives in this **p** age, *G3814*
Heb 2:8 Yet **at p** we do not see everything subject *G3814*
Heb 9:9 This is an illustration for the **p** time *G1931*
2Pe 3:7 By the same word the **p** heavens and earth *G3814*
Jude 24 from stumbling and *to* **p** you before his *G2705*

PRESENTABLE (1) [PRESENT]

1Co 12:24 while our **p** *parts* need no special *G2363*

PRESENTED (89) [PRESENT]

Ge 30:20 "God *has* **p** me *with* a precious gift. H2272
Ge 43:15 to Egypt and **p** *themselves* to Joseph. H6641
Ge 43:26 *they* **p** to him the gifts they had brought H995
Ge 47:2 his brothers and **p** them before Pharaoh H3657
Ge 47:7 Jacob in and **p** him before Pharaoh. H6641
Ex 29:18 a food offering **p to** the LORD. H4200
Ex 29:25 to the LORD, a food offering **p to** the LORD. H4200
Ex 29:27 waved and the thigh that **was p.** H9556+8123
Ex 29:41 a food offering **p to** the LORD. H4200
Ex 32:6 burnt offerings and **p** fellowship offerings. H5602
Ex 35:22 They all **p** their gold as a wave offering to H5677
Lev 2:3 holy part of the **food offerings** *p to* the LORD. AIT
Lev 2:10 holy part of the **food offerings** *p to* the LORD. AIT
Lev 2:11 honey in a food offering **p to** the LORD. H4200
Lev 2:16 incense, as a food offering **p to** the LORD. H4200
Lev 3:11 the altar as a food offering **p to** the LORD. H4200
Lev 4:35 on top of the **food offerings** *p to* the LORD. AIT
Lev 5:12 on top of the **food offerings** *p to* the LORD. AIT
Lev 6:17 it as their share of the **food offerings** *p to* me. AIT
Lev 6:18 share of the **food offerings** *p to* the LORD. AIT
Lev 7:5 the altar as a food offering **p to** the LORD. H4200
Lev 7:25 a food offering *may be* **p** to the LORD must H7928
Lev 7:34 the thigh that is **p** and have given them H9556
Lev 7:35 of the **food offerings** *p to* the LORD that AIT
Lev 7:35 on the day they *were* **p** to serve the LORD H7928
Lev 8:14 *He* then **p** the bull for the sin offering H5602
Lev 8:18 *He* then **p** the ram for the burnt offering H7928
Lev 8:21 a food offering **p to** the LORD, as the LORD H4200
Lev 8:22 *He* then **p** the other ram, the ram for the H7928
Lev 8:28 a food offering **p to** the LORD. H4200
Lev 10:12 **food offerings** prepared without yeast and *p to* AIT
Lev 10:13 share of the **food offerings** *p to* the LORD; AIT
Lev 10:14 that was waved and the thigh that was **p**. H9556
Lev 10:15 The thigh that was **p** and the breast that H9556
Lev 16:10 as the scapegoat *shall* **be p** alive before H6641
Lev 22:22 the altar as a food offering **p to** the LORD. H4200
Lev 22:27 as a food offering **p to** the LORD. H4200
Lev 23:13 a food offering **p to** the LORD, H4200
Lev 24:7 to be a food offering **p to** the LORD. H4200
Lev 24:9 share of the **food offerings** *p to* the LORD." AIT
Lev 27:8 being dedicated *is to be* **p** to the priest, H6641
Lev 27:11 the animal *must be* **p** to the priest, H6641
Nu 6:20 that was waved and the thigh that was **p**. H9556
Nu 7:3 These *they* **p** before the tabernacle H7928
Nu 7:10 its dedication and **p** them before the altar H7928
Nu 8:15 the Levites and **p** them as a wave offering H5677
Nu 8:21 Then Aaron **p** them as a wave offering H5677
Nu 15:25 intentional and they *have* **p** to the LORD H995
Nu 16:38 they *were* **p** before the LORD and have H7928
Nu 18:8 put you in charge of the **offerings** *p to* me; AIT
Nu 28:6 a food offering **p to** the LORD. H4200
Nu 28:13 a food offering **p to** the LORD. H4200
Nu 28:15 one male goat *is to* **be p** to the LORD as a H6913
Nu 29:6 They are food offerings **p to** the LORD, H4200
Nu 31:52 Moses and Eleazar **p** as a gift to the LORD H8123
Dt 18:1 shall live on the **food offerings** *p to* the LORD, AIT
Dt 31:14 came and **p themselves** at the tent of H3656
Jos 13:14 since the **food offerings** *p to* the LORD, the AIT
Jos 24:1 and *they* **p themselves** before God. H3656
Jdg 3:17 *He* **p** the tribute to Eglon king of Moab H7928
Jdg 3:18 After Ehud *had* **p** the tribute, he sent on H7928
Jdg 20:26 until evening and **p** burnt offerings and H6590
Jdg 21:4 built an altar and **p** burnt offerings and H6590
1Sa 2:28 family all the **food offerings** *p by* the AIT
2Ki 11:12 he **p** him with a copy of the covenant and NDT
2Ki 16:12 he approached it and **p offerings** on it. H6590
1Ch 6:49 were the *ones who* **p offerings** on the H7787
1Ch 16:1 and *they* **p** burnt offerings and fellowship H7928
1Ch 23:31 burnt offerings *were* **p** to the LORD on the H6590
1Ch 29:21 to the LORD and **p** burnt offerings to him: H6590
2Ch 23:11 they **p** him with a copy of the covenant and NDT
2Ch 24:14 burnt offerings were **p** continually in the H6590
2Ch 28:21 the officials and **p** them to the king of H5989
2Ch 29:24 **p** their blood on the altar **for a sin offering** H2627
Ezr 3:5 After that, they **p** the regular burnt offerings NDT
Ezr 10:19 their guilt they each **p** a ram from the flock NDT
Est 8:2 from Haman, and **p** it to Mordecai. H5989
Eze 20:28 **p** their fragrant incense and poured out H8492
Da 1:18 the chief official **p** them to H995
Da 2:46 an offering and incense *be* **p** to him. A10482
Mt 2:11 treasures and **p** him **with** gifts of gold, *G4712*
Mk 6:28 *He* **p** it to the girl, and she gave it to her *G1443*
Ac 1:3 *he* **p** himself to them and gave many *G4225*
Ac 6:6 *They* **p** these men to the apostles, who *G2705*
Ac 9:41 the widows, and **p** her to them alive. *G4225*
Ac 24:2 Tertullus **p** *his* **case** before Felix: *G806+2989*
Ac 25:2 **appeared** before him **and p** *the* **charges** *G1872*
Ro 3:25 God **p** Christ as a sacrifice of atonement *G4729*
Gal 2:2 *I* **p to** them the gospel that I preach among *G423*

PRESENTING (7) [PRESENT]

Ex 30:20 altar to minister by **p** a food offering to H7787
Ex 35:24 Those **p** an offering of silver or bronze H8123
Nu 9:7 we be kept from **p** the LORD's offering H7928
Nu 9:13 their people for not **p** the LORD's offering H7928
Nu 18:32 By **p** the best part of it you will not be H8123
Eze 46:14 The **p** of this grain offering to the LORD is a NDT
Ac 17:19 what this new teaching is that you *are* **p**? *G3281*

PRESENTS (5) [PRESENT]

Lev 22:18 **p** a gift for a burnt offering to the LORD H7928
Nu 15:14 living among you **p** a food offering as an H6913
Est 9:19 feasting, a day for giving **p** to each other. H4950
Est 9:22 joy and giving **p of food** to one another H4950
Isa 66:3 grain offering is like one who **p** pig's blood, NDT

PRESERVE (26) [PRESERVED, PRESERVES]

Ge 19:32 sleep with him and **p** our family line H2649
Ge 19:34 with him so *we can* **p** our family line H2649
Ge 45:7 me ahead of you to **p** for you a remnant H8492
Job 33:18 *to* **p** them from the pit, their lives from H3104
Ps 36:6 *You*, LORD, **p** both people and animals. H3828
Ps 79:11 your strong arm **p** those condemned to H3855
Ps 119:25 the dust; **p** my **life** according to your word. H2649
Ps 119:37 **p** my **life** according to your word. H2649
Ps 119:40 In your righteousness **p** my **life**. H2649
Ps 119:88 In your unfailing love **p** my **life**, that I may H2649
Ps 119:107 suffered much; **p** my **life**, LORD, according H2649
Ps 119:149 accordance with your love; **p** my **life**, H2649
Ps 119:154 **p** my **life** according to your promise. H2649
Ps 119:156 is great; **p** my **life** according to your laws. H2649
Ps 119:159 how I love your precepts; **p** my **life**, LORD, H2649
Ps 138:7 walk in the midst of trouble, *you* **p** my **life**. H2649
Ps 143:11 name's sake, LORD, **p** my **life**; in your H2649
Pr 3:21 **p** sound judgment and discretion H5915
Pr 5:2 discretion and your lips *may* **p** knowledge. H5915
Pr 13:3 Those who guard their lips **p** their lives H9068
Pr 16:17 those who guard their ways **p** their lives. H9068
Pr 22:5 but *those who would* **p** their life stay far H9068
Eze 7:13 their sins, not one of them *will* **p** their life. H2616
Eze 13:18 the lives of my people but **p** your own? H2649
Mal 2:7 the lips of a priest *ought to* **p** knowledge, H9068
Lk 17:33 and whoever loses their life *will* **p** it. *G2441*

PRESERVED (6) [PRESERVE]

Ex 16:34 of the covenant law, so that it might be **p**. H5466
2Sa 22:44 *you have* **p** me as the head of nations. H9068
Ps 66:9 he *has* **p** our lives and H8492+928+2021+2645
Ps 119:93 precepts, for by them *you have* **p** my **life**. H2649
Mt 9:17 wine into new wineskins, and both *are* **p**." *G5337*
Gal 2:5 the truth of the gospel *might be* **p** for you. *G1373*

PRESERVES (4) [PRESERVE]

Ps 31:23 The LORD **p** those who are true to him, but H5915
Ps 41:2 The LORD protects and **p** them—they are H2649
Ps 119:50 suffering is this: Your promise **p** my **life**. H2649
Ecc 7:12 Wisdom **p** those who have it. H2649

PRESIDENTS (KJV) ADMINISTRATORS

PRESIDES (1)

Ps 82:1 God **p** in the great assembly; he renders H5893

PRESS (13) [PRESSED, PRESSES, PRESSING, PRESSURE]

Jdg 14:17 told her, because *she continued to* **p** him. H7439
2Sa 11:25 **P** the attack against the city and destroy it H2616
Job 23:6 he *would* not **p charges** against me. H8492
Ps 56:1 all day long *they* **p** their attack. H4315
Jer 19:9 their enemies *will* **p** the siege so hard H7439
Hos 6:3 the LORD; *let us* **p on** to acknowledge him. H8103
Mic 6:15 you *will* **p** olives but not use the oil H2005
Lk 13:33 I must **p on** today and tomorrow and the *G4513*
Ac 19:38 there are proconsuls. *They can* **p charges**. *G1592*
Ac 25:5 *they can* **p charges** against him there." *G2989*
Php 3:12 *I* **p on** to take hold of that for which *G1503*
Php 3:14 *I* **p on** toward the goal to win the prize *G1503*
Rev 14:20 blood flowed out of the **p**, rising as *G3332*

PRESSED (19) [PRESS]

Ex 27:20 bring you clear oil of **p** olives for the light H4184
Ex 29:40 with a quarter of a hin of oil from **p olives**, H4184
Lev 24:2 bring you clear oil of **p** olives for the light H4184
Nu 22:25 angel of the LORD, *it* **p close** to the wall H4315
Nu 28:5 with a quarter of a hin of oil from **p olives**. H4184
Jdg 1:28 *they* **p** the Canaanites into forced labor H8492
Jdg 1:35 increased, they too were **p** into forced labor. NDT
Jdg 4:24 **p harder and harder** against H2143+2256+7997
Jdg 9:45 day Abimelek **p** *his* **attack** against the city H4309
1Sa 13:6 critical and that their army *was* **hard p**, H5601
1Sa 25:18 of raisins and two hundred **cakes of p figs**, H1811
1Sa 30:12 part of a **cake of p figs** and two cakes of H1811
2Sa 19:43 **p** their claims even more **forcefully** than H7996
1Ki 5:11 to twenty thousand baths of **p olive** oil. H4184
Ps 118:5 When **hard p**, I cried to the LORD; he H5210
Mk 5:24 A large crowd followed and **p around** him. *G5315*
Lk 6:38 A good measure, **p down**, shaken *G4390*
2Co 4:8 *We are* **hard p** on every side, but not *G2567*
2Co 8:13 might be relieved while you are **hard p**, *G2568*

PRESSES (2) [PRESS]

Isa 16:10 no one treads out wine at the **p**, for I have H3676
Jer 48:33 have stopped the flow of wine from the **p**; H3676

PRESSING (3) [PRESS]

Ex 5:13 The slave drivers *kept* **p** them, saying H237
Jdg 20:45 *They kept* **p** after the Benjamites as far as H1815
Lk 8:45 the people are crowding and **p against** you." *G632*

PRESSURE (3) [PRESS]

Ge 19:9 *They* **kept bringing p** on Lot and H7210+4394
2Co 1:8 *We were* **under** great **p**, far beyond our *G976*
2Co 11:28 I face daily the **p** of my concern for all the *G2180*

PRESUMES (1) [PRESUMPTION]

Dt 18:20 But a prophet who **p** to speak in my name H2326

PRESUMPTION (2) [PRESUMES, PRESUMPTUOUSLY]

Nu 14:44 *in their* **p** they went up toward the highest H6753
1Sa 25:28 "Please forgive your servant's **p**. The LORD H7322

PRESUMPTUOUSLY (1) [PRESUMPTION]

Dt 18:22 That prophet has spoken **p**, so do H928+2295

PRETEND (4) [PRETENDED, PRETENDING, PRETENDS, PRETENSE, PRETENSION]

2Sa 13:5 "Go to bed and **p to be ill**," Jonadab said H2703
2Sa 14:2 said to her, "**P** *you are* **in mourning**. Dress in H61
1Ki 14:5 she *will* **p to be someone else**. H5796
Pr 12:9 than **p to be somebody** and have no H3877

PRETENDED (5) [PRETEND]

Ge 42:7 but *he* **p to be a stranger** and spoke H5796
1Sa 21:13 So *he* **p to be insane** in their H9101+3248
2Sa 13:6 So Amnon lay down and **p to be ill** H2703
Ps 34:T When he **p to be insane** before H9101+3248
Lk 20:20 they sent spies, *who* **p** to be sincere. *G5693*

PRETENDING (1) [PRETEND]

Ac 27:30 **p** they were going to lower some anchors *G4733*

PRETENDS (2) [PRETEND]

Pr 13:7 *One person* **p to be rich**, yet has nothing H6947
Pr 13:7 has nothing; *another* **p to be poor**, yet has H8133

PRETENSE (2) [PRETEND]

1Ki 14:6 Why this **p**? I have been sent H5796
Jer 3:10 but only in **p**," declares the LORD. H9214

PRETENSION (1) [PRETEND]

2Co 10:5 arguments and every **p** that sets itself up *G5739*

PRETEXT (2)

Ac 23:15 him before you **on the p** of wanting more *G6055*
Ac 23:20 tomorrow **on the p** of wanting more *G6055*

PREVAIL (10) [PREVAILED, PREVAILS, PREVALENT]

2Ch 14:11 *do* not *let* mere mortals **p** against you." H6806
Ps 12:4 "By our tongues *we will* **p**; our own lips H1504
Ps 49:14 the upright *will* **p** over them in the H8097
Pr 24:5 The wise **p** through great power, and H1505
Pr 30:1 "I am weary, God, but *I can* **p**. H3523
Isa 54:17 no weapon forged against you *will* **p**, and H7503
Jer 5:22 may roll, but they cannot **p**; they may roar, H3523
Jer 20:10 then *we will* **p** over him and take our H3523
Jer 20:11 so my persecutors will stumble and not **p**. H3523
Ro 3:4 when you speak and **p** when you judge." *G3771*

PREVAILED (4) [PREVAIL]

Jdg 19:4 woman's father, **p on** him to stay; so H2616+928
Jer 20:7 deceived; you overpowered me and **p**. H3523
La 1:16 are destitute because the enemy *has* **p**." H1504
Lk 23:23 that he be crucified, and their shouts **p**. *G2996*

PREVAILS (3) [PREVAIL]

1Sa 2:9 "It is not by strength that one **p**; H1504
Pr 19:21 but it is the LORD's purpose *that* **p**. H7756
Hab 1:4 the law is paralyzed, and justice never **p**. H3655

PREVALENT (1) [PREVAIL]

Jas 1:21 the evil that is *so* **p** and humbly accept *G4353*

PREVENT (8) [PREVENTED]

2Sa 14:11 God to **p** the avenger of blood **from** H4946
1Ki 15:17 Ramah to **p** anyone *from* leaving H1194+5989
2Ch 16:1 Ramah to **p** anyone *from* leaving H1194+5989
Mal 3:11 *I will* **p** pests from devouring your crops H1721
Jn 18:36 would fight to **p** my arrest by the Jewish *G3590*
Ac 27:42 prisoners to **p** any of them **from** swimming *G3590*
2Co 3:13 his face to **p** the Israelites **from** seeing the *G3590*

P

Rev 7: 1 the earth to **p** any wind **from** blowing on *G3590*

PREVENTED (2) [PREVENT]

Ro 1:13 but *have been* **p** from doing so until now *G3266*
Heb 7:23 since death **p** them **from** continuing in *G3266*

PREVIOUS (4) [PREVIOUSLY]

Ge 26: 1 besides the **p** famine in Abraham's time H8037
Nu 6:12 The **p** days do not count, because they H8037
Jdg 3: 2 who had not had **p** battle H4200+7156
Gal 1:13 you have heard of my **p** way of life in *G4537*

PREVIOUSLY (6) [PREVIOUS]

1Sa 14:21 who had **p** been with the H3869+919+8997
1Ch 6:65 Benjamin they allotted the *p* **named** towns. AIT
Ac 21:29 They had **p seen** Trophimus the Ephesian *G4632*
Ro 9:29 It is just as Isaiah **said p**: "Unless the Lord *G4625*
Gal 3:17 the covenant **p established** by God and *G4623*
1Th 2: 2 *We had* **p suffered** and been treated *G4634*

PREY (30) [PREYS]

Ge 15:11 Then **birds of p** came down on the H6514
Ge 49: 9 Judah; you return from the **p**, my son. H3272
Ge 49:27 in the morning he devours the **p**, in the H6331
Nu 23:24 till it devours its **p** and drinks the blood of H3272
Job 4:11 The lion perishes for lack of **p**, and the H3272
Job 9:26 like eagles swooping down on their **p**. H431
Job 24:21 *They* **p on** the barren and childless H8286
Job 28: 7 No **bird of p** knows that hidden path, no H6514
Job 38:39 "Do you hunt the **p** for the lioness and H3272
Ps 17:12 They are like a lion hungry for **p**, like a H3271
Ps 22:13 Roaring lions *that* **tear** their **p** open their H3271
Ps 104:21 lions roar for their **p** and seek their food H3272
Isa 5:29 as they seize their **p** and carry it off with H3272
Isa 10: 2 making widows their **p** and robbing the H8965
Isa 18: 6 to the mountain **birds of p** and to the wild H6514
Isa 31: 4 a great lion over its **p**—and though a H3272
Isa 46:11 From the east I summon a **bird of p**; from H6514
Isa 59:15 whoever shuns evil **becomes** *a* **p**. H8964
Jer 12: 9 like a speckled **bird of p** that other birds H6514
Jer 12: 9 of prey that other **birds of p** surround and H6514
Eze 13:21 they will no longer fall **p** to your power. H5180
Eze 19: 3 learned to tear the **p** and he became a H3272
Eze 19: 6 learned to tear the **p** and he became a H3272
Eze 22:25 within her like a roaring lion tearing its **p**; H3272
Eze 22:27 within her are like wolves tearing their **p**; H3272
Am 3: 4 a lion roar in the thicket when it has no **p**? H3272
Na 2:12 his cubs and strangled the **p** for his mate, NDT
Na 2:12 lairs with the kill and his dens with the **p**. H3274
Na 2:13 I will leave you no **p** on the earth. H3272
Hab 2: 7 Then you will become their **p**. H5468

PREYS (1) [PREY]

Pr 6:26 another man's wife **p on** your very life. H7421

PRICE (32) [PRICELESS]

Ge 23: 9 it to me for the full **p** as a burial site H4084
Ge 23:13 I will pay the **p** *of* the field. Accept it H4084
Ge 23:16 out for him the **p** he had named in the H4084
Ge 34:12 Make the **p for the bride** and the gift I am H4558
Lev 25:16 you are to increase the **p**, and when the H5239
Lev 25:16 you are to decrease the **p**, because what H5239
Lev 25:50 The **p** *for* their release is to be based on H4084
Lev 25:51 a larger share of the **p** paid for them. H4084
Nu 18:16 at the redemption **p set** *at* five shekels of H6886
Dt 2:28 to eat and water to drink for their **p** in silver. NDT
1Sa 13:21 The **p** was two-thirds of a shekel for NDT
1Sa 18:25 wants no other **p for** *the* **bride** than a H4558
2Sa 3:14 to myself for the **p** of a hundred Philistine NDT
1Ki 10:28 purchased them from Kue at the **current p**. H4697
1Ch 21:22 Sell it to me at the full **p**." H4084
1Ch 21:24 I insist on paying the full **p**. H4084
2Ch 1:16 purchased them from Kue at the **current p**. H4697
Job 28:15 can its **p** be weighed out in silver. H4697
Job 28:18 the **p** *of* wisdom is beyond rubies. H5433
Pr 27:26 the goats with the **p** *of* a field. H4697
Isa 45:13 but not for a **p** or reward, says the H4697
La 5: 4 our wood can be had only at a **p**. H4697
Da 11:39 people and will distribute the land at a **p**. H4697
Am 8: 5 boosting the **p** and cheating with H9203
Mic 3:11 her priests teach for a **p**, and her prophets H4697
Zec 11:13 the handsome **p** at which they valued me! H3702
Mt 26: 9 have been **sold at a** high **p** and the *G4405*
Mt 27: 9 the **p set** *on* him by the people of *G5507+5506*
Ac 5: 8 is **this** *the p* you and Ananias got for the land AIT
Ac 5: 8 "Yes," she said, "**that** is *the p*." AIT
1Co 6:20 you were bought *at* a **p**. Therefore honor *G5507*
1Co 7:23 You were bought *at* a **p**; do not become *G5507*

PRICELESS (1) [PRICE]

Ps 36: 7 How **p** is your unfailing love, O God H3701

PRICKS (KJV) BARBS, GOADS

PRIDE (67) [PROUD]

Lev 26:19 down your stubborn **p** and make the sky H1454
2Ki 19:22 your voice and lifted your eyes *in* **p**? H5294
2Ch 26:16 powerful, his **p** led to his downfall. H1467+4213
2Ch 32:26 Hezekiah repented of the **p** *of* his heart, H1470
Job 20: 6 Though the **p** *of* the godless person H8480
Job 33:17 from wrongdoing and keep them from **p**, H1575
Ps 10: 4 In his **p** the wicked man does not H1470+678
Ps 31:18 with **p** and contempt they speak H1452
Ps 47: 4 the **p** *of* Jacob, whom he loved. H1454
Ps 56: 2 in their **p** many are attacking me. H5294
Ps 59:12 of their lips, let them be caught in their **p**. H1454
Ps 73: 6 Therefore **p** is their necklace; they clothe H1452
Pr 8:13 to hate evil; I hate **p** and arrogance, evil H1449
Pr 11: 2 When **p** comes, then comes disgrace, but H2295
Pr 13:10 is strife, there is **p**, but wisdom is found in H2295
Pr 14: 3 A fool's mouth lashes out with **p**, but the H1452
Pr 16:18 **P** goes before destruction, a haughty spirit H1454
Pr 17: 6 parents are the **p** *of* their children. H9514
Pr 29:23 **P** brings a person low, but the lowly in H1452
Ecc 7: 8 and patience is better than **p**. H1468+8120
Isa 2:11 be humbled and human **p** brought low; H8124
Isa 2:17 be brought low and human **p** humbled; H8124
Isa 4: 2 of the land will be the **p** and glory of the H1454
Isa 9: 9 who say with **p** and arrogance of heart H1452
Isa 10:12 the **willful p** *of* his heart and H7262+1542
Isa 13:11 will humble the **p** *of* the ruthless. H1452
Isa 13:19 the **p** and glory of the Babylonians H1454
Isa 16: 6 We have heard of Moab's **p**—how great H1454
Isa 16: 6 of her conceit, her **p** and her insolence H1454
Isa 23: 9 to bring down her **p** *in* all her splendor H1454
Isa 25:11 will bring down their **p** despite the H1452
Isa 28: 1 that wreath, the **p** *of* Ephraim's drunkards H1455
Isa 28: 1 to that city, the **p** of those laid low by wine! NDT
Isa 28: 3 That wreath, the **p** *of* Ephraim's drunkards H1455
Isa 37:23 your voice and lifted your eyes *in* **p**? H5294
Isa 43:14 in the ships in which they took **p**. H8262
Isa 60:15 you the everlasting **p** and the joy of all H1454
Jer 13: 9 way I will ruin the **p** *of* Judah and the H1454
Jer 13: 9 of Judah and the great **p** *of* Jerusalem. H1454
Jer 13:17 I will weep in secret because of your **p** H1575
Jer 48:29 "We have heard of Moab's **p**—how great H1454
Jer 48:29 her insolence, her **p**, her conceit and the H1454
Jer 49:16 you inspire and the **p** *of* your heart have H2295
Eze 7:20 They took **p** *in* their beautiful jewelry and H1454
Eze 7:24 I will put an end to the **p** *of* the mighty H1454
Eze 16:56 your sister Sodom in the day of your **p**, H1454
Eze 24:21 the stronghold in which you take **p**, the H1454
Eze 28: 2 " 'In *the* **p** *of* your heart you say, "I am a H1467
Eze 32:12 They will shatter the **p** *of* Egypt, and all H1454
Da 4:37 those who walk in **p** he is able to A10136
Da 5:20 became arrogant and hardened *with* **p**, A10225
Da 11:12 South *will be* **filled with p** and will H8123+4222
Am 6: 8 "I abhor the **p** *of* Jacob and detest his H1454
Am 8: 7 LORD has sworn by himself, the **P** *of* Jacob: H1454
Ob 3 The **p** *of* your heart has deceived you, you H2295
Zep 2:10 is what they will get in return for their **p**, H1454
Zec 9: 6 will put an end to the **p** *of* the Philistines. H1454
Zec 10:11 Assyria's **p** will be brought down and H1454
Ro 11:13 to the Gentiles, *I* **take p in** my ministry *G1519*
2Co 5:12 giving you an opportunity to take **p** in us, *G3017*
2Co 5:12 answer those *who take* **p** in what is seen *G3016*
2Co 7: 4 with great frankness; I take great **p** in you. *G3018*
2Co 8:24 your love and the *reason for* our **p** in you, *G3018*
Gal 6: 4 Then they can take **p** in themselves alone, *G3017*
Jas 1: 9 circumstances *ought to* **take p** in their *G3016*
Jas 1:10 the rich should take **p** in their humiliation— NDT
1Jn 2:16 of the eyes, and the **p** of life—comes not *G224*

PRIEST (476) [HIGH-PRIESTHOOD, PRIEST'S, PRIESTHOOD, PRIESTLY, PRIESTS, PRIESTS']

Ge 14:18 He was **p** of God Most High, H3913
Ge 41:45 of Potiphera, **p** *of* On, to be his wife. H3913
Ge 41:50 Asenath daughter of Potiphera, **p** *of* On. H3913
Ge 46:20 Asenath daughter of Potiphera, **p** *of* On. H3913
Ex 2:16 Now a **p** *of* Midian had seven daughters H3913
Ex 3: 1 father-in-law, the **p** *of* Midian, and he led H3913
Ex 18: 1 the **p** *of* Midian and father-in-law of H3913
Ex 28: 3 consecration, so he *may* **serve** me **as p**. H3912
Ex 29:30 who succeeds him as **p** and comes to the H3913
Ex 30:33 puts it on **anyone other than a p** must be H2424
Ex 31:10 Aaron the **p** and the garments for H3913
Ex 35:19 Aaron the **p** and the garments for H3913
Ex 38:21 direction of Ithamar son of Aaron, the **p**. H3913
Ex 39:41 Aaron the **p** and the garments for H3913
Ex 40:13 consecrate him so *he may* **serve** me **as p**. H3912
Lev 1: 7 The sons of Aaron the **p** are to put fire on H3913
Lev 1: 9 the **p** is to burn all of it on the altar. H3913
Lev 1:12 into pieces, and the **p** shall arrange them H3913
Lev 1:13 the **p** is to bring all of them and burn H3913
Lev 1:15 The **p** shall bring it to the altar, wring off H3913
Lev 1:17 then the **p** shall burn it on the wood H3913
Lev 2: 2 The **p** shall take a handful of the flour H3913
Lev 2: 8 present it to the **p**, who shall take it to H3913
Lev 2:16 The **p** shall burn the memorial portion of H3913
Lev 3:11 The **p** shall burn them on the altar as a H3913
Lev 3:16 The **p** shall burn them on the altar as a H3913
Lev 4: 3 " 'If the anointed **p** sins, bringing guilt on H3913
Lev 4: 5 Then the anointed **p** shall take some of H3913
Lev 4: 7 The **p** shall then put some of the blood on H3913
Lev 4:10 Then the **p** shall burn them on the altar of H3913
Lev 4:16 Then the anointed **p** is to take some of the H3913
Lev 4:20 In this way the **p** will make atonement H3913
Lev 4:25 Then the **p** shall take some of the blood of H3913
Lev 4:26 In this way the **p** will make atonement H3913
Lev 4:30 Then the **p** is to take some of the blood H3913
Lev 4:31 the **p** shall burn it on the altar as an H3913
Lev 4:31 In this way the **p** will make atonement H3913
Lev 4:34 Then the **p** shall take some of the blood of H3913
Lev 4:35 the **p** shall burn it on the altar on top H3913
Lev 4:35 In this way the **p** will make atonement H3913
Lev 5: 6 the **p** shall make atonement for them H3913
Lev 5: 8 They are to bring them to the **p**, who shall H3913
Lev 5:10 The **p** shall then offer the other as a burnt H3913
Lev 5:12 They are to bring it to the **p**, who shall H3913
Lev 5:13 In this way the **p** will make atonement H3913
Lev 5:13 rest of the offering will belong to the **p**, H3913
Lev 5:16 a fifth of its value and give it all to the **p**. H3913
Lev 5:16 The **p** will make atonement for them with H3913
Lev 5:18 are to bring to the **p** as a guilt offering a H3913
Lev 5:18 In this way the **p** will make atonement H3913
Lev 6: 6 And as a penalty they must bring to the **p** H3913
Lev 6: 7 In this way the **p** will make atonement H3913
Lev 6:10 The **p** shall then put on his linen clothes H3913
Lev 6:12 Every morning the **p** is to add firewood H3913
Lev 6:15 The **p** is to take a handful of the finest flour NDT
Lev 6:22 him as anointed **p** shall prepare it. H3913
Lev 6:23 Every grain offering of a **p** shall be burned H3913
Lev 6:26 The **p** who offers it shall eat it; it is to be H3913
Lev 7: 5 The **p** shall burn them on the altar as a H3913
Lev 7: 7 They belong to the **p** who makes H3913
Lev 7: 8 The **p** who offers a burnt offering for H3913
Lev 7: 9 a griddle belongs to the **p** who offers it, H3913
Lev 7:14 it belongs to the **p** who splashes the H3913
Lev 7:31 The **p** shall burn the fat on the altar, but H3913
Lev 7:32 offerings to the **p** as a contribution. H3913
Lev 7:34 them to Aaron the **p** and his sons as their H3913
Lev 12: 6 is to bring to the **p** at the entrance to the H3913
Lev 12: 8 In this way the **p** will make atonement H3913
Lev 13: 2 brought to Aaron the **p** or to one of his H3913
Lev 13: 2 the priest or to one of his sons who is a **p**. H3913
Lev 13: 3 The **p** is to examine the sore on the skin H3913
Lev 13: 3 When the **p** examines that person, he H3913
Lev 13: 4 the **p** is to isolate the affected person H3913
Lev 13: 5 the seventh day the **p** is to examine them, H3913
Lev 13: 6 the seventh day the **p** is to examine them H3913
Lev 13: 6 the **p** shall pronounce them clean H3913
Lev 13: 7 themselves to the **p** to be pronounced H3913
Lev 13: 7 they must appear before the **p** again. H3913
Lev 13: 8 The **p** is to examine that person, and if the H3913
Lev 13: 9 disease, they must be brought to the **p**. H3913
Lev 13:10 The **p** is to examine them, and if there is a H3913
Lev 13:11 disease and the **p** shall pronounce them H3913
Lev 13:12 so far as the **p** can see, it covers all H3913
Lev 13:13 the **p** is to examine them, and if the H3913
Lev 13:15 When the **p** sees the raw flesh, he shall H3913
Lev 13:16 turns white, they must go to the **p**. H3913
Lev 13:17 The **p** is to examine them, and if the sores H3913
Lev 13:17 the **p** shall pronounce the affected person H3913
Lev 13:19 they must present themselves to the **p**. H3913
Lev 13:20 The **p** is to examine it, and if it appears to H3913
Lev 13:20 the **p** shall pronounce that person H3913
Lev 13:21 when the **p** examines it, there is no H3913
Lev 13:21 then the **p** is to isolate them for seven H3913
Lev 13:22 the **p** shall pronounce them unclean H3913
Lev 13:23 the **p** shall pronounce them clean. H3913
Lev 13:25 the **p** is to examine the spot, and if the H3913
Lev 13:25 The **p** shall pronounce them unclean; it is H3913
Lev 13:26 But if the **p** examines it and there is no H3913
Lev 13:26 then the **p** is to isolate them for seven H3913
Lev 13:27 the seventh day the **p** is to examine that H3913
Lev 13:27 the **p** shall pronounce them unclean H3913
Lev 13:28 the **p** shall pronounce them clean H3913
Lev 13:30 the **p** is to examine the sore, and if it H3913
Lev 13:30 the **p** shall pronounce them unclean H3913
Lev 13:31 when the **p** examines the sore, it H3913
Lev 13:31 then the **p** is to isolate the affected H3913
Lev 13:32 the seventh day the **p** is to examine the H3913
Lev 13:33 the **p** is to keep them isolated H3913
Lev 13:34 the seventh day the **p** is to examine the H3913
Lev 13:34 the **p** shall pronounce them clean. H3913
Lev 13:36 the **p** is to examine them, and if he finds H3913
Lev 13:37 is unchanged so far as **the p** can see, H2257S
Lev 13:37 the **p** shall pronounce them clean. H3913
Lev 13:39 the **p** is to examine them, and if the spots H3913
Lev 13:43 The **p** is to examine him, and if the H3913
Lev 13:44 The **p** shall pronounce him unclean H3913
Lev 13:49 mold and must be shown to the **p**. H3913
Lev 13:50 The **p** is to examine the affected area and H3913
Lev 13:53 when the **p** examines it, the mold H3913
Lev 13:55 washed, the **p** is to examine it again H3913
Lev 13:56 when the **p** examines it, the mold has H3913
Lev 14: 2 when they are brought to the **p**: H3913
Lev 14: 3 The **p** is to go outside the camp and H3913
Lev 14: 4 the **p** shall order that two live clean birds H3913
Lev 14: 5 Then the **p** shall order that one of the H3913
Lev 14:11 The **p** who pronounces them clean shall H3913
Lev 14:12 "Then the **p** is to take one of the male H3913
Lev 14:13 the guilt offering belongs to the **p**; it is H3913
Lev 14:14 The **p** is to take some of the blood of the H3913
Lev 14:15 The **p** shall then take some of the log of H3913
Lev 14:17 The **p** is to put some of the oil remaining H3913
Lev 14:18 oil in his palm the **p** shall put on the H3913
Lev 14:19 "Then the **p** is to sacrifice the sin offering H3913
Lev 14:19 the **p** shall slaughter the burnt offering NDT
Lev 14:23 cleansing to the **p** at the entrance to the H3913
Lev 14:24 The **p** is to take the lamb for the guilt H3913
Lev 14:26 The **p** is to pour some of the oil into the H3913
Lev 14:29 oil in his palm the **p** shall put on the H3913
Lev 14:31 In this way the **p** will make atonement H3913
Lev 14:35 of the house must go and tell the **p**, H3913
Lev 14:36 The **p** is to order the house to be emptied H3913
Lev 14:36 After this the **p** is to go in and inspect the H3913

P

Lev 14:38 the p shall go out the doorway of the H3913
Lev 14:39 On the seventh day the p shall return to H3913
Lev 14:44 the p is to go and examine it and, if the H3913
Lev 14:48 "But if the p comes to examine it and the H3913
Lev 15:14 tent of meeting and give them to the p. H3913
Lev 15:15 The p is to sacrifice them, the one for a sin H3913
Lev 15:29 bring them to the p at the entrance to H3913
Lev 15:30 The p is to sacrifice one for a sin offering H3913
Lev 16:32 The p who is anointed and ordained to H3913
Lev 16:32 his father as high p is to make atonement H3912
Lev 17: 5 They must bring them to the p, that is, to H3913
Lev 17: 6 The p is to splash the blood against the H3913
Lev 19:22 guilt offering the p is to make atonement H3913
Lev 21: 1 'A p must not make himself ceremonially NDT
Lev 21:10 " 'The high p, the one among his brothers H3913
Lev 21:21 of Aaron the p who has any defect is H3913
Lev 22:10 may the guest of a p or his hired worker H3913
Lev 22:11 But if a p buys a slave with money, or if H3913
Lev 22:12 daughter marries anyone other than a p, H2424
Lev 22:14 restitution to the p for the offering and H3913
Lev 23:10 bring to the p a sheaf of the first grain you H3913
Lev 23:11 the p is to wave it on the day after the H3913
Lev 23:20 The p is to wave the two lambs before the H3913
Lev 23:20 are a sacred offering to the LORD for the p. H3913
Lev 27: 8 dedicated is to be presented to the p, H3913
Lev 27:11 the animal must be presented to the p, H3913
Lev 27:12 Whatever value the p then sets, that is H3913
Lev 27:14 the p will judge its quality as good or bad. H3913
Lev 27:14 Whatever value the p then sets, so it will H3913
Lev 27:18 the p will determine the value according H3913
Lev 27:23 the p will determine its value up to the H3913
Nu 3: 6 present them to Aaron the p to assist him. H3913
Nu 3:32 Levites was Eleazar son of Aaron, the p. H3913
Nu 4:16 son of Aaron, the p, is to have charge of H3913
Nu 4:28 direction of Ithamar son of Aaron, the p. H3913
Nu 4:33 direction of Ithamar son of Aaron, the p." H3913
Nu 5: 8 to the LORD and must be given to the p, H3913
Nu 5: 9 Israelites bring to a p will belong to him. H3913
Nu 5:10 what they give to the p will belong to the H3913
Nu 5:10 give to the priest will belong to the p. H2257S
Nu 5:15 then he is to take his wife to the p. H3913
Nu 5:16 " 'The p shall bring her and have her H3913
Nu 5:18 After the p has had the woman stand H3913
Nu 5:19 Then the p shall put the woman under H3913
Nu 5:21 here the p is to put the woman under this H3913
Nu 5:23 " 'The p is to write these curses on a scroll H3913
Nu 5:25 The p is to take from her hands the grain H3913
Nu 5:26 The p is then to take a handful of the H3913
Nu 5:30 The p is to have her stand before the LORD H3913
Nu 6:10 young pigeons to the p at the entrance to H3913
Nu 6:11 The p is to offer one as a sin offering and H3913
Nu 6:16 " 'The p is to present all these before the H3913
Nu 6:19 the p is to place in their hands a boiled H3913
Nu 6:20 The p shall then wave these before the H3913
Nu 6:20 they are holy and belong to the p H3913
Nu 7: 8 direction of Ithamar son of Aaron, the p. H3913
Nu 15:25 The p is to make atonement for the whole H3913
Nu 15:28 The p is to make atonement before the H3913
Nu 16:37 son of Aaron, the p, to remove the H3913
Nu 16:39 So Eleazar the p collected the bronze H3913
Nu 18:28 give the LORD's portion to Aaron the p. H3913
Nu 19: 3 Give it to Eleazar the p; it is to be taken H3913
Nu 19: 4 Then Eleazar the p is to take some of its H3913
Nu 19: 6 The p is to take some cedar wood, hyssop H3913
Nu 19: 7 the p must wash his clothes and bathe H3913
Nu 25: 7 the son of Aaron, the p, saw this, he left H3913
Nu 25:11 son of Aaron, the p, has turned my anger H3913
Nu 26: 1 to Moses and Eleazar son of Aaron, the p, H3913
Nu 26: 3 Eleazar the p spoke with them and H3913
Nu 26:63 Eleazar the p when they counted the H3913
Nu 26:64 Aaron the p when they counted H3913
Nu 27: 2 Eleazar the p, the leaders and the H3913
Nu 27:19 before Eleazar the p and the entire H3913
Nu 27:21 He is to stand before Eleazar the p, who H3913
Nu 27:22 before Eleazar the p and the whole H3913
Nu 31: 6 son of Eleazar, the p, who took with him H3913
Nu 31:12 Moses and Eleazar the p and the Israelite H3913
Nu 31:13 Eleazar the p and all the leaders of the H3913
Nu 31:21 Then Eleazar the p said to the soldiers H3913
Nu 31:26 "You and Eleazar the p and the family H3913
Nu 31:29 give it to Eleazar the p as the LORD's part. H3913
Nu 31:31 Moses and Eleazar the p did as the LORD H3913
Nu 31:41 tribute to Eleazar the p as the LORD's part, H3913
Nu 31:51 Eleazar the p accepted from them H3913
Nu 31:54 Eleazar the p accepted the gold H3913
Nu 32: 2 Eleazar the p and to the leaders of H3913
Nu 32:28 them to Eleazar the p and Joshua son of H3913
Nu 33:38 Aaron the p went up Mount Hor H3913
Nu 34:17 Eleazar the p and Joshua son of Nun. H3913
Nu 35:25 stay there until the death of the high p, H3913
Nu 35:28 of refuge until the death of the high p; H3913
Nu 35:28 the death of the high p may they return to H3913
Nu 35:32 own land before the death of the high p. H3913
Dt 10: 6 Eleazar his son succeeded him as p. H3912
Dt 17:12 the judge or for the p who stands H3913
Dt 20: 2 the p shall come forward and address the H3913
Dt 26: 3 say to the p in office at the time, "I H3913
Dt 26: 4 The p shall take the basket from your H3913
Jos 14: 1 which Eleazar the p, Joshua son of Nun H3913
Jos 17: 4 They went to Eleazar the p, Joshua son of H3913
Jos 19:51 are the territories that Eleazar the p, H3913
Jos 20: 6 the death of the high p who is serving at H3913
Jos 21: 1 of the Levites approached Eleazar the p, H3913
Jos 21: 4 of Aaron the p were allotted thirteen H3913
Jos 21:13 of Aaron the p they gave Hebron H3913
Jos 22:13 son of Eleazar, the p, to the land of H3913
Jos 22:30 When Phinehas the p and the leaders of H3913
Jos 22:31 son of Eleazar, the p, said to Reuben, H3913
Jos 22:32 son of Eleazar, the p, and the leaders H3913
Jdg 17: 5 installed one of his sons as his p. H3913
Jdg 17:10 "Live with me and be my father and p H3913
Jdg 17:12 young man became his p and lived in his H3913
Jdg 17:13 since this Levite has become my p." H3913
Jdg 18: 4 "He has hired me and I am his p. H3913
Jdg 18: 6 The p answered them, "Go in peace. H3913
Jdg 18:17 gods while the p and the six hundred H3913
Jdg 18:18 the p said to them, "What H3913
Jdg 18:19 be our father and p. Isn't it better that H3913
Jdg 18:19 clan in Israel as p rather than just one H3913
Jdg 18:20 The p was very pleased. He took the H3913
Jdg 18:24 gods I made, and my p, and went away. H3913
Jdg 18:27 had made, and his p, and went on to H3913
1Sa 1: 9 Now Eli the p was sitting on his chair by H3913
1Sa 2:11 before the LORD under Eli the p. H3913
1Sa 2:14 fork brought up the p would take for H3913
1Sa 2:15 "Give the p some meat to roast; he H3913
1Sa 2:28 out of all the tribes of Israel to be my p, H3913
1Sa 2:35 I will raise up for myself a faithful p, who H3913
1Sa 14: 3 the son of Eli, the LORD's p in Shiloh. H3913
1Sa 14:19 While Saul was talking to the p, the H3913
1Sa 14:19 So Saul said to the p, "Withdraw your H3913
1Sa 14:36 But the p said, "Let us inquire of God here H3913
1Sa 21: 1 to Ahimelek the p. Ahimelek trembled H3913
1Sa 21: 2 David answered Ahimelek the p, "The H3913
1Sa 21: 4 But the p answered David, "I don't have H3913
1Sa 21: 6 So the p gave him the consecrated bread H3913
1Sa 21: 9 The p replied, "The sword of Goliath the H3913
1Sa 22:11 the king sent for the p Ahimelek son of H3913
1Sa 23: 9 he said to Abiathar the p, "Bring the H3913
1Sa 30: 7 Then David said to Abiathar the p, the H3913
2Sa 15:27 The king also said to Zadok the p, "Do H3913
2Sa 20:26 Ira the Jairite was David's p. H3913
1Ki 1: 7 son of Zeruiah and with Abiathar the p, H3913
1Ki 1: 8 But Zadok the p, Benaiah son of Jehoiada H3913
1Ki 1:19 Abiathar the p and Joab the commander H3913
1Ki 1:25 of the army and Abiathar the p. H3913
1Ki 1:26 Zadok the p, and Benaiah son of H3913
1Ki 1:32 "Call in Zadok the p, Nathan the prophet H3913
1Ki 1:34 There have Zadok the p and Nathan the H3913
1Ki 1:38 So Zadok the p, Nathan the prophet H3913
1Ki 1:39 Zadok the p took the horn of oil from the H3913
1Ki 1:42 Jonathan son of Abiathar the p arrived. H3913
1Ki 1:44 The king has sent with him Zadok the p H3913
1Ki 1:45 Zadok the p and Nathan the prophet H3913
1Ki 2:22 for Abiathar the p and Joab son of H3913
1Ki 2:26 To Abiathar the p the king said, "Go back H3913
1Ki 2:35 replaced Abiathar with Zadok the p. H3913
1Ki 4: 2 Azariah son of Zadok—the p; H3913
1Ki 4: 5 of Nathan—a p and adviser to the king H3913
1Ki 13:33 become a p he consecrated for the high H3913
2Ki 11: 9 did just as Jehoiada the p ordered. H3913
2Ki 11: 9 off duty—and came to Jehoiada the p. H3913
2Ki 11:15 Jehoiada the p ordered the commanders H3913
2Ki 11:15 For the p had said, "She must not be put H3913
2Ki 11:18 killed Mattan the p of Baal in front of the H3913
2Ki 11:18 Then Jehoiada the p posted guards at the H3913
2Ki 12: 2 the years Jehoiada the p instructed him. H3913
2Ki 12: 5 Let every p receive the money from one of H3913
2Ki 12: 7 Jehoiada the p and the other priests H3913
2Ki 12: 9 Jehoiada the p took a chest and bored a H3913
2Ki 12:10 the royal secretary and the high p came H3913
2Ki 16:10 sent to Uriah the p a sketch of the altar H3913
2Ki 16:11 So Uriah the p built an altar in accordance H3913
2Ki 16:15 then gave these orders to Uriah the p: H3913
2Ki 16:16 And Uriah the p did just as King Ahaz had H3913
2Ki 22: 4 to Hilkiah the high p and have him get H3913
2Ki 22: 8 Hilkiah the high p said to Shaphan the H3913
2Ki 22:10 "Hilkiah the p has given me a book." H3913
2Ki 22:12 He gave these orders to Hilkiah the p H3913
2Ki 22:14 Hilkiah the p, Ahikam, Akbor, Shaphan H3913
2Ki 23: 4 The king ordered Hilkiah the high p, the H3913
2Ki 23:24 that Hilkiah the p had discovered in the H3913
2Ki 25:18 took as prisoners Seraiah the chief p, H3913
2Ki 25:18 Zephaniah the p next in rank and the H3913
1Ch 6:10 it was he who served as p in the temple H3912
1Ch 16:39 David left Zadok the p and his fellow H3913
1Ch 24: 6 Zadok the p, Ahimelek son of Abiathar H3913
1Ch 27: 5 was Benaiah son of Jehoiada the p. H3913
1Ch 29:22 the LORD to be ruler and Zadok to be p. H3913
2Ch 13: 9 rams may become a p of what are not H3913
2Ch 15: 3 without a p to teach and without the law. H3913
2Ch 19:11 "Amariah the chief p will be over you in H3913
2Ch 22:11 King Jehoram and wife of the p Jehoiada, H3913
2Ch 23: 8 Judah did just as Jehoiada the p ordered. H3913
2Ch 23: 8 Jehoiada the p had not released any of H3913
2Ch 23:14 Jehoiada the p sent out the commanders H3913
2Ch 23:14 For the p had said, "Do not put her to H3913
2Ch 23:17 killed Mattan the p of Baal in front of the H3913
2Ch 24: 2 the LORD all the years of Jehoiada the p. H3913
2Ch 24: 6 Jehoiada the chief p and said to him, NDT
2Ch 24:11 of the chief p would come and empty H3913
2Ch 24:20 on Zechariah son of Jehoiada the p. H3913
2Ch 24:25 murdering the son of Jehoiada the p, H3913
2Ch 26:17 Azariah the p with eighty other H3913
2Ch 26:20 Azariah the chief p and all the other H3913
2Ch 31:10 Azariah the chief p, from the family of H3913
2Ch 34: 9 to Hilkiah the high p and gave him the H3913
2Ch 34:14 Hilkiah the p found the Book of the Law of H3913
2Ch 34:18 "Hilkiah the p has given me a book." H3913
Ezr 2:63 until there was a p ministering with the H3913
Ezr 7: 5 of Eleazar, the son of Aaron the chief p— H3913
Ezr 7:11 King Artaxerxes had given to Ezra the p, H3913
Ezr 7:12 To Ezra the p, teacher of the Law A10347
Ezr 7:21 with diligence whatever Ezra the p, A10347
Ezr 8:33 hands of Meremoth son of Uriah, the p. H3913
Ezr 10:10 Then Ezra the p stood up and said to them H3913
Ezr 10:16 Ezra the p selected men who were family H3913
Ne 3: 1 Eliashib the high p and his fellow priests H3913
Ne 3:20 of the house of Eliashib the high p. H3913
Ne 7:65 there should be a p ministering with the H3913
Ne 8: 2 month Ezra the p brought the Law before H3913
Ne 8: 9 Ezra the p and teacher of the Law H3913
Ne 10:38 A p descended from Aaron is to H3913
Ne 12:26 Nehemiah the governor and of Ezra the p, H3913
Ne 13: 4 Eliashib the p had been put in charge of H3913
Ne 13:13 I put Shelemiah the p, Zadok the scribe H3913
Ne 13:28 of Eliashib the high p was son-in-law to H3913
Ps 110: 4 "You are a p forever, in the order of H3913
Isa 8: 2 called in Uriah the p and Zechariah son H3913
Isa 24: 2 it will be the same for p as for people, for H3913
Isa 61:10 as a bridegroom adorns his head like a p H3912
Jer 14:18 Both prophet and p have gone to a land H3913
Jer 18:18 of the law by the p will not cease, H3913
Jer 20: 1 When the p Pashhur son of Immer, the H3913
Jer 21: 1 of Malkijah and the p Zephaniah son of H3913
Jer 23:11 "Both prophet and p are godless; even in H3913
Jer 23:33 people, or a prophet or a p, ask you, H3913
Jer 23:34 If a prophet or a p or anyone else claims H3913
Jer 29:25 to the p Zephaniah son of Maaseiah H3913
Jer 29:26 has appointed you p in place of Jehoiada H3913
Jer 29:29 Zephaniah the p, however, read the letter H3913
Jer 37: 3 Shelemiah with the p Zephaniah son of H3913
Jer 52:24 took as prisoners Seraiah the chief p, H3913
Jer 52:24 Zephaniah the p next in rank and the H3913
La 2: 6 anger he has spurned both king and p. H3913
La 2:20 Should p and prophet be killed in the H3913
Eze 1: 3 the word of the LORD came to Ezekiel the p H3913
Eze 44:21 No p is to drink wine when he enters the H3913
Eze 44:25 " 'A p must not defile himself by going near NDT
Eze 45:19 The p is to take some of the blood of the H3913
Hos 4: 4 like those who bring charges against a p. H3913
Am 7:10 Then Amaziah the p of Bethel sent a H3913
Hag 1: 1 to Joshua son of Jozadak, the high p: H3913
Hag 1:12 of Jozadak, the high p, and the whole H3913
Hag 1:14 of Jozadak, the high p, and the spirit of H3913
Hag 2: 2 Jozadak, the high p, and to the remnant H3913
Hag 2: 4 Joshua son of Jozadak, the high p. H3913
Zec 3: 1 me Joshua the high p standing before the H3913
Zec 3: 8 " 'Listen, High P Joshua, you and your H3913
Zec 6:11 set it on the head of the high p H3913
Zec 6:13 And he will be a p on his throne. H3913
Mal 2: 7 "For the lips of a p ought to preserve H3913
Mt 8: 4 show yourself to the p and offer the gift G2636
Mt 26: 3 assembled in the palace of the high p, G797
Mt 26:51 it out and struck the servant of the high p, G797
Mt 26:57 Jesus took him to Caiaphas the high p, G797
Mt 26:58 right up to the courtyard of the high p. G797
Mt 26:62 Then the high p stood up and said to Jesus G797
Mt 26:63 The high p said to him, "I charge you G797
Mt 26:65 Then the high p tore his clothes and said G797
Mk 1:44 show yourself to the p and offer the G2636
Mk 2:26 In the days of Abiathar the high p, he G797
Mk 14:47 sword and struck the servant of the high p, G797
Mk 14:53 They took Jesus to the high p, and all the G797
Mk 14:54 right into the courtyard of the high p. G797
Mk 14:60 Then the high p stood up before them G797
Mk 14:61 Again the high p asked him, "Are you the G797
Mk 14:63 The high p tore his clothes. "Why do we G797
Mk 14:66 of the servant girls of the high p came by. G797
Lk 1: 5 of Judea there was a p named Zechariah, G2636
Lk 1: 8 duty and he was serving as p before God, G2634
Lk 5:14 show yourself to the p and offer the G2636
Lk 10:31 A p happened to be going down the same G2636
Lk 22:50 of them struck the servant of the high p, G797
Lk 22:54 took him into the house of the high p. G797
Jn 11:49 Caiaphas, who was high p that year, spoke G797
Jn 11:51 as high p that year he prophesied that G797
Jn 18:13 of Caiaphas, the high p that year. G797
Jn 18:15 this disciple was known to the high p, G797
Jn 18:16 who was known to the high p, came back, G797
Jn 18:19 the high p questioned Jesus about his G797
Jn 18:22 "Is this the way you answer the high p?" G797
Jn 18:24 sent him bound to Caiaphas the high p. G797
Ac 4: 6 Annas the high p was there, and so were G797
Ac 5:17 Then the high p and all his associates G797
Ac 5:21 When the high p and his associates arrived G797
Ac 5:27 Sanhedrin to be questioned by the high p. G797
Ac 7: 1 Then the high p asked Stephen, "Are these G797
Ac 9: 1 the Lord's disciples. He went to the high p G797
Ac 14:13 The p of Zeus, whose temple was just G2636
Ac 19:14 of Sceva, a Jewish chief p, were doing this. G797
Ac 22: 5 as the high p and all the Council can G797
Ac 23: 2 At this the high p Ananias ordered those G797
Ac 23: 4 "How dare you insult God's high p! G797
Ac 23: 5 I did not realize that he was the high p; for G797
Ac 24: 1 days later the high p Ananias went down G797

Heb 2:17 faithful **high p** in service to God, G797
Heb 3: 1 acknowledge as our apostle and **high p**. G797
Heb 4:14 we have a great **high p** who has ascended G797
Heb 4:15 we do not have a **high p** who is unable to G797
Heb 5: 1 Every **high p** is selected from among the G797
Heb 5: 5 on himself the glory of becoming a **high p**. G797
Heb 5: 6 "You are a **p** forever, in the order of G2636
Heb 5:10 by God to be **high p** in the order of G797
Heb 6:20 He has become a **high p** forever, in the G797
Heb 7: 1 king of Salem and **p** of God Most High. G2636
Heb 7: 3 the Son of God, he remains a **p** forever. G2636
Heb 7:11 there still need *for* another **p** to come, G2636
Heb 7:15 more clear if another **p** like Melchizedek G2636
Heb 7:16 one who has become a **p** not on the basis of NDT
Heb 7:17 "You are a **p** forever, in the order of G2636
Heb 7:21 he became a **p** with an oath when God NDT
Heb 7:21 change his mind: 'You are a **p** forever.'" G2636
Heb 7:26 Such a **high p** truly meets our need—one G797
Heb 8: 1 We do have such a **high p**, who sat down G797
Heb 8: 3 Every **high p** is appointed to offer both gifts G797
Heb 8: 4 he would not be a **p**, for there are already G2636
Heb 9: 7 But only the **high p** entered the inner room G797
Heb 9:11 when Christ came *as* **high p** of the good G797
Heb 9:25 the way the **high p** enters the Most Holy G797
Heb 10:11 Day after day every **p** stands and performs G2636
Heb 10:12 But when this **p** had offered for all time one NDT
Heb 10:21 we have a great **p** over the house of God G2636
Heb 13:11 The **high p** carries the blood of animals G797

PRIEST'S (12) [PRIEST]

Lev 6:29 Any male in a **p** family may eat it; it is H3913
Lev 7: 6 Any male in a **p** family may eat it, but it H3913
Lev 21: 9 " 'If a **p** daughter defiles herself by H3913
Lev 22:10 " 'No one **outside a p family** may eat the H2424
Lev 22:12 If a **p** daughter marries anyone other than H3913
Lev 22:13 But if a **p** daughter becomes a widow or is H3913
1Sa 2:13 the **p** servant would come with a H3913
1Sa 2:15 the **p** servant would come and say to the H3913
Jn 18:10 drew it and struck the **high p** servant G797
Jn 18:15 went with Jesus into the **high p** courtyard, G797
Jn 18:26 One of the **high p** servants, a relative of the G797
Ac 4: 6 Alexander and others of the **high p** family. G796

PRIESTHOOD (17) [PRIEST]

Ex 29: 9 The **p** is theirs by a lasting ordinance H3914
Ex 40:15 anointing will be to a **p** that will continue H3914
Nu 16:10 now you are trying to get the **p** too. H3914
Nu 18: 1 offenses connected with the **p**. H3914
Nu 18: 7 giving you the service of the **p** as a gift. H3914
Nu 25:13 will have a covenant of a lasting **p**, H3914
1Ki 2:27 removed Abiathar from the **p** of the LORD, H3913
Ezr 2:62 so were excluded from the **p** as unclean. H3914
Ne 7:64 so were excluded from the **p** as unclean. H3914
Ne 13:29 the covenant of the **p** and of the Levites. H3914
Lk 1: 9 according to the custom *of* the **p**, to go G2632
Heb 7:11 been attained through the Levitical **p**— G2648
Heb 7:11 law given to the people established **that** *p*— AIT
Heb 7:12 For when the **p** is changed, the law must G2648
Heb 7:24 Jesus lives forever, he has a permanent **p**. G2648
1Pe 2: 5 built into a spiritual house to be a holy **p**, G2633
1Pe 2: 9 a chosen people, a royal **p**, a holy nation, G2633

PRIESTLY (12) [PRIEST]

Lev 21:10 has been ordained to wear the **p** garments, NDT
Lev 27:21 it will become **p** property. H4200+2021+3913
Jos 18: 7 because the **p service** *of* the LORD is their H3914
1Sa 2:31 strength and the strength of your **p** house, H3S
1Sa 2:35 I will firmly establish his **p** house, and they NDT
1Sa 2:36 me to some **p office** so I can have food H3914
Ezr 2:69 5,000 minas of silver and 100 **p** garments. H3913
Ne 12:12 these were the heads of the **p** families: H3913
Ne 13:29 they defiled the **p office** and the covenant H3914
Eze 7:26 **p** instruction in the law will cease H4946+3913
Lk 1: 5 who belonged to the **p division** of Abijah G2389
Ro 15:16 He gave me the **p duty** of proclaiming the G2646

PRIESTS (424) [PRIEST]

Ge 47:22 he did not buy the land of the **p**, because H3913
Ge 47:26 the land of the **p** that did not become H3913
Ex 19: 6 me a kingdom of **p** and a holy nation. H3913
Ex 19:22 Even the **p**, who approach the LORD, must H3913
Ex 19:24 But the **p** and the people must not force H3913
Ex 28: 1 Ithamar, so they *may* **serve** me **as p**. H3912
Ex 28: 4 his sons, so they *may* **serve** me **as p**. H3912
Ex 28:41 them so *they may* **serve** me **as p**. H3912
Ex 29: 1 so *they may* **serve** me **as p**: H3912
Ex 29:44 Aaron and his sons to **serve** me **as p**. H3912
Ex 30:30 them so they *may* **serve** me **as p**. H3912
Ex 31:10 his sons when *they* **serve as p**, H3912
Ex 35:19 his sons when *they* **serve as p**. H3912
Ex 39:41 garments for his sons when **serving as p**. H3912
Ex 40:15 their father, so they *may* **serve** me **as p**. H3912
Lev 1: 5 Aaron's sons the **p** shall bring the blood H3913
Lev 1: 8 Then Aaron's sons the **p** shall arrange the H3913
Lev 1:11 Aaron's sons the **p** shall splash its H3913
Lev 2: 2 take it to Aaron's sons the **p**. H3913
Lev 3: 2 Then Aaron's sons the **p** shall splash the H3913
Lev 7:35 were presented to **serve** the LORD **as p**. H3912
Lev 16:33 for the **p** and all the members of the H3913
Lev 21: 1 "Speak to the **p**, the sons of Aaron, H3913
Lev 21: 5 " '**P** must not shave their heads or shave off NDT
Lev 21: 7 because **p** are holy to their God. H2085S
Lev 22: 9 " 'The **p** are to perform my service in such a NDT
Lev 22:15 The **p** must not desecrate the sacred NDT
Nu 3: 3 the anointed **p**, who were ordained H3913
Nu 3: 3 who were ordained to **serve as p**. H3912
Nu 3: 4 Ithamar **served as p** during the H3912
Nu 3:10 Appoint Aaron and his sons to serve as **p** H3914
Nu 10: 8 "The sons of Aaron, the **p**, are to blow the H3913
Nu 18: 7 sons may serve as **p** in connection with H3914
Dt 17: 9 Go to the Levitical **p** and to the judge who H3913
Dt 17:18 this law, taken from that of the Levitical **p**. H3913
Dt 18: 1 The Levitical **p**—indeed, the whole tribe H3913
Dt 18: 3 the share due the **p** from the people who H3913
Dt 19:17 the LORD before the **p** and the judges who H3913
Dt 21: 5 The Levitical **p** shall step forward, for the H3913
Dt 24: 8 do exactly as the Levitical **p** instruct you. H3913
Dt 27: 9 the Levitical **p** said to all Israel, H3913
Dt 31: 9 this law and gave it to the Levitical **p**, H3913
Jos 3: 3 the Levitical **p** carrying it, you are H3913
Jos 3: 6 Joshua said to the **p**, "Take up the ark of H3913
Jos 3: 8 Tell the **p** who carry the ark of the H3913
Jos 3:13 And as soon as the **p** who carry the ark of H3913
Jos 3:14 the **p** carrying the ark of the covenant H3913
Jos 3:15 Yet as soon as the **p** who carried the ark H3913
Jos 3:17 The **p** who carried the ark of the covenant H3913
Jos 4: 3 from right where the **p** are standing, and H3913
Jos 4: 9 the spot where the **p** who carried the ark H3913
Jos 4:10 Now the **p** who carried the ark remained H3913
Jos 4:11 of the LORD and the **p** came to the other H3913
Jos 4:16 "Command the **p** carrying the ark of the H3913
Jos 4:17 So Joshua commanded the **p**, "Come up H3913
Jos 4:18 And the **p** came up out of the river H3913
Jos 6: 4 Have seven **p** carry trumpets of rams' horns H3913
Jos 6: 4 with the **p** blowing the trumpets. H3913
Jos 6: 6 son of Nun called the **p** and said to them, H3913
Jos 6: 6 LORD and have seven **p** carry trumpets in H3913
Jos 6: 8 the seven **p** carrying the seven trumpets H3913
Jos 6: 9 marched ahead of the **p** who blew the H3913
Jos 6:12 next morning and the **p** took up the ark of H3913
Jos 6:13 The seven **p** carrying the seven trumpets H3913
Jos 6:16 when the **p** sounded the trumpet blast H3913
Jos 8:33 facing the Levitical **p** who carried it. H3913
Jos 21:19 The total number of towns for the **p**, the H3913
Jdg 18:30 his sons were **p** for the tribe of Dan H3913
1Sa 1: 3 the two sons of Eli, were **p** of the LORD. H3913
1Sa 2:13 Now it was the practice of the **p** that H3913
1Sa 5: 5 this day neither the **p** *of* Dagon nor any H3913
1Sa 6: 2 called for the **p** and the diviners and said, H3913
1Sa 22:11 who were the **p** at Nob, and they all H3913
1Sa 22:17 "Turn and kill the **p** *of* the LORD, because H3913
1Sa 22:17 to raise a hand to strike the **p** *of* the LORD. H3913
1Sa 22:18 "You turn and strike down the **p**. H3913
1Sa 22:19 the town of the **p**, with its men and H3913
1Sa 22:21 that Saul had killed the **p** *of* the LORD. H3913
2Sa 8:17 Ahimelek son of Abiathar were **p**; H3913
2Sa 8:18 Pelethites; and David's sons were **p**. H3913
2Sa 15:35 Won't the **p** Zadok and Abiathar be there H3913
2Sa 17:15 Abiathar, the **p**, "Ahithophel has H3913
2Sa 19:11 message to Zadok and Abiathar, the **p**: H3913
2Sa 20:25 secretary; Zadok and Abiathar were **p**; H3913
1Ki 4: 4 in chief; Zadok and Abiathar—**p**; H3913
1Ki 8: 3 Israel had arrived, the **p** took up the ark, H3913
1Ki 8: 4 The **p** and Levites carried them up, H3913
1Ki 8: 6 The **p** then brought the ark of the LORD's H3913
1Ki 8:10 When the **p** withdrew from the Holy Place, H3913
1Ki 8:11 And the **p** could not perform their service H3913
1Ki 12:31 places and appointed **p** from all sorts of H3913
1Ki 12:32 he also installed **p** *at* the high places he H3913
1Ki 13: 2 will sacrifice the **p** *of* the high places who H3913
1Ki 13:33 more appointed **p** *for* the high places H3913
2Ki 10:11 his close friends and his **p**, leaving him H3913
2Ki 10:19 of Baal, all his servants and all his **p**. H3913
2Ki 12: 4 Joash said to the **p**, "Collect all the H3913
2Ki 12: 6 of King Joash the **p** still had not repaired H3913
2Ki 12: 7 priest and the other **p** and asked them, H3913
2Ki 12: 8 The **p** agreed that they would not collect H3913
2Ki 12: 9 The **p** who guarded the entrance put into H3913
2Ki 12:16 temple of the LORD; it belonged to the **p**. H3913
2Ki 17:27 "Have one of the **p** you took captive from H3913
2Ki 17:28 So one of the **p** who had been exiled from H3913
2Ki 17:32 them as **p** in the shrines at the H3913
2Ki 19: 2 Shebna the secretary and the leading **p** H3913
2Ki 23: 2 of Jerusalem, the **p** and the prophets—all H3913
2Ki 23: 4 the **p** next in rank and the doorkeepers to H3913
2Ki 23: 5 away with the **idolatrous p** appointed by H4024
2Ki 23: 8 Josiah brought all the **p** from the towns of H3913
2Ki 23: 8 where the **p** had burned incense. H3913
2Ki 23: 9 Although the **p** *of* the high places did not H3913
2Ki 23: 9 ate unleavened bread with their fellow **p**. NDT
2Ki 23:20 slaughtered all the **p** *of* those high places H3913
1Ch 9: 2 some Israelites, **p**, Levites and temple H3913
1Ch 9:10 Of the **p**: Jedaiah; Jehoiarib; Jakin; H3913
1Ch 9:13 The **p**, who were heads of families H278+2157S
1Ch 9:30 But some of the **p** took care of mixing the H3913
1Ch 13: 2 also to the **p** and Levites who are H3913
1Ch 15:11 summoned Zadok and Abiathar the **p**, H3913
1Ch 15:14 So the **p** and Levites consecrated H3913
1Ch 15:24 Eliezer the **p** were to blow trumpets H3913
1Ch 16: 6 Jahaziel the **p** were to blow the H3913
1Ch 16:39 his fellow **p** before the tabernacle H3913
1Ch 18:16 Ahimelek son of Abiathar were **p**; H3913
1Ch 23: 2 of Israel, as well as the **p** and Levites. H3913
1Ch 24: 2 so Eleazar and Ithamar **served as** *the* **p**. H3912
1Ch 24: 6 of families of the **p** and of the Levites— H3913
1Ch 24:31 of families of the **p** and of the Levites. H3913
1Ch 28:13 the divisions of the **p** and Levites, H3913
1Ch 28:21 The divisions of the **p** and Levites are H3913
2Ch 4: 6 Sea was to be used by the **p** for washing. H3913
2Ch 4: 9 He made the courtyard of the **p**, and the H3913
2Ch 5: 5 The Levitical **p** carried them up; H3913
2Ch 5: 7 The **p** then brought the ark of the LORD's H3913
2Ch 5:11 The **p** then withdrew from the Holy Place H3913
2Ch 5:11 All the **p** who were there had consecrated H3913
2Ch 5:12 by 120 **p** sounding trumpets. H3913
2Ch 5:14 the **p** could not perform their service H3913
2Ch 6:41 May your **p**, LORD God, be clothed with H3913
2Ch 7: 2 The **p** could not enter the temple of the H3913
2Ch 7: 6 The **p** took their positions, as did the H3913
2Ch 7: 6 the Levites, the **p** blew their trumpets, and H3913
2Ch 8:14 the divisions of the **p** for their duties, H3913
2Ch 8:14 to assist the **p** according to each H3913
2Ch 8:15 commands to the **p** or to the Levites in H3913
2Ch 11:13 The **p** and Levites from all their districts H3913
2Ch 11:14 sons had rejected them as **p** of the LORD H3912
2Ch 11:15 appointed his own **p** for the high places H3913
2Ch 13: 9 But didn't you drive out the **p** *of* the LORD H3913
2Ch 13: 9 make **p** of your own as the peoples of H3913
2Ch 13:10 The **p** who serve the LORD are sons of H3913
2Ch 13:12 His **p** with their trumpets will sound the H3913
2Ch 13:14 out to the LORD. The **p** blew their trumpets H3913
2Ch 17: 8 the **p** Elishama and Jehoram. H3913
2Ch 19: 8 **p** and heads of Israelite families to H3913
2Ch 23: 4 A third of you **p** and Levites who are H3913
2Ch 23: 6 the LORD except the **p** and Levites on duty; H3913
2Ch 23:18 of the LORD in the hands of the Levitical **p**, H3913
2Ch 24: 5 called together the **p** and Levites and said H3913
2Ch 26:17 other courageous **p** of the LORD followed H3913
2Ch 26:18 That is for the **p**, the descendants of H3913
2Ch 26:19 he was raging at the **p** in their presence H3913
2Ch 26:20 priest and all the other **p** looked at him, H3913
2Ch 29: 4 He brought in the **p** and the Levites H3913
2Ch 29:16 The **p** went into the sanctuary of the LORD H3913
2Ch 29:21 The king commanded the **p**, the H3913
2Ch 29:22 the **p** took the blood and splashed it H3913
2Ch 29:24 The **p** then slaughtered the goats and H3913
2Ch 29:26 the **p** with their trumpets. H3913
2Ch 29:34 The **p**, however, were too few to skin all H3913
2Ch 29:34 until other **p** had been consecrated, H3913
2Ch 29:34 themselves than the **p** had been. H3913
2Ch 30: 3 because not enough **p** had consecrated H3913
2Ch 30:15 The **p** and the Levites were ashamed and H3913
2Ch 30:16 The **p** splashed against the altar the H3913
2Ch 30:21 while the Levites and **p** praised the LORD H3913
2Ch 30:24 A great number of **p** consecrated H3913
2Ch 30:25 along with the **p** and Levites and all who H3913
2Ch 30:27 The **p** and the Levites stood to bless the H3913
2Ch 31: 2 Hezekiah assigned the **p** and Levites to H3913
2Ch 31: 2 according to their duties as **p** or Levites— H3913
2Ch 31: 4 the portion due the **p** and Levites so they H3913
2Ch 31: 9 Hezekiah asked the **p** and Levites about H3913
2Ch 31:15 him faithfully in the towns of the **p**, H3913
2Ch 31:15 to their fellow **p** according to their divisions NDT
2Ch 31:17 they distributed to the **p** enrolled by their H3913
2Ch 31:19 As for the **p**, the descendants of Aaron H3913
2Ch 34: 5 burned the bones of the **p** on their altars, H3913
2Ch 34:30 of Jerusalem, the **p** and the Levites—all H3913
2Ch 35: 2 He appointed the **p** to their duties and H3913
2Ch 35: 8 to the people and the **p** and Levites. H3913
2Ch 35: 8 gave the **p** twenty-six hundred Passover H3913
2Ch 35:10 was arranged and the **p** stood in their H3913
2Ch 35:11 the **p** splashed against the altar the H3913
2Ch 35:14 preparations for themselves and for the **p**, H3913
2Ch 35:14 because the **p**, the descendants of H3913
2Ch 35:14 themselves and for the Aaronic **p**. H3913
2Ch 35:18 did Josiah, with the **p**, the Levites and all H3913
2Ch 36:14 the leaders of the **p** and the people H3913
Ezr 1: 5 Benjamin, and the **p** and Levites H3913
Ezr 2:36 The **p**: the descendants of Jedaiah H3913
Ezr 2:61 And from among the **p**: The descendants H3913
Ezr 2:70 The **p**, the Levites, the musicians, the H3913
Ezr 3: 2 his fellow **p** and Zerubbabel son of H3913
Ezr 3: 8 the **p** and the Levites and all who had H3913
Ezr 3:10 the **p** in their vestments and with trumpets H3913
Ezr 3:12 But many of the older **p** and Levites and H3913
Ezr 6: 9 as requested by the **p** in Jerusalem A10347
Ezr 6:16 of Israel—the **p**, the Levites and the A10347
Ezr 6:18 And they installed the **p** in their divisions A10347
Ezr 6:20 The **p** and Levites had purified themselves H3913
Ezr 6:20 their relatives the **p** and for themselves. H3913
Ezr 7: 7 Some of the Israelites, including **p**, Levites, H3913
Ezr 7:13 kingdom, including **p** and Levites, who A10347
Ezr 7:16 of the people and **p** for the temple of A10347
Ezr 7:24 tribute or duty on any of the **p**, Levites, A10347
Ezr 8:15 I checked among the people and the **p**, H3913
Ezr 8:24 Then I set apart twelve of the leading **p** H3913
Ezr 8:29 before the leading **p** and the Levites and H3913
Ezr 8:30 Then the **p** and Levites received the silver H3913
Ezr 9: 1 including the **p** and the Levites, have H3913
Ezr 9: 7 our kings and our **p** have been subjected H3913
Ezr 10: 5 put the leading **p** and Levites and all H3913
Ezr 10:18 Among the descendants of the **p**, the H3913
Ne 2:16 to the Jews or the **p** or nobles or officials H3913
Ne 3: 1 priest and his fellow **p** went to work and H3913
Ne 3:22 were made by the **p** *from* the surrounding H3913
Ne 3:28 the Horse Gate, the **p** made repairs, each H3913
Ne 5:12 I summoned the **p** and made the nobles H3913

Ne 7:39 The **p**: the descendants of Jedaiah H3913
Ne 7:63 And from among the **p**: the descendants H3913
Ne 7:70 of gold, 50 bowls and 530 garments for **p**. H3913
Ne 7:72 minas of silver and 67 garments for **p**. H3913
Ne 7:73 The **p**, the Levites, the gatekeepers, the H3913
Ne 8:13 families, along with the **p** and the Levites H3913
Ne 9:32 leaders, on our **p** and prophets, on H3913
Ne 9:34 our **p** and our ancestors did not follow H3913
Ne 9:38 our Levites and our **p** are affixing their H3913
Ne 10: 8 Bilgai and Shemaiah. These were the **p**. H3913
Ne 10:28 rest of the people—**p**, Levites H3913
Ne 10:34 the **p**, the Levites and the people H3913
Ne 10:36 of our God, to the **p** ministering there. H3913
Ne 10:37 of our God, to the **p**, the first of our H3913
Ne 10:39 the sanctuary and for the ministering **p**, H3913
Ne 11: 3 now some Israelites, **p**, Levites, temple H3913
Ne 11:10 From the **p**: Jedaiah; the son of Joiarib H3913
Ne 11:20 Israelites, with the **p** and Levites, were in H3913
Ne 12: 1 These were the **p** and Levites who H3913
Ne 12: 7 the leaders of the **p** and their associates H3913
Ne 12:22 as well as those of the **p**, were recorded H3913
Ne 12:30 When the **p** and Levites had purified H3913
Ne 12:35 as well as some **p** with trumpets, and also H3913
Ne 12:41 as well as the **p**—Eliakim, Maaseiah H3913
Ne 12:44 by the Law for the **p** and the Levites, H3913
Ne 12:44 with the ministering **p** and Levites. H3913
Ne 13: 5 as well as the contributions for the **p**. H3913
Ne 13:30 So I purified the **p** and the Levites of H3913
Job 12:19 He leads **p** away stripped and overthrows H3913
Ps 78:64 their **p** were put to the sword, and their H3913
Ps 99: 6 Moses and Aaron were among his **p** H3913
Ps 132: 9 May your **p** be clothed with your H3913
Ps 132:16 I will clothe her **p** with salvation, and her H3913
Isa 28: 7 **P** and prophets stagger from beer and are H3913
Isa 37: 2 the leading **p**, all wearing sackcloth, H3913
Isa 61: 6 And you will be called **p** *of* the LORD, you H3913
Isa 66:21 some of them also to be **p** and Levites," H3913
Jer 1: 1 one of the **p** at Anathoth in the territory of H3913
Jer 1:18 officials, its **p** and the people of the land. H3913
Jer 2: 8 The **p** did not ask, 'Where is the LORD?' H3913
Jer 2:26 their officials, their **p** and their prophets. H3913
Jer 4: 9 will lose heart, the **p** will be horrified, and H3913
Jer 5:31 the **p** rule by their own authority H3913
Jer 6:13 gain; prophets and **p** alike, all practice H3913
Jer 8: 1 the bones of the **p** and prophets, and the H3913
Jer 8:10 gain; prophets and **p** alike, all practice H3913
Jer 13:13 David's throne, the **p**, the prophets and H3913
Jer 19: 1 of the elders of the people and of the **p** H3913
Jer 26: 7 The **p**, the prophets and all the people H3913
Jer 26: 8 him to say, the **p**, the prophets and all the H3913
Jer 26:11 Then the **p** and the prophets said to the H3913
Jer 26:16 people said to the **p** and the prophets, H3913
Jer 27:16 Then I said to the **p** and all these people H3913
Jer 28: 1 the presence of the **p** and all the people: H3913
Jer 28: 5 Hananiah before the **p** and all the people H3913
Jer 29: 1 elders among the exiles and to the **p**, H3913
Jer 29:25 son of Maaseiah, and to all the other **p**. H3913
Jer 31:14 I will satisfy the **p** with abundance, and H3913
Jer 32:32 officials, their **p** and prophets, the H3913
Jer 33:18 will the Levitical **p** ever fail to have a H3913
Jer 33:21 the Levites who are **p** ministering before H3913
Jer 34:19 the **p** and all the people of the land who H3913
Jer 48: 7 together with his **p** and officials. H3913
Jer 49: 3 together with his **p** and officials. H3913
La 1: 4 are desolate, her **p** groan, her young H3913
La 1:19 My **p** and my elders perished in the city H3913
La 4:13 her prophets and the iniquities of her **p**, H3913
La 4:16 The **p** are shown no honor, the elders no H3913
Eze 22:26 Her **p** do violence to my law and profane H3913
Eze 40:45 south is for the **p** who guard the temple, H3913
Eze 40:46 north is for the **p** who guard the altar. H3913
Eze 42:13 where the **p** who approach the LORD will H3913
Eze 42:14 Once the **p** enter the holy precincts, they H3913
Eze 43:19 to the Levitical **p** of the family of Zadok, H3913
Eze 43:24 the **p** are to sprinkle salt on them and H3913
Eze 43:27 the **p** are to present your burnt offerings H3913
Eze 44:13 come near to **serve** me **as p** or come near H3912
Eze 44:15 " 'But the Levitical **p**, who are H3913
Eze 44:22 virgins of Israelite descent or widows of **p**. H3913
Eze 44:24 **the p** are to serve as judges and decide H2156S
Eze 44:28 to be the only inheritance **the p** have. H4392S
Eze 44:30 all your special gifts will belong to the **p**. H3913
Eze 44:31 The **p** must not eat anything, whether bird H3913
Eze 45: 4 the sacred portion of the land for the **p**, H3913
Eze 46: 2 The **p** are to sacrifice his burnt offering H3913
Eze 46:19 which belonged to the **p**, and showed me H3913
Eze 46:20 the place where the **p** are to cook the H3913
Eze 48:10 This will be the sacred portion for the **p**. H3913
Eze 48:11 This will be for the consecrated **p**, the H3913
Eze 48:13 "Alongside the territory of the **p**, the H3913
Hos 4: 6 I also reject you as my **p**; because you H3912
Hos 4: 7 The more **p** there were, the more they H4392S
Hos 4: 9 Like people, like **p**. I will punish both H3913
Hos 5: 1 "Hear this, you **p**! Pay attention, you H3913
Hos 6: 9 so do bands of **p**; they murder on the H3913
Hos 10: 5 so will its **idolatrous p**, those who H4024
Joel 1: 9 The **p** are in mourning, those who H3913
Joel 1:13 on sackcloth, you **p**, and mourn; wail, you H3913
Joel 2:17 Let the **p**, who minister before the LORD H3913
Mic 3:11 a bribe, her **p** teach for a price, and H3913
Zep 1: 4 names of the **idolatrous p**— H4024+6640+3913
Zep 3: 4 Her **p** profane the sanctuary and do H3913
Hag 2:11 'Ask the **p** what the law says: H3913
Hag 2:12 The **p** answered, "No." H3913
Hag 2:13 the **p** replied, "it becomes H3913
Zec 7: 3 by asking the **p** of the house of the LORD H3913
Zec 7: 5 "Ask all the people of the land and the **p** H3913
Mal 1: 6 "It is you **p** who show contempt for my H3913
Mal 2: 1 "And now, you **p**, this warning is for you. H3913
Mt 2: 4 all the people's **chief p** and teachers of the G797
Mt 12: 4 lawful for them to do, but only *for* the **p**. G2636
Mt 12: 5 in the Law that the **p** on Sabbath duty in G2636
Mt 16:21 the **chief p** and the teachers of the law G797
Mt 20:18 delivered over *to* the **chief p** and the G797
Mt 21:15 But when the **chief p** and the teachers of G797
Mt 21:23 the **chief p** and the elders of the people G797
Mt 21:45 When the **chief p** and the Pharisees heard G797
Mt 26: 3 Then the **chief p** and the elders of the G797
Mt 26:14 called Judas Iscariot—went to the **chief p** G797
Mt 26:47 sent from the **chief p** and the elders of the G797
Mt 26:59 The **chief p** and the whole Sanhedrin were G797
Mt 27: 1 all the **chief p** and the elders of the people G797
Mt 27: 3 of silver *to* the **chief p** and the elders. G797
Mt 27: 6 The **chief p** picked up the coins and said G797
Mt 27:12 was accused by the **chief p** and the elders, G797
Mt 27:20 But the **chief p** and the elders persuaded G797
Mt 27:41 In the same way the **chief p**, the teachers of G797
Mt 27:62 the **chief p** and the Pharisees went to G797
Mt 28:11 reported *to* the **chief p** everything that G797
Mt 28:12 When the chief **p** had met with the elders NDT
Mk 2:26 which is lawful only *for* **p** to eat. G2636
Mk 8:31 the **chief p** and the teachers of the law G797
Mk 10:33 delivered over *to* the **chief p** and the G797
Mk 11:18 The **chief p** and the teachers of the law G797
Mk 11:27 temple courts, the **chief p**, the teachers of G797
Mk 12:12 Then the chief **p**, the teachers of the law NDT
Mk 14: 1 the **chief p** and the teachers of the law G797
Mk 14:10 went to the **chief p** to betray Jesus to them. G797
Mk 14:43 sent from the **chief p**, the teachers of G797
Mk 14:53 and all the **chief p**, the elders and G797
Mk 14:55 The **chief p** and the whole Sanhedrin were G797
Mk 15: 1 in the morning, the **chief p**, with the elders, G797
Mk 15: 3 The **chief p** accused him of many things. G797
Mk 15:10 that the **chief p** had handed Jesus over G797
Mk 15:11 But the **chief p** stirred up the crowd to have G797
Mk 15:31 the same way the **chief p** and the teachers G797
Lk 6: 4 he ate what is lawful only *for* **p** to eat. G2636
Lk 9:22 the **chief p** and the teachers of the law G797
Lk 17:14 he said, "Go, show yourselves *to* the **p**." G2636
Lk 19:47 But the **chief p**, the teachers of the law G797
Lk 20: 1 the **chief p** and the teachers of the law G797
Lk 20:19 of the law and the **chief p** looked for a way G797
Lk 22: 2 the **chief p** and the teachers of the law G797
Lk 22: 4 And Judas went *to* the **chief p** and the G797
Lk 22:52 Then Jesus said to the **chief p**, the officers G797
Lk 22:66 both the **chief p** and the teachers of the G797
Lk 23: 4 announced to the **chief p** and the crowd, G797
Lk 23:10 The **chief p** and the teachers of the law G797
Lk 23:13 Pilate called together the **chief p**, the rulers G797
Lk 24:20 The **chief p** and our rulers handed him over G797
Jn 1:19 in Jerusalem sent **p** and Levites to ask G2636
Jn 7:32 Then the **chief p** and the Pharisees sent G797
Jn 7:45 went back to the **chief p** and the Pharisees, G797
Jn 11:47 Then the **chief p** and the Pharisees called a G797
Jn 11:57 But the **chief p** and the Pharisees had given G797
Jn 12:10 So the **chief p** made plans to kill Lazarus as G797
Jn 18: 3 officials from the **chief p** and the Pharisees. G797
Jn 18:35 own people and **chief p** handed you over G797
Jn 19: 6 As soon as the **chief p** and their officials G797
Jn 19:15 no king but Caesar," the **chief p** answered. G797
Jn 19:21 The **chief p** of the Jews protested to Pilate G797
Ac 4: 1 The **p** and the captain of the temple G2636
Ac 4:23 all that the **chief p** and the elders had G797
Ac 5:24 guard and the **chief p** were at a loss, G797
Ac 6: 7 a large number *of* **p** became obedient to G2636
Ac 9:14 authority from the **chief p** to arrest all who G797
Ac 9:21 to take them as prisoners to the **chief p**?" G797
Ac 22:30 him and ordered the **chief p** and all the G797
Ac 23:14 They went to the **chief p** and the elders G797
Ac 25: 2 where the **chief p** and the Jewish leaders G797
Ac 25:15 the **chief p** and the elders of the Jews G797
Ac 26:10 authority of the **chief p** I put many of the G797
Ac 26:12 authority and commission *of* the **chief p**. G797
Heb 7: 5 of Levi who become **p** to collect a tenth G2632
Heb 7:14 to that tribe Moses said nothing about **p**. G2636
Heb 7:20 Others became **p** without any oath, G2636
Heb 7:23 Now there have been many of those **p** G2636
Heb 7:27 Unlike the other **high p**, he does not need G797
Heb 7:28 the law appoints *as* **high p** men in all their G797
Heb 8: 4 there are already **p** who offer the gifts NDT
Heb 9: 6 the **p** entered regularly into the outer G2636
Rev 1: 6 to be a kingdom and **p** to serve his God G2636
Rev 5:10 to be a kingdom and **p** to serve our God, G2636
Rev 20: 6 they will be **p** of God and of Christ G2636

PRIESTS' (2) [PRIEST]

Eze 41:10 the **p** rooms was twenty cubits wide all NDT
Eze 42:13 temple courtyard are the **p rooms**, H4384+7731

PRIME (3)

1Sa 2:33 your descendants will die **in the p of life**. H408
Job 29: 4 the days when I was in my **p**, when H3074
Isa 38:10 "In the **p** *of* my life must I go through the H1953

PRINCE (51) [PRINCE'S, PRINCELY, PRINCES, PRINCESS]

Ge 23: 6 You are a mighty **p** among us. Bury your H5954
Ge 49:26 on the brow of the **p** *among* his brothers. H5687
Dt 33:16 on the brow of the **p** *among* his brothers. H5687
Jdg 8:18 "each one with the bearing of a **p**." H1201+4889
2Ch 11:22 of Maakah as crown **p** among his brothers H5592
Ezr 1: 8 them out to Sheshbazzar the **p** of Judah. H5954
Pr 14:28 but without subjects a **p** is ruined. H8138
Isa 9: 6 Everlasting Father, **P** *of* Peace. H8569
Eze 7:27 the **p** will be clothed with despair H5954
Eze 12:10 concerns the **p** in Jerusalem and all H5954
Eze 12:12 "The **p** among them will put his things on H5954
Eze 21:25 " 'You profane and wicked **p** *of* Israel H5954
Eze 30:13 No longer will there be a **p** in Egypt, and I H5954
Eze 34:24 my servant David will be **p** among them. H5954
Eze 37:25 David my servant will be their **p** forever. H5954
Eze 38: 2 Magog, the chief **p** *of* Meshek and Tubal H5954
Eze 38: 3 Gog, chief **p** *of* Meshek and Tubal. H5954
Eze 39: 1 Gog, chief **p** *of* Meshek and Tubal. H5954
Eze 44: 3 The **p** himself is the only one who may sit H5954
Eze 45: 7 " 'The **p** will have the land bordering H5954
Eze 45:16 give this special offering to the **p** in Israel. H5954
Eze 45:17 be the duty of the **p** to provide the burnt H5954
Eze 45:22 On that day the **p** is to provide a bull as a H5954
Eze 46: 2 The **p** is to enter from the outside through H5954
Eze 46: 4 burnt offering the **p** brings to the LORD on H5954
Eze 46: 8 When the **p** enters, he is to go in through H5954
Eze 46:10 The **p** is to be among them, going in H5954
Eze 46:12 " 'When the **p** provides a freewill offering H5954
Eze 46:16 If the **p** makes a gift from his inheritance H5954
Eze 46:17 of freedom; then it will revert to the **p**. H5954
Eze 46:18 The **p** must not take any of the inheritance H5954
Eze 48:21 property of the city will belong to the **p**. H5954
Eze 48:21 of the tribal portions will belong to the **p**, H5954
Eze 48:22 center of the area that belongs to the **p**. H5954
Eze 48:22 belonging to the **p** will lie between the H5954
Da 8:25 take his stand against the **P** *of* princes. H8569
Da 10:13 But the **p** *of* the Persian kingdom resisted H8569
Da 10:20 will return to fight against the **p** *of* Persia, H8569
Da 10:20 when I go, the **p** *of* Greece will come H8569
Da 10:21 me against them except Michael, your **p**. H8569
Da 11:22 both it and a **p** *of* the covenant will be H5592
Da 12: 1 the great **p** who protects your people H8569
Hos 3: 4 will live many days without king or **p**, H8569
Mt 9:34 "It is by the **p** of demons that he drives out G807
Mt 12:24 by Beelzebul, the **p** of demons, that this G807
Mk 3:22 By the **p** of demons he is driving out G807
Lk 11:15 "By Beelzebul, the **p** of demons, he is G807
Jn 12:31 now the **p** of this world will be driven out. G807
Jn 14:30 for the **p** of this world is coming. G807
Jn 16:11 because the **p** of this world now stands G807
Ac 5:31 his own right hand as **P** and Savior that he G795

PRINCE'S (1) [PRINCE]

SS 7: 1 your sandaled feet, O **p** daughter! H5618

PRINCELY (1) [PRINCE]

Ps 49:14 in the grave, far from their **p mansions**. H2292

PRINCES (60) [PRINCE]

Nu 21:18 about the well that the **p** dug, that the H8569
Jos 13:21 Hur and Reba—**p** *allied with* Sihon—who H5817
Jdg 5: 2 "When the **p** in Israel take the lead, when H7278
Jdg 5: 9 My heart is with Israel's **p**, with the willing H2980
Jdg 5:15 The **p** of Issachar were with Deborah; yes H8569
1Sa 2: 8 he seats them with **p** and has them H5618
2Sa 13:32 not think that they killed all the **p**; H1201+4889
2Ki 10: 6 Now the royal **p**, seventy of them, were H1201
2Ki 10: 7 men took the **p** and slaughtered H1201+4889
2Ki 10: 8 have brought the heads of the **p**." H1201+4889
2Ki 11: 2 stole him away from among the royal **p**, H1201
2Ch 22:11 among the royal **p** who were about to be H1201
Est 1: 3 Media, the **p**, and the nobles of H7312
Est 6: 9 to one of the king's most noble **p**. H8569
Job 3:15 with **p** who had gold, who filled their H8569
Job 34:19 no partiality to **p** and does not favor the H8569
Ps 45:16 you will make them **p** throughout the land H8569
Ps 68:27 there the great throng of Judah's **p**, and H8569
Ps 68:27 there the **p** *of* Zebulun and of H8569
Ps 83:11 all their **p** like Zebah and Zalmunna, H5817
Ps 105:22 to instruct his **p** as he pleased and teach H8569
Ps 113: 8 he seats them with **p**, with the princes of H5618
Ps 113: 8 with princes, with the **p** *of* his people. H5618
Ps 118: 9 take refuge in the LORD than to trust in **p**. H5618
Ps 146: 3 Do not put your trust in **p**, in human H5618
Ps 148:11 all nations, you **p** and all rulers on earth H8569
Pr 8:16 by me **p** govern, and nobles—all who rule H8569
Pr 19:10 how much worse for a slave to rule over **p**! H8569
Ecc 10: 7 horseback, while **p** go on foot like slaves. H8569
Ecc 10:16 a servant and whose **p** feast in the H8569
Ecc 10:17 birth and whose **p** eat at a proper time— H8569
Isa 23: 8 whose merchants are **p**, whose traders are H8569
Isa 34:12 a kingdom, all her **p** will vanish away. H8569
Isa 40:23 He brings **p** to naught and reduces the H8142
Isa 49: 7 stand up, **p** will see and bow down H8569
La 1: 6 Her **p** are like deer that find no pasture; in H8569
La 2: 2 her kingdom and its **p** down to the ground H8569
La 2: 9 Her king and her **p** are exiled among the H8569
La 4: 7 Their **p** were brighter than snow and H5687
La 5:12 **P** have been hung up by their hands H8569
Eze 19: 1 up a lament concerning the **p** *of* Israel H5954

P

Eze 21:12 my people; it is against all the **p** *of* Israel. H5954
Eze 22: 6 how each of the **p** *of* Israel who are in H5954
Eze 22:25 is a conspiracy of her **p** within her like a H5954
Eze 26:16 Then all the **p** *of* the coast will step down H5954
Eze 27:21 " 'Arabia and all the **p** *of* Kedar were your H5954
Eze 32:29 her kings and all her **p**; despite their H5954
Eze 32:30 "All the **p** *of* the north and all the H5817
Eze 39:18 the blood of the **p** *of* the earth as if they H5954
Eze 45: 8 And my **p** will no longer oppress my H5954
Eze 45: 9 gone far enough, **p** *of* Israel! Give up your H5954
Da 8:25 take his stand against the Prince of **p**. H8569
Da 9: 6 to our kings, our **p** and our ancestors, and H8569
Da 9: 8 our **p** and our ancestors are covered with H8569
Da 10:13 one of the chief **p**, came to help me, H8569
Hos 7: 3 their wickedness, the **p** with their lies. H8569
Hos 7: 5 of our king the **p** become inflamed with H8569
Hos 8: 4 *they* **choose p** without my approval. H8606
Hos 13:10 whom you said, 'Give me a king and **p**'? H8569
Rev 6:15 the kings of the earth, the **p**, the generals, *G3491*

PRINCESS (1) [PRINCE]

Ps 45:13 glorious is the **p** within her H1426+4889

PRINCIPAL (1)

1Ch 9:26 But the four **p** gatekeepers, who were H1475

PRINCIPLES (NIV84) FORCES

PRIOR (1)

Jos 20: 9 by the avenger of blood **p** to standing trial H6330

PRISCILLA (7)

Ac 18: 2 recently come from Italy with his wife **P**, *G4571*
Ac 18:18 Syria, accompanied by **P** and Aquila. *G4571*
Ac 18:19 at Ephesus, where Paul left **P and Aquila**. *G2797*
Ac 18:26 When **P** and Aquila heard him, they *G4571*
Ro 16: 3 Greet **P** and Aquila, my co-workers in *G4571*
1Co 16:19 Aquila and **P** greet you warmly in the Lord *G4571*
2Ti 4:19 Greet **P** and Aquila and the household of *G4571*

PRISON (74) [IMPRISON, IMPRISONED, IMPRISONMENT, IMPRISONMENTS, IMPRISONS, PRISONER, PRISONERS, PRISONS]

Ge 39:20 took him and put him in **p**, H1074+2021+6045
Ge 39:20 Joseph was there in *the* **p**, H1074+2021+6045
Ge 39:21 in the eyes of the **p** warden. H1074+2021+6045
Ge 39:22 of all those held in the **p**, H1074+2021+6045
Ge 40: 3 in the same **p** where Joseph H1074+2021+6045
Ge 40: 5 who were being held in **p** H1074+2021+6045
Ge 40:14 me to Pharaoh and get me out of this **p**. H1074
Ge 42:16 the rest of you *will* **be kept in p**, so that H673
Ge 42:19 one of your brothers stay here in **p**, H1074+5464
Jdg 16:21 set him to grinding grain in the **p**. H1074+673
Jdg 16:25 So they called Samson out of the **p** H1074+673
1Ki 22:27 this fellow in **p** and give him H1074+2021+3975
2Ki 17: 4 seized him and put him in **p**. H1074+3975
2Ki 25:27 Jehoiachin king of Judah from **p**. H1074+3975
2Ki 25:29 put aside his **p** clothes and for the rest H3975
2Ch 16:10 that he put him in **p**. H1074+2021+4551
2Ch 18:26 this fellow in **p** and give him H1074+2021+3975
Job 11:10 along and **confines** you **in p** and H6037
Ps 66:11 brought us into **p** and laid burdens on H5181
Ps 142: 7 Set me free from my **p**, that I may praise H4993
Ecc 4:14 have come from **p** to the H1074+2021+673
Isa 24:22 will be shut up in **p** and be punished after H4993
Isa 42: 7 free captives from **p** and to release from H4993
Jer 37: 4 had not yet been put in **p**. H1074+2021+3989
Jer 37:15 they had made into a **p**. H1074+2021+3975
Jer 37:18 that you have put me in **p**? H1074+2021+3975
Jer 52:11 he put him in **p** till the day H1074+2021+7213
Jer 52:31 Judah and freed him from **p**. H1074+2021+3989
Jer 52:33 put aside his **p** clothes and for the rest H3975
Eze 19: 9 They put him in **p**, so his roar was heard H5180
Mt 4:12 Jesus heard that John *had been* **put in p**, *G4140*
Mt 5:25 the officer, and you may be thrown into **p**. *G5871*
Mt 11: 2 who was in **p**, heard about the *G1303*
Mt 14: 3 him and put him in **p** because of *G5871*
Mt 14:10 had John beheaded in the **p**. *G5871*
Mt 18:30 the man thrown into **p** until he could pay *G5871*
Mt 25:36 I was in **p** and you came to visit me. *G5871*
Mt 25:39 see you sick or in **p** and go to visit you? *G5871*
Mt 25:43 I was sick and in **p** and you did not look *G5871*
Mt 25:44 stranger or needing clothes or sick or in **p**, *G5871*
Mk 1:14 After John *was* **put in p**, Jesus went into *G4140*
Mk 6:17 he had him bound and put in **p**. *G5871*
Mk 6:27 The man went, beheaded John in the **p**, *G5871*
Mk 15: 7 A man called Barabbas was **in p** with the *G1313*
Lk 3:20 this to them all: He locked John up in **p**. *G5871*
Lk 12:58 and the officer throw you into **p**. *G5871*
Lk 21:12 you over to synagogues and put you *in* **p**, *G5871*
Lk 22:33 ready to go with you to **p** and to death." *G5871*
Lk 23:19 had been thrown into **p** for an insurrection *G5871*
Lk 23:25 been thrown into **p** for insurrection and *G5871*
Jn 3:24 This was before John was put in **p**.) *G5871*
Ac 8: 3 both men and women and put them in **p**. *G5871*
Ac 12: 4 he put him in **p**, handing him over to *G5871*
Ac 12: 5 So Peter was kept in **p**, but the church was *G5871*
Ac 12: 9 Peter followed him out of the **p**, but he had NDT
Ac 12:17 how the Lord had brought him out of **p**. *G5871*
Ac 16:23 they were thrown into **p**, and the jailer *G5871*
Ac 16:26 the foundations *of* the **p** were shaken. *G1303*
Ac 16:26 At once all the **p** doors flew open, and NDT
Ac 16:27 when he saw the **p** doors open, he *G5871*
Ac 16:37 are Roman citizens, and threw us into **p**. *G5871*
Ac 16:39 them and escorted them from the **p**, NDT
Ac 16:40 After Paul and Silas came out of the **p** *G5871*
Ac 20:23 Spirit warns me that **p** and hardships are *G1301*
Ac 22: 4 women and throwing them into **p**, *G5871*
Ac 24:27 a favor to the Jews, he left Paul *in* **p**. *G1313*
Ac 26:10 I put many of the Lord's people in **p**, *G5871*
Ro 16: 7 fellow Jews who have been **in p with** me. *G5257*
2Co 11:23 much harder, been in **p** more frequently *G5871*
Heb 10:34 along with those **in p** and joyfully *G1300*
Heb 13: 3 to remember those **in p** as if you were *G1300*
Heb 13: 3 as if *you were* **together with** them **in p**, *G5279*
Rev 2:10 devil will put some of you in **p** to test you, *G5871*
Rev 20: 7 Satan will be released from his **p** *G5871*

PRISONER (20) [PRISON]

Ex 12:29 to the firstborn of the **p**, who was in the H8660
Jdg 15:10 "We have come to **take** Samson **p**," they H673
2Ki 24:12 the king of Babylon, *he* **took** Jehoiachin **p**. H4374
2Ch 33:11 Assyria, *who* **took** Manasseh **p**, put a hook H4334
Isa 22: 3 who were caught **were taken p** together, H673
Mt 27:15 to release a **p** chosen by the crowd. *G1300*
Mt 27:16 had a well-known **p** whose name was *G1300*
Mk 15: 6 festival to release a **p** whom the people *G1300*
Jn 18:39 me to release to you **one** *p* at the time of the AIT
Ac 23:18 the **p**, sent for me and asked me to *G1300*
Ac 25:14 is a man here whom Felix left *as* a **p**. *G1300*
Ac 25:27 to send a **p** on to Rome without *G1300*
Ro 7:23 my mind and **making** me **a p** of the law of *G170*
Eph 3: 1 the **p** of Christ Jesus for the sake of you *G1300*
Eph 4: 1 *As* a **p** for the Lord, then, I urge you to live *G1300*
Col 4:10 My **fellow p** Aristarchus sends you his *G5257*
2Ti 1: 8 testimony about our Lord or of me his **p**. *G1300*
Phm 1 a **p** of Christ Jesus, and Timothy our *G1300*
Phm 9 man and now also a **p** of Christ Jesus— *G1300*
Phm 23 Epaphras, my **fellow p** in Christ Jesus *G5257*

PRISONERS (30) [PRISON]

Ge 39:20 the place where the king's **p** were confined. H659
2Ki 25:18 of the guard **took as p** Seraiah the chief H4374
2Ch 28: 5 and **took** many of his people **as p** H8647+8664
2Ch 28:11 Israelites *you have* **taken as p**, H8647+8664
2Ch 28:13 "You must not bring those **p** here," they H8664
2Ch 28:14 soldiers gave up the **p** and plunder in the H8664
2Ch 28:15 The men designated by name took the **p** H8664
2Ch 28:17 attacked Judah and carried away **p**, H8660
Ps 68: 6 he leads out the **p** with singing; but the H659
Ps 79:11 May the groans of the **p** come before you H659
Ps 102:20 hear the groans of the **p** and release those H659
Ps 107:10 utter darkness, **p** suffering *in* iron chains, H659
Ps 146: 7 food to the hungry. The LORD sets **p** free, H673
Isa 24:22 together like **p** *bound* in a dungeon; H660
Isa 51:14 The **cowering p** will soon be set free; they H7579
Isa 61: 1 release from darkness for the **p**, H673
Jer 52:24 of the guard **took as p** Seraiah the chief H4374
La 3:34 To crush underfoot all **p** *in* the land, H659
Hab 1: 9 like a desert wind and gather **p** like sand. H8660
Zec 9:11 I will free your **p** from the waterless pit. H659
Zec 9:12 to your fortress, you **p** *of* hope; even now I H659
Lk 4:18 proclaim freedom *for* the **p** and recovery of *G171*
Lk 21:24 the sword and *will be* **taken as p** to all the *G170*
Ac 9: 2 he might take *them* **as p** to Jerusalem. *G1313*
Ac 9:21 here to take them **as p** to the chief priests *G1313*
Ac 16:25 the other **p** were listening to them. *G1300*
Ac 16:27 because he thought the **p** had escaped. *G1300*
Ac 22: 5 these people *as* **p** to Jerusalem to *G1639+1313*
Ac 27: 1 some other **p** were handed over to *G1304*
Ac 27:42 planned to kill the **p** to prevent any of *G1304*

PRISONS (1) [PRISON]

Isa 42:22 in pits or hidden away in **p**. H1074+3975

PRIVATE (7) [PRIVATELY]

Ge 43:30 He went into his **p room** and wept there. H2540
Ex 20:26 on steps, or your **p parts** may be exposed. H6872
Dt 25:11 reaches out and seizes him by his **p parts**, H4434
Isa 7:20 to shave your head and **p parts**, and H8552+8079
Mt 17:19 came to Jesus **in p** and asked, *G2848+2625*
Lk 9:18 Jesus was praying in **p** and his disciples *G3668*
1Co 11:21 go ahead with **your own p** suppers. *G3836+2625*

PRIVATELY (10) [PRIVATE]

1Sa 18:22 "Speak to David **p** and say H928+2021+4319
2Sa 3:27 as if to speak with him **p**. H928+2021+8952
Jer 37:17 where he asked him **p**, "Is H928+2021+6260
Jer 40:15 Kareah said **p** to Gedaliah in H928+2021+6260
Mt 14:13 withdrew by boat **p** to a solitary *G2848+2625*
Mt 24: 3 the disciples came to him **p**. *G2848+2625*
Mk 9:28 his disciples asked him **p**, "Why *G2848+2625*
Mk 13: 3 John and Andrew asked him **p**, *G2848+2625*
Lk 10:23 turned to his disciples and said **p**, *G2848+2625*
Gal 2: 2 meeting **p** with those esteemed as *G2848+2625*

PRIVILEGE (1)

2Co 8: 4 pleaded with us *for* the **p** of sharing in *G5921*

PRIZE (4)

1Co 9:24 the runners run, but only one gets the **p**? *G1092*
1Co 9:24 Run in such a way as to get the **p**. NDT
1Co 9:27 I myself will not be disqualified for the **p**. NDT
Php 3:14 the goal to win the **p** for which God has *G1092*

PROBE (5) [PROBES]

Dt 13:14 inquire, **p** and investigate it thoroughly. H2983
Job 10: 6 search out my faults and **p** after my sin— H2011
Job 11: 7 *Can you* **p** the limits of the Almighty H5162
Ps 17: 3 Though *you* **p** my heart, though you H1043
Jer 20:12 the righteous and **p** the heart and mind, H8011

PROBES (1) [PROBE]

Ps 7: 9 righteous God *who* **p** minds and hearts. H1043

PROBLEMS (3)

Dt 1:12 how can I bear your **p** and your burdens H3268
Da 5:12 explain riddles and solve **difficult p**. A10626
Da 5:16 interpretations and to solve **difficult p**. A10626

PROCEDURE (2) [PROCEED]

Ecc 8: 5 heart will know the **proper** time and **p**. H5477
Ecc 8: 6 For there is a **proper** time and **p** for every H5477

PROCEED (1) [PROCEDURE, PROCEEDED, PROCEEDINGS, PROCESSION]

Ne 12:31 One *was to* **p** on top of the wall to the H2143

PROCEEDED (9) [PROCEED]

Ge 9:20 a man of the soil, **p** to plant a vineyard. H2725
Ge 27:23 of his brother Esau; so *he p to* **bless** him. AIT
Ge 42:20 that you may not die." This *they p to* **do**. AIT
Ge 44:12 Then the steward *p to* **search**, beginning with AIT
2Ki 8: 2 The woman **p** to do as the man of God H7756
2Ki 11: 1 *she* **p** to destroy the whole royal family. H7756
2Ch 22:10 *she* **p** to destroy the whole royal family of H7756
Ne 12:38 The second choir **p** in the opposite H2143
Ac 12: 3 among the Jews, *he* **p** to seize Peter also. *G4707*

PROCEEDINGS (1) [PROCEED]

Ac 24:22 with the Way, adjourned **the p**. *G899S*

PROCESSION (10) [PROCEED]

1Sa 10: 5 you will meet a **p** *of* prophets coming H2474
1Sa 10:10 at Gibeah, a **p** *of* prophets met him H2474
Ne 12:36 Ezra the teacher of the Law led **the p**. H2157S
Ps 68:24 Your **p**, God, has come into view, the H2142
Ps 68:24 the **p** *of* my God and King into the H2142
Ps 118:27 join in the **festal p** up to the horns of the H2504
SS 6:10 as the sun, majestic as the stars **in p**? H1839
Isa 60:11 nations—their kings **led in triumphal p**. H5627
1Co 4: 9 us apostles on display *at* **the end** *of the p*, AIT
2Co 2:14 **leads** us **as captives** in Christ's **triumphal p** *G2581*

PROCLAIM (98) [PROCLAIMED, PROCLAIMING, PROCLAIMS, PROCLAMATION]

Ex 33:19 of you, and *I will* **p** my name, the H7924+928
Lev 23: 2 which *you are to* **p** as sacred assemblies. H7924
Lev 23: 4 sacred assemblies *you are to* **p** at their H7924
Lev 23:21 On that same day *you are to* **p** a sacred H7924
Lev 23:37 which *you are to* **p** as sacred assemblies H7924
Lev 25:10 the fiftieth year and **p** liberty throughout H7924
Dt 11:29 *you are to* **p** on Mount Gerizim the H5989
Dt 30:12 to get it and **p** it *to* us so we may obey H9048
Dt 30:13 sea to get it and **p** it *to* us so we may H9048
Dt 32: 3 *I will* **p** the name of the LORD. Oh, praise H7924
1Sa 31: 9 Philistines to **p the news** *in* the temple of H1413
2Sa 1:20 in Gath, **p** it not in the streets of Ashkelon H1413
1Ki 21: 9 "**P** a day of fasting and seat Naboth in a H7924
1Ch 10: 9 to **p the news** *among* their idols H1413
1Ch 16: 8 praise to the LORD, **p** his name; make H7924+928
1Ch 16:23 all the earth; **p** his salvation day after day. H1413
Ne 8:15 that *they should* **p** this word and H9048
Ps 2: 7 *I will* **p** the LORD's decree: He said to me H6218
Ps 9:11 **p** among the nations what he has done. H5583
Ps 19: 1 the skies **p** the work of his hands. H5583
Ps 22:31 *They will* **p** his righteousness, declaring to H5583
Ps 30: 9 *Will it* **p** your faithfulness? H5583
Ps 35:28 My tongue *will* **p** your righteousness, your H2047
Ps 40: 9 *I* **p** your saving acts in the great assembly H1413
Ps 50: 6 And the heavens **p** his righteousness, for H5583
Ps 64: 9 *they will* **p** the works of God and ponder H5583
Ps 68:11 the *women who* **p** it are a mighty H1413
Ps 68:34 **P** the power of God, whose majesty is H5989
Ps 71:16 I will come and **p** your mighty acts H2349
Ps 71:16 LORD; I will **p** your righteous deeds NDT
Ps 79:13 to generation *we will* **p** your praise. H6218
Ps 96: 2 his name; **p** his salvation day after day. H1413
Ps 97: 6 The heavens **p** his righteousness, and all H5583
Ps 105: 1 praise to the LORD, **p** his name; make H7924+928
Ps 106: 2 Who *can* **p** the mighty acts of the LORD H4910
Ps 118:17 and *will* **p** what the LORD has done. H6218
Ps 145: 6 works—and *I will* **p** your great deeds. H6218
Isa 12: 4 praise to the LORD, **p** his name; make H7924+928
Isa 12: 4 has done, and **p** that his name is exalted. H2349
Isa 40: 2 **p** to her that her hard service has H7924
Isa 42:12 glory to the LORD and **p** his praise in the H5583
Isa 43:21 myself *that they may* **p** my praise. H6218
Isa 44: 7 then is like me? *Let him* **p** it. Let him H7924
Isa 44: 8 *Did I* not **p** this and foretell it long ago H9048
Isa 48:20 Announce this with shouts of joy and **p** it H9048
Isa 52: 7 bring good news, *who* **p** peace, who bring H9048
Isa 52: 7 good tidings, *who* **p** salvation, who say H9048
Isa 61: 1 anointed me to **p good news** *to* the poor. H1413
Isa 61: 1 to **p** freedom for the captives and release H7924
Isa 61: 2 to **p** the year of the LORD's favor and the H7924
Isa 66:19 *They will* **p** my glory among the nations H5583

Jer 2: 2 "Go and p in the hearing of Jerusalem H7924
Jer 3:12 p this message toward the north: H7924
Jer 4: 5 in Judah and p in Jerusalem and say: H9048
Jer 4:16 to the nations, p concerning Jerusalem: H9048
Jer 5:20 descendants of Jacob and p it in Judah: H9048
Jer 7: 2 LORD's house and there p this message: H7924
Jer 11: 6 "P all these words in the towns of Judah H7924
Jer 19: 2 There p the words I tell you H7924
Jer 22: 1 king of Judah and p this message there: H1819
Jer 31:10 you nations; p it in distant coastlands: H5583
Jer 34: 8 in Jerusalem to p freedom for the slaves H7924
Jer 34:17 So I now p 'freedom' for you, declares the H7924
Jer 46:14 this in Egypt, and p it in Migdol; proclaim H9048
Jer 46:14 p it also in Memphis and Tahpanhes: H9048
Jer 50: 2 "Announce and p among the nations, lift H9048
Jer 50: 2 lift up a banner and p it; keep nothing H9048
Hos 5: 9 the tribes of Israel *I* p what is certain. H3359
Joel 3: 9 P this among the nations: Prepare for war H7924
Am 3: 9 P to the fortresses of Ashdod and to the H9048
Jnh 3: 2 city of Nineveh and p to it the message I H7924
Mic 3: 5 *they* p 'peace' if they have something to H7924
Zec 1:14 was speaking to me said, "P this word: H7924
Zec 1:17 "P further: This is what the LORD Almighty H7924
Zec 9:10 *He will* p peace to the nations H1819
Mt 10: 7 As you go, p *this* **message**: 'The kingdom G3062
Mt 10:27 is whispered in your ear, p from the roofs. G3062
Mt 12:18 and *he will* p justice to the nations. G550
Lk 4:18 anointed me *to* **p good news** to the poor. G2294
Lk 4:18 He has sent me *to* p freedom for the G3062
Lk 4:19 *to* p the year of the Lord's favor. G3062
Lk 4:43 "I must **p the good news** of the kingdom G2294
Lk 9: 2 he sent them out *to* p the kingdom of God G3062
Lk 9:60 you go and p the kingdom of God. G1334
Ac 9:15 chosen instrument *to* p my name to the G1002
Ac 17:23 this is what I *am going to* p to you. G2859
Ac 20:27 I have not hesitated *to* p to you the whole G334
Ro 10: 8 the message concerning faith that *we* p: G3062
Ro 16:25 the **message** I p about Jesus Christ G3060
1Co 11:26 *you* p the Lord's death until he comes. G2859
Php 1:14 dare all the more *to* p the gospel without G3281
Col 1:28 He is the one we p, admonishing and G2859
Col 4: 3 *so that we may* p the mystery of Christ G3281
Col 4: 4 Pray that *I may* p it clearly, as I should. G3281
1Jn 1: 1 this we p concerning the Word of life. NDT
1Jn 1: 2 testify to it, and *we* p to you the eternal life G550
1Jn 1: 3 *We* p to you what we have seen and heard G550
Rev 14: 6 the eternal gospel *to* p to those who live G2294

PROCLAIMED (49) [PROCLAIM]

Ex 9:16 that my name *might be* p in all the H6218
Ex 34: 5 there with him and p his name, H7924+928
Dt 1: 3 Moses p to the Israelites all that the LORD H1819
Dt 5:22 the LORD p in a loud voice to H1819
Dt 9:10 commandments the LORD p to you on the H1819
Dt 10: 4 Commandments *he had* p to you on the H1819
Dt 15: 2 time for canceling debts *has been* p. H7924
1Ki 16:16 p Omri, the commander of the army, **king** H4887
1Ki 21:12 *They* p a fast and seated Naboth in a H7924
2Ki 10:20 assembly in honor of Baal." So *they* p it. H7924
2Ki 11:12 a copy of the covenant and p him **king**. H4887
2Ki 23:16 word of the LORD p *by* the man of God who H7924
2Ki 24: 2 the word of the LORD p by his servants the H1819
2Ch 20: 3 of the LORD, and *he* p a fast for all Judah. H7924
2Ch 23:11 a copy of the covenant and p him **king**. H4887
Ezr 8:21 by the Ahava Canal, *I* p a fast, so that we H7924
Est 1:20 the king's edict **is** p throughout all his H9048
Est 2: 8 the king's order and edict *had* **been** p, H9048
Est 2:18 *He* p a holiday throughout the provinces H6913
Isa 43: 9 foretold this and p *to* us the former things H9048
Isa 43:12 I have revealed and saved and p—I, and H9048
Jer 23:22 *they would have* p my words *to* my people H9048
Jer 34:15 Each of you p freedom to your own H7924
Jer 34:17 you *have* not p freedom to your own H7924
Jer 36: 9 before the LORD *was* p *for* all the people in H7924
Da 3: 4 Then the herald loudly p, "Nations and A10637
Da 5:29 he *was* p the third highest ruler in A10371
Jnh 3: 5 A fast *was* p, and all of them, from the H7924
Zec 1: 4 ancestors, to whom the earlier prophets p: H7924
Zec 7: 7 the words the LORD p through the earlier H7924
Mt 11: 5 and **the good news is** p to the poor. G2294
Lk 3:18 the people and **p the good news** to them. G2294
Lk 7:22 and **the good news** *is* p to the poor. G2294
Lk 12: 3 the inner rooms *will be* p from the roofs. G3062
Lk 16:16 Law and the Prophets were p until John. NDT
Ac 8: 5 city in Samaria and p the Messiah there. G3062
Ac 8:12 Philip *as he* **p the good news** of the G2294
Ac 8:25 *After* they *had further* p the word of the G3281
Ac 13: 5 *they* p the word of God in the Jewish G2859
Ac 13:38 Jesus the forgiveness of sins *is* p to you. G2859
Ac 28:31 *He* p the kingdom of God and taught G3062
Ro 9:17 that my name *might be* p in all the G1334
Ro 15:19 I have fully **p the gospel** of Christ. G2295
1Co 2: 1 human wisdom *as I* p to you the G2859
Col 1:23 heard and that *has been* p to every G3062
2Ti 4:17 me the message *might be* **fully** *p* and all the AIT
Heb 4: 2 we also have had **the good news p** to us, G2294
Heb 4: 6 *who* formerly *had* **the good news p** *to them* G2294
Heb 9:19 *When* Moses *had* p every command of the G3281

PROCLAIMING (25) [PROCLAIM]

Ex 34: 6 he passed in front of Moses, p, "The LORD, H7924
1Sa 11: 7 throughout Israel, p, "This is what will be H606
Est 1:22 p that every man should be ruler over his H1819
Est 6: 9 the city streets, p before him, 'This is what H7924
Est 6:11 the city streets, p before him, "This is H7924
Ps 26: 7 p aloud your praise and telling of all your H9048
Ps 92: 2 p your love in the morning and your H5583
Ps 92:15 p, "The LORD is upright; he is my Rock, H5583
Isa 60: 6 gold and incense and p the praise of the H1413
Isa 63: 1 "It is I, p victory, mighty to save H1819
Jer 4:15 p disaster from the hills of Ephraim. H9048
Jer 20: 8 I cry out p violence and destruction. H7924
Jnh 3: 4 into the city, p, "Forty more days and H7924
Mt 4:23 p the good news of the kingdom G3062
Mt 9:35 p the good news of the kingdom and G3062
Mk 1:14 into Galilee, p the good news of God. G3062
Lk 8: 1 p the good news of the kingdom of God. G3062
Lk 9: 6 **p the good news** and healing people G2294
Lk 20: 1 the temple courts and **p the good news**, G2294
Ac 4: 2 p in Jesus the resurrection of the dead. G2859
Ac 5:42 and **p the good news** *that* Jesus is G2294
Ac 17: 3 "This Jesus I *am* p to you is the Messiah," G2859
Ro 15:16 the priestly duty *of* **p the gospel** of God, G2295
2Th 2: 4 up in God's temple, p himself to be God. G617
Rev 5: 2 I saw a mighty angel p in a loud voice, G3062

PROCLAIMS (3) [PROCLAIM]

Dt 18:22 If what a prophet p in the name of the H1819
Ps 6: 5 Among the dead no one p your **name** H2352
Na 1:15 one who brings good news, *who* p peace! H9048

PROCLAMATION (9) [PROCLAIM]

2Ch 24: 9 A p was then issued in Judah and H7754
2Ch 30: 5 decided to send a p throughout Israel, H7754
2Ch 36:22 of Persia to make a p throughout his H7754
Ezr 1: 1 of Persia to make a p throughout his H7754
Ezr 10: 7 A p was then issued throughout Judah H7754
Ne 6: 7 prophets to **make** *this* p about you in H7924
Isa 62:11 The LORD *has* **made** p to the ends of the H9048
Jnh 3: 7 This is **the p** *he* **issued** in Nineveh: "By the H2410
1Pe 3:19 he went and **made** p to the imprisoned G3062

PROCONSUL (6) [PROCONSULS]

Ac 13: 7 who was an attendant *of* the p, Sergius G478
Ac 13: 7 **The p**, an intelligent man, sent for G4047S
Ac 13: 8 them and tried to turn the p from the faith. G478
Ac 13:12 When the p saw what had happened, he G478
Ac 18:12 While Gallio was p of Achaia, the Jews of G478
Ac 18:17 leader and beat him in front of the p; G1037

PROCONSULS (1) [PROCONSUL]

Ac 19:38 the courts are open and there are p. G478

PROCORUS (1)

Ac 6: 5 Holy Spirit; also Philip, P, Nicanor, Timon, G4743

PRODDED (1)

Jdg 16:16 With such nagging *she* p him day after day H552

PRODUCE (43) [PRODUCED, PRODUCES, PRODUCT, PRODUCTS]

Ge 1:11 God said, "*Let* the land p vegetation: H2012
Ge 1:24 "*Let* the land p living creatures according H3655
Ge 3:18 *It will* p thorns and thistles for you, and H7541
Ge 47:26 that a fifth of the p belongs to Pharaoh. NDT
Ex 5:18 yet *you must* p your full quota of bricks." H5989
Ex 8:18 magicians tried to p gnats by their secret H3655
Dt 8:18 he who gives you the ability to p wealth, H6913
Dt 11:17 not rain and the ground will yield no p, H3292
Dt 14:22 that your fields p each year. H9311+2446+3655
Dt 14:28 tithes of that year's p and store it in your H9311
Dt 16:13 you have gathered the p of your threshing NDT
Dt 26: 2 of all that *you* p *from* the soil of the land H995
Dt 26:12 a tenth of all your p in the third year, H9311
Dt 28:33 know will eat what your land and labor p, H7262
Jos 5:11 they ate some of the p *of* the land: H6289
Jos 5:12 that year they ate the p *of* Canaan. H9311
1Ch 27:27 was in charge of **the p** of the vineyards H8611S
Job 40:20 The hills bring it their p, and all the wild H1006
Ps 78:46 to the grasshopper, their p to the locust. H3330
Ps 105:35 in their land, ate up the p *of* their soil. H7262
Pr 21: 4 the unplowed field of the wicked—p sin. NDT
Pr 25: 4 and a silversmith *can* p a vessel; H3655
Isa 5:10 A ten-acre vineyard *will* p only a bath of H6913
Jer 2: 7 a fertile land to eat its fruit and **rich** p. H3206
Jer 29: 5 plant gardens and eat *what* they p. H7262
Jer 29:28 plant gardens and eat *what* they p. H7262
Eze 17: 8 water so that *it would* p branches, H6913
Eze 17:23 *it will* p branches and bear fruit and H5951
Eze 36: 8 *will* p branches and fruit for my people H5989
Eze 48:18 Its p will supply food for the workers of the H9311
Hos 8: 7 has no head; *it will* p no flour. Were it H6913
Hab 3:17 olive crop fails and the fields p no food, H6913
Zec 8:12 the ground *will* p its crops, and the H5989
Mt 3: 8 P fruit in keeping with repentance. G4472
Mt 3:10 every tree *that does* not p good fruit G4472
Mt 21:43 given to a people *who will* p its fruit. G4472
Mk 4:20 accept it, and **p a crop**—some thirty, some G2844
Lk 3: 8 P fruit in keeping with repentance. And do G4472
Lk 3: 9 every tree *that does* not p good fruit G4472
Lk 8:15 retain it, and by persevering **p a crop**. G2844
2Ti 2:23 because you know *they* p quarrels. G1164
Jas 1:20 human anger *does* not p the G2237
Jas 3:12 Neither can a salt spring p fresh water. G4472

PRODUCED (14) [PRODUCE]

Ge 1:12 The land p vegetation: plants bearing H3655
Ge 41:47 years of abundance the land p plentifully. H6913
Ge 41:48 all the food p in those seven years H2118
Nu 17: 8 had budded, blossomed and p almonds. H1694
Dt 8:17 of my hands *have* p this wealth for me." H6913
2Ch 31: 5 oil and honey and all *that* the fields p. H9311
Eze 17: 6 became a vine and p branches and put H6913
Mt 13: 8 good soil, where *it* p a crop—a hundred, G1443
Mk 4: 8 It came up, grew and p a crop, some G1443
Ac 6:13 *They* p false witnesses, who testified G2705
Ro 7: 8 p in me every kind of coveting. G2981
2Co 7:11 See what this godly sorrow *has* p in you G2981
1Th 1: 3 our God and Father your work *p by* **faith**, AIT
Jas 5:18 gave rain, and the earth p its crops. G1056

PRODUCES (18) [PRODUCE]

Lev 25: 7 Whatever the land p may be eaten. H9311
Dt 29:18 no root among you *that* p such bitter H7238
Ne 9:36 eat its fruit and the other **good things** it *p*. AIT
Job 37:10 The breath of God p ice, and the broad H5989
Pr 13:23 An unplowed field p food for the poor H8044
Pr 30:33 For as churning cream p butter, and as H3655
Pr 30:33 as twisting the nose p blood, so H3655
Pr 30:33 so stirring up anger p strife. H3655
Hag 1:11 oil and everything else the ground p, H3655
Mt 13:23 This is the one *who* **p a crop**, yielding a G2844
Mk 4:28 All by itself the soil **p grain**—first the stalk G2844
Jn 12:24 But if it dies, *it* p many seeds. G5770
Ro 5: 3 we know that suffering p perseverance; G2981
2Co 1: 6 which p in you patient endurance of the G1919
Heb 6: 7 falling on it and *that* p a crop useful to G5503
Heb 6: 8 But land *that* p thorns and thistles is G1766
Heb 12:11 *it* p a harvest of righteousness and peace G625
Jas 1: 3 the testing of your faith p perseverance. G2981

PRODUCT (1) [PRODUCE]

Nu 18:30 to you as the p *of* the threshing floor H9311

PRODUCTS (5) [PRODUCE]

Ge 43:11 Put some of the **best** p *of* the land in your H2380
Isa 45:14 "The p *of* Egypt and the merchandise of H3330
Jer 20: 5 their enemies—all its p, all its valuables H3330
Eze 27:16 with you because of your many p; H5126
Eze 27:18 of your many p and great wealth of H5126

PROFANE (12) [PROFANED]

Lev 18:21 for *you must* not p the name of your God. H2725
Lev 19:12 by my name and so p the name of your H2725
Lev 21: 6 to their God and *must* not p the name of H2725
Lev 22: 2 so *they will* not p my holy name. H2725
Lev 22:32 *Do* not p my holy name, for I must be H2725
Eze 20:39 to me and no longer p my holy name with H2725
Eze 21:25 " 'You p and wicked prince of Israel H2729
Eze 22:26 violence to my law and p my holy things; H2725
Am 2: 7 use the same girl and so p my holy name. H2725
Zep 3: 4 Her priests p the sanctuary and do H2725
Mal 1:12 "But you p it by saying, 'The Lord's table H2725
Mal 2:10 Why *do we* p the covenant of our H2725

PROFANED (13) [PROFANE]

Lev 20: 3 my sanctuary and p my holy name. H2725
Jer 34:16 you have turned around and p my name; H2725
Eze 13:19 *You have* p me among my people for a H2725
Eze 20: 9 my name from **being** p in the eyes of H2725
Eze 20:14 would keep it from **being** p in the eyes of H2725
Eze 20:22 would keep it from **being** p in the eyes of H2725
Eze 22:26 my Sabbaths, so that *I* **am** p among them. H2725
Eze 36:20 among the nations *they* p my holy name, H2725
Eze 36:21 the people of Israel p among the nations H2725
Eze 36:22 which *you have* p among the nations H2725
Eze 36:23 which *has* **been** p among the nations H2725
Eze 36:23 the name *you have* p among them. H2725
Eze 39: 7 *I will* no longer **let** my holy name **be p** H2725

PROFESS (5) [PROFESSED]

Ro 10:10 your mouth *that you* **p** *your* **faith** and are G3933
1Ti 2:10 women *who* p to worship God. G2040
Heb 4:14 let us hold firmly *to* the **faith** we p. G3934
Heb 10:23 Let us hold unswervingly to the hope we p G3934
Heb 13:15 the fruit of lips *that* **openly** p his name. G3933

PROFESSED (1) [PROFESS]

1Ti 6:21 which some *have* p and in so doing have G2040

PROFIT (17) [PROFITABLE, PROFITS]

Lev 25:36 Do not take interest or any p from them H9552
Lev 25:37 money at interest or sell them food at a p. H5270
Job 20:18 he will not enjoy the p *from* his trading. H2657
Job 34: 9 '*There is* no p in trying to please God. H6122
Job 35: 3 ask him, 'What p *is it* to me, and what H6122
Pr 14:23 All hard work brings a p, but mere talk H4639
Pr 21: 5 of the diligent lead to p as surely as haste H4639
Pr 28: 8 taking interest or p from the poor amasses H9552
Ecc 6:11 meaning, and how does that p anyone? H3463
Isa 23:18 Yet her p and her earnings will be set H6087
Isa 44:10 casts an idol, *which can* p nothing? H3603
Eze 18: 8 to them at interest or take a p from them. H9552
Eze 18:13 He lends at interest and takes a p. H9552
Eze 18:17 poor and takes no interest or p from them. H9552
Eze 22:12 take interest and make a p from the poor. H9552
2Co 2:17 *we* do not **peddle** the word of God **for p** G1639+2836

P

Jude 11 they have rushed for p into Balaam's error; G3635

PROFITABLE (3) [PROFIT]

Pr 3:14 she is more p than silver and H3202+6087
Pr 31:18 She sees that her trading is p, and her H3202
Titus 3: 8 things are excellent and p for everyone. G6068

PROFITS (2) [PROFIT]

Ecc 5: 9 the king himself p from the fields. H6268
Isa 23:18 Her p will go to those who live before the H6087

PROFLIGATE (NIV84) GLUTTON

PROFOUND (5)

Job 9: 4 His wisdom is p, his power is vast. H4222
Ps 92: 5 your works, LORD, how p your thoughts! H6676
Ecc 7:24 exists is far off and most p— H6678+6678
Ac 24: 3 we acknowledge this with p gratitude. G4246
Eph 5:32 This is a p mystery—but I am talking about G3489

PROGRESS (4) [PROGRESSED]

Ezr 5: 8 and is making rapid p under their A10613
Jn 13: 2 The evening meal was in p, and the devil G1181
Php 1:25 all of you for your p and joy in the faith, G4620
1Ti 4:15 to them, so that everyone may see your p. G4620

PROGRESSED (1) [PROGRESS]

2Ch 24:13 diligent, and the repairs p under them. H6590

PROJECT (3) [PROJECTED, PROJECTING, PROJECTION, PROJECTIONS, PROJECTS]

1Ki 5:16 who supervised the p and directed the H4856
Ne 6: 3 on a great p and cannot go down. H4856
Eze 43:15 horns p upward from the H4200+5087+2025

PROJECTED (1) [PROJECT]

1Ki 6: 3 p ten cubits from the front of the H8145

PROJECTING (17) [PROJECT]

1Ki 7:34 one on each corner, p from the stand. H4946
Ne 3:25 angle and the tower p from the upper H3655
Ne 3:26 Gate toward the east and the p tower. H3655
Ne 3:27 from the great p tower to the wall of H3655
Eze 40: 7 the p walls between the alcoves were NDT
Eze 40:10 the faces of the p walls on each side had H382
Eze 40:14 the faces of the p walls all around the H382
Eze 40:16 The alcoves and the p walls inside the H382
Eze 40:16 The faces of the p walls were decorated H382
Eze 40:21 its p walls and its portico had the same H382
Eze 40:26 on the faces of the p walls on each side. H382
Eze 40:29 its p walls and its portico had the same H382
Eze 40:33 its p walls and its portico had the same H382
Eze 40:36 did its alcoves, its p walls and its portico H382
Eze 40:48 cubits and its p walls were three cubits H4190
Eze 41: 2 the p walls on each side of it were H4190
Eze 41: 3 the p walls on each side of it were NDT

PROJECTION (2) [PROJECT]

Ex 26:19 bases for each frame, one under each p. H3338
Ex 36:24 bases for each frame, one under each p. H3338

P

PROJECTIONS (2) [PROJECT]

Ex 26:17 with two p set parallel to each other. H3338
Ex 36:22 with two p set parallel to each other. H3338

PROJECTS (2) [PROJECT]

1Ki 9:23 chief officials in charge of Solomon's p— H4856
Ecc 2: 4 I undertook great p: I built houses for H5126

PROLONG (5) [PROLONGED]

Dt 5:33 live and prosper and p your days in the H799
Ps 85: 5 Will you p your anger through all H5432
Pr 3: 2 they will p your life many years and H802
Isa 53:10 he will see his offspring and p his days H799
La 4:22 Daughter Zion; he will not p your exile. H3578

PROLONGED (2) [PROLONG]

Dt 28:59 harsh and p disasters, and severe H586
Isa 13:22 is at hand, and her days will not be p. H5432

PROMINENT (11)

1Ki 21: 9 Naboth in a p place among the people. H8031
1Ki 21:12 Naboth in a p place among the people. H8031
2Ki 24:15 his officials and the p people of the land. H380
Est 9: 4 Mordecai was p in the palace; his H1524
Da 8: 5 a goat with a p horn between its eyes H2607
Da 8: 8 in its place four p horns grew up toward H2607
Mk 15:43 of Arimathea, a p member of the Council G2363
Lk 14: 1 went to eat in the house of a p Pharisee, G807
Ac 17: 4 Greeks and quite a few p women. G4755
Ac 17:12 also a number of p Greek women and G2363
Ac 25:23 officers and the p men of the city. G2848+2029

PROMISCUITY (5) [PROMISCUOUS]

Eze 16:25 with increasing p to anyone who passed H9373
Eze 16:26 aroused my anger with your increasing p. H9373
Eze 16:29 you increased your p to include Babylonia H9373
Eze 16:36 naked body in your p with your lovers, H9373
Eze 23:29 will be exposed. Your lewdness and p H9373

PROMISCUOUS (3) [PROMISCUITY]

Dt 22:21 thing in Israel by being p while still in her H2388
Eze 23:19 more and more p as she recalled the H9373
Hos 1: 2 marry a p woman and have children with H2393

PROMISE (68) [PROMISED, PROMISES]

Ge 47:29 under my thigh and p that you will show me NDT
Nu 23:19 Does he p and not fulfill? H1819
Nu 30: 6 after her lips utter a rash p by which she H4439
Nu 30: 8 obligates her or the rash p by which she H4439
Jos 9:21 So the leaders' p to them was kept. H1819
Jos 23:14 Every p has been fulfilled; not one has H1821
2Sa 7:25 keep forever the p you have made H1821
1Ki 2: 4 that the LORD may keep his p to me: H1821+1819
1Ki 6:12 through you the p I gave to David your H1821
1Ki 8:20 "The LORD has kept the p he made: I have H1821
1Ki 8:24 You have kept your p to your servant H1819
1Ch 16:15 covenant forever, the p he made, for a H1821
1Ch 17:23 let the p you have made concerning your H1821
2Ch 1: 9 let your p to my father David be confirmed H1821
2Ch 6:10 "The LORD has kept the p he made. I have H1821
2Ch 6:15 You have kept your p to your servant H1819
Ne 5:13 anyone who does not keep this p. H1821
Ne 9: 8 You have kept your p because you are H1821
Ne 10:30 "We p not to give our daughters in marriage NDT
Ps 77: 8 Has his p failed for all time? H608
Ps 105: 8 covenant forever, the p he made, for a H1821
Ps 105:42 remembered his holy p given to his H1821
Ps 106:24 pleasant land; they did not believe his p. H1821
Ps 119:38 Fulfill your p to your servant, so that you H614
Ps 119:41 your salvation, according to your p; H614
Ps 119:50 suffering is this: Your p preserves my life. H614
Ps 119:58 be gracious to me according to your p. H614
Ps 119:76 comfort, according to your p to your servant. H614
Ps 119:82 looking for your p; I say, "When will you H614
Ps 119:116 according to your p, and I will live; do H614
Ps 119:123 salvation, looking for your righteous p. H614
Ps 119:154 preserve my life according to your p. H614
Ps 119:162 I rejoice in your p like one who finds great H614
Ps 119:170 you; deliver me according to your p. H614
Pr 11: 7 all the p of their power comes to nothing. H9347
Jer 29:10 fulfill my good p to bring you back to H1821
Jer 33:14 fulfill the good p I made to the people H1821
Jer 34: 4 " 'Yet hear the LORD's p to you, Zedekiah H1821
Jer 34: 5 I myself make this p, declares the H1819+1821
Ac 2:39 The p is for you and your children and G2039
Ac 7:17 God to fulfill his p to G2039+4005+3933
Ac 26: 7 This is the p our twelve tribes are hoping G4005S
Ro 4:13 received the p that he would be heir G2039
Ro 4:14 means nothing and the p is worthless, G2039
Ro 4:16 Therefore, the p comes by faith, so that it G2039
Ro 4:20 through unbelief regarding the p of God, G2039
Ro 9: 8 is the children of the p who are regarded G2039
Ro 9: 9 For this was how the p was stated: "At the G2039
Gal 3:14 faith we might receive the p of the Spirit. G2039
Gal 3:17 by God and thus do away with the p. G2039
Gal 3:18 then it no longer depends on the p; but G2039
Gal 3:18 his grace gave it to Abraham through a p. G2039
Gal 3:19 Seed to whom the p referred had come. G2040
Gal 3:29 and heirs according to the p. G2039
Gal 4:23 was born as the result of a divine p. G2039
Gal 4:28 sisters, like Isaac, are children of p. G2039
Eph 2:12 foreigners to the covenants of the p, G2039
Eph 3: 6 sharers together in the p in Christ Jesus. G2039
Eph 6: 2 which is the first commandment with a p G2039
1Ti 4: 8 holding p for both the present life and the G2039
2Ti 1: 1 in keeping with the p of life that is in G2039
Heb 4: 1 since the p of entering his rest still stands G2039
Heb 6:13 When God made his p to Abraham, since G2040
Heb 11: 9 who were heirs with him of the same p. G2039
Heb 11:11 him faithful who had made the p. G2040
2Pe 2:19 They p them freedom, while they G2040
2Pe 3: 9 The Lord is not slow in keeping his p, as G2039
2Pe 3:13 in keeping with his p we are looking G2041

PROMISED (134) [PROMISE]

Ge 18:19 about for Abraham what he has p him." H1819
Ge 21: 1 the LORD did for Sarah what he had p. H1819
Ge 21: 2 old age, at the very time God had p him. H1819
Ge 24: 7 who spoke to me and p me on oath, H8678
Ge 28:15 you until I have done what I have p you." H1819
Ge 50:24 to the land he p on oath to Abraham, H8678
Ex 3:17 And I have p to bring you up out of your H606
Ex 12:25 land that the LORD will give you as he p, H1819
Ex 13:11 as he p on oath to you and your ancestors, H8678
Ex 32:13 your descendants all this land I p them, H606
Ex 33: 1 go up to the land I p on oath to Abraham, H8678
Lev 19:20 female slave who is p to another man H3072
Nu 10:29 the LORD has p good things to Israel." H1819
Nu 11:12 to the land you p on oath to their H8678
Nu 14:16 people into the land he p them on oath, H8678
Nu 14:23 ever see the land I p on oath to their H8678
Nu 14:40 are ready to go up to the land the LORD p. H606
Nu 32:11 will see the land I p on oath to Abraham, H8678
Nu 32:24 but do what you have p." H3655+4946+7023
Dt 1:11 times and bless you as he has p! H1819
Dt 6: 3 the LORD, the God of your ancestors, p you. H1819
Dt 6:18 land the LORD p on oath to your ancestors H8678
Dt 6:23 us the land he p on oath to our ancestors H8678
Dt 8: 1 the land the LORD p on oath to your H8678
Dt 9: 3 them quickly, as the LORD has p you. H1819
Dt 9:28 to take them into the land he had p them, H1819
Dt 11:25 LORD your God, as he p you, will put the H1819
Dt 12:20 has enlarged your territory as he p you, H1819
Dt 13:17 as he p on oath to your ancestors H8678
Dt 15: 6 LORD your God will bless you as he has p, H1819
Dt 18: 2 the LORD is their inheritance, as he p them. H1819
Dt 19: 8 territory, as he p on oath to your ancestors H8678
Dt 19: 8 gives you the whole land he p them, H1819
Dt 26:15 have given us as you p on oath to our H8678
Dt 26:18 his treasured possession as he p, and that H1819
Dt 26:19 people holy to the LORD your God, as he p. H1819
Dt 27: 3 the LORD, the God of your ancestors, p you. H1819
Dt 28: 9 people, as he p you on oath, if you keep H8678
Dt 29:13 may be your God as he p you and as he H1819
Dt 31:20 the land I p on oath to their ancestors H8678
Dt 31:21 them into the land I p them on oath." H8678
Dt 31:23 Israelites into the land I p them on oath, H8678
Dt 34: 4 "This is the land I p on oath to Abraham H8678
Jos 1: 3 where you set your foot, as I p Moses. H1819
Jos 5: 6 see the land he had solemnly p their H8678
Jos 13:14 are their inheritance, as he p them. H1819
Jos 13:33 is their inheritance, as he p them. H1819
Jos 14:10 just as the LORD p, he has kept me alive H1819
Jos 14:12 hill country that the LORD p me that day. H1819
Jos 22: 4 your God has given them rest as he p, H1819
Jos 23: 5 of their land, as the LORD your God p you. H1819
Jos 23:10 LORD your God fights for you, just as he p. H1819
Jos 23:15 good things the LORD your God has p you H1821
Jdg 1:20 As Moses had p, Hebron was given to H1819
Jdg 6:36 save Israel by my hand as you have p— H1819
Jdg 11:36 Do to me just as you p, now H3655+4946+7023
1Sa 2:30 'I p that members of your family H606+606
1Sa 25:30 every good thing he p concerning him H1819
2Sa 3: 9 do for David what the LORD p him on oath H8678
2Sa 3:18 the LORD p David, 'By my servant David I H606
2Sa 7:25 your servant and his house. Do as you p, H1819
2Sa 7:28 and you have p these good things to your H1819
2Sa 19:23 And the king p him on oath. H8678
1Ki 2:24 has founded a dynasty for me as he p— H1819
1Ki 5:12 Solomon wisdom, just as he had p him. H1819
1Ki 8:15 what he p with his own mouth to my H1819
1Ki 8:20 just as the LORD p, and I have built the H1819
1Ki 8:24 with your mouth you have p and with your H1819
1Ki 8:26 let your word that you p your servant H1819
1Ki 8:56 rest to his people Israel just as he p. H1819
1Ki 9: 5 as I p David your father when I said H1819
2Ki 8:19 He had p to maintain a lamp for David H606
2Ki 20: 9 to you that the LORD will do what he has p: H1819
1Ch 11: 3 as the LORD had p through Samuel. H1821
1Ch 11:10 over the whole land, as the LORD had p— H1821
1Ch 17:23 be established forever. Do as you p, H1819
1Ch 17:26 You have p these good things to your H1819
1Ch 27:23 because the LORD had p to make Israel as H606
2Ch 2:15 barley and the olive oil and wine he p, H606
2Ch 6: 4 what he p with his mouth to my father H1819
2Ch 6:10 just as the LORD p, and I have built the H1819
2Ch 6:15 with your mouth you have p and with your H1819
2Ch 6:17 let your word that you p your servant H1819
2Ch 6:42 Remember the great love p to David your AIT
2Ch 21: 7 He had p to maintain a lamp for him and H606
2Ch 23: 3 as the LORD p concerning the descendants H1819
Ne 5:12 take an oath to do what they had p. H1821
Ne 5:13 And the people did as they had p. H1821
Est 4: 7 of money Haman had p to pay into the H606
Ps 66:14 vows my lips p and my mouth spoke when H7198
Ps 119:57 LORD; I have p to obey your words. H606
Isa 38: 7 to you that the LORD will do what he has p: H1819
Isa 55: 3 with you, my faithful love p to David. AIT
Jer 32:42 them all the prosperity I have p them. H1819
Jer 44:25 what you said you would do when you p, H606
Jer 44:25 ahead then, do what you p! Keep your H5624
Mt 14: 7 that he p with an oath to give her G3933
Mk 6:23 And he p her with an oath, "Whatever you G3923
Mk 14:11 to hear this and p to give him money. G2040
Lk 1:55 just as he p our ancestors. G3281
Lk 2:29 as you have p, you may now dismiss G4839
Lk 24:49 going to send you what my Father has p; G2039
Ac 1: 4 wait for the gift my Father p, which G2039
Ac 2:30 knew that God had p him on oath that G3923
Ac 2:33 from the Father the p Holy Spirit and has G2039
Ac 3:21 as he p long ago through his holy G3281
Ac 7: 5 But God p him that he and his G2040
Ac 13:23 to Israel the Savior Jesus, as he p. G2039
Ac 13:32 What God p our ancestors G2039+1181
Ac 13:34 you the holy and sure blessings p to G4008
Ac 18:21 But as he left, he p, "I will come back if it G3306
Ac 26: 6 in what God has p our ancestors G2039+1181
Ro 1: 2 the gospel he p beforehand through his G4600
Ro 4:21 that God had power to do what he had p. G2040
2Co 9: 5 the generous gift you had p. G4600
2Co 11: 2 I p you to one husband, to Christ, so that I G764
Gal 3:22 so that what was p, being given through G2039
Eph 1:13 in him with a seal, the p Holy Spirit, G2039
Titus 1: 2 p before the beginning of time, G2040
Heb 6:12 patience inherit what has been p. G2039
Heb 6:15 patiently, Abraham received what was p. G2039
Heb 6:17 very clear to the heirs of what was p, G2039
Heb 9:15 may receive the p eternal inheritance— G2039
Heb 10:23 hope we profess, for he who p is faithful. G2040
Heb 10:36 you will receive what he has p. G2039
Heb 11: 9 his home in the p land like a stranger G2039
Heb 11:13 They did not receive the things p; they G2039
Heb 11:33 gained what was p; who shut the G2039
Heb 11:39 none of them received what had been p, G2039
Heb 12:26 the earth, but now he has p, "Once more I G2040
Jas 1:12 life that the Lord has p to those who love G2040
Jas 2: 5 the kingdom he p those who love him? G2040
2Pe 3: 4 will say, "Where is this 'coming' he p? G2039

1Jn 2:25 And this is what he **p** us—eternal *G2039+2040*

PROMISES (24) [PROMISE]

Jos 21:45 the LORD's good **p** to Israel failed; H1821+1819
Jos 23:14 one of all the good **p** the LORD your God H1821
1Ki 8:25 my father *the* **p** *you* **made** to him when H1819
1Ki 8:56 of all the good **p** he gave through his H1821
1Ch 17:19 thing and made known all these **great** *p*. AIT
1Ch 25: 5 him through the **p** *of* God to exalt him. H1821
2Ch 6:16 my father *the* **p** *you* **made** to him when H1819
Ps 85: 8 the LORD says; *he* **p** peace to his people H1819
Ps 106:12 they believed his **p** and sang his praise. H1821
Ps 119:140 Your **p** have been thoroughly tested, and H614
Ps 119:148 of the night, that I may meditate on your **p**. H614
Ps 145:13 trustworthy in all he **p** and faithful in all H1821
Hos 10: 4 *They* **make many p**, take false H1819+1821
Lk 1:45 that the Lord would fulfill his **p** to her!" *G3281*
Ro 9: 4 of the law, the temple worship and the **p**. *G2039*
Ro 15: 8 so that the **p** made to the patriarchs might *G2039*
2Co 1:20 For no matter how many **p** God has made *G2039*
2Co 7: 1 since we have these **p**, dear friends, *G2039*
Gal 3:16 The **p** were spoken to Abraham and to his *G2039*
Gal 3:21 therefore, opposed to the **p** of God? *G2039*
Heb 7: 6 blessed him who had the **p**. *G2039*
Heb 8: 6 new covenant is established on better **p**. *G2039*
Heb 11:17 who had embraced the **p** was about to *G2039*
2Pe 1: 4 given us his very great and precious **p**, *G2041*

PROMOTE (8) [PROMOTED, PROMOTES]

Ne 2:10 had come to **p** the welfare of the H1335
Pr 12:20 plot evil, but *those who* **p** peace have joy. H3619
Pr 16:21 gracious words **p** instruction. H3578
Pr 16:23 prudent, and their lips **p** instruction. H3578
Jer 5:28 *They do* not **p** the case of the fatherless H7503
Da 5:19 those he wanted to **p**, he promoted; NDT
Hab 1: 7 law to themselves and **p** their own honor. H3655
1Ti 1: 4 Such things **p** controversial speculations *G4218*

PROMOTED (4) [PROMOTE]

2Ch 28:19 for *he had* **p wickedness** in Judah and H7277
Est 10: 2 whom the king *had* **p**, are they not written H1540
Da 3:30 Then the king **p** Shadrach, Meshach A10613
Da 5:19 wanted to promote, *he* **p**; and those he A10659

PROMOTES (2) [PROMOTE]

Lk 10: 6 If **someone who p** peace is there, your *G5626*
Gal 2:17 doesn't that mean that Christ **p** sin? *G1356*[S]

PROMPT (1) [PROMPTED, PROMPTS]

Job 20: 2 thoughts **p** me **to answer** because I am H8740

PROMPTED (4) [PROMPT]

Mt 14: 8 **P** by her mother, she said, "Give me here *G4586*
Jn 13: 2 devil *had* already **p** *G965+1650+3836+2840*
1Th 1: 3 your labor *p by* **love**, and your AIT
2Th 1:11 goodness and your every deed *p by* **faith**. AIT

PROMPTS (2) [PROMPT]

Ex 25: 2 everyone whose heart **p** them **to give**. H5605
Job 15: 5 Your sin **p** your mouth; you adopt the H544

PRONE (1)

Ex 32:22 "You know how **p** these people are **to** evil. H928

PRONOUNCE (30) [PRONOUNCED, PRONOUNCES, PRONOUNCING]

Ge 48:20 "In your name *will* Israel **p** *this* **blessing**: H1385
Lev 13: 3 *he shall* **p** them **ceremonially unclean**. H3237
Lev 13: 6 the priest *shall* **p** them **clean**; it is only a H3197
Lev 13: 8 the skin, he *shall* **p** them **unclean**; it is a H3237
Lev 13:11 the priest *shall* **p** them **unclean**. H3237
Lev 13:13 their whole body, *he shall* **p** them **clean**. H3197
Lev 13:15 the raw flesh, *he shall* **p** them **unclean**. H3237
Lev 13:17 priest *shall* **p** the affected person **clean**; H3197
Lev 13:20 the priest *shall* **p** that person **unclean**. H3237
Lev 13:22 the priest *shall* **p** them **unclean**; it is a H3237
Lev 13:23 and the priest *shall* **p** them **clean**. H3197
Lev 13:25 The priest *shall* **p** them **unclean**; it is a H3237
Lev 13:27 the priest *shall* **p** them **unclean**; it is a H3237
Lev 13:28 the priest *shall* **p** them **clean**; it is H3197
Lev 13:30 the priest *shall* **p** them **unclean**; it is a H3237
Lev 13:34 skin deep, the priest *shall* **p** them **clean**. H3197
Lev 13:37 and the priest *shall* **p** them **clean**. H3197
Lev 13:44 priest *shall* **p** him **unclean** because H3237+3237
Lev 14: 7 defiling disease, and then **p** them **clean**. H3197
Lev 14:48 he *shall* **p** the house **clean**, because the H3197
Dt 10: 8 minister and to **p blessings** in his name, H1385
Dt 21: 5 to **p blessings** in the name of H1385
Dt 23: 4 in Aram Naharaim to **p a curse on** you. H7837
Dt 27:13 shall stand on Mount Ebal to **p curses**: H7839
Jdg 12: 6 because *he* could not **p** the word correctly H1819
1Ch 23:13 him and to **p blessings** in his name H1385
Job 9:20 if I were blameless, *it would* **p** me **guilty**. H6835
Ps 109:17 He loved to **p** a curse—may it come back NDT
Jer 1:16 *I will* **p** my judgments *on* my people H1819
Jer 4:12 Now I **p** my judgments against them." H1819

PRONOUNCED (20) [PRONOUNCE]

Lev 13: 7 themselves to the priest to be **p clean**, H3200
Lev 13:35 spread in the skin after they are **p clean**, H3200
Lev 14:36 nothing in the house *will be* **p unclean**. H3237
Dt 33: 1 Moses the man of God **p** *on* the Israelites H1385
Jos 6:26 At that time Joshua **p** *this* **solemn oath** H8678
1Ki 20:40 of Israel said. "*You have* **p** it yourself." H3076
2Ki 23:17 came from Judah and **p** against the altar H7924
2Ki 25: 6 where sentence *was* **p on** him. H1819+907
1Ch 16:12 his miracles, and the judgments he **p**, H7023
Ps 76: 8 From heaven *you* **p** judgment, and the H9048
Ps 105: 5 his miracles, and the judgments he **p**, H7023
Jer 19:15 around it every disaster *I* **p** against them, H1819
Jer 26:13 bring the disaster *he has* **p** against you. H1819
Jer 26:19 not bring the disaster *he* **p** against them? H1819
Jer 35:17 Jerusalem every disaster *I* **p** against them. H1819
Jer 36: 7 wrath **p** against this people *by* the LORD H1819
Jer 36:31 of Judah every disaster *I* **p** against them, H1819
Jer 39: 5 where *he* **p** sentence **on** him. H1819+907
Jer 52: 9 where *he* **p** sentence **on** him. H1819+907
Da 7:22 of Days came and **p** judgment in favor of A10314

PRONOUNCES (1) [PRONOUNCE]

Lev 14:11 The priest who **p** them **clean** shall present H3197

PRONOUNCING (1) [PRONOUNCE]

Lev 13:59 for **p** them **clean** or unclean. H3197

PROOF (7) [PROVE]

Dt 22:14 I did not find **p of** her **virginity**," H1436
Dt 22:15 elders at the gate **p that** she was **a virgin**. H1436
Dt 22:17 here is the **p of** my daughter's **virginity**." H1436
Dt 22:20 no **p of** the young woman's **virginity** can H1436
Ac 17:31 He has given **p** of this to everyone by *G4411*
2Co 8:24 show these men the **p** of your love and *G1893*
2Co 13: 3 since you are demanding **p** that Christ is *G1509*

PROOFS (1) [PROVE]

Ac 1: 3 gave many **convincing p** that he was *G5447*

PROPER (30) [PROPERLY]

Lev 5:15 without defect and of the **p value** *in* silver, H6886
Lev 5:18 one without defect and of the **p value**. H6886
Lev 6: 6 one without defect and of the **p value**. H6886
Jdg 6:26 Then build a **p kind** of altar to the LORD H5120
2Sa 15: 3 your claims are valid and **p**, but there is H5791
1Ki 4:28 to the **p place** their H5226+889+2118+9004
1Ch 23:31 regularly in the *p* **number** and in the way AIT
Ezr 4:14 palace and it is not **p** for us to see the A10071
Ps 104:27 you to give them their food at the **p time**. H6961
Ps 145:15 you give them their food at the **p time**. H6961
Pr 16: 1 the LORD comes the *p* **answer** *of* the tongue. AIT
Pr 16: 4 LORD works out everything to its **p end**— H5102
Ecc 6: 3 prosperity and does not receive **p burial**, H7690
Ecc 8: 5 heart will know the **p** time and **procedure**. H5477
Ecc 8: 6 there is a **p** time and **procedure** for every H5477
Ecc 10:17 birth and whose princes eat at a *p* **time**— AIT
Jer 30:18 the palace will stand in its **p place**. H5477
Mt 3:15 it is **p** for us to do this to fulfill all *G4560*
Mt 24:45 to give them their food at the **p time**? *G2789*
Lk 12:42 them their food allowance at the **p time**? *G2789*
Ac 13:28 Though they found no **p ground** for a death *G162*
Ro 12: 1 to God—this is your **true and p** worship. *G3358*
1Co 11:13 Is it **p** for a woman to pray to God with her *G4560*
2Co 10:13 will not boast beyond **p limits**, but will AIT
Gal 6: 9 at the **p** time we will reap a harvest if *G2625*
2Th 2: 6 so that he may be revealed at the **p** time. *G1571*
1Ti 2: 6 has now been witnessed to at the **p** time. *G2625*
1Ti 5: 3 **Give p recognition** to those widows who *G5506*
1Pe 2:17 **Show p respect** to everyone, love the *G5506*
Jude 6 authority but abandoned their *p* **dwelling**— AIT

PROPERLY (1) [PROPER]

1Ti 1: 8 know that the law is good if one uses it **p**. *G3789*

PROPERTY (67)

Ge 23: 4 Sell me *some* **p** *for* a burial site here so I H299
Ge 23:18 to Abraham as his **p** in the presence of all H5239
Ge 34:10 Live in it, trade in it, and **acquire p** in it." H296
Ge 34:23 their **p** and all their other animals H7871
Ge 47:11 Egypt and gave them **p** in the best part of H299
Ge 47:27 *They* **acquired p** there and were fruitful H296
Ex 21:21 a day or two, since the slave is their **p**. H4084
Ex 22: 8 has laid hands on the other person's **p**. H4856
Ex 22: 9 any other **lost** *p* about which somebody AIT
Ex 22:11 did not lay hands on the other person's **p**. H4856
Lev 6: 3 if they find **lost p** and lie about it, or if they H8
Lev 6: 4 entrusted to them, or the **lost p** they found, H8
Lev 25:10 is to return to your **family p** and to your own H299
Lev 25:13 Jubilee everyone is to return to their own **p**. H299
Lev 25:25 becomes poor and sells some of their **p**, H299
Lev 25:27 they can then go back to their own **p**. H299
Lev 25:28 they can then go back to their **p**. H299
Lev 25:33 So **the p** of the Levites is redeemable H889[S]
Lev 25:33 the Levites are their **p** among the Israelites. H299
Lev 25:41 own clans and to the **p** *of* their ancestors. H299
Lev 25:45 your country, and they will become your **p**. H299
Lev 25:46 children as inherited **p** and can make them H299
Lev 27:21 to the LORD; it will become priestly **p**. H299
Nu 27: 4 Give us **p** among our father's relatives." H299
Nu 27: 7 certainly give them **p** as an inheritance H299
Nu 32:32 the **p** we inherit will be on this side of H299
Nu 35:28 priest may they return to their own **p**. H824+299
Nu 36: 4 their **p** will be taken from the tribal H5709
Dt 21:16 he wills his **p** to his sons, H889+2118+4200[S]
Jdg 14:15 Did you invite us here to **steal our p**?" H3769
Ru 4: 5 the name of the dead with his **p**. H5709
Ru 4: 7 and **transfer of p** to become H9455+3972+1821
Ru 4: 9 bought from Naomi all **the p** of Elimelek, H889[S]
Ru 4:10 the name of the dead with his **p**, H5709
1Sa 25: 2 in Maon, who had **p** there at Carmel, was H5126
1Sa 25:21 over this fellow's **p** in the wilderness so H889[S]
1Ki 21:19 not murdered a man and **seized** his **p**? H3769
1Ch 9: 2 resettle on their own **p** in their own towns H299
1Ch 27:31 the officials in charge of King David's **p**. H8214
1Ch 28: 1 in charge of all the **p** and livestock H8214
2Ch 11:14 pasturelands and **p** and came to Judah H299
2Ch 31: 1 to their own towns and to their own **p**. H299
Ezr 7:26 confiscation of **p**, or imprisonment. A10479
Ezr 10: 8 within three days would forfeit all his **p**, H8214
Ne 11: 3 each on their own **p** in the various towns, H299
Ne 11:20 towns of Judah, each on their **ancestral p**. H5709
Est 8:11 to plunder the **p** *of* their enemies. H8965
Job 5:24 will take stock of your **p** and find nothing H5659
Jer 37:12 to **get** *his* **share of** *the* **p** among the H2745
Eze 7:13 will not recover the **p** *that* was **sold**— H4928
Eze 45: 6 to give the city as its **p** an area 5,000 cubits H299
Eze 45: 7 by the sacred district and the **p** *of* the city. H299
Eze 46:16 it is to be their **p** by inheritance. H299
Eze 46:18 of the people, driving them off their **p**. H299
Eze 46:18 his sons their inheritance out of his own **p**, H299
Eze 46:18 my people will be separated from their **p**. H299
Eze 48:20 sacred portion, along with the **p** *of* the city. H299
Eze 48:21 portion and the **p** *of* the city will belong H299
Eze 48:22 So the **p** *of* the Levites and the property of H299
Eze 48:22 the Levites and the **p** *of* the city will lie in H299
Lk 15:12 So he divided his **p** between them. *G1050*
Lk 15:30 has squandered your **p** with prostitutes *G1050*
Lk 16:12 been trustworthy with someone else's **p**, *G3836*[S]
Lk 16:12 who will give you **p** of your own? *G3836*[S]
Ac 2:45 They sold **p** and possessions to give to *G3228*
Ac 5: 1 his wife Sapphira, also sold a **piece of p**. *G3228*
Heb 10:34 accepted the confiscation *of* your **p**, *G5639*

PROPHECIES (5) [PROPHESY]

2Ch 24:27 his sons, the many **p** about him, and the H5363
La 2:14 The **p** they gave you were false and H5363
1Co 13: 8 But where there are **p**, they will cease *G4735*
1Th 5:20 Do not treat **p** with contempt *G4735*
1Ti 1:18 keeping with the **p** once made about you *G4735*

PROPHECY (44) [PROPHESY]

Nu 24: 3 "The **p** *of* Balaam son of Beor, the H5536
Nu 24: 3 the **p** *of* one whose eye sees clearly, H5536
Nu 24: 4 the **p** *of* one who hears the words of God H5536
Nu 24:15 "The **p** *of* Balaam son of Beor, the H5536
Nu 24:15 the **p** *of* one whose eye sees clearly H5536
Nu 24:16 the **p** *of* one who hears the words of God H5536
2Ki 9:25 when the LORD spoke this **p** against him: H5363
2Ch 9:29 in the **p** *of* Ahijah the Shilonite and in the H5553
2Ch 15: 8 these words and the **p** of Azariah son of H5553
Isa 13: 1 A **p** *against* Babylon that Isaiah son of H5363
Isa 14:28 This **p** came in the year King Ahaz died: H5363
Isa 15: 1 A **p** *against* Moab: Ar in Moab is ruined H5363
Isa 17: 1 A **p** *against* Damascus: "See, Damascus H5363
Isa 19: 1 A **p** *against* Egypt: See, the LORD rides on H5363
Isa 21: 1 A **p** *against* the Desert by the Sea: Like H5363
Isa 21:11 A **p** *against* Dumah: Someone calls to me H5363
Isa 21:13 A **p** against Arabia: You caravans of H5363
Isa 22: 1 A **p** *against* the Valley of Vision: What H5363
Isa 23: 1 A **p** *against* Tyre: Wail, you ships of H5363
Isa 30: 6 A **p** *concerning* the animals of the Negev H5363
Eze 12:10 This **p** *concerns* the prince in Jerusalem H5363
Eze 14: 9 'And if the prophet is enticed to utter a **p**, H1821
Da 9:24 to seal up vision and **p** and to anoint the H5566
Na 1: 1 A **p** *concerning* Nineveh. The book of the H5363
Hab 1: 1 The **p** that Habakkuk the prophet received. H5363
Zec 9: 1 A **p**: The word of the LORD is against the H5363
Zec 12: 1 A **p**: The word of the LORD concerning H5363
Mal 1: 1 A **p**: The word of the LORD to Israel H5363
Mt 13:14 In them is fulfilled the **p** of Isaiah: " 'You *G4735*
1Co 12:10 powers, to another **p**, to another *G4735*
1Co 13: 2 If I have the **gift of p** and can fathom all *G4735*
1Co 14: 1 desire gifts of the Spirit, especially **p**. *G4736*
1Co 14: 6 knowledge or **p** or word of instruction? *G4735*
1Co 14:22 believers but for unbelievers; **p**, however, *G4735*
2Th 2: 2 whether by a **p** or by word of mouth or by *G4460*
1Ti 4:14 given you through **p** when the body of *G4735*
2Pe 1:20 understand that no **p** of Scripture came *G4735*
2Pe 1:21 For **p** never had its origin in the human *G4735*
Rev 1: 3 one who reads aloud the words *of* this **p**, *G4735*
Rev 19:10 it is the Spirit *of* **p** who bears testimony *G4735*
Rev 22: 7 keeps the words *of* the **p** written in this *G4735*
Rev 22:10 seal up the words *of* the **p** of this scroll, *G4735*
Rev 22:18 who hears the words *of* the **p** of this scroll: *G4735*
Rev 22:19 takes words away from this scroll *of* **p**, *G4735*

PROPHESIED (36) [PROPHESY]

Nu 11:25 rested on them, *they* **p**—but did not do so H5547
Nu 11:26 rested on them, and *they* **p** in the camp. H5547
1Sa 19:20 came on Saul's men, and they also **p**. H5547
1Sa 19:21 and he sent more men, and they **p** too. H5547
1Sa 19:21 sent men a third time, and they also **p**. H5547
1Sa 19:24 he too **p** in Samuel's presence. H5547
1Ch 25: 2 who **p** under the king's supervision. H5547
1Ch 25: 3 father Jeduthun, who **p**, using the harp in H5547
2Ch 20:37 of Mareshah **p** against Jehoshaphat, H5547
Ezr 5: 1 **p** to the Jews in Judah and Jerusalem in A10451
Ne 6:12 that *he had* **p** against me H5553+1819
Jer 2: 8 The prophets **p** by Baal, following H5547
Jer 20: 6 all your friends to whom *you have* **p** lies. H5547

P

Jer 23:13 *They* **p** by Baal and led my people Israel H5547
Jer 23:21 I did not speak to them, yet they *have* **p**. H5547
Jer 25:13 in this book and **p** *by* Jeremiah against all H5547
Jer 26:11 to death because *he has* **p** against this H5547
Jer 26:18 "Micah of Moresheth **p** in the days of H5547
Jer 26:20 was another man *who* **p** in the name of H5547
Jer 26:20 *he* **p** the same things against this city H5547
Jer 28: 6 the words *you have* **p** by bringing the H5547
Jer 28: 8 who preceded you and me *have* **p** war, H5547
Jer 29:31 Because Shemaiah *has* **p** to you, even H5547
Jer 37:19 Where are your prophets who **p** to you H5547
Eze 13:16 of Israel who **p** to Jerusalem and saw H5547
Eze 37: 7 So *I* **p** as I was commanded. And as I was H5547
Eze 37:10 So *I* **p** as he commanded me, and breath H5547
Eze 38:17 At that time they **p** for years that I would H5547
Mt 11:13 all the Prophets and the Law **p** until John. *G4736*
Mt 15: 7 Isaiah was right *when he* **p** about you: *G4736*
Mk 7: 6 "Isaiah was right *when he* **p** about you *G4736*
Lk 1:67 was filled with the Holy Spirit and **p**: *G4736*
Jn 11:51 priest that year *he* **p** that Jesus would die *G4736*
Ac 19: 6 and they spoke in tongues and **p**. *G4736*
Ac 21: 9 He had four unmarried daughters *who* **p**. *G4736*
Jude 14 the seventh from Adam, **p** about them: *G4736*

PROPHESIES (13) [PROPHESY]

1Ki 22: 8 him because *he* never **p** anything good H5547
1Ki 22:18 I tell you that *he* never **p** anything good H5547
2Ch 18: 7 because he never **p** anything good about H5547
2Ch 18:17 I tell you that *he* never **p** anything good H5547
Jer 28: 9 But the prophet who **p** peace will be H5547
Eze 12:27 and he **p** about the distant future. H5547
Zec 13: 3 And if anyone still **p**, their father and H5547
Zec 13: 3 their own parents will stab the one *who* **p**. H5547
1Co 11: 4 man who prays or **p** with his head covered *G4736*
1Co 11: 5 woman who prays or **p** with her head *G4736*
1Co 14: 3 But the *one who* **p** speaks to people for *G4736*
1Co 14: 4 the *one who* **p** edifies the church. *G4736*
1Co 14: 5 The *one who* **p** is greater than the one *G4736*

PROPHESY (66) [PROPHECIES, PROPHECY, PROPHESIED, PROPHESIES, PROPHESYING, PROPHET, PROPHET'S, PROPHETESS, PROPHETIC, PROPHETS]

1Sa 10: 6 upon you, and *you will* **p** with them; and H5547
Isa 30:10 Tell us pleasant things, **p** illusions. H2600
Jer 5:31 The prophets **p** lies, the priests rule by H5547
Jer 11:21 "*Do* not **p** in the name of the LORD or you H5547
Jer 19:14 where the LORD had sent him to **p**, and H5547
Jer 23:25 the prophets say who **p** lies in my name. H5547
Jer 23:26 *who* **p** the delusions of their own minds? H5566
Jer 23:32 I am against *those who* **p** false dreams," H5547
Jer 25:30 "Now **p** all these words against them and H5547
Jer 26: 9 Why *do you* **p** in the LORD's name that this H5547
Jer 26:12 "The LORD sent me to **p** against this house H5547
Jer 27:10 They **p** lies to you that will only serve to H5547
Jer 27:15 both you and the prophets who **p** to you. H5547
Jer 32: 3 saying, "Why *do* you **p** as you do? H5547
Eze 4: 7 with bared arm **p** against her. H5547
Eze 6: 2 the mountains of Israel; **p** against them H5547
Eze 11: 4 Therefore **p** against them; prophesy, son H5547
Eze 11: 4 prophesy against them; **p**, son of man." H5547
Eze 13: 2 **p** against the prophets of Israel who are H5547
Eze 13: 2 Say to **those who p** out of their own H5566
Eze 13:17 of your people who **p** out of their own H5547
Eze 13:17 of their own imagination. **P** against them H5547
Eze 20:46 the south and **p** against the forest of H5547
Eze 21: 2 the sanctuary. **P** against the land of Israel H5547
Eze 21: 9 "Son of man, **p** and say, 'This is what the H5547
Eze 21:14 of man, **p** and strike your hands together. H5547
Eze 21:28 son of man, **p** and say, 'This is what the H5547
Eze 25: 2 the Ammonites and **p** against them. H5547
Eze 28:21 set your face against Sidon; **p** against her H5547
Eze 29: 2 king of Egypt and **p** against him and H5547
Eze 30: 2 "Son of man, **p** and say: 'This is what the H5547
Eze 34: 2 of man, **p** against the shepherds of Israel H5547
Eze 34: 2 shepherds of Israel; **p** and say to them: H5547
Eze 35: 2 your face against Mount Seir; **p** against it H5547
Eze 36: 1 **p** to the mountains of Israel and say H5547
Eze 36: 3 Therefore **p** and say, 'This is what the H5547
Eze 36: 6 Therefore **p** concerning the land of Israel H5547
Eze 37: 4 "**P** to these bones and say to them H5547
Eze 37: 9 Then he said to me, "**P** to the breath H5547
Eze 37: 9 to the breath; **p**, son of man, and say to H5547
Eze 37:12 Therefore **p** and say to them: 'This is what H5547
Eze 38: 2 of Meshek and Tubal; **p** against him H5547
Eze 38:14 son of man, **p** and say to Gog: 'This H5547
Eze 39: 1 "Son of man, **p** against Gog and say H5547
Joel 2:28 Your sons and daughters *will* **p**, your old H5547
Am 2:12 commanded the prophets not *to* **p**. H5547
Am 3: 8 LORD has spoken—who *can* but **p**? H5547
Am 7:13 Don't **p** anymore at Bethel, because this is H5547
Am 7:15 said to me, 'Go, **p** to my people Israel. H5547
Am 7:16 You say, " '*Do* not **p** against Israel, and H5547
Mic 2: 6 "*Do* not **p**," their prophets say. "Do not H5752
Mic 2: 6 "*Do* not **p** about these things; disgrace H5752
Mic 2:11 '*I will* **p** for you plenty of wine and beer H5752
Mt 7:22 *did we* not **p** in your name and in your *G4736*
Mt 26:68 said, "**P** to us, Messiah. Who hit you?" *G4736*
Mk 14:65 struck him with their fists, and said, "**P**!" *G4736*
Lk 22:64 him and demanded, "**P**! Who hit you?" *G4736*
Ac 2:17 Your sons and daughters *will* **p**, your *G4736*
Ac 2:18 my Spirit in those days, and *they will* **p**. *G4736*
Ro 12: 6 then **p** in accordance with your faith; NDT
1Co 13: 9 For we know in part and *we* **p** in part, *G4736*
1Co 14: 5 in tongues, but I would rather have *you* **p**. *G4736*
1Co 14:31 For you can all **p** in turn so that everyone *G4736*
1Co 14:39 be eager *to* **p**, and do not forbid *G4736*
Rev 10:11 "You must **p** again about many peoples *G4736*
Rev 11: 3 witnesses, and *they will* **p** for 1,260 days *G4736*

PROPHESYING (32) [PROPHESY]

Nu 11:27 "Eldad and Medad *are* **p** in the camp." H5547
1Sa 10: 5 played before them, and they *will be* **p**. H5547
1Sa 10:10 upon him, and *he* joined in their **p**. H5547
1Sa 10:11 known him saw him **p** with the prophets, H5547
1Sa 10:13 After Saul stopped **p**, he went to the high H5547
1Sa 18:10 *He was* **p** in his house, while David was H5547
1Sa 19:20 But when they saw a group of prophets **p** H5547
1Sa 19:23 he walked along **p** until he came to H5547
1Ki 18:29 and *they continued their* **frantic p** until the H5547
1Ki 22:10 with all the prophets **p** before them. H5547
1Ki 22:12 the other prophets *were* **p** the same thing. H5547
1Ch 25: 1 Heman and Jeduthun for the ministry of **p**, H5547
2Ch 18: 9 with all the prophets **p** before them. H5547
2Ch 18:11 the other prophets *were* **p** the same thing. H5547
Jer 14:14 "The prophets *are* **p** lies in my name. H5547
Jer 14:14 They *are* **p** to you false visions H5547
Jer 14:15 the prophets who *are* **p** in my name: H5547
Jer 14:16 the people they *are* **p** to will be thrown H5547
Jer 20: 1 the LORD, heard Jeremiah **p** these things, H5547
Jer 23:16 listen to what the prophets *are* **p** to you; H5547
Jer 27:14 king of Babylon,' for they *are* **p** lies to you. H5547
Jer 27:15 'They *are* **p** lies in my name H5547
Jer 27:16 from Babylon.' They *are* **p** lies to you. H5547
Jer 29: 9 They *are* **p** lies to you in my name. I have H5547
Jer 29:21 who *are* **p** lies to you in my name: H5547
Eze 11:13 Now as I *was* **p**, Pelatiah son of Benaiah H5547
Eze 13: 2 the prophets of Israel who *are now* **p**. H5547
Eze 37: 7 And as I *was* **p**, there was a noise, H5547
Am 7:12 Earn your bread there and *do your* **p** there. H5547
Ro 12: 6 If your gift is **p**, then prophesy in *G4735*
1Co 14:24 an inquirer comes in *while* everyone *is* **p**, *G4736*
Rev 11: 6 it will not rain during the time they are **p**; *G4735*

PROPHET (251) [PROPHESY]

Ge 20: 7 for he is a **p**, and he will pray for H5566
Ex 7: 1 your brother Aaron will be your **p**. H5566
Ex 15:20 Then Miriam the **p**, Aaron's sister, took a H5567
Nu 12: 6 "When there is a **p** among you, I, the LORD H5566
Dt 13: 1 If a **p**, or one who foretells by dreams H5566
Dt 13: 2 of takes place, and the **p** says, "Let us follow NDT
Dt 13: 3 listen to the words of that **p** or dreamer. H5566
Dt 13: 5 That **p** or dreamer must be put to death H5566
Dt 13: 5 That **p** or dreamer tried to turn you from the NDT
Dt 18:15 raise up for you a **p** like me from among H5566
Dt 18:18 raise up for them a **p** like you from among H5566
Dt 18:19 to my words that the **p** speaks in my name. NDT
Dt 18:20 But a **p** who presumes to speak in my H5566
Dt 18:20 a **p** who speaks in the name of other H5566
Dt 18:22 If what a **p** proclaims in the name of the H5566
Dt 18:22 That **p** has spoken presumptuously, so do H5566
Dt 34:10 no **p** has risen in Israel like Moses H5566
Jdg 4: 4 Now Deborah, a **p**, the wife of Lappidoth H5567
Jdg 6: 8 he sent them a **p**, who said, "This is what H5566
1Sa 3:20 Samuel was attested as a **p** of the LORD. H5566
1Sa 9: 9 because the **p** of today used to be called H5566
1Sa 22: 5 But the **p** Gad said to David, "Do not stay H5566
2Sa 7: 2 he said to Nathan the **p**, "Here I am, living H5566
2Sa 12:25 through Nathan the **p** to name him H5566
2Sa 24:11 word of the LORD had come to Gad the **p**, H5566
1Ki 1: 8 Nathan the **p**, Shimei and Rei and H5566
1Ki 1:10 not invite Nathan the **p** or Benaiah or the H5566
1Ki 1:22 with the king, Nathan the **p** arrived. H5566
1Ki 1:23 the king was told, "Nathan the **p** is here." H5566
1Ki 1:32 Nathan the **p** and Benaiah son of H5566
1Ki 1:34 Nathan the **p** anoint him king over H5566
1Ki 1:38 the priest, Nathan the **p**, Benaiah son of H5566
1Ki 1:44 the priest, Nathan the **p**, Benaiah son of H5566
1Ki 1:45 Nathan the **p** have anointed him H5566
1Ki 11:29 Ahijah the **p** of Shiloh met him on H5566
1Ki 13:11 there was a certain old **p** living in Bethel, H5566
1Ki 13:15 So the **p** said to him, "Come home with me NDT
1Ki 13:18 The old **p** answered, "I too am a prophet, as NDT
1Ki 13:18 answered, "I too am a **p**, as you are. H5566
1Ki 13:20 came to the old **p** who had brought him H5566
1Ki 13:23 the **p** who had brought him back saddled H5566
1Ki 13:25 it in the city where the old **p** lived. H5566
1Ki 13:26 When the **p** who had brought him back H5566
1Ki 13:27 The **p** said to his sons, "Saddle the donkey NDT
1Ki 13:29 So the **p** picked up the body of the man of H5566
1Ki 14: 2 Ahijah the **p** is there—the one who told H5566
1Ki 14:18 had said through his servant the **p** Ahijah. H5566
1Ki 16: 7 came through the **p** Jehu son of Hanani H5566
1Ki 16:12 against Baasha through the **p** Jehu— H5566
1Ki 18:36 the **p** Elijah stepped forward and prayed: H5566
1Ki 19:16 from Abel Meholah to succeed you as **p**. H5566
1Ki 20:13 Meanwhile a **p** came to Ahab king of H5566
1Ki 20:14 The **p** replied, "This is what NDT
1Ki 20:14 The **p** answered, "You will." NDT
1Ki 20:22 the **p** came to the king of Israel and said H5566
1Ki 20:36 So the **p** said, "Because you have not NDT
1Ki 20:37 The **p** found another man and said, "Strike NDT
1Ki 20:38 Then the **p** went and stood by the road H5566
1Ki 20:39 king passed by, **the p** called out to him H2085S
1Ki 20:41 Then the **p** quickly removed the headband NDT
1Ki 22: 7 there no longer a **p** of the LORD here H5566
1Ki 22: 8 is still one **p** through whom we can H408S
2Ki 3:11 "Is there no **p** of the LORD here H5566
2Ki 5: 3 would see the **p** who is in Samaria! H5566
2Ki 5: 8 he will know that there is a **p** in Israel." H5566
2Ki 5:13 if the **p** had told you to do some great H5566
2Ki 5:16 The **p** answered, "As surely as the LORD lives, NDT
2Ki 6:12 "but Elisha, the **p** who is in Israel, tells H5566
2Ki 6:16 be afraid," the **p** answered. "Those who NDT
2Ki 9: 1 The **p** Elisha summoned a man from the H5566
2Ki 9: 4 So the young **p** went to Ramoth Gilead. H5566
2Ki 9: 6 Then the **p** poured the oil on Jehu's head NDT
2Ki 14:25 son of Amittai, the **p** from Gath Hepher. H5566
2Ki 19: 2 sackcloth, to the **p** Isaiah son of Amoz. H5566
2Ki 20: 1 The **p** Isaiah son of Amoz went to him H5566
2Ki 20:11 Then the **p** Isaiah called on the LORD, and H5566
2Ki 20:14 Then Isaiah the **p** went to King Hezekiah H5566
2Ki 20:15 The **p** asked, "What did they see in your NDT
2Ki 22:14 Asaiah went to speak to the **p** Huldah, H5567
2Ki 23:18 those of the **p** who had come from H5566
1Ch 17: 1 he said to Nathan the **p**, "Here I am, H5566
1Ch 29:29 records of Nathan the **p** and the records of H5566
2Ch 9:29 not written in the records of Nathan the **p**, H5566
2Ch 12: 5 Then the **p** Shemaiah came to Rehoboam H5566
2Ch 12:15 of Shemaiah the **p** and of Iddo the seer H5566
2Ch 13:22 written in the annotations of the **p** Iddo. H5566
2Ch 15: 8 prophecy of Azariah son of Oded the **p**, H5566
2Ch 18: 6 there no longer a **p** of the LORD here H5566
2Ch 18: 7 is still one **p** through whom we can H408S
2Ch 21:12 received a letter from Elijah the **p**, H5566
2Ch 25:15 he sent a **p** to him, who said, H5566
2Ch 25:16 So the **p** stopped but said, "I know that H5566
2Ch 26:22 are recorded by the **p** Isaiah son of Amoz. H5566
2Ch 28: 9 But a **p** of the LORD named Oded was H5566
2Ch 29:25 Gad the king's seer and Nathan the **p**; H5566
2Ch 32:20 Hezekiah and the **p** Isaiah son of Amoz H5566
2Ch 32:32 in the vision of the **p** Isaiah son of Amoz H5566
2Ch 34:22 with him went to speak to the **p** Huldah, H5567
2Ch 35:18 in Israel since the days of the **p** Samuel; H5566
2Ch 36:12 humble himself before Jeremiah the **p**, H5566
Ezr 5: 1 Now Haggai the **p** and Zechariah the A10455
Ezr 5: 1 the prophet and Zechariah the **p**, A10455
Ezr 6:14 of Haggai the **p** and Zechariah, A10455
Ne 6:14 remember also the **p** Noadiah and how H5567
Ps 51: T When the **p** Nathan came to him after H5566
Isa 3: 2 the judge and the **p**, the diviner and the H5566
Isa 37: 2 sackcloth, to the **p** Isaiah son of Amoz. H5566
Isa 38: 1 The **p** Isaiah son of Amoz went to him H5566
Isa 39: 3 Then Isaiah the **p** went to King Hezekiah H5566
Isa 39: 4 The **p** asked, "What did they see in your NDT
Jer 1: 5 I appointed you as a **p** to the nations." H5566
Jer 14:18 Both **p** and priest have gone to a land H5566
Jer 20: 2 he had Jeremiah the **p** beaten and put in H5566
Jer 23:11 "Both **p** and priest are godless; even in H5566
Jer 23:28 Let the **p** who has a dream recount the H5566
Jer 23:33 these people, or a **p** or a priest, ask you, H5566
Jer 23:34 If a **p** or a priest or anyone else claims H5566
Jer 23:37 This is what you keep saying to a **p**: 'What H5566
Jer 25: 2 So Jeremiah the **p** said to all the people H5566
Jer 28: 1 of Judah, the **p** Hananiah son of Azzur H5566
Jer 28: 5 Then the **p** Jeremiah replied to the H5566
Jer 28: 5 replied to the **p** Hananiah before the H5566
Jer 28: 9 But the **p** who prophesies peace will be H5566
Jer 28:10 Then the **p** Hananiah took the yoke off H5566
Jer 28:10 off the neck of the **p** Jeremiah and broke H5566
Jer 28:11 At this, the **p** Jeremiah went on his way. H5566
Jer 28:12 After the **p** Hananiah had broken the yoke H5566
Jer 28:12 the yoke off the neck of the **p** Jeremiah, H5566
Jer 28:15 Then the **p** Jeremiah said to Hananiah H5566
Jer 28:15 prophet Jeremiah said to Hananiah the **p**, H5566
Jer 28:17 of that same year, Hananiah the **p** died. H5566
Jer 29: 1 of the letter that the **p** Jeremiah sent from H5566
Jer 29:26 put any maniac *who* **acts like a p** into the H5547
Jer 29:27 Anathoth, who **poses as a p** among you? H5547
Jer 29:29 read the letter to Jeremiah the **p**. H5566
Jer 32: 2 Jeremiah the **p** was confined in the H5566
Jer 34: 6 Then Jeremiah the **p** told all this to H5566
Jer 36: 8 everything Jeremiah the **p** told him to do; H5566
Jer 36:26 Baruch the scribe and Jeremiah the **p**. H5566
Jer 37: 2 LORD had spoken through Jeremiah the **p**. H5566
Jer 37: 3 to Jeremiah the **p** with this message: H5566
Jer 37: 6 word of the LORD came to Jeremiah the **p**: H5566
Jer 38: 9 in all they have done to Jeremiah the **p**. H5566
Jer 38:10 lift Jeremiah the **p** out of the cistern H5566
Jer 38:14 Jeremiah the **p** and had him brought H5566
Jer 42: 2 Jeremiah the **p** and said to him, "Please H5566
Jer 42: 4 have heard you," replied Jeremiah the **p**. H5566
Jer 43: 6 took Jeremiah the **p** and Baruch son of H5566
Jer 45: 1 words Jeremiah the **p** dictated in the H5566
Jer 46: 1 came to Jeremiah the **p** concerning the H5566
Jer 46:13 to Jeremiah the **p** about the coming of H5566
Jer 47: 1 came to Jeremiah the **p** concerning the H5566
Jer 49:34 came to Jeremiah the **p** concerning Elam, H5566
Jer 50: 1 Jeremiah the **p** concerning Babylon H5566
Jer 51:59 message Jeremiah the **p** gave to the staff H5566
La 2:20 Should priest and **p** be killed in the H5566
Eze 2: 5 will know that a **p** has been among them. H5566
Eze 7:26 will go searching for a vision from the **p**, H5566
Eze 14: 4 before their faces and then go to a **p**, H5566
Eze 14: 7 faces and then go to a **p** to inquire of me, H5566
Eze 14: 9 " 'And if the **p** is enticed to utter a H5566

Eze 14: 9 I the LORD have enticed that **p**, and I will H5566
Eze 14:10 the **p** will be as guilty as the one who H5566
Eze 33:33 will know that a **p** has been among them." H5566
Da 9: 2 word of the LORD given to Jeremiah the **p**, H5566
Hos 9: 7 so great, the **p** is considered a fool H5566
Hos 9: 8 The **p**, along with my God, is the H5566
Hos 12:13 The LORD used a **p** to bring Israel up from H5566
Hos 12:13 up from Egypt, by a **p** he cared for him. H5566
Am 7:14 "I was neither a **p** nor the son of a H5566
Am 7:14 was neither a prophet nor the son of a **p**, H5566
Mic 2:11 that would be just the **p** *for* this people! H5752
Hab 1: 1 prophecy that Habakkuk the **p** received. H5566
Hab 3: 1 A prayer of Habakkuk the **p**. H5566
Hag 1: 1 came through the **p** Haggai to H5566
Hag 1: 3 of the LORD came through the **p** Haggai: H5566
Hag 1:12 God and the message of the **p** Haggai, H5566
Hag 2: 1 of the LORD came through the **p** Haggai: H5566
Hag 2:10 word of the LORD came to the **p** Haggai: H5566
Zec 1: 1 the LORD came to the **p** Zechariah son of H5566
Zec 1: 7 the LORD came to the **p** Zechariah son of H5566
Zec 13: 4 "On that day every **p** will be ashamed of H5566
Zec 13: 5 will say, 'I am not a **p**. I am a farmer; the H5566
Mal 4: 5 I will send the **p** Elijah to you before that H5566
Mt 1:22 what the Lord had said through the **p**: *G4737*
Mt 2: 5 replied, "for this is what the **p** has written: *G4737*
Mt 2:15 what the Lord had said through the **p**: *G4737*
Mt 2:17 was said through the **p** Jeremiah was *G4737*
Mt 3: 3 who was spoken of through the **p** Isaiah: *G4737*
Mt 4:14 fulfill what was said through the **p** Isaiah: *G4737*
Mt 8:17 what was spoken through the **p** Isaiah: *G4737*
Mt 10:41 Whoever welcomes a **p** as a prophet will *G4737*
Mt 10:41 welcomes a prophet as a **p** will receive a *G4737*
Mt 11: 9 what did you go out to see? A **p**? Yes, *G4737*
Mt 11: 9 I tell you, and more than a **p**. *G4737*
Mt 12:17 what was spoken through the **p** Isaiah: *G4737*
Mt 12:39 be given it except the sign of the **p** Jonah. *G4737*
Mt 13:35 fulfilled what was spoken through the **p**: *G4737*
Mt 13:57 "A **p** is not without honor except in his *G4737*
Mt 14: 5 because they considered John a **p**. *G4737*
Mt 21: 4 to fulfill what was spoken through the **p**: *G4737*
Mt 21:11 is Jesus, the **p** from Nazareth in Galilee." *G4737*
Mt 21:26 they all hold that John was a **p**. *G4737*
Mt 21:46 because the people held that he was a **p**. *G4737*
Mt 24:15 spoken of through the **p** Daniel—let the *G4737*
Mt 27: 9 spoken by Jeremiah the **p** was fulfilled: *G4737*
Mk 1: 2 as it is written in Isaiah the **p**: "I will send *G4737*
Mk 6: 4 "A **p** is not without honor except in his *G4737*
Mk 6:15 others claimed, "He is a **p**, like one of the *G4737*
Mk 11:32 everyone held that John really was a **p**.) *G4737*
Lk 1:76 will be called a **p** of the Most High; for *G4737*
Lk 2:36 There was also a **p**, Anna, the daughter *G4739*
Lk 3: 4 in the book of the words of Isaiah the **p**: *G4737*
Lk 4:17 the scroll *of* the **p** Isaiah was handed *G4737*
Lk 4:24 "no **p** is accepted in his hometown. *G4737*
Lk 4:27 with leprosy in the time of Elisha the **p**, *G4737*
Lk 7:16 "A great **p** has appeared among us," *G4737*
Lk 7:26 did you go out to see? A **p**? Yes, I tell you, *G4737*
Lk 7:26 I tell you, and more than a **p**. *G4737*
Lk 7:39 "If this man were a **p**, he would know who *G4737*
Lk 13:33 surely no **p** can die outside Jerusalem! *G4737*
Lk 20: 6 they are persuaded that John was a **p**." *G4737*
Lk 24:19 "He was a **p**, powerful in word and *G467+4737*
Jn 1:21 "Are you the **P**?" He answered, *G4737*
Jn 1:23 John replied in the words of Isaiah the **p** *G4737*
Jn 1:25 are not the Messiah, nor Elijah, nor the **P**?" *G4737*
Jn 4:19 woman said, "I can see that you are a **p**. *G4737*
Jn 4:44 pointed out that a **p** has no honor in his *G4737*
Jn 6:14 "Surely this is the **P** who is to come into *G4737*
Jn 7:40 the people said, "Surely this man is the **P**." *G4737*
Jn 7:52 will find that a **p** does not come out of *G4737*
Jn 9:17 The man replied, "He is a **p**." *G4737*
Jn 12:38 This was to fulfill the word of Isaiah the **p** *G4737*
Ac 2:16 this is what was spoken by the **p** Joel: *G4737*
Ac 2:30 But he was a **p** and knew that God had *G4737*
Ac 3:22 raise up for you a **p** like me from among *G4737*
Ac 7:37 raise up for you a **p** like me from your own *G4737*
Ac 7:48 made by human hands. As the **p** says: *G4737*
Ac 7:52 Was there ever a **p** your ancestors did not *G4737*
Ac 8:28 chariot reading the Book of Isaiah the **p**. *G4737*
Ac 8:30 heard the man reading Isaiah the **p**. *G4737*
Ac 8:34 who is the **p** talking about *G4737*
Ac 13: 6 sorcerer and **false p** named Bar-Jesus, *G6021*
Ac 13:20 judges until the time of Samuel the **p**. *G4737*
Ac 21:10 a **p** named Agabus came down from *G4737*
Ac 28:25 when he said through Isaiah the **p**: *G4737*
1Co 14:37 thinks they are a **p** or otherwise gifted by *G4737*
Rev 2:20 woman Jezebel, who calls herself a **p**. *G4739*
Rev 16:13 beast and out of the mouth *of* the **false p**. *G6021*
Rev 19:20 with it the **false p** who had performed *G6021*
Rev 20:10 beast and the **false p** had been thrown. *G6021*

PROPHET'S (4) [PROPHESY]

Zec 13: 4 not put on a **p garment** *of* hair in order to H168
Mt 10:41 as a prophet will receive a **p** reward, *G4737*
2Pe 1:20 came about by the **p** own interpretation of NDT
2Pe 2:16 voice and restrained the **p** madness. *G4737*

PROPHETESS (1) [PROPHESY]

Isa 8: 3 Then I made love to the **p**, and she H5567

PROPHETIC (3) [PROPHESY]

Zec 13: 4 prophet will be ashamed of their **p** vision. H5547
Ro 16:26 made known through the **p** writings by the *G4738*
2Pe 1:19 We also have the **p** message as *G4738*

PROPHETS (248) [PROPHESY]

Nu 11:29 LORD's people were **p** and that the LORD H5566
1Sa 10: 5 a procession of **p** coming down from the H5566
1Sa 10:10 a procession of **p** met him; the Spirit of H5566
1Sa 10:11 him saw him prophesying with the **p**, H5566
1Sa 10:11 Is Saul also among the **p**?" H5566
1Sa 10:12 "Is Saul also among the **p**?" H5566
1Sa 19:20 when they saw a group of **p** prophesying, H5566
1Sa 19:24 people say, "Is Saul also among the **p**?" H5566
1Sa 28: 6 not answer him by dreams or Urim or **p**. H5566
1Sa 28:15 answers me, either by **p** or by dreams. H5566
1Ki 18: 4 While Jezebel was killing off the LORD's **p** H5566
1Ki 18: 4 taken a hundred **p** and hidden them in H5566
1Ki 18:13 Jezebel was killing the **p** *of* the LORD? H5566
1Ki 18:13 a hundred of the LORD's **p** in two caves, H5566
1Ki 18:19 hundred and fifty **p** *of* Baal and the four H5566
1Ki 18:19 Baal and the four hundred **p** *of* Asherah, H5566
1Ki 18:20 assembled the **p** on Mount Carmel. H5566
1Ki 18:22 "I am the only one of the LORD's **p** left, but H5566
1Ki 18:22 but Baal has four hundred and fifty **p**. H5566
1Ki 18:23 Let Baal's **p** choose one for themselves, and NDT
1Ki 18:25 Elijah said to the **p** *of* Baal, "Choose one H5566
1Ki 18:40 commanded them, "Seize the **p** *of* Baal. H5566
1Ki 19: 1 he had killed all the **p** with the sword. H5566
1Ki 19:10 put your **p** to death with the sword. H5566
1Ki 19:14 put your **p** to death with the sword. H5566
1Ki 20:35 the company of the **p** said to his H5566
1Ki 20:41 of Israel recognized him as one of the **p**. H5566
1Ki 22: 6 the king of Israel brought together the **p**— H5566
1Ki 22:10 with all the **p** prophesying before them. H5566
1Ki 22:12 All the other **p** were prophesying the H5566
1Ki 22:13 the other **p** without exception are H5566
1Ki 22:22 deceiving spirit in the mouths of all his **p**, H5566
1Ki 22:23 spirit in the mouths of all these **p** *of* yours. H5566
2Ki 2: 3 The company of the **p** at Bethel came out H5566
2Ki 2: 5 The company of the **p** at Jericho went up H5566
2Ki 2: 7 the company of the **p** went and stood at a H5566
2Ki 2:15 The company of the **p** from Jericho, who H5566
2Ki 3:13 Go to the **p** *of* your father and the H5566
2Ki 3:13 of your father and the **p** *of* your mother." H5566
2Ki 4: 1 the company of the **p** cried out to Elisha, H5566
2Ki 4:38 the company of the **p** was meeting with H5566
2Ki 4:38 and cook some stew for these **p**." H1201+5566
2Ki 5:22 the company of the **p** have just come to H5566
2Ki 6: 1 The company of the **p** said to Elisha H5566
2Ki 9: 1 the company of the **p** and said to him, H5566
2Ki 9: 7 of my servants the **p** and the blood of all H5566
2Ki 10:19 Now summon all the **p** *of* Baal, all his H5566
2Ki 17:13 Judah through all his **p** and seers: H5566
2Ki 17:13 to you through my servants the **p**. H5566
2Ki 17:23 had warned through all his servants the **p**. H5566
2Ki 21:10 The LORD said through his servants the **p**: H5566
2Ki 23: 2 the priests and the **p**—all the people from H5566
2Ki 24: 2 the LORD proclaimed by his servants the **p**. H5566
1Ch 16:22 my anointed ones; do my **p** no harm." H5566
2Ch 18: 5 the king of Israel brought together the **p**— H5566
2Ch 18: 9 with all the **p** prophesying before them. H5566
2Ch 18:11 All the other **p** were prophesying the H5566
2Ch 18:12 the other **p** without exception are H5566
2Ch 18:21 deceiving spirit in the mouths of all his **p**, H5566
2Ch 18:22 spirit in the mouths of these **p** *of* yours. H5566
2Ch 20:20 have faith in his **p** and you will be H5566
2Ch 24:19 Although the LORD sent **p** to the people to H5566
2Ch 29:25 commanded by the LORD through his **p**. H5566
2Ch 36:16 scoffed at his **p** until the wrath of the H5566
Ezr 5: 2 And the **p** of God were with them A10455
Ezr 9:11 your servants the **p** when you said: H5566
Ne 6: 7 have even appointed **p** to make this H5566
Ne 6:14 the rest of the **p** have been trying to H5566
Ne 9:26 They killed your **p**, who had warned them H5566
Ne 9:30 Spirit you warned them through your **p**. H5566
Ne 9:32 on our priests and **p**, on our ancestors H5566
Ps 74: 9 signs from God; no **p** are left, and none of H5566
Ps 105:15 my anointed ones; do my **p** no harm." H5566
Isa 9:15 the **p** who teach lies are the tail. H5566
Isa 28: 7 Priests and **p** stagger from beer and are H5566
Isa 29:10 your eyes (the **p**); he has covered your H5566
Isa 30:10 and to the **p**, "Give us no more visions of H2602
Isa 44:25 foils the signs of **false p** and makes fools of H967
Jer 2: 8 The **p** prophesied by Baal, following H5566
Jer 2:26 their officials, their priests and their **p**. H5566
Jer 2:30 has devoured your **p** like a ravenous lion. H5566
Jer 4: 9 be horrified, and the **p** will be appalled." H5566
Jer 5:13 The **p** are but wind and the word is not in H5566
Jer 5:31 The **p** prophesy lies, the priests rule by H5566
Jer 6:13 are greedy for gain; **p** and priests alike H5566
Jer 7:25 again I sent you my servants the **p**. H5566
Jer 8: 1 the bones of the priests and **p**, and the H5566
Jer 8:10 are greedy for gain; **p** and priests alike H5566
Jer 13:13 the **p** and all those living in Jerusalem. H5566
Jer 14:13 The **p** keep telling them, 'You will not see H5566
Jer 14:14 "The **p** are prophesying lies in my name. H5566
Jer 14:15 says about the **p** who are prophesying H5566
Jer 14:15 Those same **p** will perish by sword and H5566
Jer 18:18 from the wise, nor the word from the **p**. H5566
Jer 23: 9 Concerning the **p**: My heart is broken H5566
Jer 23:10 The **p** follow an evil course and use their H4392S
Jer 23:13 "Among the **p** *of* Samaria I saw this H5566
Jer 23:14 And among the **p** *of* Jerusalem I have H5566
Jer 23:15 the LORD Almighty says concerning the **p**: H5566
Jer 23:15 because from the **p** *of* Jerusalem H5566
Jer 23:16 listen to what the **p** are prophesying to H5566
Jer 23:21 I did not send these **p**, yet they have run H5566
Jer 23:25 have heard what the **p** say who prophesy H5566
Jer 23:26 continue in the hearts of these lying **p**, H5566
Jer 23:30 "I am against the **p** who steal from one H5566
Jer 23:31 "I am against the **p** who wag their own H5566
Jer 25: 4 all his servants the **p** to you again and H5566
Jer 26: 5 listen to the words of my servants the **p**, H5566
Jer 26: 7 the **p** and all the people heard Jeremiah H5566
Jer 26: 8 the **p** and all the people seized him and H5566
Jer 26:11 the priests and the **p** said to the officials H5566
Jer 26:16 the people said to the priests and the **p**, H5566
Jer 27: 9 So do not listen to your **p**, your diviners H5566
Jer 27:14 to the words of the **p** who say to you, H5566
Jer 27:15 both you and the **p** who prophesy to you. H5566
Jer 27:16 Do not listen to the **p** who say, 'Very soon H5566
Jer 27:18 If they are **p** and have the word of the LORD, H5566
Jer 28: 8 From early times the **p** who preceded you H5566
Jer 29: 1 the **p** and all the other people H5566
Jer 29: 8 "Do not let the **p** and diviners among you H5566
Jer 29:15 LORD has raised up **p** for us in Babylon," H5566
Jer 29:19 again and again by my servants the **p**. H5566
Jer 32:32 their priests and **p**, the people of Judah H5566
Jer 35:15 again I sent all my servants the **p** to you. H5566
Jer 37:19 Where are your **p** who prophesied to you H5566
Jer 44: 4 Again and again I sent my servants the **p** H5566
Jer 50:36 A sword against her **false p**! They will H967
La 2: 9 her **p** no longer find visions from the H5566
La 2:14 The visions of your **p** were false and H5566
La 4:13 of the sins of her **p** and the iniquities of H5566
Eze 13: 2 against the **p** *of* Israel who are now H5566
Eze 13: 3 Woe to the foolish **p** who follow their own H5566
Eze 13: 4 Your **p**, Israel, are like jackals among ruins. H5566
Eze 13: 9 will be against the **p** who see false H5566
Eze 13:16 those **p** *of* Israel who prophesied to H5566
Eze 22:28 Her **p** whitewash these deeds for them by H5566
Eze 38:17 former days by my servants the **p** *of* Israel. H5566
Da 9: 6 have not listened to your servants the **p**, H5566
Da 9:10 he gave us through his servants the **p**. H5566
Hos 4: 5 night, and the **p** stumble with you. H5566
Hos 6: 5 Therefore I cut you in pieces with my **p**, H5566
Hos 11: 6 will devour their **false p** and put an end to H967
Hos 12:10 I spoke to the **p**, gave them many visions H5566
Am 2:11 "I also raised up **p** from among your H5566
Am 2:12 commanded the **p** not to prophesy. H5566
Am 3: 7 revealing his plan to his servants the **p**. H5566
Mic 2: 6 prophesy," their **p say**. "Do not prophesy H5752
Mic 3: 5 "As for the **p** who lead my people astray H5566
Mic 3: 6 The sun will set for the **p**, and the day will H5566
Mic 3:11 and her **p** tell fortunes for money. H5566
Zep 3: 4 Her **p** are unprincipled; they are H5566
Zec 1: 4 to whom the earlier **p** proclaimed: H5566
Zec 1: 5 And the **p**, do they live forever H5566
Zec 1: 6 which I commanded my servants the **p** H5566
Zec 7: 3 the house of the LORD Almighty and the **p**, H5566
Zec 7: 7 through the earlier **p** when Jerusalem H5566
Zec 7:12 sent by his Spirit through the earlier **p**. H5566
Zec 8: 9 is also what the **p** said who were present H5566
Zec 13: 2 "I will remove both the **p** and the spirit of H5566
Mt 2:23 was fulfilled what was said through the **p**, *G4737*
Mt 5:12 persecuted the **p** who were before you *G4737*
Mt 5:17 I have come to abolish the Law or the **P**; *G4737*
Mt 7:12 for this sums up the Law and the **P**. *G4737*
Mt 7:15 "Watch out for **false p**. They come to you *G6021*
Mt 11:13 For all the **P** and the Law prophesied until *G4737*
Mt 13:17 many **p** and righteous people longed to *G4737*
Mt 16:14 still others, Jeremiah or one *of* the **p**." *G4737*
Mt 22:40 All the Law and the **P** hang on these two *G4737*
Mt 23:29 You build tombs *for* the **p** and decorate *G4737*
Mt 23:30 with them in shedding the blood *of* the **p**. *G4737*
Mt 23:31 of those who murdered the **p**. *G4737*
Mt 23:34 I am sending you **p** and sages and *G4737*
Mt 23:37 you who kill the **p** and stone those sent to *G4737*
Mt 24:11 many **false p** will appear and deceive *G6021*
Mt 24:24 messiahs and **false p** will appear and *G6021*
Mt 26:56 that the writings *of* the **p** might be *G4737*
Mk 6:15 a prophet, like one *of* the **p** *of long ago*." *G4737*
Mk 8:28 say Elijah; and still others, one *of* the **p**." *G4737*
Mk 13:22 messiahs and **false p** will appear and *G6021*
Lk 1:70 as he said through his holy **p** of long ago), *G4737*
Lk 6:23 that is how their ancestors treated the **p**. *G4737*
Lk 6:26 is how their ancestors treated the **false p**. *G6021*
Lk 9: 8 others that one *of* the **p** of long ago had *G4737*
Lk 9:19 that one *of* the **p** of long ago has come *G4737*
Lk 10:24 I tell you that many **p** and kings wanted to *G4737*
Lk 11:47 because you build tombs *for* the **p**, and it *G4737*
Lk 11:48 they killed **the p**, and you build their *G899S*
Lk 11:49 'I will send them **p** and apostles, some of *G4737*
Lk 11:50 the blood of all the **p** that has been shed *G4737*
Lk 13:28 Jacob and all the **p** in the kingdom of *G4737*
Lk 13:34 you who kill the **p** and stone those sent to *G4737*
Lk 16:16 "The Law and the **P** were proclaimed until *G4737*
Lk 16:29 'They have Moses and the **P**; let them *G4737*
Lk 16:31 'If they do not listen to Moses and the **P** *G4737*
Lk 18:31 is written by the **p** about the Son of Man *G4737*
Lk 24:25 to believe all that the **p** have spoken! *G4737*
Lk 24:27 And beginning with Moses and all the **P** *G4737*
Lk 24:44 the Law of Moses, the **P** and the Psalms." *G4737*
Jn 1:45 about whom the **p** also wrote—Jesus *G4737*
Jn 6:45 It is written in the **P**: 'They will all be *G4737*

Jn 8:52 Abraham died and so did the p, yet you G4737
Jn 8:53 and so did the p. Who do you think G4737
Ac 3:18 what he had foretold through all the p, G4737
Ac 3:21 he promised long ago through his holy p. G4737
Ac 3:24 all the p who have spoken have foretold G4737
Ac 3:25 And you are heirs *of* the p and of the G4737
Ac 7:42 with what is written in the book *of* the p: G4737
Ac 10:43 All the p testify about him that everyone G4737
Ac 11:27 During this time *some* p came down from G4737
Ac 13: 1 at Antioch there were p and teachers: G4737
Ac 13:15 After the reading from the Law and the P G4737
Ac 13:27 fulfilled the words *of* the p that are read G4737
Ac 13:40 care that what the p have said does not G4737
Ac 15:15 The words *of* the p are in agreement with G4737
Ac 15:32 who themselves were p, said much to G4737
Ac 24:14 with the Law and that is written in the P, G4737
Ac 26:22 beyond what the p and Moses said would G4737
Ac 26:27 do you believe the p? I know you do." G4737
Ac 28:23 Law of Moses and *from* the P he tried to G4737
Ro 1: 2 through his p in the Holy Scriptures G4737
Ro 3:21 to which the Law and the P testify. G4737
Ro 11: 3 have killed your p and torn down your G4737
1Co 12:28 of all apostles, second p, third teachers, G4737
1Co 12:29 Are all p? Are all teachers? G4737
1Co 14:29 Two or three p should speak, and the G4737
1Co 14:32 The spirits *of* p are subject to the control of G4737
1Co 14:32 of prophets are subject to the control *of* p. G4737
Eph 2:20 on the foundation of the apostles and p, G4737
Eph 3: 5 by the Spirit to God's holy apostles and p. G4737
Eph 4:11 gave the apostles, the p, the evangelists, G4737
1Th 2:15 Lord Jesus and the p and also drove us G4737
Titus 1:12 One of Crete's own p has said it: "Cretans G4737
Heb 1: 1 through the p at many times and in G4737
Heb 11:32 about David and Samuel and the p, G4737
Jas 5:10 take the p who spoke in the name of the G4737
1Pe 1:10 this salvation, the p, who spoke of the G4737
2Pe 1:21 in the human will, but p, though human, NDT
2Pe 2: 1 there were also **false** p among the people G6021
2Pe 3: 2 the past by the holy p and the command G4737
1Jn 4: 1 because many **false** p have gone out into G6021
Rev 10: 7 as he announced to his servants the p." G4737
Rev 11:10 because these two p had tormented those G4737
Rev 11:18 your servants the p and your people who G4737
Rev 16: 6 the blood of your holy people and your p, G4737
Rev 18:20 apostles and p! For God has judged G4737
Rev 18:24 found the blood *of* p and of God's holy G4737
Rev 22: 6 the God who inspires the p, sent his G4737
Rev 22: 9 with your fellow p and with all who G4737

PROPITIATION (KJV) ATONING SACRIFICE, SACRIFICE OF ATONEMENT

PROPORTION (3)

Nu 35: 8 to be given **in p to** the inheritance H3869+7023
Dt 16:10 offering **in p to** the blessings H5002+3869+889
Dt 16:17 must bring a gift **in p to** the way the LORD H3869

PROPOSAL (2) [PROPOSE]

Ge 34:18 Their p seemed good to Hamor and his H1821
Ac 6: 5 This p pleased the whole group. G3364

PROPOSE (2) [PROPOSAL, PROPOSED]

Dt 1:14 answered me, "What *you* p to do is good." H1819
Isa 8:10 it will be thwarted; p your plan, but it will H1819

PROPOSED (3) [PROPOSE]

Ezr 10:16 So the exiles did as was p. Ezra the priest NDT
Est 1:21 so the king did as Memukan p. H1821
Est 2: 2 Then the king's personal attendants p, "Let H606

PROPPED (2)

1Ki 22:35 the king was **p up** in his chariot H6641
2Ch 18:34 king of Israel **p** *himself* **up** in his chariot H6641

PROPRIETY (2)

1Ti 2: 9 with decency and p, adorning themselves, G5408
1Ti 2:15 in faith, love and holiness with p. G5408

PROSELYTE, PROSELYTES (KJV) CONVERT, CONVERTS

PROSPECT (1) [PROSPECTS]

Pr 10:28 The p *of* the righteous is joy, but the H9347

PROSPECTS (1) [PROSPECT]

Job 6:11 What p, that I should be H7891

PROSPER (33) [PROSPERED, PROSPERITY, PROSPEROUS, PROSPERS]

Ge 32: 9 your relatives, and *I will* **make** you p,' H3512
Ge 32:12 '*I will* **surely make** you p and will H3512+3512
Lev 25:26 them but *later on* they p and H5952+3338
Lev 25:49 Or if they p, they may redeem H5952+3338
Dt 5:33 you may live and p and prolong your days H3201
Dt 6:24 that we might always p and be kept alive, H3202
Dt 28:63 the LORD to **make** you p and increase in H3512
Dt 29: 9 so that *you may* p *in* everything you do. H8505
1Ki 2: 3 Do this so that *you may* p in all you do H8505
2Ch 24:20 *You will* not p. Because you H7503
Ezr 6:14 to build and p under the preaching of A10613
Ps 49:18 people praise you when *you* p— H3512
Ps 51:18 May it please you *to* p Zion, to build up H3512
Pr 11:10 When the righteous p, the city rejoices H3206
Pr 11:25 A generous person *will* p; whoever H2014
Pr 17:20 whose heart is corrupt *does* not p; H5162+3202
Pr 19: 8 understanding *will soon* p. H5162+3202
Pr 28:13 Whoever conceals their sins *does* not p H7503
Pr 28:25 those who trust in the LORD *will* p. H2014
Isa 53:10 the will of the LORD *will* p in his hand. H7503
Jer 10:21 so *they do* not p and all their flock is H8505
Jer 12: 1 Why *does* the way of the wicked p? Why H7503
Jer 22:30 a man *who will* not p in his lifetime H7503
Jer 22:30 none of his offspring *will* p, none will H7503
Jer 29: 7 because if it prospers, you too will p." H8934
Jer 29:11 "plans to p you and not to harm you H8934
Eze 26: 2 now that she lies in ruins *I will* p,' H4848
Eze 36:11 the past and *will* **make** you p more than H3201
Da 4: 1 live in all the earth: May you p greatly! A10720
Da 6:25 in all the earth: "May you p greatly! A10720
Da 8:25 He *will* cause deceit *to* p, and he will H7503
Mal 3:15 Certainly evildoers p, and even when they H1215
Ac 13:17 *he* **made** the people p during their stay in G5738

PROSPERED (7) [PROSPER]

Ge 39: 2 The LORD was with Joseph so that he p H7503
1Ch 29:23 *He* p and all Israel obeyed him H7503
2Ch 14: 7 rest on every side." So they built and p. H7503
2Ch 31:21 worked wholeheartedly. And so *he* p. H7503
Da 6:28 So Daniel p during the reign of Darius A10613
Da 8:12 *It* p in everything it did, and truth was H7503
Hos 10: 1 as his land p, he adorned his H3202

PROSPERITY (32) [PROSPER]

Dt 28:11 The LORD will grant you abundant p—in H3208
Dt 28:47 joyfully and gladly in the time of p, H8044+3972
Dt 30:15 I set before you today life and p, death H3202
Job 20:21 him to devour; his p will not endure. H3206
Job 21:13 spend their years in p and go down to the H3202
Job 21:16 But their p is not in their own hands, so I H3206
Job 22:21 with him; in this way p will come to you. H3208
Job 36:11 rest of their days in p and their years in H3202
Ps 4: 6 are asking, "Who will bring us p? H3202
Ps 25:13 They will spend their days in p, and their H3202
Ps 37:11 inherit the land and enjoy peace and p. H8044
Ps 72: 3 May the mountains bring p to the people H8934
Ps 72: 7 flourish and p abound till the moon H8934
Ps 73: 3 arrogant when I saw the p *of* the wicked. H8934
Ps 106: 5 I may enjoy the p *of* your chosen ones, H3208
Ps 122: 9 of the LORD our God, I will seek your p. H3202
Ps 128: 2 your labor; blessings and p will be yours. H3202
Ps 128: 5 may you see the p *of* Jerusalem all the H3206
Pr 3: 2 many years and bring you **peace and p**. H8934
Pr 8:18 riches and honor, enduring wealth and p. H7407
Pr 21:21 love finds life, p and honor. H7407
Ecc 6: 3 he cannot enjoy his p and does not H3208
Ecc 6: 6 years twice over but fails to enjoy his p. H3208
Isa 45: 7 darkness, I bring p and create disaster; I, H8934
Jer 17: 6 they will not see p when it comes. H3202
Jer 29: 7 seek the **peace and p** *of* the city to which I H8934
Jer 32:42 give them all the p I have promised them. H3208
Jer 33: 9 at the abundant p and peace I provide H3208
Jer 39:16 words concerning disaster, not p. H3208
La 3:17 of peace; I have forgotten what p is. H3208
Da 4:27 It may be that then your p will continue." A10713
Zec 1:17 'My towns will again overflow with p, and H3202

PROSPEROUS (12) [PROSPER]

Ge 30:43 the man *grew* exceedingly p and came H7287
Dt 30: 5 *He will* **make** you **more** p and numerous H3512
Dt 30: 9 will make you most p in all the work of H3208
Dt 30: 9 will again delight in you and make you p, H3202
Jos 1: 8 Then you *will be* p and successful. H7503
Jdg 18: 7 land lacked nothing, *they were* p. H3769+6807
Job 8: 6 behalf and restore you to your p state. H7406
Job 8: 7 seem humble, so p will your future be. H8436
Ps 10: 5 His ways *are* always p; your laws are H2656
Jer 31:23 'The LORD bless you, you p city, you sacred H7406
Da 4: 4 at home in my palace, contented and p. A10670
Zec 7: 7 its surrounding towns were at rest and p, H8929

PROSPERS (3) [PROSPER]

Ps 1: 3 does not wither—whatever they do p. H7503
Pr 16:20 gives heed to instruction p, H5162+3202
Jer 29: 7 because if it p, you too will prosper." H8934

PROSTITUTE (51) [PROSTITUTE'S, PROSTITUTED, PROSTITUTES, PROSTITUTING, PROSTITUTION]

Ge 34:31 he have treated our sister like a p?" H2390
Ge 38:15 he thought she *was a* p, for she had H2390
Ge 38:21 "Where is the **shrine** p who was beside H7728
Ge 38:21 "There hasn't been any **shrine** p here," H7728
Ge 38:22 'There hasn't been any **shrine** p here. H7728
Ex 34:15 when *they* p *themselves* to their gods H2388
Ex 34:16 daughters p *themselves* to their gods, H2388
Lev 17: 7 goat idols to whom they p *themselves*. H2388
Lev 19:29 degrade your daughter by **making** her **a** p, H2388
Lev 20: 6 spiritists to p *themselves* by following H2388
Lev 21: 9 daughter defiles herself by *becoming a* p, H2388
Nu 15:39 obey them and not p yourselves by H2388
Dt 23:17 man or woman is to become a **shrine** p. H7728
Dt 23:18 the earnings of a *female* p or of a male H2390
Dt 23:18 prostitute or of a **male** p into the house of H3978
Dt 31:16 people *will* soon p *themselves* to the H2388
Jos 2: 1 the house of a p named Rahab and H2390
Jos 6:17 Only Rahab the p and all who are with H2390
Jos 6:25 But Joshua spared Rahab the p, with her H2390
Jdg 11: 1 His father was Gilead; his mother was a p. H2390
Jdg 16: 1 Samson went to Gaza, where he saw a p. H2390
2Ch 21:11 *had* **caused** the people of Jerusalem **to p themselves** H2388
2Ch 21:13 *you have* **led** Judah and the people of Jerusalem **to p themselves** H2388
Pr 6:26 For a p can be had for a loaf of bread, but H2390
Pr 7:10 dressed like a p and with crafty intent. H2390
Isa 1:21 See how the faithful city has become a p H2390
Isa 23:15 happen to Tyre as in the song of the p: H2390
Isa 23:16 you forgotten p; play the harp well, H2390
Jer 2:20 every spreading tree you lay down as a p. H2390
Jer 3: 1 But you *have lived as a* p with many H2388
Jer 3: 3 Yet you have the brazen look of a p; you H2390
Eze 16:15 used your fame *to become a* p. H2388
Eze 16:30 do all these things, acting like a brazen p! H2390
Eze 16:31 you were unlike a p, because you scorned H2390
Eze 16:35 " 'Therefore, you p, hear the word of the H2390
Eze 23: 7 She gave herself as a p to all the elite of H9373
Eze 23:19 of her youth, when *she was a* p in Egypt. H2388
Eze 23:43 'Now *let them* **use** her **as a** p, for H2388+9373
Eze 23:44 As men sleep with a p, so they slept with H2390
Hos 3: 3 *you must* not *be a* p or be intimate with H2388
Hos 9: 1 you love the **wages of a** p at every H924
Am 7:17 " 'Your wife *will become a* p in the city H2388
Na 3: 4 all because of the wanton lust of a p H2390
1Co 6:15 of Christ and unite them *with* a p? G4520
1Co 6:16 unites himself with a p is one with her in G4520
Heb 11:31 By faith the p Rahab, because she G4520
Jas 2:25 not even Rahab the p considered G4520
Rev 17: 1 show you the punishment *of* the great p, G4520
Rev 17:15 you saw, where the p sits, are peoples, G4520
Rev 17:16 the ten horns you saw will hate the p. G4520
Rev 19: 2 condemned the great p who corrupted the G4520

PROSTITUTE'S (1) [PROSTITUTE]

Jos 6:22 "Go into the p house and bring her out H2390

PROSTITUTED (5) [PROSTITUTE]

Jdg 2:17 judges but p *themselves* to other gods H2388
Jdg 8:27 All Israel p *themselves* by worshiping it H2388
Jdg 8:33 again p *themselves* to the Baals. H2388
1Ch 5:25 ancestors and p *themselves* to the gods of H2388
Ps 106:39 by their deeds *they* p *themselves*. H2388

PROSTITUTES (20) [PROSTITUTE]

1Ki 3:16 Now two p came to the king and stood H2390
1Ki 14:24 were even *male* **shrine** p in the land; H7728
1Ki 15:12 expelled the *male* **shrine** p from the land H7728
1Ki 22:38 Samaria (where the p bathed), and the H2390
1Ki 22:46 rest of the *male* **shrine** p who remained H7728
2Ki 23: 7 quarters of the *male* **shrine** p that were in H7728
Job 36:14 their youth, among *male* **p of the shrines**. H7728
Pr 29: 3 a companion of p squanders his H2390
Isa 57: 3 you offspring of adulterers and p! H2388
Jer 5: 7 adultery and thronged to the houses of p. H2390
Eze 16:33 All p receive gifts, but you give gifts to all H2390
Eze 23: 3 *They became* p in Egypt, engaging in H2388
Hos 4:14 with harlots and sacrifice with **shrine** p— H7728
Joel 3: 3 lots for my people and traded boys for p; H2390
Mic 1: 7 gathered her gifts from the wages of p, H2390
Mic 1: 7 as the wages of p they will again be used." H2390
Mt 21:31 tax collectors and the p are entering the G4520
Mt 21:32 but the tax collectors and the p did. G4520
Lk 15:30 your property with p comes home, G4520
Rev 17: 5 the great THE MOTHER OF P AND OF THE G4520

PROSTITUTING (1) [PROSTITUTE]

Lev 20: 5 who follow him in p *themselves* to Molek. H2388

PROSTITUTION (36) [PROSTITUTE]

Ge 38:24 daughter-in-law Tamar *is* **guilty of p**, H2388
Lev 19:29 the land *will* **turn to** p and be filled H2388
Lev 21: 7 women defiled by p or divorced from their H2390
Lev 21:14 a woman defiled by p, but only a virgin H2390
Isa 23:17 will return to her **lucrative** p and will ply her H924
Jer 3: 2 the land with your p and wickedness. H2394
Jer 13:27 lustful neighings, your shameless p! H2394
Eze 16:16 high places, where *you* **carried on** *your* p. H2388
Eze 16:17 male idols and **engaged in** p with them. H2388
Eze 16:20 food to the idols. Was your p not enough? H9373
Eze 16:22 practices and your p you did not H9373
Eze 16:26 *You* **engaged in** p with the Egyptians, your H2388
Eze 16:28 *You* **engaged in** p with the Assyrians too H2388
Eze 16:34 So in your p you are the opposite of others; H9373
Eze 16:41 I will put a stop to your p, and you will no H2388
Eze 23: 3 in Egypt, **engaging in** p from their youth. H2388
Eze 23: 5 "Oholah **engaged in** p while she was still H2388
Eze 23: 8 did not give up the p she began in Egypt, H9373
Eze 23:11 in her lust and p she was more H9373
Eze 23:14 "But she carried her p still further. H9373
Eze 23:18 she carried on her p openly and exposed H9373
Eze 23:27 the lewdness and p you began in Egypt. H2394
Eze 23:29 the shame of your p will be exposed. H2393
Eze 23:35 consequences of your lewdness and p." H9373
Eze 43: 7 by their p and the funeral offerings for H2394
Eze 43: 9 put away from me their p and the funeral H2394
Hos 4:10 *they will* **engage in** p but not flourish H2388
Hos 4:11 to p; old wine and new wine take away H2394
Hos 4:12 A spirit of p leads them astray; they are H2393
Hos 4:13 your daughters **turn to** p and your H2388
Hos 4:14 your daughters when *they* **turn to** p, H2388
Hos 4:18 *they* **continue** *their* p; their H2388+2388

Hos 5: 3 Ephraim, *you have* now **turned to p**; Israel H2388
Hos 5: 4 A spirit of **p** is in their heart; they do not H2393
Hos 6:10 There Ephraim is given to **p**, Israel is H2394
Na 3: 4 nations by her **p** and peoples by her H2393

PROSTRATE (10) [PROSTRATED, PROSTRATING]
Nu 24: 4 the Almighty, *who* **falls p**, and whose H5877
Nu 24:16 the Almighty, *who* **falls p**, and whose H5877
Dt 9:18 Then once again *I* **fell p** before the LORD H5877
Dt 9:25 *I* **lay p** before the LORD those forty days H5877
2Sa 19:18 the Jordan, *he* **fell p** before the king H5877
1Ki 18:39 saw this, they fell **p** and cried, "The H6584+7156
Isa 15: 3 squares they all wail, **p** with weeping. H3718
Isa 51:23 '**Fall p** that we may walk on you. H8817
Da 2:46 fell **p** before Daniel and A10542+10049
Da 8:17 standing, I was terrified and fell **p**. H6584+7156

PROSTRATED (2) [PROSTRATE]
1Sa 24: 8 bowed down and **p himself** with his face H2556
1Sa 28:14 bowed down and **p himself** with his face H2556

PROSTRATING (4) [PROSTRATE]
Ge 43:28 bowed down, **p** *themselves before* him. H2556
1Ki 1:16 bowed down, **p herself** before the king. H2556
1Ki 1:31 to the ground, **p herself** before the king H2556
1Ch 29:20 **p themselves** before the LORD and the king H2556

PROTECT (26) [PROTECTED, PROTECTION, PROTECTIVE, PROTECTS]
Nu 35:25 The assembly *must* **p** the one accused of H5911
Dt 23:14 in your camp to **p** you and to deliver H5911
2Sa 18:12 '**P** the young man Absalom for my sake. H9068
Ezr 8:22 horsemen to **p** us from enemies on H6468
Est 8:11 to assemble and **p** themselves; H6641+6584
Est 9:16 also assembled *to* **p** themselves H6641+6584
Ps 12: 5 "*I will* **p** them *from* those who H8883+928+3829
Ps 12: 7 the needy safe and *will* **p** us forever from H5915
Ps 20: 1 *may* the name of the God of Jacob **p** you. H8435
Ps 25:21 *May* integrity and uprightness **p** me H5915
Ps 32: 7 *you will* **p** me from trouble and surround H5915
Ps 40:11 *may* your love and faithfulness always **p** H5915
Ps 61: 7 your love and faithfulness *to* **p** him. H5915
Ps 64: 1 **p** my life from the threat of the enemy. H5915
Ps 69:29 in pain—may your salvation, God, **p** me. H8435
Ps 91:14 "I will rescue him; *I will* **p** him, for he H8435
Ps 140: 1 from evildoers; **p** me from the violent, H5915
Ps 140: 4 of the wicked; **p** me from the violent H5915
Pr 2:11 Discretion *will* **p** you, and understanding H9068
Pr 4: 6 wisdom, and *she will* **p** you; love her, H9068
Pr 14: 3 but the lips of the wise **p** them. H9068
Da 11: 1 I took my stand to support and **p** him.) H5057
Mal 2:16 "does violence to the one he should **p**," H4230
Jn 17:11 **p** them by the power of your name G5498
Jn 17:15 the world but that *you* **p** them from the G5498
2Th 3: 3 strengthen you and **p** you from the evil G5875

PROTECTED (7) [PROTECT]
Jos 24:17 *He* **p** us on our entire journey and among H9068
1Sa 30:23 *He has* **p** us and delivered into our hands H9068
Ezr 8:31 and *he* **p** us from enemies and bandits H5911
Job 5:21 *You will* **be p** from the lash of the tongue H2461
Mk 6:20 because Herod feared John and **p** him G5337
Jn 17:12 I **p** them and kept them safe by that name G5498
2Pe 2: 5 people, but **p** Noah, a preacher of G5875

PROTECTION (9) [PROTECT]
Ge 19: 8 they have come under the **p** *of* my roof." H7498
Nu 14: 9 Their **p** is gone, but the LORD H7498
Nu 32:17 for **p from** the inhabitants of the H4946+7156
Jos 20: 3 flee there and find **p** from the avenger of H5236
Ezr 9: 9 he has given us a **wall of p** in Judah and H1555
Ps 5:11 **Spread** *your* **p** over them, that those who H6114
Ps 42: 4 of God under the **p** *of* the Mighty One H6108
Isa 30: 2 who look for help to Pharaoh's **p**, to H5057
Isa 30: 3 But Pharaoh's **p** will be to your shame H5057

PROTECTIVE (1) [PROTECT]
Na 2: 5 the city wall; the **p shield** is put in place. H6116

PROTECTS (8) [PROTECT]
Ps 34:20 *he* **p** all his bones, not one of them will H9068
Ps 41: 2 The LORD **p** and preserves them—they are H9068
Ps 116: 6 The LORD **p** the unwary; when I was H9068
Pr 2: 8 course of the just and **p** the way of his H9068
Pr 27:18 and *whoever* **p** their master will be H9068
Da 12: 1 the great prince who **p** your people, H6641+6584
Mic 1:11 Ezel is in mourning; it no longer **p** you. H6644
1Co 13: 7 *It* always **p**, always trusts, always hopes G5095

PROTEST (2) [PROTESTED]
Ecc 5: 6 And *do* not **p** to the temple messenger H606
Ac 18: 6 *he* **shook out** his clothes **in p** and said to G1759

PROTESTED (3) [PROTEST]
Isa 53: 8 Yet who of his generation **p**? For he was H8488
Jn 8:41 "We are not illegitimate children," *they* **p**. G3306
Jn 19:21 The chief priests of the Jews **p** to Pilate G3306

PROUD (40) [PRIDE, PROUDLY]
Dt 8:14 then your heart *will become* **p** and you will H8123
2Ch 25:19 and now you are arrogant and **p**. H3877
2Ch 32:25 But Hezekiah's heart *was* **p** and he did not H1467
Job 28: 8 **P beasts** do not set foot on it, and H1201+8832
Job 38:11 here is where your **p** waves halt'? H1454
Job 39:20 a locust, striking terror with its **p** snorting? H2086
Job 40:11 look at all *who* are **p** and bring them low, H1450
Job 40:12 look at all *who* are **p** and humble them H1450
Job 41:34 it is king over all that are **p**. H1201+8832
Ps 31:23 but the **p** he pays back in full. H6913+1452
Ps 36:11 the foot of the **p** not come against me H1452
Ps 40: 4 who does not look to the **p**, to those who H8107
Ps 94: 2 pay back to the **p** what they deserve. H1450
Ps 101: 5 whoever has haughty eyes and a **p** heart H8146
Ps 123: 4 from the arrogant, of contempt from the **p**. H1456
Ps 131: 1 My heart *is* not **p**, LORD, my eyes are not H1467
Pr 3:34 He mocks **p mockers** but shows favor to H4370
Pr 15:25 The LORD tears down the house of the **p** H1450
Pr 16: 5 The LORD detests all the **p** *of* heart. H1468
Pr 16:19 than to share plunder with the **p**. H1450
Pr 21: 4 Haughty eyes and a **p** heart—the H8146
Pr 21:24 The **p** and arrogant person—"Mocker" is H2294
Isa 2:12 has a day in store for all the **p** and lofty, H1450
Isa 22:18 chariots you were *so* **p** *of* will become a H3883
Eze 28: 5 of your wealth your heart *has grown* **p**. H1467
Eze 28:17 Your heart *became* **p** on account of your H1467
Eze 30: 6 Egypt will fall and her **p** strength will fail. H1454
Eze 30:18 there her **p** strength will come to an end. H1454
Eze 31:10 and because *it was* **p** of its height, H8123+4222
Eze 33:28 her **p** strength will come to an end H1454
Hos 13: 6 satisfied, they *became* **p**; then they H8123+4213
Zec 10: 3 make them like a **p** horse in battle. H2086
Lk 1:51 has scattered *those who are* **p** in their G5662
Ro 12:16 *Do* not *be* **p**, but be willing G3836+5734+5858
1Co 5: 2 And you are **p**! Shouldn't you rather have G5881
1Co 13: 4 not envy, it does not boast, *it is* not **p**. G5881
2Ti 3: 2 of money, boastful, **p**, abusive G5662
Jas 4: 6 "God opposes the **p** but shows favor to G5662
1Pe 5: 5 "God opposes the **p** but shows favor to G5662
Rev 13: 5 a mouth to utter **p** words and G3489

PROUDLY (4) [PROUD]
1Sa 2: 3 not keep talking **so p** or let your H1469+1469
Ps 140: 9 who surround me **p** rear their heads; H6147
Eze 31:14 by the waters *are ever to* **tower p** on high, H1467
Mic 2: 3 You will no longer walk **p**, for it will be a H8127

PROVE (18) [PROOF, PROOFS, PROVED, PROVEN, PROVES, PROVING]
Ge 44:16 How *can we* **p** *our* **innocence**? God H7405
Job 6:25 But what *do* your arguments **p**? H3519
Job 9: 2 how *can* mere mortals **p** *their* **innocence** H7405
Job 24:25 who *can* **p** me **false** and reduce my words H3941
Pr 29:25 Fear of man *will* **p to be** a snare, but H5989
Pr 30: 6 he will rebuke you and **p** *you* **a liar**. H3941
Isa 43: 9 in their witnesses *to* **p** *they were* **right**, H7405
Jer 17:11 in the end *they will* **p to be** fools. H2118
Mic 1:14 town of Akzib will **p** deceptive to the kings NDT
Hab 2: 3 it speaks of the end and *will* not **p false**. H3941
Jn 2:18 *can you* **show** us to **p** *your* **authority** to G1259
Jn 8:46 *Can* any of you **p** me **guilty** of sin? If I am G1794
Jn 16: 8 *he will* **p** the world **to be in the wrong** G1794
Ac 24:13 And *they* cannot **p** to you the charges they G4225
Ac 25: 7 against him, but they could not **p** them. G617
1Co 4: 2 have been given a trust *must* **p** faithful. G2351
2Co 9: 3 you in this matter *should* not **p hollow**, G3033
Heb 9:16 it is necessary *to* **p** the death of the one G5770

PROVED (25) [PROVE]
Lev 10: 3 those who approach me *I will* **be p holy**; H7727
Nu 20:13 where *he was* **p holy** among them. H7727
Dt 13:14 if it is true and *it has* **been p** that this H3922
Dt 17: 4 If it is true and *it has* **been p** that this H3922
1Ki 16:22 followers **p stronger** *than* those of Tibni H2616
Job 6:21 Now *you too have* **p to be** of no help; you H2118
Job 32:12 But not *one* of you *has* **p** Job **wrong**; none H3519
Ps 105:19 till the word of the LORD **p** him **true**. H7671
Ecc 2: 1 But that also **p** to be meaningless. NDT
Isa 5:16 the holy God *will* **be p holy** by his H7727
Eze 20:41 and *I will* **be p holy** through you in the H7727
Eze 28:22 on you and within you *am* **p to be holy**. H7727
Eze 28:25 *I will* **be p holy** through them in the sight H7727
Eze 36:23 when I *am* **p holy** through you before their H7727
Eze 38:16 know me when I *am* **p holy** through you H7727
Eze 39:27 *I will* **be p holy** through them in the sight H7727
Mt 11:19 But wisdom *is* **p right** by her deeds." G1467
Lk 7:35 But wisdom *is* **p right** by all her children." G1467
Ro 3: 4 "So that *you may be* **p right** when you G1467
2Co 7:11 At every point *you have* **p** yourselves to be G5319
2Co 7:14 you to Titus *has* **p to be** true as well. G1181
2Co 8:22 brother who *has* often **p** *to us* in many G1507
2Co 9:13 service by which you have **p** yourselves, G1509
Php 2:22 But you know that Timothy has **p** himself G1509
Col 4:11 and they *have* **p** a comfort to me. G1181

PROVEN (1) [PROVE]
1Pe 1: 7 so that the **p genuineness** of your faith— G1510

PROVENDER (KJV) FED, FEED, FODDER

PROVERB (9) [PROVERBS]
Ps 49: 4 I will turn my ear to a **p**; with the harp I H5442
Pr 26: 7 one who is lame is a **p** in the mouth of a H5442
Pr 26: 9 drunkard's hand is a **p** in the mouth of a H5442
Eze 12:22 what is this **p** you have in the land of H5442
Eze 12:23 I am going to put an end to this **p**, and H5442
Eze 16:44 proverbs *will* **quote** *this* **p** about you: H5439
Eze 18: 2 mean by quoting this **p** about the land of H5442
Eze 18: 3 you will no longer quote this **p** in Israel. H5442
Lk 4:23 "Surely you will quote this **p** to me: G4130

PROVERBS (9) [PROVERB]
1Ki 4:32 spoke three thousand **p** and his songs H5442
Job 13:12 Your maxims are **p** *of* ashes; your H5442
Pr 1: 1 The **p** *of* Solomon son of David, king of H5442
Pr 1: 6 understanding **p** and parables, the H5442
Pr 10: 1 The **p** *of* Solomon: A wise son brings joy H5442
Pr 25: 1 These are more **p** *of* Solomon, compiled H5442
Ecc 12: 9 searched out and set in order many **p**. H5442
Eze 16:44 " 'Everyone who **quotes p** will quote this H5439
2Pe 2:22 Of them the **p** are true: "A dog returns to G4231

PROVES (1) [PROVE]
Dt 19:18 if the witness **p** to be a liar, giving false NDT

PROVIDE (58) [PROVIDED, PROVIDES, PROVIDING, PROVISION, PROVISIONS]
Ge 22: 8 "God himself *will* **p** the lamb for the burnt H8011
Ge 22:14 called that place The LORD *Will* **P**. H8011
Ge 45:11 *I will* **p** *for* you there, because five years of H3920
Ge 49:16 "Dan *will* **p justice** *for* his people as one H1906
Ge 49:20 he *will* **p** delicacies fit for a king. H5989
Ge 50:21 I *will* **p** *for* you and your children. H3920
Ex 21:11 If *he does* not **p** her *with* these three H6913
Ex 27:16 the courtyard, **p** a curtain twenty cubits long NDT
Lev 25:24 *you must* **p** *for* the redemption of the land. H5989
Dt 6:11 all kinds of good things *you did* not **p**, H4848
Dt 11:15 *I will* **p** grass in the fields for your cattle H5989
Jos 9:27 **to p for the needs of** the altar of the LORD H4200
Jos 20: 4 into their city and **p** a place to live among H5989
Jdg 21: 7 "How *can we* **p** wives for those who are H6913
Jdg 21:16 how *shall we* **p** wives for the men who are H6913
2Sa 7:10 And *I will* **p** a place for my people Israel H8492
2Sa 19:33 with me in Jerusalem, and *I will* **p** *for* you." H3920
2Sa 22:37 *You* **p** a **broad** path for my feet, so that my H8143
1Ki 4: 7 one had to **p supplies** *for* one month in H3920
1Ki 5:17 to **p** a **foundation** *of* dressed stone *for* the H3569
1Ch 17: 9 And *I will* **p** a place for my people Israel H8492
1Ch 22:14 taken great pains *to* **p** for the temple of H3922
2Ch 2: 9 to **p** me *with* plenty of lumber, because H3922
Ezr 1: 4 the people *are to* **p** them with silver and H5951
Ezr 7:20 *you may* **p** from the royal treasury. A10498
Ezr 7:21 Trans-Euphrates *are to* **p** with diligence A10522
Ne 2: 7 so that *they will* **p** me **safe-conduct** until I H6296
Ps 18:36 *You* **p** a **broad** path for my feet, so that my H8143
Ps 65: 9 with water *to* **p** the people *with* grain, H3922
Pr 27:26 the lambs will **p** you **with** clothing, and H4200
Isa 4: 1 eat our own food and **p** our own clothes; H4252
Isa 43:20 because *I* **p** water in the wilderness and H5989
Isa 50:11 light fires and **p** *yourselves with* flaming H273
Isa 58: 7 and *to* **p** the poor wanderer *with* shelter— H995
Isa 61: 3 **p** for those who grieve in Zion—to H8492
Jer 33: 9 abundant prosperity and peace I **p** for it. H6913
Eze 34:29 *I will* **p** for them a land renowned for its H7756
Eze 43:25 days *you are to* **p** a male goat daily *for* a H6913
Eze 43:25 *you are* also *to* **p** a young bull and a ram H6913
Eze 45:17 duty of the prince to **p** the burnt offerings, NDT
Eze 45:17 He *will* **p** the sin offerings, grain offerings H6913
Eze 45:22 that day the prince *is to* **p** a bull as a sin H6913
Eze 45:23 of the festival *he is to* **p** seven bulls and H6913
Eze 45:24 *He is to* **p** as a grain offering an ephah H6913
Eze 46: 7 *He is to* **p** as a grain offering one ephah H6913
Eze 46:13 " 'Every day *you are to* **p** a year-old lamb H6913
Eze 46:13 morning by morning *you shall* **p** it. H6913
Eze 46:14 *You are* also *to* **p** with it morning by H6913
Lk 12:33 **P** purses for yourselves that will not wear G4472
Ac 7:46 asked *that he might* **p** a dwelling G2351
Ac 11:29 decided *to* **p** help for the brothers and G4287
Ac 23:24 **P** horses for Paul so that he may be taken G4225
Ac 27: 3 his friends *so they might* **p for** his needs. G5593
Ro 15: 4 encouragement they **p** we might have hope. NDT
1Co 10:13 *he will* also **p** a way out so that you can G4472
Col 4: 1 **p** your slaves with what is right and fair G4218
1Ti 5: 8 Anyone *who does* not **p for** their relatives G4629
Titus 3:14 in order *to* **p for** urgent needs and not live AIT

PROVIDED (40) [PROVIDE]
Ge 22:14 "On the mountain of the LORD *it will* **be p**." H8011
Ge 43:24 to wash their feet and **p** fodder for their H5989
Ge 47:12 **p** his father and his brothers and all his father's household *with* H3920
Ru 3: 1 you, where you *will be* **well p for**. H3512
1Sa 21: 4 **p** the men have kept themselves from H561+421
2Sa 9:10 grandson *may be* **p for**. H2118+4200+4312+2256+430
2Sa 15: 1 Absalom **p** himself with a chariot and H6913
2Sa 19:32 He *had* **p** *for* the king during his stay in H3920
2Sa 20: 3 *He* **p** *for* them but had no sexual relations H3920
1Ki 8:21 *I have* **p** a place there for the ark, in which H8492
1Ki 11:18 a house and land and **p** him *with* food. H606
2Ki 13: 5 The LORD **p** a deliverer for Israel, and they H5989
1Ch 22: 3 He **p** a large amount of iron to make nails H3922
1Ch 22: 4 He also **p** more cedar logs than could be NDT
1Ch 23: 5 instruments *I have* **p** for that purpose." H6913
1Ch 29: 2 all my resources *I have* **p** for the temple of H3922
1Ch 29: 3 above everything *I have* **p** for this holy H3922
1Ch 29:16 abundance that *we have* **p** for building H3922
1Ch 29:19 the palatial structure for which *I have* **p**." H3922
2Ch 2: 7 skilled workers, whom my father David **p**. H3922

P

2Ch 3: 1 the Jebusite, the place **p** *by* David. H3922
2Ch 26:14 Uzziah **p** shields, spears, helmets, coats of H3922
2Ch 28:15 *They* **p** them **with clothes** and sandals H4252
2Ch 30:24 king of Judah **p** a thousand bulls and H8123
2Ch 30:24 the officials **p** them *with* a thousand bulls H8123
2Ch 35: 7 Josiah **p** for all the lay people who were H8123
2Ch 35: 9 **p** five thousand Passover offerings and H8123
Ne 13: 5 and *he had* **p** him *with* a large room H6913
Est 2: 9 Immediately he **p** her *with* her beauty H5989
Ps 68:10 from your bounty, God, *you* **p** for the poor. H3922
Ps 111: 9 *He* **p** redemption for his people; he H8938
Eze 16:19 Also the food *I* **p** for you—the flour, olive H5989
Eze 46:15 the oil *shall be* **p** morning by H6913
Jnh 1:17 Now the LORD **p** a huge fish to swallow H4948
Jnh 4: 6 Then the LORD God **p** a leafy plant and H4948
Jnh 4: 7 But at dawn the next day God **p** a worm H4948
Jnh 4: 8 the sun rose, God **p** a scorching east wind H4948
Ro 11:22 **p that** you continue in his kindness. *G1569*
Gal 4:18 is fine to be zealous, **p** the purpose is good NDT
Heb 1: 3 *After he had* **p** purification for sins, he sat *G4472*

PROVIDENCE (1)

Job 10:12 in your **p** watched over my spirit. H7213

PROVIDES (13) [PROVIDE]

Job 5:10 He **p** rain for the earth; he sends water on H5989
Job 24: 5 the wasteland **p** food **for** their children. H4200
Job 36:31 the nations and **p** food in abundance. H5989
Job 38:41 Who **p** food for the raven when its young H3922
Ps 111: 5 *He* **p** food for those who fear him; he H5989
Ps 147: 9 *He* **p** food for the cattle and for the young H5989
Pr 31:15 *she* **p** food for her family and portions H5989
Eze 18: 7 the hungry and **p** clothing *for* the naked. H4059
Eze 18:16 the hungry and **p** clothing *for* the naked. H4059
Eze 46:12 " 'When the prince **p** a freewill offering to H6913
Ac 14:17 *he* **p** you **with plenty** of food and fills your *G1855*
1Ti 6:17 who richly **p** us with everything for our *G4218*
1Pe 4:11 they should do so with the strength God **p**, *G5961*

PROVIDING (6) [PROVIDE]

Ge 38: 9 the ground to keep from **p** offspring for his H5989
Ru 1: 6 the aid of his people by **p** food for them, H5989
1Ki 5: 8 do all you want in **p** the cedar and juniper NDT
1Ki 5: 9 grant my wish by **p** food *for* my royal H5989
Ne 13: 7 Eliashib had done *in* **p** Tobiah a room in H6913
Da 4:21 abundant fruit, **p** food for all, giving NDT

PROVINCE (42) [PROVINCES, PROVINCIAL]

Ezr 2: 1 the people of the **p** who came up from H4519
Ezr 6: 2 citadel of Ecbatana in the **p** of Media, A10406
Ezr 6: 6 other officials of **that p**, A10526+10468+10191S
Ezr 7:16 you may obtain from the **p** *of* Babylon, A10406
Ne 1: 3 are back in the **p** are in great trouble H4519
Ne 7: 6 the people of the **p** who came up from H4519
Est 1:22 to **each p** in its own script H4519+2256+4519
Est 2: 3 in every **p** *of* his realm to bring H4519
Est 3:12 script of **each p** and in the H4519+2256+4519
Est 3:14 as law in every **p** and made known to the H4519
Est 4: 3 In every **p** to which the edict and order of H4519
Est 8: 9 the script of **each p** and the H4519+2256+4519
Est 8:11 any nationality or **p** who might attack H4519
Est 8:13 as law in every **p** and made known to the H4519
Est 8:17 In every **p** and in every city to which the H4519
Est 9:28 and in **every p** and in every H4519+2256+4519
Da 2:48 over the entire **p** *of* Babylon and placed A10406
Da 2:49 administrators over the **p** *of* Babylon, A10406
Da 3: 1 on the plain of Dura in the **p** *of* Babylon. A10406
Da 3:12 set over the affairs of the **p** *of* Babylon— A10406
Da 3:30 Abednego in the **p** *of* Babylon. A10406
Da 8: 2 in the citadel of Susa in the **p** *of* Elam; H4519
Ac 10:37 has happened throughout the **p of Judea**, *G2677*
Ac 16: 6 from preaching the word in the **p of Asia**. *G823*
Ac 19:10 who lived in the **p of Asia** heard the word *G823*
Ac 19:22 he stayed in the **p of Asia** a little longer. *G823*
Ac 19:26 and *in* practically the whole **p of Asia**. *G823*
Ac 19:27 throughout the **p of Asia** and the world, *G823*
Ac 19:31 Even some *of* the **officials of the p**, friends *G825*
Ac 20: 4 Tychicus and Trophimus **from the p of Asia**. *G824*
Ac 20:16 to avoid spending time in the **p of Asia**, *G823*
Ac 20:18 from the first day I came into the **p of Asia**. *G823*
Ac 21:27 Jews from the **p of Asia** saw Paul at the *G823*
Ac 23:34 the letter and asked what **p** he was from. *G2065*
Ac 24:19 But there are some Jews from the **p of Asia** *G823*
Ac 25: 1 Three days after arriving *in* the **p**, Festus *G2065*
Ac 27: 2 ports along the coast of the **p of Asia**, *G823*
Ro 16: 5 the first convert to Christ *in* the **p of Asia**. *G823*
1Co 16:19 The churches *in* the **p of Asia** send you *G823*
2Co 1: 8 troubles we experienced in the **p of Asia**. *G823*
2Ti 1:15 everyone in the **p of Asia** has deserted me, *G823*
Rev 1: 4 To the seven churches in the **p of Asia**: *G823*

PROVINCES (24) [PROVINCE]

Ezr 4:15 troublesome to kings and **p**, a place with A10406
Est 1: 1 who ruled over 127 **p** stretching from H4519
Est 1: 3 the nobles of the **p** were present. H4519
Est 1:16 the peoples of all the **p** *of* King Xerxes. H4519
Est 2:18 throughout the **p** and distributed gifts H4519
Est 3: 8 peoples in all the **p** *of* your kingdom who H4519
Est 3:12 of the **various p** and the H4519+2256+4519
Est 3:13 to all the king's **p** with the order to destroy H4519
Est 4:11 people of the royal **p** know that for any H4519
Est 8: 5 to destroy the Jews in all the king's **p**. H4519
Est 8: 9 nobles of the 127 **p** stretching from India H4519
Est 8:12 do this in all the **p** *of* King Xerxes was the H4519
Est 9: 2 cities in all the **p** *of* King Xerxes to attack H4519
Est 9: 3 And all the nobles of the **p**, the satraps H4519
Est 9: 4 his reputation spread throughout the **p** H4519
Est 9:12 have they done in the rest of the king's **p**? H4519
Est 9:16 were in the king's **p** also assembled to H4519
Est 9:20 the Jews throughout the **p** *of* King Xerxes, H4519
Est 9:30 Jews in the 127 **p** of Xerxes' kingdom— H4519
Ecc 2: 8 and the treasure of kings and **p**. H4519
La 1: 1 queen among the **p** has now become a H4519
Da 11:24 When the richest **p** feel secure, he will H4519
Ac 6: 9 as well as the **p of Cilicia** and Asia— *G3070*
1Pe 1: 1 the **p of** Pontus, Galatia, Cappadocia, **Asia** *G823*

PROVINCIAL (8) [PROVINCE]

1Ki 20:14 officers under the **p** commanders will do it H4519
1Ki 20:15 junior officers under the **p** commanders. H4519
1Ki 20:17 officers under the **p** commanders went out H4519
1Ki 20:19 officers under the **p** commanders marched H4519
1Ki 22:47 then no king in Edom; a **p governor** ruled. H5893
Ne 11: 3 These are the **p** leaders who settled in H4519
Da 3: 2 all the other **p** officials to come to A10406
Da 3: 3 all the other **p** officials assembled A10406

PROVING (3) [PROVE]

Ac 9:22 living in Damascus *by* **p** that Jesus is the *G5204*
Ac 17: 3 explaining and **p** that the Messiah had to *G4192*
Ac 18:28 **p** from the Scriptures that Jesus was the *G2109*

PROVISION (5) [PROVIDE]

Ne 13:31 I also made **p** for contributions of wood at NDT
Ps 144:13 barns will be filled with every kind of **p**. H7049
Eze 45:25 *he is to* **make** the same **p** *for* sin offerings H6913
Ro 5:17 receive God's **abundant p** of grace and of *G4353*
Php 1:19 prayers and God's **p** of the Spirit of Jesus *G2221*

PROVISIONS (20) [PROVIDE]

Ge 42:25 and to give them **p** for their journey. H7476
Ge 45:21 he also gave them **p** for their journey. H7476
Ge 45:23 bread and *other* **p** for his journey. H4648
Jos 1:11 tell the people, 'Get your **p** ready. H7476
Jos 9:11 said to us, 'Take **p** for your journey; go H7476
Jos 9:14 sampled their **p** but did not inquire of H7474
Jdg 7: 8 who took over the **p** and trumpets of the H7476
Jdg 20:10 from ten thousand, to get **p** for the army. H7476
1Sa 22:10 he also gave him **p** and the sword of H7476
2Sa 19:42 *Have we* **eaten** any of the king's **p** H430+430
1Ki 4: 7 *who* **supplied p** *for* the king and the royal H3920
1Ki 4:22 Solomon's daily **p** were thirty cors of the H4312
1Ki 4:27 **supplied p** *for* King Solomon and all who H3920
1Ki 20:27 were also mustered and **given p**, H3920
1Ch 12:39 their families *had* **supplied p** for them. H3922
2Ch 11:23 gave them abundant **p** and took many H4648
Ps 132:15 I will bless her with abundant **p**; her poor H7474
Pr 6: 8 it stores its **p** in summer and gathers H4312
Jer 40: 5 commander gave him **p** and a present H786
Da 11:26 eat from the king's **p** will try to destroy H7329

PROVOCATION (1) [PROVOKE]

Pr 27: 3 a fool's **p** is heavier than both. H4088

PROVOKE (5) [PROVOCATION, PROVOKED, PROVOKES, PROVOKING]

Dt 2: 5 *Do* not **p** them **to war**, for I will not give H1741
Dt 2: 9 not harass the Moabites or **p** them *to* war, H1741
Dt 2:19 do not harass them or **p** them **to war**, for I H1741
Job 12: 6 and *those who* **p** God are secure H8074
Isa 65: 3 who continually **p** me to my very face, H4087

PROVOKED (3) [PROVOKE]

1Sa 1: 7 her rival **p** her till she wept and would not H4087
Ecc 7: 9 *Do* not *be* quickly **p** in your spirit, for H4087
Jer 32:32 Israel and Judah *have* **p** me by all the evil H4087

PROVOKES (2) [PROVOKE]

Pr 25:23 is a sly tongue—which **p** a horrified look. NDT
Eze 8: 3 where the idol that **p to jealousy** stood. H7861

PROVOKING (3) [PROVOKE]

1Sa 1: 6 her rival **kept p** her in order H4087+1685+4088
Jer 7:19 But am I the one they *are* **p**? declares the H4087
Gal 5:26 conceited, **p** and envying each other. *G4614*

PROWL (4) [PROWLED, PROWLING, PROWLS]

Ps 55:10 Day and night *they* **p about** on its walls H6015
Ps 59: 6 snarling like dogs, and **p about** the city. H6015
Ps 59:14 snarling like dogs, and **p about** the city. H6015
Ps 104:20 and all the beasts of the forest **p**. H8253

PROWLED (1) [PROWL]

Eze 19: 6 *He* **p** among the lions, for he was now a H2143

PROWLING (1) [PROWL]

La 5:18 which lies desolate, with jackals **p** over it. H2143

PROWLS (2) [PROWL]

Job 28: 8 do not set foot on it, and no lion **p** there. H6334
1Pe 5: 8 enemy the devil **p around** like a roaring *G4344*

PRUDENCE (8) [PRUDENT]

Pr 1: 4 giving **p** to those who are simple H6893
Pr 8: 5 are simple, gain **p**; you who are foolish H6893
Pr 8:12 dwell together with **p**; I possess H6893
Pr 12: 8 A person is praised according to their **p** H8507
Pr 15: 5 whoever heeds correction **shows p**. H6891
Pr 16:22 **P** is a fountain of life to the prudent, but H8507
Pr 19:25 the simple *will* **learn p**; rebuke the H6891
Pr 21:16 from the path of **p** comes to rest in the H8505

PRUDENT (19) [PRUDENCE]

Pr 1: 3 receiving instruction in **p behavior** H8505
Pr 10: 5 who gathers crops in summer *is* a **p** son, H8505
Pr 10:19 but the **p** hold their tongues. H8505
Pr 12:16 at once, but the **p** overlook an insult. H6874
Pr 12:23 The **p** keep their knowledge to H6874+132
Pr 13:16 All who are **p** act with knowledge, but H6874
Pr 14: 8 The wisdom of the **p** is to give thought to H6874
Pr 14:15 the **p** give thought to their steps. H6874
Pr 14:18 the **p** are crowned with knowledge. H6874
Pr 15:24 leads upward for the **p** to keep them from H8505
Pr 16:22 is a fountain of life to the **p**, H1251+2257S
Pr 16:23 hearts of the wise **make** their mouths **p**, H8505
Pr 17: 2 A **p** servant will rule over a disgraceful H8505
Pr 19:14 parents, but a **p** wife is from the LORD. H8505
Pr 22: 3 The **p** see danger and take refuge, but H6874
Pr 23: 9 to fools, for they will scorn your **p** words. H8507
Pr 27:12 The **p** see danger and take refuge, but H6874
Jer 49: 7 Has counsel perished from the **p**? Has H1067
Am 5:13 Therefore the **p** keep quiet in such times H8505

PRUNE (2) [PRUNED, PRUNES, PRUNING]

Lev 25: 3 for six years **p** your vineyards and H2377
Lev 25: 4 Do not sow your fields or **p** your vineyards. H2377

PRUNED (1) [PRUNE]

Isa 5: 6 a wasteland, neither **p** nor cultivated, and H2377

PRUNES (1) [PRUNE]

Jn 15: 2 that does bear fruit *he* **p** so that it will be *G2748*

PRUNING (4) [PRUNE]

Isa 2: 4 plowshares and their spears into **p hooks**. H4661
Isa 18: 5 he will cut off the shoots with **p knives** H4661
Joel 3:10 into swords and your **p hooks** into spears. H4661
Mic 4: 3 plowshares and their spears into **p hooks**. H4661

PSALM (60) [PSALMS]

Ps 3: T A **p** of David. When he fled from his son H4660
Ps 4: T With stringed instruments. A **p** of David. H4660
Ps 5: T director of music. For pipes. A **p** of David. H4660
Ps 6: T According to sheminith. A **p** of David. H4660
Ps 8: T According to gittith. A **p** of David. H4660
Ps 9: T of "The Death of the Son." A **p** of David. H4660
Ps 12: T According to sheminith. A **p** of David. H4660
Ps 13: T For the director of music. A **p** of David. H4660
Ps 15: T A **p** of David. H4660
Ps 19: T For the director of music. A **p** of David. H4660
Ps 20: T For the director of music. A **p** of David. H4660
Ps 21: T For the director of music. A **p** of David. H4660
Ps 22: T "The Doe of the Morning." A **p** of David. H4660
Ps 23: T A **p** of David. H4660
Ps 24: T A **p**. H4660
Ps 29: T A **p** of David. H4660
Ps 30: T A **p**. A song. For the dedication of the H4660
Ps 31: T For the director of music. A **p** of David. H4660
Ps 38: T A **p** of David. A petition. H4660
Ps 39: T For Jeduthun. A **p** of David. H4660
Ps 40: T For the director of music. Of David. A **p**. H4660
Ps 41: T For the director of music. A **p** of David. H4660
Ps 47: T Of the Sons of Korah. A **p**. H4660
Ps 47: 7 of all the earth; sing to him a **p of praise**. H5380
Ps 48: T A **p** of the Sons of Korah. H4660
Ps 49: T Of the Sons of Korah. A **p**. H4660
Ps 50: T A **p** of Asaph. H4660
Ps 51: T director of music. A **p** of David. When the H4660
Ps 62: T For Jeduthun. A **p** of David. H4660
Ps 63: T A **p** of David. When he was in the Desert H4660
Ps 64: T For the director of music. A **p** of David. H4660
Ps 65: T director of music. A **p** of David. A song. H4660
Ps 66: T For the director of music. A song. A **p**. H4660
Ps 67: T With stringed instruments. A **p**. A song. H4660
Ps 68: T director of music. Of David. A **p**. A song. H4660
Ps 73: T A **p** of Asaph. H4660
Ps 75: T "Do Not Destroy." A **p** of Asaph. A song. H4660
Ps 76: T A **p** of Asaph. A song. H4660
Ps 77: T For Jeduthun. Of Asaph. A **p**. H4660
Ps 79: T A **p** of Asaph. H4660
Ps 80: T Lilies of the Covenant." Of Asaph. A **p**. H4660
Ps 82: T A **p** of Asaph. H4660
Ps 83: T A **p** of Asaph. H4660
Ps 84: T Of the Sons of Korah. A **p**. H4660
Ps 85: T Of the Sons of Korah. A **p**. H4660
Ps 87: T Of the Sons of Korah. A **p**. A song. H4660
Ps 88: T A **p** of the Sons of Korah. For the H4660
Ps 92: T A **p**. A song. For the Sabbath day. H4660
Ps 98: T A **p**. H4660
Ps 100: T A **p**. For giving grateful praise. H4660
Ps 101: T A **p**. H4660
Ps 108: T A **p** of David. H4660
Ps 109: T For the director of music. Of David. A **p**. H4660
Ps 110: T A **p**. H4660
Ps 139: T For the director of music. Of David. A **p**. H4660
Ps 140: T For the director of music. A **p** of David. H4660
Ps 141: T A **p** of David. H4660
Ps 143: T A **p** of David. H4660
Ps 145: T A **p of praise**. Of David. H9335
Ac 13:33 As it is written in the second **P**: " 'You are *G6011*

PSALMS (5) [PSALM]
Lk 20:42 David himself declares in the Book *of* **P**: G6011
Lk 24:44 the Law of Moses, the Prophets and the **P**." G6011
Ac 1:20 said Peter, "it is written in the Book *of* **P**: G6011
Eph 5:19 speaking to one another with **p**, hymns G6011
Col 3:16 one another with all wisdom *through* **p**, G6011

PTOLEMAIS (1)
Ac 21: 7 our voyage from Tyre and landed at **P**, G4767

PUAH (5) [PUITE]
Ge 46:13 Tola, **P**, Jashub and Shimron. H7025
Ex 1:15 whose names were Shiphrah and **P**, H7045
Nu 26:23 the Tolaite clan; through **P**, the Puite clan; H7025
Jdg 10: 1 a man of Issachar named Tola son of **P** H7025
1Ch 7: 1 Tola, **P**, Jashub and Shimron H7025

PUBERTY (1)
Eze 16: 7 and developed and entered **p**. H6344+6344S

PUBLIC (25) [PUBLICLY]
Lev 5: 1 up when they hear a **p charge** to testify H460
Dt 13:16 middle of the **p square** and completely H8148
2Sa 21:12 bodies from the **p square** *at* Beth Shan, H8148
Job 29: 7 the city and took my seat in the **p square**, H8148
Pr 1:20 she raises her voice in the **p square**; H8148
Pr 5:16 your streams of water in the **p squares**? H8148
Pr 22:13 I'll be killed in the **p square**!" H8148
Isa 15: 3 roofs and in the **p squares** they all wail, H8148
Jer 9:21 the young men from the **p squares**. H8148
Jer 48:38 Moab and in the **p squares** there is H8148
Eze 16:24 made a lofty shrine in every **p square**. H8148
Eze 16:31 made your lofty shrines in every **p square**, H8148
Am 5:16 cries of anguish in every **p square**. H8148
Mt 1:19 did not want *to* **expose** her **to p disgrace**, G1258
Lk 20:26 what he had said there **in p**. G1883+3836+3295
Jn 7: 4 wants to become a **p** figure acts in G1877+4244
Ac 5:18 the apostles and put them in the **p** jail. G1323
Ac 12: 4 to bring him out *for* **p** trial after the G3295
Ac 12:21 throne and **delivered a p address** to the G1319
Ac 18:28 refuted his Jewish opponents in **p** debate, G1323
Ro 16:23 who is the city's **director of p works**, and G3874
Col 2:15 he made a **p** spectacle of them G4244
1Ti 4:13 yourself to the **p reading** *of Scripture*, G342
Heb 6: 6 again and **subjecting** him **to p disgrace**. G4136
Rev 11: 8 will lie in the **p square** of the great city— G4423

PUBLICAN, PUBLICANS (KJV) PAGAN, PAGANS, TAX COLLECTOR, TAX COLLECTORS

PUBLICLY (12) [PUBLIC]
Lev 20:17 They are to be **p** removed from H4200+6524
Lk 1:80 wilderness until he **appeared p** to Israel. G345
Lk 12: 8 whoever **p acknowledges** me before G3933
Jn 7:10 festival, he went also, not **p**, but in secret. G5747
Jn 7:13 would say anything **p** about him for fear G4244
Jn 7:26 Here he is, speaking **p**, and they are not G4244
Jn 11:54 longer moved about **p** among the people G4244
Ac 16:37 "They beat us **p** without a trial, even G1323
Ac 19: 9 believe and **p** maligned the G1967+3836+4436
Ac 19:19 together and burned them **p**. G1967+4246
Ac 20:20 have taught you **p** and from house to G1323
Heb 10:33 Sometimes *you were* **p exposed** to insult G2518

PUBLISH (1) [PUBLISHED]
Da 6:12 "*Did you* not **p** a decree that during the A10673

PUBLISHED (2) [PUBLISH]
Est 4: 8 which *had* **been p** in Susa, to show H5989
Da 6:10 learned that the decree *had* **been p**, A10673

PUBLIUS (1)
Ac 28: 7 was an estate nearby that *belonged to* **P**, G4511

PUDENS (1)
2Ti 4:21 and so do **P**, Linus, Claudia and G4545

PUFFED (3) [PUFFS]
Hab 2: 4 the enemy *is* **p up**; his desires are H6752
1Co 4: 6 Then *you* will not *be* **p up** in being a G5881
Col 2:18 *they are* **p up** with idle notions by their G5881

PUFFS (1) [PUFFED]
1Co 8: 1 But knowledge **p up** while love builds up. G5881

PUITE (1) [PUAH]
Nu 26:23 Tolaite clan; through Puah, the **P** clan; H7027

PUL (2) [TIGLATH-PILESER]
2Ki 15:19 Then **P** king of Assyria invaded the land H7040
1Ch 5:26 stirred up the spirit of **P** king of Assyria H7040

PULL (16) [PULLED, PULLING, PULLS]
Jdg 3:22 Ehud *did* not **p** the sword **out**, and the fat H8990
Ru 2:16 Even **p out** some stalks for her from H8963+8963
1Ki 13: 4 so that he could not **p** it **back**. H8740
Job 41: 1 "*Can you* **p in** Leviathan with a fishhook H5432
Pr 21:22 of the mighty and **p down** the stronghold H3718
Jer 13:26 I *will* **p up** your skirts over your face that H3106
Jer 22:24 on my right hand, *I would* still **p** you **off**. H5998
Eze 17: 9 many people to **p** it **up by the roots**. H5951
Eze 26: 4 the walls of Tyre and **p down** her towers; H2238
Eze 29: 4 *I will* **p** you **out** from among your streams H6590
Hos 7:12 *I will* **p** them **down** like the birds in the sky H3718
Am 3:11 **p down** your strongholds and plunder your H3718
Mt 9:16 the patch *will* **p away** from the garment G149
Mt 13:28 'Do you want *us to* go and **p** them **up**? G5198
Mk 2:21 the new piece *will* **p away** from the old G149
Lk 14: 5 *will you* not immediately **p** it **out**? G413

PULLED (20) [PULL]
Ge 19:10 reached out and **p** Lot **back** into the house H995
Ge 37:28 his brothers **p** Joseph up out of the cistern H5432
Jdg 8:17 *He* also **p down** the tower of Peniel and H5997
Jdg 16:14 from his sleep and **p up** the pin and the H5825
1Ki 19:13 *he* **p** his cloak **over** his face and went out H4286
2Ki 23:12 *He* **p down** the altars the kings of Judah H5997
Ezr 6:11 a beam *is to* **be p** from their house and A10481
Ezr 9: 3 **p** hair from my head and beard and sat H5307
Ne 13:25 some of the men and **p out** their **hair**. H5307
Job 4:21 **Are** not the cords of their tent **p up**, so H5825
Isa 33:20 its stakes *will* never *be* **p up**, nor any of its H5825
Isa 38:12 my house *has* **been p down** and taken H5825
Isa 50: 6 my cheeks to *those who* **p out** my **beard**; H5307
Jer 38:13 and *they* **p** him **up** with the ropes and H5432
Eze 19: 9 With hooks *they* **p** him into a cage and H5989
Mt 13:40 "As the weeds *are* **p up** and burned in the G5198
Mt 13:48 *the fishermen* **p** it **up** on the shore. G328
Mt 15:13 has not planted *will be* **p up by the roots**. G1748
Lk 5:11 So *they* **p** their boats **up** on shore, left G2864
Ac 11:10 then *it was* all **p up** to heaven again. G413

PULLING (1) [PULL]
Mt 13:29 '*because while you are* **p** the weeds G5198

PULLS (2) [PULL]
Job 20:25 *He* **p** it out of his back, the gleaming H8990
Hab 1:15 wicked foe **p** all of them **up** with hooks, H6590

PULSE (KJV) VEGETABLES

PUNISH (70) [PUNISHED, PUNISHES, PUNISHING, PUNISHMENT, PUNISHMENTS]
Ge 15:14 But I *will* **p** the nation they serve as slaves H1906
Ex 32:34 when the time comes for me *to* **p**, I will H7212
Ex 32:34 me to punish, *I will* **p** them *for* their sin." H7212
Lev 26:18 *I will* **p** you for your sins seven times over. H3579
Lev 26:28 and *I* myself *will* **p** you for your sins seven H3579
Dt 22:18 the elders shall take the man and **p** him. H3579
1Sa 15: 2 '*I will* **p** the Amalekites *for* what they did H7212
2Sa 7:14 *I will* **p** him with a rod wielded by men H3519
Job 37:13 He brings the clouds to **p** people, or to H8657
Ps 59: 5 rouse yourself to **p** all the nations; show H7212
Ps 89:32 *I will* **p** their sin with the rod, their iniquity H7212
Ps 94:10 *Does he* who disciplines nations not **p** H3519
Ps 119:84 When *will you* **p** my persecutors? H6913+5477
Ps 120: 4 He will **p** you with a warrior's sharp arrows NDT
Pr 23:13 from a child; if *you* **p** them with the rod H5782
Pr 23:14 **P** them with the rod and save them from H5782
Isa 10:12 "*I will* **p** the king of Assyria for the willful H7212
Isa 13:11 *I will* **p** the world *for* its evil, the wicked *for* H7212
Isa 24:21 that day the LORD *will* **p** the powers in the H7212
Isa 26:21 to **p** the people of the earth *for* their sins H7212
Isa 27: 1 that day, the LORD *will* **p** with his sword H7212
Isa 64:12 keep silent and **p** us beyond measure? H6700
Jer 2:19 Your wickedness *will* **p** you; your H3579
Jer 5: 9 *Should I* not **p** them for this?" declares the H7212
Jer 5:29 *Should I* not **p** them for this?" declares the H7212
Jer 6:15 they will be brought down when *I* **p** them," H7212
Jer 9: 9 *Should I* not **p** them for this?" declares the H7212
Jer 9:25 "when *I will* **p** all who are circumcised H7212
Jer 11:22 Almighty says: "I *will* **p** them. Their young H7212
Jer 14:10 their wickedness and **p** them *for* their sins." H7212
Jer 21:14 *I will* **p** you as your deeds deserve H7212
Jer 23:34 *I will* **p** them and their household. H7212
Jer 25:12 *I will* **p** the king of Babylon and his nation, the land of the Babylonians, *for* H7212
Jer 27: 8 *I will* **p** that nation with the sword H7212
Jer 29:32 I *will* surely **p** Shemaiah the Nehelamite H7212
Jer 30:20 before me; *I will* **p** all who oppress them. H7212
Jer 36:31 *I will* **p** him and his children and his attendants *for* H7212
Jer 44:13 *I will* **p** those who live in Egypt with the H7212
Jer 44:29 sign to you that I *will* **p** you in this place, H7212
Jer 49: 8 on Esau at the time when *I* **p** him. H7212
Jer 50:18 "I *will* **p** the king of Babylon and his land H7212
Jer 51:44 *I will* **p** Bel in Babylon and make him H7212
Jer 51:47 surely come when *I will* **p** the idols of H7212
Jer 51:52 the LORD, "when *I will* **p** her idols, and H7212
La 4:22 But *he will* **p** your sin, Daughter Edom H7212
Eze 7:11 has arisen, a **rod** *to* **p** the wicked. None of AIT
Eze 23:24 and *they will* **p** you according to their H9149
Eze 25:17 on them and **p** them in my wrath. H9350
Hos 1: 4 *I will* soon **p** the house of Jehu *for* the H7212
Hos 2:13 *I will* **p** her *for* the days she burned H7212
Hos 4: 9 *I will* **p** both of them *for* their ways and H7212
Hos 4:14 "*I will* not **p** your daughters when they H7212
Hos 8:13 their wickedness and **p** their sins: H7212
Hos 9: 9 their wickedness and **p** them *for* their sins. H7212
Hos 10:10 When I please, *I will* **p** them; nations will H3579
Hos 12: 2 *he will* **p** Jacob according to his ways and H7212
Am 3: 2 therefore *I will* **p** you *for* all your sins." H7212
Am 3:14 "On the day I **p** Israel for her sins, I will H7212
Hab 1:12 my Rock, have ordained them to **p**. H3519
Zep 1: 8 LORD's sacrifice *I will* **p** the officials and H7212
Zep 1: 9 On that day *I will* **p** all who avoid H7212
Zep 1:12 with lamps and **p** those who are H7212
Zec 10: 3 shepherds, and *I will* **p** the leaders; for H7212
Lk 23:16 I will **p** him and then release him. G4084
Ac 4:21 They could not decide how *to* **p** them G3134
Ac 7: 7 But I *will* **p** the nation they serve as slaves G3212
2Co 10: 6 And we will be ready *to* **p** every act of G1688
1Th 4: 6 The Lord will **p** all those who commit such G1690
2Th 1: 8 *He will* **p** those who do not know G1443+1689
1Pe 2:14 are sent by him to **p** those who do wrong G1689

PUNISHED (35) [PUNISH]
Ge 19:15 you will be swept away when the city is **p**." H6411
Ge 42:21 "Surely we are being **p** because of our H872
Ex 21:20 with a rod **must be p** if the slave H5933+5933
Ex 21:21 but *they are* not *to* **be p** if the slave H5933
Lev 18:25 was defiled; so *I* **p** it *for* its sin, and the H7212
1Sa 28:10 LORD lives, you *will* not *be* **p** for this. H6411+7936
1Ch 21: 7 evil in the sight of God; so *he* **p** Israel. H5782
Ezr 7:26 surely be **p** by death, A10522+10170+10191
Ezr 9:13 you *have* **p** us **less** than our H3104+4200+4752
Ps 99: 8 though you **p** their misdeeds. H5933
Pr 21:11 When a mocker *is* **p**, the simple gain H6740
Isa 24:22 up in prison and **be p** after many days. H7212
Isa 26:14 *You* **p** them and brought them to ruin; you H7212
Isa 53: 4 we considered him **p** *by* God, stricken H5595
Isa 53: 8 the transgression of my people he was **p**. H5596
Isa 57:17 their sinful greed; *I* **p** them, and hid my H5782
Jer 2:30 "In vain *I* **p** your people; they did not H5782
Jer 6: 6 This city *must* **be p**; it is filled with H7212
Jer 8:12 will be brought down when they are **p**, H7213
Jer 23:12 disaster on them in the year they are **p**," H7213
Jer 30:14 an enemy would and **p** you as would the H4592
Jer 44:13 famine and plague, as *I* **p** Jerusalem. H7212
Jer 46:21 upon them, the time for them to be **p**. H7213
Jer 50:18 his land as *I* **p** the king of Assyria. H7212
Jer 50:27 day has come, the time for them to be **p**. H7213
Jer 50:31 day has come, the time for you *to be* **p**. H7212
La 3:39 the living complain when **p for** their **sins**? H2628
Mk 12:40 These men *will be* **p** most severely." G3284+3210
Lk 20:47 These men *will be* **p** most severely." G3284+3210
Lk 23:22 Therefore I will *have* him **p** and then G4084
Lk 23:41 We are **p** justly, for we are getting what our NDT
Ac 22: 5 people as prisoners to Jerusalem to *be* **p**. G5512
Ac 26:11 synagogue to another *to have* them **p**, G5512
2Th 1: 9 They *will be* **p** with everlasting G1472+5514
Heb 10:29 deserves to be **p** who has trampled the G5513

PUNISHES (4) [PUNISH]
Ex 34: 7 *he* **p** the children and their children *for* H7212
Nu 14:18 *he* **p** the children *for* the sin of the parents H7212
Job 34:26 *He* **p** them for their wickedness where H6215
Job 35:15 his anger never **p** and he does not take H7212

PUNISHING (4) [PUNISH]
Ex 20: 5 **p** the children *for* the sin of the parents to H7212
Dt 5: 9 **p** the children *for* the sin of the parents to H7212
Jdg 8:16 of Sukkoth a lesson by **p** them with desert NDT
Isa 30:32 lays on them with his **p** club will be to the H4592

PUNISHMENT (55) [PUNISH]
Ge 4:13 to the LORD, "My **p** is more than I can bear. H6411
Lev 19:20 given her freedom, there must be **due p**. H1334
1Sa 14:47 he turned, *he* **inflicted p** on them. H8399
2Ki 7: 9 we wait until daylight, **p** will overtake us. H6411
Job 19:29 wrath will bring **p** *by* the sword, and H6411
Job 21:19 'God stores up the **p** *of* the wicked for their H224
Ps 81:15 before him, and their **p** would last forever. H6961
Ps 91: 8 your eyes and see the **p** *of* the wicked. H8974
Ps 149: 7 on the nations and **p** on the peoples, H9349
Pr 16:22 to the prudent, but folly brings **p** *to* fools. H4592
Isa 53: 5 the **p** *that brought* us peace was on him H4592
Jer 4:18 This is your **p**. How bitter it is! H8288
Jer 11:15 *Can* consecrated meat **avert** your *p*? When AIT
Jer 11:23 people of Anathoth in the year of their **p**." H7213
Jer 23: 2 I *will* **bestow p** on you *for* the evil you H7212
Jer 32:18 thousands but **bring** *the* **p** *for* the parents' H8966
Jer 46:25 "I *am about to* **bring p** on Amon god of H7212
Jer 48:44 I will bring on Moab the year of her **p**," H7213
La 4: 6 The **p** *of* my people is greater than that of H6411
La 4:22 Your **p** will end, Daughter Zion; he will H6411
La 5: 7 are no more, and we bear their **p**. H6411
Eze 5: 8 I will inflict **p** on you in the sight of H5477
Eze 5:10 I will inflict **p** on you and will scatter all H9150
Eze 5:15 you when I inflict **p** on you in anger and H9150
Eze 11: 9 hands of foreigners and inflict **p** on you. H9150
Eze 16:38 you to the **p** *of* women who commit H5477
Eze 16:41 houses and inflict **p** on you in the sight of H9150
Eze 21:25 whose time of **p** has reached its climax, H6411
Eze 21:29 whose time of **p** has reached its climax. H6411
Eze 23:10 women, and **p** was inflicted on her. H9144
Eze 23:24 I will turn you over to them for **p**, and they H5477
Eze 23:45 them to the **p** *of* women who commit H5477
Eze 25:11 I will inflict **p** on Moab. Then they will H9150
Eze 28:22 when I inflict **p** on you and within you am H9150
Eze 28:26 safety when I inflict **p** on all their H9150
Eze 30:14 set fire to Zoan and inflict **p** on Thebes. H9150
Eze 30:19 So I will inflict **p** on Egypt, and they will H9150
Eze 35: 5 the time their **p** reached its climax, H6411
Eze 39:21 nations will see the **p** I inflict and the H5477
Hos 9: 7 The days of **p** are coming, the days of H7213
Zep 3:15 The LORD has taken away your **p**, he has H5477
Zec 1:15 but they went too far with the **p**. H8288
Zec 14:19 This will be the **p** *of* Egypt and the H2633
Zec 14:19 of Egypt and the **p** *of* all the nations that H2633

P

Mt 25:46 "Then they will go away to eternal **p**, but *G3136*
Lk 12:48 things deserving **p** will be beaten with *G4435*
Lk 21:22 For this is the time *of* **p** in fulfillment of all *G1689*
Ro 13: 4 **agents** of wrath **to bring p** on the *G1690*
Ro 13: 5 because of possible **p** but also as a *G3973*
2Co 2: 6 The **p** inflicted on him by the majority is *G2204*
Heb 2: 2 disobedience received its just **p**, *G3632*
2Pe 2: 9 hold the unrighteous *for* **p** on the day of *G3134*
1Jn 4:18 out fear, because fear has to do with **p**. *G3136*
Jude 7 of those who suffer the **p** of eternal fire. *G1472*
Rev 17: 1 I will show you the **p** of the great *G3210*

PUNISHMENTS (2) [PUNISH]

Ps 73:14 afflicted, and every morning brings new **p**. H9350
Zep 3: 7 destroyed, nor all *my* **p come** upon her. H7212

PUNON (2)

Nu 33:42 They left Zalmonah and camped at **P**. H7044
Nu 33:43 They left **P** and camped at Oboth. H7044

PUR (3) [LOT]

Est 3: 7 the month of Nisan, the **p** (that is, the lot) H7052
Est 9:24 Jews to destroy them and had cast the **p** H7052
Est 9:26 days were called Purim, from the word **p**.) H7052

PURAH (2)

Jdg 7:10 go down to the camp with your servant **P** H7242
Jdg 7:11 So he and **P** his servant went down to the H7242

PURCHASE (6) [PURCHASED]

2Ki 22: 6 Also *have* them **p** timber and dressed H7864
2Ch 34:11 builders to **p** dressed stone, H7864
Pr 20:14 then goes off and boasts about the **p**. NDT
Jer 32:11 I took the deed of **p**—the sealed copy H5239
Jer 32:14 unsealed copies of the deed of **p**, H5239
Jer 32:16 had given the deed of **p** to Baruch son of H5239

PURCHASED (6) [PURCHASE]

1Ki 10:28 the royal merchants **p** them from Kue at H4374
2Ki 12:12 They **p** timber and blocks of dressed stone H7864
2Ch 1:16 the royal merchants **p** them from Kue at H4374
Ps 74: 2 Remember the nation *you* **p** long ago, the H7864
Rev 5: 9 with your blood *you* **p** for God persons *G60*
Rev 14: 4 They *were* **p** from among mankind and *G60*

PURE (108) [PUREST, PURIFICATION, PURIFIED, PURIFIER, PURIFIES, PURIFY, PURIFYING, PURITY]

Ex 25:11 Overlay it with **p** gold, both inside and out H3196
Ex 25:17 "Make an atonement cover of **p** gold H3196
Ex 25:24 Overlay it with **p** gold and make a gold H3196
Ex 25:29 And make its plates and dishes of **p** gold H3196
Ex 25:31 "Make a lampstand of **p** gold. Hammer H3196
Ex 25:36 the lampstand, hammered out of **p** gold. H3196
Ex 25:38 trimmers and trays are to be of **p** gold. H3196
Ex 25:39 A talent of **p** gold is to be used for the H3196
Ex 28:14 two braided chains of **p** gold, like a H3196
Ex 28:22 make braided chains of **p** gold, H3196
Ex 28:36 "Make a plate of **p** gold and engrave on it H3196
Ex 30: 3 all the sides and the horns with **p** gold, H3196
Ex 30:34 galbanum—and **p** frankincense, all H2341
Ex 30:35 It is to be salted and **p** and sacred. H3196
Ex 31: 8 the **p** gold lampstand and all its H3196
Ex 37: 2 He overlaid it with **p** gold, both inside H3196
Ex 37: 6 He made the atonement cover of **p** gold— H3196
Ex 37:11 overlaid it with **p** gold and made a gold H3196
Ex 37:16 And they made from **p** gold the articles H3196
Ex 37:17 They made the lampstand of **p** gold. H3196
Ex 37:22 the lampstand, hammered out of **p** gold. H3196
Ex 37:23 as its wick trimmers and trays, of **p** gold. H3196
Ex 37:24 its accessories from one talent of **p** gold. H3196
Ex 37:26 all the sides and the horns with **p** gold, H3196
Ex 37:29 made the sacred anointing oil and the **p**, H3196
Ex 39:15 they made braided chains of **p** gold, H3196
Ex 39:25 they made bells of **p** gold and attached H3196
Ex 39:30 emblem, out of **p** gold and engraved on it H3196
Ex 39:37 the **p** gold lampstand with its row of lamps H3196
Lev 24: 4 The lamps on the **p** gold lampstand H3196
Lev 24: 6 on the table of **p** gold before the LORD. H3196
Lev 24: 7 each stack put some **p** incense as a H2341
2Sa 22:27 to the **p** you show yourself pure, but to the H1405
2Sa 22:27 to the pure *you* **show yourself p**, but to the H1405
1Ki 6:20 He overlaid the inside with **p** gold, and H6034
1Ki 6:21 the inside of the temple with **p** gold, H6034
1Ki 7:49 the lampstands of **p** gold (five on the right H6034
1Ki 7:50 the **p** gold basins, wick trimmers H6034
1Ki 10:21 of the Forest of Lebanon were **p** gold. H6034
2Ki 2:22 And the water *has remained* **p** to this day H8324
2Ki 25:15 that were made of **p gold** or silver. H2298+2298
1Ch 28:17 the weight of **p** gold for the forks H3196
2Ch 3: 4 He overlaid the inside with **p** gold. H3196
2Ch 4:20 the lampstands of **p** gold with their lamps, H6034
2Ch 4:22 the **p** gold wick trimmers, sprinkling bowls, H6034
2Ch 9:17 with ivory and overlaid with **p** gold. H3196
2Ch 9:20 of the Forest of Lebanon were **p** gold. H6034
Job 4:17 *Can* even a strong man *be* more **p** than H3197
Job 8: 6 if you are **p** and upright, even now he will H2341
Job 11: 4 are flawless and I am **p** in your sight. H1338
Job 14: 4 Who can bring *what* is **p** from the impure H3196
Job 15:14 mortals, that *they could be* **p**, or those H2342
Job 15:15 if even the heavens *are* not **p** in his eyes, H2348
Job 16:17 been free of violence and my prayer is **p**. H2341
Job 25: 4 How *can* one born of woman *be* **p**? H2342
Job 25: 5 bright and the stars *are* not **p** in his eyes, H2348
Job 28:19 it cannot be bought with **p** gold. H3196
Job 31:24 put my trust in gold or said to **p gold**, H4188
Job 33: 9 'I am **p**, I have done no wrong; I am clean H2341
Ps 18:26 to the **p** you show yourself pure, but to the H1405
Ps 18:26 to the pure *you* **show yourself p**, but to the H1405
Ps 19: 9 The fear of the LORD is **p**, enduring forever H3196
Ps 19:10 than much **p gold**; they are sweeter H7058
Ps 21: 3 placed a crown of **p gold** on his head. H7058
Ps 24: 4 one who has clean hands and a **p** heart, H1338
Ps 51:10 Create in me a **p** heart, O God, and renew H3196
Ps 73: 1 to Israel, to *those who* are **p** *in* heart. H1338
Ps 73:13 in vain *I have* **kept** my heart **p** and have H2342
Ps 119:127 more than gold, more than **p gold**, H7058
Pr 15:26 gracious words are **p** in his sight. H3196
Pr 16: 2 All a person's ways seem **p** to them, but H2341
Pr 20: 9 can say, "*I have* **kept** my heart **p**; I am H2342
Pr 20:11 so is their conduct *really* **p** and upright? H2341
Pr 22:11 One who loves a **p** heart and who speaks H3196
Pr 30:12 those who are **p** in their own eyes and H3196
SS 5:15 pillars of marble set on bases of **p** gold. H7058
Isa 13:12 I will make people scarcer than **p gold** H7058
Isa 52:11 out from it and *be* **p**, *you* who carry the H1405
Jer 52:19 that were made of **p gold** or silver. H2298+2298
Da 2:32 head of the statue was made of **p** gold, A10294
Hab 1:13 Your eyes are too **p** to look on evil; you H3196
Mal 1:11 place incense and **p** offerings will be H3196
Mt 5: 8 Blessed are the **p** in heart, for they will *G2754*
Mk 14: 3 very expensive perfume, made of **p** nard. *G4410*
Jn 12: 3 Then Mary took about a pint of **p** nard, an *G4410*
2Co 11: 2 that I might present you as a **p** virgin to him. *G54*
2Co 11: 3 from your sincere and **p** devotion to Christ. *G55*
Php 1:10 is best and may be **p** and blameless for *G1637*
Php 2:15 so that you may become blameless and **p** *G193*
Php 4: 8 whatever is **p**, whatever is lovely, *G54*
1Ti 1: 5 which comes from a **p** heart and a good *G2754*
1Ti 5:22 share in the sins of others. Keep yourself **p**. *G54*
2Ti 2:22 who call on the Lord out of a **p** heart. *G2754*
Titus 1:15 *To* the **p**, all things are pure, but to those *G2754*
Titus 1:15 all things are **p**, but to those who *G2754*
Titus 1:15 do not believe, nothing is **p**. *G2754*
Titus 2: 5 to be self-controlled and **p**, to be busy at *G54*
Heb 7:26 blameless, **p**, set apart from sinners *G299*
Heb 10:22 having our bodies washed with **p** water. *G2754*
Heb 13: 4 the marriage bed kept **p**, for God will *G299*
Jas 1: 2 Consider it **p** joy, my brothers and sisters *G4246*
Jas 1:27 Father accepts as **p** and faultless is this *G2754*
Jas 3:17 that comes from heaven is first of all **p**; *G54*
1Pe 2: 2 newborn babies, crave **p** spiritual milk, so *G100*
1Jn 3: 3 in him purify themselves, just as he is **p**. *G54*
Rev 21:18 the city of **p** gold, as pure as glass. *G2754*
Rev 21:18 the city of pure gold, as **p** as glass. *G2754*
Rev 21:21 city was of gold, as **p** as transparent glass. *G2754*

PUREST (1) [PURE]

SS 5:11 His head is **p gold**; his hair is wavy H4188+7058

PURGE (15) [PURGED]

PURGE, PURGED, PURGETH (KJV) ATONE, ATONED, ATONEMENT, CLEANSE, CLEANSED, CLEAR, PRUNES, PURIFICATION, PURIFIED, PURIFY, REFINE, RID

Dt 13: 5 *You must* **p** the evil from among you H1278
Dt 17: 7 *You must* **p** the evil from among you H1278
Dt 17:12 *You must* **p** the evil from Israel. H1278
Dt 19:13 *You must* **p** from Israel the guilt of H1278
Dt 19:19 *You must* **p** the evil from among you H1278
Dt 21:21 *You must* **p** the evil from among you H1278
Dt 22:21 *You must* **p** the evil from among you H1278
Dt 22:22 *You must* **p** the evil from Israel H1278
Dt 22:24 *You must* **p** the evil from among you. H1278
Dt 24: 7 *You must* **p** the evil from among you. H1278
Jdg 20:13 them to death and **p** the evil from Israel." H1278
2Ch 34: 3 year he began to **p** Judah and Jerusalem H3197
Pr 20:30 away evil, and beatings **p** the inmost being. NDT
Isa 1:25 *I will* **thoroughly p away** H7671+3869+2021+1342
Eze 20:38 *I will* **p** you of those who revolt and rebel H1405

PURGED (3) [PURGE]

Dt 21: 9 you *will have* **p** from yourselves the H1278
2Ch 34: 5 and so *he* **p** Judah and Jerusalem. H3197
Jer 6:29 goes on in vain; the wicked **are not p out**. H5998

PURIFICATION (10) [PURE]

Lev 12: 4 sanctuary until the days of her **p** are over. H3198
Lev 12: 6 the days of her **p** for a son or daughter H3198
Nu 19: 9 the water of cleansing; it is for **p from sin**. H2633
Nu 19:17 from the burned **p offering** into a jar and H2633
1Ch 23:28 the **p** of all sacred things and the H3200
Ne 12:45 service of their God and the service of **p**, H3200
Lk 2:22 the time came *for* the **p rites** required by *G2752*
Ac 21:24 join in their **p rites** and pay their expenses *G49*
Ac 21:26 date when the days *of* **p** would end and the *G50*
Heb 1: 3 After he had provided **p** for sins, he sat *G2752*

PURIFIED (21) [PURE]

Lev 12: 4 days to be **p** from her bleeding. H3200
Lev 12: 5 sixty-six days to be **p** from her bleeding. H3200
Nu 8:15 "After *you have* **p** the Levites and H3197
Nu 8:21 The Levites **p themselves** and washed H2627
Nu 31:23 But *it must* also **be p** with the water of H2627
2Ch 29:18 "*We have* **p** the entire temple of the LORD H3197
2Ch 30:18 Zebulun *had* not **p themselves**, H3197
Ezr 6:20 Levites *had* **p themselves** and were H3197
Ne 12:30 Levites *had* **p themselves ceremonially**, H3197
Ne 12:30 ceremonially, *they* **p** the people, the H3197
Ne 13:30 So *I* **p** the priests and the Levites of H3197
Job 1: 5 make arrangements for them *to be* **p**. H7727
Ps 12: 6 flawless, like silver **p** in a crucible, like H7671
Eze 43:22 the altar *is to be* **p** as it was purified H2627
Eze 43:22 is to be purified as *it was* **p** with the bull. H2627
Da 11:35 **p** and made spotless until the time of the H1405
Da 12:10 Many *will* **be p**, made spotless and refined H1405
Ac 15: 9 us and them, *for he* **p** their hearts by faith. *G2751*
Ac 21:26 took the men and **p** *himself* along with them *G49*
Heb 9:23 the heavenly things *to be* **p** with these *G2751*
1Pe 1:22 *Now that you have* **p** yourselves by obeying *G49*

PURIFIER (1) [PURE]

Mal 3: 3 He will sit as a refiner and **p** *of* silver; he H3197

PURIFIES (1) [PURE]

1Jn 1: 7 blood of Jesus, his Son, **p** us from all sin. *G2751*

PURIFY (30) [PURE]

Ge 35: 2 and **p yourselves** and change your clothes. H3197
Ex 29:36 **P** the altar by making atonement for it H2627
Lev 8:15 on all the horns of the altar *to* **p** the altar. H2627
Lev 14:49 To **p** the house he is to take two birds and H2627
Lev 14:52 *He shall* **p** the house with the bird's blood H2627
Nu 8: 7 To **p** them, do this: Sprinkle the water of H3197
Nu 8: 7 And so *they will* **p themselves**. H3197
Nu 8:21 made atonement for them to **p** them. H3197
Nu 19:12 They *must* **p** themselves with the water on H2627
Nu 19:12 But if *they do* not **p themselves** on the H2627
Nu 19:13 If they fail *to* **p themselves** after touching a H2627
Nu 19:19 on the seventh day *he is to* **p** them. H2627
Nu 19:20 who are unclean *do* not **p themselves**, H2627
Nu 31:19 days you *must* **p yourselves** and your H2627
Nu 31:20 **P** every garment as well as everything H2627
2Ch 29:15 they went in to **p** the temple of the LORD H3197
2Ch 29:16 went into the sanctuary of the LORD to **p** it. H3197
2Ch 34: 8 to **p** the land and the temple H3197
Ne 13: 9 I gave orders *to* **p** the rooms, and then I H3197
Ne 13:22 the Levites *to* **p themselves** and go and H3197
Isa 66:17 **p themselves** to go into the H3197
Eze 43:20 so **p** the altar and make atonement H2627
Eze 45:18 bull without defect and **p** the sanctuary. H2627
Zep 3: 9 "Then *I will* **p** the lips of the H1359+2200
Mal 3: 3 *he will* **p** the Levites and refine them like H3197
2Co 7: 1 *let us* **p** ourselves from everything that *G2751*
Titus 2:14 all wickedness and *to* **p** for himself a *G2751*
Jas 4: 8 you sinners, and **p** your hearts, you *G49*
1Jn 1: 9 forgive us our sins and **p** us from all *G2751*
1Jn 3: 3 All who have this hope in him **p** themselves *G49*

PURIFYING (2) [PURE]

2Sa 11: 4 Now she *was* **p herself** from her monthly H7727
Eze 43:23 When you have finished **p** it, you are to H2627

PURIM (5)

Est 9:26 Therefore these days were called **P**, from H7052
Est 9:28 And these days of **P** should never fail to H7052
Est 9:29 to confirm this second letter concerning **P**. H7052
Est 9:31 these days of **P** at their designated H7052
Est 9:32 confirmed these regulations about **P**, H7052

PURITY (6) [PURE]

Ps 119: 9 can a young person stay on the path of **p**? H2342
Hos 8: 5 How long will they be incapable of **p**? H5931
2Co 6: 6 in **p**, understanding, patience and kindness *G55*
1Ti 4:12 in conduct, in love, in faith and in **p**. *G48*
1Ti 5: 2 younger women as sisters, with absolute **p**. *G48*
1Pe 3: 2 when they see the **p** and reverence of your *G54*

PURPLE (51)

Ex 25: 4 **p** and scarlet yarn and fine linen; goat H763
Ex 26: 1 linen and blue, **p** and scarlet yarn, with H763
Ex 26:31 **p** and scarlet yarn and finely twisted linen H763
Ex 26:36 **p** and scarlet yarn and finely twisted linen H763
Ex 27:16 **p** and scarlet yarn and finely twisted linen H763
Ex 28: 5 blue, **p** and scarlet yarn, and fine linen H763
Ex 28: 6 of blue, **p** and scarlet yarn, and of H763
Ex 28: 8 with blue, **p** and scarlet yarn, and with H763
Ex 28:15 of blue, **p** and scarlet yarn, and of H763
Ex 28:33 **p** and scarlet yarn around the hem of the H763
Ex 35: 6 **p** and scarlet yarn and fine linen; goat H763
Ex 35:23 had blue, **p** or scarlet yarn or fine linen H763
Ex 35:25 blue, **p** or scarlet yarn or fine linen. H763
Ex 35:35 **p** and scarlet yarn and fine linen H763
Ex 36: 8 linen and blue, **p** and scarlet yarn, with H763
Ex 36:35 **p** and scarlet yarn and finely twisted linen H763
Ex 36:37 **p** and scarlet yarn and finely twisted linen H763
Ex 38:18 **p** and scarlet yarn and finely twisted linen H763
Ex 38:23 **p** and scarlet yarn and fine linen. H763
Ex 39: 1 **p** and scarlet yarn they made woven H763
Ex 39: 2 of blue, **p** and scarlet yarn, and of H763
Ex 39: 3 the blue, **p** and scarlet yarn and fine linen H763
Ex 39: 5 with blue, **p** and scarlet yarn, and with H763
Ex 39: 8 of blue, **p** and scarlet yarn, and of H763
Ex 39:24 **p** and scarlet yarn and finely twisted linen H763
Ex 39:29 linen and blue, **p** and scarlet yarn—the H763
Nu 4:13 bronze altar and spread a **p** cloth over it. H763
Jdg 8:26 pendants and the **p** garments worn by the H763
2Ch 2: 7 iron, and in **p**, crimson and blue yarn, H760

P

2Ch 2:14 with p and blue and crimson yarn and H763
2Ch 3:14 p and crimson yarn and fine linen H763
Est 1: 6 of white linen and p material to silver rings H763
Est 8:15 crown of gold and a p robe of fine linen. H763
Pr 31:22 her bed; she is clothed in fine linen and p. H763
SS 3:10 Its seat was upholstered with p, its interior H763
Jer 10: 9 have made is then dressed in blue and p— H763
La 4: 5 brought up in royal p now lie on ash H9355
Eze 27: 7 were of blue and p from the coasts of H763
Eze 27:16 turquoise, p fabric, embroidered H763
Da 5: 7 will be clothed in p and have a gold A10066
Da 5:16 will be clothed in p and have a gold A10066
Da 5:29 Daniel was clothed in p, a gold chain A10066
Mk 15:17 They put a p robe on him, then twisted G4525
Mk 15:20 they took off the p robe and put his own G4525
Lk 16:19 who was dressed in p and fine linen and G4525
Jn 19: 2 They clothed him in a p robe G4528
Jn 19: 5 the crown of thorns and the p robe, G4528
Ac 16:14 Thyatira named Lydia, a dealer in p cloth. G4527
Rev 17: 4 The woman was dressed in p and scarlet G4528
Rev 18:12 fine linen, p, silk and scarlet cloth G4525
Rev 18:16 dressed in fine linen, p and scarlet, and G4528

PURPOSE (35) [PURPOSED, PURPOSES]

Ex 9:16 I have raised you up for this very p, H928+6288
Lev 7:24 wild animals may be used for any other p, H4856
1Ch 23: 5 instruments I have provided for that p." H2146S
Job 36: 5 no one; he is mighty, and firm in his p. H4213
Job 42: 2 all things; no p of yours can be thwarted. H4659
Pr 19:21 but it is the LORD's p that prevails. H6783
Isa 10: 7 he has in mind; his p is to destroy, to put H4222
Isa 46:10 'My p will stand, and I will do all H6783
Isa 46:11 from a far-off land, a man to fulfill my p. H6783
Isa 48:14 ally will carry out his p against Babylon; H2914
Isa 55:11 I desire and achieve the p for which I sent H7503
Jer 15:11 "Surely I will deliver you for a good p; AIT
Jer 51:11 because his p is to destroy Babylon. H4659
Jer 51:12 The LORD will carry out his p, his decree H2372
Lk 7:30 the law rejected God's p for themselves, G1087
Ac 5:38 For if their p or activity is of human origin G1087
Ac 13:36 had served God's p in his own generation G1087
Ro 8:28 who have been called according to his p. G4606
Ro 9:11 in order that God's p in election might G4606
Ro 9:17 "I raised you up for this very p, that I G1650
1Co 3: 8 plants and the one who waters have one p, AIT
2Co 5: 5 has fashioned us for this very p is God, G1650
Gal 4:18 provided the p is good, and to be so G1877
Eph 1:11 in conformity with the p of his will, G1087
Eph 2:15 His p was to create in himself one new G2671
Eph 3:11 to his eternal p that he accomplished in G4606
Eph 6:22 sending him to you for this very p, G1650+4047
Php 2:13 to act in order to fulfill his good p. G2306
Col 4: 8 to you for the express p that G1650+899+4047
1Ti 2: 7 And for this p I was appointed a herald G1650
2Ti 1: 9 done but because of his own p and grace. G4606
2Ti 3:10 my way of life, my p, faith, patience, G4606
Heb 6:17 nature of his p very clear to the G1087
Rev 17:13 They have one p and will give their power G1191
Rev 17:17 to accomplish his p by agreeing to hand G1191

PURPOSED (5) [PURPOSE]

Isa 14:24 it will be, and as I have p, so it will H3619
Isa 14:27 For the LORD Almighty has p, and who can H3619
Jer 49:20 what he has p against those who H3108+4742
Jer 50:45 what he has p against the land of H3108+4742
Eph 1: 9 his good pleasure, which he p in Christ, G4729

PURPOSES (10) [PURPOSE]

Ps 33:10 nations; he thwarts the p of the peoples. H4742
Ps 33:11 the p of his heart through all generations. H4742
Pr 20: 5 The p of a person's heart are deep waters, H6783
Jer 23:20 he fully accomplishes the p of his heart. H4659
Jer 30:24 he fully accomplishes the p of his heart. H4659
Jer 32:19 great are your p and mighty are your H6783
Jer 51:29 the LORD's p against Babylon stand H4742
Ro 9:21 some pottery for special p and some for G5507
2Ti 2:20 some are for special p and some for G5507
2Ti 2:21 the latter will be instruments for special p, G5507

PURSE (5) [PURSES]

Pr 7:20 He took his p filled with money and will H7655
Hag 1: 6 only to put them in a p with holes in it." H7655
Lk 10: 4 Do not take a p or bag or sandals; and do G964
Lk 22:35 "When I sent you without p, bag or sandals G964
Lk 22:36 to them, "But now if you have a p, take it, G964

PURSES (3) [PURSE]

Pr 16:30 whoever p their lips is bent on evil. H7975
Isa 3:22 robes and the capes and cloaks, the p H3038
Lk 12:33 Provide p for yourselves that will not wear G964

PURSUE (53) [PURSUED, PURSUER, PURSUERS, PURSUES, PURSUING, PURSUIT]

Ex 14: 4 Pharaoh's heart, and he will p them. H8103
Ex 15: 9 enemy boasted, 'I will p, I will overtake H8103
Lev 26: 7 You will p your enemies, and they will fall H8103
Lev 26:33 will draw out my sword and p you. H339
Dt 19: 6 avenger of blood might p him in a rage, H8103
Dt 28:45 They will p you and overtake you until you H8103
Jos 8: 6 They will p us until we have lured H3655+339
Jos 8:16 All the men of Ai were called to p them H8103
Jos 10:19 But don't stop; p your enemies! Attack H8103
1Sa 14:36 "Let us go down and p the Philistines by H339
1Sa 14:37 "Shall I go down and p the Philistines? H339
1Sa 30: 8 of the LORD, "Shall I p this raiding party? H8103
1Sa 30: 8 I overtake them?" "P them," he answered H8103
2Sa 20: 6 Take your master's men and p him, or he H8103
2Sa 20: 7 from Jerusalem to p Sheba son of Bikri. H8103
2Sa 20:13 went on with Joab to p Sheba son of Bikri. H8103
2Sa 24:13 from your enemies while they p you? H8103
Job 19:22 Why do you p me as God does? Will you H8103
Ps 7: 1 save and deliver me from all who p me, H8103
Ps 7: 5 then let my enemy p and overtake me; let H8103
Ps 31:15 of my enemies, from those who p me. H8103
Ps 34:14 evil and do good; seek peace and p it. H8103
Ps 35: 3 javelin against those who p me. H8103
Ps 56: 2 My adversaries p me all day long; in their H8634
Ps 57: 3 rebuking those who hotly p me—God H8634
Ps 71:11 has forsaken him; p him and seize him H8103
Ps 83:15 so p them with your tempest and terrify H8103
Ps 142: 6 rescue me from those who p me, for they H8103
Pr 15: 9 he loves those who p righteousness. H8103
Pr 19: 7 Though the poor p them with pleading H8103
Isa 51: 1 you who p righteousness and who seek H8103
Isa 59: 7 They p evil schemes; acts of violence mark NDT
Jer 2:24 Any males that p her need not tire H1335
Jer 9:16 and I will p them with the sword H8938+339
Jer 29:18 I will p them with the sword, famine and H8103
Jer 48: 2 be silenced; the sword will p you. H2143+339
Jer 49:37 "I will p them with the sword until I H8938+339
Jer 50:21 P, kill and completely destroy them," H339
La 1: 3 All who p her have overtaken her in the H8103
La 3:66 P them in anger and destroy them from H8103
La 5: 5 Those who p us are at our heels; we are H8103
Eze 5: 2 For I will p them with drawn sword. H339
Eze 5:12 to the winds and p with drawn sword. H339
Eze 12:14 I will p them with drawn sword. H339
Eze 35: 6 you over to bloodshed and it will p you. H8103
Eze 35: 6 hate bloodshed, bloodshed will p you. H8103
Hos 8: 3 what is good; an enemy will p him. H8103
Na 1: 8 he will p his foes into the realm of H8103
Mt 23:34 synagogues and p from town to town. G1503
Ro 9:30 the Gentiles, who did not p righteousness G1503
1Ti 6:11 flee from all this, and p righteousness G1503
2Ti 2:22 evil desires of youth and p righteousness, G1503
1Pe 3:11 do good; they must seek peace and p it. G1503

PURSUED (31) [PURSUE]

Ge 31:23 he p Jacob for seven days and caught up H8103
Ge 35: 5 all around them so that no one p them. H8103
Ex 14: 8 of Egypt, so that he p the Israelites, who H8103
Ex 14: 9 p the Israelites and overtook them as they H8103
Ex 14:23 The Egyptians p them, and all Pharaoh's H8103
Jos 8:16 and they p Joshua and were lured away H8103
Jos 10:10 Israel p them along the road going up to H8103
Jos 11: 8 defeated them and p them all the way to H8103
Jos 24: 6 the Egyptians p them with chariots H8103
Jdg 4:16 Barak p the chariots and army as far as H8103
Jdg 7:23 called out, and they p the Midianites. H8103
Jdg 7:25 They p the Midianites and brought the H8103
Jdg 8:12 but he p them and captured them H8103
1Sa 7:11 out of Mizpah and p the Philistines, H8103
1Sa 17:52 with a shout and p the Philistines to the H8103
2Sa 2:19 the right nor to the left as he p him. H2143+339
2Sa 2:24 But Joab and Abishai p Abner, and as the H8103
2Sa 2:28 they no longer p Israel, nor did they H8103
2Sa 20:10 his brother Abishai p Sheba son of Bikri. H8103
2Sa 22:38 "I p my enemies and crushed them; I did H8103
2Ki 25: 5 the Babylonian army p the king and H8103
2Ch 13:19 Abijah p Jeroboam and took from him the H8103
2Ch 14:13 Asa and his army p them as far as H8103
Ps 18:37 I p my enemies and overtook them; I did H8103
Jer 39: 5 the Babylonian army p them and overtook H8103
Jer 52: 8 the Babylonian army p King Zedekiah H8103
La 3:43 covered yourself with anger and p us; H8103
Am 1:11 Because he p his brother with a sword H8103
Ro 9:31 who p the law as the way of G1503
Ro 9:32 Because they p it not by faith but as if it NDT
Rev 12:13 he p the woman who had given birth to G1503

PURSUER (1) [PURSUE]

La 1: 6 in weakness they have fled before the p. H8103

PURSUERS (7) [PURSUE]

Jos 2: 7 as soon as the p had gone out, the H8103
Jos 2:16 "Go to the hills so the p will not find you. H8103
Jos 2:22 until the p had searched all along the H8103
Jos 8:20 had turned back against their p. H8103
Ne 9:11 you hurled their p into the depths, like H8103
Isa 30:16 Therefore your p will be swift! H8103
La 4:19 Our p were swifter than eagles in the sky H8103

PURSUES (9) [PURSUE]

Ps 143: 3 The enemy p me, he crushes me to the H8103
Pr 11:19 attain life, but whoever p evil finds death. H8103
Pr 13:21 Trouble p the sinner, but the righteous H8103
Pr 18: 1 An unfriendly person p selfish ends and H1335
Pr 21:21 Whoever p righteousness and love finds H8103
Pr 28: 1 The wicked flee though no one p, but the H8103
Isa 41: 3 He p them and moves on unscathed, by a H8103
Jer 8: 6 Each p their own course like a horse H8740+928
Hos 12: 1 he p the east wind all day and multiplies H8103

PURSUING (24) [PURSUE]

Ge 14:15 he routed them, p them as far as Hobah H8103
Lev 26:17 you will flee even when no one is p you. H8103
Lev 26:36 will fall, even though no one is p them. H8103
Lev 26:37 the sword, even though no one is p them. H8103
Dt 11: 4 waters of the Red Sea as they were p you, H8103
Jdg 8: 5 and I am still p Zebah and Zalmunna H8103
1Sa 14:46 Then Saul stopped p the Philistines, and H339
1Sa 24: 1 After Saul returned from p the Philistines H339
1Sa 24:14 Who are you p? A dead dog? H8103
1Sa 25:29 though someone is p you to take your H8103
1Sa 26:18 he added, "Why is my lord p his servant? H8103
2Sa 2:26 order your men to stop p their fellow H339
2Sa 2:27 have continued p them until morning." H339
2Sa 2:30 Then Joab stopped p Abner and H339
2Sa 18:16 the troops stopped p Israel, for Joab H8103
1Ki 22:33 king of Israel and stopped p him. H4946+339
2Ch 18:32 king of Israel, they stopped p him. H4946+339
Ps 35: 6 with the angel of the LORD p them. H8103
Isa 65: 2 in ways not good, p their own imaginations H339
Jer 2:33 How skilled you are at p love! Even the H1335
Hos 5:11 in judgment, intent on p idols. H2143+339
1Ti 3: 8 in much wine, and not p dishonest gain. G153
Titus 1: 7 not violent, not p dishonest gain. G153
1Pe 5: 2 not p dishonest gain, but eager to G154

PURSUIT (17) [PURSUE]

Ge 14:14 household and went in p as far as Dan. H8103
Jos 2: 7 the men set out in p of the spies on the H8103
Jos 8:17 left the city open and went in p of Israel. H8103
Jos 20: 5 If the avenger of blood comes in p, the H8103
Jdg 4:22 Just then Barak came by in p of Sisera H8103
Jdg 8: 4 exhausted yet keeping up the p, came to H8103
1Sa 14:22 on the run, they joined the battle in hot p. H339
1Sa 23:25 he went into the Desert of Maon in p of H8103
1Sa 23:28 Saul broke off his p of David and went to H8103
1Sa 30:10 the other four hundred continued the p. H8103
1Sa 31: 2 Philistines were in hot p of Saul and his H1815
2Sa 1: 6 with the chariots and their drivers in hot p. H1815
2Sa 2:23 But Asahel refused to give up the p; so H6073
2Sa 17: 1 men and set out tonight in p of David. H8103
1Ki 20:20 Arameans fled, with the Israelites in p. H8103
1Ch 10: 2 The Philistines were in hot p of Saul and H1815
Ps 56: 1 my enemies are in hot p; all day long H8634

PUSH (5) [PUSHED, PUSHES, PUSHING]

Dt 15:17 then take an awl and p it through his H5989
Jos 23: 5 God himself will p them out for your sake. H2074
2Ki 4:27 Gehazi came over to p her away, but the H2074
Ps 44: 5 Through you we p back our enemies H5590
Jer 46:15 for the LORD will p them down. H2074

PUSHED (7) [PUSH]

Jdg 16:30 Then he p with all his might, and down H5742
Ps 118:13 I was p back and about to fall, but H1890+1890
Isa 16: 2 Like fluttering birds p from the nest, so are H8938
Zec 5: 8 and he p her back into the basket and H8959
Zec 5: 8 basket and p its lead cover down on it. H8959
Ac 7:27 the other p Moses aside and said, G723
Ac 19:33 in the crowd p Alexander to the front, G4582

PUSHES (1) [PUSH]

Nu 35:22 enmity someone suddenly p another or H2074

PUSHING (2) [PUSH]

Joel 2:20 p it into a parched and barren land H5615
Mk 3:10 with diseases were p forward to touch him G2158

PUT (1021) [PUTS, PUTTING]

Ge 2: 8 there he p the man he had formed. H8492
Ge 2:15 took the man and p him in the Garden of H5663
Ge 3:12 "The woman you p here with me—she H5989
Ge 3:15 And I will p enmity between you and the H8883
Ge 4:15 Then the LORD p a mark on Cain so that no H8492
Ge 6:13 "I am going to p an end to all H4200+7156+995
Ge 6:16 P a door in the side of the ark and make H8492
Ge 10: 6 Cush, Egypt, P and Canaan. H7033
Ge 16: 5 I p my slave in your arms, and now that H5989
Ge 21:15 she p the boy under one of the bushes. H8959
Ge 24: 2 that he had, "P your hand under my thigh. H8492
Ge 24: 9 So the servant p his hand under the thigh H8492
Ge 24:47 "Then I p the ring in her nose and the H8492
Ge 26:11 his wife shall surely be p to death." H4637+4637
Ge 27:15 and p them on her younger son Jacob. H4252
Ge 28:11 he p it under his head and lay down to H8492
Ge 30:36 Then he p a three-day journey between H8492
Ge 30:40 himself and did not p them with H8883
Ge 31:17 Then Jacob p his children and his wives H5951
Ge 31:34 household gods and p them inside her H8492
Ge 31:37 P it here in front of your relatives and H8492
Ge 32:16 He p them in the care of his servants, each H5989
Ge 33: 2 He p the female servants and their H8492
Ge 34:26 They p Hamor and his son Shechem to the H2222
Ge 37:34 p on sackcloth and mourned H8492+928+5516
Ge 38: 7 LORD's sight; so the LORD p him to death. H4637
Ge 38:10 so the LORD p him to death also. H4637
Ge 38:19 off her veil and p on her widow's clothes H4252
Ge 38:28 one of them p out his hand; so H5989
Ge 39: 4 Potiphar p him in charge of his household H7212
Ge 39: 5 From the time he p him in charge of his H7212
Ge 39:20 master took him and p him in prison, H5989
Ge 39:22 So the warden p Joseph in charge of all H5989
Ge 40: 3 p them in custody in the house of the H5989
Ge 40:11 Pharaoh's cup and p the cup in his hand." H5989
Ge 40:13 and you will p Pharaoh's cup in his hand H5989
Ge 40:15 nothing to deserve being p in a dungeon H8492

P

Ge 40:21 so that he once again p the cup into H5989
Ge 41:33 wise man and p him in charge of the H8883
Ge 41:41 "I hereby p you in charge of the whole H5989
Ge 41:42 from his finger and p it on Joseph's finger H5989
Ge 41:42 of fine linen and p a gold chain around H8492
Ge 41:43 Thus he p him in charge of the whole H5989
Ge 41:48 In each city he p the food grown in the H5989
Ge 42:17 And he p them all in custody for three days. H665
Ge 42:25 to p each man's silver back in his sack H8740
Ge 42:37 "You may p both of my sons to death if I H4637
Ge 43:11 P some of the best products of the land in H4374
Ge 43:12 the silver that was p back into the mouths H8740
Ge 43:18 of the silver that was p back into our sacks H8740
Ge 43:22 We don't know who p our silver in our H8492
Ge 44: 1 p each man's silver in the mouth of H8492
Ge 44: 2 Then p my cup, the silver one, in the H8492
Ge 47: 6 p them in charge of my own livestock." H8492
Ge 47:29 p your hand under my thigh and promise H8492
Ge 48:14 his right hand and p it on Ephraim's head H8883
Ge 48:14 he p his left hand on Manasseh's head NDT
Ge 48:18 firstborn; p your right hand on his head." H8492
Ge 48:20 So he p Ephraim ahead of Manasseh H8492
Ex 1:11 So they p slave masters over them to H8492
Ex 2: 3 the child in it and p it among the reeds H8492
Ex 3:22 which you will p on your sons and H8492
Ex 4: 6 LORD said, "P your hand inside your cloak." H995
Ex 4: 6 So Moses p his hand into his cloak, and H995
Ex 4: 7 "Now p it back into your cloak," he said H8740
Ex 4: 7 So Moses p his hand back into his cloak H8740
Ex 4:15 speak to him and p words in his mouth; H8492
Ex 4:20 p them on a donkey and started back to H8206
Ex 5:21 his officials and have p a sword in their H5989
Ex 12: 7 of the blood and p it on the sides and H5989
Ex 12:22 in the basin and p some of the blood on H5595
Ex 14:31 the LORD and p their trust in him and in H586
Ex 15:25 them and p them to the test. H5814
Ex 16:33 "Take a jar and p an omer of manna in it. H5989
Ex 16:34 Aaron p the manna with the tablets of the H5663
Ex 17: 2 Why do you p the LORD to the test?" H5814
Ex 17:12 took a stone and p it under him and he H8492
Ex 19: 9 you and will always p their trust in you." H586
Ex 19:12 P limits for the people around the H1487
Ex 19:12 the mountain is to be p to death. H4637+4637
Ex 19:23 'P limits around the mountain and set it H1487
Ex 21:12 a fatal blow is to be p to death. H4637+4637
Ex 21:14 to be taken from my altar and p to death. H4637
Ex 21:15 mother is to be p to death. H4637+4637
Ex 21:16 someone is to be p to death, H4637+4637
Ex 21:17 mother is to be p to death. H4637+4637
Ex 21:29 its owner also is to be p to death. H4637
Ex 22:19 with an animal is to be p to death. H4637+4637
Ex 23: 7 do not p an innocent or honest person to death H2222
Ex 24: 6 took half of the blood and p it in bowls, H8492
Ex 25:16 Then p in the ark the tablets of the H5989
Ex 25:21 on top of the ark and p in the ark the H5989
Ex 25:25 wide and p a gold molding on H6913
Ex 25:30 P the bread of the Presence on this table H5989
Ex 26:11 bronze clasps and p them in the loops to H995
Ex 26:34 P the atonement cover on the ark of the H5989
Ex 26:35 of the tabernacle and p the lampstand H5989
Ex 27: 5 P it under the ledge of the altar so that it H5989
Ex 28:30 Also p the Urim and the Thummim in the H5989
Ex 28:41 After you p these clothes on your brother H4252
Ex 29: 3 P them in a basket and present them H5989
Ex 29: 6 P the turban on his head and attach the H8492
Ex 29:12 the bull's blood and p it on the horns of H5989
Ex 29:20 some of its blood and p it on the lobes of H5989
Ex 29:24 P all these in the hands of Aaron and his H8492
Ex 30: 6 P the altar in front of the curtain that H5989
Ex 30:18 meeting and the altar, and p water in it. H5989
Ex 31:14 desecrates it is to be p to death; H4637+4637
Ex 31:15 Sabbath day is to be p to death. H4637+4637
Ex 33: 4 mourn and no one p on any ornaments. H8883
Ex 33:22 I will p you in a cleft in the rock and cover H8492
Ex 34:33 to them, he p a veil over his face. H5989
Ex 34:35 Moses would p the veil back over his H8740
Ex 35: 2 does any work on it is to be p to death. H4637
Ex 37:12 wide and p a gold molding on H6913
Ex 37:14 The rings were p close to the rim to hold the NDT
Ex 40: 5 the covenant law and p the curtain at the H8492
Ex 40: 7 of meeting and the altar and p water in it. H5989
Ex 40: 8 around it and p the curtain at the H5989
Ex 40:18 he p the bases in place, erected H5989
Ex 40:19 the tabernacle and p the covering over H8492
Ex 40:20 to the ark and p the atonement cover H5989
Ex 40:28 Then he p up the curtain at the entrance H8492
Ex 40:30 the altar and p water in it for washing H5989
Ex 40:33 altar and p up the curtain at the H5989
Lev 1: 7 Aaron the priest are to p fire on the altar H5989
Lev 2: 1 are to pour olive oil on it, p incense on it H5989
Lev 2:15 P oil and incense on it; it is a grain H5989
Lev 4: 7 The priest shall then p some of the blood H5989
Lev 4:18 He is to p some of the blood on the horns H5989
Lev 4:25 with his finger and p it on the horns of the H5989
Lev 4:30 with his finger and p it on the horns of the H5989
Lev 4:34 with his finger and p it on the horns of the H5989
Lev 5:11 They must not p olive oil or incense on it H8492
Lev 6:10 The priest shall then p on his linen clothes H4252
Lev 6:11 to take off these clothes and p on others, H4252
Lev 8: 7 He p the tunic on Aaron, tied the sash H5989
Lev 8: 7 with the robe and p the ephod on him. H5989
Lev 8: 8 on him and p the Urim and Thummim H5989
Lev 8:13 sons forward, p tunics on them, tied H4252
Lev 8:15 with his finger he p it on all the horns H5989
Lev 8:23 some of its blood and p it on the lobe of H5989
Lev 8:24 sons forward and p some of the blood on H5989
Lev 8:26 and he p these on the fat portions and on H8492
Lev 8:27 He p all these in the hands of Aaron and H5989
Lev 9: 9 into the blood and p it on the horns of the H5989
Lev 10: 1 censers, p fire in them and added incense H5989
Lev 11:32 P it in water; it will be unclean till evening H995
Lev 11:38 But if water has been p on the seed and a H5989
Lev 14:14 guilt offering and p it on the lobe of the H5989
Lev 14:17 The priest is to p some of the oil H5989
Lev 14:18 palm the priest shall p on the head of the H5989
Lev 14:25 of its blood and p it on the lobe of the H5989
Lev 14:28 oil in his palm he is to p on the same H5989
Lev 14:28 on the same places he p the blood of the NDT
Lev 14:29 palm the priest shall p on the head of the H5989
Lev 14:34 and I p a spreading mold in a house in H5989
Lev 16: 4 He is to p on the sacred linen tunic, with H4252
Lev 16: 4 around him and p on the linen turban. H7571
Lev 16:13 He is to p the incense on the fire before H5989
Lev 16:18 the goat's blood and p it on all the horns H5989
Lev 16:21 and p them on the goat's head. H5989
Lev 16:23 linen garments he p on before he entered H4252
Lev 16:24 sanctuary area and p on his regular H4252
Lev 16:32 He is to p on the sacred linen garments H4252
Lev 19:14 curse the deaf or p a stumbling block in H5989
Lev 19:20 Yet they are not to be p to death, because H4637
Lev 19:28 bodies for the dead or p tattoo marks on H5989
Lev 20: 2 to Molek is to be p to death. H4637+4637
Lev 20: 4 Molek and if they fail to p him to death, H4637
Lev 20: 9 mother is to be p to death. H4637+4637
Lev 20:10 the adulteress are to be p to death. H4637+4637
Lev 20:11 the woman are to be p to death; H4637+4637
Lev 20:12 both of them are to be p to death. H4637+4637
Lev 20:13 They are to be p to death; their H4637+4637
Lev 20:15 animal, he is to be p to death, and H4637+4637
Lev 20:16 They are to be p to death; their H4637+4637
Lev 20:27 among you must be p to death. H4637+4637
Lev 24: 7 By each stack p some pure incense as a H5989
Lev 24:12 They p him in custody until the will of the H5663
Lev 24:16 of the LORD is to be p to death. H4637+4637
Lev 24:16 the Name they are to be p to death. H4637
Lev 24:17 a human being are to be p to death. H4637+4637
Lev 24:21 kills a human being is to be p to death. H4637
Lev 26:11 I will p my dwelling place among you, and H5989
Lev 26:36 of a windblown leaf will p them to flight. H8103
Lev 27:29 they are to be p to death. H4637+4637
Nu 1:51 who approaches it is to be p to death. H4637
Nu 3:10 the sanctuary is to be p to death. H4637
Nu 3:38 the sanctuary was to be p to death. H4637
Nu 4: 5 curtain and p it over the ark of the H4059
Nu 4: 6 blue over that and p the poles in place. H8492
Nu 4: 7 spread a blue cloth and p on it the plates, H5989
Nu 4: 8 durable leather and p the poles in place. H8492
Nu 4:10 durable leather and p it on a carrying H5989
Nu 4:11 durable leather and p the poles in place. H8492
Nu 4:12 durable leather and p them on a carrying H5989
Nu 4:14 durable leather and p the poles in place. H8492
Nu 5:15 not pour olive oil on it or p incense on it, H5989
Nu 5:17 in a clay jar and p some dust from the H5989
Nu 5:19 priest shall p the woman under oath and H8678
Nu 5:21 is to p the woman under this curse H460+8678+8652
Nu 6:18 to take the hair and p it in the fire that is H5989
Nu 6:27 "So they will p my name on the Israelites H8492
Nu 11:11 displease you that you p the burden of all H8492
Nu 11:17 the Spirit that is on you and p it on them. H8492
Nu 11:25 that was on him and p it on the seventy H5989
Nu 11:29 that the LORD would p his Spirit on H5989
Nu 14:15 If you p all these people to death, leaving H4637
Nu 16: 7 tomorrow p burning coals and incense H5989
Nu 16:17 is to take his censer and p incense in it— H5989
Nu 16:18 p burning coals and incense in it H5989
Nu 16:21 assembly so I can p an end to them at H3983
Nu 16:45 assembly so I can p an end to them at H3983
Nu 16:46 "Take your censer and p incense in it H5989
Nu 17:10 "P back Aaron's staff in front of the ark of H8740
Nu 17:10 This will p an end to their grumbling H3983
Nu 18: 7 near the sanctuary is to be p to death." H4637
Nu 18: 8 "I myself have p you in charge of the H5989
Nu 19: 9 of the heifer and p them in a H5663
Nu 19:17 p some ashes from the burned H4374
Nu 20:26 garments and p them on his son Eleazar, H4252
Nu 20:28 garments and p them on his son Eleazar. H4252
Nu 21: 8 "Make a snake and p it up on a pole H8492
Nu 21: 9 a bronze snake and p it up on a pole. H8492
Nu 21:24 p him to the sword and took over his land H5782
Nu 22: 6 Now come and p a curse on these people H826
Nu 22:11 Now come and p a curse on them for me H7686
Nu 22:12 You must not p a curse on those people H826
Nu 22:17 Come and p a curse on these people for H7686
Nu 23: 5 The LORD p a word in Balaam's mouth H8492
Nu 23:16 with Balaam and p a word in his mouth H8492
Nu 25: 5 "Each of you must p to death those of H2222
Nu 25:11 I did not p an end to them in my zeal. H3983
Nu 25:15 woman who was p to death was Kozbi H5782
Nu 31:23 withstand fire must be p through the fire, H6296
Nu 31:23 withstand fire must be p through that H6296
Nu 35:16 the murderer is to be p to death. H4637+4637
Nu 35:17 the murderer is to be p to death. H4637+4637
Nu 35:18 the murderer is to be p to death. H4637+4637
Nu 35:19 of blood shall p the murderer to death; H4637
Nu 35:19 the avenger shall p the murderer to death. H4637
Nu 35:21 that person is to be p to death; that H4637+4637
Nu 35:21 blood shall p the murderer to death when H4637
Nu 35:30 a person is to be p to death as a murderer H8357
Nu 35:30 But no one is to be p to death on the H4637
Nu 35:31 They are to be p to death. H4637+4637
Dt 1:41 So every one of you p on his weapons H2520
Dt 2: 5 not even enough to p your foot on. H4534
Dt 2:25 day I will begin to p the terror and fear H5989
Dt 6:16 Do not p the LORD your God to the test as H5814
Dt 9:28 them out to p them to death in the H4637
Dt 10: 2 Then you are to p them in the ark. H8492
Dt 10: 5 the mountain and p the tablets in the H8492
Dt 11:25 will p the terror and fear of you on the H5989
Dt 12: 5 all your tribes to p his Name there for his H8492
Dt 12: 7 in everything you have p your hand to, H5448
Dt 12:18 God in everything you p your hand to. H5448
Dt 12:21 your God chooses to p his Name is too far H8492
Dt 13: 5 dreamer must be p to death for inciting H4637
Dt 13: 9 You must certainly p them to death H2222+2222
Dt 13:15 you must certainly p to the sword all H5782+5782
Dt 14:24 LORD will choose to p his Name is so far H8492
Dt 15:10 in everything you p your hand to. H5448
Dt 15:19 Do not p the firstborn of your cows to work, H6268
Dt 16: 9 the time you begin to p the sickle to the NDT
Dt 17: 6 witnesses a person is to be p to death, H4637
Dt 17: 6 no one is to be p to death on the H4637
Dt 17:12 to the LORD your God is to be p to death. H4637
Dt 18:18 and I will p my words in his mouth. H5989
Dt 18:20 name of other gods, is to be p to death." H4637
Dt 20:13 p to the sword all the men in it. H5782
Dt 21:13 and p aside the clothes she was wearing H6073
Dt 21:22 offense is p to death and their body H4637
Dt 23:20 everything you p your hand to in the land H5448
Dt 23:24 you want, but do not p any in your basket. H5989
Dt 23:25 but you must not p a sickle to their H5677
Dt 24:16 Parents are not to be p to death for their H4637
Dt 24:16 children p to death for their parents H4637
Dt 26: 2 God is giving you and p them in a basket. H8492
Dt 28: 8 on everything you p your hand to. H5448
Dt 28:20 rebuke in everything you p your hand to, H5448
Dt 28:48 He will p an iron yoke on your neck until H5989
Dt 30: 7 The LORD your God will p all these curses H5989
Dt 32:30 two p ten thousand to flight, unless H5674
Dt 32:39 I p to death and I bring to life, I have H4637
Jos 1:18 may command them, will be p to death. H4637
Jos 4: 3 with you and p them down at the place H5663
Jos 4: 8 to their camp, where they p them down. H5663
Jos 6:23 her entire family and p them in a place H5663
Jos 6:24 they p the silver and gold and the articles of bronze and iron into H5989
Jos 7:11 they have p them with their own H8492
Jos 8:24 one of them had been p to the sword, H5877
Jos 9: 5 They p worn and patched sandals on their NDT
Jos 10:24 "Come here and p your feet on the necks H8492
Jos 10:26 p the kings to death and H5782+2256+4637
Jos 10:28 He p the city and its king to the sword H5782
Jos 10:30 everyone in it Joshua p to the sword. H5782
Jos 10:32 city and everyone in it he p to the sword, H5782
Jos 10:35 it that same day and p it to the sword H5782
Jos 10:37 They took the city and p it to the sword H5782
Jos 10:39 its villages, and p them to the sword. H5782
Jos 11:10 captured Hazor and p its king to the sword H5782
Jos 11:11 Everyone in it they p to the sword. H5782
Jos 11:12 their kings and p them to the sword. H5782
Jos 11:14 all the people they p to the sword H5782
Jos 11:17 kings and p them to death. H5782+2256+4637
Jos 13:22 the Israelites had p to the sword Balaam H2222
Jos 19:47 p it to the sword and occupied it. H5782
Jos 24: 7 and he p darkness between you and the H8492
Jos 24: 9 Balaam son of Beor to p a curse on you. H7837
Jdg 1: 8 They p the city to the sword and set it on H5782
Jdg 1:25 and they p the city to the sword but H5782
Jdg 6:31 him shall be p to death by morning! H4637
Jdg 9:26 its citizens p their confidence in him. H1053
Jdg 16:26 "P me where I can feel the pillars that H5663
Jdg 17: 4 And it was p in Micah's house H2118
Jdg 18:10 land that God has p into your hands, H5989
Jdg 19:28 Then the man p her on his donkey and H4374
Jdg 20:13 so that we may p them to death and H4637
Jdg 20:37 spread out and p the whole city to the H5782
Jdg 20:48 to Benjamin and p all the towns to the H5782
Jdg 21: 5 at Mizpah was to be p to death. H4637+4637
Jdg 21:10 Jabesh Gilead and p to the sword those H5782
Ru 2:13 "You have p me at ease by speaking H5714
Ru 3: 3 p on perfume, and get dressed in H6057
1Sa 1:14 going to stay drunk? P away your wine." H6073
1Sa 2:25 it was the LORD's will to p them to death. H4637
1Sa 5: 3 took Dagon and p him back in his place. H8740
1Sa 6: 8 the ark of the LORD and p it on the cart, H5989
1Sa 6: 8 in a chest beside it p the gold objects you H8492
1Sa 7: 4 So the Israelites p away their Baals and H6073
1Sa 11:12 to us so that we may p them to death." H4637
1Sa 11:13 "No one will be p to death today, for H4637
1Sa 14:26 yet no one p his hand to his mouth H5952
1Sa 14:45 Jonathan, and he was not p to death. H4637
1Sa 15: 3 spare them; p to death men and women H4637
1Sa 15:33 And Samuel p Agag to death before the H9119
1Sa 17:38 He p a coat of armor on him and a bronze H4252

1Sa 17:40 **p** them in the pouch of his shepherd's H8492
1Sa 17:54 *he* **p** the Philistine's weapons in his own H8492
1Sa 19: 6 LORD lives, David *will* not **be p to death**." H4637
1Sa 20:32 "Why *should he* **be p to death**? What has H4637
1Sa 22:19 *He* also **p** to the sword Nob, the town of H5782
1Sa 26:12 the LORD *had* **p** them *into* a deep sleep. H5877
1Sa 31:10 *They* **p** his armor *in* the temple of the H8492
2Sa 3:31 your clothes and **p on** sackcloth and walk H2520
2Sa 4:10 I seized him and **p** him **to death** in Ziklag. H2222
2Sa 8: 2 two lengths of them *were* **p to death**, H4637
2Sa 8: 6 He **p** garrisons in the Aramean kingdom of H8492
2Sa 8:14 *He* **p** garrisons throughout Edom, and all H8492
2Sa 10:10 *He* **p** the rest of the men under the H5989
2Sa 11:15 "**P** Uriah out in front where the fighting is H2035
2Sa 11:16 *he* **p** Uriah at a place where he knew the H5989
2Sa 12:20 **p on lotions** and changed his clothes H6057
2Sa 13:18 servant **p** her **out** and bolted H3655+2021+2575
2Sa 13:19 Tamar **p** ashes on her head and tore the H4374
2Sa 13:19 *She* **p** her hands on her head and went H8492
2Sa 14: 3 And Joab **p** the words in her mouth H8492
2Sa 14: 7 so that *we may* **p** him **to death** for the life H4637
2Sa 14: 7 *They would* **p out** the only burning coal I H3882
2Sa 14:19 to do this and who **p** all these words into H8492
2Sa 14:32 guilty of anything, *let him* **p** me **to death**." H4637
2Sa 15:14 bring ruin on us and **p** the city to the H5782
2Sa 17:23 *He* **p** his house **in order** and then hanged H7422
2Sa 18:13 And if *I had* **p** my life **in jeopardy** H6913+9214
2Sa 19:19 *May* the king **p** it out of his mind H8492
2Sa 19:21 "Shouldn't Shimei **be p to death** for this? H4637
2Sa 19:22 *Should* anyone **be p to death** in Israel H4637
2Sa 20: 3 the palace and **p** them *in* a house under H5989
2Sa 21: 1 is because *he* **p** the Gibeonites **to death**." H4637
2Sa 21: 4 the right to **p** anyone in Israel *to* **death**." H4637
2Sa 21: 9 they **were p to death** during the first days H4637
2Sa 23:23 And David **p** him in charge of his H8492
1Ki 1: 1 warm even when *they* **p** covers **over** him. H4059
1Ki 1: 5 Haggith, **p himself forward** and said, "I H5951
1Ki 1:44 and *they have* **p** him on the king's mule H8206
1Ki 1:51 that *he will* not **p** his servant **to death** with H4637
1Ki 2: 8 '*I will* not **p** you **to death** by the sword H4637
1Ki 2:24 Adonijah *shall* **be p to death** today!" H4637
1Ki 2:26 but *I will* not **p** you **to death** now H4637
1Ki 2:35 The king **p** Benaiah son of Jehoiada over H5989
1Ki 3:20 *She* **p** him by her breast and put her dead H8886
1Ki 3:20 by her breast and **p** her dead son by my H8886
1Ki 5: 3 God until the LORD **p** his enemies under H5989
1Ki 5: 5 'Your son whom *I will* **p** on the throne in H5989
1Ki 8: 6 **p** it beneath the wings of the cherubim. NDT
1Ki 10:17 The king **p** them in the Palace of the H5989
1Ki 10:24 hear the wisdom God *had* **p** in his heart. H5989
1Ki 11:28 *he* **p** him **in charge** of the whole labor H7212
1Ki 11:36 the city where I chose to **p** my Name. H8492
1Ki 12: 4 "Your father **p** *a* **heavy** yoke on us, but H7996
1Ki 12: 4 labor and the heavy yoke he **p** on us, H5989
1Ki 12: 9 'Lighten the yoke your father **p** on us'?" H5989
1Ki 12:10 'Your father **p** *a* **heavy** yoke on us, but H3877
1Ki 14:21 tribes of Israel in which to **p** his Name. H8492
1Ki 18: 9 servant over to Ahab to *be* **p to death**? H4637
1Ki 18:23 it into pieces and **p** it on the wood but not H8492
1Ki 18:23 the other bull and **p** it on the wood but H5989
1Ki 18:42 to the ground and **p** his face between his H8492
1Ki 19:10 and **p** your prophets **to death** with the H2222
1Ki 19:14 and **p** your prophets **to death** with the H2222
1Ki 19:17 Jehu *will* **p to death** any who escape the H4637
1Ki 19:17 Elisha *will* **p to death** any who H4637
1Ki 21:27 his clothes, **p on** sackcloth and fasted. H8492
1Ki 22:23 "So now the LORD *has* **p** a deceiving spirit H5989
1Ki 22:27 **P** this fellow *in* prison and give him H8492
2Ki 2:20 a new bowl," he said, "and **p** salt in it." H8492
2Ki 4: 4 and as each is filled, **p it to one side**." H5825
2Ki 4:10 room on the roof and **p** in it a bed and a H8492
2Ki 4:38 "**P on** the large pot and cook some stew H9189
2Ki 4:41 *He* **p** it into the pot and said, "Serve it to H8959
2Ki 5:24 servants and **p** them **away** in the house. H7212
2Ki 7:17 *had* **p** the officer on whose arm he leaned
in charge H7212
2Ki 9:30 *she* **p on eye makeup** H6167+928+2021+7037
2Ki 10: 7 *They* **p** their heads in baskets and sent H8492
2Ki 10: 8 "**P** them *in* two piles at the entrance of H8492
2Ki 11: 2 She **p** him and his nurse in a bedroom to NDT
2Ki 11: 4 with them and **p** them **under oath** at the H8678
2Ki 11: 8 approaches your ranks *is to* **be p to death**. H4637
2Ki 11:12 the king's son and **p** the crown on him; H5989
2Ki 11:15 the ranks and **p** to the sword anyone H4637S
2Ki 11:15 "*She must* not **be p to death** in the H4637
2Ki 11:16 grounds, and there *she* **was p to death**. H4637
2Ki 12: 9 guarded the entrance **p** into the chest all H5989
2Ki 12:10 the temple of the LORD and **p** it **into bags**. H7443
2Ki 13:16 Elisha **p** his hands on the king's hands. H8492
2Ki 14: 6 *he did* not **p** the children of the assassins **to death**
H4637
2Ki 14: 6 "Parents *are* not *to* **be p to death** for their H4637
2Ki 14: 6 children **p to death** for their parents H4637
2Ki 16: 9 its inhabitants to Kir and **p** Rezin **to death**. H4637
2Ki 16:14 **p** it on the north side of the new altar. H5989
2Ki 17: 4 seized him and **p** him *in* prison. H673
2Ki 18:23 horses—if you can **p** riders on them! H5989
2Ki 19: 1 his clothes and **p on** sackcloth and went H4059
2Ki 19:26 of power, are dismayed and **p to shame**. H1017
2Ki 19:28 *I will* **p** my hook in your nose and my bit H8492
2Ki 19:35 went out and **p to death** a hundred and H5782
2Ki 20: 1 **P** your house **in order**, because you are H7422
2Ki 21: 4 had said, "In Jerusalem *I will* **p** my Name." H8492
2Ki 21: 7 pole he had made and **p** it in the temple, H8492
2Ki 21: 7 tribes of Israel, *I will* **p** my Name forever. H8492
2Ki 23:33 Pharaoh Necho **p** him **in chains** at Riblah in H673
2Ki 25: 7 Then *they* **p out** his eyes, bound him with H6422
2Ki 25:29 So Jehoiachin **p aside** his prison clothes H9101
1Ch 1: 8 Cush, Egypt, **P** and Canaan. H7033
1Ch 2: 3 LORD's sight; so the LORD **p** him **to death**. H4637
1Ch 6:31 David **p in charge** *of* the H6641+6584+3338
1Ch 10:10 *They* **p** his armor in the temple of their H8492
1Ch 10:14 So the LORD **p** him **to death** and turned the H4637
1Ch 11:25 And David **p** him in charge of his H8492
1Ch 12:15 and *they* **p to flight** everyone living in the H1368
1Ch 13:10 down because *he had* **p** his hand on the H8938
1Ch 18: 6 He **p** garrisons in the Aramean kingdom of H8492
1Ch 18:13 *He* **p** garrisons in Edom, and all the H8492
1Ch 19:11 *He* **p** the rest of the men under the H5989
1Ch 21:27 and *he* **p** his sword **back** into its sheath. H8740
1Ch 26:32 King David **p** them **in charge** of the H7212
1Ch 28:12 all that the Spirit *had* **p** in his mind for the H2118
2Ch 3:16 chains and **p** them on top of the H5989
2Ch 5: 7 **p** it beneath the wings of the cherubim. NDT
2Ch 6:20 you said you *would* **p** your Name there. H8492
2Ch 9:16 The king **p** them in the Palace of the H5989
2Ch 9:23 hear the wisdom God *had* **p** in his heart. H5989
2Ch 10: 4 "Your father **p** *a* **heavy** yoke on us, but H7996
2Ch 10: 4 labor and the heavy yoke he **p** on us, H5989
2Ch 10: 9 'Lighten the yoke your father **p** on us'?" H5989
2Ch 10:10 'Your father **p** *a* **heavy** yoke on us, but H3877
2Ch 11:11 defenses and **p** commanders in them H5989
2Ch 11:12 He **p** shields and spears in all the cities, and NDT
2Ch 12:13 tribes of Israel in which to **p** his Name. H8492
2Ch 14: 7 to Judah, "and **p** walls **around** them, with H6015
2Ch 15:13 of Israel, *were to* **be p to death**, whether H4637
2Ch 16:10 was so enraged that *he* **p** him *in* prison. H5989
2Ch 17: 2 cities of Judah and **p** garrisons in Judah H5989
2Ch 18:22 "So now the LORD *has* **p** a deceiving spirit H5989
2Ch 18:26 **P** this fellow *in* prison and give him H8492
2Ch 21: 4 *he* **p** all his brothers to the sword along H2222
2Ch 22: 9 He was brought to Jehu and **p to death** H4637
2Ch 22:11 to be murdered and **p** him and his nurse H5989
2Ch 23: 7 who enters the temple *is to* **be p to death**. H4637
2Ch 23:11 the king's son and **p** the crown on him; H5989
2Ch 23:14 the ranks and **p** to the sword anyone H4637S
2Ch 23:14 "*Do* not **p** her **to death** *at* the temple of H4637
2Ch 23:15 grounds, and there *they* **p** her **to death**. H4637
2Ch 25: 4 Yet *he did* not **p** their children **to death** H4637
2Ch 25: 4 "Parents *shall* not *be p to* **death** for their AIT
2Ch 25: 4 children *be p to* **death** for their parents AIT
2Ch 28:15 those who were weak *they* **p on** donkeys. H5633
2Ch 29: 7 doors of the portico and **p out** the lamps. H3882
2Ch 33: 7 he had made and **p** it in God's temple, H8492
2Ch 33: 7 tribes of Israel, *I will* **p** my Name forever. H8492
2Ch 33:11 Manasseh prisoner, **p** a hook in his nose NDT
2Ch 35: 3 "**P** the sacred ark in the temple that H5989
2Ch 35:24 **p** him in his other chariot and brought H8206
2Ch 36: 7 of the LORD and **p** them in his temple H5989
2Ch 36:22 his realm and also to **p** it in writing: NDT
Ezr 1: 1 his realm and also to **p** it in writing: NDT
Ezr 7:27 who *has* **p** it into the king's heart to bring H5989
Ezr 10: 5 **p** the leading priests and Levites and
all Israel **under oath** H8678
Ezr 10:19 hands in pledge to **p away** their wives, H3655
Ne 2:12 what my God *had* **p** in my heart to do H5989
Ne 3: 3 **p** its doors and bolts and bars **in place**. H6641
Ne 3: 5 their nobles *would* not **p** their shoulders H995
Ne 3: 6 **p** its doors with their bolts and bars **in place** H6641
Ne 3:13 **p** its doors with their bolts and bars **in place** H6641
Ne 3:14 **p** its doors with their bolts and bars **in place** H6641
Ne 4:11 will kill them and **p an end** *to* the work." H8697
Ne 7: 2 *I* **p in charge** of Jerusalem my brother H7422
Ne 7: 5 So my God **p** it into my heart to assemble H5989
Ne 9:31 mercy *you did* not **p** an end to them or H6913
Ne 13: 4 the priest *had* **been p** in charge of the H5989
Ne 13: 9 then *I* **p back** *into* them the H8740
Ne 13:13 *I* **p** Shelemiah ... **in charge of the storerooms**
H732+6584+238
Est 2: 8 citadel of Susa and **p** under the care of NDT
Est 4: 1 tore his clothes, **p on** sackcloth and ashes H4252
Est 4: 4 sent clothes for him to **p on** instead of his H4252
Est 4:11 that they *be* **p to death** unless the king H4637
Est 5: 1 day Esther **p on** *her* royal **robes** and stood H4252
Est 8: 3 begged him to **p an end** *to* the evil plan H6296
Est 9:15 and *they* **p to death** in Susa three H2222
Job 1:10 "*Have* you not **p a hedge** around him and H8455
Job 1:15 *They* **p** the servants to the sword, and I H5782
Job 1:17 *They* **p** the servants to the sword, and I H5782
Job 7:12 of the deep, that *you* **p** me under guard? H8492
Job 11:14 if *you* **p away** the sin that is in your hand H8178
Job 12:18 takes off the **shackles** *p on* by kings and ties AIT
Job 13:14 *do I* **p** myself **in jeopardy** H5951+1414+928+9094
Job 14: 6 till *he has* **p** in his time like a hired H8354
Job 14: 9 it will bud and **p forth** shoots like a plant. H6913
Job 17: 3 *will* **p up security** *for* me? H9546+4200+3338
Job 28: 3 *Mortals* **p** an end to the darkness; they H8492
Job 29:14 *I* **p on** righteousness **as** *my* **clothing** H4252
Job 30: 1 have disdained to **p** with my sheep dogs. H8883
Job 31:24 "If *I have* **p** my trust *in* gold or said to pure H8492
Job 31:35 let my accuser **p** *his* indictment **in writing**. H4180
Job 31:36 my shoulder, *I would* **p** it **on** like a crown. H6698
Job 34:13 Who **p** him **in charge** *of* the whole world? H8492
Job 40: 4 *I* **p** my hand over my mouth. H8492
Job 41: 2 *Can you* **p** a cord through its nose or H8492
Job 41: 5 like a bird or **p** it **on a leash** for the young H8003
Ps 6:10 turn back and suddenly *be* **p to shame**. H1017
Ps 8: 6 *you* **p** everything under their feet: H8883
Ps 22: 4 In you our ancestors **p** *their* **trust**; they H1053
Ps 22: 5 you they trusted and *were* not **p to shame**. H1017
Ps 25: 1 In you, LORD my God, *I* **p** my **trust**. H5951+5883
Ps 25: 2 *do* not *let me be* **p to shame**, nor H1017
Ps 25: 3 hopes in you *will* ever *be* **p to shame**, H1017
Ps 25:20 *do* not *let me be* **p to shame**, for I H1017
Ps 31: 1 *let me* never *be* **p to shame** H1017
Ps 31:17 *Let me* not *be* **p to shame**, LORD, for I have H1017
Ps 31:17 but *let* the wicked *be* **p to shame** and be H1017
Ps 33:22 LORD, even as *we* **p** *our* **hope** in you. H3498
Ps 35: 4 my life be disgraced and **p to shame**; H4007
Ps 35:13 I **p on** sackcloth and humbled myself with H4230
Ps 35:26 *May* all who gloat over my distress *be* **p to shame**
H1017
Ps 39: 1 *I will* **p** a muzzle on my mouth while in H9068
Ps 40: 3 *He* **p** a new song in my mouth, a hymn of H5989
Ps 40: 4 fear the LORD and **p** *their* **trust** in him. H1053
Ps 40:14 take my life *be* **p to shame** and confusion; H1017
Ps 42: 5 **P** *your* **hope** in God, for I will yet praise H3498
Ps 42:11 **P** *your* **hope** in God, for I will yet praise H3498
Ps 43: 5 **P** *your* **hope** in God, for I will yet praise H3498
Ps 44: 6 *I* **p** no **trust** in my bow, my sword does not H1053
Ps 44: 7 enemies, *you* **p** our adversaries **to shame**. H1017
Ps 53: 5 *you* **p** them **to shame**, for God H1017
Ps 56: 3 When I am afraid, *I* **p** *my* **trust** in you. H1053
Ps 62:10 in extortion or **p vain hope** in stolen H2038
Ps 69: 6 *may* those who seek you not **be p to shame** H4007
Ps 69:11 when *I* **p on** sackcloth, people H5989+4230
Ps 69:21 *They* **p** gall in my food and gave me H5989
Ps 70: 2 *May* those who want to take my life *be* **p to shame**
H1017
Ps 71: 1 taken refuge; *let me* never **be p to shame**. H1017
Ps 71:24 to harm me *have been* **p to shame** and H1017
Ps 78: 7 Then *they would* **p** their trust in God and H8492
Ps 78:18 *They* willfully **p** God **to the test** by H5814
Ps 78:31 *he* **p to death** the sturdiest among them H2222
Ps 78:41 Again and again *they* **p** God **to the test** H5814
Ps 78:56 But *they* **p** God **to the test** and rebelled H5814
Ps 78:64 their priests *were* **p** to the sword, and their H5877
Ps 78:66 *he* **p** them to everlasting shame. H5989
Ps 85: 4 and **p away** your displeasure toward us. H7296
Ps 86: 4 Lord, for *I* **p** my **trust** in you. H5951+5883
Ps 86:17 enemies may see it and *be* **p to shame**, H1017
Ps 88: 6 *You have* **p** me in the lowest pit, in the H8883
Ps 89:44 *You have* **p an end** to his splendor and H8697
Ps 97: 7 All who worship images *are* **p to shame** H1017
Ps 101: 5 in secret, *I will* **p to silence**; whoever has H7551
Ps 101: 8 Every morning *I will* **p to silence** all the H7551
Ps 105:18 feet with shackles, his neck *was* **p in** irons, H995
Ps 106:14 in the wilderness *they* **p** God **to the test**. H5814
Ps 109:28 *may* those who attack me *be* **p to shame** H1017
Ps 119: 6 Then *I would* not *be* **p to shame** when I H1017
Ps 119:31 *do* not **let** me **be p to shame**. H1017
Ps 119:43 for *I have* **p** *my* **hope** in your laws. H3498
Ps 119:46 before kings and *will* not *be* **p to shame**, H1017
Ps 119:74 for *I have* **p** *my* **hope** in your word. H3498
Ps 119:78 *May* the arrogant *be* **p to shame** for H1017
Ps 119:80 decrees, that *I may* not *be* **p to shame**. H1017
Ps 119:81 but *I have* **p** *my* **hope** in your word. H3498
Ps 119:114 shield; *I have* **p** *my* **hope** in your word. H3498
Ps 119:147 help; *I have* **p** *my* **hope** in your word. H3498
Ps 127: 5 *They will* not *be* **p to shame** when they H1017
Ps 130: 5 being waits, and in his word *I* **p** *my* **hope**. H3498
Ps 130: 7 **p** *your* **hope** in the LORD, for with H3498
Ps 131: 3 **p** *your* **hope** in the LORD both now and H3498
Ps 143: 8 unfailing love, for *I have* **p** *my* **trust** in you. H1053
Ps 146: 3 *Do* not **p** *your* **trust** in princes, in human H1053
Ps 147:11 who **p** *their* **hope** in his unfailing love. H3498
Pr 6: 1 if *you have* **p up security** for your neighbor, H6842
Pr 21:29 The wicked **p up a bold front** H6451+928+7156
Pr 23: 2 **p** a knife to your throat if you are H8492
Pr 24:27 **P** your outdoor work **in order** and get your H3922
Pr 29:24 *they are* **p under oath** and dare not H460+9048
Ecc 10: 6 Fools **are p** in many high positions, while H5989
SS 5: 3 taken off my robe—*must I* **p** it **on** again? H4252
Isa 5:20 *who* **p** darkness for light and light for H8492
Isa 5:20 *who* **p** bitter for sweet and sweet for bitter. H8492
Isa 7:12 not ask; *I will* not **p** the LORD **to the test**." H5814
Isa 8:17 *I will* **p** *my* **trust** in him. H7747
Isa 10: 7 is to destroy, to **p an end** to many nations. H4162
Isa 11: 8 the young child *will* **p** its hand into the H2063
Isa 13:11 *I will* **p an end** *to* the arrogance of the H8697
Isa 16:10 for *I have* **p an end** *to* the shouting. H8697
Isa 20: 5 Egypt will be dismayed and **p to shame**. H1017
Isa 22:12 to tear out your hair and **p on** sackcloth. H2520
Isa 26:11 zeal for your people and *be* **p to shame**; H1017
Isa 30: 5 everyone *will be* **p to shame** because of a H1017
Isa 31: 8 their young men *will be* **p** to forced labor. H2118
Isa 36: 8 horses—if you can **p** riders on them! H5989
Isa 37: 1 his clothes and **p on** sackcloth and went H4059
Isa 37:27 of power, are dismayed and **p to shame**. H1017
Isa 37:29 *I will* **p** my hook in your nose and my bit H8492
Isa 37:36 went out and **p to death** a hundred and H5782
Isa 38: 1 **P** your house **in order**, because you are H7422
Isa 38:17 *you have* **p** all my sins behind your back. H8959
Isa 41:19 *I will* **p** in the desert the cedar and the H5989
Isa 42: 1 whom I delight; *I will* **p** my Spirit on him H5989
Isa 42: 4 his teaching the islands *will* **p** *their* **hope**." H3498

Isa 44:11 People who do that will be p to shame H1017
Isa 45:16 of idols will be p to shame and disgraced; H1017
Isa 45:17 you will never be p to shame or disgraced, H1017
Isa 45:24 him will come to him and be p to shame. H1017
Isa 49:18 ornaments; you will p them on, like a H8003
Isa 50: 7 and I know I will not be p to shame. H1017
Isa 51:16 I have p my words in your mouth and H8492
Isa 51:23 I will p it into the hands of your H8492
Isa 52: 1 P on your garments of splendor H4252
Isa 54: 4 not be afraid; you will not be p to shame. H1017
Isa 57: 8 your doorposts you have p your pagan H8492
Isa 59:17 He p on righteousness as his breastplate H4252
Isa 59:17 he p on the garments of H4252+9432
Isa 59:21 my words that I have p in your mouth H8492
Isa 65:13 will rejoice, but you will be p to shame. H1017
Isa 65:15 the Sovereign LORD will p you to death H4637
Isa 66: 5 Yet they will be p to shame. H1017
Jer 1: 9 "I have p my words in your mouth. H5989
Jer 4: 1 "If you p your detestable idols out of my H6073
Jer 4: 8 So p on sackcloth, lament and wail, for H2520
Jer 4:30 in scarlet and p on jewels of gold? H6335
Jer 6:21 "I will p obstacles before this people H5989
Jer 6:26 P on sackcloth, my people, and roll in H2520
Jer 8: 9 The wise will be p to shame; they will be H1017
Jer 13: 1 a linen belt and p it around your waist H8492
Jer 13: 2 LORD directed, and p it around my waist. H8492
Jer 15: 9 I will p the survivors to the sword before H5989
Jer 17:13 all who forsake you will be p to shame. H1017
Jer 17:18 Let my persecutors be p to shame, but H1017
Jer 18:21 let their men be p to death, their H2222+4638
Jer 20: 2 prophet beaten and p in the stocks at the H5989
Jer 20: 4 away to Babylon or p them to the sword. H5782
Jer 21: 7 He will p them to the sword; he will show H5782
Jer 25:31 on all mankind and p the wicked to the H5989
Jer 26:15 that if you p me to death, you will bring H4637
Jer 26:19 Did Hezekiah king of Judah or anyone
else in Judah p him to death H4637+4637
Jer 26:21 king was determined to p him to death. H4637
Jer 26:24 over to the people to be p to death. H4637
Jer 27: 2 straps and crossbars and p it on your neck. H5989
Jer 28:14 I will p an iron yoke on the necks of all H5989
Jer 29:21 and he will p them to death before your H5782
Jer 29:26 you should p any maniac who acts like a H5989
Jer 31:21 "Set up road signs; p up guideposts. H8492
Jer 31:33 "I will p my law in their minds and write it H5989
Jer 32:14 p them in a clay jar so they will last a H5989
Jer 36:20 After they p the scroll in the room of H7212
Jer 37: 4 he had not yet been p in prison. H5989
Jer 37:16 Jeremiah was p into a vaulted cell in a H995
Jer 37:18 this people, that you have p me in prison? H5989
Jer 38: 4 the king, "This man should be p to death. H4637
Jer 38: 6 took Jeremiah and p him into the cistern H8959
Jer 38: 7 heard that they had p Jeremiah into the H5989
Jer 38:12 "P these old rags and worn-out clothes H8492
Jer 39: 7 Then he p out Zedekiah's eyes and bound H6422
Jer 40: 7 land and had p him in charge of the men, H7212
Jer 40:10 olive oil, and p them in your storage jars H8492
Jer 46: 4 Polish your spears, p on your armor! H4252
Jer 46: 9 men of Cush and P who carry shields, men H7033
Jer 46:24 Daughter Egypt will be p to shame, given H1017
Jer 48: 2 let us p an end to that nation.' H4162
Jer 48: 9 P salt on Moab, for she will be laid waste H5989
Jer 48:35 In Moab I will p an end to those who H8697
Jer 49: 3 P on sackcloth and mourn; rush here and H2520
Jer 50: 2 captured; Bel will be p to shame, Marduk H1017
Jer 50: 2 Her images will be p to shame and her H1017
Jer 51: 3 string his bow, nor let him p on his armor. H6590
Jer 52:11 Then he p out Zedekiah's eyes, bound H6422
Jer 52:11 where he p him in prison till the day of H5989
Jer 52:33 So Jehoiachin p aside his prison clothes H9101
La 2:10 dust on their heads and p on sackcloth. H2520
La 3:65 P a veil over their hearts, and may your H5989
Eze 3:20 and I p a stumbling block before them H5989
Eze 4: 1 p it in front of you and draw the city of H5989
Eze 4: 2 camps against it and p battering rams H8492
Eze 4: 4 your left side and p the sin of the people H8492
Eze 4: 9 p them in a storage jar and use them to H5989
Eze 7:18 They will p on sackcloth and be clothed H2520
Eze 7:24 I will p an end to the pride of the mighty H8697
Eze 9: 4 of Jerusalem and p a mark on the H9344+9338
Eze 10: 7 up some of it and p it into the hands of H5989
Eze 11:19 undivided heart and p a new spirit in H5989
Eze 12: 6 P them on your shoulder as they are H5951
Eze 12:12 prince among them will p his things on H5951
Eze 12:23 I am going to p an end to this proverb H8697
Eze 14: 3 in their hearts and p wicked stumbling H5989
Eze 14: 4 in their hearts and p a wicked stumbling H8492
Eze 14: 7 in their hearts and p a wicked stumbling H8492
Eze 16: 9 blood from you and p ointments on you. H6057
Eze 16:10 and p sandals of fine leather on you. H5836
Eze 16:11 I p bracelets on your arms and a necklace H5989
Eze 16:12 and I p a ring on your nose, earrings on H5989
Eze 16:18 your embroidered clothes to p on them, H4059
Eze 16:41 I will p a stop to your prostitution, and you H8697
Eze 17: 5 of the land and p it in fertile soil. H5989
Eze 17: 6 branches and p out leafy boughs. H8938
Eze 17:16 land of the king who p him on the throne, H4887
Eze 18:13 things, he is to be p to death; his H4637+4637
Eze 19: 9 They p him in prison, so his roar was heard H995
Eze 20:17 destroy them or p an end to them in the H6913
Eze 22:15 and I will p an end to your uncleanness. H9462
Eze 22:20 my wrath and p you inside the city H5663
Eze 23:27 So I will p a stop to the lewdness and H8697
Eze 23:31 so I will p her cup into your hand. H5989
Eze 23:40 eye makeup and p on your jewelry. H6335+6344
Eze 23:42 and they p bracelets on the wrists of the H5989
Eze 23:48 "So I will p an end to lewdness in the H8697
Eze 24: 3 " 'P on the cooking pot; put it on and pour H9189
Eze 24: 3 cooking pot; p it on and pour water into it. H9189
Eze 24: 4 P into it the pieces of meat, all the choice H665
Eze 24: 8 take revenge I p her blood on the H5989
Eze 26:13 I will p an end to your noisy songs, and H8697
Eze 26:17 you p your terror on all who lived there. H5989
Eze 27:10 Lydia and P served as soldiers in your H7033
Eze 27:31 because of you and will p on sackcloth. H2520
Eze 29: 4 But I will p hooks in your jaws and make H5989
Eze 30:10 " 'I will p an end to the hordes of Egypt by H8697
Eze 30:13 the idols and p an end to the images in H8697
Eze 30:21 up to be healed or p in a splint so that it H8492
Eze 30:24 king of Babylon and p my sword in his H5989
Eze 30:25 when I p my sword into the hand of the H5989
Eze 33:31 but they do not p them into practice. H6913
Eze 33:32 words but do not p them into practice. H6913
Eze 36:26 you a new heart and p a new spirit in you; H5989
Eze 36:27 And I will p my Spirit in you and move you H5989
Eze 37: 6 you with skin; I will p breath in you, and H5989
Eze 37:14 I will p my Spirit in you and you will live H5989
Eze 37:26 and I will p my sanctuary among them H5989
Eze 38: 4 p hooks in your jaws and bring you out H5989
Eze 38: 5 Cush and P will be with them, all H7033
Eze 42:13 There they will p the most holy offerings— H5663
Eze 42:14 They are to p on other clothes before they H4252
Eze 43: 9 Now let them p away from me their H8178
Eze 43:20 of its blood and p it on the four horns H5989
Eze 44: 8 you p others in charge of my sanctuary. H8492
Eze 44:19 sacred rooms, and p on other clothes, so H4252
Eze 45:19 the sin offering and p it on the doorposts H5989
Da 1: 2 in Babylonia and p in the treasure house H995
Da 2:13 was issued to p the wise men to death, A10625
Da 2:13 his friends to p them to death. A10625
Da 2:14 gone out to p to death the wise men A10625
Da 5:19 Those the king wanted to p to death, he put NDT
Da 5:19 put to death, he p to death; those he A10625
Da 6: 8 decree and p it in writing so that A10673+10375
Da 6: 9 Darius p the decree in writing. A10673+10375
Da 6:13 to the decree you p in writing. A10673
Da 9:24 transgression, to p an end to sin, to atone H9462
Da 9:26 Anointed One will be p to death and will H4162
Da 9:27 the 'seven' he will p an end to sacrifice H8697
Da 11:18 a commander will p an end to his H8697
Hos 1: 4 and I will p an end to the kingdom of H8697
Hos 8: 1 "P the trumpet to your lips! An eagle is over NDT
Hos 10:10 against them to p them in bonds for their H673
Hos 10:11 so I will p a yoke on her fair neck. H6296
Hos 11: 6 false prophets and p an end to their plans. H430
Joel 1:13 P on sackcloth, you priests, and mourn H2520
Joel 3: 2 There I will p them on trial for what they H9149
Am 6: 3 You p off the day of disaster and bring H5612
Jnh 3: 5 the greatest to the least, p on sackcloth. H4252
Mic 7: 5 a neighbor; p no confidence in a friend. H1053
Mic 7:16 They will p their hands over their mouths H8492
Na 2: 5 the protective shield is p in place. H3922
Na 3: 9 P and Libya were among her allies. H7033
Na 3:10 great men were p in chains. H8415+2414+928
Zep 3:11 you, Jerusalem, will not be p to shame H1017
Hag 1: 6 your fill. You p on clothes, but are not H4252
Hag 1: 6 only to p them in a purse with holes in it." NDT
Zec 3: 4 and I will p fine garments on you. H4252
Zec 3: 5 "P a clean turban on his head. H8492
Zec 3: 5 So they p a clean turban on his head and H8492
Zec 9: 6 and I will p an end to the pride of the H4162
Zec 10: 5 they will p the enemy horsemen to shame H1017
Zec 13: 4 They will not p on a prophet's garment of H4252
Zec 13: 9 This third I will p into the fire; I will refine H995
Mal 3: 5 "So I will come to p you on trial. I will be H5477
Mal 3:15 even when they p God to the test H1043
Mt 4: 7 'Do not p the Lord your God to the test.'" G1733
Mt 4:12 heard that John had been p in prison, G4140
Mt 5:15 light a lamp and p it under a bowl. G5502
Mt 5:15 Instead they p it on its stand, and it gives NDT
Mt 6:17 p oil on your head and wash your face, G230
Mt 7:26 and does not p them into practice is like G4472
Mt 9:18 But come and p your hand on her, and G2202
Mt 9:25 After the crowd had been p outside, he G1675
Mt 10:21 their parents and have them p to death. G2506
Mt 12:18 whom I delight; I will p my Spirit on him G5502
Mt 12:21 In his name the nations will p their hope." G1827
Mt 12:44 unoccupied, swept clean and p in order. G3175
Mt 14: 3 bound him and p him in prison G700
Mt 15: 4 mother is to be p to death. G2505+5462
Mt 17: 4 If you wish, I will p up three shelters—one G4472
Mt 17:17 How long shall I p up with you? Bring G462
Mt 21:33 He p a wall around it, dug a winepress in G4363
Mt 22:44 right hand until I p your enemies under G5502
Mt 23: 4 loads and p them on other people's G2202
Mt 24: 9 over to be persecuted and p to death, G650
Mt 24:45 whom the master has p in charge of the G2770
Mt 24:47 he will p him in charge of all his G2770
Mt 25:16 once and p his money to work and gained G2237
Mt 25:21 I will p you in charge of many things. G2770
Mt 25:23 I will p you in charge of many things. G2770
Mt 25:27 have p my money on deposit with the G965
Mt 25:33 He will p the sheep on his right and the G2705
Mt 26:52 "P your sword back in its place," Jesus said G695
Mt 26:53 and he will at once p at my disposal more G4225
Mt 26:59 Jesus so that they could p him to death. G2506
Mt 27: 6 "It is against the law to p this into the G965
Mt 27:28 stripped him and p a scarlet robe on him, G4363
Mt 27:29 They p a staff in his right hand NDT
Mt 27:31 the robe and p his own clothes on him. G1907
Mt 27:48 with wine vinegar, p it on a staff, and G4363
Mk 1:14 After John was p in prison, Jesus went G4140
Mk 4:21 bring in a lamp to p it under a bowl or a G5502
Mk 4:21 Instead, don't you p it on its stand? G5502
Mk 5:23 come and p your hands on her so that G2202
Mk 5:40 After he p them all out, he took the G1675
Mk 6:17 he had him bound and p in prison. AIT
Mk 7:10 mother is to be p to death. G2505+5462
Mk 7:33 Jesus p his fingers into the man's ears. G965
Mk 8:23 the man's eyes and p his hands on him, G2202
Mk 8:25 more Jesus p his hands on the man's G2202
Mk 9: 5 Let us p up three shelters—one for you G4472
Mk 9:19 How long shall I p up with you? Bring G462
Mk 12: 1 He p a wall around it, dug a pit for the G4363
Mk 12:36 right hand until I p your enemies under G5502
Mk 12:41 the place where the offerings were p and G1126
Mk 12:42 a poor widow came and p in two very small G965
Mk 12:43 this poor widow has p more into the G965
Mk 12:44 out of her poverty, p in everything—all she G965
Mk 13:12 their parents and have them p to death. G2506
Mk 14:55 Jesus so that they could p him to death, G2506
Mk 15:17 They p a purple robe on him, then twisted G1898
Mk 15:20 robe and p his own clothes on him. G1907
Mk 15:36 with wine vinegar, p it on a staff, and G4363
Lk 4:12 'Do not p the Lord your God to the test.'" G1733
Lk 5: 3 asked him to p out a little from shore. G2056
Lk 5: 4 he said to Simon, "P out into deep water G2056
Lk 6:49 and does not p them into practice is like G4472
Lk 7:46 You did not p oil on my head, but she has G230
Lk 8:16 Instead, they p it on a stand, so that those G5502
Lk 8:21 hear God's word and p it into practice." G4472
Lk 9:33 Let us p up three shelters—one for you G4472
Lk 9:41 shall I stay with you and p up with you? G462
Lk 10:34 Then he p the man on his own donkey G2097
Lk 11:25 the house swept clean and p in order. G3175
Lk 11:33 Instead they p it on its stand, so that those NDT
Lk 12:44 he will p him in charge of all his G2770
Lk 13:13 Then he p his hands on her, and G2202
Lk 15:22 Bring the best robe and p it on him. Put a G1907
Lk 15:22 P a ring on his finger and sandals on his G1443
Lk 19:13 'P this money to work,' he said, 'until I G4549
Lk 19:21 take out what you did not p in and reap G5502
Lk 19:22 taking out what I did not p in, and G5502
Lk 19:23 Why then didn't you p my money on G1443
Lk 19:35 threw their cloaks on the colt and p Jesus on it. G2097
Lk 21: 2 also saw a poor widow p in two very small G965
Lk 21: 3 "this poor widow has p in more than all the G965
Lk 21: 4 out of her poverty p in all she had to live G965
Lk 21:12 you over to synagogues and p you in prison, NDT
Lk 21:16 and they will p some of you to death. G2506
Lk 23:26 and p the cross on him and made him G2202
Jn 3:24 This was before John was p in prison.) G965
Jn 8:20 the place where the offerings were p. G1126
Jn 9: 6 the saliva, and p it on the man's eyes. G2222
Jn 9:11 made some mud and p it on my eyes. G2222
Jn 9:15 "He p mud on my eyes," the man replied G2202
Jn 9:22 Messiah would be p out of the synagogue. G697
Jn 12: 6 used to help himself to what was p into it. G965
Jn 12:42 fear they would be p out of the synagogue; G697
Jn 13: 3 that the Father had p all things under G1443
Jn 13:12 he p on his clothes and returned to his G3284
Jn 16: 2 They will p you out of the synagogue; in G4472
Jn 18:11 commanded Peter, "P your sword away! G965
Jn 19: 2 a crown of thorns and p it on his head. G2202
Jn 19:29 they soaked a sponge in it, p the sponge on G4363
Jn 20: 2 we don't know where they have p him!" G5502
Jn 20:13 "and I don't know where they have p him." G5502
Jn 20:15 tell me where you have p him, and I will G5502
Jn 20:25 in his hands and p my finger where the G965
Jn 20:25 the nails were, and p my hand into his side G965
Jn 20:27 he said to Thomas, "P your finger here G5770
Jn 20:27 Reach out your hand and p it into my side G965
Ac 2:23 you, with the help of wicked men,
p him to death G359
Ac 3: 2 where he was p every day to beg from G5502
Ac 4: 3 they p them in jail until the next day. G5502
Ac 4:35 p it at the apostles' feet, and it was G5502
Ac 4:37 the money and p it at the apostles' G5502
Ac 5: 2 brought the rest and p it at the apostles' G5502
Ac 5:18 the apostles and p them in the public jail. G5502
Ac 5:25 The men you p in jail are standing in the G5502
Ac 5:33 furious and wanted to p them to death. G359
Ac 5:34 ordered that the men be p outside for a G4472
Ac 8: 3 men and women and p them in prison. G4140
Ac 12: 2 He had James, the brother of John, p to death
G359
Ac 12: 4 After arresting him, he p him in prison G5502
Ac 12: 8 "P on your clothes and sandals. G2439
Ac 14:23 the Lord, in whom they had p their trust. G4409
Ac 16:11 From Troas we p out to sea and sailed G343
Ac 16:24 he p them in the inner cell and fastened G965
Ac 20:10 young man and p his arms around him. G5227
Ac 21: 1 we p out to sea and sailed straight to Kos. G343
Ac 22:29 he had Paul, a Roman citizen, in chains
G1639+1313
Ac 26:10 of the chief priests I p many of the Lord's G2881

Ac 26:10 and when they were p to death, I cast my G359
Ac 27: 2 the province of Asia, and we p out to sea. G343
Ac 27: 4 From there we p out to sea again and G343
Ac 27: 6 ship sailing for Italy and p us on board. G1837
Ac 28: 3 brushwood and, as he p it on the fire, G2202
Ac 28:11 three months we p out to sea in a ship that G343
Ac 28:12 We p in at Syracuse and stayed there G2864
Ro 5: 5 And hope does not p us to shame G2875
Ro 7:11 through the commandment p me to death. G650
Ro 8:13 by the Spirit you p to death the misdeeds G2506
Ro 9:33 believes in him will never be p to shame." G2875
Ro 10:11 believes in him will never be p to shame." G2875
Ro 13:12 So let us p aside the deeds of darkness G700
Ro 13:12 of darkness and p on the armor of light. G1907
Ro 14:13 to p any stumbling block or obstacle in the way G5502
Ro 16:17 cause divisions and p obstacles in your G4472
1Co 4: 9 me that God has p us apostles on display G617
1Co 5: 2 gone into mourning and have p out of your G149
1Co 9:12 we p up with anything rather than hinder G5095
1Co 10:27 eat whatever is p before you without G4192
1Co 12:24 But God has p the body together, giving G5166
1Co 13:11 I p the ways of childhood behind me. G2934
1Co 14:16 who is now p in the position of an inquirer G405
1Co 15:25 must reign until he has p all his enemies G5502
1Co 15:27 For he "has p everything under his feet." G5718
1Co 15:27 "everything" has been p under him, it is G5718
1Co 15:27 himself, who p everything under Christ. G5718
1Co 15:28 to him who p everything under him, G5718
2Co 1:22 p his Spirit in our hearts as a deposit G1443
2Co 2: 5 to some extent—not to p it too severely. G2096
2Co 3:13 who would p a veil over his face to G5502
2Co 6: 3 We p no stumbling block in anyone's G1443
2Co 8:16 who p into the heart of Titus the same G1443
2Co 11: 1 I hope you will p up with me in a little G462
2Co 11: 1 Yes, please p up with me! G462
2Co 11: 4 accepted, you p up with it easily enough. G462
2Co 11:19 You gladly p up with fools since you are so G462
2Co 11:20 you even p up with anyone who enslaves G462
Gal 2:16 have p our faith in Christ Jesus that we G4409
Eph 1:10 to be p into effect when the times reach G3873
Eph 1:12 who were the first to p our hope in Christ G4598
Eph 2:16 by which he p to death their hostility. G650
Eph 4:22 former way of life, to p off your old self G700
Eph 4:24 and to p on the new self, created to be G1907
Eph 4:25 each of you must p off falsehood and G700
Eph 6:11 P on the full armor of God, so that you can G1907
Eph 6:13 Therefore p on the full armor of God, so G377
Php 1:16 knowing that I am p here for the defense G3023
Php 3: 3 and who p no confidence in the flesh G4275
Php 3: 4 have reasons to p confidence in the flesh, G4275
Php 4: 9 or seen in me—p it into practice. G4556
Col 2:11 ruled by the flesh was p off when you were G589
Col 3: 5 P to death, therefore, whatever belongs to G3739
Col 3:10 and have p on the new self, which is G1907
Col 3:14 And over all these virtues p on love, which NDT
1Th 2: 5 did we p on a mask to cover up greed G1877
1Ti 4:10 because we have p our hope in the living G1827
1Ti 5: 4 to p their religion into practice by caring for G2355
1Ti 5: 9 No widow may be p on the list of widows G2899
1Ti 5:11 do not p them on such a list. NDT
1Ti 6:17 be arrogant nor to p their hope in wealth, G1827
1Ti 6:17 so uncertain, but to p their hope in God NDT
2Ti 4: 3 when people will not p up with sound G462
Titus 1: 5 was that you might p in order what was G2114
Heb 2: 8 and p everything under their feet." In G5718
Heb 2:13 again, "I will p my trust in him." G1639+4275
Heb 8:10 I will p my laws in their minds and write G1443
Heb 9:18 covenant was not p into effect without G1590
Heb 10:16 I will p my laws in their hearts, and I will G1443
Heb 11:37 They were p to death by stoning; they G3342
Jas 3: 3 When we p bits into the mouths of horses G965
1Pe 2: 6 trusts in him will never be p to shame." G2875
1Pe 3: 5 the past who p their hope in God used to G1827
1Pe 3:18 He was p to death in the body but made G2506
2Pe 1:14 I know that I will soon p it aside, G1639+629
Rev 2:10 the devil will p some of you in prison to G965
Rev 2:13 witness, who was p to death in your city G650
Rev 3:18 salve to p on your eyes, so you G1608
Rev 7: 3 the trees until we p a seal on the G5381
Rev 17:17 For God has p it into their hearts to G1443

PUTEOLI (1)
Ac 28:13 on the following day we reached P. G4541

PUTHITES (1)
1Ch 2:53 the Ithrites, P, Shumathites and H7057

PUTIEL (1)
Ex 6:25 Aaron married one of the daughters of P, H7034

PUTS (27) [PUT]
Ex 30:33 perfume like it and p it on anyone other H5989
Lev 16: 4 himself with water before he p them on. H4252
Nu 22:38 must speak only what God p in my mouth." H8492
Nu 23:12 I not speak what the LORD p in my mouth?" H8492
2Sa 22:48 avenges me, who p the nations under me H3718
1Ki 20:11 'One who p on his armor should not boast H2520
1Ch 22:12 when he p you in command over Israel, H7422
Ps 33: 7 into jars; he p the deep into storehouses. H5989
Pr 11:15 Whoever p up security for a stranger will H6842
Pr 17:18 in pledge and p up security for a H6842+6859
Pr 20:16 of one who p up security for a stranger H6842
Pr 22:26 hands in pledge or p up security for debts; H6842
Pr 25: 8 the end if your neighbor p you to shame? H4007
Pr 27:13 of one who p up security for a stranger; H6842
Mt 7:24 of mine and p them into practice is like a G4472
Mk 4:29 grain is ripe, he p the sickle to it, because G690
Mk 13:34 leaves his house and p his servants in G1443
Lk 6:47 hears my words and p them into practice, G4472
Lk 8:16 hides it in a clay jar or p it under a bed. G5502
Lk 9:62 "No one who p a hand to the plow and G2095
Lk 11:33 lights a lamp and p it in a place where G5502
Lk 12:42 whom the master p in charge of his G2770
Lk 15: 5 he joyfully p it on his shoulders G2202
2Co 11:20 of you or p on airs or slaps you in the G2048
1Ti 5: 5 left all alone p her hope in God and G1827
Heb 6:16 what is said and p an end to all argument. NDT
3Jn 10 to do so and p them out of the church. G1675

PUTTING (27) [PUT]
Ex 29:17 p them with the head and the other H5989
Dt 13: 9 hand must be the first in p them to death, H4637
Dt 17: 7 must be the first in p that person to death, H4637
Dt 20:19 do not destroy its trees by p an ax to them, H5616
Jdg 1: 5 p to rout the Canaanites and Perizzites. H5782
Jdg 6:19 P the meat in a basket and its broth in a H8492
Jdg 16:19 After p him to sleep on her lap, she called H3822
Jdg 18:21 P their little children, their livestock and H8492
1Sa 6:19 p seventy of them to death because they H5782
1Sa 19:13 and p some goats' hair at the head. H8492
1Sa 28: 8 disguised himself, p on other clothes, and H4252
1Ki 9: 3 have built, by p my Name there forever. H8492
Ne 3:15 p its doors and bolts and bars in place. H6641
Ne 9: 1 sackcloth and p dust on their heads. NDT
Ne 9:38 agreement, p it in writing, and our H4180
Job 13:27 on all my paths by p marks on the soles of H2977
Ps 37:32 the righteous, intent on p them to death; H4637
Eze 8:17 Look at them p the branch to their nose H8938
Eze 17:13 made a treaty with him, p him under oath. H995
Mt 27:66 tomb secure by p a seal on the stone and G5381
Mk 12:41 watched the crowd p their money into the G965
Lk 18: 7 day and night? Will he keep p them off? G3428
Lk 21: 1 he saw the rich p their gifts into the temple G965
Ac 15:10 you try to test God by p on the necks of G2202
1Th 5: 8 p on faith and love as a breastplate G1907
Heb 2: 8 In p everything under them, God left G5718
2Pe 2: 4 p them in chains of darkness to be held G4140

PUZZLED (1)
Mk 6:20 heard John, he was greatly p; yet he liked G679

PYGARG (KJV) IBEX

PYRRHUS (1)
Ac 20: 4 by Sopater son of P from Berea, G4795

Q

QUAIL (4)
Ex 16:13 That evening q came and covered the H8513
Nu 11:31 from the LORD and drove q in from the sea. H8513
Nu 11:32 day the people went out and gathered q. H8513
Ps 105:40 he brought them q; he fed them well H8513

QUAKE (7) [EARTHQUAKE, EARTHQUAKES, QUAKED, QUAKING]
Job 26:11 The pillars of the heavens q, aghast at his H8344
Ps 46: 3 the mountains q with their surging. H8321
Ps 75: 3 When the earth and all its people q, it is I H4570
Isa 64: 2 and cause the nations to q before you H8074
Eze 27:28 The shorelands will q when your sailors H8321
Na 1: 5 The mountains q before him and the hills H8321
Rev 16:18 been on earth, so tremendous was the q. G4939

QUAKED (4) [QUAKE]
Jdg 5: 5 The mountains q before the LORD, the One H2362
2Sa 22: 8 The earth trembled and q, the H8321
Ps 18: 7 The earth trembled and q, and the H8321
Ps 77:18 lit up the world; the earth trembled and q. H8321

QUAKING (3) [QUAKE]
1Sa 13: 7 all the troops with him were q with fear. H3006
Ps 60: 2 torn it open; mend its fractures, for it is q. H4572
Jer 4:24 mountains, and they were q; all the hills H8321

QUALIFIED (3)
Da 1: 4 q to serve in the king's palace. H3946
Col 1:12 who has q you to share in the inheritance G2655
2Ti 2: 2 people who will also be q to teach others. G2653

QUALITIES (3) [QUALITY]
Da 6: 3 by his exceptional q that the king A10658
Ro 1:20 the creation of the world God's invisible q— AIT
2Pe 1: 8 For if you possess these q in increasing AIT

QUALITY (4) [QUALITIES]
Lev 27:12 who will judge its q as good or bad H6885
Lev 27:14 the priest will judge its q as good or bad. H6885
1Ki 7:10 were laid with large stones of good q, H3701
1Co 3:13 fire will test the q of each person's work. G3961

QUALM (1)
Jude 12 eating with you without the slightest q G925

QUANTITIES (9) [QUANTITY]
Ge 41:49 Joseph stored up huge q of grain, like the H2221
1Ki 10: 2 large q of gold, and precious H8041
1Ki 10:10 talents of gold, large q of spices, and H2221
1Ch 22:14 q of bronze and iron too great to be NDT
1Ch 29: 2 marble—all of these in large q. H4200+8044
2Ch 9: 1 spices, large q of gold, and H4200+8044
2Ch 9: 9 of gold, large q of spices, and H4200+8044
2Ch 25:13 people and carried off great q of plunder. H8041
Zec 14:14 great q of gold and silver H4200+8044+4394

QUANTITY (7) [QUANTITIES]
Lev 19:35 when measuring length, weight or q. H5374
Jos 22: 8 and a great q of clothing H2221+4394
2Sa 8: 8 David took a great q of bronze. H2221+4394
2Sa 12:30 David took a great q of plunder H2221+4394
1Ch 18: 8 David took a great q of bronze, which H8041
1Ch 20: 2 He took a great q of plunder from H2221+4394
1Ch 23:29 all measurements of q and size. H5374

QUARREL (15) [QUARRELED, QUARRELING, QUARRELS, QUARRELSOME]
Ge 45:24 he said to them, "Don't q on the way!" H8074
Ex 17: 2 replied, "Why do you q with me? Why do H8189
Ex 21:18 "If people q and one person hits another H8189
Jdg 11:25 Did he ever q with Israel or fight H8189+8189
2Ki 5: 7 See how he is trying to pick a q with me!" H628
2Ch 35:21 "What q is there, king of Judah, between H3373
Pr 15:18 the one who is patient calms a q. H8190
Pr 17:14 Starting a q is like breaching a dam; so H4506
Pr 17:19 Whoever loves a q loves sin; whoever H5175
Pr 20: 3 to avoid strife, but every fool is quick to q. H1679
Pr 26:17 who rushes into a q not their own. H8190
Pr 26:20 goes out; without a gossip a q dies down. H4506
Isa 45: 9 "Woe to those who q with their Maker H8189
Mt 12:19 He will not q or cry out; no one will hear G2248
Jas 4: 2 get what you want, so you q and fight. G3481

QUARRELED (7) [QUARREL]
Ge 26:20 the herders of Gerar q with those of Isaac H8189
Ge 26:21 but they q over that one also H8189
Ge 26:22 dug another well, and no one q over it. H8189
Ex 17: 2 So they q with Moses and said, "Give us H8189
Ex 17: 7 because the Israelites q and because they H8189
Nu 20: 3 They q with Moses and said, "If only we H8189
Nu 20:13 where the Israelites q with the LORD and H8189

QUARRELING (7) [QUARREL]
Ge 13: 7 And q arose between Abram's herders H8190
Ge 13: 8 not have any q between you and me, H5312
Isa 58: 4 Your fasting ends in q and strife, and in H8190
Ac 12:20 He had been q with the people of Tyre G2595
Ro 14: 1 without q over disputable matters. G1369
1Co 3: 3 since there is jealousy and q among you, G2251
2Ti 2:14 them before God against q about words; G3362

QUARRELS (7) [QUARREL]
Pr 18: 1 against all sound judgment starts q. H1679
Pr 22:10 out goes strife; q and insults are ended. H1907
1Co 1:11 informed me that there are q among you. G2251
1Ti 6: 4 and q about words that result in G3363
2Ti 2:23 because you know they produce q. G3480
Titus 3: 9 arguments and q about the law, G3480
Jas 4: 1 What causes fights and q among you G3480

QUARRELSOME (8) [QUARREL]
Pr 19:13 a q wife is like the constant dripping H4506
Pr 21: 9 the roof than share a house with a q wife. H4506
Pr 21:19 a desert than with a q and nagging wife. H4506
Pr 25:24 the roof than share a house with a q wife. H4506
Pr 26:21 so is a q person for kindling strife. H4506
Pr 27:15 A q wife is like the dripping of a leaky H4506
1Ti 3: 3 violent but gentle, not q, not a lover of G285
2Ti 2:24 servant must not be q but must be kind to G3481

QUARRIES (2) [QUARRY]
Jos 7: 5 gate as far as the stone q and struck them H8696
Ecc 10: 9 Whoever q stones may be injured by H5825

QUARRY (3) [QUARRIES]
1Ki 5:17 command they removed from the q large H5825
1Ki 6: 7 only blocks dressed at the q were used H5024
Isa 51: 1 and to the q from which you were H5217+1014

QUART (NIV84) POUND, POUNDS

QUARTER (16) [QUARTERS]
Ex 29:40 flour mixed with a q of a hin of oil from H8063
Ex 29:40 a q of a hin of wine as a drink H8055
Lev 23:13 its drink offering of a q of a hin of wine. H8055
Nu 15: 4 flour mixed with a q of a hin of olive oil. H8055
Nu 15: 5 prepare a q of a hin of wine as a drink H8055
Nu 28: 5 flour mixed with a q of a hin of oil from H8055
Nu 28: 7 offering is to be a q of a hin of fermented H8055
Nu 28:14 and with each lamb, a q of a hin. H8055
1Sa 9: 8 he said, "I have a q of a shekel of silver. H8063
2Ki 6:25 a q of a cab of seed pods for five H8065
2Ki 22:14 She lived in Jerusalem, in the New Q. H5467
2Ch 34:22 She lived in Jerusalem, in the New Q. H5467
Ne 9: 3 of the LORD their God for a q of the day, H8055

Ne 9: 3 spent another q in confession and in H8055
Ne 11: 9 was over the **New Q** of the city. H5467
Zep 1:10 wailing from the **New Q**, and a loud crash H5467

QUARTERS (6) [QUARTER]
2Sa 19:11 Israel has reached the king at his q? H1074
2Ki 23: 7 also tore down the q *of* the male shrine H1074
2Ki 23: 7 **the q** where women did weaving for H889S
Ne 3:30 made repairs opposite his **living q**. H5969
Isa 11:12 of Judah from the four q *of* the earth. H4053
Jer 49:36 the four winds from the four q *of* heaven; H7896

QUARTUS (1)
Ro 16:23 our brother Q send you their greetings. G3181

QUATERNIONS (KJV) SQUADS OF FOUR

QUEEN (55) [QUEEN'S, QUEENS]
1Ki 10: 1 When the q *of* Sheba heard about the H4893
1Ki 10: 4 When the q *of* Sheba saw all the wisdom H4893
1Ki 10:10 in as those the q *of* Sheba gave to King H4893
1Ki 10:13 Solomon gave the q *of* Sheba all she H4893
1Ki 11:19 of his own wife, Q Tahpenes, in marriage. H1485
1Ki 15:13 Maakah from her **position as q mother**, H1485
2Ki 10:13 families of the king and of the **q mother**." H1485
2Ch 9: 1 When the q *of* Sheba heard of Solomon's H4893
2Ch 9: 3 When the q *of* Sheba saw the wisdom of H4893
2Ch 9: 9 as those the q *of* Sheba gave to King H4893
2Ch 9:12 Solomon gave the q *of* Sheba all she H4893
2Ch 15:16 Maakah from her **position as q mother**, H1485
Ne 2: 6 the king, with the q sitting beside him H8712
Est 1: 9 Q Vashti also gave a banquet for the H4893
Est 1:11 to bring before him Q Vashti, wearing her H4893
Est 1:12 command, Q Vashti refused to come. H4893
Est 1:15 what must be done to Q Vashti? H4893
Est 1:16 the nobles, "Q Vashti has done wrong H4893
Est 1:17 Xerxes commanded Q Vashti to be H4893
Est 2: 4 *let* the young woman who pleases the king *be* q H4887
Est 2:17 on her head and **made** her q instead of H4887
Est 2:22 out about the plot and told Q Esther, H4893
Est 5: 2 When he saw Q Esther standing in the H4893
Est 5: 3 the king asked, "What is it, Q Esther? H4893
Est 5:12 "I'm the only person Q Esther invited to H4893
Est 7: 1 Haman went to Q Esther's banquet, H4893
Est 7: 2 king again asked, "Q Esther, what is your H4893
Est 7: 3 Then Q Esther answered, "If I have found H4893
Est 7: 5 King Xerxes asked Q Esther, "Who is he H4893
Est 7: 6 was terrified before the king and q. H4893
Est 7: 7 stayed behind to beg Q Esther for his life. H4893
Est 7: 8 he even molest the q while she is with H4893
Est 8: 1 King Xerxes gave Q Esther the estate of H4893
Est 8: 7 Xerxes replied to Q Esther and to H4893
Est 9:12 The king said to Q Esther, "The Jews have H4893
Est 9:29 So Q Esther, daughter of Abihail, along H4893
Est 9:31 the Jew and Q Esther had decreed H4893
Isa 47: 1 a throne, **q city** *of* the Babylonians. H1426
Isa 47: 5 go into darkness, **q city** *of* the Babylonians H1426
Isa 47: 5 no more will you be called q *of* kingdoms. H1509
Isa 47: 7 forever—the eternal q!' But you did not H1509
Jer 7:18 make cakes to offer to the Q *of* Heaven. H4906
Jer 13:18 Say to the king and to the **q mother** H1485
Jer 29: 2 after King Jehoiachin and the **q mother**, H1485
Jer 44:17 burn incense to the Q *of* Heaven and will H4906
Jer 44:18 incense to the Q *of* Heaven and pouring H4906
Jer 44:19 incense to the Q *of* Heaven and poured H4906
Jer 44:25 out drink offerings to the Q *of* Heaven. H4906
La 1: 1 She who was q among the provinces has H8576
Eze 16:13 became very beautiful and rose to be a q. H4867
Da 5:10 The q, hearing the voices of the king A10423
Mt 12:42 The Q of the South will rise at the judgment G999
Lk 11:31 The Q of the South will rise at the judgment G999
Ac 8:27 which means "q of the Ethiopians"). G999
Rev 18: 7 her heart she boasts, 'I sit enthroned *as* q. G999

QUEEN'S (2) [QUEEN]
Est 1:17 For the q conduct will become known to all H4893
Est 1:18 heard about the q conduct will respond H4893

QUEENS (4) [QUEEN]
SS 6: 8 Sixty q there may be, and eighty H4893
SS 6: 9 the q and concubines praised her. H4893
Isa 49:23 and their q your nursing mothers. H8576
Jer 44: 9 by the kings and q of Judah and the H851S

QUENCH (7) [QUENCHED]
Ps 104:11 of the field; the wild donkeys q their thirst. H8689
SS 8: 7 Many waters cannot q love; rivers cannot H3882
Isa 1:31 burn together, with no *one to* q *the* **fire**." H3882
Jer 4: 4 you have done—burn with no *one to* q it. H3882
Jer 21:12 you have done—burn with no *one to* q it. H3882
Am 5: 6 and Bethel will have no *one to* q it. H3882
1Th 5:19 *Do* not q the Spirit. G4931

QUENCHED (10) [QUENCH]
2Ki 22:17 burn against this place and *will* not *be* q. H3882
2Ch 34:25 out on this place and *will* not *be* q. H3882
Isa 34:10 *It will* not *be* q night or day; its smoke will H3882
Isa 66:24 the fire that burns them *will* not *be* q, and H3882
Jer 7:20 your land—and it will burn and not *be* q. H3882
Jer 46:10 satisfied, till *it has* **q its thirst** with blood. H8115
Eze 20:47 The blazing flame *will* not *be* q, and H3882
Eze 20:48 I the LORD have kindled it; *it will* not *be* q. H3882
Mk 9:48 eat them do not die, and the fire *is* not q. G4931
Heb 11:34 q the fury of the flames, and escaped the G4931

QUESTION (23) [QUESTIONED, QUESTIONING, QUESTIONS]
Jdg 11:12 to the Ammonite king with the q: H606
Est 5: 8 Then I will answer the king's q." H1821
Job 38: 3 like a man; *I will* q you, and you shall H8626
Job 40: 7 like a man; *I will* q you, and you shall H8626
Job 42: 4 I will speak; *I will* q you, and you H8626
Ps 35:11 *they* q me on things I know nothing about. H8626
Isa 45:11 to come, *do you* q me about my children H8626
Jer 38:27 officials did come to Jeremiah and q him, H8626
Mt 21:24 "I will also ask you one q. If you answer G3364
Mt 22:23 is no resurrection, came to him with a q. G2089
Mt 22:35 expert in the law, tested him *with this* q: G2089
Mk 8:11 Pharisees came and began *to* q Jesus. G5184
Mk 11:29 replied, "I will ask you one q. Answer me, G3364
Mk 12:18 is no resurrection, came to him *with a* q. G2089
Lk 20: 3 replied, "I will also ask you a q. Tell me: G3364
Lk 20:27 is no resurrection, came to Jesus *with a* q. G2089
Lk 22:23 They began *to* q among themselves which G5184
Jn 8: 6 *They were using* this q as a trap, in order G3306
Jn 18:21 Why q me? Ask those who heard me G2263
Ac 4: 7 before them and *began to* q them: G4785
Ac 15: 2 see the apostles and elders about this q. G2427
Ac 15: 6 elders met to consider this q. G3364
1Ti 3:16 **Beyond all q**, the mystery from which true G3935

QUESTIONED (10) [QUESTION]
Ge 43: 7 "The man q us **closely** about H8626+8626
Jdg 8:14 a young man of Sukkoth and q him, H8626
Ezr 5: 9 *We* q the elders and asked them, "Who A10689
Ne 1: 2 and *I* q them about the Jewish remnant H8626
Job 21:29 *Have you* never q those who travel? Have H8626
Da 1:20 about which the king q them, H1335
Lk 20:21 So the spies q him: "Teacher, we know G2089
Jn 1:25 q him, "Why then do you baptize if you G2263
Jn 18:19 the high priest q Jesus about his disciples G2263
Ac 5:27 the Sanhedrin *to be* q *by* the high priest. G2089

QUESTIONING (1) [QUESTION]
Jn 8: 7 When they kept on q him, he straightened G2263

QUESTIONS (17) [QUESTION]
Ge 43: 7 We simply answered his q. How were we H1821
1Ki 10: 1 she came to test Solomon with **hard q**. H2648
1Ki 10: 3 Solomon answered all her q; nothing was H1821
2Ch 9: 1 to Jerusalem to test him with **hard q**. H2648
2Ch 9: 2 Solomon answered all her q; nothing was H1821
Ecc 7:10 For it is not wise to ask **such q**. H2296S
Mt 22:46 on no one dared *to* **ask** him any more q. G2089
Mk 12:34 on no one dared **ask** him *any more* q. G2089
Lk 2:46 listening to them and **asking** them q. G2089
Lk 11:53 and *to* **besiege** him **with** q, G694+4309+4498
Lk 20:40 And no one dared *to* **ask** him any more q. G2089
Lk 23: 9 He plied him with many q, but Jesus gave G3364
Jn 16:30 not even need to *have* anyone **ask** you q. G2263
Ac 18:15 But since it involves q about words and G2427
Ac 23:29 had to do with q about their law, G2427
1Co 10:25 market without **raising** q of conscience, G373
1Co 10:27 before you without **raising** q of conscience. G373

QUICK (14) [QUICK-TEMPERED, QUICKLY]

QUICK (KJV) ALIVE, LIVING, RAW
Ge 18: 6 "Q," he said, "get three seahs of the H4554
Ge 25:30 He said to Jacob, "Q, let me have some of H5528
Ex 32: 8 *They have been* q to turn away from what I H4554
Jdg 9:48 the men with him, "Q! Do what you have H4554
1Ki 20:33 as a good sign and *were* q to pick up his H4554
Pr 6:18 schemes, feet *that are* q to rush into evil, H4554
Pr 20: 3 avoid strife, but every fool *is* **q to quarrel**. H1679
Ecc 5: 2 *Do* not *be* q with your mouth, do not be H987
Da 1: 4 informed, **q to understand**, and H1067+4529
Mal 3: 5 I will be q to testify against sorcerers H4554
Lk 15:22 to his servants, 'Q! Bring the best robe G5444
Ac 12: 7 woke him up. "Q, get up!" he said G1877+5443
Ac 22:18 saw the Lord speaking to me. 'Q!' he said. G5067
Jas 1:19 Everyone should be q to listen, slow to G5444

QUICK-TEMPERED (3) [QUICK, TEMPER]
Pr 14:17 A q *person* does foolish things, and H7920+678
Pr 14:29 but *one who* is q displays folly. H7920+8120
Titus 1: 7 not overbearing, not q, not given to G3975

QUICKEN, QUICKENED, QUICKENETH, QUICKENING (KJV) COME TO LIFE, GIVE LIFE, GIVES LIFE, LIFE-GIVING, MADE ALIVE, PRESERVE LIFE, PRESERVED LIFE, PRESERVES LIFE, RESTORE LIFE

QUICKLY (75) [QUICK]
Ge 19:22 But flee there q, because I cannot do H4554
Ge 24:18 q lowered the jar to her hands and H4554
Ge 24:20 So *she* q emptied her jar into the trough H4554
Ge 24:46 "She q lowered her jar from her shoulder H4554
Ge 27:20 "How did you find it *so* q, my son? H4554
Ge 41:14 he *was* **q brought** from the dungeon. H8132
Ge 44:11 Each of them q lowered his sack to the H4554
Ge 45:13 And bring my father down here q." H4554
Ex 10:16 Pharaoh q summoned Moses and Aaron H4554
Dt 4:26 day that you will q perish from the land H4554
Dt 7: 4 burn against you and will q destroy you. H4554
Dt 9: 3 drive them out and annihilate them q, H4554
Dt 9:12 have turned away q from what I H4554
Dt 9:16 You had turned aside q from the way that H4554
Jos 2: 5 Go after them q. You may catch up H4554
Jos 8:19 in the ambush rose q from their position H4559
Jos 8:19 city and captured it and q set it on fire. H4554
Jos 10: 6 Come up to us q and save us! Help us, H4559
Jos 23:16 you will q perish from the good land H4559
Jdg 2:17 They q turned from the ways of their H4554
1Sa 17:48 David ran q toward the battle line to meet H4554
1Sa 20:38 shouted, "Hurry! **Go q**! Don't stop!" The H2590
1Sa 23:27 came to Saul, saying, "Come q! H4554
1Sa 25:18 Abigail **acted q**. She took two hundred H4554
1Sa 25:23 *she* q got off her donkey and bowed down H4554
1Sa 25:34 if you had not come q to meet me, not H4554
1Sa 25:42 Abigail q got on a donkey and, attended H4554
2Sa 5:24 the poplar trees, **move q**, because that H3077
2Sa 15:14 or *he will* **move q** to overtake us and bring H4554
1Ki 20:41 Then the prophet q removed the H4554
2Ki 4:22 so *I can* **go** to the man of God q and H8132
2Ki 9:13 *They* q took their cloaks and spread them H4554
2Ch 29:36 people, because it was done **so q**. H928+7328
2Ch 35:13 pans and **served** them q to all the H8132
Job 8:12 they wither **more q than** grass. H4200+7156
Ps 22:19 You are my strength; **come q** to help me. H2590
Ps 31: 2 ear to me, come q to my rescue; be my H4559
Ps 38:22 **Come q** to help me, my Lord and my H2590
Ps 40:13 save me, LORD; **come q**, LORD, to help me H2590
Ps 69:17 servant; answer me q, for I am in trouble. H4554
Ps 70: 1 to save me; **come q**, LORD, to help H2590
Ps 70: 5 poor and needy; **come q** to me, O God. H2590
Ps 71:12 my God; **come q**, God, to help me H2590
Ps 79: 8 may your mercy come q to meet us, for we H4554
Ps 81:14 **how q** I would subdue their H3869+5071
Ps 90:10 sorrow, for they q pass, and we fly H2673
Ps 102: 2 your ear to me; when I call, answer me q. H4554
Ps 118:12 they were consumed as q as burning thorns; NDT
Ps 141: 1 **come q** to me; hear me when I call H2590
Ps 143: 7 Answer me q, LORD; my spirit fails. Do not H4554
Ecc 4:12 cord of three strands is not q broken. H928+4559
Ecc 7: 9 Do not be q provoked in your spirit, for H987
Ecc 8:11 sentence for a crime is not q carried out, H4559
Isa 58: 8 your healing will q appear; then your H4559
Jer 9:18 *Let them* **come** q and wail over us till our H4554
Jer 48:16 at hand; her calamity *will* **come q**. H4554+4394
Jer 49:30 "Flee q away! Stay in deep caves, you H4394
Joel 3:11 Come q, all you nations from every side H6429
Zep 1:14 LORD is near—near and **coming q**. H4554+4394
Mt 5:25 "Settle matters q with your adversary who G5444
Mt 13: 5 It sprang up q, because the soil was G2311
Mt 13:21 because of the word, they q fall away. G2317
Mt 21:20 "How did the fig tree wither **so q**?" they G4202
Mt 28: 7 Then go q and tell his disciples: 'He has G5444
Mk 1:28 News about him spread q over the whole G2317
Mk 4: 5 It sprang up q, because the soil was G2317
Mk 4:17 because of the word, they q fall away. G2317
Lk 14:21 'Go out q into the streets and alleys of the G5441
Lk 16: 6 your bill, sit down q, and make it four G5441
Lk 18: 8 see that they get justice, and q. G1877+5443
Jn 11:29 heard this, she got up q and went to him. G5444
Jn 11:31 noticed how q she got up and went out G5441
Jn 13:27 "What you are about to do, do q. G5441
Gal 1: 6 that you are so q deserting the one who G5441
2Ti 4: 9 Do your best to come to me q, G5441

QUIET (33) [QUIETED, QUIETLY, QUIETNESS]
Jdg 18:19 answered him, "*Be* q! Don't say a word. H3087
2Sa 13:20 been with you? *Be* q for now, my sister; he H3087
2Ki 2: 3 I know," Elisha replied, "so *be* q." H3120
2Ki 2: 5 I know," he replied, "so *be* q." H3120
1Ch 4:40 the land was spacious, peaceful and q. H8929
1Ch 22: 9 grant Israel peace and q during his reign. H9201
Ne 5: 8 *They kept* q, because they could find H3087
Est 7: 4 *I would have kept* q, because no H3087
Job 6:24 and I *will be* q; show me where H3087
Ps 23: 2 pastures, he leads me beside q waters, H4957
Ps 76: 8 the land feared and *was* q— H9200
Pr 17: 1 a dry crust with **peace and q** than a house H8932
Ecc 9:17 The q words of the wise are more to be H5739
Isa 18: 4 "*I will remain* q and will look on from my H9200
Isa 42:14 *I have been* q and held myself back. H3087
Isa 62: 1 Jerusalem's sake *I will* not *remain* q H9200
Am 5:13 the prudent **keep** q in such times, H1957
Mt 20:31 rebuked them and told them to *be* q, G4995
Mk 1:25 "*Be* q!" said Jesus sternly. "Come out of G5821
Mk 4:39 the wind and said to the waves, "Q! G4995
Mk 6:31 by yourselves to a q place and get some G2245
Mk 9:34 But they *kept* q because on the way they G4995
Mk 10:48 Many rebuked him and told him to *be* q G4995
Lk 4:35 "*Be* q!" Jesus said sternly. "Come out of G5821
Lk 18:39 way rebuked him and told him to *be* q, G4967
Lk 19:40 he replied, "if they *keep* q, the stones will G4995
Ac 12:17 his hand for them *to be* q and described G4967
Ac 22: 2 to them in Aramaic, they became very q. G2484
1Co 14:28 the speaker *should keep* q in the church G4967
1Th 4:11 to make it your ambition to **lead a q life**: G2483
1Ti 2: 2 may live peaceful and q lives in all G2485
1Ti 2:12 authority over a man; she must be q. G2484
1Pe 3: 4 unfading beauty of a gentle and q spirit, G2485

QUIETED (2) [QUIET]
Ps 131: 2 But I have calmed and **q** myself, I am like H1957
Ac 19:35 The city clerk **q** the crowd and said *G2948*

QUIETLY (7) [QUIET]
Jdg 4:21 and went **q** to him while he H928+2021+4319
Ru 3: 7 Ruth approached **q** H928+2021+4319
Ps 35:20 against *those who* **live q** *in* the land. H8091
La 3:26 it is good to wait **q** for the salvation of the H1876
Eze 24:17 Groan **q**; do not mourn for the dead. H1957
Mt 1:19 disgrace, he had in mind to divorce her **q**. *G3277*
Ac 16:37 And now do they want to get rid of us **q** *G3277*

QUIETNESS (4) [QUIET]
Job 3:26 I have no peace, no **q**; I have no rest, but H9200
Isa 30:15 salvation, in **q** and trust is your strength H9200
Isa 32:17 its effect *will be* **q** and confidence forever. H9200
1Ti 2:11 should learn in **q** and full submission. *G2484*

QUIRINIUS (1)
Lk 2: 2 took place while **Q** was governor of Syria *G3256*

QUITE (7)
2Sa 15:11 as guests and went **q innocently**, H4200+9448
Jn 4:18 What you have just said is *q* **true**." AIT
Ac 17: 4 Greeks and **q** a few prominent women. *G4024*s
Ro 15:15 I have written you *q* **boldly** on some points to AIT
1Co 16:12 He was **q** unwilling to go now, but he will *G4122*
1Th 3: 3 For you **know** *q well* that we are destined AIT
Heb 13:22 fact I have written to you **q briefly**. *G1328+1099*

QUIVER (6) [QUIVERED, QUIVERS]
Ge 27: 3 equipment—your **q** and bow—and go out H9437
Job 39:23 The **q** rattles against its side, along with H880
Ps 127: 5 Blessed is the man whose **q** is full of them H880
Isa 22: 6 Elam takes up the **q**, with her charioteers H880
Isa 49: 2 polished arrow and concealed me in his **q**. H880
La 3:13 He pierced my heart with arrows from his **q**. H880

QUIVERED (1) [QUIVER]
Hab 3:16 pounded, my lips **q** at the sound; decay H7509

QUIVERS (1) [QUIVER]
Jer 5:16 Their **q** are like an open grave; all of them H880

QUOTA (3) [QUOTAS]
Ex 5: 8 of bricks as before; don't reduce the **q**. NDT
Ex 5:14 you met your **q** *of* bricks yesterday or H2976
Ex 5:18 you must produce your **full q** *of* bricks." H9420

QUOTAS (1) [QUOTA]
1Ki 4:28 proper place their **q** of barley and H3869+5477

QUOTE (4) [QUOTED, QUOTES, QUOTING]
Eze 12:23 and *they will* no longer **q** it in Israel. H5439
Eze 16:44 proverbs *will* **q** *this* **proverb** about you: H5439
Eze 18: 3 you *will* no longer **q** this proverb in Israel. H5439
Lk 4:23 "Surely *you will* **q** this proverb to me: *G3306*

QUOTED (1) [QUOTE]
Heb 4: 7 as in the passage **already q**: *G4625*

QUOTES (1) [QUOTE]
Eze 16:44 'Everyone who **q proverbs** will quote this H5439

QUOTING (1) [QUOTE]
Eze 18: 2 do you people mean *by* **q** this proverb H5439

R

RAAMAH (5)
Ge 10: 7 Havilah, Sabtah, **R** and Sabteka. The sons H8311
Ge 10: 7 The sons of **R**: Sheba and Dedan. H8311
1Ch 1: 9 Havilah, Sabta, **R** and Sabteka. The sons H8309
1Ch 1: 9 The sons of **R**: Sheba and Dedan. H8309
Eze 27:22 of Sheba and **R** traded with you; H8311

RAAMIAH (1)
Ne 7: 7 Nehemiah, Azariah, **R**, Nahamani H8313

RAAMSES (KJV) RAMESES

RAB-MAG (KJV) HIGH OFFICIAL

RAB-SARIS (KJV) CHIEF OFFICER

RAB-SHAKEH (KJV) (FIELD) COMMANDER

RABBAH (15)
Dt 3:11 It is still in **R** *of* the Ammonites.) H8051
Jos 13:25 Ammonite country as far as Aroer, near **R**; H8051
Jos 15:60 and **R**—two towns and their H8051
2Sa 11: 1 the Ammonites and besieged **R**. H8051
2Sa 12:26 fought against **R** *of* the Ammonites and H8051
2Sa 12:27 have fought against **R** and taken its water H8051
2Sa 12:29 mustered the entire army and went to **R**, H8051
2Sa 17:27 son of Nahash from **R** *of* the Ammonites, H8051
1Ch 20: 1 went to **R** and besieged it, H8051
1Ch 20: 1 Joab attacked **R** and left it in ruins. H8051
Jer 49: 2 the battle cry against **R** *of* the Ammonites; H8051
Jer 49: 3 you inhabitants of **R**! Put on sackcloth H8051
Eze 21:20 to come against **R** *of* the Ammonites and H8051
Eze 25: 5 I will turn **R** into a pasture for camels and H8051
Am 1:14 fire to the walls of **R** that will consume her H8051

RABBI (16) [RABBONI]
Mt 23: 7 to be called '**R**' by others. *G4806*
Mt 23: 8 "But you are not to be called '**R**,' for you *G4806*
Mt 26:25 said, "Surely you don't mean me, **R**?" *G4806*
Mt 26:49 once to Jesus, Judas said, "Greetings, **R**!" *G4806*
Mk 9: 5 Peter said to Jesus, "**R**, it is good for us to *G4806*
Mk 10:51 The blind man said, "**R**, I want to see." *G4808*
Mk 11:21 remembered and said to Jesus, "**R**, look! *G4806*
Mk 14:45 to Jesus, Judas said, "**R**!" and kissed him. *G4806*
Jn 1:38 They said, "**R**" (which means "Teacher") *G4806*
Jn 1:49 declared, "**R**, you are the Son of *G4806*
Jn 3: 2 at night and said, "**R**, we know that you *G4806*
Jn 3:26 said to him, "**R**, that man who was *G4806*
Jn 4:31 disciples urged him, "**R**, eat something." *G4806*
Jn 6:25 they asked him, "**R**, when did you get *G4806*
Jn 9: 2 asked him, "**R**, who sinned, this man *G4806*
Jn 11: 8 "But **R**," they said, "a short while ago the *G4806*

RABBIM See BATH RABBIM

RABBIT (2)
Lev 11: 6 The **r**, though it chews the cud, does not H817
Dt 14: 7 may not eat the camel, the **r** or the hyrax. H817

RABBITH (1)
Jos 19:20 **R**, Kishion, Ebez, H8056

RABBLE (2)
Nu 11: 4 The **r** with them began to crave other food H671
Eze 23:42 desert along with men from the **r**, H8044+132

RABBONI (1) [RABBI]
Jn 20:16 toward him and cried out in Aramaic, "**R**!" *G4808*

RABSHAKEH (KJV) (FIELD) COMMANDER

RACA (1)
Mt 5:22 a brother or sister, '**R**,' is answerable to *G4819*

RACAL (NIV84) RAKAL

RACE (15) [RACED]
Ge 6: 5 wickedness of the **human r** had become on H132
Ge 6: 7 of the earth the **human r** I have created— H132
Ezr 9: 2 have mingled the holy **r** with the peoples H2446
Job 28:28 And he said to the **human r**, "The fear of H132
Ps 12: 1 have vanished from the **human r**. H1201+132
Ps 12: 8 is vile is honored by the **human r**. H1201+132
Ecc 3:10 God has laid on the **human r**. H1201+132
Ecc 9:11 The **r** is not to the swift or the battle to the H5296
Ac 20:24 aim is to finish the **r** and complete the *G1536*
Ro 9: 3 people, those **of my own r**, *G5150+2848+4922*
1Co 9:24 not know that in a **r** all the runners run, *G5084*
Gal 2: 2 and *had* not *been* **running** *my* **r** in vain. *G5556*
Gal 5: 7 *You were* **running** a good **r**. Who cut in on *G5556*
2Ti 4: 7 I have finished the **r**, I have kept the faith. *G1536*
Heb 12: 1 with perseverance the **r** marked out for us, *G74*

RACED (1) [RACE]
Jer 12: 5 "If *you have* **r** with men on foot and they H8132

RACHAB (KJV) RAHAB

RACHEL (42) [RACHEL'S]
Ge 29: 6 comes his daughter **R** with the sheep." H8162
Ge 29: 9 with them, **R** came with her father's sheep H8162
Ge 29:10 When Jacob saw **R** daughter of his uncle H8162
Ge 29:11 Then Jacob kissed **R** and began to weep H8162
Ge 29:12 He had told **R** that he was a relative of her H8162
Ge 29:16 the name of the younger was **R**. H8162
Ge 29:17 **R** had a lovely figure and was H8162
Ge 29:18 Jacob was in love with **R** and said, "I'll H8162
Ge 29:18 in return for your younger daughter **R**." H8162
Ge 29:20 So Jacob served seven years to get **R**, but H8162
Ge 29:25 I served you for **R**, didn't I? Why have H8162
Ge 29:28 gave him his daughter **R** to be his wife. H8162
Ge 29:29 Bilhah to his daughter **R** as her attendant. H8162
Ge 29:30 Jacob made love to **R** also, and his love H8162
Ge 29:30 his love for **R** was greater than his H8162
Ge 29:31 her to conceive, but **R** remained childless. H8162
Ge 30: 1 When **R** saw that she was not bearing H8162
Ge 30: 6 Then **R** said, "God has vindicated me; he H8162
Ge 30: 8 Then **R** said, "I have had a great struggle H8162
Ge 30:14 **R** said to Leah, "Please give me some of H8162
Ge 30:15 **R** said, "he can sleep with you tonight in H8162
Ge 30:22 Then God remembered **R**; he listened to H8162
Ge 30:25 After **R** gave birth to Joseph, Jacob said to H8162
Ge 31: 4 Jacob sent word to **R** and Leah to come H8162
Ge 31:14 Then **R** and Leah replied, "Do we still H8162
Ge 31:19 **R** stole her father's household gods. H8162
Ge 31:32 did not know that **R** had stolen the gods. H8162
Ge 31:34 Now **R** had taken the household gods and H8162
Ge 31:35 **R** said to her father, "Don't be angry, my NDT
Ge 33: 1 **R** and the two female servants. H8162
Ge 33: 2 and **R** and Joseph in the rear. H8162
Ge 33: 7 Last of all came Joseph and **R**, and they H8162
Ge 35:16 **R** began to give birth and had great H8162
Ge 35:19 So **R** died and was buried on the way to H8162
Ge 35:24 The sons of **R**: Joseph and Benjamin. H8162
Ge 46:19 The sons of Jacob's wife **R**: Joseph and H8162
Ge 46:22 were the sons of **R** who were born to H8162
Ge 46:25 Laban had given to his daughter **R**— H8162
Ge 48: 7 to my sorrow **R** died in the land of Canaan H8162
Ru 4:11 is coming into your home like **R** and Leah, H8162
Jer 31:15 **R** weeping for her children and refusing to H8162
Mt 2:18 **R** weeping for her children and refusing to *G4830*

RACHEL'S (5) [RACHEL]
Ge 30: 7 **R** servant Bilhah conceived again and H8162
Ge 31:33 out of Leah's tent, he entered **R** tent. H8162
Ge 35:20 to this day that pillar marks **R** tomb. H8162
Ge 35:25 The sons of **R** servant Bilhah: Dan and H8162
1Sa 10: 2 you will meet two men near **R** tomb, at H8162

RACKED (2)
Isa 21: 3 At this my body *is* **r with** pain, pangs seize H4848
La 4: 9 die of famine; **r with hunger**, they waste H1991

RADDAI (1)
1Ch 2:14 the fourth Nethanel, the fifth **R**, H8099

RADIANCE (4) [RADIANT]
Job 31:26 the sun in *its* **r** or the moon moving H2145
Eze 1:28 on a rainy day, so was the **r** around him. H5586
Eze 10: 4 court was full of the **r** *of* the glory of the H5586
Heb 1: 3 The Son is the **r** of God's glory and the *G575*

RADIANT (11) [RADIANCE]
Ex 34:29 aware that his face *was* **r** because he had H7966
Ex 34:30 saw Moses, his face *was* **r**, and they were H7966
Ex 34:35 they saw that his face *was* **r**. Then Moses H7966
Ps 19: 8 The commands of the LORD are **r**, giving H1338
Ps 34: 5 Those who look to him *are* **r**; their faces H5642
Ps 76: 4 You *are* **r with light**, more majestic than H239
Ps 132:18 his head *will be* adorned with a **r** crown." H7437
SS 5:10 My beloved is **r** and ruddy, outstanding H7456
Isa 60: 5 Then you will look and *be* **r**, your heart H5642
Eze 43: 2 and the land *was* **r** with his glory. H239
Eph 5:27 to present her to himself as a **r** church *G1902*

RAFTERS (2)
Ecc 10:18 laziness, the **r** sag; because of idle H5248
SS 1:17 of our house are cedars; our **r** are firs. H8112

RAFTS (2)
1Ki 5: 9 I will float them as **r** by sea to the place H1827
2Ch 2:16 will float them as **r** by sea down to Joppa. H8343

RAGE (28) [ENRAGED, OUTRAGED, OUTRAGEOUS, OUTRAGEOUSLY, RAGED, RAGES, RAGING]
Dt 19: 6 of blood might pursue him **in a r**, H2801+4222
2Ki 5:12 So he turned and went off in a **r**. H2779
2Ki 19:27 come and go and *how* you **r** against me. H8074
2Ki 19:28 Because you **r** against me and because H8074
2Ch 25:10 Judah and left for home in a **great r**. H3034+678
2Ch 28: 9 slaughtered them in a **r** that reaches to H2408
Est 5: 9 he was filled with **r** against Mordecai. H2779
Est 7: 7 The king got up in a **r**, left his wine and H2779
Job 15:13 that you vent your **r** against God and pour H8120
Ps 7: 6 rise up against the **r** *of* my enemies. H6301
Pr 19:12 A king's **r** is like the roar of a lion, but his H2408
Pr 29:11 Fools give full vent to their **r**, but the wise H8120
Isa 17:12 Woe to the many nations that **r**—they H2162
Isa 17:12 that rage—*they* **r** like the raging sea! H2159
Isa 37:28 come and go and *how* you **r** against me. H8074
Isa 37:29 Because you **r** against me and because H8074
Isa 41:11 "All who **r** against you will surely be H3013
Jer 51:55 Waves of enemies *will* **r** like great waters H2159
Da 3:13 Furious with **r**, Nebuchadnezzar A10654
Da 8: 6 the canal and charged at it in great **r**. H2779
Da 11:11 will march out *in a* **r** and fight against H5352
Da 11:44 will set out in a great **r** to destroy and H2779
Hab 3: 8 Did you **r** against the sea when you rode H6301
Ac 4:25 " 'Why *do* the nations **r** and the peoples *G5865*
2Co 12:20 discord, jealousy, **fits of r**, selfish ambition *G2596*
Gal 5:20 discord, jealousy, **fits of r**, selfish ambition *G2596*
Eph 4:31 rid of all bitterness, **r** and anger, brawling *G2596*
Col 3: 8 **r**, malice, slander, and filthy *G2596*

RAGED (5) [RAGE]
1Ki 22:35 All day long the battle **r**, and the king was H6590
2Ch 18:34 All day long the battle **r**, and the king of H6590
Isa 45:24 All who *have* **r** against him will come to H3013
Jer 44: 6 *it* **r** against the towns of Judah and the H1277
Am 1:11 because his anger **r** continually and his H3271

RAGES (3) [RAGE]
Ps 50: 3 and around him a **tempest r**. H8548+4394
Pr 19: 3 yet their heart **r** against the LORD. H2406
Pr 29: 9 the fool **r** and scoffs, and there H8074

RAGING (9) [RAGE]
2Ch 26:19 While he *was* **r** at the priests in their H2406
Job 40:23 A **r** river does not alarm it; it is secure H6943
Ps 124: 5 the **r** waters would have swept us away. H2327
Isa 17:12 that rage—they rage like the **r** sea! H2159
Isa 30:30 coming down with **r** anger and consuming H2408
Jnh 1:15 him overboard, and the **r** sea grew calm. H2408
Lk 8:24 rebuked the wind and the **r** waters; *G3114*
Ac 27:20 and the storm **continued r**, *G4024+3900+2130*
Heb 10:27 of judgment and of **r** fire that will *G2419*

RAGS (6)
Pr 23:21 and drowsiness clothes them in **r**. H7974
Isa 32:11 clothes and **wrap** yourselves **in r**. H2520+6584

Isa 64: 6 all our righteous acts are like filthy **r** H955
Jer 38:11 He took *some* old **r** and worn-out clothes H6080
Jer 38:12 "Put these old **r** and worn-out clothes H6080
1Co 4:11 thirsty, *we are* **in r**, we are brutally *G1217*

RAHAB (14)

Jos 2: 1 of a prostitute named **R** and stayed there. H8147
Jos 2: 3 the king of Jericho sent this message to **R**: H8147
Jos 6:17 Only **R** the prostitute and all who are with H8147
Jos 6:23 the spying went in and brought out **R**, H8147
Jos 6:25 But Joshua spared **R** the prostitute, with H8147
Job 9:13 even the cohorts of **R** cowered at his feet. H8105
Job 26:12 the sea; by his wisdom he cut **R** to pieces. H8105
Ps 87: 4 "I will record **R** and Babylon among those H8105
Ps 89:10 You crushed **R** like one of the slain; with H8105
Isa 30: 7 Therefore I call her **R** the Do-Nothing. H8105
Isa 51: 9 Was it not you who cut **R** to pieces, who H8105
Mt 1: 5 whose mother was **R**, Boaz the father of *G4829*
Heb 11:31 By faith the prostitute **R**, because she *G4805*
Jas 2:25 was not even **R** the prostitute considered *G4805*

RAHAM (2)

1Ch 2:44 Shema was the father of **R**, and Raham H8165
1Ch 2:44 of Raham, and **R** the father of Jorkeam. NDT

RAHEL (KJV) RACHEL

RAID (1) [RAIDED, RAIDERS, RAIDING]

2Sa 3:22 Joab returned from a **r** and brought with H1522

RAIDED (7) [RAID]

1Sa 27: 8 his men went up and **r** the Geshurites, H7320
1Sa 30: 1 Now the Amalekites *had* **r** the Negev and H7320
1Sa 30:14 We **r** the Negev of the Kerethites, some H7320
1Ch 14: 9 had come and **r** the Valley of Rephaim; H7320
1Ch 14:13 Once more the Philistines **r** the valley; H7320
2Ch 25:13 take part in the war **r** towns belonging to H7320
2Ch 28:18 while the Philistines *had* **r** towns in the H7320

RAIDERS (8) [RAID]

Ge 49:19 "Gad will be attacked by a **band of r**, but H1522
Jdg 2:14 into the hands of **r** who plundered them. H9115
Jdg 2:16 saved them out of the hands of these **r**. H9115
2Ki 5: 2 Now **bands of r** from Aram had gone out H1522
2Ki 13:20 Now Moabite **r** used to enter the country H1522
2Ki 13:21 suddenly they saw a **band of r**; so they H1522
2Ki 24: 2 Moabite and Ammonite **r** against him to H1522
2Ch 22: 1 his place, since the **r**, who came with the H1522

RAIDING (13) [RAID]

1Sa 13:17 **R parties** went out from the Philistine H8845
1Sa 14:15 those in the outposts and **r parties** H8845
1Sa 23:27 The Philistines *are* **r** the land." H7320
1Sa 27:10 Achish asked, "Where *did you* **go r** today?" H7320
1Sa 30: 8 of the LORD, "Shall I pursue this **r party**? H1522
1Sa 30:15 "Can you lead me down to this **r party**?" H1522
1Sa 30:23 our hands the **r party** that came against H1522
2Sa 4: 2 two men who were leaders of **r bands**. H1522
2Ki 6:23 from Aram stopped **r** Israel's territory. H995+928
1Ch 12:18 made them leaders of his **r bands**. H1522
1Ch 12:21 They helped David against **r bands**, for all H1522
Job 1:17 formed three **r parties** and swept down on H8031
Mt 11:12 violent people *have been* **r** it. *G773*

RAIL (1)

Ps 102: 8 *those who* **r** *against* me use my name as H2147

RAIMENT (KJV) CLOAK, CLOTH, CLOTHES, CLOTHING, DRESS, GARMENT, GARMENTS

RAIN (89) [RAINBOW, RAINED, RAINING, RAINS, RAINSTORM, RAINY]

Ge 2: 5 the LORD God *had* not **sent r** on the earth H4763
Ge 7: 4 days from now I *will* **send r** on the earth H4763
Ge 7:12 And **r** fell on the earth forty days and forty H1773
Ge 8: 2 the **r** had stopped falling from the sky. H1773
Ex 9:33 the **r** no longer poured down on the H4764
Ex 9:34 saw that the **r** and hail and thunder H4764
Ex 16: 4 "I *will* **r down** bread from heaven for you. H4763
Lev 26: 4 I will send you **r** in its season, and the H1773
Dt 11:11 valleys that drinks **r** *from* heaven. H4764
Dt 11:14 then I will send **r** *on* your land in its H4764
Dt 11:17 so that it will not **r** and the ground will H4764
Dt 28:12 to send **r** *on* your land in season and to H4764
Dt 28:24 The LORD will turn the **r** *of* your country H4764
Dt 32: 2 teaching fall like **r** and my words descend H4764
Dt 32: 2 like **abundant r** on tender plants. H8053
1Sa 12:17 call on the LORD to send thunder and **r**. H4764
1Sa 12:18 same day the LORD sent thunder and **r**. H4764
2Sa 1:21 may you have neither dew nor **r**, may no H4764
2Sa 21:10 the harvest till the **r** poured down from the H4784
2Sa 22:12 around him—the dark **r** clouds of the sky. H4784
2Sa 23: 4 the brightness after **r** that brings grass H4764
1Ki 8:35 up and there is no **r** because your people H4764
1Ki 8:36 send **r** on the land you gave your H4764
1Ki 17: 1 be neither dew nor **r** in the next few years H4764
1Ki 17: 7 because there had been no **r** in the land. H1773
1Ki 17:14 until the day the LORD sends **r** on the land. H1773
1Ki 18: 1 to Ahab, and I will send **r** on the land." H4764
1Ki 18:41 for there is the sound of a heavy **r**. H1773
1Ki 18:44 go down before the **r** stops you. H1773
1Ki 18:45 a heavy **r** started falling and Ahab rode H1773
2Ki 3:17 You will see neither wind nor **r**, yet this H1773
2Ch 6:26 up and there is no **r** because your people H4764
2Ch 6:27 send **r** on the land you gave your H4764
2Ch 7:13 I shut up the heavens so that there is no **r**, H4764
Ezr 10: 9 by the occasion and because of the **r**. H1773
Job 5:10 He provides **r** for the earth; he sends H4764
Job 20:23 against him and **r down** his blows on him. H4763
Job 28:26 made a decree for the **r** and a path for the H4764
Job 29:23 drank in my words as the **spring r**. H4919
Job 36:27 of water, which distill as **r** to the streams; H4764
Job 37: 6 and to the **r** shower, 'Be a mighty H4764
Job 38:25 Who cuts a channel for the **torrents of r** H8852
Job 38:28 Does the **r** have a father? Who fathers the H4764
Ps 11: 6 On the wicked *he will* **r** fiery coals and H4763
Ps 18:11 around him—the dark **r** clouds of the sky. H4784
Ps 68: 8 the heavens **poured down r**, before God, H5752
Ps 72: 6 May he be like **r** falling on a mown field H4764
Ps 105:32 He turned their **r** into hail, with lightning H1773
Ps 135: 7 lightning with the **r** and brings out the H4764
Ps 147: 8 the earth with **r** and makes grass grow on H4764
Pr 16:15 his favor is like a **r** cloud **in spring**. H4919
Pr 25:14 wind without **r** is one who boasts of H1773
Pr 25:23 that brings *unexpected* **r** is a sly tongue H1773
Pr 26: 1 Like snow in summer or **r** in harvest, honor H4764
Pr 28: 3 is like a driving **r** that leaves no crops. H4764
Ecc 11: 3 are full of water, they pour **r** on the earth. H1773
Ecc 12: 2 and the clouds return after the **r**; H1773
Isa 4: 6 hiding place from the storm and **r**. H4764
Isa 5: 6 command the clouds not *to* **r** on it." H4763+4764
Isa 28: 2 like a **driving r** and a flooding H2443+4784
Isa 30:23 will also send you **r** *for* the seed you sow H4764
Isa 44:14 planted a pine, and the **r** made it grow. H1773
Isa 45: 8 "*You* heavens above, **r down** my H8319
Isa 55:10 As the **r** and the snow come down from H1773
Jer 10:13 lightning with the **r** and brings out the H4764
Jer 14: 4 cracked because there is no **r** in the land; H1773
Jer 14:22 *Do* any of the worthless idols of the nations **bring r** H1772
Jer 51:16 lightning with the **r** and brings out the H4764
Eze 13:11 **R** will come in torrents, and I will send H1773
Eze 13:13 torrents of **r** will fall with destructive H1773
Eze 38:22 I will pour down torrents of **r**, hailstones H1773
Am 4: 7 "I also withheld **r** from you when the H1773
Am 4: 7 *I* **sent r** on one town, but withheld it from H4763
Am 4: 7 One field **had r**; another had none and H4763
Zec 10: 1 Ask the LORD for **r** in the springtime; it is H4764
Zec 10: 1 He gives showers of **r** to all people, and H1773
Zec 14:17 the LORD Almighty, they will have no **r**. H1773
Zec 14:18 not go up and take part, they will have no **r**. NDT
Mt 5:45 and **sends r** on the righteous and the *G1101*
Mt 7:25 The **r** came down, the streams rose, and *G3836*
Mt 7:27 The **r** came down, the streams rose, and *G1104*
Lk 12:54 you say, 'It's going to **r**,' and it does. *G3915*
Ac 14:17 by giving you **r** from heaven and crops *G5624*
Heb 6: 7 Land that drinks in the **r** often falling on it *G5624*
Jas 5:17 He prayed earnestly that *it would* not **r** *G1101*
Jas 5:17 and *it did* not **r** on the land for three and *G1101*
Jas 5:18 the heavens gave **r**, and the earth *G5624*
Jude 12 They are clouds **without r**, blown along by *G536*
Rev 11: 6 so that *it will* not **r** during the *G5624+1101*

RAINBOW (6) [RAIN]

Ge 9:13 I have set my **r** in the clouds, and it will be H8008
Ge 9:14 the earth and the **r** appears in the clouds, H8008
Ge 9:16 Whenever the **r** appears in the clouds, H8008
Eze 1:28 the appearance of a **r** in the clouds on a H8008
Rev 4: 3 A **r** that shone like an emerald encircled *G2692*
Rev 10: 1 in a cloud, with a **r** above his head; his *G2692*

RAINED (6) [RAIN]

Ge 19:24 Then the LORD **r down** burning sulfur on H4763
Ex 9:23 So the LORD **r** hail on the land of Egypt H4763
Ps 78:24 *he* **r down** manna for the people to eat H4763
Ps 78:27 *He* **r** meat **down** on them like dust, birds H4763
Eze 22:24 not been cleansed or **r** on in the day of H1772
Lk 17:29 fire and sulfur **r down** from heaven and *G1101*

RAINING (1) [RAIN]

Ac 28: 2 us all because it was **r** and cold. *G5624*

RAINS (11) [RAIN]

Dt 11:14 both autumn and **spring r**, so that you H4919
[Dt 11:14 both **autumn** and spring **r**, so that you H3453]
Job 24: 8 drenched by mountain **r** and hug the rocks H2443
Ps 84: 6 the **autumn r** also cover it with pools. H4620
SS 2:11 winter is past; the **r** are over and gone. H1773
Jer 3: 3 withheld, and no **spring r** have fallen. H4919
Jer 5:24 who gives autumn and spring **r** in season H1773
Hos 6: 3 he will come to us like the **winter r**, like H1773
Hos 6: 3 like the **spring r** that water the earth." H4919
Joel 2:23 has given you the **autumn r** because he is H4620
Joel 2:23 both autumn and **spring r**, as before. H4919
[Joel 2:23 both **autumn** and spring **r**, as before. H4620]
Jas 5: 7 waiting for the **autumn** and spring **r**. *G4611*
[Jas 5: 7 waiting for the autumn and **spring r**. *G4069*]

RAINSTORM (1) [RAIN]

Pr 27:15 is like the dripping of a leaky roof in a **r**; H6039

RAINY (2) [RAIN]

Ezr 10:13 many people here and it is the **r** season; H1773
Eze 1:28 of a rainbow in the clouds on a **r** day, H1773

RAISE (65) [RISE]

Ge 4:20 of those who live in tents and **r** livestock. NDT
Ge 38: 8 a brother-in-law *to* **r up** offspring for your H7756
Ex 14:16 **R** your staff and stretch out your hand over H8123
Ex 24:11 But God *did* not **r** his hand against these H8938
Dt 18:15 The LORD your God *will* **r up** for you a H7756
Dt 18:18 *I will* **r up** for them a prophet like you from H7756
Jos 6:10 give a war cry, *do* not **r** your voices, do not H9048
Jdg 8:28 the Israelites and *did* not **r** its head again. H5951
1Sa 2:35 *I will* **r up** for myself a faithful priest, who H7756
1Sa 18:17 himself, "I *will* not **r** a hand against him. H2118
1Sa 22:17 were unwilling to **r** a hand to strike the H8938
2Sa 7:12 *I will* **r up** your offspring to succeed you H7756
1Ki 14:14 "The LORD *will* **r up** for himself a king over H7756
1Ki 20:25 You *must* also **r** an army like the one you H4948
2Ki 4:28 "Didn't I tell you, 'Don't **r** my **hopes**'?" H8922
1Ch 17:11 *I will* **r up** your offspring to succeed you H7756
Job 38:34 "*Can you* **r** your voice to the clouds and H8123
Ps 41:10 LORD; **r** me **up**, that I may repay H7756
Pr 8: 1 *Does* not understanding **r** her voice H5989
Pr 8: 4 I call out; I **r** my voice to all mankind. NDT
Isa 8: 9 **R the war cry**, *you* nations, and be H8131
Isa 10:15 *Does* the ax **r itself** above the person who H6995
Isa 10:26 *he will* **r** his staff over the waters H5951
Isa 11:12 *He will* **r** a banner for the nations and H5951
Isa 13: 2 **R** a banner on a bare hilltop, shout to H5951
Isa 14:13 *I will* **r** my throne above the stars of God H8123
Isa 24:14 They **r** their voices, they shout for joy; from H5951
Isa 42: 2 cry out, or **r** his voice in the streets. H5951
Isa 42:11 *Let* the wilderness and its towns **r** their H5951
Isa 42:13 a shout *he will* **r the battle cry** and will H7658
Isa 45:13 I *will* **r up** Cyrus in my righteousness: I will H6424
Isa 58: 1 not hold back. **R** your voice like a trumpet H8123
Isa 58:12 ancient ruins and *will* **r up** the age-old H7756
Isa 62:10 **R** a banner for the nations H8123
Jer 4: 6 **R** the signal to go to Zion! Flee for safety H5951
Jer 6: 1 **R** the signal over Beth Hakkerem H5951
Jer 23: 5 "when *I will* **r up** for David a righteous H7756
Jer 30: 9 their king, whom *I will* **r up** for them. H7756
Eze 26: 8 up to your walls and **r** his shields against H7756
Eze 27:30 *They will* **r** their voice and cry bitterly over H9048
Da 11:11 of the North, *who will* **r** a large army, but H6641
Hos 5: 8 **R the battle cry** in Beth Aven; lead on H8131
Mic 5: 5 *We will* **r** against them seven shepherds H7756
Zec 1:21 Judah so that no one *could* **r** their head, H5951
Zec 2: 9 I *will* surely **r** my hand against them so H5677
Zec 11:16 For I *am going to* **r up** a shepherd over the H7756
Mt 3: 9 these stones God can **r up** children for *G1586*
Mt 10: 8 Heal the sick, **r** the dead, cleanse those *G1586*
Mt 22:24 marry the widow and **r up** offspring for him. *G482*
Mk 12:19 marry the widow and **r up** offspring for his *G1985*
Lk 3: 8 these stones God can **r up** children for *G1586*
Lk 20:28 marry the widow and **r up** offspring for his *G1985*
Jn 2:19 temple, and *I will* **r** it **again** in three days." *G1586*
Jn 2:20 you *are going to* **r** it in three days? *G1586*
Jn 6:39 given me, but **r** them **up** at the last day. *G482*
Jn 6:40 and I *will* **r** them **up** at the last day. *G482*
Jn 6:44 and I *will* **r** them **up** at the last day. *G482*
Jn 6:54 and I *will* **r** them **up** at the last day. *G482*
Ac 3:22 Lord your God *will* **r up** for you a prophet *G482*
Ac 7:37 'God *will* **r up** for you a prophet like me *G482*
1Co 6:14 Lord from the dead, and *he will* **r** us also. *G1995*
1Co 15:15 But *he did* not **r** him if in fact the dead are *G1586*
2Co 4:14 from the dead *will* also **r** us with Jesus *G1586*
Heb 11:19 reasoned that God could even **r** the dead, *G1586*
Jas 5:15 sick person well; the Lord *will* **r** them **up**. *G1586*

RAISED (125) [RISE]

Ge 14:22 "*With* **r** hand *I have* **sworn an oath** to the H8123
Ex 7:20 *He* **r** his staff in the presence of Pharaoh H8123
Ex 9:16 But *I have* **r** you **up** for this very purpose H6641
Nu 14: 1 the community **r** their voices H5951+2256+5989
Nu 20:11 Then Moses **r** his arm and struck the rock H8123
Jos 5: 7 So *he* **r up** their sons in their place, and H7756
Jos 8:29 And *they* **r** a large pile of rocks over it H7756
Jdg 2:16 Then the LORD **r up** judges, who saved H7756
Jdg 2:18 Whenever the LORD **r up** a judge for them H7756
Jdg 3: 9 to the LORD, he **r up** for them a deliverer H7756
1Sa 4: 5 Israel **r** such **a** great **shout** that the H8131+9558
1Sa 14:27 *He* **r** his hand to his mouth, and his eyes H8740
2Sa 12: 3 *He* **r** it, and it grew up with him and his H2649
2Sa 23: 8 he **r** his spear against eight hundred men H6424
2Sa 23:18 He **r** his spear against three hundred men, H6424
1Ki 11:14 Then the LORD **r up** against Solomon an H7756
1Ki 11:23 And God **r up** against Solomon another H7756
1Ki 14: 7 '*I* **r** you **up** from among the people and H8123
2Ki 3: 4 Now Mesha king of Moab **r sheep**, and he H5924
2Ki 19:22 Against whom *have you* **r** your voice and H8123
1Ch 11:11 he **r** his spear against three hundred men H6424
1Ch 11:20 He **r** his spear against three hundred men, H6424
2Ch 5:13 the singers **r** their voices in praise to the H8123
2Ch 13:15 the men of Judah **r the battle cry**. H8131
Ne 5: 1 men and their wives **r** a great outcry H2118
Job 31:21 if *I have* **r** my hand against the fatherless H5677
Ps 60: 4 *you have* **r** a banner to be unfurled H5989
Ps 80:15 planted, the son *you have* **r up** for yourself. H599
Ps 80:17 the son of man *you have* **r up** for yourself. H599
Ps 89:19 *I have* **r up** a young man from among the H8123
Ps 148:14 And *he has* **r up** for his people a horn, the H8123
Isa 5:25 his hand *is* **r** and he strikes them down. H5742
Isa 18: 3 when a banner *is* **r** on the mountains H5951
Isa 23:13 creatures; *they* **r up** their siege towers H7756

Isa 37:23 Against whom *have you* **r** your voice and H8123
Isa 40: 4 Every valley *shall* **be r up**, every mountain H5951
Isa 49:11 into roads, and my highways *will be* **r up**. H8123
Isa 52:13 *he will be* **r** and lifted up and highly H8123
Jer 12: 6 they *have* **r** a loud **cry** against you. H7924
Jer 29:15 "The LORD *has* **r up** prophets for us in H7756
La 2: 7 *they have* **r** a shout in the house of the H5989
Eze 2: 2 Spirit came into me and **r** me to my feet, H6641
Eze 3:24 Spirit came into me and **r** me to my feet. H6641
Eze 41: 8 that the temple had a **r** *base* all around it, H1470
Da 4:34 **r** my eyes toward heaven A10475
Da 7: 5 *It* **was r up** on one of its sides, and it had A10624
Da 8:18 Then he touched me and **r** me to my feet. H6641
Am 2:11 "*I* also **r up** prophets from among your H7756
Zec 5: 7 Then the cover of lead **was r**, and there in H5951
Zec 14:10 But Jerusalem *will be* **r up high** from the H8027
Mt 11: 5 the dead *are* **r**, and the good news *G1586*
Mt 16:21 be killed and on the third day *be* **r to life**. *G1586*
Mt 17: 9 the Son of Man *has been* **r** from the dead." *G1586*
Mt 17:23 on the third day *he will be* **r to life**." *G1586*
Mt 20:19 On the third day *he will be* **r to life**!" *G1586*
Mt 27:52 holy people who had died *were* **r to life**. *G1586*
Mt 27:64 the people *that he has been* **r** from the *G1586*
Mk 6:14 the Baptist *has been* **r** from the dead, *G1586*
Mk 6:16 I beheaded, *has been* **r from the dead**!" *G1586*
Lk 1:69 *He has* **r up** a horn of salvation for us in *G1586*
Lk 7:22 the dead *are* **r**, and the good news *G1586*
Lk 9: 7 that John *had been* **r** from the dead, *G1586*
Lk 9:22 be killed and on the third day *be* **r to life**." *G1586*
Lk 24: 7 crucified and on the third day *be* **r again**. *G482*
Jn 2:22 After *he was* **r** from the dead, his disciples *G1586*
Jn 12: 1 whom Jesus *had* **r** from the dead. *G1586*
Jn 12: 9 Lazarus, whom *he had* **r** from the dead. *G1586*
Jn 12:17 from the tomb and **r** him from the dead *G1586*
Jn 21:14 his disciples *after he was* **r** from the dead. *G1586*
Ac 2:14 **r** his voice and addressed the crowd: *G2048*
Ac 2:24 But God **r** him **from the dead**, freeing him *G482*
Ac 2:32 God *has* **r** this Jesus **to life**, and we are all *G482*
Ac 3:15 but God **r** him from the dead. *G1586*
Ac 3:26 *When* God **r up** his servant, he sent him first *G482*
Ac 4:10 crucified but whom God **r** from the dead, *G1586*
Ac 4:24 *they* **r** their voices together *in prayer* to God. *G149*
Ac 5:30 of our ancestors **r** Jesus **from the dead**— *G1586*
Ac 9:21 he the *man who* **r havoc** in Jerusalem *G4514*
Ac 10:40 God **r** him **from the dead** on the third *G1586*
Ac 13:30 But God **r** him from the dead, *G1586*
Ac 13:34 God **r** him from the dead so that he will *G482*
Ac 13:37 whom God **r from the dead** did not see *G1586*
Ac 22:22 Then *they* **r** their voices and shouted, "Rid *G2048*
Ro 4:24 who believe in him *who* **r** Jesus our Lord *G1586*
Ro 4:25 our sins and *was* **r to life** for our *G1586*
Ro 6: 4 just as Christ *was* **r** from the dead through *G1586*
Ro 6: 9 we know that *since* Christ *was* **r** from the *G1586*
Ro 7: 4 another, to him *who was* **r** from the dead *G1586*
Ro 8:11 the Spirit of him *who* **r** Jesus from the *G1586*
Ro 8:11 he *who* **r** Christ from the dead will also *G1586*
Ro 8:34 more than that, *who was* **r to life**—is at the *G1586*
Ro 9:17 "*I* **r** you **up** for this very purpose, that I *G1995*
Ro 10: 9 your heart that God **r** him from the dead, *G1586*
1Co 6:14 By his power God **r** the Lord **from the dead** *G1586*
1Co 15: 4 that *he was* **r** on the third day according to *G1586*
1Co 15:12 that Christ *has been* **r** from the dead, *G1586*
1Co 15:13 the dead, then not even Christ *has been* **r**. *G1586*
1Co 15:14 And if Christ *has* not *been* **r**, our preaching *G1586*
1Co 15:15 about God that *he* **r** Christ **from the dead**. *G1586*
1Co 15:15 not raise him if in fact the dead *are* not **r**. *G1586*
1Co 15:16 For if the dead *are* not **r**, then Christ has *G1586*
1Co 15:16 then Christ *has* not *been* **r** either. *G1586*
1Co 15:17 And if Christ *has* not *been* **r**, your faith is *G1586*
1Co 15:20 But Christ *has* indeed *been* **r** from the *G1586*
1Co 15:29 If the dead *are* not **r** at all, why are *G1586*
1Co 15:32 If the dead *are* not **r**, "Let us eat and drink, *G1586*
1Co 15:35 someone will ask, "How *are* the dead **r**? *G1586*
1Co 15:42 is sown is perishable, *it is* **r** imperishable; *G1586*
1Co 15:43 sown in dishonor, *it is* **r** in glory; it is sown *G1586*
1Co 15:43 it is sown in weakness, *it is* **r** in power; *G1586*
1Co 15:44 a natural body, *it is* **r** a spiritual body. *G1586*
1Co 15:52 the dead *will be* **r** imperishable *G1586*
2Co 4:14 *one who* **r** the Lord Jesus **from the dead** *G1586*
2Co 5:15 him who died for them and *was* **r again**. *G1586*
Gal 1: 1 the Father, who **r** him from the dead— *G1586*
Eph 1:20 he exerted *when he* **r** Christ from the dead *G1586*
Eph 2: 6 And God **r** us **up with** Christ and seated us *G5283*
Col 2:12 in which *you were* also **r with** him through *G5283*
Col 2:12 working of God, who **r** him from the dead. *G1586*
Col 3: 1 *you have been* **r with** Christ, set your *G5283*
1Th 1:10 from heaven, whom *he* **r** from the dead *G1586*
2Ti 2: 8 Remember Jesus Christ, **r** from the dead *G1586*
Heb 11:35 received back their dead, **r to life again**. *G414*
1Pe 1:21 who **r** him from the dead and glorified *G1586*
Rev 10: 5 the sea and on the land **r** his right hand to *G149*

RAISES (9) [RISE]

1Sa 2: 6 he brings down to the grave and **r up**. H6590
1Sa 2: 8 *He* **r** the poor from the dust and lifts the H7756
Ps 113: 7 *He* **r** the poor from the dust and lifts the H7756
Pr 1:20 *she* **r** her voice in the public square H5989
Isa 19:16 that the LORD Almighty **r** against them. H5677
Da 2:21 he deposes kings and **r up** others. A10624
Jn 5:21 For just as the Father **r** the dead and gives *G1586*
Ac 26: 8 consider it incredible that God **r** the dead? *G1586*
2Co 1: 9 on ourselves but on God, who **r** the dead. *G1586*

RAISIN (3) [RAISINS]

1Ch 12:40 of flour, fig cakes, **r cakes**, wine, olive oil, H7540
Isa 16: 7 grieve for the **r cakes** *of* Kir Hareseth. H862
Hos 3: 1 to other gods and love the sacred **r** cakes." H6694

RAISING (10) [RISE]

Jdg 21: 2 **r** their voices and weeping bitterly. H5951
1Ki 15: 4 in Jerusalem by **r up** a son to succeed H7756
Jer 4:16 **r** a war cry against the cities of Judah. H5989
Am 7:10 "Amos *is* **r a conspiracy** against you in the H8003
Hab 1: 6 I *am* **r up** the Babylonians, that ruthless H7756
Ac 10:29 sent for, I came **without r any objection**. *G395*
Ac 13:33 fulfilled for us, their children, *by* **r up** Jesus. *G482*
Ac 17:31 of this to everyone *by* **r** him from the dead." *G482*
1Co 10:25 market without **r questions** of conscience, *G373*
1Co 10:27 you without **r questions** of conscience. *G373*

RAISINS (7) [RAISIN]

Nu 6: 3 juice or eat **grapes or r**. H6694+4300+2256+3313
1Sa 25:18 a hundred **cakes of r** and two hundred H7540
1Sa 30:12 a cake of pressed figs and two **cakes of r**. H7540
2Sa 6:19 of dates and a **cake of r** to each person in H862
2Sa 16: 1 a hundred **cakes of r**, a hundred H7540
1Ch 16: 3 of dates and a **cake of r** to each Israelite H862
SS 2: 5 Strengthen me with **r**, refresh me with H862

RAKAL (1)

1Sa 30:29 **R**; to those in the towns of the H8218

RAKEM (1)

1Ch 7:16 Sheresh, and his sons were Ulam and **R**. H8388

RAKKATH (1)

Jos 19:35 Ziddim, Zer, Hammath, **R**, Kinnereth, H8395

RAKKON (1)

Jos 19:46 Me Jarkon and **R**, with the area facing H8378

RALLIED (4) [RALLY]

Ge 48: 2 Israel **r** *his* **strength** and sat up on the bed. H2616
Ex 32:26 And all the Levites **r** to him. H665
2Sa 2:25 the men of Benjamin **r** behind Abner. H7695
Ac 5:36 about four hundred men **r** to him. *G4679*

RALLY (1) [RALLIED]

Isa 11:10 peoples; the nations *will* **r** to him, and his H2011

RAM (101) [RAM'S, RAMS, RAMS']

Ge 15: 9 a goat and a **r**, each three years old, H380
Ge 22:13 in a thicket he saw a **r** caught by its horns. H380
Ge 22:13 over and took the **r** and sacrificed it as a H380
Ex 25: 5 **r** skins dyed red and another type of durable H380
Ex 26:14 the tent a covering of **r** skins dyed red, H380
Ex 29:17 Cut the **r** into pieces and wash the internal H380
Ex 29:18 Then burn the entire **r** on the altar. It is a H380
Ex 29:19 "Take the other **r**, and Aaron and his sons H380
Ex 29:22 "Take from this **r** the fat, the fat tail, the fat H380
Ex 29:22 This is the **r** *for* the ordination.) H380
Ex 29:26 the breast of the **r** for Aaron's ordination H380
Ex 29:27 of the ordination **r** that belong to Aaron H380
Ex 29:31 "Take the **r** *for* the ordination and cook the H380
Ex 29:32 eat the meat of the **r** and the bread that is H380
Ex 29:34 the meat of the **ordination r** or any bread H4854
Ex 35: 7 **r** skins dyed red and another type of durable H380
Ex 35:23 **r** skins dyed red or the other durable H380
Ex 36:19 the tent a covering of **r** skins dyed red, H380
Ex 39:34 the covering of **r** skins dyed red and the H380
Lev 5:15 to the LORD as a penalty a **r** from the flock, H380
Lev 5:16 them with the **r** as a guilt offering, H380
Lev 5:18 priest as a guilt offering a **r** from the flock, H380
Lev 6: 6 their guilt offering, a **r** from the flock, one H380
Lev 8:18 then presented the **r** *for* the burnt offering, H380
Lev 8:19 Moses slaughtered the **r** and splashed the NDT
Lev 8:20 He cut the **r** into pieces and burned the H380
Lev 8:21 water and burned the whole **r** on the altar. H380
Lev 8:22 He then presented the other **r**, the ram H380
Lev 8:22 the other ram, the **r** *for* the ordination, and H380
Lev 8:23 Moses slaughtered the **r** and took some of its NDT
Lev 8:29 which was his share of the ordination **r** H380
Lev 9: 2 sin offering and a **r** for your burnt offering H380
Lev 9: 4 an ox and a **r** for a fellowship offering H380
Lev 9:18 the ox and the **r** as the fellowship offering H380
Lev 9:19 But the fat portions of the ox and the **r**—the H380
Lev 16: 3 a sin offering and a **r** for a burnt offering. H380
Lev 16: 5 a sin offering and a **r** for a burnt offering. H380
Lev 19:21 must bring a **r** to the entrance to the tent of H380
Lev 19:22 With the **r** *of* the guilt offering the priest is H380
Nu 5: 8 along with the **r** with which atonement is H380
Nu 6:14 a **r** without defect for a fellowship offering, H380
Nu 6:17 is to sacrifice the **r** as a fellowship H380
Nu 6:19 in their hands a boiled shoulder of the **r**, H380
Nu 7:15 one **r** and one male lamb a year old for a H380
Nu 7:21 one **r** and one male lamb a year old for a H380
Nu 7:27 one **r** and one male lamb a year old for a H380
Nu 7:33 one **r** and one male lamb a year old for a H380
Nu 7:39 one **r** and one male lamb a year old for a H380
Nu 7:45 one **r** and one male lamb a year old for a H380
Nu 7:51 one **r** and one male lamb a year old for a H380
Nu 7:57 one **r** and one male lamb a year old for a H380
Nu 7:63 one **r** and one male lamb a year old for a H380
Nu 7:69 one **r** and one male lamb a year old for a H380
Nu 7:75 one **r** and one male lamb a year old for a H380
Nu 7:81 one **r** and one male lamb a year old for a H380
Nu 15: 6 " 'With a **r** prepare a grain offering of H380
Nu 15:11 Each bull or **r**, each lamb or young goat, is H380
Nu 23: 2 them offered a bull and a **r** on each altar. H380
Nu 23: 4 on each altar I have offered a bull and a **r**." H380
Nu 23:14 offered a bull and a **r** on each altar. H380
Nu 23:30 offered a bull and a **r** on each altar. H380
Nu 28:11 one **r** and seven male lambs a year old H380
Nu 28:12 with oil; with the **r**, a grain offering of H380
Nu 28:14 a hin of wine; with the **r**, a third of a hin; H380
Nu 28:19 one **r** and seven male lambs a year old H380
Nu 28:20 flour mixed with oil; with the **r**, two-tenths; H380
Nu 28:27 one **r** and seven male lambs a year old as H380
Nu 28:28 flour mixed with oil; with the **r**, two-tenths; H380
Nu 29: 2 one **r** and seven male lambs a year old H380
Nu 29: 3 mixed with olive oil; with the **r**, two-tenths; H380
Nu 29: 8 one **r** and seven male lambs a year old H380
Nu 29: 9 flour mixed with oil; with the **r**, two-tenths; H380
Nu 29:36 one **r** and seven male lambs a year old H380
Nu 29:37 With the bull, the **r** and the lambs, offer H380
Ru 4:19 Hezron the father of **R**, Ram the father of H8226
Ru 4:19 of Ram, **R** the father of Amminadab, H8226
1Ch 2: 9 to Hezron were: Jerahmeel, **R** and Caleb. H8226
1Ch 2:10 **R** was the father of Amminadab, and H8226
1Ch 2:25 **R** his firstborn, Bunah, Oren, Ozem and H8226
1Ch 2:27 The sons of **R** the firstborn of Jerahmeel H8226
Ezr 10:19 each presented a **r** *from* the flock as a guilt H380
Job 32: 2 of the family of **R**, became very angry with H8226
Eze 43:23 to offer a young bull and a **r** from the flock, H380
Eze 43:25 provide a young bull and a **r** from the flock, H380
Eze 45:24 each bull and an ephah for each **r**, H380
Eze 46: 4 day is to be six male lambs and a **r**, H380
Eze 46: 5 offering given with the **r** is to be an ephah, H380
Eze 46: 6 six lambs and a **r**, all without defect. H380
Eze 46: 7 one ephah with the **r**, and with the lambs H380
Eze 46:11 an ephah with a **r**, and with the lambs H380
Da 8: 3 there before me was a **r** with two horns, H380
Da 8: 4 I watched the **r** as it charged toward the H380
Da 8: 6 the two-horned **r** I had seen standing H380
Da 8: 7 I saw it attack the **r** furiously, striking the H380
Da 8: 7 striking the **r** and shattering its two horns. H380
Da 8: 7 The **r** was powerless to stand against it; the H380
Da 8: 7 none could rescue the **r** from its power. H380
Da 8:20 The two-horned **r** that you saw represents H380
Mt 1: 3 father of Hezron, Hezron the father of **R**, *G730*
Mt 1: 4 **R** the father of Amminadab, Amminadab *G730*
Lk 3:33 Amminadab, the son *of* **R**, the son of *G730*

RAM'S (3) [RAM]

Ex 19:13 Only when the **r horn** sounds a long blast H3413
Ps 81: 3 Sound the **r horn** at the New Moon, and H8795
Ps 98: 6 with trumpets and the blast of the **r horn**— H8795

RAMAH (34)

Jos 18:25 Gibeon, **R**, Beeroth, H8230
Jos 19: 8 as Baalath Beer (**R** *in* the Negev). H8230
Jos 19:29 turned back toward **R** and went to the H8230
Jos 19:36 Adamah, **R**, Hazor, H8230
Jdg 4: 5 of Deborah between **R** and Bethel in the H8230
Jdg 19:13 to reach Gibeah or **R** and spend the night H8230
1Sa 1:19 then went back to their home at **R**. H8230
1Sa 2:11 Then Elkanah went home to **R**, but the H8230
1Sa 7:17 But he always went back to **R**, where his H8230
1Sa 8: 4 together and came to Samuel at **R**. H8230
1Sa 15:34 Then Samuel left for **R**, but Saul went up H8230
1Sa 16:13 Samuel then went to **R**. H8230
1Sa 19:18 he went to Samuel at **R** and told him all H8230
1Sa 19:19 came to Saul: "David is in Naioth at **R**"; H8230
1Sa 19:22 he himself left for **R** and went to the great H8230
1Sa 19:22 "Over in Naioth at **R**," they said. H8230
1Sa 19:23 So Saul went to Naioth at **R**. But the Spirit H8230
1Sa 20: 1 fled from Naioth at **R** and went to H8230
1Sa 25: 1 they buried him at his home in **R**. H8230
1Sa 28: 3 him and buried him in his own town of **R**. H8230
1Ki 15:17 Judah and fortified **R** to prevent anyone H8230
1Ki 15:21 he stopped building **R** and withdrew to H8230
1Ki 15:22 carried away from **R** the stones and timber H8230
2Ch 16: 1 Judah and fortified **R** to prevent anyone H8230
2Ch 16: 5 stopped building **R** and abandoned his H8230
2Ch 16: 6 carried away from **R** the stones and timber H8230
Ezr 2:26 of **R** and Geba 621 H8230
Ne 7:30 of **R** and Geba 621 H8230
Ne 11:33 in Hazor, **R** and Gittaim, H8230
Isa 10:29 overnight at Geba." **R** trembles; Gibeah of H8230
Jer 31:15 "A voice is heard in **R**, mourning and H8230
Jer 40: 1 the imperial guard had released him at **R**. H8230
Hos 5: 8 the trumpet in Gibeah, the horn in **R**. H8230
Mt 2:18 "A voice is heard in **R**, weeping and great *G4821*

RAMATH LEHI (1) [LEHI]

Jdg 15:17 the place was called **R**. H8257

RAMATH MIZPAH (1) [MIZPAH]

Jos 13:26 from Heshbon to **R** and Betonim, H8256

RAMATHAIM (1)

1Sa 1: 1 There was a certain man from **R**, H8259

RAMATHITE (1) [RAMATH]

1Ch 27:27 Shimei the **R** was in charge of the H8258

RAMESES (5)

Ge 47:11 the district of **R**, as Pharaoh directed. H8314
Ex 1:11 they built Pithom and **R** as store cities H8314

Ex 12:37 Israelites journeyed from **R** to Sukkoth. H8314
Nu 33: 3 set out from **R** on the fifteenth day of H8314
Nu 33: 5 The Israelites left **R** and camped at H8314

RAMIAH (1)
Ezr 10:25 **R**, Izziah, Malkijah, Mijamin, Eleazar H8243

RAMOTH (7) [RAMOTH GILEAD, RAMOTH NEGEV]
Dt 4:43 the Reubenites; **R** in Gilead, for the H8030
Jos 20: 8 of Reuben, **R** in Gilead in the tribe of Gad H8030
Jos 21:38 the tribe of Gad, **R** in Gilead (a city of H8030
2Ki 8:29 had inflicted on him at **R** in his battle with H8230
1Ch 6:73 **R** and Anem, together with their H8030
1Ch 6:80 the tribe of Gad they received **R** in Gilead, H8030
2Ch 22: 6 had inflicted on him at **R** in his battle with H8230

RAMOTH GILEAD (20) [RAMOTH]
1Ki 4:13 Ben-Geber—in **R** (the settlements H8240
1Ki 22: 3 you know that **R** belongs to us H8240
1Ki 22: 4 you go with me to fight against **R**?" H8240
1Ki 22: 6 "Shall I go to war against **R**, or H8240
1Ki 22:12 "Attack **R** and be victorious," H8240
1Ki 22:15 shall we go to war against **R**, or H8240
1Ki 22:20 into attacking **R** and going to his H8240
1Ki 22:29 king of Judah went up to **R**. H8240
2Ki 8:28 against Hazael king of Aram at **R**. H8240
2Ki 9: 1 of olive oil with you and go to **R**. H8240
2Ki 9: 4 So the young prophet went to **R**. H8240
2Ki 9:14 been defending **R** against Hazael H8240
2Ch 18: 2 him and urged him to attack **R**. H8240
2Ch 18: 3 "Will you go with me against **R**?" H8240
2Ch 18: 5 "Shall we go to war against **R**, or H8240
2Ch 18:11 "Attack **R** and be victorious," H8240
2Ch 18:14 shall we go to war against **R**, or H8240
2Ch 18:19 into attacking **R** and going to his H8240
2Ch 18:28 king of Judah went up to **R**. H8240
2Ch 22: 5 against Hazael king of Aram at **R**. H8240

RAMOTH NEGEV (1) [RAMOTH]
1Sa 30:27 who were in Bethel, **R** and Jattir; H8241

RAMP (7) [RAMPS]
2Sa 20:15 They built a **siege r** up to the city, and it H6149
2Ki 19:32 it with shield or build a **siege r** against it. H6149
Job 19:12 they build a **siege r** against me and H2006
Isa 37:33 it with shield or build a **siege r** against it. H6149
Eze 4: 2 against it, build a **r** up to it, set up camps H6149
Eze 21:22 to build a **r** and to erect siege works. H6149
Eze 26: 8 build a **r** up to your walls and raise his H6149

RAMPART (1) [RAMPARTS]
Ps 91: 4 his faithfulness will be your shield and **r**. H6089

RAMPARTS (4) [RAMPART]
Ps 48:13 consider well her **r**, view her citadels, that H2658
Isa 26: 1 God makes salvation its walls and **r**. H2658
La 2: 8 He made **r** and walls lament; together H2658
Hab 2: 1 at my watch and station myself on the **r**; H5189

RAMPS (7) [RAMP]
Job 30:12 they build their **siege r** against me. H784+369
Jer 6: 6 trees and build **siege r** against Jerusalem. H6149
Jer 32:24 "See how the **siege r** are built up to take H6149
Jer 33: 4 be used against the **siege r** and the sword H6149
Eze 17:17 when **r** are built and siege works erected H6149
Da 11:15 build up **siege r** and will capture H6149
Hab 1:10 by building **earthen r** they capture them. H6760

RAMS (69) [RAM]
Ge 31:38 have I eaten **r** *from* your flocks. H380
Ge 32:14 two hundred ewes and twenty **r**, H380
Ex 29: 1 Take a young bull and two **r** without defect. H380
Ex 29: 3 them along with the bull and the two **r**. H380
Ex 29:15 "Take one of the **r**, and Aaron and his sons H380
Lev 8: 2 the two **r** and the basket containing bread H380
Lev 23:18 without defect, one young bull and two **r**. H380
Nu 7:17 two oxen, five **r**, five male goats and H380
Nu 7:23 two oxen, five **r**, five male goats and H380
Nu 7:29 two oxen, five **r**, five male goats and H380
Nu 7:35 two oxen, five **r**, five male goats and H380
Nu 7:41 two oxen, five **r**, five male goats and H380
Nu 7:47 two oxen, five **r**, five male goats and H380
Nu 7:53 two oxen, five **r**, five male goats and H380
Nu 7:59 two oxen, five **r**, five male goats and H380
Nu 7:65 two oxen, five **r**, five male goats and H380
Nu 7:71 two oxen, five **r**, five male goats and H380
Nu 7:77 two oxen, five **r**, five male goats and H380
Nu 7:83 two oxen, five **r**, five male goats and H380
Nu 7:87 twelve **r** and twelve male lambs a year old H380
Nu 7:88 sixty **r**, sixty male goats and H380
Nu 23: 1 prepare seven bulls and seven **r** for me." H380
Nu 23:29 prepare seven bulls and seven **r** for me." H380
Nu 29:13 two **r** and fourteen male lambs a year old H380
Nu 29:14 with oil; with each of the two **r**, two-tenths; H380
Nu 29:17 two **r** and fourteen male lambs a year old H380
Nu 29:18 With the bulls, **r** and lambs, offer their grain H380
Nu 29:20 two **r** and fourteen male lambs a year old H380
Nu 29:21 With the bulls, **r** and lambs, offer their grain H380
Nu 29:23 two **r** and fourteen male lambs a year old H380
Nu 29:24 With the bulls, **r** and lambs, offer their grain H380
Nu 29:26 two **r** and fourteen male lambs a year old H380
Nu 29:27 With the bulls, **r** and lambs, offer their grain H380
Nu 29:29 two **r** and fourteen male lambs a year old H380
Nu 29:30 With the bulls, **r** and lambs, offer their grain H380
Nu 29:32 two **r** and fourteen male lambs a year old H380
Nu 29:33 With the bulls, **r** and lambs, offer their grain H380
Dt 32:14 with choice **r** of Bashan and the finest H380
1Sa 15:22 to heed is better than the fat of **r**. H380
2Ki 3: 4 the wool of a hundred thousand **r**. H380
1Ch 15:26 seven bulls and seven **r** were sacrificed. H380
1Ch 29:21 a thousand **r** and a thousand male lambs H380
2Ch 13: 9 bull and seven **r** may become a priest H380
2Ch 17:11 seven hundred **r** and seven thousand H380
2Ch 29:21 seven bulls, seven **r**, seven male lambs H380
2Ch 29:22 they slaughtered the **r** and splashed their H380
2Ch 29:32 a hundred **r** and two hundred male lambs H380
Ezr 6: 9 young bulls, **r**, male lambs for burnt A10175
Ezr 6:17 two hundred **r**, four hundred male A10175
Ezr 7:17 be sure to buy bulls, **r** and male lambs A10175
Ezr 8:35 all Israel, ninety-six **r**, seventy-seven male H380
Job 42: 8 bulls and seven **r** and go to my servant H380
Ps 66:15 fat animals to you and an offering of **r**; H380
Ps 114: 4 the mountains leaped like **r**, the hills like H380
Ps 114: 6 did you leap like **r**, you hills, like lambs? H380
Isa 1:11 of **r** and the fat of fattened animals H380
Isa 34: 6 lambs and goats, fat from the kidneys of **r**. H380
Isa 60: 7 the **r** *of* Nebaioth will serve you H380
Jer 25:34 you will fall like the best of the **r**. H380
Jer 51:40 lambs to the slaughter, like **r** and goats. H380
Eze 4: 2 against it and put **battering r** around it. H4119
Eze 21:22 where he is to set up **battering r**, to give H4119
Eze 21:22 to set **battering r** against the gates H4119
Eze 26: 9 the blows of his **battering r** against your H7692
Eze 27:21 business with you in lambs, **r** and goats. H380
Eze 34:17 another, and between **r** and goats. H380
Eze 39:18 of the earth as if they were **r** and lambs, H380
Eze 45:23 seven bulls and seven **r** without defect as a H380
Mic 6: 7 the LORD be pleased with thousands of **r**, H380

RAMS' (2) [RAM]
Jos 6: 4 carry trumpets of **r horns** in front of the ark H3413
1Ch 15:28 the sounding of **r horns** and trumpets, H8795

RAN (60) [RUN]
Ge 18: 7 Then he **r** to the herd and selected a H8132
Ge 24:20 **r** back to the well to draw more water H8132
Ge 24:28 The young woman **r** and told her mother's H8132
Ge 29:12 So *she* **r** and told her father. H8132
Ge 33: 4 But Esau **r** to meet Jacob and embraced H8132
Ge 39:12 cloak in her hand and **r** out of the house. H5674
Ge 39:15 cloak beside me and **r** out of the house." H5674
Ge 39:18 cloak beside me and **r** out of the house." H5674
Ex 4: 3 it became a snake, and *he* **r** from it. H5674
Nu 11:27 A young man **r** and told Moses, "Eldad H8132
Nu 16:47 and **r** into the midst of the assembly. H8132
Jos 4:18 to their place and **r** at flood stage as H2143
Jos 7:22 messengers, and *they* **r** to the tent, and H8132
Jos 15: 3 Then *it* **r past** Hezron up to Addar and H6296
Jos 15: 8 Then it **r up** the Valley of Ben Hinnom H6590
Jos 15:10 **r** along the northern slope of Mount H6296
Jos 17: 7 The boundary **r** southward from there to H2143
Jos 18:17 and **r down** *to* the Stone of Bohan son of H3718
Jos 19:11 Going west it **r** *to* Maralah, touched H6590
Jos 19:34 The boundary **r** west *through* Aznoth H8740
Jdg 7:21 all the Midianites **r**, crying out as they fled H8132
Jdg 9:54 So his servant **r** him **through**, and he died. H1991
1Sa 3: 5 And *he* **r** to Eli and said, "Here I am; you H8132
1Sa 4:12 day a Benjamite **r** from the battle line H8132
1Sa 10:23 *They* **r** and brought him out, and as he H8132
1Sa 17:22 **r** *to* the battle lines and asked his brothers H8132
1Sa 17:48 David **r** quickly *toward* the battle line to H8132
1Sa 17:51 David **r** and stood over him. He took hold H8132
1Sa 17:51 their hero was dead, *they* **turned and r**. H5674
1Sa 20:36 *As* the boy **r**, he shot an arrow beyond H8132
2Sa 18:21 bowed down before Joab and **r off**. H8132
2Sa 18:23 Then Ahimaaz **r** by way of the plain and H8132
1Ki 2:39 of Shimei's slaves **r off** to Achish son of H1368
1Ki 18:35 The water **r down** around the altar and H2143
1Ki 18:46 *he* **r** ahead of Ahab all the way to Jezreel. H8132
1Ki 19: 3 Elijah was afraid and **r** for his life. H2143
1Ki 19:20 Elisha then left his oxen and **r** after Elijah H8132
1Ki 22:35 blood from his wound **r** onto the floor of H3668
2Ki 7: 7 the camp as it was and **r** for their lives. H5674
2Ki 9:10 Then he opened the door and **r**. H5674
Jnh 1: 3 But Jonah **r away** from the LORD and H1368
Mt 8:33 Those tending the pigs **r off**, went into the *G5771*
Mt 27:48 one of them **r** and got a sponge. *G5556*
Mt 28: 8 filled with joy, and **r** to tell his disciples. *G5556*
Mk 5: 6 *he* **r** and fell on his knees in front of him. *G5556*
Mk 5:14 tending the pigs **r off** and reported this in *G5771*
Mk 6:33 recognized them and **r** on foot from all *G5340*
Mk 6:55 *They* **r throughout** that whole region and *G4366*
Mk 9:15 with wonder and **r** to greet him. *G4708*
Mk 10:17 a man **r up to** him and fell on his knees *G4708*
Mk 15:36 Someone **r**, filled a sponge with wine *G5556*
Lk 8:34 *they* **r off** and reported this in the town *G5771*
Lk 15:20 compassion for him; *he* **r** to his son, threw *G5556*
Lk 19: 4 So *he* **r ahead** and *G4731+1650+3836+1869*
Lk 24:12 however, got up and **r** to the tomb *G5556*
Ac 8:30 Then Philip **r up to** the chariot and heard *G4708*
Ac 12:14 so overjoyed *she* **r back** without opening *G1661*
Ac 19:16 a beating that *they* **r** out of the house *G1767*
Ac 21:32 soldiers and **r down** to the crowd. *G2963*
Ac 27:41 the ship struck a sandbar and **r aground**. *G2131*

RANDOM (3)
1Ki 22:34 drew his bow **at r** and hit the king H4200+9448
2Ch 18:33 drew his bow **at r** and hit the king H4200+9448
Pr 26:10 archer who wounds **at r** is one who hires a H3972

RANG (2) [RING]
Mt 25: 6 "At midnight the cry **r out**: 'Here's the *G1181*
1Th 1: 8 Lord's message **r out** from you not only *G2010*

RANGE (5) [RANGES]
Nu 27:12 in the Abarim **R** and see the land I NDT
Dt 32:49 up into the Abarim **R** to Mount Nebo in H2215
2Ch 16: 9 the eyes of the LORD **r** throughout the earth H8763
Isa 32:20 **letting** your cattle and donkeys **r free** H8938+8079
Zec 4:10 of the LORD that **r** throughout the earth H8763

RANGES (1) [RANGE]
Job 39: 8 *It* **r** the hills *for* its pasture and searches H9365

RANK (12) [HIGH-RANKING, RANKS]
1Sa 18: 5 Saul **gave** him **a high r in** the army H8492+6584
2Ki 23: 4 the priests **next in r** and the doorkeepers H5467
2Ki 25:18 the priest **next in r** and the three H5467
1Ch 15:18 with them their relatives **next in r** H5467
1Ch 16: 5 and **next** to him **in r** were Zechariah H5467
2Ch 31:12 his brother Shimei was **next in r**. H5467
Est 10: 3 the Jew was **second in r** to King Xerxes, H5467
Pr 22:29 they will not serve before **officials of low r**. H3126
Isa 3: 3 captain of fifty and the **man of r**, H5951+7156
Isa 5:13 *those* **of high r** will die of hunger and the H3883
Jer 52:24 the priest **next in r** and the three H5467
Eze 23:23 chariot officers and **men of high r**, all H7924

RANKS (14) [RANK]
1Sa 17: 8 stood and shouted to the **r** *of* Israel, H5120
2Ki 11: 8 who approaches your **r** is to be put to H8444
2Ki 11:15 her out between the **r** and put to the H8444
1Ch 12:38 men who volunteered to serve in the **r**. H5120
2Ch 23:14 her out between the **r** and put to the H8444
Job 40:19 It **r** first among the works of God, yet its NDT
Pr 30:27 no king, yet they advance together **in r**; H2951
Isa 14:31 and there is not a straggler in its **r**. H4596
Jer 46:21 The mercenaries in her **r** are like fattened H7931
Jer 50:37 chariots and all the foreigners in her **r**! H9348
Joel 2: 8 through defenses without **breaking r**. H1298
Joel 2:20 its **eastern r** will drown in the Dead Sea H7156
Joel 2:20 the Dead Sea and its **western r** in the H6067
Gal 2: 4 believers *had* **infiltrated** our **r** to spy *G4207+4209*

RANSACKED (2)
Ob 6 But how Esau *will* **be r**, his hidden H2924
Zec 14: 2 the houses **r**, and the women raped H9116

RANSOM (15) [RANSOMED]
Ex 30:12 must pay the LORD a **r** *for* his life at the H4111
Nu 35:31 " 'Do not accept a **r** for the life of a H4111
Nu 35:32 " 'Do not accept a **r** *for* anyone who has H4111
Job 6:22 **pay a r** for me from your wealth, H8815
Job 33:24 to the pit; I have found a **r** for them— H4111
Ps 49: 7 of another or give to God a **r** *for* them— H4111
Ps 49: 8 the **r** *for* a life is costly, no payment is ever H7018
Pr 13: 8 A person's riches may **r** their life, but the H4111
Pr 21:18 The wicked become a **r** for the righteous H4111
Isa 43: 3 I give Egypt for your **r**, Cush and Seba in H4111
Isa 47:11 you that you cannot **ward off with a r**; H4105
Mt 20:28 and to give his life *as* a **r** for many." *G3389*
Mk 10:45 and to give his life as a **r** for many." *G3389*
1Ti 2: 6 who gave himself *as* a **r** for all people. *G519*
Heb 9:15 has died as a **r to set** them **free** from the *G667*

RANSOMED (2) [RANSOM]
Lev 19:20 man but *who has* not **been r** or H7009+7009
Lev 27:29 person devoted to destruction *may* **be r**; H7009

RAPE (1) [RAPED, RAPES]
Dt 28:30 another *will* take her and **r** her. H8711

RAPED (6) [RAPE]
Ge 34: 2 he took her and **r** her. H8886+2256+6700
Jdg 19:25 and *they* **r** her and abused her throughout H3359
Jdg 20: 5 *They* **r** my concubine, and she H6700
2Sa 13:14 stronger than she, *he* **r** her. H6700+2256+8886
2Sa 13:32 since the day Amnon **r** his sister Tamar. H6700
Zec 14: 2 the houses ransacked, and the women **r**. H8711

RAPES (2) [RAPE]
Dt 22:25 to be married and **r** her, H2616+2256+8886+6640
Dt 22:28 married and **r** her and H9530+2256+8886+6640

RAPHA (7) [BETH RAPHA]
2Sa 21:16 one of the descendants of **R**, whose H8335
2Sa 21:18 killed Saph, one of the descendants of **R**. H8335
2Sa 21:20 He also was descended from **R**. H8335
2Sa 21:22 These four were descendants of **R** in Gath, H8335
1Ch 8: 2 Nohah the fourth and **R** the fifth. H8325
1Ch 20: 6 He also was descended from **R**. H8325
1Ch 20: 8 These were descendants of **R** in Gath H8325

RAPHAH (1)
1Ch 8:37 father of Binea; **R** was his son, Eleasah H8334

RAPHU (1)
Nu 13: 9 from the tribe of Benjamin, Palti son of **R**; H8336

RAPID (1) [RAPIDLY]
Ezr 5: 8 and *is* **making r progress** under their A10613

RAPIDLY (2) [RAPID]
Ac 6: 7 of disciples in Jerusalem increased **r**, *G5379*
2Th 3: 1 of the Lord *may* **spread r** and be honored, *G5556*

RARE (4) [RARELY]
1Sa 3: 1 In those days the word of the LORD was **r** H3701
Pr 20:15 lips that speak knowledge are a **r** jewel. H3702
Pr 24: 4 rooms are filled with **r** and beautiful H3701
Isa 13:12 pure gold, more **r** than the gold of Ophir. NDT

RARELY (1) [RARE]
Ro 5: 7 **Very r** will anyone die for a righteous *G3660*

RASH (11) [RASHLY]
Lev 13: 2 has a swelling or a **r** or a shiny spot on H6204
Lev 13: 6 shall pronounce them clean; it is only a **r**. H5030
Lev 13: 7 But if the **r** does spread in their skin after H5030
Lev 13: 8 and if the **r** has spread in the skin H5030
Lev 13:39 it is a **harmless r** that has broken out on the H993
Lev 14:56 for a swelling, a **r** or a shiny spot, H6204
Nu 30: 6 her lips utter a **r promise** by which she H4439
Nu 30: 8 her or the **r promise** by which she H4439
Ps 106:33 and **r words came** from Moses' lips. H1051
Ac 19:36 to calm down and not do anything **r**. *G4637*
2Ti 3: 4 treacherous, **r**, conceited, lovers of *G4637*

RASHLY (2) [RASH]
Pr 13: 3 those *who* **speak r** will come to H7316+8557
Pr 20:25 is a trap *to* dedicate something **r** and only H4362

RAT (1) [RATS]
Lev 11:29 the weasel, the **r**, any kind of great H6572

RATE (1)
Lev 25:50 to be **based on the r paid** *to* a H3869+3427

RATHER (77)
Ge 27:12 a curse on myself **r than** a blessing." H2256+4202
Dt 15: 8 **R**, be openhanded and freely lend them H3954
Jdg 6:27 he did it at night **r than** in the daytime. H4946
Jdg 18:19 in Israel as priest **r than** just one man's H196
2Sa 6:21 who chose me **r than** your father or H4946
2Sa 14:14 what God desires; **r**, he devises ways so H2256
2Ki 17:39 **R**, worship the LORD your God; it is he H3954+561
2Ki 20:10 said Hezekiah. "**R**, have it go back H4202+3954
2Ch 17: 4 his commands **r than** the practices H2256+4202
Est 6: 6 that the king *would* **r** honor than me?" H2911
Job 7:15 death, **r than** this body of mine. H4946
Job 32: 2 with Job for justifying himself **r than** God. H4946
Ps 52: 3 You love evil **r than** good, falsehood H4946
Ps 52: 3 falsehood **r than** speaking the truth. H4946
Ps 84:10 *I* **would r be** a doorkeeper in the house of H1047
Pr 8:10 of silver, knowledge **r than** choice gold, H4946
Pr 16:16 than gold, to get insight **r than** silver! H4946
Pr 28:23 the end gain favor **r than** one who has a H4946
Ecc 5: 1 Go near to listen **r than** to offer the H4946
Jer 7:19 Are they not **r** harming themselves, to H2022
Jer 22:10 mourn his loss; **r**, weep bitterly for him NDT
La 3: 2 made me walk in darkness **r than** light; H4202
Eze 16: 5 **R**, you were thrown out into the open field H2256
Eze 18:23 **R**, am I not pleased when they turn from H2022
Eze 33:11 **r** that they turn from their ways and live. H561
Eze 34: 8 cared for themselves **r than** for my flock, H4202
Da 3:28 give up their lives **r than** serve or worship A10379
Hos 6: 6 of God **r than** burnt offerings. H4946
Mt 10: 6 Go **r** to the lost sheep of Israel. *G1254+3437*
Mt 10:28 **R**, be afraid of the One who can *G1254+3437*
Mk 7:15 **R**, it is what comes out of a person that *G247*
Lk 11:28 "Blessed **r** are those who hear the word of *G3528*
Lk 17: 8 Won't he **r** say, 'Prepare my supper, get *G247*
Lk 18:14 you that this man, **r than** the other, went *G4123*
Jn 14:10 **R**, it is the Father, living in me, who is *G1254*
Jn 16: 6 **R**, you are filled with grief because I have *G247*
Ac 5:29 "We must obey God **r** than human beings! *G3437*
Ac 17:25 **R**, he himself gives everyone life and breath NDT
Ro 1:25 served created things **r than** the Creator— *G4123*
Ro 3:20 works of the law; **r**, through the law we *G1142*
Ro 3:31 Not at all! **R**, we uphold the law. *G247*
Ro 6:13 **but r** offer yourselves to God as those who *G247*
Ro 8:15 you live in fear again; **r**, the Spirit you *G247*
Ro 11:11 **R**, because of their transgression, salvation *G247*
Ro 12: 3 **but r** think of yourself with sober judgment *G247*
Ro 13:14 **R**, clothe yourselves with the Lord Jesus *G247*
Ro 15:21 **R**, as it is written: "Those who were not told *G247*
1Co 5: 2 Shouldn't you **r** have gone into mourning *G3437*
1Co 6: 7 Why not **r** be wronged? Why not *G3437*
1Co 6: 7 Why not **r** be cheated? *G3437*
1Co 9:12 up with anything **r than** hinder the *G2671+3590*
1Co 9:15 I would **r** die than allow anyone to *G3437*
1Co 14: 5 tongues, but I would **r** have you prophesy. *G3437*
1Co 14:19 But in the church *I* **would r** speak five *G2527*
2Co 4: 2 **R**, we have renounced secret and shameful *G247*
2Co 5:12 in what is seen **r than** in what is in *G2779+3590*
2Co 6: 4 **R**, as servants of God we commend *G247*
2Co 7:12 **but r** that before God you could see for *G247*
2Co 10: 8 building you up **r than** tearing you *G2779+4024*
Gal 1:12 was I taught it; **r**, I received it by *G247*
Gal 4: 9 you know God—or **r** are known by God *G3437*
Gal 5:13 to indulge the flesh; **r**, serve one another *G247*
Eph 5: 4 which are out of place, but **r** thanksgiving. *G3437*
Eph 5:11 deeds of darkness, but **r** expose them. *G3437*
Php 2: 3 **R**, in humility value others above *G247*
Php 2: 7 **r**, he made himself nothing by taking the *G247*
Col 2: 8 forces of this world **r than** on Christ. *G2779+4024*
1Ti 1: 4 speculations **r** than advancing God's work *G3437*
1Ti 4: 7 old wives' tales; **r**, train yourself to be *G1254*
2Ti 1: 8 **R**, join with me in suffering for the gospel *G247*
2Ti 2: 4 **but r** tries to please his commanding *G2671*
2Ti 3: 4 lovers of pleasure **r** than lovers of God— *G3437*
Titus 1: 8 **R**, he must be hospitable, one who loves *G247*
Heb 11:25 with the people of God **r** than to enjoy the *G3437*
Heb 12:13 lame may not be disabled, but **r** healed. *G3437*
1Pe 3: 4 **R**, it should be that of your inner self, the *G247*
1Pe 4: 2 human desires, **but r** for the will of God. *G247*

RATIFIED (1)
Jos 9:15 the leaders of the assembly **r** it **by oath**. H8678

RATIONED (2)
Eze 4:16 people will eat **r** food in anxiety and H928+5486
Eze 4:16 anxiety and drink **r** water in despair, H928+5374

RATS (5) [RAT]
1Sa 6: 4 "Five gold tumors and five gold **r** H6572
1Sa 6: 5 the tumors and of the **r** that are destroying H6572
1Sa 6:11 containing the gold **r** and the models of H6572
1Sa 6:18 number of the gold **r** was according to the H6572
Isa 66:17 flesh of pigs, **r** and other unclean things H6572

RATTLES (1) [RATTLING]
Job 39:23 The quiver **r** against its side, along with H8261

RATTLING (2) [RATTLES]
Job 41:29 of straw; it laughs at the **r** *of* the lance. H8323
Eze 37: 7 was a noise, a **r sound**, and the bones H8323

RAVAGE (6) [RAVAGED, RAVAGES, RAVAGING]
Ge 41:30 forgotten, and the famine *will* **r** the land. H3983
Jdg 6: 5 their camels; they invaded the land to **r** it. H8845
Ps 80:13 Boars from the forest **r** it, and insects from H4155
Jer 5: 6 a wolf from the desert *will* **r** them, H8720
Jer 5:10 "Go through her vineyards and **r** them, but H8845
Eze 26: 8 *He will* **r** your settlements on the mainland H2222

RAVAGED (3) [RAVAGE]
Isa 6:11 left deserted and the fields ruined and **r**, H9039
Eze 26: 6 on the mainland *will* **be r** by the sword. H2222
Eze 36: 3 Because *they* **r** and crushed you from H9037

RAVAGES (2) [RAVAGE]
Ps 35:17 Rescue me from their **r**, my precious life H8738
Jer 14:18 if I go into the city, I see the **r** *of* famine. H9377

RAVAGING (1) [RAVAGE]
1Ch 21:12 the angel of the LORD **r** every part of Israel. H8845

RAVEN (6) [RAVENS]
Ge 8: 7 sent out a **r**, and it kept flying back H6854
Lev 11:15 any kind of **r**, H6854
Dt 14:14 any kind of **r**, H6854
Job 38:41 provides food for the **r** when its young cry H6854
SS 5:11 his hair is wavy and black as a **r**. H6854
Isa 34:11 the great owl and the **r** will nest there. H6854

RAVENOUS (4)
Ge 49:27 "Benjamin *is* a **r** wolf; in the morning he H3271
Ps 57: 4 I am forced to dwell among **r beasts** H4266
Isa 35: 9 will be there, nor any **r** beast; they will not H7264
Jer 2:30 has devoured your prophets like a **r** lion. H8845

RAVENS (5) [RAVEN]
1Ki 17: 4 I have directed the **r** to supply you with H6854
1Ki 17: 6 The **r** brought him bread and meat in the H6854
Ps 147: 9 cattle and for the young **r** when they call. H6854
Pr 30:17 will be pecked out by the **r** *of* the valley H6854
Lk 12:24 Consider the **r**: They do not sow or reap *G3165*

RAVIN (KJV) PREY, RAVENOUS

RAVINE (10) [RAVINES]
Jos 16: 8 west to the Kanah **R** and ended at the H5707
Jos 17: 9 boundary continued south to the Kanah **R**. H5707
Jos 17: 9 northern side of the **r** and ended at the H5707
Jos 19:11 extended to the **r** near Jokneam. H5707
1Sa 15: 5 of Amalek and set an ambush in the **r**. H5707
1Sa 25:20 came riding her donkey into a mountain **r**, H6260
1Ki 17: 3 turn eastward and hide in the Kerith **R** H5707
1Ki 17: 5 He went to the Kerith **R**, east of the H5707
Isa 15: 7 they carry away over the **R** *of* the Poplars. H5707
Zec 1: 8 standing among the myrtle trees in a **r**. H5185

RAVINES (18) [RAVINE]
Nu 21:14 Zahab in Suphah and the **r**, the Arnon H5707
Nu 21:15 the slopes of the **r** that lead to the H5707
2Sa 23:30 Pirathonite, Hiddai from the **r** *of* Gaash, H5707
1Ch 11:32 Hurai from the **r** *of* Gaash, Abiel the H5707
Job 22:24 your gold of Ophir to the rocks in the **r**, H5707
Ps 104:10 He makes springs pour water into the **r**; it H5707
Isa 7:19 settle in the steep **r** and in the crevices in H5707
Isa 57: 5 your children in the **r** and under the H5707
Isa 57: 6 smooth stones of the **r** are your portion; H5707
Jer 2: 6 through a land of deserts and **r**, a land of H8757
Eze 6: 3 mountains and hills, to the **r** and valleys: H692
Eze 31:12 branches lay broken in all the **r** *of* the land. H692
Eze 32: 6 the **r** will be filled with your flesh. H692
Eze 34:13 in the **r** and in all the settlements in the H692
Eze 35: 8 hills and in your valleys and in all your **r**. H692
Eze 36: 4 hills, to the **r** and valleys, to the H692
Eze 36: 6 mountains and hills, to the **r** and valleys: H692
Joel 3:18 all the **r** *of* Judah will run with water. H692

RAVING (1)
Jn 10:20 "He is demon-possessed and **r mad**. *G3419*

RAVISHED (1)
Jer 3: 2 any place where *you have* not **been r**? H8711

RAW (9)
Ex 12: 9 Do not eat the meat **r** or boiled in water H5529
Lev 13:10 and if there is **r** flesh in the H4695+2645
Lev 13:14 But whenever **r** flesh appears on them H2645
Lev 13:15 When the priest sees the **r** flesh, he shall H2645
Lev 13:15 The **r** flesh is unclean; they have a H2645
Lev 13:16 If the **r** flesh changes and turns white, they H2645
Lev 13:24 spot appears in the **r flesh** *of* the burn, H4695
1Sa 2:15 accept boiled meat from you, but only **r**." H2645
Eze 29:18 rubbed bare and every shoulder **made r**. H5307

RAWBONED (1)
Ge 49:14 "Issachar is a **r** donkey lying down among H1752

RAY (1) [RAYS]
Am 5:20 pitch-dark, without a **r of brightness**? H5586

RAYS (4) [RAY]
Job 3: 9 in vain and not see the **first r** *of* dawn, H6757
Job 41:18 of light; its eyes are like the **r** *of* dawn. H6757
Hab 3: 4 like the sunrise; **r** flashed from his hand H7967
Mal 4: 2 will rise with healing in its **r**. H4053

RAZOR (7)
Nu 6: 5 no **r** may be used on their head. H9509
Jdg 13: 5 to be touched by a **r** because the boy is to H4623
Jdg 16:17 "No **r** has ever been used on my head," H4623
1Sa 1:11 no **r** will ever be used on his head." H4623
Ps 52: 2 plots destruction; it is like a sharpened **r**. H9509
Isa 7:20 the Lord will use a **r** hired from beyond H9509
Eze 5: 1 use it as a barber's **r** to shave your head H9509

REACH (36) [REACHED, REACHES, REACHING]
Ge 3:22 *He must* not be allowed *to* **r out** his hand H8938
Ge 19:22 because I cannot do anything until you **r** it." H995
Ex 4: 4 "**R out** your hand and take it by the tail." H8938
Dt 30:11 not too difficult for you or **beyond** your **r**. H8158
Jos 3: 8 'When you **r** the edge of the H995+6330
Jos 10:19 rear and don't let them **r** their cities, H995+448
Jos 10:20 few survivors *managed to* **r** their H995+448
Jdg 19:13 *let's try to* **r** Gibeah or Ramah and spend H7928
1Sa 2:31 so that no *one* in it *will* **r** old age, H2118
1Sa 2:32 no *one* in your family line *will* ever **r** old H2118
1Sa 10: 3 from there until *you* **r** the great tree H995+6330
1Sa 14: 4 intended to cross **to r** the Philistine H6584
2Sa 5: 8 *will have to* use the water shaft *to* **r** those H5595
2Sa 15: 5 Absalom *would* **r out** his hand, take H8938
Job 3:22 rejoice when *they* **r** the grave? H5162
Job 29:19 My roots *will* **r** to the water, and the dew H7337
Job 37:23 Almighty is beyond *our* **r** and exalted in H5162
Ps 32: 6 rising of the mighty waters *will* not **r** them. H5595
Ps 119:48 *I* **r out** for your commands, which I H5951+4090
Ps 144: 7 **R down** your hand from on high; deliver H8938
Isa 11:11 that day the Lord *will* **r out** his hand a H3578S
Isa 49: 6 that my salvation *may* **r** to the ends of the H2118
Isa 59: 9 from us, and righteousness *does* not **r** us. H5952
Isa 65:20 the *one who* **fails** to **r** a hundred will be H2627
Jer 15: 6 So *I will* **r out** and destroy you; I am H5742+3338
Eze 31:14 well-watered *are ever to* **r** such a height; H6641
Am 9: 9 and not a pebble *will* **r** the ground. H5877
Mic 5: 4 his greatness will **r to** the ends of the H6330
Lk 13:32 on the third day *I will* **r** *my* **goal.** *G5457*
Jn 20:27 **R out** your hand and put it into my side *G5770*
Ac 17:27 him and perhaps **r out** for him and find *G6027*
Ac 20:16 he was in a hurry *to* **r** Jerusalem, *G1181+1650*
Ac 27:12 hoping *to* **r** Phoenix and winter there. *G2918*
Eph 1:10 effect when the times **r** their fulfillment— NDT
Eph 4:13 until we all **r** unity in the faith and in the *G2918*
Rev 12:14 half a time, out of the serpent's **r**. *G4725*

REACHED (102) [REACH]
Ge 8: 9 *He* **r out** his hand and took the dove and H8938
Ge 10:19 borders of Canaan **r** from Sidon toward H2118
Ge 15:16 the Amorites has not yet **r** its full measure." NDT
Ge 18:21 is as bad as the outcry that *has* **r** me. H995+448
Ge 19:10 the men inside **r out** and pulled Lot H8938+3338
Ge 19:23 By the time Lot **r** Zoar, the sun had H995+2025
Ge 22: 9 When *they* **r** the place God had told H995+448
Ge 22:10 Then he **r out** his hand and took the knife H8938
Ge 28:11 When *he* **r** a certain place, he stopped H7003
Ge 37:18 before *he* **r** them, they plotted H7928
Ge 45:16 When the news **r** Pharaoh's palace that H9048
Ge 46: 1 and when *he* **r** Beersheba, he H995+2025
Ge 48:14 But Israel **r out** his right hand and put it on H8938
Ge 50:10 When *they* **r** the threshing floor of H995+6330
Ex 3: 9 now the cry of the Israelites *has* **r** me, H995+448
Ex 4: 4 So Moses **r out** and took hold of the snake H8938
Ex 16:35 manna until they **r** the border of H995+448
Nu 13:23 When *they* **r** the Valley of Eshkol H995+6330
Nu 21:23 When *he* **r** Jahaz, he fought with H995+2025

Dt 1:19 and so *we* **r** Kadesh Barnea. H995+6330
Dt 1:20 "*You have* **r** the hill country of the H995+6330
Dt 1:31 way you went until you **r** this place." H995+6330
Dt 12: 9 since *you have* not yet **r** the resting H995+448
Dt 29: 7 When *you* **r** this place, Sihon king of H995+448
Jos 3:15 who carried the ark **r** the Jordan and H995+6330
Jos 15:11 along to Mount Baalah and **r** Jabneel. H3655
Jos 17:10 of Manasseh **r** the Mediterranean Sea H2118
Jdg 3:21 Ehud **r** *with* his left hand, drew the sword H8938
Jdg 5:26 Her hand **r** for the tent peg, her right hand H8938
Jdg 7:19 men with him **r** the edge of the camp H995+928
Jdg 16:29 Then Samson **r** **toward** the two central H4369
Jdg 19:29 When *he* **r** home, he took a knife and H995+448
1Sa 9: 5 When they **r** the district of Zuph, Saul H995+928
1Sa 9:16 on my people, for their cry *has* **r** me." H995+448
1Sa 14:27 so *he* **r** **out** the end of the staff that was in H8938
1Sa 15:13 When Samuel **r** him, Saul said, "The H995+448
1Sa 17:20 *He* **r** the camp as the army was going out H995
1Sa 30: 1 David and his men **r** Ziklag on the third day H995
1Sa 30: 3 When David and his men **r** Ziklag H995+448
1Sa 30:26 When David **r** Ziklag, he sent some of H995+448
2Sa 6: 6 Uzzah **r** **out** and took hold of the ark of H8938
2Sa 19:11 throughout Israel *has* **r** the king at his H995+448
2Sa 22:17 "*He* **r** **down** from on high and took hold of H8938
1Ki 2:28 When the news **r** Joab, who had H995+6330
1Ki 19: 8 forty days and forty nights until he **r** Horeb, NDT
2Ki 4:27 When *she* **r** the man of God at the H995+448
2Ki 4:32 When Elisha **r** the house, there was H995+2025
2Ki 6: 7 Then the man **r** **out** his hand and took it H8938
2Ki 7: 5 When *they* **r** the edge of the camp H995+6330
2Ki 7: 8 who had leprosy **r** the edge of the H995+6330
2Ki 9:18 "The messenger *has* **r** them, but he H995+6330
2Ki 9:20 reported, "*He has* **r** them, but he H995+6330
2Ki 11:16 they seized her as *she* **r** the place where H995
2Ki 19:23 *I have* **r** its remotest parts, the finest of its H995
2Ki 19:28 because your insolence *has* **r** my ears, H6590
1Ch 13: 9 Uzzah **r** **out** his hand to steady the ark H8938
2Ch 23:15 seized her as *she* **r** the entrance of H995+448
2Ch 29:17 day of the month *they* **r** the portico of the H995
2Ch 30:27 their prayer **r** heaven, his holy H995+4200
Ezr 9: 6 and our guilt *has* **r** to the heavens. H1540+6330
Ne 4: 6 the wall till all of it **r** half its **height**, H8003+6330
Job 28:22 "Only a rumor of it *has* **r** our ears." H9048+928
Ps 18:16 *He* **r** **down** from on high and took hold of H8938
Ps 80:11 Its branches **r** as far as the Sea, its shoots H8938
Isa 10:14 so my hand **r** for the wealth of the nations NDT
Isa 16: 8 *which once* **r** Jazer and spread toward the H5595
Isa 37:24 *I have* **r** its remotest heights, the finest of H995
Isa 37:29 because your insolence *has* **r** my ears, H6590
Jer 1: 9 Then the LORD **r** **out** his hand and touched H8938
Jer 37:13 But *when* he **r** the Benjamin Gate H2118+928
Jer 48:32 as far as the sea; *they* **r** as far as Jazer. H5595
Eze 10: 7 one of the cherubim **r** **out** his hand to the H8938
Eze 21:25 whose time of punishment has **r** its climax, NDT
Eze 21:29 whose time of punishment has **r** its climax. NDT
Eze 35: 5 the time their punishment **r** its climax, NDT
Eze 40:49 It *was* **r** by a flight of stairs, and H6590+448
Da 6:24 And before *they* **r** the floor of the den A10413
Da 8:10 It grew until it **r** the host of the heavens, and NDT
Jnh 3: 6 Jonah's warning **r** the king of Nineveh, H5595
Mic 1: 9 *It has* **r** the very gate of my people, even H5595
Mt 8: 3 Jesus **r** **out** his hand and touched the man *G1753*
Mt 14:31 Immediately Jesus **r** **out** his hand and *G1753*
Mt 26:51 companions **r** for his sword, *G1753+3836+5931*
Mk 1:41 *He* **r** **out** his hand and touched the man *G1753*
Mk 11:13 *When he* **r** it, he found nothing *G2262+2093*
Lk 1:44 sound of your greeting **r** my ears, *G1181+1650*
Lk 5:13 Jesus **r** **out** his hand and touched the man *G1753*
Lk 19: 5 When Jesus **r** the spot, he looked *G2262+2093*
Jn 6:21 the boat **r** the shore where they *G1181+2093*
Jn 11:32 When Mary **r** the place where Jesus was *G2262*
Jn 20: 4 outran Peter and **r** the tomb first. *G2262+1650*
Jn 20: 8 disciple, who *had* **r** the tomb first *G2262+1650*
Ac 8:40 all the towns until he **r** Caesarea. *G2262+1650*
Ac 11:22 News of this **r** the church in *G201+1650*
Ac 16: 4 the decisions **r** by the apostles and *G3212*
Ac 21: 8 *we* **r** Caesarea and stayed at the *G2262+1650*
Ac 21:31 news **r** the commander of the Roman *G326*
Ac 21:35 When Paul **r** the steps, the violence *G1181+2093*
Ac 27:44 In this way everyone **r** land safely. *G1181+2093*
Ac 28:13 on the following day *we* **r** Puteoli. *G2262+1650*
1Co 14:36 Or are you the only people *it has* **r**? *G2918*
Jas 5: 4 of the harvesters *have* **r** the ears of the *G1656*

REACHES (16) [REACH]

Ge 11: 4 with a tower that **r** to the heavens, so that H8031
Dt 25:11 and *she* **r** **out** and seizes him by his H8938+3338
2Ki 10: 2 Now as soon as this letter **r** you, H995+448
2Ch 28: 9 them in a rage *that* **r** to heaven. H5595
Job 20: 6 the godless person **r** to the heavens and H6590
Job 41:26 The sword *that* **r** it has no effect, nor does H5952
Ps 36: 5 **r** **to** the heavens, your faithfulness to H928
Ps 48:10 your praise **r** **to** the ends of the earth H6584
Ps 57:10 heavens; your faithfulness **r** **to** the skies. H6330
Ps 71:19 **r** **to** the heavens, you who have H6330
Ps 108: 4 heavens; your faithfulness **r** **to** the skies. H6330
Isa 10:14 As *one* **r** into a nest, so my hand reached H5162
Isa 15: 8 of Moab; their wailing **r** as far as Eglaim NDT
Jer 51: 9 her judgment **r** to the skies, it rises H5595
Da 4:22 greatness has grown until *it* **r** the sky, A10413
Da 12:12 who waits for and **r** the end of the 1,335 H5595

REACHING (14) [REACH]

Ge 28:12 the earth, with its top **r** to heaven, and the H5595
Ex 28:42 the body, **r** from the waist to the thigh. H2118
Jdg 3:19 But **on** **r** the stone images near Gilgal he H4946
1Sa 17:49 **R** into his bag and taking out a H8938+3338
Est 5:14 a pole set up, *r to a* **height** *of* fifty cubits, and AIT
Est 7: 9 "A pole *r to a* **height** *of* fifty cubits stands by AIT
Ps 57:10 great is your love, **r** **to** the heavens; your H6330
Isa 8: 8 passing through it and **r** up to the neck. H5595
Mk 11:15 *On* **r** Jerusalem, Jesus entered the *G2262+1650*
Lk 22:37 is written about me *is* **r** its fulfillment." *G2400*
Lk 22:40 *On* **r** the place, he said to them *G1181+2093*
2Co 4:15 *that is* **r** **more and more** *people* *G4429+1328+3836+4498*
1Ti 5:24 **r** the place of judgment **ahead of** them *G4575*
Rev 1:13 in a **robe** **r** **down** **to** his **feet** and with a *G4468*

READ (77) [READER, READING, READS]

Ex 24: 7 of the Covenant and **r** it to the people. H7924
Dt 17:19 and *he is to* **r** it all the days of his life so H7924
Dt 31:11 *you shall* **r** this law before them in their H7924
Jos 8:34 Joshua **r** all the words of the law H7924
Jos 8:35 that Joshua *did* not **r** to the whole H7924
2Ki 5: 6 The letter that he took to the king of Israel **r** H606
2Ki 5: 7 As soon as the king of Israel **r** the letter H7924
2Ki 19:14 the letter from the messengers and **r** it. H7924
2Ki 22: 8 He gave it to Shaphan, *who* **r** it. H7924
2Ki 22:10 And Shaphan **r** *from* it in the presence of H7924
2Ki 22:16 in the book the king of Judah *has* **r**. H7924
2Ki 23: 2 *He* **r** in their hearing all the words of the H7924
2Ch 30: 6 the king and from his officials, which **r**: H606
2Ch 34:18 And Shaphan **r** from it in the presence of H7924
2Ch 34:24 the book that *has been* **r** in the presence H7924
2Ch 34:30 *He* **r** in their hearing all the words of the H7924
Ezr 4:18 you sent us *has* **been** **r** and translated in A10637
Ezr 4:23 of King Artaxerxes **was** **r** to Rehum and A10637
Ezr 5: 7 The report they sent him **r** as follows: To A10374
Ne 8: 3 *He* **r** it **aloud** from daybreak till noon as he H7924
Ne 8: 8 *They* **r** from the Book of the Law of God H7924
Ne 8: 8 the people understood what was being **r**. H5246
Ne 8:18 Ezra **r** from the Book of the Law of God. H7924
Ne 9: 3 where they were and **r** from the Book of H7924
Ne 13: 1 Book of Moses **was** **r** **aloud** in the hearing H7924
Est 6: 1 of his reign, to be brought in and **r** to him. H7924
Isa 29:11 the scroll to *someone who* **can** **r**, H3359+6219
Isa 29:11 can read, and say, "**R** this, please," they H7924
Isa 29:12 to someone *who* **cannot** **r**, H4202+3359+6219
Isa 29:12 and say, "**R** this, please," they H7924
Isa 29:12 answer, "*I* don't **know** **how** **to** **r**." H3359+6219
Isa 34:16 Look in the scroll of the LORD and **r**: None H7924
Isa 37:14 the letter from the messengers and **r** it. H7924
Jer 29:29 **r** the letter to Jeremiah the prophet. H7924
Jer 36: 6 a day of fasting and **r** to the people from H7924
Jer 36: 6 **R** them to all the people of Judah who H7924
Jer 36: 8 at the LORD's temple *he* **r** the words of the H7924
Jer 36:10 Baruch **r** to all the people at the LORD's H7924
Jer 36:13 he had heard Baruch **r** to the people from H7924
Jer 36:14 scroll from which *you have* **r** to the people H7924
Jer 36:15 "Sit down, please, and **r** it to us." H7924
Jer 36:15 read it to us." So Baruch **r** it to them. H7924
Jer 36:21 the secretary and **r** it to the king and all H7924
Jer 36:23 Whenever Jehudi *had* **r** three or four H7924
Jer 51:61 see that *you* **r** all these words **aloud**. H7924
Da 5: 8 they could not **r** the writing or tell the A10637
Da 5:15 brought before me *to* **r** this writing and A10637
Da 5:16 If you can **r** this writing and tell me what A10637
Da 5:17 *I will* **r** the writing for the king and tell A10637
Mt 12: 3 "Haven't *you* **r** what David did when he *G336*
Mt 12: 5 Or haven't *you* **r** in the Law that the priests *G336*
Mt 19: 4 "Haven't *you* **r**," he replied, "that at the *G336*
Mt 21:16 "*have you* never **r**, " 'From the *G336*
Mt 21:42 "*Have you* never **r** in the Scriptures: *G336*
Mt 22:31 *have you* not **r** what God said to you, *G336*
Mk 2:25 "*Have you* never **r** what David did when he *G336*
Mk 12:10 Haven't *you* **r** this passage of Scripture: *G336*
Mk 12:26 rising—*have you* not **r** in the Book of Moses *G336*
Mk 15:26 notice of the charge against him **r**: *G1639+2108*
Lk 4:16 as was his custom. He stood up *to* **r**, *G336*
Lk 6: 3 "*Have you* never **r** what David did when he *G336*
Lk 10:26 he replied. "How *do you* **r** it?" *G336*
Lk 23:38 was a written notice above him, which **r**: NDT
Jn 19:19 to the cross. *It* **r**: JESUS OF NAZARETH, *G1639+1211*
Jn 19:20 Many of the Jews **r** this sign, for the place *G336*
Ac 13:27 of the prophets that *are* **r** every Sabbath. *G336*
Ac 15:21 earliest times and *is* **r** in the synagogues *G336*
Ac 15:31 The people **r** it and were glad for its *G336*
Ac 23:34 The governor **r** the letter and asked what *G336*
2Co 1:13 you anything *you* cannot **r** or understand. *G336*
2Co 3: 2 on our hearts, known and **r** by everyone. *G336*
2Co 3:14 veil remains when the old covenant *is* **r**. *G342*
2Co 3:15 Even to this day when Moses *is* **r**, a veil *G336*
Col 4:16 After this letter *has been* **r** to you, see that *G336*
Col 4:16 see that *it is* also **r** in the church of the *G336*
Col 4:16 that you in turn **r** the letter from *G336*
1Th 5:27 the Lord *to* **have** this letter **r** to all the *G336*

READER (2) [READ]

Mt 24:15 the prophet Daniel—let the **r** understand— *G336*
Mk 13:14 not belong—let the **r** understand—then let *G336*

READILY (2) [READY]

Job 4:19 are crushed **more** **r** **than** a moth! H4200+7156
Ro 11:24 olive tree, how much **more** *r* will these, the AIT

READINESS (2) [READY]

2Co 7:11 what concern, what **r** **to** **see** **justice** **done**. *G1689*
Eph 6:15 feet fitted with the **r** that comes from the *G2288*

READING (8) [READ]

Jer 51:63 When you finish **r** this scroll, tie a stone to H7924
Ac 8:28 sitting in his chariot **r** the Book of Isaiah the *G336*
Ac 8:30 heard the man **r** Isaiah the prophet. *G336*
Ac 8:30 "Do you understand what *you are* **r**?" Philip *G336*
Ac 8:32 the passage of Scripture the eunuch was **r**: *G336*
Ac 13:15 After the **r** from the Law and the Prophets *G342*
Eph 3: 4 *In* **r** this, then, you will be able to *G336*
1Ti 4:13 devote yourself to the **public** **r** *of Scripture* *G342*

READS (2) [READ]

Da 5: 7 "Whoever **r** this writing and tells me A10637
Rev 1: 3 Blessed is the *one who* **r** **aloud** the words of *G336*

READY (94) [ALREADY, READILY, READINESS]

Ge 24:61 her attendants **got** **r** and mounted the H7756
Ge 46:29 Joseph *had* his chariot **made** **r** and went to H673
Ge 46:30 Joseph, "Now *I am* **r** **to** **die**, since I have H4637
Ex 13:18 Israelites went up out of Egypt **r** **for** **battle**. H2821
Ex 14: 6 So *he* **had** his chariot **made** **r** and took his H673
Ex 17: 4 *They are* almost *r to* **stone** me." AIT
Ex 19:11 be **r** by the third day, because on that H3922
Ex 34: 2 Be **r** in the morning, and then come up on H3922
Nu 4:15 when the camp *is r to* **move**, only then AIT
Nu 8:11 so that *they may be* **r** to do the work of the H2118
Nu 14:40 "Now we *are r to* **go** **up** to the land the LORD AIT
Jos 1: 2 **get** **r** to cross the Jordan River into the H7756
Jos 1:11 tell the people, '**Get** your provisions **r**. H3922
Jos 1:14 fighting men, **r** **for** **battle**, must cross over H2821
Jos 4:12 crossed over, **r** **for** **battle**, in front of the H2821
Jos 22:26 we said, '*Let us* **get** **r** and build an altar H6913
1Sa 6: 7 get a new cart **r**, with two cows that H6913
1Sa 9:26 Saul on the roof, "**Get** **r**, and I will send H7756
1Sa 9:26 When Saul **got** **r**, he and Samuel went H7756
1Sa 25:41 servant and am **r** to serve you and wash H4200
2Sa 15:15 servants are **r** **to** **do** whatever our lord H2180
2Sa 15:26 with you,' then I am **r**; let him do to me H2180
1Ki 1: 5 So *he* **got** chariots and horses **r**, with fifty H6913
2Ki 22: 4 priest and **have** *him* **get** **r** the money that H9462
1Ch 5:18 44,760 men **r** **for** **military** **service**— H3655+7372
1Ch 7: 4 had 36,000 **men** **r** **for** **battle**, H1522+7372+4878
1Ch 7:11 fighting men **r** **to** **go** **out** to war. H3655+7372
1Ch 7:40 of men **r** **for** **battle**, H7372+928+2021+4878
1Ch 12: 8 **r** **for** **battle** and able to handle H408+7372+4200+2021+4878
1Ch 12:17 peace to help me, I *am r for* you *to* **join** me. AIT
1Ch 12:25 from Simeon, warriors **r** **for** battle—7,100; H4200
1Ch 12:35 from Dan, **r** *for* battle—28,600; H6885
1Ch 28:21 Levites are **r** for all the work on the NDT
2Ch 26:11 **r** **to** **go** **out** by divisions according to H3655+7372
2Ch 26:19 had a censer in his hand *r* to **burn** **incense**, AIT
2Ch 29:26 So the Levites **stood** *r* with David's AIT
Est 3:14 nationality so they would be **r** for that day. H6969
Est 8:13 the Jews would be **r** on that day to H6969
Job 3: 8 those *who are* **r** to rouse Leviathan. H6969
Job 18:12 him; disaster *is* **r** for him when he falls. H3922
Job 32:19 like new wineskins **r** **to** **burst**. H1324
Ps 7:13 weapons; *he* **makes** **r** his flaming arrows. H7188
Ps 59: 4 no wrong, yet *they are* **r** to attack me. H3922
Ps 119:173 May your hand be **r** to help me, for I have NDT
Pr 21:31 The horse **is** **made** **r** for the day of battle H3922
Pr 22:18 heart and **have** all of them **r** on your lips. H3922
Pr 24:27 work in order and **get** your fields **r**; H6963
Isa 30:33 prepared; it *has* **been** **made** **r** for the king. H3922
Jer 1:17 "**Get** yourself **r**! Stand up and say to H273+5516
Jer 9: 3 *They* **make** **r** their tongue like a bow, **to** **shoot** H2005
Jer 46:14 'Take your positions and **get** **r**, for the H3922
La 2: 4 he has strung his bow; his right hand *is* **r**. H5893
Eze 7:14 *they have* **made** all things **r**, but no H3922
Eze 21:11 **made** **r** for the hand of the slayer. H5989
Eze 38: 7 " '**Get** **r**; be prepared, you and all the H3922
Da 3:15 if you are **r** to fall down and worship the A10577
Hos 2: 9 it ripens, and my new wine when it is **r**. H4595
Na 2: 3 flashes on the day they *are* **made** **r**; H3922
Zec 5:11 When the house *is* **r**, the basket will be H3922
Mt 22: 4 have been butchered, and everything is **r**. *G2289*
Mt 22: 8 'The wedding banquet is **r**, but those I *G2289*
Mt 24:44 So you also must be **r**, because the Son of *G2289*
Mt 25:10 The virgins *who were* **r** went in with him *G2289*
Mk 3: 9 disciples to *have* a small boat **r** for him, *G4674*
Mk 14:15 a large room upstairs, furnished and **r**. *G2289*
Lk 1:17 *to* **make** **r** a people prepared for the Lord." *G2286*
Lk 1:39 At that time Mary **got** **r** and hurried to a *G482*
Lk 9:52 Samaritan village to **get** *things* **r** for him; *G2286*
Lk 12:35 "Be **dressed** **r** **for** **service** and *G3836+4019+4322*
Lk 12:38 servants whose master finds them **r**, *G4048S*
Lk 12:40 You also must be **r**, because the Son of *G2289*
Lk 12:47 will and *does* not **get** **r** or does not do *G2286*
Lk 14:17 'Come, for everything is now **r**. *G2289*
Lk 17: 8 **get** *yourself* **r** and wait on me while I eat *G4322*
Lk 22:33 I am **r** to go with you to prison and to *G2289*
Ac 16:10 *we* **got** **r** at once to leave for Macedonia *G2426*
Ac 21:13 I am **r** not only to be bound, but also to *G2290*
Ac 23:15 We are **r** to kill him before he gets here." *G2289*
Ac 23:21 They are **r** now, waiting for your consent *G2289*
Ac 23:23 "**Get** **r** a detachment of two hundred *G2286*

R

Ac 28:10 many ways; and *when we were r to* **sail**, they AIT
1Co 3: 2 not solid food, for *you were* not yet r for it. G1538
1Co 3: 2 ready for it. Indeed, *you are* still not r. G1538
1Co 14: 8 a clear call, who *will get* r for battle? G4186
2Co 9: 2 last year *you* in Achaia *were* r to give; G4186
2Co 9: 3 that you may be r, as I said you would G4186
2Co 9: 5 Then it will be r as a generous gift, not as G2289
2Co 10: 6 And we will be r to punish every act of G2289
2Co 12:14 Now I am r to visit you for the third time G2290
Titus 3: 1 obedient, to be r to do whatever is good, G2289
1Pe 1: 5 salvation that is r to be revealed in the G2289
1Pe 4: 5 account to him who is r to judge the living G2290
Rev 9:15 angels who *had been kept* r for this very G2286
Rev 19: 7 and his bride *has* **made** herself r. G2286

REAFFIRM (2) [AFFIRM]
1Sa 20:17 And Jonathan **had** David r his oath out of H3578
2Co 2: 8 I urge you, therefore, *to* r your love for him. G3263

REAFFIRMED (1) [AFFIRM]
Jos 24:25 there at Shechem *he* r for them decrees H8492

REAIAH (4)
1Ch 4: 2 **R** son of Shobal was the father of Jahath H8025
1Ch 5: 5 Micah his son, **R** his son, Baal his son, H8025
Ezr 2:47 Gahar, **R**, H8025
Ne 7:50 **R**, Rezin, Nekoda, H8025

REAL (3) [REALITIES, REALITY, REALLY]
Jn 6:55 For my flesh is r food and my blood is real G239
Jn 6:55 flesh is real food and my blood is r drink. G239
1Jn 2:27 about all things and as that anointing is r, G239

REALITIES (2) [REAL]
1Co 2:13 explaining **spiritual** *r* with Spirit-taught words. AIT
Heb 10: 1 not the r themselves. G1635+3836+4547

REALITY (1) [REAL]
Col 2:17 things that were to come; the r, however, G5393

REALIZE (38) [REALIZED, REALIZES, REALIZING]
Ge 42:23 They *did* not r that Joseph could H3359
Ex 10: 7 *Do you* not yet r that Egypt is ruined?" H3359
Lev 4:13 of the matter, when *they* r *their* **guilt** H870
Lev 4:27 LORD's commands, when *they* r *their* **guilt** H870
Lev 5: 2 then *they come to* r *their* **guilt**; H870
Lev 5: 3 but then they learn of it and r *their* **guilt**; H870
Lev 5: 4 then they learn of it and r *their* **guilt**— H870
Lev 6: 4 sin in any of these ways and r *their* **guilt**, H870
Nu 22:34 *I did* not r you were standing in the road H3359
Jdg 13:16 Manoah *did* not r that it was the angel of H3359
Jdg 15:11 "Don't *you* r that the Philistines are rulers H3359
Jdg 20:34 the Benjamites *did* not r how near H3359
1Sa 12:17 And *you will* r what an evil H3359+2256+8011
2Sa 2:26 Don't *you* r that this will end in bitterness H3359
2Sa 3:38 "*Do you* not r that a commander and a H3359
Ecc 2:14 I *came to* r that the same fate H3359
Jer 2:19 Consider then and r how evil and bitter it H8011
Jer 11:19 *I did* not r that they had plotted against H3359
Da 2: 8 because *you* r that this is what I have A10255
Hos 7: 2 but they *do* not r that I H606+4200+4222
Hos 7: 9 sap his strength, but he *does* not r it. H3359
Hos 11: 3 but *they did* not r it was I who healed H3359
Hos 14: 9 *Let them* r these things H1067
Jn 2: 9 *He did* not r where it had come from G3857
Jn 11:50 *You do* not r that it is better for you that G3357
Jn 12:16 was glorified *did they* r that these things G3630
Jn 13: 7 "You *do* not r now what I am doing G3857
Jn 14:20 On that day you *will* r that I am in my G1182
Jn 19:10 "Don't *you* r I have power either to free G3857
Jn 20:14 but *she did* not r that it was Jesus. G3857
Jn 21: 4 the disciples *did* not r that it was G3857
Ac 7:25 his own people *would* r that God was G5317
Ac 10:34 "*I now* r how true it is that God does not G2898
Ac 23: 5 *I did* not r that he was the high priest G3857
1Co 11: 3 But I want you *to* r that the head of every G3857
2Co 10:11 Such people *should* r that what we are in G3357
2Co 13: 5 *Do you* not r that Christ Jesus is in you G2105
Rev 3:17 But *you do* not r that you are wretched G3857

REALIZED (31) [REALIZE]
Ge 3: 7 were opened, and *they* r they were naked H3359
Ge 28: 8 Esau then r how displeasing the H8011
Ex 5:19 Israelite overseers r they were in trouble H8011
Jdg 6:22 When Gideon r that it was the angel of H8011
Jdg 13:21 Manoah r that it was the angel of the LORD H3359
Jdg 20:41 because *they* r that disaster had come on H8011
Ru 1:18 When Naomi r that Ruth was determined H8011
1Sa 3: 8 Then Eli r that the LORD was calling the H1067
1Sa 18:28 When Saul r that the LORD H8011+2256+3359
2Sa 10: 6 When the Ammonites r that they had H8011
2Sa 10:14 When the Ammonites r that the Arameans H8011
2Sa 12:19 themselves, and he r the child was dead. H1067
2Sa 20:12 When *he* r that everyone who came up to H8011
1Ki 3:15 awoke—and he r it had been a dream. H2180
1Ch 19: 6 When the Ammonites r that they had H8011
1Ch 19:15 When the Ammonites r that the Arameans H8011
Ne 6:12 *I* r that God had not sent him, but that he H5795
Ne 6:16 because *they* r that this work had been H3359
SS 6:12 Before *I* r it, my desire set me among the H3359
Eze 10:20 and *I* r that they were cherubim. H3359
Mt 2:16 When Herod r that he had been outwitted G3972
Mk 5:30 At once Jesus r *that* power had gone out G2105
Lk 1:22 *They* r he had seen a vision in the temple, G2105
Jn 4:53 Then the father r that this was the exact G1182
Jn 6:22 shore of the lake r that only one boat had G3972
Jn 6:24 Once the crowd r that neither Jesus nor his G3972
Ac 4:13 of Peter and John and r that they were G2898
Ac 16:19 *When* her owners r that their hope of G3972
Ac 19:34 But *when they* r he was a Jew, they all G2105
Ac 22:29 was alarmed *when he* r that he had put G2105
Heb 6:11 so that what you hope for may be **fully** r. G4443

REALIZES (1) [REALIZE]
Lev 4:22 of the LORD his God, *when he* r *his* **guilt** H870

REALIZING (3) [REALIZE]
Ge 38:16 Not r that she was his daughter-in-law, he H3359
Est 7: 7 r that the king had already decided his H8011
Ro 2: 4 **not** r that God's kindness is intended to lead G51

REALLY (46) [REAL]
Ge 3: 1 woman, "Did God r say, 'You must H677+3954
Ge 18:13 say, 'Will I r have a child, now H677+598
Ge 18:24 Will you r sweep it away and not spare the H677
Ge 20:12 she r is my sister, the daughter of H593
Ge 26: 9 Isaac and said, "She is r your wife! H421
Ge 27:21 to know whether you r are my son Esau H2296
Ge 27:24 "Are you r my son Esau?" he asked. "I am," H2296
Ge 45:12 **that** it is r I who am speaking to you. H3954
Lev 25:16 because *what is r being* **sold** to you is the AIT
Nu 22:37 Am I r not able to reward you? H598
Jdg 6:17 give me a sign that it is r you talking to me. NDT
Jdg 6:31 If Baal r is a god, he can defend himself NDT
Jdg 9:15 'If you r want to anoint me king over H928+622
Jdg 11: 9 gives them to me—*will I* r **be** your head?" AIT
Jdg 14:16 You don't r love me. You've H8370
Jdg 15: 3 with the Philistines; I will r harm them." H3954
1Ki 8:27 "But will God r dwell on earth? The H598
1Ki 18: 7 said, "Is it r you, my lord Elijah? H2296
2Ch 6:18 "But will God r dwell on earth with humans H598
Ps 78:19 "Can God *r* **spread** a table in the wilderness? AIT
Pr 20:11 so is their conduct *r* **pure** and upright? AIT
Ecc 8:17 they know, they cannot *r* **comprehend** it. AIT
Jer 7: 5 If *you* r **change** your ways and your H3512+3512
Jer 9:26 For all these nations are r uncircumcised NDT
Zec 7: 5 was it r for me that you fasted? NDT
Mk 11:32 everyone held that John r was a prophet.) G3953
Jn 4:42 we know that this man r is the Savior of the G242
Jn 7:26 the authorities r concluded that he is G3607+242
Jn 8:31 hold to my teaching, you are r my disciples. G242
Jn 13:38 "*Will you* r **lay down** your life for me? AIT
Jn 14: 7 If *you* r **know** me, you will know my Father as AIT
Ac 9:26 not believing that *he* r **was** a disciple. AIT
Ac 12: 9 the angel was doing was r happening; G239
Ro 7: 7 known what coveting r was if the law had G5445
1Co 4: 8 How I wish that you r had begun to reign G1145
1Co 5: 7 a new unleavened batch—**as** you r are. G2777
1Co 14:25 exclaiming, "God is r among you! G3953
Gal 1: 7 which **is** *r* no gospel at all. Evidently some AIT
Gal 2:18 destroyed, then I r **would be** a lawbreaker. G5319
Gal 3: 4 so much in vain—if it r was in vain? G1145
1Th 3: 8 For now *we r* **live**, since you are standing firm AIT
1Ti 5: 3 to those widows who are r *in need*. G3953
1Ti 5: 5 The widow who is r *in need* and left all G3953
1Ti 5:16 can help those widows who are r *in need*. G3953
Jas 2: 8 If you r keep the royal law found in G3530
1Jn 2:19 out from us, but they did **not** *r* belong to us. AIT

REALM (45) [REALMS]
Nu 16:30 they go down alive into the **r of the dead**, H8619
Nu 16:33 went down alive into the **r of the dead**, H8619
Dt 32:22 burns down to the **r of the dead** below. H8619
Jos 13:21 the entire r *of* Sihon king of the H4931
Jos 13:27 with the rest of the r *of* Sihon king of H4931
Jos 13:30 Bashan, the entire r *of* Og king of Bashan H4931
2Ch 36:22 throughout his r and also to put it in H4895
Ezr 1: 1 throughout his r and also to put it in H4895
Ezr 7:23 wrath fall on the r *of* the king and of his A10424
Est 1:20 is proclaimed throughout all his vast r, H4895
Est 2: 3 in every province of his r to bring all these H4895
Job 15:22 He despairs of escaping the **r of darkness** H3125
Job 17:13 if I spread out my bed in the **r of darkness**, H3125
Job 18:18 light into the **r of darkness** and is H3125
Job 26: 6 The **r of the dead** is naked before God H8619
Ps 9:17 The wicked go down to the **r of the dead** H8619
Ps 16:10 will not abandon me to the **r of the dead**, H8619
Ps 30: 3 brought me up from the **r of the dead**; you H8619
Ps 31:17 shame and be silent in the **r of the dead**. H8619
Ps 49:15 will redeem me from the **r of the dead**; H8619
Ps 55:15 them go down alive to the **r of the dead**, H8619
Ps 86:13 from the depths, from the **r of the dead**. H8619
Pr 9:18 her guests are deep in the **r of the dead**. H8619
Pr 15:24 from going down to the **r of the dead**. H8619
Ecc 9:10 in the **r of the dead**, where you are H8619
Isa 14: 9 The **r of the dead** below is all astir to H8619
Isa 14:15 are brought down to the **r of the dead**, H8619
Isa 28:15 with the **r of the dead** we have made an H8619
Isa 28:18 with the **r of the dead** will not stand. H8619
Isa 57: 9 you descended to the *very* **r of the dead**! H8619
Eze 31:14 mortals who go down to the **r of the dead**. H1014
Eze 31:15 down to the **r of the dead** I covered the H8619
Eze 31:16 it down to the **r of the dead** to be with H8619
Eze 31:17 had gone down to the **r of the dead**, to H8619
Eze 32:21 From within the **r of the dead** the mighty H8619
Eze 32:27 went down to the **r of the dead** with their H8619
Da 11: 9 North will invade the r *of* the king of the H4895
Jnh 2: 2 From deep in the **r of the dead** I called H8619
Na 1: 8 will pursue his foes into the **r of darkness**. H3125
Ac 2:27 will not abandon me to the **r of the dead**, G87
Ac 2:31 he was not abandoned to the **r of the dead**, G87
Ro 7: 5 For when we were **in the r of** the flesh, the G1877
Ro 8: 8 Those who are **in the r of** the flesh cannot G1877
Ro 8: 9 are not **in the r of** the flesh but are in the G1877
Ro 8: 9 of the flesh but are **in the r of** the Spirit, G1877

REALMS (5) [REALM]
Eph 1: 3 blessed us in the **heavenly** r with every G2230
Eph 1:20 him at his right hand in the **heavenly** r, G2230
Eph 2: 6 with him in the **heavenly** r in Christ Jesus, G2230
Eph 3:10 rulers and authorities in the **heavenly** r, G2230
Eph 6:12 spiritual forces of evil in the **heavenly** r. G2230

REAP (32) [REAPED, REAPER, REAPERS, REAPING, REAPS, REAPS']
Lev 19: 9 " 'When you r the harvest of your land, do H7917
Lev 19: 9 *do* not r *to* the very edges of your field H7917
Lev 23:10 going to give you and *you* r its harvest, H7917
Lev 23:22 " 'When you r the harvest of your land, do H7917
Lev 23:22 *do* not r *to* the very edges of your field H7917
Lev 25: 5 *Do* not r what grows of itself or H7917+7907
Lev 25:11 do not sow and *do* not r what grows of H7917
1Sa 8:12 to plow his ground and r his harvest, H7917
2Ki 19:29 But in the third year sow and r, plant H7917
Job 4: 8 plow evil and those who sow trouble r it. H7917
Job 13:26 against me and **make** me r the sins of my H3769
Ps 126: 5 sow with tears *will* r with songs of joy. H7917
Ecc 11: 4 whoever looks at the clouds *will* not r. H7917
Isa 37:30 But in the third year sow and r, plant H7917
Jer 12:13 They will sow wheat but r thorns; they will H7917
Hos 8: 7 "They sow the wind and r the whirlwind H7917
Hos 10:12 yourselves, r the fruit of unfailing love H7917
Mt 6:26 they do not sow or r or store away in barns G2545
Lk 12:24 They do not sow or r, they have no G2545
Lk 19:21 did not put in and r what you did not sow. G2545
Jn 4:38 I sent you *to* r what you have not worked G2545
Ro 6:21 What benefit *did you* r at that time from G2400
Ro 6:22 the benefit *you* r leads to holiness G2400
1Co 9:11 much if we r **a** material **harvest** from you? G2545
2Co 9: 6 sows sparingly *will* also r sparingly, G2545
2Co 9: 6 sows generously *will* also r generously. G2545
Gal 6: 8 from the flesh *will* r destruction; whoever G2545
Gal 6: 8 the Spirit, from the Spirit *will* r eternal life. G2545
Gal 6: 9 proper time *we will* **r a harvest** if we do G2545
Jas 3:18 who sow in peace r a harvest of NDT
Rev 14:15 "Take your sickle and r, because the time G2545
Rev 14:15 because the time *to* r has come, for the G2545

REAPED (3) [REAP]
Ge 26:12 land and the same year r a hundredfold, H5162
Hos 10:13 wickedness, *you have* r evil, you have H7917
Jn 4:38 you *have* r **the benefits of** their labor." G1656

REAPER (5) [REAP]
Ps 129: 7 a r cannot fill his hands with it, nor one H7917
Jer 9:22 like cut grain behind the r, with no one to H7917
Jer 50:16 and the r with his sickle at harvest. H9530
Am 9:13 "when the r will be overtaken by the H7917
Jn 4:36 the sower and the r may be glad together. G2545

REAPERS (2) [REAP]
2Ki 4:18 went out to his father, who was with the r. H7917
Isa 17: 5 It will be as when r harvest the standing H7907

REAPING (2) [REAP]
Ge 45: 6 five years there will be no plowing and r. H7907
Lk 19:22 I did not put in, and r what I did not sow? G2545

REAPPEARS (2) [APPEAR]
Lev 13:57 But if *it* r in the fabric, in the woven H8011+6388
Lev 14:43 defiling mold r in the house H8740+2256+7255

REAPS (5) [REAP]
Pr 11:18 who sows righteousness r a sure reward. NDT
Pr 22: 8 Whoever sows injustice r calamity, and H7917
Jn 4:36 Even now the *one who* r draws a wage G2545
Jn 4:37 saying 'One sows and another r' is true. G2545
Gal 6: 7 A man r what he sows. G2545

REAR (17) [REARED, REARING]
Ge 33: 2 and Rachel and Joseph *in* the r. H340
Ex 26:12 is to hang down at the r *of* the tabernacle. H294
Nu 10:25 as the **r guard** for all the units, the H665
Jos 6: 9 trumpets, and the **r guard** followed the ark. H665
Jos 6:13 of them and the **r guard** followed the ark of H665
Jos 10:19 **Attack** them **from the r** and don't let them H2386
1Sa 29: 2 men were marching at the r with Achish. H340
1Ki 6:16 twenty cubits at the r *of* the temple with H3752
2Ch 13:13 Jeroboam had sent troops around to the r, H339
2Ch 13:14 were being attacked at both front and r. H294
Ps 83: 2 how your foes r their heads. H5951
Ps 140: 9 who surround me proudly r their heads; H8123
Isa 52:12 the God of Israel will be your **r guard**. H665
Isa 58: 8 the glory of the LORD *will be* your **r guard**. H665
Eze 40:13 from the **top of the r wall** *of* one alcove to AIT
Eze 41:15 facing the courtyard at the r *of* the temple, H339
Hos 9:12 Even if *they* r children, I will bereave them H1540

R

REARED (6) [REAR]
Job 31:18 from my youth I r *them* as a father would, H1540
Isa 1: 2 "*I* r children and brought them up, but H1540
Isa 23: 4 *I have* neither r sons nor brought up H1540
Isa 51:18 all the children *she* r there was none to H1540
La 2:22 those I cared for and r my enemy has H8049
Eze 19: 2 She lay down among them and r her cubs. H8049

REARING (1) [REAR]
2Ki 10: 6 leading men of the city, *who were* r them. H1540

REASON (57) [REASONABLE, REASONED, REASONING, REASONS]
Ge 20:10 "What *was your* r for doing this? H8011
Ge 41:32 The r the dream was given to Pharaoh in H6584
1Sa 19: 5 man like David by killing him **for no** r?" H2855
Job 2: 3 me against him to ruin him **without any** r." H2855
Job 9:17 a storm and multiply my wounds **for no** r. H2855
Job 12:24 deprives the leaders of the earth of their r; H4213
Job 22: 6 security from your relatives **for no** r; H2855
Ps 35:19 who hate me **without** r maliciously wink H2855
Ps 38:19 who hate me **without** r are numerous. H9214
Ps 69: 4 who hate me **without** r outnumber the H2855
Pr 3:30 Do not accuse anyone **for no** r—when H2855
Mt 12:10 Looking *for a* r to bring charges against *G2671*
Mt 19: 3 to divorce his wife for any and every r?" *G162*
Mt 19: 5 '**For this** r a man will leave his father and *G1915*
Mk 3: 2 them were looking for a r to accuse Jesus, *G2671*
Mk 10: 7 '**For this** r a man will leave his father and *G1915*
Lk 6: 7 law were looking for a r to accuse Jesus, *G2671*
Jn 1:31 but **the** r I came baptizing with *G1328+4047*
Jn 5:18 **For this** r they tried all the more to *G1328+4047*
Jn 8:47 **The** r you do not hear is that you *G1328+4047*
Jn 10:17 **The** r my Father loves me is that I *G1328+4047*
Jn 12:27 it was **for this very** r I came to this *G1328+4047*
Jn 12:39 **For this** r they could not believe *G1328+4047*
Jn 15:25 'They hated me **without** r.' *G1562*
Jn 18:37 **the** r I was born and came into the *G1650+4047*
Ac 19:40 this commotion, since there is no r for it." *G165*
Ac 28:20 For this r I have asked to see you and talk *G162*
Ro 13: 4 rulers do not bear the sword **for no** r. *G1632*
Ro 14: 9 **For this very** r, Christ died *G1650+4047+1142*
1Co 4:17 **For this** r I have sent to you Timothy *G1328+4047*
1Co 11:10 It is **for this** r that a woman ought to *G1328+4047*
1Co 12:15 it would not **for that** r stop being *G4123+4047*
1Co 12:16 it would not **for that** r stop being *G4123+4047*
1Co 14:13 **For this** r the one who speaks in a tongue *G1475*
2Co 2: 9 Another r I wrote you was to see if *G1650+4047*
2Co 8:24 of your love and the *r for* our **pride** in you, AIT
Gal 6:12 The **only** *r* they do this is to avoid being AIT
Eph 1:15 **For this** r, ever since I heard about *G1328+4047*
Eph 3: 1 **For this** r I, Paul, the prisoner of *G4047+5920*
Eph 3:14 **For this** r I kneel before the Father, *G4047+5920*
Eph 5:31 "**For this** r a man will leave his father *G505+4047*
Col 1: 9 **For this** r, since the day we heard *G1328+4047*
1Th 3: 5 **For this** r, when I could stand it no *G1328+4047*
2Th 2:11 **For this** r God sends them a *G1328+4047*
1Ti 1:16 **for that very** r I was shown mercy *G1328+4047*
2Ti 1: 6 For this r I remind you to fan into flame the *G162*
Titus 1: 5 **The** r I left you in Crete was that *G4047+5920*
Phm 15 Perhaps **the** r he was separated *G1328+4047*
Heb 2:17 **For this** r he had to be made like them *G3854*
Heb 9:15 **For this** r Christ is the mediator of a *G1328+4047*
Heb 10: 1 **For this** r it can never, by the same *G1142*
Jas 4: 5 Scripture says **without** r that he jealously *G3036*
1Pe 3:15 asks you to give the r for the hope that *G3364*
1Pe 4: 6 For **this is the** r the gospel was *G1650+4047*
2Pe 1: 5 **For this very** r, make every effort to *G899+4047*
1Jn 3: 1 **The** r the world does not know us is *G1328+4047*
1Jn 3: 8 **The** r the Son of God appeared *G1650+4047*

REASONABLE (2) [REASON]
Ac 18:14 it would be r for me to listen to you. *G2848+3364*
Ac 26:25 "What I am saying is true and r. *G5408*

REASONED (6) [REASON]
Ac 17: 2 Sabbath days *he* r **with** them from the *G1363*
Ac 17:17 So *he* r in the synagogue **with** both Jews *G1363*
Ac 18: 4 Every Sabbath *he* r in the synagogue *G1363*
Ac 18:19 into the synagogue and r **with** the Jews. *G1363*
1Co 13:11 I thought like a child, *I* r like a child. *G3357*
Heb 11:19 Abraham r that God could even raise the *G3357*

REASONING (1) [REASON]
Job 32:11 I listened to your r; while you were H9312

REASONS (2) [REASON]
Php 3: 4 though *I myself* **have** *r for* such confidence. AIT
Php 3: 4 If someone else **thinks** *they have r* to put AIT

REASSIGN (1) [ASSIGN]
Isa 49: 8 restore the land and to r its desolate H5706

REASSURE (2) [ASSURE]
2Ki 25:24 took an oath to r them and their men. NDT
Jer 40: 9 took an oath to r them and their men. NDT

REASSURED (1) [ASSURE]
Ge 50:21 And *he* r them and spoke kindly to them H5714

REBA (2)
Nu 31: 8 Zur, Hur and R—the five kings of H8064
Jos 13:21 Hur and R—princes allied with Sihon H8064

REBECCA (KJV) REBEKAH'S

REBEKAH (30) [REBEKAH'S]
Ge 22:23 Bethuel became the father of **R**. Milkah H8071
Ge 24:15 **R** came out with her jar on her shoulder. H8071
Ge 24:29 Now **R** had a brother named Laban, and H8071
Ge 24:30 had heard **R** tell what the man said H8071
Ge 24:45 praying in my heart, **R** came out, with her H8071
Ge 24:51 Here is **R**; take her and go, and let her H8071
Ge 24:53 articles of clothing and gave them to **R**; H8071
Ge 24:58 So they called **R** and asked her, "Will you H8071
Ge 24:59 So they sent their sister **R** on her way H8071
Ge 24:60 And they blessed **R** and said to her, "Our H8071
Ge 24:61 Then **R** and her attendants got ready and H8071
Ge 24:61 So the servant took **R** and left. H8071
Ge 24:64 **R** also looked up and saw Isaac. She got H8071
Ge 24:67 of his mother Sarah, and he married **R**. H8071
Ge 25:20 when he married **R** daughter of Bethuel H8071
Ge 25:21 and his wife **R** became pregnant. H8071
Ge 25:26 sixty years old when **R** gave birth to them. NDT
Ge 25:28 loved Esau, but **R** loved Jacob. H8071
Ge 26: 7 this place might kill me on account of **R**, H8071
Ge 26: 8 saw Isaac caressing his wife **R**. H8071
Ge 26:35 They were a source of grief to Isaac and **R**. H8071
Ge 27: 5 Now **R** was listening as Isaac spoke to his H8071
Ge 27: 6 **R** said to her son Jacob, "Look, I overheard H8071
Ge 27:11 Jacob said to **R** his mother, "But my H8071
Ge 27:15 Then **R** took the best clothes of Esau her H8071
Ge 27:42 When **R** was told what her older son Esau H8071
Ge 27:46 Then **R** said to Isaac, "I'm disgusted with H8071
Ge 28: 5 the brother of **R**, who was the mother of H8071
Ge 29:12 a relative of her father and a son of **R**. H8071
Ge 49:31 there Isaac and his wife **R** were buried H8071

REBEKAH'S (2) [REBEKAH]
Ge 35: 8 Now Deborah, **R** nurse, died and was H8071
Ro 9:10 **R** children were conceived at the *G4831*

REBEL (18) [REBELLED, REBELLING, REBELLION, REBELLIOUS, REBELS]
Ex 23:21 *Do* not r against him; he will not forgive H5352
Nu 14: 9 Only *do* not r against the LORD. And do not H5277
Dt 31:27 how much more will you r after I die! NDT
Jos 22:18 " 'If you r against the LORD today H5277
Jos 22:19 But *do* not r against the LORD or against us H5277
Jos 22:29 "Far be it from us to r against the LORD H5277
1Sa 12:14 obey him and *do* not r against his H5286
1Sa 12:15 and if *you* r against his commands H5286
2Ki 18:20 you depending, that *you* r against me? H5277
Job 24:13 "There are those *who* r *against* the light H5277
Isa 1:20 if you resist and r, you will be H5286
Isa 36: 5 you depending, that *you* r against me? H5277
Isa 48: 8 you are; you were called a r from birth. H7321
Eze 2: 8 *Do* not r like that rebellious people; H2118+5308
Eze 20:38 you of those who revolt and r against me. H7321
Da 11:14 your own people *will* r in fulfillment of H5951
Mt 10:21 children *will* r against their parents and *G2060*
Mk 13:12 Children *will* r against their parents and *G2060*

REBELLED (53) [REBEL]
Ge 14: 4 in the thirteenth year *they* r. H5277
Nu 20:24 because *both of you* r against my H5286
Nu 26: 9 officials who r against Moses and Aaron H5897
Nu 26: 9 followers when they r against the LORD. H5897
Nu 27:14 when the community r at the waters in the H5312
Dt 1:26 *you* r against the command of the LORD H5286
Dt 1:43 *You* r against the LORD's command and in H5286
Dt 9:23 But *you* r against the command of the H5286
1Sa 22:13 so that he *has* r against me and lies in H7756
1Ki 11:26 son of Nebat r against the king. H8123+3338
1Ki 11:27 account of how *he* r against the H8123+3338
2Ki 1: 1 After Ahab's death, Moab r against Israel. H7321
2Ki 3: 5 the king of Moab r against the king of H7321
2Ki 3: 7 "The king of Moab *has* r against me. H7321
2Ki 8:20 Edom r against Judah and set up its own H7321
2Ki 18: 7 *He* r against the king of Assyria and did H5277
2Ki 24: 1 he turned against Nebuchadnezzar and r. H5277
2Ki 24:20 Now Zedekiah r against the king of H5277
2Ch 13: 6 son of David, r against his master. H5277
2Ch 21: 8 Edom r against Judah and set up its own H7321
2Ch 36:13 *He* also r against King Nebuchadnezzar H5277
Ne 9:26 they were disobedient and r against you; H5277
Ps 5:10 many sins, for *they have* r against you. H5286
Ps 78:40 How often *they* r *against* him in the H5286
Ps 78:56 God to the test and r against the Most H5286
Ps 105:28 for *had they* not r against his words? H5286
Ps 106: 7 kindnesses, and *they* r by the sea, the Red H5286
Ps 106:33 for *they* r against the Spirit of God, and H5286
Ps 107:11 *because they* r *against* God's commands H5286
Isa 1: 2 them up, but they *have* r against me. H7321
Isa 43:27 those I sent to teach you r against me. H7321
Isa 63:10 Yet they r and grieved his Holy Spirit. H5286
Isa 66:24 dead bodies of those who r against me; H7321
Jer 2: 8 not know me; the leaders r against me. H7321
Jer 2:29 You *have* all r against me," declares the H7321
Jer 3:13 *you have* r against the LORD your God H7321
Jer 4:17 because *she has* r against me,' " H5286
Jer 14: 7 For we have often r; we have sinned H5412
Jer 52: 3 Now Zedekiah r against the king of H5277
La 1:18 is righteous, yet *I* r *against* his command. H5286
La 3:42 "We have sinned and r and you have not H5286
Eze 2: 3 a rebellious nation that *has* r against me; H5277
Eze 5: 6 her wickedness *she has* r against my laws H5286
Eze 17:15 But the king r against him by sending his H5277
Eze 20: 8 " 'But *they* r against me and would not H5286
Eze 20:13 the people of Israel r against me in the H5286
Eze 20:21 " 'But the children r against me: They did H5286
Da 9: 5 We have been wicked and *have* r; we H5277
Da 9: 9 even though *we have* r against him; H5277
Hos 7:13 to them, because *they have* r against me! H7321
Hos 8: 1 broken my covenant and r against my law. H7321
Hos 13:16 because *they have* r against their God. H5286
Heb 3:16 Who were they who heard and r? Were *G4176*

REBELLING (3) [REBEL]
Ne 2:19 "*Are* you r against the king?" H5277
Ps 78:17 r in the wilderness *against* the Most High. H5286
Ro 13: 2 the authority *is* r **against** what God has *G468*

REBELLION (41) [REBEL]
Ex 23:21 he will not forgive your r, since my Name H7322
Ex 34: 7 forgiving wickedness, r and sin. H7322
Lev 16:16 of the uncleanness and r *of* the Israelites, H7322
Lev 16:21 the wickedness and r *of* the Israelites— H7322
Nu 14:18 abounding in love and forgiving sin and r. H7322
Dt 13: 5 death for inciting r against the LORD your H6240
Jos 22:16 yourselves an altar in r against him now? H5277
Jos 22:22 If this has been in r or disobedience to H5278
Jos 24:19 He will not forgive your r and your sins. H7322
1Sa 15:23 For r is like the sin of divination, and H5308
1Sa 24:11 that I am guilty of wrongdoing or r. H7322
1Ki 12:19 So Israel *has been* **in** r against the house H7321
1Ki 16:20 Zimri's reign, and the r he carried out, are H8004
2Ki 8:22 this day Edom *has been* **in** r against H7321
2Ch 10:19 So Israel *has been* **in** r against the house H7321
2Ch 21:10 this day Edom *has been* **in** r against H7321
Ezr 4:19 has been a place of r and sedition. A10438
Ne 9:17 in their r appointed a leader in H5308
Job 34:37 To his sin he adds r; scornfully he claps H7322
Ps 106:43 they were bent on r and they wasted away H5286
Ps 139:21 abhor *those who are* **in** r *against* you? H7756
Pr 17:11 Evildoers foster r *against God*; the H5308
Isa 1: 5 Why do you persist in r? Your whole head H6240
Isa 24:20 upon it is the **guilt of** its r that it falls— H7322
Isa 58: 1 to my people their r and to the H7322
Isa 59:13 r and treachery against the LORD, turning H7321
Jer 5: 6 their r is great and their backslidings H7322
Jer 28:16 you have preached r against the LORD. H6240
Jer 29:32 because he has preached r against me. H6240
Jer 33: 8 will forgive all their sins of r against me. H7321
Eze 21:24 brought to mind your guilt by your open r, H7322
Da 8:12 Because of r, the LORD's people and the H7322
Da 8:13 sacrifice, the r that causes desolation H7322
Mt 26:55 "Am I **leading a** r, that you have *G3334*
Mk 14:48 "Am I **leading a** r," said Jesus, "that you *G3334*
Lk 22:52 "Am I **leading a** r, that you *G6055+2093+3334*
Lk 23:14 as *one who was* **inciting** the people **to** r. *G695*
2Th 2: 3 not come until the r occurs and the man of *G686*
Heb 3: 8 not harden your hearts as you did in the r, *G4177*
Heb 3:15 not harden your hearts as you did in the r." *G4177*
Jude 11 they have been destroyed *in* Korah's r. *G517*

REBELLIOUS (42) [REBEL]
Nu 17:10 to be kept as a sign to the r. H1201+5308
Dt 9: 7 you have been r against the LORD. H5286
Dt 9:24 You have been r against the LORD ever H5286
Dt 21:18 has a stubborn and r son who does not H5286
Dt 21:20 "This son of ours is stubborn and r. H5286
Dt 31:27 For I know how r and stiff-necked you are H5308
Dt 31:27 If you have been r against the LORD while I H5286
1Sa 20:30 "You son of a perverse and r woman! H5280
Ezr 4:12 are rebuilding that r and wicked city. A10439
Ezr 4:15 you will find that this city is a r city, A10439
Ps 25: 7 the sins of my youth and my r *ways*; H7322
Ps 66: 7 let not the r rise up against him. H6253
Ps 68: 6 the r live in a sun-scorched land. H6253
Ps 68:18 from people, even from the r—that you, H6253
Ps 78: 8 a stubborn and r generation, whose H5286
Ps 107:17 fools through their r ways and suffered H7322
Pr 24:21 my son, and do not join with r *officials*, H9101
Pr 28: 2 When a country is r, it has many rulers H7322
Isa 30: 9 For these are r people, deceitful children H5308
Isa 50: 5 my ears; I *have not been* r, I have not H5286
Jer 5:23 these people have stubborn and r hearts; H5286
La 1:20 disturbed, for *I have been* **most** r. H5286+5286
Eze 2: 3 to a r nation that has rebelled against me; H5277
Eze 2: 5 they are a r people—they will know H5308
Eze 2: 6 by them, though they are a r people. H5308
Eze 2: 7 they listen or fail to listen, for they are r. H5308
Eze 2: 8 Do not rebel like that r people; open your H5308
Eze 3: 9 by them, though they are a r people." H5308
Eze 3:26 to rebuke them, for they are a r people. H5308
Eze 3:27 let them refuse; for they are a r people. H5308
Eze 12: 2 of man, you are living among a r people. H5308
Eze 12: 2 do not hear, for they are a r people. H5308
Eze 12: 3 understand, though they are a r people. H5308
Eze 12: 9 not the Israelites, that r people, ask you, H5308
Eze 12:25 For in your days, you r people, I will fulfill H5308
Eze 17:12 "Say to this r people, 'Do you not know H5308
Eze 24: 3 Tell this r people a parable and say to H5308
Eze 44: 6 Say to r Israel, 'This is what the Sovereign H5308
Hos 9:15 longer love them; all their leaders *are* r. H6253
Hos 14: 9 walk in them, but the r stumble in them. H7321
Zep 3: 1 to the city of oppressors, r and defiled! H5286

Titus 1:10 For there are many r *people*, full of G538

REBELS (14) [REBEL]
Nu 20:10 you r, must we bring you water H5286
Jos 1:18 Whoever r against your word and does not H5286
Isa 1:23 Your rulers *are* r, partners with thieves H6253
Isa 1:28 But r and sinners will both be broken, and H7321
Isa 46: 8 keep it in mind, take it to heart, you r. H7321
Isa 57: 4 Are you not a brood of r, the offspring of H7322
Jer 6:28 They are all **hardened** r, going H6253+6073
Da 8:23 when r have become completely wicked H7321
Hos 5: 2 The r are knee-deep in slaughter. I will H8473
Mt 27:38 Two r were crucified with him, one on his G3334
Mt 27:44 In the same way the r who were crucified G3334
Mk 15:27 They crucified two r with him, one on his G3334
Ro 13: 2 whoever r **against** the authority is rebelling G530
1Ti 1: 9 the righteous but for lawbreakers and r, G538

REBIRTH (1) [BEAR]
Titus 3: 5 the washing *of* r and renewal by the G4098

REBUILD (30) [BUILD]
Jos 6:26 is the one who undertakes *to* r this city, H1215
Ezr 5: 2 set to work to r the house of God in A10111
Ezr 5: 3 authorized you to r this temple and to A10111
Ezr 5: 9 authorized you to r this temple and to A10111
Ezr 5:13 issued a decree to r this house of God. A10111
Ezr 5:15 And r the house of God on its site A10111
Ezr 5:17 issue a decree to r this house of God in A10111
Ezr 6: 7 *Let* the governor of the Jews and the Jewish elders r A10111
Ezr 9: 9 us new life to r the house of our God H8123
Ne 2: 5 my ancestors are buried so that *I can* r it." H1215
Ne 2:17 *let us* r the wall of Jerusalem, and H1215
Ne 4:10 so much rubble that we cannot r the wall." H1215
Ps 69:35 will save Zion and r the cities of Judah. H1215
Ps 102:16 For the LORD *will* r Zion and appear in his H1215
Isa 9:10 but *we will* r *with* dressed stone H1215
Isa 45:13 He *will* r my city and set my exiles free H1215
Isa 54:11 I *will* r you with stones of turquoise H8069
Isa 58:12 *Your people will* r the ancient ruins and H1215
Isa 60:10 "Foreigners *will* r your walls, and their H1215
Isa 61: 4 *They will* r the ancient ruins and restore H1215
Jer 33: 7 from captivity and *will* r them as they were H1215
Da 9:25 out to restore and r Jerusalem until the H1215
Am 9:11 its ruins—and *will* r it as it used to be, H1215
Am 9:14 "*They will* r the ruined cities and live in H1215
Hag 1: 2 has not yet come to r the LORD's house. H1215
Mal 1: 4 crushed, *we will* r the ruins." H1215+8740+2256
Mt 26:61 the temple of God and r it in three days. G3868
Ac 15:16 this I will return and r David's fallen tent. G488
Ac 15:16 Its ruins *I will* r, and I will restore G488
Gal 2:18 If *I* r what I destroyed, then I really G4099+3868

REBUILDING (6) [BUILD]
Ezr 2:68 toward the r *of* the house of God on H6641
Ezr 4:12 to Jerusalem and *are* r that rebellious A10111
Ezr 5:11 we *are* r the temple that was built A10111
Ne 2:18 replied, "Let us start r." So they began this H1215
Ne 2:20 We his servants will start r, but as for you H1215
Ne 4: 1 Sanballat heard that we *were* r the wall, H1215

REBUILT (44) [BUILD]
Nu 21:27 "Come to Heshbon and *let it* **be** r; let H1215
Nu 32:37 And the Reubenites r Heshbon, Elealeh H1215
Nu 32:38 They gave names to the cities *they* r. H1215
Dt 13:16 is to remain a ruin forever, never *to* **be** r, H1215
Jdg 18:28 The Danites r the city and settled there H1215
Jdg 21:23 inheritance and r the towns and settled H1215
1Ki 9:17 And Solomon r Gezer.) He built up Lower H1215
1Ki 16:34 Hiel of Bethel r Jericho. He laid its H1215
2Ki 14:22 He was the *one who* r Elath and restored it H1215
2Ki 15:35 Jotham r the Upper Gate of the temple of H1215
2Ki 21: 3 *He* r the high places his H8740+2256+1215
2Ch 8: 2 Solomon r the villages that Hiram had H1215
2Ch 8: 5 *He* r Upper Beth Horon and Lower Beth H1215
2Ch 24:13 *They* r the temple of God according to its H6641
2Ch 26: 2 He was the one *who* r Elath and restored it H1215
2Ch 26: 6 *He* then r towns near Ashdod and H1215
2Ch 27: 3 Jotham r the Upper Gate of the temple of H1215
2Ch 33: 3 *He* r the high places his H8740+2256+1215
2Ch 33:14 Afterward *he* r the outer wall of the City of H1215
Ezr 4:21 that this city *will* not **be** r until I so order. A10111
Ezr 6: 3 *Let* the temple **be** r as a place to present A10111
Ne 3: 1 went to work and r the Sheep Gate. H1215
Ne 3: 3 The Fish Gate *was* r *by* the sons of H1215
Ne 3:13 They r it and put its doors with their bolts H1215
Ne 3:14 He r it and put its doors with their bolts H1215
Ne 3:15 He r it, roofing it over and putting its H1215
Ne 4: 6 So *we* r the wall till all of it reached half H1215
Ne 6: 1 our enemies that *I had* r the wall and not H1215
Ne 7: 1 After the wall *had* **been** r and I had set H1215
Ne 7: 4 and the houses *had* not yet **been** r. H1215
Job 12:14 What he tears down cannot **be** r; those he H1215
Isa 25: 2 a city no more; *it will* never **be** r. H1215
Isa 44:26 of Judah, '*They shall* **be** r,' and of their H1215
Isa 44:28 say of Jerusalem, "*Let it* **be** r," and of the H1215
Jer 30:18 the city *will* **be** r on her ruins, and H1215
Jer 31: 4 up again, and *you*, Virgin Israel, *will* **be** r. H1215
Jer 31:38 "when this city *will* **be** r for me from the H1215
Eze 11: 3 'Haven't our houses *been* recently r? H1215
Eze 26:14 *You will* never **be** r, for I the LORD have H1215
Eze 36:10 towns will be inhabited and the ruins r. H1215
Eze 36:33 your towns, and the ruins *will* **be** r. H1215
Eze 36:36 that I the LORD *have* r what was destroyed H1215
Da 9:25 *It will* **be** r with streets and a trench, but H1215
Zec 1:16 with mercy, and there my house *will* **be** r. H1215

REBUKE (57) [REBUKED, REBUKES, REBUKING]
Lev 19:17 **R** your neighbor **frankly** so you will H3519+3519
Dt 28:20 confusion and r in everything you put your H4486
Ru 2:16 them for her to pick up, and don't r her." H1721
1Sa 2:25 did not listen to their father's r, for it was H7754
2Sa 22:16 of the earth laid bare at the r *of* the LORD, H1722
2Ki 19: 3 is a day of distress and r and disgrace, H9349
2Ki 19: 4 that *he will* r him for the words the H3519
Job 11: 3 *Will* no *one* r you when you mock? H4007
Job 20: 3 I hear a r *that* dishonors me, and my H4592
Job 26:11 of the heavens quake, aghast at his r. H1722
Ps 6: 1 *do* not r me in your anger or discipline me H3519
Ps 18:15 of the earth laid bare at your r, H1722
Ps 38: 1 *do* not r me in your anger or discipline me H3519
Ps 39:11 When you r and discipline anyone for H9350
Ps 68:30 **R** the beast among the reeds, the herd of H1721
Ps 76: 6 At your r, God of Jacob, both horse and H1722
Ps 80:16 with fire; at your r your people perish. H1722
Ps 104: 7 But at your r the waters fled, at the sound H1722
Ps 119:21 *You* r the arrogant, who are accursed H1721
Ps 141: 5 is a kindness; *let him* r me—that is oil on H3519
Pr 1:23 Repent at my r! Then I will pour out my H9350
Pr 1:25 all my advice and do not accept my r, H9350
Pr 1:30 not accept my advice and spurned my r, H9350
Pr 3:11 LORD's discipline, and do not resent his r, H9350
Pr 9: 8 *Do* not r mockers or they will hate you H3519
Pr 9: 8 r the wise and they will love you. H3519
Pr 17:10 A r impresses a discerning person more H1722
Pr 19:25 will learn prudence; r the discerning, and H3519
Pr 25:12 of fine gold is the r *of* a wise judge to a H3519
Pr 27: 5 Better is open r than hidden love. H9350
Pr 30: 6 or *he will* r you and prove you a liar. H3519
Ecc 7: 5 better to heed the r *of* a wise person than H1722
Isa 37: 3 is a day of distress and r and disgrace, H9349
Isa 37: 4 that *he will* r him for the words the H3519
Isa 50: 2 By a mere r I dry up the sea, I turn rivers H1722
Isa 51:20 wrath of the LORD, with the r *of* your God. H1722
Isa 54: 9 to be angry with you, never *to* r you again. H1721
Isa 66:15 with fury, and his r with flames of fire. H1722
Jer 2:19 punish you; your backsliding *will* r you. H3519
Eze 3:26 you will be silent and unable *to* r them, H3519
Eze 5:15 in anger and in wrath and with stinging r. H9350
Hos 2: 2 "**R** your mother, rebuke her, for she is not H8189
Hos 2: 2 "Rebuke your mother, r her, for she is not H8189
Zep 3:17 in his love *he will* **no longer** r you, but will H3087
Zec 3: 2 said to Satan, "The LORD r you, Satan! H1721
Zec 3: 2 who has chosen Jerusalem, r you! H1721
Mal 2: 3 "Because of you I *will* r your descendants H1721
Mt 16:22 Peter took him aside and began *to* r him G2203
Mk 8:32 Peter took him aside and began *to* r him. G2203
Lk 17: 3 sins against you, r them; and if they G2203
Lk 19:39 said to Jesus, "Teacher, r your disciples!" G2203
1Ti 5: 1 *Do* not r an older man **harshly**, but exhort G2159
2Ti 4: 2 r and encourage—with great G2203
Titus 1:13 Therefore r them sharply, so that they will G1794
Titus 2:15 Encourage and r with all authority G1794
Jude 9 him for slander but said, "The Lord r you!" G2203
Rev 3:19 Those whom I love *I* r and discipline. G1794

REBUKED (32) [REBUKE]
Ge 31:42 toil of my hands, and last night *he* r you." H3519
Ge 37:10 brothers, his father r him and said, "What H1721
1Sa 24: 7 words David **sharply** r his men and did H9117
1Ki 1: 6 His father *had* never r him by asking, H6772
1Ch 16:21 to oppress them; for their sake *he* r kings: H3519
Ne 13:11 So *I* r the officials and asked them, "Why H8189
Ne 13:17 *I* r the nobles of Judah and said to them H8189
Ne 13:25 *I* r them and called curses down on them. H8189
Ps 9: 5 *You have* r the nations and destroyed the H1721
Ps 105:14 to oppress them; for their sake *he* r kings: H3519
Ps 106: 9 *He* r the Red Sea, and it dried up; he led H1721
Mt 8:26 Then he got up and r the winds and the G2203
Mt 17:18 Jesus r the demon, and it came out of the G2203
Mt 19:13 pray for them. But the disciples r them. G2203
Mt 20:31 The crowd r them **and told** them to be G2203
Mk 4:39 r the wind and said to the waves G2203
Mk 8:33 looked at his disciples, *he* r Peter. G2203
Mk 9:25 to the scene, *he* r the impure spirit. G2203
Mk 10:13 hands on them, but the disciples r them. G2203
Mk 10:48 Many r him and told him to be quiet, but G2203
Mk 14: 5 And *they* r her **harshly**. G1839
Mk 16:14 *he* r them for their lack of faith and their G3943
Lk 3:19 But *when* John r Herod the tetrarch G1794
Lk 4:39 So he bent over her and r the fever, and it G2203
Lk 4:41 But *he* r them and would not allow them G2203
Lk 8:24 He got up and r the wind and the raging G2203
Lk 9:42 But Jesus r the impure spirit, healed the G2203
Lk 9:55 But Jesus turned and r them. G2203
Lk 18:15 When the disciples saw this, *they* r them. G2203
Lk 18:39 who led the way r him and told him to G2203
Lk 23:40 But the other criminal r him. "Don't you G2203
2Pe 2:16 But *he was* r for his wrongdoing by G1792+2400

REBUKES (10) [REBUKE]
Job 22: 4 it for your piety that *he* r you and brings H3519
Ps 2: 5 *He* r them in his anger and terrifies them H1819
Pr 9: 7 *whoever* r the wicked incurs abuse. H3519
Pr 13: 1 a mocker does not respond to r. H1722
Pr 13: 8 the poor cannot respond to **threatening** r. H1722
Pr 28:23 *Whoever* r a person will in the end gain H3519
Pr 29: 1 stiff-necked after many r will suddenly be H9350
Isa 17:13 when *he* r them they flee far away H1721
Na 1: 4 *He* r the sea and dries it up; he makes all H1721
Heb 12: 5 do not lose heart *when* he r you, G1794

REBUKING (2) [REBUKE]
Ps 57: 3 saves me, r those who hotly pursue me H3070
2Ti 3:16 is useful for teaching, r, correcting and G1791

RECAB (NIV84) REKAB

RECABITE (NIV84) REKABITE

RECAH (NIV84) REKAH

RECALL (1) [RECALLED, RECALLING]
2Pe 3: 2 I want you *to* r the words spoken in the G3630

RECALLED (3) [RECALL]
Isa 63:11 Then *his people* r the days of old, the H2349
Eze 23:19 promiscuous as she r the days of her H2349
Jn 2:22 his disciples r what he had said. G3630

RECALLING (3) [RECALL]
Job 11:16 your trouble, r it only as waters gone by. H2349
1Ti 1:18 so that **by** *r* them you may fight the battle AIT
2Ti 1: 4 **R** your tears, I long to see you, so that I G3630

RECAPTURE (1) [CAPTURE]
Eze 14: 5 I will do this to r the hearts of the people H9530

RECAPTURED (1) [CAPTURE]
2Ki 13:25 of Jehoahaz r from H8740+2256+4374

RECEDE (1) [RECEDED]
Ge 8: 5 The waters continued *to* r until the tenth H2893

RECEDED (5) [RECEDE]
Ge 8: 1 a wind over the earth, and the waters r. H8896
Ge 8: 3 The water r **steadily** from H8740+2143+2256+8740
Ge 8: 8 to see if the water *had* r from the surface H7837
Ge 8:11 knew that the water *had* r from the earth. H7837
Rev 6:14 The heavens r like a scroll being rolled up G714

RECEIPT OF CUSTOM (KJV) TAX COLLECTOR'S BOOTH, TAX BOOTH

RECEIVE (111) [RECEIVED, RECEIVES, RECEIVING, RECEPTION]
Ge 4:11 opened its mouth to r your brother's blood H4374
Ge 32:20 I see him, perhaps *he will* r me." H5951+7156
Ex 25: 2 *You are to* r the offering for me from H4374
Ex 25: 3 are the offerings *you are to* r from them: H4374
Ex 30:16 **R** the atonement money from the Israelites H4374
Nu 18:23 *They will* r no **inheritance** among H5706+5709
Nu 18:26 'When *you* r from the Israelites the tithe I H4374
Nu 18:28 from all the tithes *you* r from the Israelites H4374
Nu 26:54 each *is to* r its inheritance according to H5989
Nu 32:19 *We will* not r *any* **inheritance** with them H5706
Dt 9: 9 on the mountain to r the tablets of stone, H4374
Dt 19:14 in the inheritance *you* r in the land the H5706
Dt 33: 3 all bow down, and from you r instruction, H5951
2Sa 15: 4 to me and *I would* **see that** they r **justice**." H7405
2Ki 12: 5 *Let* every priest r the money from one of H4374
Ne 10:38 the Levites when they r *the* **tithes**, H6923
Job 3:12 were there knees *to* r me and breasts that H7709
Job 35: 7 or what *does he* r from your hand? H4374
Ps 24: 5 *They will* r blessing from the LORD and H5951
Ps 27:10 mother forsake me, the LORD *will* r me. H665
Pr 8:35 find me find life and r favor from the LORD. H7049
Pr 11:31 If the righteous r *their* **due** on earth, how H8966
Pr 28:10 the blameless *will* r a good **inheritance**. H5706
Pr 28:27 who close their eyes to them r many curses. NDT
Ecc 6: 3 and *does* not r proper burial H2118+4200
Ecc 8:10 holy place and r **praise** in the city where H8655
Ecc 11: 1 after many days *you may* r a return. H5162
Isa 50:11 is what you *shall* r from my hand: H2118+4200
Isa 61: 7 of your shame you will r a double portion, NDT
Eze 16:33 All prostitutes r gifts, but you give H5989+4200
Eze 16:61 be ashamed when you r your sisters, H4374
Da 2: 6 *you will* r from me gifts and rewards and A10618
Da 7:18 of the Most High *will* r the kingdom and A10618
Da 11:34 *they will* r a little **help**, and H6468+6469
Da 12:13 days you will rise to r your allotted NDT
Hos 14: 2 "Forgive all our sins and r us graciously H4374
Mt 10:41 as a prophet *will* r a prophet's reward, G3284
Mt 10:41 a righteous person *will* r a righteous G3284
Mt 11: 5 The blind r **sight**, the lame walk, those who G329
Mt 19:29 fields for my sake *will* r a hundred times G3284
Mt 20:10 were hired first, they expected to r more. G3284
Mt 21:22 *you will* r whatever you ask for in prayer." G3284
Mk 4:16 hear the word and at once r it with joy. G3284
Mk 10:15 anyone *who will* not r the kingdom of God G1312
Mk 10:30 *will* fail to r a hundred times as much in G3284
Lk 7:22 The blind r **sight**, the lame walk, those who G329
Lk 8:13 are the ones who r the word with joy G1312
Lk 18:17 anyone *who will* not r the kingdom of God G1312
Lk 18:30 *will* fail *to* r many times as much in this age, G655
Lk 18:42 said to him, "**R** *your* **sight**; your faith has G329
Jn 1:11 was his own, but his own *did* not r him. G4161

R

Jn 1:12 Yet to all *who did* r him, to those who G3284
Jn 3:27 "A person can r only what is given them G3284
Jn 7:39 those who believed in him were later *to* r. G3284
Jn 16:14 it is from me *that he will* r what he will G3284
Jn 16:15 I said the Spirit *will* r from me what he G3284
Jn 16:24 Ask and *you will* r, and your joy will be G3284
Jn 20:22 on them and said, "R the Holy Spirit. G3284
Ac 1: 8 But *you will* r power when the Holy Spirit G3284
Ac 2:38 And *you will* r the gift of the Holy Spirit. G3284
Ac 3:21 Heaven must r him until the time comes G1312
Ac 7:59 Stephen prayed, "Lord Jesus, r my spirit." G1312
Ac 8:15 there that *they might* r the Holy Spirit, G3284
Ac 8:19 I lay my hands *may* r the Holy Spirit." G3284
Ac 19: 2 "*Did you* r the Holy Spirit when you G3284
Ac 19: 3 "Then what baptism did you r? G1650
Ac 19:25 that we r a good income from this G1639
Ac 20:35 'It is more blessed to give than *to* r.'" G3284
Ac 22:13 me and said, 'Brother Saul, r your **sight**! G329
Ac 26:18 *so that* they *may* r forgiveness of sins and G3284
Ro 5:17 more will those *who* r God's abundant G3284
Ro 11:31 that they too *may* now r **mercy** as a result G1796
Ro 16: 2 I ask you to r her in the Lord in a way G4657
1Co 3:14 built survives, the builder *will* r a reward. G3284
1Co 4: 5 At that time each *will* r their praise from G1181
1Co 4: 7 What do you have that *you did* not r? And G3284
1Co 4: 7 And if *you did* r it, why do you boast as G3284
1Co 9:14 *that* those who preach the gospel
should r *their* **living** G2409
2Co 1: 4 the comfort *we* ourselves r from God. G4151S
2Co 5:10 each of us *may* r **what is due** us for the G3152
2Co 6: 1 we urge you not *to* r God's grace in vain. G1312
2Co 6:17 no unclean thing, and I *will* r you." G1654
2Co 11: 4 if *you* r a different spirit from the Spirit G3284
Gal 1:12 I *did* not r it from any man, nor was I G4161
Gal 3: 2 *Did you* r the Spirit by the works of the law G3284
Gal 3:14 so that by faith *we might* r the promise of G3284
Gal 4: 5 that *we might* r adoption to sonship. G655
Php 2:19 may be cheered *when I* r **news** about you. G1182
Col 3:24 you know that *you will* r an inheritance G655
1Th 5: 9 suffer wrath but to r salvation through our G4348
1Ti 1:16 would believe in him and r eternal life. G1650
2Ti 2: 5 *does* not r **the victor's crown** except G5110
2Ti 2: 6 be the first *to* r **a share** of the crops. G3561
Heb 4:16 so that *we may* r mercy and find grace to G3284
Heb 9:15 those who are called *may* r the promised G3284
Heb 10:36 *you will* r what he has promised. G3152
Heb 11: 8 place he would later r as his inheritance, G3284
Heb 11:13 *They did* not r the things promised; they G3284
Heb 11:19 speaking *he did* r Isaac **back** from death G3152
Jas 1: 7 should not expect to r anything from the G3284
Jas 1:12 *that person will* r the crown of life that the G3284
Jas 4: 3 When you ask, *you do* not r, because you G3284
1Pe 2:20 your credit if *you* r **a beating** for doing G3139
1Pe 5: 4 *you will* r the crown of glory that will never G3152
2Pe 1:11 you *will* r a rich welcome into the G2220
1Jn 3:22 r from him anything we ask, because G3284
Rev 4:11 God, *to* r glory and honor and power G3284
Rev 5:12 *to* r power and wealth and wisdom and G3284
Rev 13:16 to r a mark on their right hands or on their G1443
Rev 17:12 who for one hour *will* r authority as kings G3284
Rev 18: 4 so that *you will* not r any of her plagues; G3284

RECEIVED (138) [RECEIVE]

Ge 33:10 now that *you have* r me **favorably**. H8354
Ge 43:23 treasure in your sacks; I r your silver." H995+448
Ge 47:22 because they r a regular allotment from H4200
Ex 18: 2 Zipporah, his father-in-law Jethro r her H4374
Ex 36: 3 *They* r from Moses all the offerings the H4374
Nu 23:20 *I have* r a command to bless; he has H4374
Nu 26:62 because they r no inheritance among H5989
Nu 32:18 of the Israelites *has* r their inheritance. H5706
Nu 34:14 of Manasseh *have* r their inheritance. H4374
Nu 34:15 a half tribes *have* r their inheritance H4374
Dt 18: 8 even though he has r money from the sale NDT
Jos 13: 8 the Gadites *had* r the inheritance that H4374
Jos 14: 1 Israelites r **as an inheritance** in the land H5706
Jos 14: 4 The Levites r no share of the land but only H5989
Jos 16: 4 of Joseph, r *their* **inheritance**. H5706
Jos 17: 1 who *had* r Gilead and Bashan H2118+4200
Jos 17: 6 tribe of Manasseh r an inheritance among H5706
Jos 18: 2 tribes who *had* not *yet* r their inheritance. H2745
Jos 18: 7 of Manasseh *have already* r their H4374
Jos 19: 9 Simeonites r *their* **inheritance** within the H5706
Jos 21: 7 r twelve towns from the tribes of Reuben H4200
Jos 21:23 Also from the tribe of Dan they r Eltekeh NDT
Jos 21:25 tribe of Manasseh they r Taanach and Gath NDT
1Ki 5: 8 "*I have* r the **message** you sent me and H9048
1Ki 10:14 gold that Solomon r yearly was 666 H995+4200
2Ki 12: 4 the **money** *r from* personal vows and the AIT
2Ki 19: 9 Now Sennacherib r **a report** that Tirhakah H9048
2Ki 19:14 Hezekiah r the letter from the messengers H4374
2Ki 20:13 Hezekiah r the envoys and showed them H9048
1Ch 6:71 The Gershonites r the following: From the H4200
1Ch 6:71 of Manasseh they r Golan in Bashan and NDT
1Ch 6:72 from the tribe of Issachar they r Kedesh NDT
1Ch 6:74 from the tribe of Asher they r Mashal NDT
1Ch 6:76 tribe of Naphtali they r Kedesh in Galilee, NDT
1Ch 6:77 the rest of the Levites) r the following: H4200
1Ch 6:77 From the tribe of Zebulun they r Jokneam NDT
1Ch 6:78 east of Jericho they r Bezer in the wilderness NDT
1Ch 6:80 the tribe of Gad they r Ramoth in Gilead, NDT
1Ch 11: 6 went up first, and so *he* r the command. H2118
1Ch 12:18 So David r them and made them leaders H7691
2Ch 9:13 the gold that Solomon r yearly was 666 H995
2Ch 21:12 Jehoram r a letter from Elijah the H995+448
Ezr 5: 5 go to Darius and his written reply *be* r. A10754
Ezr 8:30 priests and Levites r the silver and gold H7691
Est 6: 3 recognition *has* Mordecai r for this?" H6913
Job 15:18 hiding nothing r **from** their ancestors H4946
Ps 68:18 many captives; *you* r gifts from people H4374
Isa 37: 9 Now Sennacherib r **a report** that Tirhakah H9048
Isa 37:14 Hezekiah r the letter from the messengers H4374
Isa 39: 2 Hezekiah r the envoys **gladly** and H8523+6584
Isa 40: 2 that *she has* r from the LORD's hand H4374
Isa 47:13 All the **counsel** you have *r* has only worn you AIT
Hab 1: 1 The prophecy that Habakkuk the prophet r. H2600
Mt 6: 2 I tell you, *they have* r their reward **in full**. G600
Mt 6: 5 I tell you, *they have* r their reward **in full**. G600
Mt 6:16 I tell you, *they have* r their reward **in full**. G600
Mt 10: 8 Freely *you have* r; freely give. G3284
Mt 20: 9 afternoon came and each r a denarius. G3284
Mt 20:10 But each one of them also r a denarius. G3284
Mt 20:11 *When they* r it, they began to grumble G3284
Mt 20:34 Immediately *they* r *their* **sight** and followed G329
Mt 25:16 The *man who had* r five bags of gold went G3284
Mt 25:18 But the *man who had* r one bag went off G3284
Mt 25:20 The *man who had* r five bags of gold G3284
Mt 25:24 "Then the *man who had* r one bag of G3284
Mt 25:27 I returned *I* would have r it **back** with G3152
Mk 10:52 Immediately *he* r *his* **sight** and followed G329
Mk 11:24 believe that *you have* r it, and it will be G3284
Lk 6:24 for *you have already* r your comfort. G600
Lk 16:25 that in your lifetime *you* r your good things, G655
Lk 16:25 while Lazarus r bad things, but now G3931S
Lk 18:43 Immediately *he* r *his* **sight** and followed G329
Jn 1:16 his fullness we *have* all r grace in place of G3284
Jn 9:15 also asked him how *he had* r *his* **sight**. G329
Jn 9:18 been blind and *had* r *his* **sight** until they G329
Jn 10:18 This command *I* r from my Father." G3284
Jn 19:30 When *he had* r the drink, Jesus said, "It is G3284
Ac 1:18 With the payment he *r for* his **wickedness** AIT
Ac 2:33 *he has* r from the Father the promised G3284
Ac 5: 3 some of the money you r for the land? NDT
Ac 7:38 he r living words to pass on to us. G1312
Ac 7:53 *you* who *have* r the law that was given G3284
Ac 8:17 hands on them, and *they* r the Holy Spirit. G3284
Ac 10:47 They *have* r the Holy Spirit just as we G3284
Ac 11: 1 the Gentiles also *had* r the word of God. G1312
Ac 16:24 *When* he r these orders, he put them in G3284
Ac 17:11 *for* they r the message with great G1312
Ac 21:17 the brothers and sisters r us warmly. G622
Ac 28:21 "We *have* not r any letters from Judea G1312
Ro 1: 5 Through him *we* r grace and apostleship G3284
Ro 1:27 r in themselves the due penalty for G655
Ro 3:25 the shedding of his blood—to be *r* **by** faith. AIT
Ro 4:11 And *he* r circumcision as a sign, a seal of G3284
Ro 4:13 his offspring r the promise that he NDT
Ro 5:11 through whom *we have* now r G3284
Ro 8:15 The Spirit *you* r does not make you slaves G3284
Ro 8:15 the Spirit *you* r brought about your G3284
Ro 11:30 to God *have* now r **mercy** as a result of G1796
Ro 15:28 and *have* **made sure that** they *have* r this G5381
Ro 15:31 may be **favorably** r by the Lord's G2347
1Co 2:12 What *we have* r is not the spirit of the G3284
1Co 6:19 who is in you, whom *you have* r from God? G2400
1Co 11:23 For I r from the Lord what I also passed on G4161
1Co 15: 1 which *you* r and on which you have taken G4161
1Co 15: 3 For what *I* r I passed on to you as of first G4161
2Co 1: 9 we felt *we had* r the sentence of death. G2400
2Co 11: 4 a different spirit from the Spirit *you* r, G3284
2Co 11:24 Five times *I* r from the Jews the forty lashes G3284
Gal 1:12 I r it by revelation from Jesus Christ. NDT
Eph 4: 1 a life worthy of the calling *you have* r. G2813S
Php 4: 9 you have learned or r or heard from me, G4161
Php 4:18 *I have* r full **payment** and have more than G600
Php 4:18 *now that I have* r from Epaphroditus the G1312
Col 2: 6 So then, just as *you* r Christ Jesus as Lord G4161
Col 4:10 (*You have* r instructions about him; if he G3284
Col 4:17 the ministry *you have* r in the Lord. G4161
1Th 2:13 because, *when you* r the word of God G4161
2Th 3: 6 according to the teaching *you* r from us. G4161
1Ti 4: 3 God created to be r with thanksgiving by G3562
1Ti 4: 4 is to be rejected *if it is* r with thanksgiving, G3284
Heb 2: 2 disobedience r its just punishment, G3284
Heb 6:15 patiently, Abraham r what was promised. G2209
Heb 8: 6 the ministry Jesus *has* r is as superior to G5593
Heb 10:26 on sinning after *we have* r the knowledge G3284
Heb 10:32 earlier days *after you had r the* **light**, G5894
Heb 11:35 Women r back their dead, raised to life G3284
Heb 11:39 none of *them* r what had been G3152
1Pe 2:10 once you *had* not r **mercy**, but now you G1796
1Pe 2:10 received mercy, but now *you have* r **mercy**. G1796
1Pe 4:10 whatever gift *you have* r to serve others, G3284
2Pe 1: 1 *who* through the righteousness of our God
and Savior Jesus Christ *have* r G3275
2Pe 1:17 *He* r honor and glory from God the Father G3284
1Jn 2:27 the anointing *you* r from him remains in G3284
Rev 2:27 just as I *have* r authority from my Father. G3284
Rev 3: 3 therefore, what *you have* r and heard G3284
Rev 17:12 ten kings who *have* not yet r a kingdom, G3284
Rev 19:20 deluded those *who had* r the mark of the G3284
Rev 20: 4 its image and *had* not r its mark on G3284

RECEIVES (14) [RECEIVE]

Job 27:13 a ruthless man r from the Almighty: H4374
Pr 18:22 what is good and r favor from the LORD. H7049
Ecc 10:11 before it is charmed, the charmer r no fee. H4200
Mt 7: 8 For everyone who asks r; the one who G3284
Mt 13:20 hears the word and at once r it with joy. G3284
Lk 11:10 For everyone who asks r; the one who G3284
Ac 10:43 who believes in him r forgiveness of sins G3284
Ro 14:18 is pleasing to God and r human approval. NDT
Gal 6: 6 the *one who* r **instruction** in the word G2994
Heb 5: 4 on himself, but he r it when called by God NDT
Heb 6: 7 whom it is farmed r the blessing of God. G3561
Rev 2:17 known only *to the one who* r it. G3284
Rev 14: 9 its image and r its mark on their G3284
Rev 14:11 for anyone *who* r the mark of its name." G3284

RECEIVING (10) [RECEIVE]

Pr 1: 3 r instruction in prudent behavior, doing H4374
Ac 7:45 *After* r the tabernacle, our ancestors under G1342
Ac 21:40 *After* r the commander's **permission**, Paul G2205
Ro 9: 4 covenants, the r **of the law**, the temple G3792
2Co 7:15 obedient, r him with fear and trembling. G1312
2Co 11: 8 other churches *by* r support from them so G3284
Php 4:15 with me in the matter of giving and r, G3331
Heb 12:28 *since we are* r a kingdom that cannot be G4161
1Pe 1: 9 *for you are* r the end result of your faith G3152
3Jn 7 they went out, r no help from the pagans. G3284

RECENT (1) [RECENTLY]

1Ti 3: 6 He must not be a r **convert**, or he may G3745

RECENTLY (5) [RECENT]

Dt 24: 5 If a man has r married, he must not be H2543
Dt 32:17 gods that r appeared, gods H2543+4946+7940
Jer 34:15 R you repented and did what is H2021+3427
Eze 11: 3 'Haven't our houses been r rebuilt?' H928+7940
Ac 18: 2 who had r come from Italy with his wife G4711

RECEPTION (1) [RECEIVE]

1Th 1: 9 report what kind of r you gave us. G1658

RECESSES (2)

Job 28: 3 search out the **farthest** r for ore in H3972+9417
Job 38:16 of the sea or walked in the r *of* the deep? H2984

RECHAB, RECHABITES (KJV) REKAB, REKABITE

RECITE (4) [RECITED, RECITING]

Dt 27:14 The Levites *shall* r to all the H6699+2256+606
Jdg 5:11 *They* r the victories of the LORD, the H9480
Ps 45: 1 by a noble theme *as* I r my verses for the H606
Ps 50:16 right have you to r my laws or take my H6218

RECITED (1) [RECITE]

Dt 31:30 And Moses r the words of this song from H1819

RECITING (1) [RECITE]

Dt 32:45 When Moses finished r all these words to H1819

RECKLESS (5)

Nu 22:32 because your path *is a* r *one* before me. H3740
Jdg 9: 4 Abimelek used it to hire r scoundrels H8199
Pr 12:18 The **words** of the r pierce like swords, but H1051
Jer 23:32 lead my people astray with their r lies, H7071
1Pe 4: 4 that you do not join them in their r, G431

RECKONED (8) [RECKONING]

Ge 21:12 through Isaac that your offspring *will* **be** r. H7924
Ge 48: 5 before I came to you here will be r as mine; NDT
Ge 48: 6 they inherit *they will* **be** r under the H7924
Lev 7:18 *It will* not **be** r to their **credit**, for it has H3108
Nu 18:27 Your offering *will* **be** r to you as grain from H3108
Nu 18:30 *it will* **be** r to you as the product of the H3108
Ro 9: 7 through Isaac *that* your offspring *will be* r." G2813
Heb 11:18 through Isaac *that* your offspring *will be* r." G2813

RECKONING (3) [RECKONED]

Isa 10: 3 What will you do on the day of r, when H7213
Hos 5: 9 Ephraim will be laid waste on the day of r. H9349
Hos 9: 7 are coming, the days of r are at hand. H8936

RECLAIM (1) [CLAIM]

Isa 11:11 a second time to r the surviving remnant H7864

RECLAIMED (1) [CLAIM]

Est 8: 2 which *he had* r from Haman, and H6296

RECLINE (1) [RECLINED, RECLINING]

Lk 12:37 *will* **have** them r **at the table** and will come G369

RECLINED (3) [RECLINE]

Lk 7:36 to the Pharisee's house and r **at the table**. G2884
Lk 11:37 with him; so he went in and r **at the table**. G404
Lk 22:14 Jesus and his apostles r **at the table**. G404

RECLINING (7) [RECLINE]

Est 7: 8 falling on the couch where Esther was r. H6584
Mt 26: 7 on his head *as he was* r **at the table**. G367
Mt 26:20 Jesus *was* r **at the table** with the Twelve. G367
Mk 14: 3 r **at the table** in the home of Simon the G2879
Mk 14:18 *While* they *were* r **at** *the* **table** eating, he G367
Jn 12: 2 was among those r **at the table** with him. G367
Jn 13:23 whom Jesus loved, was r next to him. G367

RECOGNITION (3) [RECOGNIZE]

Est 6: 3 "What honor and **r** has Mordecai received H1525
1Co 16:18 spirit and yours also. Such men *deserve* **r**. *G2105*
1Ti 5: 3 **Give proper r** to those widows who are *G5506*

RECOGNIZE (15) [RECOGNITION, RECOGNIZED, RECOGNIZES, RECOGNIZING]

Ge 27:23 *He did* not **r** him, for his hands were hairy H5795
Ge 38:25 *"See if you* **r** whose seal and cord and H5795
Ge 42: 8 his brothers, they *did* not **r** him. H5795
Dt 33: 9 *He did* not **r** his brothers or acknowledge H5795
Job 2:12 a distance, *they could* hardly **r** him; they H5795
Mt 7:16 By their fruit *you will* **r** them. Do people *G2105*
Mt 7:20 by their fruit *you will* **r** them. *G2105*
Mt 17:12 and *they did* not **r** him, but have *G2105*
Lk 19:44 because *you did* not **r** the time of God's *G1182*
Jn 1:10 through him, the world *did* not **r** him. *G1182*
Jn 10: 5 him because *they do* not **r** a stranger's *G3857*
Ac 13:27 of Jerusalem and their rulers *did* **not r** Jesus, *G51*
Ac 27:39 daylight came, *they did* not **r** the land, but *G2105*
1Jn 4: 2 This is how *you can* **r** the Spirit of God *G1182*
1Jn 4: 6 This is how *we* **r** the Spirit of truth and the *G1182*

RECOGNIZED (25) [RECOGNIZE]

Ge 37:33 *He* **r** it and said, "It is my son's robe H5795
Ge 38:26 Judah **r** them and said, "She is more H5795
Ge 42: 7 saw his brothers, *he* **r** them, but he H5795
Ge 42: 8 Although Joseph **r** his brothers, they did H5795
Jdg 18: 3 they **r** the voice of the young Levite H5795
Ru 3:14 got up before anyone *could be* **r**; and H5795
1Sa 3:20 from Dan to Beersheba **r** that Samuel was H3359
1Sa 26:17 Saul **r** David's voice and said, "Is that your H5795
1Ki 14: 2 so you won't *be* **r** as the wife of Jeroboam. H3359
1Ki 18: 7 Obadiah **r** him, bowed down to the H5795
1Ki 20:41 the king of Israel **r** him as one of the H5795
Jer 28: 9 prophesies peace *will* **be r** as one truly H3359
La 4: 8 than soot; *they are* not **r** in the streets. H5795
Mt 12:33 fruit will be bad, for a tree *is* **r** by its fruit. *G1182*
Mt 14:35 And *when* the men of that place **r** Jesus *G2105*
Mk 6:33 saw them leaving **r** them and ran on foot *G2105*
Mk 6:54 they got out of the boat, *people* **r** Jesus. *G2105*
Lk 6:44 Each tree *is* **r** by its own fruit. People do *G1182*
Lk 24:31 their eyes were opened and *they* **r** him, *G2105*
Lk 24:35 how Jesus *was* **r** by them when he *G1182*
Ac 3:10 *they* **r** him as the same man who used to *G2105*
Ac 12:14 *When she* **r** Peter's voice, she was so *G2105*
Ro 7:13 in order that sin *might be* **r** as sin, it used *G5743*
Gal 2: 7 *they* **r** that I had been entrusted with the *G3972*
Gal 2: 9 of fellowship *when they* **r** the grace given *G1182*

RECOGNIZES (1) [RECOGNIZE]

Job 11:11 Surely he **r** deceivers; and when he sees H3359

RECOGNIZING (1) [RECOGNIZE]

Lk 24:16 they were kept from **r** him. *G2105*

RECOIL (1) [RECOILS]

Ps 54: 5 *Let* evil **r** on those who slander me; in H8740

RECOILS (1) [RECOIL]

Ps 7:16 The trouble they cause **r** on them; their H8740

RECOMMENDATION (1) [RECOMMENDED]

2Co 3: 1 people, letters *of* **r** to you or from you? *G5364*

RECOMMENDED (1) [RECOMMENDATION]

Est 6:10 Do not neglect anything *you have* **r**." H1819

RECOMPENSE (2)

Isa 40:10 is with him, and his **r** accompanies him. H7190
Isa 62:11 is with him, and his **r** accompanies him. H7190

RECONCILE (3) [RECONCILED, RECONCILIATION, RECONCILING]

Ac 7:26 *He tried to* **r** them by saying *G5261+1650+1645*
Eph 2:16 in one body *to* **r** both of them to God *G639*
Col 1:20 through him *to* **r** to himself all things *G639*

RECONCILED (8) [RECONCILE]

Mt 5:24 First go and *be* **r** to them; then come and *G1367*
Lk 12:58 try hard *to be* **r** on the way, or your *G557*
Ro 5:10 *we were* **r** to him through the death of his *G2904*
Ro 5:10 much more, *having been* **r**, shall we be *G2904*
1Co 7:11 unmarried or else *be* **r** to her husband. *G2904*
2Co 5:18 who **r** us to himself through Christ and *G2904*
2Co 5:20 you on Christ's behalf: *Be* **r** to God. *G2904*
Col 1:22 But now *he has* **r** you by Christ's physical *G639*

RECONCILIATION (4) [RECONCILE]

Ro 5:11 through whom we have now received **r**. *G2903*
Ro 11:15 For if their rejection brought **r** to the world *G2903*
2Co 5:18 Christ and gave us the ministry *of* **r**: *G2903*
2Co 5:19 he has committed to us the message *of* **r**. *G2903*

RECONCILING (1) [RECONCILE]

2Co 5:19 that God was **r** the world to himself in *G2904*

RECONSECRATED (1) [CONSECRATE]

Da 8:14 mornings; then the sanctuary *will* **be r**." H7405

RECONSIDER (2) [CONSIDER]

Job 6:29 do not be unjust; **r**, for my integrity H8740+6388
Jer 18:10 then *I will* **r** the good I had intended to do H5714

RECORD (15) [RECORDED, RECORDER, RECORDS]

1Ch 4:33 And they **kept a genealogical r**. H3509
1Ch 5: 1 *could* not **be listed in the genealogical r** H3509
1Ch 7: 7 Their **genealogical r listed** 22,034 H3509
1Ch 7: 9 Their **genealogical r** listed the heads of H9352
2Ch 24:27 the **r** of the restoration of the temple of NDT
Ne 7: 5 the genealogical **r** *of* those who had been H6219
Est 6: 1 of the chronicles, the **r** *of* his reign, to be H1821
Ps 56: 8 **R** my misery; list my tears on your scroll H6218
Ps 56: 8 on your scroll—are they not in your **r**? H6225
Ps 87: 4 *"I will* **r** Rahab and Babylon among those H2349
Ps 130: 3 If *you,* LORD, **kept a r** *of* sins, Lord, who H9068
Jer 22:30 "**R** this man as if childless, a man who H4180
Eze 24: 2 "Son of man, **r** this date, this very H4180+9005
Hos 13:12 is stored up, his sins *are* **kept on r**. H7621
1Co 13: 5 easily angered, *it* **keeps** no **r** of wrongs. *G3357*

RECORDED (22) [RECORD]

Ex 38:21 which **were r** at Moses' command by the H7212
Nu 33: 2 command Moses **r** the stages in their H4180
Dt 28:61 disaster not **r** in this Book of the Law, H4180
Jos 24:26 And Joshua **r** these things in the Book of H4180
1Ki 8: 5 cattle that *they could* not **be r** or counted. H6218
1Ch 9: 1 in the genealogies **r** in the book of the H4180
1Ch 24: 6 **r** their names in the presence of the king H4180
2Ch 5: 6 cattle that *they could* not **be r** or counted. H6218
2Ch 20:34 which **are r** in the book of the kings of H6590
2Ch 26:22 *are* **r** *by* the prophet Isaiah son of Amoz. H4180
2Ch 31:19 to all *who* **were r in the genealogies** of H3509
Ezr 8:34 the entire weight **was r** at that time. H4180
Ne 12:22 **were r** in the reign of Darius the Persian. H4180
Ne 12:23 son of Eliashib **were r** in the book of the H4180
Est 2:23 *All this* **was r** in the book of the annals in H4180
Est 6: 2 It was found **r** there that Mordecai had H4180
Est 9:20 Mordecai **r** these events, and he sent H4180
Job 19:23 that my words **were r**, that they were H4180
Isa 4: 3 all who *are* **r** among the living in H4180
Jer 51:60 all that *had* **been r** concerning Babylon. H4180
Jn 20:30 his disciples, which are not **r** in this book. *G1211*
Rev 20:12 to what they had done as **r** in the books. *G1211*

RECORDER (9) [RECORD]

2Sa 8:16 Jehoshaphat son of Ahilud *was* **r**; H4654
2Sa 20:24 Jehoshaphat son of Ahilud was **r**; H4654
1Ki 4: 3 secretaries; Jehoshaphat son of Ahilud—**r**; H4654
2Ki 18:18 Joah son of Asaph the **r** went out to them. H4654
2Ki 18:37 son of Asaph the **r** went to Hezekiah, H4654
1Ch 18:15 Jehoshaphat son of Ahilud was **r**; H4654
2Ch 34: 8 son of Joahaz, the **r**, to repair the temple H4654
Isa 36: 3 Joah son of Asaph the **r** went out to him. H4654
Isa 36:22 son of Asaph the **r** went to Hezekiah, H4654

RECORDS (34) [RECORD]

Ge 41:49 that he stopped **keeping r** because it was H6218
Ex 6:16 of the sons of Levi according to their **r**: H9352
Ex 6:19 were the clans of Levi according to their **r**. H9352
Nu 1:20 according to the **r** *of* their clans and H9352
Nu 1:22 according to the **r** *of* their clans and H9352
Nu 1:24 according to the **r** *of* their clans and H9352
Nu 1:26 according to the **r** *of* their clans and H9352
Nu 1:28 according to the **r** *of* their clans and H9352
Nu 1:30 according to the **r** *of* their clans and H9352
Nu 1:32 according to the **r** *of* their clans and H9352
Nu 1:34 according to the **r** *of* their clans and H9352
Nu 1:36 according to the **r** *of* their clans and H9352
Nu 1:38 according to the **r** *of* their clans and H9352
Nu 1:40 according to the **r** *of* their clans and H9352
Nu 1:42 according to the **r** *of* their clans and H9352
1Ch 4:22 (These **r** are from ancient times. H1821
1Ch 5: 7 listed according to their **genealogical r**: H9352
1Ch 5:17 these **were entered in the genealogical r** H3509
1Ch 26:31 according to the **genealogical r** of their H9352
1Ch 26:31 of David's reign a search was made in the **r**, NDT
1Ch 29:29 are written in the **r** *of* Samuel the seer, H1821
1Ch 29:29 the **r** *of* Nathan the prophet and the H1821
1Ch 29:29 the prophet and the **r** *of* Gad the seer, H1821
2Ch 9:29 not written in the **r** *of* Nathan the prophet, H1821
2Ch 12:15 not written in the **r** *of* Shemaiah the H1821
2Ch 31:16 **names** *were* **in the genealogical r**— H3509
2Ch 31:17 **enrolled** by their families **in the genealogical r** H3509
2Ch 31:18 community **listed in** *these* **genealogical r**. H3509
2Ch 33:19 all these are written in the **r** *of* the seers. H1821
Ezr 2:62 These searched for their family **r**, but they H4181
Ezr 4:15 In these **r** you will find that this A10515+10177
Ne 7:64 These searched for their family **r**, but they H4181
Est 9:32 and it was written down in the **r**. H6219
Eze 13: 9 of my people or be listed in the **r** *of* Israel, H4181

RECOUNT (2)

Ps 119:13 With my lips *I* **r** all the laws that come H6218
Jer 23:28 prophet who has a dream **r** the dream, H6218

RECOVER (13) [RECOVERED, RECOVERS, RECOVERY]

2Ki 1: 2 of Ekron, to see if *I will* **r** from this injury." H2649
2Ki 8: 8 ask him, '*Will I* **r** from this illness? H2649
2Ki 8: 9 sent me to ask, '*Will I* **r** from this illness? H2649
2Ki 8:10 say to him, '*You will* **certainly r**. H2649+2649
2Ki 8:14 told me that *you would* **certainly r**." H2649+2649
2Ki 8:29 to Jezreel to **r** from the wounds the H8324
2Ki 9:15 to Jezreel to **r** from the wounds the H8324
2Ki 20: 1 you are going to die; *you will* not **r**." H2649
2Ch 14:13 of Cushites fell that they could not **r**; H4695
2Ch 22: 6 to Jezreel to **r** *from* the wounds they had H8324
Isa 38: 1 you are going to die; *you will* not **r**." H2649
Isa 38:21 figs and apply it to the boil, and *he will* **r**." H2649
Eze 7:13 The seller *will* not **r** the property that was H8740

RECOVERED (13) [RECOVER]

Ge 14:16 *He* **r** all the goods and brought back his H8740
Ge 38:12 When Judah *had* **r from** *his* **grief**, he went H5714
1Sa 30:18 David **r** everything the Amalekites had H5911
1Sa 30:22 will not share with them the plunder *we* **r**. H5911
2Sa 14:14 which cannot **be r**, so we must die. H665
2Ki 13:25 and so *he* **r** the Israelite towns. H8740
2Ki 14:28 including how *he* **r** for Israel both H8740
2Ki 16: 6 Rezin king of Aram **r** Elath for Aram by H8740
2Ki 20: 7 did so and applied it to the boil, and *he* **r**. H2649
Jer 41:16 whom Johanan *had* **r** from Ishmael son of H8740
Jer 41:16 court officials *he had* **r** from Gibeon. H8740
Eze 38: 8 you will invade a land *that has* **r** from war, H8740
Rev 18:14 splendor have vanished, never *to be* **r**. *G2351*

RECOVERS (1) [RECOVER]

Ex 21:21 punished if the slave **r** after a day or two, H6641

RECOVERY (4) [RECOVER]

Isa 38: 9 Judah after his illness and **r**: H2649+4946+2716
Isa 39: 1 because he had heard of his illness and **r**. H2616
Lk 4:18 the prisoners and **r of sight** for the blind, *G330*
Ro 11:11 Did they stumble so as to **fall beyond r** *G4406*

RECTANGULAR (2)

1Ki 7: 5 All the doorways had **r** frames; they were H8062
Eze 41:21 The main hall had a **r** doorframe, and the H8062

RED (54) [REDDISH, REDDISH-WHITE]

Ge 25:25 The first to come out was **r**, and his whole H145
Ge 25:30 let me have some of that **r** *stew!* H137
Ex 10:19 locusts and carried them into the **R** Sea. H6068
Ex 13:18 by the desert road toward the **R** Sea. H6068
Ex 15: 4 officers are drowned in the **R** Sea. H6068
Ex 15:22 led Israel from the **R** Sea and they went H6068
Ex 23:31 your borders from the **R** Sea to the H6068
Ex 25: 5 ram skins **dyed r** and another type of H131
Ex 26:14 the tent a covering of ram skins **dyed r**, H131
Ex 35: 7 ram skins **dyed r** and another type of H131
Ex 35:23 ram skins **dyed r** or the other durable H131
Ex 36:19 the tent a covering of ram skins **dyed r**, H131
Ex 39:34 of ram skins **dyed r** and the covering of H131
Lev 11:14 the **r kite**, any kind of black kite, H1798
Nu 14:25 the desert along the route to the **R** Sea." H6068
Nu 19: 2 to bring you a **r** heifer without defect or H137
Nu 21: 4 Mount Hor along the route to the **R** Sea, H6068
Nu 33:10 They left Elim and camped by the **R** Sea. H6068
Nu 33:11 They left the **R** Sea and camped in the H6068
Dt 1:40 the desert along the route to the **R** Sea." H6068
Dt 2: 1 wilderness along the route to the **R** Sea, H6068
Dt 11: 4 with the waters of the **R** Sea as they were H6068
Dt 14:13 the **r kite**, the black kite, any kind of falcon, H8012
Jos 2:10 up the water of the **R** Sea for you when H6068
Jos 4:23 he had done to the **R** Sea when he dried H6068
Jos 24: 6 horsemen as far as the **R** Sea. H6068
Jdg 11:16 wilderness to the **R** Sea and on to Kadesh H6068
1Ki 9:26 Elath in Edom, on the shore of the **R** Sea. H6068
2Ki 3:22 the way, the water looked **r**—like blood. H137
Ne 9: 9 in Egypt; you heard their cry at the **R** Sea. H6068
Job 16:16 My face *is* **r** with weeping, dark shadows H2813
Ps 106: 7 they rebelled by the sea, the **R** Sea. H6068
Ps 106: 9 He rebuked the **R** Sea, and it dried up; he H6068
Ps 106:22 Ham and awesome deeds by the **R** Sea. H6068
Ps 136:13 him who divided the **R** Sea asunder His H6068
Ps 136:15 Pharaoh and his army into the **R** Sea; H6068
Pr 23:31 Do not gaze at wine when *it is* **r**, when it H131
Isa 1:18 as snow; though *they are* **r** as crimson, they H131
Isa 63: 2 Why are your garments **r**, like those of one H137
Jer 22:14 panels it with cedar and decorates it in **r**. H9266
Jer 49:21 their cry will resound to the **R** Sea. H6068
Eze 23:14 figures of Chaldeans portrayed in **r**, H9266
Na 2: 3 The shields of the soldiers *are* **r**; the H131
Zec 1: 8 me was a man mounted on a **r** horse. H137
Zec 1: 8 Behind him were **r**, brown and white horses H137
Zec 6: 2 The first chariot had **r** horses, the second H137
Mt 16: 2 'It will be fair weather, for the sky *is* **r**,' *G4793*
Mt 16: 3 be stormy, for the sky *is* **r** and overcast. *G4793*
Ac 7:36 at the **R** Sea and for forty years in the *G2261*
Heb 11:29 passed through the **R** Sea as on dry land; *G2261*
Rev 6: 4 another horse came out, a **fiery r** *one.* *G4794*
Rev 6:12 the whole moon turned **blood r**, *G6055+135*
Rev 9:17 Their breastplates were **fiery r**, dark blue *G4791*
Rev 12: 3 an enormous **r** dragon with seven heads *G4794*

REDDISH (2) [RED]

Lev 13:49 is greenish or **r**, it is a defiling mold H140
Lev 14:37 if it has greenish or **r** depressions that H140

REDDISH-WHITE (4) [RED, WHITE]

Lev 13:19 a white swelling or **r** spot appears H140+4237
Lev 13:24 on their skin and a **r** or white spot H140+4237
Lev 13:42 But if he has a **r** sore on his bald H140+4237
Lev 13:43 head or forehead is **r** like a defiling H140+4237

REDEDICATE (1) [DEDICATE]

Nu 6:12 *They must* **r** *themselves* to the LORD for the H5693

R

REDEEM (48) [GUARDIAN-REDEEMERS, GUARDIAN-REDEEMERS, REDEEMABLE, REDEEMED, REDEEMER, REDEEMS, REDEMPTION]
Ex 6: 6 and *I will* r you with an outstretched arm H1457
Ex 13:13 **R** with a lamb every firstborn donkey, but if H7009
Ex 13:13 donkey, but if *you do* not r it, break its H7009
Ex 13:13 **R** every firstborn among your sons. H7009
Ex 13:15 of every womb and r each of my firstborn H7009
Ex 21:30 the owner may r his life by the payment of H7018
Ex 34:20 **R** the firstborn donkey with a lamb, but if H7009
Ex 34:20 a lamb, but if *you do* not r it, break its H7009
Ex 34:20 break its neck. **R** all your firstborn sons H7009
Lev 25:25 is to come and r what they have sold. H1457
Lev 25:26 there is no *one to* r it for them but later on H1457
Lev 25:26 sufficient means to r it themselves, H1460
Lev 25:29 During that time the seller may r it. H1460
Lev 25:32 always have the **right to** r their houses in H1460
Lev 25:48 One of their relatives *may* r them: H1457
Lev 25:49 blood relative in their clan *may* r them. H1457
Lev 25:49 Or if they prosper, *they may* r **themselves**. H1457
Lev 27:13 If the owner *wishes to* r the animal H1457+1457
Lev 27:15 who dedicates their house *wishes to* r it, H1457
Lev 27:19 dedicates the field *wishes to* r it, H1457+1457
Lev 27:20 however, *they do* not r the field, or if they H1457
Lev 27:31 Whoever *would* r any of their tithe H1457+1457
Nu 3:46 *To* r the 273 firstborn Israelites who H7012
Nu 18:15 But *you* **must** r every firstborn son H7009+7009
Nu 18:16 *you must* r them at the redemption price H7009
Nu 18:17 "But *you must* not r the firstborn of a cow H7009
Ru 3:13 guardian-redeemer, good; *let him* r you. H1457
Ru 4: 4 of my people. If *you will* r it, do so. But if H1457
Ru 4: 4 I am next in line." "I *will* r it," he said. H1457
Ru 4: 6 "Then I cannot r it because I might H1457
Ru 4: 6 my own estate. You r it yourself. I cannot H1457
2Sa 7:23 that God went out to r as a people for H7009
1Ch 17:21 God went out to r a people for himself, H7009
Ps 49: 7 No one *can* r the life of another H7009+7009
Ps 49:15 But God *will* r me from the realm of the H7009
Ps 119:134 **R** me from human oppression, that I may H7009
Ps 119:154 Defend my cause and r me; preserve my H1457
Ps 130: 8 *He* himself *will* r Israel from all their sins. H7009
Isa 63: 4 the year for me to r had come. H1453
Jer 31:11 deliver Jacob and r them from the hand of H1457
Jer 32: 8 Since it is your right to r it and possess it H1460
Hos 7:13 I *long to* r them but they speak about me H7009
Hos 13:14 of the grave; *I will* r them from death. H1457
Mic 4:10 There the LORD *will* r you out of the hand H1457
Zec 10: 8 Surely *I will* r them; they will be as H7009
Lk 24:21 he was the one who was going to r Israel. G3390
Gal 4: 5 to r those under the law, that we might G1973
Titus 2:14 himself for us to r us from all wickedness G3390

REDEEMABLE (1) [REDEEM]
Lev 25:33 So the property of the Levites *is* r—that is H1457

REDEEMED (43) [REDEEM]
Ex 15:13 love you will lead the people *you have* r. H1457
Ex 21: 8 her for himself, *he must* **let** her **be** r. H7009
Lev 25:30 If *it is* not r before a full year has passed H1457
Lev 25:31 They can be r, and they are to be returned H1460
Lev 25:54 " 'Even if *someone* **is** not r in any of these H1457
Lev 27:20 sold it to someone else, *it can* never **be** r. H1457
Lev 27:27 the value to it. If *it is* not r, it is to be sold H1457
Lev 27:28 may be sold or r; everything so H1457
Lev 27:33 substitute become holy and cannot **be** r. H1457
Nu 3:49 exceeded the number r *by* the Levites. H7009
Dt 7: 8 a mighty hand and r you from the land of H7009
Dt 9:26 inheritance that *you* r by your great power H7009
Dt 13: 5 out of Egypt and r you from the land of H7009
Dt 15:15 in Egypt and the LORD your God r you. H7009
Dt 21: 8 people Israel, whom *you have* r, LORD, H7009
Dt 24:18 the LORD your God r you from there. H7009
2Sa 7:23 your people, whom *you* r from Egypt? H7009
1Ch 17:21 your people, whom *you* r from Egypt? H7009
Ne 1:10 whom *you* r by your great strength and H7009
Ps 74: 2 inheritance, whom *you* r—Mount Zion, H1457
Ps 77:15 With your mighty arm *you* r your people H1457
Ps 78:42 the day *he* r them from the oppressor, H7009
Ps 106:10 from the hand of the enemy *he* r them. H1457
Ps 107: 2 Let the r *of* the LORD tell their story—those H1457
Ps 107: 2 those *he* r from the hand of the foe H1457
Isa 29:22 what the LORD, who r Abraham, says to the H7009
Isa 35: 9 But only the r will walk there, H1457
Isa 43: 1 "Do not fear, for *I have* r you; I have H1457
Isa 44:22 Return to me, for *I have* r you." H1457
Isa 44:23 for the LORD *has* r Jacob, he displays H1457
Isa 48:20 "The LORD *has* r his servant Jacob. H1457
Isa 51:10 of the sea so that the r might cross over? H1457
Isa 52: 3 nothing, and without money *you will* **be** r." H1457
Isa 52: 9 comforted his people, *he has* r Jerusalem. H1457
Isa 62:12 Holy People, the **R** *of* the LORD; and you H1457
Isa 63: 9 In his love and mercy he r them; he lifted H1457
La 3:58 Lord, took up my case; *you* r my life. H1457
Mic 6: 4 up out of Egypt and r you from the land of H7009
Lk 1:68 come to his people and r them. G4472+3391
Gal 3:13 Christ r us from the curse of the law by G1973
Gal 3:14 He r us in order that the blessing given to NDT
1Pe 1:18 silver or gold *that you were* r from the G3390
Rev 14: 3 the 144,000 who *had been* r from the earth. G60

REDEEMER (17) [REDEEM]
Job 19:25 I know that my r lives, and that in the end H1457
Ps 19:14 in your sight, LORD, my Rock and my **R**. H1457
Ps 78:35 that God Most High was their **R**. H1457
Isa 41:14 the LORD, your **R**, the Holy One of Israel H1457
Isa 43:14 the LORD says—your **R**, the Holy One of H1457
Isa 44: 6 Israel's King and **R**, the LORD Almighty: H1457
Isa 44:24 the LORD says—your **R**, who formed you in H1457
Isa 47: 4 Our **R**—the LORD Almighty is his name—is H1457
Isa 48:17 the LORD says—your **R**, the Holy One of H1457
Isa 49: 7 LORD says—the **R** and Holy One of Israel H1457
Isa 49:26 am your Savior, your **R**, the Mighty One of H1457
Isa 54: 5 the Holy One of Israel *is* your **R**; he is H1457
Isa 54: 8 compassion on you," says the LORD your **R**. H1457
Isa 59:20 "The **R** will come to Zion, to those in H1457
Isa 60:16 am your Savior, your **R**, the Mighty One of H1457
Isa 63:16 our Father, our **R** from of old is your name. H1457
Jer 50:34 Yet their **R** is strong; the LORD Almighty is H1457

REDEEMS (1) [REDEEM]
Ps 103: 4 who r your life from the pit and crowns H1457

REDEMPTION (22) [REDEEM]
Lev 25:24 you must provide for the r of the land. H1460
Lev 25:29 city retains the **right of** r a full year after its H1460
Lev 25:48 they retain the **right of** r after they have H1460
Lev 25:51 must pay for their r a larger share of the H1460
Lev 25:52 that and pay for their r accordingly. H1460
Nu 3:48 Give the money for the r *of* the additional H7012
Nu 3:49 Moses collected the r money from those H7017
Nu 3:51 Moses gave the r money to Aaron and his H7012
Nu 18:16 redeem them at the r price set at five H7009
Ru 4: 7 the r and transfer of property to H1460
Ps 111: 9 He provided r for his people; he ordained H7014
Ps 130: 7 is unfailing love and with him is full r. H7014
Lk 2:38 looking forward to the r of Jerusalem. G3391
Lk 21:28 your heads, because your r is drawing near." G667
Ro 3:24 his grace through the r that came by Christ G667
Ro 8:23 adoption to sonship, the r of our bodies. G667
1Co 1:30 our righteousness, holiness and r. G667
Eph 1: 7 In him we have r through his blood, the G667
Eph 1:14 inheritance until the r of those who are G667
Eph 4:30 with whom you were sealed for the day *of* r. G667
Col 1:14 in whom we have r, the forgiveness of sins. G667
Heb 9:12 his own blood, thus obtaining eternal r. G3391

REDUCE (7) [REDUCED, REDUCES]
Ex 5: 8 of bricks as before; don't r the quota. H1757
Ex 5:19 "*You are* not *to* r **the number** *of* bricks H1757
2Ki 10:32 days the LORD began to r *the* **size** of Israel. H7894
Job 11: 3 *Will* your idle talk r others **to silence**? Will H3087
Job 24:25 prove me false and r my words to nothing H8492
Isa 41:15 crush them, and r the hills to chaff. H8492
Jer 10:24 in your anger, or *you will* r me **to nothing**. H5070

REDUCED (11) [REDUCE]
Ge 47:21 r the people **to servitude**, H6268+4200+6269
Ex 5:11 but your work *will* not **be** r at all. H1757
Lev 27:18 Year of Jubilee, and its set value *will* **be** r. H1757
Job 30:19 the mud, and *I am* r to dust and ashes. H5439
Ps 79: 1 temple, *they have* r Jerusalem to rubble. H8492
Ps 89:40 all his walls and r his strongholds *to* ruins. H8492
Ps 102: 5 I groan aloud and *am* r to skin and bones. H1815
Isa 25: 5 as heat is r by the shadow of a cloud NDT
Eze 16:27 my hand against you and r your territory; H1757
Eze 28:18 and *I* r you to ashes on the ground in the H5989
Am 5: 5 into exile, and Bethel will be r to nothing." NDT

REDUCES (1) [REDUCE]
Isa 40:23 princes to naught and r the rulers of this H6913

REED (12) [REEDS]
1Ki 14:15 it will be like a r swaying in the water. H7866
2Ki 18:21 that splintered r of a staff, which H7866
Isa 9:14 both palm branch and r in a single day; H109
Isa 19:15 can do—head or tail, palm branch or r. H109
Isa 36: 6 that splintered r of a staff, which H7866
Isa 42: 3 A bruised r he will not break, and a H7866
Isa 58: 5 bowing one's head like a r and for lying in H109
Eze 29: 6 have been a staff of r for the people of H7866
Mt 11: 7 A r swayed by the wind? G2812
Mt 12:20 A bruised r he will not break, and a G2812
Lk 7:24 A r swayed by the wind? G2812
Rev 11: 1 I was given a r like a measuring rod and G2812

REEDS (10) [REED]
Ge 41: 2 sleek and fat, and they grazed among the r. H286
Ge 41:18 fat and sleek, and they grazed among the r. H286
Ex 2: 3 put it among the r along the bank of H6068
Ex 2: 5 basket among the r and sent her female H6068
Job 8:11 Can r thrive without water? H286
Job 40:21 hidden among the r in the marsh. H7866
Job 41:20 as from a boiling pot over burning r. H109
Ps 68:30 Rebuke the beast among the r, the herd H7866
Isa 19: 6 The r and rushes will wither, H7866
Isa 35: 7 grass and r and papyrus will grow. H7866

REEKED (1)
Ex 8:14 piled into heaps, and the land r *of* them. H944

REEL (2) [REELED, REELING, REELS]
Isa 28: 7 also stagger from wine and r from beer: H9494
Isa 28: 7 with wine; *they* r from beer, they H9494

REELAIAH (1)
Ezr 2: 2 Nehemiah, Seraiah, **R**, Mordecai, Bilshan H8305

REELED (1) [REEL]
Ps 107:27 *They* r and staggered like drunkards; they H2510

REELING (1) [REEL]
Zec 12: 2 that sends all the surrounding peoples r. H8303

REELS (1) [REEL]
Isa 24:20 The earth r like a drunkard, it sways H5675+5675

REENTERED (1) [ENTER]
Ne 2:15 turned back and r through the H995+2256+8740

REESTABLISHED (1) [ESTABLISH]
2Ch 29:35 service of the temple of the LORD **was** r. H3922

REFER (1) [REFERRED, REFERRING, REFERS]
1Jn 5:16 I r to those whose sin does not lead to NDT

REFERRED (1) [REFER]
Gal 3:19 the Seed *to* **whom** the promise *r* had come. AIT

REFERRING (3) [REFER]
Ex 4:26 "bridegroom of blood," **r to** circumcision.) H4200
Jn 13:18 "I *am* not r to all of you; I know those I G3306
1Co 10:29 *I am* **r to** the other person's conscience G3306

REFERS (3) [REFER]
Mt 13:20 on rocky ground **r to** someone who hears G1639
Mt 13:22 among the thorns **r to** someone who G1639
Mt 13:23 on good soil **r to** someone who hears G1639

REFINE (3) [REFINED, REFINER, REFINER'S, REFINING]
Jer 9: 7 I *will* r and test them, for what else H7671
Zec 13: 9 *I will* r them like silver and test them like H7671
Mal 3: 3 purify the Levites and r them like gold H2423

REFINED (10) [REFINE]
1Ch 28:18 the weight of the r gold for the altar of H2423
1Ch 29: 4 seven thousand talents of r silver, for H2423
Job 28: 1 silver and a place where gold *is* r. H2423
Ps 12: 6 in a crucible, like gold r seven times. H2423
Ps 66:10 For you, God, tested us; *you* r us like silver. H7671
Isa 48:10 *I have* r you, though not as silver; H7671
Da 11:35 so that they *may be* r, purified and made H7671
Da 12:10 made spotless and r, but the wicked will H7671
1Pe 1: 7 which perishes even though r by fire G1507
Rev 3:18 you to buy from me gold r in the fire, G4792

REFINER (1) [REFINE]
Mal 3: 3 He will sit as a r and purifier of silver; he H7671

REFINER'S (1) [REFINE]
Mal 3: 2 For he will be like a r fire or a launderer's H7671

REFINING (1) [REFINE]
Jer 6:29 but *the* r **goes on** in vain; the H7671+7671

REFLECT (3) [REFLECTED, REFLECTION, REFLECTS]
Ecc 5:20 *They* seldom **r on** the days of their life H2349
Isa 47: 7 these things or **r on** what might happen. H2349
2Ti 2: 7 **R on** what I am saying, for the Lord will G3783

REFLECTED (1) [REFLECT]
Ecc 9: 1 So *I* **r on** all this and H5989+448+4213

REFLECTION (1) [REFLECT]
1Co 13:12 For now we see *only* a r as in a mirror; then G141

REFLECTS (2) [REFLECT]
Pr 27:19 As water r the face, so one's H4200+2021+7156
Pr 27:19 so one's life r the heart. H4200+2021+132

REFORM (4) [REFORMS]
Jer 7: 3 **R** your ways and your actions, and I will H3512
Jer 18:11 and r your ways and your actions. H3512
Jer 26:13 Now r your ways and your actions and H3512
Jer 35:15 from your wicked ways and r your actions; H3512

REFORMS (1) [REFORM]
Ac 24: 2 has brought about r in this nation. G1480

REFRAIN (7) [REFRAINED]
Dt 23:22 But if *you* **r from** making a vow, you will H2532
1Sa 18: 8 very angry; this r displeased him greatly. H1821
1Ki 22: 6 to war against Ramoth Gilead, or *shall I* r?" H2532
Job 16: 6 not relieved; and if *I* r, it does not go H2532
Ps 37: 8 **R** from anger and turn from wrath; do not H8332
Ecc 3: 5 embrace and a time to r from embracing, H8178
2Co 12: 6 But *I* r, so no one will think more of me G5767

REFRAINED (2) [REFRAIN]
2Sa 12: 4 the rich man *r from* taking one of his H2798
Job 29: 9 the chief men r from speaking and H6806

REFRESH (7) [REFRESHED, REFRESHES, REFRESHING]
Jdg 19: 5 "**R** yourself *with* something to eat H6184
Jdg 19: 8 the woman's father said, "**R** yourself. H6184
2Sa 16: 2 the wine is to r those who become H9272
SS 2: 5 me with raisins, r me with apples, for I am H8331
Jer 31:25 *I will* r the weary and satisfy the faint." H8115
Phm 20 from you in the Lord; r my heart in Christ. G399
2Pe 1:13 I think it is right *to* r your memory as long G1444

REFRESHED (11) [REFRESH]

Ge 18: 5 so you can be r and then go on H6184+4213
Ex 23:12 the foreigner living among you may be r. H5882
Ex 31:17 on the seventh day he rested and was r. H5882
2Sa 16:14 And there he r himself. H5882
Ps 68: 9 you r your weary inheritance. H3922
Pr 11:25 whoever refreshes others will be r. H3722
Ro 15:32 by God's will, and in your company be r. G5265
1Co 16:18 For they r my spirit and yours also. G399
2Co 7:13 because his spirit has been r by all of you. G399
2Ti 1:16 because he often r me and was not G434
Phm 7 have r the hearts of the Lord's people. G399

REFRESHES (3) [REFRESH]

Ps 23: 3 he r my soul. He guides me along the H8740
Pr 11:25 whoever r others will be refreshed. H8115
Pr 25:13 sends him; he r the spirit of his master. H8740

REFRESHING (2) [REFRESH]

Ps 19: 7 the LORD is perfect, r the soul. The statutes H8740
Ac 3:19 that times of r may come from the Lord G433

REFUGE (96) [REFUGEES]

Nu 35: 6 you give the Levites will be cities of r, H5236
Nu 35:11 select some towns to be your cities of r, to H5236
Nu 35:12 They will be places of r from the avenger H5236
Nu 35:13 six towns you give will be your cities of r. H5236
Nu 35:14 Jordan and three in Canaan as cities of r. H5236
Nu 35:15 towns will be a place of r for Israelites H5236
Nu 35:25 back to the city of r to which they fled. H5236
Nu 35:26 the limits of the city of r to which they fled H5236
Nu 35:28 stay in the city of r until the death of the H5236
Nu 35:32 has fled to a city of r and so allow them to H5236
Dt 19: 3 kills someone may flee for r to one of H5674
Dt 23:15 If a slave has taken r with you, do not H5911
Dt 32:37 are their gods, the rock they took r in, H2879
Dt 33:27 The eternal God is your r, and underneath H5104
Jos 20: 2 the Israelites to designate the cities of r, H5236
Jos 21:13 a city of r for one accused of murder), H5236
Jos 21:21 a city of r for one accused of murder H5236
Jos 21:27 a city of r for one accused of murder H5236
Jos 21:32 a city of r for one accused of murder), H5236
Jos 21:38 a city of r for one accused of murder), H5236
Jdg 9:15 come and take r in my shade; but H2879
Ru 2:12 whose wings you have come to take r." H2879
2Sa 22: 3 my rock, in whom I take r, my shield and H2879
2Sa 22: 3 my stronghold, my r and my savior—from H4960
2Sa 22:31 flawless; he shields all who take r in him. H2879
1Ch 6:57 given Hebron (a city of r), and Libnah, H5236
1Ch 6:67 given Shechem (a city of r), and Gezer, H5236
Ps 2:12 Blessed are all who take r in him. H2879
Ps 5:11 But let all who take r in you be glad; let H2879
Ps 7: 1 LORD my God, I take r in you; save and H2879
Ps 9: 9 The LORD is a r for the oppressed, H5369
Ps 11: 1 In the LORD I take r. How then can you say H2879
Ps 14: 6 plans of the poor, but the LORD is their r. H4726
Ps 16: 1 Keep me safe, my God, for in you I take r. H2879
Ps 17: 7 right hand those who take r in you from H2879
Ps 18: 2 my rock, in whom I take r, my shield and H2879
Ps 18:30 flawless; he shields all who take r in him. H2879
Ps 25:20 let me be put to shame, for I take r in you. H2879
Ps 31: 1 I have taken r; let me never be put H2879
Ps 31: 2 be my rock of r, a strong fortress to H5057
Ps 31: 4 trap that is set for me, for you are my r. H5057
Ps 31:19 sight of all, on those who take r in you. H2879
Ps 34: 8 blessed is the one who takes r in him. H2879
Ps 34:22 no one who takes r in him will be H2879
Ps 36: 7 People take r in the shadow of your wings. H2879
Ps 37:40 saves them, because they take r in him. H2879
Ps 46: 1 God is our r and strength, an ever-present H4726
Ps 57: 1 have mercy on me, for in you I take r. H2879
Ps 57: 1 I will take r in the shadow of your wings H2879
Ps 59:16 are my fortress, my r in times of trouble. H4960
Ps 61: 3 For you have been my r, a strong tower H4726
Ps 61: 4 tent forever and take r in the shelter of H2879
Ps 62: 7 on God; he is my mighty rock, my r. H4726
Ps 62: 8 out your hearts to him, for God is our r. H4726
Ps 64:10 will rejoice in the LORD and take r in him; H2879
Ps 71: 1 I have taken r; let me never be put H2879
Ps 71: 3 Be my rock of r, to which I can always go H5061
Ps 71: 7 a sign to many; you are my strong r. H4726
Ps 73:28 I have made the Sovereign LORD my r; H4726
Ps 91: 2 the LORD, "He is my r and my fortress, my H4726
Ps 91: 4 under his wings you will find r; his H2879
Ps 91: 9 "The LORD is my r," and you make the H4726
Ps 94:22 my God the rock in whom I take r. H4726
Ps 104:18 wild goats; the crags are a r for the hyrax. H4726
Ps 118: 8 It is better to take r in the LORD than to H2879
Ps 118: 9 It is better to take r in the LORD than to H2879
Ps 119:114 You are my r and my shield; I have put H6260
Ps 141: 8 in you I take r—do not give me over H2879
Ps 142: 4 I have no r; no one cares for my H4960
Ps 142: 5 "You are my r, my portion in the H4726
Ps 144: 2 my shield, in whom I take r, who subdues H2879
Pr 10:29 way of the LORD is a r for the blameless, H5057
Pr 14:26 for their children it will be a r. H4726
Pr 14:32 even in death the righteous seek r in God. H2879
Pr 22: 3 The prudent see danger and take r, but H6259
Pr 27:12 The prudent see danger and take r, but H6259
Pr 28:17 guilt of murder will seek r in the grave; H5674
Pr 30: 5 he is a shield to those who take r in him. H2879
Isa 4: 6 a r and hiding place from the storm H4726
Isa 14:32 in her his afflicted people will find r." H2879
Isa 25: 4 You have been a r for the poor, a refuge H5057
Isa 25: 4 the poor, a r for the needy in their distress H5057
Isa 27: 5 Or else let them come to me for r; let H5057
Isa 28:15 have made a lie our r and falsehood our H4726
Isa 28:17 hail will sweep away your r, the lie, H4726
Isa 30: 2 protection, to Egypt's shade for r. H2879
Isa 32: 2 from the wind and a r from the storm, H6260
Isa 33:16 whose r will be the mountain fortress. H5369
Isa 57:13 But whoever takes r in me will inherit the H2879
Jer 16:19 my fortress, my r in time of distress, to H4960
Jer 17:17 you are my r in the day of disaster. H4726
Jer 21:13 come against us? Who can enter our r?" H5104
Joel 3:16 But the LORD will be a r for his people, H4726
Na 1: 7 The LORD is good, a r in times of trouble H5057
Na 3:11 go into hiding and seek r from the enemy. H5057
Zep 3: 7 Then her place of r would not be H5061

REFUGEES (2) [REFUGE]

Isa 16: 3 Hide the fugitives, do not betray the r. H5610
Jer 50:28 to the fugitives and r from Babylon H7128

REFUND (1)

Lev 25:27 they sold it and r the balance to the one H8740

REFUSAL (1) [REFUSE]

Mk 16:14 their stubborn r to believe those who G4024

REFUSE (45) [REFUSAL, REFUSED, REFUSES, REFUSING]

Ge 23: 6 None of us will r you his tomb for burying H3973
Ge 24:41 go to my clan, they r to give her to you H4202
Ex 8: 2 If you r to let them go, I will send a plague H4412
Ex 9: 2 If you r to let them go and continue to H4412
Ex 10: 3 'How long will you r to humble yourself H4412
Ex 10: 4 If you r to let them go, I will bring locusts H4412
Ex 11: 9 "Pharaoh will r to listen to you—so H4202
Ex 16:28 "How long will you r to keep my H4412
Lev 26:21 toward me and r to listen to me, H4202+14
Nu 14:11 How long will they r to believe in me, in H4202
Dt 20:12 If they r to make peace and they engage H4202
1Ki 2:16 to make of you. Do not r me." "You may H8740
1Ki 2:17 King Solomon—he will not r you—to give H8740
1Ki 2:20 "Do not r me." The king replied H8740
1Ki 2:20 "Make it, my mother; I will not r you." H8740
1Ki 20: 7 my silver and my gold, I did not r him." H4979
2Ki 2:17 persisted until he was too embarrassed to r. NDT
Job 6: 7 I r to touch it; such food makes me ill. H4412
Job 34:33 you on your terms, when you r to repent? H4415
Ps 26: 5 of evildoers and r to sit with the wicked. H4202
Ps 141: 5 My head will not r it, for my prayer will H5648
Pr 1:24 But since you r to listen when I call and H4412
Pr 6:35 compensation; he will r a bribe H4202+14
Pr 21: 7 them away, for they r to do what is right. H4412
Pr 21:25 because his hands r to work. H4412
Pr 30: 7 ask of you, LORD; do not r me before I die: H4979
Isa 5:25 the dead bodies are like r in the streets. H6054
Jer 3: 3 of a prostitute; you r to blush with shame. H4412
Jer 8: 5 They cling to deceit; they r to return. H4412
Jer 9: 6 in their deceit they r to acknowledge me," H4412
Jer 13:10 people, who r to listen to my words H4412
Jer 25:28 But if they r to take the cup from your hand H4412
Jer 38:21 But if you r to surrender, this is what the H4412
La 3:45 made us scum and r among the nations. H4400
Eze 3:27 whoever will r let them refuse; for H2534
Eze 3:27 whoever will refuse let them r; for H2532
Hos 11: 5 rule over them because they r to repent? H4412
Mt 18:17 If they still r to listen, tell it to the church G4159
Mt 18:17 if they r to listen even to the church G4159
Mk 6:26 his dinner guests, he did not want to r her. G119
Jn 5:40 yet you r to come to me to have life. G4024+2527
Jn 19:10 "Do you r to speak to me?" Pilate said G4024
Ac 25:11 deserving death, I do not r to die. G4148
Heb 12:25 See to it that you do not r him who speaks G4148
Rev 11: 9 on their bodies and r them burial. G4024+918

REFUSED (56) [REFUSE]

Ge 37:35 to comfort him, but he r to be comforted. H4412
Ge 39: 8 But he r. "With me in charge," he told her, H4412
Ge 39:10 he r to go to bed with her or even H9048+4202
Ge 48:19 But his father r and said, "I know, my son H4412
Ex 4:23 But you r to let him go; so I will kill your H4412
Ex 13:15 When Pharaoh stubbornly r to let us go H7996
Nu 20:21 Since Edom r to let them go through their H4412
Nu 22:13 the LORD has r to let me go with you." H4412
Nu 22:14 said, "Balaam r to come with us. H4412
Dt 2:30 Sihon king of Heshbon r to let us pass H4202+14
Jdg 2:19 They r to give up their evil practices and H4202
Jdg 11:17 also to the king of Moab, and he r. H4202+14
1Sa 8:19 But the people r to listen to Samuel. "No!" H4412
1Sa 28:23 He r and said, "I will not eat." But his H4412
2Sa 2:23 But Asahel r to give up the pursuit; so H4412
2Sa 12:17 the ground, but he r, and he would H14+4202
2Sa 13: 9 served him the bread, but he r to eat. H4412
2Sa 13:14 But he r to listen to her, and since he H14+4202
2Sa 13:16 done to me." But he r to listen to her. H14+4202
2Sa 13:25 he still r to go but gave him his H14+4202
2Sa 14:29 the king, but Joab r to come to him. H4202+14
2Sa 14:29 sent a second time, but he r to come. H4202+14
2Sa 23:16 But he r to drink it; instead, he poured H4202+14
1Ki 12:16 Israel saw that the king r to listen to them, H4202
1Ki 20:35 "Strike me with your weapon," but he r. H4412
1Ki 21: 4 He lay on his bed sulking and r to eat. H4202
1Ki 21:15 Naboth the Jezreelite that he r to sell you. H4412
1Ki 22:49 sail with yours," but Jehoshaphat r. H4202+14
2Ki 5:16 even though Naaman urged him, he r. H4412
2Ki 15:16 because they r to open their gates. H4202
1Ch 11:18 But he r to drink it; instead, he poured H4202+14
2Ch 10:16 Israel saw that the king r to listen to them, H4202
Ne 9:17 They r to listen and failed to remember H4412
Ne 9:29 became stiff-necked and r to listen. H4202
Est 1:12 king's command, Queen Vashti r to come. H4412
Est 3: 4 day they spoke to him but he r to comply. H4202
Ps 78:10 God's covenant and r to live by his law. H4412
Ecc 2:10 my eyes desired; I r my heart no pleasure. H4979
Jer 5: 3 you crushed them, but they r correction. H4412
Jer 5: 3 faces harder than stone and r to repent. H4412
Jer 11:10 ancestors, who r to listen to my words. H4412
Zec 7:11 "But they r to pay attention; stubbornly H4412
Mt 18:30 "But he r. Instead, he went off and G4024+2527
Mt 22: 3 them to come, but they r to come. G4024+2527
Mt 27:34 after tasting it, he r to drink it. G4024+2527
Lk 15:28 became angry and r to go in. G4024+2527
Lk 18: 4 "For some time he r. But finally he G4024+2527
Ac 7:39 "But our ancestors r to obey him G4024+2527
Ac 14: 2 But the Jews who r to believe stirred up the G578
Ac 19: 9 they r to believe and publicly maligned the G578
2Th 2:10 perish because they r to love the G4024+1312
Heb 11:24 r to be known as the son of Pharaoh's G766
Heb 12:25 did not escape when they r him who G4148
Rev 13:15 and cause all who r to worship the G1569+3590
Rev 16: 9 they r to repent and glorify him. G4024
Rev 16:11 they r to repent of what they had done G4024

REFUSES (6) [REFUSE]

Ex 7:14 is unyielding; he r to let the people go. H4412
Ex 22:17 If her father absolutely r to give her H4412+4412
Dt 25: 7 "My husband's brother r to carry on his H4412
Pr 11:15 but whoever r to shake hands in pledge is H8533
Mic 3: 5 war against anyone who r to feed them. H4202
3Jn 10 he even r to welcome other believers. G4046

REFUSING (5) [REFUSE]

Jer 31:15 her children and r to be comforted, H4412
Jer 50:33 captors hold them fast, r to let them go. H4412
Da 9:11 your law and turned away, r to obey you. H1194
Mt 2:18 her children and r to be comforted, G4024+2527
Heb 11:35 r to be released so that they might G4024+4657

REFUTE (4) [REFUTED]

Job 32: 3 because they had found no way to r Job H5101
Job 32:13 found wisdom; let God, not a man, r him. H5622
Isa 54:17 and you will r every tongue that accuses H8399
Titus 1: 9 sound doctrine and r those who oppose it. G1794

REFUTED (1) [REFUTE]

Ac 18:28 he vigorously r his Jewish opponents in public debate G1352

REGAIN (4) [GAIN]

1Sa 29: 4 better could he r his master's favor than H8354
1Ki 12:21 against Israel and to r the kingdom for H8740
2Ch 11: 1 against Israel and to r the kingdom for H8740
2Ch 13:20 Jeroboam did not r power during H6806+6388

REGAINED (1) [GAIN]

Ac 9:19 after taking some food, he r his strength. G1932

REGARD (55) [REGARDED, REGARDING, REGARDLESS, REGARDS]

Ge 31:15 Does he not r us as foreigners? Not only H3108
Lev 5:15 unintentionally in r to any of the LORD's H4946
Lev 5:16 have failed to do in r to the holy things, H4946
Lev 11:10 in the water—you are to r as unclean. H4200
Lev 11:11 And since you are to r them as unclean H4200
Lev 11:11 you must r their carcasses as unclean. H9210
Lev 11:13 the birds you are to r as unclean and not H9210
Lev 11:23 have four legs you are to r as unclean. H4200
Lev 11:35 and you are to r them as unclean. H2118+4200
Lev 19:23 of fruit tree, r its fruit as forbidden. H6887+6889
Lev 21: 8 R them as holy, because they offer up the H7727
Nu 18:10 shall eat it. You must r it as holy. H2118+4200
Dt 7:26 R it as vile and utterly detest it, for H9210+9210
Dt 33: 9 father and mother, 'I have no r for them. H8011
Jos 7: 1 were unfaithful in r to the devoted things; H928
Jos 22:20 was unfaithful in r to the devoted things, H928
1Sa 2:12 scoundrels; they had no r for the LORD. H3359
Ezr 7:14 Jerusalem with r to the Law of your A10089
Est 9:31 their descendants in r to their times of NDT
Job 21:29 Have you paid no r to their accounts H5795
Job 34:27 him and had no r for any of his ways. H8505
Job 37:24 for does he not have r for all the wise in H8011
Ps 28: 5 Because they have no r for the deeds of H1067
Ps 41: 1 are those who have r for the weak; H8505
Ps 54: 3 people without r for God. H8492+4200+5584
Ps 74:20 Have r for your covenant, because H5564+4200
Ps 86:14 me—they have no r for you. H8492+4200+5584
Ps 119:117 I will always have r for your decrees. H9120
Isa 5:12 but they have no r for the deeds of the H5564
Isa 8:13 Almighty is the one you are to r as holy, H7727
Isa 17: 8 and they will have no r for the Asherah H8011
Isa 22:11 have r for the One who planned it long H8011
Isa 26:10 on doing evil and do not r the majesty of H8011
Jer 24: 5 I r as good the exiles from Judah H5795
Jer 33:24 no longer r them as a nation H2118+4200+7156
Eze 44: 8 carrying out your duty in r to my holy things, AIT

Da 11:37 *He will* **show** no r for the gods of his H1067
Da 11:37 by women, nor *will he* r any god, but will H1067
Am 5:22 offerings, *I will* **have** no r **for** them. H5564
1Co 4: 1 is how you *ought to* r us: as servants G3357
1Co 11:31 we were more discerning *with r to* **ourselves**, AIT
1Co 14:20 *In r to* **evil** be infants, but in your thinking be AIT
2Co 5:16 So from now on we r no one from a G3857
Eph 4:22 **with r to** your former way of life G2848
Php 3: 5 Hebrew of Hebrews; **in r to** the law, G2848
Col 1:24 what is still lacking *in r to* Christ's **afflictions**, AIT
Col 2:16 or **with r to** a religious festival G1877+3538
1Th 5:13 **Hold** them **in** the highest r in love because G2451
2Th 3:15 Yet *do* not r them as an enemy, but warn G2451
1Ti 1:19 have suffered shipwreck **with r to** the faith. G4309
Heb 7:14 and **in r to** that tribe Moses said nothing G1650
Heb 11:20 Jacob and Esau **in r to** their future. G4309
1Pe 4: 6 to human standards *in r to* the **body**, AIT
1Pe 4: 6 live according to God *in r to* the **spirit**. AIT
1Pe 5:12 of Silas, whom *I* r as a faithful brother G3357

REGARDED (22) [REGARD]

Ex 11: 3 himself was **highly** r in Egypt by H1524+4394
Lev 11:12 scales is to be **r as** unclean **by** you. H4200
Lev 11:20 on all fours are to be **r as** unclean **by** you. H4200
Lev 11:41 along the ground is to be **r as unclean**; H9211
Dt 24:13 it will be **r as** a righteous act in the H4200
2Sa 16:23 David and Absalom r all of Ahithophel's H4200
2Ki 5: 1 the sight of his master and **highly r**, H5951+7156
2Ch 32:23 From then on *he* **was highly** r by all the H5951
Job 18: 3 Why **are** *we* r as cattle and considered H3108
Job 31:26 if *I have* r the sun in its radiance or the H8011
Isa 40:15 a bucket; *they* **are** r as dust on the scales H3108
Isa 40:17 *they* **are** r by him as worthless and less H3108
Da 4:35 peoples of the earth **are** r as nothing. A10285
Hos 8:12 but *they* r *them* as something foreign. H3108
Mk 10:42 know that those *who are* r *as* rulers of the G1506
Ac 5:13 though they *were* **highly** r *by* the people. G3486
Ro 2:26 *will* they not *be* r as though they were G3357
Ro 9: 8 of the promise *who are* r as Abraham's G3357
2Co 5:16 Though *we once* r Christ in this way, we G1182
2Co 6: 8 good report; genuine, yet **r as** impostors; G6055
2Co 6: 9 yet **r as** unknown; dying, and yet G6055
Heb 11:26 *He* r disgrace for the sake of Christ as of G2451

REGARDING (5) [REGARD]

Lev 5: 1 charge to testify r something they have seen NDT
Eze 14:22 you will be consoled r the disaster I have H6584
Eze 44: 5 regulations and **instructions** *r* the temple of AIT
Ro 1: 3 r his Son, who as to his earthly life was a G4309
Ro 4:20 through unbelief r the promise of God, G1650

REGARDLESS (1) [REGARD]

2Ch 5:11 r of their divisions. H401+4200+9068

REGARDS (4) [REGARD]

Est 5: 8 If the king r *me with* favor and H5162+928+6524
Est 8: 5 if he r *me with* favor and H5162+4200+7156
Ro 14: 6 Whoever r one day **as special** does so to G5858
Ro 14:14 But if anyone r something as unclean G3357

REGEM (1)

1Ch 2:47 **R**, Jotham, Geshan, Pelet, Ephah and H8084

REGEM-MELEK (1)

Zec 7: 2 of Bethel had sent Sharezer and **R**, H8085

REGENERATION (KJV) REBIRTH, RENEWAL

REGIMENT (2)

Ac 10: 1 in what was known as the Italian **R**. G5061
Ac 27: 1 who *belonged to* the Imperial **R**. G5061

REGION (62) [REGIONS]

Ge 10:30 The r **where** they **lived** stretched from H4632
Ge 20: 1 from there into the r *of* the Negev and lived H824
Ge 22: 2 Isaac—and go to the r *of* Moriah. H824
Ge 35:22 While Israel was living in that r, Reuben H824
Ge 36:20 of Seir the Horite, who were living in the r: H824
Ge 45:10 shall live in the r *of* Goshen and be near H824
Ge 46:28 When they arrived in the r *of* Goshen, H824
Ge 46:34 will be allowed to settle in the r *of* Goshen, H824
Ge 47:13 in the whole r because the famine was H824
Ge 47:27 settled in Egypt in the r *of* Goshen. H824
Dt 2:18 you are to pass by the r *of* Moab at Ar. H1473
Dt 3: 4 from them—the whole r *of* Argob, Og's H2475
Dt 3:13 The whole r *of* Argob in Bashan used to H2475
Dt 3:14 took the whole r *of* Argob as far as the H2475
Dt 34: 3 Negev and the **whole** r *from* the Valley of H3971
Jos 7: 2 told them, "Go up and spy out the r." H824
Jos 10:40 So Joshua subdued the whole r, including H824
Jos 10:41 from the whole r *of* Goshen to Gibeon. H824
Jos 11: 3 Hivites below Hermon in the r *of* Mizpah. H824
Jos 11:16 the whole r *of* Goshen, the western H824
Jos 16: 3 as far as the r *of* Lower Beth Horon and on H1473
Jos 17:12 were determined to live in that r. H824
Jos 19:29 the Mediterranean Sea in the r *of* Akzib, H2475
Jdg 20: 6 one piece to each r *of* Israel's inheritance, H8441
2Sa 20:14 through the **entire** *r of* the Bikrites, AIT
2Sa 24: 6 went to Gilead and the r *of* Tahtim Hodshi, H824
1Ki 4:13 as well as the r *of* Argob in Bashan and H2475
1Ki 17: 9 to Zarephath **in the r** of Sidon and stay H4200
2Ki 4:38 to Gilgal and there was a famine in that r. H824
2Ki 10:33 land of Gilead (the r of Gad, Reuben and NDT
1Ch 5:10 throughout the entire r east of Gilead. H7156
Ne 3:22 by the priests from the **surrounding** r. H3971
Ne 12:28 together from the r around Jerusalem— H3971
Ps 78:12 in the land of Egypt, in the r *of* Zoan. H8441
Ps 78:43 in Egypt, his wonders in the r *of* Zoan. H8441
Isa 49:12 from the west, some from the r *of* Aswan." H824
Eze 47: 8 toward the eastern r and goes down into H1666
Mt 3: 5 all Judea and the whole r of the Jordan. G4369
Mt 4:25 Judea and the r **across** the Jordan G4305
Mt 8:28 the other side in the r of the Gadarenes, G6001
Mt 8:34 they pleaded with him to leave their r. G3990
Mt 9:26 News of this spread through all that r. G1178
Mt 9:31 spread the news about him all over that r. G1178
Mt 15:21 Jesus withdrew to the r of Tyre and Sidon. G3538
Mt 16:13 Jesus came to the r of Caesarea Philippi, G3538
Mt 19: 1 went into the r of Judea to the other G3990
Mk 1:28 spread quickly over the whole r of Galilee. G4369
Mk 5: 1 across the lake to the r of the Gerasenes. G6001
Mk 5:17 began to plead with Jesus to leave their r. G3990
Mk 6:55 that whole r and carried the sick G6001
Mk 7:31 of Galilee and into the r of the Decapolis. G3990
Mk 8:10 went to the r of Dalmanutha. G3538
Mk 10: 1 went into the r of Judea and across G3990
Lk 4:26 to a widow in Zarephath *in the* **r of Sidon**. G4973
Lk 6:17 from the **coastal** r around Tyre and G4163
Lk 8:26 They sailed to the r of the Gerasenes G6001
Lk 8:37 all the people *of* the r of the Gerasenes G4369
Jn 11:54 he withdrew to a r near the wilderness, G6001
Ac 13:49 of the Lord spread through the whole r. G6001
Ac 13:50 Barnabas, and expelled them from their r. G3990
Ac 16: 6 throughout the r of Phrygia and Galatia, G6001
Ac 18:23 place throughout the r of Galatia and G6001

REGIONS (10) [REGION]

Ge 36:40 by name, according to their clans and r: H5226
Jos 13: 2 all the r *of* the Philistines and Geshurites, H1666
Jos 13: 6 of the **mountain** r from Lebanon to H2215
Eze 19: 8 against him, those from r round about. H4519
Joel 3: 4 Tyre and Sidon and all you r *of* Philistia? H1666
Mk 3: 8 the **r across** the Jordan and around G4305
Ro 15:23 is no more place for me to work in these r, G3107
2Co 10:16 preach the gospel in the r **beyond** you. G5654
2Co 11:10 nobody in the r of Achaia will stop this G3107
Eph 4: 9 he also descended to the lower, earthly r? G3538

REGISTER (3) [REGISTERED, REGISTRATION]

Ps 87: 6 The LORD will write in the r *of* the peoples H4180
Lk 2: 3 And everyone went to their own town *to* r. G616
Lk 2: 5 He went there *to* r with Mary, who was G616

REGISTERED (6) [REGISTER]

Nu 1:18 The people r *their* **ancestry** by their clans H3528
1Ch 9:22 They **were r by genealogy** in their villages. H3509
1Ch 23:24 families as they **were** r under their names H7212
Ezr 8: 1 heads and *those* r *with* them who came H3509
Ezr 8: 3 Zechariah, and with him **were** r 150 men; H3509
Ezr 8:20 to assist the Levites. All **were** r by name. H5918

REGISTRATION (1) [REGISTER]

Ne 7: 5 the common people for r **by families**. H3509

REGRET (6) [REGRETTED]

Ge 6: 7 ground—for I r that I have made them." H5714
1Sa 15:11 "*I* r that I have made Saul king, because H5714
2Ch 21:20 to no one's r, and was buried in the H2775
2Co 7: 8 you sorrow by my letter, *I do* not r it. G3564
2Co 7: 8 Though *I did* r it—I see that my letter hurt G3564
2Co 7:10 that leads to salvation and leaves **no** r, G294

REGRETTED (2) [REGRET]

Ge 6: 6 The LORD r that he had made human H5714
1Sa 15:35 And the LORD r that he had made Saul H5714

REGROUPED (1) [GROUP]

2Sa 10:15 had been routed by Israel, *they* r. H665+3480

REGULAR (45) [REGULARLY]

Ge 47:22 they received a r **allotment** from Pharaoh H2976
Lev 6:20 of the finest flour as a r grain offering, H9458
Lev 14:32 who cannot afford the r offerings for their NDT
Lev 15:19 has her r **flow** *of* blood, H2307+928+1414
Lev 16:24 sanctuary area and put on his r garments. NDT
Lev 23: 7 sacred assembly and do no **r work**. H4856+6275
Lev 23: 8 sacred assembly and do no **r work**. H4856+6275
Lev 23:21 sacred assembly and do no **r work**. H4856+6275
Lev 23:25 Do no **r work**, but present a food H4856+6275
Lev 23:35 is a sacred assembly; do no **r work**. H4856+6275
Lev 23:36 special assembly; do no **r work**. H4856+6275
Nu 4:16 the r grain offering and the anointing oil. H9458
Nu 8:25 from their **r service** and work no H7372+6275
Nu 28: 3 as a r burnt offering each day. H9458
Nu 28: 6 This is the r burnt offering instituted at H9458
Nu 28:10 in addition to the r burnt offering and its H9458
Nu 28:15 Besides the r burnt offering with its drink H9458
Nu 28:18 sacred assembly and do no **r work**. H4856+6275
Nu 28:23 in addition to the r morning burnt offering H9458
Nu 28:24 in addition to the r burnt offering and its H9458
Nu 28:25 sacred assembly and do no **r work**. H4856+6275
Nu 28:26 sacred assembly and do no **r work**. H4856+6275
Nu 28:31 in addition to the r burnt offering and its H9458
Nu 29: 1 sacred assembly and do no **r work**. H4856+6275
Nu 29:11 atonement and the r burnt offering with H9458
Nu 29:12 sacred assembly and do no **r work**. H4856+6275
Nu 29:16 in addition to the r burnt offering with its H9458
Nu 29:19 in addition to the r burnt offering with its H9458
Nu 29:22 in addition to the r burnt offering with its H9458
Nu 29:25 in addition to the r burnt offering with its H9458
Nu 29:28 in addition to the r burnt offering with its H9458
Nu 29:31 in addition to the r burnt offering with its H9458
Nu 29:34 in addition to the r burnt offering with its H9458
Nu 29:35 special assembly and do no **r work**. H4856+6275
Nu 29:38 in addition to the r burnt offering with its H9458
2Ki 25:30 gave Jehoiachin a r allowance as long as H9458
2Ch 30: 3 to celebrate it at the r time because not H2085S
2Ch 30:16 they took up their *r* **positions** as prescribed in AIT
Ezr 3: 5 they presented the r burnt offerings, the H9458
Ne 10:33 the r grain offerings and burnt H9458
Job 1: 5 This was Job's r custom. H3972+2021+3427
Jer 5:24 who assures us of the r weeks of harvest. H2978
Jer 52:34 gave Jehoiachin a r allowance as long as H9458
Eze 41:17 on the walls **at r intervals** all around the H4500
Eze 46:15 morning by morning for a r burnt offering. H9458

REGULARLY (14) [REGULAR]

Ex 29:38 you are to offer on the altar r each day: H9458
Ex 29:42 is to be made r at the entrance to the H9458
Ex 30: 8 so incense will burn r before the LORD for H9458
Lev 24: 8 bread is to be set out before the LORD r, H9458
2Ki 25:29 the rest of his life ate r at the king's table. H9458
1Ch 16: 6 to blow the trumpets r before the ark of H9458
1Ch 16:37 covenant of the LORD to minister there r, H9458
1Ch 16:40 to the LORD on the altar of burnt offering r, H9458
1Ch 23:31 before the LORD r in the proper number H9458
2Ch 2: 4 setting out the consecrated bread r H9458
2Ch 24:11 did this r and collected H4200+3427+928+3427
Jer 52:33 the rest of his life ate r at the king's table. H9458
Ac 10: 2 those in need and prayed to God r. G1328+4246
Heb 9: 6 priests entered r into the outer G1328+4246

REGULATED (1) [REGULATION]

Ne 11:23 the king's orders, which r their daily activity. H591

REGULATION (3) [REGULATED, REGULATIONS]

Ne 8:18 in accordance with the r, there was an H5477
Heb 7:16 on the basis of a r as to his G3795+1953
Heb 7:18 The former r is set aside because it was G1953

REGULATIONS (43) [REGULATION]

Ex 12:43 "These are the r *for* the Passover meal: H2978
Lev 6: 9 'These are the r *for* the burnt offering H9368
Lev 6:14 " 'These are the r *for* the grain offering H9368
Lev 6:25 'These are the r *for* the sin offering H9368
Lev 7: 1 " 'These are the r *for* the guilt offering H9368
Lev 7:11 " 'These are the r *for* the fellowship H9368
Lev 7:37 are the r for the burnt offering, the H9368
Lev 11:46 " 'These are the r *concerning* animals H9368
Lev 12: 7 " 'These are the r *for* the woman who H9368
Lev 13:59 These are the r *concerning* defiling molds H9368
Lev 14: 2 "These are the r *for* any diseased person H9368
Lev 14:32 These are the r *for* anyone who has a H9368
Lev 14:54 These are the r for any defiling skin H9368
Lev 14:57 These are the r *for* defiling skin diseases H9368
Lev 15:32 These are the r *for* a man with a H9368
Lev 26:46 the laws and the r that the LORD H9368
Nu 9: 3 in accordance with all its rules and r." H5477
Nu 9:12 the Passover, they must follow all the r. H2978
Nu 9:14 in accordance with its rules and r. H5477
Nu 9:14 must have the same r for both the H2978
Nu 15:16 The same laws and r will apply both to H5477
Nu 30:16 These are the r the LORD gave Moses H2976
Nu 35:24 the avenger of blood according to these r. H5477
Nu 36:13 are the commands and r the LORD gave H5477
Dt 12:28 careful to obey all these r I am giving you, H1821
1Ki 2: 3 his laws and r, as written in the Law H6343
2Ki 17:34 the LORD nor adhere to the decrees and r, H5477
2Ki 17:37 be careful to keep the decrees and r, H5477
1Ch 6:32 according to the r *laid down* for them. H5477
1Ch 24:19 to the **r prescribed** *for* them by their H5477
2Ch 19:10 decrees or r—you are to warn them H5477
2Ch 33: 8 decrees and r given through Moses." H5477
Ne 9:13 You gave them r and laws that are just H5477
Ne 10:29 r and decrees of the LORD our Lord. H5477
Est 9:32 decree confirmed these r *about* Purim, H1821
Eze 43:11 its whole design and all its r and laws. H2978
Eze 43:11 faithful to its design and follow all its r. H2978
Eze 43:18 These will be the r *for* sacrificing burnt H2978
Eze 44: 5 you concerning all the r and instructions H2978
Eph 2:15 his flesh the law with its commands and r. G1504
Col 2:23 **Such** *r* indeed have an appearance of wisdom AIT
Heb 9: 1 first covenant had r for worship and also G1468
Heb 9:10 external r applying until the time of the G1468

REHABIAH (4)

1Ch 23:17 **R** was the first. Eliezer H8152
1Ch 23:17 the sons of **R** were very numerous. H8152
1Ch 24:21 As for **R**, from his sons: Ishiah was the first H8153
1Ch 26:25 **R** his son, Jeshaiah his son, Joram his son H8153

REHEARSE, REHEARSED (KJV) RECITE, REPEATED, REPORTED, TOLD

REHOB (10) [BETH REHOB]

Nu 13:21 land from the Desert of Zin as far as **R**, H8149
Jos 19:28 It went to Abdon, **R**, Hammon and Kanah H8149
Jos 19:30 Ummah, Aphek and **R**. There were H8149
Jos 21:31 Helkath and **R**, together with their H8149

Jdg 1:31 Ahlab or Akzib or Helbah or Aphek or **R**. H8149
2Sa 8: 3 David defeated Hadadezer son of **R**, king H8150
2Sa 8:12 plunder taken from Hadadezer son of **R**, H8150
2Sa 10: 8 of Zobah and **R** and the men of Tob H8149
1Ch 6:75 Hukok and **R**, together with their H8149
Ne 10:11 **R**, Hashabiah, H8150

REHOBOAM (49) [REHOBOAM'S]

1Ki 11:43 And **R** his son succeeded him as king H8154
1Ki 12: 1 **R** went to Shechem, for all Israel had H8154
1Ki 12: 3 of Israel went to **R** and said to him: H8154
1Ki 12: 5 **R** answered, "Go away for three days and NDT
1Ki 12: 6 Then King **R** consulted the elders who H8154
1Ki 12: 8 But **R** rejected the advice the elders gave NDT
1Ki 12:12 all the people returned to **R**, H8154
1Ki 12:17 towns of Judah, **R** still ruled over them. H8154
1Ki 12:18 King **R** sent out Adoniram, who was in H8154
1Ki 12:18 King **R**, however, managed to get into his H8154
1Ki 12:21 When **R** arrived in Jerusalem, he H8154
1Ki 12:21 regain the kingdom for **R** son of Solomon. H8154
1Ki 12:23 "Say to **R** son of Solomon king of Judah, H8154
1Ki 12:27 allegiance to their lord, **R** king of Judah. H8154
1Ki 12:27 They will kill me and return to King **R**." H8154
1Ki 14:21 **R** son of Solomon was king in Judah. H8154
1Ki 14:25 In the fifth year of King **R**, Shishak king of H8154
1Ki 14:27 So King **R** made bronze shields to replace H8154
1Ki 14:30 warfare between **R** and Jeroboam. H8154
1Ki 14:31 And **R** rested with his ancestors and was H8154
1Ch 3:10 Solomon's son was **R**, Abijah his son, Asa H8154
2Ch 9:31 And **R** his son succeeded him as king H8154
2Ch 10: 1 **R** went to Shechem, for all Israel had H8154
2Ch 10: 3 all Israel went to **R** and said to him: H8154
2Ch 10: 5 **R** answered, "Come back to me in three NDT
2Ch 10: 6 Then King **R** consulted the elders who H8154
2Ch 10: 8 But **R** rejected the advice the elders gave NDT
2Ch 10:12 all the people returned to **R**, H8154
2Ch 10:17 towns of Judah, **R** still ruled over them. H8154
2Ch 10:18 King **R** sent out Adoniram, who was in H8154
2Ch 10:18 King **R**, however, managed to get into his H8154
2Ch 11: 1 When **R** arrived in Jerusalem, he H8154
2Ch 11: 1 Israel and to regain the kingdom for **R**. H8154
2Ch 11: 3 "Say to **R** son of Solomon king of Judah H8154
2Ch 11: 5 **R** lived in Jerusalem and built up towns H8154
2Ch 11:17 Judah and supported **R** son of Solomon H8154
2Ch 11:18 **R** married Mahalath, who was the H8154
2Ch 11:21 **R** loved Maakah daughter of Absalom H8154
2Ch 11:22 **R** appointed Abijah son of Maakah as H8154
2Ch 12: 2 Jerusalem in the fifth year of King **R**. H8154
2Ch 12: 5 Shemaiah came to **R** and to the leaders H8154
2Ch 12:10 So King **R** made bronze shields to replace H8154
2Ch 12:12 Because **R** humbled himself, the LORD's H2257S
2Ch 12:13 King **R** established himself firmly in H8154
2Ch 12:15 warfare between **R** and Jeroboam. H8154
2Ch 12:16 **R** rested with his ancestors and was buried H8154
2Ch 13: 7 him and opposed **R** son of Solomon when H8154
Mt 1: 7 Solomon the father of **R**, Rehoboam the *G4850*
Mt 1: 7 of Rehoboam, **R** the father of Abijah *G4850*

REHOBOAM'S (3) [REHOBOAM]

1Ki 14:29 As for the other events of **R** reign, and all H8154
2Ch 12: 1 After **R** position as king was established H8154
2Ch 12:15 As for the events of **R** reign, from H8154

REHOBOTH (3) [REHOBOTH IR]

Ge 26:22 He named it **R**, saying, "Now the LORD has H8151
Ge 36:37 Shaul from **R** *on* the river succeeded him H8151
1Ch 1:48 Shaul from **R** *on* the river succeeded him H8151

REHOBOTH IR (1) [REHOBOTH]

Ge 10:11 where he built Nineveh, **R**, Calah H8155

REHUM (8)

Ezr 2: 2 **R** and Baanah): The list of the H8156
Ezr 4: 8 **R** the commanding officer and Shimshai A10662
Ezr 4: 9 **R** the commanding officer and Shimshai A10662
Ezr 4:17 To **R** the commanding officer, Shimshai A10662
Ezr 4:23 was read to **R** and Shimshai the A10662
Ne 3:17 made by the Levites under **R** son of Bani. H8156
Ne 10:25 **R**, Hashabnah, Maaseiah, H8156
Ne 12: 3 Shekaniah, **R**, Meremoth, H8156

REI (1)

1Ki 1: 8 Shimei and **R** and David's special guard H8298

REIGN (158) [REIGNED, REIGNING, REIGNS]

Ge 37: 8 to him, "*Do you* **intend to** r over us? H4887+4887
Dt 17:20 will r a long time **over** his kingdom in H6584
Dt 32:25 them childless; in their homes terror will **r**. NDT
1Sa 8: 9 what the king who *will* r over them will H4887
1Sa 8:11 what the king who *will* r over you will H4887
1Sa 11:12 was it that asked, '*Shall* Saul r over us? H4887
2Sa 21: 1 During the r *of* David, there was a famine H3427
1Ki 1:35 sit on my throne and r in my place. H4887
1Ki 6: 1 the fourth year of Solomon's r over Israel, H4887
1Ki 11:41 As for the other events of Solomon's r—all NDT
1Ki 14:19 The other events of Jeroboam's **r**, his wars NDT
1Ki 14:29 As for the other events of Rehoboam's r NDT
1Ki 15: 1 year of the r *of* Jeroboam son of Nebat H4889
1Ki 15: 7 As for the other events of Abijah's **r**, and all NDT
1Ki 15:23 As for all the other events of Asa's **r**, all his NDT
1Ki 15:29 As soon as he *began to* **r**, he killed H4887
1Ki 15:31 As for the other events of Nadab's **r**, and all NDT
1Ki 16: 5 As for the other events of Baasha's **r**, what NDT
1Ki 16:11 As soon as he *began to* r and was seated H4887
1Ki 16:14 As for the other events of Elah's **r**, and all NDT
1Ki 16:20 As for the other events of Zimri's **r**, and the NDT
1Ki 16:27 As for the other events of Omri's **r**, what he NDT
1Ki 22:39 As for the other events of Ahab's r NDT
1Ki 22:45 As for the other events of Jehoshaphat's r NDT
1Ki 22:46 there even after the r *of* his father Asa. H3427
2Ki 1:18 As for all the other events of Ahaziah's r NDT
2Ki 8:16 of Jehoshaphat *began his* r as king of H4887
2Ki 8:23 As for the other events of Jehoram's **r**, and NDT
2Ki 8:25 son of Jehoram king of Judah *began to* **r**. H4887
2Ki 10:34 As for the other events of Jehu's **r**, all he did NDT
2Ki 11:21 was seven years old when he *began to* **r**. H4887
2Ki 12:19 As for the other events of the r of Joash, and NDT
2Ki 13: 8 As for the other events of the r of Jehoahaz NDT
2Ki 13:12 As for the other events of the r of Jehoash NDT
2Ki 13:22 Israel throughout the r *of* Jehoahaz. H3427
2Ki 14: 1 son of Joash king of Judah *began to* **r**. H4887
2Ki 14:15 As for the other events of the r of Jehoash NDT
2Ki 14:18 As for the other events of Amaziah's **r**, are NDT
2Ki 14:28 As for the other events of Jeroboam's **r**, all NDT
2Ki 15: 1 son of Amaziah king of Judah *began to* **r**. H4887
2Ki 15: 6 As for the other events of Azariah's **r**, and NDT
2Ki 15:11 events of Zechariah's r are written in the NDT
2Ki 15:15 The other events of Shallum's **r**, and the NDT
2Ki 15:18 *During* his entire r he did not turn away H3427
2Ki 15:21 As for the other events of Menahem's **r**, and NDT
2Ki 15:26 The other events of Pekahiah's **r**, and all he NDT
2Ki 15:31 As for the other events of Pekah's **r**, and all NDT
2Ki 15:32 son of Uzziah king of Judah *began to* **r**. H4887
2Ki 15:36 As for the other events of Jotham's **r**, and NDT
2Ki 16: 1 son of Jotham king of Judah *began to* **r**. H4887
2Ki 16:19 As for the other events of the r of Ahaz, and NDT
2Ki 18: 1 son of Ahaz king of Judah *began to* **r**. H4887
2Ki 18:13 In the fourteenth year of King Hezekiah's r NDT
2Ki 20:20 As for the other events of Hezekiah's **r**, all NDT
2Ki 21:17 As for the other events of Manasseh's **r**, and NDT
2Ki 21:25 As for the other events of Amon's **r**, and NDT
2Ki 22: 3 In the eighteenth year of his **r**, King H4889
2Ki 23:28 As for the other events of Josiah's **r**, and all NDT
2Ki 23:33 so that he *might* not r in Jerusalem, H4887
2Ki 24: 1 During Jehoiakim's **r**, Nebuchadnezzar H3427
2Ki 24: 5 As for the other events of Jehoiakim's **r**, and NDT
2Ki 24:12 eighth year of the r of the king of Babylon H4887
2Ki 25: 1 So in the ninth year of Zedekiah's **r**, on H4887
1Ch 4:31 were their towns until the r *of* David. H4887
1Ch 5:10 During Saul's r they waged war against H3427
1Ch 7: 2 During the r *of* David, the descendants of H3427
1Ch 13: 3 did not inquire of it during the r *of* Saul." H3427
1Ch 22: 9 grant Israel peace and quiet during his **r**. H3427
1Ch 26:31 year of David's r a search was made in H4895
1Ch 29:29 As for the events of King David's **r**, from NDT
1Ch 29:30 with the details of his r and power, H4895
2Ch 3: 2 second month in the fourth year of his **r**. H4895
2Ch 9:29 As for the other events of Solomon's **r**, from NDT
2Ch 12:15 As for the events of Rehoboam's **r**, from NDT
2Ch 13: 1 the eighteenth year of the r *of* Jeroboam, H4889
2Ch 13:22 The other events of Abijah's **r**, what he did NDT
2Ch 15:10 month of the fifteenth year of Asa's **r**. H4895
2Ch 15:19 war until the thirty-fifth year of Asa's **r**. H4895
2Ch 16: 1 year of Asa's r Baasha king of Israel went H4895
2Ch 16:11 The events of Asa's **r**, from beginning to NDT
2Ch 16:12 year of his r Asa was afflicted with a H4895
2Ch 16:13 forty-first year of his r Asa died and rested H4887
2Ch 17: 7 the third year of his r he sent his officials H4887
2Ch 20:34 The other events of Jehoshaphat's **r**, from NDT
2Ch 22: 1 son of Jehoram king of Judah *began to* **r**. H4887
2Ch 23: 3 "The king's son *shall* **r**, as the LORD H4887
2Ch 25:26 As for the other events of Amaziah's **r**, from NDT
2Ch 26:22 The other events of Uzziah's **r**, from NDT
2Ch 27: 7 The other events in Jotham's **r**, including all NDT
2Ch 28:26 The other events of his r and all his ways NDT
2Ch 29: 3 In the first month of the first year of his r H4887
2Ch 32:32 events of Hezekiah's r and his acts of NDT
2Ch 33:18 The other events of Manasseh's **r**, including NDT
2Ch 34: 3 In the eighth year of his **r**, while he was H4887
2Ch 34: 8 In the eighteenth year of Josiah's **r**, to H4887
2Ch 35:19 in the eighteenth year of Josiah's **r**. H4895
2Ch 35:26 events of Josiah's r and his acts of devotion NDT
2Ch 36: 8 The other events of Jehoiakim's **r**, the NDT
Ezr 4: 5 during the entire r *of* Cyrus king of Persia H3427
Ezr 4: 5 down to the r *of* Darius king of Persia H4895
Ezr 4: 6 At the beginning of the r *of* Xerxes, they H4895
Ezr 4:24 second year of the r *of* Darius king of A10424
Ezr 6:15 in the sixth year of the r *of* King Darius. A10424
Ezr 7: 1 during the r *of* Artaxerxes king of Persia H4895
Ezr 8: 1 Babylon during the r *of* King Artaxerxes: H4895
Ne 12:22 recorded in the r *of* Darius the Persian. H4895
Est 1: 3 third year of his r he gave a banquet for H4887
Est 2:16 of Tebeth, in the seventh year of his **r**. H4895
Est 6: 1 the record of his **r**, to be brought in and H3427
Ps 68:16 at the mountain where God chooses to r H3782
Pr 8:15 By me kings r and rulers issue decrees H4887
Pr 28:16 ill-gotten gain *will* **enjoy a long r**. H799+3427
Isa 9: 7 He will r on David's throne and over his NDT
Isa 24:23 the LORD Almighty *will* r on Mount Zion H4887
Isa 32: 1 a king *will* r in righteousness and rulers H4887
Isa 36: 1 In the fourteenth year of King Hezekiah's r NDT
Jer 1: 2 year of the r *of* Josiah son of Amon H4887
Jer 1: 3 through the r *of* Jehoiakim son of H3427
Jer 3: 6 During the r *of* King Josiah, the LORD said H3427
Jer 23: 5 a King *who will* r wisely and do what is H4887
Jer 26: 1 Early in the r *of* Jehoiakim son of Josiah H4931
Jer 27: 1 Early in the r *of* Zedekiah son of Josiah H4930
Jer 28: 1 early in the r *of* Zedekiah king of Judah H4930
Jer 33:21 have a descendant *to* r on his throne. H4887
Jer 35: 1 the LORD during the r *of* Jehoiakim son of H3427
Jer 36: 2 speaking to you in the r *of* Josiah till now. H3427
Jer 49:34 early in the r *of* Zedekiah king of Judah: H4895
Jer 51:59 king of Judah in the fourth year of his **r**. H4887
Jer 52: 4 So in the ninth year of Zedekiah's **r**, on H4887
La 5:19 r forever; your throne endures from H3782
Eze 20:33 *I will* r over you with a mighty hand and H4887
Da 1: 1 the third year of the r *of* Jehoiakim king of H4895
Da 2: 1 In the second year of his r H4895
Da 5:26 the days of your r and brought it to an A10424
Da 6:28 prospered during the r *of* Darius and the A10424
Da 6:28 of Darius and the r *of* Cyrus the Persian. A10424
Da 8: 1 In the third year of King Belshazzar's **r**, H4895
Da 8:23 "In the latter part of their **r**, when rebels H4895
Da 9: 2 in the first year of his **r**, I, Daniel H4887
Hos 1: 1 during the r *of* Jeroboam son of H3427
Am 6: 3 day of disaster and bring near a r *of* terror. H8699
Zep 1: 1 during the r *of* Josiah son of Amon king of H3427
Lk 1:33 and *he will* r over Jacob's descendants *G996*
Lk 3: 1 the fifteenth year *of the* r of Tiberius *G2449*
Ac 11:28 This happened **during the r of** Claudius.) *G2093*
Ro 5:17 *will* those who receive God's abundant provision of grace and of the gift of righteousness r *G996*
Ro 5:21 so also grace *might* r through *G996*
Ro 6:12 Therefore *do* not *let* sin r in your mortal *G996*
1Co 4: 8 rich! *You have begun to* r—and that *G996*
1Co 4: 8 wish that *you* really *had begun to* r so that *G996*
1Co 4: 8 to reign so that we also *might* **r with** you! *G5203*
1Co 15:25 For he must r until he has put all his *G996*
2Ti 2:12 we endure, *we will* also **r with** him. If we *G5203*
Rev 5:10 serve our God, and *they will* r on the earth." *G996*
Rev 11:15 Messiah, and *he will* r for ever and ever." *G996*
Rev 11:17 your great power and *have begun to* **r**. *G996*
Rev 20: 6 God and of Christ and *will* r with him for a *G996*
Rev 22: 5 And *they will* r for ever and ever. *G996*

REIGNED (94) [REIGN]

Ge 36:31 were the kings who r in Edom before any H4887
Ge 36:31 in Edom before any Israelite king r: H4887
Nu 21:34 king of the Amorites, who r in Heshbon." H3782
Dt 1: 4 of the Amorites, who r in Heshbon, and at H3782
Dt 1: 4 Og king of Bashan, who r in Ashtaroth. H3782
Dt 3: 2 king of the Amorites, who r in Heshbon." H3782
Dt 4:46 who r in Heshbon and was defeated by H3782
Jos 9:10 Og king of Bashan, who r in Ashtaroth. NDT
Jos 12: 2 king of the Amorites, who r in Heshbon. H3782
Jos 12: 4 Rephaites, who r in Ashtaroth and Edrei. H3782
Jos 13:12 who *had* r in Ashtaroth and Edrei. H4887
Jdg 4: 2 of Jabin king of Canaan, who r in Hazor. H4887
1Sa 13: 1 and *he* r over Israel forty- two years. H4887
2Sa 2:10 king over Israel, and *he* r two years. H4887
2Sa 5: 4 he became king, and *he* r forty years. H4887
2Sa 5: 5 In Hebron *he* r over Judah seven years H4887
2Sa 5: 5 in Jerusalem *he* r over all Israel and H4887
2Sa 8:15 David r over all Israel, doing what was H4887
2Sa 16: 8 of Saul, in whose place *you have* **r**. H4887
1Ki 2:11 He *had* r forty years over Israel—seven H4887
1Ki 11:42 Solomon r in Jerusalem over all Israel forty H4887
1Ki 14:20 He r for twenty-two years and then rested H4887
1Ki 14:21 and *he* r seventeen years in Jerusalem H4887
1Ki 15: 2 and *he* r in Jerusalem three years. H4887
1Ki 15:10 and *he* r in Jerusalem forty-one years. H4887
1Ki 15:25 of Judah, and *he* r over Israel two years. H4887
1Ki 15:33 Israel in Tirzah, and he r twenty-four years. NDT
1Ki 16: 8 king of Israel, and he r in Tirzah two years. NDT
1Ki 16:15 of Judah, Zimri r in Tirzah seven days. H4887
1Ki 16:23 king of Israel, and *he* r twelve years, six of H4887
1Ki 16:29 he r in Samaria over Israel H4887
1Ki 22:42 and *he* r in Jerusalem twenty-five years. H4887
1Ki 22:51 of Judah, and *he* r over Israel two years. H4887
2Ki 3: 1 king of Judah, and *he* r twelve years. H4887
2Ki 8:17 and *he* r in Jerusalem eight years. H4887
2Ki 8:26 and *he* r in Jerusalem one year. H4887
2Ki 10:36 The time that Jehu r over Israel in Samaria H4887
2Ki 12: 1 and *he* r in Jerusalem forty years. H4887
2Ki 13: 1 Israel in Samaria, and he r seventeen years. NDT
2Ki 13:10 of Israel in Samaria, and he r sixteen years. NDT
2Ki 14: 2 and *he* r in Jerusalem twenty-nine years. H4887
2Ki 14:23 king in Samaria, and he r forty-one years. NDT
2Ki 15: 2 and *he* r in Jerusalem fifty-two years. H4887
2Ki 15: 8 of Israel in Samaria, and he r six months. NDT
2Ki 15:13 of Judah, and *he* r in Samaria one month. H4887
2Ki 15:17 king of Israel, and he r in Samaria ten years. NDT
2Ki 15:23 of Israel in Samaria, and he r two years. NDT
2Ki 15:27 of Israel in Samaria, and he r twenty years. NDT
2Ki 15:33 and *he* r in Jerusalem sixteen years. H4887
2Ki 16: 2 and *he* r in Jerusalem sixteen years. H4887
2Ki 17: 1 of Israel in Samaria, and he r nine years. NDT
2Ki 18: 2 and *he* r in Jerusalem twenty-nine years. H4887
2Ki 21: 1 and *he* r in Jerusalem fifty-five years. H4887
2Ki 21:19 and *he* r in Jerusalem two years. H4887
2Ki 22: 1 and *he* r in Jerusalem thirty-one years. H4887
2Ki 23:31 and *he* r in Jerusalem three months. H4887
2Ki 23:36 and *he* r in Jerusalem eleven years. H4887
2Ki 24: 8 and *he* r in Jerusalem three months. H4887
2Ki 24:18 and *he* r in Jerusalem eleven years. H4887
1Ch 1:43 were the kings who r in Edom before any H4887
1Ch 1:43 in Edom before any Israelite king r: H4887

1Ch 3: 4 where *he* **r** seven years and six months. H4887
1Ch 3: 4 David **r** in Jerusalem thirty-three years H4887
1Ch 18:14 David **r** over all Israel, doing what was H4887
2Ch 1:13 the tent of meeting. And *he* **r** over Israel. H4887
2Ch 9:30 Solomon **r** in Jerusalem over all Israel forty H4887
2Ch 12:13 and *he* **r** seventeen years in Jerusalem H4887
2Ch 13: 2 and *he* **r** in Jerusalem three years. H4887
2Ch 20:31 So Jehoshaphat **r** over Judah. He was H4887
2Ch 20:31 and *he* **r** in Jerusalem twenty-five years. H4887
2Ch 21: 5 and *he* **r** in Jerusalem eight years. H4887
2Ch 21:20 and *he* **r** in Jerusalem eight years. H4887
2Ch 22: 2 and *he* **r** in Jerusalem one year. H4887
2Ch 24: 1 and *he* **r** in Jerusalem forty years. H4887
2Ch 25: 1 and *he* **r** in Jerusalem twenty-nine years. H4887
2Ch 26: 3 and *he* **r** in Jerusalem fifty-two years. H4887
2Ch 27: 1 and *he* **r** in Jerusalem sixteen years. H4887
2Ch 27: 8 and *he* **r** in Jerusalem sixteen years. H4887
2Ch 28: 1 and *he* **r** in Jerusalem sixteen years. H4887
2Ch 29: 1 and *he* **r** in Jerusalem twenty-nine years. H4887
2Ch 33: 1 and *he* **r** in Jerusalem fifty-five years. H4887
2Ch 33:21 and *he* **r** in Jerusalem two years. H4887
2Ch 34: 1 and *he* **r** in Jerusalem thirty-one years. H4887
2Ch 36: 2 and *he* **r** in Jerusalem three months. H4887
2Ch 36: 5 and *he* **r** in Jerusalem eleven years. H4887
2Ch 36: 9 and *he* **r** in Jerusalem three months and H4887
2Ch 36:11 and *he* **r** in Jerusalem eleven years. H4887
Est 1: 2 time King Xerxes **r** from his royal throne H3782
Jer 37: 1 *he* **r** in place of Jehoiachin son of H4887+4889
Jer 52: 1 and *he* **r** in Jerusalem eleven years. H4887
Ro 5:14 death **r** from the time of Adam to the time G996
Ro 5:17 one man, death **r** through that one man G996
Ro 5:21 just as sin **r** in death, so also grace G996
Rev 20: 4 They came to life and **r** with Christ a G996

REIGNING (1) [REIGN]

Mt 2:22 that Archelaus *was* **r** in Judea in place G996

REIGNS (19) [REIGN]

Ex 15:18 "The LORD **r** for ever and ever. H4887
1Sa 12:14 the king who **r** over you follow the H4887
1Ki 15:16 Baasha king of Israel throughout their **r**. H3427
1Ki 15:32 Baasha king of Israel throughout their **r**. H3427
1Ch 5:17 records during the **r** *of* Jotham king of H3427
1Ch 16:31 them say among the nations, "The LORD **r**!" H4887
Ps 9: 7 The LORD **r** forever; he has established his H3782
Ps 47: 8 God **r** over the nations; God is seated on H4887
Ps 93: 1 The LORD **r**, he is robed in majesty; the H4887
Ps 96:10 nations, "The LORD **r**." The world is firmly H4887
Ps 97: 1 The LORD **r**, let the earth be glad; let the H4887
Ps 99: 1 The LORD **r**, let the nations tremble; he sits H4887
Ps 146:10 The LORD **r** forever, your God, O Zion, for H4887
Isa 1: 1 son of Amoz saw during the **r** *of* Uzziah, H3427
Isa 52: 7 salvation, who say to Zion, "Your God **r**!" H4887
Hos 1: 1 Hosea son of Beeri during the **r** *of* Uzziah, H3427
Mic 1: 1 of Moresheth during the **r** *of* Jotham, H3427
Lk 22:53 But this is your hour—when darkness **r**." G2026
Rev 19: 6 For our Lord God Almighty **r**. G996

REIMBURSE (1)

Lk 10:35 I *will* **r** you for any extra expense you may G625

REIN (2)

Job 10: 1 therefore *I will* **give free r** to my complaint H6440
Jas 1:26 and *yet do* not **keep a tight r on** their G5902

REINFORCE (2) [REINFORCED, REINFORCEMENTS]

Ps 83: 8 has joined them *to* **r** Lot's H2118+2432
Jer 51:12 **R** the guard, station the watchmen H2616

R

REINFORCED (2) [REINFORCE]

2Ch 24:13 according to its original design and **r** it. H599
2Ch 32: 5 outside that one and **r** the terraces of the H2616

REINFORCEMENTS (1) [REINFORCE]

Isa 43:17 the army and **r** together, and they H6450

REJECT (34) [REJECTED, REJECTING, REJECTION, REJECTS]

Lev 26:15 if you **r** my decrees and abhor my laws H4415
Lev 26:44 *I will* not **r** them or abhor them so as to H4415
1Sa 12:22 great name the LORD *will* not **r** his people, H5759
1Ki 9: 7 them and *will* **r** this H8938+4946+6584+7156
2Ki 23:27 removed Israel, and *I will* **r** Jerusalem, the H4415
1Ch 28: 9 if you forsake him, *he will* **r** you forever. H2396
2Ch 6:42 *do* not **r** your anointed one. H8740+7156
2Ch 7:20 and *will* **r** this temple I H8959+4946+6584+7156
Job 8:20 "Surely God *does* not **r** one who is H4415
Ps 27: 9 *Do* not **r** me or forsake me, God my Savior. H5759
Ps 36: 4 sinful course and *do* not **r** what is wrong. H4415
Ps 44:23 Rouse yourself! *Do* not **r** us forever. H2396
Ps 77: 7 "*Will* the Lord **r** forever? Will he never H2396
Ps 88:14 *do you* **r** me and hide your face from me? H2396
Ps 94:14 For the LORD *will* not **r** his people; he will H5759
Ps 119:118 *You* **r** all who stray from your decrees, for H6136
Ps 132:10 David, *do* not **r** your anointed one. H8740+7156
Isa 7:15 he knows enough *to* **r** the wrong and H4415
Isa 7:16 the boy knows enough *to* **r** the wrong and H4415
Isa 31: 7 day every one of *you will* **r** the idols of H4415
Isa 33:15 *who* **r** gain from extortion and keep their H4415
Jer 31:37 be searched out *will* I **r** all the H4415
Jer 33:26 then *I will* **r** the descendants of Jacob and H4415
Hos 4: 6 knowledge, *I* also **r** you as my priests H4415
Hos 9:17 My God *will* **r** them because they have not H4415
Lk 6:22 insult you and **r** your name as evil, G1675
Ac 13:46 Since *you* **r** it and do not consider G723
Ro 2: 8 are self-seeking and *who* **r** the truth and G578
Ro 11: 1 *Did* God **r** his people? By no G723
Ro 11: 2 God *did* not **r** his people, whom he G723
1Th 4: 8 this instruction *does* not **r** a human being G119
1Th 5:22 **r** every kind of evil. G600
Titus 1:14 human commands *of those who* **r** the truth. G695
Jude 8 **r** authority and heap abuse on celestial G119

REJECTED (79) [REJECT]

Lev 26:43 sins because they **r** my laws and abhorred H4415
Nu 11:20 because *you have* **r** the LORD, who is H4415
Nu 14:31 them in to enjoy the land *you have* **r**. H4415
Dt 32:15 who made them and **r** the Rock their H5571
Dt 32:19 LORD saw this and **r** them because he was H5540
1Sa 8: 7 it is not you *they have* **r**, but they have H4415
1Sa 8: 7 rejected, but *they have* **r** me as their king. H4415
1Sa 10:19 But you *have* now **r** your God, who saves H4415
1Sa 15:23 Because *you have* **r** the word of the LORD H4415
1Sa 15:23 word of the LORD, *he has* **r** you as king." H4415
1Sa 15:26 *You have* **r** the word of the LORD, and the H4415
1Sa 15:26 the LORD *has* **r** you as king over Israel!" H4415
1Sa 16: 1 since I *have* **r** him as king over Israel? H4415
1Sa 16: 7 appearance or his height, for *I have* **r** him. H4415
1Ki 12: 8 But Rehoboam **r** the advice the elders H6440
1Ki 19:10 The Israelites *have* **r** your covenant, torn H6440
1Ki 19:14 The Israelites *have* **r** your covenant, torn H6440
2Ki 17:15 *They* **r** his decrees and the covenant he H4415
2Ki 17:20 Therefore the LORD **r** all the people of H4415
2Ch 10: 8 But Rehoboam **r** the advice the elders H6440
2Ch 11:14 his sons *had* **r** them as priests of H2396
Ps 10: 5 your laws *are* **r** by him; he sneers at H6073
Ps 43: 2 Why *have you* **r** me? Why must I H2396
Ps 44: 9 But now *you have* **r** and humbled us; you H2396
Ps 60: 1 *You have* **r** us, God, and burst upon us H2396
Ps 60:10 *you who have now* **r** us and no longer go H2396
Ps 66:20 who *has* not **r** my prayer or withheld his H6073
Ps 74: 1 why *have you* **r** us forever? Why H2396
Ps 78:59 he was furious; *he* **r** Israel completely. H4415
Ps 78:67 Then *he* **r** the tents of Joseph, he did not H4415
Ps 89:38 But you *have* **r**, you have spurned, you H2396
Ps 108:11 *you who have* **r** us and no longer go out H2396
Ps 118:22 The stone the builders **r** has become the H4415
Isa 5:24 for *they have* **r** the law of the LORD H4415
Isa 8: 6 this people *has* **r** the gently flowing H4415
Isa 14:19 are cast out of your tomb like a **r** branch; H9493
Isa 30:12 "Because you *have* **r** this message, relied H4415
Isa 41: 9 I have chosen you and *have* not **r** you. H4415
Isa 49:21 bereaved and barren; I was exiled and **r**. H6073
Isa 53: 3 He was despised and **r** *by* mankind, H2534
Isa 54: 6 only *to* **be r**," says your God. H4415
Jer 2:37 for the LORD *has* **r** those you trust H4415
Jer 6:19 listened to my words and *have* **r** my law. H4415
Jer 6:30 They are called **r** silver, because the LORD H4415
Jer 6:30 because the LORD *has* **r** them. H4415
Jer 7:29 the LORD *has* **r** and abandoned this H4415
Jer 8: 9 Since *they have* **r** the word of the LORD H4415
Jer 14:19 *Have you* **r** Judah **completely**? Do H4415+4415
Jer 15: 6 You *have* **r** me," declares the LORD. "You H5759
Jer 33:24 'The LORD *has* **r** the two kingdoms he H4415
La 1:15 "The Lord *has* **r** all the warriors in my H6136
La 2: 7 The Lord *has* **r** his altar and abandoned H2396
La 5:22 unless *you have* **utterly r** us and are H4415+4415
Eze 5: 6 *She has* **r** my laws and has not followed H4415
Eze 20:13 did not follow my decrees but **r** my laws— H4415
Eze 20:16 because *they* **r** my laws and did not follow H4415
Eze 20:24 obeyed my laws but *had* **r** my decrees H4415
Hos 4: 6 "Because you *have* **r** knowledge, I also H4415
Hos 8: 3 But Israel *has* **r** what is good; an enemy H2396
Am 2: 4 Because they *have* **r** the law of the LORD H4415
Zec 10: 6 They will be as though *I had* not **r** them H2396
Mt 21:42 " 'The stone the builders **r** has become the G627
Mk 8:31 suffer many things and *be* **r** by the elders, G627
Mk 9:12 Son of Man must suffer much and *be* **r**? G2022
Mk 12:10 " 'The stone the builders **r** has become the G627
Lk 7:30 the experts in the law **r** God's purpose for G119
Lk 9:22 suffer many things and *be* **r** by the elders, G627
Lk 17:25 many things and *be* **r** by this generation. G627
Lk 20:17 " 'The stone the builders **r** has become the G627
Ac 4:11 Jesus is " 'the stone you builders **r**, which G2024
Ac 7:35 the same Moses *they had* **r** with the words, G766
Ac 7:39 *they* **r** him and in their hearts turned back G723
1Ti 1:19 which some *have* **r** and so have suffered G723
1Ti 4: 4 nothing is to be **r** if it is received with G612
2Ti 3: 8 as far as the faith is concerned, are **r**. G99
Heb 10:28 Anyone *who* **r** the law of Moses died G119
Heb 12:17 wanted to inherit this blessing, *he was* **r**. G627
1Pe 2: 4 **r** by humans but chosen by God and G627
1Pe 2: 7 "The stone the builders **r** has become the G627

REJECTING (3) [REJECT]

Dt 31:20 **r** me and breaking my covenant. H5540
1Ki 12:13 **R** the advice given him by the elders H6440
2Ch 10:13 them harshly. **R** the advice of the elders H6440

REJECTION (1) [REJECT]

Ro 11:15 For if their **r** brought reconciliation to the G613

REJECTS (7) [REJECT]

Lk 10:16 listens to me; whoever **r** you rejects me; but G119
Lk 10:16 whoever rejects you **r** me; but whoever G119
Lk 10:16 whoever **r** me rejects him who sent me." G119
Lk 10:16 whoever rejects me **r** him who sent me." G119
Jn 3:36 but whoever **r** the Son will not see life G578
Jn 12:48 a judge for the *one who* **r** me and does not G119
1Th 4: 8 anyone *who* **r** this instruction does not G119

REJOICE (131) [JOY]

Lev 23:40 **r** before the LORD your God for seven H8523
Dt 12: 7 shall eat and *shall* **r** in everything you H8523
Dt 12:12 And there **r** before the LORD your God— H8523
Dt 12:18 and *you are to* **r** before the LORD your God H8523
Dt 14:26 the presence of the LORD your God and **r**. H8523
Dt 16:11 And **r** before the LORD your God at the H8523
Dt 26:11 residing among you *shall* **r** in all the good H8523
Dt 32:43 **R**, *you* nations, with his people, for he will H8264
Dt 33:18 "**R**, Zebulun, in your going out, and you H8523
2Sa 1:20 lest the daughters of the uncircumcised **r**. H6600
1Ch 16:10 *let* the hearts of those who seek the LORD **r**. H8523
1Ch 16:31 *Let* the heavens **r**, let the earth be glad H8523
2Ch 6:41 *may* your faithful people **r** in your H8523
2Ch 20:27 the LORD *had* **given** them **cause to r** over H8523
Job 3:22 with gladness and **r** when they reach the H8464
Job 22:19 The righteous see their ruin and **r**; the H8523
Ps 5:11 those who love your name *may* **r** in you. H6636
Ps 9: 2 I will be glad and **r** in you; I will sing the H6636
Ps 9:14 and there **r** in your salvation. H1635
Ps 13: 4 and my foes *will* **r** when I fall. H1635
Ps 14: 7 his people, *let* Jacob **r** and Israel be glad! H1635
Ps 31: 7 I will be glad and **r** in your love, for you H8523
Ps 32:11 **R** in the LORD and be glad, you righteous H8523
Ps 33:21 In him our hearts **r**, for we trust in his holy H8523
Ps 34: 2 in the LORD; let the afflicted hear and **r**. H8523
Ps 35: 9 Then my soul *will* **r** in the LORD and H1635
Ps 40:16 But *may* all who seek you **r** and be glad in H8464
Ps 51: 8 *let* the bones you have crushed **r**. H1635
Ps 53: 6 his people, *let* Jacob **r** and Israel be glad! H1635
Ps 63:11 But the king *will* **r** in God; all who swear H8523
Ps 64:10 The righteous *will* **r** in the LORD and take H8523
Ps 66: 6 the waters on foot—*come, let us* **r** in him. H8523
Ps 68: 3 the righteous be glad and **r** before God; H6636
Ps 68: 4 on the clouds; **r** before him—his name H6600
Ps 70: 4 But *may* all who seek you **r** and be glad in H8464
Ps 85: 6 us again, that your people *may* **r** in you? H8523
Ps 89:16 *They* **r** in your name all day long; they H1635
Ps 89:42 *you have* **made** all his enemies **r**. H8523
Ps 96:11 *Let* the heavens **r**, let the earth be glad H8523
Ps 96:13 Let all creation **r** before the LORD, for he NDT
Ps 97: 1 the earth be glad; *let* the distant shores **r**. H1635
Ps 97:12 **R** in the LORD, *you* who are righteous, and H8523
Ps 104:31 *may* the LORD **r** in his works— H8523
Ps 104:34 be pleasing to him, as I **r** in the LORD. H8523
Ps 105: 3 *let* the hearts of those who seek the LORD **r**. H8523
Ps 107:42 The upright see and **r**, but all the wicked H8523
Ps 109:28 be put to shame, but *may* your servant **r**. H8523
Ps 118:24 it this very day; *let us* **r** today and be glad. H1635
Ps 119:14 *I* **r** in following your statutes as one H8464
Ps 119:74 *May* those who fear you **r** when they see H8523
Ps 119:162 I **r** in your promise like one who finds H8464
Ps 149: 2 Let Israel **r** in their Maker; let the people H8523
Ps 149: 5 *Let* his faithful people **r** in this honor and H6600
Pr 2:14 in doing wrong and **r** in the perverseness H1635
Pr 5:18 and *may you* **r** in the wife of your youth. H8523
Pr 23:16 my inmost being *will* **r** when your lips H6600
Pr 23:25 *May* your father and mother **r**; may she H8523
Pr 24:17 when they stumble, do not *let* your heart **r**, H1635
Pr 29: 2 the people **r**; when the wicked rule, H8523
SS 1: 4 *We* **r** and delight in you; we will praise H1635
Isa 9: 3 *they* **r** before you as people rejoice at the H8523
Isa 9: 3 before you as people **r** at the harvest, H8525
Isa 9: 3 as *warriors* **r** when dividing the plunder. H1635
Isa 13: 3 my wrath—*those who* **r** *in* my triumph. H6611
Isa 14:29 *Do* not **r**, all you Philistines, that the rod H8523
Isa 25: 9 *let us* **r** and be glad in his salvation." H1635
Isa 29:19 Once more the humble will **r** in the LORD H8525
Isa 29:19 the needy *will* **r** in the Holy One of Israel. H1635
Isa 30:29 your hearts will **r** as when people playing H8525
Isa 35: 1 the wilderness *will* **r** and blossom. H1635
Isa 35: 2 *it will* **r greatly** and shout for H1635+677+1638
Isa 41:16 But you *will* **r** in the LORD and glory in the H1635
Isa 42:11 let the settlements where Kedar lives **r**. NDT
Isa 49:13 you heavens; **r**, *you* earth; burst into H1635
Isa 61: 7 of disgrace *you will* **r** *in* your inheritance. H8264
Isa 62: 5 over his bride, so *will* your God **r** over you. H8464
Isa 65:13 my servants *will* **r**, but you will be H8523
Isa 65:18 But be glad and **r** forever *in* what I will H1635
Isa 65:19 *I will* **r** over Jerusalem and take delight in H1635
Isa 66:10 "**R** with Jerusalem and be glad for her, all H8523
Isa 66:10 who love her; **r greatly** with her, all H8464+5375
Isa 66:14 your heart *will* **r** and you will flourish like H8464
Jer 11:15 engage in your wickedness, then *you* **r**." H6600
Jer 31:12 *they will* **r** in the bounty of the LORD H5642
Jer 32:41 *I will* **r** in doing them good and will H8464
Jer 50:11 "Because *you* **r** and are glad, you who H8523
La 1:21 my distress; *they* **r** *at* what you have done. H8464
La 4:21 **R** and be glad, Daughter Edom, you who H8464
Eze 7:12 Let not the buyer **r** nor the seller grieve H8523
Eze 21:10 " '*Shall we* **r** *in* the scepter of my royal son H8464
Hos 9: 1 *Do* not **r**, Israel; do not be jubilant like the H8523
Joel 2:21 be afraid, land of Judah; be glad and **r**. H8523
Joel 2:23 people of Zion, **r** in the LORD your God, H8523
Am 6:13 *you who* **r** in the conquest of Lo Debar H8524
Ob 12 **r** over the people of Judah in the day H8523
Hab 3:18 I *will* **r** in the LORD, I will be joyful in H6600

Zep 3:14 Be glad and **r** with all your heart H6600
Zep 3:17 but *will* **r** over you with singing. H1635
Zec 4:10 the earth *will* **r** when they see the H8523
Zec 9: 9 **R** greatly, Daughter Zion! Shout, Daughter H1635
Zec 10: 7 be joyful; their hearts *will* **r** in the LORD. H1635
Mt 5:12 **R** and be glad, because great is your G5897
Lk 1:14 and many *will* **r** because of his birth, G5897
Lk 6:23 "**R** in that day and leap for joy, because G5897
Lk 10:20 *do* not **r** that the spirits submit to you G5897
Lk **r** that your names are written in G5897
Lk 15: 6 says, '**R with** me; I have found my G5176
Lk 15: 9 says, '**R with** me; I have found my G5176
Jn 16:22 I will see you again and you *will* **r** G5897
Ro 12:15 **R** with those who rejoice; mourn with G5897
Ro 12:15 Rejoice with *those who* **r**; mourn with G5897
Ro 15:10 it says, "**R,** *you* Gentiles, with his G2370
Ro 16:19 your obedience, so *I* **r** because of you; but G5897
2Co 2: 3 by those who should have *made* me **r**. G5897
2Co 13:11 brothers and sisters, **r**! Strive for full G5897
Php 1:18 And because of this *I* **r**. G5897
Php 1:18 Yes, and *I will continue to* **r**, G5897
Php 2:17 your faith, I am glad and **r with** all of you. G5176
Php 2:18 So you too should be glad and **r with** me. G5176
Php 3: 1 my brothers and sisters, **r** in the Lord! G5897
Php 4: 4 **R** in the Lord always. I will say it again G5897
Php 4: 4 in the Lord always. I will say it again: **R**! G5897
Col 1:24 Now *I* **r** in what I am suffering for you, G5897
1Th 5:16 **R** always, G5897
1Pe 1: 6 In all this *you* **greatly** **r**, though now for a G22
1Pe 4:13 But **r** inasmuch as you participate in the G5897
Rev 12:12 Therefore **r**, you heavens and you who G2370
Rev 18:20 "**R** over her, you heavens! Rejoice, you G2370
Rev 18:20 over her, you heavens! **R**, you people of God NDT
Rev 18:20 you people of God! **R**, apostles and NDT
Rev 19: 7 *Let us* **r** and be glad and give him glory G5897

REJOICED (17) [JOY]

1Sa 6:13 up and saw the ark, *they* **r** at the sight. H8523
2Ki 11:20 All the people of the land **r**, and the city H8523
1Ch 29: 9 The people **r** at the willing response of H8523
1Ch 29: 9 David the king also **r** greatly. H8523+8525
2Ch 15:15 All Judah **r** about the oath because they H8523
2Ch 23:21 All the people of the land **r**, and the city H8523
2Ch 29:36 all the people **r** at what God had H8523
2Ch 30:25 The entire assembly of Judah **r**, along with H8523
Ne 12:43 The women and children also **r**. H8523
Job 31:25 if *I have* **r** *over* my great wealth, the H8523
Job 31:29 "If *I have* **r** at my enemy's misfortune or H8523
Ps 122: 1 *I* **r** with those who said to me, "Let us go H8523
SS 3:11 day of his wedding, the day his heart **r**. H8525
Eze 35:15 Because you **r** when the inheritance of H8525
Hos 10: 5 *those who had* **r** over its splendor H1635
Jn 8:56 Your father Abraham **r** at the thought of G22
Php 4:10 *I* **r** greatly in the Lord that at last you G5897

REJOICES (19) [JOY]

1Sa 2: 1 "My heart **r** in the LORD; in the LORD my H6636
Ps 13: 5 my heart **r** in your salvation. H1635
Ps 16: 9 my heart is glad and my tongue **r**; H1635
Ps 21: 1 The king **r** in your strength, LORD. H8523
Ps 48:11 Mount Zion **r**, the villages of Judah are H8523
Ps 97: 8 Zion hears and **r** and the villages of H8523
Ps 119:14 your statutes as one **r** in great riches. NDT
Pr 11:10 prosper, the city **r**; when the wicked perish H6636
Pr 23:24 a man who fathers a wise son **r** in him. H8523
Isa 8: 6 of Shiloah and **r** over Rezin and the H5375
Isa 61:10 greatly in the LORD; my soul **r** in my God. H1635
Isa 62: 5 as a bridegroom **r** over his bride, so H5375
Eze 35:14 While the whole earth **r**, I will make you H8523
Hab 1:15 up in his dragnet; and so *he* **r** and is glad. H8523
Lk 1:47 my spirit **r** in God my Savior, G22
Jn 16:20 will weep and mourn *while* the world **r**. G5897
Ac 2:26 Therefore my heart is glad and my tongue **r** G22
1Co 12:26 if one part is honored, every part **r with** it. G5176
1Co 13: 6 not delight in evil but **r with** the truth. G5176

REJOICING (25) [JOY]

Nu 10:10 Also at your times of **r**—your appointed H8525
Dt 27: 7 eating them and **r** in the presence of the H8523
2Sa 6:12 of Obed-Edom to the City of David with **r**. H8525
1Ki 1:40 playing pipes and **r** greatly, so that H8524+8525
2Ki 11:14 of the land were **r** and blowing trumpets. H8524
1Ch 15:25 from the house of Obed-Edom, with **r**. H8525
2Ch 23:13 of the land were **r** and blowing trumpets, H8524
2Ch 23:18 Law of Moses, with **r** and singing, as H8525
2Ch 30:21 Bread for seven days with great **r**, H8525
Ne 12:43 **r** because God had given them great joy. H8523
Ne 12:43 The sound of **r** *in* Jerusalem could be H8525
Job 39:21 It paws fiercely, **r** in its strength, and H8464
Ps 19: 5 like a champion **r** to run his course. H8464
Ps 30: 5 the night, but **r** comes in the morning. H8262
Ps 105:43 He brought out his people with **r**, his H8607
Pr 8:30 day after day, **r** always in his presence H8471
Pr 8:31 **r** in his whole world and delighting in H8471
Pr 14:13 heart may ache, and **r** may end in grief. H8525
Jer 30:19 songs of thanksgiving and the sound of **r**. H8471
Eze 25: 6 **r** with all the malice of your heart against H8523
Lk 15: 7 there will be more **r** in heaven over one G5915
Lk 15:10 there is **r** in the presence of the angels of G5915
Ac 5:41 **r** because they had been counted worthy G5897
Ac 8:39 not see him again, but went on his way **r**. G5897
2Co 6:10 sorrowful, yet always **r**; poor, yet making G5897

REJOINED (1) [JOIN]

Jdg 14: 9 When *he* **r** his parents, he gave H2143+448

REKAB (12) [REKABITE, REKABITES]

2Sa 4: 2 One was named Baanah and the other **R** H8209
2Sa 4: 5 Now **R** and Baanah, the sons of Rimmon H8209
2Sa 4: 6 Then **R** and his brother Baanah slipped H8209
2Sa 4: 9 David answered **R** and his brother Baanah H8209
2Ki 10:15 he came upon Jehonadab son of **R**, who H8209
2Ki 10:23 Jehonadab son of **R** went into the temple H8209
Ne 3:14 Gate was repaired by Malkijah son of **R**, H8209
Jer 35: 6 Jehonadab son of **R** gave us this H8209
Jer 35: 8 Jehonadab son of **R** commanded us. H8209
Jer 35:14 'Jehonadab son of **R** ordered his H8209
Jer 35:16 of Jehonadab son of **R** have carried out H8209
Jer 35:19 'Jehonadab son of **R** will never fail to H8209

REKABITE (1) [REKAB]

Jer 35: 2 "Go to the **R** family and invite them to H8211

REKABITES (4) [REKAB]

1Ch 2:55 from Hammath, the father of the **R**. H1074+8209
Jer 35: 3 all his sons—the whole family of the **R**. H8211
Jer 35: 5 before the **R** and said to H1201+1074+8211
Jer 35:18 Then Jeremiah said to the family of the **R** H8211

REKAH (1)

1Ch 4:12 These were the men of **R**. H8212

REKEM (5)

Nu 31: 8 victims were Evi, **R**, Zur, Hur and Reba— H8390
Jos 13:21 Evi, **R**, Zur, Hur and Reba— H8390
Jos 18:27 **R**, Irpeel, Taralah, H8389
1Ch 2:43 Korah, Tappuah, **R** and Shema. H8390
1Ch 2:44 **R** was the father of Shammai H8390

RELATE (1) [RELATED, RELATING, RELATIONS, RELATIONSHIP, RELATIONSHIPS, RELATIVE, RELATIVE'S, RELATIVES]

Ps 71:15 though I know not *how to* **r** them all. H6228

RELATED (16) [RELATING, RELATION, RELATIONS, RELATIONSHIP, RELATIONSHIPS, RELATIVE, RELATIVES]

Ge 25:18 in hostility toward all the **tribes r** to them. H278
Lev 21: 4 unclean for people **r** *to* him **by marriage**, H1251
Nu 3:26 the ropes—and everything **r to** their use. H4200
Nu 3:31 the curtain, and **everything r** *to* their use. AIT
Nu 3:36 its equipment, and **everything** *r to* their use, AIT
Nu 4:32 equipment and everything **r to** their use. H4200
Dt 23: 7 an Edomite, for the Edomites are **r to** you. H278
Jdg 9: 3 Abimelek, for they said, "He is **r to** us." H278
Jdg 9:18 citizens of Shechem because he is **r to** you. H278
Ru 3:12 is another who is more **closely r** than I. H7940
2Sa 19:42 did this because the king is **closely r** to us. H7940
2Ki 8:27 he was **r by marriage** *to* Ahab's family. H3163
2Ch 4:16 shovels, meat forks and all **r** articles. H2157S
Est 8: 1 Esther had told how he was **r to** her. H4200
Ac 19:25 along with the workers in **r** *trades*, and G5525
Heb 5: 1 represent the people in matters **r to** God, G4639

RELATING (1) [RELATED]

Ne 11:24 king's agent in all affairs **r to** the people. H4200

RELATIONS (49) [RELATED]

Ex 19:15 **Abstain from sexual r**." H440+5602+448+851
Ex 22:19 "Anyone *who* **has sexual r with** an H8886+6640
Lev 15:18 When a man **has sexual r** with a woman H8886
Lev 15:24 " 'If a man **has sexual r** with her H8886+8886
Lev 15:33 a man who **has sexual r** with a woman H8886
Lev 18: 6 any close relative to **have sexual r**. H1655+6872
Lev 18: 7 *Do* not **dishonor** your father
by having sexual r with H1655+6872
Lev 18: 7 mother; *do* not **have r with** her. H1655+6872
Lev 18: 8 " '*Do* not **have sexual r with** your H1655+6872
Lev 18: 9 " '*Do* not **have sexual r with** your H1655+6872
Lev 18:10 " '*Do* not **have sexual r with** your H1655+6872
Lev 18:11 " '*Do* not **have sexual r with** the H1655+6872
Lev 18:12 " '*Do* not **have sexual r with** your H1655+6872
Lev 18:13 " '*Do* not **have sexual r with** your H1655+6872
Lev 18:14 *Do* not **dishonor** your father's brother
by approaching his wife **to have sexual r** H1655+6872
Lev 18:15 " '*Do* not **have sexual r with** your H1655+6872
Lev 18:15 son's wife; *do* not **have r with** her. H1655+6872
Lev 18:16 " '*Do* not **have sexual r with** your H1655+6872
Lev 18:17 " '*Do* not **have sexual r with** both a H1655+6872
Lev 18:17 *Do* not **have sexual r with** either H1655+6872
Lev 18:18 wife and **have sexual r** with her H1655+6872
Lev 18:19 a woman to **have sexual r** during H1655+6872
Lev 18:20 " '*Do* not **have sexual r** H5989+8888+4200+2446
Lev 18:22 " '*Do* not **have sexual r** with a man as one H8886
Lev 18:23 " '*Do* not **have sexual r** with an H5989+8888
Lev 18:23 to an animal to **have sexual r** *with* it; H8061
Lev 20:11 " 'If a man **has sexual r** with his father's H8886
Lev 20:12 " 'If a man **has sexual r** with his H8886
Lev 20:13 " 'If a man **has sexual r** with a man as H8886
Lev 20:15 " 'If a man **has sexual r** with an H5989+8888
Lev 20:16 an animal to **have sexual r with** it, H8061
Lev 20:17 and *they* **have sexual r**, it is a H8011+906+6872
Lev 20:18 a man **has sexual r with** a H1655+906+6872
Lev 20:19 " '*Do* not **have sexual r with** the H1655+6872
Lev 20:20 " 'If a man **has sexual r** with his aunt, he H8886
Nu 5:13 man **has sexual r** with her, H8886+8887+2446
Nu 5:19 no other man *has* **had sexual r** with you H8886
Nu 5:20 *by* **having sexual r with** a man H5989+928+8888
Dt 27:21 is *anyone who* **has sexual r with** H8886+6640
2Sa 20: 3 them but **had** no **sexual r with** them. H995+448
1Ki 1: 4 the king **had** no **sexual r with** her. H3359
1Ki 5:12 There were **peaceful r** between Hiram H8934
Eze 18: 6 wife or **have sexual r with** a woman H7928+448
Ro 1:26 exchanged natural **sexual r** for unnatural G5979
Ro 1:27 abandoned natural **r** with women and G5979
Ro 7: 3 if *she* **has sexual r with** another man G1181
1Co 7: 1 a man not *to* **have sexual r** with a woman G721
1Co 7: 2 man *should* **have sexual r with** his own G2400
2Co 1:12 especially **in** our **r with** you, with G4639

RELATIONSHIP (4) [RELATED]

Jdg 18: 7 Sidonians and had no **r** with anyone else. H1821
Jdg 18:28 Sidon and had no **r** with anyone else. H1821
1Ki 10: 1 fame of Solomon and his **r to** the LORD, H4200
Jn 1:18 God and is in **closest r with** the Father, G3146

RELATIONSHIPS (2) [RELATED]

Nu 30:16 concerning **r between** a man and his H1068
Php 2: 5 **In your r with one another**, have G1877+5148

RELATIVE (24) [RELATED]

Ge 14:14 Abram heard that his **r** had been taken H278
Ge 14:16 brought back his **r** Lot and his H278
Ge 29:12 Rachel that he was a **r** *of* her father and a H278
Ge 29:15 "Just because you are a **r** *of* mine, should H278
Lev 18: 6 approach any **close r** to have H8638+1414
Lev 18:12 father's sister; she is your father's **close r**. H8638
Lev 18:13 because she is your mother's **close r**. H8638
Lev 20:19 that would dishonor a **close r**; both of H8638
Lev 21: 2 except for a **close r**, such as his H8638+7940
Lev 25:25 their nearest **r** is to come and redeem H1457
Lev 25:49 a cousin or any **blood r** in their clan H8638+1414
Nu 5: 8 that person has no **close r** to whom H1457
Nu 27:11 his inheritance to the nearest **r** in his clan, H8638
Ru 2: 1 Now Naomi had a **r** on her husband's H4530
Ru 2:20 "That man is our **close r**; he is one of our H7940
Ru 3: 2 women you have worked, is a **r** *of* ours. H4531
Ru 4: 3 of land that belonged to our **r** Elimelek. H278
1Ki 16:11 spare a single male, whether **r** or friend. H1457
Pr 7: 4 my sister," and to insight, "You are my **r**." H4530
Pr 27:10 better a neighbor nearby than a **r** far away. H278
Jer 32: 7 **as nearest r** it is your right and **duty** to buy H1460
Am 6:10 And if the **r** who comes to carry the bodies H1856
Lk 1:36 Even Elizabeth your **r** is going to have a G5151
Jn 18:26 a **r** of the man whose ear Peter had cut off G5150

RELATIVE'S (1) [RELATED]

Pr 27:10 do not go to your **r** house when disaster H278

RELATIVES (94) [RELATED]

Ge 13: 8 herders and mine, for we are **close r**. H278+408
Ge 24: 4 country and my own **r** and get a wife for H4580
Ge 24:27 the journey to the house of my master's **r**." H278
Ge 27:37 you and have made all his **r** his servants, H278
Ge 31: 3 to the land of your fathers and to your **r**, H4580
Ge 31:23 Taking his **r** with him, he pursued Jacob H278
Ge 31:25 Laban and his **r** camped there too. H278
Ge 31:32 In the presence of our **r**, see for yourself H278
Ge 31:37 Put it here in front of your **r** and mine, and H278
Ge 31:46 He said to his **r**, "Gather some stones." H278
Ge 31:54 the hill country and invited his **r** to a meal. H278
Ge 32: 9 'Go back to your country and your **r**, and I H4580
Lev 10: 6 But your **r**, all the Israelites, may mourn H278
Lev 18:17 daughter's daughter; they are her **close r**. H8638
Lev 25:48 One of their **r** may redeem them: H278
Nu 27: 4 Give us property among our father's **r**." H278
Nu 27: 7 among their father's **r** and give their H278
Dt 2: 4 the territory of your **r** the descendants of H278
Dt 2: 8 we went on past our **r** the descendants of H278
Jos 17: 4 to give us an inheritance among our **r**." H278
Jdg 14: 3 woman among your **r** or among all our H278
2Sa 19:12 You are my **r**, my own flesh and blood. H278
2Ki 10:13 he met *some* **r** *of* Ahaziah king of Judah H278
2Ki 10:13 They said, "We are **r** *of* Ahaziah, and we H278
1Ch 5: 7 Their **r** by clans, listed according to their H278
1Ch 5:13 Their **r**, by families, were: Michael H278
1Ch 7: 5 The **r** who were fighting men belonging to H278
1Ch 7:22 many days, and his **r** came to comfort him. H278
1Ch 8:32 They too lived near their **r** in Jerusalem. H278
1Ch 9:38 They too lived near their **r** in Jerusalem. H278
1Ch 12: 2 they were **r** *of* Saul from the tribe of H278
1Ch 12:32 with all their **r** under their command; H278
1Ch 15: 5 of Kohath, Uriel the leader and 120 **r**; H278
1Ch 15: 6 of Merari, Asaiah the leader and 220 **r**; H278
1Ch 15: 7 of Gershon, Joel the leader and 130 **r**; H278
1Ch 15: 8 Elizaphan, Shemaiah the leader and 200 **r**; H278
1Ch 15: 9 of Hebron, Eliel the leader and 80 **r**; H278
1Ch 15:10 Amminadab the leader and 112 **r**. H278
1Ch 15:17 son of Joel; from his **r**, Asaph son of H278
1Ch 15:17 from their **r** the Merarites, Ethan son H278
1Ch 15:18 with them their **r** next in rank H278
1Ch 23:32 under their **r** the descendants of Aaron H278
1Ch 24:31 just as their **r** the descendants of Aaron did, H278
1Ch 25: 7 Along with their **r**—all of them trained and H278
1Ch 25: 9 his sons and **r** 12 the second to Gedaliah H278
1Ch 25: 9 to Gedaliah, him and his **r** and sons 12 H278
1Ch 25:10 the third to Zakkur, his sons and **r** 12 H278

R

1Ch 25:11 the fourth to Izri, his sons and **r** 12 H278
1Ch 25:12 the fifth to Nethaniah, his sons and **r** 12 H278
1Ch 25:13 the sixth to Bukkiah, his sons and **r** 12 H278
1Ch 25:14 the seventh to Jesarelah, his sons and **r** 12 H278
1Ch 25:15 the eighth to Jeshaiah, his sons and **r** 12 H278
1Ch 25:16 the ninth to Mattaniah, his sons and **r** 12 H278
1Ch 25:17 the tenth to Shimei, his sons and **r** 12 H278
1Ch 25:18 the eleventh to Azarel, his sons and **r** 12 H278
1Ch 25:19 the twelfth to Hashabiah, his sons and **r** 12 H278
1Ch 25:20 the thirteenth to Shubael, his sons and **r** 12 H278
1Ch 25:21 fourteenth to Mattithiah, his sons and **r** 12 H278
1Ch 25:22 the fifteenth to Jerimoth, his sons and **r** 12 H278
1Ch 25:23 sixteenth to Hananiah, his sons and **r** 12 H278
1Ch 25:24 to Joshbekashah, his sons and **r** 12 H278
1Ch 25:25 the eighteenth to Hanani, his sons and **r** 12 H278
1Ch 25:26 nineteenth to Mallothi, his sons and **r** 12 H278
1Ch 25:27 the twentieth to Eliathah, his sons and **r** 12 H278
1Ch 25:28 the twenty-first to Hothir, his sons and **r** 12 H278
1Ch 25:29 to Giddalti, his sons and **r** 12 H278
1Ch 25:30 to Mahazioth, his sons and **r** 12 H278
1Ch 25:31 to Romamti-Ezer, his sons and **r** 12. H278
1Ch 26: 7 his **r** Elihu and Semakiah were also able H278
1Ch 26: 8 their sons and their **r** were capable men H278
1Ch 26: 9 Meshelemiah had sons and **r**, who were H278
1Ch 26:11 The sons and **r** of Hosah were 13 in all H278
1Ch 26:12 the temple of the LORD, just as their **r** had. H278
1Ch 26:25 His **r** through Eliezer: Rehabiah his son H278
1Ch 26:26 Shelomith and his **r** were in charge of all H278
1Ch 26:28 were in the care of Shelomith and his **r**. H278
1Ch 26:30 Hashabiah and his **r**—seventeen hundred H278
1Ch 26:32 Jeriah had twenty-seven hundred **r**, who H278
2Ch 5:12 Jeduthun and their sons and **r**—stood on H278
2Ch 22: 8 of Judah and the sons of Ahaziah's **r**, H278
2Ch 29:34 so their **r** the Levites helped them until the H278
Ezr 6:20 their **r** the priests and for themselves. H278
Job 19:14 My **r** have gone away; my closest friends H7940
Job 22: 6 security from your **r** for no reason; H278
Pr 19: 7 The poor are shunned by all their **r**—how H278
Jer 12: 6 Your **r**, members of your own family—even H278
Mk 6: 4 among his **r** and in his own home. *G5150*
Lk 1:58 Her neighbors and **r** heard that the Lord *G5150*
Lk 1:61 no one among your **r** who has that name." *G5149*
Lk 2:44 looking for him among their **r** and friends. *G5150*
Lk 14:12 sisters, your **r**, or your rich neighbors; *G5150*
Lk 21:16 sisters, **r** and friends, and they *G5150*
Ac 10:24 called together his **r** and close friends. *G5150*
1Ti 5: 8 Anyone who does not provide for **their r** *G2625*

RELEASE (29) [RELEASED, RELEASES]

Lev 14: 7 *he is to* **r** the live bird in the open fields. H8938
Lev 14:53 Then *he is to* **r** the live bird in the open H8938
Lev 16:22 the man *shall* **r** it in the wilderness. H8938
Lev 25:50 The price for their **r** is to be based on the H4928
Nu 30: 5 the LORD *will* **r** her because her father has H6142
Nu 30: 8 obligates herself, and the LORD *will* **r** her. H6142
Nu 30:12 has nullified them, and the LORD *will* **r** her. H6142
Dt 15:13 And when *you* **r** them, do not send them H8938
Ps 25:15 only he *will* **r** my feet from the snare. H3655
Ps 102:20 the prisoners and **r** those condemned to H7337
Ecc 8: 8 so wickedness *will* not **r** those who H4880
Isa 42: 7 from prison and to **r** from the dungeon those NDT
Isa 61: 1 the captives and **r from darkness** for the H7223
Mt 27:15 at the festival *to* **r** a prisoner chosen by *G668*
Mt 27:17 "Which one do you want *me to* **r** to you: *G668*
Mt 27:21 of the two do you want *me to* **r** to you?" *G668*
Mk 15: 6 Now *it was the custom* at the festival *to* **r** a *G668*
Mk 15: 9 "Do you want *me to* **r** to you the king of the *G668*
Mk 15:11 up the crowd to *have* Pilate **r** Barabbas *G668*
Lk 23:16 Therefore, *I will* punish him and then **r** him." *G668*
Lk 23:18 "Away with this man! **R** Barabbas to us!" *G668*
Lk 23:20 Wanting *to* **r** Jesus, Pilate appealed to *G668*
Lk 23:22 *I will* have him punished and then **r** him." *G668*
Jn 18:39 is your custom for *me to* **r** to you one *G668*
Jn 18:39 Do you want *me to* **r** 'the king of the Jews'?" *G668*
Ac 4:23 *On their* **r**, Peter and John went back to *G668*
Ac 16:35 to the jailer with the order: "**R** those men." *G668*
Ac 28:18 They examined me and wanted *to* **r** me *G668*
Rev 9:14 "**R** the four angels who are bound at the *G3395*

RELEASED (29) [RELEASE]

Ge 24: 8 then *you will* **be r** from this oath of mine. H5927
Ge 24:41 *You will* **be r** from my oath if, when you go H5927
Ge 24:41 to you—then you will be **r** from my oath. H5929
Lev 25:41 Then they and their children *are to be* **r** H3655
Lev 25:54 their children *are to be* **r** in the Year of H3655
Lev 27:21 When the field *is* **r** in the Jubilee, it will H3655
Jos 2:20 we will be **r** from the oath you made us H5929
Jos 9:23 You *will* never **be r from** service as H4162
2Ki 25:27 *he* **r** Jehoiachin king of Judah from H5951+8031
2Ch 23: 8 Jehoiada the priest *had* not **r** any of the H7080
Job 12:14 those he imprisons cannot **be r**. H7337
Ps 105:20 The king sent and **r** him, the ruler of H6002
Jer 20: 3 when Pashhur **r** him from the stocks H3655
Jer 40: 1 the imperial guard *had* **r** him at Ramah. H8938
Jer 52:31 *he* **r** Jehoiachin king of Judah and H5951+8031
Mt 27:26 Then *he* **r** Barabbas to them. But he had *G668*
Mk 15:15 the crowd, Pilate **r** Barabbas to them. *G668*
Lk 23:25 *He* **r** the man who had been thrown into *G668*
Ac 3:14 asked that a murderer *be* **r** to you. *G5919*
Ac 16:36 have ordered that *you* and Silas *be* **r**. *G668*
Ac 22:30 So the next day *he* **r** him and ordered the *G3395*
Ro 7: 2 *she is* **r** from the law that binds her to him. *G2934*
Ro 7: 3 she is **r** from that law and is not an *G1801*
Ro 7: 6 *we have been* **r** from the law so that we *G2934*
1Co 7:27 Do not seek to be **r**. Are you free from *G3386*
Heb 11:35 refusing to be **r** so that they might gain an *G667*
Heb 13:23 know *that* our brother Timothy *has been* **r**. *G668*
Rev 9:15 month and year *were* **r** to kill a third *G3395*
Rev 20: 7 are over, Satan *will be* **r** from his prison *G3395*

RELEASES (1) [RELEASE]

Lev 16:26 "The *man who* **r** the goat as a scapegoat H8938

RELENT (22) [RELENTED, RELENTS]

Ex 32:12 **r and do not bring** disaster on your people H5714
Dt 32:36 his people and **r** concerning his servants H5714
Job 6:29 **R**, do not be unjust; reconsider, for my H8740
Ps 7:12 If *he does* not **r**, he will sharpen his sword; H8740
Ps 90:13 **R**, LORD! How long will it be? Have H8740
Isa 57: 6 In view of all this, *should I* **r**? H5714
Jer 4:28 because I have spoken and *will* not **r**, H5714
Jer 18: 8 then *I will* **r** and not inflict on it the H5714
Jer 26: 3 Then *I will* **r** and not inflict on them the H5714
Jer 26:13 the LORD *will* **r and not bring** the disaster H5714
Jer 26:19 *did* not the LORD **r, so that** he *did* **not bring** H5714
Eze 24:14 hold back; I will not have pity, nor *will I* **r**. H5714
Joel 2:14 He may turn and **r** and leave behind a H5714
Am 1: 3 of Damascus, even for four, *I will* not **r**. H8740
Am 1: 6 sins of Gaza, even for four, *I will* not **r**. H8740
Am 1: 9 sins of Tyre, even for four, *I will* not **r**. H8740
Am 1:11 sins of Edom, even for four, *I will* not **r**. H8740
Am 1:13 sins of Ammon, even for four, *I will* not **r**. H8740
Am 2: 1 sins of Moab, even for four, *I will* not **r**. H8740
Am 2: 4 sins of Judah, even for four, *I will* not **r**. H8740
Am 2: 6 sins of Israel, even for four, *I will* not **r**. H8740
Jnh 3: 9 God *may* yet **r** and with compassion turn H8740

RELENTED (9) [RELENT]

Ex 32:14 Then the LORD **r and did not** bring on his H5714
Jdg 2:18 the LORD **r** because of their groaning H5714
2Sa 24:16 the LORD **r** concerning the disaster and H5714
1Ch 21:15 the LORD saw it and **r** concerning the H5714
Ps 106:45 covenant and out of his great love *he* **r**. H5714
Jer 42:10 for *I have* **r** concerning the disaster I have H5714
Am 7: 3 So the LORD **r**. "This will not happen," H5714
Am 7: 6 the LORD **r**. "This will not happen either," H5714
Jnh 3:10 he **r** and did not bring on them the H5714

RELENTLESS (1)

Isa 14: 6 subdued nations with **r** aggression. H1172+3104

RELENTS (2) [RELENT]

Joel 2:13 and *he* **r** from sending calamity. H5714
Jnh 4: 2 a God *who* **r** from sending calamity. H5714

RELIABLE (5) [RELY]

1Sa 29: 6 you have been **r**, and I would be H3838
Isa 8: 2 son of Jeberekiah as **r** witnesses for me. H586
Jer 2:21 you like a choice vine of sound and **r** stock. H622
2Ti 2: 2 entrust to **r** people who will also *G4412*
2Pe 1:19 message *as something* **completely r**, *G1010*

RELIANCE (2) [RELY]

Ps 26: 3 have lived **in r on** your faithfulness. H928
Pr 25:19 a lame foot is **r** *on* the unfaithful in a H4440

RELIED (7) [RELY]

Jdg 20:36 because *they* **r** on the ambush they had H1053
2Ch 13:18 victorious because *they* **r** on the LORD, H9128
2Ch 16: 7 "Because you **r** on the king of Aram and H9128
2Ch 16: 8 Yet when you **r** on the LORD, he delivered H9128
Ps 71: 6 From birth *I have* **r** on you; you brought H6164
Isa 20: 6 'See what has happened to *those* we **r on**, H4438
Isa 30:12 **r** on oppression and depended on deceit H1053

RELIEF (19) [RELIEVE]

Ex 8:15 But when Pharaoh saw that there was **r**, he H8121
1Sa 8:18 cry out **for r from** the king H4946+4200+7156
1Sa 16:23 Then **r** *would* **come** to Saul; he would feel H8118
Ezr 9: 8 to our eyes and a little **r** in our bondage. H4695
Est 4:14 **r** and deliverance for the Jews will arise H8119
Est 9:16 themselves and **get r** from their enemies. H5663
Est 9:22 time when the Jews **got r** from their H5663
Job 16: 5 comfort from my lips *would* **bring** you **r**. H3104
Job 32:20 I must speak and **find r**; I must open my H8118
Job 35: 9 *they* **plead for r** from the arm of the H8775
Ps 4: 1 **Give** me **r** from my distress; have mercy on H8143
Ps 94:13 you **grant** them **r** from days of trouble, till H9200
Ps 143: 1 righteousness **come to** my **r**. H6699
Isa 14: 3 On the day the LORD **gives** you **r** from your H5663
La 2:18 give yourself no **r**, your eyes no rest. H7029
La 3:49 My eyes will flow unceasingly, without **r**, H2198
La 3:56 "Do not close your ears to my cry for **r**." H8121
Mic 1:12 in pain, waiting for **r**, because disaster H3202
2Th 1: 7 give **r** to you who are troubled, and to *G457*

RELIES (2) [RELY]

Isa 28:16 the *one who* **r on** it will never be stricken H586
Gal 3:11 Clearly no one who *r* **on** the law is justified AIT

RELIEVE (4) [RELIEF, RELIEVED, RELIEVING]

Dt 23:12 the camp where you can go to **r** yourself. NDT
Dt 23:13 and when you **r yourself**, dig a hole H3782+2575
1Sa 24: 3 went in to **r himself**. H6114+906+8079+2257
Ps 25:17 **R** the troubles of my heart and free me H8143

RELIEVED (2) [RELIEVE]

Job 16: 6 if I speak, my pain **is** not **r**; and if I refrain, H3104
2Co 8:13 that others might be **r** while you are hard *G457*

RELIEVING (1) [RELIEVE]

Jdg 3:24 "He *must be* **r himself** in H6114+906+8079+2257

RELIGION (5) [RELIGIOUS]

Ac 25:19 him about their own **r** and about a dead *G1272*
Ac 26: 5 I conformed to the strictest sect *of* our **r**, *G2579*
1Ti 5: 4 all *to* **put** *their* **r into practice by caring for** *G2355*
Jas 1:26 themselves, and their **r** is worthless. *G2579*
Jas 1:27 **R** that God our Father accepts as pure and *G2579*

RELIGIOUS (6) [RELIGION]

Am 5:21 I despise your **r festivals**; your assemblies H2504
Am 8:10 I will turn your **r festivals** into mourning H2504
Ac 17:22 I see that in every way you *are* **very r**. *G1273*
Col 2:16 with regard to a **r festival**, a New Moon *G2038*
Heb 10:11 priest stands and **performs** *his* **r duties**; *G3310*
Jas 1:26 consider themselves **r** and yet do not keep *G2580*

RELISH (1)

Hos 4: 8 my people and **r** their wickedness H5951+5883

RELUCTANTLY (1)

2Co 9: 7 to give, not **r** or under compulsion *G1666+3383*

RELY (19) [RELIABLE, RELIANCE, RELIED, RELIES, RELYING]

2Ch 14:11 LORD our God, for *we* **r** on you, and in your H9128
Job 8:14 is fragile; **what** they **r** on is a spider's web. H4440
Job 39:11 *Will you* **r** on it for its great strength? Will H1053
Ps 59:10 my God on whom I can **r**. God will go H2876
Ps 59:17 are my fortress, my God on whom I can **r**. H2876
Ps 86:11 that *I may* **r on** your faithfulness H2143+928
Isa 10:20 will no longer **r** on him who struck them H9128
Isa 10:20 them down but *will* truly **r** on the LORD, H9128
Isa 31: 1 to Egypt for help, *who* **r** on horses, who H9128
Isa 48: 2 the holy city and *claim to* **r** on the God of H6164
Isa 50:10 the name of the LORD and **r** on their God. H9128
Isa 59: 4 They **r** on empty arguments, they utter lies H1053
Jer 46:25 and on those *who* **r** on Pharaoh. H1053
Eze 33:26 *You* **r** on your sword, you do detestable H6641
Ro 2:17 if *you* **r on** the law and boast in God; *G2058*
2Co 1: 9 that *we might* not **r** on ourselves *G4275+1639*
Gal 3: 9 So those who **r on** faith are blessed along *G1666*
Gal 3:10 For all who **r on** the works of the *G1666+1639*
1Jn 4:16 so we know and **r on** the love God has *G4409*

RELYING (1) [RELY]

2Co 1:12 **r** not **on** worldly wisdom but on God's *G1877*

REMAIN (114) [REMAINDER, REMAINED, REMAINING, REMAINS]

Ge 15: 2 you give me since I **r** childless and the H2143
Ge 24:55 "*Let* the young woman **r** with us ten days H3782
Ge 36: 7 were too great for them *to* **r** together; H3782
Ge 44:33 please *let* your servant **r** here as my lord's H3782
Ex 8: 9 except for *those that* **r** in the Nile. H8636
Ex 8:11 your people; *they will* **r** only in the Nile." H8636
Ex 25:15 The poles *are to* **r** in the rings of this ark H2118
Ex 34:25 *do* not *let* any of the sacrifice from the Passover Festival **r** H4328
Lev 6: 9 The burnt offering is to **r** on the altar hearth NDT
Lev 11:37 seeds that are to be planted, they **r** clean. NDT
Lev 13:46 have the disease they **r unclean**. H3237+3238
Lev 22:27 *it is to* **r** with its mother for seven days. H2118
Lev 25:28 what was sold *will* **r** in the possession of H2118
Lev 25:51 If many years **r**, they must pay for their H6388
Lev 25:52 If only a few years **r** until the Year of H8636
Lev 26:21 " 'If *you* **r** hostile toward me and refuse to H2143
Lev 27:14 value the priest then sets, so *it will* **r**. H7756
Lev 27:18 number of years that **r** until the next Year H3855
Nu 4: 7 bread that is continually there *is to* **r** on it. H2118
Nu 6: 4 As long as they **r** under their Nazirite vow NDT
Nu 9:22 the Israelites *would* **r in camp** and not set H2837
Nu 32:26 flocks and herds *will* **r** here in the cities H2118
Nu 33:55 those *you* **allow to r** will become barbs in H3855
Dt 13:16 That town *is to* **r** a ruin forever, never to H2118
Dt 16: 4 *Do* not *let* any of the meat you sacrifice on the evening of the first day **r** H4328
Dt 31:26 There *it will* **r** as a witness against you. H2118
Jos 18: 5 Judah *is to* **r** in its territory on the south H6641
Jos 23: 4 tribes all the land of the nations that **r**— H8636
Jos 23: 7 with these nations that **r** among you; H8636
Jos 23:12 these nations that **r** among you and if you H8636
Jdg 2:23 The LORD *had* **allowed** those nations **to r** H5663
Ru 1:13 *Would you* **r unmarried** H6328+4200+1194+2118+4200+408
1Sa 16:22 "*Allow* David *to* **r** in my service, for H6641
2Sa 14:14 person *does* not **r banished** from him. AIT
2Sa 16:18 Israel—his I will be, and *I will* **r** with him. H3782
1Ki 2:45 David's throne *will* **r** secure before the H2118
1Ch 21:17 do not let this plague **r** on your people." NDT
2Ch 32:10 that you **r** in Jerusalem under siege? H3782
2Ch 33: 4 "My Name *will* **r** in Jerusalem forever." H2118
Est 4:14 For if *you* **r silent** at this time, relief H3087+3087
Job 37: 8 animals take cover; *they* **r** in their dens. H8905
Ps 27:13 I **r** confident of this: I will see the H4295
Ps 28: 1 For if *you* **r silent**, I will be like those who go AIT
Ps 49:11 Their tombs will **r** their houses forever, their NDT

Ps 83: 1 do not **r** silent; do not turn a deaf NDT
Ps 102:26 will perish, but you **r**; they will all wear H6641
Ps 102:27 But you **r** the same, and your years will NDT
Ps 109: 1 My God, whom I praise, *do* not **r silent**, AIT
Ps 109:15 *May* their sins always **r** before the LORD H2118
Ps 125: 3 of the wicked *will* not **r** over the land H5663
Pr 2:21 in the land, and the blameless *will* **r** in it; H3855
Pr 10:30 the wicked *will* not **r** *in* the land. H8905
Isa 4: 3 left in Zion, who **r** in Jerusalem, will be H3855
Isa 7:22 All who **r** in the land will eat curds and H3855
Isa 10: 4 Nothing will **r** but to cringe among the NDT
Isa 15: 9 Moab and upon *those who* **r** *in* the land. H8642
Isa 17: 6 Yet some gleanings *will* **r**, as when an H8636
Isa 18: 4 "*I will r* **quiet** and will look on from my AIT
Isa 62: 1 Jerusalem's sake *I will* not *r* **quiet**, till her AIT
Jer 24: 8 whether they **r** in this land or live in Egypt. H8636
Jer 27:11 *I will* **let** that nation **r** in its own land to till H5663
Jer 27:22 there *they will* **r** until the day I H2118
Jer 29:16 all the people who **r** in this city, H3782
Jer 32: 5 where *he will* **r** until I deal with him H2118
Jer 51:30 fighting; *they* **r** in their strongholds. H3782
Eze 36:36 around you that **r** will know that I the H8636
Eze 44: 2 LORD said to me, "This gate *is to* **r** shut. H2118
Eze 44: 2 *It is to* **r** shut because the LORD, the God of H2118
Da 2:43 will be a mixture and *will* not **r** united, A10201
Da 4:15 *let* the stump and its roots, bound with iron and bronze, **r** A10697
Da 4:23 of the field, while its roots **r** in the ground. NDT
Da 11:12 many thousands, yet *he will* not *r* **triumphant**. AIT
Hos 9: 3 *They will* not **r** in the LORD's land; Ephraim H3782
Zec 5: 4 *It will* **r** in that house and destroy it H4328
Zec 12: 6 Jerusalem will **r** intact in her place. H6388
Zec 14:10 royal winepresses, and *will* **r** in its place. H3782
Jn 1:32 from heaven as a dove and **r** on him. *G3531*
Jn 1:33 come down and **r** is the one who will *G3531*
Jn 12:34 the Law that the Messiah *will* **r** forever, *G3531*
Jn 15: 4 **R** in me, as I also remain in you. *G3531*
Jn 15: 4 as I also **r** in you. No branch can NDT
Jn 15: 4 bear fruit by itself; *it* must **r** in the vine. *G3531*
Jn 15: 4 can you bear fruit unless *you* **r** in me. *G3531*
Jn 15: 5 *If* you **r** in me and I in you, you will bear *G3531*
Jn 15: 6 If you *do* not **r** in me, you are like a branch *G3531*
Jn 15: 7 *If* you **r** in me and my words remain in you *G3531*
Jn 15: 7 If you remain in me and my words **r** in you *G3531*
Jn 15: 9 so have I loved you. *Now* **r** in my love. *G3531*
Jn 15:10 my commands, *you will* **r** in my love, just *G3531*
Jn 15:10 my Father's commands and **r** in his love. *G3531*
Jn 17:11 *I will* **r** in the world no longer, but they are *G1639*
Jn 21:22 "If I want him *to* **r** *alive* until I return, what *G3531*
Jn 21:23 "If I want him *to* **r** *alive* until I return *G3531*
Ac 11:23 encouraged them all *to* **r** true to the Lord *G4693*
Ac 14:22 encouraging them *to* **r true** to the faith. *G1844*
Ro 13: 8 *Let* no **debt r outstanding**, except the *G4053*
1Co 7:11 *she must* **r** unmarried or else be *G3531*
1Co 7:20 Each person *should* **r** in the situation they *G3531*
1Co 7:24 *should* **r** in the situation they were in *G3531*
1Co 7:26 that it is good for a man *to* **r** as he is. *G1639*
1Co 13:13 And now these three **r**: faith, hope and *G3531*
1Co 14:34 Women *should r* **silent** in the churches. AIT
Php 1:24 necessary for you *that* I **r** in the body. *G2152*
Php 1:25 I know that *I will* **r**, and I will *G3531*
1Ti 5:25 that are not obvious cannot *r* **hidden** *forever*. AIT
Heb 1:11 will perish, but you **r**; they will all wear *G1373*
Heb 1:12 But you **r** the same, and your years will *G1639*
Heb 8: 9 because they *did* not **r faithful** to my *G1844*
Heb 12:27 so that what cannot be shaken *may* **r**. *G3531*
1Jn 2:24 you also *will* **r** in the Son and in the *G3531*
1Jn 2:27 just as it has taught you, **r** in him. *G3531*
Rev 2:13 Yet *you* **r true** to my name. *G3195*
Rev 14:12 keep his commands and **r** faithful to Jesus. NDT
Rev 17:10 he must **r** for only a little while. *G3531*

REMAINDER (1) [REMAIN]

Est 9:16 the **r** *of* the Jews who were in the king's H8637

REMAINED (67) [REMAIN]

Ge 18:22 Abraham **r** standing before the LORD. H6388
Ge 29:31 her to conceive, but Rachel **r** childless. NDT
Ge 32: 4 with Laban and *have* **r** there till now. H336
Ge 49:24 But his bow **r** steady, his strong arms H3782
Ex 8:31 his officials and his people; not a fly **r**. H8636
Ex 10:15 Nothing green **r** on tree or plant in all the H3855
Ex 17:12 so that his hands **r** steady till sunset. H2118
Ex 20:21 The people **r** at a distance, while Moses H6641
Lev 10: 3 people I will be honored.'" Aaron *r* **silent**. AIT
Nu 9:18 over the tabernacle, *they* **r in camp**. H2837
Nu 9:19 When the cloud **r** over the tabernacle a H799
Nu 11:26 Eldad and Medad, *had* **r** in the camp. H8636
Nu 36:12 their inheritance **r** in their father's H2118
Jos 4:10 carried the ark *r* **standing** in the middle of AIT
Jos 5: 8 *they* **r** where they were in camp until they H3782
Jos 8:17 Not a man **r** in Ai or Bethel who did not go H8636
Jdg 5:17 Asher **r** on the coast and stayed in his H3782
Jdg 7: 3 thousand men left, while ten thousand **r**. H8636
Jdg 19: 4 him to stay; so *he* **r** with him three days H3782
Ru 2: 7 into the field and *has* **r** here from morning H6641
1Sa 5: 4 lying on the threshold; only his body **r**. H8636
1Sa 7: 2 The ark **r** at Kiriath Jearim a long time H3782
1Sa 13: 7 Saul **r** at Gilgal, and all the troops with H6388
1Sa 18:29 he **r** his enemy the rest of his days. H2118
1Sa 23:18 went home, but David **r** at Horesh. H3782
2Sa 2:10 tribe of Judah, however, **r** loyal to David. H2118
2Sa 6:11 The ark of the LORD **r** *in* the house of H3782
2Sa 11: 1 But David **r** in Jerusalem. H3782
2Sa 11:12 So Uriah **r** in Jerusalem that day and the H3782
1Ki 12:20 the tribe of Judah **r** loyal to the house of H2118
1Ki 22:46 prostitutes who **r** there even after the H8636
2Ki 2:22 And the water *has r* **pure** to this day AIT
2Ki 10:11 in Jezreel who **r** of the house of Ahab, H8636
2Ki 11: 3 *He* **r** hidden with his nurse at the temple H2118
2Ki 13: 6 the Asherah pole *r* **standing** in Samaria. AIT
2Ki 18:36 But the people *r* **silent** and said nothing in AIT
2Ki 25:11 into exile the people who **r** in the city, H8636
1Ch 12:29 most of whom *had r* **loyal** to Saul's house AIT
1Ch 13:14 The ark of God **r** with the family of H3782
1Ch 20: 1 besieged it, but David **r** in Jerusalem. H3782
2Ch 22:12 *He* **r** hidden with them at the temple of H2118
Ne 9:33 you have **r** righteous; you have NDT
Ps 39: 2 So *I r* **utterly silent**, not even saying anything AIT
Isa 36:21 But *the people r* **silent** and said nothing in AIT
Jer 35:11 So *we have* **r** in Jerusalem." H3782
Jer 37:16 in a dungeon, where he **r** a long time. H3782
Jer 37:21 So Jeremiah **r** in the courtyard of the H3782
Jer 38:13 And Jeremiah **r** in the courtyard of the H3782
Jer 38:28 And Jeremiah **r** in the courtyard of the H3782
Jer 39: 9 to Babylon the people who **r** in the city, H8636
Jer 39:14 So *he* **r** among his own people. H3782
Jer 52:15 people and those *who* **r** in the city, H8636
Eze 17: 6 turned toward him, but its roots **r** under it. H2118
Da 1:21 And Daniel **r** there until the first year of H2118
Da 2:49 while Daniel himself **r** at the royal court. NDT
Hos 10: 9 have sinned, Israel, and there *you have* **r**. H6641
Mt 11:23 in Sodom, *it* would have **r** to this day. *G3531*
Mt 26:63 But Jesus **r silent**. The high priest said to *G4995*
Mk 3: 4 to save life or to kill?" But they *r* **silent**. AIT
Mk 14:61 But Jesus *r* **silent** and gave no answer. Again AIT
Lk 1:22 signs to them but **r** unable to speak. *G1373*
Lk 1:24 pregnant and for five months *r* **in seclusion**. AIT
Lk 14: 4 But they *r* **silent**. So taking hold of the man AIT
Ac 7:45 It **r** in the land until the time of David, NDT
Ac 15:35 But Paul and Barnabas **r** in Antioch, where *G1417*
1Jn 2:19 *they* would have **r** with us; but *G3531*
Rev 14: 4 themselves with women, for they **r** virgins. *G1639*

REMAINING (15) [REMAIN]

Ex 28:10 on one stone and the **r** six on the other. H3855
Lev 10:12 Moses said to Aaron and his **r** sons H3855
Lev 10:16 Ithamar, Aaron's **r** sons, and asked, H3855
Lev 14:17 to put some of the oil **r** in his palm on the H3856
Nu 31:32 The plunder **r** *from* the spoils that the H3856
Jos 7: 6 the ark of the LORD, **r** there till evening. NDT
1Ki 9:21 of all these peoples **r** in the land— H3855
1Ch 4:43 They killed the **r** Amalekites who had H8642
2Ch 8: 8 of all these people **r** in the land— H3855
Ne 11: 1 while the **r** nine were to stay in their own H3338
Isa 10:19 And the **r** trees of his forests will be so H8637
Jer 27:18 that the articles **r** in the house of the LORD H3855
Eze 25:16 destroy those **r** *along* the coast. H8642
Eze 48:15 "The **r** *area*, 5,000 cubits wide and H3855
Jn 19:23 each of them, with the undergarment **r**. NDT

REMAINS (44) [REMAIN]

Ex 22:13 shall bring in the **r** as evidence and shall H3274
Lev 11:36 a cistern for collecting water **r** clean H2118
Lev 27:17 of Jubilee, the value that has been set **r**. H7756
Nu 15:31 must surely be cut off; their guilt **r** on them. NDT
Nu 16:37 censers from the **charred r** and scatter the H8599
Nu 19:13 are unclean; their uncleanness **r** on them. H6388
Dt 24:20 Leave what **r** for the foreigner, the fatherless NDT
Dt 24:21 Leave what **r** for the foreigner, the fatherless NDT
Jos 7:26 up a large pile of rocks, which **r** to this day. NDT
Jos 8:29 large pile of rocks over it, which **r** to this day. NDT
Jos 13: 2 "This is the land that **r**: all the regions of H8636
2Sa 7: 2 of cedar, while the ark of God **r** in a tent." H3782
1Ki 20:10 if **enough** dust *r* in Samaria to give each of AIT
2Ki 6:31 Elisha son of Shaphat **r** on his shoulders H6641
Ne 9:10 a name for yourself, which **r** to this day. H3869
Job 19: 4 gone astray, my error **r** my concern alone. H4328
Job 34:29 But if he *r* **silent**, who can condemn him? AIT
Ps 146: 6 everything in them—he **r** faithful forever. H9068
Pr 29: 1 Whoever *r* **stiff-necked** after many rebukes AIT
Ecc 1: 4 generations go, but the earth **r** forever. H6641
Isa 6:13 And though a tenth **r** in the land, it will H6388
Eze 32: 5 mountains and fill the valleys with your **r**. H8239
Eze 48:18 What **r** of the area, bordering on the H3855
Eze 48:21 "What **r** on both sides of the area formed H3855
Mic 7: 2 from the land; not one upright person **r**. NDT
Hag 1: 4 paneled houses, while this house **r** a ruin?" NDT
Hag 1: 9 of my house, which **r** a ruin, while each of NDT
Hag 2: 5 And my Spirit **r** among you. Do not H6641
Jn 3:36 not see life, for God's wrath **r** on them. *G3531*
Jn 6:56 my flesh and drinks my blood **r** in me, *G3531*
Jn 9:41 that you claim you can see, your guilt **r**. *G3531*
Jn 12:24 ground and dies, it **r** only a single seed. *G3531*
1Co 11:21 one person *r* **hungry** and another gets drunk. AIT
2Co 3:14 day the same veil **r** when the old *G3531*
2Ti 2:13 we are faithless, he **r** faithful, for he *G3531*
Heb 4: 6 Therefore since *it still* **r** for some to enter *G657*
Heb 4: 9 *There* **r**, then, a Sabbath-rest for the people *G657*
Heb 7: 3 the Son of God, *he* **r** a priest forever. *G3531*
1Jn 2:24 *see that* what you have heard from the beginning **r** *G3531*
1Jn 2:27 anointing you received from him **r** in you, *G3531*
1Jn 3: 9 because God's seed **r** in them; they *G3531*
1Jn 3:14 Anyone who does not love **r** in death. *G3531*
Rev 3: 2 Strengthen what **r** and is about to die, for *G3370*
Rev 16:15 is the one who stays awake and **r** clothed, *G5498*

REMALIAH (11) [REMALIAH'S]

2Ki 15:25 Pekah son of **R**, conspired against him H8248
2Ki 15:27 Pekah son of **R** became king of Israel in H8248
2Ki 15:30 of Elah conspired against Pekah son of **R**. H8248
2Ki 15:32 year of Pekah son of **R** king of Israel, H8248
2Ki 15:37 Aram and Pekah son of **R** against Judah.) H8248
2Ki 16: 1 In the seventeenth year of Pekah son of **R** H8248
2Ki 16: 5 Aram and Pekah son of **R** king of Israel H8248
2Ch 28: 6 day Pekah son of **R** killed a hundred and H8248
Isa 7: 1 Aram and Pekah son of **R** king of Israel H8248
Isa 7: 4 of Rezin and Aram and of the son of **R**. H8248
Isa 8: 6 rejoices over Rezin and the son of **R**, H8248

REMALIAH'S (2) [REMALIAH]

Isa 7: 5 Ephraim and **R** son have plotted your ruin H8248
Isa 7: 9 the head of Samaria is only **R** son. H8248

REMARKABLE (3)

Mk 6: 2 What are these **r miracles** he is *G1539*
Lk 5:26 said, "We have seen **r** *things* today." *G4141*
Jn 9:30 "Now that is **r**! You don't know where *G2515*

REMARKED (1) [REMARKING]

Ac 17:18 Others **r**, "He seems to be advocating NDT

REMARKING (1) [REMARKED]

Lk 21: 5 of his disciples *were* **r** about how the *G3306*

REMEDY (6)

2Ch 36:16 against his people and there was no **r**. H5340
Pr 6:15 he will suddenly be destroyed—without **r**. H5340
Pr 29: 1 will suddenly be destroyed—without **r**. H5340
Isa 3: 7 But in that day he will cry out, "I have no **r**. H2502
Jer 30:13 to plead your cause, no **r** for your sore, no H8337
Mic 2:10 it is defiled, it is ruined, **beyond all r**. H5344

REMEMBER (166) [REMEMBERED, REMEMBERING, REMEMBERS, REMEMBRANCE]

Ge 9:15 *I will* **r** my covenant between me and you H2349
Ge 9:16 I will see it and **r** the everlasting covenant H2349
Ge 31:50 **r** *that* God is a witness between you and H8011
Ge 40:14 with you, **r** me and show me kindness H2349
Ge 40:23 however, *did* not **r** Joseph; he forgot H2349
Ex 20: 8 "**R** the Sabbath day by keeping it holy. H2349
Ex 32:13 **R** your servants Abraham, Isaac and Israel H2349
Ex 33:13 **R** that this nation is your people. H8011
Lev 26:42 *I will* **r** my covenant with Jacob and my H2349
Lev 26:42 with Abraham, and *I will* **r** the land. H2349
Lev 26:45 But for their sake *I will* **r** the covenant with H2349
Nu 11: 5 *We* **r** the fish we ate in Egypt at no cost H2349
Nu 15:39 look at and so *you will* **r** all the H2349
Nu 15:40 Then *you will* **r** to obey all my commands H2349
Dt 4:10 **R** the day you stood before the LORD your NDT
Dt 5:15 **R** that you were slaves in Egypt and that H2349
Dt 7:18 **r well** what the LORD your God did H2349+2349
Dt 8: 2 **R** how the LORD your God led you all the H2349
Dt 8:18 But **r** the LORD your God, for it is he who H2349
Dt 9: 7 **R** this and never forget how you aroused H2349
Dt 9:27 **R** your servants Abraham, Isaac and Jacob H2349
Dt 11: 2 **R** today that your children were not the H3359
Dt 15:15 **R** that you were slaves in Egypt and the H2349
Dt 16: 3 of your life *you may* **r** the time of your H2349
Dt 16:12 **R** that you were slaves in Egypt, and follow H2349
Dt 24: 9 **R** what the LORD your God did to Miriam H2349
Dt 24:18 **R** that you were slaves in Egypt and the H2349
Dt 24:22 **R** that you were slaves in Egypt. That is H2349
Dt 25:17 **R** what the Amalekites did to you along H2349
Dt 32: 7 **R** the days of old; consider the H2349
Jos 1:13 "**R** the command that Moses the servant of H2349
Jos 23: 4 **R** how I have allotted as an inheritance H8011
Jdg 8:34 and *did* not **r** the LORD their God, who had H2349
Jdg 9: 2 just one man?' **R**, I am your flesh and H2349
Jdg 9:17 **R** that my father fought for you and risked NDT
Jdg 16:28 to the LORD, "Sovereign LORD, **r** me. H2349
1Sa 1:11 look on your servant's misery and **r** me, H2349
1Sa 20:23 and I discussed—**r**, the LORD is witness H2180
1Sa 25:31 brought my lord success, **r** your servant." H2349
2Sa 19:19 *Do* not **r** how your servant did wrong on H2349
1Ki 2: 8 "And **r**, you have with you Shimei son of H2180
2Ki 9:25 **R** how you and I were riding together in H2349
2Ki 20: 3 "**R**, LORD, how I have walked before you H2349
1Ch 16:12 **R** the wonders he has done, his miracles H2349
2Ch 6:42 **R** the great love promised to David your H2349
2Ch 24:22 King Joash *did* not **r** the kindness H2349
Ne 1: 8 "**R** the instruction you gave your servant H2349
Ne 4:14 **R** the Lord, who is great and awesome H2349
Ne 5:19 **R** me with favor, my God, *for* all I have H2349
Ne 6:14 **R** Tobiah and Sanballat, my God H2349
Ne 6:14 **r** also the prophet Noadiah and how she NDT
Ne 9:17 to listen and failed *to* **r** the miracles you H2349
Ne 13:14 **R** me for this, my God, and do not blot out H2349
Ne 13:22 **R** me for this also, my God, and show H2349
Ne 13:29 **R** them, my God, because they defiled the H2349
Ne 13:31 the firstfruits. **R** me with favor, my God H2349
Job 7: 7 **R**, O God, that my life is but a breath; my H2349
Job 10: 9 **R** that you molded me like clay. Will you H2349
Job 14:13 you would set me a time and then **r** me! H2349
Job 36:24 **R** to extol his work, which people have H2349
Job 41: 8 *you will* **r** the struggle and never do it H2349

R

Ps 20: 3 May he **r** all your sacrifices and accept H2349
Ps 22:27 ends of the earth will **r** and turn to the H2349
Ps 25: 6 **R**, LORD, your great mercy and love, for H2349
Ps 25: 7 Do not **r** the sins of my youth and my H2349
Ps 25: 7 according to your love **r** me, for you, H2349
Ps 42: 4 These things I **r** as I pour out my soul H2349
Ps 42: 6 therefore I will **r** you from the land of the H2349
Ps 63: 6 On my bed I **r** you; I think of you through H2349
Ps 74: 2 **R** the nation you purchased long ago, the H2349
Ps 74:18 **R** how the enemy has mocked you, LORD H2349
Ps 74:22 **r** how fools mock you all day long. H2349
Ps 77:11 I will **r** the deeds of the LORD; yes, I will H2349
Ps 77:11 I will **r** your miracles of long ago. H2349
Ps 78:42 They did not **r** his power—the day he H2349
Ps 88: 5 the grave, whom you **r** no more, who are H2349
Ps 89:47 **R** how fleeting is my life. For what futility H2349
Ps 89:50 **R**, Lord, how your servant has been H2349
Ps 103:18 his covenant and **r** to obey his precepts. H2349
Ps 105: 5 **R** the wonders he has done, his miracles H2349
Ps 106: 4 **R** me, LORD, when you show favor to your H2349
Ps 106: 7 they did not **r** your many kindnesses H2349
Ps 119:49 **R** your word to your servant, for you have H2349
Ps 119:52 I **r**, LORD, your ancient laws, and I find H2349
Ps 119:55 I **r** your name, that I may keep your H2349
Ps 132: 1 **r** David and all his self-denial. H2349
Ps 137: 6 to the roof of my mouth if I do not **r** you, H2349
Ps 137: 7 **R**, LORD, what the Edomites did on the day H2349
Ps 143: 5 I **r** the days of long ago; I meditate on all H2349
Pr 31: 7 their poverty and **r** their misery no more. H2349
Ecc 11: 8 But let them **r** the days of darkness, for H2349
Ecc 12: 1 **R** your Creator in the days of your youth H2349
Ecc 12: 6 **R** him—before the silver cord is severed NDT
Isa 38: 3 "**R**, LORD, how I have walked before you H2349
Isa 44:21 "**R** these things, Jacob, for you, Israel, are H2349
Isa 46: 8 "**R** this, keep it in mind, take it to heart H2349
Isa 46: 9 **R** the former things, those of long ago; H2349
Isa 54: 4 of your youth and **r** no more the reproach H2349
Isa 64: 5 who gladly do right, who **r** your ways. H2349
Isa 64: 9 measure, LORD; do not **r** our sins forever. H2349
Jer 2: 2 " 'I **r** the devotion of your youth, how as a H2349
Jer 14:10 he will now **r** their wickedness and punish H2349
Jer 14:21 **R** your covenant with us and do not break H2349
Jer 15:15 you understand; **r** me and care for me. H2349
Jer 17: 2 Even their children **r** their altars and H2349
Jer 18:20 **R** that I stood before you and spoke in H2349
Jer 31:20 speak against him, I still **r** him. H2349+2349
Jer 31:34 wickedness and will **r** their sins no more." H2349
Jer 44:21 "Did not the LORD **r** and call to mind the H2349
Jer 51:50 **R** the LORD in a distant land, and call to H2349
La 3:19 I **r** my affliction and my wandering, the H2349
La 3:20 I well **r** them, and my soul is H2349+2349
La 5: 1 **R**, LORD, what has happened to us; look H2349
Eze 6: 9 those who escape will **r** me—how I have H2349
Eze 16:22 prostitution you did not **r** the days of your H2349
Eze 16:43 " 'Because you did not **r** the days of your H2349
Eze 16:60 Yet I will **r** the covenant I made with you in H2349
Eze 16:61 Then you will **r** your ways and be ashamed H2349
Eze 16:63 you will **r** and be ashamed and never H2349
Eze 20:43 There you will **r** your conduct and all the H2349
Eze 23:27 things with longing or **r** Egypt anymore. H2349
Eze 36:31 Then you will **r** your evil ways and wicked H2349
Da 6:15 said to him, "**R**, Your Majesty, A10313
Hos 7: 2 do not realize that I **r** all their evil deeds. H2349
Hos 8:13 Now he will **r** their wickedness and punish H2349
Hos 9: 9 God will **r** their wickedness and punish H2349
Mic 6: 5 **r** what Balak king of Moab plotted and H2349
Mic 6: 5 **R** your journey from Shittim to Gilgal, that NDT
Hab 3: 2 time make them known; in wrath **r** mercy. H2349
Zec 10: 9 in distant lands they will **r** me. H2349
Mal 4: 4 "**R** the law of my servant Moses, the H2349
Mt 5:23 at the altar and there **r** that your brother G3630
Mt 16: 9 Don't you **r** the five loaves for the five G3648
Mt 27:63 "we **r** that while he was still alive that G3630
Mk 8:18 ears but fail to hear? And don't you **r**? G3648
Lk 1:72 our ancestors and to **r** his holy covenant, G3630
Lk 16:25 **r** that in your lifetime you received your G3630
Lk 17:32 **R** Lot's wife! G3648
Lk 23:42 **r** me when you come into your kingdom." G3630
Lk 24: 6 **R** how he told you, while he was still with G3630
Jn 15:20 **R** what I told you: 'A servant is not greater G3648
Jn 16: 4 their time comes you will **r** that I warned G3648
Ac 20:31 **R** that for three years I never stopped G3648
Ro 1: 9 is my witness how constantly I **r** you G3644+4472
1Co 1:16 I don't **r** if I baptized anyone else. G3857
2Co 9: 6 **R** this: Whoever sows sparingly will also NDT
Gal 2:10 was that we should continue to **r** the poor, G3648
Eph 2:11 **r** that formerly you who are Gentiles by G3648
Eph 2:12 **r** that at that time you were separate from NDT
Php 1: 3 I thank my God every time I **r** you. G3644
Col 4:18 in my own hand. **R** my chains. Grace be G3648
1Th 1: 3 We **r** before our God and Father your work G3648
1Th 2: 9 Surely you **r**, brothers and sisters, our toil G3648
2Th 2: 5 Don't you **r** that when I was with you I G3648
2Ti 1: 3 and day I constantly **r** you in my G2400+3644
2Ti 2: 8 **R** Jesus Christ, raised from the dead G3648
Phm 4 thank my God as I **r** you in my G3644+4472
Heb 8:12 wickedness and will **r** their sins no more." G3630
Heb 10:17 sins and lawless acts I will **r** no more." G3630
Heb 10:32 **R** those earlier days after you had received G389
Heb 13: 3 Continue to **r** those in prison as if you were G3630
Heb 13: 7 **R** your leaders, who spoke the word of G3648
Jas 5:20 **r** this: Whoever turns a sinner from the G1182
2Pe 1:15 always be able to **r** these things. G3647+4472
Jude 17 **r** what the apostles of our Lord Jesus G3630
Rev 3: 3 **R**, therefore, what you have received and G3648

REMEMBERED (55) [REMEMBER]

Ge 8: 1 But God **r** Noah and all the wild animals H2349
Ge 19:29 of the plain, he **r** Abraham, and he H2349
Ge 30:22 Then God **r** Rachel; he listened to her H2349
Ge 41:31 The abundance in the land will not **be r** H3359
Ge 42: 9 Then he **r** his dreams about them and said H2349
Ex 2:24 their groaning and he **r** his covenant with H2349
Ex 6: 5 are enslaving, and I have **r** my covenant. H2349
Ex 17:14 a scroll as **something** to be **r** and make H2355
Nu 10: 9 Then you will **be r** by the LORD your God H2349
1Sa 1:19 to his wife Hannah, and the LORD **r** her. H2349
Est 2: 1 he **r** Vashti and what she had done and H2349
Est 9:28 These days should **be r** and observed in H2349
Job 24:20 the wicked **are** no longer **r** but are broken H2349
Ps 77: 3 I **r** you, God, and I groaned; I meditated H2349
Ps 77: 6 I **r** my songs in the night. My heart H2349
Ps 78:35 They **r** that God was their Rock, that God H2349
Ps 78:39 He **r** that they were but flesh, a passing H2349
Ps 83: 4 so that Israel's name **is r** no more. H2349
Ps 98: 3 He has **r** his love and his faithfulness to H2349
Ps 105:42 For he **r** his holy promise given to his H2349
Ps 106:45 their sake he **r** his covenant and out of H2349
Ps 109:14 May the iniquity of his fathers **be r** before H2349
Ps 111: 4 He has caused his wonders to be **r**; the H2352
Ps 112: 6 never be shaken; they will be **r** forever. H2352
Ps 136:23 He **r** us in our low estate His love endures H2349
Ps 137: 1 Babylon we sat and wept when we **r** Zion. H2349
Ecc 1:11 to come will not be **r** by those who follow H2355
Ecc 2:16 will not be long **r**; the days have already H2355
Ecc 9:15 But nobody **r** that poor man. H2349
Isa 17:10 your Savior; you have not **r** the Rock, your H2349
Isa 23:16 sing many a song, so that you will **be r**." H2349
Isa 57:11 and have neither **r** me nor taken this to H2349
Isa 65:17 The former things will not **be r**, nor will H2349
Jer 3:16 It will never enter their minds or be **r**; it H2349
Jer 11:19 of the living, that his name **be r** no more." H2349
La 2: 1 he has not **r** his footstool in the day of his H2349
Eze 3:20 things that person did will not **be r**, H2349
Eze 18:22 have committed will **be r** against them. H2349
Eze 18:24 things that person has done will **be r**. H2349
Eze 21:32 in your land, you will **be r** no more; for I H2349
Eze 25:10 the Ammonites will not **be r** among the H2349
Eze 33:13 things that person has done will **be r**; H2349
Eze 33:16 has committed will **be r** against them. H2349
Jnh 2: 7 my life was ebbing away, I **r** you, LORD, H2349
Zec 13: 2 from the land, and they will **be r** no more," H2349
Mt 26:75 Then Peter **r** the word Jesus had spoken G3630
Mk 11:21 Peter **r** and said to Jesus, "Rabbi, look! The G389
Mk 14:72 Then Peter **r** the word Jesus had spoken to G389
Lk 22:61 Then Peter **r** the word the Lord had G5703
Lk 24: 8 Then they **r** his words. G3630
Jn 2:17 His disciples **r** that it is written: "Zeal for G3630
Ac 10:31 heard your prayer and **r** your gifts to the G3630
Ac 11:16 Then I **r** what the Lord had said: 'John G3630
Rev 16:19 God **r** Babylon the Great and gave her the G3630
Rev 18: 5 up to heaven, and God has **r** her crimes. G3648

REMEMBERING (4) [REMEMBER]

Lk 1:54 helped his servant Israel, **r** to be merciful G3630
Ac 20:35 **r** the words the Lord Jesus himself said: G3648
1Co 11: 2 I praise you for **r** me in everything and G3630
Eph 1:16 thanks for you, **r** you in my prayers. G3644+4472

REMEMBERS (11) [REMEMBER]

1Ch 16:15 He **r** his covenant forever, the promise he H2349
Ps 9:12 For he who avenges blood **r**; he does not H2349
Ps 103:14 how we are formed, he **r** that we are dust. H2349
Ps 103:16 it is gone, and its place **r** it no more. H5795
Ps 105: 8 He **r** his covenant forever, the promise he H2349
Ps 111: 5 who fear him; he **r** his covenant forever. H2349
Ps 115:12 The LORD **r** us and will bless us: He will H2349
Ecc 1:11 No one **r** the former generations, and H2355
Isa 43:25 my own sake, and **r** your sins no more. H2349
La 1: 7 wandering Jerusalem **r** all the treasures H2349
2Co 7:15 all the greater when he **r** that you were all G389

REMEMBRANCE (4) [REMEMBER]

Mal 3:16 A scroll of **r** was written in his presence H2355
Lk 22:19 my body given for you; do this in **r** of me." G390
1Co 11:24 which is for you; do this in **r** of me." G390
1Co 11:25 whenever you drink it, in **r** of me. G390

REMETH (1)

Jos 19:21 **R**, En Gannim, En Haddah and Beth H8255

REMIND (11) [REMINDED, REMINDER, REMINDER-OFFERING, REMINDERS, REMINDING]

Nu 16:40 This was to **r** the Israelites that no one H2355
1Ki 17:18 Did you come to **r** me of my sin and kill H2349
Eze 21:23 he will **r** them of their guilt and take H2349
Jn 14:26 you all things and will **r** you of everything G5703
Ro 15:15 on some points to **r** you of them **again**, G2057
1Co 4:17 He will **r** you of my way of life in Christ G389
1Co 15: 1 I want to **r** you of the gospel I preached to G1192
2Ti 1: 6 For this reason I **r** you to fan into flame the G389
Titus 3: 1 **R** the people to be subject to rulers and G5703
2Pe 1:12 So I will always **r** you of these things G5703
Jude 5 I want to **r** you that the Lord at one time G5703

REMINDED (2) [REMIND]

Ge 41: 9 "Today I am **r** of my shortcomings. H2349
2Ti 1: 5 I am **r** of your sincere faith, which G5704+3284

REMINDER (3) [REMIND]

Ex 13: 9 on your hand and a **r** on your forehead H2355
Eze 29:16 of Israel but will be a **r** of their sin in H2349
Heb 10: 3 But those sacrifices are an annual **r** of sins. G390

REMINDER-OFFERING (2) [OFFERING, REMIND]

Nu 5:15 a **r** to draw attention to wrongdoing H2355+4966
Nu 5:18 hair and place in her hands the **r**, H2355+4966

REMINDERS (1) [REMIND]

2Pe 3: 1 both of them as **r** to stimulate you to G5704

REMINDING (1) [REMIND]

2Ti 2:14 Keep **r** God's people of these things G5703

REMISSION (KJV) FORGIVEN, FORGIVENESS

REMNANT (65)

Ge 45: 7 preserve for you a **r** on earth and to save H8642
Jdg 5:13 "The **r** of the nobles came down; the H8586
2Ki 19: 4 Therefore pray for the **r** that still survives." H8642
2Ki 19:30 Once more a **r** of the kingdom of Judah H7129
2Ki 19:31 For out of Jerusalem will come a **r**, and H8642
2Ki 21:14 I will forsake the **r** of my inheritance and H8642
2Ch 34: 9 the entire **r** of Israel and from all H8642
2Ch 34:21 me and for the **r** in Israel and Judah H8636
2Ch 36:20 He carried into exile to Babylon the **r**, who H8642
Ezr 9: 8 in leaving us a **r** and giving us a firm H7129
Ezr 9:13 deserved and have given us a **r** like this. H7129
Ezr 9:14 to destroy us, leaving us no **r** or survivor? H8642
Ezr 9:15 We are left this day as a **r**. Here we are H7129
Ne 1: 2 about the Jewish **r** that had survived the H7129
Isa 10:20 In that day the **r** of Israel, the survivors of H8637
Isa 10:21 A **r** will return, a remnant of Jacob will H8637
Isa 10:21 a **r** of Jacob will return to the Mighty God. H8637
Isa 10:22 by the sea, Israel, only a **r** will return. H8637
Isa 11:11 reclaim the surviving **r** of his people from H8637
Isa 11:16 a highway for the **r** of his people that is H8637
Isa 17: 3 the **r** of Aram will be like the glory of the H8637
Isa 28: 5 a beautiful wreath for the **r** of his people. H8637
Isa 37: 4 Therefore pray for the **r** that still survives." H8642
Isa 37:31 Once more a **r** of the kingdom of Judah H7129
Isa 37:32 For out of Jerusalem will come a **r**, and H8642
Isa 46: 3 of Jacob, all the **r** of the people of Israel H8642
Jer 6: 9 "Let them glean the **r** of Israel as H8642
Jer 11:23 Not even a **r** will be left to them, because I H8642
Jer 23: 3 will gather the **r** of my flock out of all H8642
Jer 31: 7 save your people, the **r** of Israel. H8642
Jer 40:11 of Babylon had left a **r** in Judah and had H8642
Jer 40:15 be scattered and the **r** of Judah to perish?" H8642
Jer 42: 2 pray to the LORD your God for this entire **r**. H8642
Jer 42:15 hear the word of the LORD, you **r** of Judah. H8642
Jer 42:19 "**R** of Judah, the LORD has told you, 'Do H8642
Jer 43: 5 led away all the **r** of Judah who had come H8642
Jer 44: 7 so leave yourselves without a **r**? H8642
Jer 44:12 I will take away the **r** of Judah who were H8642
Jer 44:14 None of the **r** of Judah who have gone to H8642
Jer 44:28 Then the whole **r** of Judah who came to H8642
Jer 47: 4 the **r** from the coasts of Caphtor. H8642
Jer 47: 5 You **r** on the plain, how long will you cut H8642
Jer 50:20 be found, for I will forgive the **r** I **spare**. H8636
Jer 50:26 Completely destroy her and leave her no **r**. H8642
Eze 9: 8 to destroy the entire **r** of Israel in this H8642
Eze 11:13 you completely destroy the **r** of Israel?" H8642
Am 5:15 will have mercy on the **r** of Joseph. H8642
Am 9:12 may possess the **r** of Edom and all the H8642
Mic 2:12 I will surely bring together the **r** of Israel. H8642
Mic 4: 7 I will make the lame my **r**, those driven H8642
Mic 5: 7 The **r** of Jacob will be in the midst of H8642
Mic 5: 8 The **r** of Jacob will be among the nations H8642
Mic 7:18 transgression of the **r** of his inheritance? H8642
Zep 1: 4 I will destroy every **r** of Baal worship in H8637
Zep 2: 7 will belong to the **r** of the people of H8642
Zep 2: 9 The **r** of my people will plunder them; the H8642
Zep 3:12 The **r** of Israel will trust in the name of the H8642
Hag 1:12 the whole **r** of the people obeyed the H8642
Hag 1:14 the spirit of the whole **r** of the people. H8642
Hag 2: 2 the high priest, and to the **r** of the people. H8642
Zec 8: 6 marvelous to the **r** of this people at that H8642
Zec 8:11 not deal with the **r** of this people as I did H8642
Zec 8:12 as an inheritance to the **r** of this people. H8642
Ro 9:27 sand by the sea, only the **r** will be saved. G5698
Ro 11: 5 present time there is a **r** chosen by grace. G3307

REMORSE (1)

Mt 27: 3 he was **seized with r** and returned the G3564

REMOTE (8) [REMOTEST]

Lev 16:22 carry on itself all their sins to a **r** place; H1620
Jdg 19: 1 who lived in a **r area** in the hill country of H3752
Jdg 19:18 in Judah to a **r area** in the hill country of H3752
Mt 14:15 said, "This is a **r** place, and it's G2245
Mt 15:33 bread in this **r place** to feed such a G2244
Mk 6:35 "This is a **r** place," they said, "and it's G2245
Mk 8: 4 "But where in this **r place** can anyone get G2244
Lk 9:12 because we are in a **r** place here. G2245

REMOTEST (3) [REMOTE]

2Ki 19:23 I have reached its **r** parts, the finest of its H7891

Ne 9:22 allotting to them even the **r frontiers**. H6992
Isa 37:24 I have reached its **r** heights, the finest of H7891

REMOVAL (2) [REMOVE]

Isa 27: 9 this will be the full fruit of the **r** *of* his sin: H6073
1Pe 3:21 not the **r** of dirt from the body but the *G629*

REMOVE (58) [REMOVAL, REMOVED, REMOVES, REMOVING]

Ge 30:32 your flocks today and **r** from them every H6073
Ex 12:15 On the first day **r** the yeast from your H8697
Ex 27: 3 its pots to **r** the **ashes**, and its shovels, H2014
Ex 33:23 Then *I will* **r** my hand and you will see my H6073
Lev 1:16 *He is to* **r** the crop and the feathers and H6073
Lev 3: 4 the liver, which *you will* **r** with the kidneys. H6073
Lev 3:10 the liver, which *you will* **r** with the kidneys. H6073
Lev 3:15 the liver, which *you will* **r** with the kidneys. H6073
Lev 4: 8 *He shall* **r** all the fat from the bull of the H8123
Lev 4: 9 the liver, which *he will* **r** with the kidneys H6073
Lev 4:19 *He shall* **r** all the fat from it and burn it on H8123
Lev 4:31 *They shall* **r** all the fat, just as the fat is H6073
Lev 4:35 *They shall* **r** all the fat, just as the fat is H6073
Lev 6:10 and *shall* **r** the ashes of the burnt offering H8123
Lev 26: 6 *I will* **r** wild beasts from the land, and the H8697
Nu 4:13 "*They are to* **r** the **ashes** *from* the bronze H2014
Nu 16:37 *to* **r** the censers from the charred remains H8123
Nu 20:26 **R** Aaron's garments and put them on his H7320
Jos 7:13 against your enemies until you **r** them. H6073
1Ki 15:14 Although *he did* not **r** the high places H6073
1Ki 20:24 **R** all the kings from their commands and H6073
2Ki 23: 4 the doorkeepers to **r** from the temple of H3655
2Ki 23:27 "*I will* **r** Judah also from my presence as I H6073
2Ki 24: 3 in order to **r** them from his presence H6073
2Ch 15:17 Although *he did* not **r** the high places from H6073
2Ch 29: 5 **R** all defilement from the sanctuary H3655
2Ch 32:12 *Did* not Hezekiah himself **r** this god's high H6073
Job 9:34 *someone to* **r** God's rod from me, so that H6073
Job 22:23 If *you* **r** wickedness **far** from your tent H8178
Ps 39:10 **R** your scourge from me; I am overcome H6073
Ps 119:22 **R** from me their scorn and contempt, for I H1655
Pr 25: 4 **R** the dross from the silver, and a H2048
Pr 25: 5 **r** wicked officials from the king's presence H2048
Pr 27:22 *you will* not **r** their folly from them. H6073
Isa 1:25 away your dross and **r** all your impurities. H6073
Isa 25: 8 *he will* **r** his people's disgrace from all the H6073
Isa 57:14 **R** the obstacles out of the way of my H8123
Isa 62:10 up the highway! **R** the stones. Raise a H6232
Jer 27:10 you that *will only serve to* **r** you **far** from H8178
Jer 28:16 '*I am about to* **r** you from the face of the H8938
Jer 32:31 wrath that I *must* **r** it from my sight. H6073
Jer 47: 4 the Philistines and to **r** all survivors who H4162
Eze 11:18 will return to it and **r** all its vile images H6073
Eze 11:19 *I will* **r** from them their heart of stone and H6073
Eze 14: 8 *I will* **r** them from my people H4162
Eze 21:26 Take off the turban, **r** the crown. It will not H8123
Eze 34:10 *I will* **r** them from tending the flock so that H8697
Eze 36:26 *I will* **r** from you your heart of stone and H6073
Hos 2: 2 *Let her* **r** the adulterous look from her face H6073
Hos 2:17 *I will* **r** the names of the Baals from her H6073
Zep 3:11 because *I will* **r** from you your arrogant H6073
Zep 3:18 "*I will* **r** from you all who mourn over the H665
Zec 3: 9 'and *I will* **r** the sin of this land in a single H4631
Zec 13: 2 "*I will* **r** both the prophets and the spirit of H6296
Mal 2:12 *may* the LORD **r** him from the tents of Jacob H4162
Mt 7: 5 will see clearly *to* **r** the speck from your *G1675*
Lk 6:42 see clearly *to* **r** the speck *from* your *G1675*
Rev 2: 5 come to you and **r** your lampstand from *G3075*

REMOVED (67) [REMOVE]

Ge 8:13 Noah then **r** the covering from the ark H6073
Ge 30:35 That same day *he* **r** all the male goats that H6073
Ge 48:12 Then Joseph **r** them from Israel's knees H3655
Ex 25:15 the rings of this ark; *they are* not *to be* **r**. H6073
Ex 34:34 with him, *he* **r** the veil until he came out. H6073
Lev 4:10 just as the fat **is r** from the ox sacrificed as H8123
Lev 4:31 just as the fat **is r** from the fellowship H6073
Lev 4:35 just as the fat **is r** from the lamb of the H6073
Lev 7: 4 the liver, which *is to be* **r** with the kidneys. H6073
Lev 20:17 *They are to* **be** publicly **r from** their people H4162
Nu 20:28 Moses **r** Aaron's garments and put them H7320
Dt 26:13 "*I have* **r** from my house the sacred H1278
Dt 26:14 nor *have I* **r** any of it while I was unclean H1278
Ru 4: 8 "Buy it yourself." And *he* **r** his sandal. H8990
1Sa 21: 6 Presence that *had* **been r** from before the H6073
2Sa 7:15 from Saul, whom *I* **r** from before you. H6073
2Sa 20:13 After Amasa *had* **been r** from the road H3325
1Ki 2:27 So Solomon **r** Abiathar from the H1763
1Ki 5:17 command *they* **r from** the **quarry** large H5825
1Ki 20:41 the prophet quickly **r** the headband from H6073
1Ki 22:43 however, *were* not **r**, and the people H6073
2Ki 12: 3 however, *were* not **r**; the people H6073
2Ki 14: 4 however, *were* not **r**; the people H6073
2Ki 15: 4 however, *were* not **r**; the people H6073
2Ki 15:35 however, *were* not **r**; the people H6073
2Ki 16:17 the side panels and **r** the basins from the H6073
2Ki 16:17 *He* **r** the Sea from the bronze bulls that H3718
2Ki 16:18 built at the temple and **r** the royal entryway NDT
2Ki 17:18 angry with Israel and **r** them from his H6073
2Ki 17:23 the LORD **r** them from his presence, as H6073
2Ki 18: 4 He **r** the high places, smashed the sacred H6073
2Ki 18:22 whose high places and altars Hezekiah **r**, H6073
2Ki 23:11 *He* **r** from the entrance to the temple of H8697
2Ki 23:12 He **r** them from there, smashed them to NDT
2Ki 23:16 *he* **had** the bones **r** from H8938+2256+4374
2Ki 23:19 Josiah **r** all the shrines at the high places H6073
2Ki 23:27 Judah also from my presence as *I* **r** Israel, H6073
2Ki 24:13 Nebuchadnezzar **r** the treasures from the H3655
2Ch 14: 3 *He* **r** the foreign altars and the high places, H6073
2Ch 14: 5 *He* **r** the high places and incense altars in H6073
2Ch 15: 8 *He* **r** the detestable idols from the whole H6296
2Ch 17: 6 *he* **r** the high places and the Asherah H6073
2Ch 20:33 however, *were* not **r**, and the people still H6073
2Ch 29:19 that King Ahaz **r** in his unfaithfulness H2396
2Ch 30:14 *They* **r** the altars in Jerusalem and cleared H6073
2Ch 33:15 the foreign gods and **r** the image from the NDT
2Ch 34:33 Josiah **r** all the detestable idols from all H6073
Ezr 5:14 *He* even **r** from the temple of Babylon A10485
Job 19: 9 me of my honor and **r** the crown from my H6073
Job 34:20 the mighty *are* **r** without human hand. H6073
Ps 30:11 *you* **r** my sackcloth and clothed me with H7337
Ps 81: 6 "*I* **r** the burden from their shoulders; their H6073
Ps 103:12 *so* **far** *has he* **r** our transgressions from us. H8178
Pr 27:25 *When* the hay *is* **r** and new growth H1655
Isa 10:13 *I* **r** the boundaries of nations, I plundered H6073
Isa 14:25 his burden **r** from their shoulders. H6073
Isa 36: 7 whose high places and altars Hezekiah **r**, H6073
Isa 54:10 mountains be shaken and the hills *be* **r**, H4572
Isa 54:10 be shaken nor my covenant of peace *be* **r**," H4572
Isa 54:14 Terror will be far **r**; it will not come near NDT
Jer 8: 1 of Jerusalem *will be* **r** from their graves. H3655
Jer 9:21 *it has* **r** the children from the streets and H4162
Jer 28: 3 king of Babylon **r** from here and took to H4374
Eze 24:12 its heavy deposit *has* not *been* **r**, not even H3655
Jn 20: 1 that the stone *had been* **r** from the *G149*
2Co 3:14 *It has* not *been* **r**, because only in Christ is *G365*
Rev 6:14 mountain and island *was* **r** from its place. *G3075*

REMOVES (1) [REMOVE]

1Sa 17:26 this Philistine and **r** this disgrace from H6073

REMOVING (2) [REMOVE]

Ac 13:22 *After* **r** Saul, he made David their king *G3496*
Heb 12:27 indicate the **r** of what can be shaken *G3557*

REND (2)

Isa 64: 1 that *you would* **r** the heavens and come H7973
Joel 2:13 **R** your heart and not your garments H7973

RENDER (2) [RENDERING, RENDERS]

Isa 16: 3 "**R** a decision. Make your H6913
Zec 8:16 and **r** true and sound **judgment** in H9149+5477

RENDERING (1) [RENDER]

Isa 28: 7 they stumble when **r decisions**. H7133

RENDERS (1) [RENDER]

Ps 82: 1 *he* **r judgment** among the "gods": H9149

RENEGADES (1)

Jdg 12: 4 "You Gileadites are **r** from Ephraim and H7127

RENEW (8) [RENEWAL, RENEWED, RENEWING]

Ru 4:15 He will **r** your life and sustain you in your H8740
1Sa 11:14 us go to Gilgal and there **r** the kingship." H2542
Ps 51:10 and **r** a steadfast spirit within me. H2542
Ps 104:30 created, and *you* **r** the face of the ground. H2542
Isa 40:31 who hope in the LORD *will* **r** their strength. H2736
Isa 41: 1 **Let** the nations **r** their strength H2736
Isa 61: 4 *they will* **r** the ruined cities that have been H2542
La 5:21 that we may return; **r** our days as of old H2542

RENEWAL (4) [RENEW]

Job 14:14 hard service I will wait for my **r** to come. H2722
Isa 57:10 You found **r** *of* your strength, and so you H2652
Mt 19:28 at the **r of all things**, when the Son *G4098*
Titus 3: 5 washing of rebirth and **r** by the Holy Spirit, *G364*

RENEWED (7) [RENEW]

2Ki 23: 3 by the pillar and **r** the covenant in the H4162
2Ch 34:31 by his pillar and **r** the covenant in the H4162
Job 33:25 *let* their flesh **be r** like a child's; let them H8186
Ps 103: 5 so that your youth **is r** like the eagle's. H2542
2Co 4:16 inwardly we *are being* **r** day by day. *G363*
Php 4:10 Lord that at last *you* **r** your concern for me. *G352*
Col 3:10 which *is being* **r** in knowledge in the image *G363*

RENEWING (1) [RENEW]

Ro 12: 2 be transformed *by* the **r** of your mind. *G364*

RENOUNCE (3) [RENOUNCED, RENOUNCES]

Eze 14: 6 your idols and **r** all your detestable H8740+7156
Da 4:27 **R** your sins by doing what is right, and A10596
Rev 2:13 *You did* not **r** your faith in me, not even in *G766*

RENOUNCED (2) [RENOUNCE]

Ps 89:39 *You have* **r** the covenant with your servant H5545
2Co 4: 2 *we have* **r** secret and shameful ways *G584*

RENOUNCES (1) [RENOUNCE]

Pr 28:13 who confesses and **r** them finds mercy. H6440

RENOWN (11) [RENOWNED]

Ge 6: 4 They were the heroes of old, men of **r**. H9005
Ps 102:12 your **r** endures through all generations. H2352
Ps 135:13 endures forever, your **r**, LORD, through all H2352
Isa 26: 8 your name and **r** are the desire of our H2352
Isa 55:13 This will be for the LORD's **r**, for an H9005
Isa 63:12 to gain for himself everlasting **r**, H9005
Jer 13:11 be my people for my **r** and praise and H9005
Jer 32:20 have gained the **r** that is still yours. H9005
Jer 33: 9 Then this city will bring me **r**, joy, praise H9005
Jer 49:25 has the city of **r** not been abandoned, H9335
Eze 26:17 destroyed, city of **r**, peopled by men of the H2146

RENOWNED (4) [RENOWN]

Ps 76: 1 God **is r** in Judah; in Israel his name is H3359
Isa 23: 8 princes, whose traders *are* **r** *in* the earth? H3877
Isa 23: 9 to humble all *who are* **r** *on* the earth. H3877
Eze 34:29 them a land **r** for its crops, H4200+9005

RENT (1) [RENTED]

Mt 21:41 "and *he will* **r** the vineyard to other *G1686*

RENTED (4) [RENT]

Mt 21:33 Then *he* **r** the vineyard to some farmers *G1686*
Mk 12: 1 Then *he* **r** the vineyard to some farmers *G1686*
Lk 20: 9 **r** it to some farmers and went away for a *G1686*
Ac 28:30 there in his own **r house** and welcomed *G3637*

REOPENED (1)

Ge 26:18 Isaac **r** the wells that had H8740+2256+2916

REPAID (10) [PAY]

Ge 44: 4 to them, 'Why *have you* **r** good with evil? H8966
Jdg 9:56 Thus God **r** the wickedness that Abimelek H8740
2Sa 16: 8 The LORD *has* **r** you *for* all the blood you H8740
Ps 7: 4 if *I have* **r** my ally *with* evil or without H1694
Pr 14:14 The faithless *will be* **fully r** for their ways H8425
Jer 18:20 *Should* good **be r** with evil? Yet they have H8966
Lk 6:34 lend to sinners, expecting to *be* **r** in full. *G655*
Lk 14:12 may invite you back and so you will be **r**. *G501*
Lk 14:14 you *will be* **r** at the resurrection of the *G500*
Col 3:25 who does wrong *will be* **r** for their wrongs, *G3152*

REPAIR (14) [REPAIRED, REPAIRER, REPAIRING, REPAIRS]

2Ki 12: 5 then *use* it *to* **r** whatever damage is found H2616
2Ki 12: 8 that they *would* not **r** the temple H2616
2Ki 12:12 stone for the **r** *of* the temple of the H2616
2Ki 12:14 the workers, *who* used it *to* **r** the temple. H2616
2Ki 22: 5 the workers who **r** the temple of the H2616+981
2Ki 22: 6 timber and dressed stone to **r** the temple. H2616
1Ch 26:27 dedicated for the **r** of the temple of the H2616
2Ch 24: 5 all Israel, to **r** the temple of your God. H2616
2Ch 24:12 in iron and bronze to **r** the temple. H2616
2Ch 34: 8 to **r** the temple of the LORD his God. H2616
Ezr 9: 9 the house of our God and **r** its ruins, H6641
Eze 13: 5 in the wall *to* **r** it for the people of H1553
Am 9:11 *I will* **r** its broken walls and restore its H1553
Na 3:14 the clay, tread the mortar, **r** the brickwork! H2616

REPAIRED (24) [REPAIR]

1Ki 18:30 and *he* **r** the altar of the LORD H8324
2Ki 12: 6 the priests *still had* not **r** the temple. H2616
2Ch 15: 8 *He* **r** the altar of the LORD that was in front H2542
2Ch 29: 3 of the temple of the LORD and **r** them. H2616
2Ch 34:10 paid the workers *who* **r** and restored the H980
Ne 3: 4 the son of Hakkoz, **r** the next section. H2616
Ne 3: 5 The next section *was* **r** *by* the men of H2616
Ne 3: 6 Jeshanah Gate *was* **r** *by* Joiada son of H2616
Ne 3: 8 of the goldsmiths, **r** the next section; and H2616
Ne 3: 9 of Jerusalem, **r** the next section. H2616
Ne 3:11 son of Pahath-Moab **r** another section H2616
Ne 3:12 **r** the next section with the help of his H2616
Ne 3:13 The Valley Gate *was* **r** *by* Hanun and the H2616
Ne 3:13 They also **r** a thousand cubits of the wall as NDT
Ne 3:14 The Dung Gate *was* **r** *by* Malkijah son of H2616
Ne 3:15 Fountain Gate *was* **r** *by* Shallun son of H2616
Ne 3:15 He also **r** the wall of the Pool of Siloam, by NDT
Ne 3:19 ruler of Mizpah, **r** another section, from a H2616
Ne 3:20 son of Zabbai zealously **r** another section, H2616
Ne 3:21 the son of Hakkoz, **r** another section, from H2616
Ne 3:24 Binnui son of Henadad **r** another section H2616
Ne 3:27 the men of Tekoa **r** another section, from H2616
Ne 3:30 the sixth son of Zalaph, **r** another section. H2616
Jer 19:11 potter's jar is smashed and cannot **be r**. H8324

REPAIRER (1) [REPAIR]

Isa 58:12 you will be called **R of** Broken **Walls** H1553

REPAIRING (4) [REPAIR]

2Ki 12: 7 "Why aren't you **r** the damage done to H2616
2Ki 12: 7 treasurers, but hand it over for **r** the temple." H981
2Ch 32: 5 Then he worked hard **r** all the broken H1215
Ezr 4:12 the walls and **r** the foundations. A10253

REPAIRS (22) [REPAIR]

2Ch 24:13 diligent, and the **r** progressed under them. H776
Ne 3: 4 of Meshezabel, **made r**, and next to him H2616
Ne 3: 4 to him Zadok son of Baana also **made r**. H2616
Ne 3: 7 **r** *were* **made** *by* men from Gibeon and H2616
Ne 3: 8 the perfume-makers, **made r** next to that. H2616
Ne 3:10 son of Harumaph **made r** opposite his H2616
Ne 3:10 son of Hashabneiah **made r** next to him. H2616
Ne 3:16 **made r** up to a point opposite the tombs H2616
Ne 3:17 the **r** *were* **made** *by* the Levites under H2616
Ne 3:17 of Keilah, **carried out r** for his district. H2616
Ne 3:18 *the* **r** *were* **made** *by* their fellow Levites H2616
Ne 3:22 *The* **r** next to him *were* **made** *by* the H2616

Ne 3:23 Hasshub made r in front of their H2616
Ne 3:23 son of Ananiah, made r beside his house. H2616
Ne 3:26 hill of Ophel made r up to a point opposite NDT
Ne 3:28 the priests made r, each in front of H2616
Ne 3:29 Zadok son of Immer made r opposite his H2616
Ne 3:29 the guard at the East Gate, made r. H2616
Ne 3:30 son of Berekiah made r opposite his living H2616
Ne 3:31 made r as far as the house of the temple H2616
Ne 3:32 the goldsmiths and merchants made r. H2616
Ne 4:7 heard that the r to Jerusalem's walls H776

REPAY (49) [PAY]

Lev 25:28 But if they do not acquire the means *to* r H8740
Dt 7:10 who hate him *he will* r to their face by H8966
Dt 7:10 he will not be slow *to* r to their face those H8966
Dt 32:6 Is this the way *you* r the LORD, you foolish H1694
Dt 32:35 mine to avenge; *I will* r. In due time their H8966
Dt 32:41 my adversaries and r those who hate me. H8966
Ru 2:12 *May* the LORD r you *for* what you have H8966
2Sa 3:39 *May* the LORD r the evildoer according to H8966
1Ki 2:32 The LORD *will* r him *for* the H8740+6584+8031
1Ki 2:44 the LORD *will* r you *for* your H8740+928+8031
Job 21:19 *Let him* r the wicked, so that they H8966
Ps 28:4 R them for their deeds and for their evil H5989
Ps 28:4 r them for what their hands have done H5989
Ps 35:12 *They* r me evil for good and leave me like H8966
Ps 37:21 The wicked borrow and *do* not r, but the H8966
Ps 38:20 *Those who* r my good with evil lodge H8966
Ps 41:10 LORD; raise me up, that *I may* r them. H8966
Ps 94:23 *He will* r them *for* their sins and destroy H8740
Ps 103:10 our sins deserve or r us according to our H1694
Ps 109:5 *They* r me evil for good, and hatred for my H8492
Pr 24:12 *Will he* not r everyone according to what H8740
Isa 59:18 so *will he* r wrath to his enemies and H8966
Isa 59:18 to his foes; *he will* r the islands their due. H8966
Jer 16:18 *I will* r them double *for* their wickedness H8966
Jer 25:14 *I will* r them according to their deeds and H8966
Jer 50:29 R her for her deeds; do to her as she has H8966
Jer 51:6 he *will* r her what she deserves. H8966
Jer 51:24 *I will* r Babylon and all who live in Babylonia *for* H8966
Jer 51:56 God of retribution; *he will* r in full. H8966+8966
Eze 7:3 to your conduct and r you *for* all your H5989
Eze 7:4 *I will* surely r you *for* your conduct and H5989
Eze 7:8 to your conduct and r you *for* all your H5989
Eze 7:9 *I will* r you for your conduct and for the H5989
Eze 17:19 *I will* r him for despising my H5989+928+8031
Hos 4:9 their ways and r them *for* their deeds. H8740
Hos 12:2 to his ways and r him according to his H8740
Hos 12:14 bloodshed and *will* r him *for* his contempt H8740
Joel 2:25 "*I will* r you *for* the years the locusts have H8966
Mt 18:25 all that he had be sold *to* r *the* debt. G625
Lk 14:14 Although they cannot r you, you will be G500
Ro 2:6 God "*will* r each person according to what G625
Ro 11:35 ever given to God, that God *should* r them?" G500
Ro 12:17 *Do* not r anyone evil for evil. Be careful to G625
Ro 12:19 is mine to avenge; I *will* r," says the Lord. G500
2Ti 4:14 The Lord *will* r him for what he has done. G625
Heb 10:30 mine to avenge; I *will* r," and again, "The G500
1Pe 3:9 *Do* not r evil with evil or insult with insult G625
1Pe 3:9 On the contrary, r evil with blessing NDT
Rev 2:23 and *I will* r each of you according to your G1443

REPAYING (4) [PAY]

2Ch 20:11 See *how* they *are* r us by coming to drive H1694
Isa 66:6 sound of the LORD r his enemies all they H8966
Joel 3:4 *Are* you r me *for* something I have done H8966
1Ti 5:4 own family and so r their parents and G304+625

REPAYMENT (1) [PAY]

Lk 6:34 lend to those from whom you expect r, G3284

REPAYS (3) [PAY]

Job 21:31 Who r them for what they have done? H8966
Job 34:11 *He* r everyone *for* what they have done H8966
Ps 137:8 happy is the *one* who r you according to H8966

REPEALED (3)

Est 1:19 Media, *which* cannot *be* r, that Vashti H6296
Da 6:8 Medes and Persians, which cannot *be* r." A10528
Da 6:12 Medes and Persians, which cannot *be* r." A10528

REPEAT (4) [REPEATED, REPEATEDLY, REPEATS]

Pr 26:11 returns to its vomit, so fools r their folly. H9101
Hab 3:2 R them in our day, in our time make them H2649
2Co 11:16 *I* r: Let no one take me for a fool G4099+3306
2Co 13:2 the second time. *I* now r it while absent G4625

REPEATED (8) [REPEAT]

Ge 44:6 up with them, *he* r these words to them. H1819
Jdg 9:3 When the brothers r all this to the citizens H1819
Jdg 11:11 And he r all his words before the LORD in H1819
1Sa 8:21 the people said, *he* r it before the LORD. H1819
1Sa 11:5 Then *they* r to him what the men of H6218
1Sa 17:27 *They* r to him what they had been saying H606
1Sa 18:23 They r these words to David. But David H1819
Heb 10:1 the same sacrifices r endlessly year after G4712S

REPEATEDLY (2) [REPEAT]

Jer 46:16 *They will* stumble r; they will fall over H8049
Lk 8:31 And *they* begged Jesus *r* not to order them to AIT

REPEATS (1) [REPEAT]

Pr 17:9 but *whoever* r the matter separates close H9101

REPENT (42) [PENITENT, REPENTANCE, REPENTED, REPENTS]

1Ki 8:47 r and plead with you in the land of H8740
2Ch 6:37 r and plead with you in the land of H8740
Job 34:33 you on your terms, when you refuse to r? NDT
Job 36:10 commands them *to* r of their evil. H8740
Job 42:6 I despise myself and r in dust and ashes." H5714
Pr 1:23 R at my rebuke! Then I will pour out my H8740
Isa 59:20 to *those* in Jacob *who* r *of* their sins," H8740
Jer 5:3 faces harder than stone and refused to r. H8740
Jer 8:6 None of them r of their wickedness H5714
Jer 15:19 "If *you* r, I will restore you that you may H8740
Eze 14:6 Sovereign LORD says: R! Turn from your H8740
Eze 18:30 the Sovereign LORD. R! Turn away from all H8740
Eze 18:32 declares the Sovereign LORD. R and live! H8740
Hos 11:5 rule over them because they refuse to r? H8740
Mt 3:2 saying, "R, for the kingdom of heaven G3566
Mt 4:17 began to preach, "R, for the kingdom of G3566
Mt 11:20 been performed, because *they did* not r. G3566
Mt 21:32 saw this, *you did* not r and believe him. G3564
Mk 1:15 R and believe the good news! G3566
Mk 6:12 out and preached that *people should* r. G3566
Lk 13:3 But unless *you* r, you too will all G3566
Lk 13:5 But unless *you* r, you too will all G3566
Lk 15:7 righteous persons who do not need to r. G3567
Lk 16:30 from the dead goes to them, *they will* r. G3566
Lk 17:3 rebuke them; and if *they* r, forgive them. G3566
Lk 17:4 seven times come back to you saying '*I* r, G3566
Ac 2:38 Peter replied, "R and be baptized, every G3566
Ac 3:19 R, then, and turn to God, so that your sins G3566
Ac 8:22 R of this wickedness and pray to the Lord G3566
Ac 17:30 he commands all people everywhere *to* r. G3566
Ac 26:20 I preached *that they should* r and turn to G3566
Rev 2:5 R and do the things you did at first G3566
Rev 2:5 If *you do* not r, I will come to you and G3566
Rev 2:16 R therefore! Otherwise, I will soon come G3566
Rev 2:21 have given her time to r of her immorality, G3566
Rev 2:22 suffer intensely, unless *they* r of her ways. G3566
Rev 3:3 received and heard; hold it fast, and r. G3566
Rev 3:19 discipline. So be earnest and r. G3566
Rev 9:20 these plagues *still did* not r of the work of G3566
Rev 9:21 Nor *did they* r of their murders, their magic G3566
Rev 16:9 but *they* refused *to* r and glorify him. G3566
Rev 16:11 but *they* refused *to* r of what they had G3566

REPENTANCE (21) [REPENT]

Isa 30:15 "In r and rest is your salvation, in H8746
Mt 3:8 Produce fruit in keeping with r. G3567
Mt 3:11 "I baptize you with water for r. But after G3567
Mk 1:4 preaching a baptism *of* r for the G3567
Lk 3:3 preaching a baptism *of* r for the G3567
Lk 3:8 Produce fruit in keeping with r. And do not G3567
Lk 5:32 to call the righteous, but sinners to r." G3567
Lk 24:47 r for the forgiveness of sins will be G3567
Ac 5:31 might bring Israel to r and forgive their G3567
Ac 11:18 God has granted r that leads to life." G3567
Ac 13:24 John preached r and baptism to all the G3567
Ac 19:4 "John's baptism was a baptism *of* r. G3567
Ac 20:21 they must turn to God in r and have faith G3567
Ac 26:20 demonstrate their r by their deeds. G3567
Ro 2:4 kindness is intended to lead you to r? G3567
2Co 7:9 because your sorrow led you to r. G3567
2Co 7:10 Godly sorrow brings r that leads to G3567
2Ti 2:25 God will grant them r leading them to a G3567
Heb 6:1 the foundation *of* r from acts that lead G3567
Heb 6:6 have fallen away, to be brought back to r. G3567
2Pe 3:9 to perish, but everyone to come to r. G3567

REPENTED (9) [REPENT]

2Ch 32:26 Then Hezekiah r of the pride of his heart H4044
Jer 31:19 After I strayed, *I* r; after I came to H5714
Jer 34:15 Recently you r and did what is right in my H8740
Zec 1:6 "Then *they* r and said, 'The LORD Almighty H8740
Mt 11:21 *they* would have r long ago in sackcloth G3566
Mt 12:41 for *they* r at the preaching of Jonah G3566
Lk 10:13 Sidon, *they* would have r long ago G3566
Lk 11:32 for *they* r at the preaching of Jonah G3566
2Co 12:21 earlier and *have* not r of the impurity, G3566

REPENTS (4) [REPENT]

Jer 18:8 if that nation I warned r of its evil H8740
Eze 33:12 And if someone who is wicked r, that H8740
Lk 15:7 over one sinner *who* r than over G3566
Lk 15:10 the angels of God over one sinner *who* r." G3566

REPHAEL (1)

1Ch 26:7 R, Obed and Elzabad; his relatives H8330

REPHAH (1)

1Ch 7:25 R was his son, Resheph his son, Telah his H8338

REPHAIAH (5)

1Ch 3:21 Jeshaiah, and the sons of R, of Arnan, H8341
1Ch 4:42 Pelatiah, Neariah, R and Uzziel, the sons H8341
1Ch 7:2 R, Jeriel, Jahmai, Ibsam and H8341
1Ch 9:43 father of Binea; R was his son, Eleasah H8341
Ne 3:9 R son of Hur, ruler of a half-district of H8341

REPHAIM (8)

Jos 15:8 at the northern end of the Valley of R. H8329
Jos 18:16 of Ben Hinnom, north of the Valley of R. H8329
2Sa 5:18 come and spread out in the Valley of R; H8329
2Sa 5:22 up and spread out in the Valley of R; H8329
2Sa 23:13 was encamped in the Valley of R. H8329
1Ch 11:15 was encamped in the Valley of R. H8329
1Ch 14:9 had come and raided the Valley of R; H8329
Isa 17:5 gleans heads of grain in the Valley of R. H8329

REPHAIMS (KJV) REPHAITES

REPHAITES (10)

Ge 14:5 defeated the R in Ashteroth Karnaim H8328
Ge 15:20 Perizzites, R, H8328
Dt 2:11 they too were considered R, but the H8328
Dt 2:20 That too was considered a land of the R H8328
Dt 3:11 Og king of Bashan was the last of the R H8328
Dt 3:13 used to be known as a land of the R. H8328
Jos 12:4 one of the last of the R, who reigned in H8328
Jos 13:12 He was the last of the R.) Moses had H8328
Jos 17:15 there in the land of the Perizzites and R." H8328
1Ch 20:4 one of the descendants of the R, and the H8328

REPHAN (1)

Ac 7:43 of Molek and the star of your god R, G4818

REPHIDIM (5)

Ex 17:1 They camped at R, but there was no water H8340
Ex 17:8 came and attacked the Israelites at R. H8340
Ex 19:2 After they set out from R, they entered the H8340
Nu 33:14 They left Alush and camped at R, where H8340
Nu 33:15 They left R and camped in the Desert of H8340

REPLACE (6) [REPLACED]

Lev 14:42 other stones *to* r these and H995+448+9393
1Ki 14:27 bronze shields to r them and assigned H9393
1Ki 20:24 commands and r them *with* other H8492+9393
2Ki 17:24 in the towns of Samaria to r the Israelites. H9393
2Ch 12:10 bronze shields to r them and assigned H9393
Isa 9:10 but *we will* r them *with* cedars. H2736

REPLACED (3) [REPLACE]

1Sa 21:6 before the LORD and r *by* hot bread on the H8492
1Ki 2:35 and r Abiathar *with* Zadok the H5989+9393
Da 8:22 The four horns *that* r the one that H6641+9393

REPLANTED (1) [PLANT]

Eze 36:36 was destroyed and *have* r what was H5749

REPLENISH, REPLENISHED (KJV) ENRICHED, FILL, FILLED, FULL, PROSPER, SATISFY

REPLICA (1)

Jos 22:28 Look at the r *of* the LORD's altar, which our H9322

REPLIED (423) [REPLY]

Ge 4:9 "I don't know," *he* r. "Am I my brother's H606
Ge 19:9 out of our way," *they* r. "This fellow came H606
Ge 20:11 Abraham r, "I said to myself, 'There is H606
Ge 21:30 *He* r, "Accept these seven lambs from my H606
Ge 22:1 said to him, "Abraham!" "Here I am," *he* r. H606
Ge 22:7 Abraham r. "The fire and wood H606
Ge 22:11 Abraham!" "Here I am," *he* r. H606
Ge 23:5 The Hittites r *to* Abraham, H6699
Ge 23:10 his people and he r *to* Abraham in the H6699
Ge 24:40 "*He* r, 'The LORD, before whom I have H606
Ge 24:55 But her brother and her mother r, "Let the H606
Ge 25:31 Jacob r, "First sell me your birthright." H606
Ge 27:20 "The LORD your God gave me success," *he* r. H606
Ge 27:24 he asked. "I am," *he* r. H606
Ge 29:4 "We're from Harran," *they* r. H606
Ge 29:8 *they* r, "until all the flocks are gathered H606
Ge 29:26 Laban r, "It is not our custom here to give H606
Ge 30:31 me anything," Jacob r. "But if you will do H606
Ge 31:14 Then Rachel and Leah r, "Do we still have H6699
Ge 32:26 But Jacob r, "I will not let you go unless H606
Ge 32:29 me your name." But *he* r, "Why do you ask H606
Ge 34:13 Jacob's sons r deceitfully as they spoke to H6699
Ge 34:31 But *they* r, "Should he have treated our H606
Ge 37:13 to send you to them." "Very well," *he* r. H606
Ge 37:16 *He* r, "I'm looking for my brothers. Can you H606
Ge 41:16 Joseph r *to* Pharaoh, "but God will give H6699
Ge 42:7 the land of Canaan," *they* r, "to buy food." H606
Ge 42:13 But *they* r, "Your servants were twelve H606
Ge 42:22 Reuben r, "Didn't I tell you not to sin H6699
Ge 43:7 *They* r, "The man questioned us closely H606
Ge 43:28 *They* r, "Your servant our father is still alive H606
Ge 44:16 Judah r. "What can we say? H606
Ge 46:2 Jacob!" "Here I am," *he* r. H606
Ge 47:3 *they* r to Pharaoh, "just as our fathers were H606
Ex 4:2 "What is that in your hand?" "A staff," *he* r. H606
Ex 8:10 Moses r, "It will be as you say, so that you H606
Ex 9:29 Moses r, "When I have gone out of the city H606
Ex 10:29 as you say," Moses r. "I will never appear H606
Ex 17:2 Moses r, "Why do you quarrel H606
Ex 18:17 Moses' father-in-law r, "What you are H606
Ex 19:24 The LORD r, "Go down and bring Aaron up H606
Ex 32:18 Moses r: "It is not the sound of victory, it is H606
Ex 32:33 The LORD r to Moses, "Whoever has sinned H606
Ex 33:14 The LORD r, "My Presence will go with you H606
Lev 10:19 Aaron r to Moses, "Today they sacrificed H1819
Nu 11:29 But Moses r, "Are you jealous for my sake H606
Nu 12:14 The LORD r to Moses, "If her father had spit H606
Nu 14:20 The LORD r, "I have forgiven them, as you H606
Nu 20:19 The Israelites r: "We will go along the H606

Nu 22:38 to you now," Balaam **r**. "But I can't say H606
Dt 1:41 Then *you* **r**, "We have sinned against the H6699
Jos 2:21 "Agreed," *she* **r**. "Let it be as you say." H606
Jos 5:14 *he* **r**, "but as commander of the army of H606
Jos 5:15 The commander of the LORD's army **r**, H606
Jos 7:20 Achan **r**, "It is true! I have sinned against H6699
Jos 15:19 *She* **r**, "Do me a special favor. Since you H606
Jos 17:16 The people of Joseph **r**, "The hill country is H606
Jos 22:21 of Manasseh **r** *to* the heads of the H6699
Jos 24:22 "Yes, we are witnesses," *they* **r**. H606
Jdg 1:15 *She* **r**, "Do me a special favor. Since you H606
Jdg 6:13 my lord," Gideon **r**, "but if the LORD is with H606
Jdg 6:15 my lord," Gideon **r**, "but how can I save H606
Jdg 6:17 Gideon **r**, "If now I have found favor in your H606
Jdg 6:31 But Joash **r** to the hostile crowd around him H606
Jdg 8:7 Then Gideon **r**, "Just for that, when the H606
Jdg 8:19 Gideon **r**, "Those were my brothers, the H606
Jdg 9:11 "But the fig tree **r**, 'Should I give up my fruit H606
Jdg 9:36 Zebul **r**, "You mistake the shadows of the H606
Jdg 10:11 The LORD **r**, "When the Egyptians, the H606
Jdg 11:10 The elders of Gilead **r**, "The LORD is our H606
Jdg 11:36 *she* **r**, "you have given your word to the H606
Jdg 12:5 "Are you an Ephraimite?" If *he* **r**, "No," H606
Jdg 13:16 The angel of the LORD **r**, "Even though you H606
Jdg 13:18 He **r**, "Why do you ask my name? It is H606
Jdg 14:3 His father and mother **r**, "Isn't there an H606
Jdg 14:14 *He* **r**, "Out of the eater, something to eat H606
Jdg 14:16 my father or mother," *he* **r**, "so why should I H606
Jdg 16:13 *He* **r**, "If you weave the seven braids of my H606
Jdg 18:24 *He* **r**, "You took the gods I made, and my H606
Jdg 19:12 His master **r**, "No. We won't go into any H606
Jdg 20:18 The LORD **r**, "Judah shall go H606
Ru 1:16 But Ruth **r**, "Don't urge me to leave you H606
Ru 2:6 The overseer **r**, "She is the Moabite who H6699
Ru 2:11 Boaz **r**, "I've been told all about what you H6699
Ru 3:10 my daughter," *he* **r**. "This kindness is H606
1Sa 1:15 Hannah **r**, "I am a woman who is deeply H6699
1Sa 4:17 The man who brought the news **r**, "Israel H6699
1Sa 6:4 *They* **r**, "Five gold tumors and five gold H606
1Sa 9:6 But the servant **r**, "Look, in this town there H606
1Sa 9:19 the seer," Samuel **r**. "Go up ahead of me H6699
1Sa 10:16 Saul **r**, "He assured us that the donkeys H606
1Sa 11:2 But Nahash the Ammonite **r**, "I will make a H606
1Sa 12:4 have not cheated or oppressed us," *they* **r**. H606
1Sa 12:20 be afraid," Samuel **r**. "You have done all H606
1Sa 13:11 Saul **r**, "When I saw that the men were H606
1Sa 14:36 seems best to you," *they* **r**. But the priest H606
1Sa 14:40 "Do what seems best to you," they **r**. H606
1Sa 15:16 said to me last night." "Tell me," Saul **r**. H606
1Sa 15:22 But Samuel **r**: "Does the LORD delight in H606
1Sa 15:30 Saul **r**, "I have sinned. But please honor H606
1Sa 16:5 Samuel **r**, "Yes, in peace; I have come to H606
1Sa 17:33 Saul **r**, "You are not able to go out against H606
1Sa 17:55 Abner **r**, "As surely as you live, Your H606
1Sa 18:25 Saul **r**, "Say to David, 'The king wants no H606
1Sa 20:2 Jonathan **r**. "You are not going to H606
1Sa 21:5 David **r**, "Indeed women have been kept H6699
1Sa 21:9 The priest **r**, "The sword of Goliath the H606
1Sa 23:21 Saul **r**, "The LORD bless you for your H606
1Sa 26:14 Abner **r**, "Who are you who calls to the H6699
1Sa 26:17 David my son?" David **r**, "Yes it is, my lord H606
1Sa 28:2 Achish **r**, "Very well, I will make you my H606
1Sa 29:3 Achish **r**, "Is this not David, who was an H606
1Sa 30:23 David **r**, "No, my brothers, you must not do H606
2Sa 1:4 from the battle," *he* **r**. "Many of them fell H606
2Sa 7:3 Nathan **r** to the king, "Whatever you have H606
2Sa 9:2 "Are you Ziba?" "At your service," *he* **r**. H606
2Sa 9:6 "Mephibosheth!" "At your service," *he* **r**. H606
2Sa 12:13 Nathan **r**, "The LORD has taken away your H606
2Sa 12:19 "Yes," *they* **r**, "he is dead." H606
2Sa 13:25 the king **r**. "All of us should not H606
2Sa 14:10 The king **r**, "If anyone says anything to you H606
2Sa 14:12 a word to my lord the king." "Speak," *he* **r**. H606
2Sa 15:21 But Ittai **r** *to* the king, "As surely as the H6699
2Sa 17:7 Hushai **r** to Absalom, "The advice H606
2Sa 18:12 But the man **r**, "Even if a thousand shekels H606
2Sa 18:22 But Joab **r**, "My son, why do you want to H606
2Sa 18:32 The Cushite **r**, "May the enemies of my H606
2Sa 19:22 David **r**, "What does this have to do with H606
2Sa 20:20 Joab **r**, "Far be it from me to swallow up H6699
2Sa 24:3 But Joab **r** to the king, "May the LORD your H606
2Sa 24:24 But the king **r** to Araunah, "No, I insist on H606
1Ki 1:52 Solomon **r**, "If he shows himself to be H606
1Ki 2:14 "You may say it," *she* **r**. H606
1Ki 2:18 Bathsheba **r**, "I will speak to the king for H606
1Ki 2:20 The king **r**, "Make it, my mother; I will not H606
1Ki 11:22 "Nothing," Hadad **r**, "but do let me go!" H606
1Ki 12:7 *They* **r**, "If today you will be a servant to H1819
1Ki 12:10 young men who had grown up with him **r**, H1819
1Ki 13:14 God who came from Judah?" "I am," *he* **r**. H606
1Ki 17:12 your God lives," *she* **r**, "I don't have any H606
1Ki 17:19 me your son," Elijah **r**. He took him from H606
1Ki 18:8 *he* **r**. "Go tell your master, 'Elijah is H606
1Ki 18:18 have not made trouble for Israel," Elijah **r**. H606
1Ki 19:10 *He* **r**, "I have been very zealous for the LORD H606
1Ki 19:14 *He* **r**, "I have been very zealous for the LORD H606
1Ki 19:20 "Go back," Elijah **r**. "What have I done to H606
1Ki 20:9 So *he* **r** to Ben-Hadad's messengers, "Tell H606
1Ki 20:14 The prophet **r**, "This is what the LORD H606
1Ki 21:3 But Naboth **r**, "The LORD forbid that I H606
1Ki 22:4 Jehoshaphat **r** to the king of Israel, "I am H606
1Ki 22:8 not say such a thing," Jehoshaphat **r**. H606
1Ki 22:25 Micaiah **r**, "You will find out on the day you H606
2Ki 1:6 came to meet us," *they* **r**. "And he said to H606
2Ki 1:8 *They* **r**, "He had a garment of hair and had H606
2Ki 1:12 Elijah **r**, "may fire come down from H6699
2Ki 2:3 "Yes, I know," Elisha **r**, "so be quiet." H606
2Ki 2:4 And *he* **r**, "As surely as the LORD lives and H606
2Ki 2:5 "Yes, I know," *he* **r**, "so be quiet." H606
2Ki 2:6 And *he* **r**, "As surely as the LORD lives and H606
2Ki 2:9 a double portion of your spirit," Elisha **r**. H606
2Ki 2:16 Elisha **r**, "do not send them." H606
2Ki 3:7 "I will go with you," *he* **r**. "I am as you are, H606
2Ki 4:2 Elisha **r** to her, "How can I help you? Tell H606
2Ki 4:6 me another one." But *he* **r**, "There is not a H606
2Ki 4:13 *She* **r**, "I have a home among my own H606
2Ki 5:5 the king of Aram **r**. "I will send a letter H606
2Ki 6:3 come with your servants?" "I will," Elisha **r**. H606
2Ki 6:27 The king **r**, "If the LORD does not help you H606
2Ki 7:1 Elisha **r**, "Hear the word of the LORD. This H606
2Ki 7:19 The man of God *had* **r**, "You will see it H606
2Ki 8:14 Hazael **r**, "He told me that you would H606
2Ki 9:5 "For you, commander," *he* **r**. H606
2Ki 9:11 man and the sort of things he says," Jehu **r**. H606
2Ki 9:18 do with peace?" Jehu **r**. "Fall in behind me." H606
2Ki 9:19 Jehu **r**, "What do you have to do with H606
2Ki 9:22 Jehu **r**, "as long as all the idolatry and H606
2Ki 14:9 king of Israel **r** to Amaziah king of H8938+606
2Ki 18:27 But the commander **r**, "Was it only to your H606
2Ki 20:14 distant land," Hezekiah **r**. "They came from H606
2Ki 20:19 LORD you have spoken is good," Hezekiah **r**. H606
1Ch 17:2 Nathan **r** to David, "Whatever you have in H606
1Ch 21:3 But Joab **r**, "May the LORD multiply his H606
1Ch 21:24 But King David **r** to Araunah, "No, I insist H606
2Ch 2:11 Hiram king of Tyre **r** by letter to Solomon H606
2Ch 10:7 *They* **r**, "If you will be kind to these H1819
2Ch 10:10 young men who had grown up with him **r**, H1819
2Ch 18:3 Jehoshaphat **r**, "I am as you are, and my H606
2Ch 18:7 not say such a thing," Jehoshaphat **r**. H606
2Ch 18:24 Micaiah **r**, "You will find out on the day you H606
2Ch 25:9 The man of God **r**, "The LORD can give you H606
2Ch 25:18 king of Israel **r** to Amaziah king of H8938+606
Ne 2:18 king had said to me. *They* **r**, "Let us start H606
Est 1:16 Then Memukan **r** in the presence of the H606
Est 5:4 it pleases the king," **r** Esther, "let the king H606
Est 5:7 Esther **r**, "My petition and my request is H6699
Est 8:7 King Xerxes **r** to Queen Esther and to H606
Job 1:9 "Does Job fear God for nothing?" Satan **r**. H6699
Job 2:4 Satan **r**. "A man will give all H6699
Job 2:10 *He* **r**, "You are talking like a foolish woman. H606
Job 4:1 Then Eliphaz the Temanite **r**: H6699
Job 6:1 Then Job **r**: H6699
Job 8:1 Then Bildad the Shuhite **r**: H6699
Job 9:1 Then Job **r**: H6699
Job 11:1 Then Zophar the Naamathite **r**: H6699
Job 12:1 Then Job **r**: H6699
Job 15:1 Then Eliphaz the Temanite **r**: H6699
Job 16:1 Then Job **r**: H6699
Job 18:1 Then Bildad the Shuhite **r**: H6699
Job 19:1 Then Job **r**: H6699
Job 20:1 Then Zophar the Naamathite **r**: H6699
Job 21:1 Then Job **r**: H6699
Job 22:1 Then Eliphaz the Temanite **r**: H6699
Job 23:1 Then Job **r**: H6699
Job 25:1 Then Bildad the Shuhite **r**: H6699
Job 26:1 Then Job **r**: H6699
Job 42:1 Then Job **r** to the LORD: H6699
Isa 36:12 But the commander **r**, "Was it only to your H606
Isa 39:3 Hezekiah **r**. "They came to me from H606
Isa 39:8 LORD you have spoken is good," Hezekiah **r**. H606
Jer 1:11 "I see the branch of an almond tree," *I* **r**. H606
Jer 28:5 the prophet Jeremiah **r** to the prophet H606
Jer 35:6 But *they* **r**, "We do not drink wine, because H606
Jer 36:18 Baruch **r**, "he dictated all these words to H606
Jer 37:17 Jeremiah **r**, "you will be delivered into the H606
Jer 38:20 you over," Jeremiah **r**. "Obey the LORD by H606
Jer 42:4 "I have heard you," **r** Jeremiah the prophet H606
Da 2:5 The king **r** to the astrologers, "This is A10558
Da 2:7 Once more *they* **r**, "Let the king tell his A10558
Da 2:27 Daniel **r**, "No wise man, enchanter A10558
Da 3:16 Meshach and Abednego **r** to him, "King A10558
Da 3:24 *They* **r**, "Certainly, Your A10558
Da 12:9 *He* **r**, "Go your way, Daniel, because the H606
Joel 2:19 The LORD **r** to them: "I am sending you H6699
Am 7:8 "A plumb line," *I* **r**. Then the Lord said, H606
Jnh 1:12 me into the sea," *he* **r**, "and it will become H606
Jnh 4:4 the LORD **r**, "Is it right for you to be angry H606
Hab 2:2 Then the LORD **r**: "Write down the H6699
Hag 2:13 the priests **r**, "it becomes defiled. H6699
Zec 4:5 know what these are?" "No, my lord," *I* **r**. H606
Zec 4:13 *He* **r**, "Do you not know what these are?" H606
Zec 5:6 *He* **r**, "It is a basket." And he H606
Zec 5:11 *He* **r**, "To the country of Babylonia to build H606
Mt 2:5 they **r**, "for this is what the prophet has *G3306*
Mt 3:15 Jesus **r**, "Let it be so now; it is proper for us *G646*
Mt 8:8 The centurion **r**, "Lord, I do not deserve to *G646*
Mt 8:20 Jesus **r**, "Foxes have dens and birds have *G3306*
Mt 8:26 *He* **r**, "You of little faith, why are you so *G3306*
Mt 9:28 I am able to do this?" "Yes, Lord," *they* **r**. *G3306*
Mt 11:4 Jesus **r**, "Go back and report to John what *G646*
Mt 12:48 He **r** to him, "Who is my mother, and who *G646*
Mt 13:11 He **r**, "Because the knowledge of the *G646*
Mt 13:28 enemy did this,' *he* **r**. "The servants asked *G5774*
Mt 13:51 Jesus asked. "Yes," *they* **r**. *G3306*
Mt 14:16 Jesus **r**, "They do not need to go away *G3306*
Mt 14:28 Peter **r**, "tell me to come to you on the *G646*
Mt 15:3 Jesus **r**, "And why do you break the *G646*
Mt 15:13 He **r**, "Every plant that my heavenly Father *G646*
Mt 15:26 He **r**, "It is not right to take the children's *G646*
Mt 15:34 "Seven," they **r**, "and a few small *G3306*
Mt 16:2 He **r**, "When evening comes, you say, 'It *G646*
Mt 16:14 They **r**, "Some say John the Baptist; others *G3306*
Mt 16:17 Jesus **r**, "Blessed are you, Simon son of *G646*
Mt 17:11 Jesus **r**, "To be sure, Elijah comes and will *G646*
Mt 17:17 generation," Jesus **r**, "how long shall I stay *G646*
Mt 17:20 He **r**, "Because you have so little faith *G3306*
Mt 17:25 he does," *he* **r**. When Peter came *G3306*
Mt 19:4 he **r**, "that at the beginning the Creator *G646*
Mt 19:8 Jesus **r**, "Moses permitted you to divorce *G3306*
Mt 19:11 Jesus **r**, "Not everyone can accept this *G3306*
Mt 19:17 Jesus **r**. "There is only One *G3306S*
Mt 19:18 Jesus **r**, " 'You shall not murder, you shall *G3306*
Mt 21:16 **r** Jesus, "have you never read, *G3306*
Mt 21:21 Jesus **r**, "Truly I tell you, if you have faith *G646*
Mt 21:24 Jesus **r**, "I will also ask you one question. *G646*
Mt 21:41 " *they* **r**, "and he will rent the vineyard to *G3306*
Mt 22:21 "Caesar's," *they* **r**. Then he said to them *G3306*
Mt 22:29 Jesus **r**, "You are in error because you do *G646*
Mt 22:37 Jesus **r**: " 'Love the Lord your God with all *G5774*
Mt 22:42 "The son of David," *they* **r**. *G3306*
Mt 25:9 they **r**, 'there may not be enough for *G646*
Mt 25:12 "But he **r**, 'Truly I tell you, I don't know you. *G646*
Mt 25:21 "His master **r**, 'Well done, good and *G5774*
Mt 25:23 "His master **r**, 'Well done, good and *G5774*
Mt 25:26 "His master **r**, 'You wicked, lazy servant! *G646*
Mt 26:18 He **r**, "Go into the city to a certain man *G3306*
Mt 26:23 Jesus **r**, "The one who has dipped his hand *G646*
Mt 26:33 Peter **r**, "Even if all fall away on account of *G646*
Mt 26:50 Jesus **r**, "Do what you came for, friend." *G3306*
Mt 26:64 have said so," Jesus **r**. "But I say to all of *G3306*
Mt 27:4 "What is that to us?" they **r**. "That's your *G3306*
Mt 27:11 "You have said so," Jesus **r**. *G5774*
Mk 1:38 Jesus **r**, "Let us go somewhere else—to *G3306*
Mk 5:9 name is Legion," *he* **r**, "for we are many." *G3306*
Mk 7:6 He **r**, "Isaiah was right when he *G3306*
Mk 7:28 she **r**, "even the dogs under the table eat *G646*
Mk 8:5 Jesus asked. "Seven," they **r**. *G3306*
Mk 8:19 pieces did you pick up?" "Twelve," *they* **r**. *G3306*
Mk 8:28 They **r**, "Some say John the Baptist; others *G3306*
Mk 9:12 Jesus **r**, "To be sure, Elijah does come *G5774*
Mk 9:19 generation," Jesus **r**, "how long shall I stay *G646*
Mk 9:29 *He* **r**, "This kind can come out only by *G3306*
Mk 10:3 "What did Moses command you?" he **r**. *G646*
Mk 10:5 that Moses wrote you this law," Jesus **r**. *G3306*
Mk 10:29 Jesus **r**, "no one who has left home or *G5774*
Mk 10:37 They **r**, "Let one of us sit at your right and *G3306*
Mk 11:29 Jesus **r**, "I will ask you one question *G3306*
Mk 12:16 whose inscription?" "Caesar's," they **r**. *G3306*
Mk 12:24 Jesus **r**, "Are you not in error because you *G5774*
Mk 12:32 teacher," the man **r**. "You are right in *G3306*
Mk 13:2 great buildings?" **r** Jesus. "Not one stone *G3306*
Mk 14:20 he **r**, "one who dips bread into the bowl *G3306*
Mk 15:2 "You have said so," Jesus **r**. *G646*
Lk 3:14 *He* **r**, "Don't extort money and don't *G3306*
Lk 7:22 So *he* **r** to the messengers, "Go back and *G3306*
Lk 7:43 Simon **r**, "I suppose the one who had the *G646*
Lk 8:21 He **r**, "My mother and brothers are those *G646*
Lk 8:30 he **r**, because many demons had gone *G3306*
Lk 9:13 *He* **r**, "You give them something to eat." *G3306*
Lk 9:19 They **r**, "Some say John the Baptist; others *G646*
Lk 9:41 Jesus **r**, "how long shall I stay with you *G646*
Lk 9:58 Jesus **r**, "Foxes have dens and birds have *G3306*
Lk 9:59 But he **r**, "Lord, first let me go and bury *G3306*
Lk 9:62 Jesus **r**, "No one who puts a hand to the *G3306*
Lk 10:18 *He* **r**, "I saw Satan fall like lightning from *G3306*
Lk 10:26 he **r**. "How do you read it? *G3306*
Lk 10:28 correctly," Jesus **r**. "Do this and you will *G3306*
Lk 10:37 The expert in the law **r**, "The one who *G3306*
Lk 11:28 He **r**, "Blessed rather are those who hear *G3306*
Lk 11:46 Jesus **r**, "And you experts in the law, woe *G3306*
Lk 12:14 Jesus **r**, "Man, who appointed me a judge *G3306*
Lk 13:8 the man **r**, 'leave it alone for one *G646*
Lk 13:32 *He* **r**, "Go tell that fox, 'I will keep on *G3306*
Lk 14:16 Jesus **r**: "A certain man was preparing a *G3306*
Lk 15:27 has come,' he **r**, 'and your father has *G3306*
Lk 16:6 of olive oil,' he **r**. "The manager told him, *G3306*
Lk 16:7 bushels of wheat,' he **r**. "He told him, *G3306*
Lk 16:25 "But Abraham **r**, 'Son, remember that in *G3306*
Lk 16:29 "Abraham **r**, 'They have Moses and the *G3306*
Lk 17:6 He **r**, "If you have faith as small as a *G3306*
Lk 17:20 would come, Jesus **r**, "The coming of the *G646*
Lk 17:37 He **r**, "Where there is a dead body, there *G3306*
Lk 18:27 Jesus **r**, "What is impossible with man is *G3306*
Lk 18:41 to do for you?" "Lord, I want to see," he **r**. *G3306*
Lk 19:17 his master **r**. 'Because you have *G3306*
Lk 19:22 "His master **r**, 'I will judge you by your *G3306*
Lk 19:26 "He **r**, 'I tell you that to everyone who has NDT
Lk 19:34 They **r**, "The Lord needs it." *G3306*
Lk 19:40 "I tell you," he **r**, "if they keep quiet, the *G646*
Lk 20:3 *He* **r**, "I will also ask you a question. *G646*
Lk 20:24 inscription are on it?" "Caesar's," they **r**. *G3306*
Lk 20:34 Jesus **r**, "The people of this age marry *G3306*
Lk 21:8 He **r**: "Watch out that you are not *G3306*
Lk 22:10 He **r**, "As you enter the city, a man *G3306*
Lk 22:33 But he **r**, "Lord, I am ready to go with you *G3306*
Lk 22:38 are two swords." "That's enough!" he **r**. *G3306*

Lk 22:58 "Man, I am not!" Peter r. G5774
Lk 22:60 Peter r, "Man, I don't know what you're G3306
Lk 22:70 Son of God?" He r, "You say that I am." G5774
Lk 23: 3 "You have said so," Jesus r. G646
Lk 24:19 of Nazareth," they r. "He was a prophet, G3306
Jn 1:23 John r in the words of Isaiah the prophet G5774
Jn 1:26 John r, "but among you stands one you do G646
Jn 1:39 " *he* r, "and you will see." So they G3306
Jn 2: 4 Jesus r. "My hour has not yet G3306
Jn 2:20 They r, "It has taken forty-six years to G3306
Jn 3: 3 Jesus r, "Very truly I tell you, no one can G646
Jn 3:27 To this John r, "A person can receive only G646
Jn 4:17 have no husband," she r. Jesus said to her, G646
Jn 4:21 "Woman," Jesus r, "believe me, a time is G3306
Jn 4:50 Jesus r, "your son will live." The G3306
Jn 5: 7 the invalid r, "I have no one to help me G646
Jn 5:11 But he r, "The man who made me well G646
Jn 6:70 Then Jesus r, "Have I not chosen you, the G646
Jn 7:12 Others r, "No, he deceives G3306
Jn 7:46 the way this man does," the guards r. G646
Jn 7:52 *They* r, "Are you from Galilee, too? Look G646
Jn 8:19 do not know me or my Father," Jesus r. G646
Jn 8:25 telling you from the beginning," Jesus r. G3306
Jn 8:34 Jesus r, "Very truly I tell you, everyone who G646
Jn 8:54 Jesus r, "If I glorify myself, my glory means G646
Jn 9:11 He r, "The man they call Jesus made some G646
Jn 9:15 my eyes," the man r, "and I washed, and G3306
Jn 9:17 The man r, "He is a prophet." G3306
Jn 9:25 *He* r, "Whether he is a sinner or not, I don't G646
Jn 9:34 To this *they* r, "You were steeped in sin at G646
Jn 10:33 any good work," they r, "but for blasphemy G646
Jn 11:12 His disciples r, "Lord, if he sleeps, he will G3306
Jn 11:27 *she* r, "I believe that you are the Messiah G3306
Jn 11:34 "Come and see, Lord," *they* r. G3306
Jn 12: 7 her alone," Jesus r. "It was intended that G3306
Jn 12:23 Jesus r, "The hour has come for the Son of G646
Jn 13: 7 Jesus r, "You do not realize now what I am G646
Jn 13: 9 Simon Peter r, "not just my feet but my G3306
Jn 13:36 Jesus r, "Where I am going, you cannot G646
Jn 14:23 Jesus r, "Anyone who loves me will obey G646
Jn 16:31 "Do you now believe?" Jesus r. G646
Jn 18: 5 of Nazareth," *they* r. "I am he," Jesus G646
Jn 18:17 she asked Peter. He r, "I am not." G3306
Jn 18:20 have spoken openly to the world," Jesus r. G646
Jn 18:23 Jesus r, "testify as to what is G646
Jn 18:30 *they* r, "we would not have handed him G646
Jn 18:35 Pilate r. "Your own people G646
Ac 2:38 Peter r, "Repent and be baptized, every G4639
Ac 4:19 But Peter and John r, "Which is right in G646
Ac 5:29 Peter and the other apostles r: "We must G646
Ac 7: 2 To this he r: "Brothers and fathers, listen G5774
Ac 9: 5 am Jesus, whom you are persecuting," he r. NDT
Ac 10:14 Peter r. "I have never eaten G3306
Ac 10:22 The *men* r, "We have come from G3306
Ac 11: 8 "*I* r, 'Surely not, Lord! Nothing impure G3306
Ac 16:31 They r, "Believe in the Lord Jesus, and G3306
Ac 19: 3 "John's baptism," they r. G3306
Ac 21:37 "Do you speak Greek?" he r. G5774
Ac 22: 8 whom you are persecuting,' *he* r. G3306
Ac 22:19 I r, 'these people know that I G3306
Ac 22:28 "But I was born a citizen," Paul r. G5774
Ac 23: 5 Paul r, "Brothers, I did not realize that he G5774
Ac 24:10 governor motioned for him to speak, Paul r: G646
Ac 25:22 this man myself." *He* r, "Tomorrow you G5774
Ac 26:15 whom you are persecuting,' the Lord r. G3306
Ac 26:25 not insane, most excellent Festus," Paul r. G5774
Ac 26:29 Paul r, "Short time or long—I pray to God NDT
Ac 28:21 They r, "We have not received any letters G3306

REPLIES (2) [REPLY]

Ne 6:17 r from Tobiah kept coming to them. H8895
Isa 21:12 The watchman r, "Morning is coming, but H606

REPLY (24) [REPLIED, REPLIES]

2Ki 18:36 remained silent and **said** nothing **in** r, H6699
Ezr 4:17 The king sent this r: To Rehum the A10601
Ezr 5: 5 to Darius and his **written** r be received. A10496
Ne 6: 3 so I sent messengers to them with *this* r: "I H606
Ne 6: 8 I sent him *this* r: "Nothing like what you are H606
Est 4:15 Then Esther sent *this* r to Mordecai: H606
Job 13:22 answer, or let me speak, and *you* r *to* me. H8740
Job 20: 3 my understanding inspires me *to* r. H6699
Job 32:16 now that they stand there with no r? H6699
Job 32:20 find relief; I must open my lips and r. H6699
Job 35: 4 "I *would like to* r *to* you and to your H8740+4863
Job 40: 4 unworthy—how *can I* r *to* you? I put my H8740
Ps 38:14 not hear, whose mouth can offer no r. H9350
Pr 15:23 finds joy in **giving an apt** r— H5101+7023
Isa 36:21 remained silent and **said** nothing **in** r, H6699
Jer 18:12 But *they will* r, 'It's no use. We will continue H606
Mt 22:46 No one could **say** a word **in** r, and from that G646
Mt 25:40 "The King *will* r, 'Truly I tell you, whatever G646
Mt 25:45 "*He will* r, 'Truly I tell you, whatever you G646
Mt 27:14 But Jesus **made** no r, not even to a single G646
Mk 7:29 he told her, "For such a r, you may go; G3364
Mk 15: 5 But Jesus still **made** no r, and Pilate was G646
Lk 10:30 *In* r Jesus said: "A man was going down G5696
Lk 13:27 "But *he will* r, 'I don't know you or where G3306

REPOINTING (1)

1Sa 13:21 forks and axes and for r goads. H5893

REPORT (46) [REPORTED, REPORTING, REPORTS]

Ge 37: 2 brought their father a bad r *about* them. H1804
Nu 13:32 the Israelites a **bad** r *about* the land they H1804
Nu 14:15 who have heard this r *about* you will say, H9051
Nu 14:36 him by spreading a **bad** r about it— H1804
Nu 14:37 spreading the bad r *about* the land were H1804
Nu 22: 8 "and *I will* r **back** *to* you *with* the answer H8740
Dt 1:22 bring back a r *about* the route we are H1821
Jos 14: 7 I brought him back a r according to my H1821
Jos 22:33 were glad to hear the r and praised God. H1821
1Sa 2:24 the r I hear spreading among the LORD's H9019
2Sa 1: 5 to the young man who **brought** him *the* r, H5583
2Sa 1:13 to the young man who **brought** him *the* r, H5583
2Sa 13:30 were on their way, the r came to David: H9019
2Sa 13:33 concerned about the r that all the king's H1821
1Ki 10: 6 "The r I heard in my own country about H1821
1Ki 10: 7 you have far exceeded the r I heard. H9019
2Ki 6:13 *The* r **came back**: "He is in H5583
2Ki 7: 9 go at once and r this *to* the royal palace." H5583
2Ki 19: 7 When he hears a certain r, I will make H9019
2Ki 19: 9 Sennacherib **received a** r that Tirhakah, H9048
1Ch 21: 2 Then r **back** to me so that I may know how H995
2Ch 9: 5 "The r I heard in my own country about H1821
2Ch 9: 6 you have far exceeded the r I heard. H9019
Ezr 5: 5 not stopped until a r could go to Darius A10302
Ezr 5: 7 The r they sent him read as follows: To A10601
Ne 6: 7 Now this r will get back to the king; so H1821
Est 2:23 And when the r was investigated and H1821
Job 38:35 *Do they* r to you, 'Here we H606
Ecc 10:20 a bird on the wing *may* r what you say. H5583
Isa 21: 6 a lookout and *have him* r what he sees. H5583
Isa 23: 5 they will be in anguish at the r *from* Tyre. H9051
Isa 37: 7 When he hears a certain r, I will make H9019
Isa 37: 9 Sennacherib **received a** r that Tirhakah, H9048
Jer 10:22 The r is coming—a great commotion H9019
Jer 36:16 "*We* **must** r all these words to the H5583+5583
Jer 37: 5 Jerusalem heard the r *about* them, H9051
Mt 2: 8 soon as you find him, r to me, so that I too G550
Mt 11: 4 "Go back and r to John what you hear and G550
Mt 28:14 If this r gets to the governor, we will satisfy G201
Lk 7:22 "Go back and r to John what you have seen G550
Jn 11:57 where Jesus was *should* r it so that they G3606
Ac 5:24 On hearing this r, the captain of the G3364
2Co 6: 8 glory and dishonor, **bad** r and good report G1556
2Co 6: 8 dishonor, bad report and **good** r; genuine, G2367
Gal 1:23 *They* only **heard** *the* r: "The man who AIT
1Th 1: 9 for *they* themselves r what kind of reception G550

REPORTED (56) [REPORT]

Ge 14:13 escaped came and r this to Abram the H5583
Ex 6: 9 Moses r this to the Israelites, but they did H1819
Ex 16:22 the community came and r this to Moses. H5583
Nu 13:26 There *they* r *to* them and to the H1821+8740
Nu 14:39 When Moses r this to all the Israelites H1819
Dt 1:25 they brought it down to us and r, "It H8740+1821
Jos 22:32 in Gilead and r *to* the Israelites. H8740+1821
Jdg 9:25 passed by, and *this* **was** r to Abimelek. H5583
Jdg 9:42 to the fields, and this *was* r to Abimelek. H5583
1Sa 11: 4 to Gibeah of Saul and r these terms to the H1819
1Sa 11: 9 messengers went and r this to the men of H5583
1Sa 17:31 David said was overheard and r to Saul, H5583
1Sa 25:12 When they arrived, *they* r every word. H5583
2Sa 7:17 Nathan r to David all the words of this H1819
2Sa 18:25 watchman called out to the king and r it. H5583
2Sa 24: 9 Joab r the number of the fighting men to H5989
1Ki 2:30 Benaiah r *to* the king, "This is how H8740+1821
1Ki 13:25 they went and r it in the city where H1819
1Ki 18:44 The seventh time the servant r, "A cloud as H606
1Ki 20:17 dispatched scouts, *who* r, "Men are H5583
2Ki 7:11 the news, and *it was* r within the palace. H5583
2Ki 7:15 messengers returned and r to the king. H5583
2Ki 9:18 The lookout r, "The messenger has H5583
2Ki 9:20 The lookout r, "He has reached them, but H5583
2Ki 17:26 *It was* r to the king of Assyria: "The people H606
2Ki 22: 9 went to the king and r *to* him: H8740+1821
1Ch 17:15 Nathan r to David all the words of this H1819
1Ch 21: 5 Joab r the number of the fighting men to H5989
2Ch 29:18 Then they went in to King Hezekiah and r H606
2Ch 34:16 the book to the king and r *to* him: H8740+1821
Ne 6: 6 "*It is* r among the nations—and Geshem H9048
Est 2:22 who in turn r it to the king, giving H606
Est 4: 9 Hathak went back and r to Esther what H5583
Est 4:12 When Esther's words *were* r to Mordecai, H5583
Est 9:11 the citadel of Susa *was* r to the king that H995
Jer 36:20 in the courtyard and r everything to him. H5583
Zec 1:11 And *they* r to the angel of the LORD who H6699
Mt 8:33 went into the town and r all this, including G550
Mt 28:11 went into the city and r to the chief priests G550
Mk 5:14 the pigs ran off and r this in the town and G550
Mk 6:30 around Jesus and r to him all they had G550
Mk 16:13 These returned and r it to the rest; but they G550
Lk 8:34 they ran off and r this in the town and G550
Lk 9:10 *they* r to Jesus what they had done. G1455
Lk 14:21 servant came back and r this to his master. G550
Ac 4:23 to their own people and r all that the chief G550
Ac 5:22 find them there. So they went back and r, G550
Ac 14:27 church together and r all that God had G334
Ac 15: 4 to whom *they* r everything God had done G334
Ac 16:38 The officers r this to the magistrates, and G550
Ac 21:19 greeted them and r in detail what God G2007
Ac 22:26 he went to the commander and r it. G550
Ac 23:22 tell anyone that *you have* r this to me." G1872
Ac 28:21 come from there *has* r or said anything G550
Ro 1: 8 because your faith *is being* r all over the G2859
1Co 5: 1 *It is* actually r that there is sexual G201

REPORTING (1) [REPORT]

Ne 6:19 they kept r to me his good deeds and then H606

REPORTS (11) [REPORT]

Ex 23: 1 "Do not spread false r. Do not help a H9051
Dt 2:25 They will hear r *of* you and will tremble H9051
Jos 9: 9 For we have heard r *of* him: all that he did H9053
Ne 6: 6 according to these r you are about to H1821
Pr 22:21 you bring back truthful r to those you serve? H609
Jer 6:24 We have heard r *about* them, and our H9053
Jer 50:43 king of Babylon has heard r *about* them, H9051
Da 11:44 But r from the east and the north will H9019
Mt 14: 1 Herod the tetrarch heard the r about Jesus, G198
Ac 9:13 "I have heard **many** *r* about this man and all AIT
Ac 21:24 there is no truth in these r about you, G2994

REPOSE (2) [REPOSES]

Dt 28:65 Among those nations *you will* **find** no r, no H8089
Isa 28:12 "This is the **place of** r"—but they would H5276

REPOSES (1) [REPOSE]

Pr 14:33 Wisdom r in the heart of the discerning H5663

REPRESENT (5) [REPRESENTATION, REPRESENTATIVE, REPRESENTATIVES, REPRESENTED, REPRESENTING, REPRESENTS]

Lev 24: 7 memorial portion to r the bread and to be H4200
Jer 40:10 will stay at Mizpah to r you before the H6641
Da 8:22 that was broken off r four kingdoms that will NDT
Gal 4:24 The women r two covenants. G1639
Heb 5: 1 is appointed to r the people in G5642

REPRESENTATION (1) [REPRESENT]

Heb 1: 3 God's glory and the **exact** r of his being, G5917

REPRESENTATIVE (2) [REPRESENT]

Ex 18:19 be the people's r before God and bring NDT
2Sa 15: 3 there is no r *of* the king to hear H4946+907

REPRESENTATIVES (1) [REPRESENT]

2Co 8:23 they are r of the churches and an honor to G693

REPRESENTED (2) [REPRESENT]

Nu 17: 8 Aaron's staff, which r the tribe of Levi, H4200
Jdg 18: 2 These men r all the Danites. H4946

REPRESENTING (2) [REPRESENT]

Ex 24: 4 twelve stone pillars r the twelve tribes of H4200
Nu 1:44 leaders of Israel, each one r his family. H4200

REPRESENTS (1) [REPRESENT]

Da 8:20 ram that you saw r the kings of Media and NDT

REPRIMAND (2) [REPRIMANDED]

Ru 2:15 among the sheaves and don't r her. H4007
Pr 29:15 A rod and a r impart wisdom, but a child H9350

REPRIMANDED (1) [REPRIMAND]

Jer 29:27 So why *have you* not r Jeremiah from H1721

REPROACH (20) [REPROACHED]

Jos 5: 9 have rolled away the r *of* Egypt from you." H3075
Ne 5: 9 God to avoid the r *of* our Gentile enemies H3075
Job 27: 6 my conscience *will* not r me as long as I H3070
Ps 44:13 You have made us a r to our neighbors H3075
Ps 44:16 at the taunts of *those who* r and revile me, H3070
Pr 18: 3 does contempt, and with shame comes r. H3075
Isa 51: 7 Do not fear the r *of* mere mortals or be H3075
Isa 54: 4 no more the r *of* your widowhood. H3075
Jer 15:15 think of how I suffer r for your sake. H3075
Jer 20: 8 has brought me insult and r all day long. H7841
Jer 24: 9 of the earth, a r and a byword, a curse H3075
Jer 29:18 of scorn and r, among all the H3075
Jer 42:18 a curse and an **object of** r; you will never H3075
Jer 44: 8 a curse and an **object of** r among all the H3075
Jer 44:12 of horror, a curse and an **object of** r. H3075
Jer 49:13 an object of horror and r; and all its towns H3075
Eze 5:14 you a ruin and a r among the nations H3075
Eze 5:15 You will be a r and a taunt, a warning H3075
Zep 3:18 festivals, which is a burden and r for you. H3075
1Ti 3: 2 Now the overseer is to be **above** r, faithful G455

REPROACHED (1) [REPROACH]

Job 19: 3 Ten times now *you have* r me H4007

REPROBATE, REPROBATES (KJV) DEPRAVED, FAIL, FAILED, REJECTED, UNFIT

REPROOF, REPROOFS, REPROVE, REPROVED, REPROVETH (KJV) ACCUSE, ACCUSES, ARRAIGNED, CHARGES, COMPLAINED, CONVICT, CORRECT, CORRECTION, DECIDE, EXPOSE, EXPOSED, PROVE, REBUKE, REBUKED, REBUKES, REBUKING, REPLY, REPRIMAND, VINDICATED

REPROVE (1)

1Ti 5:20 who are sinning *you are to* r before G1794

REPTILES (5)

1Ki 4:33 spoke about animals and birds, r and fish. H8254

Ac 10:12 as well as r and birds. G2260+3836+1178
Ac 11: 6 of the earth, wild beasts, r and birds. G2260
Ro 1:23 being and birds and animals and r. G2260
Jas 3: 7 r and sea creatures are being tamed and G2260

REPULSE (2) [REPULSIVE]
2Ki 18:24 How can you r one officer of the H8740+7156
Isa 36: 9 How then can you r one officer of H8740+7156

REPULSIVE (6) [REPULSE]
1Ki 15:13 she had made a r image for the worship H5145
1Ch 21: 6 the king's command was r to him. H9493
2Ch 15:16 she had made a r image for the worship H5145
Job 33:20 that their body finds food r and their soul H2299
Ps 88: 8 friends and have made me r to them. H9359
Jer 23:13 the prophets of Samaria I saw this r thing: H9524

REPUTATION (3)
Est 9: 4 his r spread throughout the provinces H9053
1Ti 3: 7 He must also have a good r with outsiders G3456
Rev 3: 1 you have a r of being alive, but G3950

REQUEST (32) [REQUESTED, REQUESTING, REQUESTS]
Ge 19:21 I will grant this r too; I will not H1821
Jdg 6:39 Let me make just one more r. Allow H1819
Jdg 8: 8 to Peniel and made the same r of them, H1819
Jdg 8:24 he said, "I do have one r, that each H8626+8629
Jdg 11:37 But grant me this one r," she said. "Give H1821
1Sa 25:35 your words and granted your r." H5951+7156
2Sa 12:20 and at his r they served him food H8626
2Sa 14:15 perhaps he will grant his servant's r. H1821
2Sa 14:22 the king has granted his servant's r." H1821
1Ki 2:16 Now I have one r to make of you H8626+8629
1Ki 2:20 "I have one small r to make of you," H8626+8629
1Ki 2:22 "Why do you r Abishag the Shunammite H8626
1Ki 2:22 You might as well r the kingdom for him— H8626
1Ki 2:23 does not pay with his life for this r! H1819+1821
1Ch 4:10 free from pain." And God granted his r. H8626
Est 5: 3 What is your r? Even up to half H1336
Est 5: 6 And what is your r? Even up to half the H1336
Est 5: 7 replied, "My petition and my r is this: H1336
Est 5: 8 king to grant my petition and fulfill my r, H1336
Est 7: 2 What is your r? Even up to half the H1336
Est 7: 3 And spare my people—this is my r. H1336
Est 9:12 What is your r? It will also be H1336
Job 6: 8 that I might have my r, that God would H8629
Ps 21: 2 have not withheld the r of his lips. H830
Da 2:49 at Daniel's r the king appointed A10114
Da 9:20 making my r to the LORD my God H9382
Mt 14: 9 he ordered that her r be granted NDT
Mt 15:28 Your r is granted." And her G2527
Mk 6:25 the girl hurried in to the king with the r: G160
Jn 12:21 was from Bethsaida in Galilee, with a r. G2263
Ac 23:21 now, waiting for your consent to their r." AIT
Ac 24: 4 I would r that you be kind enough to hear G4151

REQUESTED (5) [REQUEST]
Ex 12:31 worship the LORD as you have r. H1819
Ezr 6: 9 olive oil, as r by the priests in Jerusalem A10397
Jer 42: 4 pray to the LORD your God as you have r; H1821
Mk 15: 6 to release a prisoner whom the people r. G4148
Ac 25: 3 They r Festus, as a favor to them, to have G4151

REQUESTING (1) [REQUEST]
Ac 16:39 from the prison, r them to leave the city. G2263

REQUESTS (6) [REQUEST]
Ne 2: 8 God was on me, the king granted my r. H5989
Ps 5: 3 the morning I lay my r before you and wait NDT
Ps 20: 5 May the LORD grant all your r. H5399
Da 9:18 We do not make r of you because we are H9384
Eph 6:18 occasions with all kinds of prayers and r. G1255
Php 4: 6 with thanksgiving, present your r to God. G161

REQUIRE (8) [REQUIRED, REQUIREMENT, REQUIREMENTS, REQUIRES, REQUIRING]
Ex 5: 8 But r them to make the same number of H8492
Dt 15: 2 They shall not r payment from anyone H5601
Dt 15: 3 You may r payment from a foreigner, but H5601
2Ki 12:15 They did not r an accounting from those to H3108
Ps 40: 6 offerings and sin offerings you did not r. H8626
Eze 18:16 anyone or r a pledge for a loan. H2471+2478
Eze 20:40 There I will r your offerings and your H2011
Mic 6: 8 And what does the LORD r of you? To H2011

REQUIRED (27) [REQUIRE]
Ge 26: 5 obeyed me and did everything I r of him, H5466
Ge 50: 3 for that was the time r for embalming. AIT
Ex 5:13 "Complete the work r of you for each day AIT
Ex 5:19 the number of bricks r of you for each day." AIT
Ex 22:11 owner is to accept this, and no restitution is r. AIT
Ex 22:13 and shall not be r to pay for the torn AIT
Lev 23:37 drink offerings r for each day. H1821
Lev 27:16 set according to the amount of seed r for it— AIT
Nu 7: 7 oxen to the Gershonites, as their work r, H7023
Nu 7: 8 oxen to the Merarites, as their work r. H7023
Nu 31:21 "This is what is r by the law that the LORD H2978
Jos 16:10 of Ephraim but are r to do forced labor. H2118
1Ki 8:31 neighbor and is r to take an H5957+460+928
2Ch 6:22 neighbor and is r to take an H5957+460+928
2Ch 24: 6 "Why haven't you r the Levites to H2011+6584
2Ch 24: 9 the servant of God had r of Israel in the H6584
2Ch 24:12 carried out the work r for the temple of the H6275
Ezr 3: 4 of Tabernacles with the r number of burnt H1821
Ne 12:44 storerooms the portions r by the Law for the AIT
Eze 45:16 of the land will be r to give this H2118+448
Lk 2:22 purification rites r by the Law of Moses, G2848
Lk 2:27 do for him what the custom of the Law r, G2848
Lk 2:39 done everything r by the Law of the Lord G2848
Lk 3:13 "Don't collect any more than you are r to," G1411
Ac 15: 5 be circumcised and r to keep the law of G4133
Ro 2:14 do by nature things r by the law, they are a AIT
1Co 4: 2 Now it is r that those who have been given G2426

REQUIREMENT (4) [REQUIRE]
Nu 19: 2 "This is a r of the law that the LORD has H2978
2Ch 8:13 according to the daily r for offerings H1821
2Ch 8:14 the priests according to each day's r. H1821
Ro 8: 4 in order that the righteous r of the law G1468

REQUIREMENTS (13) [REQUIRE]
Lev 18:30 Keep my r and do not follow any of the H5466
Dt 11: 1 Love the LORD your God and keep his r, H5466
2Ki 23:24 he did to fulfill the r of the law written in H1821
1Ch 16:37 there regularly, according to each day's r. H1821
2Ch 13:11 are observing the r of the LORD our God. H5466
Jer 5: 4 the way of the LORD, the r of their God. H5477
Jer 5: 5 the way of the LORD, the r of their God." H5477
Jer 8: 7 my people do not know the r of the LORD. H5477
Zec 3: 7 walk in obedience to me and keep my r, H5466
Mal 3:14 by carrying out his r and going about like H5466
Ac 15:28 you with anything beyond the following r: G2055
Ro 2:15 They show that the r of the law are written G2240
Ro 2:26 who are not circumcised keep the law's r, G1468

REQUIRES (11) [REQUIRE]
Lev 8:35 seven days and do what the LORD r, H5466
Nu 7: 5 them to the Levites as each man's work r." H7023
1Ki 2: 3 observe what the LORD your God r H5466
2Ki 17:26 not know what the god of that country r. H5477
2Ki 17:26 the people do not know what he r. H5477
2Ki 17:27 the people what the god of the land r." H5477
Jn 6:28 "What must we do to do the works God r?" AIT
Ro 3:27 The law that r works? No, AIT
Ro 3:27 No, because of the law that r faith. AIT
Heb 7: 5 Now the law r the G1953+2400+2848
Heb 9:22 the law r that nearly everything be G2848

REQUIRING (1) [REQUIRE]
Lev 22:16 so bring upon them guilt r payment. H873

REQUITE, REQUITED, REQUITING (KJV) CONDEMNING, PAID BACK, PAY, PAYS BACK, REPAY, REPAYING, RESTORE, SHOW

REREWARD (KJV) REAR, REAR GUARD

RESCUE (87) [RESCUED, RESCUES, RESCUING]
Ge 37:21 he tried to r him from their hands. H5911
Ge 37:22 Reuben said this to r him from them and H5911
Ex 2:17 got up and came to their r and watered H3828
Ex 3: 8 have come down to r them from the hand H5911
Dt 22:27 screamed, there was no one to r her. H4635
Dt 25:11 of them comes to r her husband from his H5911
Dt 28:29 robbed, with no one to r you. H4635
Dt 28:31 to your enemies, and no one will r them. H3828
Jdg 9:17 risked his life to r you from the hand H5911
Jdg 10:15 you think best, but please r us now." H5911
Jdg 18:28 There was no one to r them because they H5911
1Sa 7: 8 that he may r us from the hand of the H3828
1Sa 11: 3 if no one comes to r us, we will H4635
1Sa 12:21 you no good, nor can they r you, because H5911
1Sa 17:37 paw of the bear will r me from the hand H5911
1Sa 30: 8 them and succeed in the r. H5911+5911
2Sa 3:18 my servant David I will r my people Israel H3828
2Sa 10:11 then you are to come to my r; but if the H3802
2Sa 10:11 strong for you, then I will come to r you. H3828
2Sa 21:17 Abishai son of Zeruiah came to David's r; H6468
1Ch 19:12 me, then you are to r me; but if the H9591
1Ch 19:12 are too strong for you, then I will r you. H3828
2Ch 32:17 the other lands did not r their people from H5911
2Ch 32:17 god of Hezekiah will not r his people from H5911
Job 5:19 From six calamities he will r you; in seven H5911
Job 6:23 r me from the clutches of the ruthless'? H7009
Job 10: 7 that no one can r me from your hand H5911
Ps 7: 2 rip me to pieces with no one to r me. H5911
Ps 17:13 with your sword r me from the wicked. H7117
Ps 22: 8 in the LORD," they say, "let the LORD r him. H7117
Ps 22:21 R me from the mouth of the lions; save H3828
Ps 25:20 Guard my life and r me; do not let me be H5911
Ps 31: 2 ear to me, come quickly to my r; be my H5911
Ps 34:22 The LORD will r his servants; no one who H7009
Ps 35:10 You r the poor from those too strong for H5911
Ps 35:17 R me from their ravages, my precious life H8740
Ps 43: 1 R me from those who are deceitful and H7117
Ps 44:26 r us because of your unfailing love. H7009
Ps 50:22 tear you to pieces, with no one to r you: H5911
Ps 69:14 R me from the mire, do not let me sink H5911
Ps 69:18 Come near and r me; deliver me because H1457
Ps 71: 2 your righteousness, r me and deliver me H5911
Ps 71:11 him and seize him, for no one will r him." H5911
Ps 72:14 He will r them from oppression and H1457
Ps 82: 4 R the weak and the needy; deliver them H7117
Ps 91:14 says the LORD, "I will r him; I will protect H7117
Ps 140: 1 R me, LORD, from evildoers; protect me H2740
Ps 142: 6 r me from those who pursue me H5911
Ps 143: 9 R me from my enemies, LORD, for I hide H5911
Ps 144: 7 deliver me and r me from the mighty H5911
Ps 144:11 r me from the hands of foreigners whose H5911
Pr 19:19 must pay the penalty; r them, and you will H5911
Pr 24:11 R those being led away to death; hold H5911
Isa 5:29 their prey and carry it off with no one to r. H5911
Isa 19:20 a savior and defender, and he will r them. H5911
Isa 31: 5 he will 'pass over' it and will r it. H4880
Isa 42:22 plunder, with no one to r them; they have H5911
Isa 46: 2 together; unable to r the burden, they H4880
Isa 46: 4 I will sustain you and I will r you. H4880
Isa 50: 2 Do I lack the strength to r you? By a mere H5911
Jer 1: 8 I am with you and will r you," declares H5911
Jer 1:19 I am with you and will r you," declares H5911
Jer 15:20 I am with you to r and save you, H3828
Jer 21:12 r from the hand of the oppressor the one H5911
Jer 22: 3 R from the hand of the oppressor the one H5911
Jer 39:17 But I will r you on that day, declares the H5911
Eze 34:10 I will r my flock from their mouths, and it H5911
Eze 34:12 I will r them from all the places where H5911
Eze 34:27 of their yoke and r them from the hands of H5911
Da 3:15 what god will be able to r you from my A10706
Da 6:14 was determined to r Daniel and made A10706
Da 6:16 May your God, whom you serve continually, r A10706
Da 6:20 been able to r you from the lions?" A10706
Da 8: 4 and none could r from its power. H5911
Da 8: 7 none could r the ram from its power. H5911
Hos 5:14 I will carry them off, with no one to r them. H5911
Mic 5: 8 mangles as it goes, and no one can r. H5911
Zep 3:19 oppressed you. I will r the lame; I will H3828
Zec 11: 6 and I will not r anyone from their hands." H5911
Mt 27:43 Let God r him now if he wants him, for he G4861
Lk 1:74 to r us from the hand of our enemies, and G4861
Ac 7:25 that God was using him to r them, G1443+5401
Ac 26:17 I will r you from your own people and G1975
Ro 7:24 Who will r me from this body that is G4861
Gal 1: 4 our sins to r us from the present G1975
2Ti 4:18 The Lord will r me from every evil attack G4861
2Pe 2: 9 the Lord knows how to r the godly from G4861

RESCUED (40) [RESCUE]
Ex 2:19 "An Egyptian r us from the shepherds. H5911
Ex 5:23 you have not r your people at all." H5911+5911
Ex 18:10 who r you from the hand of the Egyptians H5911
Ex 18:10 who r the people from the hand of H5911
Nu 10: 9 LORD your God and r from your enemies. H3828
Jos 22:31 Now you have r the Israelites from the H5911
Jdg 6: 9 I r you from the hand of the Egyptians H5911
Jdg 8:34 who had r them from the hands of all H5911
1Sa 11: 9 the sun is hot tomorrow, you will be r. H9591
1Sa 11:13 this day the LORD has r Israel. H6913+9591
1Sa 14:45 So the men r Jonathan, and he was not H7009
1Sa 17:35 struck it and r the sheep from its mouth. H5911
1Sa 17:37 The LORD who r me from the paw of the H5911
2Sa 19: 9 he is the one who r us from the hand of H4880
2Sa 22:18 He r me from my powerful enemy, from H5911
2Sa 22:20 he r me because he delighted in me. H2740
2Sa 22:49 my foes; from a violent man you r me. H5911
2Ki 18:34 Have they r Samaria from my hand H5911
Ne 9:27 who r them from the hand of their H3828
Job 29:12 because I r the poor who cried for help H4880
Ps 18:17 He r me from my powerful enemy, from H5911
Ps 18:19 he r me because he delighted in me. H2740
Ps 18:48 my foes; from a violent man you r me. H5911
Ps 81: 7 In your distress you called and I r you, H2740
Ps 107:20 healed them; he r them from the grave. H4880
Pr 11: 8 The righteous person is r from trouble H2740
Isa 35:10 those the LORD has r will return. H7009
Isa 36:18 Have they r Samaria from my hand H5911
Isa 49:24 warriors, or captives be r from the fierce? H4880
Isa 51:11 Those the LORD has r will return. They will H7009
Da 3:28 has sent his angel and r his servants! A10706
Da 6:27 He has r Daniel from the power of the A10706
Am 3:12 will the Israelites living in Samaria be r, H5911
Mic 4:10 You will go to Babylon; there you will be r. H5911
Ac 7:10 r him from all his troubles. He gave G1975
Ac 12:11 has sent his angel and r me from Herod's G1975
Ac 23:27 I came with my troops and r him, for I G1975
Col 1:13 For he has r us from the dominion of G4861
2Ti 3:11 Yet the Lord r me from all of them. G4861
2Pe 2: 7 if he r Lot, a righteous man, who was G4861

RESCUES (7) [RESCUE]
1Sa 14:39 As surely as the LORD who r Israel lives H4635
Ps 55:18 He r me unharmed from the battle waged H7009
Pr 12: 6 the speech of the upright r them. H5911
Jer 20:13 He r the life of the needy from the hands H5911
Da 6:27 He r and he saves; he performs signs A10706
Am 3:12 "As a shepherd r from the lion's mouth H5911
1Th 1:10 who r us from the coming wrath. G4861

RESCUING (1) [RESCUE]
Ex 18: 9 done for Israel in r them from the hand of H5911

RESEMBLED (3) [RESEMBLING]
Rev 9: 7 of gold, and their faces r human faces. G6055
Rev 9:17 heads of the horses r the heads of lions, G6055
Rev 13: 2 The beast I saw r a leopard, but G1639+3927

RESEMBLING (1) [RESEMBLED]
Heb 7: 3 end of life, r the Son of God, he G2400+926

R

RESEN (1)
Ge 10:12 **R**, which is between Nineveh and H8271

RESENT (2) [RESENTFUL, RESENTMENT]
Pr 3:11 LORD's discipline, and *do* not **r** his rebuke, H7762
Pr 15:12 Mockers **r** correction, so they avoid H4202+170

RESENTFUL (1) [RESENT]
2Ti 2:24 be kind to everyone, able to teach, **not r**. *G452*

RESENTMENT (3) [RESENT]
Jdg 8: 3 At this, their **r** against him subsided H8120
Job 5: 2 **R** kills a fool, and envy slays the simple. H4089
Job 36:13 "The godless in heart harbor **r**; even when H678

RESERVE (4) [RESERVED]
Ge 41:36 food should be **held in r** for the country, H7214
Dt 32:34 "*Have* I not **kept** this **in r** and sealed it in H4022
1Ki 19:18 Yet *I* **r** seven thousand in Israel—all whose H8636
Job 38:23 which *I* **r** for times of trouble, for days of H3104

RESERVED (6) [RESERVE]
Ge 27:36 "Haven't *you* **r** any blessing for me? H724
Isa 26:11 let the **fire** *r for* your enemies consume them. AIT
Ro 11: 4 "*I have* **r** for myself seven thousand who *G2901*
2Pe 2:17 Blackest darkness *is* **r** for them. *G5498*
2Pe 3: 7 present heavens and earth are **r** for fire, *G2564*
Jude 13 blackest darkness *has been* **r** forever. *G5498*

RESERVOIR (1) [RESERVOIRS]
Isa 22:11 You built a **r** between the two walls for H5225

RESERVOIRS (2) [RESERVOIR]
Ex 7:19 over the ponds and all the **r**—and H5224+4784
Ecc 2: 6 I made **r** to water groves of H1391+4784

RESETTLE (2) [SETTLE]
1Ch 9: 2 Now the first *to* **r** on their own property in H3782
Eze 36:33 all your sins, *I will* **r** your towns, and the H3782

RESETTLED (2) [SETTLE]
2Ki 17:26 you deported and **r** in the towns of H3782
Eze 38:12 my hand against the **r** ruins and the H3782

RESHEPH (1)
1Ch 7:25 Rephah was his son, **R** his son, Telah his H8405

RESIDE (6) [RESIDED, RESIDENCE, RESIDENT, RESIDENTS, RESIDES, RESIDING]
Ge 17: 8 where you now **r as a foreigner**, I will give H4472
Ge 21:23 where *you now* **r as a foreigner** the same H1591
Ge 28: 4 the land where you now **r as a foreigner**, H4472
Lev 25:23 **r** in my land **as** foreigners and **strangers**. H9369
Dt 28:43 The **foreigners** who **r** among you will rise H1731
Job 38:19 And where does darkness **r**? H5226

RESIDED (5) [RESIDE]
Ex 6: 4 of Canaan, **where** they **r** as foreigners. H4472
Dt 23: 7 because *you* **r** as foreigners in their H2118
2Sa 4: 3 fled to Gittaim and *have* **r** there as H2118
2Ch 30:25 from Israel and also those *who* **r** in Judah. H3782
Ps 105:23 Jacob **r as a foreigner** in the land of Ham. H1591

RESIDENCE (5) [RESIDE]
2Sa 5: 9 David then **took up r** in the fortress and H3782
1Ch 11: 7 David then **took up r** in the fortress, and H3782
Ne 2: 8 the city wall and for the **r** I will occupy?" H1074
Est 2:16 Xerxes in the royal **r** in the tenth month, H1074
Da 4:30 great Babylon I have built as the royal **r**, A10103

RESIDENT (2) [RESIDE]
Ex 12:45 a **temporary r** or a hired worker may H9369
Lev 25: 6 worker and **temporary r** who live among H9369

RESIDENTS (5) [RESIDE]
Lev 25:40 hired workers or **temporary r** among you; H9369
Lev 25:45 buy some of the **temporary r** living among H9369
Ne 3:13 repaired by Hanun and the **r** *of* Zanoah. H3782
Ne 7: 3 Also appoint **r** *of* Jerusalem as guards H3782
Ac 2: 9 Medes and Elamites; **r** of Mesopotamia *G2997*

RESIDES (5) [RESIDE]
Lev 19:33 " 'When a foreigner **r** among you in your H1591
Job 18:15 Fire **r** in his tent; burning sulfur is H8905
Job 41:22 Strength **r** in its neck; dismay goes before H4328
Ecc 7: 9 your spirit, for anger **r** in the lap of fools. H5663
Eze 47:23 In whatever tribe a foreigner **r**, there you H1591

RESIDING (34) [RESIDE]
Ex 12:48 "A foreigner **r** among you who wants to H1591
Ex 12:49 to the foreigner **r** among you. H1591
Ex 20:10 animals, nor any foreigner *r* **in** your towns. AIT
Lev 16:29 native-born or a foreigner **r** among you— H1591
Lev 17: 8 any foreigner **r** among them who offers H1591
Lev 17:10 any foreigner **r** among them who eats H1591
Lev 17:12 may any foreigner **r** among you eat blood." H1591
Lev 17:13 any foreigner **r** among you who hunts H1591
Lev 18:26 the foreigners **r** among you must not H1591
Lev 19:34 The foreigner **r** among you must be H1591
Lev 20: 2 any foreigner **r** in Israel who sacrifices H1591
Lev 22:18 an Israelite or a foreigner **r** in Israel— NDT
Lev 23:22 poor and for the **foreigner r** *among* you. H1731
Lev 25:47 " 'If a foreigner **r** among you becomes rich H9369
Nu 9:14 " 'A foreigner **r** among you is also to H1591
Nu 15:15 you and for the foreigner **r** among you; H1591
Nu 15:16 to you and to the foreigner **r** among you. H1591
Nu 15:26 the foreigners **r** among them will be H1591
Nu 15:29 Israelite or a foreigner **r** among you. H1591
Nu 19:10 for the foreigners **r** among them. H1591
Nu 35:15 for foreigners **r** among them, H9369
Dt 1:16 an Israelite and a **foreigner r** *among* you. H1731
Dt 5:14 animals, nor any **foreigner r** in your towns H1731
Dt 10:18 loves the **foreigner r** *among* you H1731
Dt 14:21 it to the foreigner **r** in any of your towns, NDT
Dt 24:14 Israelite or a **foreigner r** in one of your H1731
Dt 26:11 Levites and the **foreigners r** among you H1731
Dt 31:12 the **foreigners r** in your towns—so H1731
Jos 20: 9 any foreigner **r** among them who killed H1591
1Ch 22: 2 to assemble the foreigners **r in** Israel, H928
2Ch 2:17 a census of all the **foreigners r** in Israel, H1731
Eze 14: 7 any foreigner **r** in Israel separate H1591
Eze 47:22 the foreigners **r** among you and who H1591
1Jn 3:15 that no murderer has eternal life **r** in him. *G3531*

RESIDUE (KJV) LEFT, OTHER, REMAINS, REMNANT, REST, SURVIVING, SURVIVORS

RESIN (3)
Ge 2:12 is good; **aromatic r** and onyx are also there.) H978
Ex 30:34 fragrant spices—**gum r**, onycha and H5753
Nu 11: 7 was like coriander seed and looked like **r**. H978

RESIST (14) [RESISTED]
Jdg 2:14 were no longer able to **r**. H6641+4200+7156
2Ki 10: 4 "If two kings *could* not **r** him H6641+4200+7156
2Ch 13: 7 not strong enough to **r** them. H7156
2Ch 13: 8 now you plan to **r** the kingdom of the H2616
Pr 28: 4 the wicked, but those who heed it **r** them. H1741
Isa 1:20 if *you* **r** and rebel, you will be H4412
Da 11:15 forces of the South will be powerless *to* **r**; H6641
Da 11:32 who know their God *will* firmly **r** him. H6913
Mt 5:39 But I tell you, *do* not **r** an evil person. *G468*
Lk 21:15 adversaries will be able *to* **r** or contradict. *G468*
Ac 7:51 You always **r** the Holy Spirit! *G528*
Ro 9:19 For who *is able to* **r** his will?" *G468*
Jas 4: 7 **R** the devil, and he will flee from *G468*
1Pe 5: 9 **R** him, standing firm in the faith, because *G468*

RESISTED (3) [RESIST]
Job 9: 4 Who *has* **r** him and come out unscathed? H7996
Da 10:13 kingdom **r** me twenty-one H6641+4200+5584
Heb 12: 4 *you have* not yet **r** to the point of shedding *G510*

RESOLUTE (1) [RESOLVE]
2Sa 16:21 of everyone with you *will be* **more r**." H2616

RESOLUTELY (1) [RESOLVE]
Lk 9:51 Jesus **r** set out for Jerusalem. *G3836+4725+5114*

RESOLVE (1) [RESOLUTE, RESOLUTELY, RESOLVED]
Mal 2: 2 and if *you do* not **r** to honor H8492+6584+4213

RESOLVED (4) [RESOLVE]
2Ch 20: 3 Jehoshaphat **r** to inquire of the H5989+7156
Da 1: 8 But Daniel **r** not to defile H8492+6584+4213
Mal 2: 2 you *have* not **r** to honor H8492+6584+4213
1Co 2: 2 For *I* **r** to know nothing while I was with *G3212*

RESORT (1) [RESORTED]
Nu 24: 1 *he did* not **r to** divination as H2143+4200+7925

RESORTED (1) [RESORT]
Jos 9: 4 they **r** to a ruse: They went as a delegation H6913

RESOUND (9) [RESOUNDED, RESOUNDING, RESOUNDS]
1Ch 16:32 *Let* the sea **r**, and all that is in it; let the H8306
Ps 96:11 earth be glad; *let* the sea **r**, and all that is H8306
Ps 98: 7 *Let* the sea **r**, and everything in it, the H8306
Ps 118:15 of joy and victory **r** in the tents of the H7754
Jer 6: 7 Violence and destruction **r** in her; her H9048
Jer 25:31 The tumult *will* **r** to the ends of the earth H995
Jer 49:21 tremble; their cry *will* **r** to the Red Sea. H9048
Jer 50:46 tremble; its cry *will* **r** among the nations. H9048
Jer 51:55 great waters; the roar of their voices *will* **r**. H5989

RESOUNDED (3) [RESOUND]
2Sa 22:14 from heaven; the voice of the Most High **r**. H5989
Ps 18:13 from heaven; the voice of the Most High **r**. H5989
Ps 77:17 the heavens **r** *with* thunder; your H5989

RESOUNDING (3) [RESOUND]
2Ch 30:21 LORD every day with **r** instruments H6437
Ps 150: 5 of cymbals, praise him with **r** cymbals. H9558
1Co 13: 1 I am only a **r** gong or a clanging cymbal. *G2490*

RESOUNDS (2) [RESOUND]
1Ki 1:45 gone up cheering, and the city **r** with it. H2169
Job 37: 4 When his voice **r**, he holds nothing H9048

RESOURCES (1)
1Ch 29: 2 With all my **r** I have provided for the H3946

RESPECT (32) [RESPECTABLE, RESPECTED, RESPECTFUL, RESPECTS]
Ge 41:40 Only with **r** to the throne will I be greater NDT
Lev 19: 3 " 'Each of *you must* **r** your mother and H3707
Lev 19:32 **show r** for the elderly and revere your God. H2075
Lev 22: 2 his sons *to* **treat with r** the sacred H5692
Dt 28:50 nation without **r** for the old or pity H5951+7156
2Ki 1:13 "please **have r for** my life and H3700+928+6524
2Ki 1:14 But now **have r for** my life!" H3700+928+6524
2Ki 3:14 if I *did* not **have r for** the presence of H5951
Est 1:20 all the women *will* **r** their husbands H5989+3702
Isa 5:12 of the LORD, no **r** *for* the work of his hands. H8011
La 5:12 their hands; elders **are shown** no **r**. H2075+7156
Mal 1: 6 where is the **r** *due* me?" says the LORD H4616
Mt 21:37 '*They will* **r** my son,' he said *G1956*
Mt 23: 7 they love to be **greeted with r** in the *G833*
Mk 12: 6 him last of all, saying, '*They will* **r** my son. *G1956*
Mk 12:38 robes and be **greeted with r** in the *G833*
Lk 20:13 whom I love; perhaps *they will* **r** him. *G1956*
Lk 20:46 love to be **greeted with r** in the *G833*
Ro 13: 7 then revenue; if **r**, then respect; if honor, *G5832*
Ro 13: 7 if respect, then **r**; if honor, then honor. *G5832*
Eph 4:15 to become *in* **every r** the mature *G3836+4246*
Eph 5:33 himself, and the wife must **r** her husband. *G5828*
Eph 6: 5 obey your earthly masters with **r** and fear *G5832*
1Th 4:12 daily life may **win the r** of outsiders and *G2361*
1Ti 3: 4 must do so in a manner worthy of full **r**. *G4949*
1Ti 3: 8 deacons are to be **worthy of r**, sincere, *G4948*
1Ti 3:11 the women are to be **worthy of r**, not *G4948*
1Ti 6: 1 consider their masters worthy *of* full **r**, *G5507*
Titus 2: 2 to be temperate, **worthy of r** *G4948*
1Pe 2:17 **Show proper r** to everyone, love the family *G5506*
1Pe 3: 7 treat them with **r** as the weaker *G5507*
1Pe 3:15 But do this with gentleness and **r**, *G5832*

RESPECTABLE (1) [RESPECT]
1Ti 3: 2 self-controlled, **r**, hospitable, able to *G3177*

RESPECTED (10) [RESPECT]
Dt 1:13 understanding and **r** men from each of H3359
Dt 1:15 wise and **r** men, and appointed H3359
1Sa 9: 6 man of God; he *is* **highly r**, and everything H3877
1Sa 22:14 bodyguard and **highly r** in your household H3877
Pr 31:23 Her husband **is r** at the city gate, where H3359
Isa 32: 5 noble nor the scoundrel be **highly r**. H8777
Isa 33: 8 its witnesses are despised, no one *is* **r**. H3108
Ac 10:22 man, *who is* **r** by all the Jewish people. *G3455*
Ac 22:12 of the law and **highly r** by all the Jews *G3455*
Heb 12: 9 who disciplined us and *we* **r** them for it. *G1956*

RESPECTER (KJV) FAVORITISM

RESPECTFUL (1) [RESPECT]
Lk 11:43 the synagogues and **r greetings** in the *G833*

RESPECTS (2) [RESPECT]
Pr 13:13 but *whoever* **r** a command is rewarded. H3707
Ac 25:13 arrived at Caesarea *to* **pay** *their* **r** to Festus. *G832*

RESPITE (1)
Job 20:20 "Surely he will have no **r** from his craving H8929

RESPOND (22) [RESPONDED, RESPONDING, RESPONDS, RESPONSE, RESPONSIVE]
1Sa 4:20 But *she did* not **r** or pay any attention. H6699
1Sa 14:41 my son Jonathan, **r with** Urim, but if the H2035
1Sa 14:41 of Israel are at fault, **r with** Thummim." H2035
2Ch 32:25 proud and he *did* not **r** to the kindness H8740
Est 1:18 the queen's conduct *will* **r** to all the king's H606
Ps 102:17 *He will* **r** to the prayer of the destitute; he H7155
Pr 13: 1 a mocker *does* not **r** *to* rebukes. H9048
Pr 13: 8 the poor cannot **r to** threatening H9048
Pr 29:19 though they understand, they will not **r**. H5101
Isa 14:10 They *will* all **r**, they will say to you, "You H6699
Isa 19:22 and *he will* **r** to their **pleas** and heal them. H6983
Jer 2:30 your people; *they did* not **r to** correction. H4374
Jer 17:23 would not listen or **r to** discipline. H4374
Jer 32:33 they would not listen or **r to** discipline. H4374
Hos 2:15 There *she will* **r** as in the days of her H6700
Hos 2:21 "In that day *I will* **r**," declares the LORD— H6699
Hos 2:21 the LORD—"*I will* **r** *to* the skies, and they H6699
Hos 2:21 to the skies, and they *will* **r** *to* the earth; H6699
Hos 2:22 the earth *will* **r** *to* the grain, the new H6699
Hos 2:22 the olive oil, and they *will* **r** *to* Jezreel. H6699
Ac 16:14 opened her heart *to* **r** to Paul's message. *G4668*
Rev 16: 7 And I heard the altar **r**: "Yes, Lord God *G3306*

RESPONDED (11) [RESPOND]
Ex 19: 8 The people all **r** together, "We will do H6699
Ex 24: 3 words and laws, they **r** *with* one voice H6699
Ex 24: 7 *They* **r**, "We will do everything the LORD H606
Jdg 7:14 His friend **r**, "This can be nothing other H6699
Jdg 20:28 The LORD **r**, "Go, for tomorrow I will give H606
Ezr 10:12 The whole assembly **r** with a loud voice H6699
Ne 8: 6 all the people lifted their hands and **r**, H6699
Job 9:16 Even if I summoned him and *he* **r**, I do H6699
Jer 7:28 obeyed the LORD its God or **r** to correction. H4374
Lk 20:39 Some of the teachers of the law **r**, "Well *G646*
Jn 2:18 The Jews then **r** to him, "What sign can *G646*

RESPONDING (1) [RESPOND]
Ne 12:24 one section **r to** the other, as H4200+6645

RESPONDS (1) [RESPOND]
Job 33:13 to him that *he* **r** *to* no one's words? H6699

RESPONSE (9) [RESPOND]
1Ki 18:26 But there was no **r**; no one answered. H7754
1Ki 18:29 But there was no **r**, no one answered, no H7754

2Ki 4:31 boy's face, but there was no sound or r. H7993
1Ch 29: 9 rejoiced at the willing r of their leaders, H5605
Job 19: 7 I get no r; though I call for help, there is H6699
Da 10:12 were heard, and I have come in r to them. H928
Ro 8:31 shall we say in r to these things? G4639
Gal 1:16 my immediate r was not to consult any NDT
Gal 2: 2 I went in r to a revelation and, meeting G2848

RESPONSIBILITIES (4) [RESPONSIBLE]

Nu 8:26 how you are to assign the r of the Levites." H5466
1Ch 23:32 carried out their r for the tent of meeting, H5466
2Ch 31:16 according to their r and their divisions. H5466
2Ch 31:17 according to their r and their divisions. H5466

RESPONSIBILITY (12) [RESPONSIBLE]

Nu 4:27 to them as their r all they are to carry. H5466
Nu 18: 1 bear the r for offenses connected with the H6411
Nu 18: 1 bear the r for offenses connected with the H6411
Nu 18:23 the r for any offenses they commit against H6411
1Ch 9:26 entrusted with the r for the rooms and H6584
1Ch 9:31 entrusted with the r for baking the offering H6584
1Ch 15:22 that was his r because he was skillful at it. NDT
Ne 10:32 "We assume the r for carrying out H6641+6584
Ne 10:35 "We also assume r for bringing to the house NDT
Mt 27: 4 they replied. "That's your r." G3972
Mt 27:24 this man's blood," he said. "It is your r!" G3972
Ac 6: 3 We will turn this r over to them G5970

RESPONSIBLE (44) [RESPONSIBILITIES, RESPONSIBILITY]

Ge 16: 5 "You are r for the wrong I am suffering. H6584
Ge 39:22 he was made r for all that was done H6913
Ge 43: 9 you can hold me personally r for H1335+4946+3338
Ex 21:28 the owner of the bull will not be held r. H5929
Lev 5: 1 learned about, they will be held r. H5951+6411
Lev 5:17 they are guilty and will be held r. H5951+6411
Lev 7:18 who eats any of it will be held r. H5951+6411
Lev 17:16 themselves, they will be held r. H5951+6411
Lev 19: 8 eats it will be held r because they H5951+6411
Lev 20:17 his sister and will be held r. H5951+6411
Lev 20:19 both of you would be held r. H5951+6411
Lev 20:20 They will be held r; they will die H5951+2628
Lev 24:15 who curses their God will be held r; H5951+2628
Nu 1:53 The Levites are to be r for the care of the H9068
Nu 3:25 were r for the care of the tabernacle H5466
Nu 3:28 The Kohathites were r for the care of the H5466
Nu 3:31 They were r for the care of the ark, the H5466
Nu 3:32 over those who were r for the care of the H5466
Nu 3:38 They were r for the care of the sanctuary H5466
Nu 7: 9 the holy things, for which they were r. H6275
Nu 14:37 these men who were r for spreading the bad AIT
Nu 18: 3 They are to be r to you and are to H9068+5466
Nu 18: 4 are to join you and be r for the care of the H9068
Nu 18: 5 "You are to be r for the care of the H9068
Nu 31:30 who are r for the care of the LORD's H9068
Nu 31:47 who were r for the care of the LORD's H9068
Jos 2:19 be on their own heads; we will not be r. H5929
1Sa 22:22 I am r for the death of your whole H6015+928
1Sa 23:20 we will be r for giving him into your H4200
1Ch 9:13 r for ministering in the house of God. H4856
1Ch 9:19 were r for guarding the thresholds H4856+6275
1Ch 9:19 ancestors had been r for guarding the H6584
1Ch 9:33 because they were r for the work day and H6584
1Ch 16:42 Jeduthun were r for the sounding of NDT
1Ch 26:30 were r in Israel west of the Jordan for all H7213
Ezr 7:20 God that you are r to supply, A10484+10378
Ne 11:22 the musicians r for the service of H4200+5584
Ne 13:10 musicians r for the service had gone H6913
Ne 13:13 They were made r for distributing the H6584
Jnh 1: 7 out who is r for this calamity." H928+8611+4200
Jnh 1: 8 who is r for making all this H4200+928+889
Lk 11:50 generation will be held r for the blood of G1699
Lk 11:51 this generation will be held r for it all. G1699
1Co 7:24 each person, as r to God, should remain G4123

RESPONSIVE (2) [RESPOND]

2Ki 22:19 your heart was r and you humbled H8216
2Ch 34:27 your heart was r and you humbled H8216

REST (270) [RESTED, RESTING, RESTLESS, RESTS, SABBATH-REST]

Ge 8: 4 month the ark came to r on the mountains H5663
Ge 14:10 fell into them and the r fled to the hills. H8636
Ge 18: 4 all wash your feet and r under this tree. H9128
Ge 30:36 continued to tend the r of Laban's flocks. H3855
Ge 30:40 made the r face the streaked and H7366s
Ge 42:16 the r of you will be kept in prison AIT
Ge 42:19 while the r of you go and take grain back AIT
Ge 44: 9 and the r of us will become my lord's slaves." AIT
Ge 44:10 the r of you will be free from blame. AIT
Ge 44:17 The r of you, go back to your AIT
Ge 47:30 when I r with my fathers, carry me out H8886
Ge 49:26 Let all these r on the head of Joseph, on H2118
Ex 4: 7 it was restored, like the r of his flesh. NDT
Ex 16:23 'Tomorrow is to be a day of sabbath r, H8702
Ex 23:12 so that your ox and your donkey may r H5663
Ex 29:12 pour out the r of it at the base of the H3972
Ex 31:15 seventh day is a day of sabbath r, H8701+8702
Ex 33:14 will go with you, and I will give you r." H5663
Ex 34:21 on the seventh day you shall r; even H8697
Ex 34:21 plowing season and harvest you must r. H8697
Ex 35: 2 a day of sabbath r to the LORD. H8701+8702
Lev 2: 3 The r of the grain offering belongs to H3855
Lev 2:10 The r of the grain offering belongs to H3855
Lev 4: 7 The r of the bull's blood he shall pour out H3972
Lev 4:12 all the r of the bull—he must take AIT
Lev 4:18 The r of the blood he shall pour out at the H3972
Lev 4:25 pour out the r of the blood at the base NDT
Lev 4:30 pour out the r of the blood at the H3972
Lev 4:34 pour out the r of the blood at the H3972
Lev 5: 9 the r of the blood must be drained out at H8636
Lev 5:13 The r of the offering will belong to the priest NDT
Lev 6:16 Aaron and his sons shall eat the r of it, but H3855
Lev 8:15 He poured out the r of the blood at the base NDT
Lev 8:32 Then burn up the r of the meat and the H3855
Lev 9: 9 the r of the blood he poured out at the base NDT
Lev 14: 9 their eyebrows and the r of their hair. H3972
Lev 14:18 The r of the oil in his palm the priest shall H3855
Lev 14:29 The r of the oil in his palm the priest shall H3855
Lev 16:31 It is a day of sabbath r, and you H8701+8702
Lev 23: 3 seventh day is a day of sabbath r, H8701+8702
Lev 23:24 month you are to have a day of sabbath r, H8702
Lev 23:32 It is a day of sabbath r for you, and H8701+8702
Lev 23:39 the first day is a day of sabbath r, and the H8702
Lev 23:39 the eighth day also is a day of sabbath r. H8702
Lev 25: 4 land is to have a year of sabbath r, H8701+8702
Lev 25: 5 The land is to have a year of r. H8702
Lev 26:34 then the land will r and enjoy its sabbaths H8697
Lev 26:35 the land will have the r it did not have H8697
Nu 10:12 until the cloud came to r in the Desert of H8905
Nu 10:33 those three days to find them a place to r. H4957
Nu 10:36 Whenever it came to r, he said, "Return H5663
Nu 16: 9 separated you from the r of the Israelite NDT
Nu 18:31 households may eat the r of it anywhere, NDT
Nu 23:24 like a lion that does not r till it devours its H8886
Nu 31:27 in the battle and the r of the community. H3972
Dt 3:13 The r of Gilead and also all of Bashan, the H3856
Dt 3:20 the LORD gives r to your fellow H5663
Dt 5:14 that your male and female servants may r, H5663
Dt 12:10 and he will give you r from all your H5663
Dt 19:20 The r of the people will hear of this and H8636
Dt 25:19 the LORD your God gives you r from all the H5663
Dt 31:16 "You are going to r with your ancestors H8886
Dt 33:12 "Let the beloved of the LORD r secure in H8905
Dt 33:16 Let all these r on the head of Joseph, on H995
Jos 1:13 LORD your God will give you r by giving H5663
Jos 1:15 the LORD gives them r, as he has done H5663
Jos 7:25 after they had stoned the r, they H4392s
Jos 11:23 Then the land had r from war. H9200
Jos 13:27 Zaphon with the r of the realm of Sihon H3856
Jos 14: 3 the Levites an inheritance among the r, H4392s
Jos 14:15 Then the land had r from war. H9200
Jos 17: 2 allotment was for the r of the people of H3855
Jos 17: 6 belonged to the r of the descendants of H3855
Jos 21: 5 The r of Kohath's descendants were H3855
Jos 21:20 The r of the Kohathite clans of the Levites H3855
Jos 21:26 were given to the r of the Kohathite clans. H3855
Jos 21:34 Merarite clans (the r of the Levites) were H3855
Jos 21:40 who were the r of the Levites H3855
Jos 21:44 The LORD gave them r on every side, just H5663
Jos 22: 4 LORD your God has given them r as he H5663
Jos 23: 1 the LORD had given Israel r from all H5663
Jdg 7: 6 All the r got down on their knees to drink. H3856
Jdg 7: 8 So Gideon sent the r of the Israelites H3972s
Ru 1: 9 each of you will find r in the home of H4957
Ru 2: 7 till now, except for a short r in the shelter." H3782
Ru 3:18 For the man will not r until the matter is H9200
1Sa 13: 2 The r of the men he sent back to their H3856
1Sa 15:15 your God, but we totally destroyed the r." H3463
1Sa 18:29 he remained his enemy the r of his days. H3972
1Sa 18:30 more success than the r of Saul's officers, H3972
2Sa 4: 5 while he was taking his noonday r. H8886+5435
2Sa 7: 1 the LORD had given him r from all his H5663
2Sa 7:11 I will also give you r from all your H5663
2Sa 7:12 days are over and you r with your H8886
2Sa 10:10 He put the r of the men under the H3856
2Sa 12:28 Now muster the r of the troops and H3856
2Sa 13:27 him Amnon and the r of the king's sons. H3972
1Ki 1:21 my lord the king is laid to r with his H8886
1Ki 2:33 May the guilt of their blood r on the head H8740
1Ki 5: 4 LORD my God has given me r on every side H5663
1Ki 8:56 who has given r to his people Israel just H4957
1Ki 12:23 Benjamin, and to the r of the people, H3856
1Ki 20:15 Then he assembled the r of the Israelites H3972
1Ki 20:30 The r of them escaped to the city of Aphek, H3855
1Ki 22:46 He rid the land of the r of the male shrine H3856
2Ki 13: 7 had destroyed the r and made them H4392s
2Ki 25:11 along with the r of the populace and H3856
2Ki 25:29 clothes and for the r of his life ate H3972+3427
1Ch 6:31 of the LORD after the ark came to r there. H4955
1Ch 6:61 The r of Kohath's descendants were H3855
1Ch 6:70 to the r of the Kohathite clans. H3855
1Ch 6:77 The Merarites (the r of the Levites H3855
1Ch 11: 8 while Joab restored the r of the city. H8637
1Ch 12:38 All the r of the Israelites were also of one H8642
1Ch 13: 2 far and wide to the r of our people H8636
1Ch 16:41 Jeduthun and the r of those chosen and H8637
1Ch 19:11 He put the r of the men under the H3856
1Ch 22: 9 a son who will be a man of peace and r, H4957
1Ch 22: 9 and I will give him r from all his enemies H5663
1Ch 22:18 And has he not granted you r on every H5663
1Ch 23:25 has granted r to his people and has come H5663
1Ch 24:20 As for the r of the descendants of Levi H3855
1Ch 28: 2 build a house as a place of r for the ark of H4957
2Ch 14: 6 those years, for the LORD gave him r. H5663
2Ch 14: 7 him and he has given us r on every side H5663
2Ch 15:15 So the LORD gave them r on every side. H5663
2Ch 20:30 his God had given him r on every side. H5663
2Ch 24:14 they brought the r of the money to the H8637
Ezr 2:70 the r of the Israelites settled in their H3972
Ezr 3: 8 son of Jozadak and the r of the people H8637
Ezr 4: 3 Joshua and the r of the heads of the H8637
Ezr 4: 7 Tabeel and the r of his associates wrote a H8637
Ezr 4: 9 together with the r of their associates A10692
Ezr 4:17 the secretary and the r of their associates A10692
Ezr 6:16 the Levites and the r of the exiles A10692
Ezr 7:18 seems best with the r of the silver and A10692
Ne 4:14 the officials and the r of the people H3856
Ne 4:19 the officials and the r of the people, "The H3856
Ne 6: 1 the Arab and the r of our enemies that I H3856
Ne 6:14 how she and the r of the prophets have H3856
Ne 7:72 total given by the r of the people was H8642
Ne 7:73 of the people and the r of the Israelites, H3972
Ne 9:28 "But as soon as they were at r, they again H5663
Ne 10:28 "The r of the people—priests, Levites H8637
Ne 11: 1 The r of the people cast lots to bring one H8637
Ne 11:20 The r of the Israelites, with the priests H8637
Est 9:12 they done in the r of the king's provinces H8637
Job 3:13 in peace; I would be asleep and at r H5663
Job 3:17 from turmoil, and there the weary are at r. H5663
Job 3:26 no quietness; I have no r, but only turmoil." H5663
Job 11:18 look about you and take your r in safety. H8886
Job 16:18 my blood; may my cry never be laid to r! H5226
Job 24:23 He may let them r in a feeling of security H9128
Job 30:17 my bones; my gnawing pains never r. H8886
Job 36:11 they will spend the r of their days in NDT
Ps 16: 9 rejoices; my body also will r secure, H8905
Ps 22: 2 do not answer, by night, but I find no r. H1875
Ps 55: 6 I would fly away and be at r. H8905
Ps 62: 1 Truly my soul finds r in God; my salvation H1875
Ps 62: 5 my soul, find r in God; my hope comes H1957
Ps 80:17 Let your hand r on the man at your right H2118
Ps 90:17 May the favor of the Lord our God r on us H2118
Ps 91: 1 of the Most High will r in the shadow of H4328
Ps 95:11 in my anger, 'They shall never enter my r. H4957
Ps 116: 7 Return to your r, my soul, for the LORD has H4955
Pr 4:16 For they cannot r until they do evil; they H3822
Pr 6: 3 exhaustion—and give your neighbor no r! H8104
Pr 6:10 a little folding of the hands to r— H8886
Pr 21:16 of prudence comes to r in the company H5663
Pr 24:33 a little folding of the hands to r— H8886
Pr 26: 2 an undeserved curse does not come to r. H995
Ecc 2:23 even at night their minds do not r. H8886
Ecc 6: 5 it has more r than does that man— H5739
Ecc 10: 4 calmness can lay great offenses to r. H5663
SS 1: 7 your flock and where you r your sheep at H8069
Isa 11: 2 The Spirit of the LORD will r on him—the H5663
Isa 13:20 there no shepherds will r their flocks. H8069
Isa 14: 7 All the lands are at r and at peace; they H5663
Isa 23:12 to Cyprus; even there you will find no r." H5663
Isa 25:10 hand of the LORD will r on this mountain; H5663
Isa 28:12 is the resting place, let the weary r"; H5663
Isa 30:15 "In repentance and r is your salvation, in H5739
Isa 32:18 secure homes, in undisturbed places of r. H4957
Isa 34:14 down and find for themselves places of r. H4955
Isa 38:10 death and be robbed of the r of my years?" H3856
Isa 44:17 From the r he makes a god, his idol; he H8642
Isa 57: 2 they find r as they lie in death. H5663
Isa 57:20 which cannot r, whose waves cast up H9200
Isa 62: 6 who call on the LORD, give yourselves no r, H1954
Isa 62: 7 give him no r till he establishes H1954
Isa 63:14 they were given r by the Spirit of the LORD. H5663
Jer 6:16 and you will find r for your souls. H5273
Jer 31: 2 wilderness; I will come to give r to Israel." H8089
Jer 33:12 be pastures for shepherds to r their flocks. H8069
Jer 39: 9 gone over to him, and the r of the people. H3856
Jer 41:10 captives of all the r of the people who H8642
Jer 45: 3 I am worn out with groaning and find no r. H4957
Jer 47: 6 sword of the LORD, how long till you r? H9200
Jer 47: 7 But how can it r when the LORD has H9200
Jer 48:11 "Moab has been at r from youth, like wine H8631
Jer 50:34 cause so that he may bring r to their land, H8089
Jer 52:15 along with the r of the craftsmen and H3856
Jer 52:16 left behind the r of the poorest people of H4946
Jer 52:33 clothes and for the r of his life ate H3972+3427
La 2:18 give yourself no relief, your eyes no r. H1957
La 5: 5 at our heels; we are weary and find no r. H5663
Eze 34:18 you also trample the r of your pasture with H3856
Eze 34:18 Must you also muddy the r with your feet? H3855
Eze 36: 3 possession of the r of the nations and the H8642
Eze 36: 4 ridiculed by the r of the nations around H8642
Eze 36: 5 I have spoken against the r of the nations, H8642
Eze 44:30 that a blessing may r on your household H5663
Eze 48:23 "As for the r of the tribes: Benjamin will H3856
Da 2:18 executed with the r of the wise men of A10692
Da 12:13 You will r, and then at the end of the days H5663
Mic 5: 3 the r of his brothers return to join the H3856
Na 3:18 slumber; your nobles lie down to r. H8905
Hab 2: 5 betrays him; he is arrogant and never at r. H5657
Zec 1:11 found the whole world at r and in peace." H3782
Zec 6: 8 country have given my Spirit r in the land H5663
Zec 7: 7 towns were at r and prosperous, H3782
Zec 9: 1 Hadrak and will come to r on Damascus— H4957
Zec 12:14 all the r of the clans and their wives. H8636
Zec 14: 2 the r of the people will not be taken H3856

Mt 10:13 is deserving, let your peace r on it; if it is G2262
Mt 11:28 weary and burdened, and I will give you r. G399
Mt 11:29 in heart, and you will find r for your souls. G398
Mt 12:43 arid places seeking r and does not find it. G398
Mt 22: 6 The r seized his servants, mistreated them G3370
Mt 27:49 The r said, "Now leave him alone. Let's G3370
Mk 6:31 yourselves to a quiet place and get some r." G399
Mk 16:13 These returned and reported it to the r; but G3370
Lk 10: 6 is there, your peace will r on them; if not, G2058
Lk 11:24 arid places seeking r and does not find it. G398
Lk 12:26 little thing, why do you worry about the r? G3370
Jn 11:16 said to the r of the disciples, "Let us also G5209
Ac 2: 3 separated and came to r on each of them. G2767
Ac 2:26 rejoices; my body also will r in hope, G2942
Ac 5: 2 brought the r and put it at the G3538+5516
Ac 15:17 that the r of mankind may seek the Lord G2905
Ac 16:17 She followed Paul and the r of us, shouting AIT
Ac 21:18 next day Paul and the r of us went to see AIT
Ac 27:44 The r were to get there on planks or on G3370
Ac 28: 9 the r of the sick on the island came and G3370
1Co 2: 5 that your faith might not r on human G1639
1Co 7:12 To the r I say this (I, not the Lord): G3370
2Co 7: 5 Macedonia, we had no r, but we were G457
2Co 12: 9 so that Christ's power may r on me. G2172
Eph 2: 3 Like the r, we were by nature deserving of G3370
Php 4: 3 with Clement and the r of my co-workers, G3370
1Th 4:13 you do not grieve like the r of mankind, G3370
Heb 3:11 in my anger, 'They shall never enter my r. G2923
Heb 3:18 would never enter his r if not to those who G2923
Heb 4: 1 the promise of entering his r still stands, G2923
Heb 4: 3 Now we who have believed enter that r G2923
Heb 4: 3 in my anger, 'They shall never enter my r. G2923
Heb 4: 5 he says, "They shall never enter my r." G2923
Heb 4: 6 since it still remains for some to enter that r, NDT
Heb 4: 8 For if Joshua had given them r, God G2924
Heb 4:10 who enters God's r also rests from their G2923
Heb 4:11 make every effort to enter that r, so that G2923
1Pe 4: 2 they do not live the r of their earthly lives G2145
1Jn 3:19 truth and how we set our hearts at r in his G4275
Rev 2:24 Now I say to the r of you in Thyatira, to G3370
Rev 9:20 The r of mankind who were not killed by G3370
Rev 12:17 wage war against the r of her offspring— G3370
Rev 14:11 There will be no r day or night for those G398
Rev 14:13 says the Spirit, "they will r from their labor G399
Rev 19:21 The r were killed with the sword coming G3370
Rev 20: 5 The r of the dead did not come to life until G3370

RESTED (53) [REST]

Ge 2: 2 on the seventh day he r from all his work. H8697
Ge 2: 3 because on it he r from all the work of H8697
Ex 16:30 So the people r on the seventh day. H8697
Ex 20:11 is in them, but he r on the seventh day. H5663
Ex 31:17 the seventh day he r and was refreshed H8697
Nu 11:25 When the Spirit r on them, they H5663
Nu 11:26 Yet the Spirit also r on them, and they H5663
1Ki 2:10 Then David r with his ancestors and was H8886
1Ki 7: 3 above the beams that r on the columns— H6584
1Ki 7:25 The Sea r on top of them, and their H6584
1Ki 11:21 heard that David r with his ancestors and H8886
1Ki 11:43 Then he r with his ancestors and was H8886
1Ki 14:20 years and then r with his ancestors. H8886
1Ki 14:31 And Rehoboam r with his ancestors and H8886
1Ki 15: 8 And Abijah r with his ancestors and was H8886
1Ki 15:24 Then Asa r with his ancestors and was H8886
1Ki 16: 6 Baasha r with his ancestors and was H8886
1Ki 16:28 Omri r with his ancestors and was buried H8886
1Ki 22:40 Ahab r with his ancestors. And Ahaziah H8886
1Ki 22:50 Then Jehoshaphat r with his ancestors H8886
2Ki 8:24 Jehoram r with his ancestors and was H8886
2Ki 10:35 Jehu r with his ancestors and was buried H8886
2Ki 13: 9 Jehoahaz r with his ancestors and was H8886
2Ki 13:13 Jehoash r with his ancestors, and H8886
2Ki 14:16 Jehoash r with his ancestors and was H8886
2Ki 14:22 Judah after Amaziah r with his ancestors. H8886
2Ki 14:29 Jeroboam r with his ancestors, the kings of H8886
2Ki 15: 7 Azariah r with his ancestors and was H8886
2Ki 15:22 Menahem r with his ancestors. H8886
2Ki 15:38 Jotham r with his ancestors and was H8886
2Ki 16:20 Ahaz r with his ancestors and was buried H8886
2Ki 20:21 Hezekiah r with his ancestors. H8886
2Ki 21:18 Manasseh r with his ancestors and was H8886
2Ki 24: 6 Jehoiakim r with his ancestors. H8886
2Ch 4: 4 The Sea r on top of them, and their H6584
2Ch 9:31 Then he r with his ancestors and was H8886
2Ch 12:16 Rehoboam r with his ancestors and was H8886
2Ch 14: 1 And Abijah r with his ancestors and was H8886
2Ch 16:13 reign Asa died and r with his ancestors. H8886
2Ch 21: 1 Then Jehoshaphat r with his ancestors H8886
2Ch 26: 2 Judah after Amaziah r with his ancestors. H8886
2Ch 26:23 Uzziah r with his ancestors and was buried H8886
2Ch 27: 9 Jotham r with his ancestors and was H8886
2Ch 28:27 Ahaz r with his ancestors and was buried H8886
2Ch 32:33 Hezekiah r with his ancestors and was H8886
2Ch 33:20 Manasseh r with his ancestors and was H8886
2Ch 36:21 all the time of its desolation it r, until the H8697
Ezr 8:32 in Jerusalem, where we r three days. H3782
Est 9:17 the fourteenth they r and made it a day of H5663
Est 9:18 the fifteenth they r and made it a day of H5663
Am 5:19 his house and r his hand on the wall H6164
Lk 23:56 But they r on the Sabbath in obedience to G2483
Heb 4: 4 the seventh day God r from all his works." G2924

RESTING (24) [REST]

Ge 28:12 in which he saw a stairway r on the earth, H5893
Ge 49:15 how good is his r place and how pleasant H4957
Dt 12: 9 not yet reached the r place and the H4957
Dt 28:65 no r place for the sole of your foot. H4955
1Ki 7:30 had a basin r on four supports, H4946+9393
2Ki 2:15 "The spirit of Elijah is r on Elisha. H5663
2Ki 9:16 because Joram was r there and Ahaziah H8886
2Ch 6:41 come to your r place, you and the ark H5665
Ps 132: 8 come to your r place, you and the ark H4957
Ps 132:14 "This is my r place for ever and ever; here H4957
SS 1:13 a sachet of myrrh r between my breasts. H4328
Isa 11:10 and his r place will be glorious. H4957
Isa 22:16 chiseling your r place in the rock? H5438
Isa 28:12 "This is the r place, let the weary H4957
Isa 65:10 the Valley of Achor a r place for herds, H8070
Isa 66: 1 build for me? Where will my r place be? H4957
Jer 50: 6 hill and forgot their own r place. H8070
La 1: 3 among the nations; she finds no r place. H4955
Eze 25: 5 Ammon into a r place for sheep. H5271
Eze 32:27 heads and their shields r on their bones— H2118
Mic 2:10 For this is not your r place, because it is H4957
Mt 26:45 said to them, "Are you still sleeping and r? G399
Mk 14:41 said to them, "Are you still sleeping and r? G399
Ac 7:49 Or where will my r place be? G2923

RESTITUTION (14)

Ex 22: 3 who steals must certainly make r, H8966+8966
Ex 22: 5 the offender must make r from the best of H8966
Ex 22: 6 who started the fire must make r. H8966+8966
Ex 22:11 is to accept this, and no r is required. H8966
Ex 22:12 neighbor, r must be made to the owner. H8966
Ex 22:14 is not present, they must make r. H8966+8966
Lev 5:16 They must make r for what they have H8966
Lev 6: 5 They must make r in full, add a fifth of the H8966
Lev 22:14 mistake must make r to the priest for the H5989
Lev 24:18 life of someone's animal must make r— H8966
Lev 24:21 Whoever kills an animal must make r, but H8966
Nu 5: 7 They must make full r for the H8740+928+8031
Nu 5: 8 to whom r can be made for the wrong, H8740
Nu 5: 8 the r belongs to the LORD and must H8740+871

RESTLESS (5) [REST]

Ge 4:12 You will be a r wanderer on the earth." H5675
Ge 4:14 I will be a r wanderer on the earth H5675
Ge 27:40 But when you grow r, you will throw his H8113
Jer 49:23 are disheartened, troubled like the r sea. H1796
Jas 3: 8 tame the tongue. It is a r evil, full of deadly G190

RESTORATION (2) [RESTORE]

2Ch 24:27 the record of the r of the temple of God H3572
2Co 13:11 Strive for full r, encourage one another G2936

RESTORE (62) [RESTORATION, RESTORED, RESTORER, RESTORES, RESTORING]

Ge 40:13 up your head and r you to your position, H8740
Dt 30: 3 the LORD your God will r your fortunes H8740
2Sa 8: 3 when he went to r his monument at the H8740
2Sa 9: 7 I will r to you all the land that belonged H8740
2Sa 16: 3 'Today the Israelites will r to me my H8740
2Sa 16:12 upon my misery and r to me his covenant H8740
2Ch 24: 4 Joash decided to r the temple of the LORD H2542
2Ch 24:12 carpenters to r the LORD's temple, H2542
Ne 4: 2 Will they r their wall? Will they H6441
Job 8: 6 your behalf and r you to your prosperous H8966
Job 33:26 he will r them to full well-being. H8740
Ps 51:12 R to me the joy of your salvation and H8740
Ps 60: 1 upon us; you have been angry—now r us! H8740
Ps 69: 4 I am forced to r what I did not steal H8740
Ps 71:20 bitter, you will r my life again; from H2649
Ps 80: 3 R us, O God; make your face shine on us H8740
Ps 80: 7 R us, God Almighty; make your face shine H8740
Ps 80:19 R us, LORD God Almighty; make your face H8740
Ps 85: 4 R us again, God our Savior, and put away H8740
Ps 126: 4 R our fortunes, LORD, like streams in the H8740
Isa 1:26 I will r your leaders as in days of old, your H8740
Isa 44:26 and of their ruins, 'I will r them,' H7756
Isa 49: 6 to be my servant to r the tribes of Jacob H7756
Isa 49: 8 to r the land and to reassign its desolate H7756
Isa 57:18 I will guide them and r comfort to Israel's H8966
Isa 61: 4 the ancient ruins and r the places long H7756
Jer 15:19 I will r you that you may serve me H8740
Jer 16:15 For I will r them to the land I gave their H8740
Jer 27:22 bring them back and r them to this place. H8740
Jer 30: 3 from captivity and r them to the land I H8740
Jer 30:17 But I will r you to health and heal your H6590
Jer 30:18 " 'I will r the fortunes of Jacob's tents and H8740
Jer 31:18 R me, and I will return, because you are H8740
Jer 32:44 the Negev, because I will r their fortunes H8740
Jer 33:11 For I will r the fortunes of the land as they H8740
Jer 33:26 For I will r their fortunes and have H8740
Jer 42:12 on you and r you to your land. H8740
Jer 48:47 "Yet I will r the fortunes of Moab in days H8740
Jer 49: 6 I will r the fortunes of the Ammonites," H8740
Jer 49:39 "Yet I will r the fortunes of Elam in days to H8740
La 1:16 near to comfort me, no one to r my spirit. H8740
La 5:21 R us to yourself, LORD, that we may return H8740
Eze 16:53 I will r the fortunes of Sodom and her H8740
Eze 39:25 I will now r the fortunes of Jacob and will H8740
Da 9:25 the word goes out to r and rebuild H8740
Hos 6: 2 on the third day he will r us, that we may H7756
Hos 6:11 "Whenever I would r the fortunes of my H8740
Joel 3: 1 when I r the fortunes of Judah and H8740
Am 9:11 "In that day "I will r David's fallen shelter H7756
Am 9:11 repair its broken walls and r its ruins— H7756
Na 2: 2 The LORD will r the splendor of Jacob like H8740
Zep 2: 7 will care for them; he will r their fortunes. H8740
Zep 3:20 of the earth when I r your fortunes before H8740
Zec 9:12 I announce that I will r twice as much to H8740
Zec 10: 6 I will r them because I have compassion H3782
Mt 17:11 be sure, Elijah comes and will r all things. G635
Ac 1: 6 are you at this time going to r the kingdom G635
Ac 3:21 the time comes for God to r everything, G640
Ac 9:12 place his hands on him to r his sight." G329
Ac 15:16 Its ruins I will rebuild, and I will r it, G494
Gal 6: 1 live by the Spirit should r that person G2936
1Pe 5:10 will himself r you and make you strong G2936

RESTORED (41) [RESTORE]

Ge 40:21 He r the chief cupbearer to his position, so H8740
Ge 41:13 I was r to my position, and the other man H8740
Ex 4: 7 he took it out, it was r, like the rest of H8740
Nu 21:27 let it be rebuilt; let Sihon's city be r. H3922
1Sa 7:14 had captured from Israel were r to Israel, H8740
1Ki 13: 6 pray for me that my hand may be r." H8740
1Ki 13: 6 the king's hand was r and became as it H8740
2Ki 5:10 your flesh will be r and you will be H8740
2Ki 5:14 his flesh was r and became clean like H8740
2Ki 8: 1 to the woman whose son he had r to life, H2649
2Ki 8: 5 the king how Elisha had r the dead to life, H2649
2Ki 8: 5 this is her son whom Elisha r to life." H2649
2Ki 14:22 who rebuilt Elath and r it to Judah after H8740
2Ki 14:25 He was the one who r the boundaries of H8740
1Ch 11: 8 while Joab r the rest of the city. H2649
2Ch 26: 2 who rebuilt Elath and r it to Judah after H8740
2Ch 33:16 Then he r the altar of the LORD and H1215
2Ch 34:10 workers who repaired and r the temple. H2616
Ezr 4:13 that if this city is built and its walls are r, A10354
Ezr 4:16 that if this city is built and its walls are r, A10354
Ne 3: 8 They r Jerusalem as far as the Broad Wall. H6441
Job 22:23 the Almighty, you will be r: If you remove H1215
Job 33:25 let them be r as in the days of their youth' H8740
Job 42:10 the LORD r his fortunes and gave him twice H8740
Ps 85: 1 to your land; you r the fortunes of Jacob. H8740
Ps 126: 1 When the LORD r the fortunes of Zion, we H8740
Isa 38:16 You r me to health and let me live. H2730
Eze 21:27 The crown will not be r until he to whom H2118
Da 4:26 your kingdom will be r to you when you A10629
Da 4:34 toward heaven, and my sanity was r. A10754
Da 4:36 At the same time that my sanity was r A10754
Da 4:36 and I was r to my throne and became A10771
Mic 4: 8 the former dominion will be r to you H910
Mt 9:30 their sight was r. Jesus warned them G487
Mt 12:13 he stretched it out and it was completely r, G635
Mk 3: 5 and his hand was completely r. G635
Mk 8:25 were opened, his sight was r, and he saw G635
Lk 6:10 He did so, and his hand was completely r. G635
2Co 13: 9 our prayer is that you may be fully r. G2937
Phm 22 because I hope to be r to you in answer to G5919
Heb 13:19 you to pray so that I may be r to you soon. G635

RESTORER (1) [RESTORE]

Isa 58:12 Broken Walls, R of Streets with Dwellings. H8740

RESTORES (4) [RESTORE]

Ps 14: 7 When the LORD r his people, let H8740+8654
Ps 41: 3 on their sickbed and r them from their bed H2200
Ps 53: 6 When God r his people, let Jacob H8740+8654
Mk 9:12 Elijah does come first, and r all things. G635

RESTORING (2) [RESTORE]

2Ki 12:12 all the other expenses of r the temple. H2616
Ezr 4:12 They are r the walls and repairing the A10354

RESTRAIN (5) [RESTRAINED, RESTRAINING, RESTRAINT]

1Sa 3:13 and he failed to r them. H3909
Job 9:13 God does not r his anger; even the H8740
Jer 2:24 her craving—in her heat who can r her? H8740
Jer 14:10 love to wander; they do not r their feet. H3104
Jer 31:16 "R your voice from weeping and your eyes H4979

RESTRAINED (6) [RESTRAIN]

Ex 36: 6 And so the people were r from bringing H3973
Est 5:10 Haman r himself and went home. H706
Ps 76:10 the survivors of your wrath are r. H2520
Ps 78:38 Time after time he r his anger and did not H8740
Eze 31:15 streams, and its abundant waters were r. H3973
2Pe 2:16 a human voice and r the prophet's G3266

RESTRAINING (3) [RESTRAIN]

Pr 27:16 r her is like restraining the wind or H7621
Pr 27:16 her is like r the wind or grasping H7621
Col 2:23 they lack any value in r sensual indulgence. AIT

RESTRAINT (4) [RESTRAIN]

Job 30:11 they throw off r in my presence. H8270
Pr 17:27 who has knowledge uses words with r, H3104
Pr 29:18 people cast off r; but blessed is H7277
Eze 35:13 me and spoke against me without r, H6984

RESTRICT (1) [RESTRICTED, RESTRICTION, RESTRICTIONS]

1Co 7:35 own good, not to r you, but that G1105+2095

RESTRICTED (1) [RESTRICT]
Jer 36: 5 told Baruch, "I *am* **r**; I am not allowed to H6806

RESTRICTION (1) [RESTRICT]
Job 36:16 of distress to a spacious place free from **r**, H4608

RESTRICTIONS (1) [RESTRICT]
Est 1: 8 each guest was allowed to **drink with no r**, H9276

RESTS (9) [REST]
Dt 33:12 the *one* the LORD loves **r** between his H8905
2Ch 28:11 the LORD's fierce anger **r on** you. H6584
2Ch 28:13 and his fierce anger **r on** Israel. H6584
2Ch 36:21 The land enjoyed its **sabbath r**; all the H8701
Pr 19:23 then *one* **r** content, untouched H4328
Pr 21:31 day of battle, but victory **r with** the LORD. H4200
Lk 2:14 on earth peace to those *on whom* his **favor r**." AIT
Heb 4:10 enters God's rest also **r** from their works, G2924
1Pe 4:14 the Spirit of glory and of God **r** on you. G399

RESULT (30) [RESULTED, RESULTS]
Ge 38:24 and **as a r** she is now pregnant. H4200
Ex 21:20 if the slave dies **as a direct r**, H9393+3338
Lev 7:16 their offering is the **r** of a vow or is a freewill NDT
Nu 5:27 unfaithful to her husband, this will be the **r**: NDT
Nu 25:18 the plague came **as a r of** that incident." H6584
1Ch 28:19 "I have in writing **as a r of** the LORD's hand H4946
Ezr 9:13 happened to us is **a r of** our evil deeds H928
Mic 7:13 of its inhabitants, as the **r** *of* their deeds. H7262
Mk 1:45 **As a r**, Jesus could no longer enter a town G6063
Ac 5:15 **As a r**, people brought the sick into the G6063
Ac 17:12 **As a r**, many of them believed, as G3525+4036
Ac 25:26 so that **as a r of** this investigation I may G1181
Ro 3: 8 "Let us do evil that good *may* **r**"? G2262
Ro 5:16 be compared with the **r** of one man's sin: G1328
Ro 6:21 now ashamed of? Those things **r in** death! G5465
Ro 6:22 leads to holiness, and the **r** is eternal life. G5465
Ro 11:30 received mercy *as a r of* their **disobedience**, AIT
Ro 11:31 receive mercy *as a r of* God's **mercy** to you. AIT
1Co 9: 1 Are you not the **r of** my **work** in the Lord? G2240
1Co 11:21 **As a r**, one person remains hungry and G2779
1Co 11:34 meet together it may not **r in** judgment. G1650
2Co 3: 3 letter from Christ, **the r of** our ministry G5679
2Co 9:11 us your generosity *will* **r in** thanksgiving to G2981
Gal 4:23 woman was born **as the r of a** divine G1328
Php 1:13 **As a r**, it has become clear throughout the G6063
2Th 1: 5 and **as a r** you will be counted G1650+3836
1Ti 6: 4 quarrels about words that **r in** envy, G1666+1181
1Pe 1: 7 refined by fire—*may* **r** in praise, glory and G2351
1Pe 1: 9 you are receiving the **end r** of your faith, G5465
1Pe 4: 2 **As a r**, they do not live the rest of G1650+3836

RESULTED (2) [RESULT]
Ro 5:18 just as one trespass **r in** condemnation G1650
Ro 5:18 one righteous act **r in** justification and G1650

RESULTS (1) [RESULT]
1Th 2: 1 that our visit to you was not **without r**. G3031

RESURRECTION (40)
Mt 22:23 who say there is no **r**, came to him with a G414
Mt 22:28 Now then, at the **r**, whose wife will she be G414
Mt 22:30 At the **r** people will neither marry nor be G414
Mt 22:31 But about the **r** of the dead—have you not G414
Mt 27:53 tombs after Jesus' **r** and went into the G1587
Mk 12:18 who say there is no **r**, came to him with a G414
Mk 12:23 At the **r** whose wife will she be, since the G414
Lk 14:14 you will be repaid at the **r** of the righteous." G414
Lk 20:27 who say there is no **r**, came to Jesus with a G414
Lk 20:33 Now then, at the **r** whose wife will she be G414
Lk 20:35 age to come and *in* the **r** from the dead G414
Lk 20:36 children, since they are children *of* the **r**. G414
Jn 11:24 he will rise again in the **r** at the last day." G414
Jn 11:25 "I am the **r** and the life. The one G414
Ac 1:22 must become a witness with us *of* his **r**." G414
Ac 2:31 he spoke of the **r** of the Messiah, that G414
Ac 4: 2 proclaiming in Jesus the **r** of the dead. G414
Ac 4:33 to testify *to* the **r** of the Lord Jesus. G414
Ac 17:18 the good news about Jesus and the **r**. G414
Ac 17:32 When they heard *about* the **r** of the dead G414
Ac 23: 6 because of the hope of the **r** of the dead." G414
Ac 23: 8 The Sadducees say that there is no **r**, and G414
Ac 24:15 that there will be a **r** of both the righteous G414
Ac 24:21 'It is concerning the **r** of the dead that I am G414
Ro 1: 4 of God in power by his **r** from the dead: G414
Ro 6: 5 also be united with him *in a* **r** like his. G414
1Co 15:12 of you say that there is no **r** of the dead? G414
1Co 15:13 If there is no **r** of the dead, then not even G414
1Co 15:21 the **r** of the dead comes also through a G414
1Co 15:29 Now if there is no **r**, what will those do who NDT
1Co 15:42 So will it be with the **r** of the dead. G414
Php 3:10 to know the power *of* his **r** and participation G414
Php 3:11 attaining to the **r** from the dead. G1983
2Ti 2:18 They say that the **r** has already taken place G414
Heb 6: 2 laying on of hands, the **r** of the dead, and G414
Heb 11:35 so that they might gain an even better **r**. G414
1Pe 1: 3 hope through the **r** of Jesus Christ from G414
1Pe 3:21 It saves you by the **r** of Jesus Christ, G414
Rev 20: 5 years were ended.) This is the first **r**. G414
Rev 20: 6 holy are those who share in the first **r**. G414

RETAIN (5) [RETAINS]
Lev 25:48 they **r** the right of redemption after H2118+4200
2Ch 22: 9 powerful enough to **r** the kingdom. H6806
Da 11: 6 alliance, but *she will* not **r** her power, and H6806
Lk 8:15 who hear the word, **r** it, and by G2988
Ro 1:28 think it worthwhile *to* **r** the knowledge of G2400

RETAINS (1) [RETAIN]
Lev 25:29 house in a walled city **r** the right of H2118

RETAKE (2) [TAKE]
Jdg 11:26 Why didn't *you* **r** them during that time H5911
1Ki 22: 3 are doing nothing *to* **r** it from the king of H4374

RETALIATE (1)
1Pe 2:23 insults at him, *he did* not **r**; when he G518

RETINUE (2)
1Ki 10:13 returned with her **r** to her own country. H6269
2Ch 9:12 returned with her **r** to her own country. H6269

RETIRE (1)
Nu 8:25 *they must* **r** from their regular service and H8740

RETORTED (2)
Jn 7:47 he has deceived you also?" the Pharisees **r**. G646
Jn 18:38 "What is truth?" **r** Pilate. With this he G3306

RETREAT (5) [RETREATED, RETREATING, RETREATS]
Jdg 20:32 "*Let's* **r** and draw them away from the city H5674
Job 41:25 are terrified; *they* **r** before its thrashing. H2627
Ps 44:10 *You* **made** us **r** before the enemy H8740+294
Ps 74:21 *Do* not *let* the oppressed **r** in disgrace H8740
Da 11: 9 of the South but *will* **r** to his own country. H8740

RETREATED (1) [RETREAT]
2Sa 23: 9 Dammim for battle. Then the Israelites **r**, H6590

RETREATING (1) [RETREAT]
Jer 46: 5 are terrified, *they are* **r**, their warriors H6047+294

RETREATS (1) [RETREAT]
Pr 30:30 among beasts, *who* **r** before nothing; H8740

RETRIBUTION (6)
Ps 69:22 a snare; may it become **r** and a trap. H8936
Isa 34: 8 vengeance, a year of **r**, to uphold Zion's H8936
Isa 35: 4 with divine **r** he will come to save you." H1691
Isa 59:18 wrath to his enemies and **r** to his foes; H1691
Jer 51:56 For the LORD is a God of **r**; he will repay in H1692
Ro 11: 9 a stumbling block and a **r** for them. G501

RETRIEVED (1)
Isa 49:25 plunder **r** *from* the fierce; I will H4880

RETURN (224) [RETURNED, RETURNING, RETURNS]
Ge 3:19 eat your food until you **r** to the ground, H8740
Ge 3:19 dust you are and to dust *you will* **r**. H8740
Ge 8:12 out again, but this time *it did* not **r** to him. H8740
Ge 18:10 "*I will* **surely r** to you about this H8740+8740
Ge 18:14 *I will* **r** to you at the appointed time next H8740
Ge 20: 7 Now **r** the man's wife, for he is a prophet H8740
Ge 20: 7 But if you *do* not **r** her, you may be sure H8740
Ge 28:21 so that *I* **r** safely to my father's household H8740
Ge 29: 3 Then *they would* **r** the stone to its place H8740
Ge 29:18 you seven years **in r for** your younger H928
Ge 29:27 **in r for** another seven years of work. H928
Ge 30:15 with you tonight **in r for** your son's H9393
Ge 31:30 gone off because *you* **longed** *to* **r** to your AIT
Ge 43:12 for *you must* **r** the silver that was put back H8740
Ge 44:33 and *let* the boy **r** with his brothers. H6590
Ge 45:17 your animals and **r** to the land of H2143+995
Ge 49: 9 lion's cub, Judah; *you* **r** from the prey, my H6590
Ge 50: 5 me go up and bury my father; then *I will* **r**. H8740
Ex 4:18 "*Let me* **r** to my own people H2143+2256+8740
Ex 4:21 Moses, "When you **r** to Egypt, see H2143+8740
Ex 13:17 might change their minds and **r** to Egypt." H8740
Ex 22:26 cloak as a pledge, **r** it by sunset, H8740
Ex 23: 4 wandering off, **be sure to r** it. H8740+8740
Ex 33:11 Then Moses *would* **r** to the camp, but his H8740
Lev 6: 4 *they must* **r** what they have stolen or taken H8740
Lev 14:39 day the priest *shall* **r** to inspect the house. H8740
Lev 25:10 each of *you is to* **r** to your family property H8740
Lev 25:13 of Jubilee everyone *is to* **r** to their own H8740
Nu 10:36 "**R**, LORD, *to* the countless thousands of H8740
Nu 18:21 their inheritance **in r for** the work they do H2739
Nu 32:18 *We will* not **r** to our homes until each of H8740
Nu 32:22 *you may* **r** and be free from your H8740
Nu 35:28 of the high priest *may* they **r** to their own H8740
Dt 4:30 in later days *you will* **r** to the LORD your H8740
Dt 5:30 tell them *to* **r** to their tents. H8740
Dt 16: 7 the morning **r** to your tents. H7155+2256+2143
Dt 17:16 himself or **make** the people **r** to Egypt to H8740
Dt 23:11 at sunset *he may* **r** to the camp. H995
Dt 24:13 **R** their cloak by sunset so that your H8740+8740
Dt 30: 2 your children **r** to the LORD your God H8740
Jos 2:16 yourselves there three days until they **r**, H8740
Jos 18: 4 Then *they will* **r** to me. H995
Jos 18: 8 Then **r** to me, and I will cast lots for you H8740
Jos 22: 4 **r** to your homes in the land that Moses H7155
Jos 22: 8 "**R** to your homes with your great wealth H8740
Jos 22: 9 at Shiloh in Canaan to **r** to Gilead, H8740
Jdg 6:18 the LORD said, "I will wait until you **r**." H8740
Jdg 8: 9 men of Peniel, "When I **r** in triumph, I will H8740
Jdg 11:31 to meet me when I **r** in triumph from the H8740
Jdg 19: 3 husband went to her to persuade her to **r**. H8740
Jdg 20: 8 not one of *us will* **r** to his house. H6073
Jdg 21:21 Then **r** *to* the land of Benjamin H2143
Ru 1: 6 prepared *to* **r** home from there. H8740
Ru 1:11 But Naomi said, "**R** home, my daughters H8740
Ru 1:12 **R** home, my daughters; I am too old to H8740
1Sa 6: 3 "If *you* **r** the ark of the god of Israel H8938
1Sa 18: 2 did not let him **r** home *to* his family. H8740
1Sa 29: 4 that *he may* **r** to the place you assigned H8740
2Sa 1:22 the sword of Saul *did* not **r** unsatisfied. H8740
2Sa 12:23 I will go to him, but he *will* not **r** to me." H8740
2Sa 15:27 You and Abiathar **r** with your two sons. NDT
2Sa 15:34 But if *you* **r** to the city and say to Absalom H8740
2Sa 17: 3 the man you seek will mean the **r** *of* all; H8740
2Sa 19:14 word to the king, "**R**, you and all your men H8740
2Sa 19:37 *Let* your servant **r**, that I may die in my own H8740
1Ki 11:21 that *I may* **r** to my own country. H2143
1Ki 12:27 They will kill me and **r** to King Rehoboam." H8740
1Ki 13: 9 drink water or **r** by the way you came. H8740
1Ki 13:10 another road and *did* not **r** by the way he H8740
1Ki 13:17 water there or **r** by the way you came. H8740
1Ki 17:21 "LORD my God, *let* this boy's life **r** to him!" H8740
1Ki 20:34 "*I will* **r** the cities my father took from your H8740
1Ki 22:27 nothing but bread and water until I **r** safely. H995
1Ki 22:28 declared, "If *you* **ever r** safely, the H8740+8740
2Ki 4:22 I can go to the man of God quickly and **r**." H8740
2Ki 19: 7 make him want to **r** to his own country, H8740
2Ki 19:28 and *I will* **make** you **r** by the way you H8740
2Ki 19:33 By the way that he came *he will* **r**; he will H8740
2Ch 18:26 bread and water until I **r** safely. H8740
2Ch 18:27 declared, "If *you* **ever r** safely, the H8740+8740
2Ch 30: 6 "People of Israel, **r** to the LORD, the God of H8740
2Ch 30: 6 that *he may* **r** to you who are left H8740
2Ch 30: 9 If you **r** to the LORD, then your fellow H8740
2Ch 30: 9 by their captors and *will* **r** to this land, H8740
2Ch 30: 9 not turn his face from you if *you* **r** to him." H8740
Ne 1: 9 if *you* **r** to me and obey my commands H8740
Ne 7: 5 of those *who had been* the first *to* **r**. H6590
Ne 9:17 a leader in order to **r** to their slavery. H8740
Est 2:14 in the morning **r** to another part of H8740
Est 2:14 *She would* not **r** to the king unless H995+6388
Job 7: 9 who goes down to the grave *does* not **r**. H6590
Job 10:21 before I go to the place of no **r**, to the H8740
Job 15:31 is worthless, for he will get nothing *in* **r**. H9455
Job 16:22 will pass before I take the path of no **r**. H8740
Job 22:23 If *you* **r** to the Almighty, you will be H8740
Job 34:15 together and mankind *would* **r** to the dust. H8740
Job 39: 4 in the wilds; they leave and *do* not **r**. H8740
Ps 59: 6 *They* **r** at evening, snarling like dogs, and H8740
Ps 59:14 *They* **r** at evening, snarling like dogs, and H8740
Ps 78:39 a passing breeze *that does* not **r**. H8740
Ps 80:14 **R** to us, God Almighty! Look down from H8740
Ps 90: 3 saying, "**R** to dust, *you* mortals. H8740
Ps 104:22 they **r** and lie down in their dens. NDT
Ps 104:29 their breath, they die and **r** to the dust. H8740
Ps 109: 4 **In r for** my friendship they accuse me, but H9393
Ps 116: 7 **R** to your rest, my soul, for the LORD has H8740
Ps 116:12 What *shall I* **r** to the LORD *for* all his H8740
Ps 126: 6 seed to sow, *will* **r** with songs of joy H995+995
Ps 146: 4 spirit departs, *they* **r** to the ground; on H8740
Pr 2:19 None who go to her **r** or attain the paths H8740
Ecc 1: 7 streams come from, there they **r** again. H2143
Ecc 3:20 all come from dust, and to dust all **r**. H8740
Ecc 4: 9 because they have a good **r** for their labor: H8510
Ecc 11: 1 after many days you may receive a **r**. H5647
Ecc 12: 2 grow dark, and the clouds **r** after the rain; H8740
Isa 10:21 A remnant *will* **r**, a remnant of Jacob will H8740
Isa 10:21 a remnant of Jacob will **r** to the Mighty God. NDT
Isa 10:22 by the sea, Israel, only a remnant *will* **r**. H8740
Isa 13:14 they *will all* **r** to their own people H7155
Isa 23:17 *She will* **r** to her lucrative prostitution and H8740
Isa 31: 6 **R**, *you* Israelites, to the One you have so H8740
Isa 35:10 and *those* the LORD has rescued *will* **r** H8740
Isa 37: 7 make him want to **r** to his own country, H8740
Isa 37:29 and *I will* **make** you **r** by the way you H8740
Isa 37:34 By the way that he came *he will* **r**; he will H8740
Isa 44:22 like the morning mist. **R** to me, for I have H8740
Isa 51:11 Those the LORD has rescued *will* **r**. H8740
Isa 55:10 and *do* not **r** to it without watering the H8740
Isa 55:11 *It will* not **r** to me empty, but will H8740
Isa 63:17 **R** for the sake of your servants, the tribes H8740
Jer 3: 1 another man, *should he* **r** to her again? H8740
Jer 3: 1 many lovers—*would* you now **r** to me?" H8740
Jer 3: 7 done all this *she would* **r** to me but she H8740
Jer 3:10 sister Judah *did* not **r** to me with all her H8740
Jer 3:12 " '**R**, faithless Israel,' declares the LORD, 'I H8740
Jer 3:14 "**R**, faithless people," declares the LORD H8740
Jer 3:22 "**R**, faithless people; I will cure you of H8740
Jer 4: 1 "If *you*, Israel, *will* **r**, then return to me," H8740
Jer 4: 1 will return, then **r** to me," declares the H8740
Jer 8: 4 someone turns away, *do they* not **r**? H8740
Jer 8: 5 They cling to deceit; they refuse to **r**. H8740
Jer 14: 3 *They* **r** with their jars unfilled; dismayed H8740
Jer 22:10 because *he will* never **r** nor see his native H8740
Jer 22:11 has gone from this place: "*He will* never **r**. H8740
Jer 22:27 come back to the land you long to **r** to." H8740
Jer 24: 7 for *they will* **r** to me with all their heart. H8740
Jer 31: 8 women in labor; a great throng *will* **r**. H8740
Jer 31:16 "*They will* **r** from the land of the enemy H8740
Jer 31:17 "Your children *will* **r** to their own land. H8740
Jer 31:18 Restore me, and *I will* **r**, because you are H8740
Jer 31:21 road that you take. **R**, Virgin Israel, return H8740
Jer 31:21 Return, Virgin Israel, **r** to your towns. H8740

Jer 31:22 on earth—the woman will r to the man." H6015
Jer 37: 8 Then the Babylonians will r and attack this H8740
Jer 44:14 survive to r to the land of Judah, H8740
Jer 44:14 to which they long to r and live; none will H8740
Jer 44:14 none will r except a few fugitives." H8740
Jer 44:28 the sword and r to the land of Judah H8740
Jer 47: 6 long till you rest? R to your sheath; cease H665
Jer 50: 9 warriors who do not r empty-handed. H8740
Jer 50:16 the oppressor let everyone r to their own H7155
La 3:40 test them, and let us r to the LORD. H8740
La 5:21 that we may r; renew our days as of H8740
Eze 11:18 "They will r to it and remove all its vile H995
Eze 16:55 daughters, will r to what they were before H8740
Eze 16:55 your daughters will r to what you were H8740
Eze 18:12 He does not r what he took in pledge H8740
Eze 21: 5 sword from its sheath; it will not r again. H8740
Eze 21:30 " 'Let the sword r to its sheath. In the H8740
Eze 26:20 and you will not r or take your place in the H8740
Eze 29:14 from captivity and r them to Upper Egypt, H8740
Eze 33:15 pledge for a loan, r what they have stolen H8966
Eze 46: 9 No one is to r through the gate by which H8740
Da 10:20 Soon I will r to fight against the prince of H8740
Da 11:28 king of the North will r to his own country H8740
Da 11:28 against it and then r to his own country. H8740
Da 11:30 He will r and show favor to those who H8740
Hos 3: 5 the Israelites will r and seek the LORD H8740
Hos 5: 4 do not permit them to r to their God. H8740
Hos 5:15 Then I will r to my lair until they H2143+8740
Hos 6: 1 let us r to the LORD. He has torn us H8740
Hos 7:10 all this he does not r to the LORD his H8740
Hos 8:13 punish their sins: They will r to Egypt. H8740
Hos 9: 3 Ephraim will r to Egypt and eat unclean H8740
Hos 11: 5 "Will they not r to Egypt and will not H8740
Hos 12: 6 But you must r to your God; maintain love H8740
Hos 14: 1 R, Israel, to the LORD your God. Your sins H8740
Hos 14: 2 Take words with you and r to the LORD. H8740
Joel 2:12 the LORD, "r to me with all your heart H8740
Joel 2:13 R to the LORD your God, for he is gracious H8740
Joel 3: 4 I will swiftly and speedily r on your own H8740
Joel 3: 7 and I will r on your own heads what you H8740
Ob 15 your deeds will r upon your own head. H8740
Mic 5: 3 rest of his brothers r to join the Israelites. H8740
Zep 2:10 is what they will get in r for their pride, H9393
Hag 2:17 yet you did not r to me,' declares the NDT
Zec 1: 3 'R to me,' declares the LORD Almighty H8740
Zec 1: 3 Almighty, 'and I will r to you,' says the H8740
Zec 1:16 'I will r to Jerusalem with mercy, and H8740
Zec 8: 3 "I will r to Zion and dwell in Jerusalem H8740
Zec 9:12 R to your fortress, you prisoners of hope H8740
Zec 10: 9 their children will survive, and they will r. H8740
Mal 3: 7 R to me, and I will return to you," says the H8740
Mal 3: 7 Return to me, and I will r to you," says the H8740
Mal 3: 7 "But you ask, 'How are we to r?' H8740
Mt 10:13 if it is not, let your peace r to you. G2188
Mt 12:44 Then it says, 'I will r to the house I left.' G2188
Lk 8:39 "R home and tell how much God has done G5715
Lk 10: 6 will rest on them; if not, it will r to you. G366
Lk 10:35 he said, 'and when I r, I will reimburse G2059
Lk 11:24 Then it says, 'I will r to the house I left.' G5715
Lk 12:36 their master to r from a wedding G386
Lk 19:12 himself appointed king and then to r. G5715
Jn 21:22 "If I want him to remain alive until I r G2262
Jn 21:23 "If I want him to remain alive until I r G2262
Ac 13:13 where John left them to r to Jerusalem. G5715
Ac 15:16 " 'After this I will r and rebuild David's G418
Ac 15:33 blessing of peace to r to those who had G4639
Ro 9: 9 "At the appointed time I will r, and Sarah G2262
1Co 16:11 his way in peace so that he may r to me. G2262
2Co 1:23 to spare you that I did not r to Corinth. G2262
2Co 13: 2 On my r I will not spare G2262+1650+3836+4099
1Th 3: 9 God enough for you in r for all the joy we G500
Heb 11:15 they would have had opportunity to r. G366

RETURNED (184) [RETURN]

Ge 8: 9 of the earth; so it r to Noah in the ark. H8740
Ge 8:11 When the dove r to him in the evening H995
Ge 14:17 After Abram r from defeating H8740
Ge 18:33 Abraham, he left, and Abraham r home. H8740
Ge 19:27 Abraham got up and r to the place where NDT
Ge 20:14 Abraham, and he r Sarah his wife to him. H8740
Ge 21:32 of his forces r to the land of the H8740
Ge 22:19 Then Abraham r to his servants, and they H8740
Ge 31:55 blessed them. Then he left and r home. H8740
Ge 32: 6 When the messengers r to Jacob, they H8740
Ge 35: 9 After Jacob r from Paddan Aram, God H995
Ge 37:29 When Reuben r to the cistern and saw H8740
Ge 42:28 "My silver has been r," he said to his H8740
Ge 43:10 delayed, we could have gone and r twice." H8740
Ge 44:13 all loaded their donkeys and r to the city. H8740
Ge 50:14 his father, Joseph r to Egypt, together with H8740
Ex 2:18 When the girls r to Reuel their father, he H995
Ex 2:18 "Why have you r so early today? H995
Ex 5:22 Moses r to the LORD and said, "Why, Lord H8740
Ex 18:27 his way, and Jethro r to his own country. H2143
Lev 25:28 It will be r in the Jubilee, and they can H3655
Lev 25:30 It is not to be r in the Jubilee H3655
Lev 25:31 and they are to be r in the Jubilee. H3655
Lev 25:33 they hold—and is to be r in the Jubilee H3655
Nu 11:30 the elders of Israel r to the camp. H665
Nu 13:25 end of forty days they r from exploring the H8740
Nu 14:36 who r and made the whole community H8740
Nu 16:50 Then Aaron r to Moses at the entrance to H8740
Nu 22:14 So the Moabite officials r to Balak and said, H995
Nu 24:25 Then Balaam got up and r home, and H8740
Nu 31:14 of hundreds—who r from the battle. H995
Dt 28:31 forcibly taken from you and will not be r. H8740
Jos 2:22 along the road and r without finding them H8740
Jos 4:18 waters of the Jordan r to their place and H8740
Jos 6:11 Then the army r to camp and spent the H995
Jos 6:14 around the city once and r to the camp. H8740
Jos 7: 3 When they r to Joshua, they said, "Not all H8740
Jos 8:24 all the Israelites r to Ai and killed those H8740
Jos 10:15 Then Joshua r with all Israel to the camp H8740
Jos 10:21 The whole army then r safely to Joshua in H8740
Jos 10:43 Then Joshua r with all Israel to the camp H8740
Jos 18: 9 r to Joshua in the camp at Shiloh. H995
Jos 22:32 the leaders r to Canaan from their H8740
Jdg 2:19 the people r to ways even more corrupt H8740
Jdg 7:15 He r to the camp of Israel and called out H8740
Jdg 8:13 son of Joash then r from the battle by the H8740
Jdg 11:34 When Jephthah r to his home in Mizpah H995
Jdg 11:39 the two months, she r to her father, and H8740
Jdg 14: 2 When he r, he said to his father and H6590
Jdg 14:19 with anger, he r to his father's home. H6590
Jdg 15:19 his strength r and he revived. H8740
Jdg 16:18 of the Philistines r with the silver in their H6590
Jdg 17: 3 When he r the eleven hundred shekels of H8740
Jdg 17: 4 So after he r the silver to his mother, she H8740
Jdg 18: 8 When they r to Zorah and Eshtaol, their H995
Jdg 21:14 So the Benjamites r at that time and were H8740
Jdg 21:23 Then they r to their inheritance and H8740
Ru 1:22 So Naomi r from Moab accompanied by H8740
1Sa 4: 3 When the soldiers r to camp, the elders of H995
1Sa 6:16 all this and then r that same day to Ekron. H8740
1Sa 6:21 "The Philistines have r the ark of the LORD. H8740
1Sa 17:53 When the Israelites r from chasing the H8740
1Sa 17:57 As soon as David r from killing the H8740
1Sa 20:38 picked up the arrow and r to his master. H995
1Sa 24: 1 After Saul r from pursuing the Philistines H8740
1Sa 24:22 Then Saul r home, but David and his men H2143
1Sa 26:25 David went on his way, and Saul r home. H8740
1Sa 27: 9 camels, and clothes. Then he r to Achish. H8740
2Sa 1: 1 David r from striking down the Amalekites H8740
2Sa 3:22 David's men and Joab r from a raid and H995
2Sa 3:27 Now when Abner r to Hebron, Joab took H8740
2Sa 6:20 When David r home to bless his H8740
2Sa 8:13 famous after he r from striking down H8740
2Sa 10:14 So Joab r from fighting the Ammonites H8740
2Sa 12:31 Then he and his entire army r to H8740
2Sa 17:20 found no one, so they r to Jerusalem. H8740
2Sa 19:15 Then the king r and went as far as the H8740
2Sa 19:24 day the king left until the day he r safely. H995
2Sa 19:30 my lord the king has r home safely." H995+448
2Sa 19:39 him farewell, and Barzillai r to his home. H8740
2Sa 20: 3 When David r to his palace in Jerusalem H995
2Sa 23:10 The troops r to Eleazar, but only to strip H8740
1Ki 2:41 gone from Jerusalem to Gath and had r, H8740
1Ki 3:15 He r to Jerusalem, stood before the ark of H995
1Ki 10:13 Then she left and r with her retinue to her H2143
1Ki 10:22 Once every three years it r, carrying gold H995
1Ki 12: 2 fled from King Solomon), he r from Egypt. H8740
1Ki 12:12 all the people r to Rehoboam, H995
1Ki 12:20 the Israelites heard that Jeroboam had r, H8740
1Ki 13:19 So the man of God r with him and ate H8740
1Ki 14:28 afterward they r them to the H8740
1Ki 17:22 the boy's life r to him, and he lived. H8740
2Ki 1: 5 When the messengers r to the king, he H8740
2Ki 2:18 When they r to Elisha, who was staying in H8740
2Ki 2:25 Carmel and from there r to Samaria. H8740
2Ki 3:27 they withdrew and r to their own land. H8740
2Ki 4:38 Elisha r to Gilgal and there was a famine H8740
2Ki 4:39 When he r, he cut them up into the pot of H995
2Ki 6:23 them away, and they r to their master. H2143
2Ki 7: 8 They r and entered another tent and took H8740
2Ki 7:15 So the messengers r and reported to the H8740
2Ki 8:14 Then Hazael left Elisha and r to his master H995
2Ki 8:29 so King Joram r to Jezreel to recover from H8740
2Ki 9:15 King Joram had r to Jezreel to recover H8740
2Ki 14:14 He also took hostages and r to Samaria. H8740
2Ki 16:11 finished it before King Ahaz r. H995
2Ki 19:36 He r to Nineveh and stayed there H8740
1Ch 16:43 David r home to bless his family. H6015
1Ch 20: 3 David and his entire army r to Jerusalem. H8740
2Ch 9:12 Then she left and r with her retinue to her H2143
2Ch 9:21 Once every three years it r, carrying gold H995
2Ch 10: 2 fled from King Solomon), he r from Egypt. H8740
2Ch 10:12 all the people r to Rehoboam, H995
2Ch 12:11 afterward they r them to the H8740
2Ch 14:15 Then they r to Jerusalem. H8740
2Ch 19: 1 king of Judah r safely to his palace in H8740
2Ch 20:27 Judah and Jerusalem r joyfully to H8740
2Ch 22: 6 so he r to Jezreel to recover from the H8740
2Ch 25:14 When Amaziah r from slaughtering the H995
2Ch 25:24 the hostages, and r to Samaria. H8740
2Ch 28: 9 out to meet the army when it r to Samaria. H995
2Ch 28:15 the City of Palms, and r to Samaria. H8740
2Ch 31: 1 the Israelites r to their own towns and to H8740
Ezr 2: 1 to Babylon (they r to Jerusalem and Judah H8740
Ezr 3: 8 Levites and all who had r from the captivity H995
Ezr 6: 5 are to be r to their places in the temple A10754
Ezr 6:21 the Israelites who had r from the exile ate H8740
Ezr 8:35 Then the exiles who had r from captivity H995
Ne 4:15 frustrated it, we all r to the wall, each to H8740
Ne 7: 6 captive (they r to Jerusalem and Judah H8740
Ne 8:17 whole company that had r from exile built H8740
Ne 12: 1 Levites who r with Zerubbabel son of H6590
Ne 13: 6 king of Babylon I had r to the king. H995
Est 6:12 Afterward Mordecai r to the king's gate H8740
Est 7: 8 Just as the king r from the palace garden H8740
Ps 35:13 my prayers r to me **unanswered**, H8740+2668
Ps 60: T and when Joab r and struck down twelve H8740
Isa 9:13 But the people have not r to him who H8740
Isa 37:37 He r to Nineveh and stayed there H8740
Jer 11:10 They have r to the sins of their ancestors H8740
Jer 19:14 Jeremiah then r from Topheth, where the H995
Da 2:17 Then Daniel r to his house and A10016
Da 4:36 honor and splendor were r to me for the A10754
Da 6:18 Then the king r to his palace and spent A10016
Am 4: 6 every town, yet you have not r to me," H8740
Am 4: 8 to drink, yet you have not r to me, H8740
Am 4: 9 olive trees, yet you have not r to me," H8740
Am 4:10 your camps, yet you have not r to me," H8740
Am 4:11 the fire, yet you have not r to me, H8740
Zec 4: 1 who talked with me r and woke me up, H8740
Mt 2:12 they r to their country by another route. G432
Mt 25:19 of those servants r and settled accounts G2262
Mt 25:27 so that when I r I would have received it G2262
Mt 26:40 Then he r to his disciples and found them G2262
Mt 26:45 Then he r to the disciples and said to G2262
Mt 27: 3 with remorse and r the thirty pieces of G5138
Mk 14:37 Then he r to his disciples and found them G2262
Mk 16:13 These r and reported it to the rest; but they G599
Lk 1:23 time of service was completed, he r home. G599
Lk 1:56 about three months and then r home. G5715
Lk 2:20 The shepherds r, glorifying and praising G5715
Lk 2:39 they r to Galilee to their own town of G2188
Lk 4:14 Jesus r to Galilee in the power of the G5715
Lk 7:10 who had been sent r to the house and G5715
Lk 8:40 Now when Jesus r, a crowd welcomed G5715
Lk 8:55 Her spirit r, and at once she stood up G2188
Lk 9:10 When the apostles r, they reported to G5715
Lk 10:17 The seventy-two r with joy and said, "Lord, G5715
Lk 17:18 Has no one r to give praise to God except G5715
Lk 19:15 was made king, however, and r **home**. G2059
Lk 24:33 They got up and r at once to Jerusalem G5715
Lk 24:52 worshiped him and r to Jerusalem with G5715
Jn 4:27 then his disciples r and were surprised to G2262
Jn 13:12 put on his clothes and r **to** his **place**. G404+4099
Ac 1:12 Then the apostles r to Jerusalem from the G5715
Ac 8:25 Peter and John r to Jerusalem G5715
Ac 12:25 their mission, they r from Jerusalem G5715
Ac 14:21 Then they r to Lystra, Iconium and Antioch G5715
Ac 21: 6 went aboard the ship, and they r home. G5715
Ac 22:17 "When I r to Jerusalem and was praying G5715
Ac 23:32 on with him, while they r to the barracks. G5715
Ro 14: 9 Christ died and r **to life** so that he might G2409
Gal 1:17 I went into Arabia. Later I r to Damascus. G5715
1Pe 2:25 now you have r to the Shepherd and G2188

RETURNING (11) [RETURN]

Ge 48: 7 As I was r from Paddan, to my sorrow H995
1Sa 7: 3 "If you are r to the LORD with all your H8740
1Sa 11: 5 Just then Saul was r from the fields, behind H995
1Sa 18: 6 When the men were r home after David H995
2Sa 20:22 dispersed from the city, each r to his home. NDT
Ecc 1: 6 round it goes, ever r on its course. H8740
Mic 2: 8 by without a care, like men r from battle. H8740
Mk 14:41 R the third time, he said to them, "Are G2262
Lk 2:43 while his parents were r **home**, the boy G5715
Jn 13: 3 he had come from God and was r to God; G5632
Heb 7: 1 He met Abraham r from the defeat of the G5715

RETURNS (11) [RETURN]

Lev 22:13 and she r to live in her father's household H8740
Pr 3:14 than silver and **yields** better r than gold. H9311
Pr 26:11 As a dog r to its vomit, so fools repeat H8740
Ecc 12: 7 the dust r to the ground it came from H8740
Ecc 12: 7 and the spirit r to God who gave it. H8740
Isa 52: 8 When the LORD r to Zion, they will see it H8740
Eze 18: 7 r what he took in pledge for a loan. H8740
Mt 24:46 master finds him doing so when he r. G2262
Lk 12:43 the master finds doing so when he r. G2262
2Pe 2:22 "A dog r to its vomit," and, "A sow that is G2188
2Pe 2:22 "A sow that is washed r to her wallowing in NDT

REU (6)

Ge 11:18 lived 30 years, he became the father of R. H8293
Ge 11:19 And after he became the father of R H8293
Ge 11:20 When R had lived 32 years, he became H8293
Ge 11:21 R lived 207 years and had other sons and H8293
1Ch 1:25 Eber, Peleg, R, H8293
Lk 3:35 of Serug, the son of R, the son of Peleg, G4814

REUBEN (56) [REUBENITE, REUBENITES]

Ge 29:32 She named him R, for she said, "It is H8017
Ge 30:14 R went out into the fields and found some H8017
Ge 35:22 R went in and slept with his father's H8017
Ge 35:23 R the firstborn of Jacob, Simeon, Levi H8017
Ge 37:21 When R heard this, he tried to rescue him H8017
Ge 37:22 R said this to rescue him from them and H8017
Ge 37:29 When R returned to the cistern and saw H8017
Ge 42:22 R replied, "Didn't I tell you not to sin H8017
Ge 42:37 Then R said to his father, "You may put H8017
Ge 46: 8 went to Egypt: R the firstborn of Jacob H8017
Ge 46: 9 The sons of R: Hanok, Pallu, Hezron and H8017
Ge 48: 5 be mine, just as R and Simeon are mine. H8017
Ge 49: 3 "R, you are my firstborn, my might, the H8017

Ex 1: 2 **R**, Simeon, Levi and Judah; H8017
Ex 6:14 The sons of **R** the firstborn son of Israel H8017
Ex 6:14 These were the clans of **R**. H8017
Nu 1: 5 from **R**, Elizur son of H8017
Nu 1:20 the descendants of **R** the firstborn son of H8017
Nu 1:21 number from the tribe of **R** was 46,500. H8017
Nu 2:10 of the camp of **R** under their standard. H8017
Nu 2:10 leader of the people of **R** is Elizur son of H8017
Nu 2:16 All the men assigned to the camp of **R** H8017
Nu 7:30 the leader of the people of **R**, brought his H8017
Nu 10:18 The divisions of the camp of **R** went next H8017
Nu 13: 4 from the tribe of **R**, Shammua son of H8017
Nu 26: 5 The descendants of **R**, the firstborn son of H8017
Nu 26: 7 These were the clans of **R**; those H8018
Nu 34:14 the families of the tribe of **R**, H1201+8018
Dt 27:13 **R**, Gad, Asher, Zebulun, Dan and H8017
Dt 33: 6 "Let **R** live and not die, nor his people be H8017
Jos 4:12 The men of **R**, Gad and the half-tribe of H8017
Jos 13:15 Moses had given to the tribe of **R**, H1201+8017
Jos 15: 6 Arabah to the Stone of Bohan son of **R**. H8017
Jos 18: 7 **R** and the half-tribe of Manasseh have H8017
Jos 18:17 ran down to the Stone of Bohan son of **R**. H8017
Jos 20: 8 on the plateau in the tribe of **R**, H8017
Jos 21: 7 received twelve towns from the tribes of **R** H8017
Jos 21:36 from the tribe of **R**, Bezer, Jahaz, H8017
Jos 22:13 land of Gilead—to **R**, Gad and the H1201+8017
Jos 22:15 went to Gilead—to **R**, Gad and the H1201+8017
Jos 22:21 Then **R**, Gad and the half-tribe of H1201+8017
Jos 22:30 heard what **R**, Gad and Manasseh H1201+8017
Jos 22:31 said to **R**, Gad and H1201+8017
Jdg 5:15 In the districts of **R** there was much H8017
Jdg 5:16 In the districts of **R** there was much H8017
2Ki 10:33 the region of Gad, **R** and Manasseh), H8018
1Ch 2: 1 **R**, Simeon, Levi, Judah, Issachar, Zebulun, H8017
1Ch 5: 1 The sons of **R** the firstborn of Israel (he H8017
1Ch 5: 3 the sons of **R** the firstborn of Israel: Hanok H8017
1Ch 6:63 allotted twelve towns from the tribes of **R**, H8017
1Ch 6:78 from the tribe of **R** across the Jordan east H8017
1Ch 12:37 of the Jordan, from **R**, Gad and the H8018
Eze 48: 6 "**R** will have one portion; it will border the H8017
Eze 48: 7 border the territory of **R** from east to west. H8017
Eze 48:31 on the north side will be the gate of **R**, H8017
Rev 7: 5 from the tribe *of* **R** 12,000, from the G4857

REUBENITE (2) [REUBEN]

Dt 11: 6 sons of Eliab the **R**, when the earth H1201+8017
1Ch 11:42 Adina son of Shiza the **R**, who was chief H8018

REUBENITES (30) [REUBEN]

Nu 16: 1 and certain **R**—Dathan and Abiram H1201+8017
Nu 32: 1 The **R** and Gadites, who had very H1201+8017
Nu 32: 6 Moses said to the Gadites and **R** H1201+8017
Nu 32:25 The Gadites and **R** said to Moses H1201+8017
Nu 32:29 "If the Gadites and **R**, every man H1201+8017
Nu 32:31 The Gadites and **R** answered H1201+8017
Nu 32:33 the **R** and the half-tribe of H1201+8017
Nu 32:37 And the **R** rebuilt Heshbon, Elealeh H1201+8017
Dt 3:12 I gave the **R** and the Gadites the territory H8018
Dt 3:16 But to the **R** and the Gadites I gave the H8018
Dt 4:43 plateau, for the **R**; Ramoth in Gilead, H8018
Dt 29: 8 gave it as an inheritance to the **R**, H8018
Jos 1:12 But to the **R**, the Gadites and the H8018
Jos 12: 6 of the LORD gave their land to the **R**, H8018
Jos 13: 8 the **R** and the Gadites had received the H8018
Jos 13:23 boundary of the **R** was the bank of H1201+8017
Jos 13:23 were the inheritance of the **R**, H1201+8017
Jos 22: 1 Then Joshua summoned the **R**, the H8018
Jos 22: 9 So the **R**, the Gadites and the H1201+8017
Jos 22:10 of Canaan, the **R**, the Gadites and H1201+8017
Jos 22:25 us and you—you **R** and Gadites! H1201+8017
Jos 22:32 meeting with the **R** and Gadites in H1201+8017
Jos 22:33 where the **R** and the Gadites H1201+8017
Jos 22:34 And the **R** and the Gadites gave H1201+8017
1Ch 5: 6 Beerah was a leader of the **R**. H8018
1Ch 5:18 The **R**, the Gadites and the H1201+8017
1Ch 5:26 who took the **R**, the Gadites and the H8018
1Ch 11:42 who was chief of the **R**, and the thirty with H8018
1Ch 26:32 King David put them in charge of the **R**, H8018
1Ch 27:16 over the **R**: Eliezer son of Zikri; H8018

REUEL (11)

Ge 36: 4 bore Eliphaz to Esau, Basemath bore **R**, H8294
Ge 36:10 wife Adah, and **R**, the son of Esau's H8294
Ge 36:13 The sons of **R**: Nahath, Zerah, Shammah H8294
Ge 36:17 The sons of Esau's son **R**: Chiefs Nahath H8294
Ge 36:17 the chiefs descended from **R** in Edom; H8294
Ex 2:18 When the girls returned to **R** their father H8294
Ex 2:20 "And where is he?" **R** asked his daughters NDT
Nu 10:29 said to Hobab son of **R** the Midianite, H8294
1Ch 1:35 Eliphaz, **R**, Jeush, Jalam and H8294
1Ch 1:37 The sons of **R**: Nahath, Zerah, Shammah H8294
1Ch 9: 8 the son of **R**, the son of Ibnijah. H8294

REUMAH (1)

Ge 22:24 whose name was **R**, also had sons: H8020

REVEAL (8) [REVEALED, REVEALER, REVEALING, REVEALS, REVELATION, REVELATIONS]

Nu 12: 6 *I*, the LORD, **r myself** to them in visions H3359
1Sa 2:27 '*Did I* not **clearly r myself** to your H1655+1655
Ps 19: 2 night after night *they* **r** knowledge. H2555
Da 2:11 No one *can* **r** it to the king except the A10252
Da 2:47 you were able to **r** this mystery. A10144
Mt 11:27 those to whom the Son chooses *to* **r** him. G636
Lk 10:22 those to whom the Son chooses *to* **r** him." G636
Gal 1:16 *to* **r** his Son in me so that I might preach G636

REVEALED (63) [REVEAL]

Ge 35: 7 there that God **r himself** to him when he H1655
Ge 41:25 God *has* **r** to Pharaoh what he is about to H5583
Dt 29:29 the *things* **r** belong to us and to our H1655
1Sa 3: 7 of the LORD *had* not yet **been r** to him. H1655
1Sa 3:21 there he **r himself** to Samuel through H1655
1Sa 9:15 the LORD *had* **r** this *to* Samuel: H1655+906+265
2Sa 7:27 you *have* **r** this *to* your servant H1655+265
2Ki 8:10 the LORD *has* **r** *to* me that he will in fact H8011
1Ch 17:25 *have* **r** *to* your servant that you will H1655+265
Est 2:10 Esther *had* not **r** her nationality and family H5583
Ps 98: 2 salvation known and **r** his righteousness H1655
Ps 147:19 *He has* **r** his word to Jacob, his laws and H5583
Isa 22:14 The LORD Almighty *has* **r** this in my H1655
Isa 40: 5 And the glory of the LORD *will* **be r**, and all H1655
Isa 43:12 I *have* **r** and saved and proclaimed—I H5583
Isa 53: 1 to whom *has* the arm of the LORD **been r**? H1655
Isa 56: 1 my righteousness *will* soon **be r**. H1655
Isa 65: 1 "*I* **r myself** to those who did not ask for me H2011
Jer 11:18 Because the LORD **r** their plot *to* me, I knew H3359
Jer 38:21 this is what the LORD *has* **r** *to* me: H8011
Eze 20: 5 of Jacob and **r myself** to them in Egypt. H3359
Eze 20: 9 in whose sight *I had* **r myself** to the H3359
Da 2:19 night the mystery **was r** to Daniel in a A10144
Da 2:30 this mystery *has* **been r** to me, not A10144
Hos 7: 1 are exposed and the crimes of Samaria **r**. NDT
Mt 11:25 learned, and **r** them to little children. G636
Mt 16:17 for *this was* not **r** to you by flesh and blood G636
Lk 2:26 It had been **r** to him by the Holy Spirit that G5976
Lk 2:35 that the thoughts of many hearts *will be* **r**. G636
Lk 10:21 learned, and **r** them to little children. G636
Lk 17:30 just like this on the day the Son of Man *is* **r**. G636
Jn 1:31 water was that *he might be* **r** to Israel." G5746
Jn 2:11 of the signs through which *he* **r** his glory; G5746
Jn 12:38 to whom *has* the arm of the Lord *been* **r**?" G636
Jn 17: 6 "*I have* **r** you to those whom you gave me G5746
Ro 1:17 the gospel the righteousness of God *is* **r**— G636
Ro 1:18 The wrath of God *is being* **r** from heaven G636
Ro 2: 5 *when* his righteous judgment *will be* **r**. G637
Ro 8:18 with the glory that will be **r** in us. G636
Ro 8:19 expectation for the children of God to be **r**. G637
Ro 10:20 *I* **r** *myself* to those who did not ask G1871+1181
Ro 16:26 now **r** and made known through the G5746
1Co 1: 7 wait for our Lord Jesus Christ to be **r**. G637
1Co 2:10 are the things God *has* **r** to us by his Spirit. G636
1Co 3:13 *It will be* **r** with fire, and the fire will test G636
1Co 4: 1 those entrusted with the mysteries **God** *has* **r**. AIT
2Co 4:10 life of Jesus *may* also *be* **r** in our body. G5746
2Co 4:11 so that his life *may* also *be* **r** in our mortal G5746
Gal 3:23 the faith that was to come *would be* **r**. G636
Eph 3: 5 as *it has* now *been* **r** by the Spirit G636
2Th 1: 7 the Lord Jesus is **r** from heaven in blazing G637
2Th 2: 3 occurs and the man of lawlessness *is* **r**, G636
2Th 2: 6 so that he *may be* **r** at the proper time. G636
2Th 2: 8 And then the lawless one *will be* **r**, whom G636
2Ti 1:10 but *it has* now *been* **r** through the G5746
1Pe 1: 5 that is ready *to be* **r** in the last time. G636
1Pe 1: 7 glory and honor when Jesus Christ is **r**. G637
1Pe 1:12 *It was* **r** to them that they were not serving G636
1Pe 1:13 to you when Jesus Christ *is* **r** at his coming. G637
1Pe 1:20 but *was* **r** in these last times for your sake. G5746
1Pe 4:13 you may be overjoyed when his glory is **r**. G637
1Pe 5: 1 who also will share in the glory to be **r**: G636
Rev 15: 4 for your righteous acts *have been* **r**." G5746

REVEALER (2) [REVEAL]

Da 2:29 the **r** *of* mysteries showed you what A10144
Da 2:47 the Lord of kings and a **r** *of* mysteries, A10144

REVEALING (2) [REVEAL]

Eze 21:24 rebellion, **r** your sins in all that you do H8011
Am 3: 7 does nothing without **r** his plan to his H1655

REVEALS (5) [REVEAL]

Nu 23: 3 Whatever *he* **r** *to* me I will tell you." H8011
Job 12:22 *He* **r** the deep things of darkness and H1655
Da 2:22 He **r** deep and hidden things; he knows A10144
Da 2:28 is a God in heaven *who* **r** mysteries. A10144
Am 4:13 and *who* **r** his thoughts to mankind H5583

REVELATION (16) [REVEAL]

2Sa 7:17 to David all the words of this entire **r**. H2612
1Ch 17:15 to David all the words of this entire **r**. H2606
Pr 29:18 Where there is no **r**, people cast off H2606
Da 10: 1 king of Persia, a **r** was given to Daniel H1821
Hab 2: 2 "Write down the **r** and make it plain on H2606
Hab 2: 3 For the **r** awaits an appointed time; it H2606
Lk 2:32 a light for **r** to the Gentiles, and the glory of G637
Ro 16:25 in keeping with the **r** of the mystery hidden G637
1Co 14: 6 unless I bring you some **r** or knowledge G637
1Co 14:26 a word of instruction, a **r**, a tongue or an G637
1Co 14:30 And if a **r comes** to someone who is sitting G636
Gal 1:12 rather, I received it by **r** from Jesus Christ. G637
Gal 2: 2 I went in response to a **r** and, meeting G637
Eph 1:17 may give you the Spirit of wisdom and **r**, so G637
Eph 3: 3 the mystery made known to me by **r**, as I G637
Rev 1: 1 The **r** from Jesus Christ, which God gave G637

REVELATIONS (2) [REVEAL]

2Co 12: 1 I will go on to visions and **r** from the Lord. G637
2Co 12: 7 *because of* these surpassingly great **r** G637

REVELED (2) [REVELRY]

Ne 9:25 *they* **r** in your great goodness. H6357
Ac 7:41 sacrifices to it and **r** in what their own G2370

REVELERS (3) [REVELRY]

Isa 5:14 masses with all their brawlers and **r**. H6601
Isa 24: 8 the noise of the **r** has stopped, the joyful H6611
Jer 15:17 I never sat in the company of **r**, never H8471

REVELING (3) [REVELRY]

1Sa 30:16 drinking and **r** because of the great H2510
Isa 23:12 "No more of your **r**, Virgin Daughter Sidon H6600
2Pe 2:13 **r** in their pleasures while they feast with G1960

REVELRY (7) [REVELED, REVELERS, REVELING]

Ex 32: 6 eat and drink and got up to **indulge in r**. H7464
Isa 22: 2 of commotion, you city of tumult and **r**? H6611
Isa 22:13 there is joy and **r**, slaughtering of H8525
Isa 23: 7 Is this your city of **r**, the old, old city H6611
Isa 32:13 houses of merriment and for this city of **r**. H6611
Zep 2:15 This is the city of **r** that lived in safety. H6611
1Co 10: 7 eat and drink and got up *to* **indulge in r**." G4089

REVENGE (11) [VENGEANCE]

Lev 19:18 " '*Do* not **seek r** or bear a grudge against H5933
Jdg 15: 7 that I won't stop until *I* **get** *my* **r** on you." H5933
Jdg 16:28 and *let me with* one blow **get r** on H5934+5933
1Sa 18:25 foreskins, to **take r** on his enemies. H5933
Ps 44:16 because of the enemy, *who is* **bent on r**. H5933
Pr 6:34 he will show no mercy when he takes **r**. H5934
Jer 20:10 prevail over him and take our **r** on him." H5935
Eze 24: 8 up wrath and **take r** I put her blood H5933+5934
Eze 25:12 Edom **took r** on Judah and H5933+5934
Eze 25:15 vengeance and **took r** with malice H5933+5934
Ro 12:19 *Do* not **take r**, my dear friends, but leave G1688

REVENUE (4) [REVENUES]

Isa 23: 3 the harvest of the Nile was the **r** *of* Tyre H9311
Isa 33:18 Where is the *one who* **took** *the* **r**? Where H9202
Ro 13: 7 owe taxes, pay taxes; if **r**, then revenue; if G5465
Ro 13: 7 if revenue, then **r**; if respect, then G5465

REVENUES (4) [REVENUE]

1Ki 10:15 not including the **r** from merchants and H5006
2Ch 9:14 not including the **r** brought in by merchants NDT
Ezr 4:13 eventually the royal **r** will suffer. A10063
Ezr 6: 8 treasury, from the **r** *of* Trans-Euphrates A10402

REVERE (17) [REVERED, REVERENCE, REVERENT, REVERING]

Lev 19:32 respect for the elderly and **r** your God. H3707
Dt 4:10 they may learn to **r** me as long as they H3707
Dt 13: 4 God you must follow, and him *you must* **r**. H3707
Dt 14:23 that you may learn to **r** the LORD your God H3707
Dt 17:19 he may learn to **r** the LORD his God and H3707
Dt 28:58 *do* not **r** this glorious and awesome H3707
Job 37:24 Therefore, people **r** him, for does he not H3707
Ps 22:23 **R** him, all *you* descendants of Israel H1593
Ps 33: 8 *let* all the people of the world **r** him. H1593
Ps 102:15 all the kings of the earth will **r** your glory. NDT
Isa 25: 3 cities of ruthless nations *will* **r** you. H3707
Isa 59:19 the rising of the sun, they will **r** his glory. NDT
Isa 63:17 harden our hearts so we do not **r** you? H3711
Hos 10: 3 no king because *we did* not **r** the LORD. H3707
Mal 4: 2 But for you *who* **r** my name, the sun of H3710
1Pe 3:15 But in your hearts **r** Christ as Lord. Always G39
Rev 11:18 your people who **r** your name, G5828

REVERED (2) [REVERE]

2Ki 4: 1 is dead, and you know that he **r** the LORD. H3707
Mal 2: 5 reverence and *he* **r** me and stood in H3707

REVERENCE (15) [REVERE]

Lev 19:30 my Sabbaths and **have r for** my sanctuary. H3707
Lev 26: 2 my Sabbaths and **have r** *for* my sanctuary. H3707
Jos 5:14 Joshua fell facedown to the ground *in* **r**, H2556
Ne 5:15 But out of **r** *for* God I did not act like that H3711
Ps 5: 7 in **r** I bow down toward your holy temple. H3711
Ps 130: 4 so that we *can*, **with r**, **serve** *you*. H3707
Jer 44:10 have not humbled themselves or **shown r**, H3707
Da 6:26 must fear and **r** the God of Daniel. A10167
Mal 2: 5 this called for **r** and he revered me and H4616
Ac 10:25 Cornelius met him and fell at his feet **in r**. G4686
2Co 7: 1 perfecting holiness out of **r** for God. G5832
Eph 5:21 Submit to one another out of **r** for Christ. G5832
Col 3:22 with sincerity of heart and **r** for the Lord. G5828
Heb 12:28 worship God acceptably with **r** and awe, G2325
1Pe 3: 2 they see the purity and **r** of your lives. G5832

REVERENT (5) [REVERE]

Ecc 8:12 who fear God, who *are* **r** before him. H3707
Titus 2: 3 older women to be **r** in the way they live, G2640
Heb 5: 7 was heard because of his **r submission**. G2325
1Pe 1:17 out your time as foreigners here in **r fear**. G5832
1Pe 2:18 in **r fear** of God submit yourselves G4246+5832

REVERING (2) [REVERE]

Dt 8: 6 walking in obedience to him and **r** him. H3707
Ne 1:11 your servants who delight in **r** your name. H3707

REVERSE (1) [REVERSED]
Isa 43:13 When I act, who *can* **r** it?" H8740

REVERSED (1) [REVERSE]
Eze 7:13 concerning the whole crowd *will* not *be* **r**. H8740

REVERT (3)
Lev 27:24 Jubilee the field *will* **r** to the person from H8740
1Ki 12:26 "The kingdom *will* now *likely* **r** to the H8740
Eze 46:17 of freedom; then *it will* **r** to the prince. H8697

REVIEW (1)
Isa 43:26 **R the past** *for* me, let us argue the matter H2349

REVILE (4) [REVILED, REVILES]
Ps 10:13 Why *does* the wicked man **r** God? Why H5540
Ps 44:16 taunts of those who reproach and **r** me, H1552
Ps 74:10 *Will* the foe **r** your name forever H5540
Ecc 10:20 *Do* not **r** the king even in your thoughts, or H7837

REVILED (1) [REVILE]
Ps 74:18 how foolish people *have* **r** your name. H5540

REVILES (1) [REVILE]
Ps 10: 3 he blesses the greedy and **r** the LORD. H5540

REVIVE (5) [REVIVED]
Ps 80:18 turn away from you; **r** us, and we will call H2649
Ps 85: 6 *Will* you not **r** us again, that your people H2649
Isa 57:15 to **r** the spirit of the lowly and to revive the H2649
Isa 57:15 of the lowly and to **r** the heart of the H2649
Hos 6: 2 After two days *he will* **r** us; on the third H2649

REVIVED (3) [REVIVE]
Ge 45:27 him back, the spirit of their father Jacob **r**. H2649
Jdg 15:19 his strength returned and *he* **r**. H2649
1Sa 30:12 He ate and *was* **r**, for he had not H8740+8120

REVOKE (1) [REVOKED, REVOKING]
Ps 132:11 to David, a sure oath *he will* not **r**: H8740+4946

REVOKED (3) [REVOKE]
Est 8: 8 name and sealed with his ring *can be* **r**." H8740
Isa 45:23 in all integrity a word *that will* not *be* **r**: H8740
Zec 11:11 *It* **was r** on that day, and so the oppressed H7296

REVOKING (1) [REVOKE]
Zec 11:10 **r** the covenant I had made with all the H7296

REVOLT (8) [REVOLTED]
Ezr 4:19 a long history of **r** against kings and has A10492
Ne 6: 6 that you and the Jews are plotting to **r** H5277
Pr 30:31 a he-goat, and a king secure against **r**. H7756
Isa 59:13 on our God, inciting **r** and oppression H6240
Eze 2: 3 ancestors *have been* **in r** against me to H7321
Eze 20:38 you of those *who* **r** and rebel against H5277
Ac 5:37 and **led** a band of people **in r**. G923+3958
Ac 21:38 the Egyptian who **started a r** and led four G415

REVOLTED (4) [REVOLT]
Jdg 9:18 But today you *have* **r** against my father's H7756
2Ki 8:22 Libnah **r** at the same time. H7321
2Ch 21:10 Libnah **r** at the same time, because H7321
Isa 31: 6 to the One you have so greatly **r against**. H6240

REWARD (54) [REWARDED, REWARDING, REWARDS]
Ge 15: 1 I am your shield, your very great **r**." H8510
Nu 22:17 *I will* **r** you **handsomely** and H3877+4394+3877
Nu 22:37 Am I really not able *to* **r** you?" H3877
Nu 24:11 I said *I would* **r** you **handsomely** H3877+3877
1Sa 24:19 *May* the LORD **r** you well for the way you H8966
2Sa 4:10 That was the **r** I gave him **for** his **news**! H1415
2Sa 18:22 have any news *that will* **bring** you **a r**." H5162
2Sa 19:36 why *should* the king **r** me *in* this way? H1694
Job 17: 5 If anyone denounces their friends for **r** H2750
Job 34:33 *Should* God then **r** you on your terms H8966
Ps 17:14 those of this world whose **r** is in this life. H2750
Ps 19:11 warned; in keeping them there is great **r**. H6813
Ps 37: 6 will make your **righteous r** shine like the H7406
Ps 62:12 "You **r** everyone according to what they H8966
Ps 127: 3 from the LORD, offspring a **r** from him. H8510
Pr 9:12 your wisdom will **r** you; if you are a H4200
Pr 11:18 who sows righteousness reaps a sure **r**. H8512
Pr 12:14 the work of their hands **brings** them **r**. H8740
Pr 19:17 and *he will* **r** them *for* what they have H8966
Pr 25:22 coals on his head, and the LORD *will* **r** you. H8966
Ecc 2:10 my labor, and this was the **r** for all my toil. H2750
Ecc 9: 5 they have no further **r**, and even their H8510
Isa 40:10 his **r** is with him, and his H8510
Isa 45:13 not for a price or **r**, says the LORD H8816
Isa 49: 4 LORD's hand, and my **r** is with my God." H7190
Isa 61: 8 faithfulness *I will* **r** my people and H5989+7190
Isa 62:11 his **r** is with him, and his H8510
Jer 17:10 to **r** each person according to their H5989
Jer 32:19 you **r** each person according to their H5989
Eze 29:18 his army got no **r** from the campaign H8510
Eze 29:20 given him Egypt as a **r** for his efforts H7190
Mt 5:12 because great is your **r** in heaven, for in G3635
Mt 5:46 those who love you, what **r** will you get? G3635
Mt 6: 1 you will have no **r** from your Father in G3635
Mt 6: 2 I tell you, they have received their **r** in full. G3635
Mt 6: 4 who sees what is done in secret, *will* **r** you. G625
Mt 6: 5 I tell you, they have received their **r** in full. G3635
Mt 6: 6 who sees what is done in secret, *will* **r** you. G625
Mt 6:16 I tell you, they have received their **r** in full. G3635
Mt 6:18 who sees what is done in secret, *will* **r** you. G625
Mt 10:41 as a prophet will receive a prophet's **r**, G3635
Mt 10:41 person will receive a righteous person's **r**. G3635
Mt 10:42 that person will certainly not lose their **r**." G3635
Mt 16:27 then *he will* **r** each person according to G625
Mk 9:41 the Messiah will certainly not lose their **r**. G3635
Lk 6:23 joy, because great is your **r** in heaven. G3635
Lk 6:35 Then your **r** will be great, and you will be G3635
1Co 3:14 built survives, the builder will receive a **r**. G3635
1Co 9:17 voluntarily, I have a **r**; if not voluntarily, G3635
1Co 9:18 What then is my **r**? Just this: that in G3635
Eph 6: 8 know that the Lord *will* **r** each one for G3152
Col 3:24 receive an inheritance from the Lord *as* a **r**. G502
Heb 11:26 because he was looking ahead to his **r**. G3632
Rev 22:12 My **r** is with me, and I will give to each G3635

REWARDED (16) [REWARD]
Ge 30:18 "God *has* **r** me for giving my H8510+5989
Nu 24:11 the LORD has kept you from being **r**." H3883
Ru 2:12 May you be richly **r** by the LORD, the God H5382
2Sa 22:21 the cleanness of my hands *he has* **r** me. H8740
2Sa 22:25 The LORD *has* **r** me according to my H8740
2Ch 15: 7 do not give up, for your work will be **r**." H8510
Ps 18:20 the cleanness of my hands *he has* **r** me. H8740
Ps 18:24 The LORD *has* **r** me according to my H8740
Ps 58:11 "Surely the righteous still are **r**; surely H7262
Pr 13:13 but whoever respects a command **is r**. H8966
Pr 13:21 the righteous *are* **r** *with* good things. H8966
Pr 14:14 their ways, and the good **r** for theirs. NDT
Jer 31:16 your work will be **r**," declares the LORD. H8510
1Co 3: 8 and *they will* each **be r** according G3635+3284
Heb 10:35 away your confidence; it will be richly **r**. G3632
2Jn 8 but that *you may be* **r** fully. G3635+655

REWARDING (1) [REWARD]
Rev 11:18 and *for* **r** your servants the G1443+3836+3635

REWARDS (4) [REWARD]
1Sa 26:23 The LORD **r** everyone *for* their righteousness H8740
Da 2: 6 from me gifts and **r** and great honor. A10454
Da 5:17 give your **r** to someone else. A10454
Heb 11: 6 he exists and that *he* **r** those who G3633+1181

REZEPH (2)
2Ki 19:12 **R** and the people of Eden who were in H8364
Isa 37:12 **R** and the people of Eden who were in H8364

REZIN (10) [REZIN'S]
2Ki 15:37 LORD began to send **R** king of Aram and H8360
2Ki 16: 5 Then **R** king of Aram and Pekah son of H8360
2Ki 16: 6 **R** king of Aram recovered Elath for Aram H8360
2Ki 16: 9 its inhabitants to Kir and put **R** to death. H8360
Ezr 2:48 **R**, Nekoda, Gazzam, H8360
Ne 7:50 Reaiah, **R**, Nekoda, H8360
Isa 7: 1 King **R** of Aram and Pekah son of H8360
Isa 7: 4 the fierce anger of **R** and Aram and of the H8360
Isa 7: 8 the head of Damascus is only **R**. H8360
Isa 8: 6 rejoices over **R** and the son of H8360

REZIN'S (1) [REZIN]
Isa 9:11 has strengthened **R** foes against them H8360

REZON (4)
1Ki 11:23 another adversary, **R** son of Eliada, who H8139
1Ki 11:24 **R** gathered a band of men around him and NDT
1Ki 11:25 **R** was Israel's adversary as long as Solomon NDT
1Ki 11:25 So **R** ruled in Aram and was hostile toward NDT

RHEGIUM (1)
Ac 28:13 From there we set sail and arrived at **R** G4836

RHESA (1)
Lk 3:27 son of Joanan, the son *of* **R**, the son of G4840

RHODA (1)
Ac 12:13 a servant named **R** came to answer the G4851

RHODES (2)
Eze 27:15 " 'The men of **R** traded with you, and H8102
Ac 21: 1 next day we went to **R** and from there to G4852

RIB (1) [RIBS]
Ge 2:22 a woman from the **r** he had taken out of H7521

RIBAI (2)
2Sa 23:29 Ithai son of **R** from Gibeah in Benjamin, H8192
1Ch 11:31 Ithai son of **R** from Gibeah in Benjamin H8192

RIBBON (1)
SS 4: 3 Your lips are like a scarlet **r**; your mouth is H2562

RIBLAH (11)
Nu 34:11 from Shepham to **R** on the east side of H8058
2Ki 23:33 put him in chains at **R** in the land of H8058
2Ki 25: 6 He was taken to the king of Babylon at **R** H8058
2Ki 25:20 brought them to the king of Babylon at **R**. H8058
2Ki 25:21 There at **R**, in the land of Hamath, the H8058
Jer 39: 5 king of Babylon at **R** in the land of H8058
Jer 39: 6 There at **R** the king of Babylon slaughtered H8058
Jer 52: 9 king of Babylon at **R** in the land of H8058
Jer 52:10 There at **R** the king of Babylon killed the H8058
Jer 52:26 brought them to the king of Babylon at **R**. H8058
Jer 52:27 There at **R**, in the land of Hamath, the H8058

RIBS (2) [RIB]
Ge 2:21 one of the man's **r** and then closed up H7521
Da 7: 5 it had three **r** in its mouth between A10552

RICH (97) [ENRICH, ENRICHED, RICHER, RICHES, RICHEST, RICHLY, RICHNESS]
Ge 14:23 never be able to say, 'I **made** Abram **r**. H6947
Ge 26:13 The man *became* **r**, and his wealth H1540
Ge 49:20 "Asher's food will be **r**; he will provide H9045
Ex 30:15 The **r** are not to give more than a half H6938
Lev 25:47 among you *becomes* **r** and any of H5952+3338
Ru 3:10 after the younger men, whether **r** or poor. H6938
2Sa 12: 1 a certain town, one **r** and the other poor. H6938
2Sa 12: 2 The **r** *man* had a very large number of H6938
2Sa 12: 4 "Now a traveler came to the **r** man, but H6938
2Sa 12: 4 the **r** man refrained from taking one of NDT
1Ch 4:40 They found **r**, good pasture, and the land H9045
Job 15:29 *He will* no longer *be* **r** and his wealth will H6947
Job 21:24 nourished in body, bones **r** *with* marrow. H9197
Job 34:19 does not favor the **r** over the poor, H8777
Ps 21: 3 to greet him with **r** blessings and placed a H3202
Ps 22:29 All the **r** *of* the earth will feast and H2016
Ps 49: 2 both low and high, **r** and poor alike: H6938
Ps 49:16 Do not be overawed when others *grow* **r** H6947
Ps 76: 4 more majestic than **mountains** *r with* game. AIT
Ps 145: 8 slow to anger and **r** *in* love. H1524
Pr 8:21 bestowing a **r** inheritance on those who H3780
Pr 10:15 The wealth of the **r** is their fortified city H6938
Pr 13: 7 *One person* **pretends to be r**, yet has H6947
Pr 14:20 neighbors, but the **r** have many friends. H6938
Pr 18:11 The wealth of the **r** is their fortified city H6938
Pr 18:23 plead for mercy, but the **r** answer harshly. H6938
Pr 21:17 loves wine and olive oil *will* never *be* **r**. H6947
Pr 22: 2 **R** and poor have this in common: The H6938
Pr 22: 7 The **r** rule over the poor, and the borrower H6938
Pr 22:16 wealth and one who gives gifts to the **r**— H6938
Pr 23: 4 Do not wear yourself out to *get* **r**; do not H6947
Pr 24:25 and **r** blessing will come on them. H3202
Pr 28: 6 is blameless than the **r** whose ways are H6938
Pr 28:11 The **r** are wise in their own eyes H6938+408
Pr 28:20 one eager to **get r** will not go H6947
Pr 28:22 are eager to get **r** and are unaware that H2104
Ecc 5:12 much, but as for the **r**, their abundance H6938
Ecc 10: 6 while the **r** occupy the low ones. H6938
Ecc 10:20 thoughts, or curse the **r** in your bedroom H6938
Isa 5:17 lambs will feed among the ruins of the **r**. H4671
Isa 25: 6 prepare a feast of **r food** for all peoples, H9043
Isa 30:23 from the land will be **r** and plentiful. H2015
Isa 33: 6 a **r store** *of* salvation and wisdom and H2890
Isa 53: 9 with the **r** in his death, though H6938
Jer 2: 7 a fertile land to eat its fruit and **r produce**. H3206
Jer 5:27 *they have become* **r** and powerful H6947
Jer 9:23 their strength or the **r** boast of their riches, H6938
Jer 49:19 from Jordan's thickets to a **r** pastureland, H419
Jer 50:44 from Jordan's thickets to a **r** pastureland, H419
Jer 51:13 live by many waters and are **r** *in* treasures, H8041
Eze 34:14 they will feed in a **r** pasture on the H9045
Eze 38:12 from the nations, **r** *in* livestock and goods H6913
Hos 12: 8 "*I am* very **r**; I have become H6947
Mic 2: 8 You strip off the **r** robe from those who pass H159
Mic 6:12 Your **r** *people* are violent; your inhabitants H6938
Zec 11: 3 shepherds; their **r pastures** are destroyed! H168
Zec 11: 5 sell them say, 'Praise the LORD, *I am* **r**! H6947
Mt 19:23 is hard for *someone who is* **r** to enter the G4454
Mt 19:24 needle than *for someone who is* **r** to enter G4454
Mt 27:57 there came a **r** man from Arimathea G4454
Mk 10:23 hard it is *for* the **r** to enter G3836+5975+2400
Mk 10:25 needle than *for someone who is* **r** to enter G4454
Mk 12:41 Many **r** *people* threw in large amounts G4454
Lk 1:53 things but has sent the **r** away empty. G4456
Lk 6:24 "But woe to you who are **r**, for you have G4454
Lk 12:16 ground of a certain **r** man yielded an G4454
Lk 12:21 themselves but *is* not **r** toward God." G4456
Lk 14:12 relatives, or your **r** neighbors; if you do, G4454
Lk 16: 1 "There was a **r** man whose manager was G4454
Lk 16:19 "There was a **r** man who was dressed in G4454
Lk 16:21 to eat what fell from the **r** *man's* table. G4454
Lk 16:22 The **r** *man* also died and was buried. G4454
Lk 18:24 hard it is *for* the **r** to enter G3836+5975+2400
Lk 18:25 needle than *for someone who is* **r** to enter G4454
Lk 21: 1 he saw the **r** putting their gifts into the G4454
1Co 4: 8 Already *you have become* **r**! You have G4456
2Co 6:10 yet **making** many **r**; having nothing G4457
2Co 8: 2 extreme poverty welled up in **r** generosity. G4458
2Co 8: 9 that though he was **r**, yet for your sake he G4454
2Co 8: 9 you through his poverty *might become* **r**. G4456
Eph 2: 4 great love for us, God, who is **r** in mercy, G4454
1Ti 6: 9 Those who want *to get* **r** fall into G4456
1Ti 6:17 those who are **r** in this present world G4454
1Ti 6:18 them to do good, *to be* **r** in good deeds G4456
Jas 1:10 But the **r** should take pride in their G4454
Jas 1:11 the **r** will fade away even while they go G4454
Jas 2: 5 of the world to be **r** in faith and to inherit G4454
Jas 2: 6 Is it not the **r** who are exploiting you G4454
Jas 5: 1 Now listen, you **r** *people*, weep and wail G4454
2Pe 1:11 you will receive a **r** welcome into the G4455
Rev 2: 9 afflictions and your poverty—yet you are **r**! G4454
Rev 3:17 You say, 'I am **r**; I have acquired wealth G4454
Rev 3:18 the fire, so *you can become* **r**; and white G4456
Rev 6:15 the generals, the **r**, the mighty, and G4454
Rev 13:16 great and small, **r** and poor, free and G4454
Rev 18: 3 of the earth *grew* **r** from her excessive G4456

Rev 18:19 ships on the sea became r through her G4456

RICHER (1) [RICH]
Da 11: 2 who will be far r than all the others. H6947+6948

RICHES (47) [RICH]
1Ki 10:23 was greater in r and wisdom than all H6948
2Ch 9:22 was greater in r and wisdom than all H6948
2Ch 32:29 for God had given him very great r. H8214
Job 20:15 He will spit out the r he swallowed; God H2657
Job 36:18 Be careful that no one entices you by r; do H6217
Ps 49: 6 in their wealth and boast of their great r? H6948
Ps 62:10 though your r increase, do not set H2657
Ps 112: 3 Wealth and r are in their houses, and H6948
Ps 119:14 your statutes as one rejoices in great r. H2104
Pr 3:16 in her left hand are r and honor. H6948
Pr 8:18 With me are r and honor, enduring H6948
Pr 11:28 Those who trust in their r will fall, but the H6948
Pr 12:27 diligent feed on the r of the hunt. H3701+2104
Pr 13: 8 A person's r may ransom their life, but the H6948
Pr 22: 1 name is more desirable than great r; H6948
Pr 22: 4 its wages are r and honor and life. H6948
Pr 23: 5 Cast but a glance at r, and they are gone H2257S
Pr 27:24 r do not endure forever, and a crown is H2890
Pr 30: 8 give me neither poverty nor r, but give me H6948
Isa 10: 3 run for help? Where will you leave your r? H3883
Isa 30: 6 the envoys carry their r on donkeys' backs H2657
Isa 45: 3 treasures, r stored in secret places, so H4759
Isa 60: 5 to you the r of the nations will come. H2657
Isa 61: 6 of nations, and in their r you will boast. H3883
Jer 9:23 of their strength or the rich boast of their r, H6948
Jer 17:11 lay are those who gain r by unjust means. H6948
Jer 17:11 are half gone, their r will desert them, and NDT
Jer 48: 7 Since you trust in your deeds and r, you too H238
Jer 49: 4 you trust in your r and say, 'Who will H238
Da 11:43 of gold and silver and all the r of Egypt, H2776
Joel 2:22 the fig tree and the vine yield their r. H2657
Lk 8:14 by life's worries, r and pleasures, and they G4458
Lk 16:11 who will trust you with true r? NDT
Ro 2: 4 show contempt for the r of his kindness, G4458
Ro 9:23 did this to make the r of his glory known G4458
Ro 11:12 their transgression means r for the world, G4458
Ro 11:12 their loss means r for the Gentiles G4458
Ro 11:12 how much greater r will their full inclusion NDT
Ro 11:33 the depth of the r of the wisdom and G4458
Eph 1: 7 in accordance with the r of God's grace G4458
Eph 1:18 the r of his glorious inheritance in his holy G4458
Eph 2: 7 show the incomparable r of his grace, G4458
Eph 3: 8 to the Gentiles the boundless r of Christ, G4458
Eph 3:16 out of his glorious r he may strengthen G4458
Php 4:19 according to the r of his glory in Christ G4458
Col 1:27 the Gentiles the glorious r of this mystery, G4458
Col 2: 2 they may have the full r of complete G4458

RICHEST (3) [RICH]
Ps 63: 5 as with the r of foods; H2693+2256+2016
Isa 55: 2 and you will delight in the r of fare. H2016
Da 11:24 When the r provinces feel secure, he will H5458

RICHLY (7) [RICH]
Dt 15: 4 inheritance, he will r bless you, H1385+1385
Ru 2:12 May you be r rewarded by the LORD, the H8969
Pr 28:20 A faithful person will be r blessed, but H8041
Ro 10:12 is Lord of all and r blesses all who call on G4456
Col 3:16 dwell among you r as you teach and G4455
1Ti 6:17 who r provides us with everything for our G4455
Heb 10:35 your confidence; it will be r rewarded. G3489

RICHNESS (2) [RICH]
Ge 27:28 give you heaven's dew and earth's r— H9044
Ge 27:39 dwelling will be away from the earth's r, H9044

RID (32)
Ge 21:10 "Get r of that slave woman and her son H1763
Ge 35: 2 "Get r of the foreign gods you have with H6073
Ex 8: 9 your houses may be r of the frogs, H4162
Lev 13:58 has been washed and is r of the mold, H6073
Nu 17: 5 and I will r myself of this constant H8896
Jdg 9:29 Then I would get r of him. I would H6073
Jdg 10:16 Then they got r of the foreign gods among H6073
1Sa 7: 3 then r yourselves of the foreign gods and H6073
2Sa 4:11 from your hand and r the earth of you!" H1278
2Sa 13:13 Where could I get r of my disgrace H2143
2Sa 14: 7 then we will get r of the heir as well. H9012
1Ki 15:12 from the land and got r of all the idols his H6073
1Ki 22:46 He r the land of the rest of the male shrine H1278
2Ki 3: 2 He got r of the sacred stone of Baal that H6073
2Ki 23:24 Josiah got r of the mediums and spiritists H1278
2Ch 19: 3 for you have r the land of the Asherah H1278
2Ch 33:15 He got r of the foreign gods and removed H6073
Eze 18:31 R yourselves of all the H8959+4946+6584
Eze 20: 7 get r of the vile images you have set your H8959
Eze 20: 8 they did not get r of the vile images they H8959
Eze 34:25 peace with them and r the land of savage H8697
Zec 11: 8 In one month I got r of the three H3948
Lk 2:22 looking for some way to get r of Jesus, G359
Ac 16:37 And now do they want to get r of us G1675
Ac 21:36 that followed kept shouting, "Get r of him!" G149
Ac 22:22 voices and shouted, "R the earth of him! G149
1Co 5: 7 Get r of the old yeast, so that you may be G1705
Gal 4:30 "Get r of the slave woman and her son G1675
Eph 4:31 Get r of all bitterness, rage and anger G149+608
Col 3: 8 But now you must also r yourselves of all G700
Jas 1:21 get r of all moral filth and the evil that is so G700
1Pe 2: 1 r yourselves of all malice and all deceit G700

RIDDEN (4) [RIDE]
Nu 22:30 which you have always r, to this day? H8206
Est 6: 8 king has worn and a horse the king has r, H8206
Mk 11: 2 a colt tied there, which no one has ever r. G2767
Lk 19:30 a colt tied there, which no one has ever r. G2767

RIDDLE (8) [RIDDLES]
Jdg 14:12 "Let me tell you a r," Samson said to H2648
Jdg 14:13 "Tell us your r," they said. "Let's H2648
Jdg 14:15 your husband into explaining the r for us, H2648
Jdg 14:16 You've given my people a r, but you H2648
Jdg 14:17 She in turn explained the r to her people. H2648
Jdg 14:18 you would not have solved my r. H2648
Jdg 14:19 clothes to those who had explained the r. H2648
Ps 49: 4 proverb; with the harp I will expound my r: H2648

RIDDLES (3) [RIDDLE]
Nu 12: 8 clearly and not in r; he sees the form of H2648
Pr 1: 6 parables, the sayings and r of the wise. H2648
Da 5:12 explain r and solve difficult problems. A10019

RIDE (13) [RIDDEN, RIDER, RIDERS, RIDES, RIDING, RODE]
Ge 41:43 He had him r in a chariot as his H8206
Dt 32:13 He made him r on the heights of the land H8206
Jdg 5:10 "You who r on white donkeys, sitting on H8206
2Sa 16: 2 are for the king's household to r on, H8206
2Sa 19:26 have my donkey saddled and will r on it, H8206
2Ki 10:16 Then he had him r along in his chariot H8206
Ps 45: 4 In your majesty r forth victoriously in the H8206
Ps 66:12 You let people r over our heads; we went H8206
Isa 30:16 You said, 'We will r off on swift horses H8206
Isa 33:21 No galley with oars will r them, no H2143+928
Isa 58:14 and I will cause you to r in triumph on the H8206
Jer 6:23 the roaring sea as they r on their horses; H8206
Jer 50:42 the roaring sea as they r on their horses; H8206

RIDER (11) [RIDE]
Ge 49:17 heels so that its r tumbles backward. H8206
Job 39:18 feathers to run, she laughs at horse and r. H8206
Jer 51:21 with you I shatter horse and r, with you I H8206
Zec 12: 4 horse with panic and its r with madness," H8206
Rev 6: 2 Its r held a bow, and he was given G2764+2093
Rev 6: 4 Its r was given power to take peace G2764+2093
Rev 6: 5 Its r was holding a pair of scales in G2764+2093
Rev 6: 8 Its r was named Death, and Hades G2764+2062
Rev 19:11 whose r is called Faithful and True. G2764+2093
Rev 19:19 war against the r on the horse and his G2764
Rev 19:21 out of the mouth of the r on the horse, G2764

RIDERS (8) [RIDE]
2Ki 18:23 horses—if you can put r on them! H8206
Isa 21: 7 r on donkeys or riders on camels H8207
Isa 21: 7 riders on donkeys or r on camels, let him H8207
Isa 36: 8 horses—if you can put r on them! H8206
Eze 39:20 table you will eat your fill of horses and r, H8207
Hag 2:22 horses and their r will fall, each by the H8206
Rev 9:17 The horses and r I saw in my vision G2764+2093
Rev 19:18 of horses and their r, and the flesh G2764+2093

RIDES (6) [RIDE]
Dt 33:26 who r across the heavens to help you and H8206
Ps 68: 4 his name, extol him who r on the clouds H8206
Ps 68:33 to him who r across the highest heavens H8206
Ps 104: 3 his chariot and r on the wings of the H2143
Isa 19: 1 the LORD r on a swift cloud and is coming H8206
Rev 17: 7 of the woman and of the beast she r, G1002

RIDGE (2) [RIDGES]
Ge 48:22 you I give one more r of land than to your H8900
Ge 48:22 the r I took from the Amorites with my H889S

RIDGES (1) [RIDGE]
Ps 65:10 You drench its furrows and level its r; you H1521

RIDICULE (16) [RIDICULED, RIDICULING]
Dt 28:37 a byword and an object of r among all the H9110
1Ki 9: 7 a byword and an object of r among all H9110
2Ki 19: 4 Assyria, has sent to r the living God, and H3070
2Ki 19:16 Sennacherib has sent to r the living God. H3070
2Ch 7:20 a byword and an object of r among all H9110
Job 19:18 boys scorn me; when I appear, they r me. H1819
Ps 123: 4 endured no end of r from the arrogant, H4353
Isa 37: 4 Assyria, has sent to r the living God, and H3070
Isa 37:17 Sennacherib has sent to r the living God. H3070
Jer 24: 9 a curse and an object of r, wherever I H9110
Jer 48:26 in her vomit; let her be an object of r. H8468
Jer 48:27 Was not Israel the object of your r? Was H8468
Jer 48:39 Moab has become an object of r, an H8468
Mic 2: 4 In that day people will r you; they H5442+5951
Hab 2: 6 not all of them taunt him with r and scorn, H4886
Lk 14:29 finish it, everyone who sees it will r you, G1850

RIDICULED (12) [RIDICULE]
Jdg 9:38 Aren't these the men you r? Go out and H4415
2Ki 19:22 Who is it you have r and blasphemed H3070
2Ki 19:23 By your messengers you have r the Lord H3070
2Ch 30:10 Zebulun, but people scorned and r them. H4352
Ne 2:19 heard about it, they mocked and r us. H1022
Ne 4: 1 was greatly incensed. He r the Jews, H4352
Isa 37:23 Who is it you have r and blasphemed H3070
Isa 37:24 By your messengers you have r the Lord H3070
Jer 20: 7 I am r all day long H8468
Eze 36: 4 been plundered and r by the rest of the H4353
Hos 7:16 For this they will be r in the land of Egypt. H4353
Lk 23:11 Herod and his soldiers r and mocked him. G2024

RIDICULING (1) [RIDICULE]
2Ch 32:17 The king also wrote letters r the LORD, the H3070

RIDING (14) [RIDE]
Lev 15: 9 the man sits on when r will be unclean, H8206
Nu 22:22 Balaam was r on his donkey, and his two H8206
1Sa 25:20 As she came r her donkey into a H8206
2Sa 18: 9 He was r his mule, and as the mule went H8206
2Sa 18: 9 while the mule he was r kept on going. H9393
2Ki 9:25 I were r together in chariots behind H8206
Ne 2:12 with me except the one I was r on. H8206
Est 8:14 The couriers, r the royal horses, went out H8206
Jer 17:25 their officials will come r in chariots and H8206
Jer 22: 4 of this palace, r in chariots and on horses H8206
Eze 38:15 with you, all of them r on horses, a great H8206
Zec 9: 9 victorious, lowly and r on a donkey, on a H8206
Mt 21: 5 gentle and r on a donkey, and on G2094
Rev 19:14 r on white horses and dressed in fine linen AIT

RIE (KJV) SPELT

RIGGING (2)
Pr 23:34 on the high seas, lying on top of the r. H2479
Isa 33:23 Your r hangs loose: The mast is not held H2475

RIGHT (456) [RIGHT-HANDED, RIGHTFUL, RIGHTFULLY, RIGHTLY, RIGHTS]
Ge 4: 7 If you do what is r, will you not be H3512
Ge 4: 7 But if you do not do what is r, sin is H3512
Ge 13: 9 go to the left, I'll go to the r; if you go to H3554
Ge 13: 9 if you go to the r, I'll go to the left. H3545
Ge 18:19 of the LORD by doing what is r and just, H7407
Ge 18:25 Will not the Judge of all the earth do r?" H5477
Ge 24:48 who had led me on the r road to get the H622
Ge 43:23 "It's all r," he said. "Don't be afraid. H8934
Ge 48:13 Ephraim on his r toward Israel's left hand H3545
Ge 48:13 on his left toward Israel's r hand, H3545
Ge 48:14 Israel reached out his r hand and put it on H3545
Ge 48:17 father placing his r hand on Ephraim's H3545
Ge 48:18 the firstborn; put your r hand on his head." H3545
Ex 8:26 "That would not be r. The sacrifices H3922
Ex 9:27 "The LORD is in the r, and I and my people H7404
Ex 14:22 a wall of water on their r and on their left. H3545
Ex 14:29 a wall of water on their r and on their left. H3545
Ex 15: 6 Your r hand, LORD, was majestic in power H3545
Ex 15: 6 Your r hand, LORD, shattered the H3545
Ex 15:12 "You stretch out your r hand, and the H3545
Ex 15:26 your God and do what is r in his eyes, H3838
Ex 21: 8 He has no r to sell her to foreigners H5440
Ex 29:20 on the lobes of the r ears of Aaron and H3556
Ex 29:20 on the thumbs of their r hands, and on H3556
Ex 29:20 and on the big toes of their r feet. H3556
Ex 29:22 with the fat on them, and the r thigh. H3545
Lev 7:32 You are to give the r thigh of your H3545
Lev 7:33 shall have the r thigh as his share. H3545
Lev 8:23 put it on the lobe of Aaron's r ear, H3556
Lev 8:23 on the thumb of his r hand and on the big H3556
Lev 8:23 right hand and on the big toe of his r foot. H3556
Lev 8:24 of the blood on the lobes of their r ears, H3556
Lev 8:24 the thumbs of their r hands and on the H3556
Lev 8:24 hands and on the big toes of their r feet. H3556
Lev 8:25 both kidneys and their fat and the r thigh. H3545
Lev 8:26 on the fat portions and on the r thigh. H3545
Lev 9:21 the breasts and the r thigh before the LORD H3545
Lev 14:14 it on the lobe of the r ear of the one to be H3556
Lev 14:14 the thumb of their r hand and on the big H3556
Lev 14:14 hand and on the big toe of their r foot. H3556
Lev 14:16 dip his r forefinger into the oil in his palm H3556
Lev 14:17 on the lobe of the r ear of the one to be H3556
Lev 14:17 the thumb of their r hand and on the big H3556
Lev 14:17 hand and on the big toe of their r foot, H3556
Lev 14:25 it on the lobe of the r ear of the one to be H3556
Lev 14:25 the thumb of their r hand and on the big H3556
Lev 14:25 hand and on the big toe of their r foot. H3556
Lev 14:27 with his r forefinger sprinkle some of H3556
Lev 14:28 on the lobe of the r ear of the one to be H3556
Lev 14:28 the thumb of their r hand and on the big H3556
Lev 14:28 hand and on the big toe of their r foot. H3556
Lev 25:29 city retains the r of redemption a full year H1460
Lev 25:32 always have the r to redeem their houses H1460
Lev 25:48 they retain the r of redemption after they H1460
Nu 18:18 wave offering and the r thigh are yours. H3545
Nu 20:17 not turn to the r or to the left until we H3545
Nu 22:26 room to turn, either to the r or to the left. H3545
Nu 22:29 sword in my hand, I would kill you r now." H6964
Nu 25: 6 a Midianite woman r before the eyes of H4200
Nu 25: 8 r through the Israelite man and into the NDT
Nu 27: 7 Zelophehad's daughters are saying is r. H4026
Nu 36: 5 the descendants of Joseph is saying is r. H4026
Dt 2:27 will not turn aside to the r or to the left. H3545
Dt 5:32 do not turn aside to the r or to the left. H3545
Dt 6:18 Do what is r and good in the LORD's sight H3838
Dt 11: 6 opened its mouth r in the middle of all NDT
Dt 12:25 will be doing what is r in the eyes of the H3838
Dt 12:28 what is good and r in the eyes of the H3838
Dt 13:18 you today and doing what is r in his eyes. H3838

R

Dt 17:11 what they tell you, to the **r** or to the left. H3545
Dt 17:20 turn from the law to the **r** or to the left. H3545
Dt 21: 9 you have done what is **r** in the eyes of the H3838
Dt 21:17 The **r** *of* the firstborn belongs to him. H5477
Dt 28:14 I give you today, to the **r** or to the left H3545
Jos 1: 7 do not turn from it to the **r** or to the left H3545
Jos 4: 3 from **r where** the priests are standing H2296
Jos 9:25 to us whatever seems good and **r** to you." H3838
Jos 23: 6 without turning aside to the **r** or to the left. H3545
Jdg 3:16 he strapped to his **r** thigh under his H3545
Jdg 3:21 the sword from his **r** thigh and plunged it H3545
Jdg 4:18 said to him, "Come, my lord, come **r in**. H448
Jdg 5:26 her **r** *hand* for the workman's hammer. H3545
Jdg 7:20 holding in their **r** hands the trumpets H3545
Jdg 11:23 what **r** have you to take it over? NDT
Jdg 12: 6 they said, "**All r**, say 'Shibboleth.' " If he H5528
Jdg 14: 3 "Get her for me. She's the **r** *one* for me." H3837
Jdg 15: 3 "This time *I* **have a r to get even** with the H5927
Jdg 16:29 his **r** *hand* on the one and his left hand H3545
Ru 4: 4 For no *one* **has the r to do it** except you H1457S
1Sa 6:12 they did not turn to the **r** or to the left. H3545
1Sa 11: 2 that I gouge out the **r** eye of every one of H3545
1Sa 12: 3 done any of these things, *I will* **make** it **r**." H8740
1Sa 12:23 will teach you the way that is good and **r**. H3838
1Sa 14:13 with his armor-bearer **r behind** him. H339
2Sa 2:14 "**All r**, *let them* **do it**," Joab said. H7756S
2Sa 2:19 neither to the **r** nor to the left as he H3545
2Sa 2:21 "Turn aside to the **r** or to the left; take on H3545
2Sa 8:15 what was just and **r** for all his people. H7407
2Sa 14:19 no one can **turn to the r** or to the left from H3554
2Sa 16: 6 special guard were on David's **r** and left. H3545
2Sa 18:11 you strike him to the ground **r there**? H9004
2Sa 19:22 What **r** do you have to interfere NDT
2Sa 19:28 So what **r** do I have to make any more H7407
2Sa 20: 9 by the beard with his **r** hand to kiss him. H3545
2Sa 21: 4 "We **have** no **r** to demand silver or gold H4200
2Sa 21: 4 do we **have the r** to put anyone in H4200
2Sa 23: 5 "If my house were not **r** with God, surely H4026
1Ki 1:25 **R now** they are eating and drinking with H2180
1Ki 2:19 mother, and she sat down at his **r** *hand*. H3545
1Ki 3: 9 to distinguish between **r** and wrong. H3202
1Ki 7:49 five on the **r** and five on the left H3545
1Ki 8:36 Teach them the **r** way to live, and send H3202
1Ki 11:33 done what is **r** in my eyes, nor kept H3838
1Ki 11:38 to me and do what is **r** in my eyes by H3838
1Ki 14: 8 doing only what was **r** in my eyes. H3838
1Ki 15: 5 had done what was **r** in the eyes of the H3838
1Ki 15:11 Asa did what was **r** in the eyes of the LORD, H3838
1Ki 22:19 around him on his **r** and on his left. H3545
1Ki 22:43 he did what was **r** in the eyes of the LORD. H3838
2Ki 2: 8 The water divided *to the* **r** and to the left, H2178S
2Ki 2:14 it divided *to the* **r** and to the left H2178S
2Ki 4:23 the Sabbath." "That's **all r**," she said. H8934
2Ki 4:26 to meet her and ask her, 'Are you **all r**? H8934
2Ki 4:26 Is your husband **all r**? Is your child all H8934
2Ki 4:26 husband all right? Is your child **all r**?' " H8934
2Ki 4:26 "Everything is **all r**," she said. H8934
2Ki 5:21 "Is everything **all r**?" he asked. H8934
2Ki 5:22 "Everything is **all r**," Gehazi answered H8934
2Ki 7: 9 to each other, "What we're doing is not **r**. H4026
2Ki 9:11 of them asked him, "Is everything **all r**? H8934
2Ki 10:30 what is **r** in my eyes and have H3838
2Ki 12: 2 Joash did what was **r** in the eyes of the H3838
2Ki 12: 9 on the **r** side as one enters the temple of H3545
2Ki 14: 3 He did what was **r** in the eyes of the LORD H3838
2Ki 15: 3 He did what was **r** in the eyes of the LORD H3838
2Ki 15:34 He did what was **r** in the eyes of the LORD H3838
2Ki 16: 2 did not do what was **r** in the eyes of the H3838
2Ki 17: 9 against the LORD their God that were not **r**. H4026
2Ki 18: 3 He did what was **r** in the eyes of the LORD H3838
2Ki 22: 2 He did what was **r** in the eyes of the LORD H3838
2Ki 22: 2 not turning aside to the **r** or to the left. H3545
1Ch 6:39 who served at his **r** *hand*: H3545
1Ch 13: 4 because it seemed **r** to all the people. H3837
1Ch 18:14 what was just and **r** for all his people. H7407
2Ch 6:27 Teach them the **r** way to live, and send H3202
2Ch 14: 2 what was good and **r** in the eyes of the H3838
2Ch 18:18 heaven standing on his **r** and on his left. H3545
2Ch 20:32 he did what was **r** in the eyes of the LORD. H3838
2Ch 24: 2 Joash did what was **r** in the eyes of the H3838
2Ch 25: 2 He did what was **r** in the eyes of the LORD H3838
2Ch 26: 4 He did what was **r** in the eyes of the LORD H3838
2Ch 26:18 said, "It is not **r for** you, Uzziah, H4200
2Ch 27: 2 He did what was **r** in the eyes of the LORD H3838
2Ch 28: 1 did not do what was **r** in the eyes of the H3838
2Ch 29: 2 He did what was **r** in the eyes of the LORD H3838
2Ch 30: 4 The plan seemed **r** both to the king and to H3837
2Ch 31:20 what was good and **r** and faithful before H3838
2Ch 34: 2 He did what was **r** in the eyes of the LORD H3838
2Ch 34: 2 not turning aside to the **r** or to the left. H3545
Ezr 10:12 "You are **r**! We must do as you H4026
Ne 2:20 Jerusalem or any claim or **historic r** to it." H2355
Ne 4:11 *we will* **be r there** among them and will kill H995
Ne 5: 9 I continued, "What you are doing is not **r**. H3202
Ne 8: 4 Beside him on his **r** stood Mattithiah H3545
Ne 9:13 regulations and laws that are just and **r**, H622
Ne 12:31 was to proceed on top of the wall to the **r**, H3545
Est 8: 5 with favor and **thinks** *it* the **r** thing to do, H4178
Est 8:11 Jews in every city the **r** to assemble and NDT
Job 8: 3 Does the Almighty pervert *what* is **r**? H7406
Job 27: 5 I will never **admit** you are **in the r**; till I die H7405
Job 30:12 On my **r** the tribe attacks; they lay snares H3545
Job 32: 9 only the aged who understand *what* is **r**. H5477
Job 33:12 I tell you, in this *you are* not **r**, for God is H7405
Job 33:27 I have perverted *what* is **r**, but I did not H3838
Job 34: 4 Let us discern for ourselves *what* is **r**; let H5477
Job 34: 6 Although I am **r**, I am considered a liar H5477
Job 35: 2 You say, 'I am **in the r**, not God.' H7406
Job 40:14 to you that your own **r** *hand* can save you. H3545
Ps 9: 4 For you have upheld my **r** and my cause H5477
Ps 16: 8 With him at my **r** *hand*, I will not be H3545
Ps 16:11 with eternal pleasures at your **r** *hand*. H3545
Ps 17: 2 from you; may your eyes see *what* is **r**. H4797
Ps 17: 7 who save by your **r** *hand* those who take H3545
Ps 18:35 and your **r** *hand* sustains me; your H3545
Ps 19: 8 The precepts of the LORD are **r**, giving joy H3838
Ps 20: 6 with the victorious power of his **r** *hand*. H3545
Ps 21: 8 enemies; your **r** *hand* will seize your foes. H3545
Ps 23: 3 guides me along the **r** paths for his H7406
Ps 25: 9 humble in what is **r** and teaches them his H5477
Ps 26:10 schemes, whose **r** *hands* are full of bribes. H3545
Ps 33: 4 For the word of the LORD is **r and true**; H3838
Ps 44: 3 them victory; it was your **r** *hand*, your arm, H3545
Ps 45: 4 let your **r** *hand* achieve awesome deeds. H3545
Ps 45: 9 at your **r** *hand* is the royal bride in gold of H3545
Ps 48:10 your **r** *hand* is filled with righteousness. H3545
Ps 50:16 "**What r have you** to recite H4537+4200+3870
Ps 51: 4 so *you are* **r** in your verdict and justified H7405
Ps 60: 5 Save us and help us with your **r** *hand*, that H3545
Ps 63: 8 I cling to you; your **r** *hand* upholds me. H3545
Ps 73:23 with you; you hold me by my **r** hand. H3545
Ps 74:11 do you hold back your hand, your **r** *hand*? H3545
Ps 77:10 the Most High stretched out his **r** *hand*. H3545
Ps 78:54 to the hill country his **r** *hand* had taken. H3545
Ps 80:15 the root your **r** *hand* has planted, the son H3545
Ps 80:17 your hand rest on the man at your **r** *hand*, H3545
Ps 89:13 your hand is strong, your **r** *hand* exalted. H3545
Ps 89:25 over the sea, his **r** *hand* over the rivers. H3545
Ps 89:42 You have exalted the **r** *hand of* his foes H3545
Ps 91: 7 ten thousand at your **r** *hand*, but it will not H3545
Ps 98: 1 his **r** *hand* and his holy arm have worked H3545
Ps 99: 4 in Jacob you have done what is just and **r**. H7407
Ps 106: 3 who act justly, who always do *what* is **r**. H7407
Ps 108: 6 Save us and help us with your **r** *hand*, that H3545
Ps 109: 6 let an accuser stand at his **r** *hand*. H3545
Ps 109:31 For he stands at the **r** *hand of* the needy H3545
Ps 110: 1 "Sit at my **r** *hand* until I make your H3545
Ps 110: 5 The Lord is at your **r** *hand*; he will crush H3545
Ps 118:15 "The LORD's **r** *hand* has done mighty H3545
Ps 118:16 The LORD's **r** *hand* is lifted high; H3545
Ps 118:16 the LORD's **r** *hand* has done mighty things!" H3545
Ps 119:128 because *I* **consider** all your precepts **r** H3837
Ps 119:137 are righteous, LORD, and your laws are **r**. H3838
Ps 121: 5 the LORD is your shade at your **r** hand; H3545
Ps 137: 5 Jerusalem, may my **r** *hand* forget its skill. H3545
Ps 138: 7 of my foes; with your **r** *hand* you save me. H3545
Ps 139:10 guide me, your **r** *hand* will hold me fast. H3545
Ps 142: 4 there is no one *at* my **r** *hand*; no one is H3545
Ps 144: 8 full of lies, whose **r** *hands* are deceitful. H3545
Ps 144:11 full of lies, whose **r** *hands* are deceitful. H3545
Pr 1: 3 behavior, *doing what* is **r** and just and fair H7406
Pr 2: 9 will understand *what* is **r** and just and fair H7406
Pr 3:16 Long life is in her **r** *hand*; in her left hand H3545
Pr 4:27 Do not turn to the **r** or the left; keep your H3545
Pr 8: 6 I open my lips to speak *what* is **r**. H4797
Pr 8: 9 To the discerning all of them are **r**; they H5791
Pr 12:15 The way of fools seems **r** to them, but the H3838
Pr 14:12 There is a way that appears to be **r**, but in H3838
Pr 16:13 they value the one who speaks **what** is **r**. H3838
Pr 16:25 There is a way that appears to be **r**, but in H3838
Pr 17:26 surely to flog honest officials is not **r**. H3841
Pr 18:17 In a lawsuit the first to speak seems **r** H7404
Pr 21: 2 A person may think their own ways are **r** H3838
Pr 21: 3 To do *what* is **r** and just is more H7407
Pr 21: 7 them away, for they refuse to do *what* is **r**. H5477
Pr 23:16 will rejoice when your lips speak *what* is **r**. H4797
Pr 23:19 be wise, and **set** your heart on the **r** path: H886
Pr 28: 5 Evildoers do not understand **what** is **r**, but H5477
Ecc 7:20 no one who does *what* is **r** and never sins. H3202
Ecc 10: 2 The heart of the wise inclines to the **r**, but H3545
Ecc 12:10 Teacher searched to find **just** the **r** words, H2914
SS 1: 4 *How* **r** they are to adore you H4797
SS 2: 6 my head, and his **r** *arm* embraces me. H3545
SS 8: 3 my head and his **r** *arm* embraces me. H3545
Isa 1: 7 stripped by foreigners **r before** you, H4200+5584
Isa 1:17 Learn *to* **do r**; seek justice. Defend the H3512
Isa 7:15 to reject the wrong and choose the **r**, H3202
Isa 7:16 to reject the wrong and choose the **r**, H3202
Isa 9:20 On the **r** they will devour, but still be H3545
Isa 28:26 instructs him and teaches him the **r way**. H5477
Isa 30:10 "Give us no more visions of *what* is **r**! H5791
Isa 30:21 Whether *you* **turn to the r** or to the left H3554
Isa 33:15 who walk righteously and speak *what* is **r**, H4797
Isa 40:14 and who taught him the **r** way? H5477
Isa 41:10 will uphold you with my righteous **r** *hand*. H3545
Isa 41:13 takes hold of your **r** *hand* and says to you, H3545
Isa 41:26 beforehand, so we could say, 'He was **r**'? H7404
Isa 43: 9 in their witnesses *to* **prove** *they* **were r**, H7405
Isa 44:20 "Is not this thing in my **r** *hand* a lie?" H3545
Isa 45: 1 whose **r** *hand* I take hold of to subdue H3545
Isa 45:19 speak the truth; I declare *what* is **r**. H4797
Isa 48:13 my **r** *hand* spread out the heavens H3545
Isa 51: 7 you who know *what* is **r**, you people who H7406
Isa 54: 3 you will spread out to the **r** and to the left; H3545
Isa 56: 1 "Maintain justice and do *what* is **r**, for my H7407
Isa 58: 2 a nation that does *what* is **r** and has not H7407
Isa 62: 8 has sworn by his **r** *hand* and by his mighty H3545
Isa 63:12 arm of power to be at Moses' **r** *hand*, H3545
Isa 64: 5 to the help of those who gladly do **r**, H7406
Jer 8: 6 attentively, but they do not say *what* is **r**. H4026
Jer 22: 3 Do what is just and **r**. Rescue from the H7407
Jer 22:15 He did *what* was **r** and just, so all went H5477
Jer 22:24 were a signet ring on my **r** hand, I would H3545
Jer 23: 5 do what is just and **r** in the land. H7407
Jer 26:14 with me whatever you think is good and **r**. H3838
Jer 32: 7 relative it is your **r** and duty to buy it. H5477
Jer 32: 8 Since it is your **r** to redeem it and possess H5477
Jer 33:15 he will do what is just and **r** in the land. H7407
Jer 34:15 repented and did *what* is **r** in my sight: H3838
La 2: 3 has withdrawn his **r** *hand* at the approach H3545
La 2: 4 he has strung his bow; his **r** *hand* is ready. H3545
Eze 1:10 on the **r** *side* each had the face of a H3545
Eze 4: 6 this time on your **r** side, and bear the sin H3556
Eze 18: 5 man who does what is just and **r**. H7407
Eze 18:19 what is just and **r** and has been careful H7407
Eze 18:21 my decrees and does what is just and **r**, H7407
Eze 18:27 committed and does what is just and **r**, H7407
Eze 21:16 Slash **to the r**, you sword, then to the left H3554
Eze 21:22 Into his **r** *hand* will come the lot for H3545
Eze 33:14 from their sin and do what is just and **r**— H7407
Eze 33:16 They have done what is just and **r**; they H7407
Eze 33:19 wickedness and does what is just and **r**, H7407
Eze 39: 3 make your arrows drop from your **r** hand. H3545
Eze 45: 9 oppression and do what is just and **r**. H7407
Da 4:27 Renounce your sins by doing *what* is **r** A10610
Da 4:37 he does is **r** and all his ways are A10643
Da 12: 7 lifted his **r** *hand* and his left hand toward H3545
Hos 14: 9 The ways of the LORD are **r**; the righteous H3838
Am 3:10 "They do not know how to do **r**," declares H5791
Jnh 4: 4 LORD replied, "*Is it* **r** for you to be angry?" H3512
Jnh 4: 9 "*Is it* **r** for you to be angry about the plant?" H3512
Jnh 4:11 cannot tell their **r** *hand* from their left— H3545
Mic 3: 9 despise justice and distort all that is **r**; H3838
Hab 2:16 from the LORD's **r** *hand* is coming around H3545
Zec 3: 1 standing at his **r** *side* to accuse him. H3545
Zec 4: 3 one on the **r** *of* the bowl and the other on H3545
Zec 4:11 two olive trees on the **r** and the left of the H3545
Zec 11:17 May the sword strike his arm and his **r** eye! H3545
Zec 11:17 withered, his **r** eye totally blinded! H3545
Zec 12: 6 all the surrounding peoples **r** and left, H3545
Mt 5:29 If your **r** eye causes you to stumble, gouge *G1288*
Mt 5:30 And if your **r** hand causes you to stumble *G1288*
Mt 5:39 If anyone slaps you on the **r** cheek, turn to *G1288*
Mt 6: 3 left hand know what your **r hand** is doing, *G1288*
Mt 11:19 But wisdom *is* **proved r** by her deeds." *G1467*
Mt 15: 7 Isaiah was **r** when he prophesied about *G2822*
Mt 15:26 "It is not **r** to take the children's bread *G2819*
Mt 20: 4 vineyard, and I will pay you whatever is **r**. *G1465*
Mt 20:15 Don't I **have the r** to do what I want with *G2003*
Mt 20:21 mine may sit at your **r** and the other at *G1288*
Mt 20:23 to sit at my **r** or left is not for me to *G1288*
Mt 21: 3 and he will send them **r away**. *G2317*
Mt 22:17 *Is it* **r** to pay the imperial tax to Caesar *G2003*
Mt 22:26 third brother, **r on down to** the seventh. *G2401*
Mt 22:44 "Sit at my **r hand** until I put your enemies *G1288*
Mt 24:33 you know that it is near, **r at** the door. *G2093*
Mt 25:33 the sheep on his **r** and the goats on his *G1288*
Mt 25:34 "Then the King will say to those on his **r** *G1288*
Mt 26:58 **r up to** the courtyard of the high priest. *G2401*
Mt 26:64 sitting at the **r hand** of the Mighty One *G1288*
Mt 27:29 They put a staff in his **r hand**. Then they *G1288*
Mt 27:38 with him, one on his **r** and one on his left. *G1288*
Mk 5:15 dressed and **in** *his* **r mind**; and they were *G5404*
Mk 6:25 you to give me **r now** the head of John *G1994*
Mk 7: 6 "Isaiah was **r** when he prophesied about *G2822*
Mk 7:27 "for it is not **r** to take the children's bread *G2819*
Mk 10:37 of us sit at your **r** and the other at your *G1288*
Mk 10:40 to sit at my **r** or left is not for me to *G1288*
Mk 12:14 *Is it* **r** to pay the imperial tax to Caesar *G2003*
Mk 12:32 "You are **r** in saying that God is one *G2093+237*
Mk 12:36 "Sit at my **r hand** until I put your enemies *G1288*
Mk 13:29 you know that it is near, **r at** the door. *G2093*
Mk 14:54 **r into** the courtyard of the *G2401+2276+1650*
Mk 14:62 sitting at the **r hand** of the Mighty One *G1288*
Mk 15:27 with him, one on his **r** and one on his left. *G1288*
Mk 16: 5 in a white robe sitting on the **r side**, *G1288*
Mk 16:19 heaven and he sat at the **r hand** of God. *G1288*
Lk 1:11 standing at the **r side** of the altar of *G1288*
Lk 4:30 But he **walked r through** the *G1451+1328+3545*
Lk 5:19 middle of the crowd, **r in front of** Jesus. *G1869*
Lk 6: 6 was there whose **r** hand was shriveled. *G1288*
Lk 7:29 **acknowledged** *that* God's **way** *was* **r** *G1467*
Lk 7:35 wisdom *is* **proved r** by all her children." *G1467*
Lk 8:35 dressed and **in** *his* **r mind**; and they were *G5404*
Lk 12:57 don't you judge for yourselves what is **r**? *G1465*
Lk 20:21 know that you speak and teach **what is r**, *G3987*
Lk 20:22 *Is it* **r** for us to pay taxes to Caesar or not?" *G2003*
Lk 20:42 Lord said to my Lord: "Sit at my **r hand** *G1288*
Lk 21: 9 but the end will not come **r away**. *G2311*
Lk 22:50 of the high priest, cutting off his **r** ear. *G1288*
Lk 22:69 be seated at the **r hand** of the mighty God *G1288*
Lk 23:33 criminals—one on his **r**, the other on his *G1288*
Jn 1:12 he gave the **r** to become children of God *G2026*
Jn 4:17 "You are **r** when you say you have no *G2822*
Jn 8:48 "Aren't we **r** in saying that you are a *G2822*
Jn 18:10 high priest's servant, cutting off his **r** ear. *G1288*

Jn 18:31 "But we have no r to execute anyone," G2003
Jn 21: 6 your net on the r side of the boat and G1288
Ac 2:25 Because he is at my r hand, I will not be G1288
Ac 2:33 Exalted to the r hand of God, he has G1288
Ac 2:34 Lord said to my Lord: "Sit at my r hand G1288
Ac 3: 7 Taking him by the r hand, he helped him G1288
Ac 4:19 John replied, "Which is r in God's eyes: G1465
Ac 5:31 exalted him to his own r hand as Prince G1288
Ac 6: 2 "It would not be r for us to neglect the G744
Ac 7:55 Jesus standing at the r hand of God. G1288
Ac 7:56 of Man standing at the r hand of God." G1288
Ac 8:21 because your heart is not r before God. G2318
Ac 10:35 the one who fears him and does what is r. G1466
Ac 11:11 "R then three men who had G2779+2627+1994
Ac 13:10 devil and an enemy of everything that is r! G1466
Ac 13:10 stop perverting the r ways of the Lord? G2318
Ac 25:11 no one has the r to hand me over to them. G1538
Ro 3: 4 "So that you may be proved r when you G1467
Ro 5: 6 You see, at just the r time, when we were G2848
Ro 7:21 I want to do good, evil is r there with me. AIT
Ro 8:22 pains of childbirth r up to the present time. G948
Ro 8:34 is at the r hand of God and is also G1288
Ro 9:21 the potter have the r to make out of the G2026
Ro 12:17 Be careful to do what is r in the eyes of G2819
Ro 13: 3 For rulers hold no terror for those who do r G19
Ro 13: 3 Then do what is r and you will be G19
1Co 4:13 of the world—r up to this moment. G2401
1Co 6:12 "I have the r to do anything," you say G2003
1Co 6:12 "I have the r to do anything"—but I will G2003
1Co 7:35 you may live in a r way in undivided G2363
1Co 7:37 the virgin—this man also does the r thing. G2822
1Co 7:38 he who marries the virgin does r, but he G2822
1Co 9: 4 Don't we have the r to food and drink? G2026
1Co 9: 5 Don't we have the r to take a believing G2026
1Co 9: 6 Barnabas who lack the r to not work for a G2026
1Co 9:12 If others have this r of support from you G2026
1Co 9:12 But we did not use this r. On the contrary, G2026
1Co 10:23 "I have the r to do anything," you say G2003
1Co 10:23 "I have the r to do anything"—but not G2003
2Co 5:13 is for God; if we are in our r mind, it is G5404
2Co 6: 7 righteousness in the r hand and in the left G1288
2Co 8:21 For we are taking pains to do what is r, not G2819
2Co 13: 7 you will do what is r even though we may G2819
Gal 2: 9 Barnabas the r hand of fellowship G1288
Eph 1:20 seated him at his r hand in the heavenly G1288
Eph 6: 1 obey your parents in the Lord, for this is r. G1465
Php 1: 7 It is r for me to feel this way about all of G1465
Php 4: 8 is noble, whatever is r, whatever is pure, G1465
Col 3: 1 Christ is, seated at the r hand of God. G1288
Col 4: 1 provide your slaves with what is r and fair G1465
2Th 1: 5 this is evidence that God's judgment is r, G1465
2Th 3: 9 we do not have the r to such help, G2026
Heb 1: 3 sat down at the r hand of the Majesty in G1288
Heb 1:13 "Sit at my r hand until I make your G1288
Heb 8: 1 sat down at the r hand of the throne of G1288
Heb 10:12 sins, he sat down at the r hand of God, G1288
Heb 12: 2 sat down at the r hand of the throne of G1288
Heb 13:10 at the tabernacle have no r to eat. G2026
Jas 2: 8 neighbor as yourself," you are doing r. G2822
1Pe 2:14 do wrong and to commend those who do r. G18
1Pe 3: 6 her daughters if you do what is r and do not G16
1Pe 3:14 But even if you should suffer for what is r G1466
1Pe 3:22 into heaven and is at God's r hand— G1288
2Pe 1:13 I think it is r to refresh your memory as G1465
1Jn 2:29 who does what is r has been born of him. G1466
1Jn 3: 7 The one who does what is r is righteous G1466
1Jn 3:10 who does not do what is r is not God's G1466
Rev 1:16 In his r hand he held seven stars, and G1288
Rev 1:17 he placed his r hand on me and said: G1288
Rev 1:20 you saw in my r hand and of the seven G1288
Rev 2: 1 stars in his r hand and walks among G1288
Rev 2: 7 I will give the r to eat from the tree of life AIT
Rev 3:21 I will give the r to sit with me on my throne AIT
Rev 5: 1 Then I saw in the r hand of him who sat G1288
Rev 5: 7 scroll from the r hand of him who sat on G1288
Rev 10: 2 He planted his r foot on the sea and his G1288
Rev 10: 5 on the land raised his r hand to heaven. G1288
Rev 13:16 receive a mark on their r hands or on their G1288
Rev 22:11 let the one who does r continue to do G1465
Rev 22:11 the one who does right continue to do r; G1466
Rev 22:14 that they may have the r to the tree of life G2026

RIGHT-HANDED (1) [HAND, RIGHT]

1Ch 12: 2 arrows or to sling stones r or left-handed; H3554

RIGHTEOUS (304) [OVERRIGHTEOUS, RIGHTEOUSLY, RIGHTEOUSNESS, RIGHTEOUSNESS']

Ge 6: 9 Noah was a r man, blameless among the H7404
Ge 7: 1 I have found you r in this generation. H7404
Ge 18:23 you sweep away the r with the wicked? H7404
Ge 18:24 What if there are fifty r people in the city H7404
Ge 18:24 the sake of the fifty r people in it? H7404
Ge 18:25 such a thing—to kill the r with the wicked H7404
Ge 18:25 treating the r and the wicked alike. H7404
Ge 18:26 "If I find fifty r people in the city of Sodom, H7404
Ge 18:28 if the number of the r is five less than fifty H7404
Ge 38:26 said, "She is more r than I, since I H7405
Nu 23:10 Let me die the death of the r, and may my H3838
Dt 4: 8 as to have such r decrees and laws as H7404
Dt 24:13 be regarded as a r act in the sight of the H7407
Dt 33:19 there offer the sacrifices of the r; H7406
Dt 33:21 he carried out the LORD's r will, and his H7407
1Sa 12: 7 LORD as to all the r acts performed by the H7407
1Sa 24:17 "You are more r than I," he said. "You H7404
1Ki 3: 6 faithful to you and r and upright in heart. H7407
Ezr 9:15 of Israel, you are r! We are left this day H7404
Ne 9: 8 have kept your promise because you are r. H7404
Ne 9:33 you have remained r; you have acted H7404
Job 4:17 'Can a mortal be more r than God? Can H7405
Job 12: 4 laughingstock, though r and blameless! H7404
Job 15:14 born of woman, that they could be r? H7405
Job 17: 9 Nevertheless, the r will hold to their ways H7404
Job 22: 3 would it give the Almighty if you were r? H7405
Job 22:19 The r see their ruin and rejoice; the H7404
Job 25: 4 How then can a mortal be r before God H7405
Job 27:17 what he lays up the r will wear, and the H7404
Job 32: 1 because he was r in his own eyes. H7404
Job 35: 7 If you are r, what do you give to him, or H7405
Job 36: 7 He does not take his eyes off the r; he H7404
Ps 1: 5 sinners in the assembly of the r. H7404
Ps 1: 6 For the LORD watches over the way of the r H7404
Ps 4: 1 I call to you, my r God. Give me relief H7406
Ps 4: 5 the sacrifices of the r and trust in the LORD. H7406
Ps 5:12 you bless the r; you surround them H7404
Ps 7: 9 of the wicked and make the r secure— H7404
Ps 7: 9 the r God who probes minds and hearts. H7404
Ps 7:11 God is a r judge, a God who displays his H7404
Ps 9: 4 sitting enthroned as the r judge. H7406
Ps 11: 3 are being destroyed, what can the r do?" H7404
Ps 11: 5 The LORD examines the r, but the wicked H7404
Ps 11: 7 For the LORD is r, he loves justice; the H7404
Ps 14: 5 God is present in the company of the r. H7404
Ps 15: 2 who does what is r, who speaks the H7406
Ps 19: 9 of the LORD are firm, and all of them are r. H7405
Ps 31:18 they speak arrogantly against the r. H7404
Ps 32:11 in the LORD and be glad, you r; sing, H7404
Ps 33: 1 to the LORD, you r; it is fitting for the H7404
Ps 34:15 The eyes of the LORD are on the r, and his H7404
Ps 34:17 The r cry out, and the LORD hears them; he NDT
Ps 34:19 The r person may have many troubles, but H7404
Ps 34:21 the foes of the r will be condemned. H7404
Ps 37: 6 He will make your r reward shine like the H7406
Ps 37:12 plot against the r and gnash their teeth H7404
Ps 37:16 the little that the r have than the wealth H7404
Ps 37:17 will be broken, but the LORD upholds the r. H7404
Ps 37:21 do not repay, but the r give generously; H7404
Ps 37:25 I have never seen the r forsaken or their H7404
Ps 37:29 The r will inherit the land and dwell in it H7404
Ps 37:30 The mouths of the r utter wisdom, and H7404
Ps 37:32 The wicked lie in wait for the r, intent on H7404
Ps 37:39 salvation of the r comes from the LORD; H7404
Ps 51:19 you will delight in the sacrifices of the r, H7406
Ps 52: 6 The r will see and fear; they will laugh at H7404
Ps 55:22 he will never let the r be shaken. H7404
Ps 58:10 The r will be glad when they are avenged, H7404
Ps 58:11 will say, "Surely the r still are rewarded H7404
Ps 64:10 The r will rejoice in the LORD and take H7404
Ps 65: 5 answer us with awesome and r deeds, H7406
Ps 68: 3 But may the r be glad and rejoice before H7404
Ps 69:28 book of life and not be listed with the r. H7404
Ps 71:15 My mouth will tell of your r deeds, of your H7407
Ps 71:16 I will proclaim your r deeds, yours alone. H7407
Ps 71:24 tongue will tell of your r acts all day long, H7407
Ps 72: 7 In his days may the r flourish and H7404
Ps 75:10 the horns of the r will be lifted up. H7404
Ps 88:12 your r deeds in the land of oblivion? H7407
Ps 92:12 The r will flourish like a palm tree, they H7404
Ps 94:21 together against the r and condemn the H7404
Ps 97:11 Light shines on the r and joy on the H7404
Ps 97:12 in the LORD, you who are r, and praise his H7404
Ps 112: 4 are gracious and compassionate and r. H7404
Ps 112: 6 Surely the r will never be shaken; they will H7404
Ps 116: 5 The LORD is gracious and r; our God is full H7404
Ps 118:15 victory resound in the tents of the r: H7404
Ps 118:19 Open for me the gates of the r; I will enter H7406
Ps 118:20 of the LORD through which the r may enter. H7404
Ps 119: 7 an upright heart as I learn your r laws. H7406
Ps 119:62 I rise to give you thanks for your r laws. H7406
Ps 119:75 that your laws are r, and that in H7406
Ps 119:106 it, that I will follow your r laws. H7406
Ps 119:121 I have done what is r and just; do not H7406
Ps 119:123 salvation, looking for your r promise. H7406
Ps 119:137 You are r, LORD, and your laws are right. H7404
Ps 119:138 The statutes you have laid down are r H7406
Ps 119:144 Your statutes are always r; give me H7406
Ps 119:160 words are true; all your r laws are eternal. H7406
Ps 119:164 times a day I praise you for your r laws. H7406
Ps 119:172 your word, for all your commands are r. H7406
Ps 125: 3 not remain over the land allotted to the r, H7404
Ps 125: 3 then the r might use their hands to do H7404
Ps 129: 4 But the LORD is r; he has cut me free from H7404
Ps 140:13 Surely the r will praise your name, and H7404
Ps 141: 5 Let a r man strike me—that is a kindness H7404
Ps 142: 7 Then the r will gather about me because H7404
Ps 143: 2 no one living is r before you. H7405
Ps 145:17 The LORD is r in all his ways and faithful H7404
Ps 146: 8 are bowed down, the LORD loves the r. H7404
Pr 2:20 the good and keep to the paths of the r. H7404
Pr 3:33 but he blesses the home of the r. H7404
Pr 4:18 The path of the r is like the morning sun H7404
Pr 9: 9 teach the r and they will add to their H7404
Pr 10: 3 The LORD does not let the r go hungry, but H7404
Pr 10: 6 Blessings crown the head of the r, but H7404
Pr 10: 7 The name of the r is used in blessings H7404
Pr 10:11 The mouth of the r is a fountain of life H7404
Pr 10:16 The wages of the r is life, but the H7404
Pr 10:20 The tongue of the r is choice silver, but H7404
Pr 10:21 The lips of the r nourish many, but fools H7404
Pr 10:24 what the r desire will be granted. H7404
Pr 10:25 are gone, but the r stand firm forever. H7404
Pr 10:28 The prospect of the r is joy, but the hopes H7404
Pr 10:30 The r will never be uprooted, but the H7404
Pr 10:31 From the mouth of the r comes the fruit of H7404
Pr 10:32 The lips of the r know what finds favor H7404
Pr 11: 8 The r person is rescued from trouble, and H7404
Pr 11: 9 through knowledge the r escape. H7404
Pr 11:10 When the r prosper, the city rejoices H7404
Pr 11:19 Truly the r attain life, but whoever pursues H7407
Pr 11:21 but those who are r will go free. H7404+2446
Pr 11:23 The desire of the r ends only in good, but H7404
Pr 11:28 but the r will thrive like a green leaf. H7404
Pr 11:30 The fruit of the r is a tree of life, and the H7404
Pr 11:31 If the r receive their due on earth, how H7404
Pr 12: 3 wickedness, but the r cannot be uprooted. H7404
Pr 12: 5 The plans of the r are just, but the advice H7404
Pr 12: 7 but the house of the r stands firm. H7404
Pr 12:10 The r care for the needs of their animals H7404
Pr 12:12 of evildoers, but the root of the r endures. H7404
Pr 12:21 No harm overtakes the r, but the wicked H7404
Pr 12:26 The r choose their friends carefully, but H7404
Pr 13: 5 The r hate what is false, but the wicked H7404
Pr 13: 9 The light of the r shines brightly, but the H7404
Pr 13:21 the r are rewarded with good things. H7404
Pr 13:22 a sinner's wealth is stored up for the r. H7404
Pr 13:25 The r eat to their hearts' content, but the H7404
Pr 14:19 the wicked at the gates of the r. H7404
Pr 14:32 even in death the r seek refuge in God. H7404
Pr 15: 6 The house of the r contains great treasure, H7404
Pr 15:28 The heart of the r weighs its answers, but H7404
Pr 15:29 but he hears the prayer of the r. H7404
Pr 18:10 fortified tower; the r run to it and are safe. H7404
Pr 20: 7 The r lead blameless lives; blessed are H7404
Pr 21:12 The R One takes note of the house of the H7404
Pr 21:15 it brings joy to the r but terror to evildoers. H7404
Pr 21:18 The wicked become a ransom for the r H7404
Pr 21:26 more, but the r give without sparing. H7404
Pr 23:24 The father of a r child has great joy; H7404
Pr 24:15 lurk like a thief near the house of the r, H7404
Pr 24:16 though the r fall seven times, they rise H7404
Pr 25:26 well are the r who give way to the H7404
Pr 28: 1 pursues, but the r are as bold as a lion. H7404
Pr 28:12 When the r triumph, there is great elation; H7404
Pr 28:28 when the wicked perish, the r thrive. H7404
Pr 29: 2 When the r thrive, the people rejoice H7404
Pr 29: 6 but the r shout for joy and are glad. H7404
Pr 29: 7 The r care about justice for the poor, but H7404
Pr 29:16 does sin, but the r will see their downfall. H7404
Pr 29:27 The r detest the dishonest; the wicked H7404
Ecc 3:17 into judgment both the r and the wicked, H7404
Ecc 7:15 the r perishing in their righteousness, and H7404
Ecc 7:20 there is no one on earth who is r, no one H7404
Ecc 8:14 the r who get what the wicked deserve H7404
Ecc 8:14 the wicked who get what the r deserve. H7404
Ecc 9: 1 concluded that the r and the wise and H7404
Ecc 9: 2 common destiny—the r and the wicked H7404
Isa 3:10 Tell the r it will be well with them, for H7404
Isa 5:16 holy God will be proved holy by his r acts. H7407
Isa 10:22 has been decreed, overwhelming and r. H7407
Isa 24:16 "Glory to the R One." But I said, H7404
Isa 26: 2 the gates that the r nation may enter, H7404
Isa 26: 7 The path of the r is level; you, the Upright H7404
Isa 26: 7 make the way of the r smooth. H7404
Isa 41:10 I will uphold you with my r right hand. H7406
Isa 45:21 God apart from me, a r God and a Savior H7404
Isa 53:11 by his knowledge my r servant will justify H7404
Isa 57: 1 The r perish, and no one takes it to heart H7404
Isa 57: 1 that the r are taken away to be H7404
Isa 60:21 your people will be r and they will H7404
Isa 64: 6 all our r acts are like filthy rags H7407
Jer 3:11 "Faithless Israel is more r than unfaithful H7405
Jer 4: 2 a truthful, just and r way you swear, 'As H7407
Jer 12: 1 You are always r, LORD, when I bring a H7404
Jer 20:12 who examine the r and probe the heart H7404
Jer 23: 5 "when I will raise up for David a r Branch H7404
Jer 23: 6 he will be called: The LORD Our R Savior. H7406
Jer 33:15 time I will make a r Branch sprout from H7407
Jer 33:16 it will be called: The LORD Our R Savior.' H7406
La 1:18 "The LORD is r, yet I rebelled against his H7404
La 4:13 who shed within her the blood of the r. H7404
Eze 3:20 when a r person turns from their H7404
Eze 3:20 The r things that person did will not be H7407
Eze 3:21 if you do warn the r person not to sin and H7404
Eze 13:22 you disheartened the r with your lies, H7404
Eze 16:51 and have made your sisters seem r by all H7405
Eze 16:52 than theirs, they appear more r than you. H7405
Eze 16:52 you have made your sisters appear r. H7405
Eze 18: 5 "Suppose there is a r man who does what H7404
Eze 18: 9 That man is r; he will surely live, declares H7404
Eze 18:20 righteousness of the r will be credited to H7404
Eze 18:22 Because of the r things they have done H7407
Eze 18:24 "But if a r person turns from their H7404
Eze 18:24 None of the r things that person has done H7407
Eze 18:26 If a r person turns from their righteousness H7404
Eze 21: 3 cut off from you both the r and the wicked. H7404
Eze 21: 4 I am going to cut off the r and the wicked, H7404
Eze 23:45 But r judges will sentence them to the H7404

R

Eze 33:12 'If someone who is r disobeys, that H7404
Eze 33:12 The r *person* who sins will not be allowed H7404
Eze 33:12 to live even though they were formerly r. H2023S
Eze 33:13 If I tell a r *person* that they will surely live H7404
Eze 33:13 none of the r things that person has done H7407
Eze 33:18 If a r *person* turns from their righteousness H7404
Da 9: 7 you are r, but this day we are H7407
Da 9:14 the LORD our God is r in everything he H7404
Da 9:16 in keeping with all your r acts, turn away H7407
Da 9:18 make requests of you because we are r, H7407
Hos 14: 9 LORD are right; the r walk in them, but the H7404
Mic 6: 5 that you may know the r acts *of* the LORD." H7407
Hab 1: 4 The wicked hem in the r, so that justice is H7404
Hab 1:13 swallow up *those* more r than themselves H7404
Hab 2: 4 the r *person* will live by his H7404
Zep 3: 5 The LORD within her is r; he does no wrong H7404
Zec 8: 8 will be faithful and r to them as their God." H7407
Zec 9: 9 king comes to you, r and victorious, lowly H7404
Mal 3:18 distinction between the r and the wicked, H7404
Mt 5:45 sends rain on the r and the unrighteous. G1465
Mt 9:13 For I have not come to call the r, but G1465
Mt 10:41 welcomes a r *person* as a righteous G1465
Mt 10:41 person as a r *person* will receive a G1465
Mt 10:41 person will receive a r *person's* reward. G1465
Mt 13:17 prophets and r *people* longed to see G1465
Mt 13:43 Then the r will shine like the sun in the G1465
Mt 13:49 come and separate the wicked from the r G1465
Mt 23:28 appear to people *as* r but on the inside G1465
Mt 23:29 prophets and decorate the graves *of* the r. G1465
Mt 23:35 will come all the r blood that has been G1465
Mt 23:35 from the blood of r Abel to the blood of G1465
Mt 25:37 "Then the r will answer him, 'Lord, when G1465
Mt 25:46 punishment, but the r to eternal life." G1465
Mk 2:17 I have not come to call the r, but sinners." G1465
Mk 6:20 knowing him to be a r and holy man. G1465
Lk 1: 6 Both of them were r in the sight of God G1465
Lk 1:17 the disobedient to the wisdom *of* the r— G1465
Lk 2:25 called Simeon, who was r and devout. G1465
Lk 5:32 I have not come to call the r, but sinners to G1465
Lk 14:14 will be repaid at the resurrection *of* the r." G1465
Lk 15: 7 ninety-nine r *persons* who do not need G1465
Lk 23:47 God and said, "Surely this was a r man." G1465
Jn 17:25 "R Father, though the world does not G1465
Ac 3:14 the Holy and R *One* and asked that a G1465
Ac 7:52 who predicted the coming *of* the R *One.* G1465
Ac 10:22 He is a r and God-fearing man, who is G1465
Ac 22:14 to see the R *One* and to hear words G1465
Ac 24:15 a resurrection *of* both the r and the wicked G1465
Ro 1:17 as it is written: "The r will live by faith." G1465
Ro 1:32 they know God's r decree that those who G1468
Ro 2: 5 when his r judgment will be revealed. G1464
Ro 2:13 hear the law who are r in God's sight, G1465
Ro 2:13 who obey the law *who will be* declared r. G1467
Ro 3:10 "There is no one r, not even one; G1465
Ro 3:20 no one *will be* declared r in God's sight G1467
Ro 5: 7 Very rarely will anyone die for a r *person* G1465
Ro 5:18 so also one r act resulted in justification G1468
Ro 5:19 of the one man the many will be made r. G1465
Ro 7:12 the commandment is holy, r and good. G1465
Ro 8: 4 in order that the r requirement of the law G1468
Gal 3:11 because "the r will live by faith. G1465
1Th 2:10 r and blameless we were among you who G1469
1Ti 1: 9 the law is made not *for* the r but for G1465
2Ti 4: 8 which the Lord, the r Judge, will award to G1465
Titus 3: 5 not because of r things we had done G1466
Heb 10:38 "But my r *one* will live by faith. And I G1465
Heb 11: 4 By faith he was commended as r, when G1465
Heb 12:23 to the spirits *of* the r made perfect, G1465
Jas 2:21 *Was* not our father Abraham considered r G1467
Jas 2:24 that a person *is* considered r by what they G1467
Jas 2:25 *was* not even Rahab the prostitute considered r G1467
Jas 5:16 The prayer *of* a r *person* is powerful and G1465
1Pe 3:12 of the Lord are on the r and his ears are G1465
1Pe 3:18 once for sins, the r for the unrighteous, to G1465
1Pe 4:18 "If it is hard *for* the r to be saved, what G1465
2Pe 2: 7 he rescued Lot, a r *man,* who was G1465
2Pe 2: 8 that r *man,* living among them day G1465
2Pe 2: 8 was tormented in his r soul by the lawless G1465
1Jn 2: 1 with the Father—Jesus Christ, the R *One.* G1465
1Jn 2:29 If you know that he is r, you know that G1465
1Jn 3: 7 The one who does what is right is r, just G1465
1Jn 3: 7 what is right righteous, just as he is r. G1465
1Jn 3:12 actions were evil and his brother's were r. G1465
Rev 15: 4 for your r acts have been revealed. G1468
Rev 19: 8 linen stands for the r acts of God's holy G1468

RIGHTEOUSLY (2) [RIGHTEOUS]

Isa 33:15 Those who walk r and speak what is right H7407
Jer 11:20 who judge r and test the heart and mind H7406

RIGHTEOUSNESS (218) [RIGHTEOUS]

Ge 15: 6 the LORD, and he credited it to him as r. H7407
Dt 6:25 he has commanded us, that will be our r." H7407
Dt 9: 4 possession of this land because of my r." H7407
Dt 9: 5 not because of your r or your integrity that H7407
Dt 9: 6 not because of your r that the LORD your H7407
1Sa 26:23 everyone for their r and faithfulness. H7407
2Sa 22:21 LORD has dealt with me according to my r; H7407
2Sa 22:25 LORD has rewarded me according to my r, H7407
2Sa 23: 3 'When one rules over people in r, when H7404
1Ki 10: 9 made you king to maintain justice and r." H7407
2Ch 9: 8 king over them, to maintain justice and r." H7407
Job 29:14 I put on r as my clothing; justice was my H7406
Job 35: 8 like yourself, and your r only other people. H7407
Job 37:23 in his justice and great r, he does not H7407
Ps 5: 8 in your r because of my enemies H7407
Ps 7: 8 according to my r, according to my H7406
Ps 7:17 give thanks to the LORD because of his r; H7406
Ps 9: 8 He rules the world in r and judges the H7406
Ps 18:20 LORD has dealt with me according to my r; H7406
Ps 18:24 LORD has rewarded me according to my r, H7406
Ps 22:31 They will proclaim his r, declaring to a H7407
Ps 31: 1 be put to shame; deliver me in your r. H7407
Ps 33: 5 The LORD loves r and justice; the earth is H7407
Ps 35:24 Vindicate me in your r, LORD my God; do H7406
Ps 35:28 My tongue will proclaim your r, your H7406
Ps 36: 6 Your r is like the highest mountains, your H7407
Ps 36:10 know you, your r to the upright in heart. H7407
Ps 40:10 I do not hide your r in my heart; I speak of H7407
Ps 45: 7 You love r and hate wickedness; therefore H7406
Ps 48:10 the earth; your right hand is filled with r. H7406
Ps 50: 6 And the heavens proclaim his r, for he is H7406
Ps 51:14 and my tongue will sing of your r. H7407
Ps 71: 2 In your r, rescue me and deliver me; turn H7407
Ps 71:19 Your r, God, reaches to the heavens, you H7407
Ps 72: 1 O God, the royal son with your r. H7407
Ps 72: 2 May he judge your people in r, your H7406
Ps 72: 3 to the people, the hills the fruit of r. H7407
Ps 85:10 together; r and peace kiss each other. H7406
Ps 85:11 the earth, and r looks down from heaven. H7406
Ps 85:13 R goes before him and prepares the way H7406
Ps 89:14 R and justice are the foundation of your H7406
Ps 89:16 name all day long; they celebrate your r. H7407
Ps 94:15 Judgment will again be founded on r H7406
Ps 96:13 judge the world in r and the peoples in H7406
Ps 97: 2 r and justice are the foundation of his H7406
Ps 97: 6 The heavens proclaim his r, and all H7406
Ps 98: 2 known and revealed his r to the nations. H7407
Ps 98: 9 judge the world in r and the peoples with H7406
Ps 103: 6 The LORD works r and justice for all the H7407
Ps 103:17 his r with their children's children H7407
Ps 106:31 was credited to him as r for endless H7407
Ps 111: 3 are his deeds, and his r endures forever. H7407
Ps 112: 3 their houses, and their r endures forever. H7407
Ps 112: 9 to the poor, their r endures forever; their H7407
Ps 119:40 your precepts! In your r preserve my life. H7407
Ps 119:142 Your r is everlasting and your law is true. H7407
Ps 132: 9 May your priests be clothed with your r H7406
Ps 143: 1 your faithfulness and r come to my relief. H7407
Ps 143:11 in your r, bring me out of trouble. H7407
Ps 145: 7 goodness and joyfully sing of your r. H7407
Pr 8:20 I walk in the way of r, along the paths of H7407
Pr 10: 2 lasting value, but r delivers from death. H7407
Pr 11: 4 day of wrath, but r delivers from death. H7407
Pr 11: 5 The r *of* the blameless makes their paths H7407
Pr 11: 6 The r *of* the upright delivers them, but the H7407
Pr 11:18 the one who sows r reaps a sure reward. H7407
Pr 12:28 In the way of r there is life; along that H7407
Pr 13: 6 R guards the person of integrity, but H7407
Pr 14:34 R exalts a nation, but sin condemns any H7407
Pr 15: 9 but he loves those who pursue r. H7407
Pr 16: 8 Better a little with r than much gain with H7407
Pr 16:12 a throne is established through r. H7407
Pr 16:31 of splendor; it is attained in the way of r. H7407
Pr 21:21 Whoever pursues r and love finds life H7407
Pr 25: 5 his throne will be established through r. H7406
Ecc 7:15 the righteous perishing in their r, and the H7406
Isa 1:21 was full of justice; r used to dwell in her H7406
Isa 1:26 Afterward you will be called the City of R H7406
Isa 1:27 with justice, her penitent ones with r. H7407
Isa 5: 7 saw bloodshed; for r, but heard cries of H7407
Isa 9: 7 it with justice and r from that time on and H7407
Isa 11: 4 with r he will judge the needy, with H7406
Isa 11: 5 R will be his belt and faithfulness the H7406
Isa 16: 5 seeks justice and speeds the cause of r. H7406
Isa 26: 9 the earth, the people of the world learn r. H7406
Isa 26:10 they do not learn r; even in a land of H7406
Isa 28:17 the measuring line and r the plumb line; H7407
Isa 32: 1 a king will reign in r and rulers will rule H7406
Isa 32:16 in the desert, his r live in the fertile field. H7407
Isa 32:17 The fruit of that r will be peace; its effect H7407
Isa 33: 5 he will fill Zion with his justice and r. H7407
Isa 41: 2 the east, calling him *in* r to his service? H7406
Isa 42: 6 have called you in r; I will take hold of H7406
Isa 42:21 the sake of his r to make his law great H7406
Isa 45: 8 rain down my r; let the clouds H7406
Isa 45: 8 salvation spring up, let r flourish with it; I, H7407
Isa 45:13 I will raise up Cyrus in my r: I will make all H7406
Isa 46:12 you who are now far from my r. H7407
Isa 46:13 I am bringing my r near, it is not far away H7407
Isa 48: 1 the God of Israel—but not in truth or r— H7407
Isa 51: 1 you who pursue r and who seek the LORD: H7406
Isa 51: 5 My r draws near speedily, my salvation is H7406
Isa 51: 6 will last forever, my r will never fail. H7407
Isa 51: 8 But my r will last forever, my salvation H7407
Isa 54:14 In r you will be established: Tyranny will H7407
Isa 56: 1 close at hand and my r will soon be H7407
Isa 57:12 I will expose your r and your works, and H7407
Isa 58: 8 appear; then your r will go before you H7406
Isa 59: 9 is far from us, and r does not reach us. H7407
Isa 59:14 is driven back, and r stands at a distance H7407
Isa 59:16 him, and his own r sustained him. H7407
Isa 59:17 He put on r as his breastplate, and the H7407
Isa 61: 3 They will be called oaks of r, a planting of H7406
Isa 61:10 arrayed me in a robe of his r, H7407
Isa 61:11 LORD will make r and praise spring up H7407
Jer 9:24 kindness, justice and r on earth, for in H7407
Eze 3:20 person turns from their r and does evil, H7406
Eze 14:14 they could save only themselves by their r H7407
Eze 14:20 would save only themselves by their r. H7407
Eze 18:20 The r *of* the righteous will be credited to H7407
Eze 18:24 turns from their r and commits sin and H7407
Eze 18:26 person turns from their r and commits sin, H7407
Eze 33:12 that person's former r will count for H7407
Eze 33:13 then they trust in their r and do evil H7407
Eze 33:18 person turns from their r and does evil, H7407
Da 9:24 to bring in everlasting r, to seal up vision H7406
Da 12: 3 and *those who* lead many to r, like the H7405
Hos 2:19 I will betroth you in r and justice, in love H7406
Hos 10:12 Sow r for yourselves, reap the fruit of H7407
Hos 10:12 until he comes and showers his r on you. H7406
Am 5: 7 into bitterness and cast r to the ground. H7407
Am 5:24 like a river, r like a never-failing stream! H7407
Am 6:12 poison and the fruit of r into bitterness— H7407
Mic 7: 9 bring me out into the light; I will see his r. H7407
Zep 2: 3 Seek r, seek humility; perhaps you will be H7406
Mal 3: 3 have men who will bring offerings in r, H7407
Mal 4: 2 the sun of r will rise with healing in its H7407
Mt 3:15 it is proper for us to do this to fulfill all r." G1466
Mt 5: 6 are those who hunger and thirst *for* r, G1466
Mt 5:10 those who are persecuted because of r, G1466
Mt 5:20 you that unless your r surpasses that of G1466
Mt 6: 1 not to practice your r in front of others to G1466
Mt 6:33 But seek first his kingdom and his r, and G1466
Mt 21:32 came to you to show you the way *of* r, G1466
Lk 1:75 in holiness and r before him all our days. G1466
Lk 18: 9 of their own r and looked down on G1465
Jn 16: 8 the wrong about sin and r and judgment: G1466
Jn 16:10 about r, because I am going to the Father G1466
Ac 24:25 As Paul talked about r, self-control and G1466
Ro 1:17 For in the gospel the r of God is revealed— G1466
Ro 1:17 revealed—a r that is by faith from first to last NDT
Ro 3: 5 brings out God's r more clearly, G1466
Ro 3:21 from the law the r of God has been made G1466
Ro 3:22 This r is given through faith in Jesus Christ G1466
Ro 3:25 He did this to demonstrate his r, because G1466
Ro 3:26 it to demonstrate his r at the present time, G1466
Ro 4: 3 and it was credited to him as r. G1466
Ro 4: 5 the ungodly, their faith is credited as r. G1466
Ro 4: 6 to whom God credits r apart from works: G1466
Ro 4: 9 Abraham's faith was credited to him as r. G1466
Ro 4:11 a seal *of* the r that he had by faith while G1466
Ro 4:11 in order that r might be credited to them. G1466
Ro 4:13 through the r that comes by faith. G1466
Ro 4:22 This is why "it was credited to him as r." G1466
Ro 4:24 to whom God will credit r—for us who NDT
Ro 5:17 of the gift *of* r reign in life through G1466
Ro 5:21 might reign through r to bring eternal life G1466
Ro 6:13 of yourself to him as an instrument *of* r. G1466
Ro 6:16 or to obedience, which leads to r? G1466
Ro 6:18 from sin and have become slaves *to* r. G1466
Ro 6:19 as slaves *to* r leading to holiness. G1466
Ro 6:20 you were free *from* the *control of* r. G1466
Ro 8:10 the Spirit gives life because of r. G1466
Ro 9:30 who did not pursue r, have obtained it, G1466
Ro 9:30 have obtained it, a r that is by faith; G1466
Ro 9:31 who pursued the law *as the way of* r, have G1466
Ro 10: 3 did not know the r of God and sought to G1466
Ro 10: 3 their own, they did not submit *to* God's r. G1466
Ro 10: 4 so that there may be r for everyone who G1466
Ro 10: 5 Moses writes this *about* the r that is by the G1466
Ro 10: 6 But the r that is by faith says: "Do not say G1466
Ro 14:17 drinking, but *of* r, peace and joy in G1466
1Co 1:30 from God—that is, our r, holiness and G1466
2Co 3: 9 more glorious is the ministry that *brings* r! G1466
2Co 5:21 in him we might become the r of God. G1466
2Co 6: 7 with weapons *of* r in the right hand and in G1466
2Co 6:14 For what do r and wickedness have in G1466
2Co 9: 9 gifts to the poor; their r endures forever." G1466
2Co 9:10 will enlarge the harvest *of* your r. G1466
2Co 11:15 servants also masquerade as servants *of* r. G1466
Gal 2:21 if r could be gained through the law G1466
Gal 3: 6 and it was credited to him as r. G1466
Gal 3:21 then r would certainly have come by the G1466
Gal 5: 5 await by faith the r for which we hope. G1466
Eph 4:24 to be like God in true r and holiness. G1466
Eph 5: 9 light consists in all goodness, r and truth) G1466
Eph 6:14 with the breastplate *of* r in place, G1466
Php 1:11 filled with the fruit *of* r that comes through G1466
Php 3: 6 the church; as for r based on the law G1466
Php 3: 9 not having a r of my own that comes from G1466
Php 3: 9 the r that comes from God on the basis of G1466
1Ti 6:11 and pursue r, godliness, faith, G1466
2Ti 2:22 Flee the evil desires of youth and pursue r, G1466
2Ti 3:16 rebuking, correcting and training in r, G1466
2Ti 4: 8 Now there is in store for me the crown *of* r G1466
Heb 1: 9 You have loved r and hated wickedness G1466
Heb 5:13 not acquainted with the teaching *about* r. G1466
Heb 7: 2 the name Melchizedek means "king *of* r"; G1466
Heb 11: 7 became heir *of* the r that is in G1466
Heb 12:11 produces a harvest *of* r and peace for G1466
Jas 1:20 does not produce the r that God desires. G1466
Jas 2:23 it was credited to him as r," and he G1466
Jas 3:18 who sow in peace reap a harvest *of* r. G1466
1Pe 2:24 so that we might die to sins and live *for* r G1466

2Pe 1: 1 who through the **r** of our God and Savior *G1466*
2Pe 2: 5 a preacher *of* **r**, and seven others; *G1466*
2Pe 2:21 them not to have known the way *of* **r**, *G1466*
2Pe 3:13 heaven and a new earth, where **r** dwells. *G1466*

RIGHTFULLY (1) [RIGHT]
Eze 21:27 until he to whom it **r** belongs shall come; H5477

RIGHTLY (5) [RIGHT]
Ge 27:36 "Isn't he **r** named Jacob? This is H3954
Pr 25:11 settings of silver is a ruling **r** given. H6584+698
Jn 13:13 'Lord,' and **r so**, for that is what I am. *G2822*
Ac 8:10 "This man is *r* **called** the Great Power of God." AIT
2Th 1: 3 sisters, and **r** so, because your faith is *G545*

RIGHTS (19) [RIGHT]
Ex 21: 9 he must grant her the **r** *of* a daughter. H5477
Ex 21:10 one of her food, clothing and **marital r**. H6703
Dt 21:16 not **give the r of the firstborn** *to* the son H1144
1Sa 8: 9 will reign over them will **claim as** his **r**." H5477S
1Sa 8:11 will reign over you will **claim as** his **r**: H5477S
1Sa 10:25 to the people the **r and duties** *of* kingship. H5477
1Ch 5: 1 his **r as firstborn** were given to the sons of H1148
1Ch 5: 2 the **r of the firstborn** belonged to Joseph) H1148
Job 36: 6 wicked alive but gives the afflicted their **r**. H5477
Pr 31: 5 deprive all the oppressed of their **r**. H1907
Pr 31: 8 the **r** *of* all who are destitute. H1907
Pr 31: 9 **defend** the **r** *of* the poor and needy. H1906
Ecc 5: 8 justice and **r** denied, do not be H7406
Isa 10: 2 the poor of their **r** and withhold justice H1907
La 3:35 deny people their **r** before the Most High H5477
1Co 8: 9 that the **exercise of** your **r** does not *G2026*
1Co 9:15 But I have not used any *of* **these** *r*. And I am AIT
1Co 9:18 not make full use *of* my **r** as a preacher of *G2026*
Heb 12:16 sold his **inheritance r as the oldest son**. *G4757*

RIGID (1)
Mk 9:18 gnashes his teeth and *becomes* **r**. *G3830*

RIGOUR (KJV) RUTHLESSLY

RIM (24) [RIMS]
Ex 25:25 make around it a **r** a handbreadth wide H4995
Ex 25:25 wide and put a gold molding on the **r**. H4995
Ex 25:27 to be close to the **r** to hold the poles used H4995
Ex 37:12 made around it a **r** a handbreadth wide H4995
Ex 37:12 wide and put a gold molding on the **r**. H4995
Ex 37:14 were put close to the **r** to hold the poles H4995
Dt 2:36 From Aroer on the **r** *of* the Arnon Gorge H8557
Dt 4:48 from Aroer on the **r** *of* the Arnon Gorge to H8557
Jos 12: 2 from Aroer on the **r** *of* the Arnon Gorge— H8557
Jos 13: 9 from Aroer on the **r** *of* the Arnon Gorge, H8557
Jos 13:16 from Aroer on the **r** *of* the Arnon Gorge, H8557
1Ki 7:23 ten cubits from **r** to rim and five cubits H8557
1Ki 7:23 cubits from rim to **r** and five cubits high. H8557
1Ki 7:24 Below the **r**, gourds encircled it—ten to a H8557
1Ki 7:26 its **r** was like the rim of a cup H8557
1Ki 7:26 its rim was like the **r** *of* a cup, like a H8557
2Ch 4: 2 ten cubits from **r** to rim and five cubits H8557
2Ch 4: 2 cubits from rim to **r** and five cubits high. H8557
2Ch 4: 3 Below **the r**, figures of bulls encircled it H2257S
2Ch 4: 5 its **r** was like the rim of a cup H8557
2Ch 4: 5 its rim was like the **r** *of* a cup, like a H8557
Eze 43:13 with a **r** of one span around the edge. H1473
Eze 43:17 gutter of one cubit with a **r** of half a cubit. H1473
Eze 43:20 of the upper ledge and all around the **r**, H1473

RIMMON (13) [EN RIMMON, GATH RIMMON, HADAD RIMMON, RIMMON PEREZ]
Jos 15:32 Shilhim, Ain and **R**—a total of H8234
Jos 19: 7 **R**, Ether and Ashan—four towns and H8234
Jos 19:13 it came out at **R** and turned toward Neah. H8234
Jdg 20:45 toward the wilderness to the rock of **R**, H8234
Jdg 20:47 fled into the wilderness to the rock of **R**, H8234
Jdg 21:13 peace to the Benjamites at the rock of **R**. H8234
2Sa 4: 2 they were sons of **R** the Beerothite from H8233
2Sa 4: 5 Baanah, the sons of **R** the Beerothite, set H8233
2Sa 4: 9 Baanah, the sons of **R** the Beerothite, "As H8233
2Ki 5:18 the temple of **R** to bow down and he H8235
2Ki 5:18 when I bow down in the temple of **R**, may H8235
1Ch 4:32 were Etam, Ain, **R**, Token and Ashan H8234
Zec 14:10 from Geba to **R**, south of Jerusalem, H8234

RIMMON PEREZ (2) [PEREZ, RIMMON]
Nu 33:19 They left Rithmah and camped at **R**. H8236
Nu 33:20 They left **R** and camped at Libnah. H8236

RIMMONO (1)
1Ch 6:77 **R** and Tabor, together with their H8237

RIMS (3) [RIM]
1Ki 7:33 the axles, **r**, spokes and hubs were all of H1461
Eze 1:18 Their **r** were high and awesome, and all H1461
Eze 1:18 all four **r** were full of eyes all around. H1461

RING (24) [RANG, RINGED, RINGS]
Ge 24:22 took out a gold **nose r** weighing a beka H5690
Ge 24:30 As soon as he had seen the **nose r**, and H5690
Ge 24:47 "Then I put the **r** in her nose and the H5690
Ge 41:42 Pharaoh took his **signet r** from his finger H3192
Ex 26:24 way to the top and fitted into a single **r**; H3192
Ex 27: 4 make a bronze **r** at each of the four H3192
Ex 36:29 way to the top and fitted into a single **r**; H3192
Jdg 8:25 of them threw a **r** *from* his plunder onto it H5690
Est 3:10 the king took his **signet r** from his finger H3192
Est 3:12 Xerxes himself and sealed with his own **r**. H3192
Est 8: 2 The king took off his **signet r**, which he H3192
Est 8: 8 seal it with the king's **signet r**—for no H3192
Est 8: 8 sealed with his **r** can be revoked. H3192
Est 8:10 the dispatches with the king's **signet r**, H3192
Job 13:17 to what I say; let my words *r* **in** your ears. AIT
Job 16:16 with weeping, dark shadows **r** my eyes; H6584
Job 42:11 gave him a piece of silver and a gold **r**. H5690
Pr 11:22 Like a gold **r** in a pig's snout is a beautiful H5690
Jer 22:24 were a **signet r** on my right hand H2597
Eze 16:12 I put a **r** on your nose, earrings on H5690
Da 6:17 it with his own **signet r** and with the A10536
Hag 2:23 'and I will make you like my **signet r**, for I H2597
Lk 15:22 Put a **r** on his finger and sandals on his *G1234*
Jas 2: 2 your meeting **wearing a gold r** and fine *G5993*

RINGED (1) [RING]
Job 41:14 of its mouth, **r about** *with* fearsome teeth? H6017

RINGLEADER (1) [LEAD]
Ac 24: 5 He is a **r** of the Nazarene sect *G4756*

RINGS (42) [RING]
Ge 35: 4 gods they had and the **r** in their ears, H5690
Ex 25:12 Cast four gold **r** for it and fasten them to its H3192
Ex 25:12 with two **r** on one side and two rings on H3192
Ex 25:12 rings on one side and two **r** on the other. H3192
Ex 25:14 the poles into the **r** on the sides of the ark H3192
Ex 25:15 The poles are to remain in the **r** *of* this ark H3192
Ex 25:26 Make four gold **r** for the table and fasten H3192
Ex 25:27 The **r** are to be close to the rim to hold the H3192
Ex 26:29 gold and make gold **r** to hold the H3192
Ex 27: 7 be inserted into the **r** so they will be on H3192
Ex 28:23 Make two gold **r** for it and fasten them to H3192
Ex 28:24 gold chains to the **r** at the corners of the H3192
Ex 28:26 Make two gold **r** and attach them to the H3192
Ex 28:27 Make two more gold **r** and attach them to H3192
Ex 28:28 The **r** *of* the breastpiece are to be tied to H3192
Ex 28:28 to be tied to the **r** *of* the ephod with blue H3192
Ex 30: 4 Make two gold **r** for the altar below the H3192
Ex 35:22 brooches, earrings, **r** and ornaments. H3192
Ex 36:34 gold and made gold **r** to hold the H3192
Ex 37: 3 He cast four gold **r** for it and fastened H3192
Ex 37: 3 with two **r** on one side and two rings on H3192
Ex 37: 3 rings on one side and two **r** on the other. H3192
Ex 37: 5 the poles into the **r** on the sides of the ark H3192
Ex 37:13 They cast four gold **r** for the table and H3192
Ex 37:14 The **r** were put close to the rim to hold the H3192
Ex 37:27 They made two gold **r** below the molding H3192
Ex 38: 5 They cast bronze **r** to hold the poles for the H3192
Ex 38: 7 the poles into the **r** so they would be on H3192
Ex 39:16 two gold filigree settings and two gold **r**, H3192
Ex 39:16 fastened the **r** to two of the corners of H3192
Ex 39:17 gold chains to the **r** at the corners of the H3192
Ex 39:19 They made two gold **r** and attached them H3192
Ex 39:20 made two more gold **r** and attached them H3192
Ex 39:21 They tied the **r** *of* the breastpiece to the H3192
Ex 39:21 breastpiece to the **r** *of* the ephod with H3192
Nu 31:50 bracelets, **signet r**, earrings and necklaces H3192
Jdg 8:26 weight of the gold **r** he asked for came to H5690
Est 1: 6 material to silver **r** on marble pillars. H1664
Isa 3:21 the **signet r** and nose rings, H3192
Isa 3:21 the signet rings and nose **r**, H5690
Da 6:17 signet ring and with the **r** *of* his nobles, A10536
Hos 2:13 she decked herself with **r** and jewelry, and H5690

RINGSTRAKED (KJV) STREAKED

RINNAH (1)
1Ch 4:20 Amnon, **R**, Ben-Hanan and H8263

RINSED (3) [RINSING]
Lev 6:28 the pot is to be scoured and **r** with water. H8851
Lev 15:12 any wooden article *is to* **be r** with water. H8851
2Ch 4: 6 to be used for the burnt offerings *were* **r**, H1866

RINSING (1) [RINSED]
Lev 15:11 touches without **r** his hands with water H8851

RIOT (3) [RIOTERS, RIOTING, RIOTS]
Mt 26: 5 "or there may be a **r** among the people." *G2573*
Mk 14: 2 they said, "or the people *may* **r**." *G1639+2573*
Ac 17: 5 formed a mob and **started a r** in the city. *G2572*

RIOTERS (1) [RIOT]
Ac 21:32 When the **r** saw the commander and his NDT

RIOTING (1) [RIOT]
Ac 19:40 of being charged with **r** because of what *G5087*

RIOTS (2) [RIOT]
Ac 24: 5 stirring up **r** among the Jews all over the *G5087*
2Co 6: 5 imprisonments and **r**; in hard work, *G189*

RIP (3) [RIPPED]
2Ki 8:12 and **r open** their pregnant women. H1324
Ps 7: 2 a lion and **r** me **to pieces** with no one to H7293
Hos 13: 8 them and **r** them **open**; H7973+6033+4213

RIPE (14) [RIPEN, RIPENED, RIPENING, RIPENS]
Nu 13:20 It was the season for the **first r** grapes.) H1137
2Ki 4:42 barley bread baked from the **first r grain**, H1137
Isa 28: 4 will be like **figs r** before harvest—as H1136
Joel 3:13 the sickle, for the harvest *is* **r**. Come, H1418
Am 8: 1 LORD showed me: a basket of **r fruit**. H7811
Am 8: 2 "A basket of **r fruit**," I answered. H7811
Am 8: 2 "The **time is r** for my people Israel H995+7891
Na 3:12 are like fig trees with their **first r fruit**; H1137
Zec 8: 4 again *men* and women **of r old age** will H2418
[Zec 8: 4 again men and *women* **of r old age** will H2418]
Mal 3:11 *will* **not drop** *their* **fruit before it is r**," H8897
Mk 4:29 As soon as the grain *is* **r**, he puts the sickle *G4140*
Jn 4:35 look at the fields! They are **r** for harvest. *G3328*
Rev 14:15 has come, for the harvest of the earth *is* **r**." *G3830*
Rev 14:18 the earth's vine, because its grapes *are* **r**." *G196*

RIPEN (2) [RIPE]
Ex 9:32 were not destroyed, because they **r later**.) H689
Jer 24: 2 like those that **r early**; the other basket H1136

RIPENED (3) [RIPE]
Ge 40:10 blossomed, and its clusters **r** *into* grapes. H1418
Isa 16: 9 of joy over your **r fruit** and over your H7811
Jer 48:32 has fallen on your **r fruit** and grapes. H7811

RIPENING (1) [RIPE]
Isa 18: 5 gone and the flower becomes a **r** grape, H1694

RIPENS (1) [RIPE]
Hos 2: 9 I will take away my grain when it **r**, H6961

RIPHATH (2)
Ge 10: 3 Ashkenaz, **R** and Togarmah. H8196
1Ch 1: 6 Ashkenaz, **R** and Togarmah. H8196

RIPPED (3) [RIP]
2Ki 15:16 Tiphsah and **r open** all the pregnant H1324
Hos 13:16 the ground, their pregnant women **r open**." H1324
Am 1:13 Because he **r open** the pregnant women H1324

RISE (118) [ARISE, ARISEN, ARISES, AROSE, RAISE, RAISED, RAISES, RAISING, RISEN, RISES, RISING, ROSE, UPRAISED, UPRISING, UPRISINGS]
Nu 10:35 the ark set out, Moses said, "**R up**, LORD! H7756
Nu 23:24 The people **r** like a lioness; they rouse H7756
Nu 24:17 out of Jacob; a scepter *will* **r** out of Israel. H7756
Dt 28: 7 the enemies who **r up** against you will be H7756
Dt 28:43 reside among you *will* **r** above you higher H6590
Dt 32:38 *Let them* **r up** to help you! Let H7756
Dt 33:11 Strike down *those who* **r** *against* him, his H7756
Dt 33:11 against him, his foes till *they* **r** no more." H7756
Jos 8: 7 you *are to* **r up** from ambush and take the H7756
Jdg 20:40 column of smoke began to **r** from the city, H6590
1Sa 16:12 the LORD said, "**R** and anoint him; this H7756
2Sa 18:32 king and all who **r up** to harm you be like H7756
2Sa 22:39 completely, and *they could* not **r**; they fell H7756
Ezr 10: 4 **R up**; this matter is in your hands. We will H7756
Job 14:12 so he lies down and *does* not **r**; till the H7756
Job 20:27 his guilt; the earth *will* **r up** against him. H7756
Job 24:12 *The* **groans** of the dying *r* from the city, and AIT
Job 25: 3 On whom *does* his light not **r**? H7756
Ps 2: 2 kings of the earth **r up** and the rulers band H3656
Ps 3: 1 How many **r up** against me! H7756
Ps 7: 6 **r up** against the rage of my enemies. H5951
Ps 17: 1 my prayer—it does not **r** from deceitful lips. NDT
Ps 17:13 **R up**, LORD, confront them, bring them H7756
Ps 18:38 I crushed them so that they could not **r** H7756
Ps 20: 8 fall, but we **r up** and stand firm. H7756
Ps 27:12 false witnesses **r up** against me H7756
Ps 35:23 and **r** to my defense! Contend for H7810
Ps 36:12 lie fallen—thrown down, not able *to* **r**! H7756
Ps 44:26 **R up** and help us; rescue us because of H7756
Ps 66: 7 *let* not the rebellious **r up** against him. H8123
Ps 74:22 **R up**, O God, and defend your cause H7756
Ps 82: 8 **R up**, O God, judge the earth, for all the H7756
Ps 88:10 *Do* their spirits **r up** and praise you? H7756
Ps 94: 2 **R up**, Judge of the earth; pay back to the H5951
Ps 94:16 Who *will* **r up** for me against the wicked H7756
Ps 119:62 At midnight *I* **r** to give you thanks for your H7756
Ps 119:147 *I* **r** before dawn and cry for help; I have H7709
Ps 127: 2 In vain you **r** early and stay up late, toiling H7756
Ps 135: 7 *He* **makes** clouds **r** from the ends of the H6590
Ps 139: 2 You know when I sit and *when* I **r**; you H7756
Ps 139: 9 If *I* **r** *on* the wings of the dawn, if I settle H5951
Ps 140:10 into the fire, into miry pits, never *to* **r**. H7756
Pr 24:16 fall seven times, *they* **r** again, but the H7756
Pr 28:12 when the wicked **r to power**, people H7756
Pr 28:28 When the wicked **r to power**, people go H7756
Ecc 12: 4 when *people* **r up** at the sound of birds H7756
Isa 3: 5 The young *will* **r up** against the old, the H8104
Isa 5:11 Woe to *those who* **r early** in the morning H8899
Isa 14: 9 *it* **makes** them **r** from their thrones H7756
Isa 14:21 *they are* not *to* **r** to inherit the land and H7756
Isa 14:22 "*I will* **r up** against them," declares the H7756
Isa 24:20 its rebellion that it falls—never *to* **r** again. H7756
Isa 26:14 they live no more; their spirits *do* not **r**. H7756
Isa 26:19 their bodies *will* **r**—let those who H7756
Isa 28:21 The LORD *will* **r up** as he did at Mount H7756
Isa 30:18 therefore *he will* **r up** to show you H8123
Isa 31: 2 *He will* **r up** against that wicked nation H7756
Isa 32: 9 are so complacent, **r up** and listen to me H7756
Isa 33: 3 when you **r up**, the nations scatter. H8129
Isa 34:10 night or day; its smoke *will* **r** forever. H6590
Isa 43:17 lay there, never *to* **r** *again*, extinguished, H7756
Isa 51:17 **R up**, Jerusalem, you who have drunk H7756
Isa 52: 2 Shake off your dust; **r up**, sit enthroned H7756

R

Isa 58:10 then your light *will* r in the darkness, and H2436
Jer 10:13 *he* **makes** clouds r from the ends of the H5927
Jer 25:27 fall *to* r no more because of the H7756
Jer 46: 8 She says, '*I will* r and cover the earth; H6590
Jer 49:14 yourselves to attack it! **R up** for battle!" H7756
Jer 51:16 *he* **makes** clouds r from the ends of the H6590
Jer 51:42 The sea *will* r over Babylon; its roaring H6590
Jer 51:64 will Babylon sink *to* r no more because of H7756
Eze 1:20 the wheels *would* r along with them H5951
Eze 10:16 spread their wings to r from the ground, H8123
Eze 17:14 unable *to* **r again**, surviving only by H5951
Da 7:17 are four kings *that will* r from the earth. A10624
Da 11:14 those times many *will* r against the king H6641
Da 11:23 with only a few people *he will* r to power. H6590
Da 11:31 armed forces *will* **r up** to desecrate the H6641
Da 12:13 end of the days *you will* r to receive your H6641
Hos 10:14 the roar of battle *will* r against your H7756
Joel 2:20 its smell *will* r." Surely he has H6590
Am 5: 2 Virgin Israel, never *to* r again, deserted in H7756
Am 7: 9 with my sword *I will* r against the house of H7756
Am 8: 8 The whole land *will* r like the Nile; it will H6590
Am 8:14 they will fall, never *to* r again. H7756
Ob 1 the nations to say, "**R**, let us go against H7756
Mic 4:13 "**R** and thresh, Daughter Zion, for I will H7756
Mic 7: 8 I have fallen, *I will* r. Though I sit in H7756
Mal 4: 2 of righteousness *will* r with healing in its H2436
Mt 5:45 *He* **causes** his sun **to** r on the evil and the *G422*
Mt 12:42 Queen of the South *will* r at the judgment *G1586*
Mt 24: 7 Nation *will* r against nation, and kingdom *G1586*
Mt 26:46 **R**! Let us go! Here comes my betrayer!" *G1586*
Mt 27:63 'After three days *I will* **r again**. *G1586*
Mk 8:31 must be killed and after three days **r again**. *G482*
Mk 9:31 will kill him, and after three days *he will* r." *G482*
Mk 10:34 Three days later *he will* r." *G482*
Mk 12:25 When the dead r, they will neither marry *G482*
Mk 13: 8 Nation *will* r against nation, and kingdom *G1586*
Mk 14:42 **R**! Let us go! Here comes my betrayer!" *G1586*
Lk 11:31 Queen of the South *will* r at the judgment *G1586*
Lk 17:19 Then he said to him, "**R** and go; your faith *G482*
Lk 18:33 On the third day *he will* **r again**." *G482*
Lk 20:37 even Moses showed that the dead r, for *G1586*
Lk 21:10 "Nation *will* r against nation, and *G1586*
Lk 24:38 why *do* doubts r in your minds? *G326*
Lk 24:46 will suffer and r from the dead on the *G482*
Jn 5:29 who have done what is good will r to live, *G414*
Jn 5:29 done what is evil will r to be condemned. *G414*
Jn 11:23 Jesus said to her, "Your brother *will* **r again**." *G482*
Jn 11:24 "I know *he will* **r again** in the resurrection *G482*
Jn 20: 9 Scripture that Jesus had to r from the dead.) *G482*
Ac 4:26 kings of the earth **r up** and the rulers band *G4225*
Ac 17: 3 Messiah had to suffer and r from the dead. *G482*
Ac 26:23 as the first *to* r from the dead, would *G414*
Eph 5:14 sleeper, r from the dead, and Christ will *G482*
1Th 4:16 and the dead in Christ *will* r first. *G482*
Rev 14:11 of their torment *will* r for ever and ever. *G326*

RISEN (16) [RISE]
Ge 19:23 reached Zoar, the sun *had* r over the land. H3655
Dt 34:10 no prophet *has* r in Israel like Moses H7756
2Sa 14: 7 Now the whole clan *has* **r up** against your H7756
Eze 47: 5 because the water *had* r and was deep H1448
Mic 2: 8 Lately my people *have* **r up** like an enemy. H7756
Mt 11:11 born of women *there has* not r anyone *G1586*
Mt 14: 2 John the Baptist; he *has* r from the dead! *G1586*
Mt 26:32 But after I *have* r, I will go ahead of you *G1586*
Mt 28: 6 He is not here; *he has* r, just as he said *G1586*
Mt 28: 7 '*He has* r from the dead and is going *G1586*
Mk 9: 9 the Son of Man *had* r from the dead. *G482*
Mk 14:28 But after I *have* r, I will go ahead of you *G1586*
Mk 16: 6 was crucified. *He has* r! He is not here. *G1586*
Mk 16:14 those who had seen him *after he had* r. *G1586*
Lk 24: 6 He is not here; *he has* r! Remember how *G1586*
Lk 24:34 The Lord *has* r and has appeared to *G1586*

RISES (31) [RISE]
Jos 11:17 which r *toward* Seir, to Baal Gad H6590
Jos 12: 7 to Mount Halak, which r toward Seir. H6590
Jdg 5:31 be like the sun *when it* r in its strength." H3655
Job 16: 8 my gauntness **r up** and testifies against H7756
Job 24:14 the murderer **r up**, kills the poor H7756
Job 41:25 When it **r up**, the mighty are terrified; they H8420
Ps 19: 6 It r at one end of the heavens and makes H4604
Ps 74:23 of your enemies, *which* r continually. H6590
Ps 104:22 The sun r, and they steal away; they H2436
Ecc 1: 5 The sun r and the sun sets, and hurries H2436
Ecc 1: 5 sun sets, and hurries back to where it r. H2436
Ecc 3:21 if the human spirit r upward and if the H6590
Ecc 10: 4 If a ruler's anger r against you, do not H6590
Isa 2:19 his majesty, when he r to shake the earth. H7756
Isa 2:21 his majesty, when he r to shake the earth. H7756
Isa 3:13 place in court; *he* r to judge the people. H6641
Isa 60: 1 the glory of the LORD r upon you. H2436
Isa 60: 2 the LORD r upon you and his glory H2436
Jer 46: 7 "Who is this *that* r like the Nile, like rivers H6590
Jer 46: 8 Egypt r like the Nile, like rivers of surging H6590
Jer 48:34 sound of their cry r from Heshbon to H5989
Jer 51: 9 to the skies, *it* r as **high** as the heavens. H5951
Hos 6: 3 As surely as the **sun** r, he will appear; he H8840
Hos 7: 4 from the kneading of the dough till it r. H2806
Am 9: 5 the whole land r like the Nile, then H6590
Mic 7: 6 a daughter **r up** against her mother H7756
Mal 1:11 from **where** the sun r to where it sets. H4667

Lk 16:31 even if someone r from the dead. *G482*
Eph 2:21 is joined together and r to become a holy *G889*
Jas 1:11 For the sun r with scorching heat and *G422*
2Pe 1:19 the morning star r in your hearts. *G422*

RISING (21) [RISE]
Ge 19:28 he saw dense smoke r from the land H6590
Jos 8:20 saw the smoke of the city **r up** into the sky, H6590
1Ki 18:44 small as a man's hand *is* r from the sea." H6590
Ps 32: 6 surely the r *of* the mighty waters will not H8852
Ps 50: 1 the earth from the r *of* the sun to where it H4667
Ps 55:12 endure it; if a foe *were* r against me, H1540
Ps 113: 3 From the r *of* the sun to the place where it H4667
Isa 13:10 The r sun will be darkened and the moon H3655
Isa 30:28 is like a rushing torrent, **r up** to the neck. H2936
Isa 41:25 one from the r sun who calls on my name. H4667
Isa 45: 6 so that from the r *of* the sun to the place H4667
Isa 59:19 and from the r *of* the sun, they will H4667
Jer 25:32 a mighty storm *is* r from the ends of the H6424
Jer 47: 2 "See how the waters *are* r in the north H6590
Eze 8:11 a fragrant cloud of incense *was* r. H6590
Mk 9:10 discussing what "r from the dead" meant. *G482*
Mk 12:26 Now about the dead r—have you not read *G1586*
Lk 1:78 by which the r **sun** will come to us from *G424*
Lk 2:34 to cause the falling and r of many in Israel, *G414*
Lk 12:54 "When you see a cloud r in the west *G422*
Rev 14:20 r as high as the horses' bridles for a NDT

RISK (4) [RISKED]
2Sa 17:17 for *they* **could** not r being seen entering H3523
2Sa 23:17 of men who went **at the r of** their lives?" H928
1Ch 11:19 these men who went **at the r of** their lives?" H928
La 5: 9 We get our bread **at the r of** our lives H928

RISKED (6) [RISK]
Jdg 5:18 of Zebulun r their very lives; H3070+4200+4637
Jdg 9:17 you and r his life to rescue H8959+4946+5584
1Ch 11:19 Because they r their lives to bring it back H928
Ac 15:26 men *who have* r their lives for the name *G4140*
Ro 16: 4 They r their lives for me. Not only I but all *G5719*
Php 2:30 *He* r his life to make up for the help you *G4129*

RISSAH (2)
Nu 33:21 They left Libnah and camped at **R**. H8267
Nu 33:22 They left **R** and camped at Kehelathah. H8267

RITES (3)
Lk 2:22 time came *for* the **purification** r required *G2752*
Ac 21:24 join in their **purification** r and pay their *G49*
Heb 6: 2 instruction *about* **cleansing** r, the laying on *G968*

RITHMAH (2)
Nu 33:18 They left Hazeroth and camped at **R**. H8414
Nu 33:19 They left **R** and camped at Rimmon Perez. H8414

RIVAL (4) [RIVALRY]
Lev 18:18 wife's sister as a r **wife** and have sexual H7675
1Sa 1: 6 her r kept provoking her in order to irritate H7651
1Sa 1: 7 her r provoked her till she wept and would NDT
Eze 31: 8 cedars in the garden of God *could* not r it, H6669

RIVALRY (1) [RIVAL]
Php 1:15 that some preach Christ out of envy and r, *G2251*

RIVER (106) [RIVERBANK, RIVERBED, RIVERS]
Ge 2:10 A r watering the garden flowed from Eden H5643
Ge 2:13 The name of the second r is the Gihon; it H5643
Ge 2:14 The name of the third r is the Tigris; it runs H5643
Ge 2:14 And the fourth r is the Euphrates. H5643
Ge 15:18 from the Wadi of Egypt to the great r, the H5643
Ge 31:21 crossed the **Euphrates R**, and headed H5643
Ge 36:37 from Rehoboth on the r succeeded him as H5643
Ge 41: 2 when out of the r there came up seven H3284
Ge 41:18 when out of the r there came up seven H3284
Ex 4: 9 you take from the r will become blood on H3284
Ex 7:15 in the morning as he goes out to the r. H4784
Ex 7:18 Nile will die, and the r will stink; the H3284
Ex 7:21 the r smelled so bad that the H3284
Ex 7:24 they could not drink the water of the r. H3284
Ex 8:20 as he goes to the r and say to him, H4784
Ex 23:31 from the desert to the **Euphrates R**. H5643
Nu 22: 5 near the **Euphrates R**, in his native H5643
Nu 24: 6 like gardens beside a r, like aloes planted H5643
Dt 1: 7 as far as the great r, the Euphrates. H5643
Dt 3:16 out to the Jabbok **R**, which is the H5707
Dt 11:24 from the Euphrates **R** to the H5643
Jos 1: 2 to cross the Jordan **R** into the land I am NDT
Jos 1: 4 from the great r, the Euphrates— H5643
Jos 2:23 forded the r and came to Joshua son of Nun NDT
Jos 3: 8 the Jordan's waters, go and stand in the r. H3720
Jos 4:18 came up out of the r carrying the ark of H3720
Jos 12: 2 gorge—to the Jabbok **R**, which is the H5707
Jos 13: 3 from the Shihor **R** on the east of Egypt to the NDT
Jos 24: 2 beyond the **Euphrates R** and worshiped H5643
Jos 24:14 beyond the **Euphrates R** and in Egypt, H5643
Jdg 4: 7 troops to the Kishon **R** and give him into H5707
Jdg 4:13 to the Kishon **R** all his men and his H5707
Jdg 5:21 The r Kishon swept them away, the H5707
Jdg 5:21 the age-old r, the river Kishon. H5707
Jdg 5:21 the age-old river, the r Kishon. H5707
2Sa 8: 3 restore his monument at the Euphrates **R**. H5643
2Sa 10:16 brought from beyond the **Euphrates R**; H5643
2Sa 17:21 "Set out and cross the r at once H4784

1Ki 4:21 from the **Euphrates R** to the land of H5643
1Ki 4:24 all the kingdoms west of the **Euphrates R**, H5643
1Ki 14:15 scatter them beyond the **Euphrates R**, H5643
2Ki 17: 6 Gozan on the Habor **R** and in the towns of H5643
2Ki 18:11 Gozan on the Habor **R** and in towns of the H5643
2Ki 23:29 up to the Euphrates **R** to help the king of H5643
2Ki 24: 7 the Wadi of Egypt to the Euphrates **R**. H5643
1Ch 1:48 from Rehoboth on the r succeeded him as H5643
1Ch 5: 9 desert that extends to the Euphrates **R**, H5643
1Ch 5:26 Hara and the r *of* Gozan, where they H5643
1Ch 13: 5 from the Shihor **R** in Egypt to Lebo Hamath NDT
1Ch 18: 3 set up his monument at the Euphrates **R**. H5643
1Ch 19:16 brought from beyond the **Euphrates R**, H5643
2Ch 9:26 kings from the **Euphrates R** to the land of H5643
Job 40:23 A raging r does not alarm it; it is secure H5643
Ps 36: 8 give them drink from your r *of* delights. H5707
Ps 46: 4 There is a r whose streams make glad the H5643
Ps 72: 8 to sea and from the **R** to the ends of the H5643
Ps 78:44 He turned their r into blood; they could H3284
Ps 80:11 far as the Sea, its shoots as far as the **R**. H5643
Ps 83: 9 did to Sisera and Jabin at the r Kishon, H5707
Ps 105:41 it flowed like a r in the desert. H5643
Isa 7:20 hired from beyond the **Euphrates R**— H5643
Isa 11:15 will sweep his hand over the **Euphrates R**. H5643
Isa 19: 5 The waters of the r will dry up, and the H3542
Isa 19: 7 along the Nile, at the mouth of the r. H3284
Isa 48:18 your peace would have been like a r, your H5643
Isa 66:12 "I will extend peace to her like a r, and H5643
Jer 46: 2 on the Euphrates **R** by Nebuchadnezzar H5643
Jer 46: 6 In the north by the **R** Euphrates they H5643
Jer 46:10 the land of the north by the **R** Euphrates. H5643
Jer 51:32 the r **crossings** seized, the marshes set on H5045
La 2:18 let your tears flow like a r day and night H5707
Eze 1: 1 I was among the exiles by the Kebar **R**, H5643
Eze 1: 3 by the Kebar **R** in the land of the H5643
Eze 3:15 who lived at Tel Aviv near the Kebar **R**. H5643
Eze 3:23 like the glory I had seen by the Kebar **R** H5643
Eze 10:15 living creatures I had seen by the Kebar **R**. H5643
Eze 10:20 beneath the God of Israel by the Kebar **R**, H5643
Eze 10:22 as those I had seen by the Kebar **R**. H5643
Eze 43: 3 like the visions I had seen by the Kebar **R**, H5643
Eze 47: 5 now it was a r that I could not cross H5707
Eze 47: 5 to swim in—a r that no one could cross. H5707
Eze 47: 6 Then he led me back to the bank of the r. H5707
Eze 47: 7 number of trees on each side of the r. H5707
Eze 47: 9 creatures will live wherever the r flows. H5707
Eze 47: 9 so where the r flows everything will live. H5707
Eze 47:12 all kinds will grow on both banks of the r. H5707
Da 7:10 A r of fire was flowing, coming out from A10468
Da 10: 4 I was standing on the bank of the great r, H5643
Da 12: 5 on this bank of the r and one on the H3284
Da 12: 6 who was above the waters of the r, "How H3284
Da 12: 7 who was above the waters of the r, lifted H3284
Am 5:24 But let justice roll on like a r H4784
Am 8: 8 stirred up and then sink like the r *of* Egypt. H3284
Am 9: 5 like the Nile, then sinks like the r *of* Egypt; H3284
Na 2: 6 The r gates are thrown open and the H5643
Na 3: 8 The r was her defense, the waters her H3542
Zec 9:10 to sea and from the **R** to the ends of the H5643
Mt 3: 6 were baptized by him in the Jordan **R**. *G4532*
Mk 1: 5 were baptized by him in the Jordan **R**. *G4532*
Ac 16:13 we went outside the city gate to the r, *G4532*
Rev 9:14 who are bound at the great r Euphrates." *G4532*
Rev 12:15 mouth the serpent spewed water like a r, *G4532*
Rev 12:16 swallowing the r that the dragon had *G4532*
Rev 16:12 out his bowl on the great r Euphrates, *G4532*
Rev 22: 1 angel showed me the r of the water of life *G4532*
Rev 22: 2 On each side of the r stood the tree of life, *G4532*

RIVERBANK (2) [RIVER]
Ge 41: 3 and stood beside those on the r. H8557+3284
Ex 2: 5 were walking along the r. H3284+3338

RIVERBED (2) [RIVER]
Job 14:11 lake dries up or a r becomes parched and H5643
Isa 19: 5 and the r will be parched and dry. H5643

RIVERS (29) [RIVER]
2Ki 5:12 Pharpar, the r *of* Damascus, better H5643
Job 20:17 the r *flowing with* honey and cream H5643+5707
Job 28:11 the sources of the r and bring hidden H5643
Ps 74:15 streams; you dried up the ever-flowing r. H5643
Ps 78:16 crag and made water flow down like r. H5643
Ps 89:25 over the sea, his right hand over the r. H5643
Ps 98: 8 Let the r clap their hands, let the H5643
Ps 107:33 He turned r into a desert, flowing springs H5643
Ps 137: 1 By the r *of* Babylon we sat and wept when H5643
SS 8: 7 quench love; r cannot sweep it away. H5643
Isa 18: 1 of whirring wings along the r *of* Cush, H5643
Isa 18: 2 speech, whose land is divided by r. H5643
Isa 18: 7 whose land is divided by r—the gifts will H5643
Isa 33:21 be like a place of broad r and streams. H5643
Isa 41:18 I will make r flow on barren heights, and H5643
Isa 42:15 I will turn r into islands and dry up the H5643
Isa 43: 2 when you pass through the r, they H5643
Isa 50: 2 I dry up the sea, I turn r into a desert; their H5643
Jer 46: 7 rises like the Nile, like r *of* surging waters? H5643
Jer 46: 8 rises like the Nile, like r *of* surging waters. H5643
Mic 6: 7 of rams, with ten thousand r *of* olive oil? H5707
Na 1: 4 dries it up; he makes all the r run dry. H5643
Hab 3: 8 Were you angry with the r, LORD? Was H5643
Hab 3: 9 You split the earth with r; H5643

R

Zep 3:10 From beyond the **r** *of* Cush my worshipers H5643
Jn 7:38 **r** of living water will flow from within them *G4532*
2Co 11:26 I have been in danger *from* **r**, in danger *G4532*
Rev 8:10 the sky on a third *of* the **r** and on the *G4532*
Rev 16: 4 out his bowl on the **r** and springs of water, *G4532*

RIZIA (1)

1Ch 7:39 The sons of Ulla: Arah, Hanniel and **R**. H8359

RIZPAH (4)

2Sa 3: 7 a concubine named **R** daughter of Aiah. H8366
2Sa 21: 8 the two sons of Aiah's daughter **R**, whom H8366
2Sa 21:10 **R** daughter of Aiah took sackcloth and H8366
2Sa 21:11 David was told what Aiah's daughter **R**, H8366

ROAD (97) [CROSSROADS, ROADS, ROADSIDE]

Ge 16: 7 was the spring that is beside the **r** *to* Shur. H2006
Ge 24:48 had led me on the right **r** to get the H2006
Ge 38:14 to Enaim, which is on the **r** to Timnah. H2006
Ge 38:21 prostitute who was beside the **r** at Enaim?" H2006
Ge 48: 7 I buried her there beside the **r** *to* Ephrath" H2006
Ex 13:17 lead them on the **r** *through* the Philistine H2006
Ex 13:18 by the desert **r** toward the Red Sea. H2006
Nu 20:19 "We will go along the **main r**, and if we H5019
Nu 21: 1 Israel was coming along the **r** *to* Atharim, H2006
Nu 21:33 went up along the **r** *toward* Bashan, H2006
Nu 22:22 of the LORD stood in the **r** to oppose him. H2006
Nu 22:23 LORD standing in the **r** with a drawn sword H2006
Nu 22:23 in his hand, it turned off the **r** into a field. H2006
Nu 22:23 Balaam beat it to get it back on the **r**. H2006
Nu 22:31 standing in the **r** with his sword drawn H2006
Nu 22:34 you were standing in the **r** to oppose me. H2006
Dt 1: 2 to Kadesh Barnea by the Mount Seir **r**.) H2006
Dt 2: 8 We turned from the Arabah **r**, which H2006
Dt 2: 8 traveled along the desert **r** *of* Moab. H2006
Dt 2:27 We will stay on the **main r**; we will H2006+2006
Dt 3: 1 went up along the **r** *toward* Bashan, H2006
Dt 6: 7 at home and when you walk along the **r**, H2006
Dt 11:19 at home and when you walk along the **r**, H2006
Dt 22: 4 Israelite's donkey or ox fallen on the **r**, H2006
Dt 22: 6 come across a bird's nest beside the **r**, H2006
Dt 27:18 who leads the blind astray on the **r**." H2006
Jos 2: 7 of the spies on the **r** that leads to the H2006
Jos 2:22 all along the **r** and returned without H2006
Jos 10:10 them along the **r** going up to Beth Horon H2006
Jos 10:11 Israel on the **r down** *from* Beth Horon to H4618
Jdg 5:10 you who walk along the **r**, consider H2006
Jdg 21:19 east of the **r** that goes from Bethel to H5019
Ru 1: 7 set out on the **r** that would take them H2006
1Sa 4:13 Eli sitting on his chair by the side of the **r**, H2006
1Sa 6:12 keeping on the **r** and lowing all the way H5019
1Sa 17:52 along the Shaaraim **r** to Gath and Ekron. H2006
1Sa 26: 3 his camp beside the **r** on the hill of H2006
2Sa 13:34 saw many people on the **r** west of him, H2006
2Sa 15: 2 the side of the **r** *leading to* the city gate. H2006
2Sa 16:13 continued along the **r** while Shimei was H2006
2Sa 20:12 in his blood in the middle of the **r**, H5019
2Sa 20:12 dragged him from the **r** into a field and H5019
2Sa 20:13 After Amasa had been removed from the **r**, H5019
1Ki 13:10 So he took another **r** and did not return by H2006
1Ki 13:12 showed him which **r** the man of God from H2006
1Ki 13:24 a lion met him on the **r** and killed him H2006
1Ki 13:24 his body was left lying on the **r**, with H2006
1Ki 13:28 out and found the body lying on the **r**, H2006
1Ki 20:38 stood by the **r** waiting for the king. H2006
2Ki 2:23 As he was walking along the **r**, some boys H2006
2Ki 6:19 "This is not the **r** and this is not the city. H2006
2Ki 7:15 they found the whole **r** strewn with the H2006
2Ki 9:27 he fled up the **r** *to* Beth Haggan. H2006
2Ki 12:20 him at Beth Millo, on the **r down** *to* Silla. H3718
2Ki 18:17 on the **r** *to* the Washerman's Field. H5019
1Ch 26:16 Gate on the upper **r** fell to Shuppim and H5019
1Ch 26:18 were four at the **r** and two at the court H5019
Ezr 8:22 to protect us from enemies on the **r**, H2006
Job 30:13 They break up my **r**; they succeed in H5986
Pr 26:13 "There's a lion in the **r**, a fierce lion H2006
Ecc 10: 3 Even as fools walk along the **r**, they lack H2006
Isa 7: 3 on the **r** *to* the Launderer's Field. H5019
Isa 15: 5 on the **r** *to* Horonaim they lament their H2006
Isa 36: 2 on the **r** *to* the Launderer's Field, H5019
Isa 51:10 who made a **r** in the depths of the sea so H2006
Isa 57:14 prepare the **r**! Remove the obstacles H2006
Jer 31:21 "Set up **r signs**; put up guideposts. H7483
Jer 31:21 note of the highway, the **r** *that* you take. H2006
Jer 48: 5 on the **r down** *to* Horonaim anguished H4618
Jer 48:19 Stand by the **r** and watch, you who live in H2006
Eze 21:19 a signpost where the **r** branches off to the H2006
Eze 21:20 Mark out *one* **r** for the sword to come H2006
Eze 21:21 of Babylon will stop at the fork in the **r**, H2006
Eze 47:15 Sea by the Hethlon **r** past Lebo Hamath to H2006
Eze 48: 1 will follow the Hethlon **r** to Lebo Hamath; H2006
Hos 6: 9 they murder on the **r** to Shechem, carrying H2006
Na 2: 1 the fortress, watch the **r**, brace yourselves, H2006
Mt 7:13 gate and broad is the **r** that leads to *G3847*
Mt 7:14 gate and narrow the **r** that leads to life, *G3847*
Mt 21: 8 large crowd spread their cloaks on the **r**, *G3847*
Mt 21: 8 from the trees and spread them on the **r**. *G3847*
Mt 21:19 Seeing a fig tree by the **r**, he went up to it *G3847*
Mk 9:33 "What were you arguing about on the **r**?" *G3847*
Mk 10:52 his sight and followed Jesus along the **r**. *G3847*
Mk 11: 8 Many people spread their cloaks on the **r** *G3847*
Lk 9:57 As they were walking along the **r**, a man *G3847*
Lk 10: 4 do not greet anyone on the **r**. *G3847*
Lk 10:31 happened to be going down the same **r**, *G3847*
Lk 19:36 people spread their cloaks on the **r**. *G3847*
Lk 19:37 near the **place where the r goes down** the *G2853*
Lk 24:32 he talked with us on the **r** and opened the *G3847*
Ac 8:26 "Go south to the **r**—the desert road— *G3847*
Ac 8:26 the desert **r**—that goes down from NDT
Ac 8:36 As they traveled along the **r**, they came to *G3847*
Ac 9:17 to you on the **r** as you were coming *G3847*
Ac 19: 1 Paul **took the r through** the interior and *G1451*
Ac 26:13 as I was on the **r**, I saw a light from *G3847*

ROADS (15) [ROAD]

Lev 26:22 in number that your **r** will be deserted. H2006
Jdg 20:31 men fell in the open field and on the **r**— H5019
Jdg 20:32 draw them away from the city to the **r**." H5019
Jdg 20:45 cut down five thousand men along the **r**. H5019
Isa 33: 8 are deserted, no travelers are on the **r**. H784
Isa 49: 9 will feed beside the **r** and find pasture on H2006
Isa 49:11 I will turn all my mountains into **r**, and my H2006
Isa 59: 8 They have turned them into crooked **r**; no H5986
Jer 6:25 not go out to the fields or walk on the **r**, H2006
Jer 18:15 them walk in byways, on **r** not built up. H2006
La 1: 4 The **r** *to* Zion mourn, for no one comes to H2006
Eze 21:19 mark out two **r** for the sword of the king of H2006
Eze 21:21 at the junction of the two **r**, to seek an H2006
Lk 3: 5 The **crooked** *r* shall become straight, the AIT
Lk 14:23 'Go out to the **r** and country lanes and *G3847*

ROADSIDE (6) [ROAD]

Ge 38:16 he went over to her by the **r** and said H2006
Ge 49:17 Dan will be a snake by the **r**, a viper H2006
Jer 3: 2 By the **r** you sat waiting for lovers, sat like H2006
Mt 20:30 Two blind men were sitting by the **r**, and *G3847*
Mk 10:46 Timaeus"), was sitting by the **r** begging. *G3847*
Lk 18:35 a blind man was sitting by the **r** begging. *G3847*

ROAM (4) [ROAMED, ROAMING]

Jdg 11:37 two months *to* **r** the hills and H2143+2256+3718
Isa 8:21 hungry, *they will* **r** through the land H6296
Jer 2:31 people say, '*We are free to* **r**; we will H8113
Jer 50: 6 them astray and **caused** them *to* **r** on the H8740

ROAMED (2) [ROAM]

1Sa 30:31 other places where he and his men *had* **r**. H2143
Job 30: 3 *they* **r** the parched land in desolate H6908

ROAMING (3) [ROAM]

Job 1: 7 the LORD, "From **r** throughout the earth H8763
Job 2: 2 the LORD, "From **r** throughout the earth H8763
Pr 26:13 a lion in the road, a fierce lion **r** the streets!" NDT

ROAR (39) [ROARED, ROARING, ROARS]

Job 4:10 The lions may **r** and growl, yet the teeth H8614
Job 37: 2 Listen to the **r** *of* his voice, to the rumbling H8075
Job 37: 4 After that **comes** the sound of *his* **r**; he H8613
Ps 42: 7 calls to deep in the **r** *of* your waterfalls; H7754
Ps 46: 3 though its waters **r** and foam and the H2159
Ps 104:21 The lions **r** for their prey and seek their H8613
Pr 19:12 A king's rage is like the **r** *of* a lion, but his H5638
Pr 20: 2 wrath strikes terror like the **r** *of* a lion; H5638
Isa 5:29 Their **r** is like that of the lion, they roar H8614
Isa 5:29 that of the lion, *they* **r** like young lions H8613
Isa 5:30 In that day *they will* **r** over it like the H5637
Isa 17:12 Woe to the peoples who **r**—they roar like H8623
Isa 17:12 *they* **r** like the roaring of great waters! H8616
Isa 17:13 Although the peoples **r** like the roar of H8616
Isa 17:13 peoples roar like the **r** *of* surging waters, H8623
Isa 51:15 who stirs up the sea so that its waves **r** H2159
Jer 5:22 cannot prevail; *they may* **r**, but they H2159
Jer 10:13 the waters in the heavens **r**; he makes H2162
Jer 11:16 But with the **r** *of* a mighty storm he will set H7754
Jer 25:30 " 'The LORD *will* **r** from on high; he will H8613
Jer 25:30 dwelling and **r mightily** against his H8613+8613
Jer 31:35 who stirs up the sea so that its waves **r** H2159
Jer 51:16 the waters in the heavens **r**; he makes H2162
Jer 51:38 Her *people* all **r** like young lions, they H8613
Jer 51:55 the **r** *of* their voices will resound. H8623
Eze 1:24 like the **r** *of* rushing waters, like H7754
Eze 19: 9 so his **r** was heard no longer on the H7754
Eze 43: 2 His voice was like the **r** *of* rushing waters H7754
Hos 10:14 the **r of battle** will rise against your H8623
Hos 11:10 will follow the LORD; *he will* **r** like a lion. H8613
Joel 3:16 The LORD *will* **r** from Zion and thunder H8613
Am 3: 4 *Does* a lion **r** in the thicket when it has no H8613
Zec 9:15 They will drink and **r** as with wine; they H2159
Zec 11: 3 Listen to the **r** *of* the lions; the lush thicket H8614
2Pe 3:10 The heavens will disappear *with* a **r**; the *G4853*
Rev 10: 3 he gave a loud shout like the **r** *of* a lion. *G3681*
Rev 14: 2 from heaven like the **r** of rushing waters *G5889*
Rev 19: 1 sounded like the **r** of a great *G5889+3489*
Rev 19: 6 like the **r** of rushing waters and like loud *G5889*

ROARED (4) [ROAR]

Ps 74: 4 Your foes **r** in the place where you met H8613
Jer 2:15 Lions *have* **r**; they have growled at him H8613
Am 3: 8 The lion *has* **r**—who will not fear? The H8613
Hab 3:10 the deep **r** and lifted its waves on H5989+7754

ROARING (15) [ROAR]

Jdg 14: 5 suddenly a young lion came **r** toward him. H8613
Ps 22:13 **R** lions that tear their prey open their H8613
Ps 65: 7 who stilled the **r** *of* the seas, the roaring H8623
Ps 65: 7 of the seas, the **r** *of* their waves, and the H8623
Pr 28:15 Like a **r** lion or a charging bear is a wicked H5637
Isa 5:30 they will roar over it like the **r** *of* the sea. H5639
Isa 17:12 they roar like the **r** *of* great waters! H8623
Jer 6:23 They sound like the **r** sea as they ride on H2159
Jer 50:42 They sound like the **r** sea as they ride on H2159
Jer 51:42 over Babylon; its **r** waves will cover her. H2162
Eze 19: 7 were in it were terrified by his **r**. H7754+8614
Eze 22:25 within her like a **r** lion tearing its prey; H8613
Zep 3: 3 Her officials within her are **r** lions; her H8613
Lk 21:25 perplexity *at* the **r** and tossing of the *G2492*
1Pe 5: 8 prowls around like a **r** lion looking for *G6054*

ROARS (3) [ROAR]

Jer 12: 8 *She* **r** at me; therefore I hate H5989+928+7754
Hos 11:10 When he **r**, his children will come H8613
Am 1: 2 "The LORD **r** from Zion and thunders from H8613

ROAST (4) [ROASTED, ROASTS]

Ex 12: 9 in water, but **r** it *over* a fire—with the H7507
Dt 16: 7 **R** it and eat it at the place the LORD your H1418
1Sa 2:15 "Give the priest some meat to **r**; he won't H7499
Pr 12:27 The lazy *do* not **r** any game, but the H3047

ROASTED (10) [ROAST]

Ex 12: 8 they are to eat the meat **r** *over* the fire, H7507
Lev 2:14 crushed heads of new grain **r** in the fire. H7828
Lev 23:14 not eat any bread, or **r** or new grain, until H7833
Jos 5:11 unleavened bread and **r grain**. H7828
Ru 2:14 harvesters, he offered her *some* **r grain**. H7833
1Sa 17:17 "Take this ephah of **r grain** and these ten H7833
1Sa 25:18 five seahs of **r grain**, a hundred cakes of H7833
2Sa 17:28 flour and **r grain**, beans and lentils H7833
2Ch 35:13 *They* **r** the Passover animals over the fire H1418
Isa 44:19 bread over its coals, *I* **r** meat and I ate. H7499

ROASTS (1) [ROAST]

Isa 44:16 his meal, *he* **r** his meat and eats his fill. H7499

ROB (9) [ROBBED, ROBBER, ROBBERS, ROBBERY, ROBBING, ROBS]

Lev 19:13 " 'Do not defraud or **r** your neighbor. H1608
Lev 26:22 and *they will* **r** you **of** your **children** H8897
Jdg 9:25 to ambush and **r** everyone who passed by H1608
Ps 35:10 poor and needy from *those who* **r** them." H1608
Hos 7: 1 break into houses, bandits **r** in the streets; H7320
Mic 2: 2 they **r** them of their inheritance. NDT
Mal 3: 8 "*Will* a mere mortal **r** God? Yet you rob H7693
Mal 3: 8 Yet you **r** me. "But you ask, H7693
Ro 2:22 You who abhor idols, *do you* **r temples**? *G2644*

ROBBED (15) [ROB]

Dt 28:29 day after day you will be oppressed and **r** H1608
2Sa 17: 8 as fierce as a wild bear **r of** her **cubs**. H8891
Ps 7: 4 with evil or without cause *have* **r** my foe— H2740
Pr 4:16 they **are r** *of* sleep till they make someone H1608
Pr 17:12 Better to meet a bear **r** of her cubs than a H8891
Isa 38:10 gates of death and **be r** *of* the rest of my H7212
Jer 21:12 of the oppressor the *one who has* **been r**, H1608
Jer 22: 3 of the oppressor the *one who has* **been r**. H1608
Eze 18:18 **r** his brother and did what was H1608+1609
Hos 13: 8 Like a bear **r of** *her* **cubs**, I will attack them H8891
Mk 9:17 by a spirit that has **r** him **of speech**. *G228*
Ac 19:27 the world, will be **r** of her divine majesty." *G2747*
Ac 19:37 have neither **r temples** nor blasphemed *G2645*
2Co 11: 8 *I* **r** other churches by receiving support *G5195*
1Ti 6: 5 *who have been* **r** of the truth and who think *G691*

ROBBER (1) [ROB]

Jn 10: 1 in by some other way, is a thief and a **r**. *G3334*

ROBBERS (10) [ROB]

Jer 7:11 my Name, become a den of **r** to you? H7265
Eze 7:22 **r** will desecrate the place I treasure. H7265
Ob 5 thieves came to you, if **r** *in* the night—oh, H8720
Mt 21:13 but you are making it 'a den *of* **r**. *G3334*
Mk 11:17 But you have made it 'a den *of* **r**.'" *G3334*
Lk 10:30 to Jericho, when he was attacked *by* **r**. *G3334*
Lk 10:36 to the man who fell into the hands of **r**?" *G3334*
Lk 18:11 I am not like other people—**r**, evildoers, *G774*
Lk 19:46 but you have made it 'a den *of* **r**. *G3334*
Jn 10: 8 have come before me are thieves and **r**, *G3334*

ROBBERY (5) [ROB]

Isa 61: 8 love justice; I hate **r** and wrongdoing. H1610
Eze 18: 7 *He does* not **commit r** but gives his H1608+1611
Eze 18:12 and needy. *He* **commits r**. He does H1608+1611
Eze 18:16 *He does* not **commit r** but gives his H1608+1611
Eze 22:29 practice extortion and **commit r**; H1608+1610

ROBBING (3) [ROB]

Isa 10: 2 widows their prey and **r** the fatherless. H1024
Mal 3: 8 you ask, 'How *are we* **r** you?' "In tithes H7693
Mal 3: 9 your whole nation—because you *are* **r** me. H7693

ROBE (62) [ROBED, ROBES]

Ge 37: 3 and he made an ornate **r** for him. H4189
Ge 37:23 they stripped him of his **r**—the ornate H4189
Ge 37:23 his robe—the ornate **r** he was wearing— H4189
Ge 37:31 Then they got Joseph's **r**, slaughtered a H4189
Ge 37:31 a goat and dipped the **r** in the blood. H4189
Ge 37:32 They took the ornate **r** back to their father H4189
Ge 37:32 it to see whether it is your son's **r**. H4189

Ge 37:33 recognized it and said, "It is my son's r! H4189
Ex 28: 4 an ephod, a r, a woven tunic, a turban H5077
Ex 28:31 "Make the r *of* the ephod entirely of blue H5077
Ex 28:33 scarlet yarn around the hem of **the r**, H2257s
Ex 28:34 are to alternate around the hem of the r. H5077
Ex 29: 5 with the tunic, the r *of* the ephod, the H5077
Ex 39:22 They made the r *of* the ephod entirely of H5077
Ex 39:23 in the center of the r like the opening of a H5077
Ex 39:24 twisted linen around the hem of the r. H5077
Ex 39:26 around the hem of the r to be worn for H5077
Lev 8: 7 him with the r and put the ephod on H5077
Jos 7:21 in the plunder a beautiful r *from* Babylonia, H168
Jos 7:24 the silver, the r, the gold bar, his H168
1Sa 2:19 made him a little r and took it to him H5077
1Sa 15:27 Saul caught hold of the hem of his r, and H5077
1Sa 18: 4 took off the r he was wearing and H5077
1Sa 24: 4 unnoticed and cut off a corner of Saul's r. H5077
1Sa 24: 5 having cut off a corner of his r. H889s
1Sa 24:11 look at this piece of your r in my hand! H5077
1Sa 24:11 off the corner of your r but did not kill you. H5077
1Sa 28:14 "An old man wearing a r is coming up," H5077
2Sa 13:18 She was wearing an ornate r, for this was H4189
2Sa 13:19 tore the ornate r she was wearing. H4189
2Sa 15:32 meet him, his r torn and dust on his head. H4189
1Ch 15:27 Now David was clothed in a r *of* fine linen H5077
Ne 5:13 I also shook out the **folds of** my r and said H2950
Est 6: 8 them bring a royal r the king has worn H4230
Est 6: 9 Then let the r and horse be entrusted to H4230
Est 6: 9 *Let them* r the man the king delights to H4252
Est 6:10 "Get the r and the horse and do just as H4230
Est 6:11 So Haman got the r and the horse. H4230
Est 8:15 crown of gold and a purple r *of* fine linen. H9423
Job 1:20 got up and tore his r and shaved his head H5077
Job 29:14 clothing; justice was my r and my turban. H5077
Ps 133: 2 Aaron's beard, down on the collar of his r. H4496
SS 5: 3 I have taken off my r—must I put it on H4189
Isa 6: 1 the **train of** his r filled the temple. H8767
Isa 22:21 him with your r and fasten your sash H4189
Isa 61:10 arrayed me in a r *of* his righteousness, H5077
Mic 2: 8 strip off the rich r from those who pass by H8515
Zec 8:23 of one Jew by the **hem of** his r and say, H4053
Mt 27:28 stripped him and put a scarlet r on him, G5948
Mt 27:31 they took off the r and put his own clothes G5948
Mk 15:17 They put a **purple** r on him, then twisted G4525
Mk 15:20 they took off the **purple** r and put his own G4525
Mk 16: 5 dressed in a white r sitting on the right G5124
Lk 15:22 Bring the best r and put it on him. G5124
Lk 23:11 Dressing him in an elegant r, they sent G2264
Jn 19: 2 They clothed him in a purple r G2668
Jn 19: 5 the crown of thorns and the purple r, G2668
Heb 1:12 You will roll them up like a r; like a G4316
Rev 1:13 in a r **reaching down to** his **feet** and with G4468
Rev 6:11 Then each of them was given a white r G5124
Rev 19:13 He is dressed in a r dipped in blood, and G2668
Rev 19:16 On his r and on his thigh he has this name G2668

ROBED (5) [ROBE]

Est 6:11 *He* r Mordecai, and led him on horseback H4252
Ps 93: 1 The LORD reigns, *he is* r *in* majesty; the H4252
Ps 93: 1 the LORD *is* r *in* majesty and armed with H4252
Isa 63: 1 Who is this, r in splendor, striding forward H4230
Rev 10: 1 *He was* r in a cloud, with a rainbow above G4314

ROBES (40) [ROBE]

Ge 41:42 He dressed him in r *of* fine linen and put a H955
Ge 49:11 in wine, his r in the blood of grapes. H6078
1Ki 10: 5 the attending servants in their r, his H4860
1Ki 10:25 of silver and gold, r, weapons and spices, H8515
1Ki 22:10 Dressed in their royal r, the king of Israel H955
1Ki 22:30 in disguise, but you wear your royal r." H955
2Ki 5: 7 he tore his r and said, "Am I God? H955
2Ki 5: 8 heard that the king of Israel had torn his r, H955
2Ki 5: 8 "Why have you torn your r? Have the man H955
2Ki 6:30 heard the woman's words, he tore his r. H955
2Ki 6:30 saw that, under his r, he had sackcloth on NDT
2Ki 10:22 "Bring r for all the servants of Baal." H4230
2Ki 10:22 So he brought out r for them. H4860
2Ki 11:14 Then Athaliah tore her r and called out H955
2Ki 22:11 words of the Book of the Law, he tore his r. H955
2Ki 22:19 because you tore your r and wept in my H955
2Ch 9: 4 the attending servants in their r, the H4860
2Ch 9: 4 cupbearers in their r and the burnt H4860
2Ch 9:24 gold, and r, weapons and spices, H8515
2Ch 18: 9 Dressed in their royal r, the king of Israel H955
2Ch 18:29 in disguise, but you wear your royal r." H955
2Ch 23:13 Then Athaliah tore her r and shouted H955
2Ch 34:19 heard the words of the Law, he tore his r. H955
2Ch 34:27 me and tore your r and wept in my H955
Est 5: 1 day Esther **put on** *her* royal r and stood in H4252
Job 2:12 they tore their r and sprinkled dust on H5077
Ps 45: 8 All your r are fragrant with myrrh and aloes H955
Isa 3:22 the **fine** r and the capes and cloaks, the H4711
Eze 26:16 lay aside their r and take off their H5077
Da 3:21 wearing their r, trousers, turbans A10517
Da 3:27 heads singed; their r were not scorched A10517
Jnh 3: 6 took off his **royal** r, covered himself H168
Mk 12:38 walk around in **flowing** r and be greeted G5124
Lk 20:46 to walk around in **flowing** r and love to be G5124
Ac 9:39 showing him the r and other clothing G5945
Ac 12:21 wearing his royal r, sat on his throne and G2264
Rev 7: 9 were wearing white r and were holding G5124
Rev 7:13 "These in white r—who are they, G5124
Rev 7:14 have washed their r and made them G5124
Rev 22:14 "Blessed are those who wash their r, that G5124

ROBOAM (KJV) REHOBOAM

ROBS (2) [ROB]

Pr 19:26 *Whoever* r their father and drives out their H8720
Pr 28:24 *Whoever* r their father or mother and says H1608

ROCK (115) [ROCKS, ROCKY]

Ge 49:24 because of the Shepherd, the R *of* Israel, H74
Ex 17: 6 stand there before you by the r at Horeb. H7446
Ex 17: 6 Strike the r, and water will come out of it H7446
Ex 33:21 near me where you may stand on a r. H7446
Ex 33:22 in a cleft in the r and cover you with my H7446
Nu 20: 8 Speak to that r before their eyes and it H6152
Nu 20: 8 water out of the r for the community so H6152
Nu 20:10 in front of the r and Moses said to them, H6152
Nu 20:10 must we bring you water out of this r?" H6152
Nu 20:11 arm and struck the r twice with his staff. H6152
Nu 24:21 place is secure, your nest is set in a r; H6152
Dt 8:15 He brought you water out of hard r. H7446
Dt 32: 4 He is the R, his works are perfect, and all H7446
Dt 32:13 He nourished him with honey from the r H6152
Dt 32:15 them and rejected the R their Savior. H7446
Dt 32:18 You deserted the R, who fathered you H7446
Dt 32:30 unless their R had sold them H7446
Dt 32:31 For their r is not like our Rock, as even our H7446
Dt 32:31 For their rock is not like our R, as even our H7446
Dt 32:37 are their gods, the r they took refuge in, H7446
Jdg 6:20 place them on this r, and pour out the H6152
Jdg 6:21 Fire flared from the r, consuming the meat H7446
Jdg 7:25 They killed Oreb at the r *of* Oreb, and H7446
Jdg 13:19 sacrificed it on a r to the LORD. H7446
Jdg 15: 8 stayed in a cave in the r *of* Etam. H6152
Jdg 15:11 to the cave in the r *of* Etam and said to H6152
Jdg 15:13 two new ropes and led him up from the r. H6152
Jdg 20:45 toward the wilderness to the r *of* Rimmon, H6152
Jdg 20:47 into the wilderness to the r *of* Rimmon, H6152
Jdg 21:13 to the Benjamites at the r *of* Rimmon. H6152
1Sa 2: 2 besides you; there is no R like our God. H7446
1Sa 6:14 there it stopped beside a large r. H74
1Sa 6:15 and placed them on the large r. H74
1Sa 6:18 The large r on which the Levites set the ark H74
1Sa 23:25 he went down to the r and stayed in the H6152
2Sa 20: 8 While they were at the great r in Gibeon H74
2Sa 21:10 spread it out for herself on a r. H7446
2Sa 22: 2 "The LORD is my r, my fortress and my H6152
2Sa 22: 3 my God is my r, in whom I take refuge, H7446
2Sa 22:32 And who is the R except our God? H7446
2Sa 22:47 Praise be to my R! Exalted be my God, H7446
2Sa 22:47 Exalted be my God, the R, my Savior! H7446
2Sa 23: 3 of Israel spoke, the R *of* Israel said to me: H7446
1Ch 11:15 down to David to the r at the cave of H7446
Ne 9:15 thirst you brought them water from the r; H6152
Job 14:18 crumbles and as a r is moved from its H7446
Job 19:24 iron tool on lead, or engraved in r forever! H7446
Job 28: 9 People assault the **flinty** r with their hands H2734
Job 28:10 They tunnel through the r; their eyes see H7446
Job 29: 6 with cream and the r poured out for me H7446
Job 41:24 Its chest is hard as r, hard as a lower H74
Ps 18: 2 The LORD is my r, my fortress and my H6152
Ps 18: 2 my God is my r, in whom I take refuge, H7446
Ps 18:31 And who is the R except our God? H7446
Ps 18:46 Praise be to my R! Exalted be God my H7446
Ps 19:14 your sight, LORD, my R and my Redeemer. H7446
Ps 27: 5 his sacred tent and set me high upon a r. H7446
Ps 28: 1 you are my R, do not turn a deaf ear H7446
Ps 31: 2 to my rescue; be my r *of* refuge, a strong H7446
Ps 31: 3 Since you are my r and my fortress, for the H6152
Ps 40: 2 he set my feet on a r and gave me a firm H6152
Ps 42: 9 I say to God my R, "Why have you H6152
Ps 61: 2 lead me to the r that is higher than I. H7446
Ps 62: 2 Truly he is my r and my salvation; he is H7446
Ps 62: 6 Truly he is my r and my salvation; he is H7446
Ps 62: 7 on God; he is my mighty r, my refuge. H7446
Ps 71: 3 Be my r *of* refuge, to which I can always H7446
Ps 71: 3 save me, for you are my r and my fortress. H6152
Ps 78:20 he struck the r, and water gushed H7446
Ps 78:35 They remembered that God was their R H7446
Ps 81:16 with honey from the r I would satisfy you." H7446
Ps 89:26 are my Father, my God, the R my Savior. H7446
Ps 92:15 LORD is upright; he is my R, and there is H7446
Ps 94:22 my God the r *in whom* I take refuge. H7446
Ps 95: 1 us shout aloud to the R *of* our salvation. H7446
Ps 105:41 He opened the r, and water gushed out; it H7446
Ps 114: 8 who turned the r into a pool, the hard rock H7446
Ps 114: 8 the **hard** r into springs of water. H2734
Ps 144: 1 Praise be to the LORD my R, who trains my H7446
Pr 30:19 the way of a snake on a r, the way of a H7446
SS 2:14 My dove in the clefts of the r, in the H6152
Isa 8:14 to stumble and a r *that* makes them fall. H7446
Isa 10:26 he struck down Midian at the r *of* Oreb; H7446
Isa 17:10 you have not remembered the R, your H7446
Isa 22:16 chiseling your resting place in the r? H6152
Isa 26: 4 the LORD himself, is the R eternal. H7446
Isa 30:29 mountain of the LORD, to the R *of* Israel. H7446
Isa 32: 2 the shadow of a great r in a thirsty land. H6152
Isa 44: 8 there is no other R; I know not one." H7446
Isa 48:21 he made water flow for them from the r H7446
Isa 48:21 he split the r and water gushed out. H7446
Isa 51: 1 Look to the r *from which* you were cut and H7446
Jer 23:29 like a hammer that breaks a r in pieces? H6152
Jer 51:26 No r will be taken from you for a cornerstone, H74
Eze 24: 7 She poured it on the bare r; she did not H6152
Eze 24: 8 revenge I put her blood on the bare r, H6152
Eze 26: 4 away her rubble and make her a bare r. H6152
Eze 26:14 I will make you a bare r, and you will H6152
Da 2:34 were watching, a r was cut out, but not A10006
Da 2:35 But the r that struck the statue became a A10006
Da 2:45 of the vision of the r cut out of a A10006
Da 2:45 not by human hands—a r that broke the iron NDT
Hab 1:12 judgment; you, my R, have ordained them H7446
Zec 12: 3 an immovable r for all the nations. H74
Mt 7:24 a wise man who built his house on the r. G4376
Mt 7:25 because it had its foundation on the r. G4376
Mt 16:18 and on this r I will build my church G4376
Mt 27:60 new tomb that he had cut out of the r. G4376
Mk 15:46 and placed it in a tomb cut out of r. G4376
Lk 6:48 down deep and laid the foundation on r. G4376
Lk 23:53 cloth and placed it in a tomb **cut in the r**, G3292
Ro 9:33 to stumble and a r that makes them fall, G4376
1Co 10: 4 from the spiritual r that accompanied G4376
1Co 10: 4 accompanied them, and that r was Christ. G4376
1Pe 2: 8 to stumble and a r that makes them fall." G4376

ROCKS (31) [ROCK]

Dt 8: 9 a land where the r are iron and you can dig H74
Jos 7:26 Over Achan they heaped up a large pile of r H74
Jos 8:29 And they raised a large pile of r over it H74
Jos 10:18 "Roll large r up to the mouth of the cave H74
Jos 10:27 At the mouth of the cave they placed large r H74
1Sa 13: 6 thickets, among the r, and in pits and H6152
2Sa 18:17 piled up a large heap of r over him. H74
1Ki 19:11 apart and shattered the r before the LORD, H6152
Job 8:17 its roots around a **pile of** r and looks for a H1643
Job 18: 4 Or must the r be moved from their place? H7446
Job 22:24 your gold of Ophir to the r *in* the ravines, H7446
Job 24: 8 rains and hug the r for lack of shelter. H7446
Job 28: 6 lapis lazuli comes from its r, and its dust H74
Job 30: 6 among the r and in holes in the ground. H4091
Ps 78:15 He split the r in the wilderness and gave H7446
Ps 137: 9 infants and dashes them against the r. H6152
Isa 2:10 Go into the r, hide in the ground from the H7446
Isa 2:19 flee to caves in the r and to holes in the H7446
Isa 2:21 to caverns in the r and to the overhanging H7446
Isa 7:19 steep ravines and in the crevices in the r, H6152
Jer 4:29 the thickets; some climb up among the r. H4091
Jer 13: 4 hide it there in a crevice in the r. H6152
Jer 16:16 hill and from the crevices of the r. H6152
Jer 48:28 your towns and dwell among the r, H6152
Jer 49:16 you who live in the clefts of the r, who H6152
Ob 3 in the clefts of the r and make your home H6152
Na 1: 6 like fire; the r are shattered before him. H7446
Mt 27:51 top to bottom. The earth shook, the r split G4376
Ac 27:29 we would be dashed against the r, G5550+5536
Rev 6:15 caves and among the r of the mountains. G4376
Rev 6:16 They called to the mountains and the r G4376

ROCKY (12) [ROCK]

Nu 23: 9 From the r peaks I see them, from the H7446
Job 39:28 there at night; a r crag is its stronghold. H6152
Ps 78:16 streams out of a r **crag** and made water H6152
Jer 18:14 of Lebanon ever vanish from its r slopes? H7446
Jer 21:13 live above this valley on the r plateau, H7446
Am 6:12 Do horses run on the r **crags**? Does one H6152
Mt 13: 5 Some fell on r **places**, where it did not G4378
Mt 13:20 seed falling on r **ground** refers to G4378
Mk 4: 5 Some fell on r **places**, where it did not G4378
Mk 4:16 like seed sown on r **places**, hear the word G4378
Lk 8: 6 Some fell on r **ground**, and when it came G4376
Lk 8:13 Those on the r **ground** are the ones who G4376

ROD (53) [RODS]

Ex 21:20 female slave with a r must be punished if H8657
Lev 27:32 that passes under the **shepherd's** r— H8657
1Sa 17: 7 His spear shaft was like a weaver's r, and H4962
2Sa 7:14 I will punish him with a r *wielded by* men H8657
2Sa 21:19 had a spear with a shaft like a weaver's r. H4962
1Ch 11:23 had a spear like a weaver's r in his hand, H4962
1Ch 20: 5 had a spear with a shaft like a weaver's r. H4962
Job 9:34 someone to remove God's r from me, so H8657
Job 21: 9 from fear; the r *of* God is not on them. H8657
Ps 2: 9 You will break them with a r *of* iron; you H8657
Ps 23: 4 are with me; your r and your staff, they H8657
Ps 89:32 I will punish their sin with the r, their H8657
Pr 10:13 a r is for the back of one who has no H8657
Pr 13:24 Whoever spares the r hates their children H8657
Pr 22: 8 the r they *wield in* fury will be broken. H8657
Pr 22:15 the r *of* discipline will drive it far away. H8657
Pr 23:13 if you punish them with the r, they will not H8657
Pr 23:14 them with the r and save them from H8657
Pr 26: 3 the donkey, and a r for the backs of fools! H8657
Pr 29:15 A r and a reprimand impart wisdom, but a H8657
Isa 9: 4 their shoulders, the r *of* their oppressor. H8657
Isa 10: 5 the Assyrian, the r *of* my anger, in whose H8657
Isa 10:15 As if a r were to wield the person who lifts H8657
Isa 10:24 who beat you with a r and lift up a club H8657
Isa 11: 4 strike the earth with the r *of* his mouth; H8657
Isa 14: 5 The LORD has broken the r *of* the wicked H4751
Isa 14:29 that the r that struck you is broken H8657
Isa 28:27 caraway is beaten out with a r, and cumin H4751
Isa 30:31 with his r he will strike them down. H8657
La 3: 1 seen affliction by the r *of* the LORD's wrath. H8657
Eze 7:10 has burst forth, the r has budded H4751

R

Eze 7:11 has arisen, a **r** *to punish* the wicked. H4751
Eze 20:37 take note of you as you pass under my **r**, H8657
Eze 40: 3 linen cord and a measuring **r** in his hand. H7866
Eze 40: 5 of the measuring **r** in the man's hand was H7866
Eze 40: 5 it was one **measuring r** thick and one rod H7866
Eze 40: 5 one measuring rod thick and one **r** high. H7866
Eze 40: 6 threshold of the gate; it was one **r** deep. H7866
Eze 40: 7 the guards were one **r** long and one rod H7866
Eze 40: 7 guards were one rod long and one **r** wide, H7866
Eze 40: 7 portico facing the temple was one **r** deep. H7866
Eze 41: 8 It was the length of the **r**, six long cubits. H7866
Eze 42:16 the east side with the measuring **r**; H7866
Eze 42:17 five hundred cubits by the measuring **r**. H7866
Eze 42:18 five hundred cubits by the measuring **r**. H7866
Eze 42:19 five hundred cubits by the measuring **r**. H7866
Hos 4:12 and a **diviner's r** speaks to them. H5234
Mic 5: 1 strike Israel's ruler on the cheek with a **r**. H8657
Mic 6: 9 "Heed the **r** and the One who appointed H4751
1Co 4:21 Shall I come to you with a **r of discipline** *G4811*
Rev 11: 1 a reed like a **measuring r** and was told, *G4811*
Rev 21:15 me had a measuring **r** of gold to measure *G2812*
Rev 21:16 the city *with* the **r** and found it to *G2812*

RODANITES (2)

Ge 10: 4 Elishah, Tarshish, the Kittites and the **R**. H8102
1Ch 1: 7 Elishah, Tarshish, the Kittites and the **R**. H8102

RODE (11) [RIDE]

Jdg 10: 4 He had thirty sons, *who* **r** thirty donkeys H8206
Jdg 12:14 grandsons, *who* **r** on seventy donkeys. H8206
1Sa 30:17 young men who **r off** on camels and fled. H8206
1Ki 13:14 **r** after the man of God. He found him H2143
1Ki 18:45 started falling and Ahab **r off** to Jezreel. H8206
2Ki 9:16 he got into his chariot and **r** to Jezreel, H2143
2Ki 9:18 The horseman **r off** to meet Jehu and said H2143
2Ki 9:21 of Israel and Ahaziah king of Judah **r out**, H3655
Est 8:10 *who* **r** fast horses especially bred for the H8206
Hab 3: 8 the sea when *you* **r** your horses and H8206
Rev 6: 2 and *he* **r out** as a conqueror bent on *G2002*

RODENTS (NIV84) MOLES

RODS (4) [ROD]

Job 40:18 are tubes of bronze, its limbs like **r** *of* iron. H4758
SS 5:14 His arms are **r** *of* gold set with topaz. H1664
Ac 16:22 them to be stripped and **beaten with r**. *G4810*
2Co 11:25 Three times *I was* **beaten with r**, once I *G4810*

ROE (1) [ROEBUCKS]

Dt 14: 5 the gazelle, the **r deer**, the wild goat, the H3502

ROEBUCK, ROEBUCKS, ROES (KJV) GAZELLE, GAZELLES

ROEBUCKS (1) [ROE]

1Ki 4:23 well as deer, gazelles, **r** and choice fowl. H3502

ROGEL See EN ROGEL

ROGELIM (2)

2Sa 17:27 and Barzillai the Gileadite from **R** H8082
2Sa 19:31 came down from **R** to cross the Jordan H8082

ROHGAH (1)

1Ch 7:34 Ahi, **R**, Hubbah and Aram. H8108

ROI See BEER LAHAI ROI

ROLL (16) [ROLLED, ROLLING, ROLLS]

Ge 29: 3 the shepherds *would* **r** the stone away H1670
Jos 10:18 "**R** large rocks up to the mouth of the cave, H1670
1Sa 14:33 "**R** a large stone over here at once." H1670
Pr 26:27 rolls a stone, *it will* **r back** on them. H8740
Isa 22:18 *He will* **r** you **up tightly** like a H7571+7571+7572
Jer 5:22 The waves *may* **r**, but they cannot prevail H1723
Jer 6:26 my people, and **r** in ashes; mourn with H7147
Jer 25:34 **r** in the dust, *you* leaders of the flock. H7147
Jer 51:25 my hand against you, **r** you off the cliffs H1670
Eze 27:30 dust on their heads and **r** in ashes. H7147
Da 12: 4 **r up** and seal the words of the scroll until H6258
Am 5:24 But *let* justice **r on** like a river H1670
Mic 1:10 In Beth Ophrah **r** in the dust. H7147
Mk 16: 3 "Who **will r** the stone **away** from the *G653*
Ac 9:34 Get up and **r up** your **mat**." Immediately *G5143*
Heb 1:12 *You will* **r** them **up** like a robe; like a *G1813*

ROLLED (18) [ROLL]

Ge 29: 8 the stone *has been* **r** away from the H1670
Ge 29:10 he went over and **r** the stone away from H1670
Jos 5: 9 "Today *I have* **r away** the reproach of H1670
2Ki 2: 8 **r** it **up** and struck the water with it. H1676
Isa 9: 5 every garment **r** in blood will be H1670
Isa 28:27 nor **is** the wheel of a cart **r** over cumin H6015
Isa 28:28 of a threshing cart *may be* **r over** it, H2169
Isa 34: 4 the heavens **r up** like a scroll; H1670
Isa 38:12 Like a weaver *I have* **r up** my life, and he H7886
Da 12: 9 the words *are* **r up** and sealed until H6258
Mt 27:60 *He* **r** a big stone **in front of** the entrance to *G4685*
Mt 28: 2 to the tomb, **r back** the stone and sat on it. *G653*
Mk 9:20 He fell to the ground and **r around** *G3244*
Mk 15:46 Then *he* **r** a stone against the entrance of *G4685*
Mk 16: 4 which was very large, *had been* **r away**. *G653*
Lk 4:20 Then *he* **r up** the scroll, gave it back to the *G4771*
Lk 24: 2 They found the stone **r away** from the tomb, *G653*

Rev 6:14 heavens receded like a scroll *being* **r up**, *G1813*

ROLLING (1) [ROLL]

Job 30:14 amid the ruins *they* **come r in**. H1670

ROLLS (2) [ROLL]

Pr 26:27 fall into it; if *someone* **r** a stone, it will H1670
Isa 9:18 so that *it* **r upward** *in* a column of smoke. H60

ROMAMTI-EZER (2)

1Ch 25: 4 Eliathah, Giddalti and **R**; Joshbekashah H8251
1Ch 25:31 the twenty-fourth to **R**, his sons and H8251

ROMAN (13) [ROME]

Lk 2: 1 should be taken *of* the entire **R world**. *G3876*
Jn 18:28 Caiaphas to the **palace of the R governor**. *G4550*
Ac 11:28 would spread over the entire **R world**. *G3876*
Ac 16:12 a **R colony** and the leading city of that *G3149*
Ac 16:37 even though we are **R citizens**, and *G476+4871*
Ac 16:38 heard that Paul and Silas were **R citizens**, *G4871*
Ac 21:31 the commander *of* the **R troops** that the *G5061*
Ac 22:25 you to flog a **R citizen** who hasn't *G476+4871*
Ac 22:26 he asked. "This man is a **R citizen**." *G4871*
Ac 22:27 asked, "Tell me, are you a **R citizen**?" *G4871*
Ac 22:29 he had put Paul, a **R citizen**, in chains. *G4871*
Ac 23:27 I had learned that he is a **R citizen**. *G4871*
Ac 25:16 that it is not the **R** custom to hand over *G4871*

ROMANS (3) [ROME]

Jn 11:48 then the **R** will come and take away *G4871*
Ac 16:21 unlawful for us **R** to accept or practice." *G4871*
Ac 28:17 in Jerusalem and handed over to the **R**. *G4871*

ROME (11) [ROMAN, ROMANS]

Ac 2:10 parts of Libya near Cyrene; visitors **from R** *G4871*
Ac 18: 2 Claudius had ordered all Jews to leave **R**. *G4873*
Ac 19:21 been there," he said, "I must visit **R** also." *G4873*
Ac 23:11 Jerusalem, so you must also testify in **R**." *G4873*
Ac 25:25 to the Emperor I decided to send him to **R**. NDT
Ac 25:27 send a prisoner on to **R** without specifying NDT
Ac 28:14 a week with them. And so we came to **R**. *G4873*
Ac 28:16 When we got to **R**, Paul was allowed to *G4873*
Ro 1: 7 To all in **R** who are loved by God and *G4873*
Ro 1:15 the gospel also to you who are in **R**. *G4873*
2Ti 1:17 when he was in **R**, he searched hard for *G4873*

ROOF (38) [ROOFED, ROOFING, ROOFS]

Ge 6:16 Make a **r** for it, leaving below the roof an H7415
Ge 6:16 leaving below **the r** an opening one H5626[S]
Ge 19: 8 have come under the protection of my **r**." H7771
Dt 22: 8 parapet around your **r** so that you may not H1511
Dt 22: 8 your house if someone falls from **the r**. H5647[S]
Jos 2: 6 taken them up to the **r** and hidden them H1511
Jos 2: 6 the stalks of flax she had laid out on the **r**.) H1511
Jos 2: 8 down for the night, she went up on the **r** H1511
Jdg 9:51 in and climbed up on the tower **r**. H1511
Jdg 16:27 on the **r** were about three thousand H1511
1Sa 9:25 talked with Saul on the **r of his house**. H1511
1Sa 9:26 Samuel called to Saul on the **r**, "Get H1511
2Sa 11: 2 walked around on the **r** *of* the palace. H1511
2Sa 11: 2 From the **r** he saw a woman bathing H1511
2Sa 16:22 they pitched a tent for Absalom on the **r**, H1511
2Sa 18:24 went up to the **r** *of* the gateway by the H1511
1Ki 7: 6 of that were pillars and an **overhanging r**. H6264
2Ki 4:10 a small room on the **r** and put in it a bed H7815
2Ki 19:26 like grass sprouting on the **r**, scorched H1511
2Ki 23:12 erected on the **r** *near* the upper room of H1511
Job 29:10 tongues stuck to the **r of** their **mouths**. H2674
Ps 22:15 my tongue sticks to the **r of** my **mouth**; H4918
Ps 102: 7 I have become like a bird alone on a **r**. H1511
Ps 129: 6 May they be like grass on the **r**, which H1511
Ps 137: 6 cling to the **r of** my **mouth** if I do not H2674
Pr 19:13 is like the constant dripping of a **leaky r**. H1942
Pr 21: 9 on a corner of the **r** than share a house H1511
Pr 25:24 on a corner of the **r** than share a house H1511
Pr 27:15 the dripping of a **leaky r** in a rainstorm; H1942
Isa 37:27 like grass sprouting on the **r**, scorched H1511
La 4: 4 infant's tongue sticks to the **r of** its **mouth**; H2674
Eze 3:26 stick to the **r of** your **mouth** so that you H2674
Da 4:29 was walking on the **r** of the royal palace of NDT
Mt 8: 8 not deserve to have you come under my **r**. *G5094*
Mk 2: 4 made an opening *in* the **r** above Jesus by *G5094*
Lk 5:19 they went up on the **r** and lowered him on *G1560*
Lk 7: 6 not deserve to have you come under my **r**. *G5094*
Ac 10: 9 the city, Peter went up on the **r** to pray. *G1560*

ROOFED (1) [ROOF]

1Ki 7: 3 *It* **was r** with cedar above the beams that H6211

ROOFING (2) [ROOF]

1Ki 6: 9 **r** it *with* beams and cedar planks. H6211
Ne 3:15 **r** it **over** and putting its doors and bolts H3233

ROOFS (9) [ROOF]

Ne 8:16 temporary shelters on their own **r**, H1511
Isa 15: 3 on the **r** and in the public squares they all H1511
Isa 22: 1 that you have all gone up on the **r**, H1511
Jer 19:13 burned incense on the **r** to all the starry H1511
Jer 32:29 incense on the **r** to Baal and by pouring H1511
Jer 48:38 On all the **r** *in* Moab and in the public H1511
Zep 1: 5 who bow down on the **r** to worship the H1511
Mt 10:27 in your ear, proclaim from the **r**. *G1560*
Lk 12: 3 inner rooms will be proclaimed from the **r**. *G1560*

ROOM (83) [ROOMS, STOREROOM, STOREROOMS]

Ge 24:23 is there **r** in your father's house for us to H5226
Ge 24:25 as well as **r** for you to spend the night." H5226
Ge 26:22 "Now the LORD *has* **given** us **r** and we will H8143
Ge 34:21 the land has **plenty of r** for them. H8146+3338
Ge 43:30 He went into his **private r** and wept there. H2540
Lev 26:10 move it out to **make r for** the new. H4946+7156
Nu 22:26 narrow place where there was no **r** to turn, H2006
Jdg 3:20 alone in the **upper r** *of* his palace and H6608
Jdg 3:23 the doors of the **upper r** behind him and H6608
Jdg 3:24 found the doors of the **upper r** locked. H6608
Jdg 3:24 himself in the **inner r** *of* the palace." H2540
Jdg 3:25 when he did not open the doors of the **r**, H6608
Jdg 15: 1 "I'm going to my wife's **r**." But her father H2540
Jdg 16: 9 With men hidden in the **r**, she called to H2540
Jdg 16:12 with men hidden in the **r**, she called to H2540
2Sa 18:33 He went up to the **r over** the gateway and H6608
1Ki 1:15 went to see the aged king in his **r**, H2540
1Ki 6:17 hall in front of this **r** was forty cubits long. H1074
1Ki 6:27 inside the **innermost** *r* of the temple, AIT
1Ki 6:27 touched each other in the middle of the **r**. H1074
1Ki 7:50 sockets for the doors of the innermost **r**, H1074
1Ki 17:19 carried him to the **upper r** where he was H6608
1Ki 17:23 him down from the **r** into the house. H6608
1Ki 20:30 the city and hid in an **inner r**. H2540+928+2540
1Ki 22:25 you go to hide in an **inner r**." H2540+928+2540
2Ki 1: 2 the lattice of his **upper r** in Samaria and H6608
2Ki 4:10 Let's make a small **r** *on* the roof and put in H6608
2Ki 4:11 he went up to his **r** and lay down there. H6608
2Ki 4:35 forth in the **r** and then got on the H1074
2Ki 9: 2 and take him into an **inner r**. H2540+928+2540
2Ki 23:11 the court near the **r** *of* an official named H4384
2Ki 23:12 on the roof near the **upper r** *of* Ahaz, H6608
2Ch 18:24 you go to hide in an **inner r**." H2540+928+2540
Ezr 10: 6 went to the **r** *of* Jehohanan son of H4384
Ne 2:14 was not enough **r** for my mount to get H5226
Ne 3:31 as far as the **r above** the corner; H6608
Ne 3:32 between the **r above** the corner and H6608
Ne 13: 5 him with a large **r** formerly used to store H4384
Ne 13: 7 in providing Tobiah a **r** in the courts of the H5969
Ne 13: 8 all Tobiah's household goods out of the **r**. H4384
Ps 10: 4 in all his thoughts there is no **r** for God. NDT
SS 3: 4 to the **r** *of* the one who conceived me. H2540
Jer 7:32 dead in Topheth until there is no more **r**. H5226
Jer 19:11 dead in Topheth until there is no more **r**. H5226
Jer 35: 4 into the **r** *of* the sons of Hanan son of H4384
Jer 35: 4 It was next to the **r** *of* the officials, which H4384
Jer 36:10 From the **r** *of* Gemariah son of Shaphan H4384
Jer 36:12 to the secretary's **r** in the royal palace, H4384
Jer 36:20 put the scroll in the **r** *of* Elishama the H4384
Jer 36:21 brought it from the **r** *of* Elishama the H4384
Jer 38:11 him and went to a **r** under the treasury in NDT
Eze 40:38 A **r** with a doorway was by the portico in H4384
Eze 40:45 "The **r** facing south is for the priests who H4384
Eze 40:46 the **r** facing north is for the priests who H4384
Eze 41: 5 each **side r** around the temple was H7521
Da 6:10 went home to his **upstairs r** where the A10547
Joel 2:16 bridegroom leave his **r** and the bride her H2540
Zec 10:10 and *there will* not **be r enough** for them. H5162
Mal 3:10 that there will not be **r enough to store** it. H1896
Mt 6: 6 go into your **r**, close the door and *G5421*
Mk 2: 2 large numbers that *there was* no **r** *left*, *G6003*
Mk 14:14 Where is my **guest r**, where I may eat the *G2906*
Mk 14:15 He will show you a large **r upstairs** *G333*
Lk 2: 7 was no **guest r** available *G5536+1877+3836+2906*
Lk 14:22 ordered has been done, but there is still **r**. *G5536*
Lk 22:11 Where is the **guest r**, where I may eat the *G2906*
Lk 22:12 He will show you a large **r upstairs**, all *G333*
Jn 8:37 because you **have** no **r** *for* my word. *G6003*
Jn 21:25 whole world *would* not **have r** for the *G6003*
Ac 1:13 they went **upstairs** to the **r** where they *G5673*
Ac 9:37 was washed and placed in an **upstairs r**. *G5673*
Ac 9:39 he arrived he was taken **upstairs** to the **r**. *G5673*
Ac 9:40 Peter sent them all out of the **r**; then he got NDT
Ac 20: 8 lamps in the **upstairs r** where we were *G5673*
Ac 25:23 pomp and entered the **audience r** with the *G211*
Ac 26:31 After they left the **r**, they began saying to NDT
Ro 12:19 but leave **r** for God's wrath, for it *G5536*
2Co 7: 2 **Make r for** us in your hearts. We have *G6003*
Phm 22 Prepare a **guest r** for me, because I hope *G3825*
Heb 9: 2 In its **first** *r* were the lampstand and the table AIT
Heb 9: 3 curtain was a **r** called the Most Holy *G5008*
Heb 9: 6 regularly into the outer **r** to carry on their *G5008*
Heb 9: 7 But only the high priest entered the **inner** *r* AIT

ROOMS (49) [ROOM]

Ge 6:14 make **r** in it and coat it with pitch inside H7860
1Ki 6: 5 the building, in which there were **side r**. H7521
1Ki 6:10 And he built the **side r** all along the H3666
1Ki 6:29 in both the inner and **outer** *r*, he carved AIT
1Ki 6:30 the floors of **both** the inner and **outer** *r* of the AIT
1Ch 9:26 the **r** and treasuries in the H4384
1Ch 9:33 stayed in the **r** of the temple and were H4384
1Ch 23:28 the courtyards, the **side r**, the purification H4384
1Ch 28:11 its inner **r** and the place of atonement. H2540
1Ch 28:12 of the LORD and all the surrounding **r**, H4384
Ne 13: 9 I gave orders to purify the **r**, and then I put H4384
Pr 24: 4 knowledge its **r** are filled with rare H2540
Isa 26:20 enter your **r** and shut the doors behind H2540
Jer 22:13 unrighteousness, his **upper r** by injustice H6608
Jer 22:14 a great palace with spacious **upper r**. H6608

Jer 35: 2 come to one of the **side** r of the house of H4384
Eze 40:17 There I saw *some* r and a pavement that H4384
Eze 40:17 there were thirty r along the pavement. H4384
Eze 40:44 inner court, were two r, one at the side of H4384
Eze 41: 6 The **side** r were on three levels, one above H7521
Eze 41: 6 temple to serve as supports for the **side** r, H7521
Eze 41: 7 The **side** r all around the temple were H7521
Eze 41: 7 so that the r widened as one went upward. NDT
Eze 41: 8 forming the foundation of the **side** r. H7521
Eze 41: 9 The outer wall of the **side** r was five cubits H7521
Eze 41: 9 area between the **side** r of the temple H7521
Eze 41:10 the priests' r was twenty cubits wide H4384
Eze 41:11 entrances to the **side** r from the open area H7521
Eze 41:26 The **side** r *of* the temple also had H7521
Eze 42: 1 brought me to the r opposite the temple H4384
Eze 42: 4 In front of the r was an inner passageway H4384
Eze 42: 5 Now the upper r were narrower, for the H4384
Eze 42: 5 them than from the r on the lower and NDT
Eze 42: 6 **The** r on the top floor had no pillars, as H2177S
Eze 42: 7 wall parallel to the r and the outer court; H4384
Eze 42: 7 it extended in front of the r for fifty cubits. H4384
Eze 42: 8 While the row of r on the side next to the H4384
Eze 42: 9 The lower r had an entrance on the east H4384
Eze 42:10 opposite the outer wall, were r H4384
Eze 42:11 These were like the r on the north; they H4384
Eze 42:12 were the doorways of the r on the south H4384
Eze 42:12 eastward, by which one enters **the** r. H5527S
Eze 42:13 "The north and south r facing the temple H4384
Eze 42:13 temple courtyard are the **priests'** r, H4384+7731
Eze 44:19 in and are to leave them in the sacred r, H4384
Eze 46:19 of the gate to the sacred r facing north, H4384
Mt 24:26 'Here he is, in the **inner** r,' do not believe *G5421*
Lk 12: 3 in the ear in the **inner** r will be *G5421*
Jn 14: 2 My Father's house has many r; if that were *G3665*

ROOST (1)

Zep 2:14 the screech owl *will* r on her columns. H4328

ROOSTER (14)

Job 38:36 ibis wisdom or gives the r understanding? H8498
Pr 30:31 a **strutting** r, a he-goat, and a king H2435+5516
Mt 26:34 before the r crows, you will disown *G232*
Mt 26:74 know the man!" Immediately a r crowed. *G232*
Mt 26:75 "Before the r crows, you will disown me *G232*
Mk 13:35 midnight, or **when the** r **crows**, or at dawn. *G231*
Mk 14:30 before the r crows twice you yourself will *G232*
Mk 14:72 Immediately the r crowed the second time *G232*
Mk 14:72 "Before the r crows twice you will disown *G232*
Lk 22:34 before the r crows today, you will *G232*
Lk 22:60 Just as he was speaking, the r crowed. *G232*
Lk 22:61 "Before the r crows today, you will disown *G232*
Jn 13:38 tell you, before the r crows, you will disown *G232*
Jn 18:27 and at that moment a r began to crow. *G232*

ROOT (34) [ROOTED, ROOTS]

Dt 29:18 make sure there is no r among you that H9247
2Ki 19:30 of Judah will take r below and bear fruit H9247
Job 5: 3 I myself have seen a fool **taking** r, but H9245
Job 19:28 since the r *of* the trouble lies in him H9247
Job 30: 4 their food was the r *of* the broom bush. H9247
Ps 80: 9 and *it* **took** r and filled the land. H9245+9247
Ps 80:15 the r your right hand has planted, the son H4035
Pr 12:12 the r *of* the righteous endures. H9247
Isa 11:10 In that day the **R** *of* Jesse will stand as a H9247
Isa 14:29 from the r *of* that snake will spring up a H9247
Isa 14:30 But your r I will destroy by famine; it will H9247
Isa 27: 6 In days to come Jacob *will* **take** r, Israel H9245
Isa 37:31 of Judah will take r below and bear fruit H9247
Isa 40:24 no sooner *do they* **take** r in the H9245+1614
Isa 53: 2 and like a r out of dry ground. H9247
Jer 12: 2 and *they have* **taken** r; they grow H9245
Hos 9:16 is blighted, their r is withered, they yield H9247
Mal 4: 1 "Not a r or a branch will be left to them H9247
Mt 3:10 The ax is already at the r of the trees, and *G4844*
Mt 13: 6 they withered because they had no r. *G4844*
Mt 13:21 But since they have no r, they last only a *G4844*
Mk 4: 6 they withered because they had no r. *G4844*
Mk 4:17 But since they have no r, they last only a *G4844*
Lk 3: 9 The ax is already at the r of the trees, and *G4844*
Lk 8:13 joy when they hear it, but they have no r. *G4844*
Ro 11:16 batch is holy; if the r is holy, so are the *G4844*
Ro 11:17 in the nourishing sap *from* the olive r, *G4844*
Ro 11:18 You do not support the r, but the root *G4844*
Ro 11:18 support the root, but the r supports you. *G4844*
Ro 15:12 Isaiah says, "The **R** of Jesse will spring up *G4844*
1Ti 6:10 love of money is a r of all kinds of evil. *G4844*
Heb 12:15 God and that no bitter r grows up to cause *G4844*
Rev 5: 5 tribe of Judah, the **R** of David, has *G4844*
Rev 22:16 I am the **R** and the Offspring of David *G4844*

ROOTED (2) [ROOT]

Eph 3:17 that you, *being* r and established in love *G4845*
Col 2: 7 r and built up in him, strengthened in the *G4845*

ROOTS (21) [ROOT]

Jdg 5:14 from Ephraim, whose r were in Amalek H9247
Job 8:17 it entwines its r around a pile of rocks H9247
Job 14: 8 Its r may grow old in the ground and its H9247
Job 18:16 His r dry up below and his branches H9247
Job 28: 9 lay bare the r *of* the mountains. H9247
Job 29:19 My r will reach to the water, and the dew H9247
Isa 5:24 so their r will decay and their flowers blow H9247
Isa 11: 1 from his r a Branch will bear fruit. H9247
Jer 17: 8 water that sends out its r by the stream. H9247
Eze 17: 6 toward him, but its r remained under it. H9247
Eze 17: 7 now sent out its r toward him from the H9247
Eze 17: 9 arm or many people to pull it up by the r. H9247
Eze 31: 7 its r went down to abundant waters. H9247
Da 4:15 But let the stump and its r, bound with A10743
Da 4:23 while its r remain in the ground. A10743
Da 4:26 of the tree with its r means that your A10743
Hos 14: 5 cedar of Lebanon he will send down his r; H9247
Am 2: 9 their fruit above and their r below. H9247
Jnh 2: 6 To the r *of* the mountains I sank down H7893
Mt 15:13 has not planted *will be* **pulled up by the** r. *G1748*
Mk 11:20 they saw the fig tree withered from the r. *G4844*

ROPE (6) [ROPES]

Ex 28:14 of pure gold, like a r, and attach the H6310
Ex 28:22 braided chains of pure gold, like a r. H6310
Ex 39:15 braided chains of pure gold, like a r. H6310
Jos 2:15 let them down by a r through the window, H2475
Job 41: 1 a fishhook or tie down its tongue with a r? H2475
Isa 3:24 instead of a sash, a r; instead of H5940

ROPES (28) [ROPE]

Ex 35:18 for the courtyard, and their r; H4798
Ex 39:40 the r and tent pegs for the courtyard H4798
Nu 3:26 altar, and the r—and everything H4798
Nu 3:37 with their bases, tent pegs and r. H4798
Nu 4:26 the r and all the equipment used in the H4798
Nu 4:32 tent pegs, r, all their equipment and H4798
Jdg 15:13 him with two new r and led him up from H6310
Jdg 15:14 The r on his arms became like charred H6310
Jdg 16:11 securely with new r that have never been H6310
Jdg 16:12 So Delilah took new r and tied him with H6310
Jdg 16:12 But he snapped **the** r off his arms as if H4392S
2Sa 17:13 then all Israel will bring r to that city, and H2475
1Ki 20:31 our waists and r around our heads. H2475
1Ki 20:32 their waists and r around their heads, H2475
Job 39: 5 wild donkey go free? Who untied its r? H4593
Ps 119:61 Though the wicked bind me with r, I will H2475
Isa 5:18 of deceit, and wickedness as with cart r, H6310
Isa 33:20 be pulled up, nor any of its r broken. H2475
Jer 10:20 is destroyed; all its r are snapped. H4798
Jer 38: 6 lowered Jeremiah by r into the cistern; H2475
Jer 38:11 let them down with r to Jeremiah in the H2475
Jer 38:12 clothes under your arms to pad the r." H2475
Jer 38:13 him up with the r and lifted him out of H2475
Eze 3:25 they will tie with r; you will be bound so H6310
Eze 4: 8 I will tie you up with r so that you cannot H6310
Ac 27:17 Then they passed r under the ship itself to *G1069*
Ac 27:32 the soldiers cut the r that held the lifeboat *G5389*
Ac 27:40 same time untied the r that held the *G2415*

ROSE (65) [RISE]

Ge 7:18 The waters r and increased greatly on the H1504
Ge 7:19 They r greatly on the earth, and all the H1504
Ge 7:20 The waters r and covered the mountains to H1504
Ge 23: 3 Then Abraham r from beside his dead H7756
Ge 23: 7 Then Abraham r and bowed down before H7756
Ge 32:31 The sun r above him as he passed Peniel H2436
Ge 37: 7 suddenly my sheaf r and stood upright, H7756
Ex 32: 6 next day the people r **early** and sacrificed H8899
Ex 33: 8 all the people r and stood at the H7756
Nu 16: 2 and r **up** against Moses. With them were H7756
Jos 8:19 men in the ambush r quickly from their H7756
Jdg 3:20 God for you." As the king r from his seat, H7756
Jdg 6:38 Gideon r **early** the next day; he squeezed H8899
Jdg 9:43 coming out of the city, *he* r to attack them. H7756
Jdg 10: 1 of Puah, the son of Dodo, r to save Israel. H7756
Jdg 19: 8 fifth day, when *he* r to go, the woman's H8899
Jdg 20: 8 All the men r **up** *together* as one, saying H7756
1Sa 5: 3 the people of Ashdod r **early** the next day, H8899
1Sa 5: 4 But the following morning *when they* r H8899
1Sa 9:26 *They* r about daybreak, and Samuel called H8899
2Sa 18:31 from the hand of all who r **up** against you." H7756
2Sa 22: 9 Smoke r from his nostrils; consuming fire H6590
1Ki 1:49 all Adonijah's guests r in alarm and H7756
1Ki 8:54 *he* r from before the altar of the LORD H7756
1Ki 18:45 with clouds, the wind r, a heavy rain started NDT
2Ki 3:24 the Israelites r **up** and fought them until H7756
2Ki 8:21 he r **up** and broke through by night H7756
1Ch 21: 1 Satan r **up** against Israel and incited H6641
1Ch 28: 2 King David r to his feet and said: "Listen H7756
2Ch 20:23 Moabites r **up** against the men from H6641
2Ch 21: 9 *he* r **up** and broke through by night. H7756
Ezr 9: 5 sacrifice, *I* r from my self-abasement H7756
Ezr 10: 5 So Ezra r **up** and put the leading priests H7756
Est 5: 9 observed that *he* neither r nor showed H7756
Job 29: 8 aside and the old men r to their feet; H7756
Ps 18: 8 Smoke r from his nostrils; consuming fire H6590
Ps 76: 9 r **up** to judge, to save all the H7756
Ps 78:21 and his wrath r against Israel, H6590
Ps 78:31 God's anger r against them; he put to H6590
SS 2: 1 I am a r *of* Sharon, a lily of the valleys. H2483
Eze 1:19 the living creatures r from the ground, H5951
Eze 1:19 rose from the ground, the wheels also r. H5951
Eze 1:21 when the creatures r from the ground H5951
Eze 1:21 the ground, the wheels r along with them H5951
Eze 3:12 glory of the LORD r from the place where H8123
Eze 10: 4 the glory of the LORD r from above the H8123
Eze 10:15 Then the cherubim r **upward**. These were H8250
Eze 10:17 when the cherubim r, they rose with H8123
Eze 10:17 cherubim rose, *they* r with them, because H8250
Eze 10:19 spread their wings and r from the ground, H8250
Eze 16:13 very beautiful and r to be a queen. H7503
Jnh 2: 7 and my prayer r to you, to your holy H995
Jnh 3: 6 the king of Nineveh, *he* r from his throne H7756
Jnh 4: 8 When the sun r, God provided a scorching H2436
Mt 2: 2 saw his star when *it* r and have come to *G424*
Mt 2: 9 had seen when *it* r went ahead of them *G424*
Mt 7:25 the streams r, and the winds blew *G2262*
Mt 7:27 the streams r, and the winds blew *G2262*
Mk 16: 9 *When* Jesus r early on the first day of the *G482*
Lk 22:45 *When he* r from prayer and went back to *G482*
Lk 23: 1 the whole assembly r and led him off to *G482*
Ac 10:41 drank with him after he r from the dead. *G482*
Ac 26:30 The king r, and with him the governor and *G482*
1Th 4:14 For we believe that Jesus died and r **again** *G482*
Rev 9: 2 smoke r from it like the smoke from a *G326*

ROSH (1)

Ge 46:21 Naaman, Ehi, **R**, Muppim, Huppim and H8033

ROT (7) [ROTS, ROTTED, ROTTEN]

Pr 10: 7 the name of the wicked *will* r. H8372
Isa 40:20 an offering selects wood *that will* not r; H8372
Isa 50: 2 their fish r for lack of water and die of thirst. H944
Hos 5:12 to Ephraim, like r to the people of Judah. H8373
Zec 14:12 Their flesh *will* r while they are still H5245
Zec 14:12 their eyes *will* r in their sockets, and H5245
Zec 14:12 their tongues *will* r in their mouths. H5245

ROTS (1) [ROT]

Pr 14:30 life to the body, but envy r the bones. H8373

ROTTED (1) [ROT]

Jas 5: 2 Your wealth *has* r, and moths have eaten *G4960*

ROTTEN (2) [ROT]

Job 13:28 "So man wastes away like **something** r H8373
Job 41:27 it treats like straw and bronze like r wood. H8375

ROUGH (4) [ROUGHER, ROUGHS]

Isa 40: 4 the r **ground** shall become level H6815
Isa 42:16 them and make the r **places** smooth. H5112
Lk 3: 5 shall become straight, the r ways smooth. *G5550*
Jn 6:18 wind was blowing and the waters *grew* r. *G1444*

ROUGHER (2) [ROUGH]

Jnh 1:11 *was getting* r **and rougher**. H6192+2143+2256
Jnh 1:11 *was getting* **rougher and** r. H6192+2143+2256

ROUGHS (1) [ROUGH]

Isa 44:13 *he* r it **out** with chisels and marks it with H6913

ROUND (8) [ROUNDED, ROUNDS]

Ex 29: 2 wheat flour make r **loaves** without yeast, H4312
Ex 29:23 the LORD, take one r loaf, one thick loaf H3971
Jdg 7:13 "A r **loaf** *of* barley bread came tumbling H7501
1Ki 7:31 This opening was r, and with its basework H6318
1Ki 7:31 panels of the stands were square, not r. H6318
Ecc 1: 6 turns to the north; r and round it goes H6015
Ecc 1: 6 the north; round and r it goes, ever H6015
Eze 19: 8 against him, those from regions r **about**. H6017

ROUNDABOUT (1) [AROUND]

2Ki 3: 9 After a r march of seven days, the army H6015

ROUNDED (3) [ROUND]

1Ki 10:19 had six steps, and its back had a r top. H6318
SS 7: 2 Your navel is a r goblet that never lacks H6044
Ac 17: 5 so *they* r **up** some bad characters from the *G4689*

ROUNDS (2) [ROUND]

SS 3: 3 found me *as* they **made** *their* r in the city. H6015
SS 5: 7 found me *as* they **made** *their* r in the city. H6015

ROUSE (12) [AROUSE, AROUSED, AROUSES, AROUSING, ROUSED, ROUSES]

Ge 49: 9 like a lioness—who *dares to* r him? H7756
Nu 23:24 *they* r **themselves** like a lion that does not H5951
Nu 24: 9 like a lioness—who *dares to* r them? H7756
Job 3: 8 those who are ready *to* r Leviathan. H6424
Job 8: 6 even now *he will* r *himself* on your behalf H6424
Job 41:10 No one is fierce enough *to* r it. Who then H6424
Ps 44:23 do you sleep? **R** *yourself*! Do not reject us H7810
Ps 59: 5 r yourself to punish all the nations H7810
Isa 28:21 *he will* r *himself* as in the Valley of H8074
Joel 3: 7 *I am going to* r them out of the places to H6424
Joel 3: 9 Prepare for war! **R** the warriors! Let all H6424
Zec 9:13 *I will* r your sons, Zion, against your sons H6424

ROUSED (5) [ROUSE]

Job 14:12 will not awake or **be** r from their sleep. H6424
SS 8: 5 Under the apple tree *I* r you; there your H6424
Eze 7: 6 end has come! *It has* r *itself* against you H7810
Joel 3:12 "*Let* the nations **be** r; let them advance H6424
Zec 2:13 because *he has* r **himself** from his holy H6424

ROUSES (1) [ROUSE]

Isa 14: 9 *it* r the spirits of the departed to greet you H6424

ROUT (3) [ROUTED, ROUTING, ROUTS]

Jdg 1: 5 **putting to** r the Canaanites and Perizzites. H5782
Ps 92:11 my ears have heard the r of my wicked foes. NDT
Ps 144: 6 the enemy; shoot your arrows and r them. H2169

ROUTE (8) [ROUTES]
Nu 14:25 the desert *along* the **r** *to* the Red Sea." H2006
Nu 21: 4 Mount Hor along the **r** *to* the Red Sea, H2006
Dt 1:22 a report about the **r** we are to take and H2006
Dt 1:40 the desert along the **r** *to* the Red Sea." H2006
Dt 2: 1 the wilderness along the **r** *to* the Red Sea, H2006
Jdg 8:11 went up by the **r** *of* the nomads east of H2006
2Ki 3: 8 "By what **r** shall we attack?" he asked H2006
Mt 2:12 they returned to their country by another **r**. *G3847*

ROUTED (16) [ROUT]
Ge 14:15 his men to attack them and *he* **r** them, H5782
Jos 7: 4 went up; but *they were* **r** by the men of Ai, H5674
Jos 7: 8 that Israel *has been* **r** by its H2200+6902
Jdg 4:15 the LORD **r** Sisera and all his chariots and H2169
1Sa 7:10 such a panic that *they* **were r** before the H5597
2Sa 10:15 saw that *they had* **been r** by Israel, H5597
2Sa 10:19 saw that *they had* **been r** by Israel, H5597
2Sa 18: 7 Israel's troops **were r** by David's men, H5597
2Sa 22:15 with great bolts of lightning *he* **r** them. H2169
2Ki 14:12 Judah **was r** by Israel, and every man fled H5597
1Ch 19:16 saw that *they had* **been r** by Israel, H5597
1Ch 19:19 saw that *they had* **been r** by Israel, H5597
2Ch 13:15 God **r** Jeroboam and all Israel before H5597
2Ch 25:22 Judah **was r** by Israel, and every man fled H5597
Ps 18:14 with great bolts of lightning *he* **r** them. H2169
Heb 11:34 powerful in battle and **r** foreign armies. *G3111*

ROUTES (1) [ROUTE]
Job 6:18 Caravans turn aside from their **r**; they go H2006

ROUTING (1) [ROUT]
Jdg 8:12 captured them, **r** their entire army. H3006

ROUTS (1) [ROUT]
Jos 23:10 One of you **r** a thousand, because the LORD H8103

ROVING (1)
Ecc 6: 9 the eye sees than the **r** *of* the appetite. H2143

ROW (13) [ROWED, ROWS]
Ex 28:17 The first **r** shall be carnelian, chrysolite H3215
Ex 28:18 the second **r** shall be turquoise, lapis H3215
Ex 28:19 the third **r** shall be jacinth, agate and H3215
Ex 28:20 the fourth **r** shall be topaz, onyx and jasper H3215
Ex 39:10 The first **r** was carnelian, chrysolite and H3215
Ex 39:11 the second **r** was turquoise, lapis lazuli H3215
Ex 39:12 the third **r** was jacinth, agate and amethyst H3215
Ex 39:13 the fourth **r** was topaz, onyx and jasper H3215
Ex 39:37 lampstand with its **r** of lamps and all its H5120
1Ki 7: 3 columns—forty-five beams, fifteen to a **r**. H3215
Eze 42: 8 While the **r** of rooms on the side next to the NDT
Eze 42: 8 the **r** on the side nearest the sanctuary was NDT
Jnh 1:13 the men *did their best to* **r** back to land. H3168

ROWED (1) [ROW]
Jn 6:19 *When they had* **r** about three or four miles *G1785*

ROWS (10) [ROW]
Ex 28:17 Then mount four **r** of precious stones on it H3215
Ex 39:10 they mounted four **r** *of* precious stones on H3215
1Ki 7: 2 with four **r** *of* cedar columns supporting H3215
1Ki 7:18 pomegranates in two **r** encircling each H3215
1Ki 7:20 hundred pomegranates in **r** all around. H3215
1Ki 7:24 were cast in two **r** in one piece with the H3215
1Ki 7:42 two **r** of pomegranates for each network H3215
2Ch 4: 3 were cast in two **r** in one piece with the H3215
2Ch 4:13 two **r** of pomegranates for each network H3215
Job 41:15 Its back has **r** *of* shields tightly sealed H692

ROYAL (140) [ROYALTY]
Jos 10: 2 like one of the **r** cities; it was larger H4930
Jos 11:12 Joshua took all these **r** cities and their H4889
Jos 13:31 Edrei (the **r** cities of Og in Bashan). H4931
1Sa 27: 5 your servant live in the **r** city with you?" H4930
2Sa 12:26 Ammonites and captured the **r** citadel. H4867
2Sa 14:26 two hundred shekels by the **r** standard. H4889
1Ki 1: 9 and all the **r** officials of Judah, H4889
1Ki 1:46 has taken his seat on the **r** throne. H4867
1Ki 1:47 the **r** officials have come to congratulate H4889
1Ki 4: 7 the king and the **r** household. H2257S
1Ki 5: 9 wish by providing food for my **r** household." NDT
1Ki 9: 1 the temple of the LORD and the **r** palace, H4889
1Ki 9: 5 I will establish your **r** throne over Israel H4930
1Ki 9:10 the temple of the LORD and the **r** palace— H4889
1Ki 10:12 temple of the LORD and for the **r** palace, H4889
1Ki 10:13 what he had given her out of his **r** bounty. H4889
1Ki 10:28 the **r** merchants purchased them from Kue H4889
1Ki 11: 3 hundred wives of **r birth** and three H8576
1Ki 11:14 the Edomite, from the **r** line of Edom. H4889
1Ki 11:20 Tahpenes brought up in the **r** palace. H7281
1Ki 14:26 the LORD and the treasures of the **r** palace. H4889
1Ki 14:27 on duty at the entrance to the **r** palace. H4889
1Ki 16:18 into the citadel of the **r** palace and set the H4889
1Ki 22:10 Dressed in their **r** robes, the king of Israel NDT
1Ki 22:30 in disguise, but you wear your **r** robes." NDT
2Ki 7: 9 go at once and report this to the **r** palace." H4889
2Ki 10: 6 Now the **r** princes, seventy of them, were H4889
2Ki 11: 1 proceeded to destroy the whole **r** family. H4930
2Ki 11: 2 stole him away from among the **r** princes, H4889
2Ki 11: 5 a third of you guarding the **r** palace, H4889
2Ki 11:19 king then took his place on the **r** throne. H4889
2Ki 12:10 the **r** secretary and the high priest came H4889
2Ki 12:18 temple of the LORD and of the **r** palace, H4889
2Ki 14:14 LORD and in the treasuries of the **r** palace. H4889
2Ki 15:25 in the citadel of the **r** palace at Samaria. H4889
2Ki 16: 8 treasuries of the **r** palace and sent it as H4889
2Ki 16:18 removed the **r** entryway outside the H4889
2Ki 18:15 LORD and in the treasuries of the **r** palace. H4889
2Ki 24:13 temple of the LORD and from the **r** palace, H4889
2Ki 25: 9 the **r** palace and all the houses of H4889
2Ki 25:19 of the fighting men, and five **r** advisers. H4889
2Ki 25:25 who was of **r** blood, came with ten H4867
1Ch 27:25 Adiel was in charge of the **r** storehouses. H4889
1Ch 27:34 Joab was the commander of the **r** army. H4889
1Ch 29:25 bestowed on him **r** splendor such as no H4895
2Ch 1:16 the **r** merchants purchased them from Kue H4889
2Ch 2: 1 of the LORD and a **r** palace for himself. H4895
2Ch 7:11 the temple of the LORD and the **r** palace, H4889
2Ch 7:18 I will establish your **r** throne, as I H4895
2Ch 9:11 temple of the LORD and for the **r** palace, H4889
2Ch 12: 9 the LORD and the treasures of the **r** palace. H4889
2Ch 12:10 on duty at the entrance to the **r** palace. H4889
2Ch 18: 9 Dressed in their **r** robes, the king of Israel NDT
2Ch 18:29 in disguise, but you wear your **r** robes." NDT
2Ch 22:10 to destroy the whole **r** family of the house H4930
2Ch 22:11 away from among the **r** princes who were H4889
2Ch 23: 5 a third of you at the **r** palace and a third at H4889
2Ch 23:20 Gate and seated the king on the **r** throne. H4930
2Ch 24:11 the **r** secretary and the officer of the chief H4889
2Ch 26:11 of Hananiah, one of the **r** officials. H4889
2Ch 28:21 LORD and from the **r** palace and from the H4889
Ezr 4:13 eventually the **r** revenues will suffer. A10421
Ezr 4:22 to the detriment of the **r interests**? A10421
Ezr 5:17 be made in the **r** archives of Babylon A10421
Ezr 6: 4 The costs are to be paid by the **r** treasury. A10421
Ezr 6: 8 are to be fully paid out of the **r** treasury, A10421
Ezr 7:20 you may provide from the **r** treasury. A10421
Ezr 8:36 king's orders to the **r** satraps and to the H4889
Ne 2: 8 keeper of the **r** park, so he will H4200+4889
Est 1: 2 reigned from his **r** throne in the citadel H4895
Est 1: 7 the other, and the **r** wine was abundant H4895
Est 1: 9 the women in the **r** palace of King H4895
Est 1:11 wearing her **r** crown, in order to H4895
Est 1:19 let him issue a **r** decree and let it be H4895
Est 1:19 king give her **r position** to someone else H4895
Est 2:16 to King Xerxes in the **r** residence in the H4895
Est 2:17 So he set a **r** crown on her head and H4895
Est 2:18 distributed gifts with **r** liberality. H4889
Est 3: 2 All the **r** officials at the king's gate knelt H4889
Est 3: 3 Then the **r** officials at the king's gate H4889
Est 3: 9 the king's administrators for the **r** treasury." H4889
Est 3:12 of the first month the **r** secretaries were H4889
Est 4: 7 promised to pay into the **r** treasury for the H4889
Est 4:11 the people of the **r** provinces know that H4889
Est 4:14 come to your **r position** for such a time H4895
Est 5: 1 day Esther put on her **r** robes and stood in H4895
Est 5: 1 king was sitting on his **r** throne in the hall, H4895
Est 6: 8 have them bring a **r** robe the king has H4895
Est 6: 8 one with a **r** crest placed on its head. H4895
Est 8: 9 At once the **r** secretaries were summoned H4889
Est 8:14 The couriers, riding the **r** horses, went out H350
Est 8:15 he was wearing **r** garments of blue and H4895
Ps 30: 7 you made my **r** mountain stand firm NDT
Ps 45: 9 at your right hand is the **r bride** in gold of Ophir. H8712
Ps 72: 1 the **r** son with your righteousness. H4889
SS 6:12 set me among the **r** chariots of my people H5618
SS 7: 5 Your hair is like **r** tapestry; the king is held NDT
Isa 17: 3 Ephraim, and **r power** from Damascus H4930
Isa 60:16 milk of nations and be nursed at **r** breasts. H4889
Isa 62: 3 a **r** diadem in the hand of your God. H4867
Jer 21:11 say to the **r** house of Judah, 'Hear H4889
Jer 26:10 went up from the **r** palace to the house H4889
Jer 32: 2 of the guard in the **r** palace of Judah. H4889
Jer 33: 4 in this city and the **r** palaces of Judah that H4889
Jer 36:12 to the secretary's room in the **r** palace, H4889
Jer 38: 7 an official in the **r** palace, heard that they H4889
Jer 39: 8 set fire to the **r** palace and the houses of H4889
Jer 41: 1 who was of **r** blood and had been one of H4867
Jer 43:10 he will spread his **r canopy** above them. H9188
Jer 52:13 the **r** palace and all the houses of H4889
Jer 52:25 of the fighting men, and seven **r** advisers. H4889
La 4: 5 brought up in **r purple** now lie on ash H9355
Eze 17:13 a member of the **r** family and made a H4867
Eze 21:10 'Shall we rejoice in the scepter of my **r** son? NDT
Da 1: 3 Israelites from the **r** family and the H4867
Da 1: 8 to defile himself with the **r** food and wine, H4889
Da 1:13 that of the young men who eat the **r** food, H4889
Da 1:15 any of the young men who ate the **r** food. H4889
Da 2:49 Daniel himself remained at the **r** court. A10421
Da 3:27 governors and **r** advisers crowded around A10421
Da 4:29 on the roof of the **r** palace of Babylon, A10424
Da 4:30 Babylon I have built as the **r** residence, A10424
Da 4:31 Your **r authority** has been taken from you. A10424
Da 5: 5 near the lampstand in the **r** palace. A10421
Da 5:20 deposed from his **r** throne and stripped A10424
Da 6: 7 The **r** administrators, prefects, satraps A10424
Da 6:12 spoke to him about his **r** decree: A10421
Da 11: 6 together with her **r** escort and her father NDT
Da 11:20 a tax collector to maintain the **r** splendor. H4895
Da 11:45 He will pitch his **r** tents between the seas at H683
Hos 5: 1 Listen, **r** house! This judgment H4889
Jnh 3: 6 took off his **r robes**, covered himself H168
Hag 2:22 I will overturn **r** thrones and shatter the H4930
Zec 14:10 Tower of Hananel to the **r** winepresses, H4889
Jn 4:46 was a certain **r official** whose son lay sick *G997*
Jn 4:49 The **r official** said, "Sir, come down before *G997*
Ac 12:21 day Herod, wearing his **r** robes, sat on his *G997*
Jas 2: 8 you really keep the **r** law found in Scripture *G997*
1Pe 2: 9 are a chosen people, a **r** priesthood, a holy *G994*
Rev 17:17 to hand over to the beast their **r authority**, *G993*

ROYALTY (1) [ROYAL]
Da 11:21 who has not been given the honor of **r**. H4895

RUB (1) [RUBBED]
Lk 6: 1 **r** them in their hands and eat the kernels. *G6041*

RUBBED (3) [RUB]
2Sa 1:21 the shield of Saul—no longer **r** with oil. H5417
Eze 16: 4 nor **were** *you* **r with salt** or wrapped H4873+4873
Eze 29:18 every head **was r bare** and every shoulder H7942

RUBBISH (NIV84) GARBAGE

RUBBLE (17)
1Ki 9: 8 This temple will become a **heap of r**. H6505
2Ki 23:12 pieces and threw the **r** into the Kidron H6760
2Ch 7:21 This temple will become a **heap of r**. H6505
Ezr 6:11 their house is to be made a **pile of r**. A10470
Ne 4: 2 stones back to life from those heaps of **r**— H6760
Ne 4:10 there is so much **r** that we cannot H6760
Job 15:28 no one lives, houses crumbling to **r**. H1643
Ps 79: 1 temple, they have reduced Jerusalem to **r**. H6505
Isa 25: 2 You have made the city a **heap of r**, the H1643
Jer 26:18 Jerusalem will become a **heap of r**, the H6505
Eze 26: 4 scrape away her **r** and make her a bare H6760
Eze 26:12 your stones, timber and **r** into the sea. H6760
Da 2: 5 your houses turned into **piles of r**. A10470
Da 3:29 their houses be turned into **piles of r**, A10470
Mic 1: 6 I will make Samaria a **heap of r**, H6505
Mic 3:12 Jerusalem will become a **heap of r**, the H6505
Zep 2:14 the windows, **r** will fill the doorways H2997

RUBIES (8) [RUBY]
Job 28:18 mention; the price of wisdom is beyond **r**. H7165
Pr 3:15 She is more precious than **r**; nothing you H7165
Pr 8:11 wisdom is more precious than **r**, and H7165
Pr 20:15 Gold there is, and **r** in abundance, but H7165
Pr 31:10 She is worth far more than **r**. H7165
Isa 54:12 I will make your battlements of **r**, your H3905
La 4: 7 their bodies more ruddy than **r**, their H7165
Eze 27:16 coral and **r** for your merchandise. H3905

RUBY (2) [RUBIES]
Rev 4: 3 there had the appearance of jasper and **r**. *G4917*
Rev 21:20 fifth onyx, the sixth **r**, the seventh *G4917*

RUDDER (1) [RUDDERS]
Jas 3: 4 by a very small **r** wherever the pilot *G4382*

RUDDERS (1) [RUDDER]
Ac 27:40 time untied the ropes that *held* the **r**. *G4382*

RUDDY (2)
SS 5:10 My beloved is radiant and **r**, outstanding H137
La 4: 7 their bodies more **r** than rubies, their H131

RUDIMENTS (KJV) ELEMENTAL SPIRITUAL FORCES

RUE (1)
Lk 11:42 **r** and all other kinds of garden herbs *G4379*

RUFUS (2)
Mk 15:21 the father of Alexander and **R**, was *G4859*
Ro 16:13 Greet **R**, chosen in the Lord, and his *G4859*

RUGGED (4)
Ps 68:15 mountain, Mount Bashan, **r** mountain, H1493
Ps 68:16 why gaze in envy, you **r** mountain, at the H1493
SS 2:17 gazelle or like a young stag on the **r** hills. H1441
Isa 40: 4 shall become level, the **r places** a plain. H8221

RUGS (2)
Isa 21: 5 set the tables, they spread the **r**, they eat, H7620
Eze 27:24 and multicolored **r** with cords twisted H1710

RUIN (86) [RUINED, RUINS]
Nu 11:15 and do not let me face my own **r**. H8288
Nu 24:24 Ashur and Eber, but they too will come to **r**." H7
Dt 11: 4 how the LORD **brought** lasting **r** *on* them. H6
Dt 13:16 That town is to remain a **r** forever, never H9424
Dt 28:20 destroyed and **come to** sudden **r** because of H6
Dt 28:63 so it will please him to **r** and destroy you. H6
2Sa 15:14 overtake us and bring **r** on us and put the H8288
2Sa 16: 8 You have come to **r** because you are a H8288
2Ki 3:19 **r** every good field with stones. H3872
2Ch 34:11 kings of Judah *had* **allowed to fall into r**. H8845
Est 6:13 him—*you will* **surely come to r**!" H5877+5877
Est 9:24 the lot) for their **r** and destruction. H2169
Job 2: 3 me against him to **r** him without any H1180
Job 22:19 The righteous see their **r** and rejoice; the NDT
Job 31: 3 Is it not **r** for the wicked, disaster for those H369
Ps 9: 6 Endless **r** has overtaken my enemies, you H2999
Ps 35: 4 those who plot my **r** be turned back in H8288
Ps 35: 8 may **r** overtake them by surprise—may H8739
Ps 35: 8 may they fall into the pit, to their **r**. H8739
Ps 38:12 those who would harm me talk of my **r**; all H2095
Ps 40:14 may all who desire my **r** be turned back in H8288
Ps 52: 5 God *will* **bring** you **down to** everlasting **r**: H5997

R

Ps 56: 5 my words; all their schemes are for my r. H8273
Ps 64: 8 against them and bring them to r; H4173
Ps 70: 2 may all who desire my r be turned back in H8288
Ps 73:18 slippery ground; you cast them down to r. H5397
Pr 3:25 disaster or of the r that overtakes the H8739
Pr 10: 8 a chattering fool comes to r. H4231
Pr 10:10 and a chattering fool comes to r. H4231
Pr 10:14 the mouth of a fool invites r. H4745
Pr 10:15 but poverty is the r *of* the poor. H4745
Pr 10:29 it is the r of those who do evil. H4745
Pr 11:17 the cruel bring r *on* themselves. H6579
Pr 11:29 *Whoever* brings r *on* their family will H6579
Pr 13: 3 those who speak rashly will come to r. H4745
Pr 15: 6 the income of the wicked brings r. H6579
Pr 15:27 The greedy bring r *to* their households H6579
Pr 18:24 has unreliable friends *soon* comes to r, H8318
Pr 19: 3 A person's own folly leads to their r, yet H6156
Pr 19:13 A foolish child is a father's r, and a H2095
Pr 21:12 brings the wicked to r. H6156+4200+2021+8273
Pr 26:28 and a flattering mouth works r. H4510
Pr 31: 3 women, your vigor on *those who* r kings. H4681
Ecc 4: 5 Fools fold their hands and r themselves. H430
SS 2:15 the little foxes *that* r the vineyards, our H2472
Isa 7: 5 Remaliah's son have plotted your r, H8288
Isa 23:13 its fortresses bare and turned it into a r. H5143
Isa 24: 1 *he will* r its face and scatter its inhabitants H6390
Isa 25: 2 the fortified town a r, the foreigners' H5143
Isa 26:14 punished them and brought them to r; H9012
Isa 51:19 r and destruction, famine and sword H8719
Isa 60:18 r or destruction within your borders H8719
Jer 12:10 Many shepherds *will* r my vineyard and H8845
Jer 13: 9 'In the same way *I will* r the pride of H8845
Jer 19: 7 " 'In this place *I will* r the plans of Judah H1327
Jer 22: 5 by myself that this palace will become a r. H2999
Jer 25: 9 of horror and scorn, and an everlasting r. H2999
Jer 25:18 to make them a r and an object of horror H2999
Jer 27:17 Why should this city become a r? H2999
Jer 38: 4 the good of these people but their r." H8288
Jer 48:18 up against you and r your fortified cities. H8845
Jer 49:13 "that Bozrah will become a r and a curse H9014
La 3:47 terror and pitfalls, r and destruction." H8643
Eze 5:14 "I will make you a r and a reproach H2999
Eze 21:27 A r! A ruin! I will make it a ruin! The crown H6392
Eze 21:27 A r! I will make it a ruin! The crown H6392
Eze 21:27 I will make it a r! The crown will not be H6392
Eze 23:33 the cup of r and desolation, the H9014
Eze 29:10 the land of Egypt a r and a desolate H2999
Hos 2:12 *I will* r her vines and her fig trees, which H9037
Hos 4:14 without understanding *will* come to r! H4231
Am 5: 9 brings the fortified city to r. H8719
Am 6: 6 you do not grieve over the r *of* Joseph. H8691
Mic 6:13 destroy you, *to* r you because of your sins. H9037
Mic 6:16 I will give you over to r and your people to H9014
Hab 2: 9 nest on high to escape the clutches of r! H8273
Hab 2:10 You have plotted the r *of* many peoples H7896
Zep 1:15 a day of trouble and r, a day of darkness H5409
Zep 2:15 What a r she has become, a lair for wild H9014
Hag 1: 4 houses, while this house remains a r?" H2992
Hag 1: 9 which remains a r, while each of you is H2992
Ro 3:16 r and misery mark their ways, *G5342*
1Ti 6: 9 that plunge people into r and destruction. *G3897*
Rev 17:16 *They will* bring her to r and leave *G2246+4472*
Rev 18:17 such great wealth *has been* brought to r! *G2246*
Rev 18:19 In one hour *she has been* brought to r!' *G2246*

RUINED (43) [RUIN]

Ge 41:36 the country *may* not be r by the famine." H4162
Ex 8:24 Egypt the land was r by the flies. H8845
Ex 10: 7 Do you not yet realize that Egypt *is* r?" H6
Dt 28:51 herds or lambs of your flocks until you *are* r. H6
Jdg 6: 4 on the land and r the crops all the way H8845
Job 15:28 he will inhabit r towns and houses where H3948
Ps 109:10 may they be driven from their r homes. H2999
Pr 14:28 but without subjects a prince is r. H4745
Isa 3:14 "It is you *who have* r my vineyard; the H1278
Isa 6: 5 "*I am* r! For I am a man of unclean H1950
Isa 6:11 "Until the cities lie r and without H8615
Isa 6:11 left deserted and the fields r and ravaged, H8615
Isa 15: 1 Ar in Moab *is* r, destroyed in a H1950
Isa 15: 1 Kir in Moab *is* r, destroyed in a H1950
Isa 24:10 The r city lies desolate; the entrance to H9332
Isa 49:19 "Though you *were* r and made desolate H2999
Isa 60:12 you will perish; it *will be* utterly r. H2990+2990
Isa 61: 4 they will renew the r cities that have been H2997
Jer 4:13 swifter than eagles. Woe to us! *We* are r! H8720
Jer 4:27 "The whole land will be r, though I will H9039
Jer 9:12 Why *has* the land *been* r and laid waste like H6
Jer 9:19 'How r *we are*! How great is H8720
Jer 13: 7 now it *was* r and completely useless. H8845
Jer 48: 1 to Nebo, for *it will* be r. Kiriathaim will H8720
Jer 48: 8 The valley *will be* r and the plateau destroyed H6
Eze 6: 6 your idols smashed and r, your incense H8697
Eze 29:12 will lie desolate forty years among r cities. H2990
Eze 30: 7 their cities will lie among r cities. H2990
Eze 36:38 So will the r cities be filled with flocks of H2992
Joel 1: 7 waste my vines and r my fig trees. H4200+7914
Joel 1:10 The fields *are* r, the ground is dried up H8720
Am 7: 9 the sanctuaries of Israel *will be* r; H2990
Am 9:14 "They will rebuild the r cities and live in H9037
Mic 2: 4 '*We are* utterly r; my people's H8720+8720
Mic 2:10 is defiled, *it is* r, beyond all H2472+2276+2476
Na 2: 2 laid them waste and *have* r their vines. H8845

Zec 11: 2 cedar has fallen; the stately trees *are* r! H8720
Zec 11: 3 the lush thicket of the Jordan *is* r! H8720
Mt 9:17 will run out and the wineskins *will be* r. *G660*
Mt 12:25 kingdom divided against itself *will be* r, *G2246*
Mk 2:22 both the wine and the wineskins *will be* r. *G660*
Lk 5:37 will run out and the wineskins *will be* r. *G660*
Lk 11:17 kingdom divided against itself *will be* r, *G2246*

RUINS (54) [RUIN]

Lev 26:31 turn your cities into r and lay waste your H2999
Lev 26:33 be laid waste, and your cities will lie in r. H2999
Jos 8:28 Ai and made it a permanent heap of r, H9424
1Ch 20: 1 Joab attacked Rabbah and left it in r. H2238
2Ch 34: 6 as Naphtali, and in the r around them, H2999
Ezr 9: 9 the house of our God and repair its r, H2999
Ne 2: 3 where my ancestors are buried lies in r, H2992
Ne 2:17 Jerusalem lies in r, and its gates have H2992
Job 3:14 built for themselves places now lying in r, H2999
Job 30:14 amid the r they come rolling in. H8739
Ps 74: 3 Turn your steps toward these everlasting r H5397
Ps 89:40 his walls and reduced his strongholds to r. H4745
Ps 102: 6 like a desert owl, like an owl among the r. H2999
Pr 24:31 with weeds, and the stone wall *was* in r. H2238
Isa 3: 6 our leader; take charge of this heap of r!" H4843
Isa 5:17 lambs will feed among the r *of* the rich. H2999
Isa 17: 1 be a city but will become a heap of r. H5142
Isa 24:12 The city is left in r, its gate is battered to H9014
Isa 44:26 and of their r, 'I will restore them, H2999
Isa 51: 3 will look with compassion on all her r; H2999
Isa 52: 9 of joy together, you r *of* Jerusalem, for the H2999
Isa 58:12 rebuild the ancient r and will raise up the H2999
Isa 61: 4 rebuild the ancient r and restore the H2999
Isa 64:11 and all that we treasured lies in r. H2999
Jer 4: 7 Your towns *will* lie in r without inhabitant H5898
Jer 4:20 follows disaster; the whole land lies in r. H8720
Jer 4:26 all its towns lay in r before the LORD H5997
Jer 9:11 "I will make Jerusalem a heap of r, H1643
Jer 9:19 our land because our houses *are* in r. H8959
Jer 30:18 the city will be rebuilt on her r, and the H9424
Jer 44: 2 Today they lie deserted and in r H2999
Jer 44: 6 made them the desolate r they are today. H9039
Jer 46:19 be laid waste and lie in r without H5898
Jer 49: 2 it will become a mound of r, and its H9039
Jer 49:13 all its towns will be in r forever. H2999
Jer 51:37 Babylon will be a heap of r, a haunt of H1643
Eze 13: 4 prophets, Israel, are like jackals among r. H2999
Eze 26: 2 now that *she* lies in r I will prosper H2990
Eze 26:20 as in ancient r, with those who go H2999
Eze 33:24 living in those r in the land of Israel H2999
Eze 33:27 who are left in the r will fall by the sword, H2999
Eze 35: 4 turn your towns into r and you will be H2999
Eze 36: 4 to the desolate r and the deserted towns H2999
Eze 36:10 towns will be inhabited and the r rebuilt. H2999
Eze 36:33 your towns, and the r will be rebuilt. H2999
Eze 36:35 the cities that were lying in r, desolate H2992
Eze 38:12 against the resettled r and the people H2999
Joel 1:17 The storehouses *are* in r, the granaries H9037
Am 9:11 repair its broken walls and restore its r— H2232
Na 3: 7 'Nineveh *is* in r—who will mourn H8720
Zep 2: 4 will be abandoned and Ashkelon left in r. H9039
Mal 1: 4 have been crushed, we will rebuild the r." H2999
Ac 15:16 Its r I will rebuild, and I *G2940*
2Ti 2:14 of no value, and *only* r those who listen. *G2953*

RULE (80) [RULED, RULER, RULER'S, RULERS, RULES, RULING]

Ge 1:26 so that *they may* r over the fish in the sea H8097
Ge 1:28 R over the fish in the sea and the birds in H8097
Ge 3:16 your husband, and he *will* r over you." H5440
Ge 4: 7 desires to have you, but you *must* r over it." H5440
Ge 37: 8 *Will you* actually r us?" And H5440+5440
Lev 25:43 *Do* not r over them ruthlessly, but fear your H8097
Lev 25:46 but *you must* not r over your fellow H8097
Lev 25:53 owe service *do* not r over them ruthlessly H8097
Lev 26:17 those who hate you *will* r over you, and H8097
Dt 15: 6 *You will* r over many nations but none will H5440
Dt 15: 6 many nations but none *will* r over you. H5440
Dt 19: 4 This is the r *concerning* anyone who kills H1821
Jdg 8:22 Israelites said to Gideon, "R over us—you, H5440
Jdg 8:23 told them, "I *will* not r over you, nor will H5440
Jdg 8:23 rule over you, nor *will* my son r over you. H5440
Jdg 8:23 rule over you. The LORD *will* r over you." H5440
Jdg 9: 2 *to have* all seventy of Jerub-Baal's sons r H5440
Jdg 13:12 is to be the r that governs the boy's life H5477
1Sa 12:12 we want a king *to* r over us'—even H4887
1Sa 14:47 After Saul had assumed r over Israel, he H4867
2Sa 3:21 that *you may* r over all that your heart H4887
2Sa 19:10 whom we anointed to r over us, has died H6584
1Ki 2:12 and his r was firmly established. H4895
1Ki 5: 7 a wise son to r over this great nation." H6584
1Ki 8:16 chosen David to r my people Israel. H2118+6584
1Ki 11:37 and *you will* r over all that your heart H4887
2Ch 6: 6 chosen David to r my people Israel. H2118+6584
2Ch 7:18 fail to have a successor *to* r over Israel. H5440
2Ch 9: 8 throne as king to r for the LORD your God. NDT
2Ch 20: 6 You r over all the kingdoms of the nations. H5440
Ne 9:37 *They* r over our bodies and our cattle as H5440
Ps 2:11 with fear and celebrate his r with trembling. NDT
Ps 19:13 from willful sins; *may they* not r over me. H5440
Ps 67: 4 for *you* r the peoples with equity and H9149
Ps 72: 8 *May he* r from sea to sea and from the H8097
Ps 89: 9 You r over the surging sea; when its H5440
Ps 110: 2 "R in the midst of your enemies! H8097
Ps 119:133 to your word; let no sin r over me. H8948
Pr 8:16 and nobles—all *who* r *on* earth. H9149
Pr 12:24 Diligent hands *will* r, but laziness ends in H5440
Pr 17: 2 A prudent servant *will* r over a disgraceful H5440
Pr 19:10 much worse for a slave *to* r over princes! H5440
Pr 22: 7 The rich r over the poor, and the borrower H5440
Pr 29: 2 when the wicked r, the people groan. H5440
Isa 3: 4 their officials; children *will* r over them." H5440
Isa 3:12 oppress my people, women r over them. H5440
Isa 14: 2 of their captors and r over their oppressors H8097
Isa 19: 4 a fierce king *will* r over them, H5440
Isa 28:10 Do this, do that, a r for this, a rule for that H7742
Isa 28:10 a rule for this, a r for that; a little here H7742
Isa 28:13 Do this, do that, a r for this, a rule for that H7742
Isa 28:13 a rule for this, a r for that; a little here H7742
Isa 28:14 you scoffers *who* r this people in H5440
Isa 32: 1 rulers *will* r with justice. H8606
Isa 52: 5 nothing, and *those who* r them mock," H5440
Jer 5:31 the priests r by their own authority H8097
Jer 22:30 throne of David or r anymore in Judah." H5440
Jer 33:26 one of his sons *to* r over the descendants H5440
Jer 51:28 their officials, and all the countries they r. H4939
La 5: 8 Slaves r over us, and there is no one to H5440
Eze 29:15 so weak that it *will* never again r over the H8097
Da 2:39 of bronze, *will* r over the whole earth. A10715
Da 6: 1 120 satraps to r throughout the kingdom A10542
Da 7: 6 and it was given authority to r. A10717
Da 11: 3 *who will* r *with* great power and do as he H5440
Da 11: 5 he and *will* r his own kingdom *with* great H5440
Hos 11: 5 will not Assyria r over them because they H4889
Mic 4: 7 The LORD *will* r over them in Mount Zion H4887
Mic 5: 6 *who will* r the land of Assyria with the H8286
Zec 6:13 majesty and will sit and r on his throne. H5440
Zec 9:10 His r will extend from sea to sea and from H5445
Ro 15:12 one who will arise *to* r over the nations; in *G806*
1Co 7:17 This *is* the r *I* lay down in all the churches. *G1411*
Gal 6:16 Peace and mercy to all who follow this r *G2834*
Eph 1:21 far above all r and authority, power and *G794*
Col 3:15 *Let* the peace of Christ r in your hearts *G1093*
2Th 3:10 we were with you, *we* gave you this r: *G4133*
Rev 2:27 *that one* '*will* r them with an iron scepter *G4477*
Rev 12: 5 who "will r all the nations with an iron *G4477*
Rev 19:15 "He *will* r them with an iron scepter." *G4477*

RULED (34) [RULE]

Jos 12: 2 *He* r from Aroer on the rim of the Arnon H5440
Jos 12: 3 He also r over the eastern Arabah from the NDT
Jos 12: 5 *He* r over Mount Hermon, Salekah, all of H5440
Jos 13:10 of the Amorites, who r in Heshbon, out to H4887
Jos 13:21 king of the Amorites, who r at Heshbon. H4887
Jdg 11:19 of the Amorites, *who* r *in* Heshbon, and H4889
Ru 1: 1 In the days when the judges r, there was H9149
1Ki 4: 1 So King Solomon r over all Israel. H2118+4889
1Ki 4:21 And Solomon r over all the kingdoms from H5440
1Ki 4:24 For he r over all the kingdoms west of the H8097
1Ki 9:19 throughout all the territory he r. H4939
1Ki 11:25 So Rezon r in Aram and was hostile H4887
1Ki 12:17 of Judah, Rehoboam *still* r over them. H4887
1Ki 14:19 his wars and how *he* r, are written in the H4887
1Ki 22:47 no king in Edom; a provincial governor r. H4889
2Ki 11: 3 six years while Athaliah r the land. H4887
1Ch 4:22 who r in Moab and Jashubi Lehem. H1249
1Ch 29:27 *He* r over Israel forty years—seven in H4887
2Ch 8: 6 throughout all the territory he r. H4939
2Ch 9:26 He r over all the kings from the Euphrates H5440
2Ch 10:17 of Judah, Rehoboam *still* r over them. H4887
2Ch 22:12 six years while Athaliah r the land. H4887
Ne 9:28 of their enemies so that *they* r over them. H8097
Est 1: 1 the Xerxes who r over 127 provinces H4887
Ps 106:41 of the nations, and their foes r over them. H5440
Ecc 1:16 anyone who has r over Jerusalem before H6584
Isa 26:13 other lords besides you *have* r over us, but H1249
Isa 63:19 but *you have* not r over them, they H5440
Jer 34: 1 in the empire he r were fighting H4939+3338
Jer 34: 5 the kings who r before you, so they H8037+2118
Eze 34: 4 *You have* r them harshly and brutally. H8097
Ac 13:21 of the tribe of Benjamin, who r forty years. NDT
Ro 6: 6 so that the body r *by* sin might be done away AIT
Col 2:11 Your whole self r *by* the flesh was put off AIT

RULER (87) [RULE]

Ge 34: 2 the Hivite, the r *of* that area, saw her, H5954
Ge 45: 8 of his entire household and r of all Egypt. H5440
Ge 45:26 In fact, he *is* r of all Egypt." Jacob H5440
Ex 2:14 "Who made you r and judge over us? H8569
Ex 22:28 God or curse the r of your people. H5954
Nu 24:19 A r will come out of Jacob and destroy the H8097
1Sa 9:16 Anoint him r over my people Israel; he H5592
1Sa 10: 1 LORD anointed you r over his inheritance? H5592
1Sa 13:14 heart and appointed him r of his people, H5592
1Sa 25:30 him and has appointed him r over Israel, H5592
2Sa 5: 2 and you will become their r. H5592
2Sa 6:21 when he appointed me r over the LORD's H5592
2Sa 7: 8 appointed you r over my people H5592
1Ki 1:35 I have appointed him r over Israel and H5592
1Ki 11:34 I have made him r all the days of his life H5954
1Ki 14: 7 appointed you r over my people H5592
1Ki 16: 2 appointed you r over my people H5592
1Ki 22:26 him back to Amon the r *of* the city and to H8569
2Ki 20: 5 tell Hezekiah, the r *of* my people, 'This is H5592
1Ch 5: 2 of his brothers and a r came from him, H5592

R

1Ch 11: 2 and you will become their r. H5592
1Ch 17: 7 appointed you r over my people H5592
1Ch 29:12 come from you; you *are* the r of all things. H5440
1Ch 29:22 before the LORD to be r and Zadok to be H5592
2Ch 6: 5 chosen anyone to be r over my people H5592
2Ch 18:25 him back to Amon the r *of* the city and to H8569
2Ch 34: 8 of Azaliah and Maaseiah the r *of* the city, H8569
Ne 3: 9 son of Hur, r *of* a half-district of Jerusalem H8569
Ne 3:12 Hallohesh, r *of* a half-district of Jerusalem H8569
Ne 3:14 r *of* the district of Beth Hakkerem. H8569
Ne 3:15 of Kol-Hozeh, r *of* the district of Mizpah. H8569
Ne 3:16 of Azbuk, r *of* a half-district of Beth Zur H8569
Ne 3:17 Hashabiah, r *of* half the district of Keilah H8569
Ne 3:18 r *of* the other half-district of Keilah. H8569
Ne 3:19 Ezer son of Jeshua, r *of* Mizpah, repaired H8569
Est 1:22 every man should be r over his own H8606
Job 31:37 I would present it to him as to a r. H5592
Ps 82: 7 mortals; you will fall like every other r." H8569
Ps 105:20 the r *of* peoples set him free. H5440
Ps 105:21 of his household, r over all he possessed, H5440
Pr 6: 7 It has no commander, no overseer or r, H5440
Pr 17: 7 how much worse lying lips to a r! H5618
Pr 19: 6 Many curry favor with a r, and everyone is H5618
Pr 23: 1 When you sit to dine with a r, note well H5440
Pr 25:15 Through patience a r can be persuaded H7903
Pr 28: 2 a r with discernment and knowledge H132s
Pr 28: 3 A r who oppresses the poor is like H1505+8031
Pr 28:15 bear is a wicked r over a helpless people. H5440
Pr 28:16 A tyrannical r practices extortion, but one H5592
Pr 29:12 If a r listens to lies, all his officials H5440
Pr 29:26 Many seek an audience with a r, but it is H5440
Ecc 9:17 be heeded than the shouts of a r of fools. H5440
Ecc 10: 5 the sort of error that arises from a r: H8954
Isa 16: 1 Send lambs as tribute to the r *of* the land H5440
Isa 55: 4 a r and commander of the peoples. H5592
Isa 60:17 your governor and well-being your r. H5601
Jer 30:21 their r will arise from among them. H5440
Jer 51:46 violence in the land and of r against ruler. H5440
Jer 51:46 violence in the land and of ruler against r. H5440
Eze 28: 2 of man, say to the r *of* Tyre, 'This is what H5592
Eze 31:11 it into the hands of the r *of* the nations, H380
Da 2:38 *he has* **made** you r over them all. A10715
Da 2:48 *He* **made** him r over the entire province A10715
Da 5: 7 *he will be made* the third highest r in A10715
Da 5:16 *you will be made* the third highest r in A10715
Da 5:29 the third highest r in the kingdom. A10718
Da 9: 1 who **was made** r over the Babylonian H4887
Da 9:25 until the Anointed One, the r, comes, H5592
Da 9:26 The people of the r who will come will H5592
Am 2: 3 I will destroy her r and kill all her officials H9149
Mic 4: 9 Has your r perished, that pain seizes you H3446
Mic 5: 1 will strike Israel's r on the cheek with a H9149
Mic 5: 2 come for me one who will be r over Israel, H5440
Mic 7: 3 in doing evil; the r demands gifts, the H8569
Hab 1:14 like the sea creatures that have no r. H5440
Zec 10: 4 from him the battle bow, from him every r. H5601
Mt 2: 6 of you will come a r who will shepherd my *G2451*
Lk 18:18 A certain r asked him, "Good teacher, what *G807*
Ac 7:10 Pharaoh made him r over Egypt and all *G2451*
Ac 7:27 'Who made you r and judge over us? *G807*
Ac 7:35 the words, 'Who made you r and judge? *G807*
Ac 7:35 was sent to be their r and deliverer by God *G807*
Ac 23: 5 not speak evil *about* the r of your people. *G807*
Eph 2: 2 of this world and *of* the r of the kingdom of *G807*
1Ti 6:15 the blessed and only R, the King of kings *G1541*
Rev 1: 5 and the r of the kings of the earth. *G807*
Rev 3:14 true witness, the r of God's creation. *G794*

RULER'S (4) [RULE]

Ge 49:10 the r **staff** from between his feet H2980
Ecc 10: 4 If a r anger rises against you, do not leave H5440
Eze 19:11 were strong, fit for a r scepter. It towered H5440
Eze 19:14 strong branch is left on it fit for a r scepter. H5440

RULERS (85) [RULE]

Ge 17:20 He will be the father of twelve r, and I will H5954
Ge 25:16 of the twelve tribal r according to their H5954
Jos 13: 3 held by the five Philistine r *in* Gaza, H6249
Jdg 3: 3 the five r *of* the Philistines, all the H6249
Jdg 5: 3 you kings! Listen, you r! I, even I, H8142
Jdg 15:11 realize that the Philistines *are* r over us? H5440
Jdg 16: 5 The r *of* the Philistines went to her and H6249
Jdg 16: 8 Then the r *of* the Philistines brought her H6249
Jdg 16:18 she sent word to the r *of* the Philistines H6249
Jdg 16:18 So the r *of* the Philistines returned with H6249
Jdg 16:23 Now the r *of* the Philistines assembled to H6249
Jdg 16:27 all the r *of* the Philistines were there H6249
Jdg 16:30 the temple on the r and all the people in H6249
1Sa 5: 8 together all the r *of* the Philistines and H6249
1Sa 5:11 together all the r *of* the Philistines and H6249
1Sa 6: 4 to the number of the Philistine r, H6249
1Sa 6: 4 plague has struck both you and your r. H6249
1Sa 6:12 The r *of* the Philistines followed them as H6249
1Sa 6:16 The five r *of* the Philistines saw all this H6249
1Sa 6:18 Philistine towns belonging to the five r— H6249
1Sa 7: 7 the r *of* the Philistines came up to attack H6249
1Sa 29: 2 As the Philistine r marched with their units H6249
1Sa 29: 6 but the r don't approve of you. H6249
1Sa 29: 7 do nothing to displease the Philistine r." H6249
2Sa 7: 7 to any of their r whom I commanded to H8657
1Ch 12:19 after consultation, their r sent him away. H6249
2Ch 23:20 the r of the people and all the people of H5440
2Ch 32:31 were sent by the r *of* Babylon to ask him H8569
Job 3:14 with kings and r *of* the earth, who built H3446
Job 12:17 He leads r away stripped and makes fools H3446
Ps 2: 2 rise up and the r band together against H8142
Ps 2:10 be wise; be warned, you r *of* the earth. H9149
Ps 8: 6 *You* **made** them r over the works of your H5440
Ps 58: 1 Do you r indeed speak justly? Do you judge H380
Ps 76:12 He breaks the spirit of r; he is feared by H5592
Ps 105:30 went up into the bedrooms of their r. H4889
Ps 110: 6 crushing the r of the whole earth. H8031
Ps 119:23 Though r sit together and slander me H8569
Ps 119:161 R persecute me without cause, but my H8569
Ps 141: 6 Their r will be thrown down from the cliffs H9149
Ps 148:11 nations, you princes and all r *on* earth, H9149
Pr 8:15 By me kings reign and r issue decrees that H8142
Pr 28: 2 rebellious, it has many r, but a ruler with H8569
Pr 31: 4 to drink wine, not for r to crave beer, H8142
Ecc 7:19 person more powerful than ten r in a city. H8954
Isa 1:10 of the LORD, you r *of* Sodom; listen to the H7903
Isa 1:23 Your r are rebels, partners with thieves H8569
Isa 1:26 in days of old, your r as at the beginning. H3446
Isa 14: 5 the rod of the wicked, the scepter of the r, H5440
Isa 16: 8 The r *of* the nations have trampled down H1251
Isa 32: 1 in righteousness and r will rule with H8569
Isa 40:23 reduces the r *of* this world to nothing H9149
Isa 41:25 He treads on r as if they were mortar, as if H6036
Isa 49: 7 abhorred by the nation, to the servant of r: H5440
Da 7:27 all r will worship and obey him. A10717
Da 9:12 us and against our r by bringing on us H9149
Da 11:39 *He will* **make** them r over many people H5440
Hos 4:18 their r dearly love shameful ways. H4482
Hos 7: 7 are hot as an oven; they devour their r. H9149
Hos 13:10 Where are your r in all your towns, of H9149
Mic 3: 1 you leaders of Jacob, you r *of* Israel. H7903
Mic 3: 9 of Jacob, you r *of* Israel, who despise H7903
Hab 1:10 They mock kings and scoff at r. H8142
Zep 3: 3 are roaring lions; her r are evening wolves H9149
Mt 2: 6 by no means least among the r of Judah; *G2450*
Mt 20:25 "You know that the r of the Gentiles lord it *G807*
Mk 10:42 who are regarded as r of the Gentiles lord *G806*
Lk 1:52 He has brought down r from their thrones *G1541*
Lk 12:11 before synagogues, r and authorities, do *G794*
Lk 23:13 the chief priests, the r and the people, *G807*
Lk 23:35 watching, and the r even sneered at him. *G807*
Lk 24:20 priests and our r handed him over to be *G807*
Jn 7:48 "Have any of the r or of the Pharisees *G807*
Ac 4: 5 The next day the r, the elders and the *G807*
Ac 4: 8 "R and elders of the people! *G807*
Ac 4:26 rise up and the r band together against *G807*
Ac 13:27 of Jerusalem and their r did not recognize *G807*
Ro 13: 3 For r hold no terror for those who do right *G807*
Ro 13: 4 r do not bear the sword for no reason. NDT
1Co 2: 6 wisdom of this age or *of* the r of this age, *G807*
1Co 2: 8 None *of* the r of this age understood it, for if *G807*
Eph 3:10 be made known *to* the r and authorities in *G794*
Eph 6:12 but against the r, against the *G794*
Col 1:16 thrones or powers or r or authorities; *G794*
Titus 3: 1 people to be subject *to* r and authorities, *G794*

RULES (22) [RULE]

Nu 9: 3 accordance with all its r and regulations." H2978
Nu 9:14 in accordance with its r and regulations. H2978
Nu 15:15 is to have the same r for you and for the H2978
2Sa 23: 3 '*When one* r over people *in* righteousness H5440
2Sa 23: 3 *when he* r in the fear of God, H5440
1Ki 21:18 meet Ahab king of Israel, who r in Samaria. NDT
2Ch 30:19 are not clean **according to the** r *of* the H3869
Ps 9: 8 He r the world in righteousness and H9149
Ps 22:28 to the LORD and *he* r over the nations. H5440
Ps 59:13 ends of the earth that God r over Jacob. H5440
Ps 66: 7 *He* r forever by his power, his eyes watch H5440
Ps 103:19 in heaven, and his kingdom r over all. H5440
Isa 29:13 on merely human r they have been taught H5184
Isa 40:10 with power, and *he* r with a mighty arm. H5440
Da 4:26 when you acknowledge that Heaven r. A10718
Mt 15: 9 their teachings are merely human r. *G1945*
Mk 7: 7 their teachings are merely human r. *G1945*
Lk 22:26 the *one who* r like the one who *G2451*
Col 2:20 to the world, *do you* **submit to** its r: *G1505*
Col 2:22 These r, which have to do with things that NDT
2Ti 2: 5 except by competing **according to the** r. *G3789*
Rev 17:18 the great city that r over the kings of *G2400+993*

RULING (10) [RULE]

Ex 15:25 the LORD issued a r and instruction for H2976
Jdg 14: 4 at that time they *were* r over Israel.) H5440
1Ki 3:27 Then the king **gave** *his* r: "Give the living H6699
1Ki 15:18 the king of Aram, who *was* r in Damascus. H3782
2Ch 16: 2 king of Aram, who *was* r in Damascus. H3782
Ezr 4:20 had powerful kings r over the whole of A10718
Job 34:30 to keep the godless from r, from laying H4887
Pr 25:11 in settings of silver is a r rightly given. H1821
Jn 3: 1 *who was a member of* the Jewish r **council**. *G807*
1Co 6: 4 *do you* **ask for a** r from those whose way *G2767*

RUMAH (1)

2Ki 23:36 daughter of Pedaiah; she was from R. H8126

RUMBLE (1) [RUMBLING, RUMBLINGS]

Jer 47: 3 enemy chariots and the r *of* their wheels. H2162

RUMBLING (3) [RUMBLE]

Job 37: 2 to the r that comes from his mouth. H2049
Eze 3:12 behind me a loud r sound as the glory of H8323
Eze 3:13 the wheels beside them, a loud r sound. H8323

RUMBLINGS (4) [RUMBLE]

Rev 4: 5 of lightning, r and peals of thunder. *G5889*
Rev 8: 5 peals of thunder, r, flashes of lightning *G5889*
Rev 11:19 flashes of lightning, r, peals of thunder, *G5889*
Rev 16:18 of lightning, r, peals of thunder and *G5889*

RUMOR (5) [RUMORS]

Job 28:22 "Only a r *of* it has reached our ears." H9051
Jer 51:46 heard in the land; *one* r comes this year H9019
Eze 7:26 calamity will come, and r upon rumor. H9019
Eze 7:26 calamity will come, and rumor upon r. H9019
Jn 21:23 the r spread among the believers that this *G3364*

RUMORS (4) [RUMOR]

Jer 51:46 be afraid when r are heard in the land; H9019
Jer 51:46 r of violence in the land and of ruler against NDT
Mt 24: 6 You will hear of wars and r of wars, but see *G198*
Mk 13: 7 When you hear of wars and r of wars, do *G198*

RUMP (KJV) FAT TAIL

RUN (72) [FORERUNNER, OUTRAN, OVERRAN, OVERRUN, RAN, RUNNER, RUNNERS, RUNNING, RUNS]

Ge 19:20 here is a town near enough to r to, and it H5674
Ge 31:27 Why *did you* r **off** secretly and deceive me H1368
Ge 39:13 in her hand and *had* r out of the house, H5674
Ex 23:27 all your enemies turn their backs and r. NDT
Lev 26:36 *They will* r as though fleeing from the H5674
Nu 34: 7 r **a line** from the Mediterranean Sea to H9292
Nu 34:10 r **a line** from Hazar Enan to Shepham. H204
Jos 7:12 turn their backs and r because they have NDT
Ru 3:10 You *have* not r after the younger men H2143
1Sa 8:11 and they *will* r in front of his chariots. H8132
1Sa 14:22 heard that the Philistines *were* **on the** r, H5674
1Sa 19:11 "If you don't r *for* your life tonight H4880
1Sa 20:36 to the boy, "R and find the arrows I shoot." H8132
1Sa 21:13 gate and **letting** saliva r **down** his beard. H3718
1Sa 31: 4 "Draw your sword and r me **through**, or H1991
1Sa 31: 4 come and r me **through** and abuse me H1991
2Sa 15: 1 with fifty men *to* r ahead of him. H8132
2Sa 18:19 "*Let me* r and take the news to the king H8132
2Sa 18:22 please *let* me r behind the Cushite." H8132
2Sa 18:23 what may, *I want to* r." So Joab said, H8132
2Sa 18:23 So Joab said, "R!" Then Ahimaaz ran H8132
1Ki 1: 5 with fifty men *to* r ahead of him. H8132
1Ki 17:14 the jug of oil *will* not r **dry** until the day H2893
1Ki 17:16 used up and the jug of oil *did* not r **dry**, H2893
2Ki 4:26 R to meet her and ask her, 'Are you all H8132
2Ki 4:29 your belt, take my staff in your hand and r. H2143
2Ki 5:20 *I will* r after him and get something from H8132
2Ki 9: 3 Then open the door and r; don't delay!" H5674
1Ch 10: 4 "Draw your sword and r me **through**, or H1991
Ne 6:11 "*Should* a man like me r **away**? Or H1368
Job 1: 5 When a period of feasting *had* r **its course** H5938
Job 39:18 *she* **spreads** *her* **feathers to** r H5257+928+2021+5294
Ps 16: 4 *Those who* r *after* other gods will suffer H4554
Ps 19: 5 like a champion rejoicing to r his course. H8132
Ps 119:32 *I* r in the path of your commands, for you H8132
Pr 4:12 be hampered; when *you* r, you will not H8132
Pr 18:10 the righteous r to it and are safe. H8132
Isa 5:11 early in the morning *to* r **after** their drinks, H8103
Isa 7:25 are turned loose and **where** sheep r. H5330
Isa 8: 7 all its channels, r over all its banks H2143
Isa 10: 3 To whom *will you* r for help? Where H5674
Isa 40:31 like eagles; *they will* r and not grow weary H8132
Jer 2:23 not defiled; *I have* not r after the Baals'? H2143
Jer 2:25 **Do not** r until your feet are bare and your H4979
Jer 17:16 I *have* not r away from being your shepherd H237
Jer 23:21 they *have* r with their message H8132
Jer 48: 6 R *for* your lives; become like a bush in the H4880
Jer 51: 6 from Babylon! R *for* your lives! Do not H4880
Jer 51:45 R *for* your lives! Run from the H4880
Jer 51:45 R from the fierce anger of the LORD NDT
Eze 47:15 north side it will r from the Mediterranean NDT
Eze 47:18 the boundary will r between Hauran and NDT
Eze 47:19 the south side it will r from Tamar as far as NDT
Eze 48:28 boundary of Gad *will* r south from Tamar H2118
Joel 2: 9 rush upon the city; *they* r along the wall. H8132
Joel 3:18 all the ravines of Judah *will* r *with* water. H2143
Am 6:12 *Do* horses r on the rocky crags? Does one H8132
Na 1: 4 dries it up; *he* **makes** all the rivers r **dry**. H2990
Hab 2: 2 on tablets so that a herald *may* r with it. H8132
Zec 2: 4 "R, tell that young man, 'Jerusalem will H8132
Mt 6:32 For the pagans r **after** all these things, and *G2118*
Mt 9:17 the wine *will* r **out** and the wineskins will *G1772*
Lk 5:37 the wine *will* r **out** and the wineskins will *G1772*
Jn 10: 5 *they will* r **away** from him because they do *G5771*
Ac 27:17 were afraid *they would* r **aground** on the *G1738*
Ac 27:26 we must r **aground** on some island." *G1738*
Ac 27:39 they decided *to* r the ship **aground** if they *G2034*
1Co 9:24 not know that in a race all the runners r, *G5556*
1Co 9:24 R in such a way as to get the prize *G5556*
1Co 9:26 Therefore I *do* not r like someone running *G5556*
Php 2:16 of Christ that *I did* not r or labor in vain. *G5556*
Heb 12: 1 And *let us* r with perseverance the race *G5556*

RUNNER (3) [RUN]

2Sa 18:25 And the r came closer and closer NDT

2Sa 18:26 Then the watchman saw another r, and H8132
Job 9:25 "My days are swifter than a r; they fly H8132

RUNNERS (1) [RUN]

1Co 9:24 you not know that in a race all the r run, G5556

RUNNING (31) [RUN]

Ge 16: 8 "I'm r away from my mistress Sarai," H1368
Ge 31:20 by not telling him he was r away. H1368
Ex 32:25 the people were r wild and that Aaron H7277
Lev 21:20 who has festering or r sores or damaged H3539
Lev 22:22 anything with warts or festering or r sores. H3539
Jos 8: 6 'They are r away from us as they did H5674
2Sa 3:29 be without someone who has a r sore H2307
2Sa 18:24 As he looked out, he saw a man r alone. H8132
2Sa 18:26 gatekeeper, "Look, another man r alone!" H8132
2Ki 5:21 When Naaman saw him r toward him, he H8132
2Ch 23:12 noise of the people r and cheering the H8132
Ps 133: 2 poured on the head, r down on the beard H3718
Ps 133: 2 on the beard, r down on Aaron's beard NDT
Pr 5:15 own cistern, r water from your own well. H5689
Isa 55: 5 you do not know will come r to you, H8132
Jer 2:23 a swift she-camel r here and there, H8592+2006
Eze 45: 7 r lengthwise from the western to the eastern NDT
Eze 48:18 on the sacred portion and r the length of it, NDT
Eze 48:21 Both these areas r the length of the tribal NDT
Jnh 1:10 They knew he was r away from the LORD H1368
Mk 9:25 Jesus saw that a crowd was r to the scene, G2192
Lk 6:38 shaken together and r over, will be G5658
Lk 17:23 'Here he is!' Do not go r off after them. G1503
Jn 20: 2 So she came r to Simon Peter and the G5556
Jn 20: 4 Both were r, but the other disciple outran G5556
Ac 3:11 astonished and came r to them in the G5340
Ac 21:30 the people came r from all directions. G5282
1Co 9:26 I do not run like someone r aimlessly; NDT
Gal 2: 2 to be sure I was not r and had not been G5556
Gal 2: 2 and had not been r my race in vain. G5556
Gal 5: 7 You were r a good race. Who cut in on G5556

RUNS (8) [RUN]

Ge 2:14 it r along the east side of Ashur. H2143
2Sa 18:27 me that the first one r like Ahimaaz son of H5297
Ps 147:15 command to the earth; his word r swiftly. H8132
Eze 16:34 no one r after you for your favors. H2388+339
Lk 12:30 For the pagan world r after all such things G2118
Jn 10:12 he abandons the sheep and r away. G5771
Jn 10:13 The man r away because he is a hired hand NDT
2Jn 9 Anyone who r ahead and does not G4575

RURAL (1)

Est 9:19 That is why r Jews—those living in H7253

RUSE (1)

Jos 9: 4 they resorted to a r: They went as a H6893

RUSH (7) [RUSHED, RUSHES, RUSHING]

Jdg 21:21 r from the vineyards and each of you seize H3655
Ps 39: 6 in vain they r about, heaping up H2159
Pr 1:16 their feet r into evil, they are swift to H8132
Pr 6:18 schemes, feet that are quick to r into evil, H8132
Isa 59: 7 Their feet r into sin; they are swift to shed H8132
Jer 49: 3 r here and there inside the walls H8763
Joel 2: 9 They r upon the city; they run along the H9212

RUSHED (14) [RUSH]

Jos 8:19 quickly from their position and r forward. H8132
Jdg 9:44 with him r forward to a position at H7320
1Sa 7:11 The men of Israel r out of Mizpah and H3655
2Sa 19:17 twenty servants. They r to the Jordan H7502
Est 6:12 But Haman r home, with his head covered H1894
Mt 8:32 the whole herd r down the steep G3994
Mk 5:13 r down the steep bank into the lake and G3994
Lk 8:33 the herd r down the steep bank into G3994
Ac 7:57 the top of their voices, they all r at him, G3994
Ac 14:14 tore their clothes and r out into the crowd, G1737
Ac 16:29 r in and fell trembling before Paul and G1659
Ac 17: 5 They r to Jason's house in search of Paul G2392
Ac 19:29 all of them r into the theater together. G3994
Jude 11 they have r for profit into Balaam's error G1772

RUSHES (4) [RUSH]

Dt 32:35 is near and their doom r upon them." H2590
Job 16:14 bursts upon me; he r at me like a warrior. H8132
Pr 26:17 ears is someone who r into a quarrel not H6297
Isa 19: 6 The reeds and r will wither, H6068

RUSHING (11) [RUSH]

Job 20:28 r waters on the day of God's wrath. H5599
Pr 18: 4 the fountain of wisdom is a r stream. H5580
Isa 30:28 His breath is like a r torrent, rising up to H8851
Eze 1:24 like the roar of r waters, like the voice H8041
Eze 43: 2 His voice was like the roar of r waters, and H8041
Mic 1: 4 before the fire, like water r down a slope. H5599
Na 2: 4 r back and forth through the squares. H9212
Rev 1:15 his voice was like the sound of r waters. G4498
Rev 9: 9 of many horses and chariots r into battle. G5556
Rev 14: 2 like the roar of r waters and like a loud G4498
Rev 19: 6 like the roar of r waters and like loud G5623

RUST (NIV84) VERMIN

RUTH (21) [RUTH'S]

Ru 1: 4 one named Orpah and the other R. H8134
Ru 1:14 goodbye, but R clung to her. H8134
Ru 1:16 But R replied, "Don't urge me to leave H8134
Ru 1:18 realized that R was determined to H2085S
Ru 1:22 Moab accompanied by R the Moabite, H8134
Ru 2: 2 And R the Moabite said to Naomi, "Let H8134
Ru 2: 8 So Boaz said to R, "My daughter, listen to H8134
Ru 2:17 So R gleaned in the field until evening NDT
Ru 2:18 R also brought out and gave her what she NDT
Ru 2:19 Then R told her mother-in-law about the NDT
Ru 2:21 Then R the Moabite said, "He even said H8134
Ru 2:22 Naomi said to R her daughter-in-law, "It H8134
Ru 2:23 So R stayed close to the women of Boaz to NDT
Ru 3: 5 "I will do whatever you say," R answered. NDT
Ru 3: 7 R approached quietly, uncovered his feet NDT
Ru 3: 9 "I am your servant R," she said. "Spread H8134
Ru 3:16 When R came to her mother-in-law, Naomi NDT
Ru 4: 5 you also acquire R the Moabite, the dead H8134
Ru 4:10 I have also acquired R the Moabite H8134
Ru 4:13 So Boaz took R and she became his wife H8134
Mt 1: 5 whose mother was R, Obed the father of G4858

RUTH'S (1) [RUTH]

Ru 3: 1 One day R mother-in-law Naomi said to H2023S

RUTHLESS (19) [RUTHLESSLY]

Job 6:23 rescue me from the clutches of the r'? H6883
Job 15:20 the r man through all the years stored up H6883
Job 27:13 the heritage a r man receives from the H6883
Ps 35:11 R witnesses come forward; they question H2805
Ps 37:35 seen a wicked and r man flourishing like H6883
Ps 54: 3 r people are trying to kill me H6883
Ps 86:14 r people are trying to kill me H6883
Pr 11:16 gains honor, but r men gain only wealth. H6883
Isa 13:11 will humble the pride of the r. H6883
Isa 25: 3 cities of r nations will revere you. H6883
Isa 25: 4 For the breath of the r is like a storm H6883
Isa 25: 5 of a cloud, so the song of the r is stilled. H6883
Isa 29: 5 fine dust, the r hordes like blown chaff. H6883
Isa 29:20 The r will vanish, the mockers will H6883
Eze 28: 7 against you, the most r of nations; they H6883
Eze 30:11 his army—the most r of nations—will H6883
Eze 31:12 the most r of foreign nations cut it H6883
Eze 32:12 of mighty men—the most r of all nations. H6883
Hab 1: 6 Babylonians, that r and impetuous people H5253

RUTHLESSLY (6) [RUTHLESS]

Ex 1:13 and worked them r. H928+7266
Ex 1:14 labor the Egyptians worked them r. H928+7266
Lev 25:43 Do not rule over them r, but fear your H928+7266
Lev 25:46 not rule over your fellow Israelites r. H928+7266
Lev 25:53 owe service do not rule over them r. H928+7266
Job 30:21 You turn on me r; with the might of H4200+425

S

SABACHTHANI (2)

Mt 27:46 out in a loud voice, "Eli, Eli, lema s?" G4876
Mk 15:34 out in a loud voice, "Eloi, Eloi, lema s?" G4876

SABAOTH (KJV) ALMIGHTY

SABBATH (140) [SABBATHS]

Ex 16:23 'Tomorrow is to be a day of s rest, a holy H8702
Ex 16:23 a day of sabbath rest, a holy s to the LORD. H8701
Ex 16:25 "because today is a s to the LORD. H8701
Ex 16:26 the seventh day, the S, there will not be H8701
Ex 16:29 in mind that the LORD has given you the S; H8701
Ex 20: 8 "Remember the S day by keeping it holy. H8701
Ex 20:10 seventh day is a s to the LORD your God H8701
Ex 20:11 LORD blessed the S day and made it holy H8701
Ex 31:14 " 'Observe the S, because it is holy to you H8701
Ex 31:15 the seventh day is a day of s rest, H8701+8702
Ex 31:15 does any work on the S day is to be put to H8701
Ex 31:16 The Israelites are to observe the S H8701
Ex 35: 2 holy day, a day of s rest to the LORD. H8701+8702
Ex 35: 3 fire in any of your dwellings on the S day." H8701
Lev 16:31 It is a day of s rest, and you must H8701+8702
Lev 23: 3 the seventh day is a day of s rest, H8701+8702
Lev 23: 3 wherever you live, it is a s to the LORD. H8701
Lev 23:11 priest is to wave it on the day after the S. H8701
Lev 23:15 " 'From the day after the S, the day you H8701
Lev 23:16 days up to the day after the seventh S, H8701
Lev 23:24 month you are to have a day of s rest, H8702
Lev 23:32 It is a day of s rest for you, and you H8701+8702
Lev 23:32 evening you are to observe your s." H8697+8701
Lev 23:39 the first day is a day of s rest, and the H8702
Lev 23:39 the eighth day also is a day of s rest. H8702
Lev 24: 8 regularly, S after Sabbath H928+3427+2021+8701+928+3427+2021+8701
Lev 24: 8 regularly, Sabbath after S, H928+3427+2021+8701+928+3427+2021+8701
Lev 25: 2 land itself must observe a s to the H8697+8701
Lev 25: 4 the land is to have a year of s rest, H8701+8702
Lev 25: 4 a year of sabbath rest, a s to the LORD. H8701
Lev 25: 6 yields during the s year will be food for H8701
Lev 25: 8 " 'Count off seven s years—seven times H8701
Lev 25: 8 so that the seven s years amount to a H8701
Lev 26:34 land will enjoy its s years all the time that H8701
Nu 15:32 was found gathering wood on the S day. H8701
Nu 28: 9 " 'On the S day, make an offering of two H8701
Nu 28:10 the burnt offering for every S, H8701+928+8701
Dt 5:12 "Observe the S day by keeping it holy, as H8701
Dt 5:14 seventh day is a s to the LORD your God H8701
Dt 5:15 commanded you to observe the S day. H8701
2Ki 4:23 "It's not the New Moon or the S." "That's H8701
2Ki 11: 5 that are going on duty on the S— H8701
2Ki 11: 7 that normally go off S duty are all to H8701
2Ki 11: 9 on duty on the S and those who were H8701
2Ki 16:18 He took away the S canopy that had been H8701
1Ch 9:32 of preparing for every S the bread H8701+8701
2Ch 23: 4 on duty on the S are to keep watch at H8701
2Ch 23: 8 on duty on the S and those who were H8701
2Ch 36:21 The land enjoyed its s rests; all the time of H8701
Ne 9:14 to them your holy S and gave them H8701
Ne 10:31 merchandise or grain to sell on the S, H8701
Ne 10:31 from them on the S or on any holy day. H8701
Ne 13:15 winepresses on the S and bringing in H8701
Ne 13:15 bringing all this into Jerusalem on the S. H8701
Ne 13:16 in Jerusalem on the S to the people of H8701
Ne 13:17 you are doing—desecrating the S day? H8701
Ne 13:18 wrath against Israel by desecrating the S." H8701
Ne 13:19 on the gates of Jerusalem before the S, H8701
Ne 13:19 shut and not opened until the S was over. H8701
Ne 13:19 no load could be brought in on the S day. H8701
Ne 13:21 time on they no longer came on the S. H8701
Ne 13:22 the gates in order to keep the S day holy. H8701
Ps 92: T A song. For the S day. H8701
Isa 56: 2 who keeps the S without desecrating it H8701
Isa 56: 6 all who keep the S without desecrating it H8701
Isa 58:13 from breaking the S and from doing as H8701
Isa 58:13 if you call the S a delight and the LORD's H8701
Isa 66:23 to another and from one S to another, H8701
Jer 17:21 to carry a load on the S day or bring it H8701
Jer 17:22 of your houses or do any work on the S, H8701
Jer 17:22 Sabbath, but keep the S day holy, as I H8701
Jer 17:24 through the gates of this city on the S, H8701
Jer 17:24 keep the S day holy by not doing any H8701
Jer 17:27 not obey me to keep the S day holy by not H8701
Jer 17:27 the gates of Jerusalem on the S day, H8701
Eze 46: 1 on the S day and on the day of the H8701
Eze 46: 4 to the LORD on the S day is to be six male H8701
Eze 46:12 offerings as he does on the S day. H8701
Hos 2:11 New Moons, her S days—all her H8701
Am 8: 5 the S be ended that we may market H8701
Mt 12: 1 went through the grainfields on the S. G4879
Mt 12: 2 are doing what is unlawful on the S." G4879
Mt 12: 5 that the priests on S duty in the temple G4879
Mt 12: 5 desecrate the S and yet are innocent G4879
Mt 12: 8 For the Son of Man is Lord of the S. G4879
Mt 12:10 asked him, "Is it lawful to heal on the S?" G4879
Mt 12:11 a sheep and it falls into a pit on the S, G4879
Mt 12:12 Therefore it is lawful to do good on the S." G4879
Mt 24:20 will not take place in winter or on the S. G4879
Mt 28: 1 After the S, at dawn on the first day of the G4879
Mk 1:21 when the S came, Jesus went into G4879
Mk 2:23 One S Jesus was going through the G4879
Mk 2:24 are they doing what is unlawful on the S?" G4879
Mk 2:27 said to them, "The S was made for man G4879
Mk 2:27 was made for man, not man for the S. G4879
Mk 2:28 So the Son of Man is Lord even of the S." G4879
Mk 3: 2 to see if he would heal him on the S. G4879
Mk 3: 4 asked them, "Which is lawful on the S: G4879
Mk 6: 2 When the S came, he began to teach in G4879
Mk 15:42 the day before the S). So as G4640
Mk 16: 1 When the S was over, Mary Magdalene G4879
Lk 4:16 on the S day he went into the G4879
Lk 4:31 on the S he taught the people. G4879
Lk 6: 1 One S Jesus was going through the G4879
Lk 6: 2 are you doing what is unlawful on the S?" G4879
Lk 6: 5 to them, "The Son of Man is Lord of the S." G4879
Lk 6: 6 On another S he went into the synagogue G4879
Lk 6: 7 closely to see if he would heal on the S. G4879
Lk 6: 9 "I ask you, which is lawful on the S: G4879
Lk 13:10 On a S Jesus was teaching in one of the G4879
Lk 13:14 because Jesus had healed on the S, G4879
Lk 13:14 be healed on those days, not on the S." G4879
Lk 13:15 each of you on the S untie your ox or G4879
Lk 13:16 be set free on the S day from what bound G4879
Lk 14: 1 One S, when Jesus went to eat in the G4879
Lk 14: 3 "Is it lawful to heal on the S or not?" G4879
Lk 14: 5 an ox that falls into a well on the S day, G4879
Lk 23:54 and the S was about to begin. G4879
Lk 23:56 But they rested on the S in obedience to G4879
Jn 5: 9 The day on which this took place was a S, G4879
Jn 5:10 healed, "It is the S; the law forbids you to G4879
Jn 5:16 Jesus was doing these things on the S, G4879
Jn 5:18 not only was he breaking the S, but he G4879
Jn 7:22 patriarchs), you circumcise a boy on the S. G4879
Jn 7:23 be circumcised on the S so that the law of G4879
Jn 7:23 healing a man's whole body on the S? G4879
Jn 9:14 mud and opened the man's eyes was a S. G4879
Jn 9:16 not from God, for he does not keep the S." G4879
Jn 19:31 the next day was to be a special S. G4879
Jn 19:31 bodies left on the crosses during the S, G4879
Ac 1:12 a S day's walk from the city. G1584+4879+2400+3847
Ac 13:14 On the S they entered the G2465+4879
Ac 13:27 of the prophets that are read every S. G4879
Ac 13:42 further about these things on the next S. G4879
Ac 13:44 On the next S almost the whole city G4879
Ac 15:21 is read in the synagogues on every S." G4879
Ac 16:13 On the S we went outside the city G2465+4879
Ac 17: 2 on three S days he reasoned with G4879

S

Ac 18: 4 Every **S** he reasoned in the synagogue *G4879*
Col 2:16 a New Moon celebration or a **S day**. *G4879*

SABBATH-REST (1) [REST]

Heb 4: 9 remains, then, a **S** for the people of God *G4878*

SABBATHS (28) [SABBATH]

Ex 31:13 to the Israelites, 'You must observe my **S**. H8701
Lev 19: 3 father, and you must observe my **S**. H8701
Lev 19:30 " 'Observe my **S** and have reverence for H8701
Lev 23:38 those for the LORD's **S** and in addition to H8701
Lev 26: 2 " 'Observe my **S** and have reverence for H8701
Lev 26:34 then the land will rest and enjoy its **s**. H8701
Lev 26:35 it did not have during the **s** you lived in it. H8701
Lev 26:43 will enjoy its **s** while it lies desolate H8701
1Ch 23:31 were presented to the LORD on the **S**, H8701
2Ch 2: 4 every morning and evening and on the **S**, H8701
2Ch 8:13 offerings commanded by Moses for the **S**, H8701
2Ch 31: 3 for the burnt offerings on the **S**, H8701
Ne 10:33 the offerings on the **S**, at the New H8701
Isa 1:13 New Moons, **S** and convocations—I H8701
Isa 56: 4 "To the eunuchs who keep my **S**, who H8701
La 2: 6 forget her appointed festivals and her **S**; H8701
Eze 20:12 Also I gave them my **S** as a sign between H8701
Eze 20:13 and they utterly desecrated my **S**. H8701
Eze 20:16 follow my decrees and desecrated my **S**. H8701
Eze 20:20 Keep my **S** holy, that they may be a sign H8701
Eze 20:21 live by them," and they desecrated my **S**. H8701
Eze 20:24 rejected my decrees and desecrated my **S**, H8701
Eze 22: 8 my holy things and desecrated my **S**. H8701
Eze 22:26 shut their eyes to the keeping of my **S**, H8701
Eze 23:38 my sanctuary and desecrated my **S**. H8701
Eze 44:24 festivals, and they are to keep my **S** holy. H8701
Eze 45:17 the New Moons and the **S**—at all the H8701
Eze 46: 3 On the **S** and New Moons the people of H8701

SABEANS (3)

Job 1:15 the **S** attacked and made off with H8644
Isa 45:14 those tall **S**—they will come over H6014
Joel 3: 8 they will sell them to the **S**, a nation H8645

SABTA (1)

1Ch 1: 9 Havilah, **S**, Raamah and Sabteka H6029

SABTAH (1)

Ge 10: 7 Havilah, **S**, Raamah and Sabteka H6030

SABTEKA (2)

Ge 10: 7 Sabtah, Raamah and **S**. The sons of H6031
1Ch 1: 9 Raamah and **S**. The sons of H6031

SACAR (NIV84) SAKAR

SACHET (1)

SS 1:13 My beloved is to me a **s** *of* myrrh resting H7655

SACK (10) [SACKED, SACKS]

Ge 42:25 to put each man's silver back in his **s**, and H8566
Ge 42:27 of them opened his **s** to get feed for his H8566
Ge 42:27 he saw his silver in the mouth of his **s**. H623
Ge 42:28 "Here it is in my **s**." Their hearts sank and H623
Ge 42:35 there in each man's **s** was his pouch of H8566
Ge 43:21 the exact weight—in the mouth of his **s**. H623
Ge 44: 1 put each man's silver in the mouth of his **s**. H623
Ge 44: 2 in the mouth of the youngest one's **s** H623
Ge 44:11 quickly lowered his **s** to the ground and H623
Ge 44:12 And the cup was found in Benjamin's **s**. H623

SACKBUT (KJV) LYRE

SACKCLOTH (49)

Ge 37:34 put on **s** and mourned for his son many H8566
Lev 11:32 it is made of wood, cloth, hide or **s**. H8566
2Sa 3:31 clothes and put on **s** and walk in H8566
2Sa 12:16 spent the nights lying in **s** on the ground. H8566
2Sa 21:10 of Aiah took **s** and spread it out for H8566
1Ki 20:31 king of Israel with **s** around our waists H8566
1Ki 20:32 Wearing **s** around their waists and ropes H8566
1Ki 21:27 he tore his clothes, put on **s** and fasted. H8566
1Ki 21:27 He lay in **s** and went around meekly. H8566
2Ki 6:30 under his robes, he had **s** on his body. H8566
2Ki 19: 1 his clothes and put on **s** and went into the H8566
2Ki 19: 2 all wearing **s**, to the prophet H8566
1Ch 21:16 the elders, clothed in **s**, fell facedown. H8566
Ne 9: 1 fasting and wearing **s** and putting dust on H8566
Est 4: 1 his clothes, put on **s** and ashes, and went H8566
Est 4: 2 no one clothed in **s** was allowed to enter H8566
Est 4: 3 Many lay in **s** and ashes. H8566
Est 4: 4 clothes for him to put on instead of his **s**, H8566
Job 16:15 "I have sewed **s** over my skin and buried H8566
Ps 30:11 you removed my **s** and clothed me with H8566
Ps 35:13 I put on **s** and humbled myself with H8566
Ps 69:11 when I put on **s**, people make sport of me. H8566
Isa 3:24 of fine clothing, **s**; instead of H4680+8566
Isa 15: 3 In the streets they wear **s**; on the roofs H8566
Isa 20: 2 "Take off the **s** from your body and the H8566
Isa 22:12 to tear out your hair and put on **s**. H8566
Isa 37: 1 his clothes and put on **s** and went into the H8566
Isa 37: 2 all wearing **s**, to the prophet H8566
Isa 50: 3 with darkness and make **s** its covering." H8566
Isa 58: 5 like a reed and for lying in **s** and ashes? H8566
Jer 4: 8 So put on **s**, lament and wail, for the H8566
Jer 6:26 Put on **s**, my people, and roll in ashes H8566
Jer 48:37 slashed and every waist is covered with **s**. H8566
Jer 49: 3 Put on **s** and mourn; rush here and there H8566
La 2:10 dust on their heads and put on **s**. H8566
Eze 7:18 They will put on **s** and be clothed with H8566
Eze 27:31 heads because of you and will put on **s**. H8566
Da 9: 3 petition, in fasting, and in **s** and ashes. H8566
Joel 1: 8 Mourn like a virgin in **s** grieving for the H8566
Joel 1:13 Put on **s**, you priests, and mourn; wail, you NDT
Joel 1:13 spend the night in **s**, you who minister H8566
Am 8:10 all of you wear **s** and shave your heads H8566
Jnh 3: 5 from the greatest to the least, put on **s**. H8566
Jnh 3: 6 himself with **s** and sat down in the H8566
Jnh 3: 8 let people and animals be covered with **s**. H8566
Mt 11:21 have repented long ago in **s** and ashes. *G4884*
Lk 10:13 repented long ago, sitting in **s** and ashes. *G4884*
Rev 6:12 sun turned black like **s** made of goat hair, *G4884*
Rev 11: 3 will prophesy for 1,260 days, clothed in **s**." *G4884*

SACKED (1) [SACK]

2Ki 15:16 *He* **s** Tiphsah and ripped open all the H5782

SACKS (10) [SACK]

Ge 42:35 As they were emptying their **s**, there in H8566
Ge 43:12 that was put back into the mouths of your **s**. H623
Ge 43:18 that was put back into our **s** the first time. H623
Ge 43:21 night we opened our **s** and each of us H623
Ge 43:22 We don't know who put our silver in our **s**." H623
Ge 43:23 has given you treasure in your **s**; I received H623
Ge 44: 1 "Fill the men's **s** with as much food as they H623
Ge 44: 8 silver we found inside the mouths of our **s**. H623
Jos 9: 4 with worn-out **s** and old wineskins, H8566
1Sa 9: 7 The food in our **s** is gone. We have no H3998

SACRED (131)

Ge 1:14 let them serve as signs to mark **s times**, H4595
Ex 12:16 On the first day hold a **s** assembly, and H7731
Ex 23:24 them and break their **s stones** to pieces. H5167
Ex 28: 2 Make **s** garments for your brother Aaron to H7731
Ex 28: 4 are to make these **s** garments for your H7731
Ex 28:38 guilt involved in the **s gifts** the Israelites H7731
Ex 29: 6 head and attach the **s** emblem to the H7731
Ex 29:29 "Aaron's **s** garments will belong to his H7731
Ex 29:31 cook the meat in a **s** place. H7705
Ex 29:33 else may eat them, because they are **s**. H7731
Ex 29:34 It must not be eaten, because it is **s**. H7731
Ex 30:25 Make these into a **s** anointing oil, H7731
Ex 30:25 It will be the **s** anointing oil. H7731
Ex 30:31 'This is to be my **s** anointing oil for the H7731
Ex 30:32 the same formula. It is **s**, and you are to H7731
Ex 30:32 It is sacred, and you are to consider it **s**. H7731
Ex 30:35 It is to be salted and pure and **s**. H7731
Ex 31:10 both the **s** garments for Aaron the priest H7731
Ex 34:13 smash their **s stones** and cut down their H5167
Ex 35:19 both the **s** garments for Aaron the priest H7731
Ex 35:21 all its service, and for the **s** garments. H7731
Ex 37:29 They also made the **s** anointing oil and H7731
Ex 39: 1 They also made **s** garments for Aaron, as H7731
Ex 39:30 the plate, the **s** emblem, out of pure H7731
Ex 39:41 both the **s** garments for Aaron the priest H7731
Ex 40:13 Then dress Aaron in the **s** garments H7731
Lev 8: 9 the gold plate, the **s** emblem, on the front H7731
Lev 12: 4 not touch anything **s** or go to the H7731
Lev 16: 4 He is to put on the **s** linen tunic, with linen H7731
Lev 16: 4 These are **s** garments; so he must bathe H7731
Lev 16:32 He is to put on the **s** linen garments H7731
Lev 22: 2 with respect the **s offerings** the Israelites H7731
Lev 22: 3 comes near the **s offerings** that the H7731
Lev 22: 4 he may not eat the **s offerings** until he is H7731
Lev 22: 6 eat any of the **s offerings** unless he has H7731
Lev 22: 7 after that he may eat the **s offerings** H7731
Lev 22:10 a priest's family may eat the **s offering**, H7731
Lev 22:12 she may not eat any of the **s** contributions. H7731
Lev 22:14 who eats a **s offering** by mistake must H7731
Lev 22:15 not desecrate the **s offerings** the Israelites H7731
Lev 22:16 them to eat the **s offerings** and so bring H7731
Lev 23: 2 you are to proclaim as **s** assemblies. H7731
Lev 23: 3 day of sabbath rest, a day of **s** assembly. H7731
Lev 23: 4 the **s** assemblies you are to proclaim at H7731
Lev 23: 7 the first day hold a **s** assembly and do no H7731
Lev 23: 8 seventh day hold a **s** assembly and do no H7731
Lev 23:20 They are a **s offering** to the LORD for the H7731
Lev 23:21 are to proclaim a **s** assembly and do no H7731
Lev 23:24 a **s** assembly commemorated with H7731
Lev 23:27 Hold a **s** assembly and deny yourselves H7731
Lev 23:35 The first day is a **s** assembly; do no regular H7731
Lev 23:36 eighth day hold a **s** assembly and present H7731
Lev 23:37 you are to proclaim as **s** assemblies for H7731
Lev 26: 1 up an image or a **s stone** for yourselves, H5167
Nu 5: 9 All the **s** contributions the Israelites bring H7731
Nu 5:10 **S things** belong to their owners, but what H7731
Nu 28:18 the first day hold a **s** assembly and do no H7731
Nu 28:25 seventh day hold a **s** assembly and do no H7731
Nu 28:26 hold a **s** assembly and do no regular work. H7731
Nu 29: 1 month hold a **s** assembly and do no H7731
Nu 29: 7 of this seventh month hold a **s** assembly. H7731
Nu 29:12 hold a **s** assembly and do no regular work. H7731
Dt 7: 5 smash their **s stones**, cut down their H5167
Dt 12: 3 smash their **s stones** and burn their H5167
Dt 16:22 do not erect a **s stone**, for these the H5167
Dt 26:13 my house the **s portion** and have given H7731
Dt 26:14 eaten any of **the s portion** while I was in H5647S
Jos 6:19 bronze and iron are **s** to the LORD and H7731
1Ki 1:39 horn of oil from the *s* **tent** and anointed AIT
1Ki 8: 4 of meeting and all the **s** furnishings in it. H7731
1Ki 14:23 **s stones** and Asherah poles on every high H5167
2Ki 3: 2 He got rid of the **s stone** *of* Baal that his H5167
2Ki 10:26 They brought the **s stone** out of the temple H5167
2Ki 10:27 demolished the **s stone** *of* Baal and tore H5167
2Ki 12: 4 is brought as **s offerings** to the temple of H7731
2Ki 12:18 took all the **s objects** dedicated by his H7731
2Ki 17:10 They set up **s stones** and Asherah poles H5167
2Ki 18: 4 smashed the **s stones** and cut down the H5167
2Ki 23:14 smashed the **s stones** and cut down the H5167
1Ch 16:42 playing of the other instruments for **s** song. H466
1Ch 22:19 of the LORD and the **s** articles belonging to H7731
1Ch 23:28 purification of all **s things** and the H7731
2Ch 5: 5 of meeting and all the **s** furnishings in it. H7731
2Ch 14: 3 smashed the **s stones** and cut down the H5167
2Ch 24: 7 had used even its **s objects** for the Baals. H7731
2Ch 31: 1 smashed the **s stones** and cut down the H5167
2Ch 35: 3 "Put the **s** ark in the temple that Solomon H7731
Ezr 2:63 any of the **most s** *food* until there H7731+7731
Ezr 3: 5 all the appointed **s** festivals of the LORD H7727
Ezr 8:30 silver and gold and **s** articles that had been NDT
Ezr 8:33 gold and the **s** articles into the hands NDT
Ne 7:65 any of the **most s food** until there H7731+7731
Ps 15: 1 who may dwell in your *s* **tent**? Who may live AIT
Ps 27: 5 the shelter of his *s* **tent** and set me high AIT
Ps 27: 6 at his *s* **tent** I will sacrifice with shouts of joy AIT
Ps 89:20 with my **s** oil I have anointed him. H7731
Isa 1:29 because of the **s oaks** in which you have H381
Isa 64:10 Your **s** cities have become a wasteland H7731
Isa 65: 5 come near me, for *I am too* **s** *for* you! H7727
Jer 31:23 you prosperous city, you **s** mountain. H7731
Jer 43:13 will demolish the **s pillars** and will burn H5167
La 4: 1 The **s** gems are scattered at every street H7731
Eze 44:19 in and are to leave them in the **s** rooms, H7731
Eze 45: 1 LORD a portion of the land as a **s** *district*, H7731
Eze 45: 3 In the **s** district, measure off a section 25,000 NDT
Eze 45: 4 It will be the **s** portion of the land for the H7731
Eze 45: 6 adjoining the **s** portion; it will H7731
Eze 45: 7 the area formed by the **s** district and the H7731
Eze 46:19 of the gate to the **s** rooms facing north, H7731
Eze 48:10 This will be the **s** portion for the priests. H7731
Eze 48:12 gift to them from the **s** portion of the land, NDT
Eze 48:18 bordering on the **s** portion and running H7731
Eze 48:20 gift you will set aside the **s** portion, H7731
Eze 48:21 the area formed by the **s** portion and the H7731
Eze 48:21 25,000 cubits of the **s** portion to the eastern NDT
Eze 48:21 the **s** portion with the temple H7731
Hos 3: 1 to other gods and love the **s** raisin **cakes**." H862
Hos 3: 4 without sacrifice or **s stones**, without H5167
Hos 10: 1 land prospered, he adorned his **s stones**. H5167
Hos 10: 2 their altars and destroy their **s stones**. H5167
Joel 1:14 holy fast; call a **s assembly**. Summon the H6809
Joel 2:15 declare a holy fast, call a **s assembly**. H6809
Mic 5:13 idols and your **s stones** from among you; H5167
Zec 14:20 will be like the **s bowls** in front of the altar H4670
Mt 7: 6 "Do not give dogs what is **s**; do not throw *G41*
Mt 23:17 or the temple that **makes** the gold **s**? *G39*
Mt 23:19 or the altar that **makes** the gift **s**? *G39*
Ro 14: 5 considers one day **more** *s* **than** another; AIT
1Co 3:17 God's temple is **s**, and you together are *G41*
2Pe 1:18 when we were with him on the **s** mountain. *G41*
2Pe 2:21 their backs on the **s** command that was *G41*

SACRIFICE (164) [SACRIFICED, SACRIFICES, SACRIFICIAL, SACRIFICING]

Ge 22: 2 **S** him there as a burnt offering on a H6590
Ge 31:54 He offered a **s** there in the hill country H2285
Ex 5: 8 crying out, 'Let us go and **s** to our God. H2284
Ex 5:17 keep saying, 'Let us go and **s** to the LORD. H2284
Ex 8:25 "Go, **s** to your God here in the land." H2284
Ex 12:27 'It is the Passover **s** to the LORD, who H2285
Ex 13:15 This is why I **s** to the LORD the first male H2284
Ex 20:24 altar of earth for me and **s** on it your burnt H2284
Ex 23:18 offer the blood of a **s** to me along with H2285
Ex 29:36 **S** a bull each day as a sin offering to make H6913
Ex 29:41 **S** the other lamb at twilight with the same H6913
Ex 34:15 themselves to their gods and **s** to them, H2284
Ex 34:25 offer the blood of a **s** *to* me along with H2285
Ex 34:25 do not let any of the **s** *from* the Passover H2285
Lev 7:16 the **s** shall be eaten on the day they offer H2285
Lev 7:17 Any meat of the **s** left over till the third day H2285
Lev 7:29 is to bring part of it as their **s** to the LORD. H7933
Lev 9: 4 a fellowship offering to **s** before the LORD, H2284
Lev 9: 7 to the altar and **s** your sin offering and H6913
Lev 9: 7 **s** the offering that is for the people and H6913
Lev 14:19 "Then the priest *is to* **s** the sin offering H6913
Lev 14:30 Then *he shall* **s** the doves or the young H6913
Lev 15:15 The priest *is to* **s** them, the one for a sin H6913
Lev 15:30 The priest *is to* **s** one for a sin offering H6913
Lev 16: 9 falls to the LORD and **s** it for a sin offering. H6913
Lev 16:24 he shall come out and **s** the burnt offering H6913
Lev 17: 5 tent of meeting and **s** them as fellowship H2284
Lev 17: 8 them who offers a burnt offering or **s** H2285
Lev 17: 9 tent of meeting to **s** it to the LORD must be H6913
Lev 19: 5 " 'When *you* **s** a fellowship offering to the H2284
Lev 19: 5 **s** it in such a way that it will be accepted H2284
Lev 19: 6 eaten on the day you **s** it or on the next H2285
Lev 22:29 "When *you* **s** a thank offering to the LORD H2284
Lev 22:29 **s** it in such a way that it will be accepted H2284
Lev 23:12 *you must* **s** as a burnt offering to the LORD H6913
Lev 23:19 Then **s** one male goat for a sin offering H6913
Nu 6:17 bread and *is to* **s** the ram as a H6913

S

Nu 6:18 fire that is under the **s** *of* the fellowship H2285
Nu 7:88 of animals for the **s** *of* the fellowship H2285
Nu 15: 5 each lamb for the burnt offering or the **s**, H2285
Nu 15: 8 a young bull as a burnt offering or **s**, H2285
Dt 12:13 Be careful not *to* **s** your burnt offerings H6590
Dt 15:21 *you must* not **s** it to the LORD your God. H2284
Dt 16: 2 **S** as the Passover to the LORD your God an H2284
Dt 16: 4 any of the meat *you* **s** on the evening of H2284
Dt 16: 5 You must not **s** the Passover in any town H2284
Dt 16: 6 There *you must* **s** the Passover in the H2284
Dt 17: 1 *Do* not **s** to the LORD your God an ox or a H2284
Dt 18: 3 from the people *who* **s** a bull or a H2284+2285
Dt 27: 7 **S** fellowship offerings there, eating them H2284
Jos 22:23 offerings, or to **s** fellowship offerings on it H6913
Jdg 11:31 and *I will* **s** it as a burnt offering. H6590
Jdg 16:23 to offer a great **s** to Dagon their god and H2285
1Sa 1: 3 town to worship and **s** to the LORD H2284
1Sa 1: 4 Whenever the day came for Elkanah *to* **s** H2284
1Sa 1:21 to offer the annual **s** to the LORD and to H2285
1Sa 2:13 whenever any of the people offered a **s** H2285
1Sa 2:19 up with her husband to offer the annual **s**. H2285
1Sa 2:29 Why do you scorn my **s** and offering that I H2285
1Sa 3:14 will never be atoned for by **s** or offering. H2285
1Sa 9:12 the people have a **s** at the high place. H2285
1Sa 9:13 because he must bless the **s**; afterward, H2285
1Sa 10: 8 come down to you to **s** burnt offerings H6590
1Sa 15:15 sheep and cattle to **s** to the LORD your God H2284
1Sa 15:21 in order to **s** them to the LORD your God at H2284
1Sa 15:22 To obey is better than **s**, and to heed is H2285
1Sa 16: 2 you and say, 'I have come to **s** to the LORD. H2284
1Sa 16: 3 Invite Jesse to the **s**, and I will show you H2285
1Sa 16: 5 in peace; I have come to **s** to the LORD. H2284
1Sa 16: 5 yourselves and come to the **s** with me." H2285
1Sa 16: 5 his sons and invited them to the **s**. H2285
1Sa 20: 6 because an annual **s** is being made there H2285
1Sa 20:29 family is observing a **s** in the town and my H2285
2Sa 24:24 *I will* not **s** to the LORD my God burnt H6590
1Ki 8:63 Solomon **offered a s** of fellowship H2284
1Ki 13: 2 On you *he will* **s** the priests of the high H2284
1Ki 18:29 until the time for the **evening s**. H6590+4966
1Ki 18:36 At the time of **s**, the prophet Elijah H6590+4966
1Ki 18:38 fire of the LORD fell and burned up the **s**, H6592
2Ki 3:20 about the time for offering the **s**, there it H4966
2Ki 3:27 offered him as a **s** on the city wall. H6592
2Ki 10:19 I am going to hold a great **s** for Baal. H2285
2Ki 17:35 down to them, serve them or **s** to them. H2284
2Ki 23:10 so no one *could use* it *to* **s** their son or H6296
1Ch 21:24 **s** a burnt offering that costs me nothing." H6590
2Ch 7: 5 Solomon offered a **s** *of* twenty-two H2285
2Ch 28:23 *I will* **s** to them so they will help me." H2284
2Ch 29:27 gave the order to **s** the burnt offering on H6590
2Ch 29:28 continued until the **s** of the burnt offering NDT
2Ch 33:17 continued *to* **s** at the high places H2284
Ezr 3: 2 the God of Israel to **s** burnt offerings on it, H6590
Ezr 7:17 **s** them on the altar of the temple of A10638
Ezr 9: 4 I sat there appalled until the evening **s**. H4966
Ezr 9: 5 at the evening **s**, I rose from my H4966
Job 1: 5 *he would* **s** a burnt offering *for* each of H6590
Job 42: 8 my servant Job and **s** a burnt offering for H6590
Ps 27: 6 sacred tent *I will* **s** *with* shouts of H2284+2285
Ps 40: 6 **S** and offering you did not desire—but H2285
Ps 50: 5 who made a covenant with me by **s**." H2285
Ps 50:14 "**S** thank offerings to God, fulfill your vows H2284
Ps 50:23 *Those who* **s** thank offerings honor me H2284
Ps 51:16 You do not delight in **s**, or I would bring it; H2285
Ps 51:17 My **s**, O God, is a broken spirit; a broken H2285
Ps 54: 6 *I will* **s** a freewill offering to you; I will H2284
Ps 66:15 *I will* **s** fat animals to you and an H6590+6592
Ps 107:22 *Let them* **s** thank offerings and tell of his H2284
Ps 116:17 *I will* **s** a thank offering to you and call on H2284
Ps 141: 2 up of my hands be like the evening **s**. H4966
Pr 15: 8 The LORD detests the **s** *of* the wicked, but H2285
Pr 21: 3 just is more acceptable to the LORD than **s**. H2285
Pr 21:27 The **s** *of* the wicked is detestable—how H2285
Ecc 5: 1 to listen rather than to offer the **s** of fools, H2285
Isa 34: 6 For the LORD has a **s** in Bozrah and a great H2285
Isa 57: 5 you **s** your children in the ravines and H8821
Jer 32:35 Valley of Ben Hinnom to **s** their sons and H6296
Jer 46:10 will offer **s** in the land of the north by the H2285
Eze 20:26 their gifts—the **s** *of* every firstborn—that I H6296
Eze 20:31 the **s** *of* your children in the fire H6296
Eze 39:17 all around to the **s** I am preparing for you H2285
Eze 39:17 the great **s** on the mountains of Israel. H2285
Eze 39:19 At the **s** I am preparing for you, you will H2285
Eze 43:24 salt on them and **s** them as a burnt H6590
Eze 46: 2 The priests *are to* **s** his burnt offering and H6913
Da 8:11 it took away the **daily s** from the LORD, H9458
Da 8:12 people and the **daily s** were given over to H9458
Da 8:13 the vision concerning the **daily s**, the H9458
Da 9:21 flight about the time of the evening **s**. H4966
Da 9:27 he will put an end to **s** and offering. H2285
Da 11:31 fortress and will abolish the **daily s**. H9458
Da 12:11 the time that the **daily s** is abolished and H9458
Hos 3: 4 king or prince, without **s** or sacred stones H2285
Hos 4:13 *They* **s** on the mountaintops and burn H2284
Hos 4:14 with harlots and **s** with shrine prostitutes H2284
Hos 6: 6 desire mercy, not **s**, and acknowledgment H2285
Hos 12:11 are worthless! *Do they* **s** bulls in Gilgal H2284
Jnh 1:16 they offered a **s** to the LORD and made H2285
Jnh 2: 9 shouts of grateful praise, *will* **s** to you. H2284
Zep 1: 7 The LORD has prepared a **s**; he has H2285
Zep 1: 8 the day of the LORD's **s** I will punish the H2285
Zec 14:21 all who come to **s** will take some of H2284
Mal 1: 8 When you offer blind animals for **s**, is that H2284
Mal 1: 8 When *you* **s** lame or diseased animals, is H5602
Mt 9:13 'I desire mercy, not **s**.' For I have not come G2602
Mt 12: 7 'I desire mercy, not **s**,' you would not have G2602
Mk 14:12 when *it was customary to* **s** the Passover G2604
Lk 2:24 to offer a **s** in keeping with what is G2602
Ro 3:25 God presented Christ *as a* **s of atonement** G2663
Ro 12: 1 to offer your bodies *as* a living **s**, holy G2602
1Co 10:28 "This has been **offered in s**," then do not G2638
Eph 5: 2 us as a fragrant offering and **s** to God. G2602
Php 2:17 drink offering on the **s** and service coming G2602
Php 4:18 an acceptable **s**, pleasing to God. G2602
Heb 9:26 to do away with sin by the **s** of himself. G2602
Heb 10: 5 "**S** and offering you did not desire, but a G2602
Heb 10:10 holy through the **s** of the body of Jesus G4714
Heb 10:12 had offered for all time one **s** for sins, G2602
Heb 10:14 For *by* one **s** he has made perfect forever G4714
Heb 10:18 forgiven, **s** for sin is no longer necessary. G4714
Heb 10:26 of the truth, no **s** for sins is left, G2602
Heb 11:17 God tested him, **offered** Isaac **as a s**. G4712
Heb 11:17 the promises *was about to* **s** his one and G4712
Heb 13:15 us continually offer to God a **s** of praise— G2602
1Jn 2: 2 He is the **atoning s** for our sins, and not G2662
1Jn 4:10 sent his Son *as* an **atoning s** for our sins. G2662

SACRIFICED (71) [SACRIFICE]

Ge 8:20 clean birds, *he* **s** burnt offerings on it. H6590
Ge 22:13 took the ram and **s** it as a burnt H6590
Ex 24: 5 burnt offerings and **s** young bulls as H2284
Ex 32: 6 rose early and **s** burnt offerings and H6590
Ex 32: 8 down to it and **s** to it and have said, H2284
Lev 4:10 removed from the ox **s** *as* a fellowship H2285
Lev 9:22 And *having* **s** the sin offering, the burnt H6913
Lev 10:19 "Today *they* **s** their sin offering and their H7928
Lev 18:21 give any of your children to *be* **s** to Molek, H6296
Nu 7:17 lambs a year old to be **s** as a fellowship H2285
Nu 7:23 lambs a year old to be **s** as a fellowship H2285
Nu 7:29 lambs a year old to be **s** as a fellowship H2285
Nu 7:35 lambs a year old to be **s** as a fellowship H2285
Nu 7:41 lambs a year old to be **s** as a fellowship H2285
Nu 7:47 lambs a year old to be **s** as a fellowship H2285
Nu 7:53 lambs a year old to be **s** as a fellowship H2285
Nu 7:59 lambs a year old to be **s** as a fellowship H2285
Nu 7:65 lambs a year old to be **s** as a fellowship H2285
Nu 7:71 lambs a year old to be **s** as a fellowship H2285
Nu 7:77 lambs a year old to be **s** as a fellowship H2285
Nu 7:83 lambs a year old to be **s** as a fellowship H2285
Nu 22:40 Balak **s** cattle and sheep, and gave some H2284
Dt 32:17 *They* **s** to false gods, which are not God H2284
Jos 8:31 burnt offerings and **s** fellowship offerings. H2284
Jdg 6:28 the second bull **s** on the newly built H6590
Jdg 13:19 offering, and **s** it on a rock to the LORD. H6590
1Sa 1:25 When the bull *had been* **s**, they brought H8821
1Sa 6:14 wood of the cart and **s** the cows as a burnt H6590
1Sa 7: 9 a suckling lamb and **s** it as a whole burnt H6590
1Sa 11:15 There *they* **s** fellowship offerings before H2284
2Sa 6:13 six steps, *he* **s** a bull and a fattened calf. H2284
2Sa 6:17 David **s** burnt offerings and H6590
2Sa 24:25 to the LORD there and **s** burnt offerings H6590
1Ki 1: 9 Adonijah then **s** sheep, cattle and H2284
1Ki 1:19 *He has* **s** great numbers of cattle, fattened H2284
1Ki 1:25 has gone down and **s** great numbers of H2284
1Ki 3:15 Lord's covenant and **s** burnt offerings and H6590
1Ki 9:25 a year Solomon **s** burnt offerings and H6590
2Ki 16: 3 of Israel and even **s** his son in the fire, H6296
2Ki 17:17 *They* **s** their sons and daughters in the fire H6296
2Ki 21: 6 *He* **s** his own son in the fire, practiced H6296
1Ch 15:26 seven bulls and seven rams *were* **s**. H2284
1Ch 21:26 to the LORD there and **s** burnt offerings H6590
2Ch 8:12 Solomon **s** burnt offerings to the LORD H6590
2Ch 15:11 At that time *they* **s** to the LORD seven H2284
2Ch 28: 3 of Ben Hinnom and **s** his children in the H1277
2Ch 33: 6 He **s** his children in the fire in the Valley of H6296
2Ch 33:16 altar of the LORD and **s** fellowship offerings H2284
2Ch 34: 4 the graves of those *who had* **s** to them. H2284
Ezr 3: 3 its foundation and **s** burnt offerings on it H6590
Ezr 8:35 from captivity **s** burnt offerings to the H7928
Ps 106:37 *They* **s** their sons and their daughters to H2284
Ps 106:38 whom *they* **s** to the idols of Canaan H2284
Eze 16:20 you bore to me and **s** them as food to the H2284
Eze 16:21 my children and **s** them to the H5989+928+6296
Eze 23:37 with their idols; *they* even **s** their children H6296
Eze 23:39 On the very day *they* **s** their children to H8821
Hos 11: 2 *They* **s** to the Baals and they burned H2284
Lk 22: 7 on which the Passover lamb had to *be* **s**. G2604
Ac 15:29 You are to abstain *from* **food s to idols** G1628
Ac 21:25 they should abstain *from* **food s to idols**, G1628
1Co 5: 7 For Christ, our Passover lamb, *has been* **s**. G2604
1Co 8: 1 Now about **food s to idols**: We know that G1628
1Co 8: 4 about eating **food s to idols**: We know G1628
1Co 8: 7 they think of it as having been **s to a god**, G1628
1Co 8:10 be emboldened to eat what is **s to idols**? G1628
1Co 10:19 then that **food s to an idol** is anything, G1628
Heb 7:27 *He* **s** for their sins once for all G4047+4472
Heb 9:28 so Christ *was* **s** once to take away the sins G4712
Rev 2:14 that they ate **food s to idols** and G1628
Rev 2:20 the eating *of* **food s to idols**. G1628

SACRIFICES (141) [SACRIFICE]

Ge 46: 1 he offered **s** to the God of his father Isaac. H2285
Ex 3:18 the wilderness *to* **offer s** to the LORD our H2284
Ex 5: 3 the wilderness *to* **offer s** to the LORD our H2284
Ex 8: 8 let your people go *to* **offer s** to the LORD." H2284
Ex 8:26 *The* **s** *we* **offer** the LORD our God would be H2284
Ex 8:26 And if *we* **offer s** that are detestable in H2284
Ex 8:27 the wilderness *to* **offer s** to the LORD our H2284
Ex 8:28 "I will let you go *to* **offer s** to the LORD your H2284
Ex 8:29 the people go to **offer s** to the LORD." H2284
Ex 10:25 allow us to have **s** and burnt offerings H2285
Ex 18:12 a burnt offering and other **s** to God, H2285
Ex 22:20 "*Whoever* **s** to any god other than the H2284
Ex 34:15 will invite you and you will eat their **s**. H2285
Lev 17: 3 Any Israelite who **s** an ox, a lamb or a H8821
Lev 17: 5 to the LORD the **s** they are now making H2285
Lev 17: 7 offer any of their **s** to the goat idols to H2285
Lev 20: 2 in Israel who **s** any of his children to H5989
Lev 20: 4 eyes when that man **s** one of his children H5989
Lev 23:37 **s** and drink offerings required for each day H2285
Nu 15: 3 whether burnt offerings or **s**, for special H2285
Nu 25: 2 who invited them to the **s** *to* their gods H2285
Dt 12: 6 there bring your burnt offerings and **s**, your H2285
Dt 12:11 your burnt offerings and **s**, your tithes and H2285
Dt 12:27 The blood of your **s** must be poured H2285
Dt 12:31 *They* even **burn** their sons and daughters
in the fire **as s** H8596
Dt 18:10 be found among you *who* **s** their son or H6296
Dt 32:38 ate the fat of their **s** and drank the wine of H2285
Dt 33:19 there offer the **s** *of* the righteous; H2285
Jos 22:26 an altar—but not for burnt offerings or **s**. H2285
Jos 22:27 burnt offerings, **s** and fellowship offerings. H2285
Jos 22:28 not for burnt offerings and **s**, but as a H2285
Jos 22:29 grain offerings and **s**, other than the altar H2285
Jdg 2: 5 There *they* **offered s** to the LORD. H2284
1Sa 6:15 offerings and **made s** to the LORD. H2284+2285
1Sa 15:22 burnt offerings and **s** as much as in H2285
2Sa 15:12 While Absalom was offering **s**, he also H2285
2Sa 15:24 Abiathar **offered s** until all the H6590
1Ki 3: 3 except that he **offered s** and burned H2284
1Ki 3: 4 The king went to Gibeon to **offer s**, for H2284
1Ki 8:62 Israel with him offered **s** before the LORD. H2285
1Ki 11: 8 incense and **offered s** to their gods. H2284
1Ki 12:27 go up to offer **s** at the temple of the H2285
1Ki 12:32 held in Judah, and **offered s** on the altar. H6590
1Ki 12:33 *he* **offered s** on the altar he had built at H6590
1Ki 22:43 people continued *to* **offer s** and burn H2284
2Ki 5:17 burnt offerings and **s** to any other god H2285
2Ki 10:24 went in to make **s** and burnt offerings. H2285
2Ki 12: 3 people continued *to* **offer s** and burn H2284
2Ki 14: 4 people continued *to* **offer s** and burn H2284
2Ki 15: 4 people continued *to* **offer s** and burn H2284
2Ki 15:35 people continued *to* **offer s** and burn H2284
2Ki 16: 4 *He* **offered s** and burned incense at the H2284
2Ki 16:15 the blood of all the burnt offerings and **s**. H2285
2Ki 17:31 **burned** their children in the fire **as s** to H8596
2Ki 17:36 you shall bow down and to him **offer s**. H2284
1Ch 21:28 Araunah the Jebusite, *he* **offered s** there. H2284
1Ch 23:13 holy things, to **offer s** before the LORD, to H7787
1Ch 29:21 next day *they* **made s** to the LORD H2284+2285
1Ch 29:21 other **s** in abundance for all Israel. H2285
2Ch 2: 6 except as a place to **burn s** before him? H7787
2Ch 7: 1 consumed the burnt offering and the **s**, H2285
2Ch 7: 4 all the people offered **s** before the LORD. H2285
2Ch 7:12 this place for myself as a temple for **s**. H2285
2Ch 11:16 Levites to Jerusalem to **offer s** to the LORD, H2284
2Ch 25:14 down to them and **burned s** to them. H7787
2Ch 28: 3 He **burned s** in the Valley of Ben Hinnom H7787
2Ch 28: 4 *He* **offered s** and burned incense at the H2284
2Ch 28:23 *He* **offered s** to the gods of Damascus H2284
2Ch 28:25 high places to **burn s** to other gods and H7787
2Ch 29:31 Come and bring **s** and thank offerings to H2285
2Ch 29:31 assembly brought **s** and thank offerings, H2285
2Ch 29:33 animals consecrated as **s** amounted to six NDT
2Ch 32:12 before one altar and **burn s** on it'? H7787
2Ch 33:22 worshiped and **offered s** to all the idols H2284
Ezr 3: 3 the LORD, both the morning and evening **s**. H6592
Ezr 3: 5 the New Moon **s** and the sacrifices for all NDT
Ezr 3: 5 sacrifices and the **s** for all the appointed NDT
Ezr 6: 3 be rebuilt as a place to present **s**, A10157
Ezr 6:10 so that *they may* **offer s** pleasing to the A10638
Ne 4: 2 *Will they* **offer s**? Will they H2284
Ne 12:43 And on that day they offered great **s** H2285
Ps 4: 5 Offer the **s** *of* the righteous and trust in H2285
Ps 20: 3 he remember all your **s** and accept your H4966
Ps 50: 8 you concerning your **s** or concerning your H2285
Ps 51:19 you will delight in the **s** *of* the righteous, H2285
Ps 106:28 of Peor and ate **s** *offered to* lifeless gods; H2285
Ecc 9: 2 those *who* **offer s** and those who do not. H2284
Isa 1:11 "The multitude of your **s**—what are they H2285
Isa 19:21 will worship with **s** and grain offerings; H2285
Isa 43:23 offerings, nor honored me with your **s**. H2285
Isa 43:24 or lavished on me the fat of your **s**. H2285
Isa 56: 7 burnt offerings and **s** will be accepted on H2285
Isa 57: 7 lofty hill; there you went up to offer your **s**. H2285
Isa 65: 3 **offering s** in gardens and burning incense H2284
Isa 65: 7 "Because *they* **burned s** on the mountains H7787
Isa 66: 3 But *whoever* **s** a bull is like one who kills H8821
Jer 6:20 not acceptable; your **s** do not please me." H2285
Jer 7:21 offerings to your other **s** and eat the meat H2285
Jer 7:22 commands about burnt offerings and **s**, H2285
Jer 17:26 bringing burnt offerings and **s**, grain H2285
Jer 33:18 to burn grain offerings and to present **s**. H2285
Eze 20:28 there they offered their **s**, made offerings H2285
Eze 20:40 your choice gifts, along with all your holy **s**. NDT

Eze 40:41 on which *the* s *were* **slaughtered**. H8821
Eze 40:42 the burnt offerings and the other s. H2285
Eze 44:11 burnt offerings and s for the people and H2285
Eze 44:15 before me to **offer** s *of* fat and blood, H7928
Eze 46:24 temple are to cook the s *of* the people." H2285
Hos 4:19 and their s will bring them shame. H2285
Hos 8:13 Though they offer s *as* gifts to me, and H2285
Hos 9: 4 to the LORD, nor will their s please him. H2285
Hos 9: 4 Such s will be to them like the bread of NDT
Hos 13: 2 of these people, "*They* **offer** human s! H2284
Am 4: 4 Bring your s every morning, your tithes H2285
Am 5:25 "Did you bring me s and offerings forty H2285
Hab 1:16 Therefore *he* s to his net and burns H2284
Mal 1:13 diseased animals and offer them as s, H4966
Mal 1:14 then s a blemished animal to the Lord H2284
Mal 2: 3 your faces the dung from your **festival** s, H2504
Mk 1:44 to the priest and **offer** *the* s that Moses G4712
Mk 12:33 important than all burnt offerings and s." G2602
Lk 5:14 to the priest and **offer** *the* s that Moses G4712
Lk 13: 1 blood Pilate had mixed with their s. G2602
Ac 7:41 They brought s to it and reveled in what G2602
Ac 7:42 " 'Did you bring me s and offerings forty G5376
Ac 14:13 the crowd wanted *to* **offer** s to them. G2604
1Co 10:18 not those who eat the s participate in the G2602
1Co 10:20 **the** s of pagans are offered to G4005S
Heb 5: 1 related to God, to offer gifts and s for sins. G2602
Heb 5: 3 is why he has to **offer** s for his own sins, G4712
Heb 7:27 he does not need to offer s day after day G2602
Heb 8: 3 is appointed to offer both gifts and s, G2602
Heb 9: 9 that the gifts and s being offered were not G2602
Heb 9:23 heavenly things to be purified *with* **these** *s*, AIT
Heb 9:23 themselves *with* better s than these. G2602
Heb 10: 1 *by* the same s repeated endlessly year G2602
Heb 10: 3 But **those** *s* are an annual reminder of sins. AIT
Heb 10: 8 First he said, "S and offerings, burnt G2602
Heb 10:11 again and again he offers the same s G2602
Heb 13:16 for with such s God is pleased. G2602
1Pe 2: 5 offering spiritual s acceptable to God G2602

SACRIFICIAL (2) [SACRIFICE]

Nu 25: 2 The people ate the s meal and bowed NDT
1Co 8: 7 that when they eat s food they think of it as NDT

SACRIFICING (13) [SACRIFICE]

Lev 20: 3 his people; for *by* s his children to Molek H5989
1Sa 2:15 come and say to the person who *was* s, H2284
1Sa 7:10 While Samuel was s the burnt offering H6590
2Sa 6:18 After he had finished s the burnt offerings H6590
1Ki 3: 2 however, *were still* s at the high places H2284
1Ki 8: 5 s so many sheep and cattle that they H2284
1Ki 12:32 in Bethel, s to the calves he had made. H2284
1Ch 16: 2 David had finished s the burnt offerings H6590
2Ch 5: 6 s so many sheep and cattle that they H2284
2Ch 35:14 *were* s the burnt offerings and the fat H6590
Ezr 4: 2 your God and *have been* s to him since H2284
Eze 43:18 the regulations for s burnt offerings and H6590
Ac 14:18 keeping the crowd from s to them. G2604

SAD (9) [SADDENED, SADNESS]

Ge 40: 7 "Why do you look *so* s today? H8273
Ne 2: 1 I had not been s in his presence before H8273
Ne 2: 2 does your face **look** *so* s when you are not H8273
Ne 2: 3 Why *should* my face not **look** s when the H8317
Ecc 7: 3 because a s face is good for the heart. H8278
Mt 19:22 he went away s, because he had G3382
Mt 26:22 *They were* very s and began to say to him G3382
Mk 10:22 He went away s, because he had great G3382
Lk 18:23 he became **very** s, because he was G4337

SADDENED (1) [SAD]

Mk 14:19 *They were* s, and one by one they said to G3382

SADDLE (5) [SADDLED]

Ge 31:34 inside her camel's s and was sitting on H4121
Jdg 5:10 sitting on your s **blankets**, and you who H4496
1Ki 13:13 he said to his sons, "S the donkey for me." H2502
1Ki 13:27 said to his sons, "S the donkey for me," H2502
Eze 27:20 " 'Dedan traded in s blankets with you. H8210

SADDLEBAGS (NIV84) SHEEP PENS

SADDLED (9) [SADDLE]

Nu 22:21 s his donkey and went with the Moabite H2502
Jdg 19:10 with his two s donkeys and his concubine. H2502
2Sa 16: 1 a string of donkeys s and loaded with two H2502
2Sa 17:23 *he* s his donkey and set out for his house H2502
2Sa 19:26 '*I will* **have** my donkey s and will ride on it H2502
1Ki 2:40 he s his donkey and went to Achish at H2502
1Ki 13:13 And when *they had* s the donkey for him H2502
1Ki 13:23 brought him back s his donkey for him. H2502
2Ki 4:24 *She* s the donkey and said to her servant H2502

SADDUCEES (14)

Mt 3: 7 the Pharisees and S coming to where he G4881
Mt 16: 1 The Pharisees and S came to Jesus and G4881
Mt 16: 6 against the yeast of the Pharisees and S." G4881
Mt 16:11 against the yeast of the Pharisees and S." G4881
Mt 16:12 the teaching of the Pharisees and S. G4881
Mt 22:23 That same day the S, who say there is no G4881
Mt 22:34 Hearing that Jesus had silenced the S G4881
Mk 12:18 Then the S, who say there is no G4881
Lk 20:27 Some *of* the S, who say there is no G4881
Ac 4: 1 guard and the S came up to Peter and G4881
Ac 5:17 who were members of the party *of* the S G4881
Ac 23: 6 that some of them were S and the others G4881
Ac 23: 7 out between the Pharisees and the S, G4881
Ac 23: 8 The S say that there is no resurrection, and G4881

SADNESS (1) [SAD]

Ne 2: 2 This can be nothing but s *of* heart." I was H8278

SAFE (31) [SAVE]

Dt 29:19 thinking, "I will be s, even though I persist H8934
1Sa 20: 7 he says, 'Very well,' then your servant is s. H8934
1Sa 20:21 LORD lives, you are s; there is no danger. H8934
1Sa 22:23 to kill me too. You will be s with me." H5466
2Sa 18:29 "Is the young man Absalom s? H8934
2Sa 18:32 Cushite, "Is the young man Absalom s?" H8934
2Ch 15: 5 In those days it was not s to travel about H8934
Ezr 8:21 ask him for a s journey for us and H3838
Job 21: 9 Their homes are s and free from fear; the H8934
Ps 12: 7 *will* **keep** the needy s and will protect us H9068
Ps 16: 1 **Keep** me s, my God, for in you I take H9068
Ps 27: 5 day of trouble *he will* **keep** me s in his H7621
Ps 31:20 *you* **keep** them s in your dwelling from H7621
Ps 37: 3 dwell in the land and enjoy s pasture. H575
Ps 140: 4 **Keep** me s, LORD, from the hands of the H9068
Ps 141: 9 **Keep** me s from the traps set by evildoers H9068
Pr 11:15 refuses to shake hands in pledge *is* s. H1053
Pr 18:10 the righteous run to it and *are* s. H8435
Pr 20:28 Love and faithfulness **keep** a king s H5915
Pr 28:18 one whose walk is blameless *is* **kept** s, H3828
Pr 28:26 those who walk in wisdom **are kept** s. H4880
Pr 29:25 whoever trusts in the LORD **is kept** s. H8435
Jer 7:10 say, "*We are* s"—safe to do all these H5911
Jer 7:10 —s to do all these detestable things? NDT
Jer 12: 5 If you stumble in s country, how will you H8934
Jer 12:12 of the land to the other; no one will be s. H8934
Lk 11:21 own house, his possessions are s. G1877+1645
Lk 15:27 because he has him back s **and sound**. G5617
Jn 17:12 them and **kept** them s by that name you G5875
Ro 15:31 Pray that *I may be* **kept** s from the G4861
1Jn 5:18 One who was born of God **keeps** them s, G5498

SAFE-CONDUCT (1) [CONDUCT]

Ne 2: 7 so that *they will* **provide** me s until I arrive H6296

SAFEGUARD (1) [GUARD]

Php 3: 1 things to you again, and it is a s for you. G855

SAFEKEEPING (2) [KEEP]

Ex 22: 7 silver or goods for s and they are stolen H9068
Ex 22:10 to their neighbor for s and it dies or is H9068

SAFELY (18) [SAVE]

Ge 19:16 daughters and led them s out of the city, H5663
Ge 28:21 so that I return s to my father's H928+8934
Ge 33:18 he arrived s at the city of Shechem in H8969
Lev 25:18 and you will live s in the land. H4200+1055
Jos 10:21 then returned s to Joshua in the H928+8934
2Sa 19:24 king left until the day he returned s. H928+8934
2Sa 19:30 lord the king has returned home s." H928+8934
1Ki 22:27 bread and water until I return s. H928+8934
1Ki 22:28 "If you ever return s, the LORD has not H928+8934
2Ch 18:26 bread and water until I return s. H928+8934
2Ch 18:27 "If you ever return s, the LORD has not H928+8934
2Ch 19: 1 of Judah returned s to his palace in H928+8934
Ps 78:53 He guided them s, so they were H4200+1055
Zec 8:10 their business s because of H4200+2021+8934
Ac 23:24 that he may be taken s to Governor Felix." G1407
Ac 27:44 In this way everyone reached land s. G1407
Ac 28: 1 Once s on shore, we found out that the G1407
2Ti 4:18 evil attack and *will* **bring** me s to his G5392

SAFETY (35) [SAVE]

Ge 43: 9 *I* myself *will* **guarantee** his s; you can hold H6842
Ge 44:32 Your servant **guaranteed** the boy's s to my H6842
Lev 25:19 you will eat your fill and live there in s. H1055
Lev 26: 5 food you want and live in s in your land. H1055
Dt 12:10 around you so that you will live *in* s. H1055
Dt 19: 4 who kills a person and flees there *for* s— H2649
Dt 33:28 So Israel will live *in* s; Jacob will dwell H1055
Jdg 18: 7 they saw that the people were living in s, H1055
1Sa 12:11 all around you, so that you lived **in** s. H1055
1Ki 4:25 Beersheba, lived in s, everyone under H1055
Job 5: 4 His children are far from s, crushed in H3829
Job 5:11 and those who mourn are lifted to s. H3829
Job 11:18 will look about you and take your rest in s. H1055
Job 30:15 by the wind, my s vanishes like a cloud. H3802
Ps 4: 8 you alone, LORD, make me dwell in s. H1055
Ps 141:10 fall into their own nets, while I pass by in s. NDT
Pr 1:33 listens to me will live *in* s and be at ease, H1055
Pr 3:23 Then you will go on your way in s, and H1055
Isa 14:30 pasture, and the needy will lie down in s. H1055
Jer 4: 6 to go to Zion! **Flee for** s without delay! For H6395
Jer 6: 1 "**Flee for** s, people of Benjamin! Flee from H6395
Jer 23: 6 will be saved and Israel will live in s. H1055
Jer 32:37 back to this place and let them live in s. H1055
Jer 33:16 will be saved and Jerusalem will live in s. H1055
Eze 28:26 will live there in s and will build houses H1055
Eze 28:26 they will live in s when I inflict H1055
Eze 34:25 wilderness and sleep in the forests in s. H1055
Eze 34:28 They will live in s, and no one will make H1055
Eze 38: 8 the nations, and now all of them live in s. H1055
Eze 38:14 when my people Israel are living in s, will H1055
Eze 39: 6 on those who live in s in the coastlands, H1055
Eze 39:26 when they lived in s in their land with no H1055
Hos 2:18 the land, so that all may lie down in s. H1055
Zep 2:15 This is the city of revelry that lived in s H1055
1Th 5: 3 are saying, "Peace and s," destruction will G854

SAFFRON (1)

SS 4:14 nard and s, calamus and cinnamon, with H4137

SAG (1)

Ecc 10:18 laziness, the rafters s; because of idle H4812

SAGES (1)

Mt 23:34 sending you prophets and s and teachers. G5055

SAHADUTHA See JEGAR SAHADUTHA

SAID (3195) [SAY]

Ge 1: 3 And God s, "Let there be light," and there H606
Ge 1: 6 And God s, "Let there be a vault between H606
Ge 1: 9 And God s, "Let the water under the sky be H606
Ge 1:11 Then God s, "Let the land produce H606
Ge 1:14 And God s, "Let there be lights in the vault H606
Ge 1:20 And God s, "Let the water teem with living H606
Ge 1:22 God blessed them and s, "Be fruitful and H606
Ge 1:24 And God s, "Let the land produce living H606
Ge 1:26 Then God s, "Let us make mankind in our H606
Ge 1:28 God blessed them and s to them, "Be H606
Ge 1:29 Then God s, "I give you every seed-bearing H606
Ge 2:18 The LORD God s, "It is not good for the man H606
Ge 2:23 The man s, "This is now bone of my bones H606
Ge 3: 1 *He* s to the woman, "Did God really say H606
Ge 3: 2 The woman s to the serpent, "We may eat H606
Ge 3: 4 certainly die," the serpent s to the woman. H606
Ge 3:11 And *he* s, "Who told you that you were H606
Ge 3:12 The man s, "The woman you put here with H606
Ge 3:13 Then the LORD God s to the woman, "What H606
Ge 3:13 The woman s, "The serpent deceived me H606
Ge 3:14 So the LORD God s to the serpent, "Because H606
Ge 3:16 To the woman *he* s, "I will make your pains H606
Ge 3:17 To Adam *he* s, "Because you listened to H606
Ge 3:22 And the LORD God s, "The man has now H606
Ge 4: 1 *She* s, "With the help of the LORD I have H606
Ge 4: 6 Then the LORD s to Cain, "Why are you H606
Ge 4: 8 Now Cain s to his brother Abel, "Let's go H606
Ge 4: 9 Then the LORD s to Cain, "Where is your H606
Ge 4:10 The LORD s, "What have you done? Listen H606
Ge 4:13 Cain s to the LORD, "My punishment is more H606
Ge 4:15 But the LORD s to him, "Not so; anyone who H606
Ge 4:23 Lamech s to his wives, "Adah and Zillah H606
Ge 5:29 He named him Noah and s, "He will H606
Ge 6: 3 Then the LORD s, "My Spirit will not contend H606
Ge 6: 7 So the LORD s, "I will wipe from the face of H606
Ge 6:13 So God s to Noah, "I am going to put an H606
Ge 7: 1 The LORD then s to Noah, "Go into the ark H606
Ge 8:15 Then God s to Noah, H1819
Ge 8:21 the pleasing aroma and s in his heart: H606
Ge 9: 8 Then God s to Noah and to his sons with H606
Ge 9:12 And God s, "This is the sign of the H606
Ge 9:17 So God s to Noah, "This is the sign of the H606
Ge 9:25 *he* s, "Cursed be Canaan! The lowest of H606
Ge 9:26 *He* also s, "Praise be to the LORD, the God H606
Ge 10: 9 the LORD; that is why *it is* s, "Like Nimrod, H606
Ge 11: 3 *They* s to each other, "Come, let's make H606
Ge 11: 4 Then *they* s, "Come, let us build ourselves a H606
Ge 11: 6 The LORD s, "If as one people speaking the H606
Ge 12: 1 The LORD *had* s to Abram, "Go from your H606
Ge 12: 7 The LORD appeared to Abram and s, "To H606
Ge 12:11 to enter Egypt, *he* s to his wife Sarai, "I H606
Ge 12:18 you done to me?" *he* s. "Why didn't you H606
Ge 13: 8 So Abram s to Lot, "Let's not have any H606
Ge 13:14 The LORD s to Abram after Lot had parted H606
Ge 14:21 The king of Sodom s to Abram, "Give me H606
Ge 14:22 But Abram s to the king of Sodom, "With H606
Ge 15: 2 But Abram s, "Sovereign LORD, what can H606
Ge 15: 3 And Abram s, "You have given me no H606
Ge 15: 5 He took him outside and s, "Look up at the H606
Ge 15: 5 Then he s to him, "So shall your offspring H606
Ge 15: 7 *He* also s to him, "I am the LORD, who H606
Ge 15: 8 But Abram s, "Sovereign LORD, how can I H606
Ge 15: 9 So the LORD s to him, "Bring me a heifer, H606
Ge 15:13 Then the LORD s to him, "Know for certain H606
Ge 15:18 LORD made a covenant with Abram and s, H606
Ge 16: 2 so she s to Abram, "The LORD has kept me H606
Ge 16: 2 Abram agreed to **what** Sarai s. H7754
Ge 16: 5 Then Sarai s to Abram, "You are H606
Ge 16: 6 in your hands," Abram s. "Do with her H606
Ge 16: 8 And *he* s, "Hagar, slave of Sarai, where H606
Ge 16:11 The angel of the LORD also s to her: "You H606
Ge 16:13 for *she* s, "I have now seen the One who H606
Ge 17: 1 the LORD appeared to him and s, "I am God H606
Ge 17: 3 Abram fell facedown, and God s to him, H1819
Ge 17: 9 Then God s to Abraham, "As for you, you H606
Ge 17:15 God also s to Abraham, "As for Sarai your H606
Ge 17:17 he laughed and s to himself, "Will a son H606
Ge 17:18 And Abraham s to God, "If only Ishmael H606
Ge 17:19 Then God s, "Yes, but your wife Sarah will H606
Ge 18: 3 *He* s, "If I have found favor in your eyes, H606
Ge 18: 6 *he* s, "get three seahs of the finest flour H606
Ge 18: 9 they asked him. "There, in the tent," *he* s. H606
Ge 18:10 Then *one of them* s, "I will surely return to H606
Ge 18:13 Then the LORD s to Abraham, "Why did H606
Ge 18:15 so she lied and s, "I did not laugh." H606
Ge 18:15 did not laugh." But *he* s, "Yes, you did H606

S

Book	Ref	Context	Code
Ge	18:17	Then the LORD **s**, "Shall I hide from	H606
Ge	18:20	Then the LORD **s**, "The outcry against	H606
Ge	18:23	Then Abraham approached him and **s**	H606
Ge	18:26	The LORD **s**, "If I find fifty righteous people	H606
Ge	18:28	forty-five there," *he* **s**, "I will not destroy it	H606
Ge	18:29	are found there?" *He* **s**, "For the sake of	H606
Ge	18:30	Then *he* **s**, "May the Lord not be angry, but	H606
Ge	18:31	Abraham **s**, "Now that I have been so bold	H606
Ge	18:31	*He* **s**, "For the sake of twenty, I will not	H606
Ge	18:32	Then *he* **s**, "May the Lord not be angry, but	H606
Ge	19: 2	*he* **s**, "please turn aside to your servant's	H606
Ge	19: 7	**s**, "No, my friends. Don't do this wicked	H606
Ge	19:12	The two men **s** to Lot, "Do you have	H606
Ge	19:14	*He* **s**, "Hurry and get out of this place	H606
Ge	19:17	them out, *one of them* **s**, "Flee for your	H606
Ge	19:18	But Lot **s** to them, "No, my lords, please!	H606
Ge	19:21	*He* **s** to him, "Very well, I will grant this	H606
Ge	19:31	day the older daughter **s** to the younger,	H606
Ge	19:34	day the older daughter **s** to the younger,	H606
Ge	20: 2	there Abraham **s** of his wife Sarah	H606
Ge	20: 3	in a dream one night and **s** to him,	H606
Ge	20: 4	had not gone near her, so *he* **s**, "Lord,	H606
Ge	20: 6	Then God **s** to him in the dream, "Yes,	H606
Ge	20: 9	Then Abimelek called Abraham in and **s**	H606
Ge	20:11	"*I* **s** *to myself*, 'There is surely	H606
Ge	20:13	father's household, *I* **s** to her, 'This is how	H606
Ge	20:15	And Abimelek **s**, "My land is before you	H606
Ge	20:16	To Sarah *he* **s**, "I am giving your brother a	H606
Ge	21: 1	the LORD was gracious to Sarah as *he had* **s**,	H606
Ge	21: 6	Sarah **s**, "God has brought me laughter	H606
Ge	21: 7	"Who *would have* **s** to Abraham that	H4910
Ge	21:10	and *she* **s** to Abraham, "Get rid of that slave	H606
Ge	21:12	But God **s** to him, "Do not be so distressed	H606
Ge	21:17	called to Hagar from heaven and **s** to her,	H606
Ge	21:22	the commander of his forces **s** to Abraham,	H606
Ge	21:24	Abraham **s**, "I swear it."	H606
Ge	21:26	But Abimelek **s**, "I don't know who has	H606
Ge	22: 1	tested Abraham. *He* **s** to him, "Abraham!"	H606
Ge	22: 2	Then God **s**, "Take your son, your only son	H606
Ge	22: 5	He **s** to his servants, "Stay here with the	H606
Ge	22: 7	Isaac spoke up and **s** to his father Abraham	H606
Ge	22: 7	Isaac **s**, "but where is the lamb for the	H606
Ge	22:12	a hand on the boy," *he* **s**. "Do not do	H606
Ge	22:14	And to this day **it is s**, "On the mountain of	H606
Ge	22:16	**s**, "I swear by myself, declares the LORD	H606
Ge	23: 3	dead wife and spoke to the Hittites. *He* **s**,	H606
Ge	23: 8	*He* **s** to them, "If you are willing to let me	H1819
Ge	23:11	my lord," he **s**. "Listen to me; I give	H606
Ge	23:13	and *he* **s** to Ephron in their hearing	H1819
Ge	24: 2	He **s** to the senior servant in his household	H606
Ge	24: 6	not take my son back there," Abraham **s**.	H606
Ge	24:17	The servant hurried to meet her and **s**	H606
Ge	24:18	*she* **s**, and quickly lowered the jar to her	H606
Ge	24:19	given him a drink, *she* **s**, "I'll draw water	H606
Ge	24:30	heard Rebekah tell what the man **s** to her,	H1819
Ge	24:31	you who are blessed by the LORD," *he* **s**.	H606
Ge	24:33	set before him, but *he* **s**, "I will not eat	H606
Ge	24:33	"Then tell us," Laban **s**.	H606
Ge	24:34	So *he* **s**, "I am Abraham's servant.	H606
Ge	24:37	swear an oath, and **s**, 'You must not get a	H606
Ge	24:42	I came to the spring today, *I* **s**, 'LORD,	H606
Ge	24:45	drew water, and *I* **s** to her, 'Please give	H606
Ge	24:46	lowered her jar from her shoulder and **s**,	H606
Ge	24:47	"*She* **s**, 'The daughter of Bethuel son of	H606
Ge	24:52	Abraham's servant heard **what** they **s**,	H1821
Ge	24:54	the next morning, *he* **s**, "Send me on my	H606
Ge	24:56	But *he* **s** to them, "Do not detain me, now	H606
Ge	24:57	Then *they* **s**, "Let's call the young woman	H606
Ge	24:58	you go with this man?" "I will go," *she* **s**.	H606
Ge	24:60	And they blessed Rebekah and **s** to her	H606
Ge	25:22	other within her, and *she* **s**, "Why is this	H606
Ge	25:23	The LORD **s** to her, "Two nations are in your	H606
Ge	25:30	He **s** to Jacob, "Quick, let me have some of	H606
Ge	25:32	about to die," Esau **s**. "What good is the	H606
Ge	25:33	But Jacob **s**, "Swear to me first." So he	H606
Ge	26: 2	The LORD appeared to Isaac and **s**, "Do not	H606
Ge	26: 7	him about his wife, *he* **s**, "She is my sister,"	H606
Ge	26: 9	So Abimelek summoned Isaac and **s**, "She	H606
Ge	26:10	Then Abimelek **s**, "What is this you have	H606
Ge	26:16	Then Abimelek **s** to Isaac, "Move away	H606
Ge	26:20	Gerar quarreled with those of Isaac and **s**,	H606
Ge	26:24	That night the LORD appeared to him and **s**	H606
Ge	26:28	was with you; so *we* **s**, 'There ought to be	H606
Ge	26:32	well they had dug. *They* **s**, "We've found	H606
Ge	27: 1	called for Esau his older son and **s** to him,	H606
Ge	27: 2	Isaac **s**, "I am now an old man and don't	H606
Ge	27: 6	Rebekah **s** to her son Jacob, "Look,	H606
Ge	27:11	Jacob **s** to Rebekah his mother, "But my	H606
Ge	27:13	His mother **s** to him, "My son, let the curse	H606
Ge	27:18	He went to his father and **s**, "My father."	H606
Ge	27:19	Jacob **s** to his father, "I am Esau your	H606
Ge	27:21	Then Isaac **s** to Jacob, "Come near so I can	H606
Ge	27:22	who touched him and **s**, "The voice is the	H606
Ge	27:25	Then *he* **s**, "My son, bring me some of your	H606
Ge	27:26	Then his father Isaac **s** to him, "Come here	H606
Ge	27:27	of his clothes, he blessed him and **s**, "Ah,	H606
Ge	27:31	Then *he* **s** to him, "My father, please sit up	H606
Ge	27:33	Isaac trembled violently and **s**, "Who was it	H606
Ge	27:34	a loud and bitter cry and **s** to his father,	H606
Ge	27:35	But *he* **s**, "Your brother came deceitfully	H606
Ge	27:36	Esau **s**, "Isn't he rightly named Jacob? This	H606
Ge	27:38	Esau **s** to his father, "Do you have only one	H606
Ge	27:41	He **s** to himself, "The days of mourning	H606
Ge	27:42	was told **what** her older son Esau had **s**,	H1821
Ge	27:42	her younger son Jacob and **s** to him,	H606
Ge	27:46	Then Rebekah **s** to Isaac, "I'm disgusted	H606
Ge	28:13	it stood the LORD, and *he* **s**: "I am the LORD,	H606
Ge	28:17	He was afraid and **s**, "How awesome is this	H606
Ge	29: 5	*He* **s** to them, "Do you know Laban	H606
Ge	29: 6	*they* **s**, "and here comes his daughter	H606
Ge	29: 7	*he* **s**, "the sun is still high; it is not	H606
Ge	29:14	Then Laban **s** to him, "You are my own	H606
Ge	29:15	Laban **s** to him, "Just because you are a	H606
Ge	29:18	Jacob was in love with Rachel and **s**, "I'll	H606
Ge	29:19	Laban **s**, "It's better that I give her to you	H606
Ge	29:21	Then Jacob **s** to Laban, "Give me my wife	H606
Ge	29:25	So Jacob **s** to Laban, "What is this you	H606
Ge	29:32	him Reuben, for *she* **s**, "It is because the	H606
Ge	29:33	when she gave birth to a son *she* **s**	H606
Ge	29:34	when she gave birth to a son *she* **s**	H606
Ge	29:35	when she gave birth to a son *she* **s**	H606
Ge	30: 1	So *she* **s** to Jacob, "Give me children, or I'll	H606
Ge	30: 2	Jacob became angry with her and **s**, "Am I	H606
Ge	30: 3	Then *she* **s**, "Here is Bilhah, my servant	H606
Ge	30: 6	Then Rachel **s**, "God has vindicated me; he	H606
Ge	30: 8	Then Rachel **s**, "I have had a great struggle	H606
Ge	30:11	Then Leah **s**, "What good fortune!" So she	H606
Ge	30:13	Then Leah **s**, "How happy I am! The women	H606
Ge	30:14	Rachel **s** to Leah, "Please give me some of	H606
Ge	30:15	But *she* **s** to her, "Wasn't it enough that	H606
Ge	30:15	Rachel **s**, "he can sleep with you tonight	H606
Ge	30:16	sleep with me," *she* **s**. "I have hired you	H606
Ge	30:18	Then Leah **s**, "God has rewarded me for	H606
Ge	30:20	Then Leah **s**, "God has presented me with a	H606
Ge	30:23	pregnant and gave birth to a son and **s**,	H606
Ge	30:24	him Joseph, and **s**, "May the LORD add to	H606
Ge	30:25	to Joseph, Jacob **s** to Laban, "Send me on	H606
Ge	30:27	But Laban **s** to him, "If I have found favor in	H606
Ge	30:29	Jacob **s** to him, "You know how I have	H606
Ge	30:34	"Agreed," **s** Laban. "Let it be as you have	H606
Ge	30:34	"Let it be as you have **s**."	H1821
Ge	31: 3	Then the LORD **s** to Jacob, "Go back to the	H606
Ge	31: 5	*He* **s** to them, "I see that your father's	H606
Ge	31: 8	If *he* **s**, 'The speckled ones will be your	H606
Ge	31: 8	and if *he* **s**, 'The streaked ones	H606
Ge	31:11	The angel of God **s** to me in the dream	H606
Ge	31:12	And *he* **s**, 'Look up and see that all the	H606
Ge	31:24	Aramean in a dream at night and **s** to him,	H606
Ge	31:26	Then Laban **s** to Jacob, "What have you	H606
Ge	31:29	last night the God of your father **s** to me,	H606
Ge	31:35	Rachel **s** to her father, "Don't be angry, my	H606
Ge	31:46	He **s** to his relatives, "Gather some stones."	H606
Ge	31:48	Laban **s**, "This heap is a witness between	H606
Ge	31:49	Mizpah, because *he* **s**, "May the LORD keep	H606
Ge	31:51	Laban also **s** to Jacob, "Here is this heap	H606
Ge	32: 2	Jacob saw them, *he* **s**, "This is the camp	H606
Ge	32: 6	returned to Jacob, *they* **s**, "We went to your	H606
Ge	32: 9	you who **s** to me, 'Go back to your	H606
Ge	32:12	But you *have* **s**, 'I will surely make you	H606
Ge	32:16	herd by itself, and **s** to his servants, "Go	H606
Ge	32:26	Then the man **s**, "Let me go, for it is	H606
Ge	32:28	Then the man **s**, "Your name will no longer	H606
Ge	32:29	Jacob **s**, "Please tell me your name."	H8626
Ge	33: 8	"To find favor in your eyes, my lord," *he* **s**.	H606
Ge	33: 9	But Esau **s**, "I already have plenty, my	H606
Ge	33:10	**s** Jacob. "If I have found favor in	H606
Ge	33:12	Then Esau **s**, "Let us be on our way; I'll	H606
Ge	33:13	But Jacob **s** to him, "My lord knows that the	H606
Ge	33:15	Esau **s**, "Then let me leave some of my	H606
Ge	34: 4	And Shechem **s** to his father Hamor, "Get	H606
Ge	34: 8	But Hamor **s** to them, "My son Shechem	H1819
Ge	34:11	Then Shechem **s** to Dinah's father and	H606
Ge	34:14	*They* **s** to them, "We can't do such a thing	H606
Ge	34:19	lost no time in doing what they **s**	H1821
Ge	34:21	toward us," they **s**. "Let them live in our	H606
Ge	34:30	Then Jacob **s** to Simeon and Levi, "You	H606
Ge	35: 1	Then God **s** to Jacob, "Go up to Bethel	H606
Ge	35: 2	So Jacob **s** to his household and to all who	H606
Ge	35:10	God **s** to him, "Your name is Jacob, but you	H606
Ge	35:11	And God **s** to him, "I am God Almighty; be	H606
Ge	35:17	the midwife **s** to her, "Don't despair,	H606
Ge	37: 6	*He* **s** to them, "Listen to this dream I had:	H606
Ge	37: 8	His brothers **s** to him, "Do you intend to	H606
Ge	37: 8	because of his dream and **what** he had **s**.	H1821
Ge	37: 9	*he* **s**, "I had another dream, and	H606
Ge	37:10	his father rebuked him and **s**, "What is this	H606
Ge	37:13	Israel **s** to Joseph, "As you know, your	H606
Ge	37:14	So *he* **s** to him, "Go and see if all is well	H606
Ge	37:19	comes that dreamer!" *they* **s** to each other.	H606
Ge	37:21	"Let's not take his life," *he* **s**.	H606
Ge	37:22	Reuben **s** this to rescue him from them	H606
Ge	37:26	Judah **s** to his brothers, "What will we gain	H606
Ge	37:30	He went back to his brothers and **s**, "The	H606
Ge	37:32	the ornate robe back to their father and **s**,	H606
Ge	37:33	He recognized it and **s**, "It is my son's robe	H606
Ge	37:35	*he* **s**, "I will continue to mourn until I join	H606
Ge	38: 8	Then Judah **s** to Onan, "Sleep with your	H606
Ge	38:11	Judah then **s** to his daughter-in-law Tamar,	H606
Ge	38:16	he went over to her by the roadside and **s**	H606
Ge	38:17	you a young goat from my flock," *he* **s**.	H606
Ge	38:18	*He* **s**, "What pledge should I give you?"	H606
Ge	38:21	been any shrine prostitute here," *they* **s**.	H606
Ge	38:22	So he went back to Judah and **s**, "I didn't	H606
Ge	38:22	the men who lived there **s**, 'There hasn't	H606
Ge	38:23	Then Judah **s**, "Let her keep what she has	H606
Ge	38:24	Judah **s**, "Bring her out and have her	H606
Ge	38:25	by the man who owns these," *she* **s**.	H606
Ge	38:26	Judah recognized them and **s**, "She is	H606
Ge	38:28	scarlet thread and tied it on his wrist and **s**,	H606
Ge	38:29	came out, and *she* **s**, "So this is how you	H606
Ge	39: 7	master's wife took notice of Joseph and **s**,	H606
Ge	39:12	She caught him by his cloak and **s**, "Come	H606
Ge	39:14	*she* **s** to them, "this Hebrew has been	H606
Ge	40: 8	Then Joseph **s** to them, "Do not	H606
Ge	40: 9	*He* **s** to him, "In my dream I saw a vine in	H606
Ge	40:12	it means," Joseph **s** to him. "The three	H606
Ge	40:16	interpretation, *he* **s** to Joseph, "I too had a	H606
Ge	40:18	it means," Joseph **s**. "The three baskets	H6699
Ge	40:22	*had* **s** to them **in** *his* **interpretation**.	H7354
Ge	41: 9	Then the chief cupbearer **s** to Pharaoh	H1819
Ge	41:15	Pharaoh **s** to Joseph, "I had a dream, and	H606
Ge	41:15	But I have heard *it* **s** of you that when you	H606
Ge	41:17	Then Pharaoh **s** to Joseph, "In my dream I	H1819
Ge	41:25	Then Joseph **s** to Pharaoh, "The dreams of	H606
Ge	41:28	"It is just as *I* **s** to Pharaoh: God has	H1819
Ge	41:39	Then Pharaoh **s** to Joseph, "Since God has	H606
Ge	41:41	So Pharaoh **s** to Joseph, "I hereby put you	H606
Ge	41:44	Then Pharaoh **s** to Joseph, "I am Pharaoh	H606
Ge	41:51	Joseph named his firstborn Manasseh and **s**	NDT
Ge	41:52	The second son he named Ephraim and **s**	NDT
Ge	41:54	of famine began, just as Joseph *had* **s**.	H606
Ge	42: 1	grain in Egypt, he **s** to his sons, "Why do	H606
Ge	42: 9	his dreams about them and **s** to them,	H606
Ge	42:12	*he* **s** to them. "You have come to see	H606
Ge	42:14	Joseph **s** to them, "It is just as I told you	H606
Ge	42:18	third day, Joseph **s** to them, "Do this and	H606
Ge	42:21	*They* **s** to one another, "Surely we are	H606
Ge	42:28	has been returned," *he* **s** to his brothers.	H606
Ge	42:28	they turned to each other trembling and **s**,	H606
Ge	42:29	all that had happened to them. *They* **s**,	H606
Ge	42:31	But *we* **s** to him, 'We are honest men; we	H606
Ge	42:33	the man who is lord over the land **s** to us,	H606
Ge	42:36	Their father Jacob **s** to them, "You have	H606
Ge	42:37	Then Reuben **s** to his father, "You may put	H606
Ge	42:38	But Jacob **s**, "My son will not go down	H606
Ge	43: 2	their father **s** to them, "Go back and	H606
Ge	43: 3	But Judah **s** to him, "The man warned us	H606
Ge	43: 5	because the man **s** to us, 'You will not	H606
Ge	43: 8	Then Judah **s** to Israel his father, "Send the	H606
Ge	43:11	Then their father Israel **s** to them, "If it	H606
Ge	43:16	with them, *he* **s** to the steward of his house	H606
Ge	43:20	*they* **s**, "we came down here the first time	H606
Ge	43:23	"It's all right," *he* **s**. "Don't be afraid.	H606
Ge	43:27	and then *he* **s**, "How is your aged	H606
Ge	43:29	And *he* **s**, "God be gracious to you, my	H606
Ge	43:31	controlling himself, **s**, "Serve the food."	H606
Ge	44: 2	his grain." And he did as Joseph **s**.	H1819
Ge	44: 4	from the city when Joseph **s** to his steward,	H606
Ge	44: 7	But *they* **s** to him, "Why does my lord say	H606
Ge	44:10	"Very well, then," *he* **s**, "let it be as you say.	H606
Ge	44:15	Joseph **s** to them, "What is this you have	H606
Ge	44:17	But Joseph **s**, "Far be it from me to do such	H606
Ge	44:18	Then Judah went up to him and **s**: "Pardon	H606
Ge	44:21	"Then *you* **s** to your servants, 'Bring him	H606
Ge	44:22	And *we* **s** to my lord, 'The boy cannot leave	H606
Ge	44:24	we told him **what** my lord had **s**.	H1821
Ge	44:25	"Then our father **s**, 'Go back and buy a	H606
Ge	44:26	But *we* **s**, 'We cannot go down. Only if our	H606
Ge	44:27	"Your servant my father **s** to us, 'You know	H606
Ge	44:28	away from me, and *I* **s**, "He has surely	H606
Ge	44:32	I **s**, 'If I do not bring him back to you, I will	H606
Ge	45: 3	Joseph **s** to his brothers, "I am Joseph! Is	H606
Ge	45: 4	Then Joseph **s** to his brothers, "Come close	H606
Ge	45: 4	they had done so, *he* **s**, "I am your brother	H606
Ge	45:17	Pharaoh **s** to Joseph, "Tell your brothers	H606
Ge	45:24	as they were leaving *he* **s** to them	H606
Ge	45:27	told him everything Joseph *had* **s** to them,	H1819
Ge	45:28	Israel **s**, "I'm convinced! My son Joseph	H606
Ge	46: 2	spoke to Israel in a vision at night and **s**,	H606
Ge	46: 3	God of your father," *he* **s**. "Do not be afraid	H606
Ge	46:30	Israel **s** to Joseph, "Now I am ready to die	H606
Ge	46:31	Then Joseph **s** to his brothers and to his	H606
Ge	47: 4	*They* also **s** to him, "We have come to live	H606
Ge	47: 5	Pharaoh **s** to Joseph, "Your father and your	H606
Ge	47: 9	And Jacob **s** to Pharaoh, "The years of my	H606
Ge	47:15	all Egypt came to Joseph and **s**, "Give us	H606
Ge	47:16	bring your livestock," **s** Joseph. "I will sell	H606
Ge	47:18	they came to him the following year and **s**	H606
Ge	47:23	Joseph **s** to the people, "Now that I have	H606
Ge	47:25	saved our lives," *they* **s**. "May we find favor	H606
Ge	47:29	he called for his son Joseph and **s** to him	H606
Ge	47:30	"I will do as you say," *he* **s**.	H606
Ge	47:31	"Swear to me," *he* **s**. Then Joseph swore to	H606
Ge	48: 3	Jacob **s** to Joseph, "God Almighty	H606
Ge	48: 4	**s** to me, 'I am going to make you	H606
Ge	48: 9	has given me here," Joseph **s** to his father.	H606
Ge	48: 9	Then Israel **s**, "Bring them to me so I may	H606
Ge	48:11	Israel **s** to Joseph, "I never expected to see	H606
Ge	48:15	Then he blessed Joseph and **s**, "May the	H606
Ge	48:18	Joseph **s** to him, "No, my father, this one is	H606
Ge	48:19	But his father refused and **s**, "I know, my	H606
Ge	48:20	He blessed them that day and **s**, "In your	H606
Ge	48:21	Then Israel **s** to Joseph, "I am about to die	H606
Ge	49: 1	Then Jacob called for his sons and **s**	H606
Ge	49:28	is what their father **s** to them when he	H1819
Ge	50: 4	had passed, Joseph **s** to Pharaoh's court	H1819

Ge 50: 5 'My father made me swear an oath and s, "I H606
Ge 50: 6 Pharaoh s, "Go up and bury your father, as H606
Ge 50:11 floor of Atad, they s, "The Egyptians are H606
Ge 50:15 father was dead, they s, "What if Joseph H606
Ge 50:18 "We are your slaves," they s. H606
Ge 50:19 But Joseph s to them, "Don't be afraid. H606
Ge 50:24 Then Joseph s to his brothers, "I am about H606
Ge 50:25 made the Israelites swear an oath and s, H606
Ex 1: 9 he s to his people, "the Israelites have H606
Ex 1:15 The king of Egypt s to the Hebrew H606
Ex 2: 6 "This is one of the Hebrew babies," she s. H606
Ex 2: 9 Pharaoh's daughter s to her, "Take this H606
Ex 2:14 The man s, "Who made you ruler and H606
Ex 3: 4 And Moses s, "Here I am." H606
Ex 3: 5 come any closer," God s. "Take off your H606
Ex 3: 6 Then he s, "I am the God of your father, the H606
Ex 3: 7 The LORD s, "I have indeed seen the misery H606
Ex 3:11 But Moses s to God, "Who am I that I H606
Ex 3:12 And God s, "I will be with you. And this H606
Ex 3:13 Moses s to God, "Suppose I go to the H606
Ex 3:14 God s to Moses, "I AM WHO I AM. This is H606
Ex 3:15 God also s to Moses, "Say to the Israelites H606
Ex 3:16 Isaac and Jacob—appeared to me and s: H606
Ex 4: 2 Then the LORD s to him, "What is that in H606
Ex 4: 3 The LORD s, "Throw it on the ground." H606
Ex 4: 4 Then the LORD s to him, "Reach out your H606
Ex 4: 5 s the LORD, "is so that they may believe that NDT
Ex 4: 6 Then the LORD s, "Put your hand inside your H606
Ex 4: 7 into your cloak," he s. So Moses put his H606
Ex 4: 8 Then the LORD s, "If they do not believe you NDT
Ex 4:10 Moses s to the LORD, "Pardon your servant H606
Ex 4:11 The LORD s to him, "Who gave human H606
Ex 4:13 But Moses s, "Pardon your servant, Lord H606
Ex 4:14 anger burned against Moses and he s, H606
Ex 4:18 to Jethro his father-in-law and s to him, H606
Ex 4:18 Jethro s, "Go, and I wish you H606
Ex 4:19 Now the LORD had s to Moses in Midian H606
Ex 4:21 The LORD s to Moses, "When you return to H606
Ex 4:25 are a bridegroom of blood to me," she s. H606
Ex 4:26 At that time she s "bridegroom of blood," H606
Ex 4:27 The LORD s to Aaron, "Go into the H606
Ex 4:30 them everything the LORD had s to Moses. H1819
Ex 5: 1 Moses and Aaron went to Pharaoh and s, H606
Ex 5: 2 Pharaoh s, "Who is the LORD, that I should H606
Ex 5: 3 Then they s, "The God of the Hebrews has H606
Ex 5: 4 But the king of Egypt s, "Moses and Aaron H606
Ex 5: 5 Then Pharaoh s, "Look, the people of the H606
Ex 5:10 the overseers went out and s to the people, H606
Ex 5:17 Pharaoh s, "Lazy, that's what you are—lazy H606
Ex 5:21 and they s, "May the LORD look on you and H606
Ex 5:22 Moses returned to the LORD and s, "Why H606
Ex 6: 1 Then the LORD s to Moses, "Now you will H606
Ex 6: 2 God also s to Moses, "I am the LORD. H1819
Ex 6:10 Then the LORD s to Moses, H1819
Ex 6:12 But Moses s to the LORD, "If the Israelites H1819
Ex 6:26 this Aaron and Moses to whom the LORD s, H606
Ex 6:29 he s to him, "I am the LORD. Tell Pharaoh H1819
Ex 6:30 But Moses s to the LORD, "Since I speak with H606
Ex 7: 1 Then the LORD s to Moses, "See, I have H606
Ex 7: 8 The LORD s to Moses and Aaron, H606
Ex 7:13 not listen to them, just as the LORD had s. H1819
Ex 7:14 Then the LORD s to Moses, "Pharaoh's heart H606
Ex 7:19 The LORD s to Moses, "Tell Aaron, 'Take H606
Ex 7:22 Moses and Aaron, just as the LORD had s. H1819
Ex 8: 1 Then the LORD s to Moses, "Go to Pharaoh H606
Ex 8: 5 Then the LORD s to Moses, "Tell Aaron H606
Ex 8: 8 summoned Moses and Aaron and s, H606
Ex 8: 9 Moses s to Pharaoh, "I leave to you the H606
Ex 8:10 "Tomorrow," Pharaoh s. Moses replied, "It H606
Ex 8:15 Moses and Aaron, just as the LORD had s. H1819
Ex 8:16 Then the LORD s to Moses, "Tell Aaron H606
Ex 8:19 the magicians s to Pharaoh, "This is the H606
Ex 8:19 would not listen, just as the LORD had s. H1819
Ex 8:20 Then the LORD s to Moses, "Get up early in H606
Ex 8:25 summoned Moses and Aaron and s, H606
Ex 8:26 But Moses s, "That would not be right. H606
Ex 8:28 Pharaoh s, "I will let you go to offer H606
Ex 9: 1 Then the LORD s to Moses, "Go to Pharaoh H606
Ex 9: 5 The LORD set a time and s, "Tomorrow the H606
Ex 9: 8 Then the LORD s to Moses and Aaron, "Take H606
Ex 9:12 just as the LORD had s to Moses. H1819
Ex 9:13 Then the LORD s to Moses, "Get up early in H606
Ex 9:22 Then the LORD s to Moses, "Stretch out your H606
Ex 9:27 I have sinned," he s to them. "The LORD H606
Ex 9:35 just as the LORD had s through Moses. H1819
Ex 10: 1 Then the LORD s to Moses, "Go to Pharaoh H606
Ex 10: 3 Aaron went to Pharaoh and s to him, H606
Ex 10: 7 Pharaoh's officials s to him, "How long will H606
Ex 10: 8 the LORD your God," he s. "But tell me who H606
Ex 10:10 Pharaoh s, "The LORD be with you—if I let H606
Ex 10:12 And the LORD s to Moses, "Stretch out your H606
Ex 10:16 summoned Moses and Aaron and s, H606
Ex 10:21 Then the LORD s to Moses, "Stretch out your H606
Ex 10:24 Then Pharaoh summoned Moses and s H606
Ex 10:25 But Moses s, "You must allow us to have H606
Ex 10:28 Pharaoh s to Moses, "Get out of my sight H606
Ex 11: 1 Now the LORD had s to Moses, "I will bring H606
Ex 11: 4 So Moses s, "This is what the LORD says H606
Ex 11: 9 The LORD had s to Moses, "Pharaoh will H606
Ex 12: 1 The LORD s to Moses and Aaron in Egypt, H606
Ex 12:21 all the elders of Israel and s to them, H606
Ex 12:31 summoned Moses and Aaron and s, H606
Ex 12:32 flocks and herds, as you have s, and go. H1819
Ex 12:33 "For otherwise," they s, "we will all die!" H606
Ex 12:43 The LORD s to Moses and Aaron, "These are H606
Ex 13: 1 The LORD s to Moses, H1819
Ex 13: 3 Then Moses s to the people H606
Ex 13:17 For God s, "If they face war, they might H606
Ex 13:19 He had s, "God will surely come to your aid H606
Ex 14: 1 Then the LORD s to Moses, H1819
Ex 14: 5 changed their minds about them and s, H606
Ex 14:11 They s to Moses, "Was it because there H606
Ex 14:15 Then the LORD s to Moses, "Why are you H606
Ex 14:25 And the Egyptians s, "Let's get away from H606
Ex 14:26 Then the LORD s to Moses, "Stretch out your H606
Ex 15:26 He s, "If you listen carefully to the LORD H606
Ex 16: 3 The Israelites s to them, "If only we had H606
Ex 16: 4 Then the LORD s to Moses, "I will rain down H606
Ex 16: 6 So Moses and Aaron s to all the Israelites H606
Ex 16: 8 Moses also s, "You will know that it was the H606
Ex 16:11 The LORD s to Moses, H1819
Ex 16:15 Israelites saw it, they s to each other H606
Ex 16:15 Moses s to them, "It is the bread the LORD H606
Ex 16:19 Then Moses s to them, "No one is to keep H606
Ex 16:23 He s to them, "This is what the LORD H606
Ex 16:25 Moses s, "because today is a sabbath to H606
Ex 16:28 Then the LORD s to Moses, "How long will H606
Ex 16:32 Moses s, "This is what the LORD has H606
Ex 16:33 So Moses s to Aaron, "Take a jar and put H606
Ex 17: 2 So they quarreled with Moses and s, "Give H606
Ex 17: 3 They s, "Why did you bring us up out of H606
Ex 17: 9 Moses s to Joshua, "Choose some of our H606
Ex 17:14 Then the LORD s to Moses, "Write this on a H606
Ex 17:16 He s, "Because hands were lifted up H606
Ex 18: 3 Gershom, for Moses s, "I have become a H606
Ex 18: 4 for he s, "My father's God was NDT
Ex 18:10 He s, "Praise be to the LORD, who rescued H606
Ex 18:14 the people, he s, "What is this you H606
Ex 18:24 his father-in-law and did everything he s. H606
Ex 19: 3 called to him from the mountain and s, H606
Ex 19: 8 "We will do everything the LORD has s." H1819
Ex 19: 9 The LORD s to Moses, "I am going to come H606
Ex 19: 9 told the LORD what the people had s. H1821
Ex 19:10 And the LORD s to Moses, "Go to the people H606
Ex 19:15 Then he s to the people, "Prepare H606
Ex 19:21 the LORD s to him, "Go down and warn H606
Ex 19:23 Moses s to the LORD, "The people cannot H606
Ex 20:19 s to Moses, "Speak to us yourself and H606
Ex 20:20 Moses s to the people, "Do not be afraid H606
Ex 20:22 Then the LORD s to Moses, "Tell the H606
Ex 23:13 "Be careful to do everything I have s to you H606
Ex 24: 1 Then the LORD s to Moses, "Come up to the H606
Ex 24: 3 "Everything the LORD has s we will do." H1819
Ex 24: 4 wrote down everything the LORD had s. H1821
Ex 24: 7 "We will do everything the LORD has s; we H1819
Ex 24: 8 sprinkled it on the people and s, "This is H606
Ex 24:12 The LORD s to Moses, "Come up to me on H606
Ex 24:14 He s to the elders, "Wait here for us until H606
Ex 25: 1 The LORD s to Moses, H1819
Ex 30:11 Then the LORD s to Moses, H1819
Ex 30:17 Then the LORD s to Moses, H1819
Ex 30:22 Then the LORD s to Moses, H1819
Ex 30:34 Then the LORD s to Moses, "Take fragrant H606
Ex 31: 1 Then the LORD s to Moses, H1819
Ex 31:12 Then the LORD s to Moses, H606
Ex 32: 1 they gathered around Aaron and s, "Come, H606
Ex 32: 4 Then they s, "These are your gods, Israel H606
Ex 32: 7 Then the LORD s to Moses, "Go down H1819
Ex 32: 8 down to it and sacrificed to it and have s, H606
Ex 32: 9 the LORD s to Moses, "and they are a H606
Ex 32:11 he s, "why should your anger burn against H606
Ex 32:17 people shouting, he s to Moses, "There is H606
Ex 32:21 He s to Aaron, "What did these people do H606
Ex 32:23 They s to me, 'Make us gods who will go H606
Ex 32:26 stood at the entrance to the camp and s, H606
Ex 32:27 Then he s to them, "This is what the LORD H606
Ex 32:29 Then Moses s, "You have been set apart to H606
Ex 32:30 The next day Moses s to the people, "You H606
Ex 32:31 So Moses went back to the LORD and s, "Oh H606
Ex 33: 1 Then the LORD s to Moses, "Leave this H1819
Ex 33: 5 For the LORD had s to Moses, "Tell the H606
Ex 33:12 Moses s to the LORD, "You have been H606
Ex 33:12 You have s, 'I know you by name and you H606
Ex 33:15 Then Moses s to him, "If your Presence H606
Ex 33:17 And the LORD s to Moses, "I will do the very H606
Ex 33:18 Then Moses s, "Now show me your glory." H606
Ex 33:19 And the LORD s, "I will cause all my H606
Ex 33:20 he s, "you cannot see my face, for no H606
Ex 33:21 Then the LORD s, "There is a place near me H606
Ex 34: 1 The LORD s to Moses, "Chisel out two stone H606
Ex 34: 9 he s, "if I have found favor in your H606
Ex 34:10 Then the LORD s: "I am making a covenant H606
Ex 34:27 Then the LORD s to Moses, "Write down H606
Ex 35: 1 whole Israelite community and s to them, H606
Ex 35: 4 Moses s to the whole Israelite community H606
Ex 35:30 Then Moses s to the Israelites, "See, the H606
Ex 36: 5 s to Moses, "The people are bringing H606
Ex 40: 1 Then the LORD s to Moses: H1819
Lev 1: 1 to him from the tent of meeting. He s, H606
Lev 4: 1 The LORD s to Moses, H1819
Lev 5:14 The LORD s to Moses: H1819
Lev 6: 1 The LORD s to Moses: H1819
Lev 6: 8 The LORD s to Moses: H1819
Lev 6:19 The LORD also s to Moses, H1819
Lev 6:24 The LORD s to Moses, H1819
Lev 7:22 The LORD s to Moses, H1819
Lev 7:28 The LORD s to Moses, H1819
Lev 8: 1 The LORD s to Moses, H1819
Lev 8: 5 Moses s to the assembly, "This is what the H606
Lev 8:31 Moses then s to Aaron and his sons, "Cook H606
Lev 9: 2 He s to Aaron, "Take a bull calf for your sin H606
Lev 9: 6 Then Moses s, "This is what the LORD has H606
Lev 9: 7 Moses s to Aaron, "Come to the altar and H606
Lev 10: 3 Moses then s to Aaron, "This is what the H606
Lev 10: 3 "This is what the LORD spoke of when he s: H606
Lev 10: 4 uncle Uzziel, and s to them, "Come here; H606
Lev 10: 6 Then Moses s to Aaron and his sons H606
Lev 10: 7 So they did as Moses s. H1821
Lev 10: 8 Then the LORD s to Aaron, H1819
Lev 10:12 Moses s to Aaron and his remaining sons H1819
Lev 11: 1 The LORD s to Moses and Aaron, H1819
Lev 12: 1 The LORD s to Moses, H1819
Lev 13: 1 The LORD s to Moses and Aaron, H1819
Lev 14: 1 The LORD s to Moses, H1819
Lev 14:33 The LORD s to Moses and Aaron, H1819
Lev 15: 1 The LORD s to Moses and Aaron, H1819
Lev 16: 2 The LORD s to Moses: "Tell your brother H606
Lev 17: 1 The LORD s to Moses, H1819
Lev 17:14 That is why I have s to the Israelites, "You H606
Lev 18: 1 The LORD s to Moses, H1819
Lev 19: 1 The LORD s to Moses, H1819
Lev 20: 1 The LORD s to Moses, H1819
Lev 20:24 But I s to you, "You will possess their land; H606
Lev 21: 1 The LORD s to Moses, "Speak to the priests H606
Lev 21:16 The LORD s to Moses, H1819
Lev 22: 1 The LORD s to Moses, H1819
Lev 22:17 The LORD s to Moses, H1819
Lev 22:26 The LORD s to Moses, H1819
Lev 23: 1 The LORD s to Moses, H1819
Lev 23: 9 The LORD s to Moses, H1819
Lev 23:23 The LORD s to Moses, H1819
Lev 23:26 The LORD s to Moses, H1819
Lev 23:33 The LORD s to Moses, H1819
Lev 24: 1 The LORD s to Moses, H1819
Lev 24:13 Then the LORD s to Moses: H1819
Lev 25: 1 The LORD s to Moses at Mount Sinai, H1819
Lev 27: 1 The LORD s to Moses, H1819
Nu 1: 1 the Israelites came out of Egypt. He s: H606
Nu 1:48 The LORD had s to Moses: H1819
Nu 2: 1 The LORD s to Moses and Aaron: H1819
Nu 3: 5 The LORD s to Moses, H1819
Nu 3:11 The LORD also s to Moses, H1819
Nu 3:14 The LORD s to Moses in the Desert of Sinai, H1819
Nu 3:40 The LORD s to Moses, "Count all the H606
Nu 3:44 The LORD also s to Moses, H1819
Nu 4: 1 The LORD s to Moses and Aaron: H1819
Nu 4:17 The LORD s to Moses and Aaron, H1819
Nu 4:21 The LORD s to Moses, H1819
Nu 5: 1 The LORD s to Moses, H1819
Nu 5: 5 The LORD s to Moses, H1819
Nu 5:11 Then the LORD s to Moses, H1819
Nu 6: 1 The LORD s to Moses, H1819
Nu 6:22 The LORD s to Moses, H1819
Nu 7: 4 The LORD s to Moses, H606
Nu 7:11 For the LORD had s to Moses, "Each day H606
Nu 8: 1 The LORD s to Moses, H1819
Nu 8: 5 The LORD s to Moses: H1819
Nu 8:23 The LORD s to Moses, H1819
Nu 9: 1 year after they came out of Egypt. He s, H606
Nu 9: 7 s to Moses, "We have become unclean H606
Nu 9: 9 Then the LORD s to Moses, H1819
Nu 10: 1 The LORD s to Moses: H1819
Nu 10:29 Now Moses s to Hobab son of Reuel the H606
Nu 10:29 out for the place about which the LORD s, H606
Nu 10:31 But Moses s, "Please do not leave us. H606
Nu 10:35 the ark set out, Moses s, "Rise up, H606
Nu 10:36 it came to rest, he s, "Return, LORD, H606
Nu 11: 4 again the Israelites started wailing and s, H606
Nu 11:16 The LORD s to Moses: "Bring me seventy of H606
Nu 11:21 But Moses s, "Here I am among six H606
Nu 11:24 told the people what the LORD had s. H1821
Nu 11:28 aide since youth, spoke up and s, "Moses, H606
Nu 12: 4 At once the LORD s to Moses, Aaron and H606
Nu 12: 6 he s, "Listen to my words: "When there is a H606
Nu 12:11 he s to Moses, "Please, my lord, I ask H606
Nu 13: 1 The LORD s to Moses, H1819
Nu 13:17 to explore Canaan, he s, "Go up through H606
Nu 13:30 silenced the people before Moses and s, H606
Nu 13:31 But the men who had gone up with him s H606
Nu 13:32 They s, "The land we explored devours H606
Nu 14: 2 the whole assembly s to them, "If only H606
Nu 14: 4 And they s to each other, "We should H606
Nu 14: 7 s to the entire Israelite assembly, "The H606
Nu 14:11 The LORD s to Moses, "How long will these H606
Nu 14:13 Moses s to the LORD, "Then the Egyptians H606
Nu 14:26 The LORD s to Moses and Aaron: H1819
Nu 14:31 your children that you s would be taken as H606
Nu 14:41 But Moses s, "Why are you disobeying the H606
Nu 15: 1 The LORD s to Moses, H1819
Nu 15:17 The LORD s to Moses, H1819
Nu 15:35 Then the LORD s to Moses, "The man must H606
Nu 15:37 The LORD s to Moses, H606
Nu 16: 3 to oppose Moses and Aaron and s to them, H606
Nu 16: 5 Then he s to Korah and all his followers H1819
Nu 16: 8 Moses also s to Korah, "Now listen, you H606
Nu 16:12 But they s, "We will not H606

Nu 16:15 became very angry and s to the LORD, H606
Nu 16:16 Moses s to Korah, "You and all your H606
Nu 16:20 The LORD s to Moses and Aaron, H1819
Nu 16:23 Then the LORD s to Moses, H1819
Nu 16:28 Then Moses s, "This is how you will know H606
Nu 16:36 The LORD s to Moses, H1819
Nu 16:41 have killed the LORD's people," they s. H606
Nu 16:44 the LORD s to Moses, H1819
Nu 16:46 Then Moses s to Aaron, "Take your censer H606
Nu 16:47 So Aaron did as Moses s, and ran into the H1819
Nu 17: 1 The LORD s to Moses, H1819
Nu 17:10 The LORD s to Moses, "Put back Aaron's H606
Nu 17:12 The Israelites s to Moses, "We will die! We H606
Nu 18: 1 The LORD s to Aaron, "You, your sons and H606
Nu 18: 8 Then the LORD s to Aaron, "I myself have H1819
Nu 18:20 The LORD s to Aaron, "You will have no H606
Nu 18:24 That is why I s concerning them H606
Nu 18:25 The LORD s to Moses, H1819
Nu 19: 1 The LORD s to Moses and Aaron: H1819
Nu 20: 3 They quarreled with Moses and s, "If only H606
Nu 20: 7 The LORD s to Moses, H1819
Nu 20:10 in front of the rock and Moses s to them, H606
Nu 20:12 But the LORD s to Moses and Aaron H606
Nu 20:23 of Edom, the LORD s to Moses and Aaron, H606
Nu 21: 5 against Moses, and s, "Why have you NDT
Nu 21: 7 The people came to Moses and s, "We H606
Nu 21: 8 The LORD s to Moses, "Make a snake and H606
Nu 21:16 the well where the LORD s to Moses H606
Nu 21:34 The LORD s to Moses, "Do not be afraid of H606
Nu 22: 4 The Moabites s to the elders of Midian H606
Nu 22: 5 Balak s: "A people has come H606
Nu 22: 7 Balaam, they told him **what** Balak had s. H1821
Nu 22: 8 Balaam s to them, "and I will report back H606
Nu 22:10 Balaam s to God, "Balak son of Zippor H606
Nu 22:12 But God s to Balaam, "Do not go with them H606
Nu 22:13 Balaam got up and s to Balak's officials, H606
Nu 22:14 Moabite officials returned to Balak and s, H606
Nu 22:16 They came to Balaam and s: "This is what H606
Nu 22:20 That night God came to Balaam and s H606
Nu 22:28 donkey's mouth, and it s to Balaam, "What H606
Nu 22:30 The donkey s to Balaam, "Am I not your H606
Nu 22:30 the habit of doing this to you?" "No," he s. H606
Nu 22:34 Balaam s to the angel of the LORD, "I have H606
Nu 22:35 The angel of the LORD s to Balaam, "Go H606
Nu 22:37 Balak s to Balaam, "Did I not send you an H606
Nu 23: 1 Balaam s, "Build me seven altars here, and H606
Nu 23: 2 Balak did as Balaam s, and the two of H1819
Nu 23: 3 Then Balaam s to Balak, "Stay here beside H606
Nu 23: 4 with him, and Balaam s, "I have prepared H606
Nu 23: 5 LORD put a word in Balaam's mouth and s, H606
Nu 23: 7 he s, 'curse Jacob for me; come NDT
Nu 23:11 Balak s to Balaam, "What have you done H606
Nu 23:13 Then Balak s to him, "Come with me to H606
Nu 23:15 Balaam s to Balak, "Stay here beside your H606
Nu 23:16 Balaam and put a word in his mouth and s, H606
Nu 23:23 It will now **be** s of Jacob and of Israel, 'See H606
Nu 23:25 Then Balak s to Balaam, "Neither curse H606
Nu 23:27 Then Balak s to Balaam, "Come, let me H606
Nu 23:29 Balaam s, "Build me seven altars here, and H606
Nu 23:30 Balak did as Balaam had s, and offered a H606
Nu 24:10 He struck his hands together and s to him H606
Nu 24:11 I s I would reward you handsomely, but the H606
Nu 25: 4 The LORD s to Moses, "Take all the leaders H606
Nu 25: 5 So Moses s to Israel's judges, "Each of you H606
Nu 25:10 The LORD s to Moses, H1819
Nu 25:16 The LORD s to Moses, H1819
Nu 26: 1 the plague the LORD s to Moses and Eleazar H606
Nu 26: 3 Eleazar the priest spoke with them and s, H606
Nu 26:52 The LORD s to Moses, H1819
Nu 27: 2 the entrance to the tent of meeting and s, H606
Nu 27: 6 the LORD s to him, H606
Nu 27:12 Then the LORD s to Moses, "Go up this H606
Nu 27:15 Moses s to the LORD, H1819
Nu 27:18 So the LORD s to Moses, "Take Joshua son H606
Nu 28: 1 The LORD s to Moses, H1819
Nu 30: 1 Moses s to the heads of the tribes of H1819
Nu 30: 2 but must do everything he s. H3655+4946+7023
Nu 31: 1 The LORD s to Moses, H1819
Nu 31: 3 So Moses s to the people, "Arm some of H1819
Nu 31:21 Eleazar the priest s to the soldiers who had H606
Nu 31:25 The LORD s to Moses, H606
Nu 31:49 s to him, "Your servants have counted H606
Nu 32: 2 to the leaders of the community, and s, H606
Nu 32: 5 they s, "let this land be given to your H606
Nu 32: 6 Moses s to the Gadites and Reubenites H606
Nu 32:16 Then they came up to him and s, "We H606
Nu 32:20 Then Moses s to them, "If you will do this H606
Nu 32:25 The Gadites and Reubenites s to Moses H606
Nu 32:29 He s to them, "If the Gadites and H606
Nu 32:31 "Your servants will do what the LORD has s. H1819
Nu 33:50 across from Jericho the LORD s to Moses, H1819
Nu 34: 1 The LORD s to Moses, H1819
Nu 34:16 The LORD s to Moses, H1819
Nu 35: 1 across from Jericho, the LORD s to Moses, H1819
Nu 35: 9 Then the LORD s to Moses: H1819
Nu 36: 2 They s, "When the LORD commanded my H606
Dt 1: 6 The LORD our God s to us at Horeb, "You H1819
Dt 1: 9 At that time I s to you, "You are too heavy H606
Dt 1:20 Then I s to you, "You have reached the hill H606
Dt 1:22 Then all of you came to me and s, "Let us H606
Dt 1:27 You grumbled in your tents and s, "The LORD H606
Dt 1:29 Then I s to you, "Do not be terrified; do not H606
Dt 1:34 When the LORD heard **what** you s H7754+1821
Dt 1:37 the LORD became angry with me also and s, H606
Dt 1:39 the little ones that you s would be taken H606
Dt 1:42 But the LORD s to me, "Tell them, 'Do not H606
Dt 2: 2 Then the LORD s to me, H606
Dt 2: 9 Then the LORD s to me, "Do not harass the H606
Dt 2:13 And the LORD s, "Now get up and cross the NDT
Dt 2:17 the LORD s to me, H1819
Dt 2:31 The LORD s to me, "See, I have begun to H606
Dt 3: 2 The LORD s to me, "Do not be afraid of him H606
Dt 3:26 enough," the LORD s. "Do not speak to me H606
Dt 4:10 at Horeb, when he s to me, "Assemble the H606
Dt 5: 1 Moses summoned all Israel and s: Hear H606
Dt 5: 5 did not go up the mountain.) And he s: H606
Dt 5:24 And you s, "The LORD our God has shown H606
Dt 5:28 and the LORD s to me, "I have heard H606
Dt 5:28 "I have heard what this people s to you. H1819
Dt 5:28 Everything they s was good. H1819
Dt 6:19 your enemies before you, as the LORD s. H1819
Dt 9: 2 You know about them and have heard it s NDT
Dt 9:13 And the LORD s to me, "I have seen this H606
Dt 9:23 from Kadesh Barnea, he s, "Go up and take H606
Dt 9:25 because the LORD had s he would destroy H606
Dt 9:26 I prayed to the LORD and s, "Sovereign LORD H606
Dt 10: 1 At that time the LORD s to me, "Chisel out H606
Dt 10:11 the LORD s to me, "and lead the people on H606
Dt 13:12 If you hear it s about one of the towns the H606
Dt 18:16 on the day of the assembly when you s, H606
Dt 18:17 The LORD s to me: "What they say is good. H606
Dt 22:17 Now he has slandered her and s, 'I did not H606
Dt 27: 9 the Levitical priests s to all Israel, H1819
Dt 28:68 Egypt on a journey I s you should never H606
Dt 29: 2 summoned all the Israelites and s to them: H606
Dt 31: 2 The LORD has s to me, 'You shall not cross H606
Dt 31: 3 will cross over ahead of you, as the LORD s. H1819
Dt 31: 7 summoned Joshua and s to him in the H606
Dt 31:14 The LORD s to Moses, "Now the day of your H606
Dt 31:16 And the LORD s to Moses: "You are going to H606
Dt 32:20 my face from them," he s, "and see what H606
Dt 32:26 I s I would scatter them and erase their H606
Dt 32:46 he s to them, "Take to heart all the words I H606
Dt 33: 2 He s: "The LORD came from Sinai and H606
Dt 33: 7 And this he s about Judah: "Hear, LORD, the H606
Dt 33: 8 About Levi he s: "Your Thummim and Urim H606
Dt 33: 9 He s of his father and mother, 'I have no H606
Dt 33:12 About Benjamin he s: "Let the beloved of H606
Dt 33:13 About Joseph he s: "May the LORD bless his H606
Dt 33:18 About Zebulun he s: "Rejoice, Zebulun, in H606
Dt 33:20 About Gad he s: "Blessed is he who H606
Dt 33:22 About Dan he s: "Dan is a lion's cub H606
Dt 33:23 About Naphtali he s: "Naphtali is H606
Dt 33:24 About Asher he s: "Most blessed of sons is H606
Dt 34: 4 Then the LORD s to him, "This is the land I H606
Dt 34: 4 Isaac and Jacob when I s, 'I will give it to H606
Dt 34: 5 died there in Moab, as the LORD had s. H7023
Jos 1: 1 the LORD, the LORD s to Joshua son of Nun H606
Jos 1:12 the half-tribe of Manasseh, Joshua s, H606
Jos 1:13 the servant of the LORD gave you after he s, H606
Jos 2: 1 over the land," he s, "especially Jericho." H606
Jos 2: 4 She s, "Yes, the men came to me, but I did H606
Jos 2: 9 s to them, "I know that the LORD has H606
Jos 2:16 She s to them, "Go to the hills so the H606
Jos 2:17 Now the men had s to her, "This oath you H606
Jos 2:24 They s to Joshua, "The LORD has surely H606
Jos 3: 6 Joshua s to the priests, "Take up the ark of H606
Jos 3: 7 And the LORD s to Joshua, "Today I will H606
Jos 3: 9 Joshua s to the Israelites, "Come here and H606
Jos 4: 1 crossing the Jordan, the LORD s to Joshua, H606
Jos 4: 5 s to them, "Go over before the ark of H606
Jos 4:15 Then the LORD s to Joshua, H606
Jos 4:21 He s to the Israelites, "In the future when H606
Jos 5: 2 At that time the LORD s to Joshua, "Make H606
Jos 5: 9 Then the LORD s to Joshua, "Today I have H606
Jos 6: 2 Then the LORD s to Joshua, "See, I have H606
Jos 6: 6 of Nun called the priests and s to them, H606
Jos 6:22 Joshua s to the two men who had spied H606
Jos 7: 3 to Joshua, they s, "Not all the army H606
Jos 7: 7 And Joshua s, "Alas, Sovereign LORD, why H606
Jos 7:10 The LORD s to Joshua, "Stand up! What are H606
Jos 7:19 Then Joshua s to Achan, "My son, give H606
Jos 7:25 Joshua s, "Why have you brought this H606
Jos 8: 1 Then the LORD s to Joshua, "Do not be H606
Jos 8:18 Then the LORD s to Joshua, "Hold out H606
Jos 9: 6 the camp at Gilgal and s to him and the H606
Jos 9: 7 The Israelites s to the Hivites, "But perhaps H606
Jos 9: 8 are your servants," they s to Joshua. H606
Jos 9:11 all those living in our country s to us, H606
Jos 9:22 Joshua summoned the Gibeonites and s, H1819
Jos 10: 4 he s, "because it has made peace with H606
Jos 10: 8 The LORD s to Joshua, "Do not be afraid of H606
Jos 10:12 Joshua s to the LORD in the presence of H1819
Jos 10:18 he s, "Roll large rocks up to the mouth of H606
Jos 10:22 Joshua s, "Open the mouth of the cave H606
Jos 10:24 the men of Israel and s to the army H606
Jos 10:25 Joshua s to them, "Do not be afraid; do not H606
Jos 11: 6 The LORD s to Joshua, "Do not be afraid of H606
Jos 13: 1 grown old, the LORD s to him, "You are now H606
Jos 14: 6 son of Jephunneh the Kenizzite s to him, H606
Jos 14: 6 know what the LORD s to Moses the man H1819
Jos 14:10 years since the time he s this to Moses, H1819
Jos 14:12 I will drive them out just as he s. H1819
Jos 15:16 And Caleb s, "I will give my daughter Aksah H606
Jos 17: 4 the leaders and s, "The LORD H606
Jos 17:14 The people of Joseph s to Joshua, "Why H1819
Jos 17:17 But Joshua s to the tribes of Joseph—to H606
Jos 18: 3 So Joshua s to the Israelites: "How long H606
Jos 20: 1 Then the LORD s to Joshua: H1819
Jos 21: 2 at Shiloh in Canaan and s to them, "The H1819
Jos 22: 2 s to them, "You have done all that H606
Jos 22:15 half-tribe of Manasseh—they s to them: H1819
Jos 22:26 "That is why we s, 'Let us get ready and H606
Jos 22:28 "And we s, 'If they ever say this to us, or to H606
Jos 22:31 the priest, s to Reuben, Gad and Manasseh H606
Jos 23: 2 judges and officials—and s to them: H606
Jos 24: 2 Joshua s to all the people, "This is what H606
Jos 24:19 Joshua s to the people, "You are not able H606
Jos 24:21 But the people s to Joshua, "No! We will H606
Jos 24:22 Then Joshua s, "You are witnesses against H606
Jos 24:23 s Joshua, "throw away the foreign gods NDT
Jos 24:24 And the people s to Joshua, "We will serve H606
Jos 24:27 he s to all the people. "This stone H606
Jos 24:27 heard all the words the LORD has s to us. H1819
Jdg 1: 3 The men of Judah then s to the Simeonites H606
Jdg 1: 7 Then Adoni-Bezek s, "Seventy kings with H606
Jdg 1:12 And Caleb s, "I will give my daughter H606
Jdg 1:24 coming out of the city and they s to him, H606
Jdg 2: 1 LORD went up from Gilgal to Bokim and s, H606
Jdg 2: 1 I s, 'I will never break my covenant with you H606
Jdg 2: 3 And I have also s, 'I will not drive them out H606
Jdg 2:20 the LORD was very angry with Israel and s, H606
Jdg 3:19 he himself went back to Eglon and s, H606
Jdg 3:19 The king s to his attendants H606
Jdg 3:20 in the upper room of his palace and s, H606
Jdg 3:24 They s, "He must be relieving himself in H606
Jdg 4: 6 from Kedesh in Naphtali and s to him, H606
Jdg 4: 8 Barak s to her, "If you go with me, I will go H606
Jdg 4: 9 I will go with you," s Deborah. "But H606
Jdg 4:14 Then Deborah s to Barak, "Go! This is the H606
Jdg 4:18 Jael went out to meet Sisera and s to him H606
Jdg 4:19 "I'm thirsty," he s. "Please give me some H606
Jdg 4:22 she s, "I will show you the man you're H606
Jdg 5:23 'Curse Meroz,' s the angel of the LORD H606
Jdg 6: 8 them a prophet, who s, "This is what the H606
Jdg 6:10 I s to you, 'I am the LORD your God; do not H606
Jdg 6:12 to Gideon, he s, "The LORD is with H606
Jdg 6:13 our ancestors told us about when they s, H606
Jdg 6:14 The LORD turned to him and s, "Go in the H606
Jdg 6:18 the LORD s, "I will wait until you return." H606
Jdg 6:20 The angel of God s to him, "Take the meat H606
Jdg 6:23 But the LORD s to him, "Peace! Do not be H606
Jdg 6:25 That same night the LORD s to him, "Take H606
Jdg 6:36 Gideon s to God, "If you will save Israel by H606
Jdg 6:37 you will save Israel by my hand, as you s." H1819
Jdg 6:39 Then Gideon s to God, "Do not be angry H606
Jdg 7: 2 The LORD s to Gideon, "You have too many H606
Jdg 7: 4 But the LORD s to Gideon, "There are still H606
Jdg 7: 7 The LORD s to Gideon, "With the three H606
Jdg 7: 9 During that night the LORD s to Gideon, "Get H606
Jdg 8: 5 He s to the men of Sukkoth, "Give my troops H606
Jdg 8: 6 But the officials of Sukkoth s, "Do you H606
Jdg 8: 9 So he s to the men of Peniel, "When I H606
Jdg 8:15 Then Gideon came and s to the men of H606
Jdg 8:20 to Jether, his oldest son, he s, "Kill them!" H606
Jdg 8:21 Zebah and Zalmunna s, "Come, do it H606
Jdg 8:22 The Israelites s to Gideon, "Rule over us H606
Jdg 8:24 And he s, "I do have one request, that each H606
Jdg 9: 1 in Shechem and s to them and to all his H1819
Jdg 9: 3 Abimelek, for they s, "He is related to H606
Jdg 9: 8 king for themselves. They s to the olive tree H606
Jdg 9:10 the trees s to the fig tree, 'Come and H606
Jdg 9:12 "Then the trees s to the vine, 'Come and H606
Jdg 9:14 "Finally all the trees s to the thornbush H606
Jdg 9:15 "The thornbush s to the trees, 'If you really H606
Jdg 9:28 Then Gaal son of Ebed s, "Who is H606
Jdg 9:30 of the city heard **what** Gaal son of Ebed s, H1821
Jdg 9:36 When Gaal saw them, he s to Zebul, "Look, H606
Jdg 9:38 Then Zebul s to him, "Where is your big H606
Jdg 9:38 big talk now, you who s, 'Who is Abimelek H606
Jdg 10:15 But the Israelites s to the LORD, "We have H606
Jdg 10:18 of the people of Gilead s to each other, H606
Jdg 11: 2 they s, "because you are the son of H606
Jdg 11: 6 they s, "be our commander, so we H606
Jdg 11: 7 Jephthah s to them, "Didn't you hate me H606
Jdg 11: 8 The elders of Gilead s to him H606
Jdg 11:19 in Heshbon, and s to him, 'Let us pass H606
Jdg 11:37 this one request," she s. "Give me two H606
Jdg 11:38 "You may go," he s. And he let her go H606
Jdg 12: 1 They s to Jephthah, "Why did you go to H606
Jdg 12: 4 them down because the Ephraimites had s, H606
Jdg 12: 5 whenever a survivor of Ephraim s, "Let H606
Jdg 12: 6 they s, "All right, say 'Shibboleth.'" If he H606
Jdg 12: 6 If he s, "Sibboleth," because he could H606
Jdg 13: 3 angel of the LORD appeared to her and s, H606
Jdg 13: 7 But he s to me, 'You will become pregnant H606
Jdg 13:11 came to the man, he s, "Are you the man H606
Jdg 13:11 man who talked to my wife?" "I am," he s. H606
Jdg 13:15 Manoah s to the angel of the LORD, "We H606
Jdg 13:22 doomed to die!" he s to his wife. "We have H606
Jdg 14: 2 he returned, he s to his father and mother H5583
Jdg 14: 3 But Samson s to his father, "Get her for H606
Jdg 14:12 me tell you a riddle," Samson s to them. H606
Jdg 14:13 "Tell us your riddle," they s. "Let's hear it." H606
Jdg 14:15 On the fourth day, they s to Samson's wife H606
Jdg 14:18 seventh day the men of the town s to him, H606

S

Book	Ref	Context	Number
Jdg	14:18	Samson s to them, “If you had not plowed	H606
Jdg	15: 1	to visit his wife. He s, “I’m going to my	H606
Jdg	15: 2	you hated her,” he s, “that I gave her to	H606
Jdg	15: 3	Samson s to them, “This time I have a right	H606
Jdg	15: 7	Samson s to them, “Since you’ve acted like	H606
Jdg	15:11	cave in the rock of Etam and s to Samson,	H606
Jdg	15:12	They s to him, “We’ve come to tie you up	H606
Jdg	15:12	Samson s, “Swear to me that you won’t	H606
Jdg	15:16	Then Samson s, “With a donkey’s jawbone	H606
Jdg	16: 5	rulers of the Philistines went to her and s,	H606
Jdg	16: 6	So Delilah s to Samson, “Tell me the	H606
Jdg	16:10	Then Delilah s to Samson, “You have	H606
Jdg	16:11	He s, “If anyone ties me securely with new	H606
Jdg	16:13	Delilah then s to Samson, “All this time	H606
Jdg	16:15	Then she s to him, “How can you say, ‘I	H606
Jdg	16:17	he s, “because I have been a Nazirite	H606
Jdg	16:26	Samson s to the servant who held his hand	H606
Jdg	16:30	Samson s, “Let me die with the Philistines!”	H606
Jdg	17: 2	s to his mother, “The eleven hundred	H606
Jdg	17: 2	Then his mother s, “The LORD bless you	H606
Jdg	17: 3	silver to his mother, she s, “I solemnly	H606
Jdg	17: 9	in Judah,” he s, “and I’m looking	H606
Jdg	17:10	Then Micah s to him, “Live with me and be	H606
Jdg	17:13	And Micah s, “Now I know that the LORD	H606
Jdg	18: 4	done for him, and s, “He has hired me and	NDT
Jdg	18: 5	Then they s to him, “Please inquire of God	H606
Jdg	18:14	out the land of Laish s to their fellow	H606
Jdg	18:18	the priest s to them, “What are you	H606
Jdg	18:23	the Danites turned and s to Micah, “What’s	H606
Jdg	19: 5	the woman’s father s to his son-in-law	H606
Jdg	19: 6	Afterward the woman’s father s, “Please	H606
Jdg	19: 8	the woman’s father s, “Refresh yourself.	H606
Jdg	19: 9	the woman’s father, s, “Now look, it’s	H606
Jdg	19:11	the servant s to his master, “Come,	H606
Jdg	19:20	are welcome at my house,” the old man s.	H606
Jdg	19:23	of the house went outside and s to them,	H606
Jdg	19:28	He s to her, “Get up; let’s go.” But there	H606
Jdg	20: 3	Then the Israelites s, “Tell us how this	H606
Jdg	20: 4	the murdered woman, s, “I and my	H6699
Jdg	20:18	They s, “Who of us is to go up first to fight	H606
Jdg	20:23	They s, “Shall we go up again to fight	H606
Jdg	20:39	and they s, “We are defeating them as in	H606
Jdg	21: 6	one tribe is cut off from Israel,” they s.	H606
Jdg	21:11	you are to do,” they s. “Kill every male	H606
Jdg	21:16	And the elders of the assembly s, “With the	H606
Jdg	21:17	they s, “so that a tribe of Israel will not be	H606
Ru	1: 8	Then Naomi s to her two daughters-in-law	H606
Ru	1:10	s to her, “We will go back with you to	H606
Ru	1:11	But Naomi s, “Return home, my daughters	H606
Ru	1:15	s Naomi, “your sister-in-law is going back	H606
Ru	2: 2	And Ruth the Moabite s to Naomi, “Let me	H606
Ru	2: 2	Naomi s to her, “Go ahead	H606
Ru	2: 7	She s, ‘Please let me glean and gather	H606
Ru	2: 8	So Boaz s to Ruth, “My daughter, listen to	H606
Ru	2:13	to find favor in your eyes, my lord,” she s.	H606
Ru	2:14	At mealtime Boaz s to her, “Come over	H606
Ru	2:19	man I worked with today is Boaz,” she s.	H606
Ru	2:20	Naomi s to her daughter-in-law	H606
Ru	2:21	Then Ruth the Moabite s, “He even said to	H606
Ru	2:21	Moabite said, “He even s to me, ‘Stay with	H606
Ru	2:22	Naomi s to Ruth her daughter-in-law, “It	H606
Ru	3: 1	day Ruth’s mother-in-law Naomi s to her,	H606
Ru	3: 9	servant Ruth,” she s. “Spread the corner	H606
Ru	3:14	be recognized; and he s, “No one must	H606
Ru	3:15	He also s, “Bring me the shawl you are	H606
Ru	3:18	Then Naomi s, “Wait, my daughter, until	H606
Ru	4: 1	Boaz s, “Come over here, my friend, and sit	H606
Ru	4: 2	took ten of the elders of the town and s,	H606
Ru	4: 3	Then he s to the guardian-redeemer	H606
Ru	4: 4	I am next in line.” “I will redeem it,” he s.	H606
Ru	4: 5	Then Boaz s, “On the day you buy the land	H606
Ru	4: 6	the guardian-redeemer s, “Then I cannot	H606
Ru	4: 8	So the guardian-redeemer s to Boaz, “Buy	H606
Ru	4:11	the elders and all the people at the gate s,	H606
Ru	4:14	The women s to Naomi: “Praise be to the	H606
Ru	4:17	The women living there s, “Naomi has a	H606
1Sa	1:14	s to her, “How long are you going to	H606
1Sa	1:18	She s, “May your servant find favor in your	H606
1Sa	1:22	She s to her husband, “After the boy is	H606
1Sa	1:26	and she s to him, “Pardon me, my lord.	H606
1Sa	2: 1	Then Hannah prayed and s: “My heart	H606
1Sa	2:16	If the person s to him, “Let the fat be	H606
1Sa	2:23	So he s to them, “Why do you do such	H606
1Sa	2:27	a man of God came to Eli and s to him,	H606
1Sa	3: 5	And he ran to Eli and s, “Here I am; you	H606
1Sa	3: 5	But Eli s, “I did not call; go back and lie	H606
1Sa	3: 6	And Samuel got up and went to Eli and s,	H606
1Sa	3: 6	“My son,” Eli s, “I did not call; go back	H606
1Sa	3: 8	And Samuel got up and went to Eli and s	H606
1Sa	3:10	Then Samuel s, “Speak, for your servant is	H606
1Sa	3:11	And the LORD s to Samuel: “See, I am	H606
1Sa	3:16	Eli called him and s, “Samuel, my son.”	H606
1Sa	3:17	“What was it he s to you?” Eli asked. “Do	H1819
1Sa	3:18	Then Eli s, “He is the LORD; let him do what	H606
1Sa	4: 7	has come into the camp,” they s. “Oh no!	H606
1Sa	4:20	the women attending her s, “Don’t	H1819
1Sa	4:22	She s, “The Glory has departed from Israel	H606
1Sa	5: 7	was happening, they s, “The ark of the	H606
1Sa	5:11	all the rulers of the Philistines and s,	H606
1Sa	6: 2	the priests and the diviners and s,	H606
1Sa	7: 3	So Samuel s to all the Israelites, “If you are	H606
1Sa	7: 5	Then Samuel s, “Assemble all Israel at	H606
1Sa	7: 8	They s to Samuel, “Do not stop crying out to	H606
1Sa	8: 5	They s to him, “You are old, and your sons	H606
1Sa	8: 6	But when they s, “Give us a king to lead us,”	H606
1Sa	8:11	He s, “This is what the king who will reign	H606
1Sa	8:19	“No!” they s. “We want a king	H606
1Sa	8:21	When Samuel heard all that the people s,	H1821
1Sa	8:22	Then Samuel s to the Israelites, “Everyone	H606
1Sa	9: 3	were lost, and Kish s to his son Saul, “Take	H606
1Sa	9: 5	Saul s to the servant who was with him	H606
1Sa	9: 7	Saul s to his servant, “If we go, what can	H606
1Sa	9: 8	he s, “I have a quarter of a shekel of silver.	H606
1Sa	9:10	Saul s to his servant. “Come, let’s	H606
1Sa	9:17	of Saul, the LORD s to him, “This is the	H6699
1Sa	9:23	Samuel s to the cook, “Bring the piece of	H606
1Sa	9:24	Samuel s, “Here is what has been kept	H606
1Sa	9:24	you for this occasion from the time I s,	H606
1Sa	9:27	of the town, Samuel s to Saul, “Tell the	H606
1Sa	10:14	the donkeys,” he s. “But when we saw	H606
1Sa	10:15	Saul’s uncle s, “Tell me what Samuel said	H606
1Sa	10:15	uncle said, “Tell me what Samuel s to you.”	H606
1Sa	10:16	what Samuel had s about the kingship.	H606
1Sa	10:18	s to them, “This is what the LORD, the	H606
1Sa	10:19	And you have s, ‘No, appoint a king over	H606
1Sa	10:22	And the LORD s, “Yes, he has hidden	H606
1Sa	10:24	Samuel s to all the people, “Do you see the	H606
1Sa	10:27	But some scoundrels s, “How can this fellow	H606
1Sa	11: 1	And all the men of Jabesh s to him, “Make	H606
1Sa	11: 3	The elders of Jabesh s to him, “Give us	H606
1Sa	11: 5	to him what the men of Jabesh had s.	H1821
1Sa	11:10	They s to the Ammonites, “Tomorrow we	H606
1Sa	11:12	The people then s to Samuel, “Who was it	H606
1Sa	11:13	But Saul s, “No one will be put to death	H606
1Sa	11:14	Then Samuel s to the people, “Come, let	H606
1Sa	12: 1	Samuel s to all Israel, “I have listened to	H606
1Sa	12: 1	to everything you s to me and have set a	H606
1Sa	12: 5	Samuel s to them, “The LORD is witness	H606
1Sa	12: 5	“He is witness,” they s.	H606
1Sa	12: 6	Then Samuel s to the people, “It is the	H606
1Sa	12:10	They cried out to the LORD and s, ‘We have	H606
1Sa	12:12	was moving against you, you s to me, ‘No,	H606
1Sa	12:19	The people all s to Samuel, “Pray to the	H606
1Sa	13: 3	trumpet blown throughout the land and s,	H606
1Sa	13: 9	So he s, “Bring me the burnt offering and	H606
1Sa	13:13	Samuel s. “You have not kept	H606
1Sa	13:19	because the Philistines had s, “Otherwise	H606
1Sa	14: 1	day Jonathan son of Saul s to his young	H606
1Sa	14: 6	Jonathan s to his young armor-bearer	H606
1Sa	14: 7	that you have in mind,” his armor-bearer s.	H606
1Sa	14: 8	Jonathan s, “Come on, then; we will cross	H606
1Sa	14:11	s the Philistines. “The Hebrews are	H606
1Sa	14:12	So Jonathan s to his armor-bearer, “Climb	H606
1Sa	14:17	Then Saul s to the men who were with him	H606
1Sa	14:18	Saul s to Ahijah, “Bring the ark of God.”	H606
1Sa	14:19	So Saul s to the priest, “Withdraw your	H606
1Sa	14:29	Jonathan s, “My father has made trouble	H606
1Sa	14:33	Then someone s to Saul, “Look, the men	H5583
1Sa	14:33	have broken faith,” he s. “Roll a large	H606
1Sa	14:34	Then he s, “Go out among the men and tell	H606
1Sa	14:36	Saul s, “Let us go down and pursue the	H606
1Sa	14:36	But the priest s, “Let us inquire of God here.”	H606
1Sa	14:38	Saul therefore s, “Come here, all you who	H606
1Sa	14:39	But not one of them s a word.	H6699
1Sa	14:40	Saul then s to all the Israelites, “You stand	H606
1Sa	14:42	Saul s, “Cast the lot between me and	H606
1Sa	14:43	Then Saul s to Jonathan, “Tell me what	H606
1Sa	14:44	Saul s, “May God deal with me, be it ever	H606
1Sa	14:45	But the men s to Saul, “Should Jonathan	H606
1Sa	15: 1	Samuel s to Saul, “I am the one the LORD	H606
1Sa	15: 6	Then he s to the Kenites, “Go away, leave	H606
1Sa	15:13	reached him, Saul s, “The LORD bless you!	H606
1Sa	15:14	But Samuel s, “What then is this bleating	H606
1Sa	15:16	Samuel s to Saul. “Let me tell	H606
1Sa	15:16	tell you what the LORD s to me last night.”	H1819
1Sa	15:17	Samuel s, “Although you were once small	H606
1Sa	15:20	obey the LORD,” Saul s. “I went on the	H606
1Sa	15:24	Then Saul s to Samuel, “I have sinned.	H606
1Sa	15:26	But Samuel s to him, “I will not go back	H606
1Sa	15:28	Samuel s to him, “The LORD has torn the	H606
1Sa	15:32	Then Samuel s, “Bring me Agag king of	H606
1Sa	15:33	But Samuel s, “As your sword has made	H606
1Sa	16: 1	The LORD s to Samuel, “How long will you	H606
1Sa	16: 2	But Samuel s, “How can I go? If Saul hears	H606
1Sa	16: 2	The LORD s, “Take a heifer with you and	H606
1Sa	16: 4	Samuel did what the LORD s. When he	H1819
1Sa	16: 7	But the LORD s to Samuel, “Do not consider	H606
1Sa	16: 8	But Samuel s, “The LORD has not chosen	H606
1Sa	16: 9	pass by, but Samuel s, “Nor has the LORD	H606
1Sa	16:10	Samuel, but Samuel s to him, “The LORD	H606
1Sa	16:11	Samuel s, “Send for him; we will not sit	H606
1Sa	16:12	Then the LORD s, “Rise and anoint him; this	H606
1Sa	16:15	Saul’s attendants s to him, “See, an evil	H606
1Sa	16:17	So Saul s to his attendants, “Find someone	H606
1Sa	16:19	Then Saul sent messengers to Jesse and s	H606
1Sa	17:10	Then the Philistine s, “This day I defy the	H606
1Sa	17:17	Now Jesse s to his son David, “Take this	H606
1Sa	17:29	what have I done?” s David. “Can’t I even	H606
1Sa	17:31	What David s was overheard and reported	H1819
1Sa	17:32	David s to Saul, “Let no one lose heart on	H606
1Sa	17:34	But David s to Saul, “Your servant has been	H606
1Sa	17:37	Saul s to David, “Go, and the LORD be with	H606
1Sa	17:39	he s to Saul, “because I am not used to	H606
1Sa	17:43	He s to David, “Am I a dog, that you come	H606
1Sa	17:44	he s, “and I’ll give your flesh to the birds	H606
1Sa	17:45	David s to the Philistine, “You come	H606
1Sa	17:55	the Philistine, he s to Abner, commander	H606
1Sa	17:56	The king s, “Find out whose son this young	H606
1Sa	17:58	David s, “I am the son of your servant Jesse	H606
1Sa	18:17	Saul s to David, “Here is my older daughter	H606
1Sa	18:17	For Saul s to himself, “I will not raise a	H606
1Sa	18:18	But David s to Saul, “Who am I, and what	H606
1Sa	18:21	So Saul s to David, “Now you have a	H606
1Sa	18:23	But David s, “Do you think it is a small	H606
1Sa	18:24	servants told him what David had s,	H1819
1Sa	19: 4	of David to Saul his father and s to him,	H606
1Sa	19:14	men to capture David, Michal s, “He is ill.”	H606
1Sa	19:17	Saul s to Michal, “Why did you deceive me	H606
1Sa	19:17	Michal told him, “He s to me, ‘Let me get	H606
1Sa	19:22	“Over in Naioth at Ramah,” they s.	H606
1Sa	20: 3	But David took an oath and s, “Your father	H606
1Sa	20: 3	in your eyes, and he has s to himself	H606
1Sa	20: 4	Jonathan s to David, “Whatever you want	H606
1Sa	20: 5	So David s, “Look, tomorrow is the New	H606
1Sa	20: 9	Jonathan s. “If I had the least	H606
1Sa	20:11	Jonathan s, “let’s go out into the	H606
1Sa	20:12	Then Jonathan s to David, “I swear by the	H606
1Sa	20:18	Then Jonathan s to David, “Tomorrow is	H606
1Sa	20:26	Saul s nothing that day, for he thought	H1819
1Sa	20:27	Then Saul s to his son Jonathan, “Why	H606
1Sa	20:29	He s, ‘Let me go, because our family is	H606
1Sa	20:30	flared up at Jonathan and he s to him,	H606
1Sa	20:36	and he s to the boy, “Run and find the	H606
1Sa	20:40	gave his weapons to the boy and s,	H606
1Sa	20:42	Jonathan s to David, “Go in peace, for we	H606
1Sa	21: 2	king sent me on a mission and s to me,	H606
1Sa	21: 9	David s, “There is none like it; give it to	H606
1Sa	21:11	But the servants of Achish s to him, “Isn’t	H606
1Sa	21:14	Achish s to his servants, “Look at the man	H606
1Sa	22: 3	Mizpah in Moab and s to the king of Moab,	H606
1Sa	22: 5	But the prophet Gad s to David, “Do not	H606
1Sa	22: 7	He s to them, “Listen, men of Benjamin	H606
1Sa	22: 9	with Saul’s officials, s, “I saw the son of	H6699
1Sa	22:12	Saul s, “Listen now, son of Ahitub.” “Yes	H606
1Sa	22:13	Saul s to him, “Why have you conspired	H606
1Sa	22:16	But the king s, “You will surely die	H606
1Sa	22:22	Then David s to Abiathar, “That day, when	H606
1Sa	23: 3	But David’s men s to him, “Here in Judah	H606
1Sa	23: 7	to Keilah, and he s, “God has delivered	H606
1Sa	23: 9	against him, he s to Abiathar the priest	H606
1Sa	23:10	David s, “LORD, God of Israel, your servant	H606
1Sa	23:11	And the LORD s, “He will.”	H606
1Sa	23:12	And the LORD s, “They will.”	H606
1Sa	23:17	“Don’t be afraid,” he s. “My father Saul will	H606
1Sa	23:19	Ziphites went up to Saul at Gibeah and s,	H606
1Sa	24: 4	The men s, “This is the day the LORD spoke	H606
1Sa	24: 4	the day the LORD spoke of when he s to you,	H606
1Sa	24: 6	He s to his men, “The LORD forbid that I	H606
1Sa	24: 9	He s to Saul, “Why do you listen when men	H606
1Sa	24:10	I spared you; I s, ‘I will not lay my hand	H606
1Sa	24:17	righteous than I,” he s. “You have treated	H606
1Sa	25: 5	So he sent ten young men and s to them	H606
1Sa	25:13	David s to his men, “Each of you strap on	H606
1Sa	25:21	David had just s, “It’s been useless—all my	H606
1Sa	25:24	She fell at his feet and s: “Pardon your	H606
1Sa	25:32	David s to Abigail, “Praise be to the LORD	H606
1Sa	25:35	her hand what she had brought him and s,	H606
1Sa	25:39	Nabal was dead, he s, “Praise be to the	H606
1Sa	25:40	servants went to Carmel and s to Abigail,	H1819
1Sa	25:41	down with her face to the ground and s,	H606
1Sa	26: 1	The Ziphites went to Saul at Gibeah and s	H606
1Sa	26: 6	“I’ll go with you,” s Abishai.	H606
1Sa	26: 8	Abishai s to David, “Today God has	H606
1Sa	26: 9	But David s to Abishai, “Don’t destroy him	H606
1Sa	26:10	as the LORD lives,” he s, “the LORD himself	H606
1Sa	26:15	David s, “You’re a man, aren’t you? And	H606
1Sa	26:17	Saul recognized David’s voice and s, “Is	H606
1Sa	26:19	share in the LORD’s inheritance and have s,	H606
1Sa	26:21	Then Saul s, “I have sinned. Come back	H606
1Sa	26:25	Then Saul s to David, “May you be blessed,	H606
1Sa	27: 5	Then David s to Achish, “If I have found	H606
1Sa	27:12	Achish trusted David and s to himself, “He	H606
1Sa	28: 1	Achish s to David, “You must understand	H606
1Sa	28: 2	David s, “Then you will see for yourself	H606
1Sa	28: 7	Saul then s to his attendants, “Find me a	H606
1Sa	28: 7	“There is one in Endor,” they s.	H606
1Sa	28: 8	he s, “and bring up for me the one I name	H606
1Sa	28: 9	But the woman s to him, “Surely you know	H606
1Sa	28:11	up for you?” “Bring up Samuel,” he s.	H606
1Sa	28:12	out at the top of her voice and s to Saul,	H606
1Sa	28:13	The king s to her, “Don’t be afraid.	H606
1Sa	28:13	The woman s, “I see a ghostly figure	H606
1Sa	28:14	man wearing a robe is coming up,” she s.	H606
1Sa	28:15	Samuel s to Saul, “Why have you disturbed	H606
1Sa	28:15	great distress,” Saul s. “The Philistines are	H606
1Sa	28:16	Samuel s, “Why do you consult me, now	H606
1Sa	28:21	that he was greatly shaken, she s, “Look,	H606
1Sa	28:23	He refused and s, “I will not eat.” But his	H606
1Sa	29: 4	commanders were angry with Achish and s,	H606
1Sa	29: 6	So Achish called David and s to him, “As	H606
1Sa	29: 9	the Philistine commanders have s, ‘He	H606
1Sa	30: 7	Then David s to Abiathar the priest, the	H606
1Sa	30:13	He s, “I am an Egyptian, the slave of an	H606
1Sa	30:22	troublemakers among David’s followers s,	H6699
1Sa	31: 4	Saul s to his armor-bearer, “Draw your	H606
2Sa	1: 5	Then David s to the young man who	H606

2Sa 1: 6 the young man s, "and there was Saul H606
2Sa 1: 7 called out to me, and *I* s, 'What can I do? H606
2Sa 1: 9 "Then *he* s to me, 'Stand here by me and H606
2Sa 1:13 David s to the young man who brought him H606
2Sa 1:15 Then David called one of his men and s H606
2Sa 1:16 For David *had* s to him, "Your blood be on H606
2Sa 1:16 mouth testified against you when you s, H606
2Sa 2: 1 The LORD s, "Go up." David asked H606
2Sa 2:14 Then Abner s to Joab, "Let's have some of H606
2Sa 2:14 "All right, let them do it," Joab s. H606
2Sa 2:21 Then Abner s to him, "Turn aside to the H606
2Sa 3: 7 And Ish-Bosheth s to Abner, "Why did you H606
2Sa 3: 8 very angry because of **what** Ish-Bosheth s. H1821
2Sa 3:13 s David. "I will make an H606
2Sa 3:16 Then Abner s to him, "Go back H606
2Sa 3:17 conferred with the elders of Israel and s, H606
2Sa 3:21 Then Abner s to David, "Let me go at once H606
2Sa 3:24 So Joab went to the king and s, "What H606
2Sa 3:28 heard about this, *he* s, "I and my kingdom H606
2Sa 3:31 Then David s to Joab and all the people H606
2Sa 3:38 Then the king s to his men, "Do you not H606
2Sa 4: 8 to David at Hebron and s to the king, H606
2Sa 5: 1 of Israel came to David at Hebron and s, H606
2Sa 5: 2 And the LORD s to you, 'You will shepherd H606
2Sa 5: 6 The Jebusites s to David, "You will not get H606
2Sa 5: 8 On that day David *had* s, "Anyone who H606
2Sa 5:20 *He* s, "As waters break out, the LORD has H606
2Sa 6: 9 David was afraid of the LORD that day and s H606
2Sa 6:20 of Saul came out to meet him and s, H606
2Sa 6:21 David s to Michal, "It was before the LORD H606
2Sa 7: 2 he s to Nathan the prophet, "Here I am H606
2Sa 7:18 went in and sat before the LORD, and *he* s: H606
2Sa 9: 2 and the king s to him, "Are you Ziba H606
2Sa 9: 6 David s, "Mephibosheth!" "At H606
2Sa 9: 7 David s to him, "for I will surely show you H606
2Sa 9: 8 Mephibosheth bowed down and s, "What H606
2Sa 9: 9 Saul's steward, and s to him, "I have given H606
2Sa 9:11 Then Ziba s to the king, "Your servant will H606
2Sa 10: 3 commanders s to Hanun their lord H606
2Sa 10: 5 The king s, "Stay at Jericho till your beards H606
2Sa 10:11 Joab s, "If the Arameans are too strong H606
2Sa 11: 3 *The man* s, "She is Bathsheba, the H606
2Sa 11: 8 Then David s to Uriah, "Go down to your H606
2Sa 11:11 Uriah s to David, "The ark and Israel and H606
2Sa 11:12 Then David s to him, "Stay here one more H606
2Sa 11:23 The messenger s to David, "The men H606
2Sa 12: 1 he came to him, *he* s, "There were two H606
2Sa 12: 5 anger against the man and s to Nathan, H606
2Sa 12: 7 Then Nathan s to David, "You are the man H606
2Sa 12:13 Then David s to Nathan, "I have sinned H606
2Sa 13: 4 Amnon s to him, "I'm in love with Tamar H606
2Sa 13: 5 to bed and pretend to be ill," Jonadab s. H606
2Sa 13: 6 to see him, Amnon s to him, "I would like H606
2Sa 13: 9 out of here," Amnon s. So everyone left H606
2Sa 13:10 Then Amnon s to Tamar, "Bring the food H606
2Sa 13:11 he grabbed her and s, "Come to bed with H606
2Sa 13:12 my brother!" *she* s to him. "Don't force H606
2Sa 13:15 Amnon s to her, "Get up and H606
2Sa 13:16 *she* s to him. "Sending me away H606
2Sa 13:17 He called his personal servant and s, "Get H606
2Sa 13:20 Her brother Absalom s to her, "Has that H606
2Sa 13:22 And Absalom never s **a word** to Amnon H1819
2Sa 13:24 Absalom went to the king and s, "Your H606
2Sa 13:26 Then Absalom s, "If not, please let my H606
2Sa 13:32 David's brother, s, "My lord should not H6699
2Sa 13:35 Jonadab s to the king, "See, the king's H606
2Sa 13:35 it has happened just as your servant s." H1821
2Sa 14: 2 brought from there. *He* s to her, "Pretend H606
2Sa 14: 4 to pay him honor, and *she* s, "Help me, H606
2Sa 14: 5 *She* s, "I am a widow; my husband is H606
2Sa 14: 8 The king s to the woman, "Go home, and I H606
2Sa 14: 9 But the woman from Tekoa s to him, "Let H606
2Sa 14:11 *She* s, "Then let the king invoke the LORD H606
2Sa 14:11 *he* s, "not one hair of your son's head will H606
2Sa 14:12 Then the woman s, "Let your servant speak H606
2Sa 14:13 The woman s, "Why then have you devised H606
2Sa 14:18 Then the king s to the woman, "Don't H6699
2Sa 14:18 "Let my lord the king speak," the woman s. H606
2Sa 14:21 The king s to Joab, "Very well, I will do it H606
2Sa 14:22 Joab s, "Today your servant knows that he H606
2Sa 14:24 But the king s, "He must go to his own H606
2Sa 14:30 Then *he* s to his servants, "Look, Joab's H606
2Sa 14:31 and *he* s to him, "Why have H606
2Sa 14:32 Absalom s to Joab, "Look, I sent word to H606
2Sa 14:32 I sent word to you and s, 'Come here so I H606
2Sa 15: 7 four years, Absalom s to the king, "Let me H606
2Sa 15: 9 The king s to him, "Go in peace." So he H606
2Sa 15:14 Then David s to all his officials who were H606
2Sa 15:19 The king s to Ittai the Gittite, "Why should H606
2Sa 15:22 David s to Ittai, "Go ahead, march on." H606
2Sa 15:25 Then the king s to Zadok, "Take the ark of H606
2Sa 15:27 The king also s to Zadok the priest, "Do H606
2Sa 15:33 David s to him, "If you go with me, you will H606
2Sa 16: 3 Ziba s to him, "He is staying in Jerusalem H606
2Sa 16: 4 Then the king s to Ziba, "All that belonged H606
2Sa 16: 4 "I humbly bow," Ziba s. "May I find favor in H606
2Sa 16: 7 As he cursed, Shimei s, "Get out, get out H606
2Sa 16: 9 Then Abishai son of Zeruiah s to the king H606
2Sa 16:10 But the king s, "What does this have to do H606
2Sa 16:10 If he is cursing because the LORD s to him H606
2Sa 16:11 David then s to Abishai and all his officials, H606
2Sa 16:16 went to Absalom and s to him, "Long live H606
2Sa 16:17 Absalom s to Hushai, "So this is the love H606
2Sa 16:18 Hushai s to Absalom, "No, the one chosen H606
2Sa 16:20 Absalom s to Ahithophel, "Give us your H606
2Sa 17: 1 Ahithophel s to Absalom, "I would choose H606
2Sa 17: 5 But Absalom s, "Summon also Hushai the H606
2Sa 17: 6 came to him, Absalom s, "Ahithophel has H606
2Sa 17:14 Absalom and all the men of Israel s, "The H606
2Sa 17:21 *They* s to him, "Set out and cross the river H606
2Sa 17:29 For *they* s, "The people have become H606
2Sa 18: 3 But the men s, "You must not go out; if we H606
2Sa 18:11 Joab s to the man who had told him this H606
2Sa 18:14 Joab s, "I'm not going to wait like this for H606
2Sa 18:19 Now Ahimaaz son of Zadok s, "Let me run H606
2Sa 18:21 Then Joab s to a Cushite, "Go, tell the king H606
2Sa 18:22 Ahimaaz son of Zadok again s to Joab H606
2Sa 18:23 He s, "Come what may, I want to run." NDT
2Sa 18:23 So Joab s, "Run!" Then Ahimaaz H606
2Sa 18:25 The king s, "If he is alone, he must have H606
2Sa 18:26 The king s, "He must be bringing good H606
2Sa 18:27 The watchman s, "It seems to me that the H606
2Sa 18:27 good man," the king s. "He comes with H606
2Sa 18:28 the king with his face to the ground and s, H606
2Sa 18:30 The king s, "Stand aside and wait here." H606
2Sa 18:31 Then the Cushite arrived and s, "My lord H606
2Sa 18:33 As he went, *he* s: "O my son H606
2Sa 19: 2 because on that day the troops heard *it* s H606
2Sa 19: 5 Joab went into the house to the king and s, H606
2Sa 19:11 since **what** is being s throughout Israel H1821
2Sa 19:19 s to him, "May my lord not hold me H606
2Sa 19:21 Then Abishai son of Zeruiah s, "Shouldn't H6699
2Sa 19:23 So the king s to Shimei, "You shall not die." H606
2Sa 19:26 *He* s, "My lord the king, since I your servant H606
2Sa 19:26 servant am lame, I s, 'I will have my H606
2Sa 19:29 The king s to him, "Why say more? I order H606
2Sa 19:30 Mephibosheth s to the king, "Let him take H606
2Sa 19:33 The king s to Barzillai, "Cross over with me H606
2Sa 19:38 The king s, "Kimham shall cross over with H606
2Sa 20: 4 Then the king s to Amasa, "Summon the H606
2Sa 20: 6 David s to Abishai, "Now Sheba son of H606
2Sa 20: 9 Joab s to Amasa, "How are you, my brother H606
2Sa 20:11 of Joab's men stood beside Amasa and s, H606
2Sa 20:17 *She* s, "Listen to what your servant has to H606
2Sa 20:17 servant has to say." "I'm listening," *he* s. H606
2Sa 20:21 The woman s to Joab, "His head will be H606
2Sa 21: 1 The LORD s, "It is on account of Saul and H606
2Sa 21: 6 So the king s, "I will give them to H606
2Sa 21:16 with a new sword, s he would kill David. H606
2Sa 22: 2 *He* s: "The LORD is my rock, my fortress H606
2Sa 23: 3 of Israel spoke, the Rock of Israel s to me: H1819
2Sa 23:15 David longed for water and s, "Oh, that H606
2Sa 23:17 *he* s. "Is it not the blood of men H606
2Sa 24: 2 So the king s to Joab and the army H606
2Sa 24:10 fighting men, and he s to the LORD, "I have H606
2Sa 24:13 So Gad went to David and s to him H5583
2Sa 24:14 David s to Gad, "I am in deep distress. H606
2Sa 24:16 the disaster and s to the angel who was H606
2Sa 24:17 down the people, *he* s to the LORD, "I have H606
2Sa 24:18 that day Gad went to David and s to him, H606
2Sa 24:21 Araunah s, "Why has my lord the king H606
2Sa 24:22 Araunah s to David, "Let my lord the king H606
2Sa 24:23 Araunah also s to him, "May the LORD your H606
1Ki 1: 2 So his attendants s to him, "Let us look H606
1Ki 1: 5 put himself forward and s, "I will be king." H606
1Ki 1:14 in and add my word to **what** you have s." H1821
1Ki 1:17 *She* s to him, "My lord, you yourself swore H606
1Ki 1:24 Nathan s, "Have you, my lord the king H606
1Ki 1:28 Then King David s, "Call in Bathsheba." H6699
1Ki 1:31 before the king, and s, "May my lord King H606
1Ki 1:32 King David s, "Call in Zadok the priest H606
1Ki 1:33 he s to them: "Take your lord's servants with H606
1Ki 1:42 Adonijah s, "Come in. A worthy H606
1Ki 1:48 s, 'Praise be to the LORD, the God of H606
1Ki 1:53 Solomon s, "Go to your home. H606
1Ki 2: 2 about to go the way of all the earth," he s. H606
1Ki 2:15 "As you know," *he* s, "the kingdom was H606
1Ki 2:16 not refuse me." "You may make it," *she* s. H606
1Ki 2:20 one small request to make of you," *she* s. H606
1Ki 2:21 So *she* s, "Let Abishag the Shunammite be H606
1Ki 2:26 To Abiathar the priest the king s, "Go back H606
1Ki 2:30 entered the tent of the LORD and s to Joab, H606
1Ki 2:36 Then the king sent for Shimei and s to him H606
1Ki 2:38 servant will do as my lord the king *has* s." H1819
1Ki 2:42 the king summoned Shimei and s to him H606
1Ki 2:42 At that time *you* s to me, 'What you say is H606
1Ki 2:44 The king also s to Shimei, "You know in H606
1Ki 3: 5 in a dream, and God s, "Ask for whatever H606
1Ki 3:11 So God s to him, "Since you have asked H606
1Ki 3:17 One of them s, "Pardon me, my lord. H606
1Ki 3:22 The other woman s, "No! The living one is H606
1Ki 3:23 The king s, "This one says, 'My son is alive H606
1Ki 3:24 Then the king s, "Bring me a sword." H606
1Ki 3:26 out of love for her son and s to the king, H606
1Ki 3:26 But the other s, "Neither I nor you shall H606
1Ki 5: 5 father David, when he s, 'Your son whom I H606
1Ki 5: 7 he was greatly pleased and s, "Praise be to H606
1Ki 8:12 Then Solomon s, "The LORD has said that H606
1Ki 8:12 "The LORD *has* s that he would dwell in a H606
1Ki 8:15 Then *he* s: "Praise be to the LORD, the God H606
1Ki 8:15 own mouth to my father David. For he s, H606
1Ki 8:18 But the LORD s to my father David, 'You did H606
1Ki 8:23 s: "LORD, the God of Israel, there is no H606
1Ki 8:25 the promises you made to him when you s, H606
1Ki 8:29 this place of which *you* s, 'My Name shall H606
1Ki 9: 3 The LORD s to him: "I have heard the prayer H606
1Ki 9: 5 as I promised David your father when I s H606
1Ki 10: 6 *She* s to the king, "The report I heard in my H606
1Ki 11:11 So the LORD s to Solomon, "Since this is H606
1Ki 11:21 Then Hadad s to Pharaoh, "Let me go, that H606
1Ki 11:31 Then *he* s to Jeroboam, "Take ten pieces H606
1Ki 12: 3 of Israel went to Rehoboam and s to him: H1819
1Ki 12:10 "These people *have* s to you, 'Your father H1819
1Ki 12:12 as the king *had* s, "Come back to me in H1819
1Ki 12:14 the advice of the young men and s, H1819
1Ki 12:28 *He* s to the people, "It is too much for you H606
1Ki 13: 4 stretched out his hand from the altar and s, H606
1Ki 13: 6 Then the king s to the man of God H6699
1Ki 13: 7 The king s to the man of God, "Come H1819
1Ki 13:11 told their father what *he had* s to the king. H1819
1Ki 13:13 So *he* s to his sons, "Saddle the donkey H606
1Ki 13:15 So the prophet s to him, "Come home with H606
1Ki 13:16 The man of God s, "I cannot turn back and H606
1Ki 13:18 And an angel s to me by the word of the H1819
1Ki 13:26 journey heard of it, *he* s, "It is the man of H606
1Ki 13:27 The prophet s to his sons, "Saddle the H1819
1Ki 13:30 they mourned over him and s, "Alas, NDT
1Ki 13:31 After burying him, he s to his sons, "When H606
1Ki 14: 2 Jeroboam s to his wife, "Go, disguise H606
1Ki 14: 4 wife did what he s and went to Ahijah's NDT
1Ki 14: 6 her footsteps at the door, *he* s, "Come in, H606
1Ki 14:18 as the LORD *had* s through his H1819+1821
1Ki 15:19 he s, "as there was between my father H606
1Ki 17: 1 Tishbe in Gilead, s to Ahab, "As the LORD, H606
1Ki 17:13 Elijah s to her, "Don't be afraid. Go home H606
1Ki 17:13 Go home and do as you have s. But first H1821
1Ki 17:18 *She* s to Elijah, "What do you have against H606
1Ki 17:23 He gave him to his mother and s, "Look H606
1Ki 17:24 Then the woman s to Elijah, "Now I know H606
1Ki 18: 5 Ahab *had* s to Obadiah, "Go through the H606
1Ki 18: 7 down to the ground, and s, "Is it really you, H606
1Ki 18:15 Elijah s, "As the LORD Almighty lives, H606
1Ki 18:17 he saw Elijah, he s to him, "Is that you, H606
1Ki 18:21 Elijah went before the people and s, "How H606
1Ki 18:21 But the people s nothing. H6699
1Ki 18:22 Then Elijah s to them, "I am the only one H606
1Ki 18:24 Then all the people s, "What you say is H6699
1Ki 18:25 Elijah s to the prophets of Baal, "Choose H606
1Ki 18:27 "Shout louder!" *he* s. "Surely he is a god H606
1Ki 18:30 Then Elijah s to all the people, "Come H606
1Ki 18:33 Then *he* s to them, "Fill four large jars with H606
1Ki 18:34 "Do it again," *he* s, and they did it again H606
1Ki 18:41 And Elijah s to Ahab, "Go, eat and drink H606
1Ki 18:43 is nothing there," *he* s. Seven times Elijah H606
1Ki 18:43 Seven times Elijah s, "Go back." H606
1Ki 18:44 So Elijah s, "Go and tell Ahab, 'Hitch up H606
1Ki 19: 4 had enough, LORD," *he* s. "Take my life; H606
1Ki 19: 5 All at once an angel touched him and s H606
1Ki 19: 7 a second time and touched him and s, H606
1Ki 19:11 The LORD s, "Go out and stand on the H606
1Ki 19:13 Then a voice s to him, "What are you H606
1Ki 19:15 The LORD s to him, "Go back the way you H606
1Ki 19:20 mother goodbye," *he* s, "and then I will H606
1Ki 20: 5 The messengers came again and s, "This H606
1Ki 20: 7 all the elders of the land and s to them, H606
1Ki 20:18 *He* s, "If they have come out for peace H606
1Ki 20:22 prophet came to the king of Israel and s, H606
1Ki 20:31 His officials s to him, "Look, we have heard H606
1Ki 20:32 they went to the king of Israel and s, "Your H606
1Ki 20:33 *they* s. "Go and get him, H606
1Ki 20:33 get him," the king s. When Ben-Hadad H606
1Ki 20:34 Ahab s, "On the basis of a treaty I will set NDT
1Ki 20:35 of the prophets s to his companion, H606
1Ki 20:36 So the prophet s, "Because you have not H606
1Ki 20:37 The prophet found another man and s H606
1Ki 20:39 someone came to me with a captive and s, H606
1Ki 20:40 "That is your sentence," the king of Israel s. H606
1Ki 20:42 *He* s to the king, "This is what the LORD says H606
1Ki 21: 2 Ahab s to Naboth, "Let me have your H1819
1Ki 21: 4 Naboth the Jezreelite *had* s, H1819+2021+1821
1Ki 21: 6 "Because *I* s to Naboth the Jezreelite H1819
1Ki 21: 6 But *he* s, 'I will not give you H606
1Ki 21: 7 Jezebel his wife s, "Is this how you act as H606
1Ki 21:15 to death, she s to Ahab, "Get up and H606
1Ki 21:20 Ahab s to Elijah, "So you have found me H606
1Ki 22: 3 The king of Israel *had* s to his officials H606
1Ki 22: 5 But Jehoshaphat also s to the king of Israel H606
1Ki 22: 9 of Israel called one of his officials and s, H606
1Ki 22:12 they s, "for the LORD will give it into the H606
1Ki 22:13 had gone to summon Micaiah s to him, H1819
1Ki 22:14 But Micaiah s, "As surely as the LORD lives, H606
1Ki 22:16 The king s to him, "How many times must I H606
1Ki 22:17 the LORD s, 'These people have no H606
1Ki 22:18 The king of Israel s to Jehoshaphat, "Didn't H606
1Ki 22:20 And the LORD s, 'Who will entice Ahab into H606
1Ki 22:21 stood before the LORD and s, 'I will entice H606
1Ki 22:22 in the mouths of all his prophets,' *he* s. H606
1Ki 22:22 will succeed in enticing him,' s the LORD. H606
1Ki 22:30 The king of Israel s to Jehoshaphat, "I will H606
1Ki 22:49 Ahaziah son of Ahab s to Jehoshaphat, H606
2Ki 1: 3 the angel of the LORD s to Elijah the H1819
2Ki 1: 6 "And *he* s to us, 'Go back to the king who H606
2Ki 1: 8 The king s, "That was Elijah the H606
2Ki 1: 9 top of a hill, and s to him, "Man of God, H1819
2Ki 1:11 The captain s to him, "Man of God, this is H6699
2Ki 1:15 The angel of the LORD s to Elijah, "Go H1819

2Ki 2: 2 Elijah s to Elisha, "Stay here; the LORD has H606
2Ki 2: 2 But Elisha s, "As surely as the LORD lives H606
2Ki 2: 4 Then Elijah s to him, "Stay here, Elisha H606
2Ki 2: 6 Then Elijah s to him, "Stay here; the LORD H606
2Ki 2: 9 had crossed, Elijah s to Elisha, "Tell me, H606
2Ki 2:10 Elijah s, "yet if you see me when I am H606
2Ki 2:15 who were watching, s, "The spirit of Elijah H606
2Ki 2:16 *they* s, "we your servants have fifty able H606
2Ki 2:17 So *he* s, "Send them." And they H606
2Ki 2:18 staying in Jericho, *he* s to them, "Didn't I H606
2Ki 2:19 The people of the city s to Elisha, "Look H606
2Ki 2:20 me a new bowl," *he* s, "and put salt in it." H606
2Ki 2:23 out of here, baldy!" *they* s. "Get out of here H606
2Ki 3:12 Jehoshaphat s, "The word of the LORD is H606
2Ki 3:13 Elisha s to the king of Israel, "Why do you H606
2Ki 3:14 Elisha s, "As surely as the LORD Almighty H606
2Ki 3:16 and *he* s, "This is what the LORD says: I will H606
2Ki 3:23 *they* s. "Those kings must H606
2Ki 4: 2 there at all," *she* s, "except a small jar H606
2Ki 4: 3 Elisha s, "Go around and ask all your H606
2Ki 4: 6 the jars were full, *she* s to her son, "Bring H606
2Ki 4: 7 told the man of God, and *he* s, "Go, H606
2Ki 4: 9 *She* s to her husband, "I know that this man H606
2Ki 4:12 *He* s to his servant Gehazi, "Call the H606
2Ki 4:13 Elisha s to him, "Tell her, 'You have gone H606
2Ki 4:14 Gehazi s, "She has no son, and her H606
2Ki 4:15 Then Elisha s, "Call her." So he called her H606
2Ki 4:16 next year," Elisha s, "you will hold a son H606
2Ki 4:19 *He* s to his father, "My head! My head!" H606
2Ki 4:22 She called her husband and s, "Please H606
2Ki 4:23 the Sabbath." "That's all right," *she* s. H606
2Ki 4:24 saddled the donkey and s to her servant, H606
2Ki 4:25 the man of God s to his servant Gehazi H606
2Ki 4:26 "Everything is all right," *she* s. H606
2Ki 4:27 the man of God s, "Leave her alone! H606
2Ki 4:28 a son, my lord?" *she* s. "Didn't I tell you H606
2Ki 4:29 Elisha s to Gehazi, "Tuck your cloak into H606
2Ki 4:30 But the child's mother s, "As surely as the H606
2Ki 4:36 Elisha summoned Gehazi and s, "Call the H606
2Ki 4:36 When she came, *he* s, "Take your son." H606
2Ki 4:38 meeting with him, *he* s to his servant, "Put H606
2Ki 4:41 Elisha s, "Get some flour." He put it into H606
2Ki 4:41 He put it into the pot and s, "Serve it to the H606
2Ki 4:42 "Give it to the people to eat," Elisha s. H606
2Ki 5: 3 *She* s to her mistress, "If only my master H606
2Ki 5: 4 told him what the girl from Israel *had* s. H1819
2Ki 5: 7 he tore his robes and s, "Am I God? H606
2Ki 5:11 But Naaman went away angry and s, "I H606
2Ki 5:13 Naaman's servants went to him and s H1819
2Ki 5:15 He stood before him and s, "Now I know H606
2Ki 5:17 "If you will not," s Naaman, "please let me H606
2Ki 5:19 "Go in peace," Elisha s. After Naaman had H606
2Ki 5:20 the man of God, s to himself, "My master H606
2Ki 5:23 all means, take two talents," s Naaman. H606
2Ki 5:26 But Elisha s to him, "Was not my spirit with H606
2Ki 6: 1 The company of the prophets s to Elisha H606
2Ki 6: 2 there for us to meet." And *he* s, "Go." H606
2Ki 6: 3 Then one of them s, "Won't you please H606
2Ki 6: 7 "Lift it out," *he* s. Then the man reached out H606
2Ki 6: 8 with his officers, he s, "I will set up my H606
2Ki 6:12 my lord the king," s one of his officers, "but H606
2Ki 6:20 Elisha s, "LORD, open the eyes of H606
2Ki 6:28 "This woman s to me, 'Give up your H606
2Ki 6:29 The next day *I* s to her, 'Give up your son H606
2Ki 6:31 *He* s, "May God deal with me, be it ever so H606
2Ki 6:32 he arrived, Elisha s to the elders, "Don't H606
2Ki 6:33 The king s, "This disaster is H606
2Ki 7: 2 the king was leaning s *to* the man of God, H6699
2Ki 7: 3 *They* s to each other, "Why stay here until H606
2Ki 7: 6 a great army, so that *they* s to one another H606
2Ki 7: 9 Then *they* s to each other, "What we're H606
2Ki 7:12 got up in the night and s to his officers, H606
2Ki 7:16 barley sold for a shekel, as the LORD had s. H1821
2Ki 7:18 as the man of God *had* s to the king: H1819
2Ki 7:19 The officer *had* s *to* the man of God H6699
2Ki 8: 1 Now Elisha *had* s to the woman whose H1819
2Ki 8: 2 proceeded to do as the man of God s. H1821
2Ki 8: 4 man of God, and *had* s, "Tell me about all H606
2Ki 8: 5 Gehazi s, "This is the woman, my lord the H606
2Ki 8: 6 an official to her case and s to him, H606
2Ki 8: 8 he s to Hazael, "Take a gift with you and go H606
2Ki 8: 9 before him, and s, "Your son Ben-Hadad H606
2Ki 8:13 Hazael s, "How could your servant, a mere H606
2Ki 9: 1 the company of the prophets and s to him, H606
2Ki 9: 5 a message for you, commander," *he* s. H606
2Ki 9:12 "That's not true!" *they* s. "Tell us." Jehu H606
2Ki 9:12 Jehu s, "Here is what he told me H606
2Ki 9:15 Jehu s, "If you desire to make me king H606
2Ki 9:18 The horseman rode off to meet Jehu and s H606
2Ki 9:19 When he came to them *he* s, "This is what H606
2Ki 9:25 Jehu s to Bidkar, his chariot officer, "Pick H606
2Ki 9:33 Jehu s. So they threw her H606
2Ki 9:34 cursed woman," *he* s, "and bury her, for H606
2Ki 9:36 told Jehu, *who* s, "This is the word H606
2Ki 10: 1 to the guardians of Ahab's children. He s, H606
2Ki 10: 4 But they were terrified and s, "If two kings H606
2Ki 10: 9 He stood before all the people and s, "You H606
2Ki 10:13 *They* s, "We are relatives of Ahaziah, and H606
2Ki 10:15 Jehu greeted him and s, "Are you in accord H606
2Ki 10:15 "If so," s Jehu, "give me your NDT
2Ki 10:16 Jehu s, "Come with me and see my zeal H606
2Ki 10:18 all the people together and s to them, H606
2Ki 10:20 Jehu s, "Call an assembly in honor of Baal." H606
2Ki 10:22 And Jehu s to the keeper of the wardrobe H606
2Ki 10:23 Jehu s to the servants of Baal, "Look H606
2Ki 10:30 The LORD s to Jehu, "Because you have H606
2Ki 11:15 For the priest *had* s, "She must not be put H606
2Ki 12: 4 Joash s to the priests, "Collect all the H606
2Ki 13:15 Elisha s, "Get a bow and some arrows," H606
2Ki 13:16 in your hands," *he* s to the king of Israel. H606
2Ki 13:17 the east window," *he* s, and he opened it. H606
2Ki 13:17 Elisha s, and he shot. "The LORD's H606
2Ki 13:18 Then *he* s, "Take the arrows," and the king H606
2Ki 13:19 The man of God was angry with him and s H606
2Ki 14:27 since the LORD *had* not s he would blot H1819
2Ki 17:12 though the LORD *had* s, "You shall not do H606
2Ki 18:19 The field commander s to them, "Tell H606
2Ki 18:26 Shebna and Joah s to the field H606
2Ki 18:36 remained silent and s nothing **in reply**, H6699
2Ki 18:37 told him **what** the field commander had s. H1821
2Ki 19: 6 Isaiah s to them, "Tell your master, 'This is H606
2Ki 19:23 And *you have* s, "With my many chariots I H606
2Ki 20: 1 Isaiah son of Amoz went to him and s, H606
2Ki 20: 7 Then Isaiah s, "Prepare a poultice of figs." H606
2Ki 20:10 to go forward ten steps," s Hezekiah. H606
2Ki 20:15 saw everything in my palace," Hezekiah s. H606
2Ki 20:16 Then Isaiah s to Hezekiah, "Hear the word H606
2Ki 21: 4 of which the LORD *had* s, "In Jerusalem I H606
2Ki 21: 7 of which the LORD *had* s to David and to his H606
2Ki 21:10 The LORD s through his servants the H1819
2Ki 22: 3 to the temple of the LORD. He s: H606
2Ki 22: 8 Hilkiah the high priest s to Shaphan the H606
2Ki 22:15 *She* s to them, "This is what the LORD, the H606
2Ki 23:17 The people of the city s, "It marks the tomb H606
2Ki 23:18 "Leave it alone," *he* s. "Don't let anyone H606
2Ki 23:27 So the LORD s, "I will remove Judah also H606
2Ki 23:27 about which *I* s, 'My Name shall be H606
2Ki 25:24 be afraid of the Babylonian officials," *he* s. H606
1Ch 10: 4 Saul s to his armor-bearer, "Draw your H606
1Ch 11: 1 came together to David at Hebron and s, H606
1Ch 11: 2 And the LORD your God s to you, 'You will H606
1Ch 11: 5 s to David, "You will not get in here." H606
1Ch 11: 6 David *had* s, "Whoever leads the attack on H606
1Ch 11:17 David longed for water and s, "Oh, that H606
1Ch 11:19 I should do this!" *he* s. "Should I drink the H606
1Ch 12:17 went out to meet them and s to them, H6699
1Ch 12:18 on Amasai, chief of the Thirty, and he s: NDT
1Ch 12:19 They s, "It will cost us our heads if he H606
1Ch 12:23 kingdom over to him, as the LORD had s: H7023
1Ch 13: 2 He then s to the whole assembly of Israel H606
1Ch 14:11 He s, "As waters break out, God has broken H606
1Ch 15: 2 Then David s, "No one but the Levites may H606
1Ch 15:12 *He* s to them, "You are the heads of the H606
1Ch 16:36 Then all the people s "Amen" and "Praise H606
1Ch 17: 1 in his palace, he s to Nathan the prophet H606
1Ch 17:16 went in and sat before the LORD, and *he* s: H606
1Ch 19: 3 the Ammonite commanders s to Hanun H606
1Ch 19: 5 The king s, "Stay at Jericho till your beards H606
1Ch 19:12 Joab s, "If the Arameans are too strong H606
1Ch 21: 2 So David s to Joab and the commanders of H606
1Ch 21: 8 Then David s to God, "I have sinned H606
1Ch 21: 9 The LORD s to Gad, David's seer, H1819
1Ch 21:11 So Gad went to David and s to him, "This H606
1Ch 21:13 David s to Gad, "I am in deep distress. H606
1Ch 21:15 the disaster and s to the angel who was H606
1Ch 21:17 David s to God, "Was it not I who ordered H606
1Ch 21:22 David s to him, "Let me have the site of H606
1Ch 21:23 Araunah s to David, "Take it! Let my lord H606
1Ch 22: 1 Then David s, "The house of the LORD God H606
1Ch 22: 5 David s, "My son Solomon is young and H606
1Ch 22: 7 David s to Solomon: "My son, I had it in my H606
1Ch 22:11 of the LORD your God, as *he* s you would. H1819
1Ch 22:18 He s to them, "Is not the LORD your God NDT
1Ch 23: 4 David s, "Of these, twenty-four thousand are NDT
1Ch 23:25 For David *had* s, "Since the LORD, the God H606
1Ch 28: 2 King David rose to his feet and s: "Listen to H606
1Ch 28: 3 But God s to me, 'You are not to build a H606
1Ch 28: 6 *He* s to me: 'Solomon your son is the one H606
1Ch 28:19 David s, "I have in writing as a result of the NDT
1Ch 28:20 David also s to Solomon his son, "Be H606
1Ch 29: 1 Then King David s to the whole assembly H606
1Ch 29:20 Then David s to the whole assembly H606
2Ch 1: 7 God appeared to Solomon and s to him, H606
2Ch 1:11 God s to Solomon, "Since this is your H606
2Ch 6: 1 Then Solomon s, "The LORD has said that H606
2Ch 6: 1 "The LORD *has* s that he would dwell in a H606
2Ch 6: 4 Then *he* s: "Praise be to the LORD, the God H606
2Ch 6: 4 his mouth to my father David. For he s, H606
2Ch 6: 8 But the LORD s to my father David, 'You did H606
2Ch 6:14 *He* s: "LORD, the God of Israel, there is no H606
2Ch 6:16 the promises you made to him when you s, H606
2Ch 6:20 place of which *you* s you would put your H606
2Ch 7:12 the LORD appeared to him at night and s: "I H606
2Ch 7:18 with David your father when I s, H606
2Ch 8:11 built for her, for *he* s, "My wife must not H606
2Ch 9: 5 *She* s to the king, "The report I heard in my H606
2Ch 9: 6 did not believe **what** they s until I came H1821
2Ch 10: 3 all Israel went to Rehoboam and s to him: H1819
2Ch 10:10 "The people *have* s to you, 'Your father H1819
2Ch 10:12 as the king *had* s, "Come back to me in H1819
2Ch 10:14 the advice of the young men and s, H1819
2Ch 12: 5 fear of Shishak, and *he* s to them, "This is H606
2Ch 12: 6 the king humbled themselves and s, H606
2Ch 13: 4 of Ephraim, and s, "Jeroboam and all H606
2Ch 13:22 what he did and **what** he s, are written in H1821
2Ch 14: 7 *he* s to Judah, "and put walls around H606
2Ch 14:11 Then Asa called to the LORD his God and s H606
2Ch 15: 2 He went out to meet Asa and s to him H606
2Ch 16: 3 he s, "as there was between my father H606
2Ch 16: 7 came to Asa king of Judah and s to him: H606
2Ch 18: 4 But Jehoshaphat also s to the king of Israel H606
2Ch 18: 8 of Israel called one of his officials and s, H606
2Ch 18:11 they s, "for the LORD will give it into the H606
2Ch 18:12 had gone to summon Micaiah s to him, H1819
2Ch 18:13 But Micaiah s, "As surely as the LORD lives, H606
2Ch 18:15 The king s to him, "How many times must I H606
2Ch 18:16 the LORD s, 'These people have no H606
2Ch 18:17 The king of Israel s to Jehoshaphat, "Didn't H606
2Ch 18:19 And the LORD s, 'Who will entice Ahab king H606
2Ch 18:20 stood before the LORD and s, 'I will entice H606
2Ch 18:21 in the mouths of all his prophets,' *he* s. H606
2Ch 18:21 will succeed in enticing him,' s the LORD. H606
2Ch 18:29 The king of Israel s to Jehoshaphat, "I will H606
2Ch 19: 2 went out to meet him and s to the king H606
2Ch 20: 6 s: "LORD, the God of our ancestors, are H606
2Ch 20:15 *He* s: "Listen, King Jehoshaphat and all H606
2Ch 20:20 Jehoshaphat stood and s, "Listen to me, H606
2Ch 21:12 a letter from Elijah the prophet, which s: H606
2Ch 22: 9 buried him, for *they* s, "He was a son of H606
2Ch 23: 3 Jehoiada s to them, "The king's son shall H606
2Ch 23:14 in charge of the troops, and s to them: H606
2Ch 23:14 For the priest *had* s, "Do not put her to H606
2Ch 24: 5 the priests and Levites and s to them, H606
2Ch 24: 6 Jehoiada the chief priest and s to him, H606
2Ch 24:20 He stood before the people and s, "This is H606
2Ch 24:22 killed his son, *who* s as he lay dying H606
2Ch 25: 7 But a man of God came to him and s H606
2Ch 25:15 a prophet to him, *who* s, "Why do you H606
2Ch 25:16 still speaking, the king s to him, "Have we H606
2Ch 25:16 So the prophet stopped but s, "I know that H606
2Ch 26:18 They confronted King Uzziah and s, "It is H606
2Ch 26:23 to the kings, for *people* s, "He had leprosy." H606
2Ch 28: 9 *He* s to them, "Because the LORD, the God H606
2Ch 28:13 *they* s, "or we will be guilty before the H606
2Ch 29: 5 s: "Listen to me, Levites! Consecrate H606
2Ch 29:31 Then Hezekiah s, "You have now H6699
2Ch 32: 4 come and find plenty of water?" *they* s. H606
2Ch 32: 8 from **what** Hezekiah the king of Judah s. H1821
2Ch 33: 4 of which the LORD *had* s, "My Name will H606
2Ch 33: 7 of which God *had* s to David and to his son H606
2Ch 34:15 Hilkiah s to Shaphan the secretary, "I have H6699
2Ch 34:23 *She* s to them, "This is what the LORD, the H606
2Ch 35: 3 *He* s to the Levites, who instructed all Israel H606
2Ch 35:22 not listen to **what** Necho had s at God's H1821
Ezr 4: 2 to the heads of the families and s, H606
Ezr 8:28 *I* s to them, "You as well as these articles H606
Ezr 9: 1 the leaders came to me and s, "The H606
Ezr 9:11 your servants the prophets when you s: H606
Ezr 10: 2 descendants of Elam, s to Ezra, "We have H6699
Ezr 10:10 Then Ezra the priest stood up and s to them, H606
Ne 1: 3 *They* s to me, "Those who survived the H606
Ne 1: 5 Then *I* s: "LORD, the God of heaven, the H606
Ne 2: 3 but *I* s to the king, "May the king live forever H606
Ne 2: 4 The king s to me, "What is it you want?" H606
Ne 2: 7 *I* also s to him, "If it pleases the king, may I H606
Ne 2:16 because as yet *I had* s nothing to the H5583
Ne 2:17 Then *I* s to them, "You see the trouble we H606
Ne 2:18 God on me and what the king *had* s to me. H606
Ne 4: 2 the army of Samaria, *he* s, "What are those H606
Ne 4: 3 who was at his side, s, "What they are H606
Ne 4:10 the people in Judah s, "The strength of the H606
Ne 4:11 Also our enemies s, "Before they know it H606
Ne 4:14 I stood up and s to the nobles, the H606
Ne 4:19 Then *I* s to the nobles, the officials and the H606
Ne 4:22 At that time *I* also s to the people, "Have H606
Ne 5: 8 s: "As far as possible, we have bought H606
Ne 5:12 will give it back," *they* s. "And we will not H606
Ne 5:13 I also shook out the folds of my robe and s H606
Ne 5:13 At this the whole assembly s, "Amen," H606
Ne 6:10 *He* s, "Let us meet in the house of God H606
Ne 6:11 But *I* s, "Should a man like me run away H606
Ne 6:19 good deeds and then telling him **what** I s. H1821
Ne 7: 3 *I* s to them, "The gates of Jerusalem are not H606
Ne 8: 9 were instructing the people s to them all, H606
Ne 8:10 Nehemiah s, "Go and enjoy choice food H606
Ne 9: 5 Hodiah, Shebaniah and Pethahiah—s: H606
Ne 9:18 themselves an image of a calf and s, H606
Ne 9:29 of which you s, 'The person who obeys NDT
Ne 13:17 the nobles of Judah and s to them, H606
Ne 13:21 But I warned them and s, "Why do you H606
Ne 13:25 them take an oath in God's name and s: NDT
Est 3: 8 Then Haman s to King Xerxes, "There is a H606
Est 3:11 the king s to Haman, "and do with the H606
Est 4: 9 reported to Esther **what** Mordecai had s. H1821
Est 5: 5 the king s, "so that we may do what Esther H606
Est 5:14 His wife Zeresh and all his friends s to him H606
Est 6: 4 The king s, "Who is in the court?" Now H606
Est 6:13 His advisers and his wife Zeresh s to him H606
Est 7: 6 Esther s, "An adversary and enemy! This H606
Est 7: 9 attending the king, s, "A pole reaching to a H606
Est 7: 9 The king s, "Impale him on it!" H606
Est 8: 5 *she* s, "and if he regards me with favor H606
Est 9:12 The king s to Queen Esther, "The Jews have H606
Job 1: 7 The LORD s to Satan, "Where have you come H606
Job 1: 8 Then the LORD s to Satan, "Have you H606
Job 1:12 The LORD s to Satan, "Very well, then H606

Job	1:14	a messenger came to Job and s, "The oxen	H606
Job	1:16	another messenger came and s, "The fire	H606
Job	1:17	another messenger came and s, "The	H606
Job	1:18	another messenger came and s, "Your	H606
Job	1:21	s: "Naked I came from my mother's	H606
Job	2: 2	And the LORD s to Satan, "Where have you	H606
Job	2: 3	Then the LORD s to Satan, "Have you	H606
Job	2: 6	The LORD s to Satan, "Very well, then, he is	H606
Job	2: 9	His wife s to him, "Are you still	H606
Job	2:10	In all this, Job did not sin in what he s.	H8557
Job	2:13	No one s a word to him, because they	H1819
Job	3: 2	He s:	H6699
Job	3: 3	the night that s, 'A boy is conceived	H606
Job	6:22	Have I ever s, 'Give something on my	H606
Job	21:19	It is s, 'God stores up the punishment of the	NDT
Job	22:17	They s to God, 'Leave us alone! What can	H606
Job	28:28	And he s to the human race, "The fear of	H606
Job	31:24	have put my trust in gold or s to pure gold,	H606
Job	31:31	if those of my household have never s	H606
Job	32: 6	So Elihu son of Barakel the Buzite s: "I am	H6699
Job	33: 8	"But you have s in my hearing—I heard	H606
Job	34: 1	Then Elihu s:	H6699
Job	35: 1	Then Elihu s:	H6699
Job	36: 2	that there is more to be s in God's behalf.	H4863
Job	36:23	his ways for him, or s to him, 'You have	H606
Job	38: 1	LORD spoke to Job out of the storm. He s:	H606
Job	38:11	when I s, 'This far you may come and no	H606
Job	40: 1	The LORD s to Job:	H6699
Job	42: 4	"You s, 'Listen now, and I will speak; I will	NDT
Job	42: 7	After the LORD had s these things to Job	H1819
Job	42: 7	things to Job, he s to Eliphaz the Temanite	H606
Ps	2: 7	He s to me, "You are my son; today I have	H606
Ps	18: T	enemies and from the hand of Saul. He s:	H606
Ps	30: 6	When I felt secure, I s, "I will never be	H606
Ps	31:22	In my alarm I s, "I am cut off from your	H606
Ps	32: 5	I s, "I will confess my transgressions to the	H606
Ps	38:16	For I s, "Do not let them gloat or exalt	H606
Ps	39: 1	I s, "I will watch my ways and keep my	H606
Ps	40: 7	Then I s, "Here I am, I have come—it is	H606
Ps	41: 4	I s, "Have mercy on me, LORD; heal me, for I	H606
Ps	54: T	When the Ziphites had gone to Saul and s	H606
Ps	55: 6	I s, "Oh, that I had the wings of a dove!	H606
Ps	74: 8	They s in their hearts, "We will crush them	H606
Ps	78:19	spoke against God; they s, "Can God really	H606
Ps	82: 6	"I s, 'You are "gods"; you are all sons of	H606
Ps	83:12	who s, "Let us take possession of the	H606
Ps	87: 3	Glorious things are s of you, city of God:	H1819
Ps	87: 5	of Zion it will be s, "This one and	H606
Ps	89: 3	You s, "I have made a covenant with my	NDT
Ps	89:19	in a vision, to your faithful people you s:	H606
Ps	94:18	When I s, "My foot is slipping," your	H606
Ps	95:10	that generation; I s, 'They are a people	H606
Ps	102:24	So I s: "Do not take me away, my God, in	H606
Ps	106:23	So he s he would destroy them—had not	H606
Ps	116:10	I trusted in the LORD when I s, "I am	H1819
Ps	116:11	in my alarm I s, "Everyone is a liar.	H606
Ps	122: 1	I rejoiced with those who s to me, "Let us	H606
Ps	126: 2	Then it was s among the nations, "The	H606
Ps	137: 3	songs of joy; they s, "Sing us one of the	NDT
Pr	4: 4	he taught me, and he s to me, "Take hold	H606
Pr	6: 2	have been trapped by what you s,	H609+7023
Pr	7:13	kissed him and with a brazen face she s:	H606
Ecc	1:16	I s to myself, "Look, I have increased in	H1819
Ecc	2: 1	I s to myself, "Come now, I will test you	H606
Ecc	2: 2	"Laughter," I s, "is madness. And what does	H606
Ecc	2:15	Then I s to myself, "The fate of the fool will	H606
Ecc	2:15	by being wise?" I s to myself, "This too	H1819
Ecc	3:17	I s to myself, "God will bring into judgment	H606
Ecc	3:18	I also s to myself, "As for humans, God	H606
Ecc	7:23	All this I tested by wisdom and I s, "I am	H606
Ecc	9:16	So I s, "Wisdom is better than strength."	H606
SS	2:10	My beloved spoke and s to me, "Arise, my	H606
SS	7: 8	I s, "I will climb the palm tree; I will take	H606
Isa	6: 7	With it he touched my mouth and s, "See	H606
Isa	6: 8	will go for us?" And I s, "Here am I.	H606
Isa	6: 9	He s, "Go and tell this people: " 'Be ever	H606
Isa	6:11	Then I s, "For how long, Lord?" And he	H606
Isa	7: 3	Then the LORD s to Isaiah, "Go out, you	H606
Isa	7:12	But Ahaz s, "I will not ask; I will not put the	H606
Isa	7:13	Then Isaiah s, "Hear now, you house of	H606
Isa	8: 1	The LORD s to me, "Take a large scroll and	H606
Isa	8: 3	And the LORD s to me, "Name him	H606
Isa	14:13	You s in your heart, "I will ascend to the	H606
Isa	20: 2	He s to him, "Take off the sackcloth from	H606
Isa	20: 3	Then the LORD s, "Just as my servant Isaiah	H606
Isa	22: 4	Therefore I s, "Turn away from me; let me	H606
Isa	23:12	He s, "No more of your reveling, Virgin	H606
Isa	24:16	Righteous One." But I s, "I waste away,	H606
Isa	28:12	to whom he s, "This is the resting place, let	H606
Isa	30:16	You s, 'No, we will flee on horses.'	H606
Isa	30:16	You s, 'We will ride off on	NDT
Isa	36: 4	The field commander s to them, "Tell	H606
Isa	36:11	Shebna and Joah s to the field commander	H606
Isa	36:21	remained silent and s nothing in reply,	H6699
Isa	36:22	told him what the field commander had s.	H1821
Isa	37: 6	Isaiah s to them, "Tell your master, 'This is	H606
Isa	37:24	And you have s, 'With my many chariots I	H606
Isa	38: 1	Isaiah son of Amoz went to him and s,	H606
Isa	38:10	I s, "In the prime of my life must I go	H606
Isa	38:11	I s, "I will not again see the LORD himself in	H606
Isa	38:21	Isaiah had s, "Prepare a poultice of figs	H606
Isa	39: 4	saw everything in my palace," Hezekiah s.	H606
Isa	39: 5	Then Isaiah s to Hezekiah, "Hear the word	H606
Isa	40: 6	And I s, "What shall I cry?" "All	H606
Isa	41: 9	I s, 'You are my servant'; I have chosen you	H606
Isa	45:19	I have not s to Jacob's descendants	H606
Isa	46:11	What I have s, that I will bring about	H1819
Isa	47: 7	You s, 'I am forever—the eternal queen!'	H606
Isa	47:10	trusted in your wickedness and have s,	H606
Isa	49: 3	He s to me, "You are my servant, Israel, in	H606
Isa	49: 4	But I s, "I have labored in vain; I have	H606
Isa	49:14	But Zion s, "The LORD has forsaken me, the	H606
Isa	51:23	your tormentors, who s to you, 'Fall	H606
Isa	57:14	And it will be s: "Build up, build up	H606
Isa	63: 8	He s, "Surely they are my people, children	H606
Isa	65: 1	did not call on my name, I s, 'Here am I,	H606
Isa	66: 5	of my name, have s, 'Let the LORD be	H606
Jer	1: 6	Sovereign LORD," I s, "I do not know how to	H606
Jer	1: 7	But the LORD s to me, "Do not say, 'I am too	H606
Jer	1: 9	hand and touched my mouth and s to me,	H606
Jer	1:12	The LORD s to me, "You have seen correctly	H606
Jer	1:14	The LORD s to me, "From the north disaster	H606
Jer	2:20	tore off your bonds; you s, 'I will not serve	H606
Jer	2:25	But you s, 'It's no use! I love	H606
Jer	3: 6	the LORD s to me, "Have you seen	H606
Jer	3:11	The LORD s to me, "Faithless Israel is more	H606
Jer	3:19	"I myself s, " 'How gladly would I treat you	H606
Jer	4:10	Then I s, "Alas, Sovereign LORD! How	H606
Jer	5:12	about the LORD; they s, "He will do nothing	H606
Jer	6:16	your souls. But you s, 'We will not walk	H606
Jer	6:17	I appointed watchmen over you and s	NDT
Jer	6:17	of the trumpet!' But you s, 'We will not	H606
Jer	9:13	The LORD s, "It is because they have	H606
Jer	10:19	Yet I s to myself, "This is my sickness, and I	H606
Jer	11: 4	I s, 'Obey me and do everything I	H606
Jer	11: 6	The LORD s to me, "Proclaim all these words	H606
Jer	11: 9	Then the LORD s to me, "There is a	H606
Jer	13: 1	This is what the LORD s to me: "Go and buy	H606
Jer	13: 6	Many days later the LORD s to me, "Go now	H606
Jer	14:11	Then the LORD s to me, "Do not pray for the	H606
Jer	14:13	But I s, "Alas, Sovereign LORD! The prophets	H606
Jer	14:14	Then the LORD s to me, "The prophets are	H606
Jer	15: 1	Then the LORD s to me: "Even if Moses and	H606
Jer	15:11	The LORD s, "Surely I will deliver you for a	H606
Jer	16:14	"when it will no longer be s, 'As	H606
Jer	16:15	it will be s, 'As surely as the LORD lives	NDT
Jer	17:19	This is what the LORD s to me: "Go and	H606
Jer	18: 6	He s, "Can I not do with you, Israel, as this	H606
Jer	18:18	They s, "Come, let's make plans against	H606
Jer	19:14	the LORD's temple and s to all the people,	H606
Jer	20: 3	the stocks, Jeremiah s to him, "The LORD's	H606
Jer	21: 1	priest Zephaniah son of Maaseiah. They s:	H606
Jer	22:21	you felt secure, but you s, 'I will not listen!	H606
Jer	25: 2	the prophet s to all the people of	H1819
Jer	25: 5	They s, "Turn now, each of you, from your	H606
Jer	25:15	is what the LORD, the God of Israel, s to me:	H606
Jer	26: 8	all the people seized him and s,	H606
Jer	26:11	the prophets s to the officials and all	H606
Jer	26:12	Then Jeremiah s to all the officials and all	H606
Jer	26:16	all the people s to the priests and the	H606
Jer	26:17	stepped forward and s to the entire	H606
Jer	27: 2	This is what the LORD s to me: "Make a yoke	H606
Jer	27:12	I s, "Bow your neck under the yoke of the	H606
Jer	27:16	Then I s to the priests and all these	H1819
Jer	28: 1	s to me in the house of the LORD in the	H606
Jer	28: 6	He s, "Amen! May the LORD do so! May the	H606
Jer	28:11	he s before all the people, "This is	H606
Jer	28:15	the prophet Jeremiah s to Hananiah the	H606
Jer	29: 3	to King Nebuchadnezzar in Babylon. It s:	H606
Jer	29:25	all the other priests. You s to Zephaniah,	H606
Jer	32: 6	Jeremiah s, "The word of the LORD came to	H606
Jer	32: 8	just as the LORD had s, my cousin	H1821
Jer	32: 8	to me in the courtyard of the guard and s,	H606
Jer	32:24	What you s has happened, as you now	H1819
Jer	34:13	out of Egypt, out of the land of slavery. I s,	H606
Jer	35: 5	cups before the Rekabites and s to them,	H606
Jer	35:11	of Babylon invaded this land, we s, 'Come,	H606
Jer	35:15	They s, "Each of you must turn from your	H606
Jer	35:18	Then Jeremiah s to the family of the	H606
Jer	36:15	They s to him, "Sit down, please, and read	H606
Jer	36:16	at each other in fear and s to Baruch,	H606
Jer	36:19	Then the officials s to Baruch, "You and	H606
Jer	36:29	You burned that scroll and s, "Why did you	H606
Jer	37:13	arrested him and s, "You are deserting to	H606
Jer	37:14	Jeremiah s. "I am not deserting	H606
Jer	37:18	Then Jeremiah s to King Zedekiah, "What	H606
Jer	38: 1	was telling all the people when he s,	H606
Jer	38: 4	Then the officials s to the king, "This man	H606
Jer	38: 8	went out of the palace and s to him,	H1819
Jer	38:12	Ebed-Melek the Cushite s to Jeremiah, "Put	H606
Jer	38:14	you something," the king s to Jeremiah.	H606
Jer	38:15	Jeremiah s to Zedekiah, "If I give you an	H606
Jer	38:17	Then Jeremiah s to Zedekiah, "This is what	H606
Jer	38:19	King Zedekiah s to Jeremiah, "I am afraid	H606
Jer	38:24	Then Zedekiah s to Jeremiah, "Do not let	H606
Jer	38:25	'Tell us what you s to the king and what	H1819
Jer	38:25	to the king and what the king s to you;	H1819
Jer	38:27	So they s no more to him, for no one had	H3087
Jer	40: 2	found Jeremiah, he s to him, "The LORD	H606
Jer	40: 3	he has done just as he s he would.	H1819
Jer	40: 9	be afraid to serve the Babylonians," he s.	H606
Jer	40:14	s to him, "Don't you know that Baalis	H606
Jer	40:15	son of Kareah s privately to Gedaliah	H606
Jer	40:16	son of Ahikam s to Johanan son of	H606
Jer	41: 6	When he met them, he s, "Come to	H606
Jer	41: 8	But ten of them s to Ishmael, "Don't kill us	H606
Jer	42: 2	Jeremiah the prophet and s to him, "Please	H606
Jer	42: 5	Then they s to Jeremiah, "May the LORD be	H606
Jer	42: 9	He s to them, "This is what the LORD, the	H606
Jer	42:20	you sent me to the LORD your God and s,	H606
Jer	43: 2	all the arrogant men s to Jeremiah,	H606
Jer	44: 4	the prophets, who s, 'Do not do this	H606
Jer	44:15	in Lower and Upper Egypt, s to Jeremiah,	H6699
Jer	44:17	everything we s we would:	H3655+4946+7023
Jer	44:20	Then Jeremiah s to all the people, both	H606
Jer	44:24	Then Jeremiah s to all the people	H606
Jer	44:25	what you s you would do	H1819+928+7023
Jer	45: 1	king of Judah, Jeremiah s this to Baruch:	H1819
Jer	45: 3	You s, 'Woe to me! The LORD has added	H606
Jer	50: 7	their enemies s, 'We are not guilty,	H606
Jer	51:61	He s to Seraiah, "When you get to Babylon	H606
Jer	51:62	you have s you will destroy this place	H1819
La	3:57	when I called you, and you s, "Do not fear."	H606
Eze	2: 1	He s to me, "Son of man, stand up on your	H606
Eze	2: 3	He s: "Son of man, I am sending you to the	H606
Eze	3: 1	And he s to me, "Son of man, eat what is	H606
Eze	3: 3	Then he s to me, "Son of man, eat this	H606
Eze	3: 4	He then s to me: "Son of man, go now to	H606
Eze	3:10	And he s to me, "Son of man, listen	H606
Eze	3:22	on me there, and he s to me, "Get up and	H606
Eze	3:24	me to my feet. He spoke to me and s: "Go,	H606
Eze	4:13	The LORD s, "In this way the people of Israel	H606
Eze	4:14	Then I s, "Not so, Sovereign LORD! I have	H606
Eze	4:15	he s, "I will let you bake your bread over	H606
Eze	4:16	He then s to me: "Son of man, I am about	H606
Eze	8: 5	Then he s to me, "Son of man, look toward	H606
Eze	8: 6	And he s to me, "Son of man, do you see	H606
Eze	8: 8	He s to me, "Son of man, now dig into the	H606
Eze	8: 9	And he s to me, "Go in and see the wicked	H606
Eze	8:12	He s to me, "Son of man, have you seen	H606
Eze	8:13	he s, "You will see them doing	H606
Eze	8:15	He s to me, "Do you see this, son of man	H606
Eze	8:17	He s to me, "Have you seen this, son of	H606
Eze	9: 4	s to him, "Go throughout the city of	H606
Eze	9: 5	As I listened, he s to the others, "Follow	H606
Eze	9: 7	Then he s to them, "Defile the temple	H606
Eze	10: 2	The LORD s to the man clothed in linen, "Go	H606
Eze	11: 2	The LORD s to me, "Son of man, these are	H606
Eze	11:15	people of Jerusalem have s of your fellow	H606
Eze	16: 6	as you lay there in your blood I s to you,	H606
Eze	20: 5	With uplifted hand I s to them, "I am the	H606
Eze	20: 7	And I s to them, "Each of you, get rid of the	H606
Eze	20: 8	So I s I would pour out my wrath on them	H606
Eze	20:13	So I s I would pour out my wrath on them	H606
Eze	20:18	I s to their children in the wilderness, "Do	H606
Eze	20:21	my laws, of which I s, "The person who	NDT
Eze	20:21	So I s I would pour out my wrath on them	H606
Eze	20:29	Then I s to them: What is this high place	H606
Eze	20:49	Then I s, "Sovereign LORD, they are saying	H606
Eze	23:36	The LORD s to me: "Son of man, will you	H606
Eze	23:43	Then I s about the one worn out by adultery,	H606
Eze	24:20	So I s to them, "The word of the LORD came	H606
Eze	25: 3	Because you s "Aha!" over my	H606
Eze	25: 8	'Because Moab and Seir s, "Look, Judah	H606
Eze	26: 2	because Tyre has s of Jerusalem	H606
Eze	29: 9	" 'Because you s, "The Nile is mine;	H606
Eze	33:21	from Jerusalem came to me and s,	H606
Eze	35:10	" 'Because you have s, "These two nations	H606
Eze	35:12	contemptible things you have s against the	H606
Eze	35:12	You s, "They have been laid waste and	H606
Eze	36: 2	The enemy s of you, "Aha! The	H606
Eze	36:20	my holy name, for it was s of them, 'These	H606
Eze	37: 3	these bones live?" I s, "Sovereign LORD, you	H606
Eze	37: 4	Then he s to me, "Prophesy to these bones	H606
Eze	37: 9	Then he s to me, "Prophesy to the breath	H606
Eze	37:11	Then he s to me: "Son of man, these	H606
Eze	40: 4	The man s to me, "Son of man, look	H1819
Eze	40:45	He s to me, "The room facing south is	H1819
Eze	41: 4	of the main hall. He s to me, "This is the	H606
Eze	41:22	The man s to me, "This is the table that is	H1819
Eze	42:13	Then he s to me, "The north and south	H606
Eze	43: 7	He s: "Son of man, this is the place of my	H606
Eze	43:18	Then he s to me, "Son of man, this is what	H606
Eze	44: 2	The LORD s to me, "This gate is to remain	H606
Eze	44: 5	The LORD s to me, "Son of man, look	H606
Eze	46:20	He s to me, "This is the place where the	H606
Eze	46:24	He s to me, "These are the kitchens where	H606
Eze	47: 8	He s to me, "This water flows toward the	H606
Da	1:11	Daniel then s to the guard whom the chief	H606
Da	2: 3	he s to them, "I have had a dream that	H606
Da	2:20	s: "Praise be to the name of God for	A10042
Da	2:24	men of Babylon, and s to him, "Do not	A10042
Da	2:25	took Daniel to the king at once and s,	A10042
Da	2:47	The king s to Daniel, "Surely your God is	A10558
Da	3: 9	They s to King Nebuchadnezzar, "May	A10558
Da	3:14	Nebuchadnezzar s to them, "Is it true	A10558
Da	3:25	He s, "Look! I see four men walking	A10558
Da	3:28	Then Nebuchadnezzar s, "Praise be to	A10558
Da	4: 9	I s, "Belteshazzar, chief of the magicians,	NDT
Da	4:19	So the king s, "Belteshazzar, do not let	A10558
Da	4:30	he s, "Is not this the great Babylon I	A10558
Da	4:33	Immediately what had been s about	A10418
Da	5: 7	Then he s to these wise men of Babylon	A10558
Da	5:10	she s. "Don't be alarmed!	A10558
Da	5:13	the king, and the king s to him, "Are you	A10558
Da	6: 5	Finally these men s, "We will never find	A10042

Da 6: 6 went as a group to the king and **s**: A10042
Da 6:13 Then *they* **s** to the king, "Daniel, who is A10558
Da 6:15 as a group to King Darius and **s** to him, A10042
Da 6:16 The king **s** to Daniel, "May your God A10558
Da 7: 2 Daniel **s**: "In my vision at night I looked A10558
Da 8:13 another holy one **s** to him, "How long H606
Da 8:14 *He* **s** to me, "It will take 2,300 evenings H606
Da 8:17 " *he* **s** to me, "understand that the vision H606
Da 8:19 *He* **s**: "I am going to tell you what will H606
Da 9:22 He instructed me and **s** to me, "Daniel, H1819
Da 10:11 *He* **s**, "Daniel, you who are highly H606
Da 10:11 And when he **s** this to me, I stood up H1819
Da 10:16 *I* **s** to the one standing before me, "I am H606
Da 10:19 you who are highly esteemed," *he* **s**. H606
Da 10:19 I was strengthened and **s**, "Speak, H606
Da 10:20 So *he* **s**, "Do you know why I have come to H606
Da 12: 6 *One of them* **s** to the man clothed in linen H606
Hos 1: 2 through Hosea, the LORD **s** to him, "Go, H606
Hos 1: 4 Then the LORD **s** to Hosea, "Call him Jezreel H606
Hos 1: 6 Then the LORD **s** to Hosea, "Call her H606
Hos 1: 9 Then the LORD **s**, "Call him Lo-Ammi H606
Hos 1:10 In the place where *it* **was s** to them, 'You H606
Hos 2: 5 *She* **s**, 'I will go after my lovers, who give H606
Hos 2:12 which *she* **s** were her pay from her lovers H606
Hos 3: 1 The LORD **s** to me, "Go, show your love to H606
Hos 13: 2 *It is* **s** of these people, "They offer human H606
Hos 13:10 your towns, of whom *you* **s**, 'Give me a king H606
Joel 2:32 as the LORD *has* **s**, even among the H606
Am 1: 2 *He* **s**: "The LORD roars from Zion and H606
Am 7: 3 "This will not happen," the LORD **s**. H606
Am 7: 6 not happen either," the Sovereign LORD **s**. H606
Am 7: 8 Then the Lord **s**, "Look, I am setting a H606
Am 7:12 Then Amaziah **s** to Amos, "Get out, you H606
Am 7:15 me from tending the flock and **s** to me, H606
Am 8: 2 Then the LORD **s** to me, "The time is ripe H606
Am 9: 1 the Lord standing by the altar, and *he* **s**: H606
Jnh 1: 6 The captain went to him and **s**, "How can H606
Jnh 1: 7 Then the sailors **s** to each other, "Come, let H606
Jnh 2: 2 *He* **s**: "In my distress I called to the LORD H606
Jnh 2: 4 I **s**, 'I have been banished from your sight H606
Jnh 4: 2 to the LORD, "Isn't this **what** I **s**, LORD, H1821
Jnh 4: 8 wanted to die, and **s**, "It would be better H606
Jnh 4: 9 But God **s** to Jonah, "Is it right for you to be H606
Jnh 4: 9 "It is," *he* **s**. "And I'm so angry I H606
Jnh 4:10 But the LORD **s**, "You have been concerned H606
Mic 2: 7 of Jacob, *should it* **be s**, "Does the LORD H606
Mic 3: 1 Then *I* **s**, "Listen, you leaders of Jacob, you H606
Mic 7:10 with shame, *she who* **s** to me, "Where is H606
Zep 2:15 lived in safety. She **s** to herself, "I am the H606
Hag 2:13 Then Haggai **s**, "If a person defiled by H606
Hag 2:14 Then Haggai **s**, " 'So it is with this people H6699
Zec 1: 6 "Then they repented and **s**, 'The LORD H606
Zec 1:12 Then the angel of the LORD **s**, "LORD H6699
Zec 1:14 Then the angel who was speaking to me **s** H606
Zec 2: 4 **s** to him: "Run, tell that young man H606
Zec 3: 2 The LORD **s** to Satan, "The LORD rebuke you H606
Zec 3: 4 The angel **s** to those who were standing H6699
Zec 3: 4 Then *he* **s** to Joshua, "See, I have taken H606
Zec 3: 5 Then *I* **s**, "Put a clean turban on his head." H606
Zec 4: 6 So *he* **s** to me, "This is the word of the H6699
Zec 4:13 know what these are?" "No, my lord," *I* **s**. H606
Zec 4:14 So *he* **s**, "These are the two who are H606
Zec 5: 3 And *he* **s** to me, "This is the curse that is H606
Zec 5: 5 speaking to me came forward and **s** to me, H606
Zec 5: 8 *He* **s**, "This is wickedness," and he pushed H606
Zec 6: 7 And *he* **s**, "Go throughout the H606
Zec 7: 9 "This is what the LORD Almighty **s** H606
Zec 8: 9 is also **what** the prophets **s** who H4946+7023
Zec 11: 9 **s**, "I will not be your shepherd. Let the H606
Zec 11:13 And the LORD **s** to me, "Throw it to the H606
Zec 11:15 Then the LORD **s** to me, "Take again the H606
Mal 3:13 you ask, 'What *have we* **s** against you? H1819
Mal 3:14 "*You have* **s**, 'It is futile to serve God. H606
Mt 1:20 Lord appeared to him in a dream and **s**, G3306
Mt 1:22 what the Lord *had* **s** through the prophet: G3306
Mt 2: 8 He sent them to Bethlehem and **s**, "Go G3306
Mt 2:13 *he* **s**, "take the child and his mother and G3306
Mt 2:15 what the Lord *had* **s** through the prophet: G3306
Mt 2:17 Then what *was* **s** through the prophet G3306
Mt 2:20 **s**, "Get up, take the child and his G3306
Mt 2:23 was fulfilled what *was* **s** through the G3306
Mt 3: 7 to where he was baptizing, *he* **s** to them: G3306
Mt 3:17 And a voice from heaven **s**, "This is my G3306
Mt 4: 3 The tempter came to him and **s**, "If you G3306
Mt 4: 6 are the Son of God," *he* **s**, "throw yourself G3306
Mt 4: 9 *he* **s**, "if you will bow down and worship G3306
Mt 4:10 Jesus **s** to him, "Away from me, Satan! For G3306
Mt 4:14 to fulfill what *was* **s** through the prophet G3306
Mt 4:19 Jesus **s**, "and I will send you out to fish G3306
Mt 5: 2 he began to teach them. *He* **s**: G3306
Mt 5:21 have heard that *it was* **s** to the people G3306
Mt 5:27 "You have heard that *it was* **s**, 'You shall G3306
Mt 5:31 "*It has been* **s**, 'Anyone who divorces his G3306
Mt 5:33 have heard that *it was* **s** to the people G3306
Mt 5:38 "You have heard that *it was* **s**, 'Eye for eye G3306
Mt 5:43 "You have heard that *it was* **s**, 'Love your G3306
Mt 8: 2 leprosy came and knelt before him and **s**, G3306
Mt 8: 3 "I am willing," *he* **s**. "Be clean! G3306
Mt 8: 4 Then Jesus **s** to him, "See that you don't G3306
Mt 8: 6 *he* **s**, "my servant lies at home G3306
Mt 8: 7 Jesus **s** to him, "Shall I come and heal G3306
Mt 8:10 he was amazed and **s** to those following G3306
Mt 8:13 Then Jesus **s** to the centurion, "Go! Let it G3306
Mt 8:19 a teacher of the law came to him and **s**, G3306
Mt 8:21 Another disciple **s** to him, "Lord, first let G3306
Mt 8:32 *He* **s** to them, "Go!" So they came out G3306
Mt 9: 2 saw their faith, *he* **s** to the man, "Take G3306
Mt 9: 3 of the teachers of the law **s** to themselves, G3306
Mt 9: 4 their thoughts, Jesus **s**, "Why do you G3306
Mt 9: 6 So *he* **s** to the paralyzed man, "Get up G3306
Mt 9:12 On hearing this, Jesus **s**, "It is not the G3306
Mt 9:18 leader came and knelt before him and **s**, G3306
Mt 9:21 *She* **s** to herself, "If I only touch his cloak, G3306
Mt 9:22 daughter," *he* **s**, "your faith has healed G3306
Mt 9:24 *he* **s**, "Go away. The girl is not dead but G3306
Mt 9:29 Then he touched their eyes and **s** G3306
Mt 9:33 The crowd was amazed and **s**, "Nothing G3306
Mt 9:34 But the Pharisees **s**, "It is by the prince of G3306
Mt 9:37 Then *he* **s** to his disciples, "The harvest is G3306
Mt 11:25 At that time Jesus **s**, "I praise you, Father G646
Mt 12: 2 Pharisees saw this, *they* **s** to him, "Look! G3306
Mt 12:11 He **s** to them, "If any of you has a sheep G3306
Mt 12:13 Then *he* **s** to the man, "Stretch out your G3306
Mt 12:23 All the people were astonished and **s** G3306
Mt 12:24 Pharisees heard this, *they* **s**, "It is only by G3306
Mt 12:25 Jesus knew their thoughts and **s** to them G3306
Mt 12:38 Pharisees and teachers of the law **s** to him, G646
Mt 12:49 to his disciples, *he* **s**, "Here are my G3306
Mt 13:27 "The owner's servants came to him and **s** G3306
Mt 13:36 His disciples came to him and **s**, "Explain G3306
Mt 13:52 He **s** to them, "Therefore every teacher of G3306
Mt 13:57 But Jesus **s** to them, "A prophet is not G3306
Mt 14: 2 and *he* **s** to his attendants, "This is John G3306
Mt 14: 8 by her mother, she **s**, "Give me here on a G5774
Mt 14:15 the disciples came to him and **s**, "This is G3306
Mt 14:18 "Bring them here to me," he **s**. G3306
Mt 14:26 "It's a ghost," *they* **s**, and cried out in fear G3306
Mt 14:27 But Jesus immediately **s** to them: "Take G3281
Mt 14:29 he **s**. Then Peter got down out of G3306
Mt 14:31 of little faith," *he* **s**, "why did you doubt?" G3306
Mt 15: 4 For God **s**, 'Honor your father and mother' G3306
Mt 15:10 Jesus called the crowd to him and **s** G3306
Mt 15:15 Peter **s**, "Explain the parable to us. G646
Mt 15:25 knelt before him. "Lord, help me!" *she* **s**. G3306
Mt 15:27 "Yes it is, Lord," she **s**. "Even the dogs eat G3306
Mt 15:28 Then Jesus **s** to her, "Woman, you have G646
Mt 15:32 Jesus called his disciples to him and **s**, "I G3306
Mt 16: 6 "Be careful," Jesus **s** to them. "Be on your G3306
Mt 16: 7 discussed this among themselves and **s**, G3306
Mt 16:22 *he* **s**. "This shall never happen to G3306
Mt 16:23 Jesus turned and **s** to Peter, "Get behind G3306
Mt 16:24 Then Jesus **s** to his disciples, "Whoever G3306
Mt 17: 4 Peter **s** to Jesus, "Lord, it is good for us to G646
Mt 17: 5 a voice from the cloud **s**, "This is my G3306
Mt 17: 7 "Get up," *he* **s**. "Don't be afraid. G3306
Mt 17:15 mercy on my son," *he* **s**. "He has seizures G3306
Mt 17:22 in Galilee, he **s** to them, "The Son of G3306
Mt 17:26 the children are exempt," Jesus **s** to him. G5774
Mt 18: 3 And *he* **s**: "Truly I tell you, unless you G3306
Mt 18:32 wicked servant,' *he* **s**, 'I canceled all that G3306
Mt 19: 5 **s**, 'For this reason a man will leave his G3306
Mt 19:10 The disciples **s** to him, "If this is the G3306
Mt 19:14 Jesus **s**, "Let the little children come to G3306
Mt 19:20 the young man **s**. "What do I still G3306
Mt 19:23 Then Jesus **s** to his disciples, "Truly I tell G3306
Mt 19:26 Jesus looked at them and **s**, "With man G3306
Mt 19:28 Jesus **s** to them, "Truly I tell you, at the G3306
Mt 20: 7 "*He* **s** to them, 'You also go and work in G3306
Mt 20: 8 owner of the vineyard **s** to his foreman, G3306
Mt 20:12 only one hour,' *they* **s**, 'and you have G3306
Mt 20:17 he took the Twelve aside and **s** to them, G3306
Mt 20:21 *She* **s**, "Grant that one of these two sons G3306
Mt 20:22 what you are asking," Jesus **s** to them. G646
Mt 20:23 Jesus **s** to them, "You will indeed drink G3306
Mt 20:25 Jesus called them together and **s**, "You G3306
Mt 21:13 " *he* **s** to them, " 'My house will be called G3306
Mt 21:19 Then *he* **s** to it, "May you never bear fruit G3306
Mt 21:25 discussed it among themselves and **s**, G3306
Mt 21:27 Then he **s**, "Neither will I tell you by G5774
Mt 21:28 He went to the first and **s**, 'Son, go and G3306
Mt 21:30 to the other son and **s** the same thing. G3306
Mt 21:31 Jesus **s** to them, "Truly I tell you, the tax G3306
Mt 21:37 'They will respect my son,' *he* **s**. G3306
Mt 21:38 saw the son, *they* **s** to each other, 'This G3306
Mt 21:42 Jesus **s** to them, "Have you never read in G3306
Mt 22: 4 "Then he sent some more servants and **s** G3306
Mt 22: 8 "Then *he* **s** to his servants, 'The wedding G3306
Mt 22:16 *they* **s**, "we know that you are a man of G3306
Mt 22:18 their evil intent, **s**, "You hypocrites, G3306
Mt 22:21 Then *he* **s** to them, "So give back to G3306
Mt 22:24 *they* **s**, "Moses told us that if a man dies G3306
Mt 22:31 have you not read what God **s** to you, G3306
Mt 22:43 *He* **s** to them, "How is it then that David G3306
Mt 22:44 " 'The Lord **s** to my Lord: "Sit at my right G3306
Mt 23: 1 Then Jesus **s** to the crowds and to his G3281
Mt 24: 3 "Tell us," *they* **s**, "when will this happen G3306
Mt 25: 8 The foolish ones **s** to the wise, 'Give us G3306
Mt 25:11 Lord,' *they* **s**, 'open the door for G3306
Mt 25:20 'Master,' *he* **s**, 'you entrusted me with five G3306
Mt 25:22 'Master,' *he* **s**, 'you entrusted me with two G3306
Mt 25:24 'Master,' *he* **s**, 'I knew that you are a hard G3306
Mt 26: 1 all these things, *he* **s** to his disciples, G3306
Mt 26: 5 *they* **s**, "or there may be a riot among the G3306
Mt 26:10 Aware of this, Jesus **s** to them, "Why are G3306
Mt 26:21 they were eating, *he* **s**, "Truly I tell you, G3306
Mt 26:25 who would betray him, **s**, "Surely you don't G646
Mt 26:25 Jesus answered, "You *have* **s** *so*." G3306
Mt 26:35 And all the other disciples **s** the same. G3306
Mt 26:36 Gethsemane, and *he* **s** to them, "Sit here G3306
Mt 26:38 Then *he* **s** to them, "My soul is G3306
Mt 26:45 returned to the disciples and **s** to them, G3306
Mt 26:49 at once to Jesus, Judas **s**, "Greetings, G3306
Mt 26:52 Jesus **s** to him, "for all who draw the G3306
Mt 26:55 In that hour Jesus **s** to the crowd, "Am I G3306
Mt 26:61 "This fellow **s**, 'I am able to destroy G5774
Mt 26:62 the high priest stood up and **s** to Jesus, G3306
Mt 26:63 The high priest **s** to him, "I charge you G3306
Mt 26:64 "You *have* **s** *so*," Jesus replied. "But I say G3306
Mt 26:65 the high priest tore his clothes and **s**, G3306
Mt 26:68 **s**, "Prophesy to us, Messiah. Who hit G3306
Mt 26:69 also were with Jesus of Galilee," *she* **s**. G3306
Mt 26:70 know what you're talking about," *he* **s**. G3306
Mt 26:71 girl saw him and **s** to the people there, G3306
Mt 26:73 standing there went up to Peter and **s**, G3306
Mt 27: 4 *he* **s**, "for I have betrayed innocent blood." G3306
Mt 27: 6 chief priests picked up the coins and **s**, G3306
Mt 27:11 "You *have* **s** *so*," Jesus replied G3306
Mt 27:24 of this man's blood," *he* **s**. "It is your G3306
Mt 27:29 "Hail, king of the Jews!" *they* **s**. G3306
Mt 27:42 "He saved others," *they* **s**, "but he can't G3306
Mt 27:43 if he wants him, for *he* **s**, 'I am the Son of G3306
Mt 27:47 there heard this, *they* **s**, "He's calling G3306
Mt 27:49 The rest **s**, "Now leave him alone. Let's G3306
Mt 27:63 *they* **s**, "we remember that while he was G3306
Mt 27:63 while he was still alive that deceiver **s**, G3306
Mt 28: 5 The angel **s** to the women, "Do not be G646
Mt 28: 6 has risen, just as *he* **s**. Come and see the G3306
Mt 28: 9 "Greetings," *he* **s**. They came to him G3306
Mt 28:10 Then Jesus **s** to them, "Do not be afraid G3306
Mt 28:18 Then Jesus came to them and **s**, "All G3281
Mk 1:15 time has come," *he* **s**. "The kingdom of G3306
Mk 1:17 Jesus **s**, "and I will send you out to fish G3306
Mk 1:25 **s** Jesus sternly. "Come out of G3306
Mk 1:41 "I am willing," *he* **s**. "Be clean! G3306
Mk 2: 5 saw their faith, *he* **s** to the paralyzed man G3306
Mk 2: 8 their hearts, and *he* **s** to them, "Why are G3306
Mk 2:10 earth to forgive sins." So *he* **s** to the man, G3306
Mk 2:17 On hearing this, Jesus **s** to them, "It is not G3306
Mk 2:24 The Pharisees **s** to him, "Look, why are G3306
Mk 2:27 Then *he* **s** to them, "The Sabbath was G3306
Mk 3: 3 Jesus **s** to the man with the shriveled hand G3306
Mk 3: 5 stubborn hearts, **s** to the man, "Stretch G3306
Mk 3:21 charge of him, for *they* **s**, "He is out of his G3306
Mk 3:22 law who came down from Jerusalem **s**, G3306
Mk 3:30 He **s** this because they were saying, "He has NDT
Mk 3:34 those seated in a circle around him and **s**, G3306
Mk 4: 2 things by parables, and in his teaching **s**: G3306
Mk 4: 9 Then Jesus **s**, "Whoever has ears to hear G3306
Mk 4:11 the outside everything *is* **s** in parables G1181S
Mk 4:13 Then Jesus **s** to them, "Don't you G3306
Mk 4:21 *He* **s** to them, "Do you bring in a lamp to G3306
Mk 4:26 *He* also **s**, "This is what the kingdom of G3306
Mk 4:30 Again *he* **s**, "What shall we say the G3306
Mk 4:35 when evening came, *he* **s** to his disciples G3306
Mk 4:38 The disciples woke him and **s** to him G3306
Mk 4:39 rebuked the wind and **s** to the waves G3306
Mk 4:40 *He* **s** to his disciples, "Why are you so G3306
Mk 5: 8 For Jesus *had* **s** to him, "Come out of this G3306
Mk 5:19 did not let him, but **s**, "Go home to your G3306
Mk 5:34 He **s** to her, "Daughter, your faith has G3306
Mk 5:35 is dead," *they* **s**. "Why bother the G3306
Mk 5:36 Overhearing what *they* **s**, Jesus told him G3281
Mk 5:39 He went in and **s** to them, "Why all this G3306
Mk 5:41 He took her by the hand and **s** to her G3306
Mk 6: 4 Jesus **s** to them, "A prophet is not without G3306
Mk 6:15 Others **s**, "He is Elijah." And still others G3306
Mk 6:16 Herod heard this, *he* **s**, "John, whom I G3306
Mk 6:22 The king **s** to the girl, "Ask me for G3306
Mk 6:24 She went out and **s** to her mother, "What G3306
Mk 6:31 a chance to eat, *he* **s** to them, "Come with G3306
Mk 6:35 a remote place," *they* **s**, "and it's already G3306
Mk 6:37 *They* **s** to him, "That would take more G3306
Mk 6:38 they found out, *they* **s**, "Five—and two fish G3306
Mk 6:50 Immediately he spoke to them and **s** G3306
Mk 7:10 For Moses **s**, 'Honor your father and G3306
Mk 7:14 Jesus called the crowd to him and **s**, G3306
Mk 7:34 to heaven and with a deep sigh **s** to him, G3306
Mk 7:37 everything well," *they* **s**. "He even makes G3306
Mk 8: 1 Jesus called his disciples to him and **s**, G3306
Mk 8:12 He sighed deeply and **s**, "Why does this G3306
Mk 8:16 They discussed this with one another and **s** NDT
Mk 8:21 *He* **s** to them, "Do you still not understand G3306
Mk 8:24 He looked up and **s**, "I see people; they G3306
Mk 8:33 *he* **s**. "You do not have in mind G3306
Mk 8:34 to him along with his disciples and **s**: G3306
Mk 9: 1 And *he* **s** to them, "Truly I tell you, some G3306
Mk 9: 5 Peter **s** to Jesus, "Rabbi, it is good for us to G646
Mk 9:23 " 'If you can'?" **s** Jesus. "Everything is G3306
Mk 9:25 mute spirit," *he* **s**, "I command you G3306
Mk 9:26 looked so much like a corpse that many **s**, G3306
Mk 9:31 *He* **s** to them, "The Son of Man is going G3306
Mk 9:35 Jesus called the Twelve and **s**, "Anyone G3306
Mk 9:36 the child in his arms, *he* **s** to them, G3306
Mk 9:38 **s** John, "we saw someone driving out G5774
Mk 9:39 not stop him," Jesus **s**. "For no one who G3306
Mk 10: 4 They **s**, "Moses permitted a man to write G3306

Mk 10:14 *He* s to them, "Let the little children come G3306
Mk 10:21 "One thing you lack," *he* s. "Go, G3306
Mk 10:23 looked around and s to his disciples, G3306
Mk 10:24 But Jesus s again, "Children, how hard it is G646
Mk 10:26 more amazed, and s to each other, "Who G3306
Mk 10:27 Jesus looked at them and s, "With man G3306
Mk 10:33 he s, "and the Son of Man will be NDT
Mk 10:35 *they* s, "we want you to do for us G3306
Mk 10:38 don't know what you are asking," Jesus s. G3306
Mk 10:39 Jesus s to them, "You will drink the cup I G3306
Mk 10:42 Jesus called them together and s, "You G3306
Mk 10:49 Jesus stopped and s, "Call him." So they G3306
Mk 10:51 The blind man s, "Rabbi, I want to G3306
Mk 10:52 s Jesus, "your faith has healed you." G3306
Mk 11:14 Then *he* s to the tree, "May no one ever eat G646
Mk 11:17 as he taught them, *he* s, "Is it not written: G3306
Mk 11:21 Peter remembered and s to Jesus, "Rabbi G3306
Mk 11:31 discussed it among themselves and s, G3306
Mk 11:33 Jesus s, "Neither will I tell you by what G3306
Mk 12: 7 "But the tenants s to one another, 'This is G3306
Mk 12:14 They came to him and s, "Teacher, we G3306
Mk 12:17 Then Jesus s to them, "Give back to G3306
Mk 12:19 *they* s, "Moses wrote for us that if a G3306
Mk 12:26 how God s to him, 'I am the God G3306
Mk 12:32 "Well s, teacher," the man replied. "You are NDT
Mk 12:34 answered wisely, *he* s to him, "You are G3306
Mk 12:36 " 'The Lord s to my Lord: "Sit at G3306
Mk 12:38 As he taught, Jesus s, "Watch out for the G3306
Mk 12:43 disciples to him, Jesus s, "Truly I tell you, G3306
Mk 13: 1 one of his disciples s to him, "Look, G3306
Mk 13: 5 Jesus s to them: "Watch out that no one G3306
Mk 14: 2 the festival," *they* s, "or the people may G3306
Mk 14: 6 "Leave her alone," s Jesus. "Why are you G3306
Mk 14:18 at the table eating, he s, "Truly I tell you, G3306
Mk 14:19 one by one *they* s to him, "Surely you G3306
Mk 14:24 is poured out for many," *he* s to them. G3306
Mk 14:31 And all the others s the same. G3306
Mk 14:32 Gethsemane, and Jesus s to his disciples G3306
Mk 14:34 to the point of death," *he* s to them. G3306
Mk 14:36 *he* s, "everything is possible for G3306
Mk 14:37 "Simon," *he* s to Peter, "are you G3306
Mk 14:41 the third time, *he* s to them, "Are you still G3306
Mk 14:45 to Jesus, Judas s, "Rabbi!" and kissed G3306
Mk 14:48 s Jesus, "that you have come out with G646
Mk 14:62 s Jesus. "And you will see the Son G3306
Mk 14:65 him with their fists, and s, "Prophesy!" G3306
Mk 14:67 were with that Nazarene, Jesus," *she* s. G3306
Mk 14:68 talking about," he s, and went out into G3306
Mk 14:69 *she* s again to those standing around G3306
Mk 14:70 those standing near s to Peter, "Surely G3306
Mk 15: 2 "You *have* s so," Jesus replied. G3306
Mk 15:31 "He saved others," *they* s, "but he can't G3306
Mk 15:35 standing near heard this, *they* s, "Listen, G3306
Mk 15:36 if Elijah comes to take him down," *he* s. G3306
Mk 15:39 saw how he died, *he* s, "Surely this man G3306
Mk 16: 6 be alarmed," he s. "You are looking for G3306
Mk 16: 8 *They* s nothing to anyone, because they G3306
Mk 16:15 *He* s to them, "Go into all the world and G3306
Lk 1:13 But the angel s to him: "Do not be afraid G3306
Lk 1:19 The angel s to him, "I am Gabriel. I stand G646
Lk 1:25 this for me," *she* s. "In these days he G3306
Lk 1:28 The angel went to her and s, "Greetings G3306
Lk 1:30 But the angel s to her, "Do not be afraid G3306
Lk 1:36 she who *was* **s to be** unable to G2813
Lk 1:46 And Mary s: "My soul glorifies the Lord G3306
Lk 1:60 his mother spoke up and s, "No! He is G3306
Lk 1:61 *They* s to her, "There is no one among G3306
Lk 1:70 as *he* s through his holy prophets of long G3281
Lk 2:10 But the angel s to them, "Do not be afraid G3306
Lk 2:15 heaven, the shepherds s to one another G3281
Lk 2:18 amazed at what the shepherds s to them. G3281
Lk 2:24 in keeping with what *is* s in the Law of the G3306
Lk 2:33 marveled at what *was* s about him. G3281
Lk 2:34 Then Simeon blessed them and s to Mary G3306
Lk 2:48 His mother s to him, "Son, why have you G3306
Lk 3: 7 John s to the crowds coming out to be G3306
Lk 4: 3 The devil s to him, "If you are the Son of G3306
Lk 4: 6 And he s to him, "I will give you all their G3306
Lk 4: 9 are the Son of God," *he* s, "throw yourself G3306
Lk 4:12 Jesus answered, "*It is* s: 'Do not put the G3306
Lk 4:23 Jesus s to them, "Surely you will quote G3306
Lk 4:35 Jesus s sternly. "Come out of G3306
Lk 4:36 people were amazed and s to each other, G5196
Lk 4:43 But he s, "I must proclaim the good news G3306
Lk 5: 4 finished speaking, *he* s to Simon, "Put out G3306
Lk 5: 8 he fell at Jesus' knees and s, "Go away G3306
Lk 5:10 Then Jesus s to Simon, "Don't be afraid G3306
Lk 5:13 "I am willing," *he* s. "Be clean! G3306
Lk 5:20 saw their faith, *he* s, "Friend, your sins G3306
Lk 5:24 So *he* s to the paralyzed man, "I tell you G3306
Lk 5:26 They were filled with awe and s, "We G3306
Lk 5:27 "Follow me," Jesus s to him, G3306
Lk 5:33 They s to him, "John's disciples often fast G3306
Lk 6: 5 Then Jesus s to them, "The Son of Man is G3306
Lk 6: 8 were thinking and s to the man with the G3306
Lk 6: 9 Then Jesus s to them, "I ask you, which is G3306
Lk 6:10 them all, and then s to the man, "Stretch G3306
Lk 6:20 at his disciples, *he* s: "Blessed are you G3306
Lk 7: 9 the crowd following him, *he* s, "I tell you, G3306
Lk 7:13 his heart went out to her and *he* s, "Don't G3306
Lk 7:14 *He* s, "Young man, I say G3306
Lk 7:16 prophet has appeared among us," *they* s. G3306
Lk 7:20 came to Jesus, *they* s, "John the Baptist G3306
Lk 7:39 him saw this, *he* s to himself, "If this G3306
Lk 7:40 "Tell me, teacher," he s. G5774
Lk 7:43 "You have judged correctly," Jesus s. G3306
Lk 7:44 turned toward the woman and s to Simon, G5774
Lk 7:48 Then Jesus s to her, "Your sins are G3306
Lk 7:50 Jesus s to the woman, "Your faith has G3306
Lk 8: 8 *When he* s this, he called out, "Whoever G3306
Lk 8:10 He s, "The knowledge of the secrets of the G3306
Lk 8:22 One day Jesus s to his disciples, "Let us G3306
Lk 8:45 all denied it, Peter s, "Master, the people G3306
Lk 8:46 But Jesus s, "Someone touched me; G3306
Lk 8:48 Then he s to her, "Daughter, your faith has G3306
Lk 8:49 daughter is dead," *he* s. "Don't bother the G3306
Lk 8:50 Hearing this, Jesus s to Jairus, "Don't be G646
Lk 8:52 wailing," Jesus s. "She is not dead but G3306
Lk 8:54 But he took her by the hand and s, "My G5888
Lk 9: 9 But Herod s, "I beheaded John. Who, then G3306
Lk 9:12 afternoon the Twelve came to him and s, G3306
Lk 9:14 But *he* s to his disciples, "Have them sit G3306
Lk 9:22 And *he* s, "The Son of Man must suffer G3306
Lk 9:23 Then *he* s to them all: "Whoever wants to G3306
Lk 9:28 About eight days after Jesus s this, he G3364
Lk 9:33 leaving Jesus, Peter s to him, "Master, G3306
Lk 9:43 at all that Jesus did, *he* s to his disciples, G3306
Lk 9:48 Then *he* s to them, "Whoever welcomes G3306
Lk 9:49 s John, "we saw someone driving out G646
Lk 9:50 Jesus s, "for whoever is not against you G3306
Lk 9:57 along the road, a man s to him, "I will G3306
Lk 9:59 *He* s to another man, "Follow me." But he G3306
Lk 9:60 Jesus s to him, "Let the dead bury their G3306
Lk 9:61 Still another s, "I will follow you, Lord; G3306
Lk 10:17 The seventy-two returned with joy and s G3306
Lk 10:21 through the Holy Spirit, s, "I praise you, G3306
Lk 10:23 he turned to his disciples and s privately, G3306
Lk 10:30 In reply Jesus s: "A man was going down G3306
Lk 10:35 'Look after him,' *he* s, 'and when I return G3306
Lk 10:39 at the Lord's feet listening *to* what he s. G3364
Lk 11: 1 one of his disciples s to him, "Lord, G3306
Lk 11: 2 *He* s to them, "When you pray, say: G3306
Lk 11: 5 Then Jesus s to them, "Suppose you have G3306
Lk 11:15 But some of them s, "By Beelzebul, the G3306
Lk 11:17 Jesus knew their thoughts and s to them G3306
Lk 11:29 increased, Jesus s, "This is a wicked G3306
Lk 11:39 Then the Lord s to him, "Now then, you G3306
Lk 11:49 God in his wisdom s, 'I will send them G3306
Lk 12: 3 What *you have* s in the dark will be heard G3306
Lk 12:13 Someone in the crowd s to him, "Teacher G3306
Lk 12:15 Then *he* s to them, "Watch out! Be on your G3306
Lk 12:18 "Then *he* s, 'This is what I'll do. I will tear G3306
Lk 12:20 "But God s to him, 'You fool! This very G3306
Lk 12:22 Then Jesus s to his disciples: "Therefore I G3306
Lk 12:54 *He* s to the crowd: "When you see a cloud G3306
Lk 13: 7 So *he* s to the man who took care of the G3306
Lk 13:12 he called her forward and s to her G3306
Lk 13:14 the synagogue leader s to the people G646
Lk 13:17 *When* he s this, all his opponents were G3306
Lk 13:23 going to be saved?" He s to them, G3306
Lk 13:31 Pharisees came to Jesus and s to him, G3306
Lk 14:12 Then Jesus s to his host, "When you give G3306
Lk 14:15 him heard this, *he* s to Jesus, "Blessed G3306
Lk 14:18 The first s, 'I have just bought a field, and G3306
Lk 14:19 "Another s, 'I have just bought five yoke G3306
Lk 14:20 "Still another s, 'I just got married, so I G3306
Lk 14:22 the servant s, 'what you ordered G3306
Lk 14:25 with Jesus, and turning to them *he* s: G3306
Lk 15:12 The younger one s to his father, 'Father G3306
Lk 15:17 to his senses, *he* s, 'How many of my G5774
Lk 15:21 "The son s to him, 'Father, I have sinned G3306
Lk 15:22 "But the father s to his servants, 'Quick G3306
Lk 15:31 'My son,' the father s, 'you are always G3306
Lk 16: 3 "The manager s to himself, 'What shall I G3306
Lk 16:15 *He* s to them, "You are the ones who G3306
Lk 16:30 father Abraham,' he s, 'but if someone G3306
Lk 16:31 "*He* s to him, 'If they do not listen to G3306
Lk 17: 1 Jesus s to his disciples: "Things that G3306
Lk 17: 5 The apostles s to the Lord, "Increase our G3306
Lk 17:14 When he saw them, *he* s, "Go, show G3306
Lk 17:19 Then *he* s to him, "Rise and go; your faith G3306
Lk 17:22 Then *he* s to his disciples, "The time is G3306
Lk 18: 2 *He* s: "In a certain town there was a judge G3306
Lk 18: 4 But finally *he* s to himself, 'Even though I G3306
Lk 18: 6 And the Lord s, "Listen to what the unjust G3306
Lk 18:13 heaven, but beat his breast and s, 'God, G3306
Lk 18:16 But Jesus called the children to him and s G3306
Lk 18:21 these I have kept since I was a boy," he s. G3306
Lk 18:22 Jesus heard this, *he* s to him, "You still G3306
Lk 18:24 Jesus looked at him and s, "How hard it is G3306
Lk 18:28 Peter s to him, "We have left all we had G3306
Lk 18:29 Jesus s to them, "no one who has left G3306
Lk 18:42 Jesus s to him, "Receive your sight; your G3306
Lk 19: 5 he looked up and s to him, "Zacchaeus, G3306
Lk 19: 8 But Zacchaeus stood up and s to the Lord G3306
Lk 19: 9 Jesus s to him, "Today salvation has G3306
Lk 19:12 *He* s: "A man of noble birth went to a G3306
Lk 19:13 money to work,' *he* s, 'until I come back. G3306
Lk 19:16 "The first one came and s, 'Sir, your mina G3306
Lk 19:18 "The second came and s, 'Sir, your mina G3306
Lk 19:20 "Then another servant came and s, 'Sir G3306
Lk 19:24 "Then *he* s to those standing by, 'Take his G3306
Lk 19:25 *they* s, 'he already has ten! G3306
Lk 19:28 *After* Jesus *had* s this, he went on ahead G3306
Lk 19:39 of the Pharisees in the crowd s to Jesus, G3306
Lk 19:42 s, "If you, even you, had only known G3306
Lk 19:46 " *he* s to them, " 'My house will be a G3306
Lk 20: 2 you are doing these things," *they* s. G3306
Lk 20: 5 discussed it among themselves and s, G3306
Lk 20: 8 Jesus s, "Neither will I tell you by what G3306
Lk 20:13 "Then the owner of the vineyard s, 'What G3306
Lk 20:14 'This is the heir,' *they* s. 'Let's kill him, G3306
Lk 20:16 the people heard this, *they* s, "God forbid!" G3306
Lk 20:20 hoped to catch Jesus *in* **something** he s, G3364
Lk 20:23 saw through their duplicity and s to them, G3306
Lk 20:25 He s to them, "Then give back to Caesar G3306
Lk 20:26 to trap him *in* **what** he had s there in G4839
Lk 20:28 *they* s, "Moses wrote for us that if a G3306
Lk 20:39 of the law responded, "Well s, teacher!" G3306
Lk 20:41 Then Jesus s to them, "Why is it said that G3306
Lk 20:41 "Why *is it* s that the Messiah is the son of G3306
Lk 20:42 " 'The Lord s to my Lord: "Sit at G3306
Lk 20:45 were listening, Jesus s to his disciples, G3306
Lk 21: 3 *he* s, "this poor widow has put in more G3306
Lk 21: 5 with gifts dedicated to God. But Jesus s, G3306
Lk 21:10 Then *he* s to them: "Nation will rise G3306
Lk 22:15 And *he* s to them, "I have eagerly desired G3306
Lk 22:17 he gave thanks and s, "Take this and G3306
Lk 22:25 Jesus s to them, "The kings of the Gentiles G3306
Lk 22:36 *He* s to them, "But now if you have a G3306
Lk 22:38 The disciples s, "See, Lord, here are two G3306
Lk 22:40 the place, *he* s to them, "Pray that G3306
Lk 22:49 what was going to happen, *they* s, "Lord, G3306
Lk 22:52 Then Jesus s to the chief priests, the G3306
Lk 22:56 She looked closely at him and s, "This G3306
Lk 22:57 "Woman, I don't know him," *he* s. G3306
Lk 22:58 A little later someone else saw him and s, G5774
Lk 22:65 And *they* s many other insulting things to G3306
Lk 22:67 are the Messiah," *they* s, "tell us." Jesus G3306
Lk 22:71 Then they s, "Why do we need any more G3306
Lk 23: 3 "You *have* **s so**," Jesus replied. G3306
Lk 23:14 s to them, "You brought me this man G3306
Lk 23:28 Jesus turned and s to them, "Daughters of G3306
Lk 23:34 Jesus s, "Father, forgive them, for they do G3306
Lk 23:35 *They* s, "He saved others; let him save G3306
Lk 23:37 s, "If you are the king of the Jews G3306
Lk 23:40 *he* s, "since you are under the same G5774
Lk 23:42 Then *he* s, "Jesus, remember me when G3306
Lk 23:46 " *When he had* s this, he breathed his last. G3306
Lk 23:47 praised God and s, "Surely this was a G3306
Lk 24: 5 ground, but the men s to them, "Why do G3306
Lk 24:23 a vision of angels, who s he was alive. G3306
Lk 24:24 found it just as the women *had* s, G3306
Lk 24:25 He s to them, "How foolish you are, and G3306
Lk 24:27 *he* **explained** to them **what was** s in all G1450
Lk 24:36 himself stood among them and s to them, G3306
Lk 24:38 *He* s to them, "Why are you troubled, and G3306
Lk 24:40 *When he had* s this, he showed them his G3306
Lk 24:44 *He* s to them, "This is what I told you G3306
Jn 1:15 "This is the one *I spoke about when I* s G3306
Jn 1:21 Are you Elijah?" *He* s, "I am not." "Are G3306
Jn 1:22 Finally *they* s, "Who are you? Give us an G3306
Jn 1:29 John saw Jesus coming toward him and s, G3306
Jn 1:30 This is the one I meant *when* I s, 'A man G3306
Jn 1:36 he saw Jesus passing by, *he* s, "Look, G3306
Jn 1:38 They s, "Rabbi" (which means "Teacher") G3306
Jn 1:40 who heard **what** John *had* s and who G4123S
Jn 1:42 Jesus looked at him and s, "You are G3306
Jn 1:43 Finding Philip, *he* s to him, "Follow me." G3306
Jn 1:46 "Come and see," s Philip. G3306
Jn 1:47 approaching, *he* s of him, "Here truly is G3306
Jn 1:50 Jesus s, "You believe because I told you I G646
Jn 2: 3 Jesus' mother s to him, "They have G3306
Jn 2: 5 His mother s to the servants, "Do G3306
Jn 2: 7 Jesus s to the servants, "Fill the jars with G3306
Jn 2:10 s, "Everyone brings out the choice G3306
Jn 2:16 To those who sold doves *he* s, "Get these G3306
Jn 2:22 his disciples recalled what *he had* s. G3306
Jn 3: 2 He came to Jesus at night and s, "Rabbi G3306
Jn 3:10 s Jesus, "and do you not understand these G646
Jn 3:26 They came to John and s to him, "Rabbi G3306
Jn 3:28 You yourselves can testify that *I* s, 'I am G3306
Jn 4: 7 to draw water, Jesus s to her, "Will you G3306
Jn 4: 9 The Samaritan woman s to him, "You are G3306
Jn 4:11 the woman s, "you have nothing to draw G3306
Jn 4:15 The woman s to him, "Sir, give me this G3306
Jn 4:17 Jesus s to her, "You are right when you G3306
Jn 4:18 What *you have just* s is quite true. G3306
Jn 4:19 the woman s, "I can see that you are a G3306
Jn 4:25 The woman s, "I know that Messiah" G3306
Jn 4:28 back to the town and s to the people, G3306
Jn 4:32 But he s to them, "I have food to eat that G3306
Jn 4:33 Then his disciples s to each other, "Could G3306
Jn 4:34 s Jesus, "is to do the will of him who G3306
Jn 4:42 *They* s to the woman, "We no longer G3306
Jn 4:42 longer believe just because of what you s; G3282
Jn 4:49 The royal official s, "Sir, come down G3306
Jn 4:52 son got better, *they* s to him, "Yesterday, G3306
Jn 4:53 exact time at which Jesus *had* s to him, G3306
Jn 5: 8 Then Jesus s to him, "Get up! Pick up your G3306
Jn 5:10 the Jewish leaders s to the man who had G3306
Jn 5:11 "The man who made me well s to me G3306
Jn 5:14 found him at the temple and s to him, G3306
Jn 5:17 **In** *his* **defense** Jesus s to them, "My Father G646
Jn 6: 5 toward him, *he* s to Philip, "Where G3306
Jn 6:10 Jesus s, "Have the people sit down." G3306

S

Jn	6:12	had enough to eat, *he* **s** to his disciples	G3306
Jn	6:20	But he **s** to them, "It is I; don't be afraid."	G3306
Jn	6:32	Jesus **s** to them, "Very truly I tell you, it is	G3306
Jn	6:34	*they* **s**, "always give us this bread.	G3306
Jn	6:41	to grumble about him because *he* **s**,	G3306
Jn	6:42	*They* **s**, "Is this not Jesus, the son of	G3306
Jn	6:53	Jesus **s** to them, "Very truly I tell you	G3306
Jn	6:59	*He* **s** this while teaching in the synagogue	G3306
Jn	6:60	many of his disciples **s**, "This is a hard	G3306
Jn	6:61	about this, Jesus **s** to them, "Does this	G3306
Jn	7: 3	Jesus' brothers **s** to him, "Leave Galilee	G3306
Jn	7: 9	*After he had* **s** this, he stayed in Galilee.	G3306
Jn	7:12	Some **s**, "He is a good man.	G3306
Jn	7:21	Jesus **s** to them, "I did one miracle, and	G646
Jn	7:31	*They* **s**, "When the Messiah comes, will	G3306
Jn	7:33	Jesus **s**, "I am with you for only a short	G3306
Jn	7:35	The Jews **s** to one another, "Where does	G3306
Jn	7:36	What did he mean when *he* **s**, 'You will	G3306
Jn	7:37	Jesus stood and **s** in a loud voice, "Let	G3306
Jn	7:38	as Scripture *has* **s**, rivers of living	G3306
Jn	7:40	some of the people **s**, "Surely this man is	G3306
Jn	7:41	Others **s**, "He is the Messiah." Still others	G3306
Jn	8: 4	**s** to Jesus, "Teacher, this woman was	G3306
Jn	8: 7	he straightened up and **s** to them, "Let	G3306
Jn	8:11	"No one, sir," she **s**. "Then neither do I	G3306
Jn	8:12	to the people, *he* **s**, "I am the light of	G3306
Jn	8:21	Once more Jesus **s** to them, "I am going	G3306
Jn	8:28	So Jesus **s**, "When you have lifted up the	G3306
Jn	8:31	believed him, Jesus **s**, "If you hold to my	G3306
Jn	8:39	**s** Jesus, "then you would do what	G3306
Jn	8:42	Jesus **s** to them, "If God were your Father	G3306
Jn	8:49	**s** Jesus, "but I honor my Father and you	G646
Jn	8:55	If *I* **s** I did not, I would be a liar like you	G3306
Jn	8:57	they **s** to him, "and you have seen	G3306
Jn	9: 3	**s** Jesus, "but this happened so that the	G646
Jn	9: 9	Others **s**, "No, he only looks	G3306
Jn	9:12	they asked him. "I don't know," *he* **s**.	G3306
Jn	9:16	Some of the Pharisees **s**, "This man is not	G3306
Jn	9:22	His parents **s** this because they were afraid	G3306
Jn	9:23	That was why his parents **s**, "He is of age	G3306
Jn	9:24	glory to God by telling the truth," *they* **s**.	G3306
Jn	9:28	Then they hurled insults at him and **s**	G3306
Jn	9:35	he found him, *he* **s**, "Do you believe	G3306
Jn	9:37	Jesus **s**, "You have now seen him; in fact	G3306
Jn	9:38	Then the man **s**, "Lord, I believe," and he	G5774
Jn	9:39	Jesus **s**, "For judgment I have come into	G3306
Jn	9:41	Jesus **s**, "If you were blind, you would not	G3306
Jn	10: 7	Therefore Jesus **s** again, "Very truly I tell	G3306
Jn	10:20	Many of them **s**, "He is demon-possessed	G3306
Jn	10:21	But others **s**, "These are not the sayings of	G3306
Jn	10:32	Jesus **s** to them, "I have shown you	G646
Jn	10:34	in your Law, 'I *have* **s** you are "gods" '?	G3306
Jn	10:36	you accuse me of blasphemy because *I* **s**,	G3306
Jn	10:41	*They* **s**, "Though John never performed a	G3306
Jn	10:41	all that John **s** about this man was true."	G3306
Jn	11: 4	he heard this, Jesus **s**, "This sickness will	G3306
Jn	11: 7	then *he* **s** to his disciples, "Let us go	G3306
Jn	11: 8	they **s**, "a short while ago the Jews there	G3306
Jn	11:11	After *he had* **s** this, he went on to tell	G3306
Jn	11:16	as Didymus) **s** to the rest of the disciples	G3306
Jn	11:21	Martha **s** to Jesus, "if you had	G3306
Jn	11:23	Jesus **s** to her, "Your brother will rise	G3306
Jn	11:25	Jesus **s** to her, "I am the resurrection and	G3306
Jn	11:28	*After she had* **s** this, she went back and	G3306
Jn	11:28	Teacher is here," *she* **s**, "and is asking	G3306
Jn	11:32	saw him, she fell at his feet and **s**, "Lord,	G3306
Jn	11:36	Then the Jews **s**, "See how he loved him!"	G3306
Jn	11:37	But some of them **s**, "Could not he who	G3306
Jn	11:39	away the stone," he **s**. "But, Lord," said	G3306
Jn	11:39	**s** Martha, the sister of the dead	G3306
Jn	11:40	Then Jesus **s**, "Did I not tell you that if	G3306
Jn	11:41	Then Jesus looked up and **s**, "Father,	G3306
Jn	11:42	but *I* **s** this for the benefit of the people	G3306
Jn	11:43	*When he had* **s** this, Jesus called in a	G3306
Jn	11:44	Jesus **s** to them, "Take off the grave	G3306
Jn	12:19	So the Pharisees **s** to one another, "See	G3306
Jn	12:21	"Sir," *they* **s**, "we would like to	G3306
Jn	12:29	was there and heard it **s** it had thundered;	G3306
Jn	12:29	others **s** an angel had spoken to him.	G3306
Jn	12:30	Jesus **s**, "This voice was for your benefit	G646
Jn	12:33	*He* **s** this to show the kind of death he was	G3306
Jn	12:41	Isaiah **s** this because he saw Jesus' glory	G3306
Jn	13: 6	came to Simon Peter, *who* **s** to him, "Lord,	G3306
Jn	13: 8	**s** Peter, "you shall never wash my	G3306
Jn	13:11	that was why *he* **s** not every one was	G3306
Jn	13:21	*After he had* **s** this, Jesus was troubled in	G3306
Jn	13:24	Simon Peter motioned to this disciple and **s**	NDT
Jn	13:28	meal understood why Jesus **s** this to him.	G3306
Jn	13:31	he was gone, Jesus **s**, "Now the Son of	G3306
Jn	14: 5	Thomas **s** to him, "Lord, we don't know	G3306
Jn	14: 8	Philip **s**, "Lord, show us the Father and	G3306
Jn	14:22	not Judas Iscariot) **s**, "But, Lord,	G3306
Jn	14:26	remind you of everything *I have* **s** to you.	G3306
Jn	16: 6	with grief because *I have* **s** these things.	G3281
Jn	16:15	That is why *I* **s** the Spirit will receive from	G3306
Jn	16:17	some of his disciples **s** to one another	G3306
Jn	16:19	him about this, so *he* **s** to them, "Are you	G3306
Jn	16:19	one another what I meant when *I* **s**,	G3306
Jn	16:29	Then Jesus' disciples **s**, "Now you are	G3306
Jn	17: 1	*After* Jesus **s** this, he looked toward	G3281
Jn	18: 5	"I am he," Jesus **s**. (And Judas the traitor	G3306
Jn	18: 6	When Jesus **s**, "I am he," they drew back	G3306
Jn	18: 7	"Jesus of Nazareth," they **s**.	G3306
Jn	18:20	Jews come together. *I* **s** nothing in secret.	G3281
Jn	18:21	Surely they know what I **s**."	G3306
Jn	18:22	*When* Jesus **s** this, one of the officials	G3306
Jn	18:23	"If *I* **s** something wrong," Jesus replied	G3281
Jn	18:31	Pilate **s**, "Take him yourselves and judge	G3306
Jn	18:32	fulfill what Jesus *had* **s** about the kind of	G3306
Jn	18:36	Jesus **s**, "My kingdom is not of this world.	G646
Jn	18:37	are a king, then!" **s** Pilate. Jesus	G3306
Jn	18:38	again to the Jews gathered there and **s**,	G3306
Jn	19: 4	Pilate came out and **s** to the Jews	G3306
Jn	19: 5	purple robe, Pilate **s** to them, "Here is the	G3306
Jn	19:10	Pilate **s**. "Don't you realize	G3306
Jn	19:14	"Here is your king," Pilate **s** to the Jews.	G3306
Jn	19:24	"Let's not tear it," *they* **s** to one another	G3306
Jn	19:24	that the scripture might be fulfilled that **s**,	G3306
Jn	19:26	standing nearby, *he* **s** to her, "Woman,	G3306
Jn	19:28	would be fulfilled, Jesus **s**, "I am thirsty."	G3306
Jn	19:30	received the drink, Jesus **s**, "It is finished."	G3306
Jn	20: 2	one Jesus loved, and **s**, "They have taken	G3306
Jn	20:13	*she* **s**, "and I don't know where they have	G3306
Jn	20:15	was the gardener, she **s**, "Sir, if you have	G3306
Jn	20:16	Jesus **s** to her, "Mary." She turned toward	G3306
Jn	20:17	Jesus **s**, "Do not hold on to me, for I have	G3306
Jn	20:18	told them that *he had* **s** these things to	G3306
Jn	20:19	Jesus came and stood among them and **s**,	G3306
Jn	20:20	*After he* **s** this, he showed them his hands	G3306
Jn	20:21	Again Jesus **s**, "Peace be with you! As the	G3306
Jn	20:22	And with that he breathed on them and **s**	G3306
Jn	20:25	But he **s** to them, "Unless I see the nail	G3306
Jn	20:26	Jesus came and stood among them and **s**,	G3306
Jn	20:27	Then *he* **s** to Thomas, "Put your finger	G3306
Jn	20:28	Thomas **s** to him, "My Lord and my God!"	G646
Jn	21: 3	told them, and *they* **s**, "We'll go with you	G3306
Jn	21: 6	He **s**, "Throw your net on the right side of	G3306
Jn	21: 7	the disciple whom Jesus loved **s** to Peter,	G3306
Jn	21:10	Jesus **s** to them, "Bring some of the fish	G3306
Jn	21:12	Jesus **s** to them, "Come and have	G3306
Jn	21:15	Jesus **s** to Simon Peter, "Simon	G3306
Jn	21:15	Lord," *he* **s**, "you know that I love	G3306
Jn	21:15	Jesus **s**, "Feed my lambs."	G3306
Jn	21:16	Again Jesus **s**, "Simon son of John, do	G3306
Jn	21:16	Jesus **s**, "Take care of my	G3306
Jn	21:17	The third time *he* **s** to him, "Simon son of	G3306
Jn	21:17	*He* **s**, "Lord, you know all things; you	G3306
Jn	21:17	that I love you." Jesus **s**, "Feed my sheep.	G3306
Jn	21:19	Jesus **s** this to indicate the kind of death	G3306
Jn	21:19	Then *he* **s** to him, "Follow me	G3306
Jn	21:20	against Jesus at the supper and *had* **s**,	G3306
Jn	21:23	would not die; he only **s**, "If I want him to	NDT
Ac	1: 7	*He* **s** to them: "It is not for you to know the	G3306
Ac	1: 9	*After he* **s** this, he was taken up before	G3306
Ac	1:11	they **s**, "why do you stand here looking	G3306
Ac	1:16	**s**, "Brothers and sisters, the Scripture	G3306
Ac	1:20	**s** Peter, "it is written in the Book of	NDT
Ac	2:13	made fun of them and **s**, "They have had	G3306
Ac	2:25	David **s** about him: " 'I saw the Lord	G3306
Ac	2:34	heaven, and yet he **s**, " 'The Lord said to	G3306
Ac	2:34	yet he said, " 'The Lord **s** to my Lord:	G3306
Ac	2:37	cut to the heart and **s** to Peter and the	G3306
Ac	3: 4	Then Peter **s**, "Look at us!"	G3306
Ac	3: 6	Then Peter **s**, "Silver or gold I do not have,	G3306
Ac	3:12	When Peter saw this, *he* **s** to them: "Fellow	G646
Ac	3:22	For Moses **s**, 'The Lord your God will raise	G3306
Ac	3:25	*He* **s** to Abraham, 'Through your offspring	G3306
Ac	4: 8	filled with the Holy Spirit, **s** to them:	G3306
Ac	4:23	chief priests and the elders *had* **s** to them.	G3306
Ac	4:24	*they* **s**, "you made the heavens and the	G3306
Ac	5: 3	Then Peter **s**, "Ananias, how is it that	G3306
Ac	5: 8	"Yes," she **s**, "that is the price."	G3306
Ac	5: 9	Peter **s** to her, "How could you conspire to	NDT
Ac	5:20	*he* **s**, "and tell the people all about this	G3306
Ac	5:25	Then someone came and **s**, "Look! The	G550
Ac	5:28	orders not to teach in this name," *he* **s**.	G3306
Ac	6: 2	gathered all the disciples together and **s**,	G3306
Ac	7: 3	your people,' God **s**, 'and go to the land	G3306
Ac	7: 7	as slaves,' God **s**, 'and afterward they	G3306
Ac	7:27	the other pushed Moses aside and **s**,	G3306
Ac	7:33	"Then the Lord **s** to him, 'Take off your	G3306
Ac	7:56	*he* **s**, "I see heaven open and the Son of	G3306
Ac	7:60	*When he had* **s** this, he fell	G3306
Ac	8: 6	they all paid close attention *to* what he **s**.	G3306
Ac	8:19	**s**, "Give me also this ability so that	G3306
Ac	8:24	so that nothing *you have* **s** may happen to	G3306
Ac	8:26	Now an angel of the Lord **s** to Philip, "Go	G3281
Ac	8:31	"How can I," he **s**, "unless someone	G3306
Ac	8:36	came to some water and the eunuch **s**,	G5774
Ac	9:15	But the Lord **s** to Ananias, "Go! This man	G3306
Ac	9:17	his hands on Saul, *he* **s**, "Brother Saul,	G3306
Ac	9:34	"Aeneas," Peter **s** to him, "Jesus Christ	G3306
Ac	9:40	toward the dead woman, *he* **s**, "Tabitha,	G3306
Ac	10: 3	who came to him and **s**, "Cornelius!"	G3306
Ac	10:19	the vision, the Spirit **s** to him, "Simon,	G3306
Ac	10:21	Peter went down and **s** to the men, "I'm	G3306
Ac	10:26	"Stand up," *he* **s**, "I am only a man myself	G3306
Ac	10:28	*He* **s** to them: "You are well aware that it	G5774
Ac	10:31	**s**, 'Cornelius, God has heard your	G5774
Ac	10:46	tongues and praising God. Then Peter **s**,	G646
Ac	11: 3	**s**, "You went into the house of	G3306
Ac	11:16	Then I remembered what the Lord *had* **s**	G3306
Ac	12: 7	*he* **s**, and the chains fell off Peter's wrists.	G3306
Ac	12: 8	Then the angel **s** to him, "Put on your	G3306
Ac	12:11	Then Peter came to himself and **s**, "Now I	G3306
Ac	12:15	that it was so, they **s**, "It must be his	G3306
Ac	12:17	sisters about this," *he* **s**, and then he left	G3306
Ac	13: 2	the Holy Spirit **s**, "Set apart for me	G3306
Ac	13: 9	looked straight at Elymas and **s**,	G3306
Ac	13:16	Paul motioned with his hand and **s**:	G3306
Ac	13:25	completing his work, *he* **s**: 'Who do you	G3306
Ac	13:34	As God *has* **s**, " 'I will give you the holy	G3306
Ac	13:40	the prophets *have* **s** does not happen	G3306
Ac	14:22	to enter the kingdom of God," they **s**.	NDT
Ac	15: 5	the party of the Pharisees stood up and **s**,	G3306
Ac	15:13	"Brothers," *he* **s**, "listen to me.	G3306
Ac	15:24	troubling your minds *by* **what** they **s**.	G3364
Ac	15:32	**s** much to encourage and	G1328+3364
Ac	15:36	Some time later Paul **s** to Barnabas, "Let	G3306
Ac	16:15	in the Lord," *she* **s**, "come and stay at my	G3306
Ac	16:18	that he turned around and **s** to the spirit,	G3306
Ac	16:20	them before the magistrates and **s**,	G3306
Ac	16:37	But Paul **s** to the officers: "They beat us	G5774
Ac	17: 3	proclaiming to you is the Messiah," he **s**.	NDT
Ac	17:11	every day to see if **what Paul s** was true.	G4047S
Ac	17:18	They **s** this because Paul was preaching the	NDT
Ac	17:19	Areopagus, where *they* **s** to him, "May we	G3306
Ac	17:22	in the meeting of the Areopagus and **s**:	G5774
Ac	17:28	As some of your own poets *have* **s**, 'We	G3306
Ac	17:32	sneered, but others **s**, "We want to hear	G3306
Ac	18: 6	out his clothes in protest and **s** to them,	G3306
Ac	18:14	to speak, Gallio **s** to them, "If you Jews	G3306
Ac	19: 4	Paul **s**, "John's baptism was a baptism of	G3306
Ac	19:21	have been there," *he* **s**, "I must visit Rome	G3306
Ac	19:25	with the workers in related trades, and **s**:	G3306
Ac	19:35	The city clerk quieted the crowd and **s**	G5774
Ac	19:41	*After he had* **s** this, he dismissed the	G3306
Ac	20: 1	**s goodbye** and set out for Macedonia.	G832
Ac	20:10	"Don't be alarmed," *he* **s**. "He's alive!"	G3306
Ac	20:18	When they arrived, *he* **s** to them: "You	G3306
Ac	20:35	the words the Lord Jesus himself **s**:	G3306
Ac	21:11	tied his own hands and feet with it and **s**	G3306
Ac	21:14	we gave up and **s**, "The Lord's will be	G3306
Ac	21:20	Then *they* **s** to Paul: "You	G3306
Ac	21:40	were all silent, *he* **s to** them in Aramaic:	G4715
Ac	22: 2	they became very quiet. Then Paul **s**:	G5774
Ac	22:10	" 'Get up,' the Lord **s**, 'and go into	G3306
Ac	22:13	He stood beside me and **s**, 'Brother Saul	G3306
Ac	22:14	"Then he **s**: 'The God of our ancestors has	G3306
Ac	22:18	he **s**. 'Leave Jerusalem immediately,	NDT
Ac	22:21	"Then the Lord **s** to me, 'Go; I will send	G3306
Ac	22:22	The crowd listened to Paul until he **s** this	G3364
Ac	22:25	Paul **s** to the centurion standing there	G3306
Ac	22:28	Then the commander **s**, "I had to pay a lot	G646
Ac	23: 1	looked straight at the Sanhedrin and **s**,	G3306
Ac	23: 3	Then Paul **s** to him, "God will strike you	G3306
Ac	23: 4	Those who were standing near Paul **s**	G3306
Ac	23: 7	*When* he **s** this, a dispute broke out	G3306
Ac	23: 9	find nothing wrong with this man," *they* **s**.	G3306
Ac	23:11	night the Lord stood near Paul and **s**,	G3306
Ac	23:14	to the chief priests and the elders and **s**,	G3306
Ac	23:17	Paul called one of the centurions and **s**,	G5774
Ac	23:18	The centurion **s**, "Paul, the prisoner, sent	G5774
Ac	23:20	*He* **s**: "Some Jews have agreed to ask you	G3306
Ac	23:35	*he* **s**, "I will hear your case when your	G5774
Ac	24:22	commander comes," *he* **s**, "I will decide	G3306
Ac	24:25	Felix was afraid and **s**, "That's enough	G646
Ac	25: 9	to do the Jews a favor, **s** to Paul, "Are you	G646
Ac	25:14	case with the king. *He* **s**: "There is a man	G3306
Ac	25:22	Then Agrippa **s** to Festus, "I would like to	NDT
Ac	25:24	Festus **s**: "King Agrippa, and all who are	G5774
Ac	26: 1	Then Agrippa **s** to Paul, "You have	G5774
Ac	26:22	prophets and Moses **s** would happen—	G3281
Ac	26:28	Then Agrippa **s** to Paul, "Do you think that	NDT
Ac	26:32	Agrippa **s** to Festus, "This man could have	G5774
Ac	27:11	instead of listening *to* what Paul **s**	G3306
Ac	27:21	Paul stood up before them and **s**:	G3306
Ac	27:24	**s**, 'Do not be afraid, Paul. You must	G3306
Ac	27:31	Then Paul **s** to the centurion and the	G3306
Ac	27:33	*he* **s**, "you have been in constant	G3306
Ac	27:35	*After he* **s** this, he took some bread and	G3306
Ac	28: 4	from his hand, *they* **s** to each other, "This	G3306
Ac	28: 6	changed their minds and **s** he was a god.	G3306
Ac	28:17	they had assembled, Paul **s** to them:	G3306
Ac	28:21	has reported or **s** anything bad about	G3281
Ac	28:24	Some were convinced *by* what *he* **s**, but	G3306
Ac	28:25	your ancestors *when he* **s** through Isaiah	G3306
Ro	4:18	just as it *had been* **s** to him, "So shall	G3306
Ro	7: 7	coveting really was if the law *had* not **s**,	G3306
Ro	9:26	"In the very place where *it was* **s** to them	G3306
Ro	9:29	It is just as Isaiah **s previously**: "Unless	G4625
Ro	15:18	to obey God *by* **what** I have **s** and done—	G3364
1Co	6:16	For *it is* **s**, "The two will become one flesh."	G5774
1Co	11:24	he broke it and **s**, "This is my body,	G3306
1Co	14:29	the others should weigh carefully what is **s**.	NDT
2Co	2:13	So *I* **s goodbye** to them and went on to	G698
2Co	4: 6	For God, who **s**, "Let light shine out of	G3306
2Co	6:16	As God *has* **s**: "I will live with	G3306
2Co	7: 3	*I have* **s before** that you have such a place	G4625
2Co	7:14	just as everything *we* **s** to you was true,	G3281
2Co	9: 3	you may be ready, as *I* **s** you would be.	G3306
2Co	12: 9	But *he* **s** to me, "My grace is sufficient for	G3306
Gal	1: 9	As *we have* **already s**, so now I say again	G4625
Gal	2:14	gospel, *I* **s** to Cephas in front of them all	G3306
Eph	5:14	This is why *it is* **s**: "Wake up, sleeper, rise	G3306
Titus	1:12	One of Crete's own prophets *has* **s** it	G3306

Heb 3:10 with that generation; *I* s, 'Their hearts are G3306
Heb 3:15 As *has just been* s: "Today, if you hear his G3306
Heb 4: 3 just as God *has* s, "So I declared on G3306
Heb 5: 5 But God s to him, "You are my Son; today G3281
Heb 6:16 oath confirms what is s and puts an end to NDT
Heb 7:13 of whom these things *are* s belonged to a G3306
Heb 7:14 to that tribe Moses s nothing about priests G3281
Heb 7:15 And what we have s is even more clear if NDT
Heb 7:21 a priest with an oath when God s to him: G3306
Heb 8: 8 But God found fault with the people and s G3306
Heb 9:20 *He* s, "This is the blood of the covenant G3306
Heb 10: 5 when Christ came into the world, *he* s: G3306
Heb 10: 7 Then *I* s, 'Here I am—it is written about G3306
Heb 10: 8 First *he* s, "Sacrifices and offerings, burnt G3306
Heb 10: 9 Then *he* s, "Here I am, I have come to do G3306
Heb 10:30 For we know him *who* s, "It is mine to G3306
Heb 11:18 even though God *had* s to him, "It is G3281
Heb 12:21 The sight was so terrifying *that* Moses s, "I G3306
Heb 13: 5 because God *has* s, "Never will I G3306
Jas 2:11 For he *who* s, "You shall not commit G3306
Jas 2:11 adultery," also s, "You shall not murder G3306
Jude 9 dare to condemn him for slander but s, G3306
Jude 18 *They* s to you, "In the last times there will G3306
Rev 1:11 *which* s: "Write on a scroll what you see G3306
Rev 1:17 he placed his right hand on me and s: G3306
Rev 4: 1 heard speaking to me like a trumpet s, G3306
Rev 5: 5 Then one of the elders s to me, "Do not G3306
Rev 5:14 The four living creatures s, "Amen," G3306
Rev 7:14 And *he* s, "These are they who have G3306
Rev 9:14 *It* s to the sixth angel who had the trumpet, G3306
Rev 10: 4 seven thunders *have* s and do not write G3281
Rev 10: 6 all that is in it, and s, "There will be no NDT
Rev 10: 9 the little scroll. *He* s to me, "Take it and G3306
Rev 11:15 were loud voices in heaven, *which* s: G3306
Rev 14: 7 *He* s in a loud voice, "Fear God and give G3306
Rev 14: 8 A second angel followed and s, " 'Fallen G3306
Rev 14: 9 followed them and s in a loud voice: G3306
Rev 17: 1 had the seven bowls came and s to me, G3281
Rev 17: 7 Then the angel s to me: "Why are you G3306
Rev 17:15 Then the angel s to me, "The waters you G3306
Rev 18:21 millstone and threw it into the sea, and s: G3306
Rev 19: 9 Then the angel s to me, "Write this G3306
Rev 19:10 to worship him. But *he* s to me, "Don't do G3306
Rev 21: 5 He who was seated on the throne s, "I am G3306
Rev 21: 5 Then *he* s, "Write this down, for these G3306
Rev 21: 6 *He* s to me: "It is done. I am the Alpha G3306
Rev 21: 9 the seven last plagues came and s to me, G3281
Rev 22: 6 The angel s to me, "These words are G3306
Rev 22: 9 But *he* s to me, "Don't do that! I am a G3306

SAIL (19) [FORESAIL, SAILED, SAILING, SAILORS]

1Ki 22:48 gold, but *they* never **set s**—they were H2143
1Ki 22:49 "*Let* my men s with yours H2143+928+2021+641
2Ch 20:37 were not able to **set s** to trade. H2143
Isa 33:21 will ride them, no mighty ship *will* s them. H6296
Isa 33:23 is not held secure, the s is not spread. H5812
Eze 27: 7 from Egypt was your s and served as your H5155
Eze 27:25 with heavy cargo **as** you s the sea. H928+4213[S]
Ac 18:21 Then *he* **set s** from Ephesus. G343
Ac 20: 3 him just as he was about to s for Syria, G343
Ac 20:15 The next day *we* **set s** from there and G676
Ac 20:16 Paul had decided *to* **s past** Ephesus to G4179
Ac 21: 2 over to Phoenicia, went on board and **set s**. G343
Ac 27: 1 it was decided *that* we *would* s for Italy, G676
Ac 27: 2 about to s for ports along the G4434
Ac 27:12 the majority decided *that we should* s on G343
Ac 27:21 have taken my advice not *to* s from Crete; G343
Ac 27:24 given you the lives of all who s with you. G4434
Ac 28:10 and *when we were ready to* s, they G343
Ac 28:13 From there *we* **set s** and arrived at G4311

SAILED (19) [SAIL]

1Ki 9:28 *They* s to Ophir and brought back 420 H995
2Ch 8:18 *These*, with Solomon's men, s to Ophir H995
Jnh 1: 3 he went aboard and s for Tarshish to flee H995
Lk 8:23 *As* they s, he fell asleep. A squall came G4434
Lk 8:26 *They* s to the region of the Gerasenes G2929
Ac 13: 4 to Seleucia and s from there to Cyprus G676
Ac 13:13 his companions s to Perga in G343
Ac 14:26 From Attalia *they* **s back** to Antioch, where G676
Ac 15:39 Barnabas took Mark and s for Cyprus, G1739
Ac 16:11 out to sea and s **straight** for Samothrace, G2312
Ac 18:18 the brothers and sisters and s for Syria, G1739
Ac 18:18 Before he s, he had his hair cut off at NDT
Ac 20: 6 But we s **from** Philippi after the Festival of G1739
Ac 20:13 went on ahead to the ship and s for Assos, G343
Ac 21: 1 we put out to sea and s **straight** to Kos. G2312
Ac 21: 3 to the south of it, *we* s *on* to Syria. G4434
Ac 27: 5 *When we had* s **across** the open sea off G1386
Ac 27: 7 our course, *we* **s to the lee of** Crete G5709
Ac 27:13 weighed anchor and s along the shore of G4162

SAILING (2) [SAIL]

Ac 27: 6 an Alexandrian ship s for Italy and put us G4434
Ac 27: 9 s had already become dangerous G4452

SAILORS (12) [SAIL]

1Ki 9:27 sent his men—s who knew the sea H408+641
2Ch 8:18 by his own men, s who knew the sea. H6269[S]
Eze 27: 8 skilled men, Tyre, were aboard as your s. H2480
Eze 27: 9 of the sea and their s came alongside to H4876
Eze 27:27 your mariners, s and shipwrights, your H2480
Eze 27:28 shorelands will quake when your s cry out. H2480
Eze 27:29 and all the s will stand on the H2480+3542
Jnh 1: 5 All the s were afraid and each cried out to H4876
Jnh 1: 7 Then the s said to each other, "Come, let us NDT
Ac 27:27 about midnight the s sensed they were G3731
Ac 27:30 the s let the lifeboat down into the sea G3731
Rev 18:17 travel by ship, the s, and all who earn G3731

SAINTS (NIV84) FAITHFUL PEOPLE, FAITHFUL SERVANTS, GOD'S HOLY PEOPLE, GOD'S PEOPLE, HOLY PEOPLE, LORD'S PEOPLE, LORD'S* PEOPLE

SAKAR (2)

1Ch 11:35 Ahiam son of S the Hararite, Eliphal son H8511
1Ch 26: 4 Joah the third, S the fourth, Nethanel the H8511

SAKE (109)

Ge 12:13 be treated well **for** your s and my life H928+6288
Ge 12:16 He treated Abram well **for** her s, and H928+6288
Ge 18:24 spare the place **for the s of** the fifty H4200+5100
Ge 18:26 spare the whole place **for** their s." H928+6288
Ge 18:29 He said, "**For the s of** forty, I will not H928+6288
Ge 18:31 He said, "**For the s of** twenty, I will H928+6288
Ge 18:32 He answered, "**For the s of** ten, I will H928+6288
Ge 26:24 descendants **for the s of** my servant H928+6288
Ex 18: 8 Egyptians **for** Israel's s and about H6584+128
Lev 26:45 But **for** their s I will remember the H4200
Nu 11:29 Moses replied, "Are you jealous **for** my s? H4200
Jos 23: 3 done to all these nations **for** your s; H4946+7156
Jos 23: 5 God himself will push them out for your s. H7156
1Sa 12:22 **For the s of** his great name the LORD H928+6288
2Sa 5:12 his kingdom **for the s of** his people H928+6288
2Sa 7:21 **For the s of** your word and according H928+6288
2Sa 9: 1 can show kindness **for** Jonathan's s?" H928+6288
2Sa 9: 7 you kindness **for the s of** your father H928+6288
2Sa 18: 5 with the young man Absalom **for** my s." H4200
2Sa 18:12 'Protect the young man Absalom **for** my s. H4200
1Ki 11:12 **for the s of** David your father H4200+5100
1Ki 11:13 him one tribe **for the s of** David my H4200+5100
1Ki 11:13 servant and **for the s of** Jerusalem, H4200+5100
1Ki 11:32 But **for the s of** my servant David H4200+5100
1Ki 11:34 of his life **for the s of** David my H4200+5100
1Ki 15: 4 **for** David's s the LORD his God gave H4200+5100
2Ki 8:19 **for the s of** his servant David H4200+5100
2Ki 19:34 **for** my s and for the sake of David H4200+5100
2Ki 19:34 my sake and **for the s of** David my H4200+5100
2Ki 20: 6 defend this city **for** my s and for the H4200+5100
2Ki 20: 6 my sake and **for the s of** my servant H4200+5100
1Ch 14: 2 highly exalted **for the s of** his people H928+6288
1Ch 16:21 **for** their s he rebuked kings: H6584
1Ch 17:19 **For the s of** your servant and H928+6288
Ne 10:28 peoples **for the s of** the Law of God, H448
Job 18: 4 earth to be abandoned **for** your s? H4200+5100
Ps 23: 3 the right paths **for** his name's s. H4200+5100
Ps 25:11 **For the s of** your name, LORD H4200+5100
Ps 31: 3 **for the s of** your name lead and H4200+5100
Ps 44:22 Yet **for** your s we face death all day long H6584
Ps 69: 7 For I endure scorn **for** your s, and shame H6584
Ps 79: 9 forgive our sins **for** your name's s. H4200+5100
Ps 105:14 **for** their s he rebuked kings: H6584
Ps 106: 8 Yet he saved them **for** his name's s, H4200+5100
Ps 106:45 **for** their s he remembered his covenant H4200
Ps 109:21 help me **for** your name's s; out of H4200+5100
Ps 122: 8 **For the s of** my family and friends, H4200+5100
Ps 122: 9 **For the s of** the house of the LORD H4200+5100
Ps 132:10 **For the s of** your servant David, do H928+6288
Ps 143:11 **For** your name's s, LORD, preserve H4200+5100
Isa 37:35 **for** my s and for the sake of David H4200+5100
Isa 37:35 my sake and **for the s of** David my H4200+5100
Isa 42:21 pleased the LORD **for the s of** his H4200+5100
Isa 43:14 "**For** your s I will send to Babylon H4200+5100
Isa 43:25 **for** my own s, and remembers H4200+5100
Isa 45: 4 **For the s of** Jacob my servant, of H4200+5100
Isa 48: 9 **For** my own name's s I delay my H4200+5100
Isa 48: 9 the s of my praise I hold it back from you NDT
Isa 48:11 **For** my own s, for my own sake, I do H4200+5100
Isa 48:11 own sake, **for** my own s, I do this. H4200+5100
Isa 62: 1 **For** Zion's s I will not keep silent H4200+5100
Isa 62: 1 **for** Jerusalem's s I will not remain H4200+5100
Isa 63:17 Return **for the s of** your servants H4200+5100
Jer 14: 7 **for the s of** your name. H4200+5100
Jer 14:21 **For the s of** your name do not H4200+5100
Jer 15:15 think of how I suffer reproach **for** your s. H6584
Eze 20: 9 But **for the s of** my name, I brought H4200+5100
Eze 20:14 But **for the s of** my name I did what H4200+5100
Eze 20:22 and **for the s of** my name I did H4200+5100
Eze 20:44 with you **for** my name's s and not H4200+5100
Eze 36:22 It is not **for** your s, people of Israel H4200+5100
Eze 36:22 but **for the s of** my holy name H4200
Eze 36:32 that I am not doing this **for** your s, H4200+5100
Da 9:17 **For** your s, Lord, look with favor on H4200+5100
Da 9:19 **For** your s, my God, do not delay H4200+5100
Mt 10:39 loses their life **for** my s will find it. G1915
Mt 15: 3 command of God **for the s of** your G1328
Mt 15: 6 the word of God **for the s of** your tradition. G1328
Mt 19:12 like eunuchs **for the s of** the kingdom of G1328
Mt 19:29 children or fields **for** my s will receive a G1915
Mt 24:22 but **for the s of** the elect those days will G1328
Mk 13:20 But **for the s of** the elect, whom he has G1328
Lk 18:29 children **for the s of** the kingdom of G1915
Jn 11:15 and **for** your s I am glad I was not there, so G1328
Ro 1: 5 that comes from faith **for** his name's s. G5642
Ro 8:36 "**For** your s we face death all day long; we G1915
Ro 9: 3 cut off from Christ **for the s of** my people, G5642
Ro 11:28 they are enemies **for** your s; but as far as G1328
Ro 14:20 destroy the work of God **for the s of** food. G1915
1Co 9:23 I do all this **for the s of** the gospel, that I G1328
1Co 10:28 both **for the s of** the one who told you G1328
1Co 10:28 who told you and for the s of conscience. NDT
2Co 2:10 forgiven in the sight of Christ **for** your s, G1328
2Co 4: 5 ourselves as your servants **for** Jesus' s. G1328
2Co 4:11 being given over to death **for** Jesus' s, G1328
2Co 8: 9 he was rich, yet **for** your s he became poor G1328
2Co 12:10 That is why, **for** Christ's s, I delight in G5642
Eph 3: 1 of Christ Jesus **for the s of** you Gentiles— G5642
Php 3: 7 me I now consider loss **for the s of** Christ. G1328
Php 3: 8 my Lord, **for** whose s I have lost all things. G1328
Col 1:24 afflictions, **for the s of** his body, which is G5642
1Th 1: 5 know how we lived among you **for** your s. G1328
2Ti 2:10 I endure everything **for the s of** the elect, G1328
Titus 1:11 that **for the s of** dishonest gain. G5920
Phm 6 good thing we share **for the s of** Christ. G1650
Heb 11:26 disgrace *for the s of* **Christ** as of greater AIT
1Pe 1:20 revealed in these last times **for** your s. G1328
1Pe 2:13 yourselves **for** the Lord's s to every human G1328
3Jn 7 It was **for the s of** the Name that they went G5642

SAKIA (1)

1Ch 8:10 S and Mirmah. These were his sons H8499

SALAMIS (1)

Ac 13: 5 When they arrived at S, they proclaimed G4887

SALATHIEL (KJV) SHEALTIEL

SALE (4) [SELL]

Lev 25:29 right of redemption a full year after its s. H4928
Dt 18: 8 has received **money from** the s of family H4928
Dt 28:68 There *you will* **offer yourselves for** s to H4835
Ps 44:12 a pittance, gaining nothing from their s. H4697

SALEKAH (4)

Dt 3:10 all Bashan as far as S and Edrei H6146
Jos 12: 5 over Mount Hermon, S, all of Bashan to H6146
Jos 13:11 Hermon and all Bashan as far as S— H6146
1Ch 5:11 lived next to them in Bashan, as far as S: H6146

SALEM (4)

Ge 14:18 Melchizedek king of S brought out bread H8970
Ps 76: 2 His tent is in S, his dwelling place in Zion. H8970
Heb 7: 1 was king of S and priest of God G4889
Heb 7: 2 then also, "king *of* S" means "king of G4889

SALES (1) [SELL]

Ac 4:34 sold them, brought the money *from* the s G4405

SALIM (1)

Jn 3:23 John also was baptizing at Aenon near S, G4890

SALIVA (2)

1Sa 21:13 the gate and letting s run down his beard. H8202
Jn 9: 6 made some mud with the s, and put it on G4770

SALLAI (1)

Ne 11: 8 his followers, Gabbai and S—928 men. H6144

SALLU (3) [SALLU'S]

1Ch 9: 7 S son of Meshullam, the son of Hodaviah H6132
Ne 11: 7 S son of Meshullam, the son of Joed, the H6132
Ne 12: 7 S, Amok, Hilkiah and Jedaiah. These H6139

SALLU'S (1) [SALLU]

Ne 12:20 of S, Kallai; of Amok's, Eber; H6139

SALMA (2)

1Ch 2:51 S the father of Bethlehem, and Hareph H8514
1Ch 2:54 The descendants of S: Bethlehem, the H8514

SALMON (7)

Ru 4:20 of Nahshon, Nahshon the father of S, H8517
Ru 4:21 S the father of Boaz, Boaz the father of H8517
1Ch 2:11 Nahshon was the father of S, Salmon the H8517
1Ch 2:11 father of Salmon, S the father of Boaz, H8517
Mt 1: 4 of Nahshon, Nahshon the father of S, G4891
Mt 1: 5 S the father of Boaz, whose mother was G4891
Lk 3:32 of Boaz, the son *of* S, the son of Nahshon G4891

SALMONE (1)

Ac 27: 7 we sailed to the lee of Crete, opposite S. G4892

SALOME (2)

Mk 15:40 James the younger and of Joseph, and S. G4897
Mk 16: 1 S bought spices so that they might go G4897

SALT (37) [SALTED, SALTINESS, SALTY]

Ge 19:26 and she became a pillar of s. H4875
Lev 2:13 Season all your grain offerings with s. H4875
Lev 2:13 Do not leave the s *of* the covenant of your H4875
Lev 2:13 grain offerings; add s to all your offerings. H4875
Nu 18:19 covenant of s before the LORD for H4875
Dt 29:23 will be a burning waste of s and sulfur— H4875
Jos 15:62 Nibshan, the City of S and En Gedi—six H4875
Jdg 9:45 destroyed the city and scattered s over it. H4875
2Sa 8:13 thousand Edomites in the Valley of S. H4875
2Ki 2:20 me a new bowl," he said, "and put s in it." H4875
2Ki 2:21 out to the spring and threw the s into it, H4875
2Ki 14: 7 in the Valley of S and captured Sela in H4875
1Ch 18:12 thousand Edomites in the Valley of S. H4875

2Ch 13: 5 descendants forever by a covenant of s? H4875
2Ch 25:11 led his army to the Valley of S, H4875
Ezr 6: 9 heaven, and wheat, s, wine and olive oil A10420
Ezr 7:22 baths of olive oil, and s without limit. A10420
Job 6: 6 Is tasteless food eaten without s, or is H4875
Job 30: 4 In the brush they gathered s **herbs**, and H4865
Job 39: 6 as its home, the s **flats** as its habitat. H4877
Ps 60: T thousand Edomites in the Valley of S. H4875
Ps 107:34 fruitful land into a s **waste**, because H4877
Jer 17: 6 the desert, in a s land where no one lives. H4877
Jer 48: 9 Put s on Moab, for she will be laid waste H7490
Eze 16: 4 nor **were** *you* **rubbed with** s or H4873+4873
Eze 43:24 are to sprinkle s on them and sacrifice H4875
Eze 47: 9 flows there and makes the s water fresh; NDT
Eze 47:11 not become fresh; they will be left for s. H4875
Zep 2: 9 a place of weeds and s pits, a wasteland H4875
Mt 5:13 "You are the s of the earth. But if the salt G229
Mt 5:13 But if the s loses its saltiness, how can it be G229
Mk 9:50 "S is good, but if it loses its saltiness, how G229
Mk 9:50 Have s among yourselves, and be at peace G229
Lk 14:34 "S is good, but if it loses its saltiness, how G229
Col 4: 6 of grace, seasoned *with* s, so that you may G229
Jas 3:11 fresh water and s *water* flow from the G4395
Jas 3:12 Neither can a s **spring** produce fresh water G266

SALTED (2) [SALT]

Ex 30:35 *It is to* **be** s and pure and sacred H4873
Mk 9:49 Everyone *will be* s with fire. G245

SALTINESS (3) [SALT]

Mt 5:13 But if the salt **loses** *its* s, how can it be G3701
Mk 9:50 if it **loses** its s, how can you G383+1181
Lk 14:34 is good, but if it **loses** *its* s, how can it be G3701

SALTY (4) [SALT]

Eze 47: 8 the s water there becomes fresh. NDT
Mt 5:13 its saltiness, how *can it be* **made** s again? G245
Mk 9:50 its saltiness, how *can you* **make** it s again? G789
Lk 14:34 its saltiness, how *can it be* **made** s *again*? G789

SALU (1)

Nu 25:14 the Midianite woman was Zimri son of S, H6140

SALUTATION, SALUTATIONS, SALUTE, SALUTED, SALUTETH (KJV) ASKED, CALL, GREET, GREETED, GREETING, GREETINGS, GREETS, PAY RESPECTS

SALVATION (116) [SAVE]

Ex 15: 2 my defense; he has become my s. H3802
2Sa 22: 3 my shield and the horn of my s. H3829
2Sa 23: 5 bring to fruition my s and grant me my H3829
1Ch 16:23 all the earth; proclaim his s day after day. H3802
2Ch 6:41 be clothed with s, may your faithful H9591
Ps 9:14 and there rejoice in your s. H3802
Ps 13: 5 unfailing love; my heart rejoices in your s. H3802
Ps 14: 7 that s *for* Israel would come out of Zion! H3802
Ps 18: 2 my shield and the horn of my s, my H3829
Ps 27: 1 The LORD is my light and my s—whom H3829
Ps 28: 8 a fortress of s *for* his anointed one. H3802
Ps 35: 3 who pursue me. Say to me, "I am your s." H3802
Ps 35: 9 rejoice in the LORD and delight in his s. H3802
Ps 37:39 The s *of* the righteous comes from the H9591
Ps 50:23 to the blameless I will show my s. H3829
Ps 51:12 to me the joy of your s and grant me a H3829
Ps 53: 6 that s *for* Israel would come out of Zion! H3802
Ps 62: 1 finds rest in God; my s comes from him. H3802
Ps 62: 2 Truly he is my rock and my s; he is my H3802
Ps 62: 6 Truly he is my rock and my s; he is my H3802
Ps 62: 7 My s and my honor depend on God; he is H3829
Ps 67: 2 known on earth, your s among all nations. H3802
Ps 69:13 O God, answer me with your sure s. H3829
Ps 69:27 do not let them share in your s. H7407
Ps 69:29 in pain—may your s, God, protect me. H3802
Ps 74:12 from long ago; he brings s on the earth. H3802
Ps 85: 7 unfailing love, LORD, and grant us your s. H3829
Ps 85: 9 Surely his s is near those who fear him H3829
Ps 91:16 life I will satisfy him and show him my s." H3802
Ps 95: 1 let us shout aloud to the Rock of our s. H3829
Ps 96: 2 his name; proclaim his s day after day. H3802
Ps 98: 1 his holy arm *have* **worked** s for him. H3828
Ps 98: 2 LORD has made his s known and revealed H3802
Ps 98: 3 of the earth have seen the s *of* our God. H3802
Ps 116:13 lift up the cup of s and call on the name H3802
Ps 118:14 my defense; he has become my s. H3802
Ps 118:21 answered me; you have become my s. H3802
Ps 119:41 LORD, your s, according to your H9591
Ps 119:81 My soul faints with longing for your s, but H9591
Ps 119:123 looking for your s, looking for your H3802
Ps 119:155 S is far from the wicked, for they do not H3802
Ps 119:166 I wait for your s, LORD, and I follow your H3802
Ps 119:174 I long for your s, LORD, and your law H3802
Ps 132:16 I will clothe her priests with s, and her H3829
Isa 12: 2 Surely God is my s; I will trust and not be H3802
Isa 12: 2 my defense; he has become my s. H3802
Isa 12: 3 you will draw water from the wells of s. H3802
Isa 25: 9 let us rejoice and be glad in his s. H3802
Isa 26: 1 God makes s its walls and ramparts. H3802
Isa 26:18 We have not brought s to the earth, and H3802
Isa 30:15 "In repentance and rest is *your* s, in H3828
Isa 33: 2 every morning, our s in time of distress. H3802
Isa 33: 6 a rich store of s and wisdom and H3802
Isa 45: 8 the earth open wide, let s spring up, let H3829
Isa 45:17 saved by the LORD with an everlasting s; H9591
Isa 46:13 far away; and my s will not be delayed. H9591
Isa 46:13 I will grant s to Zion, my splendor to Israel H9591
Isa 49: 6 that my s may reach to the ends of the H3802
Isa 49: 8 and in the day of s I will help you; H3802
Isa 51: 5 near speedily, my s is on the way, and my H3829
Isa 51: 6 But my s will last forever, my H3802
Isa 51: 8 last forever, my s through all generations." H3802
Isa 52: 7 who proclaim s, who say to Zion, H3802
Isa 52:10 of the earth will see the s *of* our God. H3802
Isa 56: 1 my s is close at hand and my H3802
Isa 59:16 so his own arm **achieved** s for him, and H3828
Isa 59:17 the helmet of s on his head; he put H3802
Isa 60:18 will call your walls S and your gates H3802
Isa 61:10 with garments of s and arrayed me in a H3829
Isa 62: 1 like the dawn, her s like a blazing torch. H3802
Isa 63: 5 so my own arm **achieved** s for me, and my H3828
Jer 3:23 in the LORD our God is the s *of* Israel. H9591
La 3:26 good to wait quietly for the s *of* the LORD. H9591
Jnh 2: 9 I will say, 'S comes from the LORD.'" H3802
Lk 1:69 raised up a horn *of* s for us in the house G5401
Lk 1:71 s from our enemies and from the hand of G5401
Lk 1:77 people the knowledge *of* s through the G5401
Lk 2:30 For my eyes have seen your s, G5402
Lk 3: 6 And all people will see God's s.'" G5402
Lk 19: 9 "Today s has come to this house G5401
Jn 4:22 what we do know, for s is from the Jews. G5401
Ac 4:12 S is found in no one else, for there is no G5401
Ac 13:26 us that this message *of* s has been sent. G5401
Ac 13:47 that you may bring s to the ends of the G5401
Ac 28:28 to know that God's s has been sent to the G5402
Ro 1:16 of God that brings s to everyone who G5401
Ro 11:11 s has come to the Gentiles to make Israel G5401
Ro 13:11 because our s is nearer now than when G5401
2Co 1: 6 it is for your comfort and s; if we are G5401
2Co 6: 2 and in the day *of* s I helped you. G5401
2Co 6: 2 time of God's favor, now is the day *of* s. G5401
2Co 7:10 that leads to s and leaves no regret, G5401
Eph 1:13 the message of truth, the gospel *of* your s. G5401
Eph 6:17 Take the helmet *of* s and the sword of the G5402
Php 2:12 to work out your s with fear and trembling, G5401
1Th 5: 8 the hope *of* s as a helmet. G5401
1Th 5: 9 wrath but to receive s through our Lord G5401
2Ti 2:10 too may obtain the s that is in Christ Jesus G5401
2Ti 3:15 to make you wise for s through faith in G5401
Titus 2:11 has appeared *that* **offers** s to all people. G5403
Heb 1:14 sent to serve those who will inherit s? G5401
Heb 2: 3 shall we escape if we ignore so great a s? G5401
Heb 2: 3 This s, which was first announced by the NDT
Heb 2:10 the pioneer *of* their s perfect through G5401
Heb 5: 9 the source *of* eternal s for all who obey G5401
Heb 6: 9 the things that have to do with s. G5401
Heb 9:28 to bring s to those who are waiting for G5401
1Pe 1: 5 the coming of the s that is ready to be G5401
1Pe 1: 9 result of your faith, the s of your souls. G5401
1Pe 1:10 Concerning this s, the prophets, who G5401
1Pe 2: 2 so that by it you may grow up in your s, G5401
2Pe 3:15 in mind that our Lord's patience means s, G5401
Jude 3 to write to you about the s we share, G5401
Rev 7:10 "S belongs to our God, who sits on the G5401
Rev 12:10 "Now have come the s and the power G5401
Rev 19: 1 S and glory and power belong to our God G5401

SALVE (1)

Rev 3:18 nakedness; and s to put on your eyes, so G3141

SAMARIA (119) [SAMARIA'S, SAMARITAN, SAMARITANS]

1Ki 13:32 in the towns of S will certainly come H9076
1Ki 16:24 bought the hill of S from Shemer for two H9076
1Ki 16:24 city on the hill, calling it S, after Shemer, H9076
1Ki 16:28 with his ancestors and was buried in S. H9076
1Ki 16:29 he reigned in S over Israel H9076
1Ki 16:32 in the temple of Baal that he built in S. H9076
1Ki 18: 2 Now the famine was severe in S, H9076
1Ki 20: 1 went up and besieged S and attacked it. H9076
1Ki 20:10 dust remains in S to give each of my men H9076
1Ki 20:17 reported, "Men are advancing from S." H9076
1Ki 20:34 areas in Damascus, as my father did in S." H9076
1Ki 20:43 the king of Israel went to his palace in S. H9076
1Ki 21: 1 close to the palace of Ahab king of S. H9076
1Ki 21:18 meet Ahab king of Israel, who rules in S. H9076
1Ki 22:10 floor by the entrance of the gate of S, H9076
1Ki 22:37 So the king died and was brought to S H9076
1Ki 22:38 They washed the chariot at a pool in S H9076
1Ki 22:51 king of Israel in S in the seventeenth year H9076
2Ki 1: 2 his upper room in S and injured himself. H9076
2Ki 1: 3 of the king of S and ask them, H9076
2Ki 2:25 Carmel and from there returned to S. H9076
2Ki 3: 1 king of Israel in S in the eighteenth year H9076
2Ki 3: 6 Joram set out from S and mobilized all H9076
2Ki 5: 3 master would see the prophet who is in S! H9076
2Ki 6:19 are looking for." And he led them to S. H9076
2Ki 6:20 and there they were, inside S. H9076
2Ki 6:24 army and marched up and laid siege to S. H9076
2Ki 7: 1 of barley for a shekel at the gate of S." H9076
2Ki 7:18 of barley for a shekel at the gate of S." H9076
2Ki 10: 1 Now there were in S seventy sons of the H9076
2Ki 10: 1 So Jehu wrote letters and sent them to S H9076
2Ki 10:12 Jehu then set out and went toward S. H9076
2Ki 10:17 When Jehu came to S, he killed all who H9076
2Ki 10:35 with his ancestors and was buried in S. H9076
2Ki 10:36 over Israel in S was twenty-eight years H9076
2Ki 13: 1 son of Jehu became king of Israel in S, H9076
2Ki 13: 6 the Asherah pole remained standing in S. H9076
2Ki 13: 9 with his ancestors and was buried in S. H9076
2Ki 13:10 of Jehoahaz became king of Israel in S, H9076
2Ki 13:13 Jehoash was buried in S with the kings of H9076
2Ki 14:14 He also took hostages and returned to S. H9076
2Ki 14:16 was buried in S with the kings of H9076
2Ki 14:23 Jehoash king of Israel became king in S, H9076
2Ki 15: 8 of Jeroboam became king of Israel in S, H9076
2Ki 15:13 of Judah, and he reigned in S one month. H9076
2Ki 15:14 son of Gadi went from Tirzah up to S. H9076
2Ki 15:14 He attacked Shallum son of Jabesh in S H9076
2Ki 15:17 of Israel, and he reigned in S ten years. H9076
2Ki 15:23 of Menahem became king of Israel in S, H9076
2Ki 15:25 in the citadel of the royal palace at S. H9076
2Ki 15:27 of Remaliah became king of Israel in S, H9076
2Ki 17: 1 son of Elah became king of Israel in S, H9076
2Ki 17: 5 marched against S and laid siege to it H9076
2Ki 17: 6 of Assyria captured S and deported the H9076
2Ki 17:24 them in the towns of S to replace the H9076
2Ki 17:24 They took over S and lived in its towns. H9076
2Ki 17:26 in the towns of S do not know what the H9076
2Ki 17:27 took captive from S go back to live there H9004S
2Ki 17:28 had been exiled from S came to live in H9076
2Ki 17:29 the shrines the **people of** S had made at H9085
2Ki 18: 9 marched against S and laid siege to it. H9076
2Ki 18:10 So S was captured in Hezekiah's sixth H9076
2Ki 18:34 Have they rescued S from my hand? H9076
2Ki 21:13 line used against S and the plumb line H9076
2Ki 23:18 of the prophet who had come from S. H9076
2Ki 23:19 in the towns of S and that had aroused H9076
2Ch 18: 2 later he went down to see Ahab in S. H9076
2Ch 18: 9 floor by the entrance of the gate of S, H9076
2Ch 22: 9 captured him while he was hiding in S. H9076
2Ch 25:13 belonging to Judah from S to Beth Horon. H9076
2Ch 25:24 the hostages, and returned to S. H9076
2Ch 28: 8 of plunder, which they carried back to S. H9076
2Ch 28: 9 to meet the army when it returned to S. H9076
2Ch 28:15 the City of Palms, and returned to S. H9076
Ezr 4:10 settled in the city of S and elsewhere in A10726
Ezr 4:17 associates living in S and elsewhere in A10726
Ne 4: 2 of his associates and the army of S, H9076
Isa 7: 9 The head of Ephraim is S, and the head H9076
Isa 7: 9 the head of S is only Remaliah's son. H9076
Isa 8: 4 the plunder of S will be carried off by H9076
Isa 9: 9 Ephraim and the inhabitants of S—who H9076
Isa 10: 9 Hamath like Arpad, and S like Damascus? H9076
Isa 10:10 excelled those of Jerusalem and S— H9076
Isa 10:11 images as I dealt with S and her idols? H9076
Isa 36:19 Have they rescued S from my hand? H9076
Jer 23:13 the prophets of S I saw this repulsive H9076
Jer 31: 5 you will plant vineyards on the hills of S; H9076
Jer 41: 5 Shechem, Shiloh and S, bringing grain H9076
Eze 16:46 Your older sister was S, who lived to the H9076
Eze 16:51 S did not commit half the sins you did H9076
Eze 16:53 daughters and of S and her daughters, H9076
Eze 16:55 her daughters and S with her daughters, H9076
Eze 23: 4 Oholah is S, and Oholibah is H9076
Eze 23:33 desolation, the cup of your sister S. H9076
Hos 7: 1 are exposed and the crimes of S revealed. H9076
Hos 8: 5 S, throw out your calf-idol! My anger H9076
Hos 8: 6 It will be broken in pieces, that calf of S. H9076
Hos 10: 5 people who live in S fear for the calf-idol H9076
Hos 13:16 The people of S must bear their guilt H9076
Am 3: 9 yourselves on the mountains of S; H9076
Am 3:12 will the Israelites living in S be rescued, H9076
Am 4: 1 you cows of Bashan on Mount S, you H9076
Am 6: 1 to you who feel secure on Mount S H9076
Am 8:14 Those who swear by the sin of S—who H9076
Ob 19 will occupy the fields of Ephraim and S, H9076
Mic 1: 1 he saw concerning S and Jerusalem. H9076
Mic 1: 5 Is it not S? What is Judah's high H9076
Mic 1: 6 "Therefore I will make S a heap of rubble H9076
Lk 17:11 along the border between S and Galilee. G4899
Jn 4: 4 Now he had to go through S. G4899
Jn 4: 5 So he came to a town *in* S called Sychar G4899
Ac 1: 8 in all Judea and S, and to the ends G4899
Ac 8: 1 were scattered throughout Judea and S. G4899
Ac 8: 5 down to a city *in* S and proclaimed the G4899
Ac 8: 9 the city and amazed all the people *of* S. G4899
Ac 8:14 Jerusalem heard that S had accepted the G4899
Ac 8:14 they sent Peter and John to S. G899S
Ac 9:31 Galilee and S enjoyed a time of peace G4899
Ac 15: 3 as they traveled through Phoenicia and S, G4899

SAMARIA'S (2) [SAMARIA]

Hos 10: 7 S king will be destroyed, swept away like H9076
Mic 1: 9 For S plague is incurable; it has spread H2023S

SAMARITAN (8) [SAMARIA]

Lk 9:52 who went into a S village to get things G4901
Lk 10:33 But a S, as he traveled, came where the G4901
Lk 17:16 feet and thanked him—and he was a S. G4901
Jn 4: 7 When a S woman came to G1666+3836+4899
Jn 4: 9 The S woman said to him, "You are a Jew G4902
Jn 4: 9 "You are a Jew and I am a S woman. G4902
Jn 8:48 that you are a S and demon-possessed?" G4901
Ac 8:25 preaching the gospel in many S villages. G4901

SAMARITANS (5) [SAMARIA]

Mt 10: 5 the Gentiles or enter any town *of* the S. G4901

S

Jn 4: 9 (For Jews do not associate with S.) *G4901*
Jn 4:22 You S worship what you do not know; we NDT
Jn 4:39 Many *of* the S from that town believed in *G4901*
Jn 4:40 So when the S came to him, they urged *G4901*

SAME (278)

Ge 11: 6 people speaking the s language they have H285
Ge 21:23 as a foreigner the s kindness I have H3869
Ge 26:12 in that land and the s year reaped a H2085
Ge 26:18 he gave them the s names his father had H3869
Ge 30:35 **That** s day he removed all the male goats H2085
Ge 32:19 "You are to say the s thing to Esau when H3869
Ge 40: 3 in the s prison where Joseph was confined. NDT
Ge 40: 5 had a dream the s night, and each dream H285
Ge 41:11 Each of us had a dream the s night, and H285
Ge 41:25 "The dreams of Pharaoh are **one and the s**. H285
Ge 41:26 are seven years; it is **one and the s** dream. H285
Ex 5: 6 **That** s day Pharaoh gave this order to the H2085
Ex 5: 8 to make the s number of bricks **as** before; H889
Ex 6:27 out of Egypt—**this** s Moses and Aaron. H2085
Ex 7:11 also did the s *things* by their secret arts: H4027
Ex 7:22 magicians did the s *things* by their secret H4027
Ex 8: 7 magicians did the s *things* by their secret H4027
Ex 12: 8 **That** s night they are to eat the meat H2296
Ex 12:12 "On **that** s night I will pass through Egypt H2296
Ex 12:49 The s law applies both to the native-born H285
Ex 22:30 Do the s with your cattle and your sheep H4027
Ex 23:11 Do the s with your vineyard and your olive H4027
Ex 25:33 the s for all six branches extending H4027
Ex 26: 2 All the curtains are to be the s size H285
Ex 26: 3 and **do the s** *with* the other five. H2489S
Ex 26: 4 do the s with the end curtain in the H4027
Ex 26: 8 All eleven curtains are to be the s size H285
Ex 29:41 at twilight with the s grain offering and its H3869
Ex 30:32 make any other oil using the s formula. H4017
Ex 34:16 *they will* **lead** your sons **to do the s** H2388+339+466+2177S
Ex 36: 9 All the curtains were the s size H285
Ex 36:10 and **did the s** *with* the H2489+285+448+285S
Ex 36:11 the s was done with the end curtain H4027
Ex 36:15 All eleven curtains were the s size—thirty H285
Ex 37:19 next branch and the s for all six branches H4027
Lev 7: 7 " 'The s law applies to both the sin offering H285
Lev 14:28 he is to put on the s places he put the blood NDT
Lev 16:16 He is to do the s for the tent of meeting H4027
Lev 18: 9 she was **born in the s home** or H4580+1074
Lev 22:28 cow or a sheep and its young on the s day. H285
Lev 22:30 It must be eaten **that** s day; leave none of H2085
Lev 23:21 On that s day you are to proclaim a sacred H6795
Lev 24:19 neighbor is to be injured in the s manner: H4027
Lev 24:20 injury must suffer the s injury. H3869+889+4027
Lev 24:22 You are to have the s law for the foreigner H285
Nu 2:17 will set out **in the s order** as they encamp, H4027
Nu 6:11 That s day they are to consecrate their H2085
Nu 6:12 to the LORD for the s period of dedication H2257
Nu 9: 6 they came to Moses and Aaron **that** s day H2085
Nu 9:14 You must have the s regulations for both H285
Nu 13:33 own eyes, and we looked the s to them." H4027
Nu 15:15 is to have the s rules for you and for H285
Nu 15:15 foreigner shall be the s before the LORD: H3869
Nu 15:16 The s laws and regulations will apply both H285
Nu 15:29 **One and the s** law applies to everyone who H285
Nu 26: 9 The s Dathan and Abiram were the H2085
Nu 28: 8 along with the s *kind of* grain offering H3869
Dt 2:22 LORD had done the s for the H3869+889
Dt 3:21 The LORD will do the s to all the kingdoms H4027
Dt 7:19 your God will do the s to all the peoples H4027
Dt 12:30 serve their gods? We will do the s." H4027
Dt 15:17 Do the s for your female servant H4027
Dt 18:12 because of **these** *s* detestable practices the AIT
Dt 21:23 Be sure to bury it **that** s day, because H2085
Dt 22: 3 Do the s if you find their donkey or cloak H4027
Dt 27:11 On the s day Moses commanded the H2085
Dt 32:48 On that s day the LORD told Moses, H6795
Jos 6:15 the city seven times in the s manner, H2296
Jos 7: 6 The elders of Israel did the s, and sprinkled NDT
Jos 10:35 They captured it **that** s day and put it to H2085
Jdg 6:25 **That** s night the LORD said to him, "Take H2085
Jdg 8: 8 Peniel and made the s request of them, H3869
1Sa 2:34 to you—they will both die on the s day. H285
1Sa 4:12 **That** s day a Benjamite ran from the H2085
1Sa 6: 4 because the s plague has struck both you H285
1Sa 6:16 this and then returned **that** s day to Ekron. H2085
1Sa 12:18 **that** s day the LORD sent thunder and H2085
1Sa 17:30 else and brought up the s matter, H3869
1Sa 28:25 **That** s night they got up and left H2085
1Sa 30:24 is to be the s **as** that of him who went H3869
1Sa 31: 6 all his men died together **that** s day. H2085
2Sa 2: 6 too will show you the s favor because you H2296
2Sa 16: 5 a man from the *s* **clan** *as* Saul's family came AIT
1Ki 3:17 This woman and I live in the s house, and I H285
1Ki 6:33 **In the s way**, for the entrance to the main H4027
1Ki 7:18 He did the s for each capital. H4027
1Ki 7:37 were all cast in the s molds and were H285
1Ki 8:64 On **that** s day the king consecrated the H2085
1Ki 11: 8 He did the s for all his foreign wives, who H4027
1Ki 13: 3 **That** s day the man of God gave a sign H2085
1Ki 15:26 committing the s sin his father had H2257S
1Ki 15:34 committing **the** s sin Jeroboam had H2257S
1Ki 16:19 committing **the** s sin Jeroboam had H2257S
1Ki 16:26 committing **the** s sin Jeroboam had H2257S
1Ki 22:12 prophets were prophesying the s *thing*. H4027
2Ki 4:17 next year about **that** s time she gave birth H2296
2Ki 8:22 Libnah revolted at the s time. H2085
1Ch 23:30 They were to do the s in the evening H4027
1Ch 24:31 were **treated the s as** those of H4200+6645
2Ch 16:10 At the s time Asa brutally oppressed H2085
2Ch 18:11 prophets were prophesying the s *thing*. H4027
2Ch 21:10 Libnah revolted at the s time, because H2085
2Ch 27: 5 brought him the **s amount** also in the H2296S
2Ch 35:12 They did the s with the cattle. H4027
Ne 5: 5 are of the s flesh and blood **as** our fellow H3869
Ne 6: 4 Four times they sent me the s message H3869
Ne 6: 4 each time I gave them the s answer. H3869
Ne 6: 5 sent his aide to me with the s message, H3869
Ne 9: 1 On the twenty-fourth day of the s month H2296
Ne 13:18 Didn't your ancestors do *the s things*, so H3907
Est 1:18 to all the king's nobles in the s way. NDT
Est 8: 1 **That** s day King Xerxes gave Queen Esther H2085
Est 9:11 Susa was reported to the king **that** s day. H2085
Job 9:22 It is **all the s**; that is why I say, 'He destroys H285
Job 31:15 Did not the s **one** form us both within our H285
Job 33: 6 I am **the s as** you in God's sight; H3869+7023
Ps 102:27 But you remain the s, and your years will H2085
Ecc 2:14 to realize that the s fate overtakes them H285
Ecc 3:19 the animals; the s fate awaits them both: H285
Ecc 3:19 All have the s breath; humans have no H285
Ecc 3:20 All go to the s place; all come from dust H285
Ecc 6: 6 Do not all go to the s place? H285
Ecc 9: 3 under the sun: The s destiny overtakes all H285
Isa 24: 2 it will be the s *for* priest as for people, for H3869
Jer 13: 9 **'In the s way** I will ruin the pride of Judah H3970
Jer 14:15 **Those** s prophets will perish by sword H2156
Jer 26:20 s things against this city and this land **as** H3869
Jer 27:12 I gave the s message to Zedekiah king of H3869
Jer 28: 1 In the fifth month of **that** s year, the fourth H2085
Jer 28:11 **'In the s way** I will break the yoke of H3970
Jer 28:17 In the seventh month of **that** s year H2085
Eze 4: 5 you the s number of days **as** the years of H4200
Eze 10:22 Their faces had the s appearance as those I NDT
Eze 18:24 sin and does the s detestable things the H3869
Eze 21:19 both starting from the s country. H285
Eze 23: 2 two women, daughters of the s mother. H285
Eze 23:13 both of them went the s way. H285
Eze 23:38 At **that** s time they defiled my sanctuary H2085
Eze 40:10 the three had the s measurements, and the H285
Eze 40:10 on each side had the s measurements. H285
Eze 40:21 had the s measurements **as** those of the H3869
Eze 40:22 had the s measurements **as** those of the H3869
Eze 40:24 had the s measurements **as** the others. H3869
Eze 40:28 it had the s measurements **as** the others. H3869
Eze 40:29 had the s measurements **as** the others. H3869
Eze 40:32 it had the s measurements **as** the others. H3869
Eze 40:33 had the s measurements **as** the others. H3869
Eze 40:35 It had the s measurements **as** the others, H3869
Eze 42:11 they had the s length and width H3869
Eze 44: 3 of the gateway and go out the s way." H2257S
Eze 45:11 ephah and the bath are to be the s size, H285
Eze 45:20 You are to do the s on the seventh day of H4027
Eze 45:25 he is to make the s provision for sin H3869
Eze 46: 8 he is to come out the s way. H2257S
Eze 46:22 the courts in the four corners was the s size. H285
Da 4:36 At the s time that my sanity was restored, A10192
Da 8:22 his nation but will not have the s power. H2257S
Da 11:27 will sit at the s table and lie to each other H285
Hos 3: 3 and I will *behave the s way* **toward** you." AIT
Am 2: 7 Father and son use the *s* girl and so profane AIT
Am 9: 7 you Israelites **the s** to me as the Cushites?" H3869
Zec 6:10 Go the s day to the house of Josiah son of H2085
Mt 5:12 for **in the s way** they persecuted the *G4048*
Mt 5:16 **In the s way**, let your light shine before *G4048*
Mt 7: 2 For **in the s way** you judge others, you *G3210S*
Mt 13: 1 **That** s day Jesus went out of the house *G1697*
Mt 17:12 **In the s way** the Son of Man is going to *G4048*
Mt 18:14 **In the s way** your Father in heaven is not *G4048*
Mt 20: 5 three in the afternoon and did **the s thing**. *G6058*
Mt 20:14 was hired last **the s as** I gave you. *G6055+2779*
Mt 21:30 to the other son and said **the s thing**. *G6058*
Mt 21:36 the tenants treated them **the s way**. *G6058*
Mt 22:23 **That** s day the Sadducees, who say there *G1697*
Mt 22:26 **The s thing** happened to the second and *G3931*
Mt 23:28 **In the s way**, on the outside you appear to *G4048*
Mt 26:35 And all the other disciples said **the s**. *G3931*
Mt 26:44 prayed the third time, saying the s thing. *G899*
Mt 27:41 **In the s way** the chief priests, the teachers *G3931*
Mt 27:44 **In the s way** the rebels who were *G3836+899*
Mk 12:21 It was **the s** with the third. *G6058*
Mk 14:31 And all the others said *the* **s**. *G6058*
Mk 14:39 more he went away and prayed the s thing. *G899*
Mk 15:31 **In the s way** the chief priests and the *G3931*
Lk 3:11 anyone who has food should do **the s**." *G3931*
Lk 10:31 happened to be going down the s road, *G1697*
Lk 14:33 **In the s way**, those of you who do not give *G4048*
Lk 15: 7 I tell you that **in the s way** there will be *G4048*
Lk 15:10 **In the s way**, I tell you, there is rejoicing in *G4048*
Lk 17:28 "It was **the s** in the days of Lot *G3931+2777*
Lk 20:31 and **in the s way** the seven died *G6058*
Lk 22:20 **In the s way**, after the supper he took the *G6058*
Lk 23:40 "since you are under the s sentence? *G899*
Lk 24:13 Now **that** s day two of them were going to *G899*
Jn 6:11 He did **the s** with the fish. *G3931*
Jn 9: 8 "Isn't **this** *the s man* who used to sit and beg?" AIT
Jn 11: 2 was **the** *s one* who poured perfume on the AIT
Jn 12:42 Yet **at the s time** many even among the *G3940*
Jn 21:13 it to them, and did **the s** with the fish. *G3931*
Ac 1:11 **This** s Jesus, who has been taken from *G4047*
Ac 1:11 back **in the s way** you have *G4048+4005+5573*
Ac 3:10 him as *the s man* who used to sit *G899*
Ac 7:35 "This is **the** *s* Moses they had rejected with AIT
Ac 11:17 God gave them the s gift he gave us who *G2698*
Ac 24:15 I have **the** s hope in God **as** these *G4005+2779*
Ac 24:26 **At the s time** he was hoping that Paul *G275*
Ac 27:40 in the sea and **at the s time** untied the *G275*
Ro 1:27 **In the s way** the men also abandoned *G3931*
Ro 2: 1 you who pass judgment do the s *things*. *G899*
Ro 2: 3 judgment on them and yet do *the* s *things*, *G899*
Ro 3:30 the uncircumcised through **that** s faith. *G3836*
Ro 4: 6 David says **the s thing** when he speaks of *G2749*
Ro 6:11 **In the s way**, count yourselves dead to sin *G4048*
Ro 8:26 **In the s way**, the Spirit helps us in our *G6058*
Ro 9:10 **children** *were* **conceived at the s time** *G1666+1651+3130+2400*
Ro 9:21 to make out of the s lump of clay some *G899*
Ro 10:12 the s Lord is Lord of all and richly blesses all *G899*
Ro 12: 4 members do not all have the s function, *G899*
Ro 15: 5 give you the s attitude of mind toward *G899*
1Co 2:11 **In the s way** no one knows the thoughts of *G4048*
1Co 7: 4 **In the s way**, the husband does not have *G3931*
1Co 9: 8 Doesn't the Law say **the s** *thing*? *G4047*
1Co 9:14 **In the s way**, the Lord has commanded *G4048*
1Co 10: 3 They all ate the s spiritual food *G899*
1Co 10: 4 drank the s spiritual drink; for they *G899*
1Co 11: 5 it is **the s as** having her *G1651+2779+3836+899*
1Co 11:25 **In the s way**, after supper he took the cup *G6058*
1Co 12: 4 but the s Spirit distributes them. *G899*
1Co 12: 5 are different kinds of service, but the s Lord. *G899*
1Co 12: 6 in everyone it is the s God at work. *G899*
1Co 12: 8 of knowledge by means of the s Spirit, *G899*
1Co 12: 9 to another faith by the s Spirit, to another *G899*
1Co 12:11 these are the work of one and the s Spirit, *G899*
1Co 15: 6 of the brothers and sisters **at the s time**, *G2384*
1Co 15:39 Not all flesh is the s: People have one kind *G899*
2Co 1: 6 patient endurance *of* the s sufferings we *G899*
2Co 1:17 so that *in the s breath* I *say* both "Yes, AIT
2Co 3:14 to this day the s veil remains when the *G899*
2Co 4:13 Since we have that s spirit of faith, we *G899*
2Co 8:16 heart of Titus the s concern I have for you *G899*
2Co 12:18 we not walk in the s footsteps by the same *G899*
2Co 12:18 walk in the same footsteps by the s Spirit? *G899*
Gal 4:29 power of the Spirit. It is **the s** now. *G4048+2779*
Eph 1:19 That power is **the s as** the mighty strength *G2848*
Eph 5:28 **In this s way**, husbands ought to love their *G4048*
Eph 6: 9 treat your slaves *in* the s *way*. Do not *G899*
Php 1:30 are going through the s struggle you saw I *G899*
Php 2: 2 having the s love, being one in *G899*
Php 2: 5 have *the* s mindset as Christ Jesus: *G4047*
Php 3: 1 me to write the s *things* to you *again*, *G899*
Php 4: 2 Syntyche to be of the s mind in the Lord. *G899*
Col 1: 6 **In the s way**, the gospel is bearing fruit *G2777*
1Th 2:14 own people the s *things* those churches *G899*
1Ti 3: 6 fall under the *s* judgment *as* the **devil**. AIT
1Ti 3: 8 **In the s way**, deacons are to be worthy of *G6058*
1Ti 3:11 **In the s way**, the women are to be worthy *G6058*
1Ti 5:25 **In the s way**, good deeds are obvious, and *G6058*
Heb 1:12 But you remain the s, and your years will *G899*
Heb 2:11 who are made holy are of the s *family*. *G1651*
Heb 5: 5 **In the s way**, Christ did not take on *G4048*
Heb 6:11 of you to show this s diligence to the very *G899*
Heb 9:21 **In the s way**, he sprinkled with the blood *G3931*
Heb 10: 1 by the s sacrifices repeated endlessly year *G899*
Heb 10:11 again and again he offers the s sacrifices *G899*
Heb 11: 9 who were heirs with him of the s promise. *G899*
Heb 13: 8 Jesus Christ is the s yesterday and today *G899*
Jas 1:11 **In the s way**, the rich will fade away even *G4048*
Jas 2:17 **In the s way**, faith by itself, if it is not *G4048*
Jas 2:25 **In the s way**, was not even Rahab the *G3931*
Jas 3:10 Out of the s mouth come praise and cursing. *G899*
Jas 3:11 water and salt water flow from the s spring? *G899*
1Pe 3: 1 **in the s way** submit yourselves to your *G3931*
1Pe 3: 7 **in the s way** be considerate as you live *G3931*
1Pe 4: 1 arm yourselves also with the s attitude *G899*
1Pe 5: 5 **In the s way**, you who are younger, submit *G3931*
1Pe 5: 9 is undergoing the s *kind of* sufferings. *G899*
2Pe 3: 7 By the s word the present heavens and *G899*
2Pe 3:16 He writes **the s way** in all his letters *G6055+2779*
Jude 8 **In the** very **s way**, on the strength of their *G3931*

SAMGAR (1)

Jer 39: 3 Nergal-Sharezer of S, Nebo-Sarsekim a H6161

SAMLAH (4)

Ge 36:36 S from Masrekah succeeded him as king. H8528
Ge 36:37 When S died, Shaul from Rehoboth on H8528
1Ch 1:47 S from Masrekah succeeded him as king. H8528
1Ch 1:48 When S died, Shaul from Rehoboth on H8528

SAMOS (1)

Ac 20:15 The day after that we crossed over to S *G4904*

SAMOTHRACE (1)

Ac 16:11 put out to sea and sailed straight for S, *G4903*

SAMPLE (1) [SAMPLED]

Pr 23:30 who go to s bowls of mixed wine. H2983

SAMPLED (1) [SAMPLE]

Jos 9:14 The Israelites s their provisions but did H4374

SAMSON (37) [SAMSON'S]

Jdg 13:24 gave birth to a boy and named him **S**. H9088
Jdg 14: 1 **S** went down to Timnah and saw there a H9088
Jdg 14: 3 to get a wife?" But **S** said to his father H9088
Jdg 14: 5 **S** went down to Timnah together with his H9088
Jdg 14:10 And there **S** held a feast, as was H9088
Jdg 14:12 tell you a riddle," **S** said to them. "If you H9088
Jdg 14:18 **S** said to them, "If you had not plowed with NDT
Jdg 15: 1 **S** took a young goat and went to visit his H9088
Jdg 15: 3 **S** said to them, "This time I have a right H9088
Jdg 15: 6 they were told, "**S**, the Timnite's H9088
Jdg 15: 7 **S** said to them, "Since you've acted like H9088
Jdg 15:10 "We have come to take **S** prisoner," H9088
Jdg 15:11 the cave in the rock of Etam and said to **S**, H9088
Jdg 15:12 **S** said, "Swear to me that you won't kill H9088
Jdg 15:16 Then **S** said, "With a donkey's jawbone I H9088
Jdg 15:19 When **S** drank, his strength returned and he NDT
Jdg 15:20 **S** led Israel for twenty years in the days of NDT
Jdg 16: 1 One day **S** went to Gaza, where he saw a H9088
Jdg 16: 2 of Gaza were told, "**S** is here!" So they H9088
Jdg 16: 3 But **S** lay there only until the middle of H9088
Jdg 16: 6 So Delilah said to **S**, "Tell me the secret H9088
Jdg 16: 7 **S** answered her, "If anyone ties me with H9088
Jdg 16: 9 she called to him, "**S**, the Philistines are H9088
Jdg 16:10 Then Delilah said to **S**, "You have made H9088
Jdg 16:12 she called to him, "**S**, the Philistines are H9088
Jdg 16:13 Delilah then said to **S**, "All this time you H9088
Jdg 16:14 she called to him, "**S**, the Philistines are H9088
Jdg 16:20 Then she called, "**S**, the Philistines are H9088
Jdg 16:23 "Our god has delivered **S**, our enemy, H9088
Jdg 16:25 they shouted, "Bring out **S** to entertain us." H9088
Jdg 16:25 So they called **S** out of the prison, and H9088
Jdg 16:26 **S** said to the servant who held his hand H9088
Jdg 16:27 men and women watching **S** perform. H9088
Jdg 16:28 Then **S** prayed to the LORD, "Sovereign H9088
Jdg 16:29 Then **S** reached toward the two central H9088
Jdg 16:30 **S** said, "Let me die with the Philistines!" H9088
Heb 11:32 **S** and Jephthah, about David and *G4907*

SAMSON'S (3) [SAMSON]

Jdg 14:15 they said to **S** wife, "Coax your H9088
Jdg 14:16 Then **S** wife threw herself on him H9088
Jdg 14:20 And **S** wife was given to one of his H9088

SAMUEL (140) [SAMUEL'S]

1Sa 1:20 She named him **S**, saying, "Because I H9017
1Sa 2:18 But **S** was ministering before the LORD—a H9017
1Sa 2:21 the boy **S** grew up in the presence of the H9017
1Sa 2:26 And the boy **S** continued to grow in H9017
1Sa 3: 1 The boy **S** ministered before the LORD H9017
1Sa 3: 3 **S** was lying down in the house of the H9017
1Sa 3: 4 Then the LORD called **S**. Samuel answered H9017
1Sa 3: 4 LORD called Samuel. **S** answered, "Here I NDT
1Sa 3: 6 the LORD called, "**S**!" And Samuel got up H9017
1Sa 3: 6 And **S** got up and went to Eli and said H9017
1Sa 3: 7 Now **S** did not yet know the LORD: The H9017
1Sa 3: 8 the LORD called, "**S**!" And Samuel got up H9017
1Sa 3: 8 And **S** got up and went to Eli and said NDT
1Sa 3: 9 So Eli told **S**, "Go and lie down, and if he H9017
1Sa 3: 9 So **S** went and lay down in his place H9017
1Sa 3:10 calling as at the other times, "**S**! H9017
1Sa 3:10 "Samuel! **S**!" Then Samuel said H9017
1Sa 3:10 Then **S** said, "Speak, for your servant is H9017
1Sa 3:11 And the LORD said to **S**: "See, I am about H9017
1Sa 3:15 **S** lay down until morning and then H9017
1Sa 3:16 called him and said, "**S**, my son." Samuel H9017
1Sa 3:16 "Samuel, my son." **S** answered, "Here I am." NDT
1Sa 3:18 So **S** told him everything, hiding nothing H9017
1Sa 3:19 The LORD was with **S** as he grew up, and H9017
1Sa 3:20 recognized that **S** was attested as a H9017
1Sa 3:21 revealed himself to **S** through his word. H9017
1Sa 7: 3 So **S** said to all the Israelites, "If you are H9017
1Sa 7: 5 Then **S** said, "Assemble all Israel at H9017
1Sa 7: 6 Now **S** was serving as leader of Israel at H9017
1Sa 7: 8 They said to **S**, "Do not stop crying out to H9017
1Sa 7: 9 Then **S** took a suckling lamb and sacrificed H9017
1Sa 7:10 While **S** was sacrificing the burnt offering H9017
1Sa 7:12 Then **S** took a stone and set it up H9017
1Sa 7:15 **S** continued as Israel's leader all the days H9017
1Sa 8: 1 When **S** grew old, he appointed his sons H9017
1Sa 8: 4 together and came to **S** at Ramah. H9017
1Sa 8: 6 this displeased **S**; so he prayed to the H9017
1Sa 8:10 **S** told all the words of the LORD to the H9017
1Sa 8:19 But the people refused to listen to **S**. "No!" H9017
1Sa 8:21 When **S** heard all that the people said H9017
1Sa 8:22 Then **S** said to the Israelites, "Everyone H9017
1Sa 9:14 there was **S**, coming toward them on H9017
1Sa 9:15 the LORD had revealed this to **S**: H9017
1Sa 9:17 When **S** caught sight of Saul, the LORD H9017
1Sa 9:18 Saul approached **S** in the gateway and H9017
1Sa 9:19 "I am the seer," **S** replied. "Go up ahead H9017
1Sa 9:22 Then **S** brought Saul and his servant into H9017
1Sa 9:23 **S** said to the cook, "Bring the piece of H9017
1Sa 9:24 it in front of Saul. **S** said, "Here is what has NDT
1Sa 9:24 And Saul dined with **S** that day. H9017
1Sa 9:25 **S** talked with Saul on the roof of his house. NDT
1Sa 9:26 daybreak, and **S** called to Saul on the roof H9017
1Sa 9:26 he and **S** went outside together. H9017
1Sa 9:27 the edge of the town, **S** said to Saul, "Tell H9017
1Sa 10: 1 Then **S** took a flask of olive oil and H9017
1Sa 10: 9 As Saul turned to leave **S**, God changed H9017
1Sa 10:14 they were not to be found, we went to **S**." H9017
1Sa 10:15 uncle said, "Tell me what **S** said to you." H9017
1Sa 10:16 tell his uncle what **S** had said about the H9017
1Sa 10:17 **S** summoned the people of Israel to the H9017
1Sa 10:20 When **S** had all Israel come forward by H9017
1Sa 10:24 **S** said to all the people, "Do you see the H9017
1Sa 10:25 **S** explained to the people the rights and H9017
1Sa 10:25 Then **S** dismissed the people to go to H9017
1Sa 11: 7 anyone who does not follow Saul and **S**." H9017
1Sa 11:12 The people then said to **S**, "Who was it H9017
1Sa 11:14 Then **S** said to the people, "Come, let us H9017
1Sa 12: 1 **S** said to all Israel, "I have listened to H9017
1Sa 12: 5 **S** said to them, "The LORD is witness against NDT
1Sa 12: 6 Then **S** said to the people, "It is the LORD H9017
1Sa 12:11 Jephthah and **S**, and he delivered H9017
1Sa 12:18 Then **S** called on the LORD, and that same H9017
1Sa 12:18 people stood in awe of the LORD and of **S**. H9017
1Sa 12:19 The people all said to **S**, "Pray to the LORD H9017
1Sa 12:20 "Do not be afraid," **S** replied. "You have H9017
1Sa 13: 8 the time set by **S**; but Samuel did not H9017
1Sa 13: 8 by Samuel; but **S** did not come to Gilgal H9017
1Sa 13:10 making the offering, **S** arrived, and Saul H9017
1Sa 13:11 have you done?" asked **S**. Saul replied, H9017
1Sa 13:13 a foolish thing," **S** said. "You have not H9017
1Sa 13:15 Then **S** left Gilgal and went up to Gibeah H9017
1Sa 15: 1 **S** said to Saul, "I am the one the LORD H9017
1Sa 15:10 Then the word of the LORD came to **S**: H9017
1Sa 15:11 **S** was angry, and he cried out to the LORD H9017
1Sa 15:12 Early in the morning **S** got up and went to H9017
1Sa 15:13 When **S** reached him, Saul said, "The H9017
1Sa 15:14 But **S** said, "What then is this bleating of H9017
1Sa 15:16 **S** said to Saul. "Let me tell you H9017
1Sa 15:17 **S** said, "Although you were once small in H9017
1Sa 15:22 But **S** replied: "Does the LORD delight in H9017
1Sa 15:24 Then Saul said to **S**, "I have sinned. H9017
1Sa 15:26 But **S** said to him, "I will not go back with H9017
1Sa 15:27 As **S** turned to leave, Saul caught hold of H9017
1Sa 15:28 **S** said to him, "The LORD has torn the H9017
1Sa 15:31 So **S** went back with Saul, and Saul H9017
1Sa 15:32 Then **S** said, "Bring me Agag king of the H9017
1Sa 15:33 But **S** said, "As your sword has made H9017
1Sa 15:33 And **S** put Agag to death before the LORD H9017
1Sa 15:34 Then **S** left for Ramah, but Saul went up H9017
1Sa 15:35 Until the day **S** died, he did not go to see H9017
1Sa 15:35 Saul again, though **S** mourned for him. H9017
1Sa 16: 1 The LORD said to **S**, "How long will you H9017
1Sa 16: 2 But **S** said, "How can I go? If Saul hears H9017
1Sa 16: 4 **S** did what the LORD said. When he arrived H9017
1Sa 16: 5 **S** replied, "Yes, in peace; I have come to NDT
1Sa 16: 6 When they arrived, **S** saw Eliab and thought NDT
1Sa 16: 7 But the LORD said to **S**, "Do not consider H9017
1Sa 16: 8 Abinadab and had him pass in front of **S**. H9017
1Sa 16: 8 But **S** said, "The LORD has not chosen this NDT
1Sa 16: 9 Shammah pass by, but **S** said, "Nor has the NDT
1Sa 16:10 Jesse had seven of his sons pass before **S** H9017
1Sa 16:10 before Samuel, but **S** said to him, "The H9017
1Sa 16:11 **S** said, "Send for him; we will not sit H9017
1Sa 16:13 So **S** took the horn of oil and anointed H9017
1Sa 16:13 **S** then went to Ramah. H9017
1Sa 19:18 he went to **S** at Ramah and told him all H9017
1Sa 19:18 Then he and **S** went to Naioth and stayed H9017
1Sa 19:20 with **S** standing there as their leader H9017
1Sa 19:22 "Where are **S** and David?" "Over in H9017
1Sa 25: 1 Now **S** died, and all Israel assembled H9017
1Sa 28: 3 Now **S** was dead, and all Israel had H9017
1Sa 28:11 I bring up for you?" "Bring up **S**," he said. H9017
1Sa 28:12 When the woman saw **S**, she cried out at H9017
1Sa 28:14 Then Saul knew it was **S**, and he bowed H9017
1Sa 28:15 **S** said to Saul, "Why have you disturbed H9017
1Sa 28:16 **S** said, "Why do you consult me, now that H9017
1Ch 6:27 his son, Elkanah his son and **S** his son. H9017
1Ch 6:28 The sons of **S**: Joel the firstborn and H9017
1Ch 6:33 musician, the son of Joel, the son of **S**, H9017
1Ch 7: 2 Jahmai, Ibsam and **S**—heads of their H9017
1Ch 9:22 positions of trust by David and **S** the seer. H9017
1Ch 11: 3 as the LORD had promised through **S**. H9017
1Ch 26:28 dedicated by **S** the seer and by Saul H9017
1Ch 29:29 are written in the records of **S** the seer, H9017
2Ch 35:18 in Israel since the days of the prophet **S**; H9017
Ps 99: 6 **S** was among those who called on his H9017
Jer 15: 1 "Even if Moses and **S** were to stand H9017
Ac 3:24 beginning with **S**, all the prophets who *G4905*
Ac 13:20 judges until the time of **S** the prophet. *G4905*
Heb 11:32 about David and **S** and the prophets, *G4905*

SAMUEL'S (5) [SAMUEL]

1Sa 3:19 he let none of **S** words fall to the H2257S
1Sa 4: 1 And **S** word came to all Israel. Now the H9017
1Sa 7:13 Throughout **S** lifetime, the hand of the H9017
1Sa 19:24 he too prophesied in **S** presence. H9017
1Sa 28:20 filled with fear because of **S** words. H9017

SANBALLAT (10)

Ne 2:10 When **S** the Horonite and Tobiah the H6172
Ne 2:19 But when **S** the Horonite, Tobiah the H6172
Ne 4: 1 When **S** heard that we were rebuilding H6172
Ne 4: 7 But when **S**, Tobiah, the Arabs, the H6172
Ne 6: 1 When word came to **S**, Tobiah, Geshem H6172
Ne 6: 2 **S** and Geshem sent me this message H6172
Ne 6: 5 **S** sent his aide to me with the same H6172
Ne 6:12 me because Tobiah and **S** had hired him. H6172
Ne 6:14 Remember Tobiah and **S**, my God H6172
Ne 13:28 priest was son-in-law to **S** the Horonite. H6172

SANCTIFIED (10) [SANCTIFY]

Jn 17:19 I sanctify myself, that they too may be truly **s**. *G39*
Ac 20:32 an inheritance among all those *who are* **s**. *G39*
Ac 26:18 place among those *who are* **s** by faith in me. *G39*
Ro 15:16 acceptable to God, **s** by the Holy Spirit. *G39*
1Co 1: 2 *to those* **s** in Christ Jesus and called to be *G39*
1Co 6:11 you were washed, *you were* **s**, you were *G39*
1Co 7:14 husband *has been* **s** through his wife, *G39*
1Co 7:14 the unbelieving wife *has been* **s** through her *G39*
1Th 4: 3 It is God's will that you should be **s**: that you *G40*
Heb 10:29 thing the blood of the covenant that **s** *them*, *G39*

SANCTIFY (4) [SANCTIFIED, SANCTIFYING]

Jn 17:17 **S** them by the truth; your word is truth. *G39*
Jn 17:19 For them I **s** myself, that they too may be *G39*
1Th 5:23 *May* God himself, the God of peace, **s** you *G39*
Heb 9:13 ceremonially unclean **s** them so that they *G39*

SANCTIFYING (2) [SANCTIFY]

2Th 2:13 be saved through the **s work** of the Spirit *G40*
1Pe 1: 2 through the **s work** of the Spirit, to be *G40*

SANCTUARIES (4) [SANCTUARY]

Lev 26:31 your cities into ruins and lay waste your **s**, H5219
Eze 7:24 the mighty, and their **s** will be desecrated. H5219
Eze 28:18 trade you have desecrated your **s**. H5219
Am 7: 9 be destroyed and the **s** *of* Israel will be H5219

SANCTUARY (176) [SANCTUARIES]

Ex 15:17 your dwelling, the **s**, Lord, your hands H5219
Ex 25: 8 "Then have them make a **s** for me, and I H5219
Ex 30:13 according to the **s** shekel, which weighs H7731
Ex 30:24 all according to the **s** shekel—and a hin of H7731
Ex 35:19 garments worn for ministering in the **s**— H7731
Ex 36: 1 of constructing the **s** are to do the work H7731
Ex 36: 3 to carry out the work of constructing the **s**. H7731
Ex 36: 4 all the work on the **s** left what they were H7731
Ex 36: 6 anything else as an offering for the **s**." H7731
Ex 38:24 all the work on the **s** was 29 talents and H7731
Ex 38:24 730 shekels, according to the **s** shekel. H7731
Ex 38:25 shekels, according to the **s** shekel— H7731
Ex 38:26 according to the **s** shekel, from everyone H7731
Ex 38:27 the bases for the **s** and for the curtain— H7731
Ex 39: 1 woven garments for ministering in the **s**. H7731
Ex 39:41 garments worn for ministering in the **s**, H7731
Lev 4: 6 the LORD, in front of the curtain of the **s**. H7731
Lev 5:15 value in silver, according to the **s** shekel. H7731
Lev 6:16 is to be eaten without yeast in the **s** area; H7705
Lev 6:26 it is to be eaten in the **s** area, in the H7705
Lev 6:27 a garment, you must wash it in the **s** area. H7705
Lev 7: 6 it must be eaten in the **s** area; it is H7705
Lev 10: 4 the camp, away from the front of the **s**." H7731
Lev 10:13 Eat it in the **s** area, because it is your H7705
Lev 10:17 you eat the sin offering in the **s** area? H7731
Lev 10:18 should have eaten the goat in the **s** area, H7731
Lev 12: 4 sacred or go to the **s** until the days of her H5219
Lev 14:13 the lamb in the **s** area where the sin H7731
Lev 16:24 with water in the **s** area and put on his H7705
Lev 19:30 my Sabbaths and have reverence for my **s**. H5219
Lev 20: 3 he has defiled my **s** and profaned my holy H5219
Lev 21:12 leave the **s** *of* his God or desecrate it H5219
Lev 21:23 the altar, and so desecrate my **s**. H5219
Lev 24: 9 who are to eat it in the **s** area, because it H7705
Lev 26: 2 my Sabbaths and have reverence for my **s**. H5219
Lev 27: 3 of silver, according to the **s** shekel; H7731
Lev 27:25 is to be set according to the **s** shekel, H7731
Nu 3:10 who approaches the **s** is to be put to death." NDT
Nu 3:28 were responsible for the care of the **s**. H7731
Nu 3:31 the articles of the **s** used in ministering H7731
Nu 3:32 were responsible for the care of the **s**. H7731
Nu 3:38 the care of the **s** on behalf of the H5219
Nu 3:38 who approached the **s** was to be put to NDT
Nu 3:47 according to the **s** shekel, which weighs H7731
Nu 3:50 1,365 shekels, according to the **s** shekel. H7731
Nu 4:12 the articles used for ministering in the **s**, H7731
Nu 4:19 are to go into the **s** and assign to each man NDT
Nu 7:13 both according to the **s** shekel, each filled H7731
Nu 7:19 both according to the **s** shekel, each filled H7731
Nu 7:25 both according to the **s** shekel, each filled H7731
Nu 7:31 both according to the **s** shekel, each filled H7731
Nu 7:37 both according to the **s** shekel, each filled H7731
Nu 7:43 both according to the **s** shekel, each filled H7731
Nu 7:49 both according to the **s** shekel, each filled H7731
Nu 7:55 both according to the **s** shekel, each filled H7731
Nu 7:61 both according to the **s** shekel, each filled H7731
Nu 7:67 both according to the **s** shekel, each filled H7731
Nu 7:73 both according to the **s** shekel, each filled H7731
Nu 7:79 both according to the **s** shekel, each filled H7731
Nu 7:85 shekels, according to the **s** shekel. H7731
Nu 7:86 shekels each, according to the **s** shekel. H7731
Nu 8:19 the Israelites when they go near the **s**." H7731
Nu 18: 1 offenses connected with the **s**, H5219
Nu 18: 3 near the furnishings of the **s** or the altar. H7731
Nu 18: 5 the care of the **s** and the altar, H7731
Nu 18: 7 who comes near the **s** is to be put to death." NDT
Nu 18:16 according to the **s** shekel, which weighs H7731
Nu 19:20 they have defiled the **s** *of* the LORD. H5219
Nu 28: 7 out the drink offering to the LORD at the **s**. H7731
Nu 31: 6 articles from the **s** and the trumpets for H7731
Jos 22:27 the LORD **at** his **s** with our burnt H4200+7156S
1Ki 6: 5 the main hall and **inner s** he built a H1808
1Ki 6:16 to form within the temple an **inner s**, H1808

S

1Ki 6:19 He prepared the **inner s** within the temple H1808
1Ki 6:20 The **inner s** was twenty cubits long, twenty H1808
1Ki 6:21 gold chains across the front of the **inner s**, H1808
1Ki 6:22 the altar that belonged to the **inner s**. H1808
1Ki 6:23 For the **inner s** he made a pair of H1808
1Ki 6:31 entrance to the **inner s** he made doors out H1808
1Ki 6:31 that were one fifth of the width of the **s**. NDT
1Ki 7:49 in front of the **inner s**); the gold floral H1808
1Ki 8:6 to its place in the **inner s** *of* the temple, H1808
1Ki 8:8 from the Holy Place in front of the **inner s**, H1808
1Ch 9:29 all the other articles of the **s**, H7731
1Ch 22:19 Begin to build the **s** *of* the LORD God, so H5219
1Ch 24:5 were officials of the **s** and officials of God H7731
1Ch 28:10 has chosen you to build a house as the **s**. H5219
2Ch 4:20 burn in front of the **inner s** as prescribed; H1808
2Ch 5:7 to its place in the **inner s** *of* the temple, H1808
2Ch 5:9 could be seen from in front of the **inner s** H1808
2Ch 20:8 it and have built in it a **s** for your Name, H5219
2Ch 26:18 Leave the **s**, for you have been unfaithful H5219
2Ch 29:5 Remove all defilement from the **s**. H7731
2Ch 29:7 offerings at the **s** to the God of Israel. H7731
2Ch 29:16 priests went into the **s** *of* the LORD to purify H1074
2Ch 29:21 the kingdom, for the **s** and for Judah. H5219
2Ch 30:8 Come to his **s**, which he has consecrated H5219
2Ch 30:19 not clean according to the rules of the **s**." H7731
2Ch 36:17 young men with the sword in the **s**, H1074+5219
Ezr 9:8 and giving us a firm place in his **s**, H5226+7731
Ne 10:39 the articles for the **s** and for the H5219
Ps 20:2 you help from the **s** and grant you support H7731
Ps 20:6 from his heavenly **s** with the victorious H7731
Ps 60:6 God has spoken from his **s**: "In triumph I H7731
Ps 63:2 have seen you in the **s** and beheld your H7731
Ps 68:17 the Lord has come from Sinai into his **s**. H7731
Ps 68:24 procession of my God and King into the **s**. H7731
Ps 68:35 are awesome in your **s**; the God of Israel H5219
Ps 73:17 till I entered the **s** *of* God; then I H5219
Ps 74:3 the enemy has brought on the **s**. H7731
Ps 74:7 They burned your **s** to the ground; they H5219
Ps 78:69 He built his **s** like the heights, like the H5219
Ps 96:6 strength and glory are in his **s**. H5219
Ps 102:19 "The LORD looked down from his **s** on high, H7731
Ps 108:7 God has spoken from his **s**: "In triumph I H7731
Ps 114:2 Judah became God's **s**, Israel his H7731
Ps 134:2 your hands in the **s** and praise the LORD. H7731
Ps 150:1 Praise God in his **s**; praise him in his H7731
Isa 60:13 to adorn my **s**; and I will glorify H5226+5219
Isa 62:9 grapes will drink it in the courts of my **s**." H7731
Isa 63:18 our enemies have trampled down your **s**. H5219
Jer 17:12 from the beginning, is the place of our **s**. H5219
La 1:10 she saw pagan nations enter her **s** H5219
La 2:7 rejected his altar and abandoned his **s**. H5219
La 2:20 prophet be killed in the **s** *of* the Lord? H5219
Eze 5:11 you have defiled my **s** with all your vile H5219
Eze 8:6 things that will drive me far from my **s**? H5219
Eze 9:6 Begin at my **s**." So they began with H5219
Eze 11:16 while I have been a **s** for them in the H5219
Eze 21:2 Jerusalem and preach against the **s**. H5219
Eze 23:38 time they defiled my **s** and desecrated my H5219
Eze 23:39 they entered my **s** and desecrated it. H5219
Eze 24:21 I am about to desecrate my **s**—the H5219
Eze 25:3 over my **s** when it was desecrated and H5219
Eze 37:26 I will put my **s** among them forever. H5219
Eze 37:28 when my **s** is among them forever. H5219
Eze 41:3 he went into the **inner s** and measured H7163
Eze 41:4 he measured the length of the **inner s**; H2257S
Eze 41:15 the **inner s** and the portico facing the H7164
Eze 41:17 to the inner **s** and on the walls at H1074
Eze 41:17 intervals all around the **inner** and outer **s** H7164
Eze 42:8 side nearest the **s** was a hundred cubits H2121
Eze 43:21 part of the temple area outside the **s**. H5219
Eze 44:1 me back to the outer gate of the **s**, H5219
Eze 44:5 to the temple and all the exits of the **s**. H5219
Eze 44:7 in heart and flesh into my **s**, H5219
Eze 44:8 you put others in charge of my **s**. H5219
Eze 44:9 in heart and flesh is to enter my **s**, H5219
Eze 44:11 They may serve in my **s**, having charge of H5219
Eze 44:15 who guarded my **s** when the H5219
Eze 44:16 They alone are to enter my **s**; they alone H5219
Eze 44:27 the inner court of the **s** to minister in the H7731
Eze 44:27 court of the sanctuary to minister in the **s**, H7731
Eze 45:2 500 cubits square is to be for the **s**, H7731
Eze 45:3 In it will be the **s**, the Most Holy Place. H5219
Eze 45:4 who minister in the **s** and who draw near H5219
Eze 45:4 houses as well as a holy place for the **s**. H5219
Eze 45:18 young bull without defect and purify the **s**. H5219
Eze 47:12 the water from the **s** flows to them. H5219
Eze 48:8 portions; the **s** will be in the center of it. H5219
Eze 48:10 In the center of it will be the **s** *of* the LORD. H5219
Eze 48:21 with the temple **s** will be in the center H5219
Da 8:11 from the LORD, and his **s** was thrown down. H5219
Da 8:13 the surrender of the **s** and the trampling H7731
Da 8:14 then the **s** will be reconsecrated. H7731
Da 9:17 look with favor on your desolate **s**. H5219
Da 9:26 will come will destroy the city and the **s**. H7731
Am 7:13 this is the king's **s** and the temple of the H5219
Zep 3:4 priests profane the **s** and do violence to H7731
Mal 2:11 has desecrated the **s** the LORD loves by H7731
Lk 11:51 was killed between the altar and the **s**. G3875
Heb 6:19 It enters the **inner** *s* behind the curtain, AIT
Heb 8:2 who serves *in* the **s**, the true tabernacle G41
Heb 8:5 They serve at a **s** that is a copy and shadow NDT
Heb 9:1 worship and also an earthly **s**. G41
Heb 9:24 did not enter a **s** made with human hands G41

SAND (29) [SANDY]

Ge 22:17 in the sky and as the **s** on the seashore. H2567
Ge 32:12 your descendants like the **s** *of* the sea, H2567
Ge 41:49 of grain, like the **s** *of* the sea; it was so H2567
Ex 2:12 killed the Egyptian and hid him in the **s**. H2567
Dt 33:19 the seas, on the treasures hidden in the **s**." H2567
Jos 11:4 as numerous as the **s** on the seashore. H2567
Jdg 7:12 be counted than the **s** on the seashore. H2567
1Sa 13:5 as numerous as the **s** on the seashore. H2567
2Sa 17:11 as numerous as the **s** on the seashore—be H2567
1Ki 4:20 as numerous as the **s** on the seashore; H2567
1Ki 4:29 as measureless as the **s** on the seashore. H2567
Job 6:3 would surely outweigh the **s** *of* the seas— H2567
Job 29:18 my days as numerous as the **grains of s**. H2567
Job 39:14 the ground and lets them warm in the **s**, H6760
Ps 78:27 like dust, birds like **s** *on* the seashore. H2567
Ps 139:18 they would outnumber the **grains of s** H2567
Pr 27:3 Stone is heavy and **s** a burden, but a H2567
Isa 10:22 your people be like the **s** *by* the sea, H2567
Isa 35:7 The **burning s** will become a pool, the H9220
Isa 48:19 descendants would have been like the **s**, H2567
Jer 5:22 I made the **s** a boundary for the sea, an H2567
Jer 15:8 more numerous than the **s** *of* the sea. H2567
Jer 33:22 as measureless as the **s** *on* the seashore. H2567
Hos 1:10 will be like the **s** *on* the seashore, H2567
Hab 1:9 a desert wind and gather prisoners like **s**. H2567
Mt 7:26 a foolish man who built his house on **s**. G302
Ro 9:27 of the Israelites be like the **s** by the sea, G302
Heb 11:12 as countless as the **s** on the seashore. G302
Rev 20:8 number they are like the **s** on the seashore. G302

SANDAL (6) [SANDALED, SANDALS]

Ge 14:23 not even a thread or the strap of a **s**, so H5837
Ru 4:7 one party took off his **s** and gave it to the H5837
Ru 4:8 "Buy it yourself." And he removed his **s**. H5837
Ps 60:8 on Edom I toss my **s**; over Philistia I shout H5837
Ps 108:9 on Edom I toss my **s**; over Philistia I shout H5837
Isa 5:27 at the waist, not a **s** strap is broken. H5837

SANDALED (1) [SANDAL]

SS 7:1 How beautiful your **s** feet, H928+2021+5837

SANDALS (28) [SANDAL]

Ex 3:5 "Take off your **s**, for the place where you H5837
Ex 12:11 your **s** on your feet and your staff in your H5837
Dt 25:9 take off one of his **s**, spit in his face and H5837
Dt 29:5 not wear out, nor did the **s** on your feet. H5837
Jos 5:15 "Take off your **s**, for the place where H5837
Jos 9:5 put worn and patched **s** on their feet and H5837
Jos 9:13 And our clothes and **s** are worn out by the H5837
1Ki 2:5 around his waist and the **s** on his feet. H5837
2Ch 28:15 They provided them with clothes and **s** H5836
Isa 11:15 so that anyone can cross over in **s**. H5837
Isa 20:2 from your body and the **s** from your feet." H5837
Eze 16:10 dress and **put s** of fine leather **on** you. H5836
Eze 24:17 turban fastened and your **s** on your feet; H5837
Eze 24:23 on your heads and your **s** on your feet. H5837
Am 2:6 silver, and the needy for a *pair of* **s**. H5837
Am 8:6 with silver and the needy for a *pair of* **s**, H5837
Mt 3:11 whose **s** I am not worthy to carry. G5687
Mt 10:10 the journey or extra shirt or **s** or a staff, G5687
Mk 1:7 the straps *of* whose **s** I am not worthy to G5687
Mk 6:9 Wear **s** but not an extra shirt. G4908
Lk 3:16 the straps *of* whose **s** I am not worthy to G5687
Lk 10:4 Do not take a purse or bag or **s**; and do G5687
Lk 15:22 Put a ring on his finger and **s** on his feet. G5687
Lk 22:35 without purse, bag or **s**, did you lack G5687
Jn 1:27 the straps of whose **s** I am not worthy to G5687
Ac 7:33 'Take off your **s**, for the G5687+3836+4546
Ac 12:8 said to him, "Put on your clothes and **s**." G4908
Ac 13:25 after me whose **s** I am not G5687+3836+4546

SANDBAR (1) [SANDBARS]

Ac 27:41 ship struck a **s** and ran aground. G5536+1458

SANDBARS (1) [SANDBAR]

Ac 27:17 they would run aground on the **s of Syrtis**, G5358

SANDY (1) [SAND]

Ac 27:39 they saw a bay with a **s beach**, where G129

SANG (21) [SING]

Ex 15:1 the Israelites **s** this song to the LORD: H8876
Ex 15:21 Miriam **s** to them: "Sing to the LORD, for he H6702
Nu 21:17 Then Israel **s** this song: "Spring up, O well H8876
Jdg 5:1 Barak son of Abinoam **s** *this* **song**: H8876
1Sa 18:7 As they danced, *they* **s**: "Saul has slain his H6702
1Sa 29:5 Isn't this the David *they* **s** about in their H6702
2Sa 3:33 The king **s** *this* **lament** for Abner: "Should H7801
2Sa 22:1 David **s** to the LORD the words of this song H1819
2Ch 5:13 their voices in praise to the LORD and **s**: H9048
2Ch 29:30 So *they* **s praises** with gladness and H2146
Ezr 3:11 praise and thanksgiving *they* **s** to the LORD: H6702
Ne 12:42 The choirs **s** under the direction of H9048
Job 38:7 the morning stars **s** together and all the H8264
Ps 7:T which *he* **s** to the LORD concerning Cush H8876
Ps 18:T *He* **s** to the LORD the words of this song H1819
Ps 106:12 believed his promises and **s** his praise. H8876
Mt 11:17 did not dance; *we* **s a dirge**, and you did G2577
Lk 7:32 did not dance; *we* **s a dirge**, and you did G2577
Rev 5:9 And *they* **s** a new song, saying: "You are G106
Rev 14:3 And *they* **s** a new song before the throne G106
Rev 15:3 **s** the song of God's servant Moses and G106

SANHEDRIN (20)

Mt 26:59 priests and the whole **S** were looking for G5284
Mk 14:55 priests and the whole **S** were looking for G5284
Mk 15:1 the teachers of the law and the whole **S** G5284
Jn 11:47 the Pharisees called a meeting *of* the **S**. G5284
Ac 4:15 to withdraw from the **S** and then conferred G5284
Ac 5:21 they called together the **S**—the full G5284
Ac 5:27 appear before the **S** to be questioned by G5284
Ac 5:34 stood up in the **S** and ordered that the G5284
Ac 5:35 Then he addressed **the S**: "Men of Israel G899S
Ac 5:41 The apostles left the **S**, rejoicing because G5284
Ac 6:12 Stephen and brought him before the **S**. G5284
Ac 6:15 were sitting in the **S** looked intently at G5284
Ac 7:54 When the members of the **S** heard this, they NDT
Ac 22:30 all the **members of the S** to assemble G5284
Ac 23:1 Paul looked straight at the **S** and said G5284
Ac 23:6 called out in the **S**, "My brothers, G5284
Ac 23:15 you and the **S** petition the commander to G5284
Ac 23:20 bring Paul before the **S** tomorrow on the G5284
Ac 23:28 accusing him, so I brought him to their **S**. G5284
Ac 24:20 found in me when I stood before the **S**— G5284

SANITY (2)

Da 4:34 toward heaven, and my **s** was restored. A10430
Da 4:36 At the same time that my **s** was restored A10430

SANK (12) [SINK]

Ge 42:28 Their hearts **s** and they turned to each H3655
Ex 15:5 *they* **s** to the depths like a stone. H3718
Ex 15:10 *They* **s** like lead in the mighty waters. H7510
Nu 21:18 that the nobles of the people **s**—the H4125
Jdg 3:22 Even the handle **s in** after the blade, and H995
Jdg 5:27 At her feet *he* **s**, he fell; there he lay. H4156
Jdg 5:27 At her feet *he* **s**, he fell; where he sank H4156
Jdg 5:27 where *he* **s**, there he fell—dead H4156
1Sa 17:49 The stone **s** into his forehead, and he fell H3190
SS 5:6 My heart **s** at his departure. H3655
Jer 38:6 and Jeremiah **s down** into the mud. H3190
Jnh 2:6 To the roots of the mountains *I* **s down** H3718

SANNAH See KIRIATH SANNAH

SANSANNAH (1)

Jos 15:31 Ziklag, Madmannah, **S**, H6179

SAP (5) [SAPPED]

Lev 26:16 will destroy your sight and **s** your strength. H1853
1Sa 2:33 to destroy your sight and **s** your strength, H1853
Job 6:6 is there flavor in the **s** *of* the mallow? H8202
Hos 7:9 Foreigners **s** his strength, but he does not H430
Ro 11:17 share in the **nourishing s** from the olive G4404

SAPH (1)

2Sa 21:18 time Sibbekai the Hushathite killed **S**, H6198

SAPPED (2) [SAP]

Ps 32:4 my strength **was s** as in the heat of H2200
La 1:14 my neck, and the Lord *has* **s** my strength. H4173

SAPPHIRA (1)

Ac 5:1 together with his wife **S**, also sold a piece G4912

SAPPHIRE (1) See also LAPIS LAZULI

Rev 21:19 was jasper, the second **s**, the third agate, G4913

SARAH (38) [SARAH'S, SARAI]

Ge 17:15 to call her Sarai; her name will be **S**. H8577
Ge 17:17 Will **S** bear a child at the age of ninety?" H8577
Ge 17:19 but your wife **S** will bear you a son H8577
Ge 17:21 whom **S** will bear to you by this time next H8577
Ge 18:6 So Abraham hurried into the tent to **S** H8577
Ge 18:9 "Where is your wife **S**?" they asked him H8577
Ge 18:10 next year, and **S** your wife will have a son." H8577
Ge 18:10 Now **S** was listening at the entrance to H8577
Ge 18:11 Abraham and **S** were already very old, and H8577
Ge 18:11 **S** was past the age of childbearing. H8577
Ge 18:12 So **S** laughed to herself as she thought H8577
Ge 18:13 Abraham, "Why did **S** laugh and say H8577
Ge 18:14 time next year, and **S** will have a son." H8577
Ge 18:15 **S** was afraid, so she lied and said, "I did H8577
Ge 20:2 there Abraham said of his wife **S** H8577
Ge 20:2 king of Gerar sent for **S** and took her. H8577
Ge 20:14 he returned **S** his wife to him. H8577
Ge 20:16 To **S** he said, "I am giving your brother a H8577
Ge 20:18 conceiving because of Abraham's wife **S**. H8577
Ge 21:1 the LORD was gracious to **S** as he had said, H8577
Ge 21:1 the LORD did for **S** what he had promised H8577
Ge 21:2 **S** became pregnant and bore a son to H8577
Ge 21:3 the name Isaac to the son **S** bore him. H8577
Ge 21:6 **S** said, "God has brought me laughter H8577
Ge 21:7 to Abraham that **S** would nurse children H8577
Ge 21:9 But **S** saw that the son whom Hagar the H8577
Ge 21:12 Listen to whatever **S** tells you, because it H8577
Ge 23:1 **S** lived to be a hundred and twenty-seven H8577
Ge 23:2 went to mourn for **S** and to weep over her. H8577
Ge 23:19 buried his wife **S** in the cave in the H8577
Ge 24:36 My master's wife **S** has borne him a son in H8577
Ge 24:67 brought her into the tent of his mother **S**, H8577
Ge 25:10 Abraham was buried with his wife **S**. H8577
Ge 49:31 Abraham and his wife **S** were buried, H8577
Isa 51:2 your father, and to **S**, who gave you birth. H8577

Ro 9: 9 time I will return, and S will have a son." G4925
Heb 11:11 And by faith even S, who was past G4925
1Pe 3: 6 like S, who obeyed Abraham and called G4925

SARAH'S (2) [SARAH]
Ge 25:12 son Ishmael, whom S slave, Hagar the H8577
Ro 4:19 and that S womb was also dead. G4925

SARAI (16) [SARAH]
Ge 11:29 The name of Abram's wife was S, and the H8584
Ge 11:30 Now S was childless because she was not H8584
Ge 11:31 his daughter-in-law S, the wife of his H8584
Ge 12: 5 He took his wife S, his nephew Lot, all the H8584
Ge 12:11 he said to his wife S, "I know what a H8584
Ge 12:14 Egyptians saw that S was a very H2085S
Ge 12:17 his household because of Abram's wife S. H8584
Ge 16: 1 Now S, Abram's wife, had borne him no H8584
Ge 16: 2 Abram agreed to what S said. H8584
Ge 16: 3 S his wife took her Egyptian slave Hagar H8584
Ge 16: 5 Then S said to Abram, "You are H8584
Ge 16: 6 Then S mistreated Hagar; so she fled H8584
Ge 16: 8 "Hagar, slave of S, where have you come H8584
Ge 16: 8 "I'm running away from my mistress S," H8584
Ge 17:15 said to Abraham, "*As for* S your wife, you H8584
Ge 17:15 you are no longer to call her S; her name H8584

SARAPH (1)
1Ch 4:22 Joash and S, who ruled in Moab H8598

SARDINE (KJV) RUBY

SARDIS (3)
Rev 1:11 Pergamum, Thyatira, S, Philadelphia and G4915
Rev 3: 1 "To the angel of the church in S write G4915
Rev 3: 4 a few people in S who have not soiled G4915

SARDIUS (KJV) CARNELIAN, RUBY

SARDONYX (NIV84) ONYX

SAREPTA (KJV) ZAREPHATH

SARGON (1)
Isa 20: 1 commander, sent by S king of Assyria H6236

SARID (2)
Jos 19:10 of their inheritance went as far as S. H8587
Jos 19:12 It turned east from S toward the sunrise to H8587

SASH (9) [SASHES]
Ex 28: 4 a woven tunic, a turban and a s. H77
Ex 28:39 The s is to be the work of an embroiderer H77
Ex 39:29 The s was made of finely twisted linen and H77
Lev 8: 7 on Aaron, tied the s around him, clothed H77
Lev 16: 4 is to tie the linen s around him and put on H77
Isa 3:24 will be a stench; instead of a s, a rope; H2514
Isa 11: 5 faithfulness the s *around* his waist. H258
Isa 22:21 robe and fasten your s around him and hand H77
Rev 1:13 feet and with a golden s around his chest. G2438

SASHES (6) [SASH]
Ex 28:40 s and caps for Aaron's sons to give them H77
Ex 29: 9 Then tie s on Aaron and his sons H77
Lev 8:13 tied s around them and fastened caps on H77
Pr 31:24 and supplies the merchants with s. H2512
Isa 3:20 the headdresses and anklets and s, the H8005
Rev 15: 6 wore golden s around their chests. G2438

SAT (96) [SIT]
Ge 21:16 she went off and s **down** about a bowshot H3782
Ge 21:16 And *as she* s there, she began H3782
Ge 37:25 As *they* s **down** to eat their meal, they H3782
Ge 38:14 then s **down** at the entrance to Enaim H3782
Ge 48: 2 rallied his strength and s **up** on the bed. H3782
Ex 2:15 in Midian, where *he* s **down** by a well. H3782
Ex 12:29 of Pharaoh, who s on the throne, to the H3782
Ex 16: 3 There we s around pots of meat and ate H3782
Ex 17:12 stone and put it under him and *he* s on it. H3782
Ex 32: 6 Afterward *they* s **down** to eat and drink H3782
Lev 15: 6 with a discharge s on must wash their H3782
Jdg 6:11 LORD came and s **down** under the oak in H3782
Jdg 19: 6 the two of them s **down** to eat and drink H3782
Jdg 19:15 They went and s in the city square, but no H3782
Jdg 20:26 there *they* s weeping before the LORD. H3782
Jdg 21: 2 where *they* s before God until evening H3782
Ru 2:14 When *she* s **down** with the harvesters, he H3782
Ru 4: 1 the town gate and s **down** there just as H3782
Ru 4: 1 So he went over and s **down**. H3782
1Sa 20:24 Moon feast came, the king s **down** to eat. H3782
1Sa 20:25 He s in his customary place by the wall H3782
1Sa 20:25 Jonathan, and Abner s next to Saul, but H3782
1Sa 28:23 up from the ground and s on the couch. H3782
2Sa 2:13 One group s **down** on one side of the H3782
2Sa 7:18 King David went in and s before the LORD, H3782
1Ki 2:12 So Solomon s on the throne of his father H3782
1Ki 2:19 down to her and s **down** on his throne. H3782
1Ki 2:19 mother, and *she* s **down** at his right hand. H3782
1Ki 19: 4 s **down** under it and prayed that he might H3782
1Ki 21:13 scoundrels came and s opposite him and H3782
2Ki 4:20 mother, the boy s on her lap until noon H3782
1Ch 17:16 King David went in and s before the LORD, H3782
1Ch 29:23 So Solomon s on the throne of the LORD as H3782
Ezr 9: 3 my head and beard and s **down** appalled. H3782
Ezr 9: 4 And I s there appalled until the evening H3782
Ezr 10:16 tenth month *they* s **down** to investigate H3782
Ne 1: 4 I heard these things, *I* s **down** and wept. H3782
Est 3:15 The king and Haman s **down** to drink, but H3782
Job 2: 8 himself with it as he s among the ashes. H3782
Job 2:13 Then *they* s on the ground with him for H3782
Job 29:25 the way for them and s as their chief; H3782
Ps 107:10 *Some* s *in* darkness, in utter darkness H3782
Ps 137: 1 rivers of Babylon *we* s and wept when we H3782
Jer 3: 2 By the roadside *you* s **waiting** for lovers H3782
Jer 3: 2 lovers, s like a nomad in the desert. NDT
Jer 15:17 *I* never s in the company of revelers, never H3782
Jer 15:17 *I* s alone because your hand was on me H3782
Eze 3:15 *I* s among them for seven days H3782
Eze 14: 1 came to me and s **down** in front of me. H3782
Eze 20: 1 the LORD, and *they* s **down** in front of me. H3782
Eze 23:41 *You* s on an elegant couch, with a table H3782
Jnh 3: 6 with sackcloth and s **down** in the dust. H3782
Jnh 4: 5 had gone out and s **down** at a place east H3782
Jnh 4: 5 s in its shade and waited to see what H3782
Zec 5: 7 there in the basket s a woman! H3782
Mt 5: 1 went up on a mountainside and s **down**. G2767
Mt 13: 1 went out of the house and s by the lake. G2764
Mt 13: 2 him that he got into a boat and s in it, G2764
Mt 13:48 Then *they* s **down** and collected the good G2767
Mt 15:29 went up on a mountainside and s **down**. G2764
Mt 26:55 Every day *I* s in the temple courts teaching G2757
Mt 26:58 He entered and s **down** with the guards to G2764
Mt 28: 2 rolled back the stone and s on it. G2764
Mk 4: 1 got into a boat and s in it out on the lake, G2764
Mk 6:40 So *they* s **down** in groups of hundreds and G404
Mk 11: 7 threw their cloaks over it, *he* s on it. G2767
Mk 12:41 Jesus s **down** opposite the place where G2767
Mk 14:54 There *he* s with the guards and G1639+5153
Mk 16:19 up into heaven and *he* s at the right hand G2767
Lk 4:20 gave it back to the attendant and s **down**. G2767
Lk 5: 3 Then *he* s **down** and taught the people G2767
Lk 7:15 The dead man s **up** and began to talk, and G361
Lk 9:15 The disciples did so, and everyone s **down**. G2884
Lk 10:39 who s at the Lord's feet listening to what G4149
Lk 22:55 of the courtyard and *had* s **down together**, G5154
Lk 22:55 down together, Peter s **down** with them. G2764
Jn 4: 6 was from the journey, s **down** by the well. G2757
Jn 6: 3 mountainside and s **down** with his G2764
Jn 6:10 in that place, and *they* s **down** (about five G404
Jn 8: 2 and *he* s **down** to teach them. G2767
Jn 12:14 Jesus found a young donkey and s on it G2767
Jn 19:13 Jesus out and s **down** on the judge's seat G2767
Ac 9:40 her eyes, and seeing Peter *she* s **up**. G361
Ac 12:21 s on his throne and delivered a public G2767
Ac 13:14 they entered the synagogue and s **down**. G2767
Ac 14: 8 In Lystra *there* s a man who was lame. G2764
Ac 16:13 *We* s **down** and began to speak to the G2767
1Co 10: 7 "The people s **down** to eat and drink and G2767
Heb 1: 3 *he* s **down** at the right hand of the G2767
Heb 8: 1 who s **down** at the right hand of the G2767
Heb 10:12 sins, *he* s **down** at the right hand of God, G2767
Heb 12: 2 and s **down** at the right hand of the G2767
Rev 3:21 victorious and s **down** with my Father on G2767
Rev 4: 3 And the *one who* s there had the G2764
Rev 5: 1 the right hand *of* him *who* s on the throne G2764
Rev 5: 7 the right hand *of* him *who* s on the throne G2764

SATAN (53) [SATAN'S]
1Ch 21: 1 S rose up against Israel and incited David H8477
Job 1: 6 the LORD, and S also came with them. H8477
Job 1: 7 The LORD said to S, "Where have you come H8477
Job 1: 7 S answered the LORD, "From roaming H8477
Job 1: 8 Then the LORD said to S, "Have you H8477
Job 1: 9 Job fear God for nothing?" S replied. H8477
Job 1:12 The LORD said to S, "Very well, then H8477
Job 1:12 Then S went out from the presence of the H8477
Job 2: 1 S also came with them to present H8477
Job 2: 2 And the LORD said to S, "Where have you H8477
Job 2: 2 S answered the LORD, "From roaming H8477
Job 2: 3 Then the LORD said to S, "Have you H8477
Job 2: 4 "Skin for skin!" S replied. "A man will give H8477
Job 2: 6 The LORD said to S, "Very well, then, he is H8477
Job 2: 7 So S went out from the presence of the H8477
Zec 3: 1 S standing at his right side to accuse H8477
Zec 3: 2 The LORD said to S, "The LORD rebuke you H8477
Zec 3: 2 said to Satan, "The LORD rebuke you, S! H8477
Mt 4:10 "Away from me, S! For it is written: G4928
Mt 12:26 If S drives out Satan, he is divided against G4928
Mt 12:26 If Satan drives out S, he is divided against G4928
Mt 16:23 said to Peter, "Get behind me, S! G4928
Mk 1:13 wilderness forty days, being tempted by S. G4928
Mk 3:23 "How can S drive out Satan? G4928
Mk 3:23 "How can Satan drive out S? G4928
Mk 3:26 And if S opposes himself and is divided G4928
Mk 4:15 S comes and takes away the word that G4928
Mk 8:33 "Get behind me, S!" he said. G4928
Lk 10:18 "I saw S fall like lightning from heaven. G4928
Lk 11:18 If S is divided against himself, how can his G4928
Lk 13:16 whom S has kept bound for eighteen long G4928
Lk 22: 3 Then S entered Judas, called Iscariot, one G4928
Lk 22:31 S has asked to sift all of you as wheat. G4928
Jn 13:27 Judas took the bread, S entered into him. G4928
Ac 5: 3 how is it that S has so filled your heart G4928
Ac 26:18 from the power *of* S to God, so that G4928
Ro 16:20 peace will soon crush S under your feet. G4928
1Co 5: 5 hand this man over *to* S for the destruction G4928
1Co 7: 5 again so that S will not tempt you G4928
2Co 2:11 in order that S might not outwit us. For we G4928
2Co 11:14 S himself masquerades as an angel of G4928
2Co 12: 7 a messenger *of* S, to torment me. G4928
1Th 2:18 again and again—but S blocked our way. G4928
2Th 2: 9 will be in accordance with how S works. G4928
1Ti 1:20 I have handed over *to* S to be taught not G4928
1Ti 5:15 in fact already turned away to follow S. G4928
Rev 2: 9 are not, but are a synagogue *of* S. G4928
Rev 2:13 where you live—where S has his throne. G4928
Rev 2:13 put to death in your city—where S lives. G4928
Rev 3: 9 those who are of the synagogue *of* S, G4928
Rev 12: 9 the devil, or S, who leads the whole G4928
Rev 20: 2 is the devil, or S, and bound him for a G4928
Rev 20: 7 S will be released from his prison G4928

SATAN'S (1) [SATAN]
Rev 2:24 have not learned S so-called deep G4928

SATIATE, SATIATED (KJV) SATISFIED, SATISFY

SATISFACTION (4) [SATISFY]
Est 5:13 But all this **gives** me no s as long as I see H8750
Ecc 2:24 eat and drink and find s in their own toil. H3202
Ecc 3:13 drink, and find s in all their toil—this H3202
Ecc 5:18 to drink and to find s in their toilsome H3208

SATISFIED (41) [SATISFY]
Ex 18:23 and all these people will go home s." H928+8934
Lev 10:20 Moses heard this, he *was* s. H3512+928+6524
Lev 26:26 You will eat, but *you will* not *be* s. H8425
Dt 6:11 not plant—then when you eat and *are* s, H8425
Dt 8:10 When you have eaten and *are* s, praise H8425
Dt 8:12 when you eat and *are* s, when you build H8425
Dt 11:15 your cattle, and you will eat and *be* s. H8425
Dt 14:29 your towns may come and eat and *be* s, H8425
Dt 26:12 that they may eat in your towns and *be* s. H8425
Ps 17:15 *I will be* s *with* seeing your likeness. H8425
Ps 22:26 The poor will eat and *be* s; those who H8425
Ps 59:15 wander about for food and howl if not s. H8425
Ps 63: 5 *I will be fully* s *as with* the richest of foods; H8425
Ps 104:13 the land is s by the fruit of his work. H8425
Ps 104:28 your hand, *they are* s *with* good things. H8425
Pr 13: 4 the desires of the diligent **are fully** s. H2014
Pr 18:20 *with* the harvest of their lips *they are* s. H8425
Pr 27:20 Death and Destruction *are* never s, and H8425
Pr 30:15 "There are three things *that are* never s H8425
Pr 30:16 *which is* never s *with* water, and H8425
Ecc 5:10 loves wealth is never s with their income. NDT
Ecc 6: 7 their mouth, yet their appetite **is** never s. H4848
Isa 9:20 on the left they will eat, but not *be* s. H8425
Isa 53:11 he will see the light of life and *be* s; by H8425
Isa 66:11 you will nurse and *be* s at her comforting H8425
Jer 46:10 The sword will devour till *it is* s, till it has H8425
Jer 50:19 their appetite *will be* s on the hills of H8425
Eze 16:28 even after that, *you* still *were* not s. H8425
Eze 16:29 even with this *you were* not s. H8425
Eze 27:33 out on the seas, *you* s many nations; with H8425
Hos 13: 6 I fed them, *they were* s; when they were H8425
Hos 13: 6 satisfied; when *they were* s, they became H8425
Mic 6:14 You will eat but not *be* s; your stomach H8425
Hab 2: 5 as the grave and like death is never s, H8425
Mt 14:20 They all ate and *were* s, and the disciples G5963
Mt 15:37 They all ate and *were* s. Afterward the G5963
Mk 6:42 They all ate and *were* s, G5963
Mk 8: 8 The people ate and *were* s. Afterward the G5963
Lk 6:21 you who hunger now, for *you will be* s. G5963
Lk 9:17 They all ate and *were* s, and the disciples G5963
3Jn 10 Not s with that, he even refuses to G758

SATISFIES (3) [SATISFY]
Ps 103: 5 who s your desires with good things so H8425
Ps 107: 9 for *he* s the thirsty and fills the hungry H8425
Ps 147:14 your borders and s you *with* the finest of H8425

SATISFY (18) [SATISFACTION, SATISFIED, SATISFIES]
Job 38:27 to s a desolate wasteland and make it H8425
Job 38:39 the lioness and s the hunger of the H4848
Ps 81:16 with honey from the rock *I would* s you." H8425
Ps 90:14 S us in the morning *with* your unfailing H8425
Ps 91:16 *With* long life *I will* s him and show him H8425
Ps 132:15 provisions; her poor *I will* s *with* food. H8425
Ps 145:16 open your hand and s the desires of every H8425
Pr 5:19 *may* her breasts s you always H8115
Pr 6:30 if he steals to s his hunger when he is H4848
Isa 55: 2 and your labor on *what* does not s? H8429
Isa 58:10 of the hungry and s the needs of the H8425
Isa 58:11 *he will* s your needs in a sun-scorched H8425
Jer 31:14 *I will* s the priests *with* abundance, and H8115
Jer 31:25 I will refresh the weary and s the faint." H4848
Eze 7:19 *It will* not s their hunger or fill their H8425
Joel 2:19 olive oil, *enough to* s you **fully**; never H8425
Mt 28:14 we *will* s him and keep you out of trouble." G4275
Mk 15:15 Wanting *to* s the crowd, Pilate G2653+4472

SATRAPS (13)
Ezr 8:36 orders to the royal s and to the governors of H346
Est 3:12 people all Haman's orders to the king's s, H346
Est 8: 9 the Jews, and to the s, governors and H346
Est 9: 3 of the provinces, the s, the governors and H346
Da 3: 2 He then summoned the s, prefects A10026
Da 3: 3 So the s, prefects, governors, advisers A10026
Da 3:27 the s, prefects, governors and royal A10026
Da 6: 1 to appoint 120 s to rule throughout A10026

S

Da	6: 2	The s were made accountable to them	A10026
Da	6: 3	the s by his exceptional	A10026
Da	6: 4	the s tried to find grounds	A10026
Da	6: 6	administrators and s went as a group to	A10026
Da	6: 7	prefects, s, advisers and governors have	A10026

SATYR, SATYRS (KJV) WILD GOATS

SAUL (372) [SAUL'S]

1Sa	9: 2	Kish had a son named S, as handsome a	H8620
1Sa	9: 3	Kish said to his son S, "Take one of	H8620
1Sa	9: 5	S said to the servant who was with him	H8620
1Sa	9: 7	S said to his servant, "If we go, what can	H8620
1Sa	9:10	S said to his servant. "Come, let's	H8620
1Sa	9:15	Now the day before S came, the LORD had	H8620
1Sa	9:17	When Samuel caught sight of S, the LORD	H8620
1Sa	9:18	S approached Samuel in the gateway	H8620
1Sa	9:21	S answered, "But am I not a Benjamite	H8620
1Sa	9:22	Then Samuel brought S and his servant	H8620
1Sa	9:24	with what was on it and set it in front of S.	H8620
1Sa	9:24	And S dined with Samuel that day	H8620
1Sa	9:25	Samuel talked with S on the roof of his	H8620
1Sa	9:26	Samuel called to S on the roof, "Get	H8620
1Sa	9:26	When S got ready, he and Samuel went	H8620
1Sa	9:27	Samuel said to S, "Tell the servant	H8620
1Sa	10: 9	As S turned to leave Samuel, God	H2257S
1Sa	10:11	Is S also among the prophets?	H8620
1Sa	10:12	"Is S also among the prophets?	H8620
1Sa	10:13	After S stopped prophesying, he went to the	NDT
1Sa	10:16	S replied, "He assured us that the	H8620
1Sa	10:21	Finally S son of Kish was taken	H8620
1Sa	10:26	S also went to his home in Gibeah	H8620
1Sa	10:27	brought him no gifts. But S kept silent.	NDT
1Sa	11: 4	came to Gibeah of S and reported these	H8620
1Sa	11: 5	Just then S was returning from the fields	H8620
1Sa	11: 6	When S heard their words, the Spirit of	H8620
1Sa	11: 7	who does not follow S and Samuel."	H8620
1Sa	11: 8	When S mustered them at Bezek, the men of	NDT
1Sa	11:11	The next day S separated his men into	H8620
1Sa	11:12	was it that asked, 'Shall S reign over us?	H8620
1Sa	11:13	But S said, "No one will be put to death	H8620
1Sa	11:15	to Gilgal and made S king in the	H8620
1Sa	11:15	S and all the Israelites held a great	H8620
1Sa	13: 1	S was thirty years old when he became	H8620
1Sa	13: 2	S chose three thousand men from Israel	H8620
1Sa	13: 3	Then S had the trumpet blown throughout	H8620
1Sa	13: 4	"S has attacked the Philistine outpost	H8620
1Sa	13: 4	were summoned to join S at Gilgal.	H8620
1Sa	13: 7	S remained at Gilgal, and all the troops	H8620
1Sa	13: 9	And S offered up the burnt offering	NDT
1Sa	13:10	and S went out to greet him.	H8620
1Sa	13:11	S replied, "When I saw that the men were	H8620
1Sa	13:15	S counted the men who were with	H8620
1Sa	13:16	S and his son Jonathan and the men with	H8620
1Sa	13:22	not a soldier with S and Jonathan had a	H8620
1Sa	13:22	only S and his son Jonathan had them.	H8620
1Sa	14: 1	day Jonathan son of S said to his young	H8620
1Sa	14: 2	S was staying on the outskirts of Gibeah	H8620
1Sa	14:17	Then S said to the men who were with	H8620
1Sa	14:18	S said to Ahijah, "Bring the ark of God."	H8620
1Sa	14:19	While S was talking to the priest, the	H8620
1Sa	14:19	So S said to the priest, "Withdraw your	H8620
1Sa	14:20	Then S and all his men assembled and	H8620
1Sa	14:21	Israelites who were with S and Jonathan.	H8620
1Sa	14:24	because S had bound the people under	H8620
1Sa	14:33	Then someone said to S, "Look, the men	H8620
1Sa	14:35	Then S built an altar to the LORD; it was the	H8620
1Sa	14:36	S said, "Let us go down and pursue the	H8620S
1Sa	14:37	So S asked God, "Shall I go down and	H8620
1Sa	14:38	S therefore said, "Come here, all you who	H8620
1Sa	14:40	S then said to all the Israelites, "You stand	NDT
1Sa	14:41	Then S prayed to the LORD, the God of	H8620
1Sa	14:41	Jonathan and S were taken by lot, and	H8620
1Sa	14:42	S said, "Cast the lot between me and	H8620
1Sa	14:43	Then S said to Jonathan, "Tell me what	H8620
1Sa	14:44	S said, "May God deal with me, be it ever	H8620
1Sa	14:45	But the men said to S, "Should Jonathan	H8620
1Sa	14:46	Then S stopped pursuing the Philistines	H8620
1Sa	14:47	After S had assumed rule over Israel, he	H8620
1Sa	14:52	All the days of S there was bitter war with	H8620
1Sa	14:52	whenever S saw a mighty or brave	H8620
1Sa	15: 1	Samuel said to S, "I am the one the LORD	H8620
1Sa	15: 4	So S summoned the men and mustered	H8620
1Sa	15: 5	S went to the city of Amalek and set an	H8620
1Sa	15: 7	Then S attacked the Amalekites all the	H8620
1Sa	15: 9	But S and the army spared Agag and the	H8620
1Sa	15:11	"I regret that I have made S king, because	H8620
1Sa	15:12	Samuel got up and went to meet S,	H8620
1Sa	15:12	he was told, "S has gone to Carmel.	H8620
1Sa	15:13	Samuel reached him, S said, "The LORD	H8620
1Sa	15:15	S answered, "The soldiers brought them	H8620
1Sa	15:16	Samuel said to S. "Let me tell you what	H8620
1Sa	15:16	said to me last night." "Tell me," S replied.	NDT
1Sa	15:20	did obey the LORD," S said. "I went on the	H8620
1Sa	15:24	Then S said to Samuel, "I have sinned.	H8620
1Sa	15:27	S caught hold of the hem of his robe	NDT
1Sa	15:30	S replied, "I have sinned. But please honor	NDT
1Sa	15:31	So Samuel went back with S, and Saul	H8620
1Sa	15:31	back with Saul, and S worshiped the LORD.	H8620
1Sa	15:34	S went up to his home in Gibeah of	H8620
1Sa	15:34	Saul went up to his home in Gibeah of S.	H8620
1Sa	15:35	he did not go to see S again, though	H8620
1Sa	15:35	that he had made S king over Israel.	H8620
1Sa	16: 1	"How long will you mourn for S, since I	H8620
1Sa	16: 2	"How can I go? If S hears about it, he will	H8620
1Sa	16:14	the Spirit of the LORD had departed from S,	H8620
1Sa	16:17	So S said to his attendants, "Find	H8620
1Sa	16:19	Then S sent messengers to Jesse and	H8620
1Sa	16:20	sent them with his son David to S.	H8620
1Sa	16:21	David came to S and entered his service	H8620
1Sa	16:21	S liked him very much, and David became	NDT
1Sa	16:22	Then S sent word to Jesse, saying, "Allow	H8620
1Sa	16:23	Whenever the spirit from God came on S	H8620
1Sa	16:23	Then relief would come to S; he would	H8620
1Sa	17: 2	S and the Israelites assembled and	H8620
1Sa	17: 8	are you not the servants of S?	H8620
1Sa	17:11	S and all the Israelites were dismayed	H8620
1Sa	17:13	oldest sons had followed S to the war:	H8620
1Sa	17:14	The three oldest followed S,	H8620
1Sa	17:15	back and forth from S to tend his father's	H8620
1Sa	17:19	They are with S and all the men of Israel	H8620
1Sa	17:31	said was overheard and reported to S,	H8620
1Sa	17:31	reported to Saul, and S sent for him.	NDT
1Sa	17:32	David said to S, "Let no one lose heart on	H8620
1Sa	17:33	S replied, "You are not able to go out	H8620
1Sa	17:34	But David said to S, "Your servant has	H8620
1Sa	17:37	S said to David, "Go, and the LORD be	H8620
1Sa	17:38	Then S dressed David in his own tunic	H8620
1Sa	17:39	he said to S, "because I am not used to	H8620
1Sa	17:55	As S watched David going out to meet	H8620
1Sa	17:57	Abner took him and brought him before S,	H8620
1Sa	17:58	are you, young man?" S asked him. David	H8620
1Sa	18: 1	After David had finished talking with S	H8620
1Sa	18: 2	From that day S kept David with him and	H8620
1Sa	18: 5	Whatever mission S sent him on, David	H8620
1Sa	18: 5	so successful that S gave him a high rank	H8620
1Sa	18: 6	of Israel to meet King S with singing and	H8620
1Sa	18: 7	"S has slain his thousands, and David his	H8620
1Sa	18: 8	S was very angry; this refrain displeased	H8620
1Sa	18: 9	from that time on S kept a close eye on	H8620
1Sa	18:10	evil spirit from God came forcefully on S.	H8620
1Sa	18:10	he usually did. S had a spear in his hand	H8620
1Sa	18:12	S was afraid of David, because the LORD	H8620
1Sa	18:12	was with David but had departed from S.	H8620
1Sa	18:15	When S saw how successful he was, he	H8620
1Sa	18:17	S said to David, "Here is my older	H8620
1Sa	18:17	For S said to himself, "I will not raise a	H8620
1Sa	18:18	But David said to S, "Who am I, and what	H8620
1Sa	18:20	when they told S about it, he was	H8620
1Sa	18:21	So S said to David, "Now you have a	H8620
1Sa	18:22	Then S ordered his attendants: "Speak to	H8620
1Sa	18:25	S replied, "Say to David, 'The king wants	H8620
1Sa	18:27	Then S gave him his daughter Michal in	H8620
1Sa	18:28	When S realized that the LORD was with	H8620
1Sa	18:29	S became still more afraid of him, and he	H8620
1Sa	19: 1	S told his son Jonathan and all the	H8620
1Sa	19: 2	"My father S is looking for a chance to kill	H8620
1Sa	19: 4	well of David to S his father and said to	H8620
1Sa	19: 6	S listened to Jonathan and took this oath	H8620
1Sa	19: 7	He brought him to S, and David was with	H8620
1Sa	19: 7	to Saul, and David was with S as before.	H2257S
1Sa	19: 9	the LORD came on S as he was sitting in	H8620
1Sa	19:10	S tried to pin him to the wall with his	H8620
1Sa	19:10	David eluded him as S drove the spear	H8620
1Sa	19:11	S sent men to David's house to watch it	H8620
1Sa	19:14	When S sent the men to capture David	H8620
1Sa	19:15	Then S sent the men back to see David	H8620
1Sa	19:17	S said to Michal, "Why did you deceive	H8620
1Sa	19:18	told him all that S had done to him.	H8620
1Sa	19:19	Word came to S: "David is in Naioth at	H8620
1Sa	19:21	S was told about it, and he sent more men	H8620
1Sa	19:21	S sent men a third time, and they also	H8620
1Sa	19:23	So S went to Naioth at Ramah. But the Spirit	NDT
1Sa	19:24	"Is S also among the prophets?	H8620
1Sa	20:25	Abner sat next to S, but David's place	H8620
1Sa	20:26	S said nothing that day, for he thought	H8620
1Sa	20:27	Then S said to his son Jonathan, "Why	H8620
1Sa	20:33	But S hurled his spear at him to kill him	H8620
1Sa	21:10	day David fled from S and went to Achish	H8620
1Sa	21:11	" 'S has slain his thousands, and David	H8620
1Sa	22: 6	Now S heard that David and his men had	H8620
1Sa	22: 6	And S was seated, spear in hand, under	H8620
1Sa	22:12	S said, "Listen now, son of Ahitub." "Yes	H8620
1Sa	22:13	S said to him, "Why have you conspired	H8620
1Sa	22:21	He told David that S had killed the priests	H8620
1Sa	22:22	I knew he would be sure to tell S.	H8620
1Sa	23: 7	S was told that David had gone to Keilah	H8620
1Sa	23: 8	And S called up all his forces for battle, to	H8620
1Sa	23: 9	David learned that S was plotting against	H8620
1Sa	23:10	heard definitely that S plans to come to	H8620
1Sa	23:11	Will S come down, as your servant has	H8620
1Sa	23:12	of Keilah surrender me and my men to S?"	H8620
1Sa	23:13	When S was told that David had escaped	H8620
1Sa	23:14	Day after day S searched for him, but God	H8620
1Sa	23:15	he learned that S had come out to take	H8620
1Sa	23:17	"My father S will not lay a hand on you	H8620
1Sa	23:17	Even my father S knows this."	H8620
1Sa	23:19	Ziphites went up to S at Gibeah and said,	H8620
1Sa	23:21	S replied, "The LORD bless you for your	H8620
1Sa	23:24	they set out and went to Ziph ahead of S.	H8620
1Sa	23:25	S and his men began the search, and	H8620
1Sa	23:25	When S heard this, he went into the	H8620
1Sa	23:26	S was going along one side of the	H8620
1Sa	23:26	other side, hurrying to get away from S.	H8620
1Sa	23:26	As S and his forces were closing in on	H8620
1Sa	23:27	a messenger came to S, saying, "Come	H8620
1Sa	23:28	Then S broke off his pursuit of David and	H8620
1Sa	24: 1	After S returned from pursuing the	H8620
1Sa	24: 2	So S took three thousand able young men	H8620
1Sa	24: 3	and S went in to relieve himself.	H8620
1Sa	24: 7	men and did not allow them to attack S.	H8620
1Sa	24: 7	And S left the cave and went his way	H8620
1Sa	24: 8	went out of the cave and called out to S,	H8620
1Sa	24: 8	When S looked behind him, David	H8620
1Sa	24: 9	He said to S, "Why do you listen when	H8620
1Sa	24:16	finished saying this, S asked, "Is that your	H8620
1Sa	24:22	So David gave his oath to S. Then Saul	H8620
1Sa	24:22	Then S returned home, but David and his	H8620
1Sa	25:44	But S had given his daughter Michal	H8620
1Sa	26: 1	Ziphites went to S at Gibeah and said,	H8620
1Sa	26: 2	So S went down to the Desert of Ziph	H8620
1Sa	26: 3	S made his camp beside the road on the	H8620
1Sa	26: 3	When he saw that S had followed him	H8620
1Sa	26: 4	learned that S had definitely arrived.	H8620
1Sa	26: 5	went to the place where S had camped.	H8620
1Sa	26: 5	He saw where S and Abner son of Ner	H8620
1Sa	26: 5	S was lying inside the camp, with the	H8620
1Sa	26: 6	will go down into the camp with me to S?"	H8620
1Sa	26: 7	there was S, lying asleep inside	H8620
1Sa	26:17	S recognized David's voice and said, "Is	H8620
1Sa	26:21	Then S said, "I have sinned. Come back	H8620
1Sa	26:25	Then S said to David, "May you be	H8620
1Sa	26:25	went on his way, and S returned home.	H8620
1Sa	27: 1	days I will be destroyed by the hand of S.	H8620
1Sa	27: 1	Then S will give up searching for me	H8620
1Sa	27: 4	When S was told that David had fled to	H8620
1Sa	28: 3	S had expelled the mediums and spiritists	H8620
1Sa	28: 4	while S gathered all Israel and set up	H8620
1Sa	28: 5	When S saw the Philistine army, he was	H8620
1Sa	28: 7	S then said to his attendants, "Find me a	H8620
1Sa	28: 8	So S disguised himself, putting on other	H8620
1Sa	28: 9	"Surely you know what S has done.	H8620
1Sa	28:10	S swore to her by the LORD, "As surely as	H8620
1Sa	28:12	out at the top of her voice and said to S,	H8620
1Sa	28:12	"Why have you deceived me? You are S!"	H8620
1Sa	28:14	Then S knew it was Samuel, and he	H8620
1Sa	28:15	Samuel said to S, "Why have you	H8620
1Sa	28:15	in great distress," S said. "The Philistines	H8620
1Sa	28:20	Immediately S fell full length on the	H8620
1Sa	28:21	the woman came to S and saw that he	H8620
1Sa	28:25	Then she set it before S and his men, and	H8620
1Sa	29: 3	who was an officer of S king of Israel?	H8620
1Sa	29: 3	from the day he left S until now, I have	NDT
1Sa	29: 5	" 'S has slain his thousands, and David	H8620
1Sa	31: 2	were in hot pursuit of S and his sons,	H8620
1Sa	31: 3	The fighting grew fierce around S, and	H8620
1Sa	31: 4	S said to his armor-bearer, "Draw your	H8620
1Sa	31: 4	so S took his own sword and fell on it.	H8620
1Sa	31: 5	the armor-bearer saw that S was dead,	H8620
1Sa	31: 6	So S and his three sons and his	H8620
1Sa	31: 7	had fled and that S and his sons had died	H8620
1Sa	31: 8	they found S and his three sons fallen on	H8620
1Sa	31:11	heard what the Philistines had done to S,	H8620
1Sa	31:12	down the bodies of S and his sons from	H8620
2Sa	1: 1	After the death of S, David returned from	H8620
2Sa	1: 4	And S and his son Jonathan are dead."	H8620
2Sa	1: 5	do you know that S and his son Jonathan	H8620
2Sa	1: 6	"and there was S, leaning on his	H8620
2Sa	1:12	till evening for S and his son Jonathan,	H8620
2Sa	1:17	lament concerning S and his son	H8620
2Sa	1:21	the shield of S—no longer rubbed with	H8620
2Sa	1:22	the sword of S did not return unsatisfied.	H8620
2Sa	1:23	S and Jonathan—in life they were loved	H8620
2Sa	1:24	of Israel, weep for S, who clothed you in	H8620
2Sa	2: 4	from Jabesh Gilead who had buried S,	H8620
2Sa	2: 5	this kindness to S your master by burying	H8620
2Sa	2: 7	brave, for S your master is dead	H8620
2Sa	2: 8	Ish-Bosheth son of S and brought him	H8620
2Sa	2:10	Ish-Bosheth son of S was forty years old	H8620
2Sa	2:12	with the men of Ish-Bosheth son of S,	H8620
2Sa	2:15	Benjamin and Ish-Bosheth son of S,	H8620
2Sa	3: 1	between the house of S and the house of	H8620
2Sa	3: 1	while the house of S grew weaker and	H8620
2Sa	3: 6	between the house of S and the house of	H8620
2Sa	3: 6	his own position in the house of S.	H8620
2Sa	3: 7	Now S had had a concubine named	H8620
2Sa	3: 8	house of your father S and to his family	H8620
2Sa	3:10	from the house of S and establish David's	H8620
2Sa	3:13	Michal daughter of S when you come to	H8620
2Sa	3:14	sent messengers to Ish-Bosheth son of S,	H8620
2Sa	4: 1	Ish-Bosheth son of S heard that Abner	H8620
2Sa	4: 4	Jonathan son of S had a son who was	H8620
2Sa	4: 4	the news about S and Jonathan came	H8620
2Sa	4: 8	"Here is the head of Ish-Bosheth son of S	H8620
2Sa	4: 8	lord the king against S and his offspring."	H8620
2Sa	4:10	someone told me, 'S is dead,' and	H8620
2Sa	5: 2	In the past, while S was king over us, you	H8620
2Sa	6:16	Michal daughter of S watched from a	H8620
2Sa	6:20	Michal daughter of S came out to meet	H8620
2Sa	6:23	Michal daughter of S had no children to	H8620
2Sa	7:15	as I took it away from S, whom I removed	H8620
2Sa	9: 1	left of the house of S to whom I can show	H8620
2Sa	9: 3	from the house of S to whom I can show	H8620
2Sa	9: 6	of Jonathan, the son of S, came to David,	H8620
2Sa	9: 7	land that belonged to your grandfather S,	H8620
2Sa	9: 9	that belonged to S and his family.	H8620

2Sa 12: 7 I delivered you from the hand of **S**. H8620
2Sa 16: 8 the blood you shed in the household of **S**, H8620
2Sa 21: 1 "It is on account of **S** and his H8620
2Sa 21: 2 **S** in his zeal for Israel and Judah had H8620
2Sa 21: 4 silver or gold from **S** or his family, H8620
2Sa 21: 6 exposed before the LORD at Gibeah of **S**— H8620
2Sa 21: 7 the son of **S**, because of the oath H8620
2Sa 21: 7 between David and Jonathan son of **S**. H8620
2Sa 21: 8 whom she had borne to **S**, together with H8620
2Sa 21:12 took the bones of **S** and his son Jonathan H8620
2Sa 21:12 them after they struck **S** down on Gilboa.) H8620
2Sa 21:13 the bones of **S** and his son Jonathan H8620
2Sa 21:14 buried the bones of **S** and his son H8620
2Sa 22: 1 all his enemies and from the hand of **S**. H8620
1Ch 8:33 Kish the father of **S**, and Saul the father of H8620
1Ch 8:33 of Saul, and **S** the father of Jonathan H8620
1Ch 9:39 Kish the father of **S**, and Saul the father of H8620
1Ch 9:39 of Saul, and **S** the father of Jonathan H8620
1Ch 10: 2 were in hot pursuit of **S** and his sons, H8620
1Ch 10: 3 The fighting grew fierce around **S**, and H8620
1Ch 10: 4 **S** said to his armor-bearer, "Draw your H8620
1Ch 10: 4 so **S** took his own sword and fell on it. H8620
1Ch 10: 5 the armor-bearer saw that **S** was dead, H8620
1Ch 10: 6 So **S** and his three sons died, and all his H8620
1Ch 10: 7 had fled and that **S** and his sons had died H8620
1Ch 10: 8 they found **S** and his sons fallen on H8620
1Ch 10:11 heard what the Philistines had done to **S**, H8620
1Ch 10:12 took the bodies of **S** and his sons and H8620
1Ch 10:13 **S** died because he was unfaithful to the H8620
1Ch 11: 2 the past, even while **S** was king, you were H8620
1Ch 12: 1 from the presence of **S** son of Kish H8620
1Ch 12: 2 they were relatives of **S** from the tribe of H8620
1Ch 12:19 with the Philistines to fight against **S**. H8620
1Ch 12:19 us our heads if he deserts to his master **S**." H8620
1Ch 13: 3 did not inquire of it during the reign of **S**." H8620
1Ch 15:29 Michal daughter of **S** watched from a H8620
1Ch 26:28 by Samuel the seer and by **S** son of Kish, H8620
Ps 18: T all his enemies and from the hand of **S**. H8620
Ps 52: T the Edomite had gone to **S** and told him: H8620
Ps 54: T the Ziphites had gone to **S** and said, H8620
Ps 57: T When he had fled from **S** into the cave. H8620
Ps 59: T When **S** had sent men to watch David's H8620
Isa 10:29 Ramah trembles; Gibeah of **S** flees. H8620
Ac 7:58 at the feet of a young man named **S**. *G4930*
Ac 8: 1 And **S** approved of their killing him. *G4930*
Ac 8: 3 But **S** began to destroy the church. Going *G4930*
Ac 9: 1 **S** was still breathing out murderous *G4930*
Ac 9: 4 heard a voice say to him, "**S**, Saul, *G4910*
Ac 9: 4 say to him, "Saul, **S**, why do you *G4910*
Ac 9: 5 "Who are you, Lord?" **S** asked. "I am Jesus NDT
Ac 9: 7 men traveling with **S** stood there *G899S*
Ac 9: 8 **S** got up from the ground, but when he *G4930*
Ac 9:11 ask for a man from Tarsus named **S**, *G4930*
Ac 9:17 Placing his hands on **S**, he said, "Brother *G899S*
Ac 9:17 he said, "Brother **S**, the Lord—Jesus, *G4910*
Ac 9:19 **S** spent several days with the disciples in NDT
Ac 9:22 Yet **S** grew more and more powerful and *G4930*
Ac 9:24 **S** learned of their plan. Day and night *G4930*
Ac 9:27 He told them how **S** on his journey had NDT
Ac 9:28 So **S** stayed with them and moved about NDT
Ac 11:25 Barnabas went to Tarsus to look for **S**, *G4930*
Ac 11:26 a whole year **Barnabas and S** met with *G899S*
Ac 11:30 their gift to the elders by Barnabas and **S**. *G4930*
Ac 12:25 When Barnabas and **S** had finished their *G4930*
Ac 13: 1 brought up with Herod the tetrarch) and **S**. *G4930*
Ac 13: 2 me Barnabas and **S** for the work to *G4930*
Ac 13: 7 Barnabas and **S** because he wanted to *G4930*
Ac 13: 9 Then **S**, who was also called Paul, filled *G4930*
Ac 13:21 he gave them **S** son of Kish, of the *G4910*
Ac 13:22 After removing **S**, he made David their *G899S*
Ac 22: 7 ground and heard a voice say to me, '**S**! *G4910*
Ac 22: 7 say to me, 'Saul! **S**! Why do you persecute *G4910*
Ac 22:13 said, 'Brother **S**, receive your sight!' *G4910*
Ac 26:14 a voice saying to me in Aramaic, '**S**, Saul, *G4910*
Ac 26:14 in Aramaic, 'Saul, **S**, why do you *G4910*

SAUL'S (43) [SAUL]

1Sa 9: 3 donkeys belonging to **S** father Kish were H8620
1Sa 10: 1 poured it on **S** head and kissed him, H2257S
1Sa 10: 9 Samuel, God changed **S** heart, and all H2257S
1Sa 10:14 Now **S** uncle asked him and his servant H8620
1Sa 10:15 **S** uncle said, "Tell me what Samuel said H8620
1Sa 13: 8 to Gilgal, and **S** men began to scatter. H2021S
1Sa 14:16 **S** lookouts at Gibeah in Benjamin H4200+8620
1Sa 14:49 **S** sons were Jonathan, Ishvi and H8620
1Sa 14:50 the commander of **S** army was Abner son H8620
1Sa 14:50 Abner son of Ner, and Ner was **S** uncle. H8620
1Sa 14:51 **S** father Kish and Abner's father Ner were H8620
1Sa 16:15 **S** attendants said to him, "See, an evil H8620
1Sa 17:12 eight sons, and in **S** time he was very old. H8620
1Sa 18: 5 all the troops, and **S** officers as well. H8620
1Sa 18:19 time came for Merab, **S** daughter, to be H8620
1Sa 18:20 Now **S** daughter Michal was in love with H8620
1Sa 18:24 When **S** servants told him what David had H8620
1Sa 18:25 **S** plan was to have David fall by the H8620
1Sa 18:30 more success than the rest of **S** officers, H8620
1Sa 19:20 the Spirit of God came on **S** men, and H8620
1Sa 20:30 **S** anger flared up at Jonathan and he H8620
1Sa 21: 7 Now one of **S** servants was there that day H8620
1Sa 21: 7 the Edomite, **S** chief shepherd. H4200+8620
1Sa 22: 9 who was standing with **S** officials, said, H8620
1Sa 23:16 And **S** son Jonathan went to David at H8620
1Sa 24: 4 and cut off a corner of **S** robe. H4200+8620
1Sa 26:12 took the spear and water jug near **S** head, H8620
2Sa 1: 2 a man arrived from **S** camp with his H8620
2Sa 2: 8 the commander of **S** army, had H4200+8620
2Sa 4: 2 Now **S** son had two men who were leaders H8620
2Sa 9: 2 was a servant of **S** household named Ziba H8620
2Sa 9: 9 king summoned Ziba, **S** steward, and said H8620
2Sa 16: 5 the same clan as **S** family came out from H8620
2Sa 19:17 the steward of **S** household, and his H8620
2Sa 19:24 Mephibosheth, **S** grandson, also went H8620
2Sa 21: 8 with the five sons of **S** daughter Merab, H8620
2Sa 21:11 daughter Rizpah, **S** concubine, had done, H8620
2Sa 21:14 Jonathan in the tomb of **S** father Kish, H2257S
1Ch 5:10 During **S** reign they waged war against H8620
1Ch 12:23 at Hebron to turn **S** kingdom over to him, H8620
1Ch 12:29 from Benjamin, **S** tribe—3,000, most of H8620
1Ch 12:29 had remained loyal to **S** house until then; H8620
Ac 9:18 something like scales fell from **S** eyes *G899S*

SAVAGE (2)

Eze 34:25 rid the land of **s** beasts so that they H8273
Ac 20:29 **s** wolves will come in among you and will *G987*

SAVE (183) [SAFE, SAFELY, SAFETY, SALVATION, SAVED, SAVES, SAVING, SAVIOR]

Ge 32:11 **S** me, I pray, from the hand of my brother H5911
Ge 45: 5 because it was to **s lives** that God sent me H4695
Ge 45: 7 on earth and to **s** your **lives** by a great H2649
Ex 16:23 **S** whatever is left and keep it until H5663
Nu 31:18 **s** for yourselves every girl who has H2649
Dt 4:42 into one of these cities and **s** *their* **life**. H2649
Dt 19: 5 flee to one of these cities and **s** *his* **life**. H2649
Jos 2:13 and that *you will* **s** us from death. H5911
Jos 10: 6 Come up to us quickly and **s** us! Help us, H3828
Jdg 6:14 strength you have and **s** Israel out of H3828
Jdg 6:15 Gideon replied, "but how *can I* **s** Israel? H3828
Jdg 6:31 *Are* you *trying to* **s** him? Whoever H3828
Jdg 6:36 "If you will **s** Israel by my hand as you H3828
Jdg 6:37 I will know that *you will* **s** Israel by my H3828
Jdg 7: 7 men that lapped *I will* **s** you and give the H3828
Jdg 10: 1 of Puah, the son of Dodo, rose to **s** Israel. H3828
Jdg 10:12 help, *did I* not **s** you from their hands? H3828
Jdg 10:13 other gods, so I will no longer **s** you. H3828
Jdg 10:14 *Let* them **s** you when you are in trouble!" H3828
Jdg 12: 2 *you* didn't **s** me out of their hands. H3828
1Sa 4: 3 may go with us and **s** us from the hand of H3828
1Sa 10:27 "How *can* this fellow **s** us?" H3828
1Sa 23: 2 attack the Philistines and **s** Keilah. H3828
2Sa 22: 3 my savior—from violent people *you* **s** me. H3828
2Sa 22:28 *You* **s** the humble, but your eyes are on H3828
2Sa 22:42 there was no *one to* **s** them—to the H4635
1Ki 1:12 advise you how *you can* **s** your own life H4880
2Ki 16: 7 Come up and **s** me out of the hand of the H3828
2Ki 18:35 countries *has been able to* **s** his land from H5911
2Ki 19:34 I will defend this city and **s** it, for my sake H3828
1Ch 16:35 "**S** us, God our Savior; gather us H3828
2Ch 20: 9 distress, and you will hear us and **s** us. H3828
2Ch 25:15 which *could* not **s** their own people from H5911
2Ch 32:11 'The LORD our God *will* **s** us from the hand H5911
2Ch 32:14 has been able to **s** his people from me? H5911
Ne 6:11 like me go into the temple *to* **s** *his* **life**? H2649
Job 20:20 *he* cannot **s** *himself* by his treasure. H4880
Job 22:29 then *he will* **s** the downcast. H3828
Job 40:14 to you that your own right hand *can* **s** you. H3828
Ps 6: 4 **s** me because of your unfailing love. H3828
Ps 7: 1 **s** and deliver me from all who pursue me, H3828
Ps 17: 7 you *who* **s** by your right hand those who H3828
Ps 17:14 By your hand **s** me from such people, LORD NDT
Ps 18:27 You **s** the humble but bring low those H3828
Ps 18:41 there was no *one to* **s** them—to the H3828
Ps 22:21 **s** me from the horns of the wild oxen. H6699
Ps 28: 9 **S** your people and bless your inheritance H3828
Ps 31: 2 rock of refuge, a strong fortress to **s** me. H3828
Ps 31:16 your servant; **s** me in your unfailing love. H3828
Ps 33:17 despite all its great strength *it* cannot **s**. H4880
Ps 39: 8 **S** me from all my transgressions; do not H5911
Ps 40:13 Be pleased to **s** me, LORD; come quickly H5911
Ps 54: 1 **S** me, O God, by your name; vindicate me H3828
Ps 59: 2 from evildoers and **s** me from those who H3828
Ps 60: 5 **S** us and help us with your right hand H3828
Ps 69: 1 **S** me, O God, for the waters have come H3828
Ps 69:35 God *will* **s** Zion and rebuild the cities H3828
Ps 70: 1 Hasten, O God, to **s** me; come quickly H5911
Ps 71: 2 deliver me; turn your ear to me and **s** me. H3828
Ps 71: 3 give the command to **s** me, for you are my H3828
Ps 72: 4 the people and **s** the children of the H3828
Ps 72:13 the needy and **s** the needy *from* death. H3828
Ps 76: 9 to judge, to **s** all the afflicted of the land. H3828
Ps 80: 2 Awaken your might; come and **s** us. H3802
Ps 86: 2 **s** your servant who trusts in you. H3828
Ps 86:16 of your servant; **s** me, because I serve you H3828
Ps 91: 3 Surely he *will* **s** you from the fowler's H5911
Ps 106: 4 come to my aid when you **s** them, H3802
Ps 106:47 **S** us, LORD our God, and gather us from H3828
Ps 108: 6 **S** us and help us *with* your right hand H3828
Ps 109:26 **s** me according to your unfailing love. H3828
Ps 109:31 to **s** their lives from those who would H3828
Ps 116: 4 on the name of the LORD: "LORD, **s** me!" H4880
Ps 118:25 **s** us! LORD, grant us success! H3828
Ps 119:94 **S** me, for I am yours; I have sought out H3828
Ps 119:146 **s** me and I will keep your statutes. H3828
Ps 120: 2 **S** me, LORD, from lying lips and from H5911
Ps 138: 7 of my foes; *with* your right hand *you* **s** me. H3828
Ps 146: 3 princes, in human beings, who cannot **s**. H9591
Pr 2:12 Wisdom *will* **s** you from the ways of H5911
Pr 2:16 Wisdom *will* **s** you also from the H5911
Pr 23:14 them with the rod and **s** them from death. H5911
Isa 33:22 the LORD is our king; it is he *who will* **s** us. H3828
Isa 35: 4 divine retribution he will come *to* **s** you." H3828
Isa 36:20 countries *have been able to* **s** their lands H5911
Isa 37:35 "I will defend this city and **s** it, for my sake H3828
Isa 38:20 The LORD *will* **s** me, and we will sing with H3828
Isa 44:17 to it and says, "**S** me! You are my god!" H5911
Isa 44:20 misleads him; *he* cannot **s** himself, or say, H5911
Isa 45:20 of wood, who pray to gods *that* cannot **s**. H3828
Isa 46: 7 *it* cannot **s** them from their troubles. H3828
Isa 47:13 *let them* **s** you from what is coming upon H3828
Isa 47:14 *They* cannot even **s** themselves from the H5911
Isa 47:15 their error; there is not *one that can* **s** you. H3828
Isa 49:25 with you, and your children I *will* **s**. H3828
Isa 57:13 help, *let* your collection of idols **s** you! H5911
Isa 59: 1 the arm of the LORD is not too short *to* **s**, H3828
Isa 63: 1 proclaiming victory, mighty to **s**." H3828
Jer 2:27 are in trouble, they say, 'Come and **s** us! H3828
Jer 2:28 Let them come if *they can* **s** you when you H3828
Jer 14: 9 by surprise, like a warrior powerless to **s**? H3828
Jer 15:20 I am with you to rescue and **s** you, H5911
Jer 15:21 "*I will* **s** you from the hands of the wicked H5911
Jer 17:14 I will be healed; **s** me and I will be saved H3828
Jer 30:10 '*I will* surely **s** you out of a distant place H3828
Jer 30:11 I am with you and *will* **s** you,' declares the H3828
Jer 31: 7 **s** your people, the remnant of Israel. H3828
Jer 39:18 *I will* **s** you; you will not fall by the H4880+4880
Jer 42:11 I am with you and *will* **s** you and deliver H3828
Jer 46:27 I *will* surely **s** you out of a distant place H3828
La 4:17 watched for a nation *that could* not **s** us. H3828
Eze 3:18 from their evil ways in order to **s** their **life**, H2649
Eze 13:21 off your veils and **s** my people from your H5911
Eze 13:22 from their evil ways and so **s** their **lives**, H2649
Eze 13:23 *I will* **s** my people from your hands. H5911
Eze 14:14 they *could* **s** only themselves by their H5911
Eze 14:16 *they could* not **s** their own sons or H5911
Eze 14:18 *they could* not **s** their own sons or H5911
Eze 14:20 *they could* **s** neither son nor daughter. H5911
Eze 14:20 They *would* **s** only themselves by their H5911
Eze 18:27 what is just and right, they *will* **s** their life. H2649
Eze 34:22 *I will* **s** my flock, and they will no longer be H3828
Eze 36:29 *I will* **s** you from all your uncleanness. H3828
Eze 37:23 for *I will* **s** them from all their sinful H3828
Da 3:29 no other god can **s** in this way. A10489
Da 6:14 every effort until sundown to **s** him. A10489
Hos 1: 7 to Judah; and *I will* **s** them—not by bow, H3828
Hos 1: 7 but *I*, the LORD their God, *will* **s** them." H3828
Hos 13:10 your king, that *he may* **s** you? Where are H3828
Hos 14: 3 Assyria cannot **s** us; we will not mount H3828
Am 2:14 strength, and the warrior *will* not **s** his life. H4880
Am 2:15 the horseman *will* not **s** his life. H4880
Mic 2: 3 from which *you* cannot **s** yourselves. H4631
Mic 6:14 You will store up but **s** nothing, because H7117
Mic 6:14 because what *you* **s** I will give to the H7117
Hab 1: 2 out to you, "Violence!" but *you do* not **s**? H3828
Hab 3:13 your people, to **s** your anointed one. H3829
Zep 1:18 gold will be able to **s** them on the day of H5911
Zec 8: 7 "*I will* **s** my people from the countries of H3828
Zec 8:13 the nations, so *I will* **s** you, and you will H3828
Zec 9:16 The LORD their God *will* **s** his people on H3828
Zec 10: 6 Judah and **s** the tribes of Joseph H3828
Zec 12: 7 "The LORD *will* **s** the dwellings of Judah H3828
Mt 1:21 because he *will* **s** his people from their *G5392*
Mt 8:25 went and woke him, saying, "Lord, **s** us! *G5392*
Mt 14:30 beginning to sink, cried out, "Lord, **s** me!" *G5392*
Mt 16:25 For whoever wants *to* **s** their life will lose it, *G5392*
Mt 27:40 build it in three days, **s** yourself! *G5392*
Mt 27:42 they said, "but he can't **s** himself! *G5392*
Mt 27:49 Let's see if Elijah comes *to* **s** him." *G5392*
Mk 3: 4 good or to do evil, *to* **s** life or to kill?" *G5392*
Mk 8:35 For whoever wants *to* **s** their life will lose it, *G5392*
Mk 8:35 life for me and for the gospel *will* **s** it. *G5392*
Mk 15:30 come down from the cross and **s** yourself!" *G5392*
Mk 15:31 they said, "but he can't **s** himself! *G5392*
Lk 6: 9 good or to do evil, *to* **s** life or to destroy it?" *G5392*
Lk 9:24 For whoever wants *to* **s** their life will lose it, *G5392*
Lk 9:24 whoever loses their life for me *will* **s** it. *G5392*
Lk 19:10 of Man came to seek and *to* **s** the lost." *G5392*
Lk 23:35 *let him* **s** himself if he is God's Messiah *G5392*
Lk 23:37 "If you are the king of the Jews, **s** yourself." *G5392*
Lk 23:39 you the Messiah? **S** yourself and us!" *G5392*
Jn 3:17 the world, but to **s** the world through him. *G5392*
Jn 12: 7 intended that *she should* **s** this perfume *G5498*
Jn 12:27 'Father, **s** me from this hour' *G5392*
Jn 12:47 to judge the world, but to **s** the world. *G5392*
Ac 2:40 "**S** *yourselves* from this corrupt generation." *G5392*
Ro 11:14 own people to envy and **s** some of them. *G5392*
1Co 1:21 what was preached *to* **s** those who *G5392*
1Co 7:16 whether *you will* **s** your husband? *G5392*
1Co 7:16 husband, whether *you will* **s** your wife? *G5392*
1Co 9:22 by all possible means *I might* **s** some. *G5392*
2Co 12:14 should not have *to* **s up** for their parents, *G2564*
1Ti 1:15 Jesus came into the world *to* **s** sinners— *G5392*
1Ti 4:16 *you will* **s** both yourself and your hearers. *G5392*
Heb 5: 7 to the one who could **s** him from death, *G5392*
Heb 7:25 Therefore he is able *to* **s** completely those *G5392*
Heb 11: 7 in holy fear built an ark to **s** his family. *G5401*
Jas 1:21 the word planted in you, which can **s** you. *G5392*

Jas 2:14 has no deeds? Can such faith s them? G5392
Jas 4:12 the one who is able to s and destroy. G5392
Jas 5:20 error of their way will s them from death G5392
Jude 23 s others by snatching them from the fire; to G5392

SAVED (109) [SAVE]

Ge 47:25 "You have s our lives," they said. "May we H2649
Ex 14:30 That day the LORD s Israel from the hands H3828
Ex 16:24 So they s it until morning, as Moses H5663
Ex 18: 4 he s me from the sword of Pharaoh." H5911
Ex 18: 8 the way and how the LORD had s them. H5911
Dt 33:29 is like you, a people s by the LORD? He is H3828
Jos 9:26 So Joshua s them from the Israelites, and H5911
Jdg 2:16 who s them out of the hands of these H3828
Jdg 2:18 with the judge and s them out of the H3828
Jdg 3: 9 Caleb's younger brother, who s them. H3828
Jdg 3:31 with an oxgoad. He too s Israel. H3828
Jdg 7: 2 against me, 'My own strength has s me. H3828
Jdg 8:22 because you have s us from the hand of H3828
1Sa 14:23 So on that day the LORD s Israel, and the H3828
1Sa 23: 5 the Philistines and s the people of Keilah. H3828
2Sa 19: 5 who have just s your life and the lives of H4880
2Sa 22: 4 and have **been** s from my enemies. H3828
2Ki 14:27 he s them by the hand of Jeroboam son H3828
2Ch 32:22 So the LORD s Hezekiah and the people of H3828
Job 26: 2 How you have s the arm that is feeble! H3828
Ps 18: 3 and I have **been** s from my enemies. H3828
Ps 22: 5 To you they cried out and **were** s; in you H4880
Ps 33:16 No king **is** s by the size of his army; no H3828
Ps 34: 6 he s him out of all his troubles. H3828
Ps 80: 3 your face shine on us, that we may **be** s. H3828
Ps 80: 7 your face shine on us, that we may **be** s. H3828
Ps 80:19 your face shine on us, that we may **be** s. H3828
Ps 106: 8 Yet he s them for his name's sake, to H3828
Ps 106:10 He s them from the hand of the foe; from H3828
Ps 106:21 They forgot the God who s them, who had H3828
Ps 107:13 trouble, and he s them from their distress. H3828
Ps 107:19 trouble, and he s them from their distress. H3828
Ps 116: 6 unwary; when I was brought low, he s me. H3828
Ecc 9:15 wise, and he s the city by his wisdom. H4880
Isa 25: 9 our God; we trusted in him, and he s us. H3828
Isa 43:12 I have revealed and s and proclaimed—I H3828
Isa 45:17 But Israel will be s by the LORD with an H3828
Isa 45:22 "Turn to me and **be** s, all you ends of the H3828
Isa 63: 9 the angel of his presence s them. H3828
Isa 64: 5 you were angry. How then can we **be** s? H3828
Jer 4:14 wash the evil from your heart and be s. H3828
Jer 8:20 the summer has ended, and we **are** not s." H3828
Jer 17:14 save me and I will **be** s, for you are the H3828
Jer 23: 6 In his days Judah will **be** s and Israel will H3828
Jer 30: 7 Jacob, but he will be s out of it. H3828
Jer 33:16 those days Judah will **be** s and Jerusalem H3828
Eze 3:19 their sin; but you will have s yourself. H5911
Eze 3:21 warning, and you will have s yourself." H5911
Eze 14:16 They alone would **be** s, but the land H5911
Eze 14:18 daughters. They alone would **be** s. H5911
Eze 33: 5 warning, they would have s themselves. H4880
Eze 33: 9 their sin, though you yourself will be s. H5911
Joel 2:32 calls on the name of the LORD will **be** s; H4880
Mt 10:22 one who stands firm to the end will be s. G5392
Mt 19:25 asked, "Who then can be s? G5392
Mt 24:13 one who stands firm to the end will be s. G5392
Mt 27:42 "He s others," they said, "but he can't save G5392
Mk 10:26 said to each other, "Who then can be s?" G5392
Mk 13:13 one who stands firm to the end will be s. G5392
Mk 15:31 "He s others," they said, "but he can't G5392
Mk 16:16 believes and is baptized will be s, G5392
Lk 7:50 "Your faith has s you; go in peace." G5392
Lk 8:12 so that they may not believe and be s. G5392
Lk 13:23 are only a few people going to be s?" G5392
Lk 18:26 heard this asked, "Who then can be s?" G5392
Lk 23:35 They said, "He s others; let him save G5392
Jn 2:10 to drink; but you have s the best till now." G5498
Jn 5:34 I mention it that you may be s. G5392
Jn 10: 9 whoever enters through me will be s. G5392
Ac 2:21 calls on the name of the Lord will be s. G5392
Ac 2:47 number daily those who were being s. G5392
Ac 4:12 given to mankind by which we must be s." G5392
Ac 11:14 you and all your household will be s. G5392
Ac 15: 1 custom taught by Moses, you cannot be s." G5392
Ac 15:11 the grace of our Lord Jesus that we are s, G5392
Ac 16:17 who are telling you the way to be s." G5401
Ac 16:30 asked, "Sirs, what must I do to be s?" G5392
Ac 16:31 and you will be s—you and your G5392
Ac 27:20 we finally gave up all hope of being s. G5392
Ac 27:31 men stay with the ship, you cannot be s." G5392
Ro 5: 9 how much more shall we be s from God's G5392
Ro 5:10 reconciled, shall we be s through his life! G5392
Ro 8:24 For in this hope we were s. But hope that G5392
Ro 9:27 by the sea, only the remnant will be s. G5392
Ro 10: 1 the Israelites is that they may be s. G5401
Ro 10: 9 raised him from the dead, you will be s. G5392
Ro 10:10 that you profess your faith and are s. G5401
Ro 10:13 calls on the name of the Lord will be s." G5392
Ro 11:26 in this way all Israel will be s. As it is G5392
1Co 1:18 to us who are being s it is the power G5392
1Co 3:15 builder will suffer loss but yet will be s— G5392
1Co 5: 5 that his spirit may be s on the day of the G5392
1Co 10:33 the good of many, so that they may be s. G5392
1Co 15: 2 By this gospel you are s, if you hold firmly G5392
2Co 2:15 among those who are being s and those G5392
Eph 2: 5 it is by grace you have been s. G5392
Eph 2: 8 For it is by grace you have been s, through G5392
Php 1:28 that you will be s—and that by God. G5401
1Th 2:16 to the Gentiles so that they may be s. G5392
2Th 2:10 they refused to love the truth and so be s. G5392
2Th 2:13 as firstfruits to be s through the sanctifying G5401
1Ti 2: 4 wants all people to be s and to come to a G5392
1Ti 2:15 But women will be s through childbearing G5392
2Ti 1: 9 He has s us and called us to a holy life G5392
Titus 3: 5 he s us, not because of righteous things G5392
Titus 3: 5 He s us through the washing of rebirth and NDT
Heb 10:39 who have faith and are s. G1650+4348+6034
1Pe 3:20 eight in all, were s **through** water, G1407
1Pe 4:18 "If it is hard for the righteous to be s, what G5392

SAVES (20) [SAVE]

1Sa 10:19 who s you out of all your disasters and H3828
1Sa 17:47 it is not by sword or spear that the LORD s; H3828
Job 5:15 He s the needy from the sword in their H3828
Job 5:15 he s them from the clutches of the powerful. NDT
Ps 7:10 Most High, who s the upright in heart. H3828
Ps 18:48 who s me from my enemies. You exalted H7117
Ps 34:18 brokenhearted and s those who are H3828
Ps 37:40 them from the wicked and s them, H3828
Ps 55:16 I call to God, and the LORD s me. H3828
Ps 57: 3 He sends from heaven and s me H3828
Ps 68:20 Our God is a God who s; from the H4636
Ps 88: 1 you are the God who s me; day and night H3802
Ps 145:19 fear him; he hears their cry and s them. H3828
Pr 11:30 and the one who is wise s lives. H4374
Pr 14:25 A truthful witness s lives, but a false H5911
Da 6:27 He rescues and he s; he performs signs A10489
Zep 3:17 is with you, the Mighty Warrior who s. H3828
Zec 9:16 on that day as a shepherd s his flock. NDT
1Pe 3:21 symbolizes baptism that now s you also— G5392
1Pe 3:21 It s you by the resurrection of Jesus Christ, NDT

SAVING (11) [SAVE]

Ge 50:20 is now being done, the s of many lives. H2649
1Sa 14: 6 Nothing can hinder the LORD from s H3828
2Sa 22:36 You make your s **help** my shield; your H3829
Ps 18:35 You make your s **help** my shield, and your H3829
Ps 22: 1 Why are you so far from s me, so far from H3802
Ps 40: 9 I proclaim your s **acts** in the great H7406
Ps 40:10 speak of your faithfulness and your s **help**. H9591
Ps 40:16 those who long for your s **help** always say, H9591
Ps 70: 4 those who long for your s **help** always say, H3802
Ps 71:15 of your s **acts** all day long H9591
1Co 16: 2 with your income, s it **up**, so that when I G2564

SAVIOR (58) [SAVE]

Dt 32:15 made them and rejected the Rock their S. H3802
2Sa 22: 3 my refuge and my s—from violent people H4635
2Sa 22:47 Exalted be my God, the Rock, my S! H3829
1Ch 16:35 "Save us, God our S; gather us and H3829
Ps 18:46 be to my Rock! Exalted be God my S! H3829
Ps 24: 5 the LORD and vindication from God their S. H3829
Ps 25: 5 you are God my S, and my hope is in H3829
Ps 27: 9 Do not reject me or forsake me, God my S. H3829
Ps 38:22 quickly to help me, my Lord and my S. H9591
Ps 42: 5 I will yet praise him, my S and my God. H3802
Ps 42:11 I will yet praise him, my S and my God. H3802
Ps 43: 5 I will yet praise him, my S and my God. H3802
Ps 51:14 you who are God my S, and my tongue H9591
Ps 65: 5 God our S, the hope of all the H3829
Ps 68:19 to God our S, who daily bears our H3802
Ps 79: 9 Help us, God our S, for the glory of your H3829
Ps 85: 4 us again, God our S, and put away your H3829
Ps 89:26 are my Father, my God, the Rock my S. H3802
Isa 17:10 You have forgotten God your S; you have H3829
Isa 19:20 he will send them a s and defender, and H4635
Isa 43: 3 One of Israel, your S; I give Egypt for your H4635
Isa 43:11 the LORD, and apart from me there is no s. H4635
Isa 45:15 hiding himself, the God and S of Israel. H4635
Isa 45:21 a righteous God and a S; there is none H4635
Isa 49:26 the LORD, am your S, your Redeemer, the H4635
Isa 60:16 the LORD, am your S, your Redeemer, the H4635
Isa 62:11 to Daughter Zion, 'See, your S comes! H3829
Isa 63: 8 be true to me"; and so he became their S. H4635
Jer 14: 8 hope of Israel, its S in times of distress H4635
Jer 23: 6 will be called: The LORD Our **Righteous** S. H7406
Jer 33:16 will be called: The LORD Our **Righteous** S.' H7406
Hos 13: 4 no God but me, no S except me. H4635
Mic 7: 7 I wait for God my S; my God will hear me. H3829
Hab 3:18 in the LORD, I will be joyful in God my S. H3829
Lk 1:47 my spirit rejoices in God my S, G5400
Lk 2:11 the town of David a S has been born to G5400
Jn 4:42 that this man really is the S of the world." G5400
Ac 5:31 hand as Prince and S that he might bring G5400
Ac 13:23 God has brought to Israel the S Jesus, G5400
Eph 5:23 the church, his body, of which he is the S. G5400
Php 3:20 And we eagerly await a S from there, the G5400
1Ti 1: 1 command of God our S and of Christ G5400
1Ti 2: 3 This is good, and pleases God our S, G5400
1Ti 4:10 who is the S of all people, and G5400
2Ti 1:10 revealed through the appearing of our S, G5400
Titus 1: 3 to me by the command of God our S, G5400
Titus 1: 4 God the Father and Christ Jesus our S. G5400
Titus 2:10 the teaching about God our S attractive. G5400
Titus 2:13 of the glory of our great God and S, G5400
Titus 3: 4 kindness and love of God our S appeared, G5400
Titus 3: 6 us generously through Jesus Christ our S, G5400
2Pe 1: 1 of our God and S Jesus Christ have G5400
2Pe 1:11 kingdom of our Lord and S Jesus Christ. G5400
2Pe 2:20 our Lord and S Jesus Christ and are G5400
2Pe 3: 2 by our Lord and S through your apostles G5400
2Pe 3:18 knowledge of our Lord and S Jesus Christ. G5400
1Jn 4:14 has sent his Son to be the S of the world. G5400
Jude 25 to the only God our S be glory, majesty G5400

SAVOUR (KJV) AROMA, FRAGRANCE, FRAGRANT, INCENSE, OBNOXIOUS, SALTINESS, SMELL

SAVOURY (KJV) TASTY

SAW (605) [SEE]

Ge 1: 4 God s that the light was good, and he H8011
Ge 1:10 And God s that it was good. H8011
Ge 1:12 to their kinds. And God s that it was good. H8011
Ge 1:18 And God s that it was good. H8011
Ge 1:21 And God s that it was good. H8011
Ge 1:25 to their kinds. And God s that it was good. H8011
Ge 1:31 God s all that he had made, and it was H8011
Ge 3: 6 When the woman s that the fruit of the H8011
Ge 6: 2 the sons of God s that the daughters of H8011
Ge 6: 5 The LORD s how great the wickedness of H8011
Ge 6:12 God s how corrupt the earth had become H8011
Ge 8:13 from the ark and s that the surface of the H8011
Ge 9:22 s his father naked and told his two H8011
Ge 12:14 the Egyptians s that Sarai was a very H8011
Ge 12:15 And when Pharaoh's officials s her, they H8011
Ge 13:10 looked around and s that the whole plain H8011
Ge 18: 2 looked up and s three men standing H8011
Ge 18: 2 When he s them, he hurried from the H8011
Ge 19: 1 When he s them, he got up to meet them H8011
Ge 19:28 and he s dense smoke rising from the H8011
Ge 21: 9 But Sarah s that the son whom Hagar the H8011
Ge 21:19 her eyes and she s a well of water. H8011
Ge 22: 4 looked up and s the place in the H8011
Ge 22:13 there in a thicket he s a ram caught by its H8011
Ge 24:63 he looked up, he s camels approaching. H8011
Ge 24:64 Rebekah also looked up and s Isaac. H8011
Ge 26: 8 from a window and s Isaac caressing his H8011
Ge 26:28 "We s **clearly** that the LORD was H8011+8011
Ge 28:12 a dream in which he s a stairway resting H2180
Ge 29: 2 There he s a well in the open country, with H8011
Ge 29:10 When Jacob s Rachel daughter of his H8011
Ge 29:31 When the LORD s that Leah was not loved H8011
Ge 30: 1 When Rachel s that she was not bearing H8011
Ge 30: 9 When Leah s that she had stopped H8011
Ge 31:10 I looked up and s that the male goats H2180
Ge 32: 2 When Jacob s them, he said, "This is the H8011
Ge 32:25 When the man s that he could not H8011
Ge 32:30 "It is because I s God face to face, and H8011
Ge 33: 5 Esau looked up and s the women and H8011
Ge 34: 2 ruler of that area, s her, he took her and H8011
Ge 37: 4 When his brothers s that their father loved H8011
Ge 37:18 But they s him in the distance, and before H8011
Ge 37:25 they looked up and s a caravan of H8011
Ge 37:29 to the cistern and s that Joseph was not H2180
Ge 38:14 For she s that, though Shelah had now H8011
Ge 38:15 When Judah s her, he thought she was a H8011
Ge 39: 3 When his master s that the LORD was with H8011
Ge 39:13 When she s that he had left his cloak in H8011
Ge 40: 6 morning, he s that they were dejected. H8011
Ge 40: 9 "In my dream I s a vine in front of me H2180
Ge 40:16 When the chief baker s that Joseph had H8011
Ge 41:22 "In my dream I s seven heads of grain H8011
Ge 42: 7 As soon as Joseph s his brothers, he H8011
Ge 42:21 We s how distressed he was when he H8011
Ge 42:27 and he s his silver in the mouth of his H8011
Ge 42:35 their father s the money pouches, H8011
Ge 43:16 When Joseph s Benjamin with them, he H8011
Ge 43:29 he looked about and s his brother H8011
Ge 45:27 when he s the carts Joseph had sent H8011
Ge 48: 8 When Israel s the sons of Joseph, he H8011
Ge 48:17 When Joseph s his father placing his right H8011
Ge 50:11 who lived there s the mourning at the H8011
Ge 50:15 Joseph's brothers s that their father was H8011
Ge 50:23 s the third generation of Ephraim's H8011
Ex 2: 2 When she s that he was a fine child, she H8011
Ex 2: 5 She s the basket among the reeds and H8011
Ex 2: 6 She opened it and s the baby. He was H8011
Ex 2:11 He s an Egyptian beating a Hebrew, one H8011
Ex 2:13 day he went out and s two Hebrews H2180
Ex 3: 2 Moses s that though the bush was on fire H8011
Ex 3: 4 When the LORD s that he had gone over to H8011
Ex 8:15 But when Pharaoh s that there was relief H8011
Ex 9:34 When Pharaoh s that the rain and hail H8011
Ex 14:30 Israel s the Egyptians lying dead on H8011
Ex 14:31 when the Israelites s the mighty hand of H8011
Ex 16:15 When the Israelites s it, they said to each H8011
Ex 18:14 his father-in-law s all that Moses was H8011
Ex 20:18 When the people s the thunder and H8011
Ex 20:18 the trumpet and s the mountain in smoke NDT
Ex 24:10 s the God of Israel. Under his feet was H8011
Ex 24:11 of the Israelites; they s God, and they ate H2600
Ex 32: 1 When the people s that Moses was so H8011
Ex 32: 5 When Aaron s this, he built an altar in H8011
Ex 32:19 the camp and s the calf and the H8011
Ex 32:25 Moses s that the people were running H8011
Ex 33:10 Whenever the people s the pillar of cloud H8011
Ex 34:30 Aaron and all the Israelites s Moses, H8011
Ex 34:35 they s that his face was radiant. H8011
Ex 39:43 the work and s that they had done it H2180
Lev 9:24 And when all the people s it, they H8011

S

Nu 12:10 turned toward her and **s** that she had a H2180
Nu 13:28 *We* even **s** descendants of Anak there. H8011
Nu 13:32 All the people *we* **s** there are of great size H8011
Nu 13:33 *We* **s** the Nephilim there (the descendants H8011
Nu 14:22 not one of those who **s** my glory and the H8011
Nu 17: 8 entered the tent and **s** that Aaron's staff, H2180
Nu 22: 2 Balak son of Zippor **s** all that Israel had H8011
Nu 22:23 When the donkey **s** the angel of the LORD H8011
Nu 22:25 When the donkey **s** the angel of the LORD H8011
Nu 22:27 When the donkey **s** the angel of the LORD H8011
Nu 22:31 and *he* **s** the angel of the LORD standing in H8011
Nu 22:33 The donkey **s** me and turned away from H8011
Nu 24: 1 Now when Balaam **s** that it pleased the H8011
Nu 24: 2 looked out and **s** Israel encamped tribe H8011
Nu 24:20 Then Balaam **s** Amalek and spoke his H8011
Nu 24:21 Then *he* **s** the Kenites and spoke his H8011
Nu 25: 7 son of Aaron, the priest, **s** this, he left the H8011
Nu 32: 1 **s** that the lands of Jazer and Gilead were H8011
Dt 1:28 *We* even **s** the Anakites there H8011
Dt 1:31 There *you* **s** how the LORD your God carried H8011
Dt 4: 3 You **s** with your own eyes what the LORD H8011
Dt 4:12 heard the sound of words but **s** no form; H8011
Dt 4:15 *You* **s** no form of any kind the day the LORD H8011
Dt 7:19 *You* **s** with your own eyes the great trials H8011
Dt 9:16 I **s** that you had sinned against the LORD H2180
Dt 10:21 wonders you **s** with your own eyes. H8011
Dt 11: 2 children *were* not *the ones* who **s** and H8011
Dt 11: 5 not your children who **s** what he did for you NDT
Dt 11: 7 your own eyes that **s** all these great things H8011
Dt 26: 7 the LORD heard our voice and **s** our misery, H8011
Dt 29: 3 With your own eyes *you* **s** those great trials H8011
Dt 29:17 *You* **s** among them their detestable H8011
Dt 32:19 The LORD **s** this and rejected them H8011
Jos 5:13 he looked up and **s** a man standing in H8011
Jos 7:21 When *I* **s** in the plunder a beautiful robe H8011
Jos 8:14 When the king of Ai **s** this, he and all the H8011
Jos 8:20 Ai looked back and **s** the smoke of the city H2180
Jos 8:21 all Israel **s** that the ambush had H8011
Jos 24: 7 *You* **s** with your own eyes what I did to the H8011
Jdg 1:24 the spies **s** a man coming out of the city H8011
Jdg 3:25 There they **s** their lord fallen to the floor H2180
Jdg 9:36 When Gaal **s** them, he said to Zebul H8011
Jdg 9:43 When *he* **s** the people coming out of the H8011
Jdg 9:55 When the Israelites **s** that Abimelek was H8011
Jdg 11:35 When he **s** her, he tore his clothes and H8011
Jdg 12: 3 When *I* **s** that you wouldn't help, I took my H8011
Jdg 14: 1 down to Timnah and **s** there a young H8011
Jdg 14: 8 in it he **s** a swarm of bees and some NDT
Jdg 14:11 When the people **s** him, they chose thirty H8011
Jdg 16: 1 went to Gaza, where *he* **s** a prostitute. H8011
Jdg 16:18 When Delilah **s** that he had told her H8011
Jdg 16:24 When the people **s** him, they praised H8011
Jdg 17: 6 no king; everyone did as they **s** fit. H928+6524
Jdg 18: 7 where *they* **s** that the people were living H8011
Jdg 19: 3 when her father **s** him, he gladly H8011
Jdg 19:17 When he looked and **s** the traveler in the H8011
Jdg 19:30 Everyone who **s** it was saying to one H8011
Jdg 20:36 Then the Benjamites **s** that they were H8011
Jdg 20:40 turned and **s** the whole city going H2180
Jdg 21:25 no king; everyone did as they **s** fit. H928+6524
Ru 2:18 her mother-in-law **s** how much she had H8011
1Sa 5: 7 people of Ashdod **s** what was happening, H8011
1Sa 6:13 when they looked up and **s** the ark H8011
1Sa 6:16 rulers of the Philistines **s** all this and then H8011
1Sa 10:11 formerly known him **s** him prophesying H8011
1Sa 10:14 "But when *we* **s** they were not to be found, H8011
1Sa 12:12 "But when *you* **s** that Nahash king of the H8011
1Sa 13: 6 When the Israelites **s** that their situation H8011
1Sa 13:11 "When *I* **s** that the men were scattering H8011
1Sa 14:16 Gibeah in Benjamin **s** the army melting H8011
1Sa 14:26 the woods, they **s** the honey oozing out H2180
1Sa 14:52 whenever Saul **s** a mighty or brave H8011
1Sa 16: 6 they arrived, Samuel **s** Eliab and thought H8011
1Sa 17:24 Whenever the Israelites **s** the man, they H8011
1Sa 17:42 looked David over and **s** that he was little H8011
1Sa 17:51 When the Philistines **s** that their hero was H8011
1Sa 18:15 When Saul **s** how successful he was, he H8011
1Sa 19: 5 all Israel, and *you* **s** it and were glad. H8011
1Sa 19:20 But when *they* **s** a group of prophets H8011
1Sa 22: 9 "*I* **s** the son of Jesse come to Ahimelek H8011
1Sa 25:23 When Abigail **s** David, she quickly got off H8011
1Sa 26: 3 When *he* **s** that Saul had followed him H8011
1Sa 26: 5 He **s** where Saul and Abner son of Ner H8011
1Sa 26:12 No *one* **s** or knew about it, nor did anyone H8011
1Sa 28: 5 When Saul **s** the Philistine army, he was H8011
1Sa 28:12 When the woman **s** Samuel, she cried out H8011
1Sa 28:21 came to Saul and **s** that he was greatly H8011
1Sa 31: 5 the armor-bearer **s** that Saul was dead, H8011
1Sa 31: 7 across the Jordan **s** that the Israelite army H8011
2Sa 1: 7 When he turned around and **s** me, he H8011
2Sa 6:16 And when *she* **s** King David leaping and H8011
2Sa 10: 9 Joab **s** that there were battle lines in front H8011
2Sa 10:15 After the Arameans **s** that they had been H8011
2Sa 10:19 of Hadadezer **s** that they had been H8011
2Sa 11: 2 From the roof *he* **s** a woman bathing. H8011
2Sa 13:34 looked up and **s** many people on the H8011
2Sa 17:18 But a young man **s** them and told H8011
2Sa 17:23 When Ahithophel **s** that his advice had H8011
2Sa 18:10 one of the men **s** what had happened, H8011
2Sa 18:10 "*I* just **s** Absalom hanging in an oak tree." H8011
2Sa 18:11 *You* **s** him? Why didn't you strike H8011
2Sa 18:24 he looked out, *he* **s** a man running alone. H8011
2Sa 18:26 Then the watchman **s** another runner, and H8011
2Sa 18:29 "*I* **s** great confusion just as Joab was H8011
2Sa 20:12 the man **s** that all the troops came to H8011
2Sa 24:17 When David **s** the angel who was striking H8011
2Sa 24:20 Araunah looked and **s** the king and his H8011
1Ki 3:21 I **s** that it wasn't the son I had borne." H2180
1Ki 3:28 because *they* **s** that he had wisdom from H8011
1Ki 4:27 *They* **s to it that** nothing **was lacking**. H6372
1Ki 10: 4 the queen of Sheba **s** all the wisdom of H8011
1Ki 10: 7 until I came and **s** *with* my own eyes. H8011
1Ki 11:28 when Solomon **s** how well the young H8011
1Ki 12:16 When all Israel **s** that the king refused to H8011
1Ki 13:25 who passed by **s** the body lying there H8011
1Ki 16:18 When Zimri **s** that the city was taken, he H8011
1Ki 18:17 When he **s** Elijah, he said to him, "Is that H8011
1Ki 18:39 When all the people **s** this, they fell H8011
1Ki 22:17 "*I* **s** all Israel scattered on the hills like H8011
1Ki 22:19 *I* **s** the LORD sitting on his throne with all H8011
1Ki 22:32 the chariot commanders **s** Jehoshaphat, H8011
1Ki 22:33 chariot commanders **s** that he was not the H8011
2Ki 2:12 Elisha **s** this and cried out, "My father! My H8011
2Ki 2:12 And Elisha **s** him no more. H8011
2Ki 3:26 the king of Moab **s** that the battle had H8011
2Ki 4:25 When he **s** her in the distance, the man H8011
2Ki 5:21 When Naaman **s** him running toward him, H8011
2Ki 6:17 he looked and **s** the hills full of H2180
2Ki 6:21 When the king of Israel **s** them, he asked H8011
2Ki 6:30 and they **s** *that*, under his robes, H2180
2Ki 9:17 on the tower in Jezreel **s** Jehu's troops H8011
2Ki 9:22 When Joram **s** Jehu he asked, "Have you H8011
2Ki 9:26 'Yesterday *I* **s** the blood of Naboth and the H8011
2Ki 9:27 king of Judah **s** what had happened, H8011
2Ki 11: 1 mother of Ahaziah **s** that her son was H8011
2Ki 12:10 Whenever they **s** that there was a large H8011
2Ki 13: 4 for *he* **s** how severely the king of Aram H8011
2Ki 13:21 suddenly *they* **s** a band of raiders H8011
2Ki 16:10 *He* **s** an altar in Damascus and sent to H8011
2Ki 16:12 back from Damascus and **s** the altar, H8011
2Ki 20:15 "*They* **s** everything in my palace, H8011
2Ki 23:16 when *he* **s** the tombs that were there H8011
1Ch 10: 5 the armor-bearer **s** that Saul was dead, H8011
1Ch 10: 7 in the valley **s** that the army had fled H8011
1Ch 15:29 And when *she* **s** King David dancing and H8011
1Ch 19:10 Joab **s** that there were battle lines in front H8011
1Ch 19:16 After the Arameans **s** that they had been H8011
1Ch 19:19 of Hadadezer **s** that they had been H8011
1Ch 21:15 the LORD **s** it and relented concerning the H8011
1Ch 21:16 David looked up and **s** the angel of the H8011
1Ch 21:20 he turned and **s** the angel; his four H8011
1Ch 21:21 when Araunah looked and **s** him, he H8011
1Ch 21:28 when David **s** that the LORD had answered H8011
2Ch 7: 3 all the Israelites **s** the fire coming down H8011
2Ch 9: 3 the queen of Sheba **s** the wisdom of H8011
2Ch 9: 6 said until I came and **s** *with* my own eyes. H8011
2Ch 10:16 When all Israel **s** that the king refused to H8011
2Ch 12: 7 When the LORD **s** that they humbled H8011
2Ch 13:14 Judah turned and **s** that they were being H2180
2Ch 15: 9 Israel when they **s** that the LORD his God H8011
2Ch 18:16 "*I* **s** all Israel scattered on the hills like H8011
2Ch 18:18 *I* **s** the LORD sitting on his throne with all H8011
2Ch 18:31 the chariot commanders **s** Jehoshaphat, H8011
2Ch 18:32 chariot commanders **s** that he was not the H8011
2Ch 20:24 they **s** only dead bodies lying on the H2180
2Ch 22:10 mother of Ahaziah **s** that her son was H8011
2Ch 24:11 officials and they **s** that there was a large H8011
2Ch 26:20 they **s** that he had leprosy on his forehead H2180
2Ch 31: 8 his officials came and **s** the heaps, H8011
2Ch 32: 2 When Hezekiah **s** that Sennacherib had H8011
Ezr 3:12 aloud when they **s** the foundation of H928+6524
Ne 9: 9 "*You* **s** the suffering of our ancestors in H8011
Ne 13:15 In those days *I* **s** people in Judah treading H8011
Ne 13:23 in those days *I* **s** men of Judah who had H8011
Est 2:15 won the favor of everyone *who* **s** her. H8011
Est 3: 5 When Haman **s** that Mordecai would not H8011
Est 5: 2 When he **s** Queen Esther standing in the H8011
Est 5: 9 But when he **s** Mordecai at the king's gate H8011
Job 2:12 When *they* **s** him from a H5951+906+6524
Job 2:13 because *they* **s** how great his suffering H8011
Job 3:16 like an infant *who* never **s** the light of day? H8011
Job 8:18 place disowns it and says, '*I* never **s** you. H8011
Job 10:18 I wish I had died before any eye **s** me. H8011
Job 20: 9 The eye *that* **s** him will not see him again; H8812
Job 29: 8 the young men **s** me and stepped aside H8011
Job 29:11 those *who* **s** me commended me, H8011
Job 32: 5 But when he **s** that the three men had H8011
Job 42:16 *he* **s** his children and their children to the H8011
Ps 31: 7 for *you* **s** my affliction and knew the H8011
Ps 48: 5 they **s** her and were astounded; they fled H8011
Ps 73: 3 the arrogant *when I* **s** the prosperity of H8011
Ps 77:16 The waters **s** you, God, the waters saw H8011
Ps 77:16 the waters **s** you and writhed; the H8011
Ps 107:24 They **s** the works of the LORD, his H8011
Ps 139:16 Your eyes **s** my unformed body; all the H8011
Pr 7: 7 *I* **s** among the simple, I noticed among H8011
Pr 24:32 learned a lesson from what *I* **s**: H8011
Ecc 2:13 I **s** that wisdom is better than folly, just as H8011
Ecc 3:16 And *I* **s** something else under the sun: In H8011
Ecc 3:22 So *I* **s** that there is nothing better for a H8011
Ecc 4: 1 Again I looked and **s** all the oppression H8011
Ecc 4: 1 I **s** the tears of the oppressed—and they H2180
Ecc 4: 4 And I **s** that all toil and all achievement H8011
Ecc 4: 7 Again I **s** something meaningless under H8011
Ecc 4:15 *I* **s** that all who lived and walked under the H8011
Ecc 6: 5 Though *it* never **s** the sun or knew H8011
Ecc 8: 9 All this *I* **s**, as I applied my mind to H8011
Ecc 8:10 Then too, *I* **s** the wicked buried—those H8011
Ecc 8:17 then *I* **s** all that God has done. No one can H8011
Ecc 9:13 *I* also **s** under the sun this example of H8011
SS 6: 9 The young women **s** her and called her H8011
Isa 1: 1 Isaiah son of Amoz **s** during the reigns of H2600
Isa 2: 1 Isaiah son of Amoz **s** concerning Judah H2600
Isa 5: 7 he looked for justice, but **s** bloodshed; for H2180
Isa 6: 1 King Uzziah died, *I* **s** the Lord, high and H8011
Isa 10:15 the **s** boast against the one who uses it H5373
Isa 13: 1 Babylon that Isaiah son of Amoz **s**: H2600
Isa 22: 9 *You* **s** that the walls of the City of David H8011
Isa 39: 4 "*They* **s** everything in my palace, H8011
Isa 59:16 *He* **s** that there was no one, he was H8011
Jer 3: 7 and her unfaithful sister Judah **s** it. H8011
Jer 3: 8 Yet *I* **s** that her unfaithful sister Judah had H8011
Jer 18: 3 and I **s** him working at the wheel. H2180
Jer 23:13 prophets of Samaria *I* **s** this repulsive H8011
Jer 39: 4 king of Judah and all the soldiers **s** them, H8011
Jer 41:13 Ishmael had with him **s** Johanan son of H8011
Jer 44: 2 You **s** the great disaster I brought on H8011
La 1:10 *she* **s** pagan nations enter her sanctuary H8011
Eze 1: 1 were opened and *I* **s** visions of God. H8011
Eze 1: 4 I **s** a windstorm coming out of the H2180
Eze 1:15 I **s** a wheel on the ground beside each H2180
Eze 1:27 *I* **s** that from what appeared to be his waist H8011
Eze 1:28 When *I* **s** it, I fell facedown, and I heard H8011
Eze 2: 9 I **s** a hand stretched out to me. H2180
Eze 8: 2 and I **s** a figure like that of a man. H2180
Eze 8: 5 gate of the altar I **s** this idol of jealousy. H2180
Eze 8: 7 I looked, and I **s** a hole in the wall. H2180
Eze 8: 8 I dug into the wall and **s** a doorway there. NDT
Eze 8:10 I **s** portrayed all over the walls all H2180
Eze 8:14 of the LORD, and I **s** women sitting there H2180
Eze 9: 2 And I **s** six men coming from the direction H2180
Eze 10: 1 I **s** the likeness of a throne of lapis H2180
Eze 10: 9 I **s** beside the cherubim four wheels H2180
Eze 11: 1 and *I* **s** among them Jaazaniah son of H8011
Eze 13:16 and **s visions** *of* peace for her H2600+2606
Eze 16: 6 I passed by and **s** you kicking about in H8011
Eze 16: 8 I looked at you and **s** that you were old H2180
Eze 19: 5 " 'When *she* **s** her hope unfulfilled, her H8011
Eze 20:28 to give them and *they* **s** any high hill or H8011
Eze 23:11 "Her sister Oholibah **s** this, yet in her lust H8011
Eze 23:13 *I* **s** that she too defiled herself; both of H8011
Eze 23:14 *She* **s** men portrayed on a wall, figures of H8011
Eze 23:16 As soon as she **s** them, she lusted H5260+6524
Eze 37: 2 I **s** a great many bones on the floor of H2180
Eze 40: 3 I **s** a man whose appearance was like H2180
Eze 40: 5 I **s** a wall completely surrounding the H2180
Eze 40:17 There I **s** some rooms and a pavement H2180
Eze 40:24 to the south side and I **s** the south gate. H2180
Eze 41: 8 *I* **s** that the temple had a raised base all H8011
Eze 43: 2 I **s** the glory of the God of Israel H2180
Eze 43: 3 The vision *I* **s** was like the vision I had H8011
Eze 44: 4 I looked and **s** the glory of the LORD filling H2180
Eze 46:21 I **s** in each corner another court. H2180
Eze 47: 1 I **s** water coming out from under the H2180
Eze 47: 7 I **s** a great number of trees on each side H2180
Da 2:26 able to tell me what *I* **s** in my dream A10255
Da 2:41 Just as *you* **s** that the feet and toes were A10255
Da 2:41 even as *you* **s** iron mixed with clay. A10255
Da 2:43 And just as *you* **s** the iron mixed with A10255
Da 3:27 *They* **s** that the fire had not harmed their A10255
Da 4:10 are the visions I **s** while lying in bed: A10646
Da 4:13 "In the visions I **s** while lying in bed, A10646
Da 4:20 The tree *you* **s**, which grew large and A10255
Da 4:23 "Your Majesty **s** a holy one, a messenger A10255
Da 8: 2 In my vision *I* **s** myself in the citadel of H8011
Da 8: 7 *I* **s** it attack the ram furiously, striking the H8011
Da 8:20 two-horned ram that *you* **s** represents the H8011
Da 10: 7 was the only one *who* **s** the vision; those H8011
Hos 5:13 "When Ephraim **s** his sickness, and Judah H8011
Hos 9:10 in the desert; when *I* **s** your ancestors, it H8011
Am 1: 1 **the vision** *he* **s** concerning Israel two years H2600
Am 9: 1 *I* **s** the Lord standing by the altar, and he H8011
Jnh 3:10 When God **s** what they did and how they H8011
Mic 1: 1 the **vision** *he* **s** concerning Samaria and H2600
Hab 3: 7 *I* **s** the tents of Cushan in distress, the H8011
Hab 3:10 the mountains **s** you and writhed. Torrents H8011
Hag 2: 3 'Who of you is left who **s** this house in its H8011
Mt 2: 2 *We* **s** his star when it rose and have come *G3972*
Mt 2:10 *When they* **s** the star, they were overjoyed. *G3972*
Mt 2:11 *they* **s** the child with his mother Mary *G3972*
Mt 3: 7 But *when he* **s** many of the Pharisees and *G3972*
Mt 3:16 and *he* **s** the Spirit of God descending like *G3972*
Mt 4:18 the Sea of Galilee, *he* **s** two brothers *G3972*
Mt 4:21 on from there, *he* **s** two other brothers *G3972*
Mt 5: 1 Now *when* Jesus **s** the crowds, he went up *G3972*
Mt 8:14 *he* **s** Peter's mother-in-law lying in bed *G3972*
Mt 8:18 *When* Jesus **s** the crowd around him, he *G3972*
Mt 8:34 And *when they* **s** him, they pleaded with *G3972*
Mt 9: 2 *When* Jesus **s** their faith, he said to the *G3972*
Mt 9: 8 *When* the crowd **s** this, they were filled *G3972*
Mt 9: 9 *he* **s** a man named Matthew sitting at the *G3972*
Mt 9:11 *When* the Pharisees **s** this, they asked his *G3972*
Mt 9:22 Jesus turned and **s** her. "Take heart *G3972*
Mt 9:23 leader's house and **s** the noisy crowd and *G3972*
Mt 9:36 *When he* **s** the crowds, he had *G3972*
Mt 12: 2 *When* the Pharisees **s** this, they said to *G3972*

S

Mt 14:14 When Jesus landed and **s** a large crowd G3972
Mt 14:26 *When* the disciples **s** him walking on the G3972
Mt 14:30 But *when he* **s** the wind, he was afraid and G1063
Mt 15:31 were amazed *when they* **s** the mute G1063
Mt 17: 8 looked up, *they* **s** no one except Jesus. G3972
Mt 18:31 *When* the other servants **s** what had G3972
Mt 20: 3 he went out and **s** others standing in the G3972
Mt 21:15 *when* the chief priests and the teachers of the law **s** G3972
Mt 21:20 *When* the disciples **s** this, they were G3972
Mt 21:32 And even after you **s** this, you did not G3972
Mt 21:38 "But *when* the tenants **s** the son, they said G3972
Mt 26: 8 *When* the disciples **s** this, they were G3972
Mt 26:71 another servant girl **s** him and said to the G3972
Mt 27: 3 *When* Judas, who had betrayed him, **s** G3972
Mt 27:24 *When* Pilate **s** that he was getting G3972
Mt 27:54 *When* the centurion and those with him who were guarding Jesus **s** G3972
Mt 28:17 *When they* **s** him, they worshiped him; but G3972
Mk 1:10 *he* **s** heaven being torn open and the G3972
Mk 1:16 *he* **s** Simon and his brother Andrew G3972
Mk 1:19 *he* **s** James son of Zebedee and his G3972
Mk 2: 5 *When* Jesus **s** their faith, he said to the G3972
Mk 2:14 *he* **s** Levi son of Alphaeus sitting at the G3972
Mk 2:16 *When* the teachers of the law who were Pharisees **s** G3972
Mk 3:11 Whenever the impure spirits **s** him, they G2555
Mk 5: 6 *When he* **s** Jesus from a distance, he ran G3972
Mk 5:15 *they* **s** the man who had been possessed G2555
Mk 5:22 and *when he* **s** Jesus, he fell at his G3972
Mk 5:38 Jesus **s** a commotion, with G2555
Mk 6:33 But many *who* **s** them leaving recognized G3972
Mk 6:34 When Jesus landed and **s** a large crowd G3972
Mk 6:48 *He* **s** the disciples straining at the oars G3972
Mk 6:49 but *when* they **s** him walking on the lake G3972
Mk 6:50 because *they* all **s** him and were terrified G3972
Mk 7: 2 **s** some of his disciples eating food G3972
Mk 8:25 was restored, and *he* **s** everything clearly. G1838
Mk 9: 8 *they* no longer **s** anyone with them except G3972
Mk 9:14 *they* **s** a large crowd around them and the G3972
Mk 9:15 As soon as all the people **s** Jesus, they G3972
Mk 9:20 *When* the spirit **s** Jesus, it immediately G3972
Mk 9:25 When Jesus **s** that a crowd was running to G3972
Mk 9:38 "*we* **s** someone driving out demons in G3972
Mk 10:14 When Jesus **s** this, he was indignant. G3972
Mk 11:20 *they* **s** the fig tree withered from the roots. G3972
Mk 12:34 *When* Jesus **s** that he had answered G3972
Mk 14:67 *When she* **s** Peter warming himself, she G3972
Mk 14:69 *When* the servant girl **s** him there, she G3972
Mk 15:39 *when* the centurion, who stood there in front of Jesus, **s** G3972
Mk 15:47 mother of Joseph **s** where he was laid. G2555
Mk 16: 4 they looked up, *they* **s** that the stone G2555
Mk 16: 5 *they* **s** a young man dressed in a white G3972
Lk 1:12 *When* Zechariah **s** him, he was startled G3972
Lk 2:48 *When* his parents **s** him, they were G3972
Lk 5: 2 *He* **s** at the water's edge two boats, left G3972
Lk 5: 8 *When* Simon Peter **s** this, he fell at Jesus' G3972
Lk 5:12 *When he* **s** Jesus, he fell with his face to G3972
Lk 5:20 *When* Jesus **s** their faith, he said, "Friend G3972
Lk 5:27 Jesus went out and **s** a tax collector by the G2517
Lk 7:13 *When* the Lord **s** her, his heart went out to G3972
Lk 7:39 *When* the Pharisee who had invited him **s** G3972
Lk 8:28 *When he* **s** Jesus, he cried out and fell at G3972
Lk 8:34 *When* those tending the pigs **s** what had G3972
Lk 9:32 *they* **s** his glory and the two men standing G3972
Lk 9:49 "*we* **s** someone driving out demons in G3972
Lk 9:54 *When* the disciples James and John **s** this G3972
Lk 10:18 "*I* **s** Satan fall like lightning from heaven. G2555
Lk 10:31 same road, and *when he* **s** the man, he G3972
Lk 10:32 when he came to the place and **s** him G3972
Lk 10:33 the man was; and *when he* **s** him, he took G3972
Lk 13:12 *When* Jesus **s** her, he called her forward G3972
Lk 15:20 his father **s** him and was filled with G3972
Lk 16:23 he looked up and **s** Abraham far away G3972
Lk 17:14 *When he* **s** them, he said, "Go, show G3972
Lk 17:15 One of them, *when he* **s** he was healed G3972
Lk 18:15 *When* the disciples **s** this, they rebuked G3972
Lk 18:43 *When* all the people **s** it, they also G3972
Lk 19: 7 All the people **s** this and began to mutter G3972
Lk 19:41 he approached Jerusalem and **s** the city, G3972
Lk 20:14 "But *when* the tenants **s** him, they talked G3972
Lk 20:23 *He* **s through** their duplicity and said to G2917
Lk 21: 1 *he* **s** the rich putting their gifts into the G3972
Lk 21: 2 *He* also **s** a poor widow put in two very G3972
Lk 22:49 When Jesus' followers **s** what was going G3972
Lk 22:56 A servant girl **s** him seated there in the G3972
Lk 22:58 little later someone else **s** him and said, G3972
Lk 23: 8 *When* Herod **s** Jesus, he was greatly G3972
Lk 23:48 *When* all the people who had gathered to witness this sight **s** G2555
Lk 23:55 followed Joseph and **s** the tomb and how G2517
Lk 24:12 *he* **s** the strips of linen lying by G1063
Lk 24:37 frightened, thinking *they* **s** a ghost. G2555
Jn 1:29 The next day John **s** Jesus coming toward G1063
Jn 1:32 "*I* **s** the Spirit come down from heaven as G2517
Jn 1:36 *When he* **s** Jesus passing by, he said G1838
Jn 1:38 around, Jesus **s** them following and asked G2517
Jn 1:39 So they went and **s** where he was staying G3972
Jn 1:47 *When* Jesus **s** Nathanael approaching, he G3972
Jn 1:48 "*I* **s** you while you were still under the fig G3972
Jn 1:50 because I told you *I* **s** you under the fig G3972
Jn 2:23 many people **s** the signs he was G2555
Jn 5: 6 *When* Jesus **s** him lying there and learned G3972
Jn 6: 2 him because *they* **s** the signs he had G2555
Jn 6: 5 Jesus looked up and **s** a great crowd G2517
Jn 6:14 *After* the people **s** the sign Jesus G3972
Jn 6:19 miles, *they* **s** Jesus approaching the boat G2555
Jn 6:26 not because *you* **s** the signs I performed G3972
Jn 8:56 of seeing my day; *he* **s** it and was glad." G3972
Jn 9: 1 went along, *he* **s** a man blind from birth. G3972
Jn 11:32 the place where Jesus was and **s** him, G3972
Jn 11:33 When Jesus **s** her weeping, and the Jews G3972
Jn 12:41 said this because *he* **s** Jesus' glory and G3972
Jn 16:19 Jesus **s** that they wanted to ask him about G1182
Jn 19: 6 the chief priests and their officials **s** him, G3972
Jn 19:26 *When* Jesus **s** his mother there, and the G3972
Jn 19:35 The *man who* **s** it has given testimony G3972
Jn 20: 1 to the tomb and **s** *that* the stone had G1063
Jn 20: 6 *He* **s** the strips of linen lying there G2555
Jn 20: 8 also went inside. *He* **s** and believed. G3972
Jn 20:12 **s** two angels in white, seated where G2555
Jn 20:14 turned around and **s** Jesus standing there, G2555
Jn 20:20 were overjoyed *when they* **s** the Lord. G3972
Jn 21: 9 *they* **s** a fire of burning coals there with G1063
Jn 21:20 Peter turned and **s** *that* the disciple whom G1063
Jn 21:21 When Peter **s** him, he asked, "Lord, what G3972
Ac 2: 3 They **s** what seemed to be tongues of fire G3972
Ac 2:25 " '*I* **s** the Lord always before me G4632
Ac 3: 3 *When* he **s** Peter and John about to enter G3972
Ac 3: 9 *When* all the people **s** him walking and G3972
Ac 3:12 *When* Peter **s** this, he said to them G3972
Ac 4:13 *When they* **s** the courage of Peter and G2555
Ac 6:15 and *they* **s** *that* his face was like the face G3972
Ac 7:24 *He* **s** one of them being mistreated by an G3972
Ac 7:31 *When* he **s** this, he was amazed at the G3972
Ac 7:55 up to heaven and **s** the glory of God, G3972
Ac 8: 6 heard Philip and **s** the signs he performed G1063
Ac 8:13 by the great signs and miracles *he* **s**. G2555
Ac 8:18 *When* Simon **s** that the Spirit was given at G3972
Ac 9:35 in Lydda and Sharon **s** him and turned to G3972
Ac 10: 3 *He* distinctly **s** an angel of God, who G3972
Ac 10:11 *He* **s** heaven opened and something like a G2555
Ac 11: 5 praying, and in a trance *I* **s** a vision. G3972
Ac 11: 5 I **s** something like a large sheet being let NDT
Ac 11: 6 I looked into it and **s** four-footed animals G3972
Ac 11:23 When he arrived and **s** what the grace of G3972
Ac 12: 3 *When he* **s** that this met with approval G3972
Ac 12:16 when they opened the door and **s** him, G3972
Ac 13:12 When the proconsul **s** what had happened G3972
Ac 13:45 *When* the Jews **s** the crowds, they were G3972
Ac 14: 9 **s** that he had faith to be healed G3972
Ac 14:11 *When* the crowd **s** what Paul had done G3972
Ac 16:27 and *when he* **s** the prison doors open G3972
Ac 21:27 the province of Asia **s** Paul at the temple. G2517
Ac 21:32 *When* the rioters **s** the commander and G3972
Ac 22: 9 My companions **s** the light, but they did G2517
Ac 22:18 **s** the Lord speaking to me. 'Quick!' he G3972
Ac 26:13 I was on the road, *I* **s** a light from heaven G3972
Ac 27:13 began to blow, *they* **s** their opportunity G1506
Ac 27:39 but *they* **s** a bay with a sandy beach G2917
Ac 28: 4 When the islanders **s** the snake hanging G3972
Gal 1:19 *I* **s** none of the other apostles—only James G3972
Gal 2:14 When *I* **s** that they were not acting in line G3972
Php 1:30 through the same struggle *you* **s** I had, G3972
Heb 3: 9 though for forty years *they* **s** what I did. G3972
Heb 11:13 *they* only **s** them and welcomed them G3972
Heb 11:23 because *they* **s** he was no ordinary child G3972
Heb 11:27 persevered because *he* **s** him who is G3972
2Pe 2: 8 by the lawless deeds he **s** and heard)— G1062
Rev 1: 2 who testifies to everything *he* **s**—that is G3972
Rev 1:12 And when I turned *I* **s** seven golden G3972
Rev 1:17 When *I* **s** him, I fell at his feet as though G3972
Rev 1:20 the seven stars that *you* **s** in my right hand G3972
Rev 5: 1 Then *I* **s** in the right hand of him who sat G3972
Rev 5: 2 And *I* **s** a mighty angel proclaiming in a G3972
Rev 5: 6 Then *I* **s** a Lamb, looking as if it had been G3972
Rev 6: 9 *I* **s** under the altar the souls of those who G3972
Rev 7: 1 After this *I* **s** four angels standing at the G3972
Rev 7: 2 Then *I* **s** another angel coming up from G3972
Rev 8: 2 And *I* **s** the seven angels who stand G3972
Rev 9: 1 and *I* **s** a star that had fallen from the sky G3972
Rev 9:17 horses and riders *I* **s** in my vision looked G3972
Rev 10: 1 Then *I* **s** another mighty angel coming G3972
Rev 11:11 and terror struck those *who* **s** them. G2555
Rev 12:13 When the dragon **s** that he had been G3972
Rev 13: 1 And *I* **s** a beast coming out of the sea G3972
Rev 13: 2 The beast *I* **s** resembled a leopard, but G3972
Rev 13:11 Then *I* **s** a second beast, coming out of G3972
Rev 14: 6 Then *I* **s** another angel flying in midair G3972
Rev 15: 1 *I* **s** in heaven another great and G3972
Rev 15: 2 And *I* **s** what looked like a sea of glass G3972
Rev 15: 5 this I looked, and I **s** in heaven the temple NDT
Rev 16:13 Then *I* **s** three impure spirits that looked G3972
Rev 17: 3 There *I* **s** a woman sitting on a scarlet G3972
Rev 17: 6 *I* **s** that the woman was drunk with the G3972
Rev 17: 6 *When I* **s** her, I was greatly G3972
Rev 17: 8 The beast, which *you* **s**, once was, now is G3972
Rev 17:12 "The ten horns *you* **s** are ten kings who G3972
Rev 17:15 "The waters *you* **s**, where the G3972
Rev 17:16 the ten horns *you* **s** will hate the G3972
Rev 17:18 The woman *you* **s** is the great city that G3972
Rev 18: 1 After this *I* **s** another angel coming down G3972
Rev 19:11 *I* **s** heaven standing open and there G3972
Rev 19:17 And *I* **s** an angel standing in the sun, who G3972
Rev 19:19 Then *I* **s** the beast and the kings of the G3972
Rev 20: 1 And *I* **s** an angel coming down out of G3972
Rev 20: 4 *I* **s** thrones on which were seated those G3972
Rev 20: 4 And I **s** the souls of those who had been NDT
Rev 20:11 Then *I* **s** a great white throne and him G3972
Rev 20:12 And *I* **s** the dead, great and small G3972
Rev 21: 1 Then *I* **s** "a new heaven and a new earth," G3972
Rev 21: 2 *I* **s** the Holy City, the new Jerusalem G3972
Rev 22: 8 am the one who heard and **s** these things. G1063

SAWDUST (2)

Mt 7: 3 you look at the **speck of s** in your brother's G2847
Lk 6:41 you look at the **speck of s** in your brother's G2847

SAWED (1) [SAWS]

Heb 11:37 by stoning; *they were* **s in two**; they were G4569

SAWS (2) [SAWED]

2Sa 12:31 them to labor with **s** and with iron picks H4490
1Ch 20: 3 them to labor with **s** and with iron picks H4490

SAY (940) [SAID, SAYING, SAYINGS, SAYS]

Ge 3: 1 the woman, "*Did* God really **s**, 'You must H606
Ge 3: 3 God *did* **s**, 'You must not eat fruit from H606
Ge 12:12 see you, *they will* **s**, 'This is his wife H606
Ge 12:13 **S** you are my sister, so that I will be treated H606
Ge 12:19 Why *did you* **s**, 'She is my sister,' so that I H606
Ge 14:23 so that *you will* never *be able to* **s**, 'I made H606
Ge 18: 5 they answered, "do as *you* **s**." H1819
Ge 18:13 "Why did Sarah laugh and **s**, 'Will I really H606
Ge 20: 5 *Did* he not **s** to me, 'She is my sister,' and H606
Ge 20: 5 my sister,' and *didn't* she also **s**, 'He is my H606
Ge 20:13 Everywhere we go, **s** of me, "He is my H606
Ge 24:14 May it be that when *I* **s** to a young woman H606
Ge 24:33 eat until I have told you **what I have to s**." H1821
Ge 24:43 comes out to draw water and *I* **s** to her, H606
Ge 24:50 we can **s** nothing to you one way or the H1819
Ge 26: 7 because he was afraid to **s**, "She is my wife H606
Ge 26: 9 Why *did you* **s**, 'She is my sister'? H606
Ge 27: 6 your father **s** to your brother Esau, H1819
Ge 27:13 Just do what I **s**; go and get them for H7754
Ge 27:43 my son, do **what** I **s**: Flee at once to H7754
Ge 31:24 "Be careful not *to* **s** *anything* to Jacob H1819
Ge 31:29 'Be careful not *to* **s** anything to Jacob H1819
Ge 32: 4 "This is what *you are to* **s** to my lord Esau H606
Ge 32:18 then *you are to* **s**, 'They belong to your H606
Ge 32:19 "*You are to* **s** the same thing to Esau H1819
Ge 32:20 And be sure *to* **s**, 'Your servant Jacob is H606
Ge 37:17 "I heard *them* **s**, 'Let's go to H606
Ge 37:20 these cisterns and **s** *that* a ferocious animal H606
Ge 43: 7 How were we to know *he would* **s**, 'Bring H606
Ge 44: 4 catch up with them, **s** to them, 'Why have H606
Ge 44: 7 "Why *does* my lord **s** such things? H1819
Ge 44:10 then," he said, "let it be as you **s**. H1821
Ge 44:16 "What *can we* **s** to my lord?" Judah replied H606
Ge 44:16 "What *can we* **s**? How can we H1819
Ge 45: 9 Now hurry back to my father and **s** to him H606
Ge 46:31 up and speak to Pharaoh and *will* **s** to him, H606
Ge 47:30 "I will do as you **s**," he said. H1821
Ge 50:17 'This is what *you are to* **s** to Joseph: I ask H606
Ex 3:13 I go to the Israelites and **s** to them, H606
Ex 3:14 This is what *you are to* **s** to the Israelites H606
Ex 3:15 also said to Moses, "**S** to the Israelites H606
Ex 3:16 the elders of Israel and **s** to them, H606
Ex 3:18 are to go to the king of Egypt and **s** to him, H606
Ex 4: 1 do not believe me or listen to me and **s**, H606
Ex 4:12 you speak and will teach you what *to* **s**." H1819
Ex 4:22 Then **s** to Pharaoh, 'This is what the LORD H606
Ex 4:28 everything the LORD had sent him to **s**, H1821
Ex 6: 6 "Therefore, **s** to the Israelites: 'I am the H606
Ex 7: 2 You *are to* **s** everything I command you H1819
Ex 7: 9 a miracle,' then **s** to Aaron, 'Take your H606
Ex 7:16 Then **s** to him, 'The LORD, the God of the H606
Ex 7:16 of the Hebrews, has sent me to **s** to you: H606
Ex 8: 1 "Go to Pharaoh and **s** to him, 'This is what H606
Ex 8:10 "It will be as you **s**, so that you may know H1821
Ex 8:20 as he goes to the river and **s** to him, H606
Ex 9: 1 "Go to Pharaoh and **s** to him, 'This is H1819
Ex 9:13 confront Pharaoh and **s** to him, 'This is H606
Ex 10:29 "Just as *you* **s**," Moses replied. "I will H1819
Ex 13:14 **s** to him, 'With a mighty hand the LORD H606
Ex 14:12 Didn't *we* **s** to you in Egypt, 'Leave H1819+1821
Ex 16: 9 "**S** to the entire Israelite community H606
Ex 19: 3 "This is what *you are to* **s** to the H606
Ex 23:22 to what he says and do all that *I* **s**, H1819
Ex 30:31 **S** to the Israelites, 'This is to be my sacred H1819
Ex 31:13 "**S** to the Israelites, 'You must observe my H1819
Ex 32:12 Why *should* the Egyptians **s**, 'It was with H606
Lev 1: 2 "Speak to the Israelites and **s** to them H606
Lev 4: 2 "**S** to the Israelites: 'When anyone sins H1819
Lev 6:25 "**S** to Aaron and his sons: 'These are the H1819
Lev 7:23 "**S** to the Israelites: 'Do not eat any of the H1819
Lev 7:29 "**S** to the Israelites: 'Anyone who brings a H1819
Lev 9: 3 Then **s** to the Israelites: 'Take a male goat H1819
Lev 11: 2 "**S** to the Israelites: 'Of all the animals that H1819
Lev 12: 2 "**S** to the Israelites: 'A woman who H1819
Lev 15: 2 "Speak to the Israelites and **s** to them H606
Lev 17: 2 sons and to all the Israelites and **s** to them: H606
Lev 17: 8 "**S** to them: 'Any Israelite or any foreigner H606
Lev 17:12 Therefore *I* **s** to the Israelites, "None of you H606
Lev 18: 2 "Speak to the Israelites and **s** to them: 'I am H606
Lev 19: 2 the entire assembly of Israel and **s** to them: H606

Book	Ref	Context	Code
Lev	20: 2	"S to the Israelites: 'Any Israelite or any	H606
Lev	21: 1	the sons of Aaron, and s to them:	H606
Lev	21:17	"S to Aaron: 'For the generations to come	H1819
Lev	22: 3	"S to them: 'For the generations to come, if	H606
Lev	22:18	sons and to all the Israelites and s to them:	H606
Lev	23: 2	"Speak to the Israelites and s to them	H606
Lev	23:10	"Speak to the Israelites and s to them	H606
Lev	23:24	"S to the Israelites: 'On the first day of the	H1819
Lev	23:34	"S to the Israelites: 'On the fifteenth day of	H1819
Lev	24:15	S to the Israelites: 'Anyone who curses	H1819
Lev	25: 2	"Speak to the Israelites and s to them	H606
Lev	27: 2	"Speak to the Israelites and s to them: 'If	H606
Nu	5: 6	"S to the Israelites: 'Any man or woman	H1819
Nu	5:12	"Speak to the Israelites and s to them: 'If a	H606
Nu	5:19	put the woman under oath and s to her,	H606
Nu	5:22	" 'Then the woman *is to* s, "Amen. So be it	H606
Nu	6: 2	"Speak to the Israelites and s to them: 'If a	H606
Nu	6:23	you are to bless the Israelites. S to them:	H606
Nu	8: 2	"Speak to Aaron and s to him, 'When you	H606
Nu	11:21	men on foot, and you s, 'I will give them	H606
Nu	11:23	see whether or not *what* I s will come true	H1821
Nu	14:15	have heard this report about you *will* s,	H606
Nu	14:28	will do to you the very thing I heard *you* s:	H1819
Nu	15: 2	"Speak to the Israelites and s to them	H606
Nu	15:18	"Speak to the Israelites and s to them	H606
Nu	15:38	"Speak to the Israelites and s to them	H606
Nu	16:24	"S to the assembly, 'Move away from the	H1819
Nu	18:26	"Speak to the Levites and s to them: 'When	H606
Nu	18:30	"S to the Levites: 'When you present the	H606
Nu	21:21	sent messengers to s to Sihon king of the	H606
Nu	21:27	That is why the poets s: "Come to Heshbon	H606
Nu	22:17	you handsomely and do whatever *you* s.	H606
Nu	22:38	"But I can't s whatever I please.	H1819
Nu	23:17	Balak asked him, "What *did* the LORD s?"	H1819
Nu	24:13	and *I must* s only what the LORD says'?	H1819
Nu	27: 8	"S to the Israelites, 'If a man dies and	H1819
Nu	28: 2	command to the Israelites and s to them:	H606
Nu	28: 3	S to them: 'This is the food offering you are	H606
Nu	33:51	"Speak to the Israelites and s to them	H606
Nu	34: 2	"Command the Israelites and s to them	H606
Nu	35:10	"Speak to the Israelites and s to them	H606
Dt	1:28	*They* s, 'The people are stronger and taller	H606
Dt	4: 6	will hear about all these decrees and s,	H606
Dt	7:17	*You may* s to yourselves, "These nations	H606
Dt	8:17	*You may* s to yourself, "My power and the	H606
Dt	9: 4	out before you, *do* not s to yourself, "The	H606
Dt	9:28	country from which you brought us *will* s,	H606
Dt	12:20	you crave meat and s, "I would like	H606
Dt	17:14	settled in it, and *you* s, "Let us set a king	H606
Dt	18:17	LORD said to me: "What *they* s is good.	H1819
Dt	18:21	*You may* s to yourselves, "How can we	H606
Dt	20: 3	*He shall* s: "Hear, Israel: Today you are	H606
Dt	20: 5	The officers *shall* s to the army: "Has	H1819
Dt	21:20	*They shall* s to the elders, "This son of ours	H606
Dt	22:16	Her father *will* s to the elders, "I gave my	H606
Dt	25: 7	go to the elders at the town gate and s,	H606
Dt	25: 9	spit in his face and s, "This is what is done	H606
Dt	26: 3	s to the priest in office at the time, "I	H606
Dt	26:13	Then s to the LORD your God: "I have	H606
Dt	27:15	Then all the people *shall* s	H6699+2256+606
Dt	27:16	Then all the people *shall* s, "Amen!"	H606
Dt	27:17	Then all the people *shall* s, "Amen!"	H606
Dt	27:18	Then all the people *shall* s, "Amen!"	H606
Dt	27:19	Then all the people *shall* s, "Amen!"	H606
Dt	27:20	Then all the people *shall* s, "Amen!"	H606
Dt	27:21	Then all the people *shall* s, "Amen!"	H606
Dt	27:22	Then all the people *shall* s, "Amen!"	H606
Dt	27:23	Then all the people *shall* s, "Amen!"	H606
Dt	27:24	Then all the people *shall* s, "Amen!"	H606
Dt	27:25	Then all the people *shall* s, "Amen!"	H606
Dt	27:26	Then all the people *shall* s, "Amen!"	H606
Dt	28:67	In the morning *you will* s, "If only it were	H606
Dt	32:27	lest the adversary misunderstand and s	H606
Dt	32:37	*He will* s: "Now where are their gods, the	H606
Jos	2:21	"Let it be as you s." So she sent them	H1821
Jos	6:10	*do* not s a word until the day	H3655+4946+7023
Jos	7: 8	What *can I* s, now that Israel has been	H606
Jos	8: 6	from the city, for *they will* s, 'They are	H606
Jos	9:11	go and meet them and s to them, "We are	H606
Jos	22:24	day your descendants *might* s to ours,	H606
Jos	22:27	descendants *will* not *be able to* s to ours,	H606
Jos	22:28	"And we said, 'If *they* ever s this to us, or to	H606
Jos	22:30	Gad and Manasseh *had to* s, they were	H1819
Jdg	4:20	asks you, 'Is anyone in there?' s 'No.' "	H606
Jdg	7: 4	If *I* s, 'This one shall go with you,' he shall	H606
Jdg	7: 4	he shall go; but if *I* s, 'This one shall not	H606
Jdg	9:29	*I would* s to Abimelek, 'Call out your whole	H606
Jdg	9:54	so that *they* can't s, 'A woman	H606
Jdg	11:10	our witness; we will certainly do as you s."	H1821
Jdg	12: 6	they said, "All right, s 'Shibboleth.' " If he	H606
Jdg	16:15	said to him, "How *can you* s, 'I love you,	H606
Jdg	18:19	**Don't s a word.**	H8492+3338+6584+7023
Jdg	21:22	complain to us, *we will* s to them, 'Do us	H606
Ru	3: 5	"I will do whatever *you* s," Ruth answered.	H606
1Sa	1: 8	Her husband Elkanah *would* s to her	H606
1Sa	2:15	would come and s to the person who was	H606
1Sa	3: 9	and if he calls you, s, 'Speak, LORD,	H606
1Sa	9: 9	to inquire of God, *they would* s, "Come,	H606
1Sa	9:21	Why *do you* s such a thing to me?	H1819
1Sa	10: 2	*They will* s to you, 'The donkeys you set out	H606
1Sa	11: 9	had come, "S to the men of Jabesh Gilead	H606
1Sa	14: 9	If *they* s to us, 'Wait there until we come to	H606
1Sa	14:10	But if *they* s, 'Come up to us,' we will climb	H606
1Sa	16: 2	"Take a heifer with you and s, 'I have come	H606
1Sa	18:22	"Speak to David privately and s, 'Look, the	H606
1Sa	18:25	Saul replied, "S to David, 'The king wants	H606
1Sa	19:24	This is why *people* s, "Is Saul also among	H606
1Sa	20:21	Then I will send a boy and s, 'Go, find the	NDT
1Sa	20:21	If *I* s to him, 'Look, the arrows are on	H606+606
1Sa	20:22	But if *I* s to the boy, 'Look, the arrows are	H606
1Sa	24: 9	"Why do you listen *when* men s, 'David is	H606
1Sa	25: 6	S to him: 'Long life to you! Good health to	H606
1Sa	25:24	hear **what** your servant has to s.	H1821
1Sa	27:10	David *would* s, "Against the Negev of	H606
1Sa	27:11	"They might inform on us and s, 'This is	H606
1Sa	30:24	Who will listen to **what** you s? The share	H1821
2Sa	2: 5	he sent messengers to them *to* s to them	H606
2Sa	3:11	did not dare to s another word *to* Abner,	H8740
2Sa	3:12	messengers on his behalf to s to David,	H606
2Sa	5: 8	That is why *they* s, "The 'blind and lame'	H606
2Sa	7: 7	*did I* **ever** *s to* any of their rulers	H1819+1821
2Sa	7:20	"What more *can* David s to you? For you	H1819
2Sa	7:26	Then people *will* s, 'The LORD Almighty is	H606
2Sa	11:21	he asks you this, then s to him, 'Moreover,	H606
2Sa	11:22	David everything Joab had sent him to s.	NDT
2Sa	11:25	told the messenger, "S this to Joab: 'Don't	H606
2Sa	11:25	S this to encourage Joab.	NDT
2Sa	13: 5	comes to see you, s to him, 'I would like	H606
2Sa	13:28	spirits from drinking wine and *I* s to you,	H606
2Sa	14: 7	your servant; *they* s, 'Hand over the one	H606
2Sa	14:15	now I have come to s this to my lord the	H1819
2Sa	15: 3	Then Absalom *would* s to him, "Look, your	H606
2Sa	15:10	throughout the tribes of Israel to s,	H606
2Sa	15:10	of the trumpets, then s, 'Absalom is king in	H606
2Sa	15:34	if you return to the city and s to Absalom,	H606
2Sa	17: 5	so we can hear what he has to s as well."	H7023
2Sa	17: 9	whoever hears about it *will* s, 'There has	H606
2Sa	19:10	So why *do* you s **nothing** *about* bringing	H3087
2Sa	19:13	And s to Amasa, 'Are you not my own flesh	H606
2Sa	19:29	The king said to him, "Why s more?	H1819+1821
2Sa	20:17	"Listen to **what** your servant *has to* s."	H1821
2Sa	20:18	"Long ago *they* **used to** s, 'Get your	H1819+1819
1Ki	1:13	Go in to King David and s to him, 'My lord	H606
1Ki	2:14	he added, "I have **something** to s to you."	H1821
1Ki	2:14	"*You may* s it," she replied	H1819
1Ki	2:38	answered the king, "**What** you s is good.	H1821
1Ki	2:42	time you said to me, '**What** you s is good.	H1821
1Ki	8:47	with you in the land of their captors and s,	H606
1Ki	9: 8	by will be appalled and will scoff and s,	H606
1Ki	12: 9	we answer these people who s to me,	H1819
1Ki	12:23	"S to Rehoboam son of Solomon king of	H606
1Ki	18:11	now you tell me to go to my master and s,	H606
1Ki	18:14	now you tell me to go to my master and s,	H606
1Ki	18:24	all the people said, "What you s is good."	H1821
1Ki	19: 2	So Jezebel sent a messenger to Elijah to s	H606
1Ki	20: 4	"Just as you s, my lord the king.	H1821
1Ki	21:19	S to him, 'This is what the LORD says: Have	H1819
1Ki	21:19	Then s to him, 'This is what the LORD says:	H1819
1Ki	22: 8	"The king *should* not s such a thing,"	H606
1Ki	22:27	s, 'This is what the king says: Put this	H606
2Ki	5:10	Elisha sent a messenger to s to him, "Go	H606
2Ki	5:22	"My master sent me to s, 'Two young men	H606
2Ki	7: 4	If *we* s, 'We'll go into the city'—the famine	H606
2Ki	8:10	answered, "Go and s to him, 'You will	H606
2Ki	8:14	"What *did* Elisha s to you?	H606
2Ki	9:37	so that no *one will be able to* s, 'This is	H606
2Ki	10: 5	servants and we will do anything *you* s.	H606
2Ki	16: 7	sent messengers to s to Tiglath-Pileser	H606
2Ki	18:20	You s you have the counsel and the might	NDT
2Ki	18:22	But if *you* s to me, "We are depending on	H606
2Ki	18:27	that my master sent me to s these things,	H1819
2Ki	19:10	"S to Hezekiah king of Judah: Do not let the	H606
2Ki	20:14	"What *did* those men s, and where	H606
1Ch	16:31	be glad; *let them* s among the nations	H606
1Ch	17: 6	*did I* **ever** *s to* any of their leaders	H1819+1821
1Ch	17:18	"What more can David s to you for honoring	NDT
1Ch	17:24	Then people *will* s, 'The LORD Almighty, the	H606
2Ch	6:37	with you in the land of their captivity and s,	H606
2Ch	7:21	All who pass by will be appalled and s	H606
2Ch	10: 9	we answer these people who s to me,	H1819
2Ch	11: 3	"S to Rehoboam son of Solomon king of	H606
2Ch	18: 7	"The king *should* not s such a thing,"	H606
2Ch	18:26	s, 'This is what the king says: Put this	H606
2Ch	25:19	*You* s *to yourself* that you have defeated	H606
Ezr	8:17	I told them what to s to Iddo and his	H1819
Ezr	9:10	our God, what *can we* s after this?	H606
Ezr	10:12	"You are right! We must do as you s.	H1821
Ne	5: 8	because they could find nothing to s.	H1821
Ne	5:12	We will do as you s." Then I summoned	H606
Est	1:17	so they will despise their husbands and s,	H606
Est	4:10	Then she instructed him *to* s to Mordecai,	H7422
Job	6:26	Do you mean to correct **what** I s, and treat	H4863
Job	8: 2	"How long *will you* s such things? Your	H4910
Job	9:12	Who *can* s to him, 'What are	H606
Job	9:22	the same; that is why *I* s, 'He destroys both	H606
Job	9:27	If I s, 'I will forget my complaint, I will	H606
Job	10: 2	*I* s to God: Do not declare me guilty, but	H606
Job	11: 4	*You* s to God, 'My beliefs are flawless and I	H606
Job	13:17	Listen carefully to **what I** s; let my words	H4863
Job	17:14	if *I* s to corruption, 'You are my father,'	H7924
Job	19:28	"If *you* s, 'How we will hound him, since	H606
Job	20: 7	those who have seen him *will* s, 'Where is	H606
Job	21:14	Yet *they* s to God, 'Leave us alone! We	H606
Job	21:28	*You* s, 'Where now is the house of the	H606
Job	22:13	Yet *you* s, 'What does God know? Does he	H606
Job	22:29	When people are brought low and *you* s	H606
Job	23: 5	and consider what *he would* s to me.	H606
Job	27: 4	my lips *will* not s anything wicked, and my	H1819
Job	28:22	Destruction and Death s, "Only a rumor of	H606
Job	30:13	'No one can help him,' they s.	NDT
Job	32: 5	that the three men had nothing more to s,	H5101
Job	32:10	"Therefore *I* s: Listen to me; I too will tell	H606
Job	32:13	*Do* not s, 'We have found wisdom; let God	H606
Job	32:15	are dismayed and *have* no more *to* s;	H6699
Job	32:17	I too *will* **have** my s; I too will tell	H6699+2750
Job	33: 1	my words; pay attention to everything I s.	H1821
Job	33:27	And they will go to others and s, 'I have	H606
Job	33:32	If you have **anything to** s, answer me	H4863
Job	34:16	hear this; listen to what I s.	H4863
Job	34:34	declare, wise men who hear me s to me,	H606
Job	35: 2	think this is just? *You* s, 'I am in the right	H606
Job	35:14	will he listen *when you* s that you do not	H606
Job	37:19	"Tell us what *we should* s to him; we	H606
Job	40: 5	no answer—twice, but I will s no more."	NDT
Ps	10:13	Why *does he* s to himself, "He won't call	H606
Ps	11: 1	How then *can you* s to me: "Flee	H606
Ps	12: 4	those who s, "By our tongues we will	H606
Ps	13: 4	my enemy *will* s, "I have overcome	H606
Ps	16: 2	*I* s to the LORD, "You are my Lord; apart	H606
Ps	16: 3	I s of the holy people who are in the land	NDT
Ps	22: 8	the LORD," they s, "let the LORD rescue him	NDT
Ps	31:14	I trust in you, LORD; *I* s, "You are my God."	H606
Ps	35: 3	those who pursue me. S to me, "I am your	H606
Ps	35:21	They sneer at me and s, "Aha! Aha! With	H606
Ps	35:25	or s, "We have swallowed	H606
Ps	35:27	gladness; *may they* always s, "The LORD be	H606
Ps	40:15	May those *who* s to me, "Aha! Aha!"	H606
Ps	40:16	*may* those who long for your saving help always s	H606
Ps	41: 5	My enemies s of me in malice, "When will	H606
Ps	42: 3	while *people* s to me all day long	H606
Ps	42: 9	*I* s to God my Rock, "Why have you	H606
Ps	58:11	Then people *will* s, "Surely the righteous	H606
Ps	64: 5	their snares; *they* s, "Who will see it?"	H606
Ps	64: 6	They plot injustice and s, "We have devised	NDT
Ps	66: 3	S to God, "How awesome are your deeds	H606
Ps	70: 3	May those *who* s to me, "Aha! Aha!"	H606
Ps	70: 4	*may* those who long for your saving help always s	H606
Ps	71:11	They s, "God has forsaken him; pursue him	H606
Ps	73:11	*They* s, "How would God know? Does the	H606
Ps	75: 2	You s, "I choose the appointed time; it is I	NDT
Ps	75: 4	To the arrogant *I* s, 'Boast no more,' and to	H606
Ps	79:10	Why *should* the nations s, "Where is their	H606
Ps	81: 5	I heard an unknown **voice** s:	AIT
Ps	83: 4	*they* s, "let us destroy them as a	H606
Ps	87: 4	with Cush—and will s, 'This one was born	NDT
Ps	91: 2	*I will* s of the LORD, "He is my refuge and	H606
Ps	91: 9	If you s, "The LORD is my refuge," and you	NDT
Ps	94: 7	*They* s, "The LORD does not see; the God of	H606
Ps	96:10	S among the nations, "The LORD reigns."	H606
Ps	106:48	*Let* all the people s, "Amen!	H606
Ps	115: 2	Why *do* the nations s, "Where is their God?"	H606
Ps	118: 2	*Let* Israel s: "His love endures forever."	H606
Ps	118: 3	*Let* the house of Aaron s: "His love endures	H606
Ps	118: 4	*Let* those who fear the LORD s: "His love	H606
Ps	119:82	your promise; I s, "When will you	H606
Ps	122: 8	friends, *I will* s, "Peace be within	H1819
Ps	124: 1	had not been on our side—*let* Israel s—	H606
Ps	129: 1	oppressed me from my youth," *let* Israel s;	H606
Ps	129: 8	*May* those who pass by not s to them, "The	H606
Ps	139:11	If *I* s, "Surely the darkness will hide me	H606
Ps	140: 6	*I* s to the LORD, "You are my God." Hear	H606
Ps	141: 7	They will s, "As one plows and breaks up	NDT
Ps	142: 5	I cry to you, LORD; *I* s, "You are my refuge	H606
Pr	1:11	If *they* s, "Come along with us; let's lie in	H606
Pr	3:28	*Do* not s to your neighbor, "Come back	H606
Pr	4:10	accept **what** I s, and the years of	H609
Pr	4:20	pay attention to **what** I s; turn your ear to	H1821
Pr	5: 7	do not turn aside from **what** I s.	H609+7023
Pr	5:12	*You will* s, "How I hated discipline! How	H606
Pr	7: 4	S to wisdom, "You are my sister," and to	H606
Pr	7:24	pay attention to **what** I s.	H609+7023
Pr	8: 6	for *I have* trustworthy things *to* s; I open	H1819
Pr	20: 9	Who *can* s, "I have kept my heart pure;	H606
Pr	20:22	*Do* not s, "I'll pay you back for this wrong!"	H606
Pr	23:35	"They hit me," you will s, "but I'm not hurt	NDT
Pr	24:12	If *you* s, "But we knew nothing about this,"	H606
Pr	24:29	*Do* not s, "I'll do to them as they have	H606
Pr	25: 7	it is better for him *to* s to you, "Come up	H606
Pr	30: 9	may have too much and disown you and s,	H606
Pr	30:15	never satisfied, four *that* never s, 'Enough!	H606
Ecc	1: 8	are wearisome, more than one can s.	H1819
Ecc	1:10	Is there anything of which *one can* s, "Look	H606
Ecc	5: 6	God be angry at **what** you s and destroy	H7754
Ecc	6: 3	*I* s that a stillborn child is better off than he.	H606
Ecc	7:10	*Do* not s, "Why were the old days better	H606
Ecc	7:21	not pay attention to every word *people* s,	H1819
Ecc	8: 2	king's command, I s, because you took an	NDT
Ecc	8: 4	is supreme, who *can* s to him, "What are	H606
Ecc	8:14	This too, *I* s, is meaningless.	H606
Ecc	10:20	a bird on the wing may report **what** you s.	H1821
Ecc	12: 1	the years approach when *you will* s,	H606
Isa	2: 3	Many peoples will come and s, "Come, let	H606
Isa	3: 6	his father's house, and s, "You have a cloak,	NDT
Isa	4: 1	women will take hold of one man and s,	H606

Isa 5:19 to those *who* **s**, "Let God hurry; let him H606
Isa 7:4 **S** to him, 'Be careful, keep calm and don't H606
Isa 8:4 the boy knows how *to* **s** 'My father' or 'My H7924
Isa 9:9 *who* **s** with pride and arrogance of heart H606
Isa 10:12 Jerusalem, he will **s**, "I will punish the NDT
Isa 10:29 go over the pass, and **s**, "We will camp NDT
Isa 12:1 In that day *you will* **s**: "I will praise you H606
Isa 12:4 In that day *you will* **s**: "Give praise to the H606
Isa 14:8 the cedars of Lebanon gloat over you and **s**, NDT
Isa 14:10 all respond, *they will* **s** to you, "You also H606
Isa 19:11 How *can you* **s** to Pharaoh, "I am one of H606
Isa 20:6 the people who live on this coast *will* **s**, H606
Isa 22:13 eat and drink," you **s**, "for tomorrow we die!" NDT
Isa 22:15 **s** to this steward, to Shebna the palace NDT
Isa 25:9 In that day *they will* **s**, "Surely this is our H606
Isa 28:23 my voice; pay attention and hear **what** I **s**. H614
Isa 29:11 someone who can read, and **s**, "Read this, H606
Isa 29:12 who cannot read, and **s**, "Read this, H606
Isa 29:16 *Shall* what is formed **s** to the one who H606
Isa 29:16 *Can* the pot **s** to the potter, "You know H606
Isa 30:10 *They* **s** to the seers, "See no more visions!" H606
Isa 30:22 away like a menstrual cloth and **s** to them, H606
Isa 32:9 who feel secure, hear **what I have to s**! H614
Isa 33:24 No one living in Zion *will* **s**, "I am ill"; H606
Isa 35:4 **s** to those with fearful hearts, "Be strong H606
Isa 36:5 You **s** you have counsel and might for war NDT
Isa 36:7 But if *you* **s** to me, "We are depending on H606
Isa 36:12 that my master sent me to **s** these things, H1819
Isa 37:10 "**S** to Hezekiah king of Judah: Do not let H606
Isa 38:15 But what *can I* **s**? He has spoken to me H1819
Isa 39:3 "What *did* those men **s**, and where H606
Isa 40:9 do not be afraid; **s** to the towns of Judah H606
Isa 40:27 Why *do you* **s**, Israel, "My way is hidden H1819
Isa 41:6 help each other and **s** to their companions, H606
Isa 41:26 beforehand, so *we could* **s**, 'He was right'? H606
Isa 42:17 trust in idols, who **s** to images, 'You are our H606
Isa 42:22 with no *one to* **s**, "Send them back. H606
Isa 43:6 *I will* **s** to the north, 'Give them up!' and to H606
Isa 43:9 so that others may hear and **s**, "It is true." H606
Isa 44:5 Some *will* **s**, 'I belong to the LORD'; others H606
Isa 44:19 has the knowledge or understanding to **s**, H606
Isa 44:20 save himself, or **s**, "Is not this thing in H606
Isa 44:28 that I please; he *will* **s** of Jerusalem, "Let H606
Isa 45:9 *Does* the clay **s** to the potter, 'What are you H606
Isa 45:9 Does your work **s**, 'The potter has no hands' NDT
Isa 45:24 *They will* **s** of me, 'In the LORD alone are H606
Isa 46:10 I **s**, 'My purpose will stand, and I will do all H606
Isa 47:10 mislead you when *you* **s** to yourself, H606
Isa 48:5 them to you so that *you could* not **s**, H606
Isa 48:7 So *you* cannot **s**, 'Yes, I knew H606
Isa 48:20 the ends of the earth; **s**, "The LORD has H606
Isa 49:9 to **s** to the captives, 'Come out,' and to H606
Isa 49:20 bereavement *will* yet **s** in your hearing, H606
Isa 49:21 Then *you will* **s** in your heart, 'Who bore H606
Isa 51:16 of the earth, and *who* **s** to Zion, 'You are H606
Isa 52:7 salvation, *who* **s** to Zion, "Your God H606
Isa 56:3 Let no foreigner who is bound to the LORD **s** H606
Isa 57:10 going about, but *you would* not **s**, 'It is H606
Isa 58:3 have we fasted,' they **s**, 'and you have not NDT
Isa 58:9 you will cry for help, and *he will* **s**: H606
Isa 62:11 "**S** to Daughter Zion, 'See, your Savior H606
Isa 65:5 who **s**, 'Keep away; don't come near me H606
Isa 65:8 found in a cluster of grapes and *people* **s**, H606
Jer 1:7 said to me, "*Do* not **s**, 'I am too young. H606
Jer 1:7 I send you to and **s** whatever I command H1819
Jer 1:17 Stand up and **s** to them whatever I H1819
Jer 2:23 "How *can you* **s**, 'I am not defiled; I have H606
Jer 2:27 *They* **s** to wood, 'You are my father,' and to H606
Jer 2:27 are in trouble, *they* **s**, 'Come and save us! H606
Jer 2:31 Why *do* my people **s**, 'We are free to roam H606
Jer 2:35 *you* **s**, 'I am innocent; he is not angry with H606
Jer 2:35 I will pass judgment on you because you **s**, H606
Jer 3:16 the LORD, "*people will* no longer **s**, 'The ark H606
Jer 4:5 in Judah and proclaim in Jerusalem and **s**: H606
Jer 4:5 Cry aloud and **s**: 'Gather together! H606
Jer 5:2 Although *they* **s**, 'As surely as the LORD lives H606
Jer 5:13 in them; so let what *they* **s** be done to them." NDT
Jer 5:24 *They do* not **s** to themselves, 'Let us fear H606
Jer 6:14 peace,' they **s**, when there is no H606
Jer 7:4 Do not trust in deceptive words and **s**, "This H606
Jer 7:10 bears my Name, and **s**, "We are safe"— H606
Jer 7:28 Therefore **s** to them, 'This is the nation that H606
Jer 8:4 "**S** to them, 'This is what the LORD says: H606
Jer 8:6 attentively, but *they do* not **s** what is right. H1819
Jer 8:8 " 'How *can you* **s**, "We are wise, for we H606
Jer 8:11 peace," they **s**, when there is no H606
Jer 9:22 **S**, "This is what the LORD declares: " 'Dead H1819
Jer 13:12 "**S** to them: 'This is what the LORD, the God H606
Jer 13:12 And if *they* **s** to you, 'Don't we know that H606
Jer 13:18 **S** to the king and to the queen mother H606
Jer 13:21 What *will you* **s** when the LORD sets over H606
Jer 16:11 then **s** to them, 'It is because your ancestors H606
Jer 16:19 will come from the ends of the earth and **s**, H606
Jer 17:20 **S** to them, 'Hear the word of the LORD, you H606
Jer 18:11 "Now therefore **s** to the people of Judah H606
Jer 19:3 **s**, 'Hear the word of the LORD, you kings H606
Jer 19:11 **s** to them, 'This is what the LORD H606
Jer 20:9 But if *I* **s**, "I will not mention his word or H606
Jer 21:11 "Moreover, **s** to the royal house of Judah NDT
Jer 21:13 the LORD—you who **s**, "Who can come H606
Jer 23:7 "when *people will* no longer **s**, 'As H606
Jer 23:8 they will **s**, 'As surely as the LORD lives NDT
Jer 23:17 the stubbornness of their hearts *they* **s**, H606
Jer 23:25 what the prophets **s** who prophesy lies in H606
Jer 23:25 lies in my name. They **s**, 'I had a dream! H606
Jer 23:33 from the LORD?' **s** to them, 'What message H606
Jer 25:30 these words against them and **s** to them: H606
Jer 26:4 **S** to them, 'This is what the LORD says: If H606
Jer 26:8 the LORD had commanded him to **s**, H1819
Jer 27:4 them a message for their masters and **s**, H606
Jer 27:14 to the words of the prophets who **s** to you, H606
Jer 27:16 Do not listen to the prophets *who* **s**, 'Very H606
Jer 28:7 listen to what I *have to* **s** in your hearing H1819
Jer 29:15 *You may* **s**, "The LORD has raised up H606
Jer 31:7 your praises heard, and **s**, 'LORD, save your H606
Jer 31:29 "In those days *people will* no longer **s**, 'The H606
Jer 31:34 their neighbor, or **s** *to* one another, 'Know H606
Jer 32:3 You **s**, 'This is what the LORD H606
Jer 32:7 your uncle is going to come to you and **s**, H606
Jer 32:25 Sovereign LORD, **s** to me, 'Buy the field with H606
Jer 32:43 will be bought in this land of which you **s**, H606
Jer 33:10 'You **s** about this place, "It is a desolate H606
Jer 36:14 the son of Cushi, to **s** to Baruch, "Bring the H606
Jer 38:22 Those *women will* **s** to you: H606
Jer 38:25 they come to you and **s**, 'Tell us what H606
Jer 38:27 everything the king had ordered him to **s**. H1821
Jer 42:13 "However, if you **s**, 'We will not stay in this H606
Jer 42:14 if you **s**, 'No, we will go and live in H606
Jer 43:2 The LORD our God has not sent you to **s** H606
Jer 43:10 Then **s** to them, 'This is what the LORD H606
Jer 45:4 But the LORD has told me to **s** to you, 'This H606
Jer 46:16 *They will* **s**, 'Get up, let us go back to our H606
Jer 48:14 "How *can you* **s**, 'We are warriors, men H606
Jer 48:17 who know her fame; **s**, 'How broken is the H606
Jer 49:4 you trust in your riches and **s**, 'Who will NDT
Jer 49:10 neighbors, so there is no one to **s**, NDT
Jer 49:14 an envoy was sent to the nations to **s** NDT
Jer 50:2 keep nothing back, but **s**, 'Babylon will be H606
Jer 51:35 be on Babylon," **s** the inhabitants of Zion. H606
Jer 51:62 Then **s**, 'LORD, you have said you will destroy H606
Jer 51:64 Then **s**, 'So will Babylon sink to rise no H606
La 2:12 *They* **s** to their mothers, "Where is bread H606
La 2:13 What *can I* **s** *for* you? With what can I H6386
La 2:16 they scoff and gnash their teeth and **s**, "We H606
La 3:18 So *I* **s**, "My splendor is gone and all that I H606
La 3:24 I **s** *to* myself, "The LORD is my portion H606
La 3:41 our hands to God in heaven, and **s**: NDT
La 4:15 *people* among the nations **s**, "They H606
Eze 2:4 **S** to them, 'This is what the Sovereign LORD H606
Eze 2:6 not be afraid of **what** they **s** or be terrified H1821
Eze 2:8 son of man, listen to what I **s** to you. H1819
Eze 3:11 **S** to them, 'This is what the Sovereign LORD H606
Eze 3:18 When I **s** to a wicked person, 'You will H606
Eze 3:27 open your mouth and *you shall* **s** to them, H606
Eze 6:3 **s**: 'You mountains of Israel, hear the H606
Eze 8:12 *They* **s**, 'The LORD does not see us; the LORD H606
Eze 9:9 *They* **s**, 'The LORD has forsaken the land H606
Eze 11:3 They **s**, 'Haven't our houses been recently H606
Eze 11:5 the LORD came on me, and he told me *to* **s**: H606
Eze 11:16 "Therefore **s**: 'This is what the Sovereign H606
Eze 11:17 "Therefore **s**: 'This is what the Sovereign H606
Eze 12:10 "**S** to them, 'This is what the Sovereign H606
Eze 12:11 **S** to them, 'I am a sign to you.' "As I have H606
Eze 12:19 **S** to the people of the land: 'This is what H606
Eze 12:23 **S** to them, 'This is what the Sovereign LORD H606
Eze 12:23 **S** to them, 'The days are near when every H1819
Eze 12:25 I will fulfill *whatever I* **s**, declares H1819+1821
Eze 12:28 "Therefore **s** to them, 'This is what the H606
Eze 12:28 longer; whatever *I* **s** will be fulfilled H1819+1821
Eze 13:2 **S** to those who prophesy out of their own H606
Eze 13:6 not sent them, they **s**, "The LORD declares," H606
Eze 13:7 uttered lying divinations when you **s**, H606
Eze 13:15 *I will* **s** to you, "The wall is gone and so are H606
Eze 13:18 **s**, 'This is what the Sovereign LORD says H606
Eze 14:6 "Therefore **s** to the people of Israel, 'This is H606
Eze 14:17 I bring a sword against that country and **s**, H606
Eze 16:3 **s**, 'This is what the Sovereign LORD says H606
Eze 17:3 **S** to them, 'This is what the Sovereign LORD H606
Eze 17:9 "**S** to them, 'This is what the Sovereign H606
Eze 17:12 "**S** to this rebellious people, 'Do you not H606
Eze 17:12 these things mean?' **S** to them: 'The king H606
Eze 18:25 "Yet *you* **s**, 'The way of the Lord is not just.' H606
Eze 18:29 Yet the Israelites **s**, 'The way of the Lord is H606
Eze 19:2 **s**: " 'What a lioness was your mother H606
Eze 20:3 speak to the elders of Israel and **s** to them H606
Eze 20:5 **s** to them: 'This is what the Sovereign H606
Eze 20:27 speak to the people of Israel and **s** to them, H606
Eze 20:30 "Therefore **s** to the Israelites: 'This is what H606
Eze 20:32 " 'You **s**, "We want to be like the nations H606
Eze 20:47 **S** to the southern forest: 'Hear the word of H606
Eze 21:3 **s** to her: 'This is what the LORD says: H606
Eze 21:7 *you shall* **s**, 'Because of the news that is H606
Eze 21:9 prophesy and **s**, 'This is what the H606
Eze 21:28 prophesy and **s**, 'This is what the H606
Eze 22:3 **s**: 'This is what the Sovereign LORD says H606
Eze 22:24 "Son of man, **s** to the land, 'You are a land H606
Eze 22:28 *They* **s**, 'This is what the Sovereign LORD H606
Eze 24:3 rebellious people a parable and **s** to them: H606
Eze 24:21 **S** to the people of Israel, 'This is what the H606
Eze 25:3 **S** to them, 'Hear the word of the Sovereign H606
Eze 26:17 up a lament concerning you and **s** to you: H606
Eze 27:3 **S** to Tyre, situated at the gateway to the sea H606
Eze 27:3 " 'You **s**, Tyre, "I am perfect in H606
Eze 28:2 "Son of man, **s** to the ruler of Tyre, 'This is H606
Eze 28:2 " 'In the pride of your heart *you* **s**, "I am a H606
Eze 28:9 *Will you then* **s**, "I am a god," in the H606+606
Eze 28:12 concerning the king of Tyre and **s** to him: H606
Eze 28:22 **s**: 'This is what the Sovereign LORD says H606
Eze 29:3 Speak to him and **s**: 'This is what the H606
Eze 29:3 *You* **s**, "The Nile belongs to me; I made it H606
Eze 30:2 prophesy and **s**: 'This is what the H606
Eze 30:2 " 'Wail and **s**, "Alas for that day!" NDT
Eze 31:2 **s** to Pharaoh king of Egypt and to his H606
Eze 32:2 Pharaoh king of Egypt and **s** to him: H606
Eze 32:19 **S** to them, 'Are you more favored than others NDT
Eze 32:21 the mighty leaders *will* **s** of Egypt and her H1819
Eze 33:2 speak to your people and **s** to them: H606
Eze 33:8 When I **s** to the wicked, 'You wicked person H606
Eze 33:10 "Son of man, **s** to the Israelites, 'This is H606
Eze 33:11 **S** to them, 'As surely as I live, declares the H606
Eze 33:12 son of man, **s** to your people, 'If someone H606
Eze 33:14 And if I **s** to a wicked person, 'You will H606
Eze 33:17 "Yet your people **s**, 'The way of the Lord is H606
Eze 33:20 Yet *you* Israelites **s**, 'The way of the Lord is H606
Eze 33:25 Therefore **s** to them, 'This is what the H606
Eze 33:27 "**S** this to them: 'This is what the Sovereign H606
Eze 34:2 of Israel; prophesy and **s** to them: H606
Eze 35:3 **s**: 'This is what the Sovereign LORD says H606
Eze 36:1 prophesy to the mountains of Israel and **s** H606
Eze 36:3 Therefore prophesy and **s**, 'This is what the H606
Eze 36:6 land of Israel and **s** to the mountains and H606
Eze 36:13 Because *some* **s** to you, "You devour H606
Eze 36:22 "Therefore **s** to the Israelites, 'This is what H606
Eze 36:35 *They will* **s**, "This land that was laid waste H606
Eze 37:4 "Prophesy to these bones and **s** to them H606
Eze 37:9 son of man, and **s** to it, 'This is what the H606
Eze 37:11 *They* **s**, 'Our bones are dried up and our H606
Eze 37:12 Therefore prophesy and **s** to them: 'This is H606
Eze 37:19 **s** to them, 'This is what the Sovereign H1819
Eze 37:21 **s** to them, 'This is what the Sovereign H1819
Eze 38:3 **s**: 'This is what the Sovereign LORD says H606
Eze 38:11 *You will* **s**, "I will invade a land of unwalled H606
Eze 38:13 Tarshish and all her villages *will* **s** to you, H606
Eze 38:14 son of man, prophesy and **s** to Gog: H606
Eze 39:1 prophesy against Gog and **s**: 'This is what H606
Eze 44:6 **S** to rebellious Israel, 'This is what the H606
Da 3:29 language who **s** anything against the A10042
Da 4:35 one can hold back his hand or **s** to him: A10042
Da 11:36 every god and *will* **s** unheard-of things H1819
Hos 2:1 "**S** of your brothers, 'My people,' and of H606
Hos 2:7 Then *she will* **s**, 'I will go back to my H606
Hos 2:23 *I will* **s** to those called 'Not my people,' H606
Hos 2:23 people'; and they *will* **s**, 'You are my God.' H606
Hos 10:3 Then *they will* **s**, "We have no king H606
Hos 10:8 Then *they will* **s** to the mountains, "Cover H606
Hos 14:2 return to the LORD. **S** to him: "Forgive all H606
Hos 14:3 *We will* never again **s** 'Our gods' to what H606
Joel 2:17 *Let them* **s**, "Spare your H606
Joel 2:17 Why *should they* **s** among the peoples H606
Joel 3:10 *Let* the weakling **s**, "I am H606
Am 4:1 crush the needy and **s** to your husbands, H606
Am 5:14 will be with you, just as *you* **s** he is. H606
Am 6:10 "No," then *he will go on to* **s**, "Hush! H606
Am 6:13 rejoice in the conquest of Lo Debar and **s**, H606
Am 7:16 You **s**, " 'Do not prophesy against Israel H606
Am 8:14 sin of Samaria—*who* **s**, 'As surely as your H606
Am 9:10 all those *who* **s**, 'Disaster will not H606
Ob 1 An envoy was sent to the nations to **s**, "Rise NDT
Ob 3 on the heights, you *who* **s** to yourself, 'Who H606
Jnh 2:9 I will **s**, 'Salvation comes from NDT
Mic 2:6 prophesy," their **prophets s**. "Do not H5752
Mic 3:11 Yet they look for the LORD's support and **s** H606
Mic 4:2 Many nations will come and **s**, "Come, let H606
Mic 4:11 They **s**, "Let her be defiled, let our eyes H606
Mic 6:1 let the hills hear **what** you **have to s**. H7754
Na 3:7 All who see you will flee from you and **s** H606
Hab 2:1 I will look to see what *he will* **s** to me H1819
Zep 3:16 On that day *they will* **s** to Jerusalem, "Do H606
Hag 1:2 "These people **s**, 'The time has not yet H606
Zec 8:21 of one city will go to another and **s**, H606
Zec 8:23 of one Jew by the hem of his robe and **s**, H606
Zec 11:5 Those who sell them **s**, 'Praise the LORD, H606
Zec 12:5 the clans of Judah *will* **s** in their hearts, H606
Zec 13:3 they were born, *will* **s** to them, 'You must H606
Zec 13:5 *Each will* **s**, 'I am not a prophet. I am a H606
Zec 13:9 I will answer them; *I will* **s**, 'They are my H606
Zec 13:9 and they *will* **s**, 'The LORD is our H606
Mal 1:4 Edom *may* **s**, "Though we have been H606
Mal 1:5 You will see it with your own eyes and **s** H606
Mal 1:13 And *you* **s**, 'What a burden!' and you sniff H606
Mt 3:9 And do not think you *can* **s** to yourselves *G3306*
Mt 5:11 you and falsely **s** all kinds of evil against *G3306*
Mt 5:37 All you need to **s** is simply 'Yes' or 'No' *G3364*
Mt 7:4 How *can you* **s** to your brother, 'Let me *G3306*
Mt 7:22 Many *will* **s** to me on that day, 'Lord, Lord *G3306*
Mt 8:8 But just **s** the word, and my servant will be *G3306*
Mt 8:9 I **s** to my servant, 'Do this,' NDT
Mt 8:11 *I* **s** to you that many will come from the *G3306*
Mt 9:5 *to* **s**, 'Your sins are forgiven,' or to say *G3306*
Mt 9:5 are forgiven,' or *to* **s**, 'Get up and walk'? *G3306*
Mt 10:19 not worry about what *to* **s** or how to say it. *G3281*
Mt 10:19 do not worry about what to say or how to **s** it. NDT
Mt 10:19 At that time you will be given what *to* **s**, *G3281*
Mt 11:18 drinking, and *they* **s**, 'He has a demon *G3306*
Mt 11:19 drinking, and *they* **s**, 'Here is a *G3306*
Mt 12:34 can you who are evil **s** anything good? *G3281*

Mt 13:34 he did not s anything to them without G3281
Mt 15: 5 But you s that if anyone declares that what G3306
Mt 16: 2 evening comes, you s, 'It will be fair G3306
Mt 16:13 "Who do people s the Son of Man is?" G3306
Mt 16:14 They replied, "Some s John the Baptist NDT
Mt 16:14 the Baptist; others s Elijah; and still others NDT
Mt 16:15 he asked. "Who do you s I am?" G3306
Mt 17:10 then do the teachers of the law s that G3306
Mt 17:20 mustard seed, you can s to this mountain G3306
Mt 21: 3 s that the Lord needs them G3306
Mt 21: 5 "S to Daughter Zion, 'See, your king G3306
Mt 21:21 but also you can s to this mountain G3306
Mt 21:25 said, "If we s, 'From heaven, G3306
Mt 21:26 But if we s, 'Of human origin'—we are G3306
Mt 22:23 Sadducees, who s there is no resurrection G3306
Mt 22:46 No one could s a word in reply, and from G646
Mt 23:16 You s, 'If anyone swears by the temple, it G3306
Mt 23:18 You also s, 'If anyone swears by the altar, it NDT
Mt 23:30 And you s, 'If we had lived in the days of G3306
Mt 23:39 you will not see me again until you s G3306
Mt 25:34 "Then the King will s to those on his right G3306
Mt 25:41 "Then he will s to those on his left G3306
Mt 26:22 very sad and began to s to him one after G3306
Mt 26:54 be fulfilled that s it must happen in this way NDT
Mt 26:64 Jesus replied. "But I s to all of you: From G3306
Mt 28:13 telling them, "You are to s, 'His disciples G3306
Mk 2: 9 to s to this paralyzed man, 'Your sins are G3306
Mk 2: 9 are forgiven,' or to s, 'Get up, take your G3306
Mk 4:30 shall we s the kingdom of God is like, G3929
Mk 4:34 He did not s anything to them without G3281
Mk 5:41 which means "Little girl, I s to you, get up!" G3306
Mk 7:11 But you s that if anyone declares that what G3306
Mk 8:27 he asked them, "Who do people s I am?" G3306
Mk 8:28 They replied, "Some s John the Baptist NDT
Mk 8:28 the Baptist; others s Elijah; and still others NDT
Mk 8:29 "Who do you s I am?" Peter G3306
Mk 9: 6 He did not know what to s, they were so G646
Mk 9:11 "Why do the teachers of the law s that G3306
Mk 9:39 next moment s anything bad about me, G2800
Mk 11: 3 s, 'The Lord needs it and will send it back G3306
Mk 11:14 And his disciples heard him s it. NDT
Mk 11:23 believes that what they s will happen, G3281
Mk 11:31 said, "If we s, 'From heaven, G3306
Mk 11:32 But if we s, 'Of human origin' …" (They G3306
Mk 12:18 Sadducees, who s there is no resurrection G3306
Mk 12:35 "Why do the teachers of the law s that the G3306
Mk 13:11 do not worry beforehand about what to s. G3281
Mk 13:11 Just s whatever is given you at the time G3281
Mk 13:37 What I s to you, I say to everyone: 'Watch!' G3306
Mk 13:37 What I say to you, I s to everyone: 'Watch!' G3306
Mk 14:14 S to the owner of the house he enters G3306
Mk 14:40 They did not know what to s to him. G646
Mk 14:58 "We heard him s, 'I will destroy this G3306
Lk 3: 8 And do not begin to s to yourselves, 'We G3306
Lk 5: 5 But because you s so, I will let down the G4839
Lk 5:23 to s, 'Your sins are forgiven,' or to say G3306
Lk 5:23 are forgiven,' or to s, 'Get up and walk'? G3306
Lk 5:39 wants the new, for they s, 'The old is G3306
Lk 6:27 "But to you who are listening I s: Love G3306
Lk 6:42 How can you s to your brother, 'Brother, G3306
Lk 6:46 'Lord, Lord,' and do not do what I s? G3306
Lk 7: 6 the centurion sent friends to s to him: G3306
Lk 7: 7 But s the word, and my servant will be G3306
Lk 7: 8 I s to my servant, 'Do this,' NDT
Lk 7:14 He said, "Young man, I s to you, get up!" G3306
Lk 7:31 Jesus went on to s, "To what, then, can I NDT
Lk 7:33 and you s, 'He has a demon. G3306
Lk 7:34 drinking, and you s, 'Here is a glutton G3306
Lk 7:49 guests began to s among themselves, G3306
Lk 9:18 asked them, "Who do the crowds s I am?" G3306
Lk 9:19 They replied, "Some s John the Baptist NDT
Lk 9:19 the Baptist; others s Elijah; and still others NDT
Lk 9:20 "Who do you s I am?" Peter G3306
Lk 9:61 me go back and s goodbye to my family." G698
Lk 10: 5 enter a house, first s, 'Peace to this house G3306
Lk 10:10 not welcomed, go into its streets and s, G3306
Lk 11: 2 to them, "When you pray, s: " 'Father, G3306
Lk 11: 5 you go to him at midnight and s G3306
Lk 11: 9 "So I s to you: Ask and it will be given to G3306
Lk 11:18 I s this because you claim that I drive out NDT
Lk 11:45 "Teacher, when you s these things, you G3306
Lk 11:54 in something he might s. G1666+3836+5125
Lk 12:11 will defend yourselves or what you will s, G3306
Lk 12:12 teach you at that time what you should s." G3306
Lk 12:19 And I'll s to myself, "You have plenty of G3306
Lk 12:54 immediately you s, 'It's going to G3306
Lk 12:55 south wind blows, you s, 'It's going to be G3306
Lk 13:26 "Then you will s, 'We ate and drank with G3306
Lk 13:35 you will not see me again until you s G3306
Lk 14: 6 And they had nothing to s. G503
Lk 14: 9 both of you will come and s to you, G3306
Lk 14:10 your host comes, he will s to you, 'Friend, G3306
Lk 15:18 go back to my father and s to him: G3306
Lk 17: 6 seed, you can s to this mulberry tree G3306
Lk 17: 7 Will he s to the servant when he comes in G3306
Lk 17: 8 Won't he rather s, 'Prepare my supper, get G3306
Lk 17:10 were told to do, should s, 'We are G3306
Lk 17:21 nor will people s, 'Here it is,' or 'There it is G3306
Lk 19:14 him and sent a delegation after him to s, G3306
Lk 19:31 are you untying it?' s, 'The Lord needs it.' G3306
Lk 20: 5 said, "If we s, 'From heaven, G3306
Lk 20: 6 But if we s, 'Of human origin,' all the G3306
Lk 20:27 Sadducees, who s there is no resurrection G3306
Lk 22:11 s to the owner of the house, 'The G3306
Lk 22:70 He replied, "You s that I am." G3306
Lk 23:29 For the time will come when you will s G3306
Lk 23:30 Then " 'they will s to the mountains, "Fall G3306
Jn 1:22 What do you s about yourself?" G3306
Jn 1:37 When the two disciples heard him s this G3281
Jn 4:17 "You are right when you s you have no G3306
Jn 5:47 how are you going to believe what I s?" G4839
Jn 6:14 performed, they began to s, "Surely this is G3306
Jn 6:42 How can he now s, 'I came down from G3306
Jn 6:65 He went on to s, "This is why I told you G3306
Jn 7:13 But no one would s anything publicly G3281
Jn 7:42 Does not Scripture s that the Messiah will G3306
Jn 8: 5 stone such women. Now what do you s?" G3306
Jn 8:26 "I have much to s in judgment of you. G3281
Jn 8:33 How can you s that we shall be set free?" G3306
Jn 8:43 Because you are unable to hear what I s. G3364
Jn 8:52 you s that whoever obeys your word G3306
Jn 9:17 "What have you to s about him? G3306
Jn 9:19 "Is this the one you s was born blind G3306
Jn 9:40 were with him heard him s this and asked, NDT
Jn 11:51 He did not s this on his own, but as high G3306
Jn 12: 6 He did not s this because he cared about G3306
Jn 12:27 my soul is troubled, and what shall I s? G3306
Jn 12:34 so how can you s, 'The Son of G3306
Jn 12:49 me commanded me to s all that I have G3306
Jn 12:50 So whatever I s is just what the Father has G3281
Jn 12:50 is just what the Father has told me to s." G3281
Jn 14: 9 How can you s, 'Show us the G3306
Jn 14:10 The words I s to you I do not speak on my G3306
Jn 14:11 Believe me when I s that I am in the Father NDT
Jn 14:28 "You heard me s, 'I am going away and I G3306
Jn 14:30 I will not s much more to you, for the G3281
Jn 16:12 "I have much more to s to you, more than G3306
Jn 16:16 Jesus went on to s, "In a little while you will NDT
Jn 17:13 but I s these things while I am still in the G3281
Jn 18:37 answered, "You s that I am a king. G3306
Jn 21: 7 As soon as Simon Peter heard him s, "It is NDT
Jn 21:23 But Jesus did not s that he would not die G3306
Ac 2:14 this to you; listen carefully to what I s. G4839
Ac 4:14 with them, there was nothing they could s. G515
Ac 6:11 they secretly persuaded some men to s, G3306
Ac 6:14 For we have heard him s that this Jesus of G3306
Ac 7:31 to get a closer look, he heard the Lord s: G5889
Ac 9: 4 to the ground and heard a voice s to him, G3306
Ac 10:22 so that he could hear what you have to s." G4839
Ac 11:13 seen an angel appear in his house and s, G3306
Ac 17:18 "What is this babbler trying to s? G3306
Ac 19:13 They would s, "In the name of the Jesus G3306
Ac 21:37 commander, "May I s something to you?" G3306
Ac 22: 7 to the ground and heard a voice s to me, G3306
Ac 23: 8 The Sadducees s that there is no G3306
Ac 28:26 " 'Go to this people and s, "You will be G3306
Ro 2:22 You who s that people should not commit G3306
Ro 3: 5 more clearly, what shall we s? G3306
Ro 3: 8 Why not s—as some slanderously claim that NDT
Ro 3: 8 as some slanderously claim that we s G3306
Ro 4: 1 What then shall we s that Abraham, our G3306
Ro 4: 3 What does Scripture s? "Abraham G3306
Ro 6: 1 What shall we s, then? Shall we go on G3306
Ro 7: 7 What shall we s, then? Is the law sinful G3306
Ro 8:31 shall we s in response to these things? G3306
Ro 9:14 What then shall we s? Is God unjust? Not G3306
Ro 9:19 One of you will s to me: "Then why does G3306
Ro 9:20 "Shall what is formed s to the one who G3306
Ro 9:30 What then shall we s? That the Gentiles G3306
Ro 10: 6 "Do not s in your heart, 'Who will ascend G3306
Ro 10: 8 But what does it s? "The word is near you G3306
Ro 11:19 You will s then, "Branches were broken off G3306
Ro 12: 3 the grace given me I s to every one of you G3306
1Co 1:10 of you agree with one another in what you s G3836+899+3306
1Co 1:15 so no one can s that you were baptized in G3306
1Co 6: 5 I s this to shame you. Is it possible that G3306
1Co 6:12 to do anything," you s—but not everything is NDT
1Co 6:13 You s, "Food for the stomach and the NDT
1Co 7: 6 I s this as a concession, not as a command G3306
1Co 7: 8 Now to the unmarried and the widows I s G3306
1Co 7:12 To the rest I s this (I, not the Lord): G3306
1Co 9: 8 Do I s this merely on human authority G3281
1Co 9: 8 Doesn't the Law s the same thing? G3306
1Co 10:15 people; judge for yourselves what I s. G5774
1Co 10:23 to do anything," you s—but not everything is NDT
1Co 11:22 What shall I s to you? Shall I G3306
1Co 12: 3 and no one can s, "Jesus is Lord, G3306
1Co 12:15 Now if the foot should s, "Because I am G3306
1Co 12:16 And if the ear should s, "Because I am not G3306
1Co 12:21 The eye cannot s to the hand, "I don't G3306
1Co 12:21 And the head cannot s to the feet, "I don't NDT
1Co 14:13 pray that they may interpret what they s. NDT
1Co 14:16 can someone else, who is now put in the position of an inquirer, s G3306
1Co 14:23 will they not s that you are out of your G3306
1Co 14:26 What then shall we s, brothers and sisters G1639
1Co 15:12 how can some of you s that there is no G3306
1Co 15:34 ignorant of God—I s this to your shame. G3281
2Co 1:17 so that in the same breath I s both G1639+4123
2Co 5: 8 We are confident, I s, and would prefer to be NDT
2Co 5:13 of our mind," as some s, it is for God; if we NDT
2Co 7: 3 I do not s this to condemn you; I have said G3306
2Co 9: 4 not to s anything about you—would G3306
2Co 10:10 For some s, "His letters are weighty and G5774
2Co 12: 6 than is warranted by what I do or s, G201+1666
Gal 1: 9 already said, so now I s again: If anybody G3306
Gal 3:16 Scripture does not s "and to seeds," G3306
Gal 4:30 But what does Scripture s? "Get rid of the G3306
Gal 5:16 So I s, walk by the Spirit, and you will not G3306
Php 4: 4 the Lord always. I will s it again: Rejoice! G3306
1Th 1: 8 we do not need to s anything about it, G3281
2Ti 2: 2 you have heard me s in the presence of G4123S
2Ti 2:18 They s that the resurrection has already G3306
2Ti 4: 3 to s what their itching ears want to hear G3117+198
Titus 2: 8 they have nothing bad to s about us. G3306
Titus 2:12 It teaches us to s "No" to ungodliness and G766
Heb 1: 5 For to which of the angels did God ever s G3306
Heb 1:13 To which of the angels did God ever s G3306
Heb 5:11 We have much to s about this, but it is G3364
Heb 7: 9 One might even s that Levi G6055+2229+3306
Heb 8:11 their neighbor, or s to one another, 'Know G3306
Heb 9:11 human hands, that is to s, is not a part of AIT
Heb 11:14 People who s such things show that they G3306
Heb 11:32 And what more shall I s? I do not have G3306
Heb 13: 6 So we s with confidence, "The Lord is my G3306
Jas 1:13 tempted, no one should s, "God is G3306
Jas 2: 3 to the man wearing fine clothes and s, G3306
Jas 2: 3 seat for you," but s to the poor man, "You G3306
Jas 2:18 But someone will s, "You have faith; G3306
Jas 3: 2 is never at fault in what they s is perfect, G3364
Jas 4:13 Now listen, you who s, "Today or G3306
Jas 4:15 you ought to s, "If it is the Lord's G3306
Jas 5:12 All you need to s is a simple "Yes G3992+1639
2Pe 3: 4 They will s, "Where is this 'coming' he G3306
2Jn 7 I s this because many deceivers, who do not NDT
Rev 2: 9 slander of those who s they are Jews and G3306
Rev 2:24 Now I s to the rest of you in Thyatira, to G3306
Rev 3:17 You s, 'I am rich; I have acquired wealth G3306
Rev 4:10 lay their crowns before the throne and s: G3306
Rev 6: 1 four living creatures s in a voice like G3306
Rev 6: 3 I heard the second living creature s G3306
Rev 6: 5 I heard the third living creature s, "Come!" G3306
Rev 6: 7 the voice of the fourth living creature s, G3306
Rev 10: 4 I heard a voice from heaven s, "Seal G3306
Rev 12:10 Then I heard a loud voice in heaven s G3306
Rev 14:13 Then I heard a voice from heaven s G3306
Rev 16: 5 heard the angel in charge of the waters s: G3306
Rev 18: 4 Then I heard another voice from heaven s: G3306
Rev 18:14 "They will s, 'The fruit you longed for is NDT
Rev 22:17 The Spirit and the bride s, "Come!" And G3306
Rev 22:17 And let the one who hears s, "Come!" G3306

SAYING (291) [SAY]

Ge 4:25 named him Seth, s, "God has granted NDT
Ge 9: 1 Noah and his sons, s to them, "Be fruitful H606
Ge 14:19 he blessed Abram, s, "Blessed be Abram H606
Ge 19:15 of dawn, the angels urged Lot, s, "Hurry! H606
Ge 24: 7 promised me on oath, s, 'To your offspring H606
Ge 24:21 Without s a word, the man watched her H3087
Ge 24:27 s, "Praise be to the LORD, the God of my H606
Ge 26:22 named it Rehoboth, s, "Now the LORD has H606
Ge 28:20 Jacob made a vow, s, "If God will be with H606
Ge 31: 1 Jacob heard that Laban's sons were s H1821
Ge 32:30 the place Peniel, s, "It is because I saw NDT
Ge 39:19 his wife told him, s, "This is how your slave H606
Ge 50:16 sent word to Joseph, s, "Your father left H606
Ex 2:10 named him Moses, s, "I drew him out of H606
Ex 2:22 named him Gershom, s, "I have become a H606
Ex 5:13 kept pressing them, s, "Complete the work H606
Ex 5:17 That is why you keep s, 'Let us go and H606
Ex 11: 8 bowing down before me and s, 'Go, H606
Ex 15:24 against Moses, s, "What are we to drink?" H606
Ex 17: 7 because they tested the LORD s, H606
Ex 33: 1 Isaac and Jacob, s, 'I will give it to your H606
Nu 11:20 wailed before him, s, "Why did we ever H606
Nu 14:40 in the hill country, s, "Now we are ready to H606
Nu 16:31 As soon as he finished s all this, the H1819
Nu 20:14 from Kadesh to the king of Edom, s: NDT
Nu 27: 7 "What Zelophehad's daughters are s is H1819
Nu 30:14 them by s nothing to her when he H3087
Nu 36: 5 of the descendants of Joseph is s is right. H1819
Dt 1: 5 Moses began to expound this law, s: H606
Dt 2:26 king of Heshbon offering peace and s, H606
Dt 12:30 about their gods, s, "How do these nations H606
Dt 13: 6 secretly entices you, s, "Let us go and H606
Dt 13:13 of their town astray, s, "Let us go and H606
Dt 22:14 gives her a bad name, s, "I married this H606
Dt 25: 8 If he persists in s, "I do not want to marry H606
Dt 33:27 your enemies before you, s, 'Destroy them! H606
Jos 9:22 "Why did you deceive us by s, 'We live a H606
Jos 22: 8 s, "Return to your homes with your great H606
Jdg 5:29 indeed, she keeps s to herself, H8740+609
Jdg 6:32 Jerub-Baal that day, s, "Let Baal contend H606
Jdg 7:11 listen to what they are s. Afterward H1819
Jdg 7:13 "I had a dream," he was s. "A round loaf of H606
Jdg 7:24 country of Ephraim, s, "Come down against H606
Jdg 8:15 about whom you taunted me by s, 'Do you H606
Jdg 9:31 to Abimelek, s, "Gaal son of Ebed and H606
Jdg 11:15 s: "This is what Jephthah says: Israel did H606
Jdg 11:17 to the king of Edom, s, 'Give us permission H606
Jdg 16: 2 during the night, s, "At dawn we'll kill H606
Jdg 16:23 god and to celebrate, s, "Our god has H606
Jdg 16:24 praised their god, s, "Our god has H606
Jdg 19:30 Everyone who saw it was s to one another H606

S

Jdg 20: 8 up together as one, s, "None of us will go H606
Jdg 20:12 the tribe of Benjamin, s, "What about this H606
Jdg 20:32 While the Benjamites *were* s, "We are H606
Jdg 20:32 the Israelites *were* s, "Let's retreat and H606
Jdg 21:20 the Benjamites, s, "Go and hide in the H606
Ru 3:17 measures of barley, s, 'Don't go back to H606
1Sa 1:11 And she made a vow, s, "LORD Almighty, if H606
1Sa 1:20 named him Samuel, s, "Because I asked the NDT
1Sa 2:20 Elkanah and his wife, s, "May the LORD give H606
1Sa 4:21 named the boy Ichabod, s, "The Glory has H606
1Sa 6:21 of Kiriath Jearim, s, "The Philistines have H606
1Sa 7:12 named it Ebenezer, s, "Thus far the LORD H606
1Sa 8: 7 "Listen to all that the people *are* s to you; it H606
1Sa 10: 1 head and kissed him, s, "Has not the LORD H606
1Sa 10:12 So it became a s: "Is Saul also among H5442
1Sa 14:24 under an oath, s, "Cursed be anyone H606
1Sa 14:28 under a strict oath, s, 'Cursed be anyone H606
1Sa 15:18 you on a mission, s, 'Go and completely H606
1Sa 16:22 sent word to Jesse, s, "Allow David to H606
1Sa 17:25 Now the Israelites *had been* s, "Do you see H606
1Sa 17:27 him what they had been s and told him, H1821
1Sa 18:11 he hurled it, s to himself, "I'll pin David H606
1Sa 20:16 the house of David, s, "May the LORD call NDT
1Sa 20:42 name of the LORD, s, 'The LORD is witness H606
1Sa 23: 2 inquired of the LORD, s, "Shall I go and H606
1Sa 23:27 messenger came to Saul, s, "Come quickly! H606
1Sa 24:13 As the old s goes, 'From evildoers come H5442
1Sa 24:16 When David finished s this, Saul asked H1819
1Sa 30:20 of the other livestock, s, "This is David's H606
1Sa 30:26 were his friends, s, "Here is a gift H4200+606
2Sa 3:35 David took an oath, s, "May God deal with H606
2Sa 7: 4 the word of the LORD came to Nathan, s: H606
2Sa 7:27 this to your servant, s, 'I will build a house H606
2Sa 11: 5 sent word to David, s, "I am pregnant." H606
2Sa 12:27 messengers to David, s, "I have fought H606
2Sa 19: 9 among themselves, s, "The king delivered H606
2Sa 19:41 were coming to the king and s to him, H606
2Sa 21:17 men swore to him, s, "Never again will you H606
2Sa 24: 1 David against them, s, "Go and take a H606
1Ki 1:25 are eating and drinking with him and s, H606
1Ki 1:47 our lord King David, s, 'May your God H606
1Ki 8:55 whole assembly of Israel in a loud voice, s: H606
1Ki 18:31 the LORD had come, s, "Your name shall be H606
1Ki 20: 2 to Ahab king of Israel, s, "This is what H606
1Ki 21:13 before the people, s, "Naboth has cursed H606
2Ki 1: 2 So he sent messengers, s to them, "Go H606
2Ki 2:21 the salt into it, s, "This is what the LORD H606
2Ki 10: 6 them a second letter, s, "If you are on my H606
2Ki 11: 5 He commanded them, s, "This is what you H606
2Ki 18:22 removed, s to Judah and Jerusalem H606
1Ch 4: 9 had named him Jabez, s, "I gave birth to H606
1Ch 17: 3 night the word of God came to Nathan, s: H606
1Ch 29:10 the whole assembly, s, "Praise be to you, H606
2Ch 7: 3 gave thanks to the LORD, s, "He is good; NDT
2Ch 7: 6 when he gave thanks, s, "His love endures NDT
2Ch 20: 8 built in it a sanctuary for your Name, s, H606
2Ch 20:21 as they went out at the head of the army, s: H606
2Ch 20:37 against Jehoshaphat, s, "Because you have H606
2Ch 30:18 prayed for them, s, "May the LORD, H606
2Ch 32:12 altars, s to Judah and Jerusalem H606
2Ch 32:17 the God of Israel, and s this against him: H606
2Ch 35:21 messengers to him, s, "What quarrel is H606
Ne 1: 8 your servant Moses, s, 'If you are unfaithful, H606
Ne 2:20 I answered them *by* s, "The God of heaven H606
Ne 5: 2 Some *were* s, "We and our sons and H606
Ne 5: 3 Others *were* s, "We are mortgaging our H606
Ne 5: 4 Still others *were* s, "We have had to borrow H606
Ne 6: 8 "Nothing like what you *are* s is happening H606
Ne 8:11 Levites calmed all the people, s, "Be still, H606
Job 22:19 rejoice; the innocent mock them, s, NDT
Ps 2: 2 the LORD and against his anointed, s, NDT
Ps 2: 5 his anger and terrifies them in his wrath, s, NDT
Ps 3: 2 Many *are* s of me, "God will not deliver H606
Ps 39: 2 utterly silent, **not** *even* s anything good. H3120
Ps 41: 7 they imagine the worst for me, s, NDT
Ps 42:10 as my foes taunt me, s to me all day long H606
Ps 52: 6 will see and fear; they will laugh at you, s, NDT
Ps 55: 3 because of **what** my enemy is s, because H7754
Ps 90: 3 turn people back to dust, s, "Return to dust, H606
Ps 110: 2 scepter from Zion, s, "Rule in the midst of NDT
Ps 132: 7 let us worship at his footstool, s, NDT
Ps 132:13 he has desired it for his dwelling, s, NDT
Isa 6: 8 Then I heard the voice of the Lord s H606
Isa 7: 5 Remaliah's son have plotted your ruin, s, H606
Isa 19:25 will bless them, s, "Blessed be Egypt my H606
Isa 30:21 a voice behind you, s, "This is the way; H606
Isa 36: 7 removed, s to Judah and Jerusalem H606
Isa 45:14 plead with you, s, 'Surely God is with NDT
Isa 47: 8 lounging in your security and s to yourself H606
Jer 1: 4 The word of the LORD came to me, s, H606
Jer 4:10 deceived this people and Jerusalem by s, H606
Jer 4:31 stretching out her hands and s, "Alas! NDT
Jer 8: 6 of their wickedness, s, "What have I done?" H606
Jer 11: 7 them again and again, s, "Obey me." H606
Jer 11:19 plotted against me, s, "Let us destroy the NDT
Jer 11:21 to kill you, s, "Do not prophesy in the H606
Jer 12: 4 Moreover, *the people are* s, "He will not H606
Jer 12:16 swear by my name, s, 'As surely as the NDT
Jer 14:15 send them, yet they *are* s, 'No sword or H606
Jer 17:15 They *keep* s to me, "Where is the word of H606
Jer 18:19 LORD; hear **what** my accusers are s! H7754
Jer 20:10 waiting for me to slip, s, "Perhaps he will be NDT
Jer 20:15 made him very glad, s, "A child is born to H606
Jer 23:17 *They* **keep** s to those who despise me, H606+606
Jer 23:35 is what each of *you keeps* s to your friends H606
Jer 23:37 This is what *you keep* s to a prophet: 'What H606
Jer 31: 3 to us in the past, s: "I have loved you with NDT
Jer 32: 3 him there, s, "Why do you prophesy H606
Jer 32:36 "You *are* s about this city, 'By the sword H606
Jer 33:11 house of the LORD, s, "Give thanks to the H606
Jer 33:24 you not noticed that these people *are* s, H1819
Jer 35:12 the word of the LORD came to Jeremiah, s: H606
Jer 38: 4 the people, by the things he *is* s to them. H1819
Jer 40:16 *What* you *are* s about Ishmael is not true." H1819
Eze 9:11 brought back word, s, "I have done as you H606
Eze 11: 5 That is what *you are* s, you leaders in Israel H606
Eze 12:27 the Israelites *are* s, 'The vision he H606
Eze 13:10 they lead my people astray, s, "Peace," H606
Eze 20:49 "Sovereign LORD, they *are* s of me, 'Isn't he H606
Eze 33:10 say to the Israelites, 'This is what *you are* s: H606
Eze 33:24 in those ruins in the land of Israel *are* s, H606
Eze 33:30 of the houses, s to each other, 'Come H1819
Da 4:23 coming down from heaven and s, 'Cut A10042
Da 10:15 While he *was* s this to me, I bowed with H1819
Da 12: 7 him who lives forever, s, "It will be for a NDT
Am 7:11 For this is what Amos *is* s: " 'Jeroboam will H606
Am 8: 5 s, "When will the New Moon be over that H606
Hab 2: 6 ridicule and scorn, s, " 'Woe to him who H606
Mal 1: 7 "By s that the LORD's table is contemptible. H606
Mal 1:12 "But you profane it by s, 'The Lord's table H606
Mal 2:17 By s, "All who do evil are good in the eyes H606
Mt 3: 2 s, "Repent, for the kingdom of heaven G3306
Mt 3:14 tried to deter him, s, "I need to be G3306
Mt 6:31 So do not worry, s, 'What shall we eat?' G3306
Mt 7:28 When Jesus had finished s these things G3364
Mt 8:25 went and woke him, s, "Lord, save us! G3306
Mt 9:18 *While* he *was* s this, a synagogue leader G3281
Mt 13: 3 he told them many things in parables, s: G3306
Mt 14: 4 John *had been* s to him: "It is not G3306
Mt 14:33 boat worshiped him, s, "Truly you are the G3306
Mt 19: 1 When Jesus had finished s these things G3364
Mt 21: 2 s to them, "Go to the village ahead of you G3306
Mt 21:16 "Do you hear what these children *are* s?" G3306
Mt 22: 1 Jesus spoke to them again in parables, s: G3306
Mt 26: 1 Jesus had finished s all these things, G3364
Mt 26:26 gave it to his disciples, s, "Take and eat; G3306
Mt 26:27 he gave it to them, s, "Drink from it, all of G3306
Mt 26:44 prayed the third time, s the same thing. G3306
Mt 27:40 s, "You who are going to destroy the G3306
Mk 2:12 they praised God, s, "We have never seen G3306
Mk 3:30 He said this because *they were* s, "He has G3306
Mk 6:14 *Some were* s, "John the Baptist has been G3306
Mk 6:18 For John *had been* s to Herod, "It is not G3306
Mk 7:19 out of the body." (In s this, Jesus declared NDT
Mk 8:26 Jesus sent him home, s, "Don't even go G3306
Mk 11: 2 s to them, "Go to the village ahead of you G3306
Mk 12: 6 sent him last of all, s, 'They will respect G3306
Mk 12:32 "*You are* right *in* s that God is one and G3306
Mk 14: 4 those present *were* s **indignantly** to one G24
Mk 14:22 it and gave it to his disciples, s, "Take it; G3306
Mk 15:29 shaking their heads and s, "So! G3306
Lk 2:13 with the angel, praising God and s, G3306
Lk 2:28 took him in his arms and praised God, s: G3306
Lk 2:50 not understand what *he was* s to them. G3281
Lk 4:21 He began *by* s to them, "Today this G3306
Lk 7: 1 Jesus had finished s all this to the people G4839
Lk 8:24 disciples went and woke him, s, "Master, G3306
Lk 8:38 go with him, but Jesus sent him away, s, G3306
Lk 9: 7 because some *were* s that John had been G3306
Lk 9:33 (He did not know what *he was* s.) G3306
Lk 9:35 came from the cloud, s, "This is my Son, G3306
Lk 11:27 As Jesus *was* s these things, a woman in G3306
Lk 12: 1 Jesus began to speak first to his disciples, s: NDT
Lk 14:30 s, 'This person began to build and wasn't G3306
Lk 17: 4 seven times come back to you s 'I repent, G3306
Lk 19:29 he sent two of his disciples, s to them, G3306
Lk 22: 8 sent Peter and John, s, "Go and make G3306
Lk 22:19 gave it to them, s, "This is my body G3306
Lk 22:20 he took the cup, s, "This cup is the new G3306
Lk 23: 2 to accuse him, s, "We have found this G3306
Lk 24:34 s, "It is true! The Lord has risen and G3306
Jn 1:15 He cried out, s, "This is the one I spoke G3306
Jn 3: 7 You should not be surprised at *my* s, 'You G3306
Jn 4:35 Don't you **have a** s, 'It's still four months G3306
Jn 4:37 Thus the s 'One sows and another reaps' G3364
Jn 7:26 publicly, and *they are* not s a word to him. G3306
Jn 8:48 "Aren't we right *in* s that you are a G3306
Jn 9: 6 *After* s this, he spit on the ground, made G3306
Jn 10:24 around him, s, "How long will you G3306
Jn 16:17 "What does he mean *by* s, 'In a little G3306
Jn 16:18 We don't understand what *he is* s." G3281
Jn 16:26 *I am* not s that I will ask the Father on G3306
Jn 18:25 He denied it, s, "I am not." G3306
Jn 19: 3 went up to him again and again, s, "Hail, G3306
Ac 3:18 prophets, s that his Messiah would suffer. NDT
Ac 7:26 He tried to reconcile them *by* s, "Men, you G3306
Ac 11:18 objections and praised God, s, "So then, G3306
Ac 13:15 sent word to them, s, "Brothers, G3306
Ac 13:45 what Paul *was* s and heaped abuse on G3281
Ac 17: 7 decrees, s that there is another king G3306
Ac 21: 6 *After* s **goodbye** to each other, we went G571
Ac 26:14 I heard a voice s to me in Aramaic G3306
Ac 26:22 *I am* s nothing beyond what the prophets G3306
Ac 26:25 "What *I am* s is true and reasonable G710
Ac 26:31 the room, *they began* s to one another G3281
Ro 4: 9 *We have been* s that Abraham's faith was G3306
1Co 4: 6 you may learn from us the meaning of the s, NDT
1Co 7:35 *I am* s this for your own good, not to G3306
1Co 11:25 he took the cup, s, "This cup is the new G3306
1Co 14: 9 how will anyone know what *you are* s? G3281
1Co 14:11 grasp the meaning *of* what someone is s, G5889
1Co 14:16 since they do not know what *you are* s? G3306
1Co 15:54 then the s that is written will come true: G3364
Gal 4: 1 *What I am* s is that as long as an heir is G3306
Php 4:11 *I am* not s this because I am in need, for I G3306
1Th 5: 3 While *people are* s, "Peace and safety," G3306
1Ti 1:15 Here is a trustworthy s that deserves full G3364
1Ti 3: 1 Here is a trustworthy s: Whoever aspires G3364
1Ti 4: 9 This is a trustworthy s that deserves full G3364
1Ti 5:13 talk nonsense, s things they ought not to. G3281
2Ti 2: 7 Reflect on what *I am* s, for the Lord will G3306
2Ti 2:11 Here is a trustworthy s: If we died with G3364
Titus 1:13 This s is true. Therefore rebuke them G3456
Titus 3: 8 This is a trustworthy s. And I want you to G3364
Heb 6:14 s, "I will surely bless you and give you G3306
Heb 8: 1 the main point of what we are s is this: G3306
2Pe 1:17 from the Majestic Glory, s, "This is my Son, NDT
1Jn 5:16 *I am* not s that you should pray about that. G3306
Rev 4: 8 Day and night they never stop s: " 'Holy, G3306
Rev 5: 9 sang a new song, s: "You are worthy to G3306
Rev 5:12 In a loud voice *they were* s: "Worthy is the G3306
Rev 5:13 on the sea, and all that is in them, s: G3306
Rev 6: 6 living creatures, s, "Two pounds of wheat G3306
Rev 7:12 s: "Amen! Praise and glory and wisdom G3306
Rev 11:12 a loud voice from heaven s to them, G3306
Rev 11:17 s: "We give thanks to you, Lord God G3306
Rev 16: 1 from the temple s to the seven angels, G3306
Rev 16:17 loud voice from the throne, s, "It is done!" G3306
Rev 19: 5 came from the throne, s: "Praise our God, G3306
Rev 21: 3 And I heard a loud voice from the throne s, G3306

SAYINGS (10) [SAY]

Ps 49:13 of their followers, who approve their s. H7023
Pr 1: 6 parables, the s and riddles *of* the wise. H1821
Pr 22:17 turn your ear to the s *of* the wise; H1821
Pr 22:20 Have I not written thirty s for you, sayings of NDT
Pr 22:20 sayings for you, s of counsel and knowledge NDT
Pr 24:23 These also are s of the wise: To show NDT
Pr 30: 1 The s *of* Agur son of Jakeh—an inspired H1821
Pr 31: 1 The s *of* King Lemuel—an inspired H1821
Ecc 12:11 their **collected** s like firmly H1251+670
Jn 10:21 "These are not the s of a man possessed G4839

SAYS (737) [SAY]

Ge 24:14 that I may have a drink,' and *she* s, 'Drink, H606
Ge 24:44 if *she* s to me, "Drink, and I'll draw H606
Ge 32: 4 'Your servant Jacob s, I have been staying H606
Ge 45: 9 say to him, 'This is what your son Joseph s: H606
Ex 4:22 say to Pharaoh, 'This is what the LORD s: H606
Ex 5: 1 "This is what the LORD, the God of Israel, s: H606
Ex 5:10 to the people, "This is what Pharaoh s: H606
Ex 7: 9 "When Pharaoh s to you, 'Perform a H1819
Ex 7:17 This is what the LORD s: By this you will H606
Ex 8: 1 say to him, 'This is what the LORD s: H606
Ex 8:20 say to him, 'This is what the LORD s: H606
Ex 9: 1 what the LORD, the God of the Hebrews, s: H606
Ex 9:13 what the LORD, the God of the Hebrews, s: H606
Ex 10: 3 what the LORD, the God of the Hebrews, s: H606
Ex 11: 4 "This is what the LORD s: 'About midnight I H606
Ex 22: 9 lost property about which *somebody* s, H606
Ex 23:21 attention to him and listen to **what** he s. H7754
Ex 23:22 carefully to **what** he s and do all that I H7754
Ex 32:27 "This is what the LORD, the God of Israel, s: H606
Nu 20:14 "This is what your brother Israel s: You H606
Nu 21:14 is why the Book of the Wars of the LORD s: H606
Nu 22:16 "This is what Balak son of Zippor s: Do not H606
Nu 23:26 not tell you I must do whatever the LORD s? H1819
Nu 24:13 I must say only what the LORD s'? H1819
Nu 30: 4 her vow or pledge but s **nothing** to her, H3087
Nu 30: 7 hears about it but s **nothing** to her, H3087
Nu 30:11 about it but s **nothing** to her and does H3087
Nu 30:14 husband s **nothing** to her *about* it H3087+3087
Nu 32:27 to fight before the LORD, just as our lord s." H1819
Dt 5:27 listen to all that the LORD our God s. H606
Dt 13: 2 the prophet s, "Let us follow other H606
Dt 15:16 But if your servant s to you, "I do not want H606
Dt 29: 5 Yet the LORD s, "During the forty years that NDT
Jos 7:13 this is what the LORD, the God of Israel, s: H606
Jos 22:16 "The whole assembly of the LORD s: 'How H606
Jos 24: 2 "This is what the LORD, the God of Israel, s: H606
Jdg 6: 8 "This is what the LORD, the God of Israel, s: H606
Jdg 11:15 "This is what Jephthah s: Israel did not H606
1Sa 2:27 said to him, "This is what the LORD s: H606
1Sa 9: 6 everything *he* s comes true. H1819
1Sa 10:18 "This is what the LORD, the God of Israel, s: H606
1Sa 15: 2 This is what the LORD Almighty s: 'I will H606
1Sa 20: 7 If *he* s, 'Very well,' then your servant is safe H606
2Sa 7: 5 my servant David, 'This is what the LORD s: H606
2Sa 7: 8 'This is what the LORD Almighty s: H606
2Sa 12: 7 the God of Israel, s: 'I anointed you king H606
2Sa 12:11 "This is what the LORD s: 'Out of your own H606
2Sa 14:10 replied, "If anyone s anything to you H1819
2Sa 14:13 When the king s this, does he not convict H1819
2Sa 14:17 "And now your servant s, 'May the word of H606
2Sa 14:19 the left from anything my lord the king s. H1819
2Sa 15:26 But if *he* s, 'I am not pleased with you,' H606

S

2Sa 17: 6 Should we do **what** he **s**? If not, H1821
2Sa 24:12 'This is what the LORD **s**: I am giving you H606
1Ki 1:51 *He* **s**, 'Let King Solomon swear to me today H606
1Ki 2:30 said to Joab, "The king **s**, 'Come out! H606
1Ki 2:31 king commanded Benaiah, "Do as *he* **s**. H1819
1Ki 3:23 king said, "This one **s**, 'My son is alive H606
1Ki 3:23 your son is dead,' while that one **s**, 'No! H606
1Ki 11:31 this is what the LORD, the God of Israel, **s**: H606
1Ki 12:24 'This is what the LORD **s**: Do not go up to H606
1Ki 13: 2 This is what the LORD **s**: 'A son named H606
1Ki 13:21 come from Judah, "This is what the LORD **s**: H606
1Ki 14: 7 this is what the LORD, the God of Israel, **s**: H606
1Ki 17:14 this is what the LORD, the God of Israel, **s**: H606
1Ki 20: 2 saying, "This is what Ben-Hadad **s**: H606
1Ki 20: 5 said, "This is what Ben-Hadad **s**: H606
1Ki 20:13 announced, "This is what the LORD **s**: H606
1Ki 20:14 prophet replied, "This is what the LORD **s**: H606
1Ki 20:28 the king of Israel, "This is what the LORD **s**: H606
1Ki 20:32 said, "Your servant Ben-Hadad **s**: H606
1Ki 20:42 "This is what the LORD **s**: 'You have set free H606
1Ki 21:19 'This is what the LORD **s**: Have you not H606
1Ki 21:19 'This is what the LORD **s**: In the place where H606
1Ki 21:21 He **s**, 'I am going to bring disaster on you. NDT
1Ki 21:23 "And also concerning Jezebel the LORD **s** H1819
1Ki 22:11 he declared, "This is what the LORD **s**: H606
1Ki 22:27 'This is what the king **s**: Put this fellow in H606
2Ki 1: 4 Therefore this is what the LORD **s**: 'You will H606
2Ki 1: 6 you and tell him, "This is what the LORD **s**: H606
2Ki 1: 9 "Man of God, the king **s**, 'Come down! H1819
2Ki 1:11 this is what the king **s**, 'Come down at once H606
2Ki 1:16 "This is what the LORD **s**: Is it because there H606
2Ki 2:21 salt into it, saying, "This is what the LORD **s**: H606
2Ki 3:16 is what the LORD **s**: I will fill this valley H606
2Ki 3:17 For this is what the LORD **s**: You will see H606
2Ki 4:43 For this is what the LORD **s**: 'They will eat H606
2Ki 7: 1 This is what the LORD **s**: About this time H606
2Ki 9: 3 head and declare, 'This is what the LORD **s**: H606
2Ki 9: 6 "This is what the LORD, the God of Israel, **s**: H606
2Ki 9:11 know the man and the **sort of things he s**," H8490
2Ki 9:12 'This is what the LORD **s**: I anoint you king H606
2Ki 9:18 Jehu and said, "This is what the king **s**: H606
2Ki 9:19 to them he said, "This is what the king **s**: H606
2Ki 18:19 what the great king, the king of Assyria, **s**: H606
2Ki 18:29 This is what the king **s**: Do not let Hezekiah H606
2Ki 18:30 you to trust in the LORD when he **s**, H606
2Ki 18:31 This is what the king of Assyria **s**: Make H606
2Ki 18:32 he is misleading you when he **s**, 'The H606
2Ki 19: 3 "This is what Hezekiah **s**: This day is a day H606
2Ki 19: 6 "Tell your master, 'This is what the LORD **s**: H606
2Ki 19:10 you depend on deceive you when he **s**, H606
2Ki 19:20 the God of Israel, **s**: I have heard your H606
2Ki 19:32 this is what the LORD **s** concerning the king H606
2Ki 20: 1 to him and said, "This is what the LORD **s**: H606
2Ki 20: 5 the LORD, the God of your father David, **s**: H606
2Ki 20:17 Nothing will be left, **s** the LORD. H606
2Ki 21:12 this is what the LORD, the God of Israel, **s**: H606
2Ki 22:15 "This is what the LORD, the God of Israel, **s**: H606
2Ki 22:16 'This is what the LORD **s**: I am going to bring H606
2Ki 22:18 of Israel, **s** concerning the words you heard: H606
1Ch 17: 4 my servant David, 'This is what the LORD **s**: H606
1Ch 17: 7 'This is what the LORD Almighty **s**: H606
1Ch 21:10 'This is what the LORD **s**: I am giving you H606
1Ch 21:11 said to him, "This is what the LORD **s**: H606
2Ch 11: 4 'This is what the LORD **s**: Do not go up to H606
2Ch 12: 5 "This is what the LORD **s**, 'You have H606
2Ch 18:10 he declared, "This is what the LORD **s**: H606
2Ch 18:13 I can tell him only what my God **s**. H606
2Ch 18:26 'This is what the king **s**: Put this fellow in H606
2Ch 20:15 This is what the LORD **s** to you: 'Do not be H606
2Ch 21:12 the LORD, the God of your father David, **s**: H606
2Ch 24:20 the people and said, "This is what God **s**: H606
2Ch 32:10 "This is what Sennacherib king of Assyria **s** H606
2Ch 32:11 When Hezekiah **s**, 'The LORD our God will H606
2Ch 34:23 "This is what the LORD, the God of Israel, **s**: H606
2Ch 34:24 'This is what the LORD **s**: I am going to bring H606
2Ch 34:26 of Israel, **s** concerning the words you heard: H606
2Ch 36:23 "This is what Cyrus king of Persia **s**: " 'The H606
Ezr 1: 2 "This is what Cyrus king of Persia **s**: " 'The H606
Ne 6: 6 nations—and Geshem **s** it is true—that you H606
Job 8:18 that place disowns it and **s**, 'I never saw you NDT
Job 28:14 The deep **s**, "It is not in me"; the sea says H606
Job 28:14 is not in me"; the sea **s**, "It is not with me." H606
Job 33:24 he is gracious to that person and **s** to God, H606
Job 34: 5 "Job **s**, 'I am innocent, but God denies me H606
Job 34: 9 For *he* **s**, 'There is no profit in trying to H606
Job 34:18 Is he not the *One who* **s** to kings, 'You are H606
Job 34:31 "Suppose *someone* **s** to God, 'I am guilty H606
Job 35:10 But no *one* **s**, 'Where is God my Maker H606
Job 37: 6 *He* **s** to the snow, 'Fall on the earth,' and to H606
Ps 10: 6 *He* **s** to himself, "Nothing will ever shake H606
Ps 10:11 *He* **s** to himself, "God will never notice; he H606
Ps 12: 5 needy groan, I will now arise," **s** the LORD. H606
Ps 14: 1 The fool **s** in his heart, "There is no God." H606
Ps 27: 8 My heart **s** of you, "Seek his face!" Your H606
Ps 46:10 He **s**, "Be still, and know that I am God; NDT
Ps 50:16 wicked person, God **s**: "What right have H606
Ps 53: 1 The fool **s** in his heart, "There is no God." H606
Ps 68:22 The Lord **s**, "I will bring them from Bashan H606
Ps 75:10 who **s**, "I will cut off the horns of all the NDT
Ps 85: 8 I will listen to what God the LORD **s**; he H1819
Ps 91:14 "Because he loves me," **s** the LORD, "I will NDT
Ps 110: 1 The LORD **s** to my lord: "Sit at my right H5536
Pr 9: 4 To those who have no sense *she* **s**, H606
Pr 9:16 To those who have no sense *she* **s**, H606
Pr 20:14 **s** the buyer—then goes off and boasts H606
Pr 22:13 The sluggard **s**, "There's a lion outside! I'll H606
Pr 23: 7 "Eat and drink," *he* **s** to you, but his heart is H606
Pr 24:24 *Whoever* **s** to the guilty, "You are innocent," H606
Pr 26:13 A sluggard **s**, "There's a lion in the road, H606
Pr 26:19 is one who deceives their neighbor and **s** H606
Pr 28:24 Whoever robs their father or mother and **s** H606
Pr 30:16 and fire, *which* never **s**, 'Enough! H606
Pr 30:20 She eats and wipes her mouth and **s**, 'I've H606
Ecc 1: 2 **s** the Teacher. "Utterly H606
Ecc 7:27 **s** the Teacher, "this is what I have H606
Ecc 12: 8 **s** the Teacher. "Everything is H606
Isa 1:11 what are they to me?" **s** the LORD. "I have H606
Isa 1:18 let us settle the matter," **s** the LORD. H606
Isa 3:16 The LORD **s**, "The women of Zion are H606
Isa 7: 7 Yet this is what the Sovereign LORD **s**: " 'It H606
Isa 8:11 is what the LORD **s** to me with his strong H606
Isa 10: 8 'Are not my commanders all kings?' *he* **s**. H606
Isa 10:13 For *he* **s**: " 'By the strength of my hand I H606
Isa 10:24 this is what the Lord, the LORD Almighty, **s**: H606
Isa 16: 3 up your mind," Moab **s**. "Render a decision. NDT
Isa 16:14 But now the LORD **s**: "Within three years, H1819
Isa 18: 4 This is what the LORD **s** to me: "I will H606
Isa 21: 6 This is what the Lord **s** to me: "Go, post a H606
Isa 21:16 This is what the Lord **s** to me: "Within one H606
Isa 22:14 will not be atoned for," **s** the Lord, the LORD H606
Isa 22:15 is what the Lord, the LORD Almighty, **s**: "Go, H606
Isa 28:16 So this is what the Sovereign LORD **s**: "See, H606
Isa 29:13 The Lord **s**: "These people come near to H606
Isa 29:22 Abraham, **s** to the descendants of Jacob: H606
Isa 30:12 this is what the Holy One of Israel **s**: H606
Isa 30:15 Sovereign LORD, the Holy One of Israel, **s**: H606
Isa 31: 4 This is what the LORD **s** to me: "As a lion H606
Isa 33:10 "Now will I arise," **s** the LORD. "Now will I H606
Isa 36: 4 what the great king, the king of Assyria, **s**: H606
Isa 36:14 This is what the king **s**: Do not let Hezekiah H606
Isa 36:15 you to trust in the LORD *when* he **s**, H606
Isa 36:16 This is what the king of Assyria **s**: Make H606
Isa 36:18 not let Hezekiah mislead you *when* he **s**, H606
Isa 37: 3 "This is what Hezekiah **s**: This day is a day H606
Isa 37: 6 "Tell your master, 'This is what the LORD **s**: H606
Isa 37:10 you depend on deceive you *when* he **s**, H606
Isa 37:21 the God of Israel, **s**: Because you have H606
Isa 37:33 this is what the LORD **s** concerning the king H606
Isa 38: 1 to him and said, "This is what the LORD **s**: H606
Isa 38: 5 the LORD, the God of your father David, **s**: H606
Isa 39: 6 Nothing will be left, **s** the LORD. H606
Isa 40: 1 Comfort, comfort my people, **s** your God. H606
Isa 40: 6 A voice **s**, "Cry out." And I said, "What H606
Isa 40:25 Or who is my equal?" **s** the Holy One. H606
Isa 41: 7 strikes the anvil. *One* **s** of the welding, "It is H606
Isa 41:13 takes hold of your right hand and **s** to you, H606
Isa 41:21 "Present your case," **s** the LORD. "Set forth H606
Isa 41:21 "Set forth your arguments," **s** Jacob's King. H606
Isa 42: 5 This is what God the LORD **s**—the Creator H606
Isa 43: 1 this is what the LORD **s**—he who created H606
Isa 43:14 This is what the LORD **s**—your Redeemer H606
Isa 43:16 This is what the LORD **s**—he who made a H606
Isa 44: 2 This is what the LORD **s**—he who made you, H606
Isa 44: 6 "This is what the LORD **s**—Israel's King H606
Isa 44:16 He also warms himself and **s**, "Ah! I am H606
Isa 44:17 He prays to it and **s**, "Save me! You are my H606
Isa 44:24 "This is what the LORD **s**—your Redeemer H606
Isa 44:26 of his messengers, who **s** of Jerusalem, 'It H606
Isa 44:27 who **s** to the watery deep, 'Be dry, and I H606
Isa 44:28 who **s** of Cyrus, 'He is my shepherd and will H606
Isa 45: 1 "This is what the LORD **s** to his anointed, to H606
Isa 45:10 Woe to the *one who* **s** to a father, 'What H606
Isa 45:11 "This is what the LORD **s**—the Holy One of H606
Isa 45:13 a price or reward, **s** the LORD Almighty." H606
Isa 45:14 This is what the LORD **s**: "The products of H606
Isa 45:18 For this is what the LORD **s**—he who created H606
Isa 45:18 but formed it to be inhabited—he **s**: NDT
Isa 48:17 This is what the LORD **s**—your Redeemer H606
Isa 48:22 "There is no peace," **s** the LORD, "for the H606
Isa 49: 5 And now the LORD **s**—he who formed me H606
Isa 49: 6 *he* **s**: "It is too small a thing for you to be H606
Isa 49: 7 **s**—the Redeemer and Holy One of Israel—*to* H606
Isa 49: 8 This is what the LORD **s**: "In the time of my H606
Isa 49:22 This is what the Sovereign LORD **s**: "See, H606
Isa 49:25 But this is what the LORD **s**: "Yes, captives H606
Isa 50: 1 This is what the LORD **s**: "Where is your H606
Isa 51:22 This is what your Sovereign LORD **s**, your H606
Isa 52: 3 For this is what the LORD **s**: "You were sold H606
Isa 52: 4 For this is what the Sovereign LORD **s**: "At H606
Isa 54: 1 of her who has a husband," **s** the LORD. H606
Isa 54: 6 only to be rejected," **s** your God. H606
Isa 54: 8 **s** the LORD your Redeemer. H606
Isa 54:10 of peace be removed," **s** the LORD, who has H606
Isa 56: 1 This is what the LORD **s**: "Maintain justice H606
Isa 56: 4 For this is what the LORD **s**: "To the eunuchs H606
Isa 57:15 this is what the high and exalted *One* **s**— H606
Isa 57:19 to those far and near," **s** the LORD. H606
Isa 57:21 "There is no peace," **s** my God, "for the H606
Isa 59:21 this is my covenant with them," **s** the LORD. H606
Isa 59:21 from this time on and forever," **s** the LORD. H606
Isa 65: 7 the sins of your ancestors," **s** the LORD. H606
Isa 65: 8 This is what the LORD **s**: "As when juice is H606
Isa 65:13 Therefore this is what the Sovereign LORD **s** H606
Isa 65:25 on all my holy mountain," **s** the LORD. H606
Isa 66: 1 This is what the LORD **s**: "Heaven is my H606
Isa 66: 9 not give delivery?" **s** the LORD. "Do I close H606
Isa 66: 9 when I bring to delivery?" **s** your God. H606
Isa 66:12 For this is what the LORD **s**: "I will extend H606
Isa 66:20 on mules and camels," **s** the LORD. H606
Isa 66:21 also to be priests and Levites," **s** the LORD. H606
Isa 66:23 bow down before me," **s** the LORD. H606
Jer 2: 2 "This is what the LORD **s**: " 'I remember the H606
Jer 2: 5 This is what the LORD **s**: "What fault did H606
Jer 4: 3 This is what the LORD **s** to the people of H606
Jer 4:27 This is what the LORD **s**: "The whole land H606
Jer 5:14 this is what the LORD God Almighty **s**: H606
Jer 6: 6 This is what the LORD Almighty **s**: "Cut H606
Jer 6: 9 This is what the LORD Almighty **s**: "Let H606
Jer 6:15 down when I punish them," **s** the LORD. H606
Jer 6:16 This is what the LORD **s**: "Stand at the H606
Jer 6:21 Therefore this is what the LORD **s**: "I will put H606
Jer 6:22 This is what the LORD **s**: "Look, an army is H606
Jer 7: 3 the LORD Almighty, the God of Israel, **s**: H606
Jer 7:20 this is what the Sovereign LORD **s**: H606
Jer 7:21 the LORD Almighty, the God of Israel, **s**: H606
Jer 8: 4 'This is what the LORD **s**: " 'When people H606
Jer 8:12 down when they are punished, **s** the LORD. H606
Jer 9: 7 Therefore this is what the LORD Almighty **s** H606
Jer 9:15 the LORD Almighty, the God of Israel, **s**: H606
Jer 9:17 This is what the LORD Almighty **s**: "Consider H606
Jer 9:23 This is what the LORD **s**: "Let not the wise H606
Jer 10: 1 Hear what the LORD **s** to you, people of H1819
Jer 10: 2 This is what the LORD **s**: "Do not learn the H606
Jer 10:18 For this is what the LORD **s**: "At this time I H606
Jer 11: 3 this is what the LORD, the God of Israel, **s**: H606
Jer 11:11 Therefore this is what the LORD **s**: 'I will H606
Jer 11:21 this is what the LORD **s** about the people of H606
Jer 11:22 therefore this is what the LORD Almighty **s**: H606
Jer 12:14 This is what the LORD **s**: "As for all my H606
Jer 13: 9 "This is what the LORD **s**: 'In the same way H606
Jer 13:12 the God of Israel, **s**: Every wineskin should H606
Jer 13:13 'This is what the LORD **s**: I am going to fill H606
Jer 14:10 This is what the LORD **s** about this people H606
Jer 14:15 this is what the LORD **s** about the prophets H606
Jer 15: 2 'This is what the LORD **s**: " 'Those destined H606
Jer 15:19 Therefore this is what the LORD **s**: "If you H606
Jer 16: 3 this is what the LORD **s** about the sons and H606
Jer 16: 5 For this is what the LORD **s**: "Do not enter a H606
Jer 16: 9 the LORD Almighty, the God of Israel, **s**: H606
Jer 17: 5 This is what the LORD **s**: "Cursed is the one H606
Jer 17:21 This is what the LORD **s**: Be careful not to H606
Jer 18:11 in Jerusalem, 'This is what the LORD **s**: H606
Jer 18:13 Therefore this is what the LORD **s**: "Inquire H606
Jer 18:18 pay no attention to anything he **s**. H1821
Jer 19: 1 This is what the LORD **s**: "Go and buy a clay H606
Jer 19: 3 the LORD Almighty, the God of Israel, **s**: H606
Jer 19:11 to them, 'This is what the LORD Almighty **s**: H606
Jer 19:15 the LORD Almighty, the God of Israel, **s**: H606
Jer 20: 4 For this is what the LORD **s**: 'I will make you H606
Jer 21: 4 the God of Israel, **s**: I am about to turn H606
Jer 21: 8 tell the people, 'This is what the LORD **s**: H606
Jer 21:12 This is what the LORD **s** to you, house of H606
Jer 22: 1 This is what the LORD **s**: "Go down to the H606
Jer 22: 3 This is what the LORD **s**: Do what is just and H606
Jer 22: 6 this is what the LORD **s** about the palace of H606
Jer 22:11 is what the LORD **s** about Shallum son of H606
Jer 22:14 He **s**, 'I will build myself a great palace H606
Jer 22:18 this is what the LORD **s** about Jehoiakim son H606
Jer 22:30 This is what the LORD **s**: "Record this man H606
Jer 23: 2 **s** to the shepherds who tend my people: H606
Jer 23:15 what the LORD Almighty **s** concerning the H606
Jer 23:16 This is what the LORD Almighty **s**: "Do not H606
Jer 23:17 to those who despise me, 'The LORD **s**: H1819
Jer 23:38 from the LORD,' this is what the LORD **s**: H606
Jer 24: 5 the God of Israel, **s**: 'Like these good figs, H606
Jer 24: 8 they cannot be eaten,' **s** the LORD, 'so will I H606
Jer 25: 8 Therefore the LORD Almighty **s** this H606
Jer 25:27 the LORD Almighty, the God of Israel, **s**: H606
Jer 25:28 tell them, 'This is what the LORD Almighty **s**: H606
Jer 25:32 This is what the LORD Almighty **s**: "Look H606
Jer 26: 2 "This is what the LORD **s**: Stand in the H606
Jer 26: 4 'This is what the LORD **s**: If you do not listen H606
Jer 26:18 of Judah, 'This is what the LORD Almighty **s**: H606
Jer 27: 4 the LORD Almighty, the God of Israel, **s**: H606
Jer 27:16 all these people, "This is what the LORD **s**: H606
Jer 27:19 what the LORD Almighty **s** about the pillars, H606
Jer 27:21 **s** about the things that are left in the house H606
Jer 28: 2 the LORD Almighty, the God of Israel, **s**: H606
Jer 28:11 all the people, "This is what the LORD **s**: H606
Jer 28:13 tell Hananiah, 'This is what the LORD **s**: H606
Jer 28:14 the LORD Almighty, the God of Israel, **s**: H606
Jer 28:16 Therefore this is what the LORD **s**: 'I am H606
Jer 29: 4 **s** to all those I carried into exile from H606
Jer 29: 8 the LORD Almighty, the God of Israel, **s**: H606
Jer 29:10 This is what the LORD **s**: "When seventy H606
Jer 29:16 this is what the LORD **s** about the king who H606
Jer 29:17 this is what the LORD Almighty **s**: "I will H606
Jer 29:21 **s** about Ahab son of Kolaiah and Zedekiah H606
Jer 29:25 the LORD Almighty, the God of Israel, **s**: H606
Jer 29:31 is what the LORD **s** about Shemaiah the H606
Jer 29:32 this is what the LORD **s**: I will surely punish H606
Jer 30: 2 the God of Israel, **s**: 'Write in a book all H606
Jer 30: 3 gave their ancestors to possess,' **s** the LORD." H606
Jer 30: 5 "This is what the LORD **s**: " 'Cries of fear H606
Jer 30:12 "This is what the LORD **s**: " 'Your wound is H606
Jer 30:18 "This is what the LORD **s**: " 'I will restore H606

Jer 31: 2 This is what the LORD s: “The people who H606
Jer 31: 7 This is what the LORD s: “Sing with joy for H606
Jer 31:15 This is what the LORD s: “A voice is heard H606
Jer 31:16 This is what the LORD s: “Restrain your H606
Jer 31:23 the LORD Almighty, the God of Israel, s: H606
Jer 31:35 This is what the LORD s, he who appoints H606
Jer 31:37 This is what the LORD s: “Only if the H606
Jer 32: 3 ‘This is what the LORD s: I am about to give H606
Jer 32:14 the LORD Almighty, the God of Israel, s: H606
Jer 32:15 the LORD Almighty, the God of Israel, s: H606
Jer 32:28 Therefore this is what the LORD s: I am H606
Jer 32:36 this is what the LORD, the God of Israel, s: H606
Jer 32:42 “This is what the LORD s: As I have brought H606
Jer 33: 2 “This is what the LORD s, he who made the H606
Jer 33: 4 s about the houses in this city and the royal H606
Jer 33:10 “This is what the LORD s: ‘You say about H606
Jer 33:11 of the land as they were before,’ s the LORD. H606
Jer 33:12 “This is what the LORD Almighty s: ‘In this H606
Jer 33:13 of the one who counts them,’ s the LORD. H606
Jer 33:17 For this is what the LORD s: ‘David will H606
Jer 33:20 “This is what the LORD s: ‘If you can break H606
Jer 33:25 This is what the LORD s: ‘If I have not made H606
Jer 34: 2 the God of Israel, s: Go to Zedekiah king of H606
Jer 34: 2 tell him, ‘This is what the LORD s: H606
Jer 34: 4 This is what the LORD s concerning you: H606
Jer 34:13 the God of Israel, s: I made a covenant H606
Jer 34:17 “Therefore this is what the LORD s: You H606
Jer 35:13 the LORD Almighty, the God of Israel, s: H606
Jer 35:17 the LORD God Almighty, the God of Israel, s: H606
Jer 35:18 the LORD Almighty, the God of Israel, s: H606
Jer 35:19 the LORD Almighty, the God of Israel, s: H606
Jer 36:29 king of Judah, ‘This is what the LORD s: H606
Jer 36:30 is what the LORD s about Jehoiakim king H606
Jer 37: 7 the God of Israel, s: Tell the king of Judah, H606
Jer 37: 9 “This is what the LORD s: Do not deceive H606
Jer 38: 2 “This is what the LORD s: ‘Whoever stays in H606
Jer 38: 3 And this is what the LORD s: ‘This city will H606
Jer 38:17 the LORD God Almighty, the God of Israel, s: H606
Jer 39:16 the LORD Almighty, the God of Israel, s: H606
Jer 42: 4 everything the LORD s and will keep H6699
Jer 42: 9 you sent me to present your petition, s: H606
Jer 42:15 the LORD Almighty, the God of Israel, s: H606
Jer 42:18 the LORD Almighty, the God of Israel, s: H606
Jer 42:20 tell us everything he s and we will do it. H606
Jer 43:10 the LORD Almighty, the God of Israel, s: H606
Jer 44: 2 the LORD Almighty, the God of Israel, s: H606
Jer 44: 7 the LORD God Almighty, the God of Israel, s: H606
Jer 44:11 the LORD Almighty, the God of Israel, s: H606
Jer 44:25 the LORD Almighty, the God of Israel, s: H606
Jer 44:26 by my great name,’ s the LORD, ‘that no one H606
Jer 44:30 This is what the LORD s: ‘I am going to H606
Jer 45: 2 the God of Israel, s to you, Baruch: H606
Jer 45: 4 me to say to you, ‘This is what the LORD s: H606
Jer 46: 8 *She* s, ‘I will rise and cover the earth; I will H606
Jer 46:25 the God of Israel, s: “I am about to bring H606
Jer 47: 2 This is what the LORD s: “See how the H606
Jer 48: 1 the LORD Almighty, the God of Israel, s: H606
Jer 48:40 This is what the LORD s: “Look! An eagle is H606
Jer 49: 1 This is what the LORD s: “Has Israel no sons H606
Jer 49: 2 out those who drove her out,” s the LORD. H606
Jer 49: 7 This is what the LORD Almighty s: “Is there H606
Jer 49:12 This is what the LORD s: “If those who do H606
Jer 49:18 neighboring towns,” s the LORD, “so no one H606
Jer 49:28 This is what the LORD s: “Arise, H606
Jer 49:35 This is what the LORD Almighty s: “See, H606
Jer 50:18 the LORD Almighty, the God of Israel, s: H606
Jer 50:33 This is what the LORD Almighty s: “The H606
Jer 51: 1 This is what the LORD s: “See, I will stir up H606
Jer 51:33 the LORD Almighty, the God of Israel, s: H606
Jer 51:35 those who live in Babylonia,” s Jerusalem. H606
Jer 51:36 Therefore this is what the LORD s: “See, H606
Jer 51:58 This is what the LORD Almighty s H606
Eze 2: 4 to them, ‘This is what the Sovereign LORD s. H606
Eze 3:11 ‘This is what the Sovereign LORD s,’ whether H606
Eze 3:27 to them, ‘This is what the Sovereign LORD s. H606
Eze 5: 5 “This is what the Sovereign LORD s: This is H606
Eze 5: 7 this is what the Sovereign LORD s: H606
Eze 5: 8 this is what the Sovereign LORD s: H606
Eze 6: 3 the Sovereign LORD s to the mountains and H606
Eze 6:11 “ ‘This is what the Sovereign LORD s: Strike H606
Eze 7: 2 the Sovereign LORD s to the land of Israel: H606
Eze 7: 5 “This is what the Sovereign LORD s: H606
Eze 11: 5 “This is what the LORD s: That is what you H606
Eze 11: 7 this is what the Sovereign LORD s: H606
Eze 11:16 ‘This is what the Sovereign LORD s H606
Eze 11:17 ‘This is what the Sovereign LORD s: I will H606
Eze 12:10 to them, ‘This is what the Sovereign LORD s: H606
Eze 12:19 the Sovereign LORD s about those living in H606
Eze 12:23 to them, ‘This is what the Sovereign LORD s: H606
Eze 12:28 to them, ‘This is what the Sovereign LORD s: H606
Eze 13: 3 This is what the Sovereign LORD s: Woe to H606
Eze 13: 8 this is what the Sovereign LORD s: H606
Eze 13:13 this is what the Sovereign LORD s: H606
Eze 13:18 ‘This is what the Sovereign LORD s: Woe to H606
Eze 13:20 this is what the Sovereign LORD s: H606
Eze 14: 4 ‘This is what the Sovereign LORD s: H606
Eze 14: 6 of Israel, ‘This is what the Sovereign LORD s: H606
Eze 14:21 “For this is what the Sovereign LORD s: How H606
Eze 15: 6 this is what the Sovereign LORD s: H606
Eze 16: 3 is what the Sovereign LORD s to Jerusalem: H606
Eze 16:36 This is what the Sovereign LORD s: Because H606
Eze 16:59 “ ‘This is what the Sovereign LORD s: I will H606

Eze 17: 3 to them, ‘This is what the Sovereign LORD s: H606
Eze 17: 9 to them, ‘This is what the Sovereign LORD s: H606
Eze 17:19 this is what the Sovereign LORD s: H606
Eze 17:22 “ ‘This is what the Sovereign LORD s: H606
Eze 20: 3 to them, ‘This is what the Sovereign LORD s: H606
Eze 20: 5 ‘This is what the Sovereign LORD s: On the H606
Eze 20:27 to them, ‘This is what the Sovereign LORD s: H606
Eze 20:30 ‘This is what the Sovereign LORD s: Will you H606
Eze 20:39 of Israel, this is what the Sovereign LORD s: H606
Eze 20:47 This is what the Sovereign LORD s: I am H606
Eze 21: 3 ‘This is what the LORD s: I am against you. H606
Eze 21: 9 prophesy and say, ‘This is what the Lord s: H606
Eze 21:24 this is what the Sovereign LORD s: H606
Eze 21:26 this is what the Sovereign LORD s: Take off H606
Eze 21:28 the Sovereign LORD s about the Ammonites H606
Eze 22: 3 ‘This is what the Sovereign LORD s: You city H606
Eze 22:19 Therefore this is what the Sovereign LORD s H606
Eze 22:28 ‘This is what the Sovereign LORD s’—when H606
Eze 23:22 Oholibah, this is what the Sovereign LORD s: H606
Eze 23:28 “For this is what the Sovereign LORD s: I am H606
Eze 23:32 “This is what the Sovereign LORD s: “You H606
Eze 23:35 this is what the Sovereign LORD s: H606
Eze 23:46 “This is what the Sovereign LORD s: Bring H606
Eze 24: 3 ‘This is what the Sovereign LORD s: “ ‘Put H606
Eze 24: 6 “ ‘For this is what the Sovereign LORD s: H606
Eze 24: 9 this is what the Sovereign LORD s: H606
Eze 24:21 Israel, ‘This is what the Sovereign LORD s: H606
Eze 25: 3 This is what the Sovereign LORD s: Because H606
Eze 25: 6 For this is what the Sovereign LORD s H606
Eze 25: 8 “This is what the Sovereign LORD s H606
Eze 25:12 “This is what the Sovereign LORD s H606
Eze 25:13 therefore this is what the Sovereign LORD s: H606
Eze 25:15 “This is what the Sovereign LORD s H606
Eze 25:16 therefore this is what the Sovereign LORD s: H606
Eze 26: 3 therefore this is what the Sovereign LORD s: H606
Eze 26: 7 “For this is what the Sovereign LORD s: H606
Eze 26:15 “This is what the Sovereign LORD s to Tyre H606
Eze 26:19 “This is what the Sovereign LORD s: When I H606
Eze 27: 3 ‘This is what the Sovereign LORD s: H606
Eze 28: 2 ‘This is what the Sovereign LORD s: H606
Eze 28: 6 this is what the Sovereign LORD s: H606
Eze 28:12 ‘This is what the Sovereign LORD s: “ ‘You H606
Eze 28:22 ‘This is what the Sovereign LORD s: “ ‘I am H606
Eze 28:25 “ ‘This is what the Sovereign LORD s: When H606
Eze 29: 3 ‘This is what the Sovereign LORD s: “ ‘I am H606
Eze 29: 8 this is what the Sovereign LORD s: H606
Eze 29:13 “ ‘Yet this is what the Sovereign LORD s: At H606
Eze 29:19 Therefore this is what the Sovereign LORD s H606
Eze 30: 2 ‘This is what the Sovereign LORD s: “ ‘Wail H606
Eze 30: 6 “ ‘This is what the LORD s: “ ‘The allies of H606
Eze 30:10 “ ‘This is what the Sovereign LORD s: H606
Eze 30:13 “ ‘This is what the Sovereign LORD s: H606
Eze 30:22 Therefore this is what the Sovereign LORD s H606
Eze 31:10 this is what the Sovereign LORD s: H606
Eze 31:15 “ ‘This is what the Sovereign LORD s: On H606
Eze 32: 3 “ ‘This is what the Sovereign LORD s: H606
Eze 32:11 “ ‘For this is what the Sovereign LORD s: H606
Eze 33:25 to them, ‘This is what the Sovereign LORD s: H606
Eze 33:27 ‘This is what the Sovereign LORD s: As H606
Eze 34: 2 ‘This is what the Sovereign LORD s: Woe to H606
Eze 34:10 This is what the Sovereign LORD s: I am H606
Eze 34:11 “ ‘For this is what the Sovereign LORD s: H606
Eze 34:17 my flock, this is what the Sovereign LORD s: H606
Eze 34:20 this is what the Sovereign LORD s to them: H606
Eze 35: 3 ‘This is what the Sovereign LORD s: I am H606
Eze 35:14 This is what the Sovereign LORD s: While H606
Eze 36: 2 This is what the Sovereign LORD s: The H606
Eze 36: 3 ‘This is what the Sovereign LORD s: H606
Eze 36: 4 the Sovereign LORD s to the mountains and H606
Eze 36: 5 this is what the Sovereign LORD s: In my H606
Eze 36: 6 ‘This is what the Sovereign LORD s: I speak H606
Eze 36: 7 Therefore this is what the Sovereign LORD s H606
Eze 36:13 “ ‘This is what the Sovereign LORD s H606
Eze 36:22 ‘This is what the Sovereign LORD s: H606
Eze 36:33 “ ‘This is what the Sovereign LORD s: On H606
Eze 36:37 “This is what the Sovereign LORD s: Once H606
Eze 37: 5 what the Sovereign LORD s to these bones: H606
Eze 37: 9 say to it, ‘This is what the Sovereign LORD s: H606
Eze 37:12 ‘This is what the Sovereign LORD s: My H606
Eze 37:19 to them, ‘This is what the Sovereign LORD s: H606
Eze 37:21 to them, ‘This is what the Sovereign LORD s: H606
Eze 38: 3 ‘This is what the Sovereign LORD s: I am H606
Eze 38:10 “ ‘This is what the Sovereign LORD s: On H606
Eze 38:14 ‘This is what the Sovereign LORD s: In that H606
Eze 38:17 “ ‘This is what the Sovereign LORD s: You H606
Eze 39: 1 ‘This is what the Sovereign LORD s: I am H606
Eze 39:17 this is what the Sovereign LORD s: H606
Eze 39:25 this is what the Sovereign LORD s: H606
Eze 43:18 this is what the Sovereign LORD s: H606
Eze 44: 6 ‘This is what the Sovereign LORD s: H606
Eze 44: 9 This is what the Sovereign LORD s: No H606
Eze 45: 9 “ ‘This is what the Sovereign LORD s: You H606
Eze 45:18 “ ‘This is what the Sovereign LORD s: In the H606
Eze 46: 1 “ ‘This is what the Sovereign LORD s: The H606
Eze 46:16 “ ‘This is what the Sovereign LORD s: If the H606
Eze 47:13 This is what the Sovereign LORD s: “These H606
Am 1: 3 This is what the LORD s: “For three sins of H606
Am 1: 5 Aram will go into exile to Kir,” s the LORD. H606
Am 1: 6 This is what the LORD s: “For three sins of H606
Am 1: 8 Philistines are dead,” s the Sovereign LORD. H606
Am 1: 9 This is what the LORD s: “For three sins of H606
Am 1:11 This is what the LORD s: “For three sins of H606

Am 1:13 This is what the LORD s: “For three sins of H606
Am 1:15 he and his officials together,” s the LORD. H606
Am 2: 1 This is what the LORD s: “For three sins of H606
Am 2: 3 kill all her officials with him,” s the LORD. H606
Am 2: 4 This is what the LORD s: “For three sins of H606
Am 2: 6 This is what the LORD s: “For three sins of H606
Am 3:11 Therefore this is what the Sovereign LORD s H606
Am 3:12 This is what the LORD s: “As a shepherd H606
Am 5: 3 This is what the Sovereign LORD s to Israel H606
Am 5: 4 This is what the LORD s to Israel: “Seek me H606
Am 5:16 is what the Lord, the LORD God Almighty, s: H606
Am 5:17 I will pass through your midst,” s the LORD. H606
Am 5:27 beyond Damascus,” s the LORD, whose H606
Am 6:10 and *he* s, “No,” then he will go on to say H606
Am 7:17 “Therefore this is what the LORD s: “ ‘Your H606
Am 9:15 I have given them,” s the LORD your God. H606
Ob 1 is what the Sovereign LORD s about Edom— H606
Mic 2: 3 Therefore, the LORD s: “I am planning H606
Mic 2:11 If a liar and deceiver comes and s, ‘I will NDT
Mic 3: 5 This is what the LORD s: “As for the prophets H606
Mic 6: 1 Listen to what the LORD s: “Stand up, plead H606
Na 1:12 This is what the LORD s: “Although they H606
Hab 2:19 Woe to *him who* s to wood, ‘Come to life!’ H606
Zep 2: 5 He s, “I will destroy you, and none will be NDT
Zep 3:20 fortunes before your very eyes,” s the LORD. H606
Hag 1: 2 This is what the LORD Almighty s: “These H606
Hag 1: 5 Now this is what the LORD Almighty s: H606
Hag 1: 7 This is what the LORD Almighty s: “Give H606
Hag 1: 8 pleasure in it and be honored,” s the LORD. H606
Hag 2: 6 “This is what the LORD Almighty s: ‘In a H606
Hag 2: 7 this house with glory,’ s the LORD Almighty. H606
Hag 2: 9 of the former house,’ s the LORD Almighty. H606
Hag 2:11 “This is what the LORD Almighty s: ‘Ask H606
Hag 2:11 ‘Ask the priests what the law s: H606
Zec 1: 3 This is what the LORD Almighty s: ‘Return H606
Zec 1: 3 I will return to you,’ s the LORD Almighty. H606
Zec 1: 4 This is what the LORD Almighty s: ‘Turn H606
Zec 1:14 This is what the LORD Almighty s: ‘I am H606
Zec 1:16 “Therefore this is what the LORD s: ‘I will H606
Zec 1:17 This is what the LORD Almighty s: ‘My H606
Zec 2: 8 For this is what the LORD Almighty s: “After H606
Zec 3: 7 “This is what the LORD Almighty s: ‘If you H606
Zec 3: 9 an inscription on it,’ s the LORD Almighty H5536
Zec 4: 6 by my Spirit,’ s the LORD Almighty. H606
Zec 5: 3 according to what it s on one side, every NDT
Zec 5: 3 according to what it s on the other NDT
Zec 6:12 Tell him this is what the LORD Almighty s H606
Zec 7:13 I would not listen,’ s the LORD Almighty. H606
Zec 8: 2 This is what the LORD Almighty s: “I am H606
Zec 8: 3 This is what the LORD s: “I will return to Zion H606
Zec 8: 4 This is what the LORD Almighty s: “Once H606
Zec 8: 6 This is what the LORD Almighty s: “It may H606
Zec 8: 7 This is what the LORD Almighty s: “I will H606
Zec 8: 9 This is what the LORD Almighty s: “Now H606
Zec 8:14 This is what the LORD Almighty s: “Just as I H606
Zec 8:14 angered me,” s the LORD Almighty, H606
Zec 8:19 This is what the LORD Almighty s: “The fasts H606
Zec 8:20 This is what the LORD Almighty s: “Many H606
Zec 8:23 This is what the LORD Almighty s: “In those H606
Zec 11: 4 This is what the LORD my God s: “Shepherd H606
Mal 1: 2 “I have loved you,” s the LORD. “But you H606
Mal 1: 4 But this is what the LORD Almighty s: “They H606
Mal 1: 6 the respect due me?” s the LORD Almighty H606
Mal 1: 8 Would he accept you?” s the LORD Almighty. H606
Mal 1: 9 will he accept you?”—s the LORD Almighty. H606
Mal 1:10 s the LORD Almighty, “and I will accept no H606
Mal 1:11 among the nations,” s the LORD Almighty. H606
Mal 1:13 at it contemptuously,” s the LORD Almighty. H606
Mal 1:13 accept them from your hands?” s the LORD. H606
Mal 1:14 s the LORD Almighty, “and my name is to H606
Mal 2: 2 s the LORD Almighty, “I will send a curse H606
Mal 2: 4 Levi may continue,” s the LORD Almighty. H606
Mal 2: 8 covenant with Levi,” s the LORD Almighty. H606
Mal 2:16 divorces his wife,” s the LORD, the God of H606
Mal 2:16 he should protect,” s the LORD Almighty. H606
Mal 3: 1 desire, will come,” s the LORD Almighty. H606
Mal 3: 5 do not fear me,” s the LORD Almighty. H606
Mal 3: 7 I will return to you,” s the LORD Almighty. H606
Mal 3:10 s the LORD Almighty, “and see if I will not H606
Mal 3:11 fruit before it is ripe,” s the LORD Almighty. H606
Mal 3:12 be a delightful land,” s the LORD Almighty. H606
Mal 3:13 spoken arrogantly against me,” s the LORD. H606
Mal 3:17 s the LORD Almighty, “they will be my H606
Mal 4: 1 will set them on fire,” s the LORD Almighty. H606
Mal 4: 3 the day when I act,” s the LORD Almighty. H606
Mt 5:22 anyone *who* s to a brother or sister *G3306*
Mt 5:22 And anyone *who* s, ‘You fool!’ will *G3306*
Mt 7:21 “Not everyone who s to me, ‘Lord, Lord,’ *G3306*
Mt 12:44 Then *it* s, ‘I will return to the house I left.’ *G3306*
Mt 21: 3 If anyone s anything to you, say that the *G3306*
Mt 22:43 by the Spirit, calls him ‘Lord’? *For he* s, *G3306*
Mt 24:23 At that time if anyone s to you, ‘Look, here *G3306*
Mt 24:48 that servant is wicked and s to himself, *G3306*
Mt 26:18 certain man and tell him, ‘The Teacher s: *G3306*
Mk 11:23 tell you, if anyone s to this mountain, ‘Go *G3306*
Mk 13:21 At that time if anyone s to you, ‘Look, here *G3306*
Lk 11:24 does not find it. Then *it* s, ‘I will return to *G3306*
Lk 12:45 But suppose the servant s to himself, ‘My *G3306*
Lk 15: 6 his friends and neighbors together and s, *G3306*
Lk 15: 9 her friends and neighbors together and s, *G3306*
Lk 18: 6 “Listen to what the unjust judge s. *G3306*
Jn 8:22 Is that why *he* s, ‘Where I go, you cannot *G3306*

Jn 8:47 belongs to God hears what God s. G4839
Jn 12:39 believe, because, as Isaiah s elsewhere: G3306
Jn 19:37 as another scripture s, "They will look G3306
Ac 2:17 'In the last days, God s, I will pour out my G3306
Ac 7:48 made by human hands. As the prophet s: G3306
Ac 7:49 will you build for me? s the Lord. G3306
Ac 15:17 who bear my name, s the Lord, who does G3306
Ac 19:26 He s that gods made by human hands are G3306
Ac 21:11 "The Holy Spirit s, 'In this way the G3306
Ro 3:19 Now we know that whatever the law s, it G3306
Ro 3:19 says, it s to those who are under the law G3281
Ro 4: 6 David s the same thing when he speaks of G3306
Ro 9:15 For he s to Moses, "I will have mercy on G3306
Ro 9:17 For Scripture s to Pharaoh: "I raised you G3306
Ro 9:25 As he s in Hosea: "I will call them 'my G3306
Ro 10: 6 But the righteousness that is by faith s G3306
Ro 10:11 As Scripture s, "Anyone who believes in G3306
Ro 10:16 For Isaiah s, "Lord, who has believed our G3306
Ro 10:19 Moses s, "I will make you envious by G3306
Ro 10:20 And Isaiah boldly s, "I was found by those G3306
Ro 10:21 But concerning Israel he s, "All day long I G3306
Ro 11: 2 know what Scripture s in the passage G3306
Ro 11: 9 And David s: "May their table become a G3306
Ro 12:19 mine to avenge; I will repay," s the Lord. G3306
Ro 14:11 'As surely as I live,' s the Lord, 'every knee G3306
Ro 15:10 it s, "Rejoice, you Gentiles, with G3306
Ro 15:12 And again, Isaiah s, "The Root of Jesse G3306
1Co 1:12 One of you s, "I follow Paul"; another, "I G3306
1Co 3: 4 For when one s, "I follow Paul," and G3306
1Co 9:10 Surely he s this for us, doesn't he? Yes G3306
1Co 10:28 But if someone s to you, "This has been G3306
1Co 12: 3 who is speaking by the Spirit of God s, G3306
1Co 14:21 then they will not listen to me, s the Lord." G3306
1Co 14:34 must be in submission, as the law s. G3306
1Co 15:27 Now when it s that "everything" has G3306
2Co 6: 2 For he s, "In the time of my favor I heard G3306
2Co 6:17 from them and be separate, s the Lord. G3306
2Co 6:18 sons and daughters, s the Lord Almighty." G3306
Gal 3:12 on the contrary, it s, "The person who does NDT
Gal 4:21 law, are you not aware of what the law s? G201
Eph 4: 8 This is why it s: "When he ascended on G3306
1Ti 4: 1 The Spirit clearly s that in later times G3306
1Ti 5:18 For Scripture s, "Do not muzzle an ox while G3306
Heb 1: 6 into the world, he s, "Let all God's angels G3306
Heb 1: 7 In speaking of the angels he s, "He G3306
Heb 1: 8 But about the Son he s, "Your throne, O God NDT
Heb 1:10 He also s, "In the beginning, Lord, you laid NDT
Heb 2:12 He s, "I will declare your name to my G3306
Heb 2:13 And again he s, "Here am I, and the NDT
Heb 3: 7 as the Holy Spirit s: "Today, if you hear G3306
Heb 4: 5 And again in the passage above he s, "They NDT
Heb 5: 6 And he s in another place, "You are a G3306
Heb 10:15 also testifies to us about this. First he s: G3306
Heb 10:16 with them after that time, s the Lord. G3306
Heb 12: 5 It s, "My son, do not make light of the Lord's NDT
Jas 1:22 so deceive yourselves. Do what it s. NDT
Jas 1:23 does not do what it s is like someone who NDT
Jas 2:16 If one of you s to them, "Go in peace G3306
Jas 2:23 And the scripture was fulfilled that s G3306
Jas 4: 5 you think Scripture s without reason that G3306
Jas 4: 6 That is why Scripture s: "God opposes the G3306
1Pe 2: 6 For in Scripture it s: "See, I lay a stone in G4321
1Jn 2: 4 Whoever s, "I know him," but does not do G3306
Rev 1: 8 the Omega," s the Lord God, "who is G3306
Rev 2: 7 hear what the Spirit s to the churches. G3306
Rev 2:11 hear what the Spirit s to the churches. G3306
Rev 2:17 hear what the Spirit s to the churches. G3306
Rev 2:29 hear what the Spirit s to the churches. G3306
Rev 3: 6 hear what the Spirit s to the churches. G3306
Rev 3:13 hear what the Spirit s to the churches. G3306
Rev 3:22 hear what the Spirit s to the churches." G3306
Rev 14:13 s the Spirit, "they will rest from their G3306
Rev 22:20 He who testifies to these things s, "Yes, G3306

SCAB, SCABBED (KJV) RASH, SORES

SCABBARD (NIV84) SHEATH

SCABS (1)

Job 7: 5 body is clothed with worms and s, H1599+6760

SCALE (6) [SCALES]

1Sa 17: 5 wore a coat of s armor of bronze H9234+7989
2Sa 22:30 a troop; with my God I can s a wall. H1925
2Ch 18:33 between the breastplate and the s armor. H9234
Ps 18:29 a troop; with my God I can s a wall. H1925
Pr 18:11 they imagine it a wall too high to s. H8435
Joel 2: 7 like warriors; they s walls like soldiers. H6590

SCALES (25) [SCALE]

Lev 11: 9 you may eat any that have fins and s. H7989
Lev 11:10 streams that do not have fins and s— H7989
Lev 11:12 not have fins and s is to be regarded as H7989
Lev 19:36 Use honest s and honest weights, an H4404
Dt 14: 9 you may eat any that has fins and s. H7989
Dt 14:10 does not have fins and s you may not eat; H7989
Job 6: 2 all my misery be placed on the s! H4404
Job 31: 6 weigh me in honest s and he will know H4404
Pr 11: 1 The LORD detests dishonest s, but accurate H4404
Pr 16:11 Honest s and balances belong to the LORD; H4404
Pr 20:23 dishonest s do not please him. H4404
Isa 40:12 the mountains on the s and the hills in a H7144
Isa 40:15 they are regarded as dust on the s; he H4404
Isa 46: 6 their bags and weigh out silver on the s; H7866
Jer 32:10 weighed out the silver on the s. H4404
Eze 5: 1 Then take a set of s and divide up H4404+5486
Eze 29: 4 the fish of your streams stick to your s. H7989
Eze 29: 4 streams, with all the fish sticking to your s. H7989
Eze 45:10 You are to use accurate s, an accurate H4404
Da 5:27 weighed on the s and found wanting. A10396
Hos 12: 7 uses dishonest s and loves to defraud. H4404
Am 8: 5 the price and cheating with dishonest s, H4404
Mic 6:11 Shall I acquit someone with dishonest s H4404
Ac 9:18 something like s fell from Saul's eyes G3318
Rev 6: 5 rider was holding a pair of s in his hand. G2433

SCALL (KJV) SORE

SCALP (1) [SCALPS]

Lev 13:41 from the front of his s and has a bald H7156

SCALPS (1) [SCALP]

Isa 3:17 of Zion; the LORD will make their s bald." H7327

SCAPEGOAT (4) [GOAT]

Lev 16: 8 one lot for the LORD and the other for the s. H6439
Lev 16:10 chosen by lot as the s shall be presented H6439
Lev 16:10 by sending it into the wilderness as a s. H6439
Lev 16:26 the goat as a s must wash his clothes H6439

SCAR (2)

Lev 13:23 it is only a s from the boil, and the H7648
Lev 13:28 them clean; it is only a s from the burn. H7648

SCARCE (2) [SCARCELY, SCARCER, SCARCITY]

Dt 8: 9 bread will not be s and you H430+928+5017
Eze 4:17 food and water will be s. They will be H2893

SCARCELY (4) [SCARCE]

Ge 27:30 Jacob had s left his father's presence H421
Job 29:24 smiled at them, they s believed it; the H4202
SS 3: 4 S had I passed them when I found H3869+5071
Lk 9:39 It s ever leaves him and is destroying him G3653

SCARCER (1) [SCARCE]

Isa 13:12 I will make people s than pure gold, more H3700

SCARCITY (2) [SCARCE]

Pr 6:11 you like a thief and s like an armed man. H4728
Pr 24:34 you like a thief and s like an armed man. H4728

SCARECROW (1)

Jer 10: 5 Like a s in a cucumber field, their idols H9473

SCARLET (49)

Ge 38:28 the midwife took a s thread and tied it on H9106
Ge 38:30 who had the s thread on his wrist, came H9106
Ex 25: 4 purple and s yarn and fine linen H9357+9106
Ex 26: 1 purple and s yarn, with cherubim H9357+9106
Ex 26:31 purple and s yarn and finely H9357+9106
Ex 26:36 purple and s yarn and finely H9357+9106
Ex 27:16 purple and s yarn and finely H9357+9106
Ex 28: 5 purple and s yarn, and fine linen. H9357+9106
Ex 28: 6 purple and s yarn, and of finely H9357+9106
Ex 28: 8 purple and s yarn, and with H9357+9106
Ex 28:15 purple and s yarn, and of finely H9357+9106
Ex 28:33 purple and s yarn around the hem H9357+9106
Ex 35: 6 purple and s yarn and fine linen H9357+9106
Ex 35:23 purple or s yarn or fine linen H9357+9106
Ex 35:25 purple or s yarn or fine linen. H9357+9106
Ex 35:35 purple and s yarn and fine linen H9357+9106
Ex 36: 8 purple and s yarn, with cherubim H9357+9106
Ex 36:35 purple and s yarn and finely H9357+9106
Ex 36:37 purple and s yarn and finely H9357+9106
Ex 38:18 purple and s yarn and finely H9357+9106
Ex 38:23 purple and s yarn and fine linen.) H9357+9106
Ex 39: 1 purple and s yarn they made H9357+9106
Ex 39: 2 purple and s yarn, and of finely H9357+9106
Ex 39: 3 purple and s yarn and fine linen H9357+9106
Ex 39: 5 purple and s yarn, and with H9357+9106
Ex 39: 8 purple and s yarn, and of finely H9357+9106
Ex 39:24 purple and s yarn and finely H9357+9106
Ex 39:29 purple and s yarn—the work of an H9357+9106
Lev 14: 4 s yarn and hyssop be brought for H9357+9106
Lev 14: 6 the s yarn and the hyssop H9357+9106
Lev 14:49 cedar wood, s yarn and hyssop. H9357+9106
Lev 14:51 hyssop, the s yarn and the live bird H9357+9106
Lev 14:52 the hyssop and the s yarn. H9357+9106
Nu 4: 8 are to spread a s cloth over them, H9357+9106
Nu 19: 6 hyssop and s wool and throw them H9357+9106
Jos 2:18 you have tied this s cord in the window H9106
Jos 2:21 And she tied the s cord in the window. H9106
2Sa 1:24 who clothed you in s and finery, who H9106
Pr 31:21 all of them are clothed in s. H9106
SS 4: 3 Your lips are like a s ribbon; your mouth is H9106
Isa 1:18 "Though your sins are like s, they shall be H9106
Jer 4:30 dress yourself in s and put on jewels of H9106
Na 2: 3 soldiers are red; the warriors are clad in s. H9443
Mt 27:28 stripped him and put a s robe on him, G3132
Heb 9:19 with water, s wool and branches of hyssop G3132
Rev 17: 3 a woman sitting on a s beast that was G3132
Rev 17: 4 The woman was dressed in purple and s G3132
Rev 18:12 silk and s cloth; every sort of citron G3132
Rev 18:16 purple and s, and glittering with G3132

SCATTER (39) [SCATTERED, SCATTERING, SCATTERS]

Ge 49: 7 I will s them in Jacob and disperse them H2745
Lev 26:33 I will s you among the nations and will H2430
Nu 16:37 charred remains and s the coals some H2430
Dt 4:27 The LORD will s you among the peoples H7046
Dt 28:64 Then the LORD will s you among all H7046
Dt 32:26 I said I would s them and erase their H6990
1Sa 13: 8 to Gilgal, and Saul's men began to s. H7046
1Ki 14:15 to their ancestors and s them beyond the H2430
Ne 1: 8 unfaithful, I will s you among the nations H7046
Ps 68:30 S the nations who delight in war. H1029
Ps 106:27 the nations and s them throughout the H2430
Ps 144: 6 Send forth lightning and s the enemy H7046
Ecc 3: 5 a time to s stones and a time to gather H8959
Isa 24: 1 he will ruin its face and s its inhabitants H7046
Isa 28:25 does he not sow caraway and s cumin? H2450
Isa 33: 3 when you rise up, the nations s. H5880
Jer 9:16 I will s them among nations that neither H7046
Jer 13:24 "I will s you like chaff driven by the desert H7046
Jer 18:17 I will s them before their enemies H7046
Jer 30:11 all the nations among which I s you, H7046
Jer 46:28 all the nations among which I s you, H5615
Jer 49:32 I will s to the winds those who are in H2430
Jer 49:36 of heaven; I will s them to the four winds H2430
Eze 5: 2 around the city. And s a third to the wind H2430
Eze 5:10 on you and will s all your survivors H2430
Eze 5:12 a third I will s to the winds and H2430
Eze 6: 5 and I will s your bones around your altars. H2430
Eze 10: 2 the cherubim and s them over the city." H2450
Eze 12:14 I will s to the winds all those around him— H2430
Eze 12:15 the nations and s them through the H2430
Eze 20:23 the nations and s them through the H2430
Eze 22:15 among the nations and s you through the H2430
Eze 29:12 the nations and s them through the H2430
Eze 30:23 the nations and s them through the H2430
Eze 30:26 the nations and s them through the H2430
Da 4:14 strip off its leaves and s its fruit. A10095
Hab 3:14 when his warriors stormed out to s us, H7046
Zec 1:21 against the land of Judah to s its people." H2430
Zec 10: 9 Though I s them among the peoples, yet H2445

SCATTERED (84) [SCATTER]

Ge 9:19 came the people who were s over the H5880
Ge 10:18 Later the Canaanite clans s H7046
Ge 11: 4 otherwise we will be s over the face of the H7046
Ge 11: 8 So the LORD s them from there over all the H7046
Ge 11: 9 From there the LORD s them over the face H7046
Ex 5:12 So the people s all over Egypt to gather H7046
Ex 32:20 s it on the water and made the Israelites H2430
Nu 10:35 May your enemies be s; may your foes H7046
Nu 11:31 It s them up to two cubits deep all around H5759
Dt 30: 3 from all the nations where he s you. H7046
Jdg 9:45 he destroyed the city and s salt over it. H2445
1Sa 11:11 Those who survived were s, so that no two H7046
1Sa 30:16 there they were, s over the countryside H5759
2Sa 17:19 opening of the well and s grain over it. H8848
2Sa 22:15 He shot his arrows and s the enemy, with H7046
1Ki 22:17 "I saw all Israel s on the hills like sheep H7046
2Ki 23: 6 it to powder and s the dust over the H8959
2Ki 25: 5 soldiers were separated from him and s, H7046
2Ch 18:16 "I saw all Israel s on the hills like sheep H7046
2Ch 34: 4 broke to pieces and s over the graves of H2450
Job 4:11 and the cubs of the lioness are s. H7233
Job 18:15 burning sulfur is s over his dwelling. H2430
Job 38:24 where the east winds are s over the earth? H7046
Ps 18:14 He shot his arrows and s the enemy, with H7046
Ps 44:11 like sheep and have s us among the H2430
Ps 53: 5 God s the bones of those who attacked H7061
Ps 68: 1 God arise, may his enemies be s; may his H7046
Ps 68:14 When the Almighty s the kings in the H7298
Ps 89:10 with your strong arm you s your enemies. H7061
Ps 92: 9 will perish; all evildoers will be s. H7233
Ps 112: 9 They have freely s their gifts to the poor H7061
Ps 141: 7 so our bones have been s at the mouth of H7061
Isa 11:12 assemble the s people of Judah from the H7046
Jer 3:13 you have s your favors to foreign gods H7061
Jer 10:21 they do not prosper and all their flock is s. H7046
Jer 23: 2 "Because you have s my flock and driven H7046
Jer 31:10 'He who s Israel will gather them and will H2430
Jer 40:12 all the countries where they had been s. H5615
Jer 40:15 cause all the Jews who are gathered around you to be s H7046
Jer 43: 5 all the nations where they had been s. H5615
Jer 50:17 "Israel is a s flock that lions have chased H7061
Jer 52: 8 soldiers were separated from him and s, H7046
La 4: 1 The sacred gems are s at every street H9161
La 4:16 The LORD himself has s them; he no H2745
Eze 6: 8 sword when you are s among the lands H2430
Eze 11:16 the nations and s them among the H7046
Eze 11:17 the countries where you have been s, H7046
Eze 17:21 the survivors will be s to the winds. H7298
Eze 20:34 the countries where you have been s— H7046
Eze 20:41 the countries where you have been s, H7046
Eze 28:25 from the nations where they have been s, H7046
Eze 29:13 from the nations where they were s. H7046
Eze 34: 5 So they were s because there was no H7046
Eze 34: 5 when they were s they became food H7046
Eze 34: 6 They were s over the whole earth, and no H7046
Eze 34:12 looks after his s flock when he is with H7298
Eze 34:12 the places where they were s on a day of H7046
Eze 36:19 and they were s through the countries H2430
Da 9: 7 countries where you have s us because of H5615
Joel 3: 2 because they s my people among the H7061
Na 3:18 Your people are s on the mountains with H7056

S

Zep 3:10 my worshipers, my s people, will bring me H7046
Zec 1:19 "These are the horns that s Judah, Israel H2430
Zec 1:21 are the horns that s Judah so that no one H2430
Zec 2: 6 "for *I have* s you to the four winds of H7298
Zec 7:14 '*I* s them **with a whirlwind** among all the H6192
Zec 13: 7 the sheep *will be* s, and I will turn my H7046
Mt 25:24 gathering where *you have* not s **seed**. G1399
Mt 25:26 sown and gather where *I have* not s **seed**? G1399
Mt 26:31 the sheep of the flock *will be* s. G1399
Mk 14:27 the shepherd, and the sheep *will be* s. G1399
Lk 1:51 *he has* s those who are proud in their G1399
Jn 2:15 *he* s the coins of the money changers G1772
Jn 7:35 go where **our people live** s among G3836+1402
Jn 11:52 nation but also for the s children of God, G1399
Jn 16:32 in fact has come when *you will be* s, G5025
Ac 5:37 was killed, and all his followers *were* s. G1399
Ac 8: 1 the apostles *were* s throughout Judea G1401
Ac 8: 4 Those *who had been* s preached the word G1401
Ac 11:19 Now those *who had been* s by the G1401
1Co 10: 5 *their bodies were* s in the wilderness. G2954
2Co 9: 9 "*They have* **freely** s their gifts to the poor G5025
Jas 1: 1 To the twelve tribes **s among the nations**: G1402
1Pe 1: 1 exiles **s throughout** the provinces of G1402

SCATTERING (5) [SCATTER]

1Sa 13:11 "When I saw that the men *were* s, and H5880
Jer 23: 1 who are destroying and s the sheep of my H7046
Mt 13: 4 As he *was* **s** *the* **seed**, some fell along the G5062
Mk 4: 4 As *he was* **s** *the* **seed**, some fell along the G5062
Lk 8: 5 As he *was* **s** *the* **seed**, some fell along the G5062

SCATTERS (7) [SCATTER]

Job 36:30 See how *he* s his lightning about him H7298
Job 37:11 moisture; *he* s his lightning *through* them. H7046
Ps 147:16 snow like wool and s the frost like ashes. H7061
Mt 12:30 whoever does not gather with me s. G5025
Mk 4:26 A man s seed on the ground. G965
Lk 11:23 whoever does not gather with me s. G5025
Jn 10:12 Then the wolf attacks the flock and s it. G5025

SCENE (1)

Mk 9:25 Jesus saw that a crowd was running to the s, NDT

SCENT (2)

Job 14: 9 at the s *of* water it will bud and put H8194
Job 39:25 *It* **catches the** s *of* battle from afar, the H8193

SCEPTER (26) [SCEPTERS]

Ge 49:10 The s will not depart from Judah, nor the H8657
Nu 24:17 out of Jacob; a s will rise out of Israel. H8657
Est 4:11 extends the gold s to them and spares H9222
Est 5: 2 out to her the gold s that was in his hand. H9222
Est 5: 2 approached and touched the tip of the s. H9222
Est 8: 4 extended the gold s to Esther and she H9222
Ps 45: 6 a s *of* justice will be the scepter of your H8657
Ps 45: 6 of justice will be the s *of* your kingdom. H8657
Ps 60: 7 Ephraim is my helmet, Judah is my s. H2980
Ps 108: 8 Ephraim is my helmet, Judah is my s. H2980
Ps 110: 2 LORD will extend your mighty s from Zion, H4751
Ps 125: 3 The s *of* the wicked will not remain over H8657
Isa 14: 5 the rod of the wicked, the s *of* the rulers, H8657
Jer 48:17 'How broken is the mighty s, how broken H4751
Eze 19:11 fit for a ruler's s. It towered high above H8657
Eze 19:14 strong branch is left on it fit for a ruler's s. H8657
Eze 21:10 'Shall we rejoice in the s *of* my royal son? H8657
Eze 21:13 And what if even the s, which the sword H8657
Am 1: 5 the one who holds the s in Beth Eden. H8657
Am 1: 8 the one who holds the s in Ashkelon. H8657
Zec 10:11 down and Egypt's s will pass away. H8657
Heb 1: 8 a s of justice will be the scepter of your G4811
Heb 1: 8 of justice will be the s of your kingdom. G4811
Rev 2:27 them with an iron s and will dash them to G4811
Rev 12: 5 "will rule all the nations with an iron s." G4811
Rev 19:15 "He will rule them with an iron s." He G4811

SCEPTERS (1) [SCEPTER]

Nu 21:18 the nobles with s and staffs. H2980

SCEVA (1)

Ac 19:14 Seven sons *of* S, a Jewish chief priest G5005

SCHEME (5) [SCHEMED, SCHEMER, SCHEMES, SCHEMING]

Est 9:25 orders that the evil s Haman had devised H4742
Ps 38:12 talk of my ruin; all day long *they* s and lie. H2047
Ecc 7:25 wisdom and the s **of things** and to H3113
Ecc 7:27 to another to discover the **s of things**— H3113
Eze 38:10 your mind and you will devise an evil s. H4742

SCHEMED (1) [SCHEME]

Mt 26: 4 and *they* s to arrest Jesus secretly and kill G5205

SCHEMER (1) [SCHEME]

Pr 24: 8 plots evil will be known as a s. H1251+4659

SCHEMES (26) [SCHEME]

Ex 21:14 But if anyone s and kills someone H2326
Job 5:13 the s *of* the wily are swept away. H6783
Job 18: 7 is weakened; his own s throw him down. H6783
Job 21:27 the s by which you would wrong me. H4659
Ps 10: 2 who are caught in the s he devises. H4659
Ps 21:11 plot evil against you and devise **wicked** s, H4659
Ps 26:10 in whose hands are **wicked** s, whose right H2365
Ps 37: 7 when they carry out their **wicked** s. H4659
Ps 56: 5 twist my words; all their s are for my ruin. H4742
Ps 119:150 Those who devise **wicked** s are near, but H2365
Pr 1:31 ways and be filled with the fruit of their s. H4600
Pr 6:18 a heart that devises wicked s, feet that are H4742
Pr 10:23 A fool finds pleasure in wicked s, but a H6913
Pr 12: 2 he condemns those who devise **wicked** s. H4659
Pr 14:17 the one who devises **evil** s is hated. H4659
Pr 24: 9 The s *of* folly are sin, and people detest a H2365
Ecc 7:29 they have gone in search of many s." H3115
Ecc 8:11 people's hearts are filled with s to do wrong. NDT
Isa 32: 7 they make up **evil** s to destroy the poor H2365
Isa 59: 7 They pursue evil s; acts of violence mark H4742
Jer 6:19 the fruit of their s, because they have not H4742
Jer 11:15 with many others, works out her **evil** s? H4659
Hos 6: 9 to Shechem, carrying out their **wicked** s. H2365
2Co 2:11 For we are not unaware *of* his s. G3784
Eph 6:11 can take your stand against the devil's s. G3497
Jas 4:16 you boast in your **arrogant** s. All such G224

SCHEMING (3) [SCHEME]

Ne 6: 2 But they *were* s to harm me; H3108
Mk 14: 1 teachers of the law *were* s to arrest Jesus G2426
Eph 4:14 craftiness of people in their deceitful s. G3497

SCHISM (KJV) DIVISION

SCHOOL (KJV) LECTURE HALL

SCHOOLMASTER (KJV) GUARDIAN

SCIENCE (KJV) KNOWLEDGE

SCOFF (11) [SCOFFED, SCOFFERS, SCOFFING, SCOFFS]

1Ki 9: 8 by will be appalled and *will* s and say, H9239
Ps 59: 8 at them, LORD; *you* s at all those nations. H4352
Ps 73: 8 *They* s, and speak with malice; with H4610
Jer 19: 8 be appalled and *will* s because of all its H9239
Jer 49:17 be appalled and *will* s because of all its H9239
Jer 50:13 *they will* s because of all her wounds. H9239
La 2:15 *they* s and shake their heads at Daughter H9239
La 2:16 *they* s and gnash their teeth and say H9239
Eze 27:36 merchants among the nations s at you; H9239
Hab 1:10 They mock kings and s at rulers. H5377
Zep 2:15 All who pass by her s and shake their fists. H9239

SCOFFED (1) [SCOFF]

2Ch 36:16 his words and s at his prophets until H9506

SCOFFERS (4) [SCOFF]

Isa 28:14 you s who rule this people in H408+4371
Ac 13:41 you s, wonder and perish, for I am G2970
2Pe 3: 3 that in the last days s will come, G1851
Jude 18 times there will be s who will follow their G1851

SCOFFING (1) [SCOFF]

2Pe 3: 3 s and following their own evil desires. G1848

SCOFFS (2) [SCOFF]

Ps 2: 4 in heaven laughs; the Lord s at them. H4352
Pr 29: 9 the fool rages and s, and there is no H8471

SCOOP (1) [SCOOPED, SCOOPING, SCOOPS]

Pr 6:27 *Can* a man s fire into his lap without his H3149

SCOOPED (1) [SCOOP]

Jdg 14: 9 *He* s **out** the honey with his hands and ate H8098

SCOOPING (1) [SCOOP]

Isa 30:14 from a hearth or s water out of a cistern H3106

SCOOPS (1) [SCOOP]

Ps 7:15 digs a hole and s it **out** falls into the pit H2916

SCORCH (1) [SCORCHED, SCORCHING, SUN-SCORCHED]

Rev 16: 8 the sun was allowed *to* s people with fire. G3009

SCORCHED (11) [SCORCH]

Ge 41: 6 sprouted—thin and s *by* the east wind. H8728
Ge 41:23 withered and thin and s *by* the east wind. H8728
Ge 41:27 heads of grain s *by* the east wind: H8728
2Ki 19:26 on the roof, s before it grows up. H8729
Pr 6:28 on hot coals without his feet **being** s? H3917
Isa 9:19 the land *will* **be** s and the people H6977
Isa 37:27 on the roof, s before it grows up. H8729
Eze 20:47 face from south to north *will* **be** s by it. H7646
Da 3:27 their robes *were* not s, and there was no A10731
Mt 13: 6 the plants *were* s, and they withered G3009
Mk 4: 6 sun came up, *the plants were* s, and they G3009

SCORCHING (8) [SCORCH]

Dt 28:22 with s **heat** and drought, with H3031
Ps 11: 6 burning sulfur; a s wind will be their lot. H2363
Pr 16:27 and on their lips it is like a s fire. H7647
Isa 11:15 with a s wind he will sweep his hand over H6522
Jer 4:11 "A s wind from the barren heights in the H7456
Jnh 4: 8 God provided a s east wind, and the H3046
Jas 1:11 the sun rises with s **heat** and withers the G3014
Rev 7:16 not beat down on them,' nor any s **heat**. G3008

SCORN (37) [SCORNED, SCORNFULLY, SCORNING, SCORNS]

1Sa 2:29 Why *do you* s my sacrifice and offering H1246
2Ch 29: 8 them an object of dread and horror and s, H9240
Job 16:10 strike my cheek in s and unite together H3075
Job 19:18 Even the little boys s me; when I appear H4415
Job 34: 7 anyone like Job, who drinks s like water? H4353
Ps 39: 8 do not make me the s *of* fools. H3075
Ps 44:13 the s and derision of those around us. H4353
Ps 64: 8 who see them *will* **shake** *their* **heads in** s. H5653
Ps 69: 7 For I endure s for your sake, and shame H3075
Ps 69:10 When I weep and fast, I must endure s; H3075
Ps 69:20 S has broken my heart and has left me H3075
Ps 71:13 harm me be covered with s and disgrace. H3075
Ps 79: 4 of s and derision to those around us. H4353
Ps 89:41 he has become the s of his neighbors. H3075
Ps 109:25 I am an **object of** s to my accusers; when H3075
Ps 119:22 Remove from me their s and contempt, for H3075
Pr 23: 9 to fools, for *they will* s your prudent words. H996
Isa 43:28 Jacob to destruction and Israel to s. H1526
Jer 18:16 be an object of horror and *of* lasting s; H9241
Jer 19: 8 city and make it an object of horror and s; H9240
Jer 25: 9 make them an object of horror and s, H9240
Jer 25:18 them a ruin and an object of horror and s, H9240
Jer 29:18 object of horror, of s and reproach, among H9240
Jer 48:27 that *you* **shake** *your* **head in** s whenever H5653
Jer 51:37 an object of horror and s, a place where H9240
Eze 22: 4 make you an **object of** s to the nations H3075
Eze 23:32 it will bring s and derision, for it H7465
Eze 34:29 in the land or bear the s *of* the nations. H4009
Eze 36: 6 you have suffered the s *of* the nations. H4009
Eze 36: 7 the nations around you will also suffer s. H4009
Eze 36:15 will you suffer the s *of* the peoples or H3075
Da 9:16 your people an **object of** s to all those H3075
Joel 2:17 not make your inheritance an **object of** s, H3075
Joel 2:19 I make you an **object of** s to the nations. H3075
Mic 6:16 you will bear the s *of* the nations. H3075
Hab 2: 6 all of them taunt him with ridicule and s, H2648
Gal 4:14 you did not treat me with contempt or s. G1746

SCORNED (9) [SCORN]

2Ch 30:10 people s and ridiculed them. H8471
Est 3: 6 he **s the idea** of killing only H1022+928+6524
Ps 22: 6 not a man, s *by* everyone, despised H3075
Ps 22:24 has not despised or s the suffering of the H9210
Ps 69:19 You know how I am s, disgraced and H3075
SS 8: 7 house for love, it *would be* **utterly** s. H996+996
Eze 16:31 a prostitute, because you s payment. H7840
Eze 16:57 *you are* now s *by* the daughters of Edom H3075
1Co 6: 4 those whose way of life *is* s in the church? G2024

SCORNFULLY (1) [SCORN]

Job 34:37 s *he* **claps** *his* **hands** among us and H6215

SCORNING (1) [SCORN]

Heb 12: 2 he endured the cross, s its shame, and sat G2969

SCORNS (2) [SCORN]

Pr 13:13 *Whoever* s instruction will pay for it, but H996
Pr 30:17 mocks a father, *that* s an aged mother, will H996

SCORPION (5) [SCORPIONS]

Nu 34: 4 cross south of S Pass, continue on to Zin H6832
Jos 15: 3 crossed south of S Pass, continued on to H6832
Jdg 1:36 the Amorites was from S Pass to Sela H6832
Lk 11:12 Or if he asks for an egg, will give him a s? G5026
Rev 9: 5 like that of the sting *of* a s when it strikes. G5026

SCORPIONS (9) [SCORPION]

Dt 8:15 with its venomous snakes and s. H6832
1Ki 12:11 you with whips; I will scourge you with s. H6832
1Ki 12:14 you with whips; I will scourge you with s." H6832
2Ch 10:11 you with whips; I will scourge you with s. H6832
2Ch 10:14 you with whips; I will scourge you with s." H6832
Eze 2: 6 are all around you and you live among s. H6832
Lk 10:19 on snakes and s and to overcome all G5026
Rev 9: 3 given power like that of s of the earth. G5026
Rev 9:10 with stingers, like s, and in their tails they G5026

SCOUNDREL (3) [SCOUNDRELS]

2Sa 16: 7 get out, you murderer, you s! H408+2021+1175
Pr 16:27 A s plots evil, and on their lips it is H408+1175
Isa 32: 5 noble nor the s be highly respected. H3964

SCOUNDRELS (8) [SCOUNDREL]

Jdg 9: 4 Abimelek used it to hire reckless s H7069
Jdg 11: 3 where a gang of s gathered around him H8199
1Sa 2:12 Eli's sons were s; they had no H1201+1175
1Sa 10:27 But some s said, "How can this H1201+1175
1Ki 21:10 But seat two s opposite him and H1201+1175
1Ki 21:13 Then two s came and sat opposite H1201+1175
2Ch 13: 7 Some worthless s gathered around H1201+1175
Isa 32: 7 S use wicked methods, they make up evil H3964

SCOURED (1)

Lev 6:28 the pot *is to* be s and rinsed with water. H5347

SCOURGE, SCOURGES, SCOURGETH, SCOURGING, SCOURGINGS (KJV) CHASTENS, FLOG, FLOGGED, FLOGGING, LASH, PUNISHMENT, WHIP, WHIPS

SCOURGE (8) [SCOURGED]

1Ki 12:11 you with whips; I *will* s you with scorpions. H3579
1Ki 12:14 you with whips; I *will* s you with scorpions. H3579
2Ch 10:11 you with whips; I will s you with scorpions. NDT

2Ch 10:14 you with whips; I will s you with scorpions." NDT
Job 9:23 When a s brings sudden death, he mocks H8765
Ps 39:10 Remove your s from me; I am overcome H5596
Isa 28:15 When an overwhelming s sweeps by, it H8765
Isa 28:18 When the overwhelming s sweeps by, you H8765

SCOURGED (4) [SCOURGE]
1Ki 12:11 My father s you with whips; I will scourge H3579
1Ki 12:14 My father s you with whips; I will scourge H3579
2Ch 10:11 My father s you with whips; I will scourge H3579
2Ch 10:14 My father s you with whips; I will scourge H3579

SCOUTS (2)
1Sa 26: 4 he sent out s and learned that Saul had H8078
1Ki 20:17 Now Ben-Hadad had dispatched s, who NDT

SCRAPE (1) [SCRAPED]
Eze 26: 4 *I will* s **away** her rubble and make her a H6081

SCRAPED (4) [SCRAPE]
Lev 14:41 *He must* **have** all the inside walls of the house s H7909
Lev 14:41 the material that *is* s **off** dumped into an H7894
Lev 14:43 torn out and the house s and plastered, H7894
Job 2: 8 pottery and s **himself** with it as he sat H1740

SCRAPS (2)
Jdg 1: 7 toes cut off *have* **picked up** s under my H4377
Eze 13:19 a few handfuls of barley and s *of* bread. H7336

SCRAWNY (1)
Ge 41:19 cows came up—s and very ugly and lean. H1924

SCREAM (2) [SCREAMED, SCREAMS]
Ge 39:15 he heard me **s for help**, H8123+7754+2256+7924
Dt 22:24 she was in a town and *did* not **s for help**, H7590

SCREAMED (3) [SCREAM]
Ge 39:14 to sleep with me, but *I* s. H7924+928+7754+1524
Ge 39:18 as soon as I **s for help**, H8123+7754+2256+7924
Dt 22:27 though the betrothed woman s, there H7590

SCREAMS (1) [SCREAM]
Lk 9:39 A spirit seizes him and *he* suddenly s; it *G3189*

SCREECH (4)
Lev 11:16 the horned owl, the **s owl**, the gull, any H9379
Dt 14:15 the horned owl, the **s owl**, the gull, any H9379
Isa 34:11 The desert owl and **s owl** will possess it H7887
Zep 2:14 desert owl and the **s owl** will roost on her H7887

SCRIBE (5) [SCRIBE'S, SCRIBES]
1Ch 24: 6 The s Shemaiah son of Nethanel, a Levite H6221
1Ch 27:32 was a counselor, a man of insight and a s. H6221
Ne 13:13 Zadok the s, and a Levite named H6221
Jer 36:26 to arrest Baruch the s and Jeremiah the H6221
Jer 36:32 gave it to the s Baruch son of Neriah, H6221

SCRIBE'S (1) [SCRIBE]
Jer 36:23 cut them off with a s knife and threw them H6221

SCRIBES (3) [SCRIBE]
1Ch 2:55 the clans of s who lived at Jabez: the H6221
2Ch 34:13 were secretaries, s and gatekeepers. H8853
Jer 8: 8 the lying pen of the s has handled it H6221

SCRIP (KJV) BAG, POUCH

SCRIPT (5)
Ezr 4: 7 written in Aramaic s and in the Aramaic H4181
Est 1:22 province in its own s and to each people H4181
Est 3:12 wrote out in the s *of* each province and in H4181
Est 8: 9 were written in the s *of* each province H4181
Est 8: 9 to the Jews in their own s and language. H4181

SCRIPTURE (33) [SCRIPTURES]
Mk 12:10 Haven't you read this **passage of** S: " 'The *G1210*
Lk 4:21 "Today this s is fulfilled in your hearing." *G1210*
Jn 2:22 they believed the s and the words that *G1210*
Jn 7:38 believes in me, as S has said, rivers of *G1210*
Jn 7:42 Does not S say that the Messiah will come *G1210*
Jn 10:35 God came—and S cannot be set aside— *G1210*
Jn 13:18 But this is to fulfill this **passage of** S: 'He *G1210*
Jn 17:12 to destruction so that S would be fulfilled. *G1210*
Jn 19:24 happened that the s might be fulfilled *G1210*
Jn 19:28 finished, and so that S would be fulfilled *G1210*
Jn 19:36 happened so that the s would be fulfilled: *G1210*
Jn 19:37 as another s says, "They will look on *G1210*
Jn 20: 9 not understand *from* S that Jesus had to *G1210*
Ac 1:16 the S had to be fulfilled in which the Holy *G1210*
Ac 8:32 This is the passage *of* S the eunuch was *G1210*
Ac 8:35 with that very **passage of** S and told him *G1210*
Ro 4: 3 What does S say? "Abraham believed God *G1210*
Ro 9:17 For S says to Pharaoh: "I raised you up *G1210*
Ro 10:11 As S says, "Anyone who believes in him *G1210*
Ro 11: 2 you know what S says in the passage *G1210*
Gal 3: 8 S foresaw that God would justify the *G1210*
Gal 3:16 S does not say "and to seeds," meaning NDT
Gal 3:22 But S has locked up everything under the *G1210*
Gal 4:30 But what does S say? "Get rid of the slave *G1210*
1Ti 4:13 devote yourself to the **public reading** *of* S, AIT
1Ti 5:18 For S says, "Do not muzzle an ox while it *G1210*
2Ti 3:16 All S is God-breathed and is useful for *G1210*
Jas 2: 8 If you really keep the royal law found in S *G1210*
Jas 2:23 And the s was fulfilled that says *G1210*
Jas 4: 5 Or do you think S says without reason that *G1210*
Jas 4: 6 That is why S says: "God opposes the NDT
1Pe 2: 6 For in S it says: "See, I lay a stone in Zion *G1210*
2Pe 1:20 that no prophecy *of* S came about by the *G1210*

SCRIPTURES (21) [SCRIPTURE]
Da 9: 2 understood from the S, according to the H6219
Mt 21:42 to them, "Have you never read in the S: *G1210*
Mt 22:29 do not know the S or the power of God *G1210*
Mt 26:54 how then would the S be fulfilled that say *G1210*
Mk 12:24 do not know the S or the power of God *G1210*
Mk 14:49 But the S must be fulfilled." *G1210*
Lk 24:27 was said in all the S concerning himself. *G1210*
Lk 24:32 us on the road and opened the S to us?" *G1210*
Lk 24:45 minds so they could understand the S. *G1210*
Jn 5:39 You study the S diligently because you *G1210*
Jn 5:39 These are the very S that testify about me, NDT
Ac 17: 2 days he reasoned with them from the S, *G1210*
Ac 17:11 examined the S every day to see if *G1210*
Ac 18:24 with a thorough knowledge of the S. *G1210*
Ac 18:28 proving from the S that Jesus was the *G1210*
Ro 1: 2 through his prophets in the Holy S *G1210*
Ro 15: 4 the endurance *taught in* the S and the *G1210*
1Co 15: 3 Christ died for our sins according to the S, *G1210*
1Co 15: 4 raised on the third day according to the S, *G1210*
2Ti 3:15 from infancy you have known the Holy S, *G1207*
2Pe 3:16 as they do the other S, to their own *G1210*

SCROLL (73) [SCROLLS]
Ex 17:14 "Write this on a s as something to be H6219
Nu 5:23 these curses on a s and then wash them H6219
Dt 17:18 write for himself on a s a copy of this law, H6219
Jos 18: 9 They wrote its description on a s, town by H6219
1Sa 10:25 wrote them down on a s and deposited it H6219
Ezr 6: 2 A s was found in the citadel of Ecbatana A10399
Job 19:23 recorded, that they were written on a s, H6219
Ps 40: 7 it is written about me in the s. H4479+6219
Ps 56: 8 list my tears on your s—are they not in H5532
Isa 8: 1 "Take a large s and write on it with an H1663
Isa 29:11 vision is nothing but words sealed in a s. H6219
Isa 29:11 And if you give **the** s to someone who H2257S
Isa 29:12 Or if you give the s to someone who H6219
Isa 29:18 day the deaf will hear the words of the s, H6219
Isa 30: 8 inscribe it on a s, that for the days to H6219
Isa 34: 4 the heavens rolled up like a s; H6219
Isa 34:16 Look in the s *of* the LORD and read: None H6219
Jer 36: 2 "Take a s and write on it all the H4479+6219
Jer 36: 4 Baruch wrote them on the s. H4479+6219
Jer 36: 6 the people from the s the words of the H4479
Jer 36: 8 he read the words of the LORD from the s. H6219
Jer 36:10 temple the words of Jeremiah from the s. H6219
Jer 36:11 heard all the words of the LORD from the s H6219
Jer 36:13 Baruch read to the people from the s, H6219
Jer 36:14 "Bring the s from which you have read to H4479
Jer 36:14 went to them with the s in his hand. H4479
Jer 36:18 and I wrote them in ink on the s. H6219
Jer 36:20 After they put the s in the room of H4479
Jer 36:21 The king sent Jehudi to get the s, and H4479
Jer 36:23 had read three or four columns of the s, NDT
Jer 36:23 until the entire s was burned in the fire. H4479
Jer 36:25 urged the king not to burn the s, H4479
Jer 36:27 the king burned the s containing the H4479
Jer 36:28 "Take another s and write on it all the H4479
Jer 36:28 on it all the words that were on the first s, H4479
Jer 36:29 You burned that s and said, "Why did you H4479
Jer 36:32 took another s and gave it to the H4479
Jer 36:32 all the words of the s that Jehoiakim king H6219
Jer 45: 1 Neriah wrote on a s the words Jeremiah H6219
Jer 51:60 had written on a s about all the disasters H6219
Jer 51:63 When you finish reading this s, tie a stone H6219
Eze 2: 9 stretched out to me. In it was a s, H4479+6219
Eze 3: 1 before you, eat this s; then go and speak H4479
Eze 3: 2 my mouth, and he gave me the s to eat. H4479
Eze 3: 3 eat this s I am giving you and fill your H4479
Da 12: 4 the words of the s until the time of the H6219
Zec 5: 1 there before me was a flying s. H4479
Zec 5: 2 "I see a flying s, twenty cubits long and H4479
Mal 3:16 A s *of* remembrance was written in his H6219
Lk 4:17 the s of the prophet Isaiah was *G1046*
Lk 4:20 Then he rolled up the s, gave it back to *G1046*
Heb 9:19 sprinkled the s and all the people. *G1046*
Heb 10: 7 it is written about me in the s—I *G3053+1046*
Rev 1:11 "Write on a s what you see and send it to *G1046*
Rev 5: 1 sat on the throne a s with writing on both *G1046*
Rev 5: 2 worthy to break the seals and open the s?" *G1046*
Rev 5: 3 earth could open the s or even look inside *G1046*
Rev 5: 4 was worthy to open the s or look inside. *G1046*
Rev 5: 5 is able to open the s and its seven seals." *G1046*
Rev 5: 7 He went and took the s from the right hand NDT
Rev 5: 9 worthy to take the s and to open its seals, *G1046*
Rev 6:14 heavens receded like a s being rolled up, *G1046*
Rev 10: 2 He was holding a **little** s, which lay open *G1044*
Rev 10: 8 take the s that lies open in the hand of *G1046*
Rev 10: 9 asked him to give me the **little** s. *G1044*
Rev 10:10 I took the **little** s from the angel's hand *G1044*
Rev 22: 7 the words of the prophecy *written in* this s." *G1046*
Rev 22: 9 with all who keep the words *of* this s. *G1046*
Rev 22:10 up the words of the prophecy *of* this s, *G1046*
Rev 22:18 hears the words of the prophecy *of* this s: *G1046*
Rev 22:18 person the plagues described in this s. *G1046*
Rev 22:19 takes words away from this s of prophecy, *G1046*
Rev 22:19 Holy City, which are described in this s. *G1046*

SCROLLS (3) [SCROLL]
Ac 19:19 brought their s together and burned *G1047*
Ac 19:19 When they calculated the value *of* **the** s *G899S*
2Ti 4:13 Carpus at Troas, and my s, especially the *G1046*

SCRUB (1)
Pr 20:30 Blows and wounds s **away** evil, and H9475

SCULPTURED (1)
2Ch 3:10 he made a pair of s cherubim and H5126+7589

SCUM (2)
La 3:45 You have made us s and refuse among H6082
1Co 4:13 We have become the s of the earth, the *G4326*

SCURVY (KJV) FESTERING

SCYTHIAN (1)
Col 3:11 barbarian, S, slave or free, but *G5033*

SEA (339) [SEAFARERS, SEAS, SEASHORE]
Ge 1:21 the great **creatures of the** s and every H9490
Ge 1:26 over the fish in the s and the birds in the H3542
Ge 1:28 over the fish in the s and the birds in the H3542
Ge 9: 2 on all the fish in the s; they are given H3542
Ge 14: 3 of Siddim (that is, the Dead S Valley). H3542
Ge 32:12 your descendants like the sand of the s, H3542
Ge 41:49 like the sand of the s; it was so much that H3542
Ex 10:19 locusts and carried them into the Red S. H3542
Ex 13:18 by the desert road toward the Red S. H3542
Ex 14: 2 Pi Hahiroth, between Migdol and the s. H3542
Ex 14: 2 They are to encamp by the s, directly H3542
Ex 14: 9 as they camped by the s near Pi Hahiroth, H3542
Ex 14:16 your hand over the s to divide the water H3542
Ex 14:16 can go through the s on dry ground. H3542
Ex 14:21 Moses stretched out his hand over the s, H3542
Ex 14:21 the LORD drove the s back with a strong H3542
Ex 14:22 went through the s on dry ground, H3542
Ex 14:23 horsemen followed them into the s. H3542
Ex 14:26 your hand over the s so that the waters H3542
Ex 14:27 Moses stretched out his hand over the s H3542
Ex 14:27 at daybreak the s went back to its H3542
Ex 14:27 and the LORD swept them into the s. H3542
Ex 14:28 that had followed the Israelites into the s. H3542
Ex 14:29 went through the s on dry ground, H3542
Ex 15: 1 horse and driver he has hurled into the s. H3542
Ex 15: 4 his army he has hurled into the s. H3542
Ex 15: 4 officers are drowned in the Red S. H3542
Ex 15: 8 waters congealed in the heart of the s. H3542
Ex 15:10 with your breath, and the s covered them. H3542
Ex 15:19 chariots and horsemen went into the s H3542
Ex 15:19 the waters of the s back over them, H3542
Ex 15:19 walked through the s on dry ground. H3542
Ex 15:21 horse and driver he has hurled into the s." H3542
Ex 15:22 Israel from the Red S and they went into H3542
Ex 20:11 the earth, the s, and all that is in H3542
Ex 23:31 from the Red S to the Mediterranean H3542
Ex 23:31 Red Sea to the **Mediterranean** S, H3542+7149
Nu 11:22 all the fish in the s were caught for them?" H3542
Nu 11:31 the LORD and drove quail in from the s. H3542
Nu 13:29 live near the s and along the Jordan." H3542
Nu 14:25 the desert along the route to the Red S." H3542
Nu 21: 4 Mount Hor along the route to the Red S, H3542
Nu 33: 8 passed through the s into the desert, H3542
Nu 33:10 They left Elim and camped by the Red S. H3542
Nu 33:11 They left the Red S and camped in the H3542
Nu 34: 3 east from the southern end of the Dead S, H3542
Nu 34: 5 of Egypt and end at the **Mediterranean** S. H3542
Nu 34: 6 will be the coast of the Mediterranean S. H3542
Nu 34: 7 from the Mediterranean S to Mount Hor H3542
Nu 34:11 along the slopes east of the S *of* Galilee. H3542
Nu 34:12 along the Jordan and end at the Dead S. H3542
Dt 1:40 the desert along the route to the Red S." H3542
Dt 2: 1 wilderness along the route to the Red S, H3542
Dt 3:17 from Kinnereth to the S *of* the Arabah H3542
Dt 3:17 the Dead S), below the slopes of H3542
Dt 4:49 as far as the **Dead** S, below the H3542+6858
Dt 11: 4 waters of the Red S as they were pursuing H3542
Dt 11:24 Euphrates River to the Mediterranean S. H3542
Dt 30:13 Nor is it beyond the s, so that you have to H3542
Dt 30:13 "Who will cross the s to get it and H3542
Dt 34: 2 of Judah as far as the Mediterranean S, H3542
Jos 1: 4 to the Mediterranean S in the west. H3542
Jos 2:10 the water of the Red S for you when you H3542
Jos 3:16 flowing down to the S *of* the Arabah H3542
Jos 3:16 the Dead S) was completely cut H3542
Jos 4:23 done to the Red S when he dried it up H3542
Jos 9: 1 the Mediterranean S as far as Lebanon H3542
Jos 12: 3 Arabah from the S *of* Galilee to the Sea H3542
Jos 12: 3 Sea of Galilee to the S *of* the Arabah H3542
Jos 12: 3 the Dead S), to Beth Jeshimoth H3542
Jos 13:27 territory up to the end of the S *of* Galilee). H3542
Jos 15: 2 bay at the southern end of the Dead S, H3542
Jos 15: 4 of Egypt, ending at the **Mediterranean** S. H3542
Jos 15: 5 is the Dead S as far as the mouth H3542
Jos 15: 5 from the bay of the s at the mouth of the H3542
Jos 15:11 The boundary ended at the s. H3542
Jos 15:12 is the coastline of the Mediterranean S. H3542
Jos 15:47 the coastline of the Mediterranean S. H3542
Jos 16: 3 to Gezer, ending at the **Mediterranean** S. H3542
Jos 16: 6 continued to the **Mediterranean** S H3542

S

Jos 16: 8 ended at the **Mediterranean S.** H3542
Jos 17: 9 ravine and ended at the **Mediterranean S.** H3542
Jos 17:10 reached the **Mediterranean S** and H3542
Jos 18:19 out at the northern bay of the Dead **S,** H3542
Jos 19:29 out at the **Mediterranean S** in the region H3542
Jos 23: 4 the Mediterranean **S** in the west. H3542
Jos 24: 6 you came to the **s**, and the Egyptians H3542
Jos 24: 6 horsemen as far as the Red **S.** H3542
Jos 24: 7 he brought the **s** over them and covered H3542
Jdg 11:16 to the Red **S** and on to Kadesh. H3542
2Sa 22:16 The valleys of the **s** were exposed and the H3542
1Ki 5: 9 from Lebanon to the **Mediterranean S,** H3542
1Ki 5: 9 float them as rafts by **s** to the place you H3542
1Ki 7:23 He made the **S** of cast metal, circular in H3542
1Ki 7:24 cast in two rows in one piece with the **S.** H3542
1Ki 7:25 The **S** stood on twelve bulls, three facing NDT
1Ki 7:25 The **S** rested on top of them, and their H3542
1Ki 7:39 He placed the **S** on the south side, at the H3542
1Ki 7:44 the **S** and the twelve bulls under it; H3542
1Ki 9:26 Elath in Edom, on the shore of the Red **S.** H3542
1Ki 9:27 sailors who knew the **s**—to serve in the H3542
1Ki 10:22 of trading ships at **s** along with the ships H3542
1Ki 18:43 "Go and look toward the **s**," he told his H3542
1Ki 18:44 as a man's hand is rising from the **s**." H3542
2Ki 14:25 from Lebo Hamath to the **Dead S,** H3542+6858
2Ki 16:17 He removed the **S** from the bronze bulls H3542
2Ki 25:13 stands and the bronze **S** that were at the H3542
2Ki 25:16 two pillars, the **S** and the movable stands H3542
1Ch 16:32 Let the **s** resound, and all that is in it; let H3542
1Ch 18: 8 Solomon used to make the bronze **S,** H3542
2Ch 2:16 float them as rafts by **s** down to Joppa. H3542
2Ch 4: 2 He made the **S** of cast metal, circular in H3542
2Ch 4: 3 cast in two rows in one piece with the **S.** H3542
2Ch 4: 4 The **S** stood on twelve bulls, three facing NDT
2Ch 4: 4 The **S** rested on top of them, and their H3542
2Ch 4: 6 the **S** was to be used by the priests for H3542
2Ch 4:10 He placed the **S** on the south side, at the H3542
2Ch 4:15 the **S** and the twelve bulls under it; H3542
2Ch 8:18 by his own men, sailors who knew the **s.** H3542
2Ch 20: 2 from the other side of the *Dead* **S.** H3542
Ezr 3: 7 bring cedar logs by **s** from Lebanon to H3542
Ne 9: 9 in Egypt; you heard their cry at the Red **S.** H3542
Ne 9:11 You divided the **s** before them, so that H3542
Job 7:12 Am I the **s**, or the monster of the deep H3542
Job 9: 8 heavens and treads on the waves of the **s.** H3542
Job 11: 9 than the earth and wider than the **s.** H3542
Job 12: 8 or let the fish in the **s** inform you. H3542
Job 26:12 By his power he churned up the **s**; by his H3542
Job 28:14 "It is not in me"; the **s** says, "It is not with H3542
Job 36:30 about him, bathing the depths of the **s.** H3542
Job 38: 8 "Who shut up the **s** behind doors when it H3542
Job 38:16 to the springs of the **s** or walked in the H3542
Job 41:31 stirs up the **s** like a pot of ointment. H3542
Ps 8: 8 the fish in the **s**, all that swim the H3542
Ps 18:15 The valleys of the **s** were exposed and the H4784
Ps 33: 7 He gathers the waters of the **s** into jars H3542
Ps 46: 2 the mountains fall into the heart of the **s,** H3542
Ps 66: 6 He turned the **s** into dry land, they passed H3542
Ps 68:22 I will bring them from the depths of the **s,** H3542
Ps 72: 8 May he rule from **s** to sea and from the H3542
Ps 72: 8 he rule from sea to **s** and from the River to H3542
Ps 74:13 you who split open the **s** by your power; H3542
Ps 77:19 Your path led through the **s**, your way H3542
Ps 78:13 He divided the **s** and led them through H3542
Ps 78:53 the **s** engulfed their enemies. H3542
Ps 80:11 Its branches reached as far as the **S**, its H3542
Ps 89: 9 You rule over the surging **s**; when its H3542
Ps 89:25 I will set his hand over the **s**, his right H3542
Ps 93: 4 mightier than the breakers of the **s**—the H3542
Ps 95: 5 The **s** is his, for he made it, and his hands H3542
Ps 96:11 be glad; let the **s** resound, and all that H3542
Ps 98: 7 Let the **s** resound, and everything in it, the H3542
Ps 104:25 There is the **s**, vast and spacious, teeming H3542
Ps 106: 7 they rebelled by the **s**, the Red Sea. H3542
Ps 106: 7 they rebelled by the sea, the Red **S.** H3542
Ps 106: 9 He rebuked the Red **S**, and it dried up; he H3542
Ps 106:22 Ham and awesome deeds by the Red **S.** H3542
Ps 107:23 Some went out on the **s** in ships; they H3542
Ps 107:29 whisper; the waves of the **s** were hushed. H3542
Ps 114: 3 The **s** looked and fled, the Jordan turned H3542
Ps 114: 5 Why was it, **s**, that you fled? Why, Jordan H3542
Ps 136:13 who divided the Red **S** asunder His love H3542
Ps 136:15 Pharaoh and his army into the Red **S;** H3542
Ps 139: 9 if I settle on the far side of the **s,** H3542
Ps 146: 6 earth, the **s**, and everything in H3542
Ps 148: 7 you **great s creatures** and all ocean H9490
Pr 8:29 when he gave the **s** its boundary so the H3542
Ecc 1: 7 All streams flow into the **s**, yet the sea is H3542
Ecc 1: 7 flow into the sea, yet the **s** is never full. H3542
Ecc 11: 1 Ship your grain across the **s**; after many H4784
Isa 5:30 will roar over it like the roaring of the **s.** H3542
Isa 9: 1 by the Way of the **S**, beyond the Jordan— H3542
Isa 10:22 your people be like the sand by the **s,** H3542
Isa 11: 9 of the LORD as the waters cover the **s.** H3542
Isa 11:15 LORD will dry up the gulf of the Egyptian **s;** H3542
Isa 16: 8 spread out and went as far as the **s.** H3542
Isa 17:12 that rage—they rage like the raging **s!** H3542
Isa 18: 2 sends envoys by **s** in papyrus boats over H3542
Isa 21: 1 A prophecy against the Desert by the **S** H3542
Isa 23: 4 you fortress of the **s**, for the sea has H3542
Isa 23: 4 fortress of the sea, for the **s** has spoken: H3542
Isa 23:11 his hand over the **s** and made its H3542
Isa 24:15 the God of Israel, in the islands of the **s.** H3542
Isa 27: 1 serpent; he will slay the monster of the **s.** H3542
Isa 42:10 you who go down to the **s**, and all that is H3542
Isa 43:16 he who made a way through the **s**, a path H3542
Isa 48:18 your well-being like the waves of the **s.** H3542
Isa 50: 2 By a mere rebuke I dry up the **s**, I turn H3542
Isa 51:10 Was it not you who dried up the **s**, the H3542
Isa 51:10 the depths of the **s** so that the redeemed H3542
Isa 51:15 who stirs up the **s** so that its waves roar H3542
Isa 57:20 But the wicked are like the tossing **s** H3542
Isa 63:11 is he who brought them through the **s,** H3542
Jer 5:22 I made the sand a boundary for the **s**, an H3542
Jer 6:23 like the roaring **s** as they ride on their H3542
Jer 15: 8 more numerous than the sand of the **s.** H3542
Jer 25:22 the kings of the coastlands across the **s;** H3542
Jer 27:19 the bronze **S**, the movable stands H3542
Jer 31:35 who stirs up the **s** so that its waves roar H3542
Jer 46:18 the mountains, like Carmel by the **s.** H3542
Jer 48:32 Your branches spread as far as the **s**; they H3542
Jer 49:21 their cry will resound to the Red **S.** H3542
Jer 49:23 disheartened, troubled like the restless **s.** H3542
Jer 50:42 like the roaring **s** as they ride on their H3542
Jer 51:36 I will dry up her **s** and make her springs H3542
Jer 51:42 The **s** will rise over Babylon; its roaring H3542
Jer 52:17 stands and the bronze **S** that were at the H3542
Jer 52:20 the **S** and the twelve bronze bulls under it, H3542
La 2:13 Your wound is as deep as the **s**. Who can H3542
Eze 26: 3 like the **s** casting up its waves. H3542
Eze 26: 5 Out in the **s** she will become a place to H3542
Eze 26:12 your stones, timber and rubble into the **s.** H4784
Eze 26:17 city of renown, peopled by men of the **s!** H3542
Eze 26:18 the islands in the **s** are terrified at your H3542
Eze 27: 3 situated at the gateway to the **s**, merchant H3542
Eze 27: 9 All the ships of the **s** and their sailors H3542
Eze 27:25 filled with heavy cargo as you sail the **s.** H3542
Eze 27:26 wind will break you to pieces far out at **s.** H3542
Eze 27:27 into the heart of the **s** on the day of your H3542
Eze 27:32 silenced like Tyre, surrounded by the **s**?" H3542
Eze 27:34 are shattered by the **s** in the depths of the H3542
Eze 38:20 The fish in the **s**, the birds in the sky, the H3542
Eze 39:11 valley of those who travel east of the **S.** H3542
Eze 47: 8 the Arabah, where it enters the *Dead* **S.** H3542
Eze 47: 8 When it empties into the **s**, the salty H3542
Eze 47:10 like the fish of the Mediterranean **S.** H3542
Eze 47:15 the Mediterranean **S** by the Hethlon road H3542
Eze 47:17 will extend from the **s** to Hazar Enan, H3542
Eze 47:18 to the Dead **S** and as far as Tamar. H3542
Eze 47:19 Wadi of Egypt to the Mediterranean **S.** H3542
Eze 47:20 the Mediterranean **S** will be the boundary H3542
Eze 48:28 Wadi of Egypt to the Mediterranean **S.** H3542
Da 7: 2 winds of heaven churning up the great **s.** A10322
Da 7: 3 from the others, came up out of the **s.** A10322
Hos 4: 3 sky and the fish in the **s** are swept away. H3542
Joel 2:20 drown in the Dead **S** and its western ranks H3542
Joel 2:20 its western ranks in the Mediterranean **S.** H3542
Am 5: 8 the waters of the **s** and pours them out H3542
Am 6:12 Does one plow the **s** with oxen? But you H3542
Am 8:12 will stagger from **s** to sea and wander H3542
Am 8:12 stagger from sea to **s** and wander from H3542
Am 9: 3 hide from my eyes at the bottom of the **s,** H3542
Am 9: 6 the waters of the **s** and pours them out H3542
Jnh 1: 4 Then the LORD sent a great wind on the **s** H3542
Jnh 1: 5 the cargo into the **s** to lighten the ship. H3542
Jnh 1: 9 who made the **s** and the dry land. H3542
Jnh 1:11 The **s** was getting rougher and rougher H3542
Jnh 1:11 do to you to make the **s** calm down for us?" H3542
Jnh 1:12 "Pick me up and throw me into the **s**," H3542
Jnh 1:13 the **s** grew even wilder than before. H3542
Jnh 1:15 overboard, and the raging **s** grew calm. H3542
Mic 7:12 the Euphrates and from **s** to sea and from H3542
Mic 7:12 from sea to **s** and from mountain to H3542
Mic 7:19 all our iniquities into the depths of the **s.** H3542
Na 1: 4 He rebukes the **s** and dries it up; he H3542
Hab 1:14 have made people like the fish in the **s,** H3542
Hab 1:14 like the **s creatures** that have no ruler. H8254
Hab 2:14 glory of the LORD as the waters cover the **s.** H3542
Hab 3: 8 rage against the **s** when you rode your H3542
Hab 3:15 You trampled the **s** with your horses H3542
Zep 1: 3 the birds in the sky and the fish in the **s**— H3542
Zep 2: 5 Woe to you who live by the **s**, you H3542
Zep 2: 6 The land by the **s** will become pastures H3542
Hag 2: 6 the earth, the **s** and the dry land. H3542
Zec 9: 4 destroy her power on the **s,** H3542
Zec 9:10 will extend from **s** to sea and from the H3542
Zec 9:10 extend from sea to **s** and from the River to H3542
Zec 10:11 They will pass through the **s** *of* trouble H3542
Zec 10:11 the surging **s** will be subdued and all the H3542
Zec 14: 8 of it east to the *Dead* **S** and half of it west H3542
Zec 14: 8 half of it west to the *Mediterranean* **S,** H3542
Mt 4:15 Naphtali, the Way *of* the **S**, beyond the *G2498*
Mt 4:18 was walking beside the **S** of Galilee, *G2498*
Mt 15:29 there and went along the **S** of Galilee. *G2498*
Mt 18: 6 to be drowned in the depths *of* the **s.** *G2498*
Mt 21:21 throw yourself into the **s**,' and it will be *G2498*
Mt 23:15 travel over land and **s** to win a single *G2498*
Mk 1:16 As Jesus walked beside the **S** of Galilee *G2498*
Mk 7:31 down to the **S** of Galilee and into the *G2498*
Mk 9:42 neck and they were thrown into the **s.** *G2498*
Mk 11:23 throw yourself into the **s**,' and does not *G2498*
Lk 17: 2 be thrown into the **s** with a millstone tied *G2498*
Lk 17: 6 'Be uprooted and planted in the **s**,' and it *G2498*
Lk 21:25 at the roaring and tossing *of* the **s.** *G2498*
Jn 6: 1 to the far shore *of* the **S** of Galilee *G2498*
Jn 6: 1 Sea of Galilee (that is, the **S** of Tiberias), NDT
Jn 21: 1 again to his disciples, by the **S** of Galilee. *G2498*
Ac 4:24 the heavens and the earth and the **s,** *G2498*
Ac 7:36 at the Red **S** and for forty years in the *G2498*
Ac 10: 6 the tanner, whose house is by the **s**." *G2498*
Ac 10:32 of Simon the tanner, who lives by the **s.** *G2498*
Ac 14:15 the earth and the **s** and everything in *G2498*
Ac 16:11 From Troas *we* **put out to s** and sailed *G343*
Ac 21: 1 we **put out to s** and sailed straight to Kos. *G343*
Ac 27: 2 the province of Asia, and *we* **put out to s.** *G343*
Ac 27: 4 From there *we* **put out to s** *again* and *G343*
Ac 27: 5 sailed across the **open s** off the coast of *G4283*
Ac 27:17 they lowered the **s anchor** and let the ship *G5007*
Ac 27:27 still being driven across the **Adriatic S,** *G102*
Ac 27:30 the sailors let the lifeboat down into the **s,** *G2498*
Ac 27:38 the ship by throwing the grain into the **s.** *G2498*
Ac 27:40 left them in the **s** and at the same time *G2498*
Ac 28: 4 though he escaped from the **s**, the *G2498*
Ac 28:11 three months *we* **put out to s** in a ship that *G343*
Ro 9:27 of the Israelites be like the sand *by* the **s,** *G2498*
1Co 10: 1 that they all passed through the **s.** *G2498*
1Co 10: 2 into Moses in the cloud and in the **s.** *G2498*
2Co 11:25 I spent a night and a day in the **open s,** *G1113*
2Co 11:26 in danger at **s**; and in danger from *G2498*
Heb 11:29 passed through the Red **S** as on dry land; *G2498*
Jas 1: 6 one who doubts is like a wave *of* the **s,** *G2498*
Jas 3: 7 reptiles and **s creatures** are being tamed *G1879*
Jude 13 They are wild waves *of* the **s**, foaming up *G2498*
Rev 4: 6 there was what looked like a **s** of glass, *G2498*
Rev 5:13 earth and under the earth and on the **s,** *G2498*
Rev 7: 1 on the land or on the **s** or on any tree. *G2498*
Rev 7: 2 given power to harm the land and the **s**: *G2498*
Rev 7: 3 harm the land or the **s** or the trees until *G2498*
Rev 8: 8 all ablaze, was thrown into the **s.** *G2498*
Rev 8: 8 A third *of* the **s** turned into blood, *G2498*
Rev 8: 9 a third of the living creatures in the **s** died *G2498*
Rev 10: 2 his right foot on the **s** and his left foot on *G2498*
Rev 10: 5 seen standing on the **s** and on the land *G2498*
Rev 10: 6 that is in it, and the **s** and all that is in it *G2498*
Rev 10: 8 who is standing on the **s** and on the land." *G2498*
Rev 12:12 But woe to the earth and the **s**, because *G2498*
Rev 13: 1 The dragon stood on the shore *of* the **s** *G2498*
Rev 13: 1 And I saw a beast coming out of the **s.** *G2498*
Rev 14: 7 the earth, the **s** and the springs of water." *G2498*
Rev 15: 2 what looked like a **s** of glass glowing with *G2498*
Rev 15: 2 standing beside the **s**, those who had *G2498*
Rev 16: 3 angel poured out his bowl on the **s,** *G2498*
Rev 16: 3 every living thing in the **s** died. *G2498*
Rev 18:17 "Every **s captain**, and all who travel by *G3237*
Rev 18:17 all who earn their living *from* the **s** *G2498*
Rev 18:19 had ships on the **s** became rich through *G2498*
Rev 18:21 a large millstone and threw it into the **s,** *G2498*
Rev 20:13 The **s** gave up the dead that were in it *G2498*
Rev 21: 1 and there was no longer any **s.** *G2498*

SEAFARERS (1) [SEA]

Isa 23: 2 Sidon, whom the **s** have enriched. H6296+3542

SEAH (3) [SEAHS]

2Ki 7: 1 a **s** *of* the finest flour will sell for a shekel H6006
2Ki 7:16 So a **s** *of* the finest flour sold for a shekel H6006
2Ki 7:18 a **s** *of* the finest flour will sell for a shekel H6006

SEAHS (6) [SEAH]

Ge 18: 6 "get three **s** *of* the finest flour and knead H6006
1Sa 25:18 dressed sheep, five **s** of roasted grain, H6006
1Ki 18:32 it large enough to hold *two* **s** *of* seed. H6006
2Ki 7: 1 sell for a shekel and *two* **s** of barley for a H6006
2Ki 7:16 and *two* **s** *of* barley sold for a shekel H6006
2Ki 7:18 sell for a shekel and *two* **s** of barley for a H6006

SEAL (36) [SEALED, SEALING, SEALS]

Ge 38:18 "Your **s** and its cord, and the staff in your H2597
Ge 38:25 you recognize whose **s** and cord and staff H3160
Ex 28:11 stones the way a gem cutter engraves a **s.** H2597
Ex 28:21 engraved like a **s** with the name of one H2597
Ex 28:36 of pure gold and engrave on it as on a **s**: H2597
Ex 39: 6 engraved them like a **s** with the names of H2597
Ex 39:14 engraved like a **s** with the name of one H2597
Ex 39:30 engraved on it, like an inscription on a **s**: H2597
1Ki 21: 8 name, **placed** his **s** *on* them H3159+928+2597
Est 8: 8 and **s** it with the king's signet ring H3159
Job 38:14 The earth takes shape like clay under a **s** H2597
Ps 40: 9 great assembly; *I do* not **s** my lips, LORD, H3973
SS 8: 6 Place me like a **s** over your heart, like a H2597
SS 8: 6 your heart, like a **s** on your arm; for love H2597
Isa 8:16 of warning and **s up** God's instruction H3159
Eze 28:12 " 'You *were* the **s** *of* perfection, full of H3159
Da 8:26 given you is true, but **s up** the vision, for it H6258
Da 9:24 to **s up** vision and prophecy and to anoint H3159
Da 12: 4 roll up and **s** the words of the scroll until H3159
Mt 27:66 tomb secure *by* **putting a s on** the stone *G5381*
Jn 6:27 the Father *has* **placed** *his* **s** *of* **approval.**" *G5381*
Ro 4:11 a **s** of the righteousness that he had by *G5382*
1Co 9: 2 For you are the **s** of my apostleship in the *G5382*
2Co 1:22 **set** *his* **s of ownership on** us, and put his *G5381*
Eph 1:13 *you were* **marked** in him **with a s**, the *G5381*
Rev 6: 3 When the Lamb opened the second **s,** *G5382*
Rev 6: 5 When the Lamb opened the third **s,** *G5382*
Rev 6: 7 When the Lamb opened the fourth **s,** *G5382*
Rev 6: 9 When he opened the fifth **s**, I saw under *G5382*
Rev 6:12 I watched as he opened the sixth **s**. There *G5382*

Rev 7: 2 the east, having the **s** of the living God. *G5382*
Rev 7: 3 the trees until *we* **put a s** on the *G5381*
Rev 8: 1 When he opened the seventh **s**, there *G5382*
Rev 9: 4 who did not have the **s** of God on their *G5382*
Rev 10: 4 "**S up** what the seven thunders have said *G5381*
Rev 22:10 "*Do* not **s up** the words of the prophecy of *G5381*

SEALED (23) [SEAL]
Dt 32:34 kept this in reserve and **s** it in my vaults? H3159
Ne 10: 1 Those *who* **s** it were: Nehemiah the H3159
Est 3:12 Xerxes himself and **s** with his own ring. H3159
Est 8: 8 the king's name and **s** with his ring can H3159
Est 8:10 **s** the dispatches with the king's signet H3159
Job 14:17 My offenses *will* **be s up** in a bag; you will H3159
Job 41:15 rows of shields tightly **s together**; H6037+2597
SS 4:12 you are a spring enclosed, a **s** fountain. H5835
Isa 29:10 *He has* **s** your eyes (the prophets); he has H6794
Isa 29:11 vision is nothing but words **s** in a scroll. H3159
Isa 29:11 they will answer, "I can't; it *is* **s**. H3159
Jer 32:10 I signed and **s** the deed, had it witnessed H3159
Jer 32:11 the **s** *copy* containing the terms and H3159
Jer 32:14 both the **s** and unsealed copies of the H3159
Jer 32:44 **s** and witnessed in the territory of H3159
Da 6:17 the king **s** it with his own signet ring A10291
Da 12: 9 are rolled up and **s** until the time of the H3159
Eph 4:30 with whom *you were* **s** for the day of *G5381*
2Ti 2:19 **s** with this inscription: *G2400+3836+5382*
Rev 5: 1 on both sides and **s** with seven seals. *G2958*
Rev 7: 4 I heard the number *of* those *who were* **s**: *G5381*
Rev 7: 5 From the tribe of Judah 12,000 *were* **s** *G5381*
Rev 20: 3 locked and **s** it over him, to keep *G5381*

SEALING (1) [SEAL]
Dt 29:12 with you this day and **s** with an oath, NDT

SEALS (7) [SEAL]
Ne 9:38 our priests *are* **affixing** their **s** to it. H3159
Job 9: 7 *he* **s off** the light of the stars. H3159+1237
Rev 5: 1 on both sides and sealed *with* seven **s**. *G5382*
Rev 5: 2 worthy to break the **s** and open the scroll?" *G5382*
Rev 5: 5 is able to open the scroll and its seven **s**." *G5382*
Rev 5: 9 worthy to take the scroll and to open its **s**, *G5382*
Rev 6: 1 the Lamb opened the first of the seven **s**. *G5382*

SEAM (2) [SEAMS]
Ex 28:27 close to the **s** just above the waistband of H4678
Ex 39:20 close to the **s** just above the waistband of H4678

SEAMLESS (1)
Jn 19:23 This garment was **s**, woven in one piece *G731*

SEAMS (1) [SEAM]
Eze 27: 9 on board as shipwrights to caulk your **s**. H981

SEARCH (51) [SEARCHED, SEARCHES, SEARCHING]
Ge 44:12 Then the steward *proceeded to* **s** H2924
Dt 1:33 to **s out** places for you to camp and to H9365
Jdg 17: 8 left that town *in* **s** *of* some other place to H5162
1Sa 16:16 servants here *to* **s** for someone who can H1335
1Sa 23:25 Saul and his men began the **s**, and when H1335
1Sa 26: 2 select Israelite troops, to **s** there **for** David. H1335
2Sa 5:17 they went up in full force to **s for** him, but H1335
1Ki 2:40 went to Achish at Gath **in s of** his slaves. H1335
1Ki 20: 6 send my officials *to* **s** your palace and the H2924
1Ch 4:39 east of the valley **in s of** pasture for their H1335
1Ch 14: 8 they went up in full force to **s for** him, but H1335
1Ch 26:31 David's reign *a* **s was made** in the records H2011
2Ch 22: 9 *He* then **went in s of** Ahaziah, and his H1335
Ezr 4:15 so that a **s** *may be* **made** in the archives A10118
Ezr 4:19 I issued an order and **a s** *was* **made**, and A10118
Ezr 5:17 *let* **a s be made** in the royal archives of A10118
Est 2: 2 "*Let a* **s** *be* **made for** beautiful young H1335
Job 3:21 *who* **s for** it more than for hidden treasure, H2916
Job 7:21 in the dust; *you will* **s for** me, but I will be H8838
Job 10: 6 that *you must* **s out** my faults and probe H1335
Job 28: 3 they **s out** the farthest recesses **for** ore in H2983
Job 28:11 *They* **s** the sources of the rivers and bring H2924
Ps 4: 4 your beds, **s** your hearts and be silent. H606+928
Ps 139:23 **S** me, God, and know my heart; test me H2983
Pr 2: 4 it as for silver and **s for** it as for hidden H2924
Pr 25: 2 *to* **s out** a matter is the glory of kings. H2983
Pr 25:27 is it honorable to **s out** matters that are H2984
Ecc 3: 6 a time to **s** and a time to give up, a time H1335
Ecc 7:25 investigate and *to* **s out** wisdom and the H1335
Ecc 7:29 they *have* **gone in s of** many schemes." H1335
Ecc 8:17 Despite all their efforts to **s** *it* **out**, no one H1335
SS 3: 2 *I will* **s for** the one my heart loves. H1335
Isa 41:12 Though *you* **s for** your enemies, you will H1335
Isa 41:17 "The poor and needy **s for** water, but H1335
Jer 5: 1 consider, **s** through her squares. H1335
Jer 17:10 "I the LORD **s** the heart and examine the H2983
Jer 50:20 the LORD, "**s** *will* **be made** *for* Israel's guilt H1335
La 1:11 All her people groan *as they* **s for** bread H1335
Eze 34: 8 my shepherds *did* not **s for** my flock but H2011
Eze 34:11 I myself *will* **s for** my sheep and look after H2011
Eze 34:16 *I will* **s for** the lost and bring back the H1335
Eze 39:14 *they will* **carry out a more detailed s**. H2983
Hos 7:10 not return to the LORD his God or **s for** him. H1335
Zep 1:12 At that time *I will* **s** Jerusalem with lamps H2924
Mt 2: 8 said, "Go and **s** carefully for the child. *G2004*
Mt 2:13 Herod is going to **s for** the child to kill *G2426*
Mt 10:11 **s** there **for** some worthy person and stay at *G2004*
Lk 15: 8 sweep the house and **s** carefully until she *G2426*
Jn 6:24 went to Capernaum *in* **s** *of* Jesus. *G2426*
Ac 12:19 *After* Herod *had* **a thorough s made** for *G2118*
Ac 17: 5 to Jason's house **in s of** Paul and Silas in *G2426*

SEARCHED (22) [SEARCH]
Ge 31:34 Laban **s through** everything in the tent H5491
Ge 31:35 So *he* **s** but could not find the household H2924
Ge 31:37 Now that *you have* **s through** all my goods H5491
Jos 2:22 until the pursuers *had* **s** all along the road H1335
1Sa 23:14 Day after day Saul **s for** him, but God did H1335
1Sa 27: 4 had fled to Gath, he no longer **s for** him. H1335
2Sa 17:20 The men **s** but found no one, so they H1335
1Ki 1: 3 Then *they* **s** throughout Israel **for** a H1335
2Ki 2:17 *who* **s** for three days but did not find him. H1335
Ezr 2:62 These **s for** their family records, but they H1335
Ezr 6: 1 and *they* **s** in the archives stored in the A10118
Ne 7:64 These **s for** their family records, but they H1335
Ps 139: 1 *You have* **s** me, LORD, and you know me. H2983
Ecc 12: 9 He pondered and **s** out and set in order H2983
Ecc 12:10 The Teacher **s** to find just the right words H1335
Jer 31:37 of the earth below **be s out** will I reject all H2983
La 1:19 in the city while *they* **s for** food to keep H1335
Eze 20: 6 of Egypt into a land *I had* **s out** for them, H9365
Eze 34: 4 brought back the strays or **s for** the lost. H1335
Eze 34: 6 and no *one* **s** or looked for them. H2011
2Ti 1:17 *he* **s** hard **for** me until he found me. *G2426*
1Pe 1:10 you, **s intently** and with the greatest care, *G1699*

SEARCHES (6) [SEARCH]
1Ch 28: 9 the LORD **s** every heart and understands H2011
Job 39: 8 its pasture and **s** for any green thing. H2011
Pr 11:27 but evil comes to one *who* **s for** it. H2011
Ro 8:27 And he *who* **s** our hearts knows the mind *G2236*
1Co 2:10 The Spirit **s** all things, even the deep *G2236*
Rev 2:23 that I am he *who* **s** hearts and minds *G2236*

SEARCHING (9) [SEARCH]
Jdg 5:15 of Reuben there was much **s** *of* heart. H2984
Jdg 5:16 of Reuben there was much **s** *of* heart. H2984
1Sa 27: 1 Saul will give up **s for** me anywhere in H1335
Job 32:11 reasoning; while *you were* **s for** words, H2983
Ecc 7:28 while I *was* still **s** but not finding— H1335
Eze 7:26 *They will* **go s for** a vision from the H1335
Am 8:12 north to east, **s for** the word of the LORD H1335
Lk 2:48 I *have been* anxiously **s for** you. *G2426*
Lk 2:49 "Why *were you* **s for** me?" he asked *G2426*

SEARED (2) [SEARING]
1Ti 4: 2 *have been* **s as with a hot iron**. *G3013*
Rev 16: 9 They *were* **s** by the intense heat and they *G3009*

SEARING (1) [SEARED]
Ps 38: 7 My back is filled with **s pain**; there is no H7828

SEAS (29) [SEA]
Ge 1:10 and the gathered waters he called "**s**." H3542
Ge 1:22 in number and fill the water in the **s**, H3542
Lev 11: 9 in the water of the **s** and the streams you H3542
Lev 11:10 all creatures in the **s** or streams that do H3542
Dt 33:19 they will feast on the abundance of the **s** H3542
Ne 9: 6 that is on it, the **s** and all that is in them. H3542
Job 6: 3 would surely outweigh the sand of the **s**— H3542
Ps 8: 8 the sea, all that swim the paths of the **s**. H3542
Ps 24: 2 he founded it on the **s** and established it H3542
Ps 65: 5 the ends of the earth and of the farthest **s**, H3542
Ps 65: 7 who stilled the roaring of the **s**, the H3542
Ps 69:34 the **s** and all that move in them, H3542
Ps 78:15 gave them water as abundant as the **s**; H9333
Ps 93: 3 The **s** have lifted up, LORD, the seas have H5643
Ps 93: 3 the **s** have lifted up their voice; the H5643
Ps 93: 3 the **s** have lifted up their pounding waves. H5643
Ps 135: 6 on the earth, in the **s** and all their depths. H3542
Pr 23:34 be like one sleeping on the **high s**, H4213+3542
Pr 30:19 the way of a ship on the **high s** H4213+3542
Isa 60: 5 the wealth on the **s** will be brought to you, H3542
Eze 26:17 You were a power on the **s**, you and your H3542
Eze 27: 4 Your domain was on the **high s** H4213+3542
Eze 27:26 Your oarsmen take you out to the high **s** H4784
Eze 27:33 your merchandise went out on the **s**, H3542
Eze 28: 2 the throne of a god in the heart of the **s**." H3542
Eze 28: 8 die a violent death in the heart of the **s**. H3542
Eze 32: 2 like a monster in the **s** thrashing about in H3542
Da 11:45 tents between the **s** at the beautiful holy H3542
Jnh 2: 3 into the very heart of the **s**, and the H3542

SEASHORE (13) [SEA]
Ge 22:17 in the sky and as the sand on the **s**. H8557+3542
Ge 49:13 will live by the **s** and become a H2572+3542
Jos 11: 4 as numerous as the sand on the **s**. H8557+3542
Jdg 7:12 be counted than the sand on the **s**. H8557+3542
1Sa 13: 5 as numerous as the sand on the **s**. H8557+3542
2Sa 17:11 as numerous as the sand on the **s**—be H3542
1Ki 4:20 were as numerous as the sand on the **s**; H3542
1Ki 4:29 measureless as the sand on the **s**. H8557+3542
Ps 78:27 them like dust, birds like sand on the **s**. H3542
Jer 33:22 as measureless as the sand on the **s**. H3542
Hos 1:10 Israelites will be like the sand on the **s**, H3542
Heb 11:12 as the sand on the **s**. *G5927+3836+2498*
Rev 20: 8 In number they are like the sand *on* the **s**. *G2498*

SEASON (20) [SEASONED, SEASONS]
Ge 31:10 "In breeding **s** I once had a dream in H6961
Ex 34:21 even during the **plowing s** and harvest H3045
Lev 2:13 **S** all your grain offerings with salt. Do not H4873
Lev 26: 4 I will send you rain in its **s**, and the ground H6961
Nu 13:20 It was the **s** *for* the first ripe grapes. H3427
Dt 11:14 then I will send rain on your land in its **s** H6961
Dt 28:12 rain on your land in **s** and to bless all the H6961
Ezr 10:13 many people here and it is the rainy **s**; H6961
Job 5:26 in full vigor, like sheaves gathered in **s**. H6961
Job 6:17 that stop flowing in the dry **s**, and in H6961
Ps 1: 3 yields its fruit in **s** and whose leaf does H6961
Pr 20: 4 Sluggards do not plow in **s**; so at harvest H3074
Ecc 3: 1 a **s** for every activity under the H6961
SS 2:12 on the earth; the **s** *of* singing has come H6961
Jer 5:24 who gives autumn and spring rains in **s** H6961
Eze 34:26 I will send down showers in **s**; there will H6961
Mk 11:13 because it was not the **s** for figs. *G2789*
2Ti 4: 2 be prepared **in s** and out of season *G2323*
2Ti 4: 2 be prepared in season and **out of s**; correct, *G178*
Titus 1: 3 which now *at* his **appointed s** he has *G2789*

SEASONED (1) [SEASON]
Col 4: 6 always full of grace, **s** with salt, so that you *G789*

SEASONS (6) [SEASON]
Job 38:32 in their **s** or lead out the Bear H6961
Ps 104:19 He made the moon to mark the **s**, and the H4595
Jer 8: 7 the stork in the sky knows her **appointed s**, H4595
Da 2:21 He changes times and **s**; he deposes A10232
Ac 14:17 you rain from heaven and crops *in* their **s**; *G2789*
Gal 4:10 special days and months and **s** and years! *G2789*

SEAT (25) [SEATED, SEATING, SEATS]
Ex 18:13 next day Moses **took** *his* **s** to serve as H3782
Jdg 3:20 God for you." As the king rose from his **s**, H4058
1Sa 20:18 be missed, because your **s** will be empty. H4632
2Sa 19: 8 king got up and **took** *his* **s** in the gateway. H3782
1Ki 1:46 Solomon *has* **taken** *his* **s** on the royal H3782
1Ki 10:19 both sides of the **s** were armrests, H5226+8699
1Ki 21: 9 a day of fasting and **s** Naboth in a H3782
1Ki 21:10 But **s** two scoundrels opposite him and H3782
2Ki 25:28 gave him a **s of honor** higher than H4058
2Ch 9:18 both sides of the **s** were armrests, H5226+8699
Est 3: 1 giving him a **s of honor** higher than H4058
Job 29: 7 the city and took my **s** in the public square H4632
Pr 9:14 on a **s** *at* the highest point of the city, H4058
Pr 31:23 where he **takes** his **s** among the elders of H3782
SS 3:10 Its **s** was upholstered with purple, its H5323
Isa 22:23 he will become a **s** *of* honor for the house H4058
Jer 52:32 gave him a **s of honor** higher than H4058
Da 7: 9 the Ancient of Days **took** *his* **s**. A10338
Mt 23: 2 the law and the Pharisees sit in Moses' **s**. *G2756*
Mt 27:19 While Pilate was sitting on the **judge's s** *G1037*
Lk 14: 9 say to you, 'Give this person your **s**. *G5536*
Jn 19:13 sat down on the **judge's s** at a place *G1037*
Ro 14:10 will all stand before God's **judgment s**. *G1037*
2Co 5:10 appear before the **judgment s** of Christ, *G1037*
Jas 2: 3 "Here's a good **s** for you," but say to *G2764*

SEATED (29) [SEAT]
Ge 43:33 The men *had been* **s** before him in the H3782
Ru 4: 4 the presence of these **s** here and in the H3782
1Sa 9:22 the hall and **s** them at the head H5989+5226
1Sa 22: 6 And Saul *was* **s**, spear in hand, under the H3782
1Ki 16:11 began to reign and *was* **s** on the throne, H3782
1Ki 21:12 a fast and **s** Naboth in a prominent H3782
2Ch 23:20 the Upper Gate and **s** the king on the H3782
Ps 47: 8 the nations; God *is* **s** on his holy throne. H3782
Isa 6: 1 high and exalted, **s** on a throne; and the H3782
Da 7:10 The court *was* **s**, and the books were A10338
Zec 3: 8 you and your associates **s** before you, who H3782
Mk 3:34 he looked at those **s** in a circle around *G2764*
Lk 22:56 A servant girl saw him **s** there in the *G2764*
Lk 22:69 Son of Man will be **s** at the right hand of *G2764*
Jn 6:11 distributed *to* those *who were* **s** as much as *G367*
Jn 12:15 your king is coming, **s** on a donkey's colt." *G2764*
Jn 20:12 in white, **s** where Jesus' body had been *G2757*
Ac 20: 9 **S** in a window *was* a young man named *G2757*
Eph 1:20 from the dead and **s** him at his right hand *G2767*
Eph 2: 6 up with Christ and **s** us **with** him in the *G5154*
Col 3: 1 where Christ is, **s** at the right hand of God. *G2764*
Rev 4: 4 and **s** on them *were* twenty-four elders. *G2764*
Rev 11:16 who *were* **s** on their thrones before God *G2764*
Rev 14:14 and **s** on the cloud *was one* like a son of *G2764*
Rev 14:16 So he *who was* **s** on the cloud swung his *G2764*
Rev 19: 4 worshiped God, who *was* **s** on the throne. *G2764*
Rev 20: 4 thrones on which *were* **s** those who had *G2767*
Rev 20:11 white throne and him *who was* **s** on it. *G2764*
Rev 21: 5 He *who was* **s** on the throne said, "I am *G2764*

SEATING (2) [SEAT]
1Ki 10: 5 food on his table, the **s** *of* his officials, the H4632
2Ch 9: 4 food on his table, the **s** *of* his officials, the H4632

SEATS (7) [SEAT]
1Sa 2: 8 *he* **s** them with princes and has them H3782
Ps 113: 8 he **s** them with princes, with the princes of H3782
Jer 39: 3 Babylon came and **took s** in the Middle H3782
Mt 23: 6 banquets and the **most important s** in the *G4751*
Mk 12:39 have the **most important s** in the *G4751*
Lk 11:43 you love the **most important s** in the *G4751*
Lk 20:46 have the **most important s** in the *G4751*

SEAWEED (1) [WEED]
Jnh 2: 5 **s** was wrapped around my head. H6068

SEBA (4)
Ge 10: 7 The sons of Cush: S, Havilah, Sabtah H6013
1Ch 1: 9 The sons of Cush: S, Havilah, Sabta H6013
Ps 72:10 kings of Sheba and S present him gifts. H6013
Isa 43: 3 your ransom, Cush and S in your stead. H6013

SEBAM (1)
Nu 32: 3 Heshbon, Elealeh, S, Nebo and Beon— H8423

SECACAH (NIV84) SEKAKAH

SECLUSION (1)
Lk 1:24 for five months *remained* in s. *G4332*

SECOND (160) [TWO]
Ge 1: 8 there was morning—the s day. H9108
Ge 2:13 The name of the s river is the Gihon; it H9108
Ge 7:11 on the seventeenth day of the s month H9108
Ge 8:14 day of the s month the earth was H9108
Ge 22:15 called to Abraham from heaven a s time H9108
Ge 27:36 This is the *s* time he has taken advantage of AIT
Ge 30: 7 conceived again and bore Jacob a s son. H9108
Ge 30:12 Leah's servant Zilpah bore Jacob a s son. H9108
Ge 32:19 He also instructed the s, the third and all H9108
Ge 41: 5 He fell asleep again and had a s dream H9108
Ge 41:52 The s son he named Ephraim and said, "It H9108
Ex 4: 8 to the first sign, they may believe the s. H340
Ex 16: 1 fifteenth day of the s month after they had H9108
Ex 25:19 on one end and the s cherub on the other; H285
Ex 25:35 lampstand, a s bud under the second pair NDT
Ex 25:35 a second bud under the s pair, and a third NDT
Ex 28:18 the s row shall be turquoise, lapis lazuli H9108
Ex 37: 8 on one end and the s cherub on the other; H285
Ex 37:21 lampstand, a s bud under the second pair NDT
Ex 37:21 a second bud under the s pair, and a third NDT
Ex 39:11 the s row was turquoise, lapis lazuli and H9108
Ex 40:17 first day of the first month in the s year. H9108
Lev 19:10 *Do* not go over your vineyard a s time or H6618
Nu 1: 1 the first day of the s month of the second H9108
Nu 1: 1 the second month of the s year after the H9108
Nu 1:18 together on the first day of the s month. H9108
Nu 2:16 number 151,450. They will set out s. H9108
Nu 7:18 On the s day Nethanel son of Zuar, the H9108
Nu 8: 8 you are to take a s young bull for a sin H9108
Nu 9: 1 first month of the s year after they came H9108
Nu 9:11 fourteenth day of the s month at twilight. H9108
Nu 10: 6 At the sounding of a s blast, the camps on H9108
Nu 10:11 day of the s month of the second H9108
Nu 10:11 day of the second month of the s year, H9108
Nu 28: 8 Offer the s lamb at twilight, along with the H9108
Nu 29:17 " 'On the s day offer twelve young bulls H9108
Dt 24: 3 her s husband dislikes her and writes H340
Dt 24:20 *do* not go over the branches a s time H6994+339
Jos 6:14 So on the s day they marched around the H9108
Jos 10:32 and Joshua took it on the s day. H9108
Jos 19: 1 The s lot came out for the tribe of Simeon H9108
Jdg 6:25 "Take the s bull from your father's herd H9108
Jdg 6:26 offer the s bull as a burnt offering. H9108
Jdg 6:28 it cut down and the s bull sacrificed on H9108
Jdg 20:24 drew near to Benjamin the s day. H9108
1Sa 8: 2 Joel and the name of his s was Abijah, H5467
1Sa 17:13 was Eliab; the s, Abinadab; and the third H5467
1Sa 18:21 you have a s *opportunity* to become my H9109
1Sa 20:27 the next day, the s day *of* the month H9108
1Sa 20:34 on that s day of the feast he did not eat H9108
1Sa 23:17 be king over Israel, and I will be s to you. H5467
2Sa 3: 3 his s, Kileab the son of Abigail the widow H5467
2Sa 14:29 So he sent a s time, but he refused to H9108
1Ki 6: 1 month of Ziv, the s month, he began to H9108
1Ki 6:25 The s cherub also measured ten cubits, for H9108
1Ki 9: 2 the LORD appeared to him a s time, as he H9108
1Ki 15:25 king of Israel in the s year of Asa king of H9109
1Ki 19: 7 LORD came back a s time and touched him H9108
2Ki 1:17 him as king in the s year of Jehoram son H9109
2Ki 9:19 So the king sent out a s horseman. H9108
2Ki 10: 6 Then Jehu wrote them a s letter, saying H9108
2Ki 14: 1 In the s year of Jehoash son of Jehoahaz H9109
2Ki 15:32 In the s year of Pekah son of Remaliah H9109
2Ki 19:29 the s year what springs from that. H9108
1Ch 2:13 his firstborn; the s son was Abinadab, the H9108
1Ch 3: 1 of Jezreel; the s, Daniel the son of H9108
1Ch 3:15 Jehoiakim the s son, Zedekiah the third, H9108
1Ch 5:12 the chief, Shapham the s, then Janai and H5467
1Ch 6:28 Joel the firstborn and Abijah the s son. H9108
1Ch 8: 1 Ashbel the s son, Aharah the third H9108
1Ch 8:39 Jeush the s son and Eliphelet the third. H9108
1Ch 12: 9 Obadiah the s in command, Eliab the H9108
1Ch 23:11 Jahath was the first and Ziza the s, but H9108
1Ch 23:19 the first, Amariah the s, Jahaziel the third H9108
1Ch 23:20 Micah the first and Ishiah the s. H9108
1Ch 24: 7 first lot fell to Jehoiarib, the s to Jedaiah, H9108
1Ch 24:23 the first, Amariah the s, Jahaziel the third H9108
1Ch 25: 9 sons and relatives 12 the s to Gedaliah, H9108
1Ch 26: 2 Jediael the s, Zebadiah the third, H9108
1Ch 26: 4 firstborn, Jehozabad the s, Joah the third, H9108
1Ch 26:11 Hilkiah the s, Tabaliah the third and H9108
1Ch 27: 4 division for the s month was Dodai the H9108
1Ch 29:22 Solomon son of David as king a s time, H9108
2Ch 3: 2 building on the s day of the second H9108
2Ch 3: 2 second day of the s month in the fourth H9108
2Ch 3:12 one wing of the s cherub was five cubits H337
2Ch 21:19 at the end of the s year, his bowels came H9109
2Ch 27: 5 amount also in the s and third years. H9108
2Ch 28: 7 of the palace, and Elkanah, s *to* the king. H5467
2Ch 30: 2 to celebrate the Passover in the s month. H9108
2Ch 30:13 of Unleavened Bread in the s month. H9108
2Ch 30:15 on the fourteenth day of the s month. H9108
Ezr 3: 8 In the s month of the second year after H9108
Ezr 3: 8 the second month of the s year after their H9108
Ezr 4:24 standstill until the s year of the reign of A10775
Ne 8:13 On the s day of the month, the heads of H9108
Ne 11:17 Bakbukiah, s among his associates; and H5467
Ne 12:38 The s choir proceeded in the opposite H9108
Est 2:19 the virgins were assembled a s time, H9108
Est 7: 2 as they were drinking wine on the s day, H9108
Est 9:29 to confirm this s letter concerning Purim. H9108
Est 10: 3 the Jew was s in rank to King Xerxes, H5467
Job 42:14 the s Keziah and the third Keren-Happuch H9108
Isa 11:11 reach out his hand a s time to reclaim the H9108
Isa 37:30 the s year what springs from that. H9108
Jer 13: 3 the word of the LORD came to me a s time: H9108
Jer 33: 1 the word of the LORD came to him a s time: H9108
Eze 10:14 a cherub, the s the face of a human being H9108
Eze 43:22 "On the s day you are to offer a male goat H9108
Da 2: 1 In the s year of his reign, Nebuchadnezzar H9109
Da 7: 5 "And there before me was a s beast A10765
Jnh 3: 1 word of the LORD came to Jonah a s time: H9108
Na 1: 9 to an end; trouble will not come a *s* time. AIT
Hag 1: 1 In the s year of King Darius, on the first H9109
Hag 1:15 In the s year of King Darius, H9109
Hag 2:10 ninth month, in the s year of Darius, the H9109
Hag 2:20 came to Haggai a s time on the H9108
Zec 1: 1 the eighth month of the s year of Darius, H9109
Zec 1: 7 of Shebat, in the s year of Darius, the H9109
Zec 6: 2 first chariot had red horses, the s black, H9108
Zec 11:14 Then I broke my s staff called Union H9108
Mt 22:26 thing happened *to* the s and third brother, *G1311*
Mt 22:39 And the s is like it: 'Love your neighbor as *G1311*
Mt 26:42 He went away a s time and prayed, "My *G1311*
Mk 12:21 The s *one* married the widow, but he also *G1311*
Mk 12:31 The s is this: 'Love your neighbor as *G1311*
Mk 14:72 the rooster crowed the s time. *G1666+1311*
Lk 16: 7 "Then he asked the s, 'And how much *G2283S*
Lk 19:18 "The s came and said, 'Sir, your mina has *G1311*
Lk 20:30 The s *G1311*
Jn 3: 4 they cannot enter a s time into their *G1309*
Jn 4:54 This was the s sign Jesus performed after *G1311*
Jn 9:24 A s time they summoned the man *G1666+1311*
Ac 7:13 On their s *visit*, Joseph told his brothers *G1311*
Ac 10:15 The voice spoke to him a s time *G1666+1311*
Ac 11: 9 voice spoke from heaven a s time, *G1666+1311*
Ac 12:10 passed the first and s guards and came to *G1311*
Ac 13:33 As it is written in the s Psalm: " 'You are *G1311*
1Co 12:28 first of all apostles, s prophets, third *G1309*
1Co 15:47 dust of the earth; the s man is of heaven. *G1311*
2Co 13: 2 a warning when I was with you the s time. *G1309*
Titus 3:10 and then warn them a s time. *G1311*
Heb 9: 3 Behind the s curtain was a room called the *G1311*
Heb 9:28 and he will appear a s time, not to *G1666+1311*
Heb 10: 9 He sets aside the first to establish the s. *G1311*
2Pe 3: 1 Dear friends, this is now my s letter to you. *G1311*
Rev 2:11 will not be hurt at all by the s death. *G1311*
Rev 4: 7 was like a lion, the s was like an ox, the *G1311*
Rev 6: 3 When the Lamb opened the s seal, *G1311*
Rev 6: 3 I heard the s living creature say *G1311*
Rev 8: 8 The s angel sounded his trumpet, and *G1311*
Rev 11:14 The s woe has passed; the third woe is *G1311*
Rev 13:11 Then I saw a s beast, coming out of the *G257*
Rev 13:15 The s beast was given power to give *G899S*
Rev 14: 8 A s angel followed and said, " 'Fallen *G1311*
Rev 16: 3 The s angel poured out his bowl on the *G1311*
Rev 20: 6 The s death has no power over them, but *G1311*
Rev 20:14 The lake of fire is the s death. *G1311*
Rev 21: 8 of burning sulfur. This is the s death." *G1311*
Rev 21:19 was jasper, the s sapphire, the third agate *G1311*

SECOND-IN-COMMAND (1) [COMMAND]
Ge 41:43 He had him ride in a chariot as his s, and H5467

SECRET (43) [SECRETLY, SECRETS]
Ex 7:11 also did the same things by their s arts: H4268
Ex 7:22 did the same things by their s arts, H4319
Ex 8: 7 did the same things by their s arts; H4319
Ex 8:18 tried to produce gnats by their s arts, H4319
Dt 27:15 work of skilled hands—and sets it up in s." H6260
Dt 29:29 The s *things* belong to the LORD our God H6259
Jdg 3:19 "Your Majesty, I have a s message for you." H6260
Jdg 16: 5 into showing you the s of his great H928+4537
Jdg 16: 6 "Tell me the s of your great strength H928+4537
Jdg 16: 9 So the s of his strength was not discovered NDT
Jdg 16:15 haven't told me the s of your great H928+4537
2Sa 12:12 You did it in s, but I will do this thing in H6260
2Sa 15:10 Absalom sent s messengers throughout H8078
Est 2:20 But Esther *had* kept s her family H401+5583
Ps 10: 8 His eyes watch *in* s for his victims; H7621
Ps 51: 6 you taught me wisdom in that s place. H6258
Ps 90: 8 our s sins in the light of your presence. H6623
Ps 101: 5 Whoever slanders their neighbor in s, H6260
Ps 139:15 from you when I was made in the s place, H6260
Pr 9:17 is sweet; food eaten in s is delicious!" H6260
Pr 11:13 a trustworthy person keeps a s. H1821
Pr 17:23 accept bribes in s to pervert the course H2668
Pr 21:14 A gift given in s soothes anger, and a H6260
Isa 45: 3 riches stored in s places, so that you may H5041
Isa 45:19 I have not spoken in s, from somewhere H6260
Isa 48:16 announcement I have not spoken in s; H6260
Isa 65: 4 spend their nights keeping s vigil; H5915
Jer 13:17 I will weep in s because of your pride H5041
Jer 23:24 Who can hide in s places so that I cannot H5041
Eze 28: 3 Is no s hidden from you? H6259
Mt 6: 4 so that your giving may be in s. Then your *G3220*
Mt 6: 4 who sees what is done in s, will reward *G3220*
Mt 6: 6 who sees what is done in s, will reward *G3220*
Mt 6:18 who sees what is done in s, will reward *G3224*
Mk 4:11 "The s of the kingdom of God has been *G3696*
Mk 7:24 yet he could not keep his presence s. *G3291*
Jn 7: 4 wants to become a public figure acts in s. *G3220*
Jn 7:10 he went also, not publicly, but in s. *G3220*
Jn 18:20 Jews come together. I said nothing in s. *G3220*
2Co 4: 2 we have renounced s and shameful ways *G3220*
Eph 5:12 to mention what the disobedient do *in* s. *G3225*
Php 4:12 *I have* learned the s of being content in *G3679*
2Th 2: 7 For the s *power* of lawlessness is already *G3696*

SECRETARIES (4) [SECRETARY]
1Ki 4: 3 sons of Shisha—s; Jehoshaphat son of H6221
2Ch 34:13 Some of the Levites were s, scribes and H6221
Est 3:12 first month the royal s were summoned. H6221
Est 8: 9 At once the royal s were summoned—on H6221

SECRETARY (32) [SECRETARIES, SECRETARY'S]
2Sa 8:17 of Abiathar were priests; Seraiah was s; H6221
2Sa 20:25 Sheva was s; Zadok and Abiathar were H6221
2Ki 12:10 the royal s and the high priest came H6221
2Ki 18:18 Shebna the s, and Joah son of Asaph H6221
2Ki 18:37 Shebna the s, and Joah son of Asaph H6221
2Ki 19: 2 Shebna the s and the leading priests H6221
2Ki 22: 3 King Josiah sent the s, Shaphan son of H6221
2Ki 22: 8 the high priest said to Shaphan the s, H6221
2Ki 22: 9 Then Shaphan the s went to the king and H6221
2Ki 22:10 Then Shaphan the s informed the king H6221
2Ki 22:12 Shaphan the s and Asaiah the king's H6221
2Ki 25:19 He also took the s who was chief officer in H6221
1Ch 18:16 of Abiathar were priests; Shavsha was s; H6221
2Ch 24:11 the royal s and the officer of the chief H6221
2Ch 26:11 mustered by Jeiel the s and Maaseiah the H6221
2Ch 34:15 Hilkiah said to Shaphan the s, "I have H6221
2Ch 34:18 Then Shaphan the s informed the king H6221
2Ch 34:20 Shaphan the s and Asaiah the king's H6221
Ezr 4: 8 Shimshai the s wrote a letter A10516
Ezr 4: 9 commanding officer and Shimshai the s, A10516
Ezr 4:17 Shimshai the s and the rest of their A10516
Ezr 4:23 Shimshai the s and their associates, A10516
Isa 36: 3 Shebna the s, and Joah son of Asaph H6221
Isa 36:22 Shebna the s, and Joah son of Asaph the H6221
Isa 37: 2 Shebna the s, and the leading priests, H6221
Jer 36:10 room of Gemariah son of Shaphan the s, H6221
Jer 36:12 Elishama the s, Delaiah son of Shemaiah, H6221
Jer 36:20 the scroll in the room of Elishama the s, H6221
Jer 36:21 room of Elishama the s and read it to the H6221
Jer 37:15 in the house of Jonathan the s, H6221
Jer 37:20 me back to the house of Jonathan the s, H6221
Jer 52:25 He also took the s who was chief officer in H6221

SECRETARY'S (1) [SECRETARY]
Jer 36:12 he went down to the s room in the royal H6221

SECRETLY (17) [SECRET]
Ge 31:27 Why did you run off s and deceive me H2461
Dt 13: 6 closest friend s entices you, H928+2021+6260
Dt 27:24 who kills their neighbor s." H928+2021+6260
Dt 28:57 to eat them s because of the H928+2021+6260
Jos 2: 1 Joshua son of Nun s sent two spies from H3089
2Ki 17: 9 The Israelites s did things against the LORD H2901
Job 4:12 "A word was s brought to me, my ears H1704
Job 13:10 account if you s showed H928+2021+6260
Job 31:27 my heart was s enticed and H928+2021+6260
Jer 38:16 swore this oath s to Jeremiah: H928+2021+6260
Mt 2: 7 called the Magi s and found out from *G3277*
Mt 26: 4 schemed to arrest Jesus s and kill him. *G1515*
Mk 14: 1 to arrest Jesus s and kill him. *G1877+1515*
Jn 19:38 s because he feared the Jewish *G3221*
Ac 6:11 Then *they* s persuaded some men to say *G5680*
2Pe 2: 1 They *will* s introduce destructive heresies *G4206*
Jude 4 long ago *have* s slipped in among you. *G4208*

SECRETS (7) [SECRET]
Job 11: 6 disclose to you the s *of* wisdom, for H9502
Ps 44:21 since he knows the s *of* the heart? H9502
Mt 13:11 The knowledge of the s of the kingdom of *G3696*
Lk 8:10 knowledge of the s of the kingdom of God *G3696*
Ro 2:16 God judges people's s through Jesus *G3220*
1Co 14:25 as the s of their hearts are laid bare. *G3220*
Rev 2:24 have not learned Satan's so-called deep *s*, AIT

SECT (5)
Lk 5:30 of the law *who belonged to* their *s* AIT
Ac 24: 5 He is a ringleader *of* the Nazarene s *G146*
Ac 24:14 a follower of the Way, which they call a s. *G146*
Ac 26: 5 I conformed to the strictest s of our religion, *G146*
Ac 28:22 everywhere are talking against this s." *G146*

SECTION (20) [SECTIONS]
2Ki 14:13 a s about four hundred cubits long. NDT
2Ch 25:23 a s about four hundred cubits long. NDT
Ne 3: 2 of Jericho built the adjoining s, H6584+3338
Ne 3: 4 son of Hakkoz, repaired the next s. H6584+3338

S

Ne 3: 5 The next s was repaired by the men H6584+3338
Ne 3: 8 repaired the next s; and Hananiah, H6584+3338
Ne 3: 9 of Jerusalem, repaired the next s. H6584+3338
Ne 3:11 repaired another s and the Tower of the H4500
Ne 3:12 repaired the next s with the help of H6584+3338
Ne 3:19 repaired another s, from a point facing H4500
Ne 3:20 of Zabbai zealously repaired another s, H4500
Ne 3:21 repaired another s, from the entrance of H4500
Ne 3:24 son of Henadad repaired another s, H4500
Ne 3:27 the men of Tekoa repaired another s H4500
Ne 3:30 sixth son of Zalaph, repaired another s. H4500
Ne 12:24 one s responding to the other H5464
Eze 42: 3 Both in the s twenty cubits from the inner NDT
Eze 42: 3 court and in the s opposite the pavement NDT
Eze 45: 2 a s 500 cubits square is to be for the NDT
Eze 45: 3 measure off a s 25,000 cubits long and NDT

SECTIONS (2) [SECTION]
1Ki 22:34 king of Israel between the s of his armor. H1817
2Ch 32: 5 repairing all the broken s of the wall and AIT

SECU (NIV84) SEKU

SECUNDUS (1)
Ac 20: 4 Aristarchus and S from Thessalonica G4941

SECURE (47) [SECURED, SECURELY, SECURES, SECURING, SECURITY]
Nu 24:21 "Your dwelling place is s, your nest is set in H419
Dt 33:12 "Let the beloved of the LORD rest s in him H1055
Dt 33:28 Jacob will dwell s in a land of grain and H970
Jdg 18: 7 like the Sidonians, at peace and s. H1053
Jdg 18:27 to Laish, against a people at peace and s. H1053
2Sa 14:17 'May the word of my lord the king s H2118+4200
2Sa 22:33 me with strength and keeps my way s. H9459
1Ki 2:45 throne will remain s before the LORD H3922
Job 5:24 You will know that your tent is s; you will H8934
Job 11:18 You will be s, because there is hope; you H1053
Job 12: 6 those who provoke God are s—those H1058
Job 21:23 in full vigor, completely s and at ease, H8916
Job 40:23 not alarm it; it is s, though the Jordan H1053
Ps 7: 9 of the wicked and make the righteous s— H3922
Ps 16: 5 portion and my cup; you make my lot s. H9461
Ps 16: 9 tongue rejoices; my body also will rest s, H1055
Ps 18:32 me with strength and keeps my way s. H9459
Ps 30: 6 When I felt s, I said, "I will never be H8930
Ps 39: 5 is but a breath, even those who seem s. H5893
Ps 48: 8 city of our God: God makes her s forever. H3922
Ps 93: 1 the world is established, firm and s. H1153+4572
Ps 112: 8 Their hearts are s, they will have no fear H6164
Ps 122: 6 "May those who love you be s. H8922
Pr 14:16 a fool is hotheaded and yet feels s. H1053
Pr 14:26 Whoever fears the LORD has a s fortress H4440
Pr 20:28 through love his throne is made s. H6184
Pr 27:24 a crown is not s for all generations. NDT
Pr 30:31 he-goat, and a king s against revolt. H440+6640
Isa 32: 9 you daughters who feel s, hear what I H1053
Isa 32:10 than a year you who feel s will tremble; H1053
Isa 32:11 shudder, you daughters who feel s! H1053
Isa 32:18 dwelling places, in s homes, in H4440
Isa 33:23 The mast is not held s, the sail is not H2616
Jer 22:21 I warned you when you felt s, but you said H8932
Eze 34:27 the people will be s in their land. H1055
Da 8:25 When they feel s, he will destroy many H8932
Da 11:21 the kingdom when its people feel s, H8932
Da 11:24 When the richest provinces feel s, he will H8932
Am 6: 1 to you who feel s on Mount Samaria H1053
Zec 1:15 am very angry with the nations that feel s. H8633
Zec 14:11 will it be destroyed. Jerusalem will be s. H1055
Mt 27:64 the tomb to be made s until the third G856
Mt 27:65 make the tomb as s as you know how." G856
Mt 27:66 went and made the tomb s by putting a G856
Ac 27:16 were hardly able to make the lifeboat s, G4331
Heb 6:19 as an anchor for the soul, firm and s. G1010
2Pe 3:17 the lawless and fall from your s position. G5113

SECURED (1) [SECURE]
2Sa 23: 5 arranged and s in every part; surely H9068

SECURELY (9) [SECURE]
Jos 6: 1 Jericho were s barred H6037+2256+6037
Jdg 16:11 "If anyone ties me s with new ropes H673+673
1Sa 25:29 my lord will be bound s in the bundle of H7674
1Ki 2:24 has established me s on the throne of my H3782
Pr 8:28 clouds above and fixed s the fountains of H6451
Pr 10: 9 Whoever walks in integrity walks s, but H1055
Mic 5: 4 And they will live s, for then his greatness H3782
Zec 10:12 the LORD and in his name they will live s," H2143
Ac 5:23 "We found the jail s locked G1877+4246+854

SECURES (1) [SECURE]
Ps 140:12 I know that the LORD s justice for the poor H6913

SECURING (1) [SECURE]
Ac 12:20 After s the support of Blastus, a trusted G4275

SECURITY (20) [SECURE]
Dt 24: 6 Do not take a pair of millstones—not even the upper one—as s for a debt H2471
Dt 24: 6 would be taking a person's livelihood as s H2471
2Ki 20:19 there not be peace and s in my lifetime?" H622
Job 17: 3 else will put up s for me? H9546+4200+3338
Job 18:14 He is torn from the s of his tent and H4440
Job 22: 6 You demanded s from your relatives for H2471
Job 24:23 He may let them rest in a feeling of s, but H1055
Job 31:24 gold or said to pure gold, 'You are my s,' H4440
Ps 122: 7 your walls and s within your citadels." H8932
Pr 6: 1 if you have put up s for your neighbor H6842
Pr 11:15 Whoever puts up s for a stranger will H6842
Pr 17:18 in pledge and puts up s for a H6842+6859
Pr 20:16 of one who puts up s for a stranger H6842
Pr 22:26 hands in pledge or puts up s for debts; H6842
Pr 27:13 of one who puts up s for a stranger; H6842
Isa 39: 8 "There will be peace and s in my lifetime." H622
Isa 47: 8 lounging in your s and saying to yourself H1055
Jer 30:10 Jacob will again have peace and s, and H8631
Jer 33: 6 will let them enjoy abundant peace and s. H622
Jer 46:27 Jacob will again have peace and s, and H8631

SEDITION (2)
Ezr 4:15 a place with a long history of s. A10083+10522
Ezr 4:19 has been a place of rebellion and s. A10083

SEDUCE (1) [SEDUCED, SEDUCES, SEDUCTIVE]
2Pe 2:14 stop sinning; they s the unstable; they G1284

SEDUCED (1) [SEDUCE]
Pr 7:21 she s him with her smooth talk. H5615

SEDUCES (1) [SEDUCE]
Ex 22:16 "If a man s a virgin who is not pledged to H7331

SEDUCTIVE (2) [SEDUCE]
Pr 2:16 the wayward woman with her s words, H2744
Pr 7: 5 the wayward woman with her s words. H2744

SEE (814) [NEARSIGHTED, SAW, SEEING, SEEN, SEES, SIGHT, SIGHTING, SIGHTLESS, SIGHTS]
Ge 2:19 to the man to s what he would name H8011
Ge 8: 8 he sent out a dove to s if the water had H8011
Ge 9:16 I will s it and remember the everlasting H8011
Ge 9:23 way so that they would not s their father H8011
Ge 11: 5 the LORD came down to s the city and the H8011
Ge 12:12 When the Egyptians s you, they will say H8011
Ge 13:15 All the land that you s I will give to you H8011
Ge 18:16 along with them to s them on their way. H8938
Ge 18:21 I will go down and s if what they have H8011
Ge 24:13 S, I am standing beside this spring, and H2180
Ge 24:43 S, I am standing beside this spring. H2180
Ge 27: 1 were so weak that he could no longer s, H8011
Ge 31: 5 "I s that your father's attitude toward me H8011
Ge 31:12 'Look up and s that all the male goats H8011
Ge 31:32 s for yourself whether there is anything of H5795
Ge 31:43 All you s is mine. Yet what can H8011
Ge 32:20 when I s him, perhaps he will H8011+7156
Ge 33:10 For to s your face is like seeing the face of H8011
Ge 37:14 "Go and s if all is well with your brothers H8011
Ge 37:20 Then we'll s what comes of his dreams." H8011
Ge 37:32 Examine it to s whether it is your son's H5795
Ge 38:25 "S if you recognize whose seal and cord AIT
Ge 42: 9 You have come to s where our land is H8011
Ge 42:12 "You have come to s where our land is H8011
Ge 42:16 may be tested to s if you are telling the NDT
Ge 43: 3 'You will not s my face again unless your H8011
Ge 43: 5 'You will not s my face again unless your H8011
Ge 44:21 down to me so I can s him for H6524+8492
Ge 44:23 with you, you will not s my face again. H8011
Ge 44:26 We cannot s the man's face unless our H8011
Ge 44:34 Do not let me s the misery that would H8011
Ge 45:12 "You can s for yourselves H8011+6524+4013
Ge 45:28 I will go and s him before I die." H8011
Ge 48:10 of old age, and he could hardly s. H8011
Ge 48:11 "I never expected to s your face again H8011
Ge 48:11 now God has allowed me to s your H8011
Ex 1:16 if you s that the baby is a boy H8011
Ex 2: 4 at a distance to s what would happen to H3359
Ex 3: 3 "I will go over and s this strange sight H8011
Ex 4:14 to meet you, and he will be glad to s you. H8011
Ex 4:18 people in Egypt to s if any of them are H8011
Ex 4:21 s that you perform before Pharaoh all the H8011
Ex 6: 1 "Now you will s what I will do to Pharaoh: H8011
Ex 7: 1 LORD said to Moses, "S, I have made you H8011
Ex 10:23 No one could s anyone else or move H8011
Ex 10:28 The day you s my face you will die." H8011
Ex 12:13 you are, and when I s the blood, I will H8011
Ex 12:23 he will s the blood on the top and sides H8011
Ex 14:13 Stand firm and you will s the deliverance H8011
Ex 14:13 The Egyptians you s today you will never H8011
Ex 14:13 you see today you will never s again. H8011
Ex 16: 4 I will test them and s whether they will NDT
Ex 16: 7 in the morning you will s the glory of the H8011
Ex 16:32 so they can s the bread I gave you to eat H8011
Ex 19:21 way through to s the LORD and many of H8011
Ex 21:19 s that the victim is completely healed H8324+8324
Ex 23: 5 If you s the donkey of someone who hates H8011
Ex 23: 8 a bribe blinds those who s and twists the H7221
Ex 23:20 "S, I am sending an angel ahead of you H2180
Ex 25:40 S that you make them according to the H8011
Ex 31: 2 "S, I have chosen Bezalel son of Uri, the H8011
Ex 33:20 he said, "you cannot s my face, for no one H8011
Ex 33:20 my face, for no one may s me and live." H8011
Ex 33:23 remove my hand and you will s my back; H8011
Ex 34:10 you live among will s how awesome is H8011
Ex 35:30 to the Israelites, "S, the LORD has chosen H8011
Lev 13:12 so far as the priest can s, it covers H5260+6524
Lev 13:37 is unchanged so far as the priest can s, H6524
Lev 25:53 you must s to it that those to whom H4200+6524
Nu 4:18 S that the Kohathite tribal clans are not destroyed AIT
Nu 8: 2 s that all seven light up the area in front of AIT
Nu 11: 6 we never s anything but this manna!" H6524+448
Nu 11:23 Now you will s whether or not what I say H8011
Nu 13:18 S what the land is like and whether the H8011
Nu 14:23 not one of them will ever s the land I H8011
Nu 14:23 treated me with contempt will ever s it. H8011
Nu 22:41 from there he could s the outskirts of H8011
Nu 23: 9 From the rocky peaks I s them, from the H8011
Nu 23: 9 I s a people who live apart and do not H2176
Nu 23:13 to another place where you can s them; H8011
Nu 23:13 you will not s them all but only the H8011
Nu 23:23 Jacob and of Israel, 'S what God has done! NDT
Nu 24:17 "I s him, but not now; I behold him, but H8011
Nu 27:12 the Abarim Range and s the land I have H8011
Nu 32:11 up out of Egypt will s the land I promised H8011
Dt 1: 8 S, I have given you this land. Go in and H8011
Dt 1:21 S, the LORD your God has given you the H8011
Dt 1:35 evil generation shall s the good land I H8011
Dt 1:36 He will s it, and I will give him and his H8011
Dt 2:24 S, I have given into your hand Sihon the H8011
Dt 2:31 The LORD said to me, "S, I have begun to H8011
Dt 3:25 Let me go over and s the good land H8011
Dt 3:28 them to inherit the land that you will s." H8011
Dt 4: 5 S, I have taught you decrees and laws as H8011
Dt 4:19 you look up to the sky and s the sun, H8011
Dt 4:28 which cannot s or hear or eat or smell. H8011
Dt 11:26 S, I am setting before you today a H8011
Dt 12: 8 everyone doing as they s fit, H928+6524
Dt 12:32 S that you do all I command you; do not H9068
Dt 18:16 the LORD our God nor s this great fire H8011
Dt 20: 1 your enemies and s horses and chariots H8011
Dt 21: 7 this blood, nor did our eyes s it done. H8011
Dt 22: 1 If you s your fellow Israelite's ox or sheep H8011
Dt 22: 4 If you s your fellow Israelite's donkey or ox H8011
Dt 23:14 so that he will not s among you anything H8011
Dt 28:10 peoples on earth will s that you are called H8011
Dt 28:34 The sights you s will drive you mad. H8011
Dt 28:67 hearts and the sights that your eyes will s. H8011
Dt 29: 4 eyes that s or ears that hear. H8011
Dt 29:22 from distant lands will s the calamities H8011
Dt 30:15 S, I set before you today life and H8011
Dt 32:20 he said, "and s what their end will be; for H8011
Dt 32:39 "S now that I myself am he! There is no H8011
Dt 32:52 you will s the land only from a distance H8011
Dt 34: 4 I have let you s it with your eyes, but you H8011
Jos 3: 3 "When you s the ark of the covenant of H8011
Jos 3:11 S, the ark of the covenant of the Lord of all H2180
Jos 5: 6 them that they would not s the land he H8011
Jos 6: 2 LORD said to Joshua, "S, I have delivered H8011
Jos 8: 8 has commanded. S to it; you have my H8011
Jos 9:12 But now s how dry and moldy it is H2180
Jos 9:13 were new, but s how cracked they are. H2180
Jos 24:27 "S!" he said to all the people. "This stone H2180
Jdg 1:24 city and we will s that you are treated well." AIT
Jdg 2:22 to test Israel and s whether they will keep NDT
Jdg 3: 4 test the Israelites to s whether they would H3359
Jdg 13: 4 Now s to it that you drink no wine or other H9068
Jdg 14:10 Now his father went down to s the woman NDT
Jdg 16: 5 "S if you can lure him into showing you the AIT
1Sa 2:32 and you will s distress in my dwelling H5564
1Sa 3: 2 becoming so weak that he could barely s, H8011
1Sa 3:11 "S, I am about to do something in Israel H2180
1Sa 4:15 eyes had failed so that he could not s. H8011
1Sa 10:24 "Do you s the man the LORD has chosen? H8011
1Sa 12:13 one you asked for; s, the LORD has set a H2180
1Sa 12:16 stand still and s this great thing the LORD H8011
1Sa 14: 8 cross over toward them and let them s us. H1655
1Sa 14:17 "Muster the forces and s who has left us." H8011
1Sa 14:29 S how my eyes brightened when I tasted H8011
1Sa 15:35 he did not go to s Saul again H8011
1Sa 16:15 said to him, "S, an evil spirit from God H2180
1Sa 17:18 S how your brothers are and bring back H7212
1Sa 17:25 "Do you s how this man keeps coming out H8011
1Sa 19:15 the men back to s David and told them, H8011
1Sa 20:29 let me get away to s my brothers. H8011
1Sa 24:11 S, my father, look at this piece of your robe H8011
1Sa 24:11 S that there is nothing in my hand to H8011
1Sa 25:17 Now think it over and s what you can do H8011
1Sa 25:25 servant, I did not s the men my lord sent. H8011
1Sa 28: 2 "Then you will s for yourself what your H3359
1Sa 28:13 What do you s?" The woman H8011
1Sa 28:13 "I s a ghostly figure coming up out of the H8011
2Sa 3:13 daughter of Saul when you come to s me." H8011
2Sa 13: 5 "When your father comes to s you, say to H8011
2Sa 13: 6 When the king came to s him, Amnon H8011
2Sa 13:34 "I s men in the direction of Horonaim H8011
2Sa 13:35 said to the king, "S, the king's sons have H2180
2Sa 14:24 to his own house; he must not s my face." H8011
2Sa 14:24 own house and did not s the face of the H8011
2Sa 14:32 Now then, I want to s the king's face H8011
2Sa 15: 4 and I would s that they receive justice." H7405
2Sa 15:25 bring me back and let me s it and his H8011
2Sa 19: 6 I s that you would be pleased if Absalom H3359
2Sa 24: 3 and may the eyes of my lord the king s it. H8011
1Ki 1:15 So Bathsheba went to s the aged king in his NDT
1Ki 1:48 allowed my eyes to s a successor on my H8011
1Ki 9:12 went from Tyre to s the towns that H8011
1Ki 11:31 'S, I am going to tear the kingdom out of H2180

S

1Ki 14: 4 Now Ahijah could not **s**; his sight was H8011
1Ki 15:19 **S**, I am sending you a gift of silver and H2180
1Ki 20: 7 "**S** how this man is looking H3359+2256+8011
1Ki 20:13 the LORD says: '*Do you* **s** this vast army? H8011
1Ki 20:22 position and **s** what must be H3359+2256+8011
1Ki 22: 2 of Judah went down to **s** the king of Israel. NDT
2Ki 1: 2 Ekron, to **s** if I will recover from this injury." NDT
2Ki 1:14 **S**, fire has fallen from heaven and H2180
2Ki 2:10 "yet if *you* **s** me when I am taken from you H8011
2Ki 2:19 situated, as you *can* **s**, but the water is H8011
2Ki 3:17 *You will* **s** neither wind nor rain, yet this H8011
2Ki 5: 3 master would **s** the prophet who H4200+7156
2Ki 5: 7 **S** how he is trying to pick a H3359+2256+8011
2Ki 6:17 "Open his eyes, LORD, so that *he may* **s**." H8011
2Ki 6:20 open the eyes of these men so *they can* **s**." H8011
2Ki 6:32 "Don't *you* **s** how this murderer is sending H8011
2Ki 7: 2 "You *will* **s** it with your own eyes, H8011
2Ki 7:19 replied, "You *will* **s** it with your own eyes H8011
2Ki 8:29 down to Jezreel to **s** Joram son of Ahab, H8011
2Ki 9:16 king of Judah had gone down to **s** him. H8011
2Ki 9:17 he called out, "I **s** some troops coming." H8011
2Ki 10:16 Come with me and **s** my zeal for the LORD. H8011
2Ki 10:19 **S** that no one is missing, because I am NDT
2Ki 10:23 "Look around and **s** that no one who H8011
2Ki 13:14 Israel went down to **s** him and wept over NDT
2Ki 19:16 and **s**; listen to the words H8011
2Ki 20:15 "What *did they* **s** in your palace? H8011
2Ki 22:20 Your eyes *will* not **s** all the disaster I am H8011
2Ki 23:17 king asked, "What is that tombstone I **s**?" H8011
1Ch 12:17 *may* the God of our ancestors **s** it and H8011
2Ch 16: 3 your father. **S**, I am sending you H2180
2Ch 18: 2 later he went down to **s** Ahab in Samaria. NDT
2Ch 20:11 **S** how they are repaying us by coming to H2180
2Ch 20:17 stand firm and **s** the deliverance the LORD H8011
2Ch 22: 6 down to Jezreel to **s** Joram son of Ahab H8011
2Ch 24:22 "*May* the LORD **s** this and call you to H8011
2Ch 29: 8 as you *can* **s** with your own eyes. H8011
2Ch 30: 7 made them an object of horror, as you **s**. H8011
2Ch 34:28 Your eyes *will* not **s** all the disaster I am H8011
Ezr 4:14 proper for us to **s** the king dishonored, A10255
Ezr 5:17 archives of Babylon to **s** if King Cyrus did NDT
Ne 2:17 to them, "You **s** the trouble we are in: H8011
Ne 4:11 "Before they know it or **s** us, we will be H8011
Ne 8: 5 the people could **s** him because he H4200+6524
Ne 9:36 "But **s**, we are slaves today, slaves in the H2180
Est 3: 4 Haman about it to **s** whether Mordecai's H8011
Est 5:13 as long as I **s** that Jew Mordecai sitting H8011
Est 8: 6 For how can I bear *to* **s** disaster fall on my H8011
Est 8: 6 How can I bear *to* **s** the destruction of my H8011
Job 3: 9 in vain and not **s** the first rays of dawn, H8011
Job 6:21 *you* **s** something dreadful and are afraid. H8011
Job 7: 7 my eyes *will* never **s** happiness again. H8011
Job 7: 8 that now sees me *will* **s** me no longer; H8800
Job 7:20 done to you, you *who* **s** everything we do? H5915
Job 9:11 he passes me, *I* cannot **s** him; when he H8011
Job 10: 4 eyes of flesh? *Do you* **s** as a mortal sees? H8011
Job 14:21 offspring are brought low, *they do* not **s** it. H1067
Job 17:15 is my hope—who *can* **s** any hope for me? H8800
Job 19:26 destroyed, yet in my flesh *I will* **s** God; H2600
Job 19:27 I myself *will* **s** him with my own eyes—I H2600
Job 20: 9 The eye that saw him will not **s** him again NDT
Job 21: 8 They **s** their children established H4200+7156
Job 21:20 *Let* their own eyes **s** their destruction; let H8011
Job 22:11 why it is so dark *you* cannot **s**, and why a H8011
Job 22:12 And **s** how lofty are the highest stars H8011
Job 22:14 so *he does* not **s** us as he goes about in H8011
Job 22:19 The righteous **s** their ruin and rejoice; the H8011
Job 23: 9 in the north, *I do* not **s** him; when he turns H2600
Job 24:15 'No eye *will* **s** me,' and he keeps H8800
Job 28:10 the rock; their eyes **s** all its treasures. H8011
Job 31: 4 *Does* he not **s** my ways and count my H8011
Job 33:26 *they will* **s** God's face and shout for joy H8011
Job 34:26 wickedness where *everyone can* **s** them, H8011
Job 34:29 hides his face, who *can* **s** him? Yet he is H8800
Job 34:32 Teach me what *I* cannot **s**; if I have done H2600
Job 35: 5 Look up at the heavens and **s**; gaze at the H8011
Job 35:14 listen when you say that *you do* not **s** him, H8800
Job 36:30 **S** how he scatters his lightning about him H2176
Ps 9:13 **s** how my enemies persecute me H8011
Ps 10:14 **s** the trouble of the afflicted; you H8011
Ps 11: 7 he loves justice; the upright *will* **s** his face. H2600
Ps 14: 2 on all mankind to **s** if there are any who H8011
Ps 16:10 will you let your faithful one **s** decay. H8011
Ps 17: 2 from you; *may* your eyes **s** what is right. H2600
Ps 17:15 I will be vindicated and *will* **s** your face H2600
Ps 22: 7 All *who* **s** me mock me; they hurl insults H8011
Ps 25:19 **S** how numerous are my enemies and H8011
Ps 27:13 I *will* **s** the goodness of the LORD in the H8011
Ps 31:11 *those who* **s** me on the street flee from H8011
Ps 34: 8 Taste and **s** that the LORD is good; blessed H8011
Ps 34:12 life and desires to **s** many good days, H8011
Ps 36: 9 fountain of life; in your light *we* **s** light. H8011
Ps 36:12 **S** how the evildoers lie fallen—thrown H9004
Ps 37:34 the wicked are destroyed, *you will* **s** it. H8011
Ps 40: 3 Many *will* **s** and fear the LORD and put H8011
Ps 40:12 sins have overtaken me, and I cannot **s**. H8011
Ps 41: 6 When one of them comes to **s** me, he H8011
Ps 46: 8 Come and **s** what the LORD has done, the H2600
Ps 49: 9 should live on forever and not **s** decay. H8011
Ps 49:10 For *all can* **s** that the wise die, that the H8011
Ps 49:19 *who will* never again **s** the light of life. H8011
Ps 50:18 When *you* **s** a thief, you join with him H8011
Ps 52: 6 The righteous *will* **s** and fear; they will H8011
Ps 53: 2 on all mankind to **s** if there are any who H8011
Ps 55: 9 for *I* **s** violence and strife in the city. H8011
Ps 59: 3 **S** how they lie in wait for me! Fierce men H2180
Ps 59: 7 **S** what they spew from their mouths—the H2180
Ps 64: 5 their snares; they say, "Who *will* **s** it?" H8011
Ps 64: 8 all *who* **s** them will shake their heads in H8011
Ps 66: 5 Come and **s** what God has done, his H8011
Ps 69:23 their eyes be darkened so they cannot **s**, H8011
Ps 69:32 The poor *will* **s** and be glad—you who H8011
Ps 71:20 Though *you have* **made** me **s** troubles H8011
Ps 80:14 Look down from heaven and **s**! Watch H8011
Ps 83: 2 **S** how your enemies growl, how your foes H2180
Ps 86:17 that my enemies *may* **s** it and be put to H8011
Ps 89:48 Who can live and not **s** death, or who can H8011
Ps 91: 8 with your eyes and **s** the punishment of H8011
Ps 94: 7 "The LORD *does* not **s**; the God of H8011
Ps 94: 9 *Does he* who formed the eye not **s**? H5564
Ps 97: 6 righteousness, and all peoples **s** his glory. H8011
Ps 107:42 The upright **s** and rejoice, but all the H8011
Ps 109:25 my accusers; *when they* **s** me, they shake H8011
Ps 112:10 The wicked *will* **s** and be vexed, they will H8011
Ps 115: 5 cannot speak, eyes, but cannot **s**. H8011
Ps 119:18 my eyes that *I may* **s** wonderful things H5564
Ps 119:74 who fear you rejoice *when they* **s** me, H8011
Ps 119:96 To all perfection *I* **s** a limit, but your H8011
Ps 119:159 **S** how I love your precepts; preserve my H8011
Ps 128: 5 *may you* **s** the prosperity of Jerusalem all H8011
Ps 128: 6 *May you* live to **s** your children's children H8011
Ps 135:16 cannot speak, eyes, but cannot **s**. H8011
Ps 139:24 **S** if there is any offensive way in me, and H8011
Ps 142: 4 Look and **s**, there is no one at my right H8011
Pr 1:17 to spread a net where every bird can **s** it! H6524
Pr 20:12 Ears that hear and eyes *that* **s**—the LORD H8011
Pr 22: 3 The prudent **s** danger and take refuge H8011
Pr 22:29 *Do you* **s** someone skilled in their work H2600
Pr 23:33 Your eyes *will* **s** strange *sights*, and your H8011
Pr 24:18 the LORD *will* **s** and disapprove and turn H8011
Pr 26:12 *Do you* **s** a person wise in their own eyes H8011
Pr 27:12 The prudent **s** danger and take refuge H8011
Pr 29:16 but the righteous *will* **s** their downfall. H8011
Pr 29:20 *Do you* **s** someone who speaks in haste H2600
Ecc 2: 3 *I wanted to* **s** what was good for people to H8011
Ecc 2:24 This too, I **s**, is from the hand of H8011
Ecc 3:18 them so that they *may* **s** that they are like H8011
Ecc 3:22 who can bring them to **s** what will happen H8011
Ecc 5: 8 If *you* **s** the poor oppressed in a district H8011
Ecc 7:11 thing and benefits *those who* **s** the sun. H8011
Ecc 11: 7 it pleases the eyes to **s** the sun. H8011
Ecc 11: 9 of your heart and *whatever* your eyes **s**, H5260
SS 2:11 **S**! The winter is past; the rains are over H2180
SS 6:11 to **s** if the vines had budded or the H8011
SS 7:12 to the vineyards *to* **s** if the vines have H8011
Isa 1:21 **S how** the faithful city has become a H377
Isa 3: 1 **S** now, the Lord, the LORD Almighty, is H2180
Isa 5:19 let him hasten his work so *we may* **s** it. H8011
Isa 6: 7 my mouth and said, "**S**, this has touched H2180
Isa 6:10 Otherwise *they might* **s** with their eyes H8011
Isa 8:22 toward the earth and **s** only distress and H2180
Isa 10:33 **S**, the Lord, the LORD Almighty, will lop H2180
Isa 13: 9 **S**, the day of the LORD is coming—a cruel H2180
Isa 13:17 **S**, I will stir up against them the Medes H2180
Isa 14:16 *Those who* **s** you stare at you, they ponder H8011
Isa 17: 1 "**S**, Damascus will no longer be a city H2180
Isa 18: 3 the mountains, *you will* **s** it, and when a H8011
Isa 19: 1 **S**, the LORD rides on a swift cloud and is H2180
Isa 20: 6 '**S** what has happened to those we relied H2180
Isa 21: 3 what I hear, I am bewildered by *what* I **s**. H8011
Isa 22:13 But **s**, there is joy and revelry H2180
Isa 24: 1 **S**, the LORD is going to lay waste the earth H2180
Isa 26:11 hand is lifted high, but *they do* not **s** it. H2600
Isa 26:11 *Let them* **s** your zeal for your people and H2600
Isa 26:21 **S**, the LORD is coming out of his dwelling H2180
Isa 28: 2 **S**, the Lord has one who is powerful and H2180
Isa 28: 4 as soon as people **s** them and take them H8011
Isa 28:16 "**S**, I lay a stone in Zion, a tested stone, H2180
Isa 29:18 darkness the eyes of the blind *will* **s**. H8011
Isa 29:23 When they **s** among them their children H8011
Isa 30:10 the seers, "**S** no *more* **visions**!" and to the H8011
Isa 30:20 *with* your own eyes you *will* **s** them. H8011
Isa 30:27 **S**, the Name of the LORD comes from afar H2180
Isa 30:30 voice and *will* **make** them **s** his arm H8011
Isa 32: 1 **S**, a king will reign in righteousness and H2176
Isa 32: 3 the eyes of *those who* **s** will no longer H8011
Isa 33:17 Your eyes *will* **s** the king in his beauty H2600
Isa 33:19 *You will* **s** those arrogant people no more H8011
Isa 33:20 festivals; your eyes *will* **s** Jerusalem, H8011
Isa 34: 5 fill in the heavens; **s**, it descends in H2180
Isa 35: 2 Sharon; they *will* **s** the glory of the LORD H8011
Isa 37:17 and **s**; listen to all the words H8011
Isa 38:11 "*I will* not again **s** the LORD himself in the H8011
Isa 39: 4 "What *did they* **s** in your palace? H8011
Isa 40: 5 revealed, and all people *will* **s** it together. H8011
Isa 40:10 **S**, the Sovereign LORD comes with power H2180
Isa 40:10 **S**, his reward is with him, and his H2180
Isa 41:15 "**S**, I will make you into a threshing H2180
Isa 41:20 so that people *may* **s** and know, may H8011
Isa 41:29 **S**, they are all false! Their deeds amount H2176
Isa 42: 9 **S**, the former things have taken place H2180
Isa 42:18 you deaf; look, you blind, and **s**! H8011
Isa 43:19 **S**, I am doing a new thing! Now it springs H2180
Isa 44:16 says, "Ah! I am warm; *I* **s** the fire." H8011
Isa 44:18 eyes are plastered over so they cannot **s**, H8011
Isa 48:10 **S**, I have refined you, though not as silver H2180
Isa 49: 7 "Kings *will* **s** you and stand up, princes H8011
Isa 49: 7 princes will **s** and bow down, because NDT
Isa 49:12 **S**, they will come from afar—some from H2180
Isa 49:16 **S**, I have engraved you on the palms of H2176
Isa 49:22 "**S**, I will beckon to the nations, I will lift H2180
Isa 51:22 "**S**, I have taken out of your hand the cup H2180
Isa 52: 8 to Zion, *they will* **s** it with their own eyes. H8011
Isa 52:10 ends of the earth *will* **s** the salvation of H8011
Isa 52:13 **S**, my servant will act wisely; he will be H2180
Isa 52:15 were not told, *they will* **s**, and what they H8011
Isa 53:10 *he will* **s** his offspring and prolong his H8011
Isa 53:11 *he will* **s** the light of life and be satisfied H8011
Isa 54:16 "**S**, it is I who created the blacksmith who H2180
Isa 55: 4 **S**, I have made him a witness to the H2176
Isa 58: 7 with shelter—when *you* **s** the naked, to H8011
Isa 60: 2 **S**, darkness covers the earth and thick H2180
Isa 61: 9 All *who* **s** them will acknowledge that H8011
Isa 62: 2 The nations *will* **s** your vindication, and H8011
Isa 62:11 to Daughter Zion, '**S**, your Savior comes! H2180
Isa 62:11 **S**, his reward is with him, and his H2180
Isa 63:15 Look down from heaven and **s**, from your H8011
Isa 65: 6 "**S**, it stands written before me: I will not H2180
Isa 65:17 "**S**, I will create new heavens and a new H2180
Isa 66: 5 LORD be glorified, that *we may* **s** your joy! H8011
Isa 66:14 When *you* **s** this, your heart will rejoice H8011
Isa 66:15 **S**, the LORD is coming with fire, and his H2180
Isa 66:18 they will come and **s** my glory. H8011
Jer 1:10 **S**, today I appoint you over nations and H8011
Jer 1:11 "What *do* you **s**, Jeremiah?" "I H8011
Jer 1:11 "I **s** the branch of an almond tree," I H8011
Jer 1:12 I am watching to *s that* my word *is* **fulfilled**." AIT
Jer 1:13 "What *do* you **s**?" "I see a pot H8011
Jer 1:13 "I **s** a pot that is boiling, H8011
Jer 2:10 **s** if there has ever been anything like this: H8011
Jer 2:23 **S** how you behaved in the valley; consider H8011
Jer 3: 2 "Look up to the barren heights and **s**. H8011
Jer 4:21 How long *must I* **s** the battle standard H8011
Jer 5:12 *we will* never **s** sword or famine. H8011
Jer 5:21 who have eyes but *do* not **s**, who have H8011
Jer 7:12 **s** what I did to it because of the H8011
Jer 7:17 *Do* you not **s** what they are doing in the H8011
Jer 8:17 "**S**, I will send venomous snakes among H2180
Jer 9: 7 "**S**, I will refine and test them, for what H2180
Jer 9:15 "**S**, I will make this people eat bitter food H2180
Jer 11:20 *let me* **s** your vengeance on them H8011
Jer 12: 3 *you* **s** me and test my thoughts about you. H8011
Jer 12: 4 "*He will* not **s** what happens to us. H8011
Jer 13:20 Look up and **s** those who are coming from H8011
Jer 14:13 '*You will* not **s** the sword or suffer famine. H8011
Jer 14:18 the country, I **s** those slain by the sword H2180
Jer 14:18 go into the city, I **s** the ravages of famine. H2180
Jer 16:12 **S** how all of you are following the H2180
Jer 17: 6 *they will* not **s** prosperity when it comes. H8011
Jer 20: 4 your own eyes you *will* **s** them fall by the H8011
Jer 20:12 *let me* **s** your vengeance on them H8011
Jer 20:18 out of the womb to **s** trouble and sorrow H8011
Jer 21: 8 **S**, I am setting before you the way of life H2180
Jer 22:10 never return nor **s** his native land again H8011
Jer 22:12 him captive; *he will* not **s** this land again." H8011
Jer 23:18 council of the LORD *to* **s** or to hear his word H8011
Jer 23:19 **S**, the storm of the LORD will burst out in H2180
Jer 23:24 in secret places so that I cannot **s** them?" H8011
Jer 24: 3 asked me, "What *do* you **s**, Jeremiah?" H8011
Jer 25:29 **S**, I am beginning to bring disaster on the H2180
Jer 29:32 nor *will he* **s** the good things I will do H8011
Jer 30: 6 Ask and **s**: Can a man bear children H8011
Jer 30: 6 Then why *do I* **s** every strong man with his H8011
Jer 30:23 **S**, the storm of the LORD will burst out in H2180
Jer 31: 8 **S**, I will bring them from the land of the H2180
Jer 32: 4 him face to face and **s** him with his own H8011
Jer 32:24 "**S** how the siege ramps are built up to H2180
Jer 32:24 you said has happened, as you now **s**. H8011
Jer 34: 3 You *will* **s** the king of Babylon *with* your H8011
Jer 42: 2 For as you now **s**, though we were H8011+6524
Jer 42:14 where *we will* not **s** war or hear the H8011
Jer 42:18 *you will* never **s** this place again. H8011
Jer 44:23 disaster has come upon you, as you now **s**." NDT
Jer 46: 5 What *do I* **s**? They are terrified, they are H8011
Jer 47: 2 "**S** how the waters are rising in the north H2180
Jer 49:35 "**S**, I will break the bow of Elam, the H2180
Jer 50:31 "**S**, I am against you, you arrogant one," H2180
Jer 51: 1 "**S**, I will stir up the spirit of a destroyer H2180
Jer 51:36 "**S**, I will defend your cause and avenge H2180
Jer 51:61 **s** that you read all these words aloud. H8011
La 1:12 Look around and **s**. Is any suffering H8011
La 1:20 "**S**, LORD, how distressed I am! I am in H8011
La 2:16 we have waited for; we have lived *to* **s** it." H8011
La 3:36 *would* not the Lord **s** such things? H8011
La 3:51 **What I s** brings grief to my soul because H6524
La 5: 1 happened to us; look, and **s** our disgrace. H8011
Eze 7: 5 Unheard-of disaster! **S**, it comes! H2180
Eze 7: 6 has roused itself against you. **S**, it comes! H2180
Eze 7:10 "'**S**, the day! See, it comes! Doom has H2180
Eze 7:10 **S**, it comes! Doom has burst forth, H2180
Eze 8: 6 of man, *do* you **s** what they are doing H8011
Eze 8: 6 But *you will* **s** things that are even more H8011
Eze 8: 9 "Go in and **s** the wicked and detestable H8011
Eze 8:12 'The LORD *does* not **s** us; the LORD has H8011
Eze 8:13 "*You will* **s** them doing things that are H8011
Eze 8:15 He said to me, "*Do you* **s** this, son of man H8011

Eze 8:15 *You will* **s** things that are even more H8011
Eze 9: 9 forsaken the land; the LORD *does* not **s**. H8011
Eze 12: 2 They have eyes to **s** but do not see and H8011
Eze 12: 2 eyes to see but *do* not **s** and ears to hear H8011
Eze 12: 6 your face so that *you* cannot **s** the land, H8011
Eze 12:12 so that *he* cannot **s** the H8011+4200+2021+6524
Eze 12:13 Chaldeans, but *he will* not **s** it, and there H8011
Eze 13: 9 prophets who **s** false **visions** and utter H2600
Eze 13:23 *you will* no longer **s** false **visions** or H2600
Eze 14:22 when *you* **s** their conduct and their H8011
Eze 14:23 be consoled when *you* **s** their conduct H8011
Eze 16:37 of them, and *they will* **s** you stark naked. H8011
Eze 20:48 Everyone *will* **s** that I the LORD have kindled H8011
Eze 22: 6 " '**S** how each of the princes of Israel who H2180
Eze 32:31 *will* **s** them and he will be consoled for all H8011
Eze 34:20 **S**, I myself will judge between the fat H2180
Eze 39:21 all the nations *will* **s** the punishment I H8011
Eze 40: 4 Tell the people of Israel everything you **s**." H8011
Eze 47: 6 "Son of man, *do you* **s** this?" Then he H8011
Da 1:10 Why *should he* **s** you looking worse than H8011
Da 1:13 servants in accordance with what *you* **s**." H8011
Da 3:25 I **s** four men walking around in the fire A10255
Da 5:23 which cannot **s** or hear or understand. A10255
Da 9:18 open your eyes and **s** the desolation of H8011
Da 10: 7 those who were with me *did* not **s** it, but H8011
Joel 2:28 dreams, your young men *will* **s** visions. H8011
Joel 3: 7 "**S**, I am going to rouse them out of the H2180
Am 3: 9 **s** the great unrest within her and the H8011
Am 7: 8 LORD asked me, "What *do* you **s**, Amos?" H8011
Am 8: 2 "What *do* you **s**, Amos?" he asked. "A H8011
Ob 2 "**S**, I will make you small among the H2180
Jnh 4: 5 shade and waited *to* **s** what would H8011
Mic 7: 9 into the light; *I will* **s** his righteousness. H8011
Mic 7:10 Then my enemy *will* **s** it and will be H8011
Mic 7:10 My eyes *will* **s** her downfall; even now H8011
Mic 7:16 Nations *will* **s** and be ashamed, deprived H8011
Na 3: 7 All *who* **s** you will flee from you and say H8011
Hab 2: 1 I will look to **s** what he will say to me H8011
Hab 2: 4 "**S**, the enemy is puffed up; his desires H2180
Hag 1: 9 expected much, but **s**, it turned out to be H2180
Zec 3: 4 he said to Joshua, "**S**, I have taken away H8011
Zec 3: 9 **S**, the stone I have set in front of Joshua H2180
Zec 4: 2 asked me, "What *do* you **s**?" I answered, H8011
Zec 4: 2 "*I* **s** a solid gold lampstand with a bowl at H8011
Zec 4:10 will rejoice when *they* **s** the chosen H8011
Zec 5: 2 asked me, "What *do* you **s**?" I answered, H8011
Zec 5: 2 I answered, "I **s** a flying scroll, twenty H8011
Zec 5: 5 "Look up and **s** what is appearing. H8011
Zec 9: 5 Ashkelon *will* **s** it and fear; Gaza will H8011
Zec 9: 9 **S**, your king comes to you, righteous and H2180
Zec 10: 2 diviners **s visions** that lie; they tell H2600
Zec 10: 7 Their children *will* **s** it and be joyful; their H8011
Mal 1: 5 *You will* **s** it with your own eyes and say H8011
Mal 3:10 "and **s** if I will not throw open the NDT
Mal 3:18 And *you will* again **s** the distinction H8011
Mal 4: 5 "**S**, I will send the prophet Elijah to you H2180
Mt 5: 8 are the pure in heart, for they *will* **s** God. G3972
Mt 5:16 that *they may* **s** your good deeds and G3972
Mt 6:28 **S** how the flowers of the field grow G2908
Mt 7: 5 then *you will* **s clearly** to remove the G1332
Mt 8: 4 said to him, "**S** *that* you don't tell anyone. G3972
Mt 9:30 "**S that** no one knows about this. G3972
Mt 11: 4 report to John what you hear and **s**: G1063
Mt 11: 7 did you go out into the wilderness *to* **s**? G2517
Mt 11: 8 what did you go out *to* **s**? A man dressed G3972
Mt 11: 9 Then what did you go out *to* **s**? A prophet G3972
Mt 12:22 so that he could both talk and **s**. G1063
Mt 12:38 "Teacher, we want *to* **s** a sign from you." G3972
Mt 13:13 *they do* not **s**; though hearing G1063
Mt 13:15 Otherwise *they might* **s** with their eyes G3972
Mt 13:16 But blessed are your eyes because *they* **s** G1063
Mt 13:17 people longed *to* **s** what you see but did G3972
Mt 13:17 longed to see what *you* **s** but did not see G1063
Mt 13:17 to see what you see but *did* not **s** it, G3972
Mt 15:17 "Don't *you* **s** that whatever enters the G3783
Mt 16:28 taste death before *they* **s** the Son of Man G3972
Mt 18:10 "**S** *that* you do not despise one of these G3972
Mt 18:10 in heaven always **s** the face of my Father G1063
Mt 21: 5 to Daughter Zion, '**S**, your king comes to G2627
Mt 22:11 when the king came in *to* **s** the guests, G2517
Mt 23: 5 they do is done for people *to* **s**: G2517
Mt 23:39 *you will* not **s** me again until you say G3972
Mt 24: 2 "*Do you* **s** all these things?" he asked G1063
Mt 24: 6 but **s to it** that you are not alarmed. G3972
Mt 24:15 "So when *you* **s** standing in the holy place G3972
Mt 24:25 **S**, I have told you ahead of time. G2627
Mt 24:30 will mourn when *they* **s** the Son of Man G3972
Mt 24:33 Even so, when you **s** all these things, you G3972
Mt 25:20 five bags of gold. **S**, I have gained five G2623
Mt 25:22 two bags of gold; **s**, I have gained two G2623
Mt 25:25 gold in the ground. **S**, here is what G2623
Mt 25:37 when *did we* **s** you hungry and feed you G3972
Mt 25:38 When *did we* **s** you a stranger and invite G3972
Mt 25:39 When *did we* **s** you sick or in prison and G3972
Mt 25:44 when *did we* **s** you hungry or thirsty or a G3972
Mt 26:58 down with the guards *to* **s** the outcome. G3972
Mt 26:64 From now on *you will* **s** the Son of Man G3972
Mt 27:49 *Let's* **s** if Elijah comes to save him. G3972
Mt 28: 6 Come and **s** the place where he lay G3972
Mt 28: 7 There *you will* **s** him.' Now I have G3972
Mt 28:10 to go to Galilee; there *they will* **s** me." G3972
Mk 1:44 "**S that** you don't tell this to anyone. G3972
Mk 3: 2 *so they* **watched** him **closely** *to s* if he would AIT
Mk 5:14 people went out *to* **s** what had happened. G3972
Mk 5:31 "*You* **s** the people crowding against you," G1063
Mk 5:32 kept looking around *to* **s** who had done it. G3972
Mk 6:38 "Go and **s**." When they found G3972
Mk 7:18 "Don't *you* **s** that nothing that enters a G3783
Mk 8:17 *Do you* still not **s** or understand G3783
Mk 8:18 Do you have eyes but fail *to* **s**, and ears G1063
Mk 8:23 on him, Jesus asked, "*Do you* **s** anything?" G1063
Mk 8:24 looked up and said, "*I* **s** people; they look G1063
Mk 9: 1 death before *they* **s** that the kingdom G3972
Mk 10:51 The blind man said, "Rabbi, *I* want to **s**." G329
Mk 13: 2 "*Do you* **s** all these great buildings?" G1063
Mk 13:14 "When *you* **s** 'the abomination that G3972
Mk 13:26 "At that time *people will* **s** the Son of G3972
Mk 13:29 when you **s** these things happening G3972
Mk 14:62 "And *you will* **s** the Son of Man sitting at G3972
Mk 15: 4 **S** how many things they are accusing you G2623
Mk 15:24 they cast lots to **s** what each would get. NDT
Mk 15:32 from the cross, that *we may* **s** and believe." G3972
Mk 15:36 *Let's* **s** if Elijah comes to take him down," G3972
Mk 16: 6 **S** the place where they laid him G2623
Mk 16: 7 There *you will* **s** him, just as he G3972
Lk 2:15 go to Bethlehem and **s** this thing that has G3972
Lk 3: 6 And all people *will* **s** God's salvation.' " G3972
Lk 6: 7 so *they* **watched** him **closely** *to s* if he would AIT
Lk 6:42 *when you* yourself fail *to* **s** the plank in G1063
Lk 6:42 then *you will* **s clearly** to remove the G1332
Lk 7:24 did you go out into the wilderness *to* **s**? G2517
Lk 7:25 what did you go out *to* **s**? A man dressed G3972
Lk 7:26 But what did you go out *to* **s**? A prophet G3972
Lk 7:44 said to Simon, "*Do you* **s** this woman? G1063
Lk 8:10 *they may* not **s**; though hearing G1063
Lk 8:16 so that those who come in *can* **s** the light. G1063
Lk 8:19 mother and brothers came **to s** him, G4639
Lk 8:20 are standing outside, wanting *to* **s** you." G3972
Lk 8:35 people went out *to* **s** what had happened. G3972
Lk 9: 9 such things about?" And he tried *to* **s** him. G3972
Lk 9:27 taste death before *they* **s** the kingdom of G3972
Lk 10:23 "Blessed are the eyes that **s** what you see. G1063
Lk 10:23 "Blessed are the eyes that see what *you* **s**. G1063
Lk 10:24 kings wanted *to* **s** what you see but G3972
Lk 10:24 to see what you **s** but did not see it, G1063
Lk 10:24 to see what you see but *did* not **s** it, G3972
Lk 11:33 so that those who come in *may* **s** the light. G1063
Lk 11:35 **S to it**, then, that the light within you is not G5023
Lk 12:54 "When *you* **s** a cloud rising in the west G3972
Lk 13:28 of teeth, when *you* **s** Abraham, Isaac and G3972
Lk 13:35 *you will* not **s** me again until you say G3972
Lk 14:18 just bought a field, and I must go and **s** it. G3972
Lk 14:28 estimate the cost *to s* **if** you have enough AIT
Lk 17:22 when you will long *to* **s** one of the days of G3972
Lk 17:22 of the Son of Man, but *you will* not **s** it. G3972
Lk 18: 5 *I will s that* she **gets justice**, so that she AIT
Lk 18: 8 I tell you, *he will s that* they **get** justice, and AIT
Lk 18:41 do for you?" "Lord, *I* want to **s**," he replied. G329
Lk 19: 3 He wanted *to* **s** who Jesus was, but G3972
Lk 19: 3 he was short he could not **s** over the crowd. NDT
Lk 19: 4 climbed a sycamore-fig tree to **s** him, G3972
Lk 21: 6 "As for what *you* **s** here, the time will G2555
Lk 21:20 "When *you* **s** Jerusalem being surrounded G3972
Lk 21:27 At that time *they will* **s** the Son of Man G3972
Lk 21:30 *you can* **s** for yourselves and know that G1063
Lk 21:31 when you **s** these things happening G3972
Lk 22:38 The disciples said, "**S**, Lord, here are two G2627
Lk 23: 8 long time he had been wanting *to* **s** him. G3972
Lk 23: 8 he hoped *to* **s** him perform a sign of some G3972
Lk 23:15 back to us; **as you can s**, he has G2779+2627
Lk 24:24 women had said, but *they did* not **s** Jesus." G3972
Lk 24:39 Touch me and **s**; a ghost does not have G3972
Lk 24:39 not have flesh and bones, as *you* **s** I have." G2555
Jn 1:33 'The man on whom *you* **s** the Spirit come G3972
Jn 1:39 he replied, "and *you will* **s**." So they went G3972
Jn 1:46 "Come and **s**," said Philip. G2623
Jn 1:50 *You will* **s** greater things than that. G3972
Jn 1:51 truly I tell you, *you will* **s** 'heaven open G3972
Jn 3: 3 no one can **s** the kingdom of God unless G3972
Jn 3:36 whoever rejects the Son *will* not **s** life G3972
Jn 4:19 "*I can* **s** that you are a prophet. G2555
Jn 4:29 **s** a man who told me everything I ever did G3972
Jn 4:48 "Unless *you people* **s** signs and wonders," G3972
Jn 5:14 said to him, "**S**, you are well again. G2623
Jn 6:30 will you give that *we may* **s** it and believe G3972
Jn 6:62 Then what if *you* **s** the Son of Man ascend G2555
Jn 7: 3 disciples there *may* **s** the works you do. G2555
Jn 8:51 obeys my word *will* never **s** death. G2555
Jn 9:11 I went and washed, and then *I could* **s**." G329
Jn 9:15 man replied, "and I washed, and *now I* **s**." G1063
Jn 9:19 How is it that now *he can* **s**?" G1063
Jn 9:21 But how *he can* **s** now, or who opened his G1063
Jn 9:25 thing I do know. I was blind but now *I* **s**!" G1063
Jn 9:39 so that the blind *will* **s** and those who see G1063
Jn 9:39 see and those *who* **s** will become blind G1063
Jn 9:41 now that you claim *you can* **s**, your G1063
Jn 11: 9 stumble, for *they* **s** by this world's light. G1063
Jn 11:34 "Come and **s**, Lord," they G2623
Jn 11:36 Then the Jews said, "**S** how he loved him!" G2623
Jn 11:40 if you believe, *you will* **s** the glory of God?" G3972
Jn 12: 9 only because of him but also *to* **s** Lazarus, G3972
Jn 12:15 Daughter Zion; **s**, your king is coming G2627
Jn 12:19 said to one another, "**S**, this is getting us G2555
Jn 12:21 they said, "we would like *to* **s** Jesus." G3972
Jn 12:40 so *they can* neither **s** with their eyes G3972
Jn 14:19 the world *will* not **s** me anymore G2555
Jn 14:19 not see me anymore, but you *will* **s** me. G2555
Jn 16:10 the Father, where *you can* **s** me no longer; G2555
Jn 16:16 "In a little while *you will* **s** me no more G2555
Jn 16:16 then after a little while *you will* **s** me." G3972
Jn 16:17 'In a little while *you will* **s** me no more G2555
Jn 16:17 then after a little while *you will* **s** me G3972
Jn 16:19 'In a little while *you will* **s** me no more G2555
Jn 16:19 then after a little while *you will* **s** me'? G3972
Jn 16:22 but *I will* **s** you again and you will rejoice G3972
Jn 16:30 Now *we can* **s** that you know all things G3857
Jn 17:24 where I am, and to **s** my glory, the glory G2555
Jn 18:26 "Didn't I **s** you with him in the garden?" G3972
Jn 20:25 "Unless *I* **s** the nail marks in his hands G3972
Jn 20:27 "Put your finger here; **s** my hands. G2623
Ac 2:17 your young men *will* **s** visions, your old G3972
Ac 2:27 you will not let your holy one **s** decay. G3972
Ac 2:31 of the dead, nor *did* his body **s** decay. G3972
Ac 2:33 has poured out what you now **s** and hear. G1063
Ac 3:16 this man whom *you* **s** and know was G2555
Ac 3:16 completely healed him, *as you can* all **s**. G595
Ac 4:14 But *since they could* **s** the man who had G1063
Ac 7:56 "*I* **s** heaven open and the Son of Man G2555
Ac 8:23 For *I* **s** *that* you are full of bitterness and G3972
Ac 8:39 the eunuch *did* not **s** him again, but G3972
Ac 9: 7 heard the sound but *did* not **s** anyone. G2555
Ac 9: 8 he opened his eyes *he could* **s** nothing. G1063
Ac 9:17 me so that *you may* **s again** and be filled G329
Ac 9:18 fell from Saul's eyes, and *he could* **s again**. G329
Ac 13:11 not *even able to* **s** the light of the sun." G1063
Ac 13:35 " 'You will not let your holy one **s** decay.' G3972
Ac 13:37 God raised from the dead *did* not **s** decay. G3972
Ac 15: 2 to go up to Jerusalem *to s* the apostles and AIT
Ac 15:36 word of the Lord and **s** how they are doing." NDT
Ac 17:11 every day *to s* **if** what Paul said was AIT
Ac 17:16 greatly distressed *to* **s** *that* the city was full G2555
Ac 17:22 *I* **s** *that* in every way you are very religious. G2555
Ac 18: 2 to leave Rome. Paul **went to s** them, G4665
Ac 19:26 And *you* **s** and hear how this fellow Paul G2555
Ac 20:25 the kingdom *will* ever **s** me again. G3972
Ac 20:38 that they would never **s** his face again. G2555
Ac 21:18 day Paul and the rest of us went **to** *s* James, AIT
Ac 21:20 "*You* **s**, brother, how many thousands of G2555
Ac 22:12 "A man named Ananias came **to** *s* me. AIT
Ac 22:13 at that very moment I *was* **able to s** him. G329
Ac 22:14 know his will and *to* **s** the Righteous One G3972
Ac 25:24 who are present with us, *you* **s** this man! G2555
Ac 26: 7 tribes are hoping *to* **s fulfilled** as they G2918
Ac 26:16 of what you have seen and *will* **s** of me. G3972
Ac 27:10 *I can* **s** that our voyage is going to be G2555
Ac 28: 8 Paul went in **to** *s* him and, after prayer AIT
Ac 28:20 reason I have asked *to* **s** you and talk with G3972
Ac 28:27 Otherwise *they might* **s** with their eyes G3972
Ac 28:30 house and welcomed all who came **to** *s* him. AIT
Ro 1:11 I long *to* **s** you so that I may impart to you G3972
Ro 5: 6 **You s**, at just the right time, when we G1142
Ro 7:23 but *I* **s** another law at work in me, waging G1063
Ro 9:33 "**S**, I lay in Zion a stone that causes G2627
Ro 11: 8 eyes that *could* not **s** and ears that could G1063
Ro 11:10 their eyes be darkened so *they* cannot **s**, G1063
Ro 15:21 who were not told about him *will* **s**, G3972
Ro 15:24 I hope *to* **s** you while passing through G2517
1Co 13:12 For now *we* **s** only a reflection as in a G1063
1Co 13:12 as in a mirror; then we shall **s** face to face. NDT
1Co 16: 7 For I do not want *to* **s** you now and make G3972
1Co 16:10 **s to it** that he has nothing to fear while he G1063
2Co 2: 9 I wrote you was to **s** if you would stand G1182
2Co 4: 4 so that *they* cannot **s** the light of the gospel G878
2Co 7: 8 I did regret it—*I* **s** that my letter hurt you G1063
2Co 7:11 **S** what this godly sorrow has produced in G2627
2Co 7:11 concern, what **readiness to s justice done**. G1689
2Co 7:12 that before God *you could* **s** for yourselves G5746
2Co 7:13 delighted **to s** how happy Titus was G2093
2Co 8: 7 **s that** you also excel in this grace of giving. G2671
2Co 8:24 pride in you, so that the churches can **s** it. G4725
2Co 13: 5 **Examine** yourselves *to s* whether you are in AIT
2Co 13: 7 not so that *people will* **s** *that* we have G5743
Gal 1:17 not go up to Jerusalem **to s** those who were AIT
Gal 6:11 **S** what large letters I use as I write to you G3972
Php 1:27 whether I come and **s** you or only hear G3972
Php 2:23 send him as soon as *I* **s** how things go with G927
Php 2:28 so that *when you* **s** him again you may be G3972
Col 2: 5 spirit and delight *to* **s** how disciplined you G1063
Col 2: 8 **S to it** that no one takes you captive G1063
Col 4:16 **s** that it is also read in the church of the G4472
Col 4:17 "**S to it** that you complete the ministry you G1063
1Th 2:17 longing we made every effort *to* **s** you. G3972
1Th 3: 6 memories of us and that you long *to* **s** us, G3972
1Th 3: 6 long to see us, just as we also long to **s** you. NDT
1Th 3:10 that *we may* **s** you *again* and supply G3972
1Ti 3: 4 family well and **s that** his children obey G2400
1Ti 4:15 that everyone *may* **s** your progress. G5745+1639
1Ti 6:16 whom no one has seen or can **s**. G3972
2Ti 1: 4 your tears, I long *to* **s** you, so that I may G3972
Titus 3:13 on their way and **s that** they have G2671
Heb 2: 8 Yet at present *we do* not **s** everything G3972
Heb 2: 9 But *we do* **s** Jesus, who was made lower G1063
Heb 3:12 **S to it**, brothers and sisters, that none of G1063
Heb 3:19 So *we* **s** that they were not able to enter G1063
Heb 8: 5 "**S to it** that you make everything G3972
Heb 10:25 all the more as *you* **s** the Day G1063

Heb 11: 1 assurance about what *we do* not **s**. *G1063*
Heb 12:14 without holiness no one *will* **s** the Lord. *G3972*
Heb 12:15 **S to it** that no one falls short of the grace *G2174*
Heb 12:16 **S** that no one is sexually immoral, or is NDT
Heb 12:25 **S to it** that you do not refuse him who *G1063*
Heb 13:23 *I will come* with him *to* **s** you. *G3972*
Jas 2:22 *You* **s** that his faith and his actions were *G1063*
Jas 2:24 *You* **s** that a person is considered *G3972*
Jas 5: 7 **S** how the farmer waits for the land to *G2627*
1Pe 1: 8 and *even though you do* not **s** him now *G3972*
1Pe 2: 6 "**S**, I lay a stone in Zion, a chosen and *G2627*
1Pe 2:12 *they may* **s** your good deeds and glorify *G2227*
1Pe 3: 2 *when they* **s** the purity and reverence of *G2227*
1Pe 3:10 love life and **s** good days must keep *G3972*
2Pe 1:15 And *I will* **make every effort** *to* **s** *that* after AIT
1Jn 2:24 *s that* what you have heard from the beginning **remains** AIT
1Jn 3: 1 **S** what great love the Father has lavished *G3972*
1Jn 3: 2 be like him, for *we shall* **s** him as he is. *G3972*
1Jn 4: 1 test the spirits to **s** whether they are from NDT
1Jn 5:16 If you **s** any brother or sister commit a sin *G3972*
3Jn 14 I hope *to* **s** you soon, and we will talk face *G3972*
Jude 14 "**S**, the Lord is coming with thousands *G2627*
Rev 1: 7 and "every eye *will* **s** him, even those *G3972*
Rev 1:11 on a scroll what *you* **s** and send it to the *G1063*
Rev 1:12 I turned around *to* **s** the voice that was *G1063*
Rev 3: 8 **S**, I have placed before you an open door *G2627*
Rev 3:18 salve to put on your eyes, so *you can* **s**. *G1063*
Rev 5: 5 **S**, the Lion of the tribe of Judah, the Root *G2627*
Rev 9:20 wood—idols *that* cannot **s** or hear or walk. *G1063*
Rev 17: 8 will be astonished *when they* **s** the beast, *G1063*
Rev 18: 9 shared her luxury **s** the smoke of her *G1063*
Rev 18:18 *When they* **s** the smoke of her burning *G1063*
Rev 21:22 *I did* not **s** a temple in the city, because *G3972*
Rev 22: 4 *They will* **s** his face, and his name will be *G3972*

SEED (79) [SEED-BEARING, SEEDLINGS, SEEDS, SEEDTIME]

Ge 1:11 on the land that bear fruit with **s** in it, H2446
Ge 1:12 plants bearing **s** according to their kinds H2446
Ge 1:12 bearing fruit with **s** in it according to their H2446
Ge 1:29 every tree that has fruit with **s** in it. H2445+2446
Ge 47:19 Give us **s** so that we may live and not die H2446
Ge 47:23 here is **s** for you so you can plant the H2446
Ge 47:24 you may keep as **s** *for* the fields and as H2446
Ex 16:31 white like coriander **s** and tasted like H2446
Lev 11:38 has been put on the **s** and a carcass falls H2446
Lev 19:19 *Do* not **plant** your field **with** two kinds of **s**. H2445
Lev 26:16 You will plant **s** in vain, because your H2446
Lev 27:16 to the amount of **s** *required for* it— H2446
Lev 27:16 fifty shekels of silver to a homer of barley **s**. H2446
Nu 11: 7 was like coriander **s** and looked like resin. H2446
Nu 24: 7 buckets; their **s** will have abundant water. H2446
Dt 11:10 you planted your **s** and irrigated it by H2446
Dt 22: 9 *Do* not **plant** two kinds of **s** in your H2445
Dt 28:38 You will sow much **s** in the field but you H2446
1Ki 18:32 it large enough to hold two seahs of **s**. H2446
2Ki 6:25 quarter of a cab of **s pods** for five shekels. H1807
Ps 126: 6 carrying **s to sow**, will return H5433+2446
Ecc 11: 6 Sow your **s** in the morning, and at H2446
Isa 5:10 a homer of **s** will yield only an ephah of H2446
Isa 6:13 so the holy **s** will be the stump in the land H2446
Isa 30:23 you rain for the **s** you sow in the ground H2446
Isa 32:20 you will be, **sowing** *your* **s** by every stream H2445
Isa 55:10 so that it yields **s** for the sower and bread H2446
Jer 35: 7 build houses, sow **s** or plant vineyards H2446
Hag 2:19 Is there yet any **s** left in the barn? Until H2446
Zec 8:12 "The **s** will grow well, the vine will yield H2446
Mt 13: 3 "A farmer went out *to* **sow** *his* **s**. *G5062*
Mt 13: 4 As he *was* **scattering** *the* **s**, some fell *G5062*
Mt 13: 7 Other **s** fell among thorns, which grew up NDT
Mt 13: 8 Still other **s** fell on good soil, where it NDT
Mt 13:19 This is the **s sown** along the path. *G5062*
Mt 13:20 The **s falling** on rocky ground refers to *G5062*
Mt 13:22 The **s falling** among the thorns refers to *G5062*
Mt 13:23 But the **s falling** on good soil refers to *G5062*
Mt 13:24 like a man who sowed good **s** in his field. *G5065*
Mt 13:27 didn't you sow good **s** in your field? *G5065*
Mt 13:31 kingdom of heaven is like a mustard **s**, *G3133*
Mt 13:37 who sowed the good **s** is the Son of Man. *G5065*
Mt 13:38 the good **s** stands for the people of *G5065*
Mt 17:20 if you have faith as small as a mustard **s** *G3133*
Mt 25:24 gathering where *you have* not **scattered s**. *G1399*
Mt 25:26 gather where *I have* not **scattered s**? *G1399*
Mk 4: 3 A farmer went out *to* **sow** *his* **s**. *G5062*
Mk 4: 4 As *he was* **scattering** *the* **s**, some fell *G5062*
Mk 4: 7 Other **s** fell among thorns, which grew up NDT
Mk 4: 8 Still other **s** fell on good soil. It came up NDT
Mk 4:15 Some people are like **s** along the path *G3836S*
Mk 4:16 like **s sown** on rocky places, hear *G5062*
Mk 4:18 Still others, like **s sown** among thorns *G5062*
Mk 4:20 like **s sown** on good soil, hear the *G5062*
Mk 4:26 A man scatters **s** on the ground. *G5078*
Mk 4:27 sleeps or gets up, the **s** sprouts and grows *G5078*
Mk 4:31 It is like a mustard **s**, which is the smallest *G3133*
Lk 8: 5 "A farmer went out to sow his **s**. As he was *G5078*
Lk 8: 5 As he *was* **scattering** *the* **s**, some fell *G5062*
Lk 8: 7 **Other** *s* fell among thorns, which grew up AIT
Lk 8: 8 Still **other** *s* fell on good soil. It came up and AIT
Lk 8:11 of the parable: The **s** is the word of God. *G5078*
Lk 8:14 **The s** that fell among thorns stands for *G3836S*
Lk 8:15 But **the s** on good soil stands for those *G3836S*
Lk 13:19 It is like a mustard **s**, which a man took *G3133*
Lk 17: 6 "If you have faith as small as a mustard **s** *G3133*
Jn 12:24 ground and dies, it remains only a single **s**. NDT
1Co 3: 6 I **planted** *the* **s**, Apollos watered it, but *G5885*
1Co 9:11 If we *have* **sown** spiritual **s** among you, is *G5062*
1Co 15:37 but just a **s**, perhaps of wheat or *G3133*
1Co 15:38 to each kind *of* **s** he gives its own *G5065*
2Co 9:10 Now he who supplies **s** to the sower and *G5078*
2Co 9:10 increase your **store of s** and will enlarge *G5078*
Gal 3:16 were spoken to Abraham and *to* his **s**. *G5065*
Gal 3:16 people, but "and *to* your **s**," meaning one *G5065*
Gal 3:19 until the **S** to whom the promise *G5065*
Gal 3:29 then you are Abraham's **s**, and heirs *G5065*
1Pe 1:23 not of perishable **s**, but of imperishable, *G5076*
1Jn 3: 9 because God's **s** remains in them *G5065*

SEED-BEARING (2) [SEED]

Ge 1:11 **s** plants and trees on the land that H2445+2446
Ge 1:29 give you every **s** plant on the face H2445+2446

SEEDLINGS (1) [SEED]

Eze 17: 5 'He took one of the **s** *of* the land and put H2446

SEEDS (8) [SEED]

Lev 11:37 carcass falls on any **s** that are to be H2446+2433
Nu 6: 4 the grapevine, not even the **s** or skins. H3079
Isa 61:11 come up and a garden causes **s** to grow, H2433
Joel 1:17 The **s** are shriveled beneath the clods H7237
Mt 13:32 Though it is the smallest of all **s**, yet when *G5065*
Mk 4:31 which is the smallest of all **s** on earth. *G5065*
Jn 12:24 But if it dies, it produces many **s**. *G2843*
Gal 3:16 Scripture does not say "and *to* **s**, *G5065*

SEEDTIME (1) [SEED]

Ge 8:22 the earth endures, **s** and harvest, cold H2446

SEEING (29) [SEE]

Ge 33:10 to see your face is like **s** the face of God, H8011
Ex 2:12 Looking this way and that and **s** no one H8011
Nu 35:23 without **s** them, drops on them a stone H8011
Jdg 13:20 **S** this, Manoah and his wife fell with their H8011
Jdg 18:26 **s** that they were too strong for him H8011
2Sa 14:28 in Jerusalem without **s** the king's face. H8011
Ps 17:15 I will be satisfied with **s** your likeness. NDT
Ecc 1: 8 The eye never has enough of **s**, nor the H8011
Isa 6: 9 understanding; *be* **ever s**, but never H8011+8011
Isa 28: 7 they stagger when **s visions**, they stumble H8015
Hos 9:10 it was like **s** the early fruit on the fig tree. NDT
Mt 13:13 "*Though* **s**, they do not see; though *G1063*
Mt 13:14 *you will be* **ever s** but never *G1063+1063*
Mt 15:31 the lame walking and the blind **s**. *G1063*
Mt 21:19 **S** a fig tree by the road, he went up to it *G3972*
Mk 4:12 " '*they may be* **ever s** but never *G1063+1063*
Mk 11:13 **S** in the distance a fig tree in leaf, he went *G3972*
Lk 8:10 " '*though* **s**, they may not see *G1063*
Lk 8:47 woman, **s** that she could not go unnoticed *G3972*
Lk 23:47 The centurion, **s** what had happened *G3972*
Jn 8:56 rejoiced at the thought of **s** my day; *G3972*
Jn 9: 7 went and washed, and came home **s**. *G1063*
Jn 12:45 who looks at me *is* **s** the one who sent *G2555*
Ac 2:31 **S what was to come**, he spoke of the *G4632*
Ac 9:40 opened her eyes, and **s** Peter she sat up. *G3972*
Ac 12: 9 happening; he thought *he was* **s** a vision. *G1063*
Ac 28: 6 a long time and **s** nothing unusual *G2555*
Ac 28:26 *you will be* **ever s** but never *G1063+1063*
2Co 3:13 the Israelites from **s** the end of what was *G867*

SEEK (122) [SEEKING, SEEKS, SELF-SEEKING, SOUGHT]

Ex 18:15 the people come to me to **s** God's **will**. H2011
Lev 19:18 " '*Do* not **s revenge** or bear a grudge H5933
Lev 19:26 " 'Do not practice divination or **s omens**. H6726
Lev 19:31 'Do not turn to mediums or **s out** spiritists, H1335
Dt 4:29 But if from there *you* **s** the LORD your God H1335
Dt 4:29 you will find him if *you* **s** him with all your H2011
Dt 12: 5 But *you are to* **s** the place the LORD your H2011
Dt 23: 6 *Do* not **s** a treaty of friendship with them H2011
2Sa 17: 3 of the man you **s** will mean the return H1335
1Ki 22: 5 of Israel, "First **s** the counsel of the LORD." H2011
1Ch 16:10 the hearts of *those who* **s** the LORD rejoice H1335
1Ch 16:11 LORD and his strength; **s** his face always. H1335
1Ch 28: 9 If *you* **s** him, he will be found by you; but H2011
2Ch 7:14 pray and **s** my face and turn from H1335
2Ch 14: 4 He commanded Judah to **s** the LORD, the H2011
2Ch 15: 2 If *you* **s** him, he will be found by you, but H2011
2Ch 15:12 They entered into a covenant to **s** the LORD H2011
2Ch 15:13 All who *would* not **s** the LORD, the God of H2011
2Ch 16:12 his illness *he did* not **s help** *from* the LORD, H2011
2Ch 18: 4 of Israel, "First **s** the counsel of the LORD." H2011
2Ch 20: 4 came together to **s help** from the LORD; H1335
2Ch 20: 4 came from every town in Judah to **s** him. H1335
2Ch 34: 3 he began to **s** the God of his father David. H2011
Ezr 4: 2 *we* **s** your God and have been sacrificing H2011
Ezr 6:21 Gentile neighbors in order to **s** the LORD, H2011
Ezr 9:12 *Do* not **s** a treaty of friendship with them H2011
Job 8: 5 But if you *will* **s** God **earnestly** and plead H8838
Ps 4: 2 will you love delusions and **s** false gods? H1335
Ps 9:10 have never forsaken *those who* **s** you. H2011
Ps 10: 4 his pride the wicked man *does* not **s** him; H2011
Ps 14: 2 are any who understand, *any who* **s** God. H2011
Ps 22:26 *those who* **s** the LORD will praise him H2011
Ps 24: 6 is the generation of *those who* **s** him, H2011
Ps 24: 6 who seek him, *who* **s** your face, God of H1335
Ps 27: 4 thing I ask from the LORD, this only *do I* **s**: H1335
Ps 27: 4 of the LORD and to **s** him in his temple. H1329
Ps 27: 8 heart says of you, "**S** his face!" Your face, H1335
Ps 27: 8 "Seek his face!" Your face, LORD, *I will* **s**. H1335
Ps 34:10 but *those who* **s** the LORD lack no good H2011
Ps 34:14 evil and do good; **s** peace and pursue it. H1335
Ps 35: 4 May *those who* **s** my life be disgraced H1335
Ps 37:37 a future awaits **those** *who s* peace. AIT
Ps 38:20 though I **s** *only* **to do** what is good. H8103
Ps 40:16 But may all *who* **s** you rejoice and be glad H1335
Ps 45:12 people of wealth *will* **s** your **favor**. H2704+7156
Ps 53: 2 are any who understand, *any who* **s** God. H2011
Ps 63: 1 are my God, **earnestly** *I* **s** you; I thirst for H8838
Ps 69: 4 without cause, *those who* **s to destroy** me. H7551
Ps 69: 6 may *those who* **s** you not be put to shame H1335
Ps 69:32 be glad—you *who* **s** God, may your H2011
Ps 70: 4 But may all *who* **s** you rejoice and be glad H1335
Ps 78:34 God slew them, *they would* **s** him; they H2011
Ps 83:16 so that *they will* **s** your name. H1335
Ps 104:21 their prey and **s** their food from God. H1335
Ps 105: 3 the hearts of *those who* **s** the LORD rejoice H1335
Ps 105: 4 LORD and his strength; **s** his face always. H1335
Ps 119: 2 keep his statutes and **s** him with all their H2011
Ps 119:10 *I* **s** you with all my heart; do not let me H2011
Ps 119:155 for *they do* not **s out** your decrees. H2011
Ps 119:176 **S** your servant, for I have not forgotten H1335
Ps 122: 9 the LORD our God, *I will* **s** your prosperity. H1335
Pr 8:17 love me, and *those who* **s** me find me. H8838
Pr 14:32 in death the righteous **s refuge** in God. H2879
Pr 18:15 the ears of the wise **s** it **out**. H1335
Pr 28: 5 but *those who* **s** the LORD understand it H1335
Pr 28:17 guilt of murder *will* **s refuge** in the grave; H5674
Pr 29:10 of integrity and **s to** kill the upright. H1335
Pr 29:26 Many **s an audience with** a ruler H1335+7156
Isa 1:17 Learn to do right; **s** justice. Defend the H2011
Isa 31: 1 One of Israel, or **s help** *from* the LORD. H2011
Isa 45:19 to Jacob's descendants, '**S** me in vain. H1335
Isa 51: 1 pursue righteousness and *who* **s** the LORD: H1335
Isa 55: 6 **S** the LORD while he may be found; call on H2011
Isa 56:11 to their own way, they **s** their own gain. H4200
Isa 58: 2 For day after day *they* **s** me **out**; they seem H2011
Isa 65: 1 I was found by *those who did* not **s** me. H1335
Isa 65:10 place for herds, for my people who **s** me. H2011
Jer 5:28 have no limit; *they do* not **s justice**. H1906+1907
Jer 26:19 fear the LORD and **s** his **favor**? H2704+906+7156
Jer 29: 7 **s** the peace and prosperity of the city to H2011
Jer 29:13 *You will* **s** me and find me when you seek H1335
Jer 29:13 find me when *you* **s** me with all your H2011
Jer 45: 5 *Should* you then **s** great things for yourself? H1335
Jer 45: 5 *Do* not **s** them. For I will H1335
Jer 50: 4 will go in tears *to* **s** the LORD their God. H1335
Eze 7:25 terror comes, *they will* **s** peace in vain. H1335
Eze 21:21 of the two roads, to **s an omen**: H7876+7877
Hos 3: 5 will return and **s** the LORD their God and H1335
Hos 5: 6 with their flocks and herds to **s** the LORD, H1335
Hos 5:15 have borne their guilt and **s** my face— H1335
Hos 5:15 in their misery *they will* **earnestly s** me." H8838
Hos 10:12 it is time to **s** the LORD, until he comes H2011
Am 5: 4 the LORD says to Israel: "**S** me and live; H2011
Am 5: 5 *do* not **s** Bethel, do not go to Gilgal, do H2011
Am 5: 6 **S** the LORD and live, or he will sweep H2011
Am 5:14 **S** good, not evil, that you may live. H2011
Na 3:11 go into hiding and **s** refuge from the H1335
Zep 1: 6 LORD and neither **s** the LORD nor inquire H1335
Zep 2: 3 **S** the LORD, all you humble of the land H1335
Zep 2: 3 **S** righteousness, seek humility; perhaps H1335
Zep 2: 3 Seek righteousness, **s** humility; perhaps H1335
Zec 8:21 entreat the LORD and **s** the LORD Almighty. H1335
Zec 8:22 come to Jerusalem to **s** the LORD Almighty H1335
Zec 11:16 care for the lost, or **s** the young, or heal H1335
Mal 2: 7 Almighty and *people* **s** instruction from H1335
Mal 2:15 And what *does* the one God **s**? Godly H1335
Mt 6:33 But **s** first his kingdom and his *G2426*
Mt 7: 7 will be given to you; **s** and you will find *G2426*
Lk 11: 9 will be given to you; **s** and you will find *G2426*
Lk 12:31 But **s** his kingdom, and these things will *G2426*
Lk 19:10 the Son of Man came *to* **s** and to save the *G2426*
Jn 5:30 for *I* **s** not to please myself but him who *G2426*
Jn 5:44 one another but *do* not **s** the glory that *G2426*
Ac 15:17 that the rest of mankind may **s** the Lord *G1699*
Ac 17:27 God did this *so that they would* **s** him and *G2426*
Ro 2: 7 *who* by persistence in doing good **s** glory *G2426*
Ro 10:20 "I was found by those *who did* not **s** me; *G2426*
1Co 7:27 *Do* not **s** to be released. *G2426*
1Co 10:24 No one *should* **s** their own good, but the *G2426*
Heb 11: 6 he rewards those *who* **earnestly s** him. *G1699*
1Pe 3:11 do good; *they must* **s** peace and pursue it. *G2426*
Rev 9: 6 those days people *will* **s** death but will *G2426*

SEEKING (18) [SEEK]

Jdg 14: 4 who *was* **s** an occasion to confront the H1335
Jdg 18: 1 tribe of the Danites *was* **s** a place of their H1335
1Ki 12:28 After **s advice**, the king made two golden H3619
2Ki 16:15 I will use the bronze altar for **s guidance**." H1329
1Ch 22:19 heart and soul to **s** the LORD your God. H2011
2Ch 11:16 Israel who set their hearts on **s** the LORD, H1335
2Ch 12:14 he had not set his heart on **s** the LORD. H2011
2Ch 19: 3 poles and have set your heart on **s** God." H2011
2Ch 30:19 who sets their heart *on* **s** God—the LORD H2011
Pr 20:18 Plans are established by **s** advice; so if you NDT
Jer 38: 4 This man *is* not **s** the good of these H2011
Mal 3: 1 the Lord you *are* **s** will come to his H1335

S

Mt 12:43 through arid places s rest and does not G2426
Lk 11:24 through arid places s rest and does not G2426
Jn 8:50 I *am* not s glory for myself; but there is one G2426
Ac 13:11 s someone to lead him by the hand. G2426
1Co 10:33 *For I am* not s my own good but the good G2426
Gal 2:17 *in* s to be justified in Christ, we G2426

SEEKS (12) [SEEK]

Pr 11:27 *Whoever* s good finds favor, but evil H8838
Pr 14: 6 The mocker s wisdom and finds none, but H1335
Pr 15:14 The discerning heart s knowledge, but the H1335
Isa 16: 5 one who in judging s justice and speeds H2011
Jer 5: 1 who deals honestly and s the truth, H1335
La 3:25 hope is in him, to the one *who* s him; H2011
Mt 7: 8 receives; the *one who* s finds; and to the G2426
Lk 11:10 receives; the *one who* s finds; and to the G2426
Jn 4:23 are the kind of worshipers the Father s. G2426
Jn 7:18 he *who* s the glory of the one who G2426
Jn 8:50 there is one *who* s it, and he is the G2426
Ro 3:11 understands; there is no one *who* s God. G1699

SEEM (19) [SEEMED, SEEMS]

Lev 13:31 it does not s to be more than skin deep H5260
Ne 9:32 *do* not *let* all this hardship *s* **trifling** in your AIT
Job 8: 7 Your beginnings *will* s humble, so H2118
Job 36:21 which *you s to* **prefer** to affliction. AIT
Ps 39: 5 is but a breath, even those *who s* **secure**. AIT
Pr 16: 2 All a person's ways s pure *to* them H928+6524
Isa 5:28 their horses' hooves s like flint, their H3108
Isa 29:17 field and the fertile field s like a forest? H3108
Isa 58: 2 seek me out; *they s* **eager** to know my ways AIT
Isa 58: 2 decisions and *s* **eager** *for* God to come near AIT
Eze 16:51 and *have* **made** your sisters s **righteous** by H7405
Eze 21:23 *It will* s like a false omen *to* H2118+928+6524
Hag 2: 3 Does it not s *to* you like H4017+928+6524
Zec 8: 6 "It may s marvelous *to* the remnant H6524+928
Zec 8: 6 but will it s marvelous *to* me? H6524+928
1Co 12:22 parts of the body that s to be weaker are G1506
2Co 10: 9 *I do* not want to s to be trying to frighten G1506
2Co 13: 7 even though we *may* s to *have* failed. G1639
Phm 14 favor you do *would* not s forced G6055+1639

SEEMED (15) [SEEM]

Ge 29:20 *they* s like only a few days *to* H2118+928+6524
Ge 34:18 Their proposal s good to Hamor and H928+6524
Ge 41:37 The plan s good *to* Pharaoh and to H928+6524
Nu 13:33 *We* s like grasshoppers in our own eyes H2118
Dt 1:23 The idea s good *to* me; so I selected H928+6524
2Sa 13: 2 and it s impossible for him to do H928+6524
2Sa 17: 4 This plan s good *to* Absalom and to H928+6524
1Ch 13: 4 because it s right *to* all the people. H928+6524
2Ch 30: 4 The plan s right both *to* the king and H928+6524
Jer 18: 4 shaping it as s best *to* him. H928+6524
Jnh 4: 1 But to Jonah *this* s very **wrong**, and H8317+8288
Lk 24:11 because their words s to them like G5743
Ac 2: 3 They saw **what s to be** tongues of fire that G6059
Ac 15:28 *It* s **good** to the Holy Spirit and to us not G1506
Rev 13: 3 heads of the beast s to have had a fatal G6055

SEEMLY (KJV) FITTING

SEEMS (20) [SEEM]

Jos 9:25 us whatever s good and right *to* you." H928+6524
Jos 24:15 the LORD s undesirable *to* you, H928+6524
1Sa 1:23 "Do what s best *to* you," her H928+6524
1Sa 14:36 "Do whatever s best *to* you," they H928+6524
1Sa 14:40 "Do what s best *to* you," they H928+6524
2Sa 15:26 do to me whatever s good *to* him." H928+6524
2Sa 18: 4 "I will do whatever s best *to* you." H928+6524
2Sa 18:27 "*It* s *to* me that the first one runs like H8011
1Ch 13: 2 "If it s good to you and if it is the will of the NDT
Ezr 7:18 then do whatever s **best** with the rest of A10320
Est 8: 8 behalf of the Jews as s best *to* you, H928+6524
Job 15:21 his ears; when all s well, marauders attack NDT
Job 41:29 A club s to it but a piece of straw; it H3108
Pr 12:15 The way of fools s right *to* them, but H928+6524
Pr 18:17 In a lawsuit the first to speak s right, until NDT
Isa 32:15 and the fertile field s like a forest. H3108
Ac 17:18 "*He* s to be advocating foreign gods." G1506
1Co 4: 9 For *it* s *to me* that God has put us apostles G1506
1Co 16: 4 If *it* s advisable for me to go also, they will G1639
Heb 12:11 No discipline s pleasant at the time, but G1506

SEEN (219) [SEE]

Ge 16:13 "*I have* now s the One who sees me." H8011
Ge 24:30 As soon as *he had* s the nose ring, and H8011
Ge 29:32 "It is because the LORD *has* s my misery. H8011
Ge 31:12 for *I have* s all that Laban has been doing H8011
Ge 31:42 But God *has* s my hardship and the toil of H8011
Ge 41:19 *I had* never s such ugly cows in all the H8011
Ge 44:28 And *I have* not s him since. H8011
Ge 45:13 in Egypt and about everything *you have* s. H8011
Ge 46:30 since *I have* s **for myself** that you H8011+7156
Ex 3: 7 "*I have* **indeed** s the misery of my H8011+8011
Ex 3: 9 and *I have* s the way the Egyptians are H8011
Ex 3:16 *I have* **watched over** you and *have* s H7212+7212
Ex 4:31 about them and *had* s their misery, H8011
Ex 10: 5 face of the ground so that it cannot *be* s. H8011
Ex 10: 6 your ancestors *have ever* s from the day H8011
Ex 13: 7 with yeast in it *is to* **be** s among you, H8011
Ex 13: 7 nor *shall* any yeast **be** s anywhere within H8011
Ex 19: 4 '*You* yourselves *have* s what I did to Egypt H8011
Ex 20:22 '*You have* s for yourselves that I have H8011
Ex 32: 9 "*I have* s these people," the LORD said to H8011
Ex 33:23 see my back; but my face *must* not **be** s." H8011
Ex 34: 3 to come with you or **be** s anywhere on the H8011
Lev 5: 1 something *they have* s or learned about, H8011
Lev 14:35 '*I have* s something that looks like a H8011
Nu 14:14 *have* **been** s face to face, that your H8011
Nu 23:21 "No misfortune *is* s in Jacob, no misery H5564
Nu 27:13 After *you have* s it, you too will be H8011
Dt 1:19 dreadful wilderness that *you have* s, H8011
Dt 3:21 "You *have* s *with* your own eyes all that H8011
Dt 4: 9 things your eyes *have* s or let them fade H8011
Dt 5:24 Today *we have* s that a person can live H8011
Dt 9:13 said to me, "*I have* s this people, and H8011
Dt 29: 2 Your eyes *have* s all that the LORD did in H8011
Jos 23: 3 *You* yourselves *have* s everything the LORD H8011
Jdg 2: 7 outlived him and who *had* s all the great H8011
Jdg 5: 8 a shield or spear **was** s among forty H8011
Jdg 6:22 *I have* s the angel of the LORD face to face!" H8011
Jdg 9:48 Do what *you have* s me do!" H8011
Jdg 13:22 he said to his wife. "*We have* s God!" H8011
Jdg 14: 2 "*I have* s a Philistine woman in Timnah H8011
Jdg 18: 9 *We have* s the land, and it H8011
Jdg 19:30 "Such a thing *has* never **been** s or done H8011
1Sa 16:18 "*I have* s a son of Jesse of Bethlehem H8011
1Sa 23:22 usually goes and who *has* s him there. H8011
1Sa 24:10 This day *you have* s with your own eyes H8011
2Sa 17:17 could not risk **being** s entering the city. H8011
2Sa 18:21 tell the king what *you have* s. H8011
1Ki 6:18 was cedar; no stone *was to* **be** s. H8011
1Ki 8: 8 that their ends *could* **be** s from the Holy H8011
1Ki 10:12 never been imported or s since that day.) H8011
2Ki 14:26 The LORD *had* s how bitterly everyone in H8011
2Ki 20: 5 I have heard your prayer and s your tears H8011
2Ki 23:24 detestable things s in Judah and H8011
1Ch 29:17 And now *I have* s with joy how willingly H8011
2Ch 5: 9 *could* **be** s *from* in front of the inner H8011
2Ch 9:11 like them *had* ever **been** s in Judah.) H8011
Ezr 3:12 who *had* s the former temple H8011
Est 9:26 because of what *they had* s and what had H8011
Job 5: 3 *I* myself *have* s a fool taking root, but H8011
Job 13: 1 "My eyes *have* s all this, my ears have H8011
Job 15:17 let me tell you what *I have* s, H2600
Job 20: 7 own dung; *those who have* s him will say H8011
Job 27:12 You *have* all s this yourselves. Why then H2600
Job 28: 7 that hidden path, no falcon's eye *has* s it. H8812
Job 31:19 if *I have* s anyone perishing for lack of H8011
Job 36:25 All humanity *has* s it; mortals gaze on it H2600
Job 38:17 *Have you* s the gates of the deepest H8011
Job 38:22 of the snow or s the storehouses of the H8011
Job 42: 5 heard of you but now my eyes *have* s you. H8011
Ps 35:21 *With* our own eyes *we have* s it." H8011
Ps 35:22 *you have* s this; do not be silent. H8011
Ps 37:25 yet *I have* never s the righteous forsaken H8011
Ps 37:35 *I have* s a wicked and ruthless man H8011
Ps 48: 8 so *we have* s in the city of the LORD H8011
Ps 63: 2 *I have* s you in the sanctuary and beheld H2600
Ps 77:19 though your footprints **were** not s. H3359
Ps 90:15 as many years as *we have* s trouble. H8011
Ps 92:11 My eyes *have* s the defeat of my H5564
Ps 95: 9 tried me, though *they had* s what I did. H8011
Ps 98: 3 ends of the earth *have* s the salvation of H8011
Pr 17: 8 A bribe is s **as** a charm *by* the one H928+6524
Pr 25: 7 What *you have* s *with* your eyes H8011
Ecc 1:14 *I have* s all the things that are done under H8011
Ecc 3:10 *I have* s the burden God has laid on the H8011
Ecc 4: 3 who *has* not s the evil that is done under H8011
Ecc 5:13 *I have* s a grievous evil under the sun H8011
Ecc 6: 1 *I have* s another evil under the sun, and it H8011
Ecc 7:15 life of mine *I have* s both of these: H8011
Ecc 9:11 *I have* s something else under the sun H8011
Ecc 10: 5 There is an evil *I have* s under the sun H8011
Ecc 10: 7 *I have* s slaves on horseback, while H8011
SS 3: 3 "*Have you* s the one my heart loves?" H8011
Isa 6: 5 and my eyes *have* s the King, the H8011
Isa 9: 2 walking in darkness *have* s a great light; H8011
Isa 38: 5 I have heard your prayer and s your tears H8011
Isa 41: 5 The islands *have* s it and fear; the ends of H8011
Isa 42:20 *You have* s many things, but you pay no H8011
Isa 57:18 *I have* s their ways, but I will heal them; H8011
Isa 58: 3 they say, 'and *you have* not s it? H8011
Isa 64: 4 no eye *has* s any God besides you H8011
Isa 66: 8 Who *has ever* s things like this H8011
Isa 66:19 have not heard of my fame or s my glory. H8011
Jer 1:12 said to me, "You have s correctly, for I am H8011
Jer 3: 6 "*Have you* s what faithless Israel has H8011
Jer 13:26 your face that your shame *may* **be** s— H8011
Jer 13:27 *I have* s your detestable acts on the hills H8011
Jer 23:14 of Jerusalem *I have* s something horrible: H8011
La 1: 8 for *they have all* s her naked; she H8011
La 3: 1 I am the man *who has* s affliction by the H8011
La 3:59 *you have* s the wrong done to me H8011
La 3:60 *You have* s the depth of their vengeance H8011
Eze 3:23 like the glory *I had* s by the Kebar River H8011
Eze 8: 4 as in the vision *I had* s in the plain. H8011
Eze 8:12 *have you* s what the elders of Israel are H8011
Eze 8:17 He said to me, "*Have you* s this, son of H8011
Eze 10: 8 of the cherubim *could* **be** s what looked H8011
Eze 10:15 living creatures *I had* s by the Kebar River. H8011
Eze 10:20 living creatures *I had* s beneath the God H8011
Eze 10:22 as those *I had* s by the Kebar River. H8011
Eze 11:24 Then the vision *I had* s went up from me, H8011
Eze 13: 3 follow their own spirit and *have* s nothing! H8011
Eze 13: 7 *Have you* not s false visions and uttered H2600
Eze 16:50 I did away with them as *you have* s. H8011
Eze 43: 3 like the vision *I had* s when he came to H8011
Eze 43: 3 like the visions *I had* s by the Kebar River, H8011
Da 8: 6 two-horned ram *I had* s standing beside H8011
Da 9:21 the man *I had* s in the earlier vision H8011
Da 11:19 will stumble and fall, *to* **be** s no more. H5162
Hos 6:10 *I have* s a horrible thing in Israel: There H8011
Hos 9:13 *I have* s Ephraim, like Tyre, planted in a H8011
Mt 2: 9 the star *they had* s when it rose went G3972
Mt 4:16 living in darkness *have* s a great light; G3972
Mt 6: 1 in front of others to *be* s by them. G2517
Mt 6: 5 on the street corners to *be* s by others. G5743
Mt 9:33 like this *has* ever *been* s in Israel. G5743
Mt 17: 9 "Don't tell anyone what *you have* s, until G3969
Mk 2:12 "*We have* never s anything like this!" G3972
Mk 5:16 Those *who had* s it told the people what G3972
Mk 9: 9 tell anyone what *they had* s until the Son G3972
Mk 16:11 Jesus was alive and that she *had* s *him*, G2517
Mk 16:14 to believe those *who had* s him after he G2517
Lk 1:22 They realized *he had* s a vision in the G3972
Lk 2:17 *When they had* s him, they spread the G3972
Lk 2:20 all the things they had heard and s, G3972
Lk 2:26 not die before *he had* s the Lord's G3972
Lk 2:30 For my eyes *have* s your salvation, G3972
Lk 5:26 "*We have* s remarkable things today." G3972
Lk 7:22 report to John what *you have* s and heard: G3972
Lk 8:36 Those *who had* s it told the people how G3972
Lk 9:36 tell anyone at that time what *they had* s. G3972
Lk 19:37 loud voices for all the miracles *they had* s: G3972
Lk 24:23 told us *that they had* s a vision of G3972
Jn 1:14 *We have* s his glory, the glory of the one G2517
Jn 1:18 No one *has* ever s God, but the one and G3972
Jn 1:34 I *have* s and I testify that this is God's G3972
Jn 3:11 we testify to what *we have* s, but still G3972
Jn 3:21 so that *it may be* s **plainly** that what they G5746
Jn 3:32 He testifies to what *he has* s and heard G3972
Jn 4:45 *They had* s all that he had done in G3972
Jn 5:37 have never heard his voice nor s his form, G3972
Jn 6:36 *you have* s me and still you do not G3972
Jn 6:46 No one *has* s the Father except the one G3972
Jn 6:46 who is from God; only he *has* s the Father. G3972
Jn 8:38 telling you what I *have* s in the Father's G3972
Jn 8:57 said to him, "and *you have* s Abraham!" G3972
Jn 9: 8 those *who had* formerly s him G2555
Jn 9:37 Jesus said, "*You have* now s him; in fact G3972
Jn 11:45 to visit Mary, and *had* s what Jesus did G2517
Jn 14: 7 you do know him and *have* s him. G3972
Jn 14: 9 Anyone *who has* s me has seen the G3972
Jn 14: 9 who has seen me *has* s the Father. G3972
Jn 15:24 *they have* s, and yet they have G3972
Jn 20:18 with the news: "*I have* s the Lord!" And G3972
Jn 20:25 disciples told him, "*We have* s the Lord!" G3972
Jn 20:29 "Because *you have* s me, you have G3972
Jn 20:29 are those *who have* not s and yet have G3972
Ac 1:11 in the same way *you have* s him go into G2517
Ac 4:20 about what *we have* s and heard. G3972
Ac 7:34 *I have* **indeed** s the oppression of G3972+3972
Ac 7:44 according to the pattern *he had* s. G3972
Ac 9:12 In a vision *he has* s a man named G3972
Ac 9:27 on his journey *had* s the Lord and that G3972
Ac 10:40 on the third day and caused him to be s. G1871
Ac 10:41 He was not s by all the people, but by NDT
Ac 11:13 He told us how *he had* s an angel appear G3972
Ac 13:31 many days he *was* s by those who had G3972
Ac 16:10 After Paul *had* s the vision, we got ready G3972
Ac 21:29 They had **previously** s Trophimus the G4632
Ac 22:15 all people of what *you have* s and heard. G3972
Ac 26:16 witness of what *you have* s and will see of G3972
Ro 1:20 divine nature—*have been* **clearly** s, being G2775
Ro 8:24 But hope *that is* s is no hope at all G1063
1Co 2: 9 "What no eye *has* s, what no ear has G3972
1Co 9: 1 an apostle? *Have I* not s Jesus our Lord G3972
2Co 4:18 So we fix our eyes not on what *is* s, but on G1063
2Co 4:18 unseen, since what *is* s is temporary, but G1063
2Co 5:12 who take pride in **what is** s rather than in G4725
Php 4: 9 heard from me, or s in me—put it into G3972
Col 2:18 into great detail about what *they have* s; G3972
1Ti 3:16 by the Spirit, *was* s by angels, was G3972
1Ti 6:16 whom no one *has* s or can see. G3972
Heb 11: 3 so that what *is* s was not made out of G1063
Heb 11: 7 when warned about things not yet s, in G1063
Jas 5:11 perseverance and *have* s what the Lord G3972
1Pe 1: 8 *Though you have* not s him, you love him G3972
1Jn 1: 1 which *we have* s with our eyes G3972
1Jn 1: 2 life appeared; *we have* s it and testify to it G3972
1Jn 1: 3 to you what *we have* s and heard, G3972
1Jn 2: 8 command; its truth *is* s in him and in you G1639
1Jn 3: 6 continues to sin *has* either s him or known G3972
1Jn 4:12 No one *has* ever s God; but if we love one G2517
1Jn 4:14 And we *have* s and testify that the Father G2517
1Jn 4:20 sister, whom *they have* s, cannot love G3972
1Jn 4:20 cannot love God, whom *they have* not s. G3972
3Jn 11 who does what is evil *has* not s God. G3972
Rev 1:19 therefore, what *you have* s, what is now G3972
Rev 10: 5 Then the angel *I had* s standing on the G3972
Rev 11:19 within his temple *was* s the ark of his G3972
Rev 22: 8 And when I had heard and s them, I fell G1063

SEER (20) [SEER'S, SEERS]

1Sa 9: 9 let us go to the s," because the prophet H8014
1Sa 9: 9 prophet of today used to be called a s.) H8014

1Sa 9:11 they asked them, "Is the s here? H8014
1Sa 9:19 "I am the s," Samuel replied. "Go up H8014
2Sa 24:11 had come to Gad the prophet, David's s: H2602
1Ch 9:22 of trust by David and Samuel the s. H8014
1Ch 21: 9 The LORD said to Gad, David's s, H2602
1Ch 25: 5 All these were sons of Heman the king's s. H2602
1Ch 26:28 by Samuel the s and by Saul son of Kish H8014
1Ch 29:29 are written in the records of Samuel the s, H8014
1Ch 29:29 the prophet and the records of Gad the s, H2602
2Ch 9:29 visions of Iddo the s concerning Jeroboam H2602
2Ch 12:15 prophet and of Iddo the s that deal with H2602
2Ch 16: 7 time Hanani the s came to Asa king of H8014
2Ch 16:10 Asa was angry with the s because of this H8014
2Ch 19: 2 Jehu the s, the son of Hanani, went out to H2602
2Ch 29:25 Gad the king's s and Nathan the H2602
2Ch 29:30 the words of David and of Asaph the s. H2602
2Ch 35:15 Heman and Jeduthun the king's s. H2602
Am 7:12 Amaziah said to Amos, "Get out, you s! H2602

SEER'S (1) [SEER]

1Sa 9:18 you please tell me where the s house is?" H8014

SEERS (6) [SEER]

2Ki 17:13 Judah through all his prophets and s: H2602
2Ch 33:18 the words the s spoke to him in the H2602
2Ch 33:19 all these are written in the records of the s. H2602
Isa 29:10 he has covered your heads (the s). H2602
Isa 30:10 They say to the s, "See no more visions!" H8014
Mic 3: 7 The s will be ashamed and the diviners H2602

SEES (46) [SEE]

Ge 16:13 "You are the God *who* s me," for she said H8024
Ge 16:13 "I have now seen the *One who* s me." H8011
Ge 44:31 s that the boy isn't there, he will die. H8011
Ge 49:15 When *he* s how good is his resting place H8011
Lev 13: 5 and if he s that the sore is H6524+928
Lev 13:15 When the priest s the raw flesh, he shall H8011
Nu 12: 8 not in riddles; *he* s the form of the LORD. H5564
Nu 24: 3 the prophecy of one whose eye s **clearly**, H9280
Nu 24: 4 who s a vision from the Almighty H2600
Nu 24:15 the prophecy of one whose eye s **clearly**, H9280
Nu 24:16 *who* s a vision from the Almighty H2600
Dt 32:36 his servants when *he* s their strength is H8011
Job 7: 8 The eye *that now* s me will see me no H8011
Job 10: 4 eyes of flesh? Do you see as a mortal s? H8011
Job 11:11 when *he* s evil, does he not H8011
Job 28:24 of the earth and s everything under the H8011
Job 34:21 the ways of mortals; *he* s their every step. H8011
Ps 10:11 he covers his face and never s. H8011
Ps 33:13 the LORD looks down and s all mankind; H8011
Ps 58: 8 like a stillborn child *that* never s the sun. H2600
Ps 97: 4 up the world; the earth s and trembles. H8011
Ps 138: 6 though lofty, *he* s them from afar. H3359
Pr 28:11 poor and discerning s how deluded they H2983
Pr 31:18 *She* s that her trading is profitable, and H3247
Ecc 6: 9 Better **what** the eye s than the roving of H5260
Isa 11: 3 will not judge by **what** he s *with* his eyes, H5260
Isa 21: 6 a lookout and have him report what *he* s. H8011
Isa 21: 7 When *he* s chariots with teams of horses H8011
Isa 29:15 work in darkness and think, "Who s us? H8011
Isa 47:10 wickedness and have said, 'No *one* s me. H8011
La 3:50 the LORD looks down from heaven and s. H8011
Eze 12:27 'The vision he s is for many years from H2600
Eze 18:14 this son has a son *who* s all the sins his H8011
Eze 18:14 though *he* s them, he does not H8011
Eze 33: 3 and *he* s the sword coming against the H8011
Eze 33: 6 But if the watchman s the sword coming H8011
Eze 39:15 *anyone who* s a human bone will leave a H8011
Mt 6: 4 your Father, who s what is done in secret *G1063*
Mt 6: 6 your Father, who s what is done in secret *G1063*
Mt 6:18 your Father, who s what is done in secret *G1063*
Lk 14:29 everyone who s it will ridicule you, *G2555*
Jn 5:19 he can do only what *he* s his Father doing, *G1063*
Jn 10:12 So *when he* s the wolf coming, he *G2555*
Jn 14:17 because *it* neither s him nor knows him. *G2555*
1Co 8:10 if someone with a weak conscience s you, *G3972*
1Jn 3:17 possessions and s a brother or sister in *G2555*

SEGUB (3)

1Ki 16:34 its gates at the cost of his youngest son S, H8437
1Ch 2:21 made love to her, and she bore him S. H8437
1Ch 2:22 S was the father of Jair, who controlled H8437

SEIR (39)

Ge 14: 6 the Horites in the hill country of S, as H8541
Ge 32: 3 him to his brother Esau in the land of S, H8541
Ge 33:14 the children, until I come to my lord in S." H8541
Ge 33:16 day Esau started on his way back to S. H8541
Ge 36: 8 Edom) settled in the hill country of S. H8541
Ge 36: 9 of the Edomites in the hill country of S. H8541
Ge 36:20 These were the sons of S the Horite, who H8543
Ge 36:21 These sons of S in Edom were Horite H8543
Ge 36:30 to their divisions, in the land of S. H8541
Nu 24:18 will be conquered; S, his enemy, will be H8541
Dt 1: 2 to Kadesh Barnea by the Mount S road.) H8541
Dt 1:44 beat you down from S all the way to H8541
Dt 2: 1 our way around the hill country of S. H8541
Dt 2: 4 the descendants of Esau, who live in S. H8541
Dt 2: 5 Esau the hill country of S as his own. H8541
Dt 2: 8 the descendants of Esau, who live in S. H8541
Dt 2:12 Horites used to live in S, but the H8541
Dt 2:22 who lived in S, when he destroyed H8541
Dt 2:29 of Esau, who live in S, and the Moabites, H8541
Dt 33: 2 from Sinai and dawned over them from S; H8541
Jos 11:17 which rises toward S, to Baal Gad in the H8541
Jos 12: 7 to Mount Halak, which rises toward S. H8541
Jos 15:10 curved westward from Baalah to Mount S, H8542
Jos 24: 4 I assigned the hill country of S to Esau H8541
Jdg 5: 4 went out from S, when you marched H8541
1Ch 1:38 The sons of S: Lotan, Shobal, Zibeon H8543
1Ch 4:42 sons of Ishi, invaded the hill country of S. H8541
2Ch 20:10 Moab and Mount S, whose territory you H8541
2Ch 20:22 Moab and Mount S who were invading H8541
2Ch 20:23 the men from Mount S to destroy and H8541
2Ch 20:23 finished slaughtering the men from S, H8541
2Ch 25:11 where he killed ten thousand men of S. H8541
2Ch 25:14 brought back the gods of the people of S. H8541
Isa 21:11 Someone calls to me from S, "Watchman H8541
Eze 25: 8 'Because Moab and S said, "Look, Judah H8541
Eze 35: 2 set your face against Mount S; prophesy H8541
Eze 35: 3 against you, Mount S, and I will stretch H8541
Eze 35: 7 I will make Mount S a desolate waste and H8541
Eze 35:15 be desolate, Mount S, you and all of H8541

SEIRAH (1)

Jdg 3:26 by the stone images and escaped to S. H8545

SEIZE (31) [SEIZED, SEIZES, SEIZING, SEIZURES]

Ge 43:18 overpower us and s us as slaves and H4374
Jdg 7:24 the Midianites and s the waters of the H4334
Jdg 9:33 **s the opportunity** to attack them." H5162+3338
Jdg 21:21 each of you s one of them to be your H2642
1Ki 13: 4 his hand from the altar and said, "S him!" H9530
1Ki 18:40 "S the prophets of Baal. H9530
1Ki 20: 6 *They will* s everything you H8492+928+3338
1Ch 7:21 when they went down to s their livestock. H4374
Job 3: 6 That night—*may* thick darkness s it; may it H4374
Ps 21: 8 enemies; your right hand *will* s your foes. H5162
Ps 71:11 pursue him and s him, for no one H9530
Ps 109:11 *May* a creditor s all he has; may strangers H5943
Isa 3: 6 A man *will* s one of his brothers in his H9530
Isa 5:29 they growl as *they* s their prey and carry it H296
Isa 10: 6 anger me, to s loot and snatch plunder H8964
Isa 13: 8 **Terror** *will* s *them*, pain and anguish will H987
Isa 21: 3 with pain, pangs s me, like those of a H296
Jer 12:14 wicked neighbors who s the inheritance I H5595
Eze 38:13 goods and to s much plunder? H8964
Da 11: 8 He will also s their gods, their metal images NDT
Da 11:21 and *he will* s it through intrigue. H2616
Am 9: 3 there I will hunt them down and s them. H4374
Ob 13 s their wealth in the day of their H8938
Mic 2: 2 They covet fields and s them, and houses H1608
Hab 1: 6 the whole earth to s dwellings not their H3769
Zec 14:13 *They will* s each other by the hand and H2616
Lk 21:12 *they will* s you and *G2095+2093+3836+5931*
Jn 7:30 At this they tried to s him, but no one laid *G4389*
Jn 7:44 Some wanted to s him, but no one laid a *G4389*
Jn 10:39 Again they tried to s him, but he escaped *G4389*
Ac 12: 3 the Jews, he proceeded *to* s Peter also. *G5197*

SEIZED (53) [SEIZE]

Ge 14:11 The four kings s all the goods of Sodom H4374
Ge 21:25 of water that Abimelek's servants *had* s. H1608
Ge 34:28 *They* s their flocks and herds and donkeys H4374
Ex 15:15 leaders of Moab *will be* s *with* trembling, H296
Jdg 7:24 called out and *they* s the waters of the H4334
Jdg 12: 6 *they* s him and killed him at the fords of H296
Jdg 16:21 Then the Philistines s him, gouged out his H296
1Sa 17:35 When it turned on me, *I* s it by its hair H2616
2Sa 4:10 *I* s him and put him to death in Ziklag. H296
2Sa 10: 4 So Hanun s David's envoys, shaved off H4374
1Ki 18:40 *They* s them, and Elijah had them H9530
1Ki 21:19 not murdered a man and s his **property**? H3769
2Ki 11:16 So *they* s her as she reached the H8492+3338
2Ki 17: 4 Shalmaneser s him and put him in H6806
1Ch 5:21 *They* s the livestock of the Hagrites—fifty H8647
1Ch 19: 4 So Hanun s David's envoys, shaved them H4374
2Ch 23:15 So *they* s her as she reached the H8492+3338
Est 8:17 fear of the Jews *had* s them. H5877+6584
Est 9: 3 fear of Mordecai *had* s them. H5877+6584
Job 4:14 fear and trembling s me and made all my H7925
Job 16:12 *he* s me by the neck and crushed me. H296
Job 18:20 his fate; those of the east *are* s *with* horror. H296
Job 20:19 *he has* s houses he did not build. H1608
Job 24: 9 the infant of the poor *is* s **for a debt**. H2471
Ps 48: 6 Trembling s them there, pain like that of a H296
Ps 56: T When the Philistines *had* s him in Gath. H296
Isa 10:10 As my hand s the kingdoms of the idols H5162
Jer 26: 8 all the people s him and said, H9530
Jer 49:24 anguish and pain *have* s her, pain like that H296
Jer 51:32 the river crossings s, the marshes set on H9530
Jer 51:41 captured, the boast of the whole earth s! H9530
Mt 21:35 "The tenants s his servants; they beat one, *G3284*
Mt 22: 6 The rest s his servants, mistreated them *G3195*
Mt 26:50 s Jesus and arrested him *G2095+3836+5931+2093*
Mt 27: 3 *he was* s **with remorse** and returned the *G3564*
Mk 12: 3 But *they* s him, beat him and sent him *G3284*
Mk 14:46 The men s Jesus and *G2095+3836+5931*
Mk 14:51 was following Jesus. *When they* s him, *G3195*
Lk 8:29 Many times *it had* s him, and though he *G5275*
Lk 23:26 led him away, *they* s Simon from Cyrene *G2138*
Jn 8:20 Yet no one s him, because his hour had *G4389*
Ac 4: 3 *They* s Peter and John and *G2095+3836+5931*
Ac 5: 5 And great fear s all who heard *G1181+2093*
Ac 5:11 Great fear s the whole church and *G1181+2093*
Ac 6:12 *They* s Stephen and brought him before *G5275*
Ac 16:19 *they* s Paul and Silas and dragged them *G2138*
Ac 19:17 Ephesus, they *were* all s **with** fear, and *G2158*
Ac 19:29 *The people* s Gaius and Aristarchus *G5275*
Ac 21:27 whole crowd and s him, *G2095+2093+3836+5931*
Ac 23:27 This man *was* s by the Jews and they *G5197*
Ac 24: 6 to desecrate the temple; so *we* s him. *G3195*
Ac 26:21 That is why some Jews s me in the temple *G5197*
Rev 20: 2 *He* s the dragon, that ancient serpent, who *G3195*

SEIZES (7) [SEIZE]

Dt 25:11 she reaches out and s him by his private H2616
Job 18: 9 A trap s him by the heel; a snare holds him H296
Job 21: 6 I am terrified; trembling s my body. H296
Ps 137: 9 Happy is the *one* who s your infants and H296
Mic 4: 9 that pain s you like that of a woman in H2616
Mk 9:18 Whenever *it* s him, it throws him to the *G2898*
Lk 9:39 A spirit s him and he suddenly screams; it *G3284*

SEIZING (4) [SEIZE]

Lk 22:54 Then s him, they led him away and took *G5197*
Ac 21:30 S Paul, they dragged him from the temple *G2138*
Ro 7: 8 s the opportunity afforded by the *G3284*
Ro 7:11 s the opportunity afforded by the *G3284*

SEIZURES (2) [SEIZE]

Mt 4:24 *those* **having** s, and the *G4944*
Mt 17:15 "*He* **has** s and is suffering greatly *G4944*

SEKAKAH (1)

Jos 15:61 the wilderness: Beth Arabah, Middin, S, H6117

SEKU (1)

1Sa 19:22 Ramah and went to the great cistern at S. H8497

SELA (4) [SELA HAMMAHLEKOTH]

Jdg 1:36 was from Scorpion Pass to S and beyond. H6153
2Ki 14: 7 Valley of Salt and captured S in battle, H6153
Isa 16: 1 of the land, from S, across the desert, H6153
Isa 42:11 Let the people of S sing for joy; let them H6153

SELA HAMMAHLEKOTH (1) [SELA]

1Sa 23:28 why they call this place S. H6154

SELAH (NIV84) Not Directly Translated in 2011 NIV.

See NIV footnotes at Pss 3:2; 4:2; 7:5; 9:16; 20:3; 21:2; 24:6; 32:4; 39:5; 44:8; 46:3; 47:4; 48:8; 49:13; 50:6; 52:3; 54:3; 55:7; 57:3; 59:5; 60:4; 61:4; 62:4; 66:4; 67:1; 68:7; 75:3; 76:3; 77:3; 81:7; 82:2; 83:8; 84:4; 85:2; 87:3; 88:7; 89:4; 140:3; 143:6; Hab 3:3.

SELDOM (2)

Pr 25:17 S *set* foot in your neighbor's house—too H3700
Ecc 5:20 They s reflect on the days of their H4202+2221

SELECT (8) [SELECTED, SELECTS]

Ex 12:21 "Go at once and s the animals for your H4374
Ex 18:21 But s capable men from all the people H2600
Nu 31:30 the Israelites' half, s one out of every fifty H4374
Nu 35:11 s some towns to be your cities of refuge, to H7936
Jdg 20:16 were seven hundred s troops who were H1047
1Sa 26: 2 with his three thousand s Israelite troops H1047
Est 3: 7 Haman to s **a day** and H4946+3427+4200+3427
Isa 66:21 And *I will* s some of them also to be H4374

SELECTED (12) [SELECT]

Ge 18: 7 Then he ran to the herd and s a choice H4374
Ge 32:13 what he had with him *he* s a gift for his H4374
Ex 21: 8 the master who *has* s her for himself, H3585
Nu 18: 6 *I* myself *have* s your fellow Levites from H4374
Nu 31:47 Moses s one out of every fifty people and H4374
Dt 1:23 good to me; so *I* s twelve of you, one H4374
2Sa 10: 9 so *he* s some of the best troops in Israel H1047
2Ki 7:14 So *they* s two chariots with their horses H4374
1Ch 19:10 so *he* s some of the best troops in Israel H1047
Ezr 10:16 Ezra the priest s men who were family H976
Est 2: 9 female attendants s from the king's H8011
Heb 5: 1 Every high priest *is* s from among the *G3284*

SELECTS (3) [SELECT]

Ex 21: 9 If *he* s her for his son, he must grant her H3585
Pr 31:13 *She* s wool and flax and works with eager H2011
Isa 40:20 such an offering s wood that will not rot; H1047

SELED (2)

1Ch 2:30 The sons of Nadab: S and Appaim. Seled H6135
1Ch 2:30 S died without children H6135

SELEUCIA (1)

Ac 13: 4 went down to S and sailed from there to *G4942*

SELF (10) [HERSELF, HIMSELF, ITSELF, MYSELF, ONESELF, OURSELVES, SELFISH, THEMSELVES, YOURSELF, YOURSELVES]

Ex 32:13 to whom you swore by **your own** s: H3870
Lk 9:25 and yet lose or forfeit **their very** s? *G1571*
Ro 6: 6 we know that our old s was crucified with *G476*
Eph 4:22 to put off your old s, which is being *G476*
Eph 4:24 to put on the new s, created to be like *G476*
Col 2:11 Your **whole** s ruled by the flesh was put *G5393*
Col 3: 9 have taken off your old s with its practices *G476*
Col 3:10 have put on the new s, which is being NDT
Phm 19 to mention that you owe me **your very** s. *G4932*

1Pe 3: 4 it should be that *of* your inner **s**, the G2840+476

SELF-ABASEMENT (1)
Ezr 9: 5 I rose from my **s**, with my tunic and cloak H9504

SELF-CONDEMNED (1) [CONDEMN]
Titus 3:11 people are warped and sinful; they are **s**. G896

SELF-CONFIDENCE (1) [CONFIDENCE]
Ne 6:16 afraid and **lost** their **s**, H5877+4394+928+6524

SELF-CONFIDENT (1) [CONFIDENCE]
2Co 11:17 In this **s** boasting I am not talking as the G5712

SELF-CONTROL (8) [CONTROL]
Pr 16:32 *one with* **s** than one who H5440+928+8120
Pr 25:28 is a person who lacks **s**. H5110+4200+8120
Ac 24:25 **s** and the judgment to come G1602
1Co 7: 5 not tempt you because of your **lack of s**. G202
Gal 5:23 gentleness and **s**. Against such things G1602
2Ti 3: 3 slanderous, **without s**, brutal, not lovers of G203
2Pe 1: 6 to knowledge, **s**; and to self-control G1602
2Pe 1: 6 self-control; and to **s**, perseverance; and G1602

SELF-CONTROLLED (6) [CONTROL]
1Ti 3: 2 to his wife, temperate, **s**, respectable G5409
Titus 1: 8 who loves what is good, who is **s**, upright, G5409
Titus 2: 2 worthy of respect, **s**, and sound in faith, in G5409
Titus 2: 5 to be **s** and pure, to be busy at home, to G5409
Titus 2: 6 encourage the young men *to be* **s**. G5404
Titus 2:12 passions, and to live **s**, upright and godly G5407

SELF-DENIAL (1) [DENY]
Ps 132: 1 remember David and all his **s**. H6700

SELF-DISCIPLINE (1) [DISCIPLINE]
2Ti 1: 7 us timid, but gives us power, love and **s**. G5406

SELF-IMPOSED (1) [IMPOSE]
Col 2:23 of wisdom, with their **s worship**, their false G1615

SELF-INDULGENCE (2) [INDULGE]
Mt 23:25 inside they are full of greed and **s**. G202
Jas 5: 5 You have lived on earth in luxury and **s** G5059

SELF-INTEREST (2) [INTEREST]
Mt 27:18 knew it was out of **s** that they had handed G5784
Mk 15:10 knowing it was out of **s** that the chief G5784

SELF-SEEKING (2) [SEEK]
Ro 2: 8 those who are **s** and who reject G1666+2249
1Co 13: 5 others, *it is* not **s**, it is not G2426+3836+1571

SELFISH (8) [SELF]
Ps 119:36 your statutes and not toward **s gain**. H1299
Pr 18: 1 person pursues **s ends** and against all H9294
2Co 12:20 fits of rage, **s ambition**, slander, gossip, G2249
Gal 5:20 fits of rage, **s ambition**, dissensions G2249
Php 1:17 The former preach Christ out of **s ambition** G2249
Php 2: 3 nothing out of **s ambition** or vain conceit G2249
Jas 3:14 bitter envy and **s ambition** in your hearts, G2249
Jas 3:16 For where you have envy and **s ambition** G2249

SELL (42) [SALE, SALES, SELLER, SELLERS, SELLING, SELLS, SOLD]
Ge 23: 4 **S** me some property for a burial site here H5989
Ge 23: 9 so *he will* **s** me the cave of Machpelah H5989
Ge 23: 9 Ask him *to* **s** it to me for the full price as a H5989
Ge 25:31 Jacob replied, "First **s** me your birthright." H4835
Ge 37:27 *let's* **s** him to the Ishmaelites and not lay H4835
Ge 47:16 "*I will* **s** you food in exchange for your H5989
Ge 47:22 That is why *they did* not **s** their land. H4835
Ex 21: 8 He has no right to **s** her to foreigners H4835
Ex 21:35 the two parties *are to* **s** the live one and H4835
Lev 25:14 " 'If *you* **s land** to any of your own H4835+4928
Lev 25:15 And *they are to* **s** to you on the basis of H4835
Lev 25:37 money at interest or **s** them food at a H5989
Lev 25:39 become poor and **s themselves** to you, H4835
Lev 25:47 become poor and **s themselves** to the H4835
Dt 2:28 **S** us food to eat and water to drink for their H8690
Dt 14:21 or you *may* **s** it to any other foreigner. H4835
Dt 15:12 **s themselves** to you and serve you six H4835
Dt 21:14 *You* **must** not **s** her H4835+928+2021+4084+4835
1Ki 21: 6 '**S** me your vineyard H5989+928+4084
1Ki 21:15 that he refused to **s** you. H5989+928+4084
2Ki 4: 7 he said, "Go, **s** the oil and pay your debts. H4835
2Ki 7: 1 of the finest flour will **s** for a shekel and two NDT
2Ki 7:18 finest flour *will* **s for** a shekel and H2118+928
1Ch 21:22 **S** it to me at the full price. H5989
Ne 10:31 merchandise or grain to **s** on the Sabbath, H4835
Pr 11:26 blessing on the *one who is willing to* **s**. H8690
Pr 23:23 Buy the truth and *do* not **s** it—wisdom H4835
Isa 50: 1 Or to which of my creditors *did I* **s** you H4835
Eze 30:12 of the Nile and **s** the land to an evil H4835
Eze 48:14 *They must* not **s** or exchange any of it. H4835
Joel 3: 8 *I will* **s** your sons and daughters to the H4835
Joel 3: 8 and *they will* **s** them to the Sabeans H4835
Am 2: 6 They **s** the innocent for silver, and the H4835
Am 8: 5 New Moon be over that *we may* **s** grain, H8690
Zec 11: 5 *Those who* **s** them say, 'Praise the LORD, H4835
Mt 19:21 **s** your possessions and give to the poor G4797
Mt 25: 9 go to those *who* **s** oil and buy some for G4797
Mk 10:21 **s** everything you have and give to the G4797
Lk 12:33 **S** your possessions and give to the poor G4797
Lk 18:22 **S** everything you have and give to the G4797
Lk 22:36 have a sword, **s** your cloak and buy one. G4797
Rev 13:17 could not buy or **s** unless they had the G4797

SELLER (5) [SELL]
Lev 25:29 During that time the **s** may redeem it. NDT
Isa 24: 2 as for her servant, for **s** as for buyer, for H4835
Eze 7:12 Let not the buyer rejoice nor the **s** grieve H4835
Eze 7:13 The **s** will not recover the property that H4835
Eze 7:13 as long as *both* **buyer and s** live. H4392S

SELLERS (1) [SELL]
Ne 13:20 the merchants and **s** *of* all kinds of goods H4835

SELLING (15) [SELL]
Ge 25:33 an oath to him, **s** his birthright to Jacob. H4835
Ge 45: 5 be angry with yourselves for **s** me here, H4835
Dt 24: 7 Israelite and treating or **s** them as a slave, H4835
Ru 4: 3 *is* **s** the piece of land that belonged to our H4835
Ne 5: 8 Now you *are* **s** your own people, only for H4835
Ne 13:15 I warned them against **s** food on that day. H4835
Ne 13:16 of merchandise and **s** them in Jerusalem H4835
Am 8: 6 **s** even the sweepings with the wheat. H8690
Mt 21:12 drove out all who were buying and **s** there. G60
Mt 21:12 the benches *of* those **s** doves. G4797
Mk 11:15 out those who were buying and **s** there. G60
Mk 11:15 the benches *of* those **s** doves, G4797
Lk 17:28 drinking, buying and **s**, planting and G4797
Lk 19:45 he began to drive out those *who were* **s**. G4797
Jn 2:14 temple courts he found people **s** cattle, G4797

SELLS (5) [SELL]
Ex 21: 7 "If a man **s** his daughter as a servant, she H4835
Ex 22: 1 slaughters it or **s** it must pay back five H4835
Lev 25:25 becomes poor and **s** some of their H4835
Lev 25:29 " 'Anyone *who* **s** a house in a walled city H4835
Pr 31:24 She makes linen garments and **s** them H4835

SEMAKIAH (1)
1Ch 26: 7 relatives Elihu and **S** were also able men. H6165

SEMEIN (1)
Lk 3:26 Mattathias, the son *of* **S**, the son of Josek, G4946

SEMEN (6)
Ge 38: 9 he spilled his **s** on the ground to keep from NDT
Lev 15:16 " 'When a man has an emission of **s**, he H2446
Lev 15:17 leather that has **s** on it must be washed H2446
Lev 15:18 a woman and there is an emission of **s**, H2446
Lev 15:32 made unclean by an emission of **s**, H2446
Lev 22: 4 by anyone who has an emission of **s**, H2446

SENAAH (2)
Ezr 2:35 of **S** 3,630 H6171
Ne 7:38 of **S** 3,930 H6171

SENATE (KJV) ASSEMBLY OF THE ELDERS

SEND (264) [SENDING, SENDS, SENT]
Ge 7: 4 days from now I *will* **s rain** on the earth H4763
Ge 24: 7 he *will* **s** his angel before you so that you H8938
Ge 24:40 *will* **s** his angel with you and make your H8938
Ge 24:54 he said, "**S** me **on** my **way** to my master." H8938
Ge 24:56 **S** me **on** my **way** so I may go to my master H8938
Ge 27:45 *I'll* **s word** *for* you to come back from there. H8938
Ge 30:25 "**S** me **on** my **way** so I can go back to my H8938
Ge 31:27 so *I could* **s** you **away** with joy and singing H8938
Ge 37:13 *I am going to* **s** you to them. H8938
Ge 38:17 "I'll **s** you a young goat from my flock," H8938
Ge 38:17 me something as a pledge until you **s** it?" H8938
Ge 38:23 After all, *I did* **s** her this young goat, but H8938
Ge 42: 4 But Jacob *did* not **s** Benjamin, Joseph's H8938
Ge 42:16 **S** one of your number to get your brother H8938
Ge 43: 4 If you will **s** our brother along with us, we H8938
Ge 43: 5 But if you will not **s** him, we will not go H8938
Ge 43: 8 "**S** the boy along with me and we will go H8938
Ex 4:13 servant, Lord. Please **s** someone else." H8938
Ex 8: 2 I *will* **s a plague** of frogs *on* your whole H5597
Ex 8:21 I *will* **s** swarms of flies on you and your H8938
Ex 9:14 this time I *will* **s** the full force of my H8938
Ex 9:18 time tomorrow I *will* **s** the worst hailstorm H4763
Ex 23:27 "*I will* **s** my terror ahead of you and throw H8938
Ex 23:28 *I will* **s** the hornet ahead of you to drive H8938
Ex 33: 2 *I will* **s** an angel before you and drive out H8938
Ex 33:12 not let me know whom *you will* **s** with me. H8938
Ex 33:15 not go with us, *do* not **s** us **up** from here. H6590
Lev 16:21 *He shall* **s** the goat **away** into the H8938
Lev 25:21 *I will* **s** you such a blessing in the sixth H7422
Lev 26: 4 *I will* **s** you rain in its season, and the H5989
Lev 26:22 *I will* **s** wild animals against you, and they H8938
Lev 26:25 your cities, *I will* **s** a plague among you H8938
Nu 5: 2 the Israelites *to* **s away** from the camp H8938
Nu 5: 3 **S away** male and female alike; send them H8938
Nu 5: 3 **s** them outside the camp so they will not H8938
Nu 13: 2 "**S** some men to explore the land of H8938
Nu 13: 2 each ancestral tribe **s** one of its leaders." H8938
Nu 22:37 "*Did I* not **s** you an **urgent** H8938+8938
Nu 31: 4 **S** into battle a thousand men from each of H8938
Nu 35:25 blood and **s** the accused **back** to the city H8740
Dt 1:22 "*Let us* **s** men ahead to spy out the land H8938
Dt 7:20 the LORD your God *will* **s** the hornet among H8938
Dt 11:14 then *I will* **s** rain on your land in its season, H5989
Dt 15:13 *do* not **s** them away empty-handed. H8938
Dt 28: 8 The LORD *will* **s** a blessing on your barns H7422
Dt 28:12 to **s** rain on your land in season and to H5989
Dt 28:20 The LORD *will* **s** on you curses, confusion H8938
Dt 28:59 the LORD *will* **s fearful** plagues on you and H7098
Dt 28:68 The LORD *will* **s** you **back** in ships *to* Egypt H8740
Dt 32:24 *I will* **s** wasting famine against them H8938
Dt 32:24 I will **s** against them the fangs of wild NDT
Jos 1:16 and wherever *you* **s** us we will go. H8938
Jos 7: 3 **S** two or three thousand men to take it H6590
Jos 18: 4 *I will* **s** them **out** to make a survey of the H8938
Jdg 20:38 that they *should* **s up** a great cloud H6590
1Sa 5:11 "**S** the ark of the god of Israel **away**; let H8938
1Sa 6: 2 Tell us how *we should* **s** it **back** to its H8938
1Sa 6: 3 *do* not **s** it **back** to him without a gift H8938
1Sa 6: 3 **by all means s** a guilt offering to H8740+8740
1Sa 6: 4 "What guilt offering *should we* **s** to him?" H8740
1Sa 6: 6 *did they* not **s** the Israelites **out** so they H8938
1Sa 6: 8 to him as a guilt offering. **S** it on its way, H8938
1Sa 9:16 this time tomorrow *I will* **s** you a man from H8938
1Sa 9:19 morning *I will* **s** you **on** your **way** and will H8938
1Sa 9:26 "Get ready, and *I will* **s** you **on** *your* **way**." H8938
1Sa 11: 3 us seven days so *we can* **s** messengers H8938
1Sa 12:17 will call on the LORD *to* **s** thunder and rain. H5989
1Sa 16:11 "**S for** him; we will H8938+2256+4374
1Sa 16:19 to Jesse and said, "**S** me your son David H8938
1Sa 19:17 like this and **s** my enemy **away** so that he H8938
1Sa 20:12 *will I* not **s** you **word** and let you know? H8938
1Sa 20:13 let you know and **s** you away in peace. H8938
1Sa 20:21 Then *I will* **s** a boy and say, 'Go, find the H8938
1Sa 20:31 Now **s** someone to bring him to me, for H8938
1Sa 29: 4 said, "**S** the man **back**, that he may H8740
2Sa 11: 6 this word to Joab: "**S** me Uriah the Hittite." H8938
2Sa 11:12 more day, and tomorrow *I will* **s** you **back**." H8938
2Sa 13: 9 "**S** everyone **out** of here," Amnon H3655
2Sa 14:29 sent for Joab in order to **s** him to the king, H8938
2Sa 14:32 'Come here so *I can* **s** you to the king to H8938
2Sa 15:36 **S** them to me with anything you hear." H8938
2Sa 17:16 Now **s a message** at once and tell David H8938
2Sa 18:29 as Joab was about to **s** the king's servant H8938
2Sa 19:31 king and to **s** him **on** his **way** *from* there. H8938
1Ki 8:36 **s** rain on the land you gave your H5989
1Ki 8:44 enemies, wherever *you* **s** them, and when H8938
1Ki 18: 1 to Ahab, and *I will* **s** rain on the land." H5989
1Ki 20: 6 time tomorrow *I am going to* **s** my officials H8938
1Ki 22:26 Micaiah and **s** him **back** to Amon the H8740
2Ki 2:16 Elisha replied, "*do* not **s** them." H8938
2Ki 2:17 So he said, "**S** them." And they sent H8938
2Ki 4:22 "Please **s** me one of the servants and a H8938
2Ki 5: 5 "*I will* **s** a letter to the king of Israel." H8938
2Ki 5: 7 Why *does* this fellow **s** someone to me to H8938
2Ki 6:13 ordered, "so *I can* **s** men and capture him." H8938
2Ki 7:13 So *let us* **s** them to find out what H8938
2Ki 9:17 "**S** him to meet them and ask, 'Do you H8938
2Ki 15:37 the LORD began to **s** Rezin king of Aram H8938
1Ch 13: 2 *let us* **s word** far and wide to the rest of H8938
2Ch 2: 3 "**S** me cedar logs as you did for my father NDT
2Ch 2: 7 "**S** me, therefore, a man skilled to work in H8938
2Ch 2: 8 "**S** me also cedar, juniper and algum logs H8938
2Ch 2:15 "Now *let* my lord **s** his servants the wheat H8938
2Ch 6:27 **s** rain on the land you gave your H5989
2Ch 6:34 enemies, wherever *you* **s** them, and when H8938
2Ch 7:13 devour the land or **s** a plague among my H8938
2Ch 18:25 Micaiah and **s** him **back** to Amon the H8740
2Ch 28:11 **S back** your fellow Israelites you have H8740
2Ch 30: 5 They decided to **s** a proclamation H6296
Ezr 5:17 Then *let* the king **s** us his decision in this A10714
Ezr 10: 3 our God to **s away** all these women H3655
Ne 2: 5 *let him* **s** me to the city in Judah where H8938
Ne 2: 6 It pleased the king *to* **s** me; so I set a time H8938
Ne 8:10 **s** some to those who have nothing H8938
Ne 8:12 to **s** portions of food and to celebrate with H8938
Job 14:20 their countenance and **s** them **away**. H8938
Job 21:11 *They* **s forth** their children as a flock; their H8938
Job 38:35 *Do you* **s** the lightning bolts on their way H8938
Ps 20: 2 *May he* **s** you help from the sanctuary H8938
Ps 43: 3 **S** me your light and your faithful care, let H8938
Ps 104:30 *When you* **s** your Spirit, they are created H8938
Ps 144: 6 **S forth lightning** and scatter the H1397+1398
Pr 10:26 so are sluggards to *those who* **s** them. H8938
Pr 24:22 two *will* **s** sudden destruction *on* them, H7756
SS 7:13 The mandrakes **s out** their fragrance, and H5989
Isa 6: 8 voice of the Lord saying, "Whom *shall I* **s**? H8938
Isa 6: 8 And I said, "Here am I. **S** me!" H8938
Isa 10: 6 *I* **s** him against a godless nation, H8938
Isa 10:16 *will* **s** a wasting disease upon his sturdy H8938
Isa 16: 1 **S** lambs as tribute *to* the ruler of the land H8938
Isa 19:20 *he will* **s** them a savior and defender H8938
Isa 30:23 *He will* also **s** you rain for the seed you H5989
Isa 42:19 servant, and deaf like the messenger *I* **s**? H8938
Isa 42:22 with no one to say, "**S** them **back**. H8740
Isa 43:14 "For your sake *I will* **s** to Babylon and H8938
Isa 48:20 **S** it **out** to the ends of the earth; say, "The H3655
Isa 66:19 and *I will* **s** some of those who survive to H8938
Jer 1: 7 must go to everyone *I* **s** you to and say H8938
Jer 2:10 look, **s** *to* Kedar and observe closely H8938
Jer 8:17 I *will* **s** venomous snakes among you H8938
Jer 9:17 to come; **s** for the most skillful of them. H8938
Jer 14: 3 The nobles **s** their servants for water; they H8938
Jer 14:15 I *did* not **s** them, yet they are saying, 'No H8938
Jer 14:22 *Do* the skies *themselves* **s down** showers H5989
Jer 15: 1 people. **S** them **away** from my presence H8938
Jer 15: 3 "*I will* **s** four kinds of destroyers against H7212
Jer 16:16 "But now I *will* **s** for many fishermen," H8938

Jer 16:16 After that *I will* **s** for many hunters, and H8938
Jer 22: 7 *I will* **s** destroyers against you, each man H7727
Jer 23:21 *I did* not **s** these prophets, yet they have H8938
Jer 23:32 yet I *did* not **s** or appoint them. H8938
Jer 24:10 *I will* **s** the sword, famine and plague H8938
Jer 25:15 all the nations to whom I **s** you drink it. H8938
Jer 25:16 of the sword I *will* **s** among them. H8938
Jer 25:27 because of the sword I *will* **s** among you. H8938
Jer 27: 3 Then **s word** to the kings of Edom, Moab H8938
Jer 29:17 "I *will* **s** the sword, famine and plague H8938
Jer 29:31 "**S** this message to all the exiles: 'This is H8938
Jer 29:31 even though I *did* not **s** him, and has H8938
Jer 37:20 *Do* not **s** me **back** *to* the house of H8740
Jer 38:26 the king not *to* **s** me **back** *to* Jonathan's H8740
Jer 43:10 I *will* **s for** my servant H8938+2256+4374
Jer 48:12 "when *I will* **s** men who pour from pitchers H8938
Jer 51: 2 *I will* **s** foreigners to Babylon to winnow H8938
Jer 51:27 **s up** horses like a swarm of locusts. H6590
Jer 51:53 I *will* **s** destroyers against her," H995+4946+907
Eze 5:17 *I will* **s** famine and wild beasts against you H8938
Eze 13:11 and *I will* **s** hailstones hurtling down H5989
Eze 14:13 its food supply and **s** famine upon it and H8938
Eze 14:15 "Or if *I* **s** wild beasts through that country H6296
Eze 14:19 "Or if *I* **s** a plague into that land and pour H8938
Eze 14:21 worse will it be *when I* **s** against H8938
Eze 28:23 *I will* **s** a plague upon you and make H8938
Eze 34:26 *I will* **s down** showers in season; there will H3718
Eze 39: 2 from the far north and **s** you against the H995
Eze 39: 6 *I will* **s** fire on Magog and on those who H8938
Da 11:20 "His successor *will* **s out** a tax collector to H6296
Hos 8:14 But *I will* **s** fire on their cities that will H8938
Hos 14: 5 cedar of Lebanon *he will* **s down** his roots; H5782
Joel 3: 6 that *you might* **s** them **far** from their H8178
Am 1: 4 *I will* **s** fire on the house of Hazael that H8938
Am 1: 7 *I will* **s** fire on the walls of Gaza that will H8938
Am 1:10 *I will* **s** fire on the walls of Tyre that will H8938
Am 1:12 *I will* **s** fire on Teman that will consume H8938
Am 2: 2 *I will* **s** fire on Moab that will consume the H8938
Am 2: 5 *I will* **s** fire on Judah that will consume H8938
Am 5:27 Therefore *I will* **s** you **into exile** beyond H1655
Am 8:11 "when *I will* **s** a famine through the land H8938
Zec 5: 4 declares, '*I will* **s** it **out**, and it will enter H3655
Mal 2: 2 LORD Almighty, "*I will* **s** a curse on you H8938
Mal 3: 1 "I *will* **s** my messenger, who will prepare H8938
Mal 4: 5 I *will* **s** the prophet Elijah to you before H8938
Mt 4:19 "and *I will* **s** you **out** to fish for people." *G4472*
Mt 8:31 you drive us out, **s** us into the herd of pigs." *G690*
Mt 9:38 to **s out** workers into his harvest field." *G1675*
Mt 11:10 " 'I *will* **s** my messenger ahead of you, who *G690*
Mt 13:41 The Son of Man *will* **s out** his angels, and *G690*
Mt 14:15 **S** the crowds **away**, so they can go to the *G668*
Mt 15:23 urged him, "**S** her **away**, for she keeps *G668*
Mt 15:32 I do not want *to* **s** them **away** hungry, or *G668*
Mt 19: 7 wife a certificate of divorce and **s** her **away**?" *G668*
Mt 21: 3 needs them, and *he will* **s** them right away." *G690*
Mt 24:31 And *he will* **s** his angels with a loud *G690*
Mk 1: 2 "*I will* **s** my messenger ahead of you, who *G690*
Mk 1:17 "and *I will* **s** you **out** to fish for people." *G4472*
Mk 3:14 that *he might* **s** them **out** to preach *G690*
Mk 5:10 again not to **s** them out of the area. *G690*
Mk 5:12 begged Jesus, "**S** us among the pigs *G4287*
Mk 6: 7 he began *to* **s** them **out** two by two and *G690*
Mk 6:36 **S** the people **away** so that they can go to *G668*
Mk 8: 3 If *I* **s** them home hungry, they will collapse *G668*
Mk 10: 4 a certificate of divorce and **s** her **away**." *G668*
Mk 11: 3 Lord needs it and *will* **s** it back here shortly. *G690*
Mk 12: 6 "He had one left to **s**, a son, whom he loved NDT
Mk 13:27 And *he will* **s** his angels and gather his *G690*
Lk 7:27 " '*I will* **s** my messenger ahead of you, who *G690*
Lk 9:12 "**S** the crowd **away** so they can go to the *G668*
Lk 10: 2 to **s out** workers into his harvest field. *G1675*
Lk 11:49 '*I will* **s** them prophets and apostles *G690*
Lk 14:32 *he will* **s** a delegation while the other is *G690*
Lk 16:24 have pity on me and **s** Lazarus to dip the *G4287*
Lk 16:27 I beg you, father, **s** Lazarus to my family, *G4287*
Lk 20:13 *I will* **s** my son, whom I love; perhaps they *G4287*
Lk 24:49 I *am going to* **s** you what my Father has *G690*
Jn 3:17 For God *did* not **s** his Son into the world to *G690*
Jn 13:20 whoever accepts anyone *I* **s** accepts me *G4287*
Jn 14:26 whom the Father *will* **s** in my name, will *G4287*
Jn 15:26 whom I *will* **s** to you from the Father *G4287*
Jn 16: 7 but if I go, *I will* **s** him to you. *G4287*
Ac 3:20 that *he may* **s** the Messiah, who has *G690*
Ac 7:34 Now come, *I will* **s** you back to Egypt.' *G690*
Ac 7:43 Therefore *I will* **s** you **into exile**' beyond *G3579*
Ac 10: 5 Now **s** men to Joppa to bring back a man *G4287*
Ac 10:32 **S** to Joppa for Simon who is called Peter *G4287*
Ac 11:13 'S to Joppa for Simon who is called Peter. *G690*
Ac 15:22 their own men and **s** them to Antioch with *G4287*
Ac 15:25 choose some men and **s** them to you with *G4287*
Ac 22:21 I *will* **s** you far **away** to the Gentiles. *G1990*
Ac 24:25 I find it convenient, *I will* **s for** you." *G3559*
Ac 25:21 him held until *I could* **s** him to Caesar." *G402*
Ac 25:25 the Emperor I decided *to* **s** him to Rome. *G4287*
Ac 25:27 it is unreasonable *to* **s** a prisoner on to *G4287*
Ro 16:16 All the churches of Christ **s greetings**. *G832*
Ro 16:23 our brother Quartus **s** you *their* **greetings**. *G832*
1Co 1:17 For Christ *did* not **s** me to baptize, but to *G690*
1Co 16: 3 *I will* give letters of introduction to the men
you approve and **s** *G4287*
1Co 16:11 **S** him **on** his **way** in peace so that he may *G4636*
1Co 16:19 in the province of Asia **s** you **greetings**. *G832*
1Co 16:20 brothers and sisters here **s** you **greetings**. *G832*
2Co 1:16 then *to have* you **s** me **on** my **way** to *G4636*
2Co 13:13 All God's people here **s** *their* **greetings**. *G832*
Php 2:19 in the Lord Jesus *to* **s** Timothy to you soon *G4287*
Php 2:23 *to* **s** him as soon as I see how things go *G4287*
Php 2:25 I think it is necessary *to* **s** back to you *G4287*
Php 2:28 I am all the more eager *to* **s** him, *G4287*
Php 4:21 sisters who are with me **s greetings**. *G832*
Php 4:22 All God's people here **s** you **greetings** *G832*
Col 4:14 the doctor, and Demas **s greetings**. *G832*
Titus 3:12 As soon as *I* **s** Artemas or Tychicus to you *G4287*
Heb 13:24 Those from Italy **s** you *their* **greetings**. *G832*
2Jn 13 who is chosen by God, **s** *their* **greetings**. *G832*
3Jn 6 Please **s** them **on** their **way** in a *G4472+4636*
3Jn 14 The friends here **s** *their* **greetings**. Greet *G832*
Rev 1:11 scroll what you see and **s** it to the seven *G4287*

SENDING (44) [SEND]

Ge 32: 5 Now *I am* **s** this message to my lord, that I H8938
Ge 32:20 him with these gifts *I am* **s on** ahead; H2143
Ex 3:10 *I am* **s** you to Pharaoh to bring my people H8938
Ex 23:20 I *am* **s** an angel ahead of you to guard H8938
Lev 16:10 making atonement by **s** it into the H8938
Jdg 6:14 out of Midian's hand. *Am I* not **s** you?" H8938
1Sa 6: 8 gold objects *you are* **s back** to him as a H8740
1Sa 16: 1 *I am* **s** you to Jesse of Bethlehem. H8938
1Sa 21: 2 anything about the mission *I am* **s** you *on*. H8938
2Sa 10: 3 honoring your father by **s** envoys to you to H8938
2Sa 13:16 "**S** me **away** would be a greater wrong H8938
1Ki 15:19 *I am* **s** you a gift of silver and gold H8938
2Ki 1: 6 in Israel that you *are* **s** messengers to H8938
2Ki 5: 6 this letter *I am* **s** my servant Naaman H8938
2Ki 6:32 how this murderer *is* **s** someone to cut off H8938
1Ch 19: 3 honoring your father by **s** envoys to you to H8938
2Ch 2:13 "*I am* **s** you Huram-Abi, a man of great H8938
2Ch 16: 3 See, *I am* **s** you silver and gold H8938
Ezr 4:14 *we are* **s** *this* **message** to inform the king, A10714
Ne 6:17 nobles of Judah were **s** many letters to H2143
Pr 26: 6 **S** a message by the hands of a fool is like H8938
Jer 42: 6 our God, to whom we *are* **s** you, so that it H8938
Eze 2: 3 "Son of man, I *am* **s** you to the Israelites H8938
Eze 2: 4 people to whom I *am* **s** you are obstinate H8938
Eze 17:15 him by **s** his envoys *to* Egypt to get H8938
Joel 2:13 and he relents from **s** calamity. NDT
Joel 2:19 "I *am* **s** you grain, new wine and olive oil H8938
Jnh 4: 2 a God who relents from **s** calamity. NDT
Mt 10:16 "I *am* **s** you **out** like sheep among wolves *G690*
Mt 23:34 Therefore I *am* **s** you prophets and sages *G690*
Lk 10: 3 *I am* **s** you **out** like lambs among wolves. *G690*
Jn 20:21 As the Father has sent me, I *am* **s** you." *G4287*
Ac 11:30 **s** their gift to the elders by Barnabas and *G690*
Ac 15:27 Therefore *we are* **s** Judas and Silas to *G690*
Ac 26:17 from the Gentiles. I *am* **s** you to them *G690*
Ro 8: 3 God did *by* **s** his own Son in the likeness *G4287*
2Co 8:18 And *we are* **s along** with him the brother *G5225*
2Co 8:22 *we are* **s with** them our brother who has *G5225*
2Co 9: 3 But *I am* **s** the brothers in order that our *G4287*
Eph 6:22 *I am* **s** him to you for this very purpose *G4287*
Col 4: 8 *I am* **s** him to you for the express purpose *G4287*
Phm 12 *I am* **s** him—who is my very heart—**back** to *G402*
Rev 1: 1 He made it known *by* **s** his angel to his *G690*
Rev 11:10 will celebrate *by* **s** each other gifts, *G4287*

SENDS (32) [SEND]

Dt 24: 1 gives it to her and **s** her from his house, H8938
Dt 24: 3 gives it to her and **s** her from his house, or H8938
Dt 28:48 serve the enemies the LORD **s** against you. H8938
1Sa 2: 7 The LORD **s poverty** and wealth; he H3769
1Ki 17:14 until the day the LORD **s** rain on the land. H5989
Job 5:10 the earth; *he* **s** water on the countryside. H8938
Job 37: 3 the whole heaven and **s** it to the ends of the NDT
Ps 57: 3 *He* **s** from heaven and saves me, rebuking H8938
Ps 57: 3 God **s forth** his love and his faithfulness. H8938
Ps 135: 7 *he* **s** lightning with the rain and brings out H6913
Ps 147:15 He **s** his command *to* the earth; his word H8938
Ps 147:18 *He* **s** his word and melts them; he stirs up H8938
Pr 25:13 messenger to the *one who* **s** him; H8938
Isa 18: 2 which **s** envoys by sea in papyrus boats H8938
Jer 10:13 *He* **s** lightning with the rain and brings H6913
Jer 17: 8 by the water *that* **s out** its roots by the H8938
Jer 42: 5 the LORD your God **s** you to tell us. H8938
Jer 51:16 *He* **s** lightning with the rain and brings H6913
Hos 12: 1 treaty with Assyria and **s** olive oil to Egypt. H3297
Joel 2:23 *He* **s** you abundant showers, both autumn H3718
Zec 10: 1 it is the LORD *who* **s** the thunderstorms. H6913
Zec 12: 2 to make Jerusalem a **cup** *that* **s** all the AIT
Mt 5:45 and **s rain** on the righteous and the *G1101*
Ro 16:21 my co-worker, **s** *his* **greetings** to you, as do *G832*
Ro 16:23 church here enjoy, **s** you *his* **greetings**. *G832*
Col 4:10 prisoner Aristarchus **s** you *his* **greetings**, *G832*
Col 4:11 is called Justus, also **s** greetings. These are NDT
Col 4:12 a servant of Christ Jesus, **s greetings**. *G832*
2Th 2:11 For this reason God **s** them a powerful *G4287*
Titus 3:15 Everyone with me **s** you **greetings**. Greet *G832*
Phm 23 prisoner in Christ Jesus, **s** you **greetings**. *G832*
1Pe 5:13 with you, **s** you *her* **greetings**, and so does *G832*

SENEH (1)

1Sa 14: 4 one was called Bozez and the other **S**. H6175

SENIOR (1)

Ge 24: 2 He said to the **s** servant *in* his household H2418

SENIR (4) [HERMON]

Dt 3: 9 by the Sidonians; the Amorites call it **S**.) H8536
1Ch 5:23 Hermon, that is, to **S** (Mount Hermon). H8536
SS 4: 8 from the top of **S**, the summit of Hermon, H8536
Eze 27: 5 made all your timbers of juniper from **S**; H8536

SENNACHERIB (15) [SENNACHERIB'S]

2Ki 18:13 **S** king of Assyria attacked all the fortified H6178
2Ki 19: 9 Now **S** received a report that Tirhakah, the NDT
2Ki 19:16 listen to the words **S** has sent to ridicule H6178
2Ki 19:20 your prayer concerning **S** king of Assyria. H6178
2Ki 19:36 So **S** king of Assyria broke camp and H6178
2Ch 32: 1 **S** king of Assyria came and invaded H6178
2Ch 32: 2 Hezekiah saw that **S** had come and that H6178
2Ch 32: 9 when **S** king of Assyria and all his forces H6178
2Ch 32:10 "This is what **S** king of Assyria says: On H6178
2Ch 32:22 from the hand of **S** king of Assyria and H6178
Isa 36: 1 **S** king of Assyria attacked all the fortified H6178
Isa 37: 9 Now **S** received a report that Tirhakah, the NDT
Isa 37:17 to all the words **S** has sent to ridicule H6178
Isa 37:21 to me concerning **S** king of Assyria, H6178
Isa 37:37 So **S** king of Assyria broke camp and H6178

SENNACHERIB'S (1) [SENNACHERIB]

2Ch 32:16 **S** officers spoke further against the LORD H2257S

SENSE (17) [SENSED, SENSELESS, SENSES, SENSIBLE, SENSITIVE, SENSITIVITY]

Dt 32:28 They are a nation without **s**, there is no H6783
Job 39:17 wisdom or give her a share of **good s**. H1069
Pr 6:32 But a man who commits adultery has no **s**; H4213
Pr 7: 7 the young men, a youth who had no **s**. H4213
Pr 9: 4 To those who have no **s** she says, H4213
Pr 9:16 To those who **have** no **s** she says, H4213
Pr 10:13 a rod is for the back of one who has no **s**. H4213
Pr 10:21 nourish many, but fools die for lack of **s**. H4213
Pr 11:12 Whoever derides their neighbor has no **s** H4213
Pr 12:11 those who chase fantasies have no **s**. H4213
Pr 15:21 Folly brings joy to one who has no **s**, but H4213
Pr 17:18 One who has no **s** shakes hands in H4213
Pr 24:30 the vineyard of someone who has no **s**; H4213
Ecc 10: 3 they lack **s** and show everyone how stupid H4213
Hos 13:13 he doesn't have the **s** to come out of the NDT
1Co 12:17 where would the **s of hearing** be? *G198*
1Co 12:17 where would the **s of smell** be? *G4018*

SENSED (1) [SENSE]

Ac 27:27 *when* about midnight the sailors **s** they *G5706*

SENSELESS (12) [SENSE]

Ps 49:10 that the foolish and the **s** also perish H1280
Ps 73:22 I was **s** and ignorant; I was a brute beast H1280
Ps 92: 6 **S** people do not know, fools do not H1280
Ps 94: 8 you **s** *ones* among the people H1279
Isa 19:11 wise counselors of Pharaoh **give s** advice. H1279
Jer 4:22 They are **s** children; they have no H6119
Jer 5:21 you foolish and **s** people, who have H401+4213
Jer 10: 8 *They are* all **s** and foolish; they are taught H1279
Jer 10:14 Everyone *is* **s** and without knowledge H1279
Jer 10:21 The shepherds *are* **s** and do not inquire of H1279
Jer 51:17 "Everyone *is* **s** and without knowledge H1279
Hos 7:11 easily deceived and **s**—now calling H401+4213

SENSES (3) [SENSE]

Lk 15:17 "When he came to **his s**, he said, 'How *G1571*
1Co 15:34 **Come back to** *your* **s** as you ought, and *G1729*
2Ti 2:26 and *that they will* **come to** *their* **s** and *G392*

SENSIBLE (2) [SENSE]

Job 18: 2 these speeches? *Be* **s**, and then we can H1067
1Co 10:15 I speak *to* **s** *people*; judge for yourselves *G5861*

SENSITIVE (3) [SENSE]

Dt 28:54 most gentle and **s** man among you will H6697
Dt 28:56 most gentle and **s** *woman* among you— H6697
Dt 28:56 so **s** and gentle that she would not venture H6695

SENSITIVITY (1) [SENSE]

Eph 4:19 *Having* **lost all s**, they have given *G556*

SENSUAL (2) [SENSUALITY]

Col 2:23 lack any value in restraining **s** indulgence. *G4922*
1Ti 5:11 *their* **s desires overcome** *their* **dedication** *G2952*

SENSUALITY (1) [SENSUAL]

Eph 4:19 themselves over *to* **s** so as to indulge in *G816*

SENT (652) [SEND]

Ge 2: 5 the LORD God *had* not **s rain** on the earth H4763
Ge 8: 1 in the ark, and he **s** a wind over the earth H6296
Ge 8: 7 and **s out** a raven, and it kept flying back H8938
Ge 8: 8 Then *he* **s out** a dove to see if the water H8938
Ge 8:10 days and again **s out** the dove from the H8938
Ge 8:12 more days and **s** the dove **out** again, H8938
Ge 12:20 and *they* **s** him **on** his **way**, with H8938+906
Ge 19:13 is so great that he *has* **s** us to destroy it." H8938
Ge 20: 2 king of Gerar **s for** Sarah and took her. H8938
Ge 21:14 shoulders and then **s** her **off** with the boy. H8938
Ge 24:59 So *they* **s** their sister Rebekah **on** her **way** H8938
Ge 25: 6 concubines and **s** them **away** from his son H8938
Ge 26:27 you were hostile to me and **s** me away?" H8938
Ge 26:29 you well and **s** you **away** peacefully. H8938
Ge 26:31 Then Isaac **s** them **on** their **way**, and they H8938

Ge 27:42 *she* **s for** her younger son H8938+2256+7924
Ge 28: 5 Then Isaac **s** Jacob **on** *his* **way**, and he H8938
Ge 28: 6 blessed Jacob and *had* **s** him to Paddan H8938
Ge 31: 4 So Jacob **s word** to Rachel H8938+2256+7924
Ge 31:42 *you would* surely *have* **s** me **away** H8938
Ge 32: 3 Jacob **s** messengers ahead of him to his H8938
Ge 32:18 They are a gift **s** to my lord Esau, and he H8938
Ge 32:23 After *he had* **s** them **across** the stream, he H6296
Ge 32:23 the stream, *he* **s over** all his possessions. H6296
Ge 37:14 Then *he* **s** him **off** from the Valley of H8938
Ge 38:20 Meanwhile Judah **s** the young goat by his H8938
Ge 38:25 she **s a message** to her father-in-law. H8938
Ge 41: 8 so *he* **s for** all the magicians H8938+2256+7924
Ge 41:14 So Pharaoh **s for** Joseph H8938+2256+7924
Ge 44: 3 the men **were s on** *their* **way** with their H8938
Ge 45: 5 to save lives *that* God **s** me ahead of you. H8938
Ge 45: 7 But God **s** me ahead of you to preserve H8938
Ge 45: 8 it was not you *who* **s** me here, but God. H8938
Ge 45:23 And this is what *he* **s** to his father: ten H8938
Ge 45:24 Then *he* **s** his brothers **away**, and as they H8938
Ge 45:27 the carts Joseph *had* **s** to carry him back, H8938
Ge 46: 5 carts that Pharaoh *had* **s** to transport him. H8938
Ge 46:28 Now Jacob **s** Judah ahead of him to H8938
Ge 50:16 So *they* **s word** to Joseph, saying, "Your H7422
Ex 2: 5 the reeds and **s** her female slave to H8938
Ex 3:12 the sign to you that it is I *who have* **s** you: H8938
Ex 3:13 'The God of your fathers *has* **s** me to you,' H8938
Ex 3:14 to the Israelites: 'I AM *has* **s** me to you.'" H8938
Ex 3:15 the God of Jacob—*has* **s** me to you. H8938
Ex 4:28 everything the LORD *had* **s** him to say, H8938
Ex 5:22 on this people? Is this why *you* **s** me? H8938
Ex 7:16 of the Hebrews, *has* **s** me to say to you: H8938
Ex 9:23 the LORD **s** thunder and hail, and H5989
Ex 18: 2 After Moses had **s away** his wife Zipporah, H8933
Ex 18: 6 Jethro *had* **s word** to him, "I, your H606
Ex 18:27 Moses **s** his father-in-law **on** *his* **way**, H8938
Ex 24: 5 Then *he* **s** young Israelite men, and they H8938
Ex 36: 6 and *they* **s** this word **throughout** the camp H6296
Lev 26:41 toward them so that *I* **s** them into the land H995
Nu 5: 4 *they* **s** them outside the camp. H8938
Nu 13: 3 command Moses **s** them **out** from the H8938
Nu 13:16 of the men Moses **s** to explore the land. H8938
Nu 13:17 When Moses **s** them to explore Canaan H8938
Nu 13:27 "We went into the land *to* which *you* **s** us H8938
Nu 14:36 So the men Moses *had* **s** to explore the H8938
Nu 16:28 know that the LORD *has* **s** me to do all H8938
Nu 16:29 all mankind, then the LORD *has* not **s** me. H8938
Nu 20:14 Moses **s** messengers from Kadesh to the H8938
Nu 20:16 heard our cry and **s** an angel and brought H8938
Nu 21: 6 Then the LORD **s** venomous snakes among H8938
Nu 21:21 Israel **s** messengers to say to Sihon king H8938
Nu 21:32 After Moses *had* **s** spies *to* Jazer, the H8938
Nu 22: 5 **s** messengers to summon Balaam son of H8938
Nu 22:10 king of Moab, **s** me *this* **message**: H8938
Nu 22:15 Then Balak **s** other officials, more H8938
Nu 24:12 "Did I not tell the messengers *you* **s** me, H8938
Nu 31: 6 Moses **s** them into battle, a thousand from H8938
Nu 32: 8 fathers did when I **s** them from Kadesh H8938
Dt 2:26 Desert of Kedemoth *I* **s** messengers to H8938
Dt 6:22 our eyes the LORD **s** signs and wonders— H5989
Dt 9:23 And when the LORD **s** you out from Kadesh H8938
Dt 19:12 the killer *shall be* **s** *for* by the town elders H8938
Dt 24: 5 *he must* not *be* **s** to war or have any other H3655
Dt 34:11 wonders the LORD **s** him to do in Egypt— H8938
Jos 2: 1 son of Nun secretly **s** two spies from H8938
Jos 2: 3 king of Jericho **s** *this* **message** to Rahab: H8938
Jos 2:21 So *she* **s** them **away**, and they H8938
Jos 6:17 because she hid the spies *we* **s**. H8938
Jos 6:25 hid the men Joshua *had* **s** as spies to H8938
Jos 7: 2 Now Joshua **s** men from Jericho to Ai H8938
Jos 7:22 So Joshua **s** messengers, and they ran to H8938
Jos 8: 3 best fighting men and **s** them **out** at night H8938
Jos 8: 9 Then Joshua **s** them **off**, and they went to H8938
Jos 10: 6 The Gibeonites then **s** word to Joshua in H8938
Jos 11: 1 *he* **s word** to Jobab king of Madon H8938
Jos 14: 7 servant of the LORD **s** me from Kadesh H8938
Jos 14:11 strong today as the day Moses **s** me **out**; H8938
Jos 22: 6 Joshua blessed them and **s** them **away**, H8938
Jos 22: 7 When Joshua **s** them home, he blessed H8938
Jos 22:13 So the Israelites **s** Phinehas son of H8938
Jos 22:14 With him they **s** ten of the chief men, one NDT
Jos 24: 5 " 'Then *I* **s** Moses and Aaron, and I H8938
Jos 24: 9 *he* **s for** Balaam son of H8938+2256+7924+4200
Jos 24:12 *I* **s** the hornet ahead of you, which drove H8938
Jdg 1:23 When they **s** *men* **to spy out** Bethel H9365
Jdg 3:15 The Israelites **s** him with tribute to Eglon H8938
Jdg 3:18 *he* **s on** their **way** those who had carried it. H8938
Jdg 4: 6 *She* **s for** Barak son of H8938+2256+7924+4200
Jdg 5:15 **s** under his command into the valley. H8938
Jdg 6: 8 he **s** them a prophet, who said, "This is H8938
Jdg 6:35 *He* **s** messengers throughout Manasseh H8938
Jdg 7: 8 So Gideon **s** the rest of the Israelites home H8938
Jdg 7:24 Gideon **s** messengers throughout the hill H8938
Jdg 9:31 Under cover *he* **s** messengers to Abimelek H8938
Jdg 11:12 Then Jephthah **s** messengers to the H8938
Jdg 11:14 Jephthah **s** back messengers to the H8938
Jdg 11:17 Then Israel **s** messengers to the king of H8938
Jdg 11:17 *They* **s** also to the king of Moab, and he H8938
Jdg 11:19 "Then Israel **s** messengers to Sihon king H8938
Jdg 11:28 attention to the message Jephthah **s** him. H8938
Jdg 13: 8 the man of God *you* **s** to us come again H8938
Jdg 16:18 *she* **s** word to the rulers of the Philistines H8938
Jdg 18: 2 So the Danites **s** five of their leading men H8938
Jdg 19:25 his concubine and **s** her outside to them, H3655
Jdg 19:29 into twelve parts and **s** them into all the H8938
Jdg 20: 6 her into pieces and **s** one piece to each H8938
Jdg 20:12 The tribes of Israel **s** messengers H8938
Jdg 21:10 So the assembly **s** twelve thousand H8938
Jdg 21:13 the whole assembly **s** an offer of peace to H8938
1Sa 4: 4 So the people **s** men to Shiloh, and they H8938
1Sa 4:13 had happened, the whole town **s up a cry**. H2410
1Sa 5:10 So *they* **s** the ark of God to Ekron. As the H8938
1Sa 6:17 the Philistines **s** as a guilt offering to H8740
1Sa 6:21 Then *they* **s** messengers to the people of H8938
1Sa 11: 7 **s** the pieces by messengers H8938
1Sa 12: 8 and the LORD **s** Moses and Aaron H8938
1Sa 12:11 Then the LORD **s** Jerub-Baal, Barak H8938
1Sa 12:18 same day the LORD **s** thunder and rain. H5989
1Sa 13: 2 rest of the men *he* **s back** to their homes. H8938
1Sa 14:15 the ground shook. It was a **panic** *s by* God. AIT
1Sa 15: 1 am the one the LORD **s** to anoint you king H8938
1Sa 15:18 And he **s** you on a mission, saying, 'Go H8938
1Sa 16:12 So *he* **s** *for* him and had him brought in H8938
1Sa 16:19 Then Saul **s** messengers to Jesse and H8938
1Sa 16:20 a young goat and **s** them with his son H8938
1Sa 16:22 Then Saul **s word** to Jesse, saying, "Allow H8938
1Sa 17:31 reported to Saul, and Saul **s for** him. H4374
1Sa 18: 5 Whatever mission Saul **s** him on, David H8938
1Sa 18:13 So he **s** David **away** from him and gave H6073
1Sa 19:11 Saul **s** men to David's house to watch it H8938
1Sa 19:14 When Saul **s** the men to capture David H8938
1Sa 19:15 Then Saul **s** the men **back** to see David H8938
1Sa 19:20 so he **s** men to capture him. But when they H8938
1Sa 19:21 told about it, and *he* **s** more men, and H8938
1Sa 19:21 Saul **s** men a third time, and they also H8938
1Sa 20:22 because the LORD *has* **s** you **away**. H8938
1Sa 21: 2 "The king **s** me on a mission and said to H7422
1Sa 22:11 Then the king **s for** the priest H8938+4200+7924
1Sa 25: 5 So he **s** ten young men and said to them H8938
1Sa 25:14 "David **s** messengers from the wilderness H8938
1Sa 25:25 servant, I did not see the men my lord **s**. H8938
1Sa 25:32 who *has* **s** you today to meet me. H8938
1Sa 25:39 Then David **s word** to Abigail, asking her H8938
1Sa 25:40 "David *has* **s** us to you to take you to H8938
1Sa 26: 4 he **s out** scouts and learned that Saul had H8938
1Sa 30:26 *he* **s** some of the plunder to the elders of H8938
1Sa 30:27 David **s** it to those who were in Bethel NDT
1Sa 31: 9 and *they* **s** messengers throughout the H8938
2Sa 2: 5 he **s** messengers to them to say to them H8938
2Sa 3:12 Then Abner **s** messengers on his behalf H8938
2Sa 3:14 Then David **s** messengers to Ish-Bosheth H8938
2Sa 3:21 So David **s** Abner **away**, and he went in H8938
2Sa 3:22 because David *had* **s** him **away**, and he H8938
2Sa 3:23 that the king *had* **s** him **away** and that he H8938
2Sa 3:26 then left David and **s** messengers after H8938
2Sa 5:11 Now Hiram king of Tyre **s** envoys to David H8938
2Sa 8:10 he **s** his son Joram to King David to greet H8938
2Sa 10: 2 So David **s** a delegation to express his H8938
2Sa 10: 3 Hasn't David **s** them to you only to H8938
2Sa 10: 4 at the buttocks, and **s** them **away**. H8938
2Sa 10: 5 *he* **s** messengers to meet the men H8938
2Sa 10: 7 David **s** Joab **out** with the entire army of H8938
2Sa 11: 1 David **s** Joab **out** with the king's men and H8938
2Sa 11: 3 David **s** someone to find out about H8938
2Sa 11: 4 Then David **s** messengers to get her. H8938
2Sa 11: 5 and **s word** to David, H8938+2256+5583
2Sa 11: 6 So David **s** *this* **word** to Joab: "Send me H8938
2Sa 11: 6 And Joab **s** him to David. H8938
2Sa 11: 8 a gift from the king *was* **s** after him. H3655
2Sa 11:14 wrote a letter to Joab and **s** it with Uriah. H8938
2Sa 11:18 Joab **s** David a full account of the battle. H8938
2Sa 11:22 David everything Joab *had* **s** him to say. H8938
2Sa 12: 1 The LORD **s** Nathan to David. When he H8938
2Sa 12:25 *he* **s word** through Nathan the prophet to H8938
2Sa 12:27 Joab then **s** messengers to David, saying H8938
2Sa 13: 7 David **s** word to Tamar at the palace: "Go H8938
2Sa 13:27 so *he* **s** with him Amnon and the rest of H8938
2Sa 14: 2 So Joab **s** someone to Tekoa and had a H8938
2Sa 14:29 Then Absalom **s** for Joab in order to send H8938
2Sa 14:29 So *he* **s** a second time, but he refused to H8938
2Sa 14:32 *I* **s word** to you and said, 'Come H8938
2Sa 15:10 Then Absalom **s** secret messengers H8938
2Sa 15:12 he also **s** *for* Ahithophel the Gilonite H8938
2Sa 18: 2 David **s out** his troops, a third under the H8938
2Sa 19:11 King David **s** this message to Zadok and H8938
2Sa 19:14 *They* **s word** to the king, "Return, you and H8938
2Sa 24:13 how I should answer the *one who* **s** me." H8938
2Sa 24:15 So the LORD **s** a plague on Israel from that H5989
1Ki 1:44 The king *has* **s** with him Zadok the priest H8938
1Ki 1:53 Then King Solomon **s** men, and they H8938
1Ki 2:36 the king **s for** Shimei H8938+2256+7924+4200
1Ki 4:34 **s by** all the kings of the world H4946+907
1Ki 5: 1 father David, *he* **s** his envoys to Solomon H8938
1Ki 5: 2 Solomon **s back** this message to Hiram: H8938
1Ki 5: 8 So Hiram **s** word to Solomon: "I have H8938
1Ki 5: 8 the message *you* **s** me and will do all H8938
1Ki 5:14 *He* **s** them **off** to Lebanon in shifts of ten H8938
1Ki 7:13 King Solomon **s** to Tyre and brought H8938
1Ki 8:66 the following day *he* **s** the people **away**. H8938
1Ki 9:14 Now Hiram *had* **s** to the king 120 talents H8938
1Ki 9:27 And Hiram **s** his men—sailors who knew H8938
1Ki 12: 3 So *they* **s for** Jeroboam H8938+2256+7924+4200
1Ki 12:18 King Rehoboam **s out** Adoniram, who was H8938
1Ki 12:20 *they* **s** and called him to the assembly H8938
1Ki 14: 6 I *have* **been s** to you *with* bad news. H8938
1Ki 15:18 to his officials and **s** them to Ben-Hadad H8938
1Ki 15:20 with King Asa and **s** the commanders of H8938
1Ki 18:10 where my master *has* not **s** someone to H8938
1Ki 18:20 So Ahab **s word** throughout all Israel and H8938
1Ki 19: 2 So Jezebel **s** a messenger to Elijah to say H8938
1Ki 20: 2 *He* **s** messengers into the city to Ahab king H8938
1Ki 20: 5 '*I* **s** to demand your silver and gold, your H8938
1Ki 20: 7 When *he* **s** for my wives and my children H8938
1Ki 20:10 Then Ben-Hadad **s** another message to H8938
1Ki 21: 8 **s** them to the elders and nobles who H8938
1Ki 21:14 Then *they* **s** word to Jezebel: "Naboth has H8938
2Ki 1: 2 So *he* **s** messengers, saying to them, "Go H8938
2Ki 1: 6 back to the king who **s** you and tell him, H8938
2Ki 1: 9 Then *he* **s** to Elijah a captain with his H8938
2Ki 1:11 At this the king **s** to Elijah another captain H8938
2Ki 1:13 So the king **s** a third captain with his fifty H8938
2Ki 1:16 to consult that *you have* **s** messengers to H8938
2Ki 2: 2 "Stay here; the LORD *has* **s** me to Bethel." H8938
2Ki 2: 4 Elisha; the LORD *has* **s** me *to* Jericho." H8938
2Ki 2: 6 the LORD *has* **s** me to the Jordan. H8938
2Ki 2:17 And *they* **s** fifty men, who searched for H8938
2Ki 3: 7 *He* also **s** this message to Jehoshaphat H8938
2Ki 5: 8 torn his robes, *he* **s** him this message: H8938
2Ki 5:10 Elisha **s** a messenger to say to him, "Go H8938
2Ki 5:22 "My master **s** me to say, 'Two young men H8938
2Ki 5:24 *He* **s** the men **away** and they left H8938
2Ki 6: 9 The man of God **s** word to the king of H8938
2Ki 6:14 Then *he* **s** horses and chariots and a H8938
2Ki 6:23 drinking, *he* **s** them **away**, and they H8938
2Ki 6:32 The king **s** a messenger ahead, but H8938
2Ki 7:14 the king **s** them after the Aramean H8938
2Ki 8: 9 Ben-Hadad king of Aram *has* **s** me to ask, H8938
2Ki 9:19 So the king **s out** a second horseman H8938
2Ki 10: 1 Jehu wrote letters and **s** them *to* Samaria: H8938
2Ki 10: 5 the guardians **s** this message to Jehu H8938
2Ki 10: 7 heads in baskets and **s** them to Jehu in H8938
2Ki 10:21 Then he **s word** throughout Israel, and all H8938
2Ki 11: 4 year Jehoiada **s for** the H8938+2256+4374
2Ki 12:18 and *he* **s** them to Hazael king of Aram H8938
2Ki 14: 8 Then Amaziah **s** messengers to Jehoash H8938
2Ki 14: 9 thistle in Lebanon **s** a message to a cedar H8938
2Ki 14:19 but *they* **s** men after him to Lachish and H8938
2Ki 16: 7 Ahaz **s** messengers to say to H8938
2Ki 16: 8 of the royal palace and **s** it as a gift to the H8938
2Ki 16:10 in Damascus and **s** to Uriah the priest a H8938
2Ki 16:11 that King Ahaz *had* **s** from Damascus and H8938
2Ki 17: 4 for *he had* **s** envoys to So king of Egypt H8938
2Ki 17:25 so he **s** lions among them and they killed H8938
2Ki 17:26 *He has* **s** lions among them, which are H8938
2Ki 18:14 king of Judah **s** this message to the H8938
2Ki 18:17 The king of Assyria **s** his supreme H8938
2Ki 18:27 you that my master **s** me to say these H8938
2Ki 19: 2 *He* **s** Eliakim the palace administrator H8938
2Ki 19: 4 of Assyria, *has* **s** to ridicule the living God H8938
2Ki 19: 9 So he again **s** messengers to Hezekiah H8938
2Ki 19:16 words Sennacherib *has* **s** to ridicule the H8938
2Ki 19:20 Isaiah son of Amoz **s** a message to H8938
2Ki 20:12 king of Babylon **s** Hezekiah letters and a H8938
2Ki 22: 3 **s** the secretary, Shaphan son of Azaliah, the son of Meshullam, *to* H8938
2Ki 22:15 Tell the man who **s** you to me, H8938
2Ki 22:18 of Judah, who **s** you to inquire of the LORD H8938
2Ki 24: 2 The LORD **s** Babylonian, Aramean, Moabite H8938
1Ch 6:15 LORD **s** Judah and Jerusalem **into exile** by H1655
1Ch 10: 9 and **s messengers** throughout the land of H8938
1Ch 12:19 after consultation, their rulers **s** him **away**. H8938
1Ch 14: 1 Hiram king of Tyre **s** messengers to David, H8938
1Ch 18:10 *he* **s** his son Hadoram to King David to H8938
1Ch 19: 2 So David **s** a delegation to express his H8938
1Ch 19: 4 at the buttocks, and **s** them **away**. H8938
1Ch 19: 5 the men, *he* **s** messengers to meet them H8938
1Ch 19: 6 the Ammonites **s** a thousand talents H8938
1Ch 19: 8 David **s** Joab **out** with the entire army of H8938
1Ch 19:16 *they* **s** messengers and had Arameans H8938
1Ch 21:12 how I should answer the *one who* **s** me." H8938
1Ch 21:14 So the LORD **s** a plague on Israel, and H5989
1Ch 21:15 And God **s** an angel to destroy Jerusalem H8938
2Ch 2: 3 Solomon **s** this message to Hiram king of H8938
2Ch 2: 3 father David when *you* **s** him cedar to H8938
2Ch 7:10 the seventh month *he* **s** the people to H8938
2Ch 8:18 And Hiram **s** him ships commanded by his H8938
2Ch 10: 3 So *they* **s for** Jeroboam H8938+2256+7924+4200
2Ch 10:18 King Rehoboam **s out** Adoniram, who was H8938
2Ch 13:13 Jeroboam *had* **s** troops **around** to the rear H6015
2Ch 16: 2 his own palace and **s** it to Ben-Hadad H8938
2Ch 16: 4 with King Asa and **s** the commanders of H8938
2Ch 17: 7 year of his reign *he* **s** his officials H8938
2Ch 23:14 the priest **s out** the commanders of H3655
2Ch 24:19 Although the LORD **s** prophets to the H8938
2Ch 24:23 *They* **s** all the plunder to their king in H8938
2Ch 25:10 to him from Ephraim and **s** them home. H2143
2Ch 25:13 that Amaziah *had* **s back** and had not H8740
2Ch 25:15 Amaziah, and *he* **s** a prophet to him H8938
2Ch 25:17 *he* **s** this challenge to Jehoash son of H8938
2Ch 25:18 thistle in Lebanon **s** a message to a cedar H8938
2Ch 25:27 but *they* **s** men after him to Lachish and H8938
2Ch 28:16 At that time King Ahaz **s** to the kings of H8938
2Ch 30: 1 Hezekiah **s word** to all Israel and Judah H8938
2Ch 32: 9 he **s** his officers to Jerusalem with this H8938
2Ch 32:21 And the LORD **s** an angel, who annihilated H8938
2Ch 32:31 But when envoys *were* **s** by the rulers of H8938

S

2Ch 34: 8 *he* **s** Shaphan son of Azaliah and H8938
2Ch 34:22 those the king *had* **s** with him went to H8938
2Ch 34:23 Tell the man who **s** you to me, H8938
2Ch 34:26 of Judah, who **s** you to inquire of the LORD H8938
2Ch 35:21 But Necho **s** messengers to him, saying H8938
2Ch 36:10 Nebuchadnezzar **s** *for* him and brought H8938
2Ch 36:15 **s word** to them through his messengers H8938
Ezr 4:11 This is a copy of the letter *they* **s** him.) A10714
Ezr 4:17 The king **s** this reply: To Rehum the A10714
Ezr 4:18 The letter *you* **s** us has been read and A10714
Ezr 5: 6 of Trans-Euphrates, **s** to King Darius. A10714
Ezr 5: 7 The report *they* **s** him read as follows: To A10714
Ezr 6:13 because of the decree King Darius *had* **s**, A10714
Ezr 7:14 You **are s** by the king and his seven A10714
Ne 2: 9 The king *had* also **s** army officers and H8938
Ne 6: 2 Sanballat and Geshem **s** me this message: H8938
Ne 6: 3 so *I* **s** messengers to them with this reply H8938
Ne 6: 4 Four times *they* **s** me the same message H8938
Ne 6: 5 Sanballat **s** his aide to me with the same H8938
Ne 6: 8 *I* **s** him this reply: "Nothing like what you H8938
Ne 6:12 I realized that God *had* not **s** him, but that H8938
Ne 6:19 And Tobiah **s** letters to intimidate me H8938
Ne 9:10 *You* **s** signs and wonders against Pharaoh, H5989
Est 1:22 *He* **s** dispatches to all parts of the kingdom H8938
Est 3:13 Dispatches **were s** by couriers to all the H8938
Est 4: 4 *She* **s** clothes *for* him to put on instead of H8938
Est 4:13 he **s back** this answer: "Do not think that H8740
Est 4:15 Then Esther **s** this reply to Mordecai: H8740
Est 8:10 and **s** them by mounted couriers H8938
Est 9:20 and *he* **s** letters to all the Jews throughout H8938
Est 9:30 And Mordecai **s** letters to all the Jews in H8938
Job 22: 9 And *you* **s** widows **away** empty-handed H8938
Job 33:23 a thousand, *s* **to** tell them how to be upright, AIT
Ps 59: T When Saul *had* **s** men to watch David's H8938
Ps 78:25 *he* **s** them all the food they could eat. H8938
Ps 78:45 *He* **s** swarms of flies that devoured them H8938
Ps 78:61 *He* **s** the ark of his might into captivity, his H5989
Ps 105:17 and *he* **s** a man before them—Joseph H8938
Ps 105:20 The king **s** and released him, the ruler of H8938
Ps 105:26 *He* **s** Moses his servant, and Aaron, whom H8938
Ps 105:28 *He* **s** darkness and made the land dark H8938
Ps 106:15 but **s** a wasting disease among them. H8938
Ps 107:20 *He* **s out** his word and healed them; he H8938
Ps 135: 9 *He* **s** his signs and wonders into your H8938
Pr 9: 3 *She* has **s out** her servants, and she calls H8938
Pr 17:11 of death *will* **be s** against them. H8938
Isa 6:12 the LORD *has* **s** everyone **far away** and the H8178
Isa 9: 8 The Lord *has* **s** a message against Jacob H8938
Isa 20: 1 commander, **s** *by* Sargon king of Assyria H8938
Isa 36: 2 the king of Assyria **s** his field commander H8938
Isa 36:12 you that my master **s** me to say these H8938
Isa 37: 2 *He* **s** Eliakim the palace administrator H8938
Isa 37: 4 of Assyria, *has* **s** to ridicule the living God H8938
Isa 37: 9 *he* **s** messengers to Hezekiah with this H8938
Isa 37:17 words Sennacherib *has* **s** to ridicule the H8938
Isa 37:21 Isaiah son of Amoz **s** a message to H8938
Isa 39: 1 king of Babylon **s** Hezekiah letters and a H8938
Isa 43:27 *those* I **s to teach** you rebelled against me H4885
Isa 48:16 And now the Sovereign LORD *has* **s** me H8938
Isa 50: 1 of divorce with which *I* **s** her **away**? H8938
Isa 50: 1 transgressions your mother **was s away**. H8938
Isa 55:11 achieve the purpose for which *I* **s** it. H8938
Isa 57: 9 *You* **s** your ambassadors far away; you H8938
Isa 61: 1 *He has* **s** me to bind up the H8938
Isa 63:12 *who* **s** his glorious arm of power to be at H2143
Jer 3: 8 of divorce and **s** her **away** because of all H8938
Jer 7:25 again and again *I* **s** you my servants the H8938
Jer 14:14 *I have* not **s** them or appointed them or H8938
Jer 19:14 where the LORD *had* **s** him to prophesy H8938
Jer 21: 1 when King Zedekiah **s** to him Pashhur son H8938
Jer 24: 5 whom *I* **s away** from this place *to* the land H8938
Jer 25: 4 And though the LORD *has* **s** all his servants H8938
Jer 25:17 all the nations to whom he **s** me drink it: H8938
Jer 26: 5 whom I *have* **s** to you again and again H8938
Jer 26:12 "The LORD **s** me to prophesy against this H8938
Jer 26:15 in truth the LORD *has* **s** me to you to speak H8938
Jer 26:22 however, **s** Elnathan son of Akbor to Egypt H8938
Jer 27:15 '*I have* not **s** them,' declares the LORD H8938
Jer 28: 9 as one truly **s** *by* the LORD only if his H8938
Jer 28:15 The LORD *has* not **s** you, yet you have H8938
Jer 29: 1 the prophet Jeremiah **s** from Jerusalem to H8938
Jer 29: 3 king of Judah **s** to King Nebuchadnezzar H8938
Jer 29: 9 *I have* not **s** them," declares H8938
Jer 29:19 "words that *I* **s** to them again and again H8938
Jer 29:20 exiles whom *I have* **s away** from H8938
Jer 29:25 You **s** letters in your own name to all the H8938
Jer 29:28 *He has* **s** this message to us in Babylon: It H8938
Jer 35:15 Again and again *I* **s** all my servants the H8938
Jer 36:14 all the officials **s** Jehudi son of Nethaniah H8938
Jer 36:21 The king **s** Jehudi to get the scroll, and H8938
Jer 37: 3 **s** Jehukal son of Shelemiah with the H8938
Jer 37: 7 king of Judah, who **s** you to inquire of me H8938
Jer 37:17 King Zedekiah **s for** him and had him H8938
Jer 38:14 Then King Zedekiah **s for** Jeremiah the H8938
Jer 39:14 **s** and had Jeremiah taken out of the H8938
Jer 40:14 of the Ammonites *has* **s** Ishmael son of H8938
Jer 42: 9 to whom *you* **s** me to present your petition H8938
Jer 42:20 mistake when you **s** me to the LORD your H8938
Jer 42:21 LORD your God in all *he* **s** me to tell you. H8938
Jer 43: 1 the LORD *had* **s** him to tell them— H8938
Jer 43: 2 The LORD our God *has* not **s** you to say H8938
Jer 44: 4 Again and again *I* **s** my servants the H8938

Jer 49:14 an envoy **was s** to the nations to say H8938
La 1:13 "From on high *he* **s** fire, sent it down into H8938
La 1:13 high he sent fire, **s** it **down** into my bones. H3718
Eze 3: 5 You *are* not **being s** to a people of obscure H8938
Eze 3: 6 Surely if *I had* **s** you to them, they would H8938
Eze 11:16 Although *I* **s** them **far away** among the H8178
Eze 13: 6 Even though the LORD *has* not **s** them, they H8938
Eze 17: 7 The vine now **s out** its roots toward him H4102
Eze 23:16 after them and **s** messengers to them in H8938
Eze 23:40 "*They* even **s** messengers for men who H8938
Eze 31: 4 around its base and **s** their channels to all H8938
Eze 39:28 though I **s** them **into exile** among the H1655
Da 2:13 and *men were s* to **look for** Daniel and his AIT
Da 3:28 who *has* **s** his angel and rescued his A10714
Da 5:24 Therefore he **s** the hand that wrote the A10714
Da 6:22 My God **s** his angel, and he shut the A10714
Da 10:11 stand up, for *I have* now **been s** to you." H8938
Hos 5:13 Assyria, and **s** to the great king **for help**. H8938
Joel 2:25 my great army that *I* **s** among you. H8938
Am 4: 7 *I* **s rain** on one town, but withheld it from H4763
Am 4:10 "*I* **s** plagues among you as I did to Egypt H8938
Am 7:10 the priest of Bethel **s** a message to H8938
Ob 1 An envoy **was s** to the nations to say H8938
Jnh 1: 4 Then the LORD **s** a great wind on the sea H3214
Mic 6: 4 *I* **s** Moses to lead you, also Aaron and H8938
Hag 1:12 because the LORD their God *had* **s** him. H8938
Zec 1:10 the ones the LORD *has* **s** to go throughout H8938
Zec 2: 8 the Glorious One *has* **s** me against the H8938
Zec 2: 9 know that the LORD Almighty *has* **s** me. H8938
Zec 2:11 that the LORD Almighty *has* **s** me to you. H8938
Zec 4: 9 that the LORD Almighty *has* **s** me to you. H8938
Zec 6:15 that the LORD Almighty *has* **s** me to you. H8938
Zec 7: 2 The people of Bethel *had* **s** Sharezer and H8938
Zec 7:12 the LORD Almighty *had* **s** by his Spirit H8938
Mal 2: 4 will know that *I have* **s** you this warning H8938
Mt 2: 8 *He* **s** them to Bethlehem and said, "Go *G4287*
Mt 10: 5 These twelve Jesus **s out** with the following *G690*
Mt 10:40 me welcomes the *one who* **s** me. *G690*
Mt 11: 2 deeds of the Messiah, *he* **s** his disciples *G4287*
Mt 14:35 *they* **s word** to all the surrounding country. *G690*
Mt 15:24 "*I was* **s** only to the lost sheep of Israel." *G690*
Mt 15:39 *After* Jesus *had* **s** the crowd **away**, he got *G668*
Mt 20: 2 the day and **s** them into his vineyard. *G690*
Mt 21: 1 the Mount of Olives, Jesus **s** two disciples, *G690*
Mt 21:34 *he* **s** his servants to the tenants to collect *G690*
Mt 21:36 Then *he* **s** other servants to them, more *G690*
Mt 21:37 Last of all, *he* **s** his son to them. 'They will *G690*
Mt 22: 3 *He* **s** his servants to those who had been *G690*
Mt 22: 4 "Then *he* **s** some more servants and said *G690*
Mt 22: 7 *He* **s** his army and destroyed those *G4287*
Mt 22:16 *They* **s** their disciples to him along with the *G690*
Mt 23:37 kill the prophets and stone those **s** to you, *G690*
Mt 26:47 **s from** the chief priests and the elders of *G608*
Mt 27:19 judge's seat, his wife **s** him this message: *G690*
Mk 1:12 At once the Spirit **s** him **out** into the *G1675*
Mk 1:43 Jesus **s** him **away** at once with a strong *G1675*
Mk 3:31 outside, *they* **s** someone in to call him. *G690*
Mk 6:27 So he immediately **s** an executioner with *G690*
Mk 8: 9 *After he had* **s** them **away**, *G668*
Mk 8:26 Jesus **s** him home, saying, "Don't even go *G690*
Mk 9:37 not welcome me but the *one who* **s** me." *G690*
Mk 11: 1 of Olives, Jesus **s** two of his disciples, *G690*
Mk 12: 2 At harvest time *he* **s** a servant to the tenants *G690*
Mk 12: 3 beat him and **s** him **away** empty-handed. *G690*
Mk 12: 4 Then *he* **s** another servant to them; they *G690*
Mk 12: 5 *He* **s** still another, and that one they killed *G690*
Mk 12: 5 He **s** many others; some of them they beat NDT
Mk 12: 6 *He* **s** him last of all, saying, 'They will *G690*
Mk 12:13 Later *they* **s** some of the Pharisees and *G690*
Mk 14:13 So *he* **s** two of his disciples, telling them *G690*
Mk 14:43 swords and clubs, *s* **from** the chief priests, AIT
Lk 1:19 and *I have been* **s** to speak to you and to *G690*
Lk 1:26 God **s** the angel Gabriel to Nazareth *G690*
Lk 1:53 things but *has* **s** the rich **away** empty. *G1990*
Lk 4:18 *He has* **s** me to proclaim freedom for the *G690*
Lk 4:26 Yet Elijah *was* not **s** to any of them, but to *G4287*
Lk 4:43 towns also, because that is why *I was* **s**." *G690*
Lk 7: 3 heard of Jesus and **s** some elders of the *G690*
Lk 7: 6 the house *when* the centurion **s** friends to *G4287*
Lk 7:10 Then the *men who had been* **s** returned to *G4287*
Lk 7:19 *he* **s** them to the Lord to ask, "Are you the *G4287*
Lk 7:20 "John the Baptist **s** us to you to ask, 'Are *G690*
Lk 8:38 go with him, but Jesus **s** him **away**, saying, *G668*
Lk 9: 2 and *he* **s** them **out** to proclaim the kingdom *G690*
Lk 9:48 me welcomes the *one who* **s** me. *G690*
Lk 9:52 And *he* **s** messengers on ahead, who went *G690*
Lk 10: 1 others and **s** them two by two ahead *G690*
Lk 10:16 whoever rejects me rejects him *who* **s** me." *G690*
Lk 13:34 kill the prophets and stone those **s** to you, *G690*
Lk 14: 4 he healed him and **s** him **on** his **way**. *G668*
Lk 14:17 time of the banquet *he* **s** his servant to tell *G690*
Lk 15:15 *who* **s** him to his fields to feed pigs. *G4287*
Lk 19:14 hated him and **s** a delegation after him *G690*
Lk 19:15 Then he **s for** the servants to whom *G3306+5888*
Lk 19:29 Mount of Olives, *he* **s** two of his disciples *G690*
Lk 19:32 Those *who were* **s** ahead went and found it *G690*
Lk 20:10 At harvest time *he* **s** a servant to the tenants *G690*
Lk 20:10 beat him and **s** him **away** empty-handed. *G1990*
Lk 20:11 *He* **s** another servant, but that one *G4707+4287*
Lk 20:11 shamefully and **s away** empty-handed. *G1990*
Lk 20:12 *He* **s** still a third, and they wounded *G4707+4287*
Lk 20:20 close watch on him, *they* **s** spies, who *G690*

Lk 22: 8 Jesus **s** Peter and John, saying, "Go and *G690*
Lk 22:35 asked them, "When *I* **s** you without purse *G690*
Lk 23: 7 jurisdiction, *he* **s** him to Herod, who was *G402*
Lk 23:11 an elegant robe, *they* **s** him **back** to Pilate. *G402*
Lk 23:15 has Herod, for *he* **s** him **back** to us; as you *G402*
Jn 1: 6 There was a man **s** from God whose name *G690*
Jn 1:19 leaders in Jerusalem **s** priests and Levites *G690*
Jn 1:22 an answer to take back to those *who* **s** us. *G4287*
Jn 1:24 Now the Pharisees *who had been* **s** *G690*
Jn 1:33 the *one who* **s** me to baptize with *G4287*
Jn 3:28 not the Messiah but am **s** ahead of him. *G690*
Jn 3:34 the one whom God *has* **s** speaks the words *G690*
Jn 4:34 to do the will *of* him *who* **s** me and to *G4287*
Jn 4:38 I **s** you to reap what you have not worked for *G690*
Jn 5:23 does not honor the Father, who **s** him. *G4287*
Jn 5:24 believes him *who* **s** me has eternal *G4287*
Jn 5:30 not to please myself but him *who* **s** me. *G4287*
Jn 5:33 "You *have* **s** to John and he has testified to *G690*
Jn 5:36 am doing—testify that the Father *has* **s** me. *G690*
Jn 5:37 And the Father *who* **s** me has himself *G4287*
Jn 5:38 for you do not believe the one he **s**. *G690*
Jn 6:29 to believe in the one *he has* **s**." *G690*
Jn 6:38 will but to do the will of him *who* **s** me. *G4287*
Jn 6:39 And this is the will of him *who* **s** me, that I *G4287*
Jn 6:44 unless the Father who **s** me draws them, *G4287*
Jn 6:57 as the living Father **s** me and I live because *G690*
Jn 7:16 It comes *from* the *one who* **s** me. *G4287*
Jn 7:18 the glory *of* the *one who* **s** him is a man *G4287*
Jn 7:28 own authority, but he *who* **s** me is true. *G4287*
Jn 7:29 him because I am from him and he **s** me." *G690*
Jn 7:32 the Pharisees **s** temple guards to arrest *G690*
Jn 7:33 then I am going to the *one who* **s** me. *G4287*
Jn 8:16 I stand with the Father, *who* **s** me. *G4287*
Jn 8:18 my other witness is the Father, *who* **s** me." *G4287*
Jn 8:26 But he *who* **s** me is trustworthy, and what I *G4287*
Jn 8:29 The *one who* **s** me is with me; he has not *G4287*
Jn 8:42 I have not come on my own; God **s** me. *G690*
Jn 9: 4 we must do the works of him *who* **s** me. *G4287*
Jn 9: 7 the Pool of Siloam" (this word means "**S**") *G690*
Jn 9:18 his sight until *they* **s for** the man's parents *G5888*
Jn 10:36 apart as his very own and **s** into the world? *G690*
Jn 11: 3 So the sisters **s** word to Jesus, "Lord, the *G690*
Jn 11:42 that they may believe that you **s** me." *G690*
Jn 12:44 in me only, but in the *one who* **s** me. *G4287*
Jn 12:45 looks at me is seeing the *one who* **s** me. *G4287*
Jn 12:49 the Father *who* **s** me commanded me *G4287*
Jn 13:16 greater *than* the *one who* **s** him. *G4287*
Jn 13:20 accepts me accepts the *one who* **s** me." *G4287*
Jn 14:24 they belong to the Father *who* **s** me. *G4287*
Jn 15:21 they do not know the *one who* **s** me. *G4287*
Jn 16: 5 now I am going to him *who* **s** me *G4287*
Jn 17: 3 and Jesus Christ, whom *you have* **s**. *G690*
Jn 17: 8 from you, and they believed that you **s** me. *G690*
Jn 17:18 As *you* **s** me into the world, I have sent *G690*
Jn 17:18 the world, I *have* **s** them into the world. *G690*
Jn 17:21 the world may believe that you *have* **s** me. *G690*
Jn 17:23 will know that you **s** me and have loved *G690*
Jn 17:25 and they know that you *have* **s** me. *G690*
Jn 18:24 Then Annas **s** him bound to Caiaphas the *G690*
Jn 20:21 As the Father *has* **s** me, I am sending *G690*
Ac 3:26 *he* **s** him first to you to bless you by turning *G690*
Ac 5:21 of Israel—and **s** to the jail for the apostles. *G690*
Ac 7: 4 God **s** him to this land where you are now *G3579*
Ac 7:12 *he* **s** our forefathers **on** their first **visit**. *G1990*
Ac 7:14 Joseph **s for** his father Jacob and his *G690+3559*
Ac 7:35 He *was* **s** to be their ruler and deliverer by *G690*
Ac 8:14 of God, *they* **s** Peter and John to Samaria. *G690*
Ac 9:17 *has* **s** me so that you may see again and be *G690*
Ac 9:30 down to Caesarea and **s** him **off** to Tarsus. *G1990*
Ac 9:38 *they* **s** two men to him and urged him *G690*
Ac 9:40 Peter **s** them all **out** of the room; then he *G1675*
Ac 10: 8 that had happened and **s** them to Joppa. *G690*
Ac 10:17 the men **s** by Cornelius found out where *G690*
Ac 10:20 hesitate to go with them, for I *have* **s** them." *G690*
Ac 10:29 So *when* I *was* **s for**, I came without raising *G3569*
Ac 10:29 May I ask why *you* **s for** me?" *G3569*
Ac 10:33 So *I* **s** for you immediately, and it was *G4287*
Ac 10:36 know the message God **s** to the people of *G690*
Ac 11:11 three men *who had been* **s** to me from *G690*
Ac 11:22 and *they* **s** Barnabas to Antioch. *G1990*
Ac 12:11 a doubt that the Lord *has* **s** his angel and *G1990*
Ac 13: 3 placed their hands on them and **s** them **off**. *G668*
Ac 13: 4 of them, **s on** *their* **way** by the Holy Spirit *G1734*
Ac 13: 7 **s for** Barnabas and Saul because he *G4673*
Ac 13:15 leaders of the synagogue **s** *word* to them, *G690*
Ac 13:26 that this message of salvation *has been* **s**. *G1990*
Ac 15: 3 The church **s** them **on** *their* **way**, and as *G4636*
Ac 15:23 With them *they* **s** *the following* **letter**: The *G1211*
Ac 15:30 So the men *were* **s off** and went down to *G668*
Ac 15:33 *they were* **s off** by the believers with the *G668*
Ac 15:33 peace to return to those *who had* **s** them. *G690*
Ac 16:35 the magistrates **s** their officers to the jailer *G690*
Ac 17:10 believers **s** Paul and Silas **away** to Berea. *G1734*
Ac 17:14 believers immediately **s** Paul to the coast, *G1990*
Ac 19:22 *He* **s** two of his helpers, Timothy and *G690*
Ac 19:31 **s** him *a message* begging him not to *G4287*
Ac 20: 1 had ended, Paul **s for** the disciples and *G3569*
Ac 20:17 Paul **s** to Ephesus for the elders of the *G4287*
Ac 23:18 **s for** me and asked me to bring this young *G4673*
Ac 23:30 against the man, *I* **s** him to you at once. *G4287*
Ac 24:24 *He* **s for** Paul and listened to him as he *G3569*
Ac 24:26 so *he* **s for** him frequently and talked with *G3569*

Ac 28:28 God's salvation *has been* **s** to the Gentiles, *G690*
Ro 10:15 how can anyone preach unless *they are* **s**? *G690*
1Co 4:17 For this reason *I have* **s** to you Timothy, my *G4287*
2Co 2:17 God with sincerity, as those *s* **from** God. AIT
2Co 12:17 you through any of the men *I* **s** to you? *G690*
2Co 12:18 to go to you and *I* **s** our brother **with** him. *G5273*
Gal 1: 1 an apostle—*s* not **from** men nor by a man AIT
Gal 4: 4 had fully come, God **s** his Son, born of a *G1990*
Gal 4: 6 God **s** the Spirit of his Son into our hearts *G1990*
Php 2:25 whom you **s** to take care of my needs. NDT
Php 4:16 *you* **s** me aid more than once when I was *G4287*
Php 4:18 from Epaphroditus the gifts you **s**. *G4123*
1Th 3: 2 *We* **s** Timothy, who is our brother and *G4287*
1Th 3: 5 no longer, *I* **s** to find out about your faith. *G4287*
2Ti 4:12 *I* **s** Tychicus to Ephesus. *G690*
Heb 1:14 ministering spirits **s** to serve those who will *G690*
Jas 2:25 to the spies and **s** them **off** in a different *G1675*
1Pe 1:12 to you by the Holy Spirit **s** from heaven. *G690*
1Pe 2:14 *who are* **s** by him to punish those who do *G4287*
2Pe 2: 4 but **s** them **to hell**, putting them *G5434*
1Jn 4: 9 He **s** his one and only Son into the world *G690*
1Jn 4:10 that he loved us and **s** his Son as an *G690*
1Jn 4:14 that the Father *has* **s** his Son to be the *G690*
Rev 5: 6 seven spirits of God **s** out into all the earth. *G690*
Rev 22: 6 **s** his angel to show his servants the things *G690*
Rev 22:16 *have* **s** my angel to give you this *G4287*

SENTENCE (12) [SENTENCED]
1Ki 20:40 "That is your **s**," the king of Israel said H5477
2Ki 25: 6 where **s** was pronounced on him. H5477
Ps 149: 9 to carry out the **s** written against them H5477
Ecc 8:11 When the **s** for a crime is not quickly H7330
Jer 39: 5 Hamath, where he pronounced **s** on him. H5477
Jer 52: 9 Hamath, where he pronounced **s** on him. H5477
Eze 16:38 *I will* **s** you *to* the punishment of women H9149
Eze 23:45 judges *will* **s** them *to* the punishment H9149
Lk 23:40 he said, "since you are under the same **s**? *G3210*
Ac 13:28 found no proper ground *for* a **death s**, *G2505*
Ro 9:28 will carry out his **s** on earth with speed *G3364*
2Co 1: 9 we felt we had received the **s** of death. *G645*

SENTENCED (3) [SENTENCE]
Jer 26:11 man should be **s** *to* death because he H5477
Jer 26:16 "This man should not be **s** *to* death! H5477
Lk 24:20 rulers handed him over to be **s** to death, *G3210*

SENTRIES (1)
Ac 12: 6 and **s** stood guard at the entrance. *G5874*

SEORIM (1)
1Ch 24: 8 the third to Harim, the fourth to S, H8556

SEPARATE (28) [SEPARATED, SEPARATES]
Ge 1: 6 between the waters *to* **s** water from water." H976
Ge 1:14 vault of the sky to **s** the day from the night, H976
Ge 1:18 the night, and to **s** light from darkness. H976
Ge 30:40 Thus he made **s** flocks for himself H4200+963
Ex 26:33 The curtain *will* **s** the Holy Place from the H976
Lev 15:31 "*'You must* **keep** the Israelites **s** from H5692
Nu 16:21 "**S yourselves** from this assembly so I can H976
Jdg 7: 5 "S those who lap the water H3657+4200+963
2Sa 14: 6 and no *one was there to* **s** them. H5911+1068
1Ki 5: 9 There *I will* **s** them and you can take them H5879
2Ki 15: 5 day he died, and he lived in a **s** house. H2931
2Ch 26:21 He lived in a **s** house—leprous, and H2931
Ezr 9: 1 *have* not **kept themselves s** from the H976
Ezr 10:11 **S yourselves** from the peoples around you H976
Est 3: 8 of your kingdom *who* **keep** *themselves* **s**. H7233
Eze 14: 7 in Israel **s themselves** from me and set up H5692
Eze 42:20 to **s** the holy from the common. H976
Mt 13:49 angels will come and **s** the wicked from the *G928*
Mt 19: 6 God has joined together, *let* no one **s**." *G6004*
Mt 25:32 and *he will* **s** the people one from another *G928*
Mk 10: 9 God has joined together, *let* no one **s**." *G6004*
Jn 20: 7 still lying in its place, **s from** the linen. *G6006*
Ro 8:35 Who *shall* **s** us from the love of Christ *G6004*
Ro 8:39 will be able *to* **s** us from the love of God *G6004*
1Co 7:10 A wife *must* not **s** from her husband. *G6004*
2Co 6:17 "Come out from them and *be* **s**, says the *G928*
Gal 2:12 began to draw back and **s** himself from the *G928*
Eph 2:12 that at that time you were **s** from Christ, *G6006*

SEPARATED (21) [SEPARATE]
Ge 1: 4 and he **s** the light from the darkness. H976
Ge 1: 7 made the vault and **s** the water under the H976
Ge 2:10 from there *it* **was s** into four headwaters. H7233
Ge 25:23 two peoples from within you *will* **be s**; H7233
Nu 16: 9 the God of Israel *has* **s** you from the rest of H976
1Sa 11:11 next day Saul **s** his men *into* three H8492
2Ki 2:11 appeared and **s** the two of them, H7233+1068
2Ki 25: 5 his soldiers were **s from** him and H4946+6584
1Ch 23: 6 David **s** the Levites *into* divisions H2745
1Ch 24: 3 David **s** them **into divisions** for their H2745
Ezr 6:21 with all who *had* **s themselves** from the H976
Ne 4:19 we *are* widely **s** from each other H7233
Ne 9: 2 *Those of* Israelite descent *had* **s themselves** H976
Ne 10:28 servants and all who **s themselves** from the H976
Isa 59: 2 your iniquities *have* **s** you from your God; H976
Jer 52: 8 his soldiers were **s from** him and H4946+6584
Eze 46:18 one of my people *will be* **s** from their H7046
Ac 2: 3 be tongues of fire *that* **s** and came to rest *G1374*
Eph 4:18 understanding and **s** from the life of God *G558*
1Th 2:17 orphaned by being **s from** you for a short *G608*

Phm 15 the reason *he was* **s** from you for a *G6004*

SEPARATES (4) [SEPARATE]
Ru 1:17 so severely, if even death **s** you and me." H7233
Pr 16:28 up conflict, and a gossip **s** close friends. H7233
Pr 17: 9 repeats the matter **s** close friends. H7233
Mt 25:32 as a shepherd **s** the sheep from the *G928*

SEPHAR (1)
Ge 10:30 they lived stretched from Mesha toward S, H6223

SEPHARAD (1)
Ob 20 Jerusalem who are in S will possess the H6224

SEPHARVAIM (6) [SEPHARVITES]
2Ki 17:24 Hamath and S and settled them in the H6226
2Ki 17:31 Anammelek, the gods of S. H6226
2Ki 18:34 Where are the gods of S, Hena and Ivvah? H6226
2Ki 19:13 are the kings of Lair, S, Hena and Ivvah?" H6226
Isa 36:19 Where are the gods of S? Have they H6226
Isa 37:13 are the kings of Lair, S, Hena and Ivvah?" H6226

SEPHARVITES (1) [SEPHARVAIM]
2Ki 17:31 the S burned their children in the fire H6227

SEPHER See KIRIATH SEPHER

SEPULCHRE, SEPULCHRES (KJV) BURIED, GRAVE, GRAVES, TOMB, TOMBS

SERAH (3) [TIMNATH SERAH]
Ge 46:17 Their sister was S. The sons of Beriah: H8580
Nu 26:46 Asher had a daughter named S.) H8580
1Ch 7:30 Ishvi and Beriah. Their sister was S. H8580

SERAIAH (18) [SERAIAH'S]
2Sa 8:17 of Abiathar were priests; S was secretary; H8588
2Ki 25:18 guard took as prisoners S the chief priest, H8588
2Ki 25:23 S son of Tanhumeth the Netophathite H8588
1Ch 4:13 Othniel and S. The sons of Othniel H8588
1Ch 4:14 S was the father of Joab, the father of Ge H8588
1Ch 4:35 Joshibiah, the son of S, the son of Asiel, H8588
1Ch 6:14 Azariah the father of S, and Seraiah the H8588
1Ch 6:14 of Seraiah, and S the father of Jozadak. H8588
Ezr 2: 2 Joshua, Nehemiah, S, Reelaiah H8588
Ezr 7: 1 Ezra son of S, the son of Azariah, H8588
Ne 10: 2 S, Azariah, Jeremiah, H8588
Ne 11:11 S son of Hilkiah, the son of Meshullam H8588
Ne 12: 1 with Joshua: S, Jeremiah, Ezra, H8588
Jer 36:26 S son of Azriel and Shelemiah son of H8589
Jer 40: 8 the sons of Kareah, S son of Tanhumeth H8588
Jer 51:59 gave to the staff officer S son of Neriah, H8588
Jer 51:61 He said to S, "When you get to Babylon H8588
Jer 52:24 guard took as prisoners S the chief priest, H8588

SERAIAH'S (1) [SERAIAH]
Ne 12:12 of S family, Meraiah; of Jeremiah's H8588

SERAPHIM (2)
Isa 6: 2 Above him were **s**, each with six wings H8597
Isa 6: 6 Then one of the **s** flew to me with a live H8597

SERED (2) [SEREDITE]
Ge 46:14 sons of Zebulun: S, Elon and Jahleel. H6237
Nu 26:26 through S, the Seredite clan; through Elon H6237

SEREDITE (1) [SERED]
Nu 26:26 through Sered, the S clan; through Elon H6238

SERGIUS (1) [PAULUS]
Ac 13: 7 an attendant of the proconsul, S Paulus. *G4950*

SERIOUS (9) [SERIOUSNESS]
Ge 12:17 the LORD inflicted **s** diseases on Pharaoh H1524
Ex 21:22 birth prematurely but there is no **s injury**, H656
Ex 21:23 But if there is **s injury**, you are to take life H656
Dt 15:21 blind, or has any **s** flaw, you must not H8273
Pr 5:14 And I was soon in **s** trouble in the H3972
Jer 6:14 of my people as though *it were* **not s**. H7837
Jer 8:11 of my people as though *it were* **not s**. H7837
Ac 18:14 about some misdemeanor or **s** crime, *G4505*
Ac 25: 7 They brought many **s** charges against him *G987*

SERIOUSNESS (1) [SERIOUS]
Titus 2: 7 In your teaching show integrity, **s** *G4949*

SERJEANTS (KJV) OFFICERS

SERPENT (16) [SERPENT'S, SERPENTS]
Ge 3: 1 Now the **s** was more crafty than any of the H5729
Ge 3: 2 The woman said to the **s**, "We may eat H5729
Ge 3: 4 certainly die," the **s** said to the woman. H5729
Ge 3:13 woman said, "The **s** deceived me, and I H5729
Ge 3:14 So the LORD God said to the **s**, "Because H5729
Job 26:13 his hand pierced the gliding **s**. H5729
Ps 91:13 you will trample the great lion and the **s**. H9490
Isa 14:29 its fruit will be a darting, **venomous s**. H8597
Isa 27: 1 Leviathan the gliding **s**, Leviathan the H5729
Isa 27: 1 Leviathan the coiling **s**; he will slay the H5729
Jer 46:22 hiss like a fleeing **s** as the enemy H5729
Jer 51:34 Like a **s** he has swallowed us and filled H9490
Am 9: 3 there I will command the **s** to bite them. H5729
Rev 12: 9 down—that ancient **s** called the devil, or *G4058*
Rev 12:15 from his mouth the **s** spewed water like a *G4058*
Rev 20: 2 dragon, that ancient **s**, who is the devil, *G4058*

SERPENT'S (4) [SERPENT]
Ps 140: 3 They make their tongues as sharp as a **s** H5729
Isa 65:25 like the ox, and dust will be the **s** food. H5729
2Co 11: 3 as Eve was deceived by the **s** cunning, *G4058*
Rev 12:14 times and half a time, out of the **s** reach. *G4058*

SERPENTS (3) [SERPENT]
Dt 32:33 Their wine is the venom of **s**, the deadly H9490
Job 20:14 it will become the venom of **s** within him. H7352
Job 20:16 He will suck the poison of **s**; the fangs of H7352

SERUG (6)
Ge 11:20 lived 32 years, he became the father of S. H8578
Ge 11:21 And after he became the father of S, Reu H8578
Ge 11:22 When S had lived 30 years, he became H8578
Ge 11:23 S lived 200 years and had other sons and H8578
1Ch 1:26 S, Nahor, Terah H8578
Lk 3:35 the son *of* S, the son of Reu, the son of *G4952*

SERVANT (517) [MAIDSERVANT, MAIDSERVANTS, MANSERVANT, MENSERVANTS, SERVANT'S, SERVANTS, SERVANTS']
Ge 15: 3 so a **s** *in* my household will be my heir." H1201
Ge 18: 3 your eyes, my lord, do not pass your **s** by. H6269
Ge 18: 5 now that you have come to your **s**. H6269
Ge 18: 7 tender calf and gave it to a **s**, who hurried H5853
Ge 19:19 Your **s** has found favor in your eyes, and H6269
Ge 24: 2 He said to the senior **s** in his household H6269
Ge 24: 5 The **s** asked him, "What if the woman is H6269
Ge 24: 9 So the **s** put his hand under the thigh of H6269
Ge 24:10 Then the **s** left, taking with him ten of his H6269
Ge 24:14 the one you have chosen for your **s** Isaac. H6269
Ge 24:17 The **s** hurried to meet her and said H6269
Ge 24:34 So he said, "I am Abraham's **s**. H6269
Ge 24:52 When Abraham's **s** heard what they said H6269
Ge 24:53 Then the **s** brought out gold and silver H6269
Ge 24:59 her nurse and Abraham's **s** and his men. H6269
Ge 24:61 So the **s** took Rebekah and left H6269
Ge 24:65 asked the **s**, "Who is that man in the H6269
Ge 24:65 is my master," the **s** answered. So she H6269
Ge 24:66 Then the **s** told Isaac all he had done. H6269
Ge 26:24 the sake of my **s** Abraham. H6269
Ge 29:24 And Laban gave his **s** Zilpah to his H9148
Ge 29:29 Laban gave his **s** Bilhah to his daughter H9148
Ge 30: 3 "Here is Bilhah, my **s**. Sleep with her so H563
Ge 30: 4 So she gave him her **s** Bilhah as a wife H9148
Ge 30: 7 Rachel's **s** Bilhah conceived again and H9148
Ge 30: 9 she took her **s** Zilpah and gave her to H9148
Ge 30:10 Leah's **s** Zilpah bore Jacob a son. H9148
Ge 30:12 Leah's **s** Zilpah bore Jacob a second son. H9148
Ge 30:18 me for giving my **s** to my husband. H9148
Ge 32: 4 'Your **s** Jacob says, I have been staying H6269
Ge 32:10 faithfulness you have shown your **s**. H6269
Ge 32:18 are to say, 'They belong to your **s** Jacob. H6269
Ge 32:20 'Your **s** Jacob is coming behind us. H6269
Ge 33: 5 children God has graciously given your **s**." H6269
Ge 33:14 So let my lord go on ahead of his **s**, while H6269
Ge 35:25 The sons of Rachel's **s** Bilhah: Dan and H9148
Ge 35:26 The sons of Leah's **s** Zilpah: Gad and H9148
Ge 41:12 with us, a **s** of the captain of the guard. H6269
Ge 43:28 "Your **s** our father is still alive and well." H6269
Ge 44:18 "Pardon your **s**, my lord, let me speak a H6269
Ge 44:18 Do not be angry with your **s**, though you H6269
Ge 44:24 When we went back to your **s** my father H6269
Ge 44:27 "Your **s** my father said to us, 'You know H6269
Ge 44:30 us when I go back to your **s** my father, H6269
Ge 44:32 Your **s** guaranteed the boy's safety to my H6269
Ge 44:33 please let your **s** remain here as my lord's H6269
Ex 4:10 the LORD, "Pardon your **s**, Lord. I have never NDT
Ex 4:10 past nor since you have spoken to your **s**. H6269
Ex 4:13 "Pardon your **s**, Lord. Please send NDT
Ex 14:31 put their trust in him and in Moses his **s**. H6269
Ex 20:10 your **male** or female **s**, nor your H6269
[Ex 20:10 your male or **female s**, nor your H563]
Ex 20:17 or his **male** or female **s**, his ox or H6269
[Ex 20:17 or his male or **female s**, his ox or H563]
Ex 21: 2 "If you buy a Hebrew **s**, he is to serve you H6269
Ex 21: 5 "But if the **s** declares, 'I love my master H6269
Ex 21: 6 Then *he will be* his **s** for life. H6268
Ex 21: 7 "If a man sells his daughter as a **s**, she is H563
Nu 11:11 have you brought this trouble on your **s**? H6269
Nu 12: 7 But this is not true of my **s** Moses; he is H6269
Nu 12: 8 not afraid to speak against my **s** Moses?" H6269
Nu 14:24 But because my **s** Caleb has a different H6269
Dt 3:24 to show to your **s** your greatness and H6269
Dt 5:14 your **male** or female **s**, nor your ox, H6269
[Dt 5:14 your male or **female s**, nor your ox, H563]
Dt 5:21 land, his **male** or female **s**, his ox or H6269
[Dt 5:21 land, his male or **female s**, his ox or H563]
Dt 15:16 But if your **s** says to you, "I do not want to NDT
Dt 15:17 and he will become your **s** for life. H6269
Dt 15:17 Do the same for your **female s**. H563
Dt 15:18 consider it a hardship to set your **s** free, H2257S
Dt 33: 8 Urim belong to your faithful **s**. H408
Dt 34: 5 And Moses the **s** *of* the LORD died there in H6269
Jos 1: 1 After the death of Moses the **s** *of* the LORD H6269
Jos 1: 2 "Moses my **s** is dead. Now then, you and H6269
Jos 1: 7 to obey all the law my **s** Moses gave you; H6269
Jos 1:13 that Moses the **s** *of* the LORD gave you H6269
Jos 1:15 which Moses the **s** *of* the LORD gave you H6269
Jos 5:14 message does my Lord have for his **s**?" H6269
Jos 7: 8 **Pardon your s**, Lord. What can I say, now H1065

S

Jos 8:31 as Moses the s *of* the LORD had H6269
Jos 8:33 as Moses the s *of* the LORD had formerly H6269
Jos 9:24 had commanded his s Moses to give you H6269
Jos 11:12 as Moses the s *of* the LORD had H6269
Jos 11:15 As the LORD commanded his s Moses, so H6269
Jos 12: 6 the s *of* the LORD, and the H6269
Jos 12: 6 And Moses the s *of* the LORD gave their H6269
Jos 13: 8 the s *of* the LORD, had assigned it to H6269
Jos 14: 7 old when Moses the s *of* the LORD sent me H6269
Jos 18: 7 Moses the s *of* the LORD gave it to them." H6269
Jos 22: 2 all that Moses the s *of* the LORD H6269
Jos 22: 4 that Moses the s *of* the LORD gave you H6269
Jos 22: 5 law that Moses the s *of* the LORD gave you: H6269
Jos 24:29 son of Nun, the s *of* the LORD, died at the H6269
Jdg 2: 8 son of Nun, the s *of* the LORD, died at the H6269
Jdg 7:10 go down to the camp with your s Purah H5853
Jdg 7:11 So he and Purah his s went down to the H5853
Jdg 9:54 So his s ran him through, and H5853
Jdg 13: 8 "**Pardon your** s, Lord. I beg H1065
Jdg 15:18 "You have given your s this great victory. H6269
Jdg 16:26 Samson said to the s who held his hand H5853
Jdg 19: 3 He had with him his s and two donkeys H5853
Jdg 19: 9 with his concubine and his s, got up to H5853
Jdg 19:11 was almost gone, the s said to his master H5853
Ru 2:13 me at ease by speaking kindly to your s— H9148
Ru 3: 9 "I am your s Ruth," she said H563
1Sa 1:11 not forget your s but give her a son H563
1Sa 1:16 Do not take your s for a wicked woman; H563
1Sa 1:18 "May your s find favor in your eyes." H9148
1Sa 2:13 the priest's s would come with a H5853
1Sa 2:15 the priest's s would come and say to the H5853
1Sa 2:16 you want," the s would answer, "No, hand NDT
1Sa 3: 9 'Speak, LORD, for your s is listening. H6269
1Sa 3:10 "Speak, for your s is listening. H6269
1Sa 9: 5 Saul said to the s who was with him H5853
1Sa 9: 6 But the s replied, "Look, in this town there is NDT
1Sa 9: 7 Saul said to his s, "If we go, what can we H5853
1Sa 9: 8 The s answered him again. "Look," he H5853
1Sa 9:10 Saul said to his s. "Come, let's go. H5853
1Sa 9:22 brought Saul and his s into the hall and H5853
1Sa 9:27 to Saul, "Tell the s to go on ahead of us" H5853
1Sa 9:27 the s did so—"but you stay here for a NDT
1Sa 10:10 When he and his s arrived at Gibeah, NDT
1Sa 10:14 Now Saul's uncle asked him and his s H5853
1Sa 14:41 have you not answered your s today? H6269
1Sa 17:32 Philistine; your s will go and fight him." H6269
1Sa 17:34 "Your s has been keeping his father's H6269
1Sa 17:36 Your s has killed both the lion and the H6269
1Sa 17:58 am the son of your s Jesse of Bethlehem." H6269
1Sa 19: 4 "Let not the king do wrong to his s David H6269
1Sa 20: 7 'Very well,' then your s is safe. But if he H6269
1Sa 20: 8 show kindness to your s, for you have H6269
1Sa 22: 8 son has incited my s to lie in wait for me H6269
1Sa 22:15 the king accuse your s or any of his H6269
1Sa 22:15 your s knows nothing at all about this H6269
1Sa 23:10 your s has heard definitely that Saul plans H6269
1Sa 23:11 Saul come down, as your s has heard? H6269
1Sa 23:11 of Israel, tell your s." And the LORD said, H6269
1Sa 25:24 "Pardon your s, my lord, and let me speak H563
1Sa 25:24 speak to you; hear what your s has to say. H563
1Sa 25:25 And as for me, your s, I did not see the H563
1Sa 25:27 which your s has brought to my lord H9148
1Sa 25:31 brought my lord success, remember your s." H563
1Sa 25:39 He has kept his s from doing wrong and H6269
1Sa 25:41 "I am your s and am ready to serve you H563
1Sa 26:18 he added, "Why is my lord pursuing his s? H6269
1Sa 27: 5 Why should your s live in the royal city H6269
1Sa 27:12 the Israelites, that he will be my s for life." H6269
1Sa 28: 2 will see for yourself what your s can do." H6269
1Sa 28:21 she said, "Look, your s has obeyed you. H9148
1Sa 28:22 listen to your s and let me give you H9148
1Sa 29: 8 found against your s from the day I came H6269
2Sa 3:18 'By my s David I will rescue my people H6269
2Sa 7: 5 "Go and tell my s David, 'This is what the H6269
2Sa 7: 8 "Now then, tell my s David, 'This is what H6269
2Sa 7:19 about the future of the house of your s— H6269
2Sa 7:20 For you know your s, Sovereign LORD. H6269
2Sa 7:21 great thing and made it known to your s. H6269
2Sa 7:25 made concerning your s and his house. H6269
2Sa 7:26 And the house of your s David will be H6269
2Sa 7:27 you have revealed this to your s, saying, H6269
2Sa 7:27 So your s has found courage to pray this H6269
2Sa 7:28 promised these good things to your s. H6269
2Sa 7:29 be pleased to bless the house of your s, H6269
2Sa 7:29 the house of your s will be blessed forever H6269
2Sa 9: 2 Now there was a s of Saul's household H6269
2Sa 9: 8 "What is your s, that you should H6269
2Sa 9:11 "Your s will do whatever my lord the king H6269
2Sa 9:11 my lord the king commands his s to do." H6269
2Sa 11:21 'Moreover, your s Uriah the Hittite is dead. H6269
2Sa 11:24 Moreover, your s Uriah the Hittite is dead." H6269
2Sa 13:17 He called his **personal** s and said H5853+9250
2Sa 13:18 So his s put her out and bolted the door H9250
2Sa 13:24 said, "Your s has had shearers come. H6269
2Sa 13:35 it has happened just as your s said." H6269
2Sa 14: 6 I your s had two sons. They got into a fight H9148
2Sa 14: 7 whole clan has risen up against your s; H9148
2Sa 14:12 "Let your s speak a word to my lord the H9148
2Sa 14:15 Your s thought, 'I will speak to the king H9148
2Sa 14:16 agree to deliver his s from the hand of the H563
2Sa 14:17 "And now your s says, 'May the word of H9148
2Sa 14:19 it was your s Joab who instructed me to H6269
2Sa 14:19 all these words into the mouth of your s. H9148
2Sa 14:20 Your s Joab did this to change the present H6269
2Sa 14:22 "Today your s knows that he has found H6269
2Sa 15: 2 "Your s is from one of the tribes of Israel." H6269
2Sa 15: 8 While your s was living at Geshur in Aram H6269
2Sa 15:21 means life or death, there will your s be." H6269
2Sa 15:34 I will be your s; I was your father's H6269
2Sa 15:34 I was your father's s in the past, but now I H6269
2Sa 15:34 now I will be your s,' then you can H6269
2Sa 17:17 A **female** s was to go and inform them H9148
2Sa 18:29 was about to send the king's s and me, H6269
2Sa 18:29 servant and me, your s, but I don't know H6269
2Sa 19:19 remember how your s did wrong on the H6269
2Sa 19:20 For I your s know that I have sinned, but H6269
2Sa 19:26 the king, since I your s am lame, I said, H6269
2Sa 19:26 But Ziba my s betrayed me. H6269
2Sa 19:27 has slandered your s to my lord the king. H6269
2Sa 19:28 you gave your s a place among those H6269
2Sa 19:35 Can your s taste what he eats and drinks H6269
2Sa 19:35 Why should your s be an added burden to H6269
2Sa 19:36 Your s will cross over the Jordan with the H6269
2Sa 19:37 Let your s return, that I may die in my own H6269
2Sa 19:37 But here is your s Kimham. Let him cross H6269
2Sa 20:17 "Listen to what your s has to say." "I'm H563
2Sa 24:10 I beg you, take away the guilt of your s. H6269
2Sa 24:21 "Why has my lord the king come to his s?" H6269
1Ki 1:13 the king, did you not swear to me your s: H563
1Ki 1:17 swore to me your s by the LORD your God: H563
1Ki 1:19 he has not invited Solomon your s. H6269
1Ki 1:26 But me your s, and Zadok the priest, and H6269
1Ki 1:26 your s Solomon he did not invite. H6269
1Ki 1:51 he will not put his s to death with the H6269
1Ki 2:38 Your s will do as my lord the king has said H6269
1Ki 3: 6 "You have shown great kindness to your s H6269
1Ki 3: 7 you have made your s king in place of my H6269
1Ki 3: 8 Your s is here among the people you have H6269
1Ki 3: 9 So give your s a discerning heart to govern H6269
1Ki 3:20 son from my side while I your s was asleep. H563
1Ki 8:24 your promise to your s David my father; H6269
1Ki 8:25 keep for your s David my father the H6269
1Ki 8:26 you promised your s David my father H6269
1Ki 8:28 the prayer that your s is praying in your H6269
1Ki 8:29 hear the prayer your s prays toward this H6269
1Ki 8:30 supplication of your s and of your people H6269
1Ki 8:53 declared through your s Moses when you, H6269
1Ki 8:56 promises he gave through his s Moses. H6269
1Ki 8:59 the cause of his s and the cause of his H6269
1Ki 8:66 had done for his s David and his people H6269
1Ki 11:13 the sake of David my s and for the sake of H6269
1Ki 11:32 the sake of my s David and the city of H6269
1Ki 11:34 days of his life for the sake of David my s, H6269
1Ki 11:36 son so that David my s may always have a H6269
1Ki 11:38 as David my s did, I will be with H6269
1Ki 12: 7 today you will be a s to these people and H6269
1Ki 14: 8 you have not been like my s David H6269
1Ki 14:18 said through his s the prophet Ahijah. H6269
1Ki 15:29 given through his s Ahijah the Shilonite. H6269
1Ki 18: 9 you are handing your s over to Ahab to be H6269
1Ki 18:12 Yet I your s have worshiped the LORD since H6269
1Ki 18:36 that I am your s and have done all H6269
1Ki 18:43 look toward the sea," he told his s. H5853
1Ki 18:44 The seventh time the s reported, "A cloud NDT
1Ki 19: 3 Beersheba in Judah, he left his s there, H5853
1Ki 19:21 set out to follow Elijah and *became* his s. H9250
1Ki 20: 9 'Your s will do all you demanded the first H6269
1Ki 20:32 Israel and said, "Your s Ben-Hadad says: H6269
1Ki 20:39 "Your s went into the thick of the battle H6269
1Ki 20:40 While your s was busy here and there, the H6269
2Ki 4: 1 out to Elisha, "Your s my husband is dead H6269
2Ki 4: 2 "Your s has nothing there at all," she H9148
2Ki 4:12 He said to his s Gehazi, "Call the H5853
2Ki 4:16 man of God, don't mislead your s! H9148
2Ki 4:19 His father told a s, "Carry him to his H5853
2Ki 4:20 After the s had lifted him up and carried him NDT
2Ki 4:24 She saddled the donkey and said to her s H5853
2Ki 4:25 the man of God said to his s Gehazi H5853
2Ki 4:38 he said to his s, "Put on the large H5853
2Ki 4:43 a hundred men?" his s asked. But Elisha H9250
2Ki 5: 6 I am sending my s Naaman to you so that H6269
2Ki 5:15 So please accept a gift from your s." H6269
2Ki 5:17 "please let me, your s, be given as much H6269
2Ki 5:17 your s will never again make burnt H6269
2Ki 5:18 the LORD forgive your s for this one thing: H6269
2Ki 5:18 may the LORD forgive your s for this." H6269
2Ki 5:20 the s *of* Elisha the man of God H5853
2Ki 5:25 "Your s didn't go anywhere," Gehazi H6269
2Ki 6:15 When the s *of* the man of God got up H9250
2Ki 6:15 What shall we do?" the s asked. H5853
2Ki 8: 4 to Gehazi, the s *of* the man of God, and H5853
2Ki 8:13 "How could your s, a mere dog, H6269
2Ki 8:19 the sake of his s David, the LORD was H6269
2Ki 9:36 he spoke through his s Elijah the Tishbite: H6269
2Ki 10:10 what he announced through his s Elijah." H6269
2Ki 14:25 spoken through his s Jonah son of Amittai H6269
2Ki 16: 7 king of Assyria, "I am your s and vassal. H6269
2Ki 18:12 all that Moses the s *of* the LORD H6269
2Ki 19:34 my sake and for the sake of David my s. H6269
2Ki 20: 6 my sake and for the sake of my s David. H6269
2Ki 21: 8 whole Law that my s Moses gave them." H6269
1Ch 2:34 He had an Egyptian s named Jarha. H6269
1Ch 2:35 his daughter in marriage to his s Jarha, H6269
1Ch 6:49 that Moses the s *of* God had commanded H6269
1Ch 17: 4 "Go and tell my s David, 'This is what the H6269
1Ch 17: 7 "Now then, tell my s David, 'This is what H6269
1Ch 17:17 about the future of the house of your s. H6269
1Ch 17:18 can David say to you for honoring your s? H6269
1Ch 17:18 For you know your s, H6269
1Ch 17:19 For the sake of your s and according to H6269
1Ch 17:23 made concerning your s and his house be H6269
1Ch 17:24 And the house of your s David will be H6269
1Ch 17:25 revealed to your s that you will build a H6269
1Ch 17:25 So your s has found courage to pray to H6269
1Ch 17:26 promised these good things to your s. H6269
1Ch 17:27 pleased to bless the house of your s, H6269
1Ch 21: 8 I beg you, take away the guilt of your s. H6269
2Ch 1: 3 which Moses the LORD's s had made in the H6269
2Ch 6:15 your promise to your s David my father; H6269
2Ch 6:16 keep for your s David my father the H6269
2Ch 6:17 that you promised your s David come true. H6269
2Ch 6:19 the prayer that your s is praying in your H6269
2Ch 6:20 hear the prayer your s prays toward this H6269
2Ch 6:21 supplications of your s and of your people H6269
2Ch 6:42 the great love promised to David your s." H6269
2Ch 24: 6 by Moses the s *of* the LORD and by the H6269
2Ch 24: 9 tax that Moses the s *of* God had required H6269
2Ch 32:16 the LORD God and against his s Hezekiah. H6269
Ne 1: 6 hear the prayer your s is praying before H6269
Ne 1: 7 decrees and laws you gave your s Moses. H6269
Ne 1: 8 the instruction you gave your s Moses, H6269
Ne 1:11 prayer of this your s and to the prayer of H6269
Ne 1:11 Give your s success today by granting him H6269
Ne 2: 5 the king and if your s has found favor in H6269
Ne 9:14 decrees and laws through your s Moses. H6269
Ne 10:29 through Moses the s *of* God and to obey H6269
Job 1: 8 to Satan, "Have you considered my s Job? H6269
Job 2: 3 to Satan, "Have you considered my s Job? H6269
Job 19:16 I summon my s, but he does not answer H6269
Job 42: 7 the truth about me, as my s Job has. H6269
Job 42: 8 rams and go to my s Job and sacrifice a H6269
Job 42: 8 My s Job will pray for you, and I will H6269
Job 42: 8 the truth about me, as my s Job has." H6269
Ps 4: 3 has set apart his **faithful** s for himself; H2883
Ps 18: T Of David the s *of* the LORD. He sang H6269
Ps 19:11 By them your s is warned; in keeping H6269
Ps 19:13 Keep your s also from willful sins; may H6269
Ps 27: 9 do not turn your s away in anger; you H6269
Ps 31:16 Let your face shine on your s; save me in H6269
Ps 35:27 who delights in the well-being of his s." H6269
Ps 36: T Of David the s *of* the LORD. H6269
Ps 69:17 Do not hide your face from your s; answer H6269
Ps 78:70 He chose David his s and took him from H6269
Ps 86: 2 save your s who trusts in you. H6269
Ps 86: 4 Bring joy to your s, Lord, for I put my trust H6269
Ps 86:16 show your strength in behalf of your s H6269
Ps 89: 3 chosen one, I have sworn to David my s, H6269
Ps 89:20 I have found David my s; with my sacred H6269
Ps 89:39 covenant with your s and have defiled his H6269
Ps 89:50 how your s has been mocked, how I H6269
Ps 105:26 He sent Moses his s, and Aaron, whom H6269
Ps 105:42 his holy promise given to his s Abraham. H6269
Ps 109:28 be put to shame, but may your s rejoice. H6269
Ps 116:16 Truly I am your s, LORD; I serve you just as H6269
Ps 119:17 Be good to your s while I live, that I may H6269
Ps 119:23 your s will meditate on your decrees. H6269
Ps 119:38 Fulfill your promise to your s, so that you H6269
Ps 119:49 Remember your word to your s, for you H6269
Ps 119:65 Do good to your s according to your word H6269
Ps 119:76 according to your promise to your s. H6269
Ps 119:84 How long must your s wait? When will H6269
Ps 119:124 Deal with your s according to your love H6269
Ps 119:125 I am your s; give me discernment that I H6269
Ps 119:135 face shine on your s and teach me your H6269
Ps 119:140 thoroughly tested, and your s loves them. H6269
Ps 119:176 Seek your s, for I have not forgotten your H6269
Ps 132:10 For the sake of your s David, do not reject H6269
Ps 136:22 an inheritance to his s Israel. His love H6269
Ps 143: 2 Do not bring your s into judgment, for no H6269
Ps 143:12 destroy all my foes, for I am your s. H6269
Ps 144:10 victory to kings, who delivers his s David. H6269
Pr 11:29 and the fool will be s to the wise. H6269
Pr 12: 9 yet have a s than pretend to be H6269
Pr 14:35 A king delights in a wise s, but a H6269
Pr 14:35 but a shameful s arouses his fury. NDT
Pr 17: 2 A prudent s will rule over a disgraceful H6269
Pr 29:21 A s pampered from youth will turn out to H6269
Pr 30:10 "Do not slander a s to their master, or H6269
Pr 30:22 a s who becomes king, a godless fool H6269
Pr 30:23 a s who displaces her mistress. H9148
Ecc 7:21 or you may hear your s cursing you— H6269
Ecc 10:16 whose king was a s and whose princes H5853
Isa 16:14 as a s **bound by contract** would count H8502
Isa 20: 3 "Just as my s Isaiah has gone stripped H6269
Isa 21:16 as a s **bound by contract** would count it H8502
Isa 22:20 "In that day I will summon my s, Eliakim H6269
Isa 24: 2 the master as for his s, for the mistress H6269
Isa 24: 2 the mistress as for her s, for seller as H9148
Isa 37:35 my sake and for the sake of David my s!" H6269
Isa 41: 8 "But you, Israel, my s, Jacob, whom I have H6269
Isa 41: 9 'You are my s'; I have chosen you H6269
Isa 42: 1 "Here is my s, whom I uphold, my chosen H6269
Isa 42:19 Who is blind but my s, and deaf like the H6269
Isa 42:19 with me, blind like the s *of* the LORD? H6269
Isa 43:10 the LORD, "and my s whom I have chosen H6269
Isa 44: 1 Jacob, my s, Israel, whom I have H6269

Isa 44: 2 be afraid, Jacob, my s, Jeshurun, whom I H6269
Isa 44:21 Jacob, for you, Israel, are my s. H6269
Isa 44:21 made you, you are my s; Israel, I will not H6269
Isa 45: 4 For the sake of Jacob my s, of Israel my H6269
Isa 48:20 "The LORD has redeemed his s Jacob." H6269
Isa 49: 3 "You are my s, Israel, in whom I H6269
Isa 49: 5 the womb to be his s to bring Jacob back H6269
Isa 49: 6 you to be my s to restore the tribes H6269
Isa 49: 7 abhorred by the nation, to the s *of* rulers: H6269
Isa 50:10 the LORD and obeys the word of his s? H6269
Isa 52:13 my s will act wisely; he will be raised H6269
Isa 53:11 my righteous s will justify many, H6269
Jer 2:14 Is Israel a s, a slave by birth? Why then H6269
Jer 25: 9 the north and my s Nebuchadnezzar king H6269
Jer 27: 6 the hands of my s Nebuchadnezzar king H6269
Jer 30:10 Jacob my s; do not be dismayed H6269
Jer 33:21 then my covenant with David my s—and H6269
Jer 33:22 of David my s and the Levites who H6269
Jer 33:26 Jacob and David my s and will not choose H6269
Jer 43:10 I will send for my s Nebuchadnezzar king H6269
Jer 46:27 Jacob my s; do not be dismayed H6269
Jer 46:28 be afraid, Jacob my s, for I am with you," H6269
Eze 28:25 own land, which I gave to my s Jacob. H6269
Eze 34:23 one shepherd, my s David, and he will H6269
Eze 34:24 my s David will be prince among H6269
Eze 37:24 " 'My s David will be king over them, and H6269
Eze 37:25 will live in the land I gave to my s Jacob, H6269
Eze 37:25 David my s will be their prince forever H6269
Eze 46:17 **the s** may keep it until the year of H2257S
Da 6:20 "Daniel, s *of* the living God, has your A10523
Da 9:11 Law of Moses, the s *of* God, have been H6269
Da 9:17 hear the prayers and petitions of your s. H6269
Da 10:17 How can I, your s, talk with you, my lord H6269
Hag 2:23 my s Zerubbabel son of Shealtiel H6269
Zec 3: 8 I am going to bring my s, the Branch. H6269
Mal 4: 4 "Remember the law of my s Moses, the H6269
Mt 8: 6 he said, "my s lies at home paralyzed G4090
Mt 8: 8 say the word, and my s will be healed. G4090
Mt 8: 9 I say *to* my s, 'Do this,' and he G1528
Mt 8:13 And his s was healed at that moment G4090
Mt 10:24 the teacher, nor a s above his master. G1528
Mt 12:18 "Here is my s whom I have chosen, the G4090
Mt 18:26 "At this the s fell on his knees before him G1528
Mt 18:28 "But when that s went out, he found one G1528
Mt 18:29 "His **fellow** s fell to his knees and begged G5281
Mt 18:32 "Then the master called **the s** in. 'You G899S
Mt 18:32 '*You* wicked s,' he said, 'I canceled all G1528
Mt 18:33 had mercy *on* your **fellow** s just as I had G5281
Mt 20:26 become great among you must be your s, G1356
Mt 23:11 The greatest among you will be your s. G1356
Mt 24:45 "Who then is the faithful and wise s G1528
Mt 24:46 will be good for that s whose master finds G1528
Mt 24:48 But suppose that s is wicked and says to G1528
Mt 24:50 The master *of* that s will come on a day G1528
Mt 25:21 replied, 'Well done, good and faithful s! G1528
Mt 25:23 replied, 'Well done, good and faithful s! G1528
Mt 25:26 'You wicked, lazy s! So you knew that I G1528
Mt 25:30 And throw that worthless s outside, into G1528
Mt 26:51 it out and struck the s of the high priest, G1528
Mt 26:69 in the courtyard, and a s **girl** came to him. G4087
Mt 26:71 where another s girl saw him and said to NDT
Mk 9:35 first must be the very last, and the s of all." G1356
Mk 10:43 become great among you must be your s, G1356
Mk 12: 2 harvest time he sent a s to the tenants to G1528
Mk 12: 4 Then he sent another s to them; they G1528
Mk 14:47 sword and struck the s of the high priest, G1528
Mk 14:66 one *of* the s **girls** of the high priest came G4087
Mk 14:69 When the s **girl** saw him there, she said G4087
Lk 1:38 "I am the Lord's s," Mary answered. "May G1527
Lk 1:48 been mindful of the humble state *of* his s. G1527
Lk 1:54 He has helped his s Israel, remembering G4090
Lk 1:69 us in the house of his s David G4090
Lk 2:29 you may now dismiss your s in peace. G1528
Lk 7: 2 There a centurion's s, whom his master G1528
Lk 7: 3 asking him to come and heal his s. G1528
Lk 7: 7 But say the word, and my s will be healed. G4090
Lk 7: 8 I say *to* my s, 'Do this,' and he G1528
Lk 7:10 to the house and found the s well. G1528
Lk 12:43 be good for that s whom the master finds G1528
Lk 12:45 But suppose the s says to himself, 'My G1528
Lk 12:46 The master *of* that s will come on a day G1528
Lk 12:47 "The s who knows the master's will and G1528
Lk 14:17 banquet he sent his s to tell those who G1528
Lk 14:21 "The s came back and reported this to his G1528
Lk 14:21 house became angry and ordered his s, G1528
Lk 14:22 the s said, 'what you ordered has G1528
Lk 14:23 "Then the master told his s, 'Go out to the G1528
Lk 17: 7 one of you has a s plowing or looking G1528
Lk 17: 7 Will he say *to* **the s** when he comes in G899S
Lk 17: 9 Will he thank the s because he did what G1528
Lk 19:17 'Well done, my good s!' his master G1528
Lk 19:20 "Then another s came and said, 'Sir, here is NDT
Lk 19:22 you by your own words, you wicked s! G1528
Lk 20:10 time he sent a s to the tenants so they G1528
Lk 20:11 He sent another s, but that one also they G1528
Lk 22:50 one of them struck the s of the high priest, G1528
Lk 22:56 A s **girl** saw him seated there in the G4087
Jn 12:26 and where I am, my s also will be. G1356
Jn 13:16 I tell you, no s is greater than his master G1528
Jn 15:15 because a s does not know his master's G1528
Jn 15:20 'A s is not greater than his master G1528
Jn 18:10 drew it and struck the high priest's s G1528
Jn 18:16 spoke *to* the s **girl on duty** there and G2601
Ac 3:13 of our fathers, has glorified his s Jesus. G4090
Ac 3:26 When God raised up his s, he sent him G4090
Ac 4:25 Holy Spirit through the mouth *of* your s, G4090
Ac 4:27 city to conspire against your holy s Jesus, G4090
Ac 4:30 through the name *of* your holy s Jesus." G4090
Ac 12:13 a s named Rhoda came to answer G4087
Ac 12:20 a **trusted personal** s of the G2093+3836+3131
Ac 26:16 to appoint you *as* a s and as a witness G5677
Ro 1: 1 a s of Christ Jesus, called to be an G1528
Ro 13: 4 one in authority is God's s for your good. G1356
Ro 14: 4 Who are you to judge someone else's s G3860
Ro 15: 8 Christ has become a s of the Jews on G1356
Gal 1:10 people, I would not be a s of Christ. G1528
Eph 3: 7 I became a s of this gospel by the gift of G1356
Eph 6:21 the dear brother and faithful s in the Lord G1356
Php 2: 7 nothing by taking the very nature *of* a s, G1528
Col 1: 7 Epaphras, our dear **fellow** s, who is a G5281
Col 1:23 of which I, Paul, have become a s. G1356
Col 1:25 I have become its s by the commission G1356
Col 4: 7 a faithful minister and **fellow** s in the Lord. G5281
Col 4:12 who is one of you and a s of Christ Jesus G1528
2Ti 2:24 And the Lord's s must not be quarrelsome G1528
2Ti 3:17 so that the s of God may be thoroughly G476
Titus 1: 1 a s of God and an apostle of Jesus Christ G1528
Heb 3: 5 was faithful as a s in all God's house," G2544
Jas 1: 1 a s of God and of the Lord Jesus Christ G1528
2Pe 1: 1 a s and apostle of Jesus Christ G1528
Jude 1 a s of Jesus Christ and a brother of James G1528
Rev 1: 1 known by sending his angel *to* his s John, G1528
Rev 15: 3 sang the song *of* God's s Moses and of G1528
Rev 19:10 I am a **fellow** s with you and with your G5281
Rev 22: 9 I am a **fellow** s with you and with your G5281

SERVANT'S (13) [SERVANT]

Ge 19: 2 "please turn aside to your s house. H6269
1Sa 1:11 only look on your s misery and remember H563
1Sa 25:28 "Please forgive your s presumption. H563
1Sa 26:19 let my lord the king listen to his s words. H6269
2Sa 14:15 perhaps he will grant his s request. H563
2Sa 14:22 the king has granted his s request. H6269
1Ki 8:28 attention to your s prayer and his plea H6269
1Ki 8:52 be open to your s plea and to the plea H6269
2Ki 6:17 Then the LORD opened the s eyes, and he H5853
2Ch 6:19 attention to your s prayer and his plea H6269
Ps 119:122 Ensure your s well-being; do not let the H6269
Mt 18:27 The s master took pity on him, canceled G1528
Jn 18:10 (The s name was Malchus.) G1528

SERVANTS (307) [SERVANT]

Ge 12:16 donkeys, **male** and female s, and camels. H6269
[Ge 12:16 donkeys, male and **female** s, and camels. H9148]
Ge 21:25 of water that Abimelek's s had seized. H6269
Ge 22: 3 with him two of his s and his son Isaac. H5853
Ge 22: 5 He said to his s, "Stay here with the H5853
Ge 22:19 Then Abraham returned to his s, and they H5853
Ge 24:35 gold, **male** and female s, and camels H6269
[Ge 24:35 gold, male and **female** s, and camels H9148]
Ge 26:14 flocks and herds and s that the Philistines H6276
Ge 26:15 that his father's s had dug in the time of H6269
Ge 26:19 Isaac's s dug in the valley and discovered H6269
Ge 26:25 his tent, and there his s dug a well. H6269
Ge 26:32 That day Isaac's s came and told him H6269
Ge 27:37 you and have made all his relatives his s, H6269
Ge 30:43 female and **male** s, and camels and H6269
[Ge 30:43 **female** and male s, and camels and H9148]
Ge 31:33 tent and into the tent of the two **female** s, H563
Ge 32: 5 sheep and goats, **male** and female s. H6269
[Ge 32: 5 sheep and goats, male and **female** s. H9148]
Ge 32:16 He put them in the care of his s, each herd H6269
Ge 32:16 and said to his s, "Go ahead of me, H6269
Ge 32:22 his two **female** s and his eleven sons and H9148
Ge 33: 1 Rachel and the two **female** s. H9148
Ge 33: 2 He put the **female** s and their children in H9148
Ge 33: 6 Then the **female** s and their children H9148
Ge 39:11 none of the household s was inside. H408
Ge 39:14 she called her household s. "Look," she H408
Ge 41:10 Pharaoh was once angry with his s, and he H6269
Ge 42:10 "Your s have come to buy food. H6269
Ge 42:11 Your s are honest men, not H6269
Ge 42:13 they replied, "Your s were twelve brothers H6269
Ge 44: 7 Far be it from your s to do anything like H6269
Ge 44: 9 If any of your s is found to have it, he will H6269
Ge 44:19 My lord asked his s, 'Do you have a father H6269
Ge 44:21 "Then you said to your s, 'Bring him down H6269
Ge 44:23 But you told your s, 'Unless your youngest H6269
Ge 44:31 Your s will bring the gray head of our H6269
Ge 46:34 'Your s have tended livestock from our H6269
Ge 47: 3 "Your s are shepherds," they replied to H6269
Ge 47: 4 please let your s settle in Goshen. H6269
Ge 50:17 the sins of the s *of* the God of your father H6269
Ex 5:15 "Why have you treated your s this way? H6269
Ex 5:16 Your s are given no straw, yet we are told H6269
Ex 5:16 Your s are being beaten, but the fault is H6269
Ex 21: 7 she is not to go free as **male** s do. H6269
Ex 32:13 Remember your s Abraham, Isaac and H6269
Lev 25: 6 yourself, your **male** and female s, and the H6269
[Lev 25: 6 yourself, your male and **female** s, and the H563]
Lev 25:42 Because the Israelites are my s, whom I H6269
Lev 25:55 the Israelites belong to me as s. H6269
Lev 25:55 They are my s, whom I brought out of H6269
Nu 22:22 his donkey, and his two s were with him. H5853
Nu 31:49 "Your s have counted the soldiers under H6269
Nu 32: 4 livestock, and your s have livestock. H6269
Nu 32: 5 land be given to your s as our possession. H6269
Nu 32:25 "We your s will do as our lord commands. H6269
Nu 32:27 But your s, every man who is armed for H6269
Nu 32:31 "Your s will do what the LORD has said. H6269
Dt 5:14 so that your **male** and female s may rest H6269
[Dt 5:14 so that your male and **female** s may rest H563]
Dt 9:27 Remember your s Abraham, Isaac and H6269
Dt 12:12 your **male** and female s, and the H6269
[Dt 12:12 your male and **female** s, and the H563]
Dt 12:18 your **male** and female s, and the H6269
[Dt 12:18 your male and **female** s, and the H563]
Dt 16:11 your **male** and female s, the Levites H6269
[Dt 16:11 your male and **female** s, the Levites H563]
Dt 16:14 your **male** and female s, and the H6269
[Dt 16:14 your male and **female** s, and the H563]
Dt 32:36 relent concerning his s when he sees their H6269
Dt 32:43 he will avenge the blood of his s; he H6269
Jos 9: 8 "We are your s," they said to Joshua. H6269
Jos 9: 9 "Your s have come from a very distant H6269
Jos 9:11 "We are your s; make a treaty with H6269
Jos 9:24 "Your s were clearly told how the LORD H6269
Jos 10: 6 "Do not abandon your s. Come up to us H6269
Jdg 3:24 the s came and found the doors of the H6269
Jdg 6:27 took ten of his s and did as the LORD H6269
Jdg 19:19 bread and wine for ourselves your s— H6269
Ru 2:13 do not have the standing of one of your s." H9148
1Sa 2: 9 He will guard the feet of his **faithful** s, but H2883
1Sa 8:16 Your **male** and female s and the best of H6269
[1Sa 8:16 Your male and **female** s and the best of H9148]
1Sa 9: 3 "Take one of the s with you and go and H5853
1Sa 12:19 your God for your s so that we will not H6269
1Sa 16:16 our lord command his s here to search H6269
1Sa 16:18 One of the s answered, "I have seen a H5853
1Sa 17: 8 Philistine, and are you not the s of Saul? H6269
1Sa 18:24 When Saul's s told him what David had H6269
1Sa 21: 7 Now one of Saul's s was there that day H6269
1Sa 21:11 But the s *of* Achish said to him, "Isn't this H6269
1Sa 21:14 Achish said to his s, "Look at the man! He H6269
1Sa 22:14 "Who of all your s is as loyal as David H6269
1Sa 25: 8 Ask your own s and they will tell you H5853
1Sa 25: 8 Please give your s and your son David H6269
1Sa 25:10 Nabal answered David's s, "Who is this H6269
1Sa 25:10 Many s are breaking away from their H6269
1Sa 25:14 One of the s told Abigail, Nabal's wife H5853
1Sa 25:19 Then she told her s, "Go on ahead; I'll H5853
1Sa 25:40 His s went to Carmel and said to Abigail H6269
1Sa 25:41 you and wash the feet of my lord's s." H6269
1Sa 25:42 attended by her five **female** s, went with H5855
1Sa 29:10 with your master's s who have come with H6269
2Sa 6:20 the slave girls of his s as any vulgar fellow H6269
2Sa 9:10 your sons and your s are to farm the land H6269
2Sa 9:10 Now Ziba had fifteen sons and twenty s.) H6269
2Sa 9:12 household were s of Mephibosheth. H6269
2Sa 11: 9 all his master's s and did not go down H6269
2Sa 11:13 to sleep on his mat among his master's s; H6269
2Sa 11:24 shot arrows at your s from the wall, H6269
2Sa 14:30 Then he said to his s, "Look, Joab's field is H6269
2Sa 14:30 So Absalom's s set the field on fire. H6269
2Sa 14:31 "Why have your s set my field on fire?" H6269
2Sa 15:15 "Your s are ready to do whatever our lord H6269
2Sa 19:17 his fifteen sons and twenty s. H6269
1Ki 1:27 without letting his s know who should sit H6269
1Ki 1:33 "Take your lord's s with you and have H6269
1Ki 8:23 covenant of love with your s who continue H6269
1Ki 8:32 Judge between your s, condemning the H6269
1Ki 8:36 from heaven and forgive the sin of your s, H6269
1Ki 10: 5 officials, the attending s in their robes, his H9250
1Ki 12: 7 answer, they will always be your s. H6269
2Ki 1:13 the lives of these fifty men, your s! H6269
2Ki 2:16 they said, "we your s have fifty able men. H6269
2Ki 4:22 send me one of the s and a donkey so I H5853
2Ki 5:13 Naaman's s went to him and said, "My H6269
2Ki 5:23 He gave them to two of his s, and they H5853
2Ki 5:24 the things from **the s** and put them away H4392S
2Ki 6: 3 "Won't you please come with your s?" H6269
2Ki 9: 7 the blood of my s the prophets and the H6269
2Ki 9: 7 blood of all the LORD's s shed by Jezebel. H6269
2Ki 9:28 His s took him by chariot to Jerusalem H6269
2Ki 10: 5 "We are your s and we will do anything H6269
2Ki 10:19 of Baal, all his s and all his priests. H6268
2Ki 10:19 in order to destroy the s *of* Baal. H6268
2Ki 10:21 and all the s *of* Baal came; not one H6268
2Ki 10:22 "Bring robes for all the s *of* Baal. H6268
2Ki 10:23 Jehu said to the s *of* Baal, "Look around H6268
2Ki 10:23 the LORD is here with you—only s *of* Baal." H6268
2Ki 17:13 to you through my s the prophets. H6269
2Ki 17:23 warned through all his s the prophets. H6269
2Ki 18:26 "Please speak to your s in Aramaic, since H6269
2Ki 21:10 The LORD said through his s the prophets: H6269
2Ki 23:30 Josiah's s brought his body in a chariot H6269
2Ki 24: 2 the LORD proclaimed by his s the prophets. H6269
1Ch 9: 2 Israelites, priests, Levites and **temple** s. H5987
1Ch 16:13 you his s, the descendants of Israel, his H6269
2Ch 2: 8 I know that your s are skilled in cutting H6269
2Ch 2: 8 My s will work with yours H6269
2Ch 2:10 I will give your s, the woodsmen who cut H6269
2Ch 2:15 my lord send his s the wheat and barley H6269
2Ch 6:14 covenant of love with your s who continue H6269
2Ch 6:23 Judge between your s, condemning the H6269
2Ch 6:27 from heaven and forgive the sin of your s, H6269

S

2Ch 9: 4 the attending **s** in their robes, the H9250
2Ch 9:10 The **s** *of* Hiram and the servants of H6269
2Ch 9:10 of Hiram and the **s** *of* Solomon brought H6269
2Ch 9:21 of trading ships manned by Hiram's **s**. H6269
2Ch 10: 7 answer, they will always be your **s**. H6269
2Ch 36:20 they became **s** to him and his H6269
Ezr 2:43 The **temple s**: the descendants of Ziha H5987
Ezr 2:55 The descendants of the **s** *of* Solomon: the H6269
Ezr 2:58 The **temple s** and the descendants of the H5987
Ezr 2:58 the descendants of the **s** *of* Solomon 392 H6269
Ezr 2:70 the **temple s** settled in their H5987
Ezr 4:11 From your **s** *in* Trans-Euphrates: A10523
Ezr 5:11 "We are the **s** of the God of heaven and A10523
Ezr 7: 7 gatekeepers and **temple s**, also came up H5987
Ezr 7:24 **temple s** or other workers at this house A10497
Ezr 8:17 the **temple s** in Kasiphia, so H5987
Ezr 8:20 They also brought 220 of the **temple s**—a H5987
Ezr 9:11 gave through your **s** the prophets when H6269
Ne 1: 6 before you day and night for your **s**, H6269
Ne 1:10 "They are your **s** and your people, whom H6269
Ne 1:11 to the prayer of your **s** who delight in H6269
Ne 2:20 We his **s** will start rebuilding, but as for H6269
Ne 3:26 the **temple s** living on the hill of H5987
Ne 3:31 the house of the **temple s** and the H5987
Ne 7:46 The **temple s**: the descendants of Ziha H5987
Ne 7:57 The descendants of the **s** *of* Solomon: the H6269
Ne 7:60 The **temple s** and the descendants of the H5987
Ne 7:60 the descendants of the **s** *of* Solomon 392 H6269
Ne 7:73 the musicians and the **temple s**, along H5987
Ne 10:28 **temple s** and all who separated H5987
Ne 11: 3 **temple s** and descendants of Solomon's H5987
Ne 11: 3 of Solomon's **s** lived in the towns of H6269
Ne 11:21 The **temple s** lived on the hill of Ophel H5987
Job 1: 3 donkeys, and had a large number of **s**. H6276
Job 1:15 They put the **s** to the sword, and I am the H5853
Job 1:16 burned up the sheep and the **s**, H5853
Job 1:17 They put the **s** to the sword, and I am the H5853
Job 4:18 If God places no trust in his **s**, if he H6269
Job 19:15 My guests and my **female s** count me a H563
Job 31:13 to any of my **s**, whether **male** or female, H6269
[Job 31:13 to any of my **s**, whether male or **female**, H563]
Ps 34:22 The LORD will rescue his **s**; no one who H6269
Ps 69:36 the children of his **s** will inherit it, and H6269
Ps 79: 2 dead bodies of your **s** as food for the birds H6269
Ps 79:10 avenge the outpoured blood of your **s**. H6269
Ps 85: 8 his people, his **faithful s**—but let them H2883
Ps 90:13 Have compassion on your **s**. H6269
Ps 90:16 May your deeds be shown to your **s**, your H6269
Ps 102:14 For her stones are dear to your **s**; her very H6269
Ps 102:28 The children of your **s** will live in your H6269
Ps 103:21 heavenly hosts, you his **s** who do his will. H9250
Ps 104: 4 winds his messengers, flames of fire his **s**. H9250
Ps 105: 6 you his **s**, the descendants of Abraham H6269
Ps 105:25 hate his people, to conspire against his **s**. H6269
Ps 113: 1 the LORD, you his **s**; praise the name of the H6269
Ps 116:15 of the LORD is the death of his **faithful s**. H2883
Ps 134: 1 all you **s** *of* the LORD who minister by night H6269
Ps 135: 1 of the LORD; praise him, you **s** *of* the LORD, H6269
Ps 135: 9 against Pharaoh and all his **s**. H6269
Ps 135:14 his people and have compassion on his **s**. H6269
Ps 148:14 the praise of all his **faithful s**, of Israel, H2883
Pr 9: 3 She has sent out her **s**, and she calls from H5855
Pr 27:27 your family and to nourish your **female s**. H5855
Pr 29:19 **S** cannot be corrected by mere words H6269
Pr 31:15 her family and portions for her **female s**. H5855
Isa 14: 2 make them **male** and female **s** in the H6269
[Isa 14: 2 make them male and **female s** in the H9148]
Isa 36:11 "Please speak to your **s** in Aramaic, since H6269
Isa 44:26 out the words of his **s** and fulfills the H6269
Isa 54:17 This is the heritage of the **s** *of* **the** LORD H6269
Isa 56: 6 the LORD, and to be his **s**, all who keep the H6269
Isa 63:17 Return for the sake of your **s**, the tribes H6269
Isa 65: 8 so will I do in behalf of my **s**; I will not H6269
Isa 65: 9 will inherit them, and there will my **s** live. H6269
Isa 65:13 "My **s** will eat, but you will go hungry; my H6269
Isa 65:13 will go hungry; my **s** will drink, but you H6269
Isa 65:13 will go thirsty; my **s** will rejoice, but you H6269
Isa 65:14 My **s** will sing out of the joy of their hearts, H6269
Isa 65:15 to his **s** he will give another name. H6269
Isa 66:14 of the LORD will be made known to his **s**, H6269
Jer 7:25 again I sent you my **s** the prophets. H6269
Jer 14: 3 The nobles send their **s** for water; they go H7582
Jer 25: 4 LORD has sent all his **s** the prophets to you H6269
Jer 26: 5 listen to the words of my **s** the prophets, H6269
Jer 29:19 again and again by my **s** the prophets. H6269
Jer 35:15 again I sent all my **s** the prophets to you. H6269
Jer 44: 4 Again and again I sent my **s** the prophets H6269
Eze 38:17 in former days by my **s** the prophets of H6269
Eze 46:17 a gift from his inheritance to one of his **s**, H6269
Da 1:12 "Please test your **s** for ten days: Give us H6269
Da 1:13 treat your **s** in accordance with what H6269
Da 2: 4 Tell your **s** the dream, and we will A10523
Da 2: 7 "Let the king tell his **s** the dream, and A10523
Da 3:26 Abednego, **s** *of* the Most High God A10523
Da 3:28 has sent his angel and rescued his **s**! A10523
Da 9: 6 have not listened to your **s** the prophets, H6269
Da 9:10 he gave us through his **s** the prophets. H6269
Joel 2:29 Even on my **s**, both **men** and women, H6269
Am 3: 7 revealing his plan to his **s** the prophets. H6269
Zec 1: 6 which I commanded my **s** the prophets H6269
Mt 10:25 their teachers, and **s** like their masters. *G1528*
Mt 13:27 "The owner's **s** came to him and said, 'Sir, *G1528*
Mt 13:28 "The **s** asked him, 'Do you want us to go *G1528*
Mt 18:23 who wanted to settle accounts with his **s**. *G1528*
Mt 18:28 he found one *of* his **fellow s** who owed *G5281*
Mt 18:31 When the **other s** saw what had happened *G5281*
Mt 21:34 he sent his **s** to the tenants to collect his *G1528*
Mt 21:35 "The tenants seized his **s**; they beat one *G1528*
Mt 21:36 Then he sent other **s** to them, more than *G1528*
Mt 22: 3 He sent his **s** to those who had been *G1528*
Mt 22: 4 "Then he sent some more **s** and said *G1528*
Mt 22: 6 The rest seized his **s**, mistreated them *G1528*
Mt 22: 8 "Then he said *to* his **s**, 'The wedding *G1528*
Mt 22:10 So the **s** went out into the streets and *G1528*
Mt 24:45 of the **s in** his **household** to give them *G3859*
Mt 24:49 begins to beat his **fellow s** and to eat *G5281*
Mt 25:14 who called his **s** and entrusted his wealth *G1528*
Mt 25:19 time the master *of* those **s** returned and *G1528*
Mk 13:34 leaves his house and puts his **s** in charge, *G1528*
Lk 1: 2 first were eyewitnesses and **s** of the word. *G5677*
Lk 12:36 like **s** waiting for their master to return *G476S*
Lk 12:37 be good for those **s** whose master finds *G1528*
Lk 12:38 will be good for those **s** whose master finds NDT
Lk 12:42 puts in charge of his **s** to give them their *G2542*
Lk 12:45 beat the other **s**, both **men** and women, *G4090*
Lk 15:17 of my father's **hired s** have food to spare *G3634*
Lk 15:19 make me like one *of* your **hired s**. *G3634*
Lk 15:22 "But the father said to his **s**, 'Quick! Bring *G1528*
Lk 15:26 So he called one *of* the **s** and asked him *G4090*
Lk 17:10 'We are unworthy **s**; we have only done *G1528*
Lk 19:13 So he called ten *of* his **s** and gave them *G1528*
Lk 19:15 he sent for the **s** to whom he had given *G1528*
Jn 2: 5 His mother said *to* the **s**, "Do whatever he *G1356*
Jn 2: 7 Jesus said *to* **the s**, "Fill the jars with *G899S*
Jn 2: 9 though the **s** who had drawn the water *G1356*
Jn 4:51 his **s** met him with the news that his boy *G1528*
Jn 15:15 I no longer call you **s**, because a servant *G1528*
Jn 18:18 the **s** and officials stood around a fire *G1528*
Jn 18:26 One of the high priest's **s**, a relative of the *G1528*
Jn 18:36 my **s** would fight to prevent my arrest by *G5677*
Ac 2:18 Even on my **s**, both **men** and women, *G1528*
[Ac 2:18 Even on my **s**, both men and **women**, *G1527*]
Ac 4:29 enable your **s** to speak your word with *G1528*
Ac 10: 7 Cornelius called two *of* his **s** and a devout *G3860*
Ac 16:17 "These men are **s** of the Most High God *G1528*
Ro 13: 4 They are God's **s**, agents of wrath to bring *G1356*
Ro 13: 6 the authorities are God's **s**, who give *G3313*
Ro 14: 4 To their own master, **s** stand or fall. NDT
1Co 3: 5 Only **s**, through whom you came to *G1356*
1Co 4: 1 as **s** of Christ and as those entrusted with *G5677*
2Co 4: 5 ourselves *as* your **s** for Jesus' sake. *G1528*
2Co 6: 4 as **s** of God we commend ourselves in *G1356*
2Co 11:15 if his **s** also masquerade as servants of *G1356*
2Co 11:15 also masquerade as **s** of righteousness. *G1356*
2Co 11:23 Are they **s** of Christ? (I am out of my mind *G1356*
Php 1: 1 Paul and Timothy, **s** of Christ Jesus, To all *G1528*
Heb 1: 7 his angels spirits, and his **s** flames of fire." *G3313*
Rev 1: 1 him to show his **s** what must soon take *G1528*
Rev 2:20 she misleads my **s** into sexual immorality *G1528*
Rev 6:11 until the full number of their **fellow s** *G5281*
Rev 7: 3 seal on the foreheads *of* the **s** of our God." *G1528*
Rev 10: 7 as he announced *to* his **s** the prophets." *G1528*
Rev 11:18 rewarding your **s** the prophets and your *G1528*
Rev 19: 2 He has avenged on her the blood *of* his **s**." *G1528*
Rev 19: 5 our God, all you his **s**, you who fear him, *G1528*
Rev 22: 3 be in the city, and his **s** will serve him. *G1528*
Rev 22: 6 angel to show his **s** the things that must *G1528*

SERVANTS' (2) [SERVANT]

Ge 44:16 God has uncovered your **s** guilt. We are H6269
Ge 47: 4 Canaan and your **s** flocks have no H4200+6269

SERVE (230) [SERVED, SERVES, SERVICE, SERVICES, SERVING, SERVITUDE]

Ge 1:14 and *let them* **s** as signs to mark sacred H2118
Ge 15:14 I will punish the nation *they* **s as slaves**, H6268
Ge 25:23 and the older *will* **s** the younger. H6268
Ge 27:29 *May* nations **s** you and peoples bow down H6268
Ge 27:40 by the sword and *you will* **s** your brother. H6268
Ge 31:44 and *let it* **s** as a witness between us." H2118
Ge 43:31 controlling himself, said, "**S** the food." H8492
Ex 14:12 'Leave us alone; *let us* **s** the Egyptians'? H6268
Ex 14:12 been better for us *to* **s** the Egyptians than H6268
Ex 18:13 took his seat to **s as judge** *for* the people, H9149
Ex 18:22 *Have them* **s as judges** *for* the people at H9149
Ex 21: 2 servant, *he is to* **s** you for six years. H6268
Ex 28: 1 Ithamar, so they *may* **s** me **as priests**. H3912
Ex 28: 3 consecration, so he *may* **s** me **as priest**. H3912
Ex 28: 4 his sons, so they *may* **s** me **as priests**. H3912
Ex 28:41 them so *they may* **s** me **as priests**. H3912
Ex 29: 1 so *they may* **s** me **as priests**: H3912
Ex 29:44 Aaron and his sons to **s** me **as priests**. H3912
Ex 30:30 them so they *may* **s** me **as priests**. H3912
Ex 31:10 his sons when *they* **s as priests**, H3912
Ex 35:19 his sons when *they* **s as priests**. H3912
Ex 40:13 consecrate him so *he may* **s** me **as priest**. H3912
Ex 40:15 their father, so *they may* **s** me **as priests**. H3912
Lev 7:35 were presented to **s** the LORD **as priests**. H3912
Nu 1: 3 old or more and *able to* **s** *in* the army. H3655
Nu 1:20 more *who were able to* **s** *in* the army H3655
Nu 1:22 more *who were able to* **s** *in* the army H3655
Nu 1:24 more *who were able to* **s** *in* the army H3655
Nu 1:26 more *who were able to* **s** *in* the army H3655
Nu 1:28 more *who were able to* **s** *in* the army H3655
Nu 1:30 more *who were able to* **s** *in* the army H3655
Nu 1:32 more *who were able to* **s** *in* the army H3655
Nu 1:34 more *who were able to* **s** *in* the army H3655
Nu 1:36 more *who were able to* **s** *in* the army H3655
Nu 1:38 more *who were able to* **s** *in* the army H3655
Nu 1:40 more *who were able to* **s** *in* the army H3655
Nu 1:42 more *who were able to* **s** *in* the army H3655
Nu 1:45 old or more *who were able to* **s** *in* Israel's H3655
Nu 3: 3 who were ordained to **s as priests**. H3912
Nu 3:10 Appoint Aaron and his sons *to* **s** as priests H9068
Nu 4: 3 who come to **s** *in* the work at the H6913+7372
Nu 4:23 age who come to **s** in the work at H7371+7372
Nu 4:30 of age who come to **s** in the work at the H7372
Nu 4:35 of age who came to **s** in the work at the H7372
Nu 4:39 of age who came to **s** in the work at the H7372
Nu 4:43 of age who came to **s** in the work at the H7372
Nu 18: 7 only you and your sons *may* **s** as priests in H9068
Nu 26: 2 old or more *who are able to* **s in** the army H3655
Dt 6:13 **s** him only and take your oaths in his H6268
Dt 7: 4 away from following me *to* **s** other gods, H6268
Dt 7:16 on them with pity and *do* not **s** their gods, H6268
Dt 10:12 to **s** the LORD your God with all your heart H6268
Dt 10:20 Fear the LORD your God and **s** him. H6268
Dt 11:13 LORD your God and to **s** him with all your H6268
Dt 12:30 "How *do* these nations **s** their gods? H6268
Dt 13: 4 obey him; **s** him and hold fast to him. H6268
Dt 15:12 sell themselves to you and **s** you six years H6268
Dt 18: 7 fellow Levites who **s** there in the presence H6641
Dt 28:47 Because *you did* not **s** the LORD your God H6268
Dt 28:48 *you will* **s** the enemies the LORD sends H6268
Jos 4: 6 to **s** as a sign among you. In the future H2118
Jos 22: 5 fast to him and to **s** him with all your H6268
Jos 23: 7 *You must* not **s** them or bow down to H6268
Jos 23:16 go and **s** other gods and bow down H6268
Jos 24:14 "Now fear the LORD and **s** him with all H6268
Jos 24:14 River and in Egypt, and **s** the LORD. H6268
Jos 24:15 yourselves this day whom *you will* **s**, H6268
Jos 24:15 me and my household, *we will* **s** the LORD." H6268
Jos 24:16 us to forsake the LORD to **s** other gods! H6268
Jos 24:18 We too *will* **s** the LORD, because he is our H6268
Jos 24:19 people, "You are not able to **s** the LORD. H6268
Jos 24:20 If you forsake the LORD and **s** foreign gods H6268
Jos 24:21 said to Joshua, "No! *We will* **s** the LORD." H6268
Jos 24:22 that you have chosen to **s** the LORD." H6268
Jos 24:24 "*We will* **s** the LORD our God and obey him H6268
Jdg 9:28 Zebul his deputy? **S** the family of Hamor H6268
Jdg 9:28 Why *should* we **s** Abimelek? H6268
Jdg 18:19 it better that you **s** a tribe and clan H2118+4200
1Sa 7: 3 yourselves to the LORD and **s** him only, H6268
1Sa 8:11 sons and **make** them **s** with his H8492+4200
1Sa 12:10 hands of our enemies, and *we will* **s** you. H6268
1Sa 12:14 fear the LORD and **s** and obey him and do H6268
1Sa 12:20 LORD, but **s** the LORD with all your heart. H6268
1Sa 12:24 to fear the LORD and **s** him faithfully with H6268
1Sa 17: 9 you will become our subjects and **s** us." H6268
1Sa 18:17 only **s** me bravely and fight the battles of H2118
1Sa 25:41 am ready to **s** you and wash the feet H9148
1Sa 26:19 have said, 'Go, **s** other gods. H6268
1Sa 29: 6 pleased *to have* you **s** with H3655+2256+995
2Sa 16:19 whom *should* I **s**? Should I not H6268
2Sa 16:19 Should I not **s** the son? Just as I H4200+7156
2Sa 16:19 your father, so *I will* **s** you." H2118+4200+7156
2Sa 22:44 People I did not know *now* **s** me, H6268
1Ki 1: 2 virgin *to* **s** the king and H6641+4200+7156
1Ki 9: 6 given you and go off *to* **s** other gods and H6268
1Ki 9:21 exterminate—to **s as slave** labor, as it is H6268
1Ki 9:27 to **s** in the fleet with Solomon's men. NDT
1Ki 12: 4 yoke he put on us, and *we will* **s** you." H6268
1Ki 12: 7 these people and **s** them and give them H6268
1Ki 16:31 began *to* **s** Baal and worship him. H6268
1Ki 17: 1 lives, whom *I* **s**, there will be H6641+4200+7156
1Ki 18:15 lives, whom *I* **s**, I will surely H6641+4200+7156
2Ki 3:14 lives, whom *I* **s**, if I did not H6641+4200+7156
2Ki 4:41 pot and said, "**S** it to the people to eat." H3668
2Ki 5:16 lives, whom *I* **s**, I will not H6641+4200+7156
2Ki 10:18 served Baal a little; Jehu *will* **s** him much. H6268
2Ki 17:35 down to them, **s** them or sacrifice to them. H6268
2Ki 18: 7 the king of Assyria and *did* not **s** him. H6268
2Ki 23: 9 of the high places *did* not **s** at the altar of H6590
2Ki 25:24 in the land and **s** the king of Babylon, H6268
1Ch 12:38 men *who* **volunteered to s** *in* the ranks. H6370
1Ch 23:31 They were to **s** before the LORD regularly in NDT
1Ch 28: 9 **s** him with wholehearted devotion H6268
2Ch 7:19 given you and go off *to* **s** other gods and H6268
2Ch 8: 8 had not destroyed—**to s as** slave labor, as H4200
2Ch 10: 4 yoke he put on us, and *we will* **s** you." H6268
2Ch 13:10 The priests *who* **s** the LORD are sons of H9250
2Ch 19: 9 "*You must* **s** faithfully and wholeheartedly H6913
2Ch 19:11 the Levites *will* **s as officials** before you. H8853
2Ch 29:11 you to stand before him and **s** him, H9250
2Ch 30: 8 **S** the LORD your God, so that his fierce H6268
2Ch 33:16 told Judah to **s** the LORD, the God of H6268
2Ch 34:33 *he* **had** all who were present in Israel **s** H6641
2Ch 35: 3 Now **s** the LORD your God and his people H6268
Ne 4:22 so *they can* **s** us *as* guards by night and as H2118
Ne 9:35 *they did* not **s** you or turn from their evil H6268
Est 1: 8 the wine stewards to **s** each man what he H6913
Job 21:15 is the Almighty, that *we should* **s** him? H6268
Job 36:11 If they obey and **s** him, they will spend H6268
Job 39: 9 "Will the wild ox consent *to* **s** you? Will it H6268
Ps 2:11 **S** the LORD with fear and celebrate his rule H6268
Ps 18:43 People I did not know *now* **s** me, H6268

Ps 22:30 Posterity will s him; future generations H6268
Ps 72:11 bow down to him and all nations s him. H6268
Ps 86:16 because I s you just as my mother did. H563
Ps 116:16 I s you just as my mother did; you H6269
Ps 119:91 endure to this day, for all things s you. H6269
Ps 130: 4 so that we can, with reverence, s you. H3707
Pr 22:21 bring back truthful reports to those you s? H8938
Pr 22:29 They will s before kings; they will not H3656
Pr 22:29 they will not s before officials of low rank. H3656
Isa 60: 7 the rams of Nebaioth will s you; they will H9250
Isa 60:10 your walls, and their kings will s you. H9250
Isa 60:12 kingdom that will not s you will perish; H6268
Jer 2:20 off your bonds; you said, 'I will not s you! H6268
Jer 5:19 so now you will s foreigners in a land not H6268
Jer 11:10 They have followed other gods to s them H6268
Jer 13:10 after other gods to s and worship them, H6268
Jer 15:19 you that you may s me; H6641+4200+7156
Jer 16:13 there you will s other gods day and H6268
Jer 25: 6 follow other gods to s and worship them; H6268
Jer 25:11 these nations will s the king of H6268
Jer 27: 7 All nations will s him and his son and his H6268
Jer 27: 8 kingdom will not s Nebuchadnezzar H6268
Jer 27: 9 'You will not s the king of Babylon. H6268
Jer 27:10 you that will only s to remove you far from AIT
Jer 27:11 the yoke of the king of Babylon and s him, H6268
Jer 27:12 the king of Babylon; s him and his people H6268
Jer 27:13 any nation that will not s the king of H6268
Jer 27:14 'You will not s the king of Babylon H6268
Jer 27:17 not listen to them. S the king of Babylon H6268
Jer 28:14 nations to make them s Nebuchadnezzar H6268
Jer 28:14 king of Babylon, and they will s him. H6268
Jer 30: 9 they will s the LORD their God and David H6268
Jer 35:15 do not follow other gods to s them. H6268
Jer 35:19 have a descendant to s me. H6641+4200+7156
Jer 40: 9 "Do not be afraid to s the Babylonians," H6268
Jer 40: 9 in the land and s the king of Babylon, H6268
Eze 20:32 of the world, who s wood and stone." H9250
Eze 20:39 Go and s your idols, every one H6268
Eze 20:40 the land all the people of Israel will s me, H6268
Eze 27:25 ships of Tarshish s as carriers for your wares. AIT
Eze 41: 6 wall of the temple to s as supports for the H2118
Eze 44:11 They may s in my sanctuary, having charge H2118
Eze 44:11 stand before the people and s them. H9250
Eze 44:13 come near to s me as priests or come H3912
Eze 44:16 minister before me and s me as guards. H9068
Eze 44:24 the priests are to s as judges and decide H6641
Eze 45: 5 to the Levites, who s in the temple, as H9250
Eze 47:12 Their fruit will s for food and their leaves H2118
Da 1: 4 qualified to s in the king's palace. H6641
Da 3:12 They neither s your gods nor worship the A10586
Da 3:14 that you do not s my gods or worship the A10586
Da 3:17 the God we s is able to deliver us from it, A10586
Da 3:18 that we will not s your gods or worship A10586
Da 3:28 lives rather than s or worship any god A10586
Da 6:16 your God, whom you s continually A10586
Da 6:20 your God, whom you s continually, been A10586
Zep 3: 9 name of the LORD and s him shoulder to H6268
Zec 4:14 are anointed to s the Lord of all H6641+6584
Mal 3:14 'It is futile to s God. What do we H6268
Mal 3:18 between those who s God and those who H6268
Mt 4:10 the Lord your God, and s him only. G3302
Mt 6:24 "No one can s two masters. Either you will G1526
Mt 6:24 You cannot s both God and money. G1526
Mt 20:28 to be served, but to s, and to give his life G1354
Mk 10:45 to be served, but to s, and to give his life G1354
Lk 1:74 to enable us to s him without fear G3302
Lk 4: 8 the Lord your God and s him only. G3302
Lk 12:37 tell you, he will dress himself to s, will G4322
Lk 16:13 "No one can s two masters. Either you will G1526
Lk 16:13 You cannot s both God and money." G1526
Ac 7: 7 I will punish the nation they s as slaves, G1526
Ac 26: 7 fulfilled as they earnestly s God day and G3302
Ac 27:23 I belong and whom I s stood beside me G3302
Ro 1: 9 whom I s in my spirit in preaching the G3302
Ro 7: 6 the law so that we s in the new way of the G1526
Ro 9:12 was told, "The older will s the younger." G1526
Ro 12: 7 if it is serving, then s; if it is teaching, then G1355
1Co 9:13 know that those who s in the temple get G2237
1Co 9:13 that those who s at the altar share in G4204
2Co 11: 8 support from them so as to s you. G1355
Gal 5:13 s one another humbly in love. G1526
Eph 6: 7 S wholeheartedly, as if you were serving G1526
Php 3: 3 circumcision, we who s God by his Spirit G3302
1Th 1: 9 to God from idols to s the living and true G1526
2Th 2: 9 through signs and wonders that s the lie, AIT
1Ti 3:10 against them, let them s as deacons. G1354
1Ti 6: 2 they should s them even better because G1526
2Ti 1: 3 I thank God, whom I s, as my ancestors G3302
Heb 1:14 spirits sent to s those who will inherit G1355
Heb 8: 5 They s at a sanctuary that is a copy and G3302
Heb 9:14 to death, so that we may s the living God! G3302
1Pe 4:10 should use whatever gift you have received to s G1354
1Pe 5: 2 not pursuing dishonest gain, but eager to s; NDT
Jude 7 They s as an example of those who suffer G4618
Rev 1: 6 priests to s his God and Father— AIT
Rev 5:10 to be a kingdom and priests to s our God, AIT
Rev 7:15 throne of God and s him day and night in G3302
Rev 22: 3 be in the city, and his servants will s him. G3302

SERVED (70) [SERVE]

Ge 29:20 So Jacob s seven years to get Rachel, but H6268
Ge 29:25 you have done to me? I s you for Rachel H6268
Ge 30:26 whom I have s you, and I will be H6268
Ge 43:32 They s him by himself, the brothers by H8492
Ge 43:34 When portions were s to them from H5951
Ex 18:26 They s as judges for the people at all H9149
Ex 38: 8 mirrors of the women who s at the H7371+7371
Nu 3: 4 Ithamar s as priests during the H3912
Nu 4:37 Kohathite clans who s at the tent of H6268
Nu 4:41 Gershonite clans who s at the tent of H6268
Nu 26:10 And they s as a warning sign. H2118
Jos 24:15 gods your ancestors s beyond the H6268
Jos 24:31 Israel s the LORD throughout the lifetime H6268
Jdg 2: 7 The people s the LORD throughout the H6268
Jdg 2:11 in the eyes of the LORD and s the Baals. H6268
Jdg 2:13 they forsook him and s Baal and the H6268
Jdg 3: 6 daughters to their sons, and s their gods. H6268
Jdg 3: 7 LORD their God and s the Baals and the H6268
Jdg 10: 6 They s the Baals and the Ashtoreths, and H6268
Jdg 10: 6 forsook the LORD and no longer s him, H6268
Jdg 10:13 you have forsaken me and s other gods, H6268
Jdg 10:16 foreign gods among them and s the LORD. H6268
1Sa 2:22 with the women who s at the entrance to H7371
1Sa 7: 4 Baals and Ashtoreths, and s the LORD only. H6268
1Sa 8: 2 was Abijah, and they s at Beersheba. H9149
1Sa 12:10 forsaken the LORD and s the Baals and the H6268
2Sa 12:20 at his request they s him food, and H8492
2Sa 13: 9 she took the pan and s him the bread, H3668
2Sa 16:19 serve the son? Just as I s your father, so I H6268
1Ki 11:17 Edomite officials who had s his father. H6269
1Ki 12: 6 elders who had s his father H6641+907+7156
1Ki 22:53 He s and worshiped Baal and aroused the H6268
2Ki 5: 2 and she s Naaman's wife. H2118+4200+7156
2Ki 10:18 said to them, "Ahab s Baal a little; Jehu H6268
2Ki 17:33 they also s their own gods in H6268
1Ch 6:10 it was he who s as priest in the temple H3912
1Ch 6:33 Here are the men who s, together with H6641
1Ch 6:39 associate Asaph, who s at his right hand: H6641
1Ch 23:24 old or more who s in the temple of the H6275
1Ch 24: 2 so Eleazar and Ithamar s as the priests. H3912
1Ch 27: 1 who s the king in all that concerned the H9250
2Ch 10: 6 elders who had s his father H6641+4200+7156
2Ch 17:19 These were the men who s the king H9250
2Ch 31:13 All these s by appointment of King NDT
2Ch 35:13 pans and s them quickly to all the H8132
Ne 12:26 They s in the days of Joiakim son of Joshua NDT
Est 1: 7 Wine was s in goblets of gold, each one H9197
Est 1:10 the seven eunuchs who s him— H9250
Jer 5:19 forsaken me and s foreign gods in your H6268
Jer 8: 2 have loved and s and which they have H6268
Jer 16:11 other gods and s and worshiped them. H6268
Jer 22: 9 have worshiped and s other gods. H6268
Jer 34:14 After they have s you six years, you must H6268
Jer 52:12 who s the king of Babylon H6641+4200+7156
Eze 27: 7 Egypt was your sail and s as your banner; H2118
Eze 27:10 Lydia and Put s as soldiers in your army. H2118
Eze 44:12 But because they s them in the presence H9250
Hos 12:12 of Aram; Israel s to get a wife, and to H6268
Mt 20:28 as the Son of Man did not come to be s, G1354
Mk 10:45 the Son of Man did not come to be s, G1354
Jn 12: 2 Martha s, while Lazarus was among those G1354
Ac 1:16 who s as guide for those who arrested G1181
Ac 13:36 "Now when David had s God's purpose in G5676
Ac 17:25 And he is not s by human hands, as if he G2543
Ac 20:19 I s the Lord with great humility and with G1526
Ro 1:25 worshiped and s created things rather G3302
Php 1:12 to me has actually s to advance G2262
Php 2:22 with his father he has s with me in the G1526
1Ti 3:13 Those who have s well gain an excellent G1354
Heb 7:13 one from that tribe has ever s at the altar. G4668

SERVES (11) [SERVE]

2Ki 10:23 see that no one who s the LORD is H6269
Mal 3:17 spares his son who s him. H6268
Lk 22:26 the one who rules like the one who s. G1354
Lk 22:27 one who is at the table or the one who s? G1354
Lk 22:27 But I am among you as one who s. G1354
Jn 12:26 Whoever s me must follow me; and where G1354
Jn 12:26 My Father will honor the one who s me. G1354
Ro 14:18 because anyone who s Christ in this way is G1526
1Co 9: 7 Who s as a soldier at his own expense G5129
Heb 8: 2 who s in the sanctuary, the true G3313
1Pe 4:11 If anyone s, they should do so with the G1354

SERVICE (84) [SERVE]

Ge 41:46 when he entered the s of H6641+4200+7156
Ge 50: 2 the physicians in his s to embalm his H6269
Ex 27:19 articles used in the s of the tabernacle, H6275
Ex 30:16 use it for the s of the tent of meeting. H6275
Ex 35:21 of meeting, for all its s, and for the sacred H6275
Lev 22: 9 are to perform my s in such a way that H5466
Lev 25:53 to whom they owe s do not rule over them NDT
Nu 4:24 "This is the s of the Gershonite clans in H6275
Nu 4:26 the equipment used in the s of the tent. H6275
Nu 4:27 All their s, whether carrying or doing other H6275
Nu 4:28 This is the s of the Gershonite clans at the H6275
Nu 4:31 As part of all their s at the tent, they are to H6275
Nu 4:33 This is the s of the Merarite clans as they H6275
Nu 8:25 from their regular s and work no H7372+6275
Nu 18: 7 I am giving you the s of the priesthood as H6275
Dt 15:18 because their s to you these six years has H6269
Jos 9:21 water carriers in the s of the whole H4200
Jos 9:23 be released from s as woodcutters and H6269
Jos 18: 7 because the priestly s of the LORD is their H3914
1Sa 14:52 brave man, he took him into his s. H665
1Sa 16:21 to Saul and entered his s. H6641+4200+7156
1Sa 16:22 "Allow David to remain in my s, for H4200+7156
2Sa 9: 2 "Are you Ziba?" "At your s," he replied. H6269
2Sa 9: 6 "Mephibosheth!" "At your s," he replied. H6269
1Ki 8:11 not perform their s because of the cloud, H9250
2Ki 25:14 the bronze articles used in the temple s. H9250
1Ch 5:18 44,760 men ready for military s— H3655+7372
1Ch 9:28 of the articles used in the temple s; H6275
1Ch 23:26 any of the articles used in its s. H6275
1Ch 23:28 descendants in the s of the temple of the H6275
1Ch 23:32 for the s of the temple of the LORD. H6275
1Ch 25: 1 the list of the men who performed this s: H6275
1Ch 26:30 the work of the LORD and for the king's s. H6275
1Ch 28: 1 of the divisions in the s of the king, H9250
1Ch 28:13 as for all the articles to be used in its s. H6275
1Ch 28:14 used in various kinds of s, H6275+2256+6275
1Ch 28:14 used in various kinds of s: H6275+2256+6275
1Ch 28:20 all the work for the s of the temple of the H6275
2Ch 5:14 not perform their s because of the cloud, H9250
2Ch 17:16 who volunteered himself for the s of the H5605
2Ch 24:14 articles for the s and for the burnt H9251
2Ch 25: 5 thousand men fit for military s, H3655+7372
2Ch 29:35 So the s of the temple of the LORD was H6275
2Ch 30:22 good understanding of the s of the LORD. H4200
2Ch 31:21 undertook in the s of God's temple and H6275
2Ch 35: 2 them in the s of the LORD's temple. H6275
2Ch 35:10 The s was arranged and the priests stood H6275
2Ch 35:16 that time the entire s of the LORD was H6275
Ezr 6:18 groups for the s of God at Jerusalem, A10525
Ne 10:32 each year for the s of the house of our H6275
Ne 11:22 responsible for the s of the house of God. H4856
Ne 12:45 They performed the s of their God and the H5466
Ne 12:45 of their God and the s of purification, H5466
Ne 13:10 responsible for the s had gone back to H4856
Job 7: 1 "Do not mortals have hard s on earth? Are H7372
Job 14:14 All the days of my hard s I will wait for H7372
Isa 40: 2 to her that her hard s has been completed H7372
Isa 41: 2 calling him in righteousness to his s? H8079
Jer 52:18 the bronze articles used in the temple s. H9250
Da 1: 3 bring into the king's s some of the Israelites NDT
Da 1: 5 they were to enter the king's s H6641+4200+7156
Da 1:18 time set by the king to bring them into his s, NDT
Da 1:19 so they entered the king's s. H6641+4200+7156
Lk 1:23 When his time of s was completed, he G3311
Lk 9:62 looks back is fit for s in the kingdom G2310
Lk 12:35 "Be dressed ready for s and G3836+4019+4322
Jn 16: 2 you will think they are offering a s to God. G3301
Ro 15:17 I glory in Christ Jesus in my s to God. G3836S
Ro 15:25 my way to Jerusalem in the s of the Lord's G1354
1Co 3: 9 For we are co-workers in God's s; you are G5301
1Co 12: 5 There are different kinds of s, but the G1355
1Co 16:15 themselves to the s of the Lord's people. G1355
2Co 8: 4 of sharing in this s to the Lord's people. G1355
2Co 8:18 by all the churches for his s to the gospel. AIT
2Co 9: 1 to you about this s to the Lord's people. G1355
2Co 9:12 This s that you perform is not only G1355
2Co 9:13 Because of the s by which you have proved G1355
2Co 10:13 to the sphere of s God G3586+3836+2834
Eph 4:12 to equip his people for works of s, so that G1355
Php 2:17 on the sacrifice and s coming from your G3311
1Th 3: 2 brother and co-worker in God's s in G5301
1Ti 1:12 me trustworthy, appointing me to his s. G1355
Heb 2:17 faithful high priest in s to God, G3836S
Rev 2:19 love and faith, your s and perseverance G1355

SERVICES (3) [SERVE]

Ex 14: 5 let the Israelites go and have lost their s!" H6268
Ne 12: 9 associates, stood opposite them in the s. H5466
Ne 13:14 done for the house of my God and its s. H5464

SERVILE (KJV) REGULAR

SERVING (30) [SERVE]

Ex 39:41 garments for his sons when s as priests. H3912
Nu 4:47 to do the work of s and carrying the tent H6275
Nu 18:21 work they do while s at the tent of H6275
Dt 28:14 the left, following other gods and s them. H6268
Jos 20: 6 of the high priest who is s at that time. H2118
Jos 24:15 But if s the LORD seems undesirable to you H6268
Jdg 2:19 other gods and s and worshiping them. H6268
Jdg 10:10 forsaking our God and s the Baals. H6268
1Sa 2:33 I do not cut off from s at my altar I will spare AIT
1Sa 7: 6 Now Samuel was s as leader of Israel at H9149
1Sa 8: 8 forsaking me and s other gods, so they H6268
1Ki 9: 9 worshiping and s them—that is why the H6268
1Ki 12: 8 up with him and were s him. H6641+4200+7156
2Ki 17:41 the LORD, they were s their idols. H6268
1Ch 28:13 all the work of s in the temple of the H6275
2Ch 7:22 worshiping and s them—that is why he H6268
2Ch 10: 8 up with him and were s him. H6641+4200+7156
2Ch 12: 8 difference between s me and serving the H6275
2Ch 12: 8 serving me and s the kings of other H6275
Pr 15:17 Better a small s of vegetables with love H786
Eze 44:11 of the gates of the temple and s in it; H9250
Eze 48:11 who were faithful in s me and did not go H5466
Lk 1: 8 duty and he was s as priest before God, G2634
Ro 12: 7 if it is s, then serve; if it is teaching, then G1355
Ro 12:11 keep your spiritual fervor, s the Lord. G1526
Ro 16:18 For such people are not s our Lord Christ G1526
Eph 6: 7 as if you were s the Lord, not people, NDT
Col 3:24 It is the Lord Christ you are s. G1526

2Ti 2: 4 No one s as a soldier gets entangled in G5129
1Pe 1:12 to them that *they were* not s themselves G1354

SERVITUDE (1) [SERVE]

Ge 47:21 reduced the people to s, H6268+4200+6269

SET (607) [SETS, SETTING, SETTINGS]

Ge 1:17 God s them in the vault of the sky to give H5989
Ge 9:13 *I have* s my rainbow in the clouds, and it H5989
Ge 11:31 together *they* s out from Ur of the H3655
Ge 12: 4 years old when he s out from Harran. H3655
Ge 12: 5 and *they* s out for the land of Canaan H3655
Ge 12: 9 Then Abram s out and continued toward H5825
Ge 13:11 of the Jordan and s out toward the east. H5825
Ge 15:17 When the sun *had* s and darkness had H995
Ge 18: 8 been prepared, and s these before them. H5989
Ge 21:14 *He* s them on her shoulders and then sent H8492
Ge 21:28 Abraham s apart seven ewe lambs from H5893
Ge 21:29 seven ewe lambs *you have* s apart by H5893
Ge 22: 3 *he* s out for the place God had told him H2143
Ge 22:19 *they* s off together for Beersheba. H2143
Ge 24:10 *He* s out for Aram Naharaim and made H7756
Ge 24:33 Then food was s before him, but he said H8492
Ge 28:10 Jacob left Beersheba and s out for Harran. H2143
Ge 28:11 the night because the sun *had* s. H995
Ge 28:18 under his head and s it up *as* a pillar and H8492
Ge 28:22 this stone that *I have* s up as a pillar will H8492
Ge 30:40 s apart the young of the flock by themselves H7233
Ge 31:45 Jacob took a stone and s it up as a pillar. H8123
Ge 31:51 is this pillar *I have* s up between you and H3721
Ge 33:20 There *he* s up an altar and called it El H5893
Ge 34: 8 "My son Shechem *has* his heart s on your H3137
Ge 35: 5 Then *they* s out, and the terror of God fell H5825
Ge 35:14 Jacob s up a stone pillar at the place H5893
Ge 35:20 Over her tomb Jacob s up a pillar, and to H5893
Ge 43: 9 back to you and s him here before you H3657
Ge 46: 1 So Israel s out with all that was his, and H5825
Ge 49:21 "Naphtali is a doe s free that bears H8938
Ex 9: 5 The LORD s a time and said, "Tomorrow H8492
Ex 9:17 You still s yourself against my people and H6147
Ex 16: 1 community s out from Elim and came H5825
Ex 17: 1 community s out from the Desert of H5825
Ex 19: 2 After *they* s out from Rephidim, they H5825
Ex 19: 7 of the people and s before them all the H8492
Ex 19:23 the mountain and s it apart as holy. H7727
Ex 21: 1 are the laws *you are to* s before them: H8492
Ex 24: 4 of the mountain and s up twelve stone NDT
Ex 24:13 Then Moses s out with Joshua his aide H7756
Ex 25:37 seven lamps and s them up *on* it so that H6590
Ex 26: 4 the edge of the end curtain in one s, H2501
Ex 26: 4 same with the end curtain in the other s. H4678
Ex 26: 5 loops on the end curtain of the other s, H4678
Ex 26: 9 together into one s and the other H4200+963
Ex 26: 9 set and the other six into another s. H4200+963
Ex 26:10 end curtain in one s and also along the H2501
Ex 26:10 the edge of the end curtain in the other s. H2501
Ex 26:17 two projections s parallel to each other. H8917
Ex 26:30 "S up the tabernacle according to the H7756
Ex 31: 5 to cut and s stones, to work in wood, and H4848
Ex 32:29 "You *have been* s apart to the LORD H4848+3338
Ex 35:33 to cut and s stones, to work in wood and to H4848
Ex 36:11 the edge of the end curtain in one s, H4678
Ex 36:11 done with the end curtain in the other s. H4678
Ex 36:12 loops on the end curtain of the other s, H4678
Ex 36:16 of the curtains into *one* s and the other six H963
Ex 36:16 one set and the other six into *another* s. H963
Ex 36:17 end curtain in one s and also along the H4678
Ex 36:17 the edge of the end curtain in the other s. H2501
Ex 36:22 two projections s parallel to each other. H8917
Ex 40: 2 "S up the tabernacle, the tent of meeting H7756
Ex 40: 4 in the table and s out what belongs on it. H6885
Ex 40: 4 in the lampstand and s up its lamps. H6590
Ex 40: 8 S up the courtyard around it and put the H8492
Ex 40:17 the tabernacle was s up on the first day H7756
Ex 40:18 When Moses s up the tabernacle, he put H7756
Ex 40:18 inserted the crossbars and s up the posts. H7756
Ex 40:23 and s out the bread on it before the H6885+6886
Ex 40:25 and s up the lamps before the LORD, as the H6590
Ex 40:29 *He* s the altar of burnt offering near the H8492
Ex 40:33 Then Moses s up the courtyard around the H7756
Ex 40:36 above the tabernacle, *they would* s out; H5825
Ex 40:37 *they did* not s out—until the day H5825
Lev 8: 9 on Aaron's head and s the gold plate, H8492
Lev 17:10 " '*I will* s my face against any Israelite H5989
Lev 20: 3 *I* myself *will* s my face against him and H5989
Lev 20: 5 *I* myself *will* s my face against him and his H8492
Lev 20: 6 " '*I will* s my face against anyone who H5989
Lev 20:24 who *has* s you apart from the nations. H976
Lev 20:25 those that *I have* s apart as unclean for you. H976
Lev 20:26 and *I have* s you apart from the nations to H976
Lev 24: 8 This bread *is to be* s out before the LORD H6885
Lev 26: 1 not make idols or s up an image or a H7756
Lev 26:17 *I will* s my face against you so that you will H5989
Lev 27: 3 s the value of a male between the ages of H2118
Lev 27: 4 a female, s her value at thirty shekels; H2118
Lev 27: 5 s the value of a male at twenty shekels H2118
Lev 27: 6 s the value of a male at five shekels of H2118
Lev 27: 7 s the value of a male at fifteen shekels H2118
Lev 27: 8 who *will* s *the* value according to what the H6885
Lev 27:16 its value *is to be* s according to the H2118
Lev 27:17 the value that has been s remains. NDT
Lev 27:18 Jubilee, and its s value will be reduced. H6886
Lev 27:25 Every value *is to be* s according to the H2118
Lev 27:27 it may be bought back at its s value H6886
Lev 27:27 redeemed, it is to be sold at its s value. H6886
Nu 1:51 whenever the tabernacle *is to be* s up, H2837
Nu 1:52 Israelites *are to* s up their tents by H2837
Nu 1:53 *are to* s up their tents around the H2837
Nu 2: 9 number 186,400. *They will* s out first. H5825
Nu 2:16 number 151,450. *They will* s out second. H5825
Nu 2:17 of the Levites *will* s out in the middle of H5825
Nu 2:17 *They will* s out in the same order as they H5825
Nu 2:24 number 108,100. *They will* s out third. H5825
Nu 2:31 *They will* s out last, under H5825
Nu 2:34 that is the way *they* s out, each of H5825
Nu 3:13 *I* s apart for myself every firstborn in Israel H7727
Nu 8: 2 'When you s up the lamps, see H6590
Nu 8: 3 *he* s up the lamps so that they faced H6590
Nu 8:14 this way *you are to* s the Levites apart from H976
Nu 8:17 in Egypt, *I* s them apart for myself. H7727
Nu 9:15 the covenant law, *was* s up, the cloud H7756
Nu 9:17 the Israelites s out; wherever the cloud H5825
Nu 9:18 At the LORD's command the Israelites s out H5825
Nu 9:19 obeyed the LORD's order and *did* not s out. H5825
Nu 9:20 then at his command *they would* s out. H5825
Nu 9:21 when it lifted in the morning, *they* s out. H5825
Nu 9:21 whenever the cloud lifted, *they* s out. H5825
Nu 9:22 would remain in camp and not s out; H5825
Nu 9:22 but when it lifted, *they would* s out. H5825
Nu 9:23 at the LORD's command *they* s out. H5825
Nu 10: 2 together and for having the camps s out. H5023
Nu 10: 5 tribes camping on the east *are to* s out. H5825
Nu 10: 6 the camps on the south *are to* s out. H5825
Nu 10:12 Then the Israelites s out from the Desert of H5825
Nu 10:13 *They* s out, this first time, at the LORD's H5825
Nu 10:17 Merarites, who carried it, s out. H5825
Nu 10:21 Then the Kohathites s out, carrying the H5825
Nu 10:21 The tabernacle *was to be* s up before they H7756
Nu 10:25 of the camp of Dan s out under their H5825
Nu 10:28 the Israelite divisions as *they* s out. H5825
Nu 10:33 So *they* s out from the mountain of the H5825
Nu 10:34 by day when they s out from the camp. H5825
Nu 10:35 Whenever the ark s out, Moses said, "Rise H5825
Nu 14:25 tomorrow and s out *toward* the desert H5825
Nu 14:40 next morning *they* s out for the highest H6590
Nu 16: 3 Why then *do you* s *yourselves* above the H5951
Nu 18:11 *whatever* is s aside *from* the gifts of all H9556
Nu 18:16 the redemption price s *at* five shekels of H6886
Nu 18:19 Whatever is s aside *from* the holy offerings H9556
Nu 20:22 community s out from Kadesh and H5825
Nu 21:11 Then *they* s out from Oboth and camped H5825
Nu 21:13 *They* s out from there and camped H5825
Nu 24:21 place is secure, your nest *is* s in a rock; H8492
Nu 31:28 s apart as tribute for the LORD one out of H8123
Nu 31:42 which Moses s apart from that of the H2936
Nu 33: 3 The Israelites s out from Rameses on the H5825
Dt 1:13 of your tribes, and *I will* s them over you." H8492
Dt 1:19 *we* s out from Horeb and went toward the H5825
Dt 1:36 his descendants the land *he* s *his* feet on, H2005
Dt 1:40 and s out toward the desert *along* the H5825
Dt 2: 1 and s out toward the wilderness *along* the H5825
Dt 2:24 "*S* out now and cross the Arnon Gorge. AIT
Dt 4:41 Then Moses s aside three cities east of the H976
Dt 4:44 is the law Moses s before the Israelites H8492
Dt 5:21 *You shall* not s *your* desire on your H203
Dt 7: 7 The LORD *did* not s *his* affection on you H3137
Dt 7:26 like it, will be s apart for destruction. H3051
Dt 7:26 detest it, for it is s apart for destruction. H3051
Dt 10: 8 that time the LORD s apart the tribe of Levi H976
Dt 10:15 Yet the LORD s *his* affection on your H3137
Dt 11:24 Every place where *you* s your foot will be H2005
Dt 14:22 Be sure to s aside a tenth *of* all H6923+6923
Dt 15:18 it a hardship *to* s your servant free, H2930+8938
Dt 15:19 S apart for the LORD your God every H7727
Dt 16:21 *Do* not s up any wooden Asherah pole H5749
Dt 17:14 "*Let us* s a king over us like all the nations H8492
Dt 19: 2 then s aside for yourselves three cities in H976
Dt 19: 7 I command you *to* s aside for yourselves H976
Dt 19: 9 then you are to s aside three more cities. NDT
Dt 19:14 boundary stone s up by your predecessors H1487
Dt 26: 4 your hands and s it down in front of the H5663
Dt 26:19 has declared that he *will* s you in praise, H5989
Dt 27: 2 s up some large stones and coat them H7756
Dt 27: 4 s up these stones on Mount Ebal H7756
Dt 27: 8 of this law on these stones you have s up." NDT
Dt 28: 1 the LORD your God *will* s you high above H5989
Dt 28:36 you and the king *you* s over you to a H7756
Dt 30: 1 curses *I have* s before you come on H5989
Dt 30:15 *I* s before you today life and prosperity H5989
Dt 30:19 against you that *I have* s before you life H5989
Dt 32: 8 *he* s up boundaries for the peoples H5893
Dt 32:22 its harvests and s afire the foundations of H4265
Jos 1: 3 you every place where *you* s your foot, H2005
Jos 2: 7 men s out in pursuit of the spies *on* the H8103
Jos 3: 1 all the Israelites s out from Shittim and H5825
Jos 3:13 Lord of all the earth—s foot in the Jordan H5663
Jos 4: 9 Joshua s up the twelve stones that had H7756
Jos 4:18 No sooner *had* they s their feet on the dry H5998
Jos 4:20 And Joshua s up at Gilgal the twelve H7756
Jos 6:26 cost of his youngest *he will* s up its gates." H5893
Jos 8: 2 S an ambush behind the city. H8492
Jos 8: 4 *You are to* s an ambush behind the city H741
Jos 8: 8 the city, s it on fire. H3675+928+2021+836
Jos 8:11 *They* s up camp north of Ai, with the H2837
Jos 8:12 five thousand men and s them in ambush H8492
Jos 8:14 that an ambush *had been* s against him H741
Jos 8:19 it and quickly s it on fire. H3675+928+2021+836
Jos 9:17 So the Israelites s out and on the third day H5825
Jos 16: 9 villages that were s aside for the H4426
Jos 18: 1 at Shiloh and s up the tent of meeting H8905
Jos 20: 7 So *they* s apart Kedesh in Galilee in the H7727
Jos 24:26 a large stone and s it up there under the H7756
Jdg 1: 8 put the city to the sword and s it on fire. H8938
Jdg 6:18 bring my offering and s it before you." H5663
Jdg 8:33 *They* s up Baal-Berith as their god H8492
Jdg 9:25 citizens of Shechem s men on the hilltops H8492
Jdg 9:34 all his troops s out by night and took H7756
Jdg 9:43 companies and s an ambush in the fields. H741
Jdg 9:49 and s it on fire with the H3675+928+2021+836
Jdg 9:52 the tower to s it on fire, H8596+928+2021+836
Jdg 16:21 they s *him to* grinding grain in the prison. H2118
Jdg 18:11 battle, s out from Zorah and Eshtaol. H5825
Jdg 18:12 On their way *they* s up camp near Kiriath H2837
Jdg 18:30 There the Danites s up for themselves the H7756
Jdg 19:14 the sun s as they neared Gibeah in H995
Jdg 19:28 put her on his donkey and s out for home. H2143
Jdg 20:29 Then Israel s an ambush around Gibeah. H8492
Jdg 20:36 on the ambush *they had* s near Gibeah. H8492
Jdg 20:48 the towns they came across *they* s on fire. H8938
Ru 1: 7 been living and s out on the road that H2143
1Sa 2: 8 the LORD's; on them *he has* s the world. H8883
1Sa 5: 2 Dagon's temple and s it beside Dagon. H3657
1Sa 6:18 on which the Levites s the ark of the LORD H5663
1Sa 7:12 took a stone and s it up between Mizpah H8492
1Sa 9:10 So *they* s out for the town where the man H2143
1Sa 9:24 what was on it and s it in front of Saul. H8492
1Sa 9:24 because *it* was s aside for you for this H9068
1Sa 10: 2 'The donkeys *you* s out to look for have H2143
1Sa 12: 1 to me and *have* s a king over you. H4887+4889
1Sa 12:13 see, the LORD *has* s a king over you. H5989
1Sa 13: 8 seven days, the time s by Samuel; but H4595
1Sa 13:11 you did not come at the s time, H4595+3427
1Sa 15: 5 of Amalek and s an ambush in the ravine. H741
1Sa 15:12 There *he has* s up a monument in his H5893
1Sa 17:20 loaded up and s out, as Jesse had H2143
1Sa 21: 5 kept from us, as usual whenever I s out. H3655
1Sa 23:24 So *they* s out and went to Ziph ahead of H7756
1Sa 24: 2 from all Israel and s out to look for David H2143
1Sa 26: 5 Then David s out and went to the place H7756
1Sa 28: 4 came and s up camp at Shunem, H2837
1Sa 28: 4 all Israel and s up camp at Gilboa. H2837
1Sa 28: 9 Why *have* you s a trap for my life to bring H5943
1Sa 28:25 Then *she* s it before Saul and his men H5602
2Sa 4: 5 s out for the house of Ish-Bosheth H2143
2Sa 6: 3 *They* s the ark of God on a new cart and H8206
2Sa 6:17 ark of the LORD and s it in its place inside H3657
2Sa 11:22 The messenger s out, and when he H2143
2Sa 12:30 and it was s with precious stones. NDT
2Sa 14:30 Go and s it on fire." So H3675+836+928+2021
2Sa 14:30 s the field on fire. H3675+836+928+2021
2Sa 14:31 *have* your servants s my field on fire H3675+836+928+2021
2Sa 15:16 The king s out, with his entire household H3655
2Sa 15:17 So the king s out, with all the people H3655
2Sa 15:24 *They* s down the ark of God, and Abiathar H3668
2Sa 17: 1 thousand men and s out tonight in pursuit H7756
2Sa 17:21 "S out and cross the river at once H7756
2Sa 17:22 the people with him s out and crossed the H7756
2Sa 17:23 his donkey and s out for his house in his H2143
2Sa 20: 5 than the time the king *had* s *for* him. H3585
1Ki 5: 6 you for your men whatever wages *you* s. H606
1Ki 6:19 within the temple to s the ark of the H5989
1Ki 7: 8 to live, s farther back, was H2958+2021+337
1Ki 7:16 of cast bronze to s on the tops of the H5989
1Ki 9:16 *He had* s it on fire. H8596+928+836+2021
1Ki 11:18 *They* s out from Midian and went to Paran H7756
1Ki 12:29 One *he* s up in Bethel, and the other in H8492
1Ki 14:12 When you s foot in your city, the boy will H995
1Ki 14:23 They also s up for themselves high places H1215
1Ki 16:18 and s the palace on fire H8596+928+2021+836
1Ki 16:32 *He* s up an altar for Baal in the temple of H7756
1Ki 16:34 and *he* s up its gates at the cost of his H5893
1Ki 18:23 put it on the wood but not s fire *to* it. H8492
1Ki 18:23 put it on the wood but not s fire *to* it. H8492
1Ki 19:21 Then *he* s out to follow Elijah and H7756
1Ki 20:16 *They* s out at noon while Ben-Hadad and H3655
1Ki 20:34 "*You may* s up your own market areas in H8492
1Ki 20:34 "On the basis of a treaty I *will* s you free." H8938
1Ki 20:42 '*You have* s free a man I H8938+4946+3338
1Ki 22:48 gold, but *they* never s sail—they were H2143
2Ki 2:16 him up and s him down on some H8959
2Ki 3: 6 time King Joram s out from Samaria and H3655
2Ki 3: 9 So the king of Israel s out with the king of H2143
2Ki 4:25 So *she* s out and came to the man of God H2143
2Ki 4:43 "How *can I* s this before a hundred men?" H5989
2Ki 4:44 Then *he* s it before them, and they ate H5989
2Ki 6: 8 "I will s up my camp in such and such a H9381
2Ki 6:22 S food and water before them so that they H8492
2Ki 8:12 "*You will* s fire to their H8938+928+836+2021
2Ki 8:20 Judah and s up its own king. H4887+4889
2Ki 10: 3 master's sons and s him on his father's H8492
2Ki 10:12 Jehu then s out and went toward Samaria H995
2Ki 16:17 that supported it and s it on a stone base. H5989
2Ki 17:10 *They* s up sacred stones and Asherah H5893
2Ki 17:29 and s them up in the shrines the people H5663
2Ki 25: 9 *He* s fire to the temple of the LORD, the H8596

1Ch 9:32 Sabbath the bread **s out on the table.** H5121
1Ch 16: 1 the ark of God and **s** it inside the tent that H3657
1Ch 17:14 *I will* **s** him over my house and my H6641
1Ch 18: 3 when he went to **s up** his monument at H5893
1Ch 20: 2 and it was **s with** precious stones H928
1Ch 23:13 Aaron **was s apart**, he and his descendants H976
1Ch 23:29 in charge of the bread **s out on the table,** H5121
1Ch 25: 1 **s apart** some of the sons of Asaph H976
2Ch 11:16 tribe of Israel who **s** their hearts on H5989
2Ch 12:14 did evil because *he had* not **s** his heart on H3922
2Ch 13:11 They **s out** the bread on the ceremonially H5121
2Ch 19: 3 poles and *have* **s** your heart on seeking H3922
2Ch 20:20 As they **s out**, Jehoshaphat stood and H3655
2Ch 20:22 the LORD **s** ambushes against the men of H5989
2Ch 20:33 the people still *had* not **s** their hearts on H3922
2Ch 20:37 were not able to **s sail** to trade. H2143
2Ch 21: 8 Judah and **s up** its own **king.** H4887+4889
2Ch 25:14 *He* **s** them **up** as his own gods, bowed H6641
2Ch 28:24 the LORD's temple and **s up** altars at every H6913
2Ch 29:12 Then these Levites **s to work**: from the H7756
2Ch 33:19 high places and **s up** Asherah poles and H6641
2Ch 35:12 *They* **s aside** the burnt offerings to give H6073
2Ch 35:20 when Josiah *had* **s** the temple **in order** H3922
2Ch 36:19 *They* **s fire to** God's temple and broke H8596
Ezr 4: 4 around them *s out to* **discourage** the people AIT
Ezr 5: 2 of Jozadak **s to work** to A10624+10221+10742
Ezr 8:24 Then *I* **s apart** twelve of the leading priests H976
Ezr 8:31 of the first month *we* **s out** from the Ahava H5825
Ezr 10:14 a foreign woman come at a **s** time, H2374
Ne 2: 6 the king to send me; so *I* **s** a time. H5989
Ne 2:12 **I s out** during the night with a few others. H7756
Ne 3: 1 They dedicated it and **s** its doors **in place** H6641
Ne 6: 1 up to that time *I had* not **s** the doors in H6641
Ne 7: 1 rebuilt and *I had* **s** the doors **in place,** H6641
Ne 10:33 the bread **s out on the table;** for the H5121
Ne 10:34 house of our God at **s** times each year a H2374
Ne 12:47 *They* also **s aside** the portion for the other H7727
Ne 12:47 the Levites **s aside** the portion for the H7727
Est 2:17 So *he* **s** a royal crown on her head and H8492
Est 5:14 "*Have* a pole **s up**, reaching to H6913
Est 5:14 Haman, and *he had* the pole **s up.** H6913
Est 6: 4 on the pole *he had* **s up** for him. H3922
Est 7: 9 He *had* it **s up** for Mordecai, who spoke H6913
Est 7:10 on the pole *he had* **s up** for Mordecai. H3922
Est 8: 7 they have impaled him on the pole he **s** up. NDT
Job 2:11 they **s out** from their homes and met H995
Job 14: 5 of his months and *have* **s** limits he cannot H6913
Job 14:13 If only *you would* **s** me a time and then H8883
Job 24: 1 "Why *does* the Almighty not **s** times for H7621
Job 28: 8 Proud beasts *do* not **s foot on** it, and no H2005
Job 38: 6 On what **were** its footings **s**, or who laid H3190
Job 38:10 it and **s** its doors and bars **in place,** H8492
Job 38:33 *Can you* **s up** God's dominion over the H8492
Ps 4: 3 Know that the LORD *has* **s apart** his faithful H7111
Ps 8: 1 *You have* **s** your glory in the heavens. H5989
Ps 8: 3 the stars, which *you have* **s in place,** H3922
Ps 11: 2 *they* **s** their arrows against the strings to H3922
Ps 27: 5 sacred tent and **s** me **high** upon a rock. H8123
Ps 31: 4 me free from the trap that *is* **s** for me, H3243
Ps 31: 8 of the enemy but *have* **s** my feet in a H6641
Ps 38:12 Those who want to kill me **s** *their* **traps** H5943
Ps 40: 2 *he* **s** my feet on a rock and gave me a firm H7756
Ps 41:12 you uphold me and **s** me in your presence H5893
Ps 45: 7 has **s** you above your companions by NDT
Ps 50:21 you and **s** *my* **accusations** before you. H6885
Ps 62:10 increase, *do* not **s** your heart on them. H8883
Ps 69:22 May the table **s** before them become a NDT
Ps 74: 4 with us; *they* **s up** their standards as signs. H8492
Ps 74:17 It was you *who* **s** all the boundaries of the H5893
Ps 78:60 the tent *he had* **s up** among humans. H8905
Ps 81: 6 their hands *were* **s free** from the basket. H6296
Ps 84: 5 whose hearts are **s on** pilgrimage. H928
Ps 85: 3 *You* **s aside** all your wrath and turned from H665
Ps 88: 5 I am **s apart** with the dead, like the slain H2930
Ps 89:25 *I will* **s** his hand over the sea, his right H8492
Ps 90: 8 *You have* **s** our iniquities before you, our H8883
Ps 104: 5 *He* **s** the earth on its foundations; it can H3569
Ps 104: 9 *You* **s** a boundary they cannot cross; never H8492
Ps 105:20 the ruler of peoples **s** him **free.** H7337
Ps 119:30 *I have* **s** *my* **heart** *on* your laws. H8751
Ps 119:110 The wicked *have* **s** a snare for me, but I H5989
Ps 119:112 My heart *is* **s** *on* keeping your decrees to H5742
Ps 132:17 grow for David and **s up** a lamp for my H6885
Ps 140: 5 of their net and *have* **s** traps for me along H8883
Ps 141: 2 *May* my prayer **be s** before you like H3922
Ps 141: 3 **S** a guard over my mouth, LORD; keep H8883
Ps 141: 9 Keep me safe from the **traps** *s by* evildoers AIT
Ps 142: 7 **S** me **free** from my prison, that I may H3655
Pr 1:15 with them, *do* **not s** foot on their paths; H4979
Pr 3:19 understanding *he* **s** the heavens **in place;** H3922
Pr 4:14 *Do* not **s foot** on the path of the wicked H995
Pr 7: 9 the day was fading, as the dark of night **s** in. NDT
Pr 8: 5 you who are foolish, **s** your hearts *on* it. H3922
Pr 8:27 there when he **s** the heavens **in place,** H3922
Pr 9: 1 her house; *she has* **s up** its seven pillars. H5893
Pr 9: 2 mixed her wine; *she has* also **s** her table. H6885
Pr 22:28 boundary stone **s up** *by* your ancestors. H6913
Pr 23:19 be wise, and **s** your heart on the **right** path: H886
Pr 25:17 **Seldom** *s* foot in your neighbor's house—too AIT
Pr 30:14 whose jaws are **s** with knives to devour NDT
Ecc 3:11 *He has* also **s** eternity in the human heart H5989
Ecc 12: 9 out and **s in order** many proverbs. H9545

SS 5:14 His arms are rods of gold **s** with topaz. H4848
SS 5:15 pillars of marble **s** on bases of pure gold H3569
SS 6:12 my desire **s** me *among* the royal chariots H8492
Isa 17:10 *though you* **s out** the finest plants and H5749
Isa 17:11 though on the day you **s** them **out**, you H5750
Isa 21: 5 They **s** the tables, they spread the rugs H6885
Isa 23:18 her earnings will be **s apart** for the LORD; H7731
Isa 27: 4 them in battle; *I would* **s** them all **on fire.** H7455
Isa 28: 1 **s** on the head of a fertile valley NDT
Isa 28: 4 **s on** the head of a fertile valley H6584
Isa 29: 3 you with towers and **s up** my siege works H7756
Isa 33:12 *they will be* **s ablaze.**" H3675+928+2021+836
Isa 40:20 a skilled worker to **s up** an idol that will H3922
Isa 41:19 *I will* **s** junipers in the wasteland, the fir H8492
Isa 41:21 "**S forth** your arguments," says Jacob's H5602
Isa 43: 2 burned; the flames *will* not **s** you **ablaze.** H1277
Isa 45:13 will rebuild my city and **s** my exiles **free,** H8938
Isa 46: 7 carry it; *they* **s** it **up** in its place, and H5663
Isa 50: 7 Therefore *have I* **s** my face like flint, and I H8492
Isa 50:11 fires and of the torches *you have* **s ablaze.** H1277
Isa 51:14 cowering prisoners *will* soon **be s free;** H7337
Isa 51:16 I *who* **s** the heavens **in place,** who H5749
Isa 58: 6 *to* **s** the oppressed free and break every H8938
Isa 60:20 Your sun *will* never **s** again, and your moon H995
Isa 63:11 Where is he *who* **s** his Holy Spirit among H8492
Isa 66:19 "*I will* **s** a sign among them, and I will H8492
Jer 1: 5 before you were born *I* **s** you **apart;** H7727
Jer 1:15 kings will come and **s up** their thrones in H5989
Jer 4: 7 a destroyer of nations *has* **s out.** H5825
Jer 5:26 birds and like *those who* **s** traps to catch H5893
Jer 7:30 *They have* **s up** their detestable idols in H8492
Jer 9: 8 in their hearts *they* **s** traps for them. H8492
Jer 9:13 my law, which *I* **s** before them; they H5989
Jer 10:20 now to pitch my tent or *to* **s up** my shelter. H7756
Jer 11:13 the altars *you have* **s up** to burn H8492
Jer 11:16 of a mighty storm *he will* **s** it **on fire,** H3675+836
Jer 12: 3 **S** them **apart** for the day of slaughter! H7727
Jer 15: 9 Her sun *will* **s** while it is still day; she will H995
Jer 22:17 your heart are **s** only **on** dishonest gain, H6584
Jer 26: 4 follow my law, which *I have* **s** before you, H5989
Jer 31:21 "**S up** road signs; put up guideposts. H5893
Jer 31:29 the children's teeth *are* **s on edge.** H7733
Jer 31:30 their own teeth *will be* **s on edge.** H7733
Jer 32:29 come in and **s** it **on fire;** H3675+928+2021+836
Jer 32:34 *They* **s up** their vile images in the house H8492
Jer 34:10 They agreed, and **s** them **free.** H8938
Jer 34:16 female slaves *you had* **s** free to go where H8938
Jer 35: 5 Then *I* **s** bowls full of wine and some cups H5989
Jer 39: 8 **s fire to** the royal H8596+928+2021+836
Jer 41:10 them captive and **s out** to cross over to the H2143
Jer 43:10 and *I will* **s** his throne over these stones I H8492
Jer 43:12 *He will* **s fire** to the temples of the H3675+836
Jer 44:10 the decrees *I* **s** before you and your H5989
Jer 49: 2 villages *will be* **s on fire.** H3675+928+2021+836
Jer 49:27 "*I will* **s fire** to the walls of H3675+836
Jer 49:38 *I will* **s** my throne in Elam and destroy her H8492
Jer 50:24 *I* **s** a **trap** for you, Babylon, and you were H3704
Jer 51:30 Her dwellings *are* **s on fire**; the bars of her H3675
Jer 51:32 the marshes **s on fire** H8596+928+2021+836
Jer 51:39 *I will* **s out** a feast for them and make H8883
Jer 51:58 her high gates **s on fire;** H3675+928+2021+836
Jer 52:13 *He* **s fire** to the temple of the LORD, the H8596
Eze 4: 2 **s up** camps against it and put battering H5989
Eze 4:10 day and eat it **at s times.** H4946+6961+6330+6961
Eze 4:11 and drink it **at s times.** H4946+6961+6330+6961
Eze 5: 1 Then take **a s of scales** and divide H4404+5486
Eze 5: 5 which *I have* **s** in the center of the nations, H8492
Eze 6: 2 **s** your face against the mountains of H8492
Eze 12: 3 **s out** and go from where you are to H1655
Eze 13:17 **s** your face against the daughters of your H8492
Eze 13:20 *I will* **s free** the people that you ensnare H8938
Eze 14: 3 these men *have* **s up** idols in their hearts H6590
Eze 14: 4 of the Israelites **s up** idols in their hearts H6590
Eze 14: 7 from me and **s up** idols in their hearts H6590
Eze 14: 8 *I will* **s** my face against them and make H5989
Eze 15: 7 *I will* **s** my face against them. Although H5989
Eze 15: 7 And when I **s** my face against them, you H8492
Eze 17: 2 **s forth** an allegory and tell it to the H2554
Eze 18: 2 the children's teeth *are* **s on edge**'? H7733
Eze 20: 7 of the vile images you have **s** your eyes on, NDT
Eze 20: 8 of the vile images they had **s** their eyes on, NDT
Eze 20:46 "Son of man, **s** your face toward the south H8492
Eze 20:47 I *am about to* **s fire** to you, and it H3675+836
Eze 21: 2 **s** your face against Jerusalem and preach H8492
Eze 21:22 where he is to **s up** battering rams, to give H8492
Eze 21:22 to **s** battering rams against the gates H8492
Eze 24:11 Then **s** the empty pot on the coals till it H6641
Eze 25: 2 **s** your face against the Ammonites and H8492
Eze 25: 4 *They will* **s up** their camps and pitch their H3782
Eze 26: 8 *he will* **s up** siege works against you H5989
Eze 28:21 "Son of man, **s** your face against Sidon H8492
Eze 29: 2 **s** your face against Pharaoh king of Egypt H8492
Eze 30: 8 when I **s** fire to Egypt and all her helpers H5989
Eze 30:14 **s** fire to Zoan and inflict punishment on H5989
Eze 30:16 *I will* **s** fire to Egypt; Pelusium will writhe H5989
Eze 35: 2 of man, **s** your face against Mount Seir H8492
Eze 37: 1 of the LORD and **s** me in the middle of a H5663
Eze 38: 2 "Son of man, **s** your face against Gog, of H8492
Eze 40: 2 the land of Israel and **s** me on a very high H5663
Eze 48:20 **As a special gift** *you will* **s aside** the H8123
Da 1:18 the end of the time **s** *by* the king to bring H606
Da 2:44 God of heaven *will* **s up** a kingdom that A10624

Da 3: 1 and **s** it **up** on the plain of Dura in the A10624
Da 3: 2 dedication of the image he *had* **s up.** A10624
Da 3: 3 that King Nebuchadnezzar *had* **s up,** A10624
Da 3: 5 that King Nebuchadnezzar *has* **s up.** A10624
Da 3: 7 that King Nebuchadnezzar *had* **s up.** A10624
Da 3:12 some Jews whom *you have* **s** over the A10431
Da 3:12 the image of gold *you have* **s up.** A10624
Da 3:14 worship the image of gold *I have* **s up**? A10624
Da 3:18 the image of gold *you have* **s up.** A10624
Da 5:23 *you have* **s** *yourself* **up** against the Lord A10659
Da 6: 3 king planned to **s** him over the whole A10624
Da 7: 9 "thrones **were s in place,** and the A10667
Da 7:25 try to change the **s times** and the laws. A10232
Da 8:11 *It* **s** *itself* **up to be as great** as the H1540
Da 9:27 at the temple he will **s** up an abomination NDT
Da 10:10 me and **s** me **trembling** on my hands H5675
Da 10:12 the first day that *you* **s** your mind to gain H5989
Da 11:28 his heart will be **s against** the holy H6584
Da 11:31 Then *they will* **s up** the abomination that H5989
Da 11:44 and *he will* **s out** in a great rage to H3655
Da 12:11 that causes desolation *is* **s up,** H5989
Hos 8: 4 They **s up kings** without my consent; they H4887
Am 1:14 *I will* **s fire** to the walls of Rabbah H3675+836
Ob 7 who eat your bread *will* **s** a trap for you, H8492
Ob 18 and *they will* **s** him **on fire** and destroy H1944
Mic 3: 6 The sun *will* **s** for the prophets, and the day H995
Zec 3: 9 the stone *I have* **s** in front of Joshua H5989
Zec 5:11 the basket *will* **be s** there in its place." H5663
Zec 6:11 **s** it on the head of the high priest H8492
Zec 12: 9 On that day *I will* **s out** to destroy all the H1335
Mal 4: 1 the day that is coming *will* **s** them **on fire,**" H4265
Mt 27: 9 **the price s** *on* him by the people of *G5507+5506*
Mt 27:29 a crown of thorns and **s** it **on** his head. *G2202*
Mk 15:17 a crown of thorns and **s** it **on** him. *G4363*
Lk 1:64 mouth was opened and his tongue **s** free, NDT
Lk 4:18 blind, *to* **s** the oppressed **free,** *G690+1877+912*
Lk 8:22 So they got into a boat and **s out.** *G343*
Lk 9: 6 So *they* **s out** and went from village to *G2002*
Lk 9:51 Jesus resolutely **s out** for Jerusalem. *G4513*
Lk 12:29 And *do* not **s** *your* **heart on** what you will *G2426*
Lk 13:12 "Woman, *you are* **s free** from your infirmity." *G668*
Lk 13:16 *be* **s free** on the Sabbath day from what *G3395*
Lk 15:13 **s off** for a distant country and there *G623*
Lk 15:18 *I will* **s out** and go back to my father and say *G482*
Lk 16:26 you a great chasm *has been* **s in place,** *G5114*
Jn 5:45 is Moses, on whom your **hopes** *are* **s.** *G1827*
Jn 6:17 got into a boat and **s off** across the lake *G2262*
Jn 8:32 the truth, and the truth *will* **s** you **free.**" *G1802*
Jn 8:33 How can you say that we shall be **s free**?" *G1801*
Jn 10:35 came—and Scripture cannot **be s aside**— *G3395*
Jn 10:36 the Father **s apart as** *his* **very own** and sent *G39*
Jn 13:15 *I have* **s** you an example that you should *G1443*
Jn 19:12 Pilate tried *to* **s** Jesus **free**, but the Jewish *G668*
Ac 1: 7 dates the Father *has* **s** by his own *G5502*
Ac 7: 5 not even enough ground *to* **s** his foot **on.** *G1037*
Ac 7:34 have come down *to* **s** them **free.** *G1975*
Ac 13: 2 "**S apart** for me Barnabas and Saul for the *G928*
Ac 13:39 who believes *is* **s free** from every sin, *G1467*
Ac 16:34 house and **s a meal before** them; *G4192+5544*
Ac 17:31 For *he has* **s** a day when he will judge the *G2705*
Ac 18:21 Then *he* **s sail** from Ephesus. *G343*
Ac 18:23 Paul **s out from** there and traveled from *G2002*
Ac 20: 1 said goodbye and **s out** for Macedonia. *G2002*
Ac 20:15 The next day *we* **s sail** from there and *G676*
Ac 21: 2 to Phoenicia, went on board and **s sail.** *G343*
Ac 26:32 man could have *been* **s free** if he had not *G668*
Ac 28:13 From there *we* **s sail** and arrived at *G4311*
Ro 1: 1 be an apostle and **s apart** for the gospel of *G928*
Ro 6: 7 who has died *has been* **s free** from sin. *G1467*
Ro 6:18 *You have been* **s free** from sin and have *G1802*
Ro 6:22 But now *that you have been* **s free** from sin *G1802*
Ro 8: 2 who gives life *has* **s** you **free** from the law *G1802*
Ro 8: 5 the flesh **have** *their* **minds s on** what the *G5858*
Ro 8: 5 Spirit have their minds **s** on what the Spirit NDT
1Co 16: 2 one of you *should* **s aside** a sum of *G5502*
2Co 1:10 On him *we have* **s** *our* **hope** that he will *G1827*
2Co 1:22 **s** *his* **seal of ownership** on us, and put his *G5381*
Gal 1:15 who **s** me **apart** from my mother's womb *G928*
Gal 2:21 *I do* not **s aside** the grace of God, for if *G119*
Gal 3:15 Just as no one *can* **s aside** or add to a *G119*
Gal 3:17 *does* not **s aside** the covenant previously *G218*
Gal 4: 2 trustees until the **time s** by his father. *G4607*
Gal 4: 4 But when the *s* **time** had fully come, God sent AIT
Gal 5: 1 It is for freedom *that* Christ *has* **s** us **free** *G1802*
Php 3:19 Their **mind** *is* **s** on earthly things. *G5858*
Php 4:15 the gospel, when *I* **s out** from Macedonia *G2002*
Col 3: 1 with Christ, **s** *your* **hearts on** things above *G2426*
Col 3: 2 **S** *your* **minds on** things above, not on *G5858*
1Ti 4:12 **s** an example for the believers in *G1181*
Titus 2: 7 In everything **s** them an example by doing *G4218*
Heb 1: 9 has **s** you **above** your companions by AIT
Heb 4: 7 God again **s** a certain day, calling it *G3988*
Heb 6:18 hold of the hope **s before** us may be *G4618*
Heb 7:18 regulation is **s aside** because it was weak *G120*
Heb 7:26 **s apart** from sinners, exalted above *G6004*
Heb 8: 2 the true tabernacle **s up** *by* the Lord, not *G4381*
Heb 9: 2 A tabernacle *was* **s up.** In its first room *G2941*
Heb 9:15 died as a **ransom to s** them **free** from the *G667*
Heb 12: 2 For the joy **s before** him he endured the *G4618*
Jas 3: 5 a great forest *is* **s on fire** by a small spark. *G409*
Jas 3: 6 life on fire, and *is itself* **s on fire** by hell. *G5824*
1Pe 1:13 **s** *your* **hope** on the grace to be brought to *G1827*

1Jn 3:19 how *we* s our hearts at rest in his G4275
Rev 13:14 It ordered them *to* s up an image in honor G4472
Rev 20: 3 he must *be* s free for a short time. G3395

SETH (9)

Ge 4:25 she gave birth to a son and named him S, H9269
Ge 4:26 S also had a son, and he named him H9269
Ge 5: 3 in his own image; and he named him S. H9269
Ge 5: 4 After S was born, Adam lived 800 years H9269
Ge 5: 6 When S had lived 105 years, he became H9269
Ge 5: 7 S lived 807 years and had other sons and H9269
Ge 5: 8 Altogether, S lived a total of 912 years H9269
1Ch 1: 1 S, Enosh, H9269
Lk 3:38 of Enosh, the son *of* S, the son of Adam, G4953

SETHUR (1)

Nu 13:13 from the tribe of Asher, S son of Michael; H6256

SETS (44) [SET]

Ge 45:22 shekels of silver and five s *of* clothes. H2722
Ex 36:13 to fasten the *two s of* curtains together so AIT
Lev 27:12 Whatever value the priest then s, that is NDT
Lev 27:14 Whatever value the priest then s, so it will H6885
Dt 27:15 of skilled hands—and s it up in secret." H8492
Jdg 14:12 linen garments and thirty s *of* clothes. H2722
Jdg 14:13 linen garments and thirty s *of* clothes." H2722
2Sa 3:35 bread or anything else before the sun s!" H995
2Sa 22:49 *who* s me free from my enemies. H3655
1Ki 7: 4 Its windows were placed high in s *of* three H3215
1Ki 7: 5 they were in the front part in s of three H7193
1Ki 7:41 the two *s* of network decorating the two AIT
1Ki 7:42 pomegranates for the two s of network AIT
2Ki 5: 5 shekels of gold and ten s *of* clothing. H2722
2Ki 5:22 a talent of silver and two s *of* clothing. H2722
2Ki 5:23 silver in two bags, with two s *of* clothing. H2722
2Ch 4:12 the two *s* of network decorating the two AIT
2Ch 4:13 pomegranates for the two *s of* network AIT
2Ch 30:19 *who* s their heart on seeking God—the H3922
Job 5:11 The lowly he s on high, and those who H8492
Job 34:24 the mighty and s up others in their place. H6641
Job 41:21 Its breath s coals ablaze, and flames dart H4265
Ps 50: 1 from the rising of the sun to where it s. H4427
Ps 68: 6 God s the lonely in families, he leads out H3782
Ps 83:14 forest or a flame s the mountains ablaze, H4265
Ps 113: 3 rising of the sun to the place where it s, H4427
Ps 146: 7 to the hungry. The LORD s prisoners free, H6002
Pr 15:25 *he* s the widow's boundary stones in place H5893
Pr 31:17 *She* s about her work vigorously H5516+2520
Ecc 1: 5 The sun rises and the sun s, and hurries H995
Isa 9:18 *it* s the forest thickets ablaze, so H3675
Isa 30:33 like a stream of burning sulfur, s it ablaze. H1277
Isa 64: 2 As *when* fire s twigs ablaze and causes H7706
Jer 13:21 say when the LORD s over you those you H7212
Da 4:17 anyone he wishes and s over them the A10624
Da 5:21 on earth and s over them anyone he A10624
Am 9: 6 in the heavens and s its foundation on H3569
Mal 1:11 from where the sun rises to where it s. H4427
Mt 5:19 Therefore anyone *who* s aside one of the G3395
Jn 8:36 So if the Son s you free, you will be free G1802
2Co 10: 5 pretension *that* s *itself* up against the G2048
2Th 2: 4 so that *he* s himself up in God's temple G2767
Heb 10: 9 *He* s aside the first to establish the second. G359
Jas 3: 6 s the whole course of one's life on fire G5824

SETTING (23) [SET]

Ge 15:12 As the sun *was* s, Abram fell into a deep H995
Ex 8: 9 the honor of s the time for me to H4200+5503
Nu 7: 1 When Moses finished s up the tabernacle, H7756
Nu 10: 6 The blast will be the signal for s out. H5023
Nu 10: 7 trumpets, but not with the signal for s out. NDT
Nu 10:29 "We *are* s out for the place about which H5825
Dt 4: 8 this body of laws I *am* s before you today? H5989
Dt 11:26 I *am* s before you today a blessing and a H5989
Dt 11:30 toward the s sun, near the great H4427
Dt 11:32 decrees and laws I *am* s before you today. H5989
Dt 26:12 finished s aside a tenth *of* all your H6923+5130
2Sa 2:24 and *as* the sun *was* s, they came to H995
1Ki 22:36 As the sun *was* s, a cry spread through the H995
2Ch 2: 4 s out the consecrated bread regularly NDT
2Ch 29:18 the table for s out the consecrated bread, H5121
Isa 45: 6 the sun to the place of its s people may H5115
Jer 21: 8 I *am* s before you the way of life and the H5989
Am 7: 8 I *am* s a plumb line among my people H8492
Hab 2: 9 s his nest on high to escape the clutches H8492
Mk 7: 9 "*You have* a fine way of s aside the G119
1Co 10: 6 keep us from s *our* hearts on evil things as G2122
2Co 4: 2 *by* s forth the truth plainly we commend G5748
Eph 2:15 *by* s aside in his flesh the law with its G2934

SETTINGS (12) [SET]

Ex 28:11 Then mount the stones in gold filigree s H6015
Ex 28:13 Make gold filigree s H5401
Ex 28:14 like a rope, and attach the chains to the s. H5401
Ex 28:20 Mount them in gold filigree s. H8687
Ex 28:25 the other ends of the chains to the two s, H5401
Ex 39: 6 in gold filigree s and engraved them like H6015
Ex 39:13 They were mounted in gold filigree s. H4853
Ex 39:16 made two gold filigree s and two gold H5401
Ex 39:18 the other ends of the chains to the two s, H5401
1Ch 29: 2 as well as onyx for the s, turquoise, H4854
Pr 25:11 Like apples of gold in s *of* silver is a ruling H5381
Eze 28:13 Your s and mountings were made H4856+9513

SETTLE (44) [RESETTLE, RESETTLED, SETTLED, SETTLEMENT, SETTLEMENTS, SETTLES]

Ge 34:10 *You can* s among us; the land is open to H3782
Ge 34:16 *We'll* s among you and become one H3782
Ge 34:23 to their terms, and *they will* s among us." H3782
Ge 35: 1 "Go up to Bethel and s there, and build H3782
Ge 46:34 Then *you will be allowed to* s in the H3782
Ge 47: 4 please *let* your servants s in Goshen." H3782
Ge 47: 6 s your father and your brothers in the best H3782
Nu 33:53 Take possession of the land and s in it, for H3782
Dt 8:12 when you build fine houses and s down, H3782
Dt 12:10 the Jordan and s in the land the LORD H3782
Jdg 18: 1 a place of their own where they *might* s, H3782
2Ki 25:24 "S down in the land and serve the king of H3782
2Ch 19: 8 the law of the LORD and to s disputes. NDT
Job 3: 5 it once more; *may* a cloud s over it; may H8905
Ps 69:35 Then *people will* s there and possess it H3782
Ps 107: 4 no way to a city where they could s. H4632
Ps 107: 7 a straight way to a city where they could s. H4632
Ps 107:36 they founded a city where they could s. H4632
Ps 139: 9 the dawn, if *I* s on the far side of the sea H8905
Isa 1:18 "Come now, *let us* s the matter," says the H3519
Isa 2: 4 the nations and *will* s disputes for many H3519
Isa 7:19 will all come and s in the steep ravines H5663
Isa 14: 1 choose Israel and *will* s them in their own H5663
Isa 23: 7 feet have taken her to s in far-off lands? H1591
Isa 54: 3 nations and s in their desolate cities H3782
Jer 29: 5 "Build houses and s down; plant gardens H3782
Jer 29:28 Therefore build houses and s down; plant H3782
Jer 40: 9 "S down in the land and serve the king of H3782
Jer 42:15 to go to Egypt and you do go to s there, H1591
Jer 42:17 to go to Egypt to s there will die by the H1591
Jer 42:22 in the place where you want to go to s." H1591
Jer 43: 2 'You must not go to Egypt to s there.' H1591
Jer 44:12 were determined to go to Egypt to s there. H1591
Eze 32: 4 *I will* let all the birds of the sky s on you H8905
Eze 32:14 Then *I will* let her waters s and make her H9205
Eze 36:11 *I will* s *people* on you as in the past and H3782
Eze 37:14 will live, and *I will* s you in your own land. H5663
Hos 11:11 *I will* s them in their homes," declares the H3782
Mic 4: 3 peoples and *will* s disputes for strong H3519
Na 3:17 of locusts that s in the walls on a cold H2837
Mt 5:25 "S matters quickly with your G1639+2333
Mt 18:23 a king who wanted *to* s accounts with his G5256
Ac 18:15 your own law—s the matter yourselves. G3972
2Th 3:12 Jesus Christ to s down and earn the G3552+2484

SETTLED (71) [SETTLE]

Ge 11: 2 they found a plain in Shinar and s there. H3782
Ge 11:31 when they came to Harran, *they* s there. H3782
Ge 19:30 left Zoar and s in the mountains, H3782
Ge 25:18 His descendants s in the area from H8905
Ge 26:17 in the Valley of Gerar, where *he* s. H3782
Ge 36: 8 that is, Edom) s in the hill country of Seir. H3782
Ge 47:11 So Joseph s his father and his brothers in H3782
Ge 47:27 Now the Israelites s in Egypt in the region H3782
Ex 10: 6 from the day they s in this land till now. H2118
Ex 10:14 all Egypt and s down in every area of the H5663
Ex 16:35 until they came to a land *that was* s; they H3782
Ex 22:11 between them *will be* s *by* the taking of H2118
Ex 24:16 the glory of the LORD s on Mount Sinai H8905
Ex 40:35 of meeting because the cloud *had* s on it, H8905
Nu 9:17 wherever the cloud s, the Israelites H8905
Nu 11: 9 When the dew s on the camp at night, the H3718
Nu 21:31 So Israel s in the land of the Amorites. H3782
Nu 22: 5 face of the land and *have* s next to me. H3782
Nu 31:10 all the towns where the Midianites had s, H4632
Nu 32:40 of Manasseh, and *they* s there. H3782
Dt 2:12 from before them and s in their place, H3782
Dt 2:21 who drove them out and s in their place. H3782
Dt 2:23 destroyed them and s in their place.) H3782
Dt 12:29 have driven them out and s in their land, H3782
Dt 17:14 have taken possession of it and s in it, H3782
Dt 19: 1 driven them out and s in their towns and H3782
Dt 26: 1 have taken possession of it and s in it, H3782
Jos 19:47 *They* s in Leshem and named it Dan after H3782
Jos 19:50 And he built up the town and s there. H3782
Jos 21:43 they took possession of it and s there. H3782
Jdg 7:12 other eastern peoples *had* s in the valley, H5877
Jdg 11: 3 from his brothers and s in the land of Tob, H3782
Jdg 18:28 The Danites rebuilt the city and s there. H3782
Jdg 21:23 rebuilt the towns and s in them. H3782
Ru 3:18 will not rest until the matter *is* s today." H3983
1Sa 12: 8 out of Egypt and s them in this place. H3782
1Sa 27: 3 David and his men s in Gath with Achish H3782
2Sa 2: 3 and *they* s in Hebron and its towns. H3782
2Sa 7: 1 After the king *was* s in his palace and the H3782
2Sa 20:18 'Get your answer at Abel,' and that s *it*. H9462
1Ki 11:24 Damascus, where *they* s and took control. H3782
2Ki 17: 6 *He* s them in Halah, in Gozan on the H3782
2Ki 17:24 Sepharvaim and s them in the towns H3782
2Ki 17:29 gods in the several towns where they s, H3782
2Ki 18:11 Israel to Assyria and s them in Halah, H5697
1Ch 4:41 Then *they* s in their place, because there H3782
1Ch 5: 8 They s in the area from Aroer to Nebo H3782
1Ch 5:23 *they* s in the land from Bashan to Baal H3782
1Ch 17: 1 After David *was* s in his palace, he said to H3782
2Ch 8: 2 had given him, and s Israelites in them. H3782
2Ch 15: 9 *people* from Ephraim, Manasseh and Simeon *who had* s H1591
Ezr 2:70 the temple servants s in their own towns, H3782
Ezr 2:70 the rest of the Israelites s in their towns. NDT
Ezr 3: 1 came and the Israelites had s in their towns, NDT
Ezr 4:10 deported and s in the city of Samaria A10338
Ne 7:73 rest of the Israelites, s in their own towns. H3782
Ne 7:73 came and the Israelites had s in their towns, NDT
Ne 11: 1 the leaders of the people s in Jerusalem. H3782
Ne 11: 3 provincial leaders who s in Jerusalem H3782
Ne 11:36 of the Levites of Judah s in Benjamin. NDT
Ps 68:10 Your people s in it, and from your bounty H3782
Ps 78:55 *he* s the tribes of Israel in their homes. H8905
Pr 8:25 before the mountains were s in place H3190
Isa 29: 1 Ariel, Ariel, the city where David s! H2837
Eze 31:13 All the birds s on the fallen tree, and all H8905
Zec 7: 7 Negev and the western foothills *were* s? H3782
Mt 25:19 returned and s accounts with them. G5256
Ac 7: 4 land of the Chaldeans and s in Harran. G2997
Ac 7:29 where *he* s as a foreigner and had two G1181
Ac 19:39 bring up, *it must be* s in a legal assembly. G2147
1Co 7:37 man who *has* s the matter in his G2705+1612

SETTLEMENT (3) [SETTLE]

Nu 21:15 that lead to the s *of* Ar and lie along the H8699
Isa 27:10 an abandoned s, forsaken like the H5659
Mt 18:24 As he began the s, a man who owed him G5256

SETTLEMENTS (29) [SETTLE]

Ge 25:16 rulers according to their s and camps. H2958
Ge 36:43 according to their s in the land they H4632
Nu 21:25 Heshbon and all its surrounding s. H1426
Nu 21:32 captured its surrounding s and drove out H1426
Nu 32:41 captured their s and called them Havvoth H2557
Nu 32:42 Kenath and its surrounding s and called it H1426
Jos 13:30 of Bashan—all the s *of* Jair in Bashan H2557
Jos 15:45 with its surrounding s and villages; H1426
Jos 15:47 Ashdod, its surrounding s and villages H1426
Jos 15:47 Gaza, its s and villages, as far as the H1426
Jos 17:11 together with their surrounding s (the third H1426
Jos 17:16 in Beth Shan and its s and those in the H1426
Jdg 1:27 Megiddo and their surrounding s, H1426
Jdg 11:26 the surrounding s and all the towns along H1426
1Ki 4:13 the s *of* Jair son of Manasseh in Gilead H2557
1Ch 2:23 as well as Kenath with its surrounding s H1426
1Ch 4:33 These were their s. And they kept a H4632
1Ch 6:54 the locations of their s allotted as their H4632
1Ch 7:28 Their lands and s included Bethel and its H4632
Ne 11:25 lived in Kiriath Arba and its surrounding s, H1426
Ne 11:25 in Dibon and its s, in Jekabzeel and its H1426
Ne 11:27 in Hazar Shual, in Beersheba and its s, H1426
Ne 11:28 in Ziklag, in Mekonah and its s, H1426
Ne 11:30 its fields, and in Azekah and its s. H1426
Ne 11:31 lived in Mikmash, Aija, Bethel and its s, H1426
Isa 42:11 let the s where Kedar lives rejoice. H2958
Eze 26: 6 her s on the mainland will be ravaged H1426
Eze 26: 8 He will ravage your s on the mainland H1426
Eze 34:13 in the ravines and in all the s *in* the land. H4632

SETTLES (3) [SETTLE]

2Sa 17:12 will fall on him as dew s on the ground. H5877
Ps 113: 9 *He* s the childless woman in her home as H3782
Pr 18:18 Casting the lot s disputes and keeps H8697

SEVEN (390) [SEVENFOLD, SEVENS, SEVENTH]

Ge 4:15 Cain will suffer vengeance s *times over*." H8679
Ge 4:24 If Cain is avenged s *times*, then Lamech H8679
Ge 7: 2 Take with you s pairs of every kind H8679+8679
Ge 7: 3 also s pairs of every kind of bird H8679+8679
Ge 7: 4 S days from now I will send rain on the H8679
Ge 7:10 And after the s days the floodwaters came H8679
Ge 8:10 He waited s more days and again sent out H8679
Ge 8:12 He waited s more days and sent the dove H8679
Ge 21:28 Abraham set apart s ewe lambs from the H8679
Ge 21:29 meaning of these s ewe lambs you have H8679
Ge 21:30 "Accept these s lambs from my hand as a H8679
Ge 29:18 "I'll work for you s years in return for your H8679
Ge 29:20 So Jacob served s years to get Rachel, but H8679
Ge 29:27 in return for another s years of work." H8679
Ge 29:30 And he worked for Laban another s years. H8679
Ge 31:23 pursued Jacob for s days and caught up H8679
Ge 33: 3 down to the ground s times as he H8679
Ge 41: 2 out of the river there came up s cows, H8679
Ge 41: 3 After them, s other cows, ugly and gaunt H8679
Ge 41: 4 were ugly and gaunt ate up the s sleek, H8679
Ge 41: 5 S heads of grain, healthy and good, were H8679
Ge 41: 6 s other heads of grain sprouted H8679
Ge 41: 7 of grain swallowed up the s healthy, H8679
Ge 41:18 out of the river there came up s cows, H8679
Ge 41:19 After them, s other cows came up H8679
Ge 41:20 ugly cows ate up the s fat cows that came H8679
Ge 41:22 "In my dream I saw s heads of grain, full H8679
Ge 41:23 After them, s other heads sprouted H8679
Ge 41:24 of grain swallowed up the s good heads. H8679
Ge 41:26 The s good cows are seven years, and the H8679
Ge 41:26 The seven good cows are s years, and the H8679
Ge 41:26 the s good heads of grain are seven H8679
Ge 41:26 seven good heads of grain are s years; H8679
Ge 41:27 The s lean, ugly cows that came up H8679
Ge 41:27 cows that came up afterward are s years, H8679
Ge 41:27 so are the s worthless heads of grain H8679
Ge 41:27 the east wind: They are s years of famine. H8679
Ge 41:29 S years of great abundance are coming H8679
Ge 41:30 s years of famine will follow them H8679
Ge 41:34 of Egypt during the s years of abundance. H8679
Ge 41:36 be used during the s years of famine that H8679
Ge 41:47 During the s years of abundance the land H8679

Ge 41:48 produced in those **s** years of abundance H8679
Ge 41:53 The **s** years of abundance in Egypt came H8679
Ge 41:54 the **s** years of famine began, just as H8679
Ge 46:25 given to his daughter Rachel—**s** in all. H8679
Ex 2:16 Now a priest of Midian had **s** daughters H8679
Ex 7:25 **S** days passed after the LORD struck the H8679
Ex 12:15 For **s** days you are to eat bread made H8679
Ex 12:19 For **s** days no yeast is to be found in your H8679
Ex 13:6 For **s** days eat bread made without yeast H8679
Ex 13:7 Eat unleavened bread during those **s** days H8679
Ex 22:30 Let them stay with their mothers for **s** days, H8679
Ex 23:15 **s** days eat bread made without yeast H8679
Ex 25:37 "Then make its **s** lamps and set them up H8679
Ex 29:30 in the Holy Place is to wear them **s** days. H8679
Ex 29:35 taking **s** days to ordain them. H8679
Ex 29:37 For **s** days make atonement for the altar H8679
Ex 34:18 For **s** days eat bread made without yeast H8679
Ex 37:23 They made its **s** lamps, as well as its wick H8679
Lev 4:6 sprinkle some of it **s** times before the LORD H8679
Lev 4:17 it before the LORD **s** times in front of the H8679
Lev 8:11 some of the oil on the altar **s** times, H8679
Lev 8:33 entrance to the tent of meeting for **s** days, H8679
Lev 8:33 your ordination will last **s** days. H8679
Lev 8:35 day and night for **s** days and do what the H8679
Lev 12:2 will be ceremonially unclean for **s** days, H8679
Lev 13:4 is to isolate the affected person for **s** days. H8679
Lev 13:5 he is to isolate them for another **s** days. H8679
Lev 13:21 the priest is to isolate them for **s** days. H8679
Lev 13:26 the priest is to isolate them for **s** days. H8679
Lev 13:31 is to isolate the affected person for **s** days. H8679
Lev 13:33 is to keep them isolated another **s** days. H8679
Lev 13:50 area and isolate the article for **s** days. H8679
Lev 13:54 Then he is to isolate it for another **s** days. H8679
Lev 14:7 **S** times he shall sprinkle the one to be H8679
Lev 14:8 must stay outside their tent for **s** days. H8679
Lev 14:16 some of it before the LORD **s** times. H8679
Lev 14:27 oil from his palm **s** times before the LORD H8679
Lev 14:38 of the house and close it up for **s** days. H8679
Lev 14:51 and sprinkle the house **s** times. H8679
Lev 15:13 he is to count off **s** days for his ceremonial H8679
Lev 15:19 of her monthly period will last **s** days, H8679
Lev 15:24 he will be unclean for **s** days; any bed he H8679
Lev 15:28 she must count off **s** days, and after that H8679
Lev 16:14 of it with his finger **s** times before the H8679
Lev 16:19 on it with his finger **s** times to cleanse it H8679
Lev 22:27 it is to remain with its mother for **s** days. H8679
Lev 23:6 **s** days you must eat bread made H8679
Lev 23:8 For **s** days present a food offering to the H8679
Lev 23:15 the wave offering, count off **s** full weeks. H8679
Lev 23:18 Present with this bread **s** male lambs H8679
Lev 23:34 and it lasts for **s** days. H8679
Lev 23:36 For **s** days present food offerings to the H8679
Lev 23:39 the festival to the LORD for **s** days; H8679
Lev 23:40 before the LORD your God for **s** days. H8679
Lev 23:41 a festival to the LORD for **s** days each year. H8679
Lev 23:42 Live in temporary shelters for **s** days: All H8679
Lev 25:8 " 'Count off **s** sabbath years—seven times H8679
Lev 25:8 seven sabbath years—**s** times seven years H8679
Lev 25:8 seven times **s** years—so that the H8679
Lev 25:8 so that the **s** sabbath years amount to a H8679
Lev 26:18 I will punish you for your sins **s** *times* over. H8679
Lev 26:21 I will multiply your afflictions **s** *times over* H8679
Lev 26:24 will afflict you for your sins **s** *times over.* H8679
Lev 26:28 will punish you for your sins **s** *times over.* H8679
Nu 8:2 see that *all* **s** light up the area in front of H8679
Nu 12:14 she not have been in disgrace for **s** days? H8679
Nu 12:14 Confine her outside the camp for **s** days H8679
Nu 12:15 was confined outside the camp for **s** days, H8679
Nu 13:22 had been built **s** years before Zoan in H8679
Nu 19:4 sprinkle it **s** times toward the front H8679
Nu 19:11 human corpse will be unclean for **s** days. H8679
Nu 19:14 who is in it will be unclean for **s** days, H8679
Nu 19:16 a grave, will be unclean for **s** days. H8679
Nu 23:1 Balaam said, "Build me **s** altars here, and H8679
Nu 23:1 prepare **s** bulls and seven rams for H8679
Nu 23:1 prepare seven bulls and **s** rams for me." H8679
Nu 23:4 "I have prepared **s** altars, and on each H8679
Nu 23:14 there he built **s** altars and offered a H8679
Nu 23:29 Balaam said, "Build me **s** altars here, and H8679
Nu 23:29 prepare **s** bulls and seven rams for H8679
Nu 23:29 prepare seven bulls and **s** rams for me." H8679
Nu 28:11 one ram and **s** male lambs a year old H8679
Nu 28:17 **s** days eat bread made without yeast. H8679
Nu 28:19 one ram and **s** male lambs a year old H8679
Nu 28:21 with each of the **s** lambs, one-tenth. H8679
Nu 28:24 offering every day for **s** days as an aroma H8679
Nu 28:27 one ram and **s** male lambs a year old as H8679
Nu 28:29 with each of the **s** lambs, one-tenth. H8679
Nu 29:2 one ram and **s** male lambs a year old H8679
Nu 29:4 with each of the **s** lambs, one-tenth. H8679
Nu 29:8 one ram and **s** male lambs a year old H8679
Nu 29:10 with each of the **s** lambs, one-tenth. H8679
Nu 29:12 Celebrate a festival to the LORD for **s** days. H8679
Nu 29:32 " 'On the seventh day offer **s** bulls, two H8679
Nu 29:36 one ram and **s** male lambs a year old H8679
Nu 31:19 killed must stay outside the camp **s** days. H8679
Dt 7:1 **s** nations larger and stronger than you H8679
Dt 15:1 At the end of every **s** years you must H8679
Dt 16:3 for **s** days eat unleavened bread H8679
Dt 16:4 your possession in all your land for **s** days. H8679
Dt 16:9 Count off **s** weeks from the time you begin H8679
Dt 16:13 of Tabernacles for **s** days after you have H8679
Dt 16:15 For **s** days celebrate the festival to the LORD H8679
Dt 28:7 from one direction but flee from you in **s**. H8679
Dt 28:25 one direction but flee from them in **s**, H8679
Dt 31:10 "At the end of every **s** years, in the year H8679
Jos 6:4 Have **s** priests carry trumpets of rams' H8679
Jos 6:4 march around the city **s** times, with the H8679
Jos 6:6 of the LORD and have **s** priests carry H8679
Jos 6:8 the **s** priests carrying the seven trumpets H8679
Jos 6:8 priests carrying the **s** trumpets before the H8679
Jos 6:13 The **s** priests carrying the seven trumpets H8679
Jos 6:13 priests carrying the **s** trumpets went H8679
Jos 6:15 around the city **s** times in the same H8679
Jos 6:15 on that day they circled the city **s** times. H8679
Jos 18:2 there were still **s** Israelite tribes who H8679
Jos 18:5 You are to divide the land into **s** parts H8679
Jos 18:6 descriptions of the **s** parts of the land, H8679
Jos 18:9 town by town, in **s** parts, and returned to H8679
Jdg 6:1 for **s** years he gave them into the H8679
Jdg 6:25 your father's herd, the one **s** years old. H8679
Jdg 12:9 outside his clan. Ibzan led Israel **s** years. H8679
Jdg 14:12 the answer within the **s** days of the feast, H8679
Jdg 14:17 She cried the whole **s** days of the feast. H8679
Jdg 16:7 anyone ties me with **s** fresh bowstrings H8679
Jdg 16:8 brought her **s** fresh bowstrings that H8679
Jdg 16:13 "If you weave the **s** braids of my head into H8679
Jdg 16:13 Delilah took the **s** braids of his head H8679
Jdg 16:19 to shave off the **s** braids of his hair, H8679
Jdg 20:15 in addition to **s** hundred able young men H8679
Jdg 20:16 soldiers there were **s** hundred select H8679
Ru 4:15 you and who is better to you than **s** sons, H8679
1Sa 2:5 She who was barren has borne **s** children H8679
1Sa 6:1 had been in Philistine territory **s** months, H8679
1Sa 10:8 you must wait **s** days until I come to H8679
1Sa 11:3 "Give us **s** days so we can send H8679
1Sa 13:8 He waited **s** days, the time set by Samuel H8679
1Sa 16:10 Jesse had **s** *of* his sons pass before H8679
1Sa 31:13 tree at Jabesh, and they fasted **s** days. H8679
2Sa 2:11 over Judah was **s** years and six months. H8679
2Sa 5:5 reigned over Judah **s** years and six H8679
2Sa 8:4 **s** thousand charioteers and twenty H8679
2Sa 10:18 David killed **s** hundred of their H8679
2Sa 21:6 let **s** of his male descendants be given to H8679
2Sa 21:9 *All* **s** *of* them fell together; they were put H8679
1Ki 2:11 **s** years in Hebron and thirty-three in H8679
1Ki 6:6 floor six cubits and the third floor **s**. H8679
1Ki 6:38 He had spent **s** years building it. H8679
1Ki 7:17 on top of the pillars, **s** for each capital. H8679
1Ki 8:65 LORD our God for **s** days and seven days H8679
1Ki 8:65 our God for seven days and **s** days more, H8679
1Ki 11:3 He had **s** hundred wives of royal birth and H8679
1Ki 16:15 of Judah, Zimri reigned in Tirzah **s** days. H8679
1Ki 18:43 he said. **S** times Elijah said, "Go H8679
1Ki 19:18 Yet I reserve **s** thousand in Israel—all H8679
1Ki 20:29 For **s** days they camped opposite each H8679
2Ki 3:9 After a roundabout march of **s** days, the H8679
2Ki 3:26 he took with him **s** hundred swordsmen to H8679
2Ki 4:35 The boy sneezed **s** times and opened his H8679
2Ki 5:10 wash yourself **s** times in the Jordan H8679
2Ki 5:14 dipped himself in the Jordan **s** times, H8679
2Ki 8:1 a famine in the land that will last **s** years." H8679
2Ki 8:2 in the land of the Philistines **s** years. H8679
2Ki 8:3 At the end of the **s** years she came back H8679
2Ki 11:21 Joash was **s** years old when he began to H8679
2Ki 24:16 the entire force of **s** thousand fighting H8679
1Ch 3:4 where he reigned **s** years and six months. H8679
1Ch 3:24 Johanan, Delaiah and Anani—**s** in all. H8679
1Ch 5:13 Jakan, Zia and Eber—**s** in all. H8679
1Ch 10:12 tree in Jabesh, and they fasted **s** days. H8679
1Ch 15:26 **s** bulls and seven rams were sacrificed. H8679
1Ch 15:26 seven bulls and **s** rams were sacrificed. H8679
1Ch 18:4 **s** thousand charioteers and twenty H8679
1Ch 19:18 David killed **s** thousand of their H8679
1Ch 29:4 **s** thousand talents of refined silver H8679
1Ch 29:27 **s** in Hebron and thirty-three in Jerusalem. H8679
2Ch 7:8 the festival at that time for **s** days, H8679
2Ch 7:9 of the altar for **s** days and the festival for H8679
2Ch 7:9 days and the festival for **s** days more. H8679
2Ch 13:9 a young bull and **s** rams may become a H8679
2Ch 15:11 to the LORD **s** hundred head of cattle H8679
2Ch 15:11 head of cattle and **s** thousand sheep and H8679
2Ch 17:11 **s** thousand seven hundred rams and H8679
2Ch 17:11 seven thousand **s** hundred rams and H8679
2Ch 17:11 hundred rams and **s** thousand seven H8679
2Ch 17:11 seven thousand **s** hundred goats. H8679
2Ch 24:1 Joash was **s** years old when he became H8679
2Ch 29:21 They brought **s** bulls, seven rams, seven H8679
2Ch 29:21 brought seven bulls, **s** rams, seven male H8679
2Ch 29:21 **s** male lambs and seven male goats as a H8679
2Ch 29:21 male lambs and **s** male goats as a sin H8679
2Ch 30:21 of Unleavened Bread for **s** days with great H8679
2Ch 30:22 For the **s** days they ate their assigned H8679
2Ch 30:23 to celebrate the festival **s** more days; H8679
2Ch 30:23 so for another **s** days they celebrated H8679
2Ch 30:24 thousand bulls and **s** thousand sheep H8679
2Ch 35:17 Festival of Unleavened Bread for **s** days. H8679
Ezr 6:22 For **s** days they celebrated with joy the H8679
Ezr 7:14 by the king and his **s** advisers to inquire A10696
Ne 8:18 They celebrated the festival for **s** days H8679
Est 1:5 a banquet, lasting **s** days, in the enclosed H8679
Est 1:10 he commanded the **s** eunuchs who served H8679
Est 1:14 the **s** nobles of Persia and Media who H8679
Est 2:9 He assigned to her **s** female attendants H8679
Job 1:2 He had **s** sons and three daughters, H8679
Job 1:3 he owned **s** thousand sheep, three H8679
Job 2:13 ground with him for **s** days and seven H8679
Job 2:13 with him for seven days and **s** nights. H8679
Job 5:19 rescue you; in **s** no harm will touch you. H8679
Job 42:8 So now take **s** bulls and seven rams and H8679
Job 42:8 take seven bulls and **s** rams and go to my H8679
Job 42:13 And he also had **s** sons and three H8685
Ps 12:6 in a crucible, like gold refined **s** *times*. H8679
Ps 79:12 of our neighbors **s** *times* the contempt H8679
Ps 119:164 **S** *times* a day I praise you for your H8679
Pr 6:16 LORD hates, **s** that are detestable to him: H8679
Pr 9:1 her house; she has set up its **s** pillars. H8679
Pr 24:16 though the righteous fall **s** *times*, they H8679
Pr 26:16 his own eyes than **s** people who answer H8679
Pr 26:25 for **s** abominations fill their hearts. H8679
Ecc 11:2 Invest in **s** *ventures*, yes, in eight; you do H8679
Isa 4:1 In that day **s** women will take hold of one H8679
Isa 11:15 will break it up into **s** streams so that H8679
Isa 30:26 the sunlight will be **s** *times brighter* H8679
Isa 30:26 like the light of **s** full days, when the LORD H8679
Jer 15:9 The mother of **s** will grow faint and H8679
Jer 52:25 of the fighting men, and **s** royal advisers. H8679
Eze 3:15 I sat among them for **s** days—deeply H8679
Eze 3:16 At the end of **s** days the word of the LORD H8679
Eze 39:9 For **s** years they will use them for fuel. H8679
Eze 39:12 " 'For **s** months the Israelites will be H8679
Eze 39:14 " 'After the **s** months they will carry out a H8679
Eze 40:22 **S** steps led up to it, with its portico H8679
Eze 40:26 **S** steps led up to it, with its portico H8679
Eze 41:3 on each side of it were **s** cubits wide. H8679
Eze 43:25 "For **s** days you are to provide a male goat H8679
Eze 43:26 For **s** days they are to make atonement H8679
Eze 44:26 After he is cleansed, he must wait **s** days. H8679
Eze 45:21 a festival lasting **s** days, during which you H8651
Eze 45:23 Every day during the **s** days of the festival H8679
Eze 45:23 he is to provide **s** bulls and seven rams H8679
Eze 45:23 seven bulls and **s** rams without defect as H8679
Eze 45:25 " 'During the **s** days of the festival, which H8679
Da 3:19 the furnace heated **s** times hotter than A10696
Da 4:16 of an animal, till **s** times pass by for him. A10696
Da 4:23 animals, until **s** times pass by for him. A10696
Da 4:25 **S** times will pass by for you until you A10696
Da 4:32 **S** times will pass by for you until you A10696
Da 9:25 there will be **s** 'sevens,' and H8679
Da 9:27 confirm a covenant with many *for* one '**s**. H8651
Da 9:27 In the middle of the '**s**' he will put an end H8651
Mic 5:5 We will raise against them **s** shepherds H8679
Zec 3:9 There are **s** eyes on that one stone, and I H8679
Zec 4:2 with a bowl at the top and **s** lamps on it, H8679
Zec 4:2 lamps on it, with **s** channels to the lamps. H8679
Zec 4:10 since the **s** eyes of the LORD that range H8679
Mt 12:45 goes and takes with it **s** other spirits more *G2231*
Mt 15:34 "**S**," they replied, "and a few *G2231*
Mt 15:36 Then he took the **s** loaves and the fish *G2231*
Mt 15:37 disciples picked up **s** basketfuls of broken *G2231*
Mt 16:10 Or the **s** loaves for the four thousand, and *G2231*
Mt 18:21 who sins against me? Up to **s times**?" *G2232*
Mt 18:22 "I tell you, not **s times**, but seventy-seven *G2232*
Mt 22:25 Now there were **s** brothers among us. *G2231*
Mt 22:28 whose wife will she be *of* the **s**, since all *G2231*
Mk 8:5 Jesus asked. "**S**," they replied. *G2231*
Mk 8:6 he had taken the **s** loaves and given *G2231*
Mk 8:8 disciples picked up **s** basketfuls of broken *G2231*
Mk 8:20 when I broke the **s** loaves for the four *G2231*
Mk 8:20 did you pick up?" They answered, "**S**." *G2231*
Mk 12:20 Now there were **s** brothers. The first one *G2231*
Mk 12:22 none of the **s** left any children. *G2231*
Mk 12:23 since the **s** were married to her? *G2231*
Mk 16:9 out of whom he had driven **s** demons. *G2231*
Lk 2:36 lived with her husband **s** years after her *G2231*
Lk 8:2 from whom **s** demons had come out *G2231*
Lk 11:26 Then it goes and takes **s** other spirits more *G2231*
Lk 17:4 sin against you **s times** in a day and *G2232*
Lk 17:4 in a day and **s times** come back to you *G2232*
Lk 20:29 Now there were **s** brothers. The first one *G2231*
Lk 20:31 in the same way the **s** died, leaving *G2231*
Lk 20:33 since the **s** were married to her? *G2231*
Lk 24:13 **about s miles** from Jerusalem. *G600+5084+2008*
Ac 6:3 choose **s** men from among you who are *G2231*
Ac 13:19 he overthrew **s** nations in Canaan *G2231*
Ac 19:14 **S** sons of Sceva, a Jewish chief priest *G2231*
Ac 20:6 others at Troas, where we stayed **s** days. *G2231*
Ac 21:4 there and stayed with them **s** days. *G2231*
Ac 21:8 of Philip the evangelist, one of the **S**. *G2231*
Ac 21:27 When the **s** days were nearly over, some *G2231*
Ro 11:4 myself **s thousand** who have not *G2233*
Heb 11:30 had marched around them for **s** days. *G2231*
2Pe 2:5 preacher of righteousness, **and s others**; *G3838*
Rev 1:4 To the **s** churches in the province of Asia: *G2231*
Rev 1:4 from the **s** spirits before his throne *G2231*
Rev 1:11 you see and send it to the **s** churches: *G2231*
Rev 1:12 when I turned I saw **s** golden lampstands, *G2231*
Rev 1:16 In his right hand he held **s** stars, and *G2231*
Rev 1:20 The mystery of the **s** stars that you saw in *G2231*
Rev 1:20 hand and of the **s** golden lampstands is *G2231*
Rev 1:20 The **s** stars are the angels of the seven *G2231*
Rev 1:20 stars are the angels of the **s** churches, *G2231*
Rev 1:20 the **s** lampstands are the seven *G2231*
Rev 1:20 the seven lampstands are the **s** churches. *G2231*
Rev 2:1 of him who holds the **s** stars in his right *G2231*
Rev 2:1 walks among the **s** golden lampstands. *G2231*

Rev 3: 1 of him who holds the s spirits of God and G2231
Rev 3: 1 the seven spirits of God and the s stars. G2231
Rev 4: 5 front of the throne, s lamps were blazing. G2231
Rev 4: 5 These are the s spirits of God. G2231
Rev 5: 1 on both sides and sealed with s seals. G2231
Rev 5: 5 is able to open the scroll and its s seals." G2231
Rev 5: 6 The Lamb had s horns and seven eyes G2231
Rev 5: 6 The Lamb had seven horns and s eyes G2231
Rev 5: 6 which are the s spirits of God sent out into G2231
Rev 6: 1 the Lamb opened the first of the s seals. G2231
Rev 8: 2 And I saw the s angels who stand before G2231
Rev 8: 2 and s trumpets were given to them. G2231
Rev 8: 6 Then the s angels who had the seven G2231
Rev 8: 6 angels who had the s trumpets prepared G2231
Rev 10: 3 the voices of the s thunders spoke. G2231
Rev 10: 4 And when the s thunders spoke, I was G2231
Rev 10: 4 "Seal up what the s thunders have said G2231
Rev 11:13 S thousand people were killed in the G2231
Rev 12: 3 red dragon with s heads and ten horns G2231
Rev 12: 3 ten horns and s crowns on its heads. G2231
Rev 13: 1 It had ten horns and s heads, with ten G2231
Rev 15: 1 s angels with the seven last plagues—last G2231
Rev 15: 1 seven angels with the s last plagues—last G2231
Rev 15: 6 the temple came the s angels with the G2231
Rev 15: 6 the seven angels with the s plagues. G2231
Rev 15: 7 gave to the s angels seven golden G2231
Rev 15: 7 to the seven angels s golden bowls filled G2231
Rev 15: 8 temple until the s plagues of the seven G2231
Rev 15: 8 seven plagues of the s angels were G2231
Rev 16: 1 from the temple saying to the s angels, G2231
Rev 16: 1 pour out the s bowls of God's wrath on G2231
Rev 17: 1 One of the s angels who had the seven G2231
Rev 17: 1 angels who had the s bowls came and G2231
Rev 17: 3 names and had s heads and ten horns. G2231
Rev 17: 7 which has the s heads and ten horns. G2231
Rev 17: 9 The s heads are seven hills on which the G2231
Rev 17: 9 The seven heads are s hills on which the G2231
Rev 17:10 They are also s kings. Five have fallen G2231
Rev 17:11 He belongs to the s and is going to his G2231
Rev 21: 9 One of the s angels who had the seven G2231
Rev 21: 9 angels who had the s bowls full of the G2231
Rev 21: 9 bowls full of the s last plagues came and G2231

SEVEN-DAY (2) [DAY]

Ge 50:10 Joseph observed a s period of H8679+3427
1Ch 9:25 their duties for **s periods.** H8679+2021+3427

SEVENFOLD (1) [SEVEN]

Pr 6:31 he must pay s, though it costs him H8679

SEVENS (4) [SEVEN]

Da 9:24 "Seventy 's' are decreed for your people H8651
Da 9:25 there will be seven 's,' and sixty-two H8651
Da 9:25 will be seven 'sevens,' and sixty-two 's. H8651
Da 9:26 After the sixty-two 's,' the Anointed One H8651

SEVENTEEN (8) [SEVENTEENTH]

Ge 37: 2 a young man *of* s, was tending the H8679+6926
Ge 47:28 Jacob lived in Egypt s years, and H8679+6926
Jdg 8:26 came to **s hundred** H8679+4395+2256+547
1Ki 14:21 and he reigned s years in H8679+6926
2Ki 13: 1 Samaria, and he reigned s years. H8679+6926
1Ch 26:30 **s hundred** able men H547+2256+8679+4395
2Ch 12:13 and he reigned s years in H8679+6926
Jer 32: 9 out for him s shekels of H8679+2256+6927

SEVENTEENTH (6) [SEVENTEEN]

Ge 7:11 on the s day of the second month— H8679+6925
Ge 8: 4 on the s day of the seventh H8679+6925
1Ki 22:51 in Samaria in the s year of H8679+6926
2Ki 16: 1 In the s year of Pekah son of H8679+6926
1Ch 24:15 the s to Hezir, the eighteenth to H8679+6925
1Ch 25:24 the s to Joshbekashah, his sons H8679+6925

SEVENTH (115) [SEVEN]

Ge 2: 2 By the s day God had finished the work he H8668
Ge 2: 2 so on the s day he rested from all his work H8668
Ge 2: 3 Then God blessed the s day and made it H8668
Ge 8: 4 day of the s month the ark came to H8668
Ex 12:15 first day through the s must be cut off from H8668
Ex 12:16 assembly, and another one on the s day. H8668
Ex 13: 6 yeast and on the s day hold a festival to H8668
Ex 16:26 gather it, but on the s day, the Sabbath, H8668
Ex 16:27 people went out on the s day to gather it, H8668
Ex 16:29 is to stay where they are on the s day; H8668
Ex 16:30 So the people rested on the s day. H8668
Ex 20:10 the s day is a sabbath to the LORD your H8668
Ex 20:11 is in them, but he rested on the s day. H8668
Ex 21: 2 But in the s year, he shall go free, without H8668
Ex 23:11 during the s year let the land lie H8668
Ex 23:12 but on the s day do not work, so H8668
Ex 24:16 on the s day the LORD called to Moses H8668
Ex 31:15 the s day is a day of sabbath rest H8668
Ex 31:17 on the s day he rested and was H8668
Ex 34:21 shall labor, but on the s day you shall rest H8668
Ex 35: 2 but the s day shall be your holy day H8668
Lev 13: 5 On the s day the priest is to examine them, H8668
Lev 13: 6 On the s day the priest is to examine them H8668
Lev 13:27 On the s day the priest is to examine that H8668
Lev 13:32 On the s day the priest is to examine the H8668
Lev 13:34 On the s day the priest is to examine the H8668
Lev 13:51 On the s day he is to examine it, and if the H8668
Lev 14: 9 On the s day they must shave off all their H8668
Lev 14:39 On the s day the priest shall return to H8668
Lev 16:29 tenth day of the s month you must deny H8668
Lev 23: 3 the s day is a day of sabbath rest H8668
Lev 23: 8 And on the s day hold a sacred assembly H8668
Lev 23:16 days up to the day after the s Sabbath, H8668
Lev 23:24 the first day of the s month you are to H8668
Lev 23:27 tenth day of this s month is the Day of H8668
Lev 23:34 the fifteenth day of the s month the LORD's H8668
Lev 23:39 with the fifteenth day of the s month, H8668
Lev 23:41 to come; celebrate it in the s month. H8668
Lev 25: 4 But in the s year the land is to have a year H8668
Lev 25: 9 on the tenth day of the s month; H8668
Lev 25:20 will we eat in the s year if we do not plant H8668
Nu 6: 9 they must shave their head on the s day H8668
Nu 7:48 On the s day Elishama son of Ammihud H8668
Nu 19:12 water on the third day and on the s day; H8668
Nu 19:12 purify themselves on the third and s days, H8668
Nu 19:19 who are unclean on the third and s days, H8668
Nu 19:19 on the s day he is to purify them. H8668
Nu 28:25 On the s day hold a sacred assembly and H8668
Nu 29: 1 the first day of the s month hold a sacred H8668
Nu 29: 7 tenth day of this s month hold a sacred H8668
Nu 29:12 " 'On the fifteenth day of the s month H8668
Nu 29:32 " 'On the s day offer seven bulls, two rams H8668
Nu 31:19 On the third and s days you must purify H8668
Nu 31:24 On the s day wash your clothes and you H8668
Dt 5:14 the s day is a sabbath to the LORD your H8668
Dt 15: 9 "The s year, the year for canceling debts H8679
Dt 15:12 in the s year you must let them go free. H8668
Dt 16: 8 bread and on the s day hold an assembly H8668
Jos 6: 4 On the s day, march around the city seven H8668
Jos 6:15 On the s day, they got up at daybreak H8668
Jos 6:16 The s time around, when the priests H8668
Jos 19:40 The s lot came out for the tribe of Dan H8668
Jdg 14:17 So on the s day he finally told her H8668
Jdg 14:18 Before sunset on the s day the men of the H8668
2Sa 12:18 On the s day the child died. David's H8668
1Ki 8: 2 in the month of Ethanim, the s month. H8668
1Ki 18:44 The s time the servant reported, "A cloud H8668
1Ki 20:29 on the s day the battle was joined. H8668
2Ki 11: 4 In the s year Jehoiada sent for the H8668
2Ki 12: 1 In the s year of Jehu, Joash became king H8679
2Ki 18: 9 which was the s year of Hoshea son of H8668
2Ki 25: 8 On the s day of the fifth month, in the H8679
2Ki 25:25 In the s month, however, Ishmael son of H8668
1Ch 2:15 the sixth Ozem and the s David. H8668
1Ch 12:11 Attai the sixth, Eliel the s, H8668
1Ch 24:10 the s to Hakkoz, the eighth to Abijah, H8668
1Ch 25:14 the s to Jesarelah, his sons and relatives H8668
1Ch 26: 3 Jehohanan the sixth and Eliehoenai the s. H8668
1Ch 26: 5 Issachar the s and Peullethai the eighth. H8668
1Ch 27:10 The s, for the seventh month, was Helez H8668
1Ch 27:10 seventh, for the s month, was Helez the H8668
2Ch 5: 3 at the time of the festival in the s month. H8668
2Ch 7:10 day of the s month he sent the H8668
2Ch 23: 1 In the s year Jehoiada showed his H8668
2Ch 31: 7 third month and finished in the s month. H8668
Ezr 3: 1 When the s month came and the H8668
Ezr 3: 6 the first day of the s month they began to H8668
Ezr 7: 7 up to Jerusalem in the s year of King H8679
Ezr 7: 8 in the fifth month of the s year of the king. H8668
Ne 7:73 When the s month came and the H8668
Ne 8: 2 the first day of the s month Ezra the priest H8668
Ne 8:14 shelters during the festival of the s month H8668
Ne 10:31 Every s year we will forgo working the H8668
Est 1:10 On the s day, when King Xerxes was in H8668
Est 2:16 of Tebeth, in the s year of his reign. H8679
Jer 28:17 In the s month of that same year H8668
Jer 34:14 'Every s year each of you must free any H8679
Jer 41: 1 In the s month Ishmael son of Nethaniah H8668
Jer 52:28 in the s year, 3,023 Jews; H8679
Eze 20: 1 In the s year, in the fifth month on the H8668
Eze 30:20 in the first month on the s day, the word H8679
Eze 45:20 do the same on the s day of the month H8679
Eze 45:25 which begins in the s month on the H8668
Hag 2: 1 on the twenty-first day of the s month, the H8668
Zec 7: 5 in the fifth and s months for the past H8668
Zec 8:19 s and tenth months will become joyful H8668
Mt 22:26 third brother, right on down to the s. G2231
Heb 4: 4 spoken about the s *day* in these words: G1575
Heb 4: 4 "On the s day God rested from all his G1575
Jude 14 the s from Adam, prophesied G1575
Rev 8: 1 When he opened the s seal, there was G1575
Rev 10: 7 in the days when the s angel is about to G1575
Rev 11:15 The s angel sounded his trumpet, and G1575
Rev 16:17 The s angel poured out his bowl into the G1575
Rev 21:20 the sixth ruby, the s chrysolite, the eighth G1575

SEVENTY (57) [70]

Ge 46:27 which went to Egypt, were s in all. H8679
Ge 50: 3 the Egyptians mourned for him s days. H8679
Ex 1: 5 descendants of Jacob numbered s in all; H8679
Ex 15:27 were twelve springs and s palm trees, H8679
Ex 24: 1 Abihu, and s of the elders of Israel. H8679
Ex 24: 9 and the s elders of Israel went up H8679
Nu 7:13 silver sprinkling bowl weighing s shekels, H8679
Nu 7:19 silver sprinkling bowl weighing s shekels, H8679
Nu 7:25 silver sprinkling bowl weighing s shekels, H8679
Nu 7:31 silver sprinkling bowl weighing s shekels, H8679
Nu 7:37 silver sprinkling bowl weighing s shekels, H8679
Nu 7:43 silver sprinkling bowl weighing s shekels, H8679
Nu 7:49 silver sprinkling bowl weighing s shekels, H8679
Nu 7:55 silver sprinkling bowl weighing s shekels, H8679
Nu 7:61 silver sprinkling bowl weighing s shekels, H8679
Nu 7:67 silver sprinkling bowl weighing s shekels, H8679
Nu 7:73 silver sprinkling bowl weighing s shekels, H8679
Nu 7:79 silver sprinkling bowl weighing s shekels, H8679
Nu 7:85 each sprinkling bowl s shekels. H8679
Nu 11:16 "Bring me s of Israel's elders who are H8679
Nu 11:24 He brought together s of their elders and H8679
Nu 11:25 was on him and put it on the s elders. H8679
Nu 33: 9 were twelve springs and s palm trees, H8679
Dt 10:22 who went down into Egypt were s in all, H8679
Jdg 1: 7 "S kings with their thumbs and big toes H8679
Jdg 8:30 He had s sons of his own, for he had many H8679
Jdg 9: 2 to have all s of Jerub-Baal's sons rule H8679
Jdg 9: 4 They gave him s shekels of silver from the H8679
Jdg 9: 5 on one stone murdered his s brothers, H8679
Jdg 9:18 You have murdered his s sons on a single H8679
Jdg 9:24 the crime against Jerub-Baal's s sons, H8679
Jdg 9:56 to his father by murdering his s brothers. H8679
Jdg 12:14 thirty grandsons, who rode on s donkeys. H8679
1Sa 6:19 putting s of them to death because they H8679
2Sa 24:15 s thousand of the people from Dan to H8679
1Ki 5:15 Solomon had s thousand carriers and H8679
2Ki 10: 1 were in Samaria s sons of the house of H8679
2Ki 10: 6 the royal princes, s of them, were with the H8679
2Ki 10: 7 the princes and slaughtered all s of them. H8679
1Ch 21: 5 four hundred and s thousand in Judah. H8679
1Ch 21:14 s thousand men of Israel fell dead. H8679
2Ch 29:32 the assembly brought was s bulls, H8679
2Ch 36:21 until the s years were completed in H8679
Ps 90:10 Our days may come to s years, or eighty, if H8679
Isa 23:15 that time Tyre will be forgotten for s years, H8679
Isa 23:15 But at the end of these s years, it will H8679
Isa 23:17 At the end of s years, the LORD will deal H8679
Jer 25:11 will serve the king of Babylon s years. H8679
Jer 25:12 "But when the s years are fulfilled, I will H8679
Jer 29:10 "When s years are completed for Babylon H8679
Eze 8:11 In front of them stood s elders of Israel H8679
Eze 41:12 on the west side was s cubits wide. H8679
Da 9: 2 of Jerusalem would last s years. H8679
Da 9:24 "S 'sevens' are decreed for your people H8679
Zec 1:12 you have been angry with these s years?" H8679
Zec 7: 5 seventh months for the past s years, H8679
Ac 23:23 s horsemen and two hundred spearmen G1573

SEVENTY-FIVE (5)

Ge 12: 4 Abram was s years old when H8679+2256+2822
Ge 25: 7 lived a hundred and s years. H8679+2256+2822
Est 9:16 They killed s thousand of H2822+2256+8679
Jn 19:39 myrrh and aloes, about s **pounds.** G3354+1669
Ac 7:14 and his whole family, s in all. G1573+4297

SEVENTY-SEVEN (4)

Ge 4:24 times, then Lamech s *times*." H8679+2256+8679
Jdg 8:14 names of the s officials of H8679+2256+8679
Ezr 8:35 rams, s male lambs and H8679+2256+8679
Mt 18:22 not seven times, but s **times.** G1574+2231

SEVENTY-TWO (2) [72]

Lk 10: 1 Lord appointed s others and sent G1573+1545
Lk 10:17 The s returned with joy and said G1573+1545

SEVERAL (7)

2Ki 17:29 own gods in the s **towns** where they settled AIT
Da 8:27 I lay exhausted *for* s **days.** Then I got up AIT
Da 11:13 and after *s* **years,** he will advance AIT
Ac 9:19 Saul spent s days with the disciples in G5516
Ac 16:12 And we stayed there s days. G5516
Ac 24:17 "After an absence of s years, I came to G4498
Ac 24:24 S days later Felix came with his wife G5516

SEVERE (25) [SEVERELY]

Ge 3:16 *I will* **make** your pains in childbearing **very s** H8049+8049
Ge 12:10 a while because the famine was s. H3878
Ge 41:31 the famine that follows it will be so s. H3878
Ge 41:56 the famine *was* s throughout Egypt. H2616
Ge 41:57 because the famine *was* s everywhere. H2616
Ge 43: 1 Now the famine was still s in the land. H3878
Ge 47: 4 the famine is s in Canaan and your H3878
Ge 47:13 region because the famine was s; H3878+4394
Ge 47:20 because the famine *was too* s for them. H2616
Nu 11:33 and he struck them with a s plague. H8041+4394
Dt 28:59 disasters, and s and lingering illnesses. H8273
1Ki 18: 2 Now the famine was s in Samaria, H2617
2Ki 25: 3 in the city *had become so* s that there was H2616
2Ch 16:12 Though his disease was s H4200+5087+2025
Jer 52: 6 in the city *had become so* s that there was H2616
Mt 4:24 those suffering **s pain,** the G992
Lk 4:25 there was a s famine throughout the G3489
Lk 15:14 there was a s famine in that whole G2708
Ac 11:28 predicted that a s famine would spread G3489
Ac 20:19 in the midst of **s testing** by the plots of my G4280
2Co 8: 2 In the midst of a very **s trial,** their G1509+2568
1Th 1: 6 in the midst of s suffering with the joy G4498
Rev 11:13 very hour there was a s earthquake and a G3489
Rev 11:19 thunder, an earthquake and a s hailstorm. G3489
Rev 16:18 peals of thunder and a s earthquake. G3489

SEVERED (1)

Ecc 12: 6 before the silver cord is s, and the golden H8178

S

SEVERELY (21) [SEVERE]
Ru 1:17 deal with me, *be it* ever so **s**, if even H3578
1Sa 3:17 deal with you, *be it* ever so **s**, if you hide H3578
1Sa 14:44 deal with me, *be it* ever so **s**, if you do not H3578
1Sa 20:13 with Jonathan, *be it* ever so **s**, if I do not H3578
1Sa 25:22 with David, *be it* ever so **s**, if by morning I H3578
2Sa 3:9 with Abner, *be it* ever so **s**, if I do not do H3578
2Sa 3:35 deal with me, *be it* ever so **s**, if I taste H3578
2Sa 19:13 deal with me, *be it* ever so **s**, if you are H3578
1Ki 2:23 deal with me, *be it* ever so **s**, if Adonijah H3578
1Ki 19:2 deal with me, *be it* ever so **s**, if by this H3578
1Ki 20:10 deal with me, *be it* ever so **s**, if enough H3578
2Ki 6:31 deal with me, *be it* ever so **s**, if the head H3578
2Ki 13:4 **s** the king of Aram *was* **oppressing** H4315+4316
2Ch 24:25 withdrew, they left Joash **s** wounded. H8041
Ps 118:18 The LORD *has* **chastened** me **s**, but H3579+3579
Mk 12:40 These men will be punished **most s**." *G4358*
Lk 20:47 These men will be punished **most s**." *G4358*
Ac 16:23 After they had been **s** flogged, they were *G4498*
2Co 2:5 of you to some extent—not to **put it** *too* **s**. *G2096*
2Co 11:23 been flogged **more s**, and been exposed *G5649*
Heb 10:29 How much **more s** do you think someone *G5937*

SEW (1) [SEWED, SEWS]
Eze 13:18 Woe to *the women who* **s** magic charms H9529

SEWED (2) [SEW]
Ge 3:7 so *they* **s** fig leaves **together** and made H9529
Job 16:15 "*I have* **s** sackcloth over my skin and H9529

SEWS (2) [SEW]
Mt 9:16 "No one **s** a patch of unshrunk cloth on an *G2095*
Mk 2:21 "No one **s** a patch of unshrunk cloth on an *G2165*

SEX (3) [SEXUAL, SEXUALLY]
Ge 19:5 out to us so that *we can* **have s with** them." H3359
Jdg 19:22 to your house so *we can* **have s with** him." H3359
1Co 6:9 **men who have s with men** *G3434+780*

SEXUAL (68) [SEX]
Ex 19:15 **Abstain from s relations**." H440+5602+448+851
Ex 22:19 *who* **has s relations with** an H8886+6640
Lev 15:18 When a man **has s relations** with a H8886
Lev 15:24 " 'If a man **has s relations** with her H8886+8886
Lev 15:33 a man who **has s relations** with a woman H8886
Lev 18:6 close relative to **have s relations**. H1655+6872
Lev 18:7 *Do* not **dishonor** your father
by having s relations with H1655+6872
Lev 18:8 " '*Do* not **have s relations with** your H1655+6872
Lev 18:9 " '*Do* not **have s relations with** your H1655+6872
Lev 18:10 " '*Do* not **have s relations with** your H1655+6872
Lev 18:11 " '*Do* not **have s relations with** the H1655+6872
Lev 18:12 " '*Do* not **have s relations with** your H1655+6872
Lev 18:13 " '*Do* not **have s relations with** your H1655+6872
Lev 18:14 *Do* not **dishonor** your father's brother
by approaching his wife to have s relations H1655+6872
Lev 18:15 " '*Do* not **have s relations with** your H1655+6872
Lev 18:16 " '*Do* not **have s relations with** your H1655+6872
Lev 18:17 " '*Do* not **have s relations with** both H1655+6872
Lev 18:17 *Do* not **have s relations with** either H1655+6872
Lev 18:18 wife and **have s relations** with her H1655+6872
Lev 18:19 a woman to **have s relations** during H1655+6872
Lev 18:20 '*Do* not **have s relations** H5989+8888+4200+2446
Lev 18:22 " '*Do* not **have s relations** with a man as H8886
Lev 18:23 " '*Do* not **have s relations** with an H5989+8888
Lev 18:23 to an animal to **have s relations** *with* it; H8061
Lev 20:11 " 'If a man **has s relations** with his father's H8886
Lev 20:12 " 'If a man **has s relations** with his H8886
Lev 20:13 " 'If a man **has s relations** with a man as H8886
Lev 20:15 " 'If a man **has s relations** with an H5989+8888
Lev 20:16 an animal to **have s relations with** it, H8061
Lev 20:17 and *they* **have s relations**, it is H8011+906+6872
Lev 20:18 a man **has s relations with** a H1655+906+6872
Lev 20:19 " '*Do* not **have s relations with** the H1655+6872
Lev 20:20 " 'If a man **has s relations** with his aunt H8886
Nu 5:13 man **has s relations** with her H8886+8887+2446
Nu 5:19 no other man *has* **had s relations** with you H8886
Nu 5:20 *by* **having s relations with** a H5989+928+8888
Nu 25:1 began to **indulge in s immorality** with H2388
Dt 27:21 is *anyone who* **has s relations with** H8886+6640
2Sa 20:3 but **had** no **s relations with** them. H995+448
1Ki 1:4 the king **had** no **s relations with** her. H3359
Eze 18:6 **have s relations with** a woman H7928+448
Mt 5:32 except for **s immorality**, makes her the *G4518*
Mt 15:19 adultery, **s immorality**, theft, false *G4518*
Mt 19:9 except for **s immorality**, and marries *G4518*
Mk 7:21 evil thoughts come—**s immorality**, theft, *G4518*
Ac 15:20 by idols, *from* **s immorality**, from the meat *G4518*
Ac 15:29 strangled animals and *from* **s immorality**. *G4518*
Ac 21:25 strangled animals and *from* **s immorality**." *G4518*
Ro 1:24 their hearts to **s impurity** for the degrading *G174*
Ro 1:26 natural **s relations** for unnatural *G5979*
Ro 7:3 if *she* **has s relations with** another man *G1181*
Ro 13:13 not *in* **s immorality** and debauchery *G3130*
1Co 5:1 that there is **s immorality** among you, *G4518*
1Co 6:13 is not *meant for* **s immorality** but for the *G4518*
1Co 6:18 Flee *from* **s immorality**. All other sins a *G4518*
1Co 7:1 a man not *to* **have s relations** with a *G721*
1Co 7:2 But since **s immorality** is occurring, each *G4518*
1Co 7:2 man *should* **have s relations with** his own *G2400*
1Co 10:8 *We should* not **commit s immorality**, as *G4519*
2Co 12:21 **s sin** and debauchery in which they have *G4518*
Gal 5:19 **s immorality**, impurity and *G4518*
Eph 5:3 must not be even a hint of **s immorality**, *G4518*
Col 3:5 **s immorality**, impurity, lust, evil desires *G4518*
1Th 4:3 that you should avoid **s immorality**; *G4518*
Jude 7 **gave** *themselves* **up to s immorality** and *G1745*
Rev 2:14 to idols and **committed s immorality**. *G4519*
Rev 2:20 my servants *into* **s immorality** and the *G4519*
Rev 9:21 their **s immorality** or their thefts. *G4518*

SEXUALLY (9) [SEX]
1Co 5:9 not to associate with **s immoral people**— *G4521*
1Co 5:11 sister but is **s immoral** or greedy, *G4521*
1Co 6:9 Neither the **s immoral** nor idolaters nor *G4521*
1Co 6:18 but whoever **sins s**, sins against *G4519*
1Ti 1:10 *for* the **s immoral**, for those practicing *G4521*
Heb 12:16 See that no one is **s immoral**, or is godless *G4521*
Heb 13:4 judge the adulterer and *all* the **s immoral**. *G4521*
Rev 21:8 the murderers, the **s immoral**, those who *G4521*
Rev 22:15 magic arts, the **s immoral**, the murderers, *G4521*

SHAALABBIN (1)
Jos 19:42 S, Aijalon, Ithlah, H9125

SHAALBIM (2)
Jdg 1:35 Aijalon and S, but when the power H9124
1Ki 4:9 in Makaz, S, Beth Shemesh and Elon H9124

SHAALBONITE (2)
2Sa 23:32 Eliahba the S, the sons of Jashen H9126
1Ch 11:33 Azmaveth the Baharumite, Eliahba the S, H9126

SHAALIM (1)
1Sa 9:4 They went on into the district of S, but the H9127

SHAAPH (2)
1Ch 2:47 Jotham, Geshan, Pelet, Ephah and S. H9131
1Ch 2:49 She also gave birth to S the father of H9131

SHAARAIM (3)
Jos 15:36 S, Adithaim and Gederah (or H9139
1Sa 17:52 were strewn along the S road to Gath H9139
1Ch 4:31 Markaboth, Hazar Susim, Beth Biri and S. H9139

SHAASHGAZ (1)
Est 2:14 another part of the harem to the care of S, H9140

SHABBETHAI (3)
Ezr 10:15 supported by Meshullam and S the Levite H8703
Ne 8:7 Akkub, S, Hodiah, Maaseiah H8703
Ne 11:16 S and Jozabad, two of the heads of the H8703

SHACKLES (13)
Jdg 16:21 Binding him with **bronze** *s*, they set him to AIT
2Ki 25:7 bound him with **bronze s** and took him to H5733
2Ch 33:11 bound him with **bronze s** and took him to H5733
2Ch 36:6 bound him with **bronze s** to take him to H5733
Job 12:18 He takes off the **s** *put on by* kings and ties H4591
Job 13:27 You fasten my feet in **s**; you keep close H6040
Job 33:11 He fastens my feet in **s**; he keeps close H6040
Ps 2:3 us break their chains and throw off their **s**." H6310
Ps 105:18 They bruised his feet with **s**, his neck was H3890
Ps 149:8 with fetters, their nobles with **s** *of* iron, H3890
Jer 39:7 bound him with **bronze s** to take him to H5733
Jer 52:11 bound him with **bronze s** and took him to H5733
Na 1:13 yoke from your neck and tear your **s** away." H4593

SHADE (18)
Jdg 9:15 come and take refuge in my **s**; but if not, H7498
Ne 8:15 from myrtles, palms and **s** trees, to make H6290
Ps 80:10 The mountains were covered with its **s** H7498
Ps 121:5 the LORD is your **s** at your right hand; H7498
SS 2:3 I delight to sit in his **s**, and his fruit is H7498
Isa 4:6 be a shelter and **s** from the heat of the H7498
Isa 25:4 from the storm and a **s** from the heat. H7498
Isa 30:2 protection, to Egypt's **s** for refuge. H7498
Isa 30:3 Egypt's **s** will bring you disgrace. H7498
Eze 17:23 will find shelter in the **s** *of* its branches. H7498
Eze 31:6 all the great nations lived in its **s**. H7498
Eze 31:12 earth came out from under its **s** and left it. H7498
Eze 31:17 men who lived in its **s** among the nations. H7498
Hos 4:13 terebinth, where the **s** is pleasant. H7498
Hos 14:7 People will dwell again in his **s**; they will H7498
Jnh 4:5 sat in its **s** and waited to see what would H7498
Jnh 4:6 over Jonah to give **s** for his head to ease H7498
Mk 4:32 branches that the birds can perch in its **s**." *G5014*

SHADOW (33) [SHADOWS]
2Ki 20:9 Shall the **s** go forward ten steps, or shall it H7498
2Ki 20:10 simple matter for the **s** to go forward ten H7498
2Ki 20:11 the LORD made the **s** go back the ten steps H7498
1Ch 29:15 Our days on earth are like a **s**, without H7498
Job 8:9 our days on earth are but a **s**. H7498
Job 17:7 dim with grief; my whole frame is but a **s**. H7498
Job 34:22 There is no **deep s**, no utter darkness H3125
Job 40:22 The lotuses conceal it in their **s**; the H7498
Ps 17:8 your eye; hide me in the **s** *of* your wings H7498
Ps 36:7 People take refuge in the **s** *of* your wings. H7498
Ps 57:1 take refuge in the **s** *of* your wings until the H7498
Ps 63:7 are my help, I sing in the **s** *of* your wings. H7498
Ps 91:1 High will rest in the **s** *of* the Almighty. H7498
Ps 102:11 My days are like the evening **s**; I wither H7498
Ps 109:23 I fade away like an evening **s**; I am H7498
Ps 144:4 a breath; their days are like a fleeting **s**. H7498
Ecc 6:12 days they pass through like a **s**? H7498
Ecc 8:13 their days will not lengthen like a **s**. H7498
Isa 16:3 Make your **s** like night—at high H7498
Isa 25:5 as heat is reduced by the **s** *of* a cloud, so H7498
Isa 32:2 in the desert and the **s** *of* a great rock in a H7498
Isa 34:15 her young under the **s** *of* her wings; H7498
Isa 38:8 I will make the **s** cast by the sun go back H7498
Isa 49:2 in the **s** *of* his hand he hid me; he H7498
Isa 51:16 covered you with the **s** *of* my hand— H7498
Jer 48:45 "In the **s** *of* Heshbon the fugitives stand H7498
La 4:20 that under his **s** we would live among H7498
Mt 4:16 living in the land *of* the **s** of death a light *G5014*
Lk 1:79 living in darkness and *in* the **s** of death, *G5014*
Ac 5:15 at least Peter's **s** might fall on some of *G5014*
Col 2:17 These are a **s** of the things that were to *G5014*
Heb 8:5 that is a copy and **s** of what is in heaven. *G5014*
Heb 10:1 The law is *only* a **s** of the good things that *G5014*

SHADOWS (11) [SHADOW]
Jdg 9:36 "You mistake the **s** *of* the mountains for H7498
Ne 13:19 When **evening s fell** *on* the gates of H7511
Job 7:2 Like a slave longing for the **evening s**, or H7498
Job 14:2 like fleeting **s**, they do not endure. H7498
Job 16:16 is red with weeping, **dark s** ring my eyes; H7516
Ps 11:2 to shoot from the **s** at the upright in heart. H694
SS 2:17 Until the day breaks and the **s** flee, turn H7498
SS 4:6 Until the day breaks and the **s** flee, I will H7498
Isa 59:9 brightness, but we walk in **deep s**. H696
Jer 6:4 is fading, and the **s** *of* evening grow long. H7498
Jas 1:17 who does not change like shifting **s**. *G684*

SHADRACH (14)
Da 1:7 to Hananiah, S; to Mishael, Meshach; H8731
Da 2:49 at Daniel's request the king appointed S, A10701
Da 3:12 province of Babylon—S, Meshach and A10701
Da 3:13 Nebuchadnezzar summoned S, Meshach A10701
Da 3:14 "Is it true, S, Meshach and A10701
Da 3:16 S, Meshach and Abednego replied to A10701
Da 3:19 Nebuchadnezzar was furious with S, A10701
Da 3:20 strongest soldiers in his army to tie up S, A10701
Da 3:22 the fire killed the soldiers who took up S, A10701
Da 3:26 shouted, "S, Meshach and A10701
Da 3:26 So S, Meshach and Abednego came A10701
Da 3:28 "Praise be to the God of S, Meshach A10701
Da 3:29 who say anything against the God of S, A10701
Da 3:30 Then the king promoted S, Meshach A10701

SHAFT (9)
Ex 25:31 Hammer out its base and **s**, and make its H7866
Ex 37:17 They hammered out its base and **s**, and H7866
1Sa 17:7 His spear **s** was like a weaver's rod, and its H6770
2Sa 5:8 will have to use the **water s** to reach those H7562
2Sa 21:19 had a spear with a **s** like a weaver's rod. H6770
2Sa 23:7 uses a tool of iron or the **s** *of* a spear; H6770
1Ch 20:5 had a spear with a **s** like a weaver's rod. H6770
Job 28:4 Far from human dwellings they cut a **s**, in H5707
Rev 9:1 was given the key *to* the **s** of the Abyss. *G5853*

SHAGEE (1)
1Ch 11:34 Gizonite, Jonathan son of S the Hararite, H8707

SHAGGY (1)
Da 8:21 The **s** goat is the king of Greece, and the H8537

SHAHAR See ZERETH SHAHAR

SHAHARAIM (1)
1Ch 8:8 Sons were born to S in Moab after he had H8844

SHAHAZUMAH (1)
Jos 19:22 touched Tabor, S and Beth Shemesh, and H8833

SHAKE (32) [SHAKEN, SHAKES, SHAKING, SHOOK]
Jdg 16:20 "I'll go out as before and **s myself free**." H5850
Ne 5:13 "In this way *may* God **s out** of their house H5850
Job 4:14 seized me and **made** all my bones **s**. H7064
Job 16:4 against you and **s** my head at you. H5675
Job 38:13 by the edges and **s** the wicked out of it? H5850
Ps 10:6 says to himself, "Nothing *will* ever **s** *me*." H4572
Ps 44:14 nations; the peoples **s** their heads at us. H4954
Ps 64:8 who see them *will* **s** *their* **heads in scorn**. H5653
Ps 99:1 between the cherubim, *let* the earth **s**. H5667
Ps 109:25 when they see me, *they* **s** their heads. H5675
Pr 11:15 refuses to **s hands in pledge** is safe. H9364
Isa 2:19 his majesty, when he rises to **s** the earth. H6907
Isa 2:21 his majesty, when he rises to **s** the earth. H6907
Isa 5:25 The mountains **s**, and the dead bodies H8074
Isa 10:32 *they will* **s** their fist at the mount of H5677
Isa 13:13 the earth *will* **s** from its place at the H8321
Isa 24:18 opened, the foundations of the earth **s**. H8321
Isa 52:2 **S off** your dust; rise up, sit enthroned H5850
Jer 18:16 by will be appalled and *will* **s** their heads. H5653
Jer 48:27 that *you* **s** *your* **head in scorn** whenever H5653
La 2:15 they scoff and **s** their heads at Daughter H5675
Am 9:1 tops of the pillars so that the thresholds **s**. H8321
Am 9:9 and *I will* **s** the people of Israel among all H5675
Zep 2:15 All who pass by her scoff and **s** their fists. H5675
Hag 2:6 little while I *will* once more **s** the heavens H8321
Hag 2:7 *I will* **s** all nations, and what is desired by H8321
Hag 2:21 of Judah that I *am going to* **s** the heavens H8321
Mt 10:14 home or town and **s** the dust **off** your feet. *G1759*
Mk 6:11 that place and **s** the dust **off** your feet as a *G1759*
Lk 6:48 torrent struck that house but could not **s** it, *G4888*

S

Lk 9: 5 their town and s the dust off your feet as a G701
Heb 12:26 "Once more I will s not only the earth G4940

SHAKEN (35) [SHAKE]

1Sa 28:21 to Saul and saw that he was greatly s, H987
2Sa 18:33 The king was s. He went up to the room H8074
Ne 5:13 may such a person be s out and emptied!" H5850
Job 34:20 the people are s and they pass away H1723
Ps 15: 5 does these things will never be s. H4572
Ps 16: 8 With him at my right hand, I will not be s. H4572
Ps 21: 7 love of the Most High he will not be s. H4572
Ps 30: 6 I felt secure, I said, "I will never be s." H4572
Ps 55:22 he will never let the righteous be s. H4572
Ps 60: 2 You have s the land and torn it open H8321
Ps 62: 2 he is my fortress, I will never be s. H4572
Ps 62: 6 salvation; he is my fortress, I will not be s. H4572
Ps 82: 5 all the foundations of the earth are s. H4572
Ps 109:23 evening shadow; I am s off like a locust. H5850
Ps 112: 6 Surely the righteous will never be s; they H4572
Ps 125: 1 which cannot be s but endures forever. H4572
Pr 6: 1 if you have s hands in pledge for a H9546
Isa 7: 2 the hearts of Ahaz and his people were s, H5675
Isa 7: 2 as the trees of the forest are s by the wind. H5675
Isa 24:19 asunder, the earth is violently s. H4572+4572
Isa 54:10 the mountains be s and the hills be H4631
Isa 54:10 love for you will not be s nor my covenant H4631
Am 9: 9 all the nations as grain is s in a sieve, H5675
Na 3:12 ripe fruit; when they are s, the figs fall H5675
Mt 24:29 and the heavenly bodies will be s. G4888
Mk 13:25 and the heavenly bodies will be s. G4888
Lk 6:38 s together and running over G4888
Lk 21:26 for the heavenly bodies will be s. G4888
Ac 2:25 he is at my right hand, I will not be s. G4888
Ac 4:31 the place where they were meeting was s. G4888
Ac 16:26 that the foundations of the prison were s. G4888
Heb 12:27 indicate the removing of what can be s G4888
Heb 12:27 so that what cannot be s may remain. G4888
Heb 12:28 are receiving a kingdom that cannot be s, G810
Rev 6:13 from a fig tree when s by a strong wind. G4940

SHAKES (8) [SHAKE]

Job 9: 6 He s the earth from its place and makes H8074
Job 15:25 because he s his fist at God and vaunts H5742
Ps 29: 8 The voice of the LORD s the desert; the H2655
Ps 29: 8 the LORD s the Desert of Kadesh. H2655
Pr 17:18 no sense s hands in pledge and puts up H9546
Pr 22:26 not be one who s hands in pledge or puts H9546
Isa 30:28 He s the nations in the sieve of H5677
Joel 2:10 Before them the earth s, the heavens H8074

SHAKING (3) [SHAKE]

Ps 22: 7 mock me; they hurl insults, s their heads. H5675
Mt 27:39 by hurled insults at him, s their heads G3075
Mk 15:29 insults at him, s their heads and saying G3075

SHALISHA (1)

1Sa 9: 4 Ephraim and through the area around S, H8995

SHALISHAH See BAAL SHALISHAH

SHALL (482) See Index of Articles Etc.

SHALLEKETH (1)

1Ch 26:16 West Gate and the S Gate on the upper H8962

SHALLOW (2)

Mt 13: 5 up quickly, because the soil was s. G3590+958
Mk 4: 5 because the soil was s. G3590+2400+958

SHALLUM (25) [SHALLUM'S]

2Ki 15:10 S son of Jabesh conspired against H8935
2Ki 15:13 S son of Jabesh became king in the H8935
2Ki 15:14 He attacked S son of Jabesh in Samaria H8935
2Ki 22:14 who was the wife of S son of Tikvah, the H8935
1Ch 2:40 father of Sismai, Sismai the father of S, H8935
1Ch 2:41 S the father of Jekamiah, and Jekamiah H8935
1Ch 3:15 Zedekiah the third, S the fourth. H8935
1Ch 4:25 S was Shaul's son, Mibsam his son and H8935
1Ch 6:12 father of Zadok, Zadok the father of S, H8935
1Ch 6:13 S the father of Hilkiah, Hilkiah the father H8935
1Ch 9:17 S, Akkub, Talmon, Ahiman and their H8935
1Ch 9:17 their fellow Levites, S their chief H8935
1Ch 9:19 S son of Kore, the son of Ebiasaph, the H8935
1Ch 9:31 the firstborn son of S the Korahite, was H8935
2Ch 28:12 Jehizkiah son of S, and Amasa son of H8935
2Ch 34:22 who was the wife of S son of Tokhath, the H8935
Ezr 2:42 the descendants of S, Ater, Talmon H8935
Ezr 7: 2 the son of S, the son of Zadok, the son of H8935
Ezr 10:24 From the gatekeepers: S, Telem and Uri. H8935
Ezr 10:42 S, Amariah and Joseph. H8935
Ne 3:12 S son of Hallohesh, ruler of a half-district H8935
Ne 7:45 the descendants of S, Ater, Talmon H8935
Jer 22:11 what the LORD says about S son of Josiah, H8935
Jer 32: 7 Hanamel son of S your uncle is going to H8935
Jer 35: 4 that of Maaseiah son of S the doorkeeper. H8935

SHALLUM'S (1) [SHALLUM]

2Ki 15:15 The other events of S reign, and the H8935

SHALLUN (1)

Ne 3:15 Gate was repaired by S son of Kol-Hozeh, H8937

SHALMAI (2)

Ezr 2:46 Hagab, S, Hanan, H8978
Ne 7:48 Lebana, Hagaba, S, H8978

SHALMAN (1)

Hos 10:14 as S devastated Beth Arbel on the day of H8986

SHALMANESER (3) [SHALMANESER'S]

2Ki 17: 3 S king of Assyria came up to attack H8987
2Ki 17: 4 Therefore S seized him and put H4889+855S
2Ki 18: 9 S king of Assyria marched against H8987

SHALMANESER'S (1) [SHALMANESER]

2Ki 17: 3 who had been S vassal and had H4200+2257S

SHAMA (1)

1Ch 11:44 S and Jeiel the sons of Hotham the H9052

SHAMBLES (KJV) MEAT MARKET

SHAME (133) [ASHAMED, SHAMED, SHAMEFUL, SHAMEFULLY, SHAMELESS, SHAMELESSLY, SHAMING]

Ge 2:25 wife were both naked, and they felt no s. H1017
Dt 32: 5 to their s they are a warped and crooked H4583
1Sa 20:30 Jesse to your own s and to the shame of H1425
1Sa 20:30 and to the s of the mother who H1425+6872
2Ki 19:26 of power, are dismayed and put to s. H1017
Job 8:22 Your enemies will be clothed in s, and H1425
Job 10:15 I am full of s and drowned in my H7830
Ps 4: 2 long will you people turn my glory into s? H4009
Ps 6:10 enemies will be overwhelmed with s and H1017
Ps 6:10 will turn back and suddenly be put to s. H1017
Ps 22: 5 in you they trusted and were not put to s. H1017
Ps 25: 2 do not let me be put to s, nor let H1017
Ps 25: 3 who hopes in you will ever be put to s, H1017
Ps 25: 3 but s will come on those who are H1017
Ps 25:20 rescue me; do not let me be put to s, for I H1017
Ps 31: 1 let me never be put to s; deliver H1017
Ps 31:17 Let me not be put to s, LORD, for I have H1017
Ps 31:17 but let the wicked be put to s and be H1017
Ps 34: 5 their faces are never covered with s. H2917
Ps 35: 4 seek my life be disgraced and put to s; H4007
Ps 35:26 May all who gloat over my distress be put to s H1017
Ps 35:26 over me be clothed with s and disgrace. H1425
Ps 40:14 to take my life be put to s and confusion; H1017
Ps 40:15 be appalled at their own s. H1425
Ps 44: 7 our enemies, you put our adversaries to s. H1017
Ps 44:15 day long, and my face is covered with s H1425
Ps 53: 5 attacked you; you put them to s, for God H1017
Ps 69: 6 may those who seek you not be put to s H4007
Ps 69: 7 scorn for your sake, and s covers my face. H4009
Ps 70: 2 May those who want to take my life be put to s H1017
Ps 70: 3 turn back because of their s. H1425
Ps 71: 1 taken refuge; let me never be put to s. H1017
Ps 71:13 May my accusers perish in s; may those H1017
Ps 71:24 to harm me have been put to s and H1017
Ps 78:66 his enemies; he put them to everlasting s. H3075
Ps 83:16 Cover their faces with s, LORD, so that they H7830
Ps 86:17 my enemies may see it and be put to s, H1017
Ps 89:45 you have covered him with a mantle of s. H1019
Ps 97: 7 All who worship images are put to s H1017
Ps 109:28 may those who attack me be put to s, but H1017
Ps 109:29 disgrace and wrapped in s as in a cloak. H1425
Ps 119: 6 Then I would not be put to s when I H1017
Ps 119:31 statutes, LORD; do not let me be put to s. H1017
Ps 119:46 before kings and will not be put to s, H1017
Ps 119:78 May the arrogant be put to s for wronging H1017
Ps 119:80 your decrees, that I may not be put to s. H1017
Ps 127: 5 They will not be put to s when they H1017
Ps 129: 5 all who hate Zion be turned back in s. H1017
Ps 132:18 I will clothe his enemies with s, but his H1425
Pr 3:35 wise inherit honor, but fools get only s. H7830
Pr 6:33 and his s will never be wiped away. H3075
Pr 13: 5 a stench and bring s on themselves. H2917
Pr 13:18 discipline comes to poverty and s, H7830
Pr 18: 3 contempt, and with s comes reproach. H7830
Pr 18:13 before listening—that is folly and s. H4009
Pr 19:26 is a child who brings s and disgrace. H1017
Pr 25: 8 in the end if your neighbor puts you to s? H4007
Pr 25:10 one who hears it may s you and the H2873
Isa 20: 4 with buttocks bared—to Egypt's s. H6872
Isa 20: 5 in Egypt will be dismayed and put to s. H1017
Isa 26:11 your zeal for your people and be put to s; H1017
Isa 30: 3 But Pharaoh's protection will be to your s H1425
Isa 30: 5 everyone will be put to s because of a H1017
Isa 30: 5 advantage, but only s and disgrace." H1425
Isa 37:27 of power, are dismayed and put to s. H1017
Isa 42:17 will be turned back in utter s. H1017+1425
Isa 44: 9 they are ignorant, to their own s. H1017
Isa 44:11 People who do that will be put to s; such H1017
Isa 44:11 they will be brought down to terror and s. H1017
Isa 45:16 of idols will be put to s and disgraced; H1017
Isa 45:17 you will never be put to s or disgraced H1017
Isa 45:24 him will come to him and be put to s. H1017
Isa 47: 3 will be exposed and your s uncovered. H3075
Isa 50: 7 like flint, and I know I will not be put to s. H1017
Isa 54: 4 be afraid; you will not be put to s. Do not H1017
Isa 54: 4 You will forget the s of your youth and H1425
Isa 61: 7 Instead of your s you will receive a double H1425
Isa 65:13 will rejoice, but you will be put to s. H1017
Isa 66: 5 Yet they will be put to s. H1017
Jer 3: 3 of a prostitute; you refuse to blush with s. H4007
Jer 3:25 Let us lie down in our s, and let our H1425
Jer 6:15 they have no s at all; they do H1017+1017
Jer 7:19 harming themselves, to their own s? H1425
Jer 8: 9 The wise will be put to s; they will be H1017
Jer 8:12 they have no s at all; they do H1017+1017
Jer 9:19 How great is our s! We must leave H1017
Jer 12:13 They will bear the s of their harvest H1017
Jer 13:26 over your face that your s may be seen— H7830
Jer 17:13 all who forsake you will be put to s. H1017
Jer 17:18 Let my persecutors be put to s, but keep H1017
Jer 17:18 but keep me from s; let them be H1017
Jer 20:18 sorrow and to end my days in s? H1425
Jer 23:40 everlasting s that will not be forgotten." H4010
Jer 46:12 The nations will hear of your s; your cries H7830
Jer 46:24 Daughter Egypt will be put to s, given into H1017
Jer 48:39 How Moab turns her back in s! Moab has H1017
Jer 50: 2 captured; Bel will be put to s, Marduk H1017
Jer 50: 2 Her images will be put to s and her idols H1017
Jer 51:51 been insulted and s covers our faces, H4009
Eze 7:18 Every face will be covered with s, and H1019
Eze 23:29 the s of your prostitution will be H6872
Eze 32:24 They bear their s with those who go down H4009
Eze 32:25 they bear their s with those who go down H4009
Eze 32:30 sword and bear their s with those who go H4009
Eze 39:26 They will forget their s and all the H4009
Eze 44:13 they must bear the s of their detestable H4009
Da 9: 7 this day we are covered with s—the H1425
Da 9: 8 our ancestors are covered with s, H1425
Da 12: 2 others to s and everlasting contempt. H3075
Hos 4:19 their sacrifices will bring them s. H1017
Ob 10 you will be covered with s; you will be H1019
Mic 1:11 Pass by naked and in s, you who live in H1425
Mic 7:10 will see it and will be covered with s, H1019
Na 3: 5 your nakedness and the kingdoms your s. H7830
Hab 2:16 You will be filled with s instead of glory H7830
Zep 3: 5 not fail, yet the unrighteous know no s. H1425
Zep 3:11 day you, Jerusalem, will not be put to s H1017
Zep 3:19 in every land where they have suffered s. H1425
Zec 10: 5 they will put the enemy horsemen to s. H1017
Ro 5: 5 And hope does not put us to s, because G2875
Ro 9:33 believes in him will never be put to s." G2875
Ro 10:11 believes in him will never be put to s." G2875
1Co 1:27 foolish things of the world to s the wise; G2875
1Co 1:27 weak things of the world to s the strong. G2875
1Co 4:14 am writing this not to s you but to warn G1956
1Co 6: 5 I say this to s you. Is it possible that there G1959
1Co 15:34 are ignorant of God—I say this to your s. G1959
2Co 11:21 To my s I admit that we were too weak for G871
Php 3:19 their stomach, and their glory is in their s. G158
2Ti 1:12 Yet this is no cause for s, because I know G2049
Heb 12: 2 scorning its s, and sat down at the G158
1Pe 2: 6 who trusts in him will never be put to s." G2875
Jude 13 foaming up their s; wandering stars, G158

SHAMED (5) [SHAME]

Ps 69:19 disgraced and s; all my enemies are H4009
Jer 10:14 every goldsmith is s by his idols. H1017
Jer 51:17 every goldsmith is s by his idols. H1017
Joel 2:26 you; never again will my people be s. H1017
Joel 2:27 never again will my people be s. H1017

SHAMEFACEDNESS (KJV) DECENCY

SHAMEFUL (13) [SHAME]

1Sa 20:34 at his father's s treatment of David. H4007
Pr 14:35 servant, but a s servant arouses his fury. H1017
Jer 3:24 From our youth s gods have consumed the H1425
Jer 11:13 incense to that s god Baal are as many as H1425
Hos 4:18 their rulers dearly love s ways. H7830
Hos 9:10 themselves to that s idol and became as H1425
Zep 2: 1 yourselves together, you s nation, H4202+4083
Ro 1:26 God gave them over to s lusts. G871
Ro 1:27 Men committed s acts with other men, and G859
2Co 4: 2 we have renounced secret and s ways; we G158
Eph 5:12 It is s even to mention what the disobedient G156
Rev 3:18 so you can cover your s nakedness; and G158
Rev 21:27 anyone who does what is s or deceitful, G1007

SHAMEFULLY (4) [SHAME]

Eze 22:11 another s defiles his H928+2365
Mk 12: 4 this man on the head and treated him s. G869
Lk 20:11 also they beat and treated s and sent away G869
Rev 16:15 so as not to go naked and be s exposed." G859

SHAMELESS (2) [SHAME]

Jer 13:27 lustful neighings, your s prostitution! H2365
Lk 11: 8 because of your s audacity he will surely G357

SHAMELESSLY (1) [SHAME]

Job 19: 3 reproached me; s you attack me. H4202+1017

SHAMGAR (2)

Jdg 3:31 After Ehud came S son of Anath, who H9011
Jdg 5: 6 "In the days of S son of Anath, in the days H9011

SHAMHUTH (1)

1Ch 27: 8 was the commander S the Izrahite. H9016

SHAMING (1) [SHAME]

Hab 2:10 s your own house and forfeiting your life. H1425

SHAMIR (4)

Jos 15:48 In the hill country: S, Jattir, Sokoh, H9034
Jdg 10: 1 He lived in S, in the hill country of H9034

Jdg 10: 2 then he died, and was buried in S. H9034
1Ch 24:24 Micah; from the sons of Micah: S. H9033

SHAMMA (1)
1Ch 7:37 Hod, S, Shilshah, Ithran and Beera. H9007

SHAMMAH (9)
Ge 36:13 Nahath, Zerah, S and Mizzah. These H9015
Ge 36:17 Nahath, Zerah, S and Mizzah. These H9015
1Sa 16: 9 Jesse then had S pass by, but Samuel said H9015
1Sa 17:13 the second, Abinadab; and the third, S. H9015
2Sa 23:11 Next to him was S son of Agee the H9007
2Sa 23:12 But S took his stand in the middle of the NDT
2Sa 23:25 S the Harodite, Elika the Harodite, H9015
2Sa 23:33 son of S the Hararite, Ahiam son of H9015
1Ch 1:37 Nahath, Zerah, S and Mizzah. H9015

SHAMMAI (5) [SHAMMAI'S]
1Ch 2:28 The sons of Onam: S and Jada. The sons H9025
1Ch 2:28 The sons of S: Nadab and Abishur. H9025
1Ch 2:44 Rekem was the father of S. H9025
1Ch 2:45 The son of S was Maon, and Maon was H9025
1Ch 4:17 S and Ishbah the father of Eshtemoa. H9025

SHAMMAI'S (1) [SHAMMAI]
1Ch 2:32 The sons of Jada, S brother: Jether and H9025

SHAMMOTH (1)
1Ch 11:27 S the Harorite, Helez the Pelonite, H9021

SHAMMUA (6)
Nu 13: 4 from the tribe of Reuben, S son of Zakkur; H9018
2Sa 5:14 born to him there: S, Shobab, Nathan H9018
1Ch 3: 5 born to him there: S, Shobab, Nathan H9055
1Ch 14: 4 born to him there: S, Shobab, Nathan H9018
Ne 11:17 Abda son of S, the son of Galal, H9018
Ne 12:18 of Bilgah's, S; of Shemaiah's, Jehonathan H9018

SHAMSHERAI (1)
1Ch 8:26 S, Shehariah, Athaliah, H9091

SHAN See BETH SHAN

SHAPE (12) [SHAPED, SHAPES, SHAPING]
Ex 32: 4 made it into an idol cast in the **s of a calf**. H6319
Ex 32: 8 themselves an idol cast in the **s of a calf**. H6319
Dt 4:16 an image of any **s**, whether formed like H6166
Dt 9:16 yourselves an idol cast in the **s of a calf**. H6319
1Ki 6:25 two cherubim were identical in size and **s**. H7893
1Ki 7:19 pillars in the portico were in the **s** *of* lilies, H5126
1Ki 7:22 The capitals on top were in the **s** *of* lilies H5126
1Ki 7:23 cast metal, **circular in s**, measuring H6318+6017
1Ki 7:37 molds and were identical in size and **s**. H7893
2Ki 17:16 two idols cast in the **s of calves**, H6319
2Ch 4: 2 cast metal, **circular in s**, measuring H6318+6017
Job 38:14 The earth **takes s** like clay under a seal H2200

SHAPED (5) [SHAPE]
Ex 25:33 Three cups **s like almond flowers** with H5481
Ex 25:34 four cups **s like almond flowers** with buds H5481
Ex 37:19 Three cups **s like almond flowers** with H5481
Ex 37:20 four cups **s like almond flowers** with buds H5481
Job 10: 8 "Your hands **s** me and made me. Will you H6771

SHAPES (4) [SHAPE]
Isa 44:10 Who **s** a god and casts an idol, which can H3670
Isa 44:12 it in the coals; *he* **s** an idol with hammers H3670
Isa 44:13 *He* **s** it in human form, human form in all H6913
Jer 10: 3 and a craftsman **s** it with his chisel. H5126+3338

SHAPHAM (1)
1Ch 5:12 Joel was the chief, S the second, then H9171

SHAPHAN (30)
2Ki 22: 3 sent the secretary, S son of Azaliah, the H9177
2Ki 22: 8 the high priest said to S the secretary, H9177
2Ki 22: 8 He gave it to S, who read it. H9177
2Ki 22: 9 Then S the secretary went to the king and H9177
2Ki 22:10 Then S the secretary informed the king H9177
2Ki 22:10 And S read from it in the presence of the H9177
2Ki 22:12 Ahikam son of S, Akbor son of Micaiah H9177
2Ki 22:12 S the secretary and Asaiah the king's H9177
2Ki 22:14 S and Asaiah went to speak to the H9177
2Ki 25:22 of Ahikam, the son of S, to be over the H9177
2Ch 34: 8 he sent S son of Azaliah and Maaseiah H9177
2Ch 34:15 Hilkiah said to S the secretary, "I have H9177
2Ch 34:15 the temple of the LORD." He gave it to S. H9177
2Ch 34:16 Then S took the book to the king and H9177
2Ch 34:18 Then S the secretary informed the king H9177
2Ch 34:18 And S read from it in the presence of the H9177
2Ch 34:20 Ahikam son of S, Abdon son of Micah, H9177
2Ch 34:20 S the secretary and Asaiah the king's H9177
Jer 26:24 Ahikam son of S supported Jeremiah, and H9177
Jer 29: 3 to Elasah son of S and to Gemariah son H9177
Jer 36:10 room of Gemariah son of S the secretary, H9177
Jer 36:11 the son of S, heard all the words H9177
Jer 36:12 Gemariah son of S, Zedekiah son of H9177
Jer 39:14 Ahikam, the son of S, to take him back to H9177
Jer 40: 5 of Ahikam, the son of S, whom the king of H9177
Jer 40: 9 of Ahikam, the son of S, took an oath to H9177
Jer 40:11 of Ahikam, the son of S, as governor over H9177
Jer 41: 2 of Ahikam, the son of S, with the sword, H9177
Jer 43: 6 son of Ahikam, the son of S—the men, H9177
Eze 8:11 Jaazaniah son of S was standing among H9177

SHAPHAT (8)
Nu 13: 5 from the tribe of Simeon, S son of Hori; H9151
1Ki 19:16 Elisha son of S from Abel Meholah to H9151
1Ki 19:19 from there and found Elisha son of S. H9151
2Ki 3:11 Israel answered, "Elisha son of S is here. H9151
2Ki 6:31 head of Elisha son of S remains on his H9151
1Ch 3:22 Bariah, Neariah and S—six in all. H9151
1Ch 5:12 the second, then Janai and S, in Bashan. H9151
1Ch 27:29 S son of Adlai was in charge of the herds H9151

SHAPHIR (1)
Mic 1:11 naked and in shame, you who live in S. H9160

SHAPING (2) [SHAPE]
Jer 18: 4 But the pot he *was* **s** from the clay was H6913
Jer 18: 4 another pot, **s** it as seemed best to him. H6913

SHARAI (1)
Ezr 10:40 Maknadebai, Shashai, S, H9232

SHARAR (1)
2Sa 23:33 Hararite, Ahiam son of S the Hararite, H9243

SHARE (109) [SHARED, SHARERS, SHARES, SHARING]
Ge 14:24 the **s** *that belongs to* the men who H2750
Ge 14:24 Let them have their **s**." H2750
Ge 21:10 son *will* never **s in the inheritance** with H3769
Ge 31:14 we still have any **s** in the inheritance of H2750
Ex 12: 4 they *must* **s** one with their nearest H4374
Ex 18:22 because *they will* **s** it with you. H5951
Ex 29:26 as a wave offering, and it will be your **s**. H4950
Ex 29:28 is always to be the **perpetual s** from the H2976
Lev 6:17 given it as their **s** of the food offerings H2750
Lev 6:18 it is his perpetual **s** of the food offerings H2976
Lev 6:22 the LORD's perpetual **s** and is to be burned H2976
Lev 7:33 offering shall have the right thigh as his **s**. H4950
Lev 7:34 as their perpetual **s** from the Israelites. H2976
Lev 7:36 as their perpetual **s** for the generations to H2978
Lev 8:29 which was his **s** of the ordination ram H4950
Lev 10:13 because it is your **s** and your sons' share H2976
Lev 10:13 share and your sons' **s** of the food H2976
Lev 10:14 your children as your **s** of the Israelites' H2976
Lev 10:15 will be the perpetual **s** for you and your H2976
Lev 19:17 frankly so *you will* not **s in** their H5951+6584
Lev 24: 9 of their perpetual **s** *of* the food offerings H2976
Lev 25:51 redemption a **larger s of** the price paid H4946
Nu 10:32 *we will* **s** with you whatever good things H3512
Nu 11:17 *They will* **s** the burden of the people with H5951
Nu 18: 8 sons as your portion, your perpetual **s**. H2976
Nu 18:11 sons and daughters as your perpetual **s**. H2976
Nu 18:19 sons and daughters as your perpetual **s**. H2976
Nu 18:20 will you have any **s** among them; I am H2750
Nu 18:20 I am your **s** and your inheritance among H2750
Nu 31:29 tribute from their **half s** and give it to H4734
Nu 31:36 The half **s** *of* those who fought in the H2750
Dt 10: 9 the Levites have no **s** or inheritance H2750
Dt 18: 3 This is the **s** *due* the priests from the H5477
Dt 18: 8 *He is to* **s** equally in their benefits, even H430
Dt 21:17 by giving him a double **s** of all he has. H7023
Jos 14: 4 Levites received no **s** of the land but only H2750
Jos 17: 5 Manasseh's **s** consisted of ten tracts of H2475
Jos 19: 9 was taken from the **s** *of* Judah, H2475
Jos 22:19 tabernacle stands, and **s** the land with us. H296
Jos 22:25 You have no **s** in the LORD.' So H2750
Jos 22:27 to say to ours, 'You have no **s** in the LORD. H2750
Jdg 8:24 me an earring from your **s of the plunder**." H8965
1Sa 26:19 driven me today from my **s** in the LORD's H6202
1Sa 30:22 *we will* not **s** with them the plunder we H5989
1Sa 30:24 The **s** *of* the man who stayed with the H2750
1Sa 30:24 went down to the battle. *All will* **s** alike." H2745
2Sa 20: 1 "We have no **s** in David, no part in H2750
1Ki 12:16 "What **s** do we have in David, what part H2750
1Ch 9:25 to time and **s their duties** for H6640+465
2Ch 10:16 "What **s** do we have in David, what part H2750
Ne 2:20 you have no **s** in Jerusalem or any claim H2750
Job 39:17 with wisdom or **give** her **a s** of good sense H2745
Ps 68:23 the tongues of your dogs have their **s**." H4945
Ps 69:27 *do* not *let them* **s** in your salvation. H995
Ps 106: 5 that I *may* **s** in the **joy** *of* your H8523+8525
Pr 1:14 with us; we *will* all **s** the loot" H2118+4200+285
Pr 14:10 bitterness, and no one else *can* **s** its joy. H6843
Pr 16:19 the oppressed than *to* **s** plunder with the H2745
Pr 17: 2 son and *will* **s** the inheritance as H2745
Pr 21: 9 the roof than **s** a house **with** a H2490
Pr 22: 9 for *they* **s** their food with the poor. H5989
Pr 25:24 roof than **s** a house *with* a quarrelsome H2490
Ecc 9: 2 All **s** a common destiny—the H3869+889+4200
Isa 58: 7 Is it not *to* **s** your food with the hungry H7271
Jer 37:12 to **get** *his* **s** *of the* **property** among the H2745
Eze 18:19 'Why *does* the son not **s** the guilt of H5951+928
Eze 18:20 The child *will* not **s** the guilt of the H5951+928
Eze 18:20 nor *will* the parent **s** the guilt of the H5951+928
Am 7: 1 locusts after the **king's s** had been harvested AIT
Mt 21:41 who *will* **give** him *his* **s** of the crop at *G625*
Mt 25:21 **Come and s** your master's happiness *G1656*
Mt 25:23 **Come and s** your master's happiness *G1656*
Lk 3:11 has two shirts *should* **s with** the one who *G3556*
Lk 15:12 'Father, give me my **s** of the estate. *G2095+3538*
Ac 8:21 You have no part or **s** in this ministry *G3102*
Ro 8:17 if indeed *we* **s** in his **sufferings** in order *G5224*
Ro 8:17 in order that *we may* also **s in** his **glory**. *G5280*
Ro 11:17 the others and *now* **s** in the *G5171+1181*
Ro 12:13 **S** with the Lord's people who are in need *G3125*
Ro 15:27 owe it to the Jews *to* **s** with them their *G3310*
1Co 9:13 serve at the altar **s in** what is offered on *G5211*
1Co 9:23 that *I may* **s in** its blessings. *G5171+1181*
1Co 10:17 are one body, for *we* all **s** the one loaf. *G3576*
2Co 1: 5 For just as we **s** abundantly in the *G1650*
2Co 1: 7 that just as *you* **s in** our sufferings, *G3128+1639*
2Co 1: 7 our sufferings, so also you **s** in our comfort. NDT
2Co 2: 3 in all of you, that you *would* all **s** my joy. *G1639*
Gal 4:30 son *will* never **s in the inheritance** with *G3099*
Gal 6: 6 in the word *should* **s** all good things with *G3125*
Eph 4:28 may have something *to* **s** with those in *G3556*
Php 1: 7 all of you **s in** God's grace **with** me. *G5171+1639*
Php 4:14 Yet it was good of you *to* **s in** my troubles. *G5170*
Col 1:12 has qualified you to **s** in the inheritance *G3535*
1Th 2: 8 were delighted *to* **s with** you not only the *G3556*
2Th 2:14 that you might **s in** the glory of our Lord *G4348*
1Ti 5:22 and *do* not **s in** the sins of others. *G3125*
1Ti 6:18 to be generous and **willing to s**. *G3127*
2Ti 2: 6 be the first *to* **receive a s** of the crops. *G3561*
Phm 6 every good thing we **s** for the sake of *G1877*
Heb 3: 1 sisters, *who* **s in** the heavenly calling *G3581*
Heb 3:14 We have come to **s in** Christ, if indeed we *G3581*
Heb 4: 2 *because they did* not **s** the faith of those *G5166*
Heb 12:10 in order that *we may* **s in** his holiness. *G3561*
Heb 13:16 not forget to do good and to **s with others**, *G3126*
1Pe 5: 1 who also will **s** in the glory to be *G3128*
Jude 3 to write to you about the salvation we **s**, *G3123*
Rev 18: 4 so that *you will* not **s in** her sins, so *G5170*
Rev 20: 6 holy are those *who* **s** in the first *G2400+3538*
Rev 22:19 from that person any **s** in the tree of life *G3538*

SHARED (13) [SHARE]
2Sa 12: 3 *It* **s** his food, drank from his cup and even H430
1Ki 2:26 **s** all my father's **hardships** H6700+928+889+6700
Ps 41: 9 I trusted, *one who* **s** my bread, has H430
Pr 5:17 yours alone, never to be **s with** strangers. H907
Lk 1:58 shown her great mercy, and *they* **s** her **joy**. *G5176*
Jn 13:18 'He *who* **s** my bread has turned against *G5592*
Ac 1:17 our number and **s** in our *G3275+3836+3102*
Ac 4:32 their own, but they **s** everything they had. *G3123*
Ro 15:27 For if the Gentiles *have* **s** in the Jews' *G3125*
Php 4:15 not one church **s with** me in the matter of *G3125*
Heb 2:14 he too **s in** their humanity so that by his *G3576*
Heb 6: 4 *who have* **s in** the Holy Spirit, *G3581+1181*
Rev 18: 9 with her and **s** her **luxury** see the smoke of *G5139*

SHARERS (1) [SHARE]
Eph 3: 6 and **s together** in the promise in Christ *G5212*

SHARES (3) [SHARE]
2Sa 19:43 "We have ten **s** in the king; so we H3338
Jn 19:23 dividing them into four **s**, one for each of *G3538*
2Jn 11 who welcomes them **s in** their wicked *G3125*

SHAREZER (3)
2Ki 19:37 Adrammelek and S killed him with the H8570
Isa 37:38 Adrammelek and S killed him with the H8570
Zec 7: 2 of Bethel had sent S and Regem-Melek, H8570

SHARING (5) [SHARE]
Job 31:17 to myself, not **s** it *with* the fatherless H430+4946
1Co 9:10 to do so in the hope *of* **s** in the harvest. *G3576*
2Co 8: 4 the privilege *of* **s in** this service to the *G3126*
2Co 9:13 your generosity *in* **s** with them and with *G3126*
Php 2: 1 his love, if any **common s in** the Spirit, if *G3126*

SHARON (7) [SHARONITE]
1Ch 5:16 the pasturelands of S as far as they H9227
1Ch 27:29 was in charge of the herds grazing in S. H9227
SS 2: 1 I am a rose of S, a lily of the valleys. H9227
Isa 33: 9 withers; S is like the Arabah H9227
Isa 35: 2 the splendor of Carmel and S; they will H9227
Isa 65:10 S will become a pasture for flocks, and H9227
Ac 9:35 lived in Lydda and S saw him and turned *G4926*

SHARONITE (1) [SHARON]
1Ch 27:29 Shitrai the S was in charge of the herds H9228

SHARP (20) [SHARPEN, SHARPENED, SHARPENING, SHARPENS, SHARPER, SHARPLY]
Ps 45: 5 Let your **s** arrows pierce the hearts of the H9111
Ps 57: 4 arrows, whose tongues are **s** swords. H2521
Ps 59: 7 the words from their lips are *s as* **swords**, AIT
Ps 120: 4 will punish you with a warrior's **s** arrows, H9111
Ps 140: 3 *They* **make** their tongues as **s** as a H9111
Pr 5: 4 bitter as gall, **s** as a double-edged sword. H2521
Pr 25:18 club or a sword or a **s** arrow is one who H9111
Isa 5:28 Their arrows *are* **s**, all their bows are H9111
Isa 41:15 new and **s**, with many teeth. H3023
Eze 5: 1 take a **s** sword and use it as a barber's H2521
Eze 28:24 who are painful briers and **s** thorns. H3872
Ac 15: 2 and Barnabas into **s** dispute and *G4024+3900*
Ac 15:39 They had such a **s disagreement** that they *G4237*
Rev 1:16 coming out of his mouth was a **s** *G3955*
Rev 2:12 These are the words of him who has the **s**, *G3955*
Rev 14:14 on his head and a **s** sickle in his hand. *G3955*
Rev 14:17 in heaven, and he too had a **s** sickle. *G3955*
Rev 14:18 a loud voice to him who had the **s** sickle, *G3955*
Rev 14:18 "Take your **s** sickle and gather the clusters *G3955*
Rev 19:15 of his mouth is a **s** sword with which to *G3955*

S

SHARPEN (4) [SHARP]
Dt 32:41 when *I* s my flashing sword and my hand H9111
Ps 7:12 does not relent, *he will* s his sword; he H4323
Ps 64: 3 *They* s their tongues like swords and aim H9111
Jer 51:11 "S the arrows, take up the shields! The H1406

SHARPENED (6) [SHARP]
1Sa 13:20 *have* their plow points, mattocks, ... s H4323
Ps 52: 2 plots destruction; it is like a s razor. H4323
Isa 49: 2 He made my mouth like a s sword, in the H2521
Eze 21: 9 " 'A sword, a sword, s and polished— H2523
Eze 21:10 s for the slaughter, polished to flash like H2523
Eze 21:11 with the hand; it **is** s and polished, made H2523

SHARPENING (2) [SHARP]
1Sa 13:21 of a shekel for s plow points and mattocks H7201
1Sa 13:21 third of a shekel for s forks and axes and NDT

SHARPENS (2) [SHARP]
Pr 27:17 As iron s iron, so one person sharpens H2527
Pr 27:17 sharpens iron, so one person s another. H2527

SHARPER (1) [SHARP]
Heb 4:12 S than any double-edged sword, it *G5533*

SHARPLY (3) [SHARP]
1Sa 24: 7 words David s **rebuked** his men and did H9117
Jn 6:52 Then the Jews *began to* **argue** s among *G3481*
Titus 1:13 Therefore rebuke them s, so that they will *G705*

SHARUHEN (1)
Jos 19: 6 Beth Lebaoth and S—thirteen towns and H9226

SHASHAI (1)
Ezr 10:40 Maknadebai, S, Sharai, H9258

SHASHAK (2)
1Ch 8:14 S, Jeremoth, H9265
1Ch 8:25 Iphdeiah and Penuel were the sons of S. H9265

SHATTER (13) [SHATTERED, SHATTERING, SHATTERS]
Isa 30:31 The voice of the LORD *will* s Assyria; with H3169
Jer 49:37 *I will* s Elam before their foes, before H3169
Jer 51:20 battle—with you *I* s nations, with you I H5879
Jer 51:21 with you *I* s horse and rider, with you I H5879
Jer 51:21 rider, with you *I* s chariot and driver, H5879
Jer 51:22 with you *I* s man and woman, with you I H5879
Jer 51:22 woman, with you *I* s old man and youth H5879
Jer 51:22 with you *I* s young man and young H5879
Jer 51:23 with you *I* s shepherd and flock, with you I H5879
Jer 51:23 flock, with you *I* s farmer and oxen H5879
Jer 51:23 with you *I* s governors and officials. H5879
Eze 32:12 *They will* s the pride of Egypt, and all her H8720
Hag 2:22 royal thrones and s the power of the H9012

SHATTERED (22) [SHATTER]
Ex 15: 6 Your right hand, LORD, s the enemy. H8320
Jdg 5:26 his head, *she* s and pierced his temple. H4730
Jdg 10: 8 *who* that year s and crushed them. H8320
1Ki 19:11 mountains apart and s the rocks before H8689
Job 16:12 well with me, but *he* s me; he seized me H7297
Job 17:11 passed, my plans **are** s. Yet the desires of H5998
Ps 48: 7 like ships of Tarshish s by an east wind. NDT
Ps 105:33 vines and fig trees and s the trees of their H8689
Ecc 12: 6 before the pitcher **is** s at the spring, and H8689
Isa 7: 8 years Ephraim *will* **be** too s to be a H3169
Isa 8: 9 the war cry, you nations, and *be* s! Listen, H3169
Isa 8: 9 battle, and *be* s! Prepare for battle, H3169
Isa 8: 9 Prepare for battle, and *be* s! H3169
Isa 9: 4 *you have* s the yoke that burdens them H3169
Isa 21: 9 images of its gods *lie* s on the ground! H8689
Isa 30:14 s so mercilessly that among its pieces not H4198
Jer 48: 1 the stronghold will be disgraced and s. H3169
Jer 48:20 is disgraced, for *she is* s. Wail and cry out! H3169
Jer 48:39 "How s *she is*! How they wail! How Moab H3169
Jer 50:23 How broken and s *is* the hammer of the H8689
Eze 27:34 Now *you* **are** s by the sea in the depths of H8689
Na 1: 6 out like fire; the rocks *are* s before him. H5997

SHATTERING (1) [SHATTER]
Da 8: 7 striking the ram and s its two horns. H8689

SHATTERS (2) [SHATTER]
Job 34:24 Without inquiry *he* s the mighty and sets H8318
Ps 46: 9 He breaks the bow and s the spear; he H7915

SHAUL (9) [SHAUL'S, SHAULITE]
Ge 36:37 S from Rehoboth on the river succeeded H8620
Ge 36:38 When S died, Baal-Hanan son of Akbor H8620
Ge 46:10 Zohar and S the son of a Canaanite H8620
Ex 6:15 Zohar and S the son of a Canaanite H8620
Nu 26:13 through S, the Shaulite clan. H8620
1Ch 1:48 S from Rehoboth on the river succeeded H8620
1Ch 1:49 When S died, Baal-Hanan son of Akbor H8620
1Ch 4:24 Nemuel, Jamin, Jarib, Zerah and S; H8620
1Ch 6:24 his son, Uzziah his son and S his son. H8620

SHAUL'S (1) [SHAUL]
1Ch 4:25 Shallum was S son, Mibsam his son H2257S

SHAULITE (1) [SHAUL]
Nu 26:13 Zerahite clan; through Shaul, the S clan. H8621

SHAVE (21) [SHAVED]
Lev 13:33 *the man or woman must* s **themselves**, H1662
Lev 14: 8 s **off** all their hair and bathe with water H1662
Lev 14: 9 seventh day *they must* s **off** all their hair H1662
Lev 14: 9 all their hair; *they must* s their head, their H1662
Lev 21: 5 " 'Priests **must** not s their heads H7942+7947
Lev 21: 5 their heads or s **off** the edges of their H1662
Nu 6: 9 *they must* s their head on the seventh day H1662
Nu 6:18 the Nazirite *must* s **off** the hair that H1662
Nu 8: 7 then **have** *them* s their whole H6296+9509
Dt 14: 1 cut yourselves or s the front of your H8492+7947
Dt 21:12 into your home and *have her* s her head, H1662
Jdg 16:19 someone *to* s **off** the seven braids H1662
Isa 7:20 Assyria—*to* s your head and private parts H1662
Jer 16: 6 themselves or s *their* **head** for the dead. H7942
Jer 47: 5 Gaza *will* s *her* **head in mourning** H995+7947
Eze 5: 1 a barber's razor *to* s your head and your H6296
Eze 5:11 practices, *I* myself *will* s you; I will not H1757
Eze 27:31 *They will* s *their* **heads** because of H7942+7947
Eze 44:20 " '*They must* not s their heads or let their H1662
Am 8:10 wear sackcloth and s your heads. H7947+6584
Mic 1:16 S *your* **head** in mourning for the H7942+1605

SHAVED (14) [SHAVE]
Ge 41:14 When *he had* s and changed his clothes H1662
Nu 6:19 " 'After the Nazirite *has* s **off** the hair that H1662
Jdg 16:17 If my head **were** s, my strength would H1662
Jdg 16:22 began to grow again after *it had* **been** s. H1662
2Sa 10: 4 s **off** half of each man's beard H1662
1Ch 19: 4 David's envoys, s them, cut off their H1662
Job 1:20 got up and tore his robe and s his head. H1605
Isa 15: 2 Every head is s and every beard cut off. H7947
Jer 41: 5 eighty men *who had* s **off** their beards H1662
Jer 48:37 Every head is s and every beard cut off H7947
Eze 7:18 with shame, and every head will be s. H7947
Ac 21:24 so that *they can have* their heads s. *G3834*
1Co 11: 5 it is the same as *having* her head s. *G3834*
1Co 11: 6 to have her hair cut off or her head s, *G3834*

SHAVEH (1) [SHAVEH KIRIATHAIM]
Ge 14:17 came out to meet him in the Valley of S H8753

SHAVEH KIRIATHAIM (1) [KIRIATHAIM, SHAVEH]
Ge 14: 5 in Ham, the Emites in S H8754

SHAVSHA (1)
1Ch 18:16 of Abiathar were priests; S was secretary; H8807

SHAWL (1) [SHAWLS]
Ru 3:15 "Bring me the s you are wearing and hold H4762

SHAWLS (1) [SHAWL]
Isa 3:23 the linen garments and tiaras and s. H8100

SHE (1007) [HER, HERS, HERSELF, SHE'S] See Index of Articles Etc.

SHE'S (1) [SHE]
Jdg 14: 3 "Get her for me. S the right one for me." H2085

SHE-CAMEL (1) [CAMEL]
Jer 2:23 You are a swift s running here and there, H1149

SHEAF (6) [SHEAVES]
Ge 37: 7 when suddenly my s rose and stood upright H524
Lev 23:10 the priest a s **of** the first **grain** you harvest. H6684
Lev 23:11 He is to wave the s before the LORD so it H6684
Lev 23:12 On the day you wave the s, you must H6684
Lev 23:15 you brought the s *of* the wave offering, H6684
Dt 24:19 in your field and you overlook a s, H6684

SHEAL (1)
Ezr 10:29 Adaiah, Jashub, S and Jeremoth. H8627

SHEALTIEL (13)
1Ch 3:17 of Jehoiachin the captive: S his son, H8630
Ezr 3: 2 Zerubbabel son of S and his associates H8630
Ezr 3: 8 Zerubbabel son of S, Joshua son of H8630
Ezr 5: 2 Zerubbabel son of S and Joshua son of A10691
Ne 12: 1 Zerubbabel son of S and with Joshua: H8630
Hag 1: 1 prophet Haggai to Zerubbabel son of S, H8630
Hag 1:12 Then Zerubbabel son of S, Joshua son of H9003
Hag 1:14 up the spirit of Zerubbabel son of S, H9003
Hag 2: 2 "Speak to Zerubbabel son of S, governor H9003
Hag 2:23 my servant Zerubbabel son of S,' declares H8630
Mt 1:12 Jeconiah was the father of S, Shealtiel *G4886*
Mt 1:12 of Shealtiel, S the father of Zerubbabel, *G4886*
Lk 3:27 Zerubbabel, the son *of* S, the son of Neri, *G4886*

SHEAR (3) [SHEARED, SHEARER, SHEARERS, SHEARING, SHEEP-SHEARING, SHEEPSHEARERS, SHORN]
Ge 31:19 When Laban had gone to s his sheep H1605
Ge 38:13 is on his way to Timnah to s his sheep," H1605
Dt 15:19 and *do* not s the firstborn of your sheep. H1605

SHEAR-JASHUB (1)
Isa 7: 3 you and your son S, to meet Ahaz at the H8639

SHEARED (1) [SHEAR]
Isa 22:25 will give way; *it will* **be** s **off** and will fall H1548

SHEARER (1) [SHEAR]
Ac 8:32 as a lamb before its s is silent, so he *G3025*

SHEARERS (3) [SHEAR]
1Sa 25:11 the meat I have slaughtered for my s H1605
2Sa 13:24 said, "Your servant has had s come. H1605
Isa 53: 7 as a sheep before its s is silent, so he H1605

SHEARIAH (2)
1Ch 8:38 Ishmael, S, Obadiah and Hanan. H9138
1Ch 9:44 Ishmael, S, Obadiah and Hanan. H9138

SHEARING (4) [SHEAR]
Ge 38:12 Timnah, to the *men who were* s his sheep H1605
Dt 18: 4 the first **wool from** *the* s *of* your sheep, H1600
1Sa 25: 2 which he was s in Carmel. H1605
1Sa 25: 4 he heard that Nabal *was* s sheep. H1605

SHEATH (8) [SHEATHED]
1Sa 17:51 Philistine's sword and drew it from the s. H9509
2Sa 20: 8 his waist was a belt with a dagger in its s. H9509
2Sa 20: 8 he stepped forward, it dropped out of its s. NDT
1Ch 21:27 he put his sword back into its s. H5620
Jer 47: 6 Return to your s; cease and be still.' H9509
Eze 21: 3 my sword from its s and cut off from you H9509
Eze 21: 5 I the LORD have drawn my sword from its s; H9509
Eze 21:30 " 'Let the sword return to its s. In the place H9509

SHEATHED (1) [SHEATH]
Ps 68:13 the wings of my dove **are** s with silver, its H2902

SHEAVES (9) [SHEAF]
Ge 37: 7 We were binding s **of grain** out in the field H524
Ge 37: 7 while your s gathered around mine and H524
Ru 2: 7 gather among the s behind the H6684
Ru 2:15 gather among the s and don't reprimand H6684
Job 5:26 in full vigor, like s gathered in season. H1538
Job 24:10 they carry the s, but still go hungry. H6684
Ps 126: 6 with songs of joy, carrying s *with* them. H524
Mic 4:12 gathered them like s to the threshing floor H6658
Zec 12: 6 a woodpile, like a flaming torch among s. H6658

SHEBA (34)
Ge 10: 7 The sons of Raamah: S and Dedan. H8644
Ge 10:28 Abimael, S, H8644
Ge 25: 3 Jokshan was the father of S and Dedan H8644
Jos 19: 2 Beersheba (or S), Moladah, H8681
2Sa 20: 1 Now a troublemaker named S son of Bikri H8680
2Sa 20: 2 deserted David to follow S son of Bikri. H8680
2Sa 20: 6 "Now S son of Bikri will do us more harm H8680
2Sa 20: 7 from Jerusalem to pursue S son of Bikri. H8680
2Sa 20:10 his brother Abishai pursued S son of Bikri. H8680
2Sa 20:13 on with Joab to pursue S son of Bikri. H8680
2Sa 20:14 S passed through all the tribes of Israel to NDT
2Sa 20:15 came and besieged S in Abel Beth H2257S
2Sa 20:21 A man named S son of Bikri, from the hill H8680
2Sa 20:22 cut off the head of S son of Bikri and H8680
1Ki 10: 1 When the queen of S heard about the H8644
1Ki 10: 4 When the queen of S saw all the wisdom H8644
1Ki 10:10 those the queen of S gave to King H8644
1Ki 10:13 gave the queen of S all she desired and H8644
1Ch 1: 9 The sons of Raamah: S and Dedan. H8644
1Ch 1:22 Abimael, S, H8644
1Ch 1:32 The sons of Jokshan: S and Dedan. H8644
1Ch 5:13 Michael, Meshullam, S, Jorai, Jakan, Zia H8680
2Ch 9: 1 When the queen of S heard of Solomon's H8644
2Ch 9: 3 When the queen of S saw the wisdom of H8644
2Ch 9: 9 those the queen of S gave to King H8644
2Ch 9:12 gave the queen of S all she desired and H8644
Job 6:19 the traveling merchants of S look in hope. H8644
Ps 72:10 May the kings of S and Seba present him H8644
Ps 72:15 May gold from S be given him. H8644
Isa 60: 6 And all from S will come, bearing gold H8644
Jer 6:20 about incense from S or sweet calamus H8644
Eze 27:22 " 'The merchants of S and Raamah traded H8644
Eze 27:23 Kanneh and Eden and merchants of S H8644
Eze 38:13 S and Dedan and the merchants of H8644

SHEBANIAH (6)
1Ch 15:24 S, Joshaphat, Nethanel, Amasai H8677
Ne 9: 4 Kadmiel, S, Bunni, Sherebiah H8676
Ne 9: 5 Hodiah, S and Pethahiah—said H8676
Ne 10: 4 Hattush, S, Malluk, H8676
Ne 10:10 their associates: S, Hodiah, Kelita H8676
Ne 10:12 Zakkur, Sherebiah, S, H8676

SHEBAT (1)
Zec 1: 7 the month of S, in the second year H8658

SHEBER (1)
1Ch 2:48 was the mother of S and Tirhanah. H8693

SHEBNA (9)
2Ki 18:18 palace administrator, S the secretary, and H8675
2Ki 18:26 S and Joah said to the field H8675
2Ki 18:37 palace administrator, S the secretary, and H8674
2Ki 19: 2 S the secretary and the leading priests H8674
Isa 22:15 steward, to S the palace administrator: H8674
Isa 36: 3 palace administrator, S the secretary, and H8674
Isa 36:11 S and Joah said to the field commander H8674
Isa 36:22 S the secretary and Joah son of Asaph the H8674
Isa 37: 2 palace administrator, S the secretary, and H8674

SHECANIAH (NIV84) SHEKANIAH

S

SHECHEM (61) [SHECHEM'S, SHECHEMITE, SHECHEMITES]

Ge 12: 6 as the site of the great tree of Moreh at S. H8901
Ge 33:18 at the city of S in Canaan and camped H8901
Ge 33:19 the father of S, the plot of ground H8902
Ge 34: 2 When S son of Hamor the Hivite, the ruler H8902
Ge 34: 4 And S said to his father Hamor, "Get me H8902
Ge 34: 7 because S had done an outrageous thing in NDT
Ge 34: 8 "My son S has his heart set on your H8902
Ge 34:11 Then S said to Dinah's father and H8902
Ge 34:13 as they spoke to S and his father Hamor. H8902
Ge 34:18 seemed good to Hamor and his son S. H8902
Ge 34:20 Hamor and his son S went to the gate of H8902
Ge 34:24 gate agreed with Hamor and his son S, H8902
Ge 34:26 Hamor and his son S to the sword and H8902
Ge 35: 4 Jacob buried them under the oak at S. H8901
Ge 37:12 gone to graze their father's flocks near S, H8901
Ge 37:13 your brothers are grazing the flocks near S. H8901
Ge 37:14 When Joseph arrived at S, H8901
Nu 26:31 through S, the Shechemite clan; H8903
Jos 17: 2 Asriel, S, Hepher and Shemida. H8903
Jos 17: 7 from Asher to Mikmethath east of S. H8901
Jos 20: 7 Naphtali, S in the hill country of Ephraim H8901
Jos 21:21 hill country of Ephraim they were given S H8901
Jos 24: 1 assembled all the tribes of Israel at S. H8901
Jos 24:25 there at S he reaffirmed for them H8901
Jos 24:32 were buried at S in the tract of land that H8901
Jos 24:32 from the sons of Hamor, the father of S. H8902
Jdg 8:31 who lived in S, also bore him a son, H8901
Jdg 9: 1 brothers in S and said to them and H8901
Jdg 9: 2 "Ask all the citizens of S, 'Which is better H8901
Jdg 9: 3 repeated all this to the citizens of S, H8901
Jdg 9: 6 all the citizens of S and Beth Millo H8901
Jdg 9: 6 tree at the pillar in S to crown Abimelek H8901
Jdg 9: 7 citizens of S, so that God may H8901
Jdg 9:18 over the citizens of S because he is H8901
Jdg 9:20 the citizens of S and Beth Millo, and H8901
Jdg 9:20 the citizens of S and Beth Millo, and H8901
Jdg 9:23 the citizens of S so that they acted H8901
Jdg 9:24 brother Abimelek and on the citizens of S, H8901
Jdg 9:25 him these citizens of S set men on the H8901
Jdg 9:26 son of Ebed moved with his clan into S, H8901
Jdg 9:31 clan have come to S and are stirring up H8901
Jdg 9:34 positions near S in four companies. H8901
Jdg 9:39 out the citizens of S and fought Abimelek. H8901
Jdg 9:41 Zebul drove Gaal and his clan out of S. H8901
Jdg 9:42 day the people of S went out to the fields NDT
Jdg 9:46 in the tower of S went into the stronghold H8901
Jdg 9:49 So all the people in the tower of S, about H8901
Jdg 9:57 made the people of S pay for all their H8901
Jdg 21:19 of the road that goes from Bethel to S, H8901
1Ki 12: 1 Rehoboam went to S, for all Israel had H8901
1Ki 12:25 Jeroboam fortified S in the hill country of H8901
1Ch 6:67 hill country of Ephraim they were given S H8901
1Ch 7:19 Ahian, S, Likhi and Aniam. H8903
1Ch 7:28 S and its villages all the way to H8901
2Ch 10: 1 Rehoboam went to S, for all Israel had H8901
Ps 60: 6 I will parcel out S and measure off the H8901
Ps 108: 7 I will parcel out S and measure off the H8901
Jer 41: 5 clothes and cut themselves came from S, H8901
Hos 6: 9 they murder on the road to S, carrying out H8901
Ac 7:16 were brought back to S and placed in the *G5374*
Ac 7:16 sons of Hamor at S for a certain sum of *G5374*

SHECHEM'S (3) [SHECHEM]

Ge 34: 6 Then S father Hamor went out to talk with H8902
Ge 34:26 took Dinah from S house and left. H8902
Jdg 9:28 the family of Hamor, S father! Why should H8902

SHECHEMITE (1) [SHECHEM]

Nu 26:31 through Shechem, the S clan; H8904

SHECHEMITES (1) [SHECHEM]

Jdg 9:28 why should we S be subject to him? H8902

SHED (45) [SHEDDING, SHEDS]

Ge 9: 6 by humans *shall* their blood **be s**; for in H9161
Ge 37:22 "Don't s any blood. Throw him into this H9161
Lev 17: 4 *they have* s blood and must be cut off H9161
Nu 35:33 the land on which blood *has* **been s**, H9161
Nu 35:33 except by the blood of the *one who* s it. H9161
Dt 19:10 innocent blood *will* not **be s** in your land, H9161
Dt 21: 7 "Our hands *did* not s this blood, nor did H9161
2Sa 16: 8 all the **blood** you s *in* the household H1947
1Ki 2:31 guilt of the innocent blood that Joab s. H9161
1Ki 2:32 The LORD will repay him for the blood he s NDT
2Ki 9: 7 all the LORD's servants **s by** Jezebel. H4946+3338
2Ki 21:16 Manasseh also s so much innocent blood H9161
1Ch 22: 8 '*You have* s much blood and have fought H9161
1Ch 22: 8 because *you have* s much blood on the H9161
1Ch 28: 3 you are a warrior and *have* s blood. H9161
Ps 106:38 *They* s innocent blood, the blood of their H9161
Pr 1:16 rush into evil, they are swift to s blood. H9161
Pr 6:17 tongue, hands *that* s innocent blood, H9161
Isa 26:21 The earth will disclose the **blood** *s on* it; the AIT
Isa 59: 7 they are swift to s innocent blood. H9161
Jer 7: 6 the widow and *do* not s innocent blood H9161
Jer 22: 3 and *do* not s innocent blood in this place. H9161
La 4:13 who s within her the blood of the H9161
Eze 16:38 who commit adultery and *who* s blood; H9161
Eze 21:32 your blood will be s in your land, you will NDT
Eze 22: 4 of the blood *you have* s and have become H9161
Eze 22: 6 who are in you uses his power to s blood. H9161
Eze 22:12 are people who accept bribes to s blood; H9161
Eze 22:13 at the blood *you have* s in your midst. H2118
Eze 22:27 they s blood and kill people to make H9161
Eze 23:45 women who commit adultery and s blood, H9161
Eze 24: 7 " 'For the blood she s is in her midst: She NDT
Eze 24:16 Yet do not lament or weep or s any tears. H995
Eze 33:25 in it and look to your idols and s blood, H9161
Eze 36:18 on them because *they had* s blood in the H9161
Joel 3:19 in whose land *they* s innocent blood. H9161
Mic 7: 2 Everyone lies in wait to s blood; they hunt NDT
Hab 2: 8 For you have s human blood; you have NDT
Hab 2:17 For you have s human blood; you have NDT
Mt 23:35 righteous blood *that has been* s on earth, *G1773*
Lk 11:50 the prophets that *has been* s since the *G1772*
Ac 22:20 the blood of your martyr Stephen *was* s, *G1773*
Ro 3:15 "Their feet are swift *to* s blood; *G1772*
Col 1:20 peace through his blood, *s on* the **cross**. AIT
Rev 16: 6 for *they have* s the blood of your holy *G1772*

SHEDDING (13) [SHED]

Dt 19:13 from Israel the **guilt of s** innocent **blood**, H1947
Dt 21: 9 yourselves the **guilt of s** innocent **blood**, H1947
Jdg 9:24 the **s of** their **blood**, might be H1947
1Ki 2: 5 s their blood in peacetime as if in battle H8492
2Ki 24: 4 including the s *of* innocent blood. For he H9161
Job 15:33 like an olive tree s its blossoms. H8959
Jer 22:17 on s innocent blood and on oppression H9161
Eze 22: 3 on herself doom by s blood in her midst H9161
Eze 22: 9 are slanderers who are bent on s blood; H9161
Mt 23:30 with them in s the **blood** of the prophets. *G135*
Ro 3:25 through the *s of* his **blood**—to be received by AIT
Heb 9:22 without the **s of blood** there is no *G136*
Heb 12: 4 not yet resisted to the point of s your **blood**. *G135*

SHEDEUR (5)

Nu 1: 5 from Reuben, Elizur son of S; H8725
Nu 2:10 of the people of Reuben is Elizur son of S. H8725
Nu 7:30 On the fourth day Elizur son of S, the H8725
Nu 7:35 This was the offering of Elizur son of S. H8725
Nu 10:18 Elizur son of S was in command. H8725

SHEDS (3) [SHED]

Ge 9: 6 "*Whoever* s human blood, by humans H9161
Pr 20:27 of the LORD *that* **s light on** one's inmost H2924
Eze 18:10 *who* s blood or does any of these other H9161

SHEEP (205) [SHEEP'S, SHEEPSKINS]

Ge 12:16 Abram acquired s and cattle, male H7366
Ge 20:14 Abimelek brought s and cattle and male H7366
Ge 21:27 So Abraham brought s and cattle and H7366
Ge 24:35 He has given him s and cattle, silver and H7366
Ge 29: 2 with three flocks of s lying near it because H7366
Ge 29: 3 from the well's mouth and water the s. H7366
Ge 29: 6 comes his daughter Rachel with the s." H7366
Ge 29: 7 Water the s and take them back to H7366
Ge 29: 8 Then we will water the s." H7366
Ge 29: 9 Rachel came with her father's s, for she H7366
Ge 29:10 and Laban's s, he went over and H7366
Ge 29:10 of the well and watered his uncle's s. H7366
Ge 30:32 from them every speckled or spotted s, H8445
Ge 31:19 When Laban had gone to shear his s H7366
Ge 31:38 Your s and goats have not miscarried, nor H8161
Ge 32: 5 donkeys, **s and goats**, male and H7366
Ge 38:12 to the men who were shearing his s, and H7366
Ge 38:13 is on his way to Timnah to shear his s," H7366
Ge 47:17 horses, their **s and goats**, their H5238+7366
Ge 49:14 donkey lying down among the **s pens**. H5478
Ex 9: 3 camels and on your cattle, **s and goats**. H7366
Ex 12: 5 may take them from the s or the goats. H3897
Ex 20:24 your **s and goats** and your cattle. H7366
Ex 22: 1 steals an ox or a s and slaughters it or H8445
Ex 22: 1 cattle for the ox and four s for the sheep. H7366
Ex 22: 1 cattle for the ox and four sheep for the s. H8445
Ex 22: 4 whether ox or donkey or s—they must pay H8445
Ex 22: 9 of an ox, a donkey, a s, a garment, or any H8445
Ex 22:10 a s or any other animal to their neighbor H8445
Ex 22:30 Do the same with your cattle and your s H7366
Lev 1:10 from either the s or the goats, you are H4166
Lev 7:23 not eat any of the fat of cattle, s or goats. H4166
Lev 22:19 s or goats in order that it may be accepted H4166
Lev 22:23 offering an ox or a s that is deformed or H8445
Lev 22:28 a cow or a s and its young on the H8445
Lev 27:26 whether an ox or a s, it is the LORD's. H8445
Nu 18:17 firstborn of a cow, a s or a goat; they are H4166
Nu 22:40 Balak sacrificed cattle and s, and gave H7366
Nu 27:17 will not be like s without a shepherd." H7366
Nu 31:28 whether people, cattle, donkeys or s. H7366
Nu 31:30 donkeys, s or other animals. H7366
Nu 31:32 that the soldiers took was 675,000 s, H7366
Nu 31:36 who fought in the battle was: 337,500 s, H7366
Nu 31:43 the community's half—was 337,500 s, H7366
Dt 14: 4 the ox, the s, the goat, H8445+4166
Dt 14: 5 the antelope and the **mountain** s. H2378
Dt 14:26 s, wine or other fermented drink, or H7366
Dt 15:19 do not shear the firstborn of your s. H7366
Dt 17: 1 your God an ox or a s that has any defect H8445
Dt 18: 3 the people who sacrifice a bull or a s: H8445
Dt 18: 4 the first wool from the shearing of your s, H7366
Dt 22: 1 see your fellow Israelite's ox or s straying, H8445
Dt 28:31 Your s will be given to your enemies, and H7366
Jos 6:21 young and old, cattle, s and donkeys. H8445
Jos 7:24 donkeys and s, his tent and all that H7366
Jdg 5:16 you stay among the **s pens** to hear the H5478
Jdg 6: 4 Israel, neither s nor cattle nor donkeys. H8445
1Sa 14:32 plunder and, taking s, cattle and calves, H7366
1Sa 14:34 'Each of you bring me your cattle and s H8445
1Sa 15: 3 cattle and s, camels and donkeys." H8445
1Sa 15: 9 Agag and the best of the s and cattle, H7366
1Sa 15:14 then is this bleating of s in my ears? H7366
1Sa 15:15 spared the best of the s and cattle to H7366
1Sa 15:21 The soldiers took s and cattle from the H7366
1Sa 16:11 "He is tending the s." Samuel said, H7366
1Sa 16:19 me your son David, who is with the s." H7366
1Sa 17:15 Saul to tend his father's s at Bethlehem. H7366
1Sa 17:28 you leave those few s in the wilderness? H7366
1Sa 17:34 servant has been keeping his father's s. H7366
1Sa 17:34 came and carried off a s from the flock, H8445
1Sa 17:35 struck it and rescued the s from its mouth. NDT
1Sa 22:19 infants, and its cattle, donkeys and s. H8445
1Sa 24: 3 He came to the s pens along the way; H7366
1Sa 25: 2 a thousand goats and three thousand s, H7366
1Sa 25: 4 he heard that Nabal was shearing s. H7366
1Sa 25:16 time we were herding our s near them. H7366
1Sa 25:18 of wine, five dressed s, five seahs of H7366
1Sa 27: 9 but took s and cattle, donkeys H7366
2Sa 12: 2 had a very large number of s and cattle, H7366
2Sa 12: 4 one of his own s or cattle to prepare H7366
2Sa 17:29 honey and curds, s, and cheese from cows' H7366
2Sa 24:17 These are but s. What have they done H7366
1Ki 1: 9 Adonijah then sacrificed s, cattle and H7366
1Ki 1:19 fattened calves, and s, and has invited all H7366
1Ki 1:25 numbers of cattle, fattened calves, and s. H7366
1Ki 4:23 cattle and a hundred **s and goats**, H7366
1Ki 8: 5 sacrificing so many s and cattle that they H7366
1Ki 8:63 twenty thousand **s and goats**. H7366
1Ki 22:17 on the hills like s without a shepherd, H7366
2Ki 3: 4 Now Mesha king of Moab **raised** s, and H5924
1Ch 5:21 fifty thousand s and two thousand H7366
1Ch 12:40 olive oil, cattle and s, for there was joy in H7366
1Ch 21:17 These are but s. What have they done H7366
2Ch 5: 6 sacrificing so many s and cattle that they H7366
2Ch 7: 5 twenty thousand **s and goats**. H7366
2Ch 14:15 off droves of **s and goats** and camels. H7366
2Ch 15:11 seven thousand **s and goats** from the H7366
2Ch 18: 2 slaughtered many s and cattle for him H7366
2Ch 18:16 on the hills like s without a shepherd, H7366
2Ch 29:33 bulls and three thousand **s and goats**. H7366
2Ch 30:24 seven thousand **s and goats** for the H7366
2Ch 30:24 bulls and ten thousand **s and goats**. H7366
Ne 3: 1 went to work and rebuilt the S Gate. H7366
Ne 3:32 the corner and the S Gate the goldsmiths H7366
Ne 5:18 six choice s and some poultry were H7366
Ne 12:39 of the Hundred, as far as the S Gate. H7366
Job 1: 3 he owned seven thousand s, three H7366
Job 1:16 burned up the s and the servants, H7366
Job 30: 1 have disdained to put with my s dogs. H7366
Job 31:20 warming them with the fleece from my s, H3897
Job 42:12 He had fourteen thousand s, six thousand H7366
Ps 44:11 to be devoured like s and have scattered H7366
Ps 44:22 we are considered as s to be slaughtered. H7366
Ps 49:14 They are like s and are destined to die H7366
Ps 68:13 Even while you sleep among the **s pens** H9190
Ps 74: 1 smolder against the *s of* your pasture? H7366
Ps 78:52 he led them like s through the wilderness. H6373
Ps 78:70 his servant and took him from the s pens; H7366
Ps 78:71 from tending the s he brought him to be H6402
Ps 79:13 we your people, the *s of* your pasture, will H7366
Ps 100: 3 we are his people, the *s of* his pasture. H7366
Ps 119:176 I have strayed like a lost s. Seek your H8445
Ps 144:13 Our s will increase by thousands, by tens H7366
SS 1: 7 flock and where you rest your s at midday. NDT
SS 1: 8 the tracks of the s and graze your young H7366
SS 4: 2 Your teeth are like a flock of **s just shorn** H7892
SS 6: 6 are like a flock of s coming up from the H8161
Isa 5:17 Then s will graze as in their own pasture H3897
Isa 7:25 cattle are turned loose and where s run. H8445
Isa 13:14 hunted gazelle, like s without a shepherd H7366
Isa 22:13 slaughtering of cattle and killing of s H7366
Isa 43:23 have not brought me s for burnt offerings, H8445
Isa 53: 6 like s, have gone astray, each of H7366
Isa 53: 7 as a s before its shearers is silent H8161
Jer 12: 3 Drag them off like s to be butchered! Set H7366
Jer 13:20 the *s of* which you boasted? H7366
Jer 23: 1 scattering the *s of* my pasture! H7366
Jer 50: 6 "My people have been lost s; their H7366
Eze 25: 5 Ammon into a resting place for s. H7366
Eze 34: 6 My s wandered over all the mountains H7366
Eze 34:11 will search for my s and look after them. H7366
Eze 34:12 he is with them, so will I look after my s. H7366
Eze 34:15 I myself will tend my s and have them lie H7366
Eze 34:17 I will judge between *one* s and another H8445
Eze 34:20 between the fat s and the lean sheep. H8445
Eze 34:20 between the fat sheep and the lean s. H8445
Eze 34:21 butting all the weak s with your horns until NDT
Eze 34:22 I will judge between *one* s and another. H8445
Eze 34:31 You are my s, the sheep of my pasture H7366
Eze 34:31 are my sheep, the *s of* my pasture, and I H7366
Eze 36:37 I will make their people as numerous as s, H7366
Eze 45:15 Also one s is to be taken from every flock H8445
Hos 12:12 get a wife, and to pay for her *he* **tended s**. H9068
Joel 1:18 pasture; even the flocks of s are suffering. H7366
Mic 2:12 I will bring them together like s *in* a pen H7366
Mic 5: 8 like a young lion among flocks of s, which H7366
Hab 3:17 though there are no s in the pen and no H7366

Zec 10: 2 people wander like **s** oppressed for lack of H7366
Zec 11:16 will eat the meat of the **choice s** H1374
Zec 13: 7 the shepherd, and the **s** will be scattered H7366
Mt 9:36 helpless, like **s** without a shepherd. G4585
Mt 10: 6 Go rather to the lost **s** of Israel. G4585
Mt 10:16 am sending you out like **s** among wolves. G4585
Mt 12:11 "If any of you has a **s** and it falls into a pit G4585
Mt 12:12 much more valuable is a person *than* a **s**! G4585
Mt 15:24 "I was sent only to the lost **s** of Israel." G4585
Mt 18:12 If a man owns a hundred **s**, and one of G4585
Mt 18:13 happier about **that one s** than about the G899S
Mt 25:32 shepherd separates the **s** from the goats. G4585
Mt 25:33 He will put the **s** on his right and the goats G4585
Mt 26:31 the **s** of the flock will be scattered. G4585
Mk 6:34 they were like **s** without a shepherd. G4585
Mk 14:27 the shepherd, and the **s** will be scattered. G4585
Lk 15: 4 of you has a hundred **s** and loses one of G4585
Lk 15: 4 go after the lost **s** until he finds it? NDT
Lk 15: 6 'Rejoice with me; I have found my lost **s**. G4585
Lk 17: 7 a servant plowing or **looking after the s**. G4477
Jn 2:14 selling cattle, **s** and doves, and others G4585
Jn 2:15 the temple courts, both **s** and cattle; he G4585
Jn 5: 2 is in Jerusalem near the **S Gate** a pool, G4583
Jn 10: 1 who does not enter the **s** pen by the gate, G4585
Jn 10: 2 by the gate is the shepherd *of* the **s**. G4585
Jn 10: 3 gate for him, and the **s** listen to his voice. G4585
Jn 10: 3 He calls his own **s** by name and leads G4585
Jn 10: 4 his **s** follow him because they know G4585
Jn 10: 7 truly I tell you, I am the gate *for* the **s**. G4585
Jn 10: 8 the **s** have not listened to them. G4585
Jn 10:11 shepherd lays down his life for the **s**. G4585
Jn 10:12 not the shepherd and does not own the **s**. G4585
Jn 10:12 he abandons the **s** and runs away. G4585
Jn 10:13 a hired hand and cares nothing for the **s**. G4585
Jn 10:14 I know my **s** and my sheep know me— NDT
Jn 10:14 I know my sheep and my **s** know me— NDT
Jn 10:15 Father—and I lay down my life for the **s**. G4585
Jn 10:16 I have other **s** that are not of this sheep G4585
Jn 10:16 I have other sheep that are not of this **s pen**. G885
Jn 10:26 do not believe because you are not my **s**. G4585
Jn 10:27 My **s** listen to my voice; I know them, and G4585
Jn 21:16 Jesus said, "Take care of my **s**." G4585
Jn 21:17 that I love you." Jesus said, "Feed my **s**. G4585
Ac 8:32 "He was led like a **s** to the slaughter, and G4585
Ro 8:36 we are considered as **s** to be slaughtered." G4585
Heb 13:20 Lord Jesus, that great Shepherd *of* the **s**, G4585
1Pe 2:25 For "you were like **s** going astray," but now G4585
Rev 18:13 cattle and **s**; horses and carriages G4585

SHEEP'S (1) [SHEEP]

Mt 7:15 They come to you in **s** clothing, but G4585

SHEEP-SHEARING (1) [SHEAR]

1Sa 25: 7 " 'Now I hear that *it is* **s time**. When your H1605

SHEEPCOTE, SHEEPCOTES (KJV) PASTURE, SHEEP PENS

SHEEPFOLD, SHEEPFOLDS (KJV) SHEEP PEN, SHEEP PENS

SHEEPMASTER (KJV) RAISED SHEEP

SHEEPSHEARERS (1) [SHEAR]

2Sa 13:23 when Absalom's **s** were at Baal Hazor H1605

SHEEPSKINS (1) [SHEEP]

Heb 11:37 They went about in **s** and goatskins G3603

SHEER (1)

Isa 28:19 of this message will bring **s** terror. H8370

SHEERAH (1) [UZZEN SHEERAH]

1Ch 7:24 His daughter was **S**, who built Lower and H8641

SHEET (4) [SHEETS]

Isa 25: 7 all peoples, the **s** that covers all nations H5012
Ac 10:11 like a large **s** being let down to G3855
Ac 10:16 immediately the **s** was taken back to G5007
Ac 11: 5 like a large **s** being let down from G3855

SHEETS (2) [SHEET]

Ex 39: 3 They hammered out **thin s** *of* gold and cut H7063
Nu 16:38 the censers into **s** to overlay the altar, H7063

SHEHARIAH (1)

1Ch 8:26 Shamsherai, **S**, Athaliah, H8843

SHEKANIAH (10) [SHEKANIAH'S]

1Ch 3:21 Rephaiah, of Arnan, of Obadiah and of **S**. H8908
1Ch 3:22 The descendants of **S**: Shemaiah and his H8908
1Ch 24:11 the ninth to Jeshua, the tenth to **S**, H8909
2Ch 31:15 Amariah and **S** assisted him faithfully in H8909
Ezr 8: 3 of the descendants of **S**; of the H8908
Ezr 8: 5 of Zattu, **S** son of Jahaziel, and H8908
Ezr 10: 2 Then **S** son of Jehiel, one of the H8908
Ne 3:29 Shemaiah son of **S**, the guard at the H8908
Ne 6:18 since he was son-in-law to **S** son of Arah H8908
Ne 12: 3 **S**, Rehum, Meremoth, H8908

SHEKANIAH'S (1) [SHEKANIAH]

Ne 12:14 of Malluk's, Jonathan; of **S**, Joseph; H8908

SHEKEL (41) [SHEKELS]

Ex 30:13 those already counted is to give a half **s**, H9203
Ex 30:13 according to the sanctuary **s**, which H9203
Ex 30:13 This half **s** is an offering to the LORD H9203
Ex 30:15 more than a half **s** and the poor are not H9203
Ex 30:24 all according to the sanctuary **s**—and a hin H9203
Ex 38:24 730 shekels, according to the sanctuary **s**. H9203
Ex 38:25 shekels, according to the sanctuary **s**— H9203
Ex 38:26 half a **s**, according to the sanctuary H9203
Ex 38:26 according to the sanctuary **s**, from H9203
Lev 5:15 in silver, according to the sanctuary **s**. H9203
Lev 27: 3 of silver, according to the sanctuary **s**; H9203
Lev 27:25 is to be set according to the sanctuary **s**, H9203
Lev 27:25 sanctuary shekel, twenty gerahs to the **s**. H9203
Nu 3:47 according to the sanctuary **s**, which H9203
Nu 3:50 shekels, according to the sanctuary **s**. H9203
Nu 7:13 both according to the sanctuary **s**, each H9203
Nu 7:19 both according to the sanctuary **s**, each H9203
Nu 7:25 both according to the sanctuary **s**, each H9203
Nu 7:31 both according to the sanctuary **s**, each H9203
Nu 7:37 both according to the sanctuary **s**, each H9203
Nu 7:43 both according to the sanctuary **s**, each H9203
Nu 7:49 both according to the sanctuary **s**, each H9203
Nu 7:55 both according to the sanctuary **s**, each H9203
Nu 7:61 both according to the sanctuary **s**, each H9203
Nu 7:67 both according to the sanctuary **s**, each H9203
Nu 7:73 both according to the sanctuary **s**, each H9203
Nu 7:79 both according to the sanctuary **s**, each H9203
Nu 7:85 shekels, according to the sanctuary **s**. H9203
Nu 7:86 according to the sanctuary **s**. H9203
Nu 18:16 according to the sanctuary **s**, which H9203
1Sa 9: 8 he said, "I have a quarter of a **s** *of* silver. H9203
1Sa 13:21 The price was **two-thirds of a s** for H7088
1Sa 13:21 a third of a **s** for sharpening forks and NDT
2Ki 7: 1 flour will sell for a **s** and two seahs of H9203
2Ki 7: 1 seahs of barley for a **s** at the gate of H9203
2Ki 7:16 So a seah of the finest flour sold for a **s** H9203
2Ki 7:16 two seahs of barley sold for a **s**, as H9203
2Ki 7:18 flour will sell for a **s** and two seahs of H9203
2Ki 7:18 seahs of barley for a **s** at the gate of H9203
Ne 10:32 to give a third of a **s** each year for the H9203
Eze 45:12 The **s** is to consist of twenty gerahs H9203

SHEKELS (108) [SHEKEL]

Ge 20:16 giving your brother a thousand **s** of silver. NDT
Ge 23:15 the land is worth four hundred **s** *of* silver H9203
Ge 23:16 four hundred **s** *of* silver, according to the H9203
Ge 24:22 beka and two gold bracelets weighing ten **s**. NDT
Ge 37:28 sold him for twenty **s** of silver to the NDT
Ge 45:22 he gave three hundred **s** of silver and five NDT
Ex 21:32 owner must pay thirty **s** of silver to the H9203
Ex 30:23 500 **s** of liquid myrrh, half as much (that is NDT
Ex 30:23 that is, 250 **s**) of fragrant cinnamon NDT
Ex 30:23 cinnamon, 250 **s** of fragrant calamus, NDT
Ex 30:24 500 **s** of cassia—all according to the NDT
Ex 38:24 the sanctuary was 29 talents and 730 **s**, H9203
Ex 38:25 the census was 100 talents and 1,775 **s**, H9203
Ex 38:28 They used the 1,775 **s** to make the hooks NDT
Ex 38:29 wave offering was 70 talents and 2,400 **s**. H9203
Lev 27: 3 ages of twenty and sixty at fifty **s** *of* silver, H9203
Lev 27: 4 a female, set her value at thirty **s**; H9203
Lev 27: 5 of a male at twenty **s** and of a female at H9203
Lev 27: 5 twenty shekels and of a female at ten **s**; H9203
Lev 27: 6 of a male at five **s** *of* silver and that of a H9203
Lev 27: 6 that of a female at three **s** *of* silver; H9203
Lev 27: 7 of a male at fifteen **s** and of a female at H9203
Lev 27: 7 fifteen shekels and of a female at ten **s**. H9203
Lev 27:16 fifty **s** *of* silver to a homer of barley seed. H9203
Nu 3:47 collect five **s** for each one, according to the H9203
Nu 3:50 he collected silver weighing 1,365 **s**, NDT
Nu 7:13 a hundred and thirty **s** and one silver NDT
Nu 7:13 silver sprinkling bowl weighing seventy **s**, H9203
Nu 7:14 one gold dish weighing ten **s**, filled with NDT
Nu 7:19 a hundred and thirty **s** and one silver NDT
Nu 7:19 silver sprinkling bowl weighing seventy **s**, H9203
Nu 7:20 one gold dish weighing ten **s**, filled with NDT
Nu 7:25 a hundred and thirty **s** and one silver NDT
Nu 7:25 silver sprinkling bowl weighing seventy **s**, H9203
Nu 7:26 one gold dish weighing ten **s**, filled with NDT
Nu 7:31 a hundred and thirty **s** and one silver NDT
Nu 7:31 silver sprinkling bowl weighing seventy **s**, H9203
Nu 7:32 one gold dish weighing ten **s**, filled with NDT
Nu 7:37 a hundred and thirty **s** and one silver NDT
Nu 7:37 silver sprinkling bowl weighing seventy **s**, H9203
Nu 7:38 one gold dish weighing ten **s**, filled with NDT
Nu 7:43 a hundred and thirty **s** and one silver NDT
Nu 7:43 silver sprinkling bowl weighing seventy **s**, H9203
Nu 7:44 one gold dish weighing ten **s**, filled with NDT
Nu 7:49 a hundred and thirty **s** and one silver NDT
Nu 7:49 silver sprinkling bowl weighing seventy **s**, H9203
Nu 7:50 one gold dish weighing ten **s**, filled with NDT
Nu 7:55 a hundred and thirty **s** and one silver NDT
Nu 7:55 silver sprinkling bowl weighing seventy **s**, H9203
Nu 7:56 one gold dish weighing ten **s**, filled with NDT
Nu 7:61 a hundred and thirty **s** and one silver NDT
Nu 7:61 silver sprinkling bowl weighing seventy **s**, H9203
Nu 7:62 one gold dish weighing ten **s**, filled with NDT
Nu 7:67 a hundred and thirty **s** and one silver NDT
Nu 7:67 silver sprinkling bowl weighing seventy **s**, H9203
Nu 7:68 one gold dish weighing ten **s**, filled with NDT
Nu 7:73 a hundred and thirty **s** and one silver NDT
Nu 7:73 silver sprinkling bowl weighing seventy **s**, H9203
Nu 7:74 one gold dish weighing ten **s**, filled with NDT
Nu 7:79 a hundred and thirty **s** and one silver NDT
Nu 7:79 silver sprinkling bowl weighing seventy **s**, H9203
Nu 7:80 one gold dish weighing ten **s**, filled with NDT
Nu 7:85 silver plate weighed a hundred and thirty **s**, NDT
Nu 7:85 and each sprinkling bowl seventy **s**. NDT
Nu 7:85 weighed two thousand four hundred **s**, NDT
Nu 7:86 filled with incense weighed ten **s** each, NDT
Nu 7:86 dishes weighed a hundred and twenty **s**. NDT
Nu 18:16 the redemption price set at five **s** of silver, H9203
Nu 31:52 as a gift to the LORD weighed 16,750 **s**. H9203
Dt 22:19 fine him a hundred **s** of silver and give them NDT
Dt 22:29 he shall pay her father fifty **s** of silver. NDT
Jos 7:21 two hundred **s** *of* silver and a bar of gold H9203
Jos 7:21 of silver and a bar of gold weighing fifty **s**, H9203
Jdg 8:26 he asked for came to seventeen hundred **s**, NDT
Jdg 9: 4 They gave him seventy **s** of silver from the NDT
Jdg 16: 5 us will give you eleven hundred **s** of silver." NDT
Jdg 17: 2 "The eleven hundred **s** of silver that were NDT
Jdg 17: 3 the eleven hundred **s** of silver to his mother, NDT
Jdg 17: 4 she took two hundred **s** of silver and gave NDT
Jdg 17:10 I'll give you ten **s** of silver a year, your NDT
1Sa 17: 5 armor of bronze weighing five thousand **s**; H9203
1Sa 17: 7 its iron point weighed six hundred **s**. H9203
2Sa 14:26 was two hundred **s** by the royal standard. H9203
2Sa 18:11 have had to give you ten **s** of silver and a NDT
2Sa 18:12 "Even if a thousand **s** were weighed out H4084
2Sa 21:16 three hundred **s** and who was armed NDT
2Sa 24:24 the oxen and paid fifty **s** of silver for them. H9203
1Ki 10:16 six hundred **s** of gold went into each shield. NDT
1Ki 10:29 chariot from Egypt for six hundred **s** of silver, NDT
2Ki 5: 5 six thousand **s** of gold and ten sets of NDT
2Ki 6:25 a donkey's head sold for eighty **s** of silver, NDT
2Ki 6:25 a quarter of a cab of seed pods for five **s**. H4084
2Ki 15:20 to contribute fifty **s** of silver to be given H9203
1Ch 21:25 Araunah six hundred **s** *of* gold for the site. H9203
2Ch 1:17 chariot from Egypt for six hundred **s** of silver, NDT
2Ch 3: 9 The gold nails weighed fifty **s**. He also H9203
2Ch 9:15 six hundred **s** of hammered gold went into NDT
2Ch 9:16 with three hundred **s** of gold in each shield. NDT
Ne 5:15 people and took forty **s** of silver from them H9203
SS 8:11 to bring for its fruit a thousand **s** of silver. NDT
SS 8:12 the thousand **s** are for you, Solomon, NDT
Isa 7:23 a thousand vines worth a thousand silver **s**, NDT
Jer 32: 9 weighed out for him seventeen **s** of silver. H9203
Eze 4:10 Weigh out twenty **s** of food to eat each H9203
Eze 45:12 Twenty **s** plus twenty-five shekels plus H9203
Eze 45:12 plus twenty-five **s** plus fifteen shekels H9203
Eze 45:12 shekels plus fifteen **s** equal one mina. H9203
Hos 3: 2 bought her for fifteen **s** of silver and about a NDT

SHELAH (19) [SHELANITE, SHELANITES]

Ge 10:24 Arphaxad was the father of **S**, and Shelah H8941
Ge 10:24 father of Shelah, and **S** the father of Eber. H8941
Ge 11:12 lived 35 years, he became the father of **S**. H8941
Ge 11:13 And after he became the father of **S** H8941
Ge 11:14 When **S** had lived 30 years, he became H8941
Ge 11:15 **S** lived 403 years and had other sons and H8941
Ge 38: 5 to still another son and named him **S**. H8925
Ge 38:11 household until my son **S** grows up." H8925
Ge 38:14 she saw that, though **S** had now grown up H8925
Ge 38:26 since I wouldn't give her to my son **S**." H8925
Ge 46:12 Onan, **S**, Perez and Zerah (but Er and H8925
Nu 26:20 through **S**, the Shelanite clan; through H8925
1Ch 1:18 Arphaxad was the father of **S**, and Shelah H8941
1Ch 1:18 father of Shelah, and **S** the father of Eber. H8941
1Ch 1:24 Arphaxad, **S**, H8941
1Ch 2: 3 Er, Onan and **S**. These three were H8925
1Ch 4:21 The sons of **S** son of Judah: Er the father H8925
Ne 11: 5 the son of Zechariah, a descendant of **S**. H8989
Lk 3:35 of Peleg, the son of Eber, the son *of* **S**, G4885

SHELANITE (1) [SHELAH]

Nu 26:20 through Shelah, the **S** clan; through Perez, H8989

SHELANITES (1) [SHELAH]

1Ch 9: 5 Of the **S**: Asaiah the firstborn and his sons H8872

SHELEMIAH (10)

1Ch 26:14 The lot for the East Gate fell to **S**. H8983
Ezr 10:39 **S**, Nathan, Adaiah, H8982
Ezr 10:41 **S**, Shemariah, H8983
Ne 3:30 Hananiah son of **S**, and Hanun, H8982
Ne 13:13 I put **S** the priest, Zadok the scribe, and a H8982
Jer 36:14 Nethaniah, the son of **S**, the son of Cushi, H8983
Jer 36:26 son of Azriel and **S** son of Abdeel to H8983
Jer 37: 3 sent Jehukal son of **S** with the priest H8982
Jer 37:13 whose name was Irijah son of **S**, the son H8982
Jer 38: 1 Jehukal son of **S**, and Pashhur son of H8983

SHELEPH (2)

Ge 10:26 the father of Almodad, **S**, Hazarmaveth, H8991
1Ch 1:20 the father of Almodad, **S**, Hazarmaveth, H8991

SHELESH (1)

1Ch 7:35 Zophah, Imna, **S** and Amal. H8994

SHELISHIYAH See EGLATH SHELISHIYAH

SHELOMI (1)

Nu 34:27 Ahihud son of **S**, the leader from the tribe H8979

SHELOMITH (8)
Lev 24:11 His mother's name was S, the daughter of H8985
1Ch 3:19 Hananiah. S was their sister. H8985
1Ch 23:18 The sons of Izhar: S was the first. H8984
1Ch 26:25 Joram his son, Zikri his son and S his son. H8984
1Ch 26:26 S and his relatives were in charge of all H8984
1Ch 26:28 were in the care of S and his relatives. H8984
2Ch 11:20 who bore him Abijah, Attai, Ziza and S. H8984
Ezr 8:10 descendants of Bani, S son of Josiphiah H8984

SHELOMOTH (3)
1Ch 23: 9 The sons of Shimei: S, Haziel and Haran H8977
1Ch 24:22 From the Izharites: S; from the sons of H8977
1Ch 24:22 Shelomoth; from the sons of S: Jahath. H8977

SHELTER (25) [SHELTERED, SHELTERS]
Ex 9:19 *to* **bring** your livestock and everything
you have in the field **to a place of s** H6395
Dt 32:38 to help you! *Let them* **give** you s! H2118+6261
Ru 2: 7 till now, except for a short rest in the s." H1074
Job 24: 8 rains and hug the rocks for lack of s. H4726
Ps 27: 5 will hide me in the s *of* his sacred tent H6260
Ps 31:20 In the s *of* your presence you hide them H6260
Ps 55: 8 I would hurry to my **place of s**, far from H5144
Ps 61: 4 take refuge in the s *of* your wings. H6260
Ps 91: 1 dwells in the s *of* the Most High will H6260
Ecc 7:12 Wisdom is a s as money is a shelter, but H7498
Ecc 7:12 Wisdom is a shelter as money is a s, but H7498
Isa 1: 8 Daughter Zion is left like a s in a vineyard, H6109
Isa 4: 6 It will be a s and shade from the heat of H6109
Isa 16: 4 with you; be their s from the destroyer." H6260
Isa 25: 4 a s from the storm and a shade from the H4726
Isa 32: 2 one will be like a s *from* the wind and a H4675
Isa 58: 7 to provide the poor wanderer with s— H1074
Jer 4:20 tents are destroyed, my s in a moment. H3749
Jer 10:20 left now to pitch my tent or to set up my s. H3749
Eze 17:23 *they will* **find** s in the shade of its H8905
Da 4:12 Under it the wild animals **found** s, and A10300
Da 4:21 food for all, *giving* s to the wild animals A10163
Am 9:11 that day "I will restore David's fallen s— H6109
Jnh 4: 5 There he made himself a s, sat in its H6109
Rev 7:15 *will* s them **with** *his* **presence**. *G5012+2093*

SHELTERED (1) [SHELTER]
Zep 2: 3 perhaps *you will* **be** s on the day of the H6259

SHELTERS (13) [SHELTER]
Ge 33:17 himself and made s for his livestock. H6109
Lev 23:42 Live in **temporary** s for seven days: All H6109
Lev 23:42 native-born Israelites are to live in such s H6109
Lev 23:43 live in **temporary** s when I brought H6109
Jdg 6: 2 the Israelites prepared s for themselves in H4953
Ne 8:14 were to live in **temporary** s during the H6109
Ne 8:15 to make **temporary** s"—as it is H6109
Ne 8:16 built themselves **temporary** s on their own H6109
Ne 8:17 from exile built **temporary** s and lived in H6109
Jer 49:29 their s will be carried off with all their H3749
Mt 17: 4 I will put up three s—one for you, *G5008*
Mk 9: 5 Let us put up three s—one for you, one *G5008*
Lk 9:33 Let us put up three s—one for you, one *G5008*

SHELUMIEL (5)
Nu 1: 6 from Simeon, S son of Zurishaddai; H8981
Nu 2:12 people of Simeon is S son of Zurishaddai. H8981
Nu 7:36 On the fifth day S son of Zurishaddai, the H8981
Nu 7:41 was the offering of S son of Zurishaddai. H8981
Nu 10:19 S son of Zurishaddai was over the division H8981

SHEM (19) [SHEM'S]
Ge 5:32 he became the father of S, Ham and H9006
Ge 6:10 had three sons: S, Ham and Japheth. H9006
Ge 7:13 Noah and his sons, S, Ham and Japheth, H9006
Ge 9:18 of Noah who came out of the ark were S, H9006
Ge 9:23 But S and Japheth took a garment and H9006
Ge 9:26 "Praise be to the LORD, the God of S! H9006
Ge 9:26 May Canaan be the slave of S. H4564S
Ge 9:27 may Japheth live in the tents of S, and H9006
Ge 10: 1 This is the account of S, Ham and H9006
Ge 10:21 Sons were also born to S, whose older H9006
Ge 10:21 S was the ancestor of all the sons of H2085S
Ge 10:22 The sons of S: Elam, Ashur, Arphaxad H9006
Ge 10:31 These are the sons of S by their clans H9006
Ge 11:10 the flood, when S was 100 years old, he H9006
Ge 11:11 S lived 500 years and had other sons and H9006
1Ch 1: 4 The sons of Noah: S, Ham and Japheth. H9006
1Ch 1:17 The sons of S: Elam, Ashur, Arphaxad H9006
1Ch 1:24 S, Arphaxad, Shelah, H9006
Lk 3:36 Arphaxad, the son *of* S, the son of Noah, *G4954*

SHEM'S (1) [SHEM]
Ge 11:10 This is the account of S family line. H9006

SHEMA (6)
Jos 15:26 S, Moladah, H9054
1Ch 2:43 Korah, Tappuah, Rekem and S. H9050
1Ch 2:44 S was the father of Raham, and Raham H9050
1Ch 5: 8 son of Azaz, the son of S, the son of Joel. H9050
1Ch 8:13 Beriah and S, who were heads of H9050
Ne 8: 4 on his right stood Mattithiah, S, Anaiah, H9050

SHEMAAH (1)
1Ch 12: 3 Joash the sons of S the Gibeathite; H9057

SHEMAIAH (39) [SHEMAIAH'S]
1Ki 12:22 word of God came to S the man of God: H9061
1Ch 3:22 of Shekaniah: S and his sons: Hattush, H9061
1Ch 4:37 Jedaiah, the son of Shimri, the son of S. H9061
1Ch 5: 4 S his son, Gog his son H9061
1Ch 9:14 S son of Hasshub, the son of Azrikam, the H9061
1Ch 9:16 Obadiah son of S, the son of Galal, the H9061
1Ch 15: 8 Elizaphan, S the leader and 200 relatives; H9061
1Ch 15:11 Asaiah, Joel, S, Eliel and Amminadab H9061
1Ch 24: 6 The scribe S son of Nethanel, a Levite H9061
1Ch 26: 4 S the firstborn, Jehozabad the second H9061
1Ch 26: 6 Obed-Edom's son S also had sons, who H9061
1Ch 26: 7 The sons of S: Othni, Rephael, Obed and H9061
2Ch 11: 2 of the LORD came to S the man of God: H9062
2Ch 12: 5 Then the prophet S came to Rehoboam H9061
2Ch 12: 7 this word of the LORD came to S: H9061
2Ch 12:15 in the records of S the prophet and of H9061
2Ch 17: 8 them were certain Levites—S, Nethaniah, H9062
2Ch 29:14 descendants of Jeduthun, S and Uzziel. H9061
2Ch 31:15 Jeshua, S, Amariah and Shekaniah H9062
2Ch 35: 9 Also Konaniah along with S and Nethanel, H9062
Ezr 8:13 Eliphelet, Jeuel and S, and with them 60 H9061
Ezr 8:16 Ariel, S, Elnathan, Jarib, H9061
Ezr 10:21 Maaseiah, Elijah, S, Jehiel and Uzziah. H9061
Ezr 10:31 Ishijah, Malkijah, S, Shimeon, H9061
Ne 3:29 Next to him, S son of Shekaniah, the H9061
Ne 6:10 I went to the house of S son of Delaiah, H9061
Ne 10: 8 Maaziah, Bilgai and S. These were the H9061
Ne 11:15 S son of Hasshub, the son of Azrikam, the H9061
Ne 12: 6 S, Joiarib, Jedaiah, H9061
Ne 12:34 Benjamin, S, Jeremiah, H9061
Ne 12:35 Jonathan, the son of S, the son of H9061
Ne 12:36 his associates—S, Azarel, Milalai H9061
Ne 12:42 also Maaseiah, S, Eleazar, Uzzi H9061
Jer 26:20 Now Uriah son of S from Kiriath Jearim H9062
Jer 29:24 Tell S the Nehelamite, H9061
Jer 29:31 the LORD says about S the Nehelamite: H9061
Jer 29:31 Because S has prophesied to you, even H9061
Jer 29:32 I will surely punish S the Nehelamite and H9061
Jer 36:12 Delaiah son of S, Elnathan son of Akbor, H9062

SHEMAIAH'S (1) [SHEMAIAH]
Ne 12:18 of Bilgah's, Shammua; of S, Jehonathan; H9061

SHEMARIAH (4)
1Ch 12: 5 Bealiah, S and Shephatiah the Haruphite H9080
2Ch 11:19 She bore him sons: Jeush, S and Zaham. H9079
Ezr 10:32 Benjamin, Malluk and S. H9079
Ezr 10:41 Shelemiah, S, H9079

SHEMEBER (1)
Ge 14: 2 king of Admah, S king of Zeboyim, and H9008

SHEMED (1)
1Ch 8:12 Misham, S (who built Ono and Lod with H9013

SHEMER (3)
1Ki 16:24 hill of Samaria from S for two talents of H9070
1Ki 16:24 it Samaria, after S, the name of the H9070
1Ch 6:46 of Amzi, the son of Bani, the son of S, H9070

SHEMESH See BETH SHEMESH, EN SHEMESH, IR SHEMESH

SHEMIDA (3) [SHEMIDAITE]
Nu 26:32 through S, the Shemidaite clan; through H9026
Jos 17: 2 Asriel, Shechem, Hepher and S. H9026
1Ch 7:19 The sons of S were: Ahian, Shechem H9026

SHEMIDAITE (1) [SHEMIDA]
Nu 26:32 Shemida, the S clan; through Hepher H9027

SHEMINITH (3)
1Ch 15:21 to play the harps, directing according to s. H9030
Ps 6: T According to s. A psalm of David. H9030
Ps 12: T According to s. A psalm of David. H9030

SHEMIRAMOTH (4)
1Ch 15:18 Zechariah, Jaaziel, S, Jehiel, Unni, Eliab H9035
1Ch 15:20 Zechariah, Jaaziel, S, Jehiel, Unni, Eliab H9035
1Ch 16: 5 then Jaaziel, S, Jehiel, Mattithiah, H9035
2Ch 17: 8 Zebadiah, Asahel, S, Jehonathan H9035

SHEMUEL (1)
Nu 34:20 S son of Ammihud, from the tribe of H9017

SHEN (1)
1Sa 7:12 set it up between Mizpah and S. H9095

SHENAZZAR (1)
1Ch 3:18 Pedaiah, S, Jekamiah, Hoshama H9100

SHEPHAM (2)
Nu 34:10 run a line from Hazar Enan to S. H9172
Nu 34:11 will go down from S to Riblah on the east H9172

SHEPHATIAH (13)
2Sa 3: 4 of Haggith; the fifth, S the son of Abital; H9152
1Ch 3: 3 the fifth, S the son of Abital; and the sixth, H9152
1Ch 9: 8 Meshullam son of S, the son of Reuel H9152
1Ch 12: 5 Bealiah, Shemariah and S the Haruphite; H9153
1Ch 27:16 over the Simeonites: S son of Maakah; H9153
2Ch 21: 2 Zechariah, Azariahu, Michael and S. H9153
Ezr 2: 4 of S 372 H9152
Ezr 2:57 S, Hattil, Pokereth-Hazzebaim and Ami H9152
Ezr 8: 8 of the descendants of S, Zebadiah son of H9152
Ne 7: 9 of S 372 H9152
Ne 7:59 S, Hattil, Pokereth-Hazzebaim and Amon H9152
Ne 11: 4 Amariah, the son of S, the son of H9152
Jer 38: 1 S son of Mattan, Gedaliah son of Pashhur, H9152

SHEPHER (2)
Nu 33:23 left Kehelathah and camped at Mount S. H9184
Nu 33:24 They left Mount S and camped at H9184

SHEPHERD (67) [SHEPHERD'S, SHEPHERDED, SHEPHERDS]
Ge 29: 9 with her father's sheep, for she *was a* s. H8286
Ge 48:15 the God who *has been* my s all my life to H8286
Ge 49:24 because of the S, the Rock of Israel, H8286
Nu 27:17 people will not be like sheep without a s." H8286
1Sa 17:20 David left the flock in the care of a s, H9068
1Sa 21: 7 he was Doeg the Edomite, Saul's chief s. H8286
2Sa 5: 2 said to you, 'You *will* s my people Israel H8286
2Sa 7: 7 I commanded to s my people Israel, H8286
2Sa 24:17 "I have sinned; I, the s, have done wrong. H8286
1Ki 22:17 on the hills like sheep without a s, H8286
1Ch 11: 2 said to you, 'You *will* s my people Israel H8286
1Ch 17: 6 whom I commanded to s my people, H8286
1Ch 21:17 I, the s, have sinned and H8286
2Ch 18:16 on the hills like sheep without a s, H8286
Ps 23: 1 The LORD *is* my s, I lack nothing. H8286
Ps 28: 9 *be* their s and carry them forever. H8286
Ps 49:14 death *will be* their s (but the H8286
Ps 78:71 he brought him to *be* the s of his people H8286
Ps 80: 1 Hear us, S *of* Israel, you who lead Joseph H8286
Ecc 12:11 firmly embedded nails—given by one s. H8286
Isa 13:14 like sheep without a s, they will all return H7695
Isa 40:11 He tends his flock like a s: He gathers the H8286
Isa 44:28 'He is my s and will accomplish all that I H8286
Isa 61: 5 Strangers *will* s your flocks; foreigners will H8286
Isa 63:11 through the sea, with the s *of* his flock? H8286
Jer 17:16 I have not run away from *being* your s H8286
Jer 31:10 them and will watch over his flock like a s. H8286
Jer 43:12 As a s picks his garment clean of lice, so H8286
Jer 49:19 And what s can stand against me? H8286
Jer 50:44 And what s can stand against me? H8286
Jer 51:23 with you I shatter s and flock, with you I H8286
Eze 34: 5 were scattered because *there was* no s, H8286
Eze 34: 8 my flock lacks a s and so has been H8286
Eze 34:12 As a s looks after his scattered flock when H8286
Eze 34:16 I will destroy. *I will* s the flock with justice. H8286
Eze 34:23 I will place over them one s, my servant H8286
Eze 34:23 he will tend them and be their s. H8286
Eze 37:24 over them, and they will all have one s. H8286
Am 3:12 "As a s rescues from the lion's mouth only H8286
Am 7:14 prophet, but I was a s, and I also took H1012
Mic 5: 4 will stand and s *his* **flock** in the strength H8286
Mic 7:14 S your people with your staff, the flock of H8286
Zec 9:16 his people on that day as a s saves his flock. NDT
Zec 10: 2 like sheep oppressed for lack of a s. H8286
Zec 11: 4 "S the flock marked for slaughter. H8286
Zec 11: 9 "*I will* not *be* your s. Let the H8286
Zec 11:15 "Take again the equipment of a foolish s. H8286
Zec 11:16 going to raise up a s over the land who H8286
Zec 11:17 "Woe to the worthless s, who deserts the H8286
Zec 13: 7 against my s, against the man who H8286
Zec 13: 7 "Strike the s, and the sheep will be H8286
Mt 2: 6 come a ruler who *will* s my people Israel. *G4477*
Mt 9:36 helpless, like sheep without a s. *G4478*
Mt 25:32 from another as a s separates the sheep *G4478*
Mt 26:31 " 'I will strike the s, and the sheep of the *G4478*
Mk 6:34 because they were like sheep without a s. *G4478*
Mk 14:27 " 'I will strike the s, and the sheep will be *G4478*
Jn 10: 2 enters by the gate is the s of the sheep. *G4478*
Jn 10:11 "I am the good s. The good shepherd lays *G4478*
Jn 10:11 The good s lays down his life for the *G4478*
Jn 10:12 hand is not the s and does not own the *G4478*
Jn 10:14 "I am the good s; I know my sheep and *G4478*
Jn 10:16 there shall be one flock and one s. *G4478*
Heb 13:20 our Lord Jesus, that great S of the sheep, *G4478*
1Pe 2:25 returned to the S and Overseer of your *G4478*
1Pe 5: 4 And when the **Chief** S appears, you will *G799*
Rev 7:17 at the center of the throne *will be* their s; *G4477*

SHEPHERD'S (3) [SHEPHERD]
Lev 27:32 animal that passes under the s **rod**— H8657
1Sa 17:40 put them in the pouch of his s bag and H8286
Isa 38:12 Like a s tent my house has been pulled H8286

SHEPHERDED (3) [SHEPHERD]
Ps 78:72 And David s them with integrity of heart H8286
Zec 11: 7 So *I* s the flock marked for slaughter H8286
Zec 11: 7 the other Union, and *I* s the flock. H8286

SHEPHERDS (51) [SHEPHERD]
Ge 29: 3 the s would roll the stone away from the NDT
Ge 29: 4 Jacob asked **the** s, "My brothers, where H2157S
Ge 46:32 The men *are* s; they tend livestock H8286+7366
Ge 46:34 all s are detestable to the H8286+7366
Ge 47: 3 "Your servants are s," they replied H8286+7366
Ex 2:17 Some s came along and drove them away H8286
Ex 2:19 "An Egyptian rescued us from the s. H8286
Nu 14:33 Your children will be s here for forty years H8286
1Sa 25: 7 When your s were with us, we did not H8286
2Ki 10:12 toward Samaria. At Beth Eked of the S, H8286
SS 1: 8 your young goats by the tents of the s. H8286

S

Isa 13:20 their tents, there no s will rest their flocks. H8286
Isa 31: 4 a whole band of s is called together H8286
Isa 56:11 They *are* s who lack understanding; they H8286
Jer 3:15 Then I will give you s after my own heart H8286
Jer 6: 3 S with their flocks will come against her H8286
Jer 10:21 The s are senseless and do not inquire of H8286
Jer 12:10 Many s will ruin my vineyard and trample H8286
Jer 22:22 The wind will drive all your s away, and H8286
Jer 23: 1 "Woe to the s who are destroying and H8286
Jer 23: 2 says to the s who tend my people: H8286
Jer 23: 4 I will place s over them who will tend H8286
Jer 25:34 Weep and wail, you s; roll in the dust H8286
Jer 25:35 The s will have nowhere to flee, the H8286
Jer 25:36 Hear the cry of the s, the wailing of the H8286
Jer 33:12 again be pastures for s to rest their flocks. H8286
Jer 50: 6 their s have led them astray and caused H8286
Eze 34: 2 prophesy against the s *of* Israel; prophesy H8286
Eze 34: 2 Woe to you s *of* Israel who only take care H8286
Eze 34: 2 Should not s take care of the flock? H8286
Eze 34: 7 " 'Therefore, you s, hear the word of the H8286
Eze 34: 8 because my s did not search for my H8286
Eze 34: 9 therefore, you s, hear the word of the LORD: H8286
Eze 34:10 I am against the s and will hold them H8286
Eze 34:10 the flock so that the s can no longer feed H8286
Am 1: 1 one of the s of Tekoa—the vision H5924
Am 1: 2 the pastures of the s dry up, and the top H8286
Mic 5: 5 We will raise against them seven s, even H8286
Na 3:18 of Assyria, your s slumber; your nobles H8286
Zep 2: 6 having wells for s and pens for flocks. H8286
Zec 10: 3 "My anger burns against the s, and I will H8286
Zec 11: 3 Listen to the wail of the s; their rich H8286
Zec 11: 5 Their own s do not spare them. H8286
Zec 11: 8 In one month I got rid of the three s. H8286
Lk 2: 8 And there were s living out in the fields *G4478*
Lk 2:15 into heaven, the s said to one another *G4478*
Lk 2:18 were amazed at what the s said to them. *G4478*
Lk 2:20 The s returned, glorifying and praising *G4478*
Ac 20:28 *Be* s of the church of God, which he *G4477*
1Pe 5: 2 *Be* s of God's flock that is under your care *G4477*
Jude 12 qualm—**s who feed** only themselves. *G4477*

SHEPHO (2)
Ge 36:23 Manahath, Ebal, S and Onam. H9143
1Ch 1:40 Manahath, Ebal, S and Onam. The sons H9143

SHEPHUPHAN (1)
1Ch 8: 5 S and Huram. H9146

SHERD, SHERDS (KJV) FRAGMENT, PIECES

SHEREBIAH (8) [SHEREBIAH'S]
Ezr 8:18 they brought us S, a capable man, H9221
Ezr 8:24 namely, S, Hashabiah and ten of their H9221
Ne 8: 7 Levites—Jeshua, Bani, S, Jamin, Akkub H9221
Ne 9: 4 Shebaniah, Bunni, S, Bani and Kenani. H9221
Ne 9: 5 Hashabneiah, S, Hodiah, Shebaniah H9221
Ne 10:12 Zakkur, S, Shebaniah, H9221
Ne 12: 8 Kadmiel, S, Judah, and also H9221
Ne 12:24 were Hashabiah, S, Jeshua son of H9221

SHEREBIAH'S (1) [SHEREBIAH]
Ezr 8:18 son of Israel, and S sons and brothers H2257S

SHERESH (1)
1Ch 7:16 His brother was named S, and his sons H9246

SHERIFFS (KJV) MAGISTRATES

SHESHAI (3)
Nu 13:22 where Ahiman, S, and Talmai, the H9259
Jos 15:14 three Anakites—S, Ahiman and Talmai H9259
Jdg 1:10 defeated S, Ahiman and Talmai H9259

SHESHAK (2)
Jer 25:26 all of them, the king of S will drink it too. H9263
Jer 51:41 "How S will be captured, the boast of the H9263

SHESHAN (4)
1Ch 2:31 who was the father of S. Sheshan was the H9264
1Ch 2:31 S was the father of Ahlai H9264
1Ch 2:34 S had no sons—only daughters. He had H9264
1Ch 2:35 S gave his daughter in marriage to his H9264

SHESHBAZZAR (4)
Ezr 1: 8 counted them out to S the prince of Judah H9256
Ezr 1:11 S brought all these along with the exiles H9256
Ezr 5:14 Cyrus gave them to a man named S, A10746
Ezr 5:16 "So this S came and laid the A10746

SHETH (1)
Nu 24:17 of Moab, the skulls of all the people of S. H9269

SHETHAR (1)
Est 1:14 Karshena, S, Admatha, Tarshish H9285

SHETHAR-BOZENAI (4)
Ezr 5: 3 and S and their associates went to them A10750
Ezr 5: 6 and S and their associates A10750
Ezr 6: 6 and S and you other officials of that A10750
Ezr 6:13 and S and their associates carried it out A10750

SHEVA (2)
2Sa 20:25 S was secretary; Zadok and Abiathar were H8737
1Ch 2:49 of Madmannah and to S the father of H8737

SHEWBREAD (KJV) BREAD OF THE PRESENCE, CONSECRATED BREAD

SHIBAH (1)
Ge 26:33 He called it S, and to this day the name of H8683

SHIBBOLETH (1)
Jdg 12: 6 "All right, say 'S.'" If he said H8672

SHIELD (50) [SHIELDED, SHIELDING, SHIELDS]
Ge 15: 1 I am your s, your very great reward H4482
Ex 40: 3 law in it and s the ark *with* the curtain. H6114
Dt 13: 8 Do not spare them or s them. H4059
Dt 33:29 He is your s and helper and your glorious H4482
Jdg 5: 8 not a s or spear was seen among forty H4482
1Sa 17: 7 His s bearer went ahead of him H7558
1Sa 17:41 Philistine, with his s bearer in front of him H7558
2Sa 1:21 For there the s *of* the mighty was despised H4482
2Sa 1:21 was despised, the s *of* Saul—no longer H4482
2Sa 22: 3 my s and the horn of my salvation. H4482
2Sa 22:36 You make your saving help my s; your H4482
1Ki 10:16 hundred shekels of gold went into each s. H7558
1Ki 10:17 with three minas of gold in each s. H4482
2Ki 19:32 not come before it *with* s or build a siege H4482
1Ch 5:18 men who could handle s and sword, H4482
1Ch 12: 8 able to handle the s and spear. H7558
1Ch 12:24 from Judah, carrying s and spear—6,800 H7558
2Ch 9:15 of hammered gold went into each s. H7558
2Ch 9:16 three hundred shekels of gold in each s. H4482
2Ch 25: 5 able to handle the spear and s. H7558
Job 15:26 against him with a thick, strong s. H4482
Ps 3: 3 But you, LORD, are a s around me, my glory H4482
Ps 5:12 surround them with your favor as with a s. H7558
Ps 7:10 My s is God Most High, who saves the H4482
Ps 18: 2 my s and the horn of my salvation H4482
Ps 18:35 You make your saving help my s, and your H4482
Ps 28: 7 The LORD is my strength and my s; my H4482
Ps 33:20 the LORD; he is our help and our s. H4482
Ps 35: 2 Take up s and armor; arise and come to H4482
Ps 59:11 not kill them, Lord our s, or my people will H4482
Ps 84: 9 Look on our s, O God; look with favor on H4482
Ps 84:11 For the LORD God is a sun and s; the LORD H4482
Ps 89:18 Indeed, our s belongs to the LORD, our H4482
Ps 91: 4 his faithfulness will be your s and rampart. H7558
Ps 115: 9 trust in the LORD—he is their help and s. H4482
Ps 115:10 trust in the LORD—he is their help and s. H4482
Ps 115:11 trust in the LORD—he is their help and s. H4482
Ps 119:114 You are my refuge and my s; I have put H4482
Ps 140: 7 *you* s my head in the day of battle. H6114
Ps 144: 2 my deliverer, my s, in whom I take H4482
Pr 2: 7 he is a s to those whose walk is H4482
Pr 30: 5 he is a s to those who take refuge in him. H4482
Isa 22: 6 charioteers and horses; Kir uncovers the s. H4482
Isa 31: 5 the LORD Almighty *will* s Jerusalem; he H1713
Isa 31: 5 Jerusalem; he *will* s it and deliver it H1713
Isa 37:33 not come before it *with* s or build a siege H4482
Na 2: 5 city wall; the **protective** s is put in place. H6116
Zec 9:15 the LORD Almighty *will* s them. H1713
Zec 12: 8 that day the LORD *will* s those who live in H1713
Eph 6:16 take up the s of faith, with which *G2599*

SHIELDED (3) [SHIELD]
Ex 40:21 shielding curtain and s the ark of the H6114
Dt 32:10 *He* s him and cared for him; he guarded H6015
1Pe 1: 5 who through faith *are* s by God's power *G5864*

SHIELDING (3) [SHIELD]
Ex 39:34 another durable leather and the s curtain; H5009
Ex 40:21 hung the s curtain and shielded H5009
Nu 4: 5 in and take down the s curtain and put it H5009

SHIELDS (48) [SHIELD]
Ex 27:21 the curtain that s the ark of the covenant H6584
Ex 30: 6 of the curtain that s the ark of the H6584
Ex 35:12 atonement cover and the curtain that s it; H5009
Lev 24: 3 Outside the **curtain** *that* s the ark of the AIT
Dt 33:12 secure in him, for *he* s him all day long H2910
2Sa 8: 7 David took the gold s that belonged to H8949
2Sa 22:31 flawless; he s all who take refuge in him. H4482
1Ki 10:16 made two hundred **large** s of hammered H7558
1Ki 10:17 three hundred **small** s of hammered gold, H4482
1Ki 14:26 all the gold s Solomon had made. H4482
1Ki 14:27 made bronze s to replace them and H4482
1Ki 14:28 the guards bore **the** s, and afterward H4392S
2Ki 11:10 the spears and s that had belonged to H8949
1Ch 12:34 with 37,000 men carrying s and spears; H7558
1Ch 18: 7 David took the gold s carried by the H8949
2Ch 9:15 made two hundred **large** s of hammered H7558
2Ch 9:16 three hundred **small** s of hammered gold, H4482
2Ch 11:12 He put s and spears in all the cities, and H7558
2Ch 12: 9 including the gold s Solomon had made. H4482
2Ch 12:10 made bronze s to replace them and H4482
2Ch 12:11 with him, bearing **the** s, and afterward H4392S
2Ch 14: 8 equipped with **large** s and with spears H7558
2Ch 14: 8 armed with **small** s and with bows. H4482
2Ch 17:17 200,000 men armed with bows and s; H4482
2Ch 23: 9 the **large** and small s that had belonged H4482
[2Ch 23: 9 the large and **small** s that had belonged H8949]
2Ch 26:14 Uzziah provided s, spears, helmets, coats H4482
2Ch 32: 5 made large numbers of weapons and s. H4482
2Ch 32:27 s and all kinds of valuables. H4482
Ne 4:16 equipped with spears, s, bows and armor. H4482
Job 41:15 Its back has rows of s tightly sealed H4482
Ps 18:30 flawless; he s all who take refuge in him. H4482
Ps 46: 9 the spear; he burns the s with fire. H6317
Ps 76: 3 flashing arrows, the s and the swords, the H4482
SS 4: 4 on it hang a thousand s, all of them H4482
SS 4: 4 shields, all of them s *of* warriors. H8949
Isa 21: 5 Get up, you officers, oil the s! H4482
Jer 46: 3 "Prepare your s, both **large** and small H7558
[Jer 46: 3 "Prepare your s, both large and **small** H4482]
Jer 46: 9 men of Cush and Put who carry s, men of H4482
Jer 51:11 take up the s! The LORD has stirred H8949
Eze 23:24 with **large** and small s and with helmets. H7558
[Eze 23:24 with large and **small** s and with helmets. H4482]
Eze 26: 8 to your walls and raise his s against you. H7558
Eze 27:10 They hung their s and helmets on your H4482
Eze 27:11 They hung their s around your walls; they H8949
Eze 32:27 their heads and their s resting on their H7558
Eze 38: 4 a great horde with **large** and small s H7558
[Eze 38: 4 a great horde with large and **small** s H4482]
Eze 38: 5 will be with them, all with s and helmets, H4482
Eze 39: 9 them up—the **small** and large s, the bows H4482
[Eze 39: 9 them up—the small and **large** s, the bows H7558]
Na 2: 3 The s *of* the soldiers are red; the warriors H4482

SHIFTING (1) [SHIFTS, SHIFTLESS]
Jas 1:17 who does not change like s shadows. *G5572*

SHIFTLESS (1) [SHIFTING]
Pr 19:15 deep sleep, and the s go hungry. H8244+5883

SHIFTS (1) [SHIFTING]
1Ki 5:14 off to Lebanon in s of ten thousand a H2722

SHIGGAION (1)
Ps 7: T A s of David, which he sang to the LORD H8710

SHIGIONOTH (1)
Hab 3: 1 A prayer of Habakkuk the prophet. On s. H8710

SHIHOR (3) [SHIHOR LIBNATH]
Jos 13: 3 from the S River on the east of Egypt to H8865
1Ch 13: 5 from the S River *in* Egypt to Lebo Hamath H8865
Isa 23: 3 the great waters came the grain of the S; H8865

SHIHOR LIBNATH (1) [SHIHOR]
Jos 19:26 boundary touched Carmel and S. H8866

SHIKKERON (1)
Jos 15:11 turned toward S, passed along to H8914

SHILHI (2)
1Ki 22:42 name was Azubah daughter of S. H8944
2Ch 20:31 name was Azubah daughter of S. H8944

SHILHIM (1)
Jos 15:32 Lebaoth, S, Ain and Rimmon—a total of H8946

SHILLEM (3) [SHILLEMITE]
Ge 46:24 Jahziel, Guni, Jezer and S. H8973
Nu 26:49 through S, the Shillemite clan. H8973
1Ch 7:13 Jezer and S—the descendants of H8973

SHILLEMITE (1) [SHILLEM]
Nu 26:49 Jezerite clan; through Shillem, the S clan. H8980

SHILOAH (1)
Isa 8: 6 flowing waters of S and rejoices over H8942

SHILOH (31) [TAANATH SHILOH]
Jos 18: 1 gathered at S and set up the tent of H8926
Jos 18: 8 lots for you here at S in the presence of H8926
Jos 18: 9 returned to Joshua in the camp at S. H8926
Jos 18:10 cast lots for them in S in the presence of H8926
Jos 19:51 assigned by lot at S in the presence of the H8926
Jos 21: 2 at S in Canaan and said to them, "The H8926
Jos 22: 9 the Israelites at S in Canaan to return to H8926
Jos 22:12 Israel gathered at S to go to war against H8926
Jdg 18:31 all the time the house of God was in S. H8926
Jdg 21:12 took them to the camp at S in Canaan. H8926
Jdg 21:19 is the annual festival of the LORD in S, H8931
Jdg 21:21 the young women of S come out to join in H8870
1Sa 1: 3 sacrifice to the LORD Almighty at S, H8926
1Sa 1: 9 had finished eating and drinking in S, H8926
1Sa 1:24 brought him to the house of the LORD at S. H8931
1Sa 2:14 treated all the Israelites who came to S. H8926
1Sa 3:21 The LORD continued to appear at S, and H8926
1Sa 4: 3 the ark of the LORD's covenant from S, H8926
1Sa 4: 4 So the people sent men to S, and they H8926
1Sa 4:12 line and went to S with his clothes torn H8926
1Sa 14: 3 the son of Eli, the LORD's priest in S. H8931
1Ki 2:27 LORD had spoken at S about the house of H8926
1Ki 11:29 the prophet **of S** met him on the way H8872
1Ki 14: 2 Then go to S. Ahijah the prophet H8926
1Ki 14: 4 he said and went to Ahijah's house in S. H8926
Ps 78:60 He abandoned the tabernacle of S, the H8931
Jer 7:12 now to the place in S where I first made a H8870
Jer 7:14 what I did to S I will now do to the house H8931
Jer 26: 6 make this house like S and this city a H8926
Jer 26: 9 house will be like S and this city will be H8931
Jer 41: 5 came from Shechem, S and Samaria H8926

SHILONITE (4)
1Ki 12:15 son of Nebat through Ahijah the S. H8872
1Ki 15:29 given through his servant Ahijah the S. H8872

2Ch 9:29 of Ahijah the S and in the visions of H8872
2Ch 10:15 son of Nebat through Ahijah the S. H8872

SHILSHAH (1)
1Ch 7:37 Hod, Shamma, S, Ithran and Beera. H8996

SHIMEA (4)
1Ch 2:13 second son was Abinadab, the third S, H9055
1Ch 6:30 S his son, Haggiah his son and Asaiah H9055
1Ch 6:39 Asaph son of Berekiah, the son of S, H9055
1Ch 20: 7 Jonathan son of S, David's brother, H9055

SHIMEAH (4)
2Sa 13: 3 had an adviser named Jonadab son of S, H9056
2Sa 13:32 But Jonadab son of S, David's brother H9056
2Sa 21:21 Jonathan son of S, David's brother, H9056
1Ch 8:32 who was the father of S. They too lived H9009

SHIMEAM (1)
1Ch 9:38 Mikloth was the father of S. They too lived H9010

SHIMEATH (2) [SHIMEATHITES]
2Ki 12:21 Jozabad son of S and Jehozabad son H9064
2Ch 24:26 son of S an Ammonite woman H9064

SHIMEATHITES (1) [SHIMEATH]
1Ch 2:55 the Tirathites, S and Sucathites. These H9065

SHIMEI (44) [SHIMEI'S, SHIMEITES]
Ex 6:17 of Gershon, by clans, were Libni and S. H9059
Nu 3:18 of the Gershonite clans: Libni and S. H9059
2Sa 16: 5 His name was S son of Gera, and he H9059
2Sa 16: 7 As he cursed, S said, "Get out, get out H9059
2Sa 16:13 the road while S was going along the H9059
2Sa 19:16 S son of Gera, the Benjamite from H9059
2Sa 19:18 When S son of Gera crossed the Jordan H9059
2Sa 19:21 "Shouldn't S be put to death for this? H9059
2Sa 19:23 So the king said to S, "You shall not die." H9059
1Ki 1: 8 S and Rei and David's special guard did H9059
1Ki 2: 8 you have with you S son of Gera, the H9059
1Ki 2:36 Then the king sent for S and said to him H9059
1Ki 2:38 S answered the king, "What you say is H9059
1Ki 2:38 And S stayed in Jerusalem for a long time H9059
1Ki 2:39 king of Gath, and S was told, "Your slaves H9059
1Ki 2:40 So S went away and brought the slaves H9059
1Ki 2:41 Solomon was told that S had gone from H9059
1Ki 2:42 the king summoned S and said to him H9059
1Ki 2:44 The king also said to S, "You know in your H9059
1Ki 2:46 went out and struck S down and he died. H2257S
1Ki 4:18 S son of Ela—in Benjamin; H9059
1Ch 3:19 Zerubbabel and S. The sons of H9059
1Ch 4:26 his son, Zakkur his son and S his son. H9059
1Ch 4:27 S had sixteen sons and six daughters, but H9059
1Ch 5: 4 his son, Gog his son, S his son, H9059
1Ch 6:17 of the sons of Gershon: Libni and S. H9059
1Ch 6:29 Libni his son, S his son, Uzzah his H9059
1Ch 6:42 the son of Zimmah, the son of S, H9059
1Ch 8:21 Beraiah and Shimrath were the sons of S. H9059
1Ch 23: 7 to the Gershonites: Ladan and S. H9059
1Ch 23: 9 The sons of S: Shelomoth, Haziel and H9059
1Ch 23:10 And the sons of S: Jahath, Ziza, Jeush H9059
1Ch 23:10 These were the sons of S—four in all. H9059
1Ch 25: 3 Jeshaiah, S, Hashabiah and H9059
1Ch 25:17 the tenth to S, his sons and relatives 12 H9059
1Ch 27:27 S the Ramathite was in charge of the H9059
2Ch 29:14 of Heman, Jehiel and S; from the H9059
2Ch 31:12 and his brother S was next in rank. H9059
2Ch 31:13 assistants of Konaniah and S his brother. H9059
Ezr 10:23 Jozabad, S, Kelaiah (that is, Kelita), H9059
Ezr 10:33 Eliphelet, Jeremai, Manasseh and S. H9059
Ezr 10:38 From the descendants of Binnui: S, H9059
Est 2: 5 son of Jair, the son of S, the son of Kish, H9059
Zec 12:13 their wives, the clan of S and their wives, H9060

SHIMEI'S (1) [SHIMEI]
1Ki 2:39 two of S slaves ran off to Achish H4200+9059

SHIMEITES (1) [SHIMEI]
Nu 3:21 belonged the clans of the Libnites and S; H9060

SHIMEON (1)
Ezr 10:31 Ishijah, Malkijah, Shemaiah, S, H9058

SHIMMERING (1)
Isa 18: 4 like s heat in the sunshine H7456

SHIMON (1)
1Ch 4:20 The sons of S: Amnon, Rinnah H8873

SHIMRATH (1)
1Ch 8:21 Beraiah and S were the sons of Shimei. H9086

SHIMRI (4)
1Ch 4:37 Jedaiah, the son of S, the son of H9078
1Ch 11:45 Jediael son of S, his brother Joha the H9078
1Ch 26:10 S the first (although he was not the H9078
2Ch 29:13 of Elizaphan, S and Jeiel; from the H9078

SHIMRITH (1)
2Ch 24:26 Jehozabad, son of S a Moabite woman. H9083

SHIMRON (5) [SHIMRONITE, SHIMRON MERON]
Ge 46:13 Tola, Puah, Jashub and S. H9075
Nu 26:24 through S, the Shimronite clan. H9075
Jos 11: 1 of Madon, to the kings of S and Akshaph, H9074
Jos 19:15 Kattath, Nahalal, S, Idalah and H9074
1Ch 7: 1 Puah, Jashub and S—four in all. H9075

SHIMRON MERON (1) [SHIMRON]
Jos 12:20 the king of S one H9077

SHIMRONITE (1) [SHIMRON]
Nu 26:24 through Shimron, the S clan. H9084

SHIMSHAI (4)
Ezr 4: 8 officer and S the secretary wrote a A10729
Ezr 4: 9 commanding officer and S the secretary, A10729
Ezr 4:17 S the secretary and the rest of their A10729
Ezr 4:23 read to Rehum and S the secretary and A10729

SHINAB (1)
Ge 14: 2 king of Gomorrah, S king of Admah H9098

SHINAR (4)
Ge 10:10 Akkad and Kalneh, in S. H824+9114
Ge 11: 2 found a plain in S and settled there. H824+9114
Ge 14: 1 At the time when Amraphel was king of S, H9114
Ge 14: 9 Amraphel king of S and Arioch king of H9114

SHINE (36) [SHINES, SHINING, SHINY, SHONE]
Nu 6:25 the LORD **make** his face s on you and be H239
Ne 9:19 of fire by night to s on the way they were to H239
Job 3: 4 not care about it; *may* no light s on it. H3649
Job 9: 7 He speaks to the sun and *it does* not s; he H2436
Job 22:28 be done, and light *will* s on your ways. H5585
Job 33:30 that the light of life *may* s *on* them. H239
Ps 4: 6 **Let** the light of your face s on us. H5951
Ps 31:16 *Let* your face s on your servant; save me in H239
Ps 37: 6 *He will* **make** your righteous reward s like H3655
Ps 67: 1 bless us and **make** his face s on us— H239
Ps 80: 1 enthroned between the cherubim, **s forth** H3649
Ps 80: 3 **make** your face s on us, that we H239
Ps 80: 7 God Almighty; **make** your face s on us, that H239
Ps 80:19 God Almighty; **make** your face s on us, that H239
Ps 94: 1 O God who avenges, **s forth**. H3649
Ps 104:15 oil to **make** their faces s, and bread H7413
Ps 118:27 and *he has* **made** *his* **light** s on us. H239
Ps 119:135 **Make** your face s on your servant and H239
Ps 139:12 dark to you; the night *will* s like the day, for H239
Isa 30:26 The moon *will* s like the sun, and the H2118+240
Isa 60: 1 s, for your light has come, and the H239
Isa 60:19 *will* the brightness of the moon s on H239
Jer 31:35 he who appoints the sun to s by day, who H240
Jer 31:35 decrees the moon and stars to s by night, H240
Da 12: 3 Those who are wise *will* s like the H2301
Joel 2:10 darkened, and the stars **no longer** s. H665+5586
Joel 3:15 darkened, and the stars **no longer** s. H665+5586
Mt 5:16 same way, *let* your light s before others G3290
Mt 13:43 Then the righteous *will* s like the sun in G1719
Lk 1:79 *to* s **on** those living in darkness and in the G2210
2Co 4: 6 who said, "*Let* light s out of darkness," G3290
2Co 4: 6 **made** his light s in our hearts to give us G3290
Eph 5:14 from the dead, and Christ *will* **s on** you." G2213
Php 2:15 Then *you will* s among them like stars in G5743
Rev 18:23 light of a lamp *will* never s in you again. G5743
Rev 21:23 not need the sun or the moon to s on it, G5743

SHINES (6) [SHINE]
Ps 50: 2 From Zion, perfect in beauty, God **s forth**. H3649
Ps 97:11 Light s on the righteous and joy on the H2436
Pr 13: 9 The light of the righteous s **brightly**, but H8523
Isa 62: 1 till her vindication **s out** like the dawn, her H3655
Lk 11:36 of light as when a lamp s its light on you." G5894
Jn 1: 5 The light s in the darkness, and the G5743

SHINING (12) [SHINE]
2Ki 3:22 the morning, the sun *was* s on the water. H2436
Ps 68:13 with silver, its feathers with s gold. H3768
Ps 148: 3 sun and moon; praise him, all you s stars. H240
Pr 4:18 **s ever brighter** till the full H2143+2256+239
Eze 28: 7 wisdom and pierce your **s splendor**. H3650
Eze 32: 8 All the s lights in the heavens I will darken H240
Lk 23:45 *for* the sun **stopped** s. And the curtain of G1722
Ac 10:30 Suddenly a man in s clothes stood before G3287
2Pe 1:19 as to a light s in a dark place, until G5743
1Jn 2: 8 is passing and the true light *is* already s. G5743
Rev 1:16 face was like the sun s in all its brilliance. G5743
Rev 15: 6 s linen and wore golden sashes around G3287

SHINY (3) [SHINE]
Lev 13: 2 a rash or a **s spot** on their skin that may H994
Lev 13: 4 If the **s spot** on the skin is white but does H994
Lev 14:56 for a swelling, a rash or a **s spot**, H994

SHION (1)
Jos 19:19 Hapharaim, S, Anaharath, H8858

SHIP (29) [SHIP'S, SHIPS, SHIPWRIGHTS]
Pr 30:19 the way of a s on the high seas, and H641
Ecc 11: 1 S your grain across the sea; after many H8938
Isa 2:16 every **trading** s and every stately H641+9576
Isa 33:21 will ride them, no mighty s will sail them. H7469
Jnh 1: 3 where he found a s bound for that port. H641
Jnh 1: 4 storm arose that the s threatened to break H641
Jnh 1: 5 threw the cargo into the sea to lighten the s. NDT
Ac 20:13 on ahead to the s and sailed for Assos G4450
Ac 20:38 Then they accompanied him to the s. G4450
Ac 21: 2 We found a s crossing over to Phoenicia G4450
Ac 21: 3 where our s was to unload its cargo. G4450
Ac 21: 6 we went aboard the s, and they returned G4450
Ac 27: 2 We boarded a s from Adramyttium about G4450
Ac 27: 6 found an Alexandrian s sailing for Italy G4450
Ac 27:10 bring great loss *to* s and cargo, G4450
Ac 27:11 of the pilot and *of* the **owner of the s**. G3729
Ac 27:15 The s was caught by the storm and could G4450
Ac 27:17 ropes under the s *itself* to hold it together. G4450
Ac 27:17 sea anchor and let the s be driven along. NDT
Ac 27:22 will be lost; only the s will be destroyed. G4450
Ac 27:30 In an attempt to escape from the s, the G4450
Ac 27:31 "Unless these men stay with the s, you G4450
Ac 27:38 they lightened the s by throwing the grain G4450
Ac 27:39 decided to run the s aground if they could G4450
Ac 27:41 But the s struck a sandbar and ran aground G3730
Ac 27:44 on planks or on other pieces of the s. G4450
Ac 28:11 put out to sea in a s that had wintered in G4450
Ac 28:11 it was an Alexandrian s with the figurehead NDT
Rev 18:17 and all who **travel by s**, the G2093+5536+4434

SHIP'S (1) [SHIP]
Ac 27:19 they threw the s tackle overboard with G4450

SHIPHI (1)
1Ch 4:37 Ziza son of S, the son of Allon, the H9181

SHIPHMITE (1)
1Ch 27:27 Zabdi the S was in charge of the produce H9175

SHIPHRAH (1)
Ex 1:15 whose names were S and Puah, H9186

SHIPHTAN (1)
Nu 34:24 Kemuel son of S, the leader from the tribe H9154

SHIPMASTER (KJV) CAPTAIN

SHIPMEN (KJV) SAILORS

SHIPS (30) [SHIP]
Ge 49:13 by the seashore and become a haven for s; H641
Nu 24:24 S will come from the shores of Cyprus H7469
Dt 28:68 send you back in s to Egypt on a journey H641
Jdg 5:17 why did he linger by the s? Asher remained H641
1Ki 9:26 King Solomon also built s at Ezion Geber H639
1Ki 10:11 Hiram's s brought gold from Ophir; and H639
1Ki 10:22 king had a **fleet of trading** s at sea H639+9576
1Ki 10:22 ships at sea along with the s *of* Hiram. H639
1Ki 22:48 built a **fleet of trading** s to go to H641+9576
2Ch 8:18 And Hiram sent him s commanded by his H641
2Ch 9:21 had a **fleet of trading s** H641+2143+9576
2Ch 20:36 a **fleet of trading s**. H641+4200+2143+9576
2Ch 20:37 The s were wrecked and were not able to H641
Ps 48: 7 destroyed them like s *of* Tarshish shattered H641
Ps 104:26 There the s go to and fro, and Leviathan H641
Ps 107:23 Some went out on the sea in s; they were H641
Pr 31:14 She is like the merchant s, bringing her H641
Isa 23: 1 Wail, you s *of* Tarshish! For Tyre is H641
Isa 23:14 you s *of* Tarshish; your fortress is H641
Isa 43:14 in the s *in which* they took pride. H641
Isa 60: 9 in the lead are the s *of* Tarshish, bringing H641
Eze 27: 9 All the s *of* the sea and their sailors came H641
Eze 27:25 " 'The s *of* Tarshish serve as carriers for H641
Eze 27:29 who handle the oars will abandon their s; H641
Eze 30: 9 go out from me in s to frighten Cush out H7469
Da 11:30 S *of* the western coastlands will oppose H7469
Da 11:40 chariots and cavalry and a great **fleet of s**. H641
Jas 3: 4 Or take s as an example. Although they G4450
Rev 8: 9 and a third *of* the s were destroyed. G4450
Rev 18:19 where all who had s on the sea became G4450

SHIPWRECK (2) [WRECKED]
Eze 27:27 the heart of the sea on the day of your s. H5147
1Ti 1:19 and *so have* **suffered** s with regard G3728

SHIPWRECKED (1) [WRECKED]
2Co 11:25 three times *I was* s, I spent a night G3728

SHIPWRIGHTS (2) [SHIP]
Eze 27: 9 were on board as s to caulk your seams. NDT
Eze 27:27 sailors and s, your merchants and H2616+981

SHIRT (5) [SHIRTS]
Mt 5:40 anyone wants to sue you and take your s, G5945
Mt 10:10 the journey or extra s or sandals or a staff, G5945
Mk 6: 9 Wear sandals but not an extra s. G5945
Lk 6:29 do not withhold your s from them. G5945
Lk 9: 3 no bag, no bread, no money, no extra s. G5945

SHIRTS (1) [SHIRT]
Lk 3:11 "Anyone who has two s should share with G5945

SHISHA (1)
1Ki 4: 3 Ahijah, sons of S—secretaries; H8881

SHISHAK (7)
1Ki 11:40 fled to Egypt, to S the king, and stayed H8882
1Ki 14:25 S king of Egypt attacked Jerusalem. H8882
2Ch 12: 2 S king of Egypt attacked Jerusalem in the H8882
2Ch 12: 5 had assembled in Jerusalem for fear of S, H8882
2Ch 12: 5 therefore, I now abandon you to S.' H8882
2Ch 12: 7 be poured out on Jerusalem through S. H8882
2Ch 12: 9 When S king of Egypt attacked Jerusalem H8882

SHITRAI (1)
1Ch 27:29 S the Sharonite was in charge of the H8855

SHITTAH See BETH SHITTAH

SHITTIM (4) [ABEL SHITTIM]
Nu 25: 1 While Israel was staying in S, the men H8850
Jos 2: 1 son of Nun secretly sent two spies from **S**. H8850
Jos 3: 1 set out from **S** and went to the Jordan, H8850
Mic 6: 5 Remember your journey from **S** to Gilgal H8850

SHIZA (1)
1Ch 11:42 Adina son of S the Reubenite, who was H8862

SHOA (1)
Eze 23:23 the men of Pekod and S and Koa, and all H8778

SHOBAB (4)
2Sa 5:14 Shammua, S, Nathan, Solomon, H8744
1Ch 2:18 were her sons: Jesher, S and Ardon. H8744
1Ch 3: 5 Shammua, S, Nathan and Solomon H8744
1Ch 14: 4 Shammua, S, Nathan, Solomon, H8744

SHOBAI (2)
Ezr 2:42 Talmon, Akkub, Hatita and S 139 H8662
Ne 7:45 Talmon, Akkub, Hatita and S 138 H8662

SHOBAK (2)
2Sa 10:16 with S the commander of Hadadezer's H8747
2Sa 10:18 He also struck down S the commander of H8747

SHOBAL (9)
Ge 36:20 in the region: Lotan, S, Zibeon, Anah, H8748
Ge 36:23 The sons of S: Alvan, Manahath, Ebal H8748
Ge 36:29 the Horite chiefs: Lotan, S, Zibeon, Anah, H8748
1Ch 1:38 S, Zibeon, Anah, Dishon, Ezer and H8748
1Ch 1:40 The sons of S: Alvan, Manahath, Ebal H8748
1Ch 2:50 S the father of Kiriath Jearim, H8748
1Ch 2:52 The descendants of S the father of Kiriath H8748
1Ch 4: 1 Perez, Hezron, Karmi, Hur and S. H8748
1Ch 4: 2 Reaiah son of S was the father of Jahath H8748

SHOBEK (1)
Ne 10:24 Hallohesh, Pilha, S, H8749

SHOBI (1)
2Sa 17:27 S son of Nahash from Rabbah of the H8661

SHOCKED (2) [SHOCKING, SHOCKS]
Ge 34: 7 They *were* s and furious, because H6772
Eze 16:27 who **were** s by your lewd conduct. H4007

SHOCKING (1) [SHOCKED]
Jer 5:30 "A horrible and **s thing** has happened in H9136

SHOCKS (2) [SHOCKED]
Ex 22: 6 so that it burns **s of grain** or standing H1538
Jdg 15: 5 He burned up the s and standing grain H1538

SHOD (KJV) FITTED, SANDALS, WEAR

SHOE, SHOES (KJV) SANDAL, SANDALED, SANDALS, UNSANDALED

SHOHAM (1)
1Ch 24:27 from Jaaziah: Beno, S, Zakkur and Ibri. H8733

SHOMER (3)
2Ki 12:21 son of Shimeath and Jehozabad son of **S**. H9071
1Ch 7:32 **S** and Hotham and of their sister Shua. H9071
1Ch 7:34 The sons of **S**: Ahi, Rohgah, Hubbah and H9071

SHONE (7) [SHINE]
Dt 33: 2 from Seir; *he* **s forth** from Mount Paran. H3649
Job 29: 3 when his lamp s on my head and by his H2145
Mt 17: 2 His face s like the sun, and his clothes G3290
Lk 2: 9 the glory of the Lord **s around** them G4334
Ac 12: 7 Lord appeared and a light s in the cell. G3290
Rev 4: 3 A rainbow that s like an emerald G3970
Rev 21:11 *It* **s with** the glory of God, and its G2400S

SHOOK (18) [SHAKE]
Jdg 5: 4 of Edom, the earth **s**, the heavens poured, H8321
1Sa 4: 5 such a great shout that the ground **s**. H2101
1Sa 14:15 raiding parties—and the ground **s**. H8074
2Sa 22: 8 the foundations of the heavens **s**; they H8074
1Ki 1:40 so that the ground s with the sound. H1324
Ne 5:13 *I* also **s out** the folds of my robe and said H5850
Ps 18: 7 the foundations of the mountains **s** H8074
Ps 68: 8 the earth **s**, the heavens poured down H8321
Isa 6: 4 thresholds **s** and the temple was H5675
Isa 14:16 "Is this the man *who* **s** the earth and H8074
Hab 3: 6 He stood, and **s** the earth; he looked, and H4571
Mt 27:51 top to bottom. The earth **s**, the rocks split G4940
Mt 28: 4 afraid of him *that they* **s** and became like G4940
Mk 1:26 spirit **s** the man **violently** and came out G5057
Ac 13:51 **s** the dust **off** their feet **as a warning** to G1759
Ac 18: 6 *he* **s out** his clothes **in protest** and said to G1759
Ac 28: 5 But Paul **s** the snake **off** into the fire and G701
Heb 12:26 At that time his voice **s** the earth, but now G4888

SHOOT (24) [SHOOTING, SHOOTS, SHOT]
1Sa 20:20 I *will* **s** three arrows *to* the side of it, as H3721
1Sa 20:36 to the boy, "Run and find the arrows I **s**." H3721
2Sa 11:20 you know *they would* **s arrows** from the H3721
2Ki 13:17 he opened it. "**S**!" Elisha said, and H3721
2Ki 19:32 will not enter this city or **s** an arrow here. H3721
1Ch 12: 2 were able to **s** arrows or to H928+2021+8008
2Ch 26:15 so that *soldiers could* **s** arrows and hurl H3721
Job 41:19 stream from its mouth; sparks of fire **s out**. H4880
Ps 11: 2 the strings to **s** from the shadows at H3721
Ps 64: 4 They **s** from ambush *at* the innocent; they H3721
Ps 64: 4 at the innocent; *they* **s** suddenly, without H3721
Ps 64: 7 But God *will* **s** them with his arrows; they H3721
Ps 144: 6 the enemy; **s** your arrows and rout them. H8938
Isa 11: 1 A **s** will come up from the stump of Jesse H2643
Isa 37:33 will not enter this city or **s** an arrow here. H3721
Isa 53: 2 He grew up before him like a **tender s** H3437
Isa 60:21 They are the **s** I have planted, the work of H5916
Jer 9: 3 *They* **make ready** their tongue like a bow, **to s** H2005
Jer 50:14 you who draw the bow. **S** at her! Spare no H3343
Eze 5:16 When I **s** at you with my deadly and H8938
Eze 5:16 arrows of famine, *I will* **s** to destroy you. H8938
Eze 17: 4 broke off its topmost **s** and carried it away H3566
Eze 17:22 will take a **s** from the very top *of* a cedar H7550
Ro 11:17 though a **wild olive s**, have been G66

SHOOTING (2) [SHOOT]
1Sa 20:20 side of it, as though I *were* **s** at a target. H8938
Pr 26:18 Like a maniac **s** flaming arrows of death H3721

SHOOTS (12) [SHOOT]
2Ki 19:26 in the field, like **tender** green **s**, like grass H3764
Job 8:16 sunshine, spreading its **s** over the garden; H3438
Job 14: 7 sprout again, and its **new s** will not fail. H3438
Job 14: 9 it will bud and put forth **s** like a plant. H7908
Job 15:30 a flame will wither his **s**, and the breath H3438
Ps 80:11 as far as the Sea, its **s** as far as the River. H3438
Ps 128: 3 will be like olive **s** around your table. H9277
Isa 16: 8 Their **s** spread out and went as far as the H8943
Isa 18: 5 he will cut off the **s** with pruning knives H2360
Isa 37:27 in the field, like **tender** green **s**, like grass H3764
Eze 17:22 from its topmost **s** and plant it on a high H3438
Hos 14: 6 his **young s** will grow. His splendor will be H3438

SHOPHAK (2)
1Ch 19:16 with **S** the commander of Hadadezer's H8791
1Ch 19:18 He also killed **S** the commander of their H8791

SHOPHAN See ATROTH SHOPHAN

SHORE (17) [ASHORE, SHORES]
Ex 14:30 the Egyptians lying dead on the **s**. H8557+3542
1Ki 9:26 Elath in Edom, on the **s** *of* the Red Sea. H8557
Eze 27:29 all the sailors will stand on the **s**. H824
Eze 47:10 Fishermen will stand along **the s**; from En H22578
Mt 13: 2 while all the people stood on the **s**. G129
Mt 13:48 the fishermen pulled it up on the **s**. G129
Mk 4: 1 were along the **s** at the water's edge. G1178
Lk 5: 3 asked him to put out a little from **s**. G1178
Lk 5:11 So they pulled their boats up on **s**, left G1178
Jn 6: 1 Jesus crossed **to the far s** of the Sea of G4305
Jn 6:21 the boat reached the **s** where they were G1178
Jn 6:22 had stayed **on the opposite s** of the lake G4305
Jn 21: 4 Jesus stood on the **s**, but the disciples did G129
Jn 21: 8 they were not far from **s**, about a G1178
Ac 27:13 anchor and sailed **along the s** of Crete. G839
Ac 28: 1 Once safely on **s**, we found out that the NDT
Rev 13: 1 The dragon stood on the **s** of the sea. G302

SHORELANDS (1) [LAND]
Eze 27:28 The **s** will quake when your sailors cry out. H4494

SHORES (4) [SHORE]
Nu 24:24 Ships will come from the **s** *of* Cyprus; they H3338
Est 10: 1 the empire, to its **distant s**. H362+3542
Ps 72:10 of Tarshish and of **distant s** bring tribute to H362
Ps 97: 1 the earth be glad; let the distant **s** rejoice. H362

SHORN (1) [SHEAR]
SS 4: 2 Your teeth are like a flock of **sheep just s** H7892

SHORT (33) [SHORTENED, SHORTER, SHORTLY]
Nu 11:23 answered Moses, "*Is* the LORD's arm **too s**? H7918
Ru 2: 7 till now, except for a **s** rest in the shelter." H5071
1Sa 2:31 is coming when *I will* **cut s** your strength H1548
1Sa 21:15 Am I *so* **s** *of* madmen that you have to H2894
2Sa 16: 1 David had gone a **s distance** beyond the H5071
2Sa 19:36 the Jordan with the king for a **s distance**, H5071
Job 17: 1 my days **are cut s**, the grave H2403
Ps 58: 7 they draw the bow, *let* their arrows **fall s**. H4908
Ps 89:45 *You have* **cut s** the days of his youth; you H7918
Ps 102:23 he broke my strength; *he* **cut s** my days. H7918
Pr 10:27 but the years of the wicked *are* **cut s**. H7918
Isa 28:20 The bed *is* too **s** to stretch out on, the H7918
Isa 29:17 **In a very s time**, will not H6388+5071+4663
Isa 50: 2 *Was* my arm too **s** to deliver you H7918+7918
Isa 59: 1 the arm of the LORD *is* not too **s** to save, H7918
Mic 6:10 wicked house, and the **s** ephah, which is H8137
Mt 13:21 they have no root, they last only a **s time**. G4672
Mt 24:22 "If those days *had* not *been* **cut s**, no one G3143
Mk 4:17 they have no root, they last only a **s time**. G4672
Mk 13:20 "If the Lord *had* not **cut s** those days, no G3143
Lk 19: 3 he was **s** he could not G3836+2461+3625
Jn 7:33 "I am with you for only a **s** time, and then G3625
Jn 11: 8 "**a s while ago** the Jews there tried to G3814
Ac 26:28 think that in *such a* **s** *time* you can G3900
Ac 26:29 Paul replied, "**S** *time* or long—I pray to G3900
Ac 27:28 A **s** *time* later they took soundings again G1099
Ro 3:23 all have sinned and **fall s** of the glory of G5728
1Co 7:29 brothers and sisters, is that the time is **s**. G5366
1Th 2:17 by being separated from you for a **s** time G6052
Heb 4: 1 of you be found *to have* **fallen s** of it. G5728
Heb 12:15 See to it *that* no one **falls s** of the grace of G5728
Rev 12:12 because he knows that his time is **s**." G3900
Rev 20: 3 After that, he must be set free for a **s** time. G3625

SHORTCOMINGS (1)
Ge 41: 9 Pharaoh, "Today I am reminded of my **s**. H2628

SHORTENED (2) [SHORT]
Mt 24:22 the sake of the elect those days *will be* **s**. G3143
Mk 13:20 whom he has chosen, *he has* **s** them. G3143

SHORTER (1) [SHORT]
Ex 13:17 the Philistine country, though that was **s**. H7940

SHORTLY (3) [SHORT]
Mt 14:25 **S before dawn** Jesus G5480+5871+3836+3816
Mk 6:48 **S before dawn** he went out G4309+5480+5871+3836+3816
Mk 11: 3 Lord needs it and will send it back here **s**. G2317

SHOT (9) [SHOOT]
Ge 49:23 attacked him; *they* **s** *at* him with hostility. H8046
Ex 19:13 are to be stoned or **s with arrows**; H3721+3721
1Sa 20:36 As the boy ran, he **s** an arrow beyond him. H3721
2Sa 11:24 Then the archers **s arrows** at your servants H3721
2Sa 22:15 *He* **s** his arrows and scattered the enemy H8938
2Ki 9:24 drew his bow and **s** Joram between the H5782
2Ki 13:17 Elisha said, and *he* **s**. "The LORD's arrow H3721
2Ch 35:23 Archers **s** King Josiah, and he told his H3721
Ps 18:14 *He* **s** his arrows and scattered the enemy H8938

SHOULD (363) [SHOULDN'T]
Ge 20: 9 done things to me that *s* never **be done**." AIT
Ge 27:45 Why *s I* **lose** both of you in one day? AIT
Ge 29:15 of mine, *s you* **work for** me for nothing? AIT
Ge 29:15 Tell me what your wages **s be**." NDT
Ge 34: 7 daughter—a *thing that s* not **be done**. AIT
Ge 34:31 "*S he have* **treated** our sister like a prostitute?" AIT
Ge 38:18 "What pledge *s I* **give** you?" "Your seal AIT
Ge 41:35 *They s* **collect** all the food of these good years AIT
Ge 41:36 This food *s* **be** held in reserve for the country AIT
Ge 46:34 *you s* **answer**, 'Your servants have tended AIT
Ge 47:15 Why *s we* **die** before your eyes AIT
Ge 47:19 Why *s we* **perish** before your eyes—we and AIT
Ex 3:11 "Who am I that *I s* **go** to Pharaoh and bring AIT
Ex 5: 2 the LORD, that *I s* **obey** him and let Israel go? AIT
Ex 16: 7 that *you s* **grumble** against us?" AIT
Ex 32:11 "why *s* your anger **burn** against your people AIT
Ex 32:12 Why *s* the Egyptians **say**, 'It was with evil AIT
Lev 10:18 *you s have* **eaten** the goat in the sanctuary AIT
Lev 24:12 the will of the LORD *s be* **made clear** to them. AIT
Lev 27:10 if *they s* **substitute** one animal for another AIT
Nu 9: 7 why *s we* **be kept from** presenting the AIT
Nu 10:31 You know where we *s* **camp** in the wilderness AIT
Nu 13:30 "*We s* **go up** and take possession H6590+6590
Nu 14: 4 "*We s* **choose** a leader and go back to Egypt." AIT
Nu 15:34 it was not clear what *s* **be done** to him. AIT
Nu 16:11 is Aaron that *you s* **grumble** against him?" AIT
Nu 16:40 descendant of Aaron *s* **come** to burn incense AIT
Nu 20: 4 that we and our livestock *s* **die** here? AIT
Nu 23:19 is not human, that *he s* **lie**, not a human AIT
Nu 23:19 a human being, that *he s* **change** *his* **mind**. AIT
Nu 27: 4 Why *s* our father's name **disappear** from his AIT
Nu 32: 6 "*S* your fellow Israelites **go** to war while you AIT
Dt 1:33 to camp and to show you the way *you s* **go**. AIT
Dt 5:25 why *s we* **die**? This great fire will AIT
Dt 16:16 No *one s* **appear** before the LORD AIT
Dt 20:19 the trees people, that you *s* **besiege** them? AIT
Dt 28:68 on a journey I said you *s* never **make again**. AIT
Jdg 8: 6 Why *s we* **give** bread to your troops? AIT
Jdg 8:15 Why *s we* **give** bread to your exhausted men AIT
Jdg 9: 9 tree answered, '*S I* **give up** my oil, by which AIT
Jdg 9:11 fig tree replied, '*S I* **give up** my fruit, so good AIT
Jdg 9:13 vine answered, '*S I* **give up** my wine, which AIT
Jdg 9:28 why *s* we Shechemites *be* **subject to** him? AIT
Jdg 9:28 Why *s* we **serve** Abimelek? AIT
Jdg 9:32 you and your men *s* **come** and lie in wait in AIT
Jdg 9:38 is Abimelek that *we s be* **subject to** him? AIT
Jdg 11:34 *who s* **come out** to meet him but his AIT
Jdg 14:16 he replied, "so *why s I* **explain** it to you?" AIT
Jdg 20:38 ambush that they *s* **send up** a great cloud of AIT
Jdg 21: 3 Why *s* one tribe *be* **missing** from Israel today? AIT
Ru 4: 4 *I s* **bring** the matter **to** your **attention** and AIT
1Sa 6: 2 Tell us how *we s* **send** it **back** to its place." AIT
1Sa 6: 4 "What guilt offering *s we* **send** to him?" AIT
1Sa 9:13 Go up now; *you s* **find** him about this time." AIT
1Sa 12:23 be it from me that I *s* **sin** against the LORD by AIT
1Sa 14:45 said to Saul, "*S* Jonathan **die**—he who has AIT
1Sa 15:29 a human being, that *he s* **change** *his* **mind**." AIT
1Sa 17:26 Philistine that *he s* **defy** the armies of the AIT
1Sa 18:18 that *I s* **become** the king's son-in-law?" AIT
1Sa 19:17 'Let me get away. Why *s I* **kill** you?'" AIT
1Sa 20:32 "Why *s he* **be put to death**? What has he AIT
1Sa 24: 6 LORD forbid that *I s* **do** such a thing to my AIT
1Sa 25:11 Why *s I* **take** my bread and water, and the AIT
1Sa 26:11 LORD forbid that I *s* **lay** a hand on the LORD's AIT
1Sa 27: 5 Why *s* your servant **live** in the royal city with AIT

2Sa 2:22 Why *s I* **strike** you down? How AIT
2Sa 3:33 "*S* Abner *have* **died** as the lawless die AIT
2Sa 4:11 *s I* not now **demand** his blood from your hand AIT
2Sa 9: 8 that *you s* **notice** a dead dog like me?" AIT
2Sa 12:23 now that he is dead, why *s I go on* **fasting**? AIT
2Sa 13:12 Such a thing *s* not **be done** in Israel AIT
2Sa 13:25 "All of us *s* not **go**; we would only be a AIT
2Sa 13:26 king asked him, "Why *s he* **go** with you?" AIT
2Sa 13:32 "My lord *s* not **think** that they killed all the AIT
2Sa 13:33 the king *s* not *be* **concerned about** the report AIT
2Sa 15:19 the Gittite, "Why *s* you **come** along with us? AIT
2Sa 16: 9 "Why *s* this dead dog **curse** my lord the king? AIT
2Sa 16:19 Furthermore, whom *s I* **serve**? Should I not AIT
2Sa 16:19 whom should I serve? **S** I not serve the son NDT
2Sa 16:20 "Give us your advice. What *s we* **do**?" AIT
2Sa 17: 6 given this advice. *S we* **do** what he says? If AIT
2Sa 17: 9 If *he s* **attack** your troops first, whoever hears AIT
2Sa 19:11 'Why *s you* **be** the last to bring the king back AIT
2Sa 19:12 So why *s you* **be** the last to bring back the AIT
2Sa 19:22 *S* anyone **be put to death** in Israel today AIT
2Sa 19:34 that *I s* **go up** *to* Jerusalem with the king? AIT
2Sa 19:35 Why *s* your servant **be** an added burden to AIT
2Sa 19:36 why *s* the king **reward** me *in* this way? AIT
2Sa 24:13 decide how *I s* **answer** the one who sent AIT
1Ki 1:27 servants know who *s* **sit** on the throne of my AIT
1Ki 12: 9 How *s we* **answer** these people who say to AIT
1Ki 20:11 puts on his armor *s* not **boast** like one who AIT
1Ki 20:42 set free a man I had **determined s die**. H3051
1Ki 21: 3 LORD forbid that I *s* **give** you the inheritance AIT
1Ki 22: 8 "The king *s* not **say** such a thing, AIT
2Ki 6:33 Why *s I* **wait** for the LORD any longer? AIT
2Ki 7: 2 *even if* the LORD *s* **open** the floodgates of the AIT
2Ki 7:19 *even if* the LORD *s* **open** the floodgates of the AIT
2Ki 13:19 "You *s have* **struck** the ground five or six AIT
1Ch 11:19 "God forbid that I *s* **do** this!" he said. "Should AIT
1Ch 11:19 "*S I* **drink** the blood of these men who went AIT
1Ch 12:32 the times and knew what Israel *s* **do**— AIT
1Ch 21: 3 Why *s he* **bring** guilt on Israel?" AIT
1Ch 21:12 decide how *I s* **answer** the one who sent me." AIT
1Ch 22: 5 the LORD *s be* of **great** magnificence and AIT
1Ch 29:14 that *we s be* **able** to give as generously as AIT
2Ch 10: 9 How *s we* **answer** these people who say to AIT
2Ch 18: 7 "The king *s* not **say** such a thing, AIT
2Ch 19: 2 "*S you* **help** the wicked and love those who AIT
2Ch 24: 9 Jerusalem that they *s* **bring** to the LORD the AIT
2Ch 32: 4 "Why *s* the kings of Assyria **come** and find AIT
Ezr 4:12 The king *s* **know** that the people who came AIT
Ezr 4:13 the king *s* **know** that if this city is built and its AIT
Ezr 5: 8 The king *s* **know** that we went to the district AIT
Ezr 7:23 Why *s* his wrath **fall** on the realm of the king AIT
Ne 2: 3 Why *s* my face not **look sad** when the city AIT
Ne 6: 3 Why *s* the work **stop** while I leave it and go AIT
Ne 6:11 "*S* a man like me **run away**? Or should AIT
Ne 6:11 Or *s* someone like me **go** into the temple to AIT
Ne 7:65 food until there **s** be a priest ministering NDT
Ne 8:15 that *they s* **proclaim** this word and spread AIT
Ne 13: 1 Moabite *s* ever **be admitted** into the AIT
Est 1:22 that every man *s* **be** ruler over his own AIT
Est 6: 6 "What *s be* **done** for the man the king AIT
Est 9:25 against the Jews *s* **come back** onto his own AIT
Est 9:25 that he and his sons *s be* **impaled** on poles. AIT
Est 9:27 who join them *s* without **fail** observe these AIT
Est 9:28 These days *s* **be remembered** and observed AIT
Est 9:28 days of Purim *s* never **fail** to be celebrated AIT
Est 9:28 nor *s* the memory of **these days** die out AIT
Job 4: 6 **S** not your piety be your confidence and your NDT
Job 6:11 do I have, that *I s still* **hope**? What prospects, AIT
Job 6:11 What prospects, that I *s be* **patient**? AIT
Job 9:29 already found guilty, why *s I* **struggle** in vain? AIT
Job 19:29 *you s* **fear** the sword yourselves; for wrath will AIT
Job 21: 4 to a human being? Why *s* I not *be* **impatient**? AIT
Job 21:15 Almighty, that *we s* **serve** him? What would AIT
Job 32: 7 I thought, 'Age *s* **speak**; advanced years AIT
Job 32: 7 advanced years *s* **teach** wisdom. AIT
Job 33: 7 No fear of me *s* **alarm** you, nor should my AIT
Job 33: 7 alarm you, nor *s* my hand *be* **heavy** on you. AIT
Job 34:23 that they *s* **come** before him for judgment. AIT
Job 34:33 *S* God then **reward** you on your terms, when AIT
Job 37:19 "Tell us what *we s* **say** to him; we cannot AIT
Job 37:20 *S he* **be told** that I want to speak? Would AIT
Job 40:23 though the Jordan *s* **surge** against its mouth. AIT
Ps 25:12 will instruct them in the ways they **s** choose. NDT
Ps 32: 8 you and teach you in the way *you s* **go**; AIT
Ps 49: 5 Why *s I* **fear** when evil days come, when AIT
Ps 49: 9 so that *they s* **live** on forever and not see AIT
Ps 79:10 Why *s* the nations **say**, "Where is their God?" AIT
Ps 143: 8 Show me the way *I s* **go**, for to you I entrust AIT
Pr 5:16 *S* your springs **overflow** in the streets, your AIT
Pr 17:16 Why **s** fools have money in hand to buy NDT
Pr 22: 6 Start children off on the **way** they *s go*, and AIT
Ecc 5: 6 Why *s* God *be* **angry** at what you say and AIT
Ecc 7: 2 of everyone; the living *s* **take** this to heart. AIT
SS 1: 7 Why *s I* **be** like a veiled woman beside the AIT
Isa 1: 5 Why *s you* **be beaten** anymore? Why do you AIT
Isa 8:19 *s* not a people **inquire of** their God? AIT
Isa 48:17 you, who directs you in the way *you s* **go**. AIT
Isa 53: 2 in his appearance that *we s* **desire** him. AIT
Isa 57: 6 grain offerings. In view of all this, *s I* **relent**? AIT
Jer 3: 1 another man, *s he* **return** to her again? AIT
Jer 5: 7 "Why *s I* **forgive** you? Your children have AIT
Jer 5: 9 *S I* not **punish** them for this?" declares the AIT
Jer 5: 9 "*S I* not **avenge** myself on such a nation as AIT
Jer 5:22 *S you* not **fear** me?" declares the LORD AIT
Jer 5:22 "*S you* not **tremble** in my presence AIT
Jer 5:29 *S I* not **punish** them for this?" declares the AIT
Jer 5:29 "*S I* not **avenge** myself on such a nation as AIT
Jer 9: 9 *S I* not **punish** them for this?" declares the AIT
Jer 9: 9 "*S I* not **avenge** myself on such a nation as AIT
Jer 10: 7 Who *s* not **fear** you, King of the nations? This AIT
Jer 13:12 Every wineskin *s* **be filled** *with* wine.' And if AIT
Jer 13:12 that every wineskin *s* **be filled** *with* wine? AIT
Jer 18:20 *S* good **be repaid** with evil? Yet they have AIT
Jer 26:11 "This man **s** be sentenced to death because NDT
Jer 26:16 "This man **s** not be sentenced to death! NDT
Jer 27:17 Why *s* this city **become** a ruin? AIT
Jer 29:26 *you s* **put** any maniac who acts like a prophet AIT
Jer 32:35 that they *s* **do** such a detestable thing and so AIT
Jer 38: 4 said to the king, "This man *s* **be put to death**. AIT
Jer 40:15 Why *s he* **take** your life and cause all the AIT
Jer 42: 3 tell us where *we s* **go** and what we should AIT
Jer 42: 3 us where we should go and what *we s* **do**." AIT
Jer 45: 5 *S* you then **seek** great things for yourself? Do AIT
Jer 49:12 cup must drink it, why *s* you **go unpunished**? AIT
La 2:20 *S* women **eat** their offspring, the children AIT
La 2:20 *S* priest and prophet **be killed** in the AIT
La 3:39 Why *s* the living **complain** when punished AIT
Eze 13:19 those who *s* not *have* **died** and have spared AIT
Eze 13:19 died and have spared those who *s* not **live**. AIT
Eze 14: 3 *S I* **let** them **inquire of** *me* **at all**? AIT
Eze 33:25 shed blood, *s you* then **possess** the land? AIT
Eze 33:26 wife. *S you* then **possess** the land?' AIT
Eze 34: 2 *S* not shepherds **take care of** the flock? AIT
Da 1:10 Why *s he* **see** you looking worse than the AIT
Da 6: 7 that the king *s* **issue** an edict and enforce AIT
Hos 1: 6 love to Israel, that *I s* **at all forgive** them. AIT
Joel 2:17 Why *s they* **say** among the peoples, 'Where AIT
Ob 12 *You s* not **gloat over** your brother in the day AIT
Ob 13 *You s* not **march** through the gates of my AIT
Ob 14 *You s* not **wait** at the crossroads to cut down AIT
Jnh 1:11 "What *s we* **do** to you to make the sea calm AIT
Jnh 4:11 And *s* I not **have concern** for the great city of AIT
Mic 2: 7 of Jacob, *s it* **be said**, "Does the LORD AIT
Mic 3: 1 rulers of Israel. *S* you not **embrace** justice, AIT
Zec 7: 3 "*S I* **mourn** and fast in the fifth month AIT
Mal 1:13 sacrifices, *s I* **accept** them from your hands?" AIT
Mal 2:16 "does violence to the one he **s** protect," NDT
Mt 6: 9 is how you *s* **pray**: " 'Our Father in AIT
Mt 11: 3 is to come, or *s we* **expect** someone else?" AIT
Mt 18:14 willing that any of these little ones *s* **perish**. AIT
Mt 18:34 be tortured, until *he s* **pay back** all he owed. AIT
Mt 19:12 The one who can accept this *s* **accept** it." AIT
Mt 23:23 *You* **s have** practiced the latter, without G1256
Mt 25:27 you **s have** put my money on deposit with G1256
Mk 6:12 went out and preached that *people s* **repent**. AIT
Mk 12:15 *S we* **pay** or shouldn't we?" But Jesus knew AIT
Lk 1:43 that the mother of my Lord *s* **come** to me? AIT
Lk 2: 1 decree that a **census** *s* **be taken** of the entire AIT
Lk 3:10 "What *s we* **do** then?" the crowd asked. AIT
Lk 3:11 has two shirts *s* **share with** the one who has AIT
Lk 3:11 anyone who has food *s* **do** the same. AIT
Lk 3:12 "Teacher," they asked, "what *s we* **do**?" AIT
Lk 3:14 soldiers asked him, "And what *s* we **do**?" AIT
Lk 7:19 is to come, or *s we* **expect** someone else?" AIT
Lk 7:20 is to come, or *s we* **expect** someone else? AIT
Lk 11:42 *You* **s have** practiced the latter without G1256
Lk 12: 5 I will show you whom *you s* **fear**: Fear him AIT
Lk 12:12 will teach you at that time what *you s* say." G1256
Lk 13: 7 Cut it down! Why *s it* **use up** the soil?' AIT
Lk 13:16 Then **s** not this woman, a daughter of G1256
Lk 17:10 you were told to do, *s* **say**, 'We are unworthy AIT
Lk 17:31 possessions inside, *s* **go down** to get them. AIT
Lk 17:31 no one in the field *s* **go back** *for anything*. AIT
Lk 18: 1 them that they **s** always pray and not G1256
Lk 22:26 greatest among you *s* **be like** the youngest, AIT
Lk 22:49 said, "Lord, *s we* **strike** with our swords?" AIT
Jn 3: 7 *You s* not *be* **surprised** at my saying, 'You AIT
Jn 11:57 out where Jesus was *s* **report** it so that they AIT
Jn 12: 7 was intended that *she s* **save** this perfume AIT
Jn 12:46 one who believes in me *s* **stay** in darkness. AIT
Jn 13:14 you also **s** wash one another's feet. G4053
Jn 13:15 an example that you *s* **do** as I have done AIT
Ac 4:28 will had decided beforehand *s* **happen**. AIT
Ac 10:28 shown me that *I s* not **call** anyone impure AIT
Ac 15:19 *that we s* not **make it difficult** for the Gentiles AIT
Ac 15:20 Instead *we s* **write** to them, telling them to AIT
Ac 17:26 *that they s* **inhabit** the whole earth AIT
Ac 17:29 *we* **s** not think that the divine being is like G4053
Ac 21:25 our decision *that* they *s* **abstain** from food AIT
Ac 24:20 Or these who are here *s* **state** what crime they AIT
Ac 26: 8 Why *s* any of you **consider** it incredible that AIT
Ac 26:20 I preached *that they s* **repent** and turn to God AIT
Ac 27:12 the majority decided *that we s* **sail** on AIT
Ac 27:21 *you* **s have** taken my advice not to sail G1256
Ro 2:22 who say *that people s* not **commit adultery**, AIT
Ro 6: 6 *that* we *s* no longer **be slaves** to sin— AIT
Ro 11:35 ever given to God, that God *s* **repay them**?" AIT
Ro 14: 5 Each of them *s* **be fully convinced** in their AIT
Ro 15: 2 Each of us *s* **please** our neighbors for their AIT
1Co 3:10 But each one *s* **build** with care. AIT
1Co 3:18 of this age, *you s* **become** "fools" so that you AIT
1Co 7: 2 man *s* **have sexual relations with** his own AIT
1Co 7: 3 The husband *s* **fulfill** his marital duty to his AIT
1Co 7: 9 themselves, *they s* **marry**, for it is better AIT
1Co 7:17 each person *s* **live** as a believer in whatever AIT
1Co 7:18 *He s* not *become* **uncircumcised**. Was a AIT
1Co 7:18 he was called? *He s* not *be* **circumcised**. AIT
1Co 7:20 Each person *s* **remain** in the situation they AIT
1Co 7:24 *s* **remain** in the situation they were in when AIT
1Co 7:29 those who have wives *s* **live** as if they do not; AIT
1Co 7:36 feels he ought to marry, *he s* **do** as he wants. AIT
1Co 7:36 He is not sinning. *They s get* **married**. AIT
1Co 9:10 plows and threshes **s** be able to do so in G4053
1Co 9:14 *that* those who preach the gospel
s **receive** *their* **living** AIT
1Co 10: 8 *We s* not **commit sexual immorality**, as some AIT
1Co 10: 9 *We s* not **test** Christ, as some of them did AIT
1Co 10:24 No one *s* **seek** their own good, but the good AIT
1Co 11: 6 her head shaved, then *she s* **cover** her head. AIT
1Co 11:33 you gather to eat, *you s* all eat **together**. AIT
1Co 11:34 who is hungry *s* **eat** something at home, AIT
1Co 12:15 Now if the foot *s* **say**, "Because I am not a AIT
1Co 12:16 And if the ear *s* **say**, "Because I am not an AIT
1Co 12:25 so that *there s* **be** no division in the body, but AIT
1Co 12:25 but *that* its parts *s* **have** equal **concern** for AIT
1Co 14:13 who speaks in a tongue *s* **pray** that they may AIT
1Co 14:27 at the most three—**s** speak, one at a time NDT
1Co 14:28 the speaker *s keep* **quiet** in the church and AIT
1Co 14:29 Two or three prophets *s* **speak**, and the AIT
1Co 14:29 the others *s* **weigh carefully** what is said. AIT
1Co 14:30 who is sitting down, the first **speaker** *s* **stop**. AIT
1Co 14:34 Women *s remain* **silent** in the churches. AIT
1Co 14:35 *they s* **ask** their own husbands at home AIT
1Co 14:40 But everything *s be* **done** in a fitting and AIT
1Co 16: 2 each one of you *s* **set aside** a sum of money AIT
1Co 16:11 *s* **treat** him **with contempt**. Send him AIT
2Co 2: 3 by those who **s have** made me rejoice. G1256
2Co 5:15 those who live *s* no longer **live** for AIT
2Co 9: 3 about you in this matter *s* not **prove hollow**, AIT
2Co 9: 7 Each of you **s** give what you have decided in NDT
2Co 10: 7 they *s* **consider** again that we belong to AIT
2Co 10:11 Such people *s* **realize** that what we are in our AIT
2Co 12: 6 Even if *I s* **choose** to boast, I would not be a AIT
2Co 12:14 children **s** not **have** to save up for their G4053
Gal 1: 8 from heaven *s* **preach a gospel** other than AIT
Gal 2: 9 They agreed that we **s** go to the Gentiles NDT
Gal 2:10 was that *we s continue to* **remember** the poor AIT
Gal 6: 1 live by the Spirit *s* **restore** that person gently. AIT
Gal 6: 4 Each one *s* **test** their own actions. Then they AIT
Gal 6: 5 each one *s* **carry** their own load. AIT
Gal 6: 6 in the word *s* **share** all good things with AIT
Eph 3:10 wisdom of God *s be* **made known** to the AIT
Eph 5: 4 Nor **s** there be obscenity, foolish talk or NDT
Eph 5:24 so also wives **s** submit to their husbands in NDT
Eph 6:20 that I may declare it fearlessly, as I **s**. G1256
Php 2:10 that at the name of Jesus every knee *s* **bow** AIT
Php 2:18 So you too *s be* **glad** and rejoice with me. AIT
Php 3:15 who are mature *s* **take** such a **view of things**. AIT
Col 4: 4 Pray that I may proclaim it clearly, as I **s**. G1256
1Th 4: 3 It is God's will that you **s** be sanctified: that NDT
1Th 4: 3 *that* you *s* **avoid** sexual immorality; AIT
1Th 4: 4 *that* each of you *s* **learn** to control your own AIT
1Th 4: 6 this matter no *one s* **wrong** or take advantage AIT
1Th 4:11 *You s* **mind** your own **business** and work with AIT
1Th 5: 4 so that this day *s* **surprise** you like a thief. AIT
1Ti 2:11 A woman *s* **learn** in quietness and full AIT
1Ti 5: 4 *these s* **learn** first of all to put their religion AIT
1Ti 5:16 *she s continue to* **help** them and not let the AIT
1Ti 6: 1 the yoke of slavery *s* **consider** their masters AIT
1Ti 6: 2 masters *s* not **show** them **disrespect** just AIT
1Ti 6: 2 *they s* **serve** them even better because their AIT
2Ti 2: 6 hardworking farmer **s be** the first to G1256
2Ti 4:15 You too *s be* on *your* **guard** against him AIT
Titus 2:15 are the things *you s* **teach**. Encourage and AIT
Heb 2:10 *s* **make** the pioneer of their salvation **perfect** AIT
Heb 12: 9 How much more *s we* **submit** to the Father of AIT
Heb 13: 4 Marriage **s** be honored by all, and the NDT
Jas 1: 5 you lacks wisdom, *you s* **ask** God, who gives AIT
Jas 1: 7 That person *s* not **expect** to receive anything AIT
Jas 1:10 But the rich **s** take pride in their humiliation NDT
Jas 1:13 tempted, no one *s* **say**, "God is tempting AIT
Jas 1:19 Everyone *s* **be** quick to listen, slow to speak AIT
Jas 3: 1 Not many *of you s* **become** teachers, my AIT
Jas 3:10 My brothers and sisters, this **s** not be. G5973
Jas 5:19 if one of you *s* **wander** from the truth and AIT
Jas 5:19 truth and someone *s bring* that person **back**, AIT
1Pe 2:15 doing good *you s* **silence** the ignorant **talk** of AIT
1Pe 2:21 an example, that *you s* **follow** in his steps. AIT
1Pe 3: 3 Your beauty *s* not **come** from outward AIT
1Pe 3: 4 it **s** be that of your inner self, the NDT
1Pe 3:14 But even if *you s* **suffer** for what is right, you AIT
1Pe 4:10 *s* **use** whatever gift you have received **to serve** AIT
1Pe 4:11 they **s** do so as one who speaks the very NDT
1Pe 4:11 they **s** do so with the strength God provides NDT
1Pe 4:15 it **s** not be as a murderer or thief or any NDT
1Pe 4:19 to God's will *s* **commit** themselves to their AIT
1Jn 3: 1 that *we s be* **called** children of God! AIT
1Jn 3:11 from the beginning: *We s* **love** one another. AIT
1Jn 5:16 *you s* **pray** and God will give them life. AIT
1Jn 5:16 I am not saying that *you s* **pray** about that. AIT

SHOULDER (25) [SHOULDERS]

Ge 24:15 Rebekah came out with her jar on her **s**. H8900
Ge 24:45 Rebekah came out, with her jar on her **s**. H8900
Ge 24:46 quickly lowered her jar from her **s** and said, NDT
Ge 49:15 he will bend his **s** to the burden and H8900
Ex 28: 7 It is to have two **s pieces** attached to two H4190

S

Ex 28:12 them on the **s pieces** *of* the ephod as H4190
Ex 28:25 them to the **s pieces** *of* the ephod at the H4190
Ex 28:27 the bottom of the **s pieces** on the front of H4190
Ex 39: 4 They made **s pieces** for the ephod, which H4190
Ex 39: 7 them on the **s pieces** *of* the ephod as H4190
Ex 39:18 them to the **s pieces** *of* the ephod at the H4190
Ex 39:20 the bottom of the **s pieces** on the front of H4190
Nu 6:19 place in their hands a boiled **s** of the ram, H2432
Dt 18: 3 the **s**, the internal organs and the meat H2432
Jos 4: 5 Each of you is to take up a stone on his **s** H8900
Job 31:22 then let my arm fall from the **s**, let it be H8900
Job 31:36 Surely I would wear it on my **s**, I would H8900
Isa 22:22 I will place on his **s** the key to the house of H8900
Eze 12: 6 Put them on your **s** as they are watching H4190
Eze 12:12 put his things on his **s** at dusk and leave, H4190
Eze 24: 4 all the choice pieces—the leg and the **s**. H4190
Eze 29:18 was rubbed bare and every **s** made raw. H4190
Eze 34:21 Because you shove with flank and **s** H4190
Zep 3: 9 LORD and serve him **s to shoulder**. H8900+285
Zep 3: 9 LORD and serve him **shoulder to s**. H8900+285

SHOULDERS (23) [SHOULDER]

Ge 9:23 took a garment and laid it across their **s**; H8900
Ge 21:14 He set them on her **s** and then sent her H8900
Ex 12:34 carried it on their **s** in kneading troughs H8900
Ex 28:12 the names on his **s** as a memorial before H4190
Nu 7: 9 were to carry on their **s** the holy things, H4190
Dt 33:12 one the LORD loves rests between his **s**." H4190
Jdg 9:48 some branches, which he lifted to his **s**. H8900
Jdg 16: 3 lifted them to his **s** and carried them to H4190
2Ki 6:31 son of Shaphat remains on his **s** today!" NDT
2Ki 9:24 his bow and shot Joram between the **s**. H2432
1Ch 15:15 the ark of God with the poles on their **s**, H4190
2Ch 35: 3 It is not to be carried about on your **s** H4190
Ne 3: 5 would not put their **s** to the work under H7418
Ps 81: 6 "I removed the burden from their **s**; their H8900
Isa 9: 4 the bar across their **s**, the rod of their H8900
Isa 9: 6 the government will be on his **s**. H8900
Isa 10:27 day their burden will be lifted from your **s**, H8900
Isa 14:25 his burden removed from their **s**. H8900
Isa 46: 7 They lift it to their **s** and carry it; they set it H4190
Eze 12: 7 carrying them on my **s** while they watched. H4190
Eze 29: 7 you splintered and you tore open their **s** H4190
Mt 23: 4 loads and put them on other people's **s**, *G6049*
Lk 15: 5 he finds it, he joyfully puts it on his **s** *G6049*

SHOULDN'T (6) [NOT, SHOULD]

2Sa 19:21 "**S** Shimei be put to death for this? H4202
Ne 5: 9 **S** you walk in the fear of our God to avoid H4202
Mt 18:33 **S** you have had mercy on your *G4024+1256*
Mk 12:15 Should we pay or **s** we?" But Jesus knew *G3590*
1Co 5: 2 **S** you rather have gone into mourning *G4049*
1Co 9:12 from you, **s** we have it all the more? *G4024*

SHOUT (64) [SHOUTED, SHOUTING, SHOUTS]

Nu 23:21 the **s** *of* the King is among them. H9558
Jos 6: 5 *have* the whole army **give a** loud **s** H8131+9558
Jos 6:10 not say a word until the day I tell you *to* **s**. H8131
Jos 6:10 until the day I tell you to shout. Then **s**!" H8131
Jos 6:16 Joshua commanded the army, "**S**! H8131
Jos 6:20 when the men **gave a** loud **s**, the H8131+9558
Jdg 7:18 from all around the camp blow yours and **s**, H606
1Sa 4: 5 Israel **raised** such a great **s** that the H8131+9558
1Sa 17:52 surged forward with a **s** and pursued the H8131
1Ki 1:34 Blow the trumpet and **s**, 'Long live King H606
1Ki 18:27 to taunt them. "**S** louder!" H7924+928+7754
Ezr 3:11 the people **gave a** great **s** of praise H8131+9558
Job 3: 7 be barren; may no **s of joy** be heard in it. H8265
Job 3:18 they no longer hear the slave driver's **s**. H7754
Job 33:26 they will see God's face and **s for joy**; he H9558
Job 39: 7 in the town; it does not hear a driver's **s**. H9583
Job 39:25 the **s** *of* commanders and the battle cry. H8308
Ps 20: 5 *May we* **s for joy** over your victory and lift H8264
Ps 33: 3 a new song; play skillfully, and **s for joy**. H9558
Ps 35:27 *May* those who delight in my vindication **s for joy** H8264
Ps 47: 1 all you nations; **s** to God with cries of joy. H8131
Ps 60: 8 my sandal; over Philistia *I* **s in triumph**." H8131
Ps 65:13 with grain; *they* **s for joy** and sing. H8131
Ps 66: 1 **S for joy** to God, all the earth! H8131
Ps 71:23 My lips *will* **s for joy** when I sing praise to H8264
Ps 81: 1 our strength; **s aloud** to the God of Jacob! H8131
Ps 95: 1 *let us* **s aloud** to the Rock of our salvation. H8131
Ps 98: 4 **S for joy** to the LORD, all the earth, burst H8131
Ps 98: 6 the ram's horn—**s for joy** before the LORD H8131
Ps 100: 1 **S for joy** to the LORD, all the earth. H8131
Ps 108: 9 my sandal; over Philistia *I* **s in triumph**." H8131
Pr 29: 6 the righteous **s for joy** and are glad. H8264
Isa 12: 6 **S aloud** and sing for joy, people of Zion H7412
Isa 13: 2 a bare hilltop, **s** to them; beckon to H8123+7754
Isa 24:14 their voices, *they* **s for joy**; from the west H8264
Isa 26:19 dwell in the dust wake up and **s for joy**— H8264
Isa 35: 2 it will rejoice greatly and **s for joy**. H8264
Isa 35: 6 like a deer, and the mute tongue **s for joy**. H8264
Isa 40: 9 lift up your voice with a **s**, lift it up, H3946
Isa 42: 2 *He will* not **s** or cry out, or raise his voice H7590
Isa 42:11 *let them* **s** from the mountaintops. H7423
Isa 42:13 *with a* **s** he will raise the battle cry and H8131
Isa 44:23 done this; **s aloud**, *you* earth beneath. H8131
Isa 49:13 **S for joy**, *you* heavens; rejoice, you earth H8264
Isa 52: 8 lift up their voices; together *they* **s for joy**. H8264
Isa 54: 1 **s for joy**, *you* who were never in labor H7412
Isa 58: 1 "**S** it **aloud**, do not hold back H7924+928+1744
Jer 25:30 *He will* **s** like those who tread the grapes H2116
Jer 25:30 **s** against all who live on the earth. H6699
Jer 31: 7 **s** for the foremost of the nations. H7412
Jer 31:12 will come and **s for joy** on the heights of H8264
Jer 49:29 *People will* **s** to them, 'Terror on every H7924
Jer 50:15 **S** against her on every side! She H8131
Jer 51:14 and *they will* **s in triumph** over you. H6702+2116
Jer 51:39 so that *they* **s with laughter**—then sleep H6600
Jer 51:48 that is in them *will* **s for joy** over Babylon, H8264
La 2: 7 they have raised a **s** in the house of the H7754
Eze 8:18 Although *they* **s** in my ears, H7924+7754+1524
Zep 3:14 Daughter Zion; **s aloud**, Israel! Be glad H8131
Zec 2:10 "**S** and be glad, Daughter Zion. For I am H8264
Zec 9: 9 Daughter Zion! **S**, Daughter Jerusalem H8131
Mk 10:47 Jesus of Nazareth, he began *to* **s**, "Jesus, *G3189*
Gal 4:27 bore a child; **s for joy** and cry aloud, you *G4838*
Rev 10: 3 and *he* **gave a** loud **s** like the roar *G3189+5889*

SHOUTED (54) [SHOUT]

Ge 41:43 and *people* **s** before him, "Make way H7924
Lev 9:24 *they* **s for joy** and fell facedown. H8264
Jos 6:20 sounded, the army **s**, and at the sound of H8131
Jdg 7:20 they were to blow, *they* **s**, "A sword for the H7924
Jdg 9: 7 Gerizim and **s** to them, H5951+7754+2256+7924
Jdg 16:25 in high spirits, *they* **s**, "Bring out Samson to H606
Jdg 18:23 As *they* **s** after them, the Danites turned H7924
Jdg 19:22 *they* **s** to the old man who owned the H606
1Sa 10:24 Then the people **s**, "Long live the king!" H8131
1Sa 14:12 men of the outpost **s** *to* Jonathan and his H6699
1Sa 17: 8 Goliath stood and **s** to the ranks of Israel H7924
1Sa 17:23 from his lines and **s** his usual defiance, H1819
1Sa 20:38 he **s**, "Hurry! Go quickly! Don't stop!" H7924
2Sa 20: 1 He sounded the trumpet and **s**, "We have H606
1Ki 1:39 sounded the trumpet and all the people **s**, H606
1Ki 18:26 they **s**. But there was no H606
1Ki 18:28 So *they* **s** louder and slashed H7924+928+7754
2Ki 7:11 The gatekeepers **s the news**, and it was H7924
2Ki 9:13 Then they blew the trumpet and **s**, "Jehu is H606
2Ki 11:12 the people clapped their hands and **s** H606
2Ch 23:11 They anointed him and **s**, "Long live the H606
2Ch 23:13 Then Athaliah tore her robes and **s** H606
Ezr 3:12 many others **s** for joy. H8123+7754+928+9558
Job 30: 5 **s** at as if they were thieves. H8131
Job 38: 7 sang together and all the angels **s for joy**? H8131
Isa 21: 8 And the lookout **s**, "Day after day, my lord, H7924
Da 3:26 opening of the blazing furnace and **s**, A10558
Mt 8:29 *they* **s**. "Have you come *G3189*
Mt 20:30 that Jesus was going by, *they* **s**, "Lord, *G3189*
Mt 20:31 be quiet, but they **s** all the louder, "Lord *G3189*
Mt 21: 9 ahead of him and those that followed **s**, *G3189*
Mt 27:23 But they **s** all the louder *G3189*
Mk 5: 7 *He* **s** at the top of his voice, "What do you *G3189*
Mk 10:48 to be quiet, but *he* **s** all the more, "Son *G3189*
Mk 11: 9 went ahead and those who followed **s**, *G3189*
Mk 15:13 "Crucify him!" they **s**. *G3189*
Mk 15:14 But they **s** all the louder *G3189*
Lk 18:39 to be quiet, but *he* **s** all the more, "Son *G3189*
Lk 23:18 But the whole crowd **s**, "Away with this *G371*
Jn 18:40 *They* **s** back, "No, not him! Give us *G3198*
Jn 19: 6 their officials saw him, *they* **s**, "Crucify! *G3198*
Jn 19:15 But they **s**, "Take him away! Take him *G3198*
Ac 12:22 They **s**, "This is the voice of a god, not of a *G2215*
Ac 14:11 *they* **s** in the Lycaonian *G2048+3836+5889*
Ac 16:28 But Paul **s**, "Don't harm *G5888+3489+5889*
Ac 19:33 to the front, and *they* **s instructions** to him. *G5204*
Ac 19:34 *they* all **s** in unison for about two hours: *G3189*
Ac 21:34 Some in the crowd **s** one thing and some *G2215*
Ac 22:22 Then they raised their voices and **s**, "Rid *G3306*
Ac 24:21 it was this one thing *I* **s** as I stood in their *G3189*
Ac 26:24 your mind, Paul!" *he* **s**. *G3489+3836+5889+5774*
Rev 10: 3 When *he* **s**, the voices of the seven *G3189*
Rev 18: 2 With a mighty voice *he* **s**: " 'Fallen! Fallen *G3189*
Rev 19: 3 And again *they* **s**: "Hallelujah! The smoke *G3306*

SHOUTING (26) [SHOUT]

Ex 32:17 Joshua heard the noise of the people **s**, H8275
Nu 16:34 around them fled, **s**, "The earth is going to H606
Jdg 15:14 the Philistines came toward him **s**. H8131
1Sa 4: 6 "What's all this **s** in the Hebrew H7754+9558
1Sa 17:20 out to its battle positions, **s** the war cry. H8131
2Ki 9:27 Jehu chased him, **s**, "Kill him too!" They H606
2Ch 15:14 with **s** and with trumpets and horns. H9558
Isa 16:10 the presses, for I have put an end to the **s**. H2116
Mt 21:15 the children **s** in the temple courts *G3189*
Lk 4:41 out of many people, **s**, "You are the Son *G3189*
Lk 8:28 fell at his feet, **s** at the top of his voice *G3306*
Lk 23:21 they *kept* **s**, "Crucify him! Crucify him!" *G2215*
Jn 12:13 went out to meet him, **s**, "Hosanna!" *G3198*
Jn 19:12 the Jewish leaders *kept* **s**, "If you let *G3198*
Ac 14:14 clothes and rushed out into the crowd, **s**: *G3189*
Ac 16:17 the rest of us, **s**, "These men are *G3189*
Ac 17: 6 other believers before the city officials, **s**: *G1066*
Ac 19:28 heard this, they were furious and *began* **s**: *G3189*
Ac 19:32 Some *were* **s** one thing, some *G3189*
Ac 21:28 **s**, "Fellow Israelites, help us! This is the *G3189*
Ac 21:36 The crowd that followed *kept* **s**, "Get rid of *G3189*
Ac 22:23 *As they were* **s** and throwing off their *G3198*
Ac 22:24 find out why *the people were* **s** at him like *G2215*
Ac 25:24 **s** that he ought not to live any longer. *G1066*
Rev 19: 1 the roar of a great multitude in heaven **s**: *G3306*
Rev 19: 6 waters and like loud peals of thunder, **s**: *G3306*

SHOUTS (23) [SHOUT]

2Sa 6:15 the ark of the LORD with **s** and the sound of H9558
1Ch 15:28 the ark of the covenant of the LORD with **s**, H9558
Ezr 3:13 the sound of the **s** *of* joy from the sound H9558
Job 8:21 with laughter and your lips with **s of joy**. H9558
Ps 27: 6 his sacred tent I will sacrifice with **s of joy**; H9558
Ps 42: 4 Mighty One with **s of joy** and praise H7754+8262
Ps 47: 5 God has ascended amid **s of joy**, the LORD H9558
Ps 105:43 rejoicing, his chosen ones with **s of joy**; H8262
Ps 118:15 **S of joy** and victory resound in the tents of H8262
Pr 11:10 when the wicked perish, there are **s of joy**. H8262
Ecc 9:17 be heeded than the **s** *of* a ruler of fools. H2411
Isa 16: 9 The **s of joy** over your ripened fruit and H2116
Isa 16:10 no one sings or **s** in the vineyards; no one H8131
Isa 31: 4 frightened by their **s** or disturbed by their H7754
Isa 48:20 this with **s of joy** and proclaim it. H7754+8262
Jer 48:33 presses; no one treads them with **s of joy**. H2116
Jer 48:33 Although there are **s**, they are not shouts H2116
Jer 48:33 there are shouts, they are not **s of joy**. H2116
Jnh 2: 9 with **s** *of* grateful praise, will H7754
Zep 1:14 the Mighty Warrior **s** *his* **battle cry**. H7658
Zec 4: 7 out the capstone to **s** *of* 'God bless it! H9583
Lk 23:23 But *with* loud **s** they insistently demanded *G5889*
Lk 23:23 that he be crucified, and their **s** prevailed. *G5889*

SHOVE (1) [SHOVES]

Eze 34:21 Because *you* **s** with flank and shoulder H2074

SHOVEL (1) [SHOVELS]

Isa 30:24 mash, spread out with fork and **s**. H4665

SHOVELS (9) [SHOVEL]

Ex 27: 3 the ashes, and its **s**, sprinkling bowls, H3582
Ex 38: 3 of bronze—its pots, **s**, sprinkling bowls H3582
Nu 4:14 meat forks, **s** and sprinkling bowls. H3582
1Ki 7:40 made the pots and **s** and sprinkling bowls H3582
1Ki 7:45 the pots, **s** and sprinkling bowls. All these H3582
2Ki 25:14 also took away the pots, **s**, wick trimmers, H3582
2Ch 4:11 made the pots and **s** and sprinkling bowls H3582
2Ch 4:16 the pots, **s**, meat forks and all related H3582
Jer 52:18 also took away the pots, **s**, wick trimmers, H3582

SHOVES (1) [SHOVE]

Nu 35:20 If *anyone* with malice aforethought **s** H2074

SHOW (193) [SHOWED, SHOWING, SHOWN, SHOWS]

Ge 12: 1 father's household to the land *I will* **s** you. H8011
Ge 20:13 'This is how *you can* **s** your love to me: H6913
Ge 21:23 **S** to me and the country where you now H6913
Ge 22: 2 a burnt offering on a mountain *I will* **s** you." H606
Ge 24:12 **s** kindness to my master Abraham. H6913
Ge 24:49 Now if you will **s** kindness and faithfulness H6913
Ge 40:14 remember me and **s** me kindness H6913
Ge 47:29 promise that *you will* **s** me kindness and H6913
Ex 9:16 that *I might* **s** you my power and that my H8011
Ex 18:20 **s** them the way they are to live and H3359
Ex 23: 3 and *do* not **s favoritism** *to* a poor person in H2075
Ex 25: 9 exactly like the pattern I *will* **s** you. H8011
Ex 33:18 Then Moses said, "Now **s** me your glory." H8011
Lev 19:15 *do* not **s partiality** *to* the poor or H5951+7156
Lev 19:32 **s respect** for the elderly and revere your H2075
Nu 16: 5 morning the LORD *will* **s** who belongs to H3359
Dt 1:17 *Do* not **s partiality** in judging; hear H5795+7156
Dt 1:33 you to camp and to **s** you the way you H8011
Dt 3:24 you have begun to **s** *to* your servant your H8011
Dt 4: 6 this will **s** your wisdom and H6524
Dt 7: 2 no treaty with them, and **s** them no **mercy**. H2858
Dt 13: 8 **S** them no **pity**. Do not H2571+6524
Dt 13:17 his fierce anger, *will* **s** you mercy, and will H5989
Dt 15: 9 that you *do* not **s ill will** toward the H8317+6524
Dt 16:19 Do not pervert justice or **s partiality** H5795+7156
Dt 19:13 **S** no **pity**. You must purge from H6524+2571
Dt 19:21 **S** no **pity**: life for life, eye for eye H6524+2571
Dt 25:12 cut off her hand. **S** her no **pity**. H2571+6524
Jos 2:12 by the LORD that you *will* **s** kindness to my H6913
Jdg 1:24 "**S** us how to get into the city and we will H8011
Jdg 4:22 "*I will* **s** you the man you're looking for." H8011
Jdg 8:35 *They* also failed *to* **s** any loyalty to the H6913
Jdg 13:21 LORD did not **s himself** again to Manoah H8011
Ru 1: 8 *May* the LORD **s** you kindness, as you have H6913
1Sa 16: 3 the sacrifice, and I *will* **s** you what to do. H3359
1Sa 20: 8 As for *you*, **s** kindness to your servant, for H6913
1Sa 20:14 But **s** me unfailing kindness like the LORD's H6913
2Sa 2: 6 *May* the LORD now **s** you kindness and H6913
2Sa 2: 6 I too *will* **s** you the same favor H6913
2Sa 9: 1 of Saul to whom *I can* **s** kindness for H6913
2Sa 9: 3 of Saul to whom *I can* **s** God's kindness?" H6913
2Sa 9: 7 "for *I will* **surely s** you kindness for H6913+6913
2Sa 10: 2 "*I will* **s** kindness to Hanun son of Nahash, H6913
2Sa 15:20 May the LORD **s** you kindness and H6913
2Sa 16:17 "So this is the love you **s** your friend? H907
2Sa 22:26 "To the faithful *you* **s yourself faithful**, to H2874
2Sa 22:26 to the blameless *you* **s yourself blameless**, H9462
2Sa 22:27 to the pure *you* **s yourself pure**, but to the H1405
2Sa 22:27 to the devious *you* **s yourself shrewd**. H7349
1Ki 2: 7 "But **s** kindness to the sons of Barzillai of H6913
1Ki 8:50 cause their captors *to* **s** them **mercy**; H8163
2Ki 20:13 kingdom that Hezekiah *did* not **s** them. H8011
2Ki 20:15 among my treasures that *I did* not **s** them." H8011
1Ch 19: 2 "*I will* **s** kindness to Hanun son of Nahash, H6913
Ezr 2:59 they could not **s** that their families H5583
Ne 7:61 they could not **s** that their families H5583

Ne 13:22 and s **mercy** to me according to your great H2571
Est 4: 8 to s *to* Esther and explain it to her H8011
Job 6:24 be quiet; s me where I have been wrong. H1067
Job 13: 8 *Will you* s him **partiality**? Will you H5951+7156
Job 13:23 **S** me my offense and my sin. H3359
Job 24:21 and *to* the widow *they* s no **kindness**. H3512
Job 32:21 *I will* s no **partiality**, nor will I flatter H5951+7156
Job 36: 2 a little longer and *I will* s you that there is H2555
Job 37:13 or to water his earth and s his love. NDT
Ps 17: 7 **S** me *the* **wonders** *of* your great love, you H7098
Ps 18:25 To the faithful *you* s **yourself faithful**, to H2874
Ps 18:25 to the blameless *you* s **yourself blameless**, H9462
Ps 18:26 to the pure *you* s **yourself pure**, but to the H1405
Ps 18:26 to the devious *you* s **yourself shrewd**. H7349
Ps 25: 4 **S** me your ways, LORD, teach me your H3359
Ps 39: 4 "**S** me, LORD, my life's end and the H3359
Ps 50:23 and *to* the blameless *I will* s my salvation." H8011
Ps 59: 5 the nations; s no **mercy** *to* wicked traitors. H2858
Ps 68:28 God; s us *your* **strength**, our God H6451
Ps 77: 7 *Will* he never s his **favor** again? H8354
Ps 82: 2 unjust and s **partiality** *to* the wicked H5951+7156
Ps 85: 7 **S** us your unfailing love, LORD, and grant H8011
Ps 86:16 s your strength in behalf of your servant H5989
Ps 88:10 *Do you* s your wonders to the dead? Do H6913
Ps 91:16 I will satisfy him and s him my salvation." H8011
Ps 102:13 it is time to s **favor** *to* her; the H2858
Ps 106: 4 when you s favor to your people, come NDT
Ps 106:46 all who held them captive to *s* them mercy. AIT
Ps 143: 8 **S** me the way I should go, for to you I H3359
Pr 6:34 and *he will* s no **mercy** when he takes H2798
Pr 12:16 Fools s their annoyance at once, but the H3359
Pr 24:23 *To* s **partiality** in judging is not H5795+7156
Pr 28:21 *To* s **partiality** is not good—yet a H5795+7156
Ecc 10: 3 they lack sense and s everyone how stupid H606
SS 2:14 the mountainside, s me your face, let me H8011
Isa 13:10 their constellations *will* not s their light. H2145
Isa 19:12 *Let them* s you and make known what the H5583
Isa 30:18 he will rise up to s you **compassion**. H8163
Isa 39: 2 kingdom that Hezekiah *did* not s them. H8011
Isa 39: 4 among my treasures that *I did* not s them." H8011
Isa 60:10 in favor *I will* s you **compassion**. H8163
Jer 6:23 spear; they are cruel and s no **mercy**. H8163
Jer 16: 5 do not go to mourn or s **sympathy** H5653
Jer 16:13 day and night, for *I will* s you no favor. H5989
Jer 18:17 *I will* s them my back and not my face in H8011
Jer 21: 7 *he will* s them no **mercy** or pity or H2571
Jer 32:18 You s love to thousands but bring the H6913
Jer 42:12 *I will* s you compassion so that he will H5989
La 3:32 *he will* s **compassion**, so great is H8163
Eze 36:23 *I will* s *the* **holiness** *of* my great name H7727
Eze 38:23 And so *I will* s *my* **greatness** and my H1540
Eze 40: 4 to everything I *am going to* s you, H8011
Eze 44:23 and s them **how to distinguish** between H3359
Da 1: 9 the official to s favor and H4200+7156
Da 11:30 He will return and s **favor** to those who H1067
Da 11:37 *He will* s no **regard** for the gods of his H1067
Hos 1: 6 for *I will* no longer s **love** *to* Israel, that I H8163
Hos 1: 7 Yet *I will* s **love** *to* Judah; and I will save H8163
Hos 2: 4 *I will* not s *my* **love** *to* her children H8163
Hos 2:23 *I will* s *my* **love** to the one I called 'Not my H8163
Hos 3: 1 s *your* **love** *to* your wife again, though H170
Joel 2:30 *I will* s wonders in the heavens and on H5989
Mic 7:15 out of Egypt, *I will* s them my wonders." H8011
Mic 7:18 not stay angry forever but delight to s mercy. NDT
Mic 7:20 *You will be* faithful to Jacob, and s love to H5989
Na 3: 5 *I will* s the nations your nakedness and H8011
Zec 1: 9 me answered, "*I will* s you what they are." H8011
Zec 7: 9 s mercy and compassion to one another. H6913
Mal 1: 6 you priests *who* s **contempt** *for* my name. H1022
Mt 6:16 their faces to s others they are fasting. *G5743*
Mt 8: 4 s yourself to the priest and offer the gift *G1259*
Mt 16: 1 him by asking him *to* s them a sign from *G2109*
Mt 21:32 For John came to you **to** s you the way of *G1877*
Mt 22:19 **S** me the coin used for paying the tax." *G2109*
Mk 1:44 s yourself to the priest and offer the *G1259*
Mk 12:40 widows' houses and *for a* s make lengthy *G4733*
Mk 14:15 He *will* s you a large room upstairs *G1259*
Lk 1:72 *to* s mercy to our ancestors and to *G4472*
Lk 5:14 s yourself to the priest and offer the *G1259*
Lk 6:47 practice, *I will* s you what they are like. *G5683*
Lk 12: 5 But *I will* s you whom you should fear: *G5683*
Lk 17:14 he said, "Go, s yourselves to the priests." *G2109*
Lk 18: 1 a parable **to** s them **that** they *G4639+3836*
Lk 20:21 and that *you do* not s **partiality** but *G3284+4725*
Lk 20:24 "**S** me a denarius. Whose image and *G1259*
Lk 20:47 widows' houses and *for a* s make lengthy *G4733*
Lk 22:12 He *will* s you a large room upstairs, all *G1259*
Jn 2:18 *can you* s us **to prove** *your* **authority** to *G1259*
Jn 5:20 and *he will* s him even greater works than *G1259*
Jn 7: 4 these things, s yourself to the world." *G5746*
Jn 12:33 He said this *to* s the kind of death he was *G4955*
Jn 14: 8 s us the Father and that will be enough *G1259*
Jn 14: 9 How can you say, '**S** us the Father'? *G1259*
Jn 14:21 I too will love them and s myself to them." *G1872*
Jn 14:22 why do you intend to s yourself to us and *G1872*
Ac 1:24 **S** us which of these two you have chosen *G344*
Ac 2:19 *I will* s wonders in the heavens above *G1443*
Ac 7: 3 God said, 'and go to the land *I will* s you. *G1259*
Ac 9:16 *I will* s him how much he must suffer for *G5683*
Ac 10:34 it is that God *does* not s **favoritism** *G1639+4720*
Ro 2: 4 Or *do you* s **contempt** for the riches of his *G2969*
Ro 2:11 For God *does* not s **favoritism**. *G1639+4721*
Ro 2:15 They s that the requirements of the law *G1892*
Ro 9:22 although choosing *to* s his wrath and *G1892*
Ro 12: 8 if it is *to* s **mercy**, do it cheerfully. *G1796*
1Co 11:19 among you to s which of you have *G5745+1181*
1Co 12:31 And yet *I will* s you the most excellent *G1259*
2Co 3: 3 *You* s that you are a letter from Christ, the *G5746*
2Co 4: 7 in jars of clay **to** s **that** this all-surpassing *G2671*
2Co 8:19 Lord himself and to s our eagerness to help. NDT
2Co 8:24 Therefore s these men the proof of your *G1892*
2Co 11:30 I will boast of the things that *s* my **weakness**. AIT
Gal 2: 6 God *does* not s **favoritism** *G4725+476+3284*
Eph 2: 7 the coming ages *he might* s the *G1892*
Php 2:20 who *will* s genuine **concern** for your *G3534*
Php 4:10 concerned, but *you* **had no opportunity** *to s* it. AIT
1Ti 6: 2 masters *should* not s them **disrespect** just *G2969*
2Ti 1:16 *May* the Lord s mercy to the household of *G1443*
Titus 2: 7 In your teaching s integrity, seriousness NDT
Titus 2:10 but *to* s *that* they can be fully trusted *G1892*
Heb 6:11 We want each of you *to* s this same *G1892*
Heb 11:14 who say such things s that they are *G1872*
Heb 13: 2 Do not forget to s **hospitality to strangers** *G5810*
Jas 2: 1 Lord Jesus Christ *must* not s favoritism. *G1877*
Jas 2: 3 *If you* s **special attention** to the man *G2098*
Jas 2: 9 But if *you* s **favoritism**, you sin and are *G4719*
Jas 2:18 **S** me your faith without deeds, and I will *G1259*
Jas 2:18 *I will* s you my faith by my deeds. *G1259*
Jas 3:13 *Let them* s it by their good life, by deeds *G1259*
1Pe 2:17 **S proper respect** to everyone, love the *G5506*
3Jn 8 therefore *to* s **hospitality** to such people *G5696*
Jude 23 to others s **mercy**, mixed with fear— *G1790*
Rev 1: 1 God gave him *to* s his servants what *G1259*
Rev 4: 1 and *I will* s you what must take place after *G1259*
Rev 17: 1 *I will* s you the punishment of the great *G1259*
Rev 21: 9 *I will* s you the bride, the wife of *G1259*
Rev 22: 6 sent his angel *to* s his servants the things *G1259*

SHOWED (55) [SHOW]

Ge 39:21 *he* s him kindness and granted him favor H5742
Ex 15:25 and the LORD s him a piece of wood. H3723
Nu 13:26 whole assembly and s them the fruit of H8011
Dt 4:36 On earth *he* s you his great fire, and you H8011
Dt 34: 1 There the LORD s him the whole land H8011
Jdg 1:25 So *he* s them, and they put the city to the H8011
Ru 3:10 is greater than that which you s earlier: NDT
1Sa 14:11 So both of them s **themselves** to the H1655
1Sa 15: 6 you s kindness to all the Israelites H6913
2Sa 10: 2 just as his father s kindness to me. H6913
1Ki 3: 3 Solomon s *his* **love** *for* the LORD by walking H170
1Ki 13:12 And his sons s him which road the man of H8011
2Ki 6: 6 When *he* s him the place, Elisha cut a H8011
2Ki 11: 4 Then *he* s them the king's son H8011
2Ki 13:23 and s **concern for** them because H7155+448
2Ki 20:13 the envoys and s them all that was in H8011
1Ch 19: 2 because his father s kindness to me." H6913
2Ch 23: 1 the seventh year Jehoiada s *his* **strength**. H2616
2Ch 30:22 who s good **understanding** of the H8505+8507
Est 5: 9 he neither rose nor s **fear** in his presence, H2316
Job 10:12 You gave me life and s me kindness, and H6913
Job 13:10 account if *you* secretly s **partiality**. H5951+7156
Ps 31:21 for *he* s me the **wonders** *of* his love when H7098
Ps 85: 1 *You*, LORD, s **favor** *to* your land; you H8354
Isa 39: 2 envoys gladly and s them what was in his H8011
Isa 40:14 s him the path of understanding? H3359
Isa 47: 6 into your hand, and *you* s them no mercy. H8492
Jer 11:18 at that time *he* s me what they were H8011
Jer 24: 1 the LORD s me two baskets of figs placed H8011
Jer 36:24 who heard all these words s no **fear**, H7064
Eze 35:11 anger and jealousy *you* s in your hatred of H6913
Eze 39:26 all the **unfaithfulness** *they* s toward H5085+5086
Eze 46:19 s me a place at the western end. H2180
Da 2:29 of mysteries s you what is going to A10313
Am 7: 1 This is what the Sovereign LORD s me: He H8011
Am 7: 4 This is what the Sovereign LORD s me: The H8011
Am 7: 7 This is what *he* s me: The Lord was H8011
Am 8: 1 This is what the Sovereign LORD s me: H8011
Zec 1:20 Then the LORD s me four craftsmen. H8011
Zec 3: 1 Then *he* s me Joshua the high priest H8011
Zec 8:14 disaster on you and s no **pity** when your H5714
Mt 4: 8 high mountain and s him all the *G1259*
Lk 4: 5 to a high place and s him in an instant all *G1259*
Lk 20:37 even Moses s that the dead rise, for *G3606*
Lk 24:40 said this, *he* s them his hands and feet. *G1259*
Jn 20:20 said this, *he* s them his hands and side. *G1259*
Ac 15: 8 s **that** *he* **accepted** them by giving the *G3455*
Ac 18:17 Gallio s no **concern** whatever. *G3508*
Ac 20:35 *I* s you that by this kind of hard work we *G5683*
Ac 28: 2 The islanders s us unusual kindness. *G4218*
Ac 28: 7 home and s us generous **hospitality** for *G3826*
1Jn 2:19 their going s that none of them *G5746*
1Jn 4: 9 This is how God s his love among us: He *G5746*
Rev 21:10 great and high, and s me the Holy City *G1259*
Rev 22: 1 Then the angel s me the river of the water *G1259*

SHOWER (2) [SHOWERING, SHOWERS]

Job 37: 6 and to the rain s, 'Be a mighty downpour. H1773
Isa 45: 8 righteousness; *let* the clouds s it **down**. H5688

SHOWERING (1) [SHOWER]

2Sa 16:13 stones at him and s him with dirt. H6759

SHOWERS (15) [SHOWER]

Dt 32: 2 like dew, like s on new grass, like H8540
2Sa 1:21 may no s fall on your terraced fields. NDT
Job 29:23 waited for me as for s and drank in my H4764
Job 36:28 moisture and abundant s **fall** on mankind. H8319
Ps 65:10 you soften it with s and bless its crops. H8053
Ps 68: 9 You gave abundant s, O God; you H1773
Ps 72: 6 a mown field, like s watering the earth. H8053
Jer 3: 3 Therefore the s have been withheld, and H8053
Jer 14:22 Do the skies themselves send down s? No H8053
Eze 34:26 I will send down s in season; there will be H1773
Eze 34:26 in season; there will be s *of* blessing. H1773
Hos 10:12 until he comes and s his righteousness on H3722
Joel 2:23 He sends you **abundant** s, both autumn H1773
Mic 5: 7 from the LORD, like s on the grass, which H8053
Zec 10: 1 He gives s *of* rain to all people, and H4764

SHOWING (12) [SHOW]

Ex 20: 6 s love to a thousand generations of H6913
Dt 5:10 s love to a thousand generations of H6913
Jdg 16: 5 can lure him into s *you* the secret of his H8011
Ru 2:20 "He *has* not **stopped** s his kindness *to* the H6440
2Sa 2: 5 LORD bless you for s this kindness to Saul H6913
Eze 9: 5 without s **pity** or compassion. H2571+6524
Da 1: 4 s **aptitude** for every kind of learning H8505
Jn 15: 8 much fruit, *s yourselves to* **be** my disciples. AIT
Ac 9:39 crying and s him the robes and other *G2109*
1Ti 5:10 up children, s **hospitality**, washing the *G3827*
Heb 9: 8 The Holy Spirit *was* s by this that the way *G1317*
Rev 22: 8 of the angel who *had been* s them to me. *G1259*

SHOWN (59) [SHOW]

Ge 19:19 you have s great kindness to me in H6913
Ge 21:23 the same kindness *I have* s to you. H6913
Ge 24:14 I will know that *you have* s kindness to my H6913
Ge 32:10 faithfulness *you have* s your servant. H6913
Ge 41:28 God *has* s Pharaoh what he is about to do H8011
Ex 25:40 to the pattern s *you* on the mountain. H8011
Ex 26:30 to the plan s *you* on the mountain. H8011
Ex 27: 8 made just as you *were* s on the mountain. H8011
Lev 13: 7 their skin after *they have* s themselves to H8011
Lev 13:49 defiling mold and *must* **be** s *to* the priest. H8011
Nu 8: 4 like the pattern the LORD *had* s Moses. H8011
Dt 4:35 You **were** s these things so that you might H8011
Dt 5:24 "The LORD our God *has* s us his glory and H8011
Dt 34:12 For no one has ever s the mighty power or NDT
Jos 2:12 because *I have* s kindness to you. H6913
Jdg 13:23 s us all these things or now told us H8011
Ru 1: 8 as *you have* s kindness to your dead H6913
2Sa 12:14 *you have* s **utter contempt** *for* the H5540+5540
1Ki 3: 6 "You *have* s great kindness to your servant H6913
2Ki 8:13 "The LORD *has* s me that you will become H8011
2Ch 1: 8 "You *have* s great kindness to David my H6913
2Ch 24:22 father Jehoiada *had* s him but killed his H6913
2Ch 30: 9 your children will be s compassion by their NDT
2Ch 32:25 he did not respond to the **kindness** *s* him; AIT
Ezr 9: 9 *He has* s us kindness in the sight of the H5742
Job 38:12 to the morning, or s the dawn its place, H3359
Job 38:17 *Have* the gates of death **been** s to you H1655
Ps 48: 3 *he has* s **himself** to be her fortress. H3359
Ps 60: 3 *You have* s your people desperate times H8011
Ps 78:11 he had done, the wonders *he had* s them. H8011
Ps 90:16 *May* your deeds **be** s to your servants, your H8011
Ps 111: 6 *He has* s his people the power of his H5583
Isa 21: 2 A dire vision *has* **been** s to me: The traitor H5583
Isa 26:10 But *when* **grace** is s *to* the wicked, they do H2858
Isa 66:14 servants, but *his* **fury** *will be* s *to* his foes. H2404
Jer 44:10 not humbled themselves or s **reverence**, H3707
La 4:16 The priests *are* s no **honor**, the H5951+7156
La 5:12 hands; elders **are** s no **respect**. H2075+7156
Eze 11:25 the exiles everything the LORD *had* s me. H8011
Da 2:28 *He has* s King Nebuchadnezzar what will A10313
Da 2:45 "The great God *has* s the king what will A10313
Mic 6: 8 *He has* s you, O mortal, what is good H5583
Mal 1: 6 'How *have we* s **contempt** *for* your name? H1022
Mal 2: 9 ways but *have* s **partiality** in H5951+7156
Mt 5: 7 are the merciful, for they *will be* s **mercy**. *G1796*
Lk 1:25 these days *he has* s *his* **favor** and taken *G2078*
Lk 1:58 heard that the Lord *had* s her **great** mercy, *G3486*
Lk 7:47 have been forgiven—as *her* great **love** has s. *G26*
Jn 10:32 "*I have* s you many good works from the *G1259*
Ac 4: 9 act of kindness *s to* a **man** who was lame AIT
Ac 10:28 But God *has* s me *that* I should not call *G1259*
Ac 14:17 *He has* **kindness** by giving you rain from *G14*
1Co 3:13 their work will be s **for what it is**, because *G5745*
1Ti 1:13 *I was* s **mercy** because I acted in *G1796*
1Ti 1:16 very reason *I was* s **mercy** so that in me, *G1796*
Heb 6:10 the love *you have* s him as you have *G1892*
Heb 8: 5 to the pattern s you on the mountain." *G1259*
Heb 13: 2 some people *have* s **hospitality** to angels *G3826*
Jas 2:13 mercy will be s to anyone who has not NDT

SHOWS (18) [SHOW]

Dt 10:17 who s no **partiality** and accepts no H5951+7156
Dt 17:12 Anyone who s contempt for the judge or H6913
2Sa 22:51 *he* s unfailing kindness to his anointed H6913
1Ki 1:52 "If *he* s *himself* **to be** worthy, not H2118+4200
Job 34:19 who s no **partiality** to princes and H5951+7156
Ps 18:50 *he* s unfailing love to his anointed H6913
Ps 123: 2 to the LORD our God, till *he* s us *his* **mercy**. H2858
Pr 3:34 proud mockers but s favor to the humble H5989
Pr 10:17 Whoever heeds discipline s the way to life NDT
Pr 11:22 is a beautiful woman *who* s **no** discretion. H6073
Pr 14:31 the poor s **contempt** *for* their Maker, H3070
Pr 15: 5 whoever heeds correction s **prudence**. H6891

S

Pr 17: 5 the poor s contempt *for* their Maker; H3070
Pr 19:16 but *whoever* s contempt *for* their ways will H1022
Isa 27:11 and their Creator s them no favor. H2858
Jn 5:20 loves the Son and s him all he does. G1259
Jas 4: 6 the proud but s favor to the humble." G1443
1Pe 5: 5 the proud but s favor to the humble." G1443

SHREWD (5) [SHREWDLY]
2Sa 13: 3 Jonadab was a very s man. H2682
2Sa 22:27 to the devious *you* show yourself s. H7349
Ps 18:26 to the devious *you* show yourself s. H7349
Mt 10:16 Therefore be as s as snakes and as G5861
Lk 16: 8 this world are more s in dealing with their G5861

SHREWDLY (2) [SHREWD]
Ex 1:10 *we must* deal s with them or they will H2681
Lk 16: 8 manager because he had acted s. G5862

SHRIEK (1) [SHRIEKED, SHRIEKS]
Mk 1:26 came out of him *with a* s. G5888+5889+3489

SHRIEKED (1) [SHRIEK]
Mk 9:26 The spirit s, convulsed him violently and G3189

SHRIEKS (1) [SHRIEK]
Ac 8: 7 For *with* s, impure spirits G1066+5889+3489

SHRINE (16) [SHRINES]
Ge 38:21 "Where is the s prostitute who was beside H7728
Ge 38:21 "There hasn't been any s prostitute here," H7728
Ge 38:22 'There hasn't been any s prostitute here. H7728
Dt 23:17 woman is to become a s prostitute. H7728
Jdg 17: 5 Now this man Micah had a s, and H1074+466
1Ki 14:24 were even *male* s prostitutes in the land; H7728
1Ki 15:12 expelled the *male* s prostitutes from the H7728
1Ki 22:46 rest of the *male* s prostitutes who H7728
2Ki 10:25 then entered the inner s *of* the temple of H6551
2Ki 23: 7 of the *male* s prostitutes that were in H7728
Isa 16:12 when she goes to her s to pray, it is to no H5219
Isa 44:13 in all its glory, that it may dwell in a s. H1074
Eze 8:12 darkness, each at the s *of* his own idol? H2540
Eze 16:24 yourself and made a lofty s in every public H8229
Hos 4:14 harlots and sacrifice with s prostitutes— H7728
Am 5:26 You have lifted up the s *of* your king, the H6109

SHRINES (14) [SHRINE]
1Ki 12:31 Jeroboam built s *on* high places and H1074
1Ki 13:32 against all the s *on* the high places in H1074
2Ki 17:29 the s the people of Samaria had made *at* H1074
2Ki 17:32 as priests in the s *at* the high places. H1074
2Ki 23:19 removed all the s *at* the high places that H1074
Job 36:14 among *male* prostitutes of the s. H7728
Eze 16:25 you built your lofty s and degraded your H8229
Eze 16:31 made your lofty s in every public H8229
Eze 16:39 your mounds and destroy your lofty s. H8229
Eze 18: 6 not eat at the mountain s or look to the H2215
Eze 18:11 "He eats at the mountain s. He defiles his H2215
Eze 18:15 not eat at the mountain s or look to the H2215
Eze 22: 9 who eat at the mountain s and commit H2215
Ac 19:24 who made silver s of Artemis, brought in G3724

SHRINK (2) [SHRINKS]
Heb 10:39 not belong *to those who* s back and are G5714
Rev 12:11 love their lives so much as to s from death. G948

SHRINKS (1) [SHRINK]
Heb 10:38 I take no pleasure in the one *who* s back." G5713

SHRIVEL (2) [SHRIVELED]
Isa 64: 6 filthy rags; we all s up like a leaf, and like H5570
Eze 19:12 The east wind made *it* s, it was stripped H3312

SHRIVELED (10) [SHRIVEL]
1Ki 13: 4 he stretched out toward the man s up, H3312
Job 16: 8 *You have* s me up—and it has become a H7855
Isa 34: 4 from the vine, like s figs from the fig tree. H5570
La 4: 8 Their skin *has* s on their bones; it has H7594
Joel 1:17 The seeds *are* s beneath the clods. H6308
Mt 12:10 a man with a s hand was there G3831
Mk 3: 1 a man with a s hand was there. G3830
Mk 3: 3 Jesus said to the man with the s hand G3831
Lk 6: 6 a man was there whose right hand was s. G3831
Lk 6: 8 said to the man with the s hand, G3831

SHROUD (2) [SHROUDED]
Job 40:13 dust together; s their faces in the grave. H2502
Isa 25: 7 he will destroy the s that enfolds all H4287

SHROUDED (2) [SHROUD]
Job 19: 8 *he has* s my paths *in* darkness. H8492
Ecc 6: 4 in darkness, and in darkness its name is s. H4059

SHRUB (1)
Ge 2: 5 Now no s had yet H3972+8489+2021+8441

SHUA (4)
Ge 38: 2 daughter of a Canaanite man named S. H8781
Ge 38:12 Judah's wife, the daughter of S, died. H8781
1Ch 2: 3 a Canaanite woman, the daughter of S. H8781
1Ch 7:32 Shomer and Hotham and of their sister S. H8783

SHUAH (2)
Ge 25: 2 Jokshan, Medan, Midian, Ishbak and S. H8756
1Ch 1:32 Jokshan, Medan, Midian, Ishbak and S. H8756

SHUAL (2) [HAZAR SHUAL]
1Sa 13:17 turned toward Ophrah in the vicinity of S, H8787
1Ch 7:36 Suah, Harnepher, S, Beri, Imrah, H8786

SHUBAEL (6)
1Ch 23:16 descendants of Gershom: S was the first. H8742
1Ch 24:20 the sons of Amram: S; from the sons of H8742
1Ch 24:20 Shubael; from the sons of S: Jehdeiah. H8742
1Ch 25: 4 Mattaniah, Uzziel, S and Jerimoth H8742
1Ch 25:20 the thirteenth to S, his sons and relatives H8742
1Ch 26:24 S, a descendant of Gershom son of Moses H8742

SHUDDER (7)
Isa 19:16 *They will* s with fear at the uplifted hand H3006
Isa 32:11 women; s, *you* daughters who feel secure! H8074
Jer 2:12 you heavens, and s *with* great horror," H8547
Eze 12:18 s in fear as you drink your water. H8077
Eze 27:35 their kings s *with* horror and their faces H8547
Eze 32:10 their kings *will* s *with* horror because H8547
Jas 2:19 Even the demons believe that—and s. G5857

SHUHAH'S (1)
1Ch 4:11 S brother, was the father of Mehir H8758

SHUHAM (1) [SHUHAMITE]
Nu 26:42 through S, the Shuhamite clan H8761

SHUHAMITE (2) [SHUHAM]
Nu 26:42 through Shuham, the S clan. These were H8762
Nu 26:43 All of them were S clans; and those H8762

SHUHITE (5)
Job 2:11 Bildad the S and Zophar the Naamathite H8760
Job 8: 1 Then Bildad the S replied: H8760
Job 18: 1 Then Bildad the S replied: H8760
Job 25: 1 Then Bildad the S replied: H8760
Job 42: 9 Bildad the S and Zophar the Naamathite H8760

SHULAMMITE (2)
SS 6:13 come back, O S; come back, come H8769
SS 6:13 you gaze on the S as on the dance of H8769

SHUMATHITES (1)
1Ch 2:53 Puthites, S and Mishraites. H9092

SHUN (3) [SHUNNED, SHUNS]
Job 28:28 is wisdom, and *to* s evil is understanding." H6073
Pr 3: 7 in your own eyes; fear the LORD and s evil. H6073
Pr 14:16 The wise fear the LORD and s evil, but a H6073

SHUNAMMITE (8)
1Ki 1: 3 found Abishag, a S, and brought her to H8774
1Ki 1:15 where Abishag the S was attending him. H8774
1Ki 2:17 to give me Abishag the S as my wife." H8774
1Ki 2:21 "Let Abishag the S be given in marriage H8774
1Ki 2:22 you request Abishag the S for Adonijah? H8774
2Ki 4:12 Gehazi, "Call the S." So he called her, H8774
2Ki 4:25 his servant Gehazi, "Look! There's the S! H8774
2Ki 4:36 summoned Gehazi and said, "Call the S." H8774

SHUNEM (3)
Jos 19:18 territory included: Jezreel, Kesulloth, S, H8773
1Sa 28: 4 came and set up camp at S, H8773
2Ki 4: 8 One day Elisha went to S. And a H8773

SHUNI (2) [SHUNITE]
Ge 46:16 Zephon, Haggi, S, Ezbon, Eri, Arodi and H8771
Nu 26:15 Haggite clan; through S, the Shunite clan; H8771

SHUNITE (1) [SHUNI]
Nu 26:15 Haggite clan; through Shuni, the S clan; H8772

SHUNNED (3) [SHUN]
Job 1: 1 upright; he feared God and s evil. H6073
Pr 14:20 The poor are s even by their neighbors H8533
Pr 19: 7 The poor *are* s *by* all their relatives—how H8533

SHUNS (3) [SHUN]
Job 1: 8 upright, a man who fears God and s evil." H6073
Job 2: 3 upright, a man who fears God and s evil. H6073
Isa 59:15 and *whoever* s evil becomes a prey. H6073

SHUPHAM (1) [SHUPHAMITE]
Nu 26:39 through S, the Shuphamite clan; through H8792

SHUPHAMITE (1) [SHUPHAM]
Nu 26:39 Shupham, the S clan; through Hupham H8793

SHUPPIM (1)
1Ch 26:16 on the upper road fell to S and Hosah. H9157

SHUPPITES (2)
1Ch 7:12 The S and Huppites were the H9158
1Ch 7:15 a wife from among the Huppites and S. H9158

SHUR (6)
Ge 16: 7 the spring that is beside the road to S. H8804
Ge 20: 1 Negev and lived between Kadesh and S. H8804
Ge 25:18 settled in the area from Havilah to S, H8804
Ex 15:22 Sea and they went into the Desert of S. H8804
1Sa 15: 7 Amalekites all the way from Havilah to S, H8804
1Sa 27: 8 in the land extending to S and Egypt.) H8804

SHUSHAN (KJV) SUSA

SHUT (54) [SHUTS]
Ge 7:16 Then the LORD s him in. H6037
Ge 19: 6 to meet them and s the door behind him H6037
Ge 19:10 Lot back into the house and s the door. H6037
Dt 11:17 and *he will* s up the heavens so that it H6806
Jos 2: 7 pursuers had gone out, the gate *was* s. H6037
Jdg 3:23 *he* s the doors of the upper room behind H6037
1Sa 12: 3 I accepted a bribe *to* make *me* s my eyes? H6623
1Ki 8:35 the heavens *are* s up and there is no H6806
2Ki 4: 4 Then go inside and s the door behind you H6037
2Ki 4: 5 She left him and s the door behind her H6037
2Ki 4:21 then s the door and went out. H6037
2Ki 4:33 s the door on the two of them and prayed H6037
2Ki 6:32 s the door and hold it shut against him. H6037
2Ki 6:32 shut the door and hold it s *against* him. H4315
2Ch 6:26 the heavens *are* s up and there is no H6806
2Ch 7:13 "When *I* s up the heavens so that there is H6806
2Ch 28:24 *He* s the doors of the LORD's temple and H6037
2Ch 29: 7 *They* also s the doors of the portico and H6037
Ne 6:10 of Mehetabel, who was s in at his home. H6806
Ne 7: 3 *have them* s the doors and bar them. H1589
Ne 13:19 ordered the doors *to* be s and not opened H6037
Job 3:10 *it did* not s the doors of the womb *on* me H6037
Job 24:16 by day *they* s themselves in; they want H3159
Job 38: 8 "Who s up the sea behind doors when it H6114
Ps 107:42 but all the wicked s their mouths. H7890
Isa 22:22 what he opens no *one can* s, and what he H6037
Isa 24:22 *they will* be s up in prison and be H6037
Isa 26:20 your rooms and s the doors behind you H6037
Isa 33:15 plots of murder and s their eyes against H6794
Isa 45: 1 before him so that gates *will* not be s: H6037
Isa 52:15 kings *will* s their mouths because of H7890
Isa 60:11 stand open, *they will* never be s, day or H6037
Jer 13:19 The cities in the Negev *will* be s up, and H6037
Jer 20: 9 heart like a fire, a fire s up in my bones. H6806
Eze 3:24 "Go, s yourself inside your house. H6037
Eze 22:26 and *they* s their eyes to the keeping of my H6623
Eze 44: 1 the one facing east, and it *was* s. H6037
Eze 44: 2 LORD said to me, "This gate is to remain s. H6037
Eze 44: 2 It is to remain s because the LORD, the H6037
Eze 46: 1 facing east is to be s on the six working H6037
Eze 46: 2 the gate *will* not be s until evening. H6037
Eze 46:12 after he has gone out, the gate *will be* s. H6037
Da 6:22 and *he* s the mouths of the lions. A10506
Mal 1:10 that one of you *would* s the temple doors H6037
Mt 23:13 *You* s *the door* of the kingdom of heaven G3091
Mt 25:10 wedding banquet. And the door *was* s. G3091
Lk 4:25 when the sky *was* s for three and a half G3091
Ac 21:30 immediately the gates *were* s. G3091
2Th 1: 9 destruction and *s out* from the presence of AIT
Heb 11:33 was promised; *who* s the mouths of lions, G5852
Rev 3: 7 What he opens no one *can* s, and what G3091
Rev 3: 8 you an open door that no one can s. G3091
Rev 11: 6 They have power *to* s up the heavens so G3091
Rev 21:25 On no day *will* its gates ever *be* s, for there G3091

SHUTHELAH (4) [SHUTHELAHITE]
Nu 26:35 through S, the Shuthelahite clan; through H8811
Nu 26:36 These were the descendants of S: through H8811
1Ch 7:20 S, Bered his son, Tahath his son, Eleadah H8811
1Ch 7:21 Zabad his son and S his son. Ezer and H8811

SHUTHELAHITE (1) [SHUTHELAH]
Nu 26:35 Shuthelah, the S clan; through Beker, H9279

SHUTS (5) [SHUT]
Job 5:16 poor have hope, and injustice s its mouth. H7890
Pr 21:13 *Whoever* s their ears to the cry of the poor H357
Isa 22:22 can shut, and what *he* s no one can open. H6037
La 3: 8 call out or cry for help, *he* s out my prayer. H8608
Rev 3: 7 can shut, and what *he* s no one can open. G3091

SHUTTLE (1)
Job 7: 6 "My days are swifter than a weaver's s, H756

SHY (1)
Job 39:22 *it does* not s away from the sword. H8740

SIA (1)
Ne 7:47 Keros, S, Padon, H6103

SIAHA (1)
Ezr 2:44 Keros, S, Padon, H6104

SIBBEKAI (5)
2Sa 21:18 At that time S the Hushathite killed Saph H6021
2Sa 23:27 Abiezer from Anathoth, S the Hushathite, H6021
1Ch 11:29 S the Hushathite, Ilai the Ahohite, H6021
1Ch 20: 4 At that time S the Hushathite killed H6021
1Ch 27:11 eighth month, was S the Hushathite, H6021

SIBBOLETH (1)
Jdg 12: 6 If he said, "S," because he could not H6027

SIBMAH (5)
Nu 32:38 these names were changed) and S. H8424
Jos 13:19 Kiriathaim, S, Zereth Shahar on the hill in H8424
Isa 16: 8 of Heshbon wither, the vines of S also. H8424
Isa 16: 9 as Jazer weeps, for the vines of S. H8424
Jer 48:32 you, as Jazer weeps, you vines of S. H8424

SIBRAIM (1)
Eze 47:16 Berothah and S (which lies on the border H6028

SICK (43) [SICKNESS, SICKNESSES]

Jdg 16:16 day after day until he *was* **s** to death of it. H7918
Pr 13:12 Hope deferred **makes** the heart **s**, but a H2703
Isa 10:18 destroy, as when a **s** *person* wastes away. H5823
Isa 19:10 all the wage earners will be **s** *at* heart. H108
Eze 34: 4 the weak or healed the **s** or bound up the H2703
Mt 8:16 with a word and healed all the **s**. G2809+2400
Mt 9:12 who need a doctor, but the **s**. G2809+2400
Mt 10: 8 Heal the **s**, raise the dead, cleanse those G820
Mt 14:14 compassion on them and healed their **s**. G779
Mt 14:35 People brought all their **s** to him G2809+2400
Mt 14:36 begged him to let the **s** just touch the edge NDT
Mt 25:36 me, *I was* **s** and you looked after me G820
Mt 25:39 When did we see you **s** or in prison and go G820
Mt 25:43 I was **s** and in prison and you did not look G822
Mt 25:44 needing clothes or **s** or in prison, G822
Mk 1:32 to Jesus all the **s** and G2809+2400
Mk 2:17 who need a doctor, but the **s**. G2809+2400
Mk 6: 5 hands on a few **s** *people* and heal them. G779
Mk 6:13 anointed many **s** *people* with oil and G779
Mk 6:55 and carried the **s** on mats to G2809+2400
Mk 6:56 they placed the **s** in the marketplaces. G820
Mk 16:18 they will place their hands on **s** *people* G779
Lk 5:17 of the Lord was with Jesus to **heal the s**. G2615
Lk 5:31 who need a doctor, but the **s**. G2809+2400
Lk 7: 2 highly, *was* **s** and about to die. G2809+2400
Lk 9: 2 the kingdom of God and to heal the **s**. G822
Lk 10: 9 Heal the **s** who are there and tell them G822
Jn 4:46 official whose son *lay* **s** at Capernaum. G820
Jn 6: 2 signs he had performed by healing the **s**. G820
Jn 11: 1 Now a man named Lazarus was **s**. He was G820
Jn 11: 2 whose brother Lazarus *now lay* **s**, was the G820
Jn 11: 3 word to Jesus, "Lord, the one you love *is* **s**." G820
Jn 11: 6 So when he heard that Lazarus *was* **s**, he G820
Ac 5:15 people brought the **s** into the streets and G822
Ac 5:16 bringing their **s** and those tormented by G822
Ac 9:37 About that time she *became* **s** and died G820
Ac 19:12 that had touched him were taken to the **s**, G820
Ac 28: 8 His father was **s** in bed, suffering from fever NDT
Ac 28: 9 the rest *of* the **s** on the island came G2400+819
1Co 11:30 is why many among you are weak and **s**, G779
2Ti 4:20 and I left Trophimus **s** in Miletus. G820
Jas 5:14 *Is* anyone among you **s**? Let them call the G820
Jas 5:15 in faith will make the **s** *person* well; G2827

SICKBED (1) [BED]

Ps 41: 3 them on their **s** and restores them H6911+1867

SICKLE (12) [SICKLES]

Dt 16: 9 you begin to put the **s** to the standing H3058
Dt 23:25 you must not put a **s** to their standing H3058
Jer 50:16 the reaper with his **s** at harvest. H4478
Joel 3:13 Swing the **s**, for the harvest is ripe. H4478
Mk 4:29 he puts the **s** to it, because the G1535
Rev 14:14 on his head and a sharp **s** in his hand. G1535
Rev 14:15 "Take your **s** and reap, because the G1535
Rev 14:16 on the cloud swung his **s** over the earth, G1535
Rev 14:17 in heaven, and he too had a sharp **s**. G1535
Rev 14:18 a loud voice to him who had the sharp **s**, G1535
Rev 14:18 "Take your sharp **s** and gather the clusters G1535
Rev 14:19 The angel swung his **s** on the earth G1535

SICKLES (1) [SICKLE]

1Sa 13:20 mattocks, axes and **s** sharpened. H3058

SICKNESS (11) [SICK]

Ex 23:25 I will take away **s** from among you, H4701
Dt 28:61 on you every kind of **s** and disaster not H2716
Pr 18:14 The human spirit can endure in **s**, but a H4700
Jer 6: 7 her **s** and wounds are ever before me. H2716
Jer 10:19 "This is my **s**, and I must endure it H2716
Hos 5:13 "When Ephraim saw his **s**, and Judah his H2716
Mt 4:23 every disease and **s** among the people. G3433
Mt 9:35 healing every disease and **s**. G3433
Mt 10: 1 spirits and to heal every disease and **s**. G3433
Lk 4:40 Jesus all who had various kinds *of* **s**, G820+3798
Jn 11: 4 Jesus said, "This **s** will not end in death. G819

SICKNESSES (2) [SICK]

Lk 5:15 to hear him and to be healed of their **s**. G819
Lk 7:21 who had diseases, **s** and evil spirits, and G3465

SIDDIM (3)

Ge 14: 3 kings joined forces in the Valley of **S** H8443
Ge 14: 8 up their battle lines in the Valley of **S** H8443
Ge 14:10 Now the Valley of **S** was full of tar pits H8443

SIDE (292) [ASIDE, BESIDE, SIDED, SIDES, SIDEWALLS, SIDING]

Ge 2:14 is the Tigris; it runs along the **east** *s* *of* Ashur. AIT
Ge 3:24 he placed on the **east** *s* of the Garden of AIT
Ge 6:16 Put a door in the **s** *of* the ark and make H7396
Ge 31:52 go past this heap to **your** *s* to harm you and AIT
Ge 31:52 past this heap and pillar to **my** *s* to harm me. AIT
Ex 3: 1 the flock to the **far s** *of* the wilderness and H339
Ex 14:20 darkness to the one **s** and light to the other NDT
Ex 14:20 to the one side and light to the other **s**; NDT
Ex 17:12 hands up—one on *one* **s**, one on the H2296S
Ex 25:12 two rings on one **s** and two rings on the H7521
Ex 25:32 three on one **s** and three on the other. H7396
Ex 26:18 frames for the south **s** of the tabernacle H6991
Ex 26:20 For the other **s**, the north side of the H7521
Ex 26:20 the north **s** *of* the tabernacle, make H6991
Ex 26:26 the frames on one **s** *of* the tabernacle, H7521
Ex 26:27 five for those on the other **s**, and five for H7521
Ex 26:35 on the north **s** *of* the tabernacle and H7521
Ex 26:35 the lampstand opposite it on the south **s**. H7521
Ex 27: 9 The south **s** shall be a hundred cubits H6991
Ex 27:11 The north **s** shall also be a hundred cubits H6991
Ex 27:14 long are to be on one **s** of the entrance, H4190
Ex 27:15 cubits long are to be on the other **s**, H4190
Ex 32:27 'Each man strap a sword to his **s**. Go back H3751
Ex 36:23 frames for the south **s** of the tabernacle H6991
Ex 36:25 For the other **s**, the north side of the H7521
Ex 36:25 the north **s** *of* the tabernacle, they H6991
Ex 36:31 the frames on one **s** *of* the tabernacle, H7521
Ex 36:32 five for those on the other **s**, and five for H7521
Ex 37: 3 two rings on one **s** and two rings on the H7521
Ex 37:18 three on one **s** and three on the other. H7396
Ex 38: 9 The south **s** was a hundred cubits long H6991
Ex 38:11 The north **s** was also a hundred cubits H6991
Ex 38:14 cubits long were on one **s** of the entrance, H4190
Ex 38:15 were on the other **s** of the entrance to the H4190
Ex 40:22 meeting on the north **s** *of* the tabernacle H3751
Ex 40:24 the table on the south **s** *of* the tabernacle H3751
Lev 1:11 it at the north **s** *of* the altar before the H3751
Lev 1:15 shall be drained out on the **s** *of* the altar. H7815
Lev 5: 9 the sin offering against the **s** *of* the altar; H7815
Lev 13:55 no matter *which* **s** of the fabric has been H7949
Nu 3:29 to camp on the south **s** *of* the tabernacle. H3751
Nu 3:35 to camp on the north **s** *of* the tabernacle. H3751
Nu 32:19 **on the other s of** the H4946+6298+2256+2134
Nu 32:19 to us on the east **s** *of* the Jordan." H4946+6298
Nu 32:32 will be **on this s** of the Jordan." H4946+6298
Nu 34: 3 " 'Your southern **s** will include some of H6991
Nu 34:11 to Riblah on the **east** *s* of Ain and continue AIT
Nu 34:12 your land, with its boundaries **on every s**. H6017
Nu 35: 5 two thousand cubits on the east **s**, H6991
Nu 35: 5 two thousand on the south **s**, two H6991
Nu 35:14 Give three on **this s** of the Jordan and H6298
Nu 36:11 their **cousins on their father's s**. H1201+1856
Jos 4:11 the priests **came to the other s** while the H6296
Jos 7: 7 to stay on the **other s** *of* the Jordan! H6298
Jos 12: 1 including all the **eastern** *s* *of* the Arabah: AIT
Jos 12: 7 conquered on the west **s** *of* the Jordan, H6298
Jos 13:27 of Heshbon (the east **s** *of* the Jordan, the H6298
Jos 17: 9 Manasseh was the **northern** *s* of the ravine AIT
Jos 18: 7 inheritance on the east **s** of the Jordan. H6298
Jos 18:12 On the north **s** their boundary began at H6991
Jos 18:14 along the western **s** and came out at H6991
Jos 18:14 people of Judah. This was the western **s**. H6991
Jos 18:15 The southern **s** began at the outskirts of H6991
Jos 18:20 formed the boundary on the eastern **s**. H6991
Jos 20: 8 of the Jordan (*on the other* **s** from Jericho H6298
Jos 21:44 The LORD gave them rest on **every s**, just as H6017
Jos 22: 4 gave you on the **other s** *of* the Jordan. H6298
Jos 22: 7 land on the west **s** *of* the Jordan along H6298
Jos 22:11 near the Jordan on the Israelite **s**, H6298
Jdg 8:34 of all their enemies **on every s**. H4946+6017
Jdg 10: 8 Israelites on the **east s** *of* the Jordan in H6298
Jdg 11:18 along the eastern **s** of the country of Moab, NDT
Jdg 11:18 camped on the **other s** *of* the Arnon. H6298
Ru 2: 1 Naomi had a relative **on** her husband's **s**, H4200
1Sa 4:13 Eli sitting on his chair by the **s** *of* the road, H3338
1Sa 4:18 backward off his chair by the **s** *of* the gate. H3338
1Sa 14: 1 to the Philistine outpost on the **other s**." H6298
1Sa 14: 4 On each **s** of the pass H4946+2021+6298
+4946+2296+4946+2021+6298
1Sa 14:47 fought against their enemies **on every s**: H6017
1Sa 20:20 I will shoot three arrows to the **s** *of* it, as H7396
1Sa 20:21 the arrows are **on this s** of you; bring them H2178
1Sa 20:41 got up from the south **s** of the stone and H725
1Sa 22: 6 with all his officials standing **at** his **s**. H6584
1Sa 22:17 Then the king ordered the guards **at** his **s** H6584
1Sa 23:26 was going along one **s** *of* the mountain, H7396
1Sa 23:26 David and his men were on the other **s**, H7396
1Sa 26:13 over to the **other s** and stood on top H6298
2Sa 2:13 group sat down on *one* **s** of the pool H2296S
2Sa 2:13 the pool and one group on the *other* **s**. H2296S
2Sa 2:16 thrust his dagger into his opponent's **s**, H7396
2Sa 3: 8 "Am I a dog's head—**on** Judah's **s**? H4200
2Sa 13:34 coming down the **s** *of* the hill. H7396
2Sa 13:34 direction of Horonaim, on the **s** *of* the hill." H7396
2Sa 15: 2 stand by the **s** *of* the road leading to H3338
1Ki 3:20 took my son from my **s** while I your servant H725
1Ki 5: 4 LORD my God has given me rest on **every s**, H6017
1Ki 6: 5 the building, in which there were **s rooms**. H7521
1Ki 6: 8 floor was on the south **s** *of* the temple; H4190
1Ki 6:10 And he built the **s rooms** all along the H3666
1Ki 7:28 They had **s panels** attached to uprights H4995
1Ki 7:30 four supports, cast with wreaths on each **s**. H6298
1Ki 7:39 stands on the south **s** *of* the temple and H4190
1Ki 7:39 He placed the Sea on the south **s**, at the H4190
2Ki 4: 4 and as each is filled, **put it to one s**." H5825
2Ki 6:11 Which of us is **on the s of** the king of Israel?" H448
2Ki 9:32 window and called out, "Who is **on** my **s**? H907
2Ki 10: 6 "If you are **on** my **s** and will obey me H4200
2Ki 11:11 from the south **s** to the north side of the H4190
2Ki 11:11 south side to the north **s** *of* the temple. H4190
2Ki 12: 9 on the right **s** as one enters the temple of NDT
2Ki 16:14 put it on the north **s** *of* the new altar. H3751
2Ki 16:17 cut off the **s panels** and removed the H4995
1Ch 18:17 sons were chief officials at the king's **s**. H3338
1Ch 22: 9 from all his enemies **on every s**. H4946+6017
1Ch 22:18 he not granted you rest **on every s**? H4946+6017
1Ch 23:28 courtyards, the **s rooms**, the purification H4384
2Ch 4: 6 placed five on the **south** *s* and five on the AIT
2Ch 4: 7 five on the **south** *s* and five on the north. AIT
2Ch 4: 8 five on the **south** *s* and five on the north. AIT
2Ch 4:10 He placed the Sea on the south **s**, at the H4190
2Ch 5:12 stood on the **east** *s* of the altar, dressed AIT
2Ch 14: 7 he has given us rest **on every s**." H4946+6017
2Ch 15:15 the LORD gave them rest **on every s**. H4946+6017
2Ch 20: 2 from the **other s** of the Dead Sea. H6298
2Ch 20:30 God had given him rest **on every s**. H4946+6017
2Ch 23:10 from the south **s** to the north side of the H4190
2Ch 23:10 south side to the north **s** *of* the temple. H4190
2Ch 29: 4 assembled them in the square on the **east** *s* AIT
2Ch 32:22 He took care of them **on every s**. H4946+6017
2Ch 32:30 water down to the **west** *s* of the City of David AIT
Ne 4: 3 the Ammonite, who was **at** his **s**, said, H725
Ne 4:18 wore his sword at his **s** as he worked. H5516
Job 15:10 The gray-haired and the aged are **on** our **s** H928
Job 18:11 startle him **on every s** and dog his every H6017
Job 19:10 tears me down **on every s** till I am gone; H6017
Job 21:26 **S by side** they lie in the dust, and worms H3480
Job 21:26 **Side by s** they lie in the dust, and worms H3480
Job 33:23 Yet if there is an angel **at** their **s**, H6584
Job 39:23 The quiver rattles **against** its **s**, along with H6584
Ps 3: 6 tens of thousands assail me **on every s**. H6017
Ps 31:13 whispering, "Terror **on every s**!" H4946+6017
Ps 45: 3 Gird your sword on your **s**, you mighty one; H3751
Ps 91: 7 A thousand may fall at your **s**, ten H7396
Ps 97: 3 him and consumes his foes **on every s**. H6017
Ps 118:11 They surrounded me **on every s**, but in the H6015
Ps 124: 1 If the LORD had not been **on** our **s**—let H4200
Ps 124: 2 LORD had not been **on** our **s** when people H4200
Ps 139: 9 the dawn, if I settle on the **far s** *of* the sea, H344
Pr 3:26 LORD will be at your **s** and will keep your H4073
Pr 8:30 Then I was constantly **at** his **s**. I was filled H725
Ecc 4: 1 power was on the **s** *of* their oppressors H3338
SS 3: 8 each with his sword at his **s**, prepared H3751
Jer 6:25 and there is terror **on every s**. H4946+6017
Jer 20: 3 you is not Pashhur, but Terror on **Every S**. H6017
Jer 20:10 whispering, "Terror **on every s**! H4946+6017
Jer 35: 2 to one of the **s rooms** of the house of H4384
Jer 46: 5 and there is terror **on every s**, H4946+6017
Jer 49:29 shout to them, 'Terror **on every s**! H4946+6017
Jer 49:32 will bring disaster on them from every **s**," H6298
Jer 50:15 Shout against her **on every s**! She H6017
Jer 51: 2 oppose her **on every s** in the day of H4946+6017
La 2:22 against me terrors **on every s**. H4946+6017
Eze 1:10 on the **right** *s* each had the face of a lion AIT
Eze 1:11 touching that of the creature on either **s**; NDT
Eze 4: 4 lie on your left **s** and put the sin of the H7396
Eze 4: 4 the number of days you lie on **your s**. H2257S
Eze 4: 6 this time on your right **s**, and bear the sin H7396
Eze 4: 8 cannot turn from one **s** to the other until H7396
Eze 4: 9 it during the 390 days you lie on your **s**. H7396
Eze 9: 2 in linen who had a writing kit at his **s**. H5516
Eze 9: 3 in linen who had the writing kit at his **s** H5516
Eze 9:11 the writing kit at his **s** brought back word, H5516
Eze 10: 3 standing on the **south** *s* of the temple when AIT
Eze 10:16 the wheels did not leave their **s**. H725
Eze 21:14 **closing in** on them **from every s**. H2539
Eze 23:22 will bring them against you from **every s**— H6017
Eze 23:24 against you **on every s** with large and H6017
Eze 27:11 Helek guarded your walls **on every s**; H6017
Eze 28:23 the sword against you **on every s**. H4946+6017
Eze 36: 3 crushed you **from every s** so that H4946+6017
Eze 40: 2 on whose **south** *s* were some buildings that AIT
Eze 40:10 three alcoves **on each s**;
H4946+7024+2256+4946+7024
Eze 40:10 walls **on each s** had the
H4946+7024+2256+4946+7024
Eze 40:19 cubits on the **east** *s* as well as on the AIT
Eze 40:21 three **on each s**— H4946+7024+2256+4946+7024
Eze 40:24 led me to the south **s** and I saw the south H2006
Eze 40:26 walls **on each s**. H4946+7024+4946+2256+7024
Eze 40:27 this gate to the outer gate on the south **s**; H2006
Eze 40:32 me to the inner court on the east **s**, H2006
Eze 40:34 the jambs **on either s**,
H4946+7024+2256+4946+7024
Eze 40:37 the jambs **on either s**,
H4946+7024+2256+4946+7024
Eze 40:39 two tables **on each s**,
H4946+7024+2256+4946+7024
Eze 40:40 on the other **s** of the steps were two H4190
Eze 40:41 four tables on *one* **s** of the gateway and H7024
Eze 40:44 one at the **s** *of* the north gate and facing H4190
Eze 40:44 another at the **s** *of* the south gate H4190
Eze 40:48 cubits wide **on either s**.
H4946+7024+2256+4946+7024
Eze 40:48 cubits wide **on either s**.
H4946+7024+2256+4946+7024
Eze 40:49 pillars **on each s** of the
H4946+7024+2256+4946+7024
Eze 41: 1 was six cubits **on each s**.
H4946+7024+2256+4946+7024
Eze 41: 2 walls **on each s** of it
H4946+7024+2256+4946+7024
Eze 41: 3 walls on each **s** of it were seven cubits NDT
Eze 41: 5 each **s room** around the temple was H7521
Eze 41: 6 The **s rooms** were on three levels, one H7521
Eze 41: 6 to serve as supports for the **s rooms**, H7521
Eze 41: 7 The **s rooms** all around the temple were H7521

Eze 41: 8 forming the foundation of the **s rooms**. H7521
Eze 41: 9 outer wall of the **s rooms** was five cubits H7521
Eze 41: 9 area between the **s rooms** of the temple H7521
Eze 41:11 entrances to the **s rooms** from the open H7521
Eze 41:12 courtyard *on* the west **s** was seventy H6991
Eze 41:15 its galleries **on each s**; H4946+7024+2256+4946+7024
Eze 41:19 the palm tree on one **s** and the face of a H7024
Eze 41:26 trees carved **on each s**. H4946+7024+2256+4946+7024
Eze 41:26 The **s rooms** *of* the temple also had H7521
Eze 42: 1 opposite the outer wall on the **north** *s*. AIT
Eze 42: 8 row of rooms on the **s** next to the outer court NDT
Eze 42: 8 the row on the **s** nearest the sanctuary was a NDT
Eze 42: 9 an entrance on the **east** *s* as one enters them AIT
Eze 42:10 On the south **s** along the length of the H2006
Eze 42:16 measured the east **s** with the measuring H8120
Eze 42:17 He measured the north **s**; it was five H8120
Eze 42:18 He measured the south **s**; it was five H8120
Eze 42:19 he turned to the west **s** and measured; H8120
Eze 45: 7 land **bordering each s** of H4946+2296+2256+4946+2296[S]
Eze 45: 7 from the west **s** and eastward from the H6991
Eze 45: 7 west side and eastward from the east **s**, H6991
Eze 46:19 the entrance at the **s** *of* the gate to the H4190
Eze 47: 1 from under the south **s** *of* the temple, H4190
Eze 47: 2 the water was trickling from the south **s**. H4190
Eze 47: 7 of trees **on each s** *of* the H4946+2296+2256+4946+2296[S]
Eze 47:15 "On the north **s** it will run from the H6991
Eze 47:18 "On the east **s** the boundary will run H6991
Eze 47:19 "On the south **s** it will run from Tamar as H6991
Eze 47:20 "On the west **s**, the Mediterranean Sea H6991
Eze 48: 1 of its border from the **east** *s* to the west side. AIT
Eze 48: 1 of its border from the east side to the **west** *s*. AIT
Eze 48:10 It will be 25,000 cubits long on the **north** *s* AIT
Eze 48:10 10,000 cubits wide on the **west** *s*, 10,000 AIT
Eze 48:10 cubits wide on the **east** *s* and 25,000 cubits AIT
Eze 48:10 side and 25,000 cubits long on the **south** *s*. AIT
Eze 48:16 the north **s** 4,500 cubits, the south side H6991
Eze 48:16 the south **s** 4,500 cubits, the east H6991
Eze 48:16 the east **s** 4,500 cubits, and the H6991
Eze 48:16 4,500 cubits, and the west **s** 4,500 cubits. H6991
Eze 48:18 cubits on the **east** *s* and 10,000 cubits AIT
Eze 48:18 east side and 10,000 cubits on the **west** *s*. AIT
Eze 48:20 will be a square, 25,000 cubits **on each s**. H928
Eze 48:23 extend from the east **s** to the west side. H6991
Eze 48:23 extend from the east side to the west **s**. H6991
Eze 48:30 Beginning on the north **s**, which is 4,500 H6991
Eze 48:31 three gates on the **north** *s* will be the gate of AIT
Eze 48:32 "On the east **s**, which is 4,500 cubits long H6991
Eze 48:33 "On the south **s**, which measures 4,500 H6991
Eze 48:34 "On the west **s**, which is 4,500 cubits long, H6991
Joel 3:11 all you nations **from every s**, and H4946+6017
Joel 3:12 to judge all the nations **on every s**. H4946+6017
Zec 3: 1 Satan standing at his **right** *s* to accuse him. AIT
Zec 5: 3 according to what it says on *one* **s** H2296[S]
Mt 8:18 orders to cross to the **other s of the lake**. *G4305*
Mt 8:28 he arrived at the **other s** in the region of *G4305*
Mt 14:22 go on ahead of him to the **other s**, *G4305*
Mt 19: 1 of Judea *to* the **other s** of the Jordan. *G4305*
Mk 4:35 disciples, "Let us go over to the **other s**." *G4305*
Mk 5:21 over by boat to the **other s of the lake**, *G4305*
Mk 8:13 into the boat and crossed to the **other s**. *G4305*
Mk 16: 5 in a white robe sitting on the **right s**, *G1288*
Lk 1:11 standing at the **right s** of the altar of *G1288*
Lk 8:22 "Let us go over to the **other s** of the lake." *G4305*
Lk 10:31 saw the man, *he* **passed by on the other s**. *G524*
Lk 10:32 saw him, **passed by on the other s**. *G524*
Lk 16:22 the angels carried him to Abraham's **s**. *G3146*
Lk 16:23 Abraham far away, with Lazarus by his **s**. *G3146*
Lk 19:43 encircle you and hem you in **on every s**. *G4119*
Jn 1:28 at Bethany **on the other s** of the Jordan, *G4305*
Jn 3:26 with you **on the other s** of the Jordan— *G4305*
Jn 6:25 they found him **on the other s** of the lake, *G4305*
Jn 18: 1 **On the other s** there was a garden, and *G3963[S]*
Jn 18:37 Everyone **on the s** of truth listens to me." *G1666*
Jn 19:18 **one on each s** and Jesus in *G1949+2779+1949*
Jn 19:34 the soldiers pierced Jesus' **s** with a spear, *G4433*
Jn 20:20 he showed them his hands and **s**. *G4433*
Jn 20:25 put my hand into his **s**, I will not *G4433*
Jn 20:27 Reach out your hand and put it into my **s** *G4433*
Jn 21: 6 your net on the right **s** of the boat and you *G3538*
Ac 12: 7 He struck Peter *on* the **s** and woke him up *G4433*
2Co 4: 8 We are hard pressed on **every s**, but not AIT
Php 4: 3 *since* they *have* **contended at** my **s** in *G5254*
2Ti 4:17 But the Lord **stood at** my **s** and gave me *G4225*
Heb 10:33 times you stood **s by side** with those who *G3128*
Heb 10:33 times you stood **side by s** with those who *G3128*
Rev 22: 2 **On each s** of the river stood *G1949+2779+1696*

SIDED (4) [SIDE]

1Sa 20:30 that you *have* **s with** the son of H1047+4200
1Sa 22:17 they too have **s with** David. H3338+6640
2Ch 11:13 their districts throughout Israel **s** with him. H3656
Ac 14: 4 were divided; some **s** with the Jews *G1639*

SIDES (50) [SIDE]

Ex 12: 7 put it on the **s** and tops *of* the doorframes H9109
Ex 12:22 the top and on **both s** *of* the doorframe. H9109
Ex 12:23 on the top and **s** *of* the doorframe and H9109
Ex 25:14 into the rings on the **s** *of* the ark to carry it. H7521
Ex 25:32 to extend from the **s** *of* the lampstand— H7396
Ex 26:13 a cubit longer **on both s**; H4946+2296+2256+2296[S]
Ex 26:13 will hang over the **s** *of* the tabernacle so H7396
Ex 27: 7 they will be on two **s** *of* the altar when it H7521
Ex 29:16 splash it against the **s** *of* the altar. H6017
Ex 29:20 splash blood against the **s** *of* the altar. H6017
Ex 30: 3 the top and all the **s** and the horns with H7815
Ex 30: 4 two on *each of the* **opposite s**—to H7521+7396
Ex 32:15 They were inscribed on both **s**, front and H6298
Ex 37: 5 into the rings on the **s** *of* the ark to carry it. H7521
Ex 37:18 extended from the **s** *of* the lampstand— H7396
Ex 37:26 the top and all the **s** and the horns with H7815
Ex 37:27 two on *each of the* **opposite s**—to H7521+7396
Ex 38: 7 they would be on the **s** *of* the altar for H7521
Lev 1: 5 splash it against the **s** *of* the altar at the H6017
Lev 1:11 splash its blood against the **s** *of* the altar. H6017
Lev 3: 2 the blood against the **s** *of* the altar. H6017
Lev 3: 8 splash its blood against the **s** *of* the altar. H6017
Lev 3:13 splash its blood against the **s** *of* the altar. H6017
Lev 7: 2 to be splashed against the **s** *of* the altar. H6017
Lev 8:19 the blood against the **s** *of* the altar. H6017
Lev 8:24 splashed blood against the **s** *of* the altar. H6017
Lev 9:12 he splashed it against the **s** *of* the altar. H6017
Lev 9:18 he splashed it against the **s** *of* the altar. H6017
Lev 19:27 cut the hair at the **s** *of* your head or clip H6991
Nu 22:24 with walls **on both s**. H4946+2296+2256+4946+2296[S]
Nu 33:55 barbs in your eyes and thorns in your **s**. H7396
Jos 8:22 with Israelites **on both s**. H4946+2296+2256+4946+2296[S]
Jos 8:33 **on both s** of the H4946+2296+2256+4946+2296[S]
Jos 18:20 of the clans of Benjamin **on all s**. H6017
1Ki 4:24 and had peace on all **s**. H6298+4946+6017
1Ki 5: 3 **waged against** my father David **from all s**, H6015
1Ki 10:19 **On both s** of the seat H4946+2296+2256+4946+2296[S]
1Ch 9:24 The gatekeepers were on the four **s**: east H8120
2Ch 9:18 **On both s** of the seat H4946+2296+2256+4946+2296[S]
Job 11: 6 of wisdom, for true wisdom has **two s**. H4101
Isa 29: 3 against you **on all s**; H3869+2021+1885
Jer 52:23 were ninety-six pomegranates on the **s**; H8120
Eze 1: 8 wings on their four **s** they had human H8063
Eze 2:10 **On both s** of it were written H7156+2256+294
Eze 40:18 It abutted the **s** *of* the gateways and was H4190
Eze 41:22 corners, its base and its **s** were of wood. H7815
Eze 42:20 So he measured the area on all four **s**. H8120
Eze 48:21 remains **on both s** of the H4946+2296+2256+4946+2296[S]
Da 7: 5 It was raised up on one of its **s**, and it A10680
Rev 5: 1 writing **on both s** and sealed *G2277+2779+3957*

SIDEWALLS (1) [SIDE]

Eze 41:26 On the **s** *of* the portico were narrow H4190

SIDING (1) [SIDE]

Ex 23: 2 do not pervert justice by **s** with the crowd, H5742

SIDON (32) [GREATER SIDON, SIDONIANS]

Ge 10:15 Canaan was the father of **S** his firstborn H7477
Ge 10:19 reached from **S** toward Gerar as far H7477
Ge 49:13 ships; his border will extend toward **S**. H7477
Jdg 1:31 living in Akko or **S** or Ahlab or Akzib or H7477
Jdg 10: 6 of Aram, the gods of **S**, the gods of Moab, H7477
Jdg 18:28 lived a long way from **S** and had no H7477
2Sa 24: 6 on to Dan Jaan and around toward **S**. H7477
1Ki 17: 9 in the region of **S** and stay there. H7477
1Ch 1:13 Canaan was the father of **S** his firstborn H7477
Ezr 3: 7 olive oil to the **people of S** and Tyre, H7479
Isa 23: 2 of the island and you merchants of **S**, H7477
Isa 23: 4 Be ashamed, **S**, and you fortress of the H7477
Isa 23:12 reveling, Virgin Daughter **S**, now crushed! H7477
Jer 25:22 all the kings of Tyre and **S**; the kings of the H7477
Jer 27: 3 Tyre and **S** through the envoys who have H7477
Jer 47: 4 all survivors who could help Tyre and **S**. H7477
Eze 27: 8 Men of **S** and Arvad were your oarsmen H7477
Eze 28:21 set your face against **S**; prophesy against H7477
Eze 28:22 " 'I am against you, **S**, and among you I H7477
Joel 3: 4 Tyre and **S** and all you regions of Philistia H7477
Zec 9: 2 and on Tyre and **S**, though they are H7477
Mt 11:21 in you had been performed in Tyre and **S**, *G4972*
Mt 11:22 bearable for Tyre and **S** on the day of *G4972*
Mt 15:21 withdrew to the region of Tyre and **S**. *G4972*
Mk 3: 8 across the Jordan and around Tyre and **S**. *G4972*
Mk 7:31 the vicinity of Tyre and went through **S**, *G4972*
Lk 4:26 a widow in Zarephath *in* the **region of S**. *G4973*
Lk 6:17 the coastal region *around* Tyre and **S**, *G4972*
Lk 10:13 in you had been performed in Tyre and **S**, *G4972*
Lk 10:14 Tyre and **S** at the judgment than *G4972*
Ac 12:20 quarreling with the **people of** Tyre and **S**; *G4973*
Ac 27: 3 The next day we landed at **S**; and Julius *G4972*

SIDONIANS (15) [SIDON]

Dt 3: 9 Hermon is called Sirion by the **S**; the H7479
Jos 13: 4 from Arah of the **S** as far as Aphek and H7479
Jos 13: 6 all the **S**, I myself will drive them H7479
Jdg 3: 3 the Canaanites, the **S**, and the Hivites H7479
Jdg 10:12 the **S**, the Amalekites and the Maonites H7479
Jdg 18: 7 in safety, like the **S**, at peace and secure. H7479
Jdg 18: 7 a long way from the **S** and had no H7479
1Ki 5: 6 one so skilled in felling timber as the **S**." H7479
1Ki 11: 1 Ammonites, Edomites, **S** and Hittites. H7479
1Ki 11: 5 followed Ashtoreth the goddess of the **S**, H7479
1Ki 11:33 Ashtoreth the goddess of the **S**, H7479
1Ki 16:31 Jezebel daughter of Ethbaal king of the **S**, H7479
2Ki 23:13 Ashtoreth the vile goddess of the **S**, H7479
1Ch 22: 4 the **S** and Tyrians had brought large H7479
Eze 32:30 of the north and all the **S** are there; H7479

SIEGE (51) [BESIEGE, BESIEGED, BESIEGES, BESIEGING]

Dt 20:12 engage you in battle, **lay s** to that city. H7443
Dt 20:19 When *you* **lay s** to a city for a long time H7443
Dt 20:20 use them to build **s works** until the city at H5189
Dt 28:52 *They will* **lay s** to all the cities throughout H7674
Dt 28:53 enemy will inflict on you during the **s**. H5189
Dt 28:55 on you during the **s** of all your cities. H5189
Dt 28:57 inflict on you during the **s** of your cities. H5189
2Sa 11:16 So while Joab *had* the city **under s**, he put H9068
2Sa 20:15 They built a **s ramp** up to the city, and it H6149
1Ki 16:17 from Gibbethon and **laid s** to Tirzah. H7443
2Ki 6:24 marched up and **laid s** to Samaria. H7443
2Ki 6:25 *the* **s** lasted so long that a donkey's head H7443
2Ki 17: 5 against Samaria and **laid s** to it for three H7443
2Ki 18: 9 marched against Samaria and **laid s** to it. H7443
2Ki 19:32 it with shield or build a **s ramp** against it. H6149
2Ki 24:10 and **laid s** *to* it, H995+928+2021+5189
2Ki 25: 1 the city and built **s works** all around it. H1911
2Ki 25: 2 city was kept under **s** until the eleventh H5189
2Ch 32: 1 *He* **laid s to** the fortified cities H2837+6584
2Ch 32: 9 all his forces were laying **s** to Lachish, NDT
2Ch 32:10 that you remain in Jerusalem under **s**? H5189
Job 19:12 they build a **s ramp** against me and H2006
Job 30:12 they build their **s ramps** against me. H784+369
Ps 31:21 of his love when I was in a city **under s**. H5189
Ecc 9:14 it and built huge **s works** against it. H5189
Isa 1: 8 in a cucumber field, like a city **under s**. H7443
Isa 21: 2 Media, **lay s**! I will bring to an end H7443
Isa 23:13 they raised up their **s towers**, they stripped H1032
Isa 29: 3 towers and set up my **s works** against you. H5193
Isa 37:33 it with shield or build a **s ramp** against it. H6149
Jer 6: 6 trees and build **s ramps** against H6149
Jer 10:17 to leave the land, you who live under **s**. H5189
Jer 19: 9 will press the **s** so hard against them H5189
Jer 32:24 "See how the **s ramps** are built up to take H6149
Jer 33: 4 used against the **s ramps** and the sword H6149
Jer 39: 1 with his whole army and **laid s** to it. H7443
Jer 52: 4 the city and built **s works** all around it. H1911
Jer 52: 5 city was kept under **s** until the eleventh H5189
Eze 4: 2 Then lay **s** to it: Erect siege works against H5189
Eze 4: 2 Erect **s works** against it, build a ramp up H1911
Eze 4: 3 It will be under **s**, and you shall besiege it H5189
Eze 4: 7 face toward the **s** *of* Jerusalem and with H5189
Eze 4: 8 until you have finished the days of your **s**. H5189
Eze 5: 2 When the days of your **s** come to an end H5189
Eze 17:17 are built and **s works** erected to destroy H1911
Eze 21:22 to build a ramp and to erect **s works**. H1911
Eze 24: 2 king of Babylon *has* **laid s** to Jerusalem H6164
Eze 26: 8 he will set up **s works** against you, build a H1911
Da 11:15 build up **s ramps** and will capture H6149
Mic 5: 1 city of troops, for a **s** is laid against us. H5189
Na 3:14 Draw water for the **s**, strengthen your H5189

SIEVE (2)

Isa 30:28 shakes the nations in the **s** *of* destruction; H5864
Am 9: 9 all the nations as grain is shaken in a **s**, H3895

SIFT (1)

Lk 22:31 Satan has asked *to* **s** all of you as wheat. *G4985*

SIGH (1) [SIGHED, SIGHING]

Mk 7:34 to heaven and *with a* **deep s** said to him, *G5100*

SIGHED (1) [SIGH]

Mk 8:12 He **s deeply** and said, "Why *G417+3836+4460*

SIGHING (4) [SIGH]

Job 3:24 For **s** has become my daily food; my groans H635
Ps 38: 9 Lord; my **s** is not hidden from you. H635
Isa 35:10 and sorrow and **s** will flee away. H635
Isa 51:11 and sorrow and **s** will flee away. H635

SIGHT (147) [SEE]

Ge 6:11 was corrupt in God's **s** and was full of H7156
Ge 33:18 and camped **within s of** the city. H907+7156
Ge 38: 7 was wicked in the LORD's **s**; so the LORD H6524
Ge 38:10 What he did was wicked in the LORD's **s**; H6524
Ge 43:30 Deeply moved **at the s of** his brother H448
Ex 3: 3 "I will go over and see this strange **s** H5260
Ex 4:11 Who gives them **s** or makes them blind H7221
Ex 10:28 to Moses, "Get out of **my s**! Make sure you AIT
Ex 17: 6 did this in the **s** *of* the elders of Israel H6524
Ex 19:11 on Mount Sinai in the **s** *of* all the people. H6524
Ex 40:38 in the **s** *of* all the Israelites during all their H6524
Lev 10: 3 in the **s** *of* all the people I will be H7156
Lev 26:16 will destroy your **s** and sap your strength. H6524
Lev 26:45 out of Egypt in the **s** *of* the nations to be H6524
Nu 20:12 honor me as holy in the **s** *of* the Israelites, H6524
Nu 20:27 up Mount Hor in the **s** *of* the whole H6524
Nu 32:13 who had done evil in his **s** was gone. H6524
Dt 6:18 Do what is right and good in the LORD's **s** H6524
Dt 9:18 evil in the LORD's **s** and so arousing his H6524
Dt 24:13 act in the **s** *of* the LORD your God. H7156
Dt 31:29 will do evil in the **s** *of* the LORD and arouse H6524
Dt 34:12 deeds that Moses did in the **s** *of* all Israel. H6524

Jos 4:14 LORD exalted Joshua in the **s** *of* all Israel; H6524
1Sa 2:17 men was very great **in** the LORD's **s**, H907+7156
1Sa 2:33 only to destroy your **s** and sap your H6524
1Sa 6:13 up and saw the ark, they rejoiced at the **s**. H8011
1Sa 9:17 When Samuel **caught s of** Saul, the LORD H8011
2Sa 7:19 And as if this were not enough in your **s** H6524
2Sa 7:26 David will be established in your **s**. H7156
2Sa 7:29 that it may continue forever in your **s**; for H7156
2Sa 10:12 The LORD will do what is good in his **s**." H6524
2Sa 13: 5 the food in my **s** so I may watch her and H6524
2Sa 13: 6 make some special bread in my **s**, H6524
2Sa 13: 8 made the bread in his **s** and baked it. H6524
2Sa 13:17 this woman out of **my** *s* and bolt the door AIT
2Sa 16:22 father's concubines in the **s** *of* all Israel. H6524
2Sa 22:25 according to my cleanness in his **s**. H6524
1Ki 14: 4 his **s** was gone because of his age. H6524
2Ki 5: 1 a great man in the **s** *of* his master and H7156
1Ch 2: 3 was wicked in the LORD's **s**; so the LORD H6524
1Ch 17:17 And as if this were not enough in your **s** H6524
1Ch 17:27 that it may continue forever in your **s**; for H7156
1Ch 19:13 The LORD will do what is good in his **s**." H6524
1Ch 21: 7 command was also evil in the **s** *of* God; H6524
1Ch 22: 5 splendor **in the s of** all the nations. H4200
1Ch 22: 8 shed much blood on the earth in my **s**. H7156
1Ch 28: 8 I charge you in the **s** *of* all Israel and of H6524
1Ch 29:15 We are foreigners and strangers in your **s** H7156
1Ch 29:25 exalted Solomon in the **s** *of* all Israel and H6524
Ezr 9: 9 us kindness in the **s** *of* the kings of Persia: H7156
Ne 2: 5 if your servant has found favor in his **s**, H7156
Ne 4: 5 blot out their sins from your **s**, H4200+7156
Ne 9:28 they again did what was evil in your **s**. H7156
Job 11: 4 are flawless and I am pure in your **s**. H6524
Job 18: 3 as cattle and considered stupid in your **s**? H6524
Job 33: 6 I am the same as you in God's **s**; I too am H4200
Job 41: 9 is false; the mere **s** *of* it is overpowering. H5260
Ps 18:24 to the cleanness of my hands in his **s**. H6524
Ps 19:14 of my heart be pleasing in your **s**, H7156
Ps 31:19 that you bestow **in the s of** all, on those H5584
Ps 31:22 my alarm I said, "I am cut off from your **s**!" H6524
Ps 51: 4 I sinned and done what is evil in your **s**; H6524
Ps 72:14 precious is their blood in his **s**. H6524
Ps 78:12 He did miracles **in the s of** their ancestors H5584
Ps 90: 4 years in your **s** are like a day that H6524
Ps 116:15 Precious in the **s** *of* the LORD is the death H6524
Ps 146: 8 the LORD **gives s** *to* the blind, the LORD lifts H7219
Pr 3: 4 a good name in the **s** *of* God and man. H6524
Pr 3:21 wisdom and understanding out of your **s**, H6524
Pr 4:21 Do not let them out of your **s**, keep them H6524
Pr 15:26 but gracious words are pure in his **s**. NDT
Pr 29:13 The LORD **gives s** *to* the eyes of both H239
Isa 1:16 Take your evil deeds out of my **s**; stop H6524
Isa 5:21 their own eyes and clever in their own **s**. H7156
Isa 31: 9 **at** *the s of* the battle standard their AIT
Isa 43: 4 you are precious and honored in my **s**, H6524
Isa 52:10 his holy arm in the **s** *of* all the nations, H6524
Isa 59:12 For our offenses are many **in** your **s**, and H5584
Isa 65:12 You did evil in my **s** and chose what H6524
Isa 66: 4 They did evil in my **s** and chose what H6524
Jer 4: 1 idols out of my **s** and no longer go astray, H7156
Jer 18:10 it does evil in my **s** and does not obey me H6524
Jer 18:23 blot out their sins from your **s**. H4200+7156
Jer 31:36 if these decrees vanish from my **s**," H4200+7156
Jer 32:30 nothing but evil in my **s** from their youth; H6524
Jer 32:31 wrath that I must remove it from my **s**. H7156
Jer 34:15 repented and did what is right in my **s**: H6524
Eze 4:12 bake it in the **s** *of* the people, using H6524
Eze 4:17 be appalled at the **s** of each other and will NDT
Eze 5: 8 on you in the **s** *of* the nations. H6524
Eze 5:14 around you, in the **s** *of* all who pass by. H6524
Eze 16:41 on you in the **s** *of* many women. H6524
Eze 20: 9 lived and in whose **s** I had revealed H6524
Eze 20:14 nations in whose **s** I had brought them H6524
Eze 20:22 nations in whose **s** I had brought them H6524
Eze 20:41 holy through you in the **s** *of* the nations. H6524
Eze 28:18 on the ground in the **s** *of* all who were H6524
Eze 28:25 holy through them in the **s** *of* the nations. H6524
Eze 36:17 a woman's monthly uncleanness in my **s**. H7156
Eze 36:34 desolate in the **s** *of* all who pass through H6524
Eze 38:23 myself known in the **s** *of* many nations. H6524
Eze 39:27 through them in the **s** *of* many nations. H6524
Da 6:22 because I was found innocent **in** his **s**. A10621
Joel 2: 6 At the **s** *of* them, nations are in anguish H7156
Jnh 2: 4 'I have been banished from your **s**; yet I H6524
Hag 2:14 with this people and this nation in my **s**, H7156
Mt 9:30 their **s** was restored. Jesus warned G4057
Mt 11: 5 The blind **receive s**, the lame walk, those G329
Mt 20:33 answered, "we want our **s**." G487+3836+4057
Mt 20:34 Immediately *they* **received** *their* **s** and G329
Mk 8:25 were opened, his **s** was restored, and he NDT
Mk 10:52 Immediately *he* **received** *his* **s** and G329
Lk 1: 6 of them were righteous **in the s of** God, G1883
Lk 1:15 he will be great **in the s** of the Lord. G1967
Lk 2:31 you have prepared in the **s** of all nations: G4725
Lk 4:18 prisoners and **recovery of s** for the blind, G330
Lk 7:21 gave **s** to many who were blind. G1063
Lk 7:22 The blind **receive s**, the lame walk, those G329
Lk 16:15 value highly is detestable **in** God's **s**. G1967
Lk 18:42 said to him, "**Receive** *your* **s**; your faith has G329
Lk 18:43 Immediately **he received** *his* **s** and followed G329
Lk 23:48 to witness this **s** saw what took place, G2556
Lk 24:31 and he **disappeared from** their **s**. G908+1181
Jn 3:21 done has been done **in the s of** God. G1877
Jn 9:15 also asked him how *he had* **received** *his* **s**. G329
Jn 9:18 blind and *had* **received** *his* **s** until they G329
Ac 1: 9 and a cloud hid him from their **s**. G4057
Ac 7:31 he saw this, he was amazed *at* the **s**. G3969
Ac 9:12 place his hands on him to **restore** *his* **s**." G329
Ac 22:13 me and said, 'Brother Saul, **receive** your **s**!' G329
Ac 28:15 *At the* **s** *of* these people Paul thanked G3972
Ro 2:13 the law who are righteous **in** God's **s**, G4123
Ro 3:20 righteous **in** God's **s** by the works of G1967
Ro 4:17 He is our father **in the s of** God, in whom G2978
1Co 3:19 of this world is foolishness **in** God's **s**. G4123
2Co 2:10 I have forgiven in the **s** of Christ for your G4725
2Co 4: 2 to everyone's conscience **in the s of** God. G1967
2Co 5: 7 For we live by faith, not by **s**. G1626
2Co 12:19 been speaking **in the s of** God as those in G2978
Eph 1: 4 world to be holy and blameless **in** his **s**. G2979
Col 1:22 through death to present you holy **in** his **s**, G2979
1Ti 5:21 **in the s of** God and Christ Jesus and the G1967
1Ti 6:13 **In the s of** God, who gives life to G1967
Heb 4:13 in all creation is hidden from God's **s**. G1967
Heb 12:21 The **s** was so terrifying that Moses said, "I G5751
1Pe 3: 4 which is of great worth **in** God's **s**. G1967
Rev 3: 2 your deeds unfinished **in the s of** my God. G1967

SIGHTING (1) [SEE]

Ac 21: 3 *After* **s** Cyprus and passing to the south of it G428

SIGHTLESS (1) [SEE]

Isa 29: 9 blind yourselves and *be* **s**; be drunk, H9129

SIGHTS (3) [SEE]

Dt 28:34 The **s** you see will drive you mad. H5260+6524
Dt 28:67 your hearts and the **s** that your eyes will H5260
Pr 23:33 Your eyes *will* **see** strange *s*, and your mind AIT

SIGN (89) [SIGNED, SIGNS]

Ge 9:12 "This is the **s** *of* the covenant I am making H253
Ge 9:13 it will be the **s** *of* the covenant H253
Ge 9:17 "This is the **s** *of* the covenant I have H253
Ge 17:11 it will be the **s** *of* the covenant H253
Ge 49: 3 my might, the **first** *s of* my strength, excelling AIT
Ex 3:12 And this will be the **s** to you that it is I who H253
Ex 4: 8 believe you or pay attention to the first **s**, H253
Ex 8:23 This **s** will occur tomorrow.' H253
Ex 12:13 The blood will be a **s** for you on the houses H253
Ex 13: 9 will be for you like a **s** on your hand and a H253
Ex 13:16 And it will be like a **s** on your hand and a H253
Ex 31:13 This will be a **s** between me and you for H253
Ex 31:17 It will be a **s** between me and the Israelites H253
Nu 16:38 Let them be a **s** to the Israelites." H253
Nu 17:10 to be kept as a **s** to the rebellious. H253
Nu 26:10 And they served as a **warning s**. H5812
Dt 13: 1 you and announces to you a **s** or wonder, H253
Dt 13: 2 if the **s** or wonder spoken of takes place H253
Dt 21:17 son is the first **s of** his father's **strength**. H226
Dt 28:46 They will be a **s** and a wonder to you and H253
Jos 2:12 shown kindness to you. Give me a sure **s** H253
Jos 4: 6 to serve as a **s** among you. In the future H253
Jdg 6:17 give me a **s** that it is really you talking to H253
1Sa 2:34 Phinehas, will be a **s** to you—they will both H253
1Sa 14:10 that will be our **s** that the LORD has given H253
1Ki 13: 3 That same day the man of God gave a **s** H4603
1Ki 13: 3 "This is the **s** the LORD has declared H4603
1Ki 13: 5 out according to the **s** given by the man of H4603
1Ki 20:33 The men **took** *this* **as a good s** and were H5727
2Ki 19:29 "This will be the **s** for you, Hezekiah: "This H253
2Ki 20: 8 "What will be the **s** that the LORD will heal H253
2Ki 20: 9 "This is the LORD's **s** to you that the LORD H253
2Ch 32:24 him and gave him a **miraculous s**. H4603
2Ch 32:31 ask him about the **miraculous s** that had H4603
Job 31:35 I **s** now my defense—let the Almighty H9338
Ps 71: 7 I have become a **s** to many; you are my H4603
Ps 86:17 Give me a **s** of your goodness, that my H253
Isa 7:11 "Ask the LORD your God for a **s**, whether in H253
Isa 7:14 Therefore the Lord himself will give you a **s** H253
Isa 19:20 It will be a **s** and witness to the LORD H253
Isa 20: 3 as a **s** and portent against Egypt and Cush, H253
Isa 37:30 "This will be the **s** for you, Hezekiah: "This H253
Isa 38: 7 " 'This is the LORD's **s** to you that the LORD H253
Isa 38:22 "What will be the **s** that I will go up to the H253
Isa 55:13 an everlasting **s**, that will endure forever H253
Isa 66:19 "I will set a **s** among them, and I will send H253
Jer 44:29 " 'This will be the **s** to you that I will punish H253
Eze 4: 3 This will be a **s** to the people of Israel. H253
Eze 12: 6 I have made you a **s** to the Israelites." H4603
Eze 12:11 Say to them, 'I am a **s** *to you.*' "As I have H4603
Eze 20:12 gave them my Sabbaths as a **s** between us, H253
Eze 20:20 that they may be a **s** between us. H253
Eze 24:24 Ezekiel will be a **s** to you; you will do just H4603
Eze 24:27 So you will be a **s** to them, and they will H4603
Mt 12:38 "Teacher, we want to see a **s** from you." G4956
Mt 12:39 adulterous generation asks for a **s**! G4956
Mt 12:39 given it except the **s** of the prophet Jonah. G4956
Mt 16: 1 him to show them a **s** from heaven. G4956
Mt 16: 4 adulterous generation looks for a **s**, G4956
Mt 16: 4 will be given it except the **s** of Jonah." G4956
Mt 24: 3 what will be the **s** of your coming and G4956
Mt 24:30 will appear the **s** of the Son of Man in G4956
Mk 8:11 they asked him for a **s** from heaven. G4956
Mk 8:12 "Why does this generation ask for a **s**? G4956
Mk 8:12 Truly I tell you, no **s** will be given to it." G4956
Mk 13: 4 And what will be the **s** that they are all G4956
Lk 2:12 This will be a **s** to you: You will find a G4956
Lk 2:34 to be a **s** that will be spoken against G4956
Lk 11:16 tested him by asking for a **s** from heaven. G4956
Lk 11:29 It asks for a **s**, but none will be given it G4956
Lk 11:29 will be given it except the **s** of Jonah. G4956
Lk 11:30 For as Jonah was a **s** to the Ninevites, so G4956
Lk 21: 7 And what will be the **s** that they are about G4956
Lk 23: 8 to see him perform a **s** of some sort. G4956
Jn 2:18 "What **s** can you show us to prove your G4956
Jn 4:54 This was the second **s** Jesus performed G4956
Jn 6:14 the people saw the **s** Jesus performed, G4956
Jn 6:30 "What **s** then will you give that we may G4956
Jn 10:41 "Though John never performed a **s**, all G4956
Jn 12:18 had heard that he had performed this **s**, G4956
Jn 19:20 Many of the Jews read this **s**, for the place G5518
Jn 19:20 and the **s** was written in Aramaic NDT
Ac 4:16 knows they have performed a notable **s**, G4956
Ro 4:11 And he received circumcision *as* a **s**, G4956
1Co 14:22 are a **s**, not for believers but for G4956
Php 1:28 This is a **s** to them that they will be G1893
Rev 12: 1 A great **s** appeared in heaven: a woman G4956
Rev 12: 3 Then another **s** appeared in heaven: an G4956
Rev 15: 1 in heaven another great and marvelous **s**: G4956

SIGNAL (7) [SIGNALED, SIGNALING, SIGNALS]

Nu 10: 6 The blast *will be* the **s** for setting out. H9546
Nu 10: 7 not *with* the **s** for setting out. H8131
Jer 4: 6 Raise the **s** to go to Zion! Flee for safety H5812
Jer 6: 1 Raise the **s** over Beth Hakkerem H5368
Zec 10: 8 *I will* **s** for them and gather them in H9239
Mt 26:48 the betrayer had arranged a **s** with them: G4956
Mk 14:44 the betrayer had arranged a **s** with them: G5361

SIGNALED (1) [SIGNAL]

Lk 5: 7 So *they* **s** their partners in the other boat to G2916

SIGNALING (1) [SIGNAL]

Nu 31: 6 from the sanctuary and the trumpets for **s**. H9558

SIGNALS (1) [SIGNAL]

Pr 6:13 **s** with his feet and motions with his H4911

SIGNED (3) [SIGN]

Jer 32:10 *I* **s** and sealed the deed, had it witnessed H4180
Jer 32:12 the witnesses who *had* **s** the deed and of H4180
Jer 32:44 silver, and deeds *will be* **s**, sealed and H4180

SIGNET (10)

Ge 41:42 Pharaoh took his **s ring** from his finger H3192
Nu 31:50 bracelets, **s rings**, earrings and necklaces H3192
Est 3:10 the king took his **s ring** from his finger H3192
Est 8: 2 The king took off his **s ring**, which he had H3192
Est 8: 8 seal it with the king's **s ring**—for no H3192
Est 8:10 the dispatches with the king's **s ring**, H3192
Isa 3:21 the **s rings** and nose rings, H3192
Jer 22:24 of Judah, were a **s ring** on my right hand H2597
Da 6:17 it with his own **s ring** and with the rings A10536
Hag 2:23 'and I will make you like my **s ring**, for I H2597

SIGNIFICATION (KJV) MEANING

SIGNIFIED, SIGNIFIETH, SIGNIFY, SIGNIFYING (KJV) GIVE NOTICE, INDICATE, MADE KNOWN, PETITION, POINTING, PREDICTED, SHOW, SHOWING, SPECIFYING

SIGNPOST (1)

Eze 21:19 Make a **s** where the road branches off to H3338

SIGNS (76) [SIGN]

Ge 1:14 let them serve as **s** to mark sacred times, H253
Ex 4: 9 do not believe these two **s** or listen to you, H253
Ex 4:17 your hand so you can perform the **s** with it." H253
Ex 4:28 also about all the **s** he had commanded H253
Ex 4:30 He also performed the **s** before the people H253
Ex 7: 3 I multiply my **s** and wonders in Egypt H253
Ex 10: 1 I may perform these **s** *of* mine among them H253
Ex 10: 2 how I performed my **s** among them, H253
Nu 14:11 in spite of all the **s** I have performed H253
Nu 14:22 my glory and the **s** I performed in Egypt H253
Dt 4:34 by testings, by **s** and wonders, by war, by H253
Dt 6:22 our eyes the LORD sent **s** and wonders— H253
Dt 7:19 the great trials, the **s** and wonders, the H253
Dt 11: 3 the **s** he performed and the things he did in H253
Dt 26: 8 with great terror and with **s** and wonders. H253
Dt 29: 3 great trials, those **s** and great wonders. H253
Dt 34:11 who did all those **s** and wonders the LORD H253
Jos 24:17 performed those great **s** before our eyes. H253
1Sa 10: 7 Once these **s** are fulfilled, do whatever your H253
1Sa 10: 9 all these **s** were fulfilled that day. H253
Ne 9:10 You sent **s** and wonders against Pharaoh H253
Ps 74: 4 they set up their standards as **s**. H253
Ps 74: 9 We are given no **s** *from God*; no prophets H253
Ps 78:43 the day he displayed his **s** in Egypt, his H253
Ps 105:27 They performed his **s** among them H1821+253
Ps 135: 9 He sent his **s** and wonders into your midst H253
Isa 8:18 We are **s** and symbols in Israel from the H253
Isa 44:25 who foils the **s** *of* false prophets and makes H253
Jer 10: 2 nations or be terrified by **s** in the heavens, H253
Jer 31:21 "Set up **road s**; put up guideposts. H7483
Jer 32:20 You performed **s** and wonders in Egypt H253
Jer 32:21 Israel out of Egypt with **s** and wonders, H253
Da 4: 2 you about the **miraculous s** and wonders A10084
Da 4: 3 How great are his **s**, how mighty his A10084

Da 6:27 he performs s and wonders in the A10084
Mt 16: 3 you cannot interpret the s of the times. G4956
Mt 24:24 perform great s and wonders to G4956
Mk 13:22 appear and perform s and wonders to G4956
Mk 16:17 And these s will accompany those who G4956
Mk 16:20 his word by the s that accompanied it. G4956
Lk 1:22 he kept **making** s to them but G1377
Lk 1:62 Then *they* **made** s to his father, *to find out* G1935
Lk 21:11 fearful events and great s from heaven. G4956
Lk 21:25 "There will be s in the sun, moon and G4956
Jn 2:11 was the first *of* the s through which he G4956
Jn 2:23 people saw the s he was performing G4956
Jn 3: 2 could perform the s you are doing if God G4956
Jn 4:48 "Unless you people see s and wonders," G4956
Jn 6: 2 they saw the s he had performed by G4956
Jn 6:26 because you saw the s I performed but G4956
Jn 7:31 will he perform more s than this man?" G4956
Jn 9:16 "How can a sinner perform such s? G4956
Jn 11:47 "Here is this man performing many s. G4956
Jn 12:37 performed so many s in their presence, G4956
Jn 20:30 many other s in the presence of G4956
Ac 2:19 heavens above and s on the earth below, G4956
Ac 2:22 wonders and s, which God did among G4956
Ac 2:43 the many wonders and s performed by the G4956
Ac 4:30 heal and perform s and wonders through G4956
Ac 5:12 performed many s and wonders among G4956
Ac 6: 8 great wonders and s among the people. G4956
Ac 7:36 performed wonders and s in Egypt, G4956
Ac 8: 6 heard Philip and saw the s he performed, G4956
Ac 8:13 by the great s and miracles he saw. G4956
Ac 14: 3 enabling them to perform s and wonders. G4956
Ac 15:12 telling about the s and wonders God had G4956
Ro 15:19 by the power *of* s and wonders, through G4956
1Co 1:22 Jews demand s and Greeks look for G4956
2Co 12:12 apostle, including s, wonders and G4956
2Th 2: 9 of power *through* s and wonders that G4956
Heb 2: 4 God also testified to it *by* s, wonders and G4956
Rev 13:13 And it performed great s, even causing fire G4956
Rev 13:14 Because of the s it was given power to G4956
Rev 16:14 They are demonic spirits that perform s G4956
Rev 19:20 who had performed the s on its behalf. G4956
Rev 19:20 With **these** s he had deluded those who G4005S

SIHON (34) [SIHON'S]

Nu 21:21 to say to S king of the Amorites H6095
Nu 21:23 But S would not let Israel pass through his H6095
Nu 21:26 was the city of S king of the Amorites, H6095
Nu 21:28 from Heshbon, a blaze from the city of S. H6095
Nu 21:29 as captives to S king of the Amorites. H6095
Nu 21:34 him what you did to S king of the H6095
Nu 32:33 the kingdom of S king of the Amorites H6095
Dt 1: 4 he had defeated S king of the Amorites, H6095
Dt 2:24 I have given into your hand S the Amorite, H6095
Dt 2:26 I sent messengers to S king of Heshbon H6095
Dt 2:30 But S king of Heshbon refused to let us H6095
Dt 2:31 begun to deliver S and his country over H6095
Dt 2:32 When S and all his army came out to H6095
Dt 3: 2 him what you did to S king of the H6095
Dt 3: 6 as we had done with S king of Heshbon H6095
Dt 4:46 in the land of S king of the Amorites H6095
Dt 29: 7 S king of Heshbon and Og king of Bashan H6095
Dt 31: 4 will do to them what he did to S and Og, H6095
Jos 2:10 what you did to S and Og, the two H6095
Jos 9:10 east of the Jordan—S king of Heshbon H6095
Jos 12: 2 S king of the Amorites, who reigned in H6095
Jos 12: 5 to the border of S king of Heshbon. H6095
Jos 13:10 all the towns of S king of the Amorites H6095
Jos 13:21 the entire realm of S king of the Amorites, H6095
Jos 13:21 princes allied with S—who lived in that H6095
Jos 13:27 rest of the realm of S king of Heshbon H6095
Jdg 11:19 sent messengers to S king of the Amorites H6095
Jdg 11:20 S, however, did not trust Israel to pass H6095
Jdg 11:21 gave S and his whole army into Israel's H6095
1Ki 4:19 the country of S king of the Amorites and H6095
Ne 9:22 over the country of S king of Heshbon H6095
Ps 135:11 S king of the Amorites, Og king of Bashan, H6095
Ps 136:19 S king of the Amorites His love endures H6095
Jer 48:45 a blaze from the midst of S; it burns the H6095

SIHON'S (1) [SIHON]

Nu 21:27 let it be rebuilt; let S city be restored. H6095

SILAS (21)

Ac 15:22 called Barsabbas) and S, men who were G4976
Ac 15:27 sending Judas and S to confirm by word G4976
Ac 15:32 Judas and S, who themselves were G4976
Ac 15:40 Paul chose S and left, commended by G4976
Ac 16:19 they seized Paul and S and dragged them G4976
Ac 16:22 joined in the attack against **Paul and** S, G899S
Ac 16:25 midnight Paul and S were praying and G4976
Ac 16:29 in and fell trembling before Paul and S. G4976
Ac 16:36 have ordered that you and S be released. NDT
Ac 16:38 heard that Paul and S were Roman citizens, NDT
Ac 16:40 After Paul and S came out of the prison, NDT
Ac 17: 4 were persuaded and joined Paul and S, G4976
Ac 17: 5 in search of **Paul and** S in order to bring G899S
Ac 17:10 believers sent Paul and S away to Berea. G4976
Ac 17:14 but S and Timothy stayed at Berea. G4976
Ac 17:15 with instructions for S and Timothy to join G4976
Ac 18: 5 When S and Timothy came from G4976
2Co 1:19 by me and S and Timothy—was G4977
1Th 1: 1 S and Timothy, To the church of the G4977
2Th 1: 1 S and Timothy, To the church of the G4977
1Pe 5:12 With the help of S, whom I regard as a G4977

SILENCE (18) [SILENCED, SILENCES, SILENT]

Job 11: 3 *Will* your idle talk **reduce** others **to** s? Will H3087
Job 29:21 expectantly, **waiting in** s for my counsel. H1957
Ps 8: 2 enemies, to s the foe and the avenger. H8697
Ps 12: 3 *May* the LORD s all flattering lips and every H4162
Ps 94:17 I would soon have dwelt in the s **of death**. H1872
Ps 101: 5 in secret, *I will* **put to** s; whoever has H7551
Ps 101: 8 Every morning *I will* **put to** s all the wicked H7551
Ps 115:17 those who go down to the **place of** s; H1872
Ps 143:12 your unfailing love, s my enemies; destroy H7551
Isa 25: 5 *You* s the uproar of foreigners; as heat is H4044
Isa 47: 5 "Sit *in* s, go into darkness, queen city of H1876
Jer 51:55 will destroy Babylon; *he will* s her noisy din. H6
La 2:10 of Daughter Zion sit on the ground *in* s; H1949
La 3:28 Let him sit alone *in* s, for the LORD has laid H1957
Am 8: 3 many bodies—flung everywhere! S!" H2187
Ac 19:33 He **motioned for** s in order G2939+3836+5931
1Pe 2:15 good *you should* s the ignorant **talk** of G5821
Rev 8: 1 there was s in heaven for about half an G4968

SILENCED (15) [SILENCE]

Nu 13:30 Then Caleb s the people before Moses H2188
1Sa 2: 9 the wicked *will* be s in the place of H1957
Job 23:17 Yet *I am* not s by the darkness, by the H7551
Ps 30: 9 "What is gained if I am s, if I go down to H1872
Ps 31:18 *Let* their lying lips **be** s, for with pride and H519
Ps 63:11 while the mouths of liars *will* **be** s. H6126
Pr 10:31 wisdom, but a perverse tongue *will* **be** s. H4162
Jer 47: 5 her head in mourning; Ashkelon *will* **be** s. H1949
Jer 48: 2 *You*, the people of Madmen, *will* also *be* s H1957
Jer 49:26 all her soldiers *will* **be** s in that day," H1957
Jer 50:30 all her soldiers *will* **be** s in that day," H1957
Eze 27:32 "Who was ever s like Tyre, surrounded by H1951
Mt 22:34 Hearing that Jesus *had* s the Sadducees G5821
Ro 3:19 that every mouth *may be* s and the whole G5852
Titus 1:11 They must *be* s, because they are G2187

SILENCES (1) [SILENCE]

Job 12:20 *He* s the lips of trusted advisers and takes H6073

SILENT (57) [SILENCE]

Lev 10: 3 I will be honored.' " Aaron *remained* s. H1957
Dt 27: 9 priests said to all Israel, "*Be* s, Israel, H6129
1Sa 10:27 brought him no gifts. But Saul kept s. H3087
2Ki 18:36 But the people *remained* s and said H3087
Est 4:14 For if *you* **remain** s at this time H3087+3087
Job 7:11 "Therefore I *will* not **keep** s; I will H3104+7023
Job 13: 5 If only *you would be* **altogether** s H3087+3087
Job 13:13 "*Keep* s and let me speak; then let come H3087
Job 13:19 If so, *I will be* s and die. H3087
Job 31:34 of the clans that *I kept* s and would not go H1957
Job 32:16 now that *they are* s, now that H4202+1819
Job 33:31 listen to me; *be* s, and I will speak. H3087
Job 33:33 then listen to me; *be* s, and I will teach H3087
Job 34:29 But if he *remains* s, who can condemn H9200
Ps 4: 4 on your beds, search your hearts and *be* s. H1957
Ps 28: 1 For if *you remain* s, I will be like those H3120
Ps 30:12 heart may sing your praises and not *be* s. H1957
Ps 31:17 be put to shame and *be* s in the realm of H1957
Ps 32: 3 When *I kept* s, my bones wasted away H3087
Ps 35:22 have seen this; *do* not *be* s. Do not be far H3087
Ps 39: 2 So *I remained* **utterly** s, not even H519+1875
Ps 39: 9 *I was* s; I would not open my mouth, for H519
Ps 50: 3 Our God comes and *will* not *be* s; a fire H3087
Ps 50:21 When you did these things and *I kept* s H3087
Ps 83: 1 do not remain s; do not turn a deaf H1954
Ps 109: 1 My God, whom I praise, *do* not *remain* s, H3087
Pr 17:28 Even fools are thought wise if *they* **keep** s H3087
Ecc 3: 7 a time to *be* s and a time to speak H3120
Isa 23: 2 *Be* s, *you* people of the island and you H1957
Isa 24: 8 revelers has stopped, the joyful harp *is* s. H2532
Isa 36:21 But *the people remained* s and said H3087
Isa 41: 1 "*Be* s before me, you islands! Let the H3087
Isa 42:14 "For a long time *I have kept* s, I have H3120
Isa 53: 7 as a sheep before its shearers *is* s, so H519
Isa 57:11 because I *have* long *been* s that you do H3120
Isa 62: 1 For Zion's sake *I will* not *keep* s, for H3120
Isa 62: 6 *they will* never *be* s day or night. H3120
Isa 64:12 *Will you keep* s and punish us beyond H3120
Isa 65: 6 *I will* not *keep* s but will pay back in full; H3120
Jer 4:19 heart pounds within me, *I* cannot *keep* s. H3087
Eze 3:26 mouth so that *you will be* s and unable to H519
Eze 24:27 speak with him and *will* no longer *be* s. H519
Eze 33:22 mouth was opened and *I was* no longer s. H519
Hab 1:13 Why *are you* s while the wicked swallow H3087
Hab 2:20 temple; *let* all the earth **be** s before him. H2187
Zep 1: 7 **Be** s before the Sovereign LORD, for the H2187
Mt 26:63 But Jesus **remained** s. The high priest said G4995
Mk 3: 4 save life or to kill?" But they *remained* s. G4995
Mk 14:61 But Jesus *remained* s and gave no answer G4995
Lk 1:20 And now you will be s and not able to G4995
Lk 14: 4 But they *remained* s. So taking hold of the G2483
Lk 20:26 astonished by his answer, *they became* s. G4967
Ac 8:32 as a lamb before its shearer is s, so he G936
Ac 15:12 whole assembly *became* s as they G4967
Ac 18: 9 be afraid; keep on speaking, *do* not *be* s. G4995
Ac 21:40 When they were all s, he said to them in G4968
1Co 14:34 Women *should remain* s in the churches G4967

SILK (1)

Rev 18:12 s and scarlet **cloth**; every sort of G4986

SILLA (1)

2Ki 12:20 him at Beth Millo, on the road down to S. H6133

SILLY (KJV) EASILY DECEIVED, GULLIBLE, SIMPLE

SILOAM (4)

Ne 3:15 He also repaired the wall of the Pool of S H8940
Lk 13: 4 died when the tower in S fell on them— G4978
Jn 9: 7 "wash in the Pool *of* S" (this word means G4978
Jn 9:11 He told me to go to S and wash. G4978

SILVER (346)

Ge 13: 2 wealthy in livestock and in s and gold. H4084
Ge 20:16 your brother a thousand shekels of s. H4084
Ge 23:15 land is worth four hundred shekels of s, H4084
Ge 23:16 four hundred shekels of s, according to H4084
Ge 24:35 sheep and cattle, s and gold, male and H4084
Ge 24:53 out gold and s jewelry and articles H4084
Ge 33:19 For a hundred **pieces of** s, he bought from H7988
Ge 37:28 twenty shekels of s to the Ishmaelites, H4084
Ge 42:25 to put each man's s back in his sack, and H4084
Ge 42:27 he saw his s in the mouth of his sack. H4084
Ge 42:28 "My s has been returned," he said to his H4084
Ge 42:35 in each man's sack was his pouch of s! H4084
Ge 43:12 Take double the amount of s with you, for H4084
Ge 43:12 you must return the s that was put back H4084
Ge 43:15 took the gifts and double the amount of s, H4084
Ge 43:18 here because of the s that was put back H4084
Ge 43:21 our sacks and each of us found his s— H4084
Ge 43:22 brought additional s with us to buy food. H4084
Ge 43:22 We don't know who put our s in our sacks." H4084
Ge 43:23 treasure in your sacks; I received your s." H4084
Ge 44: 1 put each man's s in the mouth of his H4084
Ge 44: 2 Then put my cup, the s one, in the mouth H4084
Ge 44: 2 one's sack, along with the s *for* his grain." H4084
Ge 44: 8 land of Canaan the s we found inside the H4084
Ge 44: 8 So why would we steal s or gold from your H4084
Ge 45:22 hundred shekels of s and five sets of H4084
Ex 3:22 house for articles of s and gold and for H4084
Ex 11: 2 their neighbors for articles of s and gold." H4084
Ex 12:35 articles of s and gold and for clothing H4084
Ex 20:23 yourselves gods of s or gods of gold. H4084
Ex 21:32 pay thirty shekels of s to the master of the H4084
Ex 22: 7 anyone gives a neighbor s or goods for H4084
Ex 25: 3 to receive from them: gold, s and bronze; H4084
Ex 26:19 make forty s bases to go under them— H4084
Ex 26:21 forty s bases—two under each frame. H4084
Ex 26:25 be eight frames and sixteen s bases— H4084
Ex 26:32 with gold and standing on four s bases. H4084
Ex 27:10 bases and with s hooks and bands on H4084
Ex 27:11 bases and with s hooks and bands on H4084
Ex 27:17 courtyard are to have s bands and hooks, H4084
Ex 31: 4 designs for work in gold, s and bronze, H4084
Ex 35: 5 LORD an offering of gold, s and bronze; H4084
Ex 35:24 an offering of s or bronze brought it as H4084
Ex 35:32 designs for work in gold, s and bronze, H4084
Ex 36:24 made forty s bases to go under them H4084
Ex 36:26 forty s bases—two under each frame. H4084
Ex 36:30 were eight frames and sixteen s bases— H4084
Ex 36:36 hooks for them and cast their four s bases. H4084
Ex 38:10 with s hooks and bands on the posts. H4084
Ex 38:11 with s hooks and bands on the posts. H4084
Ex 38:12 with s hooks and bands on the posts. H4084
Ex 38:17 The hooks and bands on the posts were s H4084
Ex 38:17 their tops were overlaid with s; so all H4084
Ex 38:17 all the posts of the courtyard had s bands. H4084
Ex 38:19 Their hooks and bands were s, and their H4084
Ex 38:19 and their tops were overlaid with s. H4084
Ex 38:25 The s *obtained from* those of the H4084
Ex 38:27 The 100 talents of s were used to cast the H4084
Lev 5:15 defect and of the proper value in s, H4084
Lev 27: 3 of twenty and sixty at fifty shekels of s, H4084
Lev 27: 6 at five shekels of s and that of a female at H4084
Lev 27: 6 that of a female at three shekels of s; H4084
Lev 27:16 fifty shekels of s to a homer of barley seed. H4084
Nu 3:50 he collected s weighing 1,365 shekels H4084
Nu 7:13 His offering was one s plate weighing a H4084
Nu 7:13 thirty shekels and one s sprinkling bowl H4084
Nu 7:19 he brought was one s plate weighing a H4084
Nu 7:19 thirty shekels and one s sprinkling bowl H4084
Nu 7:25 His offering was one s plate weighing a H4084
Nu 7:25 thirty shekels and one s sprinkling bowl H4084
Nu 7:31 His offering was one s plate weighing a H4084
Nu 7:31 thirty shekels and one s sprinkling bowl H4084
Nu 7:37 His offering was one s plate weighing a H4084
Nu 7:37 thirty shekels and one s sprinkling bowl H4084
Nu 7:43 His offering was one s plate weighing a H4084
Nu 7:43 thirty shekels and one s sprinkling bowl H4084
Nu 7:49 His offering was one s plate weighing a H4084
Nu 7:49 thirty shekels and one s sprinkling bowl H4084
Nu 7:55 His offering was one s plate weighing a H4084
Nu 7:55 thirty shekels and one s sprinkling bowl H4084
Nu 7:61 His offering was one s plate weighing a H4084
Nu 7:61 thirty shekels and one s sprinkling bowl H4084
Nu 7:67 His offering was one s plate weighing a H4084
Nu 7:67 thirty shekels and one s sprinkling bowl H4084
Nu 7:73 His offering was one s plate weighing a H4084
Nu 7:73 thirty shekels and one s sprinkling bowl H4084
Nu 7:79 His offering was one s plate weighing a H4084

Nu 7:79 thirty shekels and one **s** sprinkling bowl H4084
Nu 7:84 twelve **s** plates, twelve silver sprinkling H4084
Nu 7:84 twelve **s** sprinkling bowls and twelve gold H4084
Nu 7:85 Each **s** plate weighed a hundred and thirty H4084
Nu 7:85 the **s** dishes weighed two thousand four H4084
Nu 10: 2 "Make two trumpets of hammered **s**, and H4084
Nu 18:16 redemption price set at five shekels of **s**, H4084
Nu 22:18 Balak gave me all the **s** and gold in his H4084
Nu 24:13 Balak gave me all the **s** and gold in his H4084
Nu 31:22 **s**, bronze, iron, tin, lead H4084
Dt 2: 6 are to pay them in **s** for the food you eat H4084
Dt 2:28 eat and water to drink for their price in **s**. H4084
Dt 7:25 Do not covet the **s** and gold on them, and H4084
Dt 8:13 grow large and your **s** and gold increase H4084
Dt 14:25 then exchange your tithe for **s**, and take H4084
Dt 14:25 take the **s** with you and go to the H4084
Dt 14:26 Use the **s** to buy whatever you like: cattle H4084
Dt 17:17 accumulate large amounts of **s** and gold. H4084
Dt 22:19 hundred shekels of **s** and give them to the H4084
Dt 22:29 he shall pay her father fifty shekels of **s** H4084
Dt 29:17 idols of wood and stone, of **s** and gold. H4084
Jos 6:19 All the **s** and gold and the articles of H4084
Jos 6:24 they put the **s** and gold and the H4084
Jos 7:21 hundred shekels of **s** and a bar of gold H4084
Jos 7:21 inside my tent, with the **s** underneath." H4084
Jos 7:22 hidden in his tent, with the **s** underneath. H4084
Jos 7:24 son of Zerah, the **s**, the robe, the gold bar H4084
Jos 22: 8 of livestock, with **s**, gold, bronze and iron, H4084
Jos 24:32 a hundred **pieces of s** from the sons of H7988
Jdg 5:19 of Megiddo, they took no plunder of **s**. H4084
Jdg 9: 4 seventy shekels of **s** from the temple of H4084
Jdg 16: 5 will give you eleven hundred shekels of **s**." H4084
Jdg 16:18 returned with the **s** in their hands. H4084
Jdg 17: 2 hundred shekels of **s** that were taken from H4084
Jdg 17: 2 a curse—I have that **s** with me; I took it." H4084
Jdg 17: 3 hundred shekels of **s** to his mother, H4084
Jdg 17: 3 consecrate my **s** to the LORD for my son H4084
Jdg 17: 3 my son to make an image overlaid with **s**. NDT
Jdg 17: 4 So after he returned the **s** to his mother H4084
Jdg 17: 4 hundred shekels of **s** and gave them to a H4084
Jdg 17:10 I'll give you ten shekels of **s** a year H4084
Jdg 18:14 gods and an image **overlaid with s**? H5011
1Sa 2:36 him for a piece of **s** and a loaf of bread H4084
1Sa 9: 8 he said, "I have a quarter of a shekel of **s**. H4084
2Sa 8:10 Joram brought with him articles of **s**, of H4084
2Sa 8:11 he had done with the **s** and gold from all H4084
2Sa 18:11 you ten shekels of **s** and a warrior's belt." H4084
2Sa 21: 4 no right to demand **s** or gold from Saul H4084
2Sa 24:24 oxen and paid fifty shekels of **s** for them. H4084
1Ki 7:51 the **s** and gold and the furnishings H4084
1Ki 10:21 Nothing was made of **s**, because silver H4084
1Ki 10:21 because **s** was considered of little value in NDT
1Ki 10:22 carrying gold, **s** and ivory, and apes and H4084
1Ki 10:25 articles of **s** and gold, robes, H4084
1Ki 10:27 The king made **s** as common in Jerusalem H4084
1Ki 10:29 from Egypt for six hundred shekels of **s**, H4084
1Ki 15:15 temple of the LORD the **s** and gold and the H4084
1Ki 15:18 Asa then took all the **s** and gold that was H4084
1Ki 15:19 I am sending you a gift of **s** and gold. H4084
1Ki 16:24 two talents of **s** and built a city on the H4084
1Ki 20: 3 'Your **s** and gold are mine, and the best of H4084
1Ki 20: 5 'I sent to demand your **s** and gold, your H4084
1Ki 20: 7 my children, my **s** and my gold, I did H4084
1Ki 20:39 his life, or you must pay a talent of **s**. H4084
2Ki 5: 5 taking with him ten talents of **s**, six H4084
2Ki 5:22 give them a talent of **s** and two sets of H4084
2Ki 5:23 tied up the two talents of **s** in two bags, H4084
2Ki 6:25 donkey's head sold for eighty shekels of **s**, H4084
2Ki 7: 8 Then they took **s**, gold and clothes, and H4084
2Ki 12:13 temple was not spent for making **s** basins, H4084
2Ki 12:13 articles of gold or **s** for the temple of the H4084
2Ki 14:14 took all the gold and **s** and all the articles H4084
2Ki 15:19 a thousand talents of **s** to gain his support H4084
2Ki 15:20 fifty shekels of **s** to be given to the king of H4084
2Ki 16: 8 And Ahaz took the **s** and gold found in the H4084
2Ki 18:14 hundred talents of **s** and thirty talents of H4084
2Ki 18:15 gave him all the **s** that was found in the H4084
2Ki 20:13 was in his storehouses—the **s**, the gold, H4084
2Ki 23:33 hundred talents of **s** and a talent of gold H4084
2Ki 23:35 Pharaoh Necho the **s** and gold he H4084
2Ki 23:35 land and exacted the **s** and gold from the H4084
2Ki 25:15 that were made of pure gold or **s**. H4084+4084
1Ch 18:10 of articles of gold, of **s** and of bronze. H4084
1Ch 18:11 he had done with the **s** and gold he had H4084
1Ch 19: 6 thousand talents of **s** to hire chariots and H4084
1Ch 22:14 a million talents of **s**, quantities of bronze H4084
1Ch 22:16 in gold and **s**, bronze and iron—craftsmen H4084
1Ch 28:14 the weight of **s** for all the silver articles NDT
1Ch 28:14 of silver for all the **s** articles to be used in H4084
1Ch 28:15 the weight of **s** for each silver H4084
1Ch 28:15 of silver for each **s** lampstand and its lamps, NDT
1Ch 28:16 the weight of **s** for the silver tables H4084
1Ch 28:16 the weight of silver for the **s** tables; H4084
1Ch 28:17 the weight of **s** for each silver dish; H4084
1Ch 28:17 the weight of silver for each **s** dish; NDT
1Ch 29: 2 the gold work, **s** for the silver, bronze H4084
1Ch 29: 2 silver for the **s**, bronze for the bronze H4084
1Ch 29: 3 of gold and **s** for the temple of my H4084
1Ch 29: 4 seven thousand talents of refined **s** H4084
1Ch 29: 5 the gold work and the **s** *work*, and for H4084
1Ch 29: 7 ten thousand talents of **s**, eighteen H4084
2Ch 1:15 The king made **s** and gold as common in H4084
2Ch 1:17 from Egypt for six hundred shekels of **s**, H4084
2Ch 2: 7 a man skilled to work in gold and **s** H4084
2Ch 2:14 He is trained to work in gold and **s** H4084
2Ch 5: 1 the **s** and gold and all the furnishings H4084
2Ch 9:14 territories brought gold and **s** to Solomon. H4084
2Ch 9:20 Nothing was made of **s**, because silver H4084
2Ch 9:20 because **s** was considered of little value in NDT
2Ch 9:21 carrying gold, **s** and ivory, and apes and H4084
2Ch 9:24 articles of **s** and gold, and robes, H4084
2Ch 9:27 The king made **s** as common in Jerusalem H4084
2Ch 15:18 the temple of God the **s** and gold and the H4084
2Ch 16: 2 Asa then took the **s** and gold out of the H4084
2Ch 16: 3 I am sending you **s** and gold. Now break H4084
2Ch 17:11 Jehoshaphat gifts and **s** as tribute, H4084
2Ch 21: 3 them many gifts of **s** and gold and articles H4084
2Ch 24:14 dishes and other objects of gold and **s**. H4084
2Ch 25: 6 men from Israel for a hundred talents of **s**. H4084
2Ch 25:24 took all the gold and **s** and all the articles H4084
2Ch 27: 5 paid him a hundred talents of **s**, H4084
2Ch 32:27 treasuries for his **s** and gold and for his H4084
2Ch 36: 3 hundred talents of **s** and a talent of gold H4084
Ezr 1: 4 are to provide them with **s** and gold, H4084
Ezr 1: 6 assisted them with articles of **s** and gold, H4084
Ezr 1: 9 gold dishes 30 **s** dishes 1,000 silver pans H4084
Ezr 1: 9 gold dishes 30 silver dishes 1,000 **s** pans 29 NDT
Ezr 1:10 bowls 30 matching **s** bowls 410 other H4084
Ezr 1:11 there were 5,400 articles of gold and of **s**. H4084
Ezr 2:69 5,000 minas of **s** and 100 priestly H4084
Ezr 5:14 Babylon the gold and **s** articles of the A10362
Ezr 6: 5 the gold and **s** articles of the house of A10362
Ezr 7:15 to take with you the **s** and gold that the A10362
Ezr 7:16 together with all the **s** and gold you may A10362
Ezr 7:18 best with the rest of the **s** and gold, A10362
Ezr 7:22 up to a hundred talents of **s**, a hundred A10362
Ezr 8:25 to them the offering of **s** and gold and the H4084
Ezr 8:26 I weighed out to them 650 talents of **s** H4084
Ezr 8:26 of silver, **s** articles weighing 100 talents H4084
Ezr 8:28 The **s** and gold are a freewill offering to H4084
Ezr 8:30 received the **s** and gold and sacred H4084
Ezr 8:33 we weighed out the **s** and gold and the H4084
Ne 5:15 forty shekels of **s** from them in addition H4084
Ne 7:71 darics of gold and 2,200 minas of **s**. H4084
Ne 7:72 2,000 minas of **s** and 67 garments for H4084
Est 1: 6 purple material to **s** rings on marble H4084
Est 1: 6 couches of gold and **s** on a mosaic H4084
Est 3: 9 ten thousand talents of **s** to the king's H4084
Job 3:15 had gold, who filled their houses with **s**. H4084
Job 22:25 will be your gold, the choicest **s** for you. H4084
Job 27:16 Though he heaps up **s** like dust and H4084
Job 27:17 and the innocent will divide his **s**. H4084
Job 28: 1 There is a mine for **s** and a place where H4084
Job 28:15 can its price be weighed out in **s**. H4084
Job 42:11 one gave him a **piece of s** and a gold ring H7988
Ps 12: 6 are flawless, like **s** purified in a crucible H4084
Ps 66:10 God, tested us; you refined us like **s**. H4084
Ps 68:13 the wings of my dove are sheathed with **s** H4084
Ps 68:30 may the beast bring bars of **s**. Scatter the H4084
Ps 105:37 laden with **s** and gold, and from H4084
Ps 115: 4 But their idols are **s** and gold, made by H4084
Ps 119:72 than thousands of pieces of **s** and gold. H4084
Ps 135:15 The idols of the nations are **s** and gold H4084
Pr 2: 4 you look for it as for **s** and search for it as H4084
Pr 3:14 is more profitable than **s** and yields better H4084
Pr 8:10 Choose my instruction instead of **s** H4084
Pr 8:19 fine gold; what I yield surpasses choice **s**. H4084
Pr 10:20 The tongue of the righteous is choice **s** H4084
Pr 16:16 than gold, to get insight rather than **s**! H4084
Pr 17: 3 The crucible for **s** and the furnace for gold, H4084
Pr 22: 1 to be esteemed is better than **s** or gold. H4084
Pr 25: 4 Remove the dross from the **s**, and a H4084
Pr 25:11 of gold in settings of **s** is a ruling rightly H4084
Pr 26:23 Like a coating of **s** dross on earthenware H4084
Pr 27:21 The crucible for **s** and the furnace for gold, H4084
Ecc 2: 8 I amassed **s** and gold for myself, and the H4084
Ecc 12: 6 before the **s** cord is severed, and H4084
SS 1:11 you earrings of gold, studded with **s**. H4084
SS 3:10 Its posts he made of **s**, its base of gold. H4084
SS 8: 9 is a wall, we will build towers of **s** on her. H4084
SS 8:11 bring for its fruit a thousand shekels of **s**. H4084
Isa 1:22 Your **s** has become dross, your choice H4084
Isa 2: 7 Their land is full of **s** and gold; there is no H4084
Isa 2:20 bats their idols of **s** and idols of gold, H4084
Isa 7:23 vines worth a thousand **s** shekels, H4084
Isa 13:17 who do not care for **s** and have no delight H4084
Isa 30:22 idols overlaid with **s** and your images H4084
Isa 31: 7 reject the idols of **s** and gold your sinful H4084
Isa 39: 2 was in his storehouses—the **s**, the gold, H4084
Isa 40:19 it with gold and fashions **s** chains for it. H4084
Isa 46: 6 their bags and weigh out **s** on the scales; H4084
Isa 48:10 though not as **s**; I have tested you in H4084
Isa 60: 9 from afar, with their **s** and gold, to the H4084
Isa 60:17 will bring you gold, and **s** in place of iron. H4084
Jer 6:30 They are called rejected **s**, because the H4084
Jer 10: 4 They adorn it with **s** and gold; they fasten H4084
Jer 10: 9 Hammered **s** is brought from Tarshish H4084
Jer 32: 9 out for him seventeen shekels of **s**. H4084
Jer 32:10 weighed out the **s** on the scales. H4084
Jer 32:25 'Buy the field with **s** and have the H4084
Jer 32:44 Fields will be bought for **s**, and deeds will H4084
Jer 52:19 that were made of pure gold or **s**. H4084+4084
Eze 7:19 " 'They will throw their **s** into the streets H4084
Eze 7:19 Their **s** and gold will not be able to H4084
Eze 16:13 So you were adorned with gold and **s**; your H4084
Eze 16:17 the jewelry made of my gold and **s**, and H4084
Eze 22:18 They are but the dross of **s**. H4084
Eze 22:20 As **s**, copper, iron, lead and tin are H4084
Eze 22:22 As **s** is melted in a furnace, so you will be H4084
Eze 27:12 wealth of goods; they exchanged **s**, iron, H4084
Eze 28: 4 amassed gold and **s** in your treasuries. H4084
Eze 38:13 to carry off **s** and gold, to take H4084
Da 2:32 its chest and arms of **s**, its belly and A10362
Da 2:35 the **s** and the gold were all broken to A10362
Da 2:45 the clay, the **s** and the gold to pieces. A10362
Da 5: 2 to bring in the gold and **s** goblets that A10362
Da 5: 4 they praised the gods of gold and **s**, of A10362
Da 5:23 You praised the gods of **s** and gold, of A10362
Da 11: 8 valuable articles of **s** and gold and carry H4084
Da 11:38 ancestors he will honor with gold and **s**, H4084
Da 11:43 of gold and **s** and all the riches of H4084
Hos 2: 8 who lavished on her the **s** and gold H4084
Hos 3: 2 fifteen shekels of **s** and about a homer H4084
Hos 8: 4 With their **s** and gold they make idols H4084
Hos 9: 6 Their treasures of **s** will be taken over by H4084
Hos 13: 2 make idols for themselves from their **s**, H4084
Joel 3: 5 For you took my **s** and my gold and carried H4084
Am 2: 6 They sell the innocent for **s**, and the H4084
Am 8: 6 the poor with **s** and the needy for a H4084
Na 2: 9 Plunder the **s**! Plunder the gold! The H4084
Hab 2:19 It is covered with gold and **s**; there is no H4084
Zep 1:11 all who trade with **s** will be destroyed. H4084
Zep 1:18 Neither their **s** nor their gold will be able H4084
Hag 2: 8 'The **s** is mine and the gold is mine,' H4084
Zec 6:10 "Take **s** and gold from the exiles Heldai NDT
Zec 6:11 Take the **s** and gold and make a crown H4084
Zec 9: 3 she has heaped up **s** like dust, and gold H4084
Zec 11:12 So they paid me thirty pieces of **s**. H4084
Zec 11:13 the thirty pieces of **s** and threw them to H4084
Zec 13: 9 will refine them like **s** and test them like H4084
Zec 14:14 quantities of gold and **s** and clothing. H4084
Mal 3: 3 He will sit as a refiner and purifier of **s**; he H4084
Mal 3: 3 Levites and refine them like gold and **s**. H4084
Mt 10: 9 not get any gold or **s** or copper to take with *G738*
Mt 18:28 who owed him a hundred **s coins**. *G1324*
Mt 26:15 they counted out for him thirty **pieces of s**. *G736*
Mt 27: 3 returned the thirty **pieces of s** to the chief *G736*
Mt 27: 9 "They took the thirty **pieces of s**, the price *G736*
Lk 15: 8 a woman has ten **s coins** and loses one. *G1534*
Ac 3: 6 Then Peter said, "**S** or gold I do not have *G736*
Ac 17:29 the divine being is like gold or **s** or stone— *G738*
Ac 19:24 Demetrius, who made **s** shrines of Artemis *G739*
Ac 20:33 not coveted anyone's **s** or gold or clothing. *G736*
1Co 3:12 this foundation using gold, **s**, costly stones, *G738*
2Ti 2:20 there are articles not only of gold and **s**, *G739*
Jas 5: 3 Your gold and **s** are corroded. Their *G738*
1Pe 1:18 things such as **s** or gold that you were *G736*
Rev 9:20 idols of gold, **s**, bronze, stone and *G739*
Rev 18:12 cargoes of gold, **s**, precious stones and *G738*

SILVERSMITH (3)

Jdg 17: 4 shekels of silver and gave them to a **s**, H7671
Pr 25: 4 the silver, and a **s** can produce a vessel; H7671
Ac 19:24 A **s** named Demetrius, who made silver *G737*

SIMEON (43) [SIMEONITE, SIMEONITES]

Ge 29:33 me this one too." So she named him **S**. H9058
Ge 34:25 two of Jacob's sons, **S** and Levi, Dinah's H9058
Ge 34:30 Then Jacob said to **S** and Levi, "You have H9058
Ge 35:23 the firstborn of Jacob, **S**, Levi, Judah, H9058
Ge 42:24 He had **S** taken from them and bound H9058
Ge 42:36 Joseph is no more and **S** is no more, and H9058
Ge 43:23 Then he brought **S** out to them. H9058
Ge 46:10 The sons of **S**: Jemuel, Jamin, Ohad H9058
Ge 48: 5 be mine, just as Reuben and **S** are mine. H9058
Ge 49: 5 "**S** and Levi are brothers—their swords H9058
Ex 1: 2 Reuben, **S**, Levi and Judah; H9058
Ex 6:15 The sons of **S** were Jemuel, Jamin, Ohad H9058
Ex 6:15 These were the clans of **S**. H9058
Nu 1: 6 from **S**, Shelumiel son of Zurishaddai; H9058
Nu 1:22 From the descendants of **S**: All the men H9058
Nu 1:23 number from the tribe of **S** was 59,300. H9058
Nu 2:12 The tribe of **S** will camp next to them. H9058
Nu 2:12 of the people of **S** is Shelumiel son of H9058
Nu 7:36 the leader of the people of **S**, brought his H9058
Nu 10:19 over the division of the tribe of **S**, H1201+9058
Nu 13: 5 from the tribe of **S**, Shaphat son of Hori; H9058
Nu 26:12 The descendants of **S** by their clans were H9058
Nu 26:14 These were the clans of **S**; those H9063
Nu 34:20 of Ammihud, from the tribe of **S**; H1201+9058
Dt 27:12 **S**, Levi, Judah, Issachar, Joseph and H9058
Jos 19: 1 the tribe of **S** according to its H1201+9058
Jos 21: 4 from the tribes of Judah, **S** and Benjamin. H9063
Jos 21: 9 of Judah and **S** they allotted the H1201+9058
1Ch 2: 1 Reuben, **S**, Levi, Judah, Issachar, Zebulun, H9058
1Ch 4:24 The descendants of **S**: Nemuel, Jamin H9058
1Ch 6:65 **S** and Benjamin they allotted the H1201+9058
1Ch 12:25 from **S**, warriors ready for battle H1201+9058
2Ch 15: 9 Manasseh and **S** who had settled among H9058
2Ch 34: 6 Ephraim and **S**, as far as Naphtali, H9058
Eze 48:24 "**S** will have one portion; it will border the H9058
Eze 48:25 border the territory of **S** from east to west. H9058
Eze 48:33 the gate of **S**, the gate of Issachar and the H9058
Lk 2:25 there was a man in Jerusalem called **S**, *G5208*
Lk 2:28 **S** took him in his arms and praised God *G899S*
Lk 2:34 Then **S** blessed them and said to Mary, his *G5208*

Lk 3:30 the son *of* S, the son of Judah, the son of *G5208*
Ac 13: 1 Barnabas, S called Niger, Lucius of Cyrene *G5208*
Rev 7: 7 from the tribe *of* S 12,000, from the tribe *G5208*

SIMEONITE (1) [SIMEON]

Nu 25:14 son of Salu, the leader of a S family. H9063

SIMEONITES (8) [SIMEON]

Jos 19: 8 inheritance of the tribe of the S, H1201+9058
Jos 19: 9 of the S was taken from the H1201+9058
Jos 19: 9 So the S received their inheritance H1201+9058
Jdg 1: 3 Judah then said to the S their fellow H9058
Jdg 1: 3 you into yours." So the S went with them. H9058
Jdg 1:17 of Judah went with the S their fellow H9058
1Ch 4:42 And five hundred of these S, led by H1201+9058
1Ch 27:16 son of Zikri; over the S: Shephatiah son of H9063

SIMILAR (10) [SIMILARLY]

1Ki 7: 8 set farther back, was s *in* design. H3869
2Ki 25:17 The other pillar, with its network, was **s**. H3869
Jer 36:32 And many s words were added to them H3869
Jer 52:22 other pillar, with its pomegranates, was **s**. H3869
Eze 41:21 the Most Holy Place was s. H3869+2021+5260
Eze 42:11 width, with s exits and dimensions. H3869
Eze 42:11 S *to* the doorways on the north H3869
Zec 14:15 A s plague will strike the horses and H4027
Mk 4:33 With many s parables Jesus spoke the *G5525*
Jude 7 In a s way, Sodom and Gomorrah and the *G3927*

SIMILARLY (4) [SIMILAR]

2Ch 3:12 S one wing of the second cherub was five H2256
1Co 7:22 Lord's freed person; s, the one who was *G3931*
2Ti 2: 5 S, anyone who competes as an athlete *G2779*
Titus 2: 6 S, encourage the young men to be *G6058*

SIMON (74) [PETER, SIMON'S]

Mt 4:18 S called Peter and his brother Andrew. *G4981*
Mt 10: 2 S (who is called Peter) and his *G4981*
Mt 10: 4 S the Zealot and Judas Iscariot, who *G4981*
Mt 13:55 his brothers James, Joseph, S and Judas? *G4981*
Mt 16:16 S Peter answered, "You are the Messiah *G4981*
Mt 16:17 "Blessed are you, S son of Jonah, for this *G4981*
Mt 17:25 "What do you think, S?" he asked. *G4981*
Mt 26: 6 in Bethany in the home *of* S the Leper, *G4981*
Mt 27:32 from Cyrene, named S, and they forced *G4981*
Mk 1:16 he saw S and his brother Andrew casting *G4981*
Mk 1:29 John to the home *of* S and Andrew. *G4981*
Mk 1:36 S and his companions went to look for him *G4981*
Mk 3:16 he appointed: S (to whom he gave the *G4981*
Mk 3:18 of Alphaeus, Thaddaeus, S the Zealot *G4981*
Mk 6: 3 brother of James, Joseph, Judas and S? *G4981*
Mk 14: 3 at the table in the home *of* S the Leper, *G4981*
Mk 14:37 them sleeping. "S," he said to Peter *G4981*
Mk 15:21 man from Cyrene, S, the father of *G4981*
Lk 4:38 synagogue and went to the home *of* S. *G4981*
Lk 5: 3 the one belonging to S, and asked him to *G4981*
Lk 5: 4 speaking, he said to S, "Put out into deep *G4981*
Lk 5: 5 S answered, "Master, we've worked hard *G4981*
Lk 5: 8 When S Peter saw this, he fell at Jesus' *G4981*
Lk 5:10 Then Jesus said to S, "Don't be afraid *G4981*
Lk 6:14 S (whom he named Peter), his brother *G4981*
Lk 6:15 of Alphaeus, S who was called the Zealot *G4981*
Lk 7:40 answered him, "S, I have something to *G4981*
Lk 7:43 S replied, "I suppose the one who had *G4981*
Lk 7:44 turned toward the woman and said *to* S, *G4981*
Lk 22:31 "S, Simon, Satan has asked to sift all of *G4981*
Lk 22:31 "Simon, S, Satan has asked to sift all of *G4981*
Lk 22:32 I have prayed for you, S, that your faith may NDT
Lk 23:26 they seized S from Cyrene, who was *G4981*
Lk 24:34 The Lord has risen and has appeared *to* S." *G4981*
Jn 1:40 Andrew, S Peter's brother, was one of the *G4981*
Jn 1:41 did was to find his brother S and tell him, *G4981*
Jn 1:42 at him and said, "You are S son of John. *G4981*
Jn 6: 8 disciples, Andrew, S Peter's brother *G4981*
Jn 6:68 S Peter answered him, "Lord, to whom *G4981*
Jn 6:71 meant Judas, the *son of* S Iscariot, who, *G4981*
Jn 13: 2 prompted Judas, the *son of* S Iscariot, to *G4981*
Jn 13: 6 He came to S Peter, who said to him *G4981*
Jn 13: 9 S Peter replied, "not just my feet but my *G4981*
Jn 13:24 S Peter motioned to this disciple and said *G4981*
Jn 13:26 he gave it to Judas, the *son of* S Iscariot. *G4981*
Jn 13:36 S Peter asked him, "Lord, where are you *G4981*
Jn 18:10 Then S Peter, who had a sword, drew it *G4981*
Jn 18:15 S Peter and another disciple were *G4981*
Jn 18:25 S Peter was still standing there warming *G4981*
Jn 20: 2 came running to S Peter and the other *G4981*
Jn 20: 6 Then S Peter came along behind him and *G4981*
Jn 21: 2 S Peter, Thomas (also known as Didymus), *G4981*
Jn 21: 3 going out to fish," S Peter told them, and *G4981*
Jn 21: 7 As soon as S Peter heard him say, "It is *G4981*
Jn 21:11 So S Peter climbed back into the boat and *G4981*
Jn 21:15 Jesus said *to* S Peter, "Simon son *G4981*
Jn 21:15 to Simon Peter, "S son of John, do you *G4981*
Jn 21:16 Again Jesus said, "S son of John, do you *G4981*
Jn 21:17 he said to him, "S son of John, do you *G4981*
Ac 1:13 James son of Alphaeus and S the Zealot *G4981*
Ac 8: 9 time a man named S had practiced *G4981*
Ac 8:13 S himself believed and was baptized. *G4981*
Ac 8:18 When S saw that the Spirit was given at *G4981*
Ac 8:24 Then S answered, "Pray to the Lord for me *G4981*
Ac 9:43 some time with a tanner named S. *G4981*
Ac 10: 5 back a man named S who is called Peter. *G4981*
Ac 10: 6 He is staying with S the tanner, whose *G4981*
Ac 10:18 asking if S who was known as Peter was *G4981*
Ac 10:19 Spirit said to him, "S, three men are looking NDT
Ac 10:32 Send to Joppa for S who is called Peter *G4981*
Ac 10:32 He is a guest in the home *of* S the tanner *G4981*
Ac 11:13 'Send to Joppa for S who is called Peter. *G4981*
Ac 15:14 S has described to us how God first *G5208*
2Pe 1: 1 S Peter, a servant and apostle of Jesus *G5208*

SIMON'S (4) [SIMON]

Mk 1:30 S mother-in-law was in bed with a fever *G4981*
Lk 4:38 Now S mother-in-law was suffering from *G4981*
Lk 5:10 the sons of Zebedee, S partners. *G4981*
Ac 10:17 found out where S house was and *G4981*

SIMPLE (23) [SIMPLY]

Ex 18:22 the s cases they can decide themselves. H7785
Ex 18:26 the s ones they decided themselves. H7785
2Ki 20:10 "*It is a* s *matter* for the shadow to go H7837
Job 5: 2 kills a fool, and envy slays the s. H7331
Ps 19: 7 LORD are trustworthy, making wise the s. H7343
Ps 119:130 it gives understanding to the s. H7343
Pr 1: 4 giving prudence to *those who* are s H7343
Pr 1:22 long will you *who* are s love your simple H7343
Pr 1:22 will you who are simple love your **s ways**? H7344
Pr 1:32 the waywardness of the s will kill them, H7343
Pr 7: 7 I saw among the s, I noticed among the H7343
Pr 8: 5 You who are s, gain prudence; you who H7343
Pr 9: 4 "Let all who are s come to my house!" H7343
Pr 9: 6 Leave your **s ways** and you will live; walk H7344
Pr 9:13 woman; she is s and knows nothing. H7346
Pr 9:16 "Let all who are s come to my house!" H7343
Pr 14:15 The s believe anything, but the prudent H7343
Pr 14:18 The s inherit folly, but the prudent are H7343
Pr 19:25 a mocker, and the s will learn prudence H7343
Pr 21:11 is punished, the s gain wisdom; by paying H7343
Pr 22: 3 the s keep going and pay the penalty. H7343
Pr 27:12 the s keep going and pay the penalty. H7343
Jas 5:12 All you need to say is a s "**Yes**" or "No." AIT

SIMPLY (5) [SIMPLE]

Ge 43: 7 We s answered his questions H6584+7023
Mt 5:37 you need to say is s '**Yes**' or 'No'; *G3721+3721*
Ac 8:16 they had s been baptized in the name of *G3667*
1Co 9:17 I am s discharging the trust committed to NDT
1Th 1: 5 came to you not s with words but also *G3667*

SIN (464) [SIN'S, SINFUL, SINFULNESS, SINNED, SINNER, SINNER'S, SINNERS, SINNING, SINS]

Ge 4: 7 what is right, s is crouching at your door H2633
Ge 15:16 the s *of* the Amorites has not yet H6411
Ge 18:20 is so great and their s so grievous H2633
Ge 39: 9 such a wicked thing and s against God?" H2627
Ge 42:22 "Didn't I tell you not *to* s against the boy? H2627
Ex 10:17 Now forgive my s once more and pray to H2633
Ex 16: 1 from Elim and came to the Desert of S, H6097
Ex 17: 1 community set out from the Desert of S, H6097
Ex 20: 5 the children for the s *of* the parents to the H6411
Ex 23:33 land or *they will* **cause** you **to** s against H2627
Ex 29:14 outside the camp. It is a **s offering**. H2633
Ex 29:36 each day as a **s offering** to make H2633
Ex 30:10 of the atoning **s offering** for the H2633
Ex 32:21 that you led them into such great s?" H2631
Ex 32:30 "You *have* **committed** a great s. H2627+2631
Ex 32:30 perhaps I can make atonement for your s." H2633
Ex 32:31 what a great s these people *have* **committed** H2627+2631
Ex 32:32 please forgive their s—but if not, then H2633
Ex 32:34 to punish, I will punish them for their s." H2633
Ex 34: 7 forgiving wickedness, rebellion and s. H2632
Ex 34: 7 children for the s *of* the parents to the H6411
Ex 34: 9 forgive our wickedness and our s, and H2633
Lev 4: 3 defect as a **s offering** for the sin he has H2633
Lev 4: 3 a sin offering for the s he has committed. H2633
Lev 4: 8 all the fat from the bull of the **s offering**— H2633
Lev 4:14 the s they committed becomes known H2633
Lev 4:14 a young bull as a **s offering** and present it H2633
Lev 4:20 as he did with the bull for the **s offering**. H2633
Lev 4:21 This is the **s offering** *for* the community. H2633
Lev 4:23 the s he has committed becomes H2633
Lev 4:24 before the LORD. It is a **s offering**. H2633
Lev 4:25 the blood of the **s offering** with his finger H2633
Lev 4:26 will make atonement for the leader's **s**, H2633
Lev 4:28 the s they have committed becomes H2633
Lev 4:28 their offering for the s they committed a H2633
Lev 4:29 the head of the **s offering** and slaughter it H2633
Lev 4:32 brings a lamb as their **s** offering, H2633
Lev 4:33 slaughter it for a **s offering** at the place H2633
Lev 4:34 the blood of the **s offering** with his finger H2633
Lev 4:35 them for the s they have committed, H2633
Lev 5: 6 As a penalty for the s they have committed H2633
Lev 5: 6 goat from the flock as a **s offering**; H2633
Lev 5: 6 shall make atonement for them for their s. H2633
Lev 5: 7 to the LORD as a penalty for their s— H2627
Lev 5: 7 one for a **s offering** and the other for a H2633
Lev 5: 8 shall first offer the one for the **s offering**. H2633
Lev 5: 9 the blood of the **s offering** against the H2633
Lev 5: 9 at the base of the altar. It is a **s offering**. H2633
Lev 5:10 them for the s they have committed, H2633
Lev 5:11 an offering for their s a tenth of an ephah H2627
Lev 5:11 ephah of the finest flour for a **s offering**. H2633
Lev 5:11 incense on it, because it is a **s offering**. H2633
Lev 5:12 presented to the LORD. It is a **s offering**. H2633
Lev 6: 3 about any such s that people may commit H2627
Lev 6: 4 when *they* s in any of these ways and H2627
Lev 6:17 Like the **s offering** and the guilt offering, it H2633
Lev 6:25 are the regulations for the **s offering**: H2633
Lev 6:25 The **s offering** is to be slaughtered before H2633
Lev 6:30 But any **s offering** whose blood is brought H2633
Lev 7: 7 to both the **s offering** and the guilt H2633
Lev 7:37 grain offering, the **s offering**, the guilt H2633
Lev 8: 2 the bull for the **s offering**, the two rams H2633
Lev 8:14 then presented the bull for the **s offering**, H2633
Lev 9: 2 bull calf for your **s offering** and a ram for H2633
Lev 9: 3 'Take a male goat for a **s offering**, a calf H2633
Lev 9: 7 sacrifice your **s offering** and your burnt H2633
Lev 9: 8 the calf as a **s offering** for himself. H2633
Lev 9:10 long lobe of the liver from the **s offering**, H2633
Lev 9:15 the people's **s offering** and slaughtered H2633
Lev 9:15 it and **offered** it **for a s offering** as he did H2627
Lev 9:22 And having sacrificed the **s offering**, the H2633
Lev 10:16 the goat of the **s offering** and found that it H2633
Lev 10:17 you eat the **s offering** in the sanctuary H2633
Lev 10:19 sacrificed their **s offering** and their burnt H2633
Lev 10:19 if I had eaten the **s offering** today? H2633
Lev 12: 6 a young pigeon or a dove for a **s offering**. H2633
Lev 12: 8 offering and the other for a **s offering**. H2633
Lev 14:13 area where the **s offering** and the burnt H2633
Lev 14:13 Like the **s offering**, the guilt offering H2633
Lev 14:19 to sacrifice the **s offering** and make H2633
Lev 14:22 one for a **s offering** and the other for a H2633
Lev 14:31 one as a **s offering** and the other as a H2633
Lev 15:15 the one for a **s offering** and the other for a H2633
Lev 15:30 one for a **s offering** and the other for H2633
Lev 16: 3 young bull for a **s offering** and a ram for a H2633
Lev 16: 5 goats for a **s offering** and a ram for a H2633
Lev 16: 6 bull for his own **s offering** to make H2633
Lev 16: 9 to the LORD and sacrifice it for a **s offering**. H2633
Lev 16:11 bull for his own **s offering** to make H2633
Lev 16:11 slaughter the bull for his own **s offering**. H2633
Lev 16:15 the goat for the **s offering** for the people H2633
Lev 16:25 burn the fat of the **s offering** on the altar. H2633
Lev 16:27 The bull and the goat for the **s offerings** H2633
Lev 18:25 so I punished it for its s, and the land H6411
Lev 19:22 the LORD for the s he has committed, H2633
Lev 19:22 has committed, and his s will be forgiven. H2633
Lev 23:19 male goat for a **s offering** and two lambs, H2633
Lev 26:41 are humbled and they pay for their s, H6411
Nu 5: 7 must confess the s they have committed H2633
Nu 5:31 will bear the **consequences of** her s. H6411
Nu 6:11 offer one as a **s offering** and the other as H2633
Nu 6:14 ewe lamb without defect for a **s offering**, H2633
Nu 6:16 make the **s offering** and the burnt H2633
Nu 7:16 one male goat for a **s offering**; H2633
Nu 7:22 one male goat for a **s offering**; H2633
Nu 7:28 one male goat for a **s offering**; H2633
Nu 7:34 one male goat for a **s offering**; H2633
Nu 7:40 one male goat for a **s offering**; H2633
Nu 7:46 one male goat for a **s offering**; H2633
Nu 7:52 one male goat for a **s offering**; H2633
Nu 7:58 one male goat for a **s offering**; H2633
Nu 7:64 one male goat for a **s offering**; H2633
Nu 7:70 one male goat for a **s offering**; H2633
Nu 7:76 one male goat for a **s offering**; H2633
Nu 7:82 one male goat for a **s offering**; H2633
Nu 7:87 male goats were used for the **s offering**. H2633
Nu 8: 8 take a second young bull for a **s offering**. H2633
Nu 8:12 using one for a **s offering** to the LORD and H2633
Nu 9:13 will bear the **consequences of** their s. H2628
Nu 12:11 hold against us the s we have so foolishly H2633
Nu 14:18 in love and forgiving s and rebellion. H6411
Nu 14:18 the children for the s *of* the parents to the H6411
Nu 14:19 forgive the s *of* these people, just as H6411
Nu 15:24 offering, and a male goat for a **s offering**. H2633
Nu 15:25 wrong a food offering and a **s offering**. H2633
Nu 15:27 a year-old female goat for a **s offering**. H2633
Nu 18: 9 whether grain or s or guilt offerings, that H2633
Nu 18:22 bear the **consequences** of their s and will H2628
Nu 19: 9 of cleansing; it is for **purification from s**. H2633
Nu 27: 3 he died for his own s and left no sons. H2628
Nu 28:15 be presented to the LORD as a **s offering**. H2633
Nu 28:22 male goat as a **s offering** to make H2633
Nu 29: 5 male goat as a **s offering** to make H2633
Nu 29:11 Include one male goat as a **s offering**, in H2633
Nu 29:11 to the **s offering** *for* atonement and H2633
Nu 29:16 Include one male goat as a **s offering**, in H2633
Nu 29:19 Include one male goat as a **s offering**, in H2633
Nu 29:22 Include one male goat as a **s offering**, in H2633
Nu 29:25 Include one male goat as a **s offering**, in H2633
Nu 29:28 Include one male goat as a **s offering**, in H2633
Nu 29:31 Include one male goat as a **s offering**, in H2633
Nu 29:34 Include one male goat as a **s offering**, in H2633
Nu 29:38 Include one male goat as a **s offering**, in H2633
Nu 32:23 may be sure that your s will find you out. H2633
Nu 33:11 Red Sea and camped in the Desert of S. H6097
Nu 33:12 left the Desert of S and camped at H6097
Dt 5: 9 the children for the s *of* the parents to the H6411
Dt 9:18 because of all the s you had committed H2633
Dt 9:27 this people, their wickedness and their s. H2633
Dt 15: 9 and you will be found **guilty of s**. H2628
Dt 20:18 and *you will* s against the LORD your God. H2627
Dt 22:26 she has committed no s *deserving* death. H2628
Dt 23:21 it of you and you will be **guilty of s**. H2628
Dt 24: 4 *Do* not **bring s** *upon* the land the LORD H2627
Dt 24:15 against you, and you will be **guilty of s**. H2628

Dt 24:16 their parents; each will die for their own s. H2628
Jos 22:17 Was not the s of Peor enough for us? Up H6411
Jos 22:17 we have not cleansed ourselves from that s, NDT
Jos 22:20 was not the only one who died for his s. H6411
1Sa 2:17 This s of the young men was very great in H2633
1Sa 3:13 forever because of the s he knew about; H6411
1Sa 12:23 it from me that I should s against the LORD H2627
1Sa 14:34 Do not s against the LORD by eating meat H2627
1Sa 14:38 let us find out what s has been committed H2633
1Sa 15:23 For rebellion is like the s of divination H2633
1Sa 15:25 forgive my s and come back with me H2633
2Sa 12:13 replied, "The LORD has taken away your s. H2633
2Sa 22:24 before him and have kept myself from s. H6411
1Ki 8:34 forgive the s of your people Israel H2633
1Ki 8:35 turn from their s because you have H2633
1Ki 8:36 heaven and forgive the s of your servants, H2633
1Ki 8:46 "When they s against you—for there is no H2627
1Ki 8:46 there is no one who does not s—and H2627
1Ki 12:30 And this thing became a s; the people H2633
1Ki 13:34 This was the s of the house of Jeroboam H2633
1Ki 15:26 committing the same s his father had H2633
1Ki 15:34 the same s Jeroboam had caused H2633
1Ki 16: 2 and caused my people Israel to s and to H2627
1Ki 16:19 the same s Jeroboam had caused H2633
1Ki 16:26 the same s Jeroboam had caused H2633
1Ki 17:18 to remind me of my s and kill my son?" H6411
1Ki 21:22 my anger and have caused Israel to s. H2627
1Ki 22:52 son of Nebat, who caused Israel to s. H2627
2Ki 12:16 offerings and s offerings was not brought H2633
2Ki 14: 6 their parents; each will die for their own s." H2628
2Ki 17:21 caused them to commit a great s. H2631
2Ki 21:11 him and has led Judah into s with his H2627
2Ki 21:16 besides the s that he had caused Judah to H2633
2Ki 21:17 including the s he committed, are H2633
2Ki 23:15 who had caused Israel to s—even that H2627
2Ch 6:25 forgive the s of your people Israel H2633
2Ch 6:26 turn from their s because you have H2633
2Ch 6:27 heaven and forgive the s of your servants, H2633
2Ch 6:36 "When they s against you—for there is no H2627
2Ch 6:36 there is no one who does not s—and H2627
2Ch 7:14 I will forgive their s and will heal their H2633
2Ch 19:10 are to warn them not to s against the LORD; H870
2Ch 19:10 Do this, and you will not s. H870
2Ch 25: 4 their parents; each will die for their own s." H2628
2Ch 28:13 Do you intend to add to our s and guilt H2633
2Ch 29:21 male goats as a s offering for the H2633
2Ch 29:23 The goats for the s offering were brought H2633
2Ch 29:24 presented their blood on the altar for a s offering H2627
2Ch 29:24 offering and the s offering for all Israel. H2633
Ezr 6:17 lambs and, as a s offering for all Israel A10260
Ezr 8:35 lambs and, as a s offering, twelve male H2633
Ne 6:13 me so that I would commit a s by doing H2627
Ne 10:33 s offerings to make atonement for H2633
Ne 13:26 even he was led into s by foreign H2627
Job 1:22 Job did not s by charging God with H2627
Job 2:10 In all this, Job did not s in what he said. H2627
Job 8: 4 gave them over to the penalty of their s. H7322
Job 10: 6 out my faults and probe after my s— H2633
Job 11: 6 God has even forgotten some of your s. H6411
Job 11:14 if you put away the s that is in your hand H224
Job 13:23 Show me my offense and my s. H2633
Job 14:16 count my steps but not keep track of my s. H2633
Job 14:17 up in a bag; you will cover over my s. H6411
Job 15: 5 Your s prompts your mouth; you adopt the H6411
Job 31:11 have been wicked, a s to be judged. H6411
Job 31:30 my mouth to s by invoking a curse H2627
Job 31:33 if I have concealed my s as people do, by H7322
Job 33: 9 no wrong; I am clean and free from s. H6411
Job 34:37 To his s he adds rebellion; scornfully he H2633
Job 35: 6 If you s, how does that affect him? If your H2627
Ps 4: 4 Tremble and do not s; when you are on H2627
Ps 18:23 before him and have kept myself from s. H6411
Ps 32: 2 is the one whose s the LORD does not H6411
Ps 32: 5 I acknowledged my s to you and did not H2633
Ps 32: 5 And you forgave the guilt of my s. H2633
Ps 36: 2 too much to detect or hate their s. H6411
Ps 38: 3 soundness in my bones because of my s. H2633
Ps 38:18 my iniquity; I am troubled by my s. H2633
Ps 39: 1 my ways and keep my tongue from s; H2627
Ps 39:11 rebuke and discipline anyone for their s, H6411
Ps 40: 6 burnt offerings and s offerings you did not H2631
Ps 51: 2 all my iniquity and cleanse me from my s. H2633
Ps 51: 3 my s is always before me. H2633
Ps 59: 3 against me for no offense or s of mine, H2633
Ps 66:18 If I had cherished s in my heart, the Lord H224
Ps 78:17 But they continued to s against him H2627
Ps 89:32 I will punish their s with the rod, their H7322
Ps 106:43 rebellion and they wasted away in their s. H6411
Ps 109:14 may the s of his mother never be blotted H2633
Ps 119:11 in my heart that I might not s against you. H2627
Ps 119:133 to your word; let no s rule over me. H224
Pr 10:16 earnings of the wicked are s and death. H2633
Pr 10:19 S is not ended by multiplying words, but H7322
Pr 14: 9 Fools mock at making amends for s, but H871
Pr 14:21 It is a s to despise one's neighbor, but H2627
Pr 14:34 a nation, but s condemns any people. H2633
Pr 16: 6 love and faithfulness s is atoned for; H6411
Pr 17:19 Whoever loves a quarrel loves s; whoever H7322
Pr 20: 9 heart pure; I am clean and without s"? H2633
Pr 21: 4 unplowed field of the wicked—produce s. H2633
Pr 24: 9 The schemes of folly are s, and people H2633
Pr 29: 6 Evildoers are snared by their own s, but H7322
Pr 29:16 wicked thrive, so does s, but the righteous H7322
Ecc 5: 6 Do not let your mouth lead you into s. H2627
Isa 3: 9 they parade their s like Sodom; they do H2633
Isa 5:18 to those who draw s along with cords of H6411
Isa 6: 7 guilt is taken away and your s atoned for." H2633
Isa 22:14 your dying day this s will not be atoned H6411
Isa 27: 9 be the full fruit of the removal of his s: H2633
Isa 30: 1 not by my Spirit, heaping s upon sin; H2633
Isa 30: 1 not by my Spirit, heaping sin upon s; H2633
Isa 30:13 this s will become for you like a high wall H6411
Isa 40: 2 completed, that her s has been paid for H6411
Isa 53:10 the LORD makes his life an offering for s, H871
Isa 53:12 For he bore the s of many, and made H2628
Isa 59: 7 Their feet rush into s; they are swift to H8273
Isa 64: 5 But when we continued to s against them H2627
Jer 9: 3 They go from one s to another; they do H8288
Jer 9: 7 can I do because of the s of my people? NDT
Jer 16:10 What s have we committed against the H2633
Jer 16:17 nor is their s concealed from my eyes. H6411
Jer 16:18 double for their wickedness and their s, H2633
Jer 17: 1 "Judah's s is engraved with an iron tool H2633
Jer 17: 3 because of s throughout your country. H2633
Jer 31:30 everyone will die for their own s; whoever H6411
Jer 32:35 a detestable thing and so make Judah s. H2627
Jer 33: 8 them from all the s they have committed H6411
Jer 36: 3 I will forgive their wickedness and their s." H2633
La 2:14 they did not expose your s to ward off your H6411
La 4:22 But he will punish your s, Daughter Edom H6411
Eze 3:18 that wicked person will die for their s, and H6411
Eze 3:19 they will die for their s; but you will have H6411
Eze 3:20 not warn them, they will die for their s. H2633
Eze 3:21 person not to s and they do not sin, H2627
Eze 3:21 person not to sin and they do not s, H2627
Eze 4: 4 side and put the s of the people of Israel H6411
Eze 4: 4 You are to bear their s for the number of H6411
Eze 4: 5 number of days as the years of their s. H6411
Eze 4: 5 you will bear the s of the people of Israel. H6411
Eze 4: 6 bear the s of the people of Judah. H6411
Eze 4:17 will waste away because of their s. H6411
Eze 7:19 it has caused them to stumble into s. H6411
Eze 9: 9 "The s of the people of Israel and Judah H6411
Eze 16:49 " 'Now this was the s of your sister Sodom: H6411
Eze 18:17 He will not die for his father's s; he will H6411
Eze 18:18 But his father will die for his own s H6411
Eze 18:24 commits s and does the same H6404
Eze 18:26 from their righteousness and commits s, H6404
Eze 18:26 because of the s they have committed H6404
Eze 18:30 offenses; then s will not be your downfall. H6411
Eze 29:16 a reminder of their s in turning to her for H6411
Eze 33: 6 life will be taken because of their s, H6411
Eze 33: 8 that wicked person will die for their s, and H6411
Eze 33: 9 they will die for their s, though you H6411
Eze 33:14 turn away from their s and do what is just H2633
Eze 39:23 people of Israel went into exile for their s, H6411
Eze 40:39 s offerings and guilt offerings were H2633
Eze 42:13 the s offerings and the guilt offerings H2633
Eze 43:19 young bull as a s offering to the Levitical H2633
Eze 43:21 the bull for the s offering and burn it in H2633
Eze 43:22 male goat without defect for a s offering, H2633
Eze 43:25 provide a male goat daily for a s offering; H2633
Eze 44:10 must bear the consequences of their s. H6411
Eze 44:12 made the people of Israel fall into s, H6411
Eze 44:12 must bear the consequences of their s, H6411
Eze 44:27 he is to offer a s offering for himself H2633
Eze 44:29 the s offerings and the guilt offerings H2633
Eze 45:17 He will provide the s offerings, grain H2633
Eze 45:19 the blood of the s offering and put it on H2633
Eze 45:22 a bull as a s offering for himself and H2633
Eze 45:23 the LORD, and a male goat for a s offering. H2633
Eze 45:25 make the same provision for s offerings, H2633
Eze 46:20 offering and the s offering and bake the H2633
Da 9:20 confessing my s and the sin of my people H2633
Da 9:20 my sin and the s of my people Israel and H2633
Da 9:24 to put an end to s, to atone for H2633
Hos 5: 5 stumble in their s; Judah also stumbles H6411
Hos 8:11 Ephraim built many altars for s offerings, H2627
Hos 10: 8 will be destroyed—it is the s of Israel. H2633
Hos 10:10 to put them in bonds for their double s. H6411
Hos 12: 8 they will not find in me any iniquity or s." H2628
Hos 13: 2 Now they s more and more; they make H2627
Am 4: 4 "Go to Bethel and s; go to Gilgal and sin H7321
Am 4: 4 go to Gilgal and s yet more. H7321
Am 8:14 Those who swear by the s of Samaria H873
Mic 1:13 You are where the s of Daughter Zion H2633
Mic 3: 8 to Jacob his transgression, to Israel his s. H2633
Mic 6: 7 the fruit of my body for the s of my soul? H2633
Mic 7:18 who pardons s and forgives the H6411
Zec 3: 4 I have taken away your s, and I will put H6411
Zec 3: 9 I will remove the s of this land in a single H6411
Zec 13: 1 to cleanse them from s and impurity. H2633
Mal 2: 6 uprightness, and turned many from s. H6411
Mt 6:14 other people when they s against you, G4183
Mt 12:31 every kind of s and slander can be forgiven G281
Mt 13:41 everything that causes s and all who do G4998
Mk 3:29 be forgiven; they are guilty of an eternal s." G280
Lk 17: 4 Even if they s against you seven times in a G279
Jn 1:29 who takes away the s of the world! G281
Jn 8: 7 one of you who is without s be the first to G387
Jn 8:11 "Go now and leave your life of s." G3600+279
Jn 8:21 will look for me, and you will die in your s. G281
Jn 8:34 I tell you, everyone who sins is a slave to s. G281
Jn 8:46 Can any of you prove me guilty of s? If I am G281
Jn 9:34 "You were steeped in s at birth; how dare G281
Jn 9:41 you would not be guilty of s; but now that G281
Jn 15:22 they would not be guilty of s; but G281+2400
Jn 15:22 now they have no excuse for their s. G281
Jn 15:24 did, they would not be guilty of s. G281+2400
Jn 16: 8 in the wrong about s and righteousness G281
Jn 16: 9 about s, because people do not believe in G281
Jn 19:11 over to you is guilty of a greater s." G281+2400
Ac 7:60 "Lord, do not hold this s against them." G281
Ac 8:23 you are full of bitterness and captive to s." G94
Ac 13:39 who believes is set free from every s, AIT
Ro 2:12 All who s apart from the law will also G279
Ro 2:12 all who s under the law will be judged G279
Ro 3: 9 Gentiles alike are all under the power of s. G281
Ro 3:20 the law we become conscious of our s. G281
Ro 4: 8 is the one whose s the Lord will never G281
Ro 5:12 just as s entered the world through one G281
Ro 5:12 death through s, and in this way death G281
Ro 5:13 s was in the world before the law was G281
Ro 5:13 s is not charged against anyone's G281
Ro 5:14 over those who did not s by breaking a G279
Ro 5:16 compared with the result of one man's s: G279
Ro 5:16 judgment followed one s and brought NDT
Ro 5:20 But where s increased, grace increased all G281
Ro 5:21 just as s reigned in death, so also G281
Ro 6: 2 We are those who have died to s; how can G281
Ro 6: 6 so that the body ruled by s might be done G281
Ro 6: 6 that we should no longer be slaves to s— G281
Ro 6: 7 who has died has been set free from s. G281
Ro 6:10 he died, he died to s once for all; but the G281
Ro 6:11 yourselves dead to s but alive to God in G281
Ro 6:12 Therefore do not let s reign in your mortal G281
Ro 6:13 any part of yourself to s as an instrument of G281
Ro 6:14 For s shall no longer be your master G281
Ro 6:15 Shall we s because we are not under the G279
Ro 6:16 whether you are slaves to s, which leads to G281
Ro 6:17 though you used to be slaves to s, you G281
Ro 6:18 been set free from s and have become G281
Ro 6:20 When you were slaves to s, you were free G281
Ro 6:22 been set free from s and have become G281
Ro 6:23 For the wages of s is death, but the gift of G281
Ro 7: 7 not have known what s was had it not been G281
Ro 7: 8 But s, seizing the opportunity afforded by G281
Ro 7: 8 For apart from the law, s was dead. G281
Ro 7: 9 s sprang to life and I died. G281
Ro 7:11 For s, seizing the opportunity afforded by G281
Ro 7:13 in order that s might be recognized as sin G281
Ro 7:13 in order that sin might be recognized as s G281
Ro 7:13 the commandment s might become utterly G281
Ro 7:14 I am unspiritual, sold as a slave to s. G281
Ro 7:17 I myself who do it, but it is s living in me. G281
Ro 7:20 but it is s living in me that does it. G281
Ro 7:23 prisoner of the law of s at work within me. G281
Ro 7:25 in my sinful nature a slave to the law of s. G281
Ro 8: 2 set you free from the law of s and death. G281
Ro 8: 3 likeness of sinful flesh to be a s offering. G281
Ro 8: 3 And so he condemned s in the flesh, G281
Ro 8:10 your body is subject to death because of s, G281
Ro 14:23 that does not come from faith is s. G281
1Co 8:12 When you s against them in this way and G279
1Co 8:12 their weak conscience, you s against Christ. G279
1Co 8:13 causes my brother or sister to fall into s, G4997
1Co 14:24 they are convicted of s and are brought G1794
1Co 15:56 The sting of death is s, and the power of G281
1Co 15:56 death is sin, and the power of s is the law. G281
2Co 5:21 made him who had no s to be sin for us, G281
2Co 5:21 made him who had no sin to be s for us, G281
2Co 11: 7 Was it a s for me to lower myself in order to G281
2Co 11:29 Who is led into s, and I do not inwardly G4997
2Co 12:21 sexual s and debauchery in which they G4518
Gal 2:17 doesn't that mean that Christ promotes s? G281
Gal 3:22 locked up everything under the control of s, G281
Gal 6: 1 if someone is caught in a s, you who live G4183
Eph 4:26 "In your anger do not s": Do not let the sun G279
Heb 4:15 every way, just as we are—yet he did not s. G281
Heb 9:26 ages to do away with s by the sacrifice of G281
Heb 9:28 not to bear s, but to bring salvation G281
Heb 10: 6 and s offerings you were not G4309+281
Heb 10: 8 offerings and s offerings you did not G4309+281
Heb 10:18 sacrifice for s is no longer necessary. G281
Heb 11:25 than to enjoy the fleeting pleasures of s. G281
Heb 12: 1 that hinders and the s that so easily G281
Heb 12: 4 In your struggle against s, you have not G281
Heb 13:11 the Most Holy Place as a s offering, G4309+281
Jas 1:15 has conceived, it gives birth to s; and sin, G281
Jas 1:15 birth to sin; and s, when it is full-grown, G281
Jas 2: 9 you s and are convicted by the law G281+2237
Jas 4:17 to do and doesn't do it, it is s for them. G281
1Pe 2:22 "He committed no s, and no deceit was G281
1Pe 4: 1 whoever suffers in the body is done with s. G281
1Jn 1: 7 of Jesus, his Son, purifies us from all s. G281
1Jn 1: 8 If we claim to be without s, we deceive G281
1Jn 2: 1 I write this to you so that you will not s. G279
1Jn 2: 1 But if anybody does s, we have an G279
1Jn 3: 4 breaks the law; in fact, s is lawlessness. G281
1Jn 3: 5 take away our sins. And in him is no s. G281
1Jn 3: 6 No one who continues to s has either seen G279
1Jn 3: 9 is born of God will continue to s, G281+4472
1Jn 5:16 sister commit a s that does not G279+281
1Jn 5:16 I refer to those whose s does not lead to G279
1Jn 5:16 There is a s that leads to death. G281

1Jn 5:17 All wrongdoing is s, and there is sin that G281
1Jn 5:17 there is s that does not lead to death. G281
1Jn 5:18 anyone born of God does not continue to s; G279
Rev 2:14 to entice the Israelites to s so G965+4998+1967

SIN'S (1) [SIN]

Heb 3:13 of you may be hardened by s deceitfulness. G281

SINAI (39)

Ex 16: 1 which is between Elim and S, on the H6099
Ex 19: 1 very day—they came to the Desert of S. H6099
Ex 19: 2 they entered the Desert of S, and Israel H6099
Ex 19:11 come down on Mount S in the sight of all H6099
Ex 19:18 Mount S was covered with smoke, because H6099
Ex 19:20 to the top of Mount S and called Moses to H6099
Ex 19:23 "The people cannot come up Mount S H6099
Ex 24:16 the glory of the LORD settled on Mount S. H6099
Ex 31:18 finished speaking to Moses on Mount S, H6099
Ex 34: 2 morning, and then come up on Mount S. H6099
Ex 34: 4 went up Mount S early in the H6099
Ex 34:29 down from Mount S with the two tablets H6099
Ex 34:32 the LORD had given him on Mount S. H6099
Lev 7:38 gave Moses at Mount S in the Desert of H6099
Lev 7:38 Sinai in the Desert of S on the day he H6099
Lev 25: 1 The LORD said to Moses at Mount S, H6099
Lev 26:46 at Mount S between himself and H6099
Lev 27:34 gave Moses at Mount S for the Israelites. H6099
Nu 1: 1 in the Desert of S on the first day of the H6099
Nu 1:19 so he counted them in the Desert of S: H6099
Nu 3: 1 time the LORD spoke to Moses at Mount S. H6099
Nu 3: 4 fire before him in the Desert of S. H6099
Nu 3:14 The LORD said to Moses in the Desert of S, H6099
Nu 9: 1 in the Desert of S in the first month of H6099
Nu 9: 5 did so in the Desert of S at twilight on the H6099
Nu 10:12 out from the Desert of S and traveled from H6099
Nu 26:64 counted the Israelites in the Desert of S. H6099
Nu 28: 6 instituted at Mount S as a pleasing aroma H6099
Nu 33:15 Rephidim and camped in the Desert of S. H6099
Nu 33:16 left the Desert of S and camped at Kibroth H6099
Dt 33: 2 "The LORD came from S and dawned over H6099
Jdg 5: 5 the LORD, the One of S, before the LORD, H6099
Ne 9:13 "You came down on Mount S; you spoke H6099
Ps 68: 8 the One of S, before God, the God H6099
Ps 68:17 Lord has come from S into his sanctuary. H6099
Ac 7:30 burning bush in the desert near Mount S. G4982
Ac 7:38 the angel who spoke to him on Mount S, G4982
Gal 4:24 is from Mount S and bears children who G4982
Gal 4:25 Hagar stands for Mount S in Arabia and G4982

SINCE (273)

Ge 3:19 to the ground, s from it you were taken H3954
Ge 4:25 child in place of Abel, s Cain killed him." H3954
Ge 14:12 possessions, s he was living in Sodom. H2256
Ge 15: 2 what can you give me s I remain childless H2256
Ge 26:27 s you were hostile to me and sent me H2256
Ge 38:26 s I wouldn't give her to my H3954+6584+4027
Ge 41:39 "S God has made all this known to you H339
Ge 42:23 s he was using an interpreter. H3954
Ge 44:28 And I have not seen him s. H6330+2178
Ge 46:30 s I have seen for myself that you are still H339
Ge 47:16 your livestock, s your money is gone." H561
Ge 47:18 lord the fact that s our money is gone and H561
Ex 4:10 in the past nor s you have spoken to H4946+255
Ex 5:23 Ever s I went to Pharaoh to speak in H4946+255
Ex 6:12 listen to me, s I speak with faltering lips?" H2256
Ex 6:30 to the LORD, "S I speak with faltering lips H2176
Ex 8:18 S the gnats were on people and animals H2256
Ex 9:24 the land of Egypt s it had become a H4946+255
Ex 9:31 s the barley had headed and the flax was H3954
Ex 10:11 s that's what you have been asking for." H3954
Ex 21:21 a day or two, s the slave is their property. H3954
Ex 23:21 your rebellion, s my Name is in him. H3954
Lev 10:18 S its blood was not taken into the Holy H2176
Lev 11:11 And s you are to regard them as unclean H2256
Lev 13:13 S it has all turned white NDT
Lev 21: 3 dependent on him s she has no husband— H889
Lev 25:15 basis of the number of years s the Jubilee. H339
Lev 25:27 the value for the years s they sold it and AIT
Lev 27:26 s the firstborn already belongs to the LORD H889
Nu 5:13 s there is no witness against her and she H2256
Nu 11:28 who had been Moses' aide s youth, spoke H4946
Nu 14:25 S the Amalekites and the Canaanites are H2256
Nu 20:21 S Edom refused to let them go through H2256
Nu 22:20 "S these men have come to summon you H561
Nu 25:11 S he was as zealous for my honor among H928
Nu 35:23 then s that other person was not an H2256
Dt 3:27 s you are not going to cross this Jordan. H3954
Dt 9:24 the LORD ever s I have known H4946+3427
Dt 12: 9 s you have not yet reached the resting H3954
Dt 19: 6 s he did it to his neighbor without malice H3954
Dt 21: 9 s you have done what is right in the eyes H3954
Dt 21:14 a slave, s you have dishonored her. H9393+889
Dt 34:10 S then, no prophet has risen in Israel like H6388
Jos 3: 4 s you have never been this way before. H3954
Jos 5: 6 had died, s they had not obeyed the LORD. H889
Jos 7:26 Valley of Achor ever s. H6330+2021+3427+2021+2296
Jos 10:14 has never been a day like it before or s, H339
Jos 13:14 s the food offerings presented to the LORD NDT
Jos 14:10 forty-five years s the time he said this H4946
Jos 14:14 the Kenizzite ever s, H6330+2021+3427+2021+2296
Jos 15:19 S you have given me land in the Negev H3954
Jdg 1:15 S you have given me land in the Negev H3954
Jdg 11:23 "Now s the LORD, the God of Israel, has H2256
Jdg 15: 7 said to them, "S you've acted like this H561
Jdg 17:13 s this Levite has become my priest." H3954
Jdg 18: 7 And s their land lacked nothing, they were NDT
Jdg 19:23 S this man is my guest, don't do this H339+889
Jdg 19:30 not s the day the Israelites came up out of H4946
Jdg 21: 7 s we have taken an oath by the LORD not H2256
Jdg 21:18 s we Israelites have taken this oath: H3954
Ru 2:11 your mother-in-law s the death of your H339
Ru 3: 9 s you are a guardian-redeemer of our H3954
1Sa 16: 1 s I have rejected him as king over Israel? H2256
1Sa 21: 6 s there was no bread there except the H3954
1Sa 25: 8 my men, s we come at a festive time. H3954
1Sa 25:26 s the LORD has kept you from bloodshed H889
1Sa 27: 6 to the kings of Judah ever s. H6330+2021+3427+2021+2296
2Sa 7:11 have done ever s the time I H4946
2Sa 13:14 and s he was stronger than she H2256
2Sa 13:32 express intention ever s the day Amnon H4946
2Sa 19:11 s what is being said throughout Israel has H2256
2Sa 19:26 lord the king, s I your servant am lame H3954
1Ki 3:11 "S you have asked for this and not H3610+889
1Ki 8:16 'S the day I brought my people Israel out H4946
1Ki 8:39 to all they do, s you know their hearts H889
1Ki 10:12 never been imported or seen s that day.) H6330
1Ki 11:11 "S this is your attitude and you have H3610+889
1Ki 18:12 have worshiped the LORD s my youth. H4946
1Ki 18:25 prepare it first, s there are so many of you. H3954
1Ki 21: 2 garden, s it is close to my palace. H3954
2Ki 14:27 And s the LORD had not said he would blot H2256
2Ki 18:26 servants in Aramaic, s we understand it. H3954
1Ch 17:10 have done ever s the time I H4946
1Ch 23:25 For David had said, "S the LORD, the God of NDT
2Ch 1:11 "S this is your heart's desire and you H3610+889
2Ch 1:11 s you have not asked for a long life H1685
2Ch 2: 6 a temple for him, s the heavens, even the H3954
2Ch 6: 5 'S the day I brought my people out of H4946
2Ch 6:30 to all they do, s you know their hearts H889
2Ch 12: 7 "S they have humbled themselves, I will not NDT
2Ch 14: 6 cities of Judah, s the land was at peace. H3954
2Ch 14:14 villages, s there was much plunder there. H3954
2Ch 22: 1 king in his place, s the raiders, who came H3954
2Ch 28:23 "S the gods of the kings of Aram have H3954
2Ch 30:17 S many in the crowd had not consecrated H3954
2Ch 30:26 s the days of Solomon son of David H4946
2Ch 31:10 "S the people began to bring their H4946
2Ch 35:18 like this in Israel s the days of the prophet H4946
Ezr 4: 2 sacrificing to him s the time of H4946
Ezr 4:14 Now s we are under A10353+10619+10168
Ne 6:18 s he was son-in-law to Shekaniah son of H3954
Est 1:13 S it was customary for the king to consult H3954
Est 4:11 days have passed s I was called to go to H4202
Est 6:13 Zeresh said to him, "S Mordecai, before H561
Job 9:29 S I am already found guilty, why should I NDT
Job 19:28 s the root of the trouble lies in him H2256
Job 20: 4 ever s mankind was placed on the earth H4974
Job 21:22 s he judges even the highest? H2256
Job 30: 2 s their vigor had gone from them? NDT
Ps 22: 8 Let him deliver him, s he delights in him." H3954
Ps 31: 3 S you are my rock and my fortress, for the H3954
Ps 35: 7 S they hid their net for me without cause H3954
Ps 44:21 s he knows the secrets of the heart? H3954
Ps 45: 2 s God has blessed you forever. H6584+4027
Ps 71: 5 LORD, my confidence s my youth. H4946
Ps 71:17 S my youth, God, you have taught me H4946
Pr 1:24 But s you refuse to listen when I call and H3610
Pr 1:25 s you disregard all my advice and do not H2256
Pr 1:29 s they hated knowledge and did H9393+3954
Pr 1:30 S they would not accept my advice and NDT
Pr 6: 3 s you have fallen into your neighbor's H3954
Ecc 5:16 do they gain, s they toil for the wind? H8611
Ecc 8: 4 S a king's word is supreme, who can H928+889
Ecc 8: 7 S no one knows the future, who can tell H3954
Ecc 9: 6 their jealousy have long s vanished; H3893
Isa 7:17 unlike any s Ephraim broke H4200+4946+3427
Isa 36:11 servants in Aramaic, s we understand it. H3954
Isa 40:21 you not understood s the earth was founded NDT
Isa 43: 4 S you are precious and honored in H4946+889
Isa 44: 7 what has happened s I established my H4946
Isa 46: 3 you whom I have upheld s your birth, and H4974
Isa 46: 3 and have carried s you were born. H4974
Isa 47:12 which you have labored at s childhood. H4946
Isa 47:15 dealt with and labored with s childhood. H4946
Isa 64: 4 S ancient times no one has heard, no ear H4946
Jer 8: 9 S they have rejected the word of the LORD H2180
Jer 8:21 S my people are crushed, I am crushed; H6584
Jer 32: 8 S it is your right to redeem it and possess H3954
Jer 44:18 But ever s we stopped burning H4946+255
Jer 48: 7 S you trust in your deeds and riches H3954+3610
Jer 50:15 S this is the vengeance of the LORD, take H3954
Eze 3:20 S you did not warn them, they will die H3954
Eze 18:19 S the son has done what is just and right H2256
Eze 23:35 S you have forgotten me and turned your H3610
Eze 33: 5 S they heard the sound of the trumpet but NDT
Eze 33:25 S you eat meat with the blood still in it and NDT
Eze 35: 6 S you did not hate bloodshed, bloodshed H561
Da 10:12 S the first day that you set your mind to H4946
Da 10:19 my lord, s you have given me strength." H3954
Hos 10: 9 "S the days of Gibeah, you have sinned H4946
Hos 12: 9 LORD your God ever s you came out of Egypt; AIT
Hos 13: 4 LORD your God ever s you came out of Egypt. AIT
Mic 1: 7 S she gathered her gifts from the wages H3954
Zec 4:10 s the seven eyes of the LORD that range H2256
Zec 8:10 s I had turned everyone against their H2256
Zec 13: 5 land has been my livelihood s my youth. H4946
Mal 3: 7 Ever s the time of your ancestors H4200+4946
Mt 13:21 But s they have no root, they last only a short AIT
Mt 13:35 utter things hidden s the creation of the G608
Mt 18:25 S he was not able to pay, the master ordered AIT
Mt 22:25 died, and s he had no children, he left AIT
Mt 22:28 s all of them were married to her? G1142
Mt 25:34 prepared for you s the creation of the G608
Mt 27: 6 this into the treasury, s it is blood money." G2075
Mk 2: 4 S they could not get him to Jesus because G2779
Mk 4:17 But s they have no root, they last only a short AIT
Mk 8: 1 S they had nothing to eat, Jesus called his AIT
Mk 10:20 "all these I have kept s I was a boy." G1666
Mk 11:11 at everything, but s it was already late, he AIT
Mk 12:23 s the seven were married to her? G1142
Lk 1: 3 s I myself have carefully investigated AIT
Lk 1:34 Mary asked the angel, "s I am a virgin?" G2075
Lk 11:50 that has been shed s the beginning of the G608
Lk 12:26 S you cannot do this very little thing, G1623+4036
Lk 16:16 S that time, the good news of the kingdom G608
Lk 18:21 "All these I have kept s I was a boy," G1666
Lk 19: 4 to see him, s Jesus was coming that way. G4022
Lk 20:33 s the seven were married to her? G1142
Lk 20:36 s they are children of the resurrection. AIT
Lk 23:40 "s you are under the same sentence? G4022
Lk 24:21 it is the third day s all this took place G608+4005
Jn 5:44 can you believe s you accept glory from one AIT
Jn 5:47 But s you do not believe what he wrote G1623
Jn 7: 4 S you are doing these things, show G1623
Jn 7:39 s Jesus had not yet been glorified. G4022
Jn 13:29 S Judas had charge of the money, some G2075
Jn 19:42 of Preparation and s the tomb was nearby G4022
Ac 4:14 But s they could see the man who had been AIT
Ac 13:46 S you reject it and do not consider G2076
Ac 17:29 "Therefore s we are God's offspring, we AIT
Ac 18:15 But s it involves questions about words G1623
Ac 19:36 Therefore, s these facts are undeniable, you AIT
Ac 19:40 this commotion, s there is no reason for it." AIT
Ac 21:34 and s the commander could not get at the AIT
Ac 25:14 S they were spending many days there G6055
Ac 26: 4 the way I have lived ever s I was a child, G1666
Ac 27:12 S the harbor was unsuitable to winter in G1254
Ro 1:19 s what may be known about God is plain G1484
Ro 1:20 For s the creation of the world God's G608
Ro 3:30 s there is only one God, who will justify G1642
Ro 4:19 dead—s he was about a hundred years old AIT
Ro 5: 1 s we have been justified through faith AIT
Ro 5: 9 S we have now been justified by his G4036
Ro 6: 9 we know that s Christ was raised from the AIT
Ro 10: 3 S they did not know the righteousness of G1142
Ro 15:23 and s I have been longing for many years to AIT
1Co 1:21 For s in the wisdom of God the world G2076
1Co 3: 3 For s there is jealousy and quarreling G3963
1Co 7: 2 But s sexual immorality is occurring, each G1328
1Co 8: 7 to a god, and s their conscience is weak, it is AIT
1Co 9:16 cannot boast, s I am compelled to preach. G1142
1Co 11: 7 his head, s he is the image and glory of God AIT
1Co 14:12 S you are eager for gifts of the Spirit, try to G2075
1Co 14:16 s they do not know what you are saying? G2076
1Co 15:21 For s death came through a man, the G2076
2Co 3:12 Therefore, s we have such a hope, we are AIT
2Co 4: 1 s through God's mercy we have this G2777
2Co 4:13 " S we have that same spirit of faith, we also AIT
2Co 4:18 is unseen, s what is seen is temporary G1142
2Co 5:11 S, then, we know what it is to fear the Lord AIT
2Co 7: 1 Therefore, s we have these promises, dear AIT
2Co 8: 7 But s you excel in everything—in faith, in G6061
2Co 9: 2 telling them that s last year you in Achaia G608
2Co 11:18 S many are boasting in the way the world G2075
2Co 11:19 gladly put up with fools s you are so wise! AIT
2Co 13: 3 s you are demanding proof that Christ is G2075
Gal 4: 7 God's child; and s you are his child G1623
Gal 5:25 S we live by the Spirit, let us keep in step G1623
Eph 1:15 ever s I heard about your faith in the Lord AIT
Eph 6: 9 s you know that he who is both their Master AIT
Php 1: 7 s I have you in my heart and G1328+3836
Php 1:30 s you are going through the same struggle AIT
Php 4: 3 women s they have contended at my side in AIT
Col 1: 6 doing among you s the day you heard it G608
Col 1: 9 this reason, s the day we heard about you G608
Col 2:20 S you died with Christ to the elemental G1623
Col 3: 1 S, then, you have been raised with Christ G1623
Col 3: 9 s you have taken off your old self with its AIT
Col 3:15 s as members of one body you were G2779
Col 3:24 s you know that you will receive an AIT
1Th 3: 8 s you are standing firm in the Lord. G1569
1Th 5: 8 But s we belong to the day, let us be sober AIT
Titus 1: 7 S an overseer manages God's household G1142
Heb 2: 2 For s the message spoken through angels G1623
Heb 2:14 S the children have flesh and G2075+4036
Heb 4: 1 s the promise of entering his rest still stands AIT
Heb 4: 3 have been finished s the creation of the G608
Heb 4: 6 Therefore s it still remains for some to G2075
Heb 4: 6 s those who formerly had the good NDT
Heb 4:14 s we have a great high priest who has AIT
Heb 5: 2 s he himself is subject to weakness. G2075
Heb 6:13 s there was no one greater for him to G2075
Heb 7:23 s death prevented them from G1328+3836

S

Heb 8: 6 s the new covenant is established on better AIT
Heb 9:26 to suffer many times s the creation of the G608
Heb 10:13 and s that time he waits for his G3836+3370
Heb 10:19 s we have confidence to enter the Most Holy AIT
Heb 10:21 s we have a great priest over the house NDT
Heb 11:40 s God had planned something better for us so AIT
Heb 12: 1 s we are surrounded by such a great cloud of AIT
Heb 12:28 s we are receiving a kingdom that cannot be AIT
Jas 1:10 s they will pass away like a wild flower. G4022
1Pe 1:17 S you call on a Father who judges each G1623
1Pe 4: 1 Therefore, s Christ suffered in his body, arm AIT
2Pe 3: 4 Ever s our ancestors died, everything G608+4005
2Pe 3: 4 goes on as it has s the beginning of G608
2Pe 3:11 S everything will be destroyed in this way AIT
2Pe 3:14 s you are looking forward to this AIT
2Pe 3:17 s you have been forewarned, be on AIT
1Jn 2: 7 which you have had s the beginning. G608
1Jn 4:11 Dear friends, s God so loved us, we also G1623
Rev 3:10 S you have kept my command to endure G4022
Rev 16:18 ever occurred s mankind has been G608+4005

SINCERE (12) [SINCERITY, SINCERELY]

Da 11:34 many who are not s will join them. H2761
Lk 20:20 they sent spies, who pretended to be s. G1465
Ac 2:46 ate together with glad and s hearts, G911
Ro 12: 9 Love must be s. Hate what is evil; cling to G537
2Co 6: 6 kindness; in the Holy Spirit and in s love; G537
2Co 11: 3 from your s and pure devotion to Christ. G605
1Ti 1: 5 heart and a good conscience and a s faith. G537
1Ti 3: 8 of respect, s, not indulging in G3590+1474
2Ti 1: 5 I am reminded of your s faith, which first G537
Heb 10:22 near to God with a s heart and with the full G240
Jas 3:17 of mercy and good fruit, impartial and s. G537
1Pe 1:22 truth so that you have s love for each other, G537

SINCERELY (2) [SINCERE]

Job 33: 3 my lips s speak what I know. H1359
Php 1:17 selfish ambition, not s, supposing that they G56

SINCERITY (6) [SINCERE]

1Co 5: 8 with the unleavened bread of s and truth. G1636
2Co 1:12 with you, with integrity and godly s. G1636
2Co 2:17 in Christ we speak before God with s, as G1636
2Co 8: 8 I want to test the s of your love by G1188
Eph 6: 5 fear, and with s of heart, just as you G605
Col 3:22 with s of heart and reverence for the G605

SINEWS (3)

Job 10:11 knit me together with bones and s? H1630
Job 40:17 a cedar; the s of its thighs are close-knit. H1630
Col 2:19 held together by its ligaments and s, G5278

SINFUL (30) [SIN]

Dt 9:21 Also I took that s thing of yours, the calf H2633
Ps 36: 4 themselves to a s course and do H4202+3202
Ps 38: 5 are loathsome because of my s folly. H222
Ps 51: 5 Surely I was s at birth, sinful from the time H6411
Ps 51: 5 s from the time my mother conceived me. H2628
Pr 1:10 My son, if s men entice you, do not give H2629
Pr 12:13 Evildoers are trapped by their s talk, and H7322
Ecc 9: 2 the good, so with the s; as it is with those H2627
Isa 1: 4 Woe to the s nation, a people whose H2627
Isa 31: 7 silver and gold your s hands have made. H2628
Isa 57:17 I was enraged by their s greed; I punished H6411
Eze 37:23 will save them from all their s backsliding, H2627
Hos 9:15 Because of their s deeds, I will drive them H8278
Am 9: 8 the Sovereign LORD are on the s kingdom. H2629
Mk 8:38 words in this adulterous and s generation, G283
Lk 5: 8 "Go away from me, Lord; I am a s man!" G283
Lk 7:37 town who lived a s life learned that Jesus G283
Ro 1:24 them over in the s desires of their hearts G2123
Ro 7: 5 the s passions aroused by the law were at G281
Ro 7: 7 Is the law s? Certainly not! G281
Ro 7:13 commandment sin might become utterly s. G283
Ro 7:18 not dwell in me, that is, in my s nature. G4922
Ro 7:25 but in my s nature a slave to the law of G4922
Ro 8: 3 Son in the likeness of s flesh to be a sin G281
Gal 2:15 who are Jews by birth and not s Gentiles G283
1Ti 1: 9 the ungodly and s, the unholy and G283
Titus 3:11 be sure that such people are warped and s; G279
Heb 3:12 that none of you has a s, unbelieving G4505
1Pe 2:11 to abstain from s desires, which wage war G4920
1Jn 3: 8 The one who does what is s is of the devil G281

SINFUL NATURE (NIV84) FLESH

SINFULNESS (1) [SIN]

Ps 36: 1 my heart concerning the s of the wicked: H7322

SING (115) [SANG, SINGERS, SINGING, SINGS, SONG, SONGS, SUNG]

Ex 15: 1 "I will s to the LORD, for he is highly H8876
Ex 15:21 Miriam sang to them: "S to the LORD, for H8876
Nu 21:17 "Spring up, O well! S about it, H6702
Dt 31:19 Israelites and have them s it, H8492+928+7023
Jdg 5: 3 will s to the LORD; I will praise the H8876
1Sa 21:11 Isn't he the one they s about in their H6702
2Sa 22:50 nations; I will s the praises of your name. H2376
1Ch 16: 9 S to him, sing praise to him; tell of all his H8876
1Ch 16: 9 Sing to him, s praise to him; tell of all his H2376
1Ch 16:23 S to the LORD, all the earth; proclaim his H8876
1Ch 16:33 Let the trees of the forest s, let them sing NDT
1Ch 16:33 let them s for joy before the LORD H8264
2Ch 20:21 appointed men to s to the LORD and to H8876
2Ch 20:22 As they began to s and praise, the LORD H8262
2Ch 31: 2 thanks and to s praises at the gates of H2146
Job 21:12 They s to the music of timbrel and lyre H5951
Job 29:13 blessed me; I made the widow's heart s. H8264
Ps 5:11 in you be glad; let them ever s for joy. H8264
Ps 7:17 I will s the praises of the name of the LORD H2376
Ps 9: 2 I will s the praises of your name, H2376
Ps 9:11 S the praises of the LORD, enthroned in H2376
Ps 13: 6 I will s the LORD's praise, for he has been H8876
Ps 18:49 nations; I will s the praises of your name. H2376
Ps 21:13 we will s and praise your might. H8876
Ps 27: 6 I will s and make music to the LORD. H8876
Ps 30: 4 S the praises of the LORD, you his faithful H2376
Ps 30:12 my heart may s your praises and not be H2376
Ps 32:11 s, all you who are upright in heart! H8264
Ps 33: 1 S joyfully to the LORD, you righteous; it is H8264
Ps 33: 3 S to him a new song; play skillfully, and H8876
Ps 47: 6 S praises to God, sing praises; sing H2376
Ps 47: 6 praises to God, s praises; sing praises to H2376
Ps 47: 6 sing praises; s praises to our King, sing H2376
Ps 47: 6 sing praises to our King, s praises. H2376
Ps 47: 7 all the earth; s to him a psalm of praise. H2376
Ps 51:14 my tongue will s of your H8264
Ps 57: 7 is steadfast; I will s and make music. H8876
Ps 57: 9 I will s of you among the peoples. H2376
Ps 59:16 But I will s of your strength, in the H8876
Ps 59:16 in the morning I will s of your love; for you H8264
Ps 59:17 You are my strength, I s praise to you; you, H2376
Ps 61: 8 Then I will ever s in praise of your name H2376
Ps 63: 7 my help, I s in the shadow of your wings. H8264
Ps 65:13 with grain; they shout for joy and s. H8876
Ps 66: 2 S the glory of his name; make his praise H2376
Ps 66: 4 down to you; they s praise to you, they H2376
Ps 66: 4 they s the praises of your name. H2376
Ps 67: 4 May the nations be glad and s for joy, for H8264
Ps 68: 4 S to God, sing in praise of his name, extol H8876
Ps 68: 4 Sing to God, s in praise of his name, extol H2376
Ps 68:32 S to God, you kingdoms of the earth, sing H8876
Ps 68:32 of the earth, s praise to the Lord, H2376
Ps 71:22 my God; I will s praise to you with the lyre H2376
Ps 71:23 will shout for joy when I s praise to you— H2376
Ps 75: 9 I will s praise to the God of Jacob, H2376
Ps 81: 1 S for joy to God our strength; shout aloud H8264
Ps 87: 7 As they make music they will s, "All my H8876
Ps 89: 1 I will s of the LORD's great love forever H8876
Ps 89:12 Tabor and Hermon s for joy at your name. H8264
Ps 90:14 that we may s for joy and be glad all our H8264
Ps 92: 4 I s for joy at what your hands have done. H8264
Ps 95: 1 Come, let us s for joy to the LORD; let us H8264
Ps 96: 1 S to the LORD a new song; sing to the LORD H8876
Ps 96: 1 the LORD a new song; s to the LORD, all the H8876
Ps 96: 2 S to the LORD, praise his name; proclaim H8876
Ps 96:12 let all the trees of the forest s for joy. H8264
Ps 98: 1 S to the LORD a new song, for he has done H8876
Ps 98: 8 let the mountains s together for joy; H8264
Ps 98: 9 let them s before the LORD, for he comes to NDT
Ps 101: 1 I will s of your love and justice; to you H8876
Ps 101: 1 justice; to you, LORD, I will s praise. H2376
Ps 104:12 waters; they s among the branches. H5989+7754
Ps 104:33 I will s to the LORD all my life; I will sing H8876
Ps 104:33 I will s praise to my God as long as I live. H2376
Ps 105: 2 S to him, sing praise to him; tell of all his H8876
Ps 105: 2 Sing to him, s praise to him; tell of all his H2376
Ps 108: 1 I will s and make music with all my soul. H8876
Ps 108: 3 I will s of you among the peoples. H2376
Ps 119:172 May my tongue s of your word, for all H6702
Ps 132: 9 may your faithful people s for joy. H8264
Ps 132:16 faithful people will ever s for joy. H8264+8264
Ps 135: 3 the LORD is good; s praise to his name, for H2376
Ps 137: 3 they said, "S us one of the songs of Zion!" H8876
Ps 137: 4 How can we s the songs of the LORD while H8876
Ps 138: 1 before the "gods" I will s your praise. H2376
Ps 138: 5 May they s of the ways of the LORD, for the H8876
Ps 144: 9 I will s a new song to you, my God; on the H8876
Ps 145: 7 goodness and joyfully s of your H8264
Ps 146: 2 I will s praise to my God as long as I live. H2376
Ps 147: 1 How good it is to s praises to our God H2376
Ps 147: 7 S to the LORD with grateful praise; make H6702
Ps 149: 1 S to the LORD a new song, his praise in the H8876
Ps 149: 5 in this honor and s for joy on their beds. H8264
Isa 5: 1 I will s for the one I love a song about his H8876
Isa 12: 5 S to the LORD, for he has done glorious H2376
Isa 12: 6 Shout aloud and s for joy, people of Zion H8264
Isa 23:16 play the harp well, s many a song, so that NDT
Isa 27: 2 In that day—"S about a fruitful vineyard: H6702
Isa 30:29 And you will s as on the night you H8877
Isa 38:18 death cannot s your praise; those who go H2146
Isa 38:20 and we will s with stringed instruments all H5594
Isa 42:10 S to the LORD a new song, his praise from H8876
Isa 42:11 Let the people of Sela s for joy; let them H8264
Isa 44:23 S for joy, you heavens, for the LORD has H8264
Isa 54: 1 "S, barren woman, you who never bore a H8264
Isa 65:14 My servants will s out of the joy of their H8264
Jer 20:13 S to the LORD! Give praise to the LORD! H8876
Jer 31: 7 "S with joy for Jacob; shout for the H8264
Zep 3:14 S, Daughter Zion; shout aloud, Israel! Be H8264
Ro 15: 9 I will s the praises of your name." G6010
1Co 14:15 my understanding; I will s with my spirit G6010
1Co 14:15 but I will also s with my understanding. G6010
Eph 5:19 S and make music from your heart to the G106
Heb 2:12 in the assembly I will s your praises." G5630
Jas 5:13 Let them s songs of praise. G6010

SINGED (1)

Da 3:27 nor was a hair of their heads s; their A10283

SINGERS (8) [SING]

Jdg 5:11 the voice of the s at the watering places H2952
2Sa 19:35 hear the voices of male and female s? H8876
[2Sa 19:35 hear the voices of male and female s? H8876]
2Ch 5:13 the s raised their voices in praise to the LORD NDT
2Ch 35:25 all the male and female s commemorate H8876
[2Ch 35:25 all the male and female s commemorate H8876]
Ezr 2:65 they also had 200 male and female s. H8876
[Ezr 2:65 they also had 200 male and female s. H8876]
Ne 7:67 they also had 245 male and female s. H8876
[Ne 7:67 they also had 245 male and female s. H8876]
Ps 68:25 In front are the s, after them the H8876
Ecc 2: 8 I acquired male and female s, and a H8876
[Ecc 2: 8 I acquired male and female s, and a H8876]

SINGING (20) [SING]

Ge 31:27 you away with joy and s to the music of H8877
Ex 32:18 of defeat; it is the sound of s that I hear." H6702
1Sa 18: 6 to meet King Saul with s and dancing, H8876
1Ch 15:22 the head Levite was in charge of the s; H5362
1Ch 15:27 who was in charge of the s of the choirs. H5362
2Ch 23:18 with rejoicing and s, as David had H8877
2Ch 29:27 offering began, s to the LORD began also H8877
Ps 63: 5 with s lips my mouth will praise you. H8265
Ps 68: 6 he leads out the prisoners with s; but the H3938
Ps 98: 5 with the harp and the sound of s, H2379
SS 2:12 the season of s has come, the cooing H2369
Isa 14: 7 are at rest and at peace; they break into s. H8262
Isa 24:16 From the ends of the earth we hear s H2369
Isa 35:10 They will enter Zion with s; everlasting joy H8262
Isa 51: 3 thanksgiving and the sound of s. H2379
Isa 51:11 They will enter Zion with s; everlasting joy H8262
Am 8:10 mourning and all your s into weeping. H8877
Zep 3:17 but will rejoice over you with s. H8262
Ac 16:25 Silas were praying and s hymns to God, G5630
Col 3:16 s to God with gratitude in your hearts. G106

SINGLE (23) [SINGLED, SINGLENESS]

Ge 41: 5 good, were growing on a s stalk. H285
Ge 41:22 full and good, growing on a s stalk. H285
Ex 23:29 But I will not drive them out in a s year H285
Ex 26:24 the way to the top and fitted into a s ring; H285
Ex 36:29 the way to the top and fitted into a s ring; H285
Nu 13:23 off a branch bearing a s cluster of grapes. H285
Dt 29:21 The LORD will s them out from all the tribes H976
Jdg 9:18 seventy sons on a s stone and have made H285
1Ki 16:11 He did not spare a s male, whether relative AIT
Est 3:13 children—on a s day, the thirteenth H285
Isa 9:14 both palm branch and reed in a s day; H285
Isa 10:17 in a s day it will burn and consume his H285
Isa 47: 9 will overtake you in a moment, on a s day: H285
Eze 37:19 I will make them into a s stick of wood, and H285
Zec 3: 9 I will remove the sin of this land in a s day. H285
Mt 6:27 you by worrying add a s hour to your life? G1651
Mt 23:15 over land and sea to win a s convert, G1651
Mt 27:14 not even to a s charge—to the great G1651
Lk 12:25 by worrying can add a s hour to your life? AIT
Jn 12:24 ground and dies, it remains only a s seed. G3668
Ac 27:34 one of you will lose a s hair from his head." AIT
Heb 12:16 who for a s meal sold his inheritance G1651
Rev 21:21 each gate made of a s pearl. G1651

SINGLED (1) [SINGLE]

1Ki 8:53 For you s them out from all the nations of H976

SINGLENESS (1) [SINGLE]

Jer 32:39 I will give them s of heart and action, so H285

SINGS (3) [SING]

Pr 25:20 is one who s songs to a heavy heart. H8876
Isa 16:10 no one s or shouts in the vineyards H8264
Eze 33:32 more than one who s love songs with a NDT

SINITES (2)

Ge 10:17 Hivites, Arkites, S, H6098
1Ch 1:15 Hivites, Arkites, S, H6098

SINK (8) [SANK, SINKING, SINKS, SUNK]

Dt 28:43 but you will s lower and lower. H3718
Ps 69: 2 I s in the miry depths, where there is no H3190
Ps 69:14 from the mire, do not let me s; deliver me H3190
Jer 51:64 'So will Babylon s to rise no more H9205
Eze 27:27 else on board will s into the heart of the H5877
Am 8: 8 be stirred up and then s like the river of H9205
Mt 14:30 was afraid and, beginning to s, cried out, G2931
Lk 5: 7 both boats so full that they began to s. G1112

SINKING (1) [SINK]

Ac 20: 9 who was s into a deep sleep as Paul G2965

SINKS (2) [SINK]

Isa 5:24 as dry grass s down in the flames, H8332
Am 9: 5 like the Nile, then s like the river of Egypt; H9205

SINNED (89) [SIN]

Ex 9:27 "This time I have s," he said to H2627
Ex 9:34 thunder had stopped, he s again: H2627
Ex 10:16 "I have s against the LORD your God and H2627
Ex 32:33 "Whoever has s against me I will blot out H2627

Lev 5: 5 must confess in what way they have s. H2627
Nu 6:11 Nazirite because they s by being in the H2627
Nu 14:40 the LORD promised. Surely we have s!" H2627
Nu 16:38 of the men who s at the cost of their H2629
Nu 21: 7 "We s when we spoke against the LORD H2627
Nu 22:34 said to the angel of the LORD, "I have s. H2627
Dt 1:41 you replied, "We have s against the LORD. H2627
Dt 9:16 I saw that you had s against the LORD your H2627
Jos 7:11 Israel has s; they have violated my H2627
Jos 7:20 I have s against the LORD, the God of H2627
Jdg 10:10 out to the LORD, "We have s against you H2627
Jdg 10:15 Israelites said to the LORD, "We have s. H2627
1Sa 7: 6 confessed, "We have s against the LORD." H2627
1Sa 12:10 LORD and said, 'We have s; we have H2627
1Sa 15:24 said to Samuel, "I have s. I violated the H2627
1Sa 15:30 Saul replied, "I have s. But please honor H2627
1Sa 26:21 Then Saul said, "I have s. Come back H2627
2Sa 12:13 said to Nathan, "I have s against the LORD." H2627
2Sa 19:20 For I your servant know that I have s, but H2627
2Sa 24:10 "I have s greatly in what I have done. H2627
2Sa 24:17 to the LORD, "I have s; I, the shepherd, H2627
1Ki 8:33 enemy because they have s against you, H2627
1Ki 8:35 because your people have s against you, H2627
1Ki 8:47 say, 'We have s, we have done H2627
1Ki 8:50 your people, who have s against you H2627
1Ki 16:25 eyes of the LORD and s more than all those H8317
2Ki 17: 7 the Israelites had s against the LORD H2627
1Ch 21: 8 "I have s greatly by doing this. H2627
1Ch 21:17 the shepherd, have s and done wrong H2627
2Ch 6:24 enemy because they have s against you H2627
2Ch 6:26 because your people have s against you, H2627
2Ch 6:37 say, 'We have s, we have done H2627
2Ch 6:39 your people, who have s against you. H2627
Ezr 10:13 because we have s greatly in this thing. H7321
Ne 9:29 They s against your ordinances, of which H2627
Ne 13:26 like these that Solomon king of Israel s? H2627
Job 1: 5 my children have s and cursed God in H2627
Job 7:20 If I have s, what have I done to you, you H2627
Job 8: 4 When your children s against him, he H2627
Job 10:14 If I s, you would be watching me and H2627
Job 24:19 grave snatches away those who have s. H2627
Job 33:27 others and say, 'I have s, I have perverted H2627
Job 36: 9 have done—that they have s arrogantly. H7322
Ps 41: 4 heal me, for I have s against you. H2627
Ps 51: 4 have I s and done what is evil in your H2627
Ps 106: 6 We have s, even as our ancestors did; we H2627
Isa 42:24 it not the LORD, against whom we have s? H2627
Isa 43:27 Your first father s; those I sent to teach H2627
Jer 2:35 on you because you say, 'I have not s. H2627
Jer 3:25 We have s against the LORD our God, both H2627
Jer 8:14 to drink, because we have s against him. H2627
Jer 14: 7 often rebelled; we have s against you. H2627
Jer 14:20 ancestors; we have indeed s against you. H2627
Jer 40: 3 because you people s against the H2627
Jer 44:23 incense and have s against the LORD H2627
Jer 50: 7 are not guilty, for they s against the LORD H2627
Jer 50:14 no arrows, for she has s against the LORD. H2627
La 1: 8 Jerusalem has s greatly and so has H2627+2628
La 3:42 "We have s and rebelled and you have H7321
La 5: 7 Our ancestors s and are no more, and we H2627
La 5:16 from our head. Woe to us, for we have s! H2627
Eze 28:16 you were filled with violence, and you s. H2627
Da 9: 5 we have s and done wrong. We have H2627
Da 9: 8 because we have s against you. H2627
Da 9:11 because we have s against you. H2627
Da 9:15 to this day, we have s, we have done H2627
Hos 4: 7 the more they s against me; they H2627
Hos 10: 9 the days of Gibeah, you have s, Israel, H2627
Mic 7: 9 Because I have s against him, I will bear H2627
Zep 1:17 because they have s against the LORD. H2627
Mt 27: 4 "I have s," he said, "for I have betrayed G279
Lk 15:18 I have s against heaven and against you. G279
Lk 15:21 I have s against heaven and against you. G279
Jn 9: 2 asked him, "Rabbi, who s, this man or his G279
Jn 9: 3 "Neither this man nor his parents s," said G279
Ro 3:23 all have s and fall short of the glory of G279
Ro 5:12 death came to all people, because all s— G279
1Co 7:28 you do marry, you have not s; and if a G279
1Co 7:28 if a virgin marries, she has not s. G279
2Co 12:21 many who have s earlier and have not G4579
2Co 13: 2 not spare those who s earlier or any of the G4579
Heb 3:17 Was it not with those who s, whose bodies G279
Jas 5:15 If they have s, they will be G281+1639+4472
2Pe 2: 4 if God did not spare angels when they s, G279
1Jn 1:10 If we claim we have not s, we make him out G279

SINNER (18) [SIN]

Pr 11:31 how much more the ungodly and the s! H2627
Pr 13: 6 integrity, but wickedness overthrows the s. H2633
Pr 13:21 Trouble pursues the s, but the righteous H2629
Ecc 2:26 to the s he gives the task of gathering H2627
Ecc 7:26 escape her, but the s she will ensnare. H2627
Ecc 9:18 but one s destroys much good. H2627
Lk 7:39 what kind of woman she is—that she is a s." G283
Lk 15: 7 in heaven over one s who repents than G283
Lk 15:10 the angels of God over one s who repents." G283
Lk 18:13 said, 'God, have mercy on me, a s. G283
Lk 19: 7 "He has gone to be the guest of a s." G283+467
Jn 9:16 "How can a s perform such signs?" G476+283
Jn 9:24 "We know this man is a s." G283
Jn 9:25 "Whether he is a s or not, I don't know. G283
Ro 3: 7 his glory, why am I still condemned as a s?" G283
1Ti 2:14 who was deceived and became a s. G4126
Jas 5:20 Whoever turns a s from the error of their G283
1Pe 4:18 what will become of the ungodly and the s?" G283

SINNER'S (1) [SIN]

Pr 13:22 a s wealth is stored up for the H2627

SINNERS (44) [SIN]

Nu 32:14 you are, a brood of s, standing in the H2629
Ps 1: 1 stand in the way that s take or sit in the H2629
Ps 1: 5 s in the assembly of the righteous. H2629
Ps 25: 8 therefore he instructs s in his ways. H2629
Ps 26: 9 Do not take away my soul along with s H2629
Ps 37:38 But all s will be destroyed; there will be H7321
Ps 51:13 your ways, so that s will turn back to you. H2629
Ps 104:35 But may s vanish from the earth and the H2629
Pr 23:17 Do not let your heart envy s, but always H2629
Isa 1:28 But rebels and s will both be broken, and H2629
Isa 13: 9 land desolate and destroy the s within it. H2629
Isa 33:14 The s in Zion are terrified; trembling grips H2629
Am 9:10 All the s among my people will die by the H2629
Mt 9:10 tax collectors and s came and ate with him G283
Mt 9:11 your teacher eat with tax collectors and s?" G283
Mt 9:13 I have not come to call the righteous, but s." G283
Mt 11:19 a drunkard, a friend of tax collectors and s. G283
Mt 26:45 of Man is delivered into the hands of s. G283
Mk 2:15 tax collectors and s were eating with him G283
Mk 2:16 him eating with the s and tax collectors, G283
Mk 2:16 "Why does he eat with tax collectors and s?" G283
Mk 2:17 not come to call the righteous, but s." G283
Mk 14:41 of Man is delivered into the hands of s. G283
Lk 5:30 you eat and drink with tax collectors and s?" G283
Lk 5:32 to call the righteous, but s to repentance." G283
Lk 6:32 Even s love those who love them. G283
Lk 6:33 what credit is that to you? Even s do that. G283
Lk 6:34 Even s lend to sinners, expecting to be G283
Lk 6:34 Even sinners lend to s, expecting to be G283
Lk 7:34 a drunkard, a friend of tax collectors and s. G283
Lk 13: 2 Galileans were worse s than all the other G283
Lk 15: 1 the tax collectors and s were all gathering G283
Lk 15: 2 "This man welcomes s and eats with them." G283
Lk 24: 7 be delivered over to the hands of s, G476+283
Jn 9:31 We know that God does not listen to s. G283
Ro 5: 8 While we were still s, Christ died for us. G283
Ro 5:19 of the one man the many were made s, G283
Gal 2:17 we Jews find ourselves also among the s G283
1Ti 1:15 Christ Jesus came into the world to save s— G283
1Ti 1:16 that in me, the worst of s, Christ Jesus might NDT
Heb 7:26 set apart from s, exalted above the G283
Heb 12: 3 him who endured such opposition from s, G283
Jas 4: 8 Wash your hands, you s, and purify your G283
Jude 15 words ungodly s have spoken against G283

SINNING (22) [SIN]

Ge 13:13 wicked and were s greatly against the H2629
Ge 20: 6 so I have kept you from s against me. H2627
Ex 20:20 God will be with you to keep you from s." H2627
Lev 5:15 to the LORD by s unintentionally in regard H2627
Nu 15:28 the one who erred by s unintentionally, H2630
Nu 32:23 to do this, you will be s against the LORD H2627
1Sa 14:33 the men are s against the LORD by eating H2627
Job 35: 3 is it to me, and what do I gain by not s? H2633
Ps 78:32 of all this, they kept on s; in spite of his H2627
Jer 9: 5 they weary themselves with s. H6390
Hos 8:11 offerings, these have become altars for s. H2627
Jn 5:14 Stop s or something worse may happen to G279
Ro 6: 1 Shall we go on s so that grace may G281
1Co 7:36 do as he wants. He is not s. They should G279
1Co 11:27 manner will be guilty of s against the G1944
1Co 15:34 you ought, and stop s; for there are some G279
1Ti 5:20 But those elders who are s you are to G279
Heb 10:26 If we deliberately keep on s after we have G279
2Pe 2:14 they never stop s; they seduce the unstable G281
1Jn 3: 6 No one who lives in him keeps on s. G279
1Jn 3: 8 because the devil has been s from the G279
1Jn 3: 9 they cannot go on s, because they G279

SINS (287) [SIN]

Ge 50:17 your brothers the s and the wrongs they H7322
Ge 50:17 please forgive the s of the servants of the H7322
Lev 4: 2 'When anyone s unintentionally and does H2627
Lev 4: 3 " 'If the anointed priest s, bringing guilt H2627
Lev 4:13 community s unintentionally and does H8706
Lev 4:22 " 'When a leader s unintentionally and H2627
Lev 4:27 of the community s unintentionally and H2627
Lev 5: 1 " 'If anyone s because they do not speak H2627
Lev 5:13 any of these s they have committed, H2633
Lev 5:17 "If anyone s and does what is forbidden H2627
Lev 6: 2 "If anyone s and is unfaithful to the LORD H2627
Lev 16:16 the Israelites, whatever their s have been. H2633
Lev 16:21 all their s—and put them on the H2633
Lev 16:22 carry on itself all their s to a remote place; H6411
Lev 16:30 the LORD, you will be clean from all your s. H2633
Lev 16:34 once a year for all the s of the Israelites." H2633
Lev 26:18 punish you for your s seven times over. H2633
Lev 26:21 seven times over, as your s deserve. H2633
Lev 26:24 will afflict you for your s seven times over. H2633
Lev 26:28 punish you for your s seven times over. H2633
Lev 26:39 lands of their enemies because of their s; H6411
Lev 26:39 of their ancestors' s they will waste away. H6411
Lev 26:40 will confess their s and the sins of their H6411
Lev 26:40 their sins and the s of their ancestors— H6411
Lev 26:43 will pay for their s because they rejected H6411
Nu 14:34 will suffer for your s and know what it is H6411
Nu 15:27 " 'But if just one person s unintentionally H2627
Nu 15:29 who s unintentionally, H6913+928+8705
Nu 15:30 anyone who s defiantly, H6913+928+3338+8123
Nu 16:22 entire assembly when only one man s?" H2627
Nu 16:26 will be swept away because of all their s." H2633
Jos 24:19 will not forgive your rebellion and your s. H2633
1Sa 2:25 If one person s against another, God may H2627
1Sa 2:25 if anyone s against the LORD, who H2627
1Sa 12:19 to all our other s the evil of asking for H2633
1Ki 14:16 up because of the s Jeroboam has H2633
1Ki 14:22 By the s they committed they stirred up his H2633
1Ki 15: 3 committed all the s his father had done H2633
1Ki 15:30 because of the s Jeroboam had H2633
1Ki 16: 2 to sin and to arouse my anger by their s. H2633
1Ki 16:13 because of all the s Baasha and his son H2633
1Ki 16:19 because of the s he had committed, doing H2633
1Ki 16:31 trivial to commit the s of Jeroboam son of H2633
2Ki 3: 3 he clung to the s of Jeroboam son of H2633
2Ki 10:29 turn away from the s of Jeroboam son of H2628
2Ki 10:31 did not turn away from the s of Jeroboam, H2633
2Ki 13: 2 by following the s of Jeroboam son of H2633
2Ki 13: 6 turn away from the s of the house of H2633
2Ki 13:11 from any of the s of Jeroboam son of H2633
2Ki 14:24 from any of the s of Jeroboam son of H2633
2Ki 15: 9 turn away from the s of Jeroboam son of H2633
2Ki 15:18 turn away from the s of Jeroboam son of H2633
2Ki 15:24 turn away from the s of Jeroboam son of H2633
2Ki 15:28 turn away from the s of Jeroboam son of H2633
2Ki 17:22 persisted in all the s of Jeroboam and did H2633
2Ki 21:11 Judah has committed these detestable s. H9359
2Ki 24: 3 because of the s of Manasseh and all he H2633
2Ch 28:10 aren't you also guilty of s against the LORD H873
2Ch 33:19 as well as all his s and unfaithfulness H2633
Ezr 9: 6 because our s are higher than our heads H6411
Ezr 9: 7 Because of our s, we and our kings and H6411
Ezr 9:13 us less than our s deserved and have H6411
Ne 1: 6 I confess the s we Israelites, including H2633
Ne 4: 5 guilt or blot out their s from your sight, H2633
Ne 9: 2 confessed their s and the sins of their H2633
Ne 9: 2 their sins and the s of their ancestors. H6411
Ne 9:37 Because of our s, its abundant harvest H2633
Job 7:21 not pardon my offenses and forgive my s? H6411
Job 13:23 many wrongs and s have I committed? H2633
Job 13:26 me and make me reap the s of my youth. H6411
Job 22: 5 wickedness great? Are not your s endless? H6411
Job 31:28 then these also would be s to be judged H6411
Job 35: 6 If your s are many, what does that do to H7322
Ps 5:10 Banish them for their many s, for they H7322
Ps 19:13 Keep your servant also from willful s; may H2294
Ps 25: 7 not remember the s of my youth and my H2633
Ps 25:18 my distress and take away all my s. H2633
Ps 32: 1 are forgiven, whose s are covered. H2631
Ps 40:12 surround me; my s have overtaken me H6411
Ps 51: 9 your face from my s and blot out all my H2628
Ps 59:12 For the s of their mouths, for the words of H2633
Ps 65: 3 When we were overwhelmed by s H1821+6411
Ps 68:21 hairy crowns of those who go on in their s. H871
Ps 79: 8 hold against us the s of past generations; H6411
Ps 79: 9 us and forgive our s for your name's sake. H2633
Ps 85: 2 of your people and covered all their s. H2633
Ps 90: 8 our secret s in the light of your presence. NDT
Ps 94:23 repay them for their s and destroy them H224
Ps 103: 3 who forgives all your s and heals all your H6411
Ps 103:10 not treat us as our s deserve or repay us H2628
Ps 109:15 May their s always remain before the LORD NDT
Ps 130: 3 kept a record of s, Lord, who could stand H6411
Ps 130: 8 himself will redeem Israel from all their s. H6411
Pr 5:22 the cords of their s hold them fast. H2633
Pr 28:13 conceals their s does not prosper, H7322
Pr 29:22 a hot-tempered person commits many s. H7322
Ecc 7:20 one who does what is right and never s. H2627
Isa 1:18 "Though your s are like scarlet, they shall H2628
Isa 13:11 the world for its evil, the wicked for their s. H6411
Isa 14:21 his children for the s of their ancestors; H6411
Isa 26:21 punish the people of the earth for their s. H6411
Isa 33:24 the s of those who dwell there will be H6411
Isa 38:17 you have put all my s behind your back. H2628
Isa 40: 2 from the LORD's hand double for all her s. H2633
Isa 43:24 me with your s and wearied me with H2633
Isa 43:25 and remembers your s no more. H2633
Isa 44:22 like a cloud, your s like the morning mist. H2633
Isa 50: 1 Because of your s you were sold; because H6411
Isa 58: 1 to the descendants of Jacob their s. H2633
Isa 59: 2 your s have hidden his face from you H2633
Isa 59:12 in your sight, and our s testify against us. H2633
Isa 59:20 to those in Jacob who repent of their s," H7322
Isa 64: 6 like the wind our s sweep us away. H6411
Isa 64: 7 from us and have given us over to our s. H6411
Isa 64: 9 do not remember our s forever. H6411
Isa 65: 7 both your s and the sins of your ancestors," H6411
Isa 65: 7 both your sins and the s of your ancestors," H6411
Jer 2:13 "My people have committed two s: They H8288
Jer 5:25 your s have deprived you of good. H2633
Jer 11:10 have returned to the s of their ancestors, H6411
Jer 13:22 because of your many s that your skirts H6411
Jer 14: 7 Although our s testify against us, do H6411
Jer 14:10 wickedness and punish them for their s." H2633
Jer 15:13 because of all your s throughout your H2633
Jer 18:23 crimes or blot out their s from your sight. H2633
Jer 30:14 your guilt is so great and your s so many. H2633
Jer 30:15 great guilt and many s I have done these H2633

Jer 31:34 will remember their s no more. H2633
Jer 32:18 the parents' s into the laps of their H6411
Jer 33: 8 will forgive all their s of rebellion against H6411
Jer 50:20 be none, and for the s *of* Judah, but none H2633
Jer 51: 6 Do not be destroyed because of her s. It is H6411
La 1: 5 brought her grief because of her many s. H7322
La 1:14 "My s have been bound into a yoke; by H7322
La 1:22 have dealt with me because of all my s. H7322
La 3:39 complain when **punished for** their s? H2628
La 4:13 because of the s *of* her prophets and the H2633
Eze 7:13 Because of their s, not one of them will H6411
Eze 7:16 they will all moan, each for their own s. H6411
Eze 14:11 themselves anymore with all their s. H7322
Eze 14:13 if a country s against me by being H2627
Eze 16:51 Samaria did not commit half the s you did H2633
Eze 16:52 Because your s were more vile than theirs H2633
Eze 18: 4 The one who s is the one who will die. H2627
Eze 18:14 son who sees all the s his father commits, H2633
Eze 18:20 The one who s is the one who will die H2627
Eze 18:21 away from all the s they have committed H2633
Eze 18:24 because of the s they have H2633
Eze 21:24 revealing your s in all that you do H2633
Eze 23:49 bear the **consequences of** your s *of* H2628
Eze 24:23 away because of your s and groan among H6411
Eze 28:18 By your many s and dishonest trade you H6411
Eze 33:10 "Our offenses and s weigh us down, and H2633
Eze 33:12 person who s will not be allowed H2627
Eze 33:16 None of the s that person has committed H2633
Eze 36:31 yourselves for your s and detestable H6411
Eze 36:33 On the day I cleanse you from all your s, H6411
Eze 43:10 that they may be ashamed of their s. H6411
Eze 45:20 anyone *who* s **unintentionally** or H8706
Da 4:27 Renounce your s by doing what is right A10259
Da 9:13 by turning from our s and giving attention H6411
Da 9:16 Our s and the iniquities of our ancestors H2628
Hos 4: 8 They feed on the s *of* my people and H2633
Hos 7: 1 the s *of* Ephraim are exposed and the H6411
Hos 7: 2 Their s engulf them; they are always H5095
Hos 8:13 their wickedness and punish their s: H2633
Hos 9: 7 Because your s are so many and your H6411
Hos 9: 9 wickedness and punish them for their s. H2633
Hos 13:12 is stored up, his s are kept on record. H2633
Hos 14: 1 Your s have been your downfall! H6411
Hos 14: 2 "Forgive all our s and receive us H6411
Am 1: 3 "For three s *of* Damascus, even for four, H7322
Am 1: 6 "For three s *of* Gaza, even for four, I will H7322
Am 1: 9 "For three s *of* Tyre, even for four, I will H7322
Am 1:11 "For three s *of* Edom, even for four, I will H7322
Am 1:13 "For three s *of* Ammon, even for four, H7322
Am 2: 1 "For three s *of* Moab, even for four, I will H7322
Am 2: 4 "For three s *of* Judah, even for four, I will H7322
Am 2: 6 "For three s *of* Israel, even for four, I will H7322
Am 3: 2 therefore I will punish you for all your s." H6411
Am 3:14 "On the day I punish Israel for her s, I will H7322
Am 5:12 are your offenses and how great your s. H2633
Mic 1: 5 because of the s *of* the people of Israel. H2633
Mic 6:13 destroy you, to ruin you because of your s. H2633
Mic 7:19 you will tread our s underfoot and hurl all H6411
Mt 1:21 he will save his people from their s." G281
Mt 3: 6 Confessing their s, they were baptized by G281
Mt 6:15 But if you do not forgive others their s, G4183
Mt 6:15 your Father will not forgive your s. G4183
Mt 9: 2 "Take heart, son; your s are forgiven." G281
Mt 9: 5 'Your s are forgiven,' or to say, 'Get G281
Mt 9: 6 of Man has authority on earth to forgive s." G281
Mt 18:15 "If your brother or sister s, go and point out G279
Mt 18:21 my brother or sister *who* s against me? G279
Mt 26:28 out for many for the forgiveness *of* s. G281
Mk 1: 4 of repentance for the forgiveness *of* s. G281
Mk 1: 5 Confessing their s, they were baptized by G281
Mk 2: 5 paralyzed man, "Son, your s are forgiven." G281
Mk 2: 7 Who can forgive s but God alone?" G281
Mk 2: 9 paralyzed man, 'Your s are forgiven,' or to G281
Mk 2:10 of Man has authority on earth to forgive s." G281
Mk 3:28 be forgiven all their s and every slander G280
Mk 11:25 Father in heaven may forgive you your s." G4183
Lk 1:77 salvation through the forgiveness *of* their s, G281
Lk 3: 3 of repentance for the forgiveness *of* s. G281
Lk 5:20 he said, "Friend, your s are forgiven." G281
Lk 5:21 Who can forgive s but God alone?" G281
Lk 5:23 'Your s are forgiven,' or to say, 'Get G281
Lk 5:24 of Man has authority on earth to forgive s." G281
Lk 7:47 I tell you, her many s have been forgiven G281
Lk 7:48 Jesus said to her, "Your s are forgiven." G281
Lk 7:49 "Who is this who even forgives s? G281
Lk 11: 4 Forgive us our s, for we also forgive G281
Lk 11: 4 also forgive everyone *who* s **against** us. G4053
Lk 17: 3 "If your brother or sister s against you G279
Lk 24:47 the forgiveness *of* s will be preached in G281
Jn 8:24 I told you that you would die in your s; if G281
Jn 8:24 that I am he, you will indeed die in your s." G281
Jn 8:34 everyone who s is a slave to G4472+3836+281
Jn 20:23 If you forgive anyone's s, their sins are G281
Jn 20:23 anyone's sins, their s are forgiven; if you do NDT
Ac 2:38 of Jesus Christ for the forgiveness *of* your s. G281
Ac 3:19 so that your s may be wiped out G281
Ac 5:31 Israel to repentance and forgive their s. G281
Ac 10:43 receives forgiveness *of* s through his name." G281
Ac 13:38 the forgiveness *of* s is proclaimed to you G281
Ac 22:16 be baptized and wash your s away, calling G281
Ac 26:18 receive forgiveness *of* s and a place among G281
Ro 3:25 he had left the s committed beforehand G280
Ro 4: 7 are forgiven, whose s are covered. G281
Ro 4:25 over to death for our s and was raised to G4183
Ro 11:27 with them when I take away their s. G281
1Co 6:18 All other s a person commits are outside G280
1Co 6:18 but whoever s **sexually**, sins against G4519
1Co 6:18 sins sexually, s against their own body. G279
1Co 15: 3 that Christ died for our s according to the G281
1Co 15:17 your faith is futile; you are still in your s. G281
2Co 5:19 not counting people's s against them. G4183
Gal 1: 4 gave himself for our s to rescue us from the G281
Eph 1: 7 the forgiveness *of* s, in accordance with G4183
Eph 2: 1 you were dead in your transgressions and s, G281
Col 1:14 we have redemption, the forgiveness *of* s. G281
Col 2:13 When you were dead *in* your s and in the G4183
Col 2:13 alive with Christ. He forgave us all our s, G4183
1Th 2:16 they always heap up their s to the limit. G281
1Th 4: 6 Lord will punish all those who commit **such** s, AIT
1Ti 5:22 and do not share in the s of others. G281
1Ti 5:24 The s of some are obvious, reaching the G281
1Ti 5:24 of them; the s of others trail behind them. NDT
2Ti 3: 6 are loaded down with s and are swayed by G281
Heb 1: 3 After he had provided purification *for* s, he G281
Heb 2:17 make atonement *for* the s of the people. G281
Heb 5: 1 to offer gifts and sacrifices for s. G281
Heb 5: 3 why he has to offer sacrifices for his own s, G281
Heb 5: 3 own sins, as well as for the s of the people. NDT
Heb 7:27 first for his own s, and then for the sins G281
Heb 7:27 own sins, and then for the s of the people. NDT
Heb 7:27 He sacrificed for their s once for all when he NDT
Heb 8:12 will remember their s no more. G281
Heb 9: 7 *for* the s the people *had* **committed in ignorance** G52
Heb 9:15 set them free *from* the s committed under G4126
Heb 9:28 sacrificed once to take away the s of many; G281
Heb 10: 2 would no longer have felt guilty *for* their s. G281
Heb 10: 3 sacrifices are an annual reminder *of* s. G281
Heb 10: 4 blood of bulls and goats to take away s. G281
Heb 10:11 sacrifices, which can never take away s. G281
Heb 10:12 had offered for all time one sacrifice for s, G281
Heb 10:17 "Their s and lawless acts I will remember G281
Heb 10:26 of the truth, no sacrifice for s is left, G281
Jas 5:16 Therefore confess your s to each other and G281
Jas 5:20 from death and cover over a multitude *of* s. G281
1Pe 2:24 "He himself bore our s" in his body on the G281
1Pe 2:24 so that we might die *to* s and live for G281
1Pe 3:18 For Christ also suffered once for s, the G281
1Pe 4: 8 because love covers over a multitude *of* s. G281
2Pe 1: 9 they have been cleansed *from* their past s. G281
1Jn 1: 9 If we confess our s, he is faithful and just G281
1Jn 1: 9 will forgive us our s and purify us from all G281
1Jn 2: 2 He is the atoning sacrifice for our s, and not G281
1Jn 2: 2 ours but also for the s of the whole world. NDT
1Jn 2:12 because your s have been forgiven on G281
1Jn 3: 4 Everyone who s breaks the G4472+3836+281
1Jn 3: 5 appeared so that he might take away our s. G281
1Jn 4:10 his Son as an atoning sacrifice for our s. G281
Rev 1: 5 has freed us from our s by his blood, G281
Rev 18: 4 so that you will not share in her s, so that G281
Rev 18: 5 her s are piled up to heaven, and God G281

SION (KJV) SIRION, ZION

SIPHMOTH (1)

1Sa 30:28 to those in Aroer, S, Eshtemoa H8560

SIPPAI (1)

1Ch 20: 4 time Sibbekai the Hushathite killed S, H6205

SIR (22) [SIRS]

Ge 23: 6 "S, listen to us. You are a mighty prince H123
Mt 13:27 to him and said, 'S, didn't you sow good G3261
Mt 21:30 He answered, 'I will, s,' but he did not go. G3261
Mt 27:63 "S," they said, "we remember that while G3261
Lk 13: 8 " 'S,' the man replied, 'leave it alone G3261
Lk 13:25 pleading, 'S, open the door for us.' G3261
Lk 14:22 " 'S,' the servant said, 'what you ordered G3261
Lk 19:16 one came and said, 'S, your mina has G3261
Lk 19:18 came and said, 'S, your mina has earned G3261
Lk 19:20 came and said, 'S, here is your mina; G3261
Lk 19:25 " 'S,' they said, 'he already has ten!' G3261
Jn 4:11 "S," the woman said, "you have nothing G3261
Jn 4:15 said to him, "S, give me this water G3261
Jn 4:19 "S," the woman said, "I can see that you G3261
Jn 4:49 official said, "S, come down before my G3261
Jn 5: 7 "S," the invalid replied, "I have no one to G3261
Jn 6:34 "S," they said, "always give us this bread." G3261
Jn 8:11 "No one, s," she said. "Then neither do I G3261
Jn 9:36 "Who is he, s?" the man asked. "Tell me G3261
Jn 12:21 "S," they said, "we would like to see G3261
Jn 20:15 she said, "S, if you have carried him away, G3261
Rev 7:14 I answered, "S, you know." And he said G3261

SIRAH (1)

2Sa 3:26 brought him back from the cistern at S. H6241

SIRION (3) [HERMON]

Dt 3: 9 Hermon is called S by the Sidonians; the H8590
Dt 4:48 the rim of the Arnon Gorge to Mount S H8590
Ps 29: 6 leap like a calf, S like a young wild ox. H8590

SIRS (1) [SIR]

Ac 16:30 them out and asked, "S, what must I do to G3261

SISERA (19) [SISERA'S]

Jdg 4: 2 S, the commander of his army, was based H6102
Jdg 4: 7 I will lead S, the commander of Jabin's H6102
Jdg 4: 9 the LORD will deliver S into the hands of a H6102
Jdg 4:12 When they told S that Barak son of H6102
Jdg 4:13 S summoned from Harosheth Haggoyim to H6102
Jdg 4:14 day the LORD has given S into your hands. H6102
Jdg 4:15 the LORD routed S and all his chariots and H6102
Jdg 4:15 S got down from his chariot and fled H6102
Jdg 4:17 S, meanwhile, fled on foot to the tent of H6102
Jdg 4:18 Jael went out to meet S and said to him H6102
Jdg 4:22 Just then Barak came by in pursuit of S H6102
Jdg 4:22 there lay S with the tent peg through H6102
Jdg 5:20 from their courses they fought against S. H6102
Jdg 5:26 She struck S, she crushed his head, she H6102
Jdg 5:30 colorful garments as plunder for S H6102
1Sa 12: 9 so he sold them into the hand of S, the H6102
Ezr 2:53 Barkos, S, Temah, H6102
Ne 7:55 Barkos, S, Temah, H6102
Ps 83: 9 as you did to S and Jabin at the river H6102

SISERA'S (2) [SISERA]

Jdg 4:16 all S troops fell by the sword H6102
Jdg 5:28 "Through the window peered S mother H6102

SISMAI (2)

1Ch 2:40 Eleasah the father of S, Sismai the father H6183
1Ch 2:40 father of Sismai, S the father of Shallum H6183

SISTER (133) [SISTER-IN-LAW, SISTER'S, SISTERS]

Ge 4:22 Tubal-Cain's s was Naamah. H295
Ge 12:13 Say you are my s, so that I will be treated H295
Ge 12:19 you say, 'She is my s,' so that I took her to H295
Ge 20: 2 said of his wife Sarah, "She is my s." H295
Ge 20: 5 'She is my s,' and didn't she also H295
Ge 20:12 she really is my s, the daughter of my H295
Ge 24:59 So they sent their s Rebekah on her way H295
Ge 24:60 said to her, "Our s, may you increase to H295
Ge 25:20 Paddan Aram and s *of* Laban the Aramean H295
Ge 26: 7 he said, "She is my s," because he was H295
Ge 26: 9 you say, 'She is my s'?" Isaac answered H295
Ge 28: 9 the s *of* Nebaioth and daughter of Ishmael H295
Ge 30: 1 any children, she became jealous of her s. H295
Ge 30: 8 "I have had a great struggle with my s, and H295
Ge 34:13 Because their s Dinah had been defiled H295
Ge 34:14 we can't give our s to a man who is not H295
Ge 34:17 to be circumcised, we'll take our s and go." H1426
Ge 34:27 the city where their s had been defiled. H295
Ge 34:31 he have treated our s like a prostitute?" H295
Ge 36: 3 daughter of Ishmael and s *of* Nebaioth. H295
Ge 36:22 Hori and Homam. Timna was Lotan's s. H295
Ge 46:17 Their s was Serah. The sons of H295
Ex 2: 4 His s stood at a distance to see what would H295
Ex 2: 7 Then his s asked Pharaoh's daughter H295
Ex 6:20 Amram married his **father's** s Jochebed H1860
Ex 6:23 daughter of Amminadab and s *of* Nahshon, H295
Ex 15:20 the prophet, Aaron's s, took a timbrel in H295
Lev 18: 9 " 'Do not have sexual relations with your s H295
Lev 18:11 born to your father; she is your s. H295
Lev 18:12 have sexual relations with your father's s; H295
Lev 18:13 have sexual relations with your mother's s, H295
Lev 18:18 not take your wife's s as a rival wife and H295
Lev 20:17 " 'If a man marries his s, the daughter of H295
Lev 20:17 He has dishonored his s and will be held H295
Lev 20:19 relations with the s *of* either your mother H295
Lev 21: 3 an unmarried s who is dependent on him H295
Nu 6: 7 own father or mother or brother or s dies, H295
Nu 25:18 in the Peor incident involving their s Kozbi, H295
Nu 26:59 she bore Aaron, Moses and their s Miriam. H295
Dt 27:22 "Cursed is anyone who sleeps with his s H295
Jdg 15: 2 Isn't her younger s more attractive? Take H295
2Sa 13: 1 the beautiful s of Absalom son of David. H295
2Sa 13: 2 so obsessed with his s Tamar that he made H295
2Sa 13: 4 love with Tamar, my brother Absalom's s." H295
2Sa 13: 5 'I would like my s Tamar to come and give H295
2Sa 13: 6 "I would like my s Tamar to come and H295
2Sa 13:11 her and said, "Come to bed with me, my s." H295
2Sa 13:20 Be quiet for now, my s; he is your brother H295
2Sa 13:22 because he had disgraced his s Tamar. H295
2Sa 13:32 since the day Amnon raped his s Tamar. H295
2Sa 17:25 of Nahash and s *of* Zeruiah the mother of H295
1Ki 11:19 that he gave him a s *of* his own wife, H295
1Ki 11:20 The s *of* Tahpenes bore him a son named H295
2Ki 11: 2 of King Jehoram and s *of* Ahaziah, H295
1Ch 1:39 Hori and Homam. Timna was Lotan's s. H295
1Ch 3: 9 by his concubines. And Tamar was their s. H295
1Ch 3:19 Hananiah. Shelomith was their s. H295
1Ch 4: 3 Their s was named Hazzelelponi H295
1Ch 4:19 Hodiah's wife, the s *of* Naham: the father H295
1Ch 7:18 His s Hammoleketh gave birth to Ishhod H295
1Ch 7:30 Ishvi and Beriah. Their s was Serah. H295
1Ch 7:32 Shomer and Hotham and of their s Shua. H295
2Ch 22:11 was Ahaziah's s, she hid the child from H295
Job 17:14 to the worm, 'My mother' or 'My s,' H295
Pr 7: 4 to wisdom, "You are my s," and to insight, H295
SS 4: 9 stolen my heart, my s, my bride; you have H295
SS 4:10 is your love, my s, my bride! How much H295
SS 4:12 are a garden locked up, my s, my bride; H295
SS 5: 1 have come into my garden, my s, my bride; H295
SS 5: 2 "Open to me, my s, my darling, my dove H295
SS 8: 8 We have a little s, and her breasts are not H295
SS 8: 8 shall we do for our s on the day she is H295

Jer 3: 7 and her unfaithful **s** Judah saw it. H295
Jer 3: 8 that her unfaithful **s** Judah had no fear; H295
Jer 3:10 her unfaithful **s** Judah did not return to me H295
Jer 22:18 Alas, my **s**!' They will not H295
Eze 16:45 you are a true **s** *of* your sisters, who H295
Eze 16:46 Your older **s** was Samaria, who lived to the H295
Eze 16:46 your younger **s**, who lived to the south H295
Eze 16:48 your **s** Sodom and her daughters never did H295
Eze 16:49 " 'Now this was the sin of your **s** Sodom H295
Eze 16:56 even mention your **s** Sodom in the day of H295
Eze 22:11 another violates his **s**, his own father's H295
Eze 23: 4 named Oholah, and her **s** was Oholibah. H295
Eze 23:11 "Her **s** Oholibah saw this, yet in her lust H295
Eze 23:11 she was more depraved than her **s**. H295
Eze 23:18 just as I had turned away from her **s**. H295
Eze 23:31 You have gone the way of your **s**; so I will H295
Eze 23:33 desolation, the cup of your **s** Samaria. H295
Eze 23:42 the wrists of **the woman and her s** and H2177S
Eze 44:25 brother or unmarried **s**, then he may defile H295
Mt 5:22 who is angry *with* a **brother or s** will be G81
Mt 5:22 anyone who says *to* a **brother or s**, 'Raca, G81
Mt 5:23 that your **brother or s** has something G81
Mt 12:50 in heaven is my brother and **s** and mother." G80
Mt 18:15 "If your **brother or s** sins, go and point out G81
Mt 18:21 I forgive my **brother or s** who sins against G81
Mt 18:35 forgive your **brother or s** from your heart." G81
Mk 3:35 God's will is my brother and **s** and mother." G80
Lk 10:39 She had a **s** called Mary, who sat at the G80
Lk 10:40 you care that my **s** has left me to do the G80
Lk 17: 3 "If your **brother or s** sins against you, rebuke G81
Jn 11: 1 the village of Mary and her **s** Martha. G80
Jn 11: 5 Jesus loved Martha and her **s** and Lazarus. G80
Jn 11:28 she went back and called her **s** Mary aside. G80
Jn 11:39 said Martha, the **s** of the dead man, "by this G80
Jn 19:25 his mother's **s**, Mary the wife of G80
Ac 23:16 But when the son *of* Paul's **s** heard of this G80
Ro 14:10 why do you judge your **brother or s**? G81
Ro 14:13 block or obstacle in the way *of* a **brother or s**. G81
Ro 14:15 If your **brother or s** is distressed because of G81
Ro 14:21 else that will cause your **brother or s** to fall. G81
Ro 16: 1 I commend to you our **s** Phoebe, a deacon G80
Ro 16:15 Nereus and his **s**, and Olympas and all G80
1Co 5:11 claims to be a **brother or s** but is sexually G81
1Co 7:15 The brother or the **s** is not bound in such G80
1Co 8:11 So this weak **brother or s**, for whom Christ G81
1Co 8:13 I eat causes my **brother or s** to fall into sin, G81
1Th 4: 6 wrong or take advantage of a **brother or s**. G81
Phm 2 also to Apphia our **s** and Archippus our G80
Jas 2:15 Suppose a brother or a **s** is without clothes G80
Jas 4:11 speaks against a **brother or s** or judges them G81
1Jn 2: 9 light but hates a **brother or s** is still in the G81
1Jn 2:10 who loves their **brother and s** lives in the G81
1Jn 2:11 anyone who hates a **brother or s** is in the G81
1Jn 3:10 who does not love their **brother and s**. G81
1Jn 3:15 who hates a **brother or s** is a murderer, G81
1Jn 3:17 sees a **brother or s** in need but has no G81
1Jn 4:20 to love God yet hates a **brother or s** is a liar. G81
1Jn 4:20 whoever does not love their **brother and s**, G81
1Jn 4:21 loves God must also love their **brother and s**. G81
1Jn 5:16 If you see any **brother or s** commit a sin that G81
2Jn 13 The children *of* your **s**, who is chosen by God G80

SISTER'S (4) [SISTER]

Ge 24:30 the bracelets on his **s** arms, and had H295
Ge 29:13 news about Jacob, his **s** son, he hurried to H295
1Ch 7:15 Shuppites. His **s** name was Maakah H295
Eze 23:32 "You will drink your **s** cup, a cup large and H295

SISTER-IN-LAW (1) [SISTER]

S

Ru 1:15 "your **s** is going back to her people and H3304

SISTERS (145) [SISTER]

Jos 2:13 my brothers and **s**, and all who belong to H295
Jos 6:23 her **brothers and s** and all who belonged to H278
1Ch 2:16 Their **s** were Zeruiah and Abigail H295
Job 1: 4 invite their three **s** to eat and drink with H295
Job 42:11 All his brothers and **s** and everyone who H295
Eze 16:45 you are a true sister of your **s**, who H295
Eze 16:51 have made your **s** seem righteous by H295
Eze 16:52 have furnished some justification for your **s**. H295
Eze 16:52 you have made your **s** appear righteous. H295
Eze 16:55 And your **s**, Sodom with her daughters and H295
Eze 16:61 be ashamed when you receive your **s**, H295
Hos 2: 1 'My people,' and of your **s**, 'My loved one. H295
Mt 13:56 Aren't all his **s** with us? Where then did this G80
Mt 19:29 houses or brothers or **s** or father or mother G80
Mt 25:40 of the least *of* these **brothers and s** of mine, G81
Mk 6: 3 Aren't his **s** here with us?" And G80
Mk 10:29 home or brothers or **s** or mother or father G80
Mk 10:30 brothers, **s**, mothers, children and G80
Lk 14:12 your **brothers or s**, your relatives, G81
Lk 14:26 brothers and **s**—yes, even their own G80
Lk 18:29 home or wife or **brothers or s** or parents or G81
Lk 21:16 by parents, **brothers and s**, relatives and G81
Jn 11: 3 So the **s** sent word to Jesus, "Lord, the one G80
Ac 1:16 said, "**Brothers and s**, the Scripture G467+81
Ac 6: 3 **Brothers and s**, choose seven men from G81
Ac 11:29 provide help *for* the **brothers and s** living in G81
Ac 12:17 the *other* **brothers and s** about this, G81
Ac 16:40 met with the **brothers and s** and encouraged G81
Ac 18:18 he left the **brothers and s** and sailed for G81
Ac 18:27 the **brothers and s** encouraged him and G81
Ac 21: 7 we greeted the **brothers and s** and stayed G81
Ac 21:17 the **brothers and s** received us warmly. G81
Ac 28:14 we found *some* **brothers and s** who invited G81
Ac 28:15 The **brothers and s** there had heard that we G81
Ro 1:13 to be unaware, **brothers and s**, that I G81
Ro 7: 1 Do you not know, **brothers and s**—for I am G81
Ro 7: 4 my **brothers and s**, you also died to the G81
Ro 8:12 Therefore, **brothers and s**, we have an G81
Ro 8:29 be the firstborn among many **brothers and s**. G81
Ro 10: 1 **Brothers and s**, my heart's desire and prayer G81
Ro 11:25 of this mystery, **brothers and s**, so that you G81
Ro 12: 1 I urge you, **brothers and s**, in view of God's G81
Ro 15:14 am convinced, my **brothers and s**, that you G81
Ro 15:30 I urge you, **brothers and s**, by our Lord Jesus G81
Ro 16:14 the other **brothers and s** with them. G81
Ro 16:17 I urge you, **brothers and s**, to watch out for G81
1Co 1:10 appeal to you, **brothers and s**, in the name G81
1Co 1:11 My **brothers and s**, some from Chloe's G81
1Co 1:26 **Brothers and s**, think of what you were G81
1Co 2: 1 was with me, **brothers and s**. When I came G81
1Co 3: 1 **Brothers and s**, I could not address you as G81
1Co 4: 6 **brothers and s**, I have applied these G81
1Co 6: 8 you do this *to* your **brothers and s**. G81
1Co 7:24 **Brothers and s**, each person, as responsible G81
1Co 7:29 What I mean, **brothers and s**, is that the G81
1Co 10: 1 of the fact, **brothers and s**, that our ancestors G81
1Co 11:33 So then, my **brothers and s**, when you gather G81
1Co 12: 1 of the Spirit, **brothers and s**, I do not want G81
1Co 14: 6 **brothers and s**, if I come to you and G81
1Co 14:20 **Brothers and s**, stop thinking like children. G81
1Co 14:26 shall we say, **brothers and s**? When you G81
1Co 14:39 Therefore, my **brothers and s**, be eager to G81
1Co 15: 1 **brothers and s**, I want to remind you of G81
1Co 15: 6 hundred *of* the **brothers and s** at the same G81
1Co 15:50 declare to you, **brothers and s**, that flesh G81
1Co 15:58 my dear **brothers and s**, stand firm. G81
1Co 16:15 I urge you, **brothers and s**, G81
1Co 16:20 All the **brothers and s** here send you G81
2Co 1: 8 to be uninformed, **brothers and s**, about the G81
2Co 8: 1 And now, **brothers and s**, we want you to G81
2Co 13:11 **brothers and s**, rejoice! Strive for full G81
Gal 1: 2 all the **brothers and s** with me, To the G81
Gal 1:11 you to know, **brothers and s**, that the gospel G81
Gal 3:15 **Brothers and s**, let me take an example from G81
Gal 4:12 with you, **brothers and s**, become like me G81
Gal 4:28 Now you, **brothers and s**, like Isaac, are G81
Gal 4:31 Therefore, **brothers and s**, we are not G81
Gal 5:11 **Brothers and s**, if I am still preaching G81
Gal 5:13 my **brothers and s**, were called to be G81
Gal 6: 1 **Brothers and s**, if someone is caught in a sin, G81
Gal 6:18 Christ be with your spirit, **brothers and s**. G81
Eph 6:23 Peace *to* the **brothers and s**, and love with G81
Php 1:12 you to know, **brothers and s**, that what has G81
Php 1:14 most *of* the **brothers and s** have become G81
Php 3: 1 my **brothers and s**, rejoice in the G81
Php 3:13 **Brothers and s**, I do not consider myself yet G81
Php 3:17 my example, **brothers and s**, and just as you G81
Php 4: 1 Therefore, my **brothers and s**, you whom I G81
Php 4: 8 **brothers and s**, whatever is true G81
Php 4:21 The **brothers and s** who are with me send G81
Col 1: 2 the faithful **brothers and s** in Christ: G81
Col 4:15 greetings *to* the **brothers and s** at Laodicea G81
1Th 1: 4 For we know, **brothers and s** loved by God G81
1Th 2: 1 You know, **brothers and s**, that our visit to G81
1Th 2: 9 you remember, **brothers and s**, our toil and G81
1Th 2:14 **brothers and s**, became imitators of G81
1Th 2:17 **brothers and s**, when we were orphaned G81
1Th 3: 7 Therefore, **brothers and s**, in all our distress G81
1Th 4: 1 other matters, **brothers and s**, we instructed G81
1Th 4:10 we urge you, **brothers and s**, to do so more G81
1Th 4:13 **Brothers and s**, we do not want you to be G81
1Th 5: 1 **brothers and s**, about times and dates G81
1Th 5: 4 **brothers and s**, are not in darkness G81
1Th 5:12 we ask you, **brothers and s**, to acknowledge G81
1Th 5:14 we urge you, **brothers and s**, warn those G81
1Th 5:25 **Brothers and s**, pray for us. G81
1Th 5:27 this letter read to all the **brothers and s**. G81
2Th 1: 3 God for you, **brothers and s**, and rightly so, G81
2Th 2: 1 we ask you, **brothers and s**, G81
2Th 2:13 for you, **brothers and s** loved by the Lord G81
2Th 2:15 So then, **brothers and s**, stand firm and hold G81
2Th 3: 1 other matters, **brothers and s**, pray for us that G81
2Th 3: 6 command you, **brothers and s**, to keep away G81
2Th 3:13 And as for you, **brothers and s**, never tire of G81
1Ti 4: 6 point these things out *to* the **brothers and s**, G81
1Ti 5: 2 younger women as **s**, with absolute G80
2Ti 4:21 Claudia and all the **brothers and s**. G81
Heb 2:11 is not ashamed to call them **brothers and s**. G81
Heb 2:12 will declare your name *to* my **brothers and s**; G81
Heb 3: 1 Therefore, holy **brothers and s**, who share in G81
Heb 3:12 See to it, **brothers and s**, that none of you G81
Heb 10:19 Therefore, **brothers and s**, since we have G81
Heb 13: 1 on **loving one another as brothers and s**. G5789
Heb 13:22 **Brothers and s**, I urge you to bear with my G81
Jas 1: 2 it pure joy, my **brothers and s**, whenever you G81
Jas 1:16 Don't be deceived, my dear **brothers and s**. G81
Jas 1:19 My dear **brothers and s**, take note of this G81
Jas 2: 1 My **brothers and s**, believers in our glorious G81
Jas 2: 5 my dear **brothers and s**: Has not God G81
Jas 2:14 good is it, my **brothers and s**, if someone G81
Jas 3:10 My **brothers and s**, this should G81
Jas 3:12 My **brothers and s**, can a fig tree bear olives G81
Jas 4:11 **Brothers and s**, do not slander one another G81
Jas 5: 7 then, **brothers and s**, until the Lord's G81
Jas 5: 9 one another, **brothers and s**, or you will be G81
Jas 5:10 **Brothers and s**, as an example of patience in G81
Jas 5:12 Above all, my **brothers and s**, do not swear G81
Jas 5:19 My **brothers and s**, if one of you should G81
2Pe 1:10 Therefore, my **brothers and s**, make every G81
1Jn 3:13 be surprised, my **brothers and s**, if the world G81
1Jn 3:16 to lay down our lives for our **brothers and s**. G81
3Jn 5 in what you are doing for the **brothers and s**, G81
Rev 6:11 servants, their **brothers and s**, were killed G81
Rev 12:10 For the accuser *of* our **brothers and s**, who G81
Rev 19:10 you and *with* your **brothers and s** who hold G81

SISTRUMS (1)

2Sa 6: 5 lyres, timbrels, **s** and cymbals. H4983

SIT (109) [SAT, SITS, SITTING]

Ge 27:19 Please **s** up and eat some of my game, so H3782
Ge 27:31 *please* **s** up and eat some of my game H7756
Ex 18:14 Why *do* you alone **s as judge**, while all H3782
Nu 32: 6 Israelites go to war while you **s** here? H3782
Dt 6: 7 them when you **s** at home and when H3782
Dt 11:19 them when you **s** at home and when H3782
Ru 4: 1 "Come over here, my friend, and **s down**." H3782
Ru 4: 2 the town and said, "**S** here," and they did H3782
1Sa 16:11 *we will* not **s down** until he arrives." H6015
1Ki 1:13 after me, and he *will* **s** on my throne"? H3782
1Ki 1:17 king after me, and he *will* **s** on my throne. H3782
1Ki 1:20 learn from you who *will* **s** on the throne of H3782
1Ki 1:24 and that he *will* **s** on your throne? H3782
1Ki 1:27 know who *should* **s** on the throne of H3782
1Ki 1:30 he *will* **s** on my throne in my place." H3782
1Ki 1:35 he is to come and **s** on my throne and H3782
1Ki 3: 6 given him a son *to* **s** on his throne this H3782
1Ki 8:20 my father and now *I* **s** on the throne of H3782
1Ki 8:25 to have a successor *to* **s** before me on the H3782
2Ki 10:30 your descendants *will* **s** on the throne of H3782
2Ki 15:12 "Your descendants *will* **s** on the throne of H3782
1Ch 28: 5 my son Solomon to **s** on the throne of the H3782
2Ch 6:10 my father and now *I* **s** on the throne of H3782
2Ch 6:16 to have a successor *to* **s** before me on the H3782
Ps 1: 1 that sinners take or **s** in the company of H3782
Ps 7: 7 while *you* **s enthroned** over them on high. AIT
Ps 26: 4 *I do* not **s** with the deceitful, nor do I H3782
Ps 26: 5 evildoers and refuse *to* **s** with the wicked. H3782
Ps 50:20 *You* **s** and testify against your brother and H3782
Ps 69:12 *Those who* **s** *at* the gate mock me, and I H3782
Ps 80: 1 You *who* **s enthroned** *between* the H3782
Ps 102:12 **s enthroned** forever; your renown H3782
Ps 110: 1 "**S** at my right hand until I make your H3782
Ps 119:23 Though rulers **s** *together* and slander me H3782
Ps 123: 1 to you who **s enthroned** in heaven. H3782
Ps 132:12 then their sons *will* **s** on your throne for H3782
Ps 132:14 here *I will* **s enthroned**, for I have H3782
Ps 139: 2 You know *when* I **s** and when I rise; you H3782
Pr 23: 1 When *you* **s** to dine with a ruler, note well H3782
SS 2: 3 I delight *to* **s** in his shade, and his fruit is H3782
Isa 3:26 destitute, *she will* **s** on the ground. H3782
Isa 14:13 *I will* **s enthroned** on the mount of H3782
Isa 16: 5 in faithfulness *a man will* **s** on it—one H3782
Isa 42: 7 the dungeon *those who* **s** *in* darkness. H3782
Isa 47: 1 "Go down, **s** in the dust, Virgin Daughter H3782
Isa 47: 1 Babylon; **s** on the ground without a throne H3782
Isa 47: 5 "**S** in silence, go into darkness, queen city H3782
Isa 47:14 coals for warmth; this is not a fire to **s** by. H3782
Isa 52: 2 rise up, **s enthroned**, Jerusalem. H3782
Isa 65: 4 who **s** among the graves and spend their H3782
Jer 13:13 the kings who **s** on David's throne, H3782
Jer 16: 8 is feasting and **s down** to eat and drink. H3782
Jer 17:25 then kings *who* **s** on David's throne will H3782
Jer 22: 2 of Judah, you who **s** on David's throne H3782
Jer 22: 4 then kings *who* **s** on David's throne will H3782
Jer 22:30 none *will* **s** on the throne of David or rule H3782
Jer 33:17 fail to have a man *to* **s** on the throne of H3782
Jer 36:15 said to him, "**S down**, please, and read H3782
Jer 36:30 He will have no *one to* **s** on the throne of H3782
Jer 48:18 glory and **s** on the parched ground, *you* H3782
La 2:10 of Daughter Zion **s** on the ground in H3782
La 3:28 *Let him* **s** alone in silence, for the LORD H3782
Eze 26:16 with terror, *they will* **s** on the ground H3782
Eze 28: 2 *I* **s** *on* the throne of a god in the heart of H3782
Eze 33:31 and **s** before you to hear your words H3782
Eze 44: 3 is the only one *who may* **s** inside the H3782
Da 7:26 " 'But the court *will* **s**, and his power will A10338
Da 11:27 will **s** at the same table and lie to each NDT
Joel 3:12 there *I will* **s** to judge all the nations H3782
Mic 4: 4 Everyone *will* **s** under their own vine and H3782
Mic 7: 8 Though *I* **s** in darkness, the LORD will be H3782
Zec 3:10 your neighbor to **s** under your vine and fig NDT
Zec 6:13 with majesty and *will* **s** and rule on his H3782
Zec 8: 4 of ripe old age *will* **s** in the streets of H3782
Mal 3: 3 *He will* **s** as a refiner and purifier of silver H3782
Mt 14:19 directed the people *to* **s down** on the grass. G369
Mt 15:35 He told the crowd *to* **s down** on the ground. G404
Mt 19:28 have followed me *will* also **s** on twelve G2764
Mt 20:21 two sons of mine *may* **s** at your right and G2767
Mt 20:23 *to* **s** at my right or left is not for me to G2767
Mt 21: 7 their cloaks on them for Jesus *to* **s** on. G2125
Mt 22:44 "**S** at my right hand until I put your G2764
Mt 23: 2 law and the Pharisees **s** in Moses' seat. G2767
Mt 25:31 with him, *he will* **s** on his glorious throne. G2767

Mt 26:36 “**S** here while I go over there and pray.” *G2767*
Mk 6:39 them *to* **have** all the people **s down** in *G369*
Mk 8: 6 He told the crowd *to* **s down** on the ground *G404*
Mk 10:37 “Let one of us **s** at your right and the other *G2767*
Mk 10:40 *to* **s** at my right or left is not for me to *G2767*
Mk 12:36 “**S** at my right hand until I put your *G2764*
Mk 14:32 said to his disciples, “**S** here while I pray.” *G2767*
Lk 9:14 “*Have* them **s down** in groups of about *G2884*
Lk 14:28 Won’t *you* first **s down** and estimate the *G2767*
Lk 14:31 Won’t *he* first **s down** and consider *G2767*
Lk 16: 6 ‘Take your bill, **s down** quickly, and make *G2767*
Lk 17: 7 ‘Come along now and **s down to eat**’? *G404*
Lk 20:42 Lord said to my Lord: “**S** at my right hand *G2764*
Lk 22:30 my table in my kingdom and **s** on thrones, *G2764*
Jn 6:10 “Have the people **s down**.” There was *G404*
Jn 9: 8 the same man who *used to* **s** and beg?” *G2764*
Ac 2:34 Lord said to my Lord: “**S** at my right hand *G2764*
Ac 3:10 same man who used to **s** begging at the *G2764*
Ac 8:31 invited Philip to come up and **s** with him. *G2767*
Ac 23: 3 You **s** there to judge me according to the *G2764*
1Co 9: 3 to those *who* **s in judgment** on me. *G373*
Heb 1:13 “**S** at my right hand until I make your *G2764*
Jas 2: 3 stand there” or “**S** on the floor by my feet,” *G2764*
Rev 3:21 will give the right *to* **s** with me on my *G2767*
Rev 18: 7 heart she boasts, ‘*I* **s enthroned** as queen. *G2764*

SITE (13) [SITES]
Ge 12: 6 the land as far as the **s** *of* the great tree of H5226
Ge 23: 4 property for a **burial s** here so I can bury H7700
Ge 23: 9 the full price as a burial **s** among you.” H299
Ge 23:20 to Abraham by the Hittites as a burial **s**. H299
1Ki 6: 7 heard at the temple **s** while it was being NDT
1Ch 17: 5 I have moved from one **tent s** to another H185
1Ch 21:22 “Let me have the **s** *of* your threshing floor H5226
1Ch 21:25 six hundred shekels of gold for the **s**. H5226
Ezr 2:68 rebuilding of the house of God on its **s**. H4806
Ezr 5:15 And rebuild the house of God on its **s**.’ A10087
Ezr 6: 7 elders rebuild this house of God on its **s**. A10087
Ne 12:37 above the **s of** David’s **palace** to the H1074
Zec 14:10 Benjamin Gate to the **s** *of* the First Gate, H5226

SITES (2) [SITE]
2Ki 23:14 covered the **s** with human bones. H5226
2Ch 33:19 the **s** where he built high places and H5226

SITHRI (1)
Ex 6:22 of Uzziel were Mishael, Elzaphan and **S**. H6262

SITNAH (1)
Ge 26:21 over that one also; so he named it **S**. H8479

SITS (27) [SIT]
Ex 11: 5 son of Pharaoh, who **s** on the throne, to H3782
Lev 15: 4 anything *he* **s** on will be unclean. H3782
Lev 15: 6 Whoever **s** on anything that the man with H3782
Lev 15: 9 ‘Everything the man **s** on when riding will H5323
Lev 15:20 anything *she* **s** on will be unclean. H3782
Lev 15:22 touches anything *she* **s** on will be unclean H3782
Lev 15:26 anything *she* **s** on will be unclean H3782
Est 6:10 the Jew, who **s** at the king’s gate. H3782
Ps 29:10 The LORD **s enthroned** over the flood; the H3782
Ps 99: 1 *he* **s enthroned** *between* the cherubim H3782
Ps 113: 5 the One who **s enthroned** on high, H3782
Pr 9:14 *She* **s** at the door of her house, on a seat H3782
Pr 20: 8 *When* a king **s** on his throne to judge, he H3782
Isa 28: 6 of justice to the *one who* **s** in judgment, H3782
Isa 40:22 He **s enthroned** above the circle of the H3782
Jer 29:16 about the king who **s** on David’s throne H3782
Mt 19:28 when the Son of Man **s** on his glorious *G2767*
Mt 23:22 God’s throne and by the *one who* **s** on it. *G2764*
Rev 4: 9 thanks *to* him *who* **s** on the throne *G2764*
Rev 4:10 down before him *who* **s** on the throne *G2764*
Rev 5:13 “*To* him *who* **s** on the throne and to the *G2764*
Rev 6:16 from the face *of* him *who* **s** on the throne *G2764*
Rev 7:10 to our God, who **s** on the throne, and to *G2764*
Rev 7:15 he *who* **s** on the throne will shelter *G2764*
Rev 17: 1 great prostitute, who **s** by many waters. *G2764*
Rev 17: 9 are seven hills on which the woman **s**. *G2764*
Rev 17:15 where the prostitute **s**, are peoples, *G2764*

SITTING (76) [SIT]
Ge 18: 1 Mamre while he *was* **s** *at* the entrance to H3782
Ge 19: 1 Lot *was* **s** in the gateway of the city. H3782
Ge 23:10 the Hittite *was* **s** among his people H3782
Ge 31:34 her camel’s saddle and *was* **s** on them. H3782
Lev 15:23 it is the bed or anything she *was* **s** on, H3782
Dt 22: 6 the mother *is* **s** on the young or on H8069
Jdg 3:20 him while he *was* **s** alone in the upper H3782
Jdg 5:10 white donkeys, **s** on your saddle blankets H3782
1Sa 1: 9 Now Eli the priest *was* **s** on his chair by H3782
1Sa 4:13 there was Eli **s** on his chair by the side of H3782
1Sa 19: 9 on Saul as he *was* **s** in his house with H3782
2Sa 18:24 While David *was* **s** between the inner H3782
2Sa 19: 8 were told, “The king *is* **s** in the gateway,” H3782
1Ki 13:14 He found him **s** under an oak tree and H3782
1Ki 13:20 While they were **s** at the table, the word H3782
1Ki 22:10 king of Judah *were* **s** on their thrones at H3782
1Ki 22:19 I saw the LORD **s** on his throne with all the H3782
2Ki 1: 9 to Elijah, *who was* **s** on the top of a hill H3782
2Ki 6:32 Now Elisha *was* **s** in his house, and the H3782
2Ki 6:32 and the elders *were* **s** with him. H3782
2Ki 9: 5 he found the army officers **s** together. H3782
2Ki 18:27 not to the people **s** on the wall—who H3782
2Ch 18: 9 king of Judah *were* **s** on their thrones at H3782
2Ch 18:18 I saw the LORD **s** on his throne with all the H3782
Ezr 10: 9 all the people *were* **s** in the square before H3782
Ne 2: 6 with the queen **s** beside him, asked me H3782
Est 2:19 Mordecai *was* **s** at the king’s gate. H3782
Est 2:21 the time Mordecai *was* **s** at the king’s H3782
Est 5: 1 The king *was* **s** on his royal throne in the H3782
Est 5:13 that Jew Mordecai **s** at the king’s gate.” H3782
Ps 9: 4 **s** enthroned as the righteous judge. H3782
Isa 36:12 not to the people **s** on the wall—who H3782
Jer 8:14 Why *are* we **s** here? Gather together! Let H3782
Jer 32:12 of all the Jews **s** in the courtyard of H3782
Jer 36:12 where all the officials *were* **s**: H3782
Jer 36:22 month and the king *was* **s** in the winter H3782
Jer 38: 7 While the king *was* **s** in the Benjamin H3782
La 3:63 **S** or standing, they mock me in their H3782
Eze 8: 1 *while* I *was* **s** in my house and the elders H3782
Eze 8: 1 the elders of Judah *were* **s** before me, H3782
Eze 8:14 I saw women **s** there, mourning the H3782
Mt 9: 9 a man named Matthew **s** at the tax *G2764*
Mt 11:16 are like children **s** in the marketplaces *G2764*
Mt 20:30 Two blind men *were* **s** by the roadside *G2764*
Mt 24: 3 *As* Jesus *was* **s** on the Mount of Olives *G2764*
Mt 26:64 see the Son of Man **s** at the right hand of *G2764*
Mt 26:69 Now Peter *was* **s** out in the courtyard, and *G2764*
Mt 27:19 *While* Pilate *was* **s** on the judge’s seat *G2764*
Mt 27:36 And **s down**, they kept watch over him *G2764*
Mt 27:61 the other Mary were **s** there opposite the *G2764*
Mk 2: 6 some teachers of the law were **s** there, *G2764*
Mk 2:14 Levi son of Alphaeus **s** at the tax *G2764*
Mk 3:32 A crowd *was* **s** around him, and they told *G2764*
Mk 5:15 legion of demons, **s** there, dressed and in *G2764*
Mk 9:35 **S down**, Jesus called the Twelve and said, *G2767*
Mk 10:46 *was* **s** by the roadside begging. *G2764*
Mk 13: 3 *As* Jesus *was* **s** on the Mount of Olives *G2764*
Mk 14:62 see the Son of Man **s** at the right hand of *G2764*
Mk 16: 5 in a white robe **s** on the right side, *G2764*
Lk 2:46 the temple courts, **s** among the teachers *G2757*
Lk 5:17 teachers of the law were **s** *there*. *G2764*
Lk 5:27 by the name of Levi **s** at his tax booth. *G2764*
Lk 7:32 They are like children **s** in the marketplace *G2764*
Lk 8:35 demons had gone out, **s** at Jesus’ feet *G2764*
Lk 10:13 long ago, **s** in sackcloth and ashes. *G2764*
Lk 18:35 a blind man *was* **s** by the roadside *G2764*
Jn 2:14 others **s** at tables exchanging money. *G2764*
Ac 2: 2 filled the whole house where they were **s**. *G2764*
Ac 6:15 All who *were* **s** in the Sanhedrin looked *G2757*
Ac 8:28 on his way home was **s** in his chariot *G2764*
Ac 26:30 Bernice and those **s with** them. *G5153*
1Co 14:30 comes to someone *who is* **s down**, *G2764*
Jas 4:11 not keeping it, but **s in judgment** on it. *G3216*
Rev 4: 2 a throne in heaven with *someone* **s** on it. *G2764*
Rev 14:15 a loud voice *to* him *who was* **s** on the *G2764*
Rev 17: 3 There I saw a woman **s** on a scarlet beast *G2764*

SITUATED (3) [SITUATION]
2Ki 2:19 this town is well **s**, as you can see, H4632
Eze 27: 3 Say to Tyre, **s** at the gateway to the sea H3782
Na 3: 8 better than Thebes, **s** on the Nile, with H3782

SITUATION (11) [SITUATED, SITUATIONS]
Ge 31:40 *This* **was** *my* **s**: The heat consumed me in the AIT
1Sa 13: 6 saw that their **s** was critical and that NDT
2Sa 14:20 Joab did this to change the present **s**. H1821
Da 2: 9 wicked things, hoping the **s** will change. A10530
Da 6:17 so that Daniel’s **s** might not be changed. A10606
Mt 19:10 “If this is the **s** between a husband and *G162*
1Co 7:17 live as a believer *in* **whatever** *s* the Lord has AIT
1Co 7:20 should remain in the **s** they were in when *G3104*
1Co 7:24 should remain in **the s** they were in *G4047S*
Php 4: 6 about anything, but in **every** *s*, by prayer AIT
Php 4:12 secret of being content in any and **every** *s*, AIT

SITUATIONS (1) [SITUATION]
2Ti 4: 5 keep your head in **all** *s*, endure hardship, AIT

SIVAN (1)
Est 8: 9 day of the third month, the month of **S**. H6094

SIX (126) [SIXTH]
Ge 7: 6 Noah was **s** hundred years old when the H9252
Ge 7:11 In the **s** hundredth year of Noah’s life, on H9252
Ge 8:13 first month of Noah’s **s** hundred and first H9252
Ge 30:20 because I have borne him **s** sons. H9252
Ge 31:41 two daughters and **s** years for your flocks, H9252
Ex 12:37 There were about **s** hundred thousand H9252
Ex 14: 7 He took **s** hundred of the best chariots H9252
Ex 16:26 **S** days you are to gather it, but on the H9252
Ex 20: 9 **S** days you shall labor and do all your H9252
Ex 20:11 For in **s** days the LORD made the heavens H9252
Ex 21: 2 servant, he is to serve you for **s** years. H9252
Ex 23:10 “For **s** years you are to sow your fields H9252
Ex 23:12 “**S** days do your work, but on the seventh H9252
Ex 24:16 For **s** days the cloud covered the mountain H9252
Ex 25:32 **S** branches are to extend from the sides of H9252
Ex 25:33 the same for all **s** branches extending H9252
Ex 25:35 under the third pair—**s** branches in all. H9252
Ex 26: 9 one set and the other **s** into another set. H9252
Ex 26:22 Make **s** frames for the far end, that is, the H9252
Ex 28:10 **s** names on one stone and the remaining H9252
Ex 28:10 stone and the remaining **s** on the other. H9252
Ex 31:15 For **s** days work is to be done, but the H9252
Ex 31:17 in **s** days the LORD made the heavens H9252
Ex 34:21 “**S** days you shall labor, but on the H9252
Ex 35: 2 For **s** days, work is to be done, but the H9252
Ex 36:16 one set and the other **s** into another set. H9252
Ex 36:27 They made **s** frames for the far end, that is, H9252
Ex 37:18 **S** branches extended from the sides of the H9252
Ex 37:19 the same for all **s** branches extending H9252
Ex 37:21 under the third pair—**s** branches in all. H9252
Lev 23: 3 “ ‘There are **s** days when you may work H9252
Lev 24: 6 them in two stacks, **s** *in* each stack, on the H9252
Lev 25: 3 For **s** years sow your fields, and for six H9252
Lev 25: 3 for **s** years prune your vineyards and H9252
Nu 7: 3 gifts before the LORD **s** covered carts and H9252
Nu 11:21 “Here I am among **s** hundred thousand H9252
Nu 35: 6 “**S** *of* the towns you give the Levites will H9252
Nu 35:13 These **s** towns you give will be your cities H9252
Nu 35:15 These **s** towns will be a place of refuge H9252
Dt 5:13 **S** days you shall labor and do all your H9252
Dt 15:12 themselves to you and serve you **s** years, H9252
Dt 15:18 to you these **s** years has been worth H9252
Dt 16: 8 For **s** days eat unleavened bread and on H9252
Jos 6: 3 all the armed men. Do this for **s** days. H9252
Jos 6:14 They did this for **s** days. H9252
Jos 15:59 Eltekon—**s** towns and their villages. H9252
Jos 15:62 En Gedi—**s** towns and their villages. H9252
Jdg 3:31 who struck down **s** hundred Philistines H9252
Jdg 12: 7 Jephthah led Israel **s** years. H9252
Jdg 18:11 Then **s** hundred men of the Danites H9252
Jdg 18:16 The **s** hundred Danites, armed for battle H9252
Jdg 18:17 the priest and the **s** hundred armed men H9252
Jdg 20:47 But **s** hundred of them turned and fled into H9252
Ru 3:15 he poured into it **s** measures of barley H9252
Ru 3:17 “He gave me these **s** measures of barley H9252
1Sa 13: 5 thousand chariots, **s** thousand charioteers H9252
1Sa 13:15 They numbered about **s** hundred. H9252
1Sa 14: 2 With him were about **s** hundred men, H9252
1Sa 17: 4 His height was **s** cubits and a span. H9252
1Sa 17: 7 its iron point weighed **s** hundred shekels. H9252
1Sa 23:13 his men, about **s** hundred in number H9252
1Sa 27: 2 So David and the **s** hundred men with H9252
1Sa 30: 9 David and the **s** hundred men with him H9252
2Sa 2:11 Judah was seven years and **s** months. H9252
2Sa 5: 5 over Judah seven years and **s** months, H9252
2Sa 6:13 the ark of the LORD had taken **s** steps, H9252
2Sa 15:18 all the **s** hundred Gittites who had H9252
2Sa 21:20 was a huge man with **s** fingers on each H9252
2Sa 21:20 on each hand and **s** toes on each foot— H9252
1Ki 6: 6 the middle floor **s** cubits and the third H9252
1Ki 10:16 **s** hundred shekels of gold went into each H9252
1Ki 10:19 The throne had **s** steps, and its back had a H9252
1Ki 10:20 Twelve lions stood on the **s** steps, one at H9252
1Ki 10:29 from Egypt for **s** hundred shekels of H9252
1Ki 11:16 the Israelites stayed there for **s** months, H9252
1Ki 16:23 reigned twelve years, **s** *of* them in Tirzah. H9252
2Ki 5: 5 **s** thousand shekels of gold and ten sets of H9252
2Ki 11: 3 of the LORD for **s** years while Athaliah H9252
2Ki 13:19 have struck the ground five or **s** times; H9252
2Ki 15: 8 in Samaria, and he reigned **s** months. H9252
1Ch 3: 4 These **s** were born to David in Hebron H9252
1Ch 3: 4 he reigned seven years and **s** months. H9252
1Ch 3:22 Neariah and Shaphat—**s** in all. H9252
1Ch 4:27 Shimei had sixteen sons and **s** daughters H9252
1Ch 8:38 Azel had **s** sons, and these were their H9252
1Ch 9:44 Azel had **s** sons, and these were their H9252
1Ch 20: 6 was a huge man with **s** fingers on each H9252
1Ch 20: 6 on each hand and **s** toes on each foot— H9252
1Ch 21:25 David paid Araunah **s** hundred shekels of H9252
1Ch 23: 4 of the LORD and **s** thousand are to be H9252
1Ch 25: 3 Mattithiah, **s** in all, under the H9252
1Ch 26:17 There were **s** Levites a day on the east H9252
2Ch 1:17 from Egypt for **s** hundred shekels of H9252
2Ch 3: 8 the inside with **s** hundred talents of fine H9252
2Ch 9:15 **s** hundred shekels of hammered gold H9252
2Ch 9:18 The throne had **s** steps, and a footstool of H9252
2Ch 9:19 Twelve lions stood on the **s** steps, one at H9252
2Ch 22:12 temple of God for **s** years while Athaliah H9252
2Ch 29:33 amounted to **s** hundred bulls and H9252
Ne 5:18 **s** choice sheep and some poultry were H9252
Est 2:12 **s** months with oil of myrrh and six with H9252
Est 2:12 with oil of myrrh and **s** with perfumes and H9252
Job 5:19 From **s** calamities he will rescue you; in H9252
Job 42:12 thousand sheep, **s** thousand camels, H9252
Pr 6:16 There are **s** things the LORD hates, seven H9252
Isa 6: 2 him were seraphim, each with **s** wings: H9252
Jer 34:14 After they have served you **s** years, you H9252
Eze 9: 2 And I saw **s** men coming from the H9252
Eze 40: 5 rod in the man’s hand was **s** long cubits, H9252
Eze 40:12 the alcoves were **s** cubits square. H9252
Eze 41: 1 of the jambs was **s** cubits on each side. H9252
Eze 41: 3 The entrance was **s** cubits wide, and the H9252
Eze 41: 5 of the temple; it was **s** cubits thick, and H9252
Eze 41: 8 It was the length of the rod, **s** long cubits. H9252
Eze 46: 1 east is to be shut on the **s** working days, H9252
Eze 46: 4 day is to be **s** male lambs and a ram H9252
Eze 46: 6 offer a young bull, **s** lambs and a ram, all H9252
Da 3: 1 sixty cubits high and **s** cubits wide, and A10747
Mt 17: 1 After **s** days Jesus took with him Peter *G1971*
Mk 9: 2 After **s** days Jesus took Peter, James and *G1971*
Lk 13:14 to the people, “There are **s** days for work. *G1971*
Jn 2: 6 Nearby stood **s** stone water jars, the kind *G1971*
Jn 12: 1 **S** days before the Passover, Jesus came to *G1971*
Ac 11:12 These **s** brothers also went with me, and *G1971*
Rev 4: 8 living creatures had **s** wings and was *G1971*

Rev 6: 6 and s **pounds** of barley for a day's *G5552+5955*

SIXTEEN (18) [SIXTEENTH]
Ge 46:18 to his daughter Leah—s in all. H9252+6926
Ex 26:25 eight frames and s silver bases— H9252+6925
Ex 36:30 eight frames and s silver bases— H9252+6925
Jos 15:41 s towns and their villages. H9252+6926
Jos 19:22 There were s towns and their H9252+6926
2Ki 13:10 Samaria, and he reigned s years. H9252+6926
2Ki 14:21 Azariah, who was s years old, and H9252+6926
2Ki 15: 2 He was s years old when he H9252+6926
2Ki 15:33 he reigned in Jerusalem s years. H9252+6926
2Ki 16: 2 he reigned in Jerusalem s years. H9252+6926
1Ch 4:27 Shimei had s sons and six H9252+6925
1Ch 24: 4 s heads of families from Eleazar's H9252+6925
2Ch 13:21 twenty-two sons and s daughters. H9252+6926
2Ch 26: 1 Uzziah, who was s years old, and H9252+6926
2Ch 26: 3 Uzziah was s years old when he H9252+6926
2Ch 27: 1 he reigned in Jerusalem s years. H9252+6926
2Ch 27: 8 he reigned in Jerusalem s years. H9252+6926
2Ch 28: 1 he reigned in Jerusalem s years. H9252+6926

SIXTEENTH (3) [SIXTEEN]
1Ch 24:14 fifteenth to Bilgah, the s to Immer, H9252+6925
1Ch 25:23 the s to Hananiah, his sons and H9252+6925
2Ch 29:17 finishing on the s day of the first H9252+6925

SIXTH (38) [SIX]
Ge 1:31 there was morning—the s day. H9261
Ge 30:19 conceived again and bore Jacob a s son. H9261
Ex 16: 5 On the s day they are to prepare what they H9261
Ex 16:22 On the s day, they gathered twice as much H9261
Ex 16:29 that is why on the s day he gives you H9261
Ex 26: 9 Fold the s curtain double at the front of H9261
Lev 25:21 such a blessing in the s year that the land H9261
Nu 7:42 On the s day Eliasaph son of Deuel, the H9261
Nu 29:29 " 'On the s day offer eight bulls, two rams H9261
Jos 19:32 The s lot came out for Naphtali according H9261
2Sa 3: 5 the s, Ithream the son of David's wife H9261
2Ki 18:10 was captured in Hezekiah's s year, H9252
1Ch 2:15 the s Ozem and the seventh David. H9261
1Ch 3: 3 the son of Abital; and the s, Ithream, H9261
1Ch 12:11 Attai the s, Eliel the seventh, H9261
1Ch 24: 9 the fifth to Malkijah, the s to Mijamin, H9261
1Ch 25:13 the s to Bukkiah, his sons and relatives 12 H9261
1Ch 26: 3 Jehohanan the s and Eliehoenai the H9261
1Ch 26: 5 Ammiel the s, Issachar the seventh and H9261
1Ch 27: 9 The s, for the sixth month, was Ira the son H9261
1Ch 27: 9 The sixth, for the s month, was Ira the son H9261
Ezr 6:15 in the s year of the reign of King Darius. A10747
Ne 3:30 Hanun, the s son of Zalaph, repaired H9261
Eze 4:11 Also measure out a s *of* a hin of water H9261
Eze 8: 1 In the s year, in the sixth month on the H9261
Eze 8: 1 sixth year, in the s month on the fifth day H9261
Eze 45:13 a s *of* an ephah from each homer of H9261
Eze 45:13 of wheat and a s *of* an ephah from each H9257
Eze 46:14 consisting of a s *of* an ephah with a third H9261
Hag 1: 1 on the first day of the s month, the word H9261
Hag 1:15 on the twenty-fourth day of the s month. H9261
Lk 1:26 In the s month of Elizabeth's pregnancy *G1761*
Lk 1:36 be unable to conceive is in her s month. *G1761*
Rev 6:12 I watched as he opened the s seal. There *G1761*
Rev 9:13 The s angel sounded his trumpet, and I *G1761*
Rev 9:14 It said to the s angel who had the trumpet *G1761*
Rev 16:12 The s angel poured out his bowl on the *G1761*
Rev 21:20 the fifth onyx, the s ruby, the seventh *G1761*

SIXTY (33) [60]
Ge 25:26 Isaac was s years old when Rebekah gave H9252
Lev 27: 3 the ages of twenty and s at fifty shekels of H9252
Lev 27: 7 a person s years old or more, set the H9252
Nu 7:88 to twenty-four oxen, s rams, sixty male H9252
Nu 7:88 s male goats and sixty male lambs a year H9252
Nu 7:88 sixty male goats and s male lambs a year H9252
Dt 3: 4 was not one of the s cities that we did not H9252
Jos 13:30 settlements of Jair in Bashan, s towns, H9252
2Sa 2:31 three hundred and s Benjamites who H9252
1Ki 4:13 in Bashan and its s large walled cities H9252
1Ki 4:22 cors of the finest flour and s cors of meal, H9252
1Ki 6: 2 built for the LORD was s cubits long, H9252
2Ki 25:19 of the land and s of the conscripts who H9252
1Ch 2:21 Hezron, when he was s years old, married H9252
1Ch 2:23 with its surrounding settlements—s towns.) H9252
2Ch 3: 3 the temple of God was s cubits long and H9252
2Ch 11:21 he had eighteen wives and s concubines H9252
2Ch 11:21 twenty-eight sons and s daughters. H9252
2Ch 12: 3 chariots and s thousand horsemen H9252
Ezr 6: 3 It is to be s cubits high and sixty cubits A10749
Ezr 6: 3 to be sixty cubits high and s cubits wide, A10749
SS 3: 7 escorted by s warriors, the noblest H9252
SS 6: 8 S queens there may be, and eighty H9252
Jer 52:25 s of whom were found in the city. H9252
Eze 40:14 the inside of the gateway—s cubits. H9252
Da 3: 1 of gold, s cubits high and six cubits wide A10749
Mt 13: 8 a hundred, s or thirty times what was sown. *G2008*
Mt 13:23 hundred, s or thirty times what was sown." *G2008*
Mt 13:33 mixed into **about** s **pounds** of flour *G4929+5552*
Mk 4: 8 some s, some a hundred times. *G2008*
Mk 4:20 some thirty, some s, some a hundred *G2008*
Lk 13:21 mixed into **about** s **pounds** of flour *G4929+5552*
1Ti 5: 9 on the list of widows unless she is over s, *G2008*

SIXTY-EIGHT (1)
1Ch 16:38 and his s associates to H9252+2256+9046

SIXTY-FIVE (1) [65]
Isa 7: 8 Within s years Ephraim will H9252+2256+2822

SIXTY-SIX (2)
Ge 46:26 wives—numbered s persons. H9252+2256+9252
Lev 12: 5 she must wait s days to be H9252+2256+9252

SIXTY-TWO (3) [62]
Da 5:31 at the age of s. A10749+10221+10775
Da 9:25 'sevens,' and s 'sevens. H9252+2256+9109
Da 9:26 After the s 'sevens,' the H9252+2256+9109

SIYON (NIV84) SIRION

SIZE (15)
Ex 26: 2 All the curtains are to be the same s H4500
Ex 26: 8 All eleven curtains are to be the same s H4500
Ex 36: 9 All the curtains were the same s H4500
Ex 36:15 All eleven curtains were the same s—thirty H4500
Nu 13:32 the people we saw there are of **great** s. H4500
1Ki 6:25 cherubim were identical in s and shape. H4500
1Ki 7: 9 stone cut to s and smoothed on their H4500
1Ki 7:11 cut to s, and cedar beams. H4500
1Ki 7:37 molds and were identical in s and shape. H4500
2Ki 10:32 the LORD began to **reduce** *the* s of Israel. H7894
1Ch 23:29 all measurements of quantity and s. H4500
Ps 33:16 No king is saved by the s *of* his army; no H8044
Eze 45:11 ephah and the bath are to be the same s, H9420
Eze 46:22 courts in the four corners was the same s. H4500
Rev 18:21 up a boulder **the s of** a large millstone *G6055*

SKETCH (1)
2Ki 16:10 sent to Uriah the priest a s *of* the altar, H1952

SKIES (16) [SKY]
Ge 49:25 blesses you with blessings of the s above, H9028
Dt 28:24 come down from the s until you are H9028
Job 26: 7 spreads out the **northern** *s* over empty space; AIT
Job 26:13 By his breath the s became fair; his hand H9028
Job 37:18 can you join him in spreading out the s H8836
Job 37:21 bright as it is in the s after the wind has H8836
Ps 19: 1 the s proclaim the work of his hands. H8385
Ps 36: 5 to the heavens, your faithfulness to the s. H8836
Ps 57:10 your faithfulness reaches to the s. H8836
Ps 78:23 a command to the s above and opened H8836
Ps 89: 6 For who in the s **above** can compare with H8836
Ps 108: 4 your faithfulness reaches to the s. H8836
Ps 148: 4 heavens and you waters above the s. H9028
Jer 14:22 Do the s themselves send down showers H9028
Jer 51: 9 her judgment reaches to the s, it rises H9028
Hos 2:21 "I will respond to the s, and they will H9028

SKILL (10) [SKILLED, SKILLFUL, SKILLFULLY, SKILLS]
Ex 35:26 willing and had the s spun the goat hair. H2683
Ex 35:35 filled them with s to do all kinds of H2683+4213
Ex 36: 1 the LORD has given s and ability to know H2683
2Ch 2:13 a man of **great** s, H2682+3359+1069
Ps 137: 5 Jerusalem, *may* my right hand **forget** its *s*. AIT
Ecc 2:19 poured my effort and s under the sun. H2681
Ecc 2:21 knowledge and s, and then they must H4179
Ecc 10:10 is needed, but s will bring success. H2683
Eze 28: 5 By your great s in trading you have H2683
Ac 17:29 an image made by human design and s. *G5492*

SKILLED (43) [SKILL]
Ex 26: 1 cherubim woven into them by a s **worker**. H3110
Ex 26:31 with cherubim woven into it by a s **worker**. H3110
Ex 28: 3 Tell all the s **workers** to whom I H2682+4213
Ex 28: 6 finely twisted linen—the work of s **hands**. H3110
Ex 28:15 making decisions—the work of s **hands**. H3110
Ex 31: 6 ability to all the s **workers** to make H2682+4213
Ex 35:10 "All *who* are s among you are to H2682+4213
Ex 35:25 Every s woman spun with her hands H2682+4213
Ex 35:35 all of them s **workers** and designers. H6913+4856
Ex 36: 1 and every s person to whom H2682+4213
Ex 36: 2 and every s person to whom H2682+4213
Ex 36: 4 So all the s **workers** who were doing all H2682
Ex 36: 8 those who were s among the H2682+4213
Ex 36:35 with cherubim woven into it by a s **worker**. H3110
Ex 39: 3 yarn and fine linen—the work of s **hands**. H3110
Ex 39: 8 breastpiece—the work of a s **craftsman**. H3110
Dt 27:15 the work of s hands—and sets it up H3093
1Ki 5: 6 we have no one *so* s *in* felling timber as H3359
1Ki 7:14 from Tyre and a s **craftsman** *in* bronze. H3086
2Ki 24:14 all the s **workers** and artisans—a H3093
2Ki 24:16 a thousand s **workers** and artisans. H3093
1Ch 4:14 this because its people were s **workers**. H3093
1Ch 22:15 as well as those s in every kind of work H2682
1Ch 25: 7 of them trained and s in music for the H1067
1Ch 28:21 every willing person s in any craft will H2683
2Ch 2: 7 a man s to work in gold and silver H2682
2Ch 2: 7 Judah and Jerusalem with my s **workers**, H2682
2Ch 2: 8 that your servants *are* s *in* cutting timber H3359
2Ch 2:14 work with your s **workers** and with those H2682
2Ch 34:12 all *who were* s in playing musical H1067
Job 32:22 if *I were* s *in* flattery, my Maker would H3359
Pr 22:29 Do you see someone s in their work? They H4542
Isa 3: 3 s craftsman and clever enchanter. H2682
Isa 40:20 they look for a s worker to set up an idol H2682
Jer 2:33 How s *you are* at pursuing love H3512+2006
Jer 4:22 They are s in doing evil; they know not H2682
Jer 10: 9 blue and purple—all made by s *workers*. H2682
Jer 24: 1 the s **workers** and the artisans of Judah H3093
Jer 29: 2 the s **workers** and the artisans had gone H3093
Jer 50: 9 arrows will be like s warriors who do not H8505
Eze 21:31 of brutal men, *men* s *in* destruction. H3093
Eze 27: 8 were your oarsmen; your s *men*, Tyre, H2682
Mic 7: 3 Both hands *are* s in doing evil; the ruler H3512

SKILLFUL (7) [SKILL]
Ge 25:27 Esau became a s hunter, a man of H3359
1Ch 15:22 his responsibility because he *was* s at it. H1067
Ps 45: 1 my tongue is the pen of a s writer. H4542
Ps 58: 5 however s the enchanter may be. H2681
Ps 78:72 of heart; with s hands he led them. H9312
Jer 9:17 to come; send for the *most* s *of them*. H2682
Zec 9: 2 on Tyre and Sidon, though *they are* very s. H2681

SKILLFULLY (4) [SKILL]
Ex 28: 8 Its s **woven** waistband is to be like it—of H682
Ex 29: 5 the ephod on him by its s woven waistband. NDT
Ex 39: 5 Its s **woven** waistband was like it—of one H682
Ps 33: 3 him a new song; play s, and shout for joy. H3512

SKILLS (3) [SKILL]
Ex 31: 3 with knowledge and with all kinds of s— H4856
Ex 35:31 with knowledge and with all kinds of s— H4856
Dt 33:11 Bless all his s, LORD, and be pleased with H2657

SKIM (1)
Job 9:26 *They* s **past** like boats of papyrus, like H2736

SKIMPING (1)
Am 8: 5 s *on* the measure, boosting the price H7781

SKIN (82) [SKINNED, SKINS, SMOOTH-SKINNED]
Ge 3:21 made garments of s for Adam and his H6425
Ge 21:14 some food and a s *of* water and gave H2827
Ge 21:15 When the water in the s was gone, she H2827
Ge 21:19 went and filled the s with water and gave H2827
Ge 27:11 Esau is a hairy man while I have **smooth** *s*. AIT
Ex 4: 6 he took it out, the s was leprous—it had H3338S
Lev 1: 6 *You are to* s the burnt offering and cut it H7320
Lev 13: 2 shiny spot on their s that may be a H6425+1414
Lev 13: 2 skin that may be a defiling s **disease**, H7669
Lev 13: 3 is to examine the sore on the s, H6425+1414
Lev 13: 3 appears to be more than s deep, H6425+1414
Lev 13: 3 than skin deep, it is a defiling s **disease**. H7669
Lev 13: 4 spot on the s is white but does H6425+1414
Lev 13: 4 to be more than s deep and the hair in H6425
Lev 13: 5 is unchanged and has not spread in the s, H6425
Lev 13: 6 has faded and has not spread in the s, H6425
Lev 13: 7 does spread in their s after they have H6425
Lev 13: 8 if the rash has spread in the s, he H6425
Lev 13: 8 them unclean; it is a **defiling** s **disease**. H7669
Lev 13: 9 "When anyone has a defiling s **disease** H7669
Lev 13:10 white swelling in the s that has turned the H6425
Lev 13:11 it is a chronic s **disease** and the priest H7669
Lev 13:12 disease breaks out all over their s and, H6425
Lev 13:12 it covers all the s *of* the affected person H6425
Lev 13:18 has a boil on their s and it heals, H6425+1414
Lev 13:20 to be more than s deep and the hair in it H6425
Lev 13:20 It is a defiling s **disease** that has broken H7669
Lev 13:21 it is not more than s deep and has faded, H6425
Lev 13:22 If it is spreading in the s, the priest shall H6425
Lev 13:24 a burn on their s and a H6425+1414
Lev 13:25 it appears to be more than s deep, it H6425
Lev 13:25 them unclean; it is a defiling s **disease**. H7669
Lev 13:26 it is not more than s deep and has faded, H6425
Lev 13:27 if it is spreading in the s, the priest H6425
Lev 13:27 them unclean; it is a defiling s **disease**. H7669
Lev 13:28 has not spread in the s but has faded, H6425
Lev 13:30 to be more than s deep and the hair in it H6425
Lev 13:30 it is a **defiling** s **disease** *on* the H5999+7669
Lev 13:31 to be more than s deep and there is no H6425
Lev 13:32 does not appear to be more than s deep, H6425
Lev 13:34 not spread in the s and appears to be no H6425
Lev 13:34 appears to be no more than s deep, H6425
Lev 13:35 sore does spread in the s after they are H6425
Lev 13:36 he finds that the sore has spread in the s, H6425
Lev 13:38 woman has white spots on the s, H6425+1414
Lev 13:39 rash that has broken out on the s; H6425
Lev 13:43 like a defiling s disease, H6425+1414
Lev 14: 3 been healed of their defiling s **disease**, H7669
Lev 14:32 has a defiling s **disease** and who cannot H7669
Lev 14:54 the regulations for any defiling s **disease**, H7669
Lev 14:57 **defiling s diseases and defiling molds**. H7669
Lev 22: 4 of Aaron *has a* **defiling s disease** or a H7665
Nu 5: 2 anyone *who* **has a defiling s disease** or a H7665
Nu 12:10 above the tent, **Miriam's** *s* was leprous—it AIT
Nu 12:10 saw that *she* **had a defiling s disease**, H7665
Dt 24: 8 In cases of defiling s **diseases**, be very H5596
Jdg 4:19 She opened a s *of* milk, gave him a drink H5532
1Sa 1:24 an ephah of flour and a s *of* wine, and H5574
1Sa 10: 3 loaves of bread, and another a s *of* wine. H5574
1Sa 16:20 a s *of* wine and a young goat and sent H5532
2Sa 16: 1 a hundred cakes of figs and a s *of* wine. H5574
2Ki 5:27 Elisha's presence and *his* **s was leprous**— H7665
2Ch 29:34 were too few to s all the burnt offerings H7320
Job 2: 4 "S for skin!" Satan replied. "A man will H6425
Job 2: 4 "Skin for s!" Satan replied. "A man will H6425
Job 7: 5 scabs, my s is broken and festering. H6425
Job 10:11 clothe me with s and flesh and knit me H6425

S

Job 16:15 sackcloth over my s and buried my brow in H1654
Job 18:13 It eats away parts of his s; death's H6425
Job 19:20 I am **nothing but** s and H6425+2256+1414
Job 19:20 I have escaped only by the s *of* my teeth. H6425
Job 19:26 And after my s has been destroyed, yet in H6425
Job 30:30 My s grows black and peels; my body H6425
Ps 102: 5 aloud and am reduced to s and bones. H1414
Jer 13:23 Ethiopian change his s or a leopard its H6425
La 3: 4 He has made my s and my flesh grow old H1414
La 4: 8 Their s has shriveled on their bones; it H6425
La 5:10 Our s is hot as an oven, feverish from H6425
Eze 37: 6 come upon you and cover you with s; H6425
Eze 37: 8 appeared on them and s covered them, H6425
Mic 3: 2 who tear the s from my people and the H6425
Mic 3: 3 strip off their s and break their bones in H6425

SKINK (1)

Lev 11:30 the wall lizard, the s and the chameleon. H2793

SKINNED (1) [SKIN]

2Ch 35:11 to them, while the Levites s the animals. H7320

SKINS (11) [SKIN]

Ex 25: 5 ram s dyed red and another type of H6425
Ex 26:14 the tent a covering of ram s dyed red, H6425
Ex 35: 7 ram s dyed red and another type of H6425
Ex 35:23 ram s dyed red or the other durable H6425
Ex 36:19 the tent a covering of ram s dyed red, H6425
Ex 39:34 the covering of ram s dyed red and the H6425
Nu 6: 4 the grapevine, not even the seeds or s. H2293
1Sa 25:18 of bread, two s *of* wine, five dressed H5574
Mt 9:17 If they do, the s will burst; the wine will run *G829*
Mk 2:22 the wine will burst the s, and both the wine *G829*
Lk 5:37 the new wine will burst the s; the wine will *G829*

SKIRTED (1) [SKIRTS]

Jdg 11:18 s the lands of Edom and Moab H6015

SKIRTS (5) [SKIRTED]

Isa 47: 2 Lift up your s, bare your legs, and wade H8670
Jer 13:22 many sins that your s have been torn off H8767
Jer 13:26 I will pull up your s over your face that H8767
La 1: 9 Her filthiness clung to her s; she did not H8767
Na 3: 5 "I will lift your s over your face. I will show H8767

SKULL (7) [SKULLS]

Jdg 9:53 millstone on his head and cracked his s. H1653
2Ki 9:35 they found nothing except her s, her feet H1653
Jer 2:16 Tahpanhes have cracked your s. H7721
Mt 27:33 which means "the place *of* the s"). *G3191*
Mk 15:22 which means "the place *of* the s"). *G3191*
Lk 23:33 When they came to the place called the S *G3191*
Jn 19:17 he went out to the place *of* the S (which *G3191*

SKULLS (2) [SKULL]

Nu 24:17 of Moab, the s *of* all the people of Sheth. H7721
Jer 48:45 of Moab, the s *of* the noisy boasters. H7721

SKY (85) [SKIES]

Ge 1: 8 God called the vault "s." And there was H9028
Ge 1: 9 the water under the s be gathered to one H9028
Ge 1:14 in the vault of the s to separate the day H9028
Ge 1:15 in the vault of the s to give light on the H9028
Ge 1:17 in the vault of the s to give light on the H9028
Ge 1:20 above the earth across the vault of the s." H9028
Ge 1:26 the fish in the sea and the birds in the s, H9028
Ge 1:28 the birds in the s and over every H9028
Ge 1:30 all the birds in the s and all the creatures H9028
Ge 2:19 wild animals and all the birds in the s. H9028
Ge 2:20 the birds in the s and all the wild animals. H9028
Ge 8: 2 the rain had stopped falling from the s. H9028
Ge 9: 2 on all the birds in the s, on every H9028
Ge 15: 5 "Look up at the s and count the stars H9028
Ge 22:17 as the stars in the s and as the sand on H9028
Ge 26: 4 as the stars in the s and will give them all H9028
Ex 9:22 your hand toward the s so that hail will H9028
Ex 9:23 Moses stretched out his staff toward the s, H9028
Ex 10:21 your hand toward the s so that darkness H9028
Ex 10:22 stretched out his hand toward the s, H9028
Ex 24:10 of lapis lazuli, as bright blue as the s. H9028
Ex 32:13 as the stars in the s and I will give your H9028
Lev 26:19 make the s *above* you like iron and H9028
Dt 1:10 you are as numerous as the stars in the s. H9028
Dt 1:28 the cities are large, with walls up to the s. H9028
Dt 4:19 you look up to the s and see the sun, H9028
Dt 9: 1 large cities that have walls up to the s. H9028
Dt 10:22 you as numerous as the stars in the s. H9028
Dt 17: 3 the sun or the moon or the stars in the s, H9028
Dt 28:23 The s over your head will be bronze, the H9028
Dt 28:62 as the stars in the s will be left but few in H9028
Jos 8:20 the smoke of the city rising up into the s, H9028
Jos 10:13 in the middle of the s and delayed going H9028
2Sa 22:12 the dark rain **clouds of the** s. H6265+8836
1Ki 18:45 Meanwhile, the s grew black with clouds H9028
1Ch 27:23 Israel as numerous as the stars in the s. H9028
Ne 9:23 children as numerous as the stars in the s, H9028
Job 12: 7 the birds in the s, and they will tell you; H9028
Job 28:21 concealed even from the birds in the s. H9028
Job 35:11 makes us wiser than the birds in the s? H9028
Ps 8: 8 the birds in the s, and the fish in the sea H9028
Ps 18:11 the dark rain **clouds of the** s. H6265+8836
Ps 79: 2 your servants as food for the birds of the s, H9028
Ps 89:37 the moon, the faithful witness in the s." H8836
Ps 104:12 The birds of the s nest by the waters; they H9028
Ps 147: 8 He covers the s with clouds; he supplies H9028
Pr 23: 5 wings and fly off to the s like an eagle. H9028
Pr 30:19 the way of an eagle in the s, the way of a H9028
Ecc 10:20 a bird in the s may carry your words, H9028
Isa 34: 4 All the stars in the s will be dissolved H9028
Jer 4:25 every bird in the s had flown away. H9028
Jer 8: 7 the stork in the s knows her appointed H9028
Jer 33:22 as the stars in the s and as measureless H9028
La 4:19 pursuers were swifter than eagles in the s; H9028
Eze 29: 5 beasts of the earth and the birds of the s. H9028
Eze 31: 6 All the birds of the s nested in its boughs H9028
Eze 32: 4 all the birds of the s settle on you and all H9028
Eze 38:20 the birds in the s, the beasts of the H9028
Da 2:38 beasts of the field and the birds in the s. A10723
Da 4:11 strong and its top touched the s; A10723
Da 4:20 with its top touching the s, visible to the A10723
Da 4:22 has grown until it reaches the s, A10723
Hos 2:18 the birds in the s and the creatures that H9028
Hos 4: 3 the birds in the s and the fish in the sea H9028
Hos 7:12 will pull them down like the birds in the s. H9028
Na 3:16 more numerous than the stars in the s, H9028
Zep 1: 3 away the birds in the s and the fish in the H9028
Mt 16: 2 'It will be fair weather, for the s is red,' *G4041*
Mt 16: 3 be stormy, for the s is red and overcast.' *G4041*
Mt 16: 3 how to interpret the appearance *of* the s, *G4041*
Mt 24:29 the stars will fall from the s, and the *G4041*
Mk 13:25 the stars will fall from the s, and the *G4041*
Lk 4:25 when the s was shut for three and a half *G4041*
Lk 12:56 the appearance of the earth and the s. *G4041*
Lk 17:24 lights up the s from one end to the *G4041*
Ac 1:10 intently up into the s as he was going, *G4041*
Ac 1:11 "why do you stand here looking into the s? *G4041*
Php 2:15 will shine among them like stars in the s *G3180*
Heb 11:12 as the stars *in* the s and as countless as *G4041*
Rev 6:13 the stars *in* the s fell to earth, as figs *G4041*
Rev 8:10 fell from the s on a third of the rivers and *G4041*
Rev 9: 1 that had fallen from the s to the earth. *G4041*
Rev 9: 2 The sun and s were darkened by the smoke *G113*
Rev 12: 4 the stars out of the s and flung them to *G4041*
Rev 16:21 From the s huge hailstones, each *G4041*

SLACK (1)

Pr 18: 9 *One who is* s in his work is brother to one H8332

SLAIN (58) [SLAY]

Dt 21: 1 If someone is found s, lying in a field in H2728
Dt 32:42 the blood of the s and the captives, the H2728
Jos 11: 6 I will hand all of them, s, over to Israel. H2728
Jos 13:22 In addition to *those* s **in battle**, the H2728
Jdg 16:24 laid waste our land and multiplied our s." H2728
1Sa 18: 7 "Saul *has* s his thousands, and David his H5782
1Sa 21:11 " 'Saul *has* s his thousands, and David his H5782
1Sa 29: 5 " 'Saul *has* s his thousands, and David his H5782
2Sa 1:19 "A gazelle lies s on your heights, Israel H2728
2Sa 1:22 "From the blood of the s, from the flesh of H2728
2Sa 1:25 Jonathan lies s on your heights. H2728
2Ki 11:20 Athaliah *had been* s with the sword H4637
1Ch 5:22 many others fell s, because the battle H2728
2Ch 23:21 Athaliah *had been* s with the sword. H4637
Job 39:30 on blood, and where the s are, there it is." H2728
Ps 88: 5 the dead, like the s who lie in the grave H2728
Ps 89:10 You crushed Rahab like *one of* the s; with H2728
Pr 7:26 brought down; her s are a mighty throng. H2222
Isa 10: 4 among the captives or fall among the s. H2222
Isa 14:19 you are covered with the s, with those H2222
Isa 22: 2 Your s were not killed by the sword, nor H2728
Isa 26:21 the earth will conceal its s no longer. H2222
Isa 34: 3 Their s will be thrown out, their dead H2728
Isa 66:16 many will be *those* s *by* the LORD. H2728
Jer 9: 1 day and night for the s *of* my people. H2728
Jer 14:18 the country, I see *those* s *by* the sword; if I H2728
Jer 18:21 their young men s *by* the sword in battle. H5782
Jer 25:33 At that time *those* s *by* the LORD will be H2728
Jer 51: 4 They will fall down s in Babylon, fatally H2728
Jer 51:47 be disgraced and her s will all lie fallen H2728
Jer 51:49 "Babylon must fall because of Israel's s H2728
Jer 51:49 just as the s *in* all the earth have fallen H2728
La 2: 4 Like a foe *he has* s all who were pleasing H2222
La 2:21 *You have* s them in the day of your anger H2222
La 3:43 pursued us; *you have* s without pity. H2222
Eze 6: 7 Your people will fall s among you, and H2728
Eze 6:13 when their *people* lie s among their idols H2728
Eze 9: 7 the temple and fill the courts with the s. H2728
Eze 21:29 the necks of the wicked who are to be s, H2728
Eze 28:23 The s will fall within you, with the sword H2728
Eze 30: 4 When the s fall in Egypt, her wealth will H2728
Eze 30:11 against Egypt and fill the land with the s. H2728
Eze 32:22 is surrounded by the graves of all her s, H2728
Eze 32:23 terror in the land of the living are s, H2728
Eze 32:24 All of them are s, fallen by the sword H2728
Eze 32:25 A bed is made for her among the s, with H2728
Eze 32:25 to the pit; they are laid among the s. H2728
Eze 32:30 went down with the s in disgrace despite H2728
Eze 35: 8 I will fill your mountains with the s; those H2728
Eze 37: 9 the four winds and breathe into these s, H2222
Da 5:30 king of the Babylonians, **was** s, A10625
Da 7:11 until the beast **was** s and its body A10625
Zep 2:12 "You Cushites, too, will be s *by* my sword." H2728
Rev 5: 6 looking as if *it had been* s, standing at *G5377*
Rev 5: 9 because *you were* s, and with your *G5377*
Rev 5:12 is the Lamb, who *was* s, to receive power *G5377*
Rev 6: 9 souls *of* those *who had been* s because *G5377*
Rev 13: 8 the Lamb *who was* s from the creation of *G5377*

SLANDER (27) [SLANDERED, SLANDERER, SLANDERERS, SLANDEROUS, SLANDEROUSLY, SLANDERS]

Lev 19:16 'Do not go about **spreading** s among your H8215
Ps 15: 3 whose tongue **utters** no s, who does no H8078
Ps 41: 6 while his heart gathers s; then he goes out H224
Ps 50:20 your brother and s your own H5989+1984
Ps 54: 5 Let evil recoil on *those who* s me; in your H8806
Ps 59:10 will let me gloat over *those who* s me. H8806
Ps 119:23 Though rulers sit together and s me, your H1819
Pr 10:18 with lying lips and spreads s is a fool. H1804
Pr 30:10 "*Do* not s a servant to their master, or they H4387
Jer 6:28 are all hardened rebels, going about to s. H8215
Eze 36: 3 object of people's malicious talk and s, H1804
Mt 12:31 every kind of sin and s can be forgiven *G1060*
Mt 15:19 immorality, theft, false testimony, s. *G1060*
Mk 3:28 all their sins and every s they utter, *G1060*
Mk 7:22 lewdness, envy, s, arrogance and folly. *G1060*
2Co 12:20 selfish ambition, s, gossip, arrogance *G2896*
Eph 4:31 brawling and s, along with every *G1060*
Col 3: 8 s, and filthy language from your *G1060*
1Ti 5:14 to give the enemy no opportunity for s. *G3367*
Titus 3: 2 *to* s no one, to be peaceable and *G1059*
Jas 4:11 sisters, *do* not s one another. Anyone *G2895*
1Pe 2: 1 hypocrisy, envy, and s of every kind. *G2896*
1Pe 3:16 in Christ may be ashamed *of their* s. *G2895*
Jude 9 dare to condemn him *for* s but said, *G1060*
Jude 10 Yet these people s whatever they do not *G1059*
Rev 2: 9 I know about the s of those who say they *G1060*
Rev 13: 6 and *to* s his name and his dwelling place *G1059*

SLANDERED (5) [SLANDER]

Dt 22:17 Now he *has* s her and said, 'I H8492+6613+1821
2Sa 19:27 And *he has* s your servant to my lord the H8078
Ps 35:15 *They* s me without ceasing H7973
1Co 4:13 *when we are* s, we answer kindly. *G1555*
1Ti 6: 1 name and our teaching *may* not *be* s. *G1059*

SLANDERER (2) [SLANDER]

Jer 9: 4 is a deceiver, and every friend a s. H2143+8215
1Co 5:11 an idolater or s, a drunkard or *G3368*

SLANDERERS (5) [SLANDER]

Ps 140:11 May s not be established in the land H408+4383
Eze 22: 9 In you are s who are bent on H8215+408
Ro 1:30 s, God-haters, insolent, arrogant and *G2897*
1Co 6:10 drunkards nor s nor swindlers will *G3368*
Titus 2: 3 not to be s or addicted to much wine *G1333*

SLANDEROUS (1) [SLANDER]

2Ti 3: 3 unforgiving, s, without self-control *G1333*

SLANDEROUSLY (1) [SLANDER]

Ro 3: 8 Why not say—as some s claim that we say *G1059*

SLANDERS (2) [SLANDER]

Dt 22:14 and s her and gives her a H8492+6613+1821
Ps 101: 5 *Whoever* s their neighbor in secret, I will H4387

SLAPPED (5) [SLAPS]

1Ki 22:24 went up and s Micaiah in the face. H5782
2Ch 18:23 went up and s Micaiah in the face. H5782
Mt 26:67 struck him with their fists. Others s him *G4824*
Jn 18:22 officials nearby s him **in the face**. *G1443+4825*
Jn 19: 3 And *they* s him **in the face**. *G1443+4825*

SLAPS (3) [SLAPPED]

Mt 5:39 If anyone s you on the right cheek, turn to *G4824*
Lk 6:29 *If* someone s you on one cheek, turn to *G5597*
2Co 11:20 of you or puts on airs or s you in the face. *G1296*

SLASH (2) [SLASHED]

Eze 21:16 S to the right, *you* sword, then to the left H2523
Hos 7:14 *They* s **themselves, appealing to their gods** H1517

SLASHED (2) [SLASH]

1Ki 18:28 louder and s **themselves** with swords and H1517
Jer 48:37 every hand is s and every waist is covered H1523

SLAUGHTER (62) [SLAUGHTERED, SLAUGHTERING, SLAUGHTERS]

Ge 43:16 s an animal and prepare a meal H3180
Ex 12: 6 of Israel *must* s them at twilight. H8821
Ex 12:21 your families and s the Passover lamb. H8821
Ex 29:11 S it in the LORD's presence at the entrance H8821
Ex 29:16 S it and take the blood and splash it H8821
Ex 29:20 S it, take some of its blood and put it on H8821
Lev 1: 5 *You are to* s the young bull before the LORD H8821
Lev 1:11 *You are to* s it at the north side of the altar H8821
Lev 3: 2 of your offering and s it at the entrance to H8821
Lev 3: 8 hand on its head and s it in front of the H8821
Lev 3:13 hand on its head and s it in front of the H8821
Lev 4: 4 hand on its head and s it there before the H8821
Lev 4:24 the goat's head and s it at the place H8821
Lev 4:29 the sin offering and s it at the place of the H8821
Lev 4:33 hand on its head and s it for a sin offering H8821
Lev 14:13 *He is to* s the lamb in the sanctuary area H8821
Lev 14:19 the priest *shall* s the burnt offering H8821
Lev 14:25 *He shall* s the lamb for the guilt offering H8821
Lev 16:11 and *he is to* s the bull for his own sin H8821

Lev 16:15 "He shall then s the goat for the sin H8821
Lev 22:28 Do not s a cow or a sheep and its young H8821
Dt 12:15 you may s your animals in any of your H2284
Dt 12:21 you may s animals from the herds and H2284
1Sa 4:10 The s was very great; Israel lost thirty H4804
1Sa 14:30 Would not the s of the Philistines have H4804
1Sa 14:34 and s them here and eat them. H8821
2Sa 17: 9 'There has been a s among the troops H4487
2Ch 35: 6 S the Passover lambs, consecrate H8821
Pr 7:22 he followed her like an ox going to the s, H3181
Pr 24:11 hold back those staggering toward s. H2223
Isa 14:21 Prepare a place to s his children for the H4749
Isa 30:25 In the day of great s, when the towers fall H2223
Isa 34: 2 destroy them, he will give them over to s. H3181
Isa 34: 6 Bozrah and a great s in the land of Edom. H3181
Isa 53: 7 he was led like a lamb to the s, and as a H3181
Isa 65:12 all of you will fall in the s; for I called H3181
Jer 7:32 the Valley of S, for they will bury the H2224
Jer 11:19 I had been like a gentle lamb led to the s H3180
Jer 12: 3 Set them apart for the day of s! H2224
Jer 19: 6 Valley of Ben Hinnom, but the Valley of S. H2224
Jer 48:15 finest young men will go down in the s," H3181
Jer 50:27 young bulls; let them go down to the s! H3181
Jer 51:40 will bring them down like lambs to the s, H3180
Eze 9: 6 S the old men, the young H2222+4200+5422
Eze 21:10 sharpened for the s, polished to H3180+3181
Eze 21:14 It is a sword for s—a sword for great H2728
Eze 21:14 a sword for great s, closing in on them H2728
Eze 21:15 stationed the sword for s at all their gates. H3181
Eze 21:15 to strike like lightning, it is grasped for s. H3181
Eze 21:22 to give the command to s, to sound the H8358
Eze 21:28 drawn for the s, polished to consume H3181
Eze 26:15 groan and the s takes place in you? H2222+2223
Eze 34: 3 with the wool and s the choice animals, H2284
Eze 44:11 they may s the burnt offerings and H8821
Da 11:12 with pride and will s many thousands, H5877
Hos 5: 2 The rebels are knee-deep in s. I will H8823
Ob 9 mountains will be cut down in the s. H7780
Zec 11: 4 "Shepherd the flock marked for s. H2224
Zec 11: 5 Their buyers s them and go unpunished H2222
Zec 11: 7 So I shepherded the flock marked for s H2224
Ac 8:32 "He was led like a sheep to the s, and as G5375
Jas 5: 5 have fattened yourselves in the day of s. G5375

SLAUGHTERED (52) [SLAUGHTER]

Ge 37:31 s a goat and dipped the robe in the blood H8821
Lev 4:15 the bull shall be s before the LORD. H8821
Lev 4:24 the burnt offering is s before the LORD. H8821
Lev 4:33 at the place where the burnt offering is s. H8821
Lev 6:25 The sin offering is to be s before the LORD H8821
Lev 6:25 LORD in the place the burnt offering is s; H8821
Lev 7: 2 The guilt offering is to be s in the place H8821
Lev 7: 2 in the place where the burnt offering is s, H8821
Lev 8:15 Moses s the bull and took some of the H8821
Lev 8:19 Then Moses s the ram and splashed the H8821
Lev 8:23 Moses s the ram and took some of its H8821
Lev 9: 8 came to the altar and s the calf as a sin H8821
Lev 9:12 Then he s the burnt offering. His sons H8821
Lev 9:15 sin offering and s it and offered it for a H8821
Lev 9:18 He s the ox and the ram as the fellowship H8821
Lev 14:13 sin offering and the burnt offering are s. H8821
Nu 11:22 if flocks and herds were s for them? H8821
Nu 14:16 on oath, so he s them in the wilderness. H8821
Nu 19: 3 outside the camp and s in his presence. H8821
Dt 28:31 Your ox will be s before your eyes, but you H3180
Jdg 15: 8 them viciously and s many of them. H4804
1Sa 11:11 the Ammonites and s them until the heat H5782
1Sa 14:34 brought his ox that night and s it there. H8821
1Sa 25:11 the meat I have s for my shearers H3180
1Ki 18:40 down to the Kishon Valley and s there. H8821
1Ki 19:21 He took his yoke of oxen and s them. H2284
2Ki 3:23 kings must have fought and s each other. H5782
2Ki 3:24 invaded the land and s the Moabites. H5782
2Ki 10: 7 took the princes and s all seventy of them. H8821
2Ki 10:14 took them alive and s them by the well of H8821
2Ki 23:20 Josiah s all the priests of those high H2284
2Ch 18: 2 Ahab s many sheep and cattle for him H2284
2Ch 28: 9 But you have s them in a rage that H2222
2Ch 29:22 So they s the bulls, and the priests took H8821
2Ch 29:22 next they s the rams and splashed their H8821
2Ch 29:22 then they s the lambs and splashed their H8821
2Ch 29:24 The priests then s the goats and presented H8821
2Ch 30:15 They s the Passover lamb on the H8821
2Ch 35: 1 the Passover lamb was s on the H8821
2Ch 35:11 The Passover lambs were s, and the H8821
Ezr 6:20 The Levites s the Passover lamb for all the H8821
Ps 44:22 we are considered as sheep to be s. H3186
Jer 25:34 For your time to be s has come; you will H3180
Jer 39: 6 the king of Babylon s the sons of H8821
Jer 41: 7 who were with him s them and threw H8821
La 2:21 your anger; you have s them without pity. H3180
Eze 16:21 You s my children and sacrificed them to H8821
Eze 40:39 sin offerings and guilt offerings were s. H8821
Eze 40:41 on which the sacrifices were s. H8821
Am 1:11 with a sword and s the women of the land H8845
Ro 8:36 we are considered as sheep to be s." G5375
Rev 18:24 of all who have been s on the earth." G5377

SLAUGHTERING (5) [SLAUGHTER]

1Sa 7:11 s them along the way to a point below H5782
2Ch 20:23 After they finished s the men from Seir, they NDT
2Ch 25:14 Amaziah returned from s the Edomites, H5782
Isa 22:13 s of cattle and killing of sheep H2222
Eze 40:42 the utensils for s the burnt offerings H8821

SLAUGHTERS (1) [SLAUGHTER]

Ex 22: 1 an ox or a sheep and s it or sells it must H3180

SLAVE (94) [ENSLAVE, ENSLAVED, ENSLAVES, ENSLAVING, SLAVERY, SLAVES, SLAVING]

Ge 9:26 May Canaan be the s of Shem. H6269
Ge 9:27 may Canaan be the s of Japheth. H6269
Ge 16: 1 But she had an Egyptian s named Hagar; H9148
Ge 16: 2 sleep with my s; perhaps I can build a H9148
Ge 16: 3 took her Egyptian s Hagar and gave her to H9148
Ge 16: 5 I put my s in your arms, and now that she H9148
Ge 16: 6 "Your s is in your hands," Abram said H9148
Ge 16: 8 "Hagar, s of Sarai, where have you come H9148
Ge 21:10 "Get rid of that s woman and her son, for H563
Ge 21:12 about the boy and your s woman. H563
Ge 21:13 make the son of the s into a nation also, H563
Ge 25:12 whom Sarah's s, Hagar the Egyptian, H9148
Ge 39:17 "That Hebrew s you brought us came to H6269
Ge 39:19 "This is how your s treated me," he H6269
Ge 44:10 is found to have it will become my s; H6269
Ge 44:17 found to have the cup will become my s. H6269
Ge 44:33 here as my lord's s in place of the boy, H6269
Ex 1:11 So they put s masters over them to H4989
Ex 2: 5 the reeds and sent her female s to get it. H563
Ex 3: 7 them crying out because of their s drivers, H5601
Ex 5: 6 this order to the s drivers and overseers in H5601
Ex 5:10 Then the s drivers and the overseers went H5601
Ex 5:13 The s drivers kept pressing them, saying H5601
Ex 5:14 And Pharaoh's s drivers beat the Israelite H5601
Ex 11: 5 to the firstborn son of the female s, who is H9148
Ex 12:44 Any s you have bought may eat it after you H6269
Ex 21:20 beats their male or female s with a rod H6269
[Ex 21:20 beats their male or female s with a rod H563]
Ex 21:20 be punished if the s dies as a direct result NDT
Ex 21:21 to be punished if the s recovers after a day NDT
Ex 21:21 a day or two, since the s is their property. H2085S
Ex 21:26 who hits a male or female s in the eye H6269
[Ex 21:26 who hits a male or female s in the eye H563]
Ex 21:26 destroys it must let the s go free to H5647S
Ex 21:27 tooth of a male or female s must let the H6269
[Ex 21:27 tooth of a male or female s must let the H563]
Ex 21:27 female slave must let the s go free to H5647S
Ex 21:32 If the bull gores a male or female s, the H6269
[Ex 21:32 If the bull gores a male or female s, the H563]
Ex 21:32 shekels of silver to the master of the s, H2257S
Ex 23:12 the s born in your household and H1201+563
Lev 19:20 sleeps with a female s who is promised to H9148
Lev 22:11 But if a priest buys a s with money, or if H5883
Dt 21:14 You must not sell her or treat her as a s H6683
Dt 23:15 If a s has taken refuge with you, do not H6269
Dt 24: 7 and treating or selling them as a s, H6683
Dt 32:36 is gone and no one is left, s or free. H6806
Jdg 9:18 the son of his female s, king over the H563
1Sa 30:13 "I am an Egyptian, the s of an Amalekite. H6269
2Sa 6:20 in full view of the s girls of his servants as H563
2Sa 6:22 But by these s girls you spoke of, I will be H563
1Ki 9:21 exterminate—to serve as s labor, as it is H6268
1Ki 14:10 every last male in Israel—s or free. H6806
1Ki 21:21 Ahab every last male in Israel—s or free. H6806
2Ki 9: 8 Ahab every last male in Israel—s or free. H6806
2Ki 14:26 in Israel, whether s or free, was suffering; H6806
2Ch 8: 8 to serve as s labor, as it is to this H4989
Job 3:18 they no longer hear the s driver's shout. H5601
Job 7: 2 Like a s longing for the evening shadows H6269
Job 41: 4 you for you to take it as your s for life? H6269
Ps 105:17 a man before them—Joseph, sold as a s. H6269
Ps 123: 2 as the eyes of a female s look to the hand H9148
Pr 19:10 much worse for a s to rule over princes H6269
Pr 22: 7 and the borrower is s to the lender. H6269
Jer 2:14 a servant, a s by birth? Why then H3535+1074
La 1: 1 the provinces has now become a s. H4989
Mal 1: 6 son honors his father, and a s his master. H6269
Mt 20:27 whoever wants to be first must be your s— G1528
Mk 10:44 whoever wants to be first must be s of all. G1528
Jn 8:34 I tell you, everyone who sins is a s to sin. G1528
Jn 8:35 Now a s has no permanent place in the G1528
Ac 7: 9 of Joseph, they sold him as a s into Egypt. G625
Ac 16:16 we were met by a female s who had a G4087
Ro 7:14 I am unspiritual, sold as a s to sin. G4405
Ro 7:25 I myself in my mind am a s to God's law G1526
Ro 7:25 in my sinful nature a s to the law of sin. NDT
1Co 7:21 Were you a s when you were called G1528
1Co 7:22 the one who was a s when called to faith G1528
1Co 7:22 who was free when called is Christ's s. G1528
1Co 9:19 I have made myself a s to everyone G1530
1Co 9:27 to my body and make it my s so that after G1524
1Co 12:13 Jews or Gentiles, s or free—and we were G1528
Gal 3:28 Gentile, neither s nor free, nor is there G1528
Gal 4: 1 he is no different from a s, although he G1528
Gal 4: 7 So you are no longer a s, but God's child G1528
Gal 4:22 one by the s woman and the other by the G4087
Gal 4:23 His son by the s woman was born G4087
Gal 4:30 "Get rid of the s woman and her son, for G4087
Gal 4:30 the s woman's son will never share in G4087
Gal 4:31 we are not children of the s woman, but G4087
Eph 6: 8 good they do, whether they are s or free. G1528
Col 3:11 barbarian, Scythian, s or free, but Christ is G1528
1Ti 1:10 for s traders and liars and perjurers G435
Phm 16 no longer as a s, but better than a slave G1528
Phm 16 better than a s, as a dear brother. G1528
Rev 6:15 everyone else, both s and free, hid in G1528
Rev 13:16 poor, free and s, to receive a mark on G1528
Rev 19:18 of all people, free and s, great and small." G1528

SLAVERY (22) [SLAVE]

Ex 2:23 Israelites groaned in their s and cried out, H6275
Ex 2:23 help because of their s went up to God. H6275
Ex 13: 3 out of the land of s, because the LORD H6269
Ex 13:14 us out of Egypt, out of the land of s. H6269
Ex 20: 2 you out of Egypt, out of the land of s. H6269
Dt 5: 6 you out of Egypt, out of the land of s. H6269
Dt 6:12 you out of Egypt, out of the land of s. H6269
Dt 7: 8 redeemed you from the land of s, H6269
Dt 8:14 you out of Egypt, out of the land of s. H6269
Dt 13: 5 redeemed you from the land of s. H6269
Dt 13:10 you out of Egypt, out of the land of s. H6269
Jos 24:17 from that land of s, and performed those H6269
Jdg 6: 8 you up out of Egypt, out of the land of s. H6269
Ne 5: 5 to subject our sons and daughters to s. H6269
Ne 9:17 a leader in order to return to their s. H6285
Jer 34:13 them out of Egypt, out of the land of s. H6269
Mic 6: 4 redeemed you from the land of s. H6269
Gal 4: 3 we were in s under the elemental G1530
Gal 4:25 because she is in s with her children. G1526
Gal 5: 1 be burdened again by a yoke of s. G1525
1Ti 6: 1 are under the yoke of s should consider G1528
Heb 2:15 lives were held in s by their fear of death. G1525

SLAVES (86) [SLAVE]

Ge 9:25 The lowest of s will he be to his H6269+6269
Ge 15:14 But I will punish the nation they serve as s H6268
Ge 20:14 cattle and male and female s and gave H6269
[Ge 20:14 cattle and male and female s and gave H9148]
Ge 20:17 his wife and his female s so they could H563
Ge 43:18 us and seize us as s and take our donkeys H6269
Ge 44: 9 the rest of us will become my lord's s." H6269
Ge 44:16 We are now my lord's s—we ourselves H6269
Ge 50:18 "We are your s," they said. H6269
Ex 6: 6 I will free you from being s to them, and I H6275
Ex 9:20 hurried to bring their s and their livestock H6269
Ex 9:21 of the LORD left their s and livestock in the H6269
Lev 22:11 or if s are born in his household NDT
Lev 25:39 do not make them work as s. H6275+6269
Lev 25:42 out of Egypt, they must not be sold as s. H6269
Lev 25:44 " 'Your male and female s are to come H6269
[Lev 25:44 " 'Your male and female s are to come H563]
Lev 25:44 from them you may buy s. H6269+2256+563
Lev 25:46 property and can make them s for life, H6268
Lev 26:13 would no longer be s to the Egyptians; H6269
Nu 16:14 Do you want to treat these men like s H5941+6524
Dt 5:15 that you were s in Egypt and that the H6269
Dt 6:21 "We were s of Pharaoh in Egypt, but the H6269
Dt 15:15 that you were s in Egypt and the LORD H6269
Dt 16:12 Remember that you were s in Egypt, and H6269
Dt 24:18 that you were s in Egypt and the LORD H6269
Dt 24:22 Remember that you were s in Egypt. H6269
Dt 28:68 to your enemies as male and female s, H6269
[Dt 28:68 to your enemies as male and female s, H9148]
1Sa 8:17 you yourselves will become his s. H6269
1Ki 2:39 two of Shimei's s ran off to Achish son of H6269
1Ki 2:39 Shimei was told, "Your s are in Gath." H6269
1Ki 2:40 went to Achish at Gath in search of his s. H6269
1Ki 2:40 away and brought the s back from Gath. H6269
1Ki 9:22 But Solomon did not make s of any of the H6269
2Ki 4: 1 is coming to take my two boys as his s." H6269
2Ki 5:26 flocks and herds, or male and female s? H6269
[2Ki 5:26 flocks and herds, or male and female s? H9148]
2Ch 8: 9 Solomon did not make s of the Israelites H6269
2Ch 28:10 make the men and women of Judah and Jerusalem your s H3899+6269
Ezr 2:65 besides their 7,337 male and female s H6269
[Ezr 2:65 besides their 7,337 male and female s H563]
Ezr 9: 9 Though we are s, our God has not H6269
Ne 7:67 besides their 7,337 male and female s H6269
[Ne 7:67 besides their 7,337 male and female s H563]
Ne 9:36 "But see, we are s today, slaves in the H6269
Ne 9:36 s in the land you gave our ancestors so H6269
Est 7: 4 merely been sold as male and female s, H6269
[Est 7: 4 merely been sold as male and female s, H9148]
Job 3:19 the s are freed from their owners. H6269
Ps 123: 2 As the eyes of s look to the hand of their H6269
Ecc 2: 7 I bought male and female s and had other H6269
[Ecc 2: 7 I bought male and female s and had other H9148]
Ecc 2: 7 slaves and had other s who were born in my NDT
Ecc 10: 7 I have seen s on horseback, while princes H6269
Ecc 10: 7 horseback, while princes go on foot like s. H6269
Jer 34: 8 Jerusalem to proclaim freedom for the s. H2002
Jer 34: 9 their Hebrew s, both male and female; H6269
[Jer 34: 9 their Hebrew s, both male and female; H9148]
Jer 34:10 free their male and female s and no H6269
[Jer 34:10 free their male and female s and no H9148]
Jer 34:11 took back the s they had H6269+2256+9148
Jer 34:16 back the male and female s you had set H6269
[Jer 34:16 back the male and female s you had set H9148]
Jer 34:16 to become your s again. H6269+2256+9148
La 5: 8 S rule over us, and there is no one to free H6269
Na 2: 7 Her female s moan like doves and beat on H563
Zec 2: 9 them so that their s will plunder them. H6269
Jn 8:33 and have never been s of anyone. G1526
Ac 7: 7 But I will punish the nation they serve as s G1526
Ro 6: 6 that we should no longer be s to sin G1526

S

Ro 6:16 yourselves to someone as obedient **s**, *G1528*
Ro 6:16 you are **s** of the one you obey *G1528*
Ro 6:16 whether you are **s** to sin, which leads NDT
Ro 6:17 though you used to be **s** to sin, you have *G1528*
Ro 6:18 from sin and *have become* **s** to *G1530*
Ro 6:19 to offer yourselves *as* **s** to impurity and to *G1529*
Ro 6:19 now offer yourselves *as* **s** to righteousness *G1529*
Ro 6:20 When you were **s** to sin, you were free *G1528*
Ro 6:22 free from sin and *have become* **s** of God, *G1530*
Ro 8:15 Spirit you received does not **make** you **s**, *G1525*
1Co 7:23 do not become **s** of human beings. *G1528*
Gal 2: 4 we have in Christ Jesus and to **make** us **s**. *G2871*
Gal 4: 8 *you were* **s** to those who by nature are not *G1526*
Gal 4:24 Sinai and bears children who are to be **s**: *G1525*
Eph 6: 5 **S**, obey your earthly masters with respect *G1528*
Eph 6: 6 eye is on you, but as **s** of Christ, doing the *G1528*
Eph 6: 9 And masters, treat **your s** in the same way. *G899S*
Col 3:22 **S**, obey your earthly masters in everything *G1528*
Col 4: 1 provide your **s** with what is right and fair *G1528*
1Ti 6: 2 are devoted to the welfare of their **s**. NDT
Titus 2: 9 Teach **s** to be subject to their masters in *G1528*
1Pe 2:16 as a cover-up for evil; live as God's **s**. *G1528*
1Pe 2:18 **S**, in reverent fear of God submit *G3860*
2Pe 2:19 while they themselves are **s** of depravity *G1528*
2Pe 2:19 "people *are* **s** to whatever has *G1530*
Rev 18:13 and human beings **sold as s**. *G5393+2779+6034*

SLAVING (1) [SLAVE]

Lk 15:29 All these years *I've been* **s** for you and *G1526*

SLAY (15) [SLAIN, SLAYER, SLAYS, SLEW]

Ge 22:10 his hand and took the knife to **s** his son. H8821
Job 13:15 Though *he* **s** me, yet will I hope in him; H7779
Ps 34:21 Evil *will* **s** the wicked; the foes of the H4637
Ps 37:14 to **s** those whose ways are upright. H3180
Ps 94: 6 *They* **s** the widow and the foreigner; they H2222
Ps 139:19 If only *you*, God, *would* **s** the wicked H7779
Isa 11: 4 the breath of his lips *he will* **s** the wicked. H4637
Isa 14:30 destroy by famine; *it will* **s** your survivors. H2222
Isa 27: 1 serpent; *he will* **s** the monster of the sea. H2222
Jer 33: 5 of the people *I will* **s** in my anger and H5782
Eze 6: 4 and *I will* **s** your people in front of your H5877
Eze 28: 9 in the hands of *those who* **s** you. H2726
Hos 2: 3 into a parched land, and **s** her with thirst. H4637
Hos 9:16 children, *I will* **s** their cherished offspring." H4637
Am 9: 4 there I will command the sword *to* **s** them. H2222

SLAYER (2) [SLAY]

Eze 21:11 made ready for the hand of the **s**. H2222
Hos 9:13 will bring out their children to the **s**." H2222

SLAYS (1) [SLAY]

Job 5: 2 kills a fool, and envy **s** the simple. H4637

SLEDGE (3) [SLEDGES]

Job 41:30 a trail in the mud like a **threshing s**. H3023
Isa 28:27 Caraway is not threshed with a **s**, nor is H3023
Isa 41:15 I will make you into a **threshing s**, new H4617

SLEDGES (3) [SLEDGE]

2Sa 24:22 here are **threshing s** and ox yokes for H4617
1Ch 21:23 offerings, the **threshing s** for the wood H4617
Am 1: 3 threshed Gilead with **s** *having* iron teeth, H3023

SLEEK (6)

Ge 41: 2 up seven cows, **s** and fat, and they H3637+5260
Ge 41: 4 ugly and gaunt ate up the seven **s**, H3637+5260
Ge 41:18 fat and **s**, and they grazed H3637+9307
Dt 32:15 filled with food, they became heavy and **s**. H4170
Jer 5:28 have grown fat and **s**. Their evil H6950
Eze 34:16 the **s** and the strong I will destroy. H9045

SLEEP (79) [ASLEEP, SLEEPER, SLEEPING, SLEEPLESS, SLEEPS, SLEEPY, SLEPT]

Ge 2:21 God caused the man to fall into a **deep s**; H9554
Ge 15:12 Abram fell into a **deep s**, and a thick and H9554
Ge 16: 2 **Go, s with** my slave; perhaps I can H995+448
Ge 19:32 wine and then **s with** him and H8886+6640
Ge 19:34 you go in and **s with** him so we can H8886+6640
Ge 28:11 put it under his head and **lay down to s**. H8886
Ge 28:16 When Jacob awoke from his **s**, he thought H9104
Ge 30: 3 **S with** her so that she can bear H995+448
Ge 30:15 "*he can* **s with** you tonight in return H8886+6640
Ge 30:16 "*You must* **s with** me," she H995+448
Ge 31:40 the cold at night, and **s** fled from my eyes. H9104
Ge 38: 8 "**S with** your brother's wife and fulfill H995+448
Ge 38:16 "Come now, *let me* **s with** you. H995+448
Ge 38:16 what will you give me *to* **s with** *you*?" H995+448
Ge 38:26 And *he did* not **s with** her again. H3359
Ge 39:14 He came in here to **s with** me, but I H8886+6640
Ex 22:27 What else *can they* **s** in? When they H8886
Dt 24:12 *do* not **go to s** with their pledge in your H8886
Dt 24:13 sunset so that your neighbor *may* **s** in it. H8886
Jdg 16:14 He awoke from his **s** and pulled up the H9104
Jdg 16:19 *After* **putting** him **to s** on her lap, she H3822
Jdg 16:20 He awoke from his **s** and thought, "I'll go H9104
1Sa 26:12 the LORD had put them into a **deep s**. H9554
2Sa 3: 7 "Why *did you* **s with** my father's H995+448
2Sa 11:13 Uriah went out to **s** on his mat among his H8886
2Sa 12:11 and *he will* **s with** your wives in H8886+6640
2Sa 16:21 "**S with** your father's concubines H995+448
Est 6: 1 That night the king could not **s**; so he H9104
Job 4:13 in the night, when **deep s** falls on people, H9554
Job 14:12 will not awake or be roused from their **s**. H9104
Job 31:10 and *may* other men **s with** her. H4156+6584
Job 33:15 when **deep s** falls on people as they H9554
Ps 3: 5 I lie down and **s**; I wake again, because H3822
Ps 4: 8 In peace I will lie down and **s**, for you H3822
Ps 7: 5 to the ground and **make** me **s** in the dust. H8905
Ps 13: 3 Give light to my eyes, or *I will* **s** *in* death, H3822
Ps 44:23 Why *do you* **s**? Rouse yourself H3822
Ps 68:13 Even while *you* **s** among the sheep pens H8886
Ps 76: 5 lie plundered, *they* **s** their last sleep; not H5670
Ps 76: 5 they sleep their *last* **s**; not one of the H9104
Ps 78:65 Then the Lord awoke as from **s**, as a H3825
Ps 90: 5 sweep people away in the **s of death**— H9104
Ps 121: 4 over Israel will neither slumber nor **s**. H3822
Ps 127: 2 to eat—for he grants **s** to those he loves. H9097
Ps 132: 4 I will allow no **s** to my eyes or slumber to H9104
Pr 3:24 when you lie down, your **s** will be sweet. H9104
Pr 4:16 they are robbed of **s** till they make H9104
Pr 6: 4 Allow no **s** to your eyes, no slumber to H9104
Pr 6: 9 When will you get up from your **s**? H9104
Pr 6:10 A little **s**, a little slumber, a little folding H9104
Pr 6:22 guide you; when you **s**, they will watch H8886
Pr 19:15 Laziness brings on **deep s**, and the H9554
Pr 20:13 Do not love **s** or you will grow poor; stay H9104
Pr 24:33 A little **s**, a little slumber, a little folding H9104
Ecc 5:12 The **s** *of* a laborer is sweet, whether they H9104
Ecc 5:12 their abundance permits them no **s**. H3822
Ecc 8:16 people getting no **s** day or night— H9104
Isa 29:10 has brought over you a **deep s**: H8120+9554
Isa 56:10 they lie around and dream, they love to **s**. H5670
Jer 31:26 My **s** had been pleasant to me H9104
Jer 51:39 then **s** forever and not awake," H3822+9104
Jer 51:57 *they will* **s** forever and not awake," H3822+9104
Eze 23:44 As *men* **s with** a prostitute, so they H995+448
Eze 34:25 in the wilderness and **s** in the forests in H3822
Da 2: 1 his mind was troubled and he could not **s**. H9104
Da 6:18 brought to him. And he could not **s**. A10733
Da 8:18 *I was* **in a deep s**, with my face H8101
Da 10: 9 I **fell into a deep s**, my face to the H8101
Da 12: 2 Multitudes *who* **s** *in* the dust of the earth H3825
Jnh 1: 5 where he lay down and **fell into a deep s**. H8101
Jnh 1: 6 went to him and said, "How *can* you **s**? H8101
Zec 4: 1 like someone awakened from **s**. H9104
Jn 11:13 thought he meant **natural s**. *G3122+5678*
Ac 20: 9 was sinking *into* a deep **s** as Paul talked *G5678*
1Co 15:51 *We will* not all **s**, but we will all be *G3121*
2Co 11:27 toiled and have often **gone without s**; *G71*
1Th 4:13 uninformed about those *who* **s in death**, *G3121*
1Th 5: 7 For those who **s**, sleep at night, and those *G2761*
1Th 5: 7 For those who sleep, **s** at night, and those *G2761*

SLEEPER (1) [SLEEP]

Eph 5:14 "Wake up, **s**, rise from the dead, and *G2761*

SLEEPING (23) [SLEEP]

Ge 2:21 and while *he was* **s**, he took one of H3822
Ge 34: 7 in Israel by **s with** Jacob's daughter H8886+907
Dt 22:13 a wife and, after **s with** her, dislikes H995+448
Dt 22:22 man is found **s with** another man's H8886+6640
Jdg 16:13 So *while he was* **s**, Delilah took the H3822
Jdg 19: 4 eating and drinking, and **s** there. H4328
1Sa 26:12 They *were* all **s**, because the LORD had put H3825
1Ki 18:27 Maybe he is **s** and must be awakened." H3825
Pr 23:34 You will be like *one* **s** on the high seas H8886
Mt 8:24 swept over the boat. But Jesus *was* **s**. *G2761*
Mt 13:25 But while everyone *was* **s**, his enemy came *G2761*
Mt 26:40 to his disciples and found them **s**. *G2761*
Mt 26:43 he again found them **s**, because their *G2761*
Mt 26:45 said to them, "*Are you* still **s** and resting? *G2761*
Mk 4:38 Jesus was in the stern, **s** on a cushion. *G2761*
Mk 13:36 suddenly, do not let him find you **s**. *G2761*
Mk 14:37 to his disciples and found them **s**. *G2761*
Mk 14:40 he again found them **s**, because their *G2761*
Mk 14:41 said to them, "*Are you* still **s** and resting? *G2761*
Lk 22:46 "Why *are you* **s**?" he asked them. "Get up *G2761*
Ac 12: 6 Peter was **s** between two soldiers *G3121*
1Co 5: 1 A man *is* **s with** his father's wife. *G2400*
2Pe 2: 3 their destruction *has* not *been* **s**. *G3818*

SLEEPLESS (1) [SLEEP]

2Co 6: 5 in hard work, **s nights** and hunger; *G71*

SLEEPS (12) [SLEEP]

Ex 22:16 to be married and **s with** her, H8886+6640
Lev 14:47 Anyone *who* **s** or eats in the house must H8886
Lev 19:20 a man **s with** a female H8886+8887+2446+907
Dt 22:23 to be married and *he* **s with** her, H8886+6640
Dt 27:20 "Cursed is *anyone who* **s with** his H8886+6640
Dt 27:22 "Cursed is *anyone who* **s with** his H8886+6640
Dt 27:23 "Cursed is *anyone who* **s with** his H8886+6640
Pr 6:29 So is he *who* **s with** another man's H995+448
Pr 10: 5 but *he who* **s** during harvest is a H8101
Isa 5:27 not one slumbers or **s**; not a belt is H3822
Mk 4:27 day, whether *he* **s** or gets up, the *G2761*
Jn 11:12 replied, "Lord, if *he* **s**, he will get better." *G3121*

SLEEPY (1) [SLEEP]

Lk 9:32 and his companions were **very s**, *G976+5678*

SLEET (1)

Ps 78:47 with hail and their sycamore-figs with **s**. H2857

SLEPT (26) [SLEEP]

Ge 16: 4 *He* **s with** Hagar, and she conceived H995+448
Ge 19: 8 daughters who *have* never **s with** a man. H3359
Ge 19:33 daughter went in and **s with** him. H8886+907
Ge 19:34 "Last night *I* **s with** my father. H8886+907
Ge 19:35 daughter went in and **s with** him. H8886+6640
Ge 24:16 a virgin; no man *had ever* **s with** her. H3359
Ge 26:10 might well have **s with** your wife, H8886+907
Ge 30: 4 Bilhah as a wife. Jacob **s with** her, H995+448
Ge 30:16 So *he* **s with** her that night H8886+6640
Ge 35:22 went in and **s with** his father's H8886+907
Ge 38: 9 so whenever *he* **s with** his brother's H995+448
Ge 38:18 he gave them to her and **s with** her, H995+448
Nu 31:17 woman *who has* **s with** a H3359+4200+5435+408
Nu 31:18 girl who *has* never **s with** a man. H3359+5435
Nu 31:35 who *had* never **s with** a man H3359+5435+2351
Dt 22:22 the man who **s with** her and the H8886+6640
Jdg 21:12 who *had* never **s with** a H3359+4200+5435+2351
1Sa 2:22 and how *they* **s with** the women who H8886+907
2Sa 11: 4 came to him, and *he* **s with** her. H8886+6640
2Sa 11: 9 But Uriah **s** *at* the entrance to the palace H8886
2Sa 12: 3 drank from his cup and even **s** in his arms. H8886
2Sa 16:22 he **s with** his father's concubines H995+448
SS 5: 2 I **s** but my heart was awake. Listen! My H3825
Eze 23: 8 during her youth *men* **s with** her, H8886+907
Eze 23:44 And *they* **s with** her. As men sleep H995+448
Eze 23:44 so *they* **s with** those lewd women H995+448

SLEW (1) [SLAY]

Ps 78:34 Whenever God **s** them, they would seek H2222

SLIGHTEST (1)

Jude 12 eating with you **without the s qualm** *G925*

SLIME (1) [SLIMY]

Job 9:31 plunge me into a **s pit** so that even my H8846

SLIMEPITS (KJV) TAR PITS

SLIMY (1) [SLIME]

Ps 40: 2 He lifted me out of the **s pit**, out of H1014+8622

SLING (6) [SLINGS, SLUNG]

Jdg 20:16 each of whom *could* **s** a stone at a hair H7843
1Sa 17:40 bag and, with his **s** in his hand H7845
1Sa 17:50 over the Philistine with a **s** and a stone; H7845
1Sa 25:29 will hurl away as from the pocket of a **s**. H7845
1Ch 12: 2 arrows or to **s stones** H928+2021+74
Pr 26: 8 tying a stone in a **s** is the giving of honor H5275

SLINGS (1) [SLING]

2Ki 3:25 **men armed with s** surrounded it and H7847

SLINGSTONES (3) [STONE]

2Ch 26:14 bows and **s** for the entire army. H74+7845
Job 41:28 not make it flee; **s** are like chaff to it. H74+7845
Zec 9:15 will destroy and overcome with **s**. H74+7845

SLIP (7) [SLIPPED, SLIPPERY, SLIPPING]

Dt 32:35 In due time their foot *will* **s**; their day of H4572
1Sa 27: 1 in Israel, and *I will* **s out** of his hand." H4880
2Ki 9:15 don't *let* anyone **s out** of the city to go H3655
Ps 37:31 God is in their hearts; their feet *do* not **s**. H5048
Ps 38:16 exalt themselves over me when my feet **s**." H4572
Ps 121: 3 He will not let your foot **s**—he who H4572
Jer 20:10 All my friends are waiting for me to **s** H7520

SLIPPED (5) [SLIP]

2Sa 4: 6 Rekab and his brother Baanah **s away**. H4880
Ps 73: 2 me, my feet *had* almost **s**; I had nearly H5742
Jn 5:13 Jesus *had* **s away** into the crowd that *G1728*
2Co 11:33 in the wall and **s through** his hands. *G1767*
Jude 4 long ago *have* **secretly s** in among you. *G4208*

SLIPPERY (3) [SLIP]

Ps 35: 6 may their path be dark and **s**, with the H2761
Ps 73:18 Surely you place them on **s** *ground*; you H2747
Jer 23:12 "Therefore their path will become **s**; they H2761

SLIPPING (4) [SLIP]

Job 12: 5 as the fate of *those* whose feet *are* **s**. H5048
Ps 66: 9 our lives and kept our feet from **s**. H4572
Ps 94:18 When I said, "My foot *is* **s**," your unfailing H4572
Jn 8:59 himself, **s away** from the temple grounds. *G2002*

SLOPE (9) [SLOPES]

Jos 15: 8 along the southern **s** *of* the Jebusite city H4190
Jos 15:10 ran along the northern **s** *of* Mount Jearim H4190
Jos 15:11 It went to the northern **s** *of* Ekron, turned H4190
Jos 18:12 the northern **s** *of* Jericho and headed H4190
Jos 18:13 From there it crossed to the south **s** *of* Luz H4190
Jos 18:16 along the southern **s** *of* the Jebusite city H4190
Jos 18:18 to the northern **s** *of* Beth Arabah and on H4190
Jos 18:19 went to the northern **s** *of* Beth Hoglah H4190
Mic 1: 4 the fire, like water rushing down a **s**. H4618

SLOPES (12) [SLOPE]

Nu 21:15 the **s** *of* the ravines that lead to the H844
Nu 34:11 continue along the **s** east *of* the Sea of H4190
Dt 3:17 the Dead Sea), below the **s** *of* Pisgah. H844
Dt 4:49 far as the Dead Sea, below the **s** *of* Pisgah. H844
Dt 33: 2 ones from the south, from his **mountain s**. H850
Jos 7: 5 quarries and struck them down on the **s**. H4618
Jos 10:40 the western foothills and the **mountain s** H844

Jos 12: 3 then southward below the s of Pisgah. H844
Jos 12: 8 the Arabah, the mountain s, the wilderness H844
Jos 13:20 Beth Peor, the s of Pisgah, and Beth H844
Isa 11:14 swoop down on the s of Philistia to the H4190
Jer 18:14 of Lebanon ever vanish from its rocky s? H8442

SLOTHFUL, SLOTHFULNESS (KJV) HESITATE, LACKING, LAZINESS, LAZY, SLACK, SLUGGARD

SLOW (18) [SLOWLY, SLOWNESS]
Ex 4:10 I am s of speech and tongue. H3878
Ex 34: 6 gracious God, s to anger, abounding H800
Nu 14:18 'The LORD is s to anger, abounding in love H800
Dt 7:10 he will not be s to repay to their face those H336
Dt 23:21 LORD your God, do not be s to pay it, for the H336
2Ki 4:24 don't s down for me unless I H6806+4200+8206
Ne 9:17 s to anger and abounding in love. H800
Ps 86:15 gracious God, s to anger, abounding H800
Ps 103: 8 gracious, s to anger, abounding in H800
Ps 145: 8 compassionate, s to anger and rich in love. H800
Joel 2:13 s to anger and abounding in love H800
Jnh 4: 2 s to anger and abounding in love H800
Na 1: 3 The LORD is s to anger but great in power H800
Lk 24:25 and how s to believe all that G1096+3836+2840
Ac 27: 7 We made s headway for many days and G1095
Jas 1:19 s to speak and slow to become angry G1096
Jas 1:19 slow to speak and s to become angry, G1096
2Pe 3: 9 The Lord is not s in keeping his promise G1094

SLOWLY (1) [SLOW]
Ge 33:14 I move along s at the pace of the H4200+351

SLOWNESS (1) [SLOW]
2Pe 3: 9 his promise, as some understand s. G1097

SLUG (1)
Ps 58: 8 May they be like a s that melts away as it H8671

SLUGGARD (11) [SLUGGARD'S, SLUGGARDS]
Pr 6: 6 Go to the ant, you s; consider its ways H6789
Pr 6: 9 you lie there, you s? When will you get up H6789
Pr 15:19 The way of the s is blocked with thorns H6789
Pr 19:24 A s buries his hand in the dish; he will H6789
Pr 21:25 The craving of a s will be the death of H6789
Pr 22:13 The s says, "There's a lion outside! I'll be H6789
Pr 24:30 I went past the field of a s, past the H6789
Pr 26:13 A s says, "There's a lion in the road, H6789
Pr 26:14 on its hinges, so a s turns on his bed. H6789
Pr 26:15 A s buries his hand in the dish; he is too H6789
Pr 26:16 A s is wiser in his own eyes than seven H6789

SLUGGARD'S (1) [SLUGGARD]
Pr 13: 4 A s appetite is never filled, but the H6789

SLUGGARDS (2) [SLUGGARD]
Pr 10:26 so are s to those who send them. H6789
Pr 20: 4 S do not plow in season; so at harvest H6789

SLUMBER (9) [SLUMBERS]
Job 33:15 falls on people as they s in their beds, H9484
Ps 121: 3 he who watches over you will not s; H5670
Ps 121: 4 over Israel will neither s nor sleep. H5670
Ps 132: 4 no sleep to my eyes or s to my eyelids, H9484
Pr 6: 4 sleep to your eyes, no s to your eyelids. H9484
Pr 6:10 little sleep, a little s, a little folding of the H9484
Pr 24:33 little sleep, a little s, a little folding of the H9484
Na 3:18 your shepherds s; your nobles lie down H5670
Ro 13:11 come for you to wake up from your s, G5678

SLUMBERS (1) [SLUMBER]
Isa 5:27 stumbles, not one s or sleeps; not a H5670

SLUMPED (1)
2Ki 9:24 his heart and he s down in his chariot. H4156

SLUNG (2) [SLING]
1Sa 17: 6 a bronze javelin was s on his back. H1068+4190
1Sa 17:49 he s it and struck the Philistine on the H7843

SLUR (1)
Ps 15: 3 to a neighbor, and casts no s on others; H3075

SLY (1)
Pr 25:23 brings unexpected rain is a s tongue— H6260

SMALL (73) [SMALLER, SMALLEST]
Ge 19:20 a town near enough to run to, and it is s. H5203
Ge 19:20 me flee to it—it is very s, isn't it? Then my H5203
Ex 12: 4 If any household is too s for a whole lamb H5070
Nu 22:18 do anything great or s to go beyond the H7783
Dt 1:17 in judging; hear both s and great alike. H7783
Dt 25:14 in your house—one large, one s. H7783
Jos 17:15 the hill country of Ephraim is too s for you, H237
1Sa 15:17 you were once s in your own eyes, H7785
1Sa 18:23 "Do you think it is a s matter to become H7829
1Sa 20: 2 do anything, great or s, without letting me H7785
1Sa 20:35 He had a s boy with him, H7785
1Ki 2:20 "I have one s request to make of you," H7783
1Ki 8:64 the LORD was too s to hold the burnt H7785
1Ki 10:17 three hundred s shields of hammered H4482
1Ki 17:13 But first make a s loaf of bread for me H7783
1Ki 18:44 "A cloud as s as a man's hand is rising H7783
1Ki 20:27 opposite them like two s flocks of goats, H3105
1Ki 22:31 fight with anyone, s or great, except the H7785
2Ki 4: 2 she said, "except a s jar of olive oil." H655
2Ki 4:10 Let's make a s room on the roof and put in H7783
2Ki 6: 1 where we meet with you is too s for us. H7639
2Ch 9:16 three hundred s shields of hammered H4482
2Ch 14: 8 armed with s shields and with bows. H4482
2Ch 15:13 put to death, whether s or great, man H7785
2Ch 18:30 fight with anyone, s or great, except the H7785
2Ch 23: 9 the large and s shields that had belonged H8949
2Ch 36:18 both large and s, and the treasures H7783
Job 3:19 The s and the great are there, and the H7785
Ps 104:25 number—living things both large and s. H7783
Ps 115:13 who fear the LORD—s and great alike. H7783
Ps 148:10 all cattle, s creatures and flying birds H8254
Pr 15:17 Better a s serving of vegetables with love H786
Pr 20:11 Even s children are known by their actions, H5853
Pr 24:10 a time of trouble, how s is your strength! H7639
Pr 30:24 "Four things on earth are s, yet they are H7783
Ecc 9:14 There was once a s city with only a few H7783
Isa 49: 6 "It is too s a thing for you to be my servant H7837
Isa 49:19 now you will be too s for your people H7674
Isa 49:20 'This place is too s for us; give us more H7639
Jer 46: 3 "Prepare your shields, both large and s H4482
Jer 49:15 I will make you s among the nations, H7785
Eze 23:24 with large and s shields and with helmets H4482
Eze 38: 4 a great horde with large and s shields, H4482
Eze 39: 9 the s and large shields, the bows H4482
Da 8: 9 which started s but grew in power to the H7582
Am 6:11 into pieces and the s house into bits. H7785
Am 7: 2 How can Jacob survive? He is so s!" H7785
Am 7: 5 How can Jacob survive? He is so s!" H7785
Ob 2 I will make you s among the nations H7785
Mic 5: 2 though you are s among the clans of H7582
Zec 4:10 "Who dares despise the day of s things H7783
Mt 7:14 But s is the gate and narrow the road that G5101
Mt 15:34 "Seven," they replied, "and a few s fish." G2715
Mt 17:20 if you have faith as s as a mustard seed, you AIT
Mk 3: 9 disciples to have a s boat ready for him, G4449
Mk 8: 7 They had a few s fish as well; he gave G2715
Mk 12:42 came and put in two very s copper coins, G3321
Lk 17: 6 "If you have faith as s as a mustard seed, you AIT
Lk 19:17 have been trustworthy in a very s matter, G1788
Lk 21: 2 poor widow put in two very s copper coins. G3321
Jn 6: 9 boy with five s barley loaves and two small G788
Jn 6: 9 five small barley loaves and two s fish, G4066
Ac 12:18 there was no s commotion among the G3900
Ac 26:22 stand here and testify to s and great alike. G3625
Ac 27:16 to the lee of a s island called Cauda, G3761
Jas 3: 4 are steered by a very s rudder wherever G1788
Jas 3: 5 the tongue is a s part of the body, but it G3625
Jas 3: 5 a great forest is set on fire by a s spark. G2462
Rev 11:18 both great and s—and for destroying G3625
Rev 13:16 all people, great and s, rich and poor, G3625
Rev 19: 5 you who fear him, both great and s!" G3625
Rev 19:18 of all people, free and slave, great and s." G3625
Rev 20:12 the dead, great and s, standing before G3625

SMALLER (6) [SMALL]
Nu 26:54 to a s group a smaller one; each H5071
Nu 26:54 to a smaller group a s one; each is to H5070
Nu 26:56 by lot among the larger and s groups." H5071
Nu 33:54 to a s group a smaller one. H5071
Nu 33:54 to a smaller group a s one. H5070
Eze 42: 6 so they were s in floor space than those on H724

SMALLEST (5) [SMALL]
1Sa 9:21 Benjamite, from the s tribe of Israel, and H7783
Isa 60:22 a thousand, the s a mighty nation. H7582
Mt 5:18 disappear, not the s letter, not the least G2740
Mt 13:32 Though it is the s of all seeds, yet when it G3625
Mk 4:31 which is the s of all seeds on earth. G3625

SMASH (7) [SMASHED, SMASHES]
Ex 34:13 s their sacred stones and cut down their H8689
Dt 7: 5 down their altars, s their sacred stones H8689
Dt 12: 3 s their sacred stones and burn their H8689
Jer 13:14 I will s them one against the other H5879
Jer 19:11 I will s this nation and this city just as this H8689
Jer 48:12 they will empty her pitchers and s her jars. H5879
Am 6:11 and he will s the great house into pieces H5782

SMASHED (14) [SMASH]
Jdg 7:20 blew the trumpets and s the jars. H8689
2Ki 11:18 They s the altars and idols to pieces and H8689
2Ki 18: 4 s the sacred stones and cut down the H8689
2Ki 23:12 s them to pieces and threw the rubble H8368
2Ki 23:14 Josiah s the sacred stones and cut down H8689
2Ch 14: 3 s the sacred stones and cut down the H8689
2Ch 23:17 They s the altars and idols and killed H8689
2Ch 31: 1 s the sacred stones and cut down the H8689
2Ch 34: 4 s the Asherah poles and the idols. H8689
Ps 74: 6 They s all the carved paneling with their H2150
Jer 19:11 as this potter's jar is s and cannot be H8689
Eze 6: 4 your incense altars will be s; H8689
Eze 6: 6 devastated, your idols s and ruined, your H8689
Da 2:34 on its feet of iron and clay and s them. A10182

SMASHES (1) [SMASH]
Da 2:40 iron breaks and s everything—and as A10290

SMEAR (2) [SMEARED]
Job 13: 4 however, s me with lies; you are worthless H3260
Mal 2: 3 I will s on your faces the dung from your H2430

SMEARED (1) [SMEAR]
Ps 119:69 Though the arrogant have s me with lies H3260

SMELL (10) [SMELLED]
Ge 27:27 When Isaac caught the s of his H8193+8194
Ge 27:27 the s of my son is like the smell of a field H8194
Ge 27:27 of my son is like the s of a field that the H8194
Ex 16:20 it was full of maggots and began to s. H944
Dt 4:28 which cannot see or hear or eat or s. H8193
Ps 115: 6 cannot hear, noses, but cannot s. H8193
Ecc 10: 1 As dead flies give perfume a bad s H944+5580
Da 3:27 there was no s of fire on them. A10666
Joel 2:20 stench will go up; its s will rise." Surely he H7462
1Co 12:17 where would the sense of s be? G4018

SMELLED (2) [SMELL]
Ge 8:21 The LORD s the pleasing aroma and said in H8193
Ex 7:21 the river s so bad that the Egyptians H944

SMELTED (1)
Job 28: 2 from the earth, and copper is s from ore. H3668

SMILE (2) [SMILED]
Job 9:27 I will change my expression, and s,' H1158
Job 10: 3 while you s on the plans of the wicked? H3649

SMILED (1) [SMILE]
Job 29:24 When I s at them, they scarcely believed H8471

SMOKE (47) [SMOKING]
Ge 19:28 he saw dense s rising from the land H7798
Ge 19:28 rising from the land, like s from a furnace. H7798
Ex 19:18 Mount Sinai was covered with s, because H6939
Ex 19:18 The s billowed up from it like smoke from H6940
Ex 19:18 billowed up from it like s from a furnace, H6940
Ex 20:18 the trumpet and saw the mountain in s, H6942
Lev 16:13 the s of the incense will conceal the H6727
Jos 8:20 back and saw the s of the city rising up H6940
Jos 8:21 the city and that s was going up from it, H6940
Jdg 20:38 send up a great cloud of s from the city, H6940
Jdg 20:40 when the column of s began to rise from H6940
Jdg 20:40 saw the whole city going up in s. H5368
2Sa 22: 9 S rose from his nostrils; consuming fire H6940
Job 41:20 S pours from its nostrils as from a boiling H6940
Ps 18: 8 S rose from his nostrils; consuming fire H6940
Ps 37:20 will be consumed, they will go up in s. H6940
Ps 68: 2 May you blow them away like s—as wax H6940
Ps 102: 3 For my days vanish like s; my bones burn H6940
Ps 104:32 who touches the mountains, and they s. H6939
Ps 119:83 Though I am like a wineskin in the s, I do H7798
Ps 144: 5 touch the mountains, so that they s. H6939
Pr 10:26 As vinegar to the teeth and s to the eyes H6940
SS 3: 6 up from the wilderness like a column of s, H6940
Isa 4: 5 there a cloud of s by day and a glow of H6940
Isa 6: 4 shook and the temple was filled with s. H6940
Isa 9:18 so that it rolls upward in a column of s. H6940
Isa 14:31 A cloud of s comes from the north, and H6940
Isa 30:27 with burning anger and dense clouds of s H5366
Isa 34:10 night or day; its s will rise forever. H6940
Isa 51: 6 the heavens will vanish like s, the earth H6940
Isa 65: 5 Such people are s in my nostrils, a fire H6940
Hos 13: 3 like s escaping through a window. H6940
Joel 2:30 the earth, blood and fire and billows of s. H6940
Na 2:13 "I will burn up your chariots in s, and the H6940
Ac 2:19 blood and fire and billows of s. G2837
Rev 8: 4 The s of the incense, together with the G2837
Rev 9: 2 s rose from it like the smoke from a G2837
Rev 9: 2 rose from it like the s from a gigantic G2837
Rev 9: 2 were darkened by the s from the Abyss. G2837
Rev 9: 3 And out of the s locusts came down on the G2837
Rev 9:17 of their mouths came fire, s and sulfur. G2837
Rev 9:18 s and sulfur that came out of their mouths. G2837
Rev 14:11 And the s of their torment will rise for ever G2837
Rev 15: 8 was filled with s from the glory of God G2837
Rev 18: 9 shared her luxury see the s of her burning, G2837
Rev 18:18 When they see the s of her burning, they G2837
Rev 19: 3 The s from her goes up for ever and ever." G2837

SMOKING (1) [SMOKE]
Ge 15:17 a s firepot with a blazing torch appeared H6940

SMOLDER (2) [SMOLDERING, SMOLDERS]
Ps 74: 1 Why does your anger s against the sheep H6939
Ps 80: 4 will your anger s against the prayers of H6939

SMOLDERING (3) [SMOLDER]
Isa 7: 4 of these two s stubs of firewood— H6942
Isa 42: 3 and a s wick he will not snuff out. H3910
Mt 12:20 and a s wick he will not snuff out G5606

SMOLDERS (1) [SMOLDER]
Hos 7: 6 Their passion s all night; in the morning it H3822

SMOOTH (11) [SMOOTH-SKINNED, SMOOTHED, SMOOTHER, SMOOTHLY, SMOOTHS]
Ge 27:11 Esau is a hairy man while I have s skin. H2747
Ge 27:16 his hands and the s part of his neck with H2753
1Sa 17:40 chose five s stones from the stream H2752
Ps 55:21 His talk is s as butter, yet war is in his H2744
Pr 6:24 from the s talk of a wayward woman. H2753
Pr 7:21 she seduced him with her s talk. H2749
Isa 26: 7 you, the Upright One, make the way of the righteous s H7142

S

Isa 42:16 them and make the rough places **s**. H4793
Isa 57: 6 idols among the **s** stones *of* the ravines H2747
Lk 3: 5 shall become straight, the rough ways **s**. G3308
Ro 16:18 By **s talk** and flattery they deceive the G5981

SMOOTH-SKINNED (2) [SKIN, SMOOTH]
Isa 18: 2 to a people tall and **s**, to a people feared H5307
Isa 18: 7 LORD Almighty from a people tall and **s**, H5307

SMOOTHED (1) [SMOOTH]
1Ki 7: 9 to size and **s** on their H1760+928+2021+4490

SMOOTHER (1) [SMOOTH]
Pr 5: 3 drip honey, and her speech is **s** than oil; H2747

SMOOTHLY (1) [SMOOTH]
Pr 23:31 in the cup, when it goes down **s**! H928+4797

SMOOTHS (1) [SMOOTH]
Isa 41: 7 the *one who* **s** *with* the hammer spurs H2744

SMYRNA (2)
Rev 1:11 to Ephesus, **S**, Pergamum, Thyatira G5044
Rev 2: 8 "To the angel of the church in **S** write G5044

SNAIL (KJV) SKINK, SLUG

SNAKE (25) [SNAKES]
Ge 49:17 Dan will be a **s** by the roadside, a viper H5729
Ex 4: 3 threw it on the ground and it became a **s**, H5729
Ex 4: 4 took hold of **the s** and it turned back H2257S
Ex 7: 9 before Pharaoh,' and it will become a **s**." H9490
Ex 7:10 his officials, and it became a **s**. H9490
Ex 7:12 threw down his staff and it became a **s**. H9490
Ex 7:15 hand the staff that was changed into a **s**. H5729
Nu 21: 8 "Make a **s** and put it up on a pole H8597
Nu 21: 9 made a bronze **s** and put it up on a H5729
Nu 21: 9 was bitten by a **s** and looked at the H5729
Nu 21: 9 by a snake and looked at the bronze **s**, H5729
2Ki 18: 4 pieces the bronze **s** Moses had made, H5729
Ps 58: 4 Their venom is like the venom of a **s**, like H5729
Pr 23:32 the end it bites like a **s** and poisons like a H5729
Pr 30:19 the way of a **s** on a rock, the way of H5729
Ecc 10: 8 through a wall may be bitten by a **s**. H5729
Ecc 10:11 If a **s** bites before it is charmed, the H5729
Isa 14:29 from the root of that **s** will spring up a H5729
Am 5:19 on the wall only to have a **s** bite him. H5729
Mic 7:17 They will lick dust like a **s**, like creatures H5729
Mt 7:10 Or if he asks for a fish, will give him a **s**? G4058
Lk 11:11 asks for a fish, will give him a **s** instead? G4058
Jn 3:14 as Moses lifted up the **s** in the wilderness, G4058
Ac 28: 4 islanders saw the **s** hanging from his G2563
Ac 28: 5 But Paul shook the **s** off into the fire and G2563

SNAKES (11) [SNAKE]
Nu 21: 6 the LORD sent venomous **s** among them; H5729
Nu 21: 7 that the LORD will take the **s** away from us." H5729
Dt 8:15 with its venomous **s** and scorpions. H5729
Isa 30: 6 of adders and darting **s**, the envoys carry H8597
Jer 8:17 I will send **venomous s** among you H5729
Mt 10:16 be as shrewd as **s** and as innocent as G4058
Mt 23:33 "*You* **s**! You brood of vipers! How will you G4058
Mk 16:18 they will pick up **s** with their hands; and G4058
Lk 10:19 to trample on **s** and scorpions and to G4058
1Co 10: 9 some of them did—and were killed by **s**. G4058
Rev 9:19 their tails were like **s**, having heads G4058

SNAPPED (3) [SNAPS]
Jdg 16: 9 But *he* **s** the bowstrings as easily as a H5998
Jdg 16:12 But *he* **s** the ropes off his arms as if they H5998
Jer 10:20 all its ropes **are s**. My children are gone H5998

SNAPS (1) [SNAPPED]
Jdg 16: 9 as a piece of string **s** when it comes close H5998

SNARE (33) [ENSNARE, ENSNARED, SNARED, SNARES]
Ex 10: 7 "How long will this man be a **s** to us? H4613
Ex 23:33 of their gods will certainly be a **s** to you." H4613
Ex 34:12 are going, or they will be a **s** among you. H4613
Dt 7:16 their gods, for that will be a **s** to you. H4613
Jdg 8:27 it became a **s** to Gideon and his H4613
1Sa 18:21 that she may be a **s** to him and so that H4613
Job 18: 9 seizes him by the heel; a **s** holds him fast. H7545
Ps 25:15 only he will release my feet from the **s**. H8407
Ps 69:22 the table set before them become a **s**; H7062
Ps 91: 3 from the fowler's **s** and from the deadly H7062
Ps 106:36 their idols, which became a **s** to them. H4613
Ps 119:110 The wicked have set a **s** for me, but I H7062
Ps 124: 7 escaped like a bird from the fowler's **s**; H7062
Ps 124: 7 fowler's snare; the **s** has been broken H7062
Ps 140: 5 The arrogant have hidden a **s** for me; they H7062
Ps 142: 3 I walk people have hidden a **s** for me. H7062
Pr 6: 5 like a bird from the **s** *of* the fowler. H3338
Pr 7:23 like a bird darting into a **s**, little knowing H7062
Pr 18: 7 their lips are a **s** *to* their very lives. H4613
Pr 21: 6 tongue is a fleeting vapor and a deadly **s**. H4613
Pr 29:25 Fear of man will prove to be a **s**, but H4613
Ecc 7:26 bitter than death the woman who is a **s**, H5178
Ecc 9:12 birds are taken in a **s**, so people are H7062
Isa 8:14 of Jerusalem he will be a trap and a **s**. H4613
Isa 24:17 Terror and pit and **s** await you, people of H7062
Isa 24:18 climbs out of the pit will be caught in a **s**. H7062
Jer 5:26 in wait like **men who s birds** and like H3687
Jer 48:43 Terror and pit and **s** await you, you H7062
Jer 48:44 climbs out of the pit will be caught in a **s**; H7062
Eze 12:13 he will be caught in my **s**; I will bring H5180
Eze 17:20 him, and he will be caught in my **s**. H5180
Hos 5: 1 You have been a **s** at Mizpah, a net H7062
Ro 11: 9 "May their table become a **s** and a trap, G4075

SNARED (4) [SNARE]
Pr 3:26 side and will keep your foot from being **s**. H4335
Pr 29: 6 Evildoers are **s** by their own sin, but the H4613
Isa 8:15 be broken, *they will* **be s** and captured." H3704
Isa 28:13 they will be injured and **s** and captured. H3704

SNARES (14) [SNARE]
Jos 23:13 they will become **s** and traps for you H7062
Jdg 2: 3 and their gods will become **s** to you. H4613
2Sa 22: 6 around me; the **s** *of* death confronted me. H4613
Job 22:10 That is why **s** are all around you, why H7062
Job 30:12 tribe attacks; *they* **lay s** *for* my feet, they H8938
Job 34:30 from ruling, from laying **s** *for* the people. H4613
Ps 18: 5 around me; the **s** *of* death confronted me. H4613
Ps 64: 5 they talk about hiding their **s**; they say, H4613
Ps 141: 9 from the **s** they have laid for me. H7062
Pr 13:14 turning a person from the **s** *of* death. H4613
Pr 14:27 turning a person from the **s** *of* death. H4613
Pr 22: 5 the paths of the wicked are **s** and pitfalls, H7553
Jer 18:22 me and have hidden **s** for my feet. H7062
Hos 9: 8 **s** await him on all his paths H7062+3687

SNARLING (2)
Ps 59: 6 return at evening, **s** like dogs, and prowl H2159
Ps 59:14 return at evening, **s** like dogs, and prowl H2159

SNATCH (7) [SNATCHED, SNATCHES, SNATCHING]
Job 24:19 heat and drought **s away** the melted snow H1608
Job 30:22 *You* **s** me **up** and drive me before the H5951
Ps 52: 5 *He will* **s** you **up** and pluck you from your H3149
Isa 3:18 that day the Lord *will* **s away** their finery: H6073
Isa 10: 6 to seize loot and **s** plunder, and to H1024
Jn 10:28 no one *will* **s** them out of my hand. G773
Jn 10:29 no one can **s** them out of my Father's hand. G773

SNATCHED (9) [SNATCH]
2Sa 23:21 *He* **s** the spear from the Egyptian's hand H1608
1Ch 11:23 *He* **s** the spear from the Egyptian's hand H1608
Job 24: 9 The fatherless child *is* **s** from the breast H1608
Job 29:17 of the wicked and **s** the victims from their H8959
Pr 22:27 your very bed *will be* **s** from under you. H4374
Joel 1: 5 new wine, for *it has* **been s** from your lips. H4162
Am 4:11 were like a burning stick **s** from the fire, H5911
Zec 3: 2 this man a burning stick **s** from the fire?" H5911
Rev 12: 5 And her child *was* **s up** to God and to his G773

SNATCHES (4) [SNATCH]
Job 9:12 If *he* **s away**, who can stop him? Who can H3166
Job 24:19 so the grave **s** away those who have sinned. NDT
Job 27:20 a tempest **s** him **away** in the night. H1704
Mt 13:19 one comes and **s away** what was sown in G773

SNATCHING (1) [SNATCH]
Jude 23 save others *by* **s** them from the fire; to G773

SNEER (2) [SNEERED, SNEERING, SNEERS]
Ps 35:21 *They* **s** at me and say, "Aha! Aha H8143+7023
Isa 57: 4 At whom *do you* **s** and stick out H8143+7023

SNEERED (2) [SNEER]
Lk 23:35 watching, and the rulers even **s at** him. G1727
Ac 17:32 some of them **s**, but others said, G5949

SNEERING (1) [SNEER]
Lk 16:14 heard all this and *were* **s at** Jesus. G1727

SNEERS (1) [SNEER]
Ps 10: 5 rejected by him; *he* **s** at all his enemies. H7032

SNEEZED (1)
2Ki 4:35 The boy **s** seven times and opened his H2453

SNIFF (1) [SNIFFING]
Mal 1:13 and *you* **s** *at* it **contemptuously**," says the H5870

SNIFFING (1) [SNIFF]
Jer 2:24 to the desert, **s** the wind in her craving H8634

SNORTING (3) [SNORTS]
Job 39:20 a locust, striking terror with its proud **s**? H5724
Job 41:18 Its **s** throws out flashes of light; its eyes H6490
Jer 8:16 The **s** *of* the enemy's horses is heard from H5725

SNORTS (1) [SNORTING]
Job 39:25 At the blast of the trumpet *it* **s**, 'Aha!' It H606

SNOUT (1)
Pr 11:22 gold ring in a pig's **s** is a beautiful woman H678

SNOW (19) [SNOW-COOLED, SNOWS, SNOWY]
Ex 4: 6 leprous—it had become as **white as s**. H8920
Nu 12:10 was leprous—it became as **white as s**. H8920
2Ki 5:27 leprous—it had become as white as **s**. H8920
Job 6:16 thawing ice and swollen with melting **s**, H8920
Job 24:19 drought snatch away the melted **s**, H8920
Job 37: 6 He says to the **s**, 'Fall on the earth,' and H8920
Job 38:22 the storehouses of the **s** or seen the H8920
Ps 51: 7 wash me, and I will be whiter than **s**. H8920
Ps 68:14 *it was like* **s fallen** on Mount Zalmon. H8919
Ps 147:16 He spreads the **s** like wool and scatters H8920
Ps 148: 8 lightning and hail, **s** and clouds, stormy H8920
Pr 26: 1 Like **s** in summer or rain in harvest, honor H8920
Isa 1:18 they shall be as white as **s**; though they H8920
Isa 55:10 As the rain and the **s** come down from H8920
Jer 18:14 Does the **s** *of* Lebanon ever vanish from H8920
La 4: 7 were brighter than **s** and whiter than milk, H8920
Da 7: 9 His clothing was as white as **s**; the hair A10758
Mt 28: 3 lightning, and his clothes were white as **s**. G5946
Rev 1:14 as white as **s**, and his eyes were G5946

SNOW-COOLED (1) [COOL, SNOW]
Pr 25:13 Like a **s drink** at harvest time is a H8920+7557

SNOWS (1) [SNOW]
Pr 31:21 When it **s**, she has no fear for her H8920

SNOWY (2) [SNOW]
2Sa 23:20 down into a pit on a **s** day and killed a H8920
1Ch 11:22 down into a pit on a **s** day and killed a H8920

SNUFF (3) [SNUFFED]
Isa 42: 3 a smoldering wick *he will* not **s out**. H3882
Eze 32: 7 When I **s** you **out**, I will cover the heavens H3882
Mt 12:20 a smoldering wick *he will* not **s out** G4931

SNUFFDISHES (KJV) TRAYS

SNUFFED (6) [SNUFF]
Job 18: 5 "The lamp of a wicked man *is* **s out**; the H1980
Job 21:17 how often *is* the lamp of the wicked **s out**? H1980
Pr 13: 9 the lamp of the wicked is **s out**. H1980
Pr 20:20 their lamp *will be* **s out** in pitch darkness. H1980
Pr 24:20 the lamp of the wicked *will be* **s out**. H1980
Isa 43:17 rise again, extinguished, **s out** like a wick: H3882

SNUFFERS (KJV) WICK TRIMMERS

SO (1 of 3102) For SO as a Conjunction, see Index of Articles Etc.
2Ki 17: 4 for he had sent envoys to **S** king of Egypt, H6046

SO-CALLED (2) [CALL]
1Co 8: 5 For even if there are **s** gods, whether in G3306
Rev 2:24 not learned Satan's **s** deep secrets, G6055+3306

SOAKED (4) [SOAK]
2Ki 8:15 **s** it in water and spread it over the king's H3188
Isa 34: 3 the mountains *will* **be s** with their blood. H5022
Isa 34: 7 with blood, and the dust *will* **be s** with fat. H2014
Jn 19:29 was there, so they **s** a sponge in it, put G3550

SOAP (3)
Job 9:30 I washed myself with **s** and my hands with H8921
Jer 2:22 wash yourself with **s** and use an H6003
Mal 3: 2 be like a refiner's fire or a launderer's **s**. H1383

SOAR (4) [SOARED]
Job 39:27 *Does* the eagle **s** at your command and H1467
Isa 40:31 *They will* **s** *on* wings like eagles; they will H6590
Jer 49:22 An eagle *will* **s** and swoop down H6590
Ob 4 Though *you* **s** like the eagle and make H1467

SOARED (2) [SOAR]
2Sa 22:11 flew; *he* **s** on the wings of the wind. H1797
Ps 18:10 flew; *he* **s** on the wings of the wind. H1797

SOB (1) [SOBBING]
Ge 21:16 And as she sat there, she began *to* **s**. H1134

SOBBING (1) [SOB]
Jdg 14:16 threw herself on him, **s**, "You hate me! H1134

SOBER (7)
1Sa 25:37 when Nabal *was* **s**, his H3655+2021+3516+4946
Ro 12: 3 rather think of yourself with **s judgment**, G5404
1Th 5: 6 are asleep, but let us be awake and **s**. G3768
1Th 5: 8 to the day, *let us be* **s**, putting on faith G3768
1Pe 1:13 with minds that are alert and fully **s**, set G3768
1Pe 4: 7 be alert and **of s mind** so that you may G3768
1Pe 5: 8 Be alert and **of s mind**. Your enemy the G1213

SOBRIETY (KJV) PROPRIETY

SOCIETY (1)
Job 30: 5 They were banished from **human s** H1569

SOCKET (3) [SOCKETS]
Ge 32:25 he touched the **s** *of* Jacob's hip so that his H4090
Ge 32:32 the tendon attached to the **s** *of* the hip, H4090
Ge 32:32 because the **s** *of* Jacob's hip was touched H4090

SOCKETS (3) [SOCKET]
1Ki 6:34 each having two leaves *that* **turned in s**. H1664
1Ki 7:50 the gold **s** for the doors of the H7327
Zec 14:12 their eyes will rot in their **s**, and their H2986

SOCO (NIV84) SOKO

SOCOH (NIV84) SOKOH

SOD, SODDEN (KJV) BOILED, COOKED, COOKING

SODA (NIV84) SOAP

S

SODI (1)
Nu 13:10 the tribe of Zebulun, Gaddiel son of S; H6052

SODOM (47)
Ge 10:19 as Gaza, and then toward S, Gomorrah, H6042
Ge 13:10 the LORD destroyed S and Gomorrah.) H6042
Ge 13:12 of the plain and pitched his tents near S. H6042
Ge 13:13 Now the people of S were wicked and H6042
Ge 14: 2 kings went to war against Bera king of S, H6042
Ge 14: 8 Then the king of S, the king of Gomorrah H6042
Ge 14:10 when the kings of S and Gomorrah fled, H6042
Ge 14:11 all the goods of S and Gomorrah and all H6042
Ge 14:12 his possessions, since he was living in S. H6042
Ge 14:17 the king of S came out to meet him in the H6042
Ge 14:21 The king of S said to Abram, "Give me H6042
Ge 14:22 But Abram said to the king of S, "With H6042
Ge 18:16 they looked down toward S, and Abraham H6042
Ge 18:20 "The outcry against S and Gomorrah is so H6042
Ge 18:22 The men turned away and went toward S H6042
Ge 18:26 find fifty righteous people in the city of S, H6042
Ge 19: 1 two angels arrived at S in the evening, H6042
Ge 19: 4 the men from every part of the city of S— H6042
Ge 19:24 burning sulfur on S and Gomorrah— H6042
Ge 19:28 He looked down toward S and Gomorrah H6042
Dt 29:23 like the destruction of S and Gomorrah, H6042
Dt 32:32 from the vine of S and from the fields of H6042
Isa 1: 9 we would have become like S, we would H6042
Isa 1:10 the LORD, you rulers of S; listen to the H6042
Isa 3: 9 they parade their sin like S; they do not H6042
Isa 13:19 overthrown by God like S and Gomorrah. H6042
Jer 23:14 They are all like S to me; the people of H6042
Jer 49:18 As S and Gomorrah were overthrown H6042
Jer 50:40 As I overthrew S and Gomorrah along H6042
La 4: 6 of my people is greater than that of S, H6042
Eze 16:46 south of you with her daughters, was S. H6042
Eze 16:48 your sister S and her daughters never did H6042
Eze 16:49 " 'Now this was the sin of your sister S H6042
Eze 16:53 the fortunes of S and her daughters and H6042
Eze 16:55 S with her daughters and Samaria with H6042
Eze 16:56 mention your sister S in the day of your H6042
Am 4:11 of you as I overthrew S and Gomorrah. H6042
Zep 2: 9 "surely Moab will become like S, the H6042
Mt 10:15 more bearable for S and Gomorrah G1178+5047
Mt 11:23 in you had been performed in S, G5047
Mt 11:24 more bearable for S on the day of G1178+5047
Lk 10:12 on that day for S than for that town. G5047
Lk 17:29 But the day Lot left S, fire and sulfur rained G5047
Ro 9:29 we would have become like S, we would G5047
2Pe 2: 6 the cities of S and Gomorrah by G5047
Jude 7 S and Gomorrah and the surrounding G5047
Rev 11: 8 which is figuratively called S and Egypt G5047

SODOMITE, SODOMITES (KJV) MALE SHRINE PROSTITUTES, SHRINE PROSTITUTE

SOFTEN (1)
Ps 65:10 you s it with showers and bless its crops. H4570

SOIL (37) [SOILED]
Ge 4: 2 Abel kept flocks, and Cain worked the s. H141
Ge 4: 3 of the fruits of the s as an offering to the H141
Ge 9:20 a man of the s, proceeded to plant a H141
Ex 23:19 the firstfruits of your s to the house of the H141
Ex 34:26 the firstfruits of your s to the house of the H141
Lev 26:20 because your s will not yield its crops H824
Lev 27:30 whether grain from the s or fruit from the H824
Nu 13:20 How is the s? Is it fertile or poor? Are there H824
Dt 26: 2 you produce from the s of the land the LORD H141
Dt 26:10 now I bring the firstfruits of the s that you, H141
1Ki 18:38 the stones and the s, and also licked up H6760
2Ch 26:10 in the fertile lands, for he loved the s. H141
Job 5: 6 For hardship does not spring from the s H6760
Job 8:19 and from the s other plants grow. H6760
Job 14: 8 in the ground and its stump die in the s, H6760
Job 14:19 stones and torrents wash away the s, H6760+824
Job 21:33 The s in the valley is sweet to them H8073
Ps 105:35 in their land, ate up the produce of their s. H141
SS 5: 3 washed my feet—must I s them again? H3245
Isa 28:24 he keep on breaking up and working the s? H141
Isa 30:24 donkeys that work the s will eat fodder H141
Isa 61:11 For as the s makes the sprout come up H824
Eze 17: 5 of the land and put it in fertile s. H8441
Eze 17: 8 planted in good s by abundant water so H8441
Mt 13: 5 where it did not have much s. G1178
Mt 13: 5 up quickly, because the s was shallow. G1178
Mt 13: 8 Still other seed fell on good s, where it G1178
Mt 13:23 seed falling on good s refers to someone G1178
Mk 4: 5 where it did not have much s. G1178
Mk 4: 5 up quickly, because the s was shallow. G1178
Mk 4: 8 Still other seed fell on good s. It came up G1178
Mk 4:20 like seed sown on good s, hear the word, G1178
Mk 4:28 All by itself the s produces grain—first the G1178
Lk 8: 8 Still other seed fell on good s. It came up G1178
Lk 8:15 But the seed on good s stands for those G1178
Lk 13: 7 Why should it use up the s?' G1178
Lk 14:35 is fit neither for the s nor for the manure G1178

SOILED (1) [SOIL]
Rev 3: 4 in Sardis who have not s their clothes. G3662

SOJOURN, SOJOURNED, SOJOURNER, SOJOURNERS, SOJOURNETH, SOJOURNING
(KJV) DWELL, FOREIGNER, GUEST, LIVE, LIVED, LIVES, LIVING, RESIDED, RESIDES, RESIDING, SETTLE, SETTLED, STAY, STAYED, STAYING, STRANGER, STRANGERS, TEMPORARY RESIDENTS

SOKO (3)
1Ch 4:18 Heber the father of S, and Jekuthiel the H8459
2Ch 11: 7 Beth Zur, S, Adullam, H8459
2Ch 28:18 as well as S, Timnah and Gimzo, H8459

SOKOH (5)
Jos 15:35 Jarmuth, Adullam, S, Azekah, H8458
Jos 15:48 In the hill country: Shamir, Jattir, S, H8458
1Sa 17: 1 war and assembled at S in Judah. H8458
1Sa 17: 1 Ephes Dammim, between S and Azekah. H8458
1Ki 4:10 (S and all the land of Hepher were his); H8458

SOLD (73) [SELL]
Ge 31:15 Not only has he s us, but he has used up H4835
Ge 37:28 of the cistern and s him for twenty shekels H4835
Ge 37:36 the Midianites s Joseph in Egypt to H4835
Ge 41:56 storehouses and s grain to the Egyptians, H8690
Ge 42: 6 the person who s grain to all its people. H8690
Ge 45: 4 brother Joseph, the one you s into Egypt! H4835
Ge 47:20 one and all, s their fields, because the H4835
Ex 21:16 whether the victim has been s or is still in H4835
Ex 22: 3 they must be s to pay for their theft. H4835
Lev 25:16 because what is really being s to you is H4835
Lev 25:23 " 'The land must not be s permanently H4835
Lev 25:25 is to come and redeem what they have s. H4928
Lev 25:27 the years since they s it and refund the H4928
Lev 25:27 the balance to the one to whom they s it; H4835
Lev 25:28 what was s will remain in the possession H4928
Lev 25:33 a house s in any town they hold H4928
Lev 25:34 belonging to their towns must not be s; H4835
Lev 25:42 Egypt, they must not be s as slaves. H4835+4929
Lev 25:48 redemption after they have s themselves. H4835
Lev 25:50 the year they s themselves up to the Year H4835
Lev 27:20 or if they have s it to someone else H4835
Lev 27:27 not redeemed, it is to be s at its set value. H4835
Lev 27:28 family land—may be s or redeemed H4835
Dt 32:30 unless their Rock had s them, unless the H4835
Jdg 2:14 He s them into the hands of their H4835
Jdg 3: 8 Israel so that he s them into the hands H4835
Jdg 4: 2 So the LORD s them into the hands of Jabin H4835
Jdg 10: 7 He s them into the hands of the H4835
1Sa 12: 9 so he s them into the hand of Sisera H4835
1Ki 21:20 "because you have s yourself to do evil in H4835
1Ki 21:25 who s himself to do evil in the eyes of the H4835
2Ki 6:25 a donkey's head s for eighty shekels H2118+928
2Ki 7:16 of the finest flour s for a shekel, H2118+928
2Ki 7:16 two seahs of barley s for a shekel, as NDT
2Ki 17:17 omens and s themselves to do evil in H4835
Ne 5: 8 fellow Jews who were s to the Gentiles. H4835
Ne 5: 8 people, only for them to be s back to us!" H4835
Est 7: 4 I and my people have been s to be H4835
Est 7: 4 If we had merely been s as male and H4835
Ps 44:12 You s your people for a pittance, gaining H4835
Ps 105:17 man before them—Joseph, s as a slave. H4835
Isa 50: 1 Because of your sins you were s; because H4835
Isa 52: 3 "You were s for nothing, and without H4835
Jer 34:14 Hebrews who have s themselves to you. H4835
Eze 7:13 will not recover the property that was s— H4928
Hos 8: 9 Ephraim has s herself to lovers. H9479
Hos 8:10 Although they have s themselves among H9479
Joel 3: 3 prostitutes; they s girls for wine to drink. H4835
Joel 3: 6 You s the people of Judah and Jerusalem H4835
Joel 3: 7 out of the places to which you s them, H4835
Am 1: 6 whole communities and s them to Edom, H6037
Am 1: 9 Because she s whole communities of H6037
Mt 10:29 Are not two sparrows s for a penny? Yet G4797
Mt 13:44 in his joy went and s all he had and G4797
Mt 13:46 he went away and s everything he had G4405
Mt 18:25 all that he had be s to repay the debt. G4405
Mt 26: 9 have been s at a high price and the G4405
Mk 14: 5 It could have been s for more than a year's G4405
Lk 12: 6 Are not five sparrows s for two pennies G4797
Jn 2:16 To those who s doves he said, "Get these G4797
Jn 12: 5 this perfume s and the money given G4405
Ac 2:45 They s property and possessions to give to G4405
Ac 4:34 from time to time those who owned land or houses s G4797
Ac 4:37 s a field he owned and brought the money G4797
Ac 5: 1 wife Sapphira, also s a piece of property. G4797
Ac 5: 4 Didn't it belong to you before it was s G3531S
Ac 5: 4 And after it was s, wasn't the money at G4405
Ac 7: 9 of Joseph, they s him as a slave into Egypt. G625
Ro 7:14 I am unspiritual, s as a slave to sin. G4405
1Co 10:25 Eat anything s in the meat market without G4797
Heb 12:16 who for a single meal s his inheritance G625
Rev 18:13 human beings s as slaves. G5393+2779+6034
Rev 18:15 The merchants who s these things and G1867

SOLDIER (13) [SOLDIERS]
Nu 31:53 Each s had taken plunder for himself. H408+7372
1Sa 13:22 of the battle not a s with Saul and H6639
2Sa 17:10 Then even the bravest s, whose H1201+2657
2Ki 5: 1 He was a valiant s, but he had H1475+2657
2Ch 17:17 Eliada, a valiant s, with 200,000 H1475+2657
Am 2:15 the fleet-footed s will not get away, and H2257S
Ac 10: 7 a devout s who was one of his G5132
Ac 28:16 to live by himself, with a s to guard him. G5132
1Co 9: 7 Who serves as a s at his own expense G5129
Php 2:25 co-worker and fellow s, who is also your G5369
2Ti 2: 3 in suffering, like a good s of Christ Jesus. G5132
2Ti 2: 4 No one serving as a s gets entangled in G5129
Phm 2 our sister and Archippus our fellow s— G5369

SOLDIERS (80) [SOLDIER]
Nu 31:21 said to the s who had gone into H408+7372
Nu 31:27 between the s who took part in H9530+4878
Nu 31:28 From the s who fought in the battle H408+4878
Nu 31:32 spoils that the s took was 675,000 H6639+7372
Nu 31:49 have counted the s under our H408+4878
Dt 20: 8 go home so that his fellow s will not become AIT
Jos 8:13 So the s took up their positions—with the H6639
Jos 17: 1 because the Makirites were great s. H408+4878
Jdg 20:16 Among all these s there were seven H6639
1Sa 4: 3 When the s returned to camp, the elders H6639
1Sa 4:10 Israel lost thirty thousand foot s. H8081
1Sa 13: 5 s as numerous as the sand on the H6639
1Sa 14:28 Then one of the s told him, "Your father H6639
1Sa 15: 4 hundred thousand foot s and ten H8081
1Sa 15:15 "The s brought them from the Amalekites H6639
1Sa 15:21 The s took sheep and cattle from the H6639
1Sa 26: 7 Abner and the s were lying around him H6639
2Sa 3:23 When Joab and all the s with him arrived H7372
2Sa 8: 4 and twenty thousand foot s. H408+8081
2Sa 10: 6 Aramean foot s from Beth Rehob H8081
2Sa 10:18 forty thousand of their foot s. H8081
2Sa 11: 7 how the s were and how the war was H6639
1Ki 20:29 on the Aramean foot s in one day. H8081
2Ki 13: 7 ten chariots and ten thousand foot s, for H8081
2Ki 25: 5 All his s were separated from him and H2657
1Ch 12:33 experienced s prepared for battle H3655+7372
1Ch 12:36 experienced s prepared for battle H3655+7372
1Ch 18: 4 and twenty thousand foot s. H408+8081
1Ch 19:18 and forty thousand of their foot s. H408+8081
2Ch 26:15 so that s could shoot arrows and hurl AIT
2Ch 28: 6 and twenty thousand s in Judah— H1201+2657
2Ch 28:14 So the s gave up the prisoners and H2741
Ezr 8:22 to ask the king for s and horsemen to H2657
Jer 38: 4 is discouraging the s who are left in H408+4878
Jer 39: 4 of Judah and all the s saw them, H408+4878
Jer 41: 3 as the Babylonian s who were there. H408+4878
Jer 41:16 of Ahikam—the s, women, H1505+408+4878
Jer 49:26 all her s will be silenced in that day," H408+4878
Jer 50:30 all her s will be silenced in that day," H408+4878
Jer 51:32 set on fire, and the s terrified. H408+4878
Jer 52: 8 All his s were separated from him and H2657
Eze 27:10 and Put served as s in your army. H408+4878
Eze 27:27 your merchants and all your s, and H408+4878
Eze 39:20 mighty men and s of every kind,' H408+4878
Da 3:20 some of the strongest s in his A10132+10264
Da 3:22 the fire killed the s who took up A10131
Joel 2: 7 like warriors; they scale walls like s. H408+4878
Na 2: 3 The shields of the s are red; the warriors H1475
Mt 8: 9 a man under authority, with s under me. G5132
Mt 27:27 Then the governor's s took Jesus into the G5132
Mt 27:27 the whole company of s around him. G5061
Mt 28:12 they gave the s a large sum of money G5132
Mt 28:15 So the s took the money and did as they G3836S
Mk 15:16 The s led Jesus away into the palace (that G5132
Mk 15:16 called together the whole company of s. G5061
Lk 3:14 Then some s asked him, "And what G5129
Lk 7: 8 a man under authority, with s under me. G5132
Lk 23:11 Then Herod and his s ridiculed and G5128
Lk 23:26 As the s led him away, they seized Simon NDT
Lk 23:36 The s also came up and mocked him G5132
Jn 18: 3 guiding a detachment of s and some G5061
Jn 18:12 Then the detachment of s with its G5061
Jn 19: 2 The s twisted together a crown of thorns G5132
Jn 19:16 So the s took charge of Jesus. NDT
Jn 19:23 When the s crucified Jesus, they took his G5132
Jn 19:24 So this is what the s did. G5132
Jn 19:32 The s therefore came and broke the legs G5132
Jn 19:34 one of the s pierced Jesus' side with a G5132
Ac 12: 4 be guarded by four squads of four s each. G5132
Ac 12: 6 Peter was sleeping between two s, bound G5132
Ac 12:18 commotion among the s as to what had G5132
Ac 21:32 some officers and s and ran down to the G5132
Ac 21:32 the rioters saw the commander and his s, G5132
Ac 21:35 so great he had to be carried by the s. G5132
Ac 21:37 As the s were about to take Paul into the NDT
Ac 23:23 ready a detachment of two hundred s, G5132
Ac 23:31 So the s, carrying out their orders, took G5132
Ac 27:31 Then Paul said to the centurion and the s G5132
Ac 27:32 So the s cut the ropes that held the G5132
Ac 27:42 The s planned to kill the prisoners to G5132

SOLE (4) [SOLES]
Dt 28:56 touch the ground with the s of her foot— H4090
Dt 28:65 no resting place for the s of your foot. H4090
2Sa 14:25 of his head to the s of his foot there was H4090
Isa 1: 6 From the s of your foot to the top of your H4090

SOLEMN (6) [SOLEMNLY]
Ge 50:11 are holding a s ceremony of mourning." H3878
Jos 6:26 that time Joshua pronounced this s oath: H8678
Jdg 21: 5 they had taken a s oath that anyone who H1524
Ps 138: 2 so exalted your s decree that it surpasses H614
Eze 16: 8 I gave you my s oath and entered into a H8678

Ac 23:14 “We *have* **taken a s oath** not to eat *G353+354*

SOLEMNITIES, SOLEMNITY (KJV) FESTIVAL, FESTIVALS

SOLEMNLY (8) [SOLEMN]

Ge 43: 3 “The man **warned** us s, ‘You will H6386+6386
Dt 1:34 what you said, he was angry and **s swore**: H8678
Dt 4:21 and *he* **s swore** that I would not cross the H8678
Dt 32:40 I lift my hand to heaven and **s swear**: As H606
Dt 32:46 all the words I *have* **s declared** to you this H6386
Jos 5: 6 see the land he *had* **s promised** their H8678
Jdg 17: 3 “*I* **s consecrate** my silver to the LORD H7727+7727
1Sa 8: 9 but **warn** them s and let them know H6386+6386

SOLES (7) [SOLE]

Dt 28:35 spreading from the **s** *of* your feet to the H4090
2Ki 19:24 With the **s** *of* my feet I have dried up all H4090
Job 2: 7 sores from the **s** *of* his feet to the crown H4090
Job 13:27 by putting marks on the **s** *of* my feet. H9247
Isa 37:25 With the **s** *of* my feet I have dried up all H4090
Eze 43: 7 throne and the place for the **s** *of* my feet. H4090
Mal 4: 3 be ashes under the **s** *of* your feet on the H4090

SOLID (7)

Nu 4: 6 spread a cloth of **s** blue over that and put H4003
2Ch 4:21 lamps and tongs (they were **s** gold); H4816
Zec 4: 2 “I see a **s** gold lampstand with a bowl at H3972
1Co 3: 2 you milk, not **s food**, for you were not *G1109*
2Ti 2:19 God's **s** foundation stands firm *G5104*
Heb 5:12 all over again. You need milk, not **s** food! *G5104*
Heb 5:14 But **s** food is for the mature, who by *G5104*

SOLITARY (5)

Mt 14:13 he withdrew by boat privately to a **s** place. *G2245*
Mk 1:35 left the house and went off to a **s** place *G2245*
Mk 6:32 by themselves in a boat to a **s** place. *G2245*
Lk 4:42 Jesus went out to a **s** place. The people *G2245*
Lk 8:29 been driven by the demon into **s places**. *G2245*

SOLOMON (249) [SOLOMON'S]

2Sa 5:14 Shammua, Shobab, Nathan, S, H8976
2Sa 12:24 birth to a son, and they named him S. H8976
1Ki 1:10 the special guard or his brother S. H8976
1Ki 1:12 your own life and the life of your son S. H8976
1Ki 1:13 “Surely S your son shall be king after me H8976
1Ki 1:17 ‘S your son shall be king after me, and he H8976
1Ki 1:19 he has not invited S your servant. H8976
1Ki 1:21 I and my son S will be treated as H8976
1Ki 1:26 your servant S he did not invite. H8976
1Ki 1:30 S your son shall be king after me, and he H8976
1Ki 1:33 with you and have S my son mount my H8976
1Ki 1:34 the trumpet and shout, ‘Long live King S! H8976
1Ki 1:37 so may he be with S to make his throne H8976
1Ki 1:38 went down and had S mount King David's H8976
1Ki 1:39 oil from the sacred tent and anointed S. H8976
1Ki 1:39 all the people shouted, “Long live King S!” H8976
1Ki 1:43 “Our lord King David has made S king. H8976
1Ki 1:46 S has taken his seat on the royal throne. H8976
1Ki 1:50 Adonijah, in fear of S, went and took hold H8976
1Ki 1:51 Then S was told, “Adonijah is afraid of H8976
1Ki 1:51 is afraid of King S and is clinging to the H8976
1Ki 1:51 ‘Let King S swear to me today that he will H8976
1Ki 1:52 S replied, “If he shows himself to be H8976
1Ki 1:53 Then King S sent men, and they brought H8976
1Ki 1:53 came and bowed down to King S, H8976
1Ki 1:53 to King Solomon, and S said, “Go to your H8976
1Ki 2: 1 he gave a charge to S his son. H8976
1Ki 2:12 So S sat on the throne of his father David H8976
1Ki 2:17 “Please ask King S—he will not refuse H8976
1Ki 2:19 went to King S to speak to him for H8976
1Ki 2:22 King S answered his mother, “Why do you H8976
1Ki 2:23 Then King S swore by the LORD: “May God H8976
1Ki 2:25 So King S gave orders to Benaiah son of H8976
1Ki 2:27 So S removed Abiathar from the H8976
1Ki 2:29 King S was told that Joab had fled to the H8976
1Ki 2:29 Then S ordered Benaiah son of Jehoiada H8976
1Ki 2:41 When S was told that Shimei had gone H8976
1Ki 2:45 But King S will be blessed, and David's H8976
1Ki 3: 1 S made an alliance with Pharaoh king of H8976
1Ki 3: 3 S showed his love for the LORD by walking H8976
1Ki 3: 4 S offered a thousand burnt offerings H8976
1Ki 3: 5 the LORD appeared to S during the night in H8976
1Ki 3: 6 S answered, “You have shown great H8976
1Ki 3:10 was pleased that S had asked for this. H8976
1Ki 3:15 Then S awoke—and he realized it had H8976
1Ki 4: 1 So King S ruled over all Israel. H8976
1Ki 4: 7 S had twelve district governors over all H8976
1Ki 4:11 he was married to Taphath daughter of S); H8976
1Ki 4:15 he had married Basemath daughter of S); H8976
1Ki 4:21 And S ruled over all the kingdoms from H8976
1Ki 4:26 S had four thousand stalls for chariot H8976
1Ki 4:27 provisions for King S and all who came to H8976
1Ki 4:29 God gave S wisdom and very great insight H8976
1Ki 5: 1 of Tyre heard that S had been anointed H2257S
1Ki 5: 1 he sent his envoys to S, because he had H8976
1Ki 5: 2 S sent back this message to Hiram: H8976
1Ki 5: 8 So Hiram sent word to S: “I have received H8976
1Ki 5:10 this way Hiram kept S supplied with all H8976
1Ki 5:11 S gave Hiram twenty thousand cors of H8976
1Ki 5:11 S continued to do this for Hiram year after H8976
1Ki 5:12 The LORD gave S wisdom, just as he had H8976
1Ki 5:12 peaceful relations between Hiram and S, H8976
1Ki 5:13 King S conscripted laborers from all Israel H8976
1Ki 5:15 S had seventy thousand carriers and eighty H8976
1Ki 5:18 The craftsmen of S and Hiram and workers H8976
1Ki 6: 2 The temple that King S built for the LORD H8976
1Ki 6:11 The word of the LORD came to S: H8976
1Ki 6:14 So S built the temple and completed it. H8976
1Ki 6:21 S covered the inside of the temple with H8976
1Ki 7: 1 It took S thirteen years, however, to H8976
1Ki 7: 8 S also made a palace like this hall for H8976
1Ki 7:13 King S sent to Tyre and brought Huram, H8976
1Ki 7:14 He came to King S and did all the work H8976
1Ki 7:40 undertaken for King S in the temple of the H8976
1Ki 7:45 Huram made for King S for the temple of H8976
1Ki 7:47 S left all these things unweighed, because H8976
1Ki 7:48 S also made all the furnishings that were H8976
1Ki 7:51 all the work King S had done for the H8976
1Ki 8: 1 Then King S summoned into his presence H8976
1Ki 8: 2 came together to King S at the time of the H8976
1Ki 8: 5 King S and the entire assembly of H8976
1Ki 8:12 Then S said, “The LORD has said that he H8976
1Ki 8:22 Then S stood before the altar of the LORD H8976
1Ki 8:54 When S had finished all these prayers H8976
1Ki 8:63 S offered a sacrifice of fellowship offerings H8976
1Ki 8:65 So S observed the festival at that time H8976
1Ki 9: 1 When S had finished building the temple H8976
1Ki 9:10 during which S built these two buildings— H8976
1Ki 9:11 King S gave twenty towns in Galilee to H8976
1Ki 9:12 to see the towns that S had given him, H8976
1Ki 9:15 forced labor King S conscripted to build H8976
1Ki 9:17 And S rebuilt Gezer.) He built up Lower H8976
1Ki 9:21 S conscripted the descendants of all these H8976
1Ki 9:22 But S did not make slaves of any of the H8976
1Ki 9:24 of David to the palace S had built for her, NDT
1Ki 9:25 Three times a year S sacrificed burnt H8976
1Ki 9:26 King S also built ships at Ezion Geber H8976
1Ki 9:28 of gold, which they delivered to King S. H8976
1Ki 10: 1 about the fame of S and his relationship H8976
1Ki 10: 1 she came to test S with hard questions. H2257S
1Ki 10: 2 she came to S and talked with him about H8976
1Ki 10: 3 S answered all her questions; nothing was H8976
1Ki 10: 4 all the wisdom of S and the palace he H8976
1Ki 10:10 those the queen of Sheba gave to King S. H8976
1Ki 10:13 King S gave the queen of Sheba all she H8976
1Ki 10:14 of the gold that S received yearly was 666 H8976
1Ki 10:16 King S made two hundred large shields of H8976
1Ki 10:23 King S was greater in riches and wisdom H8976
1Ki 10:24 audience with S to hear the wisdom H8976
1Ki 10:26 S accumulated chariots and horses; he H8976
1Ki 11: 1 King S, however, loved many foreign H8976
1Ki 11: 2 Nevertheless, S held fast to them in love H8976
1Ki 11: 4 As S grew old, his wives turned his heart H8976
1Ki 11: 6 So S did evil in the eyes of the LORD; he H8976
1Ki 11: 7 S built a high place for Chemosh the H8976
1Ki 11: 9 became angry with S because his heart H8976
1Ki 11:10 he had forbidden S to follow other gods, H2257S
1Ki 11:10 S did not keep the LORD's command. NDT
1Ki 11:11 So the LORD said to S, “Since this is your H8976
1Ki 11:14 the LORD raised up against S an adversary, H8976
1Ki 11:23 raised up against S another adversary, H2257S
1Ki 11:25 was Israel's adversary as long as S lived, H8976
1Ki 11:27 S had built the terraces and had filled in H8976
1Ki 11:28 when S saw how well the young man H8976
1Ki 11:40 S tried to kill Jeroboam, but Jeroboam H8976
1Ki 11:41 not written in the book of the annals of S? H8976
1Ki 11:42 S reigned in Jerusalem over all Israel forty H8976
1Ki 12: 2 where he had fled from King S), he H8976
1Ki 12: 6 served his father S during his lifetime. H8976
1Ki 12:21 the kingdom for Rehoboam son of S. H8976
1Ki 12:23 “Say to Rehoboam son of S king of Judah H8976
1Ki 14:21 Rehoboam son of S was king in Judah H8976
1Ki 14:26 all the gold shields S had made. H8976
2Ki 21: 7 LORD had said to David and to his son S, H8976
2Ki 23:13 the ones S king of Israel had built for H8976
2Ki 24:13 the gold articles that S king of Israel had H8976
2Ki 25:16 which S had made for the temple of the H8976
1Ch 3: 5 Shobab, Nathan and S. These four were H8976
1Ch 6:10 priest in the temple S built in Jerusalem), H8976
1Ch 6:32 until S built the temple of the LORD in H8976
1Ch 14: 4 Shammua, Shobab, Nathan, S, H8976
1Ch 18: 8 which S used to make the bronze Sea H8976
1Ch 22: 5 “My son S is young and inexperienced H8976
1Ch 22: 6 called for his son S and charged him to H8976
1Ch 22: 7 David said to S: “My son, I had it in my H8976
1Ch 22: 9 His name will be S, and I will grant Israel H8976
1Ch 22:17 all the leaders of Israel to help his son S. H8976
1Ch 23: 1 he made his son S king over Israel. H8976
1Ch 28: 5 he has chosen my son S to sit on the H8976
1Ch 28: 6 ‘S your son is the one who will build my H8976
1Ch 28: 9 “And you, my son S, acknowledge the H8976
1Ch 28:11 David gave his son S the plans for the H8976
1Ch 28:20 David also said to S his son, “Be strong H8976
1Ch 29: 1 “My son S, the one whom God has H8976
1Ch 29:19 And give my son S the wholehearted H8976
1Ch 29:22 they acknowledged S son of David as king H8976
1Ch 29:23 So S sat on the throne of the LORD as king H8976
1Ch 29:24 pledged their submission to King S. H8976
1Ch 29:25 LORD highly exalted S in the sight of all H8976
1Ch 29:28 His son S succeeded him as king. H8976
2Ch 1: 1 S son of David established himself firmly H8976
2Ch 1: 2 Then S spoke to all Israel—to the H8976
2Ch 1: 3 S and the whole assembly went to the H8976
2Ch 1: 5 so S and the assembly inquired of him H8976
2Ch 1: 6 S went up to the bronze altar before the H8976
2Ch 1: 7 night God appeared to S and said to him, H8976
2Ch 1: 8 S answered God, “You have shown great H8976
2Ch 1:11 God said to S, “Since this is your heart's H8976
2Ch 1:13 Then S went to Jerusalem from the high H8976
2Ch 1:14 S accumulated chariots and horses; he H8976
2Ch 2: 1 S gave orders to build a temple for the H8976
2Ch 2: 3 S sent this message to Hiram king of Tyre H8976
2Ch 2:11 Hiram king of Tyre replied by letter to S H8976
2Ch 2:17 S took a census of all the foreigners H8976
2Ch 3: 1 Then S began to build the temple of the H8976
2Ch 3: 3 The foundation S laid for building the H8976
2Ch 4:11 undertaken for King S in the temple of H8976
2Ch 4:16 made for King S for the temple of the H8976
2Ch 4:18 these things that S made amounted to so H8976
2Ch 4:19 S also made all the furnishings that were H8976
2Ch 5: 1 When all the work S had done for the H8976
2Ch 5: 2 Then S summoned to Jerusalem the H8976
2Ch 5: 6 King S and the entire assembly of H8976
2Ch 6: 1 Then S said, “The LORD has said that he H8976
2Ch 6:12 Then S stood before the altar of the LORD in NDT
2Ch 7: 1 When S finished praying, fire came down H8976
2Ch 7: 5 And King S offered a sacrifice of H8976
2Ch 7: 7 S consecrated the middle part of the H8976
2Ch 7: 8 So S observed the festival at that time H8976
2Ch 7:10 done for David and S and for his people H8976
2Ch 7:11 When S had finished the temple of the H8976
2Ch 8: 1 during which S built the temple of the H8976
2Ch 8: 2 S rebuilt the villages that Hiram had given H8976
2Ch 8: 3 S then went to Hamath Zobah and H8976
2Ch 8: 8 S conscripted the descendants of all these H8976
2Ch 8: 9 But S did not make slaves of the Israelites H8976
2Ch 8:11 S brought Pharaoh's daughter up from the H8976
2Ch 8:12 S sacrificed burnt offerings to the LORD H8976
2Ch 8:17 Then S went to Ezion Geber and Elath on H8976
2Ch 8:18 of gold, which they delivered to King S. H8976
2Ch 9: 1 she came to S and talked with him about H8976
2Ch 9: 2 S answered all her questions; nothing was H8976
2Ch 9: 3 the queen of Sheba saw the wisdom of S, H8976
2Ch 9: 9 those the queen of Sheba gave to King S. H8976
2Ch 9:10 the servants of S brought gold from H8976
2Ch 9:12 King S gave the queen of Sheba all she H8976
2Ch 9:13 of the gold that S received yearly was 666 H8976
2Ch 9:14 the territories brought gold and silver to S. H8976
2Ch 9:15 King S made two hundred large shields of H8976
2Ch 9:22 King S was greater in riches and wisdom H8976
2Ch 9:23 audience with S to hear the wisdom H8976
2Ch 9:25 S had four thousand stalls for horses and H8976
2Ch 9:30 S reigned in Jerusalem over all Israel forty H8976
2Ch 10: 2 where he had fled from King S), he H8976
2Ch 10: 6 served his father S during his lifetime. H8976
2Ch 11: 3 to Rehoboam son of S king of Judah and H8976
2Ch 11:17 Rehoboam son of S three years, H8976
2Ch 11:17 the ways of David and S during this time. H8976
2Ch 12: 9 including the gold shields S had made. H8976
2Ch 13: 6 an official of S son of David H8976
2Ch 13: 7 Rehoboam son of S when he was young H8976
2Ch 30:26 since the days of S son of David king of H8976
2Ch 33: 7 God had said to David and to his son S, H8976
2Ch 35: 3 in the temple that S son of David king of H8976
2Ch 35: 4 by David king of Israel and by his son S. H8976
Ezr 2:55 The descendants of the servants of S: the H8976
Ezr 2:58 the descendants of the servants of S 392 H8976
Ne 7:57 The descendants of the servants of S: the H8976
Ne 7:60 the descendants of the servants of S 392 H8976
Ne 12:45 to the commands of David and his son S. H8976
Ne 13:26 like these that S king of Israel sinned? H8976
Ps 72: T Of S. H8976
Ps 127: T A song of ascents. Of S. H8976
Pr 1: 1 The proverbs of S son of David, king of H8976
Pr 10: 1 The proverbs of S: A wise son brings joy H8976
Pr 25: 1 These are more proverbs of S, compiled H8976
SS 1: 5 tents of Kedar, like the tent curtains of S. H8976
SS 3: 9 King S made for himself the carriage; he H8976
SS 3:11 Look on King S wearing a crown, the H8976
SS 8:11 S had a vineyard in Baal Hamon; he let H8976
SS 8:12 are for you, S, and two hundred are H8976
Jer 52:20 which King S had made for the temple of H8976
Mt 1: 6 David was the father of S, whose mother *G5048*
Mt 1: 7 S the father of Rehoboam, Rehoboam the *G5048*
Mt 6:29 tell you that not even S in all his splendor *G5048*
Mt 12:42 now something greater *than* S is here. *G5048*
Lk 11:31 now something greater *than* S is here. *G5048*
Lk 12:27 not even S in all his splendor was dressed *G5048*
Ac 7:47 But it was S who built a house for him. *G5048*

SOLOMON'S (41) [SOLOMON]

1Ki 1:11 asked Bathsheba, S mother, “Have you H8976
1Ki 1:47 your God make S name more famous H8976
1Ki 2:13 of Haggith, went to Bathsheba, S mother. H8976
1Ki 2:46 kingdom was now established in S hands. H8976
1Ki 4:21 tribute and were S subjects all his life. H8976
1Ki 4:22 S daily provisions were thirty cors of the H8976
1Ki 4:25 During S lifetime Judah and Israel, from H8976
1Ki 4:30 S wisdom was greater than the wisdom of H8976
1Ki 4:34 people came to listen to S wisdom, H8976
1Ki 5: 7 When Hiram heard S message, he was H8976
1Ki 6: 1 in the fourth year of S reign over Israel, in H8976
1Ki 9:16 as a wedding gift to his daughter, S wife. H8976
1Ki 9:23 officials in charge of S projects— H4200+8976
1Ki 9:27 the sea—to serve in the fleet with S men. H8976
1Ki 10:21 All King S goblets were gold, and all the H8976

S

1Ki 10:21 was considered of little value in S days. H8976
1Ki 10:28 S horses were imported from Egypt H4200+8976
1Ki 11:26 He was one of S officials, an H4200+8976
1Ki 11:31 the kingdom out of S hand and give you H8976
1Ki 11:33 decrees and laws as David, S father, did. H2257S
1Ki 11:34 take the whole kingdom out of S hand; H2257S
1Ki 11:40 the king, and stayed there until S death. H8976
1Ki 11:41 As for the other events of S reign—all he H8976
1Ch 3:10 S son was Rehoboam, Abijah his son H8976
2Ch 1:16 S horses were imported from Egypt H4200+8976
2Ch 8:10 were also King S chief officials— H4200+8976
2Ch 8:16 All S work was carried out, from the day H8976
2Ch 8:18 with S men, sailed to Ophir and H8976
2Ch 9: 1 the queen of Sheba heard of S fame, H8976
2Ch 9:20 All King S goblets were gold, and all the H8976
2Ch 9:20 was considered of little value in S day. H8976
2Ch 9:28 S horses were imported from Egypt H4200+8976
2Ch 9:29 As for the other events of S reign, from H8976
Ne 11: 3 descendants of S servants lived in the H8976
SS 1: 1 S Song of Songs. H4200+8976
SS 3: 7 It is S carriage, escorted by H8611+4200+8976
Mt 12:42 ends of the earth to listen to S wisdom, *G5048*
Lk 11:31 ends of the earth to listen to S wisdom; *G5048*
Jn 10:23 temple courts walking in S Colonnade. *G5048*
Ac 3:11 to them in the place called S Colonnade. *G5048*
Ac 5:12 used to meet together in S Colonnade. *G5048*

SOLVE (2) [SOLVED]

Da 5:12 explain riddles and s difficult problems. A10742
Da 5:16 to s difficult problems. A10742

SOLVED (1) [SOLVE]

Jdg 14:18 *you would* not *have* s my riddle. H5162

SOMBER (1)

Mt 6:16 do not look s as the hypocrites do *G5034*

SOME (578) [SOMEBODY, SOMEHOW, SOMEONE, SOMEONE'S, SOMETHING, SOMETIMES, SOMEWHAT, SOMEWHERE]

Ge 3: 6 gaining wisdom, she took s and ate it. H4946
Ge 3: 6 She also gave s to her husband, who was NDT
Ge 3:12 she gave me s fruit from the tree H4946
Ge 4: 3 of time Cain brought s *of* the fruits of the H4946
Ge 4: 4 fat portions from s *of* the firstborn of his H4946
Ge 8:20 taking s *of* all the clean animals and H4946
Ge 9:21 When he drank s *of* its wine, he became H4946
Ge 14:10 *s of the men* **fell** into them and the rest fled AIT
Ge 18: 6 finest flour and knead it and bake *s* **bread.**" AIT
Ge 18: 8 He then brought *s* **curds** and milk and the calf AIT
Ge 21:14 Abraham took *s* **food** and a skin of water AIT
Ge 22: 1 S time later God tested Abraham. H339+2021+1821+2021+465
Ge 22:20 S time later Abraham was told, H339+2021+1821+2021+465
Ge 23: 4 Sell me *s* **property** *for* a burial site here so I AIT
Ge 25:29 Once when Jacob was cooking *s* **stew,** Esau AIT
Ge 25:30 let me have s *of* that red stew! H4946
Ge 25:34 Jacob gave Esau *s* **bread** and some lentil AIT
Ge 25:34 gave Esau some bread and *s* lentil **stew.** AIT
Ge 27: 3 the open country to hunt *s* **wild game** for me. AIT
Ge 27: 7 'Bring me *s* **game** and prepare me some tasty AIT
Ge 27: 7 game and prepare me *s* **tasty food** to eat, AIT
Ge 27: 9 so I can prepare *s* **tasty food** for your father AIT
Ge 27:14 she prepared *s* **tasty food,** just the way AIT
Ge 27:19 Please sit up and eat s *of* my game, so H4946
Ge 27:25 "My son, bring me s *of* your game to eat H4946
Ge 27:25 and he brought *s* **wine** and he drank. AIT
Ge 27:31 He too prepared *s* **tasty food** and brought it to AIT
Ge 27:31 please sit up and eat s *of* my game, so H4946
Ge 29:19 that I give her to you than to *s* **other** man. AIT
Ge 30:14 into the fields and found *s* **mandrake plants,** AIT
Ge 30:14 "Please give me s *of* your son's H4946
Ge 30:21 S time later she gave birth to a daughter H339
Ge 31:46 relatives, "Gather *s* **stones.**" So they took AIT
Ge 32:16 and keep *s* **space** between the herds." AIT
Ge 33:15 "Then let me leave s *of* my men with you." H4946
Ge 35:16 were still s distance from H3896+2021+824
Ge 36: 6 to a land s distance from his H4946+7156
Ge 37:33 S ferocious animal has devoured him NDT
Ge 40: 1 S time later, the H339+2021+1821+2021+465
Ge 40: 4 After they had been in custody *for* s time, H3427
Ge 42: 2 Go down there and buy s for us, so that we NDT
Ge 43:11 Put s *of* the best products of the land in H4946
Ge 43:11 a little honey, *s* **spices** and myrrh, some AIT
Ge 43:11 myrrh, *s* **pistachio nuts** and almonds. AIT
Ge 45:19 Take s carts from Egypt for your children and AIT
Ge 48: 1 S time later Joseph was told, H339+2021+1821+2021+465
Ex 2:17 S shepherds came along and drove them H2021S
Ex 4: 9 take s water from the Nile and pour it on H4946
Ex 10:26 We have to use s *of* them in worshiping H4946
Ex 12: 7 they are to take s *of* the blood and put H4946
Ex 12:10 of it till morning; if s is left till morning H4946
Ex 12:22 in the basin and put s *of* the blood on the H4946
Ex 16:17 they were told; *s* **gathered** much, some little. AIT
Ex 16:17 were told; some gathered much, s little. NDT
Ex 16:20 s of them paid no attention to Moses H408S
Ex 16:27 s *of* the people went out on the seventh H4946
Ex 17: 5 Take with you s *of* the elders of Israel H4946
Ex 17: 9 "Choose s *of* our **men** and go out to fight the AIT
Ex 18:19 Listen now to me and *I will* **give** you *s* **advice** AIT
Ex 29:12 Take s *of* the bull's blood and put it on the H4946
Ex 29:20 take s *of* its blood and put it on the lobes H4946
Ex 29:21 And take s blood from the altar and some H4946
Ex 29:21 from the altar and s *of* the anointing oil H4946
Ex 30:36 Grind s *of* it to powder and place it in front H4946
Ex 33: 7 outside the camp s distance away, H8178+4946
Ex 34:16 And when you choose s *of* their daughters H4946
Lev 2: 7 be made of the finest flour and s olive oil. H928
Lev 4: 5 priest shall take s *of* the bull's blood and H4946
Lev 4: 6 blood and sprinkle s *of* it seven times H4946
Lev 4: 7 priest shall then put s *of* the blood on the H4946
Lev 4:16 priest is to take s *of* the bull's blood into H4946
Lev 4:18 He is to put s *of* the blood on the horns of H4946
Lev 4:25 priest shall take s *of* the blood of the sin H4946
Lev 4:30 the priest is to take s *of* the blood with his H4946
Lev 4:34 priest shall take s *of* the blood of the sin H4946
Lev 5: 9 is to splash s *of* the blood of the sin H4946
Lev 6:15 handful of the finest flour and s olive oil, H4946
Lev 8:11 He sprinkled s *of* the oil on the altar seven H4946
Lev 8:12 He poured s *of* the anointing oil on H4946
Lev 8:15 slaughtered the bull and took *s of* the **blood,** AIT
Lev 8:23 the ram and took s *of* its blood and put it H4946
Lev 8:24 forward and put s *of* the blood on the H4946
Lev 8:30 Then Moses took s *of* the anointing oil H4946
Lev 8:30 anointing oil and s *of* the blood from the H4946
Lev 11: 4 " 'There are s that only chew the cud or H4946
Lev 11:21 s flying insects that walk on all H4946+3972
Lev 11:40 Anyone who eats s *of* its carcass must H4946
Lev 14: 4 that two live clean birds and *s* cedar **wood,** AIT
Lev 14:14 The priest is to take s *of* the blood of the H4946
Lev 14:15 priest shall then take s *of* the log of oil, H4946
Lev 14:16 his finger sprinkle s *of* it before the LORD H4946
Lev 14:17 The priest is to put s *of* the oil remaining H4946
Lev 14:25 offering and take s *of* its blood and put it H4946
Lev 14:26 The priest is to pour s *of* the oil into the H4946
Lev 14:27 forefinger sprinkle s *of* the oil from his H4946
Lev 14:28 S *of* the oil in his palm he is to put on the H4946
Lev 14:49 he is to take two birds and *s* cedar **wood,** AIT
Lev 16:14 He is to take s *of* the bull's blood and with H4946
Lev 16:14 he shall sprinkle s *of* it with his finger H4946
Lev 16:18 He shall take s *of* the bull's blood and H4946
Lev 16:18 the bull's blood and s *of* the goat's blood H4946
Lev 16:19 He shall sprinkle s *of* the blood on it with H4946
Lev 24: 7 each stack put *s* pure **incense** as a memorial AIT
Lev 25:25 poor and sells s *of* their property, H4946
Lev 25:45 You may also buy s *of* the temporary H4946
Nu 2: 2 the tent of meeting s distance from it, H5584
Nu 5:17 Then he shall take s holy water in a clay jar NDT
Nu 5:17 in a clay jar and put s dust from the H4946
Nu 9: 6 But s *of them* could not celebrate the H408S
Nu 11: 1 them and consumed s *of* the outskirts of H928
Nu 11:17 I will take s of the power of the Spirit H4946
Nu 11:25 he took s of the power of the Spirit H4946
Nu 13: 2 "Send *s* **men** to explore the land of Canaan AIT
Nu 13:20 best to bring back s *of* the fruit of the land H4946
Nu 13:23 along with s pomegranates and figs. H4946
Nu 16:37 scatter the coals s distance away, H2134
Nu 19: 4 the priest is to take s *of* its blood on his H4946
Nu 19: 6 The priest is to take *s* cedar **wood,** hyssop AIT
Nu 19:17 put s ashes from the burned purification H4946
Nu 19:18 who is ceremonially clean is to take *s* **hyssop,** AIT
Nu 21: 1 the Israelites and captured s *of* them. H4946
Nu 22:40 gave s to Balaam and the officials who NDT
Nu 27:20 Give him s *of* your authority so the whole H4946
Nu 30:15 nullifies them s time after he hears about H339
Nu 31: 3 "Arm s *of* your men to go to war H4946+907
Nu 34: 3 side will include s *of* the Desert of Zin H4946
Nu 35:11 select *s* **towns** to be your cities of refuge, to AIT
Dt 1:13 Choose *s* **wise,** understanding and respected AIT
Dt 1:25 Taking with them s *of* the fruit of the land H4946
Dt 12:20 "I would like *s* **meat,**" then you may eat AIT
Dt 26: 2 take s *of* the firstfruits of all that you H4946
Dt 27: 2 set up *s* large **stones** and coat them with AIT
Jos 2: 2 s of the Israelites have come here tonight H408S
Jos 5:11 they ate s *of* the produce of the land: H4946
Jos 7: 1 of the tribe of Judah, took s of them. H4946
Jos 7:11 They have taken s *of* the devoted things H4946
Jos 10:18 of the cave, and post *s* **men** there to guard it. AIT
Jos 22:24 did it for fear that s day your descendants H4737
Jdg 4:19 "Please give me s water." She opened a H5071
Jdg 5:14 S came from Ephraim, whose roots were in NDT
Jdg 8: 5 "Give my troops *s* **bread;** they are worn out, AIT
Jdg 9:48 He took an ax and cut off *s* **branches,** which AIT
Jdg 11: 4 S time later, when the Ammonites H4946+3427
Jdg 14: 8 S time later, when he went back to H4946+3427
Jdg 14: 8 in it he saw a swarm of bees and *s* **honey.** AIT
Jdg 14: 9 he gave them s, and they too ate it. NDT
Jdg 16: 4 S time later, he fell in love with a H339+4027
Jdg 17: 5 an ephod and *s* **household gods** and AIT
Jdg 17: 8 town in search of s other place to stay. H889S
Jdg 18:14 *s* **household gods** and an image overlaid AIT
Jdg 18:22 When they *had* **gone** s distance from H8178
Jdg 18:25 or *s of* the **men** may get angry and attack you, AIT
Jdg 19:22 s *of* the wicked men of the city surrounded H408S
Ru 2:14 Have s bread and dip it in the wine H4946
Ru 2:14 the harvesters, he offered her *s* **roasted grain.** AIT
Ru 2:14 ate all she wanted and had s left over. H3855
Ru 2:16 Even pull out s stalks for her from the NDT
1Sa 2:15 "Give the priest *s* **meat** to roast; he won't AIT
1Sa 2:36 "Appoint me to s priestly office so I can H285
1Sa 6:19 But God struck down s *of* the inhabitants of H928
1Sa 8:12 S he will assign to be commanders of NDT
1Sa 9:11 they met *s* **young women** coming out to draw AIT
1Sa 10:27 But *s* **scoundrels** said, "How can this fellow AIT
1Sa 13: 7 *S* **Hebrews** even crossed the Jordan to the AIT
1Sa 14:14 armor-bearer killed s twenty men in an H3869
1Sa 14:30 had eaten today s *of* the plunder they H4946
1Sa 17:18 are and bring back *s* **assurance** *from* them. AIT
1Sa 19:13 garment and putting s goats' hair at the H2021S
1Sa 19:16 and at the head was s goats' hair. H2021S
1Sa 21: 4 there is *s* consecrated **bread** here—provided AIT
1Sa 24:10 *S* **urged** me to kill you, but I spared you; AIT
1Sa 26:13 on top of the hill s distance away; H4946+8158
1Sa 28:22 let me give you s food so you may eat H7326
1Sa 28:24 She took *s* **flour,** kneaded it and baked bread AIT
1Sa 30: 9 the Besor Valley, where s stayed behind. H3855
1Sa 30:14 s territory belonging to Judah and the H889S
1Sa 30:26 he sent s *of* the plunder to the elders of H4946
2Sa 2:14 "Let's have *s of* the **young men** get up and AIT
2Sa 3:17 "For s time you have H1685+9453+1685+8997
2Sa 4: 6 inner part of the house as if to get *s* **wheat,** AIT
2Sa 10: 9 so he selected s *of* the best troops H4946+3972
2Sa 11:17 s of the men in David's army fell H4946
2Sa 11:24 the wall, and s *of* the king's men died. H4946
2Sa 13: 6 to come and make s special bread in my H9109S
2Sa 13: 7 Amnon and prepare s food for him." H2021S
2Sa 13: 8 She took s dough, kneaded it, made the H2021S
2Sa 17: 9 he is hidden in a cave or s other place. H285S
1Ki 7:10 s measuring ten cubits and some eight. H74S
1Ki 7:10 some measuring ten cubits and s eight. H74S
1Ki 11:17 fled to Egypt with s Edomite officials who H4946
1Ki 13:25 *S* **people** who passed by saw the body lying AIT
1Ki 14: 3 of bread with you, *s* **cakes** and a jar of honey AIT
1Ki 17: 7 S time later the brook dried up because H3427
1Ki 17:17 S time later the son of the woman H339+2021+1821+2021+465
1Ki 18: 5 Maybe we can find *s* **grass** to keep the horses AIT
1Ki 19: 6 by his head was *s* **bread** baked over hot coals AIT
1Ki 20:20 on horseback with *s* of his **horsemen.** AIT
1Ki 21: 1 S time later there was an incident H339+2021+1821+2021+465
2Ki 2:16 set him down on s mountain or in some H285
2Ki 2:16 him down on some mountain or in s valley." H285
2Ki 2:23 *s* **boys** came out of the town and jeered at AIT
2Ki 4:38 large pot and cook *s* **stew** for these prophets." AIT
2Ki 4:41 Elisha said, "Get *s* **flour.**" He put it into the AIT
2Ki 4:42 ripe grain, along with *s* **heads of new grain.** AIT
2Ki 4:43 'They will eat and **have** *s* **left over.'** " AIT
2Ki 4:44 they ate and **had** *s* **left over,** according to AIT
2Ki 5:13 the prophet had told you to do *s* great **thing,** AIT
2Ki 5:19 Naaman had traveled s distance, H3896+824
2Ki 6:24 S time later, Ben-Hadad king of H339+4027
2Ki 7: 8 another tent and took s things from it and NDT
2Ki 7:13 "*Have s* **men take** five of the horses that are AIT
2Ki 9:17 he called out, "I see *s* **troops** coming." AIT
2Ki 9:33 and s *of* her blood spattered the wall and H4946
2Ki 10:13 he met s relatives *of* Ahaziah king of Judah AIT
2Ki 13:15 "Get a bow and *s* **arrows,**" and he did so. AIT
2Ki 13:21 Once while *s* **Israelites** were burying a man AIT
2Ki 17:25 them and they killed s *of* the people. H928
2Ki 20:18 And s *of* your descendants, your own flesh H4946
2Ki 25:12 left behind s *of* the poorest people H4946
1Ch 4:40 S Hamites had lived there formerly H4946
1Ch 6:66 S *of* the Kohathite clans were given as H4946
1Ch 9: 2 property in their own towns were *s* **Israelites,** AIT
1Ch 9:28 S *of* them were in charge of the articles H4946
1Ch 9:30 But s *of* the priests took care of mixing the H4946
1Ch 9:32 S *of* the Kohathites, their fellow Levites H4946
1Ch 12: 8 S Gadites defected to David at his H4946
1Ch 12:16 and *s* **men** from Judah also **came** to David in AIT
1Ch 12:19 S *of* the tribe of Manasseh defected to H4946
1Ch 16: 4 He appointed s *of* the Levites to minister H4946
1Ch 19:10 so he selected s *of* the best troops H4946+3972
1Ch 25: 1 the army, set apart s *of* the sons of Asaph H4200
1Ch 26:27 S *of* the plunder taken in battle they H4946
2Ch 11:23 dispersing s *of* his sons throughout H4946+3972
2Ch 12:12 Indeed, there was s good in Judah. H1821
2Ch 13: 7 S worthless scoundrels gathered around H408S
2Ch 16:10 Asa brutally oppressed s *of* the people. H4946
2Ch 17:11 S Philistines brought Jehoshaphat gifts H4946
2Ch 18: 2 S years later he went down H4200+7891+9102
2Ch 19: 3 however, s good in you, for you have rid H1821
2Ch 19: 8 Jehoshaphat appointed s *of* the Levites H4946
2Ch 20: 1 Ammonites with s *of* the Meunites came H4946
2Ch 20: 2 *S people* **came** and told Jehoshaphat, "A AIT
2Ch 20:19 Then s Levites from the Kohathites and H2021S
2Ch 21: 4 the sword along with s *of* the officials of H4946
2Ch 24: 4 S time later Joash decided to restore H339+4027
2Ch 28:12 Then s of the leaders in Ephraim H408S
2Ch 28:21 Ahaz **took s of the things** *from* the temple H2745
2Ch 30:11 Nevertheless, s from Asher, Manasseh and H408
2Ch 32:21 temple of his god, s *of* his sons, his own H4946
2Ch 34:13 S *of* the Levites were secretaries, scribes H4946
Ezr 2:68 s of the heads of the families gave H4946
Ezr 2:70 along with s *of* the other people H4946
Ezr 7: 7 S *of* the Israelites, including priests H4946
Ezr 9: 2 They have taken s *of* their daughters as H4946
Ezr 10:44 s *of* them had children by these wives H4946
Ne 1: 2 came from Judah with *s other* **men,** and I AIT
Ne 1: 4 *For s* **days** I mourned and fasted and prayed AIT
Ne 4:13 I stationed *s of* the **people** behind the lowest AIT
Ne 5: 2 S were saying, "We and our sons and H889S
Ne 5: 5 S *of* our daughters have already been H4946
Ne 5:18 choice sheep and *s* **poultry** were prepared AIT

Ne 7: 3 **s** at their posts and some near their own H408S
Ne 7: 3 at their posts and **s** near their own houses H408S
Ne 7:70 S *of* the heads of the families H4946+7921
Ne 7:71 S *of* the heads of the families gave to the H4946
Ne 8:10 send **s** to those who have nothing H4950S
Ne 11: 3 settled in Jerusalem (now *s* **Israelites**, priests, AIT
Ne 11:25 **s** *of* the people of Judah lived in Kiriath H4946
Ne 11:36 S *of* the divisions of the Levites of Judah H4946
Ne 12:35 as well as **s** priests with trumpets, and also H4946
Ne 13: 6 **S time** later I asked his permission H3427
Ne 13:19 I stationed **s** *of* my own men at the gates H4946
Ne 13:25 I beat **s** *of* the men and pulled out their H4946
Job 11: 6 God has even forgotten **s** *of* your sin. H4946
Job 39:15 that **s** wild animal may trample them. NDT
Ps 20: 7 **S** trust in chariots and some in horses, but H465
Ps 20: 7 Some trust in chariots and **s** in horses, but H465
Ps 107: 4 *S* **wandered** in desert wastelands, finding no AIT
Ps 107:10 *S* **sat** *in* darkness, in utter darkness, prisoners AIT
Ps 107:17 *S* became **fools** through their rebellious ways AIT
Ps 107:23 *S* **went out** *on* the sea in ships; they were AIT
Pr 1:11 let's ambush **s** harmless soul; NDT
Ecc 5:14 wealth lost through *s* **misfortune**, so that AIT
Ecc 6: 2 God gives *s* **people** wealth, possessions and AIT
Isa 1: 9 Almighty had left us **s** survivors, H3869+5071
Isa 17: 6 Yet *s* **gleanings** will remain, as when an AIT
Isa 39: 7 And **s of** your descendants, your own flesh H4946
Isa 43:12 and not *s* **foreign** god among you. AIT
Isa 44: 5 **S** will say, 'I belong to the LORD'; others H2296
Isa 44:15 **s** *of* it he takes and warms himself H4946
Isa 46: 6 **S** pour out gold from their bags and H2021S
Isa 49:12 come from afar—**s** from the north, some H465
Isa 49:12 some from the north, **s** from the west, some NDT
Isa 49:12 from the west, **s** from the region of Aswan." H465
Isa 66:19 I will send **s** *of* those who survive to H4946
Isa 66:21 And I will select **s** *of* them also to be H4946
Jer 4:29 *S* **go** into the thickets; some climb up among AIT
Jer 4:29 into the thickets; *s* **climb up** among the rocks. AIT
Jer 19: 1 Take along **s** *of* the elders of the people H4946
Jer 26:17 **S** of the elders of the land stepped H408S
Jer 26:22 of Akbor to Egypt, along with *s* other **men**. AIT
Jer 35: 5 full of wine and *s* **cups** before the Rekabites AIT
Jer 35: 5 Rekabites and said to them, "Drink *s* **wine**." AIT
Jer 38:11 He took *s* old **rags** and worn-out clothes from AIT
Jer 39:10 in the land of Judah **s** *of* the poor people, H4946
Jer 43: 9 take *s* large **stones** with you and bury them in AIT
Jer 52:15 carried into exile **s** *of* the poorest people H4946
Eze 6: 8 " 'But I will spare **s**, for some of you will NDT
Eze 6: 8 for **s** *of* you will escape the sword when H4200
Eze 10: 7 He took up **s** of it and put it into the hands NDT
Eze 14: 1 **S** of the elders of Israel came to me and H408S
Eze 14:22 Yet *there will be* **s** survivors—sons and H3855
Eze 16:16 You took **s** *of* your garments to make H4946
Eze 16:52 for *you have* **furnished** *s* **justification** for your AIT
Eze 20: 1 **s** of the elders of Israel came to inquire of H408S
Eze 36:13 Because *s* **say** to you, "You devour people AIT
Eze 40: 2 south side were *s* **buildings** that looked like a AIT
Eze 40:17 There I saw *s* **rooms** and a pavement that AIT
Eze 43:20 You are to take **s** *of* its blood and put it on H4946
Eze 45:19 The priest is to take **s** *of* the blood of the H4946
Da 1: 2 along with **s** *of* the articles from the H4946+7921
Da 1: 3 the king's service **s** *of* the Israelites from H4946
Da 1: 6 who were chosen were **s** from Judah: H1201S
Da 2:41 it will have **s** *of* the strength of iron in A10427
Da 3: 8 At this time **s** astrologers came forward A10131S
Da 3:12 But there are **s** Jews whom you have set A10131S
Da 3:20 commanded **s** *of* the strongest A10131S
Da 8:10 it threw **s** *of* the starry host down to H4946
Da 11: 6 After *s* **years**, they will become allies. AIT
Da 11: 8 *For s* **years** he will leave the king of the North AIT
Da 11:35 **S** *of* the wise will stumble, so that they H4946
Da 12: 2 **s** to everlasting life, others to shame and H465
Am 4: 1 say to your husbands, "Bring us *s* **drinks**!" AIT
Am 4:11 "I overthrew **s of** you as I overthrew Sodom H928
Hag 2:12 that fold touches **s** bread or stew H2021S
Hag 2:12 some bread or stew, **s** wine, olive oil H2021S
Zec 14:21 sacrifice will take **s** *of* the pots and cook in H4946
Mt 8:30 **S distance** from them a large herd of pigs *G3426*
Mt 9: 2 *S* **men brought** to him a paralyzed man, lying AIT
Mt 9: 3 **s** of the teachers of the law said to *G5516*
Mt 10:11 search there for **s** worthy person and stay *G5515*
Mt 12: 1 began to pick *s* **heads of grain** and eat them. AIT
Mt 12:38 Then **s** of the Pharisees and teachers of *G5516*
Mt 13: 4 the seed, **s** fell along the path *G4005+3525*
Mt 13: 5 **S** fell on rocky places, where it did *G257+1254*
Mt 14:15 go to the villages and buy themselves *s* **food**." AIT
Mt 15: 1 Then *s* **Pharisees** and teachers of the law AIT
Mt 16:14 replied, "**S** say John the Baptist *G3836+3525*
Mt 16:28 **s** who are standing here will not taste *G5516*
Mt 19: 3 *S* **Pharisees** came to him to test him. AIT
Mt 21:33 the vineyard *to s* **farmers** and moved to AIT
Mt 22: 4 "Then he sent **s more** servants and said *G257*
Mt 23:34 **S** of them you will kill and crucify; others *G1666*
Mt 25: 8 the wise, 'Give us **s of** your oil; our lamps *G1666*
Mt 25: 9 those who sell oil and buy **s** for yourselves. NDT
Mt 27:47 When **s** of those standing there heard this *G5516*
Mt 28:11 **s** of the guards went into the city and *G5516*
Mt 28:17 they worshiped him; but **s** doubted. *G3836*
Mk 2: 3 *S* **men came**, bringing to him a paralyzed AIT
Mk 2: 6 Now **s** teachers of the law were sitting *G5516*
Mk 2:18 *S* **people came** and asked Jesus, "How is it AIT
Mk 2:23 they began to pick **s** heads of grain. *G3836*
Mk 2:26 And he also gave **s** to his companions." NDT
Mk 3: 2 *S* of them *were looking* for a reason *to* **accuse** AIT
Mk 4: 4 the seed, **s** fell along the path *G4005+3525*
Mk 4: 5 **S** fell on rocky places, where it did not have *G257*
Mk 4: 8 produced a crop, **s** multiplying thirty *G1651*
Mk 4: 8 multiplying thirty, **s** sixty, some a hundred *G1651*
Mk 4: 8 some sixty, **s** a hundred times. *G1651*
Mk 4:15 **S** *people* are like seed along the path *G4047*
Mk 4:20 and produce a crop—**s** thirty, some sixty *G1651*
Mk 4:20 some thirty, **s** sixty, some a hundred times *G1651*
Mk 4:20 **s** a hundred times what was sown. *G1651*
Mk 5:35 *s people* **came** from the house of Jairus AIT
Mk 6:14 *S were* **saying**, "John the Baptist has been AIT
Mk 6:31 yourselves to a quiet place and get **s** rest." *G3900*
Mk 7: 1 The Pharisees and **s** of the teachers of the *G5516*
Mk 7: 2 saw **s** of his disciples eating food with *G5516*
Mk 7:32 There *s people* **brought** to him a man who AIT
Mk 8: 3 because **s** of them have come a long *G5516*
Mk 8:22 and *s people* **brought** a blind man and AIT
Mk 8:28 They replied, "**S** say John the Baptist; others NDT
Mk 9: 1 **s** who are standing here will not taste *G5516*
Mk 10: 2 *S* Pharisees **came** and tested him by asking AIT
Mk 11: 5 **s** *people* standing there asked, "What are *G5516*
Mk 12: 1 the vineyard *to s* **farmers** and moved to AIT
Mk 12: 2 to collect from them **s** of the fruit of the *G608*
Mk 12: 5 many others; **s** *of them* they beat *G4005+3525*
Mk 12:13 Later they sent **s** of the Pharisees and *G5516*
Mk 14: 4 **S** of those present were saying *G5516*
Mk 14:57 Then **s** stood up and gave this false *G5516*
Mk 14:65 Then **s** began to spit at him; they *G5516*
Mk 15:35 When **s** of those standing near heard this *G5516*
Mk 15:40 *S* **women** were watching from a distance AIT
Mk 15:46 So Joseph bought *s* **linen cloth**, took down AIT
Lk 3:14 Then *s* **soldiers** asked him, "And what should AIT
Lk 5:18 *S* **men** came carrying a paralyzed man on a AIT
Lk 6: 1 disciples began to pick **s** heads of grain, *G3836*
Lk 6: 2 **S** of the Pharisees asked, "Why are you *G5516*
Lk 6: 4 And he also gave **s** to his companions." NDT
Lk 7: 3 of Jesus and sent *s* **elders** of the Jews to him, AIT
Lk 8: 2 also **s** women who had been cured of *G5516*
Lk 8: 5 the seed, **s** fell along the path *G4005+3525*
Lk 8: 6 **S** fell on rocky ground, and when it came *G2283*
Lk 9: 7 perplexed because **s** were saying that *G5516*
Lk 9:19 They replied, "**S** say John the Baptist; others NDT
Lk 9:27 **s** who are standing here will not taste *G5516*
Lk 11:15 But **s** of them said, "By Beelzebul, the *G5516*
Lk 11:49 **s of** whom they will kill and others they *G1666*
Lk 13: 1 Now there were **s** present at that time *G5516*
Lk 13:31 At that time **s** Pharisees came to Jesus *G5516*
Lk 18: 4 "For *s* **time** he refused. But finally he said to AIT
Lk 18: 9 To **s** who were confident of their own *G5516*
Lk 19:39 **S** of the Pharisees in the crowd said to *G5516*
Lk 20: 9 rented it *to s* **farmers** and went away for a AIT
Lk 20:10 so they would give him **s of** the fruit of the *G608*
Lk 20:27 **S** of the Sadducees, who say there is no *G5516*
Lk 20:39 **S** of the teachers of the law responded *G5516*
Lk 21: 5 **S** of his disciples were remarking about *G5516*
Lk 21:16 they will put **s of** you to death. *G1666*
Lk 22: 2 were looking for **s way** to get rid of Jesus, *G4802*
Lk 22:55 And when **s** there had kindled a fire in the NDT
Lk 23: 8 hoped to see him perform a sign *of* **s sort**. *G5516*
Lk 24:22 In addition, **s** of our women amazed us *G5516*
Lk 24:24 Then **s** of our companions went to the *G5516*
Jn 2: 8 "Now draw **s** out and take it to the master of NDT
Jn 3:22 where *he* **spent s time** with them, and *G1417*
Jn 3:25 developed between **s of** John's disciples *G1666*
Jn 5: 1 **S time later**, Jesus went up to *G3552+4047*
Jn 6: 1 **S time after this**, Jesus crossed to *G3552+4047*
Jn 6:23 Then *s* **boats** from Tiberias landed near the AIT
Jn 6:64 Yet there are **s of** you who do not believe." *G1666*
Jn 7:12 **S** said, "He is a good *G3836+3525*
Jn 7:25 At that point **s** of the people of Jerusalem *G5516*
Jn 7:40 hearing his words, **s of** the people said *G1666*
Jn 7:44 **S** wanted to seize him, but no one laid a *G5516*
Jn 9: 6 on the ground, made *s* **mud** with the saliva AIT
Jn 9: 9 **S** claimed that he was. Others said, "No, he *G257*
Jn 9:11 they call Jesus made *s* **mud** and put it on my AIT
Jn 9:16 **S** of the Pharisees said, "This man is not *G5516*
Jn 9:40 **S** Pharisees who were with him heard him *G1666*
Jn 10: 1 climbs in **by s other way**, is a thief and *G249*
Jn 11:37 But **s** of them said, "Could not he who *G5516*
Jn 11:46 But **s** of them went to the Pharisees and *G5516*
Jn 12:20 Now there were **s** Greeks among those *G5516*
Jn 13:29 **s** thought Jesus was telling him to buy *G5516*
Jn 16:17 **s of** his disciples said to one another *G1666*
Jn 18: 3 of soldiers and *s* **officials** from the chief AIT
Jn 21: 6 the right side of the boat and you will find **s**." NDT
Jn 21: 9 coals there with fish on it, and *s* **bread**. AIT
Jn 21:10 "Bring **s of** the fish you have just caught." *G608*
Ac 2:13 **S**, however, made fun of them and said *G2283*
Ac 5: 3 have kept for yourself **s of** the money you *G608*
Ac 5: 6 Then **s** young men came forward, wrapped *G3836*
Ac 5:15 might fall on **s** of them as he passed *G5516*
Ac 5:36 **S time ago** Theudas *G4574+4047+3836+2465*
Ac 6:11 Then they secretly persuaded *s* **men** to say AIT
Ac 8: 9 Now **for s time** a man named Simon had *G4732*
Ac 8:36 they came to **s** water and the eunuch said, *G5516*
Ac 9:19 after taking *s* **food**, he regained his AIT
Ac 9:43 stayed in Joppa for **s** time with a tanner *G2653*
Ac 10:23 **s** of the believers from Joppa went *G5516*
Ac 11:20 **S** of them, however, men from Cyprus and *G5516*
Ac 11:27 During this time *s* **prophets** came down from AIT
Ac 12: 1 Herod arrested **s** who belonged to the *G5516*
Ac 14: 4 were divided; **s** sided with the Jews *G3836+3525*
Ac 14:19 Then *s* **Jews** came from Antioch and Iconium AIT
Ac 15: 2 along with **s** other believers, to *G5516*
Ac 15: 5 Then **s** of the believers who belonged to *G5516*
Ac 15: 7 that **s time ago** God made *G608+2465+792*
Ac 15:22 decided to choose **s of** their own men *G1666*
Ac 15:24 We have heard that **s** went out from us *G5516*
Ac 15:25 agreed to choose *s* **men** and send them to AIT
Ac 15:33 After spending *s* **time** there, they were sent AIT
Ac 15:36 **S** time later Paul said to Barnabas, "Let us *G5516*
Ac 17: 4 **S** of the Jews were persuaded and joined *G5516*
Ac 17: 5 so they rounded up **s** bad characters from *G5516*
Ac 17: 6 Jason and **s** *other* believers before *G5516*
Ac 17:13 of God at Berea, *s of them* **went** there too AIT
Ac 17:18 **S** *of them* asked, "What is this babbler *G5516*
Ac 17:20 You are bringing **s** strange ideas to our *G5516*
Ac 17:28 As **s** of your own poets have said, 'We *G5516*
Ac 17:32 of the dead, **s** *of them* sneered, but others *G3836*
Ac 17:34 **S** of the people became followers of Paul *G5516*
Ac 18:14 a complaint about **s** misdemeanor or *G5516*
Ac 18:18 Paul stayed on in Corinth for **s** time. *G2653*
Ac 18:23 After spending **s** time in Antioch, Paul set *G5516*
Ac 19: 1 There he found **s** disciples *G5516*
Ac 19: 9 But **s** *of them* became obstinate; they *G5516*
Ac 19:13 **S** Jews who went around driving out evil *G5516*
Ac 19:31 Even **s** of the officials of the province *G5516*
Ac 19:32 **S** were shouting one thing *G257*
Ac 19:32 shouting one thing, **s** another. Most of the NDT
Ac 20: 3 Because **s** Jews had plotted against him *G3836*
Ac 21:16 *S of* the **disciples** from Caesarea AIT
Ac 21:27 **s** Jews from the province of Asia saw Paul *G3836*
Ac 21:32 He at once took *s* **officers** and soldiers and AIT
Ac 21:34 **S** in the crowd shouted one thing and some *G257*
Ac 21:34 the crowd shouted one thing and **s** another, NDT
Ac 21:38 wilderness **s time ago**?" *G4574+4047+3836+2465*
Ac 23: 6 knowing that **s** of them were *G1651+3538*
Ac 23: 9 **s** of the teachers of the law who were *G5516*
Ac 23:12 The next morning **s** Jews formed a *G3836*
Ac 23:20 "**S** Jews have agreed to ask you to bring *G3836*
Ac 24: 1 to Caesarea with **s** of the elders and a *G5516*
Ac 24:19 But there are **s** Jews from the province of *G5516*
Ac 24:23 guard but to give him **s** freedom and permit NDT
Ac 25: 5 Let **s** of your leaders come with me, and if *G3836*
Ac 25:19 they had **s** points of dispute with him *G5516*
Ac 26:21 That is why *s* **Jews** seized me in the temple AIT
Ac 27: 1 Paul and **s** other prisoners were handed *G5516*
Ac 27:26 we must run aground on **s** island. *G5516*
Ac 27:30 were going to lower **s** anchors from the bow. NDT
Ac 27:34 Now I urge you to take *s* **food**. You need it to AIT
Ac 27:35 he took *s* **bread** and gave thanks to God in AIT
Ac 27:36 all encouraged and ate *s* **food** themselves. AIT
Ac 28:14 we found *s* **brothers and sisters** who invited AIT
Ac 28:24 **S** were convinced by what he said *G3836+3525*
Ro 1:11 I may impart to you **s** spiritual gift to make *G5516*
Ro 3: 3 What if **s** were unfaithful? Will their *G5516*
Ro 3: 8 as **s** slanderously claim that we say *G5516*
Ro 9:21 same lump of clay **s** pottery for *G4005+3525*
Ro 9:21 special purposes and **s** for common use? *G4005*
Ro 11:14 own people to envy and save **s** of them. *G5516*
Ro 11:17 If **s** of the branches have been broken off *G5516*
Ro 15:15 you quite boldly on **s** points to remind you *G608*
1Co 1:11 *s* from Chloe's household *have* **informed** me AIT
1Co 4:18 **S** of you have become arrogant, as if I *G5516*
1Co 6:11 And that is what **s** of you were. But you *G5516*
1Co 8: 7 **S** *people* are still so accustomed to idols *G5516*
1Co 9:22 that by all possible means I might save **s**. *G5516*
1Co 10: 7 not be idolaters, as **s** of them were; as it *G5516*
1Co 10: 8 immorality, as **s** of them did—and in *G5516*
1Co 10: 9 not test Christ, as **s** of them did—and *G5516*
1Co 10:10 do not grumble, as **s** of them did—and *G5516*
1Co 11:18 among you, and to **s** extent I believe it. *G5516*
1Co 11:21 **s** of you go ahead with your own private *G1667*
1Co 14: 6 unless I bring you **s** revelation or *G2445*
1Co 15: 6 still living, though **s** have fallen asleep. *G5516*
1Co 15:12 how can **s** of you say that there is no *G5516*
1Co 15:34 there are **s** who are ignorant of God *G5516*
1Co 16: 7 I hope to spend **s** time with you, if the *G5516*
2Co 2: 5 me as he has grieved all of you to *s* **extent**— AIT
2Co 3: 1 Or do we need, like **s** *people*, letters of *G5516*
2Co 5:13 "out of our mind," as **s** say, it is for God; if NDT
2Co 10: 2 to be toward **s** *people* who think that we *G5516*
2Co 10:10 For **s** say, "His letters are weighty and *G3525*
2Co 10:12 compare ourselves *with* **s** who commend *G5516*
Gal 1: 7 Evidently **s** *people* are throwing you into *G5516*
Gal 2: 4 arose because **s** false believers had *G4015*
Php 1:15 It is true that **s** preach Christ out of envy *G5516*
Php 3:15 And if *on* **s** *point* you think differently, that *G5516*
1Th 3: 5 I was afraid that **in s way** the tempter had *G4803*
2Th 3:11 We hear that **s** among you are idle and *G5516*
1Ti 1: 6 **S** have departed from these and have *G5516*
1Ti 1:19 which **s** have rejected and so have *G5516*
1Ti 4: 1 that in later times **s** will abandon the faith *G5516*
1Ti 4: 8 For physical training is of **s** value, but *G3900*
1Ti 5:15 **S** have in fact already turned away to *G5516*
1Ti 5:24 The sins *of* **s** are obvious, reaching *G5516+476*
1Ti 6:10 **S** *people*, eager for money, have *G5516*
1Ti 6:21 which **s** have professed and in so doing *G5516*
2Ti 2:18 and they destroy the faith *of* **s**. *G5516*
2Ti 2:20 **s** are for special purposes and *G4005+3525*
2Ti 2:20 special purposes and **s** for common use. *G4005*
Phm 20 *that I may* **have s benefit** from you in the Lord AIT
Heb 4: 6 it still remains *for* **s** to enter that rest, *G5516*

Heb 10:25 together, as *s* are in the habit of doing G5516
Heb 11:36 **S** faced jeers and flogging, and even G2283
Heb 13: 2 by so doing *s people* have shown G5516
2Pe 3: 9 his promise, as **s** understand slowness. G5516
2Pe 3:16 His letters contain *s* **things** that are hard to AIT
2Jn 4 me great joy to find **s** of your children G1666
3Jn 3 me great joy when *s* **believers** came and AIT
Rev 2:10 the devil will put **s of** you in prison to test G1666
Rev 2:14 There are *s* among you *who* **hold to** the AIT
Rev 2:17 victorious, I will give *s of* the hidden **manna**. AIT
Rev 11: 9 For three and a half days *s* **from** every people AIT

SOMEBODY (4) [BODY, SOME]

Ex 22: 9 any other lost property about which *s* **says** AIT
Pr 12: 9 servant than **pretend to be s** and have no H3877
Ac 5:36 claiming to be **s**, and about four hundred G5516
Heb 9:17 a will is in force only when **s** has died; NDT

SOMEHOW (5) [HOW, SOME]

Ro 11:14 the hope that I may **s** arouse my own G4803
1Co 12: 2 **s or other** you were influenced and G6055+323
2Co 11: 3 your minds may **s** be led astray from your G4803
Gal 4:11 that **s** I have wasted my efforts on you. G4803
Php 3:11 **s**, attaining to the resurrection G4803

SOMEONE (191) [ONE, SOME]

Ex 4:13 servant, Lord. Please send **s else**." H928+3338S
Ex 12:30 there was not a house without *s* **dead**. AIT
Ex 21:14 anyone schemes and kills **s** deliberately, H8276
Ex 21:16 "Anyone who kidnaps **s** is to be put to H408
Ex 21:35 bull injures **s else's** bull and it dies, H8276
Ex 22: 5 them stray and they graze in **s else's** field, H337
Ex 23: 5 the donkey of *s who* **hates** you fallen down AIT
Lev 4:32 " 'If *s* **brings** a lamb as their sin offering, they AIT
Lev 13:18 "When **s** has a boil on their skin and it H2257
Lev 13:24 "When **s** has a burn on their skin and a NDT
Lev 16:21 in the care of **s** appointed for the task. H408
Lev 25:54 " 'Even if *s* **is not redeemed** in any of these AIT
Lev 27:20 if they have sold it to **s** else, it can never H408
Nu 6: 9 " 'If **s** dies suddenly in the Nazirite's H4637S
Nu 19:16 open who touches **s** who has been killed H2021
Nu 19:16 a sword or *s who has* **died a natural death**, AIT
Nu 27:16 living things, appoint **s** over this community H408
Nu 31:19 who has killed **s** or touched someone who H5883
Nu 31:19 someone or touched **s** who was killed H2021
Nu 35: 6 to which a person who has killed **s** may flee. NDT
Nu 35:11 who has killed **s** accidentally may flee H5883
Nu 35:16 " 'If anyone strikes **s** a fatal blow with an H2084
Nu 35:17 a stone and strikes **s** a fatal blow with it, H2084
Nu 35:18 object and strikes **s** a fatal blow with it, H2084
Nu 35:22 without enmity *s* suddenly **pushes** another AIT
Nu 36: 8 tribe must marry **s** in her father's tribal H285
Dt 19: 3 so that a person *who* **kills s** may flee for H8357
Dt 19:11 But if out of hate **s** lies in wait, assaults H408
Dt 19:16 takes the stand to accuse **s** of a crime, H408
Dt 20: 5 may die in battle and **s** else may begin to H408
Dt 20: 6 he may die in battle and **s** else enjoy it. H408
Dt 20: 7 he may die in battle and **s** else marry her." H408
Dt 21: 1 If *s* **is found** slain, lying in a field in the land AIT
Dt 21:18 If **s** has a stubborn and rebellious son who H408
Dt 21:22 If **s** guilty of a capital offense is put to H408
Dt 22: 8 on your house if **s** falls from the H2021+5877S
Dt 22:26 case is like that of **s** who attacks and H408
Dt 24: 7 If **s** is caught kidnapping a fellow Israelite H408
Jos 20: 9 them who killed **s** accidentally could H5883
Jdg 4:20 "If **s** comes by and asks you, 'Is anyone in H408
Jdg 6:31 defend himself when *s* **breaks down** his altar." AIT
Jdg 16:19 she called for **s** to shave off the seven H408
Ru 2:22 because in **s else's** field you might be H337
1Sa 9: 9 in Israel, if **s** went to inquire of God H408
1Sa 14:33 Then *s* **said** to Saul, "Look, the men are AIT
1Sa 16:16 here to search for **s** who can play the lyre. H408
1Sa 16:17 "Find **s** who plays well and bring him to me H408
1Sa 17:30 turned away to **s else** and brought up the H337
1Sa 20:31 Now send **s** to bring him to me, for he must NDT
1Sa 25:29 Even though **s** is pursuing you to take your H132
1Sa 26:15 **S** came to destroy your lord H285+2021+6639
2Sa 3:29 be without *s who has a* **running sore** or AIT
2Sa 4:10 when **s** told me, 'Saul is dead,' and H2021
2Sa 11: 3 David sent **s** to find out about her. NDT
2Sa 14: 2 So Joab sent **s** to Tekoa and had a wise NDT
2Sa 23:15 that **s** would get me a drink of water from H4769
1Ki 14: 5 she arrives, she *will* **pretend to be s else**." H5796
1Ki 18:10 my master has not sent **s** to look for you. NDT
1Ki 20:39 **s** came to me with a captive and said H408
1Ki 22:34 But **s** drew his bow at random and hit the H408
2Ki 5: 7 this fellow send **s** to me to be cured of H408
2Ki 6:32 murderer is sending **s** to cut off my head? NDT
1Ch 11:17 that **s** would get me a drink of water from H4769
1Ch 19: 5 When *s* **came** and told David about the men AIT
2Ch 18:33 But **s** drew his bow at random and hit the H408
Ne 2:10 disturbed that **s** had come to promote H132
Ne 6:11 Or should **s** like me go into the temple to H4769
Est 1:19 royal position to **s else** who is better than H8295
Job 4: 2 "If *s* **ventures** a word with you, will you be AIT
Job 9:33 If only there were *s to* **mediate** between us AIT
Job 9:33 mediate between us, *s to* **bring** us together, AIT
Job 9:34 *s to* **remove** God's rod from me, so that his AIT
Job 14:14 If **s** dies, will they live again? All the days H1505
Job 31:35 that I had *s to* **hear** me! I sign now my AIT
Job 33:19 "Or *s may* **be chastened** on a bed of pain AIT
Job 34:17 *Can s who* **hates** justice govern? Will you AIT
Job 34:31 "Suppose *s* **says** to God, 'I am guilty but will AIT
Ps 41: 9 Even my close friend, **s** I trusted, one who H889
Ps 109: 6 Appoint *s* **evil** to oppose my enemy; let an AIT
Pr 4:16 robbed of sleep till they make **s** stumble. NDT
Pr 18:17 until **s** comes forward and cross-examines. H8276
Pr 20:20 If *s* **curses** their father or mother, their lamp AIT
Pr 22:29 Do you see **s** skilled in their work? They will H408
Pr 24:30 past the vineyard of **s** *who* has no sense; H132
Pr 26:17 dog by the ears is **s** who rushes into a H6296S
Pr 26:27 pit will fall into it; if *s* **rolls** a stone, it will roll AIT
Pr 27: 2 Let **s else** praise you, and not your own H2424
Pr 29:20 Do you see **s** who speaks in haste? There is H408
Ecc 5:19 when God gives **s** wealth and H3972+2021+132
Ecc 6:10 no one can contend with *s* **who** is stronger. AIT
Ecc 8: 7 who can tell **s else** what is to come? H2257S
Ecc 10:14 who can tell **s else** what will happen H2257S
Isa 8:19 When *s* **tells** you to consult mediums and AIT
Isa 17: 5 as *when s* **gleans** heads of grain in the AIT
Isa 21:11 *S* **calls** to me from Seir, "Watchman, what is AIT
Isa 29:11 And if you give the scroll to *s who* **can read** AIT
Isa 29:12 if you give the scroll to **s** who cannot read, H889
Isa 29:21 who with a word make **s** out to be guilty, H132
Isa 46: 7 Even though *s* **cries out** to it, it cannot answer AIT
Jer 8: 4 When *s* **turns away**, do they not AIT
Eze 22:30 "I looked for **s** among them who would H408
Eze 33:12 your people, 'If *s* **who** is righteous disobeys AIT
Eze 33:12 And if *s* **who** is wicked repents, that person's AIT
Eze 43: 6 I heard *s* **speaking** to me from inside the AIT
Da 5:17 yourself and give your rewards to **s else**. A10025
Mic 6:11 Shall I acquit **s** with dishonest scales, with a NDT
Hag 2:12 If **s** carries consecrated meat in the fold of H408
Zec 4: 1 woke me up, like **s** awakened from sleep. H408
Zec 13: 6 If *s* **asks**, 'What are these wounds on your AIT
Mt 11: 3 is to come, or should we expect **s else**?" G2283
Mt 12:47 **S** told him, "Your mother and brothers are G5516
Mt 13:20 ground refers to **s** who hears the word G3836
Mt 13:22 the thorns refers to **s** who hears the word, G3836
Mt 13:23 good soil refers to **s** who hears the word G3836
Mt 16:26 good will it be for **s** to gain the whole G476
Mt 19:23 it is hard for *s who is* **rich** to enter the AIT
Mt 19:24 of a needle than *for s who is* **rich** to enter the AIT
Mk 3:31 Standing outside, they sent **s** in to call him. NDT
Mk 8:36 What good is it for **s** to gain the whole G476
Mk 9:38 "we saw **s** driving out demons in your G5516
Mk 10:25 of a needle than *for s who is* **rich** to enter the AIT
Mk 15:36 **S** ran, filled a sponge with wine vinegar G5516
Lk 6:29 If **s** slaps you on one cheek, turn to them G3836
Lk 6:29 If **s** takes your coat, do not withhold your G3836
Lk 7:19 is to come, or should we expect **s else**?" G257
Lk 7:20 is to come, or should we expect **s else**? G257
Lk 8:20 *S* **told** him, "Your mother and brothers are AIT
Lk 8:46 But Jesus said, "**S** touched me; I know G5516
Lk 8:49 speaking, **s** came from the house of Jairus G5516
Lk 9:25 What good is it for **s** to gain the whole G476
Lk 9:49 "we saw **s** driving out demons in your G5516
Lk 10: 6 If **s who promotes** peace is there, your G5626
Lk 11:22 But when *s* **stronger** attacks and overpowers AIT
Lk 12:13 **S** in the crowd said to him, "Teacher, tell G5516
Lk 13:23 **S** asked him, "Lord, are only a few people G5516
Lk 14: 8 "When **s** invites you to a wedding feast G5516
Lk 16:12 not been trustworthy with **s else's** property, G259
Lk 16:30 'but if **s** from the dead goes to them G5516
Lk 16:31 convinced even if **s** rises from the dead. G5516
Lk 18:25 of a needle than *for s who is* **rich** to enter the AIT
Lk 22:58 A little later **s else** saw him and said G2283
Jn 3: 4 "How can **s** be born when they are old?" G476
Jn 4:33 "Could **s** have brought him food? G5516
Jn 5: 7 to get in, **s else** goes down ahead of me." G257
Jn 5:43 but if **s else** comes in his own name G257
Jn 21:18 and **s else** will dress you and lead you G257
Ac 5:25 Then **s** came and said, "Look! The men G5516
Ac 8: 9 He boasted that he was **s** great, G5516
Ac 8:31 he said, "unless **s** explains it to me?" G5516
Ac 8:34 prophet talking about, himself or **s else**?" G5516
Ac 13:11 seeking **s to lead** him **by the hand**. G5933
Ac 13:41 would never believe, even if **s** told you. G5516
Ro 2: 1 you who pass judgment on **s** else, for at NDT
Ro 3: 7 **S** might argue, "If my falsehood enhances NDT
Ro 5: 7 a good person **s** might possibly dare to G5516
Ro 6:16 offer yourselves *to* **s** as obedient slaves, G4005
Ro 7: 1 has authority over **s** only as long as that G476
Ro 10:14 can they hear without *s* **preaching** to them? AIT
Ro 14: 4 Who are you to judge **s else's** servant? To G259
Ro 14:15 your eating destroy **s** for whom Christ died G1697
Ro 14:20 eat anything that causes **s** else to stumble. NDT
Ro 15:20 not be building on **s else's** foundation. G259
1Co 3:10 a wise builder, and **s else** is building on it. G257
1Co 8:10 For if **s** with a weak conscience sees you G5516
1Co 9:26 I do not run like **s** running aimlessly; NDT
1Co 10:28 But if **s** says to you, "This has been offered G5516
1Co 14: 5 in tongues, unless *s* **interprets**, so that the AIT
1Co 14:11 not grasp the meaning of what **s** is saying, NDT
1Co 14:16 *can s else*, who is now put in the position of
an inquirer, **say** AIT
1Co 14:27 one at a time, and **s** must interpret. G1651
1Co 14:30 a revelation comes *to* **s** who is sitting down G257
1Co 15:35 But **s** will ask, "How are the dead raised G5516
2Co 10:16 work already done in **s else's** territory. G259
2Co 11: 4 For if **s** comes to you and preaches a Jesus G3836
Gal 6: 1 sisters, if **s** is caught in a sin, you G476
Gal 6: 4 without comparing themselves to **s else**, G2283
Php 3: 4 If **s** else thinks they have reasons to put G5516
Col 3:13 if any of you has a grievance against **s**. G5516
Heb 2: 6 But there is a place where **s** has testified G5516
Heb 3: 4 For every house is built by **s**, but God is the G5516
Heb 5:12 you need **s** to teach you the elementary G5516
Heb 6:16 People swear by **s** greater than G3836
Heb 10:29 do you think *s* **deserves** to be punished who AIT
Jas 1:23 what it says is like **s** who looks at his face G467
Jas 2:14 if **s** claims to have faith but has no deeds? G5516
Jas 2:18 But **s** will say, "You have faith; I have G5516
Jas 5:19 from the truth and **s** should bring that G5516
1Pe 2:19 is commendable if *s* **bears up** under the pain AIT
1Pe 5: 8 like a roaring lion looking for **s** to devour. G5516
Rev 1:13 the lampstands was **s** like a son of man, NDT
Rev 4: 2 was a throne in heaven with *s* **sitting** on it. AIT

SOMEONE'S (3) [ONE, SOME]

Lev 24:18 who takes the life of **s** animal must make NDT
Eze 33: 6 the sword comes and takes **s** life, H2157
Mt 15:11 What goes into **s** mouth does not defile G3836

SOMETHING (119) [SOME, THING]

Ge 18: 5 Let me get you **s to eat**, so you can H7326+4312
Ge 30:30 when *may* I **do s** for my own household?" AIT
Ge 38:17 "Will you give me **s** as a pledge until you NDT
Ex 2:20 Invite him to have **s** to eat." H4312S
Ex 10: 6 **s** neither your parents nor your ancestors H889
Ex 17:14 a scroll as **s** to be **remembered** and make H2355
Ex 24:10 his feet was **s** like a pavement **made** *of* lapis AIT
Lev 5: 1 to testify regarding **s** they have seen or NDT
Lev 6: 2 neighbor about **s entrusted** to them or left H7214
Lev 6: 2 them or left in their care or about **s stolen**, H1610
Lev 7:21 Anyone who touches **s** unclean—whether H3972
Lev 11:32 When one of them dies and falls on **s** H2257S
Lev 14:35 'I have seen **s** that looks like a defiling mold NDT
Lev 14:57 to determine when **s** is clean or unclean H2021S
Lev 22: 4 if he touches **s** defiled by a corpse H3972
Lev 27:14 their house as **s holy** to the LORD, H7731
Lev 27:23 its value on that day as **s holy** to the LORD. H7731
Nu 11: 8 And it tasted like **s made** *with* olive oil. H4382
Nu 16:30 But if the LORD brings about **s totally new** H1375
Nu 18:10 Eat it as **s** most holy; every male shall eat H2021S
Nu 35:20 another or throws **s** at them intentionally so NDT
Nu 35:22 another or throws **s** at them H3972+3998
Dt 8:16 **s** your ancestors had never known H889
Dt 23:13 part of your equipment have **s to dig with**, H3845
Dt 24: 1 because he finds **s** indecent about her, H1821
Jdg 14:14 of the eater, **s to eat**; out of the strong H4407
Jdg 14:14 something to eat; out of the strong, *s* **sweet**." AIT
Jdg 18: 9 **Aren't** you *going to* **do s**? Don't H3120
Jdg 19: 5 "Refresh yourself with **s to eat**; then H7326+4312
Jdg 19:21 their feet, *they had s to* **eat** and drink. AIT
Jdg 19:30 Just imagine! *We* **must do s**! So speak up!" H6418
Ru 3: 8 In the middle of the night *s* **startled** the man AIT
1Sa 1:18 Then she went her way and ate **s**, and her NDT
1Sa 3:11 I am about to do **s** in Israel that will make H1821
1Sa 20:26 "**S** must have **happened** to David to make H5247
2Sa 3:35 urged David to eat **s** while it was still H4312S
2Sa 12:18 child is dead? He may do **s desperate**." H8288
2Sa 13: 5 Tamar to come and give me **s** to eat. H4312S
1Ki 1:27 Is this **s** my lord the king has done without H1821
1Ki 2:14 he added, "I have **s to say** to you." "You H1821
1Ki 17:13 then make **s** for yourself and your son. NDT
2Ki 5:20 I will run after him and get **s** from him." H4399
Job 6:21 you see **s dreadful** and are afraid. H3170
Job 6:22 I ever said, 'Give **s** on my behalf, pay a NDT
Job 13:28 "So man wastes away like **s rotten**, like a H8373
Pr 20:25 is a trap to dedicate **s** rashly and only later NDT
Ecc 1:10 This is **s** new"? It was here already, long H2085S
Ecc 3:16 And I saw **s else** under the sun: In the H6388
Ecc 4: 7 Again I saw *s* **meaningless** under the sun: AIT
Ecc 8:14 There is **s** else meaningless that occurs on NDT
Ecc 9:11 I have seen **s else** under the sun: The H8740
Isa 41:23 **Do s**, whether **good** or bad, so that we will AIT
Jer 7:31 daughters in the fire—**s** I did not command H889
Jer 14: 7 our sins testify against us, **do s**, LORD, H6913
Jer 19: 5 to Baal—**s** I did not command or mention H889
Jer 23:14 of Jerusalem I have seen **s horrible**: H9136
Jer 38:14 "I am going to ask you **s**," the king said to H1821
Eze 1:22 creatures was *what* **looked s like** a vault, H1952
Eze 15: 5 it be made into **s useful** when the fire has H4856
Da 6: 5 unless it has **s to do with** the law of his A10089
Hos 4: 7 their glorious God for **s disgraceful**. AIT
Hos 8: 8 is among the nations like **s** no one wants. H3998
Hos 8:12 but they regarded them as *s* **foreign**. AIT
Joel 3: 4 Are you repaying me for **s** I have **done**? H1691
Mic 3: 5 'peace' if they **have s to eat**, H5966+928+9094
Hab 1: 5 For I am going to do **s** in your days that H7189
Mt 5:23 your brother or sister has **s** against you, G5516
Mt 12: 6 I tell you that *s* **greater** than the temple is AIT
Mt 12:41 and now *s* **greater** than Jonah is here. AIT
Mt 12:42 now *s* **greater** than Solomon is here. AIT
Mt 14:16 need to go away. You give them **s** to eat." NDT
Mt 25:35 For I was hungry and *you* **gave** me *s* to eat, AIT
Mt 25:35 I was thirsty and *you* **gave** me **s to drink**, G4540
Mt 25:37 or thirsty and **give** you **s to drink**? G4540
Mk 5:43 and told them to give her **s** to eat. NDT
Mk 6:36 villages and buy themselves **s** to eat." G5515
Mk 6:37 "You give them **s** to eat." They said to NDT
Lk 7:40 "Simon, I have **s** to tell you. G5516
Lk 8:55 Then Jesus told them to give her *s to* **eat**. AIT
Lk 9:13 "You give them *s to* **eat**." They answered, AIT
Lk 11:31 now *s* **greater** than Solomon is here. AIT

Lk 11:32 and now s greater than Jonah is here. AIT
Lk 11:54 waiting to catch him in s he might say. G5516
Lk 17:20 of God is not s that can be observed, G4191
Lk 20:20 They hoped to catch Jesus in s he said, so G3364
Jn 4:31 his disciples urged him, "Rabbi, eat s." NDT
Jn 5:14 Stop sinning or s worse may happen to G5516
Jn 13:29 the festival, or to give s to the poor. G5516
Jn 18:23 "If I said s wrong," Jesus replied, "testify as AIT
Ac 3: 5 attention, expecting to get s from them. G5516
Ac 9:18 s like scales fell from Saul's eyes AIT
Ac 10:10 He became hungry and wanted s to eat, and NDT
Ac 10:11 heaven opened and s like a large G5007+5516
Ac 11: 5 I saw s like a large sheet being let G5007+5516
Ac 13:41 I am going to do s in your days that G2240
Ac 21:37 the commander, "May I say s to you?" G5516
Ac 23:17 to the commander; he has s to tell him." G5516
Ac 23:18 man to you because he has s to tell you." G5516
Ac 25:26 of this investigation I may have s to write. G5515
Ro 4: 2 he had s to boast about—but not G3017
Ro 12:20 if he is thirsty, give him s to drink. G4540
Ro 14:14 But if anyone regards s as unclean, then G5516
1Co 7:30 were not; those who buy s, as if it were not NDT
1Co 8: 2 who think they know s do not yet know as G5516
1Co 10:30 I denounced because of s I thank God for? G4005
1Co 11:34 Anyone who is hungry should eat s at home NDT
1Co 14:35 If they want to inquire about s, they should G5516
1Co 15:37 just a seed, perhaps of wheat or of s else. G5516
2Co 11: 9 And when I was with you and needed s, I was AIT
Gal 6: 3 thinks they are s when they are not, G5516
Eph 4:28 doing s useful with their own hands G3836
Eph 4:28 that they may have s to share with those in NDT
Php 2: 6 God s to be used to his own advantage; G772
Heb 8: 3 this one also to have s to offer. G5516
Heb 11:40 since God had planned s better for us so G5516
1Pe 4:12 as though s strange were happening to you. AIT
2Pe 1:19 prophetic message as s completely reliable, AIT
Rev 8: 8 his trumpet, and s like a huge mountain, all AIT
Rev 9: 7 their heads they wore s like crowns of gold, AIT

SOMETIMES (4) [SOME]

Nu 9:20 S the cloud was over the tabernacle H3780+889
Nu 9:21 S the cloud stayed only from evening H3780+889
Ro 2:15 their thoughts s accusing them and at G2445
Heb 10:33 S you were publicly exposed to G4047+3525

SOMEWHAT (1) [SOME, WHAT]

2Co 10: 8 So even if I boast s freely about the G5516

SOMEWHERE (4) [SOME, WHERE]

Isa 45:19 in secret, from s in a land of darkness; H5226
Mk 1:38 "Let us go s else—to the nearby G250
Lk 13:31 said to him, "Leave this place and go s else. NDT
Heb 4: 4 For s he has spoken about the seventh day G4543

SON (2314) [GRANDSON, GRANDSONS, SON'S, SON-IN-LAW, SONS, SONS', SONS-IN-LAW, SONSHIP]

Ge 4:17 and he named it after his s Enoch. H1201
Ge 4:22 Zillah also had a s, Tubal-Cain, who H3528
Ge 4:25 gave birth to a s and named him Seth, H1201
Ge 4:26 Seth also had a s, and he named him H1201
Ge 5: 3 130 years, he had a s in his own likeness H3528
Ge 5:28 Lamech had lived 182 years, he had a s. H1201
Ge 9:24 out what his youngest s had done to him, H1201
Ge 11:31 Terah took his s Abram, his grandson Lot H1201
Ge 11:31 his grandson Lot s of Haran, and his H1201
Ge 11:31 the wife of his s Abram, and together H1201
Ge 15: 4 a s who is your own flesh and blood will AIT
Ge 16:11 pregnant and you will give birth to a s. H1201
Ge 16:15 So Hagar bore Abram a s, and Abram H1201
Ge 16:15 the name Ishmael to the s she had borne. H1201
Ge 17:16 her and will surely give you a s by her. H1201
Ge 17:17 "Will a s be born to a man a hundred H3528
Ge 17:19 your wife Sarah will bear you a s, and H1201
Ge 17:23 day Abraham took his s Ishmael and all H1201
Ge 17:25 his s Ishmael was thirteen; H1201
Ge 17:26 Abraham and his s Ishmael were both H1201
Ge 18:10 and Sarah your wife will have a s." H1201
Ge 18:14 time next year, and Sarah will have a s." H1201
Ge 19:37 The older daughter had a s, and she H1201
Ge 19:38 The younger daughter also had a s, and H1201
Ge 21: 2 pregnant and bore a s to Abraham in his H1201
Ge 21: 3 the name Isaac to the s Sarah bore him. H1201
Ge 21: 4 When his s Isaac was eight days old H1201
Ge 21: 5 years old when his s Isaac was born to H1201
Ge 21: 7 Yet I have borne him a s in his old age." H1201
Ge 21: 9 But Sarah saw that the s whom Hagar the H1201
Ge 21:10 "Get rid of that slave woman and her s H1201
Ge 21:10 that woman's s will never share in the H1201
Ge 21:10 share in the inheritance with my s Isaac." H1201
Ge 21:11 greatly because it concerned his s. H1201
Ge 21:13 I will make the s of the slave into a nation H1201
Ge 22: 2 God said, "Take your s, your only son, H1201
Ge 22: 2 your son, your only s, whom you love— H3495
Ge 22: 3 him two of his servants and his s Isaac. H1201
Ge 22: 6 burnt offering and placed it on his s Isaac, H1201
Ge 22: 7 "Yes, my s?" Abraham replied. H1201
Ge 22: 8 the lamb for the burnt offering, my s." H1201
Ge 22: 9 He bound his s Isaac and laid him on the H1201
Ge 22:10 his hand and took the knife to slay his s. H1201
Ge 22:12 you have not withheld from me your s, H1201
Ge 22:12 withheld from me your son, your only s." H3495
Ge 22:13 it as a burnt offering instead of his s. H1201
Ge 22:16 done this and have not withheld your s, H1201
Ge 22:16 have not withheld your son, your only s, H3495
Ge 23: 8 with Ephron s of Zohar on my behalf H1201
Ge 24: 3 get a wife for my s from the daughters of H1201
Ge 24: 4 relatives and get a wife for my s Isaac." H1201
Ge 24: 5 Shall I then take your s back to the country H1201
Ge 24: 6 sure that you do not take my s back there," H1201
Ge 24: 7 you can get a wife for my s from there. H1201
Ge 24: 8 Only do not take my s back there." H1201
Ge 24:15 was the daughter of Bethuel s of Milkah, H1201
Ge 24:24 Bethuel, the s that Milkah bore to Nahor." H1201
Ge 24:36 Sarah has borne him a s in her old age, H1201
Ge 24:37 get a wife for my s from the daughters of H1201
Ge 24:38 to my own clan, and get a wife for my s. H1201
Ge 24:40 get a wife for my s from my own clan and H1201
Ge 24:44 the LORD has chosen for my master's s. H1201
Ge 24:47 'The daughter of Bethuel s of Nahor H1201
Ge 24:48 of my master's brother for his s. H1201
Ge 24:51 her become the wife of your master's s, H1201
Ge 25: 6 them away from his s Isaac to the land of H1201
Ge 25: 9 the field of Ephron s of Zohar the Hittite, H1201
Ge 25:11 God blessed his s Isaac, who then lived H1201
Ge 25:12 of the family line of Abraham's s Ishmael, H1201
Ge 25:19 of the family line of Abraham's s Isaac. H1201
Ge 27: 1 Esau his older s and said to him, H1201
Ge 27: 1 Esau his older son and said to him, "My s." H1201
Ge 27: 5 was listening as Isaac spoke to his s Esau. H1201
Ge 27: 6 Rebekah said to her s Jacob, "Look, H1201
Ge 27: 8 my s, listen carefully and do what I H1201
Ge 27:13 said to him, "My s, let the curse fall on H1201
Ge 27:15 took the best clothes of Esau her older s, H1201
Ge 27:15 put them on her younger s Jacob. H1201
Ge 27:17 she handed to her s Jacob the tasty food H1201
Ge 27:18 "Yes, my s," he answered. "Who H1201
Ge 27:20 Isaac asked his s, "How did you find it so H1201
Ge 27:20 "How did you find it so quickly, my s?" H1201
Ge 27:21 I can touch you, my s, to know whether H1201
Ge 27:21 whether you really are my s Esau or not." H1201
Ge 27:24 "Are you really my s Esau?" he asked. "I H1201
Ge 27:25 Then he said, "My s, bring me some of H1201
Ge 27:26 "Come here, my s, and kiss me." H1201
Ge 27:27 the smell of my s is like the smell of a H1201
Ge 27:32 "I am your s," he answered, "your H1201
Ge 27:37 So what can I possibly do for you, my s?" H1201
Ge 27:42 was told what her older s Esau had said, H1201
Ge 27:42 sent for her younger s Jacob and said to H1201
Ge 27:43 Now then, my s, do what I say: Flee at H1201
Ge 28: 5 to Laban s of Bethuel the Aramean H1201
Ge 28: 9 daughter of Ishmael s of Abraham, H1201
Ge 29:12 relative of her father and a s of Rebekah. H1201
Ge 29:13 his sister's s, he hurried to meet H1201
Ge 29:32 became pregnant and gave birth to a s. H1201
Ge 29:33 when she gave birth to a s she said H1201
Ge 29:34 when she gave birth to a s she said H1201
Ge 29:35 when she gave birth to a s she said H1201
Ge 30: 5 she became pregnant and bore him a s. H1201
Ge 30: 6 has listened to my plea and given me a s." H1201
Ge 30: 7 again and bore Jacob a second s. H1201
Ge 30:10 Leah's servant Zilpah bore Jacob a s. H1201
Ge 30:12 servant Zilpah bore Jacob a second s. H1201
Ge 30:17 pregnant and bore Jacob a fifth s. H1201
Ge 30:19 conceived again and bore Jacob a sixth s. H1201
Ge 30:23 pregnant and gave birth to a s and said, H1201
Ge 30:24 "May the LORD add to me another s." H1201
Ge 34: 2 When Shechem s of Hamor the Hivite, the H1201
Ge 34: 8 "My s Shechem has his heart set on your H1201
Ge 34:18 good to Hamor and his s Shechem. H1201
Ge 34:20 So Hamor and his s Shechem went to the H1201
Ge 34:24 agreed with Hamor and his s Shechem, H1201
Ge 34:26 put Hamor and his s Shechem to the H1201
Ge 35:17 "Don't despair, for you have another s." H1201
Ge 35:18 was dying—she named her s Ben-Oni. H2257S
Ge 36:10 Eliphaz, the s of Esau's wife Adah, and H1201
Ge 36:10 Reuel, the s of Esau's wife Basemath. H1201
Ge 36:12 Esau's s Eliphaz also had a concubine H1201
Ge 36:17 The sons of Esau's s Reuel: Chiefs Nahath H1201
Ge 36:32 Bela s of Beor became king of Edom. H1201
Ge 36:33 Jobab s of Zerah from Bozrah succeeded H1201
Ge 36:35 Husham died, Hadad s of Bedad, who H1201
Ge 36:38 Baal-Hanan s of Akbor succeeded him as H1201
Ge 36:39 When Baal-Hanan s of Akbor died H1201
Ge 37:34 mourned for his s many days. H1201
Ge 37:35 to mourn until I join my s in the grave." H1201
Ge 38: 3 became pregnant and gave birth to a s, H1201
Ge 38: 4 gave birth to a s and named him Onan. H1201
Ge 38: 5 to still another s and named him Shelah. H1201
Ge 38:11 household until my s Shelah grows up." H1201
Ge 38:26 since I wouldn't give her to my s Shelah." H1201
Ge 41:52 The second s he named Ephraim and said NDT
Ge 42:38 "My s will not go down there with you H1201
Ge 43:29 Benjamin, his own mother's s, he asked, H1201
Ge 43:29 he said, "God be gracious to you, my s." H1201
Ge 44:20 is a young s born to him in his old age. H3529
Ge 45: 9 'This is what your s Joseph says: H1201
Ge 45:28 "I'm convinced! My s Joseph is still alive. H1201
Ge 46:10 Shaul the s of a Canaanite woman. H1201
Ge 46:23 The s of Dan: Hushim. H1201
Ge 47:29 he called for his s Joseph and said to him, H1201
Ge 48: 2 was told, "Your s Joseph has come to you," H1201
Ge 48:19 refused and said, "I know, my s, I know. H1201
Ge 49: 9 you return from the prey, my s. H1201
Ge 50:23 children of Makir s of Manasseh were H1201
Ex 2: 2 became pregnant and gave birth to a s. H1201
Ex 2:10 Pharaoh's daughter and he became her s. H1201
Ex 2:22 Zipporah gave birth to a s, and Moses H1201
Ex 4:22 what the LORD says: Israel is my firstborn s, H1201
Ex 4:23 I told you, "Let my s go, so he may H1201
Ex 4:23 to let him go; so I will kill your firstborn s. H1201
Ex 6:14 of Reuben the firstborn s of Israel were AIT
Ex 6:15 Shaul the s of a Canaanite woman. H1201
Ex 6:25 Eleazar s of Aaron married one of the H1201
Ex 11: 5 Every firstborn s in Egypt will die, from the AIT
Ex 11: 5 from the firstborn s of Pharaoh, who sits AIT
Ex 11: 5 to the firstborn s of the female slave AIT
Ex 13: 8 On that day tell your s, 'I do this because H1201
Ex 13:14 to come, when your s asks you, 'What H1201
Ex 18: 3 One s was named Gershom, for Moses said NDT
Ex 20:10 nor your s or daughter, nor your H1201
Ex 21: 9 If he selects her for his s, he must grant H1201
Ex 21:31 applies if the bull gores a s or daughter. H1201
Ex 29:30 The s who succeeds him as priest and H1201
Ex 31: 2 I have chosen Bezalel s of Uri, the son of H1201
Ex 31: 2 son of Uri, the s of Hur, of the tribe of H1201
Ex 31: 6 I have appointed Oholiab s of Ahisamak H1201
Ex 33:11 young aide Joshua s of Nun did not leave H1201
Ex 35:30 the LORD has chosen Bezalel s of Uri, the H1201
Ex 35:30 son of Uri, the s of Hur, of the tribe of H1201
Ex 35:34 both him and Oholiab s of Ahisamak, H1201
Ex 38:21 under the direction of Ithamar s of Aaron, H1201
Ex 38:22 Bezalel s of Uri, the son of Hur, of the tribe H1201
Ex 38:22 son of Uri, the s of Hur, of the tribe of H1201
Ex 38:23 with him was Oholiab s of Ahisamak, of H1201
Lev 6:22 The s who is to succeed him as anointed H1201
Lev 7:33 The s of Aaron who offers the blood and H1201
Lev 12: 2 gives birth to a s will be ceremonially H2351
Lev 12: 6 purification for a s or daughter are over, H1201
Lev 21: 2 mother or father, his s or daughter, his H1201
Lev 24:10 Now the s of an Israelite mother and an H1201
Lev 24:11 The s of the Israelite woman blasphemed H1201
Nu 1: 5 from Reuben, Elizur s of Shedeur; H1201
Nu 1: 6 from Simeon, Shelumiel s of Zurishaddai; H1201
Nu 1: 7 from Judah, Nahshon s of Amminadab; H1201
Nu 1: 8 from Issachar, Nethanel s of Zuar; H1201
Nu 1: 9 from Zebulun, Eliab s of Helon; H1201
Nu 1:10 Ephraim, Elishama s of Ammihud; from H1201
Nu 1:10 from Manasseh, Gamaliel s of Pedahzur; H1201
Nu 1:11 from Benjamin, Abidan s of Gideoni; H1201
Nu 1:12 from Dan, Ahiezer s of Ammishaddai; H1201
Nu 1:13 from Asher, Pagiel s of Okran; H1201
Nu 1:14 from Gad, Eliasaph s of Deuel; H1201
Nu 1:15 from Naphtali, Ahira s of Enan." H1201
Nu 1:20 of Reuben the firstborn s of Israel: AIT
Nu 2: 3 of Judah is Nahshon s of Amminadab. H1201
Nu 2: 5 people of Issachar is Nethanel s of Zuar. H1201
Nu 2: 7 the people of Zebulun is Eliab s of Helon. H1201
Nu 2:10 people of Reuben is Elizur s of Shedeur. H1201
Nu 2:12 of Simeon is Shelumiel s of Zurishaddai. H1201
Nu 2:14 the people of Gad is Eliasaph s of Deuel. H1201
Nu 2:18 of Ephraim is Elishama s of Ammihud. H1201
Nu 2:20 of Manasseh is Gamaliel s of Pedahzur. H1201
Nu 2:22 of Benjamin is Abidan s of Gideoni. H1201
Nu 2:25 of Dan is Ahiezer s of Ammishaddai. H1201
Nu 2:27 the people of Asher is Pagiel s of Okran. H1201
Nu 2:29 the people of Naphtali is Ahira s of Enan. H1201
Nu 3:24 of the Gershonites was Eliasaph s of Lael. H1201
Nu 3:30 Kohathite clans was Elizaphan s of Uzziel. H1201
Nu 3:32 of the Levites was Eleazar s of Aaron, H1201
Nu 3:35 the Merarite clans was Zuriel s of Abihail; H1201
Nu 4:16 "Eleazar s of Aaron, the priest, is to have H1201
Nu 4:28 under the direction of Ithamar s of Aaron, H1201
Nu 4:33 under the direction of Ithamar s of Aaron, H1201
Nu 7: 8 under the direction of Ithamar s of Aaron, H1201
Nu 7:12 day was Nahshon s of Amminadab of the H1201
Nu 7:17 the offering of Nahshon s of Amminadab. H1201
Nu 7:18 On the second day Nethanel s of Zuar H1201
Nu 7:23 was the offering of Nethanel s of Zuar. H1201
Nu 7:24 the third day, Eliab s of Helon, the leader H1201
Nu 7:29 This was the offering of Eliab s of Helon. H1201
Nu 7:30 On the fourth day Elizur s of Shedeur, the H1201
Nu 7:35 was the offering of Elizur s of Shedeur. H1201
Nu 7:36 the fifth day Shelumiel s of Zurishaddai, H1201
Nu 7:41 offering of Shelumiel s of Zurishaddai. H1201
Nu 7:42 On the sixth day Eliasaph s of Deuel, the H1201
Nu 7:47 was the offering of Eliasaph s of Deuel. H1201
Nu 7:48 the seventh day Elishama s of Ammihud, H1201
Nu 7:53 the offering of Elishama s of Ammihud. H1201
Nu 7:54 the eighth day Gamaliel s of Pedahzur, H1201
Nu 7:59 the offering of Gamaliel s of Pedahzur. H1201
Nu 7:60 On the ninth day Abidan s of Gideoni, the H1201
Nu 7:65 was the offering of Abidan s of Gideoni. H1201
Nu 7:66 the tenth day Ahiezer s of Ammishaddai, H1201
Nu 7:71 the offering of Ahiezer s of Ammishaddai. H1201
Nu 7:72 On the eleventh day Pagiel s of Okran H1201
Nu 7:77 This was the offering of Pagiel s of Okran H1201
Nu 7:78 On the twelfth day Ahira s of Enan, the H1201
Nu 7:83 This was the offering of Ahira s of Enan. H1201
Nu 10:14 Nahshon s of Amminadab was in H1201
Nu 10:15 Nethanel s of Zuar was over the division of H1201
Nu 10:16 Eliab s of Helon was over the division H1201
Nu 10:18 Elizur s of Shedeur was in command. H1201
Nu 10:19 Shelumiel s of Zurishaddai was over the H1201
Nu 10:20 Eliasaph s of Deuel was over the H1201
Nu 10:22 Elishama s of Ammihud was in command. H1201
Nu 10:23 Gamaliel s of Pedahzur was over the H1201

Nu 10:24 Abidan s of Gideoni was over the H1201
Nu 10:25 Ahiezer s of Ammishaddai was in H1201
Nu 10:26 Pagiel s of Okran was over the division of H1201
Nu 10:27 Ahira s of Enan was over the division H1201
Nu 10:29 Moses said to Hobab s of Reuel the H1201
Nu 11:28 Joshua s of Nun, who had been Moses' H1201
Nu 13: 4 tribe of Reuben, Shammua s of Zakkur; H1201
Nu 13: 5 the tribe of Simeon, Shaphat s of Hori; H1201
Nu 13: 6 the tribe of Judah, Caleb s of Jephunneh; H1201
Nu 13: 7 the tribe of Issachar, Igal s of Joseph; H1201
Nu 13: 8 the tribe of Ephraim, Hoshea s of Nun; H1201
Nu 13: 9 the tribe of Benjamin, Palti s of Raphu; H1201
Nu 13:10 the tribe of Zebulun, Gaddiel s of Sodi; H1201
Nu 13:11 a tribe of Joseph), Gaddi s of Susi; H1201
Nu 13:12 the tribe of Dan, Ammiel s of Gemalli; H1201
Nu 13:13 the tribe of Asher, Sethur s of Michael; H1201
Nu 13:14 the tribe of Naphtali, Nahbi s of Vophsi; H1201
Nu 13:15 from the tribe of Gad, Geuel s of Maki. H1201
Nu 13:16 Moses gave Hoshea s of Nun the name H1201
Nu 14: 6 Joshua s of Nun and Caleb son of H1201
Nu 14: 6 son of Nun and Caleb s of Jephunneh, H1201
Nu 14:30 except Caleb s of Jephunneh and Joshua H1201
Nu 14:30 son of Jephunneh and Joshua s of Nun. H1201
Nu 14:38 only Joshua s of Nun and Caleb son of H1201
Nu 14:38 of Nun and Caleb s of Jephunneh H1201
Nu 16: 1 Korah s of Izhar, the son of Kohath, the H1201
Nu 16: 1 son of Izhar, the s of Kohath, the son of H1201
Nu 16: 1 son of Kohath, the s of Levi, and certain H1201
Nu 16: 1 of Eliab, and On s of Peleth—became H1201
Nu 16:37 "Tell Eleazar s of Aaron, the priest, to H1201
Nu 18:15 redeem every firstborn s and every firstborn H132
Nu 20:25 Get Aaron and his s Eleazar and take H1201
Nu 20:26 garments and put them on his s Eleazar, H1201
Nu 20:28 garments and put them on his s Eleazar. H1201
Nu 22: 2 Now Balak s of Zippor saw all that Israel H1201
Nu 22: 4 So Balak s of Zippor, who was king of H1201
Nu 22: 5 messengers to summon Balaam s of Beor, H1201
Nu 22:10 said to God, "Balak s of Zippor, king of H1201
Nu 22:16 "This is what Balak s of Zippor says: Do H1201
Nu 23:18 and listen; hear me, s of Zippor. H1201
Nu 24: 3 "The prophecy of Balaam s of Beor, the H1201
Nu 24:15 "The prophecy of Balaam s of Beor, the H1201
Nu 25: 7 When Phinehas s of Eleazar, the son of H1201
Nu 25: 7 son of Eleazar, the s of Aaron, the priest, H1201
Nu 25:11 "Phinehas s of Eleazar, the son of Aaron H1201
Nu 25:11 son of Eleazar, the s of Aaron, the priest, H1201
Nu 25:14 the Midianite woman was Zimri s of Salu, H1201
Nu 26: 1 said to Moses and Eleazar s of Aaron, H1201
Nu 26: 5 of Reuben, the **firstborn** s of Israel, were: AIT
Nu 26: 8 The s of Pallu was Eliab, H1201
Nu 26:33 Zelophehad s of Hepher had no sons; he H1201
Nu 26:65 left except Caleb s of Jephunneh and H1201
Nu 26:65 son of Jephunneh and Joshua s of Nun. H1201
Nu 27: 1 daughters of Zelophehad s of Hepher, H1201
Nu 27: 1 son of Hepher, the s of Gilead, the son of H1201
Nu 27: 1 son of Gilead, the s of Makir, the son of H1201
Nu 27: 1 son of Makir, the s of Manasseh H1201
Nu 27: 1 to the clans of Manasseh s of Joseph. H1201
Nu 27: 4 from his clan because he had no s? H1201
Nu 27: 8 'If a man dies and leaves no s, give his H1201
Nu 27:18 "Take Joshua s of Nun, a man in whom H1201
Nu 31: 6 along with Phinehas s of Eleazar, the H1201
Nu 31: 8 also killed Balaam s of Beor with the H1201
Nu 32:12 not one except Caleb s of Jephunneh the H1201
Nu 32:12 the Kenizzite and Joshua s of Nun, H1201
Nu 32:28 the priest and Joshua s of Nun and to the H1201
Nu 32:33 of Manasseh s of Joseph the kingdom of H1201
Nu 32:39 of Makir s of Manasseh went to H1201
Nu 34:17 Eleazar the priest and Joshua s of Nun. H1201
Nu 34:19 Caleb s of Jephunneh, from the tribe of H1201
Nu 34:20 Shemuel s of Ammihud, from the tribe of H1201
Nu 34:21 Elidad s of Kislon, from the tribe of H1201
Nu 34:22 Bukki s of Jogli, the leader from the tribe H1201
Nu 34:23 Hanniel s of Ephod, the leader from the H1201
Nu 34:23 from the tribe of Manasseh s of Joseph; H1201
Nu 34:24 Kemuel s of Shiphtan, the leader from the H1201
Nu 34:24 from the tribe of Ephraim s of Joseph; NDT
Nu 34:25 Elizaphan s of Parnak, the leader from the H1201
Nu 34:26 Paltiel s of Azzan, the leader from the H1201
Nu 34:27 Ahihud s of Shelomi, the leader from the H1201
Nu 34:28 Pedahel s of Ammihud, the leader from H1201
Nu 36: 1 heads of the clan of Gilead s of Makir, H1201
Nu 36: 1 son of Makir, the s of Manasseh, who H1201
Nu 36:12 descendants of Manasseh s of Joseph, H1201
Dt 1:31 as a father carries his s, all the way you H1201
Dt 1:36 except Caleb s of Jephunneh. He will see H1201
Dt 1:38 assistant, Joshua s of Nun, will enter it. H1201
Dt 5:14 nor your s or daughter, nor your H1201
Dt 6:20 the future, when your s asks you, "What is H1201
Dt 8: 5 your heart that as a man disciplines his s, H1201
Dt 10: 6 Eleazar his s succeeded him as priest. H1201
Dt 13: 6 own brother, or your s or daughter, or the H1201
Dt 18:10 who sacrifices their s or daughter in the H1201
Dt 21:15 the firstborn is the s of the wife he does H1201
Dt 21:16 the firstborn to the s of the wife he loves H1201
Dt 21:16 the s of the wife he does not love. H1201
Dt 21:17 acknowledge the s of his unloved wife as H1201
Dt 21:17 **That** s is the first sign of his father's H2085S
Dt 21:18 rebellious s who does not obey his H1201
Dt 21:20 "This s of ours is stubborn and rebellious. H1201
Dt 23: 4 they hired Balaam s of Beor from Pethor H1201
Dt 25: 5 one of them dies without a s, H1201
Dt 25: 6 The **first** s she bears shall carry on the name AIT
Dt 28:56 she loves and her own s or daughter H1201
Dt 31:23 gave this command to Joshua s of Nun: H1201
Dt 32:44 came with Joshua s of Nun and spoke all H1201
Dt 34: 9 Now Joshua s of Nun was filled with the H1201
Jos 1: 1 the LORD said to Joshua s of Nun, Moses' H1201
Jos 2: 1 Then Joshua s of Nun secretly sent two H1201
Jos 2:23 came to Joshua s of Nun and told him H1201
Jos 6: 6 So Joshua s of Nun called the priests and H1201
Jos 6:26 "At the cost of his **firstborn** s he will lay its AIT
Jos 7: 1 Achan s of Karmi, the son of H1201
Jos 7: 1 son of Karmi, the s of Zimri, the son of H1201
Jos 7: 1 son of Zimri, the s of Zerah, of the tribe H1201
Jos 7:18 by man, and Achan s of Karmi, the son of H1201
Jos 7:18 son of Karmi, the s of Zimri, the son of H1201
Jos 7:18 son of Zimri, the s of Zerah, of the tribe H1201
Jos 7:19 said to Achan, "My s, give glory to the H1201
Jos 7:24 took Achan s of Zerah, the silver, H1201
Jos 13:22 had put to the sword Balaam s of Beor, H1201
Jos 13:31 descendants of Makir s of Manasseh— H1201
Jos 14: 1 Joshua s of Nun and the heads of the H1201
Jos 14: 6 Caleb s of Jephunneh the Kenizzite H1201
Jos 14:13 blessed Caleb s of Jephunneh and gave H1201
Jos 14:14 belonged to Caleb s of Jephunneh the H1201
Jos 15: 6 to the Stone of Bohan s of Reuben. H1201
Jos 15:13 gave to Caleb s of Jephunneh a portion H1201
Jos 15:17 Othniel s of Kenaz, Caleb's brother, took it H1201
Jos 17: 2 of Manasseh s of Joseph by their clans. H1201
Jos 17: 3 Now Zelophehad s of Hepher, the son of H1201
Jos 17: 3 son of Hepher, the s of Gilead, the son of H1201
Jos 17: 3 son of Gilead, the s of Makir, the son of H1201
Jos 17: 3 son of Makir, the s of Manasseh, had no H1201
Jos 17: 4 the priest, Joshua s of Nun, and the H1201
Jos 18:17 down to the Stone of Bohan s of Reuben. H1201
Jos 19:49 gave Joshua s of Nun an inheritance H1201
Jos 19:51 Joshua s of Nun and the heads of the H1201
Jos 21: 1 the priest, Joshua s of Nun, and the H1201
Jos 21:12 had given to Caleb s of Jephunneh as his H1201
Jos 22:13 the Israelites sent Phinehas s of Eleazar, H1201
Jos 22:20 When Achan s of Zerah was unfaithful in H1201
Jos 22:31 And Phinehas s of Eleazar, the priest, said H1201
Jos 22:32 Then Phinehas s of Eleazar, the priest H1201
Jos 24: 9 When Balak s of Zippor, the king of Moab H1201
Jos 24: 9 he sent for Balaam s of Beor to put a H1201
Jos 24:29 Joshua s of Nun, the servant of H1201
Jos 24:33 And Eleazar s of Aaron died and was H1201
Jos 24:33 been allotted to his s Phinehas in the hill H1201
Jdg 1:13 Othniel s of Kenaz, Caleb's younger H1201
Jdg 2: 8 Joshua s of Nun, the servant of the LORD H1201
Jdg 3: 9 a deliverer, Othniel s of Kenaz, Caleb's H1201
Jdg 3:11 forty years, until Othniel s of Kenaz died. H1201
Jdg 3:15 the s of Gera the Benjamite. H1201
Jdg 3:31 After Ehud came Shamgar s of Anath H1201
Jdg 4: 6 She sent for Barak s of Abinoam from H1201
Jdg 4:12 Sisera that Barak s of Abinoam had gone H1201
Jdg 5: 1 Deborah and Barak s of Abinoam sang H1201
Jdg 5: 6 "In the days of Shamgar s of Anath, in the H1201
Jdg 5:12 captive your captives, s of Abinoam.' H1201
Jdg 6:11 where his s Gideon was threshing wheat H1201
Jdg 6:29 they were told, "Gideon s of Joash did it." H1201
Jdg 6:30 demanded of Joash, "Bring out your s. H1201
Jdg 7:14 than the sword of Gideon s of Joash, H1201
Jdg 8:13 Gideon s of Joash then returned from the H1201
Jdg 8:20 to Jether, his **oldest** s, he said, "Kill them AIT
Jdg 8:22 your s and your grandson—because H1201
Jdg 8:23 rule over you, nor will my s rule over you. H1201
Jdg 8:29 Jerub-Baal s of Joash went back home to H1201
Jdg 8:31 also bore him a s, whom he named H1201
Jdg 8:32 Gideon s of Joash died at a good old age H1201
Jdg 9: 1 Abimelek s of Jerub-Baal went to his H1201
Jdg 9: 5 the youngest s of Jerub-Baal, escaped H1201
Jdg 9:18 made Abimelek, the s of his female slave H1201
Jdg 9:26 Now Gaal s of Ebed moved with his clan H1201
Jdg 9:28 Then Gaal s of Ebed said, "Who is H1201
Jdg 9:28 Isn't he Jerub-Baal's s, and isn't Zebul his H1201
Jdg 9:30 the city heard what Gaal s of Ebed said, H1201
Jdg 9:31 "Gaal s of Ebed and his clan have come H1201
Jdg 9:35 Now Gaal s of Ebed had gone out and H1201
Jdg 9:57 curse of Jotham s of Jerub-Baal came on H1201
Jdg 10: 1 a man of Issachar named Tola s of Puah H1201
Jdg 10: 1 son of Puah, the s of Dodo, rose to save H1201
Jdg 11: 2 "because you are the s of another woman." H1201
Jdg 11:25 Are you any better than Balak s of Zippor H1201
Jdg 11:34 her he had neither s nor daughter. H1201
Jdg 12:13 After him, Abdon s of Hillel, from H1201
Jdg 12:15 Then Abdon s of Hillel died and was H1201
Jdg 13: 3 to become pregnant and give birth to a s. H1201
Jdg 13: 5 have a s whose head is never H1201
Jdg 13: 7 'You will become pregnant and have a s. H1201
Jdg 17: 2 mother said, "The LORD bless you, my s!" H1201
Jdg 17: 3 to the LORD for my s to make an image H1201
Jdg 18:30 and Jonathan s of Gershom, the son H1201
Jdg 18:30 son of Gershom, the s of Moses, and his H1201
Jdg 20:28 with Phinehas s of Eleazar, the son of H1201
Jdg 20:28 son of Eleazar, the s of Aaron, ministering H1201
Ru 4:13 her to conceive, and she gave birth to a s. H1201
Ru 4:17 women living there said, "Naomi has a s!" H1201
1Sa 1: 1 whose name was Elkanah s of Jeroham H1201
1Sa 1: 1 son of Jeroham, the s of Elihu, the son of H1201
1Sa 1: 1 the son of Elihu, the s of Tohu, the son of H1201
1Sa 1: 1 son of Tohu, the s of Zuph, an Ephraimite H1201
1Sa 1:11 forget your servant but give her a s, H2446+408
1Sa 1:20 became pregnant and gave birth to a s. H1201
1Sa 1:23 home and nursed her s until she had H1201
1Sa 3: 6 "My s," Eli said, "I did not call; go back H1201
1Sa 3:16 Eli called him and said, "Samuel, my s." H1201
1Sa 4:16 Eli asked, "What happened, my s?" H1201
1Sa 4:20 despair; you have given birth to a s." H1201
1Sa 7: 1 Eleazar his s to guard the ark of the H1201
1Sa 9: 1 whose name was Kish s of Abiel, the son H1201
1Sa 9: 1 son of Abiel, the s of Zeror, the son of H1201
1Sa 9: 1 son of Zeror, the s of Bekorath, the son of H1201
1Sa 9: 1 of Bekorath, the s of Aphiah of Benjamin. H1201
1Sa 9: 2 Kish had a s named Saul, as handsome a H1201
1Sa 9: 3 Kish said to his s Saul, "Take one of H1201
1Sa 10: 2 He is asking, "What shall I do about my s?" H1201
1Sa 10:11 is this that has happened to the s of Kish? H1201
1Sa 10:21 Finally Saul s of Kish was taken H1201
1Sa 13:16 Saul and his s Jonathan and the men H1201
1Sa 13:22 only Saul and his s Jonathan had them. H1201
1Sa 14: 1 One day Jonathan s of Saul said to his H1201
1Sa 14: 3 He was a s of Ichabod's brother Ahitub H1201
1Sa 14: 3 of Ichabod's brother Ahitub s of Phinehas, H1201
1Sa 14: 3 son of Phinehas, the s of Eli, the LORD's H1201
1Sa 14:39 even if the guilt lies with my s Jonathan H1201
1Sa 14:40 I and Jonathan my s will stand over here." H1201
1Sa 14:41 If the fault is in me or my s Jonathan H1201
1Sa 14:42 the lot between me and Jonathan my s." H1201
1Sa 14:50 of Saul's army was Abner s of Ner, H1201
1Sa 16:18 "I have seen a s of Jesse of Bethlehem H1201
1Sa 16:19 "Send me your s David, who is with H1201
1Sa 16:20 sent them with his s David to Saul. H1201
1Sa 17:12 Now David was the s of an Ephrathite H1201
1Sa 17:17 Now Jesse said to his s David, "Take this H1201
1Sa 17:55 "Abner, whose s is that young man?" H1201
1Sa 17:56 "Find out whose s this young man is." H1201
1Sa 17:58 "Whose s are you, young man?" Saul H1201
1Sa 17:58 "I am the s of your servant Jesse of H1201
1Sa 19: 1 Saul told his s Jonathan and all the H1201
1Sa 20:27 Then Saul said to his s Jonathan, "Why H1201
1Sa 20:27 "Why hasn't the s of Jesse come to the H1201
1Sa 20:30 "You s of a perverse and rebellious H1201
1Sa 20:30 have sided with the s of Jesse to your own H1201
1Sa 20:31 As long as the s of Jesse lives on this H1201
1Sa 22: 7 Will the s of Jesse give all of you fields H1201
1Sa 22: 8 tells me when my s makes a covenant H1201
1Sa 22: 8 son makes a covenant with the s of Jesse. H1201
1Sa 22: 8 tells me that my s has incited my H1201
1Sa 22: 9 "I saw the s of Jesse come to Ahimelek H1201
1Sa 22: 9 come to Ahimelek s of Ahitub at Nob. H1201
1Sa 22:11 priest Ahimelek s of Ahitub and all the H1201
1Sa 22:12 "Listen now, s of Ahitub." "Yes, my H1201
1Sa 22:13 you and the s of Jesse, giving him H1201
1Sa 22:20 But one s of Ahimelek son of Ahitub H1201
1Sa 22:20 But one son of Ahimelek s of Ahitub H1201
1Sa 23: 6 Now Abiathar s of Ahimelek had brought H1201
1Sa 23:16 And Saul's s Jonathan went to David at H1201
1Sa 24:16 "Is that your voice, David my s?" H1201
1Sa 25: 8 servants and your s David whatever you H1201
1Sa 25:10 Who is this s of Jesse? Many H1201
1Sa 25:44 to Paltiel s of Laish, who was from H1201
1Sa 26: 5 He saw where Saul and Abner s of Ner H1201
1Sa 26: 6 the Hittite and Abishai s of Zeruiah, H1201
1Sa 26:14 out to the army and to Abner s of Ner, H1201
1Sa 26:17 said, "Is that your voice, David my s?" H1201
1Sa 26:21 Come back, David my s. Because you H1201
1Sa 26:25 be blessed, David my s; you will do great H1201
1Sa 27: 2 over to Achish s of Maok king of Gath. H1201
1Sa 30: 7 the priest, the s of Ahimelek, "Bring me H1201
2Sa 1: 4 And Saul and his s Jonathan are dead." H1201
2Sa 1: 5 that Saul and his s Jonathan are dead?" H1201
2Sa 1:12 till evening for Saul and his s Jonathan, H1201
2Sa 1:13 "I am the s of a foreigner, an Amalekite," H1201
2Sa 1:17 concerning Saul and his s Jonathan, H1201
2Sa 2: 8 Meanwhile, Abner s of Ner, the H1201
2Sa 2: 8 taken Ish-Bosheth s of Saul and brought H1201
2Sa 2:10 Ish-Bosheth s of Saul was forty years old H1201
2Sa 2:12 Abner s of Ner, together with the men of H1201
2Sa 2:12 with the men of Ish-Bosheth s of Saul, H1201
2Sa 2:13 Joab s of Zeruiah and David's men went H1201
2Sa 2:15 Benjamin and Ish-Bosheth s of Saul, H1201
2Sa 3: 2 was Amnon the s of Ahinoam of Jezreel; NDT
2Sa 3: 3 Kileab the s of Abigail the widow of Nabal NDT
2Sa 3: 3 Absalom the s of Maakah daughter of H1201
2Sa 3: 4 Adonijah the s of Haggith; the fifth, H1201
2Sa 3: 4 the fifth, Shephatiah the s of Abital; H1201
2Sa 3: 5 Ithream the s of David's wife Eglah. NDT
2Sa 3:14 sent messengers to Ish-Bosheth s of Saul, H1201
2Sa 3:15 away from her husband Paltiel s of Laish. H1201
2Sa 3:23 was told that Abner s of Ner had come to H1201
2Sa 3:25 You know Abner s of Ner; he came to H1201
2Sa 3:28 concerning the blood of Abner s of Ner. H1201
2Sa 3:37 no part in the murder of Abner s of Ner. H1201
2Sa 4: 1 When Ish-Bosheth s of Saul heard that H1201
2Sa 4: 2 Now Saul's s had two men who were H1201
2Sa 4: 4 Jonathan s of Saul had a son who was H1201
2Sa 4: 4 son of Saul had a s who was lame in both H1201
2Sa 4: 8 is the head of Ish-Bosheth s of Saul, H1201
2Sa 7:14 he will be my s. When he does H1201
2Sa 8: 3 David defeated Hadadezer s of Rehob H1201
2Sa 8:10 he sent his s Joram to King David to greet H1201
2Sa 8:12 taken from Hadadezer s of Rehob, H1201
2Sa 8:16 Joab s of Zeruiah was over the army H1201
2Sa 8:16 Jehoshaphat s of Ahilud was recorder; H1201

2Sa 8:17 Zadok s of Ahitub and Ahimelek son of H1201
2Sa 8:17 Ahitub and Ahimelek s of Abiathar were H1201
2Sa 8:18 Benaiah s of Jehoiada was over the H1201
2Sa 9: 3 "There is still a s of Jonathan; he is lame H1201
2Sa 9: 4 the house of Makir s of Ammiel in Lo H1201
2Sa 9: 5 from the house of Makir s of Ammiel. H1201
2Sa 9: 6 When Mephibosheth s of Jonathan, the H1201
2Sa 9: 6 of Jonathan, the s of Saul, came to David H1201
2Sa 9:12 had a young s named Mika, H1201
2Sa 10: 1 his s Hanun succeeded him as king. H1201
2Sa 10: 2 will show kindness to Hanun s of Nahash, H1201
2Sa 11:21 Who killed Abimelek s of Jerub-Besheth H1201
2Sa 11:27 she became his wife and bore him a s. H1201
2Sa 12:14 the LORD, the s born to you will die." H1201
2Sa 12:24 She gave birth to a s, and they named H1201
2Sa 13: 1 Amnon s of David fell in love with Tamar H1201
2Sa 13: 1 the beautiful sister of Absalom s of David. H1201
2Sa 13: 3 an adviser named Jonadab s of Shimeah, H1201
2Sa 13: 4 the king's s, look so haggard H1201
2Sa 13:25 my s," the king replied. "All of us H1201
2Sa 13:32 But Jonadab s of Shimeah, David's H1201
2Sa 13:37 fled and went to Talmai s of Ammihud, H1201
2Sa 13:37 King David mourned many days for his s. H1201
2Sa 14: 1 Joab s of Zeruiah knew that the king's H1201
2Sa 14:11 so that my s will not be destroyed. H1201
2Sa 14:13 king has not brought back his banished s? NDT
2Sa 14:16 off both me and my s from God's H1201
2Sa 15:27 Take your s Ahimaaz with you, and also H1201
2Sa 15:27 with you, and also Abiathar's s Jonathan. H1201
2Sa 15:36 Ahimaaz s of Zadok and Jonathan son of NDT
2Sa 15:36 son of Zadok and Jonathan s of Abiathar, NDT
2Sa 16: 5 His name was Shimei s of Gera, and he H1201
2Sa 16: 8 into the hands of your s Absalom. H1201
2Sa 16: 9 Then Abishai s of Zeruiah said to the king H1201
2Sa 16:11 all his officials, "My s, my own flesh and H1201
2Sa 16:19 Should I not serve the s? Just as I served H1201
2Sa 17:25 Amasa was the s of Jether, an Ishmaelite H1201
2Sa 17:27 Shobi s of Nahash from Rabbah of the H1201
2Sa 17:27 Makir s of Ammiel from Lo Debar H1201
2Sa 18: 2 under Joab's brother Abishai s of Zeruiah, H1201
2Sa 18:12 I would not lay a hand on the king's s. H1201
2Sa 18:18 "I have no s to carry on the memory of my H1201
2Sa 18:19 Now Ahimaaz s of Zadok said, "Let me H1201
2Sa 18:20 do so today, because the king's s is dead." H1201
2Sa 18:22 Ahimaaz s of Zadok again said to Joab H1201
2Sa 18:22 Joab replied, "My s, why do you want to H1201
2Sa 18:27 the first one runs like Ahimaaz s of Zadok." H1201
2Sa 18:33 "O my s Absalom! My son, my H1201
2Sa 18:33 my son Absalom! My s, my son Absalom H1201
2Sa 18:33 My son, my s Absalom! If only I H1201
2Sa 18:33 of you—O Absalom, my s, my son! H1201
2Sa 18:33 of you—O Absalom, my son, my s! H1201
2Sa 19: 2 "The king is grieving for his s. H1201
2Sa 19: 4 face and cried aloud, "O my s Absalom! H1201
2Sa 19: 4 son Absalom! O Absalom, my s, my son!" H1201
2Sa 19: 4 son Absalom! O Absalom, my son, my s!" H1201
2Sa 19:16 Shimei s of Gera, the Benjamite from H1201
2Sa 19:18 When Shimei s of Gera crossed the H1201
2Sa 19:21 Then Abishai s of Zeruiah said H1201
2Sa 20: 1 a troublemaker named Sheba s of Bikri, H1201
2Sa 20: 1 no share in David, no part in Jesse's s! H1201
2Sa 20: 2 deserted David to follow Sheba s of Bikri. H1201
2Sa 20: 6 "Now Sheba s of Bikri will do us more H1201
2Sa 20: 7 from Jerusalem to pursue Sheba s of Bikri. H1201
2Sa 20:10 brother Abishai pursued Sheba s of Bikri. H1201
2Sa 20:13 on with Joab to pursue Sheba s of Bikri. H1201
2Sa 20:21 A man named Sheba s of Bikri, from the H1201
2Sa 20:22 the head of Sheba s of Bikri and threw it H1201
2Sa 20:23 Benaiah s of Jehoiada was over the H1201
2Sa 20:24 Jehoshaphat s of Ahilud was recorder H1201
2Sa 21: 7 king spared Mephibosheth s of Jonathan, H1201
2Sa 21: 7 son of Jonathan, the s of Saul, because of H1201
2Sa 21: 7 between David and Jonathan s of Saul. H1201
2Sa 21: 8 she had borne to Adriel s of Barzillai the H1201
2Sa 21:12 of Saul and his s Jonathan from the H1201
2Sa 21:13 of Saul and his s Jonathan from there, H1201
2Sa 21:14 of Saul and his s Jonathan in the tomb H1201
2Sa 21:17 But Abishai s of Zeruiah came to David's H1201
2Sa 21:19 Elhanan s of Jairthe Bethlehemite killed H1201
2Sa 21:21 Jonathan s of Shimeah, David's H1201
2Sa 23: 1 inspired utterance of David s of Jesse, H1201
2Sa 23: 9 him was Eleazar s of Dodai the Ahohite H1201
2Sa 23:11 him was Shammah s of Agee the Hararite H1201
2Sa 23:18 the brother of Joab s of Zeruiah was chief H1201
2Sa 23:20 Benaiah s of Jehoiada, a valiant fighter H1201
2Sa 23:22 the exploits of Benaiah s of Jehoiada; H1201
2Sa 23:24 Elhanan s of Dodo from Bethlehem H1201
2Sa 23:26 the Paltite, Ira s of Ikkesh from Tekoa, H1201
2Sa 23:29 Heled s of Baanah the Netophathite, Ithai H1201
2Sa 23:29 Ithai s of Ribai from Gibeah in Benjamin H1201
2Sa 23:33 s of Shammah the Hararite, Ahiam son of H1201
2Sa 23:33 Hararite, Ahiam s of Sharar the Hararite H1201
2Sa 23:34 Eliphelet s of Ahasbai the Maakathite H1201
2Sa 23:34 Eliam s of Ahithophel the Gilonite H1201
2Sa 23:36 Igal s of Nathan from Zobah, the son of H1201
2Sa 23:36 son of Nathan from Zobah, the s of Hagri, H1201
2Sa 23:37 the armor-bearer of Joab s of Zeruiah, H1201
1Ki 1: 7 conferred with Joab s of Zeruiah and with H1201
1Ki 1: 8 the priest, Benaiah s of Jehoiada, Nathan H1201
1Ki 1:11 that Adonijah, the s of Haggith, has H1201
1Ki 1:12 own life and the life of your s Solomon. H1201
1Ki 1:13 "Surely Solomon your s shall be king after H1201
1Ki 1:17 'Solomon your s shall be king after me H1201
1Ki 1:21 I and my s Solomon will be treated as H1201
1Ki 1:26 Benaiah s of Jehoiada, and your H1201
1Ki 1:30 Solomon your s shall be king after me H1201
1Ki 1:32 the prophet and Benaiah s of Jehoiada." H1201
1Ki 1:33 have Solomon my s mount my own mule H1201
1Ki 1:36 Benaiah s of Jehoiada answered the king H1201
1Ki 1:38 the prophet, Benaiah s of Jehoiada, the H1201
1Ki 1:42 Jonathan s of Abiathar the priest arrived. H1201
1Ki 1:44 the prophet, Benaiah s of Jehoiada, the H1201
1Ki 2: 1 he gave a charge to Solomon his s. H1201
1Ki 2: 5 know what Joab s of Zeruiah did to me— H1201
1Ki 2: 5 Abner s of Ner and Amasa son of Jether. H1201
1Ki 2: 5 Abner son of Ner and Amasa s of Jether. H1201
1Ki 2: 8 you have with you Shimei s of Gera, the H1201
1Ki 2:13 Now Adonijah, the s of Haggith, went to H1201
1Ki 2:22 Abiathar the priest and Joab s of Zeruiah!" H1201
1Ki 2:25 gave orders to Benaiah s of Jehoiada, H1201
1Ki 2:29 Solomon ordered Benaiah s of Jehoiada, H1201
1Ki 2:32 of them—Abner s of Ner, commander of H1201
1Ki 2:32 and Amasa s of Jether, commander H1201
1Ki 2:34 So Benaiah s of Jehoiada went up and H1201
1Ki 2:35 king put Benaiah s of Jehoiada over the H1201
1Ki 2:39 slaves ran off to Achish s of Maakah, H1201
1Ki 2:46 gave the order to Benaiah s of Jehoiada, H1201
1Ki 3: 6 have given him a s to sit on his throne H1201
1Ki 3:19 night this woman's s died because she H1201
1Ki 3:20 night and took my s from my side while I H1201
1Ki 3:20 breast and put her dead s by my breast. H1201
1Ki 3:21 I got up to nurse my s—and he was dead! H1201
1Ki 3:21 I saw that it wasn't the s I had borne." H1201
1Ki 3:22 The living one is my s; the dead one is H1201
1Ki 3:23 'My s is alive and your son is dead H1201
1Ki 3:23 'My son is alive and your s is dead,' while H1201
1Ki 3:23 Your s is dead and mine is alive H1201
1Ki 3:26 The woman whose s was alive was H1201
1Ki 3:26 out of love for her s and said to the king, H1201
1Ki 4: 2 Azariah s of Zadok—the priest; H1201
1Ki 4: 3 Jehoshaphat s of Ahilud—recorder; H1201
1Ki 4: 4 Benaiah s of Jehoiada—commander in H1201
1Ki 4: 5 Azariah s of Nathan—in charge of the H1201
1Ki 4: 5 governors; Zabud s of Nathan—a priest H1201
1Ki 4: 6 Adoniram s of Abda—in charge of H1201
1Ki 4:12 Baana s of Ahilud—in Taanach and H1201
1Ki 4:13 of Jair s of Manasseh in Gilead H1201
1Ki 4:14 Ahinadab s of Iddo—in Mahanaim; H1201
1Ki 4:16 Baana s of Hushai—in Asher and in Aloth H1201
1Ki 4:17 Jehoshaphat s of Paruah—in Issachar; H1201
1Ki 4:18 Shimei s of Ela—in Benjamin; H1201
1Ki 4:19 Geber s of Uri—in Gilead (the country of H1201
1Ki 5: 5 'Your s whom I will put on the throne in H1201
1Ki 5: 7 has given David a wise s to rule over this H1201
1Ki 8:19 the temple, but your s, your own flesh H1201
1Ki 11:12 I will tear it out of the hand of your s. H1201
1Ki 11:20 Tahpenes bore him a s named Genubath, H1201
1Ki 11:23 adversary, Rezon s of Eliada, who had H1201
1Ki 11:26 Jeroboam s of Nebat rebelled against the H1201
1Ki 11:36 give one tribe to his s so that David my H1201
1Ki 11:43 And Rehoboam his s succeeded him as H1201
1Ki 12: 2 When Jeroboam s of Nebat heard this (he H1201
1Ki 12:15 spoken to Jeroboam s of Nebat through H1201
1Ki 12:16 we have in David, what part in Jesse's s? H1201
1Ki 12:21 the kingdom for Rehoboam s of Solomon. H1201
1Ki 12:23 "Say to Rehoboam s of Solomon king of H1201
1Ki 13: 2 'A s named Josiah will be born to the H1201
1Ki 14: 1 that time Abijah s of Jeroboam became H1201
1Ki 14: 5 wife is coming to ask you about her s, H1201
1Ki 14:20 And Nadab his s succeeded him as king. H1201
1Ki 14:21 Rehoboam s of Solomon was king in H1201
1Ki 14:31 And Abijah his s succeeded him as king. H1201
1Ki 15: 1 year of the reign of Jeroboam s of Nebat, H1201
1Ki 15: 4 by raising up a s to succeed him and by H1201
1Ki 15: 8 And Asa his s succeeded him as king H1201
1Ki 15:18 sent them to Ben-Hadad s of Tabrimmon, H1201
1Ki 15:18 of Tabrimmon, the s of Hezion, the king H1201
1Ki 15:24 And Jehoshaphat his s succeeded him as H1201
1Ki 15:25 Nadab s of Jeroboam became king of H1201
1Ki 15:27 Baasha s of Ahijah from the tribe of H1201
1Ki 15:33 Baasha s of Ahijah became king of all H1201
1Ki 16: 1 LORD came to Jehu s of Hanani concerning H1201
1Ki 16: 3 house like that of Jeroboam s of Nebat. H1201
1Ki 16: 6 And Elah his s succeeded him as king H1201
1Ki 16: 7 the prophet Jehu s of Hanani to Baasha H1201
1Ki 16: 8 Elah s of Baasha became king of Israel H1201
1Ki 16:13 Baasha and his s Elah had committed H1201
1Ki 16:21 half supported Tibni s of Ginath for king H1201
1Ki 16:22 stronger than those of Tibni s of Ginath. H1201
1Ki 16:26 the ways of Jeroboam s of Nebat, H1201
1Ki 16:28 And Ahab his s succeeded him as king H1201
1Ki 16:29 Ahab s of Omri became king of Israel H1201
1Ki 16:30 Ahab s of Omri did more evil in the eyes H1201
1Ki 16:31 commit the sins of Jeroboam s of Nebat, H1201
1Ki 16:34 at the cost of his **firstborn** *s* Abiram, AIT
1Ki 16:34 its gates at the cost of his **youngest** *s* Segub, AIT
1Ki 16:34 of the LORD spoken by Joshua s of Nun. H1201
1Ki 17:12 make a meal for myself and my s, H1201
1Ki 17:13 make something for yourself and your s. H1201
1Ki 17:17 Some time later the s of the woman who H1201
1Ki 17:18 to remind me of my sin and kill my s?" H1201
1Ki 17:19 "Give me your s," Elijah replied. He took H1201
1Ki 17:20 I am staying with, by causing her s to die?" H1201
1Ki 17:23 his mother and said, "Look, your s is alive!" H1201
1Ki 19:16 anoint Jehu s of Nimshi king over Israel H1201
1Ki 19:16 anoint Elisha s of Shaphat from Abel H1201
1Ki 19:19 from there and found Elisha s of Shaphat. H1201
1Ki 21:22 that of Jeroboam s of Nebat and that of H1201
1Ki 21:22 of Nebat and that of Baasha s of Ahijah, H1201
1Ki 21:29 bring it on his house in the days of his s." H1201
1Ki 22: 8 He is Micaiah s of Imlah." "The king H1201
1Ki 22: 9 "Bring Micaiah s of Imlah at once." H1201
1Ki 22:11 Now Zedekiah s of Kenaanah had made H1201
1Ki 22:24 Then Zedekiah s of Kenaanah went up H1201
1Ki 22:26 ruler of the city and to Joash the king's s H1201
1Ki 22:40 And Ahaziah his s succeeded him as king. H1201
1Ki 22:41 Jehoshaphat s of Asa became king of H1201
1Ki 22:49 At that time Ahaziah s of Ahab said to H1201
1Ki 22:50 And Jehoram his s succeeded him as king H1201
1Ki 22:51 Ahaziah s of Ahab became king of Israel H1201
1Ki 22:52 mother and of Jeroboam s of Nebat, H1201
2Ki 1:17 Because Ahaziah had no s, Joram H1201
2Ki 1:17 year of Jehoram s of Jehoshaphat king of H1201
2Ki 3: 1 Joram s of Ahab became king of Israel in H1201
2Ki 3: 3 clung to the sins of Jeroboam s of Nebat, H1201
2Ki 3:11 answered, "Elisha s of Shaphat is here. H1201
2Ki 3:27 Then he took his firstborn s, who was to H1201
2Ki 4: 6 she said to her s, "Bring me another H1201
2Ki 4:14 "She has no s, and her husband is H1201
2Ki 4:16 "you will hold a s in your arms. H1201
2Ki 4:17 that same time she gave birth to a s, H1201
2Ki 4:28 "Did I ask you for a s, my lord?" she said H1201
2Ki 4:36 When she came, he said, "Take your s." H1201
2Ki 4:37 Then she took her s and went out. H1201
2Ki 6:28 'Give up your s so we may eat him today H1201
2Ki 6:28 him today, and tomorrow we'll eat my s. H1201
2Ki 6:29 So we cooked my s and ate him. The next H1201
2Ki 6:29 'Give up your s so we may eat him,' H1201
2Ki 6:31 the head of Elisha s of Shaphat remains H1201
2Ki 8: 1 to the woman whose s he had restored to H1201
2Ki 8: 5 the woman whose s Elisha had brought H1201
2Ki 8: 5 this is her s whom Elisha restored to H1201
2Ki 8: 9 "Your s Ben-Hadad king of Aram has sent H1201
2Ki 8:16 fifth year of Joram s of Ahab king of Israel H1201
2Ki 8:16 Jehoram s of Jehoshaphat began his H1201
2Ki 8:24 And Ahaziah his s succeeded him as king. H1201
2Ki 8:25 year of Joram s of Ahab king of Israel, H1201
2Ki 8:25 Ahaziah s of Jehoram king of Judah H1201
2Ki 8:28 went with Joram s of Ahab to war against H1201
2Ki 8:29 Then Ahaziah s of Jehoram king of Judah H1201
2Ki 8:29 down to Jezreel to see Joram s of Ahab, H1201
2Ki 9: 2 look for Jehu s of Jehoshaphat, the H1201
2Ki 9: 2 Jehu son of Jehoshaphat, the s of Nimshi. H1201
2Ki 9: 9 house of Jeroboam s of Nebat and like H1201
2Ki 9: 9 like the house of Baasha s of Ahijah. H1201
2Ki 9:14 So Jehu s of Jehoshaphat, the son of H1201
2Ki 9:14 Jehoshaphat, the s of Nimshi, conspired H1201
2Ki 9:20 driving is like that of Jehu s of Nimshi— H1201
2Ki 9:29 In the eleventh year of Joram s of Ahab H1201
2Ki 10:15 he came upon Jehonadab s of Rekab H1201
2Ki 10:23 Jehu and Jehonadab s of Rekab went into H1201
2Ki 10:29 from the sins of Jeroboam s of Nebat, H1201
2Ki 10:35 And Jehoahaz his s succeeded him as H1201
2Ki 11: 1 of Ahaziah saw that her s was dead, H1201
2Ki 11: 2 took Joash s of Ahaziah and stole him H1201
2Ki 11: 4 Then he showed them the king's s. H1201
2Ki 11:12 out the king's s and put the crown on H1201
2Ki 12:21 him were Jozabad s of Shimeath and H1201
2Ki 12:21 of Shimeath and Jehozabad s of Shomer. H1201
2Ki 12:21 And Amaziah his s succeeded him as H1201
2Ki 13: 1 year of Joash s of Ahaziah king of Judah, H1201
2Ki 13: 1 Jehoahaz s of Jehu became king of Israel H1201
2Ki 13: 2 the sins of Jeroboam s of Nebat, H1201
2Ki 13: 3 king of Aram and Ben-Hadad his s. H1201
2Ki 13: 9 And Jehoash his s succeeded him as king. H1201
2Ki 13:10 Jehoash s of Jehoahaz became king of H1201
2Ki 13:11 any of the sins of Jeroboam s of Nebat, H1201
2Ki 13:24 Ben-Hadad his s succeeded him as H1201
2Ki 13:25 Then Jehoash s of Jehoahaz recaptured H1201
2Ki 13:25 from Ben-Hadad s of Hazael the towns he H1201
2Ki 14: 1 year of Jehoash s of Jehoahaz king of H1201
2Ki 14: 1 Amaziah s of Joash king of Judah began H1201
2Ki 14: 8 messengers to Jehoash s of Jehoahaz, H1201
2Ki 14: 8 son of Jehoahaz, the s of Jehu, king of H1201
2Ki 14: 9 'Give your daughter to my s in marriage. H1201
2Ki 14:13 king of Judah, the s of Joash, the son of H1201
2Ki 14:13 son of Joash, the s of Ahaziah, at Beth H1201
2Ki 14:16 And Jeroboam his s succeeded him as H1201
2Ki 14:17 Amaziah s of Joash king of Judah lived H1201
2Ki 14:17 death of Jehoash s of Jehoahaz king of H1201
2Ki 14:23 year of Amaziah s of Joash king of Judah, H1201
2Ki 14:23 Jeroboam s of Jehoash king of Israel H1201
2Ki 14:24 any of the sins of Jeroboam s of Nebat, H1201
2Ki 14:25 through his servant Jonah s of Amittai, H1201
2Ki 14:27 by the hand of Jeroboam s of Jehoash. H1201
2Ki 14:29 And Zechariah his s succeeded him as H1201
2Ki 15: 1 Azariah s of Amaziah king of Judah H1201
2Ki 15: 5 Jotham the king's s had charge of the H1201
2Ki 15: 7 And Jotham his s succeeded him as king H1201
2Ki 15: 8 Zechariah s of Jeroboam became king of H1201
2Ki 15: 9 from the sins of Jeroboam s of Nebat, H1201
2Ki 15:10 Shallum s of Jabesh conspired against H1201
2Ki 15:13 Shallum s of Jabesh became king in the H1201
2Ki 15:14 Then Menahem s of Gadi went from H1201
2Ki 15:14 attacked Shallum s of Jabesh in Samaria, H1201
2Ki 15:17 Menahem s of Gadi became king of Israel H1201

2Ki 15:18 from the sins of Jeroboam s of Nebat, H1201
2Ki 15:22 And Pekahiah his s succeeded him as H1201
2Ki 15:23 Pekahiah s of Menahem became king of H1201
2Ki 15:24 from the sins of Jeroboam s of Nebat, H1201
2Ki 15:25 officers, Pekah s of Remaliah, conspired H1201
2Ki 15:27 Pekah s of Remaliah became king of H1201
2Ki 15:28 from the sins of Jeroboam s of Nebat, H1201
2Ki 15:30 Then Hoshea s of Elah conspired against H1201
2Ki 15:30 conspired against Pekah s of Remaliah. H1201
2Ki 15:30 the twentieth year of Jotham s of Uzziah. H1201
2Ki 15:32 year of Pekah s of Remaliah king of H1201
2Ki 15:32 Jotham s of Uzziah king of Judah began H1201
2Ki 15:37 of Aram and Pekah s of Remaliah against H1201
2Ki 15:38 And Ahaz his s succeeded him as king H1201
2Ki 16: 1 seventeenth year of Pekah s of Remaliah, H1201
2Ki 16: 1 Ahaz s of Jotham king of Judah began to H1201
2Ki 16: 3 Israel and even sacrificed his s in the fire, H1201
2Ki 16: 5 of Aram and Pekah s of Remaliah king of H1201
2Ki 16:20 And Hezekiah his s succeeded him as H1201
2Ki 17: 1 Hoshea s of Elah became king of Israel in H1201
2Ki 17:21 made Jeroboam s of Nebat their king. H1201
2Ki 18: 1 year of Hoshea s of Elah king of Israel H1201
2Ki 18: 1 Hezekiah s of Ahaz king of Judah began H1201
2Ki 18: 9 year of Hoshea s of Elah king of Israel, H1201
2Ki 18:18 Eliakim s of Hilkiah the palace H1201
2Ki 18:18 Joah s of Asaph the recorder went H1201
2Ki 18:26 Then Eliakim s of Hilkiah, and Shebna H1201
2Ki 18:37 Then Eliakim s of Hilkiah the palace H1201
2Ki 18:37 Joah s of Asaph the recorder went to H1201
2Ki 19: 2 to the prophet Isaiah s of Amoz. H1201
2Ki 19:20 Then Isaiah s of Amoz sent a message to H1201
2Ki 19:37 And Esarhaddon his s succeeded him as H1201
2Ki 20: 1 The prophet Isaiah s of Amoz went to him H1201
2Ki 20:12 Marduk-Baladan s of Baladan king of H1201
2Ki 20:21 And Manasseh his s succeeded him as H1201
2Ki 21: 6 He sacrificed his own s in the fire H1201
2Ki 21: 7 had said to David and to his s Solomon, H1201
2Ki 21:18 And Amon his s succeeded him as king H1201
2Ki 21:24 they made Josiah his s king in his place. H1201
2Ki 21:26 And Josiah his s succeeded him as king H1201
2Ki 22: 3 secretary, Shaphan s of Azaliah, the son H1201
2Ki 22: 3 son of Azaliah, the s of Meshullam, to the H1201
2Ki 22:12 the priest, Ahikam s of Shaphan, Akbor H1201
2Ki 22:12 of Shaphan, Akbor s of Micaiah, Shaphan H1201
2Ki 22:14 who was the wife of Shallum s of Tikvah H1201
2Ki 22:14 son of Tikvah, the s of Harhas, keeper of H1201
2Ki 23:10 it to sacrifice their s or daughter in the fire H1201
2Ki 23:15 high place made by Jeroboam s of Nebat, H1201
2Ki 23:30 land took Jehoahaz s of Josiah and H1201
2Ki 23:34 Necho made Eliakim s of Josiah king in H1201
2Ki 24: 6 And Jehoiachin his s succeeded him as H1201
2Ki 25:22 Babylon appointed Gedaliah s of Ahikam, H1201
2Ki 25:22 son of Ahikam, the s of Shaphan, to be H1201
2Ki 25:23 at Mizpah—Ishmael s of Nethaniah H1201
2Ki 25:23 Nethaniah, Johanan s of Kareah, Seraiah H1201
2Ki 25:23 Seraiah s of Tanhumeth the Netophathite, H1201
2Ki 25:23 Jaazaniah the s of the Maakathite, and H1201
2Ki 25:25 however, Ishmael s of Nethaniah, the son H1201
2Ki 25:25 of Nethaniah, the s of Elishama, who was H1201
1Ch 1:41 The s of Anah: Dishon. The sons of H1201
1Ch 1:43 Bela s of Beor, whose city was named H1201
1Ch 1:44 Jobab s of Zerah from Bozrah succeeded H1201
1Ch 1:46 Husham died, Hadad s of Bedad, who H1201
1Ch 1:49 Baal-Hanan s of Akbor succeeded him as H1201
1Ch 2: 7 The s of Karmi: Achar, who brought H1201
1Ch 2: 8 The s of Ethan: Azariah. H1201
1Ch 2:13 firstborn; the second s was Abinadab, the NDT
1Ch 2:18 Caleb s of Hezron had children by his wife H1201
1Ch 2:31 The s of Appaim: Ishi, who was the father H1201
1Ch 2:42 of Ziph, and his s Mareshah, who was the H1201
1Ch 2:45 The s of Shammai was Maon, and Maon H1201
1Ch 3: 1 was Amnon the s of Ahinoam of Jezreel; NDT
1Ch 3: 1 Daniel the s of Abigail of Carmel; NDT
1Ch 3: 2 Absalom the s of Maakah daughter of H1201
1Ch 3: 2 the fourth, Adonijah the s of Haggith; H1201
1Ch 3: 3 Shephatiah the s of Abital; and the NDT
1Ch 3:10 Solomon's s was Rehoboam, Abijah his H1201
1Ch 3:10 was Rehoboam, Abijah his s, Asa his son, H1201
1Ch 3:10 his son, Asa his s, Jehoshaphat his son, H1201
1Ch 3:10 his son, Asa his son, Jehoshaphat his s, H1201
1Ch 3:11 Jehoram his s, Ahaziah his son, Joash his H1201
1Ch 3:11 his son, Ahaziah his s, Joash his son, H1201
1Ch 3:11 his son, Ahaziah his son, Joash his s, H1201
1Ch 3:12 Amaziah his s, Azariah his son, Jotham H1201
1Ch 3:12 his son, Azariah his s, Jotham his son, H1201
1Ch 3:12 his son, Azariah his son, Jotham his s, H1201
1Ch 3:13 Ahaz his s, Hezekiah his son, Manasseh H1201
1Ch 3:13 Hezekiah his s, Manasseh his son, H1201
1Ch 3:13 Hezekiah his son, Manasseh his s, H1201
1Ch 3:14 Amon his s, Josiah his son. H1201
1Ch 3:14 Amon his son, Josiah his s. H1201
1Ch 3:15 Jehoiakim the second s, Zedekiah the third, NDT
1Ch 3:16 Jehoiachin his s, and Zedekiah. H1201
1Ch 3:17 of Jehoiachin the captive: Shealtiel his s, H1201
1Ch 4: 2 Reaiah s of Shobal was the father of H1201
1Ch 4: 8 of the clans of Aharhel s of Harum. H1201
1Ch 4:15 The sons of Caleb s of Jephunneh: Iru H1201
1Ch 4:15 Elah and Naam. The s of Elah: Kenaz. H1201
1Ch 4:21 The sons of Shelah s of Judah: Er the H1201
1Ch 4:25 Shallum was Shaul's s, Mibsam his son H1201
1Ch 4:25 Mibsam his s and Mishma his son. H1201
1Ch 4:25 Mibsam his son and Mishma his s. H1201
1Ch 4:26 Hammuel his s, Zakkur his son and H1201
1Ch 4:26 his son, Zakkur his s and Shimei his son. H1201
1Ch 4:26 his son, Zakkur his son and Shimei his s. H1201
1Ch 4:34 Jamlech, Joshah s of Amaziah, H1201
1Ch 4:35 Jehu s of Joshibiah, the son of H1201
1Ch 4:35 of Joshibiah, the s of Seraiah, the son of H1201
1Ch 4:35 the son of Seraiah, the s of Asiel, H1201
1Ch 4:37 Ziza s of Shiphi, the son of Allon, the H1201
1Ch 4:37 son of Shiphi, the s of Allon, the son of H1201
1Ch 4:37 son of Allon, the s of Jedaiah, the son of H1201
1Ch 4:37 son of Jedaiah, the s of Shimri, the son of H1201
1Ch 4:37 the son of Shimri, the s of Shemaiah. H1201
1Ch 5: 1 given to the sons of Joseph s of Israel; H1201
1Ch 5: 4 Shemaiah his s, Gog his son, Shimei his H1201
1Ch 5: 4 his son, Gog his s, Shimei his son, H1201
1Ch 5: 4 his son, Gog his son, Shimei his s, H1201
1Ch 5: 5 Micah his s, Reaiah his son, Baal his son, H1201
1Ch 5: 5 Micah his son, Reaiah his s, Baal his son, H1201
1Ch 5: 5 Micah his son, Reaiah his son, Baal his s, H1201
1Ch 5: 6 Beerah his s, whom Tiglath-Pileser H1201
1Ch 5: 8 Bela s of Azaz, the son of Shema, the H1201
1Ch 5: 8 son of Azaz, the s of Shema, the son of H1201
1Ch 5: 8 of Azaz, the son of Shema, the s of Joel. H1201
1Ch 5:14 These were the sons of Abihail s of Huri H1201
1Ch 5:14 son of Huri, the s of Jaroah, the son of H1201
1Ch 5:14 son of Jaroah, the s of Gilead, the son of H1201
1Ch 5:14 son of Gilead, the s of Michael, the son of H1201
1Ch 5:14 son of Michael, the s of Jeshishai, the son H1201
1Ch 5:14 of Jeshishai, the s of Jahdo, the son of H1201
1Ch 5:14 Jeshishai, the son of Jahdo, the s of Buz. H1201
1Ch 5:15 Ahi s of Abdiel, the son of Guni, was H1201
1Ch 5:15 son of Abdiel, the s of Guni, was head of H1201
1Ch 6:20 Libni his s, Jahath his son, Zimmah his H1201
1Ch 6:20 his son, Jahath his s, Zimmah his son, H1201
1Ch 6:20 his son, Jahath his son, Zimmah his s, H1201
1Ch 6:21 Joah his s, Iddo his son, Zerah his son H1201
1Ch 6:21 his son, Iddo his s, Zerah his son and H1201
1Ch 6:21 his son, Zerah his s and Jeatherai his son. H1201
1Ch 6:21 his son, Zerah his son and Jeatherai his s. H1201
1Ch 6:22 Amminadab his s, Korah his son, Assir his H1201
1Ch 6:22 his son, Korah his s, Assir his son, H1201
1Ch 6:22 his son, Korah his son, Assir his s, H1201
1Ch 6:23 Elkanah his s, Ebiasaph his son, Assir his H1201
1Ch 6:23 his son, Ebiasaph his s, Assir his son, H1201
1Ch 6:23 his son, Ebiasaph his son, Assir his s, H1201
1Ch 6:24 Tahath his s, Uriel his son, Uzziah his son H1201
1Ch 6:24 his son, Uriel his s, Uzziah his son and H1201
1Ch 6:24 his son, Uzziah his s and Shaul his son. H1201
1Ch 6:24 his son, Uzziah his son and Shaul his s. H1201
1Ch 6:26 Elkanah his s, Zophai his son, Nahath his H1201
1Ch 6:26 his son, Zophai his s, Nahath his son, H1201
1Ch 6:26 his son, Zophai his son, Nahath his s, H1201
1Ch 6:27 Eliab his s, Jeroham his son, Elkanah his H1201
1Ch 6:27 Jeroham his s, Elkanah his son and H1201
1Ch 6:27 Elkanah his s and Samuel his son. H1201
1Ch 6:27 Elkanah his son and Samuel his s. H1201
1Ch 6:28 Joel the firstborn and Abijah the second s. NDT
1Ch 6:29 Libni his s, Shimei his son, Uzzah H1201
1Ch 6:29 his son, Shimei his s, Uzzah his son, H1201
1Ch 6:29 Libni his son, Shimei his son, Uzzah his s, H1201
1Ch 6:30 Shimea his s, Haggiah his son and H1201
1Ch 6:30 Haggiah his s and Asaiah his son. H1201
1Ch 6:30 Haggiah his son and Asaiah his s. H1201
1Ch 6:33 the musician, the s of Joel, the son of H1201
1Ch 6:33 the son of Joel, the s of Samuel, H1201
1Ch 6:34 the s of Elkanah, the son of Jeroham, the H1201
1Ch 6:34 son of Elkanah, the s of Jeroham, the son H1201
1Ch 6:34 son of Jeroham, the s of Eliel, the son of H1201
1Ch 6:34 Jeroham, the son of Eliel, the s of Toah, H1201
1Ch 6:35 the s of Zuph, the son of Elkanah, the son H1201
1Ch 6:35 son of Zuph, the s of Elkanah, the son of H1201
1Ch 6:35 of Elkanah, the s of Mahath, the son of H1201
1Ch 6:35 the son of Mahath, the s of Amasai, H1201
1Ch 6:36 the s of Elkanah, the son of Joel, the son H1201
1Ch 6:36 son of Elkanah, the s of Joel, the son of H1201
1Ch 6:36 son of Joel, the s of Azariah, the son of H1201
1Ch 6:36 the son of Azariah, the s of Zephaniah, H1201
1Ch 6:37 the s of Tahath, the son of Assir, the son H1201
1Ch 6:37 son of Tahath, the s of Assir, the son of H1201
1Ch 6:37 son of Assir, the s of Ebiasaph, the son of H1201
1Ch 6:37 the son of Ebiasaph, the s of Korah, H1201
1Ch 6:38 the s of Izhar, the son of Kohath, the son H1201
1Ch 6:38 son of Izhar, the s of Kohath, the son of H1201
1Ch 6:38 the son of Kohath, the s of Levi, the son of H1201
1Ch 6:38 of Kohath, the son of Levi, the s of Israel; H1201
1Ch 6:39 Asaph s of Berekiah, the son H1201
1Ch 6:39 Asaph son of Berekiah, the s of Shimea, H1201
1Ch 6:40 the s of Michael, the son of Baaseiah, the H1201
1Ch 6:40 son of Michael, the s of Baaseiah, the son H1201
1Ch 6:40 the son of Baaseiah, the s of Malkijah, H1201
1Ch 6:41 the s of Ethni, the son of Zerah, the son of H1201
1Ch 6:41 the son of Ethni, the s of Zerah, the son of H1201
1Ch 6:41 the son of Zerah, the s of Adaiah, H1201
1Ch 6:42 the s of Ethan, the son of Zimmah, the H1201
1Ch 6:42 son of Ethan, the s of Zimmah, the son of H1201
1Ch 6:42 the son of Zimmah, the s of Shimei, H1201
1Ch 6:43 the s of Jahath, the son of Gershon, the H1201
1Ch 6:43 son of Jahath, the s of Gershon, the son H1201
1Ch 6:43 the son of Gershon, the s of Levi; H1201
1Ch 6:44 Ethan s of Kishi, the son of Abdi, the son H1201
1Ch 6:44 son of Kishi, the s of Abdi, the son of H1201
1Ch 6:44 of Kishi, the son of Abdi, the s of Malluk, H1201
1Ch 6:45 the s of Hashabiah, the son of Amaziah H1201
1Ch 6:45 of Hashabiah, the s of Amaziah, the son H1201
1Ch 6:45 the son of Amaziah, the s of Hilkiah, H1201
1Ch 6:46 the s of Amzi, the son of Bani, the son of H1201
1Ch 6:46 the son of Amzi, the s of Bani, the son of H1201
1Ch 6:46 the son of Bani, the s of Shemer, H1201
1Ch 6:47 the s of Mahli, the son of Mushi, the son H1201
1Ch 6:47 son of Mahli, the s of Mushi, the son of H1201
1Ch 6:47 son of Mushi, the s of Merari, the son of H1201
1Ch 6:47 of Mushi, the son of Merari, the s of Levi. H1201
1Ch 6:50 Eleazar his s, Phinehas his son, Abishua H1201
1Ch 6:50 his son, Phinehas his s, Abishua his son, H1201
1Ch 6:50 his son, Phinehas his son, Abishua his s, H1201
1Ch 6:51 Bukki his s, Uzzi his son, Zerahiah his son, H1201
1Ch 6:51 Bukki his son, Uzzi his s, Zerahiah his son, H1201
1Ch 6:51 his son, Uzzi his son, Zerahiah his s, H1201
1Ch 6:52 Meraioth his s, Amariah his son, Ahitub H1201
1Ch 6:52 his son, Amariah his s, Ahitub his son, H1201
1Ch 6:52 his son, Amariah his son, Ahitub his s, H1201
1Ch 6:53 Zadok his s and Ahimaaz his son. H1201
1Ch 6:53 Zadok his son and Ahimaaz his s. H1201
1Ch 6:56 city were given to Caleb s of Jephunneh. H1201
1Ch 7: 3 The s of Uzzi: Izrahiah. The sons of H1201
1Ch 7:10 The s of Jediael: Bilhan. The sons of H1201
1Ch 7:16 gave birth to a s and named him Peresh. H1201
1Ch 7:17 The s of Ulam: Bedan. These were the H1201
1Ch 7:17 These were the sons of Gilead s of Makir H1201
1Ch 7:17 Gilead son of Makir, the s of Manasseh. H1201
1Ch 7:20 Shuthelah, Bered his s, Tahath his son H1201
1Ch 7:20 his son, Tahath his s, Eleadah his son, H1201
1Ch 7:20 his son, Eleadah his s, Tahath his son, H1201
1Ch 7:20 his son, Eleadah his son, Tahath his s, H1201
1Ch 7:21 Zabad his s and Shuthelah his son. H1201
1Ch 7:21 Zabad his son and Shuthelah his s. H1201
1Ch 7:23 became pregnant and gave birth to a s. H1201
1Ch 7:25 Rephah was his s, Resheph his son, Telah H1201
1Ch 7:25 was his son, Resheph his s, Telah his son, H1201
1Ch 7:25 his son, Telah his s, Tahan his son, H1201
1Ch 7:25 his son, Telah his son, Tahan his s, H1201
1Ch 7:26 Ladan his s, Ammihud his son, Elishama H1201
1Ch 7:26 Ammihud his s, Elishama his son, H1201
1Ch 7:26 Ammihud his son, Elishama his s, H1201
1Ch 7:27 Nun his s and Joshua his son. H1201
1Ch 7:27 Nun his son and Joshua his s. H1201
1Ch 7:29 descendants of Joseph s of Israel lived in H1201
1Ch 8: 1 Ashbel the second s, Aharah the third, NDT
1Ch 8:30 his firstborn s was Abdon, followed H1201
1Ch 8:34 The s of Jonathan: Merib-Baal, who was H1201
1Ch 8:37 Raphah was his s, Eleasah his son and H1201
1Ch 8:37 his son, Eleasah his s and Azel his son. H1201
1Ch 8:37 his son, Eleasah his son and Azel his s. H1201
1Ch 8:39 Jeush the second s and Eliphelet the third. NDT
1Ch 9: 4 Uthai s of Ammihud, the son of Omri, the H1201
1Ch 9: 4 son of Ammihud, the s of Omri, the son of H1201
1Ch 9: 4 the son of Omri, the s of Imri, the son of H1201
1Ch 9: 4 son of Imri, the s of Bani, a descendant H1201
1Ch 9: 4 of Bani, a descendant of Perez s of Judah. H1201
1Ch 9: 7 Sallu s of Meshullam, the son of H1201
1Ch 9: 7 of Meshullam, the s of Hodaviah, the son H1201
1Ch 9: 7 the son of Hodaviah, the s of Hassenuah; H1201
1Ch 9: 8 Ibneiah s of Jeroham; Elah son of Uzzi H1201
1Ch 9: 8 son of Jeroham; Elah s of Uzzi, the son of H1201
1Ch 9: 8 son of Uzzi, the s of Mikri; and Meshullam H1201
1Ch 9: 8 Meshullam s of Shephatiah, the son H1201
1Ch 9: 8 of Shephatiah, the s of Reuel, the son of H1201
1Ch 9: 8 the son of Reuel, the s of Ibnijah. H1201
1Ch 9:11 Azariah s of Hilkiah, the son of H1201
1Ch 9:11 of Hilkiah, the s of Meshullam, the son H1201
1Ch 9:11 of Meshullam, the s of Zadok, the son of H1201
1Ch 9:11 son of Zadok, the s of Meraioth, the son H1201
1Ch 9:11 son of Meraioth, the s of Ahitub, the H1201
1Ch 9:12 Adaiah s of Jeroham, the son of Pashhur H1201
1Ch 9:12 son of Jeroham, the s of Pashhur, the son H1201
1Ch 9:12 son of Pashhur, the s of Malkijah; and H1201
1Ch 9:12 Maasai s of Adiel, the son of H1201
1Ch 9:12 son of Adiel, the s of Jahzerah, the son of H1201
1Ch 9:12 of Jahzerah, the s of Meshullam, the son H1201
1Ch 9:12 of Meshullam, the s of Meshillemith, the H1201
1Ch 9:12 the son of Meshillemith, the s of Immer. H1201
1Ch 9:14 Shemaiah s of Hasshub, the son of H1201
1Ch 9:14 son of Hasshub, the s of Azrikam, the son H1201
1Ch 9:14 son of Azrikam, the s of Hashabiah, H1201
1Ch 9:15 Galal and Mattaniah s of Mika, the son of H1201
1Ch 9:15 son of Mika, the s of Zikri, the son of H1201
1Ch 9:15 of Mika, the son of Zikri, the s of Asaph; H1201
1Ch 9:16 Obadiah s of Shemaiah, the son of Galal H1201
1Ch 9:16 of Shemaiah, the s of Galal, the son of H1201
1Ch 9:16 the son of Galal, the s of Jeduthun; and H1201
1Ch 9:16 Berekiah s of Asa, the son of H1201
1Ch 9:16 son of Asa, the s of Elkanah, who lived in H1201
1Ch 9:19 Shallum s of Kore, the son of Ebiasaph H1201
1Ch 9:19 son of Kore, the s of Ebiasaph, the son of H1201
1Ch 9:19 son of Ebiasaph, the s of Korah, and his H1201
1Ch 9:20 times Phinehas s of Eleazar was the H1201
1Ch 9:21 Zechariah s of Meshelemiah was the H1201
1Ch 9:31 the firstborn s of Shallum the Korahite NDT
1Ch 9:36 his firstborn s was Abdon, followed H1201
1Ch 9:40 The s of Jonathan: Merib-Baal, who was H1201
1Ch 9:43 Rephaiah was his s, Eleasah his son and H1201
1Ch 9:43 his son, Eleasah his s and Azel his son. H1201
1Ch 9:43 his son, Eleasah his son and Azel his s. H1201
1Ch 10:14 the kingdom over to David s of Jesse. H1201

1Ch 11: 6 Joab s of Zeruiah went up first, and so H1201
1Ch 11:12 him was Eleazar s of Dodai the Ahohite H1201
1Ch 11:22 Benaiah s of Jehoiada, a valiant fighter H1201
1Ch 11:24 the exploits of Benaiah s of Jehoiada; H1201
1Ch 11:26 Elhanan s of Dodo from Bethlehem H1201
1Ch 11:28 Ira s of Ikkesh from Tekoa, Abiezer from H1201
1Ch 11:30 Heled s of Baanah the Netophathite H1201
1Ch 11:31 Ithai s of Ribai from Gibeah in Benjamin H1201
1Ch 11:34 Jonathan s of Shagee the Hararite H1201
1Ch 11:35 Ahiam s of Sakar the Hararite, Eliphal son H1201
1Ch 11:35 son of Sakar the Hararite, Eliphal s of Ur, H1201
1Ch 11:37 Hezro the Carmelite, Naarai s of Ezbai, H1201
1Ch 11:38 the brother of Nathan, Mibhar s of Hagri, H1201
1Ch 11:39 the armor-bearer of Joab s of Zeruiah, H1201
1Ch 11:41 Uriah the Hittite, Zabad s of Ahlai, H1201
1Ch 11:42 Adina s of Shiza the Reubenite, who was H1201
1Ch 11:43 Hanan s of Maakah, Joshaphat the H1201
1Ch 11:45 Jediael s of Shimri, his brother Joha the H1201
1Ch 12: 1 from the presence of Saul s of Kish H1201
1Ch 12:18 We are with you, s of Jesse! Success, H1201
1Ch 15:17 So the Levites appointed Heman s of Joel; H1201
1Ch 15:17 relatives, Asaph s of Berekiah; and from H1201
1Ch 15:17 the Merarites, Ethan s of Kushaiah; H1201
1Ch 16:38 Obed-Edom s of Jeduthun, and also H1201
1Ch 17:13 he will be my s. I will never take my H1201
1Ch 18:10 he sent his s Hadoram to King David to H1201
1Ch 18:12 Abishai s of Zeruiah struck down eighteen H1201
1Ch 18:15 Joab s of Zeruiah was over the army H1201
1Ch 18:15 Jehoshaphat s of Ahilud was recorder H1201
1Ch 18:16 Zadok s of Ahitub and Ahimelek son of H1201
1Ch 18:16 Ahitub and Ahimelek s of Abiathar were H1201
1Ch 18:17 Benaiah s of Jehoiada was over the H1201
1Ch 19: 1 and his s succeeded him as king. H1201
1Ch 19: 2 will show kindness to Hanun s of Nahash, H1201
1Ch 20: 5 Elhanan s of Jair killed Lahmi the brother H1201
1Ch 20: 7 Jonathan s of Shimea, David's H1201
1Ch 22: 5 "My s Solomon is young and H1201
1Ch 22: 6 he called for his s Solomon and charged H1201
1Ch 22: 7 "My s, I had it in my heart to build a H1201
1Ch 22: 9 But you will have a s who will be a man of H1201
1Ch 22:10 He will be my s, and I will be his H1201
1Ch 22:11 my s, the LORD be with you, and H1201
1Ch 22:17 leaders of Israel to help his s Solomon. H1201
1Ch 23: 1 he made his s Solomon king over Israel. H1201
1Ch 24: 6 The scribe Shemaiah s of Nethanel, H1201
1Ch 24: 6 Ahimelek s of Abiathar and the heads of H1201
1Ch 24:24 The s of Uzziel: Micah; from the sons of H1201
1Ch 24:26 The s of Jaaziah: Beno. H1201
1Ch 24:29 the s of Kish: Jerahmeel. H1201
1Ch 26: 1 Meshelemiah s of Kore, one of the sons H1201
1Ch 26: 6 Obed-Edom's s Shemaiah also had sons H1201
1Ch 26:14 Then lots were cast for his s Zechariah, H1201
1Ch 26:24 a descendant of Gershom s of Moses, was H1201
1Ch 26:25 Rehabiah his s, Jeshaiah his son, Joram H1201
1Ch 26:25 his son, Jeshaiah his s, Joram his son, H1201
1Ch 26:25 his son, Joram his s, Zikri his son and H1201
1Ch 26:25 his son, Zikri his s and Shelomith his son. H1201
1Ch 26:25 his son, Zikri his son and Shelomith his s. H1201
1Ch 26:28 by Samuel the seer and by Saul s of Kish, H1201
1Ch 26:28 Abner s of Ner and Joab son of Zeruiah H1201
1Ch 26:28 Abner son of Ner and Joab s of Zeruiah H1201
1Ch 27: 2 first month, was Jashobeam s of Zabdiel. H1201
1Ch 27: 5 was Benaiah s of Jehoiada the priest. H1201
1Ch 27: 6 His s Ammizabad was in charge of his H1201
1Ch 27: 7 of Joab; his s Zebadiah was his successor. H1201
1Ch 27: 9 was Ira the s of Ikkesh the Tekoite. H1201
1Ch 27:16 the Reubenites: Eliezer s of Zikri; over the H1201
1Ch 27:16 the Simeonites: Shephatiah s of Maakah; H1201
1Ch 27:17 Hashabiah s of Kemuel; over Aaron H1201
1Ch 27:18 over Issachar: Omri s of Michael; H1201
1Ch 27:19 Ishmaiah s of Obadiah; over H1201
1Ch 27:19 over Naphtali: Jerimoth s of Azriel; H1201
1Ch 27:20 Hoshea s of Azaziah; over half the tribe of H1201
1Ch 27:20 the tribe of Manasseh: Joel s of Pedaiah; H1201
1Ch 27:21 Iddo s of Zechariah; over H1201
1Ch 27:21 over Benjamin: Jaasiel s of Abner; H1201
1Ch 27:22 Azarel s of Jeroham. These H1201
1Ch 27:24 Joab s of Zeruiah began to count the men H1201
1Ch 27:25 Azmaveth s of Adiel was in charge of the H1201
1Ch 27:25 Jonathan s of Uzziah was in charge of the H1201
1Ch 27:26 Ezri s of Kelub was in charge of the H1201
1Ch 27:29 Shaphat s of Adlai was in charge of the H1201
1Ch 27:32 Jehiel s of Hakmoni took care of the H1201
1Ch 27:34 by Jehoiada s of Benaiah and by H1201
1Ch 28: 5 he has chosen my s Solomon to sit on the H1201
1Ch 28: 6 'Solomon your s is the one who will build H1201
1Ch 28: 6 I have chosen him to be my s, and I H1201
1Ch 28: 9 "And you, my s Solomon, acknowledge H1201
1Ch 28:11 Then David gave his s Solomon the plans H1201
1Ch 28:20 David also said to Solomon his s, "Be H1201
1Ch 29: 1 "My s Solomon, the one whom God has H1201
1Ch 29:19 And give my s Solomon the wholehearted H1201
1Ch 29:22 Solomon s of David as king a H1201
1Ch 29:26 David s of Jesse was king over all Israel. H1201
1Ch 29:28 His s Solomon succeeded him as king. H1201
2Ch 1: 1 Solomon s of David established himself H1201
2Ch 1: 5 But the bronze altar that Bezalel s of Uri H1201
2Ch 1: 5 son of Uri, the s of Hur, had made was in H1201
2Ch 2:12 He has given King David a wise s H1201
2Ch 6: 9 the temple, but your s, your own flesh H1201
2Ch 9:29 the seer concerning Jeroboam s of Nebat? H1201
2Ch 9:31 And Rehoboam his s succeeded him as H1201
2Ch 10: 2 When Jeroboam s of Nebat heard this (he H1201
2Ch 10:15 spoken to Jeroboam s of Nebat through H1201
2Ch 10:16 we have in David, what part in Jesse's s? H1201
2Ch 11: 3 "Say to Rehoboam s of Solomon king of H1201
2Ch 11:17 supported Rehoboam s of Solomon three H1201
2Ch 11:18 daughter of David's s Jerimoth and of H1201
2Ch 11:18 Abihail, the daughter of Jesse's s Eliab. H1201
2Ch 11:22 appointed Abijah s of Maakah as crown H1201
2Ch 12:16 And Abijah his s succeeded him as king H1201
2Ch 13: 6 Yet Jeroboam s of Nebat, an official of H1201
2Ch 13: 6 an official of Solomon s of David H1201
2Ch 13: 7 Rehoboam s of Solomon when he H1201
2Ch 14: 1 Asa his s succeeded him as king, and in H1201
2Ch 15: 1 Spirit of God came on Azariah s of Oded. H1201
2Ch 15: 8 of Azariah s of Oded the prophet, H1201
2Ch 17: 1 Jehoshaphat his s succeeded him as king H1201
2Ch 17:16 Amasiah s of Zikri, who volunteered H1201
2Ch 18: 7 He is Micaiah s of Imlah." "The king H1201
2Ch 18: 8 "Bring Micaiah s of Imlah at once. H1201
2Ch 18:10 Now Zedekiah s of Kenaanah had made H1201
2Ch 18:23 Then Zedekiah s of Kenaanah went up H1201
2Ch 18:25 ruler of the city and to Joash the king's s, H1201
2Ch 19: 2 Jehu the seer, the s of Hanani, went out to H1201
2Ch 19:11 and Zebadiah s of Ishmael, the H1201
2Ch 20:14 the LORD came on Jahaziel s of Zechariah, H1201
2Ch 20:14 of Zechariah, the s of Benaiah, the son of H1201
2Ch 20:14 son of Benaiah, the s of Jeiel, the son of H1201
2Ch 20:14 son of Jeiel, the s of Mattaniah, a Levite H1201
2Ch 20:34 written in the annals of Jehu s of Hanani, H1201
2Ch 20:37 Eliezer s of Dodavahu of Mareshah H1201
2Ch 21: 1 And Jehoram his s succeeded him as king H1201
2Ch 21: 3 to Jehoram because he was his **firstborn** s. AIT
2Ch 21:17 Not a s was left to him except Ahaziah H1201
2Ch 22: 1 Jehoram's youngest s, king in his place, H1201
2Ch 22: 1 So Ahaziah s of Jehoram king of Judah H1201
2Ch 22: 5 he went with Joram s of Ahab king of H1201
2Ch 22: 6 Then Ahaziah s of Jehoram king of Judah H1201
2Ch 22: 6 to see Joram s of Ahab because he had H1201
2Ch 22: 7 out with Joram to meet Jehu s of Nimshi, H1201
2Ch 22: 9 "He was a s of Jehoshaphat, who H1201
2Ch 22:10 of Ahaziah saw that her s was dead, H1201
2Ch 22:11 took Joash s of Ahaziah and stole him H1201
2Ch 23: 1 Azariah s of Jeroham, Ishmael son of H1201
2Ch 23: 1 Jeroham, Ishmael s of Jehohanan H1201
2Ch 23: 1 Jehohanan, Azariah s of Obed, Maaseiah H1201
2Ch 23: 1 son of Obed, Maaseiah s of Adaiah, and H1201
2Ch 23: 1 son of Adaiah, and Elishaphat s of Zikri. H1201
2Ch 23: 3 to them, "The king's s shall reign, as the H1201
2Ch 23:11 out the king's s and put the crown on H1201
2Ch 24:20 came on Zechariah s of Jehoiada the H1201
2Ch 24:22 Jehoiada had shown him but killed his s, H1201
2Ch 24:25 murdering the s of Jehoiada the priest, H1201
2Ch 24:26 s of Shimeath an Ammonite woman H1201
2Ch 24:26 s of Shimrith a Moabite woman. H1201
2Ch 24:27 And Amaziah his s succeeded him as H1201
2Ch 25:17 this challenge to Jehoash s of Jehoahaz, H1201
2Ch 25:17 son of Jehoahaz, the s of Jehu, king of H1201
2Ch 25:18 'Give your daughter to my s in marriage. H1201
2Ch 25:23 king of Judah, the s of Joash, the son of H1201
2Ch 25:23 son of Joash, the s of Ahaziah, at Beth H1201
2Ch 25:25 Amaziah s of Joash king of Judah lived H1201
2Ch 25:25 death of Jehoash s of Jehoahaz king of H1201
2Ch 26:21 Jotham his s had charge of the palace H1201
2Ch 26:22 recorded by the prophet Isaiah s of Amoz. H1201
2Ch 26:23 And Jotham his s succeeded him as king. H1201
2Ch 27: 9 And Ahaz his s succeeded him as king H1201
2Ch 28: 6 In one day Pekah s of Remaliah killed a H1201
2Ch 28: 7 killed Maaseiah the king's s, Azrikam the H1201
2Ch 28:12 in Ephraim—Azariah s of Jehohanan H1201
2Ch 28:12 Jehohanan, Berekiah s of Meshillemoth H1201
2Ch 28:12 Jehizkiah s of Shallum, and Amasa son H1201
2Ch 28:12 Amasa s of Hadlai—confronted H1201
2Ch 28:27 And Hezekiah his s succeeded him as H1201
2Ch 29:12 Mahath s of Amasai and Joel son of H1201
2Ch 29:12 son of Amasai and Joel s of Azariah; H1201
2Ch 29:12 Kish s of Abdi and Azariah son of H1201
2Ch 29:12 son of Abdi and Azariah s of Jehallelel; H1201
2Ch 29:12 Joah s of Zimmah and Eden son of Joah H1201
2Ch 29:12 Joah son of Zimmah and Eden s of Joah; H1201
2Ch 30:26 the days of Solomon s of David king of H1201
2Ch 31:14 Kore s of Imnah the Levite, keeper of the H1201
2Ch 32:20 the prophet Isaiah s of Amoz cried out in H1201
2Ch 32:32 the prophet Isaiah s of Amoz in the book H1201
2Ch 32:33 And Manasseh his s succeeded him as H1201
2Ch 33: 7 had said to David and to his s Solomon, H1201
2Ch 33:20 And Amon his s succeeded him as king H1201
2Ch 33:25 they made Josiah his s king in his place. H1201
2Ch 34: 8 he sent Shaphan s of Azaliah and H1201
2Ch 34: 8 the city, with Joah s of Joahaz, the H1201
2Ch 34:20 to Hilkiah, Ahikam s of Shaphan, Abdon H1201
2Ch 34:20 of Shaphan, Abdon s of Micah, Shaphan H1201
2Ch 34:22 who was the wife of Shallum s of Tokhath, H1201
2Ch 34:22 son of Tokhath, the s of Hasrah, keeper of H1201
2Ch 35: 3 temple that Solomon s of David king of H1201
2Ch 35: 4 David king of Israel and by his s Solomon. H1201
2Ch 36: 1 land took Jehoahaz s of Josiah and made H1201
2Ch 36: 8 And Jehoiachin his s succeeded him as H1201
Ezr 3: 2 Then Joshua s of Jozadak and his fellow H1201
Ezr 3: 2 Zerubbabel s of Shealtiel and his H1201
Ezr 3: 8 Zerubbabel s of Shealtiel, Joshua H1201
Ezr 3: 8 Joshua s of Jozadak and the rest of the H1201
Ezr 5: 2 Then Zerubbabel s of Shealtiel and A10120
Ezr 5: 2 Joshua s of Jozadak set to work A10120
Ezr 7: 1 of Persia, Ezra s of Seraiah, the son of H1201
Ezr 7: 1 son of Seraiah, the s of Azariah, the son H1201
Ezr 7: 1 the son of Azariah, the s of Hilkiah, H1201
Ezr 7: 2 the s of Shallum, the son of Zadok, the H1201
Ezr 7: 2 son of Shallum, the s of Zadok, the son of H1201
Ezr 7: 2 the son of Zadok, the s of Ahitub, H1201
Ezr 7: 3 the s of Amariah, the son of Azariah, the H1201
Ezr 7: 3 son of Amariah, the s of Azariah, the son H1201
Ezr 7: 3 the son of Azariah, the s of Meraioth, H1201
Ezr 7: 4 the s of Zerahiah, the son of Uzzi, the son H1201
Ezr 7: 4 son of Zerahiah, the s of Uzzi, the son of H1201
Ezr 7: 4 Zerahiah, the son of Uzzi, the s of Bukki, H1201
Ezr 7: 5 the s of Abishua, the son of Phinehas, the H1201
Ezr 7: 5 of Abishua, the s of Phinehas, the son H1201
Ezr 7: 5 of Phinehas, the s of Eleazar, the son of H1201
Ezr 7: 5 of Eleazar, the s of Aaron the chief priest H1201
Ezr 8: 4 Eliehoenai s of Zerahiah, and with him H1201
Ezr 8: 5 Shekaniah s of Jahaziel, and with H1201
Ezr 8: 6 of Adin, Ebed s of Jonathan, and with H1201
Ezr 8: 7 of Elam, Jeshaiah s of Athaliah, and with H1201
Ezr 8: 8 Zebadiah s of Michael, and with H1201
Ezr 8: 9 of Joab, Obadiah s of Jehiel, and with H1201
Ezr 8:10 of Bani, Shelomith s of Josiphiah, and H1201
Ezr 8:11 of Bebai, Zechariah s of Bebai, and with H1201
Ezr 8:12 of Azgad, Johanan s of Hakkatan, and H1201
Ezr 8:18 from the descendants of Mahli s of Levi H1201
Ezr 8:18 Mahli son of Levi, the s of Israel, and H1201
Ezr 8:33 into the hands of Meremoth s of Uriah, H1201
Ezr 8:33 Eleazar s of Phinehas was with him, and H1201
Ezr 8:33 Levites Jozabad s of Jeshua and Noadiah H1201
Ezr 8:33 son of Jeshua and Noadiah s of Binnui. H1201
Ezr 10: 2 Then Shekaniah s of Jehiel, one of the H1201
Ezr 10: 6 to the room of Jehohanan s of Eliashib. H1201
Ezr 10:15 Only Jonathan s of Asahel and Jahzeiah H1201
Ezr 10:15 son of Asahel and Jahzeiah s of Tikvah, H1201
Ezr 10:18 the descendants of Joshua s of Jozadak, H1201
Ne 1: 1 The words of Nehemiah s of Hakaliah: In H1201
Ne 3: 2 Zakkur s of Imri built next to them. H1201
Ne 3: 4 Meremoth s of Uriah, the son of Hakkoz H1201
Ne 3: 4 son of Uriah, the s of Hakkoz, repaired the H1201
Ne 3: 4 Next to him Meshullam s of Berekiah, the H1201
Ne 3: 4 of Berekiah, the s of Meshezabel, made H1201
Ne 3: 4 next to him Zadok s of Baana also made H1201
Ne 3: 6 repaired by Joiada s of Paseah and H1201
Ne 3: 6 Paseah and Meshullam s of Besodeiah. H1201
Ne 3: 8 Uzziel s of Harhaiah, one of the H1201
Ne 3: 9 Rephaiah s of Hur, ruler of a half-district of H1201
Ne 3:10 Jedaiah s of Harumaph made repairs H1201
Ne 3:10 Hattush s of Hashabneiah made H1201
Ne 3:11 Malkijah s of Harim and Hasshub son of H1201
Ne 3:11 of Harim and Hasshub s of Pahath-Moab H1201
Ne 3:12 Shallum s of Hallohesh, ruler of a H1201
Ne 3:14 Gate was repaired by Malkijah s of Rekab, H1201
Ne 3:15 was repaired by Shallun s of Kol-Hozeh, H1201
Ne 3:16 Nehemiah s of Azbuk, ruler of a H1201
Ne 3:17 by the Levites under Rehum s of Bani. H1201
Ne 3:18 fellow Levites under Binnui s of Henadad, H1201
Ne 3:19 Next to him, Ezer s of Jeshua, ruler of H1201
Ne 3:20 Baruch s of Zabbai zealously repaired H1201
Ne 3:21 Meremoth s of Uriah, the son of H1201
Ne 3:21 son of Uriah, the s of Hakkoz, repaired H1201
Ne 3:23 to them, Azariah s of Maaseiah, the son H1201
Ne 3:23 son of Maaseiah, the s of Ananiah, made H1201
Ne 3:24 Binnui s of Henadad repaired another H1201
Ne 3:25 Palal s of Uzai worked opposite the H1201
Ne 3:25 Next to him, Pedaiah s of Parosh H1201
Ne 3:29 Zadok s of Immer made repairs opposite H1201
Ne 3:29 Shemaiah s of Shekaniah, the H1201
Ne 3:30 Hananiah s of Shelemiah, and H1201
Ne 3:30 the sixth s of Zalaph, repaired H1201
Ne 3:30 Meshullam s of Berekiah made repairs H1201
Ne 6:10 to the house of Shemaiah s of Delaiah, H1201
Ne 6:10 of Delaiah, the s of Mehetabel, who was H1201
Ne 6:18 was son-in-law to Shekaniah s of Arah, H1201
Ne 6:18 his s Jehohanan had married the H1201
Ne 6:18 the daughter of Meshullam s of Berekiah. H1201
Ne 8:17 the days of Joshua s of Nun until that day, H1201
Ne 10: 1 the governor, the s of Hakaliah. H1201
Ne 10: 9 Jeshua s of Azaniah, Binnui of the sons of H1201
Ne 11: 4 Athaiah s of Uzziah, the son of Zechariah H1201
Ne 11: 4 son of Uzziah, the s of Zechariah, the son H1201
Ne 11: 4 of Zechariah, the s of Amariah, the son of H1201
Ne 11: 4 son of Amariah, the s of Shephatiah, the H1201
Ne 11: 4 son of Shephatiah, the s of Mahalalel, H1201
Ne 11: 5 Maaseiah s of Baruch, the son of H1201
Ne 11: 5 son of Baruch, the s of Kol-Hozeh, the son H1201
Ne 11: 5 of Kol-Hozeh, the s of Hazaiah, the son of H1201
Ne 11: 5 of Hazaiah, the s of Adaiah, the son of H1201
Ne 11: 5 son of Adaiah, the s of Joiarib, the son of H1201
Ne 11: 5 the son of Joiarib, the s of Zechariah, H1201
Ne 11: 7 Sallu s of Meshullam, the son of Joed H1201
Ne 11: 7 of Meshullam, the s of Joed, the son of H1201
Ne 11: 7 son of Joed, the s of Pedaiah, the son of H1201
Ne 11: 7 son of Pedaiah, the s of Kolaiah, the son H1201
Ne 11: 7 of Kolaiah, the s of Maaseiah, the son H1201
Ne 11: 7 of Maaseiah, the s of Ithiel, the son of H1201
Ne 11: 7 the son of Ithiel, the s of Jeshaiah, H1201
Ne 11: 9 Joel s of Zikri was their chief officer, and H1201
Ne 11: 9 Judah s of Hassenuah was over the H1201
Ne 11:10 Jedaiah; the s of Joiarib; Jakin; H1201
Ne 11:11 Seraiah s of Hilkiah, the son of H1201

S

Ne 11:11 of Hilkiah, the s of Meshullam, the son H1201
Ne 11:11 of Meshullam, the s of Zadok, the son of H1201
Ne 11:11 son of Zadok, the s of Meraioth, the son H1201
Ne 11:11 son of Meraioth, the s of Ahitub, the H1201
Ne 11:12 822 men; Adaiah s of Jeroham, the son of H1201
Ne 11:12 son of Jeroham, the s of Pelaliah, the son H1201
Ne 11:12 son of Pelaliah, the s of Amzi, the son of H1201
Ne 11:12 son of Amzi, the s of Zechariah, the son H1201
Ne 11:12 of Zechariah, the s of Pashhur, the son of H1201
Ne 11:12 the son of Pashhur, the s of Malkijah, H1201
Ne 11:13 242 men; Amashsai s of Azarel, the son of H1201
Ne 11:13 son of Azarel, the s of Ahzai, the son of H1201
Ne 11:13 son of Ahzai, the s of Meshillemoth, the H1201
Ne 11:13 the son of Meshillemoth, the s of Immer, H1201
Ne 11:14 officer was Zabdiel s of Haggedolim. H1201
Ne 11:15 Shemaiah s of Hasshub, the son of H1201
Ne 11:15 son of Hasshub, the s of Azrikam, the son H1201
Ne 11:15 of Azrikam, the s of Hashabiah, the son H1201
Ne 11:15 the son of Hashabiah, the s of Bunni; H1201
Ne 11:17 Mattaniah s of Mika, the son of Zabdi, the H1201
Ne 11:17 son of Mika, the s of Zabdi, the son of H1201
Ne 11:17 son of Zabdi, the s of Asaph, the director H1201
Ne 11:17 Abda s of Shammua, the son of H1201
Ne 11:17 of Shammua, the s of Galal, the son of H1201
Ne 11:17 the son of Galal, the s of Jeduthun. H1201
Ne 11:22 Levites in Jerusalem was Uzzi s of Bani, H1201
Ne 11:22 son of Bani, the s of Hashabiah, the son H1201
Ne 11:22 of Hashabiah, the s of Mattaniah, the son H1201
Ne 11:22 the son of Mattaniah, the s of Mika. H1201
Ne 11:24 Pethahiah s of Meshezabel, one of the H1201
Ne 11:24 of the descendants of Zerah s of Judah, H1201
Ne 12: 1 with Zerubbabel s of Shealtiel and with H1201
Ne 12:23 to the time of Johanan s of Eliashib were H1201
Ne 12:24 Sherebiah, Jeshua s of Kadmiel, and their H1201
Ne 12:26 served in the days of Joiakim s of Joshua, H1201
Ne 12:26 son of Joshua, the s of Jozadak, and in H1201
Ne 12:35 also Zechariah s of Jonathan, the son H1201
Ne 12:35 of Jonathan, the s of Shemaiah, the son H1201
Ne 12:35 of Shemaiah, the s of Mattaniah, the son H1201
Ne 12:35 of Mattaniah, the s of Micaiah, the son of H1201
Ne 12:35 son of Micaiah, the s of Zakkur, the son of H1201
Ne 12:35 the son of Zakkur, the s of Asaph, H1201
Ne 12:45 commands of David and his s Solomon. H1201
Ne 13:13 storerooms and made Hanan s of Zakkur, H1201
Ne 13:13 son of Zakkur, the s of Mattaniah, their H1201
Ne 13:28 the sons of Joiada s of Eliashib the high H1201
Est 2: 5 named Mordecai s of Jair, the son of H1201
Est 2: 5 son of Jair, the s of Shimei, the son of H1201
Est 2: 5 the son of Shimei, the s of Kish, H1201
Est 3: 1 honored Haman s of Hammedatha, H1201
Est 3:10 gave it to Haman s of Hammedatha, H1201
Est 8: 5 that Haman s of Hammedatha, H1201
Est 9:10 the ten sons of Haman s of Hammedatha H1201
Est 9:24 For Haman s of Hammedatha, the Agagite H1201
Job 32: 2 But Elihu s of Barakel the Buzite, of the H1201
Job 32: 6 So Elihu s of Barakel the Buzite said: "I H1201
Ps 2: 7 "You are my s; today I have H1201
Ps 2:12 Kiss his s, or he will be angry and your H1337
Ps 3: T When he fled from his s Absalom. H1201
Ps 9: T To the tune of "The Death of the S." H1201
Ps 50:20 brother and slander your own mother's s. H1201
Ps 72: 1 the royal s with your righteousness. H1201
Ps 72:20 concludes the prayers of David s of Jesse. H1201
Ps 80:15 the s you have raised up for yourself. H1201
Ps 80:17 the s of man you have raised up for H1201
Pr 1: 1 The proverbs of Solomon s of David, king H1201
Pr 1: 8 my s, to your father's instruction H1201
Pr 1:10 My s, if sinful men entice you, do not give H1201
Pr 1:15 my s, do not go along with them, do not H1201
Pr 2: 1 My s, if you accept my words and store up H1201
Pr 3: 1 My s, do not forget my teaching, but keep H1201
Pr 3:11 My s, do not despise the LORD's discipline H1201
Pr 3:12 he loves, as a father the s he delights in. H1201
Pr 3:21 My s, do not let wisdom and H1201
Pr 4: 3 For I too was a s to my father, still tender H1201
Pr 4:10 my s, accept what I say, and the H1201
Pr 4:20 My s, pay attention to what I say; turn your H1201
Pr 5: 1 My s, pay attention to my wisdom, turn H1201
Pr 5:20 my s, be intoxicated with another H1201
Pr 6: 1 My s, if you have put up security for your H1201
Pr 6: 3 So do this, my s, to free yourself, since H1201
Pr 6:20 My s, keep your father's command and do H1201
Pr 7: 1 My s, keep my words and store up my H1201
Pr 10: 1 A wise s brings joy to his father, but a H1201
Pr 10: 1 a foolish s brings grief to his mother. H1201
Pr 10: 5 gathers crops in summer is a prudent s, H1201
Pr 10: 5 sleeps during harvest is a disgraceful s. H1201
Pr 13: 1 A wise s heeds his father's instruction, but H1201
Pr 15:20 A wise s brings joy to his father, but a H1201
Pr 17: 2 over a disgraceful s and will share the H1201
Pr 17:25 A foolish s brings grief to his father and H1201
Pr 19:27 to instruction, my s, and you will stray H1201
Pr 23:15 My s, if your heart is wise, then my heart H1201
Pr 23:19 my s, and be wise, and set your H1201
Pr 23:24 a **man** *who* **fathers** a wise s rejoices in H3528
Pr 23:26 My s, give me your heart and let your eyes H1201
Pr 24:13 Eat honey, my s, for it is good; honey from H1201
Pr 24:21 the king, my s, and do not join with H1201
Pr 27:11 Be wise, my s, and bring joy to my heart H1201
Pr 28: 7 A discerning s heeds instruction, but a H1201
Pr 30: 1 The sayings of Agur s of Jakeh—an H1201
Pr 30: 4 his name, and what is the name of his s? H1201

Pr 31: 2 my s! Listen, son of my womb H1337
Pr 31: 2 Listen, s of my womb! Listen, my H1337
Pr 31: 2 Listen, my s, the answer to my H1337
Ecc 1: 1 words of the Teacher, s of David, king in H1201
Ecc 4: 8 all alone; he had neither s nor brother. H1201
Ecc 12:12 Be warned, my s, of anything in addition H1201
Isa 1: 1 that Isaiah s of Amoz saw during the H1201
Isa 2: 1 This is what Isaiah s of Amoz saw H1201
Isa 7: 1 When Ahaz s of Jotham, the son of H1201
Isa 7: 1 son of Jotham, the s of Uzziah, was king H1201
Isa 7: 1 of Aram and Pekah s of Remaliah king of H1201
Isa 7: 3 you and your s Shear-Jashub, to H1201
Isa 7: 4 Rezin and Aram and of the s of Remaliah. H1201
Isa 7: 5 Remaliah's s have plotted your ruin H1201
Isa 7: 6 make the s of Tabeel king over it. H1201
Isa 7: 9 the head of Samaria is only Remaliah's s. H1201
Isa 7:14 virgin will conceive and give birth to a s, H1201
Isa 8: 2 priest and Zechariah s of Jeberekiah as H1201
Isa 8: 3 she conceived and gave birth to a s. H1201
Isa 8: 6 rejoices over Rezin and the s of Remaliah, H1201
Isa 9: 6 a child is born, to us a s is given, and the H1201
Isa 13: 1 Babylon that Isaiah s of Amoz saw: H1201
Isa 14:12 from heaven, morning star, s of the dawn! H1201
Isa 20: 2 the LORD spoke through Isaiah s of Amoz. H1201
Isa 22:20 summon my servant, Eliakim s of Hilkiah. H1201
Isa 36: 3 Eliakim s of Hilkiah the palace H1201
Isa 36: 3 Joah s of Asaph the recorder went H1201
Isa 36:22 Then Eliakim s of Hilkiah the palace H1201
Isa 36:22 secretary and Joah s of Asaph the H1201
Isa 37: 2 to the prophet Isaiah s of Amoz. H1201
Isa 37:21 Then Isaiah s of Amoz sent a message to H1201
Isa 37:38 And Esarhaddon his s succeeded him as H1201
Isa 38: 1 The prophet Isaiah s of Amoz went to him H1201
Isa 39: 1 Marduk-Baladan s of Baladan king of H1201
Isa 66: 7 pains come upon her, she delivers a s. H2351
Jer 1: 1 The words of Jeremiah s of Hilkiah, one H1201
Jer 1: 2 reign of Josiah s of Amon king of Judah H1201
Jer 1: 3 reign of Jehoiakim s of Josiah king of H1201
Jer 1: 3 year of Zedekiah s of Josiah king of Judah H1201
Jer 6:26 mourn with bitter wailing as for an **only s** H3495
Jer 15: 4 of what Manasseh s of Hezekiah king of H1201
Jer 20: 1 When the priest Pashhur s of Immer, the H1201
Jer 20:15 saying, "A child is born to you—a s!" H2351
Jer 21: 1 sent to him Pashhur s of Malkijah and the H1201
Jer 21: 1 the priest Zephaniah s of Maaseiah. H1201
Jer 22:11 the LORD says about Shallum s of Josiah, H1201
Jer 22:18 says about Jehoiakim s of Josiah king of H1201
Jer 22:24 Jehoiachin s of Jehoiakim king of Judah H1201
Jer 24: 1 After Jehoiachin s of Jehoiakim king of H1201
Jer 25: 1 year of Jehoiakim s of Josiah king of H1201
Jer 25: 3 year of Josiah s of Amon king of Judah H1201
Jer 26: 1 reign of Jehoiakim s of Josiah king of H1201
Jer 26:20 Now Uriah s of Shemaiah from Kiriath H1201
Jer 26:22 sent Elnathan s of Akbor to Egypt, along H1201
Jer 26:24 Ahikam s of Shaphan supported Jeremiah H1201
Jer 27: 1 reign of Zedekiah s of Josiah king of H1201
Jer 27: 7 serve him and his s and his grandson H1201
Jer 27:20 carried Jehoiachin s of Jehoiakim king of H1201
Jer 28: 1 the prophet Hananiah s of Azzur, who H1201
Jer 28: 4 place Jehoiachin s of Jehoiakim king of H1201
Jer 29: 3 the letter to Elasah s of Shaphan and to H1201
Jer 29: 3 of Shaphan and to Gemariah s of Hilkiah, H1201
Jer 29:21 says about Ahab s of Kolaiah and H1201
Jer 29:21 of Kolaiah and Zedekiah s of Maaseiah, H1201
Jer 29:25 to the priest Zephaniah s of Maaseiah H1201
Jer 31: 9 Israel's father, and Ephraim is my **firstborn** *s.* AIT
Jer 31:20 Is not Ephraim my dear s, the child in H1201
Jer 32: 7 Hanamel s of Shallum your uncle is going H1201
Jer 32:12 I gave this deed to Baruch s of Neriah H1201
Jer 32:12 son of Neriah, the s of Mahseiah, in the H1201
Jer 32:16 deed of purchase to Baruch s of Neriah, H1201
Jer 35: 1 reign of Jehoiakim s of Josiah king of H1201
Jer 35: 3 So I went to get Jaazaniah s of Jeremiah H1201
Jer 35: 3 of Jeremiah, the s of Habazziniah, and H1201
Jer 35: 4 the sons of Hanan s of Igdaliah the man H1201
Jer 35: 4 over that of Maaseiah s of Shallum the H1201
Jer 35: 6 Jehonadab s of Rekab gave us this H1201
Jer 35: 8 Jehonadab s of Rekab commanded us. H1201
Jer 35:14 'Jehonadab s of Rekab ordered his H1201
Jer 35:16 of Jehonadab s of Rekab have carried out H1201
Jer 35:19 'Jehonadab s of Rekab will never fail to H1201
Jer 36: 1 year of Jehoiakim s of Josiah king of H1201
Jer 36: 4 So Jeremiah called Baruch s of Neriah H1201
Jer 36: 8 Baruch s of Neriah did everything H1201
Jer 36: 9 year of Jehoiakim s of Josiah king of H1201
Jer 36:10 the room of Gemariah s of Shaphan the H1201
Jer 36:11 When Micaiah s of Gemariah, the son of H1201
Jer 36:11 of Gemariah, the s of Shaphan, heard all H1201
Jer 36:12 secretary, Delaiah s of Shemaiah H1201
Jer 36:12 Elnathan s of Akbor, Gemariah H1201
Jer 36:12 Gemariah s of Shaphan, Zedekiah H1201
Jer 36:12 Shaphan, Zedekiah s of Hananiah, and H1201
Jer 36:14 all the officials sent Jehudi s of Nethaniah, H1201
Jer 36:14 of Nethaniah, the s of Shelemiah, the son H1201
Jer 36:14 son of Shelemiah, the s of Cushi, to say to H1201
Jer 36:14 So Baruch s of Neriah went to them with H1201
Jer 36:26 Jerahmeel, a s of the king, Seraiah son H1201
Jer 36:26 Seraiah s of Azriel and Shelemiah son of H1201
Jer 36:26 Shelemiah s of Abdeel to arrest H1201
Jer 36:32 gave it to the scribe Baruch s of Neriah, H1201
Jer 37: 1 Zedekiah s of Josiah was made king of H1201
Jer 37: 1 in place of Jehoiachin s of Jehoiakim. H1201

Jer 37: 3 sent Jehukal s of Shelemiah with the H1201
Jer 37: 3 the priest Zephaniah s of Maaseiah to H1201
Jer 37:13 whose name was Irijah s of Shelemiah H1201
Jer 37:13 of Shelemiah, the s of Hananiah, arrested H1201
Jer 38: 1 Shephatiah s of Mattan, Gedaliah son of H1201
Jer 38: 1 of Mattan, Gedaliah s of Pashhur, Jehukal H1201
Jer 38: 1 of Pashhur, Jehukal s of Shelemiah, and H1201
Jer 38: 1 Pashhur s of Malkijah heard what H1201
Jer 38: 6 of Malkijah, the king's s, which was in the H1201
Jer 39:14 turned him over to Gedaliah s of Ahikam, H1201
Jer 39:14 son of Ahikam, the s of Shaphan, to take H1201
Jer 40: 5 "Go back to Gedaliah s of Ahikam, the H1201
Jer 40: 5 of Ahikam, the s of Shaphan, whom the H1201
Jer 40: 6 went to Gedaliah s of Ahikam at Mizpah H1201
Jer 40: 7 appointed Gedaliah s of Ahikam as H1201
Jer 40: 8 at Mizpah—Ishmael s of Nethaniah H1201
Jer 40: 8 of Kareah, Seraiah s of Tanhumeth, the H1201
Jer 40: 8 Jaazaniah the s of the Maakathite H1201
Jer 40: 9 Gedaliah s of Ahikam, the son of Shaphan H1201
Jer 40: 9 son of Ahikam, the s of Shaphan, took an H1201
Jer 40:11 had appointed Gedaliah s of Ahikam, H1201
Jer 40:11 son of Ahikam, the s of Shaphan, as H1201
Jer 40:13 Johanan s of Kareah and all the army H1201
Jer 40:14 has sent Ishmael s of Nethaniah to take H1201
Jer 40:14 But Gedaliah s of Ahikam did not believe H1201
Jer 40:15 Then Johanan s of Kareah said privately H1201
Jer 40:15 me go and kill Ishmael s of Nethaniah, H1201
Jer 40:16 But Gedaliah s of Ahikam said to H1201
Jer 40:16 of Ahikam said to Johanan s of Kareah, H1201
Jer 41: 1 seventh month Ishmael s of Nethaniah, H1201
Jer 41: 1 of Nethaniah, the s of Elishama, who was H1201
Jer 41: 1 men to Gedaliah s of Ahikam at Mizpah. H1201
Jer 41: 2 Ishmael s of Nethaniah and the ten men H1201
Jer 41: 2 struck down Gedaliah s of Ahikam, H1201
Jer 41: 2 son of Ahikam, the s of Shaphan, with the H1201
Jer 41: 6 Ishmael s of Nethaniah went out from H1201
Jer 41: 6 he said, "Come to Gedaliah s of Ahikam." H1201
Jer 41: 7 Ishmael s of Nethaniah and the men who H1201
Jer 41: 9 Ishmael s of Nethaniah filled it with the H1201
Jer 41:10 had appointed Gedaliah s of Ahikam. H1201
Jer 41:10 Ishmael s of Nethaniah took them captive H1201
Jer 41:11 When Johanan s of Kareah and all the H1201
Jer 41:11 all the crimes Ishmael s of Nethaniah had H1201
Jer 41:12 went to fight Ishmael s of Nethaniah. H1201
Jer 41:13 him saw Johanan s of Kareah and the H1201
Jer 41:14 went over to Johanan s of Kareah. H1201
Jer 41:15 But Ishmael s of Nethaniah and eight of H1201
Jer 41:16 Then Johanan s of Kareah and all the H1201
Jer 41:16 from Ishmael s of Nethaniah after H1201
Jer 41:16 had assassinated Gedaliah s of Ahikam— H1201
Jer 41:18 because Ishmael s of Nethaniah had H1201
Jer 41:18 had killed Gedaliah s of Ahikam, H1201
Jer 42: 1 including Johanan s of Kareah and H1201
Jer 42: 1 of Kareah and Jezaniah s of Hoshaiah, H1201
Jer 42: 8 together Johanan s of Kareah and all the H1201
Jer 43: 2 Azariah s of Hoshaiah and Johanan son of H1201
Jer 43: 2 Johanan s of Kareah and all the H1201
Jer 43: 3 But Baruch s of Neriah is inciting you H1201
Jer 43: 4 So Johanan s of Kareah and all the army H1201
Jer 43: 5 Johanan s of Kareah and all the army H1201
Jer 43: 6 guard had left with Gedaliah s of Ahikam, H1201
Jer 43: 6 of Ahikam, the s of Shaphan—the men, H1201
Jer 43: 6 Baruch s of Neriah along with H1201
Jer 45: 1 When Baruch s of Neriah wrote on a scroll H1201
Jer 45: 1 year of Jehoiakim s of Josiah king of H1201
Jer 46: 2 year of Jehoiakim s of Josiah king of H1201
Jer 51:59 to the staff officer Seraiah s of Neriah, H1201
Jer 51:59 of Neriah, the s of Mahseiah, when he H1201
Eze 1: 3 the priest, the s of Buzi, by the Kebar H1201
Eze 2: 1 He said to me, "S of man, stand up on H1201
Eze 2: 3 "S of man, I am sending you to the H1201
Eze 2: 6 And you, s of man, do not be afraid of H1201
Eze 2: 8 s of man, listen to what I say to H1201
Eze 3: 1 And he said to me, "S of man, eat what is H1201
Eze 3: 3 he said to me, "S of man, eat this scroll H1201
Eze 3: 4 "S of man, go now to the people of Israel H1201
Eze 3:10 And he said to me, "S of man, listen H1201
Eze 3:17 "S of man, I have made you a watchman H1201
Eze 3:25 And you, s of man, they will tie with ropes H1201
Eze 4: 1 s of man, take a block of clay, put it H1201
Eze 4:16 "S of man, I am about to cut off the food H1201
Eze 5: 1 s of man, take a sharp sword and H1201
Eze 6: 2 "S of man, set your face against the H1201
Eze 7: 2 "S of man, this is what the Sovereign LORD H1201
Eze 8: 5 he said to me, "S of man, look toward the H1201
Eze 8: 6 And he said to me, "S of man, do you see H1201
Eze 8: 8 He said to me, "S of man, now dig into H1201
Eze 8:11 Jaazaniah s of Shaphan was H1201
Eze 8:12 He said to me, "S of man, have you seen H1201
Eze 8:15 "Do you see this, s of man? You will see H1201
Eze 8:17 "Have you seen this, s of man? H1201
Eze 11: 1 them Jaazaniah s of Azzur and Pelatiah H1201
Eze 11: 1 son of Azzur and Pelatiah s of Benaiah, H1201
Eze 11: 2 LORD said to me, "S of man, these are the H1201
Eze 11: 4 against them; prophesy, s of man. H1201
Eze 11:13 prophesying, Pelatiah s of Benaiah died. H1201
Eze 11:15 "S of man, the people of Jerusalem have H1201
Eze 12: 2 "S of man, you are living among a H1201
Eze 12: 3 "Therefore, s of man, pack your H1201
Eze 12: 9 "S of man, did not the Israelites, that H1201
Eze 12:18 "S of man, tremble as you eat your food H1201
Eze 12:22 "S of man, what is this proverb you have in H1201

Book	Ref	Context	Number
Eze	12:27	"S of man, the Israelites are saying, 'The	H1201
Eze	13: 2	"S of man, prophesy against the prophets	H1201
Eze	13:17	s of man, set your face against the	H1201
Eze	14: 3	"S of man, these men have set up idols in	H1201
Eze	14:13	"S of man, if a country sins against me by	H1201
Eze	14:20	they could save neither s nor daughter.	H1201
Eze	15: 2	"S of man, how is the wood of a vine	H1201
Eze	16: 2	"S of man, confront Jerusalem with her	H1201
Eze	17: 2	"S of man, set forth an allegory and tell it	H1201
Eze	18:10	"Suppose he has a violent s, who sheds	H1201
Eze	18:14	"But suppose this s has a son who sees all	NDT
Eze	18:14	this son has a s who sees all the sins	H1201
Eze	18:19	'Why does the s not share the guilt of his	H1201
Eze	18:19	Since the s has done what is just and	H1201
Eze	20: 3	"S of man, speak to the elders of Israel	H1201
Eze	20: 4	you judge them, s of man? Then confront	H1201
Eze	20:27	"Therefore, s of man, speak to the people	H1201
Eze	20:46	"S of man, set your face toward the south	H1201
Eze	21: 2	"S of man, set your face against Jerusalem	H1201
Eze	21: 6	"Therefore groan, s of man! Groan before	H1201
Eze	21: 9	"S of man, prophesy and say, 'This is what	H1201
Eze	21:10	we rejoice in the scepter of my royal s?	H1201
Eze	21:12	Cry out and wail, s of man, for it is against	H1201
Eze	21:14	"So then, s of man, prophesy and strike	H1201
Eze	21:19	"S of man, mark out two roads for the	H1201
Eze	21:28	"And you, s of man, prophesy and say	H1201
Eze	22: 2	"S of man, will you judge her? Will you	H1201
Eze	22:18	"S of man, the people of Israel have	H1201
Eze	22:24	"S of man, say to the land, 'You are a land	H1201
Eze	23: 2	"S of man, there were two women	H1201
Eze	23:36	"S of man, will you judge Oholah and	H1201
Eze	24: 2	"S of man, record this date, this very date	H1201
Eze	24:16	"S of man, with one blow I am about to	H1201
Eze	24:25	"And you, s of man, on the day I take	H1201
Eze	25: 2	"S of man, set your face against the	H1201
Eze	26: 2	"S of man, because Tyre has said of	H1201
Eze	27: 2	"S of man, take up a lament concerning	H1201
Eze	28: 2	"S of man, say to the ruler of Tyre, 'This is	H1201
Eze	28:12	"S of man, take up a lament concerning	H1201
Eze	28:21	"S of man, set your face against Sidon	H1201
Eze	29: 2	"S of man, set your face against Pharaoh	H1201
Eze	29:18	"S of man, Nebuchadnezzar king of	H1201
Eze	30: 2	"S of man, prophesy and say: 'This is what	H1201
Eze	30:21	"S of man, I have broken the arm of	H1201
Eze	31: 2	"S of man, say to Pharaoh king of Egypt	H1201
Eze	32: 2	"S of man, take up a lament concerning	H1201
Eze	32:18	"S of man, wail for the hordes of Egypt	H1201
Eze	33: 2	"S of man, speak to your people and say	H1201
Eze	33: 7	"S of man, I have made you a watchman	H1201
Eze	33:10	"S of man, say to the Israelites, 'This is	H1201
Eze	33:12	"Therefore, s of man, say to your people	H1201
Eze	33:24	"S of man, the people living in those ruins	H1201
Eze	33:30	"As for you, s of man, your people are	H1201
Eze	34: 2	"S of man, prophesy against the	H1201
Eze	35: 2	"S of man, set your face against Mount	H1201
Eze	36: 1	"S of man, prophesy to the mountains of	H1201
Eze	36:17	"S of man, when the people of Israel were	H1201
Eze	37: 3	He asked me, "S of man, can these bones	H1201
Eze	37: 9	prophesy, s of man, and say to it	H1201
Eze	37:11	"S of man, these bones are the people of	H1201
Eze	37:16	"S of man, take a stick of wood and write	H1201
Eze	38: 2	"S of man, set your face against Gog, of	H1201
Eze	38:14	"Therefore, s of man, prophesy and say to	H1201
Eze	39: 1	"S of man, prophesy against Gog and say	H1201
Eze	39:17	"S of man, this is what the Sovereign LORD	H1201
Eze	40: 4	man said to me, "S of man, look carefully	H1201
Eze	43: 7	"S of man, this is the place of my throne	H1201
Eze	43:10	"S of man, describe the temple to the	H1201
Eze	43:18	he said to me, "S of man, this is what	H1201
Eze	44: 5	LORD said to me, "S of man, look carefully,	H1201
Eze	44:25	father or mother, s or daughter, brother	H1201
Eze	47: 6	He asked me, "S of man, do you see this?"	H1201
Da	3:25	the fourth looks like a s of the gods."	A10120
Da	5:22	Belshazzar, his s, have not humbled	A10120
Da	7:13	before me was one like a s of man,	A10120
Da	8:17	"S of man," he said to me, "understand	H1201
Da	9: 1	In the first year of Darius s of Xerxes (a	H1201
Hos	1: 1	that came to Hosea s of Beeri during the	H1201
Hos	1: 1	reign of Jeroboam s of Jehoash king of	H1201
Hos	1: 3	she conceived and bore him a s.	H1201
Hos	1: 8	Lo-Ruhamah, Gomer had another s.	H1201
Hos	11: 1	loved him, and out of Egypt I called my s.	H1201
Joel	1: 1	of the LORD that came to Joel s of Pethuel.	H1201
Am	1: 1	Jeroboam s of Jehoash was king	H1201
Am	2: 7	Father and s use the same girl and so	H408
Am	7:14	neither a prophet nor the s of a prophet,	H1201
Am	8:10	mourning for an only s and the end of it	H3495
Jnh	1: 1	of the LORD came to Jonah s of Amittai:	H1201
Mic	5: 3	time when she who is in labor bears a s,	H3528
Mic	6: 5	what Balaam s of Beor answered.	H1201
Mic	7: 6	For a s dishonors his father, a daughter	H1201
Zep	1: 1	LORD that came to Zephaniah s of Cushi,	H1201
Zep	1: 1	son of Cushi, the s of Gedaliah, the son of	H1201
Zep	1: 1	of Gedaliah, the s of Amariah, the son of	H1201
Zep	1: 1	son of Amariah, the s of Hezekiah, during	H1201
Zep	1: 1	reign of Josiah s of Amon king of Judah	H1201
Hag	1: 1	Haggai to Zerubbabel s of Shealtiel,	H1201
Hag	1: 1	to Joshua s of Jozadak, the high	H1201
Hag	1:12	Then Zerubbabel s of Shealtiel, Joshua	H1201
Hag	1:12	Shealtiel, Joshua s of Jozadak, the high	H1201
Hag	1:14	up the spirit of Zerubbabel s of Shealtiel,	H1201
Hag	1:14	the spirit of Joshua s of Jozadak, the	H1201
Hag	2: 2	"Speak to Zerubbabel s of Shealtiel	H1201
Hag	2: 2	of Judah, to Joshua s of Jozadak, the high	H1201
Hag	2: 4	'Be strong, Joshua s of Jozadak, the high	H1201
Hag	2:23	my servant Zerubbabel s of Shealtiel,'	H1201
Zec	1: 1	to the prophet Zechariah s of Berekiah,	H1201
Zec	1: 1	Zechariah son of Berekiah, the s of Iddo:	H1201
Zec	1: 7	to the prophet Zechariah s of Berekiah,	H1201
Zec	1: 7	Zechariah son of Berekiah, the s of Iddo.	H1201
Zec	6:10	to the house of Josiah s of Zephaniah.	H1201
Zec	6:11	of the high priest, Joshua s of Jozadak.	H1201
Zec	6:14	Jedaiah and Hen s of Zephaniah as a	H1201
Zec	12:10	him as one grieves for a firstborn s.	AIT
Mal	1: 6	"A s honors his father, and a slave his	H1201
Mal	3:17	spares his s who serves him.	H1201
Mt	1: 1	of Jesus the Messiah the s of David,	G5626
Mt	1: 1	the son of David, the s of Abraham:	G5626
Mt	1:20	said, "Joseph s of David, do not be	G5626
Mt	1:21	She will give birth to a s, and you are to	G5626
Mt	1:23	virgin will conceive and give birth to a s,	G5626
Mt	1:25	their marriage until she gave birth to a s.	G5626
Mt	2:15	"Out of Egypt I called my s."	G5626
Mt	3:17	heaven said, "This is my S, whom I love;	G5626
Mt	4: 3	"If you are the S of God, tell these	G5626
Mt	4: 6	"If you are the S of God," he said, "throw	G5626
Mt	4:21	James s of Zebedee and his brother	G3836S
Mt	7: 9	if your s asks for bread, will	G5626
Mt	8:20	the S of Man has no place to lay his	G5626
Mt	8:29	do you want with us, S of God?" they	G5626
Mt	9: 2	the man, "Take heart, s; your sins are	G5451
Mt	9: 6	to know that the S of Man has authority	G5626
Mt	9:27	"Have mercy on us, S of David!	G5626
Mt	10: 2	Andrew; James s of Zebedee, and his	G3836S
Mt	10: 3	tax collector; James s of Alphaeus, and	G3836S
Mt	10:23	of Israel before the S of Man comes.	G5626
Mt	10:37	who loves their s or daughter more than	G5626
Mt	11:19	The S of Man came eating and drinking	G5626
Mt	11:27	No one knows the S except the Father	G5626
Mt	11:27	Father except the S and those to whom	G5626
Mt	11:27	those to whom the S chooses to reveal	G5626
Mt	12: 8	For the S of Man is Lord of the Sabbath."	G5626
Mt	12:23	said, "Could this be the S of David?"	G5626
Mt	12:32	a word against the S of Man will be	G5626
Mt	12:40	so the S of Man will be three days and	G5626
Mt	13:37	sowed the good seed is the S of Man.	G5626
Mt	13:41	The S of Man will send out his angels	G5626
Mt	13:55	"Isn't this the carpenter's s? Isn't his	G5626
Mt	14:33	saying, "Truly you are the S of God."	G5626
Mt	15:22	crying out, "Lord, S of David, have mercy	G5626
Mt	16:13	"Who do people say the S of Man is?"	G5626
Mt	16:16	are the Messiah, the S of the living God."	G5626
Mt	16:17	are you, Simon s of Jonah, for this was not	G980
Mt	16:27	For the S of Man is going to come in his	G5626
Mt	16:28	before they see the S of Man coming in	G5626
Mt	17: 5	cloud said, "This is my S, whom I love;	G5626
Mt	17: 9	until the S of Man has been raised from	G5626
Mt	17:12	In the same way the S of Man is going to	G5626
Mt	17:15	have mercy on my s," he said. "He	G5626
Mt	17:22	"The S of Man is going to be delivered	G5626
Mt	19:28	when the S of Man sits on his glorious	G5626
Mt	20:18	the S of Man will be delivered over to	G5626
Mt	20:28	just as the S of Man did not come to be	G5626
Mt	20:30	shouted, "Lord, S of David, have mercy	G5626
Mt	20:31	the louder, "Lord, S of David, have mercy	G5626
Mt	21: 9	shouted, "Hosanna to the S of David!"	G5626
Mt	21:15	"Hosanna to the S of David," they	G5626
Mt	21:28	the first and said, 'S, go and work today in	G5451
Mt	21:30	went to the other s and said the same thing.	NDT
Mt	21:37	Last of all, he sent his s to them. 'They will	G5626
Mt	21:37	'They will respect my s,' he said.	G5626
Mt	21:38	"But when the tenants saw the s, they	G5626
Mt	22: 2	prepared a wedding banquet for his s.	G5626
Mt	22:42	Whose s is he?" "The son of	G5626
Mt	22:42	Whose son is he?" "The s of David," they	NDT
Mt	22:45	calls him 'Lord,' how can he be his s?"	G5626
Mt	23:35	to the blood of Zechariah s of Berekiah,	G5626
Mt	24:27	so will be the coming of the S of Man.	G5626
Mt	24:30	appear the sign of the S of Man in	G5626
Mt	24:30	when they see the S of Man coming on	G5626
Mt	24:36	in heaven, nor the S, but only the Father.	G5626
Mt	24:37	it will be at the coming of the S of Man.	G5626
Mt	24:39	it will be at the coming of the S of Man.	G5626
Mt	24:44	because the S of Man will come at an	G5626
Mt	25:31	"When the S of Man comes in his glory	G5626
Mt	26: 2	the S of Man will be handed over to	G5626
Mt	26:24	The S of Man will go just as it is written	G5626
Mt	26:24	to that man who betrays the S of Man!	G5626
Mt	26:45	the S of Man is delivered into the	G5626
Mt	26:63	us if you are the Messiah, the S of God."	G5626
Mt	26:64	on you will see the S of Man sitting at the	G5626
Mt	27:40	from the cross, if you are the S of God!"	G5626
Mt	27:43	for he said, 'I am the S of God.	G5626
Mt	27:54	exclaimed, "Surely he was the S of God!"	G5626
Mt	28:19	of the Father and of the S and of the Holy	G5626
Mk	1: 1	about Jesus the Messiah, the S of God,	G5626
Mk	1:11	"You are my S, whom I love; with you I	G5626
Mk	1:19	he saw James s of Zebedee and his	G3836S
Mk	2: 5	to the paralyzed man, "S, your sins are	G5451
Mk	2:10	to know that the S of Man has authority	G5626
Mk	2:14	he saw Levi s of Alphaeus sitting at the	G3836S
Mk	2:28	So the S of Man is Lord even of the	G5626
Mk	3:11	him and cried out, "You are the S of God."	G5626
Mk	3:17	James s of Zebedee and his brother John	G3836S
Mk	3:18	Thomas, James s of Alphaeus	G3836S
Mk	5: 7	with me, Jesus, S of the Most High God?	G5626
Mk	6: 3	Isn't this Mary's s and the brother of	G5626
Mk	8:31	teach them that the S of Man must suffer	G5626
Mk	8:38	the S of Man will be ashamed of them	G5626
Mk	9: 7	"This is my S, whom I love. Listen	G5626
Mk	9: 9	had seen until the S of Man had risen	G5626
Mk	9:12	is it written that the S of Man must suffer	G5626
Mk	9:17	I brought you my s, who is possessed by a	G5626
Mk	9:31	"The S of Man is going to be delivered	G5626
Mk	10:33	"and the S of Man will be delivered over	G5626
Mk	10:45	For even the S of Man did not come to be	G5626
Mk	10:46	Bartimaeus (which means "s of Timaeus")	G5626
Mk	10:47	to shout, "Jesus, S of David, have mercy	G5626
Mk	10:48	all the more, "S of David, have mercy	G5626
Mk	12: 6	had one left to send, a s, whom he loved.	G5626
Mk	12: 6	last of all, saying, 'They will respect my s.	G5626
Mk	12:35	say that the Messiah is the s of David?	G5626
Mk	12:37	How then can he be his s?" The large	G5626
Mk	13:26	people will see the S of Man coming in	G5626
Mk	13:32	in heaven, nor the S, but only the Father.	G5626
Mk	14:21	The S of Man will go just as it is written	G5626
Mk	14:21	to that man who betrays the S of Man!	G5626
Mk	14:41	the S of Man is delivered into the hands	G5626
Mk	14:61	the Messiah, the S of the Blessed One?"	G5626
Mk	14:62	you will see the S of Man sitting at the	G5626
Mk	15:39	"Surely this man was the S of God!"	G5626
Lk	1:13	Your wife Elizabeth will bear you a s, and	G5626
Lk	1:31	You will conceive and give birth to a s	G5626
Lk	1:32	will be called the S of the Most High.	G5626
Lk	1:35	to be born will be called the S of God.	G5626
Lk	1:57	to have her baby, she gave birth to a s.	G5626
Lk	2: 7	to her firstborn, a s. She wrapped him in	G5626
Lk	2:48	mother said to him, "S, why have you	G5451
Lk	3: 2	of God came to John s of Zechariah in the	G5626
Lk	3:22	"You are my S, whom I love; with you I	G5626
Lk	3:23	He was the s, so it was thought, of Joseph	G5626
Lk	3:23	it was thought, of Joseph, the s of Heli,	G3836S
Lk	3:24	the s of Matthat, the son of Levi, the son	G3836S
Lk	3:24	son of Matthat, the s of Levi, the son of	G3836S
Lk	3:24	the son of Levi, the s of Melki, the son of	G3836S
Lk	3:24	the son of Melki, the s of Jannai, the son	G3836S
Lk	3:24	the son of Jannai, the s of Joseph,	G3836S
Lk	3:25	the s of Mattathias, the son of Amos, the	G3836S
Lk	3:25	of Mattathias, the s of Amos, the son	G3836S
Lk	3:25	the son of Amos, the s of Nahum, the	G3836S
Lk	3:25	the son of Nahum, the s of Esli, the son	G3836S
Lk	3:25	Nahum, the son of Esli, the s of Naggai,	G3836S
Lk	3:26	the s of Maath, the son of Mattathias	G3836S
Lk	3:26	the son of Maath, the s of Mattathias	G3836S
Lk	3:26	of Mattathias, the s of Semein, the son	G3836S
Lk	3:26	son of Semein, the s of Josek, the son	G3836S
Lk	3:26	Semein, the son of Josek, the s of Joda,	G3836S
Lk	3:27	the s of Joanan, the son of Rhesa, the	G3836S
Lk	3:27	son of Joanan, the s of Rhesa, the son	G3836S
Lk	3:27	the son of Rhesa, the s of Zerubbabel	G3836S
Lk	3:27	of Zerubbabel, the s of Shealtiel, the	G3836S
Lk	3:27	the son of Shealtiel, the s of Neri,	G3836S
Lk	3:28	the s of Melki, the son of Addi, the son	G3836S
Lk	3:28	the son of Melki, the s of Addi, the son	G3836S
Lk	3:28	the son of Addi, the s of Cosam, the son	G3836S
Lk	3:28	the son of Cosam, the s of Elmadam, the	G3836S
Lk	3:28	the son of Elmadam, the s of Er,	G3836S
Lk	3:29	the s of Joshua, the son of Eliezer, the	G3836S
Lk	3:29	the son of Joshua, the s of Eliezer, the	G3836S
Lk	3:29	the son of Eliezer, the s of Jorim, the son	G3836S
Lk	3:29	the son of Jorim, the s of Matthat, the	G3836S
Lk	3:29	the son of Matthat, the s of Levi,	G3836S
Lk	3:30	the s of Simeon, the son of Judah, the	G3836S
Lk	3:30	son of Simeon, the s of Judah, the son	G3836S
Lk	3:30	the son of Judah, the s of Joseph, the	G3836S
Lk	3:30	son of Joseph, the s of Jonam, the son	G3836S
Lk	3:30	the son of Jonam, the s of Eliakim,	G3836S
Lk	3:31	the s of Melea, the son of Menna, the	G3836S
Lk	3:31	son of Melea, the s of Menna, the son	G3836S
Lk	3:31	the son of Menna, the s of Mattatha, the	G3836S
Lk	3:31	son of Mattatha, the s of Nathan, the	G3836S
Lk	3:31	the son of Nathan, the s of David,	G3836S
Lk	3:32	the s of Jesse, the son of Obed, the son	G3836S
Lk	3:32	the son of Jesse, the s of Obed, the son	G3836S
Lk	3:32	the son of Obed, the s of Boaz, the son	G3836S
Lk	3:32	the son of Boaz, the s of Salmon, the	G3836S
Lk	3:32	the son of Salmon, the s of Nahshon,	G3836S
Lk	3:33	the s of Amminadab, the son of Ram	G3836S
Lk	3:33	of Amminadab, the s of Ram, the son	G3836S
Lk	3:33	the son of Ram, the s of Hezron, the son	G3836S
Lk	3:33	son of Hezron, the s of Perez, the son	G3836S
Lk	3:33	the son of Perez, the s of Judah,	G3836S
Lk	3:34	the s of Jacob, the son of Isaac, the son	G3836S
Lk	3:34	the son of Jacob, the s of Isaac, the son	G3836S
Lk	3:34	the son of Isaac, the s of Abraham, the	G3836S
Lk	3:34	son of Abraham, the s of Terah, the son	G3836S
Lk	3:34	the son of Terah, the s of Nahor,	G3836S
Lk	3:35	the s of Serug, the son of Reu, the son of	G3836S
Lk	3:35	the son of Serug, the s of Reu, the son of	G3836S
Lk	3:35	the son of Reu, the s of Peleg, the son of	G3836S
Lk	3:35	the son of Peleg, the s of Eber, the son	G3836S
Lk	3:35	the son of Eber, the s of Shelah,	G3836S
Lk	3:36	the s of Cainan, the son of Arphaxad	G3836S
Lk	3:36	son of Cainan, the s of Arphaxad, the	G3836S
Lk	3:36	son of Arphaxad, the s of Shem, the son	G3836S
Lk	3:36	the son of Shem, the s of Noah, the son	G3836S

Lk 3:36 the son of Noah, **the s** of Lamech, G3836S
Lk 3:37 **the s** of Methuselah, the son of Enoch G3836S
Lk 3:37 of Methuselah, **the s** of Enoch, the son G3836S
Lk 3:37 the son of Enoch, **the s** of Jared, the son G3836S
Lk 3:37 the son of Jared, **the s** of Mahalalel, the G3836S
Lk 3:37 the son of Mahalalel, **the s** of Kenan, G3836S
Lk 3:38 **the s** of Enosh, the son of Seth, the son G3836S
Lk 3:38 the son of Enosh, **the s** of Seth, the son G3836S
Lk 3:38 the son of Seth, **the s** of Adam, the son G3836S
Lk 3:38 of Seth, the son of Adam, **the s** of God. G3836S
Lk 4: 3 "If you are the **S** of God, tell this G5626
Lk 4: 9 "If you are the **S** of God," he said, "throw G5626
Lk 4:22 "Isn't this Joseph's **s**?" they asked. G5626
Lk 4:41 people, shouting, "You are the **S** of God!" G5626
Lk 5:24 to know that the **S** of Man has authority G5626
Lk 6: 5 "The **S** of Man is Lord of the Sabbath." G5626
Lk 6:15 Thomas, James *s of* **Alphaeus**, Simon who AIT
Lk 6:16 Judas *s of* **James**, and Judas Iscariot, who AIT
Lk 6:22 name as evil, because of the **S** of Man. G5626
Lk 7:12 carried out—the only **s** of his mother, and G5626
Lk 7:34 The **S** of Man came eating and drinking G5626
Lk 8:28 with me, Jesus, **S** of the Most High God? G5626
Lk 9:22 "The **S** of Man must suffer many things G5626
Lk 9:26 the **S** of Man will be ashamed of them G5626
Lk 9:35 "This is my **S**, whom I have chosen G5626
Lk 9:38 I beg you to look at my **s**, for he is my only G5626
Lk 9:41 put up with you? Bring your **s** here." G5626
Lk 9:44 The **S** of Man is going to be delivered G5626
Lk 9:58 the **S** of Man has no place to lay his G5626
Lk 10:22 one knows who the **S** is except the Father G5626
Lk 10:22 Father is except the **S** and those to whom G5626
Lk 10:22 those to whom the **S** chooses to reveal G5626
Lk 11:11 of you fathers, if your **s** asks for a fish, will G5626
Lk 11:30 so also will the **S** of Man be to this G5626
Lk 12: 8 the **S** of Man will also acknowledge G5626
Lk 12:10 a word against the **S** of Man will be G5626
Lk 12:40 because the **S** of Man will come at an G5626
Lk 12:53 father against **s** and son against father G5626
Lk 12:53 father against son and **s** against father G5626
Lk 15:13 the younger **s** got together all he had G5626
Lk 15:19 I am no longer worthy to be called your **s** G5626
Lk 15:20 he ran to his **s**, threw his arms around NDT
Lk 15:21 "The **s** said to him, 'Father, I have sinned G5626
Lk 15:21 I am no longer worthy to be called your **s** G5626
Lk 15:24 For this **s** of mine was dead and is alive G5626
Lk 15:25 "Meanwhile, the older **s** was in the field G5626
Lk 15:30 But when this **s** of yours who has G5626
Lk 15:31 " 'My **s**,' the father said, 'you are always G5451
Lk 16:25 Abraham replied, '**S**, remember that in G5451
Lk 17:22 to see one of the days *of* the **S** of Man, G5626
Lk 17:24 For the **S** of Man in his day will be like the G5626
Lk 17:26 also will it be in the days *of* the **S** of Man. G5626
Lk 17:30 this on the day the **S** of Man is revealed. G5626
Lk 18: 8 However, when the **S** of Man comes, will G5626
Lk 18:31 the prophets *about* the **S** of Man will be G5626
Lk 18:38 called out, "Jesus, **S** of David, have mercy G5626
Lk 18:39 all the more, "**S** of David, have mercy G5626
Lk 19: 9 because this man, too, is a **s** of Abraham. G5626
Lk 19:10 For the **S** of Man came to seek and to save G5626
Lk 20:13 I will send my **s**, whom I love; perhaps G5626
Lk 20:41 it said that the Messiah is the **s** of David? G5626
Lk 20:44 How then can he be his **s**?" G5626
Lk 21:27 they will see the **S** of Man coming in a G5626
Lk 21:36 be able to stand before the **S** of Man." G5626
Lk 22:22 The **S** of Man will go as it has been G5626
Lk 22:48 you betraying the **S** of Man with a kiss?" G5626
Lk 22:69 the **S** of Man will be seated at the right G5626
Lk 22:70 all asked, "Are you then the **S** of God?" G5626
Lk 24: 7 'The **S** of Man must be delivered over to G5626
Jn 1:14 the glory of the **one and only S**, who G3666
Jn 1:18 but the **one and only S**, who is G3666
Jn 1:42 him and said, "You are Simon **s** of John. G5626
Jn 1:45 Jesus of Nazareth, the **s** of Joseph. G5626
Jn 1:49 you are the **S** of God; you are the G5626
Jn 1:51 descending on' the **S** of Man. G5626
Jn 3:13 who came from heaven—the **S** of Man. G5626
Jn 3:14 so the **S** of Man must be lifted up, G5626
Jn 3:16 world that he gave his one and only **S**, G5626
Jn 3:17 God did not send his **S** into the world to G5626
Jn 3:18 in the name *of* God's one and only **S**. G5626
Jn 3:35 The Father loves the **S** and has placed G5626
Jn 3:36 Whoever believes in the **S** has eternal life G5626
Jn 3:36 whoever rejects the **S** will not see life G5626
Jn 4: 5 ground Jacob had given *to* his **s** Joseph. G5626
Jn 4:46 royal official whose **s** lay sick at G5626
Jn 4:47 begged him to come and heal his **s**, G5626
Jn 4:50 Jesus replied, "your **s** will live." The man G5626
Jn 4:52 as to the time when his **s** got better, NDT
Jn 4:53 Jesus had said to him, "Your **s** will live." G5626
Jn 5:19 I tell you, the **S** can do nothing by himself G5626
Jn 5:19 whatever the Father does the **S** also does. G5626
Jn 5:20 Father loves the **S** and shows him all he G5626
Jn 5:21 even so the **S** gives life to whom he is G5626
Jn 5:22 has entrusted all judgment *to* the **S**, G5626
Jn 5:23 that all may honor the **S** just as they honor G5626
Jn 5:23 does not honor the **S** does not honor the G5626
Jn 5:25 hear the voice *of* the **S** of God and those G5626
Jn 5:26 he has granted the **S** also to have life in G5626
Jn 5:27 to judge because he is the **S** of Man. G5626
Jn 6:27 which the **S** of Man will give you. G5626
Jn 6:40 who looks to the **S** and believes in him G5626
Jn 6:42 this not Jesus, the **s** of Joseph, whose G5626
Jn 6:53 eat the flesh *of* the **S** of Man and drink G5626
Jn 6:62 what if you see the **S** of Man ascend to G5626
Jn 6:71 He meant Judas, the *s of* **Simon** Iscariot, who AIT
Jn 8:28 "When you have lifted up the **S** of Man G5626
Jn 8:35 in the family, but a **s** belongs to it forever. G5626
Jn 8:36 So if the **S** sets you free, you will be free G5626
Jn 9:19 "Is this your **s**?" they asked. "Is this the one G5626
Jn 9:20 "We know he is our **s**," the parents G5626
Jn 9:35 he said, "Do you believe in the **S** of Man?" G5626
Jn 10:36 because I said, 'I am God's **S**'? G5626
Jn 11: 4 glory so that God's **S** may be glorified G5626
Jn 11:27 are the Messiah, the **S** of God, who is to G5626
Jn 12:23 hour has come for the **S** of Man to be G5626
Jn 12:34 you say, 'The **S** of Man must be lifted up'? G5626
Jn 12:34 Who is this '**S** of Man'?" G5626
Jn 13: 2 prompted Judas, the *s of* **Simon** Iscariot, to AIT
Jn 13:26 he gave it to Judas, the *s of* **Simon** Iscariot. AIT
Jn 13:31 "Now the **S** of Man is glorified and God is G5626
Jn 13:32 God will glorify **the S** in himself, and will G899S
Jn 14:13 that the Father may be glorified in the **S**. G5626
Jn 17: 1 Glorify your **S**, that your Son may glorify G5626
Jn 17: 1 your Son, that your **S** may glorify you. G5626
Jn 19: 7 because he claimed to be the **S** of God." G5626
Jn 19:26 he said to her, "Woman, here is your **s**," G5626
Jn 20:31 is the Messiah, the **S** of God, and that by G5626
Jn 21:15 "Simon *s of* **John**, do you love me AIT
Jn 21:16 "Simon *s of* **John**, do you love me? AIT
Jn 21:17 "Simon *s of* **John**, do you love me? AIT
Ac 1:13 James *s of* **Alphaeus** and Simon the Zealot AIT
Ac 1:13 Simon the Zealot, and Judas *s of* **James**. AIT
Ac 4:36 which means "**s** of encouragement") G5626
Ac 7:21 him and brought him up as her own **s**. G5626
Ac 7:56 open and the **S** of Man standing at G5626
Ac 9:20 synagogues that Jesus is the **S** of God. G5626
Ac 13:21 he gave them Saul **s** of Kish, of the G5626
Ac 13:22 'I have found David **s** of Jesse, a man G3836S
Ac 13:33 " 'You are my **s**; today I have become your G5626
Ac 20: 4 by Sopater *s of* **Pyrrhus** from Berea, AIT
Ac 23:16 But when the **s** of Paul's sister heard of G5626
Ro 1: 3 regarding his **S**, who as to his earthly life G5626
Ro 1: 4 was appointed the **S** of God in power by G5626
Ro 1: 9 my spirit in preaching the gospel *of* his **S**, G5626
Ro 5:10 to him through the death *of* his **S**, G5626
Ro 8: 3 by sending his own **S** in the likeness of G5626
Ro 8:29 to be conformed to the image *of* his **S**, G5626
Ro 8:32 He who did not spare his own **S**, but gave G5626
Ro 9: 9 time I will return, and Sarah will have a **s**." G5626
1Co 1: 9 has called you into fellowship *with* his **S**, G5626
1Co 4:17 to you Timothy, my **s** whom I love, who is G5451
1Co 15:28 then the **S** himself will be made subject G5626
2Co 1:19 For the **S** of God, Jesus Christ, who was G5626
Gal 1:16 to reveal his **S** in me so that I might G5626
Gal 2:20 I live by faith *in* the **S** of God, who loved G5626
Gal 4: 4 God sent his **S**, born of a woman, G5626
Gal 4: 6 God sent the Spirit *of* his **S** into our hearts, G5626
Gal 4:23 **His s** by the slave woman was born G3836S
Gal 4:23 but **his s** by the free woman was born as G3836S
Gal 4:29 At that time **the** *s* born according to the flesh AIT
Gal 4:29 the flesh persecuted **the** *s* born by the power AIT
Gal 4:30 "Get rid of the slave woman and her **s**, for G5626
Gal 4:30 the slave woman's **s** will never share in G5626
Gal 4:30 the inheritance with the free woman's **s**." G5626
Eph 4:13 in the knowledge *of* the **S** of God and G5626
Php 2:22 because as a **s** with his father he has G5451
Col 1:13 us into the kingdom *of* the **S** he loves, G5626
Col 1:15 **The S** is the image of the invisible God G4005S
1Th 1:10 to wait for his **S** from heaven, whom G5626
1Ti 1: 2 To Timothy my true **s** in the faith: Grace G5451
1Ti 1:18 Timothy, my **s**, I am giving you this G5451
2Ti 1: 2 To Timothy, my dear **s**: Grace, mercy and G5451
2Ti 2: 1 You then, my **s**, be strong in the grace G5451
Titus 1: 4 To Titus, my true **s** in our common faith G5451
Phm 10 that I appeal to you for my **s** Onesimus G5451
Phm 10 who **became** *my* **s** while I was in chains. G1164S
Heb 1: 2 last days he has spoken to us by his **S**, G5626
Heb 1: 3 **The S** is the radiance of God's glory and G4005S
Heb 1: 5 "You are my **S**; today I have become G5626
Heb 1: 5 will be his Father, and he will be my **S**"? G5626
Heb 1: 8 But about the **S** he says, "Your throne, G5626
Heb 2: 6 of them, a **s** of man that you care for him? G5626
Heb 3: 6 is faithful as the **S** over God's house. G5626
Heb 4:14 heaven, Jesus the **S** of God, let us hold G5626
Heb 5: 5 "You are my **S**; today I have G5626
Heb 5: 8 **S** though he was, he learned obedience G5626
Heb 6: 6 are crucifying the **S** of God all over again G5626
Heb 7: 3 resembling the **S** of God, he remains a G5626
Heb 7:28 appointed the **S**, who has been made G5626
Heb 10:29 who has trampled the **S** of God underfoot, G5626
Heb 11:17 was about to sacrifice his **one and only s**, G3666
Heb 11:24 to be known as the **s** of Pharaoh's G5626
Heb 12: 5 addresses you as a father addresses his **s**? G5626
Heb 12: 5 "My **s**, do not make light of the G5626
Heb 12: 6 he chastens everyone he accepts *as* his **s**." G5626
Heb 12:16 sold his **inheritance rights as the oldest s**. G4757
Jas 2:21 when he offered his **s** Isaac on the altar? G5626
1Pe 5:13 you her greetings, and so does my **s** Mark. G5626
2Pe 1:17 "This is my **S**, whom I love; with G5626
2Pe 2:15 to follow the way of Balaam **s** of Bezer, G3836S
1Jn 1: 3 is with the Father and with his **S**, G5626
1Jn 1: 7 blood of Jesus, his **S**, purifies us from all G5626
1Jn 2:22 antichrist—denying the Father and the **S**. G5626
1Jn 2:23 No one who denies the **S** has the Father G5626
1Jn 2:23 acknowledges the **S** has the Father also. G5626
1Jn 2:24 will remain in the **S** and in the Father. G5626
1Jn 3: 8 The reason the **S** of God appeared was to G5626
1Jn 3:23 to believe in the name *of* his **S**, Jesus G5626
1Jn 4: 9 his one and only **S** into the world that G5626
1Jn 4:10 loved us and sent his **S** as an atoning G5626
1Jn 4:14 Father has sent his **S** to be the Savior of G5626
1Jn 4:15 acknowledges that Jesus is the **S** of God, G5626
1Jn 5: 5 who believes that Jesus is the **S** of God. G5626
1Jn 5: 9 which he has given about his **S**. G5626
1Jn 5:10 believes in the **S** of God accepts this G5626
1Jn 5:10 the testimony God has given about his **S**. G5626
1Jn 5:11 us eternal life, and this life is in his **S**. G5626
1Jn 5:12 Whoever has the **S** has life; whoever does G5626
1Jn 5:12 does not have the **S** of God does not have G5626
1Jn 5:13 in the name *of* the **S** of God so that you G5626
1Jn 5:20 know also that the **S** of God has come G5626
1Jn 5:20 who is true by being in his **S** Jesus Christ. G5626
2Jn 3 the Father's **S**, will be with us in G5626
2Jn 9 teaching has both the Father and the **S**. G5626
Rev 1:13 lampstands was someone like a **s** of man, G5626
Rev 2:18 These are the words of the **S** of God G5626
Rev 12: 5 She gave birth *to* a **s**, a male child, who G5626
Rev 14:14 was one like a **s** of man with a crown G5626

SON'S (12) [SON]

Ge 30:14 give me some of your **s** mandrakes." H1201
Ge 30:15 Will you take my **s** mandrakes too?" "Very H1201
Ge 30:15 you tonight in return for your **s** mandrakes." H1201
Ge 30:16 "I have hired you with my **s** mandrakes." H1201
Ge 37:32 Examine it to see whether it is your **s** robe." H1201
Ge 37:33 He recognized it and said, "It is my **s** robe! H1201
Ex 4:25 cut off her **s** foreskin and touched Moses' H1201
Lev 18:10 relations with your **s** daughter or your H1201
Lev 18:15 She is your **s** wife; do not have relations H1201
Lev 18:17 relations with either her **s** daughter or her H1201
2Sa 14:11 one hair of your **s** head will fall to the H1201
1Ki 11:35 kingdom from his **s** hands and give you H1201

SON-IN-LAW (11) [SON]

Jdg 15: 6 the Timnite's **s**, because his wife was H3163
Jdg 19: 5 the woman's father said to his **s** H3163
1Sa 18:18 that I should become the king's **s**? H3163
1Sa 18:21 *you have* a second opportunity *to become* my **s** H3161
1Sa 18:22 all love you; now *become* his **s**. H3161
1Sa 18:23 is a small matter *to become* the king's **s**? H3161
1Sa 18:26 he was pleased to *become* the king's **s**. H3161
1Sa 18:27 so that David *might become* the king's **s**. H3161
1Sa 22:14 as David, the king's **s**, captain of your H3163
Ne 6:18 since he was **s** to Shekaniah son of Arah H3163
Ne 13:28 the high priest was **s** to Sanballat the H3163

SONG (77) [SING]

Ex 15: 1 the Israelites sang this **s** to the LORD: H8878
Nu 21:17 Then Israel sang this **s**: "Spring up, O well H8878
Dt 31:19 "Now write down this **s** and teach it to the H8878
Dt 31:21 on them, this **s** will testify against them H8878
Dt 31:22 wrote down this **s** that day and taught H8878
Dt 31:30 the words of this **s** from beginning to end H8878
Dt 32:44 the words of this **s** in the hearing of the H8878
Jdg 5: 1 Barak son of Abinoam **sang** *this* **s**: H8876
Jdg 5: 3 *I will* **praise** the LORD, ... **in s** H2376
Jdg 5:12 Wake up, wake up, break out in **s**! Arise, H8877
2Sa 22: 1 LORD the words of this **s** when the LORD H8878
1Ch 16:42 of the other instruments for sacred **s**. H8877
Job 30: 9 "And now those young men **mock** me **in s**; H5593
Job 36:24 his work, which people *have* **praised in s**. H8876
Ps 18: T LORD the words of this **s** when the LORD H8878
Ps 28: 7 leaps for joy, and with my **s** I praise him. H8877
Ps 30: T A **s**. *For* the dedication of the temple H8877
Ps 33: 3 Sing to him a new **s**; play skillfully, and H8877
Ps 40: 3 He put a new **s** in my mouth, a hymn of H8877
Ps 42: 8 at night his **s** is with me—a prayer H8877
Ps 45: T the Sons of Korah. A maskil. A wedding **s**. H8877
Ps 46: T According to alamoth. A **s**. H8877
Ps 48: T A **s**. A psalm of the Sons of Korah. H8877
Ps 65: T director of music. A psalm of David. A **s**. H8877
Ps 66: T For the director of music. A **s**. A psalm. H8877
Ps 67: T With stringed instruments. A psalm. A **s**. H8877
Ps 68: T director of music. Of David. A psalm. A **s**. H8877
Ps 69:12 mock me, and I am the **s** *of* the drunkards. H5593
Ps 69:30 God's name in **s** and glorify him with H8877
Ps 75: T "Do Not Destroy." A psalm of Asaph. A **s**. H8877
Ps 76: T A psalm of Asaph. A **s**. H8877
Ps 83: T A **s**. A psalm of Asaph. H8877
Ps 87: T Of the Sons of Korah. A psalm. A **s**. H8877
Ps 88: T A **s**. A psalm of the Sons of Korah. For the H8877
Ps 92: T A **s**. For the Sabbath day. H8877
Ps 95: 2 extol him with **music and s**. H2369
Ps 96: 1 Sing to the LORD a new **s**; sing to the LORD H8877
Ps 98: 1 Sing to the LORD a new **s**, for he has done H8877
Ps 98: 4 the earth, burst into **jubilant s** with music; H8264
Ps 108: T A **s**. A psalm of David. H8877
Ps 119:54 decrees are the **theme of** my **s** wherever I H2369
Ps 120: T A **s** *of* ascents. H8877
Ps 121: T A **s** of ascents. H8877
Ps 122: T A **s** *of* ascents. Of David. H8877
Ps 123: T A **s** *of* ascents. H8877
Ps 124: T A **s** *of* ascents. Of David. H8877
Ps 125: T A **s** *of* ascents. H8877
Ps 126: T A **s** *of* ascents. H8877

Ps 127: T A **s** *of* ascents. Of Solomon. H8877
Ps 128: T A **s** *of* ascents. H8877
Ps 129: T A **s** *of* ascents. H8877
Ps 130: T A **s** *of* ascents. H8877
Ps 131: T A **s** *of* ascents. Of David. H8877
Ps 132: T A **s** *of* ascents. H8877
Ps 133: T A **s** *of* ascents. Of David. H8877
Ps 134: T A **s** *of* ascents. H8877
Ps 144: 9 I will sing a new **s** to you, my God; on the H8877
Ps 149: 1 Sing to the LORD a new **s**, his praise in the H8877
Ecc 7: 5 person than to listen to the **s** *of* fools. H8877
SS 1: 1 Solomon's **S** *of* Songs. H8877
Isa 5: 1 the one I love a **s** about his vineyard: H8878
Isa 23:15 to Tyre as in the **s** *of* the prostitute: H8878
Isa 23:16 sing many a **s**, so that you will be H8877
Isa 24: 9 No longer do they drink wine with a **s**; the H8877
Isa 25: 5 a cloud, so the **s** *of* the ruthless is stilled. H2369
Isa 26: 1 In that day this **s** will be sung in the land H8877
Isa 42:10 Sing to the LORD a new **s**, his praise from H8877
Isa 44:23 Burst into **s**, you mountains, you forests H8262
Isa 49:13 you earth; burst into **s**, you mountains! H8262
Isa 54: 1 bore a child; burst into **s**, shout for joy, H8262
Isa 55:12 hills will burst into **s** before you, H8262
La 3:14 people; they **mock** me **in s** all day long. H5593
Mic 2: 4 they will taunt you with this **mournful s**: H5631
Rev 5: 9 And they sang a new **s**, saying: "You are G6046
Rev 14: 3 And they sang a new **s** before the throne G6046
Rev 14: 3 one could learn the **s** except the 144,000 G6046
Rev 15: 3 sang the **s** of God's servant Moses G6046

SONGS (34) [SING]

1Sa 18: 6 with **joyful s** and with timbrels and lyres. H8525
2Sa 23: 1 by the God of Jacob, the hero of Israel's **s**: H2369
1Ki 4:32 proverbs and his **s** numbered a thousand H8877
1Ch 13: 8 before God, with **s** and with harps, lyres, H8877
Ne 12: 8 was in charge of the **s of thanksgiving**. H2117
Ne 12:27 with **s of thanksgiving** and with the H9343
Ne 12:46 musicians and for the **s** *of* praise and H8877
Job 35:10 God my Maker, who gives **s** in the night, H2369
Ps 32: 7 surround me with **s** *of* deliverance. H8260
Ps 65: 8 evening fades, *you* **call forth s of joy**. H8264
Ps 77: 6 I remembered my **s** in the night. My heart H5593
Ps 78:63 their young women **had** no **wedding s**; H2146
Ps 100: 2 gladness; come before him with **joyful s**. H8265
Ps 107:22 tell of his works with **s of joy**. H8262
Ps 126: 2 with laughter, our tongues with **s of joy**. H8262
Ps 126: 5 who sow with tears will reap with **s of joy**. H8262
Ps 126: 6 will return with **s of joy**, carrying sheaves H8262
Ps 137: 3 there our captors asked us for **s** H1821+8877
Ps 137: 3 our tormentors demanded **s** of joy; they said NDT
Ps 137: 3 they said, "Sing us one of the **s** *of* Zion!" H8877
Ps 137: 4 can we sing the **s** *of* the LORD while in H8877
Pr 25:20 is one who sings **s** to a heavy heart. H8877
Ecc 12: 4 of birds, but all their **s** grow faint; H1426+8877
SS 1: 1 Solomon's Song of **S**. H8877
Isa 52: 9 Burst into **s of joy** together, you ruins of H8264
Jer 30:19 will come **s of thanksgiving** and the sound H9343
La 3:63 standing, they **mock me** in their **s**. H4947
Eze 26:13 I will put an end to your noisy **s**, and the H8877
Eze 33:32 one who sings love **s** with a beautiful H8877
Am 5:23 Away with the noise of your **s**! I will not H8877
Am 8: 3 "the **s** *in* the temple will turn to wailing. H8878
Eph 5:19 with psalms, hymns, and **s** from the Spirit. G6046
Col 3:16 and **s** from the Spirit, singing to G6046
Jas 5:13 anyone happy? *Let them* **sing s of praise**. G6010

SONS (799) [SON]

Ge 5: 4 800 years and had other **s** and daughters. H1201
Ge 5: 7 807 years and had other **s** and daughters. H1201
Ge 5:10 815 years and had other **s** and daughters. H1201
Ge 5:13 840 years and had other **s** and daughters. H1201
Ge 5:16 830 years and had other **s** and daughters. H1201
Ge 5:19 800 years and had other **s** and daughters. H1201
Ge 5:22 300 years and had other **s** and daughters. H1201
Ge 5:26 782 years and had other **s** and daughters. H1201
Ge 5:30 595 years and had other **s** and daughters. H1201
Ge 6: 2 the **s** *of* God saw that the daughters of H1201
Ge 6: 4 when the **s** *of* God went to the daughters H1201
Ge 6:10 Noah had three **s**: Shem, Ham and H1201
Ge 6:18 you and your **s** and your wife and your H1201
Ge 7: 7 And Noah and his **s** and his wife and his H1201
Ge 7:13 On that very day Noah and his **s**, Shem H1201
Ge 7:13 with his wife and the wives of his three **s**, H1201
Ge 8:16 your wife and your **s** and their wives. H1201
Ge 8:18 together with his **s** and his wife and his H1201
Ge 9: 1 Then God blessed Noah and his **s**, saying H1201
Ge 9: 8 God said to Noah and to his **s** with him: H1201
Ge 9:18 The **s** *of* Noah who came out of the ark H1201
Ge 9:19 These were the three **s** *of* Noah, and from H1201
Ge 10: 1 Japheth, Noah's **s**, who themselves had H1201
Ge 10: 1 who themselves had **s** after the flood. H1201
Ge 10: 2 The **s** *of* Japheth: Gomer, Magog, Madai H1201
Ge 10: 3 The **s** *of* Gomer: Ashkenaz, Riphath and H1201
Ge 10: 4 The **s** *of* Javan: Elishah, Tarshish, the H1201
Ge 10: 6 The **s** *of* Ham: Cush, Egypt, Put and H1201
Ge 10: 7 The **s** *of* Cush: Seba, Havilah, Sabtah H1201
Ge 10: 7 The **s** *of* Raamah: Sheba H1201
Ge 10:20 These are the **s** *of* Ham by their clans H1201
Ge 10:21 *S* **were** also **born** to Shem, whose older AIT
Ge 10:21 was the ancestor of all the **s** *of* Eber. H1201
Ge 10:22 The **s** *of* Shem: Elam, Ashur, Arphaxad H1201
Ge 10:23 The **s** *of* Aram: Uz, Hul, Gether and H1201
Ge 10:25 Two **s** were born to Eber: One was named H1201
Ge 10:29 All these were **s** *of* Joktan. H1201
Ge 10:31 These are the **s** *of* Shem by their clans H1201
Ge 10:32 These are the clans of Noah's **s** H1201
Ge 11:11 500 years and had other **s** and daughters. H1201
Ge 11:13 403 years and had other **s** and daughters. H1201
Ge 11:15 403 years and had other **s** and daughters. H1201
Ge 11:17 430 years and had other **s** and daughters. H1201
Ge 11:19 209 years and had other **s** and daughters. H1201
Ge 11:21 207 years and had other **s** and daughters. H1201
Ge 11:23 200 years and had other **s** and daughters. H1201
Ge 11:25 119 years and had other **s** and daughters. H1201
Ge 19:12 sons-in-law, **s** or daughters, or anyone H1201
Ge 22:20 she has borne **s** to your brother Nahor: H1201
Ge 22:23 Milkah bore **these** eight *s* to Abraham's AIT
Ge 22:24 whose name was Reumah, also **had s**: H3528
Ge 25: 4 The **s** *of* Midian were Ephah, Epher H1201
Ge 25: 6 gave gifts to the **s** *of* his concubines and H1201
Ge 25: 9 His **s** Isaac and Ishmael buried him in the H1201
Ge 25:13 These are the names of the **s** *of* Ishmael H1201
Ge 25:16 These were the **s** *of* Ishmael, and these H1201
Ge 27:29 may the **s** *of* your mother bow down H1201
Ge 29:34 because I have borne him three **s**. H1201
Ge 30:20 because I have borne him six **s**. H1201
Ge 30:35 he placed them in the care of his **s**. H1201
Ge 31: 1 Jacob heard that Laban's **s** were saying H1201
Ge 32:22 his eleven **s** and crossed the ford of H3529
Ge 33:19 he bought from the **s** *of* Hamor, the father H1201
Ge 34: 5 his **s** were in the fields with his livestock H1201
Ge 34: 7 Jacob's **s** had come in from the fields as H1201
Ge 34:13 Jacob's **s** replied deceitfully as they spoke H1201
Ge 34:25 two of Jacob's **s**, Simeon and Levi, H1201
Ge 34:27 The **s** *of* Jacob came upon the dead H1201
Ge 35:22 Israel heard of it. Jacob had twelve **s**: H1201
Ge 35:23 The **s** *of* Leah: Reuben the firstborn of H1201
Ge 35:24 The **s** *of* Rachel: Joseph and Benjamin. H1201
Ge 35:25 The **s** *of* Rachel's servant Bilhah: Dan H1201
Ge 35:26 The **s** *of* Leah's servant Zilpah: Gad and H1201
Ge 35:26 These were the **s** *of* Jacob, who were born H1201
Ge 35:29 And his **s** Esau and Jacob buried him. H1201
Ge 36: 5 These were the **s** *of* Esau, who were born H1201
Ge 36: 6 took his wives and **s** and daughters and H1201
Ge 36:10 These are the names of Esau's **s**: Eliphaz H1201
Ge 36:11 The **s** *of* Eliphaz: Teman, Omar, Zepho H1201
Ge 36:13 The **s** *of* Reuel: Nahath, Zerah, Shammah H1201
Ge 36:14 The **s** *of* Esau's wife Oholibamah H1201
Ge 36:15 The **s** *of* Eliphaz the firstborn of Esau H1201
Ge 36:17 The **s** *of* Esau's son Reuel: Chiefs Nahath H1201
Ge 36:18 The **s** *of* Esau's wife Oholibamah: Chiefs H1201
Ge 36:19 These were the **s** *of* Esau (that is, Edom), H1201
Ge 36:20 These were the **s** *of* Seir the Horite, who H1201
Ge 36:21 These **s** *of* Seir in Edom were Horite H1201
Ge 36:22 The **s** *of* Lotan: Hori and Homam. Timna H1201
Ge 36:23 The **s** *of* Shobal: Alvan, Manahath, Ebal H1201
Ge 36:24 The **s** *of* Zibeon: Aiah and Anah. This is H1201
Ge 36:26 The **s** *of* Dishon: Hemdan, Eshban, Ithran H1201
Ge 36:27 The **s** *of* Ezer: Bilhan, Zaavan and Akan. H1201
Ge 36:28 The **s** *of* Dishan: Uz and Aran. H1201
Ge 37: 2 the **s** *of* Bilhah and the sons of Zilpah H1201
Ge 37: 2 the sons of Bilhah and the **s** *of* Zilpah, his H1201
Ge 37: 3 Joseph more than any of his *other* **s**, H1201
Ge 37:35 All his **s** and daughters came to comfort H1201
Ge 41:50 two **s** were born to Joseph by Asenath H1201
Ge 42: 1 he said to his **s**, "Why do you just H1201
Ge 42: 5 So Israel's **s** were among those who went H1201
Ge 42:11 We are all the **s** *of* one man. Your servants H1201
Ge 42:13 brothers, the **s** *of* one man, who lives H1201
Ge 42:32 twelve brothers, **s** *of* one father. One is no H1201
Ge 42:37 may put both of my **s** to death if I do not H1201
Ge 44:20 he is the only one of his mother's **s** left NDT
Ge 44:27 'You know that my wife bore me **two** *s*. AIT
Ge 45:21 So the **s** *of* Israel did this. Joseph gave H1201
Ge 46: 5 Israel's **s** took their father Jacob and H1201
Ge 46: 7 him to Egypt his **s** and grandsons and his H1201
Ge 46: 8 These are the names of the **s** *of* Israel H1201
Ge 46: 9 The **s** *of* Reuben: Hanok, Pallu, Hezron H1201
Ge 46:10 The **s** *of* Simeon: Jemuel, Jamin, Ohad H1201
Ge 46:11 The **s** *of* Levi: Gershon, Kohath and Merari H1201
Ge 46:12 The **s** *of* Judah: Er, Onan, Shelah, Perez H1201
Ge 46:12 of Canaan). The **s** *of* Perez: Hezron and H1201
Ge 46:13 The **s** *of* Issachar: Tola, Puah, Jashub H1201
Ge 46:14 The **s** *of* Zebulun: Sered, Elon and H1201
Ge 46:15 These were the **s** Leah bore to Jacob in H1201
Ge 46:15 These **s** and daughters of his were H1201
Ge 46:16 The **s** *of* Gad: Zephon, Haggi, Shuni H1201
Ge 46:17 The **s** *of* Asher: Imnah, Ishvah, Ishvi and H1201
Ge 46:17 The **s** *of* Beriah: Heber and H1201
Ge 46:19 The **s** *of* Jacob's wife Rachel: Joseph and H1201
Ge 46:21 The **s** *of* Benjamin: Bela, Beker, Ashbel H1201
Ge 46:22 These were the **s** *of* Rachel who were H1201
Ge 46:24 The **s** *of* Naphtali: Jahziel, Guni, Jezer H1201
Ge 46:25 These were the **s** born to Jacob *by* Bilhah H1201
Ge 46:27 With the two **s** who had been born to H1201
Ge 48: 1 So he took his two **s** Manasseh and H1201
Ge 48: 5 your two **s** born to you in Egypt before I H1201
Ge 48: 8 When Israel saw the **s** *of* Joseph, he H1201
Ge 48: 9 "They are the **s** God has given me here," H1201
Ge 48:10 So Joseph brought **his s** close to him H4392S
Ge 49: 1 Then Jacob called for his **s** and said H1201
Ge 49: 2 listen, **s** *of* Jacob; listen to your H1201
Ge 49: 8 your father's **s** will bow down to you. H1201
Ge 49:33 had finished giving instructions to his **s**, H1201
Ge 50:12 So Jacob's **s** did as he had commanded H1201
Ex 1: 1 the names of the **s** *of* Israel who went to H1201
Ex 3:22 you will put on your **s** and daughters. H1201
Ex 4:20 So Moses took his wife and **s**, put them on H1201
Ex 6:14 The **s** *of* Reuben the firstborn son of Israel H1201
Ex 6:15 The **s** *of* Simeon were Jemuel, Jamin H1201
Ex 6:16 the names of the **s** *of* Levi according to H1201
Ex 6:17 The **s** *of* Gershon, by clans, were Libni H1201
Ex 6:18 The **s** *of* Kohath were Amram, Izhar H1201
Ex 6:19 The **s** *of* Merari were Mahli and Mushi H1201
Ex 6:21 The **s** *of* Izhar were Korah, Nepheg and H1201
Ex 6:22 The **s** *of* Uzziel were Mishael, Elzaphan H1201
Ex 6:24 The **s** *of* Korah were Assir, Elkanah and H1201
Ex 10: 9 our old, with our **s** and our daughters H1201
Ex 13:13 Redeem every firstborn among your **s**. H1201
Ex 13:15 womb and redeem each of my firstborn **s**. H1201
Ex 18: 3 her two **s**. One son was named H1201
Ex 18: 5 together with Moses' **s** and wife, came to H1201
Ex 18: 6 to you with your wife and her two **s**." H1201
Ex 21: 4 a wife and she bears him **s** or daughters, H1201
Ex 22:29 "You must give me the firstborn of your **s**. H1201
Ex 27:21 Aaron and his **s** are to keep the lamps H1201
Ex 28: 1 along with his **s** Nadab and Abihu H1201
Ex 28: 4 garments for your brother Aaron and his **s**, H1201
Ex 28: 9 on them the names of the **s** *of* Israel H1201
Ex 28:11 the names of the **s** *of* Israel on the two H1201
Ex 28:12 as memorial stones for the **s** *of* Israel. H1201
Ex 28:21 each of the names of the **s** *of* Israel, H1201
Ex 28:29 bear the names of the **s** *of* Israel over his H1201
Ex 28:40 caps for Aaron's **s** to give them dignity H1201
Ex 28:41 clothes on your brother Aaron and his **s**, H1201
Ex 28:43 Aaron and his **s** must wear them whenever H1201
Ex 29: 4 bring Aaron and his **s** to the entrance to H1201
Ex 29: 8 Bring his **s** and dress them in tunics H1201
Ex 29: 9 Then tie sashes on Aaron and his **s**. H1201
Ex 29: 9 "Then you shall ordain Aaron and his **s**. H1201
Ex 29:10 Aaron and his **s** shall lay their hands H1201
Ex 29:15 Aaron and his **s** shall lay their hands H1201
Ex 29:19 Aaron and his **s** shall lay their hands H1201
Ex 29:20 lobes of the right ears of Aaron and his **s**, H1201
Ex 29:21 on his **s** and their garments. H1201
Ex 29:21 Then he and his **s** and their garments will H1201
Ex 29:24 of Aaron and his **s** and have them wave H1201
Ex 29:27 ram that belong to Aaron and his **s**: H1201
Ex 29:28 from the Israelites for Aaron and his **s**. H1201
Ex 29:32 Aaron and his **s** are to eat the meat of the H1201
Ex 29:35 "Do for Aaron and his **s** everything I have H1201
Ex 29:44 Aaron and his **s** to serve me as priests. H1201
Ex 30:19 Aaron and his **s** are to wash their hands H1201
Ex 30:30 Aaron and his **s** and consecrate them H1201
Ex 31:10 the garments for his **s** when they serve as H1201
Ex 32: 2 your **s** and your daughters are wearing H1201
Ex 32:29 you were against your own **s** and brothers, H1201
Ex 34:16 as wives for your **s** and those daughters H1201
Ex 34:16 they will lead your **s** to do the same. H1201
Ex 34:20 Redeem all your firstborn **s**. "No one is to H1201
Ex 35:19 the garments for his **s** when they serve as H1201
Ex 39: 6 a seal with the names of the **s** *of* Israel. H1201
Ex 39: 7 as memorial stones for the **s** *of* Israel, H1201
Ex 39:14 each of the names of the **s** *of* Israel, H1201
Ex 39:27 For Aaron and his **s**, they made tunics of H1201
Ex 39:41 the garments for his **s** when serving as H1201
Ex 40:12 "Bring Aaron and his **s** to the entrance to H1201
Ex 40:14 Bring his **s** and dress them in tunics. H1201
Ex 40:31 Aaron and his **s** used it to wash their H1201
Lev 1: 5 then Aaron's **s** the priests shall bring H1201
Lev 1: 7 The **s** *of* Aaron the priest are to put fire on H1201
Lev 1: 8 Then Aaron's **s** the priests shall arrange H1201
Lev 1:11 Aaron's **s** the priests shall splash its H1201
Lev 2: 2 take it to Aaron's **s** the priests. H1201
Lev 2: 3 grain offering belongs to Aaron and his **s**; H1201
Lev 2:10 grain offering belongs to Aaron and his **s**; H1201
Lev 3: 2 Then Aaron's **s** the priests shall splash H1201
Lev 3: 5 Then Aaron's **s** are to burn it on the altar H1201
Lev 3: 8 Then Aaron's **s** shall splash its blood H1201
Lev 3:13 Then Aaron's **s** shall splash its blood H1201
Lev 6: 9 "Give Aaron and his **s** this command H1201
Lev 6:14 Aaron's **s** are to bring it before the LORD H1201
Lev 6:16 Aaron and his **s** shall eat the rest of it, but H1201
Lev 6:20 Aaron and his **s** are to bring to the H1201
Lev 6:25 "Say to Aaron and his **s**: 'These are the H1201
Lev 7:10 belongs equally to all the **s** *of* Aaron. H1201
Lev 7:31 the breast belongs to Aaron and his **s**. H1201
Lev 7:34 the priest and his **s** as their perpetual H1201
Lev 7:35 to Aaron and his **s** on the day they were H1201
Lev 8: 2 "Bring Aaron and his **s**, their garments, the H1201
Lev 8: 6 Aaron and his **s** forward and washed H1201
Lev 8:13 Then he brought Aaron's **s** forward, put H1201
Lev 8:14 Aaron and his **s** laid their hands on H1201
Lev 8:18 Aaron and his **s** laid their hands on H1201
Lev 8:22 Aaron and his **s** laid their hands on H1201
Lev 8:24 brought Aaron's **s** forward and put some H1201
Lev 8:27 all these in the hands of Aaron and his **s**, H1201
Lev 8:30 on his **s** and their garments. H1201
Lev 8:30 garments and his **s** and their garments. H1201
Lev 8:31 Moses then said to Aaron and his **s** H1201
Lev 8:31 'Aaron and his **s** are to eat it.' H1201
Lev 8:36 So Aaron and his **s** did everything the H1201
Lev 9: 1 Aaron and his **s** and the elders of H1201
Lev 9: 9 His **s** brought the blood to him, and he H1201
Lev 9:12 His **s** handed him the blood, and he H1201
Lev 9:18 His **s** handed him the blood, and he H1201

Lev 10: 1 Aaron's s Nadab and Abihu took their H1201
Lev 10: 4 Elzaphan, s of Aaron's uncle Uzziel H1201
Lev 10: 6 to Aaron and his s Eleazar and Ithamar, H1201
Lev 10: 9 "You and your s are not to drink wine or H1201
Lev 10:12 Moses said to Aaron and his remaining s H1201
Lev 10:14 But you and your s and your daughters H1201
Lev 10:16 Ithamar, Aaron's remaining s, and asked, H1201
Lev 13: 2 priest or to one of his s who is a priest. H1201
Lev 16: 1 death of the two s of Aaron who died H1201
Lev 17: 2 "Speak to Aaron and his s and to all the H1201
Lev 21: 1 to the priests, the s of Aaron, and say to H1201
Lev 21:24 this to Aaron and his s and to all the H1201
Lev 22: 2 "Tell Aaron and his s to treat with respect H1201
Lev 22:18 "Speak to Aaron and his s and to all the H1201
Lev 24: 9 It belongs to Aaron and his s, who are to H1201
Lev 26:29 the flesh of your s and the flesh of your H1201
Nu 1:10 from the s of Joseph: from Ephraim H1201
Nu 1:32 From the s of Joseph: From the H1201
Nu 3: 2 The names of the s of Aaron were Nadab H1201
Nu 3: 3 Those were the names of Aaron's s, the H1201
Nu 3: 4 They had no s, so Eleazar and Ithamar H1201
Nu 3: 9 Give the Levites to Aaron and his s; they H1201
Nu 3:10 Aaron and his s to serve as priests; H1201
Nu 3:17 These were the names of the s of Levi H1201
Nu 3:38 Aaron and his s were to camp to the H1201
Nu 3:48 additional Israelites to Aaron and his s." H1201
Nu 3:51 redemption money to Aaron and his s, H1201
Nu 4: 5 Aaron and his s are to go in and take H1201
Nu 4:15 "After Aaron and his s have finished H1201
Nu 4:19 Aaron and his s are to go into the H1201
Nu 4:27 under the direction of Aaron and his s. H1201
Nu 6:23 "Tell Aaron and his s, 'This is how you are H1201
Nu 8:13 of Aaron and his s and then present them H1201
Nu 8:18 Levites in place of all the **firstborn** *s* in Israel. AIT
Nu 8:19 to Aaron and his s to do the work at the H1201
Nu 8:22 under the supervision of Aaron and his s. H1201
Nu 10: 8 "The s of Aaron, the priests, are to blow H1201
Nu 16: 1 Abiram, s of Eliab, and On son H1201
Nu 16:12 Dathan and Abiram, the s of Eliab. H1201
Nu 18: 1 your s and your family are to bear the H1201
Nu 18: 1 you and your s alone are to bear the H1201
Nu 18: 2 when you and your s minister before the H1201
Nu 18: 7 only you and your s may serve as priests H1201
Nu 18: 8 I give to you and your s as your portion, H1201
Nu 18: 9 that part belongs to you and your s. H1201
Nu 18:11 this to you and your s and daughters as H1201
Nu 18:19 give to you and your s and daughters as H1201
Nu 21:29 He has given up his s as fugitives and his H1201
Nu 21:35 together with his s and his whole army H1201
Nu 26: 9 the s of Eliab were Nemuel, Dathan H1201
Nu 26:19 Er and Onan were s of Judah, but they H1201
Nu 26:33 Zelophehad son of Hepher had no s; he H1201
Nu 27: 3 he died for his own sin and left no s. H1201
Dt 2:33 together with his s and his whole army. H1201
Dt 7: 3 daughters to their s or take their H1201
Dt 7: 3 sons or take their daughters for your s, H1201
Dt 11: 6 Abiram, s of Eliab the Reubenite H1201
Dt 12:12 your s and daughters, your male and H1201
Dt 12:18 your s and daughters, your male and H1201
Dt 12:31 even burn their s and daughters in the H1201
Dt 16:11 your s and daughters, your male and H1201
Dt 16:14 your s and daughters, your male and H1201
Dt 21:15 both bear him s but the firstborn is H1201
Dt 21:16 when he wills his property to his s, he H1201
Dt 28:32 Your s and daughters will be given to H1201
Dt 28:41 You will have s and daughters but you will H1201
Dt 28:53 the flesh of the s and daughters the LORD H1201
Dt 32: 8 according to the number of the s of Israel. H1201
Dt 32:19 he was angered by his s and daughters. H1201
Dt 33:24 "Most blessed of s is Asher; let him be H1201
Jos 5: 7 So he raised up their s in their place, and H1201
Jos 7:24 the gold bar, his s and daughters, his H1201
Jos 13:31 half of the s of Makir, according to H1201
Jos 15:14 Ahiman and Talmai, the s of Anak. H3535
Jos 17: 3 of Manasseh, had no s but only daughters H1201
Jos 17: 6 received an inheritance among the s. H1201
Jos 24:32 pieces of silver from the s of Hamor, H1201
Jdg 1:20 who drove from it the three s of Anak. H1201
Jdg 3: 6 gave their own daughters to their s, H1201
Jdg 8:19 my brothers, the s of my own mother. H1201
Jdg 8:30 He had seventy s of his own, for he had H1201
Jdg 9: 2 all seventy of Jerub-Baal's s rule over you, H1201
Jdg 9: 5 his seventy brothers, the s of Jerub-Baal. H1201
Jdg 9:18 murdered his seventy s on a single stone H1201
Jdg 9:24 the crime against Jerub-Baal's seventy s, H1201
Jdg 10: 4 He had thirty s, who rode thirty donkeys H1201
Jdg 11: 2 Gilead's wife also bore him s, and when H1201
Jdg 12: 9 He had thirty s and thirty daughters. H1201
Jdg 12: 9 for his s he brought in thirty young H1201
Jdg 12:14 He had forty s and thirty grandsons, who H1201
Jdg 17: 5 installed one of his s as his priest. H1201
Jdg 17:11 man became like one of his s to him. H1201
Jdg 18:30 his s were priests for the tribe of Dan H1201
Ru 1: 1 together with his wife and two s, went to H1201
Ru 1: 2 the names of his two s were Mahlon and H1201
Ru 1: 3 and she was left with her two s. H1201
Ru 1: 5 left without her two s and her husband. H3529
Ru 1:11 Am I going to have any more s, who H1201
Ru 1:12 tonight and then gave birth to s— H1201
Ru 4:15 you and who is better to you than seven s, H1201
1Sa 1: 3 Phinehas, the two s of Eli, were priests of H1201
1Sa 1: 4 Peninnah and to all her s and daughters. H1201
1Sa 1: 8 Don't I mean more to you than ten s?" H1201
1Sa 2: 5 she who has had many s pines away. H1201
1Sa 2:12 Eli's s were scoundrels; they had no H1201
1Sa 2:21 gave birth to three s and two daughters. H1201
1Sa 2:22 about everything his s were doing to all H1201
1Sa 2:24 my s; the report I hear spreading H1201
1Sa 2:25 His s, however, did not listen to their NDT
1Sa 2:29 do you honor your s more than me by H1201
1Sa 2:34 " 'And what happens to your two s H1201
1Sa 3:13 he knew about; his s blasphemed God H1201
1Sa 4: 4 And Eli's two s, Hophni and Phinehas H1201
1Sa 4:11 Eli's two s, Hophni and Phinehas, H1201
1Sa 4:17 Also your two s, Hophni and Phinehas H1201
1Sa 8: 1 he appointed his s as Israel's leaders. H1201
1Sa 8: 3 But his s did not follow his ways. H1201
1Sa 8: 5 and your s do not follow your ways H1201
1Sa 8:11 He will take your s and make them serve H1201
1Sa 12: 2 old and gray, and my s are here with you. H1201
1Sa 14:49 Saul's s were Jonathan, Ishvi and H1201
1Sa 14:51 Abner's father Ner were s of Abiel. H1201
1Sa 16: 1 I have chosen one of his s to be king." H1201
1Sa 16: 5 Jesse and his s and invited them to the H1201
1Sa 16:10 had seven of his s pass before Samuel, H1201
1Sa 16:11 "Are these all the s you have? H5853
1Sa 17:12 Jesse had eight s, and in Saul's time he H1201
1Sa 17:13 Jesse's three oldest s had followed Saul to H1201
1Sa 28:19 tomorrow you and your s will be with me. H1201
1Sa 30: 3 their wives and s and daughters taken H1201
1Sa 30: 6 in spirit because of his s and daughters. H1201
1Sa 31: 2 were in hot pursuit of Saul and his s, H1201
1Sa 31: 2 they killed his s Jonathan, Abinadab H1201
1Sa 31: 6 Saul and his three s and his armor-bearer H1201
1Sa 31: 7 fled and that Saul and his s had died, H1201
1Sa 31: 8 Saul and his three s fallen on Mount H1201
1Sa 31:12 of Saul and his s from the wall of Beth H1201
2Sa 2:18 The three s of Zeruiah were there: Joab H1201
2Sa 3: 2 S were born to David in Hebron: His H1201
2Sa 3:39 these s of Zeruiah are too strong for H1201
2Sa 4: 2 they were s of Rimmon the Beerothite H1201
2Sa 4: 5 Baanah, the s of Rimmon the Beerothite H1201
2Sa 4: 9 Baanah, the s of Rimmon the Beerothite H1201
2Sa 5:13 more s and daughters were born to H1201
2Sa 6: 3 Uzzah and Ahio, s of Abinadab, were H1201
2Sa 8:18 Pelethites; and David's s were priests. H1201
2Sa 9:10 You and your s and your servants are to H1201
2Sa 9:10 Ziba had fifteen s and twenty servants H1201
2Sa 9:11 at David's table like one of the king's s. H1201
2Sa 13:23 he invited all the king's s to come there. H1201
2Sa 13:27 him Amnon and the rest of the king's s. H1201
2Sa 13:29 Then all the king's s got up, mounted H1201
2Sa 13:30 "Absalom has struck down all the king's s H1201
2Sa 13:33 the report that all the king's s are dead. H1201
2Sa 13:35 the king's s have come; it has H1201
2Sa 13:36 speaking, the king's s came in, wailing H1201
2Sa 14: 6 I your servant had two s. They got into a H1201
2Sa 14:27 Three s and a daughter were born to H1201
2Sa 15:27 You and Abiathar return with your two s. H1201
2Sa 15:36 Their two s, Ahimaaz son of Zadok and H1201
2Sa 16:10 this have to do with you, you s of Zeruiah? H1201
2Sa 19: 5 the lives of your s and daughters and the H1201
2Sa 19:17 his fifteen s and twenty servants. H1201
2Sa 19:22 this have to do with you, you s of Zeruiah? H1201
2Sa 21: 8 the two s of Aiah's daughter Rizpah H1201
2Sa 21: 8 with the five s of Saul's daughter Merab H1201
2Sa 23:32 Shaalbonite, the s of Jashen, Jonathan H1201
1Ki 1: 9 his brothers, the king's s, and all the royal H1201
1Ki 1:19 has invited all the king's s, Abiathar H1201
1Ki 1:25 He has invited all the king's s, the H1201
1Ki 2: 7 kindness to the s of Barzillai of Gilead H1201
1Ki 4: 3 Ahijah, s of Shisha—secretaries; H1201
1Ki 4:31 Kalkol and Darda, the s of Mahol. H1201
1Ki 13:11 whose s came and told him all that the H1201
1Ki 13:12 And his s showed him which road the H1201
1Ki 13:13 So he said to his s, "Saddle the donkey H1201
1Ki 13:27 The prophet said to his s, "Saddle the H1201
1Ki 13:31 he said to his s, "When I die, H1201
2Ki 4: 4 shut the door behind you and your s. H1201
2Ki 4: 5 shut the door behind her and her s. H1201
2Ki 4: 7 You and your s can live on what is left." H1201
2Ki 9:26 blood of Naboth and the blood of his s, H1201
2Ki 10: 1 in Samaria seventy s of the house of H1201
2Ki 10: 2 have your master's s with you and you H1201
2Ki 10: 3 of your master's s and set him on his H1201
2Ki 10: 6 of your master's s and come to me in H1201
2Ki 17:17 sacrificed their s and daughters in the H1201
2Ki 19:37 his s Adrammelek and Sharezer killed H1201
2Ki 25: 7 They killed the s of Zedekiah before his H1201
1Ch 1: 4 The s of Noah: Shem, Ham and Japheth. H1201
1Ch 1: 5 The s of Japheth: Gomer, Magog, Madai H1201
1Ch 1: 6 The s of Gomer: Ashkenaz, Riphath and H1201
1Ch 1: 7 The s of Javan: Elishah, Tarshish, the H1201
1Ch 1: 8 The s of Ham: Cush, Egypt, Put and H1201
1Ch 1: 9 The s of Cush: Seba, Havilah, Sabta H1201
1Ch 1: 9 The s of Raamah: Sheba H1201
1Ch 1:17 The s of Shem: Elam, Ashur, Arphaxad H1201
1Ch 1:17 Lud and Aram. The s of Aram: Uz, Hul, H1201
1Ch 1:19 Two s were born to Eber: One was named H1201
1Ch 1:23 All these were s of Joktan. H1201
1Ch 1:28 The s of Abraham: Isaac and Ishmael. H1201
1Ch 1:31 These were the s of Ishmael. H1201
1Ch 1:32 The s born to Keturah, Abraham's H1201
1Ch 1:32 The s of Jokshan: Sheba and H1201
1Ch 1:33 The s of Midian: Ephah, Epher, Hanok H1201
1Ch 1:34 father of Isaac. The s of Isaac: Esau and H1201
1Ch 1:35 The s of Esau: Eliphaz, Reuel, Jeush H1201
1Ch 1:36 The s of Eliphaz: Teman, Omar, Zepho H1201
1Ch 1:37 The s of Reuel: Nahath, Zerah, Shammah H1201
1Ch 1:38 The s of Seir: Lotan, Shobal, Zibeon H1201
1Ch 1:39 The s of Lotan: Hori and Homam. Timna H1201
1Ch 1:40 The s of Shobal: Alvan, Manahath, Ebal H1201
1Ch 1:40 The s of Zibeon: Aiah and H1201
1Ch 1:41 The s of Dishon: Hemdan H1201
1Ch 1:42 The s of Ezer: Bilhan, Zaavan and Akan H1201
1Ch 1:42 The s of Dishan: Uz and Aran H1201
1Ch 2: 1 These were the s of Israel: Reuben H1201
1Ch 2: 3 The s of Judah: Er, Onan and Shelah H1201
1Ch 2: 4 Zerah to Judah. He had five s in all. H1201
1Ch 2: 5 The s of Perez: Hezron and Hamul. H1201
1Ch 2: 6 The s of Zerah: Zimri, Ethan, Heman H1201
1Ch 2: 9 The s born to Hezron were: Jerahmeel H1201
1Ch 2:16 Zeruiah's three s were Abishai, Joab and H1201
1Ch 2:18 These were her s: Jesher, Shobab and H1201
1Ch 2:25 The s of Jerahmeel the firstborn of Hezron H1201
1Ch 2:27 The s of Ram the firstborn of Jerahmeel H1201
1Ch 2:28 The s of Onam: Shammai and Jada. H1201
1Ch 2:28 The s of Shammai: Nadab and H1201
1Ch 2:30 The s of Nadab: Seled and Appaim H1201
1Ch 2:32 The s of Jada, Shammai's brother: Jether H1201
1Ch 2:33 The s of Jonathan: Peleth and Zaza H1201
1Ch 2:34 Sheshan had no s—only daughters. H1201
1Ch 2:42 The s of Caleb the brother of Jerahmeel H1201
1Ch 2:43 The s of Hebron: Korah, Tappuah, Rekem H1201
1Ch 2:47 The s of Jahdai: Regem, Jotham, Geshan H1201
1Ch 2:50 The s of Hur the firstborn of Ephrathah H1201
1Ch 3: 1 These were the s of David born to him in H1201
1Ch 3: 9 All these were the s of David, besides his H1201
1Ch 3: 9 of David, besides his s *by* his concubines. H1201
1Ch 3:15 The s of Josiah: Johanan the firstborn H1201
1Ch 3:19 The s of Pedaiah: Zerubbabel and Shimei H1201
1Ch 3:19 The s of Zerubbabel H1201
1Ch 3:21 Jeshaiah, and the s of Rephaiah, of H1201
1Ch 3:22 Shemaiah and his s: Hattush, H1201
1Ch 3:23 The s of Neariah: Elioenai, Hizkiah and H1201
1Ch 3:24 The s of Elioenai: Hodaviah, Eliashib H1201
1Ch 4: 3 These were the s of Etam: Jezreel, Ishma H1201
1Ch 4: 7 The s of Helah: Zereth, Zohar, Ethnan, H1201
1Ch 4:13 The s of Kenaz: Othniel and Seraiah. H1201
1Ch 4:13 The s of Othniel: Hathath H1201
1Ch 4:15 The s of Caleb son of Jephunneh: Iru H1201
1Ch 4:16 The s of Jehallelel: Ziph, Ziphah, Tiria H1201
1Ch 4:17 The s of Ezrah: Jether, Mered, Epher and H1201
1Ch 4:19 The s of Hodiah's wife, the sister of H1201
1Ch 4:20 The s of Shimon: Amnon, Rinnah H1201
1Ch 4:21 The s of Shelah son of Judah: Er the H1201
1Ch 4:27 Shimei had sixteen s and six daughters H1201
1Ch 4:42 Uzziel, the s of Ishi, invaded the hill H1201
1Ch 5: 1 The s of Reuben the firstborn of Israel (he H1201
1Ch 5: 1 were given to the s of Joseph son of Israel H1201
1Ch 5: 3 the s of Reuben the firstborn of Israel H1201
1Ch 5:14 These were the s of Abihail son of Huri H1201
1Ch 6: 1 The s of Levi: Gershon, Kohath and Merari H1201
1Ch 6: 2 The s of Kohath: Amram, Izhar, Hebron H1201
1Ch 6: 3 The s of Aaron: Nadab, H1201
1Ch 6:16 The s of Levi: Gershon, Kohath and Merari H1201
1Ch 6:17 These are the names of the s of Gershon H1201
1Ch 6:18 The s of Kohath: Amram, Izhar, Hebron H1201
1Ch 6:19 The s of Merari: Mahli and Mushi. These H1201
1Ch 6:28 The s of Samuel: Joel the firstborn and H1201
1Ch 6:33 the men who served, together with their s: H1201
1Ch 7: 1 The s of Issachar: Tola, Puah, Jashub H1201
1Ch 7: 2 The s of Tola: Uzzi, Rephaiah, Jeriel H1201
1Ch 7: 3 The s of Izrahiah: Michael H1201
1Ch 7: 6 Three s of Benjamin: Bela, Beker and NDT
1Ch 7: 7 The s of Bela: Ezbon, Uzzi, Uzziel H1201
1Ch 7: 8 The s of Beker: Zemirah, Joash, Eliezer H1201
1Ch 7: 8 All these were the s of Beker. H1201
1Ch 7:10 The s of Bilhan: Jeush, Benjamin H1201
1Ch 7:11 All these s of Jediael were heads of H1201
1Ch 7:13 The s of Naphtali: Jahziel, Guni, Jezer H1201
1Ch 7:16 his s were Ulam and Rakem. H1201
1Ch 7:17 These were the s of Gilead son of Makir H1201
1Ch 7:19 The s of Shemida were: Ahian, Shechem H1201
1Ch 7:30 The s of Asher: Imnah, Ishvah, Ishvi and H1201
1Ch 7:31 The s of Beriah: Heber and Malkiel, who H1201
1Ch 7:33 The s of Japhlet: Pasak, Bimhal and H1201
1Ch 7:33 These were Japhlet's s. H1201
1Ch 7:34 The s of Shomer: Ahi, Rohgah, Hubbah H1201
1Ch 7:35 The s of his brother Helem: Zophah, Imna H1201
1Ch 7:36 The s of Zophah: Suah, Harnepher, Shual, H1201
1Ch 7:38 The s of Jether: Jephunneh, Pispah and H1201
1Ch 7:39 The s of Ulla: Arah, Hanniel and Rizia. H1201
1Ch 8: 3 The s of Bela were: Addar, Gera, Abihud, H1201
1Ch 8: 8 S were born to Shaharaim in Moab after he NDT
1Ch 8:10 These were his s, heads of families. H1201
1Ch 8:12 The s of Elpaal: Eber, Misham, Shemed H1201
1Ch 8:16 Ishpah and Joha were the s of Beriah. H1201
1Ch 8:18 Izliah and Jobab were the s of Elpaal. H1201
1Ch 8:21 Shimrath were the s of Shimei. H1201
1Ch 8:25 Penuel were the s of Shashak. H1201
1Ch 8:27 Elijah and Zikri were the s of Jeroham. H1201
1Ch 8:35 The s of Micah: Pithon, Melek, Tarea and H1201
1Ch 8:38 Azel had six s, and these were their H1201
1Ch 8:38 All these were the s of Azel. H1201
1Ch 8:39 The s of his brother Eshek: Ulam his H1201

1Ch 8:40 The s of Ulam were brave warriors who H1201
1Ch 8:40 They had many s and grandsons—150 in H1201
1Ch 9: 5 Asaiah the firstborn and his s. H1201
1Ch 9:41 The s of Micah: Pithon, Melek, Tahrea H1201
1Ch 9:44 Azel had six s, and these were their H1201
1Ch 9:44 These were the s of Azel. H1201
1Ch 10: 2 were in hot pursuit of Saul and his s, H1201
1Ch 10: 2 they killed his s Jonathan, Abinadab H1201
1Ch 10: 6 So Saul and his three s died, and all his H1201
1Ch 10: 7 fled and that Saul and his s had died, H1201
1Ch 10: 8 found Saul and his s fallen on Mount H1201
1Ch 10:12 of Saul and his s and brought them to H1201
1Ch 11:34 the s of Hashem the Gizonite, Jonathan H1201
1Ch 11:44 Shama and Jeiel the s of Hotham the H1201
1Ch 11:46 Jeribai and Joshaviah the s of Elnaam H1201
1Ch 12: 3 chief and Joash the s of Shemaah the H1201
1Ch 12: 3 Jeziel and Pelet the s of Azmaveth H1201
1Ch 12: 7 Zebadiah the s of Jeroham from H1201
1Ch 14: 3 the father of more s and daughters. H1201
1Ch 16:42 The s of Jeduthun were stationed at the H1201
1Ch 17:11 one of your own s, and I will H1201
1Ch 18:17 David's s were chief officials at the H1201
1Ch 21:20 his four s who were with him hid H1201
1Ch 23: 6 divisions corresponding to the s of Levi: H1201
1Ch 23: 8 The s of Ladan: Jehiel the first, Zetham H1201
1Ch 23: 9 The s of Shimei: Shelomoth, Haziel and H1201
1Ch 23:10 And the s of Shimei: Jahath, Ziza, Jeush H1201
1Ch 23:10 These were the s of Shimei—four in all. H1201
1Ch 23:11 Jeush and Beriah did not have many s; H1201
1Ch 23:12 The s of Kohath: Amram, Izhar, Hebron H1201
1Ch 23:13 The s of Amram: Aaron and Moses H1201
1Ch 23:14 The s of Moses the man of God were H1201
1Ch 23:15 The s of Moses: Gershom and Eliezer. H1201
1Ch 23:17 Eliezer had no other s, but the sons of H1201
1Ch 23:17 the s of Rehabiah were very numerous H1201
1Ch 23:18 The s of Izhar: Shelomith was the first. H1201
1Ch 23:19 The s of Hebron: Jeriah the first, Amariah H1201
1Ch 23:20 The s of Uzziel: Micah the first and Ishiah H1201
1Ch 23:21 The s of Merari: Mahli and Mushi. H1201
1Ch 23:21 The s of Mahli: Eleazar and H1201
1Ch 23:22 Eleazar died without having s: he had H1201
1Ch 23:22 Their cousins, the s of Kish, married them. H1201
1Ch 23:23 The s of Mushi: Mahli, Eder and Jerimoth H1201
1Ch 24: 1 The s of Aaron were Nadab, Abihu H1201
1Ch 24: 2 and they had no s; so Eleazar and H1201
1Ch 24:20 from the s of Amram: Shubael; H1201
1Ch 24:20 Shubael; from the s of Shubael: Jehdeiah H1201
1Ch 24:21 Rehabiah, from his s: Ishiah was the first. H1201
1Ch 24:22 from the s of Shelomoth: Jahath. H1201
1Ch 24:23 The s of Hebron: Jeriah the first, Amariah H1201
1Ch 24:24 from the s of Micah: Shamir. H1201
1Ch 24:25 from the s of Ishiah: Zechariah. H1201
1Ch 24:26 The s of Merari: Mahli and Mushi. H1201
1Ch 24:27 The s of Merari: from Jaaziah: Beno H1201
1Ch 24:28 Eleazar, who had no s. H1201
1Ch 24:30 And the s of Mushi: Mahli, Eder and H1201
1Ch 25: 1 set apart some of the s of Asaph, Heman H1201
1Ch 25: 2 From the s of Asaph: Zakkur, Joseph H1201
1Ch 25: 2 The s of Asaph were under the H1201
1Ch 25: 3 Jeduthun, from his s: Gedaliah, Zeri, H1201
1Ch 25: 4 Heman, from his s: Bukkiah, Mattaniah H1201
1Ch 25: 5 All these were s of Heman the king's seer. H1201
1Ch 25: 5 Heman fourteen s and three daughters H1201
1Ch 25: 9 his s and relatives 12 the second to H1201
1Ch 25: 9 Gedaliah, him and his relatives and s 12 H1201
1Ch 25:10 the third to Zakkur, his s and relatives 12 H1201
1Ch 25:11 the fourth to Izri, his s and relatives 12 H1201
1Ch 25:12 fifth to Nethaniah, his s and relatives 12 H1201
1Ch 25:13 the sixth to Bukkiah, his s and relatives 12 H1201
1Ch 25:14 to Jesarelah, his s and relatives 12 H1201
1Ch 25:15 eighth to Jeshaiah, his s and relatives 12 H1201
1Ch 25:16 ninth to Mattaniah, his s and relatives 12 H1201
1Ch 25:17 the tenth to Shimei, his s and relatives 12 H1201
1Ch 25:18 eleventh to Azarel, his s and relatives 12 H1201
1Ch 25:19 to Hashabiah, his s and relatives 12 H1201
1Ch 25:20 to Shubael, his s and relatives 12 H1201
1Ch 25:21 to Mattithiah, his s and relatives 12 H1201
1Ch 25:22 to Jerimoth, his s and relatives 12 H1201
1Ch 25:23 to Hananiah, his s and relatives 12 H1201
1Ch 25:24 to Joshbekashah, his s and relatives 12 H1201
1Ch 25:25 to Hanani, his s and relatives 12 H1201
1Ch 25:26 to Mallothi, his s and relatives 12 H1201
1Ch 25:27 to Eliathah, his s and relatives 12 H1201
1Ch 25:28 to Hothir, his s and relatives 12 H1201
1Ch 25:29 to Giddalti, his s and relatives 12 H1201
1Ch 25:30 to Mahazioth, his s and relatives 12 H1201
1Ch 25:31 to Romamti-Ezer, his s and relatives 12. H1201
1Ch 26: 1 son of Kore, one of the s of Asaph. H1201
1Ch 26: 2 Meshelemiah had s: Zechariah the H1201
1Ch 26: 4 Obed-Edom also had s: Shemaiah the H1201
1Ch 26: 6 Obed-Edom's son Shemaiah also had s H1201
1Ch 26: 7 The s of Shemaiah: Othni, Rephael, Obed H1201
1Ch 26: 8 they and their s and their relatives were H1201
1Ch 26: 9 Meshelemiah had s and relatives, who H1201
1Ch 26:10 Hosah the Merarite had s: Shimri the first H1201
1Ch 26:11 The s and relatives of Hosah were 13 in H1201
1Ch 26:15 the lot for the storehouse fell to his s. H1201
1Ch 26:22 the s of Jehieli, Zetham and his brother H1201
1Ch 26:29 Kenaniah and his s were assigned duties H1201
1Ch 27:32 son of Hakmoni took care of the king's s. H1201
1Ch 28: 1 livestock belonging to the king and his s, H1201
1Ch 28: 4 from my father's s he was pleased to H1201
1Ch 28: 5 Of all my s—and the LORD has given me H1201
1Ch 29:24 as well as all of King David's s, pledged H1201
2Ch 5:12 Jeduthun and their s and relatives—stood H1201
2Ch 11:14 Jeroboam and his s had rejected them as H1201
2Ch 11:19 She bore him s: Jeush, Shemariah and H1201
2Ch 11:21 twenty-eight s and sixty daughters. H1201
2Ch 11:23 dispersing some of his s throughout the H1201
2Ch 13: 9 of the LORD, the s of Aaron, and the H1201
2Ch 13:10 priests who serve the LORD are s of Aaron, H1201
2Ch 13:21 had twenty-two s and sixteen H1201
2Ch 21: 2 brothers, the s of Jehoshaphat, were H1201
2Ch 21: 2 All these were s of Jehoshaphat king of H1201
2Ch 21:14 strike your people, your s, your wives and H1201
2Ch 21:17 together with his s and wives. H1201
2Ch 22: 1 into the camp, had killed all the older s. NDT
2Ch 22: 8 of Judah and the s of Ahaziah's relatives, H1201
2Ch 23:11 Jehoiada and his s brought out the king's H1201
2Ch 24: 3 him, and he had s and daughters. H1201
2Ch 24: 7 Now the s of that wicked woman Athaliah H1201
2Ch 24:27 The account of his s, the many prophecies H1201
2Ch 28: 8 thousand wives, s and daughters. H1201
2Ch 29: 9 sword and why our s and daughters and H1201
2Ch 29:11 My s, do not be negligent now, for the H1201
2Ch 31:18 the s and daughters of the whole H1201
2Ch 32:21 his god, some of his s, his own flesh and H3665
Ezr 3: 9 Joshua and his s and brothers and H1201
Ezr 3: 9 sons and brothers and Kadmiel and his s H1201
Ezr 3: 9 the s of Henadad and their sons and H1201
Ezr 3: 9 of Henadad and their s and brothers— H1201
Ezr 3:10 the Levites (the s of Asaph) with cymbals H1201
Ezr 6:10 the well-being of the king and his s. A10120
Ezr 7:23 on the realm of the king and of his s? A10120
Ezr 8:18 Sherebiah's s and brothers, 18 in all H1201
Ezr 9: 2 as wives for themselves and their s, H1201
Ezr 9:12 in marriage to their s or take their H1201
Ezr 9:12 sons or take their daughters for your s. H1201
Ne 3: 3 Gate was rebuilt by the s of Hassenaah. H1201
Ne 4:14 your families, your s and your daughters H1201
Ne 5: 2 "We and our s and daughters are H1201
Ne 5: 5 we have to subject our s and daughters to H1201
Ne 10: 9 Binnui of the s of Henadad, Kadmiel, H1201
Ne 10:28 wives and all their s and daughters who H1201
Ne 10:30 us or take their daughters for our s. H1201
Ne 10:36 the firstborn of our s and of our cattle, H1201
Ne 13:25 give your daughters in marriage to their s, H1201
Ne 13:25 in marriage for your s or for yourselves. H1201
Ne 13:28 One of the s of Joiada son of Eliashib the H1201
Est 5:11 his many s, and all the ways the H1201
Est 9:10 the ten s of Haman son of Hammedatha H1201
Est 9:12 men and the ten s of Haman in the H1201
Est 9:13 let Haman's ten s be impaled on poles H1201
Est 9:14 they impaled the ten s of Haman. H1201
Est 9:25 that he and his s should be impaled H1201
Job 1: 2 He had seven s and three daughters, H1201
Job 1: 4 His s used to hold feasts in their homes H1201
Job 1:13 day when Job's s and daughters were H1201
Job 1:18 "Your s and daughters were feasting and H1201
Job 42:13 he also had seven s and three daughters. H1201
Ps 42: T A maskil of the S of Korah. H1201
Ps 44: T Of the S of Korah. A maskil. H1201
Ps 45: T Of the S of Korah. A maskil. H1201
Ps 45:16 Your s will take the place of your fathers H1201
Ps 46: T Of the S of Korah. According to H1201
Ps 47: T Of the S of Korah. A psalm. H1201
Ps 48: T A psalm of the S of Korah. H1201
Ps 49: T Of the S of Korah. A psalm. H1201
Ps 82: 6 are "gods"; you are all s of the Most High. H1201
Ps 84: T Of the S of Korah. A psalm. H1201
Ps 85: T Of the S of Korah. A psalm. H1201
Ps 87: T Of the S of Korah. A psalm. A song. H1201
Ps 88: T A psalm of the S of Korah. For the H1201
Ps 89:30 "If his s forsake my law and do not follow H1201
Ps 106:37 They sacrificed their s and their daughters H1201
Ps 106:38 the blood of their s and daughters, whom H1201
Ps 132:12 If your s keep my covenant and the H1201
Ps 132:12 then their s will sit on your throne for ever H1201
Ps 144:12 Then our s in their youth will be like H1201
Pr 4: 1 my s, to a father's instruction; pay H1201
Pr 5: 7 Now then, my s, listen to me; do not turn H1201
Pr 7:24 Now then, my s, listen to me; pay H1201
SS 1: 6 My mother's s were angry with me and H1201
Isa 23: 4 I have neither reared s nor brought up H1033
Isa 37:38 his s Adrammelek and Sharezer killed H1201
Isa 43: 6 Bring my s from afar and my daughters H1201
Isa 49:22 they will bring your s in their arms and H1201
Isa 56: 5 a name better than s and daughters; H1201
Isa 60: 4 come to you; your s come from afar, and H1201
Jer 3:24 flocks and herds, their s and daughters. H1201
Jer 5:17 devour your s and daughters; they H1201
Jer 7:31 to burn their s and daughters in the H1201
Jer 11:22 their s and daughters by famine. H1201
Jer 14:16 their wives, their s and their daughters. H1201
Jer 16: 2 not marry and have s or daughters in this H1201
Jer 16: 3 LORD says about the s and daughters born H1201
Jer 19: 9 eat the flesh of their s and daughters, H1201
Jer 29: 6 Marry and have s and daughters; find H1201
Jer 29: 6 find wives for your s and give your H1201
Jer 29: 6 that they too may have s and daughters. H1201
Jer 32:35 to sacrifice their s and daughters to Molek H1201
Jer 33:26 not choose one of his s to rule over the H2446
Jer 35: 3 his brothers and all his s—the whole H1201
Jer 35: 4 into the room of the s of Hanan son of H1201
Jer 35: 8 our wives nor our s and daughters have H1201
Jer 39: 6 slaughtered the s of Zedekiah before his H1201
Jer 40: 8 Johanan and Jonathan the s of Kareah H1201
Jer 40: 8 the s of Ephai the Netophathite H1201
Jer 48:46 your s are taken into exile and your H1201
Jer 49: 1 "Has Israel no s? Has Israel no heir? H1201
Jer 52:10 Babylon killed the s of Zedekiah before H1201
Eze 14:16 could not save their own s or daughters. H1201
Eze 14:18 could not save their own s or daughters. H1201
Eze 14:22 s and daughters who will be brought out H1201
Eze 16:20 'And you took your s and daughters whom H1201
Eze 23: 4 mine and gave birth to s and daughters. H1201
Eze 23:10 took away her s and daughters and killed H1201
Eze 23:25 They will take away your s and daughters H1201
Eze 23:47 they will kill their s and daughters and H1201
Eze 24:21 The s and daughters you left behind will H1201
Eze 24:25 their s and daughters as well— H1201
Eze 40:46 These are the s of Zadok, who are the H1201
Eze 46:16 a gift from his inheritance to one of his s, H1201
Eze 46:17 His inheritance belongs to his s only; it is H1201
Eze 46:18 He is to give his s their inheritance out of H1201
Da 11:10 His s will prepare for war and assemble a H1201
Joel 2:28 Your s and daughters will prophesy, your H1201
Joel 3: 8 I will sell your s and daughters to the H1201
Am 7:17 your s and daughters will fall by the H1201
Zep 1: 8 the king's s and all those clad in H1201
Zec 9:13 I will rouse your s, Zion, against your sons, H1201
Zec 9:13 against your s, Greece, and make H1201
Mt 20:20 the mother of Zebedee's s came to Jesus G5626
Mt 20:20 sons came to Jesus with her s and, G5626
Mt 20:21 that one of these two s of mine may sit at G5626
Mt 21:28 There was a man who had two s. He went G5451
Mt 26:37 Peter and the two s of Zebedee along G5626
Mt 27:56 Joseph, and the mother of Zebedee's s. G5626
Mk 3:17 Boanerges, which means "s of thunder") G5626
Mk 10:35 John, the s of Zebedee, came to G5626
Lk 5:10 John, the s of Zebedee, Simon's G5626
Lk 15:11 "There was a man who had two s. G5626
Jn 4:12 as did also his s and his livestock? G5626
Jn 21: 2 Cana in Galilee, the s of Zebedee, and G3836
Ac 2:17 Your s and daughters will prophesy, your G5626
Ac 7:16 bought from the s of Hamor at Shechem G5626
Ac 7:29 he settled as a foreigner and had two s. G5626
Ac 19:14 Seven s of Sceva, a Jewish chief priest G5626
2Co 6:18 you will be my s and daughters, says G5626
Gal 4: 6 Because you are his s, God sent the Spirit G5626
Gal 4:22 For it is written that Abraham had two s G5626
Heb 2:10 In bringing many **s and daughters** to glory, G5626
Heb 11:21 blessed each of Joseph's s, and G5626
Heb 12: 8 not *true* **s and daughters** at all. G5626

SONS' (5) [SON]

Ge 6:18 your wife and your s wives with you. H1201
Ge 7: 7 his wife and his s wives entered the H1201
Ge 8:18 his sons and his wife and his s wives. H1201
Ge 46:26 not counting his s wives—numbered H1201
Lev 10:13 is your share and your s share of the food H1201

SONS-IN-LAW (3) [SON]

Ge 19:12 anyone else here—s, sons or daughters, H3163
Ge 19:14 So Lot went out and spoke to his s, who H3163
Ge 19:14 But his s thought he was joking. H3163

SONSHIP (5) [SON]

Ro 8:15 brought about your **adoption to s**. G5625
Ro 8:23 as we wait eagerly *for* our **adoption to s**, G5625
Ro 9: 4 Theirs is the **adoption to s**; theirs the G5625
Gal 4: 5 that we might receive **adoption to s**. G5625
Eph 1: 5 us for **adoption to s** through Jesus G5625

SOON (108) [SOONER]

Ge 19:17 As s as they had brought them out, one of H3869
Ge 24:30 As s as he had seen the nose ring, and H3869
Ge 29:13 As s as Laban heard the news about H3869
Ge 34: 7 in from the fields as s as they heard what H3869
Ge 39:18 But as s as I screamed for help, he left his H3869
Ge 40:10 As s as it budded, it blossomed, and its H3869
Ge 41:32 decided by God, and God will do it s. H4554
Ge 42: 7 As s as Joseph saw his brothers, he H2256
Ge 46:29 As s as Joseph appeared before him, he H2256
Ex 8:29 Moses answered, "As s as I leave you, H2180
Nu 16:31 As s as he finished saying all this, the H3869
Dt 11:17 you will s perish from the good land H4559
Dt 31:16 these people will s prostitute themselves H7756
Jos 2: 7 and as s as the pursuers had gone H3869+889
Jos 3:13 And as s as the priests who carry the ark of H3869
Jos 3:15 Yet as s as the priests who carried the ark H3869
Jos 4:11 as s as all of them had crossed H3869+889
Jos 8:19 As s as he did this, the men in the H3869
1Sa 9:13 As s as you enter the town, you will H3869+4027
1Sa 17:57 As s as David returned from killing the H3869
1Sa 29:10 leave in the morning as s as it is light." H2256
2Sa 5:24 As s as you hear the sound of marching in H3869
2Sa 15:10 "As s as you hear the sound of the H3869
2Sa 19:41 S all the men of Israel were coming to the H2180
2Sa 22:45 cower before me; as s as they hear of me H4200
1Ki 1:21 as s as my lord the king is laid to rest with H3869
1Ki 14:17 As s as she stepped over the threshold of NDT
1Ki 15:29 As s as he began to reign, he killed H3869
1Ki 16:11 As s as he began to reign and was seated H928
1Ki 20:36 as s as you leave me a lion will kill you." H2180
1Ki 21:15 As s as Jezebel heard that Naboth had H3869
2Ki 5: 7 As s as the king of Israel read the letter H3869

S

2Ki 10: 2 Now **as s as** this letter reaches you H3869
2Ki 10:25 As **s as** Jehu had finished making the H3869
1Ch 14:15 **As s as** you hear the sound of marching in H3869
2Ch 12: 7 them but will **s** give them H3869+5071
2Ch 31: 5 **As s as** the order went out, the Israelites H3869
Ezr 4:23 **As s as** the copy of the A10008+10427+10168
Ne 9:28 "But **as s as** they were at rest, they again H3869
Est 7: 8 As **s** as the word left the king's mouth, they NDT
Job 7:21 For I will **s** lie down in the dust; you will H6964
Job 32:22 my Maker would **s** take me away. H3869+5071
Ps 18:44 cower before me; **as s as** they hear of me H4200
Ps 37: 2 like the grass they will **s** wither, like H4559
Ps 37: 2 like green plants they will **s** die away. NDT
Ps 37:36 but *he s* **passed away** and was no more AIT
Ps 94:17 I would **s** have dwelt in the silence H3869+5071
Ps 106:13 But they **s** forgot what he had done and H4554
Pr 5:14 And I was **s** in serious trouble in H3869+5071
Pr 18:24 who has unreliable friends *s* **comes to ruin**, AIT
Pr 19: 8 who cherishes understanding *will s* **prosper**. AIT
Pr 20:21 **claimed too s** will not H987+928+2021+8037
Isa 10:25 **Very s** my anger against you H6388+5071+4663
Isa 28: 4 **as s as** people see them and take them in H889
Isa 30:19 you cry for help! **As s as** he hears, he will H3869
Isa 51:14 The cowering prisoners will **s** be set free H4554
Isa 56: 1 my righteousness will **s** be revealed. NDT
Jer 26: 8 But **as s as** Jeremiah finished telling all H3869
Jer 27:16 '**Very s** now the articles from the LORD's H4559
Jer 51:33 the time to harvest her will **s** come." H6388+5071
Eze 16:47 ways you **s** became more H3869+5071+7775
Eze 23:16 **As s as** she saw them, she lusted after H4200
Eze 36: 8 people Israel, for they will **s** come home. H7928
Da 3: 5 **As s as** you hear the sound A10089+10530+10002+10168
Da 3: 7 **as s as** they heard the sound A10232+10002+10341+10168
Da 9:23 **As s as** you began to pray, a word went out H928
Da 10:20 **S** I will return to fight against the prince of H6964
Hos 1: 4 because I will **s** punish the house H6388+5071
Mt 2: 8 **As s as** you find him, report to me, so that *G2054*
Mt 3:16 **As s as** Jesus was baptized, he went up *G2317*
Mt 24:32 **As s as** its twigs get tender and its *G4020+2453*
Mk 1:29 **As s as** they left the synagogue, they went *G2317*
Mk 4:15 **As s as** they hear it, Satan comes *G4020+2317*
Mk 4:29 **As s as** the grain is ripe, he puts the *G4020+2317*
Mk 6:54 **As s as** they got out of the boat, people *G2317*
Mk 7:25 **as s as** she heard about him, *G2317*
Mk 9:15 **As s as** all the people saw Jesus, they *G2317*
Mk 13:28 **As s as** its twigs get tender and its *G4020+2453*
Lk 1:44 **As s as** the sound of your greeting reached *G6055*
Lk 7:11 **S afterward**, Jesus went to a *G1877+3836+2009*
Jn 13:27 **As s as** Judas took the bread, Satan *G3552*
Jn 13:30 **As s as** Judas had taken the bread, he *G2317*
Jn 19: 6 **As s as** the chief priests and their officials *G4021*
Jn 21: 7 **As s as** Simon Peter heard him say, "It is *G4036*
Ac 17:10 **As s as** it was night, the believers sent *G2311*
Ac 17:15 to join him **as s as possible**. *G6055+5441*
Ac 19:29 **S** the whole city was in an uproar. *G2779*
Ac 25: 4 and I myself am going there **s**. *G1877+5443*
Ro 16:20 of peace will **s** crush Satan under *G1877+5443*
1Co 4:19 But I will come to you **very s**, if the Lord is *G5441*
Php 2:19 the Lord Jesus to send Timothy to you **s**, *G5441*
Php 2:23 to send him **as s as** I see how *G6055+323+1994*
Php 2:24 in the Lord that I myself will come **s**. *G5441*
1Ti 3:14 Although I hope to come to you **s**, *G1877+5443*
Titus 3:12 **As s as** I send Artemas or Tychicus to you *G4020*
Heb 8:13 is obsolete and outdated will **s** disappear. *G1584*
Heb 13:19 to pray so that I may be restored to you **s**. *G5441*
Heb 13:23 If he arrives **s**, I will come with him to see *G5441*
2Pe 1:14 because I know that I will **s** put it aside, as *G5442*
3Jn 14 I hope to see you **s**, and we will talk face *G2311*
Rev 1: 1 servants what must **s** take place. *G1877+5443*
Rev 2:16 I will **s** come to you and will fight against *G5444*
Rev 3:11 I am coming **s**. Hold on to what you have *G5444*
Rev 11:14 has passed; the third woe is coming **s**. *G5444*
Rev 22: 6 the things that must **s** take place." *G1877+5443*
Rev 22: 7 I am coming **s**! Blessed is the one *G5444*
Rev 22:12 I am coming **s**! My reward is with *G5444*
Rev 22:20 to these things says, "Yes, I am coming **s**." *G5444*

SOONER (6) [SOON]

Jos 4:18 **No s** had they set their feet on the dry ground **than** H3869
Jdg 8:33 **No s** had Gideon died **than** the H3869+889
Isa 40:24 **No s** are they planted, no sooner are H677+1153
Isa 40:24 they planted, **no s** are they sown, no H677+1153
Isa 40:24 **no s** do they take root in the ground H677+1153
Isa 66: 8 Yet **no s** is Zion in labor **than** she gives H1685

SOOT (3)

Ex 9: 8 "Take handfuls of **s** *from* a furnace and H7086
Ex 9:10 So they took **s** *from* a furnace and stood H7086
La 4: 8 But now they are blacker than **s**; they are H8818

SOOTHED (1) [SOOTHES, SOOTHING]

Isa 1: 6 cleansed or bandaged or **s** with olive oil. H8216

SOOTHES (1) [SOOTHED]

Pr 21:14 A gift given in secret **s** anger, and a bribe H4092

SOOTHING (2) [SOOTHED]

Ps 55:21 his words *are* more **s** than oil, yet H8216
Pr 15: 4 The **s** tongue is a tree of life, but a H5340

SOOTHSAYER (NIV84) DIVINER, DIVINERS'

SOP (KJV) (PIECE OF) BREAD

SOPATER (1)

Ac 20: 4 was accompanied by **S** son of Pyrrhus *G5396*

SOPHERETH (1)

Ne 7:57 the descendants of Sotai, **S**, Perida, H6072

SORCERER (2) [SORCERY]

Ac 13: 6 they met a Jewish **s** and false prophet *G3407*
Ac 13: 8 But Elymas the **s** (for that is what his name *G3407*

SORCERERS (4) [SORCERY]

Ex 7:11 Pharaoh then summoned wise men and **s** H4175
Jer 27: 9 your mediums or your **s** who tell you, 'You H4177
Da 2: 2 **s** and astrologers to tell him what he had H4175
Mal 3: 5 I will be quick to testify against **s** H4175

SORCERESS (2) [SORCERY]

Ex 22:18 "Do not allow a **s** to live. H4175
Isa 57: 3 you children of a **s**, you offspring of H6726

SORCERIES (3) [SORCERY]

Isa 47: 9 in spite of your many **s** and all your potent H4176
Isa 47:12 your magic spells and with your many **s**, H4176
Na 3: 4 the mistress of **s**, who enslaved nations by H4176

SORCERY (5) [SORCERER, SORCERERS, SORCERESS, SORCERIES]

Dt 18:10 who practices divination or **s**, interprets H6726
Dt 18:14 listen to *those who* **practice s** or divination H6726
Ac 8: 9 named Simon *had* **practiced s** in the city *G3405*
Ac 8:11 amazed them for a long time *with* his **s**. *G3404*
Ac 19:19 who had practiced **s** brought their scrolls *G4319*

SORE (19) [SORES]

Lev 13: 3 The priest is to examine the **s** on the skin H5596
Lev 13: 3 if the hair in the **s** has turned white and H5596
Lev 13: 3 white and the **s** appears to be more H5596
Lev 13: 5 if he sees that the **s** is unchanged and H5596
Lev 13: 6 if the **s** has faded and has not spread H5596
Lev 13:29 a man or woman has a **s** on their head H5596
Lev 13:30 the priest is to examine the **s**, and if it H5596
Lev 13:31 when the priest examines the **s**, it H5596+5999
Lev 13:32 seventh day the priest is to examine the **s**, H5596
Lev 13:34 seventh day the priest is to examine the **s**, H5999
Lev 13:35 But if the **s** does spread in the skin after H5999
Lev 13:36 if he finds that the **s** has spread in the H5999
Lev 13:37 the **s** is unchanged so far as the priest can H5999
Lev 13:42 has a reddish-white **s** on his bald head H5596
Lev 13:43 if the swollen **s** on his head or H5596
Lev 13:44 unclean because of the **s** on his head. H5596
Lev 14:54 any defiling skin disease, for a **s**, H5999
2Sa 3:29 without *someone who has a* **running s** H2307
Jer 30:13 no remedy for your **s**, no healing for you. H4649

SOREK (1)

Jdg 16: 4 in the Valley of **S** whose name was H8604

SORES (13) [SORE]

Lev 13:17 and if the **s** have turned white, the H5596
Lev 21:20 has festering or **running s** or damaged H3539
Lev 22:22 with warts or festering or **running s**. H3539
Dt 28:27 with tumors, **festering s** and the itch H1734
Job 2: 7 Job with painful **s** from the soles of his H8825
Isa 1: 6 only wounds and welts and open **s**, not H4804
Isa 3:17 the Lord *will* **bring s on** the heads of the H8558
Hos 5:13 Judah his **s**, then Ephraim turned to H4649
Hos 5:13 able to cure you, not able to heal your **s**. H4649
Lk 16:20 a beggar named Lazarus, **covered with s** *G1815*
Lk 16:21 Even the dogs came and licked his **s**. *G1814*
Rev 16: 2 festering **s** broke out on the people who *G1814*
Rev 16:11 heaven because of their pains and their **s**, *G1814*

SORROW (35) [SORROWFUL]

Ge 42:38 my gray head down to the grave in **s**." H3326
Ge 44:31 head of our father down to the grave in **s**. H3326
Ge 48: 7 to my **s** Rachel died in the land of Canaan NDT
Est 9:22 month when their **s** was turned into joy H3326
Ps 6: 7 My eyes grow weak with **s**; they fail H4088
Ps 13: 2 day after day have **s** in my heart? H3326
Ps 31: 9 my eyes grow weak with **s**, my soul and H4088
Ps 90:10 the best of them are but trouble and **s** H224
Ps 107:39 humbled by oppression, calamity and **s**; H3326
Ps 116: 3 I was overcome by distress and **s**. H3326
Ps 119:28 My soul is weary with **s**; strengthen me H9342
Pr 23:29 Who has **s**? Who has strife? Who H16
Ecc 1:18 For with much wisdom comes much **s**; the H4088
Isa 35:10 and **s** and sighing will flee away. H3326
Isa 51:11 and **s** and sighing will flee away. H3326
Isa 60:20 everlasting light, and your days of **s** will end. H65
Jer 8:18 You who are my Comforter in **s**, my heart H3326
Jer 20:18 to see trouble and **s** and to end my days H3326
Jer 31:12 garden, and they will **s** no more. H1790
Jer 31:13 give them comfort and joy instead of **s**. H3326
Jer 45: 3 The LORD has added **s** to my pain; I am H3326
Eze 23:33 You will be filled with drunkenness and **s** H3326
Mt 26:38 "My soul is **overwhelmed with s** to the *G4337*
Mk 14:34 "My soul is **overwhelmed with s** to the *G4337*
Lk 22:45 he found them asleep, exhausted from **s**. *G3383*
Ro 9: 2 I have great **s** and unceasing anguish in *G3383*
2Co 2: 7 will not be overwhelmed by excessive **s**. *G3383*
2Co 7: 7 longing for me, your **deep s**, your ardent *G3851*
2Co 7: 8 Even if *I* **caused** you **s** by my letter, I do *G3382*
2Co 7: 9 because *your* **s** led you to repentance. *G3382*
2Co 7:10 Godly **s** brings repentance that leads to *G3383*
2Co 7:10 no regret, but worldly **s** brings death. *G3383*
2Co 7:11 See what this godly **s** has produced in you *G3382*
Php 2:27 also on me, to spare me **s** upon sorrow. *G3383*
Php 2:27 also on me, to spare me sorrow upon **s**. *G3383*

SORROWFUL (3) [SORROW]

Mt 26:37 and he began *to be* **s** and troubled. *G3382*
2Co 6:10 **s**, yet always rejoicing; poor, yet making *G3382*
2Co 7: 9 For *you became* **s** as God intended and so *G3382*

SORRY (2)

Ex 2: 6 was crying, and *she* **felt s** for him. "This is H2798
2Co 7: 9 not because *you were* **made s**, but *G3382*

SORT (4) [SORTS]

2Ki 9:11 know the man and the **s of things he says**," H8490
Ecc 10: 5 the **s** *of* error that arises from a ruler: H3869
Lk 23: 8 to see him perform a sign *of* **some s**. *G5516*
Rev 18:12 scarlet cloth; **every s** of citron wood, and AIT

SORTS (6) [SORT]

1Ki 12:31 appointed priests from **all s** *of* people, H7896
1Ki 13:33 the high places from **all s** of people. H7896
2Ki 17:32 **all s** *of* their own *people* to H4946+7896
Pr 1:13 we will get **all** *s of* valuable things and fill AIT
1Co 14:10 there are all **s** of languages in the *G1169*
2Th 2: 9 He will use **all** *s of* displays of power through AIT

SOSIPATER (1)

Ro 16:21 do Lucius, Jason and **S**, my fellow Jews. *G5399*

SOSTHENES (2)

Ac 18:17 there turned on **S** the synagogue leader *G5398*
1Co 1: 1 by the will of God, and our brother **S**, *G5398*

SOTAI (2)

Ezr 2:55 the descendants of **S**, Hassophereth H6055
Ne 7:57 the descendants of **S**, Sophereth, Perida, H6055

SOUGHT (39) [SEEK]

Ex 32:11 Moses **s the favor of** the LORD H2704+906+7156
1Sa 13:12 and *I have* not **s** the LORD's **favor**. H2704+7156
1Sa 13:14 the LORD *has* **s out** a man after his own H1335
2Sa 21: 1 so David **s** the face of the LORD. H1335
1Ki 10:24 The whole world **s** audience with Solomon H1335
2Ki 13: 4 Jehoahaz **s** the LORD's **favor**, H2704+906+7156
2Ki 17:17 divination and **s omens** and sold H5727
2Ki 21: 6 divination, **s omens**, and consulted H5727
2Ch 9:23 kings of the earth **s** audience with H1335
2Ch 14: 7 because *we have* **s** the LORD our God H2011
2Ch 14: 7 *we* **s** him and he has given us rest on H2011
2Ch 15: 4 God of Israel, and **s** him, and he was H1335
2Ch 15:15 *They* **s** God eagerly, and he was found by H1335
2Ch 17: 4 **s** the God of his father and followed H2011
2Ch 22: 9 who **s** the LORD with all his heart. H2011
2Ch 25:20 because *they* **s** the gods of Edom. H2011
2Ch 26: 5 He **s** God during the days of Zechariah H2011
2Ch 26: 5 As long as he **s** the LORD, God gave him H2011
2Ch 31:21 he **s** his God and worked wholeheartedly. H2011
2Ch 33: 6 witchcraft, **s omens**, and consulted H4175
2Ch 33:12 distress *he* **s the favor of** the H2704+906+7156
Ne 12:27 the Levites *were* **s out** from where they H1335
Ps 34: 4 *I* **s** the LORD, and he answered me; he H2011
Ps 77: 2 I was in distress, *I* **s** the Lord; at night I H2011
Ps 119:45 in freedom, for *I have* **s out** your precepts. H2011
Ps 119:58 *I have* **s** your face with all my heart; be H2704
Ps 119:94 I am yours; *I have* **s out** your precepts. H2011
Isa 9:13 nor *have they* **s** the LORD Almighty. H2011
Isa 62:12 you will be called **S After**, the City No H2011
Eze 25:15 with ancient hostility **s** to destroy Judah NDT
Eze 26:21 *You will* **be s**, but you will never again be H1335
Da 4:36 My advisers and nobles **s** me **out**, and I A10114
Da 9:13 yet *we have* not **s the favor of** H2704+7156+906
Ac 12:20 *they* now joined together and **s an audience** *G4205*
Ac 21: 4 *We* **s out** the disciples there and stayed *G461*
Ro 10: 3 of God and **s** to establish their own, *G2426*
Ro 11: 7 of Israel **s so earnestly** they did not *G2118*
Heb 8: 7 no place would *have been* **s** for another. *G2426*
Heb 12:17 Even though *he* **s** the blessing with tears *G1699*

SOUL (90) [SOULS]

Dt 4:29 him with all your heart and with all your **s**. H5883
Dt 6: 5 heart and with all your **s** and with all your H5883
Dt 10:12 with all your heart and with all your **s**, H5883
Dt 11:13 with all your heart and with all your **s**— H5883
Dt 13: 3 him with all your heart and with all your **s**. H5883
Dt 26:16 with all your heart and with all your **s**. H5883
Dt 30: 2 with all your **s** according to everything H5883
Dt 30: 6 him with all your heart and with all your **s**, H5883
Dt 30:10 with all your heart and with all your **s**. H5883
Jos 22: 5 him with all your heart and with all your **s**." H5883
Jos 23:14 all your heart and **s** that not one of all the H5883
Jdg 5:21 March on, my **s**; be strong! H5883
1Sa 1:15 I was pouring out my **s** to the LORD. H5883
1Sa 14: 7 ahead; I am with you **heart and s**." H3869+4222
1Ki 2: 4 before me with all their heart and **s**, H5883
1Ki 8:48 all their heart and **s** in the land of their H5883
2Ki 23: 3 decrees with all his heart and all his **s**, H5883

2Ki 23:25 heart and with all his s and with all his H5883
1Ch 22:19 your heart and s to seeking the LORD H5883
2Ch 6:38 all their heart and s in the land of their H5883
2Ch 15:12 their ancestors, with all their heart and s. H5883
2Ch 34:31 decrees with all his heart and all his s, H5883
Job 3:20 those in misery, and life to the bitter of s, H5883
Job 7:11 I will complain in the bitterness of my s. H5883
Job 10: 1 speak out in the bitterness of my s. H5883
Job 21:25 Another dies in bitterness of s, never H5883
Job 30:25 Has not my s grieved for the poor? H5883
Job 33:20 repulsive and their s loathes the choicest H5883
Ps 6: 3 My s is in deep anguish. How long, LORD H5883
Ps 19: 7 law of the LORD is perfect, refreshing the s. H5883
Ps 23: 3 he refreshes my s. He guides me along H5883
Ps 26: 9 Do not take away my s along with sinners H5883
Ps 31: 7 affliction and knew the anguish of my s. H5883
Ps 31: 9 with sorrow, my s and body with grief. H5883
Ps 35: 9 Then my s will rejoice in the LORD and H5883
Ps 42: 1 of water, so my s pants for you, my God. H5883
Ps 42: 2 My s thirsts for God, for the living God H5883
Ps 42: 4 things I remember as I pour out my s: H5883
Ps 42: 5 my s, are you downcast? Why so H5883
Ps 42: 6 My s is downcast within me; therefore I H5883
Ps 42:11 my s, are you downcast? Why so H5883
Ps 43: 5 my s, are you downcast? Why so H5883
Ps 57: 8 my s! Awake, harp and lyre! I will H3883
Ps 62: 1 Truly my s finds rest in God; my salvation H5883
Ps 62: 5 my s, find rest in God; my hope H5883
Ps 84: 2 My s yearns, even faints, for the courts of H5883
Ps 103: 1 Praise the LORD, my s; all my inmost being, H5883
Ps 103: 2 Praise the LORD, my s, and forget not all H5883
Ps 103:22 in his dominion. Praise the LORD, my s. H5883
Ps 104: 1 Praise the LORD, my s. LORD my God, you H5883
Ps 104:35 Praise the LORD, my s. Praise the LORD. H5883
Ps 108: 1 I will sing and make music with all my s. H3883
Ps 116: 7 to your rest, my s, for the LORD has been H5883
Ps 119:20 My s is consumed with longing for your H5883
Ps 119:28 My s is weary with sorrow; strengthen me H5883
Ps 119:81 My s faints with longing for your salvation H5883
Ps 146: 1 Praise the LORD. Praise the LORD, my s. H5883
Pr 1:11 let's ambush some **harmless** s; H5929+2855
Pr 2:10 knowledge will be pleasant to your s. H5883
Pr 13:19 A longing fulfilled is sweet to the s, but H5883
Pr 16:24 sweet to the s and healing to the bones. H5883
Pr 25:25 water to a weary s is good news from a H5883
Isa 26: 9 My s yearns for you in the night; in the H5883
Isa 38:15 my years because of this anguish of my s. H5883
Isa 61:10 in the LORD; my s rejoices in my God. H5883
Jer 32:41 them in this land with all my heart and s. H5883
La 3:20 and my s is downcast within me. H5883
La 3:51 see brings grief to my s because of all the H5883
Eze 27:31 you with anguish of s and with bitter H5883
Mic 6: 7 the fruit of my body for the sin of my s? H5883
Mt 10:28 who kill the body but cannot kill the s. G6034
Mt 10:28 who can destroy both s and body in hell. G6034
Mt 16:26 to gain the whole world, yet forfeit their s? G6034
Mt 16:26 can anyone give in exchange for their s? G6034
Mt 22:37 with all your s and with all your mind. G6034
Mt 26:38 "My s is overwhelmed with sorrow to the G6034
Mk 8:36 to gain the whole world, yet forfeit their s? G6034
Mk 8:37 can anyone give in exchange for their s? G6034
Mk 12:30 with all your s and with all your mind G6034
Mk 14:34 "My s is overwhelmed with sorrow to the G6034
Lk 1:46 And Mary said: "My s glorifies the Lord G6034
Lk 2:35 And a sword will pierce your own s too." G6034
Lk 10:27 heart and with all your s and with all your G6034
Jn 12:27 "Now my s is troubled, and what shall I G6034
1Th 5:23 s and body be kept blameless at the G6034
Heb 4:12 it penetrates even to dividing s and spirit G6034
Heb 6:19 We have this hope as an anchor *for* the s G6034
1Pe 2:11 desires, which wage war against your s. G6034
2Pe 2: 8 was tormented *in* his righteous s by the G6034
3Jn 2 even as your s is getting along well. G6034

SOULS (7) [SOUL]

Job 24:12 the s *of* the wounded cry out for help. H5883
Jer 6:16 walk in it, and you will find rest for your s. H5883
Mt 11:29 in heart, and you will find rest *for* your s. G6034
1Pe 1: 9 result of your faith, the salvation *of* your s. G6034
1Pe 2:25 to the Shepherd and Overseer *of* your s. G6034
Rev 6: 9 under the altar the s of those who had G6034
Rev 20: 4 And I saw the s of those who had been G6034

SOUND (126) [FINE-SOUNDING, SOUNDED, SOUNDING, SOUNDINGS, SOUNDNESS, SOUNDS]

Ge 3: 8 his wife heard the s *of* the LORD God as he H7754
Ex 19:19 As the s *of* the trumpet grew louder and H7754
Ex 28:35 The s *of* the bells will be heard when he H7754
Ex 32:17 "There is the s *of* war in the camp. H7754
Ex 32:18 "It is not the s *of* victory, it is not H7754+6702
Ex 32:18 it is not the s *of* defeat; it is the H7754+6702
Ex 32:18 of defeat; it is the s *of* singing that I hear." H7754
Lev 25: 9 the Day of Atonement s the trumpet H6296
Lev 26:36 enemies that the s *of* a windblown leaf H7754
Nu 10: 9 oppressing you, s **a blast** on the trumpets. H8131
Nu 10:10 *you are to* s the trumpets over your burnt H9546
Nu 29: 1 It is a day for you to **s the trumpets**. H9558
Dt 4:12 You heard the s *of* words but saw no form H7754
Jos 6: 5 When you hear them s a **long** blast on the H5432
Jos 6:20 at the s *of* the trumpet, when H7754
Jdg 11:34 his daughter, dancing to the s of timbrels! NDT
1Sa 20:12 that *I will* **surely s out** my father by this H2983
2Sa 5:24 soon as you hear the s *of* marching in the H7754
2Sa 6:15 LORD with shouts and the s *of* trumpets. H7754
2Sa 15:10 soon as you hear the s *of* the trumpets, H7754
1Ki 1:40 so that the ground shook with the s. H7754
1Ki 1:41 On hearing the s *of* the trumpet, Joab H7754
1Ki 14: 6 Ahijah heard the s *of* her footsteps at the H7754
1Ki 18:41 for there is the s *of* a heavy rain. H7754
2Ki 4:31 but there was no s or response. H7754
2Ki 6:32 Is not the s *of* his master's footsteps H7754
2Ki 7: 6 to hear the s *of* chariots and horses H7754
2Ki 7:10 one was there—not a s *of* anyone—only H7754
1Ch 14:15 soon as you hear the s *of* marching in the H7754
1Ch 15:16 make a joyful s with musical H9048+928+7754
1Ch 15:19 Ethan were to s the bronze cymbals; H9048
1Ch 16: 5 harps, Asaph *was to* s the cymbals, H9048
2Ch 13:12 with their trumpets *will* s the battle cry H8131
2Ch 13:15 At the **s of** their **battle cry**, God routed H8131
Ezr 3:13 could distinguish the s *of* the shouts of joy H7754
Ezr 3:13 of the shouts of joy from the s *of* weeping, H7754
Ezr 3:13 And the s was heard far away H7754
Ne 4:20 Wherever you hear the s *of* the trumpet H7754
Ne 12:43 *The* s of rejoicing ... *could* **be heard** H9048
Job 21:12 they make merry to the s *of* the pipe. H7754
Job 30:31 my pipe to the s *of* wailing. H7754
Job 37: 4 After that comes the s of his roar; he H7754
Ps 19: 3 use no words; no s is heard *from* them. H7754
Ps 66: 8 peoples, let the s *of* his praise be heard H7754
Ps 81: 3 S the ram's horn at the New Moon, and H9546
Ps 98: 5 with the harp and the s *of* singing, H7754
Ps 104: 7 at the s *of* your thunder they took to flight H7754
Ps 115: 7 nor *can they* **utter a s** with their throats. H2047
Pr 3:21 preserve s **judgment** and discretion H9370
Pr 4: 2 I give you s learning, so do not forsake my H3202
Pr 8:14 Counsel and s **judgment** are mine; I have H9370
Pr 18: 1 against all **s judgment** starts quarrels. H9370
Ecc 12: 4 are closed and the s *of* grinding fades; H7754
Ecc 12: 4 when people rise up at the s *of* birds, but H7754
Isa 6: 4 At the s *of* their voices the doorposts and H7754
Isa 24:18 Whoever flees at the s *of* terror will fall H7754
Isa 27:13 And in that day a great trumpet *will* s H9546
Isa 51: 3 thanksgiving and the s *of* singing. H7754
Isa 65:19 the s *of* weeping and of crying will be H7754
Isa 66: 6 It is the s *of* the LORD repaying his H7754
Jer 2:21 like a choice vine of s and reliable stock. H3972
Jer 4: 5 'S the trumpet throughout the land H9546
Jer 4:19 For I have heard the s *of* the trumpet; H7754
Jer 4:21 standard and hear the s *of* the trumpet? H7754
Jer 4:29 At the s *of* horsemen and archers every H7754
Jer 6: 1 from Jerusalem! S the trumpet in Tekoa H9546
Jer 6:17 said, 'Listen to the s *of* the trumpet!' H7754
Jer 6:23 They s like the roaring sea as they ride on H7754
Jer 9:19 The s *of* wailing is heard from Zion: 'How H7754
Jer 25:10 the s *of* millstones and the light of the H7754
Jer 30:19 of thanksgiving and the s *of* rejoicing. H7754
Jer 47: 3 at the s *of* the hooves of galloping steeds H7754
Jer 48:34 "The s *of* their cry rises from Heshbon to H7754
Jer 49: 2 "when *I will* s the battle cry against H9048
Jer 49:21 At the s *of* their fall the earth will tremble H7754
Jer 50:42 They s like the roaring sea as they ride on H7754
Jer 50:46 At the s *of* Babylon's capture the earth H7754
Jer 51:54 "The s *of* a cry comes from Babylon, the H7754
Jer 51:54 the s of great destruction from the land of NDT
Eze 1:24 I heard the s *of* their wings, like H7754
Eze 3:12 me a loud rumbling s as the glory of the H7754
Eze 3:13 It was the s *of* the wings of the living H7754
Eze 3:13 each other and the s *of* the wheels beside H7754
Eze 3:13 wheels beside them, a loud rumbling s. H7754
Eze 10: 5 The s *of* the wings of the cherubim could H7754
Eze 21:22 to slaughter, to s the battle cry, to H8123+7754
Eze 26:15 coastlands tremble at the s *of* your fall, H7754
Eze 31:16 nations tremble at the s *of* its fall when I H7754
Eze 33: 5 Since they heard the s *of* the trumpet but H7754
Eze 37: 7 was a noise, a **rattling** s, and the bones H8323
Da 3: 5 As soon as you hear the s *of* the horn A10631
Da 3: 7 as soon as they heard the s *of* the horn A10631
Da 3:10 everyone who hears the s *of* the horn, A10631
Da 3:15 Now when you hear the s *of* the horn A10631
Da 10: 6 his voice like the s *of* a multitude. H7754
Hos 5: 8 "S the trumpet in Gibeah, the horn in H9546
Joel 2: 1 in Zion; s *the* **alarm** on my holy hill. H8131
Mic 7: 4 the day your watchmen s the alarm. NDT
Hab 3:16 my lips quivered at the s; decay crept into H7754
Zec 8:16 render true and s judgment in your H8934
Zec 9:14 The Sovereign LORD *will* s the trumpet; he H9546
Mt 12:13 completely restored, just as s as the other. G5618
Lk 1:44 As soon as the s of your greeting reached G5889
Lk 15:27 calf because he has him back **safe and s**. G5617
Jn 3: 8 You hear its s, but you cannot tell where it G5889
Ac 2: 2 Suddenly a s like the blowing of a violent G2491
Ac 2: 6 When they heard this s, a crowd came G5889
Ac 9: 7 they heard the s but did not see anyone. G5889
Ac 20: 9 *When he was* **s asleep** G2965+608+3836+5678
1Co 14: 8 if the trumpet *does* not s a clear call, who G1443
1Co 15:52 For *the* **trumpet** *will* s, the dead will be G4895
1Ti 1:10 whatever else is contrary to the s doctrine G5617
1Ti 6: 3 does not agree to the s instruction of our G5617
2Ti 1:13 keep as the pattern of s teaching, with G5617
2Ti 4: 3 people will not put up with s doctrine. G5617
Titus 1: 9 encourage others by s doctrine and refute G5617
Titus 1:13 sharply, so that *they will be* s in the faith G5617
Titus 2: 1 teach what is appropriate to s doctrine. G5617
Titus 2: 2 self-controlled, and s in faith, in love and G5617
Rev 1:15 his voice was like the s of rushing waters. G5889
Rev 8: 6 the seven trumpets prepared to s them. G4895
Rev 9: 9 the s of their wings was like the G5889
Rev 10: 7 seventh angel is about to s *his* **trumpet**, G4895
Rev 14: 2 And I heard a s from heaven like the roar G5889
Rev 14: 2 The s I heard was like that of harpists G5889
Rev 18:22 The s of a millstone will never be heard G5889

SOUNDED (24) [SOUND]

Lev 25: 9 Then **have** the trumpet s everywhere on H6296
Nu 10: 3 When both *are* s, the whole community is H9546
Nu 10: 4 If only one *is* s, the leaders—the heads of H9546
Nu 10: 5 When a trumpet blast *is* s, the tribes H9546
Jos 6:16 when the priests s the trumpet **blast** H9546
Jos 6:20 When the trumpets s, the army shouted H9546
Jdg 7:22 When the three hundred trumpets s, the H9546
2Sa 18:16 Then Joab s the trumpet, and the troops H9546
2Sa 20: 1 *He* s the trumpet and shouted, "We have H9546
2Sa 20:22 So *he* s the trumpet, and his men H9546
1Ki 1:39 Then *they* s the trumpet and all the H9546
2Ch 29:28 the musicians played and the trumpets s. H2955
Ne 4:18 But the *man who* s the trumpet stayed H9546
Rev 6: 6 Then I heard what *s* **like** a voice among the AIT
Rev 8: 7 The first angel s *his* **trumpet**, and there G4895
Rev 8: 8 The second angel s *his* **trumpet**, and G4895
Rev 8:10 The third angel s *his* **trumpet**, and a great G4895
Rev 8:12 The fourth angel s *his* **trumpet**, and a G4895
Rev 8:13 blasts about to be s by the other three G4895
Rev 9: 1 The fifth angel s *his* **trumpet**, and I saw a G4895
Rev 9:13 The sixth angel s *his* **trumpet**, and I heard G4895
Rev 11:15 The seventh angel s *his* **trumpet**, and G4895
Rev 19: 1 this I heard what *s* **like** the roar of a great AIT
Rev 19: 6 Then I heard what s like a great multitude G5889

SOUNDING (8) [SOUND]

Nu 10: 6 At the s *of* a second blast, the camps on H9546
Jos 6: 9 All this time the trumpets *were* s. H9546
Jos 6:13 ark of the LORD, while the trumpets kept s. H9546
1Ch 15:28 with the s *of* rams' horns and trumpets H7754
1Ch 16:42 responsible for *the* s *of* the trumpets and H9048
2Ch 5:12 accompanied by 120 priests s trumpets. H2955
Ps 47: 5 the LORD amid the s *of* trumpets. H7754
Ps 150: 3 Praise him with the s *of* the trumpet H9547

SOUNDINGS (2) [SOUND]

Ac 27:28 *They* **took** s and found that the water was G1075
Ac 27:28 time later *they* **took** s again and found G1075

SOUNDNESS (3) [SOUND]

Ps 38: 3 there is no s in my bones because of my H8934
Isa 1: 6 to the top of your head there is no s— H5507
Titus 2: 8 s of speech that cannot be G5618

SOUNDS (11) [SOUND]

Ex 19:13 the ram's horn **s a long blast** may they H5432
Job 15:21 Terrifying s fill his ears; when all seems H7754
Job 39:24 it cannot stand still when the trumpet s. H7754
Isa 18: 3 and when a trumpet s, you will hear it. H9546
Isa 24:11 all **joyful** s are banished from the earth. H5375
Jer 7:34 bring an end to the s *of* joy and gladness H7754
Jer 16: 9 bring an end to the s *of* joy and gladness H7754
Jer 25:10 from them the s *of* joy and gladness, H7754
Jer 33:11 the s *of* joy and gladness, the voices of H7754
Am 3: 6 When a trumpet s in a city, do not the H9546
1Co 14: 7 in the case of lifeless things that make s, G5889

SOUR (6)

Job 20:14 his food will turn s in his stomach; it will NDT
Jer 31:29 'The parents have eaten s **grapes**, and H1235
Jer 31:30 whoever eats s **grapes**—their own teeth H1235
Eze 18: 2 " 'The parents eat s **grapes**, and the H1235
Rev 10: 9 *It will* **turn** your stomach s, but 'in your G4393
Rev 10:10 when I had eaten it, my stomach **turned** s. G4393

SOURCE (5) [SOURCES]

Ge 26:35 They were a **s of grief** to Isaac and H5289+8120
Lev 20:18 he has exposed the **s of** her flow, and she H5227
Isa 28: 6 a **s of strength** to those who turn back the H1476
Eze 29:16 no longer be a **s of confidence** for the H4440
Heb 5: 9 he became the s of eternal salvation for all G165

SOURCES (2) [SOURCE]

Job 28:11 They search the s *of* the rivers and bring H4441
Jer 18:14 cool waters from **distant** s ever stop H2424

SOUTH (125) [SOUTHERN, SOUTHERNMOST, SOUTHLAND, SOUTHWARD]

Ge 13:14 to the north and s, to the east and H5582+2025
Ge 28:14 to the east, to the north and to the s. H5582
Ex 26:18 for the s side of the H2025+5582+9402+2025
Ex 26:35 opposite it on the s side. H9402+2025
Ex 27: 9 The s side shall be a H5582+9402+2025
Ex 36:23 frames for the s side of the H5582+9402+2025
Ex 38: 9 The s side was a hundred H5582+9402+2025
Ex 40:24 the table on the s side of the H5582+2025
Nu 2:10 On the s will be the divisions of the camp H9402
Nu 3:29 were to camp on the s side of the H9402+2025
Nu 10: 6 the camps on the s are to set out. H9402
Nu 34: 4 cross s of Scorpion Pass, continue on to H5582
Nu 34: 4 on to Zin and go s of Kadesh Barnea. H5582
Nu 35: 5 two thousand on the s side, two thousand H5582
Dt 3:27 west and north and s and east. H9402+2025
Dt 33: 2 with myriads of holy ones from the s, H3545

S

Jos 11: 2 in the Arabah s *of* Kinnereth, in the H5582
Jos 13: 4 on the s; all the land of the Canaanites H9402
Jos 15: 1 the Desert of Zin in the extreme s. H5582+9402
Jos 15: 3 crossed s of Scorpion Pass, continued on H5582
Jos 15: 3 went over to the s of Kadesh Barnea. H5582
Jos 15: 7 Pass of Adummim s of the gorge. H4946+5582
Jos 17: 9 boundary continued s to the Kanah H5582+2025
Jos 17:10 On the s the land belonged to Ephraim H5582
Jos 18: 5 in its territory on the s and the tribes of H5582
Jos 18:13 From there it crossed to the s slope of Luz H5582
Jos 18:13 Addar on the hill s of Lower Beth H4946+5582
Jos 18:14 Beth Horon on the s the boundary turned H5582
Jos 18:14 boundary turned s along the H5582+2025
Jos 18:19 at the mouth of the Jordan in the s. H5582
Jos 19:34 It touched Zebulun on the s, Asher on the H5582
Jdg 21:19 to Shechem, and s of Lebonah." H4946+5582
1Sa 14: 5 Mikmash, the other to the s toward Geba. H5582
1Sa 20:41 got up from the s side of the stone and H5582
1Sa 23:19 the hill of Hakilah, s *of* Jeshimon? H4946+3545
1Sa 23:24 of Maon, in the Arabah s *of* Jeshimon. H3545
2Sa 24: 5 near Aroer, s *of* the town in the gorge H3545
1Ki 6: 8 floor was on the s side of the temple; H3556
1Ki 7:21 The pillar to the s he named Jakin and H3556
1Ki 7:25 three facing s and three facing east H5582+2025
1Ki 7:39 the stands on the s side of the H4946+3545
1Ki 7:39 He placed the Sea on the s side, at the H3556
2Ki 11:11 from the s side to the north side of the H3556
2Ki 23:13 east of Jerusalem on the s of the Hill of H3545
1Ch 9:24 east, west, north and s. H5582+2025
1Ch 26:15 The lot for the S Gate fell to Obed-Edom H5582
1Ch 26:17 a day on the s and two at a time H5582+2025
2Ch 3:17 temple, one to the s and one to the north. H3545
2Ch 3:17 The *one to the* s he named Jakin and the H3556
2Ch 4: 4 three facing s and three facing east H5582+2025
2Ch 4: 6 placed five on the s *side* and five on the H3545
2Ch 4: 7 five on the s *side* and five on the north. H3545
2Ch 4: 8 five on the s *side* and five on the north. H3545
2Ch 4:10 He placed the Sea on the s side, at the H3556
2Ch 23:10 from the s side to the north side of the H3556
Job 9: 9 Pleiades and the constellations of the s. H9402
Job 23: 9 when he turns to the s, I catch no glimpse H3545
Job 37:17 the land lies hushed under the **s wind**, H1999
Job 39:26 spread its wings toward the s? H9402
Ps 78:26 by his power made the **s wind** blow. H9402
Ps 89:12 You created the north and the s; Tabor H3545
Ps 107: 3 from east and west, from north and s. H3545
Ecc 1: 6 The wind blows to the s and turns to the H1999
Ecc 11: 3 a tree falls to the s or to the north, H1999
SS 4:16 and come, **s wind**! Blow on my H9402
Isa 43: 6 and to the s, 'Do not hold them H9402
Eze 10: 3 standing on the s *side* of the temple H3545
Eze 16:46 who lived to the s *of* you with her H3545
Eze 20:46 set your face toward the s; preach H9402+2025
Eze 20:46 preach against the s and prophesy H1999
Eze 20:47 every face from s to north will be H5582
Eze 21: 4 against everyone from s to north. H5582
Eze 40: 2 on whose s *side* were some H4946+5582
Eze 40:24 he led me to the s side and I saw the H1999
Eze 40:24 side and I saw the s gate. H2006+2021+1999
Eze 40:27 The inner court also had a gate facing s H1999
Eze 40:27 this gate to the outer gate on the s side; H1999
Eze 40:28 into the inner court through the s gate, H1999
Eze 40:28 he measured the s gate; it had the H1999
Eze 40:44 the north gate and facing s, H2006+2021+1999
Eze 40:44 at the side of the s gate and facing north. H1999
Eze 40:45 "The room facing s is for the H2006+2021+1999
Eze 41:11 one on the north and another on the s H1999
Eze 42:10 On the s side along the length of the wall H1999
Eze 42:12 were the doorways of the rooms on the s H1999
Eze 42:13 "The north and s rooms facing the temple H1999
Eze 42:18 He measured the s side; it was five H1999
Eze 46: 9 gate to worship is to go out the s gate; H5582
Eze 46: 9 enters by the s gate is to go out the H5582
Eze 47: 1 down from under the s side of the temple, H3556
Eze 47: 1 side of the temple, s of the altar. H4946+5582
Eze 47: 2 the water was trickling from the s side. H3556
Eze 47:19 "On the s side it will run from H5582+9402
Eze 48:10 side and 25,000 cubits long on the s *side*. H5582
Eze 48:16 4,500 cubits, the s side 4,500 cubits, the H5582
Eze 48:17 250 cubits on the s, 250 cubits on the H5582
Eze 48:28 of Gad will run s from Tamar to the H9402+2025
Eze 48:33 "On the s side, which measures 4,500 H5582
Da 8: 4 toward the west and the north and the s. H5582
Da 8: 9 in power to the s and to the east and H5582
Da 11: 5 "The king of the S will become strong, but H5582
Da 11: 6 of the king of the S will go to the king of H5582
Da 11: 9 of the king of the S but will retreat to his H5582
Da 11:11 the king of the S will march out in a H5582
Da 11:12 **the king of the S** will be filled with pride H2257S
Da 11:14 many will rise against the king of the S. H5582
Da 11:15 The forces of the S will be powerless to H5582
Da 11:17 make an alliance with **the king of the S**. H2257S
Da 11:25 courage against the king of the S. H5582
Da 11:25 The king of the S will wage war with a H5582
Da 11:29 time he will invade the S again, H5582
Da 11:40 end the king of the S will engage him in H5582
Zec 6: 6 one with the dappled horses toward the s." H9402
Zec 9:14 he will march in the storms of the s, H9402
Zec 14: 4 moving north and half moving s. H5582+2025
Zec 14:10 Geba to Rimmon, s *of* Jerusalem, will H5582
Mt 12:42 The Queen *of* the S will rise at the G3803
Lk 11:31 The Queen *of* the S will rise at the G3803
Lk 12:55 And when the **s wind** blows, you say, 'It's G3803
Lk 13:29 come from east and west and north and s, G3803
Ac 8:26 said to Philip, "Go s to the road—the G3540
Ac 21: 3 sighting Cyprus and passing *to* the s of it, G2381
Ac 27:13 When a gentle **s wind** began to blow G3803
Ac 28:13 The next day the **s wind** came up, and on G3803
Rev 21:13 three on the s and three on the west. G3803

SOUTHEAST (2) [EAST]

1Ki 7:39 at the s corner of the temple. H7711+2025+5582
2Ch 4:10 side, at the s corner. H7711+2025+5582+2025

SOUTHERN (13) [SOUTH]

Nu 34: 3 " 'Your s side will include some of the H5582
Nu 34: 3 Your s boundary will start in the east from H5582
Nu 34: 3 in the east from the s end of the Dead Sea, NDT
Jos 15: 2 Their s boundary started from the bay at H5582
Jos 15: 2 the bay at the s end of the Dead H5582+2025
Jos 15: 4 This is their s boundary. H5582
Jos 15: 8 Hinnom along the s slope of the H4946+5582
Jos 18:15 The s side began at the outskirts of H5582+2025
Jos 18:16 Valley along the s slope of the H5582+2025
Jos 18:19 This was the s boundary. H5582
Eze 20:47 Say to the s forest: 'Hear the word of the H5582
Eze 47:19 will be the s boundary. H9402+2025+5582+2025
Eze 48:28 "The s boundary of Gad will H448+6991+5582

SOUTHERNMOST (1) [SOUTH, MOST]

Jos 15:21 The s towns of the tribe of Judah in H4946+7895

SOUTHLAND (2) [SOUTH]

Isa 21: 1 Like whirlwinds sweeping through the s H5582
Eze 20:46 against the forest of the s. H8441+5582

SOUTHWARD (3) [SOUTH]

Dt 33:23 his blessing; he will inherit s to the lake." H1999
Jos 12: 3 and then s below the slopes of H4946+9402
Jos 17: 7 boundary ran s from there to H448+2021+3545

SOUTHWEST (1) [WEST]

Ac 27:12 in Crete, facing both s and northwest. G3355

SOVEREIGN (303) [SOVEREIGNTY]

Ge 15: 2 But Abram said, "S LORD, what can you give H151
Ge 15: 8 But Abram said, "S LORD, how can I know H151
Ex 23:17 the men are to appear before the S LORD. H123
Ex 34:23 your men are to appear before the S LORD, H123
Dt 3:24 "S LORD, you have begun to show to your H151
Dt 9:26 the LORD and said, "S LORD, do not destroy H151
Jos 7: 7 S LORD, why did you ever bring this H151
Jdg 6:22 of the LORD, he exclaimed, "Alas, S LORD! H151
Jdg 16:28 prayed to the LORD, "S LORD, remember me. H151
2Sa 7:18 "Who am I, S LORD, and what is my family H151
2Sa 7:19 enough in your sight, S LORD, you have also H151
2Sa 7:19 this decree, S LORD, is for a mere H151
2Sa 7:20 For you know your servant, S LORD. H151
2Sa 7:22 "How great you are, S LORD! There is no H151
2Sa 7:28 S LORD, you are God! Your covenant is H151
2Sa 7:29 your sight; for you, S LORD, have spoken H151
1Ki 2:26 the ark of the S LORD before my father H151
1Ki 8:53 Moses when you, S LORD, brought our H151
Ps 68:20 from the S LORD comes escape from death. H151
Ps 71: 5 have been my hope, S LORD, my confidence H151
Ps 71:16 your mighty acts, S LORD; I will proclaim H151
Ps 73:28 I have made the S LORD my refuge; I will H151
Ps 109:21 But you, S LORD, help me for your name's H151
Ps 140: 7 S LORD, my strong deliverer, you shield my H151
Ps 141: 8 eyes are fixed on you, S LORD; in you I take H151
Isa 7: 7 Yet this is what the S LORD says: " 'It will H151
Isa 25: 8 The S LORD will wipe away the tears from H151
Isa 28:16 So this is what the S LORD says: "See, I lay a H151
Isa 30:15 This is what the S LORD, the Holy One of H151
Isa 40:10 the S LORD comes with power, and he H151
Isa 48:16 And now the S LORD has sent me H151
Isa 49:22 This is what the S LORD says: "See, I will H151
Isa 50: 4 The S LORD has given me a well-instructed H151
Isa 50: 5 The S LORD has opened my ears; I have not H151
Isa 50: 7 Because the S LORD helps me, I will not be H151
Isa 50: 9 It is the S LORD who helps me. Who will H151
Isa 51:22 This is what your S LORD says, your God H151
Isa 52: 4 For this is what the S LORD says: "At first H151
Isa 56: 8 The S LORD declares—he who gathers the H151
Isa 61: 1 The Spirit of the S LORD is on me, because H151
Isa 61:11 so the S LORD will make righteousness and H151
Isa 65:13 Therefore this is what the S LORD says: "My H151
Isa 65:15 the S LORD will put you to death H151
Jer 1: 6 S LORD," I said, "I do not know how H151
Jer 2:22 is still before me," declares the S LORD. H151
Jer 4:10 Then I said, "Alas, S LORD! How completely H151
Jer 7:20 " 'Therefore this is what the S LORD says: H151
Jer 14:13 But I said, "Alas, S LORD! The prophets keep H151
Jer 32:17 S LORD, you have made the heavens H151
Jer 32:25 Babylonians, you, S LORD, say to me, 'Buy H151
Jer 44:26 swear, "As surely as the S LORD lives." H151
Jer 50:25 the S LORD Almighty has work to do in H151
Eze 2: 4 Say to them, 'This is what the S LORD says.' H151
Eze 3:11 'This is what the S LORD says,' whether H151
Eze 3:27 say to them, 'This is what the S LORD says. H151
Eze 4:14 Then I said, "Not so, S LORD! I have never H151
Eze 5: 5 "This is what the S LORD says: This is H151
Eze 5: 7 "Therefore this is what the S LORD says: You H151
Eze 5: 8 "Therefore this is what the S LORD says: H151
Eze 5:11 declares the S LORD, because you H151
Eze 6: 3 of Israel, hear the word of the S LORD. H151
Eze 6: 3 This is what the S LORD says to the H151
Eze 6:11 " 'This is what the S LORD says: Strike your H151
Eze 7: 2 this is what the S LORD says to the land of H151
Eze 7: 5 "This is what the S LORD says: " 'Disaster H151
Eze 8: 1 the hand of the S LORD came on me there. H151
Eze 9: 8 I fell facedown, crying out, "Alas, S LORD! H151
Eze 11: 7 "Therefore this is what the S LORD says: The H151
Eze 11: 8 will bring against you, declares the S LORD. H151
Eze 11:13 cried out in a loud voice, "Alas, S LORD! H151
Eze 11:16 'This is what the S LORD says: Although I H151
Eze 11:17 'This is what the S LORD says: I will H151
Eze 11:21 what they have done, declares the S LORD." H151
Eze 12:10 'This is what the S LORD says: This H151
Eze 12:19 'This is what the S LORD says about those H151
Eze 12:23 'This is what the S LORD says: I am going H151
Eze 12:25 fulfill whatever I say, declares the S LORD. H151
Eze 12:28 say to them, 'This is what the S LORD says: H151
Eze 12:28 I say will be fulfilled, declares the S LORD. H151
Eze 13: 3 This is what the S LORD says: Woe to the H151
Eze 13: 8 " 'Therefore this is what the S LORD says H151
Eze 13: 8 I am against you, declares the S LORD. H151
Eze 13: 9 Then you will know that I am the S LORD. H151
Eze 13:13 " 'Therefore this is what the S LORD says: In H151
Eze 13:16 there was no peace, declares the S LORD." H151
Eze 13:18 'This is what the S LORD says: Woe to the H151
Eze 13:20 " 'Therefore this is what the S LORD says: H151
Eze 14: 4 tell them, 'This is what the S LORD says: H151
Eze 14: 6 of Israel, 'This is what the S LORD says: H151
Eze 14:11 I will be their God, declares the S LORD. H151
Eze 14:14 by their righteousness, declares the S LORD. H151
Eze 14:16 as I live, declares the S LORD, even if these H151
Eze 14:18 as I live, declares the S LORD, even if these H151
Eze 14:20 as I live, declares the S LORD, even if Noah, H151
Eze 14:21 "For this is what the S LORD says: How H151
Eze 14:23 in it without cause, declares the S LORD." H151
Eze 15: 6 "Therefore this is what the S LORD says: As H151
Eze 15: 8 have been unfaithful, declares the S LORD." H151
Eze 16: 3 'This is what the S LORD says to Jerusalem: H151
Eze 16: 8 declares the S LORD, and you became H151
Eze 16:14 your beauty perfect, declares the S LORD. H151
Eze 16:19 is what happened, declares the S LORD. H151
Eze 16:23 declares the S LORD. In addition to H151
Eze 16:30 declares the S LORD, when you do all H151
Eze 16:36 This is what the S LORD says: Because you H151
Eze 16:43 what you have done, declares the S LORD. H151
Eze 16:48 declares the S LORD, your sister H151
Eze 16:59 " 'This is what the S LORD says: I will deal H151
Eze 16:63 of your humiliation, declares the S LORD. H151
Eze 17: 3 'This is what the S LORD says: A great H151
Eze 17: 9 'This is what the S LORD says: Will it H151
Eze 17:16 declares the S LORD, he shall die in H151
Eze 17:19 " 'Therefore this is what the S LORD says: H151
Eze 17:22 " 'This is what the S LORD says: I myself H151
Eze 18: 3 as I live, declares the S LORD, you will no H151
Eze 18: 9 he will surely live, declares the S LORD. H151
Eze 18:23 of the wicked? declares the S LORD. Rather, H151
Eze 18:30 to your own ways, declares the S LORD. H151
Eze 18:32 the death of anyone, declares the S LORD. H151
Eze 20: 3 say to them, 'This is what the S LORD says: H151
Eze 20: 3 let you inquire of me, declares the S LORD. H151
Eze 20: 5 'This is what the S LORD says: On the day I H151
Eze 20:27 say to them, 'This is what the S LORD says: H151
Eze 20:30 'This is what the S LORD says: Will you H151
Eze 20:31 as I live, declares the S LORD, I will not let H151
Eze 20:33 declares the S LORD, I will reign over H151
Eze 20:36 so I will judge you, declares the S LORD. H151
Eze 20:39 of Israel, this is what the S LORD says: H151
Eze 20:40 declares the S LORD, there in the H151
Eze 20:44 you people of Israel, declares the S LORD. H151
Eze 20:47 This is what the S LORD says: I am about H151
Eze 20:49 Then I said, "S LORD, they are saying of me H151
Eze 21: 7 will surely take place, declares the S LORD." H151
Eze 21:13 does not continue? declares the S LORD.' H151
Eze 21:24 "Therefore this is what the S LORD says H151
Eze 21:26 this is what the S LORD says: Take off the H151
Eze 21:28 " 'This is what the S LORD says about the H151
Eze 22: 3 'This is what the S LORD says: You city H151
Eze 22:12 you have forgotten me, declares the S LORD. H151
Eze 22:19 Therefore this is what the S LORD says H151
Eze 22:28 'This is what the S LORD says'—when the H151
Eze 22:31 all they have done, declares the S LORD." H151
Eze 23:22 Oholibah, this is what the S LORD says: H151
Eze 23:28 "For this is what the S LORD says: I am H151
Eze 23:32 "This is what the S LORD says: "You will H151
Eze 23:34 I have spoken, declares the S LORD. H151
Eze 23:35 "Therefore this is what the S LORD says H151
Eze 23:46 "This is what the S LORD says: Bring a mob H151
Eze 23:49 Then you will know that I am the S LORD." H151
Eze 24: 3 'This is what the S LORD says: " 'Put on H151
Eze 24: 6 " 'For this is what the S LORD says: " 'Woe H151
Eze 24: 9 " 'Therefore this is what the S LORD says: H151
Eze 24:14 your actions, declares the S LORD. H151
Eze 24:21 of Israel, 'This is what the S LORD says: H151
Eze 24:24 you will know that I am the S LORD. H151
Eze 25: 3 'Hear the word of the S LORD. This is what H151
Eze 25: 3 This is what the S LORD says: Because you H151
Eze 25: 6 For this is what the S LORD says: Because H151
Eze 25: 8 "This is what the S LORD says: 'Because H151
Eze 25:12 "This is what the S LORD says: 'Because H151
Eze 25:13 therefore this is what the S LORD says: I will H151
Eze 25:14 know my vengeance, declares the S LORD. H151

Eze 25:15 "This is what the **S** LORD says: 'Because the H151
Eze 25:16 therefore this is what the **S** LORD says: I am H151
Eze 26: 3 therefore this is what the **S** LORD says: I am H151
Eze 26: 5 I have spoken, declares the **S** LORD. H151
Eze 26: 7 "For this is what the **S** LORD says: From the H151
Eze 26:14 the LORD have spoken, declares the **S** LORD. H151
Eze 26:15 "This is what the **S** LORD says to Tyre: Will H151
Eze 26:19 "This is what the **S** LORD says: When I H151
Eze 26:21 never again be found, declares the **S** LORD." H151
Eze 27: 3 many coasts, 'This is what the **S** LORD says: H151
Eze 28: 2 ruler of Tyre, 'This is what the **S** LORD says: H151
Eze 28: 6 " 'Therefore this is what the **S** LORD says: H151
Eze 28:10 I have spoken, declares the **S** LORD.' " H151
Eze 28:12 'This is what the **S** LORD says: " 'You were H151
Eze 28:22 'This is what the **S** LORD says: " 'I am H151
Eze 28:24 Then they will know that I am the **S** LORD. H151
Eze 28:25 " 'This is what the **S** LORD says: When I H151
Eze 29: 3 'This is what the **S** LORD says: " 'I am H151
Eze 29: 8 " 'Therefore this is what the **S** LORD says: H151
Eze 29:13 " 'Yet this is what the **S** LORD says: At the H151
Eze 29:16 Then they will know that I am the **S** LORD.' " H151
Eze 29:19 Therefore this is what the **S** LORD says: I am H151
Eze 29:20 his army did it for me, declares the **S** LORD. H151
Eze 30: 2 'This is what the **S** LORD says: " 'Wail and H151
Eze 30: 6 the sword within her, declares the **S** LORD. H151
Eze 30:10 " 'This is what the **S** LORD says: " 'I will H151
Eze 30:13 " 'This is what the **S** LORD says: " 'I will H151
Eze 30:22 Therefore this is what the **S** LORD says: H151
Eze 31:10 " 'Therefore this is what the **S** LORD says H151
Eze 31:15 " 'This is what the **S** LORD says: On the day H151
Eze 31:18 all his hordes, declares the **S** LORD. H151
Eze 32: 3 " 'This is what the **S** LORD says: " 'With a H151
Eze 32: 8 over your land, declares the **S** LORD. H151
Eze 32:11 " 'For this is what the **S** LORD says: " 'The H151
Eze 32:14 streams flow like oil, declares the **S** LORD. H151
Eze 32:16 they will chant it, declares the **S** LORD." H151
Eze 32:31 killed by the sword, declares the **S** LORD. H151
Eze 32:32 killed by the sword, declares the **S** LORD." H151
Eze 33:11 as I live, declares the **S** LORD, I take no H151
Eze 33:25 say to them, 'This is what the **S** LORD says: H151
Eze 33:27 'This is what the **S** LORD says: As surely as H151
Eze 34: 2 'This is what the **S** LORD says: Woe to you H151
Eze 34: 8 declares the **S** LORD, because my flock H151
Eze 34:10 This is what the **S** LORD says: I am against H151
Eze 34:11 " 'For this is what the **S** LORD says: I myself H151
Eze 34:15 have them lie down, declares the **S** LORD. H151
Eze 34:17 my flock, this is what the **S** LORD says: H151
Eze 34:20 this is what the **S** LORD says to them: H151
Eze 34:30 are my people, declares the **S** LORD. H151
Eze 34:31 I am your God, declares the **S** LORD.' " H151
Eze 35: 3 'This is what the **S** LORD says: I am H151
Eze 35: 6 as I live, declares the **S** LORD, I will give you H151
Eze 35:11 as I live, declares the **S** LORD, I will treat you H151
Eze 35:14 This is what the **S** LORD says: While the H151
Eze 36: 2 This is what the **S** LORD says: The enemy H151
Eze 36: 3 'This is what the **S** LORD says: H151
Eze 36: 4 of Israel, hear the word of the **S** LORD: H151
Eze 36: 4 This is what the **S** LORD says to the H151
Eze 36: 5 this is what the **S** LORD says: In my burning H151
Eze 36: 6 'This is what the **S** LORD says: I speak in my H151
Eze 36: 7 Therefore this is what the **S** LORD says: H151
Eze 36:13 " 'This is what the **S** LORD says: Because H151
Eze 36:14 your nation childless, declares the **S** LORD. H151
Eze 36:15 your nation to fall, declares the **S** LORD. H151
Eze 36:22 the Israelites, 'This is what the **S** LORD says: H151
Eze 36:23 declares the **S** LORD, when I am H151
Eze 36:32 this for your sake, declares the **S** LORD. H151
Eze 36:33 " 'This is what the **S** LORD says: On the day I H151
Eze 36:37 "This is what the **S** LORD says: Once again I H151
Eze 37: 3 I said, "**S** LORD, you alone know. H151
Eze 37: 5 This is what the **S** LORD says to these bones H151
Eze 37: 9 say to it, 'This is what the **S** LORD says: H151
Eze 37:12 'This is what the **S** LORD says: My people, H151
Eze 37:19 'This is what the **S** LORD says: I am going H151
Eze 37:21 say to them, 'This is what the **S** LORD says: H151
Eze 38: 3 'This is what the **S** LORD says: I am H151
Eze 38:10 " 'This is what the **S** LORD says: On that day H151
Eze 38:14 'This is what the **S** LORD says: In that day H151
Eze 38:17 " 'This is what the **S** LORD says: You are the H151
Eze 38:18 anger will be aroused, declares the **S** LORD. H151
Eze 38:21 on all my mountains, declares the **S** LORD. H151
Eze 39: 1 'This is what the **S** LORD says: I am H151
Eze 39: 5 I have spoken, declares the **S** LORD. H151
Eze 39: 8 It will surely take place, declares the **S** LORD. H151
Eze 39:10 who looted them, declares the **S** LORD. H151
Eze 39:13 day for them, declares the **S** LORD. H151
Eze 39:17 this is what the **S** LORD says: Call out H151
Eze 39:20 soldiers of every kind,' declares the **S** LORD. H151
Eze 39:25 "Therefore this is what the **S** LORD says: H151
Eze 39:29 the people of Israel, declares the **S** LORD." H151
Eze 43:18 "Son of man, this is what the **S** LORD says: H151
Eze 43:19 to minister before me, declares the **S** LORD. H151
Eze 43:27 I will accept you, declares the **S** LORD." H151
Eze 44: 6 'This is what the **S** LORD says: H151
Eze 44: 9 This is what the **S** LORD says: No foreigner H151
Eze 44:12 of their sin, declares the **S** LORD. H151
Eze 44:15 of fat and blood, declares the **S** LORD. H151
Eze 44:27 sin offering for himself, declares the **S** LORD. H151
Eze 45: 9 " 'This is what the **S** LORD says: You have H151
Eze 45: 9 my people, declares the **S** LORD. H151
Eze 45:15 the people, declares the **S** LORD. H151
Eze 45:18 " 'This is what the **S** LORD says: In the first H151
Eze 46: 1 " 'This is what the **S** LORD says: The gate of H151
Eze 46:16 " 'This is what the **S** LORD says: If the prince H151
Eze 47:13 This is what the **S** LORD says: "These are the H151
Eze 47:23 their inheritance," declares the **S** LORD. H151
Eze 48:29 will be their portions," declares the **S** LORD. H151
Da 4:17 the Most High is **s** over all kingdoms on A10718
Da 4:25 the Most High is **s** over all kingdoms on A10718
Da 4:32 the Most High is **s** over all kingdoms on A10718
Da 5:21 Most High God is **s** over all kingdoms on A10718
Da 7:14 glory and **s power**; all nations and A10424
Am 1: 8 the Philistines are dead," says the **S** LORD. H151
Am 3: 7 Surely the **S** LORD does nothing without H151
Am 3: 8 The **S** LORD has spoken—who can but H151
Am 3:11 Therefore this is what the **S** LORD says: "An H151
Am 4: 2 The **S** LORD has sworn by his holiness: "The H151
Am 4: 5 what you love to do," declares the **S** LORD. H151
Am 5: 3 This is what the **S** LORD says to Isral: "Your H151
Am 6: 8 The **S** LORD has sworn by himself— H151
Am 7: 1 This is what the **S** LORD showed me: He H151
Am 7: 2 the land clean, I cried out, "**S** LORD, forgive! H151
Am 7: 4 This is what the **S** LORD showed me: The H151
Am 7: 4 The **S** LORD was calling for judgment by fire H151
Am 7: 5 Then I cried out, "**S** LORD, I beg you, stop H151
Am 7: 6 will not happen either," the **S** LORD said. H151
Am 8: 1 This is what the **S** LORD showed me: H151
Am 8: 3 declares the **S** LORD, "the songs in the H151
Am 8: 9 declares the **S** LORD, "I will make the sun H151
Am 8:11 declares the **S** LORD, "when I will send a H151
Am 9: 8 the eyes of the **S** LORD are on the sinful H151
Ob 1 This is what the **S** LORD says about Edom H151
Mic 1: 2 that the **S** LORD may bear witness against H151
Hab 3:19 The **S** LORD is my strength; he makes my H151
Zep 1: 7 Be silent before the **S** LORD, for the day of H151
Zec 9:14 The **S** LORD will sound the trumpet; he will H151
Lk 2:29 "**S Lord**, as you have promised, you may *G1305*
Ac 4:24 "**S Lord**," they said, "you made the *G1305*
2Pe 2: 1 even denying the **s Lord** who bought them *G1305*
Jude 4 deny Jesus Christ our only **S** and Lord. *G1305*
Rev 6:10 "How long, **S Lord**, holy and true *G1305*

SOVEREIGNTY (2) [SOVEREIGN]

Da 5:18 Nebuchadnezzar **s** and greatness and A10424
Da 7:27 Then the **s**, power and greatness of all A10424

SOW (31) [SOWED, SOWER, SOWING, SOWN, SOWS]

Ex 23:10 "For six years *you are to* **s** your fields and H2445
Ex 23:16 firstfruits of the crops you **s** in your field. H2445
Lev 25: 3 For six years **s** your fields, and for six years H2445
Lev 25: 4 *Do* not **s** your fields or prune your H2445
Lev 25:11 *do* not **s** and do not reap what grows of H2445
Dt 28:38 *You will* **s** much seed *in* the field but you H3655
2Ki 19:29 But in the third year **s** and reap, plant H2445
Job 4: 8 plow evil and *those who* **s** trouble reap it. H2445
Ps 126: 5 Those *who* **s** with tears will reap with H2445
Ps 126: 6 carrying **seed to s**, will return H5433+2446
Ecc 11: 6 **S** your seed in the morning, and at H2445
Isa 28:25 *does he* not **s** caraway and scatter cumin? H7046
Isa 30:23 you rain for the seed *you* **s** *in* the ground, H2445
Isa 37:30 But in the third year **s** and reap, plant H2445
Jer 4: 3 ground and *do* not **s** among thorns. H2445
Jer 12:13 *They will* **s** wheat but reap thorns; they H2445
Jer 35: 7 build houses, **s** seed or plant vineyards H2445
Hos 8: 7 "*They* **s** the wind and reap the whirlwind H2445
Hos 10:12 **S** righteousness for yourselves, reap the H2445
Mt 6:26 *they do* not **s** or reap or store away in *G5062*
Mt 13: 3 "A farmer went out *to* **s** *his* **seed**. *G5062*
Mt 13:27 didn't *you* **s** good seed in your field? *G5062*
Mk 4: 3 A farmer went out *to* **s** *his* **seed**. *G5062*
Lk 8: 5 "A farmer went out *to* **s** his seed. As he *G5062*
Lk 12:24 *They do* not **s** or reap, they have no *G5062*
Lk 19:21 not put in and reap what *you did* not **s**. *G5062*
Lk 19:22 not put in, and reaping what *I did* not **s**? *G5062*
1Co 15:36 What you **s** does not come to life unless it *G5062*
1Co 15:37 *When you* **s**, you do not plant the body *G5062*
Jas 3:18 Peacemakers *who* **s** in peace reap a *G5062*
2Pe 2:22 "A **s** that is washed returns to her *G5725*

SOWED (4) [SOW]

Ps 107:37 *They* **s** fields and planted vineyards that H2445
Mt 13:24 is like a man *who* **s** good seed in his *G5062*
Mt 13:25 his enemy came and **s** weeds among the *G2178*
Mt 13:37 "The *one who* **s** the good seed is the Son *G5062*

SOWER (5) [SOW]

Isa 55:10 it yields seed for the **s** and bread for the H2445
Jer 50:16 Cut off from Babylon the **s**, and the reaper H2445
Mt 13:18 then to what the parable *of* the **s** means: *G5062*
Jn 4:36 so that the **s** and the reaper may be glad *G5062*
2Co 9:10 who supplies seed *to* the **s** and bread *G5062*

SOWING (1) [SOW]

Isa 32:20 you will be, **s** *your* **seed** by every stream H2445

SOWN (23) [SOW]

Job 31: 8 then may others eat what *I have* **s**, and H2445
Isa 19: 7 Every **s field** *along* the Nile will become H4669
Isa 40:24 no sooner *are they* **s**, no sooner do H2445
Jer 2: 2 the wilderness, through a land not **s**. H2445
Eze 36: 9 you with favor; you will be plowed and **s**, H2445
Mt 13: 8 a hundred, sixty or thirty times what was **s**. NDT
Mt 13:19 snatches away what *was* **s** in their heart. *G5062*
Mt 13:19 This is the **seed s** along the path. *G5062*
Mt 13:23 a hundred, sixty or thirty times what was **s**." NDT
Mt 25:24 where *you have* not **s** and gathering *G5062*
Mt 25:26 I harvest where *I have* not **s** and gather *G5062*
Mk 4:15 seed along the path, where the word *is* **s**. *G5062*
Mk 4:15 takes away the word that *was* **s** in them. *G5062*
Mk 4:16 like **seed s** on rocky places, hear *G5062*
Mk 4:18 Still others, like **seed s** among thorns, hear *G5062*
Mk 4:20 like **seed s** on good soil, hear the *G5062*
Mk 4:20 some a hundred times what was **s**. NDT
Lk 8: 8 a hundred times more than was **s**. NDT
1Co 9:11 If we *have* **s** spiritual **seed** among you, is it *G5062*
1Co 15:42 The body *that is* **s** is perishable, it is *G5062*
1Co 15:43 *it is* **s** in dishonor, it is raised in glory; it is *G5062*
1Co 15:43 is raised in glory; *it is* **s** in weakness, it is *G5062*
1Co 15:44 *it is* **s** a natural body, it is raised a spiritual *G5062*

SOWS (10) [SOW]

Pr 11:18 the *one who* **s** righteousness reaps a H2445
Pr 22: 8 *Whoever* **s** injustice reaps calamity, and H2445
Mt 13:39 the enemy who **s** them is the devil *G5062*
Mk 4:14 The farmer **s** the word. *G5062*
Jn 4:37 Thus the saying 'One **s** and another reaps' *G5062*
2Co 9: 6 Whoever **s** sparingly will also reap *G5062*
2Co 9: 6 whoever **s** generously will also reap *G5062*
Gal 6: 7 A man reaps what *he* **s**. *G5062*
Gal 6: 8 Whoever **s** to please their flesh, from the *G5062*
Gal 6: 8 destruction; whoever **s** to please the Spirit *G5062*

SPACE (10) [SPACIOUS]

Ge 32:16 and keep *some* **s** between the herds." H8119
Ex 25:37 on it so that they light the **s** in front of it. H6298
1Sa 26:13 there was a wide **s** between them. H5226
1Ki 7:36 in every **available s**, with wreaths H5113
Job 26: 7 out the northern skies over **empty s**; H9332
Isa 5: 8 field to field till no **s** is left and you live H5226
Isa 49:20 too small for us; **give us more s** to live in. H5602
Eze 41:17 In the **s** above the outside of the entrance to NDT
Eze 42: 5 the galleries **took** more **s** from them than H430
Eze 42: 6 were smaller in **floor s** than those on the H824

SPACIOUS (12) [SPACE]

Ex 3: 8 out of that land into a good and **s** land, H8146
Jdg 18:10 people and a **s** land that God has H8146+3338
2Sa 22:20 He brought me out into a **s place**; he H5303
1Ch 4:40 and the land was **s**, peaceful and H8146+3338
Ne 7: 4 Now the city was large and **s**, but H8146+3338
Ne 9:35 to them in the **s** and fertile land you H8146
Job 36:16 jaws of distress to a **s place** free from H8144
Ps 18:19 He brought me out into a **s place**; he H5303
Ps 31: 8 enemy but have set my feet in a **s place**. H5303
Ps 104:25 is the sea, vast and **s**, teeming with H8146+3338
Ps 118: 5 to the LORD; he brought me into a **s place**. H5303
Jer 22:14 myself a great palace with **s** upper rooms. H8118

SPAIN (2)

Ro 15:24 I plan to do so when I go to **S**. I hope to *G5056*
Ro 15:28 I will go to **S** and visit you on the way. *G5056*

SPAN (9)

Ex 23:26 I will give you a full **life s**. H5031+3427
Ex 28:16 to be square—a **s** long and a span wide H2455
Ex 28:16 a span long and a **s** wide—and folded H2455
Ex 39: 9 It was square—a **s** long and a span wide H2455
Ex 39: 9 a span long and a **s** wide—and folded H2455
1Sa 17: 4 His height was six cubits and a **s**. H2455
Ps 39: 5 the **s of** my **years** is as nothing before you. H2698
Isa 23:15 seventy years, the **s of** a king's **life**. H3427
Eze 43:13 with a rim of one **s** around the edge. H2455

SPARE (49) [SPARED, SPARES, SPARING, SPARINGLY]

Ge 18:24 sweep it away and not **s** the place for the H5951
Ge 18:26 *I will* **s** the whole place for their sake." H5951
Dt 13: 8 *Do* not **s** them or shield them H2798
Jos 2:13 that *you will* **s** *the* **lives** *of* my father and H2649
Jos 22:22 to the LORD, *do* not **s** us this day. H3828
Jdg 6: 4 way to Gaza and *did* not **s** a living thing H8636
1Sa 2:33 at my altar I will **s** only to destroy your sight NDT
1Sa 15: 3 *Do* not **s** them; put to death men and H2798
2Sa 21: 2 the Israelites had sworn to **s** them, but Saul NDT
1Ki 16:11 *He did* not **s** a single male, whether H8636
1Ki 20:31 Perhaps *he will* **s** your life." H2649
2Ki 7: 4 If *they* **s** us, we live; if they kill us, then we H2649
2Ch 31:10 have had enough to eat and plenty *to* **s**, H3855
2Ch 36:17 and *did* not **s** young men or young H2798
Est 7: 3 And **s** my people—this is my NDT
Job 2: 6 is in your hands; but *you must* **s** his life." H9068
Job 33:24 '**S** them from going down to the pit H7021
Ps 78:50 *he did* not **s** them from death but gave H3104
Pr 20:13 stay awake and *you will* **have** food **to s**. H8425
Isa 9:19 the fire; *they will* not **s** one another. H2798
Isa 47: 3 I will take vengeance; *I will* **s** no one." H7003
Jer 50:14 **S** no arrows, for she has sinned against H2798
Jer 50:20 found, for I will forgive *the* **remnant** *I* **s**. H8636
Jer 51: 3 *Do* not **s** her young men; completely H2798
Eze 5:11 I will not look on you with pity or **s** you. H2798
Eze 6: 8 " 'But *I will* **s** some, for some of you will H3855
Eze 7: 4 not look on you with pity; *I will* not **s** you. H2798
Eze 7: 9 not look on you with pity; *I will* not **s** you. H2798
Eze 8:18 I will not look on them with pity or **s** them. H2798
Eze 9:10 I will not look on them with pity or **s** them, H2798
Eze 12:16 But *I will* **s** a few of them from the sword H3855
Da 5:19 to death; those he wanted to **s**, he spared; NDT
Joel 2:17 Let them say, "**S** your people, LORD. H2571
Am 7: 8 my people Israel; *I will* **s** them no longer. H6296

Am 8: 2 my people Israel; *I will* **s** them no longer. H6296
Zec 11: 5 Their own shepherds *do* not **s** them. H2798
Mal 3:17 *I will* **s** them, just as a father has H2798
Lk 15:17 my father's hired servants **have** food **to s**, *G4355*
Ac 20:29 in among you and *will* not **s** the flock. *G5767*
Ac 27:43 wanted *to* **s** Paul's **life** and kept them *G1407*
Ro 8:32 *He* who *did* not **s** his own Son, but gave *G5767*
Ro 11:21 For if God *did* not **s** the natural branches *G5767*
Ro 11:21 natural branches, *he will* not **s** you either. *G5767*
1Co 7:28 in this life, and I *want to* **s** you this. *G5767*
2Co 1:23 that *it was in order to* **s** you that I did not *G5767*
2Co 13: 2 On my return *I will* not **s** those who sinned *G5767*
Php 2:27 to **s** *me* sorrow upon sorrow. *G3590+2400*
2Pe 2: 4 For if God *did* not **s** angels when they *G5767*
2Pe 2: 5 if *he did* not **s** the ancient world when he *G5767*

SPARED (24) [SPARE]

Ge 12:13 sake and my life *will be* **s** because of you." H2649
Ge 19:20 isn't it? Then my life *will be* **s**." H2649
Ge 32:30 God face to face, and yet my life **was s**." H5911
Ex 12:27 in Egypt and **s** our homes when he H5911
Nu 22:33 killed you by now, but *I would have* **s** it." H2649
Jos 6:17 who are with her in her house *shall be* **s**, H2649
Jos 6:25 But Joshua **s** Rahab the prostitute, with her H2649
Jdg 1:25 to the sword but **s** the man and his whole H8938
Jdg 8:19 if *you had* **s** their **lives**, I would not H2649
Jdg 21:14 of Jabesh Gilead who *had been* **s**. H2649
1Sa 15: 9 Saul and the army **s** Agag and the best of H2798
1Sa 15:15 *they* **s** the best of the sheep and cattle to H2798
1Sa 24:10 urged me to kill you, but I **s** you; I said, H2571
2Sa 21: 7 The king **s** Mephibosheth son of Jonathan H2798
2Ki 23:18 So *they* **s** his bones and those of the H4880
Job 21:30 that the wicked **are s** from the day of H3104
Ps 30: 3 *you* **s** me from going down to the pit. H2649
Isa 57: 1 are taken away to be **s from** evil. H4946+7156
Jer 38:17 your life *will be* **s** and this city will not be H2649
Jer 38:20 go well with you, and your life *will be* **s**. H2649
Eze 6:12 who survives and **is s** will die of famine. H5915
Eze 13:19 have died and *have* **s** those who should H2649
Da 5:19 wanted to spare, *he* **s**; those he wanted A10262
Ac 27:21 then *you would have* **s** *yourselves* this *G3045*

SPARES (3) [SPARE]

Est 4:11 the gold scepter to them and **s** *their* **lives**. H2649
Pr 13:24 *Whoever* **s** the rod hates their children H3104
Mal 3:17 as a father **has compassion and s** his son H2798

SPARING (4) [SPARE]

Ge 19:19 shown great kindness to me in **s** my life. H2649
Jos 11:11 not **s** anyone that breathed H3855
Jos 11:14 not **s** anyone that breathed. H8636
Pr 21:26 more, but the righteous give without **s**. H3104

SPARINGLY (2) [SPARE]

2Co 9: 6 Whoever sows **s** will also reap sparingly *G5768*
2Co 9: 6 Whoever sows sparingly will also reap **s** *G5768*

SPARK (2) [SPARKS]

Isa 1:31 man will become tinder and his work a **s**; H5773
Jas 3: 5 a great forest is set on fire *by* a small **s**. *G4786*

SPARKLE (1) [SPARKLED, SPARKLES, SPARKLING]

Zec 9:16 *They will* **s** in his land like jewels in a H5824

SPARKLED (2) [SPARKLE]

Eze 1:16 They **s** like topaz, and all four looked H6524
Eze 10: 9 of the cherubim; the wheels **s** like topaz. H6524

SPARKLES (1) [SPARKLE]

Pr 23:31 it is red, when *it* **s** in the cup, when H5989+6524

SPARKLING (2) [SPARKLE]

Isa 54:12 your gates of **s jewels**, and all your H74+734
Eze 1:22 something like a vault, **s** like crystal, and H6524

SPARKS (2) [SPARK]

Job 5: 7 to trouble as surely as **s** fly upward. H1201+8404
Job 41:19 stream from its mouth; **s** *of* fire shoot out. H3958

SPARROW (2) [SPARROWS]

Ps 84: 3 Even the **s** has found a home, and the H7606
Pr 26: 2 Like a fluttering **s** or a darting swallow, an H7606

SPARROWS (5) [SPARROW]

Hos 11:11 from Egypt, trembling like **s**, from Assyria, H7606
Mt 10:29 Are not two **s** sold for a penny? Yet not *G5141*
Mt 10:31 you are worth more *than* many **s**. *G5141*
Lk 12: 6 Are not five **s** sold for two pennies? Yet not *G5141*
Lk 12: 7 you are worth more than many **s**. *G5141*

SPATTERED (3)

Lev 6:27 if any of the blood **is s** on a garment H5684
2Ki 9:33 some of her blood **s** the wall and the H5684
Isa 63: 3 their blood **s** my garments, and I H5684

SPEAK (314) [SPEAKER, SPEAKING, SPEAKS, SPOKE, SPOKEN, SPOKESMAN, SPOKESMEN]

Ge 18:27 I have been so bold as to **s** to the Lord, H1819
Ge 18:30 "May the Lord not be angry, but *let me* **s**. H1819
Ge 18:31 I have been so bold as to **s** to the Lord, H1819
Ge 18:32 not be angry, but *let me* **s** just once more. H1819
Ge 19:21 I will not overthrow the town *you* **s** *of*. H1819
Ge 34:20 gate of their city *to* **s** to the men of their H1819
Ge 37: 4 him and could not **s** a kind *word to* him. H1819
Ge 44:18 my lord, *let* me **s** a word to my lord. H1819
Ge 46:31 "I will go up and **s** to Pharaoh and will H5583
Ge 50: 4 favor in your eyes, **s** to Pharaoh for me. H1819
Ex 4:12 I will help you **s** and will teach you what H7023
Ex 4:14 I know he *can* **s well**. He is already H1819+1819
Ex 4:15 *You shall* **s** to him and put words in his H1819
Ex 4:15 will help both of you **s** and will teach you H7023
Ex 4:16 He *will* **s** to the people for you, and it will H1819
Ex 5:23 since I went to Pharaoh to **s** in your name, H1819
Ex 6:12 listen to me, since I **s** with faltering lips?" NDT
Ex 6:30 to the LORD, "Since I **s** with faltering lips, NDT
Ex 19: 6 are the words *you are to* **s** to the Israelites H1819
Ex 19: 7 words the LORD had commanded him to **s**. NDT
Ex 20:19 "**S** to us yourself and we will listen. H1819
Ex 20:19 But *do* not *have* God **s** to us or we will die." H1819
Ex 29:42 There I will meet you and **s** to you; H1819
Ex 33:11 The LORD *would* **s** to Moses face to face, H1819
Ex 34:34 entered the LORD's presence to **s** with him, H1819
Ex 34:35 face until he went in to **s** with the LORD. H1819
Lev 1: 2 "**S** to the Israelites and say to them H1819
Lev 5: 1 sins because *they do* not **s up** when they H5583
Lev 15: 2 "**S** to the Israelites and say to them H1819
Lev 17: 2 "**S** to Aaron and his sons and to all the H1819
Lev 18: 2 "**S** to the Israelites and say to them: 'I am H1819
Lev 19: 2 "**S** to the entire assembly of Israel and say H1819
Lev 21: 1 LORD said to Moses, "**S** to the priests, the H606
Lev 22:18 "**S** to Aaron and his sons and to all the H1819
Lev 23: 2 "**S** to the Israelites and say to them H1819
Lev 23:10 "**S** to the Israelites and say to them H1819
Lev 25: 2 "**S** to the Israelites and say to them H1819
Lev 27: 2 "**S** to the Israelites and say to them: 'If H1819
Nu 5:12 "**S** to the Israelites and say to them: 'If a H1819
Nu 6: 2 "**S** to the Israelites and say to them: 'If a H1819
Nu 7:89 the tent of meeting to **s** with the LORD, H1819
Nu 8: 2 "**S** to Aaron and say to him, 'When you set H1819
Nu 11:17 I will come down and **s** with you there H1819
Nu 12: 6 to them in visions, *I* **s** to them in dreams. H1819
Nu 12: 8 With him *I* **s** face to face, clearly and not H1819
Nu 12: 8 you not afraid to **s** against my servant H1819
Nu 15: 2 "**S** to the Israelites and say to them: 'After H1819
Nu 15:18 "**S** to the Israelites and say to them H1819
Nu 15:38 "**S** to the Israelites and say to them H1819
Nu 17: 2 "**S** to the Israelites and get twelve staffs H1819
Nu 18:26 "**S** to the Levites and say to them: 'When H1819
Nu 20: 8 **S** to that rock before their eyes and it will H1819
Nu 22:35 with the men, but **s** only what I tell you." H1819
Nu 22:38 *I must* **s** only what God puts in my mouth." H1819
Nu 23:12 "Must I not **s** what the LORD puts in my H1819
Nu 23:19 *Does* he **s** and then not act H606
Nu 33:51 "**S** to the Israelites and say to them H1819
Nu 35:10 "**S** to the Israelites and say to them H1819
Dt 3:26 "*Do* not **s** to me anymore about this H1819
Dt 18:20 who presumes to **s** in my name anything I H1819
Dt 31:28 so that *I can* **s** these words in their H1819
Dt 32: 1 you heavens, and *I will* **s**; hear, you earth, H1819
Jdg 19:30 We must do something! So **s up**!" H1819
Jdg 20: 7 **s up** and tell me what you have decided H2035
1Sa 2: 3 so proudly or *let* your mouth **s** such H3655
1Sa 3: 9 if he calls you, say, '**S**, LORD, for your H1819
1Sa 3:10 Then Samuel said, "**S**, for your servant is H1819
1Sa 17:29 said David. "Can't I even **s**?" H1821
1Sa 18:22 "**S** to David privately and say, 'Look, the H1819
1Sa 19: 3 I'll **s** to him about you and will tell you H1819
1Sa 25:24 my lord, and *let* me **s** to you; hear what H1819
2Sa 3:27 chamber, as if to **s** with him privately. H1819
2Sa 13:13 Please **s** to the king; he will not keep me H1819
2Sa 14: 3 go to the king and **s** these words to him." H1819
2Sa 14:12 "*Let* your servant **s** a word to my lord the H1819
2Sa 14:12 to my lord the king." "**S**," he replied. H1819
2Sa 14:15 servant thought, '*I will* **s** to the king H1819
2Sa 14:18 "*Let* my lord the king **s**," the H1819
2Sa 19:43 we the first to **s** *of* bringing back our king H1821
2Sa 20:16 Tell Joab to come here so *I can* **s** to him." H1819
1Ki 2:18 replied, "I *will* **s** to the king for you." H1819
1Ki 2:19 to King Solomon to **s** to him for Adonijah, H1819
1Ki 22:13 word agree with theirs, and **s** favorably." H1819
1Ki 22:24 go when he went from me to **s** *to* you?" H1819
2Ki 4:13 *Can* we **s** on your behalf to the king or the H1819
2Ki 6:12 the very words *you* **s** in your bedroom." H1819
2Ki 18:20 might for war—but *you* **s** only empty words. H606
2Ki 18:26 "Please **s** to your servants in Aramaic H1819
2Ki 18:26 Don't **s** to us in Hebrew in the hearing of H1819
2Ki 22:14 Asaiah went *to* **s** to the prophet H1819
2Ch 18:12 word agree with theirs, and **s** favorably." H1819
2Ch 18:23 go when he went from me to **s** *to* you?" H1819
2Ch 34:22 sent with him went *to* **s** to the prophet H1819
Ne 13:24 did not know how to **s** the language of H1819
Est 6: 4 the palace to **s** to the king *about* impaling H606
Job 7:11 *I will* **s out** in the anguish of my spirit H1819
Job 9:35 Then *I would* **s up** without fear of him, but H1819
Job 10: 1 my complaint and **s out** in the bitterness H1819
Job 11: 5 how I wish that God *would* **s**, that he H1819
Job 12: 8 **s** to the earth, and it will teach you, or H8488
Job 13: 3 But I desire *to* **s** to the Almighty and to H1819
Job 13: 7 *Will you* **s** wickedly on God's behalf? Will H1819
Job 13: 7 *Will you* **s** deceitfully for him? H1819
Job 13:13 "Keep silent and *let* me **s**; then let come H1819
Job 13:22 I will answer, or *let me* **s**, and you reply to H1819
Job 16: 4 I also *could* **s** like you, if you were in my H1819
Job 16: 6 "Yet if *I* **s**, my pain is not relieved; and if I H1819
Job 21: 3 Bear with me while I **s**, and after I have H1819
Job 32: 7 I thought, 'Age *should* **s**; advanced years H1819
Job 32:20 *I must* **s** and find relief; I must open my H1819
Job 33: 3 my lips sincerely **s** what I know. H4910
Job 33:14 For God *does* **s**—now one way, now H1819
Job 33:16 *he may* **s** *in* their ears and terrify them H1655
Job 33:31 listen to me; be silent, and I *will* **s**. H1819
Job 33:32 answer me; **s up**, for I want to vindicate H1819
Job 37:20 Should he be told that *I want to* **s**? Would H1819
Job 41: 3 *Will it* **s** to you **with** gentle **words**? H1819
Job 41:12 "*I will* not **fail to s** *of* Leviathan's limbs, H3087
Job 42: 4 'Listen now, and I *will* **s**; I will question H1819
Ps 17:10 and their mouths **s** with arrogance. H1819
Ps 28: 3 *who* **s** cordially with their neighbors but H1819
Ps 31:18 contempt they **s** arrogantly against H1819
Ps 35:20 *They do* not **s** peaceably, but devise false H1819
Ps 37:30 wisdom, and their tongues **s** what is just. H1819
Ps 38:13 like the mute, *who* cannot **s**; H7337+7023
Ps 40: 5 *were I to* **s** and tell of your deeds H5583
Ps 40:10 *I* **s** *of* your faithfulness and your saving help H606
Ps 49: 3 My mouth *will* **s** words of wisdom; the H1819
Ps 50: 7 my people, and *I will* **s**; I will testify H1819
Ps 58: 1 *Do you* rulers indeed **s** justly? Do you H1819
Ps 71:10 For my enemies **s** against me; those who H606
Ps 73: 8 They scoff, and **s** with malice; with H1819
Ps 75: 5 against heaven; *do* not **s** so defiantly. H1819
Ps 77: 4 eyes from closing; I was too troubled *to* **s**. H1819
Ps 109:20 to my accusers, to those *who* **s** evil of me. H1819
Ps 115: 5 mouths, but cannot **s**, eyes, but cannot H1819
Ps 119:46 *I will* **s** of your statutes before kings and H1819
Ps 120: 7 peace; but when *I* **s**, they are for war. H1819
Ps 135:16 mouths, but cannot **s**, eyes, but cannot H1819
Ps 139:20 *They* **s** *of* you with evil intent; your H606
Ps 145: 5 *They* **s** *of* the glorious splendor of your H1819
Ps 145:11 glory of your kingdom and **s** *of* your might, H1819
Ps 145:21 My mouth *will* **s** in praise of the LORD. H1819
Pr 6:22 when you awake, they *will* **s** *to* you. H8488
Pr 8: 6 I open my lips to **s** what is right. NDT
Pr 13: 3 those *who* **s rashly** will come to H7316+8557
Pr 16:10 The lips of a king **s** as an oracle, and his NDT
Pr 18:17 In a lawsuit the first to **s** seems right, until NDT
Pr 20:15 but **lips** *that* **s** knowledge are a rare jewel. AIT
Pr 22:21 you to be honest and to **s** the truth, H609
Pr 23: 9 *Do* not **s** to fools, for they will scorn your H1819
Pr 23:16 will rejoice when your lips **s** what is right. H1819
Pr 31: 8 **S up** for those who cannot speak H7337+7023
Pr 31: 8 up for **those who cannot s** *for themselves*, H522
Pr 31: 9 **S up** and judge fairly; defend the H7337+7023
Ecc 3: 7 a time to be silent and a time to **s**, H1819
Isa 8:20 If *anyone does* not **s** according to this word H606
Isa 19:18 five cities in Egypt *will* **s** the language of H1819
Isa 28:11 strange tongues God *will* **s** to this people, H1819
Isa 29: 4 Brought low, *you will* **s** from the ground H1819
Isa 32: 6 For fools **s** folly, their hearts are bent on H1819
Isa 33:15 who walk righteously and **s** what is right, H1819
Isa 36: 5 might for war—but *you* **s** only empty words. H606
Isa 36:11 "Please **s** to your servants in Aramaic H1819
Isa 36:11 Don't **s** to us in Hebrew in the hearing of H1819
Isa 40: 2 **S** tenderly *to* Jerusalem, and proclaim to H1819
Isa 41: 1 Let them come forward and **s**; let us meet H1819
Isa 44: 9 **Those who** would **s up for** them are blind H6332
Isa 45:19 the LORD, **s** the truth; I declare what is right H1819
Jer 1: 6 "I do not know how *to* **s**; I am too young." H1819
Jer 5: 5 So I will go to the leaders and **s** *to* them H1819
Jer 6:10 To whom *can I* **s** and give warning? Who H1819
Jer 9: 8 With their mouths *they all* **s** cordially to H1819
Jer 10: 5 their idols cannot **s**; they must be carried H1819
Jer 12: 1 Yet *I would* **s** with you about your justice H1819
Jer 12: 6 not trust them, though *they* **s** well of you. H1819
Jer 14:17 "**S** this word to them: " 'Let my eyes H606
Jer 20: 8 Whenever *I* **s**, I cry out proclaiming H1819
Jer 20: 9 his word or **s** anymore in his name H1819
Jer 23:16 *They* **s** visions from their own minds, not H1819
Jer 23:21 their message; *I did* not **s** to them, yet H1819
Jer 23:28 but *let* the one who has my word **s** it H1819
Jer 26: 2 LORD's house and **s** to all the people of H1819
Jer 26: 7 heard Jeremiah **s** these words in the H1819
Jer 26:15 has sent me to you to **s** all these words in H1819
Jer 31:20 Though I often **s** against him, I still H1819
Jer 32: 4 and *will* **s** *with* him face to face and see H1819
Jer 34: 3 and he *will* **s** *with* you face to face. H1819
Jer 48:27 your head in scorn whenever you **s** of her? H1821
La 3:37 Who *can* **s** and have it happen if the Lord H606
Eze 2: 1 stand up on your feet and *I will* **s** to you." H1819
Eze 2: 7 *You must* **s** my words to them, whether H1819
Eze 3: 1 then go and **s** to the people of Israel." H1819
Eze 3: 4 people of Israel and **s** my words to them. H1819
Eze 3:10 take to heart all the words *I* **s** to you. H1819
Eze 3:11 to your people in exile and **s** to them. H1819
Eze 3:17 so hear the word I **s** and give them H4946+7023
Eze 3:18 not warn them or **s out** to dissuade them H1819
Eze 3:22 out to the plain, and there *I will* **s** to you." H1819
Eze 3:27 when I **s** to you, I will open your mouth H1819
Eze 12:25 I the LORD *will* **s** what I will, and it shall H1819
Eze 14: 4 Therefore **s** to them and tell them, 'This is H1819
Eze 20: 3 **s** to the elders of Israel and say to them H1819
Eze 20:27 **s** to the people of Israel and say to them H1819
Eze 24:27 *you will* **s** with him and will no longer be H1819
Eze 29: 3 **S** to him and say: 'This is what the H1819
Eze 33: 2 of man, **s** to your people and say to them: H1819
Eze 33: 7 so hear the word I **s** and give them H4946+7023
Eze 33: 8 and *you do* not **s out** to dissuade them H1819
Eze 33:31 Their mouths **s** *of* love, but their hearts H6913
Eze 36: 6 I **s** in my jealous wrath because you have H1819

Da 7:25 *He will* **s** against the Most High A10425+10418
Da 10:11 carefully the words I *am about to* **s** to you, H1819
Da 10:16 I opened my mouth and *began to* **s**. H1819
Da 10:19 said, "**S**, my lord, since you H1819
Hos 1: 2 When the LORD began *to* **s** through Hosea H1819
Hos 2:14 into the wilderness and **s** tenderly *to* her. H1819
Hos 7:13 redeem them but they **s** about me falsely. H1819
Mic 6:12 liars and their tongues **s** deceitfully. H928+7023
Hab 2:18 own creation; he makes idols that **cannot s**. H522
Hag 2: 2 "**S** to Zerubbabel son of Shealtiel, governor H606
Zec 8:16 **S** the truth to each other, and render true H1819
Zec 10: 2 The idols **s** deceitfully, diviners see H1819
Mt 10:27 tell you in the dark, **s** in the daylight; what G3306
Mt 11: 7 Jesus began *to* **s** to the crowd about John: G3306
Mt 12:46 stood outside, wanting *to* **s** to him. G3281
Mt 12:47 are standing outside, wanting *to* **s** to you." G3281
Mt 13:10 "Why *do you* **s** to the people in parables?" G3281
Mt 13:13 This is why *I* **s** to them in parables G3281
Mt 17:25 into the house, Jesus was the first *to* **s**. G3306
Mk 1:34 not let the demons **s** because they knew G3281
Mk 3:23 over to him and *began to* **s** to them in G3306
Mk 7:35 was loosened and *he began to* **s** plainly. G3281
Mk 7:37 makes the deaf hear and the mute **s**." G3281
Mk 12: 1 Jesus then began *to* **s** to them in parables G3281
Mk 16:17 out demons; *they will* **s** in new tongues; G3281
Lk 1:19 I have been sent *to* **s** to you and to tell G3281
Lk 1:20 silent and not able *to* **s** until the day this G3281
Lk 1:22 he came out, he could not **s** to them. G3281
Lk 1:22 signs to them but remained **unable to s**. G3273
Lk 1:64 set free, and *he began to* **s**, praising God. G3281
Lk 4:41 them and would not allow them *to* **s**, G3281
Lk 7:24 Jesus began *to* **s** to the crowd about John: G3306
Lk 8:10 but to others I **s** in parables, so that, NDT
Lk 12: 1 Jesus began *to* **s** first to his disciples G3306
Lk 20:21 we know that *you* **s** and teach what is G3306
Jn 3:11 truly I tell you, *we* **s** *of* what we know, and G3281
Jn 3:12 will you believe if *I* **s** of heavenly things? G3306
Jn 7:17 from God or whether I **s** on my own. G3281
Jn 8:28 on my own but **s** just what the Father G3281
Jn 9:21 He is of age; *he will* **s** for himself." G3281
Jn 12:49 For I *did* not **s** on my own, but the Father G3281
Jn 14:10 words I say to you *I do* not **s** on my own G3281
Jn 16:13 *He will* not **s** on his own; he will speak G3281
Jn 16:13 on his own; *he will* **s** only what he hears G3281
Jn 19:10 "*Do you* refuse *to* **s** to me?" Pilate said G3281
Ac 1: 4 promised, which *you have* **heard** me **s** *about*. AIT
Ac 2: 4 Spirit and began *to* **s** in other tongues as G3281
Ac 4:17 we must warn them *to* **s** no longer to G3281
Ac 4:18 commanded them not *to* **s** or teach at all G5779
Ac 4:29 enable your servants *to* **s** your word with G3281
Ac 5:40 ordered them not *to* **s** in the name of G3281
Ac 6:11 heard Stephen **s** blasphemous words G3281
Ac 8:33 Who *can* **s of** his descendants G1455
Ac 10:34 Then Peter **began to s** G487+3836+5125+3306
Ac 11:15 "As I began *to* **s**, the Holy Spirit came on G3281
Ac 11:20 to Antioch and *began to* **s** to Greeks also, G3281
Ac 13:15 of exhortation for the people, *please* **s**." G3306
Ac 13:42 invited them *to* **s** *further* about these G3281
Ac 13:46 "We had to **s** the word of God to you first G3281
Ac 16:13 sat down and *began to* **s** to the women G3281
Ac 18:14 Just as Paul was about to **s** G487+3836+5125
Ac 18:26 He began *to* **s boldly** in the synagogue G4245
Ac 21:37 "*Do you* **s** Greek?" he replied. G1182
Ac 21:39 Please let me **s** to the people." G3281
Ac 22: 2 they heard *him* **s to** them in Aramaic G4715
Ac 23: 5 '*Do* not **s** evil about the ruler of your G3306
Ac 24:10 When the governor motioned for him *to* **s** G3306
Ac 25:18 When his accusers got up to **s**, they did not NDT
Ac 26: 1 "You have permission *to* **s** for yourself." G3306
Ac 26:26 these things, and *I can* **s** freely to him. G3281
Ro 3: 4 right when you **s** and prevail when you G3364
Ro 9: 1 *I* **s** the truth in Christ—I am not lying, my G3306
Ro 15:18 I will not venture *to* **s** of anything except G3281
1Co 2: 6 *We do*, however, **s** a message of wisdom G3281
1Co 2:13 This is what *we* **s**, not in words taught us G3281
1Co 10:15 *I* **s** to sensible people; judge for yourselves G3306
1Co 12:30 gifts of healing? *Do* all **s** in tongues? Do G3281
1Co 13: 1 If *I* **s** in the tongues of men or of angels G3281
1Co 14: 2 in a tongue *does* not **s** to people but to G3281
1Co 14: 5 like every one of you *to* **s** in tongues, G3281
1Co 14: 6 if I come to you and **s** in tongues, what G3281
1Co 14: 9 Unless *you* **s** intelligible words with your G1443
1Co 14:18 I thank God *that I* **s** in tongues more than G3281
1Co 14:19 church I would rather **s** five intelligible G3281
1Co 14:21 lips of foreigners *I will* **s** to this people, G3281
1Co 14:27 at the most three—should **s**, one at a time, NDT
1Co 14:28 in the church and **s** to himself and to God. G3281
1Co 14:29 Two or three prophets *should* **s**, and the G3281
1Co 14:34 They are not allowed *to* **s**, but must be in G3281
1Co 14:35 a woman *to* **s** in the church. G3281
2Co 2:17 in Christ *we* **s** before God with sincerity G3281
2Co 4:13 of faith, we also believe and therefore **s**, G3281
2Co 6:13 As a fair exchange—*I* **s** as to my children G3306
Eph 4:25 put off falsehood and **s** truthfully to your G3281
Eph 6:19 that whenever I **s**, words may G489+3836+5125
1Th 2: 4 *we* **s** as those approved by God to be G3281
Heb 6: 9 Even though *we* **s** like this, dear friends G3281
Jas 1:19 slow to **s** and slow to become angry G3281
Jas 2:12 **S** and act as those who are going to be G3281
1Pe 3:16 those *who* **s maliciously against** your G2092
1Jn 4: 5 world and therefore **s** from the viewpoint G3281
3Jn 12 We also **s well of** him, and you know that G3455
Rev 13:15 that the image *could* **s** and cause all who G3281

SPEAKER (6) [SPEAK]

Ac 14:12 Hermes because he was the chief **s**. G3364
1Co 14:11 I am a foreigner *to* the **s**, and the speaker G3281
1Co 14:11 speaker, and the **s** is a foreigner to me. G3281
1Co 14:28 the **s** should keep quiet in the church and NDT
1Co 14:30 is sitting down, the first **s** *should* **stop**. G4967
2Co 11: 6 I may indeed be untrained *as* a **s**, but I do G3364

SPEAKING (100) [SPEAK]

Ge 11: 6 "If as one people **s** the same language they NDT
Ge 17:22 When he had finished **s** with Abraham H1819
Ge 18:33 the LORD had finished **s** with Abraham, H1819
Ge 45:12 that it is really I who *am* **s** to you. H1819
Ex 16:10 While Aaron *was* **s** to the whole Israelite H1819
Ex 19: 9 people will hear me **s** with you and will H1819
Ex 31:18 the LORD finished **s** to Moses on Mount H1819
Ex 34:33 When Moses finished **s** to them, he put a H1819
Nu 7:89 he heard the voice **s** to him from between H1819
Dt 4:33 heard the voice of God **s** out of fire, H1819
Dt 5:26 the voice of the living God **s** out of fire, H1819
Dt 20: 9 the officers have finished **s** to the army, H1819
Jdg 15:17 When he finished **s**, he threw away the H1819
Ru 2:13 at ease by **s kindly** *to* your H1819+6584+4213
1Sa 17:28 brother, heard him **s** with the men, he H1819
2Sa 13:36 As he finished **s**, the king's sons came in H1819
1Ki 1:22 While she *was* still **s** with the king H1819
1Ki 1:42 Even as he *was* **s**, Jonathan son of H1819
2Ch 25:16 While he was still **s**, the king said to him H1819
Job 1:16 While he *was* still **s**, another messenger H1819
Job 1:17 While he *was* still **s**, another messenger H1819
Job 1:18 While he *was* still **s**, yet another H1819
Job 4: 2 be impatient? But who can keep from **s**? H4863
Job 29: 9 men refrained from **s** and covered their H4863
Job 32: 4 had waited before **s** to Job because they H1821
Ps 52: 3 falsehood rather than **s** the truth. H1819
Isa 58:13 not doing as you please or **s** idle words, H1819
Isa 65:24 answer; while they *are* still **s** I will hear. H1819
Jer 36: 2 from the time *I began* **s** to you in the H1819
Eze 1:28 facedown, and I heard the voice of *one* **s**. H1819
Eze 2: 2 me to my feet, and I heard *him* **s** to me. H1819
Eze 43: 6 I heard *someone* **s** to me from inside the H1819
Da 7:11 of the boastful words the horn *was* **s**. A10425
Da 8:13 Then I heard a holy one **s**, and another H1819
Da 8:18 While he *was* **s** to me, I was in a deep H1819
Da 9:20 While I *was* **s** and praying, confessing my H1819
Da 10: 9 Then I heard him **s**, and as I H7754+1821
Zec 1:14 Then the angel who *was* **s** to me said H1819
Zec 1:19 I asked the angel who *was* **s** to me, "What H1819
Zec 2: 3 the angel who *was* **s** to me was leaving, H1819
Zec 5: 5 Then the angel who *was* **s** to me came H1819
Zec 5:10 I asked the angel who *was* **s** to me. H1819
Zec 6: 4 I asked the angel who *was* **s** to me, "What H1819
Mt 10:20 it will not be you **s**, but the Spirit of G3281
Mt 10:20 the Spirit of your Father **s** through you. G3281
Mt 15:31 were amazed when they saw the mute **s**, G3281
Mt 17: 5 *While* he *was* still **s**, a bright cloud G3281
Mt 22:43 is it then that David, *s* **by** the Spirit, calls him AIT
Mt 26:47 While he *was still* **s**, Judas, one of the G3281
Mk 5:35 *While* Jesus *was* still **s**, some people G3281
Mk 12:36 David himself, **s** by the Holy Spirit, declared NDT
Mk 13:11 for it is not you **s**, but the Holy Spirit. G3281
Mk 14:43 Just as he *was* **s**, Judas, one of the G3281
Lk 5: 4 When he had finished **s**, he said to G3281
Lk 8:49 *While* Jesus *was* still **s**, someone came G3281
Lk 9:34 *While* he *was* **s**, a cloud appeared and G3306
Lk 11:37 When Jesus *had finished* **s**, a Pharisee G3281
Lk 22:47 *While* he *was* still **s** a crowd came up G3281
Lk 22:60 Just as he *was* **s**, the rooster G3281
Jn 4:26 declared, "I, the *one* **s** to you—I am he." G3281
Jn 7:26 Here *he is*, **s** publicly, and they are not G3281
Jn 9:37 in fact, he is the *one* **s** with you. G3281
Jn 11:13 Jesus *had been* **s** of his death, but his G3306
Jn 12:36 *When he had finished* **s**, Jesus left and G3281
Jn 16:25 "*Though I have been* **s** figuratively, a time G3281
Jn 16:29 "Now *you are* **s** clearly and without figures G3281
Ac 2: 7 "Aren't all these who are **s** Galileans? G3281
Ac 4: 1 John *while* they *were* **s** to the people G3281
Ac 4:20 we cannot help **s** about what we have G3281
Ac 6:13 never stops **s** against this holy G3281+4839
Ac 9:28 **s boldly** in the name of the Lord. G4245
Ac 10:44 *While* Peter *was* still **s** these words, the G3281
Ac 10:46 For they heard them **s** in tongues and G3281
Ac 14: 3 time there, **s boldly** for the Lord, who G4245
Ac 14: 9 He listened to Paul *as he was* **s**. G3281
Ac 18: 9 not be afraid; *keep on* **s**, do not be silent. G3281
Ac 20: 2 **s** many words of **encouragement** to the G4151
Ac 20:36 *When* Paul *had finished* **s**, he knelt down G3306
Ac 22: 9 the voice of him *who was* **s** to me. G3281
Ac 22:18 saw the Lord **s** to me. 'Quick!' he said G3306
Ro 7: 1 for *I am* **s** to those who know the law G3281
1Co 12: 3 know that no one *who is* **s** by the Spirit of G3281
1Co 12:10 to another **s in** different kinds of **tongues** G1185
1Co 14: 9 You will just be **s** into the air. G3281
1Co 14:39 prophesy, and do not forbid **s** in tongues. G3281
2Co 10:10 his **s** amounts to nothing. G3364
2Co 11:21 to boast about—*I am* **s** as a fool—I also G3306
2Co 12: 6 be a fool, because *I would be* **s** the truth. G3306
2Co 12:19 *We have been* **s** in the sight of God as G3281
2Co 13: 3 proof *that* Christ *is* **s** through me. G3281
Eph 4:15 **s the truth** in love, we will grow to G238
Eph 5:19 **s** to one another with psalms, hymns, and G3281
1Th 2:16 effort to keep us from **s** to the Gentiles so G3281
Heb 1: 7 In **s** of the angels he says, "He makes his NDT
Heb 2: 5 the world to come, about which *we are* **s**. G3281
Heb 11:19 and so **in a manner of s** he did G1877+4130
Heb 12:19 to such a voice **s words** that those who AIT
2Pe 3:16 all his letters, **s** in them of these matters. G3281
Rev 1:12 around to see the voice that *was* **s** to me. G3281
Rev 4: 1 I had first heard **s** to me like a trumpet G3281

SPEAKS (49) [SPEAK]

Ex 33:11 Moses face to face, as one **s** to a friend. H1819
Dt 5:24 a person can live even if God **s** with them. H1819
Dt 18:19 my words that the prophet **s** in my name. H1819
Dt 18:20 a prophet who **s** in the name of other H1819
1Sa 16:18 He **s** well and is a fine-looking man H1821
Job 9: 7 He **s** to the sun and it does not shine; he H606
Job 34:35 'Job **s** without knowledge; his words lack H1819
Job 36:15 *he* **s** *to* them in their affliction. H1655+265
Ps 15: 2 righteous, *who* **s** the truth from their heart H1819
Ps 41: 6 comes to see me, *he* **s** falsely, while his H1819
Ps 50: 1 **s** and summons the earth from the rising H1819
Ps 101: 7 no *one who* **s** falsely will stand in my H1819
Pr 8: 7 My mouth **s** what is true, for my lips detest H2047
Pr 16:13 they value the *one who* **s** what is right. H1819
Pr 22:11 pure heart and who **s** with grace will have H8557
Pr 29:20 Do you see someone who **s** in haste H1821
Pr 31:26 She **s** with wisdom, and faithful H7337+7023
Isa 9:17 ungodly and wicked, every mouth **s** folly. H1819
Jer 9: 5 deceives friend, and no *one* **s** the truth. H1819
Jer 9: 8 tongue is a deadly arrow; *it* **s** deceitfully. H1819
Eze 10: 5 like the voice of God Almighty when he **s**. H1819
Hos 4:12 and a diviner's rod **s** to them. H5583
Hab 2: 3 *it* **s** of the end and will not prove false. H7032
Mt 12:32 Anyone *who* **s** a word against the Son of G3306
Mt 12:32 anyone *who* **s** against the Holy Spirit G3306
Mt 12:34 For the mouth **s** what the heart is full of. G3281
Lk 5:21 "Who is this fellow who **s** blasphemy? G3281
Lk 6:26 Woe to you when everyone **s** well of you G3306
Lk 6:45 For the mouth **s** what the heart is full of. G3281
Lk 12:10 And everyone who **s** a word against the G3306
Jn 3:31 to the earth, and **s** as one from the earth. G3281
Jn 3:34 whom God has sent **s** the words of God, G3281
Jn 7:18 Whoever **s** on their own does so to gain G3281
Jn 8:44 When he lies, *he* **s** his native language G3281
Ro 4: 6 same thing when he **s** of the blessedness of NDT
1Co 14: 2 For anyone *who* **s** in a tongue does not G3281
1Co 14: 3 one who prophesies **s** to people for their G3281
1Co 14: 4 Anyone *who* **s** in a tongue edifies G3281
1Co 14: 5 is greater than the *one who* **s** in tongues, G3281
1Co 14:13 this reason the *one who* **s** in a tongue G3281
1Co 14:23 together and everyone **s** in tongues, G3281
1Co 14:27 If anyone **s** in a tongue, two—or at the G3281
Heb 11: 4 And by faith Abel still **s**, even though he G3281
Heb 12:24 blood *that* **s** a better **word** than the blood G3281
Heb 12:25 See to it that you do not refuse him *who* **s**. G3281
Jas 4:11 Anyone *who* **s against** a brother or sister G2895
Jas 4:11 judges them **s against** the law and G2895
1Pe 4:11 If anyone **s**, they should do so as one who G3281
1Pe 4:11 do so as one who **s** the very words of God. NDT

SPEAR (47) [SPEARHEAD, SPEARMEN, SPEARS]

Nu 25: 7 he left the assembly, took a **s** in his hand H8242
Nu 25: 8 He drove the **s** into both of them, right NDT
Jdg 5: 8 not a shield or **s** was seen among H8242
1Sa 13:22 Jonathan had a sword or **s** in his hand; H2851
1Sa 17: 7 His **s** shaft was like a weaver's rod, and its H2851
1Sa 17:45 against me with sword and **s** and javelin, H2851
1Sa 17:47 it is not by sword or **s** that the LORD saves; H2851
1Sa 18:10 he usually did. Saul had a **s** in his hand H2851
1Sa 19: 9 sitting in his house with his **s** in his hand. H2851
1Sa 19:10 Saul tried to pin him to the wall with his **s** H2851
1Sa 19:10 him as Saul drove the **s** into the wall. H2851
1Sa 20:33 But Saul hurled his **s** at him to kill him H2851
1Sa 21: 8 "Don't you have a **s** or a sword here? H2851
1Sa 22: 6 Saul was seated, **s** in hand, under the H2851
1Sa 26: 7 the camp with his **s** stuck in the ground H2851
1Sa 26: 8 him to the ground with one thrust of the **s**; H2851
1Sa 26:11 Now get the **s** and water jug that are near H2851
1Sa 26:12 So David took the **s** and water jug near H2851
1Sa 26:16 Where are the king's **s** and water jug that H2851
1Sa 26:22 "Here is the king's **s**," David answered H2851
2Sa 1: 6 leaning on his **s**, with the chariots H2851
2Sa 2:23 the butt of his **s** into Asahel's stomach, H2851
2Sa 2:23 the **s** came out through his back. H2851
2Sa 21:19 who had a **s** with a shaft like a weaver's H2851
2Sa 23: 7 uses a tool of iron or the shaft of a **s**; H2851
2Sa 23: 8 he raised his **s** against eight hundred H2851
2Sa 23:18 He raised his **s** against three hundred H2851
2Sa 23:21 the Egyptian had a **s** in his hand, H2851
2Sa 23:21 He snatched the **s** from the Egyptian's H2851
2Sa 23:21 hand and killed him with his own **s**. H2851
1Ch 11:11 he raised his **s** against three hundred H2851
1Ch 11:20 He raised his **s** against three hundred H2851
1Ch 11:23 the Egyptian had a **s** like a weaver's rod H2851
1Ch 11:23 He snatched the **s** from the Egyptian's H2851
1Ch 11:23 hand and killed him with his own **s**. H2851
1Ch 12: 8 able to handle the shield and **s**. H8242
1Ch 12:24 carrying shield and **s**—6,800 armed for H8242
1Ch 20: 5 who had a **s** with a shaft like a weaver's H2851
2Ch 25: 5 able to handle the **s** and shield. H8242
Job 39:23 along with the flashing **s** and lance. H2851

Job 41:26 does the **s** or the dart or the javelin. H2851
Ps 35: 3 Brandish **s** and javelin against those who H2851
Ps 46: 9 He breaks the bow and shatters the **s**; he H2851
Jer 6:23 They are armed with bow and **s**; they are H3959
Hab 3:11 at the lightning of your flashing **s**. H2851
Hab 3:14 With his own **s** you pierced his head H4751
Jn 19:34 the soldiers pierced Jesus' side *with* a **s**, *G3365*

SPEARHEAD (1) [SPEAR]
2Sa 21:16 whose bronze **s** weighed three hundred H7802

SPEARMEN (1) [SPEAR]
Ac 23:23 two hundred **s** to go to Caesarea at *G1287*

SPEARS (21) [SPEAR]
1Sa 13:19 the Hebrews will make swords or **s**!" H2851
1Ki 18:28 slashed themselves with swords and **s**, H8242
2Ki 11:10 the commanders the **s** and shields that H2851
1Ch 12:34 with 37,000 men carrying shields and **s**; H2851
2Ch 11:12 He put shields and **s** in all the cities, and H8242
2Ch 14: 8 equipped with large shields and with **s** H8242
2Ch 23: 9 of a hundred the **s** and the large and H2851
2Ch 26:14 provided shields, **s**, helmets, coats of H8242
Ne 4:13 by families, with their swords, **s** and bows. H8242
Ne 4:16 while the other half were equipped with **s**, H8242
Ne 4:21 the work with half the men holding **s**, H8242
Job 41: 7 with harpoons or its head with fishing **s**? H7528
Ps 57: 4 men whose teeth are **s** and arrows, whose H2851
Isa 2: 4 their **s** into pruning hooks. H2851
Jer 46: 4 Polish your **s**, put on your armor! H8242
Jer 50:42 They are armed with bows and **s**; they are H3959
Eze 39: 9 the bows and arrows, the war clubs and **s**. H8242
Joel 3:10 into swords and your pruning hooks into **s**. H8242
Mic 4: 3 their **s** into pruning hooks. H2851
Na 2: 3 the **s of juniper** are brandished. H1360
Na 3: 3 flashing swords and glittering **s**! H2851

SPECIAL (41) [ESPECIALLY]
Ge 47: 6 know of any among them with **s ability**, H2657
Lev 22:21 to the LORD to **fulfill** a **s vow** or as a H7098+5624
Lev 23:36 It is the **closing s assembly**; do no regular H6809
Lev 27: 2 **makes a s vow to dedicate** a H7098+5624
Nu 6: 2 woman *wants* to **make a s vow**, H5623+7098
Nu 15: 3 for **s vows** or freewill offerings or H7098+5624
Nu 15: 8 a **s vow** or a fellowship offering H7098+5624
Nu 29:35 day hold a **closing s assembly** and do no H6809
Dt 12: 6 your tithes and **s gifts**, what you H9556+3338
Dt 12:11 your tithes and **s gifts**, and all the H9556+3338
Dt 12:17 your freewill offerings or **s gifts**. H9556+3338
Jos 15:19 replied, "Do me a **s favor**. Since you have H1388
Jdg 1:15 replied, "Do me a **s favor**. Since you have H1388
2Sa 13: 6 and **make** some **s bread** in my H4221+4223
2Sa 16: 6 troops and the **s guard** were on David's H1475
1Ki 1: 8 Rei and David's **s guard** did not join H1475
1Ki 1:10 Benaiah or the **s guard** or his brother H1475
1Ch 9:29 as well as the **s flour** and wine, and the H6159
1Ch 23:29 the **s flour** for the grain offerings H6159
Est 1:14 Media *who* **had s access to the** H8011+7156
Est 2: 9 with her beauty treatments and **s food**. H4950
Jer 13:21 you those you cultivated as your **s** allies? H8031
Eze 44:30 of all your **s gifts** will belong to the H9556
Eze 45:13 " 'This is the **s gift** you are to offer: a sixth H9556
Eze 45:16 to give this **s offering** to the prince in H9556
Eze 48: 8 the **portion** you are to present **as a s gift**. H9556
Eze 48: 9 "The **s portion** you are to offer to the LORD H9556
Eze 48:12 It will be a **s gift** to them from the sacred H9557
Eze 48:20 **As a s gift** *you will* **set aside** the sacred H8123
Jn 19:31 the next day was to be a **s** Sabbath. *G3489*
Ro 9:21 some pottery for **s purposes** and some *G5507*
Ro 14: 6 Whoever **regards** one day **as s** does so to *G5858*
1Co 12:23 are less honorable we treat with **s** honor. *G4358*
1Co 12:23 unpresentable are treated with **s** modesty, *G4358*
1Co 12:24 our presentable parts need no **s** treatment. NDT
Gal 4:10 You are observing **s days** and months and AIT
2Th 3:14 **Take s note** *of* anyone who does not obey *G4957*
2Ti 2:20 some are for **s purposes** and some for *G5507*
2Ti 2:21 latter will be instruments for **s purposes**, *G5507*
Jas 2: 3 *If you* **show s attention** to the man wearing *G2098*
1Pe 2: 9 God's **s possession**, that you may *G4348*

SPECIFIC (1) [SPECIFY]
Nu 4:32 each man the **s things** he is to carry H5466+3998

SPECIFICATIONS (2) [SPECIFY]
1Ki 6:38 finished in all its details according to its **s**. H5477
2Ch 4: 7 according to the **s** *for* them and placed H5477

SPECIFIED (10) [SPECIFY]
Lev 27: 8 the vow is too poor to pay the **s amount**, H6886
Nu 1:17 these men whose names *had* **been s**, H5918
Nu 29: 6 grain offerings and drink offerings as **s**. H5477
Nu 29:18 drink offerings according to the number **s**. H5477
Nu 29:21 drink offerings according to the number **s**. H5477
Nu 29:24 drink offerings according to the number **s**. H5477
Nu 29:27 drink offerings according to the number **s**. H5477
Nu 29:30 drink offerings according to the number **s**. H5477
Nu 29:33 drink offerings according to the number **s**. H5477
Nu 29:37 drink offerings according to the number **s**. H5477

SPECIFY (1) [SPECIFIC, SPECIFICATIONS, SPECIFIED, SPECIFYING]
1Ki 5: 9 them as rafts by sea to the place *you* **s**. H8938

SPECIFYING (1) [SPECIFY]
Ac 25:27 on to Rome without **s** the charges against *G4955*

SPECK (6) [SPECKLED]
Mt 7: 3 you look at the **s of sawdust** in your *G2847*
Mt 7: 4 'Let me take the **s** out of your eye,' when *G2847*
Mt 7: 5 clearly to remove the **s** from your brother's *G2847*
Lk 6:41 you look at the **s of sawdust** in your *G2847*
Lk 6:42 let me take the **s** out of your eye,' when *G2847*
Lk 6:42 clearly to remove the **s** from your brother's *G2847*

SPECKLED (10) [SPECK]
Ge 30:32 from them every **s** or spotted sheep, H5923
Ge 30:32 lamb and every spotted or **s** goat. H5923
Ge 30:33 in my possession that is not **s** or spotted, H5923
Ge 30:35 all the **s** or spotted female goats H5923
Ge 30:39 young that were streaked or **s** or spotted. H5923
Ge 31: 8 If he said, 'The **s** *ones* will be your wages,' H5923
Ge 31: 8 then all the flocks gave birth to **s** *young* H5923
Ge 31:10 with the flock were streaked, **s** or spotted. H5923
Ge 31:12 flock are streaked, **s** or spotted, for I have H5923
Jer 12: 9 become to me like a **s** bird of prey that H7380

SPECTACLE (4)
Eze 28:17 the earth; I made a **s** of you before kings. H8019
Na 3: 6 you with contempt and make you a **s**. H8024
1Co 4: 9 We have been made a **s** to the whole *G2519*
Col 2:15 authorities, *he* **made a** public **s** of them *G1258*

SPECULATIONS (1)
1Ti 1: 4 things promote **controversial s** rather than *G1700*

SPED (1) [SPEED]
Eze 1:14 The creatures **s** back and **forth** like flashes H8351

SPEECH (31) [SPEECHES]
Ge 11: 1 had one language and a common **s**. H1821
Ex 4:10 I am slow of **s** and tongue." H7023
Ps 19: 2 Day after day they pour forth **s**; night after H608
Ps 19: 3 They have no **s**, they use no words; no H608
Pr 1:21 at the city gate *she* **makes** her **s**: H606+609
Pr 5: 3 and her **s** is smoother than oil; H2674
Pr 8:13 arrogance, evil behavior and perverse **s**. H7023
Pr 12: 6 the **s** *of* the upright rescues them. H7023
Pr 26:25 Though their **s** is charming, do not H7754
Ecc 5: 3 many words mark the **s** *of* a fool. H7754
Isa 18: 2 an aggressive nation of **strange s** H7743+7743
Isa 18: 7 an aggressive nation of **strange s** H7743+7743
Isa 29: 4 your **s** will mumble out of the dust. H614
Isa 29: 4 out of the dust your **s** will whisper. H614
Isa 33:19 people whose **s** is obscure, whose H8557
Jer 5:15 *whose* **s** you do not understand. H4537+1819
Eze 3: 5 a people of obscure **s** and strange H8557
Eze 3: 6 peoples of obscure **s** and strange H8557
Mk 9:17 by a spirit that has **robbed** him **of s**. *G228*
Jn 10: 6 Jesus used this **figure of s**, but the *G4231*
Jn 16:29 speaking clearly and without **figures of s**. *G4231*
Ac 5:40 His *s* **persuaded** *them*. They called the AIT
Ac 7:22 was powerful in **s** and action. *G3364*
1Co 1: 5 with all kinds of **s** and with all knowledge *G3364*
2Co 6: 7 in truthful **s** and in the power of God; with *G3364*
2Co 8: 7 in **s**, in knowledge, in *G3364*
1Ti 4:12 set an example for the believers in **s** *G3364*
Titus 2: 8 soundness *of* **s** that cannot be *G3364*
1Pe 3:10 from evil and their lips from deceitful **s**. *G3281*
2Pe 2:16 an animal **without s**—who spoke with *G936*
1Jn 3:18 love with words or **s** but with actions and *G1185*

SPEECHES (4) [SPEECH]
Job 15: 3 useless words, with **s** that have no value? H4863
Job 16: 3 Will your long-winded **s** never end? What H1821
Job 16: 4 *I could* **make fine s** against H2488+928+4863
Job 18: 2 "When will you end these **s**? Be sensible H4863

SPEECHLESS (3)
Da 10:15 with my face toward the ground and *was* **s**. H519
Mt 22:12 wedding clothes, friend?' The man *was* **s**. *G5821*
Ac 9: 7 The men traveling with Saul stood there **s**; *G1917*

SPEED (2) [SPED, SPEED, SPEEDS]
Ro 9:28 his sentence on earth with **s** and finality." *G5335*
2Pe 3:12 to the day of God and **s** its coming. *G5067*

SPEEDILY (3) [SPEED]
Isa 5:26 Here they come, swiftly and **s**! H7824
Isa 51: 5 My righteousness draws near **s**, my H8088
Joel 3: 4 I will swiftly and **s** return on your own H4559

SPEEDS (1) [SPEED]
Isa 16: 5 judging seeks justice and **s** the cause of H4542

SPELL (1) [SPELLS]
Rev 18:23 By your **magic s** all the nations were led *G5758*

SPELLS (4) [SPELL]
Dt 18:11 or **casts s**, or who is a medium or H2489+2490
Isa 47: 9 your many sorceries and all your potent **s**. H2490
Isa 47:12 with your **magic s** and with your many H2490
Mic 5:12 witchcraft and you will no longer **cast s**. H6726

SPELT (3)
Ex 9:32 The wheat and **s**, however, were not H4081
Isa 28:25 barley in its plot, and **s** in its field? H4081
Eze 4: 9 millet and **s**; put them in a storage H4081

SPEND (42) [SPENDING, SPENT]
Ge 19: 2 your feet and **s the night** and then go on H4328
Ge 19: 2 "*we will* **s the night** in the square. H4328
Ge 24:23 your father's house for us to **s the night**?" H4328
Ge 24:25 as well as room for you to **s the night**." H4328
Nu 22: 8 "**S** the night here," Balaam said to them H4328
Nu 22:19 Now **s** the night here so that I can find out H3782
Dt 32:23 on them and **s** my arrows against them H3983
Jdg 16: 1 *He* **went in to s the night with** her. H995+448
Jdg 19: 9 almost evening. **S the night** here; the day H4328
Jdg 19:11 this city of the Jebusites and **s the night**." H4328
Jdg 19:13 Ramah and **s the night** in one of those H4328
Jdg 19:15 There they stopped to **s the night**. H4328
Jdg 19:20 Only don't **s the night** in the square." H4328
Jdg 20: 4 to Gibeah in Benjamin to **s the night**. H4328
2Sa 17: 8 *he will* not **s the night** with the troops. H4328
2Sa 17:16 '*Do* not **s** the night at the fords in the H4328
1Ch 9:27 *They would* **s the night** stationed around H4328
Ne 13:21 "Why *do* you **s the night** by the wall? H4328
Job 21:13 *They* **s** their years in prosperity and go H3983
Job 24: 7 clothes, *they* **s the night** naked; they have H4328
Job 31:32 no stranger *had to* **s the night** in the street H4328
Job 36:11 *they will* **s** the rest of their days in H3983
Ps 25:13 They *will* **s** *their* **days** in prosperity, and H4328
Ps 37:18 The blameless **s** their days under the LORD's NDT
Pr 31: 3 *Do* not **s** your strength on women, your H5989
SS 7:11 *let us* **s the night** in the villages. H4328
Isa 55: 2 Why **s** money on what is not bread, and H9202
Isa 58:10 if *you* **s** yourselves in behalf of the H7049
Isa 65: 4 the graves and **s** *their* **nights** keeping H4328
Eze 7: 8 my wrath on you and **s** my anger against H3983
Eze 20: 8 my wrath on them and **s** my anger against H3983
Eze 20:21 my wrath on them and **s** my anger against H3983
Joel 1:13 **s the night** in sackcloth, you who H4328
Mk 6:37 Are we to go and **s** that much on bread and *G60*
Lk 21:37 he went out *to* **s the night** on the hill called *G887*
Ac 18:20 When they asked him *to* **s** more time with *G3531*
Ac 28:14 who invited us *to* **s** a week with them. *G2152*
1Co 16: 6 a while, or even **s the winter**, so that you *G4199*
1Co 16: 7 I hope *to* **s** some time with you *G2152*
2Co 12:15 *will* very gladly **s** for you **everything** *I* **have** *G1251*
Jas 4: 3 that *you may* **s** what you get on your *G1251*
Jas 4:13 to this or that city, **s** a year there, carry on *G4472*

SPENDING (5) [SPEND]
Ac 15:33 *After* **s** some time there, they were sent off *G4472*
Ac 18:23 *After* **s** some time in Antioch, Paul set out *G4472*
Ac 20:16 Ephesus to avoid **s time** in the province of *G5990*
Ac 25: 6 *After* **s** eight or ten days with them, Festus *G1417*
Ac 25:14 Since *they were* **s** many days there, Festus *G1417*

SPENT (33) [SPEND]
Ge 24:54 him ate and drank and **s the night** there. H4328
Ge 31:54 they had eaten, *they* **s the night** there. H4328
Ge 32:13 *He* **s** the night there, and from what he H4328
Ge 32:21 but *he* himself **s** the night in the camp. H4328
Lev 26:20 Your strength *will be* **s** in vain, because H9462
Dt 1:46 many days—all the time *you* **s** there. H3782
Jos 6:11 returned to camp and **s the night** there. H4328
Jos 8: 9 Joshua **s** that night with the people. H4328
Jdg 18: 2 house of Micah, where *they* **s the night**. H4328
2Sa 12:16 He fasted and **s the nights** lying in H4328
2Sa 14: 2 woman *who has* **s** many days **grieving** for the AIT
1Ki 5:14 so that *they* **s** one month in Lebanon and H2118
1Ki 6:38 *He had* **s** seven years **building** it. AIT
1Ki 19: 9 There he went into a cave and **s the night** H4328
2Ki 12:13 temple **was** not **s for making** silver H6913+4946
1Ch 12:39 *The men* **s** three days there with David H2118
Ne 9: 3 and *s* another quarter *in* **confession** and in AIT
Ne 13:20 kinds of goods **s the night** outside H4328
Pr 5:11 when your flesh and body *are* **s**. H3983
Isa 49: 4 *I have* **s** my strength for nothing at all. H3983
Eze 5:13 And when I *have* **s** my wrath on them H3983
Da 6:18 his palace and **s the night** without A10102
Mt 21:17 of the city to Bethany, where *he* **s the night**. *G887*
Mk 5:26 of many doctors and *had* **s** all she had, *G1251*
Lk 6:12 and **s the night** praying to God. *G1639+1381*
Lk 15:14 *After* he *had* **s** everything, there was a *G1251*
Jn 1:39 was staying, and *they* **s** that day with him. *G3531*
Jn 3:22 where *he* **s some time** with them, and *G1417*
Ac 9:19 Saul **s** several days with the disciples in *G1181*
Ac 14: 3 So Paul and Barnabas **s** considerable time *G1417*
Ac 17:21 who lived there **s** *their* **time** doing nothing *G2320*
2Co 11:25 *I* **s** a night and a day in the open sea *G4472*
1Pe 4: 3 For *you have* **s** enough time **in the past** *G4216*

SPEW (2) [SPEWED]
Ps 59: 7 See what *they* **s** from their mouths—the H5580
Jer 51:44 and **make** him **s out** what he H3655+4946+7023

SPEWED (3) [SPEW]
Jer 51:34 with our delicacies, and then *has* **s** us **out**. H5615
Rev 12:15 his mouth the serpent **s** water like a river, *G965*
Rev 12:16 that the dragon *had* **s** out of his mouth. *G965*

SPHERE (3)
2Co 10:13 to the **s of service** God *G3586+3836+2834*
2Co 10:13 assigned to us, a **s** that also includes you. *G3586*
2Co 10:15 our **s of activity** among you will greatly *G2834*

SPICE (4) [SPICED, SPICES]
SS 4:10 of your perfume more than any **s**! H1411

SS 5: 1 I have gathered my myrrh with my s. H1411
SS 5:13 are like beds of s yielding perfume. H1411
Rev 18:13 cargoes of cinnamon and s, of incense G319

SPICE-LADEN (1) [LOAD]

SS 8:14 like a young stag on the s mountains. H1411

SPICED (1) [SPICE]

SS 8: 2 I would give you s wine to drink, the H8380

SPICES (32) [SPICE]

Ge 37:25 Their camels were loaded with s, balm H5780
Ge 43:11 a little honey, some s and myrrh, some H5780
Ex 25: 6 s for the anointing oil and for the fragrant H1411
Ex 30:23 "Take the following fine s: 500 shekels of H1411
Ex 30:34 to Moses, "Take fragrant s—gum resin, H6160
Ex 35: 8 s for the anointing oil and for the fragrant H1411
Ex 35:28 They also brought s and olive oil for the H1411
1Ki 10: 2 with camels carrying s, large quantities of H1411
1Ki 10:10 large quantities of s, and precious stones. H1411
1Ki 10:10 again were so many s brought in as those H1411
1Ki 10:25 weapons and s, and horses and H1411
2Ki 20:13 the gold, the s and the fine olive oil—his H1411
1Ch 9:29 and the olive oil, incense and s. H1411
1Ch 9:30 of the priests took care of mixing the s. H1411
2Ch 9: 1 with camels carrying s, large quantities of H1411
2Ch 9: 9 large quantities of s, and precious stones. H1411
2Ch 9: 9 never been such s as those the queen H1411
2Ch 9:24 weapons and s, and horses and H1411
2Ch 16:14 a bier covered with s and various blended H1411
2Ch 32:27 his precious stones, s, shields and all H1411
Ps 75: 8 a cup full of foaming wine mixed with s; H5008
SS 3: 6 made from all the s of the merchant? H86
SS 4:14 with myrrh and aloes and all the finest s. H1411
SS 6: 2 garden, to the beds of s, to browse in the H1411
Isa 39: 2 the gold, the s, the fine olive oil H1411
Eze 24:10 mixing in the s; and let the bones H5350
Eze 27:22 of all kinds of s and precious stones, H1411
Mt 23:23 You give a tenth of your s—mint, dill and NDT
Mk 16: 1 Salome bought s so that they might go G808
Lk 23:56 went home and prepared s and perfumes. G808
Lk 24: 1 the women took the s they had prepared G808
Jn 19:40 wrapped it, with the s, in strips of linen. G808

SPIDER'S (2)

Job 8:14 in is fragile; what they rely on is a s web. H6571
Isa 59: 5 hatch the eggs of vipers and spin a s web. H6571

SPIED (4) [SPY]

Jos 6:22 to the two men who had s out the land, H8078
Jos 7: 2 So the men went up and s out Ai. H8078
Jdg 18:14 the five men who had s out the land of H8078
Jdg 18:17 The five men who had s out the land went H8078

SPIES (17) [SPY]

Ge 42: 9 about them and said to them, "You are s! H8078
Ge 42:11 Your servants are honest men, not s." H8078
Ge 42:14 "It is just as I told you: You are s! H8078
Ge 42:16 then as surely as Pharaoh lives, you are s!" H8078
Ge 42:31 'We are honest men; we are not s. H8078
Ge 42:34 know that you are not s but honest men. H8078
Nu 21:32 After Moses had sent s to Jazer, the H8078
Jos 2: 1 Nun secretly sent two s from Shittim. H408+8078
Jos 2: 7 out in pursuit of the s on the road that H2157S
Jos 2: 8 Before the s lay down for the night, she H2156S
Jos 6:17 be spared, because she hid the s we sent. H4855
Jos 6:25 men Joshua had sent as s to Jericho— H8078
Jdg 1:24 the s saw a man coming out of the city H9068
Lk 20:20 on him, they sent s, who pretended to be G1588
Lk 20:21 So the s questioned him: "Teacher, we know NDT
Heb 11:31 because she welcomed the s, was not G2946
Jas 2:25 she gave lodging to the s and sent them off G34

SPIKENARD (KJV) NARD, PERFUME

SPILLED (4) [SPILLS]

Ge 38: 9 he s his semen on the ground to keep H8845
2Sa 14:14 Like water s on the ground, which cannot H5599
2Sa 20:10 his intestines s out on the ground. H9161
Ac 1:18 burst open and all his intestines s out. G1772

SPILLS (1) [SPILLED]

Job 16:13 my kidneys and s my gall on the ground. H9161

SPIN (3) [SPINDLE, SPUN]

Isa 59: 5 the eggs of vipers and s a spider's web. H755
Mt 6:28 of the field grow. They do not labor or s. G3756
Lk 12:27 They do not labor or s. Yet I tell you, G3756

SPINDLE (1) [SPIN]

Pr 31:19 distaff and grasps the s with her fingers. H7134

SPIRIT (535) [SPIRIT'S, SPIRIT-TAUGHT, SPIRITIST, SPIRITISTS, SPIRITS, SPIRITUAL]

Ge 1: 2 the S of God was hovering over the H8120
Ge 6: 3 "My S will not contend with humans H8120
Ge 41:38 this man, one in whom is the s of God?" H8120
Ge 45:27 the s of their father Jacob revived. H8120
Ex 31: 3 I have filled him with the S of God H8120
Ex 35:31 he has filled him with the S of God H8120
Nu 11:17 some of the power of the S that is on you H8120
Nu 11:25 some of the power of the S that was on H8120
Nu 11:25 When the S rested on them, they H8120
Nu 11:26 Yet the S also rested on them, and they H8120
Nu 11:29 that the LORD would put his S on them!" H8120
Nu 14:24 Caleb has a different s and follows me H8120
Nu 24: 2 tribe by tribe, the S of God came on him H8120
Nu 27:18 a man in whom is the s of leadership H8120
Dt 2:30 God had made his s stubborn and his H8120
Dt 34: 9 was filled with the s of wisdom because H8120
Jdg 3:10 The S of the LORD came on him, so that he H8120
Jdg 6:34 Then the S of the LORD came on Gideon H8120
Jdg 11:29 Then the S of the LORD came on Jephthah H8120
Jdg 13:25 the S of the LORD began to stir him H8120
Jdg 14: 6 The S of the LORD came powerfully upon H8120
Jdg 14:19 Then the S of the LORD came powerfully H8120
Jdg 15:14 The S of the LORD came powerfully upon H8120
1Sa 10: 6 The S of the LORD will come powerfully H8120
1Sa 10:10 the S of God came powerfully upon him H8120
1Sa 11: 6 the S of God came powerfully upon him H8120
1Sa 16:13 from that day on the S of the LORD came H8120
1Sa 16:14 Now the S of the LORD had departed from H8120
1Sa 16:14 an evil s from the LORD tormented him H8120
1Sa 16:15 an evil s from God is tormenting you. H8120
1Sa 16:16 when the evil s from God comes on you, H8120
1Sa 16:23 Whenever the s from God came on Saul H8120
1Sa 16:23 and the evil s would leave him. H8120
1Sa 18: 1 Jonathan became one in s with David H5883
1Sa 18:10 next day an evil s from God came H8120
1Sa 19: 9 But an evil s from the LORD came on Saul H8120
1Sa 19:20 the S of God came on Saul's men H8120
1Sa 19:23 But the S of God came even on him, and H8120
1Sa 28: 8 "Consult a s for me," he said, "and bring H200
1Sa 30: 6 one was bitter in s because of his sons H5883
2Sa 23: 2 "The S of the LORD spoke through me; his H8120
1Ki 18:12 know where the S of the LORD may carry H8120
1Ki 22:21 a s came forward, stood before the H8120
1Ki 22:22 be a deceiving s in the mouths of all H8120
1Ki 22:23 has put a deceiving s in the mouths of all H8120
1Ki 22:24 way did the s from the LORD go when H8120
2Ki 2: 9 "Let me inherit a double portion of your s," H8120
2Ki 2:15 "The s of Elijah is resting on Elisha." H8120
2Ki 2:16 Perhaps the S of the LORD has picked him H8120
2Ki 5:26 "Was not my s with you when the man H4213
1Ch 5:26 stirred up the s of Pul king of Assyria H8120
1Ch 12:18 Then the S came on Amasai, chief of the H8120
1Ch 28:12 plans of all that the S had put in his mind H8120
2Ch 15: 1 The S of God came on Azariah son of H8120
2Ch 18:20 a s came forward, stood before the H8120
2Ch 18:21 be a deceiving s in the mouths of all H8120
2Ch 18:22 has put a deceiving s in the mouths of H8120
2Ch 18:23 way did the s from the LORD go when H8120
2Ch 20:14 Then the S of the LORD came on Jahaziel H8120
2Ch 24:20 Then the S of God came on Zechariah H8120
Ne 9:20 You gave your good S to instruct them H8120
Ne 9:30 By your S you warned them through your H8120
Job 4:15 A s glided past my face, and the hair on H8120
Job 6: 4 are in me, my s drinks in their poison H8120
Job 7:11 I will speak out in the anguish of my s, H8120
Job 10:12 in your providence watched over my s. H8120
Job 17: 1 My s is broken, my days are cut short, the H8120
Job 26: 4 And whose s spoke from your mouth? H5972
Job 31:39 payment or broken the s of its tenants, H5883
Job 32: 8 But it is the s in a person, the breath of H8120
Job 32:18 and the s within me compels me; H8120
Job 33: 4 The S of God has made me; the breath of H8120
Job 34:14 he withdrew his s and breath, H8120
Ps 31: 5 Into your hands I commit my s; deliver me, H8120
Ps 32: 2 against them and in whose s is no deceit. H8120
Ps 34:18 saves those who are crushed in s. H8120
Ps 51:10 and renew a steadfast s within me. H8120
Ps 51:11 presence or take your Holy S from me. H8120
Ps 51:12 of your salvation and grant me a willing s, H8120
Ps 51:17 is a broken s; a broken and H8120
Ps 73:21 heart was grieved and my s embittered, H4000
Ps 76:12 He breaks the s of rulers; he is feared by H8120
Ps 77: 3 I meditated, and my s grew faint. H8120
Ps 77: 6 My heart meditated and my s asked: H8120
Ps 104:30 When you send your S, they are created H8120
Ps 106:33 they rebelled against the S of God H8120
Ps 139: 7 Where can I go from your S? Where can I H8120
Ps 142: 3 When my s grows faint within me, it is H8120
Ps 143: 4 So my s grows faint within me; my heart H8120
Ps 143: 7 me quickly, LORD; my s fails. Do not hide H8120
Ps 143:10 may your good S lead me on level ground H8120
Ps 146: 4 When their s departs, they return to the H8120
Pr 15: 4 but a perverse tongue crushes the s. H8120
Pr 15:13 face cheerful, but heartache crushes the s. H8120
Pr 16:18 destruction, a haughty s before a fall. H8120
Pr 16:19 Better to be lowly in s along with the H8120
Pr 17:22 a crushed s dries up the bones. H8120
Pr 18:14 The human s can endure in sickness, but H8120
Pr 18:14 in sickness, but a crushed s who can bear? H8120
Pr 20:27 The human s is the lamp of the LORD that H5972
Pr 25:13 he refreshes the s of his master. H5883
Pr 29:23 person low, but the lowly in s gain honor. H8120
Ecc 3:21 knows if the human s rises upward and if H8120
Ecc 3:21 upward and if the s of the animal goes H8120
Ecc 7: 9 Do not be quickly provoked in your s, for H8120
Ecc 12: 7 the s returns to God who gave it. H8120
Isa 4: 4 from Jerusalem by a s of judgment and a H8120
Isa 4: 4 by a spirit of judgment and a s of fire. H8120
Isa 11: 2 The S of the LORD will rest on him—the H8120
Isa 11: 2 the S of wisdom and of understanding H8120
Isa 11: 2 the S of counsel and of might, the Spirit H8120
Isa 11: 2 the S of the knowledge and fear of the H8120
Isa 19:14 has poured into them a s of dizziness; H8120
Isa 26: 9 in the morning my s longs for you. H8120
Isa 28: 6 He will be a s of justice to the one who H8120
Isa 29:24 who are wayward in s will gain H8120
Isa 30: 1 not by my S, heaping sin upon sin; H8120
Isa 31: 3 not God; their horses are flesh and not s. H8120
Isa 32:15 till the S is poured on us from on high H8120
Isa 34:16 his S will gather them together. H8120
Isa 38:16 and my s finds life in them too. H8120
Isa 40:13 Who can fathom the S of the LORD, or H8120
Isa 42: 1 I will put my S on him, and he will H8120
Isa 44: 3 I will pour out my S on your offspring, and H8120
Isa 48:16 LORD has sent me, endowed with his S. H8120
Isa 54: 6 a wife deserted and distressed in s— H8120
Isa 57:15 the one who is contrite and lowly in s, H8120
Isa 57:15 to revive the s of the lowly and to revive H8120
Isa 59:21 "My S, who is on you, will not depart from H8120
Isa 61: 1 The S of the Sovereign LORD is on me H8120
Isa 61: 3 of praise instead of a s of despair. H8120
Isa 63:10 Yet they rebelled and grieved his Holy S H8120
Isa 63:11 is he who set his Holy S among them, H8120
Isa 63:14 they were given rest by the S of the LORD. H8120
Isa 65:14 of heart and wail in brokenness of s. H8120
Isa 66: 2 those who are humble and contrite in s H8120
Jer 51: 1 I will stir up the s of a destroyer against H8120
La 1:16 to comfort me, no one to restore my s. H5883
Eze 1:12 Wherever the s would go, they would go H8120
Eze 1:20 Wherever the s would go, they would go H8120
Eze 1:20 because the s of the living creatures was H8120
Eze 1:21 because the s of the living creatures was H8120
Eze 2: 2 the S came into me and raised me to my H8120
Eze 3:12 Then the S lifted me up, and I heard H8120
Eze 3:14 The S then lifted me up and took me away H8120
Eze 3:14 in bitterness and in the anger of my s, H8120
Eze 3:24 Then the S came into me and raised me H8120
Eze 8: 3 The S lifted me up between earth and H8120
Eze 10:17 because the s of the living creatures was H8120
Eze 11: 1 Then the S lifted me up and brought me H8120
Eze 11: 5 Then the S of the LORD came on me, and H8120
Eze 11:19 undivided heart and put a new s in them; H8120
Eze 11:24 The S lifted me up and brought me to the H8120
Eze 11:24 in the vision given by the S of God. H8120
Eze 13: 3 who follow their own s and have seen H8120
Eze 18:31 get a new heart and a new s. H8120
Eze 21: 7 every s will become faint and every leg H8120
Eze 36:26 you a new heart and put a new s in you; H8120
Eze 36:27 And I will put my S in you and move you H8120
Eze 37: 1 me out by the S of the LORD and set me H8120
Eze 37:14 I will put my S in you and you will live H8120
Eze 39:29 I will pour out my S on the people of H8120
Eze 43: 5 Then the S lifted me up and brought me H8120
Da 4: 8 the s of the holy gods is in him. A10658
Da 4: 9 I know that the s of the holy gods is in A10658
Da 4:18 because the s of the holy gods is in you." A10658
Da 5:11 who has the s of the holy gods in A10658
Da 5:14 heard that the s of the gods is in you A10658
Da 7:15 was troubled in s, and the visions that A10658
Hos 4:12 A s of prostitution leads them astray; they H8120
Hos 5: 4 A s of prostitution is in their heart; they do H8120
Joel 2:28 I will pour out my S on all people. H8120
Joel 2:29 I will pour out my S in those days. H8120
Mic 3: 8 with the S of the LORD, and with H8120
Hag 1:14 LORD stirred up the s of Zerubbabel son of H8120
Hag 1:14 the s of Joshua son of Jozadak H8120
Hag 1:14 the s of the whole remnant of the H8120
Hag 2: 5 And my S remains among you H8120
Zec 4: 6 by power, but by my S,' says the LORD H8120
Zec 6: 8 have given my S rest in the land of H8120
Zec 7:12 had sent by his S through the earlier H8120
Zec 12: 1 who forms the human s within a person, H8120
Zec 12:10 of Jerusalem a s of grace and H8120
Zec 13: 2 prophets and the s of impurity from the H8120
Mal 2:15 You belong to him in body and s. H8120
Mt 1:18 found to be pregnant through the Holy S. G4460
Mt 1:20 is conceived in her is from the Holy S. G4460
Mt 3:11 will baptize you with the Holy S and fire. G4460
Mt 3:16 he saw the S of God descending like G4460
Mt 4: 1 Jesus was led by the S into the wilderness G4460
Mt 5: 3 "Blessed are the poor in s, for theirs is the G4460
Mt 10:20 the S of your Father speaking through G4460
Mt 12:18 I will put my S on him, and he will G4460
Mt 12:28 But if it is by the S of God that I drive out G4460
Mt 12:31 blasphemy against the S will not be G4460
Mt 12:32 against the Holy S will not be forgiven, G4460
Mt 12:43 "When an impure s comes out of a G4460
Mt 22:43 speaking by the S, calls him 'Lord'? G4460
Mt 26:41 into temptation. The s is willing, but the G4460
Mt 27:50 again in a loud voice, he gave up his s. G4460
Mt 28:19 Father and of the Son and of the Holy S, G4460
Mk 1: 8 he will baptize you with the Holy S." G4460
Mk 1:10 torn open and the S descending on him G4460
Mk 1:12 At once the S sent him out into the G4460
Mk 1:23 was possessed by an impure s cried out, G4460
Mk 1:26 The impure s shook the man violently and G4460
Mk 2: 8 Jesus knew in his s that this was what G4460
Mk 3:29 against the Holy S will never be forgiven; G4460
Mk 3:30 they were saying, "He has an impure s." G4460
Mk 5: 2 man with an impure s came from the G4460
Mk 5: 8 "Come out of this man, you impure s!" G4460
Mk 7:25 by an impure s came and fell at his G4460
Mk 9:17 is possessed by a s that has robbed him G4460
Mk 9:18 I asked your disciples to drive out the s G899S

S

Mk 9:20 When the **s** saw Jesus, it immediately *G4460*
Mk 9:25 to the scene, he rebuked the impure **s**. *G4460*
Mk 9:25 "You deaf and mute **s**," he said, "I *G4460*
Mk 9:26 The **s** shrieked, convulsed him violently NDT
Mk 12:36 himself, speaking by the Holy **S**, declared: *G4460*
Mk 13:11 it is not you speaking, but the Holy **S**. *G4460*
Mk 14:38 into temptation. The **s** is willing, but the *G4460*
Lk 1:15 filled with the Holy **S** even before he is *G4460*
Lk 1:17 the Lord, in the **s** and power of Elijah, to *G4460*
Lk 1:35 answered, "The Holy **S** will come on you *G4460*
Lk 1:41 Elizabeth was filled with the Holy **S**. *G4460*
Lk 1:47 my **s** rejoices in God my Savior, *G4460*
Lk 1:67 filled with the Holy **S** and prophesied: *G4460*
Lk 1:80 the child grew and became strong *in* **s**; *G4460*
Lk 2:25 of Israel, and the Holy **S** was on him. *G4460*
Lk 2:26 to him by the Holy **S** that he would not *G4460*
Lk 2:27 Moved by the **S**, he went into the temple *G4460*
Lk 3:16 will baptize you with the Holy **S** and fire. *G4460*
Lk 3:22 the Holy **S** descended on him in *G4460*
Lk 4: 1 full *of* the Holy **S**, left the Jordan *G4460*
Lk 4: 1 was led by the **S** into the wilderness, *G4460*
Lk 4:14 returned to Galilee in the power *of* the **S**, *G4460*
Lk 4:18 "The **S** of the Lord is on me, because he *G4460*
Lk 4:33 man possessed by a demon, an impure **s**. *G4460*
Lk 8:29 the impure **s** to come out of the *G4460*
Lk 8:55 Her **s** returned, and at once she stood up *G4460*
Lk 9:39 A **s** seizes him and he suddenly screams *G4460*
Lk 9:42 But Jesus rebuked the impure **s**, healed *G4460*
Lk 10:21 full of joy *through* the Holy **S**, said, *G4460*
Lk 11:13 give the Holy **S** to those who ask him *G4460*
Lk 11:24 "When an impure **s** comes out of a *G4460*
Lk 12:10 against the Holy **S** will not be forgiven. *G4460*
Lk 12:12 the Holy **S** will teach you at that time *G4460*
Lk 13:11 had been crippled *by* a **s** for eighteen *G4460*
Lk 23:46 "Father, into your hands I commit my **s**." *G4460*
Jn 1:32 "I saw the **S** come down from heaven as a *G4460*
Jn 1:33 on whom you see the **S** come down and *G4460*
Jn 1:33 the one who will baptize with the Holy **S**. *G4460*
Jn 3: 5 unless they are born of water and the **S**. *G4460*
Jn 3: 6 to flesh, but the **S** gives birth to spirit. *G4460*
Jn 3: 6 to flesh, but the Spirit gives birth to **s**. *G4460*
Jn 3: 8 So it is with everyone born of the **S**." *G4460*
Jn 3:34 for God gives the **S** without limit. *G4460*
Jn 4:23 worship the Father in the **S** and in truth, *G4460*
Jn 4:24 God is **s**, and his worshipers must worship *G4460*
Jn 4:24 must worship in the **S** and in truth. *G4460*
Jn 6:63 The **S** gives life; the flesh counts for *G4460*
Jn 6:63 to you—they are full of the **S** and life. *G4460*
Jn 7:39 By this he meant the **S**, whom those who *G4460*
Jn 7:39 Up to that time the **S** had not been given *G4460*
Jn 11:33 he was deeply moved *in* **s** and troubled. *G4460*
Jn 13:21 Jesus was troubled *in* **s** and testified *G4460*
Jn 14:17 the **S** of truth. The world cannot accept *G4460*
Jn 14:26 Advocate, the Holy **S**, whom the Father *G4460*
Jn 15:26 the **S** of truth who goes out from the Father *G4460*
Jn 16:13 But when he, the **S** of truth, comes, he will *G4460*
Jn 16:15 That is why I said the **S** will receive from me NDT
Jn 19:30 he bowed his head and gave up his **s**. *G4460*
Jn 20:22 on them and said, "Receive the Holy **S**. *G4460*
Ac 1: 2 through the Holy **S** to the apostles he had *G4460*
Ac 1: 5 days you will be baptized with the Holy **S**." *G4460*
Ac 1: 8 power when the Holy **S** comes on you; *G4460*
Ac 1:16 in which the Holy **S** spoke long ago *G4460*
Ac 2: 4 filled with the Holy **S** and began to speak *G4460*
Ac 2: 4 in other tongues as the **S** enabled them. *G4460*
Ac 2:17 I will pour out my **S** on all people. *G4460*
Ac 2:18 I will pour out my **S** in those days, and *G4460*
Ac 2:33 the promised Holy **S** and has poured out *G4460*
Ac 2:38 And you will receive the gift of the Holy **S**. *G4460*
Ac 4: 8 filled with the Holy **S**, said to them: *G4460*
Ac 4:25 spoke by the Holy **S** through the mouth of *G4460*
Ac 4:31 filled with the Holy **S** and spoke the word *G4460*
Ac 5: 3 you have lied *to* the Holy **S** and have kept *G4460*
Ac 5: 9 you conspire to test the **S** of the Lord? *G4460*
Ac 5:32 so is the Holy **S**, whom God has *G4460*
Ac 6: 3 are known to be full *of* the **S** and wisdom. *G4460*
Ac 6: 5 a man full of faith and *of* the Holy **S**; also *G4460*
Ac 6:10 the wisdom the **S** gave him as he spoke. *G4460*
Ac 7:51 You always resist the Holy **S**! *G4460*
Ac 7:55 Stephen, full *of* the Holy **S**, looked up to *G4460*
Ac 7:59 Stephen prayed, "Lord Jesus, receive my **s**." *G4460*
Ac 8:15 there that they might receive the Holy **S**, *G4460*
Ac 8:16 because the Holy **S** had not yet come on any NDT
Ac 8:17 on them, and they received the Holy **S**. *G4460*
Ac 8:18 Simon saw that the **S** was given at the *G4460*
Ac 8:19 I lay my hands may receive the Holy **S**." *G4460*
Ac 8:29 The **S** told Philip, "Go to that chariot and *G4460*
Ac 8:39 the **S** of the Lord suddenly took Philip *G4460*
Ac 9:17 see again and be filled with the Holy **S**." *G4460*
Ac 9:31 of the Lord and encouraged *by* the Holy **S**, *G4460*
Ac 10:19 the vision, the **S** said to him, "Simon, *G4460*
Ac 10:38 of Nazareth *with* the Holy **S** and power, *G4460*
Ac 10:44 the Holy **S** came on all who heard the *G4460*
Ac 10:45 that the gift *of* the Holy **S** had been *G4460*
Ac 10:47 have received the Holy **S** just as we have." *G4460*
Ac 11:12 The **S** told me to have no hesitation about *G4460*
Ac 11:15 the Holy **S** came on them as he had come *G4460*
Ac 11:16 you will be baptized with the Holy **S**. *G4460*
Ac 11:24 full of the Holy **S** and faith, and a *G4460*
Ac 11:28 up and through the **S** predicted that a *G4460*
Ac 13: 2 fasting, the Holy **S** said, "Set apart for *G4460*
Ac 13: 4 sent on their way by the Holy **S**, went *G4460*
Ac 13: 9 filled with the Holy **S**, looked straight at *G4460*
Ac 13:52 were filled with joy and with the Holy **S**. *G4460*
Ac 15: 8 them by giving the Holy **S** to them, *G4460*
Ac 15:28 seemed good *to* the Holy **S** and to us not *G4460*
Ac 16: 6 kept by the Holy **S** from preaching the *G4460*
Ac 16: 7 the **S** of Jesus would not allow them *G4460*
Ac 16:16 slave who had a **s** by which she predicted *G4460*
Ac 16:18 that he turned around and said *to* the **s**, *G4460*
Ac 16:18 At that moment the **s** left her. NDT
Ac 19: 2 receive the Holy **S** when you believed?" *G4460*
Ac 19: 2 not even heard that there is a Holy **S**." *G4460*
Ac 19: 6 on them, the Holy **S** came on them, and *G4460*
Ac 19:15 One day the evil **s** answered them, "Jesus *G4460*
Ac 19:16 who had the evil **s** jumped on them and *G4460*
Ac 20:22 compelled *by* the **S**, I am going to *G4460*
Ac 20:23 every city the Holy **S** warns me that prison *G4460*
Ac 20:28 of which the Holy **S** has made you *G4460*
Ac 21: 4 Through the **S** they urged Paul not to go *G4460*
Ac 21:11 said, "The Holy **S** says, 'In this way *G4460*
Ac 23: 9 "What if a **s** or an angel has spoken to *G4460*
Ac 28:25 "The Holy **S** spoke the truth to your *G4460*
Ro 1: 4 who through the **S** of holiness was *G4460*
Ro 1: 9 whom I serve in my **s** in preaching the *G4460*
Ro 2:29 of the heart, by the **S**, not by the written *G4460*
Ro 5: 5 out into our hearts through the Holy **S**, *G4460*
Ro 7: 6 so that we serve in the new way *of* the **S**, *G4460*
Ro 8: 2 Jesus the law *of* the **S** who gives life has *G4460*
Ro 8: 4 to the flesh but according to the **S**. *G4460*
Ro 8: 5 accordance with the **S** have their minds *G4460*
Ro 8: 5 their minds set on what the **S** desires. *G4460*
Ro 8: 6 the mind *governed by* the **S** is life and *G4460*
Ro 8: 9 of the flesh but are in the realm of the **S**, *G4460*
Ro 8: 9 if indeed the **S** of God lives in you. *G4460*
Ro 8: 9 if anyone does not have the **S** of Christ, *G4460*
Ro 8:10 the **S** gives life because of righteousness. *G4460*
Ro 8:11 And if the **S** of him who raised Jesus from *G4460*
Ro 8:11 bodies because of his **S** who lives in you. *G4460*
Ro 8:13 if *by* the **S** you put to death the *G4460*
Ro 8:14 those who are led *by* the **S** of God are the *G4460*
Ro 8:15 The **S** you received does not make you *G4460*
Ro 8:15 the **S** you received brought about your *G4460*
Ro 8:16 The **S** himself testifies with our spirit that *G4460*
Ro 8:16 testifies with our **s** that we are God's *G4460*
Ro 8:23 who have the firstfruits *of* the **S**, groan *G4460*
Ro 8:26 the **S** helps us in our weakness. *G4460*
Ro 8:26 the **S** himself intercedes for us *G4460*
Ro 8:27 our hearts knows the mind *of* the **S**, *G4460*
Ro 8:27 because the **S** intercedes for God's people NDT
Ro 9: 1 confirms it through the Holy **S**— *G4460*
Ro 11: 8 "God gave them a **s** of stupor, eyes that *G4460*
Ro 14:17 peace and joy in the Holy **S**, *G4460*
Ro 15:13 with hope by the power *of* the Holy **S**. *G4460*
Ro 15:16 sanctified by the Holy **S**. *G4460*
Ro 15:19 through the power *of* the **S** of God. *G4460*
Ro 15:30 Lord Jesus Christ and by the love *of* the **S**, *G4460*
1Co 2:10 things God has revealed to us by his **S**. *G4460*
1Co 2:10 The **S** searches all things, even the deep *G4460*
1Co 2:11 thoughts except their own **s** within them? *G4460*
1Co 2:11 the thoughts of God except the **S** of God. *G4460*
1Co 2:12 we have received is not the **s** of the world, *G4460*
1Co 2:12 the world, but the **S** who is from God, so *G4460*
1Co 2:13 wisdom but in words taught *by* the **S**, *G4460*
1Co 2:14 The person **without the S** does not accept *G6035*
1Co 2:14 things that *come from* the **S** of God but *G4460*
1Co 2:14 they are discerned only *through the* **S**. *G4462*
1Co 2:15 The *person* **with the S** makes judgments *G4461*
1Co 3: 1 you as **people who live by the S** but as *G4461*
1Co 3:16 that God's **S** dwells in your midst? *G4460*
1Co 4:21 shall I come in love and *with* a gentle **s**? *G4460*
1Co 5: 3 not physically present, I am with you *in* **s**. *G4460*
1Co 5: 4 are assembled and I am with you *in* **s**, *G4460*
1Co 5: 5 so that his **s** may be saved on the day of *G4460*
1Co 6:11 Lord Jesus Christ and by the **S** of our God. *G4460*
1Co 6:17 united with the Lord is one with him *in* **s**. *G4460*
1Co 6:19 your bodies are temples of the Holy **S**, *G4460*
1Co 7:34 devoted to the Lord in both body and **s**. *G4460*
1Co 7:40 I think that I too have the **S** of God. *G4460*
1Co 12: 1 Now about the **gifts of the S**, brothers *G4461*
1Co 12: 3 one who is speaking by the **S** of God says, *G4460*
1Co 12: 3 "Jesus is Lord," except by the Holy **S**. *G4460*
1Co 12: 4 but the same **S** distributes them. *G4460*
1Co 12: 7 the manifestation *of* the **S** is given for the *G4460*
1Co 12: 8 given through the **S** a message of wisdom *G4460*
1Co 12: 8 of knowledge by means of the same **S**, *G4460*
1Co 12: 9 to another faith by the same **S**, to another *G4460*
1Co 12: 9 to another gifts of healing by that one **S**, *G4460*
1Co 12:11 are the work *of* one and the same **S**, *G4460*
1Co 12:13 all baptized by one **S** so as to form one *G4460*
1Co 12:13 we were all given the one **S** to drink. *G4460*
1Co 14: 1 of love and eagerly desire **gifts of the S**, *G4461*
1Co 14: 2 they utter mysteries *by* the **S**. *G4460*
1Co 14:12 Since you are eager *for gifts of* the **S**, try *G4460*
1Co 14:14 pray in a tongue, my **s** prays, but my mind *G4460*
1Co 14:15 I will pray *with* my **s**, but I will also pray *G4460*
1Co 14:15 I will sing *with* my **s**, but I will also sing *G4460*
1Co 14:16 when you are praising God in the **S**, *G4460*
1Co 14:37 are a prophet or otherwise **gifted by the S**, *G4461*
1Co 15:45 the last Adam, a life-giving **s**. *G4460*
1Co 16:18 For they refreshed my **s** and yours also *G4460*
2Co 1:22 put his **S** in our hearts as a deposit *G4460*
2Co 3: 3 not with ink but *with* the **S** of the living *G4460*
2Co 3: 6 not of the letter but *of* the **S**; for the letter *G4460*
2Co 3: 6 the letter kills, but the **S** gives life. *G4460*
2Co 3: 8 will not the ministry *of* the **S** be even more *G4460*
2Co 3:17 Now the Lord is the **S**, and where the Spirit *G4460*
2Co 3:17 where the **S** of the Lord is, there *G4460*
2Co 3:18 which comes from the Lord, who is the **S**. *G4460*
2Co 4:13 Since we have that same **s** of faith, we *G4460*
2Co 5: 5 who has given us the **S** as a deposit *G4460*
2Co 6: 6 in the Holy **S** and in sincere love; *G4460*
2Co 7: 1 everything that contaminates body and **s**, *G4460*
2Co 7:13 because his **s** has been refreshed by all of *G4460*
2Co 11: 4 receive a different **s** from the Spirit you *G4460*
2Co 11: 4 a different spirit from **the S** you received, *G4005S*
2Co 12:18 in the same footsteps *by* the same **S**? *G4460*
2Co 13:14 fellowship of the Holy **S** be with you all. *G4460*
Gal 3: 2 Did you receive the **S** by the works of the *G4460*
Gal 3: 3 After beginning *by means of* the **S**, are *G4460*
Gal 3: 5 God give you his **S** and work miracles *G4460*
Gal 3:14 we might receive the promise *of* the **S**. *G4460*
Gal 4: 6 God sent the **S** of his Son into our hearts *G4460*
Gal 4: 6 into our hearts, the **S** who calls out, "Abba, NDT
Gal 4:29 the son born by the power of the **S**. *G4460*
Gal 5: 5 For *through* the **S** we eagerly await by faith *G4460*
Gal 5:16 So I say, walk *by* the **S**, and you will not *G4460*
Gal 5:17 the flesh desires what is contrary to the **S**, *G4460*
Gal 5:17 the **S** what is contrary to the flesh. *G4460*
Gal 5:18 But if you are led *by* the **S**, you are not *G4460*
Gal 5:22 But the fruit *of* the **S** is love, joy, peace *G4460*
Gal 5:25 Since we live *by* the **S**, let us keep in step *G4460*
Gal 5:25 the Spirit, let us keep in step with the **S**. *G4460*
Gal 6: 1 you who **live by the S** should restore that *G4461*
Gal 6: 8 whoever sows to please the **S**, from the *G4460*
Gal 6: 8 the Spirit, from the **S** will reap eternal life. *G4460*
Gal 6:18 of our Lord Jesus Christ be with your **s**, *G4460*
Eph 1:13 in him with a seal, the promised Holy **S**, *G4460*
Eph 1:17 may give you the **S** of wisdom and *G4460*
Eph 2: 2 the **s** who is now at work in those who are *G4460*
Eph 2:18 both have access to the Father by one **S**. *G4460*
Eph 2:22 a dwelling in which God lives by his **S**. *G4460*
Eph 3: 5 been revealed by the **S** to God's holy *G4460*
Eph 3:16 power through his **S** in your inner being, *G4460*
Eph 4: 3 keep the unity *of* the **S** through the bond *G4460*
Eph 4: 4 There is one body and one **S**, just as you *G4460*
Eph 4:30 And do not grieve the Holy **S** of God, with *G4460*
Eph 5:18 Instead, be filled with the **S**, *G4460*
Eph 5:19 psalms, hymns, and songs **from the S**. *G4461*
Eph 6:17 of salvation and the sword *of* the **S**, *G4460*
Eph 6:18 And pray in the **S** on all occasions with all *G4460*
Php 1:19 God's provision *of* the **S** of Jesus Christ *G4460*
Php 1:27 will know that you stand firm in the one **S**, *G4460*
Php 2: 1 if any common sharing in the **S**, if any *G4460*
Php 2: 2 being **one in s** and of one mind. *G5249*
Php 3: 3 we who serve God *by* his **S**, who boast in *G4460*
Php 4:23 of the Lord Jesus Christ be with your **s**. *G4460*
Col 1: 8 who also told us of your love in the **S**. *G4460*
Col 1: 9 understanding **that the S gives**, *G4461*
Col 2: 5 present with you in **s** and delight to see *G4460*
Col 3:16 songs **from the S**, singing to God *G4461*
1Th 1: 5 with the Holy **S** and deep conviction. *G4460*
1Th 1: 6 suffering with the joy *given by* the Holy **S**. *G4460*
1Th 4: 8 the very God who gives you his Holy **S**. *G4460*
1Th 5:19 Do not quench the **S**. *G4460*
1Th 5:23 May your whole **s**, soul and body be kept *G4460*
2Th 2:13 sanctifying work *of* the **S** and through *G4460*
1Ti 3:16 was vindicated by the **S**, was seen by *G4460*
1Ti 4: 1 The **S** clearly says that in later times some *G4460*
2Ti 1: 7 For the **S** God gave us does not make us *G4460*
2Ti 1:14 the help of the Holy **S** who lives in us. *G4460*
2Ti 4:22 The Lord be with your **s**. Grace be with *G4460*
Titus 3: 5 of rebirth and renewal *by* the Holy **S**, *G4460*
Phm 25 of the Lord Jesus Christ be with your **s**. *G4460*
Heb 2: 4 by gifts of the Holy **S** distributed according to *G41*
Heb 3: 7 as the Holy **S** says: "Today, if you hear *G4460*
Heb 4:12 it penetrates even to dividing soul and **s** *G4460*
Heb 6: 4 who have shared in the Holy **S**, *G4460*
Heb 9: 8 The Holy **S** was showing by this that the *G4460*
Heb 9:14 who through the eternal **S** offered himself *G4460*
Heb 10:15 The Holy **S** also testifies to us about this *G4460*
Heb 10:29 who has insulted the **S** of grace? *G4460*
Jas 2:26 As the body without the **s** is dead, so faith *G4460*
Jas 4: 5 longs for the **s** he has caused to dwell *G4460*
1Pe 1: 2 through the sanctifying work *of* the **S**, to *G4460*
1Pe 1:11 to which the **S** of Christ in them was *G4460*
1Pe 1:12 to you by the Holy **S** sent from heaven. *G4460*
1Pe 3: 4 unfading beauty *of* a gentle and quiet **s**, *G4460*
1Pe 3:18 in the body but made alive *in* the **S**. *G4460*
1Pe 4: 6 live according to God *in regard to* the **s**. *G4460*
1Pe 4:14 the **S** of glory and of God rests on you. *G4460*
2Pe 1:21 as they were carried along by the Holy **S**. *G4460*
1Jn 3:24 We know it by the **S** he gave us. *G4460*
1Jn 4: 1 do not believe every **s**, but test the spirits *G4460*
1Jn 4: 2 is how you can recognize the **S** of God: *G4460*
1Jn 4: 2 Every **s** that acknowledges that Jesus *G4460*
1Jn 4: 3 every **s** that does not acknowledge *G4460*
1Jn 4: 3 This is the **s** of the antichrist, which you NDT
1Jn 4: 6 how we recognize the **S** of truth and the *G4460*
1Jn 4: 6 the Spirit of truth and the **s** of falsehood. *G4460*
1Jn 4:13 He has given us of his **S**. *G4460*
1Jn 5: 6 And it is the **S** who testifies, because the *G4460*
1Jn 5: 6 who testifies, because the **S** is the truth. *G4460*
1Jn 5: 8 the **S**, the water and the blood; and the *G4460*
Jude 19 natural instincts and do not have the **S**. *G4460*
Jude 20 most holy faith and praying in the Holy **S**, *G4460*

Rev 1:10 On the Lord's Day I was in the **S**, and I G4460
Rev 2: 7 them hear what the **S** says to the churches G4460
Rev 2:11 them hear what the **S** says to the churches G4460
Rev 2:17 them hear what the **S** says to the churches G4460
Rev 2:29 them hear what the **S** says to the churches G4460
Rev 3: 6 them hear what the **S** says to the churches G4460
Rev 3:13 them hear what the **S** says to the churches G4460
Rev 3:22 them hear what the **S** says to the churches G4460
Rev 4: 2 At once I was in the **S**, and there before G4460
Rev 14:13 says the **S**, "they will rest from their labor, G4460
Rev 17: 3 me away in the **S** into a wilderness. G4460
Rev 18: 2 demons and a haunt *for* every impure **s**, G4460
Rev 19:10 For it is the **S** of prophecy who bears G4460
Rev 21:10 me away in the **S** to a mountain great G4460
Rev 22:17 The **S** and the bride say, "Come!" And let G4460

SPIRIT'S (1) [SPIRIT]

1Co 2: 4 with a demonstration *of* the **S** power, G4460

SPIRIT-TAUGHT (1) [SPIRIT, TEACH]

1Co 2:13 explaining spiritual realities *with* **S** *words*. G4461

SPIRITIST (2) [SPIRIT]

Lev 20:27 who is a medium or **s** among you must be H3362
Dt 18:11 who is a medium or **s** or who consults the H3362

SPIRITISTS (9) [SPIRIT]

Lev 19:31 " 'Do not turn to mediums or seek out **s** H3362
Lev 20: 6 turns to mediums and **s** to prostitute H3362
1Sa 28: 3 the mediums and **s** from the land. H3362
1Sa 28: 9 cut off the mediums and **s** from the land. H3362
2Ki 21: 6 and consulted mediums and **s**. H3362
2Ki 23:24 Josiah got rid of the mediums and **s**, the H3362
2Ch 33: 6 and consulted mediums and **s**. H3362
Isa 8:19 tells you to consult mediums and **s**, H3362
Isa 19: 3 of the dead, the mediums and the **s**. H3362

SPIRITS (46) [SPIRIT]

Jdg 16:25 While they *were* **in high s**, they H3201+4213
Ru 3: 7 and drinking and *was* **in good s**, H3512+4213
1Sa 25:36 He *was* **in high s** and very drunk H3201+4213
2Sa 13:28 When Amnon *is* **in high s** from H3201+4213
Est 1:10 Xerxes *was* **in high s** from wine, H3201+4213
Est 5: 9 out that day happy and **in high s**. H3201+4213
Ps 78: 8 whose **s** were not faithful to him. H8120
Ps 88:10 Do their **s** rise up and praise you? H8327
Pr 2:18 death and her paths to the **s of the dead**. H8327
Isa 14: 9 rouses the **s of the departed** to greet you H8327
Isa 19: 3 will consult the idols and the **s of the dead**, H356
Isa 26:14 they live no more; their **s** do not rise. H8327
Zec 6: 5 "These are the four **s** *of* heaven, going H8120
Mt 8:16 he drove out the **s** with a word and G4460
Mt 10: 1 to drive out impure **s** and to heal every G4460
Mt 12:45 with it seven other **s** more wicked than G4460
Mk 1:27 gives orders *to* impure **s** and they obey G4460
Mk 3:11 Whenever the impure **s** saw him, they fell G4460
Mk 5:13 the impure **s** came out and went into G4460
Mk 6: 7 gave them authority *over* impure **s**. G4460
Lk 4:36 gives orders *to* impure **s** and they come G4460
Lk 6:18 Those troubled by impure **s** were cured, G4460
Lk 7:21 sicknesses and evil **s**, and gave sight to G4460
Lk 8: 2 had been cured of evil **s** and diseases: G4460
Lk 10:20 do not rejoice that the **s** submit to you G4460
Lk 11:26 takes seven other **s** more wicked than G4460
Ac 5:16 sick and those tormented by impure **s**, G4460
Ac 8: 7 with shrieks, impure **s** came out of many G4460
Ac 19:12 were cured and the evil **s** left them. G4460
Ac 19:13 who went around **driving out evil s** tried to G2020
Ac 23: 8 that there are neither angels nor **s** G4460
1Co 12:10 to another distinguishing between **s**, to G4460
1Co 14:32 The **s** of prophets are subject to the control G4460
1Ti 4: 1 follow deceiving **s** and things taught by G4460
Heb 1: 7 "He makes his angels **s**, and his servants G4460
Heb 1:14 angels ministering **s** sent to serve those G4460
Heb 12: 9 we submit to the Father *of* **s** and live! G4460
Heb 12:23 *to* the **s** of the righteous made perfect, G4460
1Pe 3:19 made proclamation *to* the imprisoned **s**— G4460
1Jn 4: 1 test the **s** to see whether they are from G4460
Rev 1: 4 from the seven **s** before his throne, G4460
Rev 3: 1 who holds the seven **s** of God and the G4460
Rev 4: 5 These are the seven **s** of God. G4460
Rev 5: 6 which are the seven **s** of God sent out into G4460
Rev 16:13 I saw three impure **s** that looked like frogs G4460
Rev 16:14 They are demonic **s** that perform signs G4460

SPIRITUAL (22) [SPIRIT]

Ro 1:11 impart to you some **s** gift to make you G4461
Ro 7:14 We know that the law is **s**; but I am G4461
Ro 12:11 but keep your **s** fervor, serving the G4460
Ro 15:27 have shared in the Jews' **s** *blessings*, G4461
1Co 1: 7 you do not lack any **s gift** as you eagerly G5922
1Co 2:13 explaining **s** *realities* with Spirit-taught G4461
1Co 9:11 If we have sown **s** seed among you, is it G4461
1Co 10: 3 They all ate the same **s** food G4461
1Co 10: 4 drank the same **s** drink; for they drank G4461
1Co 10: 4 they drank from the **s** rock that G4461
1Co 15:44 sown a natural body, it is raised a **s** body. G4461
1Co 15:44 is a natural body, there is also a **s** body. G4461
1Co 15:46 The **s** did not come first, but the natural G4461
1Co 15:46 but the natural, and after that the **s**. G4461
Gal 4: 3 under the **elemental s forces** of the world. G5122
Eph 1: 3 realms with every **s** blessing in Christ. G4461
Eph 6:12 against the **s** *forces* of evil in the G4461
Col 2: 8 the **elemental s forces** of this world G5122
Col 2:20 Christ to the **elemental s forces** of this G5122
1Pe 2: 2 crave pure **s** milk, so that by it you G3358
1Pe 2: 5 are being built into a **s** house to be a holy G4461
1Pe 2: 5 offering **s** sacrifices acceptable to God G4461

SPIT (15) [SPITS, SPITTING]

Nu 12:14 "If her father *had* **s** in her face H3762+3762
Dt 25: 9 one of his sandals, **s** in his face and say H3762
Job 17: 6 everyone, a man in whose face people **s**. H9531
Job 20:15 *He will* **s out** the riches he swallowed H7794
Job 30:10 they do not hesitate to **s** in my face. H8371
Mt 26:67 Then *they* **s** in his face and struck him G1870
Mt 27:30 *They* **s on** him, and took the staff and G1870
Mk 7:33 Then *he* **s** and touched the man's tongue G4772
Mk 8:23 *When he had* **s** on the man's eyes and G4772
Mk 10:34 who will mock him and **s on** him, flog him G1870
Mk 14:65 Then some began *to* **s at** him; they G1870
Mk 15:19 on the head with a staff and **s on** him. G1870
Lk 18:32 will mock him, insult him and **s on** him; G1870
Jn 9: 6 After saying this, *he* **s** on the ground G4772
Rev 3:16 I am about to **s** you **out** of my mouth. G1840

SPITE (14)

Lev 26:23 " 'If **in s of** these things you do not accept H928
Lev 26:27 " 'If **in s of** this you still do not listen to me H928
Lev 26:44 Yet **in s of** this, when they are in the land H1685
Nu 14:11 **in s of** all the signs I have performed H928
Dt 1:32 **In s of** this, you did not trust in the LORD H928
Jdg 8:35 **in s of** all the good things he had done H3869
Ezr 10: 2 But **in s of** this, there is still hope for Israel H6584
Ne 5:18 **In s of** all this, I never demanded the food H6640
Job 23: 2 his hand is heavy **in s of** my groaning. H6584
Ps 78:32 **In s of** all this, they kept on sinning; in H928
Ps 78:32 kept on sinning; **in s of** his wonders, they H928
Isa 47: 9 **in s of** your many sorceries and all your H928
Jer 2:34 catch them breaking in. Yet **in s of** all this H6584
Jer 3:10 **In s of** all this, her unfaithful sister Judah H928

SPITS (1) [SPIT]

Lev 15: 8 with the discharge **s** on anyone who is H8394

SPITTING (1) [SPIT]

Isa 50: 6 did not hide my face from mocking and **s**. H8371

SPLASH (11) [SPLASHED, SPLASHES, SPLASHING]

Ex 29:16 take the blood and **s** it against the sides H2450
Ex 29:20 Then **s** blood against the sides of the H2450
Lev 1: 5 bring the blood and **s** it against the sides H2450
Lev 1:11 sons the priests *shall* **s** its blood against H2450
Lev 3: 2 sons the priests *shall* **s** the blood against H2450
Lev 3: 8 Then Aaron's sons *shall* **s** its blood H2450
Lev 3:13 Then Aaron's sons *shall* **s** its blood H2450
Lev 5: 9 and *is to* **s** some of the blood of the sin H5684
Lev 17: 6 The priest *is to* **s** the blood against the H2450
Nu 18:17 **S** their blood against the altar and burn H2450
2Ki 16:15 **S** against this altar the blood of all the H2450

SPLASHED (12) [SPLASH]

Ex 24: 6 the other half *he* **s** against the altar. H2450
Lev 7: 2 its blood *is to be* **s** against the sides H2450
Lev 8:19 the ram and **s** the blood against the H2450
Lev 8:24 Then he **s** blood against the sides of the H2450
Lev 9:12 and *he* **s** it against the sides of the altar. H2450
Lev 9:18 and *he* **s** it against the sides of the altar. H2450
2Ki 16:13 **s** the blood of his fellowship offerings H2450
2Ch 29:22 took the blood and **s** it against the altar; H2450
2Ch 29:22 the rams and **s** their blood against the H2450
2Ch 29:22 the lambs and **s** their blood against the H2450
2Ch 30:16 The priests **s** against the altar the blood H2450
2Ch 35:11 the priests **s** against the altar the H2450

SPLASHES (1) [SPLASH]

Lev 7:14 to the priest who **s** the blood of the H2450

SPLASHING (1) [SPLASH]

Eze 43:18 burnt offerings and **s** blood against the H2450

SPLENDID (2) [SPLENDOR]

Eze 17: 8 branches, bear fruit and become a **s** vine. H168
Eze 17:23 bear fruit and become a **s** cedar. H129

SPLENDOR (78) [SPLENDID]

1Ch 16:27 **S** and majesty are before him; strength H2086
1Ch 16:29 Worship the LORD in the **s** *of* his holiness. H2079
1Ch 22: 5 fame and **s** in the sight of all the H9514
1Ch 29:11 the glory and the majesty and the **s**, H2086
1Ch 29:25 on him royal **s** such as no king over H2086
2Ch 20:21 praise him for the **s** *of* his holiness as they H2079
Est 1: 4 of his kingdom and the **s** and glory of his H3702
Job 13:11 Would not his **s** terrify you? Would not the H8420
Job 31:23 for fear of his **s** I could not do such H8420
Job 31:26 in its radiance or the moon moving *in* **s**, H3701
Job 37:22 Out of the north he comes in golden **s**; God NDT
Job 40:10 Then adorn yourself with glory and **s**, and H1470
Ps 21: 5 you have bestowed on him **s** and majesty. H2086
Ps 29: 2 worship the LORD in the **s** *of* his holiness. H2079
Ps 45: 3 clothe yourself with **s** and majesty. H2086
Ps 49:16 when the **s** *of* their houses increases H3883
Ps 49:17 their **s** will not descend with them. H3883
Ps 71: 8 your praise, declaring your **s** all day long. H9514
Ps 78:61 his **s** into the hands of the enemy. H9514
Ps 89:44 put an end to his **s** and cast his throne to H3199
Ps 90:16 to your servants, your **s** to their children. H2077
Ps 96: 6 **S** and majesty are before him; strength H2086
Ps 96: 9 Worship the LORD in the **s** *of* his holiness H2079
Ps 104: 1 you are clothed with **s** and majesty. H2086
Ps 110: 3 Arrayed in holy **s**, your young men will H2077
Ps 145: 5 speak of the glorious **s** *of* your majesty— H2077
Ps 145:12 acts and the glorious **s** *of* your kingdom. H2077
Ps 148:13 his **s** is above the earth and the heavens. H2086
Pr 16:31 Gray hair is a crown of **s**; it is attained in H9514
Pr 20:29 is their strength, gray hair the **s** *of* the old. H2077
Isa 2:10 of the LORD and the **s** *of* his majesty! H2077
Isa 2:19 of the LORD and the **s** *of* his majesty, H2077
Isa 2:21 of the LORD and the **s** *of* his majesty, H2077
Isa 10:18 The **s** *of* his forests and fertile fields it will H3883
Isa 16:14 Moab's **s** and all her many people will be H3883
Isa 21:16 all the **s** *of* Kedar will come to an end. H3883
Isa 23: 9 her pride in all her **s** and to humble all H7382
Isa 35: 2 be given to it, the **s** *of* Carmel and Sharon H2077
Isa 35: 2 see the glory of the LORD, the **s** *of* our God. H2077
Isa 46:13 will grant salvation to Zion, my **s** to Israel. H9514
Isa 49: 3 in whom *I will* **display** my **s**. H6995
Isa 52: 1 Put on your garments of **s**, Jerusalem, the H9514
Isa 55: 5 of Israel, for *he has* **endowed** you **with s**." H6995
Isa 60: 9 of Israel, for *he has* **endowed** you **with s**. H6995
Isa 60:21 work of my hands, for *the* **display** *of* my **s**. H6995
Isa 61: 3 of the LORD for *the* **display** *of* his **s**. H6995
Isa 62: 3 will be a crown of **s** in the LORD's hand, H9514
Isa 63: 1 Who is this, robed in **s**, striding forward in H2075
Jer 22:18 'Alas, my master! Alas, his **s**!' H2086
La 1: 6 All the **s** has departed from Daughter H2077
La 2: 1 hurled down the **s** *of* Israel from heaven H9514
La 3:18 "My **s** is gone and all that I had hoped H5905
Eze 16:14 because the **s** I had given you made your H2077
Eze 27:10 helmets on your walls, bringing you **s**. H2077
Eze 28: 7 wisdom and pierce your **shining s**. H3650
Eze 28:17 corrupted your wisdom because of your **s**. H3650
Eze 31:18 be compared with you in **s** and majesty? H3883
Da 4:36 my honor and **s** were returned to me A10228
Da 5:18 greatness and glory and **s**. A10199
Da 11:20 out a tax collector to maintain the royal **s**. H2078
Hos 10: 5 those who had rejoiced over its **s** H3883
Hos 14: 6 His **s** will be like an olive tree, his H2086
Na 2: 2 LORD will restore the **s** *of* Jacob like the H1454
Na 2: 2 the splendor of Jacob like the **s** *of* Israel, H1454
Hab 3: 4 His **s** was like the sunrise; rays flashed H5586
Mt 4: 8 all the kingdoms of the world and their **s**. G1518
Mt 6:29 Solomon in all his **s** was dressed like one G1518
Lk 4: 6 "I will give you all their authority and **s**; it G1518
Lk 9:30 appeared in **glorious s**, talking with G1518
Lk 12:27 Solomon in all his **s** was dressed like one G1518
1Co 15:40 the **s** of the heavenly bodies is one G1518
1Co 15:40 the **s** of the earthly bodies is another. NDT
1Co 15:41 The sun has one kind of **s**, the moon G1518
1Co 15:41 another; and star differs from star in **s**. G1518
2Th 2: 8 mouth and destroy *by* the **s** of his coming. G2211
Rev 18: 1 the earth was illuminated by his **s**. G1518
Rev 18:14 All your luxury and **s** have vanished, never G3287
Rev 21:24 kings of the earth will bring their **s** into it. G1518

SPLINT (1)

Eze 30:21 healed or put in a **s** so that it may H3151

SPLINTERED (3)

2Ki 18:21 on Egypt, that **s** reed of a staff, which H8368
Isa 36: 6 on Egypt, that **s** reed of a staff, which H8368
Eze 29: 7 *you* **s** and you tore open their shoulders H8368

SPLIT (13) [SPLITS]

Nu 16:31 the ground under them **s apart** H1324
1Ki 13: 3 The altar *will* **be s apart** and the ashes on H7973
1Ki 13: 5 the altar **was s apart** and its ashes poured H7973
1Ki 16:21 people of Israel **were s** into two factions; H2745
Ps 74:13 It was you *who* **s open** the sea by your H7297
Ps 78:15 *He* **s** the rocks in the wilderness and gave H1324
Isa 24:19 the earth **is s asunder**, the earth H7297+7297
Isa 48:21 *he* **s** the rock and water gushed out. H1324
Mic 1: 4 melt beneath him and the valleys **s apart**, H1324
Hab 3: 9 *You* **s** the earth with rivers H1324
Zec 14: 4 Mount of Olives *will* **be s** in two from east H1324
Mt 27:51 The earth shook, the rocks **s** G5387
Rev 16:19 The great city **s** into three parts, and the G1181

SPLITS (1) [SPLIT]

Ecc 10: 9 *whoever* **s** logs may be endangered by H1324

SPOIL (3) [DESPOIL, SPOILED, SPOILS]

Ps 119:162 your promise like one who finds great **s**. H8965
Jer 30:16 all *who* **make s** *of* you I will despoil. H1024
1Pe 1: 4 inheritance that can **never** perish, **s** or fade. G299

SPOILED (5) [SPOIL]

Lev 13:47 any fabric that is **s** *with* a defiling mold— H5596
Lev 13:52 any leather article that has been **s** H5596
Lev 13:54 he shall order that the **s article** be washed H5596
Lev 13:55 which side of the fabric has been **s**. H7076
Lev 13:56 he is to tear the **s part** out of the fabric H2257S

SPOILS (10) [SPOIL]

Ex 15: 9 I will divide the **s**; I will gorge myself on H8965
Nu 31:11 They took all the plunder and **s**, including H4917
Nu 31:12 **s** and plunder to Moses and Eleazar the H4917
Nu 31:27 Divide the **s** equally between the soldiers H4917
Nu 31:32 remaining from the **s** that the soldiers H4917

Jdg 5:30 'Are they not finding and dividing the s: H8965
Isa 33:23 an abundance of s will be divided and H8965
Isa 53:12 he will divide the s with the strong H8965
Jer 49:32 their large herds will be s of war. H8965
Jn 6:27 Do not work for food that s, but for food *G660*

SPOKE (194) [SPEAK, SPOKES]

Ge 16:13 gave this name to the LORD who s to her: H1819
Ge 18:27 Then Abraham s up again: "Now that I H6699
Ge 18:29 Once again *he* s to him, "What if only H1819
Ge 19:14 So Lot went out and s to his sons-in-law H1819
Ge 22:7 Isaac s up and said to his father Abraham H606
Ge 23:3 beside his dead wife and s to the Hittites. H1819
Ge 24:7 land and who s to me and promised H1819
Ge 27:5 was listening as Isaac s to his son Esau. H1819
Ge 34:3 the young woman and s tenderly to her. H1819
Ge 34:13 deceitfully as *they* s *to* Shechem and his H1819
Ge 39:10 And though she s to Joseph day after day H1819
Ge 42:7 to be a stranger and s harshly to them. H1819
Ge 42:24 then came back and s to them again. H1819
Ge 42:30 is lord over the land s harshly to us and H1819
Ge 43:19 Joseph's steward and s to him at the H1819
Ge 46:2 And God s to Israel in a vision at night H606
Ge 50:21 he reassured them and s kindly to them. H1819
Ex 6:13 Now the LORD s to Moses and Aaron about H1819
Ex 6:27 *were* the *ones who* s to Pharaoh king of Egypt *about* H1819
Ex 6:28 Now when the LORD s to Moses in Egypt, H1819
Ex 7:7 eighty-three when they s to Pharaoh. H1819
Ex 19:19 Moses s and the voice of God answered H1819
Ex 20:1 And God s all these words: H1819
Ex 32:34 lead the people to the place *I* s *of,* and H1819
Ex 33:9 the entrance, while the LORD s with Moses. H1819
Ex 34:31 came back to him, and he s to them. H1819
Lev 1:1 called to Moses and s to him from the H1819
Lev 10:3 "This is what the LORD s *of* when he said: H1819
Lev 16:1 The LORD s to Moses after the death of the H1819
Lev 24:23 Then Moses s to the Israelites, and they H1819
Nu 1:1 The LORD s to Moses in the tent of H1819
Nu 3:1 at the time the LORD s to Moses at Mount H1819
Nu 7:89 In this way the LORD s to him. H1819
Nu 9:1 The LORD s to Moses in the Desert of Sinai H1819
Nu 11:25 came down in the cloud and s with him, H1819
Nu 11:28 aide since youth, s up and said, "Moses, H6699
Nu 17:6 So Moses s to the Israelites, and their H1819
Nu 21:5 they s against God and against Moses H1819
Nu 21:7 "We sinned when *we* s against the LORD H1819
Nu 23:7 Then Balaam s his message H5951+2256+606
Nu 23:18 Then *he* s his message H5951+2256+606
Nu 24:3 and *he* s his message: "The H5951+2256+606
Nu 24:15 Then *he* s his message: "The H5951+2256+606
Nu 24:20 Amalek and s his message: H5951+2256+606
Nu 24:21 Kenites and s his message: H5951+2256+606
Nu 24:23 Then *he* s his message: "Alas H5951+2256+606
Nu 26:3 Eleazar the priest s with them and said, H1819
Nu 36:1 came and s before Moses and the leaders H1819
Dt 1:1 are the words Moses s to all Israel in the H1819
Dt 4:12 Then the LORD s to you out of the fire. H1819
Dt 4:15 the day the LORD s to you at Horeb out H1819
Dt 5:4 The LORD s to you face to face out of the H1819
Dt 5:28 The LORD heard you when you s to me H1819
Dt 31:1 Moses went out and s these words to all H1819
Dt 32:44 son of Nun and s all the words of this H1819
Jdg 9:37 But Gaal s up again: "Look, people are H1819
1Sa 3:12 Eli everything *I* s against his family— H1819
1Sa 9:17 "This is the man *I* s to you *about;* he will H606
1Sa 19:4 Jonathan s well of David to Saul his H1819
1Sa 24:4 is the day the LORD s of when he said to you, NDT
2Sa 3:19 Abner also s *to* the Benjamites in person H1819
2Sa 6:22 But by these slave girls *you* s *of,* I will be H606
2Sa 12:18 he wouldn't listen to us *when we* s to him. H1819
2Sa 21:2 summoned the Gibeonites and s to them. H606
2Sa 23:2 "The Spirit of the LORD s through me; his H1819
2Sa 23:3 The God of Israel s, the Rock of Israel said H606
1Ki 4:32 *He* s three thousand proverbs and his H1819
1Ki 4:33 *He* s about plant life, from the cedar of H1819
1Ki 4:33 *He* also s about animals and birds H1819
2Ki 9:25 father when the LORD s this prophecy H5951
2Ki 9:36 of the LORD that *he* s through his servant H1819
2Ki 25:28 *He* s kindly to him and gave him a seat of H1819
1Ch 21:27 Then the LORD s to the angel, and he put H606
2Ch 1:2 Then Solomon s to all Israel—to the H606
2Ch 30:22 Hezekiah s encouragingly *to* all the H1819
2Ch 32:16 officers s further against the H1819
2Ch 32:19 *They* s about the God of Jerusalem as they H1819
2Ch 33:10 The LORD s to Manasseh and his people H1819
2Ch 33:18 the words the seers s to him in the name H1819
2Ch 34:27 when you heard what he s against this H1821
2Ch 36:12 who s the word *of* the LORD. H4946+7023
Ne 9:13 Mount Sinai; *you* s to them from heaven. H1819
Ne 13:24 Half of their children s the language of H1819
Est 1:13 he s with the wise men who understood H606
Est 3:4 Day after day they s to him but he refused H606
Est 7:9 Mordecai, who s up to help the king." H1819
Est 10:3 of his people and s up *for* the welfare of H1819
Job 26:4 And whose spirit s from your mouth? H3655
Job 29:11 Whoever heard me s well of me, and those H887
Job 29:22 I had spoken, they s no more; my words fell NDT
Job 32:11 I waited while you s, I listened to your H1821
Job 38:1 Then the LORD s *to* Job out of the storm H6699
Job 40:5 *I* s once, but I have no answer—twice H1819
Job 40:6 Then the LORD s *to* Job out of the storm: H6699
Job 42:3 Surely *I* s *of* things I did not understand H5583
Ps 33:9 For he s, and it came to be; he H606
Ps 39:3 the fire burned; then *I* s with my tongue: H1819
Ps 66:14 my mouth s when I was in trouble H1819
Ps 78:19 *They* s against God; they said, "Can God H1819
Ps 89:19 Once *you* s in a vision, to your faithful H1819
Ps 99:7 *He* s to them from the pillar of cloud; they H1819
Ps 105:31 *He* s, and there came swarms of flies, and H606
Ps 105:34 *He* s, and the locusts came, grasshoppers H606
Ps 107:25 For *he* s and stirred up a tempest that lifted H606
SS 2:10 My beloved s and said to me, "Arise, my H6699
Isa 7:10 Again the LORD s to Ahaz, H1819
Isa 8:5 The LORD s to me again: H1819
Isa 20:2 at that time the LORD s through Isaiah son H1819
Isa 65:12 did not answer, *I* s but you did not listen. H1819
Isa 66:4 one answered, *when I* s, no one listened H1819
Jer 7:13 the LORD, *I* s to you again and again H1819
Jer 7:22 your ancestors out of Egypt and s *to* them, H1819
Jer 18:20 I stood before you and s in their behalf to H1819
Jer 30:4 the words the LORD s concerning Israel H1819
Jer 35:17 *I* s to them, but they did not listen; H1819
Jer 46:13 LORD s to Jeremiah the prophet *about* the H1819
Jer 50:1 the word the LORD s through Jeremiah the H1819
Jer 52:32 *He* s kindly to him and gave him a seat of H1819
Eze 2:2 As *he* s, the Spirit came into me and H1819
Eze 3:24 me to my feet. *He* s to me and said: "Go, H1819
Eze 24:18 So *I* s to the people in the morning, and H1819
Eze 35:13 against me and s against me without H1821
Eze 38:17 You are the one *I* s *of* in former days by H1819
Da 2:14 Daniel s to him *with* wisdom and tact. A10754
Da 6:12 went to the king and s to him about his A10042
Da 7:8 being and a mouth *that* s boastfully. A10425
Da 7:20 had eyes and a mouth *that* s boastfully. A10425
Da 9:6 prophets, who s in your name to our kings H1819
Da 10:19 When he s to me, I was strengthened H1819
Hos 12:10 *I* s to the prophets, gave them many H1819
Hos 13:1 When Ephraim s, people trembled; he H1819
Zec 1:13 LORD s kind and comforting words *to* the H6699
Mt 9:33 the man who had been mute s. *G3281*
Mt 13:34 Jesus s all these things to the crowd in *G3281*
Mt 22:1 Jesus s to them again in parables, saying: *G646*
Mk 4:33 similar parables Jesus s the word to them, *G3281*
Mk 6:50 Immediately he s to them and said, "Take *G3281*
Mk 8:32 *He* s plainly about this, and Peter took him *G3281*
Mk 10:28 Then Peter s up, "We have left everything *G3306*
Lk 1:60 his mother s up and said, "No! He is to *G646*
Lk 2:38 thanks to God and s about the child to all *G3281*
Lk 4:22 All s well of him and were amazed at the *G3455*
Lk 9:11 welcomed them and s to them about the *G3281*
Lk 9:31 *They* s about his departure, which he was *G3306*
Lk 11:14 the man who had been mute s, and the *G3281*
Lk 23:22 For the third time *he* s to them: "Why *G3306*
Jn 1:15 "This is the one *I* s *about when I* said, 'He AIT
Jn 6:8 Andrew, Simon Peter's brother, s up, *G3306*
Jn 7:46 "No *one* ever s the way this man does," *G3281*
Jn 8:12 When Jesus s again to the people, he *G3281*
Jn 8:20 *He* s these words while teaching in the *G3281*
Jn 8:30 *Even as* he s, many believed in him. *G3281*
Jn 9:29 We know that God s to Moses, but as for *G3281*
Jn 11:49 priest that year, s up, "You know nothing *G3306*
Jn 12:34 The crowd s up, "We have heard from the *G646*
Jn 12:41 he saw Jesus' glory and s about him. *G3281*
Jn 18:16 s to the servant girl on duty there and *G3306*
Jn 18:23 But if I s the truth, why did you NDT
Ac 1:3 of forty days and s about the kingdom of *G3306*
Ac 1:16 the Holy Spirit s long ago through David *G4625*
Ac 2:31 *he* s of the resurrection of the Messiah *G3281*
Ac 4:25 You s by the Holy Spirit through the mouth *G3306*
Ac 4:31 the Holy Spirit and s the word of God *G3281*
Ac 6:10 the wisdom the Spirit gave him *as he* s. *G3281*
Ac 7:6 God s to him in this way: 'For four hundred *G3281*
Ac 7:38 with the angel who s to him on Mount *G3281*
Ac 10:7 When the angel who s to him had gone *G3281*
Ac 10:15 The voice s to him a second time, "Do not NDT
Ac 11:9 "The voice s from heaven a second time *G646*
Ac 14:1 There *they* s so effectively that a great *G3281*
Ac 15:13 they finished, James s up. "Brothers," *G646*
Ac 16:2 at Lystra and Iconium s well of him. *G3455*
Ac 16:32 Then *they* s the word of the Lord to him *G3281*
Ac 18:9 One night the Lord s to Paul in a vision *G3306*
Ac 18:25 and *he* s with great fervor and taught *G3281*
Ac 19:6 and *they* s in tongues and prophesied. *G3281*
Ac 19:8 synagogue and s boldly there for three *G4245*
Ac 20:7 Paul s to the people and, because he *G1363*
Ac 24:24 listened to him as he s about faith in Christ NDT
Ac 28:25 "The Holy Spirit s the truth to your *G3281*
Heb 1:1 In the past God s to our ancestors through *G3281*
Heb 4:7 a long time later *he* s through David, *G3306*
Heb 11:4 *when* God s well of his offerings. *G3455*
Heb 11:22 s about the exodus of the Israelites from *G3648*
Heb 13:7 leaders, who s the word of God to you. *G3281*
Jas 5:10 the prophets who s in the name of the *G3281*
1Pe 1:10 who s of the grace that was to come to *G4736*
1Pe 1:12 when they s of the things that have now NDT
2Pe 1:21 s from God as they were carried along by *G3281*
2Pe 2:16 *who* s with a human voice and restrained *G5779*
Rev 10:3 the voices of the seven thunders s. *G3281*
Rev 10:4 And when the seven thunders s, I was *G3281*
Rev 10:8 heard from heaven s to me once more: *G3281*
Rev 13:11 horns like a lamb, but *it* s like a dragon. *G3281*

SPOKEN (163) [SPEAK]

Ex 4:10 past nor since you *have* s to your servant. H1819
Ex 20:22 yourselves that *I have* s to you from H1819
Ex 34:29 radiant because he *had* s with the LORD. H1819
Nu 12:2 "*Has* the LORD s only through Moses?" H1819
Nu 12:2 "Hasn't *he* also s through us?" And H1819
Nu 14:35 the LORD, *have* s, and I will surely do these H1819
Dt 13:2 if the sign or wonder s *of* takes place H1819
Dt 18:21 a message *has* not *been* s by the LORD?" H1819
Dt 18:22 that is a message the LORD *has* not s. H1819
Dt 18:22 That prophet *has* s presumptuously, so do H1819
Jos 6:8 When Joshua *had* s to the people, the H606
Jdg 2:4 angel of the LORD *had* s these things to all H1819
2Sa 2:27 God lives, if *you had* not s, the men H1819
2Sa 7:19 *you have* also s about the future of the H1819
2Sa 7:29 Sovereign LORD, *have* s, and with your H1819
1Ki 2:27 the word the LORD *had* s at Shiloh about H1819
1Ki 12:15 the word the LORD *had* s to Jeroboam son H1819
1Ki 14:11 who die in the country. The LORD *has* s!' H1819
1Ki 16:12 the word of the LORD s against Baasha H1819
1Ki 16:34 word of the LORD s by Joshua son of Nun H1819
1Ki 17:16 with the word of the LORD s by Elijah. H1819
1Ki 22:28 the LORD *has* not s through me. H1819
2Ki 1:17 to the word of the LORD that Elijah *had* s. H1819
2Ki 2:22 according to the word Elisha *had* s. H1819
2Ki 10:10 a word the LORD *has* s against the house H1819
2Ki 10:17 to the word of the LORD s to Elijah. H1819
2Ki 14:25 s through his servant Jonah son of Amittai H1819
2Ki 15:12 the word of the LORD s to Jehu was H1819
2Ki 19:21 the word that the LORD *has* s against him: H1819
2Ki 20:19 "The word of the LORD *you have* s is good," H1819
2Ki 22:19 you heard what *I have* s against this place H1819
1Ch 17:17 *you have* s about the future of the house H1819
1Ch 21:19 the word that Gad *had* s in the name of H1819
2Ch 10:15 the word the LORD *had* s to Jeroboam son H1819
2Ch 18:27 the LORD *has* not s through me. H1819
2Ch 36:21 of the word of the LORD s by Jeremiah. H7023
2Ch 36:22 fulfill the word of the LORD s by Jeremiah, H7023
Ezr 1:1 fulfill the word of the LORD s by Jeremiah, H7023
Job 15:11 not enough for you, words s gently to you? AIT
Job 21:3 while I speak, and after I *have* s, mock on. H1819
Job 29:22 After I had s, they spoke no more; my H1821
Job 42:7 because *you have* not s the truth about H1819
Job 42:8 *You have* not s the truth about me, as my H1819
Ps 60:6 God *has* s from his sanctuary: "In triumph H1819
Ps 62:11 One thing God *has* s, two things I have H1819
Ps 73:15 If *I had* s out like that, I would have H606+6218
Ps 108:7 God *has* s from his sanctuary: "In triumph H1819
Ps 109:2 *they have* s against me *with* lying tongues H1819
Ps 141:6 wicked will learn that my words were well s. NDT
SS 8:8 do for our sister on the day she is s for? H1819
Isa 1:2 For the LORD *has* s: "I reared H1819
Isa 1:20 For the mouth of the LORD *has* s. H1819
Isa 16:13 word the LORD *has* already s concerning H1819
Isa 21:17 The LORD, the God of Israel, *has* s. H1819
Isa 22:25 on it will be cut down." The LORD *has* s. H1819
Isa 23:4 you fortress of the sea, for the sea *has* s: H606
Isa 24:3 The LORD *has* s this word. H1819
Isa 25:8 from all the earth. The LORD *has* s. H1819
Isa 37:22 this is the word the LORD *has* s against him H1819
Isa 38:15 *He* has s to me, and he himself has done H606
Isa 39:8 "The word of the LORD *you have* s is good," H1819
Isa 40:5 For the mouth of the LORD *has* s." H1819
Isa 45:19 *I have* not s in secret, from somewhere in H1819
Isa 48:15 even I, *have* s; yes, I have called him. H1819
Isa 48:16 first announcement *I have* not s in secret; H1819
Isa 49:1 my mother's womb *he has* s my name. H2349
Isa 58:14 For the mouth of the LORD *has* s. H1819
Isa 59:3 Your lips *have* s falsely, and your tongue H1819
Jer 4:28 because *I have* s and will not relent H1819
Jer 5:14 "Because the people *have* s these words H1819
Jer 13:15 do not be arrogant, for the LORD *has* s. H1819
Jer 14:14 them or appointed them or s to them. H1819
Jer 23:35 LORD's answer?' or 'What *has* the LORD s?' H1819
Jer 23:37 answer to you?' or 'What *has* the LORD s?' H1819
Jer 25:3 come to me and *I have* s to you again H1819
Jer 25:13 that land all the things *I have* s against it, H1819
Jer 26:16 *He has* s to us in the name of the LORD our H1819
Jer 30:2 in a book all the words *I have* s to you. H1819
Jer 35:14 But I *have* s to you again and again, yet H1819
Jer 36:2 it all the words *I have* s to you concerning H1819
Jer 36:4 all the words the LORD *had* s to him, H1819
Jer 37:2 words the LORD *had* s through Jeremiah H1819
Jer 44:16 to the message *you have* s to us in the H1819
Jer 48:8 plateau destroyed, because the LORD *has* s. H606
Eze 5:13 know that I the LORD *have* s in my zeal. H1819
Eze 5:15 with stinging rebuke. I the LORD *have* s. H1819
Eze 5:17 the sword against you. I the LORD *have* s." H1819
Eze 13:7 "The LORD declares," though I *have* not s? H1819
Eze 17:21 Then you will know that I the LORD *have* s. H1819
Eze 17:24 " 'I the LORD *have* s, and I will do it.' " H1819
Eze 21:17 my wrath will subside. I the LORD *have* s." H1819
Eze 21:32 no more; for I the LORD *have* s. H1819
Eze 22:14 I the LORD *have* s, and I will do it. H1819
Eze 22:28 LORD says'—when the LORD *has* not s. H1819
Eze 23:34 tear your breasts. I *have* s, declares the H1819
Eze 24:14 " 'I the LORD *have* s. The time has come H1819
Eze 26:5 spread fishnets, for I *have* s, declares the H1819
Eze 26:14 for I the LORD *have* s, declares the H1819
Eze 28:10 hands of foreigners. I *have* s, declares the H1819
Eze 30:12 everything in it. I the LORD *have* s. H1819
Eze 34:24 be prince among them. I the LORD *have* s. H1819

S

Eze 36: 5 my burning zeal I have s against the rest H1819
Eze 36:36 I the LORD have s, and I will do it.' H1819
Eze 37:14 Then you will know that I the LORD have s H1819
Eze 39: 5 the open field, for I have s, declares the H1819
Eze 39: 8 This is the day I have s of. H1819
Da 9:12 fulfilled the words s against us and H1819
Joel 3: 8 a nation far away." The LORD has s. H1819
Am 3: 1 the word the LORD has s against you H1819
Am 3: 8 The Sovereign LORD has s—who can but H1819
Ob 18 no survivors from Esau." The LORD has s. H1819
Mic 4: 4 afraid, for the LORD Almighty has s. H7023+1819
Mal 3:13 "You have s arrogantly against me," H1821
Mt 3: 3 This is he who was s of through the G3306
Mt 8:17 was to fulfill what was s through the G3306
Mt 12:17 was to fulfill what was s through the G3306
Mt 12:36 every empty word they have s. G3281
Mt 13:35 was fulfilled what was s through the G3306
Mt 21: 4 to fulfill what was s through the prophet: G3306
Mt 24:15 s of through the prophet Daniel G3306
Mt 26:65 clothes and said, "He has s blasphemy! G1059
Mt 26:75 Peter remembered the word Jesus had s: G3306
Mt 27: 9 Then what was s by Jeremiah the prophet G3306
Mk 12:12 because they knew he had s the parable G3306
Mk 14:72 remembered the word Jesus had s to him: G3306
Mk 16:19 After the Lord Jesus had s to them, he G3281
Lk 2:34 to be a sign that will be s against, G515
Lk 9:36 When the voice had s, they found that G1181S
Lk 20:19 because they knew he had s this parable G3306
Lk 22:61 the word the Lord had s to him: G3306
Lk 24:25 to believe all that the prophets have s! G3281
Jn 2:21 But the temple he had s of was his body. G3306
Jn 2:22 scripture and the words that Jesus had s. G3306
Jn 3:12 I have s to you of earthly things and you G3306
Jn 6:63 The words I have s to you—they are full of G3281
Jn 12:29 others said an angel had s to him. G3281
Jn 12:48 the very words I have s will condemn G3281
Jn 12:49 commanded me to say all that I have s. G3281
Jn 14:25 "All this I have s while still with you. G3281
Jn 15: 3 clean because of the word I have s to you. G3281
Jn 15:22 If I had not come and s to them, they G3281
Jn 18: 9 so that the words he had s would be G3306
Jn 18:20 "I have s openly to the world," Jesus G3281
Ac 2: 6 one heard their own language being s. G3281
Ac 2:16 this is what was s by the prophet Joel: G3306
Ac 3:24 the prophets who have s have foretold G3281
Ac 9:27 the Lord and that the Lord had s to him, G3281
Ac 23: 9 "What if a spirit or an angel has s to him?" G3281
Ro 14:16 do not let what you know is good
be s of as evil G1059
2Co 1:20 the "Amen" is s by us to the glory of God. AIT
2Co 4:13 therefore I have s." Since we have G3281
2Co 6:11 We have s freely to you G3836+5125+487
2Co 7: 4 I have s to you with great frankness; I take NDT
Gal 3:16 The promises were s to Abraham and to G3306
Heb 1: 2 these last days he has s to us by his Son, G3281
Heb 2: 2 since the message s through angels was G3281
Heb 3: 5 to what would be s by God in the future. G3281
Heb 4: 4 For somewhere he has s about the seventh G3306
Heb 4: 8 God would not have s later about another G3281
Heb 12:19 begged that no further word be s to them, G4707
2Pe 3: 2 recall the words s in the past by the holy G4625
3Jn 12 Demetrius is well s of by everyone—and G3455
Jude 15 defiant words ungodly sinners have s G3281

SPOKES (1) [SPOKE]
1Ki 7:33 s and hubs were all of cast metal. H3140

SPOKESMAN (1) [SPEAK, MAN]
Jer 15:19 worthless, words, you will be my s. H3869+7023

SPONGE (4)
Mt 27:48 Immediately one of them ran and got a s G5074
Mk 15:36 Someone ran, filled a s with wine vinegar G5074
Jn 19:29 so they soaked a s in it, put the sponge G5074
Jn 19:29 put the s on a stalk of the hyssop plant NDT

SPOON, SPOONS (KJV) DISH, DISHES

SPORT (3)

SPORT (KJV) ENTERTAIN, JOKING, MOCKING, PERFORM, PERFORMED, PLEASURE
Ge 39:14 has been brought to us to make s of us! H7464
Ge 39:17 brought us came to me to make s of me. H7464
Ps 69:11 people make s of me. H2118+4200+5442

SPORTING (KJV) CARESSING, REVELING

SPOT (17) [SPOTLESS, SPOTS, SPOTTED]
Lev 13: 2 a rash or a shiny s on their skin that may H994
Lev 13: 4 If the shiny s on the skin is white but does H994
Lev 13:19 white swelling or reddish-white s appears, H994
Lev 13:23 But if the s is unchanged and has not H994
Lev 13:24 reddish-white or white s appears in the raw H994
Lev 13:25 the priest is to examine the s, and if the H994
Lev 13:26 no white hair in the s and if it is not more H994
Lev 13:28 the s is unchanged and has not spread in H994
Lev 14:56 for a swelling, a rash or a shiny s, H994
Jos 3:16 of the Jordan at the s where the priests H9393
2Sa 2:23 He fell there and died on the s. And every H9393
2Ki 5:11 his hand over the s and cure me of my H5226
Job 8:18 But when it is torn from its s, that place H5226
Isa 28: 8 vomit and there is not a s without filth. H5226
Isa 46: 7 From that s it cannot move. H5226
Lk 19: 5 When Jesus reached the s, he looked up G5536
1Ti 6:14 this command without s or blame until G834

SPOTLESS (3) [SPOT]
Da 11:35 purified and made s until the time of the H4235
Da 12:10 will be purified, made s and refined, but H4235
2Pe 3:14 make every effort to be found s, blameless G834

SPOTS (3) [SPOT]
Lev 13:38 a man or woman has white s on the skin, H994
Lev 13:39 and if the s are dull white, it is a H994
Jer 13:23 change his skin or a leopard its s? H2494

SPOTTED (8) [SPOT]
Ge 30:32 from them every speckled or s sheep, H3229
Ge 30:32 lamb and every s or speckled goat. H3229
Ge 30:33 in my possession that is not speckled or s, H3229
Ge 30:35 all the male goats that were streaked or s, H3229
Ge 30:35 all the speckled or s female goats (all H3229
Ge 30:39 young that were streaked or speckled or s. H3229
Ge 31:10 the flock were streaked, speckled or s. H1353
Ge 31:12 streaked, speckled or s, for I have seen all H1353

SPOUSE, SPOUSES (KJV) BRIDE, DAUGHTERS-IN-LAW

SPOUTING (1)
Ps 27:12 up against me, s malicious accusations. H3641

SPRANG (4) [SPRING]
Jnh 4:10 It s up overnight and died overnight H2118
Mt 13: 5 It s up quickly, because the soil was G1984
Mk 4: 5 It s up quickly, because the soil was G1984
Ro 7: 9 sin s to life and I died. G348

SPREAD (149) [OUTSPREAD, SPREADING, SPREADS, WIDESPREAD]
Ge 10: 5 the maritime peoples s out into their H7233
Ge 10:32 these the nations s out over the earth H7233
Ge 28:14 and you will s out to the west and to the H7287
Ge 41:56 When the famine had s over the whole H2118
Ex 1:12 the more they multiplied and s; so the H7287
Ex 9:29 I will s out my hands in prayer to the LORD. H7298
Ex 9:33 He s out his hands toward the LORD; the H7298
Ex 23: 1 "Do not s false reports. Do not help a H5951
Ex 25:20 are to have their wings s upward, H7298
Ex 37: 9 The cherubim had their wings s upward H7298
Ex 40:19 Then he s the tent over the tabernacle H7298
Lev 13: 5 is unchanged and has not s in the skin, H7313
Lev 13: 6 sore has faded and has not s in the skin, H7313
Lev 13: 7 But if the rash does s in their skin H7313+7313
Lev 13: 8 if the rash has s in the skin, he shall H7313
Lev 13:23 But if the spot is unchanged and has not s H7313
Lev 13:28 unchanged and has not s in the skin but H7313
Lev 13:32 if it has not s and there is no yellow H7313
Lev 13:34 if it has not s in the skin and appears H7313
Lev 13:35 But if the sore does s in the skin H7313+7313
Lev 13:36 if he finds that the sore has s in the skin, H7313
Lev 13:51 and if the mold has s in the fabric, the H7313
Lev 13:53 the mold has not s in the fabric, the H7313
Lev 13:55 even though it has not s, it is unclean. H7313
Lev 14:39 If the mold has s on the walls, H7313
Lev 14:44 if the mold has s in the house, it is H7313
Lev 14:48 it and the mold has not s after the house H7313
Nu 4: 6 s a cloth of solid blue over that and put H7298
Nu 4: 7 of the Presence they are to s a blue cloth H7298
Nu 4: 8 They are to s a scarlet cloth over them H7298
Nu 4:11 the gold altar they are to s a blue cloth H7298
Nu 4:13 the bronze altar and s a purple cloth over H7298
Nu 4:14 Over it they are to s a covering of the H7298
Nu 11:32 Then they s them out all around H8848+8848
Nu 13:32 And they s among the Israelites a bad H3655
Nu 24: 6 "Like valleys they s out, like gardens H5742
Jos 6:27 his fame s throughout the land. H2118
Jos 7:23 Israelites and s them out before the LORD. H3668
Jdg 8:25 So they s out a garment, and each of H7298
Jdg 20:37 s out and put the whole city to the sword. H5432
Ru 3: 9 "S the corner of your garment over me H7298
1Sa 4: 2 and as the battle s, Israel was H5759
2Sa 5:18 had come and s out in the Valley of H5759
2Sa 5:22 came up and s out in the Valley of H5759
2Sa 17:19 a covering and s it out over the opening H7298
2Sa 18: 8 The battle s out over the whole H7046
2Sa 21:10 took sackcloth and s it out for herself on a H5742
1Ki 4:31 And his fame s to all the surrounding H2118
1Ki 6:27 of the temple, with their wings s out. H7298
1Ki 8: 7 The cherubim s their wings over the place H7298
1Ki 8:22 of Israel, s out his hands toward heaven H7298
1Ki 8:54 with his hands s out toward heaven. H7298
1Ki 22:36 sun was setting, a cry s through the army: H6296
2Ki 8:15 soaked it in water and s it over the king's H7298
2Ki 9:13 their cloaks and s them under him on the H8492
2Ki 19:14 of the LORD and s it out before the LORD. H7298
1Ch 14:17 So David's fame s throughout every land H3655
1Ch 28:18 cherubim of gold that s their wings and H7298
2Ch 5: 8 The cherubim s their wings over the place H7298
2Ch 6:12 assembly of Israel and s out his hands. H7298
2Ch 6:13 of Israel and s out his hands toward H7298
2Ch 26: 8 his fame s as far as the border of H2143
2Ch 26:15 His fame s far and wide, for he was H3655
Ezr 9: 5 with my hands s out to the LORD my God H7298
Ne 4:19 "The work is extensive and s out, and we H8146
Ne 8:15 this word and s it throughout their H6296
Est 9: 4 his reputation s throughout the provinces H2143
Job 1:10 flocks and herds are s throughout the land H7287
Job 15:29 nor will his possessions s over the land. H5742
Job 17:13 if I s out my bed in the realm of darkness, H8331
Job 39:26 by your wisdom and s its wings toward the H7298
Ps 5:11 S your protection over them, that those H6114
Ps 44:20 name of our God or s out our hands to a H7298
Ps 57: 6 They s a net for my feet—I was bowed H3922
Ps 78:19 "Can God really s a table in the H6885
Ps 88: 9 every day; I s out my hands to you. H8848
Ps 105:39 He s out a cloud as a covering, and a fire H7298
Ps 136: 6 who s out the earth upon the waters, His H8392
Ps 140: 5 they have s out the cords of their net and H7298
Ps 143: 6 I s out my hands to you; I thirst for you like H7298
Pr 1:17 How useless to s a net where every bird H2430
Pr 15: 7 The lips of the wise s knowledge, but the H2430
SS 1:12 at his table, my perfume s its fragrance. H5989
SS 2:13 the blossoming vines s their fragrance. H5989
SS 4:16 that its fragrance may s everywhere. H5688
Isa 1:15 When you s out your hands in prayer, H7298
Isa 14:11 maggots are s out beneath you and H3667
Isa 16: 8 reached Jazer and s toward the desert. H9494
Isa 16: 8 Their shoots s out and went as far as the H5759
Isa 21: 5 set the tables, they s the rugs, they eat, H7596
Isa 30:24 mash, s out with fork and shovel. H2430
Isa 32: 6 ungodliness and s error concerning the H1819
Isa 33:23 mast is not held secure, the sail is not s. H7298
Isa 37:14 of the LORD and s it out before the LORD. H7298
Isa 48:13 my right hand s out the heavens H3253
Isa 54: 3 For you will s out to the right and to the H7287
Isa 65:11 who s a table for Fortune and fill bowls of H6885
Jer 23:15 ungodliness has s throughout the land." H3655
Jer 43:10 he will s his royal canopy above them. H5742
Jer 48:32 Your branches s as far as the sea; they H6296
La 1:13 He s a net for my feet and turned me back H7298
Eze 1:22 S out above the heads of the living H5742
Eze 5: 4 A fire will s from there to all Israel H3655
Eze 10:16 when the cherubim s their wings to rise H5951
Eze 10:19 the cherubim s their wings and rose from H5951
Eze 11:22 wheels beside them, s their wings, and H5951
Eze 12:13 I will s my net for him, and he will be H7298
Eze 16: 8 I s the corner of my garment over you and H7298
Eze 16:14 And your fame s among the nations on H3655
Eze 17:20 I will s my net for him, and he will be H7298
Eze 19: 8 They s their net for him, and he was H7298
Eze 19:14 Fire s from one of its main branches and H3655
Eze 23:41 with a table s before it on which you had H6885
Eze 26: 5 sea she will become a place to s fishnets, H5427
Eze 26:14 you will become a place to s fishnets. H5427
Eze 30:13 and I will s fear throughout the land. H5989
Eze 32: 5 I will s your flesh on the mountains and H5989
Eze 32:23 All who had s terror in the land of the H5989
Eze 32:24 All who had s terror in the land of the H5989
Eze 32:25 their terror had s in the land of the H5989
Eze 32:26 the sword because they s their terror in H5989
Eze 32:32 Although I had him s terror in the land of H5989
Eze 39:14 They will s out across the land and, along H6296
Hos 5: 1 a snare at Mizpah, a net s out on Tabor. H7298
Mic 1: 9 plague is incurable; it has s to Judah. H995
Mt 4:24 News about him s all over Syria, and G599
Mt 9:26 News of this s through all that region. G2002
Mt 9:31 went out and s the news about him all G1424
Mt 21: 8 A very large crowd s their cloaks on the G5143
Mt 21: 8 from the trees and s them on the road. G5143
Mk 1:28 News about him s quickly over the whole G2002
Mk 11: 8 Many people s their cloaks on the road G5143
Mk 11: 8 while others s branches they had cut in the NDT
Lk 2:17 they s the word concerning what had G1192
Lk 4:14 news about him s through the whole G2002
Lk 4:37 And the news about him s throughout the G1744
Lk 5:15 Yet the news about him s all the more, so G1451
Lk 7:17 news about Jesus s throughout Judea G2002
Lk 19:36 people s their cloaks on the road. G5716
Jn 12:17 from the dead continued to s the word. G3455
Jn 21:23 the rumor s among the believers that this G2002
Ac 6: 7 So the word of God s. The number of G889
Ac 11:28 severe famine would s over the entire G1639
Ac 12:24 word of God continued to s and flourish. G889
Ac 13:49 The word of the Lord s through the whole G1422
Ac 19:20 word of the Lord s widely and grew in G889
2Co 2:14 uses us to s the aroma of the G5746
2Th 3: 1 of the Lord may s rapidly and be honored, G5556
2Ti 2:17 Their teaching will s like gangrene G3786+2400

SPREADING (45) [SPREAD]
Lev 13:22 If it is s in the skin, the priest shall H7313+7313
Lev 13:27 person, and if it is s in the skin, the H7313+7313
Lev 13:57 it is a s mold; whatever has H7255
Lev 14:34 and I put a s mold in a house in H5596+7669
Lev 19:16 'Do not go about s slander among your H8215
Nu 14:36 against him by s a bad report about it— H3655
Nu 14:37 men who were responsible for s the bad H3655
Dt 12: 2 on the hills and under every s tree, where H8316
Dt 28:35 s from the soles of your feet to the top of your AIT
Jdg 15: 9 up and camped in Judah, s out near Lehi. H5759
1Sa 2:24 the report I hear s among the LORD's H6296
1Ki 8:38 and s out their hands toward this temple H7298
1Ki 14:23 on every high hill and under every s tree. H8316
2Ki 16: 4 on the hilltops and under every s tree. H8316
2Ki 17:10 on every high hill and under every s tree. H8316
2Ch 6:29 and s out their hands toward this temple H7298

S

2Ch 28: 4 on the hilltops and under every **s** tree. H8316
Job 8:16 the sunshine, **s** its shoots over the garden; H3655
Job 26: 9 face of the full moon, **s** his clouds over it. H7298
Job 37:18 *can you* join him in **s out** the skies, hard H8392
Ps 58: 3 from the womb they are wayward, **s** lies. H1819
Pr 29: 5 their neighbors *are* **s** nets for their feet. H7298
Isa 18: 5 cut down and take away the **s branches**. H5746
Isa 57: 5 among the oaks and under every **s** tree; H8316
Jer 2:20 under every **s** tree you lay down as H8316
Jer 3: 6 hill and under every **s** tree and has H8316
Jer 3:13 favors to foreign gods under every **s** tree, H8316
Jer 17: 2 poles beside the **s** trees and on the high H8316
Jer 25:32 Disaster *is* **s** from nation to nation; H3655
Jer 48:40 is swooping down, **s** its wings over Moab. H7298
Jer 49:22 swoop down, **s** its wings over Bozrah. H7298
Eze 1:11 They each had two wings **s out** upward H7233
Eze 6:13 under every **s** tree and every leafy oak H8316
Eze 16:25 **s** your legs with increasing promiscuity to H7316
Eze 17: 6 became a low, **s** vine. Its branches H6243
Eze 31: 5 grew long, **s** because of abundant waters. H8938
Eze 31: 7 in beauty, with its **s** boughs, for its roots H802
Eze 47:10 En Eglaim there will be **places for s** nets. H5427
Hos 10: 1 Israel *was* a **s** vine; he brought forth fruit H1328
Joel 2: 2 Like dawn **s** across the mountains a large H7298
Mk 1:45 out and began to talk freely, **s** the news. *G1424*
Ac 4:17 But to stop *this thing* from **s** any further *G1376*
Ac 11:19 Antioch, **s** the word only among Jews. *G3281*
1Th 3: 2 in God's service **in** *s* the gospel of Christ, AIT
3Jn 10 **s** malicious nonsense about us. *G4472+3364*

SPREADS (12) [SPREAD]

Ex 10:21 the sky so that darkness **s** over Egypt— H2118
Ex 22: 6 fire breaks out and **s** *into* thornbushes so H5162
Dt 32:11 *that* **s** its wings to catch them and carries H7298
Job 26: 7 *He* **s out** the northern skies over empty H5742
Job 36:29 can understand how he **s out** the clouds, H5155
Job 39:18 *she* **s** *her* **feathers to run**, H5257+928+2021+5294
Ps 41: 6 slander; then he goes out and **s** it around. H1819
Ps 147:16 He **s** the snow like wool and scatters the H5989
Pr 10:18 with lying lips and **s** slander is a fool. H3655
Isa 40:22 and **s** them **out** like a tent to live in. H5501
Isa 42: 5 *who* **s out** the earth with all that springs H8392
Isa 44:24 heavens, *who* **s out** the earth by myself H8392

SPRIG (1)

Eze 17:22 I will break off a **tender** *s* from its topmost AIT

SPRING (61) [SPRANG, SPRINGING, SPRINGS, SPRINGTIME, SPRUNG]

Ge 16: 7 Hagar near a **s** in the desert; H6524+2021+4784
Ge 16: 7 it was the **s** that is beside the road to Shur H6524
Ge 24:13 I am standing beside this **s**, and H6524+4784
Ge 24:16 She went down to the **s**, filled her jar and H6524
Ge 24:29 he hurried out to the man at the **s**. H6524
Ge 24:30 him standing by the camels near the **s**. H6524
Ge 24:42 "When I came to the **s** today, I said, 'LORD H6524
Ge 24:43 I am standing beside this **s**. H6524+4784
Ge 24:45 She went down to the **s** and drew water H6524
Ge 49:22 a fruitful vine near a **s**, whose branches H6524
Lev 11:36 A **s**, however, or a cistern for collecting H5078
Nu 21:17 sang this song: "**S up**, O well! Sing about H6590
Dt 11:14 both autumn and **s rains**, so that you may H4919
Jos 15: 9 headed toward the **s** *of* the waters of H5078
Jos 18:15 came out at the **s** *of* the waters of H5078
Jdg 7: 1 all his men camped at the **s** *of* Harod. H6524
Jdg 15:19 So **the s** was called En Hakkore, and it is H2023S
1Sa 29: 1 Israel camped by the **s** in Jezreel. H6524
2Sa 11: 1 In the **s**, at the time when kings go H9588+9102
1Ki 20:22 because next **s** the king of H9588+2021+9102
1Ki 20:26 The next **s** Ben-Hadad mustered H9588+9102
2Ki 2:21 went out to the **s** and threw the salt H4604+4784
2Ki 13:20 used to enter the country **every s**. H995+9102
1Ch 20: 1 In the **s**, at the time when H6961+9588+9102
2Ch 32:30 outlet of the Gihon **s** and channeled the H4784
2Ch 33:14 west of the Gihon **s** in the valley, as far as NDT
2Ch 36:10 In the **s**, King Nebuchadnezzar sent H9588+9102
Job 5: 6 For hardship *does* not **s** from the soil, nor H3655
Job 14: 2 *They* **s up** like flowers and wither away H3655
Job 29:23 drank in my words as the **s rain**. H4919
Ps 92: 7 though the wicked **s up** like grass and all H7255
Pr 16:15 his favor is like a **rain** cloud **in s**. H4919
Pr 25:26 Like a muddied **s** or a polluted well are H5078
Ecc 4: 4 all achievement **s** from one person's NDT
Ecc 12: 6 before the pitcher is shattered at the **s** H4432
SS 4:12 my bride; you are a **s** enclosed, a sealed H5078
Isa 14:29 the root of that snake *will* **s up** a viper, H3655
Isa 42: 9 before *they* **s into being** I announce them H7541
Isa 44: 4 *They will* **s up** like grass in a meadow H7541
Isa 45: 8 earth open wide, *let* salvation **s up**, let H7238
Isa 58:11 like a **s** whose waters never fail. H4604+4784
Isa 61:11 *will* **make** righteousness and praise **s up** H7541
Jer 2:13 forsaken me, the **s** *of* living water, and H5227
Jer 3: 3 withheld, and no **s rains** have fallen. H4919
Jer 5:24 who gives autumn and **s** rains in season H4919
Jer 9: 1 my head were a **s of water** and my eyes a H4784
Jer 15:18 like a deceptive brook, like a **s** that fails. H4784
Jer 17:13 forsaken the LORD, the **s** *of* living water. H5227
Hos 6: 3 like the **s rains** that water the earth." H4919
Hos 10: 4 therefore lawsuits **s up** like poisonous H7255
Hos 13:15 his **s** will fail and his well dry up. H5227
Joel 2:23 both autumn and **s rains**, as before. H4919
Am 3: 5 *Does* a trap **s up** from the ground if it has H6590
Jn 4:14 become in them a **s** of water welling up *G4380*
Ro 15:12 "The Root of Jesse *will* **s up**, one who will *G1639*
Col 1: 5 faith and love that *s* **from** the hope stored up AIT
1Th 2: 3 we make does not **s from** error or impure *G1666*
Jas 3:11 salt water flow from the same **s**? *G4380*
Jas 3:12 Neither can a **salt s** produce fresh water *G266*
Jas 5: 7 waiting for the autumn and **s rains**. *G4069*
Rev 21: 6 without cost from the **s** of the water of life. *G4380*

SPRINGING (1) [SPRING]

Dt 33:22 "Dan is a lion's cub, **s out** of Bashan." H2397

SPRINGS (46) [SPRING]

Ge 7:11 on that day all the **s** *of* the great deep H5078
Ge 8: 2 Now the **s** *of* the deep and the floodgates H5078
Ge 36:24 who discovered the **hot s** in the desert H3553
Ge 49:25 blessings of the **deep s** below, blessings H9333
Ex 15:27 were twelve **s** and seventy palm H6524+4784
Nu 33: 9 were twelve **s** and seventy palm H6524+4784
Dt 8: 7 and **deep s** gushing out into the valleys H9333
Jos 15:19 in the Negev, give me also **s** *of* water." H1657
Jos 15:19 So Caleb gave her the upper and lower **s**. H1657
Jos 16: 1 east of the **s** *of* Jericho, and went H4784
Jdg 1:15 in the Negev, give me also **s** *of* water." H1657
Jdg 1:15 So Caleb gave her the upper and lower **s**. H1657
1Ki 18: 5 the land to all the **s** and valleys. H5078+4784
2Ki 3:19 stop up all the **s**, and ruin every H5078+4784
2Ki 3:25 up all the **s** and cut down every H5078+4784
2Ki 19:29 the second year **what s from** *that*. H6084
2Ch 32: 3 off the water from the **s** outside the city, H6524
2Ch 32: 4 who blocked all the **s** and the stream that H5078
Job 38:16 journeyed to the **s** *of* the sea or walked H5569
Ps 74:15 It was you who opened up **s** and streams H5078
Ps 84: 6 they make it a place of **s**; the autumn H5078
Ps 85:11 Faithfulness **s forth** from the earth, and H7541
Ps 90: 6 In the morning *it* **s up** new, but by H7437
Ps 104:10 He makes **s** pour water into the ravines; it H5078
Ps 107:33 desert, **flowing s** into thirsty ground H4604+4784
Ps 107:35 the parched ground into **flowing s**; H4604+4784
Ps 114: 8 into a pool, the hard rock into **s** *of* water. H5078
Pr 5:16 Should your **s** overflow in the streets, your H5078
Pr 8:24 when there were no **s** overflowing with H5078
Pr 27: 9 of a friend **s** from their heartfelt NDT
Isa 35: 7 the thirsty ground **bubbling s**. H4432+4784
Isa 37:30 the second year **what s from** *that*. H8826
Isa 41:18 barren heights, and **s** within the valleys. H5078
Isa 41:18 and the parched ground into **s**. H4604+4784
Isa 42: 5 out the earth with **all that s from** it, H7368
Isa 43:19 Now *it* **s up**; do you not H7541
Isa 49:10 them and lead them beside **s** *of* water. H4432
Jer 51:36 I will dry up her sea and make her **s** dry. H5227
Eze 31: 4 nourished it, **deep s** made it grow tall H9333
Eze 31:15 I covered the **deep s** with mourning for H9333
1Ti 3:16 mystery *from which* **true godliness** *s* is great: AIT
2Pe 2:17 These people are **s** without water and *G4380*
Rev 7:17 'he will lead them to **s** of living water. *G4380*
Rev 8:10 third of the rivers and on the **s** of water— *G4380*
Rev 14: 7 the earth, the sea and the **s** of water." *G4380*
Rev 16: 4 out his bowl on the rivers and **s** of water, *G4380*

SPRINGTIME (1) [SPRING]

Zec 10: 1 Ask the LORD for rain in the **s**; it is H6961+4919

SPRINKLE (20) [SPRINKLED, SPRINKLES, SPRINKLING]

Ex 29:21 anointing oil and **s** it on Aaron and his H5684
Lev 4: 6 into the blood and **s** some of it seven H5684
Lev 4:17 into the blood and **s** it before the LORD H5684
Lev 14: 7 Seven times *he shall* **s** the one to be H5684
Lev 14:16 with his finger **s** some of it before the H5684
Lev 14:27 his right forefinger **s** some of the oil from H5684
Lev 14:51 fresh water, and **s** the house seven times. H5684
Lev 16:14 with his finger **s** it on the front of the H5684
Lev 16:14 then *he shall* **s** some of it with his finger H5684
Lev 16:15 *He shall* **s** it on the atonement cover and H5684
Lev 16:19 *He shall* **s** some of the blood on it with his H5684
Nu 8: 7 **S** the water of cleansing on them; then H5684
Nu 19: 4 on his finger and **s** it seven times toward H5684
Nu 19:18 it in the water and **s** the tent and all the H5684
Nu 19:18 He must also **s** anyone who has touched a NDT
Nu 19:19 man who is clean *is to* **s** those who are H5684
Isa 52:15 so *he will* **s** many nations, and kings will H5684
Eze 27:30 *they will* **s** dust on their heads and roll in H6590
Eze 36:25 *I will* **s** clean water on you, and you will be H2450
Eze 43:24 the priests *are to* **s** salt on them and H8959

SPRINKLED (15) [SPRINKLE]

Ex 24: 8 the blood, **s** it on the people and said H2450
Lev 8:11 *He* **s** some of the oil on the altar seven H5684
Lev 8:30 from the altar and **s** them on Aaron and H5684
Nu 19:13 of cleansing *has* not **been s** on them, H2450
Nu 19:20 of cleansing *has* not **been s** on them, H2450
Jos 7: 6 did the same, and **s** dust on their heads. H6590
Job 2:12 tore their robes and **s** dust on their heads. H2450
La 2:10 *they have* **s** dust on their heads and put H6590
Hos 7: 9 His hair *is* **s** *with* gray, but he does not H2450
Heb 9:13 the ashes of a heifer **s** on those who are *G4822*
Heb 9:19 **s** the scroll and all the people. *G4822*
Heb 9:21 *he* **s** with the blood both the tabernacle *G4822*
Heb 10:22 *having* our hearts **s to cleanse** us from a *G4822*
Heb 12:24 to the **s** blood that speaks a better *G4823*
1Pe 1: 2 to Jesus Christ and **s** with his blood: *G4823*

SPRINKLES (1) [SPRINKLE]

Nu 19:21 "The *man who* **s** the water of cleansing H5684

SPRINKLING (29) [SPRINKLE]

Ex 27: 3 its shovels, **s bowls**, meat forks and H4670
Ex 38: 3 shovels, **s bowls**, meat forks and H4670
Nu 4:14 firepans, meat forks, shovels and **s bowls**. H4670
Nu 7:13 one silver **s bowl** weighing seventy H4670
Nu 7:19 one silver **s bowl** weighing seventy H4670
Nu 7:25 one silver **s bowl** weighing seventy H4670
Nu 7:31 one silver **s bowl** weighing seventy H4670
Nu 7:37 one silver **s bowl** weighing seventy H4670
Nu 7:43 one silver **s bowl** weighing seventy H4670
Nu 7:49 one silver **s bowl** weighing seventy H4670
Nu 7:55 one silver **s bowl** weighing seventy H4670
Nu 7:61 one silver **s bowl** weighing seventy H4670
Nu 7:67 one silver **s bowl** weighing seventy H4670
Nu 7:73 one silver **s bowl** weighing seventy H4670
Nu 7:79 one silver **s bowl** weighing seventy H4670
Nu 7:84 twelve silver **s bowls** and twelve gold H4670
Nu 7:85 shekels, and each **s bowl** seventy shekels. H4670
1Ki 7:40 made the pots and shovels and **s bowls**. H4670
1Ki 7:45 shovels and **s bowls**. All these H4670
1Ki 7:50 wick trimmers, **s bowls**, dishes and H4670
2Ki 12:13 wick trimmers, **s bowls**, trumpets or any H4670
2Ki 25:15 took away the censers and **s bowls**— H4670
1Ch 28:17 the forks, **s bowls** and pitchers; the H4670
2Ch 4: 8 He also made a hundred gold **s bowls**. H4670
2Ch 4:11 made the pots and shovels and **s bowls**. H4670
2Ch 4:22 wick trimmers, **s bowls**, dishes and H4670
Jer 52:18 wick trimmers, **s bowls**, dishes and all the H4670
Jer 52:19 censers, **s bowls**, pots, lampstands H4670
Zec 9:15 be full like a **bowl used for s** the corners H4670

SPROUT (8) [SPROUTED, SPROUTING, SPROUTS]

Nu 17: 5 staff belonging to the man I choose *will* **s**, H7255
Job 5: 6 nor *does* trouble **s** from the ground. H7541
Job 14: 7 it is cut down, *it will* **s** again, and its new H2736
Job 38:27 wasteland and **make** it **s** *with* grass? H7541
Pr 23: 5 for *they will* **surely s** wings and fly H6913+6913
Isa 61:11 the soil makes the **s** come up and a H7542
Jer 33:15 time *I will* **make** a righteous Branch **s** from H7541
Lk 21:30 When *they* **s leaves**, you can see for *G4582*

SPROUTED (5) [SPROUT]

Ge 41: 6 seven other heads of grain **s**—thin and H7541
Ge 41:23 seven other heads **s**—withered and thin H7541
Nu 17: 8 *had* not only **s** but had budded H7255
Eze 17: 6 and *it* **s** and became a low, spreading vine H7541
Mt 13:26 When the wheat **s** and formed heads *G1056*

SPROUTING (3) [SPROUT]

Dt 29:23 planted, nothing **s**, no vegetation growing H7541
2Ki 19:26 green shoots, like **grass** *s on* the roof AIT
Isa 37:27 green shoots, like **grass** *s on* the roof AIT

SPROUTS (1) [SPROUT]

Mk 4:27 gets up, the seed **s** and grows, though he *G1056*

SPRUNG (1) [SPRING]

Ge 2: 5 on the earth and no plant *had* yet **s up**, H7541

SPUE, SPUED (KJV) SPIT, VOMIT, VOMITED

SPUN (3) [SPIN]

Ex 35:25 Every skilled woman **s** with her hands and H3211
Ex 35:25 her hands and brought **what** she had **s**— H4757
Ex 35:26 with her hands and had the skill **s** the goat hair. H3211

SPUR (1) [SPURRED, SPURS]

Heb 10:24 we may **s** one another **on** toward *G1650+4237*

SPURN (1) [SPURNED, SPURNS]

Job 10: 3 to oppress me, *to* **s** the work of your hands H4415

SPURNED (6) [SPURN]

Ps 89:38 have rejected, *you have* **s**, you have been H4415
Pr 1:30 not accept my advice and **s** my rebuke, H5540
Pr 5:12 How my heart **s** correction! H5540
Isa 1: 4 *they have* **s** the Holy One of Israel and H5540
Isa 5:24 LORD Almighty and **s** the word of the Holy H5540
La 2: 6 in his fierce anger *he has* **s** both king and H5540

SPURNS (1) [SPURN]

Pr 15: 5 A fool **s** a parent's discipline, but whoever H5540

SPURRED (3) [SPUR]

Est 3:15 went out, **s on** by the king's command H1894
Est 8:14 went out, **s on** by the king's command H1894
Isa 9:11 against them and *has* **s** their enemies **on**. H6056

SPURS (1) [SPUR]

Isa 41: 7 with the hammer **s** on the one who strikes NDT

SPY (9) [SPIED, SPIES, SPYING]

Dt 1:22 send men ahead *to* **s out** the land for us H2916
Jos 2: 2 have come here tonight to **s out** the land." H2916
Jos 2: 3 they have come to **s out** the whole land." H2916
Jos 7: 2 told them, "Go up and **s out** the region." H8078
Jdg 1:23 When they **sent** *men* **to s out** Bethel H9365
Jdg 18: 2 Zorah and Eshtaol to **s out** the land and H8078
2Sa 10: 3 the city and **s** it **out** and overthrow it?" H8078
1Ch 19: 3 only to explore and **s out** the country and H8078
Gal 2: 4 our ranks *to* **s on** the freedom we have *G2945*

SPYING (2) [SPY]
Ge 42:30 us as though we *were* **s** *on* the land. H8078
Jos 6:23 men who *had done the* **s** went in and H8078

SQUADS (1)
Ac 12: 4 be guarded by four **s of four** soldiers **each**. *G5482*

SQUALL (2)
Mk 4:37 A furious **s** came up, and the waves *G3278+449*
Lk 8:23 A **s** came down on the lake, so that *G3278+449*

SQUANDERED (2) [SQUANDERS]
Lk 15:13 country and there **s** his wealth in wild *G1399*
Lk 15:30 son of yours who *has* **s** your property with *G2983*

SQUANDERS (1) [SQUANDERED]
Pr 29: 3 a companion of prostitutes **s** his wealth. H6

SQUARE (35) [SQUARES]
Ge 19: 2 "we will spend the night in the **s**. H8148
Ex 27: 1 it is to be **s**, five cubits long and H8062
Ex 28:16 It is to be **s**—a span long and a span wide H8062
Ex 30: 2 It is to be **s**, a cubit long and a cubit wide H8062
Ex 37:25 *It was* **s**, a cubit long and a cubit wide H8062
Ex 38: 1 three cubits high; *it was* **s**, five cubits long H8062
Ex 39: 9 It was **s**—a span long and a span wide H8062
Dt 13:16 the middle of the **public s** and completely H8148
Jdg 19:15 They went and sat in the city **s**, but no H8148
Jdg 19:17 looked and saw the traveler in the city **s**, H8148
Jdg 19:20 Only don't spend the night in the **s**." H8148
2Sa 21:12 bodies from the **public s** *at* Beth Shan, H8148
1Ki 7:31 The panels of the stands *were* **s**, not H8062
2Ch 29: 4 assembled them in the **s** *on* the east side H8148
2Ch 32: 6 before him in the **s** *at* the city gate and H8148
Ezr 10: 9 sitting in the **s** *before* the house of God, H8148
Ne 8: 1 as one in the **s** before the Water Gate. H8148
Ne 8: 3 noon as he faced the **s** before the Water H8148
Ne 8:16 of God and in the **s** *by* the Water Gate H8148
Est 4: 6 Mordecai in the **open s** *of* the city in front H8148
Job 29: 7 the city and took my seat in the **public s**, H8148
Pr 1:20 she raises her voice in the **public s**; H8148
Pr 22:13 I'll be killed in the **public s**!" H8148
Eze 16:24 made a lofty shrine in every **public s**. H8148
Eze 16:31 made your lofty shrines in every **public s**, H8148
Eze 40:12 alcoves were six cubits **s**. H4946+7024+2256+4946+7024
Eze 40:47 *It was* **s**—a hundred cubits long and a H8062
Eze 41:22 cubits high and two cubits **s**; H802+2256+8145
Eze 43:16 The altar hearth *is* **s** H8062+448+752+8063
Eze 43:17 The upper ledge also is **s** H448+752+8063
Eze 45: 2 a section 500 cubits **s** is to be for the H8062
Eze 48:20 The entire portion will be a **s**, 25,000 H8055
Am 5:16 cries of anguish in every **public s**. H8148
Rev 11: 8 will lie in the **public s** of the great city— *G4423*
Rev 21:16 The city was laid out *like* a **s**, as long as it *G5481*

SQUARES (8) [SQUARE]
Pr 5:16 your streams of water in the **public s**? H8148
Pr 7:12 now in the **s**, at every corner she H8148
SS 3: 2 through its streets and **s**; I will search for H8148
Isa 15: 3 the roofs and in the **public s** they all wail, H8148
Jer 5: 1 consider, search through her **s**. H8148
Jer 9:21 the young men from the **public s**. H8148
Jer 48:38 Moab and in the **public s** there is nothing H8148
Na 2: 4 rushing back and forth through the **s**. H8148

SQUEEZED (2)
Ge 40:11 **s** them into Pharaoh's cup and put the H8469
Jdg 6:38 *he* **s** the fleece and wrung out the dew H2318

STAB (1) [STABBED]
Zec 13: 3 their own parents *will* **s** the one who H1991

STABBED (4) [STAB]
2Sa 3:27 Asahel, Joab **s** him *in* the stomach, and H5782
2Sa 4: 6 and *they* **s** him in the stomach. H5782
2Sa 4: 7 After *they* **s** and killed him, they cut off his H5782
2Sa 20:10 Without being **s** again, Amasa died NDT

STABILITY (1)
Pr 29: 4 By justice a king **gives** a country **s**, but H6641

STABLE (KJV) ESTABLISHED, PASTURE

STABLISH, STABLISHED, STABLISHETH (KJV) BUILDS, ESTABLISH, ESTABLISHED, ESTABLISHES, SET UP, STAND FIRM, STRENGTHEN, STRENGTHENED

STACHYS (1)
Ro 16: 9 co-worker in Christ, and my dear friend **S**. *G5093*

STACK (2) [STACKS]
Lev 24: 6 six in each **s**, on the table of pure H5121
Lev 24: 7 By each **s** put some pure incense as a H5121

STACKS (1) [STACK]
Lev 24: 6 Arrange them in two **s**, six in each stack H5121

STACTE (KJV) GUM RESIN

STADIA (2)
Rev 14:20 horses' bridles for a distance of 1,600 **s**. *G5084*
Rev 21:16 rod and found it to be 12,000 **s** in length, *G5084*

STAFF (69) [FLAGSTAFF, STAFFS]
Ge 32:10 I had only my **s** when I crossed this Jordan H5234
Ge 38:18 its cord, and the **s** in your hand," she H4751
Ge 38:25 whose seal and cord and **s** these are." H4751
Ge 47:31 as he leaned on the top of his **s**. H4751
Ge 49:10 the **ruler's s** from between his feet H2980
Ex 4: 2 is that in your hand?" "A **s**," he replied. H4751
Ex 4: 4 it turned back into a **s** in his hand. H4751
Ex 4:17 But take this **s** in your hand so you can H4751
Ex 4:20 And he took the **s** *of* God in his hand. H4751
Ex 7: 9 'Take your **s** and throw it down before H4751
Ex 7:10 Aaron threw his **s** down in front of H4751
Ex 7:12 one threw down his **s** and it became a H4751
Ex 7:12 But Aaron's **s** swallowed up their staffs H4751
Ex 7:15 in your hand the **s** that was changed into H4751
Ex 7:17 With the **s** that is in my hand I will strike H4751
Ex 7:19 'Take your **s** and stretch out your hand H4751
Ex 7:20 He raised his **s** in the presence of H4751
Ex 8: 5 your hand with your **s** over the streams H4751
Ex 8:16 'Stretch out your **s** and strike the dust of H4751
Ex 8:17 out his hand with the **s** and struck the dust H4751
Ex 9:23 Moses stretched out his **s** toward the sky, H4751
Ex 10:13 So Moses stretched out his **s** over Egypt H4751
Ex 12:11 on your feet and your **s** in your hand. H5234
Ex 14:16 Raise your **s** and stretch out your hand over H4751
Ex 17: 5 in your hand the **s** with which you struck H4751
Ex 17: 9 of the hill with the **s** *of* God in my hands." H4751
Ex 21:19 get up and walk around outside with a **s**; H5475
Nu 17: 2 Write the name of each man on his **s**. H4751
Nu 17: 3 On the **s** *of* Levi write Aaron's name, for H4751
Nu 17: 3 there must be one **s** for the head of each H4751
Nu 17: 5 The **s** *belonging to* the man I choose will H4751
Nu 17: 6 and Aaron's **s** was among them. H4751
Nu 17: 8 entered the tent and saw that Aaron's **s**, H4751
Nu 17: 9 each of the leaders took his own **s**. H4751
Nu 17:10 "Put back Aaron's **s** in front of the ark of H4751
Nu 20: 8 "Take the **s**, and you and your brother H4751
Nu 20: 9 So Moses took the **s** from the LORD's H4751
Nu 20:11 arm and struck the rock twice with his **s**. H4751
Nu 22:27 he was angry and beat it with his **s**. H5234
Jdg 5:14 those who bear a commander's **s**. H8657
Jdg 6:21 with the tip of the **s** that was in his hand. H5475
1Sa 14:27 out the end of the **s** that was in his hand H4751
1Sa 14:43 tasted a little honey with the end of my **s**. H4751
1Sa 17:40 Then he took his **s** in his hand, chose five H5234
2Ki 4:29 your belt, take my **s** in your hand and run. H5475
2Ki 4:29 Lay my **s** on the boy's face." H5475
2Ki 4:31 ahead and laid the **s** on the boy's face, H5475
2Ki 18:21 that splintered reed of a **s**, which pierces H5475
2Ch 32: 3 his officials and **military s** about blocking H1475
Ps 23: 4 your rod and your **s**, they comfort me. H5475
Isa 10:26 he will raise his **s** over the waters, as H4751
Isa 36: 6 that splintered reed of a **s**, which pierces H5475
Jer 48:17 mighty scepter, how broken the glorious **s**! H5234
Jer 51:59 prophet gave to the **s** officer Seraiah son H4957
Eze 12:14 around him—his **s** and all his troops H6469
Eze 29: 6 " 'You have been a **s** *of* reed for the H5475
Mic 7:14 Shepherd your people with your **s**, the H8657
Zec 11:10 Then I took my **s** called Favor and broke it H5234
Zec 11:14 Then I broke my second **s** called Union H5234
Mt 10:10 the journey or extra shirt or sandals or a **s**, *G4811*
Mt 27:29 They put a **s** in his right hand *G2812*
Mt 27:30 took the **s** and struck him on the head *G2812*
Mt 27:48 vinegar, put it on a **s**, and offered it to *G2812*
Mk 6: 8 "Take nothing for the journey except a **s** *G4811*
Mk 15:19 him on the head *with* a **s** and spit on him. *G2812*
Mk 15:36 vinegar, put it on a **s**, and offered it to *G2812*
Lk 9: 3 nothing for the journey—no **s**, no bag, *G4811*
Heb 9: 4 of manna, Aaron's **s** that had budded *G4811*
Heb 11:21 as he leaned on the top *of* his **s**. *G4811*

STAFFS (7) [STAFF]
Ex 7:12 But Aaron's staff swallowed up their **s**. H4751
Nu 17: 2 the Israelites and get twelve **s** from them, H4751
Nu 17: 6 their leaders gave him twelve **s**, one H4751
Nu 17: 7 Moses placed the **s** before the LORD in the H4751
Nu 17: 9 brought out all the **s** from the LORD's H4751
Nu 21:18 the nobles with scepters and **s**. H5475
Zec 11: 7 Then I took two **s** and called one Favor H5234

STAG (3)
SS 2: 9 is like a gazelle or a **young s**. H6762+385
SS 2:17 like a **young s** on the rugged H6762+385
SS 8:14 gazelle or like a **young s** on the H6762+385

STAGE (2) [STAGES]
Jos 3:15 Jordan *is* **at flood s** all H4848+6584+3972+1536
Jos 4:18 and ran **at flood s** as before. H6584+3972+1536

STAGES (4) [STAGE]
Nu 33: 1 Here are the **s in** the **journey** *of* the H5023
Nu 33: 2 Moses recorded the **s** in their journey. H4604
Nu 33: 2 in their journey. This is their journey by **s**: H4604
Eze 41: 7 temple was built **in ascending s**, H4200+5087+2025+4200+5087+2025

STAGGER (12) [STAGGERED, STAGGERING, STAGGERS]
Job 12:25 no light; *he* **makes** them **s** like drunkards. H9494
Ps 60: 3 you have given us wine *that* **makes** us **s**. H9570
Isa 19:14 *they* **make** Egypt **s** in all that she does H9494
Isa 28: 7 And these also **s** from wine and reel from H8706
Isa 28: 7 Priests and prophets **s** from beer and are H8706
Isa 28: 7 reel from beer, *they* **s** when seeing visions H8706
Isa 29: 9 not from wine, **s**, but not from beer. H5675
Isa 51:17 its dregs the goblet that **makes** people **s**. H9570
Isa 51:22 out of your hand the cup that **made** you **s**; H9570
Jer 25:16 *they will* **s** and go mad because of the H1723
La 5:13 millstones; boys **s** under loads of wood. H4173
Am 8:12 *People will* **s** from sea to sea and wander H5675

STAGGERED (3) [STAGGER]
Ps 107:27 They reeled and **s** like drunkards; they H5675
Isa 21: 3 a woman in labor; *I* **am s** by what I hear, H6390
Am 4: 8 People **s** from town to town for water but H5675

STAGGERING (2) [STAGGER]
1Sa 25:31 the **s burden** of needless H7050+2256+4842
Pr 24:11 hold back *those* **s** toward slaughter. H4572

STAGGERS (2) [STAGGER]
Isa 3: 8 Jerusalem **s**, Judah is falling; their words H4173
Isa 19:14 as a drunkard **s around** in his vomit. H9494

STAIN (2) [STAINED]
Jer 2:22 the **s** of your guilt *is still* before me," H4187
Eph 5:27 without **s** or wrinkle or any other blemish *G5070*

STAINED (6) [STAIN]
1Ki 2: 5 and *with* that blood *he* **s** the belt around H5989
Isa 59: 3 For your hands **are s** with blood, your H1458
Isa 63: 1 from Bozrah, with his garments **s crimson**? H2808
Isa 63: 3 my garments, and *I* **s** all my clothing. H1458
Hos 6: 8 a city of evildoers, *s with* **footprints** of blood. AIT
Jude 23 even the clothing **s** by corrupted flesh. *G5071*

STAIRS (2) [DOWNSTAIRS, STAIRWAY, UPSTAIRS]
Ne 9: 4 Standing on the **s** *of* the Levites were H5090
Eze 40:49 It was reached by a **flight of s**, and there H5092

STAIRWAY (5) [STAIRS]
Ge 28:12 in which he saw a **s** resting on the earth, H6150
1Ki 6: 8 a **s** led up to the middle level and from H4294
2Ki 20:11 steps it had gone down on the **s** *of* Ahaz. H5092
Isa 38: 8 steps it has gone down on the **s** *of* Ahaz. H5092
Eze 41: 7 A **s** went up from the lowest floor to the top NDT

STAKE (2) [STAKES]
Job 6:29 reconsider, for my integrity is **at s**. H928
2Co 1:23 witness—and I **s** my life **on** it—that it was *G2093*

STAKES (2) [STAKE]
Isa 33:20 be moved; its **s** will never be pulled up H3845
Isa 54: 2 lengthen your cords, strengthen your **s**. H3845

STALK (6) [STALKED, STALKS]
Ge 41: 5 good, were growing on a single **s**. H7866
Ge 41:22 full and good, growing on a single **s**. H7866
Job 10:16 *you* **s** me like a lion and again display H7421
Hos 8: 7 The **s** has no head; it will produce no H7850
Mk 4:28 produces grain—first the **s**, then the head, *G5965*
Jn 19:29 put the sponge on a **s of the hyssop plant** *G5727*

STALKED (1) [STALK]
La 4:18 *People* **s** us *at* every step, so we could not H7421

STALKS (3) [STALK]
Jos 2: 6 them under the **s** *of* flax she had laid H6770
Ru 2:16 Even pull out some **s** for her from the NDT
Ps 91: 6 the pestilence *that* **s** in the darkness H2143

STALL (2) [STALLS]
Ps 50: 9 of a bull from your **s** or of goats from your H1074
Lk 13:15 ox or donkey from the **s** and lead it out to *G5764*

STALL-FED (1) [FEED]
1Ki 4:23 ten head of **s** cattle, twenty of pasture-fed H1374

STALLIONS (3)
Jer 5: 8 are well-fed, lusty **s**, each neighing for H6061
Jer 8:16 the neighing of their **s** the whole land H52
Jer 50:11 a heifer threshing grain and neigh like **s**, H52

STALLS (4) [STALL]
1Ki 4:26 had four thousand **s** for chariot horses, H774
2Ch 9:25 had four thousand **s** *for* horses and chariots H774
2Ch 32:28 he made **s** for various kinds of cattle H774
Hab 3:17 sheep in the pen and no cattle in the **s**, H8348

STAMMERING (1)
Isa 32: 4 the **s** tongue will be fluent and clear. H6589

STAMP (1) [STAMPED]
Eze 6:11 hands together and **s** your feet and cry out H8392

STAMPED (1) [STAMP]
Eze 25: 6 have clapped your hands and **s** your feet, H8392

STAND (260) [STANDING, STANDS, STOOD]
Ge 31:35 that I cannot **s up** in your presence H7756
Ex 9:11 magicians could not **s** before Moses H6641
Ex 14:13 **S firm** and you will see the deliverance H3656
Ex 17: 6 I *will* **s** there before you by the rock at H6641
Ex 17: 9 Tomorrow I *will* **s** on top of the hill with H5893
Ex 18:14 while all these people **s** around you from H5893
Ex 18:23 you will be able *to* **s the strain**, and all H6641
Ex 30:18 with its bronze **s**, for washing. H4029

S

Ex 30:28 all its utensils, and the basin with its s. H4029
Ex 31: 9 all its utensils, the basin with its s— H4029
Ex 33:21 place near me where you may s on a rock. H5893
Ex 35:16 its utensils; the bronze basin with its s; H4029
Ex 38: 8 basin and its bronze s from the mirrors of H4029
Ex 39:39 all its utensils; the basin with its s; H4029
Ex 40:11 the basin and its s and consecrate them. H4029
Lev 8:11 all its utensils and the basin with its s, H4029
Lev 19:32 " 'S up in the presence of the aged, show H7756
Lev 26:37 So you will not be able to s before your H9538
Nu 5:16 bring her and have her s before the LORD. H6641
Nu 5:18 the priest has had the woman s before H6641
Nu 5:30 The priest is to have her s before the LORD H6641
Nu 8:13 Have the Levites s in front of Aaron and H6641
Nu 11:16 meeting, that they may s there with you. H3656
Nu 11:24 elders and had them s around the tent H6641
Nu 16: 9 tabernacle and to s before the community H6641
Nu 27:19 Have him s before Eleazar the priest and H6641
Nu 27:21 He is to s before Eleazar the priest, who H6641
Nu 27:22 took Joshua and had him s before Eleazar H6641
Nu 30: 4 by which she obligated herself will s. H7756
Nu 30: 5 by which she obligated herself will s; H7756
Nu 30: 7 by which she obligated herself will s. H7756
Nu 30:11 by which she obligated herself will s. H7756
Nu 30:12 pledges that came from her lips will s. H7756
Nu 35:12 may not die before they s trial before the H6641
Dt 7:24 No one will be able to s up against you H3656
Dt 9: 2 "Who can s up against the Anakites?" H3656
Dt 10: 8 to s before the LORD to minister and to H6641
Dt 11:25 No one will be able to s against you. H3656
Dt 18: 5 of all your tribes to s and minister in the H6641
Dt 19:16 witness takes the s to accuse H7756+928
Dt 19:17 in the dispute must s in the presence of H6641
Dt 27:12 these tribes shall s on Mount Gerizim to H6641
Dt 27:13 And these tribes shall s on Mount Ebal to H6641
Jos 1: 5 No one will be able to s against you all H3656
Jos 3: 8 the Jordan's waters, go and s in the river. H6641
Jos 3:13 will be cut off and s up in a heap. H6641
Jos 7:10 said to Joshua, "S up! What are you H7756
Jos 7:12 Israelites cannot s against their enemies H7756
Jos 7:13 You cannot s against your enemies until H7756
Jos 10:12 s still over Gibeon, and you, moon H1957
Jos 20: 4 they are to s in the entrance of the city H6641
Jdg 4:20 "S in the doorway of the tent," he told her. H6641
1Sa 6:20 "Who can s in the presence of the LORD H6641
1Sa 12: 3 Here I s. Testify against me in the presence NDT
1Sa 12: 7 Now then, s here, because I am going to H3656
1Sa 12:16 s still and see this great thing the LORD is H3656
1Sa 14:40 all the Israelites, "You s over there; I and H2118
1Sa 14:40 I and Jonathan my son will s over here." H2118
1Sa 17:16 morning and evening and took his s. H3656
1Sa 19: 3 I will go out and s with my father in the H6641
2Sa 1: 9 he said to me, 'S here by me and kill me! H6641
2Sa 2:25 into a group and took their s on top of a H6641
2Sa 15: 2 get up early and s by the side of the H6641
2Sa 18:30 The king said, "S aside and wait here." H6015
2Sa 22:34 he causes me to s on the heights. H6641
2Sa 23:12 But Shammah took his s in the middle of H3656
1Ki 7:30 Each s had four bronze wheels with bronze H4807
1Ki 7:31 On the inside of the s there was an H2084S
1Ki 7:32 of the wheels were attached to the s. H4807
1Ki 7:34 Each s had four handles, one on each H4807
1Ki 7:34 one on each corner, projecting from the s. H4807
1Ki 7:35 At the top of the s there was a circular H4807
1Ki 7:35 panels were attached to the top of the s. H4807
1Ki 10: 8 who continually s before you and hear H6641
1Ki 19:11 "Go out and s on the mountain in the H6641
2Ki 5:11 come out to me and s and call on the H6641
1Ch 11:14 But they took their s in the middle of the H3656
1Ch 23:30 They were also to s every morning to thank H6641
2Ch 9: 7 who continually s before you and hear H6641
2Ch 20: 9 we will s in your presence before this H6641
2Ch 20:17 s firm and see the deliverance the LORD H6641
2Ch 29:11 has chosen you to s before him and serve H6641
2Ch 35: 5 "S in the holy place with a group of H6641
Ezr 9:15 of it not one of us can s in your presence." H6641
Ezr 10:13 the rainy season; so we cannot s outside. H6641
Ne 9: 5 "S up and praise the LORD your God, who H7756
Est 6:13 origin, you cannot s against him H3523+4202
Est 9: 2 No one could s against them, because H6641
Job 11:15 your face; you will s firm and without fear. H2118
Job 19:25 that in the end he will s on the earth. H7756
Job 21:16 so I s aloof from the plans of the wicked. H8178
Job 22:18 so I s aloof from the plans of the wicked. H8178
Job 30:20 you do not answer; I s up, but you merely H6641
Job 30:28 I s up in the assembly and cry for help. H7756
Job 32:16 now that they s there with no reply? H6641
Job 33: 5 s up and argue your case before me. H6885
Job 38:14 its features s out like those of a garment. H3656
Job 39:24 it cannot s still when the trumpet sounds. H586
Job 40:12 crush the wicked where they s. H9393
Job 41:10 Who then is able to s against me? H3656
Ps 1: 1 with the wicked or s in the way that H6641
Ps 1: 5 the wicked will not s in the judgment, H7756
Ps 5: 5 The arrogant cannot s in your presence H3656
Ps 10: 1 LORD, do you s far off? Why do you H6641
Ps 18:33 he causes me to s on the heights. H6641
Ps 20: 8 knees and fall, but we rise up and s firm. H6386
Ps 24: 3 Who may s in his holy place? H7756
Ps 26:12 My feet s on level ground; in the great H6641
Ps 30: 7 you made my royal mountain s firm; but H6641
Ps 33:11 But the plans of the LORD s firm forever H6641
Ps 40: 2 on a rock and gave me a firm place to s. H892
Ps 76: 7 Who can s before you when you are angry H6641
Ps 78:13 he made the water s up like a wall. H5893
Ps 83: 1 not turn a deaf ear, do not s aloof, O God. H9200
Ps 93: 5 s firm; holiness adorns your H586+4394
Ps 94:16 Who will take a s for me against evildoers H3656
Ps 101: 7 who speaks falsely will s in my presence. H3922
Ps 109: 6 let an accuser s at his right hand. H6641
Ps 119:120 in fear of you; I s in awe of your laws. H3707
Ps 122: 5 There s the thrones for judgment, the H3782
Ps 127: 1 over the city, the guards s watch in vain. H9193
Ps 130: 3 kept a record of sins, Lord, who could s? H6641
Pr 8: 2 where the paths meet, she takes her s; H5893
Pr 10:25 are gone, but the righteous s firm forever. H3572
Pr 25:10 and the charge against you will s. H4202+8740
Pr 27: 4 who can s before jealousy? H6641
Ecc 8: 3 Do not s up for a bad cause, for he will do H6641
Isa 7: 9 If you do not s firm in your faith, you will H586
Isa 7: 9 stand firm in your faith, you will not s at all. H586
Isa 8:10 your plan, but it will not s, for God is with H7756
Isa 11:10 the Root of Jesse will s as a banner for H6641
Isa 21: 8 my lord, I s on the watchtower; every night H6641
Isa 28:18 with the realm of the dead will not s. H7756
Isa 29:23 and will s in awe of the God of Israel. H6907
Isa 32: 8 noble plans, and by noble deeds they s. H7756
Isa 44:11 them all come together and take their s; H6641
Isa 46:10 'My purpose will s, and I will do all H7756
Isa 48:13 I summon them, they all s up together. H6641
Isa 49: 7 "Kings will see you and s up, princes will H7756
Isa 60:11 Your gates will always s open, they will never AIT
Jer 1:17 S up and say to them whatever I H7756
Jer 1:18 a bronze wall to s against the whole NDT
Jer 6:16 "S at the crossroads and look; ask for the H6641
Jer 7: 2 "S at the gate of the LORD's house and H6641
Jer 7:10 then come and s before me in this H6641
Jer 14: 6 Wild donkeys s on the barren heights H6641
Jer 15: 1 Moses and Samuel were to s before me, H6641
Jer 17:19 "Go and s at the Gate of the People H6641
Jer 17:19 s also at all the other gates of Jerusalem. NDT
Jer 26: 2 S in the courtyard of the LORD's house and H6641
Jer 30:18 the palace will s in its proper place. H3782
Jer 33:18 to have a man to s before me continually NDT
Jer 44:28 in Egypt will know whose word will s— H7756
Jer 44:29 of harm against you will surely s. H7756+7756
Jer 46:15 They cannot s, for the LORD will push them H6641
Jer 46:21 they will not s their ground, for the H6641
Jer 48:19 S by the road and watch, you who live in H6641
Jer 48:45 of Heshbon the fugitives s helpless, H6641
Jer 49:19 And what shepherd can s against me?" H6641
Jer 50:44 And what shepherd can s against me?" H6641
Jer 51:29 the LORD's purposes against Babylon s— H7756
Eze 2: 1 s up on your feet and I will speak to you." H6641
Eze 13: 5 Israel so that it will s firm in the battle on H6641
Eze 22:30 up the wall and s before me in the gap H6641
Eze 27:29 all the sailors will s on the shore. H6641
Eze 44:11 the people and s before the people H6641
Eze 44:15 they are to s before me to offer sacrifices H6641
Eze 46: 2 of the gateway and s by the gatepost. H6641
Eze 47:10 Fishermen will s along the shore; from En H6641
Da 8: 4 No animal could s against it, and none H6641
Da 8: 7 The ram was powerless to s against it; the H6641
Da 8:25 destroy many and take his s against the H6641
Da 10:11 to you, and s up, for I have H6641+6584+6642
Da 11: 1 I took my s to support and protect him.) H6641
Da 11:15 best troops will not have the strength to s. H6641
Da 11:16 no one will be able to s against him. H6641
Da 11:25 but he will not be able to s because of H6641
Am 2:15 The archer will not s his ground, the H6641
Mic 5: 4 He will s and shepherd his flock in the H6641
Mic 6: 1 "S up, plead my case before the H7756
Hab 2: 1 I will s at my watch and station myself on H6641
Hab 3: 2 of your fame; I s in awe of your deeds H3707
Zep 3: 8 the LORD, "for the day I will s up to testify. H7756
Zec 14: 4 On that day his feet will s on the Mount of H6641
Mal 3: 2 Who can s when he appears H6641
Mt 4: 5 the holy city and had him s on the highest G2705
Mt 5:15 Instead they put it on its s, and it gives G3393
Mt 12:25 divided against itself will not s. G2705
Mt 12:26 How then can his kingdom s? G2705
Mt 12:41 men of Nineveh will s up at the judgment G482
Mk 3: 3 shriveled hand, "S up in front of everyone." G1586
Mk 3:24 against itself, that kingdom cannot s. G2705
Mk 3:25 against itself, that house cannot s. G2705
Mk 3:26 is divided, he cannot s; his end has come. G2705
Mk 4:21 Instead, don't you put it on its s? G3393
Mk 11:25 And when you s praying, if you hold G5112
Mk 13: 9 On account of me you will s before G2705
Lk 1:19 I s in the presence of God, and I have G4225
Lk 4: 9 Jerusalem and had him s on the highest G2705
Lk 6: 8 "Get up and s in front of everyone." G2705
Lk 8:16 they put it on a s, so that those who come G3393
Lk 9:47 a little child and had him s beside him. G2705
Lk 11:18 against himself, how can his kingdom s? G2705
Lk 11:32 men of Nineveh will s up at the judgment G482
Lk 11:33 Instead they put it on its s, so that those G3393
Lk 13:25 you will s outside knocking and pleading G2705
Lk 21:19 S firm, and you will win life. G5705
Lk 21:28 to take place, s up and lift up your heads G376
Lk 21:36 you may be able to s before the Son of G2705
Jn 8: 3 They made her s before the group G2705
Jn 8:16 I am not alone. I s with the Father, who sent NDT
Ac 1:11 "why do you s here looking into the sky? G2705
Ac 5:20 s in the temple courts," he said, "and G2705
Ac 6:10 they could not s up against the wisdom the G468
Ac 8:36 What can s in the way of my being G3266
Ac 10:26 made him get up. "S up," he said, "I am G482
Ac 10:47 no one can s in the way of their being G3266
Ac 11:17 was I to think that I could s in God's way?" G3266
Ac 14:10 called out, "S up on your feet!" At that G482
Ac 22:30 brought Paul and had him s before them. G2705
Ac 23: 6 I s on trial because of the hope of the G3212
Ac 25: 9 to Jerusalem and s trial before me there G3212
Ac 25:20 go to Jerusalem and s trial there on these G3212
Ac 26: 2 myself fortunate to s before you today as I AIT
Ac 26:16 'Now get up and s on your feet. I have G2705
Ac 26:22 so I s here and testify to small and great G2705
Ac 27:24 You must s trial before Caesar; and God G4225
Ro 5: 2 by faith into this grace in which we now s. G2705
Ro 9:11 that God's purpose in election might s: G3531
Ro 11:20 because of unbelief, and you s by faith. G2705
Ro 14: 4 own master, servants s or fall. And they G5112
Ro 14: 4 And they will s, for the Lord is able to G2705
Ro 14: 4 for the Lord is able to make them s. G2705
Ro 14:10 For we will all s before God's judgment G4225
1Co 15: 1 on which you have taken your s. G2705
1Co 15:58 my dear brothers and sisters, s firm. G1612+1181
1Co 16:13 Be on your guard; s firm in the faith; be G5112
2Co 1:21 God who makes both us and you s firm in G1011
2Co 1:24 your joy, because it is by faith you s firm. G2705
2Co 2: 9 if you would s the test and be obedient G1509
Gal 5: 1 S firm, then, and do not let yourselves be G5112
Eph 6:11 so that you can take your s against the G2705
Eph 6:13 you may be able to s your ground, and G468
Eph 6:13 after you have done everything, to s. G2705
Eph 6:14 S firm then, with the belt of truth buckled G2705
Php 1:27 I will know that you s firm in the one Spirit G5112
Php 4: 1 crown, s firm in the Lord in this way G5112
Col 4:12 that you may s firm in all the will of God G2705
1Th 3: 1 So when we could s it no longer, we G5095
1Th 3: 5 this reason, when I could s it no longer, G5095
2Th 2:15 s firm and hold fast to the teachings we G5112
Jas 2: 3 the poor man, "You s there" or "Sit on the G2705
Jas 5: 8 be patient and s firm G5114+3836+2840
1Pe 5:12 this is the true grace of God. S fast in it. G2705
Rev 3:20 I s at the door and knock. G2705
Rev 8: 2 I saw the seven angels who s before God, G2705
Rev 11: 4 "they s before the Lord of the earth." G2705
Rev 18:10 at her torment, they will s far off and cry: G2705
Rev 18:15 gained their wealth from her will s far off, G2705
Rev 18:17 their living from the sea, will s far off. G2705

STANDARD (16) [STANDARDS]

Nu 1:52 of them in their own camp under their s. H1840
Nu 2: 2 of them under their s and holding the H1840
Nu 2: 3 of Judah are to encamp under their s. H1840
Nu 2:10 of the camp of Reuben under their s. H1840
Nu 2:17 each in their own place under their s. H1840
Nu 2:18 of the camp of Ephraim under their s. H1840
Nu 2:25 of the camp of Dan under their s. H1840
Nu 10:14 camp of Judah went first, under their s. H1840
Nu 10:18 camp of Reuben went next, under their s. H1840
Nu 10:22 camp of Ephraim went next, under their s. H1840
Nu 10:25 of the camp of Dan set out under their s. H1840
2Sa 14:26 was two hundred shekels by the royal s. H74
2Ch 3: 3 cubits wide (using the cubit of the old s). H4500
Isa 31: 9 the sight of the battle s their commanders H5812
Jer 4:21 must I see the battle s and hear the H5812
Eze 45:11 the homer is to be the s measure for both. H5504

STANDARDS (13) [STANDARD]

Lev 19:35 use dishonest s when measuring length, H5477
Nu 2:31 They will set out last, under their s. H1840
Nu 2:34 is the way they encamped under their s, H1840
Ps 74: 4 met with us; they set up their s as signs. H253
Eze 5: 7 conformed to the s of the nations around H5477
Eze 7:27 by their own s I will judge them. H5477
Eze 11:12 conformed to the s of the nations around H5477
Eze 23:24 they will punish you according to their s. H5477
Jn 8:15 You judge by human s; I pass judgment G4922
1Co 1:26 Not many of you were wise by human s G4922
1Co 3:18 think you are wise by the s of this age, G1877
2Co 10: 2 that we live by the s of this world. G6055+2848
1Pe 4: 6 according to human s in regard to the G476

STANDING (157) [STAND]

Ge 18: 2 looked up and saw three men s nearby, H5893
Ge 18:22 Abraham remained s before the LORD. H6641
Ge 24:13 I am s beside this spring, and the H5893
Ge 24:30 the man and found him s by the camels H6641
Ge 24:31 "Why are you s out here? I have H6641
Ge 24:43 I am s beside this spring. If a young H5893
Ge 41: 1 had a dream: He was s by the Nile, H6641
Ge 41:17 "In my dream I was s on the bank of the H6641
Ex 3: 5 the place where you are s is holy ground." H6641
Ex 22: 6 of grain or s grain or the whole field H7850
Ex 26:32 with gold and s on four silver bases. NDT
Ex 33:10 the pillar of cloud s at the entrance to the H6641
Nu 16:27 had come out and were s with their wives, H5893
Nu 22:23 the angel of the LORD s in the road with a H5893
Nu 22:31 angel of the LORD s in the road with his H5893
Nu 22:34 I did not realize you were s in the road to H5893
Nu 23: 6 to him and found him s beside his H5893
Nu 23:17 him and found him s beside his offering, H5893
Nu 32:14 s in the place of your fathers and making H7756

Dt 16: 9 you begin to put the sickle to the **s grain**. H7850
Dt 23:25 you must not put a sickle to their **s grain**. H7850
Dt 29:10 All of you *are* s today in the presence of H5893
Dt 29:12 You are s here in order to enter into a NDT
Dt 29:15 who are s here with us today in the H6641
Jos 4: 3 right where the priests *are* s, H5163+8079+3922
Jos 4:10 carried the ark *remained* s in the middle H6641
Jos 5:13 up and saw a man s in front of him with a H6641
Jos 5:15 the place where you *are* s is holy. H6641
Jos 8:33 *were* s on both sides of the ark of the H6641
Jos 20: 9 of blood prior *to* **s trial** before the H6641
Jdg 9:35 gone out and *was* s *at* the entrance of H6641
Jdg 15: 5 loose in the **s grain** *of* the Philistines. H7850
Jdg 15: 5 He burned up the shocks and **s grain** H7850
Ru 2: 1 a man of s from the clan of H1475+2657
Ru 2:13 I do not have the s *of* one of your servants H3869
Ru 4:11 May you have s in Ephrathah and be H2657
1Sa 9: 1 Benjamite, a man of s, whose name was H2657
1Sa 17:26 David asked the men s near him, "What H6641
1Sa 19:20 with Samuel s there as their leader H6641
1Sa 22: 6 Gibeah, with all his officials s at his side. H5893
1Sa 22: 9 Edomite, who *was* s with Saul's officials H5893
2Sa 13:34 Now the man **s watch** looked up and saw H7595
1Ki 8:14 the whole assembly of Israel *was* s there, H6641
1Ki 10:19 with a lion s beside each of them. H6641
1Ki 11:28 Now Jeroboam was a man of s, and H1475+2657
1Ki 13: 1 as Jeroboam *was* s by the altar to make H6641
1Ki 13:24 both the donkey and the lion s beside it. H6641
1Ki 13:25 with the lion s beside the body, and H6641
1Ki 13:28 with the donkey and the lion s beside it. H6641
1Ki 22:19 multitudes of heaven s around him on his H6641
2Ki 9:17 When the lookout s on the tower in H6641
2Ki 11:14 there was the king, s by the pillar, as the H6641
2Ki 13: 6 the Asherah pole *remained* s in Samaria. H6641
1Ch 21:15 of the LORD *was* then s at the threshing H6641
1Ch 21:16 angel of the LORD s between heaven and H6641
2Ch 6: 3 the whole assembly of Israel *was* s there, H6641
2Ch 7: 6 trumpets, and all the Israelites *were* s. H6641
2Ch 9:18 with a lion s beside each of them. H6641
2Ch 18:18 of heaven s on his right and on H6641
2Ch 23:13 the king, s by his pillar at the entrance. H6641
Ne 8: 5 see him because *he was* s above them; H2118
Ne 8: 7 in the Law while the people were s there. H6642
Ne 9: 4 **S** on the stairs of the Levites were Jeshua H7756
Ne 11: 6 lived in Jerusalem totaled 468 men of s. H2657
Ne 11:14 who were **men of s**—128. H1475+2657
Est 5: 2 When he saw Queen Esther s in the court H6641
Est 6: 5 answered, "Haman *is* s in the court." H6641
Ps 122: 2 Our feet are s in your gates, Jerusalem. H6641
Isa 17: 5 be as when reapers harvest the **s grain**, H7850
Isa 27: 9 poles or incense altars *will be left* s. H7756
Jer 28: 5 all the people who *were* s in the house of H6641
Jer 36:21 the king and all the officials s beside him. H6641
La 3:63 Sitting or s, they mock me in H7800
Eze 3:12 LORD rose from the **place where** it was s. H5226
Eze 3:23 And the glory of the LORD *was* s there, like H6641
Eze 8:11 son of Shaphan *was* s among them. H6641
Eze 10: 3 Now the cherubim *were* s on the south H6641
Eze 40: 3 he *was* s in the gateway with a linen cord H6641
Eze 43: 6 While the man was s beside me, I heard H6641
Da 7:16 one of *those* s there and asked A10624
Da 8: 3 ram with two horns, s beside the canal H6641
Da 8: 6 ram I had seen s beside the canal and H6641
Da 8:17 As he came near the **place where** I was s H6642
Da 10: 4 as I was s on the bank of the great river NDT
Da 10:16 I said to the *one* s before me, "I am H6641
Am 7: 7 The Lord *was* s by a wall that had been H5893
Am 9: 1 I saw the Lord s by the altar, and he said H5893
Zec 1: 8 He *was* s among the myrtle trees in a H6641
Zec 1:10 Then the man s among the myrtle trees H6641
Zec 1:11 of the LORD who *was* s among the myrtle H6641
Zec 3: 1 the high priest s before the angel of H6641
Zec 3: 1 Satan s at his right side to accuse H6641
Zec 3: 4 said to those *who were* s before him, H6641
Zec 3: 7 will give you a place among these s here. H6641
Zec 6: 5 going out from s in the presence of the H3656
Zec 14:12 will rot while they *are still* s on their feet, H6641
Mt 6: 5 they love to pray s in the synagogues and G2705
Mt 12:47 "Your mother and brothers *are* s outside G2705
Mt 16:28 some who are s here will not taste death G2705
Mt 20: 3 out and saw others s in the marketplace G2705
Mt 20: 6 went out and found still others **s around**. G2705
Mt 20: 6 'Why *have you been* s here all day long G2705
Mt 24:15 "So when you see s in the holy place 'the G2705
Mt 26:73 those s there went up to Peter and said G2705
Mt 27:47 *When* some of those s there heard this G2705
Mk 3:31 **S** outside, they sent someone in to call G5112
Mk 9: 1 some who are s here will not taste death G2705
Mk 11: 5 some people s there asked, "What are you G2705
Mk 13:14 causes desolation' s where it does not G2705
Mk 14:47 Then one *of* those **s near** drew his sword G4225
Mk 14:69 she said again *to* those **s around**, "This G4225
Mk 14:70 a little while, those **s near** said to Peter G4225
Mk 15:35 When some *of* those **s near** heard this G4225
Lk 1:11 s at the right side of the altar of incense. G2705
Lk 5: 1 One day as Jesus was s by the Lake of G2705
Lk 8:20 "Your mother and brothers *are* s outside G2705
Lk 9:27 some who are s here will not taste death G2705
Lk 9:32 saw his glory and the two men s **with** him. G5319
Lk 19:24 "Then he said *to* those **s by**, 'Take his G4225
Lk 23:10 the teachers of the law *were* s there, G2705
Jn 8: 9 was left, with the woman *still* s there. G1639
Jn 11:42 this for the benefit of the people **s here**, G4325
Jn 18: 5 Judas the traitor *was* **s there** with them.) G2705
Jn 18:18 Peter also was s with them, warming G2705
Jn 18:25 Simon Peter was *still* **s there** warming G2705
Jn 19:26 the disciple whom he loved **s nearby** G4225
Jn 20:14 she turned around and saw Jesus s there G2705
Ac 4:14 who had been healed s there with them, G2705
Ac 5:23 with the guards s at the doors; but when G2705
Ac 5:25 you put in jail are s in the temple courts G2705
Ac 7:33 the place where *you are* s is holy ground. G2705
Ac 7:55 Jesus s at the right hand of God. G2705
Ac 7:56 the Son of Man s at the right hand of G2705
Ac 13:16 **S up**, Paul motioned with his hand and G482
Ac 13:50 women *of* **high** s and the leading G2363
Ac 16: 9 a man of Macedonia s and begging him, G2705
Ac 22:25 Paul said to the centurion s there, "Is it G2705
Ac 23: 2 ordered those s **near** Paul to strike him G4225
Ac 23: 4 Those *who were* **s near** Paul said, "How G4225
Ac 25:10 "I am *now* s before Caesar's court, where I G2705
1Co 10:12 if you think you *are* **s firm**, be careful that G2705
1Th 3: 8 really live, since you *are* **s firm** in the Lord. G5112
1Ti 3:13 gain an excellent s and great assurance in G957
Jas 5: 9 The Judge *is* s at the door! G2705
1Pe 5: 9 Resist him, **s firm** in the faith, because you G5104
Rev 4: 1 before me *was* a door **s open** in heaven. G487
Rev 5: 6 been slain, s at the center of the throne G2705
Rev 7: 1 I saw four angels s at the four corners of G2705
Rev 7: 9 s before the throne and before the Lamb. G2705
Rev 7:11 All the angels *were* s around the throne G2705
Rev 10: 5 the angel I had seen s on the sea and on G2705
Rev 10: 8 of the angel who *is* s on the sea and on G2705
Rev 14: 1 me was the Lamb, s on Mount Zion, and G2705
Rev 15: 2 with fire and, s beside the sea, those G2705
Rev 19:11 I saw heaven **s open** and there before me G487
Rev 19:17 And I saw an angel s in the sun, who G2705
Rev 20:12 great and small, s before the throne, and G2705

STANDS (47) [STAND]

Dt 17:12 for the priest who s ministering there to H6641
Jos 22:19 where the LORD's tabernacle s, and share H8905
Jos 22:29 LORD our God that s before his tabernacle NDT
Jdg 6:24 To this day it s in Ophrah of the Abiezrites H6388
1Sa 16: 6 the LORD's anointed s here before the LORD." NDT
1Ki 7:27 He also made ten **movable s** of bronze H4807
1Ki 7:28 This is how the s were made: They had H4807
1Ki 7:31 The panels of **the s** were square, not H2157S
1Ki 7:37 This is the way he made the ten s. H4807
1Ki 7:38 one basin to go on each of the ten s. H4807
1Ki 7:39 placed five of the s on the south side of H4807
1Ki 7:43 the ten s with their ten basins; H4807
2Ki 16:17 removed the basins from the **movable s**. H4807
2Ki 25:13 the **movable** s and the bronze Sea that H4807
2Ki 25:16 the Sea and the **movable** s, which H4807
2Ch 4:14 the s with their basins; H4807
Est 7: 9 height of fifty cubits s by Haman's house. H6641
Job 9:35 but as it now s with me, I cannot. NDT
Job 23:13 "But he s alone, and who can oppose him NDT
Ps 89: 2 I will declare that your love s **firm** forever H1215
Ps 109:31 For *he* s at the right hand of the needy, to H6641
Ps 119:89 is eternal; *it* **s firm** in the heavens. H5893
Pr 12: 7 the house of the righteous s **firm**. H6641
SS 2: 9 There *he* s behind our wall, gazing H6641
Isa 27:10 The fortified city s desolate, an abandoned NDT
Isa 46: 7 they set it up in its place, and there *it* s. H6641
Isa 59:14 righteousness s at a distance; truth H6641
Isa 65: 6 *it* **s written** before me: I will not keep AIT
Jer 27:19 the **movable** s and the other articles that H4807
Jer 52:17 the **movable** s and the bronze Sea that H4807
Jer 52:20 under it, and the **movable** s, which King H4807
Da 6:12 "The decree s—in accordance with A10327
Mt 10:22 the *one who* **s firm** to the end will be G5702
Mt 13:38 the good seed **s for** the people of the G1639
Mt 24:13 the *one who* **s firm** to the end will be G5702
Mk 13:13 the *one who* **s firm** to the end will be G5702
Lk 8:14 fell among thorns **s for** those who hear, G1639
Lk 8:15 seed on good soil **s for** those with a noble G1639
Jn 1:26 "but among you s one you do not know. G2705
Jn 3:18 not believe *s* **condemned** already because AIT
Jn 16:11 prince of this world *now* **s condemned**. G3212
Ac 4:10 that this man s before you healed. G4225
Gal 4:25 Now Hagar **s for** Mount Sinai in Arabia G1639
2Ti 2:19 God's solid foundation **s firm**, sealed with G2705
Heb 4: 1 *since* the promise of entering his rest *still* s G2901
Heb 10:11 after day every priest s and performs his G2705
Rev 19: 8 Fine linen **s for** the righteous acts of God's G1639

STANDSTILL (1)

Ezr 4:24 God in Jerusalem **came to a s** until the A10098

STAR (17) [STARGAZERS, STARRY, STARS]

Nu 24:17 A s will come out of Jacob; a scepter will H3919
Isa 14:12 from heaven, **morning** s, son of the dawn! H2122
Am 5:26 of your idols, the s *of* your god—which H3919
Mt 2: 2 We saw his s when it rose and have come G843
Mt 2: 7 them the exact time the s had appeared. G843
Mt 2: 9 the s they had seen when it rose went G843
Mt 2:10 When they saw the s, they were overjoyed. G843
Ac 7:43 of Molek and the s of your god Rephan, G849
1Co 15:41 another; and s differs from star in splendor. G843
1Co 15:41 another; and star differs *from* s in splendor. G843
2Pe 1:19 day dawns and the **morning** s rises in your G5892
Rev 2:28 I will also give that one the morning s. G843
Rev 8:10 trumpet, and a great s, blazing like a torch, G843
Rev 8:11 the name *of* the s is Wormwood. A third of G843
Rev 9: 1 I saw a s that had fallen from the sky G843
Rev 9: 1 **The** s was given the key to the shaft of the G899S
Rev 22:16 of David, and the bright Morning **S**. G843

STARE (4) [STARES]

Ps 22:17 on display; people s and gloat over me. H5564
SS 1: 6 *Do* not s *at* me because I am dark H8011
Isa 14:16 Those who see you s at you, they ponder H8708
Ac 3:12 Why *do you* s at us as if by our own power G867

STARED (3) [STARE]

2Ki 8:11 s *at* him **with a fixed gaze** H6641+906+7156+2256+8492
Jn 13:22 His disciples s at one another, at a loss to G1063
Ac 10: 4 Cornelius s at him in fear. "What is it, Lord?" G867

STARGAZERS (1) [STAR]

Isa 47:13 those s who make predictions H2600+928+3919

STARK (4)

Eze 16: 7 yet you were **s naked**. H6567+2256+6880
Eze 16:37 and they will see you **s naked**. H3972+6872
Eze 16:39 and leave you **s naked**. H6567+2256+6880
Eze 23:29 They will leave you **s naked** H6567+2256+6880

STARRY (15) [STAR]

2Ki 17:16 They bowed down to all the s hosts, and H9028
2Ki 21: 3 down to all the s hosts and worshiped H9028
2Ki 21: 5 the LORD, he built altars to all the s hosts. H9028
2Ki 23: 4 Baal and Asherah and all the s hosts. H9028
2Ki 23: 5 to the constellations and to all the s hosts. H9028
2Ch 33: 3 down to all the s hosts and worshiped H9028
2Ch 33: 5 the LORD, he built altars to all the s hosts. H9028
Ne 9: 6 all their **s host**, the earth and all H7372
Ps 33: 6 their **s host** by the breath of his mouth. H7372
Isa 34: 4 all the **s host** will fall like withered leaves H7372
Isa 40:26 who brings out the **s host** one by one and H7372
Isa 45:12 the heavens; I marshaled their **s hosts**. H7372
Jer 19:13 the roofs to all the s hosts and poured out H9028
Da 8:10 it threw some of the s host down to the H9028
Zep 1: 5 down on the roofs to worship the s host, H9028

STARS (56) [STAR]

Ge 1:16 to govern the night. He also made the s. H3919
Ge 15: 5 "Look up at the sky and count the s—if H3919
Ge 22:17 as numerous as the s *in* the sky and as H3919
Ge 26: 4 as numerous as the s *in* the sky and will H3919
Ge 37: 9 moon and eleven s were bowing down to H3919
Ex 32:13 as numerous as the s *in* the sky and I will H3919
Dt 1:10 you are as numerous as the s *in* the sky. H3919
Dt 4:19 the moon and the s—all the heavenly H3919
Dt 10:22 you as numerous as the s *in* the sky. H3919
Dt 17: 3 to the sun or the moon or the s *in* the sky, H7372
Dt 28:62 as numerous as the s *in* the sky will be H3919
Jdg 5:20 From the heavens the s fought, from their H3919
1Ch 27:23 Israel as numerous as the s *in* the sky. H3919
Ne 4:21 the first light of dawn till the s came out. H3919
Ne 9:23 children as numerous as the s *in* the sky, H3919
Job 3: 9 May its morning s become dark; may it H3919
Job 9: 7 not shine; he seals off the light of the s. H3919
Job 22:12 And see how lofty are the highest s! H3919
Job 25: 5 is not bright and the s are not pure in his H3919
Job 38: 7 while the morning s sang together and all H3919
Ps 8: 3 the moon and the s, which you have set H3919
Ps 136: 9 the moon and s to govern the night; His H3919
Ps 147: 4 the number of the s and calls them each H3919
Ps 148: 3 moon; praise him, all you shining s. H3919
Ecc 12: 2 light and the moon and the s grow dark, H3919
SS 6:10 as the sun, majestic as the s in procession? NDT
Isa 13:10 The s *of* heaven and their constellations H3919
Isa 14:13 I will raise my throne above the s *of* God H3919
Isa 34: 4 All the s *in* the sky will be dissolved and H7372
Jer 8: 2 the moon and all the s *of* the heavens, H7372
Jer 31:35 decrees the moon and s to shine by night, H3919
Jer 33:22 me as countless as the s *in* the sky and as H7372
Eze 32: 7 will cover the heavens and darken their s; H3919
Da 12: 3 righteousness, like the s for ever and ever. H3919
Joel 2:10 are darkened, and the s no longer shine. H3919
Joel 3:15 be darkened, and the s no longer shine. H3919
Ob 4 eagle and make your nest among the s, H3919
Na 3:16 are more numerous than the s *in* the sky, H3919
Mt 24:29 not give its light; the s will fall from the sky G843
Mk 13:25 the s will fall from the sky, and the G843
Lk 21:25 will be signs in the sun, moon and s. G849
Ac 7:42 *of* the **sun, moon and s**. G5131+3836+4041
Ac 27:20 When neither sun nor s appeared for many G849
1Co 15:41 the moon another and the s another; and G843
Php 2:15 will shine among them like s in the sky G5891
Heb 11:12 as numerous as the s in the sky and as G849
Jude 13 wandering s, for whom blackest G843
Rev 1:16 In his right hand he held seven s, and G843
Rev 1:20 The mystery *of* the seven s that you saw in G843
Rev 1:20 The seven s are the angels of the seven G843
Rev 2: 1 who holds the seven s in his right hand G843
Rev 3: 1 the seven spirits of God and the seven s. G843
Rev 6:13 the s in the sky fell to earth, as figs G843
Rev 8:12 and a third *of* the s, so that a third G843
Rev 12: 1 feet and a crown *of* twelve s on her head. G843
Rev 12: 4 tail swept a third *of* the s out of the sky G843

START (6) [STARTED, STARTING, STARTS]
Nu 34: 3 southern boundary *will* **s** in the east from H2118
1Sa 9: 5 about the donkeys and **s worrying** about us." AIT
1Ki 20:14 "And who *will* **s** the battle?" he H673
Ne 2:18 They replied, "*Let us* **s** rebuilding." So H7756
Ne 2:20 We his servants *will* **s** rebuilding, but as H7756
Pr 22: 6 **S** children **off** on the way they should go H2852

STARTED (25) [START]
Ge 33:16 So that day Esau **s** on his way **back** to Seir. H8740
Ex 4:20 put them on a donkey and **s back** to Egypt. H8740
Ex 22: 6 the *one who* **s** the fire must make H1277
Nu 11: 4 again the Israelites *s* **wailing** and said AIT
Nu 16:46 come out from the LORD; the plague *has* **s**." H2725
Nu 16:47 The plague *had already* **s** among the H2725
Jos 2:23 Then the two men **s back**. They went down H8740
Jos 15: 2 southern boundary **s** from the bay at the H2118
Jos 15: 5 boundary **s** from the bay of H4200+6991
Jos 18: 8 *As* the men **s** on their way to map out the H7756
1Ki 18:45 a heavy rain **s falling** and Ahab rode off H2118
Est 6:13 before whom your downfall *has* **s**, is of H2725
Jer 37:12 Jeremiah *s to* **leave** the city to go to the AIT
Da 8: 9 which **s** small but grew in power to the H4946
Mt 23:32 complete **what** your ancestors **s**! G3836+3586S
Mk 10:17 *As* Jesus **s** on his way, a man ran up to G1744
Lk 9:46 An argument **s** among the disciples as to G1656
Lk 23: 5 *He* **s** in Galilee and has come all the way G806
Jn 8: 6 bent down and *s to* **write** on the ground with AIT
Jn 20: 3 the other disciple **s** for the tomb. G2002
Ac 8:27 So *he* **s out**, and on his way he met an G4513
Ac 10:23 The next day Peter *s* **out** with them, and AIT
Ac 17: 5 formed a mob and **s a riot** in the city. G2572
Ac 21:15 *we* **s** on our way up to Jerusalem. G2171
Ac 21:38 the Egyptian who **s a revolt** and led four G415

STARTING (5) [START]
2Ki 15:16 time Menahem, **s out from** Tirzah H4946
Pr 17:14 **S** a quarrel is like breaching a dam; so H8040
Eze 21:19 both **s** from the same country. H3655
Mt 27:24 that instead an uproar *was* **s**, he took G1181
Ac 11: 4 **S from the beginning**, Peter told them the G806

STARTLE (1) [STARTLED]
Job 18:11 Terrors **s** him on every side and dog his H1286

STARTLED (3) [STARTLE]
Ru 3: 8 middle of the night *something* **s** the man; H3006
Lk 1:12 *he was* **s** and was gripped with fear. G5429
Lk 24:37 They were **s** and frightened, thinking they G4765

STARTS (1) [START]
Pr 18: 1 against all sound judgment **s quarrels**. H1679

STARVATION (2) [STARVE]
Jer 15: 2 the sword; those for **s**, to starvation; those H8280
Jer 15: 2 starvation, to **s**; those for captivity, H8280

STARVE (2) [STARVATION, STARVING]
Ex 16: 3 into this desert to **s** this entire assembly to H8280
Jer 38: 9 where he will **s** to death when there is no H8280

STARVING (5) [STARVE]
Ge 42:19 take grain back for your **s** households. H8282
Ge 42:33 take food for your **s** households and go. H8282
2Ki 7:12 They know we are **s**; so they have left the H8281
Pr 6:30 steals to satisfy his hunger when *he is* **s**. H8279
Lk 15:17 food to spare, and here I am **s** to death! G3350

STATE (7) [STATED, STATEMENT, STATEMENTS]
Jos 20: 4 of the city gate and **s** their case before the H1819
Job 8: 6 restore you to your prosperous **s**. H5661
Job 23: 4 *I would* **s** my case before him and fill my H6885
Isa 14:18 kings of the nations **lie in s**, H8886+928+3883
Isa 43:26 together; **s** the case for your innocence. H6218
Lk 1:48 mindful of the **humble s** of his servant. G5428
Ac 24:20 who are here *should* **s** what crime they G3306

STATED (2) [STATE]
Ac 13:35 So *it is* also **s** elsewhere: " 'You will not G3306
Ro 9: 9 For this was how the promise was **s**: "At G3364

STATELY (4)
Pr 30:29 are three things *that are* **s** *in* their stride, H3512
Pr 30:29 their stride, four that move *with* **s bearing**: H3512
Isa 2:16 every trading ship and every **s** vessel. H2775
Zec 11: 2 the cedar has fallen; the **s** trees are ruined! H129

STATEMENT (2) [STATE]
Ac 20:38 them most was his **s** that they would G3364
Ac 28:25 *after* Paul *had* **made** this final **s**: G3306+4839

STATEMENTS (1) [STATE]
Mk 14:56 against him, but their **s** did not agree. G3456

STATION (4) [STATIONED]
2Ki 11: 8 **S yourselves** around the king, each of you H5938
2Ch 23: 7 The Levites *are to* **s themselves** around the H5938
Jer 51:12 Reinforce the guard, **s** the watchmen H7756
Hab 2: 1 at my watch and **s myself** on the ramparts; H3656

STATIONED (16) [STATION]
Jdg 20:22 where *they had* **s** *themselves* the first day. H6885
2Ki 3:21 arms was called up and **s** on the border. H6641
2Ki 11:11 in hand, **s** *themselves* around the king H6641
1Ch 9:18 being **s at** the King's Gate on the east, up H928
1Ch 9:27 spend the night **s around** the house of H6017
1Ch 16:42 The sons of Jeduthun were **s at** the gate. H4200
2Ch 17: 2 *He* **s** troops in all the fortified cities of H5989
2Ch 17:19 besides those he **s** in the fortified cities H5989
2Ch 23:10 *He* **s** all the men, each with his weapon in H6641
2Ch 23:19 *He* also **s** gatekeepers at the gates of the H6641
2Ch 29:25 *He* **s** the Levites in the temple of the LORD H6641
2Ch 33:14 *He* **s** military commanders in all the H8492
Ne 4:13 Therefore *I* **s** some of the people behind H6641
Ne 13:11 them together and **s** them at their posts. H6641
Ne 13:19 *I* **s** some of my own men at the gates so H6641
Eze 21:15 *I have* **s** the sword for slaughter at all their H5989

STATUE (5)
Da 2:31 there before you stood a large **s** A10614
Da 2:31 an enormous, dazzling **s**, awesome in A10614
Da 2:32 The head of the **s** was made of pure gold A10614
Da 2:34 It struck the **s** on its feet of iron and clay A10614
Da 2:35 rock that struck the **s** became a huge A10614

STATURE (3)
1Sa 2:26 continued to grow *in* **s** and in favor with H1541
SS 7: 7 Your **s** is like that of the palm, and your H7757
Lk 2:52 And Jesus grew in wisdom and **s**, and in G2461

STATUTE (3) [STATUTES]
1Sa 30:25 David made this a **s** and ordinance for H2976
Ps 81: 5 he established it as a **s** for Joseph. H6343
Ps 122: 4 the LORD according to the **s** given to Israel. H6343

STATUTES (39) [STATUTE]
2Ki 17:15 ancestors and the **s** he had warned them H6343
2Ki 23: 3 **s** and decrees with all his heart and all H6343
1Ch 29:19 **s** and decrees and to do everything to H6343
2Ch 34:31 **s** and decrees with all his heart and all H6343
Ne 9:34 commands or the **s** you warned them to H6343
Ps 19: 7 The **s** *of* the LORD are trustworthy, making H6343
Ps 78: 5 He decreed **s** for Jacob and established H6343
Ps 78:56 the Most High; they did not keep his **s**. H6343
Ps 89:30 forsake my law and do not follow my **s**, H5477
Ps 93: 5 Your **s**, LORD, stand firm; holiness adorns H6343
Ps 99: 7 they kept his **s** and the decrees he gave H6343
Ps 119: 2 those who keep his **s** and seek him with H6343
Ps 119:14 in following your **s** as one rejoices in H6343
Ps 119:22 scorn and contempt, for I keep your **s**. H6343
Ps 119:24 Your **s** are my delight; they are my H6343
Ps 119:31 I hold fast to your **s**, LORD; do not let me H6343
Ps 119:36 my heart toward your **s** and not toward H6343
Ps 119:46 I will speak of your **s** before kings and will H6343
Ps 119:59 ways and have turned my steps to your **s**. H6343
Ps 119:79 turn to me, those who understand your **s**. H6343
Ps 119:88 that I may obey the **s** *of* your mouth. H6343
Ps 119:95 to destroy me, but I will ponder your **s**. H6343
Ps 119:99 all my teachers, for I meditate on your **s**. H6343
Ps 119:111 Your **s** are my heritage forever; they are H6343
Ps 119:119 discard like dross; therefore I love your **s**. H6343
Ps 119:125 discernment that I may understand your **s**. H6343
Ps 119:129 Your **s** are wonderful; therefore I obey H6343
Ps 119:138 The **s** you have laid down are righteous H6343
Ps 119:144 Your **s** are always righteous; give me H6343
Ps 119:146 out to you; save me and I will keep your **s**. H6343
Ps 119:152 I learned from your **s** that you established H6343
Ps 119:157 but I have not turned from your **s**. H6343
Ps 119:167 I obey your **s**, for I love them greatly. H6343
Ps 119:168 I obey your precepts and your **s**, for all H6343
Ps 132:12 keep my covenant and the **s** I teach them, H6343
Isa 24: 5 violated the **s** and broken the everlasting H2976
Eze 20:18 "Do not follow the **s** *of* your parents or H2976
Eze 20:25 So I gave them other **s** that were not good H2976
Mic 6:16 have observed the **s** *of* Omri and all the H2978

STAVES (KJV) CLUBS, POLES, SPEAR, STAFF, STAFFS, STICKS

STAY (128) [STAYED, STAYING, STAYS]
Ge 13: 6 that they were not able to **s** together. H3782
Ge 19:30 mountains, for he was afraid to **s** in Zoar. H3782
Ge 22: 5 "**S** here with the donkey while I and the H3782
Ge 25:27 content *to* **s at home** *among* the tents. H3782
Ge 26: 3 **S** in this land **for a while**, and I will be H1591
Ge 27:44 **S** with him for a while until your brother's H3782
Ge 29:19 to some other man. **S** *here* with me." H3782
Ge 30:27 "If I have found favor in your eyes, please **s**. NDT
Ge 38: 1 went down *to* **s** with a man of H5742
Ge 42:19 *let* one of your brothers **s** here in prison H673
Ex 2:21 Moses agreed to **s** with the man, who H3782
Ex 9:28 let you go; *you* don't *have to* **s** any longer." H6641
Ex 16:29 Everyone *is to* **s** where they are on the H3782
Ex 22:30 *Let them* **s** with their mothers for seven H2118
Ex 24:12 up to me on the mountain and **s** here, H2118
Ex 33: 9 would come down and **s** at the entrance, H6641
Lev 8:35 *You must* **s** at the entrance to the tent of H3782
Lev 14: 8 but *they must* **s** outside their tent for H3782
Nu 23: 3 "**S** here beside your offering while I go H3656
Nu 23:15 "**S** here beside your offering while I meet H3656
Nu 31:19 who was killed *must* **s** outside the camp H2837
Nu 35:25 The accused *must* **s** there until the death H3782
Nu 35:28 The accused *must* **s** in the city of refuge H3782
Dt 2:27 *We will* **s** on the main road; we will not H2143
Dt 3:19 *may* **s** in the towns I have given you H3782
Dt 5:31 But you **s** here with me so that I may give H6641
Dt 23:10 to go outside the camp and **s** there. H4202+995
Dt 24: 5 year he is to be free to **s** at home and bring NDT
Dt 24:11 **S** outside and let the neighbor to whom H6641
Jos 1:14 your livestock *may* **s** in the land that H3782
Jos 4: 3 down at the place where *you* **s** tonight." H4328
Jos 7: 7 had been content *to* **s** on the other side H3782
Jos 20: 6 *They are to* **s** in that city until they have H3782
Jdg 5:16 Why *did you* **s** among the sheep pens to H3782
Jdg 13:15 "*We would like* you *to* **s** until we prepare H6806
Jdg 17: 8 town in search of some other place to **s**. H1591
Jdg 17: 9 he said, "and I'm looking for a place to **s**." H1591
Jdg 19: 4 prevailed on him to **s**; so he remained with NDT
Jdg 19: 6 "Please **s tonight** and enjoy yourself." H4328
Jdg 19: 9 day is nearly over. **S** and enjoy yourself H4328
Jdg 19:10 unwilling to **s** another **night**, the man left H4328
Ru 1:16 go I will go, and where *you* **s** I will stay. H4328
Ru 1:16 go I will go, and where you stay *I will* **s**. H4328
Ru 2: 8 **S** here with the women who work for me H1815
Ru 2:21 '**S** with my workers until they finish H1815
Ru 3:13 **S** here for the night, and in the morning if H4328
1Sa 1:14 "How long *are you going to* **s drunk**? H8910
1Sa 1:23 "**S** here until you have weaned him; only H3782
1Sa 5: 7 the god of Israel *must* not **s** here with us, H3782
1Sa 9:27 did so—"but you **s** here for a while, so H6641
1Sa 14: 9 *we will* **s** where we are and not go up to H6641
1Sa 19: 2 morning; go into hiding and **s there**. H2461
1Sa 22: 3 mother come and **s** with you until I NDT
1Sa 22: 5 said to David, "*Do* not **s** in the stronghold. H3782
1Sa 22:23 **S** with me; don't be afraid. The man who H3782
2Sa 10: 5 "**S** at Jericho till your beards have grown H3782
2Sa 11:12 David said to him, "**S** here one more day H3782
2Sa 15:19 Go back and **s** with King Absalom H3782
2Sa 19:32 the king during his **s** in Mahanaim, H8859
2Sa 19:33 over with me and **s** with me in Jerusalem, NDT
1Ki 17: 9 in the region of Sidon and **s** there. H3782
2Ki 2: 2 Elijah said to Elisha, "**S** here; the LORD H3782
2Ki 2: 4 Elijah said to him, "**S** here, Elisha; the H3782
2Ki 2: 6 Elijah said to him, "**S** here; the LORD has H3782
2Ki 4: 8 who urged him to **s for a meal**. H430+4312
2Ki 4:10 Then *he can* **s** there whenever he comes H6073
2Ki 7: 3 to each other, "Why **s** here until we die? H3782
2Ki 7: 4 And if *we* **s** here, we will die H3782
2Ki 8: 1 your family and **s for a while** wherever you H1591
2Ki 11: 8 **S** close to the king wherever he goes." H2118
2Ki 14:10 in your victory, but **s** at home! Why ask H3782
1Ch 19: 5 "**S** at Jericho till your beards have grown H3782
2Ch 23: 7 **S** close to the king wherever he goes." H2118
2Ch 25:19 But **s** at home! Why ask for H3782
Ezr 6: 6 of that province, **s** away from there. A10201
Ne 4:22 *Have* every man and his helper **s** inside Jerusalem **at night** H4328
Ne 5: 2 in order for us to eat and **s alive**, we must H2649
Ne 11: 1 nine were to **s** in their own towns. NDT
Job 24:13 who do not know its ways or **s** in its paths. H3782
Job 39: 9 *Will it* **s** by your manger **at night**? H4328
Ps 30: 5 lifetime; weeping *may* **s** for the night, but H4328
Ps 38:11 of my wounds; my neighbors **s** far away. H6641
Ps 55: 7 I would flee far away and **s** in the desert; H4328
Ps 92:14 in old age, *they will* **s** fresh and green, H2118
Ps 119: 9 How *can* a young person **s on the path** *of* H784
Ps 119:148 My eyes **s open** *through* the watches of H7709
Ps 127: 2 In vain you rise early and **s up** late, toiling H3782
Pr 7:11 defiant, her feet never **s** at home; H8905
Pr 14: 7 **S** away from a fool, for you will not find H2143
Pr 20:13 **s awake** and you will have food to H7219+6524
Pr 22: 5 would preserve their life **s far** from them. H8178
Isa 5:11 *who* **s up late** at night till they are inflamed H336
Isa 16: 4 *Let* the Moabite fugitives **s** with you; be H1591
Isa 21: 8 the watchtower; every night I **s** at my post. H5893
Jer 25: 5 and *you can* **s** in the land the LORD gave to H3782
Jer 40:10 *I* myself *will* **s** at Mizpah to represent you H3782
Jer 42:10 'If *you* **s** in this land, I will build you H3782+3782
Jer 42:13 if you say, '*We will* not **s** in this land,' H3782
Jer 43: 4 LORD's command to **s** in the land of Judah. H3782
Jer 49:30 **S in** deep caves, you who live in Hazor," H3782
La 4:15 nations say, "*They can* **s** here no longer." H1591
Mic 7:18 *You do* not **s** angry forever but delight to H2616
Mt 2:13 **S** there until I tell you, for Herod is going G1639
Mt 10:11 worthy person and **s** at their house until G3531
Mt 17:17 replied, "how long *shall I* **s** with you? G1639
Mt 26:38 **S** here and keep watch with me. G3531
Mk 6:10 a house, **s** there until you leave that town. G3531
Mk 9:19 replied, "how long *shall I* **s** with you? G1639
Mk 14:34 he said to them. "**S** here and keep watch." G3531
Lk 9: 4 **s** there until you leave that town. G3531
Lk 9:41 "how long *shall I* **s** with you and put up G1639
Lk 10: 7 **S** there, eating and drinking whatever they G3531
Lk 19: 5 I must **s** at your house today. G3531
Lk 24:29 urged him strongly, "**S** with us, for it is G3531
Lk 24:29 So he went in *to* **s** with them. G3531
Lk 24:49 **s** in the city until you have been G2767
Jn 4:40 they urged him *to* **s** with them, and he G3531
Jn 12:46 who believes in me *should* **s** in darkness. G3531
Ac 8:29 "Go to that chariot and **s near** it. G3140
Ac 10:48 they asked Peter *to* **s** *with* them for a few G2152
Ac 13:17 the people prosper during their **s** in Egypt; G4229
Ac 16:15 she said, "come and **s** at my house." G3531
Ac 21:16 the home of Mnason, where *we were to* **s**. G3826
Ac 27:31 "Unless these men **s** with the ship, you G3531
1Co 7: 8 It is good for them *to* **s** unmarried, as I do. G3531
1Co 16: 6 Perhaps *I will* **s** with you **for a while**, or G4169
1Co 16: 8 But *I will* **s on** at Ephesus until Pentecost, G2152
1Ti 1: 3 **s** there in Ephesus so that you may G4693

STAYED (94) [STAY]

Ge 13: 6 not support them while they **s** together, H3782
Ge 20: 1 **For a while** *he* **s** in Gerar, H1591
Ge 21:34 And Abraham **s** in the land of the H1591
Ge 22:19 And Abraham **s** in Beersheba. H3782
Ge 26: 6 So Isaac **s** in Gerar. H3782
Ge 29:14 After Jacob *had* **s** with him *for* a whole H3782
Ge 35:27 Hebron), where Abraham and Isaac *had* **s**. H1591
Ge 37: 1 lived in the land where his father *had* **s**, H4472
Ge 49:24 his strong arms *s* **limber**, because of the AIT
Ge 50:22 Joseph **s** in Egypt, along with all his H3782
Ex 20:18 trembled with fear. *They* **s** at a distance H6641
Ex 24:18 And he **s** on the mountain forty days and H2118
Nu 9:18 long as the cloud **s** over the tabernacle, H8905
Nu 9:21 Sometimes the cloud **s** only from evening H2118
Nu 9:22 Whether the cloud **s** over the H799+8905
Nu 11:35 people traveled to Hazeroth and **s** there. H2118
Nu 20: 1 at the Desert of Zin, and they **s** at Kadesh. H3782
Nu 22: 8 So the Moabite officials **s** with him. H3782
Dt 1: 6 "You *have* **s** long enough at this H3782
Dt 1:46 And so *you* **s** in Kadesh many days—all H3782
Dt 3:29 So *we* **s** in the valley near Beth Peor. H3782
Dt 9: 9 *I* **s** on the mountain forty days and forty H3782
Dt 10:10 Now I *had* **s** on the mountain forty days H6641
Jos 2: 1 of a prostitute named Rahab and **s** there. H8886
Jos 2:22 went into the hills and **s** there three days, H3782
Jdg 5:17 Gilead **s** beyond the Jordan. And Dan H8905
Jdg 5:17 remained on the coast and **s** in his coves. H8905
Jdg 9:41 Then Abimelek **s** in Arumah, and Zebul H3782
Jdg 11:17 he refused. So Israel **s** at Kadesh. H3782
Jdg 15: 8 he went down and **s** in a cave in the rock H3782
Jdg 19: 7 so *he* **s** there *that* **night**. H3782+2256+4328
Jdg 20:47 of Rimmon, where *they* **s** four months. H3782
Ru 2:23 So Ruth **s close** to the women of Boaz to H1815
1Sa 1:23 So the woman **s at home** and nursed her H3782
1Sa 19:18 Samuel went to Naioth and **s** there. H3782
1Sa 22: 4 and *they* **s** with him as long as David was H3782
1Sa 23:14 David **s** in the wilderness strongholds H3782
1Sa 23:25 down to the rock and **s** in the Desert of H3782
1Sa 25:13 while two hundred **s** with the supplies. H3782
1Sa 26: 3 Jeshimon, but David **s** in the wilderness. H3782
1Sa 30: 9 to the Besor Valley, where some **s behind**. H6641
1Sa 30:24 The share of the *man* *who* **s** with the H3782
2Sa 1: 1 the Amalekites and **s** in Ziklag two days. H3782
2Sa 13:38 went to Geshur, *he* **s** there three years. H2118
2Sa 15:29 ark of God back to Jerusalem and **s** there. H3782
2Sa 20: 2 But the men of Judah **s** by their king all H1815
1Ki 2:38 And Shimei **s** in Jerusalem for a long H3782
1Ki 11:16 all the Israelites **s** there for six months, H3782
1Ki 11:40 and **s** there until Solomon's death. H2118
1Ki 17: 5 east of the Jordan, and **s** there. H3782
2Ki 8: 2 family went away and **s** in the land of the H1591
2Ki 10:21 of Baal came; not one **s away**. H4202+995
2Ki 15:20 withdrew and **s** in the land no *longer*. H6641
2Ki 19:36 He returned to Nineveh and **s** there. H3782
1Ch 4:23 *they* **s** there and worked for the king. H3782
1Ch 9:33 **s** in the rooms of the temple and were NDT
Ne 4:18 man who sounded the trumpet **s** with me. NDT
Est 7: 7 **s behind** to beg Queen Esther for his life. H6641
Ecc 2: 9 In all this my wisdom **s** with me. H6641
Isa 37:37 He returned to Nineveh and **s** there. H3782
Jer 40: 6 at Mizpah and **s** with him among the H3782
Mt 2:15 where *he* **s** until the death of Herod. G1639
Mk 1:45 a town openly but **s** outside in lonely G1639
Lk 1:21 why he **s so long** in the temple. G5988
Lk 1:56 Mary **s** with Elizabeth for about three G3531
Lk 2:43 the boy Jesus **s behind** in Jerusalem, but G5702
Lk 24:53 And *they* **s** continually at the temple G1639
Jn 2:12 There *they* **s** for a few days. G3531
Jn 4:40 him to stay with them, and *he* **s** two days. G3531
Jn 6:22 day the crowd that *had* **s** on the opposite G2705
Jn 7: 9 After he had said this, he **s** in Galilee. G3531
Jn 10:40 baptizing in the early days. There *he* **s**, G3531
Jn 11: 6 *he* **s** where he was two more days G3531
Jn 11:20 out to meet him, but Mary **s** at home. G2757
Jn 11:54 Ephraim, where *he* **s** with his disciples. G3531
Ac 9:28 So Saul **s** with them and moved about G1639
Ac 9:43 Peter **s** in Joppa for some time with a G3531
Ac 12:19 went from Judea to Caesarea and **s** there. G1417
Ac 14:28 And *they* **s** there a long time with the G1417
Ac 16:12 And *we* **s** there several days G1417
Ac 17:14 but Silas and Timothy **s** at Berea. G5702
Ac 18: 3 as they were, *he* **s** and worked with them. G3531
Ac 18:11 So Paul **s** in Corinth for a year and a half G2767
Ac 18:18 Paul **s on** in Corinth for some time. G4693
Ac 19:22 *while* he **s** in the province of Asia a little G2091
Ac 20: 3 where *he* **s** three months. Because some G4472
Ac 20: 6 others at Troas, where *we* **s** seven days. G1417
Ac 21: 4 disciples there and **s** with them seven G2152
Ac 21: 7 sisters and **s** with them for a day. G3531
Ac 21: 8 reached Caesarea and **s** at the house of G3531
Ac 28:12 put in at Syracuse and **s** there three days. G2152
Ac 28:30 years Paul **s** there **in** his own rented G1844
Gal 1:18 with Cephas and **s** with him fifteen days. G2152
2Ti 4:20 Erastus **s** in Corinth, and I left Trophimus G3531

STAYING (23) [STAY]

Ge 32: 4 *I have been* **s** with Laban and have H1591
Ge 36: 7 land where they were **s** could not support H4472
Nu 25: 1 While Israel *was* **s** in Shittim, the men H3782
Jdg 19:26 back to the house where her master was **s**, NDT
1Sa 13:16 the men with them *were* **s** in Gibeah in H3782
1Sa 14: 2 Saul *was* **s** on the outskirts of Gibeah H3782
2Sa 11:11 ark and Israel and Judah *are* **s** in tents, H3782
2Sa 16: 3 Ziba said to him, "*He is* **s** in Jerusalem H3782
2Sa 17:17 Ahimaaz *were* **s** at En Rogel. H6641
1Ki 17:19 him to the upper room where he *was* **s**, H3782
1Ki 17:20 tragedy even on this widow I *am* **s** with, H1591
2Ki 2:18 to Elisha, who *was* **s** in Jericho, he said to H3782
Ne 2:11 to Jerusalem, and after **s** there three days H2118
Mt 24:48 'My master *is* **s away a long time**,' G5988
Jn 1:38 means "Teacher"), "where *are you* **s**?" G3531
Jn 1:39 So they went and saw where *he was* **s** G3531
Jn 20:10 disciples went back to **where they were** **s**. G899S
Ac 1:13 upstairs to the room where they were **s**. G2910
Ac 2: 5 Now there were **s** in Jerusalem G2997
Ac 10: 6 He *is* **s** with Simon the tanner, whose G3826
Ac 10:18 who was known as Peter *was* **s** there. G3826
Ac 11:11 stopped at the house where *I was* **s**. G1639
Ac 28:23 numbers to the **place where** he was **s**. G3825

STAYS (7) [STAY]

Nu 14:14 that your cloud **s** over them, and that H6641
Job 39:28 It dwells on a cliff and **s** there **at night**; H4328
Jer 14: 8 like a traveler who **s only a night**? H5742+4328
Jer 21: 9 Whoever **s** in this city will die by the sword, H3782
Jer 38: 2 'Whoever **s** in this city will die by the H3782
1Co 7:40 she is happier if *she* **s** as she is—and I G3531
Rev 16:15 is the *one who* **s awake** and remains G1213

STEAD (1) [INSTEAD]

Isa 43: 3 your ransom, Cush and Seba **in** your **s**. H9393

STEADFAST (9) [STEADFASTLY]

Ps 51:10 and renew a **s** spirit within me. H3922
Ps 57: 7 My heart, O God, *is* **s**, my heart is H3922
Ps 57: 7 steadfast, my heart *is* **s**; I will sing and H3922
Ps 108: 1 *is* **s**; I will sing and make music H3922
Ps 112: 7 their hearts *are* **s**, trusting in the H3922
Ps 119: 5 that my ways *were* **s** in obeying your H3922
Pr 4:26 your feet and *be* **s** *in* all your ways. H3922
Isa 26: 3 in perfect peace those whose minds *are* **s**, H6164
1Pe 5:10 you and make you strong, firm and **s**. G2530

STEADFASTLY (1) [STEADFAST]

2Ch 27: 6 because he walked **s** before the LORD his H3922

STEADILY (2) [STEADY]

Ge 8: 3 The water **receded** **s** from H8740+2143+2256+8740
2Co 3: 7 Israelites could not **look** **s** at the face of G867

STEADY (4) [STEADILY]

Ge 49:24 But his bow remained **s**, his strong arms H419
Ex 17:12 so that his hands remained **s** till sunset. H575
1Ch 13: 9 Uzzah reached out his hand to **s** the ark H296
Isa 35: 3 the feeble hands, **s** the knees that give way H599

STEAL (26) [STEALING, STEALS, STOLE, STOLEN]

Ge 31:30 But why *did you* **s** my gods?" H1704
Ge 44: 8 So why *would we* **s** silver or gold from H1704
Ex 20:15 "*You shall* not **s**. H1704
Lev 19:11 " '*Do* not **s**. " 'Do not lie. H1704
Dt 5:19 "*You shall* not **s**. H1704
Jdg 14:15 Did you invite us here to **s** our **property**?" H3769
2Sa 19: 3 that day as men **s** **in** who are ashamed H1704
2Sa 19:41 *did* our brothers, the men of Judah, **s** the king **away** H1704
Ps 69: 4 I am forced to restore what *I did* not **s**. H1608
Ps 104:22 sun rises, and *they* **s** **away**; they return and H665
Pr 30: 9 Or I may become poor and **s**, and so H1704
Jer 7: 9 " '*Will you* **s** and murder, commit adultery H1704
Jer 23:30 the prophets *who* **s** from one another H1704
Jer 49: 9 *would they* not **s** only as much as they H8845
Ob 5 *would they* not **s** only as much as they H1704
Mt 6:19 destroy, and where thieves break in and **s**. G3096
Mt 6:20 where thieves do not break in and **s**. G3096
Mt 19:18 adultery, *you shall* not **s**, you shall not G3096
Mt 27:64 may come and **s** the body and tell the G3096
Mk 10:19 adultery, *you shall* not **s**, you shall not G3096
Lk 18:20 not murder, *you shall* not **s**, you shall not G3096
Jn 10:10 thief comes only to **s** and kill and destroy; G3096
Ro 2:21 who preach against stealing, *do you* **s**? G3096
Ro 13: 9 not murder," "*You shall* not **s**," "You shall G3096
Eph 4:28 who has been stealing *must* **s** no longer, G3096
Titus 2:10 not *to* **s** from them, but to show that G3802

STEALING (3) [STEAL]

Hos 4: 2 lying and murder, **s** and adultery; they H1704
Ro 2:21 You who preach against **s**, do you steal? G3096
Eph 4:28 Anyone *who has been* **s** must steal no G3096

STEALS (4) [STEAL]

Ex 22: 1 "Whoever **s** an ox or a sheep and H1704
Ex 22: 3 "Anyone who **s** must certainly make NDT
Job 24:14 and in the night **s** **forth** like a thief. H2118
Pr 6:30 despise a thief if *he* **s** to satisfy his hunger H1704

STEDFAST, STEDFASTLY (KJV) BINDING, DETERMINED, DEVOTED, DIRECTLY, ENDURES, FAITHFUL, FIRM, FIRMLY, FIXED, INTENTLY, RESOLUTELY, SECURE, SETTLED, STEADILY

STEEDS (3)

Jdg 5:22 galloping, galloping go his mighty **s**. NDT
Jer 46: 4 mount the **s**! Take your positions H7304
Jer 47: 3 at the sound of the hooves of galloping **s**, at H52

STEEL (KJV) BRONZE, BRONZE-TIPPED

STEEP (4) [STEEPED]

Isa 7:19 settle in the **s** ravines and in the H1431
Mt 8:32 rushed down the **s bank** into the lake and G3204
Mk 5:13 rushed down the **s bank** into the lake and G3204
Lk 8:33 rushed down the **s bank** into the lake and G3204

STEEPED (1) [STEEP]

Jn 9:34 replied, "You were **s** in sin at birth; how G3910

STEERED (1)

Jas 3: 4 *they are* **s** by a very small rudder wherever G3555

STEM (KJV) STUMP

STENCH (5) [STINK]

Pr 13: 5 the wicked **make** *themselves* **a s** and bring H944
Isa 3:24 Instead of fragrance there will be a **s** H5215
Joel 2:20 And its **s** will go up; its smell will H945
Am 4:10 filled your nostrils with the **s** *of* your camps, H945
Am 5:21 your assemblies *are* **a s** *to me*. H4202+8193

STEP (15) [FOOTSTEPS, OVERSTEP, STEPPED, STEPPING, STEPS]

Dt 21: 5 The Levitical priests *shall* **s forward**, for H5602
1Sa 5: 5 temple at Ashdod **s** on the threshold. H2005
1Sa 20: 3 there is only a **s** between me and death." H7315
1Ki 10:20 on the six steps, one at either end of each **s**. NDT
2Ch 9:19 on the six steps, one at either end of each **s**. NDT
Job 18: 7 The vigor of his **s** is weakened; his own H7576
Job 18:11 him on every side and dog his *every* **s**. H8079
Job 31: 4 he not see my ways and count my every **s**? H7576
Job 31:37 I would give him an account of my *every* **s**; H7576
Job 34:21 the ways of mortals; he sees their every **s**. H7576
Ps 1: 1 does not walk **in s with** the wicked H928+6783
Ps 89:51 have mocked *every* **s** *of* your anointed H6811
La 4:18 People stalked us at *every* **s**, so we could H7576
Eze 26:16 of the coast *will* **s down** from their thrones H3718
Gal 5:25 the Spirit, *let us* **keep in s with** the Spirit. G5123

STEPHANAS (3)

1Co 1:16 I also baptized the household *of* **S** G5107
1Co 16:15 that the household *of* **S** were the first G5107
1Co 16:17 I was glad when **S**, Fortunatus and G5107

STEPHEN (12)

Ac 6: 5 They chose **S**, a man full of faith and of G5108
Ac 6: 8 Now **S**, a man full of God's grace and G5108
Ac 6: 9 Asia—who began to argue with **S**. G5108
Ac 6:11 "We have heard **S** speak blasphemous G899S
Ac 6:12 They seized **S** and brought him before the G899S
Ac 6:15 in the Sanhedrin looked intently at **S**, G899S
Ac 7: 1 Then the high priest asked **S**, "Are these NDT
Ac 7:55 But **S**, full of the Holy Spirit, looked up to NDT
Ac 7:59 were stoning him, **S** prayed, "Lord Jesus, G5108
Ac 8: 2 Godly men buried **S** and mourned deeply G5108
Ac 11:19 that broke out when **S** was killed traveled G5108
Ac 22:20 the blood of your martyr **S** was shed, G5108

STEPPED (14) [STEP]

Lev 9:22 the fellowship offering, *he* **s down**. H3718
Nu 12: 5 When the two of them **s forward**, H3655
Jdg 8:21 So Gideon **s forward** and killed them H7756
Jdg 19:27 of the house and **s out** to continue on his H3655
1Sa 17:23 **s out** from his lines and shouted his usual H6590
2Sa 18:30 So *he* **s aside** and stood there H6015
2Sa 20: 8 As he **s forward**, it dropped out of its H3655
1Ki 14:17 As soon as she **s** over the threshold of the H995
1Ki 18:36 the prophet Elijah **s forward** and prayed: H5602
Job 29: 8 men saw me and **s aside** and the old H2461
Jer 26:17 of the land **s forward** and said to the H7756
Mt 9: 1 Jesus **s into** a boat, crossed over and G1832
Mt 26:50 Then *the men* **s forward**, seized Jesus G4665
Lk 8:27 *When* Jesus **s** ashore, he was met by a G2002

STEPPING (2) [STEP]

Pr 7:22 the slaughter, like a deer **s** into a noose H6576
Zep 1: 9 punish all who **avoid** **s** on the threshold, H1925

STEPS (46) [STEP]

Ex 20:26 And do not go up to my altar on **s**, or your H5092
2Sa 6:13 the ark of the LORD *had* **taken** six **s**, H7575+7576
1Ki 10:19 The throne had six **s**, and its back had a H5092
1Ki 10:20 Twelve lions stood on the six **s**, one at H5092
2Ki 9:13 spread them under him on the bare **s**. H5092
2Ki 20: 9 Shall the shadow go forward ten **s**, or H5092
2Ki 20: 9 ten steps, or shall it go back ten **s**? H5092
2Ki 20:10 matter for the shadow to go forward ten **s**," H5092
2Ki 20:10 "Rather, have it go back ten **s**." H5092
2Ki 20:11 go back the ten **s** it had gone down on H5092
2Ch 9:11 algumwood to make **s** for the temple of H5019
2Ch 9:18 The throne had six **s**, and a footstool of H5092
2Ch 9:19 Twelve lions stood on the six **s**, one at H5092
Ne 3:15 as far as the **s** going down from the City of H5092
Ne 12:37 directly up the **s** *of* the City of David on H5092
Job 14:16 you will count my **s** but not keep track of H7576
Job 23:11 My feet have closely followed his **s**; I have H892
Job 31: 7 if my **s** have turned from the path, if my H892
Ps 17: 5 My **s** have held to your paths; my feet have H892
Ps 37:23 LORD makes firm the **s** *of* the one who H5202

S

Ps 56: 6 they watch my **s**, hoping to take my H6811
Ps 74: 3 Turn your **s** toward these everlasting ruins H7193
Ps 85:13 before him and prepares the way for his **s**. H7193
Ps 119:59 have turned my **s** to your statutes. H8079
Pr 4:12 you walk, your **s** will not be hampered H7576
Pr 5: 5 to death; her **s** lead straight to the grave. H7576
Pr 14:15 the prudent give thought to their **s**. H892
Pr 16: 9 but the LORD establishes their **s**. H7576
Pr 20:24 A person's **s** are directed by the LORD. H5202
Ecc 5: 1 Guard your **s** when you go to the house of H8079
Isa 38: 8 go back the ten **s** it has gone down on H5092
Isa 38: 8 went back the ten **s** it had gone down. H5092
Jer 10:23 it is not for them to direct their **s**. H7576
Eze 40: 6 He climbed its **s** and measured the H5092
Eze 40:22 Seven **s** led up to it, with its portico H5092
Eze 40:26 Seven **s** led up to it, with its portico H5092
Eze 40:31 its jambs, and eight **s** led up to it. H5092
Eze 40:34 on either side, and eight **s** led up to it. H5092
Eze 40:37 on either side, and eight **s** led up to it. H5092
Eze 40:40 near the **s** at the entrance of the north H6590
Eze 40:40 on the other side of the **s** were two tables. NDT
Eze 43:17 The **s** *of* the altar face east. H5092
Hab 3: 5 before him; pestilence followed his **s**. H8079
Ac 21:35 When Paul reached the **s**, the violence of *G325*
Ac 21:40 Paul stood on the **s** and motioned to the *G325*
1Pe 2:21 example, that you should follow *in* his **s**. *G2717*

STERN (4) [STERNLY, STERNNESS]

Pr 15:10 **S** discipline awaits anyone who leaves H8273
Mk 4:38 Jesus was in the **s**, sleeping on a cushion *G4744*
Ac 27:29 four anchors from the **s** and prayed for *G4744*
Ac 27:41 the **s** was broken to pieces by the *G4744*

STERNLY (3) [STERN]

Mt 9:30 Jesus **warned** them **s**, "See that no one *G1839*
Mk 1:25 said Jesus **s**. "Come out of him! *G2203*
Lk 4:35 Jesus said **s**. "Come out of him! *G2203*

STERNNESS (2) [STERN]

Ro 11:22 therefore the kindness and **s** of God: *G704*
Ro 11:22 **s** to those who fell, but kindness to you *G704*

STEW (7)

Ge 25:29 Once when Jacob was cooking *some* **s** H5686
Ge 25:30 let me have some of that **red** *s*! AIT
Ge 25:34 gave Esau some bread and *some* lentil **s**. H5686
2Ki 4:38 large pot and cook *some* **s** for these H5686
2Ki 4:39 he cut them up into the pot of **s**, though H5686
2Ki 4:40 The **s** was poured out for the men, but as H5686
Hag 2:12 that fold touches some bread or **s** H5686

STEWARD (10) [STEWARDS]

Ge 43:16 he said to **the s** *of* his house H889+6584[S]
Ge 43:19 went up to Joseph's **s** and spoke H2021+408+889+6584+1074[S]
Ge 43:24 The **s** took the men into Joseph's house H408[S]
Ge 44: 1 instructions to **the s** *of* his house: H889+6584[S]
Ge 44: 4 when Joseph said to his **s**, H889+6584+1074[S]
Ge 44:12 Then the **s** proceeded to search, beginning NDT
2Sa 9: 9 Saul's **s**, and said to him, H5853
2Sa 16: 1 there was Ziba, the **s** *of* Mephibosheth H5853
2Sa 19:17 with Ziba, the **s** *of* Saul's household H5853
Isa 22:15 say to this **s**, to Shebna the palace H6125

STEWARDS (2) [STEWARD]

Est 1: 8 all the **wine s** to serve each man H8042+1074
1Pe 4:10 as faithful **s** of God's grace in its various *G3874*

STICK (17) [STICKING, STICKS, STUCK]

2Ki 6: 6 Elisha cut a **s** and threw it there H6770
Job 33:21 their bones, once hidden, now **s out**. H9142
Job 38:38 hard and the clods of earth **s together**? H1815
Isa 28:27 out with a rod, and cumin with a **s**. H8657
Isa 57: 4 whom do you sneer and **s out** your tongue? H799
La 4: 8 their bones; it has become as dry as a **s**. H6770
Eze 3:26 *I will* **make** your tongue **s** to the roof of H1815
Eze 21:10 The sword despises every such **s**. H6770
Eze 29: 4 and **make** the fish of your streams **s** to H1815
Eze 37:16 of man, take a **s of wood** and write on it H6770
Eze 37:16 Then take another **s of wood**, and write H6770
Eze 37:17 them together into one **s** so that they will H6770
Eze 37:19 I am going to take the **s** *of* Joseph—which H6770
Eze 37:19 with him, and join it to Judah's **s**. H6770
Eze 37:19 I will make them into a single **s of wood** H6770
Am 4:11 You were like a **burning s** snatched from H202
Zec 3: 2 Is not this man a **burning s** snatched from H202

STICKING (1) [STICK]

Eze 29: 4 streams, with all the fish **s** to your scales. H1815

STICKS (7) [STICK]

1Sa 17:43 "Am I a dog, that you come at me with **s**?" H5234
1Ki 17:10 a widow was there gathering **s**. H6770
1Ki 17:12 I am gathering a few **s** to take home and H6770
Ps 22:15 my tongue **s** *to* the roof of my mouth H1815
Pr 18:24 is a friend *who* **s closer** than a brother. H1816
La 4: 4 the infant's tongue **s** to the roof of its H1815
Eze 37:20 their eyes the **s** you have written on H6770

STIFF-NECKED (19) [NECK]

Ex 32: 9 Moses, "and they are a **s** people. H7997+6902
Ex 33: 3 because you are a **s** people and I H7997+6902
Ex 33: 5 the Israelites, 'You are a **s** people. H7997+6902
Ex 34: 9 Although this is a **s** people, forgive H7997+6902
Dt 9: 6 to possess, for you are a **s** people. H7997+6902
Dt 9:13 and they are a **s** people indeed! H7997+6902
Dt 10:16 and *do* not *be* **s** any longer. H7996+6902
Dt 31:27 know how rebellious and **s** you are. H7997+6902
2Ki 17:14 not listen and *were* as **s** as their H7996+6902
2Ch 30: 8 *Do* not *be* **s**, as your ancestors were H7996+6902
2Ch 36:13 *He became* **s** and hardened his H7996+6902
Ne 9:16 became arrogant and **s**, and they H7996+6902
Ne 9:17 *They became* **s** and in their H7996+6902
Ne 9:29 *became* **s** and refused to listen. H7996+6902
Pr 29: 1 Whoever *remains* **s** after many H7996+6902
Jer 7:26 *They were* **s** and did more evil than H7996+6902
Jer 17:23 *they were* **s** and would not listen H7996+6902
Jer 19:15 because *they were* **s** and would not H7996+6902
Ac 7:51 "*You* **s** *people*! Your hearts and ears are *G5019*

STILL (292) [STILLED]

Ge 9: 4 not eat meat that has its lifeblood **s** in it. NDT
Ge 11:28 **While** his father Terah was **s alive** H6584+7156
Ge 16:14 Beer Lahai Roi; **it is s there**, between H2180
Ge 25: 6 But while he was **s** living, he gave gifts to H6388
Ge 29: 7 he said, "the sun is **s** high; it is not time H6388
Ge 29: 9 **While** he was **s** talking with them, Rachel H6388
Ge 31:14 "Do we **s** have any share in the H6388
Ge 34:25 while all of them were *s* **in pain**, two of AIT
Ge 35:16 While they were **s** some distance from H6388
Ge 38: 5 gave birth to **s another** son and H3578+6388
Ge 43: 1 Now the famine was **s** severe in the land. NDT
Ge 43: 7 'Is your father **s** living?' he asked us. H6388
Ge 43:27 father you told me about? Is he **s** living?" H6388
Ge 43:28 servant our father is **s** alive and well." H6388
Ge 44:14 Joseph was **s** in the house when Judah H6388
Ge 45: 3 Is my father **s** living?" But his H6388
Ge 45:11 five years of famine are **s** *to come*. H6388
Ge 45:26 told him, "Joseph is **s** alive! In fact, he is H6388
Ge 45:28 My son Joseph is **s** alive. I will go and see H6388
Ge 46:30 I have seen for myself that you are **s** alive." H6388
Ge 47:26 land in Egypt—**s in force** today—that a H6330
Ge 48: 7 of Canaan while we were **s** on the way, H6388
Ex 4:18 in Egypt to see if any of them are **s** alive." H6388
Ex 9:17 You **s** set yourself against my people and H6388
Ex 9:19 been brought in and *is* **s out** in the field, H5162
Ex 9:30 your officials **s** do **not** fear the LORD God H3270
Ex 14:14 will fight for you; you *need only to be* **s**." H3087
Ex 15:16 of your arm *they will be* as **s** as a stone— H1957
Ex 21:16 has been sold or **is** *s* in the kidnapper's AIT
Ex 22:17 *he must s* **pay** the bride-price for virgins. AIT
Lev 10: 5 came and carried them, **s** in their tunics NDT
Lev 19:26 " 'Do not eat any meat with the blood **s** in it. NDT
Lev 26:10 *You will s be* **eating** last year's harvest when AIT
Lev 26:27 in spite of this *you s do* not **listen** to me but AIT
Nu 9:10 *they are s to* **celebrate** the LORD's Passover AIT
Nu 11:33 But **while** the meat was **s** between their H6388
Nu 30: 3 "When a young woman **s** living in her NDT
Nu 30:16 his young daughter **s** living at home. NDT
Dt 3:11 It is **s** in Rabbah of the Ammonites. NDT
Dt 4: 4 fast to the LORD your God are **s** alive today. NDT
Dt 10: 8 blessings in his name, as they **s** do today. H6330
Dt 22:21 promiscuous while **s** in her father's house. NDT
Dt 31:27 the LORD while I am **s** alive and with you, H6388
Jos 5: 7 They were **s** uncircumcised because they H3954
Jos 10:12 **stand s** over Gibeon, and you H1957
Jos 10:13 So the sun **stood s**, and the moon H1957
Jos 13: 1 and *there are* **s** very large areas of land to H8636
Jos 14:11 I am **s** as strong today as the day Moses H6388
Jos 18: 2 but *there were* **s** seven Israelite tribes who H3855
Jdg 7: 4 to Gideon, "There are **s** too many men. H6388
Jdg 8: 5 *I am s* **pursuing** Zebah and Zalmunna AIT
Jdg 9:49 set it on fire **with** the people **s inside**. H6584
Jdg 15:19 and it is **s** there in Lehi. H6330+2021+3427+2021+2296
Ru 1:12 Even if I thought there was **s** hope for me NDT
1Sa 8:12 **s** others to make weapons of war and NDT
1Sa 12:16 **stand s** and see this great thing the LORD H3656
1Sa 14:34 the LORD by eating meat with blood **s** in it. NDT
1Sa 16:11 "*There is* **s** the youngest," Jesse H8636+6388
1Sa 17:57 with David **s** holding the Philistine's head. NDT
1Sa 18:29 Saul became **s** more afraid of him, and he H6388
2Sa 1: 9 the throes of death, but I'm **s** alive. H3972+6388
2Sa 3:35 to eat something while it was **s** day; H6388
2Sa 9: 1 "Is there anyone **s** left of the house of H6388
2Sa 9: 3 "Is there no one **s** alive from the house of H6388
2Sa 9: 3 the king, "There is **s** a son of Jonathan H6388
2Sa 12:18 "While the child **was** *s* living, he wouldn't AIT
2Sa 12:22 "While the child was **s** alive, I fasted and H6388
2Sa 13:25 *he s* **refused** to go but gave him his blessing. AIT
2Sa 14:32 It would be better for me if I were **s** there!" H6388
2Sa 18:14 heart **while** Absalom was **s** alive in the H6388
2Sa 19:35 Can I **s** hear the voices of male and H6388
2Sa 21:20 In **s another** battle, which took place at H6388
1Ki 1:14 **While** you are **s** there talking to the king, H6388
1Ki 1:22 **While** she was **s** speaking with the king H6388
1Ki 3: 2 however, *were s* **sacrificing** at the high places AIT
1Ki 8: 8 Holy Place; and they are **s** there today. H6330
1Ki 9:20 *There were* **s** people **left** from the H3855
1Ki 11:17 But Hadad, **s** only a boy, fled to Egypt with NDT
1Ki 12: 2 heard this (he was **s** in Egypt, where he H6388
1Ki 12:17 of Judah, Rehoboam **s ruled** over them. AIT
1Ki 20:32 king answered, "Is he **s** alive? He is my H6388
1Ki 22: 8 "There is **s** one prophet through whom we H6388
2Ki 6:33 **While** he was **s** talking to them, the H6388
2Ki 12: 6 the priests *s had* not **repaired** the temple. AIT
2Ki 17:23 and they are **s** there. H6330+2021+3427+2021+2296
2Ki 19: 4 pray for the remnant that *s* **survives**." AIT
2Ki 25:19 Of *those* **s** in the city, he took the officer in H5162
1Ch 20: 6 In **s another** battle, which took place at H6388
2Ch 5: 9 Holy Place; and they are **s** there today. H6330
2Ch 8: 7 There were **s** people **left** from the Hittites H3855
2Ch 10:17 of Judah, Rehoboam *s* **ruled** over them. AIT
2Ch 14: 7 The land is **s** ours, because we have H6388
2Ch 18: 7 "There is **s** one prophet through whom we H6388
2Ch 20:33 the people **s** had not set their hearts H6388
2Ch 25:16 **While** he was *s* speaking, the king said to AIT
2Ch 34: 3 of his reign, **while** he was **s** young, he H6388
Ezr 10: 2 But in spite of this, **there is** *s* hope for Israel. AIT
Ne 5: 4 **S** others were saying, "We have had to H2256
Ne 7: 3 While the gatekeepers *are s* **on duty**, have AIT
Ne 8:11 the people, saying, "**Be s**, for this is a holy H2187
Est 6:14 **While** they were **s** talking with him, the H6388
Job 1:16 **While** he was **s** speaking, another H6388
Job 1:17 **While** he was **s** speaking, another H6388
Job 1:18 **While** he was **s** speaking, yet another H6330
Job 2: 3 And he **s** maintains his integrity, though H6388
Job 2: 9 "Are you **s** maintaining your integrity? H6388
Job 6:10 Then I would **s** have this consolation H6388
Job 6:11 strength do I have, that *I should s* **hope**? AIT
Job 8:12 **While s** growing and uncut, they wither H6388
Job 9:28 *I s* **dread** all my sufferings, for I know you AIT
Job 23:14 and many such plans he **s** has in store. NDT
Job 24:10 they carry the sheaves, but **s** go hungry. NDT
Job 29: 5 when the Almighty was **s** with me and my H6388
Job 39:24 *it* cannot **stand s** when the trumpet sounds. H586
Ps 37: 7 **Be s** before the LORD and wait patiently H1957
Ps 46:10 He says, "*Be* **s**, and know that I am God; H8332
Ps 58:11 "Surely the righteous **s** are rewarded; surely NDT
Ps 67: 7 *May* God **bless** us *s*, so that all the ends of AIT
Ps 76: 6 God of Jacob, both horse and chariot **lie s**. H8101
Ps 78:30 even **while** the food was **s** in their mouths, H6388
Ps 89: 9 when its waves mount up, you **s** them. H8656
Ps 92:14 They will **s** bear fruit in old age, they will H6388
Ps 139:18 of sand—when I awake, I am **s** with you. H6388
Ps 141: 5 my prayer will **s** be against the deeds H6388
Pr 4: 3 a son to my father, **s** tender, and cherished NDT
Pr 9: 9 Instruct the wise and they will be wiser **s** H6388
Pr 31:15 She gets up while it is **s** night; she H6388
Ecc 2: 3 my mind *s* **guiding** me with wisdom. AIT
Ecc 4: 2 happier than the living, who are **s** alive. H6364
Ecc 5: 8 over them both are others higher **s**. NDT
Ecc 7:28 **while** I was **s** searching but not finding—I H6388
Isa 5:25 is not turned away, his hand is **s** upraised. H6388
Isa 9:12 is not turned away, his hand is **s** upraised. H6388
Isa 9:17 is not turned away, his hand is **s** upraised. H6388
Isa 9:20 will devour, but *s be* **hungry**; on the left they AIT
Isa 9:21 is not turned away, his hand is **s** upraised. H6388
Isa 10: 4 is not turned away, his hand is **s** upraised. H6388
Isa 15: 9 I will bring **s more** upon Dimon—a H3578
Isa 22: 3 having fled while the enemy was **s** far away. NDT
Isa 29: 8 awakens **hungry** *s*; as when a thirsty AIT
Isa 29: 8 of drinking, but awakens faint and **thirsty** *s*. AIT
Isa 37: 4 pray for the remnant that *s* **survives**." AIT
Isa 44: 5 of Jacob; **s** others will write on their hand H2256
Isa 46:10 ancient times, what *is* **s to come**. H4202+6913
Isa 56: 8 "I will gather *s* **others** to them besides those AIT
Isa 65: 8 "As when juice **is** *s* **found** in a cluster of AIT
Isa 65: 8 destroy it, there is **s** a blessing in it,' so H3954
Isa 65:24 **while** they are **s** speaking I will hear. H6388
Jer 2:22 the **stain** of your guilt *is s* before me, AIT
Jer 5: 2 **s** they are swearing falsely. H4200+4027
Jer 15: 9 Her sun will set while it is **s** day; she will H6388
Jer 22:24 on my right hand, I would **s** pull you off. H3954
Jer 31:20 speak against him, I **s** remember him. H6388
Jer 32:20 renown that is **s** yours. H3869+2021+3427+2021+2296
Jer 33: 1 **While** Jeremiah was **s** confined in the H6388
Jer 34: 7 cities of Judah that *were s* **holding out**— AIT
Jer 40: 7 their men who were **s** in the open country NDT
Jer 40:13 all the army officers **s** in the open country NDT
Jer 42:21 but *you s have* not **obeyed** the LORD your God AIT
Jer 47: 6 Return to your sheath; cease and **be s**.' H1957
Jer 52:25 Of those **s** in the city, he took the officer in H5162
Eze 1:21 when the creatures **stood s**, they also H6641
Eze 1:21 stood still, *they* also **stood s**; and when H6641
Eze 1:24 When they **stood s**, they lowered their H6641
Eze 10:17 When the cherubim **stood s**, they also H6641
Eze 10:17 stood still, *they* also **stood s**; and when H6641
Eze 16:28 after that, you **s** were not satisfied. H2256+1685
Eze 23: 5 in prostitution while she was **s** mine; NDT
Eze 23:14 "But *she* **carried** her prostitution **s further** H3578
Eze 33:25 meat with the blood **s** in it and look to your NDT
Da 6:13 *He s* **prays** three times a day. AIT
Da 9:21 **while** I was **s** in prayer, Gabriel, the man I H6388
Da 11:27 because an end will **s** come at the H6388
Da 11:35 it will **s** come at the appointed time. H6388
Am 4: 7 the harvest was **s** three months away. H6388
Jnh 4: 2 what I said, LORD, when I was **s** at home? H6330
Mic 6:10 Am I **s** to forget your ill-gotten treasures H6388
Mic 6:14 be satisfied; your stomach will **s** be empty. NDT
Hab 3:11 Sun and moon **stood s** in the heavens at H6641
Zep 3: 7 But *they were s* **eager** to act corruptly in all AIT
Zec 2:13 **Be s** before the LORD, all mankind, because H2187
Zec 13: 3 And if anyone **s** prophesies, their father H6388
Zec 14:12 rot while they *are s* **standing** on their feet, AIT

Mt 5:25 Do it while you are s together on G2401+4015
Mt 12:46 While Jesus was s talking to the crowd G2285
Mt 13: 8 S other seed fell on good soil, where it G1254
Mt 13:33 He told them s another parable: "The AIT
Mt 15:16 "Are you s so dull?" Jesus asked them. G197
Mt 16: 9 Do you s not understand? Don't you G4037
Mt 16:14 say Elijah; and s others, Jeremiah or one of AIT
Mt 17: 5 While he was s speaking, a bright cloud G2285
Mt 18:17 If they s refuse to listen, tell it to the church AIT
Mt 19:20 the young man said. "What do I s lack?" G2285
Mt 20: 6 out and found s others standing around. AIT
Mt 24: 6 must happen, but the end is s to come. G4037
Mt 26:45 "Are you s sleeping and resting? G3836+3370
Mt 26:47 While he was s speaking, Judas, one of the AIT
Mt 27:63 that while he was s alive that deceiver G2285
Mk 1:35 morning, while it was s dark, Jesus got G1939
Mk 1:45 Yet the people s came to him from AIT
Mk 4: 8 S other seed fell on good soil. It came up G2779
Mk 4:18 S others, like seed sown among thorns G2779
Mk 4:39 Be s!" Then the wind died down G5821
Mk 4:40 you so afraid? Do you s have no faith?" G4037
Mk 5:35 While Jesus was s speaking, some G2285
Mk 6:15 And s others claimed, "He is a prophet, like AIT
Mk 8:17 Do you s not see or understand G4037
Mk 8:21 said to them, "Do you s not understand?" G4037
Mk 8:28 say Elijah; and s others, one of the prophets." AIT
Mk 12: 5 He sent s another, and that one they killed G2779
Mk 13: 7 must happen, but the end is s to come. G4037
Mk 14:41 "Are you s sleeping and resting? G3836+3370
Mk 15: 5 But Jesus s made no reply, and Pilate was G4033
Lk 7:14 carrying him on, and the bearers stood s. G2705
Lk 8: 8 S other seed fell on good soil. It came up G2779
Lk 8:49 While Jesus was s speaking, someone G2285
Lk 9: 8 and s others that one of the prophets of long AIT
Lk 9:19 say Elijah; and s others, that one of the AIT
Lk 9:61 S another said, "I will follow you, Lord G2779
Lk 14:20 "S another said, 'I just got married, so I G2779
Lk 14:22 has been done, but there is s room. G2285
Lk 14:32 while the other is s a long way off and G2285
Lk 15:20 "But while he was s a long way off, his G2285
Lk 18:22 he said to him, "You s lack one thing. G2285
Lk 20:12 He sent s a third, and they wounded him G2779
Lk 22:47 While he was s speaking a crowd came G2285
Lk 24: 6 while he was s with you in Galilee: G2285
Lk 24:17 you walk along?" They stood s, their faces G2705
Lk 24:36 While they were s talking about this, Jesus AIT
Lk 24:41 And while they s did not believe it G2285
Lk 24:44 is what I told you while I was s with you: G2285
Jn 1:48 "I saw you while you were s under the fig AIT
Jn 3:11 but s you people do not accept our testimony. AIT
Jn 4:35 a saying, 'It's s four months until harvest'? G2285
Jn 4:51 While he was s on the way, his servants G2453
Jn 6:36 you have seen me and s you do not believe. AIT
Jn 7:28 Then Jesus, s teaching in the temple courts AIT
Jn 7:31 S, many in the crowd believed in him G1254
Jn 7:41 S others asked, "How can the G3836+1254
Jn 8: 9 was left, with the woman s standing there. AIT
Jn 9:18 They s did not believe that he had been AIT
Jn 11:30 was s at the place where Martha had G2285
Jn 12:37 presence, they s would not believe in him. AIT
Jn 14:25 "All this I have spoken while s with you. G3531
Jn 17:11 no longer, but they are s in the world, and I AIT
Jn 17:13 I say these things while I am s in the world, AIT
Jn 18:25 Simon Peter was s standing there warming AIT
Jn 20: 1 while it was s dark, Mary G2285
Jn 20: 7 The cloth was s lying in its place, separate AIT
Jn 20: 9 They s did not understand from Scripture G4031
Ac 7: 2 father Abraham while he was s in AIT
Ac 7:51 Your hearts and ears are s uncircumcised NDT
Ac 9: 1 Saul was s breathing out murderous G2285
Ac 9:39 Dorcas had made while she was s with them. AIT
Ac 10:19 While Peter was s thinking about the vision AIT
Ac 10:44 While Peter was s speaking these words G2285
Ac 27:27 we were s being driven across the Adriatic AIT
Ro 3: 7 why am I s condemned as a sinner?" G2285
Ro 4:11 had by faith while he was s uncircumcised. NDT
Ro 5: 6 when we were s powerless, Christ G2285
Ro 5: 8 While we were s sinners, Christ died for G2285
Ro 7: 3 another man while her husband is s alive, AIT
Ro 9:19 "Then why does God s blame us? For who G2285
1Co 1:12 follow Cephas"; s another, "I follow Christ G1254
1Co 3: 1 the Spirit but as people who are s worldly— AIT
1Co 3: 2 Indeed, you are s not ready. G2285+3814
1Co 3: 3 You are s worldly. For since there is G2285
1Co 8: 7 Some people are s so accustomed G2401+785
1Co 12:10 and to s another the interpretation of G1254
1Co 15: 6 most of whom are s living, though G2401+785
1Co 15:17 your faith is futile; you are s in your sins. G2285
2Co 2:13 I s had no peace of mind, because I did not AIT
Gal 1:10 If I were s trying to please people, I would G2285
Gal 5:11 if I am s preaching circumcision G2285
Gal 5:11 why am I s being persecuted? G2285
Eph 4:26 let the sun go down while you are s angry, NDT
Php 1:30 you saw I had, and now hear that I s have. NDT
Col 1:24 up in my flesh what is s lacking in regard to NDT
Col 2:20 as though you s belonged to the world AIT
1Th 4:15 we tell you that we who are s alive, who are AIT
1Th 4:17 we who are s alive and are left will be AIT
Heb 4: 1 since the promise of entering his rest s stands AIT
Heb 4: 6 Therefore since it s remains for some to enter AIT
Heb 5:13 who lives on milk, being s an infant, is not AIT
Heb 7:10 Levi was s in the body of his ancestor. G2285
Heb 7:11 why was there s need for another priest to G2285
Heb 9: 8 as long as the first tabernacle was s G2285
Heb 11: 4 And by faith Abel s speaks, even though G2285
Heb 11:13 All these people were s living by faith when NDT
1Jn 2: 9 brother or sister is s in the darkness. G2401+785
Rev 9:20 these plagues s did not repent of the work of AIT
Rev 14:18 S another angel, who had charge of the G2779

STILLBORN (4) [BEAR]

Nu 12:12 let her be like a s infant coming from its H4637
Job 3:16 hidden away in the ground like a s child, H5878
Ps 58: 8 like a s child that never sees the sun. H5878+851
Ecc 6: 3 I say that a s child is better off than he. H5878

STILLED (6) [STILL]

Ps 65: 7 who s the roaring of the seas, the roaring H8656
Ps 107:29 He s the storm to a whisper; the waves of H7756
Isa 16: 9 fruit and over your harvests have been s. H5877
Isa 24: 8 The joyful timbrels are s, the noise of the H8697
Isa 25: 5 of a cloud, so the song of the ruthless is s. H6700
1Co 13: 8 are tongues, they will be s; where there is G4264

STIMULATE (1)

2Pe 3: 1 them as reminders to s you to wholesome G1444

STING (3) [STINGERS, STINGING]

1Co 15:55 Where, O death, is your s?" G3034
1Co 15:56 The s of death is sin, and the power of sin G3034
Rev 9: 5 was like that of the s of a scorpion when it G990

STINGERS (1) [STING]

Rev 9:10 They had tails with s, like scorpions, and G3034

STINGING (1) [STING]

Eze 5:15 in anger and in wrath and with s rebuke. H2779

STINGY (1)

Pr 28:22 The s are eager to get rich H8273+6524+408

STINK (4) [STENCH]

Ex 7:18 and the river will s; the Egyptians will H944
Ex 16:24 and it did not s or get maggots in it. H944
Isa 19: 6 The canals will s; the streams of Egypt H2395
Isa 34: 3 their dead bodies will s; the H6590+945

STINKWEED (1) [WEED]

Job 31:40 instead of wheat and s instead of barley." H947

STIPULATIONS (4)

Dt 4:45 These are the s, decrees and laws Moses H6343
Dt 6:17 your God and the s and decrees he has H6343
Dt 6:20 "What is the meaning of the s, decrees H6343
Jer 44:23 followed his law or his decrees or his s, H6343

STIR (18) [ASTIR, STIRRED, STIRRING, STIRS]

Jdg 13:25 the LORD began to s him while he was in H7192
Ne 4: 8 Jerusalem and s up trouble against it. H6913
Ps 78:38 his anger and did not s up his full wrath. H6424
Ps 140: 2 in their hearts and s up war every day. H1592
Pr 28:25 The greedy s up conflict, but those who H1741
Pr 29: 8 Mockers s up a city, but the wise turn H7032
Isa 13:17 I will s up against them the Medes H6424
Isa 19: 2 "I will s up Egyptian against Egyptian H6056
Isa 42:13 like a warrior he will s up his zeal; with a H6424
Jer 50: 9 For I will s up and bring against Babylon H6424
Jer 51: 1 I will s up the spirit of a destroyer against H6424
Eze 23:22 I will s up your lovers against you, those H6424
Eze 24: 8 To s up wrath and take revenge I put her H6590
Da 11: 2 he will s up everyone against the H6424
Da 11:25 a large army he will s up his strength and H6424
Hos 7: 4 the baker need not s from the kneading of H6424
Am 6:14 declares, "I will s up a nation against you H7756
Php 1:17 supposing that they can s up trouble for G1586

STIRRED (23) [STIR]

Jdg 9:23 God s up animosity between Abimelek H8938
Ru 1:19 the whole town was s because of them H2101
1Ki 14:22 they s up his jealous anger more H7861
1Ch 5:26 So the God of Israel s up the spirit of Pul H6424
Ps 45: 1 My heart is s by a noble theme as I recite H8180
Ps 107:25 For he spoke and s up a tempest that H6641
Ecc 12: 5 itself along and desire no longer is s. H7296
Isa 41: 2 "Who has s up one from the east, calling H6424
Isa 41:25 "I have s up one from the north, and he H6424
Jer 6:22 a great nation is being s up from the ends H6424
Jer 50:41 many kings are being s up from the ends H6424
Jer 51:11 The LORD has s up the kings of the Medes H6424
Eze 32:13 no longer to be s by the foot of man H1931
Am 8: 8 it will be s up and then sink like the river H1764
Hag 1:14 So the LORD s up the spirit of Zerubbabel H6424
Mt 21:10 the whole city was s and asked, "Who is G4940
Mk 15:11 But the chief priests s up the crowd to have G411
Jn 5: 7 me into the pool when the water is s. G5015
Ac 6:12 So they s up the people and the elders G5167
Ac 13:50 They s up persecution against Paul and G2074
Ac 14: 2 refused to believe s up the other Gentiles G2074
Ac 21:27 They s up the whole crowd and seized G5177
2Co 9: 2 enthusiasm has s most of them to action. G2241

STIRRING (6) [STIR]

Jdg 9:31 to Shechem and are s up the city against H7443
Ne 13:18 Now you are s up more wrath against H3578
Pr 30:33 so s up anger produces strife. H4790
Ac 17:13 agitating the crowds and s them up. G5429
Ac 24: 5 s up riots among the Jews all over the G3075
Ac 24:12 or s up a crowd in the synagogues G2180+4472

STIRS (13) [STIR]

Dt 32:11 like an eagle that s up its nest and hovers H6424
Job 41:31 caldron and s up the sea like a pot H8492
Ps 147:18 melts them; he s up his breezes, and H5959
Pr 6:14 in his heart—he always s up conflict. H8938
Pr 6:19 out lies and a person who s up conflict in H8938
Pr 10:12 Hatred s up conflict, but love covers over H6424
Pr 15: 1 away wrath, but a harsh word s up anger. H6590
Pr 15:18 A hot-tempered person s up conflict, but H1741
Pr 16:28 A perverse person s up conflict, and a H8938
Pr 29:22 An angry person s up conflict, and a H1741
Isa 51:15 who s up the sea so that its waves roar H8088
Jer 31:35 who s up the sea so that its waves roar H8088
Lk 23: 5 "He s up the people all over Judea by his G411

STOCK (2) [STOCKS]

Job 5:24 you will take s of your property and find H7212
Jer 2:21 like a choice vine of sound and reliable s. H2446

STOCKS (4) [STOCK]

Jer 20: 2 put in the s at the Upper Gate of H4551
Jer 20: 3 when Pashhur released him from the s H4551
Jer 29:26 like a prophet into the s and neck-irons. H4551
Ac 16:24 inner cell and fastened their feet in the s. G3833

STOIC (1)

Ac 17:18 of Epicurean and S philosophers began to G5121

STOLE (6) [STEAL]

Ge 31:19 Rachel s her father's household gods. H1704
2Sa 15: 6 so he s the hearts of the people of H1704
2Sa 19: 3 The men s into the city that H1704+4200+995
2Ki 11: 2 of Ahaziah and s him away from among H1704
2Ch 22:11 of Ahaziah and s him away from among H1704
Mt 28:13 the night and s him away while we were G3096

STOLEN (17) [STEAL]

Ge 30:33 is not dark-colored, will be considered s." H1704
Ge 31:32 did not know that Rachel had s the gods. H1704
Ge 31:39 from me for whatever was s by day or H1704
Ex 22: 4 If the s animal is found alive in their H1706
Ex 22: 7 safekeeping and they are s from the H1704
Ex 22:12 But if the animal was s from the H1704+1704
Lev 6: 2 left in their care or about something s, H1610
Lev 6: 4 return what they have s or taken by H1611+1608
Jos 7:11 they have s, they have lied H1704
2Sa 21:12 They had s their bodies from the public H1704
Job 24: 2 they pasture flocks they have s. H1608
Ps 62:10 in extortion or put vain hope in s goods; H1610
Pr 9:17 "S water is sweet; food eaten in secret is H1704
SS 4: 9 You have s my heart, my sister, my bride H4220
SS 4: 9 you have s my heart with one glance of H4220
Eze 33:15 return what they have s, follow the H1611
Hab 2: 6 piles up s goods and makes H4202+4200+2257

STOMACH (21) [STOMACHS]

Nu 25: 8 the Israelite man and into the woman's s. H7687
2Sa 2:23 thrust the butt of his spear into Asahel's s, H2824
2Sa 3:27 Joab stabbed him in the s, and he died. H2824
2Sa 4: 6 and they stabbed him in the s. H2824
Job 20:14 his food will turn sour in his s; it will H5055
Job 20:15 God will make his s vomit them up. H1061
Pr 13:25 the s of the wicked goes hungry. H1061
Pr 18:20 fruit of their mouth a person's s is filled; H1061
Jer 30: 6 his hands on his s like a woman in labor H2743
Jer 51:34 us and filled his s with our delicacies, H4160
Eze 3: 3 I am giving you and fill your s with it." H5055
Mic 6:14 not be satisfied; your s will still be empty. H7931
Mt 15:17 mouth goes into the s and then out of the G3120
Mk 7:19 doesn't go into their heart but into their s, G3120
Lk 15:16 He longed to fill his s with the pods that G3120
1Co 6:13 "Food for the s and the stomach for food G3120
1Co 6:13 "Food for the stomach and the s for food G3120
Php 3:19 their god is their s, and their glory is in G3120
1Ti 5:23 wine because of your s and your frequent G5126
Rev 10: 9 It will turn your s sour, but 'in your mouth G3120
Rev 10:10 when I had eaten it, my s turned sour. G3120

STOMACHS (2) [STOMACH]

Eze 7:19 It will not satisfy their hunger or fill their s H5055
Am 4: 6 "I gave you empty s in every city H5931+9094

STONE (189) [CAPSTONE, CORNERSTONE, CORNERSTONES, FIELDSTONES, MILLSTONE, MILLSTONES, SLINGSTONES, STONE'S, STONECUTTERS, STONED, STONEMASONS, STONES, STONING, TOMBSTONE]

Ge 11: 3 They used brick instead of s, and tar for H74
Ge 28:18 Jacob took the s he had placed under H74
Ge 28:22 this s that I have set up as a pillar will H74
Ge 29: 2 The s over the mouth of the well was large H74
Ge 29: 3 would roll the s away from the well's H74
Ge 29: 3 they would return the s to its place over the H74
Ge 29: 8 gathered and the s has been rolled away H74
Ge 29:10 over and rolled the s away from the mouth H74
Ge 31:45 So Jacob took a s and set it up as a pillar. H74
Ge 35:14 Jacob set up a s pillar at the place where H74
Ex 7:19 in Egypt, even in vessels of wood and s." H74
Ex 8:26 in their eyes, will they not s us? H6232
Ex 15: 5 they sank to the depths like a s. H74

Ex 15:16 of your arm they will be as still as a **s**— H74
Ex 17: 4 *They are* almost *ready to* **s** me." H6232
Ex 17:12 they took a **s** and put it under him and he H74
Ex 21:18 hits another with a **s** or with their fist and the H74
Ex 24: 4 set up twelve **s pillars** representing the H5167
Ex 24:12 give you the tablets of **s** with the law and H74
Ex 28:10 six names on one **s** and the remaining six on H74
Ex 31:18 the tablets of **s** inscribed by the finger of H74
Ex 34: 1 "Chisel out two **s** tablets like the first ones H74
Ex 34: 4 Moses chiseled out two **s** tablets like the first H74
Ex 34: 4 he carried the two **s** tablets in his hands. H74
Lev 20: 2 community *are to* **s** him. H8083+928+2021+74
Lev 20:27 *You are to* **s** them; their H8083+928+2021+74
Lev 24:14 and the entire assembly *is to* **s** him. H8083
Lev 24:16 The entire assembly **must s** them H8083+8083
Lev 26: 1 up an image or a **sacred s** for yourselves, H5167
Lev 26: 1 do not place a carved **s** in your land to bow H74
Nu 15:35 assembly *must* **s** him H8083+928+2021+74
Nu 35:17 anyone is holding a **s** and strikes someone a H74
Nu 35:23 drops on them a **s** heavy enough to kill them H74
Dt 4:13 follow and then wrote them on two **s** tablets. H74
Dt 4:28 will worship man-made gods of wood and **s**, H74
Dt 5:22 he wrote them on two **s** tablets and gave H74
Dt 9: 9 on the mountain to receive the tablets of **s**, H74
Dt 9:10 The LORD gave me two **s** tablets inscribed by H74
Dt 9:11 the LORD gave me the two **s** tablets, the H74
Dt 10: 1 "Chisel out two **s** tablets like the first ones H74
Dt 10: 3 chiseled out two **s** tablets like the first H74
Dt 13:10 **S** them to death, because they tried to turn H6232
Dt 16:22 do not erect a **sacred s**, for these the H5167
Dt 17: 5 gate and **s** that person H6232+928+2021+74
Dt 19:14 your neighbor's **boundary s** set up by your H1473
Dt 21:21 his town *are to* **s** him to H8083+928+2021+74
Dt 22:21 of her town *shall* **s** her to H6232+928+2021+74
Dt 22:24 town and **s** them to death H6232+928+2021+74
Dt 27:17 who moves their neighbor's **boundary s**." H1473
Dt 28:36 will worship other gods, gods of wood and **s**. H74
Dt 28:64 gods of wood and **s**, which neither you H74
Dt 29:17 detestable images and idols of wood and **s**, H74
Jos 4: 5 Each of you is to take up a **s** on his shoulder H74
Jos 7: 5 as far as the **s quarries** and struck them H8696
Jos 15: 6 Beth Arabah to the **S** *of* Bohan son of H74
Jos 18:17 ran down to the **S** *of* Bohan son of H74
Jos 24:26 Then he took a large **s** and set it up there H74
Jos 24:27 "This **s** will be a witness against us H74
Jdg 3:19 on reaching the **s images** near Gilgal he H7178
Jdg 3:26 passed by the **s images** and escaped to H7178
Jdg 9: 5 Ophrah and on one **s** murdered his seventy H74
Jdg 9:18 sons on a single **s** and have made Abimelek H74
Jdg 20:16 of whom could sling a **s** at a hair and not H74
1Sa 7:12 Then Samuel took a **s** and set it up between H74
1Sa 14:33 "Roll a large **s** over here at once." H74
1Sa 17:49 Reaching into his bag and taking out a **s**, he H74
1Sa 17:49 The **s** sank into his forehead, and he fell H74
1Sa 17:50 over the Philistine with a sling and a **s**; H74
1Sa 20:19 this trouble began, and wait by the **s** Ezel. H74
1Sa 20:41 south side of the **s** and bowed down before NDT
1Sa 25:37 his heart failed him and he became like a **s**. H74
1Ki 1: 9 fattened calves at the **S** *of* Zoheleth near En H74
1Ki 5:17 blocks of high-grade **s** to provide a H74
1Ki 5:17 a foundation of dressed **s** for the temple. H74
1Ki 5:18 the timber and **s** for the building of the H74
1Ki 6:18 Everything was cedar; no **s** was to be seen. H74
1Ki 6:36 three courses of **dressed s** and one course H1607
1Ki 7: 9 made of *blocks of* high-grade **s** cut to size H74
1Ki 7:12 three courses of **dressed s** and one course H1607
1Ki 8: 9 ark except the two **s** tablets that Moses had H74
1Ki 21:10 Then take him out and **s** him to death." H6232
2Ki 3: 2 He got rid of the **sacred s** *of* Baal that his H5167
2Ki 3:25 each man threw a **s** on every good field H74
2Ki 10:26 They brought the **sacred s** out of the H5167
2Ki 10:27 demolished the **sacred s** *of* Baal and tore H5167
2Ki 12:12 timber and **blocks of** dressed **s** for the repair H74
2Ki 16:17 bulls that supported it and set it on a **s** base. H74
2Ki 19:18 they were not gods but only wood and **s** H74
2Ki 19:25 turned fortified cities into **piles of s**. H1643+5898
2Ki 22: 6 timber and dressed **s** to repair the temple. H74
1Ch 22: 2 to prepare dressed **s** for building the house H74
1Ch 22:14 too great to be weighed, and wood and **s**. H74
1Ch 29: 2 all kinds of fine **s** and marble—all of H74
2Ch 2:14 bronze and iron, **s** and wood, and with H74
2Ch 34:11 builders to purchase dressed **s**, H74
Ne 9:11 into the depths, like a **s** into mighty waters. H74
Job 6:12 Do I have the strength of **s**? Is my flesh H74
Job 38:30 when the waters become hard as **s**, when H74
Ps 91:12 that you will not strike your foot against a **s**. H74
Ps 118:22 The **s** the builders rejected has become the H74
Pr 22:28 an ancient **boundary s** set up by your H1473
Pr 23:10 an ancient **boundary s** or encroach on H1473
Pr 24:31 with weeds, and the **s** wall was in ruins. H74
Pr 26: 8 Like tying a **s** in a sling is the giving of honor H74
Pr 26:27 if someone rolls a **s**, it will roll back on H74
Pr 27: 3 **S** is heavy and sand a burden, but a fool's H74
SS 4: 4 built with **courses of s**; on it hang a H9444
Isa 8:14 Judah he will be a **s** *that* causes people to H74
Isa 9:10 we will rebuild with **dressed s**; the fig H1607
Isa 28:16 I lay a **s** in Zion, a tested stone, H74
Isa 28:16 a tested **s**, a precious cornerstone H74
Isa 37:19 they were not gods but only wood and **s** H74
Isa 37:26 turned fortified cities into **piles of s**. H1643+5898
Jer 2:27 are my father,' and to **s**, 'You gave me birth. H74
Jer 3: 9 committed adultery with **s** and wood. H74
Jer 5: 3 faces harder than **s** and refused to repent. H6152
Jer 51:26 a cornerstone, nor any **s** for a foundation, for H74
Jer 51:63 tie a **s** to it and throw it into the Euphrates. H74
La 3: 9 He has barred my way with **blocks of s**; he H1607
Eze 3: 9 make your forehead like the **hardest s**, H9032
Eze 11:19 them their heart of **s** and give them a heart H74
Eze 16:40 *who will* **s** you and hack H8083+928+2021+74
Eze 20:32 peoples of the world, who serve wood and **s**." H74
Eze 23:47 The mob *will* **s** them and cut them H8083+74
Eze 28:13 every precious **s** adorned you: H74
Eze 36:26 from you your heart of **s** and give you a heart H74
Eze 40:42 four tables of dressed **s** for the burnt H74
Eze 46:23 each of the four courts was a **ledge of s**, H3215
Da 5: 4 silver, of bronze, iron, wood and **s**. A10006
Da 5:23 wood and **s**, which cannot see or A10006
Da 6:17 A **s** was brought and placed over the A10006
Am 5:11 though you have built **s** mansions, you H1607
Hab 2:19 Or to lifeless **s**, 'Wake up!' Can it give H74
Hag 2:15 were before one **s** was laid on another in H74
Zec 3: 9 the **s** I have set in front of Joshua! There H74
Zec 3: 9 There are seven eyes on that one **s**, and I H74
Mt 4: 6 you will not strike your foot against a **s**. *G3345*
Mt 7: 9 your son asks for bread, will give him a **s**? *G3345*
Mt 21:42 " 'The **s** the builders rejected has become *G3345*
Mt 21:44 who falls on this **s** will be broken to *G3345*
Mt 23:37 kill the prophets and **s** those sent to you, *G3344*
Mt 24: 2 not one **s** here will be left on another *G3345*
Mt 27:60 He rolled a big **s** in front of the entrance *G3345*
Mt 27:66 a seal on the **s** and posting the guard *G3345*
Mt 28: 2 the tomb, rolled back the **s** and sat on it. *G3345*
Mk 12:10 " 'The **s** the builders rejected has become *G3345*
Mk 13: 2 "Not one **s** here will be left on another *G3345*
Mk 15:46 Then he rolled a **s** against the entrance of *G3345*
Mk 16: 3 "Who will roll the **s** away from the *G3345*
Mk 16: 4 they saw that the **s**, which was very large *G3345*
Lk 4: 3 Son of God, tell this **s** to become bread." *G3345*
Lk 4:11 you will not strike your foot against a **s**. *G3345*
Lk 13:34 kill the prophets and **s** those sent to you, *G3344*
Lk 19:44 They will not leave one **s** on another *G3345*
Lk 20: 6 all the people *will* **s** us, because they are *G2902*
Lk 20:17 " 'The **s** the builders rejected has become *G3345*
Lk 20:18 who falls on that **s** will be broken to *G3345*
Lk 21: 6 will come when not *one* **s** will be left on *G3345*
Lk 24: 2 They found the **s** rolled away from the *G3345*
Jn 2: 6 Nearby stood six **s** water jars, the kind *G3343*
Jn 8: 5 Moses commanded us *to* **s** such women. *G3342*
Jn 8: 7 without sin be the first to throw a **s** at her." *G3345*
Jn 8:59 they picked up stones to **s** him, but *G965+2093*
Jn 10:31 opponents picked up stones to **s** him, *G3342*
Jn 10:32 For which of these *do you* **s** me?" *G3342*
Jn 11: 8 while ago the Jews there tried to **s** you, *G3342*
Jn 11:38 It was a cave with a **s** laid across the *G3345*
Jn 11:39 "Take away the **s**," he said. "But, Lord," *G3345*
Jn 11:41 So they took away the **s**. Then Jesus *G3345*
Jn 19:13 at a place known as the **S Pavement** *G3346*
Jn 20: 1 saw that the **s** had been removed *G3345*
Ac 4:11 Jesus is " 'the **s** you builders rejected *G3345*
Ac 5:26 they feared that the people *would* **s** them. *G3342*
Ac 7:58 him out of the city and *began to* **s** him. *G3344*
Ac 14: 5 leaders, to mistreat them and **s** them. *G3344*
Ac 17:29 divine being is like gold or silver or **s**— *G3345*
Ro 9:32 They stumbled over the stumbling **s**. *G3345*
Ro 9:33 I lay in Zion a **s** that causes people to *G3345*
2Co 3: 3 not on tablets *of* **s** but on tablets of *G3343*
2Co 3: 7 which was engraved in letters *on* **s**, came *G3345*
Heb 9: 4 the **s tablets** of the covenant. *G4419*
1Pe 2: 4 the living **S**—rejected by humans *G3345*
1Pe 2: 6 I lay a **s** in Zion, a chosen and *G3345*
1Pe 2: 7 to you who believe, this **s** is precious. But to NDT
1Pe 2: 7 "The **s** the builders rejected has become *G3345*
1Pe 2: 8 "A **s** that causes people to stumble and a *G3345*
Rev 2:17 that person a white **s** with a new name *G6029*
Rev 9:20 **s** and wood—idols that cannot *G3343*
Rev 21:19 decorated *with* every kind of precious **s**. *G3345*

STONE'S (1) [STONE]

Lk 22:41 He withdrew about a **s** throw beyond them, *G3345*

STONECUTTERS (6) [STONE]

1Ki 5:15 carriers and eighty thousand **s** in the hills, H2935
2Ki 12:12 the masons and **s**. They purchased H2935+74
1Ch 22: 2 them he appointed **s** to prepare dressed H2935
1Ch 22:15 **s**, masons and carpenters, as well as H2935
2Ch 2: 2 80,000 as **s** in the hills and 3,600 H2935
2Ch 2:18 be carriers and 80,000 to be **s** in the hills, H2935

STONED (17) [STONE]

Ex 19:13 *They are to* **be s** or shot with arrows H6232+6232
Ex 21:28 the bull *is to* **be s to death**, and its H6232+6232
Ex 21:29 the bull *is to* **be s** and its owner also is to H6232
Ex 21:32 the slave, and the bull *is to* **be s to death**. H6232
Lev 24:23 outside the camp and **s** him. H8083+74
Nu 15:36 camp and **s** him to death H8083+928+2021+74
Jos 7:25 Then all Israel **s** him, and after they H8083+74
Jos 7:25 after *they had* **s** the rest H6232+928+2021+74
1Ki 12:18 but all Israel **s** him to death. H8083+74
1Ki 21:13 city and **s** him to death H6232+928+2021+74
1Ki 21:14 "Naboth *has* **been s** to death." H6232
1Ki 21:15 heard that Naboth *had* **been s** to death, H6232
2Ch 10:18 the Israelites **s** him to death. H8083+74
2Ch 24:21 of the king *they* **s** him **to death** in the H8083+74
Mt 21:35 beat one, killed another, and **s** a third. *G3344*
Ac 14:19 *They* **s** Paul and dragged him outside the *G3342*
Heb 12:20 the mountain, *it must be* **s to death**." *G3344*

STONEMASONS (2) [STONE]

2Sa 5:11 logs and carpenters and **s**, H3093+74+7815
1Ch 14: 1 **s** and carpenters to build a palace H3093+7815

STONES (129) [STONE]

Ge 28:11 Taking one of the **s** there, he put it under his H74
Ge 31:46 relatives, "Gather *some* **s**." So they took H74
Ge 31:46 So they took **s** and piled them in a heap H74
Ex 20:25 If you make an altar of **s** for me, do not build H74
Ex 20:25 do not build it with **dressed s**, for you will H1607
Ex 23:24 them and break their **sacred s** to pieces. H5167
Ex 25: 7 onyx **s** and other gems to be mounted H74
Ex 28: 9 "Take two onyx **s** and engrave on them the H74
Ex 28:11 of Israel on the two **s** the way a gem cutter H74
Ex 28:11 Then mount **the s** in gold filigree H4392S
Ex 28:12 the ephod as memorial **s** for the sons of H74
Ex 28:17 Then mount four rows of precious **s** on it. H74
Ex 28:21 There are to be twelve **s**, one for each of the H74
Ex 31: 5 to cut and set **s**, to work in wood, and to H74
Ex 34:13 smash their **sacred s** and cut down their H5167
Ex 35: 9 onyx **s** and other gems to be mounted H74
Ex 35:27 leaders brought onyx **s** and other gems to be H74
Ex 35:33 to cut and set **s**, to work in wood and to H74
Ex 39: 6 They mounted the onyx **s** in gold filigree H74
Ex 39: 7 the ephod as memorial **s** for the sons of H74
Ex 39:10 they mounted four rows of precious **s** on it. H74
Ex 39:14 There were twelve **s**, one for each of the H74
Lev 14:40 that the contaminated **s** be torn out and H74
Lev 14:42 they are to take other **s** to replace these H74
Lev 14:43 the house after the **s** have been torn out H74
Lev 14:45 be torn down—its **s**, timbers and all the H74
Dt 7: 5 smash their **sacred s**, cut down their H5167
Dt 12: 3 smash their **sacred s** and burn their H5167
Dt 27: 2 set up *some* large **s** and coat them with H74
Dt 27: 4 set up these **s** on Mount Ebal, as I H74
Dt 27: 5 an altar to the LORD your God, an altar of **s**. H74
Dt 27: 8 words of this law on these **s** you have set up." H74
Jos 4: 3 to take up twelve **s** from the middle of the H74
Jos 4: 6 children ask you, 'What do these **s** mean? H74
Jos 4: 7 These **s** are to be a memorial to the people H74
Jos 4: 8 They took twelve **s** from the middle of the H74
Jos 4: 9 set up the twelve **s** that had been in the H74
Jos 4:20 at Gilgal the twelve **s** they had taken out of H74
Jos 4:21 ask their parents, 'What do these **s** mean? H74
Jos 8:31 an altar of uncut **s**, on which no iron tool H74
Jos 8:32 Joshua wrote on **s** a copy of the law of H74
1Sa 17:40 chose five smooth **s** from the stream, put H74
2Sa 12:30 talent of gold, and it was set with precious **s**. H74
2Sa 16: 6 David and all the king's officials with **s**, H74
2Sa 16:13 went and throwing **s** at him and showering H74
1Ki 7:10 were laid with large **s** of good quality, H74
1Ki 7:11 Above were high-grade **s**, cut to size, and H74
1Ki 10: 2 and precious **s**—she came to Solomon H74
1Ki 10:10 large quantities of spices, and precious **s**. H74
1Ki 10:11 great cargoes of almugwood and precious **s**. H74
1Ki 10:27 made silver as common in Jerusalem as **s**, H74
1Ki 14:23 **sacred s** and Asherah poles on every high H5167
1Ki 15:22 carried away *from* Ramah the **s** and timber H74
1Ki 18:31 Elijah took twelve **s**, one for each of the H74
1Ki 18:32 With the **s** he built an altar in the name of H74
1Ki 18:38 the wood, the **s** and the soil, and also licked H74
2Ki 3:19 the springs, and ruin every good field with **s**." H74
2Ki 3:25 Only Kir Hareseth was left with its **s** in place H74
2Ki 17:10 They set up **sacred s** and Asherah poles H5167
2Ki 18: 4 smashed the **sacred s** and cut down the H5167
2Ki 23:14 smashed the **sacred s** and cut down the H5167
1Ch 12: 2 arrows or to **sling s** right-handed H928+2021+74
1Ch 20: 2 it was set with precious **s**—and it was H74
1Ch 29: 2 turquoise, **s** *of* various colors, and all kinds H74
1Ch 29: 8 Anyone who had precious **s** gave them to the H74
2Ch 1:15 gold as common in Jerusalem as **s**, H74
2Ch 3: 6 He adorned the temple with precious **s**. H74
2Ch 9: 1 and precious **s**—she came to Solomon H74
2Ch 9: 9 large quantities of spices, and precious **s**. H74
2Ch 9:10 also brought algumwood and precious **s**. H74
2Ch 9:27 made silver as common in Jerusalem as **s**, H74
2Ch 14: 3 smashed the **sacred s** and cut down the H5167
2Ch 16: 6 carried away *from* Ramah the **s** and timber H74
2Ch 26:15 shoot arrows and hurl large **s** from the walls. H74
2Ch 31: 1 smashed the **sacred s** and cut down the H5167
2Ch 32:27 his silver and gold and for his precious **s**, H74
Ezr 5: 8 it with **large s** and placing the A10006+10146
Ezr 6: 4 courses of **large s** and one of A10006+10146
Ne 4: 2 Can they bring the **s** back to life from those H74
Ne 4: 3 up on it would break down their wall of **s**!" H74
Est 1: 6 mother-of-pearl and other **costly s**. H6090
Job 5:23 will have a covenant with the **s** *of* the field, H74
Job 8:17 of rocks and looks for a place among the **s**. H74
Job 14:19 as water wears away **s** and torrents wash H74
Job 24: 2 There are those who move **boundary s** H1474
Ps 102:14 For her **s** are dear to your servants; her very H74
Pr 15:25 he sets the widow's **boundary s** in place. H1473
Ecc 3: 5 a time to scatter **s** and a time to gather them H74
Ecc 10: 9 Whoever quarries **s** may be injured by them H74
Isa 5: 2 dug it up and **cleared** it **of s** and planted H6232
Isa 14:19 those who descend to the **s** *of* the pit. H74
Isa 27: 9 he makes all the altar **s** to be like limestone H74
Isa 54:11 I will rebuild you with **s** *of* turquoise, your H74
Isa 54:12 and all your walls of precious **s**. H74

Isa 57: 6 idols among the smooth **s** of the ravines are NDT
Isa 60:17 will bring you bronze, and iron in place of **s**. H74
Isa 62:10 Remove the **s**. Raise a banner for H74
Jer 43: 9 take *some* large **s** with you and bury them in H74
Jer 43:10 his throne over these **s** I have buried here; H74
La 3:53 to end my life in a pit and threw **s** at me; H74
Eze 26:12 demolish your fine houses and throw your **s**, H74
Eze 27:22 finest of all kinds of spices and precious **s**, H74
Eze 28:14 you walked among the fiery **s**. H74
Eze 28:16 guardian cherub, from among the fiery **s**. H74
Da 11:38 silver, with precious **s** and costly gifts. H74
Hos 3: 4 without sacrifice or **sacred s**, without H5167
Hos 5:10 are like those who move **boundary s**. H1473
Hos 10: 1 land prospered, he adorned his **sacred s**. H5167
Hos 10: 2 their altars and destroy their **sacred s**. H5167
Hos 12:11 will be like **piles of s** on a plowed field. H1643
Mic 1: 6 I will pour her **s** into the valley and lay bare H74
Mic 5:13 idols and your **sacred s** from among you; H5167
Hab 2:11 The **s** of the wall will cry out, and the beams H74
Zec 5: 4 it completely, both its timbers and its **s**. H74
Mt 3: 9 you that out of these **s** God can raise up *G3345*
Mt 4: 3 Son of God, tell these **s** to become bread." *G3345*
Mk 5: 5 he would cry out and cut himself *with* **s**. *G3345*
Mk 13: 1 What massive **s**! What magnificent *G3345*
Lk 3: 8 you that out of these **s** God can raise up *G3345*
Lk 19:40 "if they keep quiet, the **s** will cry out." *G3345*
Lk 21: 5 was adorned *with* beautiful **s** and with *G3345*
Jn 8:59 they picked up **s** to stone him, but *G3345*
Jn 10:31 opponents picked up **s** to stone him, *G3345*
1Co 3:12 silver, costly **s**, wood, hay or straw, *G3345*
2Co 11:25 once *I was* **pelted with s**, three times *G3342*
1Pe 2: 5 you also, like living **s**, are being built into *G3345*
Rev 17: 4 glittering with gold, precious **s** and pearls. *G3345*
Rev 18:12 precious **s** and pearls; fine linen *G3345*
Rev 18:16 glittering with gold, precious **s** and pearls! *G3345*

STONING (5) [STONE]

Nu 14:10 talked about **s** them. H8083+928+2021+74
1Sa 30: 6 because the men were talking of **s** him; H6232
Jn 10:33 "*We are* not **s** you for any good work," *G3342*
Ac 7:59 *While they were* **s** him, Stephen prayed *G3344*
Heb 11:37 *They were* **put to death by s**; they were *G3342*

STOOD (217) [STAND]

Ge 18: 8 they ate, he **s** near them under a tree. H6641
Ge 19:27 the place where *he had* **s** before the LORD. H6641
Ge 28:13 There above it **s** the LORD, and he said: "I H5893
Ge 37: 7 suddenly my sheaf rose and **s upright**, H5893
Ge 41: 3 out of the Nile and **s** beside those on the H6641
Ex 2: 4 His sister **s** at a distance to see what H3656
Ex 9:10 soot from a furnace and **s** before Pharaoh. H6641
Ex 14:19 moved from in front and **s** behind them, H6641
Ex 15: 8 The surging waters **s up** like a wall; the H5893
Ex 18:13 they **s** around him from morning till H6641
Ex 19:17 and *they* **s** at the foot of the mountain. H3656
Ex 32:26 So he **s** at the entrance to the camp and H6641
Ex 33: 8 the people rose and **s** at the entrances to H5893
Ex 33:10 to the tent, they all **s** and worshiped, each H7756
Ex 34: 5 in the cloud and **s** there with him and H3656
Lev 9: 5 came near and **s** before the LORD. H6641
Nu 12: 5 *he* **s** *at* the entrance to the tent and H6641
Nu 16:18 **s** with Moses and Aaron at the H6641
Nu 16:48 *He* **s** between the living and the dead H6641
Nu 22:22 angel of the LORD **s** in the road to oppose H3656
Nu 22:24 the angel of the LORD **s** in a narrow path H6641
Nu 22:26 moved on ahead and **s** in a narrow place H6641
Nu 27: 2 **s** before Moses, Eleazar the priest, the H6641
Dt 4:10 Remember the day *you* **s** before the LORD H6641
Dt 4:11 You came near and **s** at the foot of the H6641
Dt 5: 5 At that time I **s** between the LORD and you H6641
Dt 31:15 the cloud **s** over the entrance to the H6641
Jos 3:17 middle of the Jordan and **s** on dry ground, H6641
Jos 4: 9 the ark of the covenant had **s**. H5163+8079
Jos 4:14 and *they* **s in awe** *of* him all the days of H3707
Jos 4:14 just as *they had* **s in awe** *of* Moses. H3707
Jos 8:33 Half of the people **s** in front of Mount NDT
Jos 10:13 So the sun **s still**, and the moon stopped H1957
Jos 20: 6 that city until they *have* **s** trial before the H6641
Jdg 16:25 When *they* **s** him among the pillars H6641
Jdg 16:29 two central pillars on which the temple **s**. H3922
Jdg 18:16 battle, **s** *at* the entrance of the gate. H5893
Jdg 18:17 hundred armed men **s** *at* the entrance of H5893
1Sa 1: 9 drinking in Shiloh, Hannah **s up**. H7756
1Sa 1:26 I am the woman who **s** here beside you H5893
1Sa 3:10 The LORD came and **s** there, calling as at H3656
1Sa 10:23 and *as he* **s** among the people he was a H3656
1Sa 12:18 the people **s in awe** *of* the LORD H3707+4394
1Sa 14: 5 One cliff **s** to the north toward Mikmash H5187
1Sa 17: 8 Goliath **s** and shouted to the ranks of H6641
1Sa 17:51 David ran and **s** over him. He took hold of H6641
1Sa 26:13 to the other side and **s** on top of the hill H6641
2Sa 1:10 "So *I* **s** beside him and killed him H6641
2Sa 2:15 So *they* **s up** and were counted off H7756
2Sa 12:17 of his household **s** beside him to get him H7756
2Sa 13:31 The king **s up**, tore his clothes and lay H7756
2Sa 13:31 all his attendants **s by** with their clothes H5893
2Sa 18: 4 So the king **s** beside the gate while all his H6641
2Sa 18:30 So he stepped aside and **s** there. H6641
2Sa 20:11 One of Joab's men **s** beside Amasa and H6641
2Sa 20:15 and *it* **s** against the outer fortifications. H6641
2Sa 23:10 Eleazar **s** *his* **ground** and struck down H7756
1Ki 1:28 into the king's presence and **s** before him. H6641
1Ki 2: 7 *They* **s** by me when I fled from your H7928
1Ki 2:19 Adonijah, the king **s up** to meet her H7756
1Ki 3:15 **s** before the ark of the Lord's covenant H6641
1Ki 3:16 came to the king and **s** before him. H6641
1Ki 7:25 The Sea **s** on twelve bulls, three facing H6641
1Ki 8:22 Then Solomon **s** before the altar of the H6641
1Ki 8:55 *He* **s** and blessed the whole assembly of H6641
1Ki 8:64 altar that **s before** the LORD was too H4200+7156
1Ki 10:20 Twelve lions **s** on the six steps, one at H6641
1Ki 19:13 went out and **s** at the mouth of the H6641
1Ki 20:38 went and **s** by the road **waiting** for the H6641
1Ki 22:21 came forward, **s** before the LORD and said H6641
2Ki 2: 7 of the prophets went and **s** at a distance, H6641
2Ki 2:13 went back and **s** on the bank of the H6641
2Ki 4:12 So he called her, and *she* **s** before him. H6641
2Ki 4:15 he called her, and *she* **s** in the doorway. H6641
2Ki 5:15 *He* **s** before him and said, "Now I know H6641
2Ki 5:25 When he went in and **s** before his master H6641
2Ki 8: 9 He went in and **s** before him, and said H6641
2Ki 10: 9 *He* **s** before all the people and said, "You H6641
2Ki 13:21 the man came to life and **s up** on his feet. H7756
2Ki 16:14 As for the bronze altar that **s** before the LORD NDT
2Ki 18:28 Then the commander **s** and called out in H6641
2Ki 23: 3 The king **s** by the pillar and renewed the H6641
2Ch 3:13 twenty cubits. They **s** on their feet, facing H6641
2Ch 4: 4 The Sea **s** on twelve bulls, three facing H6641
2Ch 5:12 relatives—**s** on the east side of the altar H6641
2Ch 6:12 Then Solomon **s** before the altar of the H6641
2Ch 6:13 *He* **s** on the platform and then knelt down H6641
2Ch 9:19 Twelve lions **s** on the six steps, one at H6641
2Ch 13: 4 Abijah **s** on Mount Zemaraim, in the hill H7756
2Ch 18:20 came forward, **s** before the LORD and said H6641
2Ch 20: 5 Then Jehoshaphat **s up** in the assembly H6641
2Ch 20:13 little ones, **s** there before the LORD. H6641
2Ch 20:14 of Asaph, as he **s** in the assembly. NDT
2Ch 20:19 Korahites **s up** and praised the LORD, H7756
2Ch 20:20 Jehoshaphat **s** and said, "Listen to H6641
2Ch 24:20 *He* **s** before the people and said, "This is H6641
2Ch 29:26 So the Levites **s** *ready* with David's H6641
2Ch 30:27 the Levites **s** to bless the people, H7756
2Ch 34:31 The king **s** by his pillar and renewed the H6641
2Ch 35:10 the priests **s** in their places with the H6641
Ezr 10:10 Then Ezra the priest **s up** and said to them, H7756
Ne 4:14 things over, *I* **s up** and said to the nobles H7756
Ne 8: 4 teacher of the Law **s** on a high wooden H6641
Ne 8: 4 Beside him on his right **s** Mattithiah H6641
Ne 8: 5 as he opened it, the people all **s up**. H6641
Ne 9: 2 *They* **s in** *their* **places** and confessed their H6641
Ne 9: 3 *They* **s** where they were and read from the H7756
Ne 12: 9 associates, **s** opposite them in the services. NDT
Ne 12:24 who **s** opposite them to give praise and NDT
Est 5: 1 her royal robes and **s** in the inner court of H6641
Est 8: 4 to Esther and she arose and **s** before him. H6641
Job 4:15 and the hair on my body **s on end**. H6169
Job 4:16 A form **s** before my eyes, and I heard a NDT
Ps 33: 9 came to be; he commanded, and *it* **s firm**. H6641
Ps 104: 6 the waters **s** above the mountains. H6641
Ps 106:23 *had* not Moses, his chosen one, **s** in the H6641
Ps 106:30 But Phinehas **s up** and intervened, and H6641
Isa 36:13 Then the commander **s** and called out in H6641
Jer 18:20 Remember that I **s** before you and spoke H6641
Jer 19:14 **s** in the court of the LORD's temple H6641
Jer 23:18 But which of *them has* **s** in the council of H6641
Jer 23:22 But if *they had* **s** in my council, they would H6641
Eze 1:21 when the creatures **s still**, they also stood H6641
Eze 1:21 stood still, *they* also **s still**; and when the H6641
Eze 1:24 When they **s still**, they lowered their H6641
Eze 1:25 their heads as they **s** with lowered wings. H6641
Eze 8: 3 where the idol that provokes to jealousy **s**. H4632
Eze 8:11 In front of them **s** seventy elders of Israel H6641
Eze 9: 2 They came in and **s** beside the bronze H6641
Eze 10: 6 the man went in and **s** beside a wheel. H6641
Eze 10:17 When the cherubim **s still**, they also stood H6641
Eze 10:17 stood still, *they* also **s still**; and when the H6641
Eze 37:10 they came to life and **s up** on their feet H6641
Da 2: 2 When they came in and **s** before the king H6641
Da 2:31 there before you **s** a large statue A10624
Da 3: 3 had set up, and *they* **s** before it. A10624
Da 4:10 there before me **s** a tree in the middle NDT
Da 7: 4 the ground so that *it* **s** on two feet like a A10624
Da 7:10 times ten thousand **s** before him. A10624
Da 8:15 there before me **s** one who looked like a H6641
Da 10:11 when he said this to me, *I* **s up** trembling. H6641
Da 12: 5 there before me **s** two others, one on H6641
Ob 11 On the day you **s** aloof while strangers H6641
Hab 3: 6 *He* **s**, and shook the earth; he looked, and H6641
Hab 3:11 Sun and moon **s still** in the heavens at H6641
Zec 3: 3 in filthy clothes as *he* **s** before the angel. H6641
Zec 3: 5 while the angel of the LORD **s by**. H6641
Mal 2: 5 he revered me and **s in awe** of my name. H3169
Mt 12:46 his mother and brothers **s** outside *G2705*
Mt 13: 2 *while* all the people **s** on the shore. *G2705*
Mt 26:62 Then the high priest **s up** and said to Jesus, *G482*
Mt 27:11 Meanwhile Jesus **s** before the governor *G2705*
Mk 5:42 the girl **s up** and began to walk *G482*
Mk 9:27 lifted him to his feet, and *he* **s up**. *G482*
Mk 14:57 Then some **s up** and gave this false *G482*
Mk 14:60 Then the high priest **s up** before them and *G482*
Mk 15:39 centurion, who **s there** in front of Jesus *G4225*
Lk 4:16 as was his custom. *He* **s up** to read, *G482*
Lk 5:25 Immediately *he* **s up** in front of them, took *G482*
Lk 6: 8 So he got up and **s** there. *G2705*
Lk 6:17 down with them and **s** on a level place. *G2705*
Lk 7:14 carrying him on, and the bearers **s still**. *G2705*
Lk 7:38 *As she* **s** behind him at his feet weeping *G2705*
Lk 8:55 at once *she* **s up**. Then Jesus told *G482*
Lk 10:25 an expert in the law **s up** to test Jesus. *G482*
Lk 17:12 had leprosy met him. They **s** at a distance *G2705*
Lk 18:11 The Pharisee **s** by himself and prayed *G2705*
Lk 18:13 "But the tax collector **s** at a distance. *G2705*
Lk 19: 8 But Zacchaeus **s up** and said to the Lord *G2705*
Lk 22:28 You are those *who have* **s** by me in my *G1373*
Lk 23:35 The people **s** watching, and the rulers *G2705*
Lk 23:49 him from Galilee, **s** at a distance *G2705*
Lk 24: 4 gleamed like lightning **s beside** them. *G2392*
Lk 24:17 you walk along?" *They* **s still**, their faces *G2705*
Lk 24:36 Jesus himself **s** among them and said to *G2705*
Jn 2: 6 Nearby **s** six stone water jars, the *G1639+3023*
Jn 7:37 festival, Jesus **s** and said in a loud voice *G2705*
Jn 11:56 and *as they* **s** in the temple courts they *G2705*
Jn 18:18 officials **s** around a fire they had *G2705*
Jn 19:25 Near the cross of Jesus **s** his mother, his *G2705*
Jn 20:11 Now Mary **s** outside the tomb crying. *G2705*
Jn 20:19 Jesus came and **s** among them and said *G2705*
Jn 20:26 Jesus came and **s** among them and said *G2705*
Jn 21: 4 the morning, Jesus **s** on the shore, but the *G2705*
Ac 1:10 two men dressed in white **s beside** them. *G4225*
Ac 1:15 In those days Peter **s up** among the *G482*
Ac 2:14 Then Peter **s up** with the Eleven, raised *G2705*
Ac 5:34 **s up** in the Sanhedrin and ordered that the *G482*
Ac 9: 7 traveling with Saul **s** *there* speechless; *G2705*
Ac 9:39 All the widows **s around** him, crying and *G4225*
Ac 10:30 a man in shining clothes **s** before me *G2705*
Ac 11:28 **s up** and through the Spirit predicted that a *G482*
Ac 12: 6 sentries **s** guard at the entrance. *G5498*
Ac 15: 5 the party of the Pharisees **s up** and said, *G1985*
Ac 17:22 Paul then **s up** in the meeting of the *G2705*
Ac 21:40 Paul **s** on the steps and motioned to the *G2705*
Ac 22:13 *He* **s beside** me and said, 'Brother Saul *G2392*
Ac 22:20 I **s there** giving my approval and *G1639+2392*
Ac 23: 9 who were Pharisees **s up** and argued *G482*
Ac 23:11 night the Lord **s near** Paul and said, *G2392*
Ac 24:20 they found in me *when I* **s** before the *G2705*
Ac 24:21 thing I shouted *as I* **s** in their presence: *G2705*
Ac 25: 7 come down from Jerusalem **s around** him. *G4325*
Ac 27:21 Paul **s up** before them and said: *G2705*
Ac 27:23 I belong and whom I serve **s beside** me *G4225*
Ro 16:10 whose fidelity to Christ has **s the test**. *G1511*
2Co 13: 7 see that we have **s the test** but so that you *G1511*
Gal 2:11 to his face, because *he* **s** condemned. *G1639*
Col 2:14 which **s** against us and condemned us *G1639*
2Ti 4:17 But the Lord **s at** my **side** and gave me *G4225*
Heb 10:33 at other times *you* **s** side by side with *G1181*
Jas 1:12 under trial because, *having* **s** the test, that *G1181*
Rev 8: 3 a golden censer, came and **s** at the altar. *G2705*
Rev 11:11 entered them, and *they* **s** on their feet *G2705*
Rev 12: 4 The dragon **s** in front of the woman who *G2705*
Rev 13: 1 The dragon **s** on the shore of the sea *G2705*
Rev 22: 2 On each side of the river **s** the tree of life NDT

STOOL (1) [FOOTSTOOL]

Ex 1:16 women during childbirth on the **delivery s**, H78

STOOP (3) [STOOPED, STOOPS]

Ecc 12: 3 the strong men **s**, when the grinders H6430
Isa 46: 2 *They* **s** and bow down together; unable to H7970
Mk 1: 7 I am not worthy *to* **s down** and untie. *G3252*

STOOPED (1) [STOOP]

Jn 8: 8 Again *he* **s down** and wrote on the ground. *G2893*

STOOPS (2) [STOOP]

Ps 113: 6 who **s down** to look on the heavens and H9164
Isa 46: 1 bows down, Nebo **s low**; their idols are H7970

STOP (73) [STOPPED, STOPPING, STOPS]

Ge 19:17 and don't **s** anywhere in the plain! H6641
Ex 9:29 The thunder *will* **s** and there will be no H2532
Nu 11:28 up and said, "Moses, my lord, **s** them!" H3973
Jos 10:19 But don't **s**; pursue your enemies! Attack H6641
Jos 22:25 descendants *might* **cause** ours **to s** fearing H8697
Jdg 15: 7 *I swear that I* won't **s** until I get my H2532
Jdg 19:11 *let's* **s** at this city of the Jebusites and H6073
1Sa 7: 8 "*Do* not **s** crying out to the LORD our God H3087
1Sa 9: 5 my father *will* **s** thinking about the H2532
1Sa 20:38 Don't **s**!" The boy picked up H6641
2Sa 2:21 But Asahel would not **s** chasing him. H6073
2Sa 2:22 Abner warned Asahel, "**S** chasing me! H6073
2Sa 2:26 order your men to **s** pursuing their fellow H8740
2Ki 3:19 every good tree, **s up** all the springs, and H6258
2Ki 18: 6 to the LORD and *did* not **s** following him; H6073
2Ch 25:16 **S**! Why be struck down? H2532
2Ch 35:21 me to hurry; so **s** opposing God, who is H2532
Ezr 4:21 issue an order to these men to **s work**, A10098
Ezr 4:23 compelled them by force *to* **s**. A10098
Ezr 6: 8 so that the work *will* not **s**. A10098
Ne 5:10 But *let us* **s** charging interest! H6440
Ne 6: 3 Why *should* the work **s** while I leave it H8697
Job 6:17 that **s flowing** in the dry season, and H7551
Job 9:12 who *can* **s** him? Who can say H8740
Job 13:21 and **s** frightening me with your terrors. H440
Job 37:14 Job; **s** and consider God's wonders. H6641
Pr 19:27 **S** listening to instruction, my son, and you H2532
Isa 1:13 **S** bringing meaningless offerings H4202+3578
Isa 1:16 evil deeds out of my sight; **s** doing wrong. H2532

Isa 2:22 **S trusting in** mere humans, who H2532+4946
Isa 28:22 Now s your mocking, or your chains will H440
Isa 30:11 s confronting us with the Holy One of H8697
Isa 33: 1 When you s destroying, you will be H9462
Isa 33: 1 destroyed; when you s betraying, you will H5801
Isa 33:15 *who* s their ears against plots of murder H357
Jer 15: 5 Who *will* s to ask how you are? H6073
Jer 18:14 *Do* its cool waters from distant sources *ever* s H5980
Jer 32:40 *I will* never s doing good to them, and I H8740
Jer 44: 5 their wickedness or s burning incense to H1194
Eze 16:41 *I will* **put a** s to your prostitution, and you H8697
Eze 21:21 the king of Babylon *will* s at the fork in the H6641
Eze 23:27 So *I will* **put a** s *to* the lewdness and H8697
Eze 45: 9 S dispossessing my people, declares the H8123
Hos 2:11 *I will* s all her celebrations: her yearly H8697
Am 7: 5 I cried out, "Sovereign LORD, I beg you, s! H2532
Am 7:16 s preaching against the descendants H4202
Na 2: 8 whose water is draining away. "S! Stop!" H6641
Na 2: 8 draining away. "Stop! S!" they cry, but no H6641
Mk 9:38 in your name and *we* **told** him **to** s, G3266
Mk 9:39 "*Do* not s him," Jesus said. "For no one G3266
Lk 8:52 mourning for her. "S wailing," Jesus said G3590
Lk 9:49 in your name and *we tried to* s him, G3266
Lk 9:50 "*Do* not s him," Jesus said, "for whoever G3266
Jn 2:16 S turning my Father's house into a market!" G3590
Jn 5:14 S sinning or something worse may G3600
Jn 6:43 "S grumbling among yourselves," Jesus G3590
Jn 7:24 S judging by mere appearances, but G3590
Jn 20:27 S doubting and believe. G3590+1181
Ac 4:17 But to s this thing *from* spreading any G3590
Ac 5:39 you will not be able *to* s these men; you G2907
Ac 8:38 And he gave orders *to* s the chariot. G2705
Ac 13:10 *Will you* never s perverting the right ways G4264
Ro 14:13 Therefore let us s passing judgment on G3600
1Co 12:15 not for that reason s being part of the G4024
1Co 12:16 not for that reason s being part of the G4024
1Co 14:20 sisters, s thinking like children. G3590
1Co 14:30 is sitting down, the first **speaker** *should* s. G4967
1Co 15:34 as you ought, and s sinning; for there are G3590
2Co 11:10 regions of Achaia *will* s this boasting of G5852
1Ti 5:23 S drinking only water, and use a little G3600
2Pe 2:14 of adultery, they **never** s sinning; they G188
Rev 4: 8 Day and night *they* never s saying: G398+2400
Rev 9:20 they did not s worshiping demons NDT

STOPPED (79) [STOP]

Ge 8: 2 the rain *had* s **falling** from the sky. H3973
Ge 11: 8 all the earth, and *they* s building the city. H2532
Ge 26:15 the Philistines s **up**, filling them with H6258
Ge 26:18 the Philistines *had* s **up** after Abraham H6258
Ge 28:11 *he* s **for the night** because the sun had set H4328
Ge 29:35 Then *she* s having children. H6641
Ge 30: 9 Leah saw that *she had* s having children, H6641
Ge 41:49 it was so much that *he* s keeping records H2532
Ge 42:27 the **place where they** s **for the night** one H4869
Ge 43:21 at the **place where we** s **for the night** we H4869
Ex 9:33 the thunder and hail s, and the rain no H2532
Ex 9:34 that the rain and hail and thunder *had* s, H2532
Nu 16:48 the living and the dead, and the plague s. H6806
Nu 16:50 the tent of meeting, for the plague *had* s. H6806
Nu 25: 8 the plague against the Israelites **was** s; H6806
Jos 3:16 the water from upstream s flowing. It piled H6641
Jos 3:17 of the LORD s in the middle of the H3922
Jos 5:12 The manna s the day after they ate this H8697
Jos 10:13 and the moon s, till the nation H6641
Jos 10:13 The sun s in the middle of the sky and H6641
Jdg 19:15 There *they* s to spend the night. They went H6073
Ru 1:18 to go with her, *she* s urging her. H2532
Ru 2:20 "He *has* not s **showing** his kindness *to* the H6440
1Sa 6:14 there *it* s beside a large rock. H6641
1Sa 7:13 and *they* s invading H4202+3578+6388
1Sa 10: 2 your father *has* s **thinking** *about* them H5759
1Sa 10:13 After Saul s prophesying, he went to the H3983
1Sa 14:46 Then Saul s pursuing the H6590+4946
2Sa 2:23 And every man s when he came to the H6641
2Sa 2:30 Then Joab s pursuing Abner and H8740+4946
2Sa 18:16 the troops s pursuing Israel, for H8740
2Sa 20:12 that everyone who came up to Amasa s, H6641
2Sa 24:21 that the plague on the people *may* **be** s." H6806
2Sa 24:25 the land, and the plague on Israel **was** s. H6806
1Ki 15:21 *he* s building Ramah and withdrew to H2532
1Ki 17:17 and worse, and finally s breathing. H4202+3855
1Ki 22:33 not the king of Israel and s pursuing him. H8740
2Ki 2: 7 Elijah and Elisha *had* s at the Jordan. H6641
2Ki 3:25 *They* s **up** all the springs and cut down H6258
2Ki 4: 6 is not a jar left." Then the oil s flowing. H6641
2Ki 4: 8 whenever he came by, *he* s there to eat. H6073
2Ki 5: 9 chariots and s at the door of Elisha's H6641
2Ki 6:23 bands from Aram s raiding H4202+3578+6388
2Ki 13:18 He struck it three times and s. H6641
2Ki 18:17 up to Jerusalem and s at the aqueduct of H6641
1Ch 21:22 that the plague on the people *may* **be** s. H6806
2Ch 16: 5 *he* s building Ramah and abandoned his H2532
2Ch 18:32 not the king of Israel, *they* s pursuing him. H8740
2Ch 25:16 So the prophet s but said, "I know that H2532
Ezr 5: 5 they *were* not s until a report could A10098
Ne 12:39 At the Gate of the Guard *they* s. H6641
Job 4:16 *It* s, but I could not tell what it was. H6641
Job 32: 1 So these three men s answering Job H8697
Ps 58: 4 like that of a cobra *that has* s its ears, H357
Isa 24: 8 the noise of the revelers *has* s, the joyful H8697
Isa 36: 2 the commander s at the aqueduct of H6641
Jer 44:18 But ever since *we* s burning incense to the H2532
Jer 48:33 *I have* s the flow of wine from the presses H8697
Jer 51:30 Babylon's warriors *have* s fighting; they H2532
La 5:14 the young men have s their music. H4946
Eze 10:18 of the temple and s above the cherubim. H6641
Eze 10:19 *They* s at the entrance of the east gate of H6641
Eze 11:23 within the city and s above the mountain H6641
Mt 2: 9 ahead of them until *it* s over the place G2705
Mt 20:32 Jesus s and called them. "What do you G2705
Mk 5:29 her bleeding s and she felt in her G3830
Mk 10:49 Jesus s and said, "Call him." So they G2705
Lk 7:45 time I entered, *has* not s kissing my feet. G1364
Lk 8:44 and immediately her bleeding s. G2705
Lk 18:40 Jesus s and ordered the man to be G2705
Lk 23:45 *for* the sun s **shining**. And the curtain of G1722
Ac 5:42 *they* never s teaching and proclaiming the G4264
Ac 10:17 Simon's house was and s at the gate. G2392
Ac 11:11 me from Caesarea s at the house where G2392
Ac 20:31 three years *I* never s warning each of G4264
Ac 21:32 his soldiers, *they* s beating Paul. G4264
Eph 1:16 *I have* not s giving thanks for you G4264
Col 1: 9 about you, we *have* not s praying for you. G4264
Heb 10: 2 would *they* not have s being offered? G4264

STOPPING (2) [STOP]

Ex 5: 5 and *you are* s them from working. H8697
Jer 41:17 s at Geruth Kimham near Bethlehem on H3782

STOPS (7) [STOP]

1Ki 18:44 go down before the rain s you. H6806
Job 18: 5 the flame of his fire s burning. H4202
Job 30:27 The churning inside me never s; days of H1957
Job 37: 7 his work, *he* s all people from their labor. H3159
Isa 44:19 No one s **to think**, no one has H8740+448+4213
Ac 6:13 "This fellow never s speaking against this G4264
3Jn 10 *He* also s those who want to do so and G3266

STORAGE (2) [STORE]

Jer 40:10 put them in your s **jars**, and live in H3998
Eze 4: 9 put them in a s **jar** and use them to make H3998

STORE (31) [STORAGE, STORED, STORES, STORING]

Ge 6:21 is to be eaten and s it **away** as food for you H665
Ge 41:35 that are coming and s **up** the grain under H7392
Ex 1:11 Rameses as s cities for Pharaoh. H5016
Dt 14:28 that year's produce and s it in your towns, H5663
1Ki 9:19 as well as all his s cities and the towns H5016
2Ch 8: 4 desert and all the s cities he had built in H5016
2Ch 8: 6 as well as Baalath and all his s cities, and H5016
2Ch 16: 4 Maim and all the s cities of Naphtali. H5016
2Ch 17:12 he built forts and s cities in Judah H5016
2Ch 32:28 He also made **buildings to** s the harvest of H5016
Ne 13: 5 room formerly used *to* s the grain H5989
Job 23:14 and many such plans he still has **in** s. H6640
Pr 2: 1 my words and s **up** my commands within H7621
Pr 2: 7 *He* **holds** success **in** s for the upright, he is H7621
Pr 7: 1 keep my words and s **up** my commands H7621
Pr 10:14 The wise s **up** knowledge, but the mouth H7621
Pr 21:20 The wise s **up** choice food and H238+928+5659
Pr 30:25 yet *they* s **up** their food in the summer; H3922
Isa 2:12 has a day **in** s **for** all the proud and H6584
Isa 10:28 Migron; *they* s supplies at Mikmash. H7212
Isa 33: 6 a **rich** s *of* salvation and wisdom and H2890
Am 3:10 "who s **up** in their fortresses what they have H732
Mic 6:14 *You will* s **up** but save nothing, because H6047
Mal 3:10 that there will not be **room enough to** s it. H1896
Mt 6:19 "*Do* not s **up** for yourselves treasures on G2564
Mt 6:20 But s **up** for yourselves treasures in heaven, G2564
Mt 6:26 do not sow or reap or s **away** in barns, G5251
Lk 12:17 I have no place *to* s my crops.' G5251
Lk 12:18 and there *I will* s my surplus grain. G5251
2Co 9:10 increase your s **of seed** and will enlarge G5078
2Ti 4: 8 Now *there is* **in** s for me the crown of G641

STORED (20) [STORE]

Ge 41:48 abundance in Egypt and s it in the cities. H5989
Ge 41:49 Joseph s **up** huge quantities of grain, like H7392
2Ki 20:17 your predecessors *have* s **up** until this day, H732
Ezr 6: 1 in the archives s in the treasury at A10474
Job 15:20 man through all the years s **up** for him. H7621
Ps 17:14 May *what you have* s **up** for the wicked fill H7621
Ps 31:19 things that *you have* s **up** for those who H7621
Pr 13:22 a sinner's wealth **is** s **up** for the righteous. H7621
SS 7:13 new and old, that *I have* s **up** for you, my H7621
Isa 15: 7 have acquired and s **up** they carry away H7213
Isa 22: 9 *you* s **up** water in the Lower Pool. H7695
Isa 23:18 the LORD; *they will* not **be** s **up** or hoarded. H732
Isa 39: 6 your predecessors *have* s **up** until this day, H732
Isa 45: 3 hidden treasures, **riches** *s in* secret places, so AIT
Hos 13:12 The guilt of Ephraim *is* s **up**, his sins are H7674
Mt 12:35 good things out of the good s **up** in him, G2565
Mt 12:35 evil things out of the evil s **up** in him. G2565
Lk 6:45 things out of the good s **up** in his heart, G2565
Lk 6:45 evil things out of the evil s **up** in his heart. G2565
Col 1: 5 from the hope s **up** for you in heaven G641

STOREHOUSE (5) [HOUSE]

Dt 28:12 the heavens, the s *of* his bounty, to send H238
1Ch 26:15 and the lot for the s fell to his sons. H1074+667
1Ch 26:17 on the south and two at a time at the s. H667
Hos 13:15 His s will be plundered of all its treasures H238
Mal 3:10 Bring the whole tithe into the s, that H1074+238

STOREHOUSES (12) [HOUSE]

Ge 41:56 opened all **the** s and sold H889+928+2157S
2Ki 20:13 them all that was in his s— H1074+5800
1Ch 27:25 son of Adiel was in charge of the royal s. H238
1Ch 27:25 was in charge of the s in the outlying H238
Job 38:22 you entered the s *of* the snow or seen the H238
Job 38:22 of the snow or seen the s *of* the hail, H238
Ps 33: 7 the sea into jars; he puts the deep into s. H238
Ps 135: 7 the rain and brings out the wind from his s. H238
Isa 39: 2 showed them what was in his s— H1074+5800
Jer 10:13 the rain and brings out the wind from his s. H238
Jer 51:16 the rain and brings out the wind from his s. H238
Joel 1:17 The s are in ruins, the granaries have been H238

STOREROOM (2) [ROOM]

Mt 13:52 brings out of his s new treasures as well G2565
Lk 12:24 reap, they have no s or barn; yet God G5421

STOREROOMS (11) [ROOM]

1Ch 28:11 its buildings, its s, its upper parts, its H1711
2Ch 31:11 orders to prepare s in the temple of the H4384
Ne 10:37 we will bring to the s *of* the house of our H4384
Ne 10:38 house of our God, to the s of the treasury. H4384
Ne 10:39 new wine and olive oil to the s, where the H4384
Ne 12:25 who guarded the s *at* the gates. H667
Ne 12:44 be in charge of the s for the H5969+4200+238
Ne 12:44 were to bring into **the** s the portions H2157S
Ne 13: 4 put in charge of the s *of* the house of our H4384
Ne 13:12 of grain, new wine and olive oil into the s. ... H238
Ne 13:13 *I* **put** Shelemiah the priest, Zadok the scribe, ... **in charge of the** s H732+6584+238

STORES (3) [STORE]

Job 21:19 'God s **up** the punishment of the wicked H7621
Pr 6: 8 yet *it* s its provisions in summer and H3922
Lk 12:21 how it will be *with* whoever s **up** things G2564

STORIES (2) [STORY]

2Pe 1:16 cleverly devised s when we told you about G3680
2Pe 2: 3 teachers will exploit you *with* fabricated s. G3364

STORING (2) [STORE]

Ecc 2:26 gathering and s **up wealth** to hand it over H4043
Ro 2: 5 *you are* s **up** wrath against yourself for the G2564

STORK (6)

Lev 11:19 the s, any kind of heron, the hoopoe and H2884
Dt 14:18 the s, any kind of heron, the hoopoe and H2884
Job 39:13 with the wings and feathers of the s. H2884
Ps 104:17 the s has its home in the junipers. H2884
Jer 8: 7 Even the s in the sky knows her appointed H2884
Zec 5: 9 They had wings like those of a s, and they H2884

STORM (33) [STORMED, STORMS, STORMY, THUNDERSTORM, THUNDERSTORMS, WINDSTORM]

Ex 9:24 It was the worst s in all the land of Egypt H1352
Job 9:17 would crush me with a s and multiply my H8554
Job 30:22 the wind; you toss me about in the s. H9583
Job 36:33 His thunder announces **the coming** s H2257S
Job 38: 1 Then the LORD spoke to Job out of the s H6194
Job 40: 6 Then the LORD spoke to Job out of the s: H6194
Ps 55: 8 of shelter, far from the tempest and s." H6193
Ps 83:15 your tempest and terrify them with your s. H6070
Ps 107:29 He stilled the s to a whisper; the waves of H6194
Pr 1:27 when calamity overtakes you like a s H8739
Pr 10:25 When the s has swept by, the wicked are H6070
Isa 4: 6 hiding place from the s and rain. H2443
Isa 25: 4 a shelter from the s and a shade from the H2443
Isa 25: 4 ruthless is like a s *driving against* a wall H2443
Isa 32: 2 from the wind and a refuge from the s, H2443
Jer 11:16 the roar of a mighty s he will set it on fire, H2167
Jer 23:19 the s *of* the LORD will burst out in wrath H6194
Jer 25:32 a mighty s is rising from the ends of the H6193
Jer 30:23 the s *of* the LORD will burst out in wrath H6194
Eze 30:16 Thebes will be **taken by** s; Memphis will H1324
Eze 38: 9 advancing like a s; you will be like a H8739
Da 11:40 of the North *will* s **out** against him with H8548
Jnh 1: 4 such a violent s arose that the ship H6193
Jnh 1:12 fault that this great s has come upon you." H6193
Na 1: 3 His way is in the whirlwind and the s, and H8554
Na 2: 4 The chariots s through the streets, rushing H2147
Mt 8:24 Suddenly a furious s came up on the lake G4939
Lk 8:24 raging waters; the s subsided, and all was NDT
Ac 27:15 was caught by the s and could not head NDT
Ac 27:18 **took such a** violent **battering from the** s G5928
Ac 27:20 many days and the s continued raging, G5930
Heb 12:18 with fire; to darkness, gloom and s; G2590
2Pe 2:17 without water and mists driven by a s. G3278

STORMED (1) [STORM]

Hab 3:14 head when his warriors s **out** to scatter us, H6192

STORMS (2) [STORM]

Isa 54:11 **lashed by** s and not comforted H6192
Zec 9:14 he will march in the s *of* the south, H6194

STORMY (3) [STORM]

Ps 148: 8 clouds, s winds that do his bidding, H6194
Am 1:14 of battle, amid violent winds on a s day. H6070
Mt 16: 3 'Today it will be s, for the sky is red and G5930

STORY (6) [STORIES]
Ge 39:17 Then she told him this s: "That Hebrew H1821
Ge 39:19 his master heard the s his wife told him, H1821
Ps 107: 2 *Let* the redeemed of the LORD **tell** their s H606
Mt 28:15 And this s has been widely circulated *G3364*
Ac 11: 4 beginning, Peter told them **the whole** s: *G2759*
Ac 20: 9 ground from the **third** s and was picked up *G5566*

STRAGGLER (1)
Isa 14:31 the north, and there is not a s in its ranks. H969

STRAIGHT (40) [STRAIGHTEN, STRAIGHTENED]
Jos 6: 5 the army will go up, everyone **s in**. H5584
Jos 6:20 so everyone charged **s in**, and they took H5584
1Sa 6:12 Then the cows **went s** *up* toward Beth H3837
2Sa 5:23 he answered, "*Do* not **go s up**, but circle H6590
Job 10:19 carried **s** from the womb **to** the grave! H4200
Ps 5: 8 enemies—**make** your way **s** before me. H3837
Ps 27:11 lead me in a **s** path because of my H4793
Ps 107: 7 He led them by a **s** way to a city where H3838
Pr 2:13 who have left the **s** paths to walk in dark H3841
Pr 3: 6 and he *will* **make** your paths **s**. H3837
Pr 4:11 of wisdom and lead you along **s** paths. H3841
Pr 4:25 Let your eyes look **s ahead**; fix your H4200+5790
Pr 5: 5 to death; her steps **lead s** *to* the grave. H9461
Pr 9:15 who pass by, who **go s** *on* their way, H3837
Pr 11: 5 of the blameless **makes** their paths **s**, H3837
Pr 15:21 has understanding **keeps** a **s** course. H3837
SS 7: 9 May the wine go **s** to my beloved, flowing H4797
Isa 40: 3 **make s** in the desert a highway for our H3837
Isa 45:13 *I will* **make** all his ways **s**. He will H3837
Jer 31:39 stretch from there **s** to the hill of Gareb H5584
Eze 1: 7 Their legs were **s**; their feet were like H3838
Eze 1: 9 Each one went **s ahead**; they H448+6298+7156
Eze 1:12 Each one went **s ahead** H448+6298+7156
Eze 10:22 Each one went **s ahead.** H448+6298+7156
Joel 2: 8 jostle each other; each marches **s ahead**. H5019
Am 4: 3 will each go **s** out **through** breaches in the H5584
Mt 3: 3 way for the Lord, make **s** paths for him. *G2318*
Mk 1: 3 way for the Lord, make **s** paths for him. *G2318*
Lk 3: 4 way for the Lord, make **s** paths for him. *G2318*
Lk 3: 5 The crooked roads shall become **s**, the *G2318*
Lk 22:61 The Lord turned and **looked s at** Peter *G1838*
Jn 1:23 wilderness, '**Make s** the way for the Lord.' *G2316*
Jn 20: 6 behind him and **went s into** the tomb. *G1656*
Ac 3: 4 Peter **looked s** at him, as did John. *G867*
Ac 9:11 house of Judas on **S** Street and ask for a *G2318*
Ac 13: 9 the Holy Spirit, **looked s at** Elymas and said *G867*
Ac 16:11 out to sea and **sailed s** for Samothrace, *G2312*
Ac 21: 1 we put out to sea and **sailed s** to Kos. *G2312*
Ac 23: 1 Paul **looked s at** the Sanhedrin and said *G867*
2Pe 2:15 They have left the **s** way and wandered off *G2318*

STRAIGHTEN (2) [STRAIGHT]
Ecc 7:13 Who can **s** what he has made crooked? H9545
Lk 13:11 was bent over and could not **s up** at all. *G376*

STRAIGHTENED (4) [STRAIGHT]
Ecc 1:15 What is crooked cannot *be* **s**; what is H9545
Lk 13:13 immediately *she* **s up** and praised God *G494*
Jn 8: 7 questioning him, *he* **s up** and said to them *G376*
Jn 8:10 Jesus **s up** and asked her, "Woman, where *G376*

STRAIGHTWAY (KJV) AS SOON AS, AT ONCE, IMMEDIATELY, JUST AS, RIGHT AWAY, SHORTLY, WITHOUT DELAY

STRAIN (2) [STRAINING]
Ex 18:23 you will be able *to* **stand the s**, and all H6641
Mt 23:24 You **s out** a gnat but swallow a camel *G1494*

STRAINING (3) [STRAIN]
Zec 6: 7 *they were* **s** to go throughout the earth. H1335
Mk 6:48 He saw the disciples **s** at the oars, because *G989*
Php 3:13 is behind and **s toward** what is ahead, *G2085*

STRANDS (2)
Ex 39: 3 of gold and cut **s** to be worked into the H7348
Ecc 4:12 A cord of **three** *s* is not quickly broken AIT

STRANGE (12) [ESTRANGED, STRANGER, STRANGER'S, STRANGERS]
Ex 3: 3 "I will go over and see this **s** sight—why H1524
Pr 23:33 Your eyes will see **s** sights, and your mind H2424
Isa 18: 2 an aggressive nation of **s speech** H7743+7743
Isa 18: 7 an aggressive nation of **s speech** H7743+7743
Isa 28:11 with foreign lips and **s** tongues God will H337
Isa 28:21 to do his work, his **s** work, and perform his H2424
Isa 33:19 whose language is **s** and H4352
Eze 3: 5 of obscure speech and **s** language, H3878
Eze 3: 6 of obscure speech and **s** language, H3878
Ac 17:20 You are bringing some **s** *ideas* to our ears *G3826*
Heb 13: 9 carried away by all kinds of **s** teachings. *G3828*
1Pe 4:12 as though *something* **s** were happening *G3828*

STRANGER (20) [STRANGE]
Ge 23: 4 "I am a foreigner and **s** among you. H9369
Ge 42: 7 but *he* **pretended to be a s** and spoke H5796
Lev 25:35 help them as you would a foreigner and **s**, H9369
Job 19:15 a foreigner; they look on me as on a **s**. H5799
Job 29:16 needy; I took up the case of the **s**. H4202+3359
Job 31:32 no **s** had to spend the night in the H1731
Ps 39:12 as a foreigner, a **s**, as all my ancestors H9369
Ps 69: 8 a **s** to my own mother's children; H5799
Ps 119:19 I am a **s** on earth; do not hide your H1731
Pr 6: 1 you have shaken hands in pledge for a **s**, H2424
Pr 11:15 puts up security for a **s** will surely suffer, H2424
Pr 20:16 of one who puts up security for a **s**; H2424
Pr 27:13 of one who puts up security for a **s**; H2424
Jer 14: 8 why are you like a **s** in the land, like a H1731
Mt 25:35 to drink, I was a **s** and you invited me in, *G3828*
Mt 25:38 did we see you a **s** and invite you in, *G3828*
Mt 25:43 I was a **s** and you did not invite me in, *G3828*
Mt 25:44 thirsty or a **s** or needing clothes or *G3828*
Jn 10: 5 But they will never follow a **s**; in fact, they *G259*
Heb 11: 9 promised land like a **s in a foreign country**; *G259*

STRANGER'S (1) [STRANGE]
Jn 10: 5 because they do not recognize a **s** voice." *G259*

STRANGERS (20) [STRANGE]
Ge 15:13 descendants will be **s** in a country not H1731
Lev 25:23 you **reside** in my land **as** foreigners and **s**. H9369
1Ch 16:19 few in number, few indeed, and **s** in it, H1591
1Ch 29:15 We are foreigners and **s** in your sight, as H9369
Ps 105:12 few in number, few indeed, and **s** in it, H1591
Ps 109:11 may **s** plunder the fruits of his labor. H2424
Pr 5:10 lest **s** feast on your wealth and your toil H2424
Pr 5:17 be yours alone, never to be shared with **s**. H2424
Ecc 6: 2 and **s** enjoy them instead. H408+5799
Isa 1: 7 laid waste as when overthrown by **s**. H2424
Isa 61: 5 **S** will shepherd your flocks; foreigners will H2424
La 5: 2 Our inheritance has been turned over to **s** H2424
Eze 16:32 You prefer **s** to your own husband! H2424
Ob 11 you stood aloof while **s** carried off his H2424
Zec 7:14 all the nations, where they *were* **s**. H3359+4202
Ac 7: 6 descendants will be **s** in a country not *G4230*
Eph 2:19 you are no longer foreigners and **s**, but *G4230*
Heb 11:13 that they were foreigners and **s** on earth. *G4215*
Heb 13: 2 Do not forget to **show hospitality to s**, for *G5810*
3Jn 5 sisters, even though they are **s** to you. *G3828*

STRANGLED (4) [STRANGLING]
Na 2:12 his cubs and **s** the prey for his mate, H2871
Ac 15:20 *from the meat of* **s** *animals* and from *G4465*
Ac 15:29 *from the meat of* **s** *animals* and from *G4465*
Ac 21:25 *from the meat of* **s** *animals* and from *G4465*

STRANGLING (1) [STRANGLED]
Job 7:15 so that I prefer **s** and death, rather than H4725

STRAP (4) [STRAPPED, STRAPS]
Ge 14:23 not even a thread or the **s** *of* a sandal, so H8579
Ex 32:27 'Each man **s** a sword to his side. H8492
1Sa 25:13 to his men, "Each *of you* **s on** your sword!" H2520
Isa 5:27 at the waist, not a sandal **s** is broken. H8579

STRAPPED (3) [STRAP]
Jdg 3:16 which *he* **s** to his right thigh under his H2520
1Sa 25:13 and David **s** his **on** as well. About H2520
2Sa 20: 8 **s** over it at his waist was a belt with a H7537

STRAPS (4) [STRAP]
Jer 27: 2 "Make a **yoke** *out* **of s** and crossbars and H4593
Mk 1: 7 the **s** of whose sandals I am not worthy to *G2666*
Lk 3:16 the **s** of whose sandals I am not worthy to *G2666*
Jn 1:27 the **s** of whose sandals I am not worthy to *G2666*

STRATEGY (1)
Isa 8:10 Devise your **s**, but it will be thwarted H6783

STRAW (23)
Ge 24:25 "We have plenty of **s** and fodder, as well H9320
Ge 24:32 **S** and fodder were brought for the camels H9320
Ex 5: 7 the people with **s** for making bricks; H9320
Ex 5: 7 let them go and gather their own **s**. H9320
Ex 5:10 'I will not give you any more **s**. H9320
Ex 5:11 Go and get your own **s** wherever you can H9320
Ex 5:12 over Egypt to gather stubble to use for **s**. H9320
Ex 5:13 you for each day, just as when you had **s**." H9320
Ex 5:16 Your servants are given no **s**, yet we are H9320
Ex 5:18 You will not be given any **s**, yet you must H9320
Jdg 19:19 We have both **s** and fodder for our H9320
1Ki 4:28 quotas of barley and **s** for the chariot H9320
Job 21:18 How often are they like **s** before the wind H9320
Job 41:27 Iron it treats like **s** and bronze like rotten H9320
Job 41:29 A club seems to it but a **piece of s**; it H7990
Isa 5:24 of fire lick up **s** and as dry grass sinks H7990
Isa 11: 7 the lion will eat **s** like the ox. H9320
Isa 25:10 in their land as **s** is trampled down in the H5495
Isa 33:11 you give birth to **s**; your breath is a fire H7990
Isa 65:25 the lion will eat **s** like the ox, and H9320
Jer 23:28 For what has **s** to do with grain? H9320
Am 5:11 You **levy a s tax** on the poor and impose a H1424
1Co 3:12 silver, costly stones, wood, hay or **s**, *G2811*

STRAWED (KJV) SCATTERED, SPREAD

STRAY (10) [ASTRAY, STRAYED, STRAYING, STRAYS]
Ex 22: 5 vineyard and **lets** them **s** and they graze H8938
1Ki 22:43 of his father Asa and *did* not **s** from them; H6073
2Ch 20:32 of his father Asa and *did* not **s** from them; H6073
Ps 119:10 *do* not **let** me **s** from your commands. H8706
Ps 119:21 those *who* **s** from your commands. H8706
Ps 119:118 You reject all *who* **s** from your decrees, H8706
Pr 7:25 heart turn to her ways or **s** into her paths. H9494
Pr 19:27 you *will* **s** from the words of H8706
Pr 26:17 Like one who grabs a *s* **dog** by the ears is AIT
Eze 14:11 people of Israel *will* no longer **s** from me, H9494

STRAYED (6) [STRAY]
Ps 44:18 our feet *had* not **s** from your path. H5742
Ps 119:110 but *I have* not **s** from your precepts. H9494
Ps 119:176 *I have* **s** like a lost sheep. Seek your H9494
Jer 2: 5 find in me, that *they* **s so far** from me? H8178
Jer 31:19 After I **s**, I repented; after I came to H8740
Hos 7:13 to them, because *they have* **s** from me! H5610

STRAYING (1) [STRAY]
Dt 22: 1 see your fellow Israelite's ox or sheep **s**, H5615

STRAYS (3) [STRAY]
Pr 21:16 Whoever **s** from the path of prudence H9494
Eze 34: 4 not brought back the **s** or searched for the H5615
Eze 34:16 search for the lost and bring back the **s**. H5615

STREAKED (7)
Ge 30:35 all the male goats that were **s** or spotted, H6819
Ge 30:39 bore young that were **s** or speckled or H6819
Ge 30:40 made the rest face the **s** and dark-colored H6819
Ge 31: 8 if he said, 'The **s** *ones* will be your wages H6819
Ge 31: 8 then all the flocks bore **s** *young*. H6819
Ge 31:10 male goats mating with the flock were **s**, H6819
Ge 31:12 male goats mating with the flock are **s**, H6819

STREAM (18) [DOWNSTREAM, STREAMING, STREAMS, UPSTREAM]
Ge 32:23 After he had sent them across the **s**, he H5707
Dt 9:21 the dust into a **s** that flowed down the H5707
Dt 21: 4 planted and where there is a **flowing s**. H419
1Sa 17:40 chose five smooth stones from the **s**, put H5707
2Ch 32: 4 the springs and the **s** that flowed through H5707
Job 30: 6 They were forced to live in the dry **s beds** H5707
Job 40:22 shadow; the poplars by the **s** surround it. H5707
Job 41:19 Flames **s** from its mouth; sparks of fire H2143
Pr 18: 4 the fountain of wisdom is a rushing **s**. H5707
Pr 21: 1 the king's heart is a **s** *of* water that he H7104
Isa 2: 2 above the hills, and all nations *will* **s** to it. H5641
Isa 30:33 of the LORD, like a **s** *of* burning sulfur, sets H5707
Isa 32:20 sowing your seed by every **s**, and letting H4784
Isa 66:12 the wealth of nations like a flooding **s**; H5707
Jer 17: 8 the water that sends out its roots by the **s**. H3414
Jer 51:44 The nations *will* no longer **s** to him. H5641
Am 5:24 righteousness like a never-failing **s**! H5707
Mic 4: 1 above the hills, and peoples *will* **s** to it. H5641

STREAMING (1) [STREAM]
SS 4:15 of flowing water **s down** from Lebanon. H5688

STREAMS (58) [STREAM]
Ge 2: 6 **s** came up from the earth and watered H116
Ex 7:19 of Egypt—over the **s** and canals, over the H5643
Ex 8: 5 your staff over the **s** and canals and ponds H5643
Lev 11: 9 of the seas and the **s** you may eat any H5707
Lev 11:10 in the seas or **s** that do not have fins H5707
Dt 8: 7 a land with brooks, **s**, and deep springs H6524
Dt 10: 7 on to Jotbathah, a land with **s** *of* water. H5707
2Ki 19:24 my feet I have dried up all the **s** *of* Egypt." H3284
Job 6:15 are as undependable as **intermittent s**, H5707
Job 6:15 streams, as the **s** that overflow H692+5707
Job 20:17 He will not enjoy the **s**, the rivers flowing H7106
Job 29: 6 the rock poured out for me **s** *of* olive oil. H7104
Job 36:27 drops of water, which distill as rain to the **s**; H116
Ps 1: 3 person is like a tree planted by **s** *of* water, H7104
Ps 42: 1 As the deer pants for **s** *of* water, so my soul H692
Ps 46: 4 is a river whose **s** make glad the city of H7104
Ps 65: 9 The **s** *of* God are filled with water to H7104
Ps 74:15 It was you who opened up springs and **s** H5707
Ps 78:16 he brought **s** out of a rocky crag and made H5689
Ps 78:20 water gushed out, **s** flowed abundantly H5707
Ps 78:44 they could not drink from their **s**. H5689
Ps 119:136 **S** *of* tears flow from my eyes, for your H7104
Ps 126: 4 our fortunes, LORD, like **s** in the Negev. H692
Pr 5:16 your **s** *of* water in the public squares? H7104
Ecc 1: 7 All **s** flow into the sea, yet the sea is H5707
Ecc 1: 7 To the place the **s** come from, there they H5707
SS 5:12 His eyes are like doves by the water **s** H692
Isa 11:15 it up into seven **s** so that anyone can H5707
Isa 19: 6 the **s** *of* Egypt will dwindle and dry up. H3284
Isa 30:25 **s** *of* water will flow on every high H7104
Isa 32: 2 like **s** *of* water in the desert and the H7104
Isa 33:21 It will be like a place of broad rivers and **s**. H3284
Isa 34: 9 Edom's **s** will be turned into pitch, her H5707
Isa 35: 6 forth in the wilderness and **s** in the desert. H5707
Isa 37:25 my feet I have dried up all the **s** *of* Egypt. H3284
Isa 43:19 in the wilderness and **s** in the wasteland. H5643
Isa 43:20 in the wilderness and **s** in the wasteland, H5643
Isa 44: 3 the thirsty land, and **s** on the dry ground; H5689
Isa 44: 4 like poplar trees by **flowing s**. H3298+4784
Isa 44:27 'Be dry, and I will dry up your **s**,' H5643
Isa 47: 2 bare your legs, and wade through the **s**. H5643
Jer 9:18 with tears and water **s** *from* our eyelids. H5688
Jer 31: 9 lead them beside **s** *of* water on a level H5707
La 3:48 **S** *of* tears flow from my eyes because my H7104
Eze 29: 3 you great monster lying among your **s**. H3284
Eze 29: 4 make the fish of your **s** stick to your scales. H3284
Eze 29: 4 I will pull you out from among your **s**, with H3284
Eze 29: 5 the desert, you and all the fish of your **s**. H3284
Eze 29:10 I am against you and against your **s**, H3284
Eze 31: 4 their **s** flowed all around its base and sent H5643

Eze 31:15 I held back its s, and its abundant H5643
Eze 32: 2 in the seas thrashing about in your s, H5643
Eze 32: 2 water with your feet and muddying the s. H5643
Eze 32:14 waters settle and make her s flow like oil, H5643
Joel 1:20 the s *of* water have dried up and fire has H692
Hab 3: 8 Was your wrath against the s? Did you H5643
Mt 7:25 came down, the s rose, and the winds *G4532*
Mt 7:27 came down, the s rose, and the winds *G4532*

STREET (24) [STREETS]

Dt 32:25 In the s the sword will make them H2575
Jos 2:19 of them go outside your house into the s, H2575
2Ch 28:24 up altars at every s **corner** in Jerusalem. H7157
Job 31:32 stranger had to spend the night in the s, H2575
Ps 31:11 those who see me on the s flee from me. H2575
Pr 7: 8 He was going down the s near her corner H8798
Pr 7:12 now in the s, now in the squares, at every H2575
Ecc 12: 4 the doors to the s are closed and the H8798
Isa 51:20 they lie at every s corner, like antelope H2575
Isa 51:23 like the ground, like a s to be walked on." H2575
Jer 6:11 the children in the s and on the young H2575
Jer 37:21 of bread from the s *of* the bakers each day H2575
La 2:19 who faint from hunger at every s corner. H2575
La 4: 1 gems are scattered at every s corner. H2575
Eze 16:25 At every s corner you built your lofty H2006
Eze 16:31 mounds at every s corner and made your H2006
Na 3:10 were dashed to pieces at every s corner. H2575
Mt 6: 5 on the s corners to be seen by *G4423*
Mt 22: 9 So go to the s corners and invite to the *G3847*
Mk 11: 4 went and found a colt outside in the s, *G316*
Ac 9:11 of Judas on Straight S and ask for a man *G4860*
Ac 12:10 they had walked the length of one s, *G4860*
Rev 21:21 The **great** s of the city was of gold, as *G4423*
Rev 22: 2 down the middle *of* the **great** s of the city *G4423*

STREETS (63) [STREET]

2Sa 1:20 proclaim it not in the s *of* Ashkelon, lest H2575
2Sa 22:43 trampled them like mud in the s. H2575
Est 6: 9 lead him on the horse through the city s, H8148
Est 6:11 led him on horseback through the city s, H8148
Ps 18:42 I trampled them like mud in the s. H2575
Ps 55:11 the city; threats and lies never leave its s. H8148
Ps 144:14 into captivity, no cry of distress in our s. H8148
Pr 5:16 Should your springs overflow in the s, your H2575
Pr 26:13 in the road, a fierce lion roaming the s!" H8148
Ecc 12: 5 afraid of heights and of dangers in the s; H2006
Ecc 12: 5 home and mourners go about the s. H8798
SS 3: 2 the city, through its s and squares; I will H8798
Isa 5:25 the dead bodies are like refuse in the s. H2575
Isa 10: 6 to trample them down like mud in the s. H2575
Isa 15: 3 In the s they wear sackcloth; on the roofs H2575
Isa 24:11 In the s they cry out for wine; all joy turns H2575
Isa 33: 7 their brave men cry aloud in the s; the H2575
Isa 42: 2 shout or cry out, or raise his voice in the s. H2575
Isa 58:12 Restorer of S with Dwellings. H5986
Isa 59:14 truth has stumbled in the s, honesty H8148
Jer 5: 1 "Go up and down the s *of* Jerusalem, look H2575
Jer 7:17 towns of Judah and in the s *of* Jerusalem? H2575
Jer 7:34 towns of Judah and the s *of* Jerusalem, H2575
Jer 9:21 children from the s and the young men H2575
Jer 11: 6 towns of Judah and in the s *of* Jerusalem: H2575
Jer 11:13 Baal are as many as the s *of* Jerusalem. H2575
Jer 14:16 out into the s *of* Jerusalem because H2575
Jer 33:10 of Judah and the s *of* Jerusalem that are H2575
Jer 44: 6 of Judah and the s *of* Jerusalem and H2575
Jer 44: 9 the land of Judah and the s *of* Jerusalem? H2575
Jer 44:17 towns of Judah and in the s *of* Jerusalem. H2575
Jer 44:21 of Judah and the s *of* Jerusalem by you H2575
Jer 49:26 her young men will fall in the s; all her H8148
Jer 50:30 her young men will fall in the s; all her H8148
Jer 51: 4 slain in Babylon, fatally wounded in her s. H2575
La 2:11 infants faint in the s *of* the city. H8148
La 2:12 faint like the wounded in the s *of* the city, H8148
La 2:21 old lie together in the dust of the s; H2575
La 4: 5 once ate delicacies are destitute in the s. H2575
La 4: 8 they are not recognized in the s. H2575
La 4:14 grope through the s as if they were blind. H2575
La 4:18 every step, so we could not walk in our s. H8148
Eze 7:19 " 'They will throw their silver into the s H2575
Eze 11: 6 in this city and filled its s with the dead. H2575
Eze 26:11 of his horses will trample all your s; H2575
Eze 28:23 upon you and make blood flow in your s. H2575
Da 9:25 It will be rebuilt with s and a trench, but H8148
Hos 7: 1 break into houses, bandits rob in the s; H2575
Am 5:16 wailing in all the s and cries of anguish H2575
Mic 7:10 be trampled underfoot like mire in the s. H2575
Na 2: 4 The chariots storm through the s, rushing H2575
Zep 3: 6 I have left their s deserted, with no one H2575
Zec 8: 4 ripe old age will sit in the s *of* Jerusalem, H8148
Zec 8: 5 The city s will be filled with boys and girls H8148
Zec 9: 3 like dust, and gold like the dirt of the s. H2575
Zec 10: 5 their enemy into the mud of the s. H2575
Mt 6: 2 do in the synagogues and on the s, *G4860*
Mt 12:19 no one will hear his voice in the s. *G4423*
Mt 22:10 went out into the s and gathered all the *G3847*
Lk 10:10 are not welcomed, go into its s and say, *G4423*
Lk 13:26 drank with you, and you taught in our s. *G4423*
Lk 14:21 out quickly into the s and alleys of the *G4423*
Ac 5:15 the sick into the s and laid them on beds *G4423*

STRENGTH (180) [STRONG]

Ge 31: 6 I've worked for your father with all my s, H3946
Ge 48: 2 Israel **rallied** *his* s and sat up on the bed. H2616
Ge 49: 3 the first sign of my s, excelling in honor, H226
Ex 15: 2 "The LORD is my s and my defense; he has H6437
Ex 15:13 In your s you will guide them to your holy H6437
Lev 26:16 that will destroy your sight and sap your s. H5883
Lev 26:20 Your s will be spent in vain, because your H3946
Nu 14:17 "Now may the Lord's s be displayed, just H3946
Nu 23:22 out of Egypt; they have the s *of* a wild ox. H9361
Nu 24: 8 out of Egypt; they have the s *of* a wild ox. H9361
Dt 4:37 of Egypt by his Presence and his great s, H3946
Dt 6: 5 with all your soul and with all your s. H4394
Dt 8:17 "My power and the s *of* my hands have H6797
Dt 11: 8 so that *you may* **have** *the* s *to* go in and H2616
Dt 21:17 That son is the first **sign** of his father's s H226
Dt 32:36 when he sees their s is gone and no one H3338
Dt 33:25 and your s will equal your days. H1801
Dt 34: 7 his eyes were not weak nor his s gone. H4301
Jdg 5:31 you be like the sun when it rises in its s." H1476
Jdg 6:14 "Go in the s you have and save Israel out H3946
Jdg 7: 2 against me, 'My own s has saved me.' H3338
Jdg 8:21 do it yourself. 'As is the man, so is his s.' " H1476
Jdg 15:19 his s returned and he revived. H8120
Jdg 16: 5 the secret of his great s and how we can H3946
Jdg 16: 6 secret of your great s and how you can be H3946
Jdg 16: 9 So the secret of his s was not discovered. H3946
Jdg 16:15 haven't told me the secret of your great s." H3946
Jdg 16:17 were shaved, my s would leave me, and H3946
Jdg 16:19 began to subdue him. And his s left him. H3946
1Sa 2: 4 those who stumbled are armed with s. H2657
1Sa 2: 9 "It is not by s that one prevails; H3946
1Sa 2:10 "He will give s to his king and exalt the H6437
1Sa 2:31 I will cut short your s and the strength of H2432
1Sa 2:31 strength and the s *of* your priestly house, H2432
1Sa 2:33 only to destroy your sight and sap your s, H5883
1Sa 23:16 and **helped** him **find** s in God H2616+906+3338
1Sa 28:20 His s was gone, for he had eaten nothing H3946
1Sa 28:22 eat and have the s to go on your way." H3946
1Sa 30: 4 aloud until they had no s left to weep. H3946
1Sa 30: 6 But David **found** s in the LORD his God H2616
2Sa 15:12 And so the conspiracy gained s, and H579
2Sa 22:33 who arms me with s and keeps my way H2657
2Sa 22:40 You armed me with s for battle; you H2657
2Ki 19: 3 of birth and there is no s to deliver them. H3946
2Ki 23:25 with all his soul and with all his s, H4394
1Ch 16:11 Look to the LORD and his s; seek his face H6437
1Ch 16:27 s and joy are in his dwelling place. H6437
1Ch 16:28 of nations, ascribe to the LORD glory and s. H6437
1Ch 26: 8 capable men with the s to do the work— H3946
1Ch 29:12 In your hands are s and power to exalt H3946
1Ch 29:12 power to exalt and **give** s to all. H2616
2Ch 13:21 But Abijah **grew in** s. He married fourteen H2616
2Ch 23: 1 the seventh year Jehoiada **showed** *his* s. H2616
2Ch 25:11 then **marshaled** *his* s and led his H2616
Ne 1:10 by your great s and your mighty hand. H3946
Ne 4:10 "The s *of* the laborers is giving out H3946
Ne 8:10 for the joy of the LORD is your s." H5057
Job 6:11 "What s do I have, that I should still hope H3946
Job 6:12 Do I have the s *of* stone? Is my flesh H3946
Job 9:19 If it is a matter of s, he is mighty! And if it H3946
Job 12:16 To him belong s and insight; both H6437
Job 22: 9 broke the s *of* the fatherless. H2432
Job 30: 2 what use was the s *of* their hands to me, H3946
Job 39:11 Will you rely on it for its great s? Will you H3946
Job 39:19 you give the horse its s or clothe its neck H1476
Job 39:21 rejoicing in its s, and charges into the fray H3946
Job 40:16 What s it has in its loins, what power in H3946
Job 41:12 its s and its graceful form. H1476
Job 41:22 S resides in its neck; dismay goes before H6437
Ps 10:10 they collapse; they fall under his s. H6786
Ps 18: 1 I love you, LORD, my s. H2619
Ps 18:32 who arms me with s and keeps my way H2657
Ps 18:39 You armed me with s for battle; you H2657
Ps 21: 1 The king rejoices in your s, LORD. H6437
Ps 21:13 Be exalted in your s, LORD; we will sing H6437
Ps 22:19 You are my s; come quickly to H394
Ps 28: 7 The LORD is my s and my shield; my heart H6437
Ps 28: 8 The LORD is the s of his people, a fortress H6437
Ps 29: 1 ascribe to the LORD glory and s. H6437
Ps 29:11 The LORD gives s to his people; the LORD H6437
Ps 31:10 my s fails because of my affliction H3946
Ps 32: 4 my s was sapped as in the heat of H4382
Ps 33:16 no warrior escapes by his great s. H3946
Ps 33:17 despite all its great s it cannot save. H2657
Ps 38:10 My heart pounds, my s fails me; even the H3946
Ps 46: 1 God is our refuge and s, an ever-present H6437
Ps 59: 9 You are my s, I watch for you; you, God H6437
Ps 59:16 But I will sing of your s, in the morning I H6437
Ps 59:17 You are my s, I sing praise to you; you H6437
Ps 65: 6 your power, having armed yourself with s, H1476
Ps 68:28 God; **show** us *your* s, our God, as H6451
Ps 68:35 of Israel gives power and s to his people. H9508
Ps 71: 9 do not forsake me when my s is gone. H3946
Ps 73:26 God is the s *of* my heart and my H7446
Ps 81: 1 Sing for joy to God our s; shout aloud to H6437
Ps 84: 5 Blessed are those whose s is in you H6437
Ps 84: 7 They go from s to strength, till each H2657
Ps 84: 7 They go from strength to s, till each H2657
Ps 86:16 show your s in behalf of your servant H6437
Ps 88: 4 go down to the pit; I am like one without s. H384
Ps 89:17 For you are their glory and s, and by your H6437
Ps 89:19 "I have bestowed s on a warrior; I have H6469
Ps 90:10 eighty, if our s endures; yet the best of H1476
Ps 93: 1 is robed in majesty and armed with s; H6437
Ps 96: 6 s and glory are in his sanctuary. H6437
Ps 96: 7 of nations, ascribe to the LORD glory and s. H6437
Ps 102:23 In the course of my life he broke my s; he H3946
Ps 105: 4 Look to the LORD and his s; seek his face H6437
Ps 118:14 The LORD is my s and my defense; he has H6437
Ps 147:10 His pleasure is not in the s *of* the horse H1476
Pr 14: 4 from the s *of* an ox come abundant H3946
Pr 20:29 The glory of young men is their s, gray H3946
Pr 24: 5 those who have knowledge muster their s. H3946
Pr 24:10 in a time of trouble, how small is your s! H3946
Pr 30:25 Ants are creatures of little s, yet they store H6434
Pr 31: 3 Do not spend your s on women, your vigor H2657
Pr 31:25 She is clothed with s and dignity; she can H6437
Ecc 9:16 "Wisdom is better than s." But the poor H1476
Ecc 10:10 edge unsharpened, *more* s is needed, but H2657
Ecc 10:17 for s and not for drunkenness. H1476
Isa 10:13 " 'By the s *of* my hand I have done this H3946
Isa 12: 2 LORD himself, is my s and my defense; he H6437
Isa 28: 6 a **source of** s to those who turn back the H1476
Isa 30:15 in quietness and trust is your s, but you H1476
Isa 31: 1 in the great s of their horsemen, H6793
Isa 33: 2 Be our s every morning, our salvation in H2432
Isa 37: 3 of birth and there is no s to deliver them. H3946
Isa 40:26 Because of his great power and mighty s H3946
Isa 40:29 He gives s to the weary and increases the H3946
Isa 40:31 who hope in the LORD will renew their s. H3946
Isa 41: 1 Let the nations renew their s! Let them H3946
Isa 44:12 He gets hungry and loses his s; he drinks H3946
Isa 45:24 'In the LORD alone are deliverance and s. H6437
Isa 49: 4 I have spent my s for nothing at all. H3946
Isa 49: 5 of the LORD and my God has been my s— H6437
Isa 50: 2 Do I lack the s to rescue you? By a H3946
Isa 51: 9 arm of the LORD, clothe yourself with s! H6437
Isa 52: 1 Zion, clothe yourself with s! H6437
Isa 57:10 You found renewal of your s, and so you H3338
Isa 63: 1 striding forward in the greatness of his s? H3946
Jer 9:23 strong boast of their s or the rich boast of H1476
Jer 16:19 my s and my fortress, my refuge in H6437
Jer 17: 5 who draws s from mere flesh and whose H2432
Jer 51:30 Their s is exhausted; they have become H1476
La 1:14 my neck, and the Lord has sapped my s. H3946
Eze 30: 6 of Egypt will fall and her proud s will fail. H6437
Eze 30:18 there her proud s will come to an end. H6437
Eze 33:28 her proud s will come to an end H6437
Da 2:41 it will have some of the s of iron in it A10487
Da 10: 8 I had no s left, my face turned H3946
Da 10:17 My s is gone and I can hardly breathe." H3946
Da 10:18 like a man touched me and **gave** me s. H2616
Da 10:19 my lord, since *you have* **given** me s." H2616
Da 11:15 best troops will not have the s to stand. H3946
Da 11:25 he will stir up his s and courage against H3946
Hos 7: 9 Foreigners sap his s, but he does not H3946
Hos 10:13 on your own s and on your many H2006
Am 2:14 the strong will not muster their s, and the H3946
Am 6:13 "Did we not take Karnaim by our own s?" H2620
Mic 5: 4 shepherd his flock in the s *of* the LORD, H6437
Na 2: 1 brace yourselves, marshal all your s! H3946
Na 3: 9 Cush and Egypt were her boundless s; Put H6797
Hab 1:11 guilty people, whose own s is their god." H3946
Hab 3:19 The Sovereign LORD is my s; he makes my H2657
Mk 12:30 with all your mind and with all your s. *G2709*
Mk 12:33 all your understanding and with all your s, *G2709*
Lk 10:27 soul and with all your s and with all your *G2709*
Ac 9:19 after taking some food, *he* **regained** *his* s. *G1932*
1Co 1:25 weakness of God is stronger than human s. NDT
Eph 1:19 That power is the same as the mighty s *G2709*
Php 4:13 do all this through him *who* **gives** me s. *G1904*
1Ti 1:12 our Lord, who *has* **given** me s, that he *G1904*
2Ti 4:17 the Lord stood at my side and **gave** me s, *G1904*
Heb 11:34 whose weakness *was* **turned to** s; and *G1540*
1Pe 4:11 they should do so with the s God provides, *G2709*
Jude 8 **on the** s **of** their **dreams** these ungodly *G1965*
Rev 3: 8 I know that you have little s, yet you have *G1539*
Rev 5:12 wisdom and s and honor and glory *G2709*
Rev 7:12 honor and power and s be to our God *G2709*
Rev 14:10 has been poured **full** s into the cup of his *G204*

STRENGTHEN (32) [STRONG]

Dt 3:28 encourage and s him, for he will lead H599
Jdg 16:28 s me just once more, and let me H2616
1Ki 20:22 "S *your* **position** and see what must be H2616
2Ki 15:19 his support and s his own hold on the H2616
2Ch 16: 9 the earth to s those whose hearts are H2616
Ne 6: 9 But I prayed, "Now s my hands." H2616
Job 8:20 who is blameless or s the hands of H2616
Ps 89:21 will sustain him; surely my arm *will* s him. H599
Ps 119:28 with sorrow; s me according to your word. H7756
SS 2: 5 S me with raisins, refresh me with apples H6164
Isa 22:10 tore down houses to s the wall. H1307
Isa 35: 3 S the feeble hands, steady the knees that H2616
Isa 41:10 *I will* s you and help you; I will uphold you H599
Isa 45: 5 *I will* s you, though you have not H273
Isa 54: 2 lengthen your cords, s your stakes. H2616
Isa 58:11 sun-scorched land and *will* s your frame. H2741
Jer 23:14 *They* s the hands of evildoers, so that not H2616
Eze 30:24 *I will* s the arms of the king of Babylon H2616
Eze 30:25 *I will* s the arms of the king of Babylon, H2616
Eze 34:16 I will bind up the injured and s the weak H2616
Na 3:14 water for the siege, s your defenses! Work H2616
Zec 10: 6 "*I will* s Judah and save the tribes of H1504
Zec 10:12 *I will* s them in the LORD and in his name H1504

S

Lk 22:32 you have turned back, s your brothers." G5114
Ac 15:32 much to encourage and s the believers. G2185
Eph 3:16 riches *he may* s you with power G1443+3194
1Th 3: 2 to s and encourage you in your faith G5114
1Th 3:13 *May he* s your hearts so that you will be G5114
2Th 2:17 your hearts and s you in every good deed G5114
2Th 3: 3 he *will* s you and protect you from the G5114
Heb 12:12 s your feeble arms and weak knees. G494
Rev 3: 2 S what remains and is about to die, for I G5114

STRENGTHENED (17) [STRONG]

1Ki 19: 8 S by that food, he traveled forty days and H3946
2Ch 11:11 *He* s their defenses and put commanders H2616
2Ch 11:17 *They* s the kingdom of Judah and H2616
2Ch 17: 1 him as king and s **himself** against Israel. H2616
Job 4: 3 how *you have* s feeble hands. H2616
Job 4: 4 who stumbled; *you have* s faltering knees. H599
Isa 9:11 But the LORD *has* s Rezin's foes against H8435
Eze 34: 4 *You have* not s the weak or healed the sick H2616
Da 10:19 he spoke to me, *I* **was** s and said, "Speak, H2616
Hos 7:15 I trained them and s their arms, but they H2616
Lk 22:43 from heaven appeared to him and s him. G1932
Ac 9:31 enjoyed a time of peace and *was* s. G3868
Ac 16: 5 So the churches *were* s in the faith and G5105
Ro 4:20 but *was* s in his faith and gave glory to G1904
Col 1:11 *being* s with all power according to his G1540
Col 2: 7 s in the faith as you were taught G1011
Heb 13: 9 It is good for our hearts *to be* s by grace G1011

STRENGTHENING (6) [STRONG]

2Sa 3: 6 had been s **his own position** in the house H2616
Ac 14:22 s the disciples and G2185+3836+6034
Ac 15:41 through Syria and Cilicia, s the churches. G2185
Ac 18:23 of Galatia and Phrygia, s all the disciples. G2185
1Co 14: 3 prophesies speaks to people *for* their s, G3869
2Co 12:19 dear friends, is for your s. G3869

STRENGTHENS (1) [STRONG]

Ps 147:13 *He* s the bars of your gates and blesses H2616

STRENUOUSLY (1)

Col 1:29 To this end I s contend with all the energy G3159

STRESS (1)

Titus 3: 8 And I want you *to* s these things, so that G1331

STRETCH (39) [OUTSTRETCHED, STRETCHED, STRETCHES, STRETCHING]

Ex 3:20 So *I will* s **out** my hand and strike the H8938
Ex 7: 5 am the LORD when I s **out** my hand against H5742
Ex 7:19 your staff and s **out** your hand over the H5742
Ex 8: 5 'S **out** your hand with your staff over the H5742
Ex 8:16 'S **out** your staff and strike the dust of the H5742
Ex 9:22 "S **out** your hand toward the sky so that H5742
Ex 10:12 "S **out** your hand over Egypt so that H5742
Ex 10:21 "S **out** your hand toward the sky so that H5742
Ex 14:16 your staff and s **out** your hand over the H5742
Ex 14:26 "S **out** your hand over the sea so that the H5742
Ex 15:12 "*You* s **out** your right hand, and the earth H5742
2Ki 21:13 *I will* s **out** over Jerusalem the measuring H5742
Job 1:11 But now s **out** your hand and strike H8938
Job 2: 5 But now s **out** your hand and strike his H8938
Job 11:13 heart to him and s **out** your hands to him, H7298
Ps 138: 7 *You* s **out** your hand against the anger of H8938
Pr 1:24 one pays attention *when I* s **out** my hand, H5742
Isa 25:11 *They will* s **out** their hands in it, as H7298
Isa 25:11 as swimmers s **out** their hands to swim. H7298
Isa 28:20 The bed is too short *to* s **out** *on*, the H8594
Isa 34:11 God *will* s **out** over Edom the measuring H5742
Isa 54: 2 your tent, s your tent curtains **wide**, do not H5742
Jer 6:12 when *I* s **out** my hand against those who H5742
Jer 31:39 measuring line *will* s *from* there straight H3655
Jer 51:25 "*I will* s **out** my hand against you, roll you H5742
Eze 6:14 And *I will* s **out** my hand against them H5742
Eze 14: 9 and *I will* s **out** my hand against him and H5742
Eze 14:13 unfaithful and *I* s **out** my hand against it H5742
Eze 25: 7 therefore I *will* s **out** my hand against you H5742
Eze 25:13 *I will* s **out** my hand against Edom and kill H5742
Eze 25:16 I *am about to* s **out** my hand against the H5742
Eze 35: 3 and *I will* s **out** my hand against you and H5742
Zep 1: 4 "*I will* s **out** my hand against Judah and H5742
Zep 2:13 *He will* s **out** his hand against the north H5742
Mt 12:13 he said to the man, "S **out** your hand." G1753
Mk 3: 5 said to the man, "S **out** your hand." G1753
Lk 6:10 then said to the man, "S **out** your hand." G1753
Jn 21:18 you are old *you will* s **out** your hands, G1753
Ac 4:30 S **out** your hand to heal and perform signs G1753

STRETCHED (34) [STRETCH]

Ge 10:30 where they lived s from Mesha toward H2118
Ex 8: 6 So Aaron s **out** his hand over the waters H5742
Ex 8:17 when Aaron s **out** his hand with the H5742
Ex 9:15 For by now *I could have* s **out** my hand H8938
Ex 9:23 When Moses s **out** his staff toward the sky H5742
Ex 10:13 So Moses s **out** his staff over Egypt, and H5742
Ex 10:22 So Moses s **out** his hand toward the sky H5742
Ex 14:21 Then Moses s **out** his hand over the sea H5742
Ex 14:27 Moses s **out** his hand over the sea, and at H5742
2Sa 24:16 When the angel s **out** his hand to destroy H8938
1Ki 13: 4 *he* s **out** his hand from the altar and said H8938
1Ki 13: 4 But the hand *he* s **out** toward the man H8938
1Ki 17:21 Then *he* s **himself out** on the boy three H4499
2Ki 4:34 As *he* s *himself* **out** on him, the boy's H1566
2Ki 4:35 on the bed and s **out** on him once more. H1566
Job 38: 5 Who s a measuring line across it H5742
Ps 77: 2 at night I s **out** untiring hands, and H5599
Ps 77:10 when the Most High s out his right hand. NDT
Isa 14:26 this is the hand s **out** over all nations. H5742
Isa 14:27 His hand *is* s **out**, and who can turn it H5742
Isa 23:11 The LORD *has* s **out** his hand over the sea H5742
Isa 45:12 My own hands s **out** the heavens; H5742
Jer 10:12 by his wisdom and s **out** the heavens by H5742
Jer 51:15 by his wisdom and s **out** the heavens by H5742
La 2: 8 *He* s **out** a measuring line and did not H5742
Eze 1:23 their wings were s **out** one toward the H3838
Eze 2: 9 I looked, and I saw a hand s **out** to me. H8938
Eze 8: 3 *He* s **out** what looked like a hand and took H8938
Eze 16:27 So *I* s **out** my hand against you and H5742
Eze 17: 7 it was planted and s **out** its branches to H8938
Zec 1:16 measuring line *will* **be** s **out** over H5742
Mt 12:13 So *he* s it **out** and it was completely G1753
Mk 3: 5 *He* s it **out**, and his hand was completely G1753
Ac 22:25 As *they* s him **out** to flog him, Paul said to G4727

STRETCHES (10) [STRETCH]

Job 9: 8 He alone s **out** the heavens and treads on H5742
Ps 104: 2 garment; *he* s **out** the heavens like a tent H5742
Isa 31: 3 When the LORD s **out** his hand, those who H5742
Isa 33:17 in his beauty and view a land that s **afar**. H5305
Isa 40:22 He s **out** the heavens like a canopy, and H5742
Isa 42: 5 heavens, *who* s them **out**, who spreads H5742
Isa 44:24 of all things, *who* s **out** the heavens, who H5742
Isa 51:13 *who* s **out** the heavens and who lays the H5742
La 1:17 Zion s **out** her hands, but there is no one H7298
Zec 12: 1 The LORD, *who* s **out** the heavens, who H5742

STRETCHING (3) [STRETCH]

Est 1: 1 over 127 provinces s **from** India to Cush: AIT
Est 8: 9 of the 127 provinces *s* **from** India to Cush. AIT
Jer 4:31 breath, s **out** her hands and saying H7298

STREWN (2)

1Sa 17:52 Their dead *were* s along the Shaaraim H5877
2Ki 7:15 the whole road s **with** the clothing and H4849

STRICKEN (3) [STRIKE]

Isa 28:16 who relies on it *will* never *be* s **with panic**. H2591
Isa 53: 4 punished by God, s *by* him, and afflicted. H5782
Zec 14:13 people will be *s* by the LORD *with* **great** panic. AIT

STRICT (5) [STRICTEST, STRICTLY]

1Sa 14:28 **bound** the army **under a** s **oath**, H8678+8678
Mk 3:12 But he gave them s orders not to tell G4498
Mk 5:43 He gave s orders not to let anyone know G4498
Ac 5:28 "*We* **gave** you s **orders** not to teach G4132+4133
1Co 9:25 in the games goes into s training. G4246

STRICTEST (1) [STRICT]

Ac 26: 5 I conformed to the s sect of our religion, G207

STRICTLY (2) [STRICT]

Lk 9:21 Jesus s **warned** them not to tell this G2203+4133
Jas 3: 1 that we who teach will be judged **more** *s*. AIT

STRIDE (1) [STRIDING, STRODE]

Pr 30:29 are three things that are stately in their s, H7576

STRIDING (1) [STRIDE]

Isa 63: 1 s **forward** in the greatness of his strength? H7579

STRIFE (13) [STRIVE]

Ps 55: 9 for I see violence and s in the city. H8190
Pr 13:10 Where there is s, there is pride, but H5175
Pr 17: 1 quiet than a house full of feasting, with s. H8190
Pr 18: 6 The lips of fools bring them s, and their H8190
Pr 20: 3 It is to one's honor to avoid s, but every H8190
Pr 22:10 mocker, and out goes s; quarrels and H4506
Pr 23:29 Who has s? Who has complaints H4506
Pr 26:21 so is a quarrelsome person for kindling s. H8190
Pr 30:33 so stirring up anger produces s. H8190
Isa 58: 4 Your fasting ends in quarreling and s, and H5175
Hab 1: 3 before me; there is s, and conflict H8190
Ro 1:29 full of envy, murder, s, deceit and malice. G2251
1Ti 6: 4 words that result in envy, s, malicious talk, G2251

STRIKE (83) [STRICKEN, STRIKES, STRIKING, STROKE, STRUCK]

Ge 3:15 crush your head, and you *will* s his heel." H8790
Ex 3:20 out my hand and s the Egyptians with all H5782
Ex 5: 3 or *he may* s us with plagues or with the H7003
Ex 7:17 that is in my hand I *will* s the water of the H5782
Ex 8:16 out your staff and s the dust of the ground H5782
Ex 12:12 through Egypt and s **down** every firstborn H5782
Ex 12:13 plague will touch you when I s Egypt. H5782
Ex 12:23 through the land to s **down** the Egyptians, H5597
Ex 12:23 to enter your houses and s you **down**. H5597
Ex 17: 6 S the rock, and water will come out of it H5782
Nu 8:19 that no plague *will* s the Israelites H2118+928
Nu 14:12 *I will* s them **down** with a plague and H5782
Dt 28:22 The LORD *will* s you with wasting disease H5782
Dt 33:11 S **down** those who rise against him, H4730+5516
Jdg 6:16 and *you will* s **down** all the Midianites H5782
1Sa 17:46 and *I'll* s you **down** and cut off your head. H5782
1Sa 22:17 to raise a hand to s the priests of the LORD. H7003
1Sa 22:18 "You turn and s **down** the priests. H7003
1Sa 26: 8 thrust of the spear; *I* won't s him **twice**." H9101
1Sa 26:10 "the LORD *himself will* s him, or his H5597
2Sa 1:15 of his men and said, "Go, s him **down**!" H7003
2Sa 2:22 Why *should I* s you down? How H5782
2Sa 5:24 out in front of you to s the Philistine army." H5782
2Sa 13:28 I say to you, 'S Amnon **down**,' then kill H5782
2Sa 17: 2 *I would* s him **with terror**, and then all the H3006
2Sa 17: 2 *I would* s **down** only the king H5782
2Sa 18:11 Why didn't *you* s him to the ground right H5782
1Ki 2:29 son of Jehoiada, "Go, s him **down**!" H7003
1Ki 2:31 S him **down** and bury him, and so clear H7003
1Ki 14:15 And the LORD *will* s Israel, so that it will be H5782
1Ki 20:35 his companion, "S me with your weapon," H5782
1Ki 20:37 another man and said, "S me, please." H5782
2Ki 6:18 to the LORD, "S this army with blindness." H5782
2Ki 13:18 Elisha told him, "S the ground." He struck H5782
1Ch 14:15 out in front of you to s the Philistine army." H5782
2Ch 21:14 So now the LORD *is about to* s your people H5597
Job 1:11 out your hand and s everything he has, H5595
Job 2: 5 out your hand and s his flesh and bones, H5595
Job 16:10 *they* s my cheek in scorn and unite H5782
Job 36:32 lightning and commands it *to* s its **mark**. H7003
Ps 3: 7 S all my enemies *on* the jaw; break the H5782
Ps 9:20 S them *with* terror, LORD; let the nations H8883
Ps 10:18 earthly mortals *will* never again s **terror**. H6907
Ps 81: 2 Begin the music, s the timbrel, play the H5989
Ps 89:23 before him and s **down** his adversaries. H5597
Ps 91:12 so that *you will* not s your foot against a H5597
Ps 141: 5 *Let* a righteous man s me—that is a H2150
Isa 11: 4 *He will* s the earth with the rod of his H5782
Isa 13:18 Their bows *will* s **down** the young men H8187
Isa 19:22 The LORD *will* s Egypt **with a plague**; he H5597
Isa 19:22 a plague; *he will* s them and heal them. H5597
Isa 30:31 Assyria; with his rod *he will* s them **down**. H5782
Jer 21: 6 *I will* s **down** those who live in this city H5782
La 3:30 offer his cheek to *one who would* s him, H5782
Eze 5: 2 Take a third and s it with the sword all H5782
Eze 6:11 S your hands **together** and stamp your H5782
Eze 21:14 prophesy and s your hands together. H5782
Eze 21:14 *Let* the sword s **twice**, even three H4100
Eze 21:15 It is forged to s **like lightning**, it is grasped H1398
Eze 21:17 I too *will* s my hands together, and my H5782
Eze 22:13 " '*I will* surely s my hands **together** at the H5782
Eze 32:15 when I s **down** all who live there H5782
Eze 39: 3 Then *I will* s your bow from your left hand H5782
Am 9: 1 "S the tops of the pillars so that the H5782
Mic 5: 1 *They will* s Israel's ruler on the cheek with H5782
Zec 11:17 May the sword s his arm and his right eye H6584
Zec 12: 4 On that day *I will* s every horse with panic H5782
Zec 13: 7 "S the shepherd, and the sheep will be H5782
Zec 14:12 with which the LORD *will* s all the nations H5597
Zec 14:15 A similar plague *will* s the horses and H2118
Mal 4: 6 I will come and s the land *with* total H5782
Mt 4: 6 so that *you will* not s your foot against a G4684
Mt 26:31 " '*I will* s the shepherd, and the sheep of G4250
Mk 14:27 " '*I will* s the shepherd, and the sheep G4250
Lk 4:11 so that *you will* not s your foot **against** a G4684
Lk 22:49 "Lord, *should we* s with our swords?" G4250
Jn 18:23 if I spoke the truth, why *did you* s me?" G1296
Ac 23: 2 near Paul *to* s him on the mouth. G5597
Ac 23: 3 "God will s you, you whitewashed G5597
1Co 9:27 *I* s **a blow** to my body and make it my G5724
Rev 2:23 *I will* s her children **dead** G650+1877+2505
Rev 11: 6 into blood and *to* s the earth with every G4250
Rev 19:15 sword with which to s **down** the nations. G4250

STRIKER (KJV) VIOLENT

STRIKES (16) [STRIKE]

Ex 21:12 "*Anyone who* s a person with a fatal blow H5782
Nu 35:16 " 'If *anyone* s someone **a** fatal **blow** with H5782
Nu 35:17 stone and s someone **a** fatal **blow** with it, H5782
Nu 35:18 object and s someone **a** fatal **blow** with it, H5782
Job 4: 5 you are discouraged; *it* s you, and you are H5595
Ps 29: 7 The voice of the LORD s with flashes of H2934
Pr 1:26 I in turn will laugh when **disaster** *s* you; I will AIT
Pr 20: 2 A king's wrath s terror like the roar of a lion NDT
Pr 24:16 the wicked stumble **when** calamity *s*. AIT
Pr 27:10 your relative's house when disaster s you— NDT
Isa 5:25 his hand is raised and *he* s them **down**. H5782
Isa 41: 7 hammer spurs on the *one who* s the anvil. H2150
Jer 11:12 will not help them at all when disaster s. NDT
Eze 7: 9 will know that it is I the LORD *who* s you. H5782
Eze 17:10 completely when the east wind s it— H5595
Rev 9: 5 that of the sting of a scorpion when *it* s. G4091

STRIKING (7) [STRIKE]

1Sa 14:20 s each other with their swords. H2118+928
2Sa 1: 1 returned from s **down** the Amalekites and H5782
2Sa 8:13 he returned from s **down** eighteen H5782
2Sa 24:17 the angel who *was* s **down** the people, H5782
Job 39:20 like a locust, s terror with its proud snorting? NDT
Isa 58: 4 *in* s *each other* with wicked fists. H5782
Da 8: 7 s the ram and shattering its two horns. H5782

STRING (4) [STRINGED, STRINGS, STRUNG, TEN-STRINGED]

Jdg 16: 9 easily as a **piece of** s snaps when it H7348+5861
2Sa 16: 1 He had a s *of* donkeys saddled and H7538
Ps 7:12 his sword; he will bend and s his bow. H3922
Jer 51: 3 *Let* not the archer s his bow, nor let him H2005

STRINGED (10) [STRING]

Ge 4:21 of all who play s **instruments** and pipes. H4036

S

Ps 4: T With **s instruments**. A psalm of H5593
Ps 6: T With **s instruments**. According to H5593
Ps 54: T With **s instruments**. A maskil of H5593
Ps 55: T With **s instruments**. A maskil of H5593
Ps 61: T With **s instruments**. Of David. H5593
Ps 67: T With **s instruments**. A psalm. H5593
Ps 76: T With **s instruments**. A psalm of H5593
Isa 38:20 will sing with **s instruments** all the days of H5593
Hab 3:19 director of music. On my **s instruments**. H5593

STRINGS (4) [STRING]
Ps 11: 2 arrows against the **s** to shoot from the H3857
Ps 45: 8 with ivory the **music** of the **s** makes you H4944
Ps 150: 4 dancing, praise him with the **s** and pipe, H4944
SS 1:10 with earrings, your neck with **s of jewels**. H3016

STRIP (19) [STRIPPED, STRIPS]
1Sa 31: 8 when the Philistines came to **s** the dead H7320
2Sa 2:21 the young men and **s** him of his weapons." H4374
2Sa 23:10 to Eleazar, but only to **s the dead**. H7320
1Ch 10: 8 when the Philistines came to **s** the dead H7320
Job 41:13 Who *can* **s off** its outer coat? Who can H1655
Isa 27:10 they lie down; *they* **s** its branches **bare**. H3983
Isa 32:11 **S off** *your* **fine clothes** and H7320+2256+6910
Isa 45: 1 before him and *to* **s** kings *of* their armor, H7337
Jer 5:10 **S off** her branches, for these people do H6073
Jer 49:10 But I *will* **s** Esau **bare**; I will uncover his H3106
Eze 16:37 all around and *will* **s** you in front of H1655+6872
Eze 16:39 *They will* **s** you *of* your clothes and take H7320
Eze 23:26 *They will* also **s** you *of* your clothes and H7320
Eze 32:15 Egypt desolate and **s** the land of H9037
Da 4:14 **s off** its leaves and scatter its fruit. A10499
Hos 2: 3 Otherwise *I will* **s** her naked and make her H7320
Mic 2: 8 *You* **s** off the rich robe from those who H7320
Mic 3: 3 **s off** their skin and break their bones in H7320
Na 3:16 like locusts *they* **s** the land and then H7320

STRIPE, STRIPES (KJV) BEATINGS, BLOWS, BRUISE, FLOGGED, FLOGGING, FLOGGINGS, LASHES, WOUNDS

STRIPES (1)
Ge 30:37 made white **s** on them by peeling H7203

STRIPPED (33) [STRIP]
Ge 37:23 his brothers, *they* **s** him *of* his robe—the H7320
Ex 9:25 growing in the fields and **s** every tree. H8689
Ex 33: 6 So the Israelites **s off** their ornaments at H5911
Jdg 14:19 **s** them *of* everything and gave their H4374
1Sa 19:24 He **s off** his garments, and he too H7320
1Sa 31: 9 They cut off his head and **s off** his armor H7320
2Ki 18:16 king of Judah **s off** the gold with which H7915
1Ch 10: 9 *They* **s** him and took his head and his H7320
Job 12:17 He leads rulers away **s** and makes fools of H8768
Job 12:19 He leads priests away **s** and overthrows H8768
Job 15:33 will be like a vine **s** *of* its unripe grapes, H2803
Job 19: 9 *He has* **s** me *of* my honor and removed H7320
Job 22: 6 no reason; *you* **s** people *of* their clothing H7320
Isa 1: 7 your fields *are being* **s** *by* foreigners right H430
Isa 20: 2 he did so, going around **s** and barefoot. H6873
Isa 20: 3 Isaiah has gone **s** and barefoot for three H6873
Isa 20: 4 Assyria will lead away **s** and barefoot the H6873
Isa 22: 8 The Lord **s away** the defenses of Judah H1655
Isa 23:13 *they* **s** its fortresses **bare** and turned it into H6910
La 4:21 be passed; you will be drunk and **s naked**. H6867
Eze 12:19 their land *will be* **s** of everything in it H9037
Eze 17: 9 not be uprooted and **s** *of* its fruit so that it H7878
Eze 19:12 made it shrivel, *it* **was s** *of* its fruit; its H7293
Eze 23:10 They **s** her naked, took away her sons and H1655
Da 5:20 from his royal throne and **s** of his glory. A10528
Da 7:12 The other beasts *had been* **s** *of* their A10528
Joel 1: 7 *It has* **s off** their **bark** and thrown it H3106+3106
Am 7: 2 When *they had* **s** the land **clean**, I cried out H430
Na 2:10 She is pillaged, plundered, **s**! Hearts melt, H1191
Hab 3:13 wickedness, *you* **s** him from head to foot. H6867
Mt 27:28 *They* **s** him and put a scarlet robe on him, G1694
Lk 10:30 They **s** him **of** his **clothes**, beat him and G1694
Ac 16:22 them *to be* **s** and beaten G4351+3836+2668

STRIPS (6) [STRIP]
Ps 29: 9 LORD twists the oaks and **s** the forests **bare**. H3106
Lk 24:12 he saw the **s of linen** lying by themselves G3856
Jn 11:44 hands and feet wrapped *with* **s of linen**, G3024
Jn 19:40 wrapped it, with the spices, *in* **s of linen**. G3856
Jn 20: 5 looked in *at* the **s of linen** lying there G3856
Jn 20: 6 He saw the **s of linen** lying there, G3856

STRIVE (4) [STRIFE, STRIVES, STRIVING]
Ac 24:16 So I **s** always to keep my conscience clear G828
2Co 13:11 **S for full restoration**, encourage one G2936
1Th 5:15 always **s to do** what is good for each G1503
1Ti 4:10 That is why we labor and **s**, because we have G76

STRIVES (2) [STRIVE]
Isa 64: 7 calls on your name or **s** to lay hold of you; H6424
Jer 15:10 whom the whole land **s** and contends! H8190

STRIVING (2) [STRIVE]
Ecc 2:22 the toil and **anxious s** with which H8301+4213
Php 1:27 **s together** as one for the faith of the G5254

STRODE (1) [STRIDE]
Hab 3:12 In wrath *you* **s through** the earth and in H7575

STROKE (4) [STRIKE]

STROKE, STROKES (KJV) ASSAULT, ASSAULTS, BEATING, BLOW, BLOWS, BRUISES, SCOURGE
Job 5:20 in battle from the **s** *of* the sword. H3338
Isa 30:32 Every **s** the LORD lays on them with his H5044
Mt 5:18 not the **least s of a pen**, will by any G3037
Lk 16:17 than *for* the **least s of a pen** to drop out G3037

STRONG (159) [STRENGTH, STRENGTHEN, STRENGTHENED, STRENGTHENING, STRENGTHENS, STRONGER, STRONGEST, STRONGLY]
Ge 30:42 went to Laban and the **s** *ones* to Jacob. H8003
Ge 49:24 steady, his **s arms** stayed limber H2432+3338
Ex 10:19 changed the wind to a very **s** west wind, H2617
Ex 14:21 the sea back with a **s** east wind and H6434
Nu 13:18 the people who live there are **s** or weak, H2617
Nu 24:18 will be conquered, but Israel will grow **s**. H2657
Dt 2:10 a people **s** and numerous, and H1524
Dt 2:21 They were a people **s** and numerous, and H1524
Dt 2:36 as Gilead, not one town was too **s** for us. H8435
Dt 3:24 servant your greatness and your **s** hand. H2617
Dt 9: 2 The people are **s** and tall—Anakites! You H1524
Dt 31: 6 *Be* **s** and courageous. Do not be afraid H2616
Dt 31: 7 of all Israel, "*Be* **s** and courageous, for H2616
Dt 31:23 "*Be* **s** and courageous, for you will bring H2616
Jos 1: 6 *Be* **s** and courageous, because you will H2616
Jos 1: 7 "*Be* **s** and very courageous. Be careful to H2616
Jos 1: 9 commanded you? *Be* **s** and courageous H2616
Jos 1:18 Only *be* **s** and courageous!" H2616
Jos 10:25 not be discouraged. *Be* **s** and courageous H2616
Jos 14:11 I am still as **s** today as the day Moses sent H2617
Jos 17:18 fitted with iron and though they are **s**, H2617
Jos 23: 6 "*Be* very **s**; be careful to obey all that is H2616
Jdg 1:28 When Israel *became* **s**, they pressed the H2616
Jdg 3:29 all vigorous and **s**; not one escaped. H2657
Jdg 5:21 the river Kishon. March on, my soul; be **s**! H6437
Jdg 9:51 however, was a **s** tower, to which all the H6437
Jdg 14:14 out of the **s**, something sweet. H6434
Jdg 18:26 seeing that they were too **s** for him H2617
1Sa 4: 9 *Be* **s**, Philistines! Be men, or you will be H2616
2Sa 2: 7 Now then, *be* **s** and brave, for Saul H2616+3338
2Sa 3:39 these sons of Zeruiah are too **s** for me. H7997
2Sa 10:11 "If the Arameans *are* too **s** for me, then H2616
2Sa 10:11 if the Ammonites *are* too **s** for you H2616
2Sa 10:12 *Be* **s**, and let us fight bravely for our H2616
2Sa 13:28 I given you this order? *Be* **s** and brave." H2616
2Sa 22:18 from my foes, *who were* too **s** for me. H599
1Ki 2: 2 he said. "So *be* **s**, act like a man, H2616
1Ki 15: 4 succeed him and by **making** Jerusalem **s**. H6641
1Ki 20:23 That is why *they were* too **s** for us. But if H2616
2Ki 6:14 horses and chariots and a **s** force there. H3878
2Ki 24:16 fighting men, **s** and fit for war, and a H1475
1Ch 11:10 **gave** his kingship **s support** to H2616+6640
1Ch 19:12 "If the Arameans *are* too **s** for me, then H2616
1Ch 19:12 if the Ammonites *are* too **s** for you H2616
1Ch 19:13 *Be* **s**, and let us fight bravely for our H2616
1Ch 22:13 Moses for Israel. *Be* **s** and courageous. H2616
1Ch 28:10 as the sanctuary. *Be* **s** and do the work." H2616
1Ch 28:20 Solomon his son, "*Be* **s** and courageous H2616
2Ch 11:12 in all the cities, and **made** them very **s**. H2616
2Ch 12: 1 was established and he had **become s**, H2621
2Ch 13: 7 not **s** *enough* to resist them. H2616
2Ch 15: 7 But as for you, *be* **s** and do not give up, for H2616
2Ch 32: 7 "*Be* **s** and courageous. Do not be afraid H2616
Ezr 9:12 that *you may be* **s** and eat the good H2616
Job 4:17 Can even a **s man** be more pure than his H1505
Job 10: 5 mortal or your years like those of a **s man**, H1505
Job 15:26 against him with a thick, **s** shield. H1461
Job 39: 4 Their young thrive and **grow s** in the wilds; H2730
Ps 18:17 from my foes, *who were* too **s** for me. H599
Ps 22:12 surround me; **s** bulls *of* Bashan encircle me. H52
Ps 24: 8 The LORD **s** and mighty, the LORD mighty H6450
Ps 27:14 *be* **s** and take heart and wait for the LORD. H2616
Ps 31: 2 of refuge, a **s fortress** to save me. H1074+5181
Ps 31:24 *Be* **s** and take heart, all you who hope in H2616
Ps 35:10 rescue the poor from *those* too **s** for them, H2617
Ps 52: 7 his great wealth and *grew* **s** by destroying H6451
Ps 61: 3 my refuge, a **s** tower against the foe. H6437
Ps 71: 7 a sign to many; you are my **s** refuge. H6437
Ps 73: 4 struggles; their bodies are healthy and **s**. H9447
Ps 79:11 with your **s** arm preserve those H1542
Ps 89:10 with your **s** arm you scattered your H6437
Ps 89:13 your hand *is* **s**, your right hand H6451
Ps 140: 7 Sovereign LORD, my **s** deliverer, you shield H6437
Ps 142: 6 who pursue me, for *they are* too **s** for me. H599
Pr 18:18 disputes and keeps **s** *opponents* apart. H6786
Pr 23:11 their Defender is **s**; he will take up H2617
Pr 31:17 vigorously; her arms *are* **s** for her tasks. H599
Ecc 9:11 is not to the swift or the battle to the **s**, H1475
Ecc 12: 3 tremble, and the **s** men stoop, when the H2657
SS 8: 6 for love is as **s** as death, its jealousy H6434
Isa 8:11 LORD says to me with his **s** hand upon me, H2621
Isa 17: 9 In that day their **s** cities, which they left H5057
Isa 25: 3 Therefore **s** peoples will honor you; cities H6434
Isa 26: 1 We have a **s** city; God makes salvation its H6434
Isa 28: 2 the Lord has one who is powerful and **s**. H579
Isa 35: 4 with fearful hearts, "*Be* **s**, do not fear; H2616
Isa 41: 6 other and say to their companions, "*Be* **s**!" H2616
Isa 53:12 he will divide the spoils with the **s** H6786
Isa 59:10 twilight; among the **s**, we are like the dead H875
Jer 4:12 a wind too **s** for that comes from me. H4849
Jer 9:23 of their wisdom or the **s** boast of their H1475
Jer 23: 9 like a **s man** overcome by wine H1505
Jer 30: 6 do I see every **s man** with his hands on H1505
Jer 46: 6 "The swift cannot flee nor the **s** escape. H1475
Jer 50:34 Yet their Redeemer is **s**; the LORD Almighty H2617
Eze 3:14 with the **s** hand of the LORD on me. H2617
Eze 17: 9 It will not take a **s** arm or many people to H1524
Eze 19: 3 one of her cubs, and he became a **s lion**. H4097
Eze 19: 5 of her cubs and made him a **s lion**. H4097
Eze 19: 6 among the lions, for he was now a **s lion**. H4097
Eze 19:11 Its branches were **s**, fit for a ruler's scepter. H6437
Eze 19:12 its **s** branches withered and fire consumed H6437
Eze 19:14 No **s** branch is left on it fit for a ruler's H6437
Eze 22:14 your hands *be* **s** in the day I deal H2616
Eze 26:11 your **s** pillars will fall to the ground. H6437
Eze 30:21 so that it *may become* **s** *enough* to hold a H2616
Eze 34:16 the sleek and the **s** I will destroy. H2617
Da 2:40 be a fourth kingdom, **s** as iron—for iron A10768
Da 2:42 will be partly **s** and partly brittle. A10768
Da 4:11 grew large and **s** and its top touched A10772
Da 4:20 which grew large and **s**, with its top A10772
Da 4:22 You have become great and **s**; your A10772
Da 8:24 *He will become* **very s**, but not by H6793+3946
Da 10:19 *Be* **s** now; be strong." When he H2616
Da 10:19 Be strong now; *be* **s**." When he spoke to H2616
Da 11: 5 "The king of the South *will become* **s**, but H2616
Joel 3:10 Let the weakling say, "I am **s**!" H1475
Am 2: 9 were tall as the cedars and **s** as the oaks. H2891
Am 2:14 the **s** will not muster their strength H2617
Am 5: 3 marches out a thousand **s** will have only a NDT
Am 5: 3 marches out a hundred **s** will have only ten NDT
Am 8:13 young women and **s young men** will faint H1033
Mic 4: 3 settle disputes for **s** nations far and wide. H6786
Mic 4: 7 remnant, those driven away a **s** nation. H6786
Hag 2: 4 But now *be* **s**, Zerubbabel,' declares the H2616
Hag 2: 4 '*Be* **s**, Joshua son of Jozadak, the high H2616
Hag 2: 4 *Be* **s**, all you people of the land,' declares H2616
Zec 8: 9 '*Let* your hands *be* **s** so that the temple H2616
Zec 8:13 not be afraid, but *let* your hands *be* **s**." H2616
Zec 12: 5 'The people of Jerusalem are **s**, because H602
Mt 12:29 anyone enter a **s** *man's* house and carry G2708
Mt 12:29 unless he first ties up the **s** *man*? G2708
Mk 1:43 sent him away at once *with a* **s warning**: G1839
Mk 3:27 no one can enter a **s** *man's* house without G2708
Mk 3:27 Then he can plunder the **s man's** house. G899S
Mk 5: 4 No one *was* **s** *enough* to subdue him G2710
Lk 1:80 And the child grew and *became* **s** in spirit; G3194
Lk 2:40 And the child grew and *became* **s**; he was G3194
Lk 11:21 "When a **s** *man*, fully armed, guards his G2708
Lk 16: 3 *I'm* not **s** *enough* to dig, and I'm G2710
Jn 6:18 A **s** wind was blowing and the waters grew G3489
Ac 3: 7 the man's feet and ankles *became* **s**. G5105
Ac 3:16 whom you see and know *was* **made s**. G5105
Ro 1:11 to you some spiritual gift to **make** you **s**— G5114
Ro 15: 1 We who are **s** ought to bear with the G1543
1Co 1:27 weak things of the world to shame the **s**. G2708
1Co 4:10 are weak, but you are **s**! You are honored, G2708
1Co 7:36 if his **passions** are **too s** and he feels G5644
1Co 16:13 firm in the faith; be courageous; *be* **s**. G3194
2Co 12:10 For when I am weak, then I am **s**. G1543
2Co 13: 9 glad whenever we are weak but you are **s**; G1543
Eph 6:10 *be* **s** in the Lord and in his mighty power. G1904
1Th 2: 2 you his gospel in the face of **s** opposition. G4498
2Ti 2: 1 *be* **s** in the grace that is in Christ Jesus. G1904
Jas 3: 4 are so large and are driven by **s** winds, G5017
1Pe 5:10 will himself restore you and **make** you **s** G5114
1Jn 2:14 because you are **s**, and the word of God G2708
Rev 6:13 from a fig tree when shaken by a **s** wind. G3489
Rev 12: 8 But *he was* not **s** *enough*, and they lost G2710

STRONGER (28) [STRONG]
Ge 25:23 one people *will be* **s** than the other, and H599
Ge 30:41 Whenever the **s** *females* were in heat H8003
Nu 13:31 those people; they are **s** than we are." H2617
Nu 14:12 you into a nation greater and **s** than they." H6786
Dt 1:28 'The people are **s** and taller than we are H1524
Dt 4:38 nations greater and **s** than you and to H6786
Dt 7: 1 seven nations larger and **s** than you— H6786
Dt 7:17 "These nations are **s** than we are. H8041
Dt 9: 1 nations greater and **s** than you, H6786
Dt 9:14 you into a nation **s** and more numerous H6786
Dt 11:23 dispossess nations larger and **s** than you. H6786
Jos 17:13 when the Israelites *grew* **s**, they subjected H2616
Jdg 14:18 What is **s** than a lion? H6434
2Sa 1:23 than eagles, *they were* **s** than lions. H1504
2Sa 3: 1 David **grew s and stronger** H2143+2256+2618
2Sa 3: 1 David **grew stronger and s** H2143+2256+2618
2Sa 13:14 and since *he was* **s** than she, he H2616
1Ki 16:22 followers **proved s** *than* those of Tibni H2616
1Ki 20:23 the plains, surely *we will be* **s** than they. H2616
1Ki 20:25 Then surely *we will be* **s** than they." H2616
Job 17: 9 *those with* clean hands *will* **grow s**. H601+3578
Ecc 6:10 one can contend with someone who is **s**. H9544
Jer 31:11 them from the hand of *those* **s** than they. H2617
Da 11: 5 commanders *will become even* **s** than he H2616
Lk 11:22 But when *someone* **s** attacks and G2708
1Co 1:25 weakness of God is **s** than human G2708
1Co 10:22 the Lord's jealousy? Are we **s** than he? G2708
2Pe 2:11 although they are **s** and more powerful G2709

STRONGEST (3) [STRONG]
2Sa 11:16 he knew the **s defenders** were. H408+2657

1Ch 5: 2 though Judah *was the* **s** of his H1504
Da 3:20 some of the **s soldiers** in his A10132+10264

STRONGHOLD (33) [STRONGHOLDS]

Jdg 9:46 Shechem went into the **s** *of* the temple of H7663
Jdg 9:49 piled them against the **s** and set it on fire H7663
1Sa 22: 4 with him as long as David was in the **s**. H5181
1Sa 22: 5 Gad said to David, "Do not stay in the **s**. H5181
1Sa 24:22 David and his men went up to the **s**. H5181
2Sa 5:17 heard about it and went down to the **s**. H5181
2Sa 22: 3 He is my **s**, my refuge and my savior H5369
2Sa 23:14 At that time David was in the **s**, and the H5181
1Ch 11:16 At that time David was in the **s**, and the H5181
1Ch 12: 8 to David at his **s** in the wilderness. H5171
1Ch 12:16 from Judah also came to David in his **s**. H5171
Job 39:28 stays there at night; a rocky crag is its **s**. H5181
Ps 8: 2 have established a **s** against your H6437
Ps 9: 9 the oppressed, a **s** in times of trouble. H5369
Ps 18: 2 shield and the horn of my salvation, my **s**. H5369
Ps 27: 1 The LORD is the **s** *of* my life—of whom H5057
Ps 37:39 the LORD; he is their **s** in time of trouble. H5057
Ps 43: 2 You are God my **s**. Why have you rejected H5057
Ps 52: 7 did not make God his **s** but trusted in his H5057
Ps 144: 2 my fortress, my **s** and my deliverer H5369
Pr 12:12 The wicked desire the **s** *of* evildoers, but H5178
Pr 21:22 pull down the **s** in which they trust. H6437
Isa 25: 2 the foreigners' **s** a city no more; it will H810
Isa 31: 9 Their **s** will fall because of terror; at the H6152
Jer 48: 1 the **s** will be disgraced and shattered. H5369
Jer 51:53 to the heavens and fortifies her lofty **s**, H6437
Eze 24:21 sanctuary—the **s** *in which* you take pride H6437
Eze 24:25 on the day I take away their **s**, their joy H5057
Eze 30:15 on Pelusium, the **s** *of* Egypt, and wipe out H5057
Joel 3:16 his people, a **s** for the people of Israel. H5057
Am 5: 9 flash he destroys the **s** and brings the H6434
Mic 4: 8 of the flock, **s** *of* Daughter Zion, the H6755
Zec 9: 3 Tyre has built herself a **s**; she has heaped H5190

STRONGHOLDS (19) [STRONGHOLD]

Jdg 6: 2 in mountain clefts, caves and **s**. H5171
1Sa 23:14 in the wilderness **s** and in the hills of the H5171
1Sa 23:19 hiding among us in the **s** at Horesh, H5171
1Sa 23:29 from there and lived in the **s** of En Gedi. H5171
2Sa 22:46 they come trembling from their **s**. H4995
Ps 18:45 they come trembling from their **s**. H4995
Ps 89:40 all his walls and reduced his **s** to ruins. H4448
Isa 13:22 Hyenas will inhabit her **s**, jackals her H528
Isa 34:13 her citadels, nettles and brambles her **s**. H4448
Jer 48:41 Kerioth will be captured and the **s** taken H5171
Jer 51:30 stopped fighting; they remain in their **s**. H5171
La 2: 2 has torn down the **s** *of* Daughter Judah. H4448
La 2: 5 up all her palaces and destroyed her **s**. H4448
Eze 19: 7 He broke down their **s** and devastated their H528
Eze 33:27 those in **s** and caves will die of a H5171
Am 3:11 pull down your **s** and plunder your H6437
Mic 5:11 of your land and tear down all your **s**. H4448
Zep 3: 6 destroyed nations; their **s** are demolished. H7157
2Co 10: 4 they have divine power to demolish **s**. G4065

STRONGLY (4) [STRONG]

Ge 19: 3 But he insisted *so* **s** that they did go with H4394
Lk 24:29 But *they* **urged** him **s**, "Stay with us, for it G4128
1Co 16:12 I **s** urged him to go to you with the G4498
2Ti 4:15 because he **s** opposed our message. G3336

STRUCK (140) [STRIKE]

Ge 19:11 Then *they* **s** the men who were at the door H5782
Ex 7:20 his officials and **s** the water of the Nile H5782
Ex 7:25 days passed after the LORD **s** the Nile. H5782
Ex 8:17 with the staff and **s** the dust of the ground H5782
Ex 9:15 out my hand and **s** you and your people H5782
Ex 9:25 Throughout Egypt hail **s** everything in the H5782
Ex 12:27 homes when he **s down** the Egyptians. H5597
Ex 12:29 midnight the LORD **s down** all the firstborn H5782
Ex 17: 5 hand the staff with which *you* **s** the Nile, H5782
Ex 21:19 the *one who* **s the blow** will not be held H5782
Ex 22: 2 breaking in at night and **is s** a fatal blow, H5782
Ex 32:35 LORD **s** the people **with a plague** because H5597
Nu 3:13 When I **s down** all the firstborn in Egypt, H5782
Nu 8:17 When I **s down** all the firstborn in Egypt, H5782
Nu 11:33 he **s** them *with* a severe plague. H5782
Nu 14:37 the land *were* **s down and died** of a H4637
Nu 20:11 raised his arm and **s** the rock twice with H5782
Nu 21:35 So *they* **s** him **down**, together with his H5782
Nu 24:10 *He* **s** his hands **together** and said to him H6215
Nu 31:16 so that a plague **s** the LORD's people. H2118+928
Nu 33: 4 whom the LORD *had* **s down** among them H5782
Dt 2:33 him over to us and *we* **s** him **down**, H5782
Dt 3: 3 *We* **s** them **down**, leaving no H5782
Jos 7: 5 quarries and **s** them **down** on the slopes. H5782
Jdg 1: 4 and *they* **s down** ten thousand men at H5782
Jdg 3:29 At that time *they* **s down** about ten H5782
Jdg 3:31 *who* **s down** six hundred Philistines with H5782
Jdg 5:26 *She* **s** Sisera, she crushed his head, she H2150
Jdg 7:13 *It* **s** the tent with such force that the tent H5782
Jdg 9:44 those in the fields and **s** them **down**. H5782
Jdg 12: 4 The Gileadites **s** them **down** because the H5782
Jdg 14:19 to Ashkelon, **s down** thirty of their men H5782
Jdg 15:15 grabbed it and **s down** a thousand men. H5782
Jdg 20:35 the Israelites **s down** 25,100 Benjamites H8845
Jdg 20:45 far as Gidom and **s down** two thousand H5782
1Sa 4: 8 are the gods who **s** the Egyptians with H5782
1Sa 6: 4 the same plague has **s** both you and your H4200
1Sa 6: 9 was not his hand that **s** us but that it H5595
1Sa 6:19 But God **s down** some of the inhabitants H5782
1Sa 14:15 Then panic **s** the whole army—those H2118+928
1Sa 14:31 the Israelites *had* **s down** the Philistines H5782
1Sa 17:35 **s** it and rescued the sheep from its mouth. H5782
1Sa 17:35 I seized it by its hair, **s** it and killed it. H5782
1Sa 17:49 he slung it and **s** the Philistine on the H5782
1Sa 17:50 in his hand *he* **s down** the Philistine H5782
1Sa 19: 8 *He* **s** them *with* such force that they fled H5782
1Sa 22:18 the Edomite turned and **s** them **down**. H7003
1Sa 25:38 days later, the LORD **s** Nabal and he died. H5597
2Sa 1:15 So *he* **s** him **down**, and he died H5782
2Sa 5:25 and *he* **s down** the Philistines all the way H5782
2Sa 6: 7 therefore God **s** him **down**, and he died H5782
2Sa 8: 5 David **s down** twenty-two thousand of H5782
2Sa 10:18 *He* also **s down** Shobak the commander H5782
2Sa 11:15 from him so *he will* **be s down** and die." H5782
2Sa 12: 9 *You* **s down** Uriah the Hittite with the H5782
2Sa 12:15 the LORD **s** the child that Uriah's wife had H5597
2Sa 13:30 "Absalom *has* **s down** all the king's sons H5782
2Sa 14: 6 One **s** the other and killed him H5782
2Sa 14: 7 over the *one who* **s** his brother **down**, H5782
2Sa 18:15 Absalom, **s** him and killed him. H5782
2Sa 21:12 them after they **s** Saul **down** on Gilboa.) H5782
2Sa 21:17 *he* **s** the Philistine **down** and killed him. H5782
2Sa 23:10 his ground and **s down** the Philistines H5782
2Sa 23:12 defended it and **s** the Philistines **down**, H5782
2Sa 23:20 He **s down** Moab's two mightiest warriors H5782
2Sa 23:21 And he **s down** a huge Egyptian. Although H5782
1Ki 2:25 and *he* **s down** Adonijah and he died. H7003
1Ki 2:34 went up and **s down** Joab and killed him H7003
1Ki 2:46 went out and **s** Shimei **down** and he died. H7003
1Ki 11:15 *had* **s down** all the men in Edom. H5782
1Ki 15:27 and he **s** him **down** at Gibbethon, H5782
1Ki 16:10 **s** him **down** and killed him in the H5782
1Ki 20:20 each one **s down** his opponent. H5782
1Ki 20:37 So the man **s** him and wounded H5782+5782
2Ki 2: 8 rolled it up and **s** the water with it. H5782
2Ki 2:14 fallen from Elijah and **s** the water *with* it. H5782
2Ki 2:14 When *he* **s** the water, it divided to the H5782
2Ki 6:18 So *he* **s** them with blindness, as Elisha H5782
2Ki 13:18 *He* **s** it three times and stopped H5782
2Ki 13:19 "You *should have* **s** the ground five or six H5782
1Ch 11:14 defended it and **s** the Philistines **down**, H5782
1Ch 11:22 He **s down** Moab's two mightiest warriors H5782
1Ch 11:23 And he **s down** an Egyptian who was five H5782
1Ch 13:10 and *he* **s** him **down** because he had put H5782
1Ch 14:16 and *they* **s down** the Philistine army H5782
1Ch 18: 5 David **s down** twenty-two thousand of H5782
1Ch 18:12 son of Zeruiah **s down** eighteen thousand H5782
2Ch 13:20 And the LORD **s** him **down** and he died. H5597
2Ch 14:12 The LORD **s down** the Cushites before Asa H5597
2Ch 25:16 Why *be* **s down**?" So the prophet H5782
Est 9: 5 **s down** all their enemies *with* the H5782+4804
Job 1:19 from the desert and **s** the four corners of H5595
Job 19:21 have pity, for the hand of God *has* **s** me. H5595
Ps 60: T returned and **s down** twelve thousand H5782
Ps 64: 7 his arrows; they will suddenly be **s down**. H4804
Ps 78:20 *he* **s** the rock, and water gushed out H5782
Ps 78:51 *He* **s down** all the firstborn of Egypt, the H5782
Ps 105:33 *he* **s down** their vines and fig trees and H5782
Ps 105:36 Then *he* **s down** all the firstborn in their H5782
Ps 135: 8 He **s down** the firstborn of Egypt, the H5782
Ps 135:10 He **s down** many nations and killed H5782
Ps 136:10 to *him who* **s down** the firstborn of Egypt H5782
Ps 136:17 to *him who* **s down** great kings, His love H5782
Isa 9:13 have not returned to him *who* **s** them, H5782
Isa 10:20 rely on *him who* **s** them **down** but will H5782
Isa 10:26 as when he **s down** Midian at the rock of H4804
Isa 14: 6 *which* in anger **s down** peoples *with* H5782
Isa 14:29 that the rod *that* **s** you is broken; from the H5782
Isa 27: 7 *Has* the LORD **s** her as he struck down H5782
Isa 27: 7 struck her as he **s down** those who struck H4804
Isa 27: 7 her as he struck down *those who* **s** her? H5782
Isa 60:10 Though in anger *I* **s** you, in favor I will H5782
Jer 5: 3 *You* **s** them, but they felt no pain; you H5782
Jer 26:23 *who* **had** him **s down** with a sword and his H5782
Jer 30:14 *I have* **s** you as an enemy would and H5782
Jer 41: 2 him got up and **s down** Gedaliah son of H5782
Da 2:34 *It* **s** the statue on its feet of iron and clay A10411
Da 2:35 But the rock that **s** the statue became a A10411
Am 4: 9 "Many times *I* **s** your gardens and H5782
Hag 2:17 *I* **s** all the work of your hands with blight H5782
Zec 13: 8 "two-thirds *will* **be s down** and perish; yet H4162
Mt 26:51 drew it out and **s** the servant of the high G4250
Mt 26:67 spit in his face and **s** him **with** *their* **fists**. G3139
Mt 27:30 and **s** him on the head *again and again*. G5597
Mk 12: 4 *they* **s** this man **on the head** and treated G3052
Mk 14:47 drew his sword and **s** the servant of the G4091
Mk 14:65 **s** him **with** *their* **fists**, and said, G3139
Mk 15:19 *Again and again they* **s** him on the head G5597
Lk 6:48 the torrent **s** that house but could not G4703
Lk 6:49 The moment the torrent **s** that house, it G4703
Lk 22:50 And one of them **s** the servant of the high G4250
Jn 18:10 drew it and **s** the high priest's servant G4091
Ac 7:11 "Then a famine **s** all Egypt and G2262+2093
Ac 12: 7 *He* **s** Peter on the side and woke him up G4250
Ac 12:23 an angel of the Lord **s** him **down**, and he G4250
Ac 23: 3 the law by commanding *that* I **be s**!" G5597
Ac 27:41 But the ship **s** a sandbar and ran aground G4346
2Co 4: 9 not abandoned; **s down**, but not G2850
Rev 8:12 a third of the sun *was* **s**, a third of the G4448
Rev 11:11 and terror **s** those who saw them. G2158

STRUCTURE (5) [STRUCTURES]

1Ki 6: 5 he built a **s** around the building, H3666
1Ch 29: 1 because this **palatial s** is not for man but H1072
1Ch 29:19 to build the **palatial s** for which I have H1072
Eze 1:16 was the appearance and **s** *of* the wheels: H5126
Eze 41: 7 The *s* **surrounding** the temple was built in AIT

STRUCTURES (1) [STRUCTURE]

1Ki 7: 9 All **these** *s*, from the outside to the great AIT

STRUGGLE (8) [STRUGGLED, STRUGGLES]

Ge 30: 8 "*I have* **had** a great **s** with my sister, H7349+5887
Jdg 12: 2 engaged in a great **s** with the Ammonites H8190
Job 9:29 found guilty, why *should I* **s** in vain? H3333
Job 41: 8 will remember the **s** and never do it again H4878
Ro 15:30 *to* **join** me **in** my **s** by praying to God for G5253
Eph 6:12 For our **s** is not against flesh and blood G4097
Php 1:30 are going through the same **s** you saw I had, G74
Heb 12: 4 *In your* **s against** sin, you have not yet G497

STRUGGLED (3) [STRUGGLE]

Ge 32:28 because *you have* **s** with God and with H8575
Hos 12: 3 brother's heel; as a man *he* **s** with God. H8575
Hos 12: 4 *He* **s** with the angel and overcame him H8575

STRUGGLES (1) [STRUGGLE]

Ps 73: 4 They have no **s**; their bodies are healthy H3078

STRUM (1)

Am 6: 5 *You* **s away** on your harps like David and H7260

STRUNG (2) [STRING]

Isa 5:28 all their bows *are* **s**; their horses' H2005
La 2: 4 Like an enemy *he has* **s** his bow; his right H2005

STRUT (1) [STRUTTING]

Ps 12: 8 who **freely s** about when what is vile is H2143

STRUTTING (2) [STRUT]

Pr 30:31 a **s rooster**, a he-goat, and a king H2435+5516
Isa 3:16 **s along with swaying hips** H2143+2256+3262

STUBBLE (7)

Ex 5:12 all over Egypt to gather **s** to use for straw. H7990
Ex 15: 7 burning anger; it consumed them like **s**. H7990
Isa 47:14 Surely they are like **s**; the fire will burn H7990
Joel 2: 5 like a crackling fire consuming **s**, like a H7990
Ob 18 a flame; Esau will be **s**, and they will set H7990
Na 1:10 they will be consumed like dry **s**. H7990
Mal 4: 1 the arrogant and every evildoer will be **s**, H7990

STUBBORN (15) [STUBBORN-HEARTED, STUBBORNLY, STUBBORNNESS]

Lev 26:19 break down your **s** pride and make the H6437
Dt 2:30 your God *had* **made** his spirit **s** and his H7996
Dt 21:18 If someone has a **s** and rebellious son H6253
Dt 21:20 "This son of ours *is* **s** and rebellious. H6253
Jdg 2:19 to give up their evil practices and **s** ways. H7997
Ps 78: 8 ancestors—a **s** and rebellious generation H6253
Ps 81:12 them over to their **s** hearts to follow their H9244
Isa 48: 4 For I knew how **s** you were; your neck H7997
Jer 5:23 these people have **s** and rebellious hearts H6253
Jer 7:24 they followed the **s** inclinations of their H9244
Eze 2: 4 sending you are obstinate and **s**. H2617+4213
Hos 4:16 The Israelites *are* **s**, like a stubborn heifer H6253
Hos 4:16 stubborn, like a **s** heifer. How then can H6253
Mk 3: 5 deeply distressed at their **s** hearts, said to G4801
Mk 16:14 lack of faith and their **s** refusal to believe G5016

STUBBORN-HEARTED (1) [HEART, STUBBORN]

Isa 46:12 Listen to me, you **s**, you who are now H52+4213

STUBBORNLY (3) [STUBBORN]

Ex 13:15 When Pharaoh **s refused** to let us go, the H7996
Ne 9:29 **S** they turned their backs on you, became H6253
Zec 7:11 **s** they turned their backs and covered their H6253

STUBBORNNESS (9) [STUBBORN]

Dt 9:27 Overlook the **s** *of* this people, their H8001
Jer 3:17 will they follow the **s** *of* their evil hearts. H9244
Jer 9:14 they have followed the **s** *of* their hearts H9244
Jer 11: 8 they followed the **s** *of* their evil hearts, H9244
Jer 13:10 who follow the **s** *of* their hearts and go H9244
Jer 16:12 you are following the **s** *of* your evil hearts H9244
Jer 18:12 we will all follow the **s** *of* our evil hearts. H9244
Jer 23:17 to all who follow the **s** *of* their hearts they H9244
Ro 2: 5 But because of your **s** and your G5018

STUBS (1)

Isa 7: 4 of these two smoldering **s** *of* firewood— H2387

STUCK (3) [STICK]

1Sa 26: 7 camp with his spear **s** in the ground near H5080
Job 29:10 their tongues **s** to the roof of their H1815
Ac 27:41 The bow **s fast** and would not move, and G2242

STUDDED (1)

SS 1:11 make you earrings of gold, **s** with silver. H5925

STUDENT (3) [STUDY]

1Ch 25: 8 teacher as well as **s**, cast lots for their H9441
Mt 10:24 "The **s** is not above the teacher, nor a G3412

Lk 6:40 The **s** is not above the teacher, but *G3412*

STUDENTS (1) [STUDY]
Mt 10:25 It is enough for **s** to be like their teachers *G3412*

STUDIED (1) [STUDY]
Ac 22: 3 I **s** under Gamaliel and was thoroughly NDT

STUDY (4) [STUDENT, STUDENTS, STUDIED]

STUDY (KJV) AMBITION, DO BEST
Ezr 7:10 himself to the **s** and observance of the H2011
Ecc 1:13 I applied my mind to **s** and to explore by H2011
Ecc 12:12 is no end, and much **s** wearies the body. H4261
Jn 5:39 *You* **s** the Scriptures **diligently** because you *G2236*

STUFF (KJV) BELONGINGS, GOODS, POSSESSIONS, SUPPLIES, THINGS

STUMBLE (63) [STUMBLED, STUMBLES, STUMBLING]
Lev 26:37 *They will* **s** over one another as though H4173
Ps 9: 3 turn back; *they* **s** and perish before you. H4173
Ps 27: 2 enemies and my foes who *will* **s** and fall. H4173
Ps 37:24 though *he may* **s**, he will not fall, for the H5877
Ps 119:165 your law, and nothing can **make** them **s**. H4842
Pr 3:23 way in safety, and your foot *will* not **s**. H5597
Pr 4:12 hampered; when you run, *you will* not **s**. H4173
Pr 4:16 robbed of sleep till *they* **make** someone **s**. H4173
Pr 4:19 they do not know what *makes them* **s**. H4173
Pr 24:16 the wicked **s** when calamity strikes. H4173
Pr 24:17 when they **s**, do not let your heart H4173
Isa 8:14 a stone that **causes** people **to s** and a rock H5598
Isa 8:15 Many of them *will* **s**; they will fall and be H4173
Isa 28: 7 *they* **s** when rendering decisions. H7048
Isa 31: 3 those who help *will* **s**, those who are H4173
Isa 40:30 weary, and young men **s and fall**; H4173+4173
Isa 59:10 At midday *we* **s** as if it were twilight H4173
Isa 63:13 a horse in open country, *they did* not **s**; H4173
Jer 6:21 children alike *will* **s** over them; H4173
Jer 12: 5 If you **s** in safe country, how will you H1054
Jer 13:16 before your feet **s** on the darkening hills. H5597
Jer 18:15 *which* **made** them **s** in their ways H4173
Jer 20:11 so my persecutors *will* **s** and not prevail. H4173
Jer 31: 9 on a level path where *they will* not **s**, H4173
Jer 46: 6 by the River Euphrates *they* **s** and fall. H4173
Jer 46:12 One warrior *will* **s** over another; both will H4173
Jer 46:16 They will **s** repeatedly; they will fall over H4173
Jer 50:32 The arrogant one *will* **s** and fall and no H4173
Eze 7:19 it has caused them to **s** *into* sin. H4842
Da 11:19 of his own country but *will* **s** and fall, H4173
Da 11:35 Some of the wise *will* **s**, so that they may H4173
Hos 4: 5 *You* **s** day and night, and the prophets H4173
Hos 4: 5 night, and the prophets **s** with you. H4173
Hos 5: 5 even Ephraim, **s** in their sin; Judah also H4173
Hos 14: 9 in them, but the rebellious **s** in them. H4173
Na 2: 5 her picked troops, yet *they* **s** on their way. H4173
Zep 1: 3 the **idols that cause** the wicked **to s**." H4843
Mal 2: 8 by your teaching *have* **caused** many to **s**; H4173
Mt 5:29 If your right eye **causes** you **to s**, gouge it *G4997*
Mt 5:30 And if your right hand **causes** you **to s**, cut *G4997*
Mt 11: 6 is anyone *who does* not **s** on account of *G4997*
Mt 18: 6 *If* anyone **causes** one of these little ones— those who believe in me—**to s** *G4997*
Mt 18: 7 of the **things that cause** people **to s**! *G4998*
Mt 18: 8 If your hand or your foot **causes** you **to s** *G4997*
Mt 18: 9 And if your eye **causes** you **to s**, gouge it *G4997*
Mk 9:42 **causes** one of these little ones— those who believe in me—**to s** *G4997*
Mk 9:43 If your hand **causes** you **to s**, cut it off. *G4997*
Mk 9:45 And if your foot **causes** you **to s**, cut it off *G4997*
Mk 9:47 And if your eye **causes** you **to s**, pluck it *G4997*
Lk 7:23 is anyone *who does* not **s** on account of *G4997*
Lk 17: 1 "**Things that cause people to s** are bound *G4998*
Lk 17: 2 than to **cause** one of these little ones **to s**. *G4997*
Jn 11: 9 who walks in the daytime *will* not **s**, *G4684*
Jn 11:10 when a person walks at night that *they* **s**, *G4684*
Ro 9:33 a stone that **causes** people **to s** and a rock *G4682*
Ro 11:11 *Did they* **s** so as to fall beyond recovery *G4760*
Ro 14:20 anything that causes someone else to **s**. *G4682*
1Co 10:32 Do **not cause** anyone **to s**, whether Jews *G718*
Jas 3: 2 *We* all **s** in many ways. Anyone who is *G4760*
1Pe 2: 8 stone that **causes** people **to s** and a rock *G4682*
1Pe 2: 8 They **s** because they disobey the message *G4684*
2Pe 1:10 For if you do these things, *you will* never **s**, *G4760*
1Jn 2:10 there is nothing in them *to* **make** them **s**. *G4998*

STUMBLED (9) [STUMBLE]
1Sa 2: 4 but *those who* **s** are armed with strength. H4173
2Sa 6: 6 of the ark of God, because the oxen **s**. H9023
1Ch 13: 9 to steady the ark, because the oxen **s**. H9023
Job 4: 4 Your words have supported *those who* **s** H4173
Ps 17: 5 held to your paths; my feet *have* not **s**. H4572
Ps 35:15 But when I **s**, they gathered in glee H7520
Ps 107:12 to bitter labor; *they* **s**, and there was no H4173
Isa 59:14 at a distance; truth *has* **s** in the streets H4173
Ro 9:32 *They* **s over** the stumbling stone. *G4684*

STUMBLES (3) [STUMBLE]
Isa 5:27 Not one of them grows tired or **s**, not one H4173
Hos 5: 5 in their sin; Judah also **s** with them. H4173
Jas 2:10 whole law and yet **s** at just one point is *G4760*

STUMBLING (16) [STUMBLE]
Lev 19:14 the deaf or put a **s block** in front of the H4842
Ps 56:13 me from death and my feet from **s**, H1892
Ps 116: 8 my eyes from tears, my feet from **s**, H1892
Eze 3:20 and I put a **s block** before them, they H4842
Eze 14: 3 put wicked **s blocks** before their faces. H4842
Eze 14: 4 put a wicked **s block** before their H4842
Eze 14: 7 put a wicked **s block** before their H4842
Na 3: 3 number, *people* **s** over the corpses H4173
Mt 16:23 You are a **s block** to me; you do not have *G4998*
Ro 9:32 They stumbled over the **s** stone. *G4682*
Ro 11: 9 a **s block** and a retribution for them. *G4998*
Ro 14:13 not to put any **s block** or obstacle in the *G4682*
1Co 1:23 a **s block** to Jews and foolishness to *G4998*
1Co 8: 9 does not become a **s block** to the weak. *G4682*
2Co 6: 3 We put no **s block** in anyone's path, so *G4683*
Jude 24 able to keep you **from s** and to present you *G720*

STUMBLINGBLOCK, STUMBLINGBLOCKS (KJV) OBSTACLES, STUMBLING BLOCK, STUMBLING BLOCKS

STUMP (6) [STUMPS]
Job 14: 8 old in the ground and its **s** die in the soil, H1614
Isa 6:13 so the holy seed will be the **s** *in* the land." H5169
Isa 11: 1 A shoot will come up from the **s** *of* Jesse H1614
Da 4:15 But let the **s** and its roots, bound with A10567
Da 4:23 but leave the **s**, bound with iron and A10567
Da 4:26 to leave the **s** of the tree with its A10567

STUMPS (1) [STUMP]
Isa 6:13 oak leave **s** when they are cut down, H5169

STUNNED (2)
Ge 45:26 Jacob *was* **s**; he did not believe H7028+4213
Isa 29: 9 *Be* **s** and amazed, blind yourselves and H9449

STUNTED (1)
Lev 22:23 an ox or a sheep that is deformed or **s**, H7832

STUPID (4) [STUPIDITY]
Job 18: 3 as cattle and **considered s** in your sight? H3241
Pr 12: 1 whoever hates correction is **s**. H1280
Ecc 10: 3 sense and show everyone *how* **s** they are. H6119
2Ti 2:23 to do with foolish and **s** arguments, *G553*

STUPIDITY (1) [STUPID]
Ecc 7:25 to understand the **s** of wickedness and the H4073

STUPOR (2)
Ps 78:65 as a warrior **wakes from** *the* **s** of wine. H8130
Ro 11: 8 "God gave them a spirit *of* **s**, eyes that *G2919*

STURDIEST (1) [STURDY]
Ps 78:31 he put to death the **s** among them H5458

STURDY (1) [STURDIEST]
Isa 10:16 a wasting disease upon his **s** *warriors*; H5458

SUAH (1)
1Ch 7:36 The sons of Zophah: S, Harnepher, Shual H6053

SUBDIVISION (1) [DIVIDE]
2Ch 35: 5 of Levites for *each* **s** *of* the families of H7107

SUBDIVISIONS (1) [DIVIDE]
2Ch 35:12 to give them to the **s** of the families of the H5141

SUBDUE (11) [SUBDUED, SUBDUES, SUBDUING]
Ge 1:28 increase in number; fill the earth and **s** it. H3899
Nu 24:24 of Cyprus; *they will* **s** Ashur and Eber H6700
Dt 9: 3 destroy them; he *will* **s** them before you. H4044
Jdg 16: 5 him so we may tie him up and **s** him. H6700
Jdg 16:19 braids of his hair, and so began to **s** him. H6700
1Ch 17:10 *I will* also **s** all your enemies H4044
Ps 81:14 how quickly *I would* **s** their enemies and H4044
Isa 11:14 They *will* **s** Edom and Moab, and H5447+3338
Isa 45: 1 I take hold of to **s** nations before him and H8096
Da 7:24 the earlier ones; *he will* **s** three kings. A10737
Mk 5: 4 No one was strong enough *to* **s** him. *G1238*

SUBDUED (19) [SUBDUE]
Nu 32: 4 the land the LORD **s** before the people of H5782
Nu 32:22 then when the land is **s** before the LORD H3899
Nu 32:29 then when the land **is s** before you, you H3899
Jos 10:40 So Joshua **s** the whole region, including H5782
Jos 10:41 Joshua **s** them from Kadesh Barnea to H5782
Jdg 4:23 On that day God **s** Jabin king of Canaan H4044
Jdg 8:28 Thus Midian **was s** before the Israelites H4044
Jdg 11:33 as Abel Keramim. Thus Israel **s** Ammon. H4044
Jdg 16: 6 how you can be tied up and **s**. H6700
1Sa 7:13 the Philistines **were s** and they stopped H4044
2Sa 8: 1 defeated the Philistines and **s** them, H4044
2Sa 8:11 gold from all the nations *he had* **s**: H3899
1Ch 18: 1 defeated the Philistines and **s** them, H4044
2Ch 13:18 The Israelites **were s** on that occasion, and H4044
Ne 9:24 *You* **s** before them the Canaanites, who H4044
Ps 47: 3 *He* **s** nations under us, peoples under our H1818
Isa 10:13 treasures; like a mighty one *I* **s** their kings. H3718
Isa 14: 6 in fury **s** nations with relentless H8097
Zec 10:11 the surging sea *will be* **s** and all the H5782

SUBDUES (3) [SUBDUE]
Ps 18:47 avenges me, *who* **s** nations under me H1818
Ps 144: 2 I take refuge, who **s** peoples under me. H8096
Isa 41: 2 over to him and **s** kings before him. H8097

SUBDUING (1) [SUBDUE]
Job 41: 9 Any hope of **s** it is false; the mere sight of it NDT

SUBJECT (43) [SUBJECTED, SUBJECTING, SUBJECTS]
Ge 14: 4 *For* twelve years *they had been* **s to** H6268
Dt 20:11 people in it shall be **s to** forced labor and H4200
Jdg 1:30 Zebulun *did* **s** *them* to forced labor. H2118S
Jdg 3: 8 **to** whom the Israelites *were* **s** for eight H6268
Jdg 3:14 The Israelites *were* **s to** Eglon king of H6268
Jdg 3:30 Moab *was* **made s to** Israel, H4044+9393+3338
Jdg 9:28 why *should we* Shechemites *be* **s to** him? H6268
Jdg 9:38 is Abimelek that *we should be* **s to** him? H6268
1Sa 4: 9 Be men, or *you will be* **s** to the Hebrews H6268
1Sa 11: 1 a treaty with us, and *we will be* **s to** you." H6268
2Sa 8: 2 the Moabites became **s** to David and H6269
2Sa 8: 6 Arameans became **s** to him and brought H6269
2Sa 8:14 all the Edomites became **s** to David. H6269
2Sa 10:19 with the Israelites and *became* **s** *to* them. H6268
1Ch 18: 2 they became **s** to him and brought H6269
1Ch 18: 6 Arameans became **s** to him and brought H6269
1Ch 18:13 all the Edomites became **s** to David. H6269
1Ch 19:19 peace with David and *became* **s** *to* him. H6268
1Ch 22:18 the land **is s** to the LORD and to his H3899
2Ch 12: 8 however, become **s** to him, so that they H6269
Ne 5: 5 we *have to* **s** our sons and daughters H3899
Isa 11:14 the Ammonites will be **s to** them. H5463
Jer 27: 6 will make even the wild animals **s to** him. H6268
Mt 5:21 who murders will be **s** to judgment. *G1944*
Mt 5:22 a brother or sister will be **s** to judgment. *G1944*
Mt 9:20 a woman *who had been* **s to bleeding** *G137*
Mk 5:25 there *who had been* **s to** bleeding *G1639+1877*
Lk 8:43 had been **s to bleeding** for *G1877+4868+135*
Ac 13:34 dead *so that* he *will* never *be* **s to** *G5715+1650*
Ac 17:32 "We want to hear you again on **this** *s*." AIT
Ro 7:24 rescue me from this body that is *s to* **death**? AIT
Ro 8:10 your body is **s to death** because of sin, *G3738*
Ro 13: 1 *Let* everyone *be* **s** to the governing *G5718*
1Co 2:15 *is* not **s to** *merely human* **judgments**, *G373*
1Co 14:32 of prophets *are* **s** to *the* **control** of *G5718*
1Co 15:28 Son himself *will be* **made s** to him who *G5718*
Gal 4: 2 The heir is **s to** guardians and trustees *G5679*
Titus 2: 5 to be kind, and *to be* **s** to their husbands *G5718*
Titus 2: 9 Teach slaves *to be* **s** to their masters in *G5718*
Titus 3: 1 Remind the people *to be* **s** to rulers and *G5718*
Heb 2: 8 God left nothing that is **not s** to them. *G538*
Heb 2: 8 we do not see everything **s** to them. *G5718*
Heb 5: 2 since *he* himself *is* **s** to weakness. *G4329*

SUBJECTED (8) [SUBJECT]
Jos 17:13 *they* **s** the Canaanites to forced labor but H5989
Ezr 9: 7 our priests *have* **been s** to the sword H5989
Ps 106:42 them and **s** *them* to their power. H4044
Ps 107:12 So *he* **s** them to bitter labor; they H4044
Mt 11:12 of heaven *has been* **s to violence**, *G1041*
Ro 8:20 For the creation *was* **s** to frustration, not by *G5718*
Ro 8:20 by the will of the *one who* **s** it, in *G5718*
Heb 2: 5 is not to angels *that he has* **s** the world to *G5718*

SUBJECTING (2) [SUBJECT]
Dt 26: 6 made us suffer, **s** us *to* harsh labor. H5989
Heb 6: 6 over again and **s** him **to public disgrace**. *G4136*

SUBJECTS (7) [SUBJECT]
1Sa 17: 9 we will become your **s**; but if I overcome H6269
1Sa 17: 9 you will become our **s** and serve us." H6269
1Ki 4:21 tribute and *were* Solomon's **s** all his life. H6268
1Ch 21: 3 lord the king, are they not all my lord's **s**? H6269
Pr 14:28 but without **s** a prince is ruined. H4211
Mt 8:12 But the **s** of the kingdom will be thrown *G5626*
Lk 19:14 "But his **s** hated him and sent a *G4489*

SUBJUGATE (1) [SUBJUGATED]
Jer 27: 7 many nations and great kings *will* **s** him. H6268

SUBJUGATED (1) [SUBJUGATE]
1Ch 20: 4 the Rephaites, and the Philistines **were s**. H4044

SUBMISSION (6) [SUBMIT]
1Ch 29:24 pledged their **s** *to* King Solomon. H9393
Da 11:43 with the Libyans and Cushites in **s**. H5202
1Co 14:34 to speak, but *must be* **in s**, as the law says *G5718*
1Ti 2:11 should learn in quietness and full **s**. *G5717*
Heb 5: 7 he was heard because of his **reverent s**. *G2325*
1Pe 3:22 authorities and powers **in s** to him. *G5718*

SUBMISSIVE (1) [SUBMIT]
Jas 3:17 considerate, **s**, full of mercy and good fruit *G2340*

SUBMIT (26) [SUBMISSION, SUBMISSIVE, SUBMITS, SUBMITTED]
Ge 16: 9 "Go back to your mistress and **s** to her." H6700
Ge 41:40 all my people are *to* **s** to your orders. H5976
Ge 49:15 to the burden and **s** to forced labor. H6268
2Ch 30: 8 your ancestors were; **s** to the LORD. H5989+3338
Job 22:21 "**S** to God and be at peace with him; in H6122
Ps 68:31 Cush *will* **s** herself to God. H8132+3338
Ps 81:11 not listen to me; Israel *would* not **s** to me. H14
Pr 3: 6 in all your ways **s** *to* him, and he will H3359
Lk 10:17 even the demons **s** to us in your name." *G5718*
Lk 10:20 do not rejoice that the spirits **s** to you, but *G5718*

Ro 8: 7 hostile to God; *it does* not **s** to God's law *G5718*
Ro 10: 3 *they did* not **s** to God's righteousness. *G5718*
Ro 13: 5 it is necessary *to* **s** to the authorities, not *G5718*
1Co 16:16 to **s** to such people and to everyone who *G5718*
Eph 5:21 **S** to one another out of reverence for *G5718*
Eph 5:22 **s** yourselves to your own husbands as you NDT
Eph 5:24 so also wives should **s** to their husbands in NDT
Col 2:20 to the world, *do you* **s to** its **rules**: *G1505*
Col 3:18 **s** *yourselves* to your husbands, as *G5718*
Heb 12: 9 How much more *should we* **s** to the Father *G5718*
Heb 13:17 in your leaders and **s to** their **authority**, *G5640*
Jas 4: 7 **S** *yourselves*, then, to God. Resist the *G5718*
1Pe 2:13 **S** *yourselves* for the Lord's sake to every *G5718*
1Pe 2:18 fear of God **s** *yourselves* to your masters, *G5718*
1Pe 3: 1 in the same way **s** *yourselves* to your own *G5718*
1Pe 5: 5 *you* who are younger, **s** *yourselves* to your *G5718*

SUBMITS (1) [SUBMIT]
Eph 5:24 Now as the church **s** to Christ, so also *G5718*

SUBMITTED (2) [SUBMIT]
La 5: 6 *We* **s** *to* Egypt and Assyria to get H5989+3338
1Pe 3: 5 *They* **s** *themselves* to their own husbands, *G5718*

SUBORDINATES (1)
1Ki 11:11 from you and give it to one of your **s**. H6269

SUBSCRIBE, SUBSCRIBED (KJV) SIGNED, WRITE

SUBSIDE (3) [SUBSIDED, SUBSIDES]
Eze 5:13 cease and my wrath against them *will* **s**, H5663
Eze 16:42 wrath against you *will* **s** and my jealous H5663
Eze 21:17 my hands together, and my wrath *will* **s**. H5663

SUBSIDED (5) [SUBSIDE]
Jdg 8: 3 At this, their resentment against him **s**. H8332
Est 2: 1 Later when King Xerxes' fury *had* **s**, he H8896
Est 7:10 up for Mordecai. Then the king's fury **s**. H8896
Eze 24:13 again until my wrath against you *has* **s**. H5663
Lk 8:24 the storm **s**, and all was calm. *G4264*

SUBSIDES (1) [SUBSIDE]
Ge 27:44 him for a while until your brother's fury **s**. H8740

SUBSTANCE (1)
Da 7: 1 wrote down the **s** of his dream. A10646+10418

SUBSTITUTE (4) [SUBSTITUTION]
Lev 27:10 not exchange it or **s** a good one for a bad H4614
Lev 27:10 if *they should* **s** one animal for H4614+4614
Lev 27:10 another, both it and the **s** become holy. H9455
Lev 27:33 the animal and its **s** become holy and H9455

SUBSTITUTION (2) [SUBSTITUTE]
Lev 27:33 out the good from the bad or **make** any **s**. H4614
Lev 27:33 If *anyone does* **make a s**, both the H4614+4614

SUBTIL, SUBTILTY (KJV) CONSPIRE, CRAFTY, CUNNING, DECEIT, DECEITFULLY, DECEPTIVELY, PRUDENCE, SECRETLY, SHREWD, TREACHEROUSLY

SUBTRACT (1)
Dt 4: 2 what I command you and *do* not **s** from it, H1757

SUBURBS (KJV) COURT, FARMLANDS, OPEN LAND, PASTURELAND, PASTURELANDS, SHORELANDS

SUBVERT, SUBVERTED, SUBVERTING (KJV) DEPRIVE, DISRUPTING, RUINS, TROUBLING, WARPED

SUBVERTING (1)
Lk 23: 2 "We have found this man **s** our nation. *G1406*

SUCATHITES (1)
1Ch 2:55 Shimeathites and **S**. These are the H8460

SUCCEED (27) [SUCCEEDED, SUCCEEDS, SUCCESS, SUCCESSFUL, SUCCESSFULLY, SUCCESSIVE, SUCCESSOR, SUCCESSORS]
Lev 6:22 The son who is to **s** him as anointed priest H9393
Lev 16:32 ordained to **s** his father as high H9393
Nu 14:41 the LORD's command? This *will* not **s**! H7503
1Sa 30: 8 overtake them and **s in the rescue**." H5911+5911
2Sa 7:12 I will raise up your offspring to **s** you, your H339
1Ki 5: 1 been anointed king to **s** his father David, H9393
1Ki 15: 4 by raising up a son to **s** him and by making H339
1Ki 19:16 from Abel Meholah to **s** you as prophet. H9393
1Ki 22:22 " '*You will* **s** in enticing him,' said the H3523
2Ki 3:27 who was to **s** him as king, and H9393
1Ch 17:11 I will raise up your offspring to **s** you, one H339
2Ch 13:12 God of your ancestors, for *you will* not **s**." H7503
2Ch 18:21 " '*You will* **s** in enticing him,' said the H3523
Job 30:13 up my road; *they* **s** in destroying me. H3603
Ps 20: 4 of your heart and **make** all your plans **s**. H4848
Ps 21:11 devise wicked schemes, *they* cannot **s**. H3523
Ps 37: 7 do not fret when people **s** *in* their ways H7503
Ps 140: 8 their desires, LORD; *do* not **let** their plans **s**. H7049
Pr 15:22 of counsel, but with many advisers *they* **s**. H7756
Pr 21:30 no plan that can **s against** the LORD. H4200+5584
Ecc 11: 6 you do not know which *will* **s**, whether H4178
Isa 47:12 Perhaps you will **s**, perhaps you will cause H3603
Isa 48:15 bring him, and *he will* **s** in his mission. H7503
Jer 32: 5 against the Babylonians, *you will* not **s**. H7503
Eze 17:15 *Will he* **s**? Will he who does H7503
Da 8:24 devastation and *will* **s** in whatever he H7503
Da 11:17 his plans *will* not **s** or help him. H6641

SUCCEEDED (74) [SUCCEED]
Ge 36:33 son of Zerah from Bozrah **s** him as king. H9393
Ge 36:34 the land of the Temanites **s** him as king. H9393
Ge 36:35 in the country of Moab, **s** him as king. H9393
Ge 36:36 Samlah from Masrekah **s** him as king. H9393
Ge 36:37 from Rehoboth on the river **s** him as king. H9393
Ge 36:38 Baal-Hanan son of Akbor **s** him as king. H9393
Ge 36:39 son of Akbor died, Hadad **s** him as king. H9393
Dt 10: 6 Eleazar his son **s** him as priest. H9393
2Sa 10: 1 and his son Hanun **s** him as king. H9393
1Ki 8:20 *I have* **s** David my father and now I H7756+9393
1Ki 11:43 And Rehoboam his son **s** him as king. H9393
1Ki 14:20 And Nadab his son **s** him as king. H9393
1Ki 14:31 And Abijah his son **s** him as king. H9393
1Ki 15: 8 And Asa his son **s** him as king. H9393
1Ki 15:24 And Jehoshaphat his son **s** him as king. H9393
1Ki 15:28 of Asa king of Judah and **s** him as king. H9393
1Ki 16: 6 And Elah his son **s** him as king. H9393
1Ki 16:10 Asa king of Judah. Then he **s** him as king. H9393
1Ki 16:28 And Ahab his son **s** him as king. H9393
1Ki 22:40 And Ahaziah his son **s** him as king. H9393
1Ki 22:50 And Jehoram his son **s** him as king. H9393
2Ki 1:17 Joram **s** him as king in the second year of H9393
2Ki 8:15 Then Hazael **s** him as king. H9393
2Ki 8:24 And Ahaziah his son **s** him as king. H9393
2Ki 10:35 And Jehoahaz his son **s** him as king. H9393
2Ki 12:21 And Amaziah his son **s** him as king. H9393
2Ki 13: 9 And Jehoash his son **s** him as king. H9393
2Ki 13:13 Jeroboam **s** him on the throne. H3782
2Ki 13:24 Ben-Hadad his son **s** him as king. H9393
2Ki 14:16 And Jeroboam his son **s** him as king. H9393
2Ki 14:29 And Zechariah his son **s** him as king. H9393
2Ki 15: 7 And Jotham his son **s** him as king. H9393
2Ki 15:10 assassinated him and **s** him as king. H9393
2Ki 15:14 assassinated him and **s** him as king. H9393
2Ki 15:22 And Pekahiah his son **s** him as king. H9393
2Ki 15:25 Pekah killed Pekahiah and **s** him as king. H9393
2Ki 15:30 then **s** him as king in the twentieth H9393
2Ki 15:38 And Ahaz his son **s** him as king. H9393
2Ki 16:20 And Hezekiah his son **s** him as king. H9393
2Ki 19:37 And Esarhaddon his son **s** him as king. H9393
2Ki 20:21 And Manasseh his son **s** him as king. H9393
2Ki 21:18 And Amon his son **s** him as king. H9393
2Ki 21:26 And Josiah his son **s** him as king. H9393
2Ki 24: 6 And Jehoiachin his son **s** him as king. H9393
1Ch 1:44 son of Zerah from Bozrah **s** him as king. H9393
1Ch 1:45 the land of the Temanites **s** him as king. H9393
1Ch 1:46 in the country of Moab, **s** him as king. H9393
1Ch 1:47 Samlah from Masrekah **s** him as king. H9393
1Ch 1:48 from Rehoboth on the river **s** him as king. H9393
1Ch 1:49 Baal-Hanan son of Akbor **s** him as king. H9393
1Ch 1:50 Baal-Hanan died, Hadad **s** him as king. H9393
1Ch 19: 1 and his son **s** him as king. H9393
1Ch 27:34 Ahithophel was **s** *by* Jehoiada son of H339
1Ch 29:28 His son Solomon **s** him as king. H9393
2Ch 6:10 *I have* **s** David my father and now I H7756+9393
2Ch 7:11 *had* **s in carrying out** all he had in H7503
2Ch 9:31 And Rehoboam his son **s** him as king. H9393
2Ch 12:16 And Abijah his son **s** him as king. H9393
2Ch 14: 1 Asa his son **s** him as king, and in his days H9393
2Ch 17: 1 Jehoshaphat his son **s** him as king and H9393
2Ch 21: 1 And Jehoram his son **s** him as king. H9393
2Ch 24:27 And Amaziah his son **s** him as king. H9393
2Ch 26:23 And Jotham his son **s** him as king. H9393
2Ch 27: 9 And Ahaz his son **s** him as king. H9393
2Ch 28:27 And Hezekiah his son **s** him as king. H9393
2Ch 32:30 He **s** in everything he undertook H7503
2Ch 32:33 And Manasseh his son **s** him as king. H9393
2Ch 33:20 And Amon his son **s** him as king. H9393
2Ch 36: 8 And Jehoiachin his son **s** him as king. H9393
Isa 37:38 And Esarhaddon his son **s** him as king. H9393
Jer 22:11 who **s** his father as king of Judah but has H9393
Da 11:21 "He *will be* **s** *by* a H6641+6584+4030
Mt 23:15 when *you have* **s**, you make them *G1181*
Ac 24:27 Felix *was* **s** *by* Porcius Festus *G3284+1345*

SUCCEEDS (1) [SUCCEED]
Ex 29:30 The son who **s** him as priest and comes to H9393

SUCCESS (26) [SUCCEED]
Ge 24:40 with you and **make** your journey **a s**, H7503
Ge 24:42 please **grant s** *to* the journey on which I H7503
Ge 24:56 that the LORD *has* **granted s** *to* my journey. H7503
Ge 27:20 "The LORD your God **gave** me **s**," he H7936
Ge 39: 3 that the LORD **gave** him **s** *in* everything he H7503
Ge 39:23 Joseph and **gave** him **s** *in* whatever he H7503
1Sa 18:14 In everything he did he **had great s** H8505
1Sa 18:30 David **met with** more **s** than the rest of H8505
1Sa 25:31 the LORD your God *has* **brought** my lord **s**, H3512
1Ki 22:13 exception are predicting **s** for the king. H3202
1Ch 12:18 **S**, success to you, and success to those H8934
1Ch 12:18 Success, **s** to you, and success to those H8934
1Ch 12:18 and **s** to those who help you H8934
1Ch 22:11 and *may you* **have s** and build the house H7503
1Ch 22:13 Then *you will* **have s** if you are careful to H7503
2Ch 18:12 exception are predicting **s** for the king. H3202
2Ch 26: 5 as he sought the LORD, God **gave** him **s**. H7503
Ne 1:11 **Give** your servant **s** today by granting him H7503
Ne 2:20 "The God of heaven *will* **give** us **s**. H7503
Job 5:12 so that their hands achieve no **s**. H9370
Job 6:13 now that **s** has been driven from me? H9370
Ps 118:25 save us! LORD, **grant** us **s**! H7503
Pr 2: 7 He holds **s** in store for the upright, he is a H9370
Pr 17: 8 they think **s** *will* **come** at every turn. H8505
Ecc 10:10 strength is needed, but skill will bring **s**. H3862
Da 11:14 in fulfillment of the vision, but **without s**. H4173

SUCCESSFUL (10) [SUCCEED]
Ge 24:12 master Abraham, **make** me **s** today, and H7936
Ge 24:21 not the LORD *had* **made** his journey **s**. H7503
Jos 1: 7 that *you may be* **s** wherever you go. H8505
Jos 1: 8 Then you will be prosperous and **s**. H8505
Jdg 18: 5 to learn whether our journey *will be* **s**." H7503
1Sa 18: 5 David was *so* **s** that Saul gave him a high H8505
1Sa 18:15 When Saul saw how **s** he *was*, he was H8505
2Ki 18: 7 *he was* **s** in whatever he undertook. H8505
2Ch 20:20 faith in his prophets and *you will be* **s**." H7503
Da 11:36 *He will be* **s** until the time of wrath is H7503

SUCCESSFULLY (1) [SUCCEED]
Pr 21:28 a careful listener will testify **s**. H4200+5905

SUCCESSIVE (2) [SUCCEED]
2Sa 21: 1 a famine *for* three **s years**; H9102+339+9102
Eze 41: 7 wider **at each s level**. H4200+5087+2025+4200+5087+2025

SUCCESSOR (11) [SUCCEED]
1Ki 1:48 my eyes to see a **s** on my throne today. H3782
1Ki 2: 4 never fail to have a **s** on the throne of H408[S]
1Ki 8:25 never fail to have a **s** to sit before me on H408
1Ki 9: 5 never fail to have a **s** on the throne of H408
1Ch 27: 7 of Joab; his son Zebadiah was his **s**. H339
2Ch 6:16 never fail to have a **s** to sit before me on H408
2Ch 7:18 never fail to have a **s** to rule over Israel. H408
Ecc 2:12 the king's **s** do than what H132+8611+995+339
Ecc 4:15 followed the youth, the king's **s**. H6641+9393
Ecc 4:16 came later were not pleased with the **s**. H2257[S]
Da 11:20 "His **s** will send out a tax H6641+6584+4030

SUCCESSORS (2) [SUCCEED]
1Ch 3:16 The **s** *of* Jehoiakim: Jehoiachin his son H1201
2Ch 36:20 to him and his **s** until the kingdom of H1201

SUCCOTH (NIV84) SUKKOTH

SUCCOTH BENOTH (NIV84) SUKKOTH BENOTH

SUCCOUR, SUCCOURED, SUCCOURER (KJV) BENEFACTOR, HELP, HELPED, RESCUE, SUPPORT

SUCH (239)
Ge 18:25 Far be it from you to do **s** a thing—to kill H3869
Ge 20: 9 you have brought **s great** guilt upon me and AIT
Ge 34:14 to them, "We can't do **s** a thing; we can't H2296
Ge 39: 9 then could I do **s** a wicked thing H2296+1524
Ge 41:19 I had never seen **s** ugly cows in all the H3869
Ge 44: 7 "Why does my lord say **s** things? H3869
Ge 44:17 "Far be it from me to do **s** *a thing*! H2296
Ex 10:14 had there been **s** a plague of H4027+4017
Ex 28: 3 have given wisdom in **s** matters that they NDT
Ex 32:21 do to you, that you led them into **s great** sin?" AIT
Lev 6: 3 falsely about any **s** sin that people may H2179
Lev 10:19 but **s** things **as** this have happened to me. H3869
Lev 11:34 contact with water from **any** *s* pot is unclean, AIT
Lev 11:34 liquid that is drunk from **s** a pot is unclean. NDT
Lev 13:45 "Anyone with **s** a defiling disease must H889
Lev 14:22 two young pigeons, **s as** they can afford H889
Lev 14:30 young pigeons, **s as** the person can afford, H889
Lev 15: 2 discharge, **s** a discharge is unclean. H2257[S]
Lev 18:29 **s** persons must be cut off from H2021+6913[S]
Lev 19: 5 sacrifice it **in s a way that** it will be H4200
Lev 21: 2 a close relative, **s as** his mother or father H4200
Lev 22: 6 who touches **any s thing** will be unclean H2257[S]
Lev 22: 9 my service **in s a way that** they do not H2256
Lev 22:25 must not accept **s** animals from the H4946+3972
Lev 22:29 sacrifice it **in s a way that** it will be H4200
Lev 23:42 Israelites are to live in **s** shelters H2021
Lev 25:21 I will send you **s** a blessing in the sixth year NDT
Lev 27: 9 **s** an animal given to the LORD becomes H889
Dt 4: 8 have **s** righteous decrees and laws **as** this H3869
Dt 13:11 among you will do **s** an evil thing again. H3869
Dt 19:20 never again will **s** an evil thing be H3869
Dt 29:18 among you that produces **s** bitter poison. NDT
Dt 29:19 When **s** a person hears the words of this NDT
Dt 33:17 **S** are the ten thousands of Ephraim H2156[S]
Dt 33:17 **s** are the thousands of Manasseh." H2156[S]
Jdg 7:13 It struck the tent with **s force** that the tent H5877[S]
Jdg 16:16 With **s** nagging she prodded him day H1821[S]
Jdg 19:24 this man, don't do **s** an outrageous thing." H2296
Jdg 19:30 "**S** a thing has never been seen or done H3869
Ru 2:10 "Why have I found **s** favor in your eyes that NDT
1Sa 2: 3 proudly or let your mouth speak **s** arrogance, NDT
1Sa 2:23 said to them, "Why do you do **s** things? H3869
1Sa 4: 5 all Israel raised **s** a great shout that the NDT
1Sa 6:10 They took two **s** cows and hitched them H6402[S]
1Sa 7:10 and **threw** them **into** *s* **a panic** that they were AIT
1Sa 8: 5 to lead us, **s as** all the other nations have." H3869
1Sa 9:21 Why do you say **s** a thing to me?" H3869
1Sa 19: 8 He struck them with **s** force that they fled H1524
1Sa 24: 6 that I should do **s** a thing to my master, H2296
1Sa 25:17 He is **s** a wicked man that no one can talk to NDT
1Sa 27:11 And **s** was his practice as long as he lived H3907

S

2Sa 11:11 surely as you live, I will not do s a thing!" H2296
2Sa 12: 6 because he did s a thing and had no pity." H2296
2Sa 13:12 S a thing should not be done in Israel H4027
2Sa 17:15 elders of Israel to do s and s, H3869+2296
2Sa 17:15 elders of Israel to do such and s, H3869+2296
2Sa 17:21 has advised s and such against you." H3970
2Sa 17:21 has advised such and s against you." H3970
2Sa 23:17 S were the exploits of the three mighty H465
2Sa 23:22 S were the exploits of Benaiah son of H465
2Sa 24: 3 my lord the king want to do s a thing?" H2296
1Ki 9: 8 the LORD done s a thing to this land and H3970
1Ki 14: 5 are to give her s and such an H3869+2297
1Ki 14: 5 to give her such and s an answer. H3869+2296
1Ki 22: 8 "The king should not say s a thing," H4027
2Ki 6: 8 up my camp in s and such a place." H7141+532
2Ki 6: 8 up my camp in such and s a place." H7141+532
2Ki 6:10 so that he was on his guard in s places. H9004S
2Ki 8:13 servant, a mere dog, accomplish s a feat?" H2296
2Ki 18:21 S is Pharaoh king of Egypt to all who H4027
2Ki 21:12 I am going to bring s disaster on Jerusalem NDT
2Ki 23:22 of Judah had any s Passover been H3869
1Ch 11:19 S were the exploits of the three mighty H465
1Ch 11:24 S were the exploits of Benaiah son of H465
1Ch 29:25 on him royal splendor s as no king over Israel AIT
2Ch 1:12 s as no king who was before you ever had H4027
2Ch 7:21 the LORD done s a thing to this land and H3970
2Ch 9: 9 had never been s spices as those the H3869
2Ch 14:13 S a great number of Cushites fell that they NDT
2Ch 18: 7 "The king should not say s a thing," H4027
2Ch 35:18 had ever celebrated s a Passover as did H3869
Ezr 9:14 peoples who commit s detestable practices H465
Ne 5:13 So may s a person be shaken out and AIT
Est 4:14 to your royal position for s a time as this?" H3869
Est 7: 4 because no s distress would justify H2021
Est 7: 5 the man who has dared to do s a thing?" H4027
Job 6: 7 I refuse to touch it; s food makes me ill. H3869
Job 8: 2 "How long will you say s things? Your H465
Job 8:13 S is the destiny of all who forget God; so H4027
Job 15:13 God and pour out s words from your mouth? AIT
Job 18:21 Surely s is the dwelling of an evil man H465
Job 18:21 s is the place of one who does not know H2296
Job 20:29 S is the fate God allots the wicked, the H2296
Job 22:13 Does he judge through s darkness? NDT
Job 23:14 many s plans he still has in store. H3869
Job 24: 1 who know him look in vain for s days? H2257S
Job 31:23 fear of his splendor I could not do s things. NDT
Ps 16: 4 of blood to s gods or take up their H2157S
Ps 17:14 By your hand save me from s people, LORD AIT
Ps 24: 6 S is the generation of those who seek him H2296
Ps 139: 6 S knowledge is too wonderful for me, too AIT
Pr 1:19 S are the paths of all who go after H4027
Pr 29: 7 the poor, but the wicked have no s concern. AIT
Ecc 5: 8 do not be surprised at s things; for one H2296S
Ecc 7:10 For it is not wise to ask s questions. H2296S
Isa 36: 6 S is Pharaoh king of Egypt to all who H4027
Isa 38:16 by s things people live; and my H2157S
Isa 38:17 was for my benefit that I suffered s anguish. AIT
Isa 40:20 too poor to present s an offering selects AIT
Isa 44:11 s craftsmen are only human beings. H2156
Isa 44:20 S a person feeds on ashes; a deluded heart AIT
Isa 57:10 You wearied yourself by s going about H8044S
Isa 65: 5 S people are smoke in my nostrils, a fire H465
Isa 66: 8 Who has ever heard of s things? Who has H3869
Jer 5: 9 I not avenge myself on s a nation as this? H3869
Jer 5:29 I not avenge myself on s a nation as this? H3869
Jer 9: 9 I not avenge myself on s a nation as this?" H3869
Jer 16:10 has the LORD decreed s a great disaster H2296
Jer 22: 8 has the LORD done s a thing to this great H3970
Jer 32:35 that they should do s a detestable thing H2296
Jer 40:16 son of Kareah, "Don't do s a thing! H2296
Jer 44: 7 Why bring s great disaster on yourselves by AIT
La 3:36 of justice—would not the Lord see s things? NDT
Eze 1:11 S were their faces. They each had two wings NDT
Eze 17:15 Will he who does s things escape? Will he H465
Eze 18:13 Will s a man live? He will not! AIT
Eze 18:14 he sees them, he does not do s things: H3869
Eze 21:10 The sword despises every s stick. NDT
Eze 31:14 so well-watered are ever to reach s a height; AIT
Eze 43:12 be most holy. S is the law of the temple H2296
Da 2:10 has ever asked s a thing of any A10341+10180
Da 2:15 "Why did the king issue s a harsh decree?" AIT
Da 10: 7 s terror overwhelmed them that they H1524
Da 12: 1 a time of distress s as has not happened H889
Hos 9: 4 S sacrifices will be to them like the bread of NDT
Joel 2: 2 s as never was in ancient times nor ever H4017
Am 5:13 the prudent keep quiet in s times, H2085
Jnh 1: 4 s a violent storm arose that the ship NDT
Mic 2: 7 Does he do s things?" "Do not my words H465
Zep 1:17 "I will bring s distress on all people that they AIT
Mal 1: 9 With s offerings from your hands, will he H2296S
Mt 8:10 found anyone in Israel with s great faith. G5537
Mt 9: 8 who had given s authority to man. G5525
Mt 13: 2 S large crowds gathered around him that he AIT
Mt 15:33 in this remote place to feed s a crowd?" G5537
Mt 18: 5 welcomes one s child in my name G5525
Mt 18: 7 S things must come, but woe to the G4998S
Mt 19:14 kingdom of heaven belongs to s as these." G5525
Mt 24: 6 S things must happen, but the end is still to AIT
Mk 2: 2 in s large numbers that there was G6063
Mk 4:32 with s big branches that the birds can G6063
Mk 7: 4 other traditions, s as the washing of cups NDT
Mk 7:29 he told her, "For s a reply, you may go; G4047
Mk 10:14 kingdom of God belongs to s as these. G5525
Mk 13: 7 S things must happen, but the end is still to NDT
Lk 5: 6 caught s a large number of fish that their G1254
Lk 7: 9 I have not found s great faith even in G5537
Lk 9: 9 is this I hear s things about?" And he G5525
Lk 12:30 For the pagan world runs after all s things G4047
Lk 14:26 own life—s a person cannot be my disciple. AIT
Lk 18:16 kingdom of God belongs to s as these. G5525
Jn 7:15 "How did this man get s learning without AIT
Jn 7:32 the crowd whispering s things about him. G4047
Jn 8: 5 Moses commanded us to stone s women. G5525
Jn 8:40 Abraham did not do s things. G4047
Jn 9:16 "How can a sinner perform s signs?" G5525
Jn 14: 9 I have been among you s a long time? G5537
Jn 15: 6 withers; s branches are picked up G899S
Jn 16: 3 They will do s things because they have not AIT
Ac 5: 4 What made you think of doing s a thing G4047
Ac 8:22 you for having s a thought in your heart AIT
Ac 15:39 They had s a sharp disagreement that they G6063
Ac 16:26 there was s a violent earthquake that the G6063
Ac 17:30 In the past God overlooked s ignorance G3836
Ac 18:15 I will not be a judge of s things." G4047
Ac 19:16 He gave them s a beating that they ran G6063
Ac 25:20 was at a loss how to investigate s matters; G4047
Ac 26:28 think that in s a short time you can persuade AIT
Ac 27:18 took s a violent battering from the storm G5928
Ro 1:32 that those who do s things deserve death, G5525
Ro 2: 2 those who do s things is based on truth. G5525
Ro 2:29 S a person's praise is not from other G4005
Ro 16:18 For s people are not serving our Lord Christ, G5525
1Co 7:15 but s a person is not subject to merely G899
1Co 5:11 Do not even eat with s people. G5525
1Co 6: 4 if you have disputes about s matters, do G1053S
1Co 7:15 the sister is not bound in s circumstances; G5525
1Co 7:27 Are you free from s a commitment? Do G1222S
1Co 9:15 the hope that you will do s things for me, G4048
1Co 9:24 Run in s a way as to get the prize G4048
1Co 11:31 we would not come under s judgment. AIT
1Co 14: 7 that make sounds, s as the pipe or harp G1664
1Co 16:16 to submit to s people and to everyone who G5525
1Co 16:18 S men deserve recognition. G5525
2Co 1:10 He has delivered us from s a deadly peril G5496
2Co 2:16 And who is equal to s a task? G4047
2Co 3: 4 S confidence we have through Christ G5525
2Co 3:12 since we have s a hope, we are very bold G5525
2Co 7: 3 s a place in our hearts that we G1650+3836
2Co 10:11 S people should realize that what we are G5525
2Co 11:13 For s people are false apostles, deceitful G5525
Gal 5:23 Against s things there is no law. G5525
Eph 5: 5 greedy person—s a person is an idolater G4005
Eph 5: 6 because of s things God's wrath comes G4047
Php 3: 4 have reasons for s confidence. G1877+4922S
Php 3:15 are mature should take s a view of things. G4047
Php 4: 8 praiseworthy—think about s things. G4047
Col 2:18 S a person also goes into great detail about AIT
Col 2:23 S regulations indeed have an G4015S
Col 3: 8 also rid yourselves of all s things as these: AIT
1Th 4: 6 will punish all those who commit s sins, G4047
2Th 3: 9 because we do not have the right to s help, NDT
2Th 3:12 S people we command and urge in the G5525
1Ti 1: 4 S things promote controversial G4015
1Ti 4: 2 S teachings come through hypocritical liars NDT
1Ti 5:10 her good deeds, s as bringing up children G1623
1Ti 5:11 younger widows, do not put them on s a list. NDT
2Ti 3: 5 Have nothing to do with s people. G4047
Titus 3:11 be sure that s people are warped and G5525
Heb 7:26 S a high priest truly meets our need—one G5525
Heb 8: 1 We do have s a high priest, who sat down G5525
Heb 11:14 People who say s things show that they G5525
Heb 12: 1 are surrounded by s a great cloud of G5537
Heb 12: 3 him who endured s opposition from G5525
Heb 12:19 trumpet blast or to s a voice speaking words AIT
Heb 13:16 for with s sacrifices God is pleased. G5525
Jas 1: 8 S a person is double-minded and unstable in AIT
Jas 2:14 has no deeds? Can s faith save them? G3836
Jas 3:15 S "wisdom" does not come down from G4047
Jas 4:16 arrogant schemes. All s boasting is evil. G5525
1Pe 1:18 perishable things s as silver or gold that NDT
1Pe 2:12 Live s good lives among the pagans that G2671
1Pe 3: 3 s as elaborate hairstyles and the wearing of NDT
2Pe 2:11 not heap abuse on s beings when bringing G899
1Jn 2:22 S a person is the antichrist—denying the G4047
2Jn 7 Any s person is the deceiver and the G4047
3Jn 8 hospitality to s people so that we may G5525
Rev 18:17 In one hour s great wealth has been G5537
Rev 18:21 "With s violence the great city of Babylon G4048

SUCK, SUCKED, SUCKING (KJV) FEAST, INFANT, NOURISHED, NURSE, NURSED, NURSING

SUCK (1) [SUCKLING]

Job 20:16 He will s the poison of serpents; the fangs H3567

SUCKLING, SUCKLINGS (KJV) INFANT, INFANTS

SUCKLING (1) [SUCK]

1Sa 7: 9 Then Samuel took a s lamb and sacrificed H2692

SUDDEN (10) [SUDDENLY]

Lev 26:16 I will bring on you s terror, wasting H988
Dt 28:20 come to s ruin because of the H4554
Jdg 20:37 in ambush made a s dash into Gibeah, H2590
Job 9:23 When a scourge brings s death, he mocks H7328
Job 22:10 all around you, why s peril terrifies you, H7328
Pr 3:25 Have no fear of s disaster or of the ruin H7328
Pr 24:22 those two will send s destruction on them, H7328
Isa 17:14 In the evening, s terror! Before the H1166
Zep 1:18 he will make a s end of all who live on H987
Jn 19:34 bringing a s flow of blood and water. G2317

SUDDENLY (47) [SUDDEN]

Ge 37: 7 out in the field when s my sheaf rose and H2180
Nu 6: 9 'If someone dies s in the H928+7353+7328
Nu 16:42 s the cloud covered it and the glory of the H2180
Nu 35:22 enmity someone s pushes another H928+7353
Jos 11: 7 came against them s at the Waters of H7328
Jdg 14: 5 s a young lion came roaring toward him. H2180
2Ki 2:11 s a chariot of fire and horses of fire appeared H2180
2Ki 13:21 s they saw a band of raiders H2180
Job 1:19 when s a mighty wind swept in from the H2180
Job 5: 3 taking root, but s his house was cursed. H7328
Ps 6:10 they will turn back and s be put to shame. H8092
Ps 64: 4 at the innocent; they shoot s, without fear. H7328
Ps 64: 7 with his arrows; they will s be struck down. H7328
Ps 73:19 How s are they destroyed H3869+8092
Pr 6:15 an instant; he will s be destroyed H7353
Pr 29: 1 after many rebukes will s be destroyed— H7353
Isa 29: 5 hordes like blown chaff. S, in an instant, H7328
Isa 30:13 bulging, that collapses s, in an instant. H7328
Isa 47:11 you cannot foresee will s come upon you. H7328
Isa 48: 3 them known; then s I acted, and they H7328
Jer 6:26 for s the destroyer will come upon us. H7328
Jer 15: 8 s I will bring down on them anguish and H7328
Jer 18:22 their houses when you s bring invaders H7328
Jer 51: 8 Babylon will s fall and be broken. H7328
Da 5: 5 S the fingers of a human hand A10734+10191
Da 8: 5 s a goat with a prominent horn between H2180
Hab 2: 7 Will not your creditors s arise? Will they H7353
Mal 3: 1 Then s the Lord you are seeking will come H7328
Mt 8:24 S a furious storm came up on the G2779+2627
Mt 28: 9 S Jesus met them. "Greetings," G2779+2627
Mk 9: 8 S, when they looked around, they no G1988
Mk 13:36 If he comes s, do not let him find you G1978
Lk 2:13 S a great company of the heavenly host G1978
Lk 9:39 A spirit seizes him and he s screams; it G1978
Lk 21:34 that day will close on you s like a trap. G167
Lk 24: 4 s two men in clothes that gleamed G2779+2627
Ac 1:10 when s two men dressed in white stood G2627
Ac 2: 2 S a sound like the blowing of a violent wind G924
Ac 8:39 the Spirit of the Lord s took Philip away G773
Ac 9: 3 s a light from heaven flashed around him. G1978
Ac 10:30 S a man in shining clothes stood before G2627
Ac 12: 7 S an angel of the Lord appeared and a G2627
Ac 12:10 length of one street, s the angel left him. G2311
Ac 16:26 S there was such a violent earthquake that G924
Ac 22: 6 s a bright light from heaven flashed G1978
Ac 28: 6 expected him to swell up or s fall dead; G924
1Th 5: 3 destruction will come on them s, as labor G167

SUE (1)

Mt 5:40 if anyone wants to s you and take your G3212

SUFFER (50) [LONG-SUFFERING, SUFFERED, SUFFERING, SUFFERINGS, SUFFERS]

Ge 4:15 kills Cain will s vengeance seven times H5933
Lev 24:20 inflicted the injury must s the same injury. H5989
Nu 14:34 you will s for your sins and know what it is H5951
Nu 16:29 a natural death and s the fate of all H7212
Dt 26: 6 Egyptians mistreated us and made us s, H6700
Ezr 4:13 and eventually the royal revenues will s. A10472
Job 24:11 they tread the winepresses, yet s thirst. H7532
Job 36:15 But those who s he delivers in their H6714
Ps 16: 4 run after other gods will s more and more. H6780
Ps 42:10 My bones s mortal agony as my foes taunt H928
Pr 9:12 if you are a mocker, you alone will s. H5951
Pr 11:15 security for a stranger will surely s, H8317+8273
Isa 47: 8 never be a widow or s the loss of children. H3359
Isa 53:10 will to crush him and cause him to s, H2703
Jer 14:13 'You will not see the sword or s famine. H2118
Jer 15:15 think of how I s reproach for your sake. H5951
Eze 23:49 You will s the penalty for your H5989+6584
Eze 36: 7 the nations around you will also s scorn. H5951
Eze 36:15 no longer will you s the scorn of the H5951
Eze 36:30 so that you will no longer s disgrace H4374
Da 6: 2 to them so that the king might not s loss. A10472
Mt 16:21 go to Jerusalem and s many things at the G4248
Mt 17:12 Son of Man is going to s at their hands." G4248
Mk 8:31 Son of Man must s many things and be G4248
Mk 9:12 that the Son of Man must s much and be G4248
Lk 9:22 Son of Man must s many things and be G4248
Lk 17:25 But first he must s many things and be G4248
Lk 22:15 to eat this Passover with you before I s. G4248
Lk 24:26 the Messiah have to s these things and G4248
Lk 24:46 The Messiah will s and rise from the dead G4248
Ac 3:18 saying that his Messiah would s. G4248
Ac 9:16 him how much he must s for my name." G4248
Ac 17: 3 the Messiah had to s and rise from the G4248
Ac 26:23 that the Messiah would s and, as the first G4078
1Co 3:15 the builder will s loss but yet will be G2423
2Co 1: 6 endurance of the same sufferings we s. G4248
Php 1:29 to believe in him, but also to s for him, G4248
1Th 5: 9 did not appoint us to s wrath but to receive AIT
Heb 9:26 would have had to s many times since the G4248
1Pe 1: 6 you may have had to s grief in all kinds of G3382

S

1Pe 2:20 But if *you* s for doing good and you G4248
1Pe 3:14 But even if *you should* s for what is right G4248
1Pe 3:17 *to* s for doing good than for doing evil. G4248
1Pe 4:15 *If* you s, it should not be as a murderer G4248
1Pe 4:16 However, if you s as a Christian, do not be NDT
1Pe 4:19 those *who* s according to God's will G4248
Jude 7 as an example *of those who* s the G5674
Rev 2:10 not be afraid of what you are about to s. G4248
Rev 2:10 and *you will* s persecution for ten days. G2400
Rev 2:22 who commit adultery with her s intensely, G2568

SUFFERED (31) [SUFFER]

1Sa 4:17 and the army *has* s heavy losses. H2118+928
Ps 88:15 From my youth I have s and been close to H6714
Ps 107:17 ways and s **affliction** because of their H6700
Ps 119:107 *I have* s much; preserve my life, LORD H6700
Isa 38:17 it was for my benefit that I s such anguish. H5352
Isa 53:11 After he *has* s, he will see the light of life H6662
Jer 14:17 my people, *has* s a grievous wound, H8689
Jer 44:17 of food and were well off and s no harm. H8011
La 3:47 We *have* s terror and pitfalls, ruin H2118+4200
Eze 36:6 wrath because *you have* s the scorn of the H5951
Zep 3:19 in every land where they have s shame. NDT
Mt 27:19 for *I have* s a great deal today in a dream G4248
Mk 5:26 *She had* s a great deal under the care of G4248
Lk 13:2 other Galileans because *they* s this way? G4248
Ac 28:5 snake off into the fire and s no ill effects. G4248
1Th 2:2 *We had* **previously** s and been treated G4634
1Th 2:14 You s from your own people the same G4248
1Th 2:14 same things those churches s from the Jews NDT
1Ti 1:19 and *so have* s **shipwreck** with regard G3728
Heb 2:9 with glory and honor because he s death, G4077
Heb 2:10 their salvation perfect through *what* he s. G4077
Heb 2:18 Because *he* himself s when he was G4248
Heb 5:8 he learned obedience from what *he* s G4248
Heb 10:34 *You* s **along with** those in prison and G5217
Heb 13:12 And so Jesus also s outside the city gate G4248
1Pe 2:21 because Christ s for you, leaving you G4248
1Pe 2:23 did not retaliate; *when he* s, he made no G4248
1Pe 3:18 For Christ also s once for sins, the G4248
1Pe 4:1 Therefore, *since* Christ s in his body, arm G4248
1Pe 5:10 in Christ, *after you have* s a little while G4248
Rev 9:5 And the **agony** they *s* was like that of the AIT

SUFFERING (54) [SUFFER]

Ge 16:5 "You are responsible for the **wrong** I am *s*. AIT
Ge 41:52 has made me fruitful in the land of my s." H6715
Ex 3:7 and I am concerned about their s. H4799
Nu 5:24 a curse and causes **bitter** s will enter her. H5253
Nu 5:27 that brings a curse and causes **bitter** s, H5253
Nu 14:33 forty years, s **for** your unfaithfulness H5951
Dt 28:53 Because of the s your enemy will inflict on H5186
Dt 28:55 left because of the s your enemy will H5186
Dt 28:57 because of the s your enemy will inflict H5186
2Ki 13:14 Now Elisha *had been* s *from* the illness H2703
2Ki 14:26 slave or free, was s; there was no one to H6715
Ne 9:9 "You saw the s *of* our ancestors in Egypt H6715
Job 2:13 because they saw how great his s was. H3873
Job 30:16 now my life ebbs away; days of s grip me. H6715
Job 30:27 me never stops; days of s confront me. H6715
Job 36:15 But those who suffer he delivers in their s H6715
Ps 22:24 scorned the s *of* the afflicted one; H6713
Ps 55:3 they bring down s on me and assail me H224
Ps 107:10 utter darkness, prisoners s in iron chains, H6715
Ps 119:50 My comfort in my s is this: Your promise H6715
Ps 119:153 Look on my s and deliver me, for I have H6715
Isa 14:3 relief from your s and turmoil and from H6778
Isa 53:3 by mankind, a man of s, and familiar with H4799
Isa 53:4 Surely he took up our pain and bore our s H4799
La 1:12 Is any s like my suffering that was inflicted H4799
La 1:12 suffering like my s that was inflicted on H4799
La 1:18 look on my s. My young men and H4799
Joel 1:18 no pasture; even the flocks of sheep *are* s. H870
Mt 4:24 various diseases, *those* s severe pain, the G5309
Mt 8:6 servant lies at home paralyzed, s terribly." G989
Mt 15:22 is demon-possessed and s **terribly**." G2809
Mt 17:15 "He has seizures and *is* s greatly. G4248
Mk 5:29 in her body that she was freed from her s. G3465
Mk 5:34 Go in peace and be freed from your s." G3465
Lk 4:38 mother-in-law was s from a high fever, G5309
Lk 14:2 s **from abnormal swelling of** *his* **body**. G5622
Ac 1:3 After his s, he presented himself to them G4248
Ac 5:41 counted worthy *of* s **disgrace** for the Name. G869
Ac 7:11 bringing great s, and our ancestors G2568
Ac 28:8 sick in bed, s **from** fever and dysentery. G5309
Ro 5:3 because we know that s produces G2568
Col 1:24 Now I rejoice in what I am s for you, and I G4077
1Th 1:6 the midst of severe s with the joy given by G2568
2Th 1:5 the kingdom of God, for which *you are* s. G4248
2Ti 1:8 **join with** me in s for the gospel G5155
2Ti 1:12 That is why *I am* s as I am. Yet this is no G4248
2Ti 2:3 **Join with** **me in** s, like a good soldier of G5155
2Ti 2:9 which *I am* s even to the point of being G2802
Heb 10:32 you endured in a great conflict *full of* s. G4077
Heb 13:3 as if you yourselves were s. G1877+5393S
Jas 5:10 an example of patience *in the face of* s, G2801
1Pe 2:19 under the pain *of* unjust s because they G4248
Rev 1:9 companion in the s and kingdom and G2568
Rev 2:22 So I will cast her on a bed of s, and I will NDT

SUFFERINGS (14) [SUFFER]

Job 9:28 I still dread all my s, for I know you will H6780
Ro 5:3 we also glory in our s, because we G2568
Ro 8:17 if indeed *we* **share in** his s in order that G5224
Ro 8:18 that our present s are not worth G4077
2Co 1:5 as we share abundantly in the s of Christ, G4077
2Co 1:6 endurance of the same s we suffer. G4077
2Co 1:7 we know that just as you share in our s, G4077
Eph 3:13 be discouraged because of my s for you, G2568
Php 3:10 his resurrection and participation *in* his s, G4077
2Ti 3:11 persecutions, s—what kinds of things G4077
1Pe 1:11 he predicted the s of the Messiah and G4077
1Pe 4:13 as you participate in the s of Christ, G4077
1Pe 5:1 a witness *of* Christ's s who also will G4077
1Pe 5:9 world is undergoing the same kind *of* s. G4077

SUFFERS (5) [SUFFER]

Job 15:20 All his days the wicked man s **torment** H2655
Pr 13:20 for a companion of fools s **harm**. H8317
1Co 12:26 If one part s, every part suffers with it; if G4248
1Co 12:26 every part s **with** it; if one part is G5224
1Pe 4:1 because whoever s in the body is done G4248

SUFFICE, SUFFICED, SUFFICETH (KJV) ENOUGH, WANTED

SUFFICIENT (5)

Lev 25:26 and acquire s **means** *to* redeem it H3869+1896
Isa 40:16 Lebanon is not s *for* altar fires, nor its H1896
2Co 2:6 inflicted on him by the majority is s. G2653
2Co 12:9 said to me, "My grace *is* s for you, for my G758
Php 1:20 will have s courage so that now as G4246

SUGGEST (1) [SUGGESTED, SUGGESTION]

Ru 4:4 to your attention and s that you buy it in H606

SUGGESTED (5) [SUGGEST]

1Ki 22:20 "One s this, and another that H606
2Ch 18:19 "One s this, and another that H606
Ezr 10:5 to do what had been s. H2021+1821+2021+2296
Est 2:15 eunuch who was in charge of the harem, s. H606
Est 6:10 do just as *you have* s for Mordecai H1819

SUGGESTION (1) [SUGGEST]

Est 5:14 This s delighted Haman, and he had the H1821

SUIT (1) [SUITABLE]

2Ti 4:3 Instead, **to** s their own desires, they will G2848

SUITABLE (4) [SUIT]

Ge 2:18 I will make a helper s **for** him." H3869+5584
Ge 2:20 But for Adam no s helper was H3869+5584
Nu 32:1 of Jazer and Gilead were s *for* livestock. H5226
Nu 32:4 of Israel—are s *for* livestock, and your H824

SUKKITES (1)

2Ch 12:3 S and Cushites that came with him from H6113

SUKKOTH (18) [SUKKOTH BENOTH]

Ge 33:17 however, went to S, where he built a H6111
Ge 33:17 That is why the place is called S. H6111
Ex 12:37 Israelites journeyed from Rameses to S. H6111
Ex 13:20 After leaving S they camped at Etham on H6111
Nu 33:5 Israelites left Rameses and camped at S. H6111
Nu 33:6 They left S and camped at Etham, on the H6111
Jos 13:27 S and Zaphon with the rest of the realm H6111
Jdg 8:5 He said to the men of S, "Give my troops H6111
Jdg 8:6 But the officials of S said, "Do you already H6111
Jdg 8:8 they answered as the men of S had. H6111
Jdg 8:14 a young man of S and questioned him, H6111
Jdg 8:14 names of the seventy-seven officials of S, H6111
Jdg 8:15 Gideon came and said to the men of S, H6111
Jdg 8:16 taught the men of S a lesson by H6111
1Ki 7:46 of the Jordan between S and Zarethan. H6111
2Ch 4:17 of the Jordan between S and Zarethan. H6111
Ps 60:6 Shechem and measure off the Valley of S. H6111
Ps 108:7 Shechem and measure off the Valley of S. H6111

SUKKOTH BENOTH (1) [SUKKOTH]

2Ki 17:30 The people from Babylon made S H6112

SULFUR (15)

Ge 19:24 rained down burning s on Sodom and H1730
Dt 29:23 will be a burning waste of salt and s— H1730
Job 18:15 **burning** s is scattered over his dwelling. H1730
Ps 11:6 he will rain fiery coals and **burning** s; H1730
Isa 30:33 like a stream of **burning** s, sets it ablaze. H1730
Isa 34:9 her dust into **burning** s; her land will H1730
Eze 38:22 burning s on him and on his H1730
Lk 17:29 fire and s rained down from heaven and G2520
Rev 9:17 were fiery red, dark blue, and **yellow as** s. G2523
Rev 9:17 of their mouths came fire, smoke and s. G2520
Rev 9:18 smoke and s that came out of their G2520
Rev 14:10 with burning s in the presence of the G2520
Rev 19:20 alive into the fiery lake of burning s. G2520
Rev 20:10 was thrown into the lake *of* burning s G2520
Rev 21:8 consigned to the fiery lake *of* burning s. G2520

SULKING (1)

1Ki 21:4 on his bed s and refused to H6015+906+7156

SULLEN (3)

1Ki 20:43 S and angry, the king of Israel went to his H6234
1Ki 21:4 s and angry because Naboth the H6234
1Ki 21:5 in and asked him, "Why are you so s? H6234

SUM (4) [SUMMED, SUMS]

Ps 139:17 thoughts, God! How vast is the s *of* them! H8031
Mt 28:12 they gave the soldiers a **large** s of money G2653
Ac 7:16 at Shechem *for a certain* s of money. G5507
1Co 16:2 set aside a s **of money** in keeping G4123+1571S

SUMMED (1) [SUM]

Ro 13:9 may be, *are* s **up** in this one command: G368

SUMMER (18)

Ge 8:22 cold and heat, s and winter, day and H7811
Ps 32:4 strength was sapped as in the heat of s. H7811
Ps 74:17 of the earth; you made both s and winter. H7811
Pr 6:8 its provisions in s and gathers its food at H7811
Pr 10:5 who gathers crops in s is a prudent son, H7811
Pr 26:1 Like snow in s or rain in harvest, honor is H7811
Pr 30:25 they store up their food in the s; H7811
Isa 18:6 the birds *will* feed on them **all** s, the wild H7810
Jer 8:20 harvest is past, the s has ended, and we H7811
Jer 40:10 harvest the wine, s **fruit** and olive oil, and H7811
Jer 40:12 an abundance of wine and s **fruit**. H7811
Da 2:35 like chaff on a threshing floor in the s. A10627
Am 3:15 the winter house along with the s house; H7811
Mic 7:1 one who gathers s **fruit** at the gleaning of H7811
Zec 14:8 Mediterranean Sea, in s and in winter. H7811
Mt 24:32 leaves come out, you know that s is near. G2550
Mk 13:28 leaves come out, you know that s is near. G2550
Lk 21:30 see for yourselves and know that s is near. G2550

SUMMIT (4)

2Sa 15:32 When David arrived at the s, where H8031
2Sa 16:1 had gone a short distance beyond the s, H8031
SS 4:8 the top of Senir, the s of Hermon, from the NDT
Jer 22:6 Gilead to me, like the s *of* Lebanon, I will H8031

SUMMON (26) [SUMMONED, SUMMONING, SUMMONS]

Nu 22:5 sent messengers to s Balaam son of Beor H7924
Nu 22:20 "Since these men have come to s you, go H7924
Dt 25:8 elders of his town *shall* s him and talk to H7924
Dt 33:19 *They will* s peoples *to* the mountain and H7924
2Sa 17:5 Absalom said, "S also Hushai the Arkite H7924
2Sa 20:4 "S the men of Judah to come to me H2410
2Sa 20:5 But when Amasa went to s Judah, he took H2410
1Ki 18:19 Now s the people from all over Israel to H8938
1Ki 22:13 who had gone to s Micaiah said to him, H7924
2Ki 10:19 Now s all the prophets of Baal, all his H7924
2Ch 18:12 who had gone to s Micaiah said to him, H7924
Job 13:22 Then s me and I will answer, or let me H7924
Job 19:16 *I* s my servant, but he does not answer H7924
Ps 68:28 S your power, God; show us your strength H7422
Isa 22:20 "In that day *I will* s my servant, Eliakim H7924
Isa 45:4 *I* s you by name and bestow on you a title H7924
Isa 46:11 From the east I s a bird of prey; from a H7924
Isa 48:13 out the heavens; *when* I s them, they all H7924
Isa 55:5 Surely *you will* s nations you know not H7924
Jer 1:15 *I am about to* s all the peoples of the H7924
Jer 25:9 *I will* s all the peoples of the H8938+2256+4374
Jer 50:29 "S archers against Babylon, all those who H9048
Jer 51:27 s against her these kingdoms: H9048
La 2:22 "As *you* s *to* a feast day, so you H7924
Eze 38:21 *I will* s a sword against Gog on all my H7924
Joel 1:14 S the elders and all who live in the land to H665

SUMMONED (68) [SUMMON]

Ge 12:18 So Pharaoh s Abram. "What have you H7924
Ge 20:8 next morning Abimelek s all his officials, H7924
Ge 26:9 So Abimelek s Isaac and said, "She is H7924
Ex 1:18 Then the king of Egypt s the midwives H7924
Ex 7:11 Pharaoh then s wise men and sorcerers H7924
Ex 8:8 Pharaoh s Moses and Aaron and said H7924
Ex 8:25 Then Pharaoh s Moses and Aaron and H7924
Ex 9:27 Then Pharaoh s Moses and H8938+2256+7924
Ex 10:16 Pharaoh quickly s Moses and Aaron and H7924
Ex 10:24 Then Pharaoh s Moses and said, "Go H7924
Ex 12:21 Then Moses s all the elders of Israel and H7924
Ex 12:31 the night Pharaoh s Moses and Aaron H7924
Ex 19:7 Moses went back and s the elders of the H7924
Ex 36:2 Then Moses s Bezalel and Oholiab and H7924
Lev 9:1 eighth day Moses s Aaron and his sons H7924
Lev 10:4 Moses s Mishael and Elzaphan, sons of H7924
Nu 12:5 to the tent and s Aaron and Miriam. H7924
Nu 16:12 Then Moses s Dathan and H8938+4200+7924
Nu 24:10 said to him, "*I* s you to curse my enemies H7924
Dt 5:1 Moses s all Israel and said: Hear, Israel H7924
Dt 29:2 Moses s all the Israelites and said to H7924
Dt 31:7 Then Moses s Joshua and said to him in H7924
Jos 9:22 Then Joshua s the Gibeonites and said H7924
Jos 10:24 he s all the men of Israel and said to the H7924
Jos 22:1 Then Joshua s the Reubenites, the H7924
Jos 23:2 s all Israel—their elders, leaders, judges H7924
Jos 24:1 *He* s the elders, leaders, judges and H7924
Jdg 4:10 There Barak s Zebulun and Naphtali, and H2410
Jdg 4:13 Sisera s from Harosheth Haggoyim to the H2410
1Sa 10:17 Samuel s the people of Israel to the LORD H7590
1Sa 13:4 And the people **were** s to join Saul at H7590
1Sa 15:4 So Saul s the men and mustered them at H9048
2Sa 9:2 *They* s him to appear before David, and H7924
2Sa 9:9 Then the king s Ziba, Saul's steward, and H7924
2Sa 14:33 Then the king s Absalom, and he came in H7924
2Sa 21:2 The king s the Gibeonites and spoke to H7924
1Ki 2:42 the king s Shimei and said to H8938+2256+7924

S

1Ki 8: 1 Then King Solomon **s** into his presence at H7735
1Ki 18: 3 Ahab *had* **s** Obadiah, his palace H7924
1Ki 20: 7 The king of Israel **s** all the elders of the H7924
1Ki 20:15 So Ahab **s** the 232 junior officers under H7212
2Ki 4:36 Elisha **s** Gehazi and said, "Call the H7924
2Ki 6:11 *He* **s** his officers and demanded of them H7924
2Ki 9: 1 The prophet Elisha **s** a man from the H7924
2Ki 12: 7 Therefore King Joash **s** Jehoiada the priest H7924
1Ch 15:11 Then David **s** Zadok and Abiathar the H7924
1Ch 28: 1 **s** all the officials of Israel **to assemble** at H7735
2Ch 5: 2 Then Solomon **s** to Jerusalem the elders H7735
2Ch 24: 6 Therefore the king **s** Jehoiada the chief H7924
Ezr 8:16 So *I* **s** Eliezer, Ariel, Shemaiah, Elnathan H8938
Ne 5:12 Then *I* **s** the priests and made the nobles H7924
Est 2:14 was pleased with her and **s** *her* by name. H7924
Est 3:12 first month the royal secretaries **were s**. H7924
Est 4: 5 Then Esther **s** Hathak, one of the king's H7924
Est 4:11 court without **being s** the king has but H7924
Est 8: 9 At once the royal secretaries **were s**—on H7924
Job 9:16 Even if *I* **s** him and he responded, I do not H7924
Isa 13: 3 *I have* **s** my warriors to carry out my wrath H7924
Isa 43: 1 redeemed you; *I have* **s** you by name; you H7924
La 1:15 *he has* **s** an army against me to crush my H7924
La 2:22 so you **s** against me terrors on every side. NDT
Da 2: 2 So the king **s** the magicians, enchanters H7924
Da 3: 2 He then **s** the satraps A10714+10378+10359
Da 3:13 **s** Shadrach, Meshach and A10042+10378+10085
Da 5: 7 The king **s** the enchanters, A10637+10089+10264+10378+10549
Am 5:16 The farmers *will be* **s** to weep and the H7924
Jn 9:24 A second time *they* **s** the man who had G5888
Jn 18:33 inside the palace, **s** Jesus and asked him G5888

SUMMONING (2) [SUMMON]
Jdg 6:34 a trumpet, **s** the Abiezrites to follow him. H2410
Mk 15:44 **S** the centurion, he asked him if Jesus G4673

SUMMONS (5) [SUMMON]
Nu 22:37 Balaam, "Did I not send you an urgent **s**? H7924
Ps 50: 1 speaks and **s** the earth from the rising of H7924
Ps 50: 4 *He* **s** the heavens above, and the earth H7924
Isa 45: 3 the God of Israel, who **s** you by name. H7924
Na 2: 5 Nineveh **s** her picked troops, yet they H2349

SUMS (1) [SUM]
Mt 7:12 this **s up** the Law and the Prophets. G1639

SUN (146) [SUNDOWN, SUNRISE, SUNSET, SUNSHINE]
Ge 15:12 As the **s** was setting, Abram fell into a H9087
Ge 15:17 When the **s** had set and darkness had H9087
Ge 19:23 the **s** had risen over the land. H9087
Ge 28:11 the night because the **s** had set. H9087
Ge 29: 7 he said, "the **s** is still high; it is not time H3427
Ge 32:31 The **s** rose above him as he passed H9087
Ge 37: 9 this time the **s** and moon and eleven H9087
Ex 16:21 when the **s** grew hot, it melted H9087
Lev 22: 7 When the **s** goes down, he will be clean H9087
Dt 4:19 you look up to the sky and see the **s**, H9087
Dt 11:30 toward the setting **s**, near the great trees H9087
Dt 16: 6 evening, when the **s** goes down, on the H9087
Dt 17: 3 to them or to the **s** or the moon or the H9087
Dt 33:14 with the best the **s** brings forth and the H9087
Jos 10:12 "**S**, stand still over Gibeon, and you H9087
Jos 10:13 So the **s** stood still, and the moon H9087
Jos 10:13 The **s** stopped in the middle of the sky H9087
Jdg 5:31 love you be like the **s** when it rises in its H9087
Jdg 19:14 the **s** set as they neared Gibeah in H9087
1Sa 11: 9 'By the time the **s** is hot tomorrow, you H9087
2Sa 2:24 and as the **s** was setting, they H9087
2Sa 3:35 bread or anything else before the **s** sets!" H9087
1Ki 22:36 As the **s** was setting, a cry spread through H9087
2Ki 3:22 morning, the **s** was shining on the water. H9087
2Ki 23: 5 incense to Baal, to the **s** and moon, to the H9087
2Ki 23:11 the kings of Judah had dedicated to the **s**. H9087
2Ki 23:11 burned the chariots dedicated to the **s**. H9087
Ne 7: 3 are not to be opened until the **s** is hot. H9087
Job 9: 7 He speaks to the **s** and it does not shine H3064
Job 30:28 not by the **s**; I stand up in the H2780
Job 31:26 I have regarded the **s** in its radiance or the H240
Job 37:21 Now no one can look at the **s**, bright as it is H240
Ps 19: 4 heavens God has pitched a tent for the **s**. H9087
Ps 37: 6 your vindication like the **noonday s**. H7416
Ps 50: 1 from the rising of the **s** to where it sets. H9087
Ps 58: 8 like a stillborn child that never sees the **s**. H9087
Ps 72: 5 May he endure as long as the **s**, as long H9087
Ps 72:17 may it continue as long as the **s**. H9087
Ps 74:16 you established the **s** and moon. H9087
Ps 84:11 For the LORD God is a **s** and shield; the H9087
Ps 89:36 his throne endure before me like the **s**; H9087
Ps 104:19 the **s** knows when to go down. H9087
Ps 104:22 The **s** rises, and they steal away; they H9087
Ps 113: 3 the rising of the **s** to the place where it H9087
Ps 121: 6 the **s** will not harm you by day, nor the H9087
Ps 136: 8 the **s** to govern the day, His love endures H9087
Ps 148: 3 Praise him, **s** and moon; praise him, all H9087
Pr 4:18 path of the righteous is like the morning **s**, H240
Ecc 1: 3 their labors at which they toil under the **s**? H9087
Ecc 1: 5 The **s** rises and the sun sets, and hurries H9087
Ecc 1: 5 The sun rises and the **s** sets, and hurries H9087
Ecc 1: 9 there is nothing new under the **s**. H9087
Ecc 1:14 all the things that are done under the **s**; H9087
Ecc 2:11 nothing was gained under the **s**. H9087
Ecc 2:17 is done under the **s** was grievous to me. H9087
Ecc 2:18 all the things I had toiled for under the **s**, H9087
Ecc 2:19 poured my effort and skill under the **s**. H9087
Ecc 2:20 over all my toilsome labor under the **s**. H9087
Ecc 2:22 striving with which they labor under the **s**? H9087
Ecc 3:16 And I saw something else under the **s**: In H9087
Ecc 4: 1 that was taking place under the **s**: H9087
Ecc 4: 3 not seen the evil that is done under the **s**. H9087
Ecc 4: 7 saw something meaningless under the **s**: H9087
Ecc 4:15 walked under the **s** followed the youth, H9087
Ecc 5:13 I have seen a grievous evil under the **s** H9087
Ecc 5:18 labor under the **s** during the few days of H9087
Ecc 6: 1 I have seen another evil under the **s**, and H9087
Ecc 6: 5 it never saw the **s** or knew anything, H9087
Ecc 6:12 happen under the **s** after they are gone? H9087
Ecc 7:11 thing and benefits those who see the **s**. H9087
Ecc 8: 9 my mind to everything done under the **s**. H9087
Ecc 8:15 a person under the **s** than to eat and drink H9087
Ecc 8:15 the life God has given them under the **s**. H9087
Ecc 8:17 comprehend what goes on under the **s**. H9087
Ecc 9: 3 in everything that happens under the **s**: H9087
Ecc 9: 6 part in anything that happens under the **s**. H9087
Ecc 9: 9 life that God has given you under the **s**— H9087
Ecc 9: 9 in your toilsome labor under the **s**. H9087
Ecc 9:11 I have seen something else under the **s** H9087
Ecc 9:13 I also saw under the **s** this example of H9087
Ecc 10: 5 There is an evil I have seen under the **s** H9087
Ecc 11: 7 it pleases the eyes to see the **s**. H9087
Ecc 12: 2 before the **s** and the light and the moon H9087
SS 1: 6 am dark, because I am darkened by the **s**. H9087
SS 6:10 bright as the **s**, majestic as the H2780
Isa 5:30 even the **s** will be darkened by clouds. H240
Isa 13:10 The rising **s** will be darkened and the H9087
Isa 19:18 of them will be called the City of the **S**. H3064
Isa 24:23 be dismayed, the **s** ashamed; for the LORD H2780
Isa 30:26 The moon will shine like the **s**, and the H2780
Isa 38: 8 shadow cast by the **s** go back the ten H9087
Isa 41:25 one from the rising **s** who calls on my H9087
Isa 45: 6 from the rising of the **s** to the place of its H9087
Isa 49:10 desert heat or the **s** beat down on them. H9087
Isa 59:19 from the rising of the **s**, they will H9087
Isa 60:19 The **s** will no more be your light by day H9087
Isa 60:20 Your **s** will never set again, and your H9087
Jer 8: 2 be exposed to the **s** and the moon and all H9087
Jer 15: 9 Her **s** will set while it is still day; she will H9087
Jer 31:35 he who appoints the **s** to shine by day H9087
Jer 43:13 in the temple of the **s** in Egypt he will H9087
Eze 8:16 were bowing down to the **s** in the east. H9087
Eze 32: 7 I will cover the **s** with a cloud, and the H9087
Hos 6: 3 As surely as the **s rises**, he will appear; he H8840
Hos 6: 5 then my judgments go forth like the **s**. H240
Joel 2:10 tremble, the **s** and moon are darkened H9087
Joel 2:31 The **s** will be turned to darkness and the H9087
Joel 3:15 The **s** and moon will be darkened, and H9087
Am 8: 9 "I will make the **s** go down at noon and H9087
Jnh 4: 8 When the **s** rose, God provided a H9087
Jnh 4: 8 the **s** blazed on Jonah's head so that H9087
Mic 3: 6 The **s** will set for the prophets, and the H9087
Na 3:17 when the **s** appears they fly away H9087
Hab 3:11 **S** and moon stood still in the heavens at H9087
Mal 1:11 from where the **s** rises to where it sets. H9087
Mal 4: 2 the **s** *of* righteousness will rise with H9087
Mt 5:45 He causes his **s** to rise on the evil and the G2463
Mt 13: 6 But when the **s** came up, the plants were G2463
Mt 13:43 will shine like the **s** in the kingdom of G2463
Mt 17: 2 His face shone like the **s**, and his clothes G2463
Mt 24:29 of those days " 'the **s** will be darkened, G2463
Mk 4: 6 But when the **s** came up, the plants were G2463
Mk 13:24 distress, " 'the **s** will be darkened, and G2463
Lk 1:78 by which the **rising s** will come to us from G424
Lk 21:25 "There will be signs in the **s**, moon and G2463
Lk 23:45 the **s** stopped shining. And the curtain G2463
Ac 2:20 The **s** will be turned to darkness and the G2463
Ac 7:42 *of* the **s**, **moon and stars**. G5131+3836+4041
Ac 13:11 not even able to see the **light of the s**." G2463
Ac 26:13 brighter than the **s**, blazing around me G2463
Ac 27:20 When neither **s** nor stars appeared for G2463
1Co 15:41 The **s** has one kind of splendor, the moon G2463
Eph 4:26 Do not let the **s** go down while you are G2463
Jas 1:11 For the **s** rises with scorching heat and G2463
Rev 1:16 His face was like the **s** shining in all its G2463
Rev 6:12 The **s** turned black like sackcloth made of G2463
Rev 7:16 The **s** will not beat down on them,' nor G2463
Rev 8:12 a third *of* the **s** was struck, a third G2463
Rev 9: 2 The **s** and sky were darkened by the G2463
Rev 10: 1 his face was like the **s**, and his legs were G2463
Rev 12: 1 a woman clothed with the **s**, with the G2463
Rev 16: 8 fourth angel poured out his bowl on the **s**, G2463
Rev 16: 8 and **the s** was allowed to scorch people G899S
Rev 19:17 And I saw an angel standing in the **s** G2463
Rev 21:23 does not need the **s** or the moon to shine G2463
Rev 22: 5 the light of a lamp or the light *of* the **s**, G2463

SUN-SCORCHED (2) [SCORCH]
Ps 68: 6 the rebellious live in a **s land**. H7461
Isa 58:11 your needs in a **s land** and will strengthen H7463

SUNDER, SUNDERED (KJV) AWAY, PARTED, PIECES, SHATTERS, THROUGH

SUNDOWN (1) [SUN]
Da 6:14 effort until **s** to save him. A10436+10728+10002

SUNG (3) [SING]
Isa 26: 1 that day this song *will* **be s** in the land of H8876
Mt 26:30 *When they had* **s a hymn**, they went out G5630
Mk 14:26 *When they had* **s a hymn**, they went out G5630

SUNK (3) [SINK]
Jer 38:22 Your feet *are* **s** in the mud; your friends H3190
La 2: 9 Her gates *have* **s** into the ground; their H3190
Hos 9: 9 *They have* **s deep** *into* corruption, as in H6676

SUNLIGHT (3) [LIGHT]
Isa 30:26 and the **s** will be seven times H240+2780
Isa 38: 8 So the **s** went back the ten steps it had H9087
Zec 14: 6 On that day there will be neither **s** nor cold H240

SUNRISE (13) [SUN]
Ex 22: 3 if it happens *after* **s**, the H2436+2021+9087
Ex 27:13 east end, toward the **s**, the courtyard shall H4667
Ex 38:13 east end, toward the **s**, was also fifty H4667
Nu 2: 3 the east, toward the **s**, the divisions of the H4667
Nu 3:38 toward the **s**, in front of the tent H4667
Nu 21:11 that faces Moab toward the **s**. H4667+9087
Nu 34:15 Jordan across from Jericho, toward the **s**." H4667
Jos 1:15 east of the Jordan toward the **s**." H4667+9087
Jos 19:12 east from Sarid *toward* the **s** to the H4667+9087
Jdg 9:33 In the morning at **s**, advance H2436+2021+9087
2Sa 23: 4 light of morning at **s** *on* a cloudless H2436+9087
Hab 3: 4 His splendor was like the **s**; rays flashed H240
Mk 16: 2 the week, **just after s**, they G422+3836+2463

SUNSET (11) [SUN]
Ex 17:12 hands remained steady till **s**. H995+2021+9087
Ex 22:26 as a pledge, return it by **s**, H995+2021+9087
Dt 23:11 and at **s** he may return to the H995+2021+9087
Dt 24:13 their cloak by **s** so that your H995+2021+9087
Dt 24:15 wages each day before **s**, H995+2021+9087
Jos 8:29 At **s**, Joshua ordered them to H995+2021+9087
Jos 10:27 At **s** Joshua gave the H6961+995+2021+9087
Jdg 14:18 Before **s** on the seventh day H995+2021+3064
2Ch 18:34 Then at **s** he died. H6961+995+2021+9087
Mk 1:32 evening after **s** the people brought G1544+2463
Lk 4:40 *At* **s**, the people brought to G1544+3836+2463

SUNSHINE (2) [SUN]
Job 8:16 are like a well-watered plant in the **s**, H9087
Isa 18: 4 like shimmering heat in the **s**, like a cloud H240

SUP, SUPPED (KJV) EAT, SUPPER

SUPER-APOSTLES (2) [APOSTLE]
2Co 11: 5 I am in the least inferior to those "**s**." G5663+693
2Co 12:11 am not in the least inferior *to* the "**s**," G5663+693

SUPERFLUITY, SUPERFLUOUS (KJV) DEFORMED, NO NEED, PREVALENT

SUPERIOR (7)
Da 8:25 to prosper, and *he will* consider himself **s**. H1540
Ro 2:18 approve of what *is* **s** because you are G1422
Ro 11:18 *do* not **consider** *yourself* **to be s** to those G2878
Heb 1: 4 So he became as much **s** to the angels as G3202
Heb 1: 4 the name he has inherited is **s** to theirs. G1427
Heb 8: 6 Jesus has received is *as* **s** to theirs as the G1427
Heb 8: 6 which he is mediator is **s** to the old one, G3202

SUPERSCRIPTION (KJV) INSCRIPTION, WRITTEN NOTICE

SUPERSTITIONS (1)
Isa 2: 6 They are full of **s** from the East; they practice NDT

SUPERVISE (4) [SUPERVISED, SUPERVISING, SUPERVISION, SUPERVISORS]
2Ki 12:11 to the men appointed *to* **s** the work on the H6913
2Ki 22: 5 to the men appointed *to* **s** the work on the H6913
2Ch 34:10 to the men appointed *to* **s** the work on the H6913
Ezr 3: 8 old and older to **s** the building of the H5904

SUPERVISED (2) [SUPERVISE]
1Ki 5:16 hundred foremen who **s** the project and H6584
2Ch 34:13 of the laborers and **s** all the workers from H5904

SUPERVISING (3) [SUPERVISE]
1Ki 9:23 550 officials **s** those who did the work. H928
2Ch 8:10 two hundred and fifty officials **s** the men. H928
Ezr 3: 9 joined together in **s** those working on the H5904

SUPERVISION (6) [SUPERVISE]
Nu 8:22 meeting **under** the **s** *of* Aaron and H4200+7156
1Ch 25: 2 sons of Asaph were under the **s** *of* Asaph, H3338
1Ch 25: 2 who prophesied under the king's **s**. H3338
1Ch 25: 3 under the **s** *of* their father Jeduthun H3338
1Ch 25: 6 men were under the **s** *of* their father for H3338
1Ch 25: 6 Heman were under the **s** *of* the king. H3338

SUPERVISORS (3) [SUPERVISE]
2Ki 22: 9 it to the workers and **s** at the temple." H7212
2Ch 34:17 have entrusted it to the **s** and workers." H7212
Ne 3: 5 their shoulders to the work under their **s**. H123

SUPH (1)
Dt 1: 1 Arabah—opposite **S**, between Paran and H6069

SUPHAH (1)
Nu 21:14 Zahab in S and the ravines, the H6071

SUPPER (7) [SUPPERS]
Lk 17: 8 'Prepare *my* s, get yourself *G5515+1268*
Lk 22:20 same way, after the s he took the cup *G1268*
Jn 21:20 back against Jesus at the s and had said, *G1270*
1Co 11:20 together, it is not the Lord's S you eat, *G1270*
1Co 11:25 In the same way, after s he took the cup *G1268*
Rev 19: 9 are invited to the wedding s of the Lamb!" *G1270*
Rev 19:17 gather together for the great s of God, *G1270*

SUPPERS (1) [SUPPER]
1Co 11:21 of you go ahead with your own private **s**. *G1270*

SUPPLICATION (5) [SUPPLICATIONS]
1Ki 8:30 Hear the s *of* your servant and of your H9382
1Ki 8:33 praying and **making** s to you in this H2858
2Ch 6:24 praying and **making** s before you in this H2858
Ps 119:170 May my s come before you; deliver me H9382
Zec 12:10 of Jerusalem a spirit of grace and **s**. H9384

SUPPLICATIONS (2) [SUPPLICATION]
1Ki 8:54 all these prayers and s to the LORD, H9382
2Ch 6:21 Hear the s *of* your servant and of your H9384

SUPPLIED (14) [SUPPLY]
Nu 31: 5 each tribe, *were* s from the clans of Israel. H5034
1Ki 4: 7 *who* **s provisions** *for* the king and the royal H3920
1Ki 4:27 **s provisions** *for* King Solomon and all who H3920
1Ki 5:10 way Hiram *kept* Solomon **s** *with* all the H5989
1Ki 9:11 because Hiram *had* **s** him with all the H5951
1Ki 18: 4 and *had* **s** them *with* food and water.) H3920
1Ki 18:13 in each, and **s** them *with* food and water. H3920
1Ch 12:39 their families *had* **s provisions** for them. H3922
Isa 33:16 Their bread *will* **be s**, and water will not H5989
Jer 5: 7 *I* **s all** their **needs**, yet they committed H8425
Ac 20:34 hands of mine *have* **s** my own needs and *G5676*
1Co 16:17 because they *have* **s** what was lacking from *G405*
2Co 11: 9 came from Macedonia **s** what I needed. *G4650*
Php 4:18 *I am* **amply s**, now that I have received *G4444*

SUPPLIES (18) [SUPPLY]
1Sa 10:22 he has hidden himself among the **s**." H3998
1Sa 17:22 David left his things with the keeper of **s** H3998
1Sa 25:13 while two hundred stayed with the **s**. H3998
1Sa 30:24 who stayed with the **s** is to be the same H3998
1Ki 4: 7 one had to **provide s** *for* one month in H3920
1Ch 12:40 There were plentiful **s** of flour, fig cakes H4407
1Ch 27:28 Joash was in charge of the **s** *of* olive oil. H238
2Ch 11:11 in them, with **s** *of* food, olive oil and H238
2Ch 17:13 had large **s** in the towns of Judah. H4856
Ne 13:13 responsible for **distributing** *the* **s** to their H2745
Ps 105:16 the land and destroyed all their **s** *of* food; H4751
Ps 147: 8 he **s** the earth *with* rain and makes grass H3922
Pr 31:24 and **s** the merchants *with* sashes. H5989
Isa 3: 1 all **s** *of* food and all supplies of water, H5472
Isa 3: 1 all supplies of food and all **s** *of* water, H5472
Isa 10:28 through Migron; they store **s** at Mikmash. H3998
Ac 28:10 they furnished us *with* **the s** we needed. AIT
2Co 9:10 Now he *who* **s** seed to the sower and *G2220*

SUPPLY (23) [SUPPLIED, SUPPLIES, SUPPLYING]
Ex 5: 7 no longer to **s** the people *with* straw for H5989
Lev 26:26 When I cut off your **s** *of* bread, ten women H4751
Nu 4: 9 all its jars for the olive oil used *to* **s** it. H9250
Dt 15:14 **S** them **liberally** from your flock H6735+6735
Jos 9: 5 bread of their **food** was dry and moldy H7474
Jdg 19:20 "Let me **s** whatever you need NDT
2Sa 12:27 against Rabbah and taken its **water s**. H4784
1Ki 17: 4 the ravens to **s** you with food there." H3920
1Ki 17: 9 directed a widow there to **s** you **with food**." H3920
Ezr 7:20 your God that you are responsible to **s**, A10498
Ne 5:18 ten days an **abundant s** of wine of all H2221
Ps 78:20 *Can he* **s** meat for his people? H3922
Isa 3: 1 Jerusalem and Judah both **s** and support: H5473
Eze 4:16 about to cut off the food **s** in Jerusalem. H4751
Eze 5:16 upon you and cut off your **s** *of* food. H4751
Eze 14:13 to cut off its food **s** and send famine upon H4751
Eze 48:18 Its produce *will* **s** food for the H2118+4200
Na 2: 9 The **s** is endless, the wealth from all its H9414
Ac 12:20 on the king's country *for* their **food s**. *G5555*
2Co 8:14 time your plenty will **s** what they need, *G1650*
2Co 8:14 their plenty *will* **s** what you need. *G1181+1650*
2Co 9:10 bread for food *will* also **s** and increase *G5961*
1Th 3:10 see you again and **s** what is lacking in *G2936*

SUPPLYING (1) [SUPPLY]
2Co 9:12 perform is not only **s** the needs of the *G4650*

SUPPORT (24) [SUPPORTED, SUPPORTING, SUPPORTS]
Ge 13: 6 But the land *could* not **s** them while they H5951
Ge 36: 7 staying could not **s** them both because of H5951
Lev 25:35 poor and *are* **unable to s** H4572+3338
Jdg 16:26 I can feel the pillars that **s** the temple, H3922
2Sa 18: 3 now for you to **give** us **s** from the city." H6468
2Sa 22:19 day of my disaster, but the LORD was my **s**. H5472
1Ki 1: 7 the priest, and *they* **gave** him *their* **s**. H6468+339
2Ki 15:19 of silver to **gain** his **s** and H2118+3338+907
1Ch 11:10 **gave** his kingship **strong s** to H2616+6640
2Ch 26:13 a powerful force to **s** the king against his H6468
Ezr 10: 4 We will **s** you, so take H6640
Ps 18:18 day of my disaster, but the LORD was my **s**. H5472
Ps 20: 2 the sanctuary and **grant** you **s** from Zion. H6184
Isa 3: 1 Jerusalem and Judah both supply and **s**: H5474
Isa 63: 5 I was appalled that no *one* **gave s**; so my H6164
Jer 37: 7 which has marched out to **s** you, will go H6476
Da 11: 1 I took my stand to **s** and protect him.) H2616
Mic 3:11 Yet *they* **look for** the LORD's **s** and say, "Is H9128
Lk 8: 3 These women *were* **helping to s** them out *G1354*
Ac 12:20 *After* **securing** *the* **s** *of* Blastus, a trusted *G4275*
Ro 11:18 You *do* not **s** the root, but the root *G1002*
1Co 9:12 If others **have** this right of **s** from you *G3576*
2Co 11: 8 churches by receiving **s** from them so as to *G4072*
2Ti 4:16 no one **came to** my **s**, but everyone *G4134*

SUPPORTED (11) [SUPPORT]
1Ki 16:21 half **s** Tibni son of Ginath for king H2118+339
1Ki 16:21 Ginath for king, and the other half **s** Omri. H339
2Ki 16:17 the bronze bulls that **s** it and set it on a H9393
2Ch 11:17 kingdom of Judah and **s** Rehoboam son of H599
Ezr 10:15 **s** *by* Meshullam and Shabbethai the H6468
Job 4: 4 Your words *have* **s** those who stumbled H7756
Ps 89:43 of his sword and *have* not **s** him in battle. H7756
Ps 94:18 slipping," your unfailing love, LORD, **s** me. H6184
Jer 26:24 son of Shaphan **s** Jeremiah, H3338+2118+907
Da 11: 6 her father and the *one who* **s** her. H2616
Col 2:19 **s** and held together by its ligaments and *G2220*

SUPPORTING (3) [SUPPORT]
1Ki 7: 2 of cedar columns **s** trimmed cedar beams. H6584
Ezr 5: 2 prophets of God were with them, **s** them. A10514
Eph 4:16 held together by every **s** ligament, *G2221*

SUPPORTS (8) [SUPPORT]
1Ki 7:30 each had a basin resting on four **s**, H7193+4190
1Ki 7:35 The **s** and panels were attached to the H3338
1Ki 7:36 the surfaces of the **s** and on the panels, H3338
1Ki 10:12 almugwood to make **s** for the temple of H5026
Eze 41: 6 the temple to serve as **s** for the side rooms, H296
Eze 41: 6 so that the **s** were not inserted into the wall H296
Da 10:21 No one **s** me against them except H2616+6640
Ro 11:18 do not support the root, but the root **s** you. NDT

SUPPOSE (23) [SUPPOSED, SUPPOSEDLY, SUPPOSING]
Ex 3:13 "**S** I go to the Israelites and say to them H2180
Nu 36: 3 Now **s** they marry men from other Israelite NDT
Jdg 11: 9 "**S** you take me back to fight the H561
Job 34:31 "**S** someone says to God, 'I am guilty but H3954
Eze 18: 5 "**S** there is a righteous man who does H3954
Eze 18:10 "**S** he has a violent son, who sheds blood H2256
Eze 18:14 "But **s** this son has a son who sees all the H2180
Mt 10:34 "*Do* not **s** that I have come to bring peace *G3787*
Mt 24:48 But **s** that servant is wicked and says to *G1569*
Lk 7:43 "*I* **s** the one who had the bigger debt *G5696*
Lk 11: 5 said to them, "*S* you **have** a friend, and you AIT
Lk 11: 7 And *s* the one inside **answers**, 'Don't bother AIT
Lk 12:45 But **s** the servant says to himself, 'My *G1569*
Lk 14:28 "**S** one of you wants to build a tower *G1142*
Lk 14:31 "Or *s* a king *is* **about to** go to war against AIT
Lk 15: 4 "*S* one of you **has** a hundred sheep and loses AIT
Lk 15: 8 "Or **s** a woman has ten silver coins and *G1569*
Lk 17: 7 "*S* one of you **has** a servant plowing or AIT
Jn 21:25 *I* **s** *that* even the whole world would not *G3887*
Ac 2:15 are not drunk, as you **s**. It's only nine in *G5696*
Ac 13:25 'Who *do* you **s** I am? I am not the *G5706*
Jas 2: 2 **S** a man comes into your meeting wearing *G1569*
Jas 2:15 **S** a brother or a sister is without clothes *G1569*

SUPPOSED (1) [SUPPOSE]
1Sa 20: 5 and I *am* **s to dine** with the H3782+3782+430

SUPPOSEDLY (1) [SUPPOSE]
Jer 23:30 steal from one another words **s** from me. NDT

SUPPOSING (2) [SUPPOSE]
Jn 11:31 **s** she was going to the tomb to mourn *G1506*
Php 1:17 **s** that they can stir up trouble for me while *G3887*

SUPPRESS (1)
Ro 1:18 who **s** the truth by their wickedness *G2988*

SUPREMACY (1) [SUPREME]
Col 1:18 so that in everything he might have the **s**. *G4750*

SUPREME (4) [SUPREMACY]
2Ki 18:17 The king of Assyria sent his **s commander** H9580
Ecc 8: 4 Since a king's word is **s**, who can say to H8950
Isa 20: 1 In the year that the **s commander**, sent by H9580
1Pe 2:13 to the emperor, as the **s authority**, *G5660*

SUR (1)
2Ki 11: 6 a third at the S Gate, and a third at the H6075

SURE (60) [SURELY]
Ge 20: 7 *you may* **be s** that you and all who belong H3359
Ge 24: 6 "**Make s** *that* you do not take my son back H9068
Ge 32:20 And **be s** to say, 'Your servant Jacob is H2180
Ex 8:29 *let* Pharaoh *be s that he does* not **act deceitfully** AIT
Ex 10:28 **Make s** you do not appear before me H9068
Ex 17:14 **make s** *that* Joshua **hears** it H8492+928+265
Ex 23: 4 wandering off, **be s to return** it. H8740+8740
Ex 23: 5 it there; **be s** *you* **help** them with it. H6441+6441
Nu 26:55 **Be s** that the land is distributed by lot. H421
Nu 28: 2 '**Make s** that you present to me at the H9068
Nu 28:31 Be **s** the animals are without defect NDT
Nu 32:23 and *you may* **be s** that your sin will find H3359
Dt 5: 1 Learn them and **be s** to follow them. H9068
Dt 6:17 **Be s to keep** the commands of the H9068+9068
Dt 11:32 **be s** that you obey all the decrees and H9068
Dt 12:23 But **be s** you do not eat the blood H2616
Dt 14:22 **Be s to set aside a tenth** *of* all that H6923+6923
Dt 17:15 **be s to appoint** over you a king the H8492+8492
Dt 21:23 **Be s to bury** it that same day H7699+7699
Dt 22: 1 it but **be s to take** it **back** to its H8740+8740
Dt 22: 7 but **be s to let** the mother **go**, so H8938+8938
Dt 23:23 your lips utter *you must* **be s** to do, H9068
Dt 28:66 both night and day, never **s** of your life. H586
Dt 29:18 Make **s** there is no man or woman, clan or NDT
Dt 29:18 make **s** there is no root among you that NDT
Dt 31:29 *you are* **s to become utterly corrupt** H8845+8845
Jos 2:12 shown kindness to you. Give me a **s** sign H622
Jos 13: 6 **Be s** to allocate this land to Israel for an H8370
Jos 23:13 then *you may* **be s** that the LORD H3359+3359
Jdg 15: 2 "*I was* **so s** you hated her," he said H606+606
1Sa 12:24 But *be s to* **fear** the LORD and serve him AIT
1Sa 20: 7 *you can* **be s** that he is determined to H3359
1Sa 22:22 I knew *he would* **be s to tell** Saul. H5583+5583
1Ki 2:37 Valley, *you can* **be s** you will die H3359+3359
1Ki 2:42 *you can* **be s** you will die'? H3359+3359
Ezr 7:17 With this money **be s** to buy bulls, rams A10056
Ps 69:13 answer me with your **s** salvation. H622
Ps 132:11 oath to David, a **s** oath he will not revoke: H622
Pr 11:18 who sows righteousness reaps a **s** reward. H622
Pr 11:21 **Be s of this**: The wicked will H3338+4200+3338
Pr 16: 5 **Be s of this**: They will not H3338+4200+3338
Pr 27:23 **Be s** *you* **know** the condition of your H3359+3359
Isa 28:16 a precious cornerstone for a **s** foundation H3569
Isa 33: 6 He will be the **s foundation** *for* your times H575
Jer 42:19 go to Egypt.' **Be s** *of* this: I warn H3359+3359
Jer 42:22 So now, **be s** *of* this: You will die by H3359+3359
Eze 30: 9 day of Egypt's doom, for it is **s** to come. H2180
Mt 17:11 Jesus replied, "**To be s**, Elijah comes and *G3525*
Mk 9:12 Jesus replied, "**To be s**, Elijah does come *G3525*
Lk 1:18 asked the angel, "How *can I be* **s** of this? *G1182*
Lk 10:11 Yet **be s** of this: The kingdom *G1182*
Ac 13:34 you the holy and **s** blessings promised to *G4412*
Ro 5:13 **To be s**, sin was in the world before the *G1142*
Ro 15:28 and *have* **made s that** they *have* **received** *G5381*
2Co 13: 4 For **to be s**, he was crucified in weakness *G2779*
Gal 2: 2 I **wanted to be s** I was **not** running *G3590+4803*
Eph 5: 5 For of this you can be **s**: No immoral *G1182*
1Th 5:15 **Make s** that nobody pays back wrong for *G3972*
Titus 3:11 *You may be* **s** that such people are warped *G3857*
Heb 13:18 *We are* **s** that we have a clear conscience *G4275*

SURELY (309) [SURE]
Ge 6:13 I am **s** going to destroy both them and the H2180
Ge 9: 5 lifeblood I will **s** demand an accounting. H421
Ge 17:16 bless her and will **s** give you a son by her. H1685
Ge 17:20 I will **s** bless him; I will make him fruitful H2180
Ge 18:10 "*I will* **s return** to you about this H8740+8740
Ge 18:18 Abraham *will* **s become** a great and H2118+2118
Ge 20:11 'There is **s** no fear of God in this place H8370
Ge 22:17 *I will* **s bless** you and make your H1385+1385
Ge 26:11 his wife *shall* **s be put to death**." H4637+4637
Ge 28:16 he thought, "**S** the LORD is in this place, and H434
Ge 29:32 **S** my husband will love me now. H3954
Ge 31:16 **S** all the wealth that God took away from H3954
Ge 31:42 you would **s** have sent me away H3954+6964
Ge 32:12 '*I will* **s make** you **prosper** and will H3512+3512
Ge 37:33 Joseph *has* **s been torn to pieces**." H3271+3271
Ge 42:15 **As s as** Pharaoh **lives**, you will not leave H2644
Ge 42:16 then **as s as** Pharaoh **lives**, you are H2644
Ge 42:21 "**S** we are being punished because of our H66
Ge 44:28 I said, "He has **s** been torn to pieces." H421
Ge 46: 4 and I *will* **s bring** you **back** again. H6590+6590
Ge 50:24 God *will* **s come to** your **aid** and H7212+7212
Ge 50:25 "God *will* **s come to** your **aid**, and H7212+7212
Ex 4:25 "**S** you are a bridegroom of blood to me," H3954
Ex 13:19 "God *will* **s come to** your **aid**, and H7212+7212
Nu 14:21 **as s as I live** and as surely as the glory of H2644
Nu 14:21 surely as I live and as **s** as the glory of the NDT
Nu 14:28 So tell them, '**As s as I live**, declares the H2644
Nu 14:35 and I will **s** do these things to this H561+4202
Nu 14:40 the LORD promised. **S** we have sinned!" H3954
Nu 15:31 they **must s be cut off**; their guilt H4162+4162
Nu 26:65 Israelites *they would* **s die** in the H4637+4637
Dt 4: 6 "**S** this great nation is a wise and H8370
Dt 8:19 you today that *you will* **s be destroyed**. H6+6
Dt 32:40 solemnly swear: **As s as I live** forever, H2645
Dt 33: 3 **S** it is you who love the people; all the holy H677
Jos 2:24 "The LORD has **s** given the whole land into H3954
Jos 10:14 **S** the LORD was fighting for Israel H3954
Jdg 8:19 **As s as** the LORD **lives**, if you had spared H2644
Ru 3:13 **as s as** the LORD **lives** I will do it. H2644
1Sa 1:26 **As s as** you **live**, I am the woman H2644+5883
1Sa 10: 8 I will **s** come down to you to sacrifice H2180
1Sa 14:39 **As s as** the LORD who rescues Israel **lives** H2644
1Sa 14:45 **As s as** the LORD **lives**, not a hair of his H2644
1Sa 15:32 thought, "**S** the bitterness of death is past." H434
1Sa 16: 6 "**S** the LORD's anointed stands here before H421
1Sa 17:55 replied, "**As s as** you **live**, Your Majesty, H2644
1Sa 19: 6 "**As s as** the LORD **lives**, David will not be H2644
1Sa 20: 3 Yet **as s as** the LORD **lives** and as you live H2644
1Sa 20:12 that *I will* **s sound out** my father by this H2983

1Sa 20:21 because, as s as the LORD lives, you are H2644
1Sa 20:26 ceremonially unclean—s he is unclean." H3954
1Sa 22:16 "You will s die, Ahimelek, H4637+4637
1Sa 24:20 that you will s be king and that H4887+4887
1Sa 25:26 as s as the LORD your God lives and as you H2644
1Sa 25:34 as s as the LORD, the God of Israel, lives H2644
1Sa 26:10 As s as the LORD lives," he said, "the LORD H2644
1Sa 26:16 As s as the LORD lives, you and your men H2644
1Sa 26:21 S I have acted like a fool and have been H2180
1Sa 26:24 As s as I valued your life today, so may the H2180
1Sa 26:25 will do great things and s triumph." H3523+3523
1Sa 28: 9 "S you know what Saul has done. H2180
1Sa 28:10 the LORD, "As s as the LORD lives, you will H2644
1Sa 29: 6 "As s as the LORD lives, you have H2644
2Sa 2:27 answered, "As s as God lives, if you had H2644
2Sa 4: 9 "As s as the LORD lives, who has H2644
2Sa 5:19 for I will s deliver the Philistines H5989+5989
2Sa 9: 7 "for I will s show you kindness for H6913+6913
2Sa 11:11 As s as you live, I will H2644+2256+2644+5883
2Sa 12: 5 Nathan, "As s as the LORD lives, the man H2644
2Sa 14:11 "As s as the LORD lives," he said, "not H2644
2Sa 14:19 "As s as you live, my lord H2644+5883
2Sa 15:21 "As s as the LORD lives, and as my H2644
2Sa 18: 2 I myself will s march out with you. H3655+3655
2Sa 23: 5 s he would not have made with me an H3954
2Sa 23: 5 s he would not bring to fruition my H3954
1Ki 1:13 "S Solomon your son shall be king after H3954
1Ki 1:29 "As s as the LORD lives, who has delivered H2644
1Ki 1:30 I will s carry out this very day what I swore H3954
1Ki 2:24 And now, as s as the LORD lives—he who H2644
1Ki 11: 2 because they will s turn your hearts after H434
1Ki 17:12 "As s as the LORD your God lives," she H2644
1Ki 18:10 As s as the LORD your God lives, there is H2644
1Ki 18:15 I will s present myself to Ahab today." H3954
1Ki 18:27 "S he is a god! Perhaps he is H3954
1Ki 20:23 s we will be stronger than they. H561+4202
1Ki 20:25 Then s we will be stronger than they." H561+4202
1Ki 22:14 "As s as the LORD lives, I can tell H2644
1Ki 22:32 they thought, "S this is the king of Israel." H421
2Ki 2: 2 "As s as the LORD lives and as you live H2644
2Ki 2: 4 "As s as the LORD lives and as you live H2644
2Ki 2: 6 "As s as the LORD lives and as you live H2644
2Ki 3:14 "As s as the LORD Almighty lives, whom H2644
2Ki 4:30 "As s as the LORD lives and as you live H2644
2Ki 5:11 that he would s come out to me H3655+3655
2Ki 5:16 answered, "As s as the LORD lives, whom I H2644
2Ki 5:20 As s as the LORD lives, I will run after him H2644
2Ki 7:12 thinking, 'They will s come out, and then H3954
2Ki 9:26 and I will s make you pay for it on H561+4202
2Ki 18:30 'The LORD will s deliver us; this city H5911+5911
2Ki 19:11 S you have heard what the kings of Assyria H2180
2Ki 20:17 The time will s come when everything in H2180
2Ki 24: 3 S these things happened to Judah H421
2Ch 18:13 "As s as the LORD lives, I can tell H2644
Ezr 7:26 of the king must s be punished by death A10056
Est 6:13 him—you will s come to ruin!" H5877+5877
Job 1:11 and he will s curse you to your face." H4202+561
Job 2: 5 and he will s curse you to your face." H561+4202
Job 5: 7 born to trouble as s as sparks fly upward. H2256
Job 6: 3 It would s outweigh the sand of the seas H3954
Job 8:19 S its life withers away, and from the soil H2176
Job 8:20 "S God does not reject one who is H2176
Job 11:11 S he recognizes deceivers; and when he H3954
Job 11:16 You will s forget your trouble, recalling it H3954
Job 13:10 He would s call you to account if H3519+3519
Job 13:15 I will s defend my ways to his face. H421
Job 14:16 S then you will count my steps but not H3954
Job 16: 7 S, God, you have worn me out; you H421+6964
Job 17: 2 S mockers surround me; my eyes H561+4202
Job 18:21 S such is the dwelling of an evil man; such H421
Job 20: 4 "S you know how it has been from of old H2022
Job 20:20 "S he will have no respite from his craving H3954
Job 22:20 'S our foes are destroyed, and fire H561+4202
Job 22:26 S then you will find delight in the H3954
Job 27: 2 "As s as God lives, who has denied me H2644
Job 30:24 "S no one lays a hand on a broken man H421
Job 31:36 S I would wear it on my shoulder, H561+4202
Job 38: 5 off its dimensions? S you know! Who H3954
Job 38:21 S you know, for you were already born H3954
Job 42: 3 S I spoke of things I did not H4200+4027
Ps 5:12 S, LORD, you bless the righteous; you H3954
Ps 16: 6 s I have a delightful inheritance. H677
Ps 21: 6 S you have granted him unending H3954
Ps 23: 6 S your goodness and love will follow me H421
Ps 32: 6 s the rising of the mighty waters will not H8370
Ps 39: 6 "S everyone goes around like a mere H421
Ps 39:11 like a moth—s everyone is but a breath. H421
Ps 49:15 of the dead; he will s take me to himself. H3954
Ps 51: 5 S I was sinful at birth, sinful from the time H2176
Ps 52: 5 S God will bring you down to everlasting H1685
Ps 54: 4 S God is my help; the Lord is the one who H2180
Ps 58:11 will say, "S the righteous still are rewarded H421
Ps 58:11 s there is a God who judges the earth." H421
Ps 62: 4 S they intend to topple me from my lofty H421
Ps 62: 9 S the lowborn are but a breath, the H421
Ps 64: 6 S the human mind and heart are cunning. H2256
Ps 66:19 God has s listened and has heard my H434
Ps 68:21 S God will crush the heads of his enemies H421
Ps 73: 1 S God is good to Israel, to those who are H421
Ps 73:13 S in vain I have kept my heart pure and H421
Ps 73:18 S you place them on slippery ground; you H421
Ps 76:10 S your wrath against mankind brings you H3954
Ps 85: 9 S his salvation is near those who fear him H421
Ps 89:21 sustain him; s my arm will strengthen him. H677
Ps 91: 3 S he will save you from the fowler's snare H3954
Ps 92: 9 For s your enemies, LORD, surely your H2180
Ps 92: 9 s your enemies will perish; all H2180
Ps 112: 6 S the righteous will never be shaken; they H3954
Ps 139:11 "S the darkness will hide me and the light H421
Ps 140:13 S the righteous will praise your name, and H421
Pr 2:18 S her house leads down to death and her H3954
Pr 11:15 security for a stranger will s suffer, H8317+8273
Pr 17:26 s to flog honest officials is not right. H1685
Pr 21: 5 lead to profit as s as haste leads to poverty. H421
Pr 23: 5 for they will s sprout wings and fly H6913+6913
Pr 23:18 There is s a future hope for you, and H3954+561
Pr 24: 6 S you need guidance to wage war, and H3954
Pr 30: 2 S I am only a brute, not a man; I do not H3954
Pr 30: 4 what is the name of his son? S you know! H3954
Ecc 3:19 S the fate of human beings is like that of H3954
Isa 5: 9 "S the great houses will become H561+4202
Isa 9:18 S wickedness burns like a fire; it H3954
Isa 12: 2 S God is my salvation; I will trust and not H2180
Isa 14:24 has sworn, "S, as I have planned, H561+4202
Isa 25: 9 day they will say, "S this is our God; we H2180
Isa 36:15 'The LORD will s deliver us; this city H5911+5911
Isa 37:11 S you have heard what the kings of Assyria H2180
Isa 38:17 S it was for my benefit that I suffered such H2180
Isa 39: 6 The time will s come when everything in H2180
Isa 40: 7 LORD blows on them. S the people are grass H434
Isa 40:15 S the nations are like a drop in a bucket H2176
Isa 41:11 rage against you will s be ashamed and NDT
Isa 45:14 'S God is with you, and there is no H421
Isa 47:14 S they are like stubble; the fire will burn H2180
Isa 49:18 As s as I live," declares the LORD, "you will H2644
Isa 51: 3 The LORD will s comfort Zion and will look H3954
Isa 53: 4 S he took up our pain and bore our H434
Isa 55: 5 S you will summon nations you know not H2176
Isa 56: 3 "The LORD will s exclude me from his H976+976
Isa 59: 1 S the arm of the LORD is not too short to H2176
Isa 60: 9 S the islands look to me; in the lead are H3954
Isa 63: 8 He said, "S they are my people, children H421
Jer 3:23 S the idolatrous commotion on the hills H434
Jer 3:23 s in the LORD our God is the salvation of H434
Jer 4: 2 'As s as the LORD lives,' then the H2644
Jer 5: 2 they say, 'As s as the LORD lives,' still they H2644
Jer 5: 5 to them; s they know the way of the LORD H3954
Jer 12:16 'As s as the LORD lives'—even as H2644
Jer 15:11 "S I will deliver you for a good H561+4202
Jer 15:11 s I will make your enemies plead H561+4202
Jer 16:14 be said, 'As s as the LORD lives, who H2644
Jer 16:15 be said, 'As s as the LORD lives, who H2644
Jer 22: 6 I will s make you like a wasteland H561+4202
Jer 22:24 "As s as I live," declares the LORD, "even if H2644
Jer 23: 7 'As s as the LORD lives, who brought H2644
Jer 23: 8 will say, 'As s as the LORD lives, who H2644
Jer 23:39 I will s forget you and cast you out H5960+5960
Jer 29:32 I will s punish Shemaiah the Nehelamite H2180
Jer 30:10 'I will s save you out of a distant place H3954
Jer 31:18 "I have s heard Ephraim's moaning H9048+9048
Jer 32:37 I will s gather them from all the lands H2180
Jer 34: 3 grasp but will s be captured and H9530+9530
Jer 37: 9 will s leave us. H2143+4946+6584+2143
Jer 38:16 "As s as the LORD lives, who has given us H2644
Jer 44:26 "As s as the Sovereign LORD lives. H2644
Jer 44:29 of harm against you will s stand. H7756+7756
Jer 46:18 "As s as I live," declares the King, whose H2644
Jer 46:27 I will s save you out of a distant place H3954
Jer 49:26 S, her young men will fall in the H4200+4027
Jer 51:14 I will s fill you with troops, as with a H3954+561
Jer 51:47 For the time will s come when I will H2180
Eze 3: 6 S if I had sent you to them, they would H4202
Eze 3:18 person, 'You will s die,' and you do H4637+4637
Eze 3:21 they will s live because they took H2649+2649
Eze 5:11 Therefore as s as I live, declares the H2644
Eze 7: 4 I will s repay you for your conduct and H3954
Eze 14:16 as s as I live, declares the Sovereign LORD H2644
Eze 14:18 as s as I live, declares the Sovereign LORD H2644
Eze 14:20 as s as I live, declares the Sovereign LORD H2644
Eze 16:43 I will s bring down on your head what you H2026
Eze 16:48 As s as I live, declares the Sovereign LORD H2644
Eze 17:16 " 'As s as I live, declares the Sovereign H2644
Eze 17:19 As s as I live, I will repay him for H2644
Eze 18: 3 "As s as I live, declares the Sovereign H2644
Eze 18: 9 righteous; he will s live, declares H2649+2649
Eze 18:17 his father's sin; he will s live. H2649+2649
Eze 18:19 keep all my decrees, he will s live. H2649+2649
Eze 18:21 that person will s live; they H2649+2649
Eze 18:28 that person will s live; they H2649+2649
Eze 20: 3 As s as I live, I will not let you inquire of H2644
Eze 20:31 As s as I live, declares the Sovereign LORD H2644
Eze 20:33 As s as I live, declares the Sovereign LORD H2644
Eze 20:39 afterward you will s listen to me and H561+401
Eze 21: 7 It will s take place, declares the Sovereign H2118
Eze 21:13 " 'Testing will s come. And what if even H3954
Eze 22:13 " 'I will s strike my hands together at the H2180
Eze 33: 8 person, you will s die,' and you do H4637+4637
Eze 33:11 Say to them, 'As s as I live, declares the H2644
Eze 33:13 person that they will s live, H2649+2649
Eze 33:14 person, 'You will s die,' but they H4637+4637
Eze 33:15 evil—that person will s live; they H2649+2649
Eze 33:16 is just and right; they will s live. H2649+2649
Eze 33:24 s the land has been given to us as our NDT
Eze 33:27 As s as I live, those who are left in the H2644
Eze 33:33 comes true—and it s will—then they will H2180
Eze 34: 8 As s as I live, declares the Sovereign LORD H2644
Eze 35: 6 therefore as s as I live, declares the H2644
Eze 35:11 therefore as s as I live, declares the H2644
Eze 39: 8 It will s take place, declares the Sovereign H2180
Da 2:47 "S your God is the God A10427+10643+10168
Hos 4:15 And do not swear, 'As s as the LORD lives!' H2644
Hos 6: 3 As s as the sun rises, he will appear; he H3869
Joel 1:12 S the people's joy is withered away H3954
Joel 2:20 S he has done great things H3954
Joel 2:21 S the LORD has done great things! H3954
Am 3: 7 S the Sovereign LORD does nothing H3954
Am 4: 2 "The time will s come when you will be H3954
Am 5: 5 For Gilgal will s go into exile, and H1655+1655
Am 7:11 and Israel will s go into exile, away H1655+1655
Am 7:17 And Israel will s go into exile H1655+1655
Am 8:14 who say, 'As s as your god lives, Dan,' or, H2644
Am 8:14 'As s as the god of Beersheba lives' H2644
Am 9: 8 "S the eyes of the Sovereign LORD are on H2180
Mic 2:12 "I will s gather all of you, Jacob; I will H665+665
Mic 2:12 I will s bring together the remnant H7695+7695
Zep 2: 9 Therefore, as s as I live," declares the H2644
Zep 2: 9 "s Moab will become like Sodom H3954
Zep 3: 7 'S you will fear me and accept correction! H421
Zec 2: 9 I will s raise my hand against them so that H3954
Zec 10: 8 S I will redeem them; they will be as H3954
Mal 4: 1 "S the day is coming; it will burn H3954+2180
Mt 26:22 the other, "S you don't mean me, Lord?" G3614
Mt 26:25 said, "S you don't mean me, Rabbi?" G3614
Mt 26:73 to Peter and said, "S you are one of them G242
Mt 27:54 exclaimed, "S he was the Son of God!" G242
Mt 28:20 And s I am with you always, to the very G2627
Mk 14:19 they said to him, "S you don't mean me?" G3614
Mk 14:70 near said to Peter, "S you are one of them G242
Mk 15:39 he said, "S this man was the Son of God!" G242
Lk 4:23 "S you will quote this proverb to me: G4122
Lk 11: 8 audacity he will s get up and give you as AIT
Lk 13:33 for s no prophet can die outside Jerusalem! AIT
Lk 23:47 said, "S this was a righteous man. G3953
Jn 3: 4 "S they cannot enter a second time G3590+1538
Jn 6:14 "S this is the Prophet who is to come into G242
Jn 7:40 people said, "S this man is the Prophet." G242
Jn 18:21 who heard me. S they know what I said." G2623
Ac 10:14 "S not, Lord!" Peter replied. "I have never G3592
Ac 10:47 "S no one can stand in the way of their G3614
Ac 11: 8 "I replied, 'S not, Lord! Nothing impure G3592
Ro 14:11 " 'As s as I live,' says the Lord, 'every knee AIT
1Co 9: 2 an apostle to others, s I am to you! G247+1145
1Co 9:10 S he says this for us, doesn't he? Yes, this G4122
1Co 15:31 yes, just as s as I boast about you in Christ G3755
2Co 1:18 But as s as God is faithful, our message to G1254
2Co 11:10 As s as the truth of Christ is in me, nobody in AIT
Eph 3: 2 S you have heard about the G1623+1145
1Th 2: 9 S you remember, brothers and sisters, our G1142
Heb 2:16 For s it is not angels he helps, but G1327
Heb 6:14 "I will s bless you and give you G1623+3605

SURETY (KJV) CERTAIN, ENSURE, GUARANTEE, GUARANTEED, GUARANTOR, PLEDGE, REALLY, SECURITY, WITHOUT A DOUBT

SURF (1)

Ac 27:41 broken to pieces by the pounding of the s. G3246

SURFACE (11) [SURFACES]

Ge 1: 2 darkness was over the s of the deep, and H7156
Ge 2: 6 watered the whole s of the ground. H7156
Ge 7:18 the ark floated on the s of the water. H7156
Ge 8: 8 had receded from the s of the ground. H7156
Ge 8: 9 there was water over all the s of the earth; H7156
Ge 8:13 saw that the s of the ground was dry. H7156
Lev 14:37 appear to be deeper than the s of the wall, NDT
Job 24:18 "Yet they are foam on the s of the water H7156
Job 38:30 when the s of the deep is frozen? H7156
Isa 28:25 When he has leveled the s, does he not H7156
Hos 10: 7 away like a twig on the s of the waters. H7156

SURFACES (1) [SURFACE]

1Ki 7:36 palm trees on the s of the supports and H4283

SURGE (2) [SURGED, SURGING]

Job 40:23 though the Jordan should s against its H1631
Isa 54: 8 In a s of anger I hid my face from you H9192

SURGED (1) [SURGE]

1Sa 17:52 Israel and Judah s forward with a shout H7756

SURGING (7) [SURGE]

Ex 15: 8 The s waters stood up like a wall; the H5689
Ps 46: 3 the mountains quake with their s. H1452
Ps 89: 9 You rule over the s sea; when its waves H1455
Isa 17:13 the peoples roar like the roar of s waters, H8041
Jer 46: 7 rises like the Nile, like rivers of s waters? H1723
Jer 46: 8 rises like the Nile, like rivers of s waters. H1723
Zec 10:11 the s sea will be subdued and all the H1644

SURLY (1)

1Sa 25: 3 her husband was s and mean in his H7997

SURMOUNTED (1)

Eze 40:16 the gateway were s by narrow parapet H448

SURNAME, SURNAMED (KJV) BESTOW, CALLED, KNOWN, NAME, TAKE

SURPASS (1) [ALL-SURPASSING, SURPASSED, SURPASSES, SURPASSING, SURPASSINGLY]
Pr 31:29 do noble things, but you s them all." H6590

SURPASSED (2) [SURPASS]
Jn 1:15 after me has s me because he G1869+1181
Jn 1:30 after me has s me because he G1869+1181

SURPASSES (4) [SURPASS]
Ps 138: 2 solemn decree that it s your fame. H6584+3972
Pr 8:19 than fine gold; what I yield s choice silver. H4946
Mt 5:20 your righteousness s that of the G4355+4498
Eph 3:19 to know this love that s knowledge G5650

SURPASSING (4) [SURPASS]
Ps 150: 2 of power; praise him for his s greatness. H8044
2Co 3:10 glory now in comparison with the s glory. G5650
2Co 9:14 because of the s grace God has given you. G5650
Php 3: 8 because of the s worth of knowing Christ G5660

SURPASSINGLY (1) [SURPASS]
2Co 12: 7 because of these s great revelations G5651

SURPLUS (1)
Lk 12:18 there I will store my s grain. G4246+2779+19

SURPRISE (6) [SURPRISED, SURPRISING]
Jos 10: 9 march from Gilgal, Joshua took them by s. H7328
Ps 35: 8 may ruin overtake them by s—may H4202+3359
Ps 55:15 Let death take my enemies by s; let them H5958
Jer 14: 9 Why are you like a man taken by s, like a H1850
Ac 3:12 why does this s you? Why do you G2513
1Th 5: 4 so that this day should s you like a thief. G2898

SURPRISED (8) [SURPRISE]
Ecc 5: 8 rights denied, do not be s at such things H9449
Mk 15:44 Pilate was s to hear that he was already G2513
Lk 11:38 But the Pharisee was s when he noticed G2513
Jn 3: 7 You should not be s at my saying, 'You G2513
Jn 4:27 returned and were s to find him talking G2513
1Pe 4: 4 They are s that you do not join them in G3826
1Pe 4:12 do not be s at the fiery ordeal that has G3826
1Jn 3:13 Do not be s, my brothers and sisters, if the G2513

SURPRISING (1) [SURPRISE]
2Co 11:15 It is not s, then, if his servants also G3489

SURRENDER (11) [SURRENDERED, SURRENDERS]
Jos 20: 5 the elders must not s the H6037+928+3338
1Sa 11: 3 one comes to rescue us, we will s to you." H3655
1Sa 11:10 "Tomorrow we will s to you, and you can H3655
1Sa 23:11 Will the citizens of Keilah s me to him H6037
1Sa 23:12 "Will the citizens of Keilah s me and my H6037
2Ki 7: 4 over to the camp of the Arameans and s. H5877
Isa 54:15 whoever attacks you will s to you. H5877
Jer 38:17 'If you s to the officers of the king H3655+3655
Jer 38:18 But if you will not s to the officers of the H3655
Jer 38:21 But if you refuse to s, this is what the LORD H3655
Da 8:13 the s of the sanctuary and the trampling H5989

SURRENDERED (2) [SURRENDER]
2Ki 24:12 his nobles and his officials all s to him. H3655
Lk 23:25 they asked for, and s Jesus to their will. G4140

SURRENDERS (2) [SURRENDER]
Jer 21: 9 goes out and s to the Babylonians H5877
Jer 50:15 She s, her towers fall, her walls are H5989+3338

SURROUND (21) [SURROUNDED, SURROUNDING, SURROUNDS]
Jos 7: 9 about this and they will s us and wipe out H6015
Job 16:13 his archers s me. Without pity, he pierces H6015
Job 17: 2 Surely mockers s me; my eyes must dwell H6643
Job 40:22 shadow; the poplars by the stream s it. H6015
Ps 5:12 you s them with your favor as with a H6496
Ps 17: 9 from my mortal enemies who s me. H5938
Ps 17:11 me down, they now s me, with eyes H6015
Ps 22:12 Many bulls s me; strong bulls of Bashan H6015
Ps 22:16 Dogs s me, a pack of villains encircles me; H6015
Ps 27: 6 be exalted above the enemies who s me; H6017
Ps 32: 7 me from trouble and s me with songs of H6015
Ps 40:12 For troubles without number s me; my sins H705
Ps 49: 5 when wicked deceivers s me— H6015
Ps 88:17 All day long they s me like a flood; they H6015
Ps 89: 7 he is more awesome than all who s him. H6017
Ps 97: 2 Clouds and thick darkness s him H6017
Ps 109: 3 With words of hatred they s me; they H6015
Ps 125: 2 As the mountains s Jerusalem, so the H6017
Ps 140: 9 Those who s me proudly rear their heads H4990
Jer 4:17 They s her like men H2118+6017+4946
Jer 12: 9 prey that other birds of prey s and attack? H6017

SURROUNDED (27) [SURROUND]
Ge 19: 4 both young and old—s the house. H6015
Jdg 16: 2 So they s the place and lay in wait for him H6015
Jdg 19:22 of the wicked men of the city s the house. H6015
Jdg 20: 5 Gibeah came after me and s the house, H6015
Jdg 20:43 They s the Benjamites, chased them and H4193
2Sa 18:15 ten of Joab's armor-bearers s Absalom, H6015
1Ki 7:12 great courtyard was s by a wall of three H6017
2Ki 3:25 armed with slings s it and attacked it. H6015
2Ki 6:14 They went by night and s the city. H5938
2Ki 6:15 with horses and chariots had s the city. H6015
2Ki 8:21 The Edomites s him and his chariot H6015
1Ch 29:30 circumstances that s him and Israel and H6296
2Ch 21: 9 The Edomites s him and his chariot H6015
Ps 118:10 All the nations s me, but in the name of H6015
Ps 118:11 They s me on every side, but in the name H6015
Ecc 9:14 s it and built huge siege works against it. H6015
La 3: 5 me and s me with bitterness and H5938
Eze 1: 4 flashing lightning and s by brilliant light. H6017
Eze 1:27 looked like fire; and brilliant light s him. H6017
Eze 27:32 ever silenced like Tyre, s by the sea?" H928+9348
Eze 32:22 she is s by the graves of all her slain H6017
Hos 11:12 Ephraim has s me with lies, Israel with H6015
Jnh 2: 5 the deep s me; seaweed was H6015
Lk 21:20 you see Jerusalem being s by armies, G3240
Jn 5: 2 Bethesda and which is s by five covered G2400
Heb 12: 1 since we are s by such a great cloud of G4329
Rev 20: 9 of the earth and s the camp of God's G3238

SURROUNDING (58) [SURROUND]
Ge 41:48 he put the food grown in the fields s it. H6017
Ex 38:20 of the s courtyard were bronze H6017
Ex 38:31 the bases for the s courtyard and those H6017
Ex 38:31 tabernacle and those for the s courtyard. H6017
Nu 3:26 to the courtyard s the tabernacle and altar H6017
Nu 3:37 as the posts of the s courtyard with their H6017
Nu 4:26 of the courtyard s the tabernacle and altar H6017
Nu 4:32 as the posts of the s courtyard with their H6017
Nu 21:25 Heshbon and all its s settlements. H1426
Nu 21:32 captured its s settlements and drove out H1426
Nu 32:42 Kenath and its s settlements and called it H1426
Jos 15:45 with its s settlements and villages; H1426
Jos 15:47 Ashdod, its s settlements and villages H1426
Jos 17:11 together with their s settlements (the third H1426
Jos 21:11 with its s pastureland, in the hill country H6017
Jos 21:42 Each of these towns had pasturelands s it H6017
Jdg 1:27 Megiddo and their s settlements, H1426
Jdg 11:26 the s settlements and all the towns along H1426
1Ki 4:31 And his fame spread to all the s nations. H6017
2Ki 25: 4 though the Babylonians were s the city. H6017
1Ch 2:23 as well as Kenath with its s settlements H1426
1Ch 4:32 Their s villages were Etam, Ain, Rimmon H2958
1Ch 6:55 Hebron in Judah with its s pasturelands. H6017
1Ch 7:28 included Bethel and its s villages, H1426
1Ch 8:12 who built Ono and Lod with its s villages), H1426
1Ch 11: 8 from the terraces to the s wall, while Joab H6017
1Ch 18: 1 Gath and its s villages from the control H1426
1Ch 28:12 temple of the LORD and all the s rooms, H6017
2Ch 13:19 Ephron, with their s villages. H1426
2Ch 17:10 on all the kingdoms of the lands s Judah, H6017
2Ch 20:29 came on all the s kingdoms when they H824S
2Ch 28:18 Timnah and Gimzo, with their s villages. H1426
Ne 3:22 made by the priests from the s region. H3971
Ne 5:17 those who came to us from the s nations. H6017
Ne 6:16 all the s nations were afraid and lost their H6017
Ne 11:25 lived in Kiriath Arba and its s settlements, H1426
Jer 1:15 come against all her s walls and against H6017
Jer 25: 9 inhabitants and against all the s nations. H6017
Jer 34: 1 against Jerusalem and all its s towns, NDT
Jer 49: 2 and its s villages will be set on fire. H1426
Jer 52: 7 though the Babylonians were s the city. H6017
Jer 52:23 above the s network was a hundred. H6017
Eze 34:26 make them and the places s my hill a H6017
Eze 40: 5 saw a wall completely s the temple H6017+6017
Eze 41: 7 The structure s the temple was built in H6015
Eze 43:12 All the s area on top of the H6017+6017
Zec 7: 7 Jerusalem and its s towns were at rest H6017
Zec 12: 2 a cup that sends all the s peoples reeling. H6017
Zec 12: 6 will consume all the s peoples right and H6017
Zec 14:14 The wealth of all the s nations will be H6017
Mt 14:35 they sent word to all the s country. G4369
Mk 6:36 that they can go to the s countryside and G3241
Lk 4:37 about him spread throughout the s area. G4369
Lk 7:17 throughout Judea and the s country. G4369
Lk 9:12 so they can go to the s villages and G3241
Ac 14: 6 of Lystra and Derbe and to the s country, G4369
Jude 7 Gomorrah and the s towns gave G4309
Rev 4: 4 S the throne were twenty-four other G3239

SURROUNDS (3) [SURROUND]
Ps 32:10 unfailing love s the one who trusts in H6015
Ps 89: 8 are mighty, and your faithfulness s you. H6017
Ps 125: 2 so the LORD s his people both now and H6017

SURVEY (2) [SURVEYED]
Jos 18: 4 them out to make a s of the land H2143+928
Jos 18: 8 "Go and make a s of the land and H2143+928

SURVEYED (1) [SURVEY]
Ecc 2:11 Yet when I s all that my hands had done H7155

SURVIVE (15) [SURVIVED, SURVIVES, SURVIVING, SURVIVOR, SURVIVORS]
Dt 4:27 only a few of you will s among the H8636
Jos 11:22 only in Gaza, Gath and Ashdod did any s. H8636
2Sa 1:10 that after he had fallen he could not s. H2649
Job 27:15 The plague will bury those who s him H8586
Isa 66:19 some of those who s to the nations— H7128
Jer 21: 7 the people in this city who s the plague, H8636
Jer 31: 2 "The people who s the sword will find H8586
Jer 42:17 not one of them will s or escape the H8586
Jer 44:14 Egypt will escape or s to return to the land H8586
Am 7: 2 How can Jacob s? He is so small! H7756
Am 7: 5 How can Jacob s? He is so H7756
Zec 10: 9 They and their children will s, and they H2649
Mt 24:22 no one would s, but for the sake of G5392
Mk 13:20 not cut short those days, no one would s. G5392
Ac 27:34 You need it to s. Not one of you will G5401

SURVIVED (9) [SURVIVE]
Ex 14:28 Israelites into the sea. Not one of them s. H8636
Nu 14:38 of Nun and Caleb son of Jephunneh s. H2649
Dt 5:26 speaking out of fire, as we have, and s? H2649
1Sa 11:11 Those who s were scattered, so that no H8636
Ne 1: 2 the Jewish remnant that had s the exile, H8636
Ne 1: 3 "Those who s the exile and are back in H8636
Ps 106:11 their adversaries; not one of them s. H3855
Jer 41:16 away all the people of Mizpah who had s, H8642
La 2:22 of the LORD's anger no one escaped or s; H8586

SURVIVES (4) [SURVIVE]
2Ki 19: 4 Therefore pray for the remnant that still s." H5162
Isa 37: 4 Therefore pray for the remnant that still s." H5162
Eze 6:12 anyone who s and is spared will die H8636
1Co 3:14 If what has been built s, the builder will G3531

SURVIVING (4) [SURVIVE]
Dt 28:54 he loves or his s children, H3856+889+3855
Isa 11:11 time to reclaim the s remnant of his H8636
Jer 29: 1 from Jerusalem to the s elders among the H3856
Eze 17:14 to rise again, s only by keeping his treaty. H6641

SURVIVOR (5) [SURVIVE]
Jdg 12: 5 whenever a s of Ephraim said, "Let H7127
2Ki 10:11 friends and his priests, leaving him no s. H8586
2Ki 10:14 forty-two of them. He left no s. H8636
Ezr 9:14 to destroy us, leaving us no remnant or s? H7129
Job 18:19 his people, no s where once he lived. H8586

SURVIVORS (41) [SURVIVE]
Nu 21:35 his whole army, leaving them no s. H8586
Nu 24:19 out of Jacob and destroy the s of the city." H8586
Dt 2:34 women and children. We left no s. H8586
Dt 3: 3 We struck them down, leaving no s. H8586
Dt 7:20 them until even the s who hide from you H8636
Jos 8:22 leaving them neither s nor fugitives. H8586
Jos 10:20 a few s managed to reach their H8572
Jos 10:28 He left no s. And he did to the king H8586
Jos 10:30 He left no s there. And he did to H8586
Jos 10:33 him and his army—until no s were left. H8586
Jos 10:37 They left no s. Just as at Eglon, H8586
Jos 10:39 They left no s. They did to Debir and H8586
Jos 10:40 He left no s. He totally destroyed H8586
Jos 11: 8 Mizpah on the east, until no s were left. H8586
Jos 23:12 yourselves with the s of these nations that H3856
Jdg 21:17 The Benjamite s must have heirs," they H7129
2Sa 21: 2 a part of Israel but were s of the Amorites; H3856
2Ki 19:31 out of Mount Zion a band of s. H7129
Ezr 1: 4 in any locality where s may now be living, H8636
Ps 76:10 the s of your wrath are restrained. H8642
Isa 1: 9 the LORD Almighty had left us some s, H8586
Isa 4: 2 be the pride and glory of the s in Israel. H7129
Isa 10:20 of Israel, the s of Jacob, will no longer H7129
Isa 14:22 "I will wipe out Babylon's name and s H8637
Isa 14:30 I will destroy by famine; it will slay your s. H8642
Isa 16:14 her s will be very few and feeble. H8637
Isa 21:17 The s of the archers, the warriors of Kedar H8637
Isa 37:32 out of Mount Zion a band of s. H7129
Jer 8: 3 all the s of this evil nation will prefer H8642
Jer 15: 9 I will put the s to the sword before their H8642
Jer 24: 8 his officials and the s from Jerusalem H8642
Jer 47: 4 to remove all s who could help Tyre H8586
Eze 5:10 will scatter all your s to the winds. H8642
Eze 14:22 Yet there will be some s—sons and H7129
Eze 17:21 the s will be scattered to the winds. H8636
Joel 2:32 even among the s whom the LORD calls. H8586
Ob 14 hand over their s in the day of their H8586
Ob 18 There will be no s from Esau." The LORD H8586
Zep 2: 9 the s of my nation will inherit their land." H3856
Zec 14:16 Then the s from all the nations that have H3855
Rev 11:13 the s were terrified and gave glory to G3370

SUSA (22)
Ezr 4: 9 Uruk and Babylon, the Elamites of S, A10704
Ne 1: 1 while I was in the citadel of S, H8809
Est 1: 2 from his royal throne in the citadel of S, H8809
Est 1: 5 the greatest who were in the citadel of S. H8809
Est 2: 3 women into the harem at the citadel of S. H8809
Est 2: 5 in the citadel of S a Jew of the tribe of H8809
Est 2: 8 to the citadel of S and put under the care H8809
Est 3:15 the edict was issued in the citadel of S. H8809
Est 3:15 to drink, but the city of S was bewildered. H8809
Est 4: 8 which had been published in S, to show H8809
Est 4:16 gather together all the Jews who are in S H8809
Est 8:14 the edict was issued in the citadel of S. H8809
Est 8:15 And the city of S held a joyous H8809
Est 9: 6 In the citadel of S, the Jews killed and H8809
Est 9:11 in the citadel of S was reported to the H8809
Est 9:12 the ten sons of Haman in the citadel of S. H8809
Est 9:13 "give the Jews in S permission to carry out H8809
Est 9:14 An edict was issued in S, and they H8809
Est 9:15 The Jews in S came together on the H8809
Est 9:15 they put to death in S three hundred men, H8809
Est 9:18 The Jews in S, however, had assembled H8809

Da 8: 2 in the citadel of **S** in the province of Elam; H8809

SUSAH See HAZAR SUSAH

SUSANNA (1)

Lk 8: 3 Herod's household; **S**; and many others. *G5052*

SUSI (1)

Nu 13:11 a tribe of Joseph), Gaddi son of **S**; H6064

SUSIM See HAZAR SUSIM

SUSPECTS (3) [SUSPICIONS]

Nu 5:14 her husband and *he* **s** his wife and she is H7861
Nu 5:14 if he is jealous and **s** her even though she H7861
Nu 5:30 come over a man because *he* **s** his wife. H7861

SUSPENDS (1)

Job 26: 7 empty space; *he* **s** the earth over nothing. H9434

SUSPENSE (3)

Dt 28:66 You will live *in* constant **s**, filled with H9428
Jn 10:24 long *will you* **keep** us **in s**? *G3836+6034+149*
Ac 27:33 "*you have been* **in** *constant* **s** and have *G4659*

SUSPICIONS (1) [SUSPECTS]

1Ti 6: 4 result in envy, strife, malicious talk, evil **s** *G5707*

SUSTAIN (9) [SUSTAINED, SUSTAINING, SUSTAINS]

Ru 4:15 renew your life and **s** you *in* your old age. H3920
Job 36:19 *Would* your wealth or even ... efforts **s** H6885
Ps 51:12 grant me a willing spirit, *to* **s** me. H6164
Ps 55:22 your cares on the LORD and he *will* **s** you; H3920
Ps 89:21 My hand *will* **s** him; surely my arm will H3922
Ps 119:116 **S** me, my God, according to your promise H6164
Ps 119:175 may praise you, and *may* your laws **s** me. H6468
Isa 46: 4 hairs I am he, I am he *who will* **s** you. H6022
Isa 46: 4 I *will* **s** you and I will rescue you. H6022

SUSTAINED (4) [SUSTAIN]

Ge 27:37 and *I have* **s** him *with* grain and new wine H6164
Ne 9:21 For forty years *you* **s** them in the H3920
Isa 59:16 him, and his own righteousness **s** him. H6164
Isa 63: 5 salvation for me, and my own wrath **s** me. H6164

SUSTAINING (1) [SUSTAIN]

Heb 1: 3 **s** all things by his powerful word. *G5770*

SUSTAINS (8) [SUSTAIN]

Ps 3: 5 I wake again, because the LORD **s** me. H6164
Ps 18:35 your right hand **s** me; your help has H6184
Ps 41: 3 The LORD **s** them on their sickbed and H6184
Ps 54: 4 is my help; the Lord is the *one who* **s** me. H6164
Ps 104:15 faces shine, and bread *that* **s** their hearts. H6184
Ps 146: 9 the foreigner and **s** the fatherless and the H6386
Ps 147: 6 The LORD **s** the humble but casts the H6386
Isa 50: 4 to know the word *that* **s** the weary. H6431

SWADDLED, SWADDLING, SWADDLINGBAND (KJV) CARED FOR, WRAPPED (IN CLOTHS)

SWALLOW (14) [SWALLOWED, SWALLOWING, SWALLOWS]

Nu 16:34 shouting, "The earth *is going to* **s** us too!" H1180
2Sa 20:19 Why *do you want to* **s up** the LORD's H1180
2Sa 20:20 "Far be it from me *to* **s up** or destroy! H1180
Ps 21: 9 The LORD *will* **s** them **up** in his wrath, and H1180
Ps 69:15 me or the depths **s** me **up** or the pit close H1180
Ps 84: 3 found a home, and the **s** a nest for herself H2000
Pr 1:12 *let's* **s** them alive, like the grave, and H1180
Pr 26: 2 Like a fluttering sparrow or a darting **s**, an H2000
Isa 25: 8 *he will* **s up** death forever. The Sovereign H1180
Isa 28: 4 them and take them in hand, *they* **s** them. H1180
Hos 8: 7 it to yield grain, foreigners *would* **s** it **up**. H1180
Jnh 1:17 the LORD provided a huge fish to **s** Jonah, H1180
Hab 1:13 while the wicked **s up** those more H1180
Mt 23:24 You strain out a gnat but **s** a camel. *G2927*

SWALLOWED (22) [SWALLOW]

Ge 41: 7 heads of grain **s up** the seven healthy, H1180
Ge 41:24 thin heads of grain **s up** the seven good H1180
Ex 7:12 But Aaron's staff **s up** their staffs. H1180
Nu 16:32 opened its mouth and **s** them and their H1180
Nu 26:10 opened its mouth and **s** them along with H1180
Dt 11: 6 of all Israel and **s** them **up** with their H1180
2Sa 17:16 all the people with him *will* **be s up**. H1180
2Sa 18: 8 the forest **s up** more men that day than H430
Job 20:15 He will spit out the riches *he* **s**; God will H1180
Job 37:20 Would anyone ask *to* **be s up**? H1180
Ps 35:25 or say, "*We have* **s** him **up**." H1180
Ps 106:17 The earth opened up and **s** Dathan; it H1180
Ps 124: 3 *they would have* **s** us alive when their H1180
Jer 51:34 Like a serpent *he has* **s** us and filled his H1180
Jer 51:44 make him spew out **what** he has **s**. H1183
La 2: 2 pity the Lord *has* **s up** all the dwellings of H1180
La 2: 5 Lord is like an enemy; *he has* **s up** Israel. H1180
La 2: 5 *He has* **s up** all her palaces and destroyed H1180
La 2:16 their teeth and say, "*We have* **s** her **up**. H1180
Hos 8: 8 Israel **is s up**; now she is among the H1180
1Co 15:54 "Death *has been* **s up** in victory." *G2927*
2Co 5: 4 so that what is mortal *may be* **s up** by life. *G2927*

SWALLOWING (1) [SWALLOW]

Rev 12:16 opening its mouth and **s** the river that the *G2927*

SWALLOWS (2) [SWALLOW]

Ex 15:12 right hand, and the earth **s** your enemies. H1180
Nu 16:30 the earth opens its mouth and **s** them, H1180

SWAMPED (2) [SWAMPLAND, SWAMPS]

Mk 4:37 over the boat, so that it *was* nearly **s**. *G1153*
Lk 8:23 so that the boat *was being* **s**, and they *G5230*

SWAMPLAND (1) [SWAMPED]

Isa 14:23 her into a place for owls and into **s**; H106+4784

SWAMPS (1) [SWAMPED]

Eze 47:11 But the **s** and marshes will not become H1289

SWAN (KJV) WHITE OWL

SWARM (11) [SWARMED, SWARMING, SWARMS]

Ge 7:21 all the creatures that **s** over the earth, and H9237
Ex 10:12 Egypt so that locusts **s** over the land and H6590
Dt 1:44 you like a **s of bees** and beat you down H1805
Jdg 14: 8 in it he saw a **s** *of* bees and some H6337
Isa 33: 4 like a **s** *of* locusts people pounce on it. H5480
Jer 12:12 heights in the desert destroyers *will* **s**, H995
Jer 51:14 as with a **s of locusts**, and they will H3540
Jer 51:27 send up horses like a **s** of locusts. H6170
Joel 1: 4 What the **locust s** has left the great H1612
Joel 2:25 the other locusts and the **locust s**—my H1612
Na 3:15 they will devour you like a **s of locusts**. H3540

SWARMED (1) [SWARM]

Ps 118:12 *They* **s around** me like bees, but they H6015

SWARMING (1) [SWARM]

Lev 11:10 among all the **s things** or among all the H9238

SWARMS (10) [SWARM]

Ex 8:21 I will send **s of flies** on you and your H6856
Ex 8:22 people live; no **s of flies** will be there, so H6856
Ex 8:24 Dense **s of flies** poured into Pharaoh's H6856
Dt 28:42 **S of locusts** will take over all your trees H7526
Jdg 6: 5 livestock and their tents like **s** *of* locusts. H1896
Ps 78:45 He sent **s of flies** that devoured them, and H6856
Ps 105:31 there came **s of flies**, and gnats H6856
Eze 47: 9 **S** of living creatures will live wherever the H9237
Am 7: 1 He was preparing **s of locusts** after the H1479
Na 3:17 your officials like **s** *of* locusts that settle in H1571

SWAY (5) [SWAYED, SWAYING, SWAYS]

Jdg 9: 9 are honored, to **hold s** over the trees? H5675
Jdg 9:11 good and sweet, to **hold s** over the trees? H5675
Jdg 9:13 humans, to **hold s** over the trees? H5675
Job 28: 4 far from other people they dangle and **s**. H5675
Ps 72:16 the land; on the tops of the hills *may it* **s**. H8321

SWAYED (5) [SWAY]

Mt 11: 7 wilderness to see? A reed **s** by the wind? *G4888*
Mt 22:16 You aren't **s** by others, because you pay *G3508*
Mk 12:14 You aren't **s** by others, because you pay *G3508*
Lk 7:24 wilderness to see? A reed **s** by the wind? *G4888*
2Ti 3: 6 down with sins and *are* **s** by all kinds of evil *G72*

SWAYING (3) [SWAY]

1Ki 14:15 so that it will be like a reed **s** in the water. H5653
Isa 3:16 **strutting along with s hips** H2143+2256+3262
Jer 4:24 they were quaking; all the hills *were* **s**. H7837

SWAYS (2) [SWAY]

Job 40:17 Its tail **s** like a cedar; the sinews of its H2912
Isa 24:20 like a drunkard, *it* **s** like a hut in the wind H5653

SWEAR (58) [SWEARING, SWEARS, SWORE, SWORN]

Ge 21:23 Now **s** to me here before God *that* you will H8678
Ge 21:24 Abraham said, "I **s** it." H8678
Ge 22:16 "*I* **s** by myself, declares the LORD H8678
Ge 24: 3 *I* **want** you *to* **s** by the LORD, the God of H8678
Ge 24:37 And my master **made** me **s an oath**, and H8678
Ge 25:33 But Jacob said, "**S** to me first." So he H8678
Ge 47:31 "**S** to me," he said. Then Joseph swore to H8678
Ge 50: 5 'My father **made** me **s an oath** and said, "I H8678
Ge 50: 6 bury your father, as *he* **made** you **s** *to do*." H8678
Ge 50:25 Joseph **made** the Israelites **s an oath** and H8678
Ex 13:19 *had* **made** the Israelites **s an oath**. H8678+8678
Lev 5: 4 in any matter one might carelessly **s** about) H8652
Lev 6: 3 if *they* **s** falsely about any such sin that H8678
Lev 19:12 " '*Do* not **s** falsely by my name and so H8678
Dt 32:40 I lift my hand to heaven and **solemnly s**: As H606
Jos 2:12 please **s** to me by the LORD that you will H8678
Jos 2:17 "This oath *you* **made** us **s** will not be H8678
Jos 2:20 be released from the oath *you* **made** us **s**." H8678
Jos 23: 7 the names of their gods or **s** by them. H8678
Jdg 15: 7 *I* **s** *that* I won't **stop** until I get my revenge on AIT
Jdg 15:12 "**S** to me that you won't kill me yourselves." H8678
1Sa 20:12 said to David, "*I* **s** *by* **the** LORD, the God of AIT
1Sa 24:21 Now **s** to me by the LORD that you will not H8678
1Sa 30:15 "**S** to me before God that you will not kill H8678
2Sa 19: 7 *I* **s** by the LORD that if you don't go out, not H8678
1Ki 1:13 the king, *did* you not **s** to me your servant: H8678
1Ki 1:51 '*Let* King Solomon **s** to me today that he H8678
1Ki 2:42 "*Did* I not **make** you **s** by the LORD and H8678
1Ki 8:31 they come and **s the oath** before your H457
1Ki 18:10 *he* **made** them **s** they could not find you. H8678
1Ki 22:16 many times *must* I **make** you **s** to tell me H8678
2Ch 6:22 they come and **s the oath** before your H457
2Ch 18:15 many times *must* I **make** you **s** to tell me H8678
Ps 24: 4 not trust in an idol or **s** by a false god. H8678
Ps 63:11 all who **s** by God will glory in him H8678
Isa 19:18 of Canaan and **s allegiance** to the LORD H8678
Isa 45:23 knee will bow; by me every tongue *will* **s**. H8678
Isa 65:16 oath in the land *will* **s** by the one true H8678
Jer 4: 2 just and righteous way *you* **s**, 'As surely as H8678
Jer 12:16 the ways of my people and **s** by my name, H8678
Jer 12:16 once taught my people to **s** by Baal— H8678
Jer 22: 5 *I* **s** by myself that this palace will become H8678
Jer 44:26 '*I* **s** by my great name,' says the LORD, H8678
Jer 44:26 Egypt will ever again invoke my name or **s**, H606
Jer 49:13 *I* **s** by myself," declares the LORD, "that H8678
Eze 36: 7 **I s with uplifted** hand that the nations H5951
Da 12: 7 I heard him **s** by him who lives H8678
Hos 4:15 to Beth Aven. And *do* not **s**, 'As surely as H8678
Am 8:14 Those *who* **s** by the sin of Samaria—who H8678
Zep 1: 5 who bow down and **s** by the LORD and who H8678
Zep 1: 5 by the LORD and who also **s** by Molek, H8678
Zec 8:17 each other, and do not love to **s** falsely. H8652
Mt 5:34 I tell you, *do* not **s an oath** at all: either *G3923*
Mt 5:36 And *do* not **s** by your head, for you cannot *G3923*
Heb 3:18 And to whom *did* God **s** that they would *G3923*
Heb 6:13 there was no one greater for him *to* **s** by, *G3923*
Heb 6:16 People **s** by someone greater than *G3923*
Jas 5:12 sisters, *do* not **s**—not by heaven or by *G3923*

SWEARING (1) [SWEAR]

Jer 5: 2 as the LORD lives,' still *they are* **s** falsely." H8678

SWEARS (13) [SWEAR]

Ps 10: 6 ever shake me." *He* **s**, "No one will ever H457
Zec 5: 3 everyone who **s falsely** will be banished. H8678
Zec 5: 4 house of anyone *who* **s** falsely by my H8678
Mt 23:16 You say, 'If anyone **s** by the temple, it *G3923*
Mt 23:16 anyone who **s** by the gold of the *G3923*
Mt 23:18 also say, 'If anyone **s** by the altar, it *G3923*
Mt 23:18 anyone who **s** by the gift on the altar *G3923*
Mt 23:20 anyone *who* **s** by the altar swears by it *G3923*
Mt 23:20 swears by the altar **s** by it and by *G3923*
Mt 23:21 And anyone *who* **s** by the temple swears *G3923*
Mt 23:21 by the temple **s** by it and by the one *G3923*
Mt 23:22 And anyone *who* **s** by heaven swears by *G3923*
Mt 23:22 swears by heaven **s** by God's throne and *G3923*

SWEAT (2)

Ge 3:19 By the **s** *of* your brow you will eat your H2399
Lk 22:44 his **s** was like drops of blood falling *G2629*

SWEEP (23) [SWEEPING, SWEEPINGS, SWEEPS, SWEPT]

Ge 18:23 "*Will you* **s away** the righteous with the H6200
Ge 18:24 *Will you* really **s** it **away** and not spare the H6200
Ps 90: 5 Yet *you* **s** people **away** in the sleep of H2441
SS 8: 7 quench love; rivers cannot **s** it **away**. H8851
Isa 8: 8 and **s on** into Judah, swirling over it H2736
Isa 11:15 a scorching wind *he will* **s** his hand over H5677
Isa 14:23 *I will* **s** her with the broom of destruction," H3173
Isa 28:17 plumb line; hail *will* **s away** your refuge H3589
Isa 28:19 by day and by night, *it will* **s through**." H6296
Isa 43: 2 through the rivers, *they will* not **s over** you. H8851
Isa 64: 6 and like the wind our sins **s** us **away**. H5951
Eze 5:17 Plague and bloodshed *will* **s** through you H6296
Da 11:10 *which will* **s on** like an irresistible H995+995
Da 11:40 countries and **s through** them like a flood H6296
Hos 4:19 A whirlwind *will* **s** them **away** H7674+928+4053
Am 5: 6 or *he will* **s through** the tribes of Joseph H7502
Hab 1: 6 who **s** across the whole earth to seize H2143
Hab 1:11 Then *they* **s past** like the wind and go on H2736
Zep 1: 2 "*I will* **s away** everything from the H6066+665
Zep 1: 3 "*I will* **s away** both man and beast; I will H6066
Zep 1: 3 *I will* **s away** the birds in the sky and the H6066
Lk 15: 8 **s** the house and search carefully until she *G4924*
Rev 12:15 and **s** her **away with the torrent**. *G4533+4472*

SWEEPING (1) [SWEEP]

Isa 21: 1 Like whirlwinds **s** through the southland H2736

SWEEPINGS (1) [SWEEP]

Am 8: 6 selling even the **s** *with* the wheat. H5139

SWEEPS (6) [SWEEP]

Job 27:21 he is gone; *it* **s** him **out** of his place. H8548
Pr 1:27 when disaster **s over** you like a whirlwind H910
Pr 13:23 food for the poor, but injustice **s** it **away**. H6200
Isa 28:15 When an overwhelming scourge **s by**, it H6296
Isa 28:18 When the overwhelming scourge **s by** H6296
Isa 40:24 a whirlwind **s** them **away** like chaff. H5951

SWEET (24) [SWEETER, SWEETNESS]

Jdg 9:11 my fruit, so good and **s**, to hold sway over H5519
Jdg 14:14 out of the strong, *something* **s**. H5498
Ne 8:10 "Go and enjoy choice food and **s** drinks H4941
Job 20:12 "Though evil *is* **s** in his mouth and he H5517
Job 21:33 The soil in the valley *is* **s** to them H5517
Ps 55:14 with whom *I once* **enjoyed s** fellowship at H5517
Ps 119:103 How **s** *are* your words to my taste, H4914
Pr 3:24 when you lie down, your sleep *will be* **s**. H6844
Pr 9:17 "Stolen water *is* **s**; food eaten in secret is H5517
Pr 13:19 A longing fulfilled *is* **s** to the soul, but H6844
Pr 16:24 **s** to the soul and healing to the bones. H5498
Pr 20:17 Food gained by fraud **tastes s**, but one H6853
Pr 24:13 honey from the comb is **s** to your taste. H5498
Pr 27: 7 to the hungry even what is bitter tastes **s**. H5498

Ecc 5:12 The sleep of a laborer is s, whether they H5498
Ecc 11: 7 Light is s, and it pleases the eyes to see H5498
SS 2: 3 in his shade, and his fruit is s to my taste. H5498
SS 2:14 your voice is s, and your face is lovely H6853
Isa 5:20 who put bitter for s and sweet for bitter. H5498
Isa 5:20 who put bitter for sweet and s for bitter. H5498
Jer 6:20 incense from Sheba or s calamus from a H3203
Eze 3: 3 it tasted as s as honey in my mouth. H5498
Rev 10: 9 'in your mouth it will be as s as honey. *G1184*
Rev 10:10 It tasted as s as honey in my mouth, but *G1184*

SWEETER (3) [SWEET]
Jdg 14:18 town said to him, "What is s than honey? H5498
Ps 19:10 pure gold; they are s than honey, than H5498
Ps 119:103 to my taste, s than honey to my mouth! NDT

SWEETNESS (2) [SWEET]
SS 4:11 Your lips drop **s as the honeycomb**, my H5885
SS 5:16 His mouth is s *itself*; he is altogether H4941

SWELL (5) [SWELLING, SWELLS, SWOLLEN]
Nu 5:21 your womb miscarry and your abdomen s. H7379
Nu 5:27 her abdomen *will* s and her womb will H7377
Dt 8: 4 out and your feet *did* not s during these H1301
Isa 60: 5 your heart will throb and **s with joy**; the H8143
Ac 28: 6 expected him to **s up** or suddenly fall *G4399*

SWELLING (7) [SWELL]
Lev 13: 2 "When anyone has a s or a rash or a shiny H8421
Lev 13:10 if there is a white s in the skin that has H8421
Lev 13:10 white and if there is raw flesh in the s, H8421
Lev 13:19 a white s or reddish-white spot appears H8421
Lev 13:28 has faded, it is a s *from* the burn, and the H8421
Lev 14:56 for a s, a rash or a shiny spot, H8421
Lk 14: 2 **suffering from abnormal s of *his* body**. *G5622*

SWELLS (1) [SWELL]
Nu 5:22 so that your abdomen s or your womb H7377

SWELTER (1)
Job 37:17 You who s in your clothes when the land H2768

SWEPT (33) [SWEEP]
Ge 19:15 or *you will* **be s away** when the city is H6200
Ge 19:17 to the mountains or *you will* **be s away**!" H6200
Ex 14:27 and the LORD s them into the sea. H5850
Nu 16:26 or *you will* **be s away** because of all their H6200
Jdg 5:21 The river Kishon s them **away**, the H1759
1Ch 21:12 three months of **being s away** before your H6200
Job 1:17 parties and s **down** on your camels and H7320
Job 1:19 a mighty wind s **in** from the desert and H995
Job 5:13 the schemes of the wily **are s away**. H4554
Job 21:18 the wind, like chaff s **away** *by* a gale? H1704
Job 37:21 the skies after the wind *has* s them clean. H6296
Ps 42: 7 your waves and breakers *have* s over me. H6296
Ps 58: 9 green or dry—the wicked *will be* **s away**. H8548
Ps 73:19 destroyed, completely s **away** by terrors! H6200
Ps 88:16 Your wrath *has* s over me; your terrors H6296
Ps 124: 4 the torrent *would have* s over us, H6296
Ps 124: 5 the raging waters *would have* s us **away**. H6296
Ps 136:15 s Pharaoh and his army into the Red H5850
Pr 10:25 When the storm *has* **s by**, the wicked are H6296
Isa 44:22 *I have* **s away** your offenses like a cloud H4681
Da 2:35 The wind s them **away** without leaving a A10492
Da 11:22 army *will* **be s away** before him; H8851
Da 11:26 his army *will be* **s away**, and many H8851
Hos 4: 3 the sky and the fish in the sea *are* **s away**. H665
Hos 10: 7 s away like a twig on the surface of the NDT
Jnh 2: 3 all your waves and breakers s over me. H6296
Mic 7: 2 The faithful *have been* s from the land; not H6
Hab 3:10 Torrents of water **s by**; the deep roared H6296
Mt 8:24 so that the waves **s over** the boat. *G2821*
Mt 12:44 unoccupied, **s clean** and put in order. *G4924*
Lk 11:25 it finds the house **s clean** and put in order. *G4924*
Ac 27:14 the Northeaster, **s down** from the island. *G965*
Rev 12: 4 Its tail s a third of the stars **out of** the sky *G5359*

SWERVING (1)
Joel 2: 7 all march in line, not s *from* their course. H6293

SWIFT (16) [SWIFTER, SWIFTLY]
1Ch 12: 8 they were as s as gazelles in the H4554
Pr 1:16 rush into evil, *they are* s to shed blood. H4554
Ecc 9:11 The race is not to the s or the battle to the H7824
Isa 18: 2 s messengers, to a people tall and H7824
Isa 19: 1 the LORD rides on a s cloud and is coming H7824
Isa 30:16 'We will ride off on s horses.' Therefore H7824
Isa 30:16 Therefore your pursuers *will be* s! H7837
Isa 38:14 I cried like a s or thrush, I moaned like a H6101
Isa 59: 7 *they are* s to shed innocent blood. H4554
Jer 2:23 You are a s she-camel running here and H7824
Jer 8: 7 the s and the thrush observe the time of H6101
Jer 46: 6 "The s cannot flee nor the strong escape H7824
Da 9:21 came to me in s **flight** about the H3618+3616
Am 2:14 The s will not escape, the strong will not H7824
Ro 3:15 "Their feet are s to shed blood; *G3955*
2Pe 2: 1 bringing s destruction on themselves. *G5442*

SWIFTER (6) [SWIFT]
2Sa 1:23 *They were* s than eagles, they were H7837
Job 7: 6 "My days *are* s than a weaver's shuttle H7837
Job 9:25 "My days *are* s than a runner; they fly H7837
Jer 4:13 a whirlwind, his horses *are* s than eagles. H7837
La 4:19 Our pursuers were s than eagles in the sky H7824
Hab 1: 8 Their horses *are* s than leopards, fiercer H7837

SWIFTLY (4) [SWIFT]
Ps 147:15 to the earth; his word runs s. H6330+4559
Isa 5:26 Here they come, s and speedily! H4559
Isa 60:22 I am the LORD; in its time *I will* **do** this s." H2590
Joel 3: 4 I will s and speedily return on your own H7824

SWIM (4) [SWIMMERS, SWIMMING]
Ps 8: 8 in the sea, all *that* s the paths of the seas. H6296
Isa 25:11 as swimmers stretch out their hands to s. H8466
Eze 47: 5 had risen and was **deep enough to s in**— H8467
Ac 27:43 those who could s to jump overboard first *G3147*

SWIMMERS (1) [SWIM]
Isa 25:11 as s stretch out their hands to swim. H8466

SWIMMING (1) [SWIM]
Ac 27:42 prevent any *of them* from **s away** and *G1713*

SWINDLER (1) [SWINDLERS]
1Co 5:11 an idolater or slanderer, a drunkard or s. *G774*

SWINDLERS (2) [SWINDLER]
1Co 5:10 immoral, or the greedy and s, or idolaters. *G774*
1Co 6:10 slanderers nor s will inherit the *G774*

SWINE, SWINE'S (KJV) PIG, PIG'S, PIGS

SWING (3) [SWINGS, SWUNG]
Ex 28:28 breastpiece *will* not **s out** from the ephod H2322
Ex 39:21 breastpiece *would* not **s out** from the H2322
Joel 3:13 S the sickle, for the harvest is ripe. H8938

SWINGS (2) [SWING]
Dt 19: 5 cut wood, and as he s his ax to fell a tree H5616
Isa 10:15 ax raise itself above the *person who* s it, H2933

SWIRL (1) [SWIRLED, SWIRLING]
Job 37:12 his direction they s around over the face H2200

SWIRLED (2) [SWIRL]
2Sa 22: 5 The waves of death **s about** me; the H705
Jnh 2: 3 the currents **s about** me; all your H6015

SWIRLING (4) [SWIRL]
Isa 8: 8 on into Judah, **s over** it, passing through H8851
Jer 23:19 a whirlwind **s down** on the heads of the H2565
Jer 30:23 a driving wind **s down** on the heads of the H2565
Hos 13: 3 like chaff s from a threshing floor H6192

SWOLLEN (3) [SWELL]
Lev 13:43 if the s sore on his head or forehead H8421
Ne 9:21 not wear out nor *did* their feet *become* s. H1301
Job 6:16 by thawing ice and s with melting snow, H6623

SWOOP (3) [SWOOPING]
Isa 11:14 *They will* **s down** on the slopes of Philistia H6414
Jer 49:22 An eagle will soar and **s down**, spreading H1797
Am 3: 5 *Does* a bird **s down** to a trap on the H5877

SWOOPING (4) [SWOOP]
Dt 28:49 like an eagle **s down**, a nation whose H1797
Job 9:26 papyrus, like eagles **s down** on their prey. H3216
Jer 48:40 An eagle *is* **s down**, spreading its wings H1797
Hab 1: 8 They fly like an eagle s to devour; H2590

SWORD (403) [SWORDS, SWORDSMEN]
Ge 3:24 a flaming s flashing back and H2995
Ge 27:40 You will live by the s and you will serve H2995
Ge 34:26 son Shechem to the s and took Dinah H2995
Ge 48:22 from the Amorites with my s and my bow." H2995
Ex 5: 3 may strike us with plagues or with the s." H2995
Ex 5:21 have put a s in their hand to kill us H2995
Ex 15: 9 I will draw my s and my hand will destroy H2995
Ex 17:13 overcame the Amalekite army with the s. H2995
Ex 18: 4 he saved me from the s *of* Pharaoh." H2995
Ex 22:24 I will kill you with the s; your wives H2995
Ex 32:27 'Each man strap a s to his side. Go back H2995
Lev 26: 6 the s will not pass through your H2995
Lev 26: 7 they will fall by the s before you. H2995
Lev 26: 8 your enemies will fall by the s before you. H2995
Lev 26:25 And I will bring the s on you to avenge the H2995
Lev 26:33 will draw out my s and pursue you. H2995
Lev 26:36 They will run as though fleeing from the s, H2995
Lev 26:37 one another as though fleeing from the s, H2995
Nu 14: 3 us to this land only to let us fall by the s? H2995
Nu 14:43 not be with you and you will fall by the s." H2995
Nu 19:16 been killed with a s or someone who has H2995
Nu 20:18 will march out and attack you with the s." H2995
Nu 21:24 put him to the s and took over his land H2995
Nu 22:23 in the road with a drawn s in his hand, H2995
Nu 22:29 If only I had a s in my hand, I would kill H2995
Nu 22:31 standing in the road with his s drawn. H2995
Nu 31: 8 also killed Balaam son of Beor with the s. H2995
Dt 13:15 certainly put to the s all who live in that H2995
Dt 20:13 your hand, put to the s all the men in it. H2995
Dt 32:25 In the street the s will make them H2995
Dt 32:41 my flashing s and my hand grasps H2995
Dt 32:42 with blood, while my s devours flesh: H2995
Dt 33:29 shield and helper and your glorious s. H2995
Jos 5:13 in front of him with a drawn s in his hand. H2995
Jos 6:21 destroyed with the s every living thing in H2995
Jos 8:24 every one of them had been put to the s, H2995
Jos 10:28 its king to the s and totally destroyed H2995
Jos 10:30 city and everyone in it Joshua put to the s. H2995
Jos 10:32 The city and everyone in it he put to the s H2995
Jos 10:35 put it to the s and totally destroyed H2995
Jos 10:37 They took the city and put it to the s H2995
Jos 10:39 its villages, and put them to the s. H2995
Jos 11:10 captured Hazor and put its king to the s. H2995
Jos 11:11 Everyone in it they put to the s. H2995
Jos 11:12 their kings and put them to the s. H2995
Jos 11:14 they put to the s until they completely H2995
Jos 13:22 had put to the s Balaam son of Beor, H2995
Jos 19:47 put it to the s and occupied it. H2995
Jos 24:12 did not do it with your own s and bow. H2995
Jdg 1: 8 They put the city to the s and set it on fire H2995
Jdg 1:25 put the city to the s but spared the man H2995
Jdg 3:16 a double-edged s about a cubit long, H2995
Jdg 3:21 drew the s from his right thigh and H2995
Jdg 3:22 Ehud did not pull the s out, and the fat H2995
Jdg 4:15 all his chariots and army by the s, H2995
Jdg 4:16 all Sisera's troops fell by the s; not a H2995
Jdg 7:14 other than the s *of* Gideon son of Joash, H2995
Jdg 7:20 "A s for the LORD and for Gideon!" H2995
Jdg 8:20 But Jether did not draw his s, because he H2995
Jdg 9:54 "Draw your s and kill me, so that H2995
Jdg 18:27 them with the s and burned down their H2995
Jdg 20:37 spread out and put the whole city to the s. H2995
Jdg 20:48 Benjamin and put all the towns to the s, H2995
Jdg 21:10 Gilead and put to the s those living there, H2995
1Sa 13:22 Jonathan had a s or spear in his H2995
1Sa 15: 8 his people he totally destroyed with the s. H2995
1Sa 15:33 "As your s has made women childless H2995
1Sa 17:39 David fastened on his s over the tunic and H2995
1Sa 17:45 come against me with s and spear and H2995
1Sa 17:47 that it is not by s or spear that the LORD H2995
1Sa 17:50 without a s in his hand he struck down the H2995
1Sa 17:51 of the Philistine's s and drew it from the H2995
1Sa 17:51 killed him, he cut off his head with **the s**. H2023S
1Sa 18: 4 and even his s, his bow and his belt H2995
1Sa 21: 8 "Don't you have a spear or a s here? H2995
1Sa 21: 8 haven't brought my s or any other weapon H2995
1Sa 21: 9 replied, "The s *of* Goliath the Philistine H2995
1Sa 21: 9 take it; there is no s here but that one." H337S
1Sa 22:10 him provisions and the s *of* Goliath the H2995
1Sa 22:13 him bread and a s and inquiring of God H2995
1Sa 22:19 He also put to the s Nob, the town of the H2995
1Sa 25:13 to his men, "Each of you strap on your s!" H2995
1Sa 31: 4 "Draw your s and run me through, or H2995
1Sa 31: 4 so Saul took his own s and fell on it. H2995
1Sa 31: 5 he too fell on his s and died with him. H2995
2Sa 1:12 because they had fallen by the s. H2995
2Sa 1:22 the s *of* Saul did not return unsatisfied. H2995
2Sa 2:26 out to Joab, "Must the s devour forever? H2995
2Sa 3:29 who falls by the s or who lacks food." H2995
2Sa 11:25 the s devours one as well as another. H2995
2Sa 12: 9 the Hittite with the s and took his wife to H2995
2Sa 12: 9 killed him with the s *of* the Ammonites. H2995
2Sa 12:10 the s will never depart from your house H2995
2Sa 15:14 bring ruin on us and put the city to the s." H2995
2Sa 18: 8 up more men that day than the s. H2995
2Sa 21:16 shekels and who was armed with a new s, NDT
2Sa 23:10 till his hand grew tired and froze to the s. H2995
2Sa 24: 9 able-bodied men who could handle a s, H2995
1Ki 1:51 not put his servant to death with the s. H2995
1Ki 2: 8 'I will not put you to death by the s.' H2995
1Ki 2:32 two men and killed them with the s. H2995
1Ki 3:24 "Bring me a s." So they brought a H2995
1Ki 3:24 So they brought a s for the king. H2995
1Ki 19: 1 he had killed all the prophets with the s. H2995
1Ki 19:10 put your prophets to death with the s. H2995
1Ki 19:14 put your prophets to death with the s. H2995
1Ki 19:17 to death any who escape the s *of* Hazael, H2995
1Ki 19:17 to death any who escape the s *of* Jehu. H2995
2Ki 6:22 have captured with your own s or bow? H2995
2Ki 8:12 kill their young men with the s, dash their H2995
2Ki 10:25 So they cut them down with the s. H2995
2Ki 11:15 ranks and put to the s anyone who follows H2995
2Ki 11:20 had been slain with the s at the palace. H2995
2Ki 19: 7 there I will have him cut down with the s. H2995
2Ki 19:37 Sharezer killed him with the s, H2995
1Ch 5:18 men who could handle shield and s, H2995
1Ch 10: 4 "Draw your s and run me through, or H2995
1Ch 10: 4 so Saul took his own s and fell on it. H2995
1Ch 10: 5 was dead, he too fell on his s and died. H2995
1Ch 21: 5 thousand men who could handle a s, H2995
1Ch 21:12 three days of the s *of* the LORD—days of H2995
1Ch 21:16 with a drawn s in his hand extended over H2995
1Ch 21:27 he put his s back into its sheath. H2995
1Ch 21:30 he was afraid of the s *of* the angel of the H2995
2Ch 20: 9 whether the s *of* judgment, or plague H2995
2Ch 21: 4 his brothers to the s along with some of H2995
2Ch 23:14 ranks and put to the s anyone who follows H2995
2Ch 23:21 Athaliah had been slain with the s. H2995
2Ch 29: 9 have fallen by the s and why our sons H2995
2Ch 32:21 flesh and blood, cut him down with the s. H2995
2Ch 36:17 young men with the s in the sanctuary, H2995
2Ch 36:20 who escaped from the s, and they H2995
Ezr 9: 7 been subjected to the s and captivity, H2995
Ne 4:18 the builders wore his s at his side as he H2995
Est 9: 5 struck down all their enemies with the s, H2995
Job 1:15 They put the servants to the s, and I am H2995
Job 1:17 They put the servants to the s, and I am H2995

S

Job 5:15 saves the needy from the s in their mouth; H2995
Job 5:20 in battle from the stroke of the s. H2995
Job 15:22 realm of darkness; he is marked for the s. H2995
Job 19:29 you should fear the s yourselves; for wrath H2995
Job 19:29 wrath will bring punishment by the s H2995
Job 27:14 their fate is the s; his offspring will never H2995
Job 33:18 their lives from perishing by the s. H8939
Job 36:12 they will perish by the s and die without H8939
Job 39:22 nothing; it does not shy away from the s. H2995
Job 40:19 its Maker can approach it with his s. H2995
Job 41:26 The s that reaches it has no effect, nor H2995
Ps 7:12 he will sharpen his s; he will bend and H2995
Ps 17:13 with your s rescue me from the wicked. H2995
Ps 22:20 Deliver me from the s, my precious life H2995
Ps 37:14 wicked draw the s and bend the bow to H2995
Ps 44: 3 It was not by their s that they won the H2995
Ps 44: 6 in my bow, my s does not bring me victory H2995
Ps 45: 3 Gird your s on your side, you mighty one H2995
Ps 63:10 given over to the s and become food for H2995
Ps 78:62 He gave his people over to the s; he was H2995
Ps 78:64 their priests were put to the s, and their H2995
Ps 89:43 back the edge of his s and have not H2995
Ps 144:10 his servant David. From the deadly s H2995
Ps 149: 6 a double-edged s in their hands, H2995
Pr 5: 4 bitter as gall, sharp as a double-edged s. H2995
Pr 25:18 Like a club or a s or a sharp arrow is one H2995
SS 3: 8 all of them wearing the s, all experienced H2995
SS 3: 8 each with his s at his side, prepared H2995
Isa 1:20 rebel, you will be devoured by the s." H2995
Isa 2: 4 Nation will not take up s against nation H2995
Isa 3:25 Your men will fall by the s, your warriors H2995
Isa 13:15 all who are caught will fall by the s. H2995
Isa 14:19 with those pierced by the s, those who H2995
Isa 21:15 They flee from the s, from the drawn H2995
Isa 21:15 from the drawn s, from the bent bow H2995
Isa 22: 2 Your slain were not killed by the s, nor did H2995
Isa 27: 1 the LORD will punish with his s—his fierce, H2995
Isa 27: 1 great and powerful s—Leviathan the NDT
Isa 31: 8 "Assyria will fall by no human s; a sword H2995
Isa 31: 8 by no human sword; a s, not of mortals, H2995
Isa 31: 8 will flee before the s and their young men H2995
Isa 34: 5 My s has drunk its fill in the heavens; see H2995
Isa 34: 6 The s of the LORD is bathed in blood, it is H2995
Isa 37: 7 there I will have him cut down with the s. H2995
Isa 37:38 Sharezer killed him with the s, H2995
Isa 41: 2 He turns them to dust with his s, to H2995
Isa 49: 2 He made my mouth like a sharpened s, in H2995
Isa 51:19 famine and s—who can console you? H2995
Isa 65:12 I will destine you for the s, and all of you H2995
Isa 66:16 fire and with his s the LORD will execute H2995
Jer 2:30 Your s has devoured your prophets like a H2995
Jer 4:10 have peace,' when the s is at our throats!" H2995
Jer 5:12 come to us; we will never see s or famine. H2995
Jer 5:17 With the s they will destroy the fortified H2995
Jer 6:25 the enemy has a s, and there is terror H2995
Jer 9:16 them with the s until I have made an H2995
Jer 11:22 Their young men will die by the s, their H2995
Jer 12:12 the s of the LORD will devour from one H2995
Jer 14:12 I will destroy them with the s, famine and H2995
Jer 14:13 'You will not see the s or suffer famine. H2995
Jer 14:15 'No s or famine will touch this land.' H2995
Jer 14:15 prophets will perish by s and famine. H2995
Jer 14:16 Jerusalem because of the famine and s. H2995
Jer 14:18 I see those slain by the s; if I go into the H2995
Jer 15: 2 those for the s, to the sword; those H2995
Jer 15: 2 the sword, to the s; those for starvation H2995
Jer 15: 3 "the s to kill and the dogs to drag away H2995
Jer 15: 9 the survivors to the s before their enemies H2995
Jer 16: 4 They will perish by s and famine, and H2995
Jer 18:21 hand them over to the power of the s. H2995
Jer 18:21 their young men slain by the s in battle. H2995
Jer 19: 7 them fall by the s before their enemies, H2995
Jer 20: 4 see them fall by the s *of* their enemies. H2995
Jer 20: 4 away to Babylon or put them to the s. H2995
Jer 21: 7 survive the plague, s and famine, into the H2995
Jer 21: 7 He will put them to the s; he will show H2995
Jer 21: 9 Whoever stays in this city will die by the s H2995
Jer 24:10 I will send the s, famine and plague H2995
Jer 25:16 mad because of the s I will send among H2995
Jer 25:27 more because of the s I will send among H2995
Jer 25:29 I am calling down a s on all who live on H2995
Jer 25:31 all mankind and put the wicked to the s,' H2995
Jer 25:38 because of the s *of* the oppressor and H2995
Jer 26:23 struck down with a s and his body thrown H2995
Jer 27: 8 I will punish that nation with the s H2995
Jer 27:13 Why will you and your people die by the s H2995
Jer 29:17 "I will send the s, famine and plague H2995
Jer 29:18 I will pursue them with the s, famine and H2995
Jer 31: 2 who survive the s will find favor in the H2995
Jer 32:24 Because of the s, famine and plague, the H2995
Jer 32:36 this city, 'By the s, famine and plague it H2995
Jer 33: 4 used against the siege ramps and the s H2995
Jer 34: 4 concerning you: You will not die by the s; H2995
Jer 34:17 'freedom' to fall by the s, plague and H2995
Jer 38: 2 stays in this city will die by the s, H2995
Jer 39:18 will not fall by the s but will escape with H2995
Jer 41: 2 of Shaphan, with the s, killing the one H2995
Jer 42:16 then the s you fear will overtake you there H2995
Jer 42:17 to Egypt to settle there will die by the s, H2995
Jer 42:22 You will die by the s, famine and plague H2995
Jer 43:11 the s to those destined for the sword. H2995
Jer 43:11 the sword to those destined for the s. H2995
Jer 44:12 they will fall by the s or die from famine. H2995
Jer 44:12 the greatest, they will die by s or famine. H2995
Jer 44:13 punish those who live in Egypt with the s, H2995
Jer 44:18 have been perishing by s and famine." H2995
Jer 44:27 Egypt will perish by s and famine until H2995
Jer 44:28 Those who escape the s and return to the H2995
Jer 46:10 The s will devour till it is satisfied, till it H2995
Jer 46:14 for the s devours those around you.' H2995
Jer 46:16 away from the s *of* the oppressor.' H2995
Jer 47: 6 s of the LORD, how long till you H2995
Jer 48: 2 also be silenced; the s will pursue you. H2995
Jer 48:10 who keeps their s from bloodshed! H2995
Jer 49:37 them with the s until I have made an H2995
Jer 50:16 Because of the s *of* the oppressor let H2995
Jer 50:35 "A s against the Babylonians!" declares H2995
Jer 50:36 A s against her false prophets! They will H2995
Jer 50:36 become fools. A s against her warriors H2995
Jer 50:37 A s against her horses and chariots and H2995
Jer 50:37 A s against her treasures! H2995
Jer 51:50 You who have escaped the s, leave and H2995
La 1:20 Outside, the s bereaves; inside, there is H2995
La 2:21 young women have fallen by the s. H2995
La 4: 9 Those killed by the s are better off than H2995
La 5: 9 of our lives because of the s *in* the desert. H2995
Eze 5: 1 take a sharp s and use it as a barber's H2995
Eze 5: 2 strike it with the s all around the city. H2995
Eze 5: 2 For I will pursue them with drawn s. H2995
Eze 5:12 a third will fall by the s outside your walls H2995
Eze 5:12 to the winds and pursue with drawn s. H2995
Eze 5:17 and I will bring the s against you. H2995
Eze 6: 3 I am about to bring a s against you, and I H2995
Eze 6: 8 you will escape the s when you are H2995
Eze 6:11 they will fall by the s, famine and H2995
Eze 6:12 one who is near will fall by the s, and H2995
Eze 7:15 Outside is the s; inside are plague and H2995
Eze 7:15 Those in the country will die by the s H2995
Eze 11: 8 You fear the s, and the sword is what I will H2995
Eze 11: 8 the s is what I will bring against you H2995
Eze 11:10 You will fall by the s, and I will execute H2995
Eze 12:14 I will pursue them with drawn s. H2995
Eze 12:16 But I will spare a few of them from the s H2995
Eze 14:17 "Or if I bring a s against that country and H2995
Eze 14:17 'Let the s pass throughout the land H2995
Eze 14:21 s and famine and wild beasts and plague H2995
Eze 17:21 All his choice troops will fall by the s, and H2995
Eze 21: 3 I will draw my s from its sheath and cut off H2995
Eze 21: 4 my s will be unsheathed against everyone H2995
Eze 21: 5 the LORD have drawn my s from its sheath; H2995
Eze 21: 9 " 'A s, a sword, sharpened and polished— H2995
Eze 21: 9 " 'A sword, a s, sharpened and polished— H2995
Eze 21:10 The s despises every such stick. NDT
Eze 21:11 " 'The s is appointed to be polished, to H2995
Eze 21:12 are thrown to the s along with my people. H2995
Eze 21:13 the scepter, which the s despises, does not NDT
Eze 21:14 Let the s strike twice, even H2995
Eze 21:14 It is a s *for* slaughter—a sword for great H2995
Eze 21:14 slaughter—a s *for* great slaughter H2995
Eze 21:15 I have stationed the s for slaughter at all H2995
Eze 21:16 Slash to the right, you s, then to the left NDT
Eze 21:19 two roads for the s *of* the king of Babylon H2995
Eze 21:20 out one road for the s to come against H2995
Eze 21:28 " 'A s, a sword, drawn for the slaughter H2995
Eze 21:28 " 'A sword, a s, drawn for the slaughter H2995
Eze 21:30 " 'Let the s return to its sheath. In the place NDT
Eze 23:10 daughters and killed her with the s. H2995
Eze 23:25 those of you who are left will fall by the s. H2995
Eze 24:21 you left behind will fall by the s. H2995
Eze 25:13 Teman to Dedan they will fall by the s. H2995
Eze 26: 6 on the mainland will be ravaged by the s. H2995
Eze 26: 8 settlements on the mainland with the s; H2995
Eze 26:11 he will kill your people with the s, and H2995
Eze 28:23 with the s against you on every side. H2995
Eze 29: 8 I will bring a s against you and kill both H2995
Eze 30: 4 A s will come against Egypt, and anguish H2995
Eze 30: 5 land will fall by the s along with Egypt. H2995
Eze 30: 6 to Aswan they will fall by the s within her, H2995
Eze 30:17 Heliopolis and Bubastis will fall by the s, H2995
Eze 30:21 it may become strong enough to hold a s. H2995
Eze 30:22 and make the s fall from his hand. H2995
Eze 30:24 king of Babylon and put my s in his hand, H2995
Eze 30:25 when I put my s into the hand of the king H2995
Eze 31:17 to those killed by the s, along with the H2995
Eze 31:18 uncircumcised, with those killed by the s. H2995
Eze 32:10 of you when I brandish my s before them. H2995
Eze 32:11 " 'The s *of* the king of Babylon will come H2995
Eze 32:20 They will fall among those killed by the s H2995
Eze 32:20 The s is drawn; let her be dragged off H2995
Eze 32:21 uncircumcised, with those killed by the s.' H2995
Eze 32:22 all her slain, all who have fallen by the s. H2995
Eze 32:23 of the living are slain, fallen by the s. H2995
Eze 32:24 fallen by the s. All who had spread H2995
Eze 32:25 of them are uncircumcised, killed by the s. H2995
Eze 32:26 killed by the s because they spread their H2995
Eze 32:28 uncircumcised, with those killed by the s. H2995
Eze 32:29 they are laid with those killed by the s. H2995
Eze 32:30 those killed by the s and bear their shame H2995
Eze 32:31 all his hordes that were killed by the s, H2995
Eze 32:32 with those killed by the s, declares the H2995
Eze 33: 2 'When I bring the s against a land, and H2995
Eze 33: 3 he sees the s coming against the land H2995
Eze 33: 4 the warning and the s comes and takes H2995
Eze 33: 6 watchman sees the s coming and does H2995
Eze 33: 6 the people and the s comes and takes H2995
Eze 33:26 You rely on your s, you do detestable H2995
Eze 33:27 who are left in the ruins will fall by the s, H2995
Eze 35: 5 Israelites over to the s at the time of their H2995
Eze 35: 8 those killed by the s will fall on your hills H2995
Eze 38:21 I will summon a s against Gog on all my H2995
Eze 38:21 Every man's s will be against his brother. H2995
Eze 39:23 their enemies, and they all fell by the s. H2995
Da 11:33 they will fall by the s or be burned or H2995
Hos 1: 7 not by bow, s or battle, or by horses and H2995
Hos 2:18 Bow and s and battle I will abolish from H2995
Hos 7:16 leaders will fall by the s because of their H2995
Hos 11: 6 A s will flash in their cities; it will devour H2995
Hos 13:16 They will fall by the s; their little ones will H2995
Am 1:11 his brother with a s and slaughtered the H2995
Am 4:10 I killed your young men with the s, along H2995
Am 7: 9 with my s I will rise against the house of H2995
Am 7:11 " 'Jeroboam will die by the s, and Israel H2995
Am 7:17 your sons and daughters will fall by the s. H2995
Am 9: 1 those who are left I will kill with the s. H2995
Am 9: 4 there I will command the s to slay them. H2995
Am 9:10 among my people will die by the s, H2995
Mic 4: 3 Nation will not take up s against nation H2995
Mic 5: 6 will rule the land of Assyria with the s, H2995
Mic 5: 6 the land of Nimrod with **drawn** s. H7347
Mic 6:14 because what you save I will give to the s. H2995
Na 2:13 the s will devour your young lions. H2995
Na 3:15 will consume you; the s will cut you down H2995
Zep 2:12 "You Cushites, too, will be slain by my s." H2995
Hag 2:22 will fall, each by the s *of* his brother. H2995
Zec 9:13 Greece, and make you like a warrior's s. H2995
Zec 11:17 May the s strike his arm and his right eye H2995
Zec 13: 7 "Awake, s, against my shepherd, against H2995
Mt 10:34 I did not come to bring peace, but a s. *G3479*
Mt 26:51 of Jesus' companions reached *for* his s, *G3479*
Mt 26:52 "Put your s back in its place," Jesus said *G3479*
Mt 26:52 all who draw the s will die by the sword *G3479*
Mt 26:52 all who draw the sword will die by the s. *G3479*
Mk 14:47 near drew his s and struck the servant *G3479*
Lk 2:35 And a s will pierce your own soul too." *G4855*
Lk 21:24 They will fall *by* the s and will be *G5125+3479*
Lk 22:36 if you don't have a s, sell your cloak *G3479*
Jn 18:10 who had a s, drew it and struck *G3479*
Jn 18:11 commanded Peter, "Put your s away! *G3479*
Ac 12: 2 brother of John, put to death *with* the s. *G3479*
Ac 16:27 he drew his s and was about to kill *G3479*
Ro 8:35 famine or nakedness or danger or s? *G3479*
Ro 13: 4 rulers do not bear the s for no reason. *G3479*
Eph 6:17 helmet of salvation and the s of the Spirit, *G3479*
Heb 4:12 Sharper than any double-edged s, it *G3479*
Heb 11:34 escaped the edge *of* the s; whose *G3479*
Heb 11:37 sawed in two; they were killed *by* the s. *G3479*
Rev 1:16 his mouth was a sharp, double-edged s. *G4855*
Rev 2:12 him who has the sharp, double-edged s. *G4855*
Rev 2:16 against them with the s of my mouth. *G4855*
Rev 6: 4 To him was given a large s. *G3479*
Rev 6: 8 over a fourth of the earth to kill by s, *G4855*
Rev 13:10 If anyone is to be killed with the s, with *G3479*
Rev 13:10 the sword, with the s they will be killed." *G3479*
Rev 13:14 who was wounded by the s and yet lived. *G3479*
Rev 19:15 his mouth is a sharp s with which to strike *G4855*
Rev 19:21 were killed with the s coming out of the *G4855*

SWORDS (38) [SWORD]

Ge 34:25 took their s and attacked the unsuspecting H2995
Ge 49: 5 their s are weapons of violence. H4839
Jos 10:11 than were killed by the s of the Israelites. H2995
Jdg 7:22 camp to turn on each other with their s. H2995
Jdg 20: 2 four hundred thousand men armed with s. H2995
Jdg 20:25 Israelites, all of them armed with s. H2995
Jdg 20:35 25,100 Benjamites, all armed with s. H2995
1Sa 13:19 the Hebrews will make s or spears!" H2995
1Sa 14:20 confusion, striking each other with their s. H2995
1Ki 18:28 slashed themselves with s and spears, H2995
1Ch 21:12 enemies, with their s overtaking you, or H2995
Ne 4:13 by families, with their s, spears and bows. H2995
Ps 37:15 But their s will pierce their own hearts H2995
Ps 55:21 soothing than oil, yet they are **drawn** s. H7347
Ps 57: 4 arrows, whose tongues are sharp s. H2995
Ps 59: 7 the words from their lips are *sharp as* s H2995
Ps 64: 3 their tongues like s and aim cruel words H2995
Ps 76: 3 the shields and the s, the weapons of war H2995
Pr 12:18 The words of the reckless pierce like s, but H2995
Pr 30:14 whose teeth are s and whose jaws are H2995
Isa 2: 4 They will beat their s into plowshares H2995
Eze 16:40 you and hack you to pieces with their s. H2995
Eze 23:47 them and cut them down with their s; H2995
Eze 28: 7 they will draw their s against your beauty H2995
Eze 30:11 They will draw their s against Egypt and H2995
Eze 32:12 hordes to fall by the s *of* mighty men— H2995
Eze 32:27 their s placed under their heads and their H2995
Eze 38: 4 shields, all of them brandishing their s. H2995
Joel 3:10 your plowshares into s and your pruning H2995
Mic 4: 3 They will beat their s into plowshares H2995
Na 3: 3 flashing s and glittering spears! H2995
Mt 26:47 a large crowd armed with s and clubs, *G3479*
Mt 26:55 have come out with s and clubs to capture *G3479*
Mk 14:43 him was a crowd armed with s and clubs, *G3479*
Mk 14:48 have come out with s and clubs to capture *G3479*
Lk 22:38 disciples said, "See, Lord, here are two s." *G3479*
Lk 22:49 "Lord, should we strike with our s? *G3479*
Lk 22:52 that you have come with s and clubs? *G3479*

SWORDSMEN (5) [SWORD]
Jdg 8:10 twenty thousand **s** had fallen. H408+8990+2995
Jdg 20:15 thousand **s** from their towns, H408+8990+2995
Jdg 20:17 four hundred thousand **s**, H408+8990+2995
Jdg 20:46 thousand Benjamite **s** fell, H408+8990+2995
2Ki 3:26 seven hundred **s** to break H408+8990+2995

SWORE (60) [SWEAR]
Ge 21:31 because the two men **s an oath** there. H8678
Ge 24: 9 Abraham and **s an oath** to him H8678
Ge 25:33 So *he* **s an oath** to him, selling his H8678
Ge 26: 3 will confirm the oath *I* **s** to your father H8678
Ge 26:31 next morning *the men* **s an oath** to each H8678
Ge 47:31 Then Joseph **s** to him, and Israel H8678
Ex 6: 8 to the land I **s with uplifted** hand to give H5951
Ex 13: 5 the land *he* **s** to your ancestors to give you H8678
Ex 32:13 to whom *you* **s** by your own self: H8678
Lev 6: 5 whatever it was *they* **s** falsely about H8678
Nu 14:30 the land I **s with uplifted** hand to make H5951
Nu 32:10 was aroused that day and *he* **s** *this* **oath**: H8678
Dt 1: 8 of the land the LORD **s** he would give to H8678
Dt 1:34 you said, he was angry and **solemnly s**: H8678
Dt 1:35 see the good land *I* **s** to give your H8678
Dt 4:21 and *he* **solemnly s** that I would not cross H8678
Dt 6:10 you into the land *he* **s** to your fathers, H8678
Dt 7: 8 kept the oath *he* **s** to your ancestors H8678
Dt 7:12 of love with you, as *he* **s** to your ancestors. H8678
Dt 7:13 flocks in the land *he* **s** to your ancestors to H8678
Dt 8:18 his covenant, which *he* **s** to your ancestors H8678
Dt 9: 5 to accomplish what he **s** to your fathers, to H8678
Dt 10:11 possess the land *I* **s** to their ancestors H8678
Dt 11: 9 in the land the LORD **s** to your ancestors to H8678
Dt 11:21 in the land the LORD **s** to give your H8678
Dt 26: 3 to the land the LORD **s** to our ancestors to H8678
Dt 28:11 in the land he **s** to your ancestors to give H8678
Dt 29:13 promised you and as *he* **s** to your fathers, H8678
Dt 30:20 years in the land he **s** to give to your H8678
Dt 31: 7 land that the LORD **s** to their ancestors to H8678
Jos 1: 6 to inherit the land *I* **s** to their ancestors to H8678
Jos 9:20 on us for breaking the oath *we* **s** to them." H8678
Jos 14: 9 So on that day Moses **s** to me, 'The land H8678
Jdg 2: 1 led you into the land *I* **s** to give to your H8678
1Sa 3:14 Therefore *I* **s** to the house of Eli, 'The guilt H8678
1Sa 28:10 Saul **s** to her by the LORD, "As surely as the H8678
2Sa 21:17 Then David's men **s** to him, saying H8678
1Ki 1:17 *you* yourself **s** to me your servant by the H8678
1Ki 1:30 this very day what *I* **s** to you by the LORD, H8678
1Ki 2: 8 me at the Jordan, *I* **s** to him by the LORD: H8678
1Ki 2:23 Then King Solomon **s** by the LORD: "May H8678
1Ch 16:16 with Abraham, the **oath** he **s** to Isaac. H8652
Ps 89:49 *which* in your faithfulness *you* **s** to David? H8678
Ps 105: 9 made with Abraham, the oath he **s** to Isaac. NDT
Ps 106:26 So *he* **s** to them **with uplifted** hand that H5951
Ps 132: 2 He **s an oath** to the LORD, he made a vow H8678
Ps 132:11 The LORD **s an oath** to David, a sure oath H8678
Isa 54: 9 when *I* **s** that the waters of Noah would H8678
Jer 11: 5 I will fulfill the oath *I* **s** to your ancestors, H8678
Jer 38:16 But King Zedekiah **s** *this* **oath** secretly to H8678
Eze 20: 5 I **s with uplifted** hand to the descendants H5951
Eze 20: 6 On that day *I* **s** to them that I would H5951+3338
Eze 20:15 Also **with uplifted** hand I **s** to them in the H5951
Eze 20:23 Also **with uplifted** hand I **s** to them in the H5951
Eze 47:14 Because I **s with uplifted** hand to give it to H5951
Mt 26:74 down curses, and *he* **s** to them, "I don't G3923
Mk 14:71 down curses, and *he* **s** to them, "I don't G3923
Lk 1:73 the oath *he* **s** to our father Abraham: G3923
Heb 6:13 him to swear by, *he* **s** by himself, G3923
Rev 10: 6 And *he* **s** by him who lives for ever and G3923

SWORN (32) [SWEAR]
Ge 14:22 "*With* **raised** hand *I have* **s an oath** to the H8123
Ge 26:28 ought to be a **s agreement** between us'— H460
Nu 30:13 vow she makes or any **s** pledge to deny H8652
Dt 2:14 from the camp, as the LORD *had* **s** to them. H8678
Jos 5: 6 For the LORD *had* **s** to them that they would H8678
Jos 9:18 the assembly *had* **s an oath** to them by H8678
Jos 21:43 Israel all the land *he had* **s** to give their H8678
Jos 21:44 just as *he had* **s** to their ancestors. H8678
Jdg 2:15 to defeat them, just as he *had* **s** to them. H8678
1Sa 20:42 we *have* **s** friendship with each other H8678
2Sa 21: 2 the Israelites *had* **s** to spare them, but H8678
2Ch 15:15 the oath because *they had* **s** it H8678
Ne 9:15 the land *you had* **s with uplifted** hand to H5951
Ps 89: 3 chosen one, *I have* **s** to David my servant H8678
Ps 89:35 Once for all, *I have* **s** by my holiness H8678
Ps 110: 4 The LORD *has* **s** and will not change his H8678
Isa 14:24 The LORD Almighty *has* **s**, "Surely, as I H8678
Isa 45:23 By myself *I have* **s**, my mouth has uttered H8678
Isa 54: 9 So now *I have* **s** not to be angry with you H8678
Isa 62: 8 The LORD *has* **s** by his right hand and by H8678
Jer 5: 7 forsaken me and **s** by gods that are not H8678
Jer 32:22 them this land *you had* **s** to give their H8678
Jer 51:14 The LORD Almighty *has* **s** by himself: I will H8678
Eze 20:28 the land I *had* **s** to give them H5951+906+3338
Eze 20:42 the land I *had* **s with uplifted** hand to give H5951
Eze 21:23 those *who have* **s allegiance** to H8678+8652
Eze 44:12 therefore I *have* **s with uplifted** hand that H5951
Da 9:11 the curses and **s judgments** written in the H8652
Am 4: 2 The Sovereign LORD *has* **s** by his holiness H8678
Am 6: 8 The Sovereign LORD *has* **s** by himself—the H8678
Am 8: 7 The LORD *has* **s** by himself, the Pride of H8678
Heb 7:21 "The Lord *has* **s** and will not change his G3923

SWUNG (3) [SWING]
Eze 26: 2 its doors *have* **s open** to me; now that H6015
Rev 14:16 seated on the cloud **s** his sickle over the G965
Rev 14:19 The angel **s** his sickle on the earth G965

SYCAMORE-FIG (6) [FIG]
1Ki 10:27 as plentiful as **s trees** in the foothills. H9204
1Ch 27:28 of the olive and **s trees** in the western H9204
2Ch 1:15 as plentiful as **s trees** in the foothills. H9204
2Ch 9:27 as plentiful as **s trees** in the foothills. H9204
Am 7:14 shepherd, and I also took care of **s trees**. H9204
Lk 19: 4 ahead and climbed a **s tree** to see him, G5191

SYCAMORE-FIGS (1) [FIG]
Ps 78:47 their vines with hail and their **s** with sleet. H9204

SYCHAR (1)
Jn 4: 5 So he came to a town in Samaria called **S** G5373

SYCOMORE (KJV) SYCAMORE-FIG

SYENE (KJV) ASWAN

SYMBOL (2) [SYMBOLIC, SYMBOLIZES, SYMBOLS]
Ex 13:16 on your hand and a **s** on your forehead H3213
Nu 6: 7 the **s of** their **dedication** *to* God is on H5694

SYMBOLIC (1) [SYMBOL]
Zec 3: 8 who are men **s of things to come**: H4603

SYMBOLIZES (4) [SYMBOL]
Nu 6: 9 thus defiling the **hair** *that* **s** their dedication AIT
Nu 6:18 shave off the **hair** *that* **s** their dedication. AIT
Nu 6:19 shaved off the hair that **s** their dedication, NDT
1Pe 3:21 this water **s** baptism that now saves you G531

SYMBOLS (4) [SYMBOL]
Dt 6: 8 Tie them as **s** on your hands and bind them H253
Dt 11:18 tie them as **s** on your hands and bind them H253
Isa 8:18 We are signs and **s** in Israel from the LORD H4603
Isa 57: 8 your doorposts you have put your **pagan s**. H2355

SYMPATHETIC (1) [SYMPATHY]
1Pe 3: 8 be like-minded, be **s**, love one another G5218

SYMPATHIZE (1) [SYMPATHY]
Job 2:11 agreement to go and **s** with him and H5653

SYMPATHY (7) [SYMPATHETIC, SYMPATHIZE]
2Sa 10: 2 a delegation to **express** his **s** to Hanun H5714
2Sa 10: 3 by sending envoys to you *to* **express s**? H5714
1Ch 19: 2 a delegation to **express** his **s** *to* Hanun H5714
1Ch 19: 2 of the Ammonites to **express s** *to* him, H5714
1Ch 19: 3 by sending envoys to you *to* **express s**? H5714
Ps 69:20 I looked for **s**, but there was none, H5653
Jer 16: 5 do not go to mourn or **show s**, because I H5653

SYNAGOGUE (46) [SYNAGOGUES]
Mt 9:18 a **s leader** came and knelt before him and G807
Mt 9:23 entered the **s leader's** house and saw G807
Mt 12: 9 on from that place, he went into their **s**, G5252
Mt 13:54 he began teaching the people in their **s** G5252
Mk 1:21 Jesus went into the **s** and began to teach. G5252
Mk 1:23 then a man in their **s** who was possessed G5252
Mk 1:29 As soon as they left the **s**, they went with G5252
Mk 3: 1 Another time Jesus went into the **s**, and a G5252
Mk 5:22 Then one *of* the **s leaders**, named Jairus G801
Mk 5:35 from the house of Jairus, the **s leader**. G801
Mk 5:38 they came to the home *of* the **s leader**, G801
Mk 6: 2 he began to teach in the **s**, and many G5252
Lk 4:16 on the Sabbath day he went into the **s**, G5252
Lk 4:20 of everyone in the **s** were fastened on him G5252
Lk 4:28 All the people in the **s** were furious when G5252
Lk 4:33 In the **s** there was a man possessed by a G5252
Lk 4:38 Jesus left the **s** and went to the home of G5252
Lk 6: 6 he went into the **s** and was teaching, G5252
Lk 7: 5 he loves our nation and has built our **s**." G5252
Lk 8:41 man named Jairus, a **s** leader, came and G5252
Lk 8:49 from the house of Jairus, the **s leader**. G801
Lk 13:14 Sabbath, the **s leader** said to the people G801
Jn 6:59 while teaching in the **s** in Capernaum. G5252
Jn 9:22 was the Messiah would be **put out of the s**. G697
Jn 12:42 faith for fear they would be **put out of the s**; G697
Jn 16: 2 They will put you **out of the s**; in fact, the G697
Ac 6: 9 from members of the **S** of the Freedmen G5252
Ac 13:14 Sabbath they entered the **s** and sat down. G5252
Ac 13:15 the **leaders of the s** sent word to them G801
Ac 13:42 As Paul and Barnabas were leaving the **s** NDT
Ac 14: 1 Barnabas went as usual into the Jewish **s**. G5252
Ac 17: 1 where there was a Jewish **s**. G5252
Ac 17: 2 Paul went into **the s**, and on three G899S
Ac 17:10 arriving there, they went to the Jewish **s**. G5252
Ac 17:17 he reasoned in the **s** with both Jews and G5252
Ac 18: 4 Every Sabbath he reasoned in the **s**, trying G5252
Ac 18: 7 Then Paul left the **s** and went next door to G5252
Ac 18: 8 the **s leader**, and his entire G801
Ac 18:17 on Sosthenes the **s leader** and beat him in G801
Ac 18:19 went into the **s** and reasoned with the G5252
Ac 18:26 He began to speak boldly in the **s**. G5252
Ac 19: 8 Paul entered the **s** and spoke boldly there G5252
Ac 22:19 that I went from one **s** to another to G5252
Ac 26:11 time I went from one **s** to another to have G5252
Rev 2: 9 Jews and are not, but are a **s** of Satan. G5252
Rev 3: 9 will make those who are of the **s** of Satan, G5252

SYNAGOGUES (23) [SYNAGOGUE]
Mt 4:23 teaching in their **s**, proclaiming the good G5252
Mt 6: 2 hypocrites do in the **s** and on the streets, G5252
Mt 6: 5 to pray standing in the **s** and on the street G5252
Mt 9:35 teaching in their **s**, proclaiming the good G5252
Mt 10:17 the local councils and be flogged in the **s**. G5252
Mt 23: 6 the most important seats in the **s**; G5252
Mt 23:34 will flog in your **s** and pursue from town G5252
Mk 1:39 preaching in their **s** and driving out G5252
Mk 12:39 important seats in the **s** and the places of G5252
Mk 13: 9 to the local councils and flogged in the **s**. G5252
Lk 4:15 He was teaching in their **s**, and everyone G5252
Lk 4:44 he kept on preaching in the **s** of Judea. G5252
Lk 11:43 important seats in the **s** and respectful G5252
Lk 12:11 "When you are brought before **s**, rulers G5252
Lk 13:10 Jesus was teaching in one *of* the **s**, G5252
Lk 20:46 important seats in the **s** and the places of G5252
Lk 21:12 hand you over to **s** and put you in prison G5252
Jn 18:20 "I always taught in **s** or at the temple G5252
Ac 9: 2 him for letters to the **s** in Damascus, G5252
Ac 9:20 to preach in the **s** that Jesus is the Son G5252
Ac 13: 5 the word of God in the Jewish **s**. G5252
Ac 15:21 is read in the **s** on every Sabbath. G5252
Ac 24:12 up a crowd in the **s** or anywhere else in G5252

SYNTYCHE (1)
Php 4: 2 I plead with **S** to be of the same G5345

SYRACUSE (1)
Ac 28:12 We put in at **S** and stayed there three days G5352

SYRIA (KJV) ARAM

SYRIA (8) [SYRIAN, SYRIAN PHOENICIA]
Mt 4:24 News about him spread all over **S**, and G5353
Lk 2: 2 place while Quirinius was governor *of* **S**.) G5353
Ac 15:23 believers in Antioch, **S** and Cilicia: G5353
Ac 15:41 He went through **S** and Cilicia G5353
Ac 18:18 the brothers and sisters and sailed for **S**, G5353
Ac 20: 3 him just as he was about to sail for **S**, G5353
Ac 21: 3 to the south of it, we sailed on to **S**. G5353
Gal 1:21 I went to **S** and Cilicia. G3836+3107+3836+5353

SYRIAN, SYRIANS (KJV) ARAMEAN, ARAMEANS

SYRIAN (1) [SYRIA]
Lk 4:27 them was cleansed—only Naaman the **S**." G5354

SYRIAN PHOENICIA (1) [PHOENICIA, SYRIA]
Mk 7:26 woman was a Greek, born in **S**. G5355

SYRTIS (1)
Ac 27:17 would run aground on the **sandbars of S**, G5358

T

TAANACH (7)
Jos 12:21 the king of **T** one the king of Megiddo one H9505
Jos 17:11 **T** and Megiddo, together with their H9505
Jos 21:25 they received **T** and Gath Rimmon, H9505
Jdg 1:27 of Beth Shan or **T** or Dor or Ibleam or H9505
Jdg 5:19 At **T**, by the waters of Megiddo, they took H9505
1Ki 4:12 son of Ahilud—in **T** and Megiddo, and in H9505
1Ch 7:29 were Beth Shan, **T**, Megiddo and Dor, H9505

TAANATH SHILOH (1)
Jos 16: 6 the north it curved eastward to **T**, H9304

TABALIAH (1)
1Ch 26:11 **T** the third and Zechariah the fourth. H3189

TABBAOTH (2)
Ezr 2:43 the descendants of Ziha, Hasupha, **T**, H3191
Ne 7:46 the descendants of Ziha, Hasupha, **T**, H3191

TABBATH (1)
Jdg 7:22 far as the border of Abel Meholah near **T**. H3195

TABEEL (2)
Ezr 4: 7 **T** and the rest of his associates wrote a H3175
Isa 7: 6 make the son of **T** king over it. H3174

TABERAH (2)
Nu 11: 3 So that place was called **T**, because fire H9323
Dt 9:22 You also made the LORD angry at **T**, at H9323

TABERNACLE (113) [TABERNACLES]
Ex 25: 9 Make this **t** and all its furnishings exactly H5438
Ex 26: 1 "Make the **t** with ten curtains of finely H5438
Ex 26: 6 curtains together so that the **t** is a unit. H5438
Ex 26: 7 of goat hair for the tent over the **t**— H5438
Ex 26:12 over is to hang down at the rear of the **t**. H5438
Ex 26:13 over the sides of the **t** so as to cover it. H5438
Ex 26:15 upright frames of acacia wood for the **t**. H5438
Ex 26:17 Make all the frames of the **t** in this way. H5438
Ex 26:18 twenty frames for the south side of the **t** H5438
Ex 26:20 the north side of the **t**, make twenty H5438
Ex 26:22 the far end, that is, the west end of the **t**, H5438
Ex 26:26 five for the frames on one side of the **t**, H5438
Ex 26:27 frames on the west, at the far end of the **t**. H5438
Ex 26:30 "Set up the **t** according to the plan shown H5438

Ex 26:35 north side of the **t** and put the lampstand H5438
Ex 27: 9 "Make a courtyard for the **t**. The south H5438
Ex 27:19 other articles used in the service of the **t**, H5438
Ex 35:11 the **t** with its tent and its covering, clasps H5438
Ex 35:15 the doorway at the entrance to the **t**; H5438
Ex 35:18 the tent pegs for the **t** and for the courtyard H5438
Ex 36: 8 workers made the **t** with ten curtains of H5438
Ex 36:13 curtains together so that the **t** was a unit. H5438
Ex 36:14 of goat hair for the tent over the **t**— H5438
Ex 36:20 upright frames of acacia wood for the **t**. H5438
Ex 36:22 made all the frames of the **t** in this way. H5438
Ex 36:23 twenty frames for the south side of the **t** H5438
Ex 36:25 the north side of the **t**, they made twenty H5438
Ex 36:27 the far end, that is, the west end of the **t**, H5438
Ex 36:28 the corners of the **t** at the far end. H5438
Ex 36:31 five for the frames on one side of the **t**, H5438
Ex 36:32 frames on the west, at the far end of the **t**. H5438
Ex 38:20 the tent pegs of the **t** and of the H5438
Ex 38:21 amounts of the materials used for the **t**, H5438
Ex 38:21 the tabernacle, the **t** *of* the covenant law H5438
Ex 38:31 the tent pegs for the **t** and those for the H5438
Ex 39:32 So all the work on the **t**, the tent of H5438
Ex 39:33 Then they brought the **t** to Moses: the tent H5438
Ex 39:40 all the furnishings for the **t**, the tent of H5438
Ex 40: 2 "Set up the **t**, the tent of meeting, on the H5438
Ex 40: 5 put the curtain at the entrance to the **t**. H5438
Ex 40: 6 offering in front of the entrance to the **t**, H5438
Ex 40: 9 oil and anoint the **t** and everything in it; H5438
Ex 40:17 So the **t** was set up on the first day of the H5438
Ex 40:18 When Moses set up the **t**, he put the H5438
Ex 40:19 the tent over the **t** and put the covering H5438
Ex 40:21 the ark into the **t** and hung the shielding H5438
Ex 40:22 the north side of the **t** outside the curtain H5438
Ex 40:24 the table on the south side of the **t** H5438
Ex 40:28 put up the curtain at the entrance to the **t**. H5438
Ex 40:29 burnt offering near the entrance to the **t**, H5438
Ex 40:33 around the **t** and altar and put up H5438
Ex 40:34 the glory of the LORD filled the **t**. H5438
Ex 40:35 and the glory of the LORD filled the **t**. H5438
Ex 40:36 the cloud lifted from above the **t**, H5438
Ex 40:38 cloud of the LORD was over the **t** by day, H5438
Lev 8:10 oil and anointed the **t** and everything in it H5438
Lev 17: 4 to the LORD in front of the **t** *of* the LORD— H5438
Nu 1:50 in charge of the **t** *of* the covenant law— H5438
Nu 1:50 They are to carry the **t** and all its H5438
Nu 1:51 Whenever the **t** is to move, the Levites are H5438
Nu 1:51 whenever the **t** is to be set up, the H5438
Nu 1:53 tents around the **t** *of* the covenant law so H5438
Nu 1:53 the care of the **t** *of* the covenant law." H5438
Nu 3: 7 tent of meeting by doing the work of the **t**. H5438
Nu 3: 8 of the Israelites by doing the work of the **t**. H5438
Nu 3:23 were to camp on the west, behind the **t**. H5438
Nu 3:25 responsible for the care of the **t** and tent, H5438
Nu 3:26 the courtyard surrounding the **t** and altar, H5438
Nu 3:29 were to camp on the south side of the **t**. H5438
Nu 3:35 were to camp on the north side of the **t**. H5438
Nu 3:36 to take care of the frames of the **t**, H5438
Nu 3:38 his sons were to camp to the east of the **t**, H5438
Nu 4:16 charge of the entire **t** and everything in it, H5438
Nu 4:25 They are to carry the curtains of the **t**, that H5438
Nu 4:26 the courtyard surrounding the **t** and altar, H5438
Nu 4:31 they are to carry the frames of the **t**, its H5438
Nu 5:17 some dust from the **t** floor into the water. H5438
Nu 7: 1 When Moses finished setting up the **t**, he H5438
Nu 7: 3 These they presented before the **t**. H5438
Nu 9:15 On the day the **t**, the tent of the covenant H5438
Nu 9:15 the cloud above the **t** looked like fire. H5438
Nu 9:18 As long as the cloud stayed over the **t** H5438
Nu 9:19 cloud remained over the **t** a long time, H5438
Nu 9:20 the cloud was over the **t** only a few days; H5438
Nu 9:22 cloud stayed over the **t** for two days or a H5438
Nu 10:11 from above the **t** *of* the covenant law. H5438
Nu 10:17 Then the **t** was taken down, and the H5438
Nu 10:21 The **t** was to be set up before they arrived. H5438
Nu 16: 9 work at the LORD's **t** and to stand before H5438
Nu 17:13 even comes near the **t** *of* the LORD will die. H5438
Nu 19:13 a human corpse, they defile the LORD's **t**. H5438
Nu 31:30 responsible for the care of the LORD's **t**." H5438
Nu 31:47 responsible for the care of the LORD's **t**. H5438
Jos 22:19 where the LORD's **t** stands, and share the H5438
Jos 22:29 the LORD our God that stands before his **t**." H5438
1Ch 6:32 They ministered with music before the **t** H5438
1Ch 6:48 assigned to all the other duties of the **t**, H5438
1Ch 16:39 priests before the **t** *of* the LORD at the high H5438
1Ch 21:29 The **t** *of* the LORD, which Moses had made H5438
1Ch 23:26 need to carry the **t** or any of the articles H5438
2Ch 1: 5 was in Gibeon in front of the **t** *of* the LORD; H5438
Ps 78:60 He abandoned the **t** *of* Shiloh, the tent he H5438
Ac 7:43 have taken up the **t** of Molek and the star *G5008*
Ac 7:44 ancestors had the **t** of the covenant law *G5008*
Ac 7:45 After receiving **the t**, our ancestors under *G4005S*
Heb 8: 2 sanctuary, the true **t** set up by the Lord *G5008*
Heb 8: 5 warned when he was about to build the **t**: *G5008*
Heb 9: 2 A **t** was set up. In its first room were the *G5008*
Heb 9: 8 as long as the first **t** was still functioning. *G5008*
Heb 9:11 more perfect **t** that is not made with *G5008*
Heb 9:21 the blood both the **t** and everything used *G5008*
Heb 13:10 who minister *at* the **t** have no right to *G5008*
Rev 15: 5 the **t** of the covenant law—and it *G5008*

TABERNACLES (10) [TABERNACLE]

Lev 23:34 month the LORD's Festival of **T** begins, H6109
Dt 16:13 the Festival of **T** for seven days after you H6109
Dt 16:16 Festival of Weeks and the Festival of **T**. H6109
Dt 31:10 canceling debts, during the Festival of **T**, H6109
2Ch 8:13 Festival of Weeks and the Festival of **T**. H6109
Ezr 3: 4 the Festival of **T** with the required number H6109
Zec 14:16 to celebrate the Festival of **T**. H6109
Zec 14:18 not go up to celebrate the Festival of **T**. H6109
Zec 14:19 not go up to celebrate the Festival of **T**. H6109
Jn 7: 2 when the Jewish Festival *of* **T** was near, *G5009*

TABITHA (2)

Ac 9:36 In Joppa there was a disciple named **T** (in *G5412*
Ac 9:40 the dead woman, he said, "**T**, get up." *G5412*

TABLE (86) [TABLES]

Ge 43:34 were served to them from Joseph's **t**, H7156S
Ex 25:23 "Make a **t** *of* acacia wood—two cubits H8947
Ex 25:26 gold rings for **the t** and fasten them to H2257S
Ex 25:27 to hold the poles used in carrying the **t**. H8947
Ex 25:28 them with gold and carry the **t** with them. H8947
Ex 25:30 the Presence on this **t** to be before me at H8947
Ex 26:35 Place the **t** outside the curtain on the north H8947
Ex 30:27 the **t** and all its articles, the lampstand H8947
Ex 31: 8 the **t** and its articles, the pure gold H8947
Ex 35:13 the **t** with its poles and all its articles and H8947
Ex 37:10 They made the **t** of acacia wood—two H8947
Ex 37:13 gold rings for **the t** and fastened them H2257S
Ex 37:14 to hold the poles used in carrying the **t**. H8947
Ex 37:15 carrying the **t** were made of acacia H8947
Ex 37:16 from pure gold the articles for the **t**— H8947
Ex 39:36 the **t** with all its articles and the bread of H8947
Ex 40: 4 Bring in the **t** and set out what belongs on H8947
Ex 40:22 Moses placed the **t** in the tent of meeting H8947
Ex 40:24 opposite the **t** on the south side of H8947
Lev 24: 6 on the **t** of pure gold before the LORD. H8947
Nu 3:31 the care of the ark, the **t**, the lampstand, H8947
Nu 4: 7 "Over the **t** *of* the Presence they are to H8947
Jdg 1: 7 cut off have picked up scraps under my **t**. H8947
1Sa 20:29 is why he has not come to the king's **t**." H8947
1Sa 20:34 Jonathan got up from the **t** in fierce anger; H8947
2Sa 9: 7 and you will always eat at my **t**. H8947
2Sa 9:10 of your master, will always eat at my **t**." H8947
2Sa 9:11 ate at David's **t** like one of the king's sons H8947
2Sa 9:13 because he always ate at the king's **t**; he H8947
2Sa 19:28 a place among those who eat at your **t**. H8947
1Ki 2: 7 them be among those who eat at your **t**. H8947
1Ki 4:27 all who came to the king's **t**. H8947
1Ki 7:48 the golden **t** on which was the bread of H8947
1Ki 10: 5 the food on his **t**, the seating of his H8947
1Ki 13:20 While they were sitting at the **t**, the word H8947
1Ki 18:19 of Asherah, who eat at Jezebel's **t**." H8947
2Ki 4:10 on the roof and put in it a bed and a **t**, H8947
2Ki 25:29 life ate regularly **at** the king's **t**. H4200+7156S
1Ch 9:32 every Sabbath the bread **set out on the t**. H5121
1Ch 23:29 in charge of the bread **set out on the t**, H5121
1Ch 28:16 of gold for **each t** for H8947+2256+8947
2Ch 9: 4 the food on his **t**, the seating of his H8947
2Ch 13:11 ceremonially clean **t** and light the lamps H8947
2Ch 29:18 the **t** *for* setting out the consecrated H8947
Ne 5:17 fifty Jews and officials ate at my **t**, H8947
Ne 10:33 the bread **set out on the t**; for the H5121
Job 36:16 the comfort of your **t** laden with choice H8947
Ps 23: 5 You prepare a **t** before me in the H8947
Ps 69:22 May the **t** set before them become a H8947
Ps 78:19 God really spread a **t** in the wilderness? H8947
Ps 128: 3 will be like olive shoots around your **t**. H8947
Pr 9: 2 mixed her wine; she has also set her **t**. H8947
SS 1:12 While the king was at his **t**, my perfume H4990
Isa 65:11 who spread a **t** for Fortune and fill bowls H8947
Jer 52:33 life ate regularly **at** the king's **t**. H4200+7156S
Eze 23:41 with a **t** spread before it on which you had H8947
Eze 39:20 At my **t** you will eat your fill of horses and H8947
Eze 41:22 "This is the **t** that is before the LORD." H8947
Eze 44:16 are to come near my **t** to minister before H8947
Da 1: 5 of food and wine from the king's **t**. H5492
Da 11:27 will sit at the same **t** and lie to each other, H8947
Mal 1: 7 saying that the LORD's **t** is contemptible. H8947
Mal 1:12 it by saying, 'The Lord's **t** is defiled,' and, H8947
Mt 15:27 the crumbs that fall from their master's **t**." *G5544*
Mt 26: 7 on his head *as he was* **reclining at the t**. *G367*
Mt 26:20 Jesus *was* **reclining at the t** with the Twelve *G367*
Mk 7:28 the dogs under the **t** eat the children's *G5544*
Mk 14: 3 **reclining at the t** in the home of Simon *G2879*
Mk 14:18 *While* they *were* **reclining at** *the* **t** eating *G367*
Lk 7:36 Pharisee's house and **reclined at the t**. *G2884*
Lk 11:37 so he went in and **reclined at the t**. *G404*
Lk 12:37 *will* **have** them **recline at the t** and will *G369*
Lk 14: 7 guests picked the **places of honor at the t**, *G4752*
Lk 14:15 one of those **at the t with** him heard this, *G5263*
Lk 16:21 to eat what fell from the rich man's **t**. *G5544*
Lk 22:14 Jesus and his apostles **reclined at the t**. *G404*
Lk 22:21 going to betray me is with mine on the **t**. *G5544*
Lk 22:27 the *one who is* **at the t** or the one who *G367*
Lk 22:27 Is it not the *one who is* **at the t**? But I am *G367*
Lk 22:30 eat and drink at my **t** in my kingdom and *G5544*
Lk 24:30 When he *was* **at the t** with them, he took *G2884*
Jn 12: 2 among those **reclining at the t** with him. *G367*
Ro 11: 9 "May their **t** become a snare and a trap, *G5544*
1Co 10:21 in both the Lord's **t** and the table of *G5544*
1Co 10:21 both the Lord's table and the **t** of demons. *G5544*
Heb 9: 2 lampstand and the **t** with its consecrated *G5544*

TABLES (18) [TABLE]

1Ch 28:16 the weight of silver for the silver **t**; H8947
2Ch 4: 8 He made ten **t** and placed them in the H8947
2Ch 4:19 the **t** on which was the bread of the H8947
Est 9: 1 now **the t were turned** and the Jews H2200
Isa 21: 5 They set the **t**, they spread the rugs, they H8947
Isa 28: 8 All the **t** are covered with vomit and there H8947
Eze 40:39 of the gateway were two **t** on each side, H8947
Eze 40:40 entrance of the north gateway were two **t**, H8947
Eze 40:40 on the other side of the steps were two **t**. H8947
Eze 40:41 So there were four **t** on one side of the H8947
Eze 40:41 on the other—eight **t** in all—on which the H8947
Eze 40:42 There were also four **t** of dressed stone H8947
Eze 40:43 The **t** were for the flesh of the offerings H8947
Mt 21:12 He overturned the **t** of the money *G5544*
Mk 11:15 He overturned the **t** of the money *G5544*
Jn 2:14 others sitting at **t** exchanging money. NDT
Jn 2:15 money changers and overturned their **t**. *G5544*
Ac 6: 2 of the word of God in order to wait on **t**. *G5544*

TABLET (4) [TABLETS]

Pr 3: 3 write them on the **t** *of* your heart. H4283
Pr 7: 3 write them on the **t** *of* your heart. H4283
Isa 30: 8 Go now, write it on a **t** for them, inscribe it H4283
Lk 1:63 He asked for a **writing t**, and to everyone's *G4400*

TABLETS (42) [TABLET]

Ex 16:34 the manna with the **t of the covenant law**, H6343
Ex 24:12 I will give you the **t** *of* stone with the law H4283
Ex 25:16 put in the ark the **t of the covenant law**. H6343
Ex 25:21 the ark the **t of the covenant law** that I will H6343
Ex 30: 6 that is over the **t of the covenant law**— H6343
Ex 31:18 gave him the two **t** *of* the covenant law, H4283
Ex 31:18 the **t** *of* stone inscribed by the finger of H4283
Ex 32:15 with the two **t** *of* the covenant law in H4283
Ex 32:16 The **t** were the work of God; the writing H4283
Ex 32:16 was the writing of God, engraved on the **t**. H4283
Ex 32:19 he threw the **t** out of his hands, H4283
Ex 34: 1 "Chisel out two stone **t** like the first ones H4283
Ex 34: 1 on them the words that were on the first **t**, H4283
Ex 34: 4 chiseled out two stone **t** like the first ones H4283
Ex 34: 4 he carried the two stone **t** in his hands. H4283
Ex 34:28 And he wrote on the **t** the words of the H4283
Ex 34:29 Sinai with the two **t** *of* the covenant law in H4283
Ex 40:20 took the **t of the covenant law** and placed H6343
Lev 16:13 cover above the **t of the covenant law**, H6343
Dt 4:13 then wrote them on two stone **t**. H4283
Dt 5:22 them on two stone **t** and gave them to me H4283
Dt 9: 9 on the mountain to receive the **t** *of* stone, H4283
Dt 9: 9 the **t** *of* the covenant that the LORD had H4283
Dt 9:10 LORD gave me two stone **t** inscribed by the H4283
Dt 9:11 the LORD gave me the two stone **t**, the H4283
Dt 9:11 two stone tablets, the **t** *of* the covenant. H4283
Dt 9:15 And the two **t** *of* the covenant were in my H4283
Dt 9:17 So I took the two **t** and threw them out of H4283
Dt 10: 1 "Chisel out two stone **t** like the first ones H4283
Dt 10: 2 I will write on the **t** the words that were on H4283
Dt 10: 2 tablets the words that were on the first **t**, H4283
Dt 10: 3 chiseled out two stone **t** like the first ones, H4283
Dt 10: 3 the mountain with the two **t** in my hands. H4283
Dt 10: 4 LORD wrote on these **t** what he had written H4283
Dt 10: 5 mountain and put the **t** in the ark I had H4283
1Ki 8: 9 except the two stone **t** that Moses had H4283
2Ch 5:10 ark except the two **t** that Moses had H4283
Jer 17: 1 on the **t** *of* their hearts and on the horns H4283
Hab 2: 2 make it plain on **t** so that a herald may H4283
2Co 3: 3 not on **t** of stone but on tablets of human *G4419*
2Co 3: 3 tablets of stone but on **t** of human hearts. *G4419*
Heb 9: 4 budded, and the **stone t** of the covenant. *G4419*

TABOR (10) [AZNOTH TABOR, KISLOTH TABOR]

Jos 19:22 The boundary touched **T**, Shahazumah H9314
Jdg 4: 6 Zebulun and lead them up to Mount **T**. H9314
Jdg 4:12 son of Abinoam had gone up to Mount **T**, H9314
Jdg 4:14 So Barak went down Mount **T**, with ten H9314
Jdg 8:18 "What kind of men did you kill at **T**?" H9314
1Sa 10: 3 there until you reach the great tree of **T**. H9314
1Ch 6:77 Rimmono and **T**, together with H9314
Ps 89:12 **T** and Hermon sing for joy at your name. H9314
Jer 46:18 come who is like **T** among the mountains, H9314
Hos 5: 1 a snare at Mizpah, a net spread out on **T**. H9314

TABRET, TABRETS (KJV) TIMBRELS

TABRIMMON (1)

1Ki 15:18 sent them to Ben-Hadad son of **T**, H3193

TACHES (KJV) CLASPS

TACKLE (1)

Ac 27:19 threw the ship's **t** overboard with their *G5006*

TACT (1)

Da 2:14 Daniel spoke to him with wisdom and **t**. A10302

TADMOR (2)

1Ki 9:18 Baalath, and **T** in the desert, within his H9330
2Ch 8: 4 He also built up **T** in the desert and all the H9330

TAHAN (2) [TAHANITE]

Nu 26:35 through **T**, the Tahanite clan. H9380
1Ch 7:25 his son, Telah his son, **T** his son, H9380

TAHANITE (1) [TAHAN]
Nu 26:35 Bekerite clan; through Tahan, the **T** clan. H9385

TAHASH (1)
Ge 22:24 Tebah, Gaham, **T** and Maakah. H9392

TAHATH (6)
Nu 33:26 They left Makheloth and camped at **T**. H9395
Nu 33:27 They left **T** and camped at Terah. H9395
1Ch 6:24 **T** his son, Uriel his son, Uzziah his son H9394
1Ch 6:37 the son of **T**, the son of Assir, the son of H9394
1Ch 7:20 Bered his son, **T** his son, Eleadah his son H9394
1Ch 7:20 his son, Eleadah his son, **T** his son, H9394

TAHKEMONITE (1)
2Sa 23: 8 Josheb-Basshebeth, a **T**, was chief of the H9376

TAHPANHES (7)
Jer 2:16 men of Memphis and **T** have cracked your H9387
Jer 43: 7 to the LORD and went as far as **T**. H9387
Jer 43: 8 In **T** the word of the LORD came to H9387
Jer 43: 9 at the entrance to Pharaoh's palace in **T**. H9387
Jer 44: 1 in Migdol, **T** and Memphis—and in Upper H9387
Jer 46:14 proclaim it also in Memphis and **T**: H9387
Eze 30:18 will be the day at **T** when I break the yoke H9387

TAHPENES (3)
1Ki 11:19 of his own wife, Queen **T**, in marriage. H9388
1Ki 11:20 The sister of **T** bore him a son named H9388
1Ki 11:20 whom **T** brought up in the royal palace. H9388

TAHREA (1)
1Ch 9:41 Pithon, Melek, **T** and Ahaz. H9390

TAHTIM HODSHI (1)
2Sa 24: 6 to Gilead and the region of **T**, H9398

TAIL (15) [TAILS]
Ex 4: 4 "Reach out your hand and take it by the **t**." H2387
Ex 29:22 this ram the fat, the **fat t**, the fat on the H487
Lev 3: 9 the entire **fat t** cut off close to the backbone H487
Lev 7: 3 the **fat t** and the fat that covers the internal H487
Lev 8:25 he took the fat, the **fat t**, all the fat around H487
Lev 9:19 ox and the ram—the **fat t**, the layer of fat, H487
Dt 28:13 The LORD will make you the head, not the **t**. H2387
Dt 28:44 will be the head, but you will be the **t**. H2387
Jdg 15: 4 foxes and tied them **t** to tail in pairs. H2387
Jdg 15: 4 foxes and tied them tail to **t** in pairs. H2387
Job 40:17 Its **t** sways like a cedar; the sinews of its H2387
Isa 9:14 will cut off from Israel both head and **t**, H2387
Isa 9:15 the prophets who teach lies are the **t**. H2387
Isa 19:15 can do—head or **t**, palm branch or reed. H2387
Rev 12: 4 Its **t** swept a third of the stars out of the sky *G4038*

TAILS (5) [TAIL]
Jdg 15: 4 He then fastened a torch to every pair of **t**, H2387
Rev 9:10 They had **t** with stingers, like scorpions *G4038*
Rev 9:10 in their **t** they had power to torment *G4038*
Rev 9:19 horses was in their mouths and in their **t**; *G4038*
Rev 9:19 their tails; for their **t** were like snakes *G4038*

TAKE (860) [RETAKE, TAKEN, TAKES, TAKING, TOOK]
Ge 2:15 Garden of Eden to work it and **t care of** it. H9068
Ge 3:22 out his hand and **t** also from the tree of H4374
Ge 6:21 You *are to* **t** every kind of food that is to be H4374
Ge 7: 2 **T** with you seven pairs of every kind of H4374
Ge 12:19 here is your wife. **T** her and go!" H4374
Ge 15: 7 to give you this land to **t possession** *of* it." H3769
Ge 19:15 **T** your wife and your two daughters who H4374
Ge 21:18 Lift the boy up and **t** him by the hand, for I H2616
Ge 22: 2 Then God said, "**T** your son, your only son, H4374
Ge 22:17 descendants *will* **t possession** *of* the cities H3769
Ge 24: 5 *Shall I then* **t** your son **back** to the H8740+8740
Ge 24: 6 sure that you *do* not **t** my son **back** there," H8740
Ge 24: 8 Only *do* not **t** my son **back** there." H8740
Ge 24:51 Here is Rebekah; **t** her and go, and let her H4374
Ge 27:10 Then **t** it to your father to eat, so that he H995
Ge 28: 2 **T** a wife for yourself there, from among H4374
Ge 28: 4 so that you *may* **t possession** *of* the land H3769
Ge 28: 6 to Paddan Aram to **t** a wife from there, H4374
Ge 29: 7 the sheep and **t** them **back** to pasture." H2143
Ge 30:15 *Will you* **t** my son's mandrakes too?" H4374
Ge 31:31 *you* would **t** your daughters away from me **by force** H1608
Ge 31:32 of yours here with me; and if so, **t** it." H4374
Ge 31:50 my daughters or if *you* **t** any wives besides H4374
Ge 34: 9 us your daughters and **t** our daughters H4374
Ge 34:16 our daughters and **t** your daughters for H4374
Ge 34:17 be circumcised, *we'll* **t** our sister and go." H4374
Ge 37:21 "*Let's* not **t** his life," he said H5782
Ge 37:22 from them and **t** him **back** to his father. H8740
Ge 37:25 on their way to **t** them **down** to Egypt. H3718
Ge 41:34 over the land *to* **t a fifth** *of* the harvest of H2821
Ge 42:19 of you go and **t** grain **back** *for* your starving H995
Ge 42:33 and **t** food *for* your starving households H4374
Ge 42:36 and now *you want to* **T** Benjamin. H4374
Ge 43:11 and **t** them **down** to the man *as* a gift— H3718
Ge 43:12 **T** double the amount of silver with you, for H4374
Ge 43:13 **T** your brother also and go back to the H4374
Ge 43:16 of his house, "**T** these men to my house H995
Ge 43:18 us and seize us as slaves and **t** our donkeys." NDT
Ge 44:29 If *you* **t** this one from me too and harm H4374
Ge 45:19 **T** some carts from Egypt for your children H4374
Ge 48:21 be with you and **t** you **back** to the land of H8740
Ge 50:24 to your aid and **t** you **up** out of this land to H6590
Ex 2: 9 "**T** this baby and nurse him for me H2143
Ex 3: 5 "**T off** your sandals, for the place where H5970
Ex 3:18 *Let us* **t** a three-day journey into the H2143
Ex 4: 4 "Reach out your hand and **t** it by the tail." H296
Ex 4: 9 **t** some water from the Nile and pour it on H4374
Ex 4: 9 The water *you* **t** from the river will become H4374
Ex 4:17 But **t** this staff in your hand so you can H4374
Ex 5: 3 Now *let us* **t** a three-day journey into the H2143
Ex 6: 7 *I will* **t** you as my own people, and I will H4374
Ex 7: 9 '**T** your staff and throw it down before H4374
Ex 7:15 **t** in your hand the staff that was H4374
Ex 7:19 '**T** your staff and stretch out your hand H4374
Ex 7:23 and *did* not **t** even this *to* heart. H8883
Ex 8: 8 the LORD *to* **t** the frogs **away** from me and H6073
Ex 8:27 *We must* **t** a three-day journey into the H2143
Ex 9: 8 "**T** handfuls of soot from a furnace and H4374
Ex 10:17 God *to* **t** this deadly plague **away** from me H6073
Ex 12: 3 this month each man *is to* **t** a lamb for his H4374
Ex 12: 5 and *you may* **t** them from the sheep or the H4374
Ex 12: 6 **T care of** them until the H2118+4200+5466
Ex 12: 7 Then *they are to* **t** some of the blood and H4374
Ex 12:22 **T** a bunch of hyssop, dip it into the blood H4374
Ex 12:32 **T** your flocks and herds, as you have said H4374
Ex 12:46 **t** none of the meat outside the house. H3655
Ex 12:48 then *he may* **t part** like one born in H6913+7928
Ex 16:16 **T** an omer for each person you have in H4374
Ex 16:32 '**T** an omer of manna and keep it for the H4850
Ex 16:33 "**T** a jar and put an omer of manna in it. H4374
Ex 17: 5 **T** with you some of the elders of Israel H4374
Ex 17: 5 elders of Israel and **t** in your hand the H4374
Ex 21: 6 then his master *must* **t** him before the H5602
Ex 21: 6 *He shall* **t** him to the door or the doorpost H5602
Ex 21:23 is serious injury, *you are to* **t** life for life, H5989
Ex 21:34 loss and **t** the dead animal **in exchange**. H2118
Ex 21:36 and **t** the dead animal **in exchange**. H2118
Ex 22:22 "*Do* not **t advantage of** the widow or the H6700
Ex 22:26 *you* **t** your neighbor's cloak **as a pledge** H2471+2471
Ex 23:25 *I will* **t away** sickness from among you H6073
Ex 23:30 enough *to* **t possession** *of* the land. H5706
Ex 28: 9 "**T** two onyx stones and engrave on them H4374
Ex 29: 1 **T** a young bull and two rams without H4374
Ex 29: 5 **T** the garments and dress Aaron with the H4374
Ex 29: 7 **T** the anointing oil and anoint him by H4374
Ex 29:12 **T** some of the bull's blood and put it on H4374
Ex 29:13 Then **t** all the fat on the internal organs H4374
Ex 29:15 "**T** one of the rams, and Aaron and his H4374
Ex 29:16 Slaughter it and **t** the blood and splash it H4374
Ex 29:19 "**T** the other ram, and Aaron and his sons H4374
Ex 29:20 **t** some of its blood and put it on the lobes H4374
Ex 29:21 And **t** some blood from the altar and some H4374
Ex 29:22 "**T** from this ram the fat, the fat tail, the H4374
Ex 29:23 is before the LORD, **t** one round loaf, one NDT
Ex 29:25 Then **t** them from their hands and burn H4374
Ex 29:26 After *you* **t** the breast of the ram for H4374
Ex 29:31 "**T** the ram for the ordination and cook the H4374
Ex 30:12 "When *you* **t a census** *of* the H5951+906+8031
Ex 30:23 "**T** the following fine spices: 500 shekels H4374
Ex 30:34 said to Moses, "**T** fragrant spices—gum H4374
Ex 32: 2 "**T off** the gold earrings that your wives H7293
Ex 32:24 'Whoever has any gold jewelry, **t** it **off**. H7293
Ex 33: 5 Now **t off** your ornaments H3718+4946+6584
Ex 33: 7 Now Moses *used to* **t** a tent and pitch it H4374
Ex 34: 9 our sin, and **t** us **as** *your* **inheritance**." H5706
Ex 35: 5 what you have, **t** an offering for the LORD. H4374
Ex 40: 9 "**T** the anointing oil and anoint the H4374
Lev 2: 2 **t** it to Aaron's sons the priests. H995
Lev 2: 2 priest *shall* **t a handful** of H7858+4850+7859
Lev 2: 8 it to the priest, *who shall* **t** it to the altar. H5602
Lev 2: 9 He *shall* **t out** the memorial portion from H8123
Lev 4: 5 anointed priest *shall* **t** some of the bull's H4374
Lev 4:12 *he must* **t** outside the camp to a place H3655
Lev 4:16 anointed priest *is to* **t** some of the bull's H995
Lev 4:21 Then *he shall* **t** the bull outside the camp H3655
Lev 4:25 Then the priest *shall* **t** some of the blood H4374
Lev 4:30 Then the priest *is to* **t** some of the blood H4374
Lev 4:34 Then the priest *shall* **t** some of the blood H4374
Lev 5:12 who *shall* **t a handful** of it as H7858+4850+7859
Lev 6:11 Then *he is to* **t off** these clothes and put H7320
Lev 6:15 The priest *is to* **t** a handful of the finest H8123
Lev 9: 2 "**T** a bull calf for your sin offering and a H4374
Lev 9: 3 '**T** a male goat for a sin offering, a calf H4374
Lev 10:12 "**T** the grain offering left over from the H4374
Lev 10:17 was given to you to **t away** the guilt of the H5951
Lev 14: 6 *He is* then *to* **t** the live bird and dip it H4374
Lev 14:12 "Then the priest *is to* **t** one of the male H4374
Lev 14:14 The priest *is to* **t** some of the blood of the H4374
Lev 14:15 The priest *shall* then **t** some of the log of H4374
Lev 14:21 *they must* **t** one male lamb as a guilt H4374
Lev 14:24 The priest *is to* **t** the lamb for the guilt H4374
Lev 14:25 guilt offering and **t** some of its blood and H4374
Lev 14:42 Then *they are to* **t** other stones to replace H4374
Lev 14:42 replace these and **t** new clay and plaster H4374
Lev 14:49 To purify the house *he is to* **t** two birds H4374
Lev 14:51 Then *he is to* **t** the cedar wood, the hyssop, H4374
Lev 15:14 On the eighth day *he must* **t** two doves H4374
Lev 15:29 On the eighth day *she must* **t** two doves H4374
Lev 16: 5 community *he is to* **t** two male goats for H4374
Lev 16: 7 Then *he is to* **t** the two goats and present H4374
Lev 16:12 *He is to* **t** a censer full of burning coals H4374
Lev 16:12 fragrant incense and **t** them behind the H995
Lev 16:14 *He is to* **t** some of the bull's blood and H4374
Lev 16:15 the people and **t** its blood behind the H995
Lev 16:18 *He shall* **t** some of the bull's blood and H4374
Lev 16:23 of meeting and **t off** the linen garments H7320
Lev 18:18 " '*Do* not **t** your wife's sister as a rival wife H4374
Lev 23:40 On the first day *you are to* **t** branches from H4374
Lev 24: 5 "**T** fine flour and bake twelve loaves H4374
Lev 24:14 "**T** the blasphemer outside the camp. H3655
Lev 25:14 *do* not **t advantage of** each other. H3561
Lev 25:17 *Do* not **t advantage of** each other, but fear H3561
Lev 25:36 *Do* not **t** interest or any profit from them H4374
Lev 26:31 and *I will* **t** no **delight** in the pleasing H8193
Nu 1: 2 "**T a census** *of* the whole Israelite H5951+8031
Nu 1:50 they *are to* **t care of** it and encamp around H9250
Nu 1:51 the Levites *are to* **t** it **down**, and whenever H3718
Nu 3: 8 *They are to* **t care of** all the furnishings of H9068
Nu 3:36 were appointed to **t care of** the frames of H5466
Nu 3:41 **T** the Levites for me in place of all the H4374
Nu 3:45 "**T** the Levites in place of all the firstborn H4374
Nu 4: 2 "**T a census** *of* the Kohathite H5951+906+8031
Nu 4: 5 are to go in and **t down** the shielding H3718
Nu 4: 9 "*They are to* **t** a blue cloth and cover the H4374
Nu 4:12 "*They are to* **t** all the articles used for H4374
Nu 4:22 "**T a census** also *of* the Gershonites H5951+8031
Nu 5:15 then he *is to* **t** his wife to the priest. H995
Nu 5:15 *He must* also **t** an offering of a tenth of an H995
Nu 5:17 Then he *shall* **t** some holy water in a clay H4374
Nu 5:25 The priest *is to* **t** from her hands the grain H4374
Nu 5:26 The priest *is* then *to* **t a handful** of the H7858
Nu 6:18 *They are to* **t** the hair and put it in the fire H4374
Nu 8: 6 "**T** the Levites from among all the H4374
Nu 8: 8 *Have them* **t** a young bull with its grain H4374
Nu 8: 8 then *you are to* **t** a second young bull H4374
Nu 8:24 shall come to **t part** in the work at H7371+7372
Nu 11:17 and *I will* **t** some of the power of the Spirit H724
Nu 13:30 go up and **t possession** *of* the land, H3769
Nu 16: 6 all your followers are to do this: **T** censers H4374
Nu 16:17 Each man *is to* **t** his censer and put H4374
Nu 16:46 "**T** your censer and put incense in it H4374
Nu 19: 4 Eleazar the priest *is to* **t** some of its blood H4374
Nu 19: 6 The priest *is to* **t** some cedar wood, hyssop H4374
Nu 19:18 is ceremonially clean *is to* **t** some hyssop, H4374
Nu 20: 8 "**T** the staff, and you and your brother H4374
Nu 20:25 his son Eleazar and **t** them **up** Mount Hor. H6590
Nu 21: 7 the LORD *will* **t** the snakes **away** from us." H6073
Nu 23:27 *let me* **t** you to another place. H4374
Nu 25: 4 "**T** all the leaders of these people H4374
Nu 26: 2 "**T a census** *of* the whole H5951+906+8031
Nu 26: 4 "**T** a census of the men twenty years old NDT
Nu 27:18 said to Moses, "**T** Joshua son of Nun, H4374
Nu 31: 2 "**T vengeance** on the Midianites *for* H5933+5935
Nu 31:29 **T** this tribute from their half share and give H4374
Nu 33:53 **T possession** *of* the land and settle in it H3769
Nu 35: 8 **T many** towns from a tribe that has many H8049
Dt 1: 8 Go in and **t possession** *of* the land the H3769
Dt 1:21 Go up and **t possession** *of* it as the LORD H3769
Dt 1:22 about the route *we are to* **t** and the towns H6590
Dt 1:39 it to them and they *will* **t possession** *of* it. H3769
Dt 2:24 Begin *to* **t possession** *of* it and engage H3769
Dt 3: 4 sixty cities that *we did* not **t** from them— H4374
Dt 3:18 given you this land to **t possession** *of* it. H3769
Dt 4: 1 go in and **t possession** *of* the land the H3769
Dt 4: 5 land you are entering to **t possession** *of* it. H3769
Dt 4:22 cross over and **t possession** *of* that good H3769
Dt 4:34 any god ever tried to **t** for himself one H4374
Dt 4:39 Acknowledge and **t** to heart this day that H8740
Dt 6:13 him only and **t** *your* **oaths** in his name. H8678
Dt 6:18 you may go in and **t over** the good land H3769
Dt 7: 3 to their sons or **t** their daughters for your H4374
Dt 7:11 Therefore, **t care** to follow the commands H9068
Dt 7:25 on them, and *do* not **t** it for yourselves H4374
Dt 9: 4 me here to **t possession** *of* this land H3769
Dt 9: 5 are going in to **t possession** *of* their land; H3769
Dt 9:23 "Go up and **t possession** *of* the land I H3769
Dt 9:28 LORD was not able to **t** them into the land H995
Dt 10:20 fast to him and **t** *your* **oaths** in his name. H8678
Dt 11: 8 to go in and **t over** the land that you H3769
Dt 11:10 you are entering to **t over** is not like the H3769
Dt 11:11 the Jordan to **t possession** *of* is a land of H3769
Dt 11:31 to enter and **t possession** *of* the land the H3769
Dt 12:26 But **t** your consecrated things and H5951
Dt 12:32 do not add to it or **t away** from it. H1757
Dt 14:25 **t** the silver with you and go to the H7443
Dt 15:17 then **t** an awl and push it through his H4374
Dt 17: 5 **t** the man or woman who has done this H3655
Dt 17: 8 **t** them to the place the LORD your God will H6590
Dt 17:17 *He must* not **t many** wives, or his heart will H8049
Dt 18:22 of the LORD *does* not **t place** or come true, H2118
Dt 20:14 *you may* **t** these as plunder for yourselves. H1024
Dt 21: 3 nearest the body *shall* **t** a heifer that has H4374
Dt 21:10 into your hands and *you* **t captives**, H8647+8660
Dt 21:11 *you may* **t** her as your wife. H4374
Dt 21:19 mother *shall* **t hold** of him and bring H9530
Dt 22: 1 it but **be sure to t** it **back** to its H8740+8740
Dt 22: 2 **t** it home with you and keep it until they H665
Dt 22: 6 *do* not **t** the mother with the young. H4374
Dt 22: 7 You *may* **t** the young, but be sure to let the H4374
Dt 22:18 the elders *shall* **t** the man and punish H4374
Dt 22:24 *you shall* **t** both of them to the gate of that H3655
Dt 24: 6 *Do* not **t** a pair of millstones—not even the upper one—**as security for a debt** H2471

Dt 24:14 *Do* not **t advantage** *of* a hired worker who H6943
Dt 24:17 **t** the cloak of the widow **as a pledge**. H2471
Dt 25: 1 *they are to* **t** it to court and the judges will H5602
Dt 25: 5 brother *shall* **t** her and marry H995+6584
Dt 25: 9 of the elders, **t off** one of his sandals H2740
Dt 26: 2 **t** some of the firstfruits of all that you H4374
Dt 26: 4 The priest *shall* **t** the basket from your H4374
Dt 28:30 but another will **t** her and rape her. NDT
Dt 28:42 Swarms of locusts *will* **t over** all your trees H3769
Dt 30: 1 you come on you and *you* **t** them to heart H8740
Dt 30: 5 ancestors, and *you will* **t possession** *of* it. H3769
Dt 31: 3 and *you will* **t possession** *of* their land. H3769
Dt 31:26 "**T** this Book of the Law and place it beside H4374
Dt 32:41 *I will* **t vengeance** on my H8740+5934
Dt 32:43 *he will* **t vengeance** on his H8740+5934
Dt 32:46 "**T** to heart all the words I have solemnly H8492
Jos 1:11 to go in and **t possession** *of* the land the H3769
Jos 3: 6 "**T up** the ark of the covenant and pass on H5951
Jos 4: 3 tell them *to* **t up** twelve stones from H5951
Jos 4: 5 Each of you *is to* **t up** a stone on his H8123
Jos 5:15 army replied, "**T off** your sandals, for the H5970
Jos 6: 6 "**T up** the ark of the covenant of the LORD H5951
Jos 7: 3 three thousand men *to* **t** it and do not H5782
Jos 8: 1 **T** the whole army with you, and go up H4374
Jos 8: 7 are to rise up from ambush and **t** the city. H3769
Jos 8:29 ordered them *to* **t** the body from the H3718
Jos 9:11 said to us, '**T** provisions for your journey H4374
Jos 18: 3 you begin to **t possession** *of* the land that H3769
Jos 23: 5 and *you will* **t possession** *of* their land H3769
Jdg 2: 6 they went to **t possession** *of* the land H3769
Jdg 4: 6 **t** with you ten thousand men of Naphtali H4374
Jdg 5: 2 "When the princes in Israel **t the lead** H7276
Jdg 5:12 **T captive** your captives, son of H8647
Jdg 6:20 "**T** the meat and the unleavened bread H4374
Jdg 6:25 "**T** the second bull from your father's herd H4374
Jdg 7: 4 **T** them **down** to the water, and I will thin H3718
Jdg 9:15 come and **t refuge** in my shade; but H2879
Jdg 10:18 "Whoever *will* **t the lead** in attacking the H2725
Jdg 11: 9 "Suppose you **t** me **back** to fight the H8740
Jdg 11:15 Israel *did* not **t** the land of Moab or the H4374
Jdg 11:23 what right have you *to* **t** it **over**? H3769
Jdg 11:24 *Will you* not **t** what your god Chemosh H3769
Jdg 13: 5 He *will* **t the lead** in delivering Israel from H2725
Jdg 15: 2 more attractive? **T** *her* instead." H2118+4200
Jdg 15:10 "We have come to **t** Samson **prisoner**," H673
Jdg 18: 9 Don't hesitate to go there and **t** it **over**. H3769
Jdg 20:10 *We'll* **t** ten men out of every hundred from H4374
Ru 1: 7 road that *would* **t** them **back** to the land H8740
Ru 2:12 whose wings you have come to **t refuge**." H2879
1Sa 1:16 *Do* not **t** your servant **for** a H5989+4200+7156
1Sa 1:22 *I will* **t** him and present him before the LORD H995
1Sa 2:14 brought up the priest *would* **t** for himself. H4374
1Sa 2:16 and then **t** whatever you want, H4374
1Sa 2:16 it over now; if you don't, *I'll* **t** it by force." H4374
1Sa 2:20 this woman to **t the place of** the one she H9393
1Sa 6: 7 but **t** their calves **away** and pen them up. H8740
1Sa 6: 8 **T** the ark of the LORD and put it on the cart H4374
1Sa 6:21 Come down and **t** it **up** to your town." H6590
1Sa 8:11 *He will* **t** your sons and make them serve H4374
1Sa 8:13 *He will* **t** your daughters to be perfumers H4374
1Sa 8:14 *He will* **t** the best of your fields and H4374
1Sa 8:15 *He will* **t a tenth** *of* your grain and of your H6923
1Sa 8:16 donkeys *he will* **t** for his own use. H4374
1Sa 8:17 *He will* **t a tenth** *of* your flocks, and you H6923
1Sa 9: 3 "**T** one of the servants with you and go H4374
1Sa 9: 6 Perhaps he will tell us what way *to* **t**." H2143
1Sa 9: 7 We have no gift to **t** to the man of God H995
1Sa 9: 8 of God so that he will tell us what way to **t**." NDT
1Sa 16: 2 LORD said, "**T** a heifer with you and say H4374
1Sa 16:23 David *would* **t up** his lyre and play. H4374
1Sa 17:17 "**T** this ephah of roasted grain and these H4374
1Sa 17:18 **T along** these ten cheeses to the H995
1Sa 18:25 foreskins, to **t revenge** on his enemies. H5933
1Sa 21: 9 If you want it, **t** it; there is no sword here H4374
1Sa 23:15 that Saul had come out to **t** his life. H1335
1Sa 24:11 you are hunting me down to **t** my life. H4374
1Sa 25:11 Why *should I* **t** my bread and water, and H4374
1Sa 25:29 someone is pursuing you to **t** your life, H1335
1Sa 25:40 has sent us to you to **t** you to become his H4374
1Sa 30:15 my master, and *I will* **t** you **down** to them." H3718
1Sa 30:22 each man *may* **t** his wife and children H5627
2Sa 2:21 **t on** one of the young men and strip him of H296
2Sa 6:10 He was not willing to **t** the ark of the LORD H6073
2Sa 12:11 your very eyes *I will* **t** your wives and give H4374
2Sa 12:28 Otherwise I *will* **t** the city, and it will be H4334
2Sa 13:20 Don't **t** this thing *to* heart." And H8883
2Sa 15: 5 out his hand, **t hold** of him and kiss him. H2616
2Sa 15:16 left ten concubines to **t care of** the palace. H9068
2Sa 15:20 Go back, and **t** your people with you H8740
2Sa 15:25 "**T** the ark of God **back** *into* the city. H8740
2Sa 15:27 *T* your son Ahimaaz **with** you, and also AIT
2Sa 16:21 whom he left to **t care of** the palace. H9068
2Sa 18:19 me run and **t the news** to the king that H1413
2Sa 18:20 "You are not the one to **t** the news today," NDT
2Sa 18:20 "*You may* **t the news** another time, but H1413
2Sa 19:18 ford to **t** the king's household **over** and to H6296
2Sa 19:30 to the king, "*Let him* **t** everything, now H4374
2Sa 20: 3 he had left to **t care of** the palace and put H9068
2Sa 20: 6 **T** your master's men and pursue him, or H4374
2Sa 22: 3 in whom *I* **t refuge**, my shield and H2879
2Sa 22:31 he shields all who **t refuge** in him. H2879
2Sa 24: 1 "Go and **t a census** *of* Israel and Judah." H4948
2Sa 24:10 I beg you, **t away** the guilt of your servant. H6296
2Sa 24:22 "*Let* my lord the king **t** whatever he wishes H4374
1Ki 1: 2 to serve the king and **t care of** him. H2118+6125
1Ki 1:33 "**T** your lord's servants with you and have H4374
1Ki 1:33 my own mule and **t** him **down** to Gihon. H3718
1Ki 5: 9 separate them and you *can* **t** them **away**. H5951
1Ki 8:31 is required to **t an oath** and they come H457
1Ki 8:46 *who* **t** them **captive** to their own H8647+8647
1Ki 11:31 to Jeroboam, "**T** ten pieces for yourself H4374
1Ki 11:34 " 'But *I will* not **t** the whole kingdom out H4374
1Ki 11:35 *I will* **t** the kingdom from his son's hands H4374
1Ki 11:37 as for you, *I will* **t** you, and you will rule H4374
1Ki 14: 3 **T** ten loaves of bread with you, some H4374
1Ki 17:12 a few sticks *to* **t home** and make a meal H995
1Ki 19: 4 "**T** my life; I am no better than my H4374
1Ki 20:18 come out for peace, **t** them alive; if they H9530
1Ki 20:18 they have come out for war, **t** them alive." H9530
1Ki 21:10 Then **t** him **out** and stone him to death." H3655
1Ki 21:15 "Get up and **t possession** *of* the vineyard H3769
1Ki 21:16 went down to **t possession** *of* Naboth's H3769
1Ki 21:18 where he has gone to **t possession** *of* it. H3769
1Ki 22:26 "**T** Micaiah and send him back to Amon H4374
2Ki 2: 1 the LORD *was about to* **t** Elijah **up** to H6590
2Ki 2: 3 that the LORD *is going to* **t** your master H4374
2Ki 2: 5 that the LORD *is going to* **t** your master H4374
2Ki 4: 1 creditor is coming to **t** my two boys as his H4374
2Ki 4:29 your belt, **t** my staff in your hand and run. H4374
2Ki 4:36 When she came, he said, "**T** your son." H5951
2Ki 5:23 "By all means, **t** two talents," said H4374
2Ki 5:26 Is this the time to **t** money or to accept H4374
2Ki 7:12 then *we will* **t** them alive and get into H9530
2Ki 7:13 "*Have some men* **t** five of the horses that H4374
2Ki 8: 8 "**T** a gift with you and go to meet the man H4374
2Ki 9: 1 **t** this flask of olive oil with you and go to H4374
2Ki 9: 2 companions and **t** him **into** an inner room. H995
2Ki 9: 3 Then **t** the flask and pour the oil on his H4374
2Ki 9:34 "**T care of** that cursed woman," he said H7212
2Ki 10: 6 **t** the heads of your master's sons and H4374
2Ki 10:14 "**T** them alive!" he ordered. So they took H9530
2Ki 11: 6 who **t turns** guarding the temple H5005
2Ki 12: 7 **T** no more money from your treasurers H4374
2Ki 13:16 "**T** the bow in your hands," he said to the H8206
2Ki 13:18 Then he said, "**T** the arrows," and the H4374
2Ki 18:32 I come and **t** you to a land like your H4374
2Ki 19:30 kingdom of Judah will **t** root below and bear NDT
1Ch 9:29 were assigned to **t care of** the furnishings H6584
1Ch 13:13 He *did* not **t** the ark to be with him in the H6073
1Ch 17:13 *I will* never **t** my love **away** from him, as I H6073
1Ch 21: 1 incited David to **t a census** *of* Israel. H4948
1Ch 21: 8 I beg you, **t away** the guilt of your servant. H6296
1Ch 21:11 is what the LORD says: '**T** your **choice**: H7691
1Ch 21:23 said to David, "**T** it! Let my lord the H4374
1Ch 21:24 *I will* not **t** for the LORD what is yours, or H5951
1Ch 27:23 David *did* not **t** the number of the men H5951
2Ch 2:16 You *can* then **t** them **up** *to* Jerusalem." H6590
2Ch 6:22 is required to **t an oath** and they come H457
2Ch 18:25 "**T** Micaiah and send him back to Amon H4374
2Ch 20:17 **T up** *your* **positions**; stand firm and see H3656
2Ch 20:25 more than *they could* **t away**. H5911+5362
2Ch 25:13 and *had* not *allowed to* **t part** in H2143+6640
2Ch 35:23 his officers, "**T** me **away**; I am badly H6296
2Ch 36: 6 with bronze shackles to **t** him to Babylon. H2143
2Ch 36:13 who *had* **made** him **t an oath** in God's H8678
Ezr 5:15 '**T** these articles and go and deposit A10492
Ezr 7:15 you are to **t** with you the silver and gold A10308
Ezr 9:12 to their sons or **t** their daughters for your H5951
Ezr 10: 4 will support you, so **t courage** and do it." H2616
Ne 2: 6 "How long *will* your journey **t**, and when H2118
Ne 5:12 **made** the nobles and officials **t an oath** to H8678
Ne 9:12 give them light on the way *they were to* **t**. H2143
Ne 9:15 to go in and **t possession** *of* the land you H3769
Ne 9:19 night to shine on the way *they were to* **t**. H2143
Ne 10:30 peoples around us or **t** their daughters H4374
Ne 13:25 *I* **made** them **t an oath** in God's name H8678
Ne 13:25 *are you to* **t** their daughters **in marriage** H5951
Est 2:13 was given her to **t** with her from the harem H995
Job 5:24 *you will* **t stock of** your property and find H7212
Job 11:11 when he sees evil, *does he* not **t note**? H1067
Job 11:18 look about you and **t** *your* **rest** in safety. H8886
Job 13:14 in jeopardy and **t** my life in my hands? H8492
Job 16:22 will pass before *I* **t** the path of no return H2143
Job 23:10 But he knows the way that I **t**; when he has NDT
Job 24: 3 donkey and **t** the widow's ox **in pledge**. H2471
Job 32:22 my Maker *would* soon **t** me **away**. H5951
Job 35:15 and *he does* not **t** the least **notice** of H3359
Job 36: 7 *He does* not **t** his eyes off the righteous H1757
Job 37: 8 The animals **t** cover; they remain in H995+1198
Job 38:13 that *it might* **t** the earth by the edges and H296
Job 38:20 *Can you* **t** them to their places? Do you H4374
Job 39:26 "*Does* the hawk **t flight** by your wisdom and H87
Job 41: 4 with you for *you to* **t** it as your slave for H4374
Job 42: 8 So now **t** seven bulls and seven rams and H4374
Ps 1: 1 stand in the **way** *that* sinners *t* or sit in the AIT
Ps 2:12 Blessed are all *who* **t refuge** in him. H2879
Ps 5:11 But let all *who* **t refuge** in you be glad; let H2879
Ps 7: 1 LORD my God, *I* **t refuge** in you; save and H2879
Ps 10:14 you consider their grief and **t** it in hand. H5989
Ps 11: 1 In the LORD *I* **t refuge**. How then can you H2879
Ps 16: 1 me safe, my God, for in you *I* **t refuge**. H2879
Ps 16: 4 to such gods or **t up** their names on my H5951
Ps 17: 7 right hand *those who* **t refuge** in you from H2879
Ps 18: 2 in whom *I* **t refuge**, my shield and H2879
Ps 18:30 he shields all who **t refuge** in him. H2879
Ps 25:18 my distress and **t away** all my sins. H5951
Ps 25:20 me be put to shame, for *I* **t refuge** in you. H2879
Ps 26: 9 *Do* not **t away** my soul along with sinners H665
Ps 27:14 be strong and **t heart** and wait for H599+4213
Ps 31:13 conspire against me and plot to **t** my life. H4374
Ps 31:19 sight of all, on those *who* **t refuge** in you. H2879
Ps 31:24 Be strong and **t heart**, all you who H599+4222
Ps 35: 2 **T up** shield and armor; arise and come to H2616
Ps 36: 7 People **t refuge** in the shadow of your H2879
Ps 37: 4 **T delight** in the LORD, and he will give you H6695
Ps 37:40 saves them, because *they* **t refuge** in him. H2879
Ps 40:14 May all who want to **t** my life be put to H6200
Ps 45:16 Your sons *will* **t the place of** your H2118+9393
Ps 49:15 the dead; *he will* surely **t** me to himself. H4374
Ps 49:17 for *they will* **t** nothing with them when H4374
Ps 50:16 to recite my laws or **t** my covenant on your H5951
Ps 51:11 your presence or **t** your Holy Spirit from H4374
Ps 51:16 *you do* not **t pleasure in** burnt offerings. H8354
Ps 55:15 *Let* death **t** my enemies **by surprise**; let H5958
Ps 56: 6 they watch my steps, **hoping** *to t* my life. AIT
Ps 57: 1 have mercy on me, for in you I **t refuge**. H2879
Ps 57: 1 *I will* **t refuge** in the shadow of your wings H2879
Ps 61: 4 tent forever and **t refuge** in the shelter of H2879
Ps 62: 4 from my lofty place; *they* **t delight** in lies. H8354
Ps 64:10 rejoice in the LORD and **t refuge** in him; H2879
Ps 70: 2 May *those who* **want to t** my life be put to H1335
Ps 72:13 *He will* **t pity** on the weak and the needy H2571
Ps 73: 9 their tongues **t possession** of the earth. H2143
Ps 73:24 afterward *you will* **t** me *into* glory. H4374
Ps 74:11 **T** it from the folds of your garment and NDT
Ps 83:12 "*Let us* **t possession** *of* the pasturelands of H3769
Ps 89:33 but *I will* not **t** my love from him, nor will I H7296
Ps 94: 8 **T notice**, *you* senseless ones among the H1067
Ps 94:16 Who *will* **t a stand** for me against H3656
Ps 94:22 my God the rock in whom I **t** refuge. NDT
Ps 102:24 "*Do* not **t** me **away**, my God, in the midst H6590
Ps 104:29 are terrified; *when you* **t away** their breath H665
Ps 109: 8 *may* another **t** his place of leadership. H4374
Ps 109:12 kindness to him or **t pity** on his fatherless H2858
Ps 118: 8 It is better to **t refuge** in the LORD than to H2879
Ps 118: 9 It is better to **t refuge** in the LORD than to H2879
Ps 119:39 **T away** the disgrace I dread, for your laws H6296
Ps 119:43 Never **t** your word of truth from my mouth H5911
Ps 119:109 Though I constantly **t** my life in my hands, NDT
Ps 141: 4 is evil so that I **t part in** wicked deeds H6618
Ps 141: 8 in you *I* **t refuge**—do not give me H2879
Ps 144: 2 in whom *I* **t refuge**, who subdues H2879
Pr 3:18 is a tree of life to those *who* **t hold** of her; H2616
Pr 4: 4 "**T hold** *of* my words *with* all your heart H9461
Pr 13:10 wisdom is found in *those who* **t advice**. H3619
Pr 16:13 Kings **t** pleasure in honest lips; they value NDT
Pr 20:16 **T** the garment of one who puts up security H4374
Pr 22: 3 The prudent see danger and **t refuge**, but H6259
Pr 22:23 the LORD *will* **t up** their case and will H8189
Pr 23:11 he *will* **t up** their case against you. H8189
Pr 25: 9 If *you* **t** your neighbor **to court**, do H8189+8190
Pr 27:12 The prudent see danger and **t refuge**, but H6259
Pr 27:13 **T** the garment of one who puts up security H4374
Pr 30: 5 is a shield to those *who* **t refuge** in him. H2879
Ecc 5:15 *They* **t** nothing from their toil that they can H5951
Ecc 7: 2 everyone; the living *should* **t** this to heart. H5989
Ecc 9: 2 as it is with those *who* **t oaths**, so with H8678
Ecc 9: 2 so with those who are afraid to **t** them. NDT
SS 1: 4 **T** me **away** with you—let us hurry! Let the H5432
SS 1: 6 me and made me **t care of** the vineyards; H5757
SS 7: 8 climb the palm tree; *I will* **t hold** of its fruit." H296
Isa 1:16 **T** your evil deeds out of my sight; stop H6073
Isa 1:17 **T up the cause** *of* the fatherless; plead H9149
Isa 2: 4 Nation *will* not **t up** sword against nation H5951
Isa 3: 1 *is about to* **t** from Jerusalem and Judah H6073
Isa 3: 6 **t charge** of this heap of ruins!" H9393+3338
Isa 4: 1 seven women *will* **t hold** of one man and H2616
Isa 4: 1 by your name. **T away** our disgrace!" H665
Isa 5: 5 I *will* **t away** its hedge, and it will be H6073
Isa 7: 7 " '*It will* not **t place**, it will not H7756
Isa 8: 1 "**T** a large scroll and write on it with an H4374
Isa 9:17 the Lord *will* **t** no **pleasure** in the young H8523
Isa 10:31 is in flight; the people of Gebim **t cover**. H6395
Isa 14: 2 Nations *will* **t** them and bring them to H4374
Isa 14: 2 And Israel *will* **t possession** *of* the nations H5706
Isa 14: 4 *you will* **t up** this taunt against the king of H5951
Isa 18: 5 cut down and **t away** the spreading H6073
Isa 20: 2 "**T off** the sackcloth from your body and H7337
Isa 22:17 LORD *is about to* **t firm hold** *of* you H6487+6487
Isa 23:16 "**T up** a harp, walk through the city, you H4374
Isa 27: 6 In days to come Jacob *will* **t root**, Israel H9245
Isa 28: 4 as people see them and **t** them in hand, NDT
Isa 31: 2 disaster; *he does* not **t back** his words. H6073
Isa 36:17 I come and **t** you to a land like your H4374
Isa 37:31 kingdom of Judah will **t** root below and bear NDT
Isa 40:24 no sooner *do they* **t root** in the H9245+1614
Isa 42: 6 righteousness; *I will* **t hold** of your hand. H2616
Isa 42:25 but *they did* not **t** it to heart. H8492
Isa 44: 5 'The LORD's,' and *will* **t** the name Israel. H4033
Isa 44:11 them all come together and **t** *their* **stand**; H6641
Isa 45: 1 whose right hand *I* **t hold** *of* to subdue H2616
Isa 45:21 present it—*let them* **t counsel** together. H3619
Isa 46: 8 keep it in mind, **t** it to heart, *you* rebels. H8740
Isa 47: 2 **T** millstones and grind flour; take off your H4374
Isa 47: 2 millstones and grind flour; **t off** your veil. H1655
Isa 47: 3 shame uncovered. *I will* **t** vengeance; H4374

Isa 48: 1 you who t oaths in the name of the LORD H8678
Isa 51:18 there was none to t her by the hand. H2616
Isa 62: 4 the LORD will t delight in you, and your H2911
Isa 65:19 Jerusalem and t delight in my people; H8464
Jer 6: 8 T warning, Jerusalem, or I will turn away H3579
Jer 7:29 t up a lament on the barren heights H5951
Jer 8:13 " 'I will t away their harvest, declares the H665
Jer 9:10 the mountains and t up a lament NDT
Jer 13: 4 "T the belt you bought and are wearing H4374
Jer 15:15 do not t me away; think of how H4374
Jer 19: 1 T along some of the elders of the people NDT
Jer 20: 5 They will t it away as plunder and carry it H4374
Jer 20:10 over him and t our revenge on him." H4374
Jer 25:15 "T from my hand this cup filled with the H4374
Jer 25:28 But if they refuse to t the cup from your H4374
Jer 27:20 king of Babylon did not t away when he H4374
Jer 31: 4 Again you will t up your timbrels and go H6335
Jer 31:21 T note of the highway, the road H8883+4213
Jer 31:21 note of the highway, the road that you t. H2143
Jer 32: 5 He will t Zedekiah to Babylon, where he H2143
Jer 32:14 T these documents, both the sealed and H4374
Jer 32:24 the siege ramps are built up to t the city. H4334
Jer 34:22 will fight against it, t it and burn it down. H4334
Jer 36: 2 "T a scroll and write on it all the words I H4374
Jer 36:28 "T another scroll and write on it all the H4374
Jer 38:10 "T thirty men from here with you and lift H4374
Jer 39: 7 with bronze shackles to t him to Babylon. H995
Jer 39:12 "T him and look after him; don't harm him H4374
Jer 39:14 of Shaphan, to t him back to his home. H3655
Jer 40:14 Ishmael son of Nethaniah to t your life?" H5782
Jer 40:15 Why should he t your life and cause all H5782
Jer 43: 9 t some large stones with you and bury H4374
Jer 43:12 their temples and t their gods captive. H8647
Jer 44:12 I will t away the remnant of Judah who H4374
Jer 46: 4 T your positions with helmets on H3656
Jer 46:14 'T your positions and get ready, for the H3656
Jer 50: 9 They will t up their positions against her H6885
Jer 50:14 "T up your positions around Babylon, all H6885
Jer 50:15 of the LORD, t vengeance on her; do to her H5933
Jer 51:11 "Sharpen the arrows, t up the shields! The H4848
Jer 51:11 The LORD will t vengeance, vengeance for NDT
Eze 3:10 listen carefully and t to heart all the words H4374
Eze 4: 1 son of man, t a block of clay, put it in front H4374
Eze 4: 3 Then t an iron pan, place it as an iron wall H4374
Eze 4: 9 "T wheat and barley, beans and lentils H4374
Eze 5: 1 t a sharp sword and use it as a barber's H4374
Eze 5: 1 Then t a set of scales and divide up the H4374
Eze 5: 2 T a third and strike it with the sword all H4374
Eze 5: 3 But t a few hairs and tuck them away in H4374
Eze 5: 4 t a few of these and throw them into the H4374
Eze 7:24 of nations to t possession of their houses. H3769
Eze 10: 6 in linen, "T fire from among the wheels H4374
Eze 12: 5 wall and t your belongings out through it. H3655
Eze 16:39 of your clothes and t your fine jewelry H4374
Eze 17: 9 It will not t a strong arm or many people to NDT
Eze 17:22 I myself will t a shoot from the very top of H4374
Eze 18: 8 to them at interest or t a profit from them. H4374
Eze 18:23 Do I t any pleasure in the death of H2911+2911
Eze 18:32 For I t no pleasure in the death of anyone H2911
Eze 19: 1 "T up a lament concerning the princes of H5951
Eze 20:37 I will t note of you as you pass under my H6296
Eze 21: 7 It will surely t place, declares the H2118
Eze 21:19 the sword of the king of Babylon to t, H995
Eze 21:23 them of their guilt and t them captive. H9530
Eze 21:26 T off the turban, remove H6073
Eze 22:12 you t interest and make a profit from the H4374
Eze 22:25 t treasures and precious things and make H4374
Eze 23:24 they will t up positions against you on H8492
Eze 23:25 They will t away your sons and daughters H4374
Eze 23:26 you of your clothes and t your fine jewelry. H4374
Eze 23:29 you in hatred and t away everything you H4374
Eze 23:48 that all women may t warning and not H3579
Eze 24: 5 t the pick of the flock. Pile wood beneath H4374
Eze 24: 6 T the meat out piece by piece in whatever H3655
Eze 24: 8 up wrath and t revenge I put her H5933+5934
Eze 24:16 one blow I am about to t away from you H4374
Eze 24:21 the stronghold in which you t pride, the NDT
Eze 24:25 on the day I t away their stronghold H4374
Eze 25:14 I will t vengeance on Edom by the hand of H5989
Eze 25:17 the LORD, when I t vengeance on them. H5989
Eze 26:16 their robes and t off their embroidered H7320
Eze 26:17 Then they will t up a lament concerning H5951
Eze 26:20 not return or t your place in the land of H3656
Eze 27: 2 of man, t up a lament concerning Tyre. H5951
Eze 27:26 Your oarsmen t you out to the high seas H995
Eze 27:32 they will t up a lament concerning you: H7801
Eze 28:12 t up a lament concerning the king of Tyre H5951
Eze 30: 9 Anguish will t hold of them on the H2118+928
Eze 32: 2 t up a lament concerning Pharaoh king of H5951
Eze 33:11 I t no pleasure in the death of the wicked H2911
Eze 34: 2 of Israel who only t care of yourselves! H8286
Eze 34: 2 Should not shepherds t care of the flock? H8286
Eze 34: 3 animals, but you do not t care of the flock. H8286
Eze 35:10 be ours and we will t possession of them," H3769
Eze 36:24 " 'For I will t you out of the nations; I will H4374
Eze 37:16 of man, t a stick of wood and write on it H4374
Eze 37:16 Then t another stick of wood, and write H4374
Eze 37:19 I am going to t the stick of Joseph—which H4374
Eze 37:21 I will t the Israelites out of the nations H4374
Eze 38: 7 and t command of them. H2118+4200+5464
Eze 38:13 to t away livestock and goods and to seize H4374
Eze 38:14 living in safety, will you not t notice of it? H3359

Eze 39: 8 It will surely t place, declares the H2118
Eze 43:20 You are to t some of its blood and put it H4374
Eze 43:21 You are to t the bull for the sin offering H4374
Eze 44:19 they are to t off the clothes they have H7320
Eze 45:18 on the first day you are to t a young bull H4374
Eze 45:19 The priest is to t some of the blood of the H4374
Eze 46:18 The prince must not t any of the H4374
Da 2:24 T me to the king, and I will interpret his A10549
Da 2:45 the king what will t place in the future. A10201
Da 8:13 "How long will it t for the vision to be NDT
Da 8:14 "It will t 2,300 evenings and mornings NDT
Da 8:25 destroy many and t his stand against the H6641
Da 11: 7 from her family line will arise to t her place. NDT
Da 11:18 to the coastlands and will t many of them, H4334
Da 11:28 He will t action against it and then return H6913
Da 11:36 what has been determined must t place. H6913
Hos 2: 9 "Therefore I will t away my grain when it H4374
Hos 2: 9 I will t back my wool and my linen H5911
Hos 2:10 no one will t her out of my hands. H5911
Hos 4:11 wine and new wine t away their H4374
Hos 10: 4 t false oaths and make agreements H457
Hos 14: 2 T words with you and return to the LORD H4374
Am 5: 1 this lament I t up concerning you: H5951
Am 5:12 the innocent and t bribes and deprive the H4374
Am 6:13 "Did we not t Karnaim by our own H4374
Am 9: 2 from there my hand will t them. H4374
Jnh 1: 6 Maybe he will t notice of us so that we H6951
Jnh 4: 3 t away my life, for it is better for me H4374
Mic 2: 2 seize them, and houses, and t them. H5951
Mic 2: 9 You t away my blessing from their H4374
Mic 4: 3 Nation will not t up sword against nation H5951
Mic 5:15 I will t vengeance in anger and wrath on H6913
Zep 3:17 He will t great delight in you H8464+928+8525
Hag 1: 8 so that I may t pleasure in it and be H8354
Hag 2:23 LORD Almighty, 'I will t you, my servant H4374
Zec 3: 4 before him, "T off his filthy clothes." H6073
Zec 6:10 "T silver and gold from the exiles Heldai H4374
Zec 6:11 T the silver and gold and make a crown H4374
Zec 8:23 nations will t firm hold of one Jew by H2616
Zec 9: 4 the Lord will t away her possessions and H3769
Zec 9: 7 I will t the blood from their mouths, the H6073
Zec 9:10 I will t away the chariots from Ephraim H4162
Zec 11:15 "T again the equipment of a foolish H4374
Zec 14:18 Egyptian people do not go up and t part, H995
Zec 14:21 come to sacrifice will t some of the pots H4374
Mt 1:20 not be afraid to t Mary home as your wife, G4161
Mt 2:13 "t the child and his mother and escape to G4161
Mt 2:20 t the child and his mother and go to the G4161
Mt 2:20 those who were trying to t the child's G2426
Mt 5:40 anyone wants to sue you and t your shirt, G3284
Mt 7: 4 'Let me t the speck out of your eye G1675
Mt 7: 5 first t the plank out of your own eye G1675
Mt 8:11 and will t their places at the feast with G369
Mt 9: 2 said to the man, "T heart, son; your sins G2510
Mt 9: 6 "Get up, t your mat and go home." G149
Mt 9:22 "T heart, daughter," he said, "your faith G2510
Mt 10: 9 silver or copper to t with you in your belts NDT
Mt 10:38 Whoever does not t up their cross and G3284
Mt 11:29 T my yoke upon you and learn from me, for G149
Mt 12:11 will you not t hold of it and lift it out? G3195
Mt 14:27 "T courage! It is I. G2510
Mt 15:26 "It is not right to t the children's bread G3284
Mt 16: 5 the lake, the disciples forgot to t bread. G3284
Mt 16:24 deny themselves and t up their cross and G149
Mt 17:27 T the first fish you catch; open its mouth G149
Mt 17:27 T it and give it to them for my tax and G3284
Mt 18:16 t one or two others along, so that G4161
Mt 20:14 T your pay and go. I want to give the one G149
Mt 21:38 let's kill him and t his inheritance.' G2400
Mt 24:17 housetop go down to t anything out of the G149
Mt 24:20 your flight will not t place in winter or on G1181
Mt 25: 3 their lamps but did not t any oil with them G3284
Mt 25:28 " 'So t the bag of gold from him and give it G149
Mt 25:34 my Father; t your inheritance, the kingdom G3099
Mt 26:26 disciples, saying, "T and eat; this is my G3284
Mt 27:65 "T a guard," Pilate answered. "Go, make G2400
Mk 2: 9 to say, 'Get up, t your mat and walk'? G149
Mk 2:11 "I tell you, get up, t your mat and go home." G149
Mk 3:21 they went to t charge of him, for they G3195
Mk 6: 8 "T nothing for the journey except a staff G149
Mk 6:37 "That would t more than half a year's wages NDT
Mk 6:50 he spoke to them and said, "T courage! G2510
Mk 7:27 "for it is not right to t the children's bread G3284
Mk 8:34 deny themselves and t up their cross and G149
Mk 9:22 can do anything, t pity on us and help us." G5072
Mk 13:15 down or enter the house to t anything out. G149
Mk 13:18 Pray that this will not t place in winter, G1181
Mk 14:22 his disciples, saying, "T it; this is my body." G3284
Mk 14:36 is possible for you. T this cup from me G4195
Mk 15:23 wine mixed with myrrh, but he did not t it. G3284
Mk 15:36 Let's see if Elijah comes to t him down," G2747
Lk 1:15 He is never to t wine or other fermented G4403
Lk 5:18 tried to t him into the house to lay G1662
Lk 5:24 "I tell you, get up, t your mat and go home." G149
Lk 6:42 let me t the speck out of your eye,' G1675
Lk 6:42 hypocrite, first t the plank out of your eye G1675
Lk 9: 3 "T nothing for the journey—no staff, no G149
Lk 9:23 deny themselves and t up their cross daily G149
Lk 10: 4 Do not t a purse or bag or sandals; and do G1002
Lk 12:19 many years. T life easy; eat, drink and G399
Lk 13:29 and will t their places at the feast in the G369
Lk 14: 8 do not t the place of honor G2884+1650

Lk 14: 9 you will have to t the least important G2988
Lk 14:10 you are invited, t the lowest place G404+1650
Lk 16: 6 manager told him, 'T your bill, sit down G1312
Lk 16: 7 'T your bill and make it eight hundred. G1312
Lk 19:17 small matter, t charge of ten cities. G1639+2400
Lk 19:19 'You t charge of five cities. G2062+1181
Lk 19:21 You t out what you did not put in and reap G149
Lk 19:24 'T his mina away from him and give it to G149
Lk 21: 7 be the sign that they are about to t place?" G1181
Lk 21:28 When these things begin to t place, stand G1181
Lk 22:17 said, "T this and divide it among you. G3284
Lk 22:36 if you have a purse, t it, and also a bag; G149
Lk 22:42 if you are willing, t this cup from me; yet G4195
Jn 1:22 Give us an answer to t back to those who G1443
Jn 2: 8 draw some out and t it to the master of G5770
Jn 6: 7 "It would t more than half a year's wages to NDT
Jn 6:21 they were willing to t him into the boat, G3284
Jn 10:17 I lay down my life—only to t it up again. G3284
Jn 10:18 lay it down and authority to t it up again. G3284
Jn 11:39 "T away the stone," he said. "But, Lord," G149
Jn 11:44 "T off the grave clothes and let him go." G3395
Jn 11:48 will come and t away both our temple and G149
Jn 11:53 So from that day on they plotted to t his life. G650
Jn 14: 3 I will come back and t you to be with me G4161
Jn 16:22 and no one will t away your joy. G149
Jn 16:33 But t heart! I have overcome G2510
Jn 17:15 My prayer is not that you t them out of the G149
Jn 18:31 "T him yourselves and judge him by your G3284
Jn 19: 6 answered, "You t him and crucify him. G3284
Jn 19:15 they shouted, "T him away! Take him away G149
Jn 19:15 "Take him away! T him away! Crucify him!" G149
Jn 21:16 Jesus said, "T care of my sheep." G4477
Ac 1:20 " 'May another t his place of leadership. G3284
Ac 1:25 to t over this apostolic G3284+3836+5536
Ac 7:33 Lord said to him, 'T off your sandals, for G3395
Ac 9: 2 he might t them as prisoners to Jerusalem. G72
Ac 9:21 he come here to t them as prisoners to G72
Ac 13:40 T care that what the prophets have said G1063
Ac 15:37 to t John, also called Mark, with them, G5221
Ac 15:38 Paul did not think it wise to t him G5221
Ac 16: 3 Paul wanted to t him along on the journey, G2002
Ac 20:13 where we were going to t Paul aboard. G377
Ac 21:24 T these men, join in their purification rites G4161
Ac 21:37 were about to t Paul into the barracks, G1652
Ac 23:10 and t him away from them by force and G773
Ac 23:11 stood near Paul and said, "T courage! G2510
Ac 23:17 "T this young man to the commander G552
Ac 24:23 permit his friends to t care of his needs. G5676
Ac 27:34 Now I urge you to t some food. You need G3561
Ro 2:16 This will t place on the day when God NDT
Ro 11:13 to the Gentiles, I t pride in my ministry G1519
Ro 11:27 with them when I t away their sins. G904
Ro 12:19 Do not t revenge, my dear friends, but G1688
Ro 15:31 that the contribution I t to Jerusalem may be AIT
1Co 6: 1 to t it before the ungodly for judgment G3212
1Co 6:15 Shall I then t the members of Christ and G149
1Co 9: 5 right to t a believing wife along with us, G4310
1Co 10:30 If I t part in the meal with thankfulness G3576
2Co 5:12 giving you an opportunity to t pride in us, NDT
2Co 5:12 can answer those who t pride in what is seen AIT
2Co 7: 4 with great frankness; I t great pride in you. NDT
2Co 10: 5 and we t captive every thought to make it G170
2Co 11:16 Let no one t me for a fool G1506+1639
2Co 12: 8 pleaded with the Lord to t it away from me. G923
Gal 3:15 let me t an example from everyday life. G3306
Gal 5:10 in the Lord that you will t no other view. G5858
Gal 6: 4 Then they can t pride in themselves alone G2400
Eph 6:11 so that you can t your stand against the G2705
Eph 6:16 addition to all this, t up the shield of faith G377
Eph 6:17 T the helmet of salvation and the sword of G1312
Php 2:25 whom you sent to t care of my needs. G3313
Php 3:12 I press on to t hold of that for which G2898
Php 3:15 are mature should t such a view of things. G5858
1Th 4: 6 wrong or t advantage of a brother or G4430
2Th 3:14 T special note of anyone who does not G4957
1Ti 3: 5 how can he t care of God's church? G2150
1Ti 5:20 so that the others may t warning. G2400
1Ti 6: 7 the world, and we can t nothing out of it. G1766
1Ti 6:12 T hold of the eternal life to which you G2138
1Ti 6:19 so that they may t hold of the life that is G2138
Phm 13 that he could t your place in helping me G5642
Heb 5: 5 Christ did not t on himself the glory of G1519
Heb 6:18 who have fled to t hold of the hope set G3195
Heb 9:28 sacrificed once to t away the sins of many; G429
Heb 10: 4 the blood of bulls and goats to t away sins. G904
Heb 10:11 sacrifices, which can never t away sins. G4311
Heb 10:38 And I t no pleasure in the one who G2305
Jas 1: 9 circumstances ought to t pride in their G3016
Jas 1:10 But the rich should t pride in their NDT
Jas 1:19 My dear brothers and sisters, t note of this: G3857
Jas 3: 4 Or t ships as an example. Although they G2627
Jas 5:10 t the prophets who spoke in the name of G3284
1Jn 3: 5 appeared so that he might t away our sins. G149
2Jn 10 do not t them into your house or welcome G3284
Rev 1: 1 show his servants what must soon t place. G1181
Rev 1: 3 who hear it and t to heart what is written G5498
Rev 1:19 what is now and what will t place later. G1181
Rev 3:11 you have, so that no one will t your crown. G3284
Rev 4: 1 will show you what must t place after this." G1181
Rev 5: 9 "You are worthy to t the scroll and to open G3284
Rev 6: 4 rider was given power to t peace from the G3284
Rev 10: 8 t the scroll that lies open in the hand of G3284

T

Rev 10: 9 He said to me, "T it and eat it. It will G3284
Rev 14:15 on the cloud, "T your sickle and reap G4287
Rev 14:18 "T your sharp sickle and gather the G4287
Rev 22: 6 servants the things that must soon **t place**." G1181
Rev 22:17 and *let* the one who wishes t the free gift G3284
Rev 22:19 God *will* **t away** from that person any share G904

TAKEN (270) [TAKE]

Ge 2:22 from the rib *he had* t out of the man, H4374
Ge 2:23 called 'woman,' for she **was t** out of man." H4374
Ge 3:19 since from it *you* **were t**; for dust you are H4374
Ge 3:23 the ground from which *he had* **been t**. H4374
Ge 12:15 to Pharaoh, and she **was t** *into* his palace. H4374
Ge 14:14 heard that his relative *had* **been t captive**, H8647
Ge 20: 3 dead because of the woman *you have* **t**; H4374
Ge 25: 1 Abraham *had* t another wife, whose H4374
Ge 27:36 second time *he has* **t advantage of** me: H6810
Ge 27:36 my birthright, and now *he's* t my blessing!" H4374
Ge 30:23 said, "God *has* **t away** my disgrace. H665
Ge 31: 1 "Jacob *has* t everything our father owned H4374
Ge 31: 9 So God *has* **t away** your father's livestock H5911
Ge 31:34 Now Rachel *had* t the household gods H4374
Ge 39: 1 Now Joseph *had* **been t down** to Egypt H3718
Ge 39: 1 from the Ishmaelites who *had* t him there. H3718
Ge 42:24 *He had* Simeon t from them and bound H4374
Ge 43:18 frightened when *they* **were t** *to* his house. H995
Ex 12: 4 having **t into account** the number of people H928
Ex 21:14 that person *is to be* t from my altar and H4374
Ex 22:10 is injured or **is t away** while no one is H8647
Lev 6: 4 they have stolen or **t by extortion**, H6943+6945
Lev 7:34 *I have* t the breast that is waved and the H4374
Lev 10:18 Since its blood **was** not **t** into the Holy Place H995
Lev 14:45 and **t out** of the town to an unclean place. H3655
Lev 16:27 atonement, *must be* t outside the camp H3655
Lev 25:12 eat only **what is t** directly from the fields. H9311
Nu 3:12 "*I have* t the Levites from among the H4374
Nu 8:16 *I have* t them as my own in place of the H4374
Nu 8:18 And *I have* t the Levites in place of all the H4374
Nu 10:17 Then the tabernacle **was t down**, and the H3718
Nu 14: 3 wives and children *will be* t as plunder. H2118
Nu 14:31 that you said *would be* t as plunder, H2118
Nu 16:15 *I have* not t so much as a donkey from H5951
Nu 19: 3 it *is to be* t outside the camp and H3655
Nu 21:26 king of Moab and *had* t from him all his H4374
Nu 30: 9 "Any vow or **obligation** t by a widow or H673
Nu 31:53 Each soldier *had* **t plunder** for himself. H1024
Nu 36: 3 their inheritance *will* **be t** from our H1757
Nu 36: 3 inheritance allotted to us *will* **be t away**. H1757
Nu 36: 4 their property *will* **be t** from the tribal H1757
Dt 1:39 ones that you said would be **t captive**, H1020
Dt 3:20 they too *have* **t over** the land that the H3769
Dt 11:31 When *you have* t it **over** and are living H3769
Dt 17:14 giving you and *have* **t possession** *of* it H3769
Dt 17:18 **t from** that of the Levitical H4946+4200+7156
Dt 23:15 If a slave *has* **t refuge** with you, do not H5911
Dt 26: 1 and *have* **t possession** *of* it and settled H3769
Dt 28:31 Your donkey *will* **be forcibly t** from you H1608
Jos 1:15 they too *have* **t possession** *of* the land the H3769
Jos 2: 4 But the woman *had* t the two men and H4374
Jos 2: 6 But she *had* t them **up** to the roof and H6590
Jos 4:20 twelve stones *they had* t out of the Jordan H4374
Jos 7:11 *They have* t some of the devoted things H4374
Jos 8: 8 When you *have* t the city, set it on fire. H9530
Jos 8:12 Joshua *had* t about five thousand men H4374
Jos 8:21 that the ambush *had* t the city and that H4334
Jos 10: 1 heard that Joshua *had* t Ai and totally H4334
Jos 13: 1 still very large areas of land to *be* **t over**. H3769
Jos 13:12 had defeated them and **t over** their land. H3769
Jos 19: 9 of the Simeonites **was t** from the share of NDT
Jdg 14: 9 not tell them that *he had* t the honey from H8098
Jdg 17: 2 of silver that **were t** from you and about H4374
Jdg 19:18 No one *has* t me in for the night H665
Jdg 21: 1 men of Israel *had* **t an oath** at Mizpah: H8678
Jdg 21: 5 For they *had* t a solemn oath that anyone H2118
Jdg 21: 7 since we *have* **t an oath** by the LORD not H8678
Jdg 21:18 since we Israelites *have* t *this* **oath**: H8678
1Sa 10:20 the tribe of Benjamin **was t by lot**. H4334
1Sa 10:21 clan by clan, and Matri's clan **was t**. H4334
1Sa 10:21 Finally Saul son of Kish **was t**. But when H4334
1Sa 12: 3 Whose ox *have I* t? Whose donkey H4374
1Sa 12: 3 Whose donkey *have I* t? Whom have I H4374
1Sa 12: 4 "*You have* not t anything from anyone's H4374
1Sa 14:41 Jonathan and Saul **were t** by lot, and the H4334
1Sa 14:42 Jonathan my son." And Jonathan **was t**. H4334
1Sa 19: 1 But Jonathan *had* t a great **liking** to David H2911
1Sa 21: 6 by hot bread on the day it **was t away**. H4374
1Sa 30: 2 and *had* **t captive** the women and H8647
1Sa 30: 3 wives and sons and daughters **t captive**. H8647
1Sa 30:16 of plunder *they had* t from the land of H4374
1Sa 30:18 everything the Amalekites *had* t, H4374
1Sa 30:19 plunder or anything else *they had* t. H4374
2Sa 2: 8 *had* t Ish-Bosheth son of Saul and H4374
2Sa 3:15 gave orders and *had* her **t away** from her H4374
2Sa 6:13 the ark of the LORD *had* t six **steps**, H7575+7576
2Sa 7:15 But my love *will* never **be t away** from him, H6073
2Sa 8:12 the plunder t from Hadadezer son of NDT
2Sa 12:13 replied, "The LORD *has* **t away** your sin. H6296
2Sa 12:27 against Rabbah and t its water supply. H4334
2Sa 18:18 his lifetime Absalom *had* t a pillar and H4374
2Sa 19:24 He *had* not **t care of** his feet or trimmed H6913
2Sa 19:40 the troops of Israel *had* t the king **over**. H6296
2Sa 19:42 *Have we* **t anything** for ourselves?" H5951+5951

1Ki 1:46 Solomon *has* t *his* **seat** on the royal H3782
1Ki 13:12 road the man of God from Judah *had* **t**. H2143
1Ki 16:18 When Zimri saw that the city **was t**, he H4334
1Ki 18: 4 Obadiah *had* t a hundred prophets and H4374
2Ki 2: 9 can I do for you before *I* **am t** from you?" H4374
2Ki 2:10 "yet if you see me when I **am t** from you H4374
2Ki 5: 2 gone out and *had* **t captive** a young girl H8647
2Ki 13:16 When *he had* t it, Elisha put his hands on H8206
2Ki 13:25 Hazael the towns *he had* t in battle from H4374
2Ki 17:23 *were* t from their homeland **into exile** in H1655
2Ki 20:18 born to you, *will be* **t away**, and they will H4374
2Ki 24: 7 the king of Babylon *had* t all his territory, H4374
2Ki 25: 6 He *was* t to the king of Babylon at Riblah H6590
1Ch 9: 1 **They were t captive** to Babylon because H1655
1Ch 9:28 brought in and *when* they *were* **t out**. H3655
1Ch 18:11 the silver and gold *he had* t from all these H5951
1Ch 22:14 "I have **t great pains** to provide for H928+6715
1Ch 24: 6 one family **being** t from Eleazar and then H296
1Ch 26:27 Some of the plunder t *in* battle they H4946
2Ch 2:17 the **census** his father David *had* t; H6222+6218
2Ch 6:38 land of their captivity where they *were* t, H8647
2Ch 28:11 Israelites *you have* **t as prisoners**, H8647+8664
2Ch 34:14 money that *had* **been t into** the temple of H995
Ezr 2: 1 king of Babylon *had* **t captive** to Babylon H1655
Ezr 5:14 Nebuchadnezzar *had* t from the temple A10485
Ezr 8:30 been weighed out to *be* t to the house of H995
Ezr 9: 2 *They have* t some of their daughters **as wives** H5951
Ezr 10:13 this matter cannot be t care of in a day or NDT
Ne 7: 6 king of Babylon *had* **t captive** H1655
Est 1:15 that the eunuchs have t to her." H928+3338
Est 2: 6 among those t **captive** with Jehoiachin H1655
Est 2: 7 Mordecai *had* t her as his own daughter H4374
Est 2: 8 Esther also **was** t to the king's palace and H4374
Est 2:16 She **was** t to King Xerxes in the royal H4374
Job 1:21 The LORD gave and the LORD *has* **t away** H4374
Job 28: 2 Iron **is** t from the earth, and copper is H4374
Job 36:17 judgment and justice *have* **t hold** of you. H9461
Ps 31: 1 *I have* **t refuge**; let me never be put H2879
Ps 71: 1 *I have* **t refuge**; let me never be put H2879
Ps 78:54 to the hill country his right hand *had* **t**. H7864
Ps 88: 8 *You have* t from me my closest friends H8178
Ps 88:18 *You have* t from me friend and neighbor— H8178
Ps 102:10 for *you have* t me **up** and thrown me H5951
Ps 119:106 *I have* **t an oath** and confirmed it, that I H8678
Pr 27:14 in the morning, *it will* **be t** as a curse. H3108
Ecc 3:14 can be added to it and nothing t from it. H1757
Ecc 5: 9 The increase from the land is t by all; the NDT
Ecc 9:12 cruel net, or birds **are t** in a snare, so H296
SS 5: 3 *I have* **t off** my robe—must I put it on H7320
Isa 6: 6 which *he had* t with tongs from the altar. H4374
Isa 6: 7 your guilt **is t away** and your sin atoned H6073
Isa 14:25 His yoke *will be* t from my people, and his H6073
Isa 16:10 Joy and gladness **are t away** from the H665
Isa 22: 3 who were caught **were t prisoner** together, H673
Isa 23: 7 whose feet *have* t her to settle in far-off H3297
Isa 28: 9 their milk, to *those just* t from the breast? H6972
Isa 38:12 has been pulled down and t from me. H1655
Isa 39: 7 born to you, *will be* **t away**, and they will H4374
Isa 42: 9 the former things *have* **t place**, and new H995
Isa 49:24 *Can* plunder **be t** from warriors, or captives H4374
Isa 49:25 captives *will be* t *from* warriors, and H4374
Isa 51: 7 people who have *t* my instruction to heart: AIT
Isa 51:22 *I have* t out of your hand the cup that H4374
Isa 52: 5 my people *have* **been t away** for nothing, H4374
Isa 53: 8 oppression and judgment *he* **was t away**. H4374
Isa 57: 1 to heart; the devout **are t away**, and no one H665
Isa 57: 1 the righteous **are t away** to be spared from H665
Isa 57:11 remembered me nor **t** this to heart? H8492
Jer 8:13 I have given them *will be* **t from** them. H6296
Jer 12: 2 and *they have* **t root**; they grow and H9245
Jer 13:17 because the LORD's flock *will* **be t captive**. H8647
Jer 14: 9 Why are you like a man **t by surprise**, like H1850
Jer 27:18 in Jerusalem not *be* t to Babylon. H995
Jer 27:22 '*They will* **be t** to Babylon and there they H995
Jer 34:16 each of *you has* **t back** the male and H8740
Jer 38:28 This is how Jerusalem **was t**: H4334
Jer 39:14 sent and *had* Jeremiah t out of the H4374
Jer 40:10 and live in the towns *you have* **t over**." H9530
Jer 41:14 people Ishmael *had* **t captive** at Mizpah H8647
Jer 48: 7 you too *will* **be t captive**, and Chemosh H4334
Jer 48:41 will be captured and the strongholds **t**. H9530
Jer 48:46 your sons **are t** into exile and your H4374
Jer 49: 1 Why then *has* Molek **t possession** *of* Gad H3769
Jer 49:29 Their tents and their flocks *will be* **t**; their H4374
Jer 50:28 Zion how the LORD our God has t vengeance, NDT
Jer 51:26 No rock *will* **be t** from you for a H4374
Jer 52: 9 He *was* t to the king of Babylon at Riblah H6590
Jer 52:30 745 Jews **t into exile** *by* Nebuzaradan the H1655
Eze 15: 3 **Is** wood *ever* t from it to make anything H4374
Eze 21:24 *you will* **be t captive**. H9530+928+2021+4090
Eze 30:16 Thebes will be **t by storm**; Memphis will H1324
Eze 33: 6 that person's life *will* **be t** because of their H4374
Eze 45:15 Also one sheep is to be t from every flock of NDT
Da 4:31 Your royal authority *has been* t from you. A10528
Da 5: 2 his father *had* t from the temple in A10485
Da 5: 3 goblets that *had been* t from the temple A10485
Da 7:26 his power *will be* **t away** and A10528
Hos 9: 6 treasures of silver *will be* **t over** *by* briers, H3769
Hos 10: 5 because *it is* t from them **into exile**. H1655
Am 2: 8 every altar on garments **t in pledge**. H2471
Am 2: 8 house of their god they drink **wine** *t as* fines. AIT
Am 4: 2 come when you *will* **be t away** with hooks, H5951

Na 3:10 Yet she was t captive and went into exile H4200
Zep 3:15 The LORD *has* **t away** your punishment, he H6073
Zec 3: 4 *I have* **t away** your sin, and I will put H6296
Zec 14: 2 of the people *will* not **be t** from the city. H4162
Mt 9:15 when the bridegroom *will be* t from them; G554
Mt 13:12 even what they have *will be* t from them. G149
Mt 21:43 of God *will be* **t away** from you and G149
Mt 23:30 *we* would not have **t part** with them G1639+3128
Mt 24:40 the field; one *will be* t and the other left. G4161
Mt 24:41 hand mill; one *will be* t and the other left. G4161
Mt 25:29 even what they have *will be* t from them. G149
Mt 26:39 if it is possible, *may* this cup *be* t from me. G4216
Mt 26:42 this cup *to be* **t away** unless I drink it, G4216
Mt 26:56 But this *has* all **t place** that the writings of G1181
Mk 2:20 when the bridegroom *will be* **t from** them, G554
Mk 4:25 even what they have *will be* t from them." G149
Mk 8: 6 *When he had* t the seven loaves and G3284
Mk 16:19 *he was* **t up** into heaven and he sat at the G377
Lk 1:25 his favor and **t away** my disgrace among G904
Lk 2: 1 decree that a **census** *should* **be t** of the G616
Lk 5: 9 astonished at the catch of fish *they had* t, G5197
Lk 5:35 when the bridegroom *will be* t from them; G554
Lk 8:18 they think they have *will be* t from them." G149
Lk 9:51 approached for him *to be* **t up to heaven**, G378
Lk 10:42 is better, and it *will* not **be t away** from her." G904
Lk 11:52 because *you have* **t away** the key to G149
Lk 17:34 one bed; one *will be* t and the other left. G4161
Lk 17:35 together; one *will be* t and the other left." G4161
Lk 19:26 even what they have *will be* **t away**. G149
Lk 21:24 sword and *will be* **t as prisoners** to all the G170
Lk 24:51 he left them and *was* **t up** into heaven. G429
Jn 2:20 "*It has t* forty-six years to **build** this temple AIT
Jn 13:30 As soon as Judas *had* t the bread, he went G3284
Jn 18:40 Barabbas *had* **t part in an uprising**. G1639+3334
Jn 19:31 the legs broken and the bodies **t down**. G149
Jn 20: 2 "*They have* t the Lord out of the tomb G149
Jn 20:13 "*They have* t my Lord **away**," she said G149
Jn 21: 7 for he had **t it off**) and jumped into G1218
Ac 1: 2 the day *he was* **t up** *to heaven*, after G377
Ac 1: 9 *he was* **t up** before their very eyes G2048
Ac 1:11 who *has been* t from you into heaven G377
Ac 1:22 to the time when Jesus *was* **t up** from us. G377
Ac 7:43 *You have* **t up** the tabernacle of Molek G377
Ac 8:33 For his life *was* t from the earth." G149
Ac 9:39 when he arrived *he was* t upstairs to the G343
Ac 10:16 the sheet *was* **t back** to heaven. G377
Ac 18:18 at Cenchreae because of a vow *he had* t. G2400
Ac 19:12 that had touched him *were* t to the sick, G708
Ac 21:34 he ordered *that* Paul *be* t into the barracks. G72
Ac 22:24 ordered *that* Paul *be* **t into** the barracks. G1652
Ac 23:14 "We *have* **t a solemn oath** not to eat G353+354
Ac 23:21 They *have* **t an oath** not to eat or drink G354
Ac 23:24 Paul so that *he may be* t safely to G2097
Ac 27:21 you should have t my **advice** not to sail G4272
1Co 15: 1 on which *you have* t *your* **stand**. G2705
2Co 3:14 because only in Christ *is it* **t away**. G2934
2Co 3:16 turns to the Lord, the veil *is* **t away**. G4311
Gal 4:24 These things are *being* **t figuratively**: The G251
Php 3:13 consider myself yet *to have* **t hold of** it. G2898
Col 2:14 condemned us; *he has* t it away, nailing G149
Col 3: 9 *since you have* **t off** your old self with its G588
2Th 2: 7 to do so till *he is* t out of the way. G1181
1Ti 3:16 believed on in the world, *was* **t up** in glory. G377
2Ti 2:18 *that* the resurrection *has* already **t place**, G1181
2Ti 2:26 who has **t** *them* **captive** to do his will. G2436
Heb 6: 1 about Christ and *be* t forward to maturity, G5770
Heb 11: 5 By faith Enoch *was* **t from** *this life*, so that G3572
Heb 11: 5 be found, because God *had* t him **away**." G3572
Heb 11: 5 For before he was **t**, he was commended G3557
Jude 11 *They have* t the way of Cain; they have G4513
Rev 5: 8 And when *he had* t it, the four living G3284
Rev 11:17 because *you have* t your great power and G3284
Rev 12: 6 where *she might be* **t care of** for 1,260 G5555
Rev 12:14 where *she would be* **t care of** for a time G5555

TAKES (69) [TAKE]

Ge 27:46 If Jacob t a wife from among the women H4374
Lev 5: 4 thoughtlessly **t an oath** to do anything, H8678
Lev 24:17 'Anyone *who* t the **life** *of* a human H5782+5883
Lev 24:18 *Anyone who* t the **life** *of* someone's H5782+5883
Nu 24:22 be destroyed when Ashur t you **captive**." H8647
Nu 30: 2 to the LORD or **t an oath** to obligate H8678+8652
Dt 1: 2 It t eleven days to go from Horeb to Kadesh NDT
Dt 13: 2 if the sign or wonder spoken of **t place** H995
Dt 17:18 When he t the throne of his H3782+6584
Dt 19:16 witness **t the stand** to accuse H7756+928
Dt 22:13 If a man t a wife and, after sleeping with H4374
2Sa 15: 8 'If the LORD t me **back** *to* Jerusalem H8740+8740
1Ki 20:11 should not boast like *one who* **t** *it* **off**. H7337
2Ch 6:36 *who* t them **captive** to a land far H8647+8647
Job 12:18 *He* **t off** the shackles put on by kings and H7337
Job 12:20 advisers and **t away** the discernment of H4374
Job 27: 8 are cut off, when God **t away** their life? H8923
Job 34:25 Because *he* **t note of** their deeds, he H5795
Job 38:14 The earth **t shape** like clay under a seal H2200
Ps 34: 8 blessed is the one *who* **t refuge** in him. H2879
Ps 34:22 no one who **t refuge** in him will be H2879
Ps 94: 7 not see; the God of Jacob **t no notice**." H1067
Ps 149: 4 For the LORD **t delight** in his people; he H8354
Pr 1:19 *it* **t away** the life of those who get it. H4374
Pr 3:32 the perverse but **t** the upright into his NDT
Pr 6:34 he will show no mercy when he **t** revenge. NDT

Pr 8: 2 where the paths meet, *she* t *her* **stand**; H5893
Pr 10: 9 but *whoever* **t crooked** paths will be found H6835
Pr 16: 7 When the LORD **t pleasure** *in* anyone's way H8354
Pr 16:32 with self-control than *one who* t a city. H4334
Pr 21:12 The Righteous One **t note** of the house of H8505
Pr 25:20 Like *one who* **t away** a garment on a cold H6334
Pr 31:23 where he t his **seat** among the elders of H3782
Isa 3:13 The LORD t *his* **place** in court; he rises to H5893
Isa 21: 2 The traitor betrays, the looter **t loot**. Elam, H8720
Isa 22: 6 Elam **t up** the quiver, with her charioteers H5951
Isa 41:13 LORD your God *who* **t hold** *of* your right H2616
Isa 44:12 The blacksmith t a tool and works with it in NDT
Isa 44:15 some of it *he* t and warms himself H4374
Isa 57: 1 and no one t it to heart; the H8492
Isa 57:13 But whoever **t refuge** in me will inherit the H2879
Isa 65:16 whoever **t an oath** in the land will swear H8678
Jer 4:29 archers every town **t to flight**. H1368
Eze 18:13 He lends at interest and t a profit. H4374
Eze 18:17 poor and t no interest or profit *from* them. H4374
Eze 26:15 and *the* **slaughter t place** in you? H2222+2223
Eze 33: 4 the sword comes and t their **life**, H4374
Eze 33: 6 the sword comes and t someone's life, H4374
Mic 2: 4 is divided up. *He* t it from me! He assigns H4631
Na 1: 2 the LORD **t vengeance** and is filled with H5933
Na 1: 2 The LORD **t vengeance** on his foes and H5933
Hab 2: 5 the nations and **t captive** all the peoples. H7695
Zep 2: 2 before the decree **t effect** and that day H3528
Mt 12:45 Then it goes and t with it seven other *G4161*
Mt 18: 4 whoever **t the lowly position** of this child *G5427*
Mk 4:15 Satan comes and **t away** the word that was *G149*
Lk 6:29 *If* someone t your coat, do not withhold *G149*
Lk 6:30 and *if* anyone t what belongs to you *G149*
Lk 8:12 the devil comes and **t away** the word from *G149*
Lk 11:22 *he* **t away** the armor in which the man *G149*
Lk 11:26 Then it goes and t seven other spirits more *G4161*
Jn 1:29 who **t away** the sin of the world! *G149*
Jn 10:18 No one t it from me, but I lay it down of my *G149*
1Co 6: 6 *one* brother t another **to court**—and *G3552+3212*
2Co 11:20 you or **t advantage** *of* you or puts on *G3284*
Col 2: 8 it *that* no one t you **captive** *G1639+3836+5194*
Heb 5: 4 And no one t this honor on himself, but he *G3284*
Heb 9:17 *it* never **t effect** while the one who made *G2710*
Rev 22:19 And if anyone t words **away** from this scroll *G904*

TAKING (57) [TAKE]

Ge 8:20 t some of all the clean animals and clean H4374
Ge 24:10 t with him ten of his master's camels H4374
Ge 28:11 T one of the stones there, he put it under H4374
Ge 28:20 on this journey I *am* t and will give me H2143
Ge 31:23 T his relatives with him, he pursued Jacob H4374
Ge 34:29 **t as plunder** everything in the houses. H1024
Ge 42:38 comes to him on the journey *you are* t, H2143
Ge 46: 6 t with them their livestock and the H4374
Ge 50: 3 t a **full** forty days, for that was the time H4848
Ex 5: 4 why *are you* t the people **away** from their H7277
Ex 22:11 will be settled by the t of an oath before the NDT
Ex 29:35 t seven days to ordain them. NDT
Nu 15:18 you enter the land to which I *am* t you H995
Nu 22: 7 **t with** them the fee for divination. H928+3338
Dt 1:25 T with them some of the fruit of the land H4374
Dt 24: 6 *would be* t a person's livelihood **as security** H2471
Jos 6:18 your own destruction *by* t any of them. H4374
Jdg 4: 9 "But because of the course you *are* t, the H2143
1Sa 14:32 on the plunder and, t sheep, cattle and H4374
1Sa 17:49 Reaching into his bag and t out a stone H4374
1Sa 29: 4 favor than by t the heads of our own NDT
2Sa 4: 5 while he *was* t his noonday **rest**. H8886+5435
2Sa 4: 7 T it with them, they traveled all night by H4374
2Sa 12: 4 man refrained from t one of his own H4374
1Ki 11:18 Then t people from Paran with them, they H4374
2Ki 5: 5 t with him ten talents of silver H4374
2Ki 8: 9 t with him as a gift forty camel-loads of H4374
2Ki 15:25 T fifty men of Gilead with him, he NDT
1Ch 2: 7 by violating the ban on t devoted things. NDT
2Ch 17: 9 t with them the Book of the Law of the LORD NDT
Job 5: 3 I myself have seen a fool **t root**, but H9245
Job 5: 5 his harvest, t it even from among thorns H4374
Pr 28: 8 wealth by **t interest** or profit from the H5968
Ecc 4: 1 that *was* **t place** under the sun: H6913
Isa 30:14 will be found for t coals from a hearth H3149
Eze 17: 3 **T hold** *of* the top of a cedar H4374
Hos 11: 3 Ephraim to walk, t them by the arms; but H4374
Jnh 1:14 do not let us die for t this man's life. NDT
Zec 5:10 "Where *are* they t the basket?" I asked the H2143
Mt 5:25 *with* your **adversary who is t** you **to court**. *G508*
Mt 14:19 T the five loaves and the two fish and *G3284*
Mk 6:41 T the five loaves and the two fish and *G3284*
Mk 9:36 T the child **in** *his* **arms**, he said to *G1878*
Lk 6: 4 and t the consecrated bread *G3284*
Lk 9:16 T the five loaves and the two fish and *G3284*
Lk 12:45 'My master *is* **t a long time** in coming,' *G5988*
Lk 14: 4 So **t hold** of the man, he healed him and *G2138*
Lk 16: 3 My master *is* **t away** my job. I'm not *G904*
Lk 19:22 I am a hard man, **t out** what I did not put in *G149*
Lk 20:35 considered worthy *of* **t part** in the age to *G5593*
Lk 22:17 *After* t the cup, he gave thanks and said *G1312*
Jn 19:40 T Jesus' body, the two of them wrapped it *G3284*
Ac 3: 7 T him by the right hand, he helped him up *G4389*
Ac 9:19 and *after* t some food, he regained his *G3284*
Ac 12:25 from Jerusalem, **t with** them John, also *G5221*
2Co 8:21 For *we are* **t pains** to do what is right, not *G4629*
Php 2: 7 himself nothing *by* t the very nature of a *G3284*

TALE (KJV) COUNTED, NUMBER, QUOTA

TALEBEARER (KJV) GOSSIP, SPREADING SLANDER

TALENT (9) [TALENTS]

Ex 25:39 A t *of* pure gold is to be used for the H3971
Ex 37:24 all its accessories from *one* t *of* pure gold. H3971
Ex 38:27 from the 100 talents, one t for each base. H3971
2Sa 12:30 It weighed a t *of* gold, and it was set with H3971
1Ki 20:39 his life, or you must pay a t *of* silver. H3971
2Ki 5:22 Please give them a t *of* silver and two sets H3971
2Ki 23:33 a hundred talents of silver and a t *of* gold. H3971
1Ch 20: 2 its weight was found to be a t *of* gold, and H3971
2Ch 36: 3 a hundred talents of silver and a t *of* gold. H3971

TALENTS (39) [TALENT]

Ex 38:24 the sanctuary was 29 t and 730 shekels, H3971
Ex 38:25 the census was 100 t and 1,775 shekels, H3971
Ex 38:27 The 100 t *of* silver were used to cast the H3971
Ex 38:27 100 bases from the 100 t, one talent for H3971
Ex 38:29 wave offering was 70 t and 2,400 shekels. H3971
1Ki 9:14 Hiram had sent to the king 120 t *of* gold. H3971
1Ki 9:28 to Ophir and brought back 420 t of gold, H3971
1Ki 10:10 And she gave the king 120 t *of* gold H3971
1Ki 10:14 that Solomon received yearly was 666 t, H3971
1Ki 16:24 from Shemer for *two* t *of* silver and built a H3971
2Ki 5: 5 taking with him ten t *of* silver, six H3971
2Ki 5:23 all means, take *two* t," said Naaman. H3971
2Ki 5:23 then tied up the *two* t of silver in two H3971
2Ki 15:19 gave him a thousand t *of* silver to gain his H3971
2Ki 18:14 Judah three hundred t *of* silver and thirty H3971
2Ki 18:14 talents of silver and thirty t *of* gold. H3971
2Ki 23:33 a levy of a hundred t *of* silver and a talent H3971
1Ch 19: 6 sent a thousand t *of* silver to hire chariots H3971
1Ch 22:14 of the LORD a hundred thousand t *of* gold, H3971
1Ch 22:14 of gold, a million t of silver, quantities of H3971
1Ch 29: 4 three thousand t *of* gold (gold of Ophir H3971
1Ch 29: 4 seven thousand t *of* refined silver, for H3971
1Ch 29: 7 of God five thousand t and ten thousand H3971
1Ch 29: 7 of gold, ten thousand t of silver, eighteen H3971
1Ch 29: 7 eighteen thousand t of bronze and a H3971
1Ch 29: 7 bronze and a hundred thousand t of iron. H3971
2Ch 3: 8 the inside with six hundred t of fine gold. H3971
2Ch 8:18 back four hundred and fifty t *of* gold, H3971
2Ch 9: 9 Then she gave the king 120 t *of* gold H3971
2Ch 9:13 that Solomon received yearly was 666 t, H3971
2Ch 25: 6 men from Israel for a hundred t *of* silver. H3971
2Ch 25: 9 what about the hundred t I paid for these H3971
2Ch 27: 5 paid him a hundred t *of* silver, H3971
2Ch 36: 3 a levy of a hundred t *of* silver and a talent H3971
Ezr 7:22 up to a hundred t of silver, a hundred A10352
Ezr 8:26 I weighed out to them 650 t of silver, silver H3971
Ezr 8:26 silver articles weighing 100 t, 100 talents H3971
Ezr 8:26 weighing 100 talents, 100 t of gold, H3971
Est 3: 9 give ten thousand t *of* silver to the king's H3971

TALES (1)

1Ti 4: 7 to do with godless myths and old wives' t; NDT

TALITHA (1)

Mk 5:41 her by the hand and said to her, "T koum!" *G5420*

TALK (46) [TALKED, TALKER, TALKERS, TALKING, TALKS]

Ge 34: 6 father Hamor went out to t with Jacob. H1819
Nu 12: 1 Aaron *began to* t against Moses H1819
Dt 6: 7 T about them when you sit at home and H1819
Dt 25: 8 his town shall summon him and t to him. H1819
Jdg 9:38 "Where is your **big** t now, you who said, H7023
1Sa 25:17 a wicked man that no *one can* t to him." H1819
Job 11: 3 Will your **idle** t reduce others to silence H966
Job 18: 2 Be sensible, and then *we can* t. H1819
Job 27:12 Why then this **meaningless** t? H2038+2039
Job 35:16 So Job opens his mouth with **empty t**; H2039
Ps 38:12 those who would harm me t *of* my ruin H1819
Ps 55:21 His t is smooth as butter, yet war is in his H7023
Ps 64: 5 evil plans, *they* t *about* hiding their snares H6218
Ps 69:26 those you wound and t about the pain of H6218
Pr 4:24 keep **corrupt** t far from your lips. H4299
Pr 6:24 from the smooth t *of* a wayward woman. H4383
Pr 7:21 she seduced him with her smooth t. H8557
Pr 12:13 Evildoers are trapped by their sinful t, and H8557
Pr 14:23 but **mere** t leads only to poverty. H1821+8557
Pr 24: 2 their lips t *about* making trouble. H1819
Isa 58: 9 with the pointing finger and malicious t, H1819
Jer 3: 5 This is how *you* t, but you do all the evil H1819
Eze 36: 3 *the* **object of** people's **malicious t** H6590+6584+8557+4383
Da 10:17 your servant, t with you, my lord? H1819
Mt 9:32 and **could not** t was brought to *G3273*
Mt 12:22 so that he *could* both t and see. *G3281*
Mk 1:45 Instead he went out and began *to* t freely *G3062*
Mk 2: 7 "Why *does* this fellow t like that? He's *G3281*
Mk 7:32 a man who was deaf and **could hardly** t, *G3652*
Lk 7:15 The dead man sat up and began *to* t, and *G3281*
Jn 18:34 "or *did* others t to you about me? *G3306*
Ac 28:20 I have asked to see you and **t with** you. *G4688*
Ro 9:20 are you, a human being, *to* **t back** to God? *G503*
Ro 16:18 By **smooth** t and flattery they deceive the *G5981*
1Co 4:20 of God is not a matter of t but of power. *G3364*
2Co 11:23 (*I am* out of my mind *to* t like this. *G3281*
Eph 4:29 let any unwholesome t come out of your *G3364*
Eph 5: 4 be obscenity, **foolish** t or coarse joking *G3703*
1Ti 1: 6 these and have turned to **meaningless t**. *G3467*
1Ti 5:13 also busybodies *who* **t nonsense** *G4319*
1Ti 6: 4 in envy, strife, **malicious** t, evil suspicions *G1060*
Titus 1:10 **full of meaningless t** and deception *G3468*
Titus 2: 9 to try to please them, not *to* **t back** to them, *G515*
1Pe 2:15 good *you should* **silence** the ignorant t of *G5821*
2Jn 12 to visit you and t with you face to face *G3281*
3Jn 14 see you soon, and *we will* t face to face. *G3281*

TALKED (28) [TALK]

Ge 35:13 him at the place where *he had* t with him. H1819
Ge 35:14 at the place where God *had* t with him, H1819
Ge 35:15 place where God *had* t with him Bethel. H1819
Ge 45:15 Afterward his brothers t with him. H1819
Nu 14:10 the whole assembly t *about* stoning them. H606
Jos 22:33 And *they* t no more *about* going to war H606
Jdg 13:11 "Are you the man who t to my wife?" H1819
Jdg 14: 7 Then he went down and t with the woman, H1819
1Sa 9:25 Samuel t with Saul on the roof of his H1819
1Ki 10: 2 Solomon and t with him *about* all that H1819
2Ch 9: 1 Solomon and t with him *about* all she H1819
Jer 38:25 If the officials hear that *I* t with you, and H1819
Da 1:19 The king t with them, and he found none H1819
Hos 12: 4 him at Bethel and t with him there— H1819
Zec 1:13 words to the angel who t with me. H1819
Zec 4: 1 Then the angel who t with me returned H1819
Zec 4: 4 I asked the angel who t with me, "What H1819
Mal 3:16 who feared the LORD t with each other, H1819
Lk 20:14 *they* **t the matter over**. *G1368+4639+253*
Lk 24:15 As they t and discussed these things with *G3917*
Lk 24:32 within us while *he* t with us on the road *G3281*
Ac 9:29 *He* t and debated with the Hellenistic *G3281*
Ac 13:43 who **t with** them and urged them to *G4688*
Ac 20: 9 into a deep sleep *as* Paul t on and on. *G1363*
Ac 24:25 *As* Paul t about righteousness, self-control *G1363*
Ac 24:26 he sent for him frequently and t with him. *G3917*
1Co 13:11 When I was a child, *I* t like a child, *G3281*
Rev 21:15 The angel *who* t with me had a *G3281*

TALKER (1) [TALK]

Job 11: 2 Is this t to be vindicated? H408+8557

TALKERS (1) [TALK]

1Ti 3:11 not **malicious** t but temperate and *G1333*

TALKING (47) [TALK]

Ge 29: 9 While he *was* still t with them, Rachel H1819
Dt 11:19 t about them when you sit at home and H1819
Jdg 6:17 give me a sign that it is really you t to me. H1819
1Sa 2: 3 "Do not keep t so proudly or let your H1819
1Sa 14:19 While Saul *was* t to the priest, the tumult H1819
1Sa 17:23 As he *was* t with them, Goliath, the H1819
1Sa 18: 1 After David had finished t with Saul H1819
1Sa 30: 6 because the men *were* t *of* stoning him; H606
1Ki 1:14 While you *are* still there t to the king, I will H1819
2Ki 2:11 they were walking along and t together, H1819
2Ki 6:33 While he *was* still t to them, the H1819
2Ki 8: 4 The king *was* t to Gehazi, the servant of H1819
Est 6:14 While they *were* still t with him, the king's H1819
Job 2:10 replied, "*You are* t like a foolish woman. H1819
Eze 33:30 your people *are* **t together** about you by H1819
Zec 1: 9 The angel who *was* t with me answered H1819
Mt 12:46 *While* Jesus *was* still t to the crowd, his *G3281*
Mt 16: 8 why *are you* t among yourselves about *G1368*
Mt 16:11 understand that *I was* not t to you about *G3306*
Mt 17: 3 them Moses and Elijah, **t with** Jesus. *G5196*
Mt 17:13 understood that *he was* t to them about *G3306*
Mt 21:45 parables, they knew *he was* t about them. *G3306*
Mt 26:70 "I don't know what *you're* **t about**," he *G3306*
Mk 7:36 he did so, the more they *kept* **t about** it. *G3062*
Mk 8:17 "Why *are you* **t about** having no bread *G1368*
Mk 9: 4 Elijah and Moses, who were **t with** Jesus. *G5196*
Mk 14:68 know or understand what you're **t about**," *G3306*
Mk 14:71 "I don't know this man *you're* **t about**." *G3306*
Lk 1:65 of Judea *people were* **t about** all these *G1362*
Lk 9:30 in glorious splendor, **t with** Jesus. *G5196*
Lk 18:34 they did not know what *he was* **t about**. *G3306*
Lk 22:60 I don't know what *you're* **t about**! *G3306*
Lk 24:14 They *were* t with each other about *G3917*
Lk 24:36 *While* they *were still* t about this, Jesus *G3281*
Jn 4:27 surprised to find *him* t with a woman. *G3281*
Jn 4:27 or "Why *are you* t with her?" *G3281*
Ac 8:34 who *is* the prophet t about *G3306*
Ac 10:27 *While* **t with** him, Peter went inside and *G5326*
Ac 17:21 doing nothing but t *about* and listening to *G3306*
Ac 20: 7 the next day, kept on t until midnight. *G3364*
Ac 20:11 bread and ate. *After* t until daylight, he *G3917*
Ac 28:22 that *people* everywhere *are* **t against** this *G515*
Ro 11:13 *I am* t to you Gentiles. Inasmuch as I am *G3306*
1Co 4:19 not only how these arrogant people are t, *G3364*
2Co 11:17 boasting *I am* not t as the Lord would, *G3281*
Eph 5:32 I *am* t about Christ and the church. *G3306*
1Ti 1: 7 know what *they are* **t** *about* or what they *G3306*

TALKS (1) [TALK]

Pr 20:19 so avoid *anyone who* **t too much**. H7331+8557

TALL (14) [TALLER, TALLEST]

Dt 2:10 numerous, and as t as the Anakites. H8123
Dt 2:21 numerous, and as t as the Anakites. H8123
Dt 9: 2 The people *are* strong and t—Anakites H8123
1Ch 11:23 down an Egyptian who was five cubits **t**. H4500
Job 8:11 *Can* papyrus **grow** t where there is no H1448

Isa 2:13 cedars of Lebanon, **t** and lofty, and all the H8123
Isa 10:33 be felled, the **t** *ones* will be brought low. H1469
Isa 18: 2 to a people **t** and smooth-skinned, to H5432
Isa 18: 7 from a people **t** and smooth-skinned, H5432
Isa 45:14 and those **t** Sabeans—they H408+4500
Eze 17:24 LORD bring down the **t** tree and make the H1469
Eze 17:24 the tall tree and **make** the low tree **grow t**. H1467
Eze 31: 4 deep springs **made** it **grow t**; their streams H8123
Am 2: 9 though they were **t** as the cedars and H1470

TALLER (3) [TALL]

Dt 1:28 people are stronger and **t** than we are; H8123
1Sa 9: 2 he was a head **t** than anyone else. H1469
1Sa 10:23 the people *he was* a head **t** than any of H1467

TALLEST (2) [TALL]

2Ki 19:23 I have cut down its **t** cedars, the choicest H7757
Isa 37:24 I have cut down its **t** cedars, the choicest H7757

TALMAI (6)

Nu 13:22 Sheshai and **T**, the descendants of H9440
Jos 15:14 Sheshai, Ahiman and **T**, the sons of Anak. H9440
Jdg 1:10 defeated Sheshai, Ahiman and **T**. H9440
2Sa 3: 3 of Maakah daughter of **T** king of Geshur; H9440
2Sa 13:37 fled and went to **T** son of Ammihud, H9440
1Ch 3: 2 of Maakah daughter of **T** king of Geshur; H9440

TALMON (5)

1Ch 9:17 **T**, Ahiman and their fellow Levites, H3236
Ezr 2:42 of Shallum, Ater, **T**, Akkub, Hatita and H3236
Ne 7:45 of Shallum, Ater, **T**, Akkub, Hatita and H3236
Ne 11:19 **T** and their associates, who kept H3236
Ne 12:25 **T** and Akkub were gatekeepers who H3236

TAMAR (26) [BAAL TAMAR, HAZEZON TAMAR]

Ge 38: 6 his firstborn, and her name was **T**. H9470
Ge 38:11 Judah then said to his daughter-in-law **T** H9470
Ge 38:11 So **T** went to live in her father's H9470
Ge 38:13 When **T** was told, "Your father-in-law is H9470
Ge 38:24 "Your daughter-in-law **T** is guilty of H9470
Ru 4:12 like that of Perez, whom **T** bore to Judah." H9470
2Sa 13: 1 Amnon son of David fell in love with **T** H9470
2Sa 13: 2 with his sister **T** that he made himself ill H9470
2Sa 13: 4 "I'm in love with **T**, my brother Absalom's H9470
2Sa 13: 5 like my sister **T** to come and give me H9470
2Sa 13: 6 would like my sister **T** to come and make H9470
2Sa 13: 7 David sent word to **T** at the palace: "Go to H9470
2Sa 13: 8 So **T** went to the house of her brother H9470
2Sa 13:10 Then Amnon said to **T**, "Bring the food H9470
2Sa 13:10 And **T** took the bread she had prepared H9470
2Sa 13:19 **T** put ashes on her head and tore the H9470
2Sa 13:20 And **T** lived in her brother Absalom's H9470
2Sa 13:22 because he had disgraced his sister **T**. H9470
2Sa 13:32 since the day Amnon raped his sister **T**. H9470
2Sa 14:27 His daughter's name was **T**, and she H9470
1Ch 2: 4 daughter-in-law **T** bore Perez and Zerah H9470
1Ch 3: 9 by his concubines. And **T** was their sister. H9470
Eze 47:18 of Israel, to the Dead Sea and as far as **T**. H9471
Eze 47:19 side it will run from **T** as far as the waters H9471
Eze 48:28 Gad will run south from **T** to the waters of H9471
Mt 1: 3 whose mother was **T**, Perez the father of *G2500*

TAMARISK (3)

Ge 21:33 Abraham planted a **t tree** in Beersheba H869
1Sa 22: 6 under the **t tree** on the hill at Gibeah H869
1Sa 31:13 buried them under a **t tree** at Jabesh, H869

TAMBOURINE (NIV84) TIMBREL

TAME (1) [TAMED]

Jas 3: 8 no human being can **t** the tongue. It is *G1238*

TAMED (2) [TAME]

Jas 3: 7 sea creatures *are being* **t** and have been *G1238*
Jas 3: 7 tamed and *have been* **t** by mankind, *G1238*

TAMMUZ (1)

Eze 8:14 women sitting there, mourning the **god T**. H9452

TANHUMETH (2)

2Ki 25:23 Seraiah son of **T** the Netophathite H9489
Jer 40: 8 Seraiah son of **T**, the sons of Ephai the H9489

TANNER (3)

Ac 9:43 some time with a **t** named Simon. *G1114*
Ac 10: 6 He is staying with Simon the **t**, whose *G1114*
Ac 10:32 He is a guest in the home of Simon the **t** *G1114*

TAPESTRY (1)

SS 7: 5 Your hair is like royal **t**; the king is held H763

TAPHATH (1)

1Ki 4:11 he was married to **T** daughter of Solomon); H3264

TAPPUAH (6) [BETH TAPPUAH, EN TAPPUAH]

Jos 12:17 the king of **T** one the king of Hepher one H9517
Jos 15:34 Zanoah, En Gannim, **T**, Enam, H9517
Jos 16: 8 From **T** the border went west to the Kanah H9517
Jos 17: 8 Manasseh had the land of **T**, but Tappuah H9517
Jos 17: 8 land of Tappuah, but **T** itself, on the H9517
1Ch 2:43 Korah, **T**, Rekem and Shema. H9516

TAR (3)

Ge 11: 3 brick instead of stone, and **t** for mortar. H2819
Ge 14:10 Now the Valley of Siddim was full of **t** pits H2819
Ex 2: 3 him and coated it with **t** and pitch. H2819

TARALAH (1)

Jos 18:27 Rekem, Irpeel, **T**, H9550

TAREA (1)

1Ch 8:35 Pithon, Melek, **T** and Ahaz. H9308

TARES (KJV) WEEDS

TARGET (4)

1Sa 20:20 as though I were shooting at a **t**. H4766
Job 7:20 Why have you made me your **t**? Have I H5133
Job 16:12 crushed me. He has made me his **t**; H4766
La 3:12 his bow and made me the **t** for his arrows. H4766

TARRIED, TARRIEST, TARRIETH, TARRY, TARRYING (KJV) DELAY, DELAYED, HALTED, LEFT, REMAINED, REST, SPEND, SPENT, STAY, STAYED, STAYING, STOPPED, WAIT, WAITED

TARSHISH (19)

Ge 10: 4 Elishah, **T**, the Kittites and the H9578
1Ch 1: 7 Elishah, **T**, the Kittites and the H9578
1Ch 7:10 Kenaanah, Zethan, **T** and Ahishahar. H9578
Est 1:14 Shethar, Admatha, **T**, Meres, Marsena H9578
Ps 48: 7 them like ships of **T** shattered by an east H9576
Ps 72:10 May the kings of **T** and of distant shores H9576
Isa 23: 1 you ships of **T**! For Tyre is destroyed H9576
Isa 23: 6 Cross over to **T**; wail, you people of the H9576
Isa 23:10 the Nile, Daughter **T**, for you no longer H9576
Isa 23:14 you ships of **T**; your fortress is H9576
Isa 60: 9 in the lead are the ships of **T**, bringing H9576
Isa 66:19 to the nations—to **T**, to the Libyans and H9576
Jer 10: 9 is brought from **T** and gold from Uphaz. H9576
Eze 27:12 " '**T** did business with you because of your H9576
Eze 27:25 " 'The ships of **T** serve as carriers for your H9576
Eze 38:13 the merchants of **T** and all her villages H9576
Jnh 1: 3 ran away from the LORD and headed for **T**. H9576
Jnh 1: 3 sailed for **T** to flee from the LORD H9576
Jnh 4: 2 is what I tried to forestall by fleeing to **T**. H9576

TARSUS (5)

Ac 9:11 ask for a *man* **from T** named Saul, *G5432*
Ac 9:30 down to Caesarea and sent him off to **T**. *G5433*
Ac 11:25 Then Barnabas went to **T** to look for Saul, *G5433*
Ac 21:39 "I am a Jew, **from T** in Cilicia, a citizen of *G5432*
Ac 22: 3 "I am a Jew, born in **T** of Cilicia, but *G5433*

TARTAK (1)

2Ki 17:31 the Avvites made Nibhaz and **T**, and the H9581

TARTAN (KJV) SUPREME COMMANDER

TASK (16) [TASKS]

Ge 31:36 Jacob was angry and **took** Laban **to t** H8189
Lev 16:21 the care of someone **appointed for the t**. H6967
1Ch 29: 1 The **t** is great, because this palatial H4856
2Ch 29:34 helped them until the **t** was finished and H4856
Ne 13:30 assigned them duties, each to his own **t**. H4856
Ecc 2:26 the sinner he gives the **t** of gathering and H6721
Isa 28:21 and perform his **t**, his alien task. H6275
Isa 28:21 and perform his task, his alien **t**. H6275
Mk 13:34 each *with* their **assigned t**, and tells *G2240*
Ac 20:24 complete the **t** the Lord Jesus has *G1355*
Ac 20:24 the **t** of testifying to the good news of God's NDT
Ro 15:28 I have completed **this** *t* and have made sure AIT
1Co 3: 5 as the Lord *has* **assigned** to each his **t**. *G1443*
2Co 2:16 that brings life. And who is equal to **such** *a t*? AIT
Gal 2: 7 that *I had been* **entrusted with** *the* **t** of *G4409*
1Ti 3: 1 to be an overseer desires a noble **t**. *G2240*

TASKMASTERS (KJV) SLAVE DRIVERS, SLAVE MASTERS

TASKS (2) [TASK]

2Ch 31:16 perform the daily duties of their *various* **t**, H6275
Pr 31:17 vigorously; her arms are strong for her **t**. NDT

TASSEL (1) [TASSELS]

Nu 15:38 your garments, with a blue cord on each **t**. H7492

TASSELS (4) [TASSEL]

Nu 15:38 come you are to make **t** on the corners of H7492
Nu 15:39 You will have these **t** to look at and so you H7492
Dt 22:12 Make **t** on the four corners of the cloak H1544
Mt 23: 5 wide and the **t on** their **garments** long; *G3192*

TASTE (16) [TASTED, TASTELESS, TASTES, TASTING, TASTY]

Ge 25:28 who had a **t** *for* wild game, loved H7023
2Sa 3:35 if *I* **t** bread or anything else before the sun H3247
2Sa 19:35 *Can* your servant **t** what he eats and drinks H3247
Ps 34: 8 **T** and see that the LORD is good; blessed H3247
Ps 119:103 How sweet are your words to my **t** H2674
Pr 24:13 honey from the comb is sweet to your **t**. H2674
SS 2: 3 in his shade, and his fruit is sweet to my **t**. H2674
SS 4:16 come into his garden and **t** its choice fruits. H430
Jnh 3: 7 *Do* not *let* people or animals, herds ..., **t** H3247
Mt 16:28 are standing here *will* not **t** death before *G1174*
Mk 9: 1 are standing here *will* not **t** death before *G1174*
Lk 9:27 standing here *will* not **t** death before they *G1174*
Lk 14:24 were invited *will* **get a t** of my banquet. *G1174*
Jn 8:52 obeys your word *will* never **t** death. *G1174*
Col 2:21 "Do not handle! *Do* not **t**! Do not touch!" *G1174*
Heb 2: 9 the grace of God *he might* **t** death for *G1174*

TASTED (11) [TASTE]

Ex 16:31 coriander seed and **t** like wafers made H3248
Nu 11: 8 And it **t** like something made with olive H3248
1Sa 14:24 So none of the troops **t** food. H3247
1Sa 14:29 eyes brightened when *I* **t** a little of this H3247
1Sa 14:43 "*I* **t** a little honey with the end of H3247+3247
Eze 3: 3 and *it* **t** as sweet as honey in my mouth. H2118
Jn 2: 9 of the banquet **t** the water that had *G1174*
Heb 6: 4 enlightened, *who have* **t** the heavenly gift *G1174*
Heb 6: 5 *who have* **t** the goodness of the word of *G1174*
1Pe 2: 3 now *that you have* **t** that the Lord is good. *G1174*
Rev 10:10 *It* **t** as sweet as honey in my mouth, but *G1639S*

TASTELESS (1) [TASTE]

Job 6: 6 Is **t** *food* eaten without salt, or is there H9522

TASTES (5) [TASTE]

Job 12:11 the ear test words as the tongue **t** food? H3247
Job 34: 3 the ear tests words as the tongue **t** food. H3247
Pr 20:17 Food gained by fraud **t sweet**, but one H6853
Pr 27: 7 to the hungry even what is bitter **t** sweet. NDT
Jer 48:11 So she **t** as she did, and her aroma is H3248

TASTING (1) [TASTE]

Mt 27:34 with gall; but *after* **t** it, he refused to *G1174*

TASTY (6) [TASTE]

Ge 27: 4 me the kind of **t food** I like and bring it H4761
Ge 27: 7 game and prepare me *some* **t food** to eat, H4761
Ge 27: 9 I can prepare *some* **t food** for your father, H4761
Ge 27:14 she prepared *some* **t food**, just the H4761
Ge 27:17 her son Jacob the **t food** and the bread H4761
Ge 27:31 He too prepared *some* **t food** and brought H4761

TATTENAI (4)

Ezr 5: 3 At that time **T**, governor of A10779
Ezr 5: 6 This is a copy of the letter that **T** A10779
Ezr 6: 6 Now then, **T**, governor of A10779
Ezr 6:13 King Darius had sent, **T**, governor of A10779

TATTOO (1)

Lev 19:28 the dead or put **t** marks on yourselves. H7882

TAUGHT (58) [TEACH]

Dt 4: 5 *I have* **t** you decrees and laws as the LORD H4340
Dt 31:22 this song that day and **t** it *to* the Israelites. H4340
Jdg 8:16 and **t** the men of Sukkoth **a lesson** by H3359
2Sa 1:18 people of Judah *be* **t** this lament of the H4340
2Ki 17:28 live in Bethel and **t** them how to H2118+3723
2Ch 17: 9 *They* **t** throughout Judah, taking with them H4340
2Ch 17: 9 all the towns of Judah and **t** the people. H4340
Ps 51: 6 *you* **t** me wisdom in that secret place. H3359
Ps 71:17 *you have* **t** me, and to this day I H4340
Ps 119:102 your laws, for *you* yourself *have* **t** me. H3723
Pr 4: 4 Then *he* **t** me, and he said to me, "Take H3723
Pr 31: 1 an inspired utterance his mother **t** him. H3579
SS 8: 2 my mother's house—*she who has* **t** me. H4340
Isa 29:13 on merely human rules *they have* **been t**. H4340
Isa 40:14 and *who* **t** him the right way? H4340
Isa 40:14 *Who* was it that **t** him knowledge, or H4340
Isa 54:13 All your children will be **t** *by* the LORD, H4341
Jer 9: 5 *They have* **t** their tongues to lie; they H4340
Jer 9:14 the Baals, as their ancestors **t** them." H4340
Jer 10: 8 they are **t** *by* worthless wooden idols. H4592
Jer 12:16 even as *they once* **t** my people to swear by H4340
Jer 32:33 though I **t** them again and again H4340
Hos 11: 3 It was I *who* **t** Ephraim **to walk**, taking H8078
Mt 7:29 because *he* **t** as one who had *G1639+1438*
Mk 1:22 because *he* **t** them as one who had *G1639+1438*
Mk 4: 2 *He* **t** them many things by parables, and in *G1438*
Mk 6:30 reported to him all they had done and **t**. *G1438*
Mk 10: 1 and as was his custom, *he* **t** them. *G1438*
Mk 11:17 And *as he* **t** them, he said, "Is it not *G1438*
Mk 12:38 As he **t**, Jesus said, "Watch out for the *G1439*
Lk 1: 4 certainty of the things *you have been* **t**. *G2994*
Lk 4:31 on the Sabbath *he* **t** the people. *G1639+1438*
Lk 5: 3 he sat down and **t** the people from the *G1438*
Lk 11: 1 us to pray, just as John **t** his disciples." *G1438*
Lk 13:26 drank with you, and *you* **t** in our streets. *G1438*
Jn 6:45 'They will all be **t** by God.' Everyone who *G1435*
Jn 7:15 get such learning without *having been* **t**?" *G3443*
Jn 8:28 speak just what the Father *has* **t** me. *G1438*
Jn 18:20 "I always **t** in synagogues or at the temple *G1438*
Ac 11:26 with the church and **t** great numbers of *G1438*
Ac 15: 1 according to the custom *t by* **Moses**, you AIT
Ac 15:35 where *they* and many others **t** and *G1438*
Ac 18:25 with great fervor and **t** about Jesus *G1438*
Ac 20:20 helpful to you but *have* **t** you publicly and *G1438*
Ac 28:31 kingdom of God and **t** about the Lord *G1438*
Ro 15: 4 the endurance *t in* the **Scriptures** and the AIT
1Co 2:13 not in words **t** us by human wisdom but in *G1435*
1Co 2:13 wisdom but in words **t** by the Spirit, *G1435*
Gal 1:12 it from any man, nor *was I* **t** it; rather, *G1438*
Eph 4:21 about Christ and *were* **t** in him in *G1438*
Eph 4:22 You were **t**, with regard to your former way NDT
Col 2: 7 strengthened in the faith as *you were* **t** *G1438*
1Th 4: 9 have been **t by God** to love each other. *G2531*
1Ti 1:20 over to Satan to *be* **t** not to blaspheme. *G4084*
1Ti 4: 1 deceiving spirits and **things t** by demons. *G1436*

T

Titus 1: 9 the trustworthy message as it has been t, G1439
1Jn 2:27 just as it has t you, remain in him G1438
Rev 2:14 who t Balak to entice the Israelites to sin G1438

TAUNT (8) [TAUNTED, TAUNTS]
Dt 32:27 I dreaded the t of the enemy, lest the H4088
1Ki 18:27 At noon Elijah began to t them. "Shout H2252
Ps 42:10 suffer mortal agony as my foes t me, H3070
Ps 102: 8 All day long my enemies t me; those who H3070
Isa 14: 4 you will take up this t against the king of H5442
Eze 5:15 You will be a reproach and a t, a warning H1527
Mic 2: 4 they will t you with this mournful song: H5629
Hab 2: 6 "Will not all of them t him with H5951+5442

TAUNTED (4) [TAUNT]
Jdg 8:15 about whom you t me by saying, 'Do H3070
2Sa 21:21 When he t Israel, Jonathan son of H3070
2Sa 23: 9 with David when they t the Philistines H3070
1Ch 20: 7 When he t Israel, Jonathan son of Shimea, H3070

TAUNTS (6) [TAUNT]
Ps 44:16 at the t of those who reproach and revile H7754
Ps 89:50 I bear in my heart the t of all the nations, H8190
Ps 89:51 the t with which your enemies, LORD, have NDT
Ps 119:42 then I can answer anyone who t me, for I H3070
Eze 36:15 will I make you hear the t of the nations, H4009
Zep 2: 8 of Moab and the t of the Ammonites, H1526

TAVERNS See THREE TAVERNS

TAX (37) [TAXED, TAXES]
2Ch 24: 6 Jerusalem the t imposed by Moses the H5368
2Ch 24: 9 to bring to the LORD the t that Moses the H5368
Ne 5: 4 to pay the king's t on our fields and H4501
Da 11:20 will send out a t collector to maintain the H5601
Am 5:11 You levy a straw t on the poor and impose H1424
Am 5:11 on the poor and impose a t on their grain. H5368
Mt 5:46 Are not even the t collectors doing that? G5467
Mt 9: 9 Matthew sitting at the t collector's booth. G5468
Mt 9:10 many t collectors and sinners came and G5467
Mt 9:11 teacher eat with t collectors and sinners?" G5467
Mt 10: 3 Thomas and Matthew the t collector G5467
Mt 11:19 a friend of t collectors and sinners. G5467
Mt 17:24 of the two-drachma temple t came to G1440
Mt 17:24 "Doesn't your teacher pay the temple t?" G1440
Mt 17:27 it and give it to them for my t and yours." NDT
Mt 18:17 as you would a pagan or a t collector. G5467
Mt 21:31 the t collectors and the prostitutes are G5467
Mt 21:32 the t collectors and the prostitutes did. G5467
Mt 22:17 right to pay the imperial t to Caesar or not G3056
Mt 22:19 Show me the coin used for paying the t." G3056
Mk 2:14 Alphaeus sitting at the t collector's booth. G5468
Mk 2:15 many t collectors and sinners were eating G5467
Mk 2:16 eating with the sinners and t collectors, G5467
Mk 2:16 does he eat with t collectors and sinners?" G5467
Mk 12:14 right to pay the imperial t to Caesar or not G3056
Lk 3:12 Even t collectors came to be baptized G5467
Lk 5:27 out and saw a t collector by the name of G5467
Lk 5:27 by the name of Levi sitting at his t booth. G5468
Lk 5:29 a large crowd of t collectors and others G5467
Lk 5:30 drink with t collectors and sinners? G5467
Lk 7:29 people, even the t collectors, when they G5467
Lk 7:34 a friend of t collectors and sinners. G5467
Lk 15: 1 Now the t collectors and sinners were all G5467
Lk 18:10 one a Pharisee and the other a t collector. G5467
Lk 18:11 adulterers—or even like this t collector. G5467
Lk 18:13 "But the t collector stood at a distance. G5467
Lk 19: 2 he was a chief t collector and was wealthy. G803

TAXED (1) [TAX]
2Ki 23:35 he t the land and exacted the silver and H6885

TAXES (10) [TAX]
1Sa 17:25 and will exempt his family from t in H6913+2930
Ezr 4:13 restored, no more t, tribute or duty will A10402
Ezr 4:20 Trans-Euphrates, and t, tribute and duty A10402
Ezr 7:24 that you have no authority to impose t, A10402
Mt 17:25 the kings of the earth collect duty and t— G3056
Lk 20:22 Is it right for us to pay t to Caesar or not?" G5843
Lk 23: 2 He opposes payment of t to Caesar and G5843
Ro 13: 6 This is also why you pay t, for the G5843
Ro 13: 7 If you owe t, pay taxes; if revenue, then G5843
Ro 13: 7 If you owe taxes, pay t; if revenue, then G5843

TAXING (KJV) CENSUS

TEACH (123) [SPIRIT-TAUGHT, TAUGHT, TEACHER, TEACHERS, TEACHES, TEACHING, TEACHINGS]
Ex 4:12 help you speak and will t you what to say." H3723
Ex 4:15 of you speak and will t you what to do. H3723
Ex 18:20 T them his decrees and instructions, and H2302
Ex 33:13 t me your ways so I may know you and H3359
Ex 35:34 of the tribe of Dan, the ability to t others. H3723
Lev 10:11 so you can t the Israelites all the H3723
Dt 4: 1 the decrees and laws I am about to t you. H4340
Dt 4: 9 T them to your children and to their H3359
Dt 4:10 the land and may t them to their children H4340
Dt 4:14 me at that time to t you the decrees and H4340
Dt 5:31 laws you are to t them to follow H4340
Dt 6: 1 God directed me to t you to observe in the H4340
Dt 8: 3 to t you that man does not live on bread H3359
Dt 11:19 T them to your children, talking about H4340
Dt 17:11 to whatever they t you and the decisions H3723
Dt 20:18 they will t you to follow all the detestable H4340
Dt 31:19 down this song and t it to the Israelites H4340
Jdg 3: 2 this only to t warfare to the descendants H4340
Jdg 13: 8 to us come again to t us how to bring up H3723
1Sa 12:23 And I will t you the way that is good and H3723
1Sa 14:12 "Come up to us and we'll t you a lesson." H3359
1Ki 8:36 T them the right way to live, and send H3723
2Ki 17:27 to live there and t the people what the H3723
2Ch 6:27 T them the right way to live, and send H3723
2Ch 15: 3 without a priest to t and without the law. H3723
2Ch 17: 7 Micaiah to t in the towns of Judah. H4340
Ezr 7:25 And you are to t any who do not know A10313
Job 6:24 "T me, and I will be quiet; show me H3723
Job 12: 7 the animals, and they will t you, or the H3723
Job 12: 8 to the earth, and it will t you, or let the H3723
Job 21:22 "Can anyone t knowledge to God, since H4340
Job 27:11 "I will t you about the power of God; the H3723
Job 32: 7 advanced years should t wisdom. H3359
Job 33:33 be silent, and I will t you wisdom. H544
Job 34:32 T me what I cannot see; if I have done H3723
Ps 25: 4 Show me your ways, LORD, t me your paths. H4340
Ps 25: 5 Guide me in your truth and t me, for you H4340
Ps 27:11 T me your way, LORD; lead me in a straight H3723
Ps 32: 8 I will instruct you and t you in the way you H3723
Ps 34:11 I will t you the fear of the LORD. H4340
Ps 51:13 Then I will t transgressors your ways, so H4340
Ps 78: 5 our ancestors to t their children, H3359
Ps 86:11 T me your way, LORD, that I may rely on H3723
Ps 90:12 T us to number our days, that we may H3359
Ps 94:12 the one you t from your law; H4340
Ps 105:22 as he pleased and t his elders wisdom. H2681
Ps 119:12 Praise be to you, LORD; t me your decrees. H4340
Ps 119:26 you answered me; t me your decrees. H4340
Ps 119:29 be gracious to me and t me your law. NDT
Ps 119:33 T me, LORD, the way of your decrees, that I H3723
Ps 119:64 with your love, LORD; t me your decrees. H4340
Ps 119:66 T me knowledge and good judgment, for H4340
Ps 119:68 what you do is good; t me your decrees. H4340
Ps 119:108 praise of my mouth, and t me your laws. H4340
Ps 119:124 to your love and t me your decrees. H4340
Ps 119:135 on your servant and t me your decrees. H4340
Ps 119:171 with praise, for you t me your decrees. H4340
Ps 132:12 my covenant and the statutes I t them, H4340
Ps 143:10 T me to do your will, for you are my God H4340
Pr 9: 9 t the righteous and they will add to their H3359
Pr 22:17 of the wise; apply your heart to what I t, H1981
Pr 22:19 be in the LORD, I t you today, even you H3359
Isa 2: 3 He will t us his ways, so that we may walk H3723
Isa 9:15 the prophets who t lies are the tail. H3723
Isa 28: 9 "Who is it he is trying to t? To H3723+1978
Isa 43:27 those I sent to t you rebelled against me. H4885
Jer 9:20 T your daughters how to wail; teach one H4340
Jer 9:20 how to wail; t one another a lament. NDT
Jer 16:21 "Therefore I will t them—this time I will H3359
Jer 16:21 this time I will t them my power and H3359
Jer 31:34 No longer will they t their neighbor, or say H4340
Eze 22:26 they t that there is no difference between H3359
Eze 44:23 They are to t my people the difference H3723
Da 1: 4 He was to t them the language and H4340
Mic 3:11 a bribe, her priests t for a price, and her H3723
Mic 4: 2 He will t us his ways, so that we may walk H3723
Mt 5: 2 he began to t them. He said: G1438
Mt 11: 1 went on from there to t and preach in the G1438
Mt 22:16 integrity and that you t the way of God in G1438
Mk 1:21 went into the synagogue and began to t. G1438
Mk 2:13 came to him, and he began to t them. G1438
Mk 4: 1 Again Jesus began to t by the lake. G1438
Mk 6: 2 he began to t in the synagogue G1438
Mk 8:31 He then began to t them that the Son of G1438
Mk 12:14 but you t the way of God in accordance G1438
Lk 11: 1 t us to pray, just as John taught his G1438
Lk 12:12 the Holy Spirit will t you at that time G1438
Lk 20:21 know that you speak and t what is right, G1438
Lk 20:21 not show partiality but t the way of God in G1438
Jn 7:14 go up to the temple courts and begin to t. G1438
Jn 7:35 among the Greeks, and t the Greeks? G1438
Jn 8: 2 around him, and he sat down to t them. G1438
Jn 14:26 will t you all things and will remind you of G1438
Ac 1: 1 about all that Jesus began to do and to t G1438
Ac 4:18 them not to speak or t at all in the name G1438
Ac 5:21 been told, and began to t the people. G1438
Ac 5:28 you strict orders not to t in this name," G1438
Ac 21:21 informed that you t all the Jews who live G1438
Ro 2:21 who t others, do you not teach G1438
Ro 2:21 who teach others, do you not t yourself? G1438
Ro 12: 7 then serve; if it is teaching, then t; G1436
Ro 15: 4 was written in the past was written to t us, G1436
1Co 4:17 agrees with what I t everywhere in every G1438
1Co 11:14 Does not the very nature of things t you G1438
Col 3:16 among you richly as you t and admonish G1438
1Ti 1: 3 people not to t false doctrines any longer G2281
1Ti 2:12 I do not permit a woman to t or to assume G1438
1Ti 3: 2 respectable, hospitable, able to t, G1434
1Ti 4:11 Command and t these things. G1438
1Ti 6: 2 are the things you are to t and insist on. G1438
2Ti 2: 2 who will also be qualified to t others. G1438
2Ti 2:24 kind to everyone, able to t, not resentful. G1434
Titus 1:11 by teaching things they ought not to t— NDT
Titus 2: 1 must t what is appropriate to sound G3281
Titus 2: 2 T the older men to be temperate, worthy of NDT
Titus 2: 3 t the older women to be reverent in the way NDT
Titus 2: 3 to much wine, but to t what is good. G2815
Titus 2: 9 T slaves to be subject to their masters in NDT
Titus 2:15 are the things you should t. Encourage G3281
Heb 5:12 you need someone to t you the G1438
Heb 8:11 No longer will they t their neighbor, or say G1438
Jas 3: 1 you know that we who t will be judged more NDT
1Jn 2:27 you do not need anyone to t you. G1438

TEACHER (73) [TEACH]
1Ch 25: 8 Young and old alike, t as well as student H1067
Ezr 7: 6 He was a t well versed in the Law of H6221
Ezr 7:11 the priest, a t of the Law, a man learned H6221
Ezr 7:12 t of the Law of the God of heaven: A10516
Ezr 7:21 the t of the Law of the God of heaven A10516
Ne 8: 1 told Ezra the t of the Law to bring out the H6221
Ne 8: 4 Ezra the t of the Law stood on a high H6221
Ne 8: 9 Ezra the priest and t of the Law, and the H6221
Ne 8:13 around Ezra the t to give attention to the H6221
Ne 12:26 of Ezra the priest, the t of the Law. H6221
Ne 12:36 Ezra the t of the Law led the procession H6221
Job 36:22 exalted in his power. Who is a t like him? H4621
Ecc 1: 1 The words of the T, son of David, king in H7738
Ecc 1: 2 says the T. "Utterly meaningless! H7738
Ecc 1:12 the T, was king over Israel in Jerusalem. H7738
Ecc 7:27 says the T, "this is what I have H7738
Ecc 12: 8 Meaningless!" says the T. "Everything is H7738
Ecc 12: 9 Not only was the T wise, but he also H7738
Ecc 12:10 The T searched to find just the right words H7738
Mt 8:19 Then a t of the law came to him and said G1208
Mt 8:19 to him and said, "T, I will follow you G1437
Mt 9:11 "Why does your t eat with tax collectors G1437
Mt 10:24 "The student is not above the t, nor a G1437
Mt 12:38 the law said to him, "T, we want to see a G1437
Mt 13:52 every t of the law who has become G1208
Mt 17:24 "Doesn't your t pay the temple tax?" G1437
Mt 19:16 to Jesus and asked, "T, what good thing G1437
Mt 22:16 "T," they said, "we know that you are a G1437
Mt 22:24 "T," they said, "Moses told us that if a G1437
Mt 22:36 "T, which is the greatest commandment in G1437
Mt 23: 8 you have one T, and you are all G1437
Mt 26:18 a certain man and tell him, 'The T says: G1437
Mk 4:38 said to him, "T, don't you care if we G1437
Mk 5:35 "Why bother the t anymore?" G1437
Mk 9:17 the crowd answered, "T, I brought you my G1437
Mk 9:38 "T," said John, "we saw someone driving G1437
Mk 10:17 "Good t," he asked, "what must I do to G1437
Mk 10:20 "T," he declared, "all these I have kept G1437
Mk 10:35 "T," they said, "we want you to do for us G1437
Mk 12:14 to him and said, "T, we know that you are G1437
Mk 12:19 "T," they said, "Moses wrote for us that if a G1437
Mk 12:32 "Well said, t," the man replied. "You are G1437
Mk 13: 1 one of his disciples said to him, "Look, T! G1437
Mk 14:14 of the house he enters, 'The T asks: G1437
Lk 3:12 to be baptized. "T," they asked, "what G1437
Lk 6:40 The student is not above the t, but G1437
Lk 6:40 who is fully trained will be like their t. G1437
Lk 7:40 "Tell me, t," he said. G1437
Lk 8:49 "Don't bother the t anymore." G1437
Lk 9:38 crowd called out, "T, I beg you to look at G1437
Lk 10:25 "T," he asked, "what must I do to inherit G1437
Lk 11:45 law answered him, "T, when you say G1437
Lk 12:13 crowd said to him, "T, tell my brother to G1437
Lk 18:18 asked him, "Good t, what must I do to G1437
Lk 19:39 crowd said to Jesus, "T, rebuke your G1437
Lk 20:21 "T, we know that you speak and teach G1437
Lk 20:28 "T," they said, "Moses wrote for us that if a G1437
Lk 20:39 of the law responded, "Well said, t!" G1437
Lk 21: 7 "T," they asked, "when will these things G1437
Lk 22:11 to the owner of the house, 'The T asks: G1437
Jn 1:38 which means "T"), "where are you G1437
Jn 3: 2 know that you are a t who has come from G1437
Jn 3:10 "You are Israel's t," said Jesus, "and do G1437
Jn 8: 4 said to Jesus, "T, this woman was G1437
Jn 11:28 "The T is here," she said, "and is asking G1437
Jn 13:13 "You call me 'T' and 'Lord,' and rightly so G1437
Jn 13:14 your Lord and T, have washed your G1437
Jn 20:16 Aramaic, "Rabboni!" (which means "T") G1437
Ac 5:34 Gamaliel, a t of the law, who was G3791
Ro 2:20 of the foolish, a t of little children G1437
1Co 1:20 Where is the t of the law? Where is the G1208
1Ti 2: 7 a true and faithful t of the Gentiles. G1437
2Ti 1:11 a herald and an apostle and a t. G1437

TEACHERS (77) [TEACH]
Ps 119:99 I have more insight than all my t, for I H4340
Pr 5:13 I would not obey my t or turn my ear to my H4621
Isa 30:20 of affliction, your t will be hidden no more H4621
Mt 2: 4 the people's chief priests and t of the law, G1208
Mt 5:20 that of the Pharisees and the t of the law, G1208
Mt 7:29 authority, and not as their t of the law. G1208
Mt 9: 3 some of the t of the law said to G1208
Mt 10:25 It is enough for students to be like their t G1437
Mt 12:38 Pharisees and t of the law said to him, G1208
Mt 15: 1 Pharisees and t of the law came to Jesus G1208
Mt 16:21 the chief priests and the t of the law, and G1208
Mt 17:10 then do the t of the law say that Elijah G1208
Mt 20:18 to the chief priests and the t of the law. G1208
Mt 21:15 priests and the t of the law saw the G1208
Mt 23: 2 "The t of the law and the Pharisees sit in G1208
Mt 23:13 "Woe to you, t of the law and Pharisees G1208
Mt 23:15 "Woe to you, t of the law and Pharisees G1208
Mt 23:23 "Woe to you, t of the law and Pharisees G1208
Mt 23:25 "Woe to you, t of the law and Pharisees G1208

T

Mt 23:27 "Woe to you, **t of the law** and Pharisees *G1208*
Mt 23:29 "Woe to you, **t of the law** and Pharisees *G1208*
Mt 23:34 sending you prophets and sages and **t**. *G1208*
Mt 26:57 where the **t of the law** and the elders had *G1208*
Mt 27:41 the **t of the law** and the elders mocked *G1208*
Mk 1:22 who had authority, not as the **t of the law**. *G1208*
Mk 2: 6 Now some **t of the law** were sitting there *G1208*
Mk 2:16 When the **t of the law** who were Pharisees *G1208*
Mk 3:22 And the **t of the law** who came down from *G1208*
Mk 7: 1 some *of* the **t of the law** who had *G1208*
Mk 7: 5 Pharisees and **t of the law** asked Jesus, *G1208*
Mk 8:31 the chief priests and the **t of the law**, and *G1208*
Mk 9:11 "Why do the **t of the law** say that Elijah *G1208*
Mk 9:14 them and the **t of the law** arguing with *G1208*
Mk 10:33 to the chief priests and the **t of the law**. *G1208*
Mk 11:18 priests and the **t of the law** heard this *G1208*
Mk 11:27 the **t of the law** and the elders came to *G1208*
Mk 12:12 the **t** of the law and the elders looked for a NDT
Mk 12:28 One *of* the **t of the law** came and heard *G1208*
Mk 12:35 "Why do the **t of the law** say that the *G1208*
Mk 12:38 Jesus said, "Watch out for the **t of the law**. *G1208*
Mk 14: 1 the **t of the law** were scheming *G1208*
Mk 14:43 the **t of the law**, and the elders. *G1208*
Mk 14:53 elders and the **t of the law** came together. *G1208*
Mk 15: 1 the **t of the law** and the whole Sanhedrin *G1208*
Mk 15:31 priests and the **t of the law** mocked him *G1208*
Lk 2:46 sitting among the **t**, listening to them *G1437*
Lk 5:17 Pharisees and **t of the law** were sitting *G3791*
Lk 5:21 the **t of the law** began thinking *G1208*
Lk 5:30 the **t of the law** who belonged to *G1208*
Lk 6: 7 the **t of the law** were looking for *G1208*
Lk 6:11 But **the Pharisees and the t of the law** *G899S*
Lk 9:22 the chief priests and the **t of the law**, and *G1208*
Lk 11:53 the **t of the law** began to oppose *G1208*
Lk 15: 2 Pharisees and the **t of the law** muttered, *G1208*
Lk 19:47 the **t of the law** and the leaders among *G1208*
Lk 20: 1 the chief priests and the **t of the law** *G1208*
Lk 20:19 The **t of the law** and the chief priests *G1208*
Lk 20:39 Some *of* the **t of the law** responded *G1208*
Lk 20:46 "Beware of the **t of the law**. They like to *G1208*
Lk 22: 2 priests and the **t of the law** were looking *G1208*
Lk 22:66 both the chief priests and the **t of the law** *G1208*
Lk 23:10 priests and the **t of the law** were standing *G1208*
Jn 8: 3 The **t of the law** and the Pharisees brought *G1208*
Ac 4: 5 elders and the **t of the law** met in *G1208*
Ac 6:12 the elders and the **t of the law**. *G1208*
Ac 13: 1 at Antioch there were prophets and **t**: *G1437*
Ac 23: 9 some *of* the **t of the law** who were *G1208*
1Co 12:28 prophets, third **t**, then miracles, then *G1437*
1Co 12:29 Are all **t**? Do all work miracles *G1437*
Eph 4:11 the evangelists, the pastors and **t**, *G1437*
1Ti 1: 7 They want to be **t of the law**, but they do *G3791*
2Ti 3: 8 so also these **t** oppose the truth. NDT
2Ti 4: 3 them a great number *of* **t** to say what their *G1437*
Heb 5:12 though by this time you ought to be **t**, you *G1437*
Jas 3: 1 Not many of you should become **t**, my *G1437*
2Pe 2: 1 just as there will be **false t** among you. *G6015*
2Pe 2: 3 In their greed these **t** will exploit you with NDT

TEACHES (14) [TEACH]

Dt 33:10 *He* **t** your precepts to Jacob and your law H3723
Job 35:11 *who* **t** us more than he teaches the beasts H544
Job 35:11 us more than he **t** the beasts of the earth NDT
Ps 25: 9 in what is right and **t** them his way. H4340
Ps 94:10 Does *he who* **t** mankind lack knowledge H4340
Isa 28:26 God instructs him and **t** him the right way. H3723
Isa 48:17 your God, *who* **t** you what is best for you H4340
Hab 2:18 Or an image *that* **t** lies? For the one who H3723
Mt 5:19 these commands and **t** others accordingly *G1438*
Mt 5:19 practices and **t** these commands will *G1438*
Ac 21:28 is the man who **t** everyone everywhere *G1438*
1Ti 6: 3 If anyone **t otherwise** and does not agree *G2281*
Titus 2:12 *It* **t** us to say "No" to ungodliness and *G4084*
1Jn 2:27 But as his anointing **t** you about all things *G1438*

TEACHING (89) [TEACH]

Dt 32: 2 Let my **t** fall like rain and my words H4375
Ezr 7:10 to **t** its decrees and laws in Israel. H4340
Ps 60: T For **t**. When he fought Aram H4340
Ps 78: 1 My people, hear my **t**; listen to the words H9368
Pr 1: 8 do not forsake your mother's **t**. H9368
Pr 3: 1 do not forget my **t**, but keep my H9368
Pr 4: 2 sound learning, so do not forsake my **t**. H9368
Pr 6:20 do not forsake your mother's **t**. H9368
Pr 6:23 command is a lamp, this **t** is a light, and H9368
Pr 13:14 The **t** *of* the wise is a fountain of life H9368
Pr 22:21 **t** you to be honest and to speak the truth H3359
Isa 42: 4 In his **t** the islands will put their hope." H9368
Jer 18:18 the **t of the law** by the priest will not H9368
Mal 2: 8 way and by your **t** have caused many to H9368
Mt 4:23 throughout Galilee, **t** in their synagogues *G1438*
Mt 7:28 the crowds were amazed at his **t**, *G1439*
Mt 9:35 towns and villages, **t** in their synagogues *G1438*
Mt 13:54 *he began* **t** the people in their synagogue, *G1438*
Mt 16:12 against the **t** of the Pharisees and *G1439*
Mt 21:23 *while he was* **t**, the chief priests and *G1438*
Mt 22:33 heard this, they were astonished at his **t**. *G1439*
Mt 26:55 Every day I sat in the temple courts **t**, and *G1438*
Mt 28:20 **t** them to obey everything I have *G1438*
Mk 1:22 The people were amazed at his **t**, because *G1439*
Mk 1:27 A new **t**—and with authority *G1439*
Mk 4: 2 things by parables, and in his **t** said: *G1439*
Mk 6: 6 Then Jesus went around **t** from village to *G1438*
Mk 6:34 So he began **t** them many things. *G1438*
Mk 9:31 because *he was* **t** his disciples. He said to *G1438*
Mk 11:18 the whole crowd was amazed at his **t**. *G1439*
Mk 12:35 *While* Jesus *was* **t** in the temple courts *G1438*
Mk 14:49 day I was with you, **t** in the temple courts *G1438*
Lk 4:15 He *was* **t** in their synagogues, and *G1438*
Lk 4:32 They were amazed at his **t**, because his *G1439*
Lk 5:17 One day Jesus was **t**, and Pharisees and *G1438*
Lk 6: 6 he went into the synagogue and *was* **t**, *G1438*
Lk 13:10 On a Sabbath Jesus was **t** in one of the *G1438*
Lk 13:22 **t** as he made his way to Jerusalem. *G1438*
Lk 19:47 Every day he was **t** at the temple. But the *G1438*
Lk 20: 1 One day *as* Jesus *was* **t** the people in the *G1438*
Lk 21:37 Each day Jesus was **t** at the temple, and *G1438*
Lk 23: 5 stirs up the people all over Judea *by his* **t**. *G1438*
Jn 6:59 He said this *while* **t** in the synagogue in *G1438*
Jn 6:60 of his disciples said, "This is a hard **t**. *G3364*
Jn 7:16 Jesus answered, "My **t** is not my own. *G1439*
Jn 7:17 find out whether my **t** comes from God *G1439*
Jn 7:28 Then Jesus, *still* **t** in the temple courts *G1438*
Jn 8:20 spoke these words *while* **t** in the temple *G1438*
Jn 8:31 "If you hold to my **t**, you are really my *G3364*
Jn 14:23 "Anyone who loves me will obey my **t**. *G3364*
Jn 14:24 who does not love me will not obey my **t**. *G3364*
Jn 15:20 If they obeyed my **t**, they will obey yours *G3364*
Jn 18:19 Jesus about his disciples and his **t**. *G1439*
Ac 2:42 to the apostles' **t** and to fellowship, *G1439*
Ac 4: 2 because the apostles *were* **t** the people, *G1438*
Ac 5:25 in the temple courts **t** the people. *G1438*
Ac 5:28 Jerusalem with your **t** and are determined *G1439*
Ac 5:42 they never stopped **t** and proclaiming the *G1438*
Ac 13:12 he was amazed at the **t** about the Lord. *G1439*
Ac 15: 1 to Antioch and *were* **t** the believers: *G1438*
Ac 17:19 we know what this new **t** is that you are *G1439*
Ac 18:11 a year and a half, **t** them the word of God. *G1438*
Ro 6:17 heart the pattern *of* **t** that has now *G1439*
Ro 12: 7 is serving, then serve; if it is **t**, then teach; *G1438*
Ro 16:17 are contrary to the **t** you have learned. *G1439*
Eph 4:14 by every wind *of* **t** and by the cunning *G1436*
Col 1:28 admonishing and **t** everyone with all *G1438*
2Th 2: 2 alarmed by the **t** allegedly from us— *G3808*
2Th 3: 6 according to the **t** you received from us. *G4142*
1Ti 4: 6 the faith and *of* the good **t** that you have *G1436*
1Ti 4:13 of Scripture, to preaching and *to* **t**. *G1436*
1Ti 5:17 those whose work is preaching and **t**. *G1436*
1Ti 6: 1 God's name and our **t** may not be *G1436*
1Ti 6: 3 of our Lord Jesus Christ and to godly **t**, *G1436*
2Ti 1:13 keep as the pattern *of* sound **t**, with faith *G3364*
2Ti 2:17 Their **t** will spread like gangrene. Among *G3364*
2Ti 3:10 know all about my **t**, my way of life, *G1436*
2Ti 3:16 is God-breathed and is useful for **t**, *G1436*
Titus 1:11 whole households *by* **t** things they ought *G1438*
Titus 2: 7 what is good. In your **t** show integrity *G1436*
Titus 2:10 they will make the **t** about God our Savior *G1436*
Heb 5:13 acquainted with the **t** about righteousness *G3364*
2Jn 9 not continue in the **t** of Christ does not *G1439*
2Jn 9 continues in the **t** has both the Father *G1439*
2Jn 10 comes to you and does not bring this **t**, *G1439*
Rev 2:14 among you who hold to the **t** of Balaam, *G1439*
Rev 2:15 those who hold to the **t** of the Nicolaitans. *G1439*
Rev 2:20 *By her* **t** she misleads my servants into *G1438*
Rev 2:24 do not hold to her **t** and have not learned *G1439*

TEACHINGS (9) [TEACH]

Pr 1:23 I will make known to you my **t**. H1821
Pr 7: 2 guard my **t** as the apple of your eye. H9368
Mt 15: 9 *their* **t** *are* merely human rules. *G1438+1436*
Mk 7: 7 *their* **t** are merely human rules. *G1438+1436*
Col 2:22 on merely human commands and **t**. *G1436*
2Th 2:15 hold fast *to* the **t** we passed on to *G4142*
1Ti 4: 2 Such **t** come through hypocritical liars, NDT
Heb 6: 1 the elementary **t** about Christ and be *G3364*
Heb 13: 9 be carried away *by* all kinds of strange **t**. *G1439*

TEAM (1) [TEAMS]

Isa 21: 9 a man in a chariot with a **t** *of* horses. H7538

TEAMS (1) [TEAM]

Isa 21: 7 When he sees chariots with **t** *of* horses H7538

TEAR (55) [TEARING, TEARS, TORE, TORN]

Ex 28:32 around this opening, so that it *will* not **t**. H7973
Ex 39:23 this opening, so that *it would* not **t**. H7973
Lev 1:17 *He shall* **t** it **open** by the wings, not H9117
Lev 10: 6 unkempt and *do* not **t** your clothes, H7268
Lev 13:56 *he is to* **t** the spoiled part out of the fabric H7973
Lev 21:10 his hair become unkempt or **t** his clothes. H7268
Jdg 6:25 **T down** your father's altar to Baal and cut H2238
Jdg 8: 7 *I will* **t** your flesh with desert thorns and H1889
Jdg 8: 9 return in triumph, *I will* **t down** this tower." H5997
2Sa 3:31 "**T** your clothes and put on sackcloth and H7973
1Ki 11:11 *I will* **most certainly t** the kingdom **away** H7973+7973
1Ki 11:12 *I will* **t** it out of the hand of your son H7973
1Ki 11:13 Yet *I will* not **t** the whole kingdom from H7973
1Ki 11:31 *I am going to* **t** the kingdom out of H7973
Job 18: 4 You *who* **t** yourself **to pieces** in your anger, H3271
Ps 7: 2 or *they will* **t** me **apart** like a lion and rip H3271
Ps 22:13 Roaring lions *that* **t** their **prey** open their H3271
Ps 28: 5 *he will* **t** them **down** and never build them H2238
Ps 50:22 or *I will* **t** you **to pieces**, with no one H3271
Ps 58: 6 LORD, **t out** the fangs of those lions! H5997
Ps 137: 7 "**T** it **down**," they cried, "tear it down to H6867
Ps 137: 7 they cried, "**t** it **down** to its foundations!" H6867
Pr 29: 4 those who are greedy for bribes **t** it **down**. H2238
Ecc 3: 3 a time to **t down** and a time to build H7287
Ecc 3: 7 a time to **t** and a time to mend, a time to H7973
Isa 7: 6 *let us* **t** it **apart** and divide it among H7763
Isa 22:12 to **t out** your **hair** and put on sackcloth. H7947
Jer 1:10 kingdoms to uproot and **t down**, H5997
Jer 5: 6 their towns *to* **t to pieces** any who venture H3271
Jer 24: 6 I will build them up and not **t** them **down** H2238
Jer 30: 8 off their necks and *will* **t off** their bonds; H5998
Jer 31:28 watched over them to uproot and **t down**, H5997
Jer 36:24 no fear, nor *did they* **t** their clothes. H7973
Jer 42:10 I will build you up and not **t** you **down**; H2238
La 2: 8 determined to **t down** the wall around H8845
Eze 13:14 *I will* **t down** the wall you have covered H2238
Eze 13:20 like birds and *I will* **t** them from your arms; H7973
Eze 13:21 *I will* **t off** your veils and save my people H7973
Eze 16:39 and *they will* **t down** your mounds and H2238
Eze 19: 3 He learned to **t** the prey and he became a H3271
Eze 19: 6 He learned to **t** the prey and he became a H3271
Eze 23:34 on its pieces—and *you will* **t** your breasts. H5998
Hos 5:14 I *will* **t** them **to pieces** and go away; I will H3271
Hos 13: 8 a wild animal *will* **t** them **apart**. H1324
Am 3:15 *I will* **t down** the winter house along with H5782
Mic 3: 2 *who* **t** the skin from my people and the H1608
Mic 5:11 of your land and **t down** all your H2238
Na 1:13 from your neck and **t** your shackles **away**." H5998
Mt 7: 6 their feet, and turn and **t** you to **pieces**. *G4838*
Mt 9:16 from the garment, making the **t** worse. *G5388*
Mk 2:21 away from the old, making the **t** worse. *G5388*
Lk 12:18 *I will* **t down** my barns and build bigger *G2747*
Jn 19:24 "*Let's* not **t** it," they said to one another *G5387*
Rev 7:17 will wipe away every **t** from their eyes. *G1232*
Rev 21: 4 'He will wipe every **t** from their eyes. *G1232*

TEARING (6) [TEAR]

Dt 33:20 lives there like a lion, **t** *at* arm or head. H3271
Eze 22:25 within her like a roaring lion **t** its prey; H3271
Eze 22:27 within her are like wolves **t** their prey; H3271
Zec 11:16 of the choice sheep, **t off** their hooves. H7293
2Co 10: 8 building you up rather than **t** you **down**, *G2746*
2Co 13:10 building you up, not for **t** you **down**. *G2746*

TEARS (43) [TEAR]

2Ki 20: 5 I have heard your prayer and seen your **t**; H1965
Job 12:14 What *he* **t down** cannot be rebuilt; those H2238
Job 16: 9 God assails me and **t** me in his anger H3271
Job 16:20 is my friend *as* my eyes **pour out t** to God; H1940
Job 19:10 *He* **t** me **down** on every side till I am gone H5997
Job 31:38 me and all its furrows *are* **wet with t**, H1134
Ps 6: 6 with weeping and drench my couch with **t**. H1965
Ps 42: 3 My **t** have been my food day and night H1965
Ps 56: 8 my misery; list my **t** on your scroll—are H1965
Ps 80: 5 You have fed them with the bread of **t** H1965
Ps 80: 5 have made them drink **t** by the bowlful. H1965
Ps 102: 9 as my food and mingle my drink with **t** H1140
Ps 116: 8 my eyes from **t**, my feet from H1965
Ps 119:136 Streams of **t** flow from my eyes, for your H4784
Ps 126: 5 Those who sow with **t** will reap with songs H1965
Pr 14: 1 own hands the foolish one **t** hers **down**. H2238
Pr 15:25 The LORD **t down** the house of the proud H5815
Ecc 4: 1 I saw the **t** *of* the oppressed—and they H1965
Isa 16: 9 I drench you with **t**! The shouts of joy over H1965
Isa 25: 8 LORD will wipe away the **t** from all faces; H1965
Isa 38: 5 I have heard your prayer and seen your **t**; H1965
Jer 9: 1 of water and my eyes a fountain of **t**! H1965
Jer 9:18 eyes overflow with **t** and water streams H1965
Jer 13:17 overflowing with **t**, because the LORD's H1965
Jer 14:17 eyes overflow with **t** night and day without H1965
Jer 31:16 voice from weeping and your eyes from **t**, H1965
Jer 50: 4 together will go *in* **t** to seek the LORD H1134
La 1: 2 she weeps at night, **t** are on her cheeks. H1965
La 1:16 why I weep and my eyes overflow with **t**. H4784
La 2:18 let your **t** flow like a river day and night H1965
La 3:48 Streams of **t** flow from my eyes because H4784
Eze 24:16 Yet do not lament or weep or shed any **t**. H1965
Mal 2:13 You flood the LORD's altar with **t**. H1965
Lk 5:36 "No one **t** a piece out of a new garment *G5387*
Lk 7:38 she began to wet his feet *with* her **t**. *G1232*
Lk 7:44 wet my feet *with* her **t** and wiped them *G1232*
Ac 20:19 great humility and *with* **t** and in the midst *G1232*
Ac 20:31 warning each of you night and day with **t**. *G1232*
2Co 2: 4 anguish of heart and with many **t**, *G1232*
Php 3:18 now tell you again even **with t**, *G3081*
2Ti 1: 4 Recalling your **t**, I long to see you, so that I *G1232*
Heb 5: 7 fervent cries and **t** to the one who could *G1232*
Heb 12:17 though he sought the blessing with **t**, *G1232*

TEATS (KJV) BREASTS

TEBAH (3)

Ge 22:24 also had sons: **T**, Gaham, Tahash and H3182
2Sa 8: 8 From **T** and Berothai, towns that belonged H3183
1Ch 18: 8 From **T** and Kun, towns that belonged to H3187

TEBETH (1)

Est 2:16 the month of **T**, in the seventh H3194

TEEM (2) [TEEMED, TEEMING, TEEMS]

Ge 1:20 "*Let* the water **t** *with* living H9237+9238
Ex 8: 3 The Nile *will* **t** *with* frogs. They will come H9237

TEEMED (1) [TEEM]
Ps 105:30 Their land t *with* frogs, which went up into H9237

TEEMING (1) [TEEM]
Ps 104:25 spacious, t with **creatures** beyond number H8254

TEEMS (1) [TEEM]
Ge 1:21 which the water t and that moves about H9237

TEETH (42) [TOOTH]
Ge 49:12 darker than wine, his t whiter than milk. H9094
Nu 11:33 still between their t and before it could be H9094
Job 4:10 the t *of* the great lions are broken. H9094
Job 16: 9 me in his anger and gnashes his t at me; H9094
Job 19:20 I have escaped only by the skin of my t. H9094
Job 29:17 snatched the victims from their t. H9094
Job 41:14 its mouth, ringed about with fearsome t? H9094
Ps 3: 7 on the jaw; break the t *of* the wicked. H9094
Ps 35:16 mocked; they gnashed their t at me. H9094
Ps 37:12 the righteous and gnash their t at them; H9094
Ps 57: 4 men whose t are spears and arrows H9094
Ps 58: 6 Break the t in their mouths, O God; LORD H9094
Ps 112:10 they will gnash their t and waste away H9094
Ps 124: 6 who has not let us be torn by their t. H9094
Pr 10:26 As vinegar to the t and smoke to the eyes H9094
Pr 30:14 those whose t are swords and whose jaws H9094
SS 4: 2 Your t are like a flock of sheep just shorn H9094
SS 6: 6 Your t are like a flock of sheep coming up H9094
SS 7: 9 beloved, flowing gently over lips and t. H9094
Isa 41:15 new and sharp, with **many** t. H7092
Jer 31:29 the children's t are set on edge. H9094
Jer 31:30 grapes—their own t will be set on edge. H9094
La 2:16 they scoff and gnash their t and say, "We H9094
La 3:16 He has broken my t with gravel; he has H9094
Eze 18: 2 the children's t are set on edge'? H9094
Da 7: 5 had three ribs in its mouth between its t. A10730
Da 7: 7 It had large iron t; it crushed and A10730
Da 7:19 with its iron t and bronze claws—the A10730
Joel 1: 6 number; it has the t *of* a lion, the fangs of H9094
Am 1: 3 threshed Gilead with sledges having iron t, NDT
Zec 9: 7 the forbidden food from between their t. H9094
Mt 8:12 there will be weeping and gnashing *of* t." G3848
Mt 13:42 there will be weeping and gnashing *of* t. G3848
Mt 13:50 there will be weeping and gnashing *of* t. G3848
Mt 22:13 there will be weeping and gnashing *of* t. G3848
Mt 24:51 there will be weeping and gnashing *of* t. G3848
Mt 25:30 there will be weeping and gnashing *of* t. G3848
Mk 9:18 gnashes his t and becomes rigid. G3848
Lk 13:28 and gnashing *of* t, when you see G3848
Ac 7:54 were furious and gnashed their t at him. G3848
Rev 9: 8 and their t were like lions' teeth. G3848
Rev 9: 8 and their teeth were like lions' t. NDT

TEHINNAH (1)
1Ch 4:12 Paseah and T the father of Ir Nahash. H9383

TEKEL (2)
Da 5:25 that was written: MENE, MENE, T, PARSIN A10770
Da 5:27 T: You have been weighed on the scales A10770

TEKOA (13) [TEKOITE]
2Sa 14: 2 sent someone to T and had a wise H9541
2Sa 14: 4 When the woman **from** T went to the king, H9542
2Sa 14: 9 But the woman **from** T said to him, "Let H9542
2Sa 23:26 Helez the Paltite, Ira son of Ikkesh **from** T, H9542
1Ch 2:24 Hezron bore him Ashhur the father of T. H9541
1Ch 4: 5 Ashhur the father of T had two wives H9541
1Ch 11:28 Ira son of Ikkesh **from** T, Abiezer from H9542
2Ch 11: 6 Bethlehem, Etam, T, H9541
2Ch 20:20 the morning they left for the Desert of T. H9541
Ne 3: 5 section was repaired by the **men of** T, H9542
Ne 3:27 the **men of** T repaired another section H9542
Jer 6: 1 Sound the trumpet in T! Raise the signal H9541
Am 1: 1 one of the shepherds of T—the vision he H9541

TEKOITE (1) [TEKOA]
1Ch 27: 9 was Ira the son of Ikkesh the T. H9542

TEL ASSAR (2)
2Ki 19:12 the people of Eden who were in T? H9431
Isa 37:12 the people of Eden who were in T? H9431

TEL AVIV (1) [AVIV]
Eze 3:15 exiles who lived at T near the Kebar H9425

TEL HARSHA (2) [HARSHA]
Ezr 2:59 the towns of Tel Melah, T, Kerub, H9426
Ne 7:61 the towns of Tel Melah, T, Kerub, H9426

TEL MELAH (2)
Ezr 2:59 came up from the towns of T, H9427
Ne 7:61 came up from the towns of T, H9427

TELAH (1)
1Ch 7:25 Resheph his son, T his son, Tahan his son H9436

TELAIM (1)
1Sa 15: 4 the men and mustered them at T— H3230

TELEM (2)
Jos 15:24 Ziph, T, Bealoth, H3234
Ezr 10:24 the gatekeepers: Shallum, T and Uri. H3235

TELL (569) [TELLING, TELLS, TOLD]
Ge 12:18 "Why didn't *you* t me she was your wife? H5583
Ge 21:26 You *did* not t me, and I heard about it H5583
Ge 24:23 Please t me, is there room in your father's H5583
Ge 24:30 heard Rebekah t what the man said H606+1821
Ge 24:33 "Then t us," Laban said. H1819
Ge 24:49 to my master, t me; and if not, H5583
Ge 24:49 if not, t me, so I may know which way H5583
Ge 26: 2 live in the land where *I* t you to live. H606
Ge 27: 8 listen carefully and do what I t you: H7422
Ge 29:15 T me what your wages should be. H5583
Ge 31:27 Why didn't *you* t me, so I could send you H5583
Ge 32:29 Jacob said, "Please t me your name." H5583
Ge 37:16 *Can you* t me where they are grazing their H5583
Ge 40: 8 belong to God? T me your dreams." H6218
Ge 41:21 no *one could* t that they had done so H3359
Ge 42:22 "Didn't *I* t you not to sin against the boy? H606
Ge 45:13 T my father *about* all the honor accorded H5583
Ge 45:17 said to Joseph, "T your brothers, 'Do this H606
Ge 45:19 "You are also directed to t them, 'Do this NDT
Ge 49: 1 "Gather around so *I can* t you what will H5583
Ge 50: 4 your eyes, speak to Pharaoh for me. T him, H606
Ex 3:13 Then what *shall I* t them?" H606
Ex 6:11 t Pharaoh king of Egypt to let the H1819
Ex 6:29 T Pharaoh king of Egypt everything I tell H1819
Ex 6:29 Pharaoh king of Egypt everything I t you." H1819
Ex 7: 2 your brother Aaron *is to* t Pharaoh to let H1819
Ex 7:19 LORD said to Moses, "T Aaron, 'Take your H606
Ex 8: 5 LORD said to Moses, "T Aaron, 'Stretch out H606
Ex 8:16 LORD said to Moses, "T Aaron, 'Stretch out H606
Ex 10: 2 that *you may* t your children H6218+928+265
Ex 10: 8 "But t me who will be going. NDT
Ex 11: 2 T the people that men and H1819+928+265
Ex 12: 3 T the whole community of Israel that on H1819
Ex 12:27 then t them, 'It is the Passover sacrifice to H606
Ex 13: 8 On that day t your son, 'I do this because H5583
Ex 14: 2 "T the Israelites to turn back and encamp H1819
Ex 14:15 T the Israelites to move on H1819
Ex 16:12 T them, 'At twilight you will eat meat H1819
Ex 19: 3 Jacob and what *you are to* t the people of H5583
Ex 19:12 people around the mountain and t them, H606
Ex 20:22 LORD said to Moses, "T the Israelites this: H606
Ex 25: 2 "T the Israelites to bring me an offering H1819
Ex 28: 3 T all the skilled workers to whom I have H1819
Ex 33: 5 had said to Moses, "T the Israelites, 'You H606
Lev 14:35 of the house must go and t the priest, H5583
Lev 16: 2 "T your brother Aaron that he is not to H1819
Lev 22: 2 "T Aaron and his sons to treat with respect H1819
Nu 6:23 "T Aaron and his sons, 'This is how you H1819
Nu 9:10 "T the Israelites: 'When any of you or your H1819
Nu 11:12 Why *do you* t me to carry them in my arms H606
Nu 11:18 "T the people: 'Consecrate yourselves in H606
Nu 14:14 *they will* t the inhabitants of this land *about* H606
Nu 14:28 So t them, 'As surely as I live, declares the H606
Nu 16:37 "T Eleazar son of Aaron, the priest, to H606
Nu 19: 2 T the Israelites to bring you a red heifer H1819
Nu 22:19 can find out what else the LORD *will* t me." H1819
Nu 22:20 go with them, but do only what *I* t you." H1819
Nu 22:35 with the men, but speak only what *I* t you." H1819
Nu 23: 3 Whatever he reveals to me *I will* t you." H5583
Nu 23:26 "*Did I* not t you I must do whatever the H1819
Nu 24:12 "*Did I* not t the messengers you sent me, H1819
Nu 25:12 Therefore t him I am making my covenant H606
Dt 1:42 LORD said to me, "T them, 'Do not go up H606
Dt 5:27 Then t us whatever the LORD our God tells H1819
Dt 5:30 t them to return to their tents. H606
Dt 6:21 t him: "We were slaves of Pharaoh in Egypt H606
Dt 17:11 Do not turn aside from what *they* t you, to H5583
Dt 18:18 *He will* t them everything I command him. H1819
Dt 32: 7 Ask your father and *he will* t you, your H5583
Jos 1:11 "Go through the camp and t the people H7422
Jos 2:14 "If *you* don't t what we are doing, we will H5583
Jos 2:20 But if *you* t what we are doing, we will be H5583
Jos 3: 8 T the priests who carry the ark of the H7422
Jos 4: 3 t them to take up twelve stones from H7422
Jos 4: 7 t them that the flow of the Jordan was cut H606
Jos 4:22 t them, 'Israel crossed the Jordan on dry H3359
Jos 6:10 say a word until the day I t you to shout. H606
Jos 7:13 T them, 'Consecrate yourselves in H606
Jos 7:19 T me what you have done; do not hide it H5583
Jos 20: 2 "T the Israelites to designate the cities of H1819
Jdg 13: 6 came from, and *he* didn't t me his name. H5583
Jdg 13:10 The woman hurried *to* t her husband H5583
Jdg 14: 9 But *he did* not t them that he had taken H5583
Jdg 14:12 "*Let me* t you a riddle," Samson said to H2554
Jdg 14:13 If you can't t me *the* **answer**, you must give H5583
Jdg 14:13 sets of clothes." "T us your riddle," they H2554
Jdg 16: 6 "T me the secret of your great strength H5583
Jdg 16:10 Come now, t me how you can be tied." H5583
Jdg 16:13 T me how you can be tied. H5583
Jdg 20: 3 "T us how this awful thing happened." H1819
Jdg 20: 7 speak up and t me what you have H1821
Ru 3: 4 lie down. He *will* t you what to do." H5583
Ru 4: 4 But if you will not, t me, so I will know. H5583
1Sa 3:15 He was afraid *to* t Eli the vision, H5583
1Sa 6: 2 T us how we should send it back to its H3359
1Sa 9: 6 Perhaps *he will* t us what way to take." H5583
1Sa 9: 8 of God so that *he will* t us what way to H5583
1Sa 9:18 "*Would you* please t me where the seer's H5583
1Sa 9:19 on your way and *will* t you all that is in H5583
1Sa 9:27 "T the servant to go on ahead of us"— H606
1Sa 10: 8 I come to you and t you what you are to H3359
1Sa 10:15 "T me what Samuel said to you. H5583
1Sa 10:16 But *he did* not t his uncle what Samuel H5583
1Sa 14: 1 But *he did* not t his father. H5583
1Sa 14:34 "Go out among the men and t them, 'Each H606
1Sa 14:43 to Jonathan, "T me what you have done." H5583
1Sa 15:16 "*Let me* t you what the LORD said to me H5583
1Sa 15:16 to me last night." "T me," Saul replied. H1819
1Sa 19: 3 him about you and *will* t you what I find H5583
1Sa 20: 6 misses me at all, t him, 'David earnestly H606
1Sa 20: 9 determined to harm you, wouldn't *I* t you?" H5583
1Sa 20:10 "Who *will* t me if your father answers you H5583
1Sa 22:17 fleeing, yet *they did* not t me." H1655+906+265
1Sa 22:22 I knew *he would* **be sure to** t Saul. H5583+5583
1Sa 23:11 God of Israel, t your servant." And H5583
1Sa 23:22 seen him there. *They* t me he is very crafty H606
1Sa 25: 8 Ask your own servants and *they will* t you H5583
1Sa 25:19 But *she did* not t her husband Nabal H5583
1Sa 28:15 I have called on you to t me what to do." H3359
2Sa 1: 4 "T me." "The men fled from H5583
2Sa 1:20 "T it not in Gath, proclaim it not in the H5583
2Sa 3:19 he went to Hebron to t David everything H1819
2Sa 7: 5 "Go and t my servant David, 'This is what H606
2Sa 7: 8 "Now then, t my servant David, 'This is H606
2Sa 12:18 were afraid to t him that the child was H5583
2Sa 12:18 How *can we* now t him the child is dead H606
2Sa 13: 4 Won't *you* t me?" Amnon said H5583
2Sa 15:35 T them anything you hear in the king's H5583
2Sa 17:16 Now send a message at once and t David H5583
2Sa 17:17 they were to go and t King David, for H5583
2Sa 18:21 t the king what you have seen. H5583
2Sa 19:35 *Can I* t **the difference** between what is H3359
2Sa 20:16 T Joab to come here so I can speak to him." H606
2Sa 24:12 "Go and t David, 'This is what the LORD H1819
1Ki 12:10 Now t them, 'My little finger is thicker H1819
1Ki 14: 3 He *will* t you what will happen to the boy." H5583
1Ki 14: 7 t Jeroboam that this is what the LORD H606
1Ki 18: 8 "Go t your master, 'Elijah is H606
1Ki 18:11 But now you t me to go to my master and H606
1Ki 18:12 If I go and t Ahab and he doesn't find you H5583
1Ki 18:14 And now you t me to go to my master and H606
1Ki 18:44 Elijah said, "Go and t Ahab, 'Hitch up your H606
1Ki 20: 9 messengers, "T my lord the king, 'Your H606
1Ki 20:11 of Israel answered, "T him: 'One who puts H1819
1Ki 22:14 *I can* t him only what the LORD tells me." H1819
1Ki 22:16 I make you swear *to* t me nothing but the H1819
1Ki 22:18 "Didn't *I* t you that he never prophesies H606
2Ki 1: 6 back to the king who sent you and t him, H1819
2Ki 2: 9 said to Elisha, "T me, what can I do for H8626
2Ki 2:18 he said to them, "Didn't *I* t you not to go?" H606
2Ki 4: 2 can I help you? T me, what do you have H5583
2Ki 4:13 Elisha said to him, "T her, 'You have gone H606
2Ki 4:24 don't slow down for me unless *I* t you." H606
2Ki 4:28 "Didn't *I* t you, 'Don't raise my H606
2Ki 6:11 officers and demanded of them, "T me! H5583
2Ki 7:12 "*I will* t you what the Arameans have H5583
2Ki 8: 4 "T me *about* all the great things Elisha H6218
2Ki 9:12 "T us." Jehu said, "Here is H5583
2Ki 9:15 of the city to go and t **the news** in Jezreel." H5583
2Ki 18:19 commander said to them, "T Hezekiah: H606
2Ki 19: 6 Isaiah said to them, "T your master, 'This is H606
2Ki 20: 5 "Go back and t Hezekiah, the ruler of my H606
2Ki 22:15 T the man who sent you to me H606
2Ki 22:18 T the king of Judah, who sent you to inquire H606
1Ch 16: 9 praise to him; t of all his wonderful acts. H8488
1Ch 17: 4 "Go and t my servant David, 'This is what H606
1Ch 17: 7 "Now then, t my servant David, 'This is H606
1Ch 21:10 "Go and t David, 'This is what the LORD H1819
1Ch 21:18 LORD ordered Gad to t David to go up and H606
2Ch 10:10 Now t them, 'My little finger is thicker than H606
2Ch 18:13 *I can* t him only what my God says." H1819
2Ch 18:15 I make you swear *to* t me nothing but the H1819
2Ch 18:17 "Didn't *I* t you that he never prophesies H606
2Ch 34:23 T the man who sent you to me H606
2Ch 34:26 T the king of Judah, who sent you to inquire H606
Job 1:15 the only one who has escaped to t you!" H5583
Job 1:16 the only one who has escaped to t you!" H5583
Job 1:17 the only one who has escaped to t you!" H5583
Job 1:19 the only one who has escaped to t you!" H5583
Job 4:16 It stopped, but *I could* not t what it was. H5795
Job 8:10 Will they not instruct you and t you? Will H606
Job 10: 2 t me what charges you have against H3359
Job 12: 7 the birds in the sky, and *they will* t you; H5583
Job 15:17 *let me* t you what I have seen, H6218
Job 32: 6 not daring to t you what I know. H2555
Job 32:10 Listen to me; I too *will* t you what I know. H2555
Job 32:17 will have my say; I too *will* t what I know. H2555
Job 33:12 "But *I* t you, in this you are not right, for H6699
Job 33:23 sent to t them how to be upright, H5583
Job 34:33 not I; so t me what you know. H1819
Job 37:19 "T us what we should say to him; we H3359
Job 38: 4 earth's foundation? T me, if you H5583
Job 38:18 T me, if you know all H5583
Ps 5: 6 you destroy *those who* t lies. H1819
Ps 5: 9 open grave; *with* their tongues *they* t **lies**. H2744
Ps 9: 1 *I will* t of all your wonderful deeds. H6218
Ps 40: 5 were I to speak and t of your deeds, they H1819
Ps 48:13 that *you may* t of them to the next H6218
Ps 50:12 If I were hungry *I would* not t you, for the H606
Ps 66:16 *let me* t you what he has done for me. H6218
Ps 71:15 My mouth *will* t *of* your righteous deeds H6218
Ps 71:24 My tongue *will* t *of* your righteous acts all H2047
Ps 73:28 LORD my refuge; *I will* t *of* all your deeds. H6218

Ps 75: 1 *people* **t** *of* your wonderful deeds. H6218
Ps 78: 4 we *will* **t** the next generation the H6218
Ps 78: 6 and *they* in turn *would* **t** their children. H6218
Ps 105: 2 praise to him; **t** of all his wonderful acts. H8488
Ps 107: 2 *Let* the redeemed of the LORD **t** their **story** H606
Ps 107:22 thank offerings and **t** *of* his works with H6218
Ps 142: 2 my complaint; before him *I* **t** my trouble. H5583
Ps 145: 4 to another; *they* **t** *of* your mighty acts. H5583
Ps 145: 6 *They* **t** *of* the power of your awesome works H606
Ps 145:11 *They* **t** *of* the glory of your kingdom and H606
Ecc 6:12 Who *can* **t** them what will happen under H5583
Ecc 8: 7 who *can* **t** someone else what is to come? H5583
Ecc 10:14 who *can* **t** someone else what will H5583
SS 1: 7 **T** me, you whom I love, where you graze H5583
SS 5: 8 you find my beloved, what *will you* **t** him? H5583
SS 5: 8 will you tell him? **T** him I am faint with love. NDT
Isa 3:10 **T** the righteous it will be well with them H606
Isa 5: 5 Now *I will* **t** you what I am going to do to H3359
Isa 6: 9 He said, "Go and **t** this people: " 'Be ever H606
Isa 21:10 *I* **t** you what I have heard from the LORD H5583
Isa 30:10 of what is right! **T** us pleasant things H1819
Isa 36: 4 commander said to them, "**T** Hezekiah: H606
Isa 37: 6 Isaiah said to them, "**T** your master, 'This is H606
Isa 38: 5 "Go and **t** Hezekiah, 'This is what the LORD H606
Isa 38:19 parents **t** their children about your H3359
Isa 41:22 "**T** us, you idols, what is going to happen H5583
Isa 41:22 **T** us what the former things were, so that H5583
Isa 41:23 **t** us what the future holds, so we may H5583
Isa 41:27 I was the first to **t** Zion, 'Look, here they are!' NDT
Isa 48: 6 now on *I will* **t** you *of* new things, *of* H9048
Isa 63: 7 *I will* **t** *of* the kindnesses of the LORD, the H2349
Jer 4:16 "**T** this to the nations, proclaim H2349
Jer 5:19 *you will* **t** them, 'As you have forsaken me H606
Jer 7:27 "When *you* **t** them all this, they will not H1819
Jer 10:11 "**T** them this: 'These gods, who did not A10042
Jer 11: 2 of this covenant and **t** them to the people H1819
Jer 11: 3 **T** them that this is what the LORD, the God H606
Jer 13:13 then **t** them, 'This is what the LORD says: H606
Jer 15: 2 'Where shall we go?' **t** them, 'This is what H606
Jer 16:10 "When *you* **t** these people all this and H5583
Jer 19: 2 There proclaim the words *I* **t** you, H1819
Jer 21: 3 Jeremiah answered them, "**T** Zedekiah, H606
Jer 21: 8 "Furthermore, **t** the people, 'This is what H606
Jer 23:27 think the dreams *they* **t** one another will H6218
Jer 23:32 "*They* **t** them and lead my people astray H6218
Jer 25:27 "Then **t** them, 'This is what the LORD H606
Jer 25:28 your hand and drink, **t** them, 'This is what H606
Jer 26: 2 **T** them everything I command you; do not H1819
Jer 27: 4 God of Israel, says: "**T** this to your masters: H606
Jer 27: 9 your mediums or your sorcerers who **t** you H606
Jer 28:13 "Go and **t** Hananiah, 'This is what the LORD H606
Jer 29:24 **T** Shemaiah the Nehelamite, H606
Jer 33: 3 I will answer you and **t** you great and H5583
Jer 34: 2 Go to Zedekiah king of Judah and **t** him H606
Jer 35:13 Go and **t** the people of Judah and those H606
Jer 36:17 they asked Baruch, "**T** us, how did you H5583
Jer 36:29 Also **t** Jehoiakim king of Judah, 'This is H606
Jer 37: 7 **T** the king of Judah, who sent you to H606
Jer 38:20 "Obey the LORD by doing what I **t** you H1819
Jer 38:25 '**T** us what you said to the king and what H5583
Jer 38:26 then **t** them, 'I was pleading with the king H606
Jer 39:16 "Go and **t** Ebed-Melek the Cushite, 'This is H606
Jer 42: 3 the LORD your God *will* **t** us where we H5583
Jer 42: 4 *I will* **t** you everything the LORD says and H5583
Jer 42: 5 the LORD your God sends you to **t** us. NDT
Jer 42:20 **t** us everything he says and we will do it. H5583
Jer 42:21 the LORD your God in all he sent me to **t** you. NDT
Jer 43: 1 everything the LORD had sent him to **t** them NDT
Jer 51:10 *let us* **t** in Zion what the LORD our God has H6218
Eze 13:11 therefore **t** those who cover it with H606
Eze 14: 4 Therefore speak to them and **t** them, 'This H606
Eze 17: 2 and **t** it to the Israelites *as* a parable. H5439
Eze 24: 3 **T** this rebellious people a parable and say H5439
Eze 24:19 "Won't *you* **t** us what these things have to H5583
Eze 24:26 day a fugitive will come to **t** you the news. NDT
Eze 33:13 If I **t** a righteous person that they will surely H606
Eze 37:18 'Won't *you* **t** us what you mean by this? H5583
Eze 40: 4 **T** the people of Israel everything you see." H5583
Eze 44: 5 to everything I **t** you concerning all the H1819
Da 2: 2 astrologers to **t** him what he had H5583
Da 2: 4 **T** your servants the dream, and we will A10042
Da 2: 5 If *you do* not **t** me what my dream was A10313
Da 2: 6 But if *you* **t** me the dream and explain it A10252
Da 2: 6 So **t** me the dream and interpret it for A10252
Da 2: 7 "*Let* the king **t** his servants the dream A10042
Da 2: 9 If *you do* not **t** me the dream, there is A10313
Da 2: 9 have conspired to **t** me misleading and A10042
Da 2: 9 So then, **t** me the dream, and I will know A10042
Da 2:25 from Judah who *can* **t** the king what his A10313
Da 2:26 "Are you able to **t** me what I saw in my A10313
Da 4: 2 my pleasure to **t** you *about* the A10252
Da 4:18 Belteshazzar, **t** me what it means, for A10042
Da 5: 8 read the writing or **t** the king what it A10313
Da 5:12 and *he will* **t** you what the writing means A10252
Da 5:15 this writing and **t** me what it means, A10313
Da 5:16 this writing and **t** me what it means, A10313
Da 5:17 the king and **t** him what it means. A10313
Da 8:16 **t** this man **the meaning** *of* the vision." H1067
Da 8:19 "I *am going to* **t** you what will happen H3359
Da 9:23 which I have come to **t** you, for you are H5583
Da 10:21 first *I will* **t** you what is written in the H5583
Da 11: 2 "Now then, *I* **t** you the truth: Three more H5583
Joel 1: 3 **T** it to your children, and let your children H6218
Joel 1: 3 let your children **t** it to their children NDT
Jnh 1: 8 So they asked him, "**T** us, who is H5583
Jnh 4:11 people who cannot **t** their right hand from H3359
Mic 1:10 **T** it not in Gath; weep not at all. In Beth H5583
Mic 3:11 her prophets **t fortunes** for money. H7876
Zep 3:13 will do no wrong; *they will* **t** no lies. H1819
Hag 2:21 "**T** Zerubbabel governor of Judah that I am H606
Zec 1: 3 Therefore **t** the people: This is what the H606
Zec 2: 4 **t** that young man, 'Jerusalem will H1819
Zec 6:12 **T** him this is what the LORD Almighty says H606
Zec 10: 2 that lie; *they* **t** dreams that are false H1819
Mt 2:13 Stay there until *I* **t** you, for Herod is going G3306
Mt 3: 9 '*I* **t** you that out of these stones God can G3306
Mt 4: 3 **t** these stones to become bread. G3306
Mt 5:18 For truly *I* **t** you, until heaven and earth G3306
Mt 5:20 For *I* **t** you that unless your righteousness G3306
Mt 5:22 But I **t** you that anyone who is angry with a G3306
Mt 5:26 Truly *I* **t** you, you will not get out until you G3306
Mt 5:28 But I **t** you that anyone who looks at a G3306
Mt 5:32 But I **t** you that anyone who divorces his G3306
Mt 5:34 But I **t** you, do not swear an oath at all G3306
Mt 5:39 But I **t** you, do not resist an evil person. G3306
Mt 5:44 But I **t** you, love your enemies and pray G3306
Mt 6: 2 Truly *I* **t** you, they have received their G3306
Mt 6: 5 Truly *I* **t** you, they have received their G3306
Mt 6:16 Truly *I* **t** you, they have received their G3306
Mt 6:25 "Therefore *I* **t** you, do not worry about your G3306
Mt 6:29 Yet *I* **t** you that not even Solomon in all his G3306
Mt 7:23 Then *I will* **t** them **plainly**, 'I never knew G3933
Mt 8: 4 said to him, "See that *you* don't **t** anyone. G3306
Mt 8: 9 *I* **t** this one, 'Go,' and he goes; and that G3306
Mt 8:10 following him, "Truly *I* **t** you, I have not G3306
Mt 10:15 Truly *I* **t** you, it will be more bearable for G3306
Mt 10:23 Truly *I* **t** you, you will not finish going G3306
Mt 10:27 What *I* **t** you in the dark, speak in the G3306
Mt 10:42 is my disciple, truly *I* **t** you, that person G3306
Mt 11: 9 Yes, *I* **t** you, and more than a G3306
Mt 11:11 Truly *I* **t** you, among those born of women G3306
Mt 11:22 But *I* **t** you, it will be more bearable for G3306
Mt 11:24 But *I* **t** you that it will be more bearable G3306
Mt 12: 6 *I* **t** you that something greater than the G3306
Mt 12:16 them not *to* **t** others **about** him. G5745+4472
Mt 12:31 And so *I* **t** you, every kind of sin and G3306
Mt 12:36 But *I* **t** you that everyone will have to give G3306
Mt 13:17 For truly *I* **t** you, many prophets and G3306
Mt 13:30 At that time *I will* **t** the harvesters G3306
Mt 14:28 "**t** me to come to you on the water." G3027
Mt 16:18 And I **t** you that you are Peter, and on this G3306
Mt 16:20 his disciples not to **t** anyone that he was G3306
Mt 16:28 "Truly *I* **t** you, some who are standing G3306
Mt 17: 9 "Don't **t** anyone what you have seen G3306
Mt 17:12 But *I* **t** you, Elijah has already come, and G3306
Mt 17:20 Truly *I* **t** you, if you have faith as small as G3306
Mt 18: 3 "Truly *I* **t** you, unless you change and G3306
Mt 18:10 For *I* **t** you that their angels in heaven G3306
Mt 18:13 if he finds it, truly *I* **t** you, he is happier G3306
Mt 18:17 still refuse to listen, **t** it to the church; and G3306
Mt 18:18 "Truly *I* **t** you, whatever you bind on earth G3306
Mt 18:19 truly *I* **t** you that if two of you on earth G3306
Mt 18:22 Jesus answered, "*I* **t** you, not seven times G3306
Mt 19: 9 *I* **t** you that anyone who divorces his wife G3306
Mt 19:23 to his disciples, "Truly *I* **t** you, it is hard G3306
Mt 19:24 Again *I* **t** you, it is easier for a camel to go G3306
Mt 19:28 said to them, "Truly *I* **t** you, at the renewal G3306
Mt 21:21 Jesus replied, "Truly *I* **t** you, if you have G3306
Mt 21:24 I *will* **t** you by what authority I am doing G3306
Mt 21:27 "Neither *will* I **t** you by what authority I am G3306
Mt 21:31 said to them, "Truly *I* **t** you, the tax G3306
Mt 21:43 "Therefore *I* **t** you that the kingdom of G3306
Mt 22: 3 invited to the banquet *to* **t** them **to come**, G2813
Mt 22: 4 '**T** those who have been invited that I G3306
Mt 22:17 **T** us then, what is your opinion? Is it right G3306
Mt 23: 3 be careful to do everything *they* **t** you. G3306
Mt 23:36 Truly *I* **t** you, all this will come on this G3306
Mt 23:39 For *I* **t** you, you will not see me again until G3306
Mt 24: 2 "Truly *I* **t** you, not one stone here will be G3306
Mt 24: 3 "**T** us," they said, "when will this happen G3306
Mt 24:34 Truly *I* **t** you, this generation will certainly G3306
Mt 24:47 Truly *I* **t** you, he will put him in charge of G3306
Mt 25:12 he replied, 'Truly *I* **t** you, I don't know you. G3306
Mt 25:40 will reply, 'Truly *I* **t** you, whatever you did G3306
Mt 25:45 will reply, 'Truly *I* **t** you, whatever you did G3306
Mt 26:13 Truly *I* **t** you, wherever this gospel is G3306
Mt 26:18 into the city to a certain man and **t** him, G3306
Mt 26:21 he said, "Truly *I* **t** you, one of you will G3306
Mt 26:29 *I* **t** you, I will not drink from this fruit of G3306
Mt 26:34 "Truly *I* **t** you," Jesus answered, "this very G3306
Mt 26:63 **T** us if you are the Messiah, the Son of G3306
Mt 27:64 steal the body and **t** the people that he G3306
Mt 28: 7 Then go quickly and **t** his disciples: 'He G3306
Mt 28: 8 filled with joy, and ran *to* **t** his disciples. G550
Mt 28:10 Go and **t** my brothers to go to Galilee G550
Mk 1:44 "See that *you* don't **t** this to anyone. G3306
Mk 2:11 "*I* **t** you, get up, take your mat and go G3306
Mk 3:12 orders not to **t** others **about** him. G5745+4472
Mk 3:28 Truly *I* **t** you, people can be forgiven all G3306
Mk 5:19 your own people and **t** them how much the G550
Mk 5:20 away and began *to* **t** in the Decapolis G3062
Mk 7:36 Jesus commanded them not to **t** anyone G3306
Mk 8:12 Truly *I* **t** you, no sign will be G3306
Mk 8:30 warned them not to **t** anyone about him. G3306
Mk 9: 1 said to them, "Truly *I* **t** you, some who are G3306
Mk 9: 9 them orders not to **t** anyone what they G1455
Mk 9:13 But *I* **t** you, Elijah has come, and they have G3306
Mk 9:41 Truly *I* **t** you, anyone who gives you a cup G3306
Mk 10:15 Truly *I* **t** you, anyone who will not receive G3306
Mk 10:29 "Truly *I* **t** you," Jesus replied, "no one who G3306
Mk 11:23 "Truly *I* **t** you, if anyone says to this G3306
Mk 11:24 Therefore *I* **t** you, whatever you ask for in G3306
Mk 11:29 and *I will* **t** you by what authority I am G3306
Mk 11:30 from heaven, or of human origin? **T** me!" G646
Mk 11:33 "Neither *will* I **t** you by what authority I G3306
Mk 12:43 Jesus said, "Truly *I* **t** you, this poor widow G3306
Mk 13: 4 "**T** us, when will these things happen G3306
Mk 13:30 Truly *I* **t** you, this generation will certainly G3306
Mk 14: 9 Truly *I* **t** you, wherever the gospel is G3306
Mk 14:18 he said, "Truly *I* **t** you, one of you will G3306
Mk 14:25 "Truly *I* **t** you, I will not drink again from G3306
Mk 14:30 "Truly *I* **t** you," Jesus answered, "today G3306
Mk 16: 7 **t** his disciples and Peter, 'He is G3306
Lk 1:19 speak to you and *to* **t** you this **good news**. G2294
Lk 3: 8 For *I* **t** you that out of these stones God G3306
Lk 4: 3 Son of God, **t** this stone to become bread." G3306
Lk 4:23 And you will **t** me, 'Do here in your NDT
Lk 4:24 "Truly *I* **t** you," he continued, "no prophet G3306
Lk 5:14 ordered him, "Don't **t** anyone, but go, G3306
Lk 5:24 to the paralyzed man, "*I* **t** you, get up, G3306
Lk 7: 8 *I* **t** this one, 'Go,' and he goes; and that G3306
Lk 7: 9 he said, "*I* **t** you, I have not found such G3306
Lk 7:26 Yes, *I* **t** you, and more than a G3306
Lk 7:28 *I* **t** you, among those born of women there G3306
Lk 7:40 "Simon, I have something *to* **t** you." G3306
Lk 7:40 "**T** me, teacher," he said. G3306
Lk 7:47 Therefore, *I* **t** you, her many sins have G3306
Lk 8:39 "Return home and **t** how much God has G1455
Lk 8:56 ordered them not *to* **t** anyone what had G3306
Lk 9:21 warned them not *to* **t** this to anyone. G3306
Lk 9:27 "Truly *I* **t** you, some who are standing G3306
Lk 9:36 to themselves and *did* not **t** anyone at that G550
Lk 9:44 carefully to what I am about to **t** you: G3364
Lk 10: 9 Heal the sick who are there and **t** them G3306
Lk 10:12 *I* **t** you, it will be more bearable on that G3306
Lk 10:24 For *I* **t** you that many prophets and kings G3306
Lk 10:40 do the work by myself? **T** her to help me!" G3306
Lk 11: 8 *I* **t** you, even though he will not get up G3306
Lk 11:51 *I* **t** you, this generation will be held G3306
Lk 12: 4 "*I* **t** you, my friends, do not be afraid of G3306
Lk 12: 5 throw you into hell. Yes, *I* **t** you, fear him. G3306
Lk 12: 8 "*I* **t** you, whoever publicly acknowledges G3306
Lk 12:13 **t** my brother to divide the inheritance with G3306
Lk 12:22 "Therefore *I* **t** you, do not worry about G3306
Lk 12:27 Yet *I* **t** you, not even Solomon in all his G3306
Lk 12:37 Truly *I* **t** you, he will dress himself to serve, G3306
Lk 12:44 Truly *I* **t** you, he will put him in charge of G3306
Lk 12:51 peace on earth? No, *I* **t** you, but division. G3306
Lk 12:59 *I* **t** you, you will not get out until you have G3306
Lk 13: 3 *I* **t** you, no! But unless you repent, you too G3306
Lk 13: 5 *I* **t** you, no! But unless you repent, you too G3306
Lk 13:24 because many, *I* **t** you, will try to enter G3306
Lk 13:32 He replied, "Go **t** that fox, 'I will keep on G3306
Lk 13:35 *I* **t** you, you will not see me again until G3306
Lk 14:17 sent his servant *to* **t** those who had been G3306
Lk 14:24 *I* **t** you, not one of those who were invited G3306
Lk 15: 7 *I* **t** you that in the same way there will be G3306
Lk 15:10 In the same way, *I* **t** you, there is rejoicing G3306
Lk 16: 9 I **t** you, use worldly wealth to gain friends G3306
Lk 17:23 *People will* **t** you, 'There he is!' or 'Here G3306
Lk 17:34 *I* **t** you, on that night two people will be in G3306
Lk 18: 8 *I* **t** you, he will see that they get justice G3306
Lk 18:14 "*I* **t** you that this man, rather than the G3306
Lk 18:17 Truly *I* **t** you, anyone who will not receive G3306
Lk 18:29 "Truly *I* **t** you," Jesus said to them, "no G3306
Lk 19:11 he went on *to* **t** them a parable G3306
Lk 19:26 replied, '*I* **t** you that to everyone who has G3306
Lk 19:40 "*I* **t** you," he replied, "if they keep quiet G3306
Lk 20: 2 "**T** us by what authority you are doing G3306
Lk 20: 3 "I will also ask you a question. **T** me: G3306
Lk 20: 8 "Neither *will* I **t** you by what authority I G3306
Lk 20: 9 He went on *to* **t** the people this parable G3306
Lk 21: 3 "Truly *I* **t** you," he said, "this poor widow G3306
Lk 21:32 "Truly *I* **t** you, this generation will certainly G3306
Lk 22:16 For *I* **t** you, I will not eat it again until it G3306
Lk 22:18 For *I* **t** you I will not drink again from the G3306
Lk 22:34 Jesus answered, "*I* **t** you, Peter, before the G3306
Lk 22:37 and *I* **t** you that this must be fulfilled in G3306
Lk 22:67 they said, "**t** us." Jesus answered, G3306
Lk 22:67 Jesus answered, "If *I* **t** you, you will not G3306
Lk 23:43 "Truly *I* **t** you, today you will G3306
Jn 1:41 was to find his brother Simon and **t** him, G3306
Jn 1:51 "Very truly *I* **t** you, you will see G3306
Jn 3: 3 replied, "Very truly *I* **t** you, no one can see G3306
Jn 3: 5 answered, "Very truly *I* **t** you, no one can G3306
Jn 3: 8 but *you* cannot **t** where it comes from or G3857
Jn 3:11 Very truly *I* **t** you, we speak of what we G3306
Jn 4:35 *I* **t** you, open your eyes and look at the G3306
Jn 5:19 "Very truly *I* **t** you, the Son can do nothing G3306
Jn 5:24 "Very truly *I* **t** you, whoever hears my word G3306
Jn 5:25 Very truly *I* **t** you, a time is coming and has G3306
Jn 6:26 "Very truly *I* **t** you, you are looking G3306
Jn 6:32 to them, "Very truly *I* **t** you, it is not Moses G3306
Jn 6:47 Very truly *I* **t** you, the one who believes has G3306
Jn 6:53 to them, "Very truly *I* **t** you, unless you eat G3306
Jn 8:26 what I have heard from him *I* **t** the world." G3281

Jn 8:34 replied, "Very truly *I* t you, everyone who *G3306*
Jn 8:45 Yet because I t the truth, you do not *G3306*
Jn 8:51 Very truly *I* t you, whoever obeys my word *G3306*
Jn 8:58 "Very truly *I* t you," Jesus answered *G3306*
Jn 9:36 "T me so that I may believe in him. NDT
Jn 10: 1 "Very truly *I* t you Pharisees, anyone who *G3306*
Jn 10: 7 "Very truly *I* t you, I am the gate for *G3306*
Jn 10:24 If you are the Messiah, t us plainly." *G3306*
Jn 10:25 Jesus answered, "*I did* t you, but you do *G3306*
Jn 11:11 had said this, *he went on to* t them, "Our *G3306*
Jn 11:40 "*Did I* not t you that if you believe *G3306*
Jn 12:22 Philip went *to* t Andrew; Andrew and *G3306*
Jn 12:24 Very truly *I* t you, unless a kernel of wheat *G3306*
Jn 13:16 Very truly *I* t you, no servant is greater than *G3306*
Jn 13:20 Very truly *I* t you, whoever accepts anyone I *G3306*
Jn 13:21 testified, "Very truly *I* t you, one of you is *G3306*
Jn 13:33 just as I told the Jews, so *I* t you now: *G3306*
Jn 13:38 Very truly *I* t you, before the rooster crows *G3306*
Jn 14:12 Very truly *I* t you, whoever believes in me *G3306*
Jn 16: 4 *I did* not t you this from the beginning *G3306*
Jn 16: 7 But very truly I t you, it is for your good *G3306*
Jn 16:13 and *he will* t you what is yet to come. *G334*
Jn 16:20 Very truly *I* t you, you will weep and mourn *G3306*
Jn 16:23 Very truly *I* t you, my Father will give you *G3306*
Jn 16:25 of language but *will* t you plainly about *G550*
Jn 20:15 him away, t me where you have put him *G3306*
Jn 20:17 Go instead to my brothers and t them, 'I *G3306*
Jn 21:18 Very truly *I* t you, when you were younger *G3306*
Ac 2:29 I can t you confidently that the patriarch *G3306*
Ac 5: 8 Peter asked her, "T me, is this the price *G3306*
Ac 5:20 "and t the people all about this new life." *G3281*
Ac 8:34 asked Philip, "T *me*, **please**, who is the *G1289*
Ac 10:33 the Lord has commanded you to t us." NDT
Ac 12:17 "T James and the other brothers and sisters *G550*
Ac 13:32 "We t you **the good news**: What God *G2294*
Ac 21:23 so do what *we* t you. There are four men *G3306*
Ac 22:27 Paul and asked, "T me, are you a Roman *G3306*
Ac 23:17 commander; he has something *to* t him." *G550*
Ac 23:18 you because he has something *to* t you." *G3281*
Ac 23:19 asked, "What is it you want to t me?" *G550*
Ac 23:22 "Don't t anyone that you have reported *G1718*
Ro 15: 8 For *I* t you that Christ has become a servant *G3306*
1Co 15:51 *I* t you a mystery: We will not all *G3306*
2Co 6: 2 I t you, now is the time of God's favor, now NDT
2Co 12: 4 things that no one is permitted *to* t. *G3281*
Gal 4:21 T me, you who want to be under the law *G3306*
Gal 5: 2 I t you that if you let yourselves be *G3306*
Eph 4:17 So *I* t you this, and insist on it in the Lord *G3306*
Eph 6:21 in the Lord, *will* t you everything, so *G1192*
Php 3:18 you before and now t you again even with *G3306*
Col 2: 4 *I* t you this so that no one may deceive you *G3306*
Col 4: 7 Tychicus *will* t you all the news about me *G1192*
Col 4: 9 *They will* t you everything that is *G1192*
Col 4:17 T Archippus: "See to it that you complete *G3306*
1Th 1: 9 They t how you turned to God from idols to NDT
1Th 2: 2 of our God we dared *to* t you his gospel in *G3281*
1Th 4:15 *we* t you that we who are still alive *G3306*
2Th 2: 5 I was with you *I used to* t you these things *G3306*
Heb 11:32 I do not have time *to* t about Gideon *G1455*
Rev 2:10 **I t you**, the devil will put some of you in *G2627*

TELLING (38) [TELL]

Ge 31:20 the Aramean by not t him he was running H5583
Ge 42:16 may be tested to see if you are t the truth. NDT
Ge 43: 6 this trouble on me by t the man you had H5583
Ex 33:12 the LORD, "You *have been* t me, 'Lead these H606
Jdg 7:13 just as a man *was* t a friend his dream. H6218
2Ki 8: 5 Just as Gehazi was t the king how Elisha H6218
Ne 6:19 good deeds and then t him what I said. H3655
Ps 26: 7 your praise and t *of* all your wonderful H6218
Ps 34:13 tongue from evil and your lips from t lies. H1819
Jer 14:13 The prophets *keep* t them, 'You will not H606
Jer 26: 8 as Jeremiah finished t all the people H1819
Jer 38: 1 heard what Jeremiah *was* t all the people H1819
Jer 43: 1 had finished t the people all the H1819
Eze 20:49 are saying of me, 'Isn't he *just* t parables? H5439
Mt 16:12 that *he was* not t them to guard *G3306*
Mt 28:13 t them, "You are to say, 'His disciples *G3306*
Mk 14:13 two of his disciples, t them, "Go into the *G3306*
Lk 12:41 *are you* t this parable to us, or to *G3306*
Jn 8:25 "Just what *I have been* t you from the *G3281*
Jn 8:27 understand that *he was* t them about his *G3306*
Jn 8:38 *I am* t you what I have seen in the Father's *G3281*
Jn 8:46 If *I am* t the truth, why don't you believe *G3306*
Jn 9:24 "Give **glory** to God **by t the truth**," they *G1518*
Jn 10: 6 did not understand what he was t them. *G3281*
Jn 13:19 "*I am* t you now before it happens, so that *G3306*
Jn 13:29 thought Jesus *was* t him to buy what *G3306*
Ac 11: 7 Then I heard a voice t me, 'Get up, Peter *G3306*
Ac 11:20 t them **the good news** about the Lord *G2294*
Ac 14:15 t you to turn from these worthless things to NDT
Ac 15:12 Barnabas and Paul t **about** the signs and *G2007*
Ac 15:20 t them to abstain from food polluted by NDT
Ac 16:17 who *are* t you the way to be saved." *G2859*
Ac 21:21 t them not to circumcise their children *G3306*
2Co 9: 2 t them that since last year you in Achaia NDT
Gal 4:16 now become your enemy *by* t you **the truth**? *G238*
1Th 3: 4 *we kept* t you that we would be *G4625*
1Ti 2: 7 an apostle—*I am* t the truth, I am not *G3306*
3Jn 3 to the truth, t how you continue to walk in it. NDT

TELLS (19) [TELL]

Ge 21:12 Listen to whatever Sarah t you, because it H606
Ge 41:55 "Go to Joseph and do what *he* t you." H606
Dt 5:27 tell us whatever the LORD our God t you. H1819
1Sa 22: 8 No *one* t me when my son H1655+906+265
1Sa 22: 8 about me or t me that my son H1655+906+265
1Ki 22:14 I can tell him only what the LORD t me." H606
2Ki 5:13 when *he* t you, 'Wash and be H606
2Ki 6:12 t the king of Israel the very words you H5583
Job 36: 9 *he* t them what they have done—that H5583
Pr 12:17 An honest witness t the truth, but a false H5583
Pr 12:17 tells the truth, but a false witness t lies. NDT
Isa 8:19 When *someone* t you to consult mediums H606
Da 5: 7 this writing and t me what it means will A10252
Am 5:10 court and detest the *one who* t the truth. H1819
Mt 24:26 "So if *anyone* t you, 'There he is, out in *G3306*
Mk 13:34 t the one at the door to keep watch. *G1948*
Jn 2: 5 to the servants, "Do whatever *he* t you." *G3306*
Jn 19:35 He knows that *he* t the truth, and he *G3306*
Ac 3:22 you must listen to everything he t you. *G3281*

TEMA (5)

Ge 25:15 T, Jetur, Naphish and Kedemah. H9401
1Ch 1:30 Mishma, Dumah, Massa, Hadad, T, H9401
Job 6:19 The caravans of T look for water, the H9401
Isa 21:14 you who live in T, bring food for the H824+9401
Jer 25:23 T, Buz and all who are in distant H9401

TEMAH (2)

Ezr 2:53 Sisera, T, H9457
Ne 7:55 Sisera, T, H9457

TEMAN (11) [TEMANITE, TEMANITES]

Ge 36:11 sons of Eliphaz: T, Omar, Zepho, Gatam H9403
Ge 36:15 Chiefs T, Omar, Zepho, Kenaz, H9403
Ge 36:42 T, Mibzar, H9403
1Ch 1:36 T, Omar, Zepho, Gatam and Kenaz; by H9403
1Ch 1:53 T, Mibzar, H9403
Jer 49: 7 "Is there no longer wisdom in T? Has H9403
Jer 49:20 has purposed against those who live in T: H9403
Eze 25:13 from T to Dedan they will fall by the H9403
Am 1:12 I will send fire on T that will consume the H9403
Ob 9 Your warriors, T, will be terrified, and H9403
Hab 3: 3 God came from T, the Holy One from H9403

TEMANITE (6) [TEMAN]

Job 2:11 Eliphaz the T, Bildad the Shuhite H9404
Job 4: 1 Then Eliphaz the T replied: H9404
Job 15: 1 Then Eliphaz the T replied: H9404
Job 22: 1 Then Eliphaz the T replied: H9404
Job 42: 7 he said to Eliphaz the T, "I am angry with H9404
Job 42: 9 So Eliphaz the T, Bildad the Shuhite and H9404

TEMANITES (2) [TEMAN]

Ge 36:34 from the land of the T succeeded him as H9404
1Ch 1:45 from the land of the T succeeded him as H9404

TEMENI (1)

1Ch 4: 6 Ahuzzam, Hepher, T and Haahashtari. H9405

TEMPER (1) [EVEN-TEMPERED, HOT-TEMPERED, QUICK-TEMPERED]

1Sa 20: 7 But if *he* **loses** his t, you can be H3013+3013

TEMPERANCE (KJV) SELF-CONTROL

TEMPERATE (3)

1Ti 3: 2 faithful to his wife, t, self-controlled *G3767*
1Ti 3:11 malicious talkers but t and trustworthy in *G3767*
Titus 2: 2 Teach the older men to be t, worthy of *G3767*

TEMPEST (7)

Job 27:20 a t snatches him away in the night. H6070
Job 37: 9 The t comes out from its chamber, the H6070
Ps 50: 3 and around him a **t rages**. H8548+4394
Ps 55: 8 of shelter, far from the t and storm." H8120+6185
Ps 83:15 them with your t and terrify them with H6193
Ps 107:25 and stirred up a t that lifted high H8120+6194
Isa 29: 6 with windstorm and t and flames of a H6194

TEMPLE (683) [TEMPLES]

Jdg 4:21 the peg through his t into the ground, H8377
Jdg 4:22 Sisera with the tent peg through his t— H8377
Jdg 5:26 his head, she shattered and pierced his t. H8377
Jdg 9: 4 shekels of silver from the t *of* Baal-Berith, H1074
Jdg 9:27 they held a festival in the t *of* their god. H1074
Jdg 9:46 into the stronghold of the t *of* El-Berith. H1074
Jdg 16:26 I can feel the pillars that support the t, H1074
Jdg 16:27 Now the t was crowded with men and H1074
Jdg 16:29 two central pillars on which the t stood. H1074
Jdg 16:30 down came the t on the rulers and all H1074
1Sa 5: 2 the ark into Dagon's t and set it beside H1074
1Sa 5: 5 who enter Dagon's t at Ashdod step on H1074
1Sa 31: 9 the news in the t *of* their idols and among H1074
1Sa 31:10 his armor in the t *of* the Ashtoreths and H1074
2Sa 22: 7 From his t he heard my voice; my cry came H2121
1Ki 3: 1 building his palace and the t *of* the LORD, H1074
1Ki 3: 2 because a t had not yet been built for the H1074
1Ki 5: 3 he could not build a t for the Name of the H1074
1Ki 5: 5 to build a t for the Name of the LORD my H1074
1Ki 5: 5 in your place will build the t for my Name. H1074
1Ki 5:17 a foundation of dressed stone for the t. H1074
1Ki 5:18 timber and stone for the building of the t. H1074
1Ki 6: 1 he began to build the t of the LORD. H1074
1Ki 6: 2 The t that King Solomon built for the LORD H1074
1Ki 6: 3 the main hall of the t extended the width H1074
1Ki 6: 3 of the temple extended the width of the t, H1074
1Ki 6: 3 projected ten cubits from the front of the t. H1074
1Ki 6: 4 narrow windows high up in the t *walls*. H1074
1Ki 6: 6 the outside of the t so that nothing would H1074
1Ki 6: 6 would be inserted into the t walls. H1074
1Ki 6: 7 In building the t, only blocks dressed at H1074
1Ki 6: 7 tool was heard at the t site while it was H1074
1Ki 6: 8 floor was on the south side of the t; H1074
1Ki 6: 9 So he built the t and completed it, roofing H1074
1Ki 6:10 he built the side rooms all along the t. H1074
1Ki 6:10 were attached to the t by beams of cedar. H1074
1Ki 6:12 "As for this t you are building, if you H1074
1Ki 6:14 So Solomon built the t and completed it. H1074
1Ki 6:15 them from the floor of the t to the ceiling, H1074
1Ki 6:15 the floor of the t with planks of juniper. H1074
1Ki 6:16 at the rear of the t with cedar boards from H1074
1Ki 6:16 to form within the t an inner sanctuary, H1074
1Ki 6:18 The inside of the t was cedar, carved with H1074
1Ki 6:19 sanctuary within the t to set the ark of the H1074
1Ki 6:21 covered the inside of the t with pure gold, H1074
1Ki 6:27 inside the innermost room of the t, H1074
1Ki 6:29 On the walls all around the t, in both the H1074
1Ki 6:30 inner and outer rooms of the t with gold. H1074
1Ki 6:37 foundation of the t *of* the LORD was laid in H1074
1Ki 6:38 the t was finished in all its details H1074
1Ki 7:12 inner courtyard of the t *of* the LORD with H1074
1Ki 7:21 erected the pillars at the portico of the t. H2121
1Ki 7:39 south side of the t and five on the north H1074
1Ki 7:39 at the southeast corner of the t. H1074
1Ki 7:40 King Solomon in the t *of* the LORD: H1074
1Ki 7:45 King Solomon for the t *of* the LORD were H1074
1Ki 7:48 the furnishings that were in the LORD's t: H1074
1Ki 7:50 the doors of the main hall of the t. H1074
1Ki 7:51 had done for the t *of* the LORD was H1074
1Ki 7:51 them in the treasuries of the LORD's t. H1074
1Ki 8: 6 to its place in the inner sanctuary of the t, H1074
1Ki 8:10 the cloud filled the t *of* the LORD. H1074
1Ki 8:11 for the glory of the LORD filled his t. H1074
1Ki 8:13 I have indeed built a magnificent t for you H1074
1Ki 8:16 of Israel to have a t built so that my Name H1074
1Ki 8:17 his heart to build a t for the Name of the H1074
1Ki 8:18 it in your heart to build a t for my Name. H1074
1Ki 8:19 you are not the one to build the t, but H1074
1Ki 8:19 the one who will build the t for my Name. H1074
1Ki 8:20 I have built the t for the Name of the H1074
1Ki 8:27 How much less this t I have built! H1074
1Ki 8:29 eyes be open toward this t night and day, H1074
1Ki 8:31 swear the oath before your altar in this t, H1074
1Ki 8:33 making supplication to you in this t, H1074
1Ki 8:38 spreading out their hands toward this t— H1074
1Ki 8:42 when they come and pray toward this t, H1074
1Ki 8:44 have chosen and the t I have built for your H1074
1Ki 8:48 have chosen and the t I have built for your H1074
1Ki 8:63 the Israelites dedicated the t *of* the LORD. H1074
1Ki 8:64 the courtyard in front of the t *of* the LORD, H1074
1Ki 9: 1 finished building the t *of* the LORD and the H1074
1Ki 9: 3 I have consecrated this t, which you have H1074
1Ki 9: 7 will reject this t I have consecrated for H1074
1Ki 9: 8 This t will become a heap of rubble. H1074
1Ki 9: 8 such a thing to this land and to this t? H1074
1Ki 9:10 the t *of* the LORD and the royal palace H1074
1Ki 9:15 Solomon conscripted to build the LORD's t, H1074
1Ki 9:25 and so fulfilled the t obligations. H1074
1Ki 10: 5 offerings he made at the t *of* the LORD, H1074
1Ki 10:12 supports for the t *of* the LORD and for the H1074
1Ki 12:27 sacrifices at the t *of* the LORD in Jerusalem, H1074
1Ki 14:26 the treasures of the t *of* the LORD and the H1074
1Ki 14:28 Whenever the king went to the LORD's t H1074
1Ki 15:15 He brought into the t *of* the LORD the silver H1074
1Ki 15:18 of the LORD's t and of his own palace. H1074
1Ki 16:32 altar for Baal in the t *of* Baal that he built H1074
2Ki 5:18 master enters the t *of* Rimmon to bow H1074
2Ki 5:18 when I bow down in the t *of* Rimmon, may H1074
2Ki 10:21 crowded into the t *of* Baal until it was H1074
2Ki 10:23 son of Rekab went into the t *of* Baal. H1074
2Ki 10:25 entered the inner shrine of the t *of* Baal. H1074
2Ki 10:26 stone out of the t *of* Baal and burned it. H1074
2Ki 10:27 stone of Baal and tore down the t *of* Baal, H1074
2Ki 11: 3 with his nurse at the t *of* the LORD for six H1074
2Ki 11: 4 them brought to him at the t *of* the LORD. H1074
2Ki 11: 4 put them under oath at the t *of* the LORD. H1074
2Ki 11: 6 who take turns guarding the t— H1074
2Ki 11: 7 duty are all to guard the t for the king. H1074
2Ki 11:10 David and that were in the t *of* the LORD. H1074
2Ki 11:11 near the altar and the t, from the south H1074
2Ki 11:11 the south side to the north side of the t. H1074
2Ki 11:13 went to the people at the t *of* the LORD. H1074
2Ki 11:15 not be put to death in the t *of* the LORD." H1074
2Ki 11:18 the land went to the t *of* Baal and tore it H1074
2Ki 11:18 priest posted guards at the t *of* the LORD. H1074
2Ki 11:19 king down from the t *of* the LORD and went H1074
2Ki 12: 4 as sacred offerings to the t *of* the LORD— H1074
2Ki 12: 4 the money brought voluntarily to the t. H1074
2Ki 12: 5 repair whatever damage is found in the t." H1074
2Ki 12: 6 the priests still had not repaired the t. H1074
2Ki 12: 7 you repairing the damage done to the t? H1074
2Ki 12: 7 hand it over for repairing the t. H1074
2Ki 12: 8 they would not repair the t themselves. H1074
2Ki 12: 9 right side as one enters the t *of* the LORD. H1074

2Ki 12: 9 that was brought to the **t** *of* the LORD. H1074
2Ki 12:10 brought into the **t** *of* the LORD and put it H1074
2Ki 12:11 appointed to supervise the work on the **t**. H1074
2Ki 12:11 those who worked on the **t** *of* the LORD— H1074
2Ki 12:12 stone for the repair of the **t** *of* the LORD, H1074
2Ki 12:12 all the other expenses of restoring the **t**. H1074
2Ki 12:13 brought into the **t** was not spent for H1074
2Ki 12:13 of gold or silver for the **t** *of* the LORD; H1074
2Ki 12:14 to the workers, who used it to repair the **t**. H1074
2Ki 12:16 was not brought into the **t** *of* the LORD; H1074
2Ki 12:18 treasuries of the **t** *of* the LORD and of the H1074
2Ki 14:14 found in the **t** *of* the LORD and in the H1074
2Ki 15:35 rebuilt the Upper Gate of the **t** *of* the LORD. H1074
2Ki 16: 8 gold found in the **t** *of* the LORD and in the H1074
2Ki 16:14 he brought it from the front of the **t**—from H1074
2Ki 16:14 the new altar and the **t** *of* the LORD— H1074
2Ki 16:18 been built at the **t** and removed the royal H1074
2Ki 16:18 royal entryway outside the **t** *of* the LORD, H1074
2Ki 18:15 was found in the **t** *of* the LORD and in the H1074
2Ki 18:16 doors and doorposts of the **t** *of* the LORD, H2121
2Ki 19: 1 sackcloth and went into the **t** *of* the LORD. H1074
2Ki 19:14 he went up to the **t** *of* the LORD and spread H1074
2Ki 19:37 was worshiping in the **t** *of* his god Nisrok, H1074
2Ki 20: 5 now you will go up to the **t** *of* the LORD. H1074
2Ki 20: 8 I will go up to the **t** *of* the LORD on the H1074
2Ki 21: 4 He built altars in the **t** *of* the LORD, of which H1074
2Ki 21: 5 In the two courts of the **t** *of* the LORD, he H1074
2Ki 21: 7 pole he had made and put it in the **t**, H1074
2Ki 21: 7 son Solomon, "In this **t** and in Jerusalem H1074
2Ki 22: 3 the son of Meshullam, to the **t** *of* the LORD. H1074
2Ki 22: 4 has been brought into the **t** *of* the LORD, H1074
2Ki 22: 5 appointed to supervise the work on the **t**. H1074
2Ki 22: 5 the workers who repair the **t** *of* the LORD— H1074
2Ki 22: 6 timber and dressed stone to repair the **t**. H1074
2Ki 22: 8 the Book of the Law in the **t** *of* the LORD." H1074
2Ki 22: 9 that was in the **t** *of* the LORD and have H1074
2Ki 22: 9 it to the workers and supervisors at the **t**." H1074
2Ki 23: 2 He went up to the **t** *of* the LORD with the H1074
2Ki 23: 2 which had been found in the **t** *of* the LORD. H1074
2Ki 23: 4 to remove from the **t** *of* the LORD all the H2121
2Ki 23: 6 Asherah pole from the **t** *of* the LORD to the H1074
2Ki 23: 7 prostitutes that were in the **t** *of* the LORD, H1074
2Ki 23:11 the entrance to the **t** *of* the LORD the H1074
2Ki 23:12 built in the two courts of the **t** *of* the LORD. H1074
2Ki 23:24 priest had discovered in the **t** *of* the LORD. H1074
2Ki 23:27 city I chose, and this **t**, about which I said, H1074
2Ki 24:13 treasures from the **t** *of* the LORD and from H1074
2Ki 24:13 of Israel had made for the **t** *of* the LORD. H2121
2Ki 25: 9 He set fire to the **t** *of* the LORD, the royal H1074
2Ki 25:13 Sea that were at the **t** *of* the LORD and they H1074
2Ki 25:14 all the bronze articles used in the **t** service. NDT
2Ki 25:16 Solomon had made for the **t** *of* the LORD, H1074
1Ch 6:10 served as priest in the **t** Solomon built in H1074
1Ch 6:32 Solomon built the **t** *of* the LORD in H1074
1Ch 9: 2 Israelites, priests, Levites and **t servants**. H5987
1Ch 9:28 charge of the articles used in the **t** service; NDT
1Ch 9:33 in the rooms of the **t** and were exempt from NDT
1Ch 10:10 his armor in the **t** *of* their gods and hung H1074
1Ch 10:10 hung up his head in the **t** *of* Dagon. H1074
1Ch 22:14 to provide for the **t** *of* the LORD a hundred H1074
1Ch 22:19 to God into the **t** that will be built for H1074
1Ch 23: 4 of the work of the **t** *of* the LORD and six H1074
1Ch 23:24 more who served in the **t** *of* the LORD. H1074
1Ch 23:28 in the service of the **t** *of* the LORD: H1074
1Ch 23:32 for the service of the **t** *of* the LORD. H1074
1Ch 24:19 when they entered the **t** *of* the LORD, H1074
1Ch 25: 6 father for the music of the **t** *of* the LORD, H1074
1Ch 26:12 duties for ministering in the **t** *of* the LORD, H1074
1Ch 26:22 of the treasuries of the **t** *of* the LORD. H1074
1Ch 26:27 the repair of the **t** *of* the LORD. H1074
1Ch 26:29 sons were assigned duties away from the **t**, NDT
1Ch 28:11 Solomon the plans for the portico of the **t**, NDT
1Ch 28:12 the courts of the **t** *of* the LORD and all the H1074
1Ch 28:12 the treasuries of the **t** *of* God and for the H1074
1Ch 28:13 all the work of serving in the **t** *of* the LORD, H1074
1Ch 28:20 the service of the **t** *of* the LORD is finished. H1074
1Ch 28:21 are ready for all the work on the **t** *of* God, H1074
1Ch 29: 2 I have provided for the **t** *of* my God— H1074
1Ch 29: 3 my devotion to the **t** *of* my God I now give H1074
1Ch 29: 3 of gold and silver for the **t** *of* my God, H1074
1Ch 29: 3 everything I have provided for this holy **t**: H1074
1Ch 29: 7 the work on the **t** *of* God five thousand H1074
1Ch 29: 8 to the treasury of the **t** *of* the LORD in the H1074
1Ch 29:16 building you a **t** for your Holy Name H1074
2Ch 2: 1 orders to build a **t** for the Name of the H1074
2Ch 2: 4 am about to build a **t** for the Name of the H1074
2Ch 2: 5 "The **t** I am going to build will be great H1074
2Ch 2: 6 But who is able to build a **t** for him, since H1074
2Ch 2: 6 Who then am I to build a **t** for him, except H1074
2Ch 2: 9 because the **t** I build must be large and H1074
2Ch 2:12 who will build a **t** for the LORD and a H1074
2Ch 3: 1 began to build the **t** *of* the LORD in H1074
2Ch 3: 3 building the **t** *of* God was sixty cubits H1074
2Ch 3: 4 at the front of the **t** was twenty cubits long NDT
2Ch 3: 6 He adorned the **t** with precious stones H1074
2Ch 3: 7 walls and doors of the **t** with gold, and he H1074
2Ch 3: 8 corresponding to the width of the **t**— H1074
2Ch 3:11 five cubits long and touched the **t** wall, H1074
2Ch 3:12 cubits long and touched the other **t** wall, H1074
2Ch 3:15 For the front of the **t** he made two pillars H1074
2Ch 3:17 He erected the pillars in the front of the **t** H2121
2Ch 4: 7 them and placed them in the **t**, H2121
2Ch 4: 8 ten tables and placed them in the **t**, H2121
2Ch 4:11 King Solomon in the **t** *of* God: H1074
2Ch 4:16 King Solomon for the **t** *of* the LORD were H1074
2Ch 4:19 all the furnishings that were in God's **t**: H1074
2Ch 4:22 censers; and the gold doors of the **t**: H1074
2Ch 5: 1 had done for the **t** *of* the LORD was H1074
2Ch 5: 1 placed them in the treasuries of God's **t**. H1074
2Ch 5: 7 to its place in the inner sanctuary of the **t**, H1074
2Ch 5:13 Then the **t** *of* the LORD was filled with the H1074
2Ch 5:14 the glory of the LORD filled the **t** *of* God. H1074
2Ch 6: 2 I have built a magnificent **t** for you, H1074
2Ch 6: 5 of Israel to have a **t** built so that my Name H1074
2Ch 6: 7 his heart to build a **t** for the Name of the H1074
2Ch 6: 8 it in your heart to build a **t** for my Name. H1074
2Ch 6: 9 you are not the one to build the **t**, but H1074
2Ch 6: 9 the one who will build the **t** for my Name. H1074
2Ch 6:10 I have built the **t** for the Name of the H1074
2Ch 6:18 How much less this **t** I have built! H1074
2Ch 6:20 eyes be open toward this **t** day and night, H1074
2Ch 6:22 swear the oath before your altar in this **t**, H1074
2Ch 6:24 making supplication before you in this **t**, H1074
2Ch 6:29 spreading out their hands toward this **t**— H1074
2Ch 6:32 when they come and pray toward this **t**, H1074
2Ch 6:34 have chosen and the **t** I have built for your H1074
2Ch 6:38 toward the **t** I have built for your H1074
2Ch 7: 1 the glory of the LORD filled the **t**. H1074
2Ch 7: 2 could not enter the **t** *of* the LORD because H1074
2Ch 7: 3 the glory of the LORD above the **t**, H1074
2Ch 7: 5 all the people dedicated the **t** *of* God. H1074
2Ch 7: 7 the courtyard in front of the **t** *of* the LORD, H1074
2Ch 7:11 had finished the **t** *of* the LORD and the H1074
2Ch 7:11 mind to do in the **t** *of* the LORD and in his H1074
2Ch 7:12 this place for myself as a **t** *for* sacrifices. H1074
2Ch 7:16 consecrated this **t** so that my Name may H1074
2Ch 7:20 will reject this **t** I have consecrated for H1074
2Ch 7:21 This **t** will become a heap of rubble. H1074
2Ch 7:21 such a thing to this land and to this **t**? H1074
2Ch 8: 1 Solomon built the **t** *of* the LORD and his H1074
2Ch 8:16 foundation of the **t** *of* the LORD was laid H1074
2Ch 8:16 So the **t** *of* the LORD was finished H1074
2Ch 9: 4 offerings he made at the **t** *of* the LORD, H1074
2Ch 9:11 make steps for the **t** *of* the LORD and for H1074
2Ch 12: 9 the treasures of the **t** *of* the LORD and the H1074
2Ch 12:11 Whenever the king went to the LORD's **t** H1074
2Ch 15: 8 was in front of the portico of the LORD's **t**. NDT
2Ch 15:18 He brought into the **t** *of* God the silver H1074
2Ch 16: 2 of the LORD's **t** and of his own palace H1074
2Ch 20: 5 Jerusalem at the **t** *of* the LORD in the H1074
2Ch 20: 9 before this **t** that bears your Name H1074
2Ch 20:28 went to the **t** *of* the LORD with harps H1074
2Ch 22:12 with them at the **t** *of* God for six years H1074
2Ch 23: 3 a covenant with the king at the **t** *of* God. H1074
2Ch 23: 5 to be in the courtyards of the **t** *of* the LORD. H1074
2Ch 23: 6 one is to enter the **t** *of* the LORD except the H1074
2Ch 23: 7 who enters the **t** is to be put to death H1074
2Ch 23: 9 King David and that were in the **t** *of* God. H1074
2Ch 23:10 near the altar and the **t**, from the south H1074
2Ch 23:10 the south side to the north side of the **t**. H1074
2Ch 23:12 she went to them at the **t** *of* the LORD. H1074
2Ch 23:14 not put her to death at the **t** *of* the LORD." H1074
2Ch 23:17 people went to the **t** *of* Baal and tore it H1074
2Ch 23:18 the oversight of the **t** *of* the LORD in the H1074
2Ch 23:18 David had made assignments in the **t**, H1074
2Ch 23:19 gates of the LORD's **t** so that no one who H1074
2Ch 23:20 the king down from the **t** *of* the LORD. H1074
2Ch 24: 4 Joash decided to restore the **t** *of* the LORD. H1074
2Ch 24: 5 from all Israel, to repair the **t** *of* your God. H1074
2Ch 24: 7 broken into the **t** *of* God and had used H1074
2Ch 24: 8 outside, at the gate of the **t** *of* the LORD. H1074
2Ch 24:12 out the work required for the **t** *of* the LORD. H1074
2Ch 24:12 carpenters to restore the LORD's **t**, H1074
2Ch 24:12 workers in iron and bronze to repair the **t**. H1074
2Ch 24:13 They rebuilt the **t** *of* God according to its H1074
2Ch 24:14 with it were made articles for the LORD's **t**: H1074
2Ch 24:14 presented continually in the **t** *of* the LORD. H1074
2Ch 24:16 he had done in Israel for God and his **t**. H1074
2Ch 24:18 They abandoned the **t** *of* the LORD, the God H1074
2Ch 24:21 to death in the courtyard of the LORD's **t**. H1074
2Ch 24:27 restoration of the **t** *of* God are written in H1074
2Ch 25:24 found in the **t** *of* God that had been in H1074
2Ch 26:16 entered the **t** *of* the LORD to burn H2121
2Ch 26:19 before the incense altar in the LORD's **t**, H1074
2Ch 26:21 and banned from the **t** *of* the LORD. H1074
2Ch 27: 2 him he did not enter the **t** *of* the LORD. H2121
2Ch 27: 3 Upper Gate of the **t** *of* the LORD and did H1074
2Ch 28:21 the things from the **t** *of* the LORD and from H1074
2Ch 28:24 from the **t** *of* God and cut them in H1074
2Ch 28:24 doors of the LORD's **t** and set up altars at H1074
2Ch 29: 3 the doors of the **t** *of* the LORD and repaired H1074
2Ch 29: 5 now and consecrate the **t** *of* the LORD, H1074
2Ch 29:15 they went in to purify the **t** *of* the LORD, as H1074
2Ch 29:16 of the LORD's **t** everything unclean that H1074
2Ch 29:16 that they found in the **t** *of* the LORD. H2121
2Ch 29:17 they consecrated the **t** *of* the LORD *itself*, H1074
2Ch 29:18 "We have purified the entire **t** *of* the LORD H1074
2Ch 29:20 together and went up to the **t** *of* the LORD. H1074
2Ch 29:25 the Levites in the **t** *of* the LORD with H1074
2Ch 29:31 thank offerings to the **t** *of* the LORD. H1074
2Ch 29:35 So the service of the **t** *of* the LORD was H1074
2Ch 30: 1 them to come to the **t** *of* the LORD in H1074
2Ch 30:15 burnt offerings to the **t** *of* the LORD. H1074
2Ch 31:10 their contributions to the **t** *of* the LORD, H1074
2Ch 31:11 to prepare storerooms in the **t** *of* the LORD, H1074
2Ch 31:13 the official in charge of the **t** *of* God. H1074
2Ch 31:16 who would enter the **t** *of* the LORD to H1074
2Ch 31:21 the service of God's **t** and in obedience to H1074
2Ch 32:21 And when he went into the **t** *of* his god H1074
2Ch 33: 4 He built altars in the **t** *of* the LORD, of which H1074
2Ch 33: 5 In both courts of the **t** *of* the LORD, he built H1074
2Ch 33: 7 image he had made and put it in God's **t**, H1074
2Ch 33: 7 son Solomon, "In this **t** and in Jerusalem H1074
2Ch 33:15 removed the image from the **t** *of* the LORD, H1074
2Ch 33:15 he had built on the **t** hill and in H1074
2Ch 34: 8 to purify the land and the **t**, he sent H1074
2Ch 34: 8 to repair the **t** *of* the LORD his God. H1074
2Ch 34: 9 that had been brought into the **t** *of* God, H1074
2Ch 34:10 to supervise the work on the LORD's **t**. H1074
2Ch 34:10 workers who repaired and restored the **t**. H1074
2Ch 34:14 that had been taken into the **t** *of* the LORD, H1074
2Ch 34:15 the Book of the Law in the **t** *of* the LORD." H1074
2Ch 34:17 that was in the **t** *of* the LORD and have H1074
2Ch 34:30 He went up to the **t** *of* the LORD with the H1074
2Ch 34:30 which had been found in the **t** *of* the LORD. H1074
2Ch 35: 2 them in the service of the LORD's **t**. H1074
2Ch 35: 3 sacred ark in the **t** that Solomon son of H1074
2Ch 35: 8 the officials in charge of God's **t**, gave the H1074
2Ch 35:20 when Josiah had set the **t** in order, Necho H1074
2Ch 36: 7 articles from the **t** *of* the LORD and put H1074
2Ch 36: 7 of the LORD and put them in his **t** there. H2121
2Ch 36:10 articles of value from the **t** *of* the LORD, H1074
2Ch 36:14 the nations and defiling the **t** *of* the LORD, H1074
2Ch 36:18 Babylon all the articles from the **t** *of* God, H1074
2Ch 36:18 of the LORD's **t** and the treasures of H1074
2Ch 36:19 set fire to God's **t** and broke down the H1074
2Ch 36:23 me to build a **t** for him at Jerusalem in H1074
Ezr 1: 2 me to build a **t** for him at Jerusalem in H1074
Ezr 1: 3 in Judah and build the **t** *of* the LORD, H1074
Ezr 1: 4 offerings for the **t** *of* God in Jerusalem. H1074
Ezr 1: 7 the articles belonging to the **t** *of* the LORD, H1074
Ezr 1: 7 had placed in the **t** *of* his god. H1074
Ezr 2:42 The gatekeepers of the **t**: the descendants NDT
Ezr 2:43 The **t servants**: the descendants of Ziha H5987
Ezr 2:58 The **t servants** and the descendants of the H5987
Ezr 2:70 the **t servants** settled in their H5987
Ezr 3: 6 of the LORD's **t** had not yet been laid. H2121
Ezr 3:10 laid the foundation of the **t** *of* the LORD, H2121
Ezr 3:12 who had seen the former **t**, wept aloud H1074
Ezr 3:12 saw the foundation of this **t** being laid, H1074
Ezr 4: 1 the exiles were building a **t** for the LORD, H2121
Ezr 4: 3 no part with us in building a **t** to our God. H1074
Ezr 5: 3 you to rebuild this **t** and to finish it?" A10103
Ezr 5: 8 of Judah, to the **t** *of* the great God. A10103
Ezr 5: 9 you to rebuild this **t** and to finish it?" A10103
Ezr 5:11 are rebuilding the **t** that was built many A10103
Ezr 5:12 who destroyed this **t** and deported the A10103
Ezr 5:14 removed from the **t** of Babylon the gold A10206
Ezr 5:14 had taken from the **t** in Jerusalem and A10206
Ezr 5:14 brought to the **t** in Babylon. A10206
Ezr 5:15 deposit them in the **t** in Jerusalem. A10206
Ezr 6: 3 concerning the **t** *of* God in Jerusalem: A10103
Ezr 6: 3 Let the **t** be rebuilt as a place to present A10103
Ezr 6: 5 took from the **t** in Jerusalem and brought A10206
Ezr 6: 5 to their places in the **t** in Jerusalem; A10206
Ezr 6: 7 interfere with the work on this **t** *of* God. A10103
Ezr 6:12 decree or to destroy this **t** in Jerusalem. A10103
Ezr 6:14 finished building the **t** according to the NDT
Ezr 6:15 The **t** was completed on the third day of A10103
Ezr 7: 7 gatekeepers and **t servants**, also came up H5987
Ezr 7:16 priests for the **t** *of* their God in A10103
Ezr 7:17 on the altar of the **t** *of* your God in A10103
Ezr 7:19 to you for worship in the **t** *of* your God. A10103
Ezr 7:20 needed for the **t** *of* your God that you A10103
Ezr 7:23 diligence for the **t** *of* the God of heaven. A10103
Ezr 7:24 **t servants** or other workers at this house A10497
Ezr 8:17 the **t servants** in Kasiphia, so H5987
Ezr 8:20 They also brought 220 of the **t servants**— H5987
Ne 2: 8 of the citadel by the **t** and for the city wall H1074
Ne 3:26 the **t servants** living on the hill of H5987
Ne 3:31 the house of the **t servants** and the H5987
Ne 6:10 inside the **t**, and let us close the H2121
Ne 6:10 let us close the **t** doors, because men H2121
Ne 6:11 like me go into the **t** to save his life? H2121
Ne 7:46 The **t servants**: the descendants of Ziha H5987
Ne 7:60 The **t servants** and the descendants of the H5987
Ne 7:73 the musicians and the **t servants**, along H5987
Ne 10:28 **t servants** and all who separated H5987
Ne 11: 3 **t servants** and descendants of Solomon's H5987
Ne 11:12 who carried on work for the **t**—822 men; H1074
Ne 11:21 The **t servants** lived on the hill of Ophel H5987
Ne 13: 5 grain offerings and incense and **t** articles, NDT
Ps 5: 7 reverence I bow down toward your holy **t**. H2121
Ps 11: 4 The LORD is in his holy **t**; the LORD is on H2121
Ps 18: 6 From his **t** he heard my voice; my cry came H2121
Ps 27: 4 of the LORD and to seek him in his **t**. H2121
Ps 29: 9 And in his **t** all cry, "Glory!" H2121
Ps 30: T For the dedication of the **t**. Of David. H1074
Ps 48: 9 Within your **t**, O God, we meditate on H2121
Ps 65: 4 good things of your house, of your holy **t**. H2121
Ps 66:13 I will come to your **t** with burnt offerings H1074
Ps 68:29 Because of your **t** at Jerusalem kings will H2121
Ps 79: 1 they have defiled your holy **t**, they have H2121
Ps 138: 2 toward your holy **t** and will praise your H2121
Ecc 5: 6 And do not protest to the *t* **messenger**, "My AIT
Isa 2: 2 of the LORD's **t** will be established as H1074

Isa 2: 3 of the LORD, to the **t** *of* the God of Jacob. H1074
Isa 6: 1 the train of his robe filled the **t**. H2121
Isa 6: 4 shook and the **t** was filled with smoke. H1074
Isa 15: 2 Dibon goes up to its **t**, to its high places H1074
Isa 37: 1 sackcloth and went into the **t** *of* the LORD. H1074
Isa 37:14 he went up to the **t** *of* the LORD and spread H1074
Isa 37:38 was worshiping in the **t** *of* his god Nisrok, H1074
Isa 38:20 the days of our lives in the **t** *of* the LORD. H1074
Isa 38:22 sign that I will go up to the **t** *of* the LORD?" H1074
Isa 43:28 So I disgraced the dignitaries of your **t**; H7731
Isa 44:28 and of the **t**, "Let its foundations H2121
Isa 56: 5 I will give within my **t** and its walls a H1074
Isa 60: 7 my altar, and I will adorn my glorious **t**. H1074
Isa 64:11 Our holy and glorious **t**, where our H1074
Isa 66: 6 from the city, hear that noise from the **t**! H2121
Isa 66:20 to the **t** *of* the LORD in ceremonially clean H1074
Jer 7: 4 "This is the **t** *of* the LORD, the temple H2121
Jer 7: 4 of the LORD, the **t** *of* the LORD, the temple H2121
Jer 7: 4 the temple of the LORD, the **t** *of* the LORD!" H2121
Jer 7:14 that bears my Name, **the t** you trust in, the H889S
Jer 11:15 "What is my beloved doing in my **t** as she, H1074
Jer 19:14 the court of the LORD's **t** and said to all the H1074
Jer 20: 1 the official in charge of the **t** *of* the LORD H1074
Jer 20: 2 Upper Gate of Benjamin at the LORD's **t**. H1074
Jer 23:11 even in my **t** I find their wickedness," H1074
Jer 24: 1 of figs placed in front of the **t** *of* the LORD. H2121
Jer 26:18 the **t** hill a mound overgrown with thickets. H1074
Jer 36: 5 I am not allowed to go to the LORD's **t**. H1074
Jer 36: 8 at the LORD's **t** he read the words of the H1074
Jer 36:10 at the entrance of the New Gate of the **t**, H1074
Jer 36:10 people at the LORD's **t** the words of H1074
Jer 38:14 to the third entrance to the **t** *of* the LORD. H1074
Jer 43:13 There in the **t** *of* the sun in Egypt he will H1074
Jer 50:28 has taken vengeance, vengeance for his **t**. H2121
Jer 51:11 will take vengeance, vengeance for his **t**. H2121
Jer 52:13 He set fire to the **t** *of* the LORD, the royal H1074
Jer 52:17 Sea that were at the **t** *of* the LORD and they H1074
Jer 52:18 all the bronze articles used in the **t** service. NDT
Jer 52:20 Solomon had made for the **t** *of* the LORD, H1074
Eze 8:16 there at the entrance to the **t** H2121
Eze 8:16 backs toward the **t** *of* the LORD and their H2121
Eze 9: 3 moved to the threshold of the **t**. H1074
Eze 9: 6 the old men who were in front of the **t**. H1074
Eze 9: 7 "Defile the **t** and fill the courts with the H1074
Eze 10: 3 south side of the **t** when the man went in, H1074
Eze 10: 4 moved to the threshold of the **t**. H1074
Eze 10: 4 The cloud filled the **t**, and the court was H1074
Eze 10:18 the threshold of the **t** and stopped above H1074
Eze 40: 5 a wall completely surrounding the **t** area. H1074
Eze 40: 7 the portico facing the **t** was one rod deep. H1074
Eze 40: 9 The portico of the gateway faced the **t**. H1074
Eze 40:45 south is for the priests who guard the **t**, H1074
Eze 40:47 And the altar was in front of the **t**. H1074
Eze 40:48 to the portico of the **t** and measured the H1074
Eze 41: 5 Then he measured the wall of the **t**; it H1074
Eze 41: 5 room around the **t** was four cubits wide H1074
Eze 41: 6 the wall of the **t** to serve as supports H1074
Eze 41: 6 were not inserted into the wall of the **t**. H1074
Eze 41: 7 rooms all around the **t** were wider at each NDT
Eze 41: 7 surrounding the **t** was built in ascending H1074
Eze 41: 8 I saw that the **t** had a raised base all H1074
Eze 41: 9 area between the side rooms of the **t** H1074
Eze 41:10 was twenty cubits wide all around the **t**. H1074
Eze 41:12 building facing the **t** courtyard on the west NDT
Eze 41:13 Then he measured the **t**; it was a hundred H1074
Eze 41:13 the **t** courtyard and the building with its NDT
Eze 41:14 The width of the **t** courtyard on the east NDT
Eze 41:14 including the front of the **t**, was a hundred H1074
Eze 41:15 facing the courtyard at the rear of **the t**, H2023S
Eze 41:19 They were carved all around the whole **t**. H1074
Eze 41:26 side rooms of the **t** also had overhangs. H1074
Eze 42: 1 rooms opposite the **t** courtyard and opposite NDT
Eze 42:10 adjoining the **t** courtyard and opposite the NDT
Eze 42:13 south rooms facing the **t** courtyard are the NDT
Eze 42:15 measuring what was inside the **t area**, H1074
Eze 43: 4 the LORD entered the **t** through the gate H1074
Eze 43: 5 and the glory of the LORD filled the **t**. H1074
Eze 43: 6 speaking to me from inside the **t**. H1074
Eze 43:10 describe the **t** to the people of Israel H1074
Eze 43:11 make known to them the design of the **t** H1074
Eze 43:12 "This is the law of the **t**: All the H1074
Eze 43:12 be most holy. Such is the law of the **t**. H1074
Eze 43:21 part of the **t area** outside the sanctuary H1074
Eze 44: 4 way of the north gate to the front of the **t**. H1074
Eze 44: 4 glory of the LORD filling the **t** *of* the LORD, H1074
Eze 44: 5 instructions regarding the **t** *of* the LORD. H1074
Eze 44: 5 to the entrance to the **t** and all the exits of H1074
Eze 44: 7 desecrating my **t** while you offered me H1074
Eze 44:11 of the gates of the **t** and serving in it; H1074
Eze 44:14 them to guard the **t** for all the work that is H1074
Eze 44:17 the gates of the inner court or inside the **t**. H1074
Eze 45: 5 who serve in the **t**, as their possession H1074
Eze 45:19 put it on the doorposts of the **t**, H1074
Eze 45:20 so you are to make atonement for the **t**. H1074
Eze 46:24 those who minister at the **t** are to cook the H1074
Eze 47: 1 brought me back to the entrance to the **t**, H1074
Eze 47: 1 the threshold of the **t** toward the east H1074
Eze 47: 1 the east (for the **t** faced east). The water H1074
Eze 47: 1 down from under the south side of the **t**, H1074
Eze 48:21 portion with the **t** sanctuary will be in H1074
Da 1: 2 some of the articles from the **t** *of* God. H1074
Da 1: 2 carried off to the **t** *of* his god in Babylonia H1074
Da 5: 2 father had taken from the **t** in Jerusalem, A10206
Da 5: 3 taken from the **t** of God in Jerusalem A10206
Da 5:23 the goblets from his **t** brought to you, A10103
Da 9:27 And at the **t** he will set up an H1074
Da 11:31 rise up to desecrate the **t** fortress and will H5219
Hos 9: 4 it will not come into the **t** *of* the LORD. H1074
Am 7:13 king's sanctuary and the **t** *of* the kingdom." H1074
Am 8: 3 "the songs in the **t** will turn to wailing. H2121
Jnh 2: 4 I will look again toward your holy **t**. H2121
Jnh 2: 7 my prayer rose to you, to your holy **t**. H2121
Mic 1: 2 against you, the Lord from his holy **t**. H2121
Mic 1: 7 all her **t gifts** will be burned with fire H924
Mic 3:12 the **t** hill a mound overgrown with thickets. H1074
Mic 4: 1 of the LORD's **t** will be established as H1074
Mic 4: 2 of the LORD, to the **t** *of* the God of Jacob. H1074
Na 1:14 idols that are in the **t** *of* your gods. H1074
Hab 2:20 The LORD is in his holy **t**; let all the earth H2121
Zep 1: 9 who fill the **t** *of* their gods with violence H1074
Hag 2:15 stone was laid on another in the LORD's **t**. H2121
Hag 2:18 the foundation of the LORD's **t** was laid. H2121
Zec 4: 9 have laid the foundation of this **t**; H1074
Zec 6:12 from his place and build the **t** *of* the LORD. H2121
Zec 6:13 It is he who will build the **t** *of* the LORD H2121
Zec 6:14 as a memorial in the **t** *of* the LORD. H2121
Zec 6:15 come and help to build the **t** *of* the LORD, H2121
Zec 8: 9 be strong so that the **t** may be built. H2121
Zec 9: 8 I will encamp at my **t** to guard it against H1074
Mal 1:10 that one of you would shut the **t** doors, so NDT
Mal 3: 1 Lord you are seeking will come to his **t**; H2121
Mt 4: 5 him stand on the highest point *of* the **t**. G2639
Mt 12: 5 Sabbath duty in the **t** desecrate the G2639
Mt 12: 6 that something greater *than* the **t** is here. G2639
Mt 17:24 *of* the **two-drachma t tax** came to G1440
Mt 17:24 "Doesn't your teacher pay the **t tax**?" G1440
Mt 21:12 Jesus entered the **t courts** and drove out G2639
Mt 21:14 blind and the lame came to him at the **t**, G2639
Mt 21:15 the children shouting in the **t courts**, G2639
Mt 21:23 Jesus entered the **t courts**, and, while he G2639
Mt 23:16 'If anyone swears by the **t**, it means G3724
Mt 23:16 by the gold *of* the **t** is bound by that G3724
Mt 23:17 or the **t** that makes the gold sacred? G3724
Mt 23:21 who swears by the **t** swears by it and by G3724
Mt 23:35 murdered between the **t** and the altar. G3724
Mt 24: 1 Jesus left the **t** and was walking away G2639
Mt 26:55 Every day I sat in the **t courts** teaching G2639
Mt 26:61 able to destroy the **t** of God and rebuild it G3724
Mt 27: 5 Judas threw the money into the **t** and left. G3724
Mt 27:40 going to destroy the **t** and build it in three G3724
Mt 27:51 the curtain *of* the **t** was torn in two G3724
Mk 11:11 Jerusalem and went into the **t courts**. G2639
Mk 11:15 Jesus entered the **t courts** and began G2639
Mk 11:16 to carry merchandise through the **t courts**. G2639
Mk 11:27 while Jesus was walking in the **t courts**, G2639
Mk 12:35 While Jesus was teaching in the **t courts** G2639
Mk 12:41 putting their money into the **t treasury**. G1126
Mk 13: 1 As Jesus was leaving the **t**, one of his G2639
Mk 13: 3 on the Mount of Olives opposite the **t**, G2639
Mk 14:49 teaching in the **t courts**, and you did not G2639
Mk 14:58 'I will destroy this **t** made with human G3724
Mk 15:29 going to destroy the **t** and build it in three G3724
Mk 15:38 The curtain *of* the **t** was torn in two from G3724
Lk 1: 9 to go into the **t** of the Lord and burn G3724
Lk 1:21 wondering why he stayed so long in the **t**. G3724
Lk 1:22 realized he had seen a vision in the **t**, G3724
Lk 2:27 by the Spirit, he went into the **t courts**. G2639
Lk 2:37 She never left the **t** but worshiped night G2639
Lk 2:46 three days they found him in the **t courts**, G2639
Lk 4: 9 him stand on the highest point *of* the **t**. G2639
Lk 18:10 "Two men went up to the **t** to pray, one a G2639
Lk 19:45 When Jesus entered the **t courts**, he G2639
Lk 19:47 Every day he was teaching at the **t**. G2639
Lk 20: 1 the people in the **t courts** and proclaiming G2639
Lk 21: 1 rich putting their gifts into the **t treasury**. G1126
Lk 21: 5 about how the **t** was adorned with G2639
Lk 21:37 Each day Jesus was teaching at the **t**, and G2639
Lk 21:38 early in the morning to hear him at the **t**. G2639
Lk 22: 4 the **officers of the t guard** and G5130
Lk 22:52 the officers of the **t** guard, and the elders, G2639
Lk 22:53 Every day I was with you in the **t courts** G2639
Lk 23:45 And the curtain *of* the **t** was torn in two. G3724
Lk 24:53 And they stayed continually at the **t** G2639
Jn 2:14 In the **t courts** he found people selling G2639
Jn 2:15 drove all from the **t courts**, both G2639
Jn 2:19 "Destroy this **t**, and I will raise it G3724
Jn 2:20 "It has taken forty-six years to build this **t** G3724
Jn 2:21 But the **t** he had spoken of was his body. G3724
Jn 5:14 Jesus found him at the **t** and said to him, G2639
Jn 7:14 Jesus go up to the **t courts** and begin to G2639
Jn 7:28 still teaching in the **t courts**, cried out, G2639
Jn 7:32 the Pharisees sent **t guards** to arrest him. G5677
Jn 7:45 Finally the **t guards** went back to the chief G5677
Jn 8: 2 dawn he appeared again in the **t courts**, G2639
Jn 8:20 teaching in the **t courts** near the place G2639
Jn 8:59 himself, slipping away from the **t grounds**. G2639
Jn 10:23 Jesus was in the **t courts** walking in G2639
Jn 11:48 take away both our **t** and our nation." G5536S
Jn 11:56 they stood in the **t courts** they asked one G2639
Jn 18:20 "I always taught in synagogues or at the **t** G2639
Ac 2:46 continued to meet together in the **t courts**. G2639
Ac 3: 1 were going up to the **t** at the time of G2639
Ac 3: 2 being carried to the **t** gate called G2639
Ac 3: 2 to beg from those going into the **t courts**. G2639
Ac 3: 8 Then he went with them into the **t courts** G2639
Ac 3:10 sit begging at the **t** gate called Beautiful G2639
Ac 4: 1 the captain of the **t** guard and the G2639
Ac 5:20 stand in the **t courts**," he said, "and G2639
Ac 5:21 At daybreak they entered the **t courts**, as G2639
Ac 5:24 the captain of the **t** guard and the chief G2639
Ac 5:25 are standing in the **t courts** teaching the G2639
Ac 5:42 in the **t courts** and from house to house G2639
Ac 14:13 of Zeus, **whose t** was just outside the city G3836S
Ac 19:27 also that the **t** of the great goddess G2639
Ac 19:35 is the **guardian of the t** of the great G3753
Ac 21:26 Then he went to the **t** to give notice of the G2639
Ac 21:27 the province of Asia saw Paul at the **t**. G2639
Ac 21:28 Greeks into the **t** and defiled this holy G2639
Ac 21:29 that Paul had brought him into the **t**.) G2639
Ac 21:30 they dragged him from the **t**, and G2639
Ac 22:17 to Jerusalem and was praying at the **t**, G2639
Ac 24: 6 even tried to desecrate the **t**; so we G2639
Ac 24:12 not find me arguing with anyone at the **t**, G2639
Ac 24:18 they found me in the **t courts** doing this. G2639
Ac 25: 8 law or against the **t** or against Caesar." G2639
Ac 26:21 seized me in the **t courts** and tried to kill G2639
Ro 9: 4 the law, the **t worship** and the promises. G3301
1Co 3:16 yourselves are God's **t** and that God's G3724
1Co 3:17 If anyone destroys God's **t**, God will G3724
1Co 3:17 that person; for God's **t** is sacred, and you G3724
1Co 3:17 is sacred, and you together are **that t**. G4015S
1Co 8:10 eating in an **idol's t**, won't that person be G1627
1Co 9:13 those who serve *in* the **t** get their food G2641
1Co 9:13 in the temple get their food from the **t**, G2639
2Co 6:16 is there between the **t** of God and idols? G3724
2Co 6:16 For we are the **t** of the living God. G3724
Eph 2:21 rises to become a holy **t** in the Lord. G3724
2Th 2: 4 so that he sets himself up in God's **t** G3724
Rev 3:12 I will make a pillar in the **t** of my God. G3724
Rev 7:15 God and serve him day and night in his **t**; G3724
Rev 11: 1 "Go and measure the **t** of God and the G3724
Rev 11:19 Then God's **t** in heaven was opened, and G3724
Rev 11:19 within his **t** was seen the ark of his G3724
Rev 14:15 came out of the **t** and called in a loud G3724
Rev 14:17 angel came out of the **t** in heaven, G3724
Rev 15: 5 I saw in heaven the **t**—that is, G3724
Rev 15: 6 Out of the **t** came the seven angels with G3724
Rev 15: 8 And the **t** was filled with smoke from the G3724
Rev 15: 8 no one could enter the **t** until the seven G3724
Rev 16: 1 loud voice from the **t** saying to the seven G3724
Rev 16:17 out of the **t** came a loud voice from G3724
Rev 21:22 I did not see a **t** in the city, because the G3724
Rev 21:22 Lord God Almighty and the Lamb are its **t**. G3724

TEMPLES (10) [TEMPLE]

SS 4: 3 Your **t** behind your veil are like the halves H8377
SS 6: 7 Your **t** behind your veil are like the halves H8377
Jer 43:12 will set fire to the **t** *of* the gods of Egypt; H1074
Jer 43:12 he will burn **their t** and take their gods H4392S
Jer 43:13 will burn down the **t** *of* the gods of Egypt. H1074
Joel 3: 5 carried off my finest treasures to your **t**. H2121
Ac 17:24 does not live in **t** built by human hands G3724
Ac 19:37 have neither **robbed t** nor blasphemed G2645
Ro 2:22 You who abhor idols, *do you* **rob t**? G2644
1Co 6:19 that your bodies are **t** of the Holy Spirit, G3724

TEMPORARY (11)

Ex 12:45 a **t resident** or a hired worker may not H9369
Lev 23:42 Live in **t shelters** for seven days: All H6109
Lev 23:43 Israelites live in **t shelters** when I brought H6109
Lev 25: 6 worker and **t resident** who live among H9369
Lev 25:40 as hired workers or **t residents** among you; H9369
Lev 25:45 buy some of the **t residents** living among H9369
Ne 8:14 were to live in **t shelters** during the H6109
Ne 8:15 to make **t shelters**"—as it is written. H6109
Ne 8:16 built themselves **t shelters** on their own H6109
Ne 8:17 from exile built **t shelters** and lived in H6109
2Co 4:18 since what is seen is **t**, but what is unseen G4672

TEMPT (2) [TEMPTATION, TEMPTED, TEMPTER, TEMPTING]

1Co 7: 5 so that Satan *will* not **t** you because of G4279
Jas 1:13 tempted by evil, nor *does* he **t** anyone; G4279

TEMPTATION (8) [TEMPT]

Mt 6:13 And lead us not into **t**, but deliver us from G4280
Mt 26:41 pray so that you will not fall into **t**. G4280
Mk 14:38 pray so that you will not fall into **t**. G4280
Lk 11: 4 sins against us. And lead us not into **t**.'" G4280
Lk 22:40 to them, "Pray that you will not fall into **t**." G4280
Lk 22:46 up and pray so that you will not fall into **t**." G4280
1Co 10:13 No **t** has overtaken you except what is G4280
1Ti 6: 9 to get rich fall into **t** and a trap and into G4280

TEMPTED (13) [TEMPT]

Mt 4: 1 into the wilderness *to be* **t** by the devil. G4279
Mk 1:13 wilderness forty days, *being* **t** by Satan. G4279
Lk 4: 2 where for forty days *he was* **t** by the devil G4279
1Co 10:13 he will not let you *be* **t** beyond what you G4279
1Co 10:13 But when you are **t**, he will also provide a G4280
Gal 6: 1 watch yourselves, or you also *may be* **t**. G4279
1Th 3: 5 way the tempter *had* **t** you and that our G4279
Heb 2:18 he himself suffered when *he was* **t**, G4279
Heb 2:18 he is able to help those *who are being* **t**. G4279
Heb 4:15 we have *one who has been* **t** in every G4279
Jas 1:13 *When* **t**, no one should say, "God is G4279
Jas 1:13 For God **cannot** be **t** by evil, nor does he G585

Jas 1:14 each person *is* t when they are *G4279*

TEMPTER (2) [TEMPT]

Mt 4: 3 The t came to him and said, "If you are *G4279*
1Th 3: 5 in some way the t had tempted you and *G4279*

TEMPTING (2) [TEMPT]

Lk 4:13 When the devil had finished all this t, he *G4280*
Jas 1:13 no one should say, "God *is* t *me*. *G4279*

TEN (202) [ONE-TENTH, TENS, TENTH, TITHE, TITHES, TWO-TENTHS]

Ge 16: 3 Abram had been living in Canaan t years, H6924
Ge 18:32 What if only t can be found there? H6927
Ge 18:32 "For the sake of t, I will not destroy it." H6927
Ge 24:10 taking with him t of his master's camels H6927
Ge 24:22 two gold bracelets weighing t shekels. H6927
Ge 24:55 young woman remain with us t days or so; H6917
Ge 31: 7 me by changing my wages t times. H6930
Ge 31:41 you changed my wages t times. H6930
Ge 32:15 forty cows and t bulls, and twenty H6927
Ge 32:15 female donkeys and t male donkeys. H6927
Ge 42: 3 Then t of Joseph's brothers went down to H6927
Ge 45:23 t donkeys loaded with the best things of H6927
Ge 45:23 t female donkeys loaded with grain H6924
Ge 50:22 He lived a hundred and t years H6924
Ge 50:26 died at the age of a hundred and t. H6924
Ex 26: 1 the tabernacle with t curtains of finely H6924
Ex 26:16 Each frame is to be t cubits long and a H6924
Ex 27:12 have curtains, with t posts and ten bases. H6927
Ex 27:12 have curtains, with ten posts and t bases. H6924
Ex 34:28 of the covenant—the T Commandments. H6930
Ex 36: 8 the tabernacle with t curtains of finely H6924
Ex 36:21 Each frame was t cubits long and a cubit H6924
Ex 38:12 had curtains, with t posts and ten bases H6927
Ex 38:12 with ten posts and t bases, with silver H6927
Lev 26: 8 a hundred of you will chase t **thousand**, H8047
Lev 26:26 t women will be able to bake your bread H6924
Lev 27: 5 shekels and of a female at t shekels; H6930
Lev 27: 7 shekels and of a female at t shekels. H6927
Nu 7:14 one gold dish weighing t shekels, filled H6927
Nu 7:20 one gold dish weighing t shekels, filled H6927
Nu 7:26 one gold dish weighing t shekels, filled H6927
Nu 7:32 one gold dish weighing t shekels, filled H6927
Nu 7:38 one gold dish weighing t shekels, filled H6927
Nu 7:44 one gold dish weighing t shekels, filled H6927
Nu 7:50 one gold dish weighing t shekels, filled H6927
Nu 7:56 one gold dish weighing t shekels, filled H6927
Nu 7:62 one gold dish weighing t shekels, filled H6927
Nu 7:68 one gold dish weighing t shekels, filled H6927
Nu 7:74 one gold dish weighing t shekels, filled H6927
Nu 7:80 one gold dish weighing t shekels, filled H6927
Nu 7:86 with incense weighed t shekels each, H6927
Nu 11:19 or two days, or five, t or twenty days, H6927
Nu 11:32 No one gathered less than t homers H6927
Nu 14:22 disobeyed me and tested me t times— H6924
Nu 29:23 " 'On the fourth day offer t bulls, two rams H6927
Dt 4:13 his covenant, the T Commandments H6930
Dt 10: 4 the T Commandments he had proclaimed H6930
Dt 32:30 two put t **thousand** to flight, unless H8047
Dt 33:17 Such are the t **thousands** *of* Ephraim; such H8047
Jos 15:57 Timnah—t towns and their villages. H6924
Jos 17: 5 share consisted of t tracts of land besides H6927
Jos 21: 5 were allotted t towns from the clans of H6924
Jos 21:26 All these t towns and their pasturelands H6924
Jos 22:14 With him they sent t *of* the chief men, one H6927
Jos 24:29 died at the age of a hundred and t. H6924
Jdg 1: 4 they struck down t thousand men at H6930
Jdg 2: 8 died at the age of a hundred and t. H6924
Jdg 3:29 struck down about t thousand Moabites, H6930
Jdg 4: 6 take with you t thousand men of Naphtali H6930
Jdg 4:10 t thousand men went up under his H6930
Jdg 4:14 with t thousand men following him. H6930
Jdg 6:27 So Gideon took t of his servants and did H6927
Jdg 7: 3 men left, while t thousand remained. H6930
Jdg 12:11 Elon the Zebulunite led Israel t years. H6924
Jdg 17:10 I'll give you t shekels of silver a year H6930
Jdg 20:10 We'll take t men out of every hundred H6924
Jdg 20:10 a thousand from t **thousand**, to get H8047
Jdg 20:34 Then t thousand of Israel's able young H6930
Ru 1: 4 After they had lived there about t years, H6924
Ru 4: 2 Boaz took t of the elders of the town and H6927
1Sa 1: 8 Don't I mean more to you than t sons?" H6924
1Sa 15: 4 foot soldiers and t thousand from Judah. H6930
1Sa 17:17 grain and these t loaves of bread for H6927
1Sa 17:18 Take along these t cheeses to the H6930
1Sa 25: 5 So he sent t young men and said to them H6927
1Sa 25:38 About t days later, the LORD struck Nabal H6930
2Sa 15:16 he left t concubines to take care of the H6924
2Sa 18: 3 but you are worth t thousand of us. H6927
2Sa 18:11 have had to give you t shekels of silver H6927
2Sa 18:15 And t of Joab's armor-bearers surrounded H6927
2Sa 19:43 of Judah, "We have t shares in the king H6924
2Sa 20: 3 he took the t concubines he had left to H6924
1Ki 4:23 t head of stall-fed cattle, twenty of H6927
1Ki 5:14 Lebanon in shifts of t thousand a month, H6930
1Ki 6: 3 projected t cubits from the front of the H6924
1Ki 6:23 out of olive wood, each t cubits high. H6924
1Ki 6:24 cubits—t cubits from wing tip to wing tip. H6924
1Ki 6:25 The second cherub also measured t cubits H6924
1Ki 6:26 The height of each cherub was t cubits. H6924
1Ki 7:10 some measuring t cubits and some eight. H6924
1Ki 7:23 measuring t cubits from rim to rim and H6924
1Ki 7:24 the rim, gourds encircled it—t to a cubit. H6924
1Ki 7:27 He also made t movable stands of bronze; H6924
1Ki 7:37 This is the way he made the t stands. H6924
1Ki 7:38 He then made t bronze basins, each H6927
1Ki 7:38 one basin to go on each of the t stands. H6924
1Ki 7:43 the t stands with their ten basins; H6924
1Ki 7:43 the ten stands with their t basins; H6927
1Ki 11:31 to Jeroboam, "Take t pieces for yourself H6927
1Ki 11:31 of Solomon's hand and give you t tribes. H6927
1Ki 11:35 from his son's hands and give you t tribes. H6930
1Ki 14: 3 Take t loaves of bread with you, some H6927
2Ki 5: 5 taking with him t talents of silver, six H6924
2Ki 5: 5 shekels of gold and t sets of clothing. H6924
2Ki 13: 7 t chariots and ten thousand foot soldiers H6927
2Ki 13: 7 ten chariots and t thousand foot soldiers H6930
2Ki 14: 7 one who defeated t thousand Edomites in H6930
2Ki 15:17 and he reigned in Samaria t years. H6924
2Ki 20: 9 Shall the shadow go forward t steps, or H6924
2Ki 20: 9 ten steps, or shall it go back t steps?" H6924
2Ki 20:10 the shadow to go forward t steps, H6924
2Ki 20:10 "Rather, have it go back t steps." H6924
2Ki 20:11 shadow go back the t steps it had gone H6924
2Ki 24:14 artisans—a total of t thousand. H6930
2Ki 25:25 came with t men and assassinated H6927
1Ch 6:61 were allotted t towns from the clans of H6924
1Ch 29: 7 talents and t **thousand** darics of gold, H8052
1Ch 29: 7 darics of gold, t thousand talents of silver H6930
2Ch 4: 1 twenty cubits wide and t cubits high. H6924
2Ch 4: 2 measuring t cubits from rim to rim and H6924
2Ch 4: 3 figures of bulls encircled it—t to a cubit. H6924
2Ch 4: 6 He then made t basins for washing and H6927
2Ch 4: 7 He made t gold lampstands according to H6924
2Ch 4: 8 He made t tables and placed them in the H6927
2Ch 14: 1 days the country was at peace for t years. H6924
2Ch 25:11 where he killed t thousand men of Seir. H6930
2Ch 25:12 also captured t thousand men alive, H6930
2Ch 27: 5 t thousand cors of wheat and ten H6930
2Ch 27: 5 cors of wheat and t thousand cors of H6930
2Ch 30:24 thousand bulls and t thousand sheep H6930
2Ch 36: 9 in Jerusalem three months and t days. H6930
Ezr 8:24 Hashabiah and t of their brothers, H6927
Ne 4:12 near them came and told us t times over, H6924
Ne 5:18 every t days an abundant supply of H6930
Ne 11: 1 bring one out of every t of them to live in H6927
Est 3: 9 I will give t thousand talents of silver H6930
Est 9:10 the t sons of Haman son of Hammedatha H6930
Est 9:12 hundred men and the t sons of Haman in H6930
Est 9:13 let Haman's t sons be impaled on H6930
Est 9:14 they impaled the t sons of Haman. H6930
Job 19: 3 T times now you have reproached me H6924
Ps 91: 7 at your side, t **thousand** at your right hand H8047
Ecc 7:19 more powerful than t rulers in a city. H6927
SS 5:10 outstanding among t **thousand**. H8047
Isa 38: 8 the sun go back the t steps it has gone H6924
Isa 38: 8 went back the t steps it had gone down H6924
Jer 41: 1 came with t men to Gedaliah son of H6927
Jer 41: 2 Nethaniah and the t men who were with H6930
Jer 41: 8 But t of them said to Ishmael, "Don't kill H6927
Jer 42: 7 T days later the word of the LORD came to H6930
Eze 40:11 it was t cubits and its length was thirteen H6924
Eze 41: 2 The entrance was t cubits wide, and the H6924
Eze 42: 4 an inner passageway t cubits wide and a H6924
Eze 45:14 which consists of t baths or one homer H6930
Eze 45:14 t baths are equivalent to a homer). H6930
Da 1:12 "Please test your servants for t days: Give H6927
Da 1:14 agreed to this and tested them for t days. H6927
Da 1:15 At the end of the t days they looked H6927
Da 1:20 he found them t times better than all the H6927
Da 7: 7 all the former beasts, and it had t horns. A10573
Da 7:10 t **thousand** *times* ten thousand stood A10649
Da 7:10 thousand times t **thousand** stood before A10649
Da 7:20 to know about the t horns on its head A10573
Da 7:24 The t horns are ten kings who will come A10573
Da 7:24 The ten horns are t kings who will come A10573
Am 5: 3 out a hundred strong will have only t left." H6927
Am 6: 9 If t people are left in one house, they too H6927
Mic 6: 7 of rams, with t **thousand** rivers of olive oil? H8047
Hag 2:16 of twenty measures, there were only t. H6927
Zec 5: 2 twenty cubits long and t cubits wide." H6924
Zec 8:23 "In those days t people from all H6927
Mt 18:24 who owed him t **thousand** bags of gold *G3691*
Mt 20:24 When the t heard about this, they were *G1274*
Mt 25: 1 heaven will be like t virgins who took their *G1274*
Mt 25:28 give it to the one who has t bags. *G1274*
Mk 10:41 When the t heard about this, they *G1274*
Lk 14:31 he is able with t thousand men to oppose *G1274*
Lk 15: 8 suppose a woman has t silver coins and *G1274*
Lk 17:12 t men who had leprosy met him. *G1274*
Lk 17:17 "Were not all t cleansed? Where are *G1274*
Lk 19:13 So he called t of his servants and gave *G1274*
Lk 19:13 of his servants and gave them t minas. *G1274*
Lk 19:16 'Sir, your mina has earned t more.' *G1274*
Lk 19:17 a very small matter, take charge of t cities.' *G1274*
Lk 19:24 give it to the one who has t minas.' *G1274*
Lk 19:25 they said, 'he already has t!' *G1274*
Ac 25: 6 After spending eight or t days with them *G1274*
1Co 4:15 Even if you had t **thousand** guardians in *G3692*
1Co 14:19 others than t **thousand** words in a tongue. *G3692*
Rev 2:10 you will suffer persecution for t days. *G1274*
Rev 5:11 and t **thousand** times ten thousand. *G5942*
Rev 5:11 ten thousand *times* t **thousand**. *G5942*
Rev 9:16 troops was **twice** t **thousand** times ten *G1490*
Rev 9:16 was twice ten thousand *times* t **thousand**. *G3689*
Rev 12: 3 with seven heads and t horns and seven *G1274*
Rev 13: 1 It had t horns and seven heads, with ten *G1274*
Rev 13: 1 seven heads, with t crowns on its horns *G1274*
Rev 17: 3 names and had seven heads and t horns. *G1274*
Rev 17: 7 which has the seven heads and t horns. *G1274*
Rev 17:12 "The t horns you saw are ten kings who *G1274*
Rev 17:12 horns you saw are t kings who have not *G1274*
Rev 17:16 The beast and the t horns you saw will *G1274*

TEN-ACRE (1) [ACRE]

Isa 5:10 A t vineyard will produce only a H6930+7538

TEN-STRINGED (3) [STRING]

Ps 33: 2 the harp; make music to him on the t lyre. H6917
Ps 92: 3 to the music of the t lyre and the melody H6917
Ps 144: 9 on the t lyre I will make music to you H6917

TENANTS (15)

Job 31:39 payment or broken the spirit of its t, H1251
SS 8:11 Baal Hamon; he let out his vineyard to t. H5757
Mt 21:34 his servants to the t to collect his fruit. *G1177*
Mt 21:35 "The t seized his servants; they beat one *G1177*
Mt 21:36 and the t treated them the same way. NDT
Mt 21:38 "But when the t saw the son, they said to *G1177*
Mt 21:40 what will he do *to* those t? *G1177*
Mt 21:41 "and he will rent the vineyard *to* other t *G1177*
Mk 12: 2 sent a servant to the t to collect from them *G1177*
Mk 12: 7 "But the t said to one another, 'This is the *G1177*
Mk 12: 9 come and kill those t and give the *G1177*
Lk 20:10 sent a servant to the t so they would give *G1177*
Lk 20:10 But the t beat him and sent him away *G1177*
Lk 20:14 "But when the t saw him, they talked the *G1177*
Lk 20:16 come and kill those t and give the *G1177*

TEND (12) [TENDED, TENDING, TENDS]

Ge 30:36 while Jacob *continued to* t the rest of H8286
Ge 46:32 *they* t **livestock**, and they H408+5238+2118
Lev 24: 3 Aaron *is to* t the lamps before the LORD H6885
1Sa 17:15 forth from Saul to t his father's sheep at H8286
SS 8:12 two hundred are for *those who* t its fruit. H5757
Jer 23: 2 says to the shepherds who t my people: H8286
Jer 23: 4 shepherds over them *who will* t them, H8286
Eze 34:14 *I will* t them in a good pasture, and the H8286
Eze 34:15 *I* myself *will* t my sheep and have them lie H8286
Eze 34:23 servant David, and *he will* t them; he will H8286
Eze 34:23 he *will* t them and be their shepherd. H8286
Jnh 4:10 though *you did* not t it or make it grow. H6661

TENDED (3) [TEND]

Ge 46:34 servants *have* t **livestock** from H408+5238+2118
Lev 24: 4 before the LORD *must be* t continually. H6885
Hos 12:12 get a wife, and to pay for her *he* t **sheep**. H9068

TENDER (12) [TENDERLY, TENDERNESS]

Ge 18: 7 a choice, t calf and gave it to a servant H8205
Ge 33:13 that the children are t and that I must care H8205
Dt 32: 2 new grass, like abundant rain on t **plants**. H6912
2Ki 19:26 in the field, like t green **shoots**, like grass H3764
Pr 4: 3 to my father, still t, and cherished by my H8205
Isa 37:27 in the field, like t green **shoots**, like grass H3764
Isa 47: 1 No more will you be called t or delicate. H8205
Isa 53: 2 He grew up before him like a t **shoot**, and H3437
Eze 17:22 I will break off a t *sprig* from its topmost H8205
Mt 24:32 soon as its twigs get t and its leaves come *G559*
Mk 13:28 soon as its twigs get t and its leaves come *G559*
Lk 1:78 because of the t **mercy** of our God *G5073+1799*

TENDERHEARTED (KJV) COMPASSIONATE, INDECISIVE

TENDERLY (3) [TENDER]

Ge 34: 3 young woman and spoke t *to* her. H6584+4213
Isa 40: 2 Speak t to Jerusalem, and proclaim H6584+4213
Hos 2:14 the wilderness and speak t to her. H6584+4213

TENDERNESS (2) [TENDER]

Isa 63:15 Your t and compassion are H2162+5055
Php 2: 1 in the Spirit, if any t and compassion, *G5073*

TENDING (13) [TEND]

Ge 30:31 I will go on t your flocks and watching H8286
Ge 37: 2 was t the flocks with his brothers H8286
Ex 3: 1 Now Moses was t the flock of Jethro his H8286
1Sa 16:11 Jesse answered. "*He is* t the sheep." H8286
2Sa 7: 8 from the pasture, from t the flock, and H339
1Ch 17: 7 from the pasture, from t the flock, and H339
Ps 78:71 from t the sheep he brought him to be the H339
Jer 6: 3 tents around her, each t his own portion." H8286
Eze 34:10 remove them from t the flock so that the H8286
Am 7:15 LORD took me from t the flock and said to H339
Mt 8:33 Those t the pigs ran off, went into the *G1081*
Mk 5:14 Those t the pigs ran off and reported this *G1081*
Lk 8:34 When those t the pigs saw what had *G1081*

TENDON (2) [TENDONS]

Ge 32:32 do not eat the t attached to the H1630+5962
Ge 32:32 Jacob's hip was touched near the t. H1630+5962

TENDONS (2) [TENDON]

Eze 37: 6 I will attach t to you and make flesh come H1630
Eze 37: 8 t and flesh appeared on them and H1630

TENDS (3) [TEND]

Ex 30: 7 altar every morning when he t the lamps. H3512
Isa 40:11 *He* t his flock like a shepherd: He gathers H8286
1Co 9: 7 Who t a flock and does not drink the milk? *G4477*

TENONS (KJV) PROJECTIONS

TENS (10) [TEN]

Ex 18:21 over thousands, hundreds, fifties and t. H6930
Ex 18:25 over thousands, hundreds, fifties and t. H6930
Dt 1:15 of fifties and of t and as tribal officials. H6930
1Sa 18: 7 thousands, and David his **t of thousands**." H8047
1Sa 18: 8 have credited David with **t of thousands**," H8047
1Sa 21:11 thousands, and David his **t of thousands**'?" H8047
1Sa 29: 5 thousands, and David his **t of thousands**'?" H8047
Ps 3: 6 fear though **t of thousands** assail me on H8047
Ps 68:17 of God are **t of thousands** and thousands H8052
Ps 144:13 thousands, *by* **t of thousands** in our fields H8045

TENT (286) [TENT-DWELLING, TENTMAKER, TENTS]

Ge 9:21 drunk and lay uncovered inside his t. H185
Ge 12: 8 the hills east of Bethel and pitched his t, H185
Ge 13: 3 Bethel and Ai where his t had been earlier H185
Ge 18: 1 the entrance to his t in the heat of the day H185
Ge 18: 2 the entrance of his t to meet them and H185
Ge 18: 6 So Abraham hurried into the t to Sarah H185
Ge 18: 9 they asked him. "There, in the t," he said. H185
Ge 18:10 was listening at the entrance to the t, H185
Ge 24:67 brought her into the t *of* his mother Sarah, H185
Ge 26:25 There he pitched his t, and there his H185
Ge 31:25 Jacob had pitched his t in the hill country H185
Ge 31:33 went into Jacob's t and into Leah's tent H185
Ge 31:33 tent and into Leah's t and into the tent of H185
Ge 31:33 tent and into the t *of* the two female H185
Ge 31:33 After he came out of Leah's t, he entered H185
Ge 31:33 out of Leah's tent, he entered Rachel's t. H185
Ge 31:34 everything in the t but found nothing. H185
Ge 33:19 the plot of ground where he pitched his t. H185
Ge 35:21 pitched his t beyond Migdal Eder. H185
Ex 16:16 an omer for each person you have in your t. H185
Ex 18: 7 each other and then went into the t. H185
Ex 26: 7 of goat hair for the t over the tabernacle— H185
Ex 26: 9 the sixth curtain double at the front of the t. H185
Ex 26:11 the loops to fasten the t together as a unit. H185
Ex 26:12 As for the additional length of the t curtains, H185
Ex 26:13 The t curtains will be a cubit longer on both H185
Ex 26:14 Make for the t a covering of ram skins dyed H185
Ex 26:36 the entrance to the t make a curtain of blue H185
Ex 27:19 including all the **t pegs** *for* it and those H3845
Ex 27:21 In the t *of* meeting, outside the curtain that H185
Ex 28:43 they enter the t *of* meeting or approach H185
Ex 29: 4 the entrance to the t *of* meeting and wash H185
Ex 29:10 the bull to the front of the t *of* meeting, H185
Ex 29:11 at the entrance to the t *of* meeting. H185
Ex 29:30 comes to the t *of* meeting to minister H185
Ex 29:32 At the entrance to the t *of* meeting, Aaron H185
Ex 29:42 at the entrance to the t *of* meeting, H185
Ex 29:44 I will consecrate the t *of* meeting and the H185
Ex 30:16 use it for the service of the t *of* meeting. H185
Ex 30:18 Place it between the t *of* meeting and the H185
Ex 30:20 Whenever they enter the t *of* meeting, they H185
Ex 30:26 Then use it to anoint the t *of* meeting, the H185
Ex 30:36 ark of the covenant law in the t *of* meeting, H185
Ex 31: 7 the t *of* meeting, the ark of the covenant H185
Ex 31: 7 and all the other furnishings of the t— H185
Ex 33: 7 Moses used to take a t and pitch it outside H185
Ex 33: 7 distance away, calling it the "t *of* meeting." H185
Ex 33: 7 would go to the t *of* meeting outside the H185
Ex 33: 8 And whenever Moses went out to the t, all H185
Ex 33: 8 watching Moses until he entered the t. H185
Ex 33: 9 As Moses went into the t, the pillar of cloud H185
Ex 33:10 of cloud standing at the entrance to the t, H185
Ex 33:10 worshiped, each at the entrance to their t. H185
Ex 33:11 aide Joshua son of Nun did not leave the t. H185
Ex 35:11 the tabernacle with its t and its covering H185
Ex 35:18 the **t pegs** *for* the tabernacle and for the H3845
Ex 35:21 to the LORD for the work on the t *of* meeting, H185
Ex 36:14 of goat hair for the t over the tabernacle— H185
Ex 36:18 clasps to fasten the t together as a unit. H185
Ex 36:19 Then they made for the t a covering of ram H185
Ex 36:37 the entrance to the t they made a curtain of H185
Ex 38: 8 served at the entrance to the t *of* meeting. H185
Ex 38:20 All the **t pegs** of the tabernacle and of the H3845
Ex 38:30 bases for the entrance to the t *of* meeting, H185
Ex 38:31 all the **t pegs** *for* the tabernacle and H3845
Ex 39:32 on the tabernacle, the t *of* meeting, was H185
Ex 39:33 the t and all its furnishings, its clasps H185
Ex 39:38 the curtain for the entrance to the t; H185
Ex 39:40 the ropes and **t pegs** *for* the courtyard; all H3845
Ex 39:40 the tabernacle, the t *of* meeting; H185
Ex 40: 2 the tabernacle, the t *of* meeting, on the H185
Ex 40: 6 to the tabernacle, the t *of* meeting; H185
Ex 40: 7 basin between the t *of* meeting and the H185
Ex 40:12 the entrance to the t *of* meeting and wash H185
Ex 40:19 Then he spread the t over the tabernacle H185
Ex 40:19 tabernacle and put the covering over the t, H185
Ex 40:22 the table in the t *of* meeting on the north H185
Ex 40:24 the lampstand in the t *of* meeting opposite H185
Ex 40:26 the gold altar in the t *of* meeting in front of H185
Ex 40:29 the tabernacle, the t *of* meeting, and H185
Ex 40:30 basin between the t *of* meeting and the H185
Ex 40:32 they entered the t *of* meeting or H185
Ex 40:34 Then the cloud covered the t *of* meeting H185
Ex 40:35 could not enter the t *of* meeting because H185
Lev 1: 1 spoke to him from the t *of* meeting. H185
Lev 1: 3 the entrance to the t *of* meeting so that it H185
Lev 1: 5 altar at the entrance to the t *of* meeting. H185
Lev 3: 2 it at the entrance to the t *of* meeting. H185
Lev 3: 8 slaughter it in front of the t *of* meeting. H185
Lev 3:13 slaughter it in front of the t *of* meeting. H185
Lev 4: 4 the entrance to the t *of* meeting before the H185
Lev 4: 5 blood and carry it into the t *of* meeting. H185
Lev 4: 7 that is before the LORD in the t *of* meeting. H185
Lev 4: 7 offering at the entrance to the t *of* meeting. H185
Lev 4:14 present it before the t *of* meeting. H185
Lev 4:16 of the bull's blood into the t *of* meeting. H185
Lev 4:18 that is before the LORD in the t *of* meeting. H185
Lev 4:18 offering at the entrance to the t *of* meeting. H185
Lev 6:16 eat it in the courtyard of the t *of* meeting. H185
Lev 6:26 in the courtyard of the t *of* meeting. H185
Lev 6:30 is brought into the t *of* meeting to make H185
Lev 8: 3 at the entrance to the t *of* meeting. H185
Lev 8: 4 at the entrance to the t *of* meeting. H185
Lev 8:31 the entrance to the t *of* meeting and eat it H185
Lev 8:33 the entrance to the t *of* meeting for seven H185
Lev 8:35 the entrance to the t *of* meeting day and H185
Lev 9: 5 to the front of the t *of* meeting, H185
Lev 9:23 Aaron then went into the t *of* meeting. H185
Lev 10: 7 the entrance to the t *of* meeting or you will H185
Lev 10: 9 whenever you go into the t *of* meeting, H185
Lev 12: 6 the entrance to the t *of* meeting a year-old H185
Lev 14: 8 must stay outside their t for seven days. H185
Lev 14:11 LORD at the entrance to the t *of* meeting. H185
Lev 14:23 priest at the entrance to the t *of* meeting, H185
Lev 15:14 the entrance to the t *of* meeting and give H185
Lev 15:29 priest at the entrance to the t *of* meeting. H185
Lev 16: 7 LORD at the entrance to the t *of* meeting. H185
Lev 16:16 He is to do the same for the t *of* meeting H185
Lev 16:17 No one is to be in the t *of* meeting from the H185
Lev 16:20 Holy Place, the t *of* meeting and the altar H185
Lev 16:23 is to go into the t *of* meeting and take off H185
Lev 16:33 for the t *of* meeting and the altar H185
Lev 17: 4 the entrance to the t *of* meeting to present H185
Lev 17: 5 the entrance to the t *of* meeting and H185
Lev 17: 6 the entrance to the t *of* meeting and burn H185
Lev 17: 9 the entrance to the t *of* meeting to sacrifice H185
Lev 19:21 the entrance to the t *of* meeting for a guilt H185
Lev 24: 3 ark of the covenant law in the t *of* meeting, H185
Nu 1: 1 spoke to Moses in the t *of* meeting in the H185
Nu 2: 2 to camp around the t *of* meeting some H185
Nu 2:17 Then the t *of* meeting and the camp of the H185
Nu 3: 7 community at the t *of* meeting by doing the H185
Nu 3: 8 of all the furnishings of the t *of* meeting, H185
Nu 3:25 At the t *of* meeting the Gershonites were H185
Nu 3:25 the care of the tabernacle and t, H185
Nu 3:25 curtain at the entrance to the t *of* meeting, H185
Nu 3:37 with their bases, **t pegs** and ropes. H3845
Nu 3:38 the sunrise, in front of the t *of* meeting. H185
Nu 4: 3 to serve in the work at the t *of* meeting. H185
Nu 4: 4 work of the Kohathites at the t *of* meeting: H185
Nu 4:15 those things that are in the t *of* meeting. H185
Nu 4:23 to serve in the work at the t *of* meeting. H185
Nu 4:25 the t *of* meeting, its covering and its H185
Nu 4:25 the entrance to the t *of* meeting, H185
Nu 4:26 the equipment used in the service of the t. NDT
Nu 4:28 of the Gershonite clans at the t *of* meeting. H185
Nu 4:30 to serve in the work at the t *of* meeting. H185
Nu 4:31 As part of all their service at the t, they are H185
Nu 4:32 courtyard with their bases, **t pegs**, ropes, H3845
Nu 4:33 as they work at the t *of* meeting under the H185
Nu 4:35 to serve in the work at the t *of* meeting, H185
Nu 4:37 clans who served at the t *of* meeting. H185
Nu 4:39 to serve in the work at the t *of* meeting, H185
Nu 4:41 clans who served at the t *of* meeting. H185
Nu 4:43 to serve in the work at the t *of* meeting, H185
Nu 4:47 of serving and carrying the t *of* meeting H185
Nu 6:10 priest at the entrance to the t *of* meeting. H185
Nu 6:13 brought to the entrance to the t *of* meeting. H185
Nu 6:18 " 'Then at the entrance to the t *of* meeting H185
Nu 7: 5 be used in the work at the t *of* meeting. H185
Nu 7:89 Moses entered the t *of* meeting to speak H185
Nu 8: 9 to the front of the t *of* meeting and H185
Nu 8:15 come to do their work at the t *of* meeting. H185
Nu 8:19 do the work at the t *of* meeting on behalf H185
Nu 8:22 do their work at the t *of* meeting under the H185
Nu 8:24 to take part in the work at the t *of* meeting, H185
Nu 8:26 performing their duties at the t *of* meeting, H185
Nu 9:15 the tabernacle, the t *of* the covenant law H185
Nu 9:17 Whenever the cloud lifted from above the t H185
Nu 10: 3 you at the entrance to the t *of* meeting. H185
Nu 11:16 Have them come to the t *of* meeting, that H185
Nu 11:24 elders and had them stand around the t. H185
Nu 11:26 the elders, but did not go out to the t. H185
Nu 12: 4 "Come out to the t *of* meeting, all three of H185
Nu 12: 5 the entrance to the t and summoned Aaron H185
Nu 12:10 When the cloud lifted from above the t H185
Nu 14:10 LORD appeared at the t *of* meeting to all the H185
Nu 16:18 Aaron at the entrance to the t *of* meeting. H185
Nu 16:19 to them at the entrance to the t *of* meeting, H185
Nu 16:42 Aaron and turned toward the t *of* meeting, H185
Nu 16:43 Aaron went to the front of the t *of* meeting, H185
Nu 16:50 Moses at the entrance to the t *of* meeting, H185
Nu 17: 4 Place them in the t *of* meeting in front of H185
Nu 17: 7 the LORD in the t *of* the covenant law. H185
Nu 17: 8 Moses entered the t and saw that Aaron's H185
Nu 18: 2 minister before the t *of* the covenant law. H185
Nu 18: 3 are to perform all the duties of the t, H185
Nu 18: 4 the care of the t *of* meeting— H185
Nu 18: 4 all the work at the t—and no one else may H185
Nu 18: 6 the LORD to do the work at the t *of* meeting. H185
Nu 18:21 they do while serving at the t *of* meeting. H185
Nu 18:22 must not go near the t *of* meeting, H185
Nu 18:23 do the work at the t *of* meeting and bear H185
Nu 18:31 wages for your work at the t *of* meeting. H185
Nu 19: 4 times toward the front of the t *of* meeting. H185
Nu 19:14 law that applies when a person dies in a t: H185
Nu 19:14 who enters the t and anyone who is in H185
Nu 19:18 water and sprinkle the t and all the H185
Nu 20: 6 to the entrance to the t *of* meeting and fell H185
Nu 25: 6 at the entrance to the t *of* meeting. H185
Nu 25: 8 followed the Israelite into the t. H7688
Nu 27: 2 the entrance to the t *of* meeting and said, H185
Nu 31:54 brought it into the t *of* meeting as a H185
Dt 31:14 present yourselves at the t *of* meeting, H185
Dt 31:14 presented themselves at the t *of* meeting. H185
Dt 31:15 LORD appeared at the t in a pillar of cloud, H185
Dt 31:15 the cloud stood over the entrance to the t. H185
Jos 7:21 They are hidden in the ground inside my t H185
Jos 7:22 they ran to the t, and there it was, H185
Jos 7:22 hidden in his t, with the silver H185
Jos 7:23 They took the things from the t, brought H185
Jos 7:24 sheep, his t and all that he had H185
Jos 18: 1 at Shiloh and set up the t *of* meeting there. H185
Jos 19:51 LORD at the entrance to the t *of* meeting. H185
Jdg 4:11 pitched his t by the great tree in H185
Jdg 4:17 fled on foot to the t *of* Jael, the wife of H185
Jdg 4:18 So he entered her t, and she covered him H185
Jdg 4:20 "Stand in the doorway of the t," he told her. H185
Jdg 4:21 picked up a t peg and a hammer and went H185
Jdg 4:22 Sisera with the **t peg** through his temple H3845
Jdg 5:26 Her hand reached for the **t peg**, her right H3845
Jdg 7:13 It struck the t with such force that the tent H185
Jdg 7:13 such force that the t overturned and H185
1Sa 2:22 served at the entrance to the t *of* meeting. H185
1Sa 4:10 were defeated and every man fled to his t. H185
1Sa 17:54 put the Philistine's weapons in his own t. H185
2Sa 6:17 its place inside the t that David had H185
2Sa 7: 2 while the ark of God remains in a t." H3749
2Sa 7: 6 place to place with a t as my dwelling. H185
2Sa 16:22 So they pitched a t for Absalom on the roof H185
2Sa 20: 1 in Jesse's son! Every man to his t, Israel!" H185
1Ki 1:39 horn of oil from the *sacred* t and anointed H185
1Ki 2:28 he fled to the t *of* the LORD and took hold of H185
1Ki 2:29 Joab had fled to the t *of* the LORD and was H185
1Ki 2:30 Benaiah entered the t *of* the LORD and said H185
1Ki 8: 4 of the LORD and the t *of* meeting and all the H185
2Ki 7: 8 entered another t and took some H185
1Ch 6:32 the tabernacle, the t *of* meeting, until H185
1Ch 9:19 the thresholds of the t just as their H185
1Ch 9:21 at the entrance to the t *of* meeting. H185
1Ch 9:23 the house called the t of meeting. H185
1Ch 15: 1 the ark of God and pitched a t for it. H185
1Ch 16: 1 set it inside the t that David had H185
1Ch 17: 1 of the covenant of the LORD is under a t." H3749
1Ch 17: 5 I have moved from one t **site** to another H185
1Ch 23:32 their responsibilities for the t *of* meeting, H185
2Ch 1: 3 at Gibeon, for God's t *of* meeting was there H185
2Ch 1: 4 he had pitched a t for it in Jerusalem. H185
2Ch 1: 6 the LORD in the t *of* meeting and offered a H185
2Ch 1:13 at Gibeon, from before the t *of* meeting. H185
2Ch 5: 5 up the ark and the t *of* meeting and all the H185
2Ch 24: 6 of Israel for the t *of* the covenant law?" H185
Job 4:21 Are not the **cords of** their t pulled up, so H3857
Job 5:24 You will know that your t is secure; you will H185
Job 11:14 hand and allow no evil to dwell in your t, H185
Job 18: 6 The light in his t becomes dark; the lamp H185
Job 18:14 the security of his t and marched off to the H185
Job 18:15 Fire resides in his t; burning sulfur is H185
Job 19:12 ramp against me and encamp around my t. H185
Job 20:26 him and devour what is left in his t. H185
Job 22:23 If you remove wickedness far from your t H185
Ps 15: 1 who may dwell in your *sacred* t? Who may H185
Ps 19: 4 heavens God has pitched a t for the sun. H185
Ps 27: 5 the shelter of his *sacred* t and set me high H185
Ps 27: 6 at his *sacred* t I will sacrifice with shouts of H185
Ps 52: 5 snatch you up and pluck you from your t; H185
Ps 61: 4 long to dwell in your t forever and take H185
Ps 76: 2 His t is in Salem, his dwelling place in H6108
Ps 78:60 the t he had set up among humans. H185
Ps 91:10 no disaster will come near your t. H185
Ps 104: 2 he stretches out the heavens like a t H3749
Pr 14:11 the t *of* the upright will flourish. H185
SS 1: 5 of Kedar, like the **t curtains** *of* Solomon. H3749
Isa 33:20 peaceful abode, a t that will not be moved H185
Isa 38:12 Like a shepherd's t my house has been H185
Isa 40:22 spreads them out like a t to live in. H185
Isa 54: 2 "Enlarge the place of your t, stretch your H185
Isa 54: 2 stretch your t curtains wide, do not H5438
Jer 10:20 My t is destroyed; all its ropes are snapped H185
Jer 10:20 left now to pitch my t or to set up my H185
La 2: 4 wrath like fire on the t *of* Daughter Zion. H185
Zec 10: 4 from him the **t peg**, from him the battle H3845
Ac 15:16 I will return and rebuild David's fallen t. *G5008*
2Co 5: 1 that if the earthly t we live in is destroyed, *G5011*
2Co 5: 4 For while we are in this t, we groan and *G5011*
2Pe 1:13 as long as I live in the t *of* this *body*, *G5013*

TENT-DWELLING (1) [DWELL, TENT]
Jdg 5:24 most blessed of t women. H928+2021+185

TENTH (66) [TEN]
Ge 8: 5 continued to recede until the t month, H6920
Ge 8: 5 the first day of the t month the tops of the H6920
Ge 14:20 Then Abram gave him a t of everything. H5130
Ge 28:22 *of* all that you give me *I will* **give** you **a t** H6923+6923
Ex 12: 3 of Israel that on the t day of this month H6917
Ex 29:40 the first lamb offer a t *of* an ephah of the H6928
Lev 5:11 their sin a t *of* an ephah of the finest H6920
Lev 6:20 a t *of* an ephah of the finest flour as a H6920
Lev 14:21 together with a t of an ephah of the finest H6928
Lev 16:29 On the t day of the seventh month you H6917
Lev 23:27 "The t day of this seventh month is the H6917
Lev 25: 9 everywhere on the t day of the seventh H6917
Lev 27:32 every t animal that passes under the H6920
Nu 5:15 an offering of a t *of* an ephah of barley H6920
Nu 7:66 On the t day Ahiezer son of Ammishaddai H6920
Nu 15: 4 a grain offering of a t *of* an ephah of the H6928
Nu 18:26 you must present a t of that tithe as the H5130
Nu 28: 5 a grain offering of a t *of* an ephah of the H6920
Nu 28:13 a grain offering of a t of an ephah of the H6928
Nu 29: 7 " 'On the t day of this seventh month hold H6917
Dt 14:22 **Be sure to set aside a t** *of* all that H6923+6923
Dt 23: 2 of the LORD, not even in the t generation. H6920
Dt 23: 3 of the LORD, not even in the t generation. H6920
Dt 26:12 finished **setting aside a t** *of* all your H6923+5130
Jos 4:19 On the t day of the first month the people H6917
1Sa 8:15 *He will* **take a t** *of* your grain and of your H6923
1Sa 8:17 *He will* **take a t** *of* your flocks, and you H6923
2Ki 25: 1 on the t day of the tenth month H6917
2Ki 25: 1 on the tenth day of the t month H6920
1Ch 12:13 Jeremiah the t and Makbannai the H6920
1Ch 24:11 the ninth to Jeshua, the t to Shekaniah, H6920
1Ch 25:17 the t to Shimei, his sons and relatives 12 H6920
1Ch 27:13 The t, for the tenth month, was Maharai H6920
1Ch 27:13 The tenth, for the t month, was Maharai H6920
Ezr 10:16 the first day of the t month they sat down H6920
Ne 10:38 are to bring a t *of* the tithes up to the H5130
Est 2:16 in the royal residence in the t month, H6920
Isa 6:13 And though a t remains in the land, it will H6920
Jer 32: 1 from the LORD in the t year of Zedekiah H6920
Jer 39: 1 of Judah, in the t month, Nebuchadnezzar H6920
Jer 52: 4 on the t day of the tenth month H6917
Jer 52: 4 on the tenth day of the t month H6920
Jer 52:12 On the t day of the fifth month, in the H6917
Eze 20: 1 in the fifth month on the t day, some of H6917
Eze 24: 1 in the t month on the tenth day H6920
Eze 24: 1 in the tenth month on the t day, the word H6917
Eze 29: 1 In the t year, in the tenth month on the H6920
Eze 29: 1 in the t month on the twelfth day H6920
Eze 33:21 our exile, in the t month on the fifth day H6920
Eze 40: 1 of the year, on the t of the month, in the H6917
Eze 45:11 bath containing a t *of* a homer and the H5130
Eze 45:11 of a homer and the ephah a t *of* a homer; H6920
Eze 45:14 by the bath, is a t *of* a bath from each cor H5130
Zec 8:19 seventh and t months will become joyful H6920
Mt 23:23 *You* **give a t** of your spices—mint, dill and *G620*
Lk 11:42 because *you* **give** God **a t** of your mint, rue *G620*
Lk 18:12 I fast twice a week and **give a t** of all I get.' *G620*
Heb 7: 2 Abraham gave him a t of everything *G1281*
Heb 7: 4 Abraham gave him a t of the plunder! *G1281*
Heb 7: 5 become priests *to* **collect a t** from the *G620*
Heb 7: 6 *yet he* **collected a t** from Abraham and *G1282*
Heb 7: 8 the t is collected by people who die *G1281*
Heb 7: 9 who collects the t, paid the tenth *G1281*
Heb 7: 9 the tenth, **paid the t** through Abraham, *G1282*
Rev 11:13 earthquake and a t of the city collapsed. *G1281*
Rev 21:20 the ninth topaz, the t turquoise, the *G1281*

TENTMAKER (1) [TENT]
Ac 18: 3 he was a t as they were, *G5010+3836+5492*

TENTS (59) [TENT]
Ge 4:20 of those who live in t and raise livestock. H185
Ge 9:27 may Japheth live in the t *of* Shem, and H185
Ge 13: 5 also had flocks and herds and t. H185
Ge 13:12 of the plain and **pitched** *his* t near Sodom. H182
Ge 13:18 Mamre at Hebron, where *he* **pitched** *his* t. H182
Ge 25:27 was content to stay at home among the t. H185
Ex 33: 8 rose and stood at the entrances to their t, H185
Nu 1:52 Israelites *are to* **set up** their t by divisions H2837
Nu 1:53 *are to* **set up** their t around the tabernacle H2837
Nu 11:10 family wailing at the entrance to their t. H185
Nu 16:24 'Move away from the t *of* Korah, Dathan H5438
Nu 16:26 "Move back from the t *of* these wicked men! H185
Nu 16:27 So they moved away from the t *of* Korah H5438
Nu 16:27 little ones at the entrances to their t. H185
Nu 24: 5 "How beautiful are your t, Jacob, your H185
Dt 1:27 You grumbled in your t and said, "The LORD H185
Dt 5:30 tell them to return to their t. H185
Dt 11: 6 their t and every living thing that belonged H185
Dt 16: 7 Then in the morning return to your t. H185
Dt 33:18 your going out, and you, Issachar, in your t. H185
Jdg 6: 5 livestock and their t like swarms of locusts. H185
2Sa 11:11 ark and Israel and Judah are staying in t, H6109
1Ki 12:16 in Jesse's son? To your t, Israel! Look after H185
1Ki 20:12 he and the kings were drinking in their t, H6109
1Ki 20:16 with him were in their t getting drunk. H6109
2Ki 7: 7 abandoned their t and their horses H185
2Ki 7: 8 entered one of the t and ate and drank. H185
2Ki 7:10 donkeys, and the t left just as they were." H185
2Ch 10:16 in Jesse's son? To your t, Israel! Look after H185
Job 8:22 the t *of* the wicked will be no more. H185
Job 12: 6 The t of marauders are undisturbed, and H185
Job 15:34 fire will consume the t *of* those who love H185
Job 21:28 of the great, the t where the wicked lived? H185
Ps 69:25 let there be no one to dwell in their t. H185
Ps 78:28 down inside their camp, all around their t. H5438
Ps 78:51 the firstfruits of manhood in the t *of* Ham. H185
Ps 78:67 Then he rejected the t *of* Joseph, he did H185
Ps 83: 6 the t *of* Edom and the Ishmaelites, of H185
Ps 84:10 my God than dwell in the t *of* the wicked. H185
Ps 106:25 grumbled in their t and did not obey the H185
Ps 118:15 victory resound in the t *of* the righteous: H185
Ps 120: 5 in Meshek, that I live among the t *of* Kedar! H185
SS 1: 5 dark like the t *of* Kedar, like the tent H185
SS 1: 8 young goats by the t *of* the shepherds. H5438
Isa 13:20 there no nomads *will* **pitch** *their* t, there no H182
Jer 4:20 In an instant my t are destroyed, my shelter H185
Jer 6: 3 they will pitch their t around her, each H185
Jer 30:18 fortunes of Jacob's t and have compassion H185
Jer 35: 7 of these things, but must always live in t. H185
Jer 35:10 We have lived in t and have fully obeyed H185
Jer 37:10 only wounded men were left in their t, H185
Jer 49:29 Their t and their flocks will be taken; their H185
Eze 25: 4 their camps and pitch their t among you; H5438
Da 11:45 He will pitch his royal t between the seas at H185
Hos 9: 6 by briers, and thorns will overrun their t. H185
Hos 12: 9 I will make you live in t again, as in the H185
Hab 3: 7 I saw the t *of* Cushan in distress, the H185
Mal 2:12 the LORD remove him from the t *of* Jacob— H185
Heb 11: 9 country; he lived in t, as did Isaac and *G5008*

TERAH (12) [TERAH'S]
Ge 11:24 lived 29 years, he became the father of T. H9561
Ge 11:25 And after he became the father of T H9561
Ge 11:26 After T had lived 70 years, he became the H9561
Ge 11:27 T became the father of Abram, Nahor H9561
Ge 11:28 While his father T was still alive, Haran H9561
Ge 11:31 T took his son Abram, his grandson Lot H9561
Ge 11:32 T lived 205 years, and he died in Harran. H9561
Nu 33:27 They left Tahath and camped at T. H9562
Nu 33:28 They left T and camped at Mithkah. H9562
Jos 24: 2 including T the father of Abraham and H9561
1Ch 1:26 Nahor, T H9561
Lk 3:34 Abraham, the son *of* T, the son of Nahor, *G2508*

TERAH'S (1) [TERAH]
Ge 11:27 This is the account of T family line. Terah H9561

TEREBINTH (2)
Isa 6:13 But as the t and oak leave stumps when H461
Hos 4:13 poplar and t, where the shade is H461

TERESH (2)
Est 2:21 Bigthana and T, two of the king's H9575
Est 6: 2 Mordecai had exposed Bigthana and T, H9575

TERMS (14)
Ge 23:16 Abraham **agreed** to Ephron's *t* and weighed AIT
Ge 34:23 So *let us* **agree to** their t, and they will H252
Dt 29: 1 These are the t *of* the covenant the LORD H1821
Dt 29: 9 Carefully follow the t *of* this covenant, so H1821
1Sa 11: 4 Saul and reported these t to the people, H1821
1Ki 5: 1 had always been **on friendly** t with David. H170
Job 34:33 God then reward you on your t, H4946+6640
Jer 11: 2 "Listen to the t *of* this covenant and tell H1821
Jer 11: 3 does not obey the t *of* this covenant— H1821
Jer 11: 4 **the t** I commanded your ancestors when I H889[S]
Jer 11: 6 'Listen to the t *of* this covenant and follow H1821
Jer 32:11 copy containing the t and conditions, H5184
Jer 34:18 not fulfilled the t *of* the covenant they H1821
Lk 14:32 a long way off and will ask *for* t of peace. *G3836*

TERRACED (2) [TERRACES]
Jdg 5:18 very lives; so did Naphtali on the t fields. H5294
2Sa 1:21 may no showers fall on your t fields. H9556

TERRACES (8) [TERRACED]
2Sa 5: 9 up the area around it, from the t inward. H4864
1Ki 9:15 his own palace, the t, the wall of H4864
1Ki 9:24 had built for her, he constructed the t. H4864
1Ki 11:27 had built the t and had filled in the H4864
1Ch 11: 8 from the t to the surrounding wall H4864
2Ch 32: 5 reinforced the t *of* the City of David. H4864
Job 24:11 They crush olives among the t; they tread H8805
Jer 31:40 all the t out to the Kidron Valley on H8727

TERRESTRIAL (KJV) EARTHLY

TERRIBLE (10) [TERROR]
Ex 9: 3 LORD will bring a t plague on your H3878+4394
Nu 20: 5 bring us up out of Egypt to this t place? H8273
Dt 6:22 wonders—great and t—on Egypt and H8273
Ne 13:27 are doing all this t wickedness and are H1524
Jer 4: 6 disaster from the north, even t destruction." H1524
Jer 6: 1 looms out of the north, even t destruction. H1524
Jer 21: 6 beast—and they will die of a t plague. H1524
Jer 26:19 are about to bring a t disaster on H1524
2Ti 3: 1 There will be t times in the last days. *G5901*
Rev 16:21 because the plague was so t. *G3489*

TERRIBLY (3) [TERROR]
1Sa 26:21 like a fool and have been t wrong." H2221+4394
Mt 8: 6 lies at home paralyzed, suffering t." *G1267*
Mt 15:22 is demon-possessed and **suffering t**." *G2809*

TERRIFIED (49) [TERROR]
Ge 45: 3 because *they were* t at his presence. H987
Ex 14:10 *They were* t and cried out to the H3707+4394
Ex 15:15 The chiefs of Edom *will be* t, the leaders of H987
Nu 22: 3 Moab *was* t because there were so H1593
Dt 1:29 I said to you, "Do not *be* t; do not be H6907
Dt 7:21 *Do* not *be* t by them, for the LORD your God H6907
Dt 20: 3 afraid; do not panic or *be* t by them. H6907
Dt 31: 6 Do not be afraid or t because of them, for H6907
Jdg 20:41 the Benjamites *were* t, because they H987
1Sa 17:11 the Israelites were dismayed and t. H3707+4394
1Sa 31: 4 armor-bearer *was* t and would not H3707+4394
2Ki 10: 4 But *they were* t and said, "If H3707+4394+4394
1Ch 10: 4 armor-bearer *was* t and would not H3707+4394
Est 7: 6 Then Haman *was* t before the king and H1286
Job 21: 6 I think about this, *I am* t; trembling seizes H987
Job 23:15 That is why *I am* t before him; when I think H987
Job 23:16 my heart faint; the Almighty *has* t me. H987
Job 41:25 rises up, the mighty *are* t; they retreat H1593
Ps 90: 7 by your anger and t by your indignation. H987
Ps 104:29 hide your face, *they are* t; when you take H987
Isa 19:17 to whom Judah is mentioned *will be* t, H7064
Isa 33:14 The sinners in Zion *are* t; trembling grips H7064
Isa 51: 7 of mere mortals or *be* t by their insults. H3169
Jer 1:17 *Do* not *be* t by them, or I will terrify you H3169
Jer 10: 2 ways of the nations or *be* t by signs in the H3169
Jer 10: 2 though the nations *are* t by them. H3169
Jer 17:18 from shame; *let* them *be* t, but keep me H3169
Jer 23: 4 they will no longer be afraid or t, nor H3169
Jer 46: 5 They are t, they are retreating, their H3146
Jer 51:32 the marshes set on fire, and the soldiers t." H987
Eze 2: 6 be afraid of what they say or *be* t by them, H3169
Eze 3: 9 Do not be afraid of them or t by them H3169
Eze 19: 7 all who were in it **were** t by his roaring. H9037
Eze 26:18 the islands in the sea *are* t at your collapse. H987
Da 4: 5 that passed through my mind t me. A10097
Da 4:19 a time, and his thoughts t him. A10097
Da 5: 9 Belshazzar *became* even more t and his A10097
Da 8:17 I was standing, *I was* t and fell prostrate. H1286
Ob 9 Teman, *will be* t, and everyone in Esau's H3169
Jnh 1:10 This t them and they asked H3707+1524+3711
Mt 14:26 saw him walking on the lake, *they were* t. *G5429*
Mt 17: 6 they fell facedown to the ground, t. *G5828+5379*
Mt 27:54 had happened, *they were* t, and *G5828+5379*
Mk 4:41 *They were* t and asked each *G5828+5832+3489*
Mk 6:50 because they all saw him and *were* t *G5429*
Lk 2: 9 them, and *they were* t. *G5828+5832+3489*
Rev 11:13 the survivors were t and gave glory to the *G1873*
Rev 18:10 T at her torment, they will stand far off *G5832*
Rev 18:15 her will stand far off, t at her torment. *G5832*

TERRIFIES (2) [TERROR]
Job 22:10 are all around you, why sudden peril t you, H987
Ps 2: 5 them in his anger and t them in his wrath, H987

TERRIFY (8) [TERROR]
2Ch 32:18 to t them and make them afraid in order H3707
Job 7:14 me with dreams and t me with visions, H1286
Job 13:11 *Would* not his splendor t you? Would not H1286
Job 33:16 in their ears and t them with warnings, H3169
Ps 83:15 your tempest and t them with your storm. H987
Jer 1:17 by them, or *I will* t you before them. H3169
Hab 2:17 your destruction of animals *will* t you. H3169
Zec 1:21 have come to t them and throw down H3006

TERRIFYING (4) [TERROR]
Job 15:21 T sounds fill his ears; when all seems H7065
Da 7: 7 t and frightening and very powerful. A10167
Da 7:19 different from all the others and most t, A10167
Heb 12:21 The sight was so t that Moses said, "I am *G5829*

TERRITORIES (7) [TERRITORY]
Ge 10: 5 spread out into their t by their clans within H824
Ge 10:20 languages, in their t and nations. H824
Ge 10:31 languages, in their t and nations. H824
Jos 19:51 These are the t that Eleazar the priest H5709
1Ki 10:15 Arabian kings and the governors of the t. H824
1Ch 13: 2 of our people throughout the t *of* Israel, H824
2Ch 9:14 the governors of the t brought gold and H824

TERRITORY (97) [TERRITORIES]
Ge 9:27 *May* God **extend** Japheth's t; may Japheth H7332
Ge 14: 7 conquered the whole t *of* the Amalekites, H8441
Ge 48: 6 in the t they **inherit** they will be reckoned H5709
Ex 34:24 out nations before you and enlarge your t, H1473
Nu 20:16 at Kadesh, a town on the edge of your t. H1473
Nu 20:17 left until we have passed through your t." H1473
Nu 20:21 refused to let them go through their t, H1473
Nu 21:13 the wilderness extending into Amorite t. H1473
Nu 21:22 until we have passed through your t." H1473
Nu 21:23 would not let Israel pass through his t. H1473
Nu 22:36 on the Arnon border, at the edge of his t. H1473
Nu 32:33 land with its cities and the t around them. H1474
Dt 1: 5 East of the Jordan in the t *of* Moab, Moses H824
Dt 2: 4 to pass through the t *of* your relatives the H1473
Dt 3: 8 of the Amorites the t east of the Jordan, H824
Dt 3:12 the Gadites the t north of Aroer by H889[S]

Dt 3:16 Gadites I gave the t extending from Gilead NDT
Dt 11:24 Your t will extend from the desert to H1473
Dt 11:30 in the t *of* those Canaanites living in the H824
Dt 12:20 has enlarged your t as he promised you, H1473
Dt 19: 8 If the LORD your God enlarges your t, as he H1473
Dt 34: 2 Naphtali, the t *of* Ephraim and Manasseh H824
Jos 1: 4 Your t will extend from the desert to H1473
Jos 11:22 No Anakites were left in Israelite t; only in H824
Jos 12: 1 defeated and whose t they took over east H824
Jos 12: 4 And the t *of* Og king of Bashan, one of H1473
Jos 13: 3 of Egypt to the t *of* Ekron on the north, H1473
Jos 13: 3 Gath and Ekron; the t of the Avvites NDT
Jos 13:11 the t *of* the people of Geshur and Maakah H1473
Jos 13:16 The t from Aroer on the rim of the Arnon H1473
Jos 13:25 The t *of* Jazer, all the towns of Gilead H1473
Jos 13:26 from Mahanaim to the t *of* Debir; H1473
Jos 13:27 the t up to the end of the Sea of Galilee). H1473
Jos 13:30 The t extending from Mahanaim and H1473
Jos 15: 1 extended down to the t *of* Edom, to the H1473
Jos 16: 2 crossed over to the t *of* the Arkites in H1473
Jos 16: 3 westward to the t *of* the Japhletites as far H1473
Jos 16: 5 This was the t *of* Ephraim, according to its H1473
Jos 17: 7 The t *of* Manasseh extended from Asher H1473
Jos 17:10 The t *of* Manasseh reached the H1473
Jos 18: 5 is to remain in its t on the south and the H1473
Jos 18: 5 the tribes of Joseph in their t on the north. H1473
Jos 18:11 Their allotted t lay between the tribes of H1473
Jos 19: 1 Their inheritance lay within the t *of* Judah. H5709
Jos 19: 9 their inheritance within the t *of* Judah. H5709
Jos 19:12 the sunrise to the t *of* Kisloth Tabor and H1473
Jos 19:18 Their t included: Jezreel, Kesulloth H1473
Jos 19:25 Their t included: Helkath, Hali, Beten H1473
Jos 19:41 The t *of* their inheritance included: Zorah H1473
Jos 19:47 When the t *of* the Danites was lost to H1473
Jos 21:41 the Levites in the t *held by* the Israelites H299
Jdg 1: 3 "Come up with us into the t **allotted** *to* us H1598
Jdg 1:18 Ashkelon and Ekron—each city with its t. H1473
Jdg 11:18 They did not enter the t *of* Moab, for the H1473
Jdg 11:20 did not trust Israel to pass through his t. H1473
1Sa 6: 1 had been in Philistine t seven months, H8441
1Sa 6: 9 If it goes up to its own t, toward Beth H1473
1Sa 7:13 they stopped invading Israel's t. H1473
1Sa 7:14 delivered the **neighboring** t from the H1473
1Sa 9: 4 Then he passed through the t *of* Benjamin H824
1Sa 27: 7 lived in Philistine t a year and four H8441
1Sa 27:11 practice as long as he lived in Philistine t. H8441
1Sa 30:14 **some** t belonging to Judah and the H889S
1Ki 9:19 Lebanon and throughout all the t he ruled. H824
1Ki 15:17 entering the t of Asa king of Judah. NDT
2Ki 6:23 bands from Aram stopped raiding Israel's t. H824
2Ki 10:32 the Israelites throughout their t H1473
2Ki 18: 8 the Philistines, as far as Gaza and its t. H1473
2Ki 24: 7 the king of Babylon had taken all his t, H889S
1Ch 4:10 you would bless me and enlarge my t! H1473
1Ch 6:54 of their settlements **allotted** as their t H1473
1Ch 6:66 were given as their t towns from the tribe H1473
2Ch 8: 6 Lebanon and throughout all the t he ruled. H824
2Ch 16: 1 entering the t of Asa king of Judah. NDT
2Ch 20:10 whose t you would not allow Israel to H889S
2Ch 34:33 idols from all the t belonging to the H824
Jer 1: 1 priests at Anathoth in the t *of* Benjamin. H824
Jer 17:26 from the t *of* Benjamin and the western H824
Jer 32: 8 my field at Anathoth in the t *of* Benjamin. H824
Jer 32:44 sealed and witnessed in the t *of* Benjamin H824
Jer 33:13 of the Negev, in the t *of* Benjamin, in the H824
Jer 37:12 the city to go to the t *of* Benjamin to get his H824
Eze 16:27 my hand against you and reduced your t; H2976
Eze 48: 2 it will border the t *of* Dan from east to H1473
Eze 48: 3 it will border the t *of* Asher from east to H1473
Eze 48: 4 it will border the t *of* Naphtali from east to H1473
Eze 48: 5 it will border the t *of* Manasseh from east H1473
Eze 48: 6 it will border the t *of* Ephraim from east to H1473
Eze 48: 7 it will border the t *of* Reuben from east to H1473
Eze 48: 8 "Bordering the t *of* Judah from east to H1473
Eze 48:12 portion, bordering the t *of* the Levites. H1473
Eze 48:13 "Alongside the t *of* the priests, the Levites H1473
Eze 48:24 it will border the t *of* Benjamin from east H1473
Eze 48:25 it will border the t *of* Simeon from east to H1473
Eze 48:26 it will border the t *of* Issachar from east to H1473
Eze 48:27 it will border the t *of* Zebulun from east to H1473
2Co 10:16 work already done in someone else's t. *G2834*

TERROR (76) [TERRIBLE, TERRIBLY, TERRIFIED, TERRIFIES, TERRIFY, TERRIFYING, TERRORISTS, TERRORIZED, TERRORS]

Ge 35: 5 the t *of* God fell on the towns all H3150
Ex 15:16 t and dread will fall on them. By the power H399
Ex 23:27 "I will send my t ahead of you and throw H399
Lev 26:16 I will bring on you **sudden** t, wasting H988
Dt 2:25 will begin to put the t and fear of you on H7065
Dt 11:25 will put the t and fear of you on the whole H7065
Dt 26: 8 with great t and with signs and wonders. H4616
Dt 28:67 because of the t that will fill your hearts H7065
Dt 32:25 them childless; in their homes t will reign. H399
1Sa 14:15 Then the t *of* the LORD fell on the people H7065
1Sa 28: 5 he was afraid; t **filled** his heart. H3006+4394
2Sa 17: 2 *I would* **strike** him **with** t, and then all the H3006
2Ch 14:14 the t *of* the LORD had fallen on them. H7065
Job 9:34 so that his t would frighten me no more. H399
Job 15:24 Distress and anguish **fill** him **with** t H1286
Job 39:20 a locust, striking t with its proud snorting? H399
Ps 9:20 Strike them with t, LORD; let the nations H4616
Ps 10:18 earthly mortals *will* never again **strike** t. H6907
Ps 31:13 I hear many whispering, "T on every side!" H4471
Ps 48: 5 saw her and were astounded; they fled *in* t. H987
Ps 78:33 their days in futility and their years in t. H988
Ps 91: 5 You will not fear the t *of* night, nor the H7065
Pr 20: 2 A king's wrath strikes t like the roar of a lion NDT
Pr 21:15 joy to the righteous but t to evildoers. H4745
Isa 13: 8 T *will* **seize** *them*, pain and anguish will H987
Isa 17:14 In the evening, **sudden** t! Before the H1166
Isa 19:17 of Judah will bring t to the Egyptians; H2505
Isa 21: 1 comes from the desert, from a land of t. H3707
Isa 22: 5 trampling and t in the Valley of H4428
Isa 24:17 T and pit and snare await you, people of H7065
Isa 24:18 flees at the sound of t will fall into a pit; H7065
Isa 28:19 of this message will bring sheer t. H2317
Isa 31: 9 Their stronghold will fall because of t; at H4471
Isa 33:18 your thoughts you will ponder the former t: H399
Isa 44:11 they *will be* **brought down to** t and shame. H7064
Isa 47:12 will succeed, perhaps *you will* **cause** t. H6907
Isa 51:13 that *you* **live in** constant t every day H7064
Isa 54:14 T will be far removed; it will not come H4745
Jer 6:25 has a sword, and there is t on every side. H4471
Jer 8:15 a time of healing but there is only t. H1287
Jer 14:19 a time of healing but there is only t. H1287
Jer 15: 8 I will bring down on them anguish and t. H988
Jer 17:17 Do not be a t to me; you are my refuge in H4745
Jer 17:18 let them be terrified, but *keep* me from t. H3169
Jer 20: 3 you is not Pashhur, but T on Every Side. H4474
Jer 20: 4 'I will make you a t to yourself and to all H4471
Jer 20:10 hear many whispering, "T on every side H4471
Jer 30: 5 " 'Cries of fear are heard—t, not peace. H7065
Jer 32:21 an outstretched arm and with great t. H4616
Jer 46: 5 and there is t on every side, H4471
Jer 48:43 T and pit and snare await you, you H7065
Jer 48:44 flees from the t will fall into a pit, H7065
Jer 49: 5 I will bring t on you from all those around H7065
Jer 49:16 The t you inspire and the pride of your H9526
Jer 49:29 will shout to them, 'T on every side!' H4471
Jer 50: 2 will be put to shame, Marduk **filled with** t. H3169
Jer 50: 2 put to shame and her idols **filled with** t. H3169
Jer 50:36 *They will be* **filled with** t. H3169
Jer 50:38 land of idols, idols that will go mad with t. H399
La 3:47 We have suffered t and pitfalls, ruin and H7065
Eze 7:18 put on sackcloth and be clothed with t. H7146
Eze 7:25 When t comes, they will seek peace in H7888
Eze 23:46 give them over to t and plunder. H2400
Eze 26:16 Clothed with t, they will sit on the ground H3010
Eze 26:17 you put your t on all who lived there. H3154
Eze 32:23 All who had spread t in the land of the H3154
Eze 32:24 All who had spread t in the land of the H3154
Eze 32:25 Because their t had spread in the land of H3154
Eze 32:26 they spread their t in the land of the living H3154
Eze 32:30 disgrace despite the t caused by their H3154
Eze 32:32 I had him spread t in the land of the H3154
Da 10: 7 such t overwhelmed them that they H3010
Am 6: 3 day of disaster and bring near a reign of t. H2805
Lk 21:26 People will faint from t, apprehensive of *G5832*
Ro 13: 3 For rulers hold no t for those who do right *G5832*
Rev 11:11 and t struck those who saw them. *G5832+3489*

TERRORISTS (1) [TERROR]

Ac 21:38 four thousand t out into the *G467+3836+4974*

TERRORIZED (1) [TERROR]

Eze 32:27 warriors also had t the land of the H3154+928

TERRORS (14) [TERROR]

Job 6: 4 God's t are marshaled against me. H1243
Job 13:21 and stop frightening me with your t. H399
Job 18:11 T startle him on every side and dog his H1166
Job 18:14 his tent and marched off to the king of t. H1166
Job 20:25 point out of his liver. T will come over him; H399
Job 24:17 they make friends with the t *of* darkness. H1166
Job 27:20 T overtake him like a flood; a tempest H1166
Job 30:15 T overwhelm me; my dignity is driven H1166
Ps 55: 4 the t *of* death have fallen on me. H399
Ps 73:19 destroyed, completely swept away by t! H1166
Ps 88:15 I have borne your t and am in despair. H399
Ps 88:16 swept over me; your t have destroyed me. H1243
SS 3: 8 at his side, prepared for the t of the night. H7065
La 2:22 you summoned *against* me t on every H4471

TERTIUS (1)

Ro 16:22 T, who wrote down this letter, greet you *G5470*

TERTULLUS (2)

Ac 24: 1 of the elders and a lawyer named T, *G5472*
Ac 24: 2 T presented his case before Felix: *G5472*

TEST (60) [TESTED, TESTER, TESTING, TESTINGS, TESTS]

Ex 15:25 instruction for them and **put** them **to the** t. H5814
Ex 16: 4 In this way *I will* t them and see whether H5814
Ex 17: 2 Why *do you* **put** the LORD **to the** t?" H5814
Ex 20:20 God has come to t you, so that the fear of H5814
Dt 6:16 *Do* not **put** the LORD your God **to the** t as H5814
Dt 8: 2 to humble and t you in order to know H5814
Dt 8:16 to humble and t you so that in the end it H5814
Jdg 2:22 I will use them to t Israel and see whether H5814
Jdg 3: 1 the LORD left to t all those Israelites who H5814
Jdg 3: 4 They were left to t the Israelites to see H5814
Jdg 6:39 *Allow me* one more t with the fleece, but H5814
1Ki 10: 1 she came to t Solomon with hard H5814
1Ch 29:17 that you t the heart and are pleased with H1043
2Ch 9: 1 came to Jerusalem to t him with hard H5814
2Ch 32:31 God left him to t him and to know H5814
Job 7:18 every morning and t them every moment? H1043
Job 12:11 *Does* not the ear t words as the tongue H1043
Ps 17: 3 you examine me at night and t me, H7671
Ps 26: 2 T me, LORD, and try me, examine my heart H1043
Ps 78:18 *They* willfully **put** God **to the** t by H5814
Ps 78:41 Again and again *they* **put** God **to the** t H5814
Ps 78:56 But *they* **put** God **to the** t and rebelled H5814
Ps 106:14 in the wilderness *they* **put** God **to the** t. H5814
Ps 139:23 t me and know my anxious thoughts. H1043
Ecc 2: 1 *I will* t you with pleasure to find out what H5814
Isa 7:12 not ask; *I will* not **put** the LORD **to the** t." H5814
Jer 6:27 that you may observe and t their ways. H1043
Jer 9: 7 I will refine and t them, for what else can H1043
Jer 11:20 righteously and t the heart and mind, H1043
Jer 12: 3 you see me and t my thoughts about you. H1043
La 3:40 Let us examine our ways and t them, and H2983
Da 1:12 "Please t your servants for ten days: Give H5814
Zec 13: 9 them like silver and t them like gold. H1043
Mal 3:10 T me in this," says the LORD Almighty H1043
Mal 3:15 even *when they* **put** God **to the** t, they H1043
Mt 4: 7 '*Do* not **put** the Lord your God **to the** t.'" *G1733*
Mt 19: 3 Some Pharisees came to him *to* t him *G4279*
Mk 8:11 *To* t him, they asked him for a sign from *G4279*
Lk 4:12 '*Do* not **put** the Lord your God **to the** t.'" *G1733*
Lk 10:25 an expert in the law stood up *to* t Jesus. *G1733*
Jn 6: 6 He asked this only *to* t him, for he already *G4279*
Ac 5: 9 could you conspire *to* t the Spirit of the *G4279*
Ac 15:10 why *do you try to* t God by putting on the *G4279*
Ro 12: 2 will be able to **t and approve** what God's *G1507*
Ro 16:10 whose fidelity to Christ has **stood the** t. *G1511*
1Co 3:13 the fire *will* t the quality of each *G1507*
1Co 10: 9 *We should* not t Christ, as some of them *G1733*
2Co 2: 9 if you would **stand the** t and be obedient *G1509*
2Co 8: 8 but *I want to* t the sincerity of your love by *G1507*
2Co 13: 5 whether you are in the faith; t yourselves. *G1507*
2Co 13: 5 unless, of course, *you* **fail the** t? *G99+1639*
2Co 13: 6 discover that we *have* not **failed the** t. *G1639+99*
2Co 13: 7 that we have **stood the** t but so that you *G1511*
Gal 6: 4 Each one *should* t their own actions. *G1507*
1Th 5:21 t them all; hold on to what is good, *G1507*
Jas 1:12 having stood the t, that person will *G1511*
1Pe 4:12 fiery ordeal that has come on you to t you, *G4280*
1Jn 4: 1 t the spirits to see whether they are *G1507*
Rev 2:10 will put some of you in prison to t *you*, *G4279*
Rev 3:10 on the whole world *to* t the inhabitants of *G4279*

TESTATOR (KJV) ONE WHO MADE IT

TESTED (26) [TEST]

Ge 22: 1 Some time later God t Abraham. He said H5814
Ge 42:15 And this is how *you will* **be** t: As surely as H1043
Ge 42:16 that your words *may* **be** t to see if you are H1043
Ex 17: 7 because they t the LORD saying, H5814
Nu 14:22 who disobeyed me and t me ten times— H5814
Dt 33: 8 *You* t him at Massah; you contended with H5814
Job 23:10 that I take; *when he has* t me, I will come H1043
Job 28:27 appraised it; he confirmed it and t it. H2983
Job 34:36 that Job *might* **be** t to the utmost for H1043
Ps 66:10 For you, God, t us; you refined us like H1043
Ps 81: 7 *I* t you at the waters of Meribah. H1043
Ps 95: 9 where your ancestors t me; they tried me H5814
Ps 119:140 Your promises *have* **been** thoroughly t H7671
Pr 27:21 gold, but people are t by their praise. NDT
Ecc 7:23 All this *I* t by wisdom and I said, "I am H5814
Isa 28:16 I lay a stone in Zion, a t stone, a precious H1046
Isa 48:10 *I have* t you in the furnace of affliction. H1047
Da 1:14 he agreed to this and t them for ten days. H5814
Mt 16: 1 came to Jesus and t him by asking him to *G4279*
Mt 22:35 expert in the law, t him with this question: *G4279*
Mk 10: 2 Pharisees came and t him by asking, *G4279*
Lk 11:16 Others t him by asking for a sign from *G4279*
1Ti 3:10 They *must* first *be* t; and then if there is *G1507*
Heb 3: 9 where your ancestors t and tried me *G4279*
Heb 11:17 Abraham, *when* God t *him*, offered Isaac *G4279*
Rev 2: 2 that *you have* t those who claim to be *G4279*

TESTER (1) [TEST]

Jer 6:27 made you a **t of metals** and my people H1031

TESTICLES (2)

Lev 21:20 festering or running sores or damaged t. H863
Lev 22:24 to the LORD an animal whose t are bruised, NDT

TESTIFIED (16) [TESTIFY]

2Sa 1:16 Your own mouth t against you when you H6699
2Ch 24:19 and though *they* t against them H6386
Mk 14:56 Many t **falsely** against him, but their *G6018*
Jn 1:15 John t concerning him. He cried out *G3455*
Jn 3:26 of the Jordan—the one you t about—look, *G3455*
Jn 5:33 sent to John and *he has* t to the truth. *G3455*
Jn 5:37 who sent me *has* himself t concerning me *G3455*
Jn 13:21 Jesus was troubled in spirit and t, "Very *G3455*
Ac 6:13 false witnesses, *who* t, "This fellow never *G3306*
Ac 8:25 the word of the Lord and t about Jesus, *G1371*
Ac 13:22 David their king. God t concerning him: 'I *G3455*
Ac 23:11 As *you have* t about me in Jerusalem, so *G1371*
1Co 15:15 for *we have* t about God that he raised *G3455*
Heb 2: 4 God also t to it by signs, wonders and *G5296*
Heb 2: 6 But there is a place where someone *has* t *G1371*
3Jn 3 came and t **about** your faithfulness *G3455*

TESTIFIES (15) [TESTIFY]

Job 16: 8 my gauntness rises up and t against me. H6699
Isa 3: 9 The look on their faces t against them H6699
Hos 5: 5 Israel's arrogance t against them; the H6699
Hos 7:10 Israel's arrogance t against him, but H6699
Jn 3:32 He t to what he has seen and heard, but G3455
Jn 5:32 There is another who t in my favor, and I G3455
Jn 8:18 I am one *who* t for myself; my other G3455
Jn 19:35 and he t so that you also may believe. NDT
Jn 21:24 is the disciple who t to these things and G3455
Ro 8:16 The Spirit himself t **with** our spirit that we G5210
2Co 1:12 Our conscience t that we have conducted G3457
Heb 10:15 The Holy Spirit also t to us about this. First G3455
1Jn 5: 6 And it is the Spirit who t, because the G3455
Rev 1: 2 who t to everything he saw—that is, the G3455
Rev 22:20 He *who* t to these things says, "Yes, I am G3455

TESTIFY (49) [TESTIFIED, TESTIFIES, TESTIFYING, TESTIMONY]

Ge 30:33 And my honesty *will* t for me in the future H6699
Lev 5: 1 a public charge to t regarding something H6332
Dt 8:19 *I* t against you today that you will surely H6386
Dt 31:21 this song *will* t against them, H6699+4200+6332
Dt 31:28 and **call** the heavens and the earth **to** t H6386
1Sa 12: 3 T against me in the presence of the LORD H6699
Job 15: 6 not mine; your own lips t against you. H6699
Ps 50: 7 I will speak; *I will* t against you, Israel H6386
Ps 50:20 You sit and t against your brother and H1819
Pr 21:28 a careful listener *will* t successfully. H1818
Pr 24:28 *Do* not t against your neighbor H2118+6332
Pr 29:24 they are put under oath and *dare* not t. H5583
Isa 59:12 in your sight, and our sins t against us. H6699
Jer 14: 7 Although our sins t against us, do H6699
Am 3:13 "Hear this and t against the descendants H6386
Zep 3: 8 the LORD, "for the day I will stand up to t. H6332
Mal 3: 5 I will be quick to t against sorcerers H6332
Mt 23:31 So *you* t against yourselves that you are G3455
Lk 11:48 So *you* t that you approve of what G3459+1639
Jn 1: 7 came as a witness to t concerning that G3455
Jn 1:34 I have seen and *I* t that this is God's G3455
Jn 3:11 we know, and *we* t *to* what we have seen G3455
Jn 3:28 You yourselves *can* t that I said, 'I am not G3455
Jn 5:31 "If I t about myself, my testimony is not G3455
Jn 5:36 am doing—t that the Father has sent me. G3455
Jn 5:39 are the very Scriptures that t about me, G3455
Jn 7: 7 it hates me because I t that its works are G3455
Jn 8:14 "Even if I t on my own behalf, my G3455
Jn 10:25 I do in my Father's name t about me, G3455
Jn 15:26 out from the Father—he *will* t about me. G3455
Jn 15:27 And you also *must* t, for you have been G3455
Jn 18:23 Jesus replied, "t as to what is wrong. G3455
Jn 18:37 came into the world is to t to the truth. G3455
Ac 4:33 apostles *continued to* t to the G625+3836+3457
Ac 10:42 to the people and *to* t that he is the one G1371
Ac 10:43 the prophets t about him *that* everyone G3455
Ac 22: 5 all the Council *can themselves* t. G3455
Ac 23:11 in Jerusalem, so you must also t in Rome." G3455
Ac 26: 5 have known me for a long time and *can* t, G3455
Ac 26:22 so I stand here and t to small and great G3458
Ro 3:21 to which the Law and the Prophets t. G3455
Ro 10: 2 For *I can* t about them that they are G3455
2Co 8: 3 For *I* t that they gave as much as they were G3455
Gal 4:15 *I can* t that, if you could have done so G3455
Php 1: 8 God can t how I long for all of you with the G3459
Jas 5: 3 corrosion *will* t against you G1650+3457+1639
1Jn 1: 2 we have seen it and t to it, and we G3455
1Jn 4:14 we have seen and t that the Father has G3455
1Jn 5: 7 For there are three that t: G3455

TESTIFYING (4) [TESTIFY]

Ac 18: 5 t to the Jews that Jesus was the Messiah. G1371
Ac 20:24 the task of t to the good news of God's G1371
1Ti 6:13 who *while* t before Pontius Pilate made G3455
1Pe 5:12 encouraging you and t that this is the true G2148

TESTIMONY (73) [TESTIFY]

Ex 20:16 shall not give false t against your H6332
Ex 23: 2 When *you* **give** t in a lawsuit, do not H6699
Nu 35:30 as a murderer only on the t *of* witnesses. H7023
Nu 35:30 be put to death *on the* t *of* only one H6699
Dt 5:20 shall not give false t against your H6332
Dt 17: 6 On the t *of* two or three witnesses a person H7023
Dt 17: 6 put to death on the t *of* only one witness. H7023
Dt 19:15 be established by the t *of* two or three H7023
Dt 19:18 **giving** false t against a fellow Israelite H6699
Pr 25:18 one who gives false t against a neighbor. H6332
Isa 8:16 Bind up this t **of warning** and seal up H9496
Isa 8:20 God's instruction and the t **of warning**. H9496
Isa 29:21 court and with false t deprive the innocent NDT
Mt 8: 4 gift Moses commanded, as a t to them." G3457
Mt 15:19 sexual immorality, theft, **false** t, slander. G6019
Mt 18:16 be established by the t of two or three G5125
Mt 19:18 shall not steal, *you shall* not **give false** t, G6018
Mt 24:14 in the whole world as a t to all nations, G3457
Mt 26:62 *is this* t that these men *are* **bringing against** G2909
Mt 27:13 hear *the* t *they are* **bringing against** you?" G2909
Mk 1:44 your cleansing, as a t to them. G3457
Mk 6:11 the dust off your feet as a t against them." G3457
Mk 10:19 *you shall* not **give false** t, you shall G6018
Mk 14:57 stood up and **gave** *this* **false** t against him G6018
Mk 14:59 Yet even then their t did not agree. G3456
Mk 14:60 *this* t that these men *are* **bringing against** G2909
Lk 5:14 your cleansing, as a t to them. G3457
Lk 9: 5 the dust off your feet as a t against them." G3457
Lk 18:20 not steal, *you shall* not **give false** t, honor G6018
Lk 21:13 And so you *will* **bear** t to me. G609+1650+3457
Lk 22:71 they said, "Why do we need any more t? G3456
Jn 1:19 Now this was John's t when the Jewish G3456
Jn 1:32 Then John **gave this** t: "I saw the Spirit G3455
Jn 2:25 He did not need any t about mankind, for G3455
Jn 3:11 still you people do not accept our t. G3456
Jn 3:32 seen and heard, but no one accepts his t. G3456
Jn 4:39 in him because of the woman's t, G3364+3455
Jn 5:31 "If I testify about myself, my t is not true. G3456
Jn 5:32 I know that his t about me is true. G3456
Jn 5:34 Not that I accept human t; but I mention it G3456
Jn 5:36 "I have t weightier than that of John. G3456
Jn 8:13 as your own witness; your t is not valid." G3456
Jn 8:14 on my own behalf, my t is valid, for I know G3456
Jn 8:17 it is written that the t of two witnesses is G3456
Jn 19:35 The man who saw it *has* **given** t, and his G3455
Jn 19:35 it has given testimony, and his t is true. G3456
Jn 21:24 We know that his t is true. G3456
Ac 14:17 Yet he has not left himself **without** t: He has G282
Ac 22:18 here will not accept your t about me. G3456
1Co 1: 6 thus confirming our t about Christ among G3457
1Co 2: 1 as I proclaimed to you the t about God. G3457
2Co 13: 1 be established by the t of two or three G5125
2Th 1:10 because you believed our t to you. G3457
2Ti 1: 8 not be ashamed *of* the t about our Lord G3457
Heb 10:28 mercy on the t **of** two or three **witnesses**. G3459
1Jn 5: 9 We accept human t, but God's testimony G3456
1Jn 5: 9 God's t is greater because it is the G3456
1Jn 5: 9 is greater because it is the t of God, G3456
1Jn 5:10 believes in the Son of God accepts this t. G3456
1Jn 5:10 not believed the t God has given about G3456
1Jn 5:11 And this is the t: God has given us eternal G3456
3Jn 12 and you know that our t is true. G3456
Rev 1: 2 the word of God and the t of Jesus Christ. G3456
Rev 1: 9 of the word of God and the t of Jesus. G3456
Rev 6: 9 of God and the t they had maintained G3456
Rev 11: 7 Now when they have finished their t, the G3456
Rev 12:11 of the Lamb and by the word *of* their t; G3456
Rev 12:17 hold fast their t about Jesus. G3456
Rev 17: 6 the blood *of* those *who* **bore** t to Jesus. G3459
Rev 19:10 sisters who hold to the t of Jesus. G3456
Rev 19:10 Spirit of prophecy who **bears** t to Jesus." G3456
Rev 20: 4 because of their t about Jesus and G3456
Rev 22:16 sent my angel *to* **give** you this t for the G3455

TESTING (6) [TEST]

Dt 13: 3 The LORD your God *is* t you to find out H5814
Eze 21:13 " 'T *will* surely *come*. And what if even H1043
Lk 8:13 but in the time *of* t they fall away. G4280
Ac 20:19 in the midst of **severe** t by the plots of my G4280
Heb 3: 8 during the time *of* t in the wilderness, G4280
Jas 1: 3 you know that the t of your faith produces G1510

TESTINGS (1) [TEST]

Dt 4:34 another nation, by t, by signs and H4999

TESTS (4) [TEST]

Job 34: 3 For the ear t words as the tongue tastes H1043
Pr 17: 3 furnace for gold, but the LORD t the heart. H1043
Ecc 3:18 God t them so that they may see that they H1405
1Th 2: 4 please people but God, who t our hearts. G1507

TETHER (1) [TETHERED]

Ge 49:11 *He will* t his donkey to a vine, his colt to H673

TETHERED (1) [TETHER]

2Ki 7:10 of anyone—only t horses and donkeys H673

TETRARCH (7)

Mt 14: 1 At that time Herod the t heard the reports G5490
Lk 3: 1 of Judea, Herod t of Galilee, his brother G5489
Lk 3: 1 his brother Philip t of Iturea and Traconitis G5489
Lk 3: 1 Traconitis, and Lysanias t of Abilene— G5489
Lk 3:19 John rebuked Herod the t because of his G5490
Lk 9: 7 Now Herod the t heard about all that was G5490
Ac 13: 1 had been brought up with Herod the t) G5490

TEXT (4)

Est 3:14 A copy of the t of the edict was to be H4181
Est 4: 8 him a copy of the t *of* the edict for their H4181
Est 8:13 A copy of the t of the edict was to be H4181
Jer 29: 1 This is the t *of* the letter that the prophet H1821

THADDAEUS (2)

Mt 10: 3 collector; James son of Alphaeus, and T; G2497
Mk 3:18 son of Alphaeus, T, Simon the Zealot G2497

THAN (538)

Ge 3: 1 the serpent was **more** crafty t any of the H4946
Ge 4:13 "My punishment is more t I can bear. H4946
Ge 7:20 to a depth of **more** t fifteen cubits. H4946
Ge 18:28 the **number** of the righteous **is** five **less** t H2893
Ge 19: 9 We'll treat you worse t them." They kept H4946
Ge 25:23 one people will be stronger t the other H4946
Ge 27:12 curse on myself **rather** t a blessing." H2256+4202
Ge 28:17 This is none **other** t the house of H3954+561
Ge 29:19 that I give her to you t to some other man. H4946
Ge 29:30 Rachel was **greater** t his love for Leah. H4946
Ge 37: 3 loved Joseph **more** t any of his other H4946
Ge 37: 4 their father loved him **more** t any of them, H4946
Ge 38:26 "She is **more** righteous t I, since I H4946
Ge 39: 9 No one is greater in this house t I am. H4946
Ge 41:40 to the throne will I be greater t you." H4946
Ge 48:19 his younger brother will be greater t he H4946
Ge 48:22 you I give one **more** ridge of land t to your H6584
Ge 49:12 His eyes will be darker t wine, his teeth H4946
Ge 49:12 darker than wine, his teeth whiter t milk. H4946
Ge 49:26 are greater t the blessings of the H6584
Ge 49:26 mountains, t the bounty of the age-old hills. NDT
Ex 11: 6 **worse** *t* there has ever been or ever will be AIT
Ex 14:12 serve the Egyptians t to die in the desert!" H4946
Ex 18:11 that the LORD is greater t all other gods, H4946
Ex 22:20 to any god **other** t the LORD H1194+4200+963
Ex 30:15 are not to give more t a half shekel and H4946
Ex 30:33 puts it on **anyone other** t **a priest** must be H2424
Ex 36: 5 are bringing more t enough for doing the H4946
Ex 36: 7 already had *was* **more** *t* enough to do all AIT
Lev 13: 3 the sore appears to be **more** t skin deep, H4946
Lev 13: 4 not appear to be **more** t skin deep and H4946
Lev 13:20 it appears to be **more** t skin deep and the H4946
Lev 13:21 it and it is not **more** t skin deep and has H4946
Lev 13:25 it appears to be **more** t skin deep, it H4946
Lev 13:26 if it is not **more** t skin deep and has H4946
Lev 13:30 it appears to be **more** t skin deep and the H4946
Lev 13:31 not seem to be **more** t skin deep and H4946
Lev 13:32 it does not appear to be **more** t skin deep, H4946
Lev 13:34 appears to be no **more** t skin deep, H4946
Lev 14:37 appear to be deeper t the surface of the H4946
Lev 15:25 days at a time **other** t her monthly period H4202
Lev 22:12 daughter marries **anyone other** t **a priest**, H2424
Nu 5:20 with a man **other** t your husband"— H4946+1187
Nu 11:32 **No** one gathered **less** t ten homers H5070
Nu 12: 3 **more** humble t anyone else on the face of H4946
Nu 13:31 those people; they are stronger t we are." H4946
Nu 14:12 into a nation greater and stronger t they." H4946
Nu 22:15 and **more** distinguished t the first. H4946
Nu 24: 7 "Their king will be greater t Agag; their H4946
Dt 1:28 people are stronger and taller t we are; H4946
Dt 3:11 iron and was *more t* nine cubits long and AIT
Dt 4:38 stronger t you and to bring you H4946
Dt 7: 1 seven nations larger and stronger t you— H4946
Dt 7: 7 you were **more** numerous t other peoples, H4946
Dt 7:14 will be blessed **more** t any other people; H4946
Dt 7:17 "These nations are stronger t we are. H4946
Dt 9: 1 nations greater and stronger t you, H4946
Dt 9:14 stronger and **more** numerous t they." H4946
Dt 11:23 nations larger and stronger t you. H4946
Dt 17:20 himself better t his fellow Israelites H4946
Dt 20: 1 chariots and an army greater t yours, H4946
Dt 25: 3 judge must not impose **more** *t* forty lashes. AIT
Dt 25: 3 If the guilty party is flogged more t that H6584
Dt 30: 5 numerous t your ancestors. H4946
Jos 4:18 **No sooner** had they set their feet on the dry ground t H3869
Jos 10: 2 it was larger t Ai, and all its men H4946
Jos 10:11 died from the hail t were killed by the H4946
Jos 19: 9 Judah's portion was more t they needed. H4946
Jos 22:19 **other** t the altar of the LORD our God H4946+1187
Jos 22:29 **other** t the altar of the LORD H4946+4200+963
Jdg 2:19 to ways **even more** corrupt t those of their H4946
Jdg 6:27 he did it at night **rather** t in the daytime. H4946
Jdg 7:12 no more be counted t the sand on the H3869
Jdg 7:14 can be nothing **other** t the sword of Gideon H561
Jdg 8: 2 grapes better t the full grape harvest H4946
Jdg 8:33 **No sooner** had Gideon died t the H3869+889
Jdg 11:25 Are you any better t Balak son of Zippor H4946
Jdg 14:18 said to him, "What is sweeter t honey? H4946
Jdg 14:18 What is stronger t a lion?" Samson said to H4946
Jdg 16:30 many **more** when he died t while he H4946
Jdg 18:19 in Israel as priest **rather** t just one man's H196
Ru 1:13 It is more bitter for me t for you, because H4946
Ru 3:10 kindness is greater t that which you H4946
Ru 3:12 is another who is **more** closely related t I. H4946
Ru 4:15 you and who is better to you t seven sons, H4946
1Sa 1: 8 Don't I mean more to you t ten sons?" H4946
1Sa 2:29 honor your sons **more** t me by fattening H4946
1Sa 9: 2 he was a head taller t anyone else. H4946
1Sa 10:23 he was a head taller t any of the others. H4946
1Sa 15:22 To obey is better t sacrifice, and to heed H4946
1Sa 15:22 to heed is **better** t the fat of rams. H4946
1Sa 15:28 of your neighbors—to one better t you. H4946
1Sa 17:42 over and saw that he was little more t a boy, NDT
1Sa 18:25 wants no **other** price for the bride t a H3954
1Sa 18:30 David met with **more** success t the rest of H4946
1Sa 24:17 "You are **more** righteous t I," he said. "You H4946
1Sa 29: 4 **better** could he regain his master's favor t H4202
2Sa 1:23 They were swifter t eagles, they were H4946
2Sa 1:23 than eagles, they were stronger t lions. H4946
2Sa 1:26 **more** wonderful t that of women. H4946
2Sa 6:21 who chose me **rather** t your father or H4946
2Sa 6:22 I will become even **more** undignified t this, H4946
2Sa 13:14 since he was stronger t she, he raped H4946
2Sa 13:15 he hated her more t he had loved her. H4946
2Sa 13:16 be a greater wrong t what you have H4946
2Sa 17:14 the Arkite is better t that of Ahithophel." H4946
2Sa 18: 8 up more men that day t the sword. H4946
2Sa 19: 7 will be worse for you t all the calamities H4946
2Sa 19:43 have a **greater** claim on David t you have H4946
2Sa 19:43 claims **even more** forcefully t the men of H4946
2Sa 20: 5 he took longer t the time the king had set H4946
2Sa 20: 6 Bikri will do us **more** harm t Absalom did. H4946
2Sa 23:19 he not held in greater honor t the Three? H4946

2Sa 23:23 He was held in **greater** honor **t** any of the H4946
1Ki 1:37 throne even greater **t** the throne of my H4946
1Ki 1:47 name **more** famous **t** yours and his H4946
1Ki 1:47 than yours and his throne greater **t** yours! H4946
1Ki 2:32 were better men and **more** upright **t** he. H4946
1Ki 4:30 wisdom was greater **t** the wisdom of all H4946
1Ki 4:30 greater **t** all the wisdom of Egypt. H4946
1Ki 4:31 He was wiser **t** anyone else, including H4946
1Ki 4:31 the Ezrahite—wiser **t** Heman, Kalkol and NDT
1Ki 10:23 in riches and wisdom **t** all the other kings H4946
1Ki 12:10 little finger is thicker **t** my father's waist. H4946
1Ki 14: 9 You have done **more** evil **t** all who lived H4946
1Ki 14:22 his jealous anger **more t** those who were H4946
1Ki 16:22 followers **proved stronger** *t* those of Tibni AIT
1Ki 16:25 LORD and sinned **more t** all those before H4946
1Ki 16:30 did **more** evil in the eyes of the LORD **t** any H4946
1Ki 16:33 **t** did all the kings of Israel before him. H4946
1Ki 19: 4 I am no better **t** my ancestors. H4946
1Ki 20:23 surely we will be stronger **t** they. H4946
1Ki 20:25 Then surely we will be stronger **t** they." H4946
2Ki 5:12 better **t** all the waters of Israel? H4946
2Ki 6:16 are with us are more **t** those who are with H4946
2Ki 21: 9 that they did **more** evil **t** the nations the H4946
2Ki 21:11 has done more evil **t** the Amorites who H4946
2Ki 25:16 of the LORD, was **more t** could be weighed. H4202
2Ki 25:28 seat of honor **higher t** those of the H4946+6584
1Ch 4: 9 Jabez was **more** honorable **t** his brothers H4946
1Ch 11:25 He was held in **greater** honor **t** any of the H4946
1Ch 22: 3 more bronze **t** could be weighed. H401
1Ch 22: 4 provided **more** cedar logs **t** could be H4200+401
1Ch 24: 4 Eleazar's descendants **t** among Ithamar's, H4946
2Ch 2: 5 our God is greater **t** all other gods. H4946
2Ch 9:12 he gave her **more t** she had H4946+4200+963
2Ch 9:22 in riches and wisdom **t** all the other kings H4946
2Ch 10:10 little finger is thicker **t** my father's waist. H4946
2Ch 11:21 of Absalom **more t** any of his other H4946
2Ch 17: 4 his commands **rather t** the practices H2256+4202
2Ch 20:25 of value—**more** *t* they could take away. AIT
2Ch 21:13 own family, men who were better **t** you. H4946
2Ch 25: 9 "The LORD can give you much **more t** that." H4946
2Ch 29:34 **more** conscientious in consecrating themselves **t** H4946
2Ch 32: 7 is a greater power with us **t** with him. H4946
2Ch 33: 9 that they did **more** evil **t** the nations the H4946
Ezr 9: 6 our sins *are* **higher t** our H8049+4200+5087+2025
Ezr 9:13 us less **t** our sins **deserved** and have given H4946
Ne 7: 2 feared God **more t** most people do. H4946
Est 1:19 to someone else who is better **t** she. H4946
Est 2:15 nothing **other t** what Hegai, H3954+561
Est 2:17 attracted to Esther **more t** to any of the H4946
Est 2:17 favor and approval **more t** any of the other H4946
Est 3: 1 a seat of honor **higher t** that of all H6584+4946
Est 6: 6 the king would rather honor **t** me?" H3463+4946
Job 3:21 who search for it **more t** for hidden H4946
Job 4:17 'Can a mortal be **more** righteous **t** God H4946
Job 4:17 a strong man be **more** pure **t** his Maker? H4946
Job 4:19 are crushed **more readily t** a moth! H4200+7156
Job 7: 6 "My days are swifter **t** a weaver's shuttle H4974
Job 7:15 death, **rather t** this body of mine. H4946
Job 8:12 they wither **more quickly t** grass. H4200+7156
Job 9:25 "My days are swifter **t** a runner; they fly H4974
Job 11: 8 They are **higher** *t* the heavens above—what AIT
Job 11: 8 They are deeper **t** the depths below H4946
Job 11: 9 measure is longer **t** the earth and wider H4946
Job 11: 9 longer than the earth and wider **t** the sea. H4974
Job 11:12 witless can **no more** become wise **t** a wild H2256
Job 11:17 Life will be brighter **t** noonday, and H4946
Job 15:10 on our side, men even older **t** your father. H4946
Job 23:12 words of his mouth **more t** my daily bread. H4946
Job 30: 1 men younger **t** I, whose fathers I H4946
Job 32: 2 Job for justifying himself **rather t** God. H4946
Job 32: 4 to Job because they were older **t** he. H4946
Job 33:12 not right, for God is greater **t** any mortal. H4946
Job 35:11 who teaches us **more t** he teaches the H4946
Job 35:11 makes us wiser **t** the birds in the sky? H4946
Job 42:12 part of Job's life **more t** the former part. H4946
Ps 8: 5 them a little lower **t** the angels and H4946
Ps 19:10 They are **more** precious **t** gold, than much H4946
Ps 19:10 precious than gold, **t** much pure gold H4946
Ps 19:10 they are sweeter **t** honey, than honey from H4946
Ps 19:10 than honey, **t** honey from the honeycomb. NDT
Ps 37:16 the righteous have **t** the wealth of many H4946
Ps 40:12 They are more **t** the hairs of my head, and H4946
Ps 51: 7 wash me, and I will be whiter **t** snow. H4946
Ps 52: 3 You love evil **rather t** good, falsehood H4946
Ps 52: 3 falsehood **rather t** speaking the truth. H4946
Ps 55:21 his words are **more** soothing **t** oil, yet they H4946
Ps 61: 2 lead me to the rock that is higher **t** I. H4946
Ps 63: 3 Because your love is better **t** life, my lips H4946
Ps 69:31 This will please the LORD **more t** an ox H4946
Ps 69:31 more **t** a bull with its horns and hooves. NDT
Ps 76: 4 **more** majestic **t** mountains rich with game H4946
Ps 81: 9 shall not worship any god **other t** me. H5797S
Ps 84:10 day in your courts **t** a thousand elsewhere; H4946
Ps 84:10 the house of my God **t** dwell in the tents H4946
Ps 87: 2 the gates of Zion **more t** all the other H4946
Ps 89: 7 he is more awesome **t** all who surround H6584
Ps 93: 4 Mightier **t** the thunder of the great waters H4946
Ps 93: 4 mightier **t** the breakers of the sea NDT
Ps 108: 4 is your love, **higher t** the heavens H4946+6584
Ps 118: 8 refuge in the LORD **t** to trust in humans. H4946
Ps 118: 9 take refuge in the LORD **t** to trust in princes. H4946
Ps 119:72 mouth is **more** precious to me **t** thousands H4946
Ps 119:98 me and make me wiser **t** my enemies. H4946
Ps 119:99 I have **more** insight **t** all my teachers, for I H4946
Ps 119:100 I have **more** understanding **t** the elders H4946
Ps 119:103 my taste, sweeter **t** honey to my mouth! H4946
Ps 119:127 I love your commands **more t** gold, H4946
Ps 119:127 more than gold, **more t** pure gold, H4946
Ps 130: 6 wait for the Lord **more t** watchmen wait H4946
Ps 130: 6 more **t** watchmen wait for the morning. NDT
Ps 135: 5 is great, that our Lord is **greater t** all gods. H4946
Pr 3:14 she is **more** profitable **t** silver and H4946
Pr 3:14 than silver and yields **better** returns **t** gold. H4946
Pr 3:15 She is **more** precious **t** rubies; nothing you H4946
Pr 5: 3 and her speech is smoother **t** oil; H4946
Pr 8:10 of silver, knowledge **rather t** choice gold, H4946
Pr 8:11 wisdom is **more** precious **t** rubies, and H4946
Pr 8:19 My fruit is better **t** fine gold; what I yield H4946
Pr 12: 9 have a servant **t** pretend to be H4946
Pr 15:16 the fear of the LORD **t** great wealth with H4946
Pr 15:17 vegetables with love **t** a fattened calf with H4946
Pr 16: 8 with righteousness **t** much gain with H4946
Pr 16:16 How much better to get wisdom **t** gold, to H4946
Pr 16:16 than gold, to get insight **rather t** silver! H4946
Pr 16:19 with the oppressed **t** to share plunder with H4946
Pr 16:32 Better a patient person **t** a warrior, one H4946
Pr 16:32 with self-control **t** one who takes a city. H4946
Pr 17: 1 with peace and quiet **t** a house full of H4946
Pr 17:10 person **more t** a hundred lashes H4946
Pr 17:12 **Better** to meet a bear robbed of her cubs **t** H440
Pr 18:19 wronged is **more** unyielding **t** a fortified H4946
Pr 18:24 is a friend who sticks closer **t** a brother. H4946
Pr 19: 1 walk is blameless **t** a fool whose lips are H4946
Pr 19:22 is unfailing love; better to be poor **t** a liar. H4946
Pr 21: 3 just is **more** acceptable to the LORD **t** H4946
Pr 21: 9 a corner of the roof **t** share a house with a H4946
Pr 21:19 to live in a desert **t** with a quarrelsome H4946
Pr 22: 1 good name is **more** desirable **t** great H4946
Pr 22: 1 to be esteemed is better **t** silver or gold. H4946
Pr 25: 7 **t** for him to humiliate you before his H4946
Pr 25:24 a corner of the roof **t** share a house with a H4946
Pr 26:12 There is **more** hope for a fool **t** for them. H4946
Pr 26:16 wiser in his own eyes **t** seven people who H4946
Pr 27: 3 a fool's provocation is heavier **t** both. H4946
Pr 27: 5 Better is open rebuke **t** hidden love. H4946
Pr 27:10 a neighbor nearby **t** a relative far away. H4946
Pr 28: 6 walk is blameless **t** the rich whose ways H4946
Pr 28:23 the end gain favor **rather t** one who has a H4946
Pr 29:20 There is more hope for a fool **t** for them. H4946
Pr 31:10 She is worth far **more t** rubies. H4946
Ecc 1: 8 are wearisome, **more t** one can say. H4202
Ecc 1:16 in wisdom **more t** anyone who has H6584
Ecc 2: 7 herds and flocks **t** anyone in Jerusalem H4946
Ecc 2: 9 greater by far **t** anyone in Jerusalem H4946
Ecc 2:12 king's successor do **t** what has already been NDT
Ecc 2:13 I saw that wisdom is better **t** folly, just as H4946
Ecc 2:13 than folly, just as light is better **t** darkness. H4946
Ecc 2:24 do nothing better **t** to eat and drink and H8611
Ecc 3:12 better for people **t** to be happy and H3954+561
Ecc 3:22 a person **t** to enjoy their work H4946+889
Ecc 4: 2 are happier **t** the living, who are still H4946
Ecc 4: 3 But better **t** both is the one who has never H4946
Ecc 4: 6 with tranquillity **t** two handfuls with toil H4946
Ecc 4: 9 Two are better **t** one, because they have a H4946
Ecc 4:13 a poor but wise youth **t** an old but foolish H4946
Ecc 5: 1 Go near to listen **rather t** to offer the H4946
Ecc 5: 5 not to make a vow **t** to make one and not H4946
Ecc 6: 3 I say that a stillborn child is better off **t** he. H4946
Ecc 6: 5 it has **more** rest **t** does that man— H4946
Ecc 6: 9 what the eye sees **t** the roving of the H4946
Ecc 7: 1 A good name is better **t** fine perfume H4946
Ecc 7: 1 the day of death **better t** the day of birth. H4946
Ecc 7: 2 a house of mourning **t** to go to a house of H4946
Ecc 7: 3 Frustration is better **t** laughter, because a H4946
Ecc 7: 5 of a wise person **t** to listen to the song H4946
Ecc 7: 8 end of a matter is better **t** its beginning, H4946
Ecc 7: 8 beginning, and patience is better **t** pride. H4946
Ecc 7:10 "Why were the old days better **t** these?" H4946
Ecc 7:19 wise person **more** powerful **t** ten rulers in H4946
Ecc 7:26 I find **more** bitter **t** death the woman who H4946
Ecc 8:15 under the sun **t** to eat and drink and H3954+561
Ecc 9: 4 even a live dog is better off **t** a dead lion! H4946
Ecc 9:16 "Wisdom is better **t** strength." But the H4946
Ecc 9:17 wise are **more** to be heeded **t** the shouts H4946
Ecc 9:18 Wisdom is better **t** weapons of war, but H4946
SS 1: 2 your love is **more** delightful **t** wine. H4946
SS 1: 4 we will praise your love **more t** wine. H4946
SS 4:10 How **much more** pleasing is your love **t** H4946
SS 4:10 of your perfume **more t** any spice! H4946
SS 5: 9 How is your beloved **better t** others, most H4946
SS 5: 9 How is your beloved **better t** others, that H4946
Isa 1:11 "*I* **have more t enough** *of* burnt offerings H8425
Isa 5: 4 my vineyard **t** I have done for it? H2256+4202
Isa 13:12 I will make people scarcer **t** pure gold H4946
Isa 13:12 pure gold, **more** rare **t** the gold of Ophir. H4946
Isa 32:10 **In little more t** a year you who feel H3427+6584
Isa 40:17 by him as worthless and **less t** nothing. H4946
Isa 40:24 **t** he blows on them and they wither H2256+1685
Isa 41:24 But you are **less t** nothing and your works H4946
Isa 54: 1 of the desolate woman **t** of her who has a H4946
Isa 55: 9 "As the heavens are higher **t** the earth, so H4946
Isa 55: 9 so are my ways higher **t** your ways and my H4946
Isa 55: 9 ways and my thoughts **t** your thoughts. H4946
Isa 56: 5 a name better **t** sons and daughters; H4946
Isa 66: 8 Yet **no sooner** is Zion in labor **t** she gives H1685
Jer 3:11 Israel is **more** righteous **t** unfaithful Judah H4946
Jer 4:13 whirlwind, his horses are swifter **t** eagles. H4946
Jer 5: 3 their faces harder **t** stone and refused to H4946
Jer 7:26 did **more** evil **t** their ancestors. H4946
Jer 15: 8 their widows **more** numerous **t** the sand of H4946
Jer 16:12 have behaved **more** wickedly **t** your H4946
Jer 31:11 from the hand of those stronger **t** they. H4946
Jer 46:23 They are **more** numerous **t** locusts, they H4946
Jer 52:20 of the LORD, was **more t** could be weighed. H4202
Jer 52:32 a seat of honor higher **t** those of the other H4200
La 3: 2 made me walk in darkness **rather t** light; H4202
La 4: 6 of my people is greater **t** that of Sodom, H4946
La 4: 7 were brighter **t** snow and whiter than H4946
La 4: 7 were brighter than snow and whiter **t** milk, H4946
La 4: 7 their bodies **more** ruddy **t** rubies, their H4946
La 4: 8 But now they are blacker **t** soot; they are H4946
La 4: 9 sword are better off **t** those who die of H4946
La 4:19 pursuers were swifter **t** eagles in the sky; H4946
Eze 3: 9 like the hardest stone, harder **t** flint. H4946
Eze 5: 6 laws and decrees **more t** the nations and H4946
Eze 5: 7 You have been **more** unruly **t** the nations H4946
Eze 8:15 that are even more detestable **t** this." H4946
Eze 16:47 you soon became **more** depraved **t** they. H4946
Eze 16:51 have done more detestable things **t** they, H4946
Eze 16:52 Because your sins were **more** vile **t** theirs H4946
Eze 16:52 they appear **more** righteous **t** you. H4946
Eze 16:61 those who are older **t** you and those who H4946
Eze 23:11 she was **more** depraved **t** her sister. H4946
Eze 28: 3 Are you wiser **t** Daniel? Is no secret H4946
Eze 31: 5 So it towered higher **t** all the trees of the H4946
Eze 32:19 to them, 'Are you more favored **t** others? H4946
Eze 33:32 them you are **nothing more t** one who H3869
Eze 34: 8 cared for themselves **rather t** for my flock, H4202
Eze 36:11 will make you prosper **more t** before. H4946
Eze 42: 5 took **more** space from them **t** from the H4946
Eze 42: 6 in floor space **t** those on the lower and H4946
Da 1:10 you looking worse **t** the other young men H4946
Da 1:15 and **better** nourished **t** any of the H4946
Da 1:20 them ten times **better t** all the magicians H6584
Da 2:30 I have **greater** wisdom **t** anyone else A10427
Da 2:43 **any more t** iron mixes A10195+10341+10168
Da 3:19 heated seven times hotter **t** usual A10542
Da 3:28 up their lives **rather t** serve or worship A10379
Da 4:36 throne and became even greater **t** before. NDT
Da 7:20 that looked **more** imposing **t** the others A10427
Da 8: 3 the horns was longer **t** the other but grew H4946
Da 11: 2 who will be far richer **t** all the others. H4946
Da 11: 5 even stronger **t** he and will rule his H6584
Da 11:13 another army, larger **t** the first; and after H4946
Hos 2: 7 as at first, for then I was better off **t** now. H4946
Hos 6: 6 of God **rather t** burnt offerings. H4946
Am 6: 2 Are they better off **t** your two kingdoms? H4946
Am 6: 2 two kingdoms? Is their land larger **t** yours? H4946
Jnh 1:13 for the sea grew even wilder **t** before. NDT
Jnh 4: 3 for it is better for me to die **t** to live." H4946
Jnh 4: 8 "It would be better for me to die **t** to live." H4946
Jnh 4:11 there are more **t** a hundred and twenty H4946
Mic 7: 4 the most upright **worse t** a thorn hedge. H4946
Na 3: 8 Are you better **t** Thebes, situated on the H4946
Na 3:16 till they are **more numerous t** the stars in H4946
Hab 1: 8 Their horses are swifter **t** leopards, fiercer H4946
Hab 1: 8 than leopards, fiercer **t** wolves at dusk. H4946
Hab 1:13 up those **more** righteous **t** themselves? H4946
Hag 2: 9 house will be greater **t** the glory of the H4946
Zec 12: 7 may not be greater **t** that of Judah. H6584
Mt 3:11 after me comes one who is **more powerful** *t* I, AIT
Mt 5:29 part of your body **t** for your whole *G2779+3590*
Mt 5:30 part of your body **t** for your whole *G2779+3590*
Mt 5:47 what are you doing more **t** others? NDT
Mt 6:25 Is not life **more** *t* food, and the body more AIT
Mt 6:25 than food, and the body more **t** clothes? NDT
Mt 6:26 Are you not much more valuable *t* **they**? AIT
Mt 10:15 on the day of judgment **t** for that town. *G2445*
Mt 10:31 you are worth more *t* many **sparrows.** AIT
Mt 10:37 father or mother **more t** me is not worthy *G5642*
Mt 10:37 son or daughter **more t** me is not worthy *G5642*
Mt 11: 9 I tell you, and **more t** a prophet. *G4358*
Mt 11:11 not risen anyone greater *t* **John** the Baptist; AIT
Mt 11:11 in the kingdom of heaven is greater *t* **he.** AIT
Mt 11:22 Sidon on the day of judgment **t** for you. *G2445*
Mt 11:24 Sodom on the day of judgment **t** for you." *G2445*
Mt 12: 6 that something greater *t* **the temple** is here. AIT
Mt 12:12 much more valuable is a person *t* **a sheep**! AIT
Mt 12:41 now something greater *t* **Jonah** is here. AIT
Mt 12:42 now something greater *t* **Solomon** is here. AIT
Mt 12:45 with it seven other spirits more wicked *t* **itself**, AIT
Mt 12:45 condition of that person is worse *t* **the first.** AIT
Mt 18: 8 maimed or crippled **t** to have two hands *G2445*
Mt 18: 9 life with one eye **t** to have two eyes and *G2445*
Mt 18:13 about that one sheep **t** about the *G2445*
Mt 19:24 the eye of a needle **t** for someone who is *G2445*
Mt 21:36 to them, more *t* **the first** *time*, and the AIT
Mt 26:53 my disposal more *t* **twelve** legions of angels? AIT
Mt 27:64 This last deception will be worse *t* **the first.**" AIT
Mk 1: 7 "After me comes the one more powerful *t* **I.** AIT
Mk 6:37 take **more t half a year's wages**! *G1324+1357*
Mk 9: 3 whiter **t** anyone in the world could bleach *G3888*
Mk 9:43 enter life maimed **t** with two hands to go *G2445*
Mk 9:45 enter life crippled **t** to have two feet and *G2445*
Mk 9:47 of God with one eye **t** to have two eyes *G2445*

Mk 10:25 the eye of a needle t for someone who is G2445
Mk 12:31 There is no commandment greater t these." AIT
Mk 12:33 is more important t all burnt offerings and AIT
Mk 12:43 put more into the treasury t all the others. AIT
Mk 14: 5 have been sold for more t a year's wages G2062
Lk 3:13 collect any more t you are required to," G4123
Lk 3:16 But one who is more powerful t I will come AIT
Lk 7:26 I tell you, and more t a prophet. G4358
Lk 7:28 of women there is no one greater t John; AIT
Lk 7:28 is least in the kingdom of God is greater t he." AIT
Lk 8: 8 a hundred times more t was sown. NDT
Lk 10:12 on that day for Sodom t for that town. G2445
Lk 10:14 Tyre and Sidon at the judgment t for you. G2445
Lk 11:26 takes seven other spirits more wicked t itself, AIT
Lk 11:26 condition of that person is worse t the first." AIT
Lk 11:31 now something greater t Solomon is here. AIT
Lk 11:32 now something greater t Jonah is here. AIT
Lk 12: 7 you are worth more t many sparrows. G1422
Lk 12:23 For life is more t food, and the body more AIT
Lk 12:23 more than food, and the body more t clothes. AIT
Lk 12:24 And how much more valuable you are t birds! AIT
Lk 13: 2 were worse sinners t all the other G4123
Lk 13: 4 think they were more guilty t all the others G4123
Lk 14: 8 more distinguished t you may have been AIT
Lk 15: 7 more rejoicing in heaven over one sinner who repents t G2445
Lk 16: 8 more shrewd in dealing with their own kind t G5642
Lk 16:17 earth to disappear t for the least stroke G2445
Lk 17: 2 around their neck t to cause one of these G2445
Lk 18:14 you that this man, rather t the other, went G4123
Lk 18:25 the eye of a needle t for someone who is G2445
Lk 21: 3 poor widow has put in more t all the others. AIT
Jn 1:50 You will see greater things t that." AIT
Jn 4: 1 baptizing more disciples t John— G2445
Jn 4:12 Are you greater t our father Jacob, who gave AIT
Jn 5:20 he will show him even greater works t these, AIT
Jn 5:36 "I have testimony weightier t that of John. AIT
Jn 6: 7 take more t half a year's wages to G1357+1324
Jn 7:31 will he perform more signs t this man?" AIT
Jn 8:53 Are you greater t our father Abraham? He AIT
Jn 10:29 is greater t all; no one can snatch AIT
Jn 11:18 was less t two miles from G6055+5084+1278
Jn 11:50 the people t that the whole G2779+3590
Jn 12:43 human praise more t praise from God. G2472
Jn 13:16 no servant is greater t his master, nor is a AIT
Jn 13:16 a messenger greater t the one who sent him. AIT
Jn 14:12 they will do even greater things t these AIT
Jn 14:28 to the Father, for the Father is greater t I. AIT
Jn 15:13 Greater love has no one t this: to lay down AIT
Jn 15:20 'A servant is not greater t his master.' If they AIT
Jn 16:12 say to you, more t you can now bear. G247+4024
Jn 17:14 of the world any more t I am of the G2777+4024
Jn 21:15 son of John, do you love me more t these?" AIT
Ac 5:29 must obey God rather t human beings! G2445
Ac 17:11 Jews were of more noble character t those in AIT
Ac 20:35 'It is more blessed to give t to receive.'" G2445
Ac 23:13 More t forty men were involved in this plot. AIT
Ac 23:21 because more t forty of them are waiting in AIT
Ac 24:11 that no more t twelve days ago I went up AIT
Ac 26:13 from heaven, brighter t the sun, blazing G5642
Ro 1:25 created things rather t the Creator— G4123
Ro 8:34 Jesus who died—more t that, who was G3437
Ro 8:37 things we are more t conquerors through G5664
Ro 12: 3 think of yourself more highly t you ought, G4123
Ro 13:11 is nearer now t when we first believed. G2445
Ro 14: 5 considers one day more sacred t another; G4123
1Co 1:25 foolishness of God is wiser t human wisdom, AIT
1Co 1:25 of God is stronger t human strength. AIT
1Co 3:11 foundation other t the one already laid G4123
1Co 7: 9 it is better to marry t to burn with passion. G2445
1Co 9:12 up with anything rather t hinder the G2671+3590
1Co 9:15 I would rather die t allow anyone to G2445
1Co 10:22 the Lord's jealousy? Are we stronger t he? AIT
1Co 11:17 your meetings do more harm t good. G4024+247
1Co 14: 5 is greater t the one who speaks in G2445
1Co 14:18 God that I speak in tongues more t all of you. AIT
1Co 14:19 to instruct others t ten thousand words in G2445
1Co 15: 6 he appeared to more t five hundred of the G2062
1Co 15:10 I worked harder t all of them—yet not I, but AIT
1Co 15:15 More t that, we are then found to be false G2779
1Co 15:32 in Ephesus with no more t human hopes, AIT
2Co 5:12 what is seen rather t in what is in G2779+3590
2Co 7: 7 so that my joy was greater t ever. G3437
2Co 10: 8 building you up rather t tearing you G2779+4024
2Co 11: 4 preaches a Jesus other t the Jesus we G257
2Co 12: 6 think more of me t is warranted by what I G5642
Gal 1: 8 preach a gospel other t the one we G4123
Gal 1: 9 to you a gospel other t what you accepted G4123
Gal 3:20 however, implies more t one party; but G4024
Gal 4:27 desolate woman t of her who has a G3437+2445
Eph 3: 8 Although I am less t the least of all the G1788
Eph 3:20 do immeasurably more t all we ask or G5642
Eph 4:10 one who ascended higher t all the heavens, AIT
Php 4:16 me aid more t once when I G562+2779+1489
Php 4:18 full payment and have more t enough. G4355
Col 2: 8 of this world rather t on Christ. G2779+4024
1Ti 1: 4 speculations rather t advancing God's G2445
1Ti 5: 8 the faith and is worse t an unbeliever. AIT
2Ti 3: 4 lovers of pleasure rather t lovers of God— G2445
Phm 9 It is as none other t Paul—an old man G5525
Phm 16 as a slave, but better t a slave, as a dear G5642
Phm 21 that you will do even more t I ask. G5642
Heb 2: 7 You made them a little lower t the angels; G4123
Heb 2: 9 who was made lower t the angels for a G4123
Heb 3: 3 found worthy of greater honor t Moses, G4123
Heb 3: 3 a house has greater honor t the house itself. AIT
Heb 4:12 Sharper t any double-edged sword, it G5642
Heb 6:16 swear by someone greater t themselves, NDT
Heb 9:23 themselves with better sacrifices t these. G4123
Heb 11: 4 brought God a better offering t Cain did. G4123
Heb 11:25 people of God rather t to enjoy the G2445
Heb 11:26 as of greater value t the treasures of Egypt, AIT
Heb 12:24 speaks a better word t the blood of Abel. G4123
1Pe 1: 7 of greater worth t gold, which perishes even AIT
1Pe 3:17 to suffer for doing good t for doing evil. G2445
2Pe 2:20 off at the end t they were at the beginning. AIT
2Pe 2:21 t to have known it and then to turn their G2445
1Jn 3:20 we know that God is greater t our hearts, AIT
1Jn 4: 4 is in you is greater t the one who is in the G2445
3Jn 4 I have no greater joy t to hear that my AIT
Rev 2:19 you are now doing more t you did at first. AIT

THANK (35) [THANKED, THANKFUL, THANKFULNESS, THANKING, THANKS, THANKSGIVING]

Lev 7:12 then along with this t offering they are to H9343
Lev 22:29 you sacrifice a t offering to the LORD, H9343
Dt 24:13 Then they will t you, and it will be H1385
1Ch 16: 4 the LORD, to extol, t, and praise the LORD H3344
1Ch 23:30 every morning to t and praise the LORD. H3344
2Ch 29:31 sacrifices and t offerings to the temple of H9343
2Ch 29:31 brought sacrifices and t offerings, H9343
2Ch 33:16 fellowship offerings and t offerings on it, H9343
Ps 50:14 "Sacrifice t offerings to God, fulfill your H9343
Ps 50:23 Those who sacrifice t offerings honor me H9343
Ps 56:12 I will present my t offerings to you. H9343
Ps 107:22 Let them sacrifice t offerings and tell of H9343
Ps 116:17 I will sacrifice a t offering to you and call H9343
Jer 17:26 bringing t offerings to the house of H9343
Jer 33:11 those who bring t offerings to the house H9343
Da 2:23 I t and praise you, God of my ancestors A10312
Am 4: 5 bread as a t offering and brag about H9343
Lk 17: 9 Will he t the servant because he G2400+5921
Lk 18:11 I t you that I am not like other people G2373
Jn 11:41 "Father, I t you that you have heard me. G2373
Ro 1: 8 I t my God through Jesus Christ for all of G2373
1Co 1: 4 I always t my God for you because of his G2373
1Co 1:14 I t God that I did not baptize any of you G2373
1Co 10:30 because of something I t God for? G2373
1Co 14:18 I t God that I speak in tongues more than G2373
Php 1: 3 I t my God every time I remember you. G2373
Col 1: 3 We always t God, the Father of our Lord G2373
1Th 1: 2 We always t God for all of you and G2373
1Th 2:13 And we also t God continually because G2373
1Th 3: 9 How can we t God enough for you in G2374
2Th 1: 3 We ought always to t God for you G2373
2Th 2:13 But we ought always to t God for you G2373
1Ti 1:12 I t Christ Jesus our Lord, who has G5921+2400
2Ti 1: 3 I t God, whom I serve, as my G5921+2400
Phm 4 I always t my God as I remember you in G2373

THANKED (2) [THANK]

Lk 17:16 threw himself at Jesus' feet and t him— G2373
Ac 28:15 of these people Paul t God and was G2373

THANKFUL (3) [THANK]

Col 3:15 body you were called to peace. And be t. G2375
Col 4: 2 yourselves to prayer, being watchful and t. G2374
Heb 12:28 shaken, let us be t, and so worship God G5921

THANKFULNESS (3) [THANK]

Lev 7:12 " 'If they offer it as an expression of t H9343
1Co 10:30 If I take part in the meal with t, why am I G5921
Col 2: 7 you were taught, and overflowing with t. G2374

THANKING (1) [THANK]

1Ch 25: 3 using the harp in t and praising the LORD. H3344

THANKS (72) [THANK]

1Ch 16:34 Give t to the LORD, for he is good; his love H3344
1Ch 16:35 that we may give t to your holy name H3344
1Ch 16:41 designated by name to give t to the LORD, H3344
1Ch 29:13 our God, we give you t, and praise your H3344
2Ch 5:13 in unison to give praise and t to the LORD. H3344
2Ch 7: 3 they worshiped and gave t to the LORD, H3344
2Ch 7: 6 which were used when he gave t, H2146
2Ch 20:21 "Give t to the LORD, for his love endures H3344
2Ch 31: 2 to give t and to sing praises at the gates H3344
Ne 12:31 I also assigned two large choirs to give t H9343
Ne 12:40 The two choirs that gave t then took their H9343
Ps 7:17 I will give t to the LORD because of his H3344
Ps 9: 1 I will give t to you, LORD, with all my heart H3344
Ps 35:18 I will give you t in the great assembly H3344
Ps 100: 4 give t to him and praise his name. H3344
Ps 106: 1 Give t to the LORD, for he is good; his love H3344
Ps 106:47 that we may give t to your holy name and H3344
Ps 107: 1 Give t to the LORD, for he is good; his love H3344
Ps 107: 8 Let them give t to the LORD for his H3344
Ps 107:15 Let them give t to the LORD for his H3344
Ps 107:21 Let them give t to the LORD for his H3344
Ps 107:31 Let them give t to the LORD for his H3344
Ps 118: 1 Give t to the LORD, for he is good; his love H3344
Ps 118:19 I will enter and give t to the LORD. H3344
Ps 118:21 I will give you t, for you answered me; you H3344
Ps 118:29 Give t to the LORD, for he is good; his love H3344
Ps 119:62 midnight I rise to give you t for your H3344
Ps 136: 1 Give t to the LORD, for he is good. His love H3344
Ps 136: 2 Give t to the God of gods. His love H3344
Ps 136: 3 Give t to the Lord of lords: His love H3344
Ps 136:26 Give t to the God of heaven. His love H3344
Jer 33:11 "Give t to the LORD Almighty, for H3344
Da 6:10 prayed, giving t to his God, just A10312
Mt 14:19 heaven, he gave t and broke the loaves. G2328
Mt 15:36 and when he had given t, he broke G2373
Mt 26:26 and when he had given t, he broke G2328
Mt 26:27 and when he had given t, he gave G2373
Mk 6:41 heaven, he gave t and broke the loaves. G2328
Mk 8: 6 had taken the seven loaves and given t, G2373
Mk 8: 7 he gave t for them also and told the G2328
Mk 14:22 and when he had given t, he broke G2328
Mk 14:23 and when he had given t, he gave G2373
Lk 2:38 she gave t to God and spoke about the G469
Lk 9:16 up to heaven, he gave t and broke them. G2328
Lk 22:17 taking the cup, he gave t and said, "Take G2373
Lk 22:19 he took bread, gave t and broke it, and G2373
Lk 24:30 he took bread, gave t, broke it and began G2328
Jn 6:11 took the loaves, gave t, and distributed to G2373
Jn 6:23 the bread after the Lord had given t. G2373
Ac 27:35 some bread and gave t to God in front of G2373
Ro 1:21 glorified him as God nor gave t to him, G2373
Ro 6:17 But t be to God that, though you used to G5921
Ro 7:25 T be to God, who delivers me through G5921
Ro 14: 6 so to the Lord, for they give t to God; and G2373
Ro 14: 6 does so to the Lord and gives t to God. G2373
1Co 10:16 which we give t a participation in G2328
1Co 11:24 and when he had given t, he broke it and G2373
1Co 14:17 You are giving t well enough, but no one G2373
1Co 15:57 But t be to God! He gives us the victory G5921
2Co 1:11 Then many will give t on our behalf for G2373
2Co 2:14 But t be to God, who always leads us as G5921
2Co 8:16 T be to God, who put into the heart of G5921
2Co 9:12 in many expressions of t to God. G2374
2Co 9:15 T be to God for his indescribable gift! G5921
Eph 1:16 I have not stopped giving t for you G2373
Eph 5:20 always giving t to God the Father for G2373
Col 1:12 and giving joyful t to the Father, who has G2373
Col 3:17 giving t to God the Father through him. G2373
1Th 5:18 give t in all circumstances; for this is God's G2373
Rev 4: 9 honor and t to him who sits on the throne G2374
Rev 7:12 wisdom and t and honor and power G2374
Rev 11:17 "We give t to you, Lord God Almighty, the G2373

THANKSGIVING (22) [THANK]

Lev 7:13 offering of t they are to present an H9343
Lev 7:15 offering of t must be eaten on the H9343
Ezr 3:11 With praise and t they sang to the LORD H3344
Ne 11:17 the director who led in t and prayer; H3344+9378
Ne 12: 8 was in charge of the songs of t. H2117
Ne 12:24 stood opposite them to give praise and t, H3344
Ne 12:27 dedication with songs of t and with the H9343
Ne 12:46 for the songs of praise and t to God. H3344
Ps 69:30 name in song and glorify him with t. H9343
Ps 95: 2 before him with t and extol him with H9343
Ps 100: 4 Enter his gates with t and his courts with H9343
Isa 51: 3 found in her, t and the sound of singing. H9343
Jer 30:19 them will come songs of t and the sound H9343
1Co 10:16 Is not the cup of t for which we give thanks G2330
1Co 14:16 say "Amen" to your t, since they do not G2374
2Co 4:15 people may cause t to overflow to the G2374
2Co 9:11 us your generosity will result in t to God. G2374
Eph 5: 4 which are out of place, but rather t. G2374
Php 4: 6 petition, with t, present your requests G2374
1Ti 2: 1 intercession and t be made for all people G2374
1Ti 4: 3 to be received with t by those who believe G2374
1Ti 4: 4 is to be rejected if it is received with t, G2374

THARSHISH (KJV) TRADING, TARSHISH

THAT (5820) [THAT'S] See Index of Articles Etc.

THAT'S (12) [BE, THAT]

Ge 42:21 t why this distress has come on us." H6584+4027
Ex 5:17 Pharaoh said, "Lazy, t what you are—lazy NDT
Ex 10:11 since t what you have been asking for." H2023
1Ki 1:45 resounds with it. T the noise you hear. H2085
2Ki 3:23 "T blood!" they said. "Those kings must H2296
2Ki 4:23 the Sabbath." "T all right," she said. NDT
2Ki 9:12 "T not true!" they said. "Tell us." Jehu said NDT
Est 5:12 "And t not all," Haman added. "I'm the only NDT
Jer 37:14 "T not true!" Jeremiah said. "I am not NDT
Mt 27: 4 they replied. "T your responsibility." AIT
Lk 22:38 are two swords." "T enough!" he replied. G1639
Ac 24:25 Felix was afraid and said, "T enough for now! AIT

THAWING (1)

Job 6:16 when darkened by t ice and swollen with NDT

THE (55924) See Index of Articles Etc.

THEATER (2)

Ac 19:29 all of them rushed into the t together. G2519
Ac 19:31 begging him not to venture into the t. G2519

THEBES (5)

Jer 46:25 to bring punishment on Amon god of T, H5530
Eze 30:14 fire to Zoan and inflict punishment on T. H5530
Eze 30:15 of Egypt, and wipe out the hordes of T. H5530
Eze 30:16 T will be taken by storm; Memphis will be H5530
Na 3: 8 Are you better than T, situated on the H5531

THEBEZ (2)
Jdg 9:50 Abimelek went to T and besieged it and H9324
2Sa 11:21 him from the wall, so that he died in T? H9324

THEFT (3) [THIEF]
Ex 22: 3 they must be sold to pay for their t. H1706
Mt 15:19 sexual immorality, t, false testimony G3113
Mk 7:21 come—sexual immorality, t, murder, G3113

THEFTS (1) [THIEF]
Rev 9:21 their sexual immorality or their t. G3092

THEIR (4400) [THEY] See Index of Articles Etc.

THEIRS (23) [THEY] See Index of Articles Etc.

THEM (5584) [THEY] See Index of Articles Etc.

THEME (3)
Ps 22:25 you comes the t of my praise in the great H9335
Ps 45: 1 is stirred by a noble t as I recite my verses H1821
Ps 119:54 decrees are the t of my song wherever I H2369

THEMSELVES (316) [SELF, THEY] See Index of Articles Etc.

THEN (2968) See Index of Articles Etc.

THEOPHILUS (2)
Lk 1: 3 orderly account for you, most excellent T, G2541
Ac 1: 1 In my former book, T, I wrote about all G2541

THERE (1894) [THERE'S] See Index of Articles Etc.

THERE'S (3) [BE, THERE]
2Ki 4:25 Gehazi, "Look! T the Shunammite! H2137
Pr 22:13 The sluggard says, "T a lion outside! I'll be NDT
Pr 26:13 A sluggard says, "T a lion in the road, NDT

THEREFORE (446)
Ge 32:32 T to this day the Israelites do not H6584+4027
Ex 6: 6 "T, say to the Israelites: 'I am the H4200+4027
Ex 9:18 T, at this time tomorrow I will send the H2180
Ex 20:11 T the LORD blessed the Sabbath day H6584+4027
Lev 11:45 to be your God; t be holy, because I am H2256
Lev 17:12 T I say to the Israelites, "None of H6584+4027
Lev 20:25 " 'You must t make a distinction between H2256
Nu 11:34 T the place was named Kibroth Hattaavah H2256
Nu 25:12 T tell him I am making my covenant H4200+4027
Dt 4:15 T watch yourselves very carefully, H2256
Dt 5:15 T the LORD your God has H6584+4027
Dt 7: 9 Know t that the LORD your God is God; H2256
Dt 7:11 T, take care to follow the commands H2256
Dt 10:16 Circumcise your hearts, t, and do not be H2256
Dt 11: 8 Observe t all the commands I am giving H2256
Dt 15:11 T I command you to be H6584+4027
Dt 28:48 t in hunger and thirst, in nakedness and H2256
Dt 29:27 T the LORD's anger burned against this H2256
Dt 32:52 T, you will see the land only from a H3954
Jos 7:26 T that place has been called the H6584+4027
Jdg 1:17 T it was called Hormah. H2256
Jdg 2:20 T the LORD was very angry with Israel and H2256
1Sa 2:30 "T the LORD, the God of Israel H4200+4027
1Sa 3:14 T I swore to the house of Eli, 'The H4200+4027
1Sa 14:38 Saul t said, "Come here, all you who are H2256
1Sa 25: 8 T be favorable toward my men, since we H2256
2Sa 6: 7 his irreverent act; t God struck him down H2256
2Sa 12:10 t, the sword will never depart from H2256
2Sa 22:50 T I will praise you, LORD, among the H6584+4027
1Ki 5: 5 I intend, t, to build a temple for the Name H2256
1Ki 13:22 T your body will not be buried in the tomb NDT
1Ki 20:42 T it is your life for his life, your people H2256
1Ki 22:19 "T hear the word of the LORD: H4200+4027
2Ki 1: 4 T this is what the LORD says: 'You H4200+4027
2Ki 1: 6 T you will not leave the bed you H4200+4027
2Ki 12: 7 T King Joash summoned Jehoiada the H2256
2Ki 17: 4 T Shalmaneser seized him and put him in H2256
2Ki 17:20 T the LORD rejected all the people of Israel H2256
2Ki 19: 4 T pray for the remnant that still survives." H2256
2Ki 19:32 "T this is what the LORD says H4200+4027
2Ki 21:12 T this is what the LORD, the God of H4200+4027
2Ki 22:20 T I will gather you to your ancestors H4200+4027
1Ch 22: 5 T I will make preparations for it. H5528
2Ch 1:12 t wisdom and knowledge will be given you NDT
2Ch 2: 7 "Send me, t, a man skilled to work in gold H6964
2Ch 12: 5 abandoned me; t, I now abandon you H2256
2Ch 18:18 "T hear the word of the LORD: H4200+4027
2Ch 24: 6 T the king summoned Jehoiada the chief H2256
2Ch 28: 5 T the LORD his God delivered him into the H2256
2Ch 29: 8 T, the anger of the LORD has fallen on H2256
2Ch 32:25 t the LORD's wrath was on him and on H2256
2Ch 32:26 t the LORD's wrath did not come on them H2256
Ezr 9:12 T, do not give your daughters in marriage H6964
Ne 4:13 T I stationed some of the people behind H2256
Ne 6: 6 and t you are building the wall. H6584+4027
Ne 7:65 The governor, t, ordered them not to eat H2256
Ne 9:17 T you did not desert them, H2256
Ne 9:32 "Now t, our God, the great God, mighty H2256
Ne 13:15 T I warned them against selling food on H2256
Est 1:19 "T, if it pleases the king, let him issue a NDT
Est 3: 4 T they told Haman about it to see H2256
Est 9:26 T these days were called Purim H6584+4027
Job 7:11 "T I will not keep silent; I will speak out in H1685
Job 10: 1 t I will give free rein to my complaint and NDT
Job 17: 4 t you will not let them triumph. H6584+4027
Job 32:10 "T I say: Listen to me; I too will tell H4200+4027
Job 37:24 T, people revere him, for does he H4200+4027
Job 42: 6 T I despise myself and repent in H6584+4027
Ps 1: 5 T the wicked will not stand in the H6584+4027
Ps 2:10 T, you kings, be wise; be warned, you H6964
Ps 16: 9 T my heart is glad and my tongue H4200+4027
Ps 18:49 T I will praise you, LORD, among the H6584+4027
Ps 25: 8 t he instructs sinners in his ways. H6584+4027
Ps 32: 6 T let all the faithful pray to you H6584+2296
Ps 42: 6 t I will remember you from the land H6584+4027
Ps 45: 7 hate wickedness; t God, your God, H6584+4027
Ps 45:17 t the nations will praise you for H6584+4027
Ps 46: 2 T we will not fear, though the earth H6584+4027
Ps 73: 6 T pride is their necklace; they H4200+4027
Ps 73:10 T their people turn to them and H4200+4027
Ps 106:40 T the LORD was angry with his people and H2256
Ps 119:104 precepts; t I hate every wrong path. H6584+4027
Ps 119:119 like dross; t I love your statutes. H4200+4027
Ps 119:129 are wonderful; t I obey them. H6584+4027
Pr 6:15 T disaster will overtake him in an H6584+4027
Ecc 5: 7 many words are meaningless. T fear God. H3954
Ecc 7:14 T, no one can discover H6584+1826+8611
Isa 1:24 T the Lord, the LORD Almighty, the H4200+4027
Isa 3:17 T the Lord will bring sores on the heads of H2256
Isa 5:13 T my people will go into exile for H4200+4027
Isa 5:14 T Death expands its jaws, opening H4200+4027
Isa 5:24 T, as tongues of fire lick up straw H4200+4027
Isa 5:25 T the LORD's anger burns against H6584+4027
Isa 7:14 T the Lord himself will give you a H4200+4027
Isa 8: 7 t the Lord is about to bring against H4200+4027
Isa 9:17 T the Lord will take no pleasure in H6584+4027
Isa 10:16 T, the Lord, the LORD Almighty, will H4200+4027
Isa 10:24 T this is what the Lord, the LORD H4200+4027
Isa 13:13 T I will make the heavens tremble H6584+4027
Isa 15: 4 T the armed men of Moab cry out H6584+4027
Isa 16: 7 T the Moabites wail, they wail H4200+4027
Isa 17:10 T, though you set out the finest H6584+4027
Isa 22: 4 T I said, "Turn away from me; let H6584+4027
Isa 24: 6 T a curse consumes the earth; its H6584+4027
Isa 24: 6 T earth's inhabitants are burned up H6584+4027
Isa 24:15 T in the east give glory to the LORD H6584+4027
Isa 25: 3 T strong peoples will honor you H6584+4027
Isa 28:14 T hear the word of the LORD, you H4200+4027
Isa 29:14 T once more I will astound these H4200+4027
Isa 29:22 T this is what the LORD, who H4200+4027
Isa 30: 7 T I call her Rahab the Do-Nothing H4200+4027
Isa 30:12 T this is what the Holy One of H4200+4027
Isa 30:16 flee on horses.' T you will flee! You H6584+4027
Isa 30:16 T your pursuers will be swift H6584+4027
Isa 30:18 t he will rise up to show you H4200+4027
Isa 37: 4 T pray for the remnant that still survives." H2256
Isa 37:33 "T this is what the LORD says H4200+4027
Isa 48: 5 T I told you these things long ago; before H2256
Isa 50: 7 T have I set my face like flint, and I H6584+4027
Isa 51:21 T hear this, you afflicted one H4200+4027
Isa 52: 6 T my people will know my name H4200+4027
Isa 52: 6 t in that day they will know that it is H4200+4027
Isa 53:12 T I will give him a portion among H4200+4027
Isa 65:13 T this is what the Sovereign LORD H4200+4027
Jer 2: 9 "T I bring charges against you H4200+4027
Jer 3: 3 T the showers have been withheld, and H2256
Jer 4:28 T the earth will mourn and the H6584+2296
Jer 5: 6 T a lion from the forest will attack H6584+4027
Jer 5:14 T this is what the LORD God H4200+4027
Jer 6:18 T hear, you nations; you who are H4200+4027
Jer 6:21 T this is what the LORD says: "I will H4200+4027
Jer 7:14 T, what I did to Shiloh I will now do to the H2256
Jer 7:20 " 'T this is what the Sovereign LORD H4200+4027
Jer 7:28 T say to them, 'This is the nation that has H2256
Jer 8:10 T I will give their wives to other H4200+4027
Jer 9: 7 T this is what the LORD Almighty H4200+4027
Jer 9:15 T this is what the LORD Almighty, H4200+4027
Jer 11:11 T this is what the LORD says: 'I will H4200+4027
Jer 11:21 T this is what the LORD says about H4200+4027
Jer 11:22 t this is what the LORD Almighty says: H4200+4027
Jer 12: 8 She roars at me; t I hate her. H6584+4027
Jer 14:15 T this is what the LORD says about H4200+4027
Jer 14:22 T our hope is in you, for you are the one H2256
Jer 15:19 T this is what the LORD says: "If you H4200+4027
Jer 16:21 "T I will teach them—this time I H4200+4027
Jer 18:11 "Now t say to the people of Judah and H2256
Jer 18:13 T this is what the LORD says H4200+4027
Jer 22:18 T this is what the LORD says about H4200+4027
Jer 23: 2 T this is what the LORD, the God of H4200+4027
Jer 23:12 "T their path will become slippery H4200+4027
Jer 23:15 T this is what the LORD Almighty H4200+4027
Jer 23:30 "T," declares the LORD, "I am H4200+4027
Jer 23:39 T, I will surely forget you and cast H4200+4027
Jer 25: 8 T the LORD Almighty says this H4200+4027
Jer 27:15 T, I will banish you and you will H4200+5100
Jer 28:16 T this is what the LORD says: 'I am H4200+4027
Jer 29:20 T, hear the word of the LORD, all you exiles H2256
Jer 29:28 T build houses and settle down; plant NDT
Jer 31:20 T my heart yearns for him; I have H6584+4027
Jer 32:28 T this is what the LORD says: I am H4200+4027
Jer 34:17 "T this is what the LORD says: You H4200+4027
Jer 35:17 "T this is what the LORD God H4200+4027
Jer 35:19 T this is what the LORD Almighty, H4200+4027
Jer 36:30 T this is what the LORD says about H4200+4027
Jer 44: 6 T, my fierce anger was poured out; it H2256
Jer 44:11 "T this is what the LORD Almighty H4200+4027
Jer 48:31 T I wail over Moab, for all Moab I H6584+4027
Jer 49:20 T, hear what the LORD has planned H4200+4027
Jer 50:18 T this is what the LORD Almighty H4200+4027
Jer 50:30 T, her young men will fall in the H4200+4027
Jer 50:45 T, hear what the LORD has planned H4200+4027
Jer 51: 7 t they have now gone mad. H6584+4027
Jer 51:36 T this is what the LORD says: "See, H4200+4027
La 3:21 I call to mind and t I have hope: H6584+4027
La 3:24 is my portion; t I will wait for him." H6584+4027
Eze 5: 7 "T this is what the Sovereign LORD H4200+4027
Eze 5: 8 "T this is what the Sovereign LORD H4200+4027
Eze 5:10 T in your midst parents will eat their H4200+4027
Eze 5:11 T as surely as I live, declares the H4200+4027
Eze 7:20 t I will make it a thing unclean for H6584+4027
Eze 8:18 T I will deal with them in anger; H2256+1685
Eze 11: 4 T prophesy against them; prophesy H4200+4027
Eze 11: 7 "T this is what the Sovereign LORD H4200+4027
Eze 11:16 "T say: 'This is what the Sovereign H4200+4027
Eze 11:17 "T say: 'This is what the Sovereign H4200+4027
Eze 12: 3 "T, son of man, pack your belongings H2256
Eze 12:28 "T say to them, 'This is what the H4200+4027
Eze 13: 8 " 'T this is what the Sovereign LORD H4200+4027
Eze 13:11 t tell those who cover it with whitewash that NDT
Eze 13:13 " 'T this is what the Sovereign LORD H4200+4027
Eze 13:20 " 'T this is what the Sovereign LORD H4200+4027
Eze 13:23 t you will no longer see false H4200+4027
Eze 14: 4 T speak to them and tell them H4200+4027
Eze 14: 6 "T say to the people of Israel, 'This H4200+4027
Eze 15: 6 "T this is what the Sovereign LORD H4200+4027
Eze 16:35 " 'T, you prostitute, hear the word H4200+4027
Eze 16:37 t I am going to gather all your H4200+4027
Eze 16:50 T I did away with them as you have seen. H2256
Eze 17:19 " 'T this is what the Sovereign LORD H4200+4027
Eze 18:30 "T, you Israelites, I will judge each H4200+4027
Eze 20:10 T I led them out of Egypt and brought H2256
Eze 20:27 "T, son of man, speak to the H4200+4027
Eze 20:30 "T say to the Israelites: 'This is H4200+4027
Eze 21: 6 "T groan, son of man! Groan before them H2256
Eze 21:12 with my people. T beat your breast. H4200+4027
Eze 21:24 "T this is what the Sovereign LORD H4200+4027
Eze 22: 4 T I will make you an object of scorn H6584+4027
Eze 22:19 T this is what the Sovereign LORD H4200+4027
Eze 23: 9 "T I delivered her into the hands of H4200+4027
Eze 23:22 "T, Oholibah, this is what the H4200+4027
Eze 23:35 "T this is what the Sovereign LORD H4200+4027
Eze 24: 9 " 'T this is what the Sovereign LORD H4200+4027
Eze 25: 4 t I am going to give you to the H4200+4027
Eze 25: 7 t I will stretch out my hand against H4200+4027
Eze 25: 9 t I will expose the flank of Moab H4200+4027
Eze 25:13 t this is what the Sovereign LORD H4200+4027
Eze 25:16 t this is what the Sovereign LORD H4200+4027
Eze 26: 3 t this is what the Sovereign LORD H4200+4027
Eze 28: 6 " 'T this is what the Sovereign LORD H4200+4027
Eze 29: 8 " 'T this is what the Sovereign LORD H4200+4027
Eze 29:10 t I am against you and against your H4200+4027
Eze 29:19 T this is what the Sovereign LORD H4200+4027
Eze 30:22 T this is what the Sovereign LORD H4200+4027
Eze 31:10 " 'T this is what the Sovereign LORD H4200+4027
Eze 31:14 T no other trees by the waters are H4200+5100
Eze 33:12 "T, son of man, say to your people, 'If H2256
Eze 33:25 T say to them, 'This is what the H4200+4027
Eze 34: 7 " 'T, you shepherds, hear the word H4200+4027
Eze 34: 9 t, you shepherds, hear the word of H4200+4027
Eze 34:20 " 'T this is what the Sovereign LORD H4200+4027
Eze 35: 6 t as surely as I live, declares the H4200+4027
Eze 35:11 t as surely as I live, declares the H4200+4027
Eze 36: 3 T prophesy and say, 'This is what H4200+4027
Eze 36: 4 t, mountains of Israel, hear the H4200+4027
Eze 36: 6 T prophesy concerning the land of H4200+4027
Eze 36: 7 T this is what the Sovereign LORD H4200+4027
Eze 36:14 t you will no longer devour people H4200+4027
Eze 36:22 "T say to the Israelites, 'This is H4200+4027
Eze 37:12 T prophesy and say to them: 'This is H4200+4027
Eze 38:14 "T, son of man, prophesy and say H4200+4027
Eze 39:25 "T this is what the Sovereign LORD H4200+4027
Eze 44:12 t I have sworn with uplifted hand H6584+4027
Da 3: 7 T, as soon as they heard A10353+10619+10180
Da 3:29 T I decree that the people of any nation A10221
Da 4:27 T, Your Majesty, be pleased to accept A10385
Da 5:24 T he sent the hand that wrote the A10089+10008
Da 9:11 "T the curses and sworn judgments H2256
Da 9:23 T, consider the word and understand the H2256
Hos 2: 6 T I will block her path with H4200+4027
Hos 2: 9 "T I will take away my grain when H4200+4027
Hos 2:14 "T I am now going to allure her; H4200+4027
Hos 4:13 T your daughters turn to H6584+4027
Hos 6: 5 T I cut you in pieces with my H6584+4027
Hos 10: 4 t lawsuits spring up like poisonous weeds H2256
Hos 13: 3 T they will be like the morning mist H4027+4200
Am 3: 2 t I will punish you for all your sins." H6584+4027
Am 3:11 T this is what the Sovereign LORD H4200+4027
Am 4:12 "T this is what I will do to you H4200+4027
Am 5:11 T, though you have built H4200+4027+3610
Am 5:13 T the prudent keep quiet in such H4200+4027
Am 5:16 T this is what the Lord, the LORD H4200+4027
Am 5:27 T I will send you into exile beyond H2256
Am 6: 7 T you will be among the first to go H4200+4027
Am 7:17 "T this is what the LORD says: H4200+4027
Mic 1: 6 "T I will make Samaria a heap of rubble H2256
Mic 1:14 T you will give parting gifts to H4200+4027
Mic 2: 3 T, the LORD says: "I am planning H4200+4027
Mic 2: 5 T you will have no one in the H4200+4027

T

Mic 3: 6 **T** night will come over you, without H4200+4027
Mic 3:12 **T** because of you, Zion will be H4200+4027
Mic 5: 3 **T** Israel will be abandoned until H4200+4027
Mic 6:13 **T**, I have begun to destroy you, to H2256+1685
Mic 6:16 **T** I will give you over to ruin and H4200+5100
Hab 1: 4 **T** the law is paralyzed, and justice H6584+4027
Hab 1:16 **T** he sacrifices to his net and burns H6584+4027
Zep 2: 9 **T**, as surely as I live," declares the H4200+4027
Zep 3: 8 **T** wait for me," declares the LORD H4200+4027
Hag 1:10 **T**, because of you the heavens have H6584+4027
Zec 1: 3 **T** tell the people: This is what the LORD H2256
Zec 1:16 "**T** this is what the LORD says: 'I will H4200+4027
Zec 8:19 **T** love truth and peace. H2256
Zec 10: 2 **T** the people wander like sheep H6584+4027
Mt 5:19 **T** anyone who sets aside one of the least *G4036*
Mt 5:23 "**T**, if you are offering your gift at the altar *G4036*
Mt 5:48 Be perfect, **t**, as your heavenly Father is *G4036*
Mt 6:25 "**T** I tell you, do not worry about *G1328+4047*
Mt 6:34 **T** do not worry about tomorrow, for *G4036*
Mt 7:24 "**T** everyone who hears these words of *G4036*
Mt 9:38 Lord of the harvest, **t**, to send out workers *G4036*
Mt 10:16 **T** be as shrewd as snakes and as innocent *G4036*
Mt 12:12 **T** it is lawful to do good on the Sabbath." *G6063*
Mt 13:52 "**T** every teacher of the law who *G1328+4047*
Mt 18: 4 **T**, whoever takes the lowly position of this *G4036*
Mt 18:23 "**T**, the kingdom of heaven is like a *G1328+4047*
Mt 19: 6 **T** what God has joined together, let no *G4036*
Mt 21:40 "**T**, when the owner of the vineyard comes *G4036*
Mt 21:43 "**T** I tell you that the kingdom of *G1328+4047*
Mt 23:20 **T**, anyone who swears by the altar swears *G4036*
Mt 23:34 **T** I am sending you prophets and *G1328+4047*
Mt 24:42 "**T** keep watch, because you do not know *G4036*
Mt 25:13 "**T** keep watch, because you do not know *G4036*
Mt 28:19 **T** go and make disciples of all nations *G4036*
Mk 10: 9 **T** what God has joined together, let no *G4036*
Mk 11:24 **T** I tell you, whatever you ask for in *G1328+4047*
Mk 13:35 "**T** keep watch because you do not know *G4036*
Lk 7:47 **T**, I tell you, her many sins have *G4005+5920*
Lk 8:18 **T** consider carefully how you listen *G4036*
Lk 10: 2 Lord of the harvest, **t**, to send out workers *G4036*
Lk 11:36 **T**, if your whole body is full of light, and *G4036*
Lk 11:50 **T** this generation will be held responsible *G2671*
Lk 12:22 "**T** I tell you, do not worry about *G1328+4047*
Lk 23:16 **T**, I will punish him and then release him." *G4036*
Lk 23:22 **T** I will have him punished and then *G4036*
Jn 7: 6 **T** Jesus told them, "My time is not yet *G4036*
Jn 9:15 **T** the Pharisees also asked him how he *G4036*
Jn 10: 7 **T** Jesus said again, "Very truly I tell you, *G4036*
Jn 11:45 **T** many of the Jews who had come to visit *G4036*
Jn 11:54 **T** Jesus no longer moved about publicly *G4036*
Jn 19:11 **T** the one who handed me over to *G1328+4047*
Jn 19:32 The soldiers **t** came and broke the legs of *G4036*
Ac 1:21 **T** it is necessary to choose one of the men *G4036*
Ac 2:26 **T** my heart is glad and my tongue *G1328+4047*
Ac 2:36 "**T** let all Israel be assured of this: God *G4036*
Ac 5:38 **T**, in the present case I advise you: Leave *G2779*
Ac 7:43 **T** I will send you into exile' beyond *G2779*
Ac 13:38 "**T**, my friends, I want you to know that *G4036*
Ac 15:19 "It is my judgment, **t**, that we should not *G1475*
Ac 15:27 **T** we are sending Judas and Silas to *G4036*
Ac 17:29 "**T** since we are God's offspring, we *G1475*
Ac 19:36 **T**, since these facts are undeniable, you *G4036*
Ac 20:26 **T**, I declare to you today that I am *G1484*
Ac 25:26 **T** I have brought him before all of you *G1475*
Ac 26: 3 controversies. **T**, I beg you to listen to *G1475*
Ac 28:28 "**T** I want you to know that God's salvation *G4036*
Ro 1:24 **T** God gave them over in the sinful *G1475*
Ro 2: 1 **t**, have no excuse, you who pass *G1475*
Ro 3:20 **T** no one will be declared righteous in *G1484*
Ro 4:16 **T**, the promise comes by faith, so *G1328+4047*
Ro 5: 1 **T**, since we have been justified through *G4036*
Ro 5:12 **T**, just as sin entered the world *G1328+4047*
Ro 6: 4 We were **t** buried with him through *G4036*
Ro 6:12 **T** do not let sin reign in your mortal body *G4036*
Ro 8: 1 **T**, there is now no condemnation for those *G726*
Ro 8:12 **T**, brothers and sisters, we have an *G726+4036*
Ro 9:16 It does not, **t**, depend on human *G726+4036*
Ro 9:18 **T** God has mercy on whom he wants *G726+4036*
Ro 11:22 Consider **t** the kindness and sternness of *G4036*
Ro 12: 1 **T**, I urge you, brothers and sisters, in view *G4036*
Ro 13: 5 **T**, it is necessary to submit to the *G1475*
Ro 13:10 **T** love is the fulfillment of the law. *G4036*
Ro 14:13 **T** let us stop passing judgment on one *G4036*
Ro 14:16 **T** do not let what you know is good be *G4036*
Ro 14:19 Let us **t** make every effort to do what *G726+4036*
Ro 15: 9 "**T** I will praise you among the *G1328+4047*
Ro 15:17 **T** I glory in Christ Jesus in my service to *G4036*
1Co 1: 7 **T** you do not lack any spiritual gift as you *G6063*
1Co 1:31 **T**, as it is written: "Let the one who boasts *G2671*
1Co 4: 5 **T** judge nothing before the appointed *G6063*
1Co 4:16 **T** I urge you to imitate me. *G4036*
1Co 5: 8 **T** let us keep the Festival, not with the old *G6063*
1Co 6: 4 **T**, if you have disputes about such matters *G4036*
1Co 6:20 **T** honor God with your bodies. *G1314*
1Co 8:13 **T**, if what I eat causes my brother or sister *G1478*
1Co 9:26 **T** I do not run like someone running *G5523*
1Co 10:14 **T**, my dear friends, flee from idolatry. *G1478*
1Co 12: 3 **T** I want you to know that no one who is *G1475*
1Co 14:39 **T**, my brothers and sisters, be eager to *G6063*
1Co 15:58 **T**, my dear brothers and sisters, stand firm. *G6063*
2Co 2: 8 I urge you, **t**, to reaffirm your love for him. *G1475*
2Co 3:12 **T**, since we have such a hope, we are very *G4036*
2Co 4: 1 **T**, since through God's mercy we *G1328+4047*
2Co 4:13 "I believed; **t** I have spoken." Since *G1475*
2Co 4:13 of faith, we also believe and **t** speak, *G1475*
2Co 4:16 **T** we do not lose heart. Though outwardly *G1475*
2Co 5: 6 **T** we are always confident and know that *G4036*
2Co 5:14 that one died for all, and **t** all died. *G726*
2Co 5:17 **T**, if anyone is in Christ, the new creation *G6063*
2Co 5:20 We are **t** Christ's ambassadors, as though *G4036*
2Co 6:17 **T**, "Come out from them and be separate *G1475*
2Co 7: 1 **T**, since we have these promises, dear *G4036*
2Co 8:24 **T** show these men the proof of your love *G4036*
2Co 12: 7 **T**, in order to keep me from becoming *G1475*
2Co 12: 9 **T** I will boast all the more gladly about *G4036*
Gal 3:21 Is the law, **t**, opposed to the promises of *G4036*
Gal 4:31 **T**, brothers and sisters, we are not children *G1475*
Gal 6:10 **T**, as we have opportunity, let us do *G726+4036*
Eph 2:11 **T**, remember that formerly you who are *G1475*
Eph 3:13 I ask you, **t**, not to be discouraged because *G1475*
Eph 4:25 **T** each of you must put off falsehood and *G1475*
Eph 5: 1 Follow God's example, **t**, as dearly loved *G4036*
Eph 5: 7 **T** do not be partners with them. *G4036*
Eph 5:17 **T** do not be foolish, but understand *G1328+4047*
Eph 6:13 **T** put on the full armor of God, so *G1328+4047*
Php 2: 1 **T** if you have any encouragement from *G4036*
Php 2: 9 **T** God exalted him to the highest place *G1475*
Php 2:12 **T**, my dear friends, as you have always *G6063*
Php 2:23 **t**, to send him as soon as I see *G4036*
Php 2:28 **T** I am all the more eager to send him, so *G4036*
Php 4: 1 **T**, my brothers and sisters, you whom I *G6063*
Col 2:16 **T** do not let anyone judge you by what *G4036*
Col 3: 5 Put to death, **t**, whatever belongs to your *G4036*
Col 3:12 **T**, as God's chosen people, holy and *G4036*
1Th 1: 8 **T** we do not need to say anything about it, *G6063*
1Th 3: 7 **T**, brothers and sisters, in all our *G1328+4047*
1Th 4: 8 **T**, anyone who rejects this instruction does *G5521*
1Th 4:18 **T** encourage one another with these words *G6063*
1Th 5:11 **T** encourage one another and build each *G1475*
2Th 1: 4 **T**, among God's churches we boast about *G6063*
1Ti 2: 8 **T** I want the men everywhere to pray *G4036*
2Ti 2:10 **T** I endure everything for the sake of *G1328+4047*
Titus 1:13 **T** rebuke them sharply, so *G1328+4005+162*
Phm 8 **T**, although in Christ I could be bold and *G1475*
Heb 1: 9 hated wickedness; **t** God, your God, *G1328+4047*
Heb 2: 1 attention, **t**, to what we have *G1328+4047*
Heb 3: 1 **T**, holy brothers and sisters, who share in *G3854*
Heb 4: 1 **T**, since the promise of entering his rest *G4036*
Heb 4: 6 **T** since it still remains for some to enter *G4036*
Heb 4:11 **t**, make every effort to enter that *G4036*
Heb 4:14 **T**, since we have a great high priest who *G4036*
Heb 6: 1 **T** let us move beyond the elementary *G1475*
Heb 7:25 **T** he is able to save completely those who *G3854*
Heb 10: 5 **T**, when Christ came into the world, he *G1475*
Heb 10:19 **T**, brothers and sisters, since we have *G4036*
Heb 11:16 **T** God is not ashamed to be called their *G1475*
Heb 12: 1 **T**, since we are surrounded by such a *G5521*
Heb 12:12 **T**, strengthen your feeble arms and weak *G1475*
Heb 12:28 **T**, since we are receiving a kingdom that *G1475*
Heb 13:15 Through Jesus, **t**, let us continually offer *G4036*
Jas 1:21 **T**, get rid of all moral filth and the evil that *G1475*
Jas 4: 4 **T**, anyone who chooses to be a friend of *G4036*
Jas 5:16 **T** confess your sins to each other and pray *G4036*
1Pe 1:13 **T**, with minds that are alert and fully *G1475*
1Pe 2: 1 **T**, rid yourselves of all malice and all *G4036*
1Pe 4: 1 **T**, since Christ suffered in his body, arm *G4036*
1Pe 4: 7 **T** be alert and of sober mind so that you *G4036*
1Pe 5: 6 Humble yourselves, **t**, under God's mighty *G4036*
2Pe 1:10 **T**, my brothers and sisters, make every *G1475*
2Pe 3:17 **T**, dear friends, since you have been *G4036*
1Jn 4: 5 the world and **t** speak from the *G1328+4047*
3Jn 8 We ought **t** to show hospitality to such *G4036*
Rev 1:19 **t**, what you have seen, what is *G4036*
Rev 2:16 Repent **t**! Otherwise, I will soon come to *G4036*
Rev 3: 3 Remember, **t**, what you have received *G4036*
Rev 7:15 **T**, "they are before the throne of *G1328+4047*
Rev 12:12 **T** rejoice, you heavens and you *G1328+4047*
Rev 18: 8 **T** in one day her plagues will *G1328+4047*

THESE (1112) [THIS] See Index of Articles Etc.

THESSALONIANS (2) [THESSALONICA]

1Th 1: 1 To the church *of* the **T** in God the Father *G2552*
2Th 1: 1 To the church *of* the **T** in God our Father *G2552*

THESSALONICA (7) [THESSALONIANS]

Ac 17: 1 they came to **T**, where there was a *G2553*
Ac 17:11 of more noble character than those in **T**, *G2553*
Ac 17:13 But when the Jews in **T** learned that Paul *G2553*
Ac 20: 4 Aristarchus and Secundus **from T**, Gaius *G2552*
Ac 27: 2 a Macedonian **from T**, was with us. *G2552*
Php 4:16 even when I was in **T**, you sent me aid *G2553*
2Ti 4:10 has deserted me and has gone to **T**. *G2553*

THEUDAS (1)

Ac 5:36 Some time ago **T** appeared, claiming to *G2554*

THEY (7211) [THEIR, THEIRS, THEM, THEMSELVES] See Index of Articles Etc.

THICK (37) [THICKER, THICKNESS]

Ge 15:12 a **t** and dreadful darkness came over H1524
Ex 19:16 with a **t** cloud over the mountain H3878
Ex 20:21 the **t darkness** where God was H6906
Ex 29: 2 **t loaves** without yeast and with olive oil H2705
Ex 29:23 one **t loaf** *with* olive oil *mixed in* H2705+4312
Lev 2: 4 either **t loaves** *made* without yeast and H2705
Lev 7:12 they are to offer **t loaves** made without H2705
Lev 7:12 and **t loaves** *of* the finest flour H2705
Lev 7:13 offering with **t loaves** *of* bread made with H2705
Lev 8:26 he took one **t loaf**, one thick loaf H2705
Lev 8:26 one **t loaf** *with* olive oil *mixed in*, and one H2705
Nu 6:15 yeast—**t loaves** with olive oil mixed in H2705
Nu 6:19 one **t loaf** and one thin loaf from the H2705
Jdg 7:12 had settled in the valley, **t** as locusts. H8044
2Sa 18: 9 went under the **t branches** *of* a large oak, H8449
1Ki 20:39 "Your servant went into the **t** *of* the battle H7931
2Ki 8:15 But the next day he took a **t cloth**, soaked H4802
Job 3: 6 That night—may **t darkness** seize it; may it H694
Job 15:26 defiantly charging against him with a **t** H6295
Job 22:14 **T clouds** veil him, so he does not see us H6265
Job 23:17 by the **t darkness** that covers my face. H694
Job 38: 9 its garment and wrapped it in **t darkness**, H6906
Ps 97: 2 Clouds and **t darkness** surround him H6906
Isa 60: 2 the earth and **t darkness** is over the H6906
Jer 51:58 "Babylon's **t** wall will be leveled and her H8146
Jer 52:21 each was four fingers **t**, and hollow. H6295
Eze 19:11 It towered high above the **t foliage** H6291
Eze 31: 3 on high, its top above the **t foliage.** H6291
Eze 31:10 the great cedar towered over the **t foliage**, H6291
Eze 31:14 lifting their tops above the **t foliage.** H6291
Eze 40: 5 one measuring rod **t** and one rod high. H8145
Eze 40: 7 walls between the alcoves were five cubits **t**. NDT
Eze 40: 9 cubits deep and its jambs were two cubits **t**. NDT
Eze 41: 5 it was six cubits **t**, and each side room NDT
Eze 41: 9 wall of the side rooms was five cubits **t**. H8145
Eze 41:12 the building was five cubits **t** all around, H8145
Rev 21:17 measurement, and it was 144 cubits **t**. NDT

THICKER (2) [THICK]

1Ki 12:10 'My little finger *is* **t** than my father's waist. H6286
2Ch 10:10 'My little finger *is* **t** than my father's waist. H6286

THICKET (6) [THICKETS]

Ge 22:13 up and there in a **t** he saw a ram caught H6019
Job 38:40 crouch in their dens or lie in wait in a **t**? H6109
Ps 74: 5 wielding axes to cut through a **t** *of* trees. H6020
Hos 2:12 I will make them a **t**, and wild animals H3623
Am 3: 4 a lion roar in the **t** when it has no prey? H3623
Zec 11: 3 the **lush t** *of* the Jordan is ruined! H1454

THICKETS (11) [THICKET]

1Sa 13: 6 they hid in caves and **t**, among the rocks, H2560
Isa 9:18 it sets the forest **t** ablaze, so that it rolls H6019
Isa 10:34 He will cut down the forest **t** with an ax H6019
Isa 17: 9 places abandoned to **t** and undergrowth. H3091
Isa 21:13 Dedanites, who camp in the **t** of Arabia, H3623
Jer 4:29 Some go into the **t**; some climb up H6266
Jer 12: 5 will you manage in the **t** *by* the Jordan? H1454
Jer 26:18 the temple hill a mound overgrown with **t**. H3623
Jer 49:19 up from Jordan's **t** to a rich pastureland, H1454
Jer 50:44 up from Jordan's **t** to a rich pastureland, H1454
Mic 3:12 the temple hill a mound overgrown with **t**. H3623

THICKNESS (2) [THICK]

1Ki 7:26 It was a handbreadth *in* **t**, and its rim was H6295
2Ch 4: 5 It was a handbreadth *in* **t**, and its rim was H6295

THIEF (24) [THEFT, THEFTS, THIEVES]

Ex 22: 2 "If a **t** is caught breaking in at night and is H1705
Ex 22: 7 the neighbor's house, the **t**, if caught, H1705
Ex 22: 8 But if the **t** is not found, the owner of the H1705
Job 24:14 in the night steals forth like a **t**. H1705
Ps 50:18 When you see a **t**, you join with him; you H1705
Pr 6:11 come on you like a **t** and scarcity like an H2143
Pr 6:30 do not despise a **t** if he steals to satisfy H1705
Pr 24:15 Do not lurk like a **t** near the house of the H8401
Pr 24:34 come on you like a **t** and scarcity like an H2143
Jer 2:26 "As a **t** is disgraced when he is caught, so H1705
Zec 5: 3 on one side, every **t** will be banished, and H1704
Zec 5: 4 enter the house of the **t** and the house of H1705
Mt 24:43 at what time of night the **t** was coming, *G3095*
Lk 12:33 where no **t** comes near and no moth *G3095*
Lk 12:39 known at what hour the **t** was coming, *G3095*
Jn 10: 1 in by some other way, is a **t** and a robber. *G3095*
Jn 10:10 The **t** comes only to steal and kill and *G3095*
Jn 12: 6 about the poor but because he was a **t**; *G3095*
1Th 5: 2 of the Lord will come like a **t** in the night. *G3095*
1Th 5: 4 that this day should surprise you like a **t**. *G3095*
1Pe 4:15 be as a murderer or **t** or any other kind of *G3095*
2Pe 3:10 But the day of the Lord will come like a **t** *G3095*
Rev 3: 3 I will come like a **t**, and you will not know *G3095*
Rev 16:15 I come like a **t**! Blessed is the one *G3095*

THIEVES (13) [THIEF]

Job 24:16 In the dark, *t* **break into** houses, but by day AIT
Job 30: 5 shouted at as if they were **t**. H1705
Pr 29:24 The accomplices of **t** are their own H1705
Isa 1:23 partners with **t**; they all love bribes H1705
Jer 48:27 Was she caught among **t**, that you shake H1705
Jer 49: 9 If **t** came during the night, would they not H1705
Hos 7: 1 They practice deceit, **t** break into houses H1705
Joel 2: 9 like **t** they enter through the windows. H1705
Ob 5 "If **t** came to you, if robbers in the night H1705
Mt 6:19 destroy, and where **t** break in and steal. *G3095*
Mt 6:20 where **t** do not break in and steal. *G3095*
Jn 10: 8 have come before me are **t** and robbers, *G3095*
1Co 6:10 **t** nor the greedy nor drunkards nor *G3095*

T

THIGH (20) [THIGHS]

Ge 24: 2 that he had, "Put your hand under my **t**. H3751
Ge 24: 9 his hand under the **t** *of* his master H3751
Ge 47:29 your hand under my **t** and promise that H3751
Ex 28:42 the body, reaching from the waist to the **t**. H3751
Ex 29:22 with the fat on them, and the right **t**. H8797
Ex 29:27 was waved and the **t** that was presented. H8797
Lev 7:32 are to give the right **t** of your fellowship H8797
Lev 7:33 offering shall have the right **t** as his share. H8797
Lev 7:34 is waved and the **t** that is presented and H8797
Lev 8:25 both kidneys and their fat and the right **t**. H8797
Lev 8:26 on the fat portions and on the right **t**. H8797
Lev 9:21 the right **t** before the LORD as a H8797
Lev 10:14 was waved and the **t** that was presented. H8797
Lev 10:15 The **t** that was presented and the breast H8797
Nu 6:20 was waved and the **t** that was presented. H8797
Nu 18:18 wave offering and the right **t** are yours. H8797
Jdg 3:16 strapped to his right **t** under his clothing. H3751
Jdg 3:21 sword from his right **t** and plunged it into H3751
1Sa 9:24 the cook took up the **t** with what was on it H8797
Rev 19:16 On his robe and on his **t** he has this name *G3611*

THIGHS (2) [THIGH]

Job 40:17 a cedar; the sinews of its **t** are close-knit. H7066
Da 2:32 arms of silver, its belly and **t** of bronze, A10334

THIN (17)

Ge 41: 6 **t** and scorched by the east wind. H1987
Ge 41: 7 The **t** heads of grain swallowed up the H1987
Ge 41:23 withered and **t** and scorched by the east H1987
Ge 41:24 The **t** heads of grain swallowed up the H1987
Ex 16:14 **t** flakes like frost on the ground appeared H1987
Ex 29: 2 and **t loaves** without yeast and brushed H8386
Ex 29:23 with olive oil mixed in, and one **t loaf**. H8386
Ex 39: 3 hammered out **t sheets** *of* gold and cut H7063
Lev 2: 4 mixed in or **t loaves** *made* without yeast H8386
Lev 7:12 **t loaves** made without yeast and brushed H8386
Lev 8:26 mixed in, and one **t loaf**, and he put H8386
Lev 13:30 deep and the hair in it is yellow and **t**, H1987
Nu 6:15 and **t loaves** brushed with olive oil. H8386
Nu 6:19 thick loaf and one **t loaf** from the basket, H8386
Jdg 7: 4 and *I will* **t** them **out** for you there. H7671
1Ch 23:29 offerings, the **t loaves** made without yeast H8386
Ps 109:24 way from fasting; my body *is* **t** and gaunt. H3950

THING (148) [SOMETHING, THINGS]

Ge 1:21 every living **t** with which the water H5883
Ge 7:16 in were male and female of every **living t**, H1414
Ge 7:21 Every **living t** that moved on land perished H1414
Ge 7:23 Every **living t** on the face of the earth was H3685
Ge 18:25 Far be it from you to do such a **t**—to kill H1821
Ge 19: 7 my friends. Don't **do** *this* **wicked t**. H8317
Ge 30:31 "But if you will do this *one* **t** for me, I will H1821
Ge 31:28 You have done a **foolish** *t*. AIT
Ge 32:19 are to say the same **t** to Esau when you H1821
Ge 34: 7 had done an **outrageous t** in Israel by H5576
Ge 34: 7 daughter—a *t that should* not **be done**. AIT
Ge 34:14 "We can't do such a **t**; we can't give our H1821
Ge 39: 9 could I do such a **wicked t** and sin against H8288
Ge 44: 5 *This is a* **wicked** *t* you have done.' AIT
Ge 44:17 "Far be it from me to do **such** *a t*! AIT
Ex 33:17 "I will do the very **t** you have asked H1821
Lev 11:46 every living **t** that moves about in the H5883
Lev 22: 5 he touches any **crawling t** that makes him H9238
Lev 22: 6 who touches **any such t** will be unclean H2257S
Nu 14:28 to you the **very t** I heard you H3869+889+4027
Dt 7:26 Do not bring a **detestable t** into your H9359
Dt 9:21 Also I took that **sinful t** *of* yours, the calf H2633
Dt 11: 6 tents and every **living t** that belonged to H3685
Dt 13:11 among you will do such an evil **t** again. H1821
Dt 13:14 that this **detestable t** has been done H9359
Dt 14: 3 Do not eat any **detestable t**. H9359
Dt 17: 4 that this **detestable t** has been done in H9359
Dt 19:20 will such an evil **t** be done among you. H1821
Dt 22:21 She has done an **outrageous t** in Israel by H5576
Dt 27:15 an idol—a **t detestable** *to* the LORD, the H9359
Dt 28:25 you will become a **t of horror** to all the H2400
Dt 28:37 You will become a **t of horror**, a byword H9014
Jos 6:21 with the sword every **living t** in it— H889S
Jos 7:15 has done an **outrageous t** in Israel! H5576
Jdg 6: 4 did not spare a **living t** for Israel, H4695
Jdg 13:19 the LORD did an **amazing** *t* while Manoah AIT
Jdg 19:23 is my guest, don't do this **outrageous t**. H5576
Jdg 19:24 this man, don't do such an outrageous **t**." H1821
Jdg 19:30 "Such a **t** has never been seen or done H2296S
Jdg 20: 3 "Tell us how this **awful t** happened." H8288
1Sa 9:21 Why do you say such a **t** to me?" H1821
1Sa 12:16 see this great **t** the LORD is about to H1821
1Sa 12:17 realize what an **evil t** you did in the eyes H8288
1Sa 13:13 "*You have* **done a foolish t**," Samuel said H6118
1Sa 24: 6 that I should do such a **t** to my master, H1821
1Sa 25:30 my lord every **good t** he promised H3208
1Sa 27: 1 The **best** *t* I can do is to escape to the land of AIT
2Sa 3:13 But I demand one **t** of you: Do not come H1821
2Sa 7:21 have done this **great t** and made it known H1525
2Sa 11:11 As surely as you live, I will not do such a **t**!" H1821
2Sa 11:27 But the **t** David had done displeased the H1821
2Sa 12: 6 because he did such a **t** and had no pity." H1821
2Sa 12:12 I will do this **t** in broad daylight before H1821
2Sa 13:12 **Such** *a t* should not be done in Israel AIT
2Sa 13:12 be done in Israel! Don't do this **wicked t**. H5576
2Sa 13:20 Don't take this **t** to heart." And Tamar H1821
2Sa 14:13 have you devised a **t** like this against the NDT
2Sa 24: 3 does my lord the king want to do such a **t**?" H1821
2Sa 24:10 *I have* **done** a very **foolish t**." H6118
1Ki 9: 8 has the LORD done **such** *a t* to this land and to AIT
1Ki 12:30 And this **t** became a sin; the people came H1821
1Ki 22: 8 "The king should not say **such a t**, H4027
1Ki 22:12 other prophets were prophesying the **same** *t*. AIT
2Ki 2:10 "You have asked a **difficult** *t*," Elijah said AIT
2Ki 3:18 This *is an* **easy** *t* in the eyes of the LORD; he AIT
2Ki 5:13 prophet had told you to do *some* great **t**, H1821
2Ki 5:16 whom I serve, I will not accept a **t**. NDT
2Ki 5:18 the LORD forgive your servant for this one **t**: H1821
1Ch 17:19 have done this **great t** and made known H1525
1Ch 21: 8 *I have* **done** a very **foolish t**." H6118
2Ch 7:21 the LORD done **such a t** to this land and H3970
2Ch 16: 9 *You have* **done a foolish t**, and from now H6118
2Ch 18: 7 "The king should not say **such a t**, H4027
2Ch 18:11 other prophets were prophesying the **same** *t*. AIT
Ezr 10:13 because we have sinned greatly in this **t**. H1821
Ne 13: 7 learned about the **evil t** Eliashib had H8288
Ne 13:17 "What is this wicked **t** you are doing H1821
Est 7: 5 the man who has dared to do **such** *a t*?" AIT
Est 8: 5 with favor and thinks it the right **t** to do, H1821
Job 28:21 It is hidden from the eyes of every **living t** H2645
Job 39: 8 its pasture and searches for any **green t**. H3728
Ps 16: 2 my Lord; apart from you I have no **good t**." H3208
Ps 27: 4 **One** *t* I ask from the LORD, this only do I seek AIT
Ps 34:10 those who seek the LORD lack no **good** *t*. AIT
Ps 62:11 **One** *t* God has spoken, two things I have AIT
Ps 84:11 no **good** *t* does he withhold from those AIT
Ps 105:35 they ate up every **green t** in their land, ate H6912
Ps 145:16 hand and satisfy the desires of every **living** *t*. AIT
Ecc 7:11 is a **good** *t* and benefits those who see the AIT
Ecc 7:27 "Adding **one** *t* to another to discover the AIT
Ecc 12:14 including every **hidden** *t*, whether it is good AIT
Isa 43:19 I am doing a **new** *t*! Now it springs up AIT
Isa 44:19 Shall I make a **detestable t** from what is H9359
Isa 44:20 "Is not this **t** in my right hand a lie? NDT
Isa 49: 6 "*It is* too **small** *a t for* you to be my servant to AIT
Isa 52:11 Touch no **unclean** *t*! Come out from it AIT
Jer 5:30 "A horrible and **shocking t** has happened H9136
Jer 18:13 A most **horrible t** has been done by Virgin H9137
Jer 22: 8 has the LORD done **such a t** to this great H3970
Jer 23:13 prophets of Samaria I saw this **repulsive t**: H9524
Jer 31:22 The LORD will create a **new** *t* on earth—the AIT
Jer 32:35 do such a **detestable t** and so make H9359
Jer 40:16 son of Kareah, "Don't do such a **t**! H1821
Jer 44: 4 'Do not do this detestable **t** that I hate! H1821
La 1:17 has become an **unclean t** among them. H5614
Eze 7:19 their gold will be treated as a **t unclean**. H5614
Eze 7:20 I will make it a **t unclean** for them. H5614
Da 2:10 ever asked such a **t** of any magician or A10418
Hos 6:10 I have seen a **horrible t** in Israel: There H9137
Hos 9:10 became as vile as the **t** they **loved**. H171
Mal 2:11 A **detestable t** has been committed in H9359
Mal 2:13 Another **t** you do: You flood the LORD's H2296S
Mt 19:16 what **good** *t* must I do to get eternal life?" AIT
Mt 20: 5 three in the afternoon and did **the same t**. *G6058*
Mt 21:30 to the other son and said **the same t**. *G6058*
Mt 22:26 **The same t** happened to the second and *G3931*
Mt 26:10 She has done a beautiful **t** to me. *G2240*
Mt 26:44 prayed the third time, saying the same **t**. *G3364*
Mk 10:21 him and loved him. "**One** *t* you lack," he said AIT
Mk 14: 6 She has done a beautiful **t** to me. *G2240*
Mk 14:39 he went away and prayed the same **t**. *G3364*
Lk 2:15 see this **t** that has happened, *G4839*
Lk 12:26 Since you cannot do this **very little** *t*, why do AIT
Lk 18:22 he said to him, "You still lack **one** *t*. AIT
Jn 1:41 The **first** *t* Andrew did was to find his brother AIT
Jn 9:25 **One** *t* I do know. I was blind but AIT
Ac 4:17 But to stop *this t* from **spreading** any further AIT
Ac 5: 4 What made you think *of doing* such a **t** *G4547*
Ac 17:23 are ignorant *of the very* **t** you worship— *G4005*
Ac 19:32 Some were shouting *one* **t**, some another *G5516*
Ac 21:34 the crowd shouted **one** *t* and some another, AIT
Ac 24:21 it was this one **t** I shouted as I stood *G5889S*
Ro 4: 6 David says **the same t** when he speaks of *G2749*
1Co 7:37 the virgin—this man also does **the right t**. *G2822*
1Co 9: 8 Doesn't the Law say **the same** *t*? AIT
2Co 6:17 Touch no **unclean** *t*, and I will AIT
Gal 2:10 the very **t** I had been eager to do all *G4047*
Gal 3: 2 I would like to learn just **one** *t* from you: AIT
Gal 5: 6 **The only t that counts** is faith expressing *G247*
Php 1:18 The **important t** is that in every way *G4440*
Php 3:13 taken hold of it. But one *t* I do: Forgetting AIT
Phm 6 understanding *of* every **good** *t* we share for AIT
Phm 22 And **one t more**: Prepare a guest room *G275*
Heb 10:29 has treated as an **unholy** *t* the blood of the AIT
Heb 10:31 It is a **dreadful** *t* to fall into the hands of the AIT
2Pe 3: 8 But do not forget this **one** *t*, dear friends AIT
Rev 3:17 acquired wealth and do **not need a t**. *G4029*
Rev 16: 3 and every **living t** in the sea died. *G6034+2437*

THINGS (600) [THING]

Ge 20: 9 You have done **t** to me that should never H5126
Ge 24:10 with all kinds of **good t** *from* his master. H3206
Ge 24:28 her mother's household about these **t**. H1821
Ge 29:13 there Jacob told him all these **t**. H1821
Ge 41:13 And *t* **turned out** exactly as he interpreted AIT
Ge 44: 7 "Why does my lord say such **t**? H1821
Ge 44:15 me *can* **find t out by divination**?" H5727+5727
Ge 45:23 donkeys loaded with the **best t** *of* Egypt, H3206
Ex 7:11 also did the **same** *t* by their secret arts: AIT
Ex 7:22 magicians did the **same** *t* by their secret arts, AIT
Ex 8: 7 magicians did the **same** *t* by their secret arts AIT
Ex 18: 9 about all the **good t** the LORD had done H3208
Ex 21:11 If he does not provide her with these **three** *t* AIT
Ex 35: 1 "These are the **t** the LORD has commanded H1821
Lev 2: 8 grain offering made of **these** *t* to the LORD; AIT
Lev 5:15 in regard to any of the LORD's **holy t**, H7731
Lev 5:16 have failed to do in regard to the **holy t**, H7731
Lev 6: 7 any of **the t** they did that made H3972S
Lev 9: 5 They took the **t** Moses commanded to the H889
Lev 10:19 such *t* as **this** have happened to me. AIT
Lev 11:10 among all the **swarming t** or among all H9238
Lev 15:10 whoever touches **any** *of the t* that were under AIT
Lev 15:10 whoever picks up *those* **t** must wash their H4392S
Lev 15:31 separate from **t that make** them **unclean**, H3240
Lev 18:26 you must not do any of these **detestable t**, H9359
Lev 18:27 all these **t** were done by the people H9359S
Lev 18:29 who does any of these **detestable t**— H9359
Lev 20:23 Because they did all **these** *t*, I abhorred them. AIT
Lev 26:23 " 'If in spite of **these** *t* you do not accept my AIT
Nu 4: 4 the care of the **most holy t**. H7731+7731
Nu 4:15 must not touch the **holy t** or they will die. H7731
Nu 4:15 are to carry **those** *t* that are in the tent AIT
Nu 4:19 they come near the **most holy t**, H7731+7731
Nu 4:20 must not go in to look at the **holy t**, H7731
Nu 4:26 all that needs to be done with **these t**. H2157S
Nu 4:32 each man the **specific t** he is to H5466+3998
Nu 5:10 **Sacred t** belong to their owners, but what H7731
Nu 7: 9 were to carry on their shoulders the **holy t**, H7731
Nu 10:21 the Kohathites set out, carrying the **holy t**. H5219
Nu 10:29 the LORD has promised **good** *t* to Israel." AIT
Nu 10:32 you whatever good **t** the LORD gives us." H2085S
Nu 14:35 I will surely do **these** *t* to this whole AIT
Nu 15:13 native-born must do **these** *t* in this way when AIT
Nu 16:22 the God who gives breath to all **living t** H1414
Nu 16:28 me to do all these **t** and that it was not H5126
Nu 27:16 *May* the LORD, the God who gives breath to all **living t** H1414
Dt 4: 9 do not forget the **t** your eyes have seen H1821
Dt 4:19 them and worshiping **t** the LORD your God H4392S
Dt 4:30 all these **t** have happened to you, H1821
Dt 4:34 like all the **t** the LORD your God did for you H889
Dt 4:35 You were shown these **t** so that you might NDT
Dt 6:11 with all kinds of **good t** you did not H3206
Dt 11: 3 performed and the **t** he **did** in the heart of H5126
Dt 11: 7 saw all these great **t** the LORD has done. H5126
Dt 12:26 But take your **consecrated t** and whatever H7731
Dt 12:31 do all kinds of **detestable t** the LORD hates. H9359
Dt 13:17 none of the **condemned t** are to be H3051
Dt 18:12 Anyone who does **these** *t* is detestable to the AIT
Dt 20:18 to follow all the **detestable t** they do in H9359
Dt 25:16 your God detests anyone who does **these** *t*, AIT
Dt 26:11 rejoice in all the **good** *t* the LORD your God AIT
Dt 29:29 The **secret** *t* belong to the LORD our God, but AIT
Dt 29:29 the *t* **revealed** belong to us and to our AIT
Jos 3: 5 the LORD will do **amazing** *t* among you." AIT
Jos 6:18 But keep away from the **devoted t**, so that H3051
Jos 7: 1 were unfaithful in regard to the **devoted t**; H3051
Jos 7:11 They have taken some of the **devoted t** H3051
Jos 7:13 There are **devoted t** among you H3051
Jos 7:15 is caught with the **devoted t** shall be H3051
Jos 7:23 They took **the t** from the tent, brought H4392S
Jos 9: 1 west of the Jordan heard about these **t**— NDT
Jos 22:20 was unfaithful in regard to the **devoted t**, H3051
Jos 23:15 **t** the LORD your God has **promised** you H1821
Jos 23:15 on you all the evil **t** he has **threatened**, H1821
Jos 24:26 Joshua recorded these **t** in the Book of the H1821
Jos 24:29 After these **t**, Joshua son of Nun, the H1821
Jdg 2: 4 had spoken these **t** to all the Israelites H1821
Jdg 2: 7 seen all the great **t** the LORD had done H5126
Jdg 8:35 in spite of all the **good t** he had done H3208
Jdg 13:23 shown us all **these** *t* or now told us this." AIT
Jdg 18: 8 Danites asked them, "**How** did you **find t**?" H4537
1Sa 2:23 he said to them, "Why do you do such **t**? H1821
1Sa 12: 3 If I have done any of these **t**, I will make it NDT
1Sa 12:24 consider what **great t** *he has* **done** for you. H1540
1Sa 16: 7 LORD does not look at the **t** people look at. H889
1Sa 17:22 David left his **t** with the keeper of supplies H3998
1Sa 18:26 When the attendants told David these **t** H1821
1Sa 25:37 his wife told him all these **t**, and his heart H1821
1Sa 26:25 *you will* **do great t** and surely H6913+6913
2Sa 7:28 promised these **good t** to your servant. H3208
1Ki 2:15 But *t* **changed**, and the kingdom has gone to AIT
1Ki 7:47 Solomon left all these **t** unweighed H3998
1Ki 7:51 in the **t** his father David had **dedicated**— H7731
1Ki 8:66 heart for all the **good t** the LORD had done H3208
1Ki 10: 7 not believe these **t** until I came and saw H1821
1Ki 16: 7 arousing his anger by the **t** he **did** H5126+3338
1Ki 16:27 what he did and the **t** he achieved, are H1476S
1Ki 18:36 have done all these **t** at your command. H1821
1Ki 22:45 the **t** he achieved and his military H1476S
2Ki 5:24 he took the **t** from the servants and put them NDT
2Ki 7: 8 tent and took some **t** from it and hid them NDT
2Ki 8: 4 me about all the **great** *t* Elisha has done." AIT
2Ki 9:11 know the man and the **sort of t he says**," H8490
2Ki 17: 9 secretly did **t** against the LORD their H1821
2Ki 17:11 They did wicked **t** that aroused the LORD's H1821
2Ki 18:27 you that my master sent me to say these **t**, H1821
2Ki 23:16 by the man of God who foretold these **t**. H1821
2Ki 23:17 of Bethel the very **t** you have done to it." H1821
2Ki 23:24 all the other **detestable t** seen in Judah H9199

2Ki 24: 3 Surely *these t* **happened** to Judah according AIT
1Ch 2: 7 by violating the ban on taking **devoted t**. H3051
1Ch 17:26 promised these **good t** to your servant. H3208
1Ch 23:13 to consecrate the **most holy t**, to H7731+7731
1Ch 23:28 purification of all **sacred t** and the H7731
1Ch 26:20 the treasuries for the **dedicated t**. H7731
1Ch 26:26 the treasuries for the **t** dedicated by King H7731S
1Ch 26:28 all the other **dedicated** *t* were in the care AIT
1Ch 28:12 for the treasuries for the **dedicated t**. H7731
1Ch 29:12 come from you; you are the ruler of **all** *t*. AIT
1Ch 29:17 All **these** *t* I have given willingly and with AIT
2Ch 4: 6 In them the **t** to be *used for* the burnt H5126
2Ch 4:18 All these **t** that Solomon made amounted H3998
2Ch 5: 1 in the **t** his father David had **dedicated**— H7731
2Ch 7:10 in heart for the **good t** the LORD had done H3208
2Ch 27: 7 all his wars and the other **t** he **did**, H2006
2Ch 28:21 Ahaz **took some of the** *t from* the temple H2745
2Ch 31: 6 a tithe of the **holy t** dedicated to the H7731
2Ch 31:12 was the overseer in charge of **these** *t*, and his AIT
2Ch 36: 8 the **detestable t** he did and all that was H9359
Ezr 7: 1 After these **t**, during the reign of H1821
Ezr 9: 1 After **these** *t* had been done, the leaders AIT
Ezr 9:12 strong and eat the **good t** *of* the land and H3206
Ne 1: 4 When I heard these **t**, I sat down and H1821
Ne 4:14 After *I* **looked t over**, I stood up and said to H8011
Ne 9:25 of houses filled with all kinds of **good t**, H3206
Ne 9:36 its fruit and the other **good t** it *produces*. H3206
Ne 13:18 Didn't your ancestors do *the* **same** *t*, so that AIT
Job 8: 2 "How long will you say **such** *t*? Your words AIT
Job 12: 3 Who does not know all **these** *t*? AIT
Job 12:22 He reveals the **deep** *t* of darkness and brings AIT
Job 13:20 "Only grant me these **two** *t*, God, and then I AIT
Job 13:26 For you write down **bitter t** against me H5353
Job 16: 2 "I have heard **many** *t* like these; you are AIT
Job 22:18 it was he who filled their houses with **good** *t*, AIT
Job 28:11 of the rivers and bring **hidden t** to light. H9502
Job 31:23 fear of his splendor I could not do such **t**. NDT
Job 33:29 "God does all **these** *t* to a person—twice AIT
Job 37: 5 he does **great** *t* beyond our understanding. AIT
Job 42: 2 "I know that you can do **all** *t*; no purpose of AIT
Job 42: 3 Surely I spoke of **t** I did not understand NDT
Job 42: 3 understand, *t* too **wonderful** for me to know. AIT
Job 42: 7 After the LORD had said these **t** to Job, he H1821
Ps 15: 5 Whoever does **these** *t* will never be shaken. AIT
Ps 31:19 How abundant are the **good** *t* that you have AIT
Ps 35:11 they question me on **t** I know nothing H889
Ps 40: 5 you have done, the **t** you **planned** for us. H4742
Ps 42: 4 **These** *t* I remember as I pour out my soul AIT
Ps 50:21 When you did **these** *t* and I kept silent, you AIT
Ps 62:11 thing God has spoken, two **t** I have heard: H2306
Ps 65: 4 with the **good t** *of* your house, *of* your holy H3206
Ps 71:19 to the heavens, you who have done **great** *t*. AIT
Ps 78: 2 I will utter **hidden t**, things from of old— H2648
Ps 78: 2 I will utter hidden things, **t** from of old— NDT
Ps 78: 3 **t** we have heard and known, things our H889
Ps 78: 3 known, **t** our ancestors have told us. NDT
Ps 87: 3 **Glorious** *t* are said of you, city of God: AIT
Ps 98: 1 he has done **marvelous** *t*; his right hand AIT
Ps 103: 5 your desires with **good** *t* so that your youth is AIT
Ps 104:25 number—**living t** both large and small. H2651
Ps 104:28 your hand, they are satisfied with **good** *t*. AIT
Ps 106:21 saved them, who had done **great** *t* in Egypt, AIT
Ps 107: 9 the thirsty and fills the hungry with **good** *t*. AIT
Ps 107:43 one who is wise heed **these** *t* and ponder the AIT
Ps 118:15 "The LORD's right hand has done **mighty t**! H2657
Ps 118:16 the LORD's right hand has done **mighty t**!" H2657
Ps 119:18 eyes that I may see **wonderful** *t* in your law. AIT
Ps 119:37 Turn my eyes away from **worthless t** H8736
Ps 119:91 laws endure to this day, for **all** *t* serve you. AIT
Ps 126: 2 "The LORD has done **great** *t* for them. AIT
Ps 126: 3 The LORD has done **great** *t* for us, and we are AIT
Ps 131: 1 with great matters or *t* too **wonderful** for me. AIT
Pr 1:13 all sorts of **valuable t** and fill our H2104+3701
Pr 6:16 There are six **t** the LORD hates, seven that H2179S
Pr 8: 6 I have **trustworthy t** to say; I open my H5592
Pr 12:14 of their lips people are filled with **good** *t*, AIT
Pr 13: 2 the fruit of their lips people enjoy **good** *t*, AIT
Pr 13:21 the righteous are rewarded with **good** *t*. AIT
Pr 14:17 A quick-tempered person does **foolish** *t*, and AIT
Pr 23:33 your mind will imagine **confusing t**. H9337
Pr 30: 7 "**Two** *t* I ask of you, LORD; do not refuse me AIT
Pr 30:15 "There are three **t** that are never H2179S
Pr 30:18 "There are three **t** that are too amazing H2156S
Pr 30:21 "Under **three** *t* the earth trembles, under four AIT
Pr 30:24 "Four **t** on earth are small, yet they are H2156S
Pr 30:29 "There are three **t** that are stately in their H2156S
Pr 31:29 "Many women do **noble** *t*, but you surpass AIT
Ecc 1: 8 All **t** are wearisome, more than one can H1821
Ecc 1:14 I have seen all the **t** that are done under H5126
Ecc 2:18 I hated all the **t** I had toiled for under the H6662S
Ecc 5: 8 do not be surprised at **such t**; for one H2914S
Ecc 7:25 wisdom and the **scheme of t** and to H3113
Ecc 7:27 to another to discover the **scheme of t**— H3113
Ecc 8: 1 Who knows the explanation of **t**? H1821
Ecc 11: 5 the work of God, the Maker of **all** *t*. AIT
Ecc 11: 9 know that for all **these** *t* God will bring you AIT
Isa 1:19 obedient, you will eat the **good** *t of* the land; AIT
Isa 12: 5 he has done **glorious t**; let this be H1455
Isa 25: 1 faithfulness you have done **wonderful t**, H7099
Isa 25: 1 done wonderful things, *t* **planned** long ago. AIT
Isa 29:16 You turn **t** upside down, as if the potter were NDT
Isa 30:10 Tell us **pleasant** *t*, prophesy illusions. AIT
Isa 36:12 you that my master sent me to say these **t**, H1821
Isa 38:16 by **such t** people live; and my spirit H2157S
Isa 41:22 Tell us what the **former** *t* were, so that we AIT
Isa 41:22 Or declare to us the *t to* **come**, AIT
Isa 42: 9 the **former** *t* have taken place, and new AIT
Isa 42: 9 have taken place, and **new** *t* I declare; before AIT
Isa 42:16 These are the **t** I will do; I will not forsake H1821
Isa 42:20 You have seen **many** *t*, but you pay no AIT
Isa 43: 9 this and proclaimed to us the **former** *t*? AIT
Isa 43:18 "Forget the **former** *t*; do not dwell on the past. AIT
Isa 44: 9 the *t* they **treasure** are worthless. AIT
Isa 44:21 "Remember **these** *t*, Jacob, for you, Israel AIT
Isa 44:24 the LORD, the Maker of **all** *t*, who stretches out AIT
Isa 45: 7 create disaster; I, the LORD, do all **these** *t*. AIT
Isa 45:11 Concerning **t to come**, do you question me H910
Isa 46: 9 Remember the **former** *t*, those of long ago; AIT
Isa 47: 7 did not consider **these** *t* or reflect on what AIT
Isa 48: 3 I foretold the **former** *t* long ago, my mouth AIT
Isa 48: 5 Therefore I told you these **t** long ago; before NDT
Isa 48: 6 You have heard these **t**; look at them all NDT
Isa 48: 6 "From now on I will tell you of **new** *t*, of AIT
Isa 48: 6 of new things, of **hidden** *t* unknown to you. AIT
Isa 48:14 Which of the idols has foretold **these** *t*? The AIT
Isa 59: 3 and your tongue mutters **wicked** *t*. AIT
Isa 63: 7 the many **good t** he has done for Israel H3206
Isa 64: 3 For when you did **awesome** *t* that we did not AIT
Isa 65:17 The **former** *t* will not be remembered, nor AIT
Isa 66: 2 Has not my hand made all **these** *t*, and so AIT
Isa 66: 8 Who has ever heard of such **t**? Who has H2296S
Isa 66: 8 Who has ever seen *t* like **this**? Can a country AIT
Isa 66:17 rats and other **unclean t**—they will meet H9211
Jer 7:10 safe to do all these **detestable t**? H9359
Jer 7:13 While you were doing all these **t**, declares H5126
Jer 10:16 he is the Maker of **all** *t*, including Israel, AIT
Jer 17: 9 is deceitful above **all** *t* and beyond cure. AIT
Jer 20: 1 heard Jeremiah prophesying these **t**, H1821
Jer 25:13 on that land all the **t** I have spoken H1821
Jer 26:10 the officials of Judah heard about these **t**, H1821
Jer 26:12 this city all the **t** you have heard. H1821
Jer 26:20 prophesied the same **t** against this city H1821
Jer 27:21 says about the **t** that are left in the house H3998
Jer 29:23 For they have done **outrageous t** in Israel H5576
Jer 29:32 will he see the **good** *t* I will do for my AIT
Jer 30:15 many sins I have done **these** *t* to you. AIT
Jer 33: 3 you great and **unsearchable** *t* you do not AIT
Jer 33: 9 earth that hear of all the **good t** I do for it; H3208
Jer 35: 7 you must never have any of these **t**, but NDT
Jer 38: 4 the people, by the **t** he is saying to them. H1821
Jer 44:22 actions and the **detestable t** you did, H9359
Jer 45: 5 Should you then seek **great** *t* for yourself? AIT
Jer 51:19 he is the Maker of **all** *t*, including the AIT
La 3:36 of justice—would not the Lord see such **t**? NDT
La 3:38 High that both calamities and **good** *t* come? AIT
La 5:17 because of **these** *t* our eyes grow dim AIT
Eze 3:20 The **righteous t** that person did will not be H7407
Eze 7:14 they have made **all** *t* ready, but no one will AIT
Eze 8: 6 the utterly **detestable t** the Israelites are H9359
Eze 8: 6 **t** that will drive me far from my sanctuary? NDT
Eze 8: 6 will see **t** *that* are even more **detestable**." H9359
Eze 8: 9 the wicked and **detestable t** they are H9359
Eze 8:10 walls all kinds of **crawling t** and unclean H8254
Eze 8:13 doing **t** *that* are even more **detestable**." H9359
Eze 8:15 see **t** *that* are even more **detestable** than H9359
Eze 8:17 to do the **detestable t** they are doing H9359
Eze 9: 4 over all the **detestable t** that are done in H9359
Eze 12: 7 day I brought out my **t** packed for exile. H3998
Eze 12:12 them will put his **t** on his shoulder at dusk NDT
Eze 15: 3 make pegs from it to hang **t** on? H3972+3998
Eze 16: 5 enough to do any of **these** *t* for you. AIT
Eze 16:30 when you do all **these** *t*, acting like a AIT
Eze 16:43 your youth but enraged me with all **these** *t*, AIT
Eze 16:50 haughty and did **detestable t** before me. H9359
Eze 16:51 have done more **detestable t** than they, H9359
Eze 16:51 righteous by all these **t** you have done. H9359S
Eze 17:12 'Do you not know what **these** *t* mean? AIT
Eze 17:15 Will he who does **such** *t* escape? Will he AIT
Eze 17:18 his hand in pledge and yet did all **these** *t*, AIT
Eze 18:10 who sheds blood or does any of **these** other *t* AIT
Eze 18:12 looks to the idols. He does **detestable t**. H9359
Eze 18:13 he has done all these **detestable t**, H9359
Eze 18:14 he sees them, he does not do such **t**: H2177
Eze 18:22 Because of the **righteous t** they have done H7407
Eze 18:24 does the same **detestable t** the wicked H9359
Eze 18:24 None of the **righteous t** that person has H7407
Eze 22: 8 have despised my **holy t** and desecrated H7731
Eze 22:25 treasures and **precious t** and make many H3702
Eze 22:26 violence to my law and profane my **holy t**; H7731
Eze 23:27 You will not look on **these** *t* with longing AIT
Eze 24:19 you tell us what **these** *t* have to do with us? AIT
Eze 33:13 none of the **righteous t** that person has H7407
Eze 33:26 you do **detestable t**, and each of H9359
Eze 33:29 of all the **detestable t** they have done. H9359
Eze 35:12 heard all the **contemptible t** you have H5542
Eze 36:22 that I am going to do these **t**, but for the NDT
Eze 44: 8 out your duty in regard to my **holy t**, H7731
Eze 44:13 near any of my **holy t** or my most holy H7731
Da 2: 9 to tell me misleading and wicked **t**, A10418
Da 2:22 He reveals deep and **hidden** *t*; he knows AIT
Da 2:29 your mind turned to **t** to come, and the A10408
Da 2:40 as iron breaks **t** to pieces, so it will crush NDT
Da 7:16 gave me the interpretation of these **t**: A10418
Da 11:36 will say **unheard-of** *t* against the God AIT
Da 12: 6 before these **astonishing t** are fulfilled?" H7099
Da 12: 7 finally broken, all **these** *t* will be completed." AIT
Hos 8:12 I wrote for them the **many** *t of* my law, but AIT
Hos 14: 9 Let them realize **these** *t*. Who is discerning? AIT
Joel 2:20 Surely he has done **great** *t*! AIT
Joel 2:21 Surely the LORD has done **great** *t*! AIT
Am 9:12 declares the LORD, who will do **these** *t*. AIT
Mic 2: 6 "Do not prophesy about **these** *t*; disgrace will AIT
Mic 2: 7 Does he do **such** *t*?" "Do not my words AIT
Hag 2:13 with a dead body touches one of **these** *t*, AIT
Hag 2:15 consider how **t** were before one stone was NDT
Zec 3: 8 who are men **symbolic of t to come**: H4603
Zec 4:10 "Who dares despise the day of **small** *t*, since AIT
Zec 8:12 I will give all **these** *t* as an inheritance to the AIT
Zec 8:16 These are the **t** you are to do: Speak the H1821
Mt 6:32 For the pagans run after all **these** *t*, and your AIT
Mt 6:33 all **these** *t* will be given to you as well. AIT
Mt 7:28 When Jesus had finished saying **these** *t*, the AIT
Mt 11:25 you have hidden **these** *t* from the wise and AIT
Mt 11:27 "**All** *t* have been committed to me by my AIT
Mt 12:35 A good man brings **good** *t* out of the good AIT
Mt 12:35 an evil man brings **evil** *t* out of the evil AIT
Mt 13: 3 Then he told them **many** *t* in parables, saying: AIT
Mt 13:34 Jesus spoke all **these** *t* to the crowd in AIT
Mt 13:35 I will utter *t* **hidden** since the creation of the AIT
Mt 13:51 "Have you understood all **these** *t*?" Jesus AIT
Mt 13:56 Where then did this man get all **these** *t*?" AIT
Mt 15:18 But the *t that* **come out** of a person's mouth AIT
Mt 16:21 suffer **many** *t* at the hands of the AIT
Mt 17:11 Elijah comes and will restore **all** *t*. AIT
Mt 18: 7 of the **t that cause** people **to stumble**! *G4998*
Mt 18: 7 **Such t** must come, but woe to the person *G4998S*
Mt 19: 1 When Jesus had finished saying **these** *t*, he AIT
Mt 19:26 is impossible, but with God **all** *t* are possible." AIT
Mt 19:28 at the **renewal of all t**, when the Son *G4098*
Mt 21:15 the law saw the **wonderful** *t* he did and the AIT
Mt 21:23 "By what authority are you doing **these** *t*?" AIT
Mt 21:24 tell you by what authority I am doing **these** *t*. AIT
Mt 21:27 tell you by what authority I am doing **these** *t*. AIT
Mt 24: 2 "Do you see all **these** *t*?" he asked. "Truly I AIT
Mt 24: 6 *Such t* must **happen**, but the end is still to AIT
Mt 24:33 when you see all **these** *t*, you know that it AIT
Mt 24:34 pass away until all **these** *t* have happened. AIT
Mt 25:21 You have been faithful with a **few** *t*; I will put AIT
Mt 25:21 few things; I will put you in charge of **many** *t*. AIT
Mt 25:23 You have been faithful with a **few** *t*; I will put AIT
Mt 25:23 few things; I will put you in charge of **many** *t*. AIT
Mt 26: 1 When Jesus had finished saying all **these** *t* AIT
Mk 2: 8 said to them, "Why are you thinking **these** *t*? AIT
Mk 4: 2 He taught them **many** *t* by parables, and in AIT
Mk 4:19 the desires for **other** *t* come in and choke AIT
Mk 6: 2 "Where did this man get **these** *t*?" they asked AIT
Mk 6:34 So he began teaching them **many** *t*. AIT
Mk 7:13 And you do **many** *t* like that." AIT
Mk 8:31 of Man must suffer **many** *t* and be rejected by AIT
Mk 9:12 Elijah does come first, and restores **all** *t*. AIT
Mk 10:27 not with God; **all** *t* are possible with God." AIT
Mk 11:28 "By what authority are you doing **these** *t*?" AIT
Mk 11:29 tell you by what authority I am doing **these** *t*. AIT
Mk 11:33 tell you by what authority I am doing **these** *t*." AIT
Mk 13: 4 when will **these** *t* happen? And what AIT
Mk 13: 7 Such **t** must happen, but the end is still to NDT
Mk 13:29 when you see **these** *t* happening, you AIT
Mk 13:30 pass away until all **these** *t* have happened. AIT
Mk 14:16 the city and found **t** just as Jesus had told NDT
Mk 15: 3 The chief priests accused him *of* **many** *t*. AIT
Mk 15: 4 See **how many** *t* they are accusing you of." AIT
Lk 1: 1 up an account of the **t** that have been *G4547*
Lk 1: 4 certainty of the **t** you have been taught *G3364*
Lk 1:49 the Mighty One has done **great** *t* for me AIT
Lk 1:53 filled the hungry *with* **good** *t* but has sent the AIT
Lk 1:65 people were talking about all these **t**. *G4839*
Lk 2:19 up all these **t** and pondered them in *G4839*
Lk 2:20 praising God for all **the** *t* they had heard AIT
Lk 2:51 mother treasured all these **t** in her heart. *G4839*
Lk 3:19 and all the other **evil** *t* he had done, AIT
Lk 5:22 "Why are you thinking these **t** in your hearts? NDT
Lk 5:26 said, "We have seen **remarkable** *t* today." AIT
Lk 6:45 A good man brings **good** *t* out of the good AIT
Lk 6:45 an evil man brings **evil** *t* out of the evil stored AIT
Lk 7:18 John's disciples told him about all **these** *t* AIT
Lk 9: 9 is this I hear **such** *t* about?" And he AIT
Lk 9:22 of Man must suffer **many** *t* and be rejected by AIT
Lk 9:52 a Samaritan village to **get** *t* **ready** for him; AIT
Lk 10:21 you have hidden **these** *t* from the wise and AIT
Lk 10:22 "**All** *t* have been committed to me by my AIT
Lk 10:41 "you are worried and upset about **many** *t*, AIT
Lk 10:42 but **few** *t* are needed—or indeed only one AIT
Lk 11:27 As Jesus was saying **these** *t*, a woman in the AIT
Lk 11:45 when you say **these** *t*, you insult us also." AIT
Lk 12:21 whoever stores up **t** for themselves but is NDT
Lk 12:30 For the pagan world runs after all **such** *t*, and AIT
Lk 12:31 and **these** *t* will be given to you as well. AIT
Lk 12:48 know and does *t* **deserving** punishment will AIT
Lk 13:17 with all the **wonderful** *t* he was doing. AIT
Lk 16:25 that in your lifetime you received your **good** *t*, AIT
Lk 16:25 while Lazarus received **bad** *t*, but now he is AIT
Lk 17: 1 "**T that cause people to stumble** are *G4998*
Lk 17:25 first he must suffer **many** *t* and be rejected by AIT
Lk 20: 2 us by what authority you are doing **these** *t*," AIT
Lk 20: 8 tell you by what authority I am doing **these** *t*." AIT
Lk 21: 7 they asked, "when will **these** *t* happen? AIT

Lk 21: 9 These t must happen first, but the end will AIT
Lk 21:28 When these t begin to take place, stand up AIT
Lk 21:31 when you see these t happening, you AIT
Lk 21:32 pass away until all these t have happened. AIT
Lk 22:13 They left and found t just as Jesus had told NDT
Lk 22:65 And they said many other insulting t to him. AIT
Lk 23:31 For if people do these t when the tree is AIT
Lk 23:49 stood at a distance, watching these t. AIT
Lk 24: 9 they told all these t to the Eleven and to all AIT
Lk 24:15 discussed these t with each other, NDT
Lk 24:18 not know the t that have happened there in AIT
Lk 24:19 "What t?" he asked. "About Jesus of AIT
Lk 24:26 have to suffer these t and then enter his AIT
Lk 24:48 You are witnesses of these t. AIT
Jn 1: 3 Through him all t were made; without him AIT
Jn 1:50 You will see greater t than that." AIT
Jn 3:10 "and do you not understand these t? AIT
Jn 3:12 spoken to you of earthly t and you do not G2103
Jn 3:12 will you believe if I speak of heavenly t? G2230
Jn 5:16 Jesus was doing these t on the Sabbath, AIT
Jn 7: 4 Since you are doing these t, show yourself to AIT
Jn 7:32 the crowd whispering such t about him. AIT
Jn 8:40 heard from God. Abraham did not do such t. AIT
Jn 12:16 did they realize that these t had been written AIT
Jn 12:16 about him and that these t had been done to AIT
Jn 13: 3 that the Father had put all t under his power, AIT
Jn 13:17 Now that you know these t, you will be G4047
Jn 14:12 they will do even greater t than these AIT
Jn 14:26 will teach you all t and will remind you of AIT
Jn 16: 3 They will do such t because they have not G4047
Jn 16: 6 filled with grief because I have said these t. AIT
Jn 16:30 see that you know all t and that you do not AIT
Jn 16:33 "I have told you these t, so that in me you AIT
Jn 17:13 I say these t while I am still in the world AIT
Jn 19:36 These t happened so that the scripture would AIT
Jn 20:18 she told them that he had said these t to her. AIT
Jn 21:17 you know all t; you know that I love AIT
Jn 21:24 who testifies to these t and who wrote them AIT
Jn 21:25 Jesus did many other t as well. If every one AIT
Ac 5:32 We are witnesses of these t, and so is the G4839
Ac 7:50 Has not my hand made all these t? AIT
Ac 13:42 to speak further about these t on the next G4839
Ac 14:15 turn from these worthless t to the living God, AIT
Ac 15:17 my name, says the Lord, who does these t'— AIT
Ac 15:18 t known from long ago. NDT
Ac 15:29 You will do well to avoid these t. Farewell. AIT
Ac 18:15 I will not be a judge of such t." AIT
Ac 23: 8 the Pharisees believe all these t. G317
Ac 24: 9 accusation, asserting that these t were true. AIT
Ac 26:26 The king is familiar with these t, and I can AIT
Ro 1:25 served created t rather than the G3232
Ro 1:32 that those who do such t deserve death, AIT
Ro 1:32 continue to do these very t but also approve AIT
Ro 2: 1 you who pass judgment do the same t. AIT
Ro 2: 2 those who do such t is based on truth. AIT
Ro 2: 3 judgment on them and yet do the same t, AIT
Ro 2:14 do by nature t required by the law G3836
Ro 4:17 dead and calls into being t that were not. G3836
Ro 6:21 at that time from the t you are now ashamed AIT
Ro 6:21 are now ashamed of? Those t result in death! AIT
Ro 8:28 And we know that in all t God works for the AIT
Ro 8:31 shall we say in response to these t? AIT
Ro 8:32 with him, graciously give us all t? G3836+4246
Ro 8:37 in all these t we are more than conquerors AIT
Ro 10: 5 person who does these t will live by them." AIT
Ro 11:36 through him and for him are all t. G3836+4246
Ro 14:22 believe about these t keep between yourself NDT
1Co 1:27 But God chose the foolish t of the world to AIT
1Co 1:27 God chose the weak t of the world to shame AIT
1Co 1:28 God chose the lowly t of this world and the AIT
1Co 1:28 things of this world and the despised t— AIT
1Co 1:28 things—and the t that are not—to nullify the AIT
1Co 1:28 things that are not—to nullify the t that are, AIT
1Co 2: 9 the t God has prepared for those who love AIT
1Co 2:10 these are the t God has revealed to us by NDT
1Co 2:10 The Spirit searches all t, even the deep AIT
1Co 2:10 searches all things, even the deep t of God. AIT
1Co 2:14 does not accept the t that come from the AIT
1Co 2:15 with the Spirit makes judgments about all t, AIT
1Co 3: 7 anything, but only God, who makes t grow. NDT
1Co 3:21 about human leaders! All t are yours, AIT
1Co 4: 6 I have applied these t to myself and Apollos AIT
1Co 6: 3 How much more the t of this life! G1053
1Co 7:31 those who use the t of the world, as if not G3180
1Co 8: 6 from whom all t came and for G3836+4246
1Co 8: 6 through whom all t came and G3836+4246
1Co 9:15 in the hope that you will do such t for me, AIT
1Co 9:22 I have become all t to all people so that by AIT
1Co 10: 6 Now these t occurred as examples to keep us AIT
1Co 10: 6 from setting our hearts on evil t as they did. AIT
1Co 10:11 These t happened to them as examples AIT
1Co 11:14 not the very nature of t teach you that G5882
1Co 14: 7 in the case of lifeless t that make sounds, AIT
2Co 5:10 what is due us for the t done while in the AIT
2Co 9: 8 so that in all t at all times, having AIT
2Co 11:12 equal with us in the t they boast about. AIT
2Co 11:30 I will boast of the t that show my weakness. AIT
2Co 12: 4 up to paradise and heard inexpressible t, G4839
2Co 12: 4 t that no one is permitted to tell. AIT
2Co 13:10 This is why I write these t when I am absent AIT
Gal 3:12 person who does these t will live by them." AIT
Gal 4:24 These t are being taken figuratively: The AIT
Gal 5:23 Against such t there is no law. AIT
Gal 6: 6 word should share all good t with their AIT
Eph 1:10 to bring unity to all t in heaven and G3836+4246
Eph 1:22 And God placed all t under his feet and AIT
Eph 3: 9 hidden in God, who created all t. G3836+4246
Eph 5: 6 because of such t God's wrath comes on AIT
Php 2:23 him as soon as I see how t go with me. G3836
Php 3: 1 me to write the same t to you again, AIT
Php 3: 8 whose sake I have lost all t. G3836+4246
Php 3:15 are mature should take such a view of t. G5858
Php 3:19 Their mind is set on earthly t. G3836
Php 4: 8 excellent or praiseworthy—think about such t. AIT
Col 1:16 For in him all t were created: things G3836+4246
Col 1:16 t in heaven and on earth, visible and NDT
Col 1:16 all t have been created through G3836+4246
Col 1:17 He is before all t, and in him all things hold AIT
Col 1:17 and in him all t hold together. G3836+4246
Col 1:20 him to reconcile to himself all t, G3836+4246
Col 1:20 whether t on earth or things in heaven G3836
Col 1:20 whether things on earth or t in heaven, by G3836
Col 2:17 are a shadow of the t that were to come; AIT
Col 2:22 have to do with t that are all destined G4005
Col 3: 1 set your hearts on t above, where Christ is, G3836
Col 3: 2 Set your minds on t above, not on earthly G3836
Col 3: 2 minds on things above, not on earthly t. G3836
Col 3: 8 rid yourselves of all such t as these: G3836+4246
1Th 2:14 your own people the same t those churches AIT
2Th 2: 5 I was with you I used to tell you these t? AIT
2Th 3: 4 will continue to do the t we command. AIT
1Ti 1: 4 Such t promote controversial speculations AIT
1Ti 4: 1 deceiving spirits and t taught by demons. G1436
1Ti 4: 6 If you point these t out to the brothers and AIT
1Ti 4: 8 godliness has value for all t, holding AIT
1Ti 4:11 Command and teach these t. AIT
1Ti 5:13 talk nonsense, saying t they ought not to. G3836
1Ti 6: 2 These are the t you are to teach and insist on AIT
2Ti 2: 2 And the t you have heard me say in the AIT
2Ti 2:14 Keep reminding God's people of these t. AIT
2Ti 3:11 what kinds of t happened to me in Antioch AIT
Titus 1:11 by teaching t they ought not to G4005
Titus 1:15 To the pure, all t are pure, but to those who AIT
Titus 2:15 These, then, are the t you should teach AIT
Titus 3: 5 not because of righteous t we had done G2240
Titus 3: 8 And I want you to stress these t, so that those AIT
Titus 3: 8 These t are excellent and profitable for AIT
Heb 1: 2 whom he appointed heir of all t, and through AIT
Heb 1: 3 sustaining all t by his powerful G3836+4246
Heb 6: 9 we are convinced of better t in your case AIT
Heb 6: 9 the t that have to do with salvation. NDT
Heb 6:18 by two unchangeable t in which it is G4547
Heb 7:13 He of whom these t are said belonged to a AIT
Heb 9: 5 But we cannot discuss these t in detail now. AIT
Heb 9:11 as high priest of the good t that are now AIT
Heb 9:23 the copies of the heavenly t to be purified AIT
Heb 9:23 the heavenly t themselves with better AIT
Heb 10: 1 only a shadow of the good t that are coming AIT
Heb 11: 7 when warned about t not yet seen, in holy G3836
Heb 11:13 They did not receive the t promised; they AIT
Heb 11:14 People who say such t show that they are AIT
Heb 12:27 created t—so that what cannot be AIT
1Pe 1:12 they spoke of the t that have now been G899
1Pe 1:12 Even angels long to look into these t. AIT
1Pe 1:18 that it was not with perishable t such as silver AIT
1Pe 4: 7 The end of all t is near. Therefore be alert AIT
1Pe 4:11 so that in all t God may be praised through AIT
2Pe 1:10 For if you do these t, you will never AIT
2Pe 1:12 So I will always remind you of these t, even AIT
2Pe 1:15 you will always be able to remember these t. AIT
2Pe 1:20 by the prophet's own interpretation of t. AIT
2Pe 3:16 His letters contain some t that are hard to G5516
1Jn 2:26 I am writing these t to you about those who AIT
1Jn 2:27 teaches you about all t and as that anointing AIT
1Jn 5:13 I write these t to you who believe in the AIT
Jude 10 and the very t they do understand by G4012
Rev 2: 5 Repent and do the t you did at first. If you do AIT
Rev 2:14 I have a few t against you: There AIT
Rev 4:11 you created all t, and by your G3836+4246
Rev 17: 4 filled with abominable t and the filth of her AIT
Rev 18:15 merchants who sold these t and gained their AIT
Rev 21: 4 the old order of t has passed away." G4755
Rev 22: 6 to show his servants the t that must soon take AIT
Rev 22: 8 am the one who heard and saw these t. AIT
Rev 22:20 He who testifies to these t says, "Yes, I am AIT

THINK (86) [AFORETHOUGHT, THINKING, THINKS, THOUGHT, THOUGHTLESSLY, THOUGHTS]

Ge 16: 6 "Do with her whatever you t best." H928+6524
Ex 14: 3 Pharaoh will t, 'The Israelites are H606
Jdg 10:15 Do with us whatever you t best, but H928+6524
1Sa 18:23 "Do you t it is a small matter to H928+6524
1Sa 25:17 Now t it over and see what you can do H3359
2Sa 10: 3 "Do you t David is honoring your H928+6524
2Sa 13:32 "My lord should not t that they killed all the H606
2Sa 24:13 t it over and decide how I should answer H3359
1Ki 20:28 the Arameans t the LORD is a god of H606
2Ki 10: 5 as king; you do whatever you t best." H928+6524
1Ch 19: 3 "Do you t David is honoring your H928+6524
Est 4:13 "Do not t that because you are in the H1948
Job 4: 3 T how you have instructed many, how you H2180
Job 7: 4 When I lie down I t, 'How long before I get H606
Job 7:13 When I t my bed will comfort me and my H606
Job 21: 6 When I t about this, I am terrified H2349
Job 23:15 before him; when I t of all this, I fear H1067
Job 35: 2 "Do you t this is just? You say, 'I am in the H3108
Job 41:32 one would t the deep had white hair. H3108
Ps 35:25 Do not let them t, "Aha, just H606+928+4213
Ps 40:17 am poor and needy; may the Lord t of me. H3108
Ps 59: 7 as swords, and they t, "Who can hear us?" NDT
Ps 63: 6 I t of you through the watches of the night. H2047
Ps 144: 3 them, mere mortals that you t of them? H3108
Pr 17: 8 they t success will come at every turn. NDT
Pr 21: 2 A person may t their own ways are H928+6524
Isa 29:15 who do their work in darkness and t, "Who H606
Isa 44:19 No one stops to t, no one has H8740+448+4213
Jer 15:15 t of how I suffer reproach for your sake. H3359
Jer 23:27 They t the dreams they tell one another H3108
Jer 26:14 me whatever you t is good and right. H928+6524
Eze 28: 2 though you t you are as wise as a H5989+4213
Eze 28: 6 " 'Because you t you are wise, as H5989+4222
Zep 1:12 its dregs, who t, 'The LORD will H606+928+4222
Zec 11:12 told them, "If you t it best, give me H928+6524
Mt 3: 9 And do not t you can say to yourselves G1506
Mt 5:17 "Do not t that I have come to abolish the G3787
Mt 6: 7 for they t they will be heard because of G1506
Mt 17:25 "What do you t, Simon?" he G1506
Mt 18:12 "What do you t? If a man owns a hundred G1506
Mt 21:28 "What do you t? There was a man who G1506
Mt 22:42 "What do you t about the Messiah G1506
Mt 26:53 Do you t I cannot call on my Father, and G1506
Mt 26:66 What do you t?" "He is worthy of death," G1506
Mk 14:64 the blasphemy. What do you t?" They all G5743
Lk 8:18 even what they t they have will be taken G1506
Lk 10:36 of these three do you t was a neighbor to G1506
Lk 12:51 Do you t I came to bring peace on earth G1506
Lk 13: 2 "Do you t that these Galileans were worse G1506
Lk 13: 4 do you t they were more guilty than all the G1506
Lk 18: 4 I don't fear God or care what people t, G1956
Jn 5:39 because you t that in them you have G1506
Jn 5:45 "But do not t I will accuse you before the G1506
Jn 8:53 did the prophets. Who do you t you are?" G4472
Jn 11:56 they asked one another, "What do you t? G1506
Jn 16: 2 who kills you will t they are offering a G1506
Ac 5: 4 What made you t of G5502+1877+3836+2840
Ac 11:17 who was I to t that I could stand in God's NDT
Ac 15:38 Paul did not t it wise to take him G546
Ac 17:29 we should not t that the divine being is G3787
Ac 25:27 For I t it is unreasonable to send a prisoner G1506
Ac 26:28 "Do you t that in such a short time you can NDT
Ro 1:28 just as they did not t it worthwhile to G1507
Ro 2: 3 do you t you will escape God's judgment? G3357
Ro 12: 3 Do not t of yourself more highly than you G5672
Ro 12: 3 rather t of yourself with sober G5858
Ro 13:14 and do not t about how to gratify G4630+4472
1Co 1:26 t of what you were when you were called. G1063
1Co 3:18 If any of you t you are wise by the G1506
1Co 7:26 I t that it is good for a man to remain as G3787
1Co 7:40 and I t that I too have the Spirit of God. G1506
1Co 8: 2 Those who t they know something do not G1506
1Co 8: 7 sacrificial food they t of it as having been NDT
1Co 10:12 if you t you are standing firm, be G1506
1Co 12:23 the parts that we t are less honorable G1506
2Co 10: 2 some people who t that we live by the G3357
2Co 11: 5 I do not t I am in the least inferior to G3357
2Co 12: 6 so no one will t more of me than is G3357
Php 2:25 But I t it is necessary to send back to you G2451
Php 3:15 And if on some point you t differently G5858
Php 4: 8 praiseworthy—t about such things. G3357
1Ti 6: 5 of the truth and who t that godliness is a G3787
Heb 7: 4 Just t how great he was: Even the G2555
Heb 10:29 more severely do you t someone deserves G1506
Jas 4: 5 Or do you t Scripture says without reason G1506
2Pe 1:13 I t it is right to refresh your memory as long G2451

THINKING (34) [THINK]

Ex 2:14 Are you t of killing me as you killed the H606
Dt 1:41 t it easy to go up into the hill country. H2103
Dt 29:19 on themselves, t, "I will be H606+928+4222
1Sa 9: 5 my father will stop t about the donkeys and NDT
1Sa 10: 2 your father has stopped t about them and H5759
2Ki 7:12 in the countryside, t, 'They will surely come H606
2Ch 32: 1 t to conquer them for himself. H606
Ne 6: 9 trying to frighten us, t, "Their hands will get H606
Job 1: 5 each of them, t, "Perhaps my children H606
Job 21:27 "I know full well what you are t, the H4742
Pr 23: 7 kind of person who is always t about the H9132
Jer 37: 9 deceive yourselves, t, 'The Babylonians will H606
Da 7: 8 "While I was t about the horns, there A10683
Da 8: 5 As I was t about this, suddenly a goat H1067
Mk 2: 6 law were sitting there, t to themselves, G1368
Mk 2: 8 this was what they were t in their hearts, G1368
Mk 2: 8 to them, "Why are you t these things? G1368
Lk 2:44 T he was in their company, they traveled G3787
Lk 5:21 of the law began t to themselves, G1368
Lk 5:22 Jesus knew what they were t and asked G1369
Lk 5:22 "Why are you t these things in your hearts G1368
Lk 6: 8 what they were t and said to the man G1369
Lk 24:37 frightened, t they saw a ghost. G1506
Jn 20:15 T he was the gardener, she said, "Sir, if G1506
Ac 7:28 Are you t of killing me as you killed the G2527
Ac 10:19 While Peter was still t about the vision G1445
Ac 14:19 him outside the city, t he was dead. G3787
Ro 1:21 their t became futile and their foolish G1369
1Co 14:20 sisters, stop t like children. G1181+3836+5856
1Co 14:20 to evil be infants, but in your t be adults. G5856

T

2Co 12:19 *Have you been* t all along that we have G1506
Eph 4:17 as the Gentiles do, in the futility *of* their t. G3808
Heb 11:15 If *they had been* t of the country they had G3648
2Pe 3: 1 to stimulate you *to* wholesome t. G1379

THINKS (6) [THINK]

2Sa 16: 3 in Jerusalem, because *he* t, 'Today the H606
Est 8: 5 with favor and t *it* the **right** thing to do, H4178
Job 24:15 watches for dusk; he t, 'No eye will see me, H606
1Co 14:37 If anyone t they are a prophet or otherwise G1506
Gal 6: 3 If anyone t they are something when they G1506
Php 3: 4 someone else t *they have reasons* to put G1506

THIRD (177) [THREE]

Ge 1:13 there was morning—the t day. H8958
Ge 2:14 The name of the t river is the Tigris; it runs H8958
Ge 22: 4 On the t day Abraham looked up and saw H8958
Ge 31:22 On the t day Laban was told that Jacob H8958
Ge 32:19 the t and all the others who followed the H8958
Ge 40:20 Now the t day was Pharaoh's birthday H8958
Ge 42:18 On the t day, Joseph said to them, "Do H8958
Ge 50:23 saw the **t generation** of Ephraim's H9000
Ex 19: 1 On the first day of the t month after the H8958
Ex 19:11 be ready by the t day, because on that H8958
Ex 19:15 people, "Prepare yourselves for the t day. H8993
Ex 19:16 the morning of the t day there was H8958
Ex 20: 5 the parents to the t and fourth generation H9000
Ex 25:35 second pair, and a t bud under the third pair NDT
Ex 25:35 a third bud under the t pair—six NDT
Ex 28:19 the t row shall be jacinth, agate and H8958
Ex 34: 7 the parents to the t and fourth generation H9000
Ex 37:21 second pair, and a t bud under the third pair NDT
Ex 37:21 a third bud under the t pair—six NDT
Ex 39:12 the t row was jacinth, agate and amethyst; H8958
Lev 7:17 left over till the t day must be burned up. H8958
Lev 7:18 fellowship offering is eaten on the t day, H8958
Lev 19: 6 left over until the t day must be burned up H8958
Lev 19: 7 If any of it is eaten on the t day, it is H8958
Nu 2:24 number 108,100. They will set out t. H8958
Nu 7:24 On the t day, Eliab son of Helon, the H8958
Nu 14:18 the parents to the t and fourth generation H9000
Nu 15: 6 flour mixed with a t *of* a hin of olive oil, H8958
Nu 15: 7 a t *of* a hin of wine as a drink offering H8958
Nu 19:12 with the water on the t day and on the H8958
Nu 19:12 themselves on the t and seventh days, H8958
Nu 19:19 are unclean on the t and seventh days, H8958
Nu 28:14 with the ram, a t *of* a hin; and with each H8958
Nu 29:20 " 'On the t day offer eleven bulls, two H8958
Nu 31:19 On the t and seventh days you must purify H8958
Dt 5: 9 the parents to the t and fourth generation H9000
Dt 23: 8 The t generation of children born to them H8958
Dt 26:12 a tenth of all your produce in the t year, H8958
Jos 9:17 set out and on the t day came to their H8958
Jos 17:11 settlements (the t in the list is Naphoth). H8993
Jos 19:10 The t lot came up for Zebulun according H8958
Jdg 16:15 This is the t time you have made a fool of H8993
Jdg 20:30 the Benjamites on the t day and took up H8958
1Sa 3: 8 A t *time* the LORD called, "Samuel!" And H8958
1Sa 13:18 the t toward the borderland H285S
1Sa 13:21 a t *of* a shekel for sharpening forks H8993
1Sa 17:13 second, Abinadab; and the t, Shammah. H8958
1Sa 19:21 Saul sent men a t *time*, and they also H8958
1Sa 30: 1 his men reached Ziklag on the t day. H8958
2Sa 1: 2 On the t day a man arrived from Saul's H8958
2Sa 3: 3 of Carmel; the t, Absalom the son of H8958
2Sa 8: 2 the t length was allowed to live. H4850S
2Sa 18: 2 a t under the command of Joab H8958
2Sa 18: 2 a t under Joab's brother Abishai son of H8958
2Sa 18: 2 of Zeruiah, and a t under Ittai the Gittite. H8958
1Ki 3:18 The t day after my child was born, this H8958
1Ki 6: 6 floor six cubits and the t floor seven. H8958
1Ki 6: 8 the middle level and from there to the t. H8958
1Ki 15:28 killed Nadab in the t year of Asa king of H8993
1Ki 15:33 In the t year of Asa king of Judah, Baasha H8993
1Ki 18: 1 a long time, in the t year, the word of the H8958
1Ki 18:34 "**Do** *it* **a t time**," he ordered, and they did H8992
1Ki 18:34 he ordered, and *they* **did** *it* **the t time**. H8992
1Ki 22: 2 But in the t year Jehoshaphat king of H8958
2Ki 1:13 So the king sent a t captain with his fifty H8958
2Ki 1:13 This t captain went up and fell on his H8958
2Ki 11: 5 a t of you guarding the royal palace, H8958
2Ki 11: 6 a t at the Sur Gate, and a third at the gate H8958
2Ki 11: 6 a t at the gate behind the guard H8958
2Ki 18: 1 In the t year of Hoshea son of Elah king of H8993
2Ki 19:29 But in the t year sow and reap, plant H8958
2Ki 20: 5 On the t day from now you will go up to H8958
2Ki 20: 8 temple of the LORD on the t day from now? H8958
1Ch 2:13 second son was Abinadab, the t Shimea, H8958
1Ch 3: 2 the t, Absalom the son of Maakah H8958
1Ch 3:15 Zedekiah the t, Shallum the fourth. H8958
1Ch 8: 1 Ashbel the second son, Aharah the t, H8958
1Ch 8:39 Jeush the second son and Eliphelet the t. H8958
1Ch 12: 9 the second in command, Eliab the t, H8958
1Ch 23:19 Jahaziel the t and Jekameam the fourth. H8958
1Ch 24: 8 the t to Harim, the fourth to Seorim, H8958
1Ch 24:23 Jahaziel the t and Jekameam the fourth. H8958
1Ch 25:10 the t to Zakkur, his sons and relatives 12 H8958
1Ch 26: 2 Zebadiah the t, Jathniel the fourth H8958
1Ch 26: 4 the second, Joah the t, Sakar the fourth, H8958
1Ch 26:11 Tabaliah the t and Zechariah the fourth. H8958
1Ch 27: 5 The t army commander, for the third H8958
1Ch 27: 5 commander, for the t month, was Benaiah H8958
2Ch 15:10 at Jerusalem in the t month of the H8958
2Ch 17: 7 In the t year of his reign he sent his H8993
2Ch 23: 4 A t of you priests and Levites who are H8958
2Ch 23: 5 a t of you at the royal palace and a third at H8958
2Ch 23: 5 royal palace and a t at the Foundation H8958
2Ch 27: 5 amount also in the second and t years. H8958
2Ch 31: 7 doing this in the t month and finished in H8958
Ezr 6:15 completed on the t day of the month A10760
Ne 10:32 commands to give a t *of* a shekel each H8958
Est 1: 3 in the t year of his reign he gave a H8993
Est 5: 1 On the t day Esther put on her royal robes H8958
Est 8: 9 on the twenty-third day of the t month, the H8958
Job 42:14 second Keziah and the t Keren-Happuch. H8958
Isa 19:24 In that day Israel will be the t, along with H8958
Isa 37:30 But in the t year sow and reap, plant H8958
Jer 38:14 him brought to the t entrance to the H8958
Eze 5: 2 an end, burn a t of the hair inside the city. H8958
Eze 5: 2 Take a t and strike it with the sword all H8958
Eze 5: 2 And scatter a t to the wind. For I will H8958
Eze 5:12 A t *of* your *people* will die of the plague H8958
Eze 5:12 a t will fall by the sword outside your H8958
Eze 5:12 a t I will scatter to the winds and H8958
Eze 10:14 of a human being, the t the face of a lion H8958
Eze 31: 1 in the t month on the first day H8958
Eze 46:14 of an ephah with a t *of* a hin of oil to H8958
Da 1: 1 In the t year of the reign of Jehoiakim H8993
Da 2:39 a t kingdom, one of bronze, will A10759
Da 5: 7 will be made the **t highest** ruler in the A10761
Da 5:16 will be made the **t highest** ruler in the A10761
Da 5:29 was proclaimed the **t highest** ruler in the A10761
Da 8: 1 In the t year of King Belshazzar's reign, H8993
Da 10: 1 In the t year of Cyrus king of Persia, H8993
Hos 6: 2 revive us; on the t day he will restore us H8958
Zec 6: 3 the t white, and the fourth dappled—all of H8958
Zec 13: 9 This t I will put into the fire; I will refine H8958
Mt 16:21 be killed and on the t day be raised to life G5569
Mt 17:23 on the t day he will be raised to life." G5569
Mt 20:19 *On* the t day he will be raised to life!" G5569
Mt 21:35 beat one, killed another, and stoned a t. G4005S
Mt 22:26 happened to the second and t brother, G5569
Mt 26:44 away once more and prayed the **t time**, G5569
Mt 27:64 tomb to be made secure until the t day. G5569
Mk 12:21 It was the same with the t. G5569
Mk 14:41 Returning the **t time**, he said to them G5568
Lk 9:22 be killed and on the t day be raised to life G5569
Lk 13:32 and *on* the t day I will reach my goal. G5569
Lk 18:33 On the t day he will rise again. G5569
Lk 20:12 He sent still a t, and they wounded him G5569
Lk 20:31 then the t married her, and in the G5569
Lk 23:22 *For* the t *time* he spoke to them: "Why G5568
Lk 24: 7 on the t day be raised again. G5569
Lk 24:21 it is the t day since all this took place. G5569
Lk 24:46 suffer and rise from the dead on the t day, G5569
Jn 2: 1 On the t day a wedding took place at G5569
Jn 21:14 This was now the **t time** Jesus appeared to G5568
Jn 21:17 The **t time** he said to him, "Simon son of G5568
Jn 21:17 hurt because Jesus asked him the **t time**, G5568
Ac 10:40 the dead on the t day and caused him G5569
Ac 20: 9 ground from the **t story** and was picked up G5566
Ac 27:19 *On* the t *day*, they threw the ship's tackle G5569
1Co 12:28 second prophets, t teachers, then miracles G5568
1Co 15: 4 was raised on the t day according to the G5569
2Co 12: 2 years ago was caught up to the t heaven. G5569
2Co 12:14 Now I am ready to visit you *for* the **t time** G5568
2Co 13: 1 This will be my t visit to you. "Every matter G5568
Rev 4: 7 like an ox, the t had a face like a man G5569
Rev 6: 5 When the Lamb opened the t seal, G5569
Rev 6: 5 third seal, I heard the t living creature say G5569
Rev 8: 7 A t of the earth was burned up, a third of G5569
Rev 8: 7 a t of the trees were burned up G5569
Rev 8: 8 A t of the sea turned into blood, G5569
Rev 8: 9 a t of the living creatures in the sea died G5569
Rev 8: 9 and a t of the ships were destroyed. G5569
Rev 8:10 The t angel sounded his trumpet, and a G5569
Rev 8:10 fell from the sky on a t of the rivers and on G5569
Rev 8:11 A t of the waters turned bitter, and many G5569
Rev 8:12 his trumpet, and a t of the sun was struck G5569
Rev 8:12 the sun was struck, a t of the moon, and a G5569
Rev 8:12 of the moon, and a t of the stars, so that a G5569
Rev 8:12 the stars, so that a t of them turned dark. G5569
Rev 8:12 A t of the day was without light, and also G5569
Rev 8:12 was without light, and also a t of the night. NDT
Rev 9:15 year were released to kill a t of mankind. G5569
Rev 9:18 A t of mankind was killed by the three G5569
Rev 11:14 has passed; the t woe is coming soon. G5569
Rev 12: 4 Its tail swept a t of the stars out of the sky G5569
Rev 14: 9 A t angel followed them and said in a G5569
Rev 16: 4 The t angel poured out his bowl on the G5569
Rev 21:19 second sapphire, the t agate, the fourth G5569

THIRST (25) [THIRSTS, THIRSTY]

Ex 17: 3 us and our children and livestock die of t?" H7533
Dt 28:48 therefore in hunger and t, in nakedness H7533
Jdg 15:18 Must I now die of t and fall into the hands H7533
2Ch 32:11 to let you die of hunger and t. H7533
Ne 9:15 heaven and in their t you brought them H7533
Ne 9:20 you gave them water for their t. H7533
Job 24:11 they tread the winepresses, yet **suffer** t. H7532
Ps 63: 1 I seek you; I t for you, my whole being H7532
Ps 69:21 in my food and gave me vinegar for my t. H7533
Ps 104:11 the field; the wild donkeys quench their t. H7533
Ps 143: 6 hands to you; I t for you like a parched land. NDT
Isa 5:13 common people will be parched with t. H7533
Isa 41:17 is none; their tongues are parched with t. H7533
Isa 48:21 *They did* not t when he led them through H7532
Isa 49:10 They will neither hunger nor t, nor will the H7532
Isa 50: 2 their fish rot for lack of water and die of t. H7533
Jer 46:10 till *it has* **quenched its** t with blood. H8115
La 4: 4 Because of t the infant's tongue sticks to H7533
Hos 2: 3 into a parched land, and slay her with t. H7533
Am 8:11 not a famine of food or a t for water, but a H7533
Am 8:13 strong young men will faint because of t. H7533
Mt 5: 6 those who hunger and t for righteousness, G1498
Jn 4:14 drinks the water I give them *will* never t. G1498
2Co 11:27 known hunger and t and have often gone G1499
Rev 7:16 will they hunger; never again *will they* t. G1498

THIRSTS (1) [THIRST]

Ps 42: 2 My soul t for God, for the living God H7532

THIRSTY (34) [THIRST]

Ex 17: 3 But the people *were* t for water there, and H7532
Dt 8:15 wilderness, that t and waterless land, with H7536
Jdg 4:19 "*I'm* t," he said. "Please give me some H7532
Jdg 15:18 Because *he was* very t, he cried out to the H7532
Ru 2: 9 And *whenever you are* t, go and get a H7532
2Sa 17:29 hungry and t in the wilderness. H7534
Job 5: 5 and the t pant after his wealth. H7534
Ps 107: 5 They were hungry and t, and their lives H7534
Ps 107: 9 he satisfies the t and fills the H5883+8799
Ps 107:33 a desert, flowing springs into **t ground**, H7536
Pr 25:21 food to eat; if he is t, give him water to H7534
Isa 21:14 bring water for the t; you who live in H7534
Isa 29: 8 as when a t *person* dreams of drinking H7534
Isa 29: 8 awakens faint and t *still*. H8799+5883
Isa 32: 2 the shadow of a great rock in a t land. H6546
Isa 32: 6 empty and from the t they withhold water. H7534
Isa 35: 7 the **t ground** bubbling springs. H7536
Isa 44: 3 For I will pour water on the t land, and H7534
Isa 55: 1 all you *who* are t, come to the H7534
Isa 65:13 but you *will go* t; my servants will H7532
Eze 19:13 planted in the desert, in a dry and t land. H7533
Mt 25:35 *I was* t and you gave me something to G1498
Mt 25:37 or t and give you something to drink? G1498
Mt 25:42 *I was* t and you gave me nothing to drink, G1498
Mt 25:44 we see you hungry or t or a stranger or G1498
Jn 4:13 who drinks this water *will be* t again, G1498
Jn 4:15 water so that I won't *get* t and have to G1498
Jn 6:35 whoever believes in me *will* never *be* t. G1498
Jn 7:37 "Let anyone *who is* t come to me and G1498
Jn 19:28 would be fulfilled, Jesus said, "*I am* t." G1498
Ro 12:20 feed him; if *he is* t, give him something to G1498
1Co 4:11 To this very hour we go hungry and t, we G1498
Rev 21: 6 *To* the t I will give water without cost from G1498
Rev 22:17 Let the *one who is* t come; and let the G1498

THIRTEEN (12) [THIRTEENTH, 13]

Ge 17:25 his son Ishmael was t; H8993+6926
Nu 29:13 of a burnt offering of t young bulls, H8993+6925
Nu 29:14 With each of the t bulls offer a H8993+6925
Jos 19: 6 t towns and their villages H8993+6926
Jos 21: 4 were allotted t towns from the H8993+6926
Jos 21: 6 were allotted t towns from the H8993+6926
Jos 21:19 of Aaron, came to t, together with H8993+6926
Jos 21:33 of the Gershonite clans came to t, H8993+6926
1Ki 7: 1 It took Solomon t years, however H8993+6926
1Ch 6:60 the Kohathite clans came to t. H8993+6926
1Ch 6:62 were allotted t towns from the H8993+6926
Eze 40:11 cubits and its length was t cubits. H8993+6926

THIRTEENTH (11) [THIRTEEN]

Ge 14: 4 in the t year they rebelled. H8993+6926
1Ch 24:13 the t to Huppah, the fourteenth to H8993+6925
1Ch 25:20 the t to Shubael, his sons and H8993+6925
Est 3:12 Then on the t day of the first month H8993+6925
Est 3:13 the t day of the twelfth month H8993+6925
Est 8:12 Xerxes was the t day of the twelfth H8993+6925
Est 9: 1 On the t day of the twelfth month H8993+6925
Est 9:17 happened on the t day of the H8993+6925
Est 9:18 assembled on the t and fourteenth, H8993+6925
Jer 1: 2 to him in the t year of the reign H8993+6926
Jer 25: 3 from the t year of Josiah son of H8993+6926

THIRTIETH (1) [THIRTY]

Eze 1: 1 In my t year, in the fourth month on the H8993

THIRTY (95) [THIRTIETH, 30]

Ge 6:15 fifty cubits wide and t cubits high. H8993
Ge 18:30 What if only t can be found there? H8993
Ge 18:30 answered, "I will not do it if I find t there." H8993
Ge 32:15 t female camels with their young, forty H8993
Ge 41:46 Joseph was t years old when he entered H8993
Ge 47: 9 of my pilgrimage are a hundred and t. H8993
Ex 21:32 the owner must pay t shekels of silver to H8993
Ex 26: 8 size—t cubits long and four cubits wide. H8993
Ex 36:15 size—t cubits long and four cubits wide. H8993
Lev 27: 4 a female, set her value at t shekels; H8993
Nu 4: 3 all the men from t to fifty years of age H8993
Nu 4:23 all the men from t to fifty years of age H8993
Nu 4:30 all the men from t to fifty years of age H8993
Nu 4:35 All the men from t to fifty years of age who H8993
Nu 4:39 All the men from t to fifty years of age who H8993
Nu 4:43 All the men from t to fifty years of age who H8993
Nu 4:47 All the men from t to fifty years of age who H8993
Nu 7:13 a hundred and t shekels and one silver H8993

Nu 7:19 a hundred and **t** shekels and one silver H8993
Nu 7:25 a hundred and **t** shekels and one silver H8993
Nu 7:31 a hundred and **t** shekels and one silver H8993
Nu 7:37 a hundred and **t** shekels and one silver H8993
Nu 7:43 a hundred and **t** shekels and one silver H8993
Nu 7:49 a hundred and **t** shekels and one silver H8993
Nu 7:55 a hundred and **t** shekels and one silver H8993
Nu 7:61 a hundred and **t** shekels and one silver H8993
Nu 7:67 a hundred and **t** shekels and one silver H8993
Nu 7:73 a hundred and **t** shekels and one silver H8993
Nu 7:79 a hundred and **t** shekels and one silver H8993
Nu 7:85 plate weighed a hundred and **t** shekels, H8993
Nu 20:29 all the Israelites mourned for him **t** days. H8993
Dt 34: 8 Moses in the plains of Moab **t** days, H8993
Jos 8: 3 He chose **t** thousand of his best fighting H8993
Jdg 10: 4 He had **t** sons, who rode thirty donkeys H8993
Jdg 10: 4 thirty sons, who rode **t** donkeys. H8993
Jdg 10: 4 They controlled **t** towns in Gilead, which H8993
Jdg 12: 9 He had **t** sons and thirty daughters. H8993
Jdg 12: 9 He had thirty sons and **t** daughters. H8993
Jdg 12: 9 sons he brought in **t** young women as H8993
Jdg 12:14 He had forty sons and **t** grandsons, who H8993
Jdg 14:11 they chose **t** *men* to be his companions. H8993
Jdg 14:12 I will give you **t** linen garments and thirty H8993
Jdg 14:12 thirty linen garments and **t** sets of clothes. H8993
Jdg 14:13 you must give me **t** linen garments and H8993
Jdg 14:13 thirty linen garments and **t** sets of clothes." H8993
Jdg 14:19 Ashkelon, struck down **t** of their men H8993
Jdg 20:31 so that about **t** men fell in the open field H8993
Jdg 20:39 on the Israelites (about **t**), and they said, H8993
1Sa 4:10 Israel lost **t** thousand foot soldiers. H8993
1Sa 9:22 who were invited—about **t** in number. H8993
1Sa 11: 8 thousand and those of Judah **t** thousand. H8993
1Sa 13: 1 Saul was **t** years old when he became H8993
2Sa 5: 4 David was **t** years old when he became H8993
2Sa 6: 1 able young men of Israel—**t** thousand. H8993
2Sa 23:13 three of the **t** chief warriors came down to H8993
2Sa 23:23 held in greater honor than any of the **T**, H8993
2Sa 23:24 Among the **T** were: Asahel the brother of H8993
1Ki 4:22 daily provisions were **t** cors of the finest H8993
1Ki 5:13 laborers from all Israel—**t** thousand men. H8993
1Ki 6: 2 sixty cubits long, twenty wide and **t** high. H8993
1Ki 7: 2 fifty wide and **t** high, with four rows H8993
1Ki 7: 6 a colonnade fifty cubits long and **t** wide. H8993
1Ki 7:23 It took a line of **t** cubits to measure H8993
2Ki 18:14 talents of silver and **t** talents of gold. H8993
1Ch 11:15 Three of the **t** chiefs came down to David H8993
1Ch 11:25 held in greater honor than any of the **T**, H8993
1Ch 11:42 of the Reubenites, and the **t** with him, H8993
1Ch 12: 4 a mighty warrior among the **T**, who was a H8993
1Ch 12: 4 who was a leader of the **T**; Jeremiah, H8993
1Ch 12:18 on Amasai, chief of the **T**, and he said: H8993
1Ch 23: 3 The Levites **t** years old or more were H8993
1Ch 27: 6 warrior among the **T** and was over the H8993
1Ch 27: 6 among the Thirty and was over the **T**. H8993
2Ch 4: 2 It took a line of **t** cubits to measure H8993
2Ch 24:15 he died at the age of a hundred and **t**. H8993
2Ch 35: 7 there a total of **t** thousand lambs and H8993
Est 4:11 But **t** days have passed since I was called H8993
Pr 22:20 Have I not written **t** sayings for you H8993
Jer 38:10 "Take **t** men from here with you and lift H8993
Eze 40:17 there were **t** rooms along the pavement. H8993
Eze 41: 6 one above another, **t** on each level. H8993
Eze 46:22 forty cubits long and **t** cubits wide; each of H8993
Da 6: 7 human being during the next **t** days, A10762
Da 6:12 that during the next **t** days anyone who A10762
Zec 11:12 So they paid me **t** *pieces of* silver. H8993
Zec 11:13 So I took the **t** *pieces of* silver and threw H8993
Mt 13: 8 a hundred, sixty or **t** *times* what was sown. G5558
Mt 13:23 a hundred, sixty or **t** *times* what was sown." G5558
Mt 26:15 they counted out for him **t** pieces of silver. G5558
Mt 27: 3 returned the **t** pieces of silver to the G5558
Mt 27: 9 "They took the **t** pieces of silver, the price G5558
Mk 4: 8 some multiplying **t**, some sixty, G5558
Mk 4:20 a crop—some **t**, some sixty, some a G5558
Lk 3:23 himself was about **t** years old when he G5558
Jn 2: 6 holding from twenty to **t gallons**. G3583+5552

THIRTY-EIGHT (3) [THIRTY-EIGHTH]

Dt 2:14 **T** years passed from the H8993+2256+9046
1Ch 23: 3 of men was **t** thousand. H8993+2256+9046
Jn 5: 5 had been an invalid for **t** years. G5558+3893

THIRTY-EIGHTH (2) [THIRTY-EIGHT]

1Ki 16:29 In the **t** year of Asa king of H8993+2256+9046
2Ki 15: 8 In the **t** year of Azariah king H8993+2256+9046

THIRTY-FIFTH (1) [THIRTY-FIVE]

2Ch 15:19 war until the **t** year of Asa's H8993+2256+2822

THIRTY-FIRST (1)

1Ki 16:23 In the **t** year of Asa king of H8993+2256+285

THIRTY-FIVE (3) [THIRTY-FIFTH, 35]

1Ki 22:42 was **t** years old when H8993+2256+2822
2Ch 3:15 together were **t** cubits long, H8993+2256+2822
2Ch 20:31 He was **t** years old when he H8993+2256+2822

THIRTY-NINTH (3)

2Ki 15:13 king in the **t** year of Uzziah H8993+2256+9596
2Ki 15:17 In the **t** year of Azariah king H8993+2256+9596
2Ch 16:12 In the **t** year of his reign Asa H8993+2256+9596

THIRTY-ONE (3)

Jos 12:24 of Tirzah one **t** kings in all. H8993+2256+285
2Ki 22: 1 reigned in Jerusalem **t** years. H8993+2256+285
2Ch 34: 1 reigned in Jerusalem **t** years. H8993+2256+285

THIRTY-SECOND (2)

Ne 5:14 until his **t** year—twelve H8993+2256+9109
Ne 13: 6 in the **t** year of Artaxerxes H8993+2256+9109

THIRTY-SEVEN (2) [THIRTY-SEVENTH]

Ge 25:17 lived a hundred and **t** years. H8993+2256+8679
2Sa 23:39 There were **t** in all. H8993+2256+8679

THIRTY-SEVENTH (3) [THIRTY-SEVEN]

2Ki 13:10 In the **t** year of Joash king of H8993+2256+8679
2Ki 25:27 In the **t** year of the exile of H8993+2256+8679
Jer 52:31 In the **t** year of the exile of H8993+2256+8679

THIRTY-SIX (1) [THIRTY-SIXTH]

Jos 7: 5 who killed about **t** of them H8993+2256+9252

THIRTY-SIXTH (1) [THIRTY-SIX]

2Ch 16: 1 In the **t** year of Asa's reign H8993+2256+9252

THIRTY-THREE (7)

Ge 46:15 of his were **t** in all. H8993+2256+8993
Lev 12: 4 must wait **t** days to be H8993+2256+8993
2Sa 5: 5 all Israel and Judah **t** years. H8993+2256+8993
1Ki 2:11 Hebron and **t** in Jerusalem. H8993+2256+8993
1Ki 5:16 well as **t hundred** H8993+547+2256+8993+4395
1Ch 3: 4 in Jerusalem **t** years, H8993+2256+8993
1Ch 29:27 Hebron and **t** in Jerusalem. H8993+2256+8993

THIRTY-TWO (6) [32]

1Ki 20: 1 Accompanied by **t** kings with H8993+2256+9109
1Ki 22:31 had ordered his **t** chariot H8993+2256+9109
2Ki 8:17 He was **t** years old when he H8993+2256+9109
1Ch 19: 7 They hired **t** thousand H8993+2256+9109
2Ch 21: 5 Jehoram was **t** years old H8993+2256+9109
2Ch 21:20 Jehoram was **t** years old H8993+2256+9109

THIS (3729) [THESE] See Index of Articles Etc.

THISTLE (4) [THISTLES]

2Ki 14: 9 "A **t** in Lebanon sent a message to a H2560
2Ki 14: 9 came along and trampled the **t** underfoot. H2560
2Ch 25:18 "A **t** in Lebanon sent a message to a H2560
2Ch 25:18 came along and trampled the **t** underfoot. H2560

THISTLES (4) [THISTLE]

Ge 3:18 It will produce thorns and **t** for you, and H1998
Hos 10: 8 Thorns and **t** will grow up and cover their H1998
Mt 7:16 grapes from thornbushes, or figs from **t**? *G5560*
Heb 6: 8 produces thorns and **t** is worthless and is *G5560*

THOMAS (11)

Mt 10: 3 **T** and Matthew the tax collector *G2605*
Mk 3:18 Bartholomew, Matthew, **T**, James son of *G2605*
Lk 6:15 Matthew, **T**, James son of Alphaeus *G2605*
Jn 11:16 Then **T** (also known as Didymus) said to *G2605*
Jn 14: 5 **T** said to him, "Lord, we don't know where *G2605*
Jn 20:24 Now **T** (also known as Didymus), one of *G2605*
Jn 20:26 in the house again, and **T** was with them. *G2605*
Jn 20:27 Then he said *to* **T**, "Put your finger here *G2605*
Jn 20:28 **T** said to him, "My Lord and my God!" *G2605*
Jn 21: 2 Simon Peter, **T** (also known as Didymus), *G2605*
Ac 1:13 Andrew; Philip and **T**, Bartholomew and *G2605*

THONG (NIV84) STRAP, STRAPS

THORN (2) [THORNBUSH, THORNBUSHES, THORNS]

Mic 7: 4 the most upright worse than a **t hedge**. H5004
2Co 12: 7 I was given a **t** in my flesh, a messenger *G5022*

THORNBUSH (5) [THORN]

Jdg 9:14 "Finally all the trees said to the **t**, 'Come H353
Jdg 9:15 "The **t** said to the trees, 'If you really want H353
Jdg 9:15 fire come out of the **t** and consume the H353
Pr 26: 9 Like a **t** in a drunkard's hand is a proverb H2560
Isa 55:13 Instead of the **t** will grow the juniper, and H5848

THORNBUSHES (6) [THORN]

Ex 22: 6 out and spreads into **t** so that it burns H7764
Isa 7:19 on all the **t** and at all the water holes. H5848
Isa 33:12 to ashes; like cut **t** they will be set ablaze." H7764
Hos 2: 6 Therefore I will block her path with **t**; I will H6106
Mt 7:16 Do people pick grapes from **t**, or figs from *G180*
Lk 6:44 People do not pick figs from **t**, or grapes *G180*

THORNS (41) [THORN]

Ge 3:18 It will produce **t** and thistles for you, and H7764
Nu 33:55 barbs in your eyes and **t** in your sides. H7564
Jos 23:13 whips on your backs and **t** in your eyes H7564
Jdg 8: 7 tear your flesh with desert **t** and briers." H7764
Jdg 8:16 punishing them with desert **t** and briers. H7764
2Sa 23: 6 But evil men are all to be cast aside like **t** H7764
2Sa 23: 7 Whoever touches **t** uses a tool of iron H2157S
Job 5: 5 taking it even from among **t**, and the H7553
Ps 58: 9 Before your pots can feel the heat of the **t**— H353
Ps 118:12 were consumed as quickly as burning **t**; H7764
Pr 15:19 The way of the sluggard is blocked with **t** H2537
Pr 24:31 **t** had come up everywhere, the ground H7853
Ecc 7: 6 Like the crackling of **t** under the pot, so is H6106
SS 2: 2 Like a lily among **t** is my darling among H2560
Isa 5: 6 briers and **t** will grow there. H8885
Isa 7:23 shekels, there will be only briers and **t**. H8885
Isa 7:24 the land will be covered with briers and **t**. H8885
Isa 7:25 longer go there for fear of the briers and **t**; H8885
Isa 9:18 it consumes briers and **t**, it sets the forest H8885
Isa 10:17 burn and consume his **t** and his briers. H8885
Isa 27: 4 there were briers and **t** confronting me! H8885
Isa 32:13 a land overgrown with **t** and briers—yes, H7764
Isa 34:13 **T** will overrun her citadels, nettles and H6106
Jer 4: 3 ground and do not sow among **t**. H7764
Jer 12:13 They will sow wheat but reap **t**; they will H7764
Eze 2: 6 though briers and **t** are all around you H6141
Eze 28:24 who are painful briers and sharp **t**. H7764
Hos 9: 6 by briers, and **t** will overrun their tents. H2560
Hos 10: 8 **T** and thistles will grow up and cover their H7764
Na 1:10 be entangled among **t** and drunk from H6106
Mt 13: 7 Other seed fell among **t**, which grew up *G180*
Mt 13:22 falling among the **t** refers to someone who *G180*
Mt 27:29 together a crown of **t** and set it on his head *G180*
Mk 4: 7 Other seed fell among **t**, which grew up *G180*
Mk 4:18 like seed sown among **t**, hear the word; *G180*
Mk 15:17 together a crown **of t** and set it on him. *G181*
Lk 8: 7 Other seed fell among **t**, which grew up *G180*
Lk 8:14 seed that fell among **t** stands for those who *G180*
Jn 19: 2 together a crown of **t** and put it on his head *G180*
Jn 19: 5 wearing the crown **of t** and the purple robe, *G181*
Heb 6: 8 But land that produces **t** and thistles is *G180*

THOROUGH (3) [THOROUGHLY]

Dt 19:18 The judges must make a **t** investigation H3512
Ac 12:19 *After* Herod *had* **a t search made** for him *G2118*
Ac 18:24 with a **t knowledge** of the Scriptures. *G1543*

THOROUGHLY (9) [THOROUGH]

Ge 11: 3 bricks and **bake** them **t**. H8596+4200+8599
Dt 13:14 must inquire, probe and investigate it **t**. H3512
Dt 17: 4 attention, then you must investigate it **t**. H3512
Ps 119:140 Your promises have been **t** tested, and H4394
Isa 1:25 *I will* **t purge away** your H7671+3869+2021+1342
Jer 6: 9 *Let them* **glean** the remnant of Israel as **t** H6618+6618
Jer 20:11 They will fail and be **t** disgraced; their H4394
Ac 22: 3 Gamaliel and was **t** trained in the *G2848+205*
2Ti 3:17 of God may be **t** equipped for every *G1992*

THOSE (1488) [THAT] See Index of Articles Etc.

THOUGH (337) [ALTHOUGH]

Ge 8:21 **even t** every inclination of the human H3954
Ge 18:27 **t** I am nothing but dust and ashes, H2256
Ge 20:12 daughter of my father **t** not of my mother; H421
Ge 28:19 **t** the city used to be called Luz. H219
Ge 31:50 my daughters, even **t** no one is with us NDT
Ge 38:14 *t* And Shelah *had* now **grown up**, she had AIT
Ge 39:10 And **t** she spoke to Joseph day after day H3869
Ge 42:30 us and treated us **as t** we were spying on H3869
Ge 44:18 **t** you are equal to Pharaoh himself. H3954
Ge 48:14 on Ephraim's head, **t** he was the younger H2256
Ge 48:14 **even t** Manasseh was the firstborn. H3954
Ex 3: 2 Moses saw that **t** the bush was on fire it H2180
Ex 7: 3 **and t** I multiply my signs and wonders in H2256
Ex 13:17 the Philistine country, **t** that was shorter. H3954
Lev 4:13 **even t** the community is unaware of the H2256
Lev 5: 3 unclean) **even t** they are unaware of it H2256
Lev 5: 4 swear about) **even t** they are unaware of it H2256
Lev 5:17 commands, **even t** they do not know it H2256
Lev 11: 4 The camel, **t** it chews the cud, does not H3954
Lev 11: 5 The hyrax, **t** it chews the cud, does not H3954
Lev 11: 6 The rabbit, **t** it chews the cud, does not H3954
Lev 11: 7 And the pig, **t** it has a divided hoof, does H3954
Lev 13:55 its appearance, **even t** it has not spread, it H2256
Lev 26:36 They will run as **t** fleeing from the sword NDT
Lev 26:36 will fall, **even t** no one is pursuing them. H2256
Lev 26:37 over one another as **t** fleeing from the H3869
Lev 26:37 **even t** no one is pursuing them. H2256
Nu 5:14 suspects her **even t** she is not impure H2256
Nu 14:44 **t** neither Moses nor the ark of the LORD's H2256
Dt 18: 8 **even t** he has received money from H4200+963
Dt 19: 6 kill him **even t** he is not deserving of H2256
Dt 22:27 **t** the betrothed woman screamed NDT
Dt 29:19 **even t** I persist in going my own way," H3954
Jos 13: 3 of it counted as Canaanite **t** held by the five NDT
Jos 17:18 **t** the Canaanites have chariots fitted with H3954
Jos 17:18 fitted with iron and **t** they are strong, H3954
Jos 22:17 **even t** a plague fell on the community of H2256
Jdg 13:16 the LORD replied, "**Even t** you detain me, H561
Jdg 18:29 to Israel—**t** the city used to be called Laish. H219
Ru 2:13 **t** I do not have the standing of one of your H2256
1Sa 12:12 **even t** the LORD your God was your king. H2256
1Sa 15:35 Saul again, **t** Samuel mourned for him. H3954
1Sa 20:20 side of it, as **t** I were shooting at a target. NDT
1Sa 25:29 **Even t** someone is pursuing you to take H2256
2Sa 3:39 And today, **t** I am the anointed king, I am H2256
2Sa 16: 6 **t** all the troops and the special guard H2256
2Sa 23:19 **even t** he was not included among them. H2256
1Ki 2:28 with Adonijah **t** not with Absalom, H2256
1Ki 12:31 of people, **even t** they were not Levites. H889
2Ki 4:39 of stew, **t** no one knew what they were. H3954
2Ki 5:16 **And even t** Naaman urged him, he H2256
2Ki 17:12 They worshiped idols, **t** the LORD had said H889
2Ki 18:24 **even t** you are depending on Egypt for H2256
2Ki 25: 4 **t** the Babylonians were surrounding the H2256
1Ch 5: 2 **t** Judah was the strongest of his H3954

T

1Ch 11:21 **even** t he was not included among them. H2256
1Ch 17:17 have looked on me **as** t I were the most H3869
2Ch 16:12 T his disease was severe, even in his H6330
2Ch 24:19 **and** t they testified against them H2256
Ezr 3: 6 t the foundation of the LORD's temple had H2256
Ezr 9: 9 T we are slaves, our God has not forsaken H3954
Ezr 9:15 t because of it not one of us can stand in H3954
Ne 5: 5 as our fellow Jews and t our children are as NDT
Ne 6: 1 t up to that time I had not set the doors in H1685
Est 4:16 go to the king, **even** t it is against the law. H889
Job 2: 3 t you incited me against him to ruin him H2256
Job 9: 3 T they wished to dispute with him, they H561
Job 9:15 T I were innocent, I could not answer him; H561
Job 10: 7 t you know that I am not guilty and that H6584
Job 12: 4 t I called on God and he answered NDT
Job 12: 4 laughingstock, t righteous and blameless! NDT
Job 13:15 T he slay me, yet will I hope in him; I will H2176
Job 15:27 "T his face is covered with fat and his H3954
Job 19: 7 "T I cry, 'Violence!' I get no response H2176
Job 19: 7 I get no response; t I call for help, there is NDT
Job 19:16 not answer, t I beg him with my own mouth. NDT
Job 20: 6 T the pride of the godless person reaches H561
Job 20:12 "T evil is sweet in his mouth and he hides H561
Job 20:13 t he cannot bear to let it go and lets it linger NDT
Job 20:24 T he flees from an iron weapon, NDT
Job 22: 8 t you were a powerful man, owning land H2256
Job 24:22 by his power; t they become established H2256
Job 27:16 T he heaps up silver like dust and clothes H561
Job 33:14 now another—t no one perceives it. NDT
Job 39:13 t they cannot compare with the wings and NDT
Job 40:23 t the Jordan should surge against its H3954
Ps 3: 6 I will not fear t tens of thousands assail H4946
Ps 14: 4 They devour my people *as t* **eating** bread AIT
Ps 17: 3 T you probe my heart, though you examine NDT
Ps 17: 3 t you examine me at night and test me NDT
Ps 17: 4 T people tried to bribe me, I have kept H4200
Ps 21:11 T they plot evil against you and devise H3954
Ps 23: 4 Even t I walk through the darkest valley, H3954
Ps 25:11 forgive my iniquity, t it is great. H3954
Ps 27: 3 T an army besiege me, my heart will not H561
Ps 27: 3 will not fear; t war break out against me H561
Ps 27:10 T my father and mother forsake me, the H3954
Ps 31:12 I am forgotten **as** t I were dead; I have H3869
Ps 35:14 went about mourning **as** t for my friend H3869
Ps 35:14 my head in grief **as** t weeping for my H3869
Ps 37:10 will be no more; t you look for them, they H2256
Ps 37:20 T the LORD's enemies are like the flowers H2256
Ps 37:24 t he may stumble, he will not fall, for the H3954
Ps 37:36 was no more; t I looked for him, he H2256
Ps 38:20 t I seek only to do what is good. H9393
Ps 44:17 came upon us, t we had not forgotten you H2256
Ps 46: 2 t the earth give way and the mountains fall H928
Ps 46: 3 t its waters roar and foam and the NDT
Ps 49:11 t they had named lands after themselves. NDT
Ps 49:18 T while they live they count themselves H3954
Ps 53: 4 They devour my people *as t* **eating** bread AIT
Ps 55:18 against me, **even** t many oppose me. H3954
Ps 62:10 in stolen goods; t your riches increase H3954
Ps 71:15 t I know not how to relate them all. H3954
Ps 71:20 T you have made me see troubles, many H889
Ps 77:19 t your footprints were not seen. H2256
Ps 78: 9 The men of Ephraim, t armed with bows NDT
Ps 92: 7 that t the wicked spring up like grass and H928
Ps 95: 9 they tried me, t they had seen what I did. H1685
Ps 99: 8 t you punished their misdeeds. H2256
Ps 119:23 T rulers sit together and slander me, your H1685
Ps 119:61 T the wicked bind me with ropes, I will not NDT
Ps 119:69 T the arrogant have smeared me with lies, NDT
Ps 119:83 T I am like a wineskin in the smoke, I do H3954
Ps 119:109 T I constantly take my life in my hands, NDT
Ps 119:141 T I am lowly and despised, I do not forget NDT
Ps 138: 6 T the LORD is exalted, he looks kindly on H3954
Ps 138: 6 kindly on the lowly; t lofty, he sees them H2256
Ps 138: 7 T I walk in the midst of trouble, you H561
Pr 4: 7 T it cost all you have, get H2256
Pr 6:31 t it costs him all the wealth of his house. NDT
Pr 19: 7 T the poor pursue them with pleading, they NDT
Pr 24:16 **for** *t* the righteous fall seven times, they rise AIT
Pr 26:25 T their speech is charming, do not believe H3954
Pr 27:22 T you grind a fool in a mortar, grinding H561
Pr 28: 1 The wicked flee t no one pursues, but the H2256
Pr 29:19 by mere words; t they understand, they H3954
Ecc 4:12 T one may be overpowered, two can H561
Ecc 6: 5 T it never saw the sun or knew anything, it H1685
Ecc 8: 6 t a person may be weighed down by H3954
Isa 1:18 "T your sins are like scarlet, they shall be H561
Isa 1:18 as white as snow; t they are red as crimson H561
Isa 6:13 **And** t a tenth remains in the land, it will H2256
Isa 10:22 T your people be like the sand by H3954+561
Isa 17:10 *t you* **set out** the finest plants and plant AIT
Isa 17:11 t on the day you set them out, you make NDT
Isa 30: 4 T they have officials in Zoan and their H3954
Isa 31: 4 t a whole band of shepherds is called H889
Isa 32:19 T hail flattens the forest and the city is H2256
Isa 36: 9 **even** t you are depending on Egypt for H2256
Isa 40:15 weighs the islands **as** t they were fine H3869
Isa 41:12 T you search for your enemies, you will not NDT
Isa 45: 4 of honor, t you do not acknowledge me. H2256
Isa 45: 5 t you have not acknowledged me H2256
Isa 46: 7 **Even** t someone cries out to it, it cannot H677
Isa 48:10 I have refined you, t not as silver; I have H2256
Isa 49:15 child she has borne? T she may forget, H1685
Isa 49:19 "T you were ruined and made desolate H3954
Isa 53: 9 in his death, t he had done no violence H6584
Isa 53:10 t the LORD makes his life an offering for H561
Isa 54:10 T the mountains be shaken and the hills H3954
Isa 60:10 T in anger I struck you, in favor I will show H3954
Isa 63:16 t Abraham does not know us or Israel H3954
Jer 2:34 t you did not catch them breaking in. NDT
Jer 4:27 t I will not destroy it completely. H2256
Jer 6:14 wound of my people **as** t it were not H6584
Jer 8:11 wound of my people **as** t it were not H6584
Jer 10: 2 t the nations are terrified by them. H3954
Jer 12: 6 not trust them, t they speak well of you. H3954
Jer 14:12 t they offer burnt offerings and grain H3954
Jer 22: 6 "T you are like Gilead to me, like the NDT
Jer 23:38 **even** t I told you that you must not claim H2256
Jer 25: 4 **And** t the LORD has sent all his servants H2256
Jer 26: 5 again and again (t you have not listened), H2256
Jer 29:31 **even** t I did not send him H2256
Jer 30:11 'T I completely destroy all the nations H3954
Jer 31:20 T I often speak against him, I still H3954
Jer 31:32 my covenant, t I was a husband to them," H2256
Jer 32:25 **And** t the city will be given into the hands H2256
Jer 32:33 t I taught them again and again H2256
Jer 32:35 daughters to Molek, t I never commanded H889
Jer 36:25 Even t Elnathan, Delaiah and Gemariah H2256
Jer 42: 2 For as you now see, t we were once many NDT
Jer 46:23 declares the LORD, "dense t it be. H3954
Jer 46:28 "T I completely destroy all the nations H3954
Jer 49:16 T you build your nest as high as the H3954
Jer 51: 5 t their land is full of guilt before the Holy H3954
Jer 52: 7 t the Babylonians were surrounding the H2256
La 3:32 T he brings grief, he will show H3954+561
Eze 2: 6 t briers and thorns are all around you and H3954
Eze 2: 6 by them, t they are a rebellious people. H3954
Eze 3: 9 by them, t they are a rebellious people." H3954
Eze 12: 3 t they are a rebellious people. H3954
Eze 13: 6 **Even** t the LORD has not sent them, they H2256
Eze 13: 7 "The LORD declares," t I have not spoken? H2256
Eze 18:11 t the father has done none of them): H2256
Eze 18:14 father commits, **and** t he sees them, he H2256
Eze 28: 2 t you think you are as wise as a god. H2256
Eze 32:27 t these warriors also had terrorized the H3954
Eze 33: 9 their sin, t you yourself will be saved. H2256
Eze 33:12 be allowed to live **even** t they were H928
Eze 35:10 of them," **even** t I the LORD was there H2256
Eze 39:28 t I sent them into exile among the H928
Da 5:22 t you knew all this. A10353+10619+10168
Da 9: 9 **even** t we have rebelled against him; H3954
Da 11:33 t for a time they will fall by the sword or H2256
Hos 3: 1 t she is loved by another man and is an NDT
Hos 3: 1 t they turn to other gods and love the H2256
Hos 4:15 "T you, Israel, commit adultery, do not let H561
Hos 8:11 "T Ephraim built many altars for sin H3954
Hos 8:13 *T they* offer sacrifices as gifts to me, and AIT
Hos 8:13 gifts to me, and *t they* **eat** the meat, the LORD AIT
Hos 11: 7 **Even** t they call me God Most High, I will H2256
Hos 13:15 **even** t he thrives among his brothers. H3954
Am 2: 9 t they were tall as the cedars and strong as H889
Am 5:11 Therefore, t you have built stone mansions NDT
Am 5:11 in them; t you have planted lush vineyards NDT
Am 5:19 It will be **as** t a man fled from a lion H3869+889
Am 5:19 as t he entered his house and rested his NDT
Am 5:22 Even t you bring me burnt offerings and H561
Am 5:22 T you bring choice fellowship offerings, H2256
Am 9: 2 T they dig down to the depths below, from H561
Am 9: 2 T they climb up to the heavens above, from H561
Am 9: 3 T they hide themselves on the top of H561
Am 9: 3 T they hide from my eyes at the bottom of H561
Am 9: 4 T they are driven into exile by their H561
Ob 4 T you soar like the eagle and make your H561
Jnh 4:10 t you did not tend it or make it grow. H889
Mic 5: 2 t you are small among the clans of Judah NDT
Mic 7: 8 T I have fallen, I will rise H3954
Mic 7: 8 T I sit in darkness, the LORD will be my H3954
Na 2: 2 t destroyers have laid them waste and H3954
Hab 2: 3 T it linger, wait for it; it will certainly come H561
Hab 3:14 gloating **as** t about to devour the H4017
Hab 3:17 T the fig tree does not bud and there are H3954
Hab 3:17 t the olive crop fails and the fields produce NDT
Hab 3:17 t there are no sheep in the pen and no NDT
Zep 1:13 T they build houses, they will not live in H2256
Zep 1:13 not live in them; t they plant vineyards H2256
Zec 9: 2 on Tyre and Sidon, t they are very skillful. H3954
Zec 10: 6 They will be as t I had not rejected them H889
Zec 10: 9 T I scatter them among the peoples, yet H2256
Mal 1: 4 may say, "*T we have* **been crushed**, we will AIT
Mal 2:12 **even** t he brings an offering to the LORD H2256
Mal 2:14 unfaithful to her, t she is your partner H2256
Mt 7:11 *t you* **are** evil, know how to give good AIT
Mt 13:13 "*T* **seeing**, they do not see; though hearing AIT
Mt 13:13 they do not see; *t* **hearing**, they do not hear AIT
Mt 13:32 T it is the smallest of all seeds, yet when it G3525
Mt 26:60 *t* many false witnesses **came forward**. AIT
Mk 4:27 grows, t he does not know how. G6055
Lk 8:10 " '*t* **seeing**, they may not see AIT
Lk 8:10 they may not see; *t* **hearing**, they may not AIT
Lk 8:29 and *t he was* **chained hand** and foot and AIT
Lk 11: 8 even t he will not get up and give you the G1623
Lk 11:13 If you then, *t you* **are** evil, know how to give AIT
Lk 18: 4 'Even t I don't fear God or care what G1623
Jn 1:10 and *t* the world *was* **made** through him AIT
Jn 2: 9 t the servants who had drawn the water G1254
Jn 6:71 t one of the Twelve, was later to betray NDT
Jn 7:22 (t **actually** it did not come from Moses G4022
Jn 8:55 T you do not know him, I know him. G2779
Jn 10:38 I do them, *even t you do* not **believe** me AIT
Jn 10:41 "T John never performed a sign G3525
Jn 11:25 believes in me will live, **even** t they die; G2829
Jn 13:10 And you are clean, t not every one of you." G247
Jn 16:25 "*T I have been* **speaking** figuratively, a time AIT
Jn 17:25 t the world does not know you G2779
Jn 20:26 *T* the doors *were* **locked**, Jesus came and AIT
Ac 3:13 before Pilate, *t he had* **decided** to let him go. AIT
Ac 5:13 **even** t they were highly regarded by the G247
Ac 7: 5 *even t at that time* Abraham **had** no child. AIT
Ac 13:28 T they found no proper ground for a death G2779
Ac 16:37 without a trial, *even t we* **are** Roman citizens AIT
Ac 17:27 t he is not far from any one of us. G2779+1145
Ac 18:25 *t he* **knew** only the baptism of John. AIT
Ac 19:37 *t they have* neither robbed temples nor **blasphemed** AIT
Ac 28: 4 be a murderer; *for t he* **escaped** from the sea AIT
Ro 2:14 themselves, *even t they do* not **have** the law. AIT
Ro 2:25 you have become as t you had not been NDT
Ro 2:26 they not be regarded **as** t they were G1650
Ro 2:27 even t you have the written code and NDT
Ro 5: 7 t for a good person someone might G1142
Ro 6:17 be to God that, *t you used to* **be** slaves to sin AIT
Ro 8:10 then **even** t your body is subject to death G3525
Ro 9: 6 It is not as t God's word had failed. G4022
Ro 9:27 "T the number of the Israelites be like the G1569
Ro 11:17 t a wild olive shoot, have been G1639
Ro 12: 5 so in Christ we, t many, form one body, and NDT
1Co 3:15 **even** t only as one escaping through the G1254
1Co 4: 7 why do you boast **as** t you did not? G6055
1Co 5: 3 **even** t I am not physically present G3525+1142
1Co 9: 2 **Even** t I may not be an apostle to others G1623
1Co 9:19 *T I* **am** free and belong to no one, I have AIT
1Co 9:20 the law (*t I* myself **am** not under the law), AIT
1Co 9:21 *t I* **am** not free from God's law but am under AIT
1Co 12:12 Just as a body, t one, has many parts, but G1639
1Co 15: 6 are still living, t some have fallen asleep. G1254
2Co 3: 7 because of its glory, **transitory** *t it was*, AIT
2Co 4:16 T outwardly we are wasting away G247+1623
2Co 5:16 T we once regarded Christ in this way, we G1623
2Co 5:20 **as** t God were making his appeal through G6055
2Co 7: 8 T I did regret it—I see that my letter hurt G1623
2Co 7:12 So even t I wrote to you, it was neither on G1623
2Co 8: 9 Jesus Christ, that *t he* **was** rich, yet for your AIT
2Co 10: 3 For *t we* **live** in the world, we do not wage war AIT
2Co 12:11 the "super-apostles," even t I am nothing. G1623
2Co 13: 7 what is right even t we may seem to have G6055
Gal 2: 3 to be circumcised, *even t he* **was** a Greek. AIT
Gal 4:14 even t my illness was a trial to you, you NDT
Php 3: 4 t I myself have reasons for such confidence G2788
Col 2: 5 For t I am absent from you in body, I am G1623
Col 2:20 **as** t you still belonged to the world G6055
1Th 2: 6 *even t* as apostles of Christ *we* **could** *have* AIT
1Ti 1:13 *Even t I* **was** once a blasphemer and a AIT
Heb 3: 9 t for forty years they saw what I did. G2779
Heb 5: 8 Son t he was, he learned obedience from G2788
Heb 5:12 *t* by this time *you* **ought** to be teachers AIT
Heb 6: 9 Even t we speak like this, dear friends, we G1623
Heb 7: 5 **even** t they also are descended from G2788
Heb 10: 8 *t they were* **offered** in accordance with the law AIT
Heb 11: 4 by faith Abel still speaks, *even t he is* **dead**. AIT
Heb 11: 8 *even t he did* not **know** where he was going. AIT
Heb 11:18 even t God had said to him, "It is through NDT
Heb 12:17 **Even** t he sought the blessing with tears G2788
1Pe 1: 6 t now for a little while you may have had G1623
1Pe 1: 7 which perishes **even** t refined by fire G1254
1Pe 1: 8 *T you have* not **seen** him, you love him; and AIT
1Pe 1: 8 and *even t you do* not **see** him now, you AIT
1Pe 2:12 t they accuse you of doing wrong G1877+4005
1Pe 4:12 **as** t something strange were happening G6055
2Pe 1:12 **even** t you know them and are firmly G2788
2Pe 1:21 prophets, *t* **human**, spoke from God as AIT
3Jn 5 sisters, **even** t they are strangers to you. G2779
Jude 5 *T you already* **know** all this, I want to remind AIT
Rev 1:17 I saw him, I fell at his feet **as** t dead. G6055
Rev 3: 9 who claim to be Jews t they are not, but G2779

THOUGHT (92) [THINK]

Ge 18:12 So Sarah laughed to herself *as she* t, "After H606
Ge 19:14 But his sons-in-law t he was joking. H928+6524
Ge 21:16 a bowshot away, for *she* t, "I cannot watch H606
Ge 26: 7 He t, "The men of this place might kill me NDT
Ge 26: 9 "Because *I* t I might lose my life on account H606
Ge 28:16 from his sleep, *he* t, "Surely the LORD is H606
Ge 31:31 because *I* t you would take your daughters H606
Ge 32: 8 *He* t, "If Esau comes and attacks one group H606
Ge 32:20 For *he* t, "I will pacify him with these gifts H606
Ge 38:11 For *he* t, "He may die too, just like his H606
Ge 38:15 Judah saw her, *he* t she was a prostitute H3108
Ge 43:18 *They* t, "We were brought here because of H606
Ex 2:14 Then Moses was afraid and t, "What I did H606
Ex 3: 3 So Moses t, "I will go over and see this H606
Dt 15: 9 Be careful not to harbor this wicked t: "The H1821
Jdg 16:20 He awoke from his sleep and t, "I'll go out H606
Ru 1:12 Even if *I* t there was still hope for me H606
Ru 4: 4 I t I should bring the matter to your H606
1Sa 1:13 voice was not heard. Eli t she was drunk H3108
1Sa 13:12 *I* t, 'Now the Philistines will come down H606
1Sa 15:32 And *he* t, "Surely the bitterness of death is H606

1Sa 16: 6 Samuel saw Eliab and **t**, "Surely the LORD's H606
1Sa 18: 8 tens of thousands," *he* **t**, "but me with only H606
1Sa 18:21 he **t**, "so that she may be a snare to him H606
1Sa 20:26 nothing that day, for *he* **t**, "Something must H606
1Sa 27: 1 But David **t** to himself, "One of these days I H606
1Sa 27:11 to Gath, for *he* **t**, "They might inform H606
2Sa 4:10 and **t** he was bringing good news H928+6524
2Sa 5: 6 They **t**, "David cannot get in H606
2Sa 10: 2 David **t**, "I will show kindness to Hanun son H606
2Sa 12:18 child was dead, for *they* **t**, "While the child H606
2Sa 12:22 I fasted and wept. *I* **t**, 'Who knows? The H606
2Sa 14:15 Your servant **t**, 'I will speak to the king H606
2Sa 18:18 to himself, for *he* **t**, "I have no son to H606
1Ki 12:26 Jeroboam **t** to himself, "The kingdom will H606
1Ki 18:27 Perhaps he is **deep in t**, or busy, or H8490
1Ki 22:32 saw Jehoshaphat, they **t**, "Surely this is the H606
2Ki 5:11 "*I* **t** that he would surely come H606+448+3276
2Ki 20:19 For *he* **t**, "Will there not be peace and H606
1Ch 19: 2 David **t**, "I will show kindness to Hanun son H606
1Ch 28: 9 understands every desire and every **t**. H4742
2Ch 18:31 Jehoshaphat, they **t**, "This is the king of H606
2Ch 28:23 defeated him; for *he* **t**, "Since the gods of H606
Est 6: 6 Now Haman **t** to himself, "Who is there H606
Job 29:18 "*I* **t**, 'I will die in my own house, my days as H606
Job 32: 7 *I* **t**, 'Age should speak; advanced years H606
Ps 50:21 I kept silent, *you* **t** I was exactly like you. H1948
Ps 77: 5 *I* **t** *about* the former days, the years of H3108
Ps 77:10 Then *I* **t**, "To this I will appeal: the years H606
Ps 106: 7 in Egypt, *they* **gave** no **t** *to* your miracles H8505
Ps 109:16 For *he* never **t** *of* doing a kindness, but H2349
Pr 4:26 **Give careful t** *to* the paths for your feet H7143
Pr 5: 6 *She* **gives** no **t** *to* the way of life; her paths H7143
Pr 14: 8 of the prudent is *to* **give t** *to* their ways, H1067
Pr 14:15 the prudent **give t** to their steps. H1067
Pr 17:28 Even fools **are t** wise if they keep silent H3108
Pr 21:29 but the upright **give t** *to* their ways. H1067
Isa 29:16 as if the potter **were t** to be like the clay! H3108
Isa 39: 8 For *he* **t**, "There will be peace and security H606
Isa 65:20 dies at a hundred will be **t** a mere child; NDT
Jer 3: 7 *I* **t** that after she had done all this she H606
Jer 3:19 *I* **t** you would call me 'Father' and not turn H606
Jer 5: 4 I **t**, "These are only the poor; they are H606
La 3:54 over my head, and *I* **t** I was about to perish. H606
La 4:20 *We* **t** that under his shadow we would live H606
Zep 3: 7 Of Jerusalem *I* **t**, 'Surely you will fear me H606
Hag 1: 5 "**Give careful t** to your ways. H8492+4222
Hag 1: 7 "**Give careful t** to your ways. H8492+4222
Hag 2:15 " 'Now **give careful t** to this from H8492+4222
Hag 2:18 **give careful t** to the day when the H8492+4222
Hag 2:18 temple was laid. **Give careful t**: H8492+4222
Mk 5:28 because *she* **t**, "If I just touch his clothes, *G3306*
Mk 6:49 on the lake, *they* **t** he was a ghost. *G1506*
Lk 3:23 He was the son, so *it was* **t**, of Joseph, the *G3787*
Lk 12:17 *He* **t** to himself, 'What shall I do? I have *G1368*
Lk 18: 2 feared God nor **cared what** people **t**. *G1956*
Lk 19:11 the people **t** that the kingdom of God *G1506*
Jn 8:56 rejoiced **at the t** of seeing my day; *G2671*
Jn 11:13 his disciples **t** he meant natural sleep. *G1506*
Jn 13:29 some **t** Jesus was telling him to buy what *G1506*
Ac 7:25 Moses **t** *that* his own people would realize *G3787*
Ac 8:20 because *you* **t** you could buy the gift of *G3787*
Ac 8:22 you for having such a **t** in your heart. *G2154*
Ac 12: 9 happening; *he* **t** he was seeing a vision. *G1506*
Ac 16:27 to kill himself *because he* **t** the prisoners *G3787*
1Co 1:10 that you be perfectly united in mind and **t**. *G1191*
1Co 13:11 I talked like a child, *I* **t** like a child, *G5858*
2Co 9: 5 So *I* **t** it necessary to urge the brothers to *G2451*
2Co 10: 5 take captive every **t** to make it obedient *G3784*
1Th 2:17 in person, not *in* **t**), out of our intense *G2840*
1Th 3: 1 *we* **t it best** to be left by ourselves in *G2305*
Heb 12:10 us for a little while as they **t** *best*; *G1506*

THOUGHTLESSLY (1) [THINK]

Lev 5: 4 if anyone **t** takes an H4200+1051+928+8557

THOUGHTS (44) [THINK]

Ge 6: 5 inclination of the **t** *of* the human heart H4742
1Ch 29:18 these desires and **t** *in* the hearts of your H4742
Job 20: 2 "My **troubled t** prompt me to answer H8546
Ps 10: 4 in all his **t** there is no room for God. H4659
Ps 13: 2 with my **t** and day after H6783+928+5883
Ps 55: 2 My **t** trouble me and I am distraught H8490
Ps 92: 5 your works, LORD, how profound your **t**! H4742
Ps 139: 2 when I rise; you perceive my **t** from afar. H8277
Ps 139:17 How precious to me are your **t**, God! How H8277
Ps 139:23 my heart; test me and know my **anxious t**. H8595
Pr 1:23 Then I will pour out my **t** to you, I will H8120
Pr 15:26 The LORD detests the **t** *of* the wicked, but H4742
Ecc 2:12 Then I turned my **t** to consider wisdom, and NDT
Ecc 10:20 Do not revile the king even in your **t**, or H4529
Isa 33:18 In your **t** you will ponder the former terror H4213
Isa 55: 7 their ways and the unrighteous their **t**. H4742
Isa 55: 8 "For my **t** are not your thoughts, neither H4742
Isa 55: 8 "For my thoughts are not your **t**, neither H4742
Isa 55: 9 your ways and my **t** than your thoughts. H4742
Isa 55: 9 your ways and my thoughts than your **t**. H4742
Jer 4:14 How long will you harbor wicked **t**? H4742
Jer 12: 3 you see me and test my **t** about you. H4213
Eze 38:10 On that day **t** will come into your mind H1821
Da 4:19 a time, and his **t** terrified him. A10669
Da 7:28 was deeply troubled by my **t**, and my A10669
Am 4:13 who reveals his **t** to mankind, who H8465
Mic 4:12 But they do not know the **t** *of* the LORD H4742
Mt 9: 4 Knowing their **t**, Jesus said, "Why do you *G1927*
Mt 9: 4 "Why *do you* **entertain** evil **t** in your hearts *G1926*
Mt 12:25 Jesus knew their **t** and said to them *G1927*
Mt 15:19 For out of the heart come evil **t**—murder *G1369*
Mk 7:21 that evil **t** come—sexual immorality *G1369*
Lk 1:51 those who are proud *in* their inmost **t**. *G1379*
Lk 2:35 so that the **t** of many hearts will be *G1369*
Lk 9:47 knowing their **t**, took a little *G1369+2840*
Lk 11:17 Jesus knew their **t** and said to them: "Any *G1378*
Ro 2:15 their **t** sometimes accusing them and *G3361*
1Co 2:11 who knows a person's **t** except their own *G3836S*
1Co 2:11 way no one knows **the** *t* of God except the AIT
1Co 3:20 Lord knows that the **t** of the wise are futile *G1369*
Eph 2: 3 our flesh and following its desires and **t**. *G1379*
Heb 3: 1 calling, **fix your t on** Jesus, whom we *G2917*
Heb 4:12 it judges the **t** and attitudes of the heart. *G1927*
Jas 2: 4 yourselves and become judges *with* evil **t**? *G1369*

THOUSAND (274) [THOUSANDS, 1000]

Ge 20:16 am giving your brother a **t** shekels *of* silver. H547
Ex 12:37 were about six hundred **t** men on foot, H547
Ex 20: 6 love to a **t generations** of those who H547
Ex 32:28 that day about three **t** of the people died. H547
Lev 26: 8 a hundred of you will chase **ten t** H8047
Nu 7:85 dishes weighed *two* **t** four hundred shekels H547
Nu 11:21 I am among six hundred **t** men on foot, H547
Nu 31: 4 Send into battle a **t** *men* from each of the H547
Nu 31: 5 So twelve **t** men armed for battle, H547
Nu 31: 5 armed for battle, a **t** from each tribe, were H547
Nu 31: 6 them into battle, a **t** from each tribe, along H547
Nu 35: 4 Levites will extend *a* **t** cubits from the town H547
Nu 35: 5 measure *two* **t** cubits on the east side H547
Nu 35: 5 on the east side, *two* **t** on the south side H547
Nu 35: 5 *two* **t** on the west and two thousand on the H547
Nu 35: 5 on the west and *two* **t** on the north, H547
Dt 1:11 increase you a **t** times and bless you as he H547
Dt 5:10 love to a **t generations** of those who H547
Dt 7: 9 covenant of love to a **t** generations of those H547
Dt 32:30 How could one man chase a **t**, or two put H547
Dt 32:30 thousand, or two put **ten t** to flight, unless H8047
Jos 3: 4 distance of about *two* **t** cubits between you H547
Jos 4:13 About forty **t** armed for battle crossed over H547
Jos 7: 3 Send *two* or three **t** men to take it and do H547
Jos 7: 4 So about three **t** went up; but they were H547
Jos 8: 3 He chose thirty **t** of his best fighting men H547
Jos 8:12 had taken about five **t** men and set them in H547
Jos 8:25 Twelve **t** men and women fell that day—all H547
Jos 23:10 One of you routs a **t**, because the LORD your H547
Jdg 1: 4 they struck down ten **t** men at Bezek. H547
Jdg 3:29 they struck down about ten **t** Moabites, H547
Jdg 4: 6 take with you ten **t** men of Naphtali and H547
Jdg 4:10 ten **t** men went up under his command H547
Jdg 4:14 with ten **t** men following him. H547
Jdg 5: 8 spear was seen among forty **t** in Israel. H547
Jdg 7: 3 So twenty-two **t** men left, while ten H547
Jdg 7: 3 thousand men left, while ten **t** remained. H547
Jdg 8:10 Karkor with a force of about fifteen **t** men, H547
Jdg 8:10 hundred and twenty **t** swordsmen had H547
Jdg 9:49 Shechem, about a **t** men and women, also H547
Jdg 12: 6 Forty-two **t** Ephraimites were killed at that H547
Jdg 15:11 Then three **t** men from Judah went down to H547
Jdg 15:15 he grabbed it and struck down a **t** men. H547
Jdg 15:16 a donkey's jawbone I have killed a **t** men." H547
Jdg 16:27 roof were about three **t** men and women H547
Jdg 20: 2 four hundred **t** men armed with swords. H547
Jdg 20:10 a hundred from a **t**, and a thousand H547
Jdg 20:10 a thousand, and a **t** from ten thousand, to H547
Jdg 20:10 a thousand from **ten t**, to get H8047
Jdg 20:15 twenty-six **t** swordsmen from their H547
Jdg 20:17 mustered four hundred **t** swordsmen, all of H547
Jdg 20:21 cut down twenty-two **t** Israelites on the H547
Jdg 20:25 they cut down another eighteen **t** Israelites H547
Jdg 20:34 Then ten **t** of Israel's able young men made H547
Jdg 20:44 Eighteen **t** Benjamites fell, all of them H547
Jdg 20:45 cut down five **t** men along the roads. H547
Jdg 20:45 far as Gidom and struck down *two* **t** more. H547
Jdg 20:46 day twenty-five **t** Benjamite swordsmen H547
Jdg 21:10 assembly sent twelve **t** fighting men with H547
1Sa 4: 2 who killed about four **t** of them on the H547
1Sa 4:10 very great; Israel lost thirty **t** foot soldiers. H547
1Sa 11: 8 three hundred **t** and those of Judah H547
1Sa 11: 8 thousand and those of Judah thirty **t**. H547
1Sa 13: 2 Saul chose three **t** *men* from Israel; two H547
1Sa 13: 2 *two* **t** were with him at Mikmash and in the H547
1Sa 13: 2 a **t** were with Jonathan at Gibeah in H547
1Sa 13: 5 with three **t** chariots, six thousand H547
1Sa 13: 5 thousand chariots, six **t** charioteers, and H547
1Sa 15: 4 two hundred **t** foot soldiers and ten H547
1Sa 15: 4 foot soldiers and ten **t** *from* Judah. H547
1Sa 17: 5 armor of bronze weighing five **t** shekels; H547
1Sa 18:13 him and gave him command over a **t** *men*, H547
1Sa 24: 2 So Saul took three **t** able young men from H547
1Sa 25: 2 He had a **t** goats and three thousand H547
1Sa 25: 2 had a thousand goats and three **t** sheep, H547
1Sa 26: 2 with his three **t** select Israelite troops H547
2Sa 6: 1 all the able young men of Israel—thirty **t**. H547
2Sa 8: 4 David captured a **t** of his chariots, seven H547
2Sa 8: 4 seven **t** charioteers and twenty thousand H547
2Sa 8: 4 charioteers and twenty **t** foot soldiers. H547
2Sa 8: 5 David struck down twenty-two **t** of them. H547
2Sa 8:13 down eighteen **t** Edomites in the Valley H547
2Sa 10: 6 they hired twenty **t** Aramean foot soldiers H547
2Sa 10: 6 as well as the king of Maakah with a **t** men, H547
2Sa 10: 6 and also twelve **t** men from Tob. H547
2Sa 10:18 charioteers and forty **t** *of* their foot soldiers. H547
2Sa 17: 1 "I would choose twelve **t** men and set out H547
2Sa 18: 3 won't care; but you are worth ten **t** of us. H547
2Sa 18: 7 that day were great—twenty **t** men. H547
2Sa 18:12 "Even if a **t** shekels were weighed out into H547
2Sa 19:17 With him were a **t** Benjamites, along with H547
2Sa 24: 9 were eight hundred **t** able-bodied men H547
2Sa 24: 9 a sword, and in Judah five hundred **t**. H547
2Sa 24:15 seventy **t** of the people from Dan to H547
1Ki 3: 4 Solomon offered a **t** burnt offerings on H547
1Ki 4:26 Solomon had four **t** stalls for chariot horses H547
1Ki 4:26 chariot horses, and twelve **t** horses. H547
1Ki 4:32 He spoke three **t** proverbs and his songs H547
1Ki 4:32 his songs numbered a **t** and five. H547
1Ki 5:11 gave Hiram twenty **t** cors of wheat as food H547
1Ki 5:11 in addition to twenty **t** baths of pressed H547
1Ki 5:13 laborers from all Israel—thirty **t** men. H547
1Ki 5:14 off to Lebanon in shifts of ten **t** a month, H547
1Ki 5:15 Solomon had seventy **t** carriers and eighty H547
1Ki 5:15 carriers and eighty **t** stonecutters in the hills H547
1Ki 7:26 like a lily blossom. It held *two* **t** baths. H547
1Ki 8:63 twenty-two **t** cattle and a hundred and H547
1Ki 8:63 a hundred and twenty **t** sheep and goats. H547
1Ki 10:26 hundred chariots and twelve **t** horses, H547
1Ki 12:21 a hundred and eighty **t** able young men—to H547
1Ki 19:18 Yet I reserve seven **t** in Israel—all whose H547
1Ki 20:29 inflicted a hundred **t** casualties on the H547
1Ki 20:30 wall collapsed on twenty-seven **t** of them. H547
2Ki 3: 4 tribute of a hundred **t** lambs and the wool H547
2Ki 3: 4 lambs and the wool of a hundred **t** rams. H547
2Ki 5: 5 six **t** shekels of gold and ten sets of H547
2Ki 13: 7 ten chariots and ten **t** foot soldiers, for the H547
2Ki 14: 7 one who defeated ten **t** Edomites in the H547
2Ki 15:19 Menahem gave him a **t** talents of silver to H547
2Ki 18:23 I will give you *two* **t** horses—if you can put H547
2Ki 19:35 eighty-five **t** in the Assyrian camp. H547
2Ki 24:14 workers and artisans—a total of ten **t**. H547
2Ki 24:16 the entire force of seven **t** fighting men, H547
2Ki 24:16 and a **t** skilled workers and artisans. H547
1Ch 5:21 of the Hagrites—fifty **t** camels, two hundred H547
1Ch 5:21 two hundred fifty **t** sheep and two thousand H547
1Ch 5:21 fifty thousand sheep and *two* **t** donkeys. H547
1Ch 5:21 also took one hundred **t** people captive, H547
1Ch 12:14 a hundred, and the greatest for a **t**. H547
1Ch 12:20 leaders of **units of a t** in Manasseh. H547
1Ch 15:25 commanders of **units of a t** went to bring H547
1Ch 16:15 the promise he made, for a **t** generations, H547
1Ch 18: 4 David captured a **t** of his chariots, seven H547
1Ch 18: 4 seven **t** charioteers and twenty thousand H547
1Ch 18: 4 charioteers and twenty **t** foot soldiers. H547
1Ch 18: 5 David struck down twenty-two **t** of them. H547
1Ch 18:12 struck down eighteen **t** Edomites in the H547
1Ch 19: 6 the Ammonites sent a **t** talents of silver to H547
1Ch 19: 7 They hired thirty-two **t** chariots and H547
1Ch 19:18 David killed seven **t** of their charioteers H547
1Ch 19:18 charioteers and forty **t** *of* their foot soldiers. H547
1Ch 21: 5 million one hundred **t** men who could H547
1Ch 21: 5 four hundred and seventy **t** in Judah. H547
1Ch 21:14 seventy **t** men of Israel fell dead. H547
1Ch 22:14 of the LORD a hundred **t** talents of gold, H547
1Ch 23: 3 the total number of men was thirty-eight **t**. H547
1Ch 23: 4 twenty-four **t** are to be in charge of the H547
1Ch 23: 4 of the LORD and six **t** are to be officials and H547
1Ch 23: 5 Four **t** are to be gatekeepers and four H547
1Ch 23: 5 gatekeepers and four **t** are to praise the H547
1Ch 29: 4 three **t** talents of gold (gold of Ophir) and H547
1Ch 29: 4 and seven **t** talents of refined silver H547
1Ch 29: 7 the temple of God five **t** talents and ten H547
1Ch 29: 7 thousand talents and ten **t** darics of gold, H8052
1Ch 29: 7 darics of gold, ten **t** talents of silver H547
1Ch 29: 7 **eighteen t** talents of H8052+2256+9046+547
1Ch 29: 7 of bronze and a hundred **t** talents of iron. H547
1Ch 29:21 a **t** bulls, a thousand rams and a thousand H547
1Ch 29:21 a **t** rams and a thousand male lambs H547
1Ch 29:21 a thousand rams and a **t** male lambs H547
2Ch 1: 6 offered a **t** burnt offerings on it H547
2Ch 1:14 hundred chariots and twelve **t** horses, H547
2Ch 2:10 the timber, twenty **t** cors of ground wheat H547
2Ch 2:10 ground wheat, twenty **t** cors of barley H547
2Ch 2:10 twenty **t** baths of wine and twenty thousand H547
2Ch 2:10 of wine and twenty **t** baths of olive oil." H547
2Ch 4: 5 like a lily blossom. It held three **t** baths. H547
2Ch 7: 5 of twenty-two **t** head of cattle and a H547
2Ch 7: 5 a hundred and twenty **t** sheep and goats. H547
2Ch 9:25 Solomon had four **t** stalls for horses and H547
2Ch 9:25 chariots, and twelve **t** horses, which he kept H547
2Ch 11: 1 a hundred and eighty **t** able young men—to H547
2Ch 12: 3 chariots and sixty **t** horsemen and the H547
2Ch 13: 3 army of four hundred **t** able fighting men, H547
2Ch 13: 3 him with eight hundred **t** able troops. H547
2Ch 13:17 there were five hundred **t** casualties among H547
2Ch 14: 8 army of three hundred **t** men from Judah, H547
2Ch 14: 8 two hundred and eighty **t** from Benjamin, H547
2Ch 15:11 of cattle and seven **t** sheep and goats from H547
2Ch 17:11 seven **t** seven hundred rams and seven H547
2Ch 17:11 rams and seven **t** seven hundred goats. H547
2Ch 25: 5 were three hundred **t** men fit for military H547
2Ch 25: 6 also hired a hundred **t** fighting men from H547
2Ch 25:11 where he killed ten **t** men of Seir. H547

2Ch 25:12 of Judah also captured ten **t** men alive, H547
2Ch 25:13 They killed three **t** people and carried off H547
2Ch 27: 5 ten **t** cors of wheat and ten thousand cors H547
2Ch 27: 5 cors of wheat and ten **t** cors of barley. H547
2Ch 28: 6 a hundred and twenty **t** soldiers in Judah— H547
2Ch 28: 8 who were from Judah two hundred **t** wives, H547
2Ch 29:33 hundred bulls and three **t** sheep and goats. H547
2Ch 30:24 of Judah provided a **t** bulls and seven H547
2Ch 30:24 bulls and seven **t** sheep and goats for the H547
2Ch 30:24 provided them with a **t** bulls and ten H547
2Ch 30:24 thousand bulls and ten **t** sheep and goats. H547
2Ch 35: 7 a total of thirty **t** lambs and goats for the H547
2Ch 35: 7 also three **t** cattle—all from the H547
2Ch 35: 9 provided five **t** Passover offerings and five H547
Ne 3:13 They also repaired a **t** cubits of the wall as H547
Est 3: 9 I will give ten **t** talents of silver to the H547
Est 9:16 killed seventy-five **t** of them but did not lay H547
Job 1: 3 he owned seven **t** sheep, three H547
Job 1: 3 three **t** camels, five hundred H547
Job 9: 3 could not answer him one time out of a **t**. H547
Job 33:23 one out of a **t**, sent to tell them how H547
Job 42:12 He had fourteen **t** sheep, six thousand H547
Job 42:12 thousand sheep, six **t** camels, a thousand H547
Job 42:12 a **t** yoke of oxen and a thousand donkeys. H547
Job 42:12 a thousand yoke of oxen and a **t** donkeys. H547
Ps 50:10 forest is mine, and the cattle on a **t** hills. H547
Ps 60: T struck down twelve **t** Edomites in the Valley H547
Ps 84:10 one day in your courts than a **t** elsewhere; H547
Ps 90: 4 A **t** years in your sight are like a day that H547
Ps 91: 7 A **t** may fall at your side, ten thousand at H547
Ps 91: 7 fall at your side, **ten t** at your right hand H8047
Ps 105: 8 the promise he made, for a **t** generations, H547
Ecc 6: 6 even if he lives a **t** years twice over but fails H547
Ecc 7:28 I found one upright man among a **t**, but H547
SS 4: 4 of stone; on it hang a **t** shields, all of them H547
SS 5:10 ruddy, outstanding among **ten t**. H8047
SS 8:11 was to bring for its fruit a **t** shekels *of* silver. H547
SS 8:12 is mine to give; the **t** shekels are for you H547
Isa 7:23 where there were a **t** vines worth a H547
Isa 7:23 a thousand vines worth a **t** silver shekels, H547
Isa 30:17 A **t** will flee at the threat of one; at the H547
Isa 36: 8 I will give you *two* **t** horses—if you can put H547
Isa 37:36 eighty-five **t** in the Assyrian camp. H547
Isa 60:22 The least of you will become a **t**, the H547
Eze 47: 3 he measured off a **t** cubits and then led me H547
Eze 47: 4 measured off another **t** cubits and led me H547
Eze 47: 4 measured off another **t** and led me through H547
Eze 47: 5 He measured off another **t**, but now it was a H547
Da 5: 1 a great banquet for a **t** of his nobles A10038
Da 7:10 **ten t** *times* ten thousand stood before A10649
Da 7:10 thousand times **ten t** stood before him. A10649
Am 5: 3 that marches out a **t** strong will have only a H547
Jnh 4:11 than a **hundred and twenty t** H8052+9109+6926
Mic 6: 7 of rams, with **ten t** rivers of olive oil? H8047
Mt 14:21 of those who ate was about **five t** men, *G4295*
Mt 15:38 number of those who ate was **four t** men, *G5483*
Mt 16: 9 remember the five loaves *for* the **five t**, *G4295*
Mt 16:10 Or the seven loaves *for* the **four t**, and how *G5483*
Mt 18:24 man who owed him **ten t** bags of gold *G3691*
Mk 5:13 about **two t in number**, rushed down *G1493*
Mk 6:44 of the men who had eaten was **five t**. *G4295*
Mk 8: 9 About **four t** were present. After he had *G5483*
Mk 8:19 When I broke the five loaves for the **five t** *G4295*
Mk 8:20 I broke the seven loaves for the **four t**, *G5483*
Lk 9:14 About **five t** men were there.) But he said *G4295*
Lk 14:31 is able with ten **t** *men* to oppose the one *G5942*
Lk 14:31 one coming against him with twenty **t**? *G5942*
Lk 16: 7 " 'A **t bushels** of wheat,' he *G1669+3174*
Jn 6:10 sat down (about **five t** men were there). *G4295*
Ac 2:41 about **three t** were added to their *G5567*
Ac 4: 4 of men who believed grew to about five **t**. *G5942*
Ac 19:19 the total came to **fifty t** drachmas. *G3689+4297*
Ac 21:38 a revolt and led **four t** terrorists out into *G5483*
Ro 11: 4 myself **seven t** who have not bowed *G2233*
1Co 4:15 Even if you had **ten t** guardians in Christ *G3692*
1Co 10: 8 in one day twenty-three **t** of them died. *G5942*
1Co 14:19 others than **ten t** words in a tongue. *G3692*
2Pe 3: 8 With the Lord a day is like a **t** years, and a *G5943*
2Pe 3: 8 and a **t** years are like a day. *G5943*
Rev 5:11 thousands, and **ten t** times ten thousand. *G5942*
Rev 5:11 thousands, and ten thousand *times* **ten t**. *G5942*
Rev 9:16 mounted troops was **twice ten t** times ten *G1490*
Rev 9:16 troops was twice ten thousand *times* **ten t**. *G3689*
Rev 11:13 Seven **t** people were killed in the *G5942*
Rev 20: 2 Satan, and bound him for a **t** years. *G5943*
Rev 20: 3 anymore until the **t** years were ended. *G5943*
Rev 20: 4 to life and reigned with Christ a **t** years. *G5943*
Rev 20: 5 come to life until the **t** years were ended.) *G5943*
Rev 20: 6 Christ and will reign with him for a **t** years. *G5943*
Rev 20: 7 When the **t** years are over, Satan will be *G5943*

THOUSANDS (55) [THOUSAND]

Ge 24:60 may you increase to **t** *upon* thousands; may H547
Ge 24:60 may you increase to thousands upon **t** H8047
Ex 18:21 appoint them as officials over **t**, H547
Ex 18:25 of the people, officials over **t**, hundreds, H547
Ex 34: 7 maintaining love to **t**, and forgiving H547
Nu 10:36 "Return, LORD, to the countless **t** *of* Israel." H547
Nu 31:14 the commanders of **t** and commanders of H547
Nu 31:48 the commanders of **t** and commanders of H547
Nu 31:52 the commanders of **t** and commanders of H547
Nu 31:54 the commanders of **t** and commanders of H547
Dt 1:15 as commanders of **t**, of hundreds, H547
Dt 33:17 Such are the **ten t** *of* Ephraim; such are H8047
Dt 33:17 of Ephraim; such are the **t** *of* Manasseh." H547
1Sa 8:12 to be commanders of **t** and commanders of H547
1Sa 18: 7 "Saul has slain his **t**, and David his **tens of t**." H547
1Sa 18: 7 his thousands, and David his **tens of t**." H8047
1Sa 18: 8 "They have credited David with **tens of t**," H8047
1Sa 18: 8 he thought, "but me with only **t**. H547
1Sa 21:11 " 'Saul has slain his **t**, and David his tens H547
1Sa 21:11 his thousands, and David his **tens of t**'?" H8047
1Sa 22: 7 you commanders of **t** and commanders of H547
1Sa 29: 2 marched with their units of hundreds and **t**, H547
1Sa 29: 5 " 'Saul has slain his **t**, and David his tens H547
1Sa 29: 5 his thousands, and David his **tens of t**'?" H8047
2Sa 18: 1 them commanders of **t** and commanders of H547
2Sa 18: 4 marched out in units of hundreds and of **t**. H547
1Ch 13: 1 the commanders of **t** and commanders of H547
1Ch 26:26 the commanders of **t** and commanders of H547
1Ch 27: 1 commanders of **t** and commanders of H547
1Ch 28: 1 the commanders of **t** and commanders of H547
1Ch 29: 6 the commanders of **t** and commanders of H547
2Ch 1: 2 to the commanders of **t** and commanders of H547
2Ch 14: 9 with an army of **t** *upon* thousands and H547
2Ch 14: 9 of thousands upon **t** and three hundred H547
2Ch 25: 5 to commanders of **t** and commanders of H547
Ps 3: 6 not fear though **tens of t** assail me on H8047
Ps 68:17 of God are **tens of t** and thousands of H8052
Ps 68:17 are tens of thousands and **t** *of* thousands; H547
Ps 68:17 are tens of thousands and thousands of **t**; H9099
Ps 119:72 to me than **t** *of pieces of* silver and gold. H547
Ps 144:13 Our sheep *will* **increase by t**, by tens of H545
Ps 144:13 by thousands, *by* **tens of t** in our fields; H8045
Jer 32:18 You show love to **t** but bring the H547
Da 7:10 **T** *upon* thousands attended him; ten A10038
Da 7:10 Thousands upon **t** attended him; ten A10038
Da 11:12 with pride and will slaughter **many t**, H8052
Mic 6: 7 Will the LORD be pleased with **t** *of* rams H547
Lk 12: 1 when a crowd *of* **many t** had gathered, so *G3689*
Ac 21:20 how many **t** of Jews have believed *G3689*
Heb 12:22 have come to **t upon thousands** of angels *G3689*
Heb 12:22 have come to **thousands upon t** of angels *G3689*
Jude 14 coming with **t upon thousands** of his holy *G3689*
Jude 14 coming with **thousands upon t** of his holy *G3689*
Rev 5:11 numbering **t** upon thousands, and *G3689*
Rev 5:11 numbering thousands *upon* **t**, and ten *G3689*

THRASHING (2)

Job 41:25 are terrified; they retreat before its **t**. H8691
Eze 32: 2 in the seas **t about** in your streams, H1631

THREAD (3) [THREADS]

Ge 14:23 not even a **t** or the strap of a sandal H2562
Ge 38:28 the midwife took a **scarlet t** and tied it on H9106
Ge 38:30 who had the **scarlet t** on his wrist, came H9106

THREADS (1) [THREAD]

Jdg 16:12 the ropes off his arms as if they were **t**. H2562

THREAT (5) [THREATEN, THREATENED, THREATENING, THREATS]

Ezr 4:22 Why let this **t** grow, to the detriment of A10244
Ne 4: 9 a guard day and night to meet **this t**. H2157S
Ps 64: 1 protect my life from the **t** *of* the enemy. H7065
Isa 30:17 A thousand will flee at the **t** *of* one; at the H1722
Isa 30:17 at the **t** *of* five you will all flee away H1722

THREATEN (3) [THREAT]

Ps 73: 8 with arrogance *they* **t** oppression. H1819
Eze 6:10 *I did* not **t** in vain to bring this calamity on H1819
Eph 6: 9 Do not **t** them, since you know that he who *G581*

THREATENED (7) [THREAT]

Ex 32:14 bring on his people the disaster *he had* **t**. H1819
Jos 23:15 bring on you all the evil **things** he has **t**, H1821
Isa 38:14 I am being **t**; Lord, come to my H6946
Jer 27:13 with which the LORD *has* **t** any nation that H1819
Jnh 1: 4 storm arose that the ship **t** to break up. H3108
Jnh 2: 5 The engulfing waters **t** me, the H6330+5883
Jnh 3:10 bring on them the destruction *he had* **t**. H1819

THREATENING (2) [THREAT]

Pr 13: 8 the poor cannot respond to **t rebukes**. H1722
Jer 11:21 of Anathoth who *are* **t** to **kill** you, H1335+5883

THREATS (10) [THREAT]

Ps 10: 7 His mouth is full of lies and **t**; trouble H9412
Ps 55: 3 because of the **t** *of* the wicked; for they H6821
Ps 55:11 the city; **t** and lies never leave its streets. H9412
Jer 44:29 will know that my **t** of harm against you H1821
Zep 2: 8 my people and **made t** against their land. H1540
Ac 4:21 *After* **further t** they let them go. *G4653*
Ac 4:29 consider their **t** and enable your servants to *G581*
Ac 9: 1 out murderous **t** against the Lord's *G581*
1Pe 2:23 retaliate; when he suffered, *he* **made** no **t**. *G580*
1Pe 3:14 "Do not fear their **t**; do not be frightened." *G5832*

THREE (395) [THIRD, THREE TAVERNS, THREE-DAY, THREE-PRONGED, THREE-TENTHS, THREE-YEAR-OLD, TWO-THIRDS]

Ge 6:10 Noah had **t** sons: Shem, Ham and Japheth H8993
Ge 6:15 The ark is to be **t** hundred cubits long, fifty H8993
Ge 7:13 with his wife and the wives of his **t** sons, H8993
Ge 9:19 These were the **t** sons of Noah, and from H8993
Ge 15: 9 a ram, each **t years old**, along with a H8992
Ge 18: 2 looked up and saw **t** men standing nearby H8993
Ge 18: 6 "get **t** seahs of the finest flour and knead H8993
Ge 29: 2 with **t** flocks of sheep lying near it H8993
Ge 29:34 because I have borne him **t** sons. H8993
Ge 34:25 **T** days later, while all of them were still in H8958
Ge 38:24 About **t** months later Judah was told H8993
Ge 40:10 on the vine were **t** branches. As soon H8993
Ge 40:12 "The **t** branches are three days. H8993
Ge 40:12 "The three branches are **t** days. H8993
Ge 40:13 Within **t** days Pharaoh will lift up your H8993
Ge 40:16 On my head were **t** baskets of bread. H8993
Ge 40:18 "The **t** baskets are three days. H8993
Ge 40:18 "The three baskets are **t** days. H8993
Ge 40:19 Within **t** days Pharaoh will lift off your H8993
Ge 42:17 And he put them all in custody for **t** days. H8993
Ge 45:22 to Benjamin he gave **t** hundred shekels of H8993
Ex 2: 2 was a fine child, she hid him for **t** months. H8993
Ex 10:22 total darkness covered all Egypt for **t** days. H8993
Ex 10:23 see anyone else or move about for **t** days. H8993
Ex 15:22 For **t** days they traveled in the desert H8993
Ex 21:11 does not provide her with these **t** *things*, H8993
Ex 23:14 "**T** times a year you are to celebrate a H8993
Ex 23:17 "**T** times a year all the men are to appear H8993
Ex 25:32 **t** on one side and three on the other. H8993
Ex 25:32 three on one side and **t** on the other. H8993
Ex 25:33 **T** cups shaped like almond flowers with H8993
Ex 25:33 to be on one branch, **t** on the next branch H8993
Ex 27: 1 altar of acacia wood, **t** cubits high; it is to H8993
Ex 27:14 entrance, with **t** posts and three bases, H8993
Ex 27:14 entrance, with three posts and **t** bases, H8993
Ex 27:15 other side, with **t** posts and three bases. H8993
Ex 27:15 other side, with three posts and **t** bases. H8993
Ex 32:28 that day about **t** thousand of the H8993
Ex 34:23 **T** times a year all your men are to appear H8993
Ex 34:24 land when you go up **t** times each year to H8993
Ex 37:18 **t** on one side and three on the other. H8993
Ex 37:18 three on one side and **t** on the other. H8993
Ex 37:19 **T** cups shaped like almond flowers with H8993
Ex 37:19 **t** on the next branch and the same for all H8993
Ex 38: 1 of acacia wood, **t** cubits high; it was H8993
Ex 38:14 entrance, with **t** posts and three bases, H8993
Ex 38:14 entrance, with three posts and **t** bases, H8993
Ex 38:15 courtyard, with **t** posts and three bases. H8993
Ex 38:15 courtyard, with three posts and **t** bases. H8993
Lev 19:23 For **t** years you are to consider it forbidden; H8993
Lev 25:21 that the land will yield enough for **t** years. H8993
Lev 27: 6 that of a female at **t** shekels of silver; H8993
Nu 10:33 of the LORD and traveled for **t** days. H8993
Nu 10:33 them during those **t** days to find them a H8993
Nu 12: 4 out to the tent of meeting, *all* **t** *of* you." H8993
Nu 12: 4 So the **t** *of* them went out. H8993
Nu 22:28 you to make you beat me these **t** times?" H8993
Nu 22:32 you beaten your donkey these **t** times? H8993
Nu 22:33 turned away from me these **t** times. H8993
Nu 24:10 you have blessed them these **t** times. H8993
Nu 33: 8 had traveled for **t** days in the Desert of H8993
Nu 35:14 Give **t** on this side of the Jordan and three H8993
Nu 35:14 of the Jordan and **t** in Canaan as cities of H8993
Dt 4:41 Then Moses set aside **t** cities east of the H8993
Dt 14:28 At the end of every **t** years, bring all the H8993
Dt 16:16 **T** times a year all your men must appear H8993
Dt 17: 6 testimony of two or **t** witnesses a person is H8993
Dt 19: 2 aside for yourselves **t** cities in the land the H8993
Dt 19: 3 involved and **divide into t** parts the land H8992
Dt 19: 7 you to set aside for yourselves **t** cities. H8993
Dt 19: 9 then you are to set aside **t** more cities. H8993
Dt 19:15 by the testimony of two or **t** witnesses. H8993
Jos 1:11 **T** days from now you will cross the Jordan H8993
Jos 2:16 Hide yourselves there **t** days until they H8993
Jos 2:22 into the hills and stayed there **t** days, H8993
Jos 3: 2 After **t** days the officers went throughout H8993
Jos 7: 3 Send two or **t** thousand men to take it H8993
Jos 7: 4 So about **t** thousand went up; but they H8993
Jos 9:16 **T** days after they made the treaty with the H8993
Jos 15:14 Hebron Caleb drove out the **t** Anakites— H8993
Jos 18: 4 Appoint **t** men from each tribe. I will send H8993
Jos 21:32 together with their pasturelands—**t** towns. H8993
Jdg 1:20 who drove from it the **t** sons of Anak. H8993
Jdg 7: 6 **T** hundred of them drank from cupped H8993
Jdg 7: 7 "With the **t** hundred men that lapped I H8993
Jdg 7: 8 Israelites home but kept the **t** hundred, H8993
Jdg 7:16 Dividing the **t** hundred men into three H8993
Jdg 7:16 the three hundred men into **t** companies, H8993
Jdg 7:20 The **t** companies blew the trumpets and H8993
Jdg 7:22 When the **t** hundred trumpets sounded H8993
Jdg 8: 4 Gideon and his **t** hundred men H8993
Jdg 9:22 Abimelek had governed Israel **t** years, H8993
Jdg 9:43 divided them into **t** companies and set an H8993
Jdg 11:26 For **t** hundred years Israel occupied H8993
Jdg 14:14 For **t** days they could not give the answer H8993
Jdg 15: 4 went out and caught **t** hundred foxes and H8993
Jdg 15:11 Then **t** thousand men from Judah went H8993
Jdg 16:27 the roof were about **t** thousand men and H8993
Jdg 19: 4 so he remained with him **t** days, eating H8993
1Sa 2:21 she gave birth to **t** sons and two H8993
1Sa 9:20 As for the donkeys you lost **t** days ago, do H8993
1Sa 10: 3 **T** men going up to worship God at Bethel H8993
1Sa 10: 3 One will be carrying **t** young goats H8993
1Sa 10: 3 another **t** loaves of bread, and H8993
1Sa 11: 8 of Israel numbered **t** hundred thousand H8993
1Sa 11:11 Saul separated his men into **t** divisions; H8993

1Sa 13: 2 Saul chose t thousand men from Israel H8993
1Sa 13: 5 to fight Israel, with t thousand chariots, six H8993
1Sa 13:17 the Philistine camp in t detachments. H8993
1Sa 17:13 Jesse's t oldest sons had followed Saul to H8993
1Sa 17:14 the youngest. The t oldest followed Saul H8993
1Sa 20:20 I will shoot t arrows to the side of it, as H8993
1Sa 20:41 bowed down before Jonathan t times, H8993
1Sa 24: 2 So Saul took t thousand able young men H8993
1Sa 25: 2 a thousand goats and t thousand sheep, H8993
1Sa 26: 2 with his t thousand select Israelite troops H8993
1Sa 30:12 drunk any water for t days and three H8993
1Sa 30:12 any water for three days and t nights. H8993
1Sa 30:13 me when I became ill t days *ago*. H8993
1Sa 31: 6 So Saul and his t sons and his H8993
1Sa 31: 8 found Saul and his t sons fallen on Mount H8993
2Sa 2:18 The t sons of Zeruiah were there: Joab H8993
2Sa 2:31 men had killed t hundred and sixty H8993
2Sa 6:11 of Obed-Edom the Gittite for t months, H8993
2Sa 13:38 went to Geshur, he stayed there t years. H8993
2Sa 14:27 T sons and a daughter were born to H8993
2Sa 18:14 So he took t javelins in his hand and H8993
2Sa 20: 4 of Judah to come to me within t days, H8993
2Sa 21: 1 there was a famine for t successive years H8993
2Sa 21:16 spearhead weighed t hundred shekels H8993
2Sa 23: 8 was chief of the T; he raised his spear H8998
2Sa 23: 9 As one of the t mighty warriors, he was H8993
2Sa 23:13 t of the thirty chief warriors came down to H8993
2Sa 23:16 So the t mighty warriors broke through the H8993
2Sa 23:17 were the exploits of the t mighty warriors. H8993
2Sa 23:18 of Joab son of Zeruiah was chief of the T. H8998
2Sa 23:18 raised his spear against t hundred men, H8993
2Sa 23:18 so he became as famous as the T. H8993
2Sa 23:19 he not held in greater honor than the T? H8993
2Sa 23:22 was as famous as the t mighty warriors. H8993
2Sa 23:23 he was not included among the T. H8993
2Sa 24:12 I am giving you t *options*. Choose one of H8993
2Sa 24:13 there come on you t years of famine in H8993
2Sa 24:13 Or t months of fleeing from your enemies H8993
2Sa 24:13 Or t days of plague in your land H8993
1Ki 2:39 But t years later, two of Shimei's slaves H8993
1Ki 4:32 He spoke t thousand proverbs and his H8993
1Ki 6:36 the inner courtyard of t courses of dressed H8993
1Ki 7: 4 Its windows were placed high in sets of t H8993
1Ki 7: 5 they were in the front part in sets of t H8993
1Ki 7:12 by a wall of t courses of dressed H8993
1Ki 7:25 stood on twelve bulls, t facing north, three H8993
1Ki 7:25 three facing north, t facing west, three H8993
1Ki 7:25 t facing south and three facing east. H8993
1Ki 7:25 three facing south and t facing east. H8993
1Ki 7:27 was four cubits long, four wide and t high. H8993
1Ki 9:25 T times a year Solomon sacrificed burnt H8993
1Ki 10:17 He also made t hundred small shields of H8993
1Ki 10:17 with t minas of gold in each shield. H8993
1Ki 10:22 Once every t years it returned, carrying H8993
1Ki 11: 3 of royal birth and t hundred concubines, H8993
1Ki 12: 5 "Go away for t days and then come back H8993
1Ki 12:12 T days later Jeroboam and all the people H8958
1Ki 12:12 had said, "Come back to me in t days." H8958
1Ki 15: 2 he reigned in Jerusalem t years. H8993
1Ki 17:21 out on the boy t times and cried out to H8993
1Ki 22: 1 For t years there was no war between H8993
2Ki 2:17 who searched for t days but did not find H8993
2Ki 3:10 the LORD called us t kings together only to H8993
2Ki 3:13 the LORD who called us t kings together to H8993
2Ki 9:32 Two or t eunuchs looked down at him H8993
2Ki 11: 5 You who are in the t companies that are NDT
2Ki 13:18 He struck it t times and stopped. H8993
2Ki 13:19 But now you will defeat it only t times." H8993
2Ki 13:25 T times Jehoash defeated him, and so he H8993
2Ki 17: 5 Samaria and laid siege to it for t years. H8993
2Ki 18:10 At the end of t years the Assyrians took it H8993
2Ki 18:14 king of Judah t hundred talents of H8993
2Ki 23:31 he reigned in Jerusalem t months. H8993
2Ki 24: 1 Jehoiakim became his vassal for t years. H8993
2Ki 24: 8 he reigned in Jerusalem t months. H8993
2Ki 25:17 of one pillar was t cubits high and was H8993
2Ki 25:18 priest next in rank and the t doorkeepers. H8993
1Ch 2: 3 These t were born to him by a Canaanite H8993
1Ch 2:16 Zeruiah's t sons were Abishai, Joab and H8993
1Ch 3:23 Elioenai, Hizkiah and Azrikam—t in all. H8993
1Ch 7: 6 T sons of Benjamin: Bela, Beker and H8993
1Ch 10: 6 So Saul and his t sons died, and all his H8993
1Ch 11:11 raised his spear against t hundred men, H8993
1Ch 11:12 the Ahohite, one of the t mighty warriors. H8993
1Ch 11:15 T of the thirty chiefs came down to David H8993
1Ch 11:18 So the T broke through the Philistine lines H8993
1Ch 11:19 were the exploits of the t mighty warriors. H8993
1Ch 11:20 the brother of Joab was chief of the T. H8993
1Ch 11:20 raised his spear against t hundred men, H8993
1Ch 11:20 so he became as famous as the T. H8993
1Ch 11:21 honored above the T and became their H8993
1Ch 11:24 was as famous as the t mighty warriors. H8993
1Ch 11:25 he was not included among the T. H8993
1Ch 12:39 The men spent t days there with David H8993
1Ch 13:14 of Obed-Edom in his house for t months, H8993
1Ch 21:10 I am giving you t *options*. Choose one of H8993
1Ch 21:12 t years of famine, three months of being H8993
1Ch 21:12 t months of being swept away before your H8993
1Ch 21:12 or t days of the sword of the LORD H8993
1Ch 23: 8 the first, Zetham and Joel—t in all. H8993
1Ch 23: 9 Haziel and Haran—t in all. These were H8993
1Ch 23:23 Eder and Jerimoth—t in all. H8993
1Ch 25: 5 Heman fourteen sons and t daughters.) H8993
1Ch 29: 4 t thousand talents of gold (gold of Ophir H8993
2Ch 4: 4 stood on twelve bulls, t facing north, three H8993
2Ch 4: 4 three facing north, t facing west, three H8993
2Ch 4: 4 t facing south and three facing east. H8993
2Ch 4: 4 three facing south and t facing east. H8993
2Ch 4: 5 a lily blossom. It held t thousand baths. H8993
2Ch 6:13 five cubits wide and t cubits high, and H8993
2Ch 8:13 New Moons and the t annual festivals— H8993
2Ch 9:16 He also made t hundred small shields of H8993
2Ch 9:16 with t hundred shekels of gold in each H8993
2Ch 9:21 Once every t years it returned, carrying H8993
2Ch 10: 5 answered, "Come back to me in t days." H8993
2Ch 10:12 T days later Jeroboam and all the people H8958
2Ch 10:12 had said, "Come back to me in t days." H8958
2Ch 11:17 Rehoboam son of Solomon t years, H8993
2Ch 13: 2 he reigned in Jerusalem t years. H8993
2Ch 14: 8 Asa had an army of t hundred thousand H8993
2Ch 14: 9 upon thousands and t hundred chariots, H8993
2Ch 20:25 plunder that it took t days to collect it. H8993
2Ch 25: 5 that there were t hundred thousand men H8993
2Ch 25:13 They killed t thousand people and carried H8993
2Ch 29:33 hundred bulls and t thousand sheep and H8993
2Ch 31:16 to the males t years old or more whose H8993
2Ch 35: 7 offerings, and also t thousand cattle—all H8993
2Ch 35: 8 Passover offerings and t hundred cattle. H8993
2Ch 36: 2 he reigned in Jerusalem t months. H8993
2Ch 36: 9 in Jerusalem t months and ten days. H8993
Ezr 6: 4 with t courses of large stones and one of A10760
Ezr 8:15 and we camped there t days. H8993
Ezr 8:32 in Jerusalem, where we rested t days. H8993
Ezr 10: 8 to appear within t days would forfeit all H8993
Ezr 10: 9 Within the t days, all the men of Judah H8993
Ne 2:11 Jerusalem, and after staying there t days H8993
Est 4:16 Do not eat or drink for t days, night or day H8993
Est 9:15 they put to death in Susa t hundred men, H8993
Job 1: 2 He had seven sons and t daughters, H8993
Job 1: 3 thousand sheep, t thousand camels, five H8993
Job 1: 4 they would invite their t sisters to eat and H8993
Job 1:17 Chaldeans formed t raiding parties and H8993
Job 2:11 When Job's t friends, Eliphaz the H8993
Job 32: 1 So these t men stopped answering Job H8993
Job 32: 3 He was also angry with the t friends H8993
Job 32: 5 he saw that the t men had nothing more H8993
Job 33:29 to a person—twice, even t *times*— H8993
Job 42:13 he also had seven sons and t daughters. H8993
Pr 30:15 "There are t things that are never satisfied H8993
Pr 30:18 "There are t things that are too amazing H8993
Pr 30:21 "Under t *things* the earth trembles, under H8993
Pr 30:29 "There are t things that are stately in their H8993
Ecc 4:12 A cord of t *strands* is not quickly broken H8992
Isa 16:14 "Within t years, as a servant bound by H8993
Isa 17: 6 leaving two or t olives on the topmost H8993
Isa 20: 3 gone stripped and barefoot for t years, H8993
Jer 36:23 Jehudi had read t or four columns of the H8993
Jer 52:24 priest next in rank and the t doorkeepers. H8993
Eze 14:14 even if these t men—Noah, Daniel and H8993
Eze 14:16 even if these t men were in it, they H8993
Eze 14:18 even if these t men were in it, they H8993
Eze 21:14 strike twice, even t *times*. It is a sword H8958
Eze 40:10 the east gate were t alcoves on each side; H8993
Eze 40:10 the t had the same measurements H8993
Eze 40:21 Its alcoves—t on each side—its projecting H8993
Eze 40:48 walls were t cubits wide on either H8993
Eze 41: 6 The side rooms were on t levels, one H8993
Eze 41:16 galleries around the t *of* them— H8993
Eze 41:22 was a wooden altar t cubits high and two H8993
Eze 42: 3 gallery faced gallery at the t *levels*. H8958
Eze 48:31 The t gates on the north side will be the H8993
Eze 48:32 which is 4,500 cubits long, will be t gates: H8993
Eze 48:33 measures 4,500 cubits, will be t gates: H8993
Eze 48:34 which is 4,500 cubits long, will be t gates: H8993
Da 1: 5 They were to be trained for t years, and H8993
Da 3:23 these t men, firmly tied, fell into the A10760
Da 3:24 "Weren't there t men that we tied up A10760
Da 6: 2 with t administrators over them, one of A10760
Da 6:10 T times a day he got down on his knees A10760
Da 6:13 He still prays t times a day." A10760
Da 7: 5 it had t ribs in its mouth between its A10760
Da 7: 8 t of the first horns were uprooted A10760
Da 7:20 before which t of them fell—the horn A10760
Da 7:24 the earlier ones; he will subdue t kings. A10760
Da 10: 2 that time I, Daniel, mourned for t weeks. H8993
Da 10: 3 lotions at all until the t weeks were over. H8993
Da 11: 2 T more kings will arise in Persia, and then H8993
Am 1: 3 "For t sins of Damascus, even for four, H8993
Am 1: 6 "For t sins of Gaza, even for four, I will not H8993
Am 1: 9 "For t sins of Tyre, even for four, I will not H8993
Am 1:11 "For t sins of Edom, even for four, I will H8993
Am 1:13 "For t sins of Ammon, even for four, I will H8993
Am 2: 1 "For t sins of Moab, even for four, I will H8993
Am 2: 4 "For t sins of Judah, even for four, I will H8993
Am 2: 6 "For t sins of Israel, even for four, I will H8993
Am 4: 4 every morning, your tithes every t years. H8993
Am 4: 7 when the harvest was still t months away. H8993
Jnh 1:17 belly of the fish t days and three nights H8993
Jnh 1:17 belly of the fish three days and t nights. H8993
Jnh 3: 3 large city; it took t days to go through it. H8993
Zec 11: 8 In one month I got rid of the t shepherds H8993
Mt 12:40 For as Jonah was t days and three nights G5552
Mt 12:40 was three days and t nights in the belly of G5552
Mt 12:40 Son of Man will be t days and three G5552
Mt 12:40 be three days and t nights in the heart of G5552
Mt 15:32 already been with me t days and have G5552
Mt 17: 4 I will put up t shelters—one for you, G5552
Mt 18:16 by the testimony of two or t witnesses. G5552
Mt 18:20 For where two or t gather in my name G5552
Mt 20: 5 about **t in the afternoon** and did the G1888
Mt 26:34 rooster crows, you will disown me **t times**." G5565
Mt 26:61 the temple of God and rebuild it in t days. G5552
Mt 26:75 rooster crows, you will disown me **t times**." G5565
Mt 27:40 destroy the temple and build it in t days, G5552
Mt 27:45 until **t in the afternoon** darkness G6052+1888
Mt 27:46 About **t in the afternoon** Jesus cried G1888+6052
Mt 27:63 'After t days I will rise again. G5552
Mk 8: 2 already been with me t days and have G5552
Mk 8:31 must be killed and after t days rise again. G5552
Mk 9: 5 Let us put up t shelters—one for you, one G5552
Mk 9:31 will kill him, and after t days he will rise." G5552
Mk 10:34 him and kill him. T days later he will rise." G5552
Mk 14:30 twice you yourself will disown me **t times**." G5565
Mk 14:58 human hands and in t days will build G5552
Mk 14:72 crows twice you will disown me **t times**." G5565
Mk 15:29 destroy the temple and build it in t days, G5552
Mk 15:33 whole land until **t in the afternoon**. G6052+1888
Mk 15:34 And *at* **t in the afternoon** G3836+1888+6052
Lk 1:56 Elizabeth for about t months and then G5552
Lk 2:46 After t days they found him in the temple G5552
Lk 4:25 shut for **t and a half years** G2291+5552+2779+3604+1971
Lk 9:33 Let us put up t shelters—one for you, one G5552
Lk 10:36 "Which of these t do you think was a G5552
Lk 11: 5 'Friend, lend me t loaves of bread; G5552
Lk 12:52 t against two and two against three. G5552
Lk 12:52 three against two and two against t. G5552
Lk 13: 7 '*For* t years now I've been coming to look G5552
Lk 22:34 you will deny **t times** that you know me." G5565
Lk 22:61 crows today, you will disown me **t times**." G5565
Lk 23:44 whole land until **t in the afternoon**, G6052+1888
Jn 2:19 temple, and I will raise it again in t days." G5552
Jn 2:20 you are going to raise it in t days? G5552
Jn 6:19 rowed about t or four **miles**, G5084+1633+4297
Jn 13:38 rooster crows, you will disown me **t times**! G5565
Ac 2:41 about **t thousand** were added to their G5567
Ac 3: 1 of prayer—*at* **t in the afternoon**. G3836+1888
Ac 5: 7 About t hours later his wife came in, not G5552
Ac 7:20 For t months he was cared for by his G5552
Ac 9: 9 For t days he was blind, and did not eat G5552
Ac 10: 3 **t in the afternoon** he G6052+1888+3836+2465
Ac 10:16 This happened **t times**, and G2093+5565
Ac 10:19 "Simon, t men are looking for you. G5552
Ac 10:30 "**T days ago** I was in my house G608+5480
Ac 10:30 at this hour, *at* **t in the afternoon**. G3836+1888
Ac 11:10 This happened **t times**, and then it G2093+5565
Ac 11:11 "Right then t men who had been sent to G5552
Ac 17: 2 on t Sabbath days he reasoned with G5552
Ac 19: 8 spoke boldly there for t months, G5552
Ac 20: 3 where he stayed t months. Because some G5552
Ac 20:31 Remember that *for* **t years** I never stopped G5562
Ac 25: 1 T days after arriving in the province G5552
Ac 28: 7 showed us generous hospitality for t days. G5552
Ac 28:11 After t months we put out to sea in a ship G5552
Ac 28:12 put in at Syracuse and stayed there t days. G5552
Ac 28:17 T days later he called together the local G5552
1Co 13:13 And now these t remain: faith, hope and G5552
1Co 14:27 or at the most t—should speak, one G5552
1Co 14:29 Two or t prophets should speak, and the G5552
2Co 11:25 **T times** I was beaten with rods, once I was G5565
2Co 11:25 with stones, **t times** I was shipwrecked G5565
2Co 12: 8 **T times** I pleaded with the Lord to take it G5565
2Co 13: 1 by the testimony of two or t witnesses." G5552
Gal 1:18 Then after t years, I went up to Jerusalem G5552
1Ti 5:19 unless it is brought by two or t witnesses. G5552
Heb 10:28 on the testimony of two or t witnesses. G5552
Heb 11:23 parents hid him **for t months** after he was G5564
Jas 5:17 not rain on the land for t and a half years. G5552
1Jn 5: 7 For there are t that testify: G5552
1Jn 5: 8 the blood; and the t are in agreement. G5552
Rev 8:13 to be sounded by the other t angels!" G5552
Rev 9:18 was killed by the t plagues of fire, G5552
Rev 11: 9 For t and a half days some from every G5552
Rev 11:11 But after the t and a half days the breath G5552
Rev 16:13 Then I saw t impure spirits that looked like G5552
Rev 16:19 The great city split into t parts, and the G5552
Rev 21:13 There were t gates on the east, three on G5552
Rev 21:13 gates on the east, t on the north, three on G5552
Rev 21:13 t on the south and three on the west. G5552
Rev 21:13 three on the south and t on the west. G5552

THREE TAVERNS (1) [THREE]

Ac 28:15 Forum of Appius and the T to meet us. G5553

THREE-DAY (4) [DAY, THREE]

Ge 30:36 Then he put a t journey between H8993+3427
Ex 3:18 Let us take a t journey into the H8993+3427
Ex 5: 3 Now let us take a t journey into the H8993+3427
Ex 8:27 We must take a t journey into the H8993+3427

THREE-PRONGED (1) [THREE]

1Sa 2:13 come with a t fork in his hand H8993+9094

THREE-TENTHS (8) [TEN, THREE]

Lev 14:10 along with t of an ephah of the H6928+8993
Nu 15: 9 grain offering of t of an ephah of H8993+6928
Nu 28:12 grain offering of t of an ephah of H8993+6928

Nu 28:20 grain offering of **t** of an ephah of H8993+6928
Nu 28:28 grain offering of **t** of an ephah of H8993+6928
Nu 29: 3 grain offering of **t** of an ephah of H8993+6928
Nu 29: 9 grain offering of **t** of an ephah of H8993+6928
Nu 29:14 grain offering of **t** of an ephah of H8993+6928

THREE-YEAR-OLD (1) [THREE, YEAR]

1Sa 1:24 he was, along with a **t** bull, an ephah of H8992

THRESH (4) [THRESHED, THRESHES, THRESHING]

Isa 27:12 In that day the LORD *will* **t** from the flowing H2468
Isa 41:15 *You will* **t** the mountains and crush them H1889
Hos 10:11 Ephraim is a trained heifer that loves to **t** H1889
Mic 4:13 "Rise and **t**, Daughter Zion, for I will give H1889

THRESHED (4) [THRESH]

Ru 2:17 Then *she* **t** the barley she had gathered H2468
Isa 28:27 Caraway **is** not **t** with a sledge, nor is the H1889
Am 1: 3 Because she **t** Gilead with sledges having H1889
Hab 3:12 the earth and in anger *you* **t** the nations. H1889

THRESHES (1) [THRESH]

1Co 9:10 whoever plows and **t** should be able to do *G262*

THRESHING (51) [THRESH]

Ge 50:10 When they reached the **t floor** *of* Atad H1755
Ge 50:11 saw the mourning at the **t floor** *of* Atad, H1755
Lev 26: 5 Your **t** will continue until grape harvest H1912
Nu 15:20 present it as an offering from the **t floor**. H1755
Nu 18:27 as grain from the **t floor** or juice from the H1755
Nu 18:30 the product of the **t floor** or the winepress. H1755
Dt 15:14 your flock, your **t floor** and your winepress. H1755
Dt 16:13 produce of your **t floor** and your winepress H1755
Jdg 6:11 where his son Gideon *was* **t** wheat in a H2468
Jdg 6:37 I will place a wool fleece on the **t floor**. H1755
Ru 3: 2 will be winnowing barley on the **t floor**. H1755
Ru 3: 3 Then go down to the **t floor**, but don't let H1755
Ru 3: 6 went down to the **t floor** and did H1755
Ru 3:14 know that a woman came to the **t floor**." H1755
1Sa 23: 1 Keilah and are looting the **t floors**, H1755
2Sa 6: 6 When they came to the **t floor** *of* Nakon H1755
2Sa 24:16 was then at the **t floor** *of* Araunah the H1755
2Sa 24:18 to the LORD on the **t floor** *of* Araunah the H1755
2Sa 24:21 "To buy your **t floor**," David answered H1755
2Sa 24:22 here are **t sledges** and ox yokes for H4617
2Sa 24:24 David bought the **t floor** and the oxen H1755
1Ki 22:10 thrones at the **t floor** *by* the entrance of H1755
2Ki 6:27 From the **t floor**? From the H1755
2Ki 13: 7 made them like the dust at **t time**. H1889
1Ch 13: 9 When they came to the **t floor** *of* Kidon H1755
1Ch 21:15 standing at the **t floor** *of* Araunah the H1755
1Ch 21:18 to the LORD on the **t floor** *of* Araunah the H1755
1Ch 21:20 While Araunah *was* **t** wheat, he turned H1889
1Ch 21:21 he left the **t floor** and bowed down before H1755
1Ch 21:22 the site of your **t floor** so I can build an H1755
1Ch 21:23 offerings, the **t sledges** for the wood, and H4617
1Ch 21:28 him on the **t floor** *of* Araunah the H1755
2Ch 3: 1 It was on the **t floor** *of* Araunah the H1755
2Ch 18: 9 thrones at the **t floor** *by* the entrance of H1755
Job 39:12 in your grain and bring it to your **t floor**? H1755
Job 41:30 leaving a trail in the mud like a **t sledge**. H3023
Pr 20:26 the wicked; he drives the *t* **wheel** over them. AIT
Isa 21:10 My people who are crushed on the **t floor** H1755
Isa 28:28 so *one does* not **go on t** it forever. H1889+1889
Isa 28:28 The wheels of a **t cart** may be rolled over H6322
Isa 41:15 I will make you into a **t sledge**, new and H4617
Jer 50:11 frolic like a heifer **t grain** and neigh like H1889
Jer 51:33 Babylon is like a **t floor** at the time it is H1755
Da 2:35 like chaff on a **t floor** *in* the summer. A10010
Hos 9: 1 of a prostitute at every **t floor**. H1755+1841
Hos 9: 2 **T floors** and winepresses will not feed the H1755
Hos 13: 3 like chaff swirling from a **t floor**, like H1755
Joel 2:24 The **t floors** will be filled with grain; the H1755
Mic 4:12 gathered them like sheaves to the **t floor**. H1755
Mt 3:12 he will clear his **t floor**, gathering his *G272*
Lk 3:17 hand to clear his **t floor** and to gather the *G272*

THRESHOLD (15) [THRESHOLDS]

Jdg 19:27 of the house, with her hands on the **t**. H6197
1Sa 5: 4 been broken off and were lying on the **t**; H5159
1Sa 5: 5 Dagon's temple at Ashdod step on the **t**. H5159
1Ki 14:17 as she stepped over the **t** *of* the house, H6197
Eze 9: 3 and moved to the **t** *of* the temple. H5159
Eze 10: 4 moved to the **t** *of* the temple. H5159
Eze 10:18 from over the **t** *of* the temple and H5159
Eze 40: 6 its steps and measured the **t** *of* the gate; H6197
Eze 40: 7 And the **t** *of* the gate next to the portico H6197
Eze 41:16 including the **t** was covered with H6197
Eze 43: 8 they placed their **t** next to my threshold H6197
Eze 43: 8 threshold next to my **t** and their doorposts H6197
Eze 46: 2 in worship at the **t** *of* the gateway and H5159
Eze 47: 1 out from under the **t** *of* the temple toward H5159
Zep 1: 9 punish all who avoid stepping on the **t**, H5159

THRESHOLDS (5) [THRESHOLD]

1Ch 9:19 guarding the **t** of the tent just as their H6197
1Ch 9:22 to be gatekeepers at the **t** numbered 212. H6197
Isa 6: 4 the doorposts and **t** shook and the temple H6197
Eze 41:16 as well as the **t** and the narrow windows H6197
Am 9: 1 the tops of the pillars so that the **t** shake. H6197

THREW (70) [THROW]

Ge 33: 4 *he* **t** *his* **arms around** his neck and H5877+6584
Ge 37:24 they took him and **t** him into the cistern H8959
Ge 44:14 and *they* **t** *themselves* to the ground H5877
Ge 45:14 *he* **t** *his* **arms around** his H5877+6584+7418
Ge 46:29 *he* **t** *his* **arms around** his H5877+6584+7418
Ge 50: 1 Joseph **t** *himself* on his father and wept H5877
Ge 50:18 came and **t** *themselves* **down** before him. H5877
Ex 4: 3 Moses **t** it on the ground and it became a H8959
Ex 7:10 Aaron **t** his staff **down** in front of Pharaoh H8959
Ex 7:12 Each one **t down** his staff and it became a H8959
Ex 14:24 the Egyptian army and **t** it **into confusion**. H2169
Ex 15: 7 of your majesty *you* **t down** those who H2238
Ex 15:25 *He* **t** it into the water, and the water H8959
Ex 32:19 anger burned and *he* **t** the tablets out of H8959
Ex 32:24 gave me the gold, and *I* **t** it into the fire H8959
Dt 9:17 the two tablets and **t** them out of my H8959
Dt 9:21 as fine as dust and **t** the dust into a H8959
Jos 10:10 The LORD **t** them **into confusion** before H2169
Jos 10:27 from the poles and **t** them into the cave H8959
Jdg 8:25 each of them **t** a ring from his H8959
Jdg 14:16 Then Samson's wife **t** herself on him NDT
Jdg 15:17 speaking, *he* **t away** the jawbone; and H8959
1Sa 7:10 and **t** them **into** *such* **a panic** that they H2169
2Sa 18:17 **t** him into a big pit in the forest and piled H8959
2Sa 20:12 into a field and **t** a garment over him. H8959
2Sa 20:22 of Sheba son of Bikri and **t** it to Joab. H8959
1Ki 19:19 went up to him and **t** his cloak around H8959
2Ki 2:21 out to the spring and **t** the salt into it, H8959
2Ki 3:25 each man **t** a stone *on* every good H8959
2Ki 6: 6 Elisha cut a stick and **t** it there, and made H8959
2Ki 9:33 So *they* **t** her **down**, and some of her H9023
2Ki 10:25 officers **t** the bodies **out** and then H8959
2Ki 13:21 so *they* **t** the man's body into Elisha's H8959
2Ki 23:12 them to pieces and **t** the rubble into the H8959
2Ch 25:12 top of a cliff and **t** them down so that all H8959
2Ch 30:14 incense altars and **t** them into the Kidron H8959
2Ch 33:15 Jerusalem; and *he* **t** them out of the city. H8959
Ne 13: 8 displeased and **t** all Tobiah's household H8959
Jer 36:23 a scribe's knife and **t** them into the firepot H8959
Jer 41: 7 slaughtered them and **t** them into a cistern. NDT
Jer 41: 9 the cistern where he **t** all the bodies of H8959
La 3:53 to end my life in a pit and **t** stones at me; H3343
Eze 28:17 So *I* **t** you to the earth; I made a spectacle H8959
Da 3:24 men that *we* tied up and **t** into the fire A10667
Da 6:16 brought Daniel and **t** him into the lions' A10667
Da 8:10 and *it* **t** some of the starry host **down** to H5877
Jnh 1: 5 And *they* **t** the cargo into the sea to H3214
Jnh 1:15 Then they took Jonah and **t** him overboard, H3214
Zec 11:13 pieces of silver and **t** them to the potter at H8959
Mt 13:48 good fish in baskets, but **t** the bad away. *G965*
Mt 21:39 took him and **t** him **out** of the vineyard *G1675*
Mt 27: 5 So Judas **t** the money into the temple *G4849*
Mk 9:20 *it* immediately **t** the boy **into a convulsion**. *G5360*
Mk 11: 7 the colt to Jesus and **t** their cloaks **over** it, *G2095*
Mk 12: 8 killed him, and **t** him **out** of the vineyard. *G1675*
Mk 12:41 Many rich people **t in** large amounts. *G965*
Lk 4:35 the demon **t** the man **down** before them *G4849*
Lk 9:42 the demon **t** him **to the ground** in a *G4838*
Lk 15:20 **t** *his* **arms around** him *G2158+2093+3836+5549*
Lk 17:16 *He* **t himself** at Jesus' feet *G4406+2093+4725*
Lk 19:35 **t** their cloaks **on** the colt and put Jesus on *G2166*
Lk 20:12 they wounded him and **t** him **out**. *G1675*
Lk 20:15 So *they* **t** him **out** of the vineyard and *G1675*
Jn 9:34 dare you lecture us!" And *they* **t** him **out**. *G1675*
Ac 16:37 are Roman citizens, and **t** us into prison. *G965*
Ac 20:10 **t** *himself* **on** the young man and put his *G2158*
Ac 27:19 *they* **t** the ship's tackle **overboard** with *G4849*
Rev 14:19 its grapes and **t** them into the great *G965*
Rev 18:21 of a large millstone and **t** it into the sea, *G965*
Rev 20: 3 *He* **t** him into the Abyss, and locked and *G965*

THRIVE (11) [THRIVES, THRIVING]

Dt 31:20 when they eat their fill and **t**, they H2014
Job 8:11 *Can* reeds **t** without water? H8436
Job 39: 4 Their young **t** and grow strong in the wilds H8049
Ps 72:16 like Lebanon and **t** like the grass of the H6658
Pr 11:28 the righteous *will* **t** like a green leaf. H7255
Pr 28:28 when the wicked perish, the righteous **t**. H8049
Pr 29: 2 When the righteous **t**, the people rejoice H8049
Pr 29:16 When the wicked **t**, so does sin, but the H8049
Eze 17: 9 *Will it* **t**? Will it not be H7503
Eze 17:10 been planted, but *will it* **t**? Will it not H7503
Zec 9:17 Grain *will* **make** the young men **t**, and H5649

THRIVES (1) [THRIVE]

Hos 13:15 even though he **t** among his brothers. H7229

THRIVING (1) [THRIVE]

Jer 11:16 The LORD called you a **t** olive tree with fruit H8316

THROAT (4) [THROATS]

Ps 5: 9 Their **t** is an open grave; with their H1744
Ps 69: 3 worn out calling for help; my **t** is parched. H1744
Pr 23: 2 put a knife to your **t** if you are given to H4350
Jer 2:25 until your feet are bare and your **t** is dry. H1744

THROATS (3) [THROAT]

Ps 115: 7 can they utter a sound with their **t**. H1744
Jer 4:10 have peace,' when the sword is at our **t**!" H5883
Ro 3:13 "Their **t** are open graves; their tongues *G3296*

THROB (1)

Isa 60: 5 your heart *will* **t** and swell with joy H7064

THROES (1)

2Sa 1: 9 I'm in the **t of death**, but I'm still H8688

THRONE (169) [DETHRONED, ENTHRONED, ENTHRONES, THRONES]

Ge 41:40 with respect to the **t** will I be greater than H4058
Ex 11: 5 who sits on the **t**, to the firstborn son of H4058
Ex 12:29 who sat on the **t**, to the firstborn of H4058
Ex 17:16 were lifted up against the **t** *of* the LORD, H4058
Dt 17:18 When he takes the **t** *of* his kingdom, he is H4058
1Sa 2: 8 princes and has them inherit a **t** *of* honor. H4058
2Sa 3:10 establish David's **t** over Israel and Judah H4058
2Sa 7:13 will establish the **t** *of* his kingdom forever H4058
2Sa 7:16 your **t** will be established forever. H4058
2Sa 14: 9 let the king and his **t** be without guilt." H4058
1Ki 1:13 he will sit on my **t**"? Why then has H4058
1Ki 1:17 be king after me, and he will sit on my **t**. H4058
1Ki 1:20 who will sit on the **t** *of* my lord the king H4058
1Ki 1:24 after you, and that he will sit on your **t**? H4058
1Ki 1:27 who should sit on the **t** *of* my lord the king H4058
1Ki 1:30 and he will sit on my **t** in my place." H4058
1Ki 1:35 come and sit on my **t** and reign in my H4058
1Ki 1:37 Solomon to make his **t** even greater than H4058
1Ki 1:37 greater than the **t** *of* my lord King David!" H4058
1Ki 1:46 Solomon has taken his seat on the royal **t**. H4058
1Ki 1:47 than yours and his **t** greater than yours! H4058
1Ki 1:48 my eyes to see a successor on my **t** today. H4058
1Ki 2: 4 fail to have a successor on the **t** *of* Israel. H4058
1Ki 2:12 Solomon sat on the **t** *of* his father David, H4058
1Ki 2:19 bowed down to her and sat down on his **t**. H4058
1Ki 2:19 He had a **t** brought for the king's mother H4058
1Ki 2:24 me securely on the **t** *of* my father David H4058
1Ki 2:33 his house and his **t**, may there be the H4058
1Ki 2:45 David's **t** will remain secure before H4058
1Ki 3: 6 him a son to sit on his **t** this very day. H4058
1Ki 5: 5 whom I will put on the **t** in your place will H4058
1Ki 7: 7 He built the **t** hall, the Hall of Justice H4058
1Ki 8:20 my father and now I sit on the **t** *of* Israel, H4058
1Ki 8:25 to sit before me on the **t** *of* Israel, H4058
1Ki 9: 5 establish your royal **t** over Israel forever, H4058
1Ki 9: 5 fail to have a successor on the **t** *of* Israel. H4058
1Ki 10: 9 in you and placed you on the **t** *of* Israel. H4058
1Ki 10:18 made a great **t** *covered with* ivory and H4058
1Ki 10:19 The **t** had six steps, and its back had a H4058
1Ki 16:11 began to reign and was seated on the **t**, H4058
1Ki 22:19 LORD sitting on his **t** with all the multitudes H4058
2Ki 10: 3 sons and set him on his father's **t**. H4058
2Ki 10:30 will sit on the **t** *of* Israel to the fourth H4058
2Ki 11:19 king then took his place on the royal **t**. H4058
2Ki 13:13 Jeroboam succeeded him on the **t**. H4058
2Ki 15:12 will sit on the **t** *of* Israel to the fourth H4058
1Ch 17:12 me, and I will establish his **t** forever. H4058
1Ch 17:14 his **t** will be established forever. H4058
1Ch 22:10 I will establish the **t** *of* his kingdom over H4058
1Ch 28: 5 to sit on the **t** *of* the kingdom of the H4058
1Ch 29:23 Solomon sat on the **t** *of* the LORD as king H4058
2Ch 6:10 my father and now I sit on the **t** *of* Israel, H4058
2Ch 6:16 to sit before me on the **t** *of* Israel, H4058
2Ch 7:18 I will establish your royal **t**, as I H4058
2Ch 9: 8 placed you on his **t** as king to rule for H4058
2Ch 9:17 made a great **t** *covered with* ivory and H4058
2Ch 9:18 The **t** had six steps, and a footstool of gold H4058
2Ch 18:18 LORD sitting on his **t** with all the multitudes H4058
2Ch 23:20 Gate and seated the king on the royal **t**. H4058
Est 1: 2 from his royal **t** in the citadel of Susa H4058
Est 5: 1 king was sitting on his royal **t** in the hall, H4058
Ps 9: 7 he has established his **t** for judgment. H4058
Ps 11: 4 holy temple; the LORD is on his heavenly **t**. H4058
Ps 45: 6 Your **t**, O God, will last for ever and ever H4058
Ps 47: 8 the nations; God is seated on his holy **t**. H4058
Ps 89: 4 forever and make your **t** firm through all H4058
Ps 89:14 justice are the foundation of your **t**; H4058
Ps 89:29 his **t** as long as the heavens endure. H4058
Ps 89:36 forever and his **t** endure before me like H4058
Ps 89:44 his splendor and cast his **t** to the ground. H4058
Ps 93: 2 Your **t** was established long ago; you are H4058
Ps 94:20 Can a corrupt **t** be allied with you—a H4058
Ps 94:20 a **t** that brings on misery by its decrees? NDT
Ps 97: 2 justice are the foundation of his **t**. H4058
Ps 103:19 The LORD has established his **t** in heaven H4058
Ps 132:11 own descendants I will place on your **t**. H4058
Ps 132:12 sons will sit on your **t** for ever and ever." H4058
Pr 16:12 a **t** is established through H4058
Pr 20: 8 When a king sits on his **t** to judge, he H4058
Pr 20:28 through love his **t** is made secure. H4058
Pr 25: 5 his **t** will be established through H4058
Pr 29:14 fairness, his **t** will be established forever. H4058
Isa 6: 1 exalted, seated on a **t**; and the train of his H4058
Isa 9: 7 reign on David's **t** and over his kingdom, H4058
Isa 14:13 I will raise my **t** above the stars of God H4058
Isa 16: 5 In love a **t** will be established; in H4058
Isa 47: 1 sit on the ground without a **t**, queen city H4058
Isa 63:15 from your **lofty t**, holy and H2292
Isa 66: 1 "Heaven is my **t**, and the earth is my H4058
Jer 3:17 they will call Jerusalem The **T** *of* the LORD, H4058
Jer 13:13 including the kings who sit on David's **t** H4058
Jer 14:21 do not dishonor your glorious **t**. H4058
Jer 17:12 A glorious **t**, exalted from the beginning H4058
Jer 17:25 who sit on David's **t** will come through the H4058
Jer 22: 2 of Judah, you who sit on David's **t**—you, H4058
Jer 22: 4 who sit on David's **t** will come through the H4058
Jer 22:30 none will sit on the **t** *of* David or rule H4058

Jer 29:16 who sits on David's **t** and all the people H4058
Jer 33:17 fail to have a man to sit on the **t** *of* Israel, H4058
Jer 33:21 have a descendant to reign on his **t**. H4058
Jer 36:30 will have no one to sit on the **t** *of* David; H4058
Jer 43:10 I will set his **t** over these stones I H4058
Jer 49:38 I will set my **t** in Elam and destroy her H4058
La 5:19 your **t** endures from generation to H4058
Eze 1:26 was what looked like a **t** of lapis lazuli, H4058
Eze 1:26 high above on the **t** was a figure like H4058
Eze 10: 1 the likeness of a **t** of lapis lazuli above H4058
Eze 17:16 the land of the king who **put** him **on** *the* **t**, H4887
Eze 28: 2 I sit on the **t** *of* a god in the heart of the H4632
Eze 43: 7 is the place of my **t** and the place for the H4058
Da 4:36 I was restored to my **t** and became even A10424
Da 5:20 from his royal **t** and stripped of his A10372
Da 7: 9 His **t** was flaming with fire, and its A10372
Jnh 3: 6 he rose from his **t**, took off his royal robes H4058
Zec 6:13 with majesty and will sit and rule on his **t**. H4058
Zec 6:13 And he will be a priest on his **t**. And there H4058
Mt 5:34 either by heaven, for it is God's **t**; *G2585*
Mt 19:28 the Son of Man sits on his glorious **t**, *G2585*
Mt 23:22 swears by God's **t** and by the one who *G2585*
Mt 25:31 with him, he will sit on his glorious **t**. *G2585*
Lk 1:32 will give him the **t** of his father David, *G2585*
Ac 2:30 place one of his descendants on his **t**. *G2585*
Ac 7:49 " 'Heaven is my **t**, and the earth is my *G2585*
Ac 12:21 sat on his **t** and delivered a public *G1037*
Heb 1: 8 But about the Son he says, "Your **t**, O God, *G2585*
Heb 4:16 us then approach God's **t** of grace with *G2585*
Heb 8: 1 at the right hand *of* the **t** of the Majesty in *G2585*
Heb 12: 2 sat down at the right hand *of* the **t** of God. *G2585*
Rev 1: 4 from the seven spirits before his **t**, *G2585*
Rev 2:13 where you live—where Satan has his **t**. *G2585*
Rev 3:21 I will give the right to sit with me on my **t** *G2585*
Rev 3:21 sat down with my Father on his **t**. *G2585*
Rev 4: 2 there before me was a **t** in heaven with *G2585*
Rev 4: 3 shone like an emerald encircled the **t**. *G2585*
Rev 4: 4 Surrounding the **t** were twenty-four other *G2585*
Rev 4: 5 From the **t** came flashes of lightning *G2585*
Rev 4: 5 In front of the **t**, seven lamps were blazing *G2585*
Rev 4: 6 Also in front of the **t** there was what *G2585*
Rev 4: 6 the center, around the **t**, were four living *G2585*
Rev 4: 9 him who sits on the **t** and who lives for *G2585*
Rev 4:10 who sits on the **t** and worship him who *G2585*
Rev 4:10 They lay their crowns before the **t** and say *G2585*
Rev 5: 1 him who sat on the **t** a scroll with writing *G2585*
Rev 5: 6 standing at the center of the **t**, encircled *G2585*
Rev 5: 7 the right hand of him who sat on the **t**. *G2585*
Rev 5:11 They encircled the **t** and the living *G2585*
Rev 5:13 him who sits on the **t** and to the Lamb be *G2585*
Rev 6:16 him who sits on the **t** and from the wrath *G2585*
Rev 7: 9 before the **t** and before the Lamb *G2585*
Rev 7:10 who sits on the **t**, and to the Lamb." *G2585*
Rev 7:11 standing around the **t** and around the *G2585*
Rev 7:11 faces before the **t** and worshiped God, *G4725*
Rev 7:15 are before the **t** of God and serve him *G2585*
Rev 7:15 he who sits on the **t** will shelter them with *G2585*
Rev 7:17 at the center of the **t** will be their *G2585*
Rev 8: 3 on the golden altar in front of the **t**. *G2585*
Rev 12: 5 child was snatched up to God and to his **t**. *G2585*
Rev 13: 2 his power and his **t** and great authority. *G2585*
Rev 14: 3 new song before the **t** and before the four *G2585*
Rev 16:10 poured out his bowl on the **t** of the beast, *G2585*
Rev 16:17 the temple came a loud voice from the **t**, *G2585*
Rev 19: 4 worshiped God, who was seated on the **t**. *G2585*
Rev 19: 5 Then a voice came from the **t**, saying *G2585*
Rev 20:11 I saw a great white **t** and him who was *G2585*
Rev 20:12 standing before the **t**, and books were *G2585*
Rev 21: 3 And I heard a loud voice from the **t** saying *G2585*
Rev 21: 5 He who was seated on the **t** said, "I am *G2585*
Rev 22: 1 flowing from the **t** of God and of the Lamb *G2585*
Rev 22: 3 The **t** of God and of the Lamb will be in *G2585*

THRONES (17) [THRONE]

1Ki 22:10 were sitting on their **t** at the threshing H4058
2Ch 18: 9 were sitting on their **t** at the threshing H4058
Ps 122: 5 There stand the **t** for judgment, the H4058
Ps 122: 5 judgment, the **t** of the house of David. H4058
Isa 14: 9 it makes them rise from their **t**—all those H4058
Jer 1:15 come and set up their **t** in the entrance of H4058
Jer 13:18 "Come down from *your* **t**, for your glorious H3782
Eze 26:16 step down from their **t** and lay aside their H4058
Da 7: 9 "As I looked, "**t** were set in place, and A10372
Hag 2:22 I will overturn royal **t** and shatter the power H4058
Mt 19:28 have followed me will also sit on twelve **t**, *G2585*
Lk 1:52 rulers from their **t** but has lifted up the *G2585*
Lk 22:30 at my table in my kingdom and sit on **t**, *G2585*
Col 1:16 whether **t** or powers or rulers or authorities *G2585*
Rev 4: 4 the throne were twenty-four other **t**, *G2585*
Rev 11:16 who were seated on their **t** before God *G2585*
Rev 20: 4 I saw **t** on which were seated those who *G2585*

THRONG (10) [THRONGED, THRONGS]

Job 21:33 and a countless **t** goes before them. NDT
Ps 42: 4 of joy and praise among the festive **t**. H2162
Ps 68:11 women who proclaim it are a mighty **t**: H7372
Ps 68:27 there the **great** **t** *of* Judah's princes H8086
Ps 109:30 in the **great** *t of worshipers* I will praise him. AIT
Pr 7:26 brought down; her slain are a mighty **t**. H3972
Jer 31: 8 women in labor; a great **t** will return. H7736
Eze 23:24 wagons and with a **t** *of* people; H7736
Eze 32: 3 " 'With a great **t** *of* people I will cast my H7736
Mic 2:12 in its pasture; the place *will* **t** with people. H2101

THRONGED (1) [THRONG]

Jer 5: 7 committed adultery and **t** *to* the houses of H1518

THRONGS (1) [THRONG]

Ps 35:18 among the **t** I will praise you. H6786+6639

THROUGH (746) [THROUGHOUT]

Ge 2:11 it **winds** **t** the entire land of Havilah H6015
Ge 2:13 it **winds** **t** the entire land of Cush. H6015
Ge 3:17 **t** painful toil you will eat food from it all H928
Ge 12: 3 all peoples on earth will be blessed **t** you." H928
Ge 12: 6 Abram traveled **t** the land as far as the site H928
Ge 13:17 walk **t** the length and breadth of the land H4200
Ge 16: 2 perhaps I can build a family **t** her. H4946
Ge 18:18 all nations on earth will be blessed **t** him. H928
Ge 19:32 preserve our family line **t** our father." H4946
Ge 19:34 can preserve our family line **t** our father." H4946
Ge 21:12 because it is **t** Isaac that your offspring will H928
Ge 22:18 **t** your offspring all nations on earth will H928
Ge 26: 4 **t** your offspring all nations on earth H928
Ge 28:14 earth will be blessed **t** you and your H928
Ge 30: 3 me and I too can build a family **t** her." H4946
Ge 30:32 Let me go **t** all your flocks today and remove H928
Ge 31:34 Laban **searched** **t** everything in the tent H5491
Ge 31:37 Now that *you have* **searched** **t** all my H5491
Ge 47:17 And he brought them **t** that year with food H928
Ex 9:35 just as the LORD had said **t** Moses. H928+3338
Ex 12:12 night I will pass **t** Egypt and strike down H928
Ex 12:15 it from the first day **t** the seventh must be H6330
Ex 12:23 When the LORD **goes** **t** the land to strike H6296
Ex 13:17 not lead them on the **road** *t* the Philistine AIT
Ex 14: 4 gain glory for myself **t** Pharaoh and all his H928
Ex 14:16 Israelites can go **t** the sea on dry H928+9348
Ex 14:17 And I will gain glory **t** Pharaoh and all his H928
Ex 14:17 his army, **t** his chariots and his horsemen. H928
Ex 14:18 I am the LORD when I gain glory **t** Pharaoh, H928
Ex 14:22 the Israelites went **t** the sea on dry H928+9348
Ex 14:29 the Israelites went **t** the sea on dry H928+9348
Ex 15:19 Israelites walked **t** the sea on dry H928+9348
Ex 19:21 so *they do* not **force** *their* **way** **t** to see H2238
Ex 19:24 people *must* not **force** *their* **way** **t** to come H2238
Ex 32:27 Go back and forth **t** the camp from one end H928
Ex 35:29 the work the LORD **t** Moses had H928+3338
Lev 8:36 the LORD commanded **t** Moses. H928+3338
Lev 10:11 the LORD has given them **t** Moses." H928+3338
Lev 22: 8 wild animals, and so become unclean **t** it. H928
Lev 26: 6 the sword will not pass **t** your country. H928
Lev 26:46 himself and the Israelites **t** Moses. H928+3338
Nu 4:37 to the LORD's command **t** Moses. H928+3338
Nu 4:45 to the LORD's command **t** Moses. H928+3338
Nu 4:49 At the LORD's command **t** Moses H928+3338
Nu 9:23 with his command **t** Moses. H928+3338
Nu 10:13 at the LORD's command **t** Moses. H928+3338
Nu 12: 2 "Has the LORD spoken only **t** Moses?" they H928
Nu 12: 2 "Hasn't he also spoken **t** us?" And the LORD H928
Nu 13:17 "Go up **t** the Negev and on into the hill H928
Nu 13:22 They went up **t** the Negev and came to H928
Nu 14: 7 "The land we passed **t** and explored is H928
Nu 15:23 the LORD's commands to you **t** him, H928+3338
Nu 15:23 them and continuing **t** the generations to H4200
Nu 16:40 as the LORD directed him **t** Moses H928+3338
Nu 20:17 Please let us pass **t** your country. We will H928
Nu 20:17 We will not go **t** any field or vineyard, or H928
Nu 20:17 the left until *we have* **passed** **t** your H6296
Nu 20:18 "You may not pass **t** here; if you try, we will H928
Nu 20:19 *We* only *want to* **pass** **t** on foot—nothing H6296
Nu 20:20 "*You may* not **pass** **t**." Then H6296
Nu 20:21 refused to let them go **t** their territory, H928
Nu 21:22 "Let us pass **t** your country. We will not turn H928
Nu 21:22 Highway until *we have* **passed** **t** your H6296
Nu 21:23 would not let Israel pass **t** his territory. H928
Nu 22:24 LORD stood in a **narrow path** *t* the vineyards, AIT
Nu 25: 8 right **t** the Israelite man and into the NDT
Nu 26: 5 **t** Hanok, the Hanokite clan; through Pallu NDT
Nu 26: 5 the Hanokite clan; **t** Pallu, the Palluite H4200
Nu 26: 6 **t** Hezron, the Hezronite clan; through H4200
Nu 26: 6 the Hezronite clan; **t** Karmi, the Karmite H4200
Nu 26:12 **t** Nemuel, the Nemuelite clan; through H4200
Nu 26:12 the Nemuelite clan; **t** Jamin, the Jaminite H4200
Nu 26:12 the Jaminite clan; **t** Jakin, the Jakinite H4200
Nu 26:13 **t** Zerah, the Zerahite clan; through Shaul H4200
Nu 26:13 the Zerahite clan; **t** Shaul, the Shaulite H4200
Nu 26:15 **t** Zephon, the Zephonite clan; through H4200
Nu 26:15 the Zephonite clan; **t** Haggi, the Haggite H4200
Nu 26:15 the Haggite clan; **t** Shuni, the Shunite H4200
Nu 26:16 **t** Ozni, the Oznite clan; through Eri, the H4200
Nu 26:16 the Oznite clan; **t** Eri, the Erite clan; H4200
Nu 26:17 **t** Arodi, the Arodite clan; through Areli H4200
Nu 26:17 the Arodite clan; **t** Areli, the Arelite clan. H4200
Nu 26:20 **t** Shelah, the Shelanite clan; through H4200
Nu 26:20 the Shelanite clan; **t** Perez, the Perezite H4200
Nu 26:20 the Perezite clan; **t** Zerah, the Zerahite H4200
Nu 26:21 **t** Hezron, the Hezronite clan; through H4200
Nu 26:21 the Hezronite clan; **t** Hamul, the Hamulite H4200
Nu 26:23 **t** Tola, the Tolaite clan; through Puah, the NDT
Nu 26:23 the Tolaite clan; **t** Puah, the Puite clan; H4200
Nu 26:24 **t** Jashub, the Jashubite clan; through H4200
Nu 26:24 the Jashubite clan; **t** Shimron, the H4200
Nu 26:26 **t** Sered, the Seredite clan; through Elon H4200
Nu 26:26 the Seredite clan; **t** Elon, the Elonite clan H4200
Nu 26:26 the Elonite clan; **t** Jahleel, the Jahleelite H4200
Nu 26:28 by their clans **t** Manasseh and Ephraim NDT
Nu 26:29 **t** Makir, the Makirite clan (Makir was the H4200
Nu 26:29 father of Gilead); **t** Gilead, the Gileadite H4200
Nu 26:30 **t** Iezer, the Iezerite clan; through Helek, the NDT
Nu 26:30 the Iezerite clan; **t** Helek, the Helekite H4200
Nu 26:31 **t** Asriel, the Asrielite clan; through Shechem NDT
Nu 26:31 the Asrielite clan; **t** Shechem, the NDT
Nu 26:32 **t** Shemida, the Shemidaite clan; through NDT
Nu 26:32 the Shemidaite clan; **t** Hepher, the NDT
Nu 26:35 **t** Shuthelah, the Shuthelahite clan H4200
Nu 26:35 Shuthelahite clan; **t** Beker, the Bekerite H4200
Nu 26:35 the Bekerite clan; **t** Tahan, the Tahanite H4200
Nu 26:36 of Shuthelah: **t** Eran, the Eranite clan. H4200
Nu 26:38 **t** Bela, the Belaite clan; through Ashbel H4200
Nu 26:38 the Belaite clan; **t** Ashbel, the Ashbelite H4200
Nu 26:38 the Ashbelite clan; **t** Ahiram, the H4200
Nu 26:39 **t** Shupham, the Shuphamite clan; through H4200
Nu 26:39 the Shuphamite clan; **t** Hupham, the H4200
Nu 26:40 of Bela **t** Ard and Naaman were NDT
Nu 26:40 **t** Ard, the Ardite clan; through Naaman H4200
Nu 26:40 the Ardite clan; **t** Naaman, the Naamite H4200
Nu 26:42 Dan by their clans: **t** Shuham, the H4200
Nu 26:44 **t** Imnah, the Imnite clan; through Ishvi H4200
Nu 26:44 the Imnite clan; **t** Ishvi, the Ishvite clan H4200
Nu 26:44 the Ishvite clan; **t** Beriah, the Beriite clan H4200
Nu 26:45 **t** the descendants of Beriah: through H4200
Nu 26:45 **t** Heber, the Heberite clan; through H4200
Nu 26:45 the Heberite clan; **t** Malkiel, the H4200
Nu 26:48 **t** Jahzeel, the Jahzeelite clan; through H4200
Nu 26:48 the Jahzeelite clan; **t** Guni, the Gunite H4200
Nu 26:49 **t** Jezer, the Jezerite clan; through Shillem H4200
Nu 26:49 the Jezerite clan; **t** Shillem, the Shillemite H4200
Nu 26:57 **t** Gershon, the Gershonite clan; through H4200
Nu 26:57 the Gershonite clan; **t** Kohath, the H4200
Nu 26:57 the Kohathite clan; **t** Merari, the Merarite H4200
Nu 27:23 as the LORD instructed **t** Moses. H928+3338
Nu 31:23 can withstand fire must be put **t** the fire, H928
Nu 31:23 withstand fire must be put **t** that water. H928
Nu 33: 8 and passed **t** the sea into the H928+9348
Nu 36:13 the LORD gave **t** Moses to the H928+3338
Dt 1:19 **went** toward the hill country of the Amorites *t* AIT
Dt 2: 4 'You are about to pass **t** the territory of your H928
Dt 2: 7 watched over your **journey** *t* this vast AIT
Dt 2:27 "Let us pass **t** your country. We will stay on H928
Dt 2:28 price in silver. Only *let us* **pass** **t** on foot— H6296
Dt 2:30 king of Heshbon refused to let us pass **t**. H928
Dt 8:15 He led you **t** the vast and dreadful H928
Dt 15:17 an awl and push it **t** his earlobe into the H928
Dt 29: 5 forty years that I led you **t** the wilderness, H928
Dt 29:16 how we passed **t** the countries on H928+7931
Jos 1:11 "Go **t** the camp and tell the people H928+7931
Jos 2:15 let them down by a rope **t** the window, H1237
Jos 2:18 cord in the window **t** which you let us down H928
Jos 14: 2 the LORD had commanded **t** Moses. H928+3338
Jos 16: 1 went up from there **t** the desert into the NDT
Jos 18: 9 So the men left and went **t** the land. H928
Jos 19:34 The boundary **ran** west *t* Aznoth Tabor and AIT
Jos 20: 2 refuge, as I instructed you **t** Moses, H928+3338
Jos 21: 2 LORD commanded **t** Moses that you H928+3338
Jos 21: 8 the LORD had commanded **t** Moses. H928+3338
Jos 22: 9 the command of the LORD **t** Moses. H928+3338
Jos 24:17 all the nations **t** which we traveled. H928+7931
Jdg 3: 4 had given their ancestors **t** Moses. H928+3338
Jdg 4:21 She drove the peg **t** his temple into the H928
Jdg 4:22 lay Sisera with the tent peg **t** his temple— H928
Jdg 5:28 "**T** the window peered Sisera's mother H1237
Jdg 9:54 So his servant **ran** him **t**, and he died. H1991
Jdg 11:16 Israel went **t** the wilderness to the Red Sea H928
Jdg 11:17 'Give us permission to go **t** your country,' H928
Jdg 11:18 "Next they traveled **t** the wilderness, skirted H928
Jdg 11:19 'Let us pass **t** your country to our own place. H928
Jdg 11:20 did not trust Israel to pass **t** his territory. H928
Jdg 11:29 Manasseh, **passed** **t** Mizpah of Gilead H6296
Ru 4:12 **T** the offspring the LORD gives you by this H4946
1Sa 3:21 he revealed himself to Samuel **t** his word. H928
1Sa 9: 4 So he passed **t** the hill country of Ephraim H928
1Sa 9: 4 country of Ephraim and **t** the area around H928
1Sa 9: 4 Then he passed **t** the territory of Benjamin H928
1Sa 19:12 So Michal let David down **t** a window, and H1237
1Sa 28:17 has done what he predicted **t** me. H928+3338
1Sa 31: 4 "Draw your sword and **run** me **t**, or these H1991
1Sa 31: 4 will come and **run** me **t** and abuse me." H1991
1Sa 31:12 valiant men marched **t** the night to Beth H3972
2Sa 2:23 the spear came out **t** his back. H4946
2Sa 2:29 Abner and his men marched **t** the Arabah. H928
2Sa 2:29 continued **t** the morning hours and came H3972
2Sa 12:25 he sent word **t** Nathan the prophet H928+3338
2Sa 20:14 Sheba passed **t** all the tribes of Israel to H928
2Sa 20:14 Abel Beth Maakah and **t** the entire region of NDT
2Sa 23: 2 "The Spirit of the LORD spoke **t** me; his word H928
2Sa 23:16 mighty warriors broke **t** the Philistine lines, H928
2Sa 24: 5 and then went **t** Gad and on to Jazer. NDT
2Sa 24: 8 After they had gone **t** the entire land, they H928
2Sa 24:19 as the LORD had commanded **t** Gad. H3869+1821
1Ki 6:12 I will fulfill **t** you the promise I gave to H907
1Ki 8:53 as you declared **t** your servant Moses H928+3338
1Ki 8:56 promises he gave **t** his servant H928+3338
1Ki 12:15 son of Nebat **t** Ahijah the Shilonite. H928+3338
1Ki 14:18 as the LORD had said **t** his servant the H928+3338
1Ki 15:29 of the LORD given **t** his servant Ahijah H928+3338
1Ki 16: 7 of the LORD came **t** the prophet Jehu H928+3338

T

1Ki 16:12 against Baasha **t** the prophet Jehu— H928+3338
1Ki 18: 5 "Go **t** the land to all the springs and valleys H928
1Ki 22: 8 still one prophet **t** whom we can H4946+907
1Ki 22:28 return safely, the LORD has not spoken **t** me." H928
1Ki 22:36 sun was setting, a cry spread **t** the army: H928
2Ki 1: 2 Now Ahaziah had fallen **t** the lattice of his H1237
2Ki 3: 8 "**T** the Desert of Edom," he H2006
2Ki 3:11 **t** whom we may inquire of the LORD?" H4946+907
2Ki 3:26 swordsmen to **break t** to the king of Edom H1324
2Ki 5: 1 because **t** him the LORD had given victory to H928
2Ki 8: 8 Consult the LORD **t** him; ask him H4946+907
2Ki 8:21 he rose up and **broke t** by night; his H5782
2Ki 9:36 that he spoke **t** his servant Elijah H928+3338
2Ki 10:10 what he announced **t** his servant H928+3338
2Ki 10:33 by the Arnon Gorge **t** Gilead to Bashan. H2256
2Ki 14:25 spoken **t** his servant Jonah son of H928+3338
2Ki 17:13 Israel and Judah **t** all his prophets H928+3338
2Ki 17:13 I delivered to you **t** my servants the H928+3338
2Ki 17:23 as he had warned **t** all his servants H928+3338
2Ki 21:10 The LORD said **t** his servants the H928+3338
2Ki 25: 4 Then the city wall **was broken t**, and the H1324
2Ki 25: 4 army fled at night **t** the gate between the H2006
1Ch 7:14 Asriel *was his* **descendant** *t* his Aramean AIT
1Ch 10: 4 "Draw your sword and **run** me **t**, or these H1991
1Ch 11: 3 as the LORD had promised **t** Samuel. H928+3338
1Ch 11:18 So the Three broke **t** the Philistine lines H928
1Ch 25: 5 They were given him **t** the promises of God H928
1Ch 26:12 of the gatekeepers, **t** their leaders, had H4200
1Ch 26:21 were Gershonites **t** Ladan and who were H4200
1Ch 26:25 His relatives **t** Eliezer: Rehabiah his son H4200
2Ch 10:15 son of Nebat **t** Ahijah the Shilonite. H928+3338
2Ch 12: 7 poured out on Jerusalem **t** Shishak. H928+3338
2Ch 18: 7 still one prophet **t** whom we can H4946+907
2Ch 18:27 return safely, the LORD has not spoken **t** me." H928
2Ch 21: 9 he rose up and **broke t** by night. H5782
2Ch 22: 7 **T** Ahaziah's visit to Joram, God brought NDT
2Ch 23:20 into the palace **t** the Upper Gate H928+9348
2Ch 29:25 by the LORD **t** his prophets. H928+3338
2Ch 32: 4 the stream that flowed **t** the land. H928+9348
2Ch 33: 8 and regulations given **t** Moses." H928+3338
2Ch 34:14 LORD that had been given **t** Moses. H928+3338
2Ch 35: 6 what the LORD commanded **t** Moses." H928+3338
2Ch 36:15 sent word to them **t** his messengers H928+3338
Ezr 2: 6 (**t** the line of Jeshua and Joab H4200
Ezr 2:16 of Ater (**t** Hezekiah) 98 H4200
Ezr 2:36 of Jedaiah (**t** the family of Jeshua H4200
Ezr 9:11 you gave **t** your servants the H928+3338
Ne 2:13 By night I went out **t** the Valley Gate toward H928
Ne 2:14 not enough room for my mount to **get t**; H6296
Ne 2:15 back and reentered **t** the Valley Gate. H928
Ne 7:11 (**t** the line of Jeshua and Joab H4200
Ne 7:21 of Ater (**t** Hezekiah) 98 H4200
Ne 7:39 of Jedaiah (**t** the family of Jeshua H4200
Ne 7:43 (**t** Kadmiel through the line of Hodaviah H4200
Ne 7:43 through Kadmiel **t** the line of Hodaviah H4200
Ne 8:14 the LORD had commanded **t** Moses, H928+3338
Ne 9:11 that they passed **t** it on dry ground, H928+9348
Ne 9:14 decrees and laws **t** your servant H928+3338
Ne 9:30 you warned them **t** your prophets. H928+3338
Ne 10:29 Law of God given **t** Moses the H928+3338
Est 6: 9 lead him on the horse **t** the city streets H928
Est 6:11 led him on horseback **t** the city streets H928
Job 15:20 the ruthless man **t** all the years stored up NDT
Job 22:13 Does he judge **t** such darkness? H1237
Job 22:30 will be delivered **t** the cleanness of your H928
Job 28:10 They tunnel **t** the rock; their eyes see all its H928
Job 29: 3 my head and by his light *I* **walked** *t* darkness! AIT
Job 30:14 *They* **advance** as *t* a gaping breach; amid the AIT
Job 37:11 moisture; *he* **scatters** his lightning *t* them. AIT
Job 41: 2 Can you put a cord **t** its nose or pierce its H928
Ps 8: 2 **T** the praise of children and infants you H4946
Ps 17: 4 ways of the violent **t** what your lips have H928
Ps 21: 5 **T** the victories you gave, his glory is great H928
Ps 21: 7 **t** the unfailing love of the Most High he H928
Ps 23: 4 Even though I walk **t** the darkest valley, H928
Ps 32: 3 bones wasted away **t** my groaning all day H928
Ps 33:11 the purposes of his heart **t** all generations. H4200
Ps 44: 5 **T** you we push back our enemies; through H928
Ps 44: 5 enemies; **t** your name we trample our foes. H928
Ps 45:17 perpetuate your memory **t** all generations; H928
Ps 63: 6 I think of you **t** the watches of the night. H928
Ps 66: 6 dry land, they passed **t** the waters on foot H928
Ps 66:12 our heads; we went **t** fire and water, but H928
Ps 68: 7 when you marched **t** the wilderness, H928
Ps 72: 5 as the moon, **t all generations**. H1887+1887
Ps 72:17 Then all nations will be blessed **t** him, and H928
Ps 74: 5 wielding axes to cut **t** a thicket of trees. H928
Ps 77:19 Your path led **t** the sea, your way through H928
Ps 77:19 the sea, your way **t** the mighty waters H928
Ps 78:13 He divided the sea and **led** them **t**; he H6296
Ps 78:52 he led them like sheep **t** the wilderness. H928
Ps 84: 6 As they pass **t** the Valley of Baka, they H928
Ps 85: 5 you prolong your anger **t** all generations? H4200
Ps 89: 1 your faithfulness known **t** all generations. H4200
Ps 89: 4 make your throne firm **t** all generations. H4200
Ps 89:24 **t** my name his horn will be exalted. H928
Ps 89:40 *You have* **broken t** all his walls and H7287
Ps 100: 5 faithfulness continues **t** all generations. H6330
Ps 102:12 your renown endures **t** all generations. H4200
Ps 102:24 my days; your years go on **t** all generations. H928
Ps 106: 9 he led them **t** the depths as through a H928
Ps 106: 9 led them through the depths as **t** a desert. NDT
Ps 107:16 gates of bronze and **cuts t** bars of iron. H1548
Ps 107:17 Some became fools **t** their rebellious H4946
Ps 118:20 the gate of the LORD **t** which the righteous H928
Ps 119:90 faithfulness continues **t** all generations; H4200
Ps 119:148 My eyes **stay open** *t* the watches of the night AIT
Ps 135:13 your renown, LORD, **t** all generations. H4200
Ps 136:14 brought Israel **t** the midst of it, His love H928
Ps 136:16 to him who led his people **t** the wilderness H928
Ps 145:13 your dominion endures **t** all generations. H928
Pr 7: 6 of my house I looked down **t** the lattice. H1237
Pr 9:11 For **t** wisdom your days will be many, and H928
Pr 11: 9 **t** knowledge the righteous escape. H928
Pr 11:11 **T** the blessing of the upright a city is H928
Pr 11:14 but victory is won **t** many advisers. H928
Pr 12: 3 No one can be established **t** wickedness H928
Pr 16: 6 **T** love and faithfulness sin is atoned for H928
Pr 16: 6 **t** the fear of the LORD evil is avoided. H928
Pr 16:12 a throne is established **t** righteousness. H928
Pr 20:28 king safe; **t** love his throne is made secure. H928
Pr 24: 3 and **t** understanding it is established H928
Pr 24: 4 **t** knowledge its rooms are filled with rare H928
Pr 24: 5 The wise prevail **t** great power, and those H928
Pr 24: 6 and victory is won **t** many advisers. H928
Pr 25: 5 throne will be established **t** righteousness. H928
Pr 25:15 **T** patience a ruler can be persuaded, and a H928
Pr 25:28 whose walls **are broken t** is a person who H7287
Ecc 5:14 wealth lost **t** some misfortune, so that H928
Ecc 6:12 days *they* **pass t** like a shadow? H6913
Ecc 10: 8 *whoever* **breaks t** a wall may be bitten by H7287
Ecc 10:18 **T** laziness, the rafters sag; because of idle H928
Ecc 12: 3 those looking **t** the windows grow dim H928
SS 2: 9 our wall, gazing **t** the windows, peering H4946
SS 2: 9 the windows, peering **t** the lattice. H4946
SS 3: 2 go about the city, **t** its streets and squares H928
SS 5: 4 thrust his hand **t** the latch-opening; H4946
Isa 8: 8 **passing t** it and reaching up to the neck. H6296
Isa 8:21 they will roam **t** the land; when they H928
Isa 10:28 enter Aiath; they pass **t** Migron; they store H928
Isa 13:15 Whoever is captured *will* **be thrust t**; all H1991
Isa 13:20 be inhabited or lived in **t** all generations; H6330
Isa 20: 2 the LORD spoke **t** Isaiah son of Amoz. H928+3338
Isa 21: 1 Like whirlwinds sweeping **t** the southland H928
Isa 22: 9 **walls** of the City of David were **broken t** in H1323
Isa 23:16 **walk t** the city, *you* forgotten prostitute H6015
Isa 28:19 by day and by night, *it will* **sweep t**." H6296
Isa 30: 6 **T** a land of hardship and distress, of lions H928
Isa 34:10 desolate; no one will ever pass **t** it again. H928
Isa 38:10 of my life must I go **t** the gates of death H928
Isa 41: 4 Who has done this and **carried** *it* **t**, calling H6913
Isa 43: 2 When you pass **t** the waters, I will be with H928
Isa 43: 2 when you pass **t** the rivers, they will H928
Isa 43: 2 When you walk **t** the fire, you will not be H1198
Isa 43:16 he who made a way **t** the sea, a path H928
Isa 43:16 the sea, a path **t** the mighty waters, H928
Isa 45: 2 gates of bronze and **cut t** bars of iron. H1548
Isa 47: 2 bare your legs, and **wade t** the streams. H6296
Isa 48:21 not thirst when he led them **t** the deserts; H928
Isa 51: 8 my salvation **t** all generations. H4200
Isa 51: 9 to pieces, *who* **pierced** that monster **t**? H2726
Isa 60:15 with no *one* **traveling t**, I will make H6296
Isa 62:10 **Pass t**, pass through the gates! Prepare H6296
Isa 62:10 Pass through, **pass t** the gates! Prepare H6296
Isa 63:11 where is he who brought them **t** the sea H4946
Isa 63:13 who led them **t** the depths? Like a horse in H928
Jer 1: 3 **t** the reign of Jehoiakim son of Josiah H928
Jer 2: 2 me and followed me **t** the wilderness, H928
Jer 2: 2 through the wilderness, **t** a land not sown. H928
Jer 2: 6 of Egypt and led us **t** the barren wilderness, H928
Jer 2: 6 wilderness, **t** a land of deserts and ravines H928
Jer 5: 1 around and consider, search **t** her squares. H928
Jer 5:10 "Go **t** her vineyards and ravage them, but H928
Jer 7: 2 of Judah who come **t** these gates to H928
Jer 9:21 has climbed in **t** our windows and has H928
Jer 17: 4 **T** your own **fault** you will lose the H928
Jer 17:19 **t** which the kings of Judah go in and out H928
Jer 17:20 in Jerusalem who come **t** these gates. H928
Jer 17:21 day or bring it **t** the gates of Jerusalem. H928
Jer 17:24 bring no load **t** the gates of this city on H928
Jer 17:25 throne will come **t** the gates of this city H928
Jer 17:27 any load as you come **t** the gates of H928
Jer 22: 2 your people who come **t** these gates. H928
Jer 22: 4 throne will come **t** the gates of this palace H928
Jer 23:27 ancestors forgot my name **t** Baal worship. H928
Jer 27: 3 Tyre and Sidon **t** the envoys who H928+3338
Jer 37: 2 the LORD had spoken **t** Jeremiah the H928+3338
Jer 39: 2 eleventh year, the city wall **was broken t**. H1324
Jer 39: 4 **t** the gate between the two walls H928
Jer 39:11 about Jeremiah **t** Nebuzaradan H928+3338
Jer 50: 1 word the LORD spoke **t** Jeremiah the H928+3338
Jer 51:43 where no one lives, **t** which no one travels. H928
Jer 52: 7 Then the city wall **was broken t**, and the H1324
Jer 52: 7 the city at night **t** the gate between the H2006
La 3:44 with a cloud so that no prayer *can* **get t**. H6296
La 4:14 Now they grope **t** the streets as if they were H928
Eze 5:17 Plague and bloodshed will sweep **t** you H928
Eze 9: 5 the others, "Follow him **t** the city and kill H928
Eze 11: 5 I know **what is going t** your mind. H5091
Eze 12: 5 dig **t** the wall and take your belongings out H928
Eze 12: 5 the wall and take your belongings out **t** it. H928
Eze 12: 7 in the evening I dug **t** the wall with my H928
Eze 12:12 hole will be dug in the wall for him to go **t**. H928
Eze 12:15 nations and scatter them **t** the countries. H928
Eze 14:15 if I send wild beasts **t** that country and they H928
Eze 14:15 so that no *one can* **pass t** it because of H6296
Eze 14:19 pour out my wrath on it **t** bloodshed, H928
Eze 20:23 nations and scatter them **t** the countries, H928
Eze 20:25 not good and laws **t** which they could not H928
Eze 20:26 I defiled them **t** their gifts—the sacrifice of H928
Eze 20:41 I will be proved holy **t** you in the sight of H928
Eze 22:15 the nations and scatter you **t** the countries; H928
Eze 26:10 a city whose walls *have* **been broken t**. H1324
Eze 28:16 **T** your widespread trade you were filled H928
Eze 28:25 I will be proved holy **t** them in the sight of H928
Eze 29:11 foot of neither man nor beast will pass **t** it; H928
Eze 29:12 nations and scatter them **t** the countries. H928
Eze 30:23 nations and scatter them **t** the countries. H928
Eze 30:26 nations and scatter them **t** the countries. H928
Eze 36:19 they were scattered **t** the countries; H928
Eze 36:23 I am proved holy **t** you before their eyes H928
Eze 36:34 desolate in the sight of all *who* **pass t** it. H6296
Eze 38:16 I am proved holy **t** you before their eyes H928
Eze 39:15 As they go **t** the land, anyone who sees a H928
Eze 39:27 I will be proved holy **t** them in the sight of H928
Eze 40:28 me into the inner court **t** the south gate, H928
Eze 41: 7 floor to the top floor **t** the middle floor. H4200
Eze 43: 4 entered the temple **t** the gate facing east. H2006
Eze 44: 2 must not be opened; no one may enter **t** it. H928
Eze 44: 2 the LORD, the God of Israel, has entered **t** it. H928
Eze 44:19 consecrated **t contact with** their garments. H928
Eze 45:20 who sins unintentionally or **t** ignorance; H4946
Eze 46: 2 enter from the outside **t** the portico of the H2006
Eze 46: 8 he is to go in **t** the portico of the gateway H2006
Eze 46: 9 No one is to return **t** the gate by which H2006
Eze 46:19 the man brought me **t** the entrance at the H928
Eze 47: 2 then brought me out **t** the north gate and H2006
Eze 47: 3 cubits and then led me **t** water that was H928
Eze 47: 4 cubits and led me **t** water that was H928
Eze 47: 4 thousand and led me **t** water that was up H6296
Da 2:28 the **visions** *that passed t* your mind as AIT
Da 2:30 you may understand what went **t** your mind. NDT
Da 4: 5 images and **visions** *that passed t* my mind AIT
Da 7: 1 and **visions** *passed t* his mind as he was AIT
Da 7:15 the **visions** *that passed t* my mind AIT
Da 9:10 laws he gave us **t** his servants the H928+3338
Da 11:21 feel secure, and he will seize it **t** intrigue. H928
Da 11:40 countries and **sweep t** them like a flood H6296
Hos 1: 2 When the LORD began to speak **t** Hosea H928
Hos 12:10 visions and told parables **t** them." H928+3338
Hos 13: 3 like smoke escaping **t** a window. H4946
Joel 2: 8 They plunge **t** defenses without breaking H1237
Joel 2: 9 like thieves they enter **t** the windows. H1237
Joel 3:20 forever and Jerusalem **t** all generations. H4200
Am 4: 3 will each go **straight** out **t** breaches in the H5584
Am 5: 6 or *he will* **sweep t** the tribes of Joseph like H7502
Am 5:17 I will pass **t** your midst," says the LORD H928
Am 8:11 "when I will send a famine **t** the land—not H928
Ob 13 You should not march **t** the gates of my H928
Jnh 3: 3 very large city; it took three days to **go t** it. H4544
Mic 2:13 they will break **t** the gate and go out. H6296
Mic 2:13 Their King *will* **pass t** before them, the H6296
Mic 5: 5 invade our land and march **t** our fortresses. H928
Na 2: 4 The chariots storm **t** the streets, rushing H928
Na 2: 4 rushing back and forth **t** the squares. H928
Hab 3:12 In wrath *you* **strode t** the earth and in H7575
Zep 2:14 Their hooting will echo **t** the windows H928
Zep 3: 6 streets deserted, with no *one* **passing t**. H6296
Hag 1: 1 of the LORD came **t** the prophet H928+3338
Hag 1: 3 of the LORD came **t** the prophet H928+3338
Hag 2: 1 of the LORD came **t** the prophet H928+3338
Zec 7: 7 the LORD proclaimed **t** the earlier H928+3338
Zec 7:12 sent by his Spirit **t** the earlier H928+3338
Zec 7:14 that no *one* **traveled t** it. H6296+2256+8740
Zec 10:11 They will pass **t** the sea of trouble; the H928
Mal 1: 1 word of the LORD to Israel **t** Malachi. H928+3338
Mt 1:18 found to be pregnant **t** the Holy Spirit. *G1666*
Mt 1:22 what the Lord had said **t** the prophet: *G1328*
Mt 2:15 what the Lord had said **t** the prophet: *G1328*
Mt 2:17 Then what was said **t** the prophet *G1328*
Mt 2:23 was fulfilled what was said **t** the prophets, *G1328*
Mt 3: 3 who was spoken of **t** the prophet Isaiah: *G1328*
Mt 4:14 fulfill what was said **t** the prophet Isaiah: *G1328*
Mt 7:13 "Enter **t** the narrow gate. For wide is the *G1328*
Mt 7:13 leads to destruction, and many enter **t** it. *G1328*
Mt 8:17 what was spoken **t** the prophet Isaiah: *G1328*
Mt 9:26 News of this spread **t** all that region. *G1650*
Mt 9:35 Jesus *went* **t** all the towns and villages *G4310*
Mt 10:20 the Spirit of your Father speaking **t** you. *G1877*
Mt 10:23 *you will* not **finish** *going t* the towns of Israel AIT
Mt 12: 1 that time Jesus went **t** the grainfields on *G1328*
Mt 12:17 what was spoken **t** the prophet Isaiah: *G1328*
Mt 12:20 till *he has* **brought** justice **t** to victory. *G1675*
Mt 12:43 *it* **goes t** arid places seeking rest and does *G1451*
Mt 13:33 of flour until *it* **worked** all **t the dough**." *G2435*
Mt 13:35 fulfilled what was spoken **t** the prophet: *G1328*
Mt 18: 7 woe to the person **t** whom they come! *G1328*
Mt 19:24 easier for a camel *to* **go t** the eye of a *G1451*
Mt 21: 4 to fulfill what was spoken **t** the prophet: *G1328*
Mt 24:15 spoken of **t** the prophet Daniel—let *G1328*
Mk 2: 4 roof above Jesus *by* **digging t** it and then *G2021*
Mk 2:23 Jesus was going **t** the grainfields, *G1328*
Mk 7:31 left the vicinity of Tyre and went **t** Sidon, *G1328*
Mk 9:30 They left that place and passed **t** Galilee *G1328*
Mk 10:25 easier for a camel *to* **go t** the eye of a *G1451*
Mk 11:16 anyone to **carry** merchandise **t** the temple *G1422*

Lk 1:70 as he said t his holy prophets of G1328+5125
Lk 1:77 of salvation t the forgiveness of G1877
Lk 4:14 about him spread t the whole countryside G2848
Lk 4:30 But he **walked right** t the G1451+1328+3545
Lk 5:19 lowered him on his mat t the tiles into the G1328
Lk 6: 1 Sabbath Jesus *was* **going** t the grainfields G1388
Lk 10:21 time Jesus, full of joy *t* the Holy **Spirit**, said, AIT
Lk 11:24 *it* **goes** t arid places seeking rest and does G1451
Lk 13:21 of flour until *it* **worked** all **t the dough**." G2435
Lk 13:22 Then Jesus **went** t the towns and villages G1388
Lk 13:24 every effort to enter t the narrow door, G1328
Lk 17: 1 woe to anyone t whom they come. G1328
Lk 18:25 a camel to go t the eye of a needle G1328
Lk 19: 1 Jesus entered Jericho and *was* **passing t**. G1451
Lk 20:23 *He* **saw** t their duplicity and said to them, G2917
Jn 1: 3 **T** him all things were made; without him G1328
Jn 1: 7 that light, so that t him all might believe. G1328
Jn 1:10 though the world was made t him G1328
Jn 1:17 For the law was given t Moses; grace and G1328
Jn 1:17 grace and truth came t Jesus Christ. G1328
Jn 2:11 the first of the signs t which he revealed his NDT
Jn 3:17 the world, but to save the world t him. G1328
Jn 4: 4 Now he had to **go t** Samaria. G1451
Jn 7:14 Not until **halfway** t the festival did Jesus G3548
Jn 10: 9 whoever enters t me will be saved. G1328
Jn 11: 4 so that God's Son may be glorified t it." G1328
Jn 14: 6 No one comes to the Father except t me. G1328
Jn 17:10 And glory has come to me t them. G1877
Jn 17:20 who will believe in me t their message, G1328
Ac 1: 2 giving instructions t the Holy Spirit to the G1328
Ac 1:16 spoke long ago t David concerning G1328+5125
Ac 2:22 which God did among you t him, as you G1328
Ac 3:16 the faith that *comes* t him that has G1328
Ac 3:18 he had foretold t all the prophets, G1328+5125
Ac 3:21 long ago t his holy prophets G1328+5125
Ac 3:25 '**T** your offspring all peoples on earth will G1877
Ac 4:25 by the Holy Spirit *t* the **mouth** of your servant, AIT
Ac 4:30 signs and wonders t the name of your G1328
Ac 7:35 t the angel who appeared to him G5250+5931
Ac 7:53 law that was given t angels but have not G1650
Ac 9:25 him in a basket t *an opening* in the wall. G1328
Ac 10:36 the good news of peace t Jesus Christ, G1328
Ac 10:43 receives forgiveness of sins t his name." G1328
Ac 11:14 bring you a message t which you and all G1877
Ac 11:28 stood up and t the Spirit predicted that a G1328
Ac 12:10 them by itself, and *they* **went** t it. G2002
Ac 13: 6 *They* **traveled** t the whole island until they G1451
Ac 13:38 you to know that t Jesus the forgiveness G1328
Ac 13:39 **T** him everyone who believes is set free G1877
Ac 13:49 of the Lord spread t the whole region. G1328
Ac 14:22 "We must *go* t many hardships to enter G1328
Ac 14:24 *After* **going** t Pisidia, they came into G1451
Ac 14:27 that God had done t them and how he G3552
Ac 15: 3 and *as they* **traveled** t Phoenicia and G1451
Ac 15: 4 reported everything God had done t them. G3552
Ac 15:11 We believe it is t the grace of our Lord G1328
Ac 15:12 had done among the Gentiles t them. G1328
Ac 15:41 *He* **went** t Syria and Cilicia, strengthening G1451
Ac 17: 1 *When* Paul and his companions *had* **passed** t G1476
Ac 19: 1 Paul **took the road** t the interior and G1451
Ac 19:11 extraordinary miracles t Paul, G1328+3836+5931
Ac 19:21 **passing** t Macedonia and Achaia. G1451
Ac 20: 2 *He* **traveled** t that area, speaking many G1451
Ac 20: 3 he decided to go back t Macedonia. G1328
Ac 21: 4 **T** the Spirit they urged Paul not to go on G1328
Ac 21:19 done among the Gentiles t his ministry. G1328
Ac 28:25 when he said t Isaiah the prophet: G1328
Ro 1: 2 promised beforehand t his prophets in the G1328
Ro 1: 4 who t the Spirit of holiness was G2848
Ro 1: 5 **T** him we received grace and apostleship G1328
Ro 1: 8 I thank my God t Jesus Christ for all of you, G1328
Ro 2:16 judges people's secrets t Jesus Christ, G1328
Ro 3:20 t the law we become conscious of our sin. G1328
Ro 3:22 This righteousness is *given* t faith in Jesus G1328
Ro 3:24 freely by his grace t the redemption that G1328
Ro 3:25 of atonement, t the shedding of his blood G1877
Ro 3:30 the uncircumcised t that same faith. G1328
Ro 4:13 It was not t the law that Abraham and his G1328
Ro 4:13 t the righteousness that comes by G1328
Ro 4:20 Yet he did not waver *t* **unbelief** regarding the AIT
Ro 5: 1 since we have been justified t faith, we G1666
Ro 5: 1 have peace with God t our Lord Jesus G1328
Ro 5: 2 t whom we have gained access by faith G1328
Ro 5: 5 out into our hearts t the Holy Spirit, G1328
Ro 5: 9 shall we be saved from God's wrath t him! G1328
Ro 5:10 reconciled to him t the death of his Son, G1328
Ro 5:10 reconciled, shall we be saved t his life! G1877
Ro 5:11 we also boast in God t our Lord Jesus G1328
Ro 5:11 t whom we have now received G1328
Ro 5:12 just as sin entered the world t one man G1328
Ro 5:12 one man, and death t sin, and in this way G1328
Ro 5:17 death reigned t that one man, how G1328
Ro 5:17 righteousness reign in life t the one man, G1328
Ro 5:19 For just as t the disobedience of the one G1328
Ro 5:19 so also t the obedience of the one man G1328
Ro 5:21 grace might reign t righteousness to bring G1328
Ro 5:21 to bring eternal life t Jesus Christ our Lord. G1328
Ro 6: 4 buried with him t baptism into death in G1328
Ro 6: 4 raised from the dead t the glory of the G1328
Ro 7: 4 also died to the law t the body of Christ, G1328
Ro 7:11 t the commandment put me to death. G1328
Ro 7:13 so that t the commandment sin might G1328
Ro 7:25 who delivers me t Jesus Christ our Lord! G1328
Ro 8: 2 because t Christ Jesus the law of the Spirit G1877
Ro 8:26 himself intercedes for us *t* wordless **groans**. AIT
Ro 8:37 more than conquerors t him who loved us. G1328
Ro 9: 1 conscience confirms it t the Holy Spirit— G1877
Ro 9: 7 "It is t Isaac that your offspring will be G1877
Ro 10:17 the message is heard t the word about G1328
Ro 11:36 For from him and t him and for him are all G1328
Ro 15: 4 so that t the endurance taught in the G1328
Ro 15:18 has accomplished t me in leading the G1328
Ro 15:19 wonders, t the power of the Spirit of God. G1877
Ro 15:24 to see you *while* **passing** t and to have G1388
Ro 16:26 made known t the prophetic writings G1328
Ro 16:27 wise God be glory forever t Jesus Christ! G1328
1Co 1:21 of God the world t its wisdom did not G1328
1Co 1:21 God was pleased t the foolishness of G1328
1Co 2:14 because they are discerned only *t the* **Spirit**. AIT
1Co 3: 5 servants, t whom you came to believe G1328
1Co 3:15 though only as one *escaping* t the flames. G1328
1Co 4:15 Jesus I became your father t the gospel. G1328
1Co 7:14 husband has been sanctified t his wife, G1877
1Co 7:14 has been sanctified t her believing G1877
1Co 8: 6 t whom all things came and through G1328
1Co 8: 6 all things came and t whom we live. G1328
1Co 10: 1 cloud and that *they* all **passed** t the sea. G1451
1Co 12: 8 one there is given t the Spirit a message G1328
1Co 14:21 other tongues and t the lips of foreigners G1877
1Co 15:21 For since death came t a man, the G1328
1Co 15:21 of the dead comes also t a man. G1328
1Co 15:57 gives us the victory t our Lord Jesus Christ. G1328
1Co 16: 5 After *I* **go t** Macedonia, I will come to you G1451
1Co 16: 5 to you—for *I will be* **going** t Macedonia. G1451
2Co 1: 5 so also our comfort abounds t Christ. G1328
2Co 1:20 And so t him the "Amen" is spoken by us G1328
2Co 3: 4 confidence we have t Christ before God. G1328
2Co 4: 1 since *t* God's **mercy** we have this ministry AIT
2Co 5:18 us to himself t Christ and gave us the G1328
2Co 5:20 though God were making his appeal t us. G1328
2Co 6: 8 t glory and dishonor, bad report and good G1328
2Co 8: 9 so that you *t* his **poverty** might become rich. AIT
2Co 9:11 t us your generosity will result in G1328
2Co 11:33 in the wall and **slipped** t his hands. G1767
2Co 12:17 Did I exploit you t any of the men I sent to G1328
2Co 13: 3 proof that Christ is speaking t me. G1877
Gal 2:19 "For t the law I died to the law so that I G1328
Gal 2:21 righteousness could be gained t the law, G1328
Gal 3: 8 "All nations will be blessed t you." G1877
Gal 3:14 might come to the Gentiles t Christ Jesus, G1877
Gal 3:18 his grace gave it to Abraham t a promise. G1328
Gal 3:19 The law was given t angels and entrusted G1328
Gal 3:22 being **given** t faith in Jesus Christ G1666
Gal 3:26 Jesus you are all children of God t faith, G1328
Gal 5: 5 For *t* the **Spirit** we eagerly await by faith the AIT
Gal 5: 6 that counts is faith expressing itself t love. G1328
Gal 5: 9 "A little yeast **works** t the whole batch of G2435
Gal 6:14 t which the world has been crucified to G1328
Eph 1: 5 us for adoption to sonship t Jesus Christ, G1328
Eph 1: 7 In him we have redemption t his blood G1328
Eph 2: 8 you have been saved, t faith—and this is G1328
Eph 2:16 reconcile both of them to God t the cross, G1328
Eph 2:18 For t him we both have access to the G1328
Eph 3: 6 This mystery is that t the gospel the G1328
Eph 3: 7 God's grace given me t the working of his G2848
Eph 3:10 His intent was that now, t the church, the G1328
Eph 3:12 In him and t faith in him we may approach G1328
Eph 3:16 you with power t his Spirit in your inner G1328
Eph 3:17 that Christ may dwell in your hearts t faith. G1328
Eph 4: 3 the unity of the Spirit t the bond of peace. G1877
Eph 4: 6 who is over all and t all and in all. G1328
Eph 5:26 her by the washing with water t the word, G1877
Php 1:11 righteousness that *comes* t Jesus Christ— G1328
Php 1:19 I know that t your prayers and God's G1328
Php 1:26 so that t my being with you again your G1328
Php 1:30 *since* you *are* **going** t the same struggle G2400
Php 3: 9 but that which is t faith in Christ—the G1328
Php 4:13 I can do all this t him who gives me G1877
Col 1: 9 of his will t all the wisdom and G1877
Col 1:16 have been created t him and for him. G1328
Col 1:20 t him to reconcile to himself all things, G1328
Col 1:20 by making peace t his blood, shed on the G1328
Col 1:22 physical body t death to present you G1328
Col 2: 8 takes you captive t hollow and deceptive G1328
Col 2:12 also raised with him t your faith in the G1328
Col 3:16 one another with all wisdom *t* **psalms**, AIT
Col 3:17 giving thanks to God the Father t him. G1328
1Th 5: 9 to receive salvation t our Lord Jesus Christ. G1328
1Th 5:23 God of peace, sanctify you **t and through**. G3911
1Th 5:23 God of peace, sanctify you **through and t**. G3911
2Th 2: 9 of displays of power *t* **signs** and wonders that AIT
2Th 2:13 to be saved t the sanctifying work of G1877
2Th 2:13 work of the Spirit and *t* **belief** in the truth. AIT
2Th 2:14 He called you to this t our gospel, that you G1328
1Ti 2:15 But women will be saved t childbearing G1328
1Ti 4: 2 Such teachings *come* t hypocritical liars G1877
1Ti 4:14 which was given you t prophecy when the G1328
2Ti 1: 6 which is in you t the laying on of my G1328
2Ti 1:10 now been revealed t the appearing of our G1328
2Ti 1:10 life and immortality to light t the gospel. G1328
2Ti 3:15 wise for salvation t faith in Christ Jesus. G1328
2Ti 4:17 so that t me the message might be fully G1328
Titus 1: 3 has brought to light t the preaching G1877
Titus 3: 5 He saved us t the washing of rebirth and G1328
Titus 3: 6 out on us generously t Jesus Christ our G1328
Heb 1: 1 to our ancestors t the prophets at many G1877
Heb 1: 2 t whom also he made the universe. G1328
Heb 2: 2 the message spoken t angels was binding G1328
Heb 2:10 whom and t whom everything exists G1328
Heb 2:10 their salvation perfect t what he suffered. G1328
Heb 4: 7 when a long time later he spoke t David, G1877
Heb 6:12 to imitate those who t faith and patience G1328
Heb 7: 9 the tenth, paid the tenth t Abraham, G1328
Heb 7:11 have been attained t the Levitical G1328
Heb 7:25 completely those who come to God t him, G1328
Heb 9:11 he *went* t the greater and more perfect G1328
Heb 9:14 who t the eternal Spirit offered himself G1328
Heb 10:10 have been made holy t the sacrifice of the G1328
Heb 10:20 living way opened for us t the curtain, G1328
Heb 11:18 "It is t Isaac that your offspring will be G1877
Heb 11:29 By faith *the people* **passed** t the Red Sea G1329
Heb 11:33 who t faith conquered kingdoms G1328
Heb 13:12 to make the people holy t his own blood. G1328
Heb 13:15 **T** Jesus, therefore, let us continually offer G1328
Heb 13:20 who t the blood of the eternal covenant G1877
Heb 13:21 is pleasing to him, t Jesus Christ, to whom G1328
Jas 1:18 He chose to give us birth *t* the **word** of truth AIT
1Pe 1: 2 t the sanctifying work of the Spirit G1877
1Pe 1: 3 into a living hope t the resurrection of G1328
1Pe 1: 5 who t faith are shielded by God's power G1328
1Pe 1:21 **T** him you believe in God, who raised him G1328
1Pe 1:23 t the living and enduring word of God. G1328
1Pe 2: 5 sacrifices acceptable to God t Jesus Christ. G1328
1Pe 3:20 people, eight in all, *were* **saved** t water, G1407
1Pe 4:11 things God may be praised t Jesus Christ. G1328
2Pe 1: 1 To those who t the righteousness of our G1877
2Pe 1: 2 yours in abundance t the knowledge of G1877
2Pe 1: 3 a godly life t our knowledge of him G1328
2Pe 1: 4 **T** these he has given us his very great and G1328
2Pe 1: 4 so that t them you may participate in the G1328
2Pe 3: 2 given by our Lord and Savior *t* your **apostles**. AIT
1Jn 4: 9 into the world that we might live t him. G1328
Jude 25 authority, t Jesus Christ our Lord G1328
Rev 18:19 on the sea became rich t her wealth! G1666
Rev 22:14 of life and may go *t* the **gates** into the city. AIT

THROUGHLY (KJV) ALL, PERFECTLY, REALLY, THOROUGHLY, VIGOROUSLY

THROUGHOUT (135) [THROUGH]

Ge 7: 3 kinds alive t the earth. H6584+7156+3972
Ge 41:29 are coming t the land of Egypt, H928+3972
Ge 41:45 And Joseph went t the land of Egypt. H6584
Ge 41:46 presence and traveled t Egypt. H928+3972
Ge 41:56 the famine was severe t Egypt. H928
Ex 8:16 and t the land of Egypt the dust will H928+3972
Ex 8:17 All the dust t the land of Egypt H928+3972
Ex 8:24 t Egypt the land was ruined by the H928+3972
Ex 9: 9 on people and animals t the land." H928+3972
Ex 9:25 **T** Egypt hail struck everything in the H928+3972
Ex 11: 4 'About midnight I will go t Egypt. H928+9348
Ex 11: 6 There will be loud wailing t Egypt H928+3972
Ex 14:20 *T* the **night** the cloud brought darkness to the AIT
Ex 36: 6 order and *they* **sent** this word t the camp: H6296
Ex 40:15 that will continue t their generations." H4200
Lev 6: 9 to remain on the altar hearth t the night, H3972
Lev 25: 9 sound the trumpet t your land. H928+3972
Lev 25:10 proclaim liberty t the land to all its H928
Lev 25:24 **T** the land that you hold as a H928+3972
Nu 6: 6 " '**T** the period of their dedication to the H3972
Nu 6: 8 **T** the period of their dedication, they are H3972
Nu 15:21 **T** the generations to come you are to give H4200
Nu 15:38 '**T** the generations to come you are to H4200
Nu 35:29 force of law for you t the generations to H4200
Dt 28:40 have olive trees t your country but H928+3972
Dt 28:52 to all the cities t your land until the H928+3972
Dt 28:52 all the cities t the land the LORD your H928+3972
Jos 3: 2 days the officers went t the camp, H928+7931
Jos 6:27 and his fame spread t the land. H928+3972
Jos 24: 3 and led him t Canaan and gave him H928+3972
Jos 24:31 served the LORD t the lifetime of Joshua H3972
Jdg 2: 7 served the LORD t the lifetime of Joshua H3972
Jdg 6:35 He sent messengers t Manasseh H928+3972
Jdg 7:22 caused the men t the camp to turn H928+3972
Jdg 7:24 sent messengers t the hill country of H928+3972
Jdg 19:25 raped her and abused her t the night, H3972
Jdg 20:12 sent messengers t the tribe of H928+3972
Ru 4:14 May he become famous t Israel! H928
1Sa 7:13 **T** Samuel's lifetime, the hand of the LORD H3972
1Sa 11: 3 can send messengers t Israel; H928+3972+1473
1Sa 11: 7 pieces by messengers t Israel, H928+3972+1473
1Sa 13: 3 trumpet blown t the land and said H928+3972
1Sa 31: 9 sent messengers t the land of the H928+6017
2Sa 8:14 He put garrisons t Edom, and all the H928+3972
2Sa 15:10 secret messengers t the tribes of H928+3972
2Sa 19: 9 **T** the tribes of Israel, all the people H928+3972
2Sa 19:11 what is being said t Israel has reached H3972
2Sa 24: 2 "Go t the tribes of Israel from Dan to H928+3972
1Ki 1: 3 they searched t Israel for a H928+3972+1473
1Ki 9:19 in Lebanon and t all the territory he ruled. H928
1Ki 15: 6 Abijah and Jeroboam t Abijah's lifetime. H3972
1Ki 15:16 Baasha king of Israel t their reigns. H3972
1Ki 15:32 Baasha king of Israel t their reigns. H3972
1Ki 18:20 So Ahab sent word t all Israel and H928
2Ki 10:21 Then he sent word t Israel, and all H928+3972
2Ki 10:32 the Israelites t their territory H928+3972

T

2Ki 13:22 oppressed Israel t the reign of Jehoahaz H3972
1Ch 5:10 of the Hagrites t the entire region east of H6584
1Ch 10: 9 sent messengers t the land of the H928+6017
1Ch 13: 2 rest of our people t the territories of H928+3972
1Ch 14:17 So David's fame spread t every land, and H928
1Ch 21: 4 Joab left and went t Israel and then H928+3972
1Ch 27: 1 on duty month by month t the year. H4200+3972
2Ch 8: 6 in Lebanon and t all the territory he ruled. H928
2Ch 11:13 all their districts t Israel sided with H928+3972
2Ch 11:23 some of his sons t the districts of H4200+3972
2Ch 16: 9 eyes of the LORD range t the earth to H928+3972
2Ch 17: 9 They taught t Judah, taking with them the H928
2Ch 17:19 in the fortified cities t Judah. H928+3972
2Ch 23: 2 They went t Judah and gathered the H6015
2Ch 30: 5 to send a proclamation t Israel, H928+3972
2Ch 30: 6 couriers went t Israel and Judah with H928+3972
2Ch 31: 1 and the altars t Judah and H4946+3972
2Ch 31:20 This is what Hezekiah did t Judah H928+3972
2Ch 34: 7 pieces all the incense altars t Israel. H928+3972
2Ch 36:22 a proclamation t his realm and also H928+3972
Ezr 1: 1 a proclamation t his realm and also H928+3972
Ezr 10: 7 was then issued t Judah and Jerusalem H928
Ne 8:15 and spread it t their towns and in H928+3972
Est 1:20 edict is proclaimed t all his vast realm, H928
Est 2:18 proclaimed a holiday t the provinces and H4200
Est 3: 6 the Jews, t the whole kingdom of Xerxes. H928
Est 9: 4 his reputation spread t the provinces, H928+3972
Est 9:20 to all the Jews t the provinces of H928+3972
Est 10: 1 King Xerxes imposed tribute t the empire H6584
Job 1: 7 "From roaming t the earth, going back H928
Job 1:10 his flocks and herds are spread t the land. H928
Job 2: 2 "From roaming t the earth, going back H928
Ps 45:16 will make them princes t the land. H928+3972
Ps 72:16 May grain abound t the land; on the tops H928
Ps 90: 1 been our dwelling place t all generations. H928
Ps 105:31 of flies, and gnats t their country. H928+3972
Ps 105:32 rain into hail, with lightning t their land; H928
Ps 106:27 the nations and scatter them t the lands. H928
Jer 4: 5 'Sound the trumpet t the land!' Cry aloud H928
Jer 15:13 of all your sins t your country. H928+3972
Jer 17: 3 places, because of sin t your country. H928+3972
Jer 23:15 ungodliness has spread t the land." H4200+3972
Jer 45: 4 uproot what I have planted, t the earth. H3972
Jer 51:52 and t her land the wounded will H928+3972
Eze 9: 4 "Go t the city of Jerusalem and put a H928+9348
Eze 9: 7 they went out and began killing t the city. H928
Eze 14:17 'Let the sword pass t the land,' and I kill H928
Eze 30:13 in Egypt, and I will spread fear t the land. H928
Da 6: 1 satraps to rule t the kingdom, A10089+10353
Zec 1:10 ones the LORD has sent to go t the earth." H928
Zec 1:11 "We have gone t the earth and found the H928
Zec 4:10 the LORD that range t the earth will H928+3972
Zec 5: 6 the iniquity of the people t the land." H928+3972
Zec 6: 7 they were straining to go t the earth. H928
Zec 6: 7 And he said, "Go t the earth!" So they H928
Zec 6: 7 So they went t the earth. H928
Mt 4:23 Jesus went t Galilee, teaching in G1877+3910
Mt 26:13 this gospel is preached t the world, G1877+3910
Mk 1:39 So he traveled t Galilee, preaching G1650+3910
Mk 6:55 They ran t that whole region and carried G4366
Mk 14: 9 the gospel is preached t the world, G1650+3910
Lk 1:65 and t the hill country of Judea G1877+3910
Lk 4:25 was a severe famine t the land. G2093+4246
Lk 4:37 about him spread t the surrounding G1650+4246
Lk 7:17 Jesus spread t Judea and the G1877+3910
Ac 8: 1 were scattered t Judea and Samaria. G2848
Ac 9:31 Then the church t Judea, Galilee G2848+3910
Ac 10:37 has happened t the province of G2848+3910
Ac 11: 1 the believers t Judea heard that the G2848
Ac 16: 6 his companions traveled t the region of G1451
Ac 18:23 and traveled from place to place t the G1451
Ac 19:27 who is worshiped t the province of Asia G3910
2Co 1: 1 with all his holy people t Achaia: G1877+3910
Eph 3:21 in Christ Jesus t all generations, G1650
Php 1:13 it has become clear t the whole palace G1877
Col 1: 6 fruit and growing t the whole world— G1877
1Th 4:10 all of God's family t Macedonia. G1877+3910
1Pe 1: 1 exiles scattered t the provinces of Pontus G1402
1Pe 5: 9 family of believers t the world is G1877

THROW (68) [THREW, THROWING, THROWN, THROWS]

Ge 27:40 you will t his yoke from off your neck." H7293
Ge 37:20 let's kill him and t him into one of these H8959
Ge 37:22 T him into this cistern here in the H8959
Ex 1:22 boy that is born you must t into the Nile, H8959
Ex 4: 3 The LORD said, "T it on the ground. H8959
Ex 7: 9 your staff and t it down before Pharaoh, H8959
Ex 22:31 torn by wild beasts; t it to the dogs. H8959
Ex 23:27 of you and t into confusion every nation H2169
Lev 1:16 the feathers and t them down east of the H8959
Nu 19: 6 scarlet wool and t them onto the H8959
Jos 8:29 the pole and t it down at the entrance H8959
Jos 24:14 T away the gods your ancestors worshiped H6073
Jos 24:23 "t away the foreign gods that are among H6073
2Ki 9:25 "Pick him up and t him on the field that H8959
2Ki 9:26 pick him up and t him on that plot, in H8959
2Ki 9:33 "T her down!" Jehu said. So they threw her H9023
Job 18: 7 weakened; his own schemes t him down. H8959
Job 30:11 they t off restraint in my presence. H8938
Ps 2: 3 break their chains and t off their shackles." H8959
Ps 17:11 with eyes alert, to t me to the ground. H5742
Ps 50:18 with him; you t in your lot with adulterers. NDT
Ps 62: 3 Would all of you t me down—this H8132
Ecc 3: 6 a time to keep and a time to t away, H8959
Isa 2:20 that day people will t away to the moles H8959
Isa 19: 8 those who t nets on the water will pine H7298
Isa 22:18 tightly like a ball and t you into a large NDT
Isa 28: 2 he will t it forcefully to the ground. H5663
Isa 30:22 you will t them away like a menstrual H2430
Jer 7:29 " 'Cut off your hair and t it away; take up a H8959
Jer 16:13 So I will t you out of this land into a land H3214
Jer 22: 7 fine cedar beams and t them into the fire. H5877
Jer 51:63 tie a stone to it and t it into the Euphrates. H8959
Eze 5: 4 a few of these and t them into the fire H8959
Eze 7:19 " 'They will t their silver into the streets H8959
Eze 26:12 your fine houses and t your stones, H8492
Eze 32: 4 I will t you on the land and hurl you on H5759
Da 3:20 Abednego and t them into the A10667
Hos 7:12 When they go, I will t my net over them; H7298
Hos 8: 5 Samaria, t out your calf-idol! My anger H2396
Jnh 1:12 "Pick me up and t me into the sea," H3214
Zec 1:21 terrify them and t down these horns of the H3343
Zec 11:13 LORD said to me, "T it to the potter"—the H8959
Mal 3:10 "and see if I will not t open the H7337
Mt 4: 6 the Son of God," he said, "t yourself down. G965
Mt 5:29 you to stumble, gouge it out and t it away. G965
Mt 5:30 you to stumble, cut it off and t it away. G965
Mt 7: 6 what is sacred; do not t your pearls to pigs. G965
Mt 13:42 They will t them into the blazing furnace G965
Mt 13:50 t them into the blazing furnace, where G965
Mt 17:27 offense, go to the lake and t out your line. G965
Mt 18: 8 you to stumble, cut it off and t it away. G965
Mt 18: 9 you to stumble, gouge it out and t it away. G965
Mt 21:21 t yourself into the sea,' and it will be G965
Mt 22:13 hand and foot, and t him outside, into the G1675
Mt 25:30 And t that worthless servant outside, into G1675
Mk 11:23 t yourself into the sea,' and does not G965
Lk 4: 9 he said, "t yourself down from here. G965
Lk 4:29 was built, in order to t him off the cliff. G2889
Lk 12: 5 has authority to t you into hell. G1833
Lk 12:58 the officer, and the officer t you into prison. G965
Lk 22:41 withdrew about a stone's t beyond them, G1074
Jn 8: 7 Let any one of you who is without sin be the first to t G965
Jn 21: 6 "T your net on the right side of the boat G965
Ac 7:19 by forcing them to t out their newborn G1704
Ac 27:18 day they began to t the cargo overboard. G1678
Heb 10:35 So do not t away your confidence; it will be G610
Heb 12: 1 let us t off everything that hinders and the G700
Rev 18:19 They will t dust on their heads, and with G965

THROWING (11) [THROW]

Dt 7:23 t them into great confusion until H2169+4539
1Sa 5: 9 was against that city, t it into a great panic. NDT
2Sa 16:13 as he went and t stones at him and H6232
Ezr 10: 1 weeping and t himself down before the H5877
Mk 10:50 T his cloak aside, he jumped to his feet G610
Ac 16:20 are Jews, and are t our city into an uproar G1752
Ac 22: 4 men and women and t them into prison, G4140
Ac 22:23 were shouting and t off their cloaks and G4848
Ac 27:38 lightened the ship by t the grain into the G1675
Gal 1: 7 people are t you into confusion and are G5429
Gal 5:10 The one who is t you into confusion G5429

THROWN (74) [THROW]

Lev 4:12 where the ashes are t, and burn it H9162
Lev 14:40 be torn out and t into an unclean place H8959
2Sa 20:21 "His head will be t to you from the wall." H8959
2Ki 7:15 the Arameans had t away in their H8959
2Ki 19:18 They have t their gods into the fire and H5989
Ne 4: 5 for they have t insults in the face of the H4087
Job 16:11 to the ungodly and t me into the clutches H3740
Ps 36:12 lie fallen—t down, not able to rise! H1890
Ps 102:10 you have taken me up and t me aside. H8959
Ps 140:10 fall on them; may they be t into the fire H5877
Ps 141: 6 Their rulers will be t down from the cliffs H9023
Isa 34: 3 Their slain will be t out, their dead bodies H8959
Isa 37:19 They have t their gods into the fire and H5989
Jer 14:16 to will be t out into the streets of H8959
Jer 22:19 dragged away and t outside the gates of H8959
Jer 26:23 a sword and his body t into the burial H8959
Jer 31:40 valley where dead bodies and ashes are t, NDT
Jer 36:30 his body will be t out and exposed to the H8959
Jer 38: 9 They have t him into a cistern, where he H8959
Jer 51:34 he has t us into confusion, he has H2169
Eze 11: 7 The bodies you have t there are the meat H8492
Eze 15: 4 And after it is t on the fire as fuel and the H5989
Eze 16: 5 you were t out into the open field H8959
Eze 19:12 was uprooted in fury and t to the ground. H8959
Eze 21:12 They are t to the sword along with my H4489
Da 3: 6 worship will immediately be t into a A10667
Da 3:11 worship will be t into a blazing A10667
Da 3:15 you will be t immediately into a blazing A10667
Da 3:17 If we are t into the blazing furnace, the God NDT
Da 3:21 were bound and t into the blazing A10667
Da 6: 7 Majesty, shall be t into the lions' den. A10667
Da 6:12 Majesty, would be t into the lions' den?" A10667
Da 6:24 were brought in and t into the lions' den A10667
Da 7:11 body destroyed and t into the blazing A10314
Da 8:11 the LORD, and his sanctuary was t down. H8959
Da 8:12 and truth was t to the ground. H8959
Joel 1: 7 It has stripped off their bark and t it away H8959
Na 2: 6 The river gates are t open and the palace H7337
Mt 3:10 fruit will be cut down and t into the fire. G965
Mt 5:13 except to be t out and trampled underfoot. G965
Mt 5:25 to the officer, and you may be t into prison. G965
Mt 5:29 than for your whole body to be t into hell. G965
Mt 6:30 here today and tomorrow is t into the fire, G965
Mt 7:19 good fruit is cut down and t into the fire. G965
Mt 8:12 subjects of the kingdom will be t outside, G1675
Mt 18: 8 hands or two feet and be t into eternal fire. G965
Mt 18: 9 to have two eyes and be t into the fire of G965
Mt 18:30 he went off and had the man t into prison G965
Mt 24: 2 left on another; every one will be t down." G2907
Mk 9:22 "It has often t him into fire or water to kill G965
Mk 9:42 their neck and they were t into the sea. G965
Mk 9:45 than to have two feet and be t into hell. G965
Mk 9:47 than to have two eyes and be t into hell, G965
Mk 13: 2 left on another; every one will be t down." G2907
Lk 3: 9 fruit will be cut down and t into the fire." G965
Lk 12:28 and tomorrow is t into the fire, how G965
Lk 13:28 kingdom of God, but you yourselves t out. G1675
Lk 14:35 the soil nor for the manure pile; it is t out. G965
Lk 17: 2 better for them to be t into the sea with G4849
Lk 21: 6 every one of them will be t down. G2907
Lk 23:19 Barabbas had been t into prison for an G965
Lk 23:25 the man who had been t into prison G965
Jn 9:35 Jesus heard that they had t him out, and G1675
Jn 15: 6 are like a branch that is t away and withers; G965
Jn 15: 6 are picked up, t into the fire and burned. G965
Ac 16:23 flogged, they were t into prison, and G965
Ac 17: 8 the city officials were t into turmoil. G5429
Rev 8: 8 mountain, all ablaze, was t into the sea. G965
Rev 18:21 the great city of Babylon will be t down, G965
Rev 19:20 The two of them were t alive into the fiery G965
Rev 20:10 them, was t into the lake of burning sulfur G965
Rev 20:10 the beast and the false prophet had been t. NDT
Rev 20:14 death and Hades were t into the lake of G965
Rev 20:15 in the book of life was t into the lake of fire G965

THROWS (6) [THROW]

Nu 35:20 shoves another or t something at them H8959
Nu 35:22 pushes another or t something at them H8959
Job 30:19 He t me into the mud, and I am reduced H3721
Job 41:18 Its snorting t out flashes of light; its eyes H2145
Mk 9:18 it seizes him, it t him to the ground. G4838
Lk 9:39 it t him into convulsions so that he foams G5057

THRUSH (2)

Isa 38:14 I cried like a swift or t, I moaned like a H6315
Jer 8: 7 the swift and the t observe the time of H6315

THRUST (13) [THRUSTING]

Dt 29:28 from their land and t them into another H8959
1Sa 26: 8 him to the ground with one t of the spear; H7193
2Sa 2:16 by the head and t his dagger into his NDT
2Sa 2:23 so Abner t the butt of his spear into H5782
2Ki 17:20 until he t them from his presence. H8959
2Ki 24:20 in the end he t them from his H8959
Job 18: 8 His feet t him into a net; he wanders into H8938
Job 24: 4 They t the needy from the path and force H5742
SS 5: 4 My beloved t his hand through the H8938
Isa 8:22 and they will be t into utter darkness. H5615
Isa 13:15 Whoever is captured will be t through; all H1991
Jer 7:15 I will t you from my presence, just as I did H8959
Jer 52: 3 in the end he t them from his H8959

THRUSTING (1) [THRUST]

Dt 6:19 t out all your enemies before you, as the H2074

THUMB (5) [THUMBS]

Lev 8:23 on the t of his right hand and on the big H991
Lev 14:14 on the t of their right hand and on the big H991
Lev 14:17 on the t of their right hand and on the big H991
Lev 14:25 on the t of their right hand and on the big H991
Lev 14:28 on the t of their right hand and on the big H991

THUMBS (4) [THUMB]

Ex 29:20 his sons, on the t of their right hands H991
Lev 8:24 on the t of their right hands and on the big H991
Jdg 1: 6 and cut off his t and big toes. H984+3338
Jdg 1: 7 kings with their t and big toes cut off H984+3338

THUMMIM (6)

Ex 28:30 put the Urim and the T in the breastpiece, H9460
Lev 8: 8 put the Urim and T in the breastpiece. H9460
Dt 33: 8 "Your T and Urim belong to your faithful H9460
1Sa 14:41 men of Israel are at fault, respond with T." H9459
Ezr 2:63 a priest ministering with the Urim and T. H9460
Ne 7:65 a priest ministering with the Urim and T. H9460

THUNDER (29) [THUNDERED, THUNDERING, THUNDERS, THUNDERSTORM, THUNDERSTORMS]

Ex 9:23 the LORD sent t and hail, and H7754
Ex 9:28 for we have had enough t and hail. H7754
Ex 9:29 The t will stop and there will be no more H7754
Ex 9:33 toward the LORD; the t and hail stopped H7754
Ex 9:34 that the rain and hail and t had stopped, H7754
Ex 19:16 of the third day there was t and lightning, H7754
Ex 20:18 the people saw the t and lightning and H7754
1Sa 2:10 The Most High will t from heaven; the H8306
1Sa 7:10 thundered with loud t against the H7754
1Sa 12:17 I will call on the LORD to send t and rain H7754
1Sa 12:18 that same day the LORD sent t and rain. H7754
Job 26:14 then can understand the t of his power?" H8308
Job 36:33 His t announces the coming storm; even H8275

T

Job 40: 9 like God's, and *can* your voice **t** like his? H8306
Ps 77:17 the heavens resounded with **t**; your arrows H7754
Ps 77:18 Your **t** was heard in the whirlwind, your H8308
Ps 93: 4 Mightier than the **t** *of* the great waters H7754
Ps 104: 7 at the sound of your **t** they took to flight; H8308
Isa 29: 6 will come with **t** and earthquake and H8308
Jer 25:30 *he will* **t** from his holy dwelling and H5989+7754
Joel 3:16 from Zion and **t** from Jerusalem; H5989+7754
Mk 3:17 Boanerges, which means "sons *of* **t**") *G1103*
Rev 4: 5 of lightning, rumblings and **peals of t**. *G1103*
Rev 6: 1 four living creatures say in a voice like **t**, *G1103*
Rev 8: 5 there came **peals of t**, rumblings, *G1103*
Rev 11:19 rumblings, **peals of t**, an earthquake and *G1103*
Rev 14: 2 rushing waters and like a loud peal *of* **t**. *G1103*
Rev 16:18 **peals of t** and a severe earthquake. *G1103*
Rev 19: 6 of rushing waters and like loud peals *of* **t**, *G1103*

THUNDERCLOUD (1) [CLOUD]

Ps 81: 7 I answered you out of a **t**; I tested H6260+8308

THUNDERED (5) [THUNDER]

Jdg 5:22 Then **t** the horses' hooves—galloping H2150
1Sa 7:10 But that day the LORD **t** with loud thunder H8306
2Sa 22:14 The LORD **t** from heaven; the voice of the H8306
Ps 18:13 The LORD **t** from heaven; the voice of the H8306
Jn 12:29 there and heard it said *it had* **t**; *G1103+1181*

THUNDERING (1) [THUNDER]

Rev 9: 9 wings was like the **t** of many horses and *G5889*

THUNDERS (13) [THUNDER]

Job 36:29 the clouds, how he **t** *from* his pavilion? H9583
Job 37: 4 of his roar; *he* **t** with his majestic voice. H8306
Job 37: 5 God's voice **t** in marvelous ways; he does H8306
Ps 29: 3 the God of glory **t**, the LORD thunders over H8306
Ps 29: 3 thunders, the LORD **t** over the mighty waters. NDT
Ps 68:33 *who* **t** *with* mighty voice. H5989+928+7754
Jer 10:13 When he **t**, the waters in the H5989+7754
Jer 51:16 When he **t**, the waters in the H5989+7754
Joel 2:11 The LORD **t** at the head of his army H5989+7754
Am 1: 2 from Zion and **t** from Jerusalem; H5989+7754
Rev 10: 3 shouted, the voices *of* the seven **t** spoke. *G1103*
Rev 10: 4 And when the seven **t** spoke, I was about *G1103*
Rev 10: 4 up what the seven **t** have said and do not *G1103*

THUNDERSTORM (3) [STORM, THUNDER]

Job 28:26 the rain and a path for the **t**, H2613+7754
Job 38:25 of rain, and a path for the **t**, H2613+7754
Isa 30:30 with cloudburst, **t** and hail. H2443

THUNDERSTORMS (1) [STORM, THUNDER]

Zec 10: 1 springtime; it is the LORD who sends the **t**. H2613

THUS (28)

Ge 2: 1 **T** the heavens and the earth were H2256
Ge 19:25 **T** he overthrew those cities and the entire H2256
Ge 30:40 **T** he made separate flocks for himself H2256
Ge 41:43 **T** he put him in charge of the whole land H2256
Ex 28:30 **T** Aaron will always bear the means of H2256
Nu 4:49 **T** they were counted, as the LORD H2256
Nu 6: 9 **t** defiling the hair that symbolizes their H2256
Jdg 8:28 **T** Midian was subdued before the H2256
Jdg 9:56 **T** God repaid the wickedness that H2256
Jdg 11:33 Abel Keramim. **T** Israel subdued Ammon. H2256
Jdg 16:30 **T** he killed many more when he died than H2256
1Sa 7:12 "**T far** the LORD has helped us." H6330+2178
2Ki 23: 3 **t** confirming the words of the covenant H4200
Ezr 4:24 **T** the work on the house of God A10089+10008
Pr 2:20 **T** you will walk in the ways of the H4200+5100
SS 8:10 **T** I have become in his eyes like one H255
Eze 43:26 altar and cleanse it; **t** they will dedicate it. H2256
Mt 1:17 **T** there were fourteen generations in all *G4036*
Mt 7:20 **T**, by their fruit you will recognize *G726+1145*
Mt 15: 6 **T** you nullify the word of God for the sake *G2779*
Mk 7:13 **T** you nullify the word of God by your NDT
Jn 4:37 **T** the saying 'One sows and another *G1877+4047*
Jn 7:43 **T** the people were divided because of *G4036*
1Co 1: 6 God **t** confirming our testimony about *G2777*
Gal 3:17 by God **and t** to do away with the *G1650+3836*
Eph 2:15 humanity out of the two, ***t*** **making** peace, AIT
1Ti 5:12 **T** they bring judgment on themselves NDT
Heb 9:12 own blood, ***t*** **obtaining** eternal redemption. AIT

THWART (1) [THWARTED, THWARTS]

Isa 14:27 has purposed, and who *can* **t** him? H7296

THWARTED (2) [THWART]

Job 42: 2 all things; no purpose of yours *can* **be t**. H1307
Isa 8:10 your strategy, but *it will* **be t**; propose your H7296

THWARTS (3) [THWART]

Job 5:12 *He* **t** the plans of the crafty, so that their H7296
Ps 33:10 nations; *he* **t** the purposes of the peoples. H5648
Pr 10: 3 but *he* **t** the craving of the wicked. H2074

THYATIRA (4)

Ac 16:14 a woman from the city *of* **T** named Lydia, *G2587*
Rev 1:11 Smyrna, Pergamum, **T**, Sardis *G2587*
Rev 2:18 "To the angel of the church in **T** write *G2587*
Rev 2:24 Now I say to the rest of you in **T**, to you *G2587*

TIARAS (1)

Isa 3:23 the linen garments and **t** and shawls. H7566

TIBERIAS (2) [GALILEE]

Jn 6: 1 the Sea of Galilee (that is, the Sea *of* **T**), *G5500*
Jn 6:23 Then some boats from **T** landed near the *G5500*

TIBERIUS (1)

Lk 3: 1 fifteenth year of the reign *of* **T** Caesar— *G5501*

TIBNI (3)

1Ki 16:21 half supported **T** son of Ginath for king H9321
1Ki 16:22 stronger than those of **T** son of Ginath. H9321
1Ki 16:22 So **T** died and Omri became king H9321

TIDAL (2)

Ge 14: 1 king of Elam and **T** king of Goyim, H9331
Ge 14: 9 king of Elam, **T** king of Goyim, Amraphel H9331

TIDINGS (1)

Isa 52: 7 *who* **bring** good **t**, who proclaim H1413

TIE (15) [TIED, TIES, TYING]

Ex 29: 9 Then **t** sashes *on* Aaron and his sons H2520
Lev 16: 4 *he is to* **t** the linen sash **around** him and H2520
Dt 6: 8 **T** them as symbols on your hands and H8003
Dt 11:18 **t** them as symbols on your hands and H8003
Jdg 15:12 "We've come to **t** you **up** and hand you H673
Jdg 15:13 "*We will* only **t** you **up** and hand you H673+673
Jdg 16: 5 him so *we may* **t** him **up** and subdue him. H673
Job 41: 1 a fishhook or **t down** its tongue with a H9205
Jer 51:63 **t** a stone to it and throw it into the H8003
Eze 3:25 of man, *they will* **t** *with* ropes; you H5989+6584
Eze 4: 8 *I will* **t** you **up** *with* ropes so that you H5989
Da 3:20 soldiers in his army to **t up** Shadrach, A10366
Mt 13:30 the weeds and **t** them in bundles to be *G1313*
Mt 22:13 told the attendants, '**T** him hand and foot *G1313*
Mt 23: 4 *They* **t up** heavy, cumbersome loads and *G1297*

TIED (24) [TIE]

Ge 38:28 a scarlet thread and **t** it on his wrist and H8003
Ex 28:28 the breastpiece *are to be* **t** to the rings of H8220
Ex 39:21 *They* **t** the rings of the breastpiece to the H8220
Lev 8: 7 on Aaron, **t** the sash **around** him, clothed H2520
Lev 8: 7 waistband, which *he* **t** around him. H679
Lev 8:13 **t** sashes **around** them and fastened caps H2520
Jos 2:18 *you have* **t** this scarlet cord in the window H8003
Jos 2:21 And *she* **t** the scarlet cord in the window. H8003
Jdg 15: 4 hundred foxes and **t** them tail to tail in H7155
Jdg 16: 6 how *you can* **be t up** and subdued. H673
Jdg 16: 8 not been dried, and *she* **t** him with them. H673
Jdg 16:10 Come now, tell me how *you can* **be t**." H673
Jdg 16:12 took new ropes and **t** him with them. H673
Jdg 16:13 Tell me how *you can* **be t**." He replied, H673
2Ki 5:23 then **t up** the two talents of silver in H7443
Ps 109:19 like a belt **t** forever **around** him. H2520
Da 3:23 these three men, **firmly t**, fell into the A10366
Da 3:24 three men that we **t up** and threw into A10366
Mt 21: 2 at once you will find a donkey **t** there *G1313*
Mk 11: 2 you will find a colt **t** there, which no one *G1313*
Mk 11: 4 a colt outside in the street, **t** at a doorway. *G1313*
Lk 17: 2 with a millstone **t around** their neck than *G4329*
Lk 19:30 you will find a colt **t** there, which no one *G1313*
Ac 21:11 **t** his own hands and feet with it and said *G1313*

TIES (5) [TIE]

Jdg 16: 7 "If *anyone* **t** me with seven fresh bowstrings H673
Jdg 16:11 "If *anyone* **t** me **securely** with new H673+673
Job 12:18 put on by kings and **t** a loincloth around H673
Hos 11: 4 cords of human kindness, with **t** *of* love. H6310
Mt 12:29 unless *he* first **t up** the strong man? *G1313*

TIGHT (1) [TIGHTEN, TIGHTENED, TIGHTFISTED, TIGHTLY]

Jas 1:26 and *yet do* not **keep a t rein on** their *G5902*

TIGHTEN (1) [TIGHT]

Jdg 16:13 fabric on the loom and **t** it with the pin, H9546

TIGHTENED (1) [TIGHT]

Jdg 16:14 **t** it with the pin. Again she called to H9546

TIGHTFISTED (1) [FIST, TIGHT]

Dt 15: 7 hardhearted or **t** toward them. H7890+906+3338

TIGHTLY (4) [TIGHT]

Job 41:15 has rows of shields **t** sealed together; H7639
Job 41:23 The folds of its flesh *are* **t joined**; they are H1815
Isa 22:18 *He will* **roll** you **up t** like a H7571+7571+7572
Eze 27:24 rugs with cords twisted and **t knotted**. H775

TIGLATH-PILESER (6) [PUL]

2Ki 15:29 **T** king of Assyria came and took Ijon H9325
2Ki 16: 7 messengers to say to **T** king of Assyria, H9325
2Ki 16:10 to Damascus to meet **T** king of Assyria. H9325
1Ch 5: 6 whom **T** king of Assyria took into exile. H9433
1Ch 5:26 **T** king of Assyria), who took the H9433
2Ch 28:20 **T** king of Assyria came to him, but he gave H9433

TIGRIS (2)

Ge 2:14 The name of the third river is the **T**; it runs H2538
Da 10: 4 on the bank of the great river, the **T**, H2538

TIKVAH (2)

2Ki 22:14 who was the wife of Shallum son of **T**, the H9537
Ezr 10:15 son of Asahel and Jahzeiah son of **T**, H9537

TILES (1)

Lk 5:19 his mat through the **t** into the middle of *G3041*

TILGATH-PILNESER (KJV) TIGLATH-PILESER

TILL (130)

Ge 32: 4 Laban and have remained there **t** now. H6330
Ge 32:24 a man wrestled with him **t** daybreak. H6330
Ex 9:18 from the day it was founded **t** now. H6330
Ex 10: 6 the day they settled in this land **t** now. H6330
Ex 12:10 Do not leave any of it **t** morning; if some is H6330
Ex 12:10 if some is left **t** morning, you must burn H6330
Ex 17:12 that his hands remained steady **t** sunset. H6330
Ex 18:13 around him from morning **t** evening. H6330
Ex 18:14 around you from morning **t** evening?" H6330
Ex 27:21 before the LORD from evening **t** morning. H6330
Ex 29:34 ram or any bread is left over **t** morning, H6330
Lev 6: 9 the night, **t** morning, and the fire H6330
Lev 7:15 they must leave none of it **t** morning. H6330
Lev 7:17 sacrifice left over **t** the third day must be H928
Lev 11:24 their carcasses will be unclean **t** evening. H6330
Lev 11:25 they will be unclean **t** evening. H6330
Lev 11:27 their carcasses will be unclean **t** evening. H6330
Lev 11:28 they will be unclean **t** evening. H6330
Lev 11:31 they are dead will be unclean **t** evening. H6330
Lev 11:32 it will be unclean **t** evening, and then it H6330
Lev 11:39 its carcass will be unclean **t** evening. H6330
Lev 11:40 they will be unclean **t** evening. H6330
Lev 11:40 they will be unclean **t** evening. H6330
Lev 14:46 it is closed up will be unclean **t** evening. H6330
Lev 15: 5 and they will be unclean **t** evening. H6330
Lev 15: 6 and they will be unclean **t** evening. H6330
Lev 15: 7 and they will be unclean **t** evening. H6330
Lev 15: 8 and they will be unclean **t** evening. H6330
Lev 15:10 under him will be unclean **t** evening; H6330
Lev 15:10 and they will be unclean **t** evening. H6330
Lev 15:11 and they will be unclean **t** evening. H6330
Lev 15:16 and he will be unclean **t** evening. H6330
Lev 15:17 and it will be unclean **t** evening. H6330
Lev 15:18 and they will be unclean **t** evening. H6330
Lev 15:19 touches her will be unclean **t** evening. H6330
Lev 15:21 and they will be unclean **t** evening. H6330
Lev 15:22 and they will be unclean **t** evening. H6330
Lev 15:23 touches it, they will be unclean **t** evening. H6330
Lev 15:27 and they will be unclean **t** evening. H6330
Lev 17:15 will be ceremonially unclean **t** evening; H6330
Lev 22: 6 any such thing will be unclean **t** evening. H6330
Lev 22:30 that same day; leave none of it **t** morning. H6330
Lev 24: 3 before the LORD from evening **t** morning, H6330
Nu 9:12 not leave any of it **t** morning or break any H6330
Nu 9:15 From evening **t** morning the cloud above H6330
Nu 9:21 cloud stayed only from evening **t** morning, H6330
Nu 12:15 did not move on **t** she was brought back. H6330
Nu 19: 7 will be ceremonially unclean **t** evening. H6330
Nu 19: 8 he too will be unclean **t** evening. H6330
Nu 19:10 he too will be unclean **t** evening. H6330
Nu 19:21 of cleansing will be unclean **t** evening. H6330
Nu 19:22 touches it becomes unclean **t** evening." H6330
Nu 23:24 that does not rest **t** it devours its prey and H6330
Dt 33:11 against him, his foes **t** they rise **no more**." H4946
Jos 7: 6 ark of the LORD, remaining there **t** evening. H6330
Jos 10:13 **t** the nation avenged itself on its enemies, H6330
Jdg 19: 8 Wait **t** afternoon!" So the two H6330
Ru 2: 7 has remained here from morning **t** now, H6330
1Sa 1: 7 rival provoked her **t** she wept and would H2256
1Sa 14:36 by night and plunder them **t** dawn, H6330
2Sa 1:12 wept and fasted **t** evening for Saul H6330
2Sa 10: 5 "Stay at Jericho **t** your beards have grown H6330
2Sa 19: 7 have come on you from your youth **t** now." H6330
2Sa 20: 3 kept in confinement **t** the day of their H6330
2Sa 21:10 of the harvest **t** the rain poured down H6330
2Sa 22:38 I did not turn back **t** they were destroyed. H6330
2Sa 23:10 the Philistines **t** his hand grew tired H6330+3954
1Ki 18:26 the name of Baal from morning **t** noon. H6330
1Ch 19: 5 "Stay at Jericho **t** your beards have H6330+889
Ne 4: 6 we rebuilt the wall **t** all of it reached half H2256
Ne 4:21 the first light of dawn **t** the stars came out. H6330
Ne 8: 3 aloud from daybreak **t** noon as he faced H6330
Job 14: 6 **t** he has put in his time like a hired H6330
Job 14:12 does not rise; **t** the heavens are no more H6330
Job 14:13 grave and conceal me **t** your anger has H6330
Job 19:10 tears me down on every side **t** I am gone; H2256
Job 27: 5 you are in the right; **t** I die, I will not deny H6330
Job 39: 2 Do you count the months **t** they bear? Do NDT
Job 39:10 *Will it* **t** the valleys behind you H8440
Ps 18:37 I did not turn back **t** they were destroyed. H6330
Ps 59:13 consume them **t** they are no more. H2256
Ps 71:18 **t** I declare your power to the next H6330
Ps 72: 7 prosperity abound **t** the moon is no more. H6330
Ps 73:17 **t** I entered the sanctuary of God; then I H6330
Ps 78:29 They ate **t** they were gorged—he had H2256
Ps 84: 7 strength, **t** each appears before God in Zion. NDT
Ps 94:13 of trouble, **t** a pit is dug for the wicked. H6330
Ps 105:19 **t** what he foretold came to pass, till H6330+6961
Ps 105:19 **t** the word of the LORD proved him true. NDT
Ps 123: 2 our God, **t** he shows us his mercy. H6330+8611
Ps 132: 5 **t** I find a place for the LORD, a dwelling H6330
Pr 4:16 robbed of sleep **t** they make H561+4202
Pr 4:18 shining ever brighter **t** the full light of day. H6330
Pr 7:18 let's drink deeply of love **t** morning; let's H6330
Pr 7:20 money and will not be home **t** full moon." H4200
Pr 7:23 **t** an arrow pierces his liver, like a bird H6330

T

SS 3: 4 not let him go **t** I had brought him H6330+8611
Isa 5: 8 join field to field **t** no space is left and H6330
Isa 5:11 late at night *t* they *are* **inflamed** *with* wine. AIT
Isa 22:14 "**T** your dying *day* this sin will not be H6330
Isa 23:10 **T** your land as they do along the Nile H6268
Isa 30:17 **t** you are left like a flagstaff on a H6330+561
Isa 32:15 **t** the Spirit is poured on us from on high H6330
Isa 38:13 I waited patiently **t** dawn, but like a lion H6330
Isa 42: 4 be discouraged **t** he establishes justice H6330
Isa 62: 1 **t** her vindication shines out like the dawn H6330
Isa 62: 7 give him no rest **t** he establishes H6330
Jer 3:25 from our youth **t** this day we have not H6330
Jer 9:18 wail over us **t** our eyes overflow with H2256
Jer 27:11 in its own land *to* **t** it and to live there, H6268
Jer 36: 2 to you in the reign of Josiah **t** now. H6330
Jer 46:10 The sword will devour **t** it is satisfied, till it H2256
Jer 46:10 **t** it has quenched its thirst with blood. H2256
Jer 47: 6 sword of the LORD, how long **t** you rest? H4202
Jer 52:11 he put him in prison **t** the day of his death H6330
Jer 52:34 as long as he lived, **t** the day of his death. H6330
Eze 24:11 pot on the coals **t** it becomes hot H4200+5100
Eze 28:15 you were created **t** wickedness was found H6330
Eze 39:19 you will eat fat **t** you are glutted and drink H4200
Eze 39:19 glutted and drink blood **t** you are drunk. H4200
Da 4:16 animal, **t** seven times pass by for him. A10221
Da 12:13 you, go your way **t** the end. You will H4200
Hos 7: 4 from the kneading of the dough **t** it rises. H6330
Am 1: 8 **t** the last of the Philistines are dead," H2256
Na 3:16 of your merchants **t** they are more numerous NDT
Hab 2:15 it from the wineskin **t** they are drunk, H2256+677
Mt 12:20 **t** he has brought justice through to *G2401+323*
Jn 2:10 but you have saved the best **t** now." *G2401*
Ac 28:23 to them from morning **t** evening, *G2401*
2Th 2: 7 continue to do so **t** he is taken out of the *G2401*

TILLAGE, TILLED, TILLER, TILLEST, TILLETH

(KJV) CULTIVATED, FARMED, PLOWED, UNPLOWED FIELD, WORK, WORKED

TILON (1)

1Ch 4:20 Ben-Hanan and **T**. The descendants of H9400

TILTING (1)

Jer 1:13 "It is **t toward** us from the north. H7156

TIMAEUS (1) [BARTIMEAUS]

Mk 10:46 which means "son *of* **T**"), was sitting by *G5505*

TIMBER (12) [TIMBERS]

1Ki 5: 6 so skilled in felling **t** as the Sidonians." H6770
1Ki 5:18 cut and prepared the **t** and stone for the H6770
1Ki 15:22 Ramah the stones and **t** Baasha had been H6770
2Ki 12:12 They purchased **t** and blocks of dressed H6770
2Ki 22: 6 have them purchase **t** and dressed stone H6770
2Ch 2: 8 your servants are skilled in cutting **t** there. H6770
2Ch 2:10 the woodsmen who cut the **t**, twenty H6770
2Ch 16: 6 Ramah the stones and **t** Baasha had been H6770
2Ch 34:11 **t** for joists and beams for the H6770
Ne 2: 8 so he will give me **t** to make beams for H6770
Eze 26:12 your stones, **t** and rubble into the sea. H6770
Hag 1: 8 bring down **t** and build my house, H6770

TIMBERS (5) [TIMBER]

Lev 14:45 its stones, **t** and all the plaster—and taken H6770
Ezr 5: 8 stones and placing the **t** in the walls. A10058
Ezr 6: 4 courses of large stones and one of **t**. A10058
Eze 27: 5 They made all your **t** of juniper from Senir; H4283
Zec 5: 4 it completely, both its **t** and its stones. H6770

TIMBREL (5) [TIMBRELS]

Ex 15:20 took a **t** in her hand, and all H9512
Job 21:12 They sing to the **music of t** and lyre; they H9512
Ps 81: 2 the music, strike the **t**, play the melodious H9512
Ps 149: 3 make music to him with **t** and harp. H9512
Ps 150: 4 praise him with **t** and dancing, praise him H9512

TIMBRELS (12) [TIMBREL]

Ge 31:27 singing to the **music of t** and harps? H9512
Ex 15:20 women followed her, with **t** and dancing. H9512
Jdg 11:34 his daughter, dancing to the sound of **t**! H9512
1Sa 10: 5 place with lyres, **t**, pipes and harps being H9512
1Sa 18: 6 with joyful songs and with **t** and lyres. H9512
2Sa 6: 5 lyres, **t**, sistrums and cymbals. H9512
1Ch 13: 8 with harps, lyres, **t**, cymbals and trumpets. H9512
Ps 68:25 them are the young women **playing** the **t**. H9528
Isa 5:12 banquets, pipes and **t** and wine, but they H9512
Isa 24: 8 The joyful **t** are stilled, the noise of the H9512
Isa 30:32 club will be to the **music of t** and harps," H9512
Jer 31: 4 will take up your **t** and go out to dance H9512

TIME (763) [TIMELY, TIMES]

Ge 4: 3 In the course of **t** Cain brought some of the H3427
Ge 4:26 **At that t** people began to call on the name H255
Ge 6: 5 of the human heart was only evil all the **t**. H3427
Ge 6: 9 blameless among the **people of** his **t**, and H1887
Ge 8:12 out again, but this **t** it did not return to him. NDT
Ge 10:25 because in his **t** the earth was divided H3427
Ge 12: 6 **At that t** the Canaanites were in the land H255
Ge 13: 7 were also living in the land **at that t**. H255
Ge 14: 1 At *the* **t** *when* Amraphel was king of H3427
Ge 17:21 Sarah will bear to you by this **t** next year." H4595
Ge 18:10 surely return to you about this **t** next year, H6961
Ge 18:14 return to you at the appointed **t** next year, H6961
Ge 19:23 **By the t** Lot reached Zoar, the sun had H2256
Ge 21: 2 at the very **t** God had promised him. H4595
Ge 21:22 At that **t** Abimelek and Phicol the H6961
Ge 21:34 in the land of the Philistines *for* a long **t**. H3427
Ge 22: 1 **Some t later** God tested Abraham H339+2021+1821+2021+465
Ge 22:15 to Abraham from heaven a **second t** H9108
Ge 22:20 **Some t later** Abraham was told, H339+2021+1821+2021+465
Ge 24:11 the **t** the women go out to draw water. H6961
Ge 25:24 When the **t** came *for* her to give birth H3427
Ge 26: 1 the previous famine in Abraham's **t**— H3427
Ge 26: 8 When Isaac had been there a long **t** H3427
Ge 26:15 had dug in the **t** *of* his father Abraham, H3427
Ge 26:18 been dug in the **t** *of* his father Abraham H3427
Ge 27:36 This is the *second* **t** he has taken H7193
Ge 29: 7 it is not **t** *for* the flocks to be gathered. H6961
Ge 29:21 My **t** is completed, and I want to make H3427
Ge 29:35 she said, "This **t** I will praise the LORD." H7193
Ge 30:20 This **t** my husband will treat me with H7193
Ge 30:21 **Some t later** she gave birth to a daughter H339
Ge 34:19 **lost** no **t** in doing what they said H336
Ge 37: 9 this **t** the sun and moon and eleven NDT
Ge 38: 1 At that **t**, Judah left his brothers and went H6961
Ge 38:12 After a long **t** Judah's wife, the daughter H3427
Ge 38:27 When the **t** came *for* her to give birth H6961
Ge 39: 5 From *the* **t** he put him in charge of his H255
Ge 40: 1 **Some t later**, the H339+2021+1821+2021+465
Ge 40: 4 After they had been in custody *for* **some t**, H3427
Ge 43:18 that was put back into our sacks the **first t**. H9378
Ge 43:20 came down here the **first t** to buy food. H9378
Ge 46:29 around his father and wept *for* a **long t**. H6388
Ge 47:29 When the **t** drew near *for* Israel to die, he H3427
Ge 48: 1 **Some t later** Joseph was told H339+2021+1821+2021+465
Ge 50: 3 that was the **t** *required for* embalming. H3427
Ex 4:26 (**At that t** she said "bridegroom of blood," H255
Ex 8: 9 the honor of **setting the t** for me to H4200+5503
Ex 8:32 But this **t** also Pharaoh hardened his heart H7193
Ex 9: 5 The LORD set a **t** and said, "Tomorrow the H4595
Ex 9:14 this **t** I will send the full force of my H7193
Ex 9:18 at this **t** tomorrow I will send the worst H6961
Ex 9:27 "This **t** I have sinned," he H7193
Ex 12:39 Egypt and *did* not **have t** to prepare H4538+3523
Ex 12:40 Now the **length of t** the Israelite people H4632
Ex 13:10 at the **appointed t** year after year H4595
Ex 21:19 person for any **loss of t** and see that the H8700
Ex 23:15 Do this at the **appointed t** in the month of H4595
Ex 30:12 a ransom for his life **at the t** he is counted. H928
Ex 32:34 when the **t** comes for me to punish H3427
Ex 34:18 Do this at the **appointed t** *in* the month of H4595
Lev 14: 2 person at the **t** *of* their ceremonial H3427
Lev 15:25 many days at a **t** other than her H6961
Lev 16:17 tent of meeting **from the t** Aaron goes in to H928
Lev 19:10 *Do* not **go over** your vineyard **a second t** H6618
Lev 25:29 **During that t** the seller may redeem it H3427
Lev 25:50 buyer are to count the **t** from the year they NDT
Lev 26:34 years all the **t** *that* it lies desolate and H3427
Lev 26:35 All the **t** that it lies desolate, the land will H3427
Nu 3: 1 Moses at the **t** the LORD spoke to H3427
Nu 9: 2 celebrate the Passover at the **appointed t**. H4595
Nu 9: 3 Celebrate it at the **appointed t**, at twilight H4595
Nu 9: 7 the other Israelites at the **appointed t**?" H4595
Nu 9:13 the LORD's offering at the **appointed t**. H4595
Nu 9:19 remained over the tabernacle a long **t**, H3427
Nu 10:13 They set out, this **first** *t*, at the LORD's AIT
Nu 14:19 them from the **t** they left Egypt until NDT
Nu 22: 4 who was king of Moab at that **t**, H6961
Nu 28: 2 to me at the **appointed t** my food H4595
Nu 30:15 nullifies them **some t after** he hears about H339
Dt 1: 9 At that **t** I said to you, "You are too heavy H6961
Dt 1:16 And I charged your judges at that **t**, "Hear H6961
Dt 1:18 And at that **t** I told you everything you H6961
Dt 1:46 many days—all the **t** you spent there. H3427
Dt 2: 1 *For* a long **t** we made our way around the H3427
Dt 2:14 passed from the **t** we left Kadesh Barnea H3427
Dt 2:34 At that **t** we took all his towns and H6961
Dt 3: 4 At that **t** we took all his cities. There was H6961
Dt 3: 8 So at that **t** we took from these two kings H6961
Dt 3:12 Of the land that we took over at that **t**, H6961
Dt 3:18 I commanded you at that **t**: "The LORD H6961
Dt 3:21 At that **t** I commanded Joshua: "You have H6961
Dt 3:23 At that **t** I pleaded with the LORD: H6961
Dt 4:14 directed me at that **t** to teach you the H6961
Dt 4:25 and *have* **lived** in the land **a long t**— H3823
Dt 4:32 long before your **t**, from the day God NDT
Dt 4:40 land the LORD your God gives you *for* all **t**. H3427
Dt 5: 5 At that **t** I stood between the LORD and you H6961
Dt 9:20 but at that **t** I prayed for Aaron too. H6961
Dt 10: 1 At that **t** the LORD said to me, "Chisel out H6961
Dt 10: 8 At that **t** the LORD set apart the tribe of Levi H6961
Dt 10:10 as I did the first **t**, and the LORD listened to H3427
Dt 10:10 the LORD listened to me at this **t** also. H7193
Dt 15: 2 the LORD's **t for canceling debts** has been H9024
Dt 16: 3 may remember the **t** *of* your departure H3427
Dt 16: 9 seven weeks from the **t** you begin to put the NDT
Dt 17: 9 to the judge who is in office at that **t**. H3427
Dt 17:20 will reign a long **t** over his kingdom in H3427
Dt 19:17 the judges who are in office at the **t**. H3427
Dt 20:19 When you lay siege to a city *for* a long **t** H3427
Dt 24:20 *do* not **go over the branches a second t** H6994+339
Dt 26: 3 say to the priest in office at the **t**, "I H3427
Dt 28:47 God joyfully and gladly in the **t** of prosperity, NDT
Dt 32:35 In **due t** their foot will slip; their day of H6961
Dt 34: 8 until the **t** *of* weeping and mourning was H3427
Jos 2: 5 when it was **t** to close the city gate NDT
Jos 5: 2 At that **t** the LORD said to Joshua, "Make H6961
Jos 6: 9 **All this t** the trumpets were sounding. H2143
Jos 6:16 The seventh **t** around, when the priests H7193
Jos 6:26 At that **t** Joshua pronounced this solemn H6961
Jos 11: 6 because by this **t** tomorrow I will hand all H6961
Jos 11:10 At that **t** Joshua turned back and captured H6961
Jos 11:18 war against all these kings *for* a long **t**. H3427
Jos 11:21 At that **t** Joshua went and destroyed the H6961
Jos 14:10 years since the **t** he said this to Moses, H255
Jos 20: 6 of the high priest who is serving at that **t**. H3427
Jos 22: 3 *For* a long **t** now—to this very day—you H3427
Jos 23: 1 After a long **t** had passed and the LORD H3427
Jos 24: 7 you lived in the wilderness *for* a long **t**. H3427
Jdg 3:29 At that **t** they struck down about ten H6961
Jdg 4: 4 of Lappidoth, was leading Israel at that **t**. H6961
Jdg 6:39 this **t** make the fleece dry and let the NDT
Jdg 10: 1 **After the t** of Abimelek, a man of Issachar H339
Jdg 11: 4 **Some t later**, when the Ammonites H4946+3427
Jdg 11:26 Why didn't you retake them during that **t**? H6961
Jdg 12: 6 Ephraimites were killed at that **t**. H6961
Jdg 14: 4 at that **t** they were ruling over Israel.) H6961
Jdg 14: 8 **Some t later**, when he went back to H4946+3427
Jdg 15: 1 Later on, at the **t** *of* wheat harvest H3427
Jdg 15: 3 "This **t** I have a right to get even with the H7193
Jdg 16: 4 **Some t later**, he fell in love with a H339+4027
Jdg 16:13 "**All this t** you have been making a H6330+2178
Jdg 16:15 This is the third **t** you have made a fool of H7193
Jdg 18:30 of Dan until the **t** *of* the captivity of the H3427
Jdg 18:31 all the **t** the house of God was in Shiloh. H3427
Jdg 20:25 This **t**, when the Benjamites came out H3427
Jdg 21:14 returned at that **t** and were given the H6961
Jdg 21:24 At that **t** the Israelites left that place and H6961
1Sa 1:20 So in the course of **t** Hannah became H3427
1Sa 2:31 The **t** is coming when I will cut short your H3427
1Sa 3: 8 A **third** *t* the LORD called, "Samuel!" And AIT
1Sa 3:12 At that **t** I will carry out against Eli H3427
1Sa 4:19 was pregnant and **near the t of delivery**. H3528
1Sa 7: 2 ark remained at Kiriath Jearim a long **t**— H3427
1Sa 9:13 up now; you should find him about this **t**." H3427
1Sa 9:16 "About this **t** tomorrow I will send you a H6961
1Sa 9:24 you for this occasion from the **t** I said, NDT
1Sa 11: 9 '**By the t** the sun is hot tomorrow H3869
1Sa 13: 8 seven days, the **t set** by Samuel; but H4595
1Sa 13:11 that you did not come at the **set t**, H4595+3427
1Sa 13:13 your kingdom over Israel for **all t**. H6409
1Sa 14:18 At that **t** it was with the Israelites. H3427
1Sa 14:35 it *was the* **first t** he had done this. H2725
1Sa 17:12 and in Saul's **t** he was very old. H3427
1Sa 18: 9 And from that **t** on Saul kept a close eye H3427
1Sa 18:19 So when the **t** came *for* Merab, Saul's H6961
1Sa 18:26 So before the **allotted t** elapsed, H3427
1Sa 19:21 Saul sent men a **third** *t*, and they also AIT
1Sa 20:12 out my father by this **t** the day after H6961
1Sa 22:15 *Was* that day *the* **first t** I inquired of God H2725
1Sa 25: 7 " 'Now I hear that *it is* **sheep-shearing t** H1605
1Sa 25: 7 the whole **t** they were at Carmel H3427
1Sa 25: 8 my men, since we come at a festive **t**. H3427
1Sa 25:15 the whole **t** we were out in the fields H3427
1Sa 25:16 us the whole **t** we were herding our H3427
1Sa 26:10 or his **t** will come and he will die H3427
2Sa 2: 1 **In the course of t**, David inquired of H339+4027
2Sa 2:11 The length of **t** David was king in Hebron H3427
2Sa 3: 1 the house of David lasted a **long t**. H801
2Sa 3:17 "**For some t** you have H1685+9453+1685+8997
2Sa 7:11 done ever since the **t** I appointed leaders H3427
2Sa 8: 1 **In the course of t**, David defeated H339+4027
2Sa 10: 1 **In the course of t**, the king of the H339+4027
2Sa 11: 1 at the **t** *when* kings go off to war H6961
2Sa 11:27 After the **t of mourning** was over, David had H65
2Sa 13: 1 **In the course of t**, Amnon son of H339+4027
2Sa 14:29 So he sent a second **t**, but he refused to H6388
2Sa 15: 1 **In the course of t**, Absalom H4946+339+4027
2Sa 17: 7 Ahithophel has given is not good this **t**. H7193
2Sa 18:20 "You may take the news another **t**, but H3427
2Sa 20: 5 took longer than the **t** the king had set H4595
2Sa 21:18 **In the course of t**, there was another H339+4027
2Sa 21:18 **At that t** Sibbekai the Hushathite killed H255
2Sa 23:13 During **harvest t**, three of the thirty chief H7907
2Sa 23:14 **At that t** David was in the stronghold, and H255
2Sa 24:15 morning until the end of the **t** designated, H6961
1Ki 2: 1 When the **t** drew near *for* David to die, he H3427
1Ki 2:38 Shimei stayed in Jerusalem *for* a long **t**. H3427
1Ki 2:42 **At that t** you said to me, 'What you say is H2256
1Ki 8: 2 to King Solomon **at the t of** the festival in H928
1Ki 8:40 will fear you all the **t** they live in the land H3427
1Ki 8:61 obey his commands, as at this **t**. H3427
1Ki 8:65 So Solomon observed the festival at that **t**, H6961
1Ki 9: 2 the LORD appeared to him a **second t**, as H9108
1Ki 11:29 About that **t** Jeroboam was going out of H6961
1Ki 14: 1 At that **t** Abijah son of Jeroboam became H6961
1Ki 16: 9 Elah was in Tirzah at the **t**, getting drunk in NDT
1Ki 16:34 In Ahab's **t**, Hiel of Bethel rebuilt Jericho H3427
1Ki 17: 7 **Some t** later the brook dried up because H3427
1Ki 17:17 **Some t later** the son of the woman H339+2021+1821+2021+465
1Ki 18: 1 After a long **t**, in the third year, the word H3427
1Ki 18:29 prophesying **until the t for** the evening H6330

1Ki 18:34 "**Do** *it* **a third t**," he ordered, and they did H8992
1Ki 18:34 he ordered, and *they* **did** *it* **the third t.** H8992
1Ki 18:36 **At the t of** sacrifice, the prophet Elijah H928
1Ki 18:44 The seventh **t** the servant reported, "A cloud NDT
1Ki 19: 2 if by this **t** tomorrow I do not make your H6961
1Ki 19: 7 came back a **second t** and touched him H9108
1Ki 20: 6 But about this **t** tomorrow I am going to H6961
1Ki 20: 9 servant will do all you demanded the **first** *t*, AIT
1Ki 21: 1 **Some t later** there was an incident H339+2021+1821+2021+465
1Ki 22:49 **At that t** Ahaziah son of Ahab said to H255
2Ki 3: 6 So at that **t** King Joram set out from H3427
2Ki 3:20 about the **t** for offering the sacrifice NDT
2Ki 4:16 "About this **t** next year," Elisha said, "you H4595
2Ki 4:17 year about that same **t** she gave birth to a H4595
2Ki 5:26 Is this the **t** to take money or to accept H6961
2Ki 6:10 **T and again** Elisha H4202+285+2256+4202+9109
2Ki 6:24 **Some t later**, Ben-Hadad king of H339+4027
2Ki 7: 1 About this **t** tomorrow, a seah of the finest H6961
2Ki 7:18 "About this **t** tomorrow, a seah of the H6961
2Ki 8:20 In the **t** *of* Jehoram, Edom rebelled H3427
2Ki 8:22 Libnah revolted at the same **t.** H6961
2Ki 10: 6 come to me in Jezreel by this **t** tomorrow." H6961
2Ki 10:36 The **t** that Jehu reigned over Israel in H3427
2Ki 12:17 **About this t** Hazael king of Aram went up H255
2Ki 13: 3 and *for* a long **t** he kept them under the H3427
2Ki 13: 7 made them like the dust at **threshing t.** H1889
2Ki 15:16 **At that t** Menahem, starting out from Tirzah H255
2Ki 15:29 In the **t** *of* Pekah king of Israel H3427
2Ki 16: 6 At that **t**, Rezin king of Aram recovered H6961
2Ki 18: 4 up to that **t** the Israelites had been H3427
2Ki 18:16 At this **t** Hezekiah king of Judah stripped H6961
2Ki 20:12 At that **t** Marduk-Baladan son of Baladan H6961
2Ki 20:17 The **t** will surely come when everything in H3427
2Ki 24:10 At that **t** the officers of Nebuchadnezzar H6961
1Ch 1:19 because in his **t** the earth was divided H3427
1Ch 9:18 Gate on the east, up to **the present t.** H2178
1Ch 9:25 had to come from **t** to time and share H6961
1Ch 9:25 to come from time to **t** and share their H6961
1Ch 11:16 **At that t** David was in the stronghold, and H255
1Ch 15:13 bring it up the **first** *t* that the LORD our God AIT
1Ch 17:10 done ever since the **t** I appointed leaders H3427
1Ch 18: 1 **In the course of t**, David defeated H339+4027
1Ch 19: 1 **In the course of t**, Nahash king of H339+4027
1Ch 20: 1 at the **t** *when* kings go off to war H6961
1Ch 20: 4 **In the course of t**, war broke out with H339+4027
1Ch 20: 4 **At that t** Sibbekai the Hushathite killed H255
1Ch 21:28 At that **t**, when David saw that the LORD H6961
1Ch 21:29 were at that **t** on the high place at H6961
1Ch 26:17 on the south and **two at a t** at the H9109+9109
1Ch 28: 7 laws, as is being done at this **t.** H3427
1Ch 29:22 Solomon son of David as king a **second t**, H9108
2Ch 5: 3 to the king **at the t of** the festival in the H928
2Ch 6:31 to you all the **t** they live in the land H3427
2Ch 7: 8 the festival at that **t** for seven days, H6961
2Ch 11:17 David and Solomon during **this t.** H9102+8993S
2Ch 13:20 not regain power during the **t** *of* Abijah. H3427
2Ch 15: 3 *For* a long **t** Israel was without the true H3427
2Ch 15:11 At that **t** they sacrificed to the LORD seven H3427
2Ch 16: 7 At that **t** Hanani the seer came to Asa H6961
2Ch 16:10 At the same **t** Asa brutally oppressed H6961
2Ch 21: 8 In the **t** *of* Jehoram, Edom rebelled H3427
2Ch 21:10 Libnah revolted at the same **t**, because H6961
2Ch 21:19 **In the course of t**, at the H4200+3427+4946+3427
2Ch 24: 4 **Some t later** Joash decided to H339+4027
2Ch 25:27 From the **t** that Amaziah turned away from H6961
2Ch 28:16 At that **t** King Ahaz sent to the kings of H6961
2Ch 28:22 In his **t** *of* trouble King Ahaz became even H6961
2Ch 30: 3 it at the regular **t** because not enough H6961
2Ch 35:16 So at that **t** the entire service of the LORD H3427
2Ch 35:17 the Passover at that **t** and observed the H6961
2Ch 35:21 It is not you I am attacking **at this t** H2021+3427
2Ch 36:21 all the **t** *of* its desolation it rested H3427
Ezr 4: 2 to him since the **t** *of* Esarhaddon king of H3427
Ezr 5: 3 At that **t** Tattenai, governor of A10232
Ezr 8:34 the entire weight was recorded at that **t.** H6961
Ezr 9:12 a treaty of friendship with them at **any t**, H6409
Ezr 10:14 married a foreign woman come at a set **t**, H6961
Ne 2: 6 pleased the king to send me; so I set a **t.** H2375
Ne 4:22 At that **t** I also said to the people, "Have H6961
Ne 6: 1 though up to that **t** I had not set the doors H6961
Ne 6: 4 each **t** I gave them the same answer. NDT
Ne 6: 5 the fifth **t**, Sanballat sent his aide H7193
Ne 9:28 you delivered them **t after time.** H8041+6961
Ne 9:28 you delivered them **time after t.** H8041+6961
Ne 12:23 of Levi up to the **t** *of* Johanan son of H3427
Ne 12:44 At that **t** men were appointed to be in H3427
Ne 13: 6 **Some t** later I asked his permission H3427
Ne 13:21 From that **t** on they no longer came on the H6961
Est 1: 1 is what happened during the **t** *of* Xerxes, H3427
Est 1: 2 At that **t** King Xerxes reigned from his H3427
Est 2:19 the virgins were assembled a **second t**, H9108
Est 2:21 During the **t** Mordecai was sitting at the H3427
Est 4:14 For if you remain silent at this **t**, relief and H6961
Est 4:14 to your royal position for such a **t** as this?" H6961
Est 8:16 For the Jews it was a **t of happiness** and joy H245
Est 9:22 as the **t** when the Jews got relief from their H3427
Est 9:27 way prescribed and at the **t appointed.** H2375
Job 9: 3 not answer him one *t* out of a thousand. AIT
Job 14: 6 till he has put in his **t** like a hired laborer. H3427
Job 14:13 you would set me a **t** and then remember H2976
Job 15:32 Before his **t** he will wither, and his H3427
Job 22:16 They were carried off before their **t**, their H6961
Job 39: 2 Do you know the **t** they give birth? H6961
Ps 37:39 he is their stronghold in **t** *of* trouble. H6961
Ps 51: 5 sinful from the **t** my mother conceived me. NDT
Ps 69:13 in the **t** *of* your favor; in your great H6961
Ps 75: 2 "I choose the **appointed t**; it is I who H4595
Ps 77: 8 his promise failed for **all t**? H1887+2256+1887
Ps 78:38 **T after time** he restrained his anger and H8049
Ps 78:38 **Time after t** he restrained his anger and H8049
Ps 102:13 on Zion, for it is **t** to show favor to her; the H6961
Ps 102:13 favor to her; the **appointed t** has come. H4595
Ps 104:27 to give them their food at the **proper t.** H6961
Ps 119:126 It is **t** for you to act, LORD; your law is H6961
Ps 145:15 you give them their food at the **proper t.** H6961
Pr 17:17 a brother is born for a **t** of adversity. NDT
Pr 20: 4 so at **harvest t** they look but find nothing. H7907
Pr 24:10 If you falter in a **t** *of* trouble, how small is H3427
Pr 25:13 drink at harvest **t** is a trustworthy H3427
Pr 25:19 reliance on the unfaithful in a **t** *of* trouble. H3427
Ecc 1:10 it was here **before** our **t.** H4946+4200+7156
Ecc 3: 1 There is a **t** for everything, and a season H2375
Ecc 3: 2 a **t** to be born and a time to die, a time to H6961
Ecc 3: 2 a time to be born and a **t** to die, a time to H6961
Ecc 3: 2 a **t** to plant and a time to uproot, H6961
Ecc 3: 2 a time to plant and a **t** to uproot, H6961
Ecc 3: 3 a **t** to kill and a time to heal, a time to H6961
Ecc 3: 3 a time to kill and a **t** to heal, a time to H6961
Ecc 3: 3 a **t** to tear down and a time to build H6961
Ecc 3: 3 a time to tear down and a **t** to build, H6961
Ecc 3: 4 a **t** to weep and a time to laugh, a time to H6961
Ecc 3: 4 a time to weep and a **t** to laugh, a time to H6961
Ecc 3: 4 a **t** to mourn and a time to dance H6961
Ecc 3: 4 a time to mourn and a **t** to dance, H6961
Ecc 3: 5 a **t** to scatter stones and a time to gather H6961
Ecc 3: 5 to scatter stones and a **t** to gather them, H6961
Ecc 3: 5 a **t** to embrace and a time to refrain from H6961
Ecc 3: 5 a time to embrace and a **t** to refrain from H6961
Ecc 3: 6 a **t** to search and a time to give up, a time H6961
Ecc 3: 6 a time to search and a **t** to give up, a time H6961
Ecc 3: 6 a **t** to keep and a time to throw away H6961
Ecc 3: 6 a time to keep and a **t** to throw away, H6961
Ecc 3: 7 a **t** to tear and a time to mend, a time to H6961
Ecc 3: 7 a time to tear and a **t** to mend, a time to H6961
Ecc 3: 7 a **t** to be silent and a time to speak H6961
Ecc 3: 7 a time to be silent and a **t** to speak, H6961
Ecc 3: 8 a **t** to love and a time to hate, a time for H6961
Ecc 3: 8 a time to love and a **t** to hate, a time for H6961
Ecc 3: 8 to hate, a **t** *for* war and a time for peace. H6961
Ecc 3: 8 to hate, a time for war and a **t** *for* peace. H6961
Ecc 3:11 He has made everything beautiful in its **t** H6961
Ecc 3:17 there will be a **t** for every activity, H6961
Ecc 3:17 every activity, a **t** to judge every deed." NDT
Ecc 7:17 do not be a fool—why die before your **t**? H6961
Ecc 8: 5 will know the proper **t** and procedure. H6961
Ecc 8: 6 For there is a proper **t** and procedure for H6961
Ecc 8: 8 one has power over the **t** *of* their death. H3427
Ecc 8: 8 As no one is discharged in **t of war**, so H4878
Ecc 8: 9 There is a **t** when a man lords it over H6961
Ecc 8:12 a hundred crimes *may* **live a long t**, H799
Ecc 9:11 **t** and chance happen to them all. H6961
Ecc 10:17 whose princes eat at a *proper* **t**— H6961
Isa 7:17 house of your father a **t** unlike any since H3427
Isa 9: 7 righteousness from **that t on** and forever. H6964
Isa 11:11 out his hand a **second t** to reclaim the H9108
Isa 13:22 Her **t** is at hand, and her days will not be H6961
Isa 18: 7 At that **t** gifts will be brought to the LORD H6961
Isa 20: 2 at that **t** the LORD spoke through Isaiah son H6961
Isa 23:15 At that **t** Tyre will be forgotten for seventy H3427
Isa 29:17 **In a very short t**, will not H6388+5071+4663
Isa 33: 2 morning, our salvation in **t** *of* distress. H6961
Isa 39: 1 At that **t** Marduk-Baladan son of Baladan H6961
Isa 39: 6 The **t** will surely come when everything in H3427
Isa 42:14 "For a **long t** I have kept silent, I have H6409
Isa 42:23 to this or pay close attention in **t to come**? H294
Isa 48:16 in secret; at the **t** it happens, I am there." H6961
Isa 49: 8 "In the **t** *of* my favor I will answer you, and H6961
Isa 59:21 descendants—from **this t on** and forever," H6964
Isa 60:22 I am the LORD; in its **t** I will do this swiftly. H6961
Jer 2:24 themselves; at **mating t** they will find her. H2544
Jer 3:17 At that **t** they will call Jerusalem The H6961
Jer 4:11 At that **t** this people and Jerusalem will H6961
Jer 7:25 From the **t** your ancestors left Egypt until H3427
Jer 8: 1 " 'At that **t**, declares the LORD, the bones H6961
Jer 8: 7 the thrush observe the **t** *of* their migration. H6961
Jer 8:15 a **t** *of* healing but there is only terror. H6961
Jer 10:18 "At this **t** I will hurl out those who live in H7193
Jer 11: 7 From the **t** I brought your ancestors up from H3427
Jer 11:14 they call to me in the **t** *of* their distress. H6961
Jer 11:18 for **at that t** he showed me what they were H255
Jer 13: 3 word of the LORD came to me a **second t**: H9108
Jer 14:19 a **t** *of* healing but there is only terror. H6961
Jer 16:19 my refuge in **t** *of* distress, to you the H3427
Jer 16:21 this **t** I will teach them my power and H7193
Jer 18: 7 If **at any t** I announce that a nation or H8092
Jer 18: 9 And if **at another t** I announce that a H8092
Jer 18:23 deal with them in the **t** *of* your anger. H6961
Jer 25:33 At that **t** those slain by the LORD will be H3427
Jer 25:34 For your **t** to be slaughtered has come H3427
Jer 27: 7 grandson until the **t** *for* his land comes; H6961
Jer 29:28 It will be a **long t.** Therefore build H801
Jer 30: 7 It will be a **t** *of* trouble for Jacob, but he H6961
Jer 31: 1 "At that **t**," declares the LORD, "I will be H6961
Jer 31:33 make with the people of Israel after that **t**," H3427
Jer 32:14 in a clay jar so they will last a long **t.** H3427
Jer 33: 1 word of the LORD came to him a **second t**: H9108
Jer 33:15 those days and at that **t** I will make a H6961
Jer 33:20 night no longer come at their **appointed t**, H6961
Jer 35: 7 you will live a long **t** in the land where H3427
Jer 36: 2 nations from the **t** I began speaking to H3427
Jer 36: 9 a **t of fasting** before the LORD was H7427
Jer 37:16 a dungeon, where he remained a long **t.** H3427
Jer 39:10 at that **t** he gave them vineyards and H3427
Jer 39:16 At that **t** they will be fulfilled before your H3427
Jer 44:17 **At that t** we had plenty of food and were H2256
Jer 46:21 upon them, the **t** *for* them to be punished. H6961
Jer 49: 8 on Esau *at* the **t** *when* I punish him. H6961
Jer 50: 4 those days, at that **t**," declares the LORD, H6961
Jer 50:20 In those days, at that **t**," declares the LORD H6961
Jer 50:27 has come, the **t** *for* them to be punished. H6961
Jer 50:31 has come, the **t** *for* you to be punished. H6961
Jer 51: 6 It is **t** *for* the LORD's vengeance; he will H6961
Jer 51:13 has come, the **t** *for* you to be destroyed. H564
Jer 51:33 a threshing floor at the **t** it is trampled; H6961
Jer 51:33 the **t** to harvest her will soon come." H6961
Jer 51:47 For the **t** will surely come when I will H3427
Eze 4: 6 lie down again, **this t** on your right side H9108
Eze 7: 7 The **t** has come! The day is near! H6961
Eze 7:12 The **t** has come! The day has arrived! Let H6961
Eze 21:25 whose **t** *of* punishment has reached its H6961
Eze 21:29 whose **t** *of* punishment has reached its H6961
Eze 23:38 At that same **t** they defiled my sanctuary H3427
Eze 24:14 The **t** has come for me to act NDT
Eze 24:27 At that **t** your mouth will be opened; you H3427
Eze 30: 3 day of clouds, a **t** *of* doom *for* the nations. H6961
Eze 35: 5 over to the sword at the **t** *of* their calamity, H6961
Eze 35: 5 the **t** their punishment reached its climax, H6961
Eze 38:17 At that **t** they prophesied for years that I H3427
Eze 38:19 declare that at that **t** there shall be a H3427
Eze 48:35 the name of the city from that **t** on will be: H3427
Da 1:18 At the end of the **t** set by the king to bring H3427
Da 2: 8 "I am certain that you are trying to gain **t**, A10530
Da 2:16 went in to the king and asked for **t**, A10232
Da 2:44 "In the **t** of those kings, the God of A10317
Da 3: 8 At this **t** some astrologers came forward A10232
Da 4:19 was greatly perplexed for a **t**, and his A10734
Da 4:34 At the end of that **t**, I, Nebuchadnezzar A10317
Da 4:36 At the same **t** that my sanity was A10232
Da 5:11 In the **t** *of* your father he was found to A10317
Da 7:12 to live for a **period of t.**) A10232+10221+10530
Da 7:22 the **t** came when they possessed the A10232
Da 7:25 will be delivered into his hands for a **t**, A10530
Da 7:25 his hands for a time, times and half a **t.** A10530
Da 8:17 that the vision concerns the **t** *of* the end." H6961
Da 8:19 will happen **later in** the **t** *of* wrath, H928+344
Da 8:19 concerns the **appointed t** *of* the end. H4595
Da 9:21 flight about the **t** *of* the evening sacrifice H6961
Da 9:25 **From** *the t* the word goes out to restore and AIT
Da 10: 2 At that **t** I, Daniel, mourned for three H3427
Da 10:14 the vision concerns a **t** yet to come." H3427
Da 11:24 overthrow of fortresses—but only for a **t.** H6961
Da 11:27 an end will still come at the **appointed t.** H4595
Da 11:29 "At the **appointed t** he will invade the H4595
Da 11:29 this **t** the outcome will be different from H340
Da 11:33 though *for* a **t** they will fall by the sword H3427
Da 11:35 made spotless until the **t** *of* the end, H6961
Da 11:35 it will still come at the **appointed t.** H4595
Da 11:36 successful until the **t** of wrath is completed, NDT
Da 11:40 "At the **t** *of* the end the king of the South H6961
Da 12: 1 "At that **t** Michael, the great prince who H6961
Da 12: 1 There will be a **t** *of* distress such as has H6961
Da 12: 1 But at that **t** your people—everyone H6961
Da 12: 4 words of the scroll until the **t** *of* the end. H6961
Da 12: 7 "It will be for a **t**, times and half a time. H4595
Da 12: 7 "It will be for a time, times and half a **t.** NDT
Da 12: 9 up and sealed until the **t** *of* the end. H6961
Da 12:11 "From the **t** *that* the daily sacrifice is H6961
Hos 10:12 ground; for it is **t** to seek the LORD, until he H6961
Hos 13:13 wisdom; when the **t** arrives, he doesn't H6961
Joel 3: 1 "In those days and at that **t**, when I H6961
Am 4: 2 "The **t** will surely come when you will be H3427
Am 8: 2 "The **t is ripe** for my people Israel H995+7891
Am 8:10 I will make **that t** like mourning for an H2023S
Jnh 3: 1 of the LORD came to Jonah a **second t**: H9108
Mic 2: 3 walk proudly, for it will be a **t** *of* calamity. H6961
Mic 3: 4 At that **t** he will hide his face from them H6961
Mic 5: 3 abandoned until the **t** when she who is in H6961
Mic 7: 4 Now is the **t** of your confusion. NDT
Na 1: 9 an end; trouble will not come a *second* **t.** H7193
Hab 2: 3 For the revelation awaits an **appointed t** H4595
Hab 3: 2 in our day, in our **t** make them known; in H9102
Zep 1:12 At that **t** I will search Jerusalem with H6961
Zep 3:19 At that **t** I will deal with all who H6961
Zep 3:20 At that **t** I will gather you; at that time I H6961
Zep 3:20 gather you; at that **t** I will bring you home. H6961
Hag 1: 2 'The **t** has not yet come to rebuild the H6961
Hag 1: 4 "Is it a **t** for you yourselves to be living in H6961
Hag 2:20 came to Haggai a **second t** on the H9108
Zec 8: 6 to the remnant of this people at that **t**, H3427
Zec 8:10 Before that **t** there were no wages for H3427
Mal 3: 7 Ever since the **t** of your ancestors you have H3427
Mt 1:11 his brothers **at the t of** the exile to *G2093*
Mt 2: 1 during the **t** of King Herod, Magi *G2465*
Mt 2: 7 from them the exact **t** the star had *G5989*
Mt 2:16 with the **t** he had learned from *G5989*

T

Mt 4:17 From **that t on** Jesus began to preach G5538
Mt 7: 4 **when** *all the t* there is a plank in your own AIT
Mt 8:29 here to torture us before the **appointed t**?" G2789
Mt 9:15 The **t** will come when the bridegroom will G2465
Mt 10:19 At that **t** you will be given what to say, G6052
Mt 11:25 At that **t** Jesus said, "I praise you, Father G2789
Mt 12: 1 At that **t** Jesus went through the G2789
Mt 13:21 they have no root, they last only a **short t**. G4672
Mt 13:30 At that **t** I will tell the harvesters G2789
Mt 14: 1 At that **t** Herod the tetrarch heard the G2789
Mt 16:21 From **that t on** Jesus began to explain to G5538
Mt 18: 1 At that **t** the disciples came to Jesus and G6052
Mt 21:34 When the harvest **t** approached, he sent G2789
Mt 21:36 to them, more *than* the **first** *t*, and the AIT
Mt 21:41 give him his share of the crop at harvest **t**." G2789
Mt 24:10 **At that t** many will turn away from the faith G5538
Mt 24:23 **At that t** if anyone says to you, 'Look, here G5538
Mt 24:25 *I have* **told** you **ahead of t**. G4625
Mt 24:43 had known at what **t of night** the thief was G5871
Mt 24:45 to give them their food at the **proper t**? G2789
Mt 24:48 'My master *is* **staying away a long t**,' G5988
Mt 25: 1 "**At that t** the kingdom of heaven will be G5538
Mt 25: 5 The bridegroom *was* **a long t in coming** G5988
Mt 25:19 "After a long **t** the master of those G5989
Mt 26:18 My **appointed t** is near. G2789
Mt 26:42 He went away a **second t** and prayed, "My G1311
Mt 26:44 away once more and prayed the **third t**, G5569
Mt 27:16 **At that t** they had a well-known prisoner G5538
Mk 1: 9 At that **t** Jesus came from Nazareth in G2465
Mk 1:15 "The **t** has come," he said. "The kingdom G2789
Mk 2:20 But the **t** will come when the bridegroom G2465
Mk 3: 1 **Another t** Jesus went into the synagogue G4099
Mk 4:17 they have no root, they last only a **short t**. G4672
Mk 6:21 Finally the opportune **t** came. On his G2465
Mk 6:35 **By this t** it was late in the day, so his G2453
Mk 12: 2 *At* **harvest t** he sent a servant to the G2789
Mk 13:11 Just say whatever is given you at the **t**, for G6052
Mk 13:21 **At that t** if anyone says to you, 'Look, here G5538
Mk 13:23 *I have* **told** you everything **ahead of t**. G4625
Mk 13:26 "**At that t** people will see the Son of Man G5538
Mk 13:33 You do not know when that **t** will come. G2789
Mk 14: 7 you can help them **any t** you want. G4020
Mk 14:41 Returning the **third t**, he said to them G5568
Mk 14:72 the rooster crowed the **second t**. G1666+1311
Lk 1: 5 In the **t** of Herod king of Judea there was G2465
Lk 1:10 And *when* the **t** for the burning of incense G6052
Lk 1:20 which will come true at their **appointed t**." G2789
Lk 1:23 When his **t** of service was completed, he G2465
Lk 1:39 At that **t** Mary got ready and hurried to a G2465
Lk 1:57 When it was **t** for Elizabeth to have her G5989
Lk 2: 6 the **t** came for the baby to be born, G2465
Lk 2:21 when *it was* **t** to circumcise the child G4398
Lk 2:22 When the **t** came for the purification rites G2465
Lk 4:13 he left him until an **opportune t**. G2789
Lk 4:25 were many widows in Israel in Elijah's **t**, G2465
Lk 4:27 with leprosy **in the t of** Elisha the prophet G2093
Lk 5:35 But the **t** will come when the bridegroom G2465
Lk 7:21 At that very **t** Jesus cured many who had G6052
Lk 7:45 this woman, **from the t** I entered G608+4005
Lk 8:13 in the **t** of testing they fall away. G2789
Lk 8:27 *For* a long **t** this man had not worn clothes G5989
Lk 9:36 tell anyone at that **t** what they had seen. G2465
Lk 9:51 As the **t** approached for him to be taken G2465
Lk 10:21 At that **t** Jesus, full of joy through the Holy G6052
Lk 12:12 teach you at that **t** what you should say." G6052
Lk 12:42 them their food allowance at the **proper t**? G2789
Lk 12:45 'My master *is* **taking a long t** in coming,' G5988
Lk 12:56 don't know how to interpret this **present t**? G2789
Lk 13: 1 present at that **t** who told Jesus about G2789
Lk 13:31 At that **t** some Pharisees came to Jesus G6052
Lk 14:17 *At* the **t** of the banquet he sent his servant G6052
Lk 16:16 Since **that t**, the good news of the G5538
Lk 16:22 "**The t came** when the beggar died and G1181
Lk 17:22 "The **t** is coming when you will long to G2465
Lk 18: 4 "For *some* **t** he refused. But finally he said G5989
Lk 19:44 did not recognize the **t** of God's coming to G2789
Lk 20: 9 some farmers and went away *for* a long **t**. G5989
Lk 20:10 *At* **harvest t** he sent a servant to the G2789
Lk 21: 6 the **t** will come when not one stone will G2465
Lk 21: 8 claiming, 'I am he,' and, 'The **t** is near. G2789
Lk 21:22 For this is the **t** of punishment in G2465
Lk 21:27 **At that t** they will see the Son of Man G5538
Lk 23: 7 who was also in Jerusalem at that **t**. G2465
Lk 23: 8 because for a long **t** he had been wanting G5989
Lk 23:22 *For* the **third** *t* he spoke to them: "Why? AIT
Lk 23:29 For the **t** will come when you will say G2465
Jn 2:13 When it was **almost t** for the Jewish G1584
Jn 3: 4 they cannot enter a **second t** into their G1309
Jn 3:22 where *he* **spent some t** with them, and G1417
Jn 4:21 a **t** is coming when you will worship the G6052
Jn 4:23 Yet a **t** is coming and has now come when G6052
Jn 4:52 he inquired as to the **t** when his son got G6052
Jn 4:53 this was the exact **t** at which Jesus had G6052
Jn 5: 1 **Some t later**, Jesus went up to G3552+4047
Jn 5: 6 he had been in this condition *for* a long **t**, G5989
Jn 5:25 a **t** is coming and has now come when G6052
Jn 5:28 a **t** is coming when all who are in their G6052
Jn 5:35 you chose for a **t** to enjoy his light. G6052
Jn 6: 1 **Some t after this**, Jesus crossed to G3552+4047
Jn 6:66 From **this** *t* many of his disciples turned back AIT
Jn 7: 6 Jesus told them, "My **t** is not yet here; for G2789
Jn 7: 6 time is not yet here; for you any **t** will do. G2789
Jn 7: 8 because my **t** has not yet fully come." G2789
Jn 7:33 "I am with you for only a short **t**, and then G5989
Jn 7:39 **Up to that t** the Spirit had **not** been given G4037
Jn 8: 9 to go away **one at a t**, G1651+2848+1651
Jn 9:24 A **second t** they summoned the G1666+1311
Jn 11:39 dead man, "**by this t** there is a bad odor G2453
Jn 11:55 When it was **almost t for** the Jewish G1584
Jn 12:31 **Now** is *the t for* judgment on this world; now AIT
Jn 12:42 Yet **at the same t** many even among the G3940
Jn 14: 9 I have been among you such a long **t**? G5989
Jn 16: 2 the **t** is coming when anyone who kills G6052
Jn 16: 4 so that when their **t** comes you will G6052
Jn 16:21 a child has pain because her **t** has come; G6052
Jn 16:22 Now is your **t of grief**, but I will see you G3383
Jn 16:25 a **t** is coming when I will no longer use G6052
Jn 16:32 "A **t** is coming and in fact has come when G6052
Jn 18:39 you one prisoner **at the t of** the Passover. G1877
Jn 19:27 From that **t** on, this disciple took her into G6052
Jn 21:14 This was now the **third t** Jesus appeared to G5568
Jn 21:17 The **third t** he said to him, "Simon son of G5568
Jn 21:17 hurt because Jesus asked him the **third t**, G5568
Ac 1: 6 are you at this **t** going to restore the G5989
Ac 1:21 with us the whole **t** the Lord Jesus was G5989
Ac 1:22 baptism to the **t** when Jesus was taken G2465
Ac 3: 1 up to the temple at the **t** of prayer— G6052
Ac 3:21 receive him until the **t** comes for God to G5989
Ac 4:34 *from t to time* those who owned land or houses **sold** AIT
Ac 4:34 *from time to t* those who owned land or houses **sold** AIT
Ac 5:36 **Some t ago** Theudas G4574+4047+3836+2465
Ac 7: 5 *even though at that t* Abraham **had** no child. AIT
Ac 7:17 "As the **t** drew near for God to fulfill his G5989
Ac 7:20 "At that **t** Moses was born, and he was no G2789
Ac 7:41 **That was the t** they made G1877+3836+2465+1697
Ac 7:45 remained in the land until the **t** of David, G2465
Ac 8: 9 Now **for some t** a man named Simon had G4732
Ac 8:11 had amazed them *for* a long **t** with his G5989
Ac 9:31 Samaria enjoyed a *t of* **peace** and was AIT
Ac 9:37 About that **t** she became sick and died G2465
Ac 9:43 stayed in Joppa *for* some **t** with a tanner G2465
Ac 10:15 The voice spoke to him a **second t** G1666+1311
Ac 11: 9 spoke from heaven a **second t**, G1666+1311
Ac 11:27 During this **t** some prophets came down G2465
Ac 12: 1 It was about this **t** that King Herod G2789
Ac 13:11 You are going to be blind for a **t**, not even G2789
Ac 13:20 them judges **until the t of** Samuel the G2401
Ac 14: 3 Barnabas spent considerable **t** there, G5989
Ac 14:28 stayed there a long **t** with the disciples. G5989
Ac 15: 7 that **some t ago** God made G608+2465+792
Ac 15:33 After spending *some* **t** there, they were G5989
Ac 15:36 Some **t** later Paul said to Barnabas, "Let G2465
Ac 17:21 lived there **spent** *their* **t** doing nothing G2320
Ac 18:18 Paul stayed on in Corinth for some **t**. G2465
Ac 18:20 asked him to spend more **t** with them, G5989
Ac 18:23 After spending some **t** in Antioch, Paul G5989
Ac 19:23 About that **t** there arose a great G2789
Ac 20:16 to avoid **spending t** in the province G5990
Ac 20:18 how I lived the whole **t** I was with you, G5989
Ac 21: 5 When it was **t** to leave, we left and G2465
Ac 21:38 into the wilderness **some t ago**?" G4574+4047+3836+2465
Ac 24:26 **At the same t** he was hoping that Paul G275
Ac 26: 5 have known me **for a long t** and can testify, G540
Ac 26:11 **Many a t** I went from one synagogue to G4490
Ac 26:28 think that in *such a* **short** *t* you can persuade AIT
Ac 26:29 Paul replied, "**Short** *t* or long—I pray to God AIT
Ac 27: 9 Much **t** had been lost, and sailing had G5989
Ac 27:21 After they had gone a **long** *t* without food AIT
Ac 27:28 A **short** *t* later they took soundings again AIT
Ac 27:40 in the sea and **at the same t** untied the G275
Ac 28: 6 after waiting a **long** *t* and seeing nothing AIT
Ro 3:26 his righteousness at the present **t**, G2789
Ro 5: 6 at just the right **t**, when we were still G2789
Ro 5:14 death reigned **from the t of** Adam to the G608
Ro 5:14 from the time of Adam **to the t of** Moses, G3588
Ro 6:21 did you reap **at that t** from the things you G5538
Ro 8:22 of childbirth right up to the **present t**. G3814
Ro 9: 9 "At the appointed **t** I will return, and G2789
Ro 9:10 **children** *were* **conceived at the same t** G1666+1651+3130+2400
Ro 11: 5 at the present **t** there is a remnant chosen G2789
Ro 11:30 as you who were **at one t** disobedient to G4537
Ro 13: 6 *who* **give** *their* **full t** to governing. G4674
Ro 13:11 understanding the *present* **t**: The hour has G2789
1Co 2: 7 God destined for our glory before **t** began. G172
1Co 4: 5 judge nothing before the **appointed t**; G2789
1Co 4: 5 **At that t** each will receive their praise G5538
1Co 7: 5 perhaps by mutual consent and for a **t**, G2789
1Co 7:29 brothers and sisters, is that the **t** is short. G2789
1Co 14:27 **one at a t**, and someone G324+3538
1Co 15: 6 of the brothers and sisters **at the same t**, G2384
1Co 16: 7 I hope to spend some **t** with you, if the G5989
2Co 6: 2 he says, "*In* the **t** of my favor I heard you G2789
2Co 6: 2 tell you, now is the **t** of God's favor, now G2789
2Co 8:14 At the present **t** your plenty will supply G2789
2Co 12:14 Now I am ready to visit you *for* the **third t** G5568
2Co 13: 2 when I was with you the **second t**. G1309
Gal 2: 1 up again to Jerusalem, this **t** with Barnabas. NDT
Gal 4: 2 trustees until the **t set** by his father. G4607
Gal 4: 4 But when the *set* **t** had fully come, God G5989
Gal 4:29 **At that t** the son born according to the G5538
Gal 6: 9 for *at* the proper **t** we will reap a harvest if G2789
Eph 2: 3 All of us also lived among them **at one t** G4537
Eph 2:12 remember that *at* that **t** you were separate G2789
Php 1: 3 I thank my God **every** *t* I remember you. AIT
1Th 2:17 by being separated from you for a short **t** G2789
2Th 2: 6 that he may be revealed at the proper **t**. G2789
1Ti 2: 6 now been witnessed to *at* the proper **t**. G2789
1Ti 6:15 which God will bring about *in* his own **t** G2789
2Ti 1: 9 Jesus before the **beginning of t**, G5989+173
2Ti 4: 3 For the **t** will come when people will not G2789
2Ti 4: 6 the **t** for my departure is near. G2789
Titus 1: 2 promised before the **beginning of t**, G5989+173
Titus 3: 3 **At one t** we too were foolish, disobedient G4537
Titus 3:10 and then warn them a **second t**. G1311
Heb 3: 8 during the **t** of testing in the wilderness G2465
Heb 4: 7 he did when a long **t** later he spoke G5989
Heb 4:16 find grace to help us in our **t of need**. G2322
Heb 5:12 though by this **t** you ought to be teachers G5989
Heb 8:10 with the people of Israel after that **t**, G2465
Heb 9: 9 This is an illustration for the present **t** G2789
Heb 9:10 applying until the **t** of the new order. G2789
Heb 9:28 and he will appear a **second t**, not G1666+1311
Heb 10:12 had offered **for all t** one G1650+3836+1457
Heb 10:13 and **since that t** he waits for his G3836+3370
Heb 10:16 I will make with them after that **t**, G2465
Heb 11:32 I do not have **t** to tell about Gideon, Barak G5989
Heb 12:11 No discipline seems pleasant at the **t**, but G4205
Heb 12:26 **At that t** his voice shook the earth, but G5538
1Pe 1: 5 that is ready to be revealed in the last **t**. G2789
1Pe 1:11 to find out the **t** and circumstances to G2789
1Pe 1:17 live out your **t** as foreigners here in G5989
1Pe 4: 3 have spent enough **t** in the past doing G5989
1Pe 4:17 For it is **t** for judgment to begin with God's G2789
1Pe 5: 6 that he may lift you up in *due* **t**. G2789
2Pe 3: 6 also the world **of that t** was deluged and G5538
Jude 5 you that the Lord **at one t** delivered his G562
Rev 1: 3 what is written in it, because the **t** is near. G2789
Rev 2:21 I have given her **t** to repent of her G5989
Rev 3: 3 you will not know *at* what **t** I will come to G6052
Rev 11: 6 it will not rain *during* the **t** they are G2465
Rev 11:18 The **t** has come for judging the dead, and G2789
Rev 12:12 because he knows that his **t** is short." G2789
Rev 12:14 where she would be taken care of *for* a **t** G2789
Rev 12:14 times and half a **t**, out of the serpent's G2789
Rev 14:15 because the **t** to reap has come, for G6052
Rev 20: 3 After that, he must be set free *for* a short **t**. G5989
Rev 22:10 of this scroll, because the **t** is near. G2789

TIMELY (1) [TIME]

Pr 15:23 reply—and how good is a **t** word! H928+6961

TIMES (183) [TIME]

Ge 1:14 let them serve as signs to mark **sacred t**, H4595
Ge 4:15 kills Cain will suffer vengeance **seven** *t over*." AIT
Ge 4:24 If Cain is avenged **seven** *t*, then Lamech AIT
Ge 4:24 seven times, then Lamech **seventy-seven** *t*." AIT
Ge 31: 7 cheated me by changing my wages ten **t**. H4951
Ge 31:41 and you changed my wages ten **t**. H4951
Ge 33: 3 to the ground seven **t** as he approached H7193
Ge 43:34 portion was five **t** as much as anyone H3338
Ex 18:22 serve as judges for the people at all **t**, H6961
Ex 18:26 served as judges for the people at all **t**. H6961
Ex 23:14 "Three **t** a year you are to celebrate a H8079
Ex 23:17 "Three **t** a year all the men are to appear H7193
Ex 25:30 on this table to be before me **at all t**. H9458
Ex 34:23 Three **t** a year all your men are to appear H7193
Ex 34:24 you go up three **t** each year to appear H7193
Lev 4: 6 some of it seven **t** before the LORD, H7193
Lev 4:17 before the LORD seven **t** in front of the H7193
Lev 8:11 some of the oil on the altar seven **t**, H7193
Lev 14: 7 Seven **t** he shall sprinkle the one to be H7193
Lev 14:16 some of it before the LORD seven **t**. H7193
Lev 14:27 oil from his palm seven **t** before the LORD. H7193
Lev 14:51 and sprinkle the house seven **t**. H7193
Lev 16:14 his finger seven **t** before the atonement H7193
Lev 16:19 with his finger seven **t** to cleanse it and to H7193
Lev 23: 4 you are to proclaim at their **appointed t**: H4595
Lev 25: 8 seven **t** seven years—so that H7193
Lev 26:18 I will punish you for your sins **seven** *t* over. AIT
Lev 26:21 I will multiply your afflictions **seven** *t over*, AIT
Lev 26:24 will afflict you for your sins **seven** *t over*. AIT
Lev 26:28 will punish you for your sins **seven** *t over*. AIT
Nu 10:10 Also at your *t of* rejoicing—your appointed H3427
Nu 14:22 who disobeyed me and tested me ten **t**— H7193
Nu 19: 4 sprinkle it seven **t** toward the front of H7193
Nu 22:28 to you to make you beat me these three **t**?" H8079
Nu 22:32 you beaten your donkey these three **t**? H8079
Nu 22:33 turned away from me these three **t**. H8079
Nu 24: 1 to divination as **at other t**, H7193+928+7193
Nu 24:10 you have blessed them these three **t**. H7193
Dt 1:11 you a thousand **t** and bless you as he has H7193
Dt 16:16 Three **t** a year all your men must appear H7193
Jos 6: 4 march around the city seven **t**, with the H7193
Jos 6:15 the city seven **t** in the same manner, H7193
Jos 6:15 on that day they circled the city seven **t**. H7193
Ru 4: 7 Now in **earlier t** in Israel, for the H7156
1Sa 3:10 calling as at the other **t**, "Samuel! H7193
1Sa 20:41 bowed down before Jonathan three **t**, H7193
1Sa 27: 8 From **ancient t** these peoples had lived in H6409
2Sa 12: 6 He must pay for that lamb **four** *t over* AIT
2Sa 24: 3 God multiply the troops a hundred **t** *over*, H7193

1Ki 9:25 Three **t** a year Solomon sacrificed burnt H7193
1Ki 17:21 out on the boy three **t** and cried out to the H7193
1Ki 18:43 Seven **t** Elijah said, "Go back. H7193
1Ki 22:16 "How many **t** must I make you swear to H7193
2Ki 4:35 boy sneezed seven **t** and opened his eyes H7193
2Ki 5:10 wash yourself seven **t** in the Jordan, and H7193
2Ki 5:14 dipped himself in the Jordan seven **t**, H7193
2Ki 13:18 He struck it three **t** and stopped. H7193
2Ki 13:19 should have struck the ground five or six **t**; H7193
2Ki 13:19 But now you will defeat it only three **t**." H7193
2Ki 13:25 Three **t** Jehoash defeated him, and so he H7193
1Ch 4:22 These records are **from ancient t**.) H6972
1Ch 9:20 **In earlier t** Phinehas son of Eleazar H4200+7156
1Ch 12:32 who understood the **t** and knew what H6961
1Ch 21:3 LORD multiply his troops a hundred **t** *over*. H7193
2Ch 18:15 "How many **t** must I make you swear to H7193
Ne 4:12 near them came and told us ten **t** *over*, H7193
Ne 6:4 Four **t** they sent me the same message H7193
Ne 10:34 house of our God at set **t** each year a H6961
Ne 13:31 contributions of wood at designated **t**, H6961
Est 1:13 with the wise men who understood the **t** H6961
Est 9:31 these days of Purim at their **designated t**, H2375
Est 9:31 in regard to their **t** *of* fasting and H1821
Job 19:3 Ten **t** now you have reproached me H7193
Job 24:1 does the Almighty not set **t** for judgment? H6961
Job 27:10 Will they call on God at all **t**? H6961
Job 33:29 things to a person—twice, even **three** *t*— AIT
Job 38:23 which I reserve for **t** *of* trouble, for days of H6961
Ps 9:9 oppressed, a stronghold in **t** *of* trouble. H6961
Ps 10:1 Why do you hide yourself in **t** *of* trouble? H6961
Ps 12:6 in a crucible, like gold refined **seven** *t*. AIT
Ps 31:15 My **t** are in your hands; deliver me from H6961
Ps 34:1 I will extol the LORD at all **t**; his praise will H6961
Ps 37:19 In **t** *of* disaster they will not wither; in days H6961
Ps 41:1 the LORD delivers them in **t** *of* trouble. H3427
Ps 59:16 are my fortress, my refuge in **t** *of* trouble. H3427
Ps 60:3 You have shown your people **desperate t** H7997
Ps 62:8 Trust in him at all **t**, you people; pour out H6961
Ps 79:12 of our neighbors **seven** *t* the contempt they AIT
Ps 106:43 Many **t** he delivered them, but they were H7193
Ps 119:20 with longing for your laws at all **t**. H6961
Ps 119:164 **Seven** *t* a day I praise you for your righteous AIT
Pr 17:17 A friend loves at all **t**, and a brother is H6961
Pr 24:16 though the righteous fall **seven** *t*, they rise AIT
Ecc 7:14 When **t** are good, be happy; but when H3427
Ecc 7:14 be happy; but when **t** are bad, consider H3427
Ecc 7:22 your heart that many **t** you yourself have H7193
Ecc 9:12 are trapped by evil **t** that fall unexpectedly H6961
Isa 30:26 the sunlight will be **seven** *t brighter*, like AIT
Isa 33:6 He will be the sure foundation for your **t** H6961
Isa 46:10 beginning, from **ancient t**, what is still to H7710
Isa 64:4 Since **ancient t** no one has heard, no ear H6409
Jer 14:8 its Savior in **t** *of* distress, why are H6961
Jer 15:11 plead with you in **t** *of* disaster and times H6961
Jer 15:11 you in times of disaster and **t** *of* distress. H6961
Jer 21:2 **us as in t past** so that he H3869+3972
Jer 28:8 From **early t** the prophets who preceded H6409
Jer 46:26 Egypt will be inhabited as *in* **t** *past*," H3427
Eze 4:10 day and eat it **at set t**. H4946+6961+6330+6961
Eze 4:11 and drink it **at set t**. H4946+6961+6330+6961
Eze 21:14 strike twice, even **three** *t*. It is a sword for AIT
Da 1:20 he found them ten **t** better than all the H3338
Da 2:21 He changes **t** and seasons; he deposes A10530
Da 3:19 furnace heated seven **t** hotter than usual A10248
Da 4:16 of an animal, till seven **t** pass by for him. A10530
Da 4:23 animals, until seven **t** pass by for him. A10530
Da 4:25 Seven **t** will pass by for you until you A10530
Da 4:32 Seven **t** will pass by for you until you A10530
Da 6:10 Three **t** a day he got down on his knees A10232
Da 6:13 He still prays three **t** a day." A10232
Da 7:10 **ten thousand** *t* ten thousand stood before AIT
Da 7:25 try to change the **set t** and the laws. A10232
Da 7:25 his hands for a time, **t** and half a time. A10530
Da 9:25 streets and a trench, but in **t** of trouble. H6961
Da 11:14 "In those **t** many will rise against the king H6961
Da 12:7 "It will be for a time, **t**, and half a time. H4595
Joel 2:2 as never was in **ancient t** nor ever will be H6409
Am 4:9 "**Many t** I struck your gardens and H8049
Am 5:13 the prudent keep quiet in such **t**, H6961
Am 5:13 keep quiet in such times, for the **t** are evil. H6961
Mic 5:2 origins are from of old, from ancient **t**." H3427
Na 1:7 is good, a refuge in **t** *of* trouble. He cares H3427
Mt 13:8 a hundred, sixty or **thirty** *t* what was sown. AIT
Mt 13:23 a hundred, sixty or **thirty** *t* what was sown." AIT
Mt 16:3 you cannot interpret the signs *of* the **t**. G2789
Mt 18:21 **how many t** shall I forgive my brother or G4529
Mt 18:21 who sins against me? Up to **seven t**?" G2232
Mt 18:22 "I tell you, not **seven t**, but seventy-seven G2232
Mt 18:22 seven times, but **seventy-seven t**. G1574+2231
Mt 19:29 will receive a **hundred t** *as much* and will G1671
Mt 26:34 rooster crows, you will disown me **three t**." G5565
Mt 26:75 rooster crows, you will disown me **three t**." G5565
Mk 4:8 some sixty, some a **hundred** *t*. AIT
Mk 4:20 sixty, some a **hundred** *t* what was sown." AIT
Mk 10:30 to receive a **hundred t** *as much* in this G1671
Mk 14:30 twice you yourself will disown me **three t**." G5565
Mk 14:72 crows twice you will disown me **three t**." G5565
Lk 8:8 a **hundred t** *more* than was sown. G1671
Lk 8:29 Many **t** it had seized him, and though he G5989
Lk 17:4 sin against you **seven t** in a day and G2232
Lk 17:4 in a day and **seven t** come back to you G2232
Lk 18:30 fail to receive **many t as much** in this age, G4491
Lk 19:8 I will pay back **four t** *the amount*. G5487
Lk 21:24 the Gentiles until the **t** of the Gentiles are G2789
Lk 22:34 you will deny **three t** that you know me." G5565
Lk 22:61 crows today, you will disown me **three t**." G5565
Jn 13:38 rooster crows, you will disown me **three t**! G5565
Ac 1:7 you to know the **t** or dates the Father G5989
Ac 3:19 that **t** of refreshing may come from the G2789
Ac 10:16 This happened **three t**, and G2093+5565
Ac 11:10 This happened **three t**, and then it G2093+5565
Ac 15:21 city from the earliest **t** and is read in the G1155
Ac 17:26 their appointed **t in history** and the G2789
Ro 1:10 in my prayers **at all t**; and I pray that now G4121
Ro 1:13 that I planned **many t** to come to you (but G4490
Ro 2:15 accusing them **and** *at other t even* defending AIT
2Co 9:8 so that in all things **at all t**, having all that G4121
2Co 11:24 **Five t** I received from the Jews the forty G4294
2Co 11:25 **Three t** I was beaten with rods, once I was G5565
2Co 11:25 with stones, **three t** I was shipwrecked G5565
2Co 12:8 **Three t** I pleaded with the Lord to take it G5565
Eph 1:10 into effect when the **t** reach their G2789
1Th 5:1 about **t** and dates we do not need to write G5989
2Th 3:16 give you peace **at all t** and in every G1328+4246
1Ti 4:1 says that in later **t** some will abandon the G2789
2Ti 3:1 There will be terrible **t** in the last days. G2789
Heb 1:1 the prophets **at many t** and in various G4495
Heb 9:26 have had to suffer **many t** since the G4490
Heb 10:33 **at other t** you stood side by side G4047+1254
1Pe 1:20 was revealed in these last **t** for your sake. G5989
Jude 18 "In the last **t** there will be scoffers who G5989
Rev 5:11 thousands, and ten thousand *t* **ten thousand**. AIT
Rev 9:16 was twice ten thousand *t* **ten thousand**. AIT
Rev 12:14 care of for a time, **t** and half a time, out of G2789

TIMID (2)
2Co 10:1 who am "**t**" when face to face with G5424
2Ti 1:7 Spirit God gave us does not make us **t**, G1261

TIMNA (6)
Ge 36:12 Eliphaz also had a concubine named **T**, H9465
Ge 36:22 Hori and Homam. **T** was Lotan's sister. H9465
Ge 36:40 clans and regions: **T**, Alvah, Jetheth, H9465
1Ch 1:36 Zepho, Gatam and Kenaz; *by* **T**: H9465
1Ch 1:39 Hori and Homam. **T** was Lotan's sister. H9465
1Ch 1:51 chiefs of Edom were: **T**, Alvah, Jetheth, H9465

TIMNAH (11) [TIMNITE'S]
Ge 38:12 he went up to **T**, to the men who were H9463
Ge 38:13 is on his way to **T** to shear his sheep," H9463
Ge 38:14 to Enaim, which is on the road to **T**. H9463
Jos 15:10 down to Beth Shemesh and crossed to **T**. H9463
Jos 15:57 Gibeah and **T**—ten towns and their H9463
Jos 19:43 **T**, Ekron, H9463
Jdg 14:1 Samson went down to **T** and saw there a H9463
Jdg 14:2 "I have seen a Philistine woman in **T** H9463
Jdg 14:5 Samson went down to **T** together with his H9463
Jdg 14:5 As they approached the vineyards of **T** H9463
2Ch 28:18 as well as Soko, **T** and Gimzo, with their H9463

TIMNATH HERES (1) [HERES]
Jdg 2:9 at **T** in the hill country of Ephraim H9466

TIMNATH SERAH (2) [SERAH]
Jos 19:50 **T** in the hill country of Ephraim. H9467
Jos 24:30 at **T** in the hill country of Ephraim H9467

TIMNITE'S (1) [TIMNAH]
Jdg 15:6 "Samson, the **T** son-in-law, because his H9464

TIMON (1)
Ac 6:5 Procorus, Nicanor, **T**, Parmenas, and G5511

TIMOTHEUS (KJV) TIMOTHY

TIMOTHY (25)
Ac 16:1 where a disciple named **T** lived, whose G5510
Ac 17:14 the coast, but Silas and **T** stayed at Berea. G5510
Ac 17:15 Silas and **T** to join him as soon as G5510
Ac 18:5 When Silas and **T** came from Macedonia G5510
Ac 19:22 sent two of his helpers, **T** and Erastus, to G5510
Ac 20:4 Gaius from Derbe, **T** also, and Tychicus G5510
Ro 16:21 **T**, my co-worker, sends his greetings to G5510
1Co 4:17 For this reason I have sent to you **T**, my G5510
1Co 16:10 When **T** comes, see to it that he has G5510
2Co 1:1 the will of God, and **T** our brother, To the G5510
2Co 1:19 by me and Silas and **T**—was not "Yes" G5510
Php 1:1 Paul and **T**, servants of Christ Jesus, To all G5510
Php 2:19 in the Lord Jesus to send **T** to you soon, G5510
Php 2:22 But you know that **T** has proved himself NDT
Col 1:1 by the will of God, and **T** our brother, G5510
1Th 1:1 Silas and **T**, To the church of the G5510
1Th 3:2 We sent **T**, who is our brother and G5510
1Th 3:6 But **T** has just now come to us from you G5510
2Th 1:1 Silas and **T**, To the church of the G5510
1Ti 1:2 *To* **T** my true son in the faith: Grace G5510
1Ti 1:18 **T**, my son, I am giving you this command G5510
1Ti 6:20 **T**, guard what has been entrusted to your G5510
2Ti 1:2 *To* **T**, my dear son: Grace, mercy and G5510
Phm 1 of Christ Jesus, and **T** our brother, To G5510
Heb 13:23 that our brother **T** has been released. G5510

TIN (4)
Nu 31:22 silver, bronze, iron, **t**, lead H974
Eze 22:18 of them are the copper, **t**, iron and lead left H974
Eze 22:20 lead and **t** are gathered into a furnace to H974
Eze 27:12 **t** and lead for your merchandise. H974

TINDER (1)
Isa 1:31 man will become **t** and his work a spark; H5861

TINGLE (3)
1Sa 3:11 *will make* the ears of everyone who hears about it **t** H7509
2Ki 21:12 the ears of everyone who hears of it *will* **t**. H7509
Jer 19:3 *will* **make** the ears of everyone who hears of it **t** H7509

TINKLING (KJV) BANGLES, CLANGING, JINGLING

TIP (7)
Jdg 6:21 bread with the **t** *of* the staff that was in H7895
1Ki 6:24 cubits—ten cubits from wing **t** to wing tip. H7896
1Ki 6:24 cubits—ten cubits from wing tip to wing **t**. H7896
Est 5:2 touched the **t** *of* the scepter. H8031
Job 33:2 are **on the t** of my **tongue**. H4383+928+2674
Job 38:37 Who *can* **t over** the water jars of the H8886
Lk 16:24 Lazarus to dip the **t** of his finger in water G216

TIPHSAH (3)
1Ki 4:24 Euphrates River, from **T** to Gaza, and had H9527
2Ki 15:16 attacked **T** and everyone in the city and its H9527
2Ki 15:16 He sacked **T** and ripped open all the NDT

TIRAS (2)
Ge 10:2 Javan, Tubal, Meshek and **T**. H9410
1Ch 1:5 Javan, Tubal, Meshek and **T**. H9410

TIRATHITES (1)
1Ch 2:55 lived at Jabez: the **T**, Shimeathites and H9571

TIRE (2) [TIRED]
Jer 2:24 that pursue her *need* not **t** *themselves*; H3615
2Th 3:13 sisters, never **t** of doing what is good. G1591

TIRED (7) [TIRE]
Ex 17:12 When Moses' hands grew **t**, they took a H3878
2Sa 23:10 till his hand *grew* **t** and froze to the sword. H3333
Isa 5:27 Not *one* of them grows **t** or stumbles, not H6546
Isa 40:28 *He will* not *grow* **t** or weary, and his H3615
Isa 40:30 Even youths *grow* **t** and weary, and young H3615
Jer 15:6 destroy you; *I* **am t** *of* holding back. H4206
Jn 4:6 Jesus, **t** *as he was* from the journey G3159

TIRHAKAH (2)
2Ki 19:9 Now Sennacherib received a report that **T** H9555
Isa 37:9 Now Sennacherib received a report that **T** H9555

TIRHANAH (1)
1Ch 2:48 Maakah was the mother of Sheber and **T**. H9563

TIRIA (1)
1Ch 4:16 Ziph, Ziphah, **T** and Asarel. H9409

TIRSHATHA (KJV) GOVERNOR

TIRZAH (18)
Nu 26:33 Mahlah, Noah, Hoglah, Milkah and **T**.) H9573
Nu 27:1 Mahlah, Noah, Hoglah, Milkah and **T**. H9573
Nu 36:11 daughters—Mahlah, **T**, Hoglah, Milkah H9573
Jos 12:24 the king of **T** one thirty-one kings in all. H9574
Jos 17:3 Mahlah, Noah, Hoglah, Milkah and **T**. H9573
1Ki 14:17 wife got up and left and went to **T**. H9574
1Ki 15:21 building Ramah and withdrew to **T**. H9574
1Ki 15:33 of Ahijah became king of all Israel in **T**, H9574
1Ki 16:6 with his ancestors and was buried in **T**. H9574
1Ki 16:8 of Israel, and he reigned in **T** two years. H9574
1Ki 16:9 Elah was in **T** at the time, getting drunk in H9574
1Ki 16:9 of Arza, the palace administrator at **T**. H9574
1Ki 16:15 of Judah, Zimri reigned in **T** seven days. H9574
1Ki 16:17 from Gibbethon and laid siege to **T**. H9574
1Ki 16:23 he reigned twelve years, six of them in **T**. H9574
2Ki 15:14 son of Gadi went from **T** up to Samaria. H9574
2Ki 15:16 starting out from **T**, attacked Tiphsah and H9574
SS 6:4 You are as beautiful as **T**, my darling, as H9574

TISHBE (1) [TISHBITE]
1Ki 17:1 the Tishbite, from **T** *in* Gilead, said to H9586

TISHBITE (6) [TISHBE]
1Ki 17:1 Now Elijah the **T**, from Tishbe in Gilead H9585
1Ki 21:17 the word of the LORD came to Elijah the **T**: H9585
1Ki 21:28 the word of the LORD came to Elijah the **T**: H9585
2Ki 1:3 the angel of the LORD said to Elijah the **T**, H9585
2Ki 1:8 The king said, "That was Elijah the **T**." H9585
2Ki 9:36 he spoke through his servant Elijah the **T**: H9585

TITHE (15) [TEN]
Lev 27:30 " 'A **t** *of* everything from the land, whether H5130
Lev 27:31 redeem any of their **t** must add a fifth of H5130
Lev 27:32 Every **t** *of* the herd and flock—every tenth H5130
Nu 18:26 from the Israelites the **t** I give you as your H5130
Nu 18:26 a tenth of that **t** as the LORD's offering. H5130
Dt 12:17 your own towns the **t** *of* your grain and H5130
Dt 14:23 Eat the **t** *of* your grain, new wine and olive H5130
Dt 14:24 LORD your God and cannot carry **your t** H2257S
Dt 14:25 then exchange your **t** for silver, and take the NDT
Dt 26:12 the year of the **t**, you shall give it to H5130
2Ch 31:5 brought a great amount, a **t** *of* everything. H5130
2Ch 31:6 Judah also brought a **t** *of* their herds and H5130
2Ch 31:6 herds and flocks and a **t** *of* the holy things H5130

Ne 10:37 And we will bring a t *of* our crops to the H5130
Mal 3:10 Bring the whole t into the storehouse, that H5130

TITHES (16) [TEN]

Nu 18:21 to the Levites all the t in Israel as their H5130
Nu 18:24 their inheritance the t that the Israelites H5130
Nu 18:28 LORD from all the t you receive from the H5130
Nu 18:28 From **these** t you must give the LORD's H5647S
Dt 12: 6 sacrifices, your t and special gifts H5130
Dt 12:11 sacrifices, your t and special gifts H5130
Dt 14:28 bring all the t of that year's produce and H5130
2Ch 31:12 in the contributions, t and dedicated gifts. H5130
Ne 10:37 the Levites who **collect** *the* t in all the H6923
Ne 10:38 the Levites when they **receive** *the* t, H6923
Ne 10:38 bring a tenth of the t up to the house of H5130
Ne 12:44 the contributions, firstfruits and t. H5130
Ne 13: 5 also the t *of* grain, new wine and H5130
Ne 13:12 All Judah brought the t *of* grain, new H5130
Am 4: 4 every morning, your t every three years. H5130
Mal 3: 8 are we robbing you?' "In t and offerings. H5130

TITIUS (1) [JUSTUS]

Ac 18: 7 went next door to the house *of* T Justus, *G5517*

TITLE (1)

Isa 45: 4 by name and **bestow** *on* you **a** t **of honor**, H4033

TITTLE (KJV) LEAST STROKE OF A PEN

TITUS (14)

2Co 2:13 because I did not find my brother T there. *G5519*
2Co 7: 6 comforted us by the coming *of* T, *G5519*
2Co 7:13 delighted to see how happy T was, *G5519*
2Co 7:14 about you to T has proved to be true *G5519*
2Co 8: 6 So we urged T, just as he had earlier *G5519*
2Co 8:16 put into the heart *of* T the same concern I *G5519*
2Co 8:17 For T not only welcomed our appeal, but he NDT
2Co 8:23 As for T, he is my partner and co-worker *G5519*
2Co 12:18 I urged T to go to you and I sent our *G5519*
2Co 12:18 our brother with him. T did not exploit you *G5519*
Gal 2: 1 time with Barnabas. I took T along also. *G5519*
Gal 2: 3 Yet not even T, who was with me, was *G5519*
2Ti 4:10 has gone to Galatia, and T to Dalmatia. *G5519*
Titus 1: 4 *To* T, my true son in our common faith *G5519*

TIZITE (1)

1Ch 11:45 son of Shimri, his brother Joha the T, H9407

TO (21090) [TOWARD] See Index of Articles Etc.

TOAH (1)

1Ch 6:34 of Jeroham, the son of Eliel, the son of T, H9346

TOB (4)

Jdg 11: 3 his brothers and settled in the land of T, H3204
Jdg 11: 5 went to get Jephthah from the land of T. H3204
2Sa 10: 6 also twelve thousand men from T. H3204
2Sa 10: 8 the men of T and Maakah were by H3204

TOB-ADONIJAH (1)

2Ch 17: 8 Adonijah, Tobijah and T—and the priests H3207

TOBIAH (14) [TOBIAH'S]

Ezr 2:60 of Delaiah, T and Nekoda 652 H3209
Ne 2:10 the Horonite and T the Ammonite official H3209
Ne 2:19 T the Ammonite official and Geshem the H3209
Ne 4: 3 T the Ammonite, who was at his side H3209
Ne 4: 7 But when Sanballat, T, the Arabs, the H3209
Ne 6: 1 came to Sanballat, T, Geshem the Arab H3209
Ne 6:12 against me because T and Sanballat had H3209
Ne 6:14 Remember T and Sanballat, my God H3209
Ne 6:17 of Judah were sending many letters to T, H3209
Ne 6:17 replies from T kept coming to them. H3209
Ne 6:19 And T sent letters to intimidate me H3209
Ne 7:62 of Delaiah, T and Nekoda 642 H3209
Ne 13: 4 He was closely associated with T, H3209
Ne 13: 7 done in providing T a room in the courts H3209

TOBIAH'S (1) [TOBIAH]

Ne 13: 8 threw all T household goods out of H3209

TOBIJAH (3)

2Ch 17: 8 Adonijah, T and Tob-Adonijah—and the H3210
Zec 6:10 the exiles Heldai, T and Jedaiah, who H3209
Zec 6:14 be given to Heldai, T, Jedaiah and Hen H3209

TODAY (215)

Ge 4:14 T you are driving me from the land H2021+3427
Ge 19:37 is the father of the Moabites of t. H2021+3427
Ge 19:38 is the father of the Ammonites of t. H2021+3427
Ge 21:26 tell me, and I heard about it only t." H2021+3427
Ge 24:12 make me successful t, and show H2021+3427
Ge 24:42 "When I came to the spring t, H2021+3427
Ge 30:32 all your flocks t and remove from H2021+3427
Ge 31:43 Yet what can I do t about these H2021+3427
Ge 31:48 is a witness between you and me t." H2021+3427
Ge 40: 7 house, "Why do you look so sad t?" H2021+3427
Ge 41: 9 "T I am reminded of my H2021+3427
Ge 47:23 you and your land t for Pharaoh, H2021+3427
Ge 47:26 law ... still in force t— H2021+3427+2021+2296
Ex 2:18 "Why have you returned so early t?" H2021+3427
Ex 5:14 your quota of bricks yesterday or t, H2021+3427
Ex 13: 4 T, in the month of Aviv, you are H2021+3427
Ex 14:13 the LORD will bring you t. H2021+3427
Ex 14:13 Egyptians you see t you will never H2021+3427
Ex 16:25 "Eat it t," Moses said, "because H2021+3427
Ex 16:25 "because t is a sabbath to the LORD. H2021+3427
Ex 16:25 not find any of it on the ground t. H2021+3427
Ex 19:10 consecrate them t and tomorrow. H2021+3427
Ex 32:29 have been set apart to the LORD t, H2021+3427
Ex 34:11 Obey what I command you t. I will H2021+3427
Lev 8:34 been done t was H2021+3427+2021+2296
Lev 9: 4 For t the LORD will appear to you H2021+3427
Lev 10:19 "T they sacrificed their sin offering H2021+3427
Lev 10:19 if I had eaten the sin offering t?" H2021+3427
Dt 1:10 numbers so that t you are as H2021+3427
Dt 2:18 "T you are to pass by the region of H2021+3427
Dt 4: 4 the LORD your God are still alive t. H2021+3427
Dt 4: 8 of laws I am setting before you t? H2021+3427
Dt 4:38 inheritance, as it is t. H2021+3427+2021+2296
Dt 4:40 which I am giving you t, so that it H2021+3427
Dt 5: 1 laws I declare in your hearing t. H2021+3427
Dt 5: 3 with all of us who are alive here t. H2021+3427
Dt 5:24 T we have seen that a H2021+3427+2021+2296
Dt 6: 6 that I give you t are to be on your H2021+3427
Dt 6:24 alive, as is the case t. H2021+3427+2021+2296
Dt 7:11 decrees and laws I give you t. H2021+3427
Dt 8: 1 every command I am giving you t, H2021+3427
Dt 8:18 your ancestors, as it is t. H2021+3427+2021+2296
Dt 8:19 testify against you t that you will H2021+3427
Dt 9: 3 But be assured t that the LORD your H2021+3427
Dt 10: 8 name, as they still do t. H2021+3427+2021+2296
Dt 10:13 I am giving you t for your own good H2021+3427
Dt 10:15 the nations—as it is t. H2021+3427+2021+2296
Dt 11: 2 Remember t that your children were H2021+3427
Dt 11: 8 the commands I am giving you t, H2021+3427
Dt 11:13 the commands I am giving you t— H2021+3427
Dt 11:26 before you t a blessing and a H2021+3427
Dt 11:27 your God that I am giving you t; H2021+3427
Dt 11:28 I command you t by following other H2021+3427
Dt 11:32 and laws I am setting before you t. H2021+3427
Dt 12: 8 You are not to do as we do here t H2021+3427
Dt 13:18 I am giving you t and doing what is H2021+3427
Dt 15: 5 these commands I am giving you t. H2021+3427
Dt 15:15 is why I give you this command t. H2021+3427
Dt 19: 9 all these laws I command you t— H2021+3427
Dt 20: 3 T you are going into battle against H2021+3427
Dt 26: 3 "I declare t to the LORD your God H2021+3427
Dt 27: 1 these commands that I give you t. H2021+3427
Dt 27: 4 as I command you t, and coat them H2021+3427
Dt 27:10 and decrees that I give you t. H2021+3427
Dt 28: 1 all his commands I give you t, H2021+3427
Dt 28:14 any of the commands I give you t, H2021+3427
Dt 28:15 and decrees I am giving you t, H2021+3427
Dt 29:10 you are standing t in the presence H2021+3427
Dt 29:15 here with us t in the presence of H2021+3427
Dt 29:15 also with those who are not here t. H2021+3427
Dt 29:18 tribe among you t whose heart H2021+3427
Dt 30: 2 to everything I command you t, H2021+3427
Dt 30: 8 his commands I am giving you t. H2021+3427
Dt 30:11 I am commanding you t is not too H2021+3427
Dt 30:15 I set before you t life and prosperity H2021+3427
Dt 30:16 I command you t to love the LORD H2021+3427
Jos 3: 7 "T I will begin to exalt H2021+3427+2021+2296
Jos 5: 9 "T I have rolled away the reproach H2021+3427
Jos 7:25 bring trouble on you t." H2021+3427+2021+2296
Jos 14:10 So here I am t, eighty-five years H2021+3427
Jos 14:11 still as strong t as the day Moses H2021+3427
Jos 22:18 " 'If you rebel against the LORD t H2021+3427
Jos 22:29 away from him t by building an H2021+3427
Jos 22:31 "T we know that the LORD is with us H2021+3427
Jdg 9:18 But t you have revolted against my H2021+3427
Jdg 9:19 and his family t? H2021+3427+2021+2296
Jdg 12: 3 come up t to fight me H2021+3427+2021+2296
Jdg 21: 3 one tribe be missing from Israel t?" H2021+3427
Jdg 21: 6 "T one tribe is cut off from Israel," H2021+3427
Ru 2:19 asked her, "Where did you glean t? H2021+3427
Ru 2:19 of the man I worked with t is Boaz," H2021+3427
Ru 3:18 not rest until the matter is settled t." H2021+3427
Ru 4: 9 "T you are witnesses that I have H2021+3427
Ru 4:10 hometown. T you are witnesses!" H2021+3427
1Sa 4: 3 bring defeat on us t before the H2021+3427
1Sa 9: 9 the prophet of t used to be called a H2021+3427
1Sa 9:12 he has just come to our town t, for H2021+3427
1Sa 9:19 for t you are to eat with me H2021+3427
1Sa 10: 2 When you leave me t, you will H2021+3427
1Sa 11:13 will be put to death t, H2021+3427+2021+2296
1Sa 14:28 'Cursed be anyone who eats food t! H2021+3427
1Sa 14:30 the men had eaten t some of the H2021+3427
1Sa 14:38 out what sin has been committed t. H2021+3427
1Sa 14:41 you not answered your servant t? H2021+3427
1Sa 14:45 he did this t with God's H2021+3427+2021+2296
1Sa 15:28 of Israel from you t and has given it H2021+3427
1Sa 20:27 to the meal, either yesterday or t?" H2021+3427
1Sa 21: 5 How much more so t!" H2021+3427
1Sa 22: 8 for me, as he does t." H2021+3427+2021+2296
1Sa 22:13 for me, as he does t?" H2021+3427+2021+2296
1Sa 24:19 way you treated me t. H2021+3427+2021+2296
1Sa 25:32 sent you t to meet me. H2021+3427+2021+2296
1Sa 26: 8 "T God has delivered your enemy H2021+3427
1Sa 26:19 have driven me t from my share in H2021+3427
1Sa 26:21 my life precious t, H2021+3427+2021+2296
1Sa 26:23 LORD delivered you into my hands t, H2021+3427
1Sa 26:24 as I valued your life t, H2021+3427+2021+2296
1Sa 27:10 "Where did you go raiding t?" H2021+3427
1Sa 28:18 has done this to you t. H2021+3427+2021+2296
1Sa 29: 6 you came to me until t, H2021+3427+2021+2296
2Sa 3:39 And t, though I am the anointed H2021+3427
2Sa 6:20 Israel has distinguished himself t, H2021+3427
2Sa 14:22 "T your servant knows that he has H2021+3427
2Sa 15:20 And t shall I make you wander H2021+3427
2Sa 16: 3 'T the Israelites will restore to me H2021+3427
2Sa 16:12 instead of his curse t." H2021+3427+2021+2296
2Sa 18:20 one to take the news t," H2021+3427+2021+2296
2Sa 18:20 but you must not do so t H2021+3427+2021+2296
2Sa 18:31 vindicated you t by delivering you H2021+3427
2Sa 19: 5 "T you have humiliated all your H2021+3427
2Sa 19: 6 have made it clear t that the H2021+3427
2Sa 19: 6 were alive t and all of us were H2021+3427
2Sa 19:20 t I have come here as the first H2021+3427
2Sa 19:22 anyone be put to death in Israel t? H2021+3427
2Sa 19:22 Don't I know that t I am king over H2021+3427
1Ki 1:25 T he has gone down and sacrificed H2021+3427
1Ki 1:48 to see a successor on my throne t. H2021+3427
1Ki 1:51 swear to me t that he will not H2021+3427
1Ki 2:24 Adonijah shall be put to death t!" H2021+3427
1Ki 5: 7 "Praise be to the LORD t, for he has H2021+3427
1Ki 8: 8 and they are still there t. H2021+3427+2021+2296
1Ki 8:24 fulfilled it—as it is t. H2021+3427+2021+2296
1Ki 12: 7 "If t you will be a servant to these H2021+3427
1Ki 18:15 surely present myself to Ahab t." H2021+3427
1Ki 18:36 let it be known t that you are God H2021+3427
1Ki 20:13 I will give it into your hand t, and H2021+3427
2Ki 2: 3 to take your master from you t?" H2021+3427
2Ki 2: 5 to take your master from you t?" H2021+3427
2Ki 4:23 "Why go to him t?" he asked. "It's H2021+3427
2Ki 6:28 up your son so we may eat him t, H2021+3427
2Ki 6:31 remains on his shoulders t! H2021+3427
1Ch 29: 5 themselves to the LORD t? H2021+3427
2Ch 5: 9 and they are still there t. H2021+3427+2021+2296
2Ch 6:15 fulfilled it—as it is t. H2021+3427+2021+2296
Ezr 9: 7 foreign kings, as it is t. H2021+3427+2021+2296
Ne 1:11 servant success t by granting him H2021+3427
Ne 9:32 kings of Assyria until t. H2021+3427+2021+2296
Ne 9:36 we are slaves t, slaves in the H2021+3427
Est 5: 4 come t to a banquet I have H2021+3427
Job 23: 2 "Even t my complaint is bitter; his H2021+3427
Ps 2: 7 t I have become your father. H2021+3427
Ps 95: 7 under his care. T, if only you would H2021+3427
Ps 118:24 very day; let us rejoice t and be glad. H2257S
Pr 7:14 "T I fulfilled my vows, and I have H2021+3427
Pr 22:19 in the LORD, I teach you t, even you. H2021+3427
Isa 38:19 as I am doing t; parents tell H2021+3427
Isa 48: 7 you have not heard of them before t. H3427
Isa 56:12 And tomorrow will be like t, or H2296+3427
Isa 58: 4 fast as you do t and expect your H2021+3427
Jer 1:10 t I appoint you over H2021+3427+2021+2296
Jer 1:18 T I have made you a fortified city H2021+3427
Jer 11: 5 the land you possess t." H2021+3427+2021+2296
Jer 11: 7 up from Egypt until t, H2021+3427+2021+2296
Jer 25:18 a curse—as they are t; H2021+3427+2021+2296
Jer 40: 4 But t I am freeing you from the H2021+3427
Jer 42:19 Be sure of this: I warn you t H2021+3427
Jer 42:21 I have told you t, but you still have H2021+3427
Jer 44: 2 T they lie deserted and H2021+3427+2021+2296
Jer 44: 6 desolate ruins they are t. H2021+3427+2021+2296
Jer 44:22 inhabitants, as it is t. H2021+3427+2021+2296
Mt 6:11 Give us t our daily bread. *G4958*
Mt 6:30 which is here t and tomorrow is thrown *G4958*
Mt 16: 3 in the morning, 'T it will be stormy, for *G4958*
Mt 21:28 'Son, go and work t in the vineyard. *G4958*
Mt 27:19 a great deal t in a dream because of *G4958*
Mk 14:30 Jesus answered, "t—yes, tonight—before *G4958*
Lk 2:11 T in the town of David a Savior has been *G4958*
Lk 4:21 "T this scripture is fulfilled in your hearing." *G4958*
Lk 5:26 "We have seen remarkable things t." *G4958*
Lk 12:28 which is here t, and tomorrow is *G4958*
Lk 13:32 healing people t and tomorrow, *G4958*
Lk 13:33 I must press on t and tomorrow and the *G4958*
Lk 19: 5 I must stay at your house t." *G4958*
Lk 19: 9 "T salvation has come to this house *G4958*
Lk 22:34 before the rooster crows t, you will deny *G4958*
Lk 22:61 "Before the rooster crows t, you will *G4958*
Lk 23:43 tell you, t you will be with me in paradise." *G4958*
Ac 4: 9 called to account t for an act of kindness *G4958*
Ac 13:33 are my son; t I have become your father. *G4958*
Ac 19:40 with rioting because of what happened t. *G4958*
Ac 20:26 to you t that I am *G1877+3836+4958+2465*
Ac 22: 3 as zealous for God as any of you are t. *G4958*
Ac 24:21 of the dead that I am on trial before you t. *G4958*
Ac 26: 2 to stand before you t as I make my *G4958*
Ac 26: 6 promised our ancestors that I am on trial t. NDT
Ac 26:29 are listening to me t may become what I *G4958*
Heb 1: 5 are my Son; t I have become your Father"? *G4958*
Heb 3: 7 Holy Spirit says: "T, if you hear his voice *G4958*
Heb 3:13 as long as it is called "T," so that none of *G4958*
Heb 3:15 "T, if you hear his voice, do not harden *G4958*
Heb 4: 7 calling it "T." This he did when a *G4958*
Heb 4: 7 "T, if you hear his voice, do not harden *G4958*
Heb 5: 5 are my Son; t I have become your Father." *G4958*
Heb 13: 8 is the same yesterday and t and forever. *G4958*
Jas 4:13 "T or tomorrow we will go to this or that *G4958*

TOE (5) [TOES]

Lev 8:23 right hand and on the **big** t *of* his right foot. H991
Lev 14:14 hand and on the **big** t *of* their right foot. H991
Lev 14:17 hand and on the **big** t *of* their right foot, H991
Lev 14:25 hand and on the **big** t *of* their right foot. H991

T

Lev 14:28 hand and on the **big t** *of* their right foot. H991

TOES (8) [TOE]

Ex 29:20 and on the **big t** *of* their right feet. H991
Lev 8:24 hands and on the **big t** *of* their right feet. H991
Jdg 1: 6 and cut off his thumbs and **big t**. H8079
Jdg 1: 7 their thumbs and **big t** cut off have picked H8079
2Sa 21:20 on each hand and six **t** *on* each foot— H720
1Ch 20: 6 on each hand and six **t** on each foot— NDT
Da 2:41 that the feet and **t** were partly of baked A10064
Da 2:42 As the **t** were partly iron and A10064+10655

TOGARMAH (2) [BETH TOGARMAH]

Ge 10: 3 sons of Gomer: Ashkenaz, Riphath and **T**. H9328
1Ch 1: 6 sons of Gomer: Ashkenaz, Riphath and **T**. H9328

TOGETHER (394) [ALTOGETHER]

Ge 3: 7 so *they* **sewed** fig leaves **t** and made H9529
Ge 7:13 **t with** his wife and the wives of his three H2256
Ge 8:18 **t with** his sons and his wife and his sons' H2256
Ge 11:31 **t** they set out from Ur of the Chaldeans H907
Ge 13: 6 not support them while they stayed **t**, H3481
Ge 13: 6 so great that they were not able to stay **t**. H3481
Ge 14:16 **t with** the women and the other H2256+1685
Ge 22: 6 As the two of them went on **t**, H3481
Ge 22: 8 And the two of them went on **t**. H3481
Ge 22:19 servants, and they set off **t** for Beersheba. H3481
Ge 29:22 So Laban **brought t** all the people of the H665
Ge 36: 7 were too great for them to remain **t**; H3481
Ge 50:14 **t with** his brothers and all the others who H2256
Ex 4:29 Moses and Aaron **brought t** all the elders H665
Ex 18: 5 father-in-law, **t with** Moses' sons and wife H2256
Ex 19: 8 The people all responded **t**, "We will do H3481
Ex 26: 3 Join five of the curtains **t**, and do H851+448+295
Ex 26: 6 fasten the curtains **t** so that the H851+448+295
Ex 26: 9 **Join** five of the curtains **t** into one set and H2489
Ex 26:11 in the loops *to* **fasten** the tent **t** as a unit. H2489
Ex 36:10 of the curtains **t** and did the H285+448+285
Ex 36:13 two sets of curtains **t** so that the H448+285+285
Ex 36:18 clasps to **fasten** the tent **t** as a unit. H2489
Lev 2: 2 the flour and oil, **t with** all the incense H6584
Lev 2:16 grain and the oil, **t with** all the incense H6584
Lev 6:15 **t with** all the incense on the grain offering H2256
Lev 7:30 to bring the fat, **t with** the breast, and H6584
Lev 9: 4 **t with** a grain offering mixed with olive oil. H2256
Lev 14: 6 bird and dip it, **t with** the cedar wood, the H2256
Lev 14:20 it on the altar, **t with** the grain offering H2256
Lev 14:21 **t with** a tenth of an ephah of the finest H2256
Lev 14:24 the guilt offering, **t with** the log of oil, and H2256
Lev 14:31 a burnt offering, **t with** the grain offering. H6584
Lev 20: 5 off from their people **t** with all who follow H2256
Lev 23:13 **t with** its grain offering of two-tenths of an H2256
Lev 23:18 **t with** their grain offerings and drink H2256
Lev 23:20 offering, **t with** the bread of the firstfruits. H6584
Nu 1:18 and *they* **called** the whole community **t** on H7735
Nu 4: 9 that is for light, **t with** its lamps, its wick H2256
Nu 6:15 **t with** their grain offerings and drink H2256
Nu 6:17 **t with** its grain offering and drink offering. H2256
Nu 6:20 **t with** the breast that was waved and the H6584
Nu 7:87 a year old, **t with** their grain offering. H2256
Nu 9:11 **t with** unleavened bread and bitter herbs. H6584
Nu 10: 2 them for **calling** the community **t** and for H5246
Nu 11:24 *He* **brought t** seventy of their elders and H665
Nu 14:35 which *has* **banded t** against me. H3585
Nu 16:11 you and all your followers *have* **banded t**. H3585
Nu 16:32 with Korah, **t with** their possessions. H2256
Nu 20: 8 your brother Aaron **gather** the assembly **t**. H7735
Nu 20:10 Aaron **gathered** the assembly **t** in front H7735
Nu 21:16 "**Gather** the people **t** and I will give them H665
Nu 21:35 **t with** his sons and his whole army H2256
Nu 24:10 *He* **struck** his hands **t** and said to him, "I H6215
Nu 27: 3 followers, who **banded t** against the LORD H3585
Nu 28: 5 **t with** a grain offering of a tenth of an H2256
Nu 28: 9 **t with** its drink offering and a grain H2256
Nu 28:31 Offer these **t with** their drink offerings, in H2256
Nu 35: 7 **t with** their pasturelands. H2256
Dt 2:33 down, **t with** his sons and his whole army. H2256
Dt 3:12 the hill country of Gilead, **t with** its towns. H2256
Dt 22:10 not plow with an ox and a donkey yoked **t**. H3481
Dt 22:11 wear clothes of wool and linen woven **t**. H3481
Dt 25: 5 brothers are living **t** and one of them dies H3481
Dt 29:11 **t** with your children and your wives, and the NDT
Jos 4: 4 So Joshua **called t** the twelve men he had H7924
Jos 7:24 Then Joshua, **t with** all Israel, took Achan H6640
Jos 9: 2 *they* **came t** to wage war against H7695+3481
Jos 10:37 put it to the sword, **t with** its king, its H2256
Jos 10:40 the mountain slopes, **t with** all their kings. H2256
Jos 11: 5 forces and made camp **t** at the Waters of H3481
Jos 15:46 vicinity of Ashdod, **t with** their villages; H2256
Jos 17:11 **t with** their surrounding settlements H2256
Jos 21:16 Beth Shemesh, **t with** their pasturelands H2256
Jos 21:18 Almon, **t with** their pasturelands H2256
Jos 21:19 came to thirteen, **t with** their pasturelands. H2256
Jos 21:22 Beth Horon, **t with** their pasturelands H2256
Jos 21:24 Gath Rimmon, **t with** their pasturelands H2256
Jos 21:25 Gath Rimmon, **t with** their pasturelands H2256
Jos 21:27 Be Eshterah, **t with** their pasturelands H2256
Jos 21:29 En Gannim, **t with** their pasturelands H2256
Jos 21:31 Rehob, **t with** their pasturelands H2256
Jos 21:32 Dor and Kartan, **t with** their pasturelands H2256
Jos 21:33 to thirteen, **t with** their pasturelands. H2256
Jos 21:35 Nahalal, **t with** their pasturelands H2256
Jos 21:37 Mephaath, **t with** their pasturelands H2256
Jos 21:39 Jazer, **t with** their pasturelands H2256
Jos 21:41 forty-eight in all, **t with** their pasturelands. H2256
Jdg 12: 4 Jephthah then **called t** the men of Gilead H7695
Jdg 13:19 a young goat, **t with** the grain offering H2256
Jdg 14: 5 down to Timnah **t with** his father and H2256
Jdg 15: 5 **t with** the vineyards and olive H2256+6330
Jdg 16: 3 of the city gate, **t with** the two posts, and H2256
Jdg 18:22 near Micah **were called t** and overtook H2410
Jdg 19: 6 two of them sat down to eat and drink **t**. H3481
Jdg 19: 8 So the two of them ate **t**. NDT
Jdg 20: 1 the land of Gilead **came t** as one and H3655
Jdg 20: 8 All the men **rose up** *t* as one, saying, "None AIT
Jdg 20:11 So all the Israelites **got t** and united as one H665
Jdg 20:14 their towns they **came t** at Gibeah to fight H665
Ru 1: 1 in Judah, **t with** his wife and two sons H2256
Ru 4:11 who **t** built up the family of Israel. H9109
1Sa 5: 8 So *they* **called t** all the rulers H8938+2256+665
1Sa 5:11 So *they* **called t** all the rulers H8938+2256+665
1Sa 6:15 **t with** the chest containing the gold H2256
1Sa 8: 4 elders of Israel **gathered t** and came to H7695
1Sa 9:26 got ready, he and Samuel went outside **t**. H9109
1Sa 11: 7 the people, and *they* **came out t** as one. H3655
1Sa 11:11 so that no two of them were left **t**. H3480
1Sa 14:32 ground and ate them, **t with** the blood. H6584
1Sa 20:11 out into the field." So they went there **t**. H9109
1Sa 20:41 each other and wept **t**— H408+907+8276+2084
1Sa 31: 6 all his men died **t** that same day. H3481
2Sa 2:12 **t with** the men of Ish-Bosheth son of Saul H2256
2Sa 2:16 his opponent's side, and they fell down **t**. H3481
2Sa 6: 1 David again **brought t** all the able young H665
2Sa 19:41 across the Jordan, **t with** all his men?" H6640
2Sa 20:14 *who* **gathered t** and followed him. H7735
2Sa 21: 8 **t with** the five sons of Saul's daughter H2256
2Sa 21: 9 All seven of them fell **t**; they were put to H3480
2Sa 23:11 **banded t** at a place H665+4200+2021+2653
1Ki 8: 2 All the Israelites **came t** to King Solomon H7735
1Ki 22: 6 the king of Israel **brought t** the prophets— H7695
2Ki 2:11 As they were **walking along** and talking *t* AIT
2Ki 3:10 "*Has* the LORD **called** us three kings **t** only H7924
2Ki 3:13 the LORD *who* **called** us three kings **t** to H7924
2Ki 9: 5 he found the army officers sitting **t**. NDT
2Ki 9:25 you and I were riding **t** in chariots behind H7538
2Ki 10:18 Jehu **brought** all the people **t** and said H7695
2Ki 11:19 and *t they* **brought** the king **down** from the AIT
2Ki 23: 1 Then the king **called t** all the H8938+2256+665
2Ki 25:26 to the greatest, **t with** the army officers H2256
1Ch 6:33 are the men who served, **t with** their sons: H2256
1Ch 6:59 Beth Shemesh, **t with** their pasturelands. H2256
1Ch 6:60 Anathoth, **t with** their pasturelands. H2256
1Ch 6:69 Gath Rimmon, **t with** their pasturelands. H2256
1Ch 6:70 Bileam, **t with** their pasturelands H2256
1Ch 6:71 also Ashtaroth, **t with** their pasturelands H2256
1Ch 6:73 Anem, **t with** their pasturelands H2256
1Ch 6:75 Rehob, **t with** their pasturelands H2256
1Ch 6:76 Kiriathaim, **t with** their pasturelands. H2256
1Ch 6:77 Tabor, **t with** their pasturelands H2256
1Ch 6:79 Mephaath, **t with** their pasturelands; H2256
1Ch 6:81 Jazer, **t with** their pasturelands. H2256
1Ch 7:29 Megiddo and Dor, **t with** their villages. H2256
1Ch 10: 6 three sons died, and all his house died **t**. H3481
1Ch 11: 1 All Israel **came t** to David at Hebron and H7695
1Ch 11:10 **t with** all Israel, gave his kingship H6640
1Ch 12:34 **t with** 37,000 men carrying shields and H6640
1Ch 15: 4 *He* **called t** the descendants of Aaron and H665
1Ch 23: 2 *He* also **gathered t** all the leaders of Israel H665
1Ch 25: 1 **t with** the commanders of the army H2256
1Ch 28: 1 his sons, **t with** the palace officials H6640
1Ch 29:21 male lambs, **t with** their drink offerings H2256
1Ch 29:30 **t with** the details of his reign and power H6640
2Ch 3:15 which **t** were thirty-five cubits long NDT
2Ch 5: 3 all the Israelites **came t** to the king at the H7735
2Ch 18: 5 the king of Israel **brought t** the prophets— H7695
2Ch 20: 4 people of Judah **came t** to seek help from H7695
2Ch 21:17 palace, **t with** his sons and wives. H2256+1685
2Ch 24: 5 *He* **called t** the priests and Levites and H7695
2Ch 25: 5 **called** the people of Judah **t** and H7695
2Ch 25:24 **t with** the palace treasures and the H2256
2Ch 28:24 Ahaz **gathered t** the furnishings from the H665
2Ch 29:20 **gathered** the city officials **t** and went H665
2Ch 29:35 **t with** the fat of the fellowship offerings H928
2Ch 34:29 Then the king **called t** all the H8938+2256+665
2Ch 36:10 **t with** articles of value from the temple of H6640
Ezr 3: 1 the people **assembled t** as one in H665
Ezr 3: 9 **joined t** in supervising those H6641+3869+285
Ezr 4: 9 **t with** the rest of their associates A10221
Ezr 6:21 **t with** all who had separated themselves H2256
Ezr 7:16 **t with** all the silver and gold you may A10221
Ezr 7:17 **t with** their grain offerings and drink A10221
Ezr 8:19 **t with** Jeshaiah from the descendants of H907
Ne 4: 8 They all plotted **t** to come and fight H3481
Ne 5: 7 So *I* **called t** a large meeting to deal with H5989
Ne 6: 2 let us meet **t** in one of the villages on the H3481
Ne 6: 7 back to the king; so come, let us meet **t**." H3481
Ne 8: 1 all the people **came t** as one in the square H665
Ne 9: 1 the Israelites **gathered t**, fasting and H665
Ne 10:28 **t** with their wives and all their sons and NDT
Ne 12: 8 **t with** his associates, was in charge H2256
Ne 12:28 musicians also **were brought t** from the H665
Ne 12:38 on top of the wall, **t with** half the people H2256
Ne 12:40 so did I, **t with** half the officials, H6640
Ne 13:11 Then *I* **called** them **t** and stationed them H7695
Ne 13:15 it on donkeys, **t with** wine, grapes, H2256+677
Est 4:16 **gather t** all the Jews who are in Susa H4043
Est 5: 4 "let the king, **t with** Haman, come today H2256
Est 5:10 **Calling t** his friends and H8938+2256+995
Est 9:15 The Jews in Susa **came t** on the fourteenth H7735
Est 10: 2 **t with** a full account of the greatness of H2256
Job 2:11 homes and met **t** by agreement to go H3481
Job 9:33 between us, someone to bring us **t**, H9109
Job 10:11 flesh and **knit** me **t** with bones and H6115
Job 16:10 my cheek in scorn and unite **t** against me. H3480
Job 17:16 Will we descend **t** into the dust?" H3480
Job 34: 4 what is right; let us learn **t** what is good. H1068
Job 34:15 would perish **t** and mankind would H3480
Job 38: 7 morning stars sang **t** and all the angels H3480
Job 38:38 hard and the clods of earth **stick t**? H1815
Job 40:13 Bury them all in the dust **t**; shroud their H3480
Job 41:15 has rows of shields tightly **sealed t**; H6037+2597
Job 41:17 *they* **cling t** and cannot be parted. H4334
Ps 2: 2 the rulers band **t** against the LORD and H3480
Ps 34: 3 the LORD with me; let us exalt his name **t**. H3481
Ps 41: 7 All my enemies whisper **t** against me H3480
Ps 48: 4 joined forces, when they advanced **t**, H3481
Ps 62: 9 they are nothing; **t** they are only a breath. H3480
Ps 71:10 those who wait to kill me conspire **t**. H3481
Ps 83: 5 With one mind they plot **t**; they form an H3481
Ps 85:10 Love and faithfulness **meet t** H7008
Ps 94:21 The wicked **band t** against the righteous H1518
Ps 98: 8 let the mountains sing **t** for joy; H3480
Ps 119:23 Though rulers **sit** *t* and slander me, your AIT
Ps 122: 3 built like a city that is closely compacted **t**. H3481
Ps 133: 1 it is when God's people live **t in unity**! H3480
Ps 139:13 *you* **knit** me **t** in my mother's womb. H6115
Ps 139:15 *when I* **was woven t** in the depths of the H8387
Pr 8:12 wisdom, **dwell** *t with* prudence; I possess AIT
Pr 30:27 have no king, yet they advance **t** in ranks; H3972
Ecc 4:11 if two **lie down** *t*, they will keep warm AIT
Isa 1:31 both will burn **t**, with no one to H3481
Isa 9:21 Manasseh; **t** they will turn against Judah. H3481
Isa 11: 6 the calf and the lion and the yearling **t** H3481
Isa 11: 7 their young will lie down **t**, and the lion H3481
Isa 11:14 **t** they will plunder the people to the east. H3481
Isa 13: 4 the kingdoms, like nations **massing t**! H665
Isa 16: 7 the Moabites wail, they wail **t** for Moab. H3972
Isa 19:23 The Egyptians **and** Assyrians will worship **t** H907
Isa 22: 3 All your leaders have fled **t**; they have H3480
Isa 22: 3 who were caught were taken prisoner **t**, H3481
Isa 24:22 *They will* **be herded t** like prisoners H665+669
Isa 31: 3 who are helped will fall; all will perish **t**. H3481
Isa 31: 4 band of shepherds **is called t** against it, H7924
Isa 34:16 and his Spirit *will* **gather** them **t**. H7695
Isa 40: 5 be revealed, and all people will see it **t**. H3481
Isa 41: 1 let us meet **t** at the place of judgment. H3481
Isa 41:19 in the wasteland, the fir and the cypress **t**, H3481
Isa 43: 9 All the nations gather **t** and the peoples H3481
Isa 43:17 the army and reinforcements **t**, and they H3481
Isa 43:26 let us argue the matter **t**; state the case H3480
Isa 44:11 *Let* them all **come t** and take their stand H7695
Isa 45:16 disgraced; they will go off into disgrace **t**. H3481
Isa 45:20 "**Gather t** and come; assemble, you H7695
Isa 45:21 present it—let them take counsel **t**. H3481
Isa 46: 2 They stoop and bow down **t**; unable to H3481
Isa 48:13 when I summon them, they all stand up **t**. H3481
Isa 48:14 "**Come t**, all of you, and listen: Which of H7695
Isa 52: 8 lift up their voices; **t** they shout for joy. H3481
Isa 52: 9 Burst into songs of joy **t**, you ruins of H3481
Isa 60:13 the fir and the cypress **t**, to adorn my H3481
Isa 65:25 The wolf and the lamb will feed **t** H3869+285
Isa 66:17 will meet their end **t** with the one they H3481
Jer 3:18 **t** they will come from a northern land H3481
Jer 4: 5 aloud and say: '**Gather t**! Let us flee to the H665
Jer 6:11 street and on the young men gathered **t**; H3481
Jer 6:12 **t with** their fields and their wives H3481
Jer 8:14 we sitting here? **Gather t**! Let us flee to the H665
Jer 17: 3 away as plunder, **t** with your high places NDT
Jer 31:24 People will live **t** in Judah and all its H3481
Jer 41: 1 While they were eating **t** there, H3481
Jer 42: 8 So *he* **called t** Johanan son of Kareah and H7924
Jer 46:12 over another; both will fall down **t**. H3481
Jer 46:21 They too will turn and flee **t**, they will not H3481
Jer 48: 7 into exile, **t with** his priests and officials. H3481
Jer 49: 3 go into exile, **t** with his priests and officials. NDT
Jer 50: 4 the people of Judah **t** will go in tears to H3481
La 1:14 by his hands *they were* **woven t**. H8571
La 2: 8 walls lament; **t** they wasted away. H3481
La 2:21 "Young and old **lie** *t* in the dust of the streets; AIT
Eze 6:11 **Strike** your hands **t** and stamp your feet H5782
Eze 21:14 and strike your **hands t**. H4090+448+4090
Eze 21:17 I too will strike my **hands t** H4090+448+4090
Eze 22:13 " '*I will* surely **strike** my hands **t** at the H5782
Eze 33:30 your people *are* **talking t** about you by the H1819
Eze 37: 7 the bones **came t**, bone to bone. H7928
Eze 37:17 Join them **t** into one stick so that H285+448+285
Eze 39:17 'Assemble and come **t** from all around to H665
Da 11: 6 **t with** her royal escort and her father and H2256
Hos 1:11 the people of Israel *will* **come t**; H7695+3481
Hos 7:12 When I hear them **flocking t**, I will catch H6337
Hos 8:10 the nations, *I will* now **gather** them **t**. H7695
Joel 2:16 the assembly; **bring t** the elders, gather H7695
Am 1:15 he and his officials **t**," says the LORD. H3481
Am 3: 3 Do two walk **t** unless they have agreed to H3481
Mic 2:12 *I will* **surely bring t** the remnant of H7695+7695
Mic 2:12 I will bring them **t** like sheep in a pen H3480

Mic 7: 3 dictate what they desire—*they all* **conspire** *t*. AIT
Zep 2: 1 **Gather** t, gather yourselves together, you H8006
Zep 2: 1 together, **gather** *yourselves* t, you H8006
Zec 7: 2 Regem-Melek, **t with** their men, to H2256
Zec 10: 5 **T** they will be like warriors in battle H3481
Mt 1:18 before they **came** t, she was found to *G5302*
Mt 2: 4 *When he had* **called** t all the people's *G5251*
Mt 5:25 Do it while you are still t on the way, or *G3552*
Mt 13:30 Let both **grow** t until the harvest. At that *G5277*
Mt 17:22 *When* they **came** t in Galilee, he said to *G5370*
Mt 19: 6 Therefore what God *has joined* t, let no *G5183*
Mt 20:25 Jesus **called** them t and said, "You know *G4673*
Mt 22:34 the Pharisees **got** t. *G5251+2093+3836+899*
Mt 22:41 *While* the Pharisees *were* **gathered t** *G5251*
Mt 23:37 I have longed *to* **gather** your children t, *G2190*
Mt 27:29 then **twisted t** a crown of thorns and *G4428*
Mk 10: 9 Therefore what God *has* **joined** t, let no *G5183*
Mk 10:42 Jesus **called** them t and said, "You know *G4673*
Mk 10:46 his disciples, **t with** a large crowd *G2779*
Mk 14:53 elders and the teachers of the law **came** t. *G5302*
Mk 15:16 and **called** t the whole company of *G5157*
Mk 15:17 then **twisted** t a crown of thorns and set it *G4428*
Lk 6:38 pressed down, **shaken** t and running over *G4888*
Lk 9: 1 *When* Jesus *had* **called** the Twelve **t**, he *G5157*
Lk 13:34 I have longed *to* **gather** your children t, *G2190*
Lk 15: 6 *he* **calls** his friends and neighbors t and *G5157*
Lk 15: 9 *she* **calls** her friends and neighbors t and *G5157*
Lk 15:13 the younger son **got** t all he had, set off *G5251*
Lk 17:35 will be grinding grain t; *G2093+3836+899*
Lk 20: 1 of the law, **t with** the elders, came up *G5250*
Lk 22:55 of the courtyard and *had* **sat down** t, *G5154*
Lk 22:66 of the law, **met** t, and Jesus was led *G5251*
Lk 23:13 Pilate **called** t the chief priests, the rulers *G5157*
Lk 24:17 you discussing t as you walk along?" *G4639+253*
Lk 24:33 Eleven and those with them, **assembled** t *G125*
Jn 4:36 the sower and the reaper may be glad t. *G3938*
Jn 11:52 *to* **bring** them t and make them one. *G5251*
Jn 18:20 at the temple, where all the Jews **come** t. *G5302*
Jn 19: 2 The soldiers **twisted** t a crown of thorns *G4428*
Jn 20:19 when the disciples were t, with the doors *G3963*
Jn 21: 2 Zebedee, and two other disciples were t. *G3938*
Ac 1:14 They all joined t constantly in prayer *G3924*
Ac 2: 1 they were all t in one place. *G3938*
Ac 2: 6 a crowd **came** t in bewilderment *G5302*
Ac 2:44 believers were t and had *G2093+3836+899*
Ac 2:46 continued to meet t in the temple courts. *G3924*
Ac 2:46 homes and **ate** t with glad and *G3561+5575*
Ac 4:15 the Sanhedrin and then conferred t. *G4639+253*
Ac 4:24 they raised their voices t in prayer to God. *G3924*
Ac 4:26 the rulers band t against the *G2093+3836+899*
Ac 4:27 Pontius Pilate **met** t with the Gentiles *G5251*
Ac 5: 1 named Ananias, **t with** his wife Sapphira *G5250*
Ac 5:12 used to meet t in Solomon's Colonnade *G3924*
Ac 5:21 *they* **called** t the Sanhedrin—the *G5157*
Ac 6: 2 Twelve **gathered** all the disciples t and *G4673*
Ac 10:24 them and *had* **called** t his relatives and *G5157*
Ac 12:20 they now **joined** t and sought an *G3924*
Ac 14: 5 Gentiles and Jews, **t with** their leaders, to *G5250*
Ac 14:27 *they* **gathered** the church t and reported *G5251*
Ac 15:30 where *they* **gathered** the church t and *G5251*
Ac 19:19 sorcery **brought** their scrolls t and burned *G5237*
Ac 19:25 *He* **called** them t, along with the workers *G5255*
Ac 19:29 and **all** of them rushed into the theater t. *G3924*
Ac 20: 7 of the week we **came** t to break bread. *G5251*
Ac 27:17 ropes **under** the ship itself to **hold** it t. *G5690*
Ac 28:17 days later he **called** t the local Jewish *G5157*
Ro 3:12 turned away, they have t become worthless *G275*
1Co 1: 2 **t with** all those everywhere who call on *G5250*
1Co 3:17 temple is sacred, and **you** *t* are that temple. AIT
1Co 7: 5 Then come t again so that *G2093+3836+899*
1Co 11:18 I hear *that when* you **come** t as a church *G5302*
1Co 11:20 *when* you **come** t, it *G5302+2093+3836+899*
1Co 11:33 you gather to eat, *you should* all eat t. *G1683*
1Co 11:34 so that *when you* **meet** t it may not result *G5302*
1Co 12:24 But God *has* **put** the body t, giving greater *G5166*
1Co 14:23 church **comes** t and *G5302+2093+3836+899*
1Co 14:26 When *you* **come** t, each of you has a *G5302*
2Co 1: 1 **t with** all his holy people throughout *G5250*
2Co 6:14 Do not be **yoked** t with unbelievers. *G2282*
Eph 2:21 the whole building *is* **joined** t and rises to *G5274*
Eph 2:22 him you too *are being* **built** t to become a *G5325*
Eph 3: 6 gospel the Gentiles are **heirs** t with Israel, *G5169*
Eph 3: 6 **members t of one body**, and *G5362*
Eph 3: 6 and **sharers** t in the promise in Christ *G5212*
Eph 3:18 **t with** all the Lord's holy people *G5250*
Eph 4:16 joined and **held** t by every supporting *G5204*
Php 1: 1 **t with** the overseers and deacons: *G5250*
Php 1:27 **striving** t as one for the faith of the gospel *G5254*
Php 3:17 **Join t in following** my **example** *G5213+1181*
Col 1:17 all things, and in him all things **hold** t. *G5319*
Col 2:19 supported and **held** t by its ligaments *G5204*
Col 3:14 which **binds** them all t in perfect *G1639+5278*
1Th 4:17 left will be caught up t with them in the *G275*
1Th 5:10 awake or asleep, we may live t with him. *G275*
Heb 9:19 blood of calves, **t with** water, scarlet wool *G3552*
Heb 10:25 not giving up **meeting** t, as some are in *G2191*
Heb 11:40 us so that *only* **t with** us would they *G3590+6006*
Heb 13: 3 as if *you were* **t with** them **in prison**, *G5279*
Jas 2:22 his faith and his actions *were* **working** t, *G5300*
1Pe 5:13 is in Babylon, **chosen** t with you, sends *G5293*
3Jn 8 so that *we may* **work** t for the truth *G5301+1181*
Rev 8: 4 incense, *t with* the **prayers** of God's people AIT
Rev 16:16 Then *they* **gathered** the kings **t** to the *G5251*
Rev 19:17 **gather** t for the great supper of God, *G5251*
Rev 19:19 their armies **gathered** t to wage war *G5251*

TOHU (1)

1Sa 1: 1 of Elihu, the son of **T**, the son of Zuph, H9375

TOIL (25) [TOILED, TOILING, TOILSOME]

Ge 3:17 through **painful** t you will eat food from it H6779
Ge 5:29 the labor and **painful** t *of* our hands H6779
Ge 31:42 seen my hardship and the t *of* my hands, H3330
Dt 26: 7 saw our misery, t and oppression. H6662
Jos 24:13 land on which *you did* not t and cities you H3333
Pr 5:10 your wealth and your t enrich the house of H6776
Pr 10:22 brings wealth, without **painful** t for it. H6776
Ecc 1: 3 their labors at which *they* t under the sun? H6661
Ecc 2:10 and this was the reward for all my t. H6662
Ecc 2:19 over all the **fruit of** my t into which I have H6662
Ecc 2:22 get for all the t and anxious striving H6662
Ecc 2:24 drink and find satisfaction in their own t. H6662
Ecc 3: 9 What do workers gain from their t? H6665
Ecc 3:13 find satisfaction in all their t—this is H6662
Ecc 4: 4 And I saw that all t and all achievement H6662
Ecc 4: 6 two handfuls with t and chasing after the H6662
Ecc 4: 8 There was no end to his t, yet his eyes H6662
Ecc 5:15 nothing from their t that they can carry in H6662
Ecc 5:16 do they gain, since *they* t for the wind? H6661
Ecc 5:19 accept their lot and be happy in their t— H6662
Ecc 6: 7 Everyone's t is for their mouth, yet their H6662
Ecc 8:15 them in their t all the days of the H6662
Ecc 10:15 The t *of* fools wearies them; they do not H6662
La 5:13 Young men t *at* the millstones; boys H5951
1Th 2: 9 sisters, our t and hardship; we worked *G3160*

TOILED (7) [TOIL]

Job 20:18 **What** he t **for** he must give back uneaten H3334
Ps 105:44 they fell heir to **what** others had **t for**— H6662
Ecc 2:11 had done and what *I had* t to achieve, H6661
Ecc 2:18 all the things I had **t for** under the sun, H6665
Ecc 2:21 they own to another who *has* not t for it. H6661
Isa 62: 8 drink the new wine for which *you have* t; H3333
2Co 11:27 I have labored and t and have often gone *G3677*

TOILING (3) [TOIL]

Ps 127: 2 stay up late, t for food to eat—for he H6776
Ecc 4: 8 "For whom am I t," he asked, "and why H6665
2Th 3: 8 laboring and t so that we would not be a *G3677*

TOILSOME (3) [TOIL]

Ecc 2:20 despair over all my t labor under the sun. H6662
Ecc 5:18 satisfaction in their t labor under the sun H6662
Ecc 9: 9 in life and in your t labor under the sun. H6665

TOKEN (1)

1Ch 4:32 Rimmon, **T** and Ashan—five towns— H9421

TOKHATH (1)

2Ch 34:22 who was the wife of Shallum son of **T**, the H9534

TOLA (6) [TOLAITE]

Ge 46:13 The sons of Issachar: **T**, Puah, Jashub H9356
Nu 26:23 through **T**, the Tolaite clan; through Puah H9356
Jdg 10: 1 a man of Issachar named **T** son of Puah H9356
1Ch 7: 1 The sons of Issachar: **T**, Puah, Jashub H9356
1Ch 7: 2 The sons of **T**: Uzzi, Rephaiah, Jeriel H9356
1Ch 7: 2 the descendants of **T** listed as fighting H9356

TOLAD (1)

1Ch 4:29 Bilhan, Ezem, **T**, H9351

TOLAITE (1) [TOLA]

Nu 26:23 through Tola, the **T** clan; through Puah H9358

TOLD (451) [TELL]

Ge 3:11 he said, "Who t you that you were naked? H5583
Ge 9:22 his father naked and t his two brothers H5583
Ge 12: 4 as the LORD *had* t him; and Lot went H1819
Ge 16: 9 Then the angel of the LORD t her, "Go back H606
Ge 17:23 circumcised them, as God t him. H1819
Ge 20: 8 and when *he* t them all that H1819+928+265
Ge 22: 3 set out for the place God *had* t him *about*. H606
Ge 22: 9 reached the place God *had* t him *about*, H606
Ge 22:20 Some time later Abraham **was** t, "Milkah H5583
Ge 24:28 young woman ran and t her mother's H5583
Ge 24:33 will not eat until *I have* t you what I have H1819
Ge 24:66 Then the servant t Isaac all he had done. H6218
Ge 26:32 servants came and t him about the well H5583
Ge 27:19 I have done as *you* t me. Please sit up H1819
Ge 27:42 When Rebekah **was** t what her older son H5583
Ge 29:12 He *had* t Rachel that he was a relative of H5583
Ge 29:12 So she ran and t her father. H5583
Ge 29:13 there Jacob t him all these things. H6218
Ge 31:16 So do whatever God *has* t you." H606
Ge 31:22 the third day Laban **was** t that Jacob had H5583
Ge 37: 5 a dream, and when *he* t it to his brothers H5583
Ge 37: 9 another dream, and *he* t it to his brothers. H6218
Ge 37:10 When *he* t his father as well as his H6218
Ge 38:13 When Tamar **was** t, "Your father-in-law is H5583
Ge 38:24 About three months later Judah **was t** H5583
Ge 39: 8 *he* t her, "my master does not concern H606
Ge 39:17 Then *she* t him this story: "That Hebrew H1819
Ge 39:19 his master heard the story his wife t him, H1819
Ge 40: 9 the chief cupbearer t Joseph his dream. H6218
Ge 41: 8 Pharaoh t them his dreams, but no one H6218
Ge 41:12 *We* t him our dreams, and he interpreted H6218
Ge 41:24 *I* t this to the magicians, but none of them H606
Ge 41:55 Then Pharaoh t all the Egyptians, "Go to H606
Ge 42:14 "It is just as *I* t you: You are spies! H1819
Ge 42:29 *they* t him all that had happened to them. H5583
Ge 43:17 man did as Joseph t him and took the men H606
Ge 43:27 "How is your aged father *you* t me *about*? H606
Ge 43:29 youngest brother, the one *you* t me *about*?" H606
Ge 44:23 But *you* t your servants, 'Unless your H606
Ge 44:24 *we* t him what my lord had said. H5583
Ge 45:26 *They* t him, "Joseph is still alive! In fact H5583
Ge 45:27 But when *they* t him everything Joseph H1819
Ge 47: 1 Joseph went and t Pharaoh, "My father H5583
Ge 48: 1 Some time later Joseph *was* t, "Your father H606
Ge 48: 2 When Jacob *was* t, "Your son Joseph has H5583
Ex 1:17 what the king of Egypt *had* t them to do; H1819
Ex 4:23 and *I* t you, "Let my son go, so he may H606
Ex 4:28 t Aaron everything the LORD had sent him to say, and also *about* H5583
Ex 4:30 Aaron t them everything the LORD had H1819
Ex 5:16 given no straw, yet we *are* t, 'Make bricks! H606
Ex 5:19 they were in trouble *when* they *were* t, H606
Ex 14: 5 the king of Egypt **was** t that the people H5583
Ex 16: 9 Then Moses t Aaron, "Say to the entire H606
Ex 16:17 The Israelites did as they were t; some NDT
Ex 18: 8 Moses t his father-in-law *about* everything H6218
Ex 19: 9 Then Moses t the LORD what the people H5583
Ex 19:25 went down to the people and t them. H606
Ex 24: 3 Moses went and t the people all the H6218
Ex 32:24 So *I* t them, 'Whoever has any gold jewelry H606
Ex 34:34 he came out and t the Israelites what H1819
Lev 21:24 So Moses t this to Aaron and his sons H1819
Nu 4:49 was assigned his work and t what to carry. NDT
Nu 9: 4 So Moses t the Israelites to celebrate the H1819
Nu 11:24 Moses went out and t the people what H1819
Nu 11:27 A young man ran and t Moses, "Eldad H5583
Nu 22: 7 Balaam, *they* t him what Balak had said. H1819
Nu 26:65 For the LORD *had* t those Israelites they H606
Nu 29:40 Moses t the Israelites all that the LORD H606
Dt 1:18 And at that time *I* t you everything you H7422
Dt 1:21 the LORD, the God of your ancestors, t you. H1819
Dt 1:43 So *I* t you, but you would not listen. H1819
Dt 9:12 Then the LORD t me, "Go down from here at H606
Dt 10: 9 inheritance, as the LORD your God t them.) H1819
Dt 17:16 for the LORD *has* t you, "You are not H606
Dt 32:48 On that same day the LORD t Moses, H1819
Jos 2: 2 The king of Jericho **was** t, "Look, some of H606
Jos 2:23 son of Nun and t him everything that H6218
Jos 3: 5 Joshua t the people, "Consecrate H606
Jos 4: 8 as the LORD *had* t Joshua; and they H1819
Jos 7: 2 east of Bethel, and t them, "Go up and spy H606
Jos 9:24 **were clearly** t how the LORD H5583+5583
Jos 10:17 When Joshua **was** t that the five kings had H5583
Jdg 4:12 When *they* t Sisera that Barak son of H5583
Jdg 4:20 "Stand in the doorway of the tent," *he* t her. H606
Jdg 6:13 our ancestors t us *about* when they said, H6218
Jdg 6:27 of his servants and did as the LORD t him. H1819
Jdg 6:29 investigated, *they were* t, "Gideon son of H606
Jdg 7: 5 There the LORD t him, "Separate those who H606
Jdg 7:17 "Watch me," *he* t them. "Follow my lead H606
Jdg 8:23 But Gideon t them, "I will not rule over you H606
Jdg 9: 7 When Jotham was t *about* this, he H5583
Jdg 13: 6 the woman went to her husband and t him, H606
Jdg 13:13 "Your wife must do all that *I have* t her. H606
Jdg 13:23 shown us all these things or now t us this." H9048
Jdg 14: 6 But *he* t neither his father nor his mother H5583
Jdg 14:16 a riddle, but *you* haven't t me *the* **answer**." H5583
Jdg 14:17 So on the seventh day *he* finally t her H5583
Jdg 15: 6 *they were* t, "Samson, the Timnite's H606
Jdg 16: 2 The people of Gaza *were* t, "Samson is H606
Jdg 16:15 of me and haven't t me the secret of your H5583
Jdg 16:17 So *he* t her everything. "No razor has ever H5583
Jdg 16:18 Delilah saw that *he had* t her everything, H5583
Jdg 16:18 back once more; *he has* t me everything." H5583
Jdg 18: 2 all the Danites. *They* t them, "Go, explore H606
Jdg 18: 4 *He* t them what Micah had done for him H606
Ru 1:20 call me Naomi," *she* t them. "Call me Mara H606
Ru 2: 9 *I have* t the men not to lay a hand on you H7422
Ru 2:11 "I've **been** t all **about** what you H5583+5583
Ru 2:19 Ruth t her mother-in-law *about* the one H5583
Ru 3: 6 everything her mother-in-law t her to do. H7422
Ru 3:16 Then *she* t her everything Boaz had done H5583
1Sa 1:23 best to you," her husband Elkanah t her. H606
1Sa 3: 9 So Eli t Samuel, "Go and lie down, and if H606
1Sa 3:13 For *I* t him that I would judge his family H5583
1Sa 3:17 if you hide from me anything *he* t you." H1819
1Sa 3:18 So Samuel t him everything, hiding H5583
1Sa 4:13 the town and t what had happened, H5583
1Sa 4:16 He t Eli, "I have just come from the battle H606
1Sa 8: 7 And the LORD t him: "Listen to all that the H606
1Sa 8:10 Samuel t all the words of the LORD to the H606
1Sa 9:23 I gave you, the one *I* t you to lay aside." H606
1Sa 11: 9 *They* t the messengers who had come H606
1Sa 14:28 Then one of the soldiers t him, "Your H6699
1Sa 14:43 So Jonathan t him, "I tasted a little H5583
1Sa 15:12 meet Saul, but he **was** t, "Saul has gone H5583
1Sa 17:27 him what they had been saying and t him, H606
1Sa 18:20 when *they* t Saul *about* it, he was H5583
1Sa 18:24 Saul's servants t him what David had H5583
1Sa 18:26 When the attendants t David these things, H5583
1Sa 19: 1 Saul t his son Jonathan and all the H1819
1Sa 19: 7 called David and t him the whole H5583

1Sa 19:15 the men back to see David and **t** them, H606
1Sa 19:17 Michal **t** him, "He said to me, 'Let me get H606
1Sa 19:18 Samuel at Ramah and **t** him all that Saul H5583
1Sa 19:21 Saul *was* **t** *about* it, and he sent more men H5583
1Sa 21: 2 *I have* **t** them to meet me at a certain H3359
1Sa 22:21 He **t** David that Saul had killed the priests H5583
1Sa 23: 1 When David *was* **t**, "Look, the Philistines H5583
1Sa 23: 7 Saul *was* **t** that David had gone to Keilah H5583
1Sa 23:13 When Saul **was t** that David had escaped H5583
1Sa 23:25 when David *was* **t** *about* it, he went H5583
1Sa 24: 1 the Philistines, he *was* **t**, "David is in the H5583
1Sa 24:18 You *have* just now **t** me *about* the good H5583
1Sa 25:14 One of the servants **t** Abigail, Nabal's H5583
1Sa 25:19 Then *she* **t** her servants, "Go on ahead; I'll H606
1Sa 25:36 So *she* **t** him nothing at all until daybreak H5583
1Sa 25:37 was sober, his wife **t** him all these things H5583
1Sa 27: 4 When Saul **was t** that David had fled to H5583
1Sa 28:21 in my hands and did what *you* **t** me to do. H1819
2Sa 2: 4 When David *was* **t** that it was the men H5583
2Sa 3:23 he *was* **t** that Abner son of Ner had come H5583
2Sa 4:10 when someone **t** me, 'Saul is dead,' and H5583
2Sa 6:12 Now King David **was t**, "The LORD has H5583
2Sa 10: 5 When David **was t** *about* this, he sent H5583
2Sa 10:17 When David **was t** *of* this, he gathered all H5583
2Sa 11:10 David *was* **t**, "Uriah did not go home." H5583
2Sa 11:22 when he arrived *he* **t** David everything H5583
2Sa 11:25 David **t** the messenger, "Say this to Joab H606
2Sa 13:34 The watchman went and **t** the king, "I see H5583
2Sa 14:33 So Joab went to the king and **t** him this H5583
2Sa 15:13 A messenger came and **t** David, "The H606
2Sa 15:31 Now David *had been* **t**, "Ahithophel is H5583
2Sa 16:11 let him curse, for the LORD *has* **t** him to. H606
2Sa 17:15 Hushai **t** Zadok and Abiathar, the priests H606
2Sa 17:18 a young man saw them and **t** Absalom. H5583
2Sa 18: 2 The king **t** the troops, "I myself will surely H606
2Sa 18:10 had happened, *he* **t** Joab, "I just saw H5583
2Sa 18:11 Joab said to the man who *had* **t** him this H5583
2Sa 18:20 one to take the news today," Joab **t** him. H606
2Sa 19: 1 Joab **was t**, "The king is weeping and H5583
2Sa 19: 8 When the men *were* **t**, "The king is sitting H5583
2Sa 21:11 When David **was t** what Aiah's daughter H5583
1Ki 1:23 And the king *was* **t**, "Nathan the prophet is H5583
1Ki 1:51 Then Solomon **was t**, "Adonijah is afraid H5583
1Ki 2:29 King Solomon **was t** that Joab had fled to H5583
1Ki 2:39 and Shimei *was* **t**, "Your slaves are H5583
1Ki 2:41 When Solomon **was t** that Shimei had H5583
1Ki 5: 5 my God, as the LORD **t** my father David H1819
1Ki 10: 7 not even half **was t** me; in wisdom and H5583
1Ki 11: 2 about which the LORD *had* **t** the Israelites, H606
1Ki 13:11 whose sons came and **t** him all that the H6218
1Ki 13:11 *They* also **t** their father what he had said H6218
1Ki 13:17 I have been **t** by the word of the LORD: 'You H1821
1Ki 13:22 in the place where *he* **t** you not to eat H1819
1Ki 14: 2 the one *who* **t** me I would be king over this H1819
1Ki 14: 5 But the LORD *had* **t** Ahijah, "Jeroboam's wife H606
1Ki 17: 5 So he did what the LORD had **t** him. H1821
1Ki 17:15 went away and did as Elijah had **t** her. H1821
1Ki 18:16 Obadiah went to meet Ahab and **t** him, H5583
1Ki 18:43 look toward the sea," *he* **t** his servant. H606
1Ki 19: 1 Now Ahab **t** Jezebel everything Elijah had H5583
1Ki 20:28 of God came up and **t** the king of Israel, H606
1Ki 22:34 The king **t** his chariot driver, "Wheel H606
2Ki 1: 7 it who came to meet you and **t** you this?" H1819
2Ki 1:16 *He* **t** the king, "This is what the LORD says H1819
2Ki 4: 7 She went and **t** the man of God, and he H5583
2Ki 4:17 birth to a son, just as Elisha *had* **t** her. H1819
2Ki 4:19 His father **t** a servant, "Carry him to his H606
2Ki 4:27 hidden it from me and *has* not **t** me why." H5583
2Ki 4:31 went back to meet Elisha and **t** him, H5583
2Ki 5: 4 to his master and **t** him what the girl from H5583
2Ki 5:13 if the prophet *had* **t** you to do some great H1819
2Ki 5:14 as the man of God had **t** him, and his H1821
2Ki 6:19 Elisha **t** them, "This is not the road and this H606
2Ki 7:10 out to the city gatekeepers and **t** them, H5583
2Ki 8: 6 asked the woman about it, and *she* **t** him. H6218
2Ki 8: 7 When the king **was t**, "The man of God H5583
2Ki 8:14 "*He* **t** me that you would certainly recover." H606
2Ki 9:12 "Here is what *he* **t** me: 'This is what H606
2Ki 9:36 They went back and **t** Jehu, who said H5583
2Ki 10: 8 messenger arrived, *he* **t** Jehu, "They have H5583
2Ki 13:18 king took them. Elisha **t** him, "Strike the H606
2Ki 18:25 The LORD *himself* **t** me to march against this H606
2Ki 18:37 **t** him what the field commander had H5583
2Ki 19: 3 *They* **t** him, "This is what Hezekiah says H606
1Ch 15:16 David **t** the leaders of the Levites to H606
1Ch 19: 5 someone came and **t** David about the H5583
1Ch 19:17 When David **was t** *of* this, he gathered all H5583
2Ch 9: 6 the greatness of your wisdom **was t** me; H5583
2Ch 18:33 The king **t** the chariot driver, "Wheel H606
2Ch 19: 6 *He* **t** them, "Consider carefully what you do H606
2Ch 20: 2 Some people came and **t** Jehoshaphat H5583
2Ch 33:16 and **t** Judah to serve the LORD H606
2Ch 35:21 God *has* **t** me to hurry; so stop opposing H606
2Ch 35:23 King Josiah, and he **t** his officers, "Take me H606
Ezr 5:15 and *he* **t** him, 'Take these articles and A10042
Ezr 8:17 *I* **t** them what to say to Iddo H8492+928+7023
Ezr 8:22 the road, because *we had* **t** the king, "The H606
Ne 2:12 *I had* not **t** anyone what my God had put H5583
Ne 2:18 *I* also **t** them *about* the gracious hand of H5583
Ne 4:12 near them came and **t** us ten times over, H606
Ne 5: 7 *I* **t** them, "You are charging your own H606
Ne 8: 1 *They* **t** Ezra the teacher of the Law to bring H606
Ne 9:15 *you* **t** them to go in and take possession of H606
Ne 9:23 into the land that *you* **t** their parents to H606
Est 2:20 just as Mordecai *had* **t** her to do, H7422
Est 2:22 out about the plot and **t** Queen Esther, H5583
Est 3: 4 Therefore *they* **t** Haman *about* it to see H5583
Est 3: 4 for *he had* **t** them he was a Jew. H5583
Est 4: 4 came and **t** her *about* Mordecai, H5583
Est 4: 7 Mordecai **t** him everything that had H5583
Est 4: 8 he **t** him to instruct her to go into the NDT
Est 6:13 **t** Zeresh his wife and all his friends H6218
Est 8: 1 Esther *had* **t** how he was related to her. H5583
Job 37:20 *Should* he **be t** that I want to speak H6218
Job 42: 9 the Naamathite did what the LORD **t** them; H1819
Ps 22:30 generations *will* **be t** about the Lord. H6218
Ps 44: 1 our ancestors *have* **t** us what you did in H6218
Ps 52: T the Edomite had gone to Saul and **t** him: H5583
Ps 78: 3 things our ancestors *have* **t** us. H6218
Isa 7: 2 Now the house of David **was t**, "Aram has H5583
Isa 28:22 *has* **t** *me of* the destruction H9048+4946+907
Isa 36:10 The LORD *himself* **t** me to march against this H606
Isa 36:22 **t** him what the field commander had H5583
Isa 37: 3 *They* **t** him, "This is what Hezekiah says H606
Isa 40:21 *Has it* not **been t** you from the beginning H5583
Isa 41:26 Who **t** *of* this from the beginning, so we H5583
Isa 41:26 No *one* **t** *of* this, no one foretold it, no H5583
Isa 48: 5 Therefore *I* **t** you these things long ago H5583
Isa 52:15 For what they **were** not **t**, they will see H6218
Jer 4:11 time this people and Jerusalem *will* **be t**, H606
Jer 13: 5 hid it at Perath, as the LORD **t** me. H7422
Jer 13: 6 get the belt *I* **t** you to hide there. H7422
Jer 23:38 even though *I* **t** you that you H8938+4200+606
Jer 26:18 *He* **t** all the people of Judah, 'This is what H606
Jer 34: 6 the prophet **t** all this to Zedekiah H1819
Jer 36: 5 Then Jeremiah **t** Baruch, "I am restricted; H7422
Jer 36: 8 Jeremiah the prophet **t** him to do; H7422
Jer 36:13 After Micaiah **t** them everything he had H5583
Jer 38:27 and *he* **t** them everything the king had H5583
Jer 42:19 of Judah, the LORD *has* **t** you, 'Do not go to H1819
Jer 42:21 *I have* **t** you today, but you still have not H5583
Jer 45: 4 But the LORD has **t** me to say to you, 'This is NDT
Eze 11: 5 the LORD came on me, and *he* **t** me to say: H606
Eze 11:25 and *I* **t** the exiles everything the LORD had H1819
Da 1:10 the official **t** Daniel, "I am afraid of my H606
Da 4: 7 diviners came, I **t** them the dream, but A10042
Da 4: 8 into my presence and *I* **t** him the dream. A10042
Da 7: 5 It *was* **t**, 'Get up and eat A10042
Da 7:16 "So *he* **t** me and gave me the A10042
Hos 3: 3 Then *I* **t** her, "You are to live with me many H606
Hos 12:10 visions and **t parables** through them." H1948
Jnh 1:10 because *he had already* **t** them so.) H5583
Hab 1: 5 you would not believe, even if *you* **were t**. H6218
Zec 11:12 *I* **t** them, "If you think it best, give me my H606
Zec 13: 3 because *you have* **t** lies in the LORD's H1819
Mt 8:22 But Jesus **t** him, "Follow me, and let the *G3306*
Mt 9: 9 " *he* **t** him, and Matthew got up and *G3306*
Mt 12:47 Someone **t** him, "Your mother and *G3306*
Mt 13: 3 Then *he* **t** them many things in parables *G3281*
Mt 13:24 Jesus **t** them another parable: "The *G4192*
Mt 13:31 *He* **t** them another parable: "The kingdom *G4192*
Mt 13:33 *He* **t** them still another parable: "The *G3281*
Mt 14:12 Then they went and **t** Jesus. *G550*
Mt 15:35 *He* **t** the crowd to sit down on the ground. *G4133*
Mt 18:31 outraged and went and **t** their master *G1397*
Mt 20: 4 *He* **t** them, 'You also go and work in my *G3306*
Mt 20:31 The crowd **rebuked** them **and t** them to be *G2203*
Mt 22:13 "Then the king **t** the attendants, 'Tie him *G3306*
Mt 22:24 "Moses **t** us that if a man dies without *G3306*
Mt 24:25 *I have* **t** you **ahead of time**. *G4625*
Mt 26:13 what she has done *will* also *be* **t**, in *G3281*
Mt 26:31 Then Jesus **t** them, "This very night you *G3306*
Mt 28: 7 you will see him.' Now *I have* **t** you." *G3306*
Mt 28:16 mountain where Jesus *had* **t** them to go. *G5435*
Mk 1:30 and *they* immediately **t** Jesus about her. *G3306*
Mk 2:14 Jesus **t** him, and Levi got up and *G3306*
Mk 3: 9 Because of the crowd *he* **t** his disciples to *G3306*
Mk 3:32 around him, and *they* **t** him, "Your mother *G3306*
Mk 4:11 *He* **t** them, "The secret of the kingdom of *G3306*
Mk 5:16 who had seen it **t** the people what had *G1455*
Mk 5:16 and **t** about the pigs as well. NDT
Mk 5:33 trembling with fear, **t** him the whole truth. *G3306*
Mk 5:36 they said, Jesus **t** him, "Don't be afraid *G3306*
Mk 5:43 **t** them to give her something to eat. *G3306*
Mk 7:27 *he* **t** her, "for it is not right to take the *G3306*
Mk 7:29 Then *he* **t** her, "For such a reply, you may *G3306*
Mk 8: 6 *He* **t** the crowd to sit down on the ground *G4133*
Mk 8: 7 thanks for them also and **t** the disciples to *G3306*
Mk 9:38 in your name and *we* **t** him **to stop**, *G3266*
Mk 10:32 Twelve aside and **t** them what was going *G3306*
Mk 10:48 Many rebuked him and **t** him to be quiet NDT
Mk 11: 6 They answered as Jesus *had* **t** them to *G3306*
Mk 13:23 *I have* **t** you everything **ahead of time**. *G4625*
Mk 14: 9 what she has done *will* also *be* **t**, in *G3281*
Mk 14:16 found things just as Jesus *had* **t** them. *G3306*
Mk 14:27 all fall away," Jesus **t** them, "for it is *G3306*
Mk 16: 7 There you will see him, just as *he* **t** you.' " *G3306*
Mk 16:10 She went and **t** those who had been with *G550*
Lk 2:15 happened, which the Lord *has* **t** us **about**." *G1192*
Lk 2:17 concerning what *had been* **t** them about *G3281*
Lk 2:20 which were just as they *had been* **t**. *G3281*
Lk 3:13 than you are required to," he **t** them. *G3306*
Lk 5:36 *He* **t** them this parable: "No one tears a *G3306*
Lk 6:39 *He* also **t** them this parable: "Can the *G3306*
Lk 7:18 John's disciples **t** him about all these *G550*
Lk 8: 4 from town after town, *he* **t** this parable: *G3306*
Lk 8:20 *Someone* **t** him, "Your mother and brothers *G550*
Lk 8:36 who had seen it **t** the people how the *G550*
Lk 8:39 man went away and **t** all over town how *G3062*
Lk 8:47 *she* **t** why she had touched him and how *G550*
Lk 8:55 Then Jesus **t** them to give her something *G1411*
Lk 9: 3 *He* **t** them: "Take nothing for the journey *G3306*
Lk 10: 2 *He* **t** them, "The harvest is plentiful, but *G3306*
Lk 10:37 mercy on him." Jesus **t** him, "Go and do *G3306*
Lk 12:16 And *he* **t** them this parable: "The ground *G3306*
Lk 13: 1 present at that time *who* **t** Jesus about the *G550*
Lk 13: 6 Then *he* **t** this parable: "A man had a fig *G3306*
Lk 14: 7 honor at the table, *he* **t** them this parable: *G3306*
Lk 14:23 "Then the master **t** his servant, 'Go out to *G3306*
Lk 15: 3 Then Jesus **t** them this parable: *G3306*
Lk 16: 1 Jesus **t** his disciples: "There was a rich *G3306*
Lk 16: 6 "The manager **t** him, 'Take your bill, sit *G3306*
Lk 16: 7 "*He* **t** him, 'Take your bill and make it *G3306*
Lk 17: 9 because he did what *he was* **t to do**? *G1411*
Lk 17:10 have done everything you *were* **t to do**, *G1411*
Lk 18: 1 Then Jesus **t** his disciples a parable to *G3306*
Lk 18: 9 on everyone else, Jesus **t** this parable: *G3306*
Lk 18:31 Jesus took the Twelve aside and **t** them *G3306*
Lk 18:37 *They* **t** him, "Jesus of Nazareth is passing by *G550*
Lk 18:39 the way rebuked him and **t** him to be quiet, NDT
Lk 19:32 went and found it just as *he had* **t** them. *G3306*
Lk 21:29 *He* **t** them this parable: "Look at the fig *G3306*
Lk 22:13 found things just as Jesus *had* **t** them. *G3306*
Lk 24: 6 Remember how *he* **t** you, while he was *G3281*
Lk 24: 9 *they* **t** all these things to the Eleven and to *G550*
Lk 24:10 the others with them *who* **t** this to the *G3306*
Lk 24:23 They came and **t** us that they had seen a *G3306*
Lk 24:35 Then the two **t** what had happened on the *G2007*
Lk 24:44 "This is what *I* **t** you while I was still with *G3281*
Lk 24:46 *He* **t** them, "This is what is written: The *G3306*
Jn 1:33 who sent me to baptize with water **t** me, *G3306*
Jn 1:45 Philip found Nathanael and **t** him, "We *G3306*
Jn 1:50 believe because *I* **t** you I saw you under *G3306*
Jn 2: 8 Then *he* **t** them, "Now draw some out *G3306*
Jn 4:16 *He* **t** her, "Go, call your husband and *G3306*
Jn 4:29 see a man who **t** me everything I ever did. *G3306*
Jn 4:39 testimony, "*He* **t** me everything I ever did." *G3306*
Jn 4:48 wonders," Jesus **t** him, "you will *G3306*
Jn 5:12 is this fellow who **t** you to pick it up and *G3306*
Jn 5:15 man went away and **t** the Jewish leaders *G334*
Jn 6:36 But *as I* **t** you, you have seen me and still *G3306*
Jn 6:65 "This is why *I* **t** you that no one can come *G3306*
Jn 7: 6 Therefore Jesus **t** them, "My time is not *G3306*
Jn 8:24 *I* **t** you that you would die in your sins; if *G3306*
Jn 8:40 a man who *has* **t** you the truth that I heard *G3281*
Jn 9: 7 *he* **t** him, "wash in the Pool of *G3306*
Jn 9:11 *He* **t** me to go to Siloam and wash *G3306*
Jn 9:27 "*I have* **t** you already and you did not *G3306*
Jn 11:14 So then he **t** them plainly, "Lazarus is *G3306*
Jn 11:46 the Pharisees and **t** them what Jesus had *G3306*
Jn 12:22 Andrew and Philip in turn **t** Jesus. *G3306*
Jn 12:35 Then Jesus **t** them, "You are going to *G3306*
Jn 12:50 say is just what the Father *has* **t** me to say." *G3306*
Jn 13:27 So Jesus **t** him, "What you are about to *G3306*
Jn 13:33 me, and just as *I* **t** the Jews, so I tell *G3306*
Jn 14: 2 would *I have* **t** you that I am going there *G3306*
Jn 14:29 *I have* **t** you now before it happens, so that *G3306*
Jn 15:11 *I have* **t** you this so that my joy may be in *G3281*
Jn 15:20 Remember what I **t** you: 'A servant is not *G3306*
Jn 16: 1 "All this *I have* **t** you so that you will not *G3281*
Jn 16: 4 *I have* **t** you this, so that when their time *G3281*
Jn 16:33 "*I have* **t** you these things, so that in me *G3281*
Jn 18: 8 Jesus answered, "*I* **t** you that I am he. *G3306*
Jn 20:18 And she **t** them that he had said these NDT
Jn 20:25 So the other disciples **t** him, "We have *G3306*
Jn 20:29 Then Jesus **t** him, "Because you have *G3306*
Jn 21: 3 Simon Peter **t** them, and they said *G3306*
Ac 5:21 *as they had been* **t**, and began to *G201*
Ac 7:13 Joseph **t** his brothers **who** *he* **was**, and *G341*
Ac 7:37 "This is the Moses who **t** the Israelites *G3306*
Ac 7:40 *They* **t** Aaron, 'Make us gods who will go *G3306*
Ac 8:29 The Spirit **t** Philip, "Go to that chariot and *G3306*
Ac 8:35 and **t** him **the good news** about Jesus. *G2294*
Ac 9: 6 and you *will be* **t** what you must do." *G3281*
Ac 9:11 The Lord **t** him, "Go to the house of Judas NDT
Ac 9:27 *He* **t** them how Saul on his journey had *G1455*
Ac 10: 8 *He* **t** them everything that had happened *G2007*
Ac 10:13 Then a voice **t** him, "Get up, Peter *G1181+4639*
Ac 10:22 A holy angel **t** him **to ask** you to come to *G5976*
Ac 11: 4 beginning, Peter **t** them the whole story: *G1758*
Ac 11:12 The Spirit **t** me to have no hesitation *G3306*
Ac 11:13 *He* **t** us how he had seen an angel appear *G550*
Ac 12: 8 you and follow me," the angel **t** him. *G3306*
Ac 12:15 of your mind," they **t** her. When she kept *G3306*
Ac 13:41 never believe, even if someone **t** you. *G1687*
Ac 15: 3 *they* **t** *how* the Gentiles had been *G1687*
Ac 16:36 The jailer **t** Paul, "The *G550+3836+3364+4047*
Ac 19: 4 *He* **t** the people to believe in the one *G3306*
Ac 22:10 There you *will be* **t** all that you have been *G3281*
Ac 23:16 he went into the barracks and **t** Paul. *G550*
Ac 25:16 "*I* **t** them that it is not the Roman custom to *G646*
Ac 27:25 in God that it will happen just as *he* **t** me. *G3281*
Ro 9:12 him who calls—she *was* **t**, "The older will *G3306*
Ro 15:21 "Those *who were* not **t** about him will see *G334*
1Co 10:28 the sake of the one *who* **t** you and for the *G3606*
1Co 16: 1 Do what *I* **t** the Galatian churches **to do**. *G1411*

T

2Co 7: 7 *He* t us **about** your longing for me, your G334
Php 3:18 *as I have* often t you *before* and now tell G3306
Col 1: 8 who also t us of your love in the Spirit. G1317
1Th 3: 6 He has t us that you always have pleasant NDT
1Th 4: 6 as *we* t you and warned you **before.** G4625
1Th 4:11 work with your hands, just as *we* t you, G4133
1Pe 1:12 things that *have* now *been* t you by those G334
2Pe 1:16 stories *when we* t you *about* the coming G1192
3Jn 6 They *have* t the church **about** your love G3455
Rev 6:11 they *were* t to wait a little longer G3306
Rev 9: 4 They *were* t not to harm the grass of the G3306
Rev 10:11 Then I *was* t, "You must prophesy again G3306
Rev 11: 1 a reed like a measuring rod and *was* t, G3306
Rev 22:10 Then *he* t me, "Do not seal up the words G3306

TOLERATE (9) [TOLERATED]

Est 3: 8 is not in the king's best interest to t them. H5663
Ps 101: 5 eyes and a proud heart, *I will* not t. H3523
Hab 1: 3 Why *do you* t wrongdoing H5564
Hab 1:13 to look on evil; you cannot t wrongdoing. H5564
Hab 1:13 Why then *do you* t the treacherous H5564
1Co 5: 1 of a kind that even pagans do not t: G1877
2Co 11:16 then t me just as you would a fool G1312
Rev 2: 2 I know that you cannot t wicked people G1002
Rev 2:20 *You* t that woman Jezebel, who calls G918

TOLERATED (1) [TOLERATE]

Est 3: 4 whether Mordecai's behavior *would be* t, H6641

TOMB (64) [TOMBS]

Ge 23: 6 refuse you his t for burying your dead." H7700
Ge 35:20 Over her t Jacob set up a pillar, and to this H7690
Ge 35:20 to this day that pillar marks Rachel's t. H7690
Ge 50: 5 bury me in the t I dug for myself in the H7700
Jdg 8:32 was buried in the t *of* his father Joash in H7700
Jdg 16:31 Eshtaol in the t *of* Manoah his father. H7700
1Sa 10: 2 you will meet two men near Rachel's t, at H7690
2Sa 2:32 buried him in his father's t at Bethlehem. H7700
2Sa 3:32 the king wept aloud at Abner's t. H7700
2Sa 4:12 buried it in Abner's t at Hebron. H7700
2Sa 17:23 he died and was buried in his father's t. H7700
2Sa 19:37 my own town near the t *of* my father and H7700
2Sa 21:14 son Jonathan in the t *of* Saul's father Kish H7700
1Ki 13:22 not be buried in the t *of* your ancestors. H7700
1Ki 13:30 Then he laid the body in his own t, and H7700
2Ki 9:28 his ancestors in his t in the City of David. H7690
2Ki 13:21 they threw the man's body into Elisha's t. H7700
2Ki 21:26 He was buried in his t in the garden of H7690
2Ki 23:17 "It marks the t *of* the man of God who H7700
2Ki 23:30 to Jerusalem and buried him in his own t. H7690
2Ch 16:14 buried him in the t that he had cut out H7700
Isa 14:18 the nations lie in state, each in his own t. H1074
Isa 14:19 are cast out of your t like a rejected H7700
Mt 27:60 it in his own new t that he had cut out of G3646
Mt 27:60 of the entrance *to* the t and went away. G3646
Mt 27:61 Mary were sitting there opposite the t. G5439
Mt 27:64 give the order for the t to be made secure G5439
Mt 27:65 make the t as secure as you know how." NDT
Mt 27:66 went and made the t secure by putting a G5439
Mt 28: 1 the other Mary went to look at the t. G5439
Mt 28: 2 going to the t, rolled back the stone NDT
Mt 28: 8 So the women hurried away from the t G3646
Mk 6:29 came and took his body and laid it in a t. G3646
Mk 15:46 and placed it in a t cut out of rock. G3646
Mk 15:46 a stone against the entrance *of* the t. G3646
Mk 16: 2 sunrise, they were on their way to the t G3646
Mk 16: 3 the stone away from the entrance *of* the t?" G3646
Mk 16: 5 As they entered the t, they saw a young G3646
Mk 16: 8 the women went out and fled from the t. G3646
Lk 23:53 cloth and placed it in a t cut in the rock, G3645
Lk 23:55 Joseph and saw the t and how his body G3646
Lk 24: 1 they had prepared and went to the t. G3645
Lk 24: 2 found the stone rolled away from the t, G3646
Lk 24: 9 When they came back from the t, they G3646
Lk 24:12 got up and ran to the t. Bending over, G3646
Lk 24:22 They went to the t early this morning G3646
Lk 24:24 went to the t and found it just as G3646
Jn 11:17 had already been in the t for four days. G3646
Jn 11:31 she was going to the t to mourn there. G3646
Jn 11:38 once more deeply moved, came to the t. G3646
Jn 12:17 Lazarus from the t and raised him from G3646
Jn 19:41 in the garden a new t, in which no G3646
Jn 19:42 of Preparation and since the t was nearby, G3646
Jn 20: 1 Magdalene went to the t and saw that the G3646
Jn 20: 2 "They have taken the Lord out of the t G3646
Jn 20: 3 the other disciple started for the t. G3646
Jn 20: 4 outran Peter and reached the t first. G3646
Jn 20: 6 behind him and went straight into the t. G3646
Jn 20: 8 who had reached the t first, also went G3646
Jn 20:11 Now Mary stood outside the t crying. G3646
Jn 20:11 she wept, she bent over to look into the t G3646
Ac 2:29 was buried, and his t is here to this day. G3645
Ac 7:16 placed in the t that Abraham had G3645
Ac 13:29 down from the cross and laid him in a t. G3646

TOMBS (21) [TOMB]

Ge 23: 6 Bury your dead in the choicest of our t H7700
2Ki 23:16 when he saw the t that were there on H7700
2Ch 21:20 City of David, but not in the t *of* the kings. H7700
2Ch 24:25 City of David, but not in the t *of* the kings. H7700
2Ch 28:27 not placed in the t *of* the kings of Israel. H7700
2Ch 32:33 the hill where the t *of* David's H7700
2Ch 35:24 He was buried in the t *of* his ancestors H7700
Ne 3:16 up to a point opposite the t *of* David, H7700
Job 21:32 the grave, and watch is kept over their t. H1539
Ps 49:11 Their t will remain their houses forever H7700
Mt 8:28 men coming from the t met him. G3646
Mt 23:27 You are like whitewashed t, which look G5439
Mt 23:29 You build t for the prophets and decorate G5439
Mt 27:52 the t broke open. The bodies of many G3646
Mt 27:53 They came out of the t after Jesus' G3646
Mk 5: 2 spirit came from the t to meet him. G3646
Mk 5: 3 This man lived in the t, and no one could G3645
Mk 5: 5 day among the t and in the hills he G3645
Lk 8:27 lived in a house, but had lived in the t. G3645
Lk 11:47 because you build t for the prophets, and G3646
Lk 11:48 killed the prophets, and you build their t. NDT

TOMBSTONE (1) [STONE]

2Ki 23:17 "What is that t I see?" The people H7483

TOMORROW (58)

Ex 8:10 "T," Pharaoh said. Moses replied, "It will H4737
Ex 8:23 your people. This sign will occur t.'" H4737
Ex 8:29 t the flies will leave Pharaoh and his H4737
Ex 9: 5 "T the LORD will do this in the land." H4737
Ex 9:18 at this time t I will send the worst H4737
Ex 10: 4 I will bring locusts into your country t. H4737
Ex 16:23 'T is to be a day of sabbath rest, a holy H4737
Ex 17: 9 T I will stand on top of the hill with the H4737
Ex 19:10 people and consecrate them today and t. H4737
Ex 32: 5 "T there will be a festival to the LORD." H4737
Nu 11:18 'Consecrate yourselves in preparation for t, H4737
Nu 14:25 turn back t and set out toward the desert H4737
Nu 16: 7 t put burning coals and incense in H4737
Nu 16:16 are to appear before the LORD t— H4737
Jos 3: 5 t the LORD will do amazing things H4737
Jos 7:13 'Consecrate yourselves in preparation for t; H4737
Jos 11: 6 because by this time t I will hand all of H4737
Jos 22:18 t he will be angry with the whole H4737
Jdg 19: 9 Early t morning you can get up and be on H4737
Jdg 20:28 for t I will give them into your hands." H4737
1Sa 9:16 "About this time t I will send you a man H4737
1Sa 11: 9 'By the time the sun is hot t, you will be H4737
1Sa 11:10 Ammonites, "T we will surrender to you H4737
1Sa 19: 2 Be on your guard t morning; go into H2021[S]
1Sa 19:11 run for your life tonight, t you'll be killed." H4737
1Sa 20: 5 t is the New Moon feast, and I am H4737
1Sa 20: 5 field until the evening of the **day after** t. H8958
1Sa 20:12 out my father by this time the day after t! H4737
1Sa 20:18 said to David, "T is the New Moon feast. H4737
1Sa 20:19 **The day after** t, toward evening, go to the H8992
1Sa 28:19 t you and your sons will be with me. H4737
2Sa 11:12 one more day, and t I will send you back." H4737
1Ki 19: 2 if by this time t I do not make your life like H4737
1Ki 20: 6 But about this time t I am going to send H4737
2Ki 6:28 eat him today, and t we'll eat my son. H4737
2Ki 7: 1 About this time t, a seah of the finest H4737
2Ki 7:18 "About this time t, a seah of the finest H4737
2Ki 10: 6 come to me in Jezreel by this time t." H4737
2Ch 20:16 T march down against them. They will be H4737
2Ch 20:17 Go out to face them t, and the LORD will H4737
Est 5: 8 king and Haman come t to the banquet I H4737
Est 5:12 she has invited me along with the king t. H4737
Est 9:13 to carry out this day's edict t also, H4737
Pr 3:28 "Come back t and I'll give it to you"— H4737
Pr 27: 1 Do not boast about t, for you do H3427+4737
Isa 22:13 us eat and drink," you say, "for t we die!" H4737
Isa 56:12 our fill of beer! And t will be like today, or H4737
Mt 6:30 is here today and t is thrown into the fire G892
Mt 6:34 Therefore do not worry about t, for tomorrow G892
Mt 6:34 about tomorrow, for t will worry about itself. G892
Lk 12:28 is here today, and t is thrown into the fire G892
Lk 13:32 demons and healing people today and t, G892
Lk 13:33 press on today and t and the next day— G892
Ac 23:20 before the Sanhedrin t on the pretext of G892
Ac 25:22 He replied, "T you will hear him." G892
1Co 15:32 "Let us eat and drink, for t we die." G892
Jas 4:13 "Today or t we will go to this or that city G892
Jas 4:14 you do not even know what will happen t. G892

TONE (1)

Gal 4:20 I could be with you now and change my t, G5889

TONGS (3)

1Ki 7:49 the gold floral work and lamps and t; H4920
2Ch 4:21 the gold floral work and lamps and t (they H4920
Isa 6: 6 which he had taken with t from the altar. H4920

TONGUE (85) [TONGUES]

Ex 4:10 I am slow of speech and t." H4383
2Sa 23: 2 spoke through me; his word was on my t. H4383
Est 1:22 his own household, using his native t. H4383
Job 5:21 will be protected from the lash of the t, H4383
Job 12:11 not the ear test words as the t tastes food? H2674
Job 15: 5 your mouth; you adopt the t *of* the crafty. H4383
Job 20:12 in his mouth and he hides it under his t, H4383
Job 27: 4 and my t will not utter lies. H4383
Job 33: 2 words are **on the tip of** my t. H4383+928+2674
Job 34: 3 For the ear tests words as the t tastes food. H2674
Job 41: 1 a fishhook or tie down its t with a rope? H4383
Ps 10: 7 trouble and evil are under his t. H4383
Ps 12: 3 all flattering lips and every boastful t— H4383
Ps 15: 3 whose t utters no slander, who does no H4383
Ps 16: 9 my heart is glad and my t rejoices; H3883
Ps 22:15 my t sticks to the roof of my mouth H4383
Ps 34:13 keep your t from evil and your lips from H4383
Ps 35:28 My t will proclaim your righteousness H4383
Ps 39: 1 watch my ways and keep my t from sin; H4383
Ps 39: 3 the fire burned; then I spoke with my t: H4383
Ps 45: 1 my t is the pen of a skillful writer. H4383
Ps 50:19 evil and harness your t to deceit. H4383
Ps 51:14 my t will sing of your righteousness. H4383
Ps 52: 2 practice deceit, your t plots destruction; it H4383
Ps 52: 4 love every harmful word, you deceitful t! H4383
Ps 66:17 with my mouth; his praise was on my t. H4383
Ps 71:24 My t will tell of your righteous acts all day H4383
Ps 114: 1 Jacob from a people of **foreign** t, H4357
Ps 119:172 May my t sing of your word, for all your H4383
Ps 120: 3 what more besides, you deceitful t? H4383
Ps 137: 6 May my t cling to the roof of my mouth if I H4383
Ps 139: 4 Before a word is on my t you, LORD, know H4383
Pr 6:17 haughty eyes, a lying t, hands that shed H4383
Pr 10:20 The t *of* the righteous is choice silver, but H4383
Pr 10:31 wisdom, but a perverse t will be silenced. H4383
Pr 11:12 one who has understanding **holds** *their* t. H3087
Pr 12:18 the t *of* the wise brings healing. H4383
Pr 12:19 but a lying t lasts only a moment. H4383
Pr 15: 2 The t *of* the wise adorns knowledge, but H4383
Pr 15: 4 The soothing t is a tree of life, but a H4383
Pr 15: 4 but a perverse t crushes the spirit. H2023[S]
Pr 16: 1 the LORD comes the proper answer of the t. H4383
Pr 17: 4 a liar pays attention to a destructive t. H4383
Pr 17:20 one whose t is perverse falls into trouble. H4383
Pr 18:21 The t has the power of life and death H4383
Pr 21: 6 made by a lying t is a fleeting vapor and H4383
Pr 25:15 a gentle t can break a bone. H4383
Pr 25:23 that brings unexpected rain is a sly t— H4383
Pr 26:28 A lying t hates those it hurts, and a H4383
Pr 28:23 rather than one who has a flattering t. H4383
Pr 31:26 faithful instruction is on her t. H4383
SS 4:11 my bride; milk and honey are under your t. H4383
Isa 30:27 full of wrath, and his t is a consuming fire. H4383
Isa 32: 4 the stammering t will be fluent and H4383
Isa 35: 6 like a deer, and the mute t shout for joy. H4383
Isa 45:23 knee will bow; by me every t will swear. H4383
Isa 50: 4 LORD has given me a well-instructed t, H4383
Isa 54:17 you will refute every t that accuses you. H4383
Isa 57: 4 whom do you sneer and stick out your t? H4383
Isa 59: 3 and your t mutters wicked things. H4383
Jer 9: 3 "They make ready their t like a bow, to H4383
Jer 9: 8 Their t is a deadly arrow; it speaks H4383
La 4: 4 of thirst the infant's t sticks to the roof of H4383
Eze 3:26 I will make your t stick to the roof of your H4383
Zep 3:13 A deceitful t will not be found in their H4383
Mk 7:33 Then he spit and touched the man's t. G1185
Mk 7:35 his t was loosened and he began to G1185
Lk 1:64 his mouth was opened and his t set free, G1185
Lk 16:24 tip of his finger in water and cool my t, G1185
Ac 2:26 my heart is glad and my t rejoices; G1185
Ro 14:11 before me; every t will acknowledge God. G1185
1Co 14: 2 anyone who speaks *in a* t does not speak G1185
1Co 14: 4 Anyone who speaks *in a* t edifies G1185
1Co 14: 9 you speak intelligible words with your t, G1185
1Co 14:13 one who speaks *in a* t should pray that G1185
1Co 14:14 For if I pray *in a* t, my spirit prays, but my G1185
1Co 14:19 others than ten thousand words in a t. G1185
1Co 14:26 a revelation, a t or an interpretation. G1185
1Co 14:27 If anyone speaks *in a* t, two—or at the G1185
Php 2:11 every t acknowledge that Jesus Christ G1185
Jas 3: 5 Likewise, the t is a small part of the body G1185
Jas 3: 6 The t also is a fire, a world of evil among G1185
Jas 3: 8 no human being can tame the t. It is a G1185
Jas 3: 9 With **the** t we praise our Lord and Father G899[S]
1Pe 3:10 days must keep their t from evil and their G1185

TONGUES (50) [TONGUE]

Jdg 7: 5 the water with their t as a dog laps from H4383
Job 29:10 their t stuck to the roof of their H4383
Ps 5: 9 is an open grave; with their t they tell lies. H4383
Ps 12: 4 who say, "By our t we will prevail; our H4383
Ps 31:20 safe in your dwelling from accusing t. H4383
Ps 37:30 wisdom, and their t speak what is just. H4383
Ps 57: 4 arrows, whose t are sharp swords. H4383
Ps 64: 3 They sharpen their t like swords and aim H4383
Ps 64: 8 will turn their own t against them and H4383
Ps 68:23 while the t *of* your dogs have their share." H4383
Ps 73: 9 their t take possession of the earth. H4383
Ps 78:36 their mouths, lying to him with their t; H4383
Ps 109: 2 they have spoken against me with lying t. H4383
Ps 120: 2 from lying lips and from deceitful t. H4383
Ps 126: 2 with laughter, our t with songs of joy. H4383
Ps 140: 3 They make their t as sharp as a serpent's H4383
Pr 10:19 but the prudent hold their t. H8557
Pr 17:28 and discerning if they hold their t. H8557
Pr 21:23 mouths and their t keep themselves from H4383
Isa 5:24 as t *of* fire lick up straw and as dry grass H4383
Isa 28:11 lips and strange t God will speak to this H4383
Isa 41:17 is none; their t are parched with thirst. H4383
Jer 9: 5 They have taught their t to lie; they weary H4383
Jer 18:18 attack him with our t and pay no attention H4383
Jer 23:31 who wag their own t and yet declare, H4383
Mic 6:12 are liars and their t speak deceitfully. H4383
Zec 14:12 their t will rot in their mouths. H4383
Mk 16:17 out demons; they will speak *in* new t; G1185
Ac 2: 3 saw what seemed to be t *of fire* that G1185
Ac 2: 4 began to speak *in* other t as the Spirit G1185
Ac 2:11 the wonders of God *in* our own t! G1185

T

Ac 10:46 them speaking *in* t and praising God. *G1185*
Ac 19: 6 they spoke *in* t and prophesied. *G1185*
Ro 3:13 are open graves; their t practice deceit." *G1185*
1Co 12:10 to another **speaking in** different kinds of t *G1185*
1Co 12:10 to still another the interpretation *of* t. *G1185*
1Co 12:28 of guidance, and of different kinds *of* t. *G1185*
1Co 12:30 Do all speak *in* t? Do all interpret? *G1185*
1Co 13: 1 If I speak *in* the t of men or of angels, but *G1185*
1Co 13: 8 where there are t, they will be stilled; *G1185*
1Co 14: 5 I would like every one of you to speak *in* t *G1185*
1Co 14: 5 is greater than the one who speaks *in* t, *G1185*
1Co 14: 6 if I come to you and speak *in* t, what good *G1185*
1Co 14:18 God that I speak *in* t more than all of you. *G1185*
1Co 14:21 "With **other** t and through the lips of *G2280*
1Co 14:22 T, then, are a sign, not for believers but *G1185*
1Co 14:23 comes together and everyone speaks *in* t, *G1185*
1Co 14:39 prophesy, and do not forbid speaking *in* t. *G1185*
Jas 1:26 a tight rein on their t deceive themselves, *G1185*
Rev 16:10 People gnawed their t in agony *G1185*

TONIGHT (12)

Ge 19: 5 are the men who came to you t? H2021+4326
Ge 19:34 Let's get him to drink wine again t H2021+4326
Ge 30:15 sleep with you t in return for your H2021+4326
Jos 2: 2 have come here t to spy out the H2021+4326
Jos 4: 3 down at the place where you stay t." H2021+4326
Jdg 19: 6 "Please **stay** t and enjoy yourself. H4328
Ru 1:12 if I had a husband t and then gave H2021+4326
Ru 3: 2 T he will be winnowing barley on H2021+4326
1Sa 19:11 "If you don't run for your life t H2021+4326
2Sa 17: 1 men and set out t in pursuit of H2021+4326
Mk 14:30 "today—**yes,** t—before the *G4047+3836+3816*
Ac 23:23 spearmen to go to Caesarea at nine t. *G3816*

TOO (269)

Ge 9: 5 **And** from each human being, t, I will H2256
Ge 16:10 that they will be t numerous to count." H4946
Ge 18:14 Is anything t hard *for* the LORD? I will H4946
Ge 19:21 I will grant this request t; I will not H1685
Ge 24:14 I'll water your camels t'—let her be H1685
Ge 24:19 "I'll draw water for your camels t, until H1685
Ge 24:44 I'll draw water for your camels t," let H1685
Ge 24:46 'Drink, and I'll water your camels t.' H1685
Ge 26:16 you have become t powerful for us." H4394
Ge 27:31 He t prepared some tasty food and H1685
Ge 27:34 to his father, "Bless me—me t, my father!" H1685
Ge 27:38 Bless me t, my father!" Then H1685
Ge 29:33 I am not loved, he gave me this one t." H1685
Ge 30: 3 children for me and I t can build a family H1685
Ge 30:15 Will you take my son's mandrakes t?" H1685
Ge 31:25 Laban and his relatives camped there t. NDT
Ge 33: 7 Rachel, **and** they t bowed down. H2256
Ge 36: 7 were t great *for* them to remain H4946
Ge 38:11 thought, "He may die t, just like his H1685
Ge 40:16 he said to Joseph, "I t had a dream: H677
Ge 44:29 this one from me t and harm comes to H1685
Ge 47:20 because the famine *was t* **severe** for them. AIT
Ge 48:11 has allowed me to see your children t." H1685
Ge 48:19 He t will become a people, and he too H1685
Ge 48:19 a people, and he t will become great. H1685
Ex 1: 9 become **far t numerous** for H8041+2256+6786
Ex 10:26 Our livestock t must go with us; not a hoof H1685
Ex 12: 4 household is t small *for* a whole lamb, H4946
Ex 16:18 who gathered much *did* not **have t much,** H6369
Ex 16:18 who gathered little *did* not **have t little.** H2893
Ex 18:18 The work is t heavy *for* you; you cannot H4946
Ex 23:29 the wild animals t numerous *for* you. H6584
Lev 27: 8 making the vow is t poor to pay the H4946
Nu 11:14 by myself; the burden is t heavy *for* me. H4946
Nu 11:23 "*Is* the LORD's arm t **short**? H7918
Nu 16: 3 said to them, "You have **gone t far**! H8041
Nu 16: 7 You Levites have **gone t far**!" H8041
Nu 16:10 now you are trying to get the priesthood t. H1685
Nu 16:34 "The earth is going to swallow us t!" H7153
Nu 19: 8 **and** he t will be unclean till evening. H2256
Nu 19:10 **and** he t will be unclean till evening. H2256
Nu 22: 6 because they are t powerful *for* me. H4946
Nu 24:24 Eber, but they t will come to ruin. H1685
Nu 27:13 you t will be gathered to your people H1685
Dt 1: 9 *are* **t heavy a burden** for me **to carry** H4202+3523+5951
Dt 1:17 Bring me any case t hard *for* you, and I H4946
Dt 2:11 Anakites, they t were considered Rephaites H677
Dt 2:20 That t was considered a land of the H677
Dt 2:36 not one town was t strong *for* us. H4946
Dt 3:20 they t have taken over the land that H1685
Dt 9:20 but at that time I prayed for Aaron t. H1685
Dt 12:21 to put his Name *is t* **far away** from you, AIT
Dt 14:24 But if that place is t distant and you have H4946
Dt 17: 8 courts that are t difficult *for* you to judge— H4946
Dt 19: 6 overtake him if the distance *is t* **great**, and AIT
Dt 20: 8 soldiers will not become disheartened t." H3869
Dt 30:11 today is not t difficult *for* you or beyond H4946
Jos 1:15 until they t have taken possession of H1685
Jos 17:15 the hill country of Ephraim *is t* **small** for you, AIT
Jos 24:18 We t will serve the LORD, because he is H1685
Jdg 1:33 **but** the Naphtalites t lived among the H2256
Jdg 1:35 they t were pressed into forced labor. H2256
Jdg 3:31 with an oxgoad. He t saved Israel. H1685
Jdg 6:35 so that they t went up to meet them. NDT
Jdg 7: 2 LORD said to Gideon, "You have *t* **many** men. AIT
Jdg 7: 4 said to Gideon, "There are still t many men. NDT
Jdg 9:19 be your joy, and may you be his, t! H1685
Jdg 14: 9 he gave them some, **and** they t ate it. H2256
Jdg 18:26 seeing that they were t strong *for* him H4946
Ru 1:12 I am t old to have another husband. H4946
1Sa 19:21 he sent more men, and they prophesied t. H1685
1Sa 19:24 he t prophesied in Samuel's H1685
1Sa 22:17 because they t have sided with David. H1685
1Sa 22:23 who wants to kill you is trying to kill me t. NDT
1Sa 30:10 of them were t exhausted to cross H4946
1Sa 30:21 men who had been t exhausted to follow H4946
1Sa 31: 5 he t fell on his sword and died with him. H1685
2Sa 2: 6 I t will show you the same favor H1685
2Sa 3:39 these sons of Zeruiah are t strong *for* me. H4946
2Sa 10:11 "If the Arameans are t strong *for* me, then H4946
2Sa 10:11 if the Ammonites are t strong *for* you H4946
2Sa 12: 8 And if all this had been **t little**, I would H5071
2Sa 13:36 The king, t, and all his attendants H2256+1685
2Sa 14:26 year because it became t heavy *for* him— H6584
2Sa 15:24 Zadok was there, t, and all the Levites H1685
2Sa 15:30 their heads t and were weeping as H2256
2Sa 18:26 "He must be bringing good news, t." H1685
2Sa 22:18 from my foes, who were t strong *for* me. H4946
2Sa 23:22 he t was as famous as the three mighty H2256
1Ki 3: 8 people, t numerous to count or number. H4946
1Ki 8:64 before the LORD was t small to hold the H4946
1Ki 10: 3 nothing was t hard *for* the king to explain H4946
1Ki 12:28 "It is t much for you to go up to Jerusalem. H4946
1Ki 13:18 answered, "I t am a prophet, as you H1685
1Ki 19: 7 for the journey is t much *for* you. H4946
1Ki 19:10 one left, and now they are trying to kill me t." NDT
1Ki 19:14 one left, and now they are trying to kill me t." NDT
1Ki 20:23 That is why they were t strong *for* us. But if H4946
2Ki 2:17 he was t embarrassed to refuse. NDT
2Ki 5:20 "My master *was* **t easy on** Naaman, this H3104
2Ki 6: 1 where we meet with you is t small *for* us. H4946
2Ki 9:27 shouting, "Kill him t!" They wounded him H1685
1Ch 8:32 They t lived near their relatives in H2256+677
1Ch 9:38 They t lived near their relatives in H2256+677
1Ch 10: 5 was dead, he t fell on his sword and died. H1685
1Ch 11:24 he t was as famous as the three mighty H2256
1Ch 19:12 "If the Arameans are t strong *for* me, then H4946
1Ch 19:12 if the Ammonites are t strong *for* you H4946
1Ch 19:15 they t fled before his brother Abishai and H1685
1Ch 22:14 of bronze and iron t great to be weighed, H401
2Ch 9: 2 nothing was t hard *for* him to explain to H4946
2Ch 22: 3 He t followed the ways of the house of H1685
2Ch 29:34 were **t few** to skin all the burnt offerings H5071
Ezr 9: 6 "*I am t* **ashamed** and disgraced, my God, to AIT
Ezr 10: 1 gathered around him. They t wept bitterly. H3954
Ne 6: 9 "Their hands will get t weak *for* the work H4946
Ne 13:27 we hear now that you t are doing all this H2256
Job 6:21 Now you t have proved to be of no help H3954
Job 32:10 Listen to me; I t will tell you what I know. H677
Job 32:17 I t will have my say; I too will tell what I H677
Job 32:17 will have my say; I t will tell what I know. H677
Job 33: 6 you in God's sight; I t am a piece of clay. H1685
Job 42: 3 things t wonderful *for* me to know. H4946
Ps 18:17 from my foes, who were t strong *for* me. H4946
Ps 35:10 the poor from those t strong *for* them, H4946
Ps 36: 2 own eyes *they* **flatter** themselves *t* **much** to AIT
Ps 38: 4 me like a burden t heavy to bear. H4946
Ps 40: 5 they would be t many to declare. H4946
Ps 77: 4 from closing; I was t troubled to speak. H4202
Ps 87: 4 acknowledge me—Philistia t, and Tyre, H2180
Ps 89: 5 your faithfulness t, in the assembly of the H677
Ps 105:24 he made them t numerous *for* their foes, H4946
Ps 120: 6 **T long** have I lived among those who H8041
Ps 131: 1 great matters or things t wonderful *for* me. H4946
Ps 139: 6 Such knowledge is t wonderful *for* me, too H4946
Ps 139: 6 too wonderful for me, t lofty for me to attain. NDT
Ps 142: 6 pursue me, for they are t strong *for* me. H4946
Pr 4: 3 For I t was a son to my father, still tender NDT
Pr 18:11 they imagine it a wall **t high to scale**. H8435
Pr 20:19 so avoid *anyone who* **talks t much**. H7331+8557
Pr 20:21 **claimed t soon** will not H987+928+2021+8037
Pr 23:20 not join *those who* **drink t much** wine or H6010
Pr 24: 7 Wisdom *is t* **high** for fools; in the assembly AIT
Pr 25:16 just enough—**t much** *of* it, and you will H8425
Pr 25:17 house—**t much** *of* you, and they H8425
Pr 25:27 It is not good to eat **t much** honey, nor is H8049
Pr 25:27 to search out matters that are *t* **deep**. AIT
Pr 26:15 *he is t* **lazy** to bring it back to his mouth. AIT
Pr 30: 9 *I may* **have t much** and disown you and H8425
Pr 30:18 three things that are t amazing *for* me, H4946
Ecc 1:17 I learned that this, t, is a chasing after the H1685
Ecc 2:15 I said to myself, "This t is meaningless." H1685
Ecc 2:16 Like the fool, the wise t must die! H375
Ecc 2:19 skill under the sun. This t is meaningless. H1685
Ecc 2:21 This t is meaningless and a great H1685
Ecc 2:23 minds do not rest. This t is meaningless. H1685
Ecc 2:24 in their own toil. This t, I see, is from the H1685
Ecc 2:26 This t is meaningless, a chasing after the H1685
Ecc 4: 4 This t is meaningless, a chasing after the H1685
Ecc 4: 8 This t is meaningless—a miserable H1685
Ecc 4:16 This t is meaningless, a chasing after the H1685
Ecc 5:10 with their income. This t is meaningless. H1685
Ecc 5:16 This t is a grievous evil: As H2256+1685
Ecc 6: 9 This t is meaningless, a chasing after the H1685
Ecc 7: 6 This t is meaningless. H2256+1685
Ecc 8:10 Then t, I saw the wicked buried—those H4027
Ecc 8:10 This t is meaningless. H1685
Ecc 8:14 This t, I say, is meaningless. H1685
Isa 7: 8 years Ephraim will be t shattered to be a H4946
Isa 28:20 The bed is t short to stretch out on, the H4946
Isa 28:20 the blanket *t* **narrow** to wrap around you. AIT
Isa 31: 2 Yet he t is wise and can bring disaster; he H1685
Isa 38:16 **and** my spirit finds life in them t. H2256
Isa 40:20 A *person* **t poor** *to* present such an H6123
Isa 49: 6 "It is t small a thing for you to be my H4946
Isa 49:19 now you will be t small *for* your people H4946
Isa 49:20 hearing, 'This place is t small for us; give us NDT
Isa 50: 2 Was my arm t short to deliver you H4946
Isa 59: 1 the arm of the LORD is not t short to save, H4946
Isa 59: 1 short to save, nor his ear t dull to hear. H4946
Isa 63: 9 In all their distress he t was distressed, and NDT
Isa 65: 5 don't come near me, for *I am t* **sacred** *for* you! AIT
Jer 1: 6 do not know how to speak; I am **t young**." H5853
Jer 1: 7 said to me, "Do not say, 'I am **t young**. H5853
Jer 4:12 a wind t strong *for* that comes from me H4946
Jer 5: 5 **But** with one accord they t had broken off H421
Jer 25:26 of them, the king of Sheshak will drink it t. NDT
Jer 29: 6 so that they t may have sons and daughters. NDT
Jer 29: 7 because if it prospers, you t will prosper." NDT
Jer 32:17 Nothing is t hard *for* you. H4946
Jer 32:27 of all mankind. Is anything t hard *for* me? H4946
Jer 46:21 They t will turn and flee together, they H1685
Jer 48: 7 riches, you t will be taken captive H1685
Jer 49:11 Your widows t can depend on me.' H2256
Eze 16:28 in prostitution with the Assyrians t, H2256
Eze 21:17 I t will strike my hands together H2256+1685
Eze 23:12 She t lusted after the Assyrians—governors NDT
Eze 23:13 I saw that she t defiled herself; both of them NDT
Eze 24: 9 city of bloodshed! I, t, will pile the wood H1685
Eze 31:17 They t, like the great cedar, had gone H1685
Eze 31:18 t, will be brought down with the NDT
Eze 32:28 "You t, Pharaoh, will be broken and will H2256
Da 2:11 What the king asks is **t difficult**. No one A10330
Da 4: 9 is in you, and no mystery is *t* **difficult** for you. AIT
Am 6: 9 are left in one house, they t will die. H2256
Na 3:11 You t will become drunk; you will go into H1685
Hab 1:13 Your eyes are t pure to look on evil; you H4946
Zep 2:12 "You Cushites, t, will be slain by my sword H1685
Zec 1:15 they **went t far** with the punishment. H6468
Zec 9: 2 on Hamath t, which borders on it H1685
Zec 9: 5 writhe in agony, **and** Ekron t, for her hope H2256
Zec 14:14 Judah t will fight at Jerusalem. The wealth H1685
Mt 2: 8 so that **I t** may go and worship him." *G2743*
Mt 7: 1 "Do not judge, or you t will be judged. NDT
Mk 12:22 Last of all, the woman died t. *G2779*
Lk 1: 3 **I t** decided to write an orderly account *G2743*
Lk 2:35 And a sword will pierce your own soul t." *G1254*
Lk 3:21 being baptized, Jesus was baptized t. *G2779*
Lk 10:32 So t, a Levite, when he came to the place *G1254*
Lk 13: 3 But unless you repent, you t will all perish. *G3931*
Lk 13: 5 But unless you repent, you t will all perish." *G6058*
Lk 19: 9 because this man, t, is a son of Abraham. *G2779*
Lk 20:32 the woman died t. *G2779*
Jn 2:10 after the guests **have had t much to drink**; *G3499*
Jn 5:17 work to this very day, **and I t** am working." *G2743*
Jn 6:67 "You do not want to leave t, do you?" *G2779*
Jn 7:52 "Are you from Galilee, t? Look into it, *G2779*
Jn 9:27 Do you want to become his disciples t?" *G2779*
Jn 9:40 this and asked, "What? Are we blind t?" *G2779*
Jn 10:16 They t will listen to my voice, and there *G2779*
Jn 14:21 **and I t** will love them and show myself to *G2743*
Jn 17:19 that they t may be truly sanctified. *G2779*
Jn 18:17 "You aren't one of this man's disciples t *G2779*
Jn 18:25 "You aren't one of his disciples t, are you?" *G2779*
Ac 2:13 said, "They have **had t much** wine." *G3551*
Ac 5:37 **He t** was killed, and all his followers were *G2797*
Ac 14:15 you doing this? We t are only human, like *G2779*
Ac 17:13 some of them went **there t**, agitating the *G2795*
Ac 26: 9 "I t was convinced that I ought to do all *G4036*
Ro 3:29 Is he not the God of Gentiles t? Yes, *G2779*
Ro 3:29 God of Gentiles too? Yes, of Gentiles t, *G2779*
Ro 6: 4 of the Father, we t may live a new life. *G2779*
Ro 11: 5 So t, at the present time there is a *G2779*
Ro 11:31 so they t have now become disobedient in *G2779*
Ro 11:31 in order that they t may now receive mercy *G2779*
Ro 16:13 mother, who has been a mother to me, t. *G2779*
1Co 7:36 if his **passions** are **t strong** and he *G5644*
1Co 7:40 I think that **I t** have the Spirit of God. *G2743*
1Co 9:11 is it *t* **much** if we reap a material harvest from AIT
1Co 10:21 cup of the Lord **and** the cup of demons t; *G2779*
2Co 2: 5 you to some extent—not to **put it** *t* **severely**. AIT
2Co 8:15 who gathered much *did* not **have t much,** *G4429*
2Co 8:15 who gathered little *did* not **have t little.**" *G1782*
2Co 10:14 *We are* not **going t far** in our boasting, as *G2391*
2Co 11:18 in the way the world does, **I t** will boast. *G2743*
2Co 11:21 shame I admit that we *were t* **weak** for that! AIT
Gal 2:16 **So** we, t, have put our faith in Christ Jesus *G2779*
Eph 2:22 And in him you t are being built together *G2779*
Php 2:18 So you t should be glad and *G3836+899+2779*
Php 3:15 that t God will make clear to you. *G2779*
Col 4: 3 And pray for us, t, that God may open a *G2779*
2Ti 2:10 that they t may obtain the salvation that is *G2779*
2Ti 4:15 You t should be on your guard against him *G2779*
Titus 3: 3 At one time we t were foolish *G2779*
Heb 2:14 he t shared in their humanity so that by *G4181*
Jas 5: 8 You t, be patient and stand firm, because *G2779*
2Pe 2:12 like animals they t will perish. *G2779*
Rev 14:10 t, will drink the wine of God's fury *G2779*
Rev 14:17 in heaven, **and** he t had a sharp sickle. *G2779*

TOOK (669) [TAKE]

Ge 2:15 The LORD God t the man and put him in H4374
Ge 2:21 he t one of the man's ribs and then H4374
Ge 3: 6 gaining wisdom, she t some and ate it. H4374
Ge 5:24 was no more, because God t him away. H4374
Ge 8: 9 out his hand and t the dove and brought H4374
Ge 9:23 Shem and Japheth t a garment and laid H4374
Ge 11:31 Terah t his son Abram, his grandson Lot H4374
Ge 12: 5 He t his wife Sarai, his nephew Lot, all the H4374
Ge 12:19 is my sister,' so that I t her to be my wife? H4374
Ge 15: 5 He t him outside and said, "Look up at the H3655
Ge 16: 3 Sarai his wife t her Egyptian slave Hagar H4374
Ge 17:23 very day Abraham t his son Ishmael and H4374
Ge 20: 2 king of Gerar sent for Sarah and t her. H4374
Ge 21:14 morning Abraham t some food and a skin H4374
Ge 22: 3 He t with him two of his servants and his H4374
Ge 22: 6 Abraham t the wood for the burnt offering H4374
Ge 22:10 out his hand and t the knife to slay his H4374
Ge 22:13 He went over and t the ram and sacrificed H4374
Ge 24:22 the man t out a gold nose ring weighing H4374
Ge 24:61 So the servant t Rebekah and left. H4374
Ge 24:65 So she t her veil and covered herself H4374
Ge 27:15 Then Rebekah t the best clothes of Esau H4374
Ge 27:35 came deceitfully and t your blessing." H4374
Ge 27:36 He t my birthright, and now he's taken my H4374
Ge 28:18 next morning Jacob t the stone he had H4374
Ge 29:23 he t his daughter Leah and brought her to H4374
Ge 30: 9 she t her servant Zilpah and gave her to H4374
Ge 30:15 it enough that you t away my husband? H4374
Ge 30:37 however, t fresh-cut branches from poplar H4374
Ge 31:16 wealth that God t away from our father H5911
Ge 31:36 Jacob was angry and t Laban to task H8189
Ge 31:45 So Jacob t a stone and set it up as a pillar H4374
Ge 31:46 So they t stones and piled them in a heap H4374
Ge 31:53 So Jacob t an oath in the name of the H8678
Ge 32:22 night Jacob got up and t his two wives, H4374
Ge 34: 2 saw her, he t her and raped her. H4374
Ge 34:25 t their swords and attacked the H4374
Ge 34:26 to the sword and t Dinah from Shechem's H4374
Ge 36: 2 Esau t his wives from the women of H4374
Ge 36: 6 Esau t his wives and sons and daughters H4374
Ge 37:24 and they t him and threw him into the H4374
Ge 37:28 to the Ishmaelites, who t him to Egypt. H995
Ge 37:32 They t the ornate robe back to H8938+2256+995
Ge 38:14 she t off her widow's clothes, covered H6073
Ge 38:19 she t off her veil and put on her widow's H6073
Ge 38:28 so the midwife t a scarlet thread and tied H4374
Ge 39: 7 master's wife t notice of Joseph H5951+6524
Ge 39:20 Joseph's master t him and put him in H4374
Ge 40:11 was in my hand, and I t the grapes H4374
Ge 41:42 Then Pharaoh t his signet ring from his H6073
Ge 43:15 So the men t the gifts and double the H4374
Ge 43:17 Joseph told him and t the men to Joseph's H995
Ge 43:24 The steward t the men into Joseph's house, H995
Ge 46: 5 Israel's sons t their father Jacob and H5951
Ge 48: 1 So he t his two sons Manasseh and H4374
Ge 48:13 And Joseph t both of them, Ephraim on H4374
Ge 48:17 so he t hold of his father's hand to move H9461
Ge 48:22 the ridge I t from the Amorites with my H4374
Ex 2: 9 So the woman t the baby and nursed him. H4374
Ex 2:10 she t him to Pharaoh's daughter and he H995
Ex 4: 4 reached out and t hold of the snake and it H2616
Ex 4: 6 and when he t it out, the skin was H3655
Ex 4: 7 and when he t it out, it was H3655
Ex 4:20 So Moses t his wife and sons, put them on H4374
Ex 4:20 And he t the staff of God in his hand H4374
Ex 4:25 But Zipporah t a flint knife, cut off her H4374
Ex 9:10 So they t soot from a furnace and stood H4374
Ex 12:34 So the people t their dough before the H5951
Ex 13:19 Moses t the bones of Joseph with him H4374
Ex 14: 6 made ready and t his army with him. H4374
Ex 14: 7 He t six hundred of the best chariots H4374
Ex 15:20 Aaron's sister, t a timbrel in her hand H4374
Ex 17:12 they t a stone and put it under him and H4374
Ex 18:13 next day Moses t his seat to serve as H3782
Ex 24: 6 Moses t half of the blood and put it in H4374
Ex 24: 7 Then he t the Book of the Covenant and H4374
Ex 24: 8 Moses then t the blood, sprinkled it on H4374
Ex 32: 3 So all the people t off their earrings and H7293
Ex 32: 4 He t what they handed him and made it H4374
Ex 32:20 And he t the calf the people had made H4374
Ex 40:20 He t the tablets of the covenant law and H4374
Lev 8:10 Then Moses t the anointing oil and H4374
Lev 8:15 the bull and t some of the blood, H4374
Lev 8:16 Moses also t all the fat around the internal H4374
Lev 8:23 the ram and t some of its blood and H4374
Lev 8:25 After that, he t the fat, the fat tail, all the H4374
Lev 8:26 before the LORD, he t one thick loaf, one H4374
Lev 8:28 Then Moses t them from their hands and H4374
Lev 8:29 Moses also t the breast, which was his H4374
Lev 8:30 Then Moses t some of the anointing oil H4374
Lev 9: 5 They t the things Moses commanded to H4374
Lev 9:15 He t the goat for the people's sin offering H4374
Lev 9:17 t a handful of it and burned it on H4848+4090
Lev 10: 1 sons Nadab and Abihu t their censers, H4374
Lev 24:23 and they t the blasphemer outside the H3655
Nu 1:17 Moses and Aaron t these men whose H4374
Nu 7: 6 So Moses t the carts and oxen and gave H4374
Nu 11:25 and he t some of the power of the Spirit H724
Nu 15:36 So the assembly t him outside the camp H3655
Nu 16:18 So each of them t his censer, put burning H4374
Nu 17: 9 each of the leaders t his own staff. H4374
Nu 20: 9 So Moses t the staff from the LORD's H4374
Nu 21:24 to the sword and t over his land from the H3769
Nu 21:35 And they t possession of his land. H3769
Nu 22:41 next morning Balak t Balaam up to H4374
Nu 23:14 So he t him to the field of Zophim on the H4374
Nu 23:28 And Balak t Balaam to the top of Peor H4374
Nu 25: 7 he left the assembly, t a spear in his hand H4374
Nu 27:22 He t Joshua and had him stand before H4374
Nu 31: 6 who t with him articles from the H928+3338
Nu 31: 9 t all the Midianite herds, ... as plunder H1024
Nu 31:11 They t all the plunder and spoils H4374
Nu 31:27 soldiers who t part in the battle H3655+4200
Nu 31:32 that the soldiers t was 675,000 sheep, H1024
Dt 1:15 So I t the leading men of your tribes, wise H4374
Dt 2:34 At that time we t all his towns and H4334
Dt 3: 4 At that time we t all his cities. There was H4334
Dt 3: 8 So at that time we t from these two kings H4374
Dt 3:10 We t all the towns on the plateau, and all NDT
Dt 3:12 Of the land that we t over at that time, H3769
Dt 3:14 t the whole region of Argob as far as the H4374
Dt 4:20 the LORD t you and brought you out of the H4374
Dt 4:47 They t possession of his land and the land H3769
Dt 9:17 So I t the two tablets and threw them out H9530
Dt 9:21 Also I t that sinful thing of yours, the calf H4374
Dt 29: 8 We t their land and gave it as an H4374
Dt 32:37 are their gods, the rock they t refuge in, H2879
Jos 3: 6 So they t it up and went ahead of them H5951
Jos 4: 8 They t twelve stones from the middle of H5951
Jos 6:12 the priests t up the ark of the LORD. H5951
Jos 6:20 charged straight in, and they t the city. H4334
Jos 7: 1 of the tribe of Judah, t some of them. H4374
Jos 7:21 fifty shekels, I coveted them and t them. H4374
Jos 7:23 They t the things from the tent, brought H4374
Jos 7:24 with all Israel, t Achan son of Zerah, the H4374
Jos 8:13 So the soldiers t up their positions—with H8492
Jos 8:23 But they t the king of Ai alive and brought H9530
Jos 10: 5 troops and t up positions against Gibeon H2837
Jos 10: 9 Joshua t them by surprise. H995+448
Jos 10:27 the order and they t them down from the H3718
Jos 10:28 That day Joshua t Makkedah. He put the H4334
Jos 10:31 he t up positions against it and attacked it H2837
Jos 10:32 and Joshua t it on the second day. H4334
Jos 10:34 they t up positions against it and attacked H2837
Jos 10:37 They t the city and put it to the sword H4334
Jos 10:39 They t the city, its king and its villages H4334
Jos 11:12 Joshua t all these royal cities and their H4334
Jos 11:16 So Joshua t this entire land: the hill H4374
Jos 11:19 the Israelites, who t them all in battle. H4374
Jos 11:23 So Joshua t the entire land, just as the H4374
Jos 12: 1 whose territory they t over east of the H3769
Jos 15:17 Caleb's brother, t it; so Caleb gave his H4334
Jos 19:47 attacked Leshem, t it, put it to the H4334
Jos 21:43 and they t possession of it and settled H3769
Jos 24: 3 But I t your father Abraham from the land H4374
Jos 24: 8 and you t possession of their land. H3769
Jos 24:26 Then he t a large stone and set it up H4374
Jdg 1: 8 of Judah attacked Jerusalem also and t it. H4334
Jdg 1:13 younger brother, t it; so Caleb gave his H4334
Jdg 1:18 Judah also t Gaza, Ashkelon and Ekron H4334
Jdg 1:19 They t possession of the hill country, but H3769
Jdg 3: 6 They t their daughters in marriage H4374+4200+851
Jdg 3:13 and they t possession of the City of Palms. H3769
Jdg 3:25 the room, they t a key and unlocked them. H4374
Jdg 3:28 him down and t possession of the fords of H4334
Jdg 5: 6 abandoned; travelers t to winding paths. H2143
Jdg 5:19 of Megiddo, they t no plunder of silver. H4374
Jdg 6:27 So Gideon t ten of his servants and did as H4374
Jdg 7: 5 So Gideon t the men down to the water H3718
Jdg 7: 8 who t over the provisions and trumpets of H4374
Jdg 8:16 He t the elders of the town and taught the H4374
Jdg 8:21 t the ornaments off their camels' H4374
Jdg 9:34 by night and t up concealed positions near H741
Jdg 9:43 So he t his men, divided them into three H4374
Jdg 9:48 He t an ax and cut off some branches H4374
Jdg 11:13 they t away my land from the Arnon to the H4374
Jdg 11:21 Israel t over all the land of the Amorites H3769
Jdg 12: 3 I t my life in my hands and crossed over to H8492
Jdg 13:19 Then Manoah t a young goat, together H4374
Jdg 15: 1 Samson t a young goat and went to visit H928
Jdg 16: 3 Then he got up and t hold of the doors of H296
Jdg 16:12 So Delilah t new ropes and tied him with H4374
Jdg 16:13 Delilah t the seven braids of his head NDT
Jdg 16:21 out his eyes and t him down to Gaza. H3718
Jdg 17: 2 a curse—I have that silver with me; I t it." H4374
Jdg 17: 4 she t two hundred shekels of silver and H4374
Jdg 18:17 went inside and t the idol, H4374+2256+5011
Jdg 18:18 went into Micah's house and t the idol, H4374
Jdg 18:20 He t the ephod, the household gods and H4374
Jdg 18:24 He replied, "You t the gods I made, and H4374
Jdg 18:27 Then they t what Micah had made, and H4374
Jdg 19: 1 hill country of Ephraim t a concubine from H4374
Jdg 19: 3 She t him into her parents' home, and H995
Jdg 19:15 but no one t them in for the night. H665
Jdg 19:21 So he t him into his house and fed his H995
Jdg 19:25 So the man t his concubine and sent her H2616
Jdg 19:29 he t a knife and cut up his concubine H4374
Jdg 20: 2 of Israel t their places in the assembly H3656
Jdg 20: 6 I t my concubine, cut her into pieces and H296
Jdg 20:20 t up battle positions against them H6885
Jdg 20:22 again t up their positions where they H6885
Jdg 20:30 third day and t up positions against H6885
Jdg 20:33 places and t up positions at Baal Tamar, H6885
Jdg 21:12 and they t them to the camp at Shiloh in H995
Ru 2:19 Blessed be the man who t notice of you!" H5795
Ru 4: 2 Boaz t ten of the elders of the town and H4374
Ru 4: 7 one party t off his sandal and gave it to H8990
Ru 4:13 So Boaz t Ruth and she became his wife H4374
Ru 4:16 Then Naomi t the child in her arms and H4374
1Sa 1:24 he was weaned, she t the boy with her H6590
1Sa 2:19 him a little robe and t it to him when she H6590
1Sa 5: 1 they t it from Ebenezer to Ashdod. H995
1Sa 5: 3 They t Dagon and put him back in his H4374
1Sa 6:10 They t two such cows and hitched them to H4374
1Sa 6:15 The Levites t down the ark of the LORD H3718
1Sa 7: 1 Jearim came and t up the ark of the LORD. H6590
1Sa 7: 9 Then Samuel t a suckling lamb and H4374
1Sa 7:12 Then Samuel t a stone and set it up H4374
1Sa 9:24 So the cook t up the thigh with what was H8123
1Sa 10: 1 Then Samuel t a flask of olive oil and H4374
1Sa 11: 7 He t a pair of oxen, cut them into pieces H4374
1Sa 14:30 of the plunder they t from their enemies. H5162
1Sa 14:52 brave man, he t him into his service. H665
1Sa 15: 8 He t Agag king of the Amalekites alive H9530
1Sa 15:21 The soldiers t sheep and cattle from the H4374
1Sa 16:13 So Samuel t the horn of oil and anointed H4374
1Sa 16:20 So Jesse t a donkey loaded with bread, H4374
1Sa 17:16 morning and evening and t his stand. H3656
1Sa 17:39 I am not used to them." So he t them off. H6073
1Sa 17:40 Then he t his staff in his hand, chose five H4374
1Sa 17:51 He t hold of the Philistine's sword and H4374
1Sa 17:54 David t the Philistine's head and brought H4374
1Sa 17:57 Abner t him and brought him before Saul H4374
1Sa 18: 4 Jonathan t off the robe he was wearing H7320
1Sa 18:27 David t his men with him and went out and AIT
1Sa 19: 5 He t his life in his hands when he killed H8492
1Sa 19: 6 Saul listened to Jonathan and t this oath H8678
1Sa 19:13 Then Michal t an idol and laid it on the H4374
1Sa 20: 3 But David t an oath and said, "Your father H8678
1Sa 21:12 David t these words to heart and was very H8492
1Sa 24: 2 So Saul t three thousand able young men H4374
1Sa 25:18 She t two hundred loaves of bread, two H4374
1Sa 26:12 So David t the spear and water jug near H4374
1Sa 27: 9 woman alive, but t sheep and cattle H4374
1Sa 28:21 I t my life in my hands and did what you H8492
1Sa 28:24 She t some flour, kneaded it and baked H4374
1Sa 30:20 He t all the flocks and herds, and his men H4374
1Sa 31: 4 so Saul t his own sword and fell on it. H4374
1Sa 31:12 They t down the bodies of Saul and his H4374
1Sa 31:13 Then they t their bones and buried them H4374
2Sa 1:10 And I t the crown that was on his head H4374
2Sa 1:11 the men with him t hold of their clothes H2616
2Sa 1:17 David t up this lament concerning H7801+7806
2Sa 2: 3 David also t the men who were with him H6590
2Sa 2:25 into a group and t their stand on top of a H6641
2Sa 2:32 They t Asahel and buried him in his H5951
2Sa 3:27 Joab t him aside into an inner chamber H5742
2Sa 3:35 was still day; but David t an oath, saying, H8678
2Sa 3:36 All the people t note and were pleased H5795
2Sa 4:12 But they t the head of Ish-Bosheth and H4374
2Sa 5: 9 David then t up residence in the fortress H3782
2Sa 5:13 David t more concubines and wives in H4374
2Sa 6: 6 reached out and t hold of the ark of God, H296
2Sa 6:10 he t it to the house of Obed-Edom the H5742
2Sa 7: 8 I t you from the pasture, from tending the H4374
2Sa 7:15 from him, as I t it away from Saul, whom H6073
2Sa 8: 1 he t Metheg Ammah from the control H4374
2Sa 8: 7 David t the gold shields that belonged to H4374
2Sa 8: 8 King David t a great quantity of bronze. H4374
2Sa 12: 4 he t the ewe lamb that belonged to the H4374
2Sa 12: 9 with the sword and t his wife to be your H4374
2Sa 12:10 you despised me and t the wife of Uriah H4374
2Sa 12:30 David t the crown from their king's head H4374
2Sa 12:30 t a great quantity of plunder from the H3655
2Sa 13: 8 She t some dough, kneaded it, made the H4374
2Sa 13: 9 Then she t the pan and served him the H4374
2Sa 13:10 And Tamar t the bread she had prepared H4374
2Sa 13:11 But when she t it to him to eat, he H5602
2Sa 15:29 Abiathar t the ark of God back to H8740
2Sa 17:19 His wife t a covering and spread it out over H4374
2Sa 18: 6 the battle t place in the forest of H2118
2Sa 18:14 So he t three javelins in his hand and H4374
2Sa 18:17 They t Absalom, threw him into a big pit H4374
2Sa 19: 8 king got up and t his seat in the gateway. H3782
2Sa 20: 3 he t the ten concubines he had left to H4374
2Sa 20: 5 he t longer than the time the king had set H336
2Sa 20: 9 Then Joab t Amasa by the beard with his H296
2Sa 21: 8 But the king t Armoni and Mephibosheth H4374
2Sa 21:10 daughter of Aiah t sackcloth and spread it H4374
2Sa 21:12 he went and t the bones of Saul and his H4374
2Sa 21:20 which t place at Gath, there H2118
2Sa 22:17 down from on high and t hold of me; H4374
2Sa 23:12 But Shammah t his stand in the middle of H3656
1Ki 1: 4 she t care of the king and waited H2118+6125
1Ki 1:29 The king then t an oath: "As surely as the H8678
1Ki 1:39 Zadok the priest t the horn of oil from the H4374
1Ki 1:50 went and t hold of the horns of the altar. H2616
1Ki 2:28 of the LORD and t hold of the horns of the H2616
1Ki 3:20 of the night and t my son from my side H4374
1Ki 7: 1 It t Solomon thirteen years, however, to NDT
1Ki 7:23 It t a line of thirty cubits to measure around NDT
1Ki 8: 3 Israel had arrived, the priests t up the ark, H5951
1Ki 8:48 land of their enemies who t them captive, H8647
1Ki 11:24 where they settled and t control. H4887

1Ki 11:30 Ahijah t hold of the new cloak he was H9530
1Ki 13:10 So he t another road and did not return by H2143
1Ki 14:26 He t everything, including all the gold H4374
1Ki 15:18 Asa then t all the silver and gold that was H4374
1Ki 17:19 He t him from her arms, carried him to the H4374
1Ki 18:26 So they t the bull given them and H4374
1Ki 18:31 Elijah t twelve stones, one for each of the H4374
1Ki 19:21 He t his yoke of oxen and slaughtered H4374
1Ki 20: 9 left and t the answer back to Ben-Hadad. H8740
1Ki 20:33 The men t this as a good sign and were H5727
1Ki 20:34 the cities my father t from your father," H4374
1Ki 21:13 So they t him outside the city and stoned H3655
2Ki 2: 8 Elijah t his cloak, rolled it up and struck H4374
2Ki 2:12 Then he t hold of his garment and tore it H2616
2Ki 2:14 He t the cloak that had fallen from Elijah H4374
2Ki 3:26 he t with him seven hundred swordsmen H4374
2Ki 3:27 Then he t his firstborn son, who was to H4374
2Ki 4:27 at the mountain, she t hold of his feet. H2616
2Ki 4:37 Then she t her son and went out H5951
2Ki 5: 6 The letter that he t to the king of Israel read: H995
2Ki 5:24 he t the things from the servants and put H4374
2Ki 6: 7 the man reached out his hand and t it. H4374
2Ki 7: 8 Then they t silver, gold and clothes, and H5951
2Ki 7: 8 another tent and t some things from it H5951
2Ki 8:15 But the next day he t a thick cloth, soaked H4374
2Ki 9:13 They quickly t their cloaks and spread H4374
2Ki 9:28 His servants t him by chariot to Jerusalem H8206
2Ki 10: 7 these men t the princes and slaughtered H4374
2Ki 10:14 So they t them alive and slaughtered H9530
2Ki 11: 2 t Joash son of Ahaziah and stole him H4374
2Ki 11: 9 Each one t his men—those who were H4374
2Ki 11:19 He t with him the commanders of H4374
2Ki 11:19 The king then t his place on the royal H3782
2Ki 12: 9 Jehoiada the priest t a chest and bored a H4374
2Ki 12:18 Joash king of Judah t all the sacred H4374
2Ki 13:18 "Take the arrows," and the king t them. H4374
2Ki 14:14 He t all the gold and silver and all the H4374
2Ki 14:14 He also t hostages and returned to Samaria NDT
2Ki 14:21 Then all the people of Judah t Azariah H4374
2Ki 15:29 king of Assyria came and t Ijon, H4374
2Ki 15:29 He t Gilead and Galilee, including all the NDT
2Ki 16: 8 And Ahaz t the silver and gold found in H4374
2Ki 16:18 He t away the Sabbath canopy that had H6015
2Ki 17: 7 All this t place because the Israelites had H2118
2Ki 17:24 They t over Samaria and lived in its towns. H3769
2Ki 17:27 of the priests you t captive from Samaria go AIT
2Ki 18:10 At the end of three years the Assyrians t it H4334
2Ki 21: 7 He t the carved Asherah pole he had made NDT
2Ki 22:20 So they t her answer back to the king. H8740
2Ki 23: 4 Kidron Valley and t the ashes to Bethel. H5951
2Ki 23: 6 He t the Asherah pole from the temple of H3655
2Ki 23:30 people of the land t Jehoahaz son of H4374
2Ki 23:34 But he t Jehoahaz and carried him off to H4374
2Ki 24:12 king of Babylon, he t Jehoiachin prisoner. H4374
2Ki 24:15 t Jehoiachin captive to Babylon. H1655
2Ki 24:15 He also t from Jerusalem to H2143+1583
2Ki 25: 7 with bronze shackles and t him to Babylon. H995
2Ki 25:14 They also t away the pots, shovels, wick H4374
2Ki 25:15 the imperial guard t away the censers H4374
2Ki 25:18 of the guard t as prisoners Seraiah the H4374
2Ki 25:19 he t the officer in charge of the fighting H4374
2Ki 25:19 He also t the secretary who was chief officer NDT
2Ki 25:20 the commander t them all and brought H4374
2Ki 25:24 Gedaliah t an oath to reassure them and H8678
1Ch 5: 6 Tiglath-Pileser king of Assyria t into exile. H1655
1Ch 5:21 They also t one hundred thousand people NDT
1Ch 5:26 who t the Reubenites, the Gadites and
the half-tribe of Manasseh into exile H1655
1Ch 5:26 He t them to Halah, Habor, Hara and the H995
1Ch 7:15 Makir t a wife from among the Huppites H4374
1Ch 9:30 priests t care of mixing the spices H8379+5351
1Ch 10: 4 so Saul t his own sword and fell on it. H4374
1Ch 10: 9 They stripped him and t his head and his H5951
1Ch 10:12 valiant men went and t the bodies of Saul H5951
1Ch 11: 7 David then t up residence in the fortress H3782
1Ch 11:14 But they t their stand in the middle of the H3656
1Ch 13:13 he t it to the house of Obed-Edom the H5742
1Ch 14: 3 In Jerusalem David t more wives and H4374
1Ch 17: 7 I t you from the pasture, from tending the H4374
1Ch 17:13 as I t it away from your predecessor. H6073
1Ch 18: 1 and he t Gath and its surrounding villages H4374
1Ch 18: 7 David t the gold shields carried by the H4374
1Ch 18: 8 David t a great quantity of bronze H4374
1Ch 20: 2 David t the crown from the head of their H4374
1Ch 20: 2 He t a great quantity of plunder from the H3655
1Ch 20: 6 which t place at Gath, there H2118
1Ch 27:32 son of Hakmoni t care of the king's sons. H6640
2Ch 2:17 Solomon t a census of all the foreigners H6218
2Ch 4: 2 It t a line of thirty cubits to measure around NDT
2Ch 5: 4 had arrived, the Levites t up the ark, H5951
2Ch 7: 6 The priests t their positions, as did the H6641
2Ch 11:23 provisions and t many wives for them. H8626
2Ch 12: 9 He t everything, including the gold H4374
2Ch 13:19 Jeroboam and t from him the towns H4334
2Ch 14:10 and they t up battle positions in the H6885
2Ch 15: 8 son of Oded the prophet, he t courage. H2616
2Ch 15:14 They t an oath to the LORD with loud H8678
2Ch 16: 2 Asa then t the silver and gold out of the H3655
2Ch 20:25 much plunder that it t three days to collect NDT
2Ch 22:11 t Joash son of Ahaziah and stole him H4374
2Ch 23: 8 Each one t his men—those who were H4374
2Ch 23:20 He t with him the commanders of H4374
2Ch 25:12 t them to the top of a cliff and threw them H995
2Ch 25:24 He t all the gold and silver and all the NDT
2Ch 26: 1 Then all the people of Judah t Uzziah H4374
2Ch 28: 5 t many of his people as prisoners H8647+8664
2Ch 28: 8 The men of Israel t captive from their H8647
2Ch 28: 8 They also t a great deal of plunder, which H1024
2Ch 28:15 men designated by name t the prisoners, H2616
2Ch 28:15 So they t them back to their fellow H995
2Ch 28:21 Ahaz t some of the things from the temple H2745
2Ch 29:16 The Levites t it and carried it out to the H7691
2Ch 29:22 the priests t the blood and splashed H7691
2Ch 30:16 Then they t up their regular H6641+6584
2Ch 32:22 He t care of them on every side H5633
2Ch 33: 7 He t the image he had made and put it in NDT
2Ch 33:11 Assyria, who t Manasseh prisoner, put a H4334
2Ch 33:11 bronze shackles and t him to Babylon. H2143
2Ch 34:16 Then Shaphan t the book to the king and H995
2Ch 34:28 So they t her answer back to the king. H8740
2Ch 35:24 So they t him out of his chariot, put him in H6296
2Ch 36: 1 people of the land t Jehoahaz son of H4374
2Ch 36: 4 But Necho t Eliakim's brother Jehoahaz H4374
2Ch 36: 7 Nebuchadnezzar also t to Babylon articles H995
Ezr 3:10 cymbals, t their places to praise the LORD H6641
Ezr 6: 5 Nebuchadnezzar t from the temple in A10485
Ezr 7:28 I t courage and gathered leaders from H2616
Ezr 10: 5 been suggested. And they t the oath. H8678
Ne 2: 1 I t the wine and gave it to the king. H5951
Ne 4:23 the guards with me t off our clothes; H7320
Ne 5:15 on the people and t forty shekels of silver H4374
Ne 9:22 They t over the country of Sihon king of H3769
Ne 9:24 went in and t possession of the land. H3769
Ne 9:25 they t possession of houses filled with all H3769
Ne 12:40 thanks then t their places in the house of H6641
Est 3:10 So the king t his signet ring from his H6073
Est 8: 2 The king t off his signet ring, which he had H6073
Est 9:27 the Jews t it on themselves to establish H7691
Job 2: 8 Then Job t a piece of broken pottery and H4374
Job 29: 7 gate of the city and t my seat in the public H3922
Job 29:16 the needy; I t up the case of the stranger. H2983
Ps 18:16 down from on high and t hold of me; H4374
Ps 68:18 on high, you t many captives; you H8647+8660
Ps 78:70 his servant and t him from the sheep H4374
Ps 80: 9 and it t root and filled the land. H9245+9247
Ps 104: 7 the sound of your thunder they t to flight; H2905
Ps 106:44 Yet he t note of their distress when he H8011
Pr 7:13 She t hold of him and kissed him and H2616
Pr 7:20 He t his purse filled with money and will H4374
Ecc 2:10 My heart t delight in all my labor, and this AIT
Ecc 8: 2 because you t an oath before God. NDT
SS 5: 7 they bruised me; they t away my cloak H5951
Isa 33:18 Where is the one who t the revenue H9202
Isa 41: 9 I t you from the ends of the earth, from its H2616
Isa 43:14 in the ships in which they t pride. NDT
Isa 44:14 or perhaps t a cypress or oak. H4374
Isa 53: 4 Surely he t up our pain and bore our H5951
Jer 13: 7 dug up the belt and t it from the place H4374
Jer 25:17 So I t the cup from the LORD's hand and H4374
Jer 26:10 of the LORD and t their places at the H3782
Jer 26:23 out of Egypt and t him to King Jehoiakim, H995
Jer 28: 3 removed from here and t to Babylon. H995
Jer 28:10 the prophet Hananiah t the yoke off the H4374
Jer 31:32 ancestors when I t them by the hand to H2616
Jer 32:11 I t the deed of purchase—the sealed copy H4374
Jer 32:23 They came in and t possession of it, but H3769
Jer 34:11 their minds and t back the slaves they had H8740
Jer 36:32 So Jeremiah t another scroll and gave it H4374
Jer 38: 6 So they t Jeremiah and put him into the H4374
Jer 38:11 So Ebed-Melek t the men with him and H4374
Jer 38:11 He t some old rags and worn-out clothes H4374
Jer 39: 3 Babylon came and t seats in the Middle H3782
Jer 39: 5 captured him and t him to H6590
Jer 40: 9 t an oath to reassure them and their men. H8678
Jer 41:10 of Nethaniah t them captive and set out H8647
Jer 41:12 they t all their men and went to fight H4374
Jer 43: 6 And they t Jeremiah the prophet and Baruch NDT
Jer 52:11 with bronze shackles and t him to Babylon, H995
Jer 52:18 They also t away the pots, shovels, wick H4374
Jer 52:19 of the imperial guard t away the basins, H4374
Jer 52:24 of the guard t as prisoners Seraiah the H4374
Jer 52:25 he t the officer in charge of the fighting H4374
Jer 52:25 He also t the secretary who was chief officer NDT
Jer 52:26 the commander t them all and brought H4374
La 3:58 You, Lord, t up my case; you redeemed H8189
Eze 3:14 Spirit then lifted me up and t me away, H4374
Eze 3:21 will surely live because they t warning, H2302
Eze 7:20 They t pride in their beautiful jewelry and H8492
Eze 8: 3 like a hand and t me by the hair of my H4374
Eze 8: 3 in visions of God he t me to Jerusalem, H995
Eze 10: 7 He t up some of it and put it into the H5951
Eze 10: 7 the man in linen, who t it and went out. H4374
Eze 12: 7 I t my belongings out at dusk, carrying H3655
Eze 16:16 You t some of your garments to make H4374
Eze 16:17 You also t the fine jewelry I gave you, the H4374
Eze 16:18 And you t your embroidered clothes to put H4374
Eze 16:20 " 'And you t your sons and daughters H4374
Eze 17: 5 " 'He t one of the seedlings of the land H4374
Eze 17:13 Then he t a member of the royal family H4374
Eze 18: 7 returns what he t in pledge for a loan. H2481
Eze 18:12 He does not return what he t in pledge H2478
Eze 19: 5 she t another of her cubs and made him a H4374
Eze 23:10 t away her sons and daughters and killed H4374
Eze 25:12 Edom t revenge on Judah and H5933+5934
Eze 25:15 and t revenge with malice H5933+5934
Eze 27: 5 they t a cedar from Lebanon to make a H4374
Eze 33:15 give back what they t in pledge for a loan, H2478
Eze 40: 1 of the LORD was on me and he t me there. H995
Eze 40: 2 In visions of God he t me to the land of H995
Eze 40: 3 He t me there, and I saw a man whose H995
Eze 42: 5 the galleries t more space from them than H430
Da 1:16 So the guard t away their choice food and H5951
Da 2:25 Arioch t Daniel to the king at once and A10549
Da 3:22 killed the soldiers who t up Shadrach, A10513
Da 5:31 Darius the Mede t over the kingdom A10618
Da 7: 9 the Ancient of Days t his seat. A10338
Da 8:11 it t away the daily sacrifice from the LORD H8123
Da 11: 1 I t my stand to support and protect him.) H6641
Hos 13:11 you a king, and in my wrath I t him away. H4374
Joel 2:18 his land and t pity on his people. H2798
Joel 3: 5 For you t my silver and my gold and carried H4374
Am 1: 6 Because she t captive whole communities H1655
Am 7:14 I also t care of sycamore-fig trees. H1179
Am 7:15 But the LORD t me from tending the flock H4374
Jnh 1:15 Then they t Jonah and threw him H5951
Jnh 3: 3 large city; it t three days to go through it. NDT
Jnh 3: 6 rose from his throne, t off his royal robes H6296
Zec 11: 7 Then I t two staffs and called one Favor H4374
Zec 11:10 Then I t my staff called Favor and broke it H4374
Zec 11:13 So I t the thirty pieces of silver and threw H4374
Mt 1:22 All this t place to fulfill what the Lord had G1181
Mt 1:24 him and t Mary home as his wife. G4161
Mt 2:14 t the child and his mother during the G4161
Mt 2:21 t the child and his mother and went to the G4161
Mt 4: 5 Then the devil t him to the holy city and G4161
Mt 4: 8 the devil t him to a very high mountain G4161
Mt 8:17 "He t up our infirmities and bore our G3284
Mt 9:25 he went in and t the girl by the hand G3195
Mt 13:31 which a man t and planted in his field. G3284
Mt 13:33 yeast that a woman t and mixed into G3284
Mt 13:57 And they t offense at him. But Jesus said G4997
Mt 14:12 disciples came and t his body and buried it G149
Mt 15:36 Then he t the seven loaves and the fish G3284
Mt 16:22 Peter t him aside and began to rebuke G4689
Mt 17: 1 After six days Jesus t with him Peter G4161
Mt 18:27 The servant's master t pity on him G5072
Mt 20:17 he t the Twelve aside and said to them G4161
Mt 21: 4 This t place to fulfill what was spoken G1181
Mt 21:39 So they t him and threw him out of the G3284
Mt 24:39 the flood came and t them all away. G149
Mt 25: 1 ten virgins who t their lamps and went G3284
Mt 25: 3 The foolish ones t their lamps but did not G3284
Mt 25: 4 t oil in jars along with their lamps. G3284
Mt 26:26 were eating, Jesus t bread, and when he G3284
Mt 26:27 Then he t a cup, and when he had given G3284
Mt 26:37 He t Peter and the two sons of Zebedee along with G4161
Mt 26:57 had arrested Jesus t him to Caiaphas the G552
Mt 27: 9 "They t the thirty pieces of silver, the price G3284
Mt 27:24 he t water and washed his hands in front G3284
Mt 27:27 the governor's soldiers t Jesus into the G4161
Mt 27:30 t the staff and struck him on the head G3284
Mt 27:31 they t off the robe and put his own clothes G1694
Mt 27:59 Joseph t the body, wrapped it in a clean G3284
Mt 28:15 So the soldiers t the money and did as G3284
Mk 1:31 t her hand and helped her up. G3195
Mk 2:12 t his mat and walked out in full view of G149
Mk 4:36 crowd behind, they t him along, just as he G4161
Mk 5:40 he t the child's father and mother and the G4161
Mk 5:41 He t her by the hand and said to her G3195
Mk 6: 3 And they t offense at him. G4997
Mk 6:29 disciples came and t his body and laid it in G149
Mk 7:33 After he t him aside, away from the crowd G655
Mk 8:23 He t the blind man by the hand and led G2138
Mk 8:32 Peter t him aside and began to G4689
Mk 9: 2 Jesus t Peter, James and John with him G4161
Mk 9:27 But Jesus t him by the hand and lifted him G3195
Mk 9:36 He t a little child whom he placed among G3284
Mk 10:16 And he t the children in his arms, placed G1878
Mk 10:32 Again he t the Twelve aside and told G4161
Mk 12: 8 So they t him and killed him, and threw G3284
Mk 14:22 were eating, Jesus t bread, and when he G3284
Mk 14:23 Then he t a cup, and when he had given G3284
Mk 14:33 He t Peter, James and John along with G4161
Mk 14:53 They t Jesus to the high priest, and all the G552
Mk 14:65 And the guards t him and beat him. G3284
Mk 15:20 they t off the purple robe and put his own G1694
Mk 15:46 linen cloth, t down the body, wrapped G2747
Lk 2: 2 first census that t place while Quirinius G1181
Lk 2:22 Joseph and Mary t him to Jerusalem to G343
Lk 2:28 Simeon t him in his arms and praised God, G1312
Lk 4:29 t him to the brow of the hill on which G72
Lk 5:25 t what he had been lying on and went G149
Lk 8:54 But he t her by the hand and said, "My G3195
Lk 9:10 Then he t them with him and they G4161
Lk 9:28 he t Peter, John and James with him and G4161
Lk 9:47 t a little child and had him stand beside G2138
Lk 10:33 when he saw him, he t pity on him. G5072
Lk 10:34 brought him to an inn and t care of him. G2150
Lk 10:35 The next day he t out two denarii and G1675
Lk 13: 7 said to the man who t care of the vineyard, G307
Lk 13:19 which a man t and planted in his garden. G3284
Lk 13:21 yeast that a woman t and mixed into G3284
Lk 18:31 Jesus t the Twelve aside and told them G4161
Lk 22:19 And he t bread, gave thanks and broke it G3284
Lk 22:20 after the supper he t the cup, saying, NDT

Lk 22:54 led him away and **t** him **into** the house of *G1652*
Lk 23:48 to witness this sight saw what **t place,** *G1181*
Lk 23:53 Then *he* **t** it **down**, wrapped it in linen *G2747*
Lk 24: 1 the women **t** the spices they had prepared *G5770*
Lk 24:21 it is the third day since all this **t place**. *G1181*
Lk 24:30 table with them, *he* **t** bread, gave thanks, *G3284*
Lk 24:43 and *he* **t** it and ate it in their presence. *G3284*
Jn 2: 1 day a wedding **t place** at Cana in Galilee *G1181*
Jn 4:50 man **t** Jesus **at** *his* **word** and *G4409+3836+3364*
Jn 5: 9 day on which this **t** place was a Sabbath, NDT
Jn 6:11 Jesus then **t** the loaves, gave thanks, and *G3284*
Jn 11:41 So *they* **t away** the stone. Then Jesus *G149*
Jn 12: 3 Then Mary **t** about a pint of pure nard, an *G3284*
Jn 12:13 *They* **t** palm branches and went out to *G3284*
Jn 13: 4 up from the meal, **t off** his outer clothing *G5502*
Jn 13:27 As soon as Judas **t** the bread, Satan entered NDT
Jn 18:28 the Jewish leaders **t** Jesus from Caiaphas to *G72*
Jn 18:32 This **t** place to fulfill what Jesus had said NDT
Jn 19: 1 Then Pilate **t** Jesus and had him flogged. *G3284*
Jn 19:16 So the soldiers **t charge of** Jesus. *G4161*
Jn 19:23 crucified Jesus, *they* **t** his clothes, dividing *G3284*
Jn 19:27 time on, this disciple **t** her into his home. *G3284*
Jn 19:38 permission, he came and **t** the body **away**. *G149*
Jn 21:13 **t** the bread and gave it to them *G3284*
Ac 4:13 astonished and *they* **t note** that these *G2105*
Ac 7:21 Pharaoh's daughter **t** him and brought him *G359*
Ac 7:45 it with them when they **t** the land from the *G2959*
Ac 8:39 Spirit of the Lord **suddenly t** Philip **away**, *G773*
Ac 9:25 But his followers **t** him by night and *G3284*
Ac 9:27 But Barnabas **t** him and brought him to the *G2138*
Ac 9:30 *they* **t** him **down** to Caesarea and sent *G2864*
Ac 9:41 *He* **t** her by the hand and helped her to *G1443*
Ac 13:20 All this **t** about 450 years. "After this, God NDT
Ac 13:29 *they* **t** him **down** from the cross and laid *G2747*
Ac 15:39 Barnabas **t** Mark and sailed for Cyprus *G4161*
Ac 16:33 the night the jailer **t** them and washed *G4161*
Ac 17:19 Then *they* **t** him and brought him to a *G2138*
Ac 19: 1 Paul **t the road through** the interior and *G1451*
Ac 19: 9 *He* **t** the disciples *with* him and had *G928*
Ac 20:12 *The people* **t** the young man **home** alive *G72*
Ac 20:14 *we* **t** him **aboard** and went on to Mitylene. *G377*
Ac 21:11 Coming over to us, *he* **t** Paul's belt, tied his *G149*
Ac 21:26 The next day Paul **t** the men and purified *G4161*
Ac 21:32 He at once **t** some officers and soldiers *G4161*
Ac 23:18 So he **t** him to the commander. *G72*
Ac 23:19 The commander **t** the young man by the *G2138*
Ac 23:31 **t** Paul with them during the night and *G377*
Ac 27:18 **t such a** violent **battering from the storm** *G5928*
Ac 27:28 *They* **t soundings** and found that the water *G1075*
Ac 27:28 time later *they* **t soundings** again and *G1075*
Ac 27:35 *he* **t** some bread and gave thanks to God *G3284*
1Co 11:23 on the night he was betrayed, **t** bread, *G3284*
1Co 11:25 same way, after supper he **t** the cup, saying, NDT
Gal 2: 1 time with Barnabas. *I* **t** Titus **along** also. *G5221*
Eph 4: 8 *he* **t many captives** and gave gifts to *G169+168*
Php 3:12 of that for which Christ Jesus **t hold of** *me*. *G2898*
Heb 8: 9 ancestors when I **t** them **by** the hand to *G2138*
Heb 9:19 to all the people, *he* **t** the blood of calves *G3284*
Rev 5: 7 He went and **t** the scroll from the right *G3284*
Rev 8: 5 Then the angel **t** the censer, filled it with *G3284*
Rev 10:10 *I* **t** the little scroll from the angel's hand *G3284*

TOOL (9) [TOOLS]

Ex 20:25 you will defile it if you use a **t** on it. H2995
Ex 32: 4 the shape of a calf, fashioning it with a **t**. H3032
Dt 27: 5 Do not use any **iron t** on them. H1366
Jos 8:31 on which no **iron t** had been used. H1366
2Sa 23: 7 thorns uses a **t of iron** or the shaft of a H1366
1Ki 6: 7 any other iron **t** was heard at the H3998
Job 19:24 they were inscribed with an iron **t** on lead, H6485
Isa 44:12 blacksmith takes a **t** and works with it in H5108
Jer 17: 1 "Judah's sin is engraved with an iron **t** H6485

TOOLS (1) [TOOL]

Ge 4:22 forged all kinds of **t** out of bronze and iron H3086

TOOTH (11) [TEETH]

Ex 21:24 eye for eye, **t** for tooth, hand for hand, foot H9094
Ex 21:24 eye for eye, tooth for **t**, hand for hand, foot H9094
Ex 21:27 who knocks out the **t** *of* a male or female H9094
Ex 21:27 the slave go free to compensate for the **t**. H9094
Lev 24:20 eye for eye, **t** for tooth. The one who H9094
Lev 24:20 eye for eye, tooth for **t**. The one who has H9094
Dt 19:21 life, eye for eye, **t** for tooth, hand for H9094
Dt 19:21 eye, tooth for **t**, hand for hand, foot H9094
Pr 25:19 Like a broken **t** or a lame foot is reliance H9094
Mt 5:38 it was said, 'Eye for eye, and **t** for tooth. *G3848*
Mt 5:38 it was said, 'Eye for eye, and tooth for **t**. *G3848*

TOP (89) [HOUSETOP, TOPMOST, TOPS]

Ge 22: 9 laid him on the altar, on **t** of the wood. H5087
Ge 28:12 on the earth, with its **t** reaching to heaven H8031
Ge 28:18 it up as a pillar and poured oil on **t** *of* it. H8031
Ge 40:17 In the **t** basket were all kinds of baked H6609
Ge 47:31 as he leaned on the **t** *of* his staff. H8031
Ex 12:22 of the blood on the **t** and on both sides of H5485
Ex 12:23 see the blood on the **t** and sides of the H5485
Ex 17: 9 I will stand on **t** *of* the hill with the staff H8031
Ex 17:10 Aaron and Hur went to the **t** *of* the hill. H8031
Ex 19:20 descended to the **t** *of* Mount Sinai and H8031
Ex 19:20 called Moses to the **t** *of* the mountain. H8031
Ex 24:17 a consuming fire on **t** *of* the mountain. H8031
Ex 25:21 cover **on t of** the ark H4946+4200+5087+2025
Ex 26:24 all the way to the **t** and fitted into a single H8031
Ex 30: 3 Overlay the **t** and all the sides and the H1511
Ex 34: 2 yourself to me there on **t** *of* the mountain. H8031
Ex 36:29 all the way to the **t** and fitted into a single H8031
Ex 37:26 They overlaid the **t** and all the sides and H1511
Lev 3: 5 it on the altar **on t of** the burnt offering H6584
Lev 4:35 it on the altar **on t of** the food offerings H6584
Lev 5:12 it on the altar **on t of** the food offerings H6584
Lev 8:28 them on the altar **on t of** the burnt H6584
Lev 9:14 burned them **on t of** the burnt H6584
Lev 14:17 **on t of** the blood of the guilt offering. H6584
Nu 20:28 Aaron died there on **t** *of* the mountain. H8031
Nu 21:20 in Moab where the **t** *of* Pisgah overlooks H8031
Nu 23:14 to the field of Zophim on the **t** *of* Pisgah, H8031
Nu 23:28 And Balak took Balaam to the **t** *of* Peor H8031
Dt 3:27 Go up to the **t** *of* Pisgah and look west H8031
Dt 28:13 you will always be at the **t**, never at H5087+2025
Dt 28:35 soles of your feet to the **t of** your **head**. H7721
Dt 34: 1 the plains of Moab to the **t** *of* Pisgah, H8031
Jos 15: 8 it climbed to the **t** *of* the hill west of the H8031
Jdg 6:26 the LORD your God on the **t** *of* this height. H8031
Jdg 9: 7 climbed up on the **t** *of* Mount Gerizim H8031
Jdg 16: 3 carried them to the **t** *of* the hill that faces H8031
1Sa 26:13 side and stood on **t** *of* the hill some H8031
1Sa 28:12 she cried out at the **t** of her voice and said H1524
2Sa 2:25 a group and took their stand on **t** *of* a hill. H8031
2Sa 14:25 From the **t of** his **head** to the sole of his H7721
1Ki 7:17 adorned the capitals on **t** *of* the pillars, H8031
1Ki 7:18 to decorate the capitals on **t** *of* the pillars. H8031
1Ki 7:19 The capitals on **t** *of* the pillars in the H8031
1Ki 7:22 The capitals on **t** were in the shape of H8031
1Ki 7:25 Sea rested on **t** *of* them, H4946+4200+5087+2025
1Ki 7:35 At the **t** *of* the stand there was a circular H8031
1Ki 7:35 were attached to the **t** *of* the stand. H8031
1Ki 7:41 bowl-shaped capitals on **t** *of* the pillars; H8031
1Ki 7:41 bowl-shaped capitals on **t** *of* the pillars; H8031
1Ki 7:42 bowl-shaped capitals on **t** *of* the pillars); H7156
1Ki 10:19 six steps, and its back had a rounded **t**. H8031
1Ki 18:42 Elijah climbed to the **t** *of* Carmel, bent H8031
2Ki 1: 9 who was sitting on the **t** *of* a hill, and said H8031
2Ki 25:17 The bronze capital **on t of** one pillar was H6584
2Ch 3:16 chains and put them on **t** *of* the pillars. H8031
2Ch 4: 4 Sea rested on **t** *of* them, H4946+4200+5087+2025
2Ch 4:12 bowl-shaped capitals on **t** *of* the pillars; H8031
2Ch 4:12 bowl-shaped capitals on **t** *of* the pillars; H8031
2Ch 4:13 bowl-shaped capitals on **t** *of* the pillars); H7156
2Ch 25:12 took them to the **t** *of* a cliff and threw H8031
Ne 12:31 leaders of Judah go up on **t** of the wall. H6584
Ne 12:31 One was to proceed on **t** of the wall to the H6584
Ne 12:38 I followed them on **t** of the wall, together H6584
Pr 1:21 on **t** *of* the wall she cries out, at the city H8031
Pr 23:34 on the high seas, lying on **t** *of* the rigging. H8031
SS 4: 8 of Amana, from the **t** *of* Senir, the summit H8031
Isa 1: 6 of your foot to the *t of* your **head** there is no AIT
Jer 52:22 The bronze capital **on t of** one pillar was H6584
Eze 17: 3 Taking hold of the **t** *of* a cedar, H7550
Eze 17:22 a shoot from the **very t** of a cedar and H8123
Eze 31: 3 on high, its **t** above the thick foliage. H7550
Eze 40:13 from the **t of the** *rear* **wall** *of* one alcove to H1511
Eze 40:13 of one alcove to the **t** *of* the opposite one; H1511
Eze 41: 7 floor to the **t** *floor* through the middle H6609
Eze 42: 6 The rooms *on the* **t** *floor* had no pillars H8992S
Eze 43:12 area on **t** *of* the mountain will H8031
Da 4:11 strong and its **t** touched the sky; A10660
Da 4:20 strong, with its **t** touching the sky A10660
Am 1: 2 and the **t** *of* Carmel withers. H8031
Am 9: 3 they hide themselves on the **t** *of* Carmel, H8031
Zec 4: 2 with a bowl at the **t** and seven lamps on it H8031
Mt 27:51 temple was torn in two from **t** to bottom. *G540*
Mk 5: 7 He shouted **at the t of** his voice, "What do *G3489*
Mk 15:38 temple was torn in two from **t** to bottom. *G540*
Lk 4:33 He cried out **at the t of** his voice, *G3489*
Lk 8:28 shouting **at the t of** his voice, "What *G3489*
Jn 19:23 woven in one piece from **t** to bottom. *G540*
Ac 7:57 ears and, yelling **at the t of** their voices *G3489*
Heb 11:21 as he leaned on the **t** of his staff. *G216*

TOPAZ (9)

Ex 28:20 the fourth row shall be **t**, onyx and jasper H9577
Ex 39:13 the fourth row was **t**, onyx and jasper. H9577
Job 28:19 The **t** *of* Cush cannot compare with it; it H7077
SS 5:14 His arms are rods of gold set with **t**. H9577
Eze 1:16 They sparkled like **t**, and all four looked H9577
Eze 10: 9 cherubim; the wheels sparkled like **t**. H74+9577
Eze 28:13 chrysolite and emerald, **t**, onyx and jasper, H9577
Da 10: 6 His body was like **t**, his face like lightning H9577
Rev 21:20 the ninth **t**, the tenth turquoise, *G5535*

TOPHEL (1)

Dt 1: 1 between Paran and **T**, Laban, H9523

TOPHETH (10)

2Ki 23:10 He desecrated **T**, which was in the Valley H9532
Isa 30:33 **T** has long been prepared; it has been H9533
Jer 7:31 the high places of **T** in the Valley of Ben H9532
Jer 7:32 will no longer call it **T** or the Valley of Ben H9532
Jer 7:32 will bury the dead in **T** until there is no H9532
Jer 19: 6 call this place **T** or the Valley of Ben H9532
Jer 19:11 will bury the dead in **T** until there is no H9532
Jer 19:12 I will make this city like **T**. H9532
Jer 19:13 like this place, **T**—all the houses where H9532
Jer 19:14 Jeremiah then returned from **T**, where the H9532

TOPMOST (3) [TOP, MOST]

Isa 17: 6 two or three olives on the **t** branches, H8031
Eze 17: 4 he broke off its **t** shoot and carried it away H8031
Eze 17:22 tender sprig from its **t** shoots and plant it H8031

TOPPLE (3)

Ps 62: 4 Surely they intend to **t** me from my lofty H5615
Isa 40:20 worker to set up an idol *that will* not **t**. H4572
Isa 41: 7 other nails down the idol so *it will* not **t**. H4572

TOPS (14) [TOP]

Ge 8: 5 the tenth month the **t** *of* the mountains H8031
Ex 12: 7 it on the sides and **t** of the doorframes of H5485
Ex 36:38 They overlaid the **t** *of* the posts and their H8031
Ex 38:17 and their **t** were overlaid with silver H8031
Ex 38:19 and their **t** were overlaid with silver. H8031
Ex 38:28 to overlay the **t** *of* the posts, and to H8031
Jdg 9:36 coming down from the **t** *of* the mountains!" H8031
2Sa 5:24 of marching in the **t** *of* the poplar trees, H8031
1Ki 7:16 of cast bronze to set on the **t** *of* the pillars; H8031
1Ch 14:15 of marching in the **t** *of* the poplar trees, H8031
Ps 72:16 the land; on the **t** *of* the hills may it sway. H8031
Isa 14:14 I will ascend above the **t** *of* the clouds; H1195
Eze 31:14 lifting their **t** above the thick foliage. H7550
Am 9: 1 "Strike the **t of the pillars** so that the H4117

TORCH (5) [TORCHES]

Ge 15:17 with a blazing **t** appeared and passed H4365
Jdg 15: 4 He then fastened a **t** to every pair of tails, H4365
Isa 62: 1 the dawn, her salvation like a blazing **t**. H4365
Zec 12: 6 like a flaming **t** among sheaves. H4365
Rev 8:10 blazing like a **t**, fell from the sky on a *G3286*

TORCHES (9) [TORCH]

Jdg 7:16 in the hands of all of them, with **t** inside. H4365
Jdg 7:20 Grasping the **t** in their left hands and H4365
Jdg 15: 5 lit the **t** and let the foxes loose in the H4365
Isa 50:11 provide yourselves with **flaming t**, H2338
Isa 50:11 fires and of the **t** you have set ablaze. H2338
Eze 1:13 was like burning coals of fire or like **t**. H4365
Da 10: 6 his eyes like flaming **t**, his arms and legs H4365
Na 2: 4 They look like **flaming t**; they dart about H4365
Jn 18: 3 They were carrying **t**, lanterns and *G5749*

TORE (44) [TEAR]

Ge 37:29 Joseph was not there, *he* **t** his clothes. H7973
Ge 37:34 Then Jacob **t** his clothes, put on sackcloth H7973
Ge 44:13 *they* **t** their clothes. Then they all H7973
Nu 14: 6 who had explored the land, **t** their clothes H7973
Jos 7: 6 Then Joshua **t** his clothes and fell H7973
Jdg 11:35 he saw her, *he* **t** his clothes and cried H7973
Jdg 14: 6 him so that *he* **t** the lion **apart** with his H9117
Jdg 16: 3 two posts, and **t** them **loose**, bar and all. H5825
1Sa 15:27 hold of the hem of his robe, and *it* **t**. H7973
2Sa 1:11 him took hold of their clothes and **t** them. H7973
2Sa 13:19 on her head and **t** the ornate robe she H7973
2Sa 13:31 **t** his clothes and lay down on the ground H7973
1Ki 11:30 was wearing and **t** it *into* twelve pieces. H7973
1Ki 14: 8 *I* **t** the kingdom **away** from the house of H7973
1Ki 19:11 powerful wind **t** the mountains **apart** and H7293
1Ki 21:27 heard these words, *he* **t** his clothes, put H7973
2Ki 2:12 hold of his garment and **t** it in two. H7973+7974
2Ki 5: 7 read the letter, *he* **t** his robes and said H7973
2Ki 6:30 heard the woman's words, *he* **t** his robes. H7973
2Ki 10:27 stone of Baal and **t down** the temple of H5997
2Ki 11:14 Then Athaliah **t** her robes and called out H7973
2Ki 11:18 went to the temple of Baal and **t** it **down**. H5997
2Ki 17:21 When *he* **t** Israel **away** from the house of H7973
2Ki 19: 1 *he* **t** his clothes and put on sackcloth and H7973
2Ki 22:11 of the Book of the Law, *he* **t** his robes. H7973
2Ki 22:19 because *you* **t** your robes and wept in H7973
2Ki 23: 7 *He* also **t down** the quarters of the male H5997
2Ch 23:13 Then Athaliah **t** her robes and shouted H7973
2Ch 23:17 went to the temple of Baal and **t** it **down**. H5997
2Ch 34: 7 *he* **t down** the altars and the Asherah H5997
2Ch 34:19 the words of the Law, *he* **t** his robes. H7973
2Ch 34:27 before me and **t** your robes and wept in H7973
Ezr 9: 3 When I heard this, *I* **t** my tunic and cloak H7973
Est 4: 1 had been done, he **t** his clothes, put on H7973
Job 1:20 Job got up and **t** his robe and shaved his H7973
Job 2:12 and *they* **t** their robes and sprinkled dust H7973
Isa 22:10 in Jerusalem and **t down** houses to H5997
Isa 37: 1 *he* **t** his clothes and put on sackcloth and H7973
Jer 2:20 broke off your yoke and **t off** your bonds; H5998
Eze 29: 7 splintered and *you* **t open** their shoulders; H1324
Mt 26:65 Then the high priest **t** his clothes and said *G1396*
Mk 5: 4 he **t** the chains **apart** and broke the *G1400*
Mk 14:63 The high priest **t** his clothes. "Why do we *G1396*
Ac 14:14 *they* **t** their clothes and rushed out into *G1396*

TORMENT (14) [TORMENTED, TORMENTING, TORMENTORS]

Job 13:25 *Will you* **t** a windblown leaf? Will you H6907
Job 15:20 All his days the wicked man **suffers t**, the H2655
Job 19: 2 "How long *will you* **t** me and crush me H3324
Isa 50:11 from my hand: You will lie down in **t**. H5107
La 1:20 I *am* **in t** within, and in my heart I am H2813
La 2:11 from weeping, I *am* **in t** within; my heart H2813
Lk 16:23 where he was in **t**, he looked up and saw *G992*
Lk 16:28 they will not also come to this place *of* **t**. *G992*
2Co 12: 7 my flesh, a messenger of Satan, to **t** me. *G3139*
Rev 9:10 tails they had power *to* **t** people for five *G92*

Rev 14:11 And the smoke *of* their t will rise for ever *G990*
Rev 18: 7 Give her as much t and grief as the glory *G990*
Rev 18:10 Terrified *at* her t, they will stand far off and *G990*
Rev 18:15 from her will stand far off, terrified *at* her t. *G990*

TORMENTED (7) [TORMENT]

1Sa 16:14 an evil spirit from the LORD t him. H1286
Pr 28:17 Anyone t by the guilt of murder will seek H6943
Ac 5:16 their sick and *those* t by impure spirits, *G4061*
2Pe 2: 8 *was* t in his righteous soul by the lawless *G989*
Rev 11:10 these two prophets *had* t those who live on *G989*
Rev 14:10 *They will be* t with burning sulfur in the *G989*
Rev 20:10 *They will be* t day and night for ever and *G989*

TORMENTING (1) [TORMENT]

1Sa 16:15 "See, an evil spirit from God *is* t you. H1286

TORMENTORS (2) [TORMENT]

Ps 137: 3 us for songs, our t demanded songs of joy H9354
Isa 51:23 I will put it into the hands of your t, who H3324

TORN (58) [TEAR]

Ge 31:39 not bring you **animals t by wild beasts**; H3274
Ge 37:33 Joseph *has* **surely been t to pieces**." H3271+3271
Ge 44:28 "*He has* surely **been t to pieces**." H3271+3271
Ex 22:13 *it* **was t to pieces by a wild animal**, H3271+3271
Ex 22:13 shall not be required to pay for the t animal. NDT
Ex 22:31 the meat of an **animal t** by wild **beasts**; H3274
Lev 7:24 dead or **t by wild animals** may be used H3274
Lev 13:45 a defiling disease must wear t clothes, H7268
Lev 14:40 stones *be* **t out** and thrown into an H2740
Lev 14:43 the stones *have been* **t out** and the house H2740
Lev 14:45 It *must be* **t down**—its stones, timbers and H5997
Lev 17:15 dead or **t by wild animals** must wash H3274
Lev 22: 8 anything found dead or **t by wild animals**, H3274
Lev 22:24 testicles are bruised, crushed, t or cut. H5998
Jdg 14: 6 hands as *he might have* t a young goat H9117
1Sa 4:12 to Shiloh **with** his clothes t and dust on H7973
1Sa 15:28 "The LORD *has* t the kingdom of Israel H7973
1Sa 28:17 The LORD *has* t the kingdom out of your H7973
2Sa 1: 2 with his clothes t and dust on his head. H7973
2Sa 13:31 attendants stood by with their clothes t. H7973
2Sa 15:32 his robe t and dust on his head. H7973
1Ki 18:30 altar of the LORD, which *had* **been t down**. H2238
1Ki 19:10 your covenant, **t down** your altars, and put H2238
1Ki 19:14 your covenant, **t down** your altars, and put H2238
2Ki 5: 8 that the king of Israel *had* t his robes, H7973
2Ki 5: 8 "Why *have you* t your robes H7973
2Ki 18:37 with their clothes t, and told him what the H7973
2Ch 34: 4 the altars of the Baals *were* **t down**; H5997
Ezr 9: 5 with my tunic and cloak t, and fell on my H7973
Job 8:18 But when it *is* t from its spot, that place H1180
Job 18:14 He **is t** from the security of his tent and H5998
Ps 60: 2 You have shaken the land and **t it open** H7204
Ps 124: 6 who has not let us be t by their teeth. H3272
Pr 2:22 and the unfaithful *will be* t from it. H5815
Isa 36:22 with their clothes t, and told him what the H7973
Jer 5: 5 broken off the yoke and **t off** the bonds. H5998
Jer 13:22 your skirts *have* **been t off** and your body H1655
Jer 18: 7 is to be uprooted, **t down** and destroyed, H5997
Jer 33: 4 Judah that *have* **been t down** to be used H5997
Jer 41: 5 t their clothes and cut themselves came H7973
Jer 50:15 her towers fall, her walls **are t down**. H2238
La 2: 2 in his wrath *he has* **t down** the H2238
Eze 4:14 anything found dead or **t by wild animals**. H3274
Eze 30: 4 carried away and her foundations **t down**. H2238
Eze 44:31 animal, found dead or **t by wild animals**. H3274
Da 7: 4 until its wings **were t off** and it was lifted A10440
Hos 6: 1 He *has* **t** us **to pieces** but he will heal us H3271
Mt 27:51 of the temple *was* t in two from top to *G5387*
Mk 1:10 he saw heaven *being* **t open** and the *G5387*
Mk 15:38 of the temple *was* t in two from top to *G5387*
Lk 5:36 *they will have* t the new garment *G5387*
Lk 23:45 the curtain of the temple *was* t in two. *G5387*
Jn 21:11 even with so many the net *was* not t. *G5387*
Ac 21: 1 After *we had* t *ourselves* **away** from them *G685*
Ac 23:10 afraid Paul *would be* **t to pieces** by them. *G1400*
Ro 11: 3 your prophets and **t down** your altars; *G2940*
Gal 4:15 *you would have* **t out** your eyes and given *G2021*
Php 1:23 *I am* t between the two: I desire to depart *G5309*

TORRENT (6) [TORRENTS]

Ps 124: 4 the t would have swept over us H5707
Isa 30:28 His breath is like a rushing t, rising up to H5707
Jer 47: 2 they will become an overflowing t. H5707
Lk 6:48 the t struck that house but could not shake *G4532*
Lk 6:49 The moment the t struck that house, it *G4532*
Rev 12:15 and **sweep** her **away with the t**. *G4533+4472*

TORRENTS (8) [TORRENT]

2Sa 22: 5 the t *of* destruction overwhelmed me. H5707
Job 14:19 away stones and t wash away the soil, H6207
Job 38:25 Who cuts a channel for the **t of rain**, and H8852
Ps 18: 4 the t *of* destruction overwhelmed me. H5707
Eze 13:11 Rain will come *in* t, and I will send H8851
Eze 13:13 hailstones and t *of* rain will fall with H8851
Eze 38:22 I will pour down t *of* rain, hailstones and H8851
Hab 3:10 T *of* water swept by; the deep roared and H2443

TORTURE (4) [TORTURED]

Mt 8:29 "Have you come here *to* t us before the *G989*
Mk 5: 7 In God's name don't t me!" *G989*
Lk 8:28 Most High God? I beg you, don't t me!" *G989*
Rev 9: 5 kill them but only to t them for five months. *G989*

TORTURED (2) [TORTURE]

Mt 18:34 handed him over *to* the **jailers to be t**, *G991*
Heb 11:35 There were others *who were* t, refusing to *G5594*

TOSS (7) [TOSSED, TOSSES, TOSSING]

Ex 9: 8 a furnace and *have* Moses t it into the air H2450
Job 7: 4 and *I* **t and turn** until dawn. H8425+5611
Job 30:22 the wind; *you* t me **about** in the storm. H4570
Ps 60: 8 washbasin, on Edom *I* t my sandal; over H8959
Ps 108: 9 washbasin, on Edom *I* t my sandal; over H8959
Mt 15:26 the children's bread and t it to the dogs." *G965*
Mk 7:27 the children's bread and t it to the dogs." *G965*

TOSSED (3) [TOSS]

Ex 9:10 Moses t it into the air, and festering boils H2450
Eph 4:14 infants, **t back and forth by the waves**, *G3115*
Jas 1: 6 wave of the sea, blown and t by the wind. *G4847*

TOSSES (2) [TOSS]

2Ki 19:21 Daughter Jerusalem t her head as you H5675
Isa 37:22 Daughter Jerusalem t her head as you H5675

TOSSING (2) [TOSS]

Isa 57:20 But the wicked are like the t sea, which H1764
Lk 21:25 perplexity at the roaring and t of the sea. *G4893*

TOTAL (39) [TOTALED, TOTALLY]

Ge 5: 5 **Altogether**, Adam lived **a t** *of* 930 H3972+3427
Ge 5: 8 **Altogether**, Seth lived **a t** *of* 912 years H3972
Ge 5:11 **Altogether**, Enosh lived **a t** *of* 905 years H3972
Ge 5:14 **Altogether**, Kenan lived **a t** *of* 910 years H3972
Ge 5:17 **Altogether**, Mahalalel lived **a t** *of* 895 H3972
Ge 5:20 **Altogether**, Jared lived **a t** *of* 962 years H3972
Ge 5:23 **Altogether**, Enoch lived **a t** *of* 365 years. H3972
Ge 5:27 **Altogether**, Methuselah lived **a t** *of* 969 H3972
Ge 5:31 **Altogether**, Lamech lived **a t** *of* 777 years H3972
Ge 9:29 Noah lived a t *of* 950 years, and then he H3972
Ex 10:22 and **t darkness** covered all Egypt for H3125+696
Ex 38:24 The t *amount of* the gold from the wave H3972
Ex 38:26 years old or more, a t *of* 603,550 men. H4200
Nu 1:46 The t number was 603,550. H3972
Nu 3:39 The t number of Levites counted at the H3972
Nu 3:43 The t number of firstborn males a month H3972
Nu 4:37 This was the t *of* all those in the Kohathite H7212
Nu 4:41 This was the t *of those in* the H3972+7212
Nu 4:45 This was the t *of those in* the Merarite H7212
Nu 7:87 The t *number of* animals for the burnt H3972
Nu 7:88 The t *number of* animals for the sacrifice H3972
Nu 26:51 **The t** number of the men of Israel was H4655
Jos 15:32 a t *of* twenty-nine towns and their villages. H3972
Jos 21:19 The t *number of* towns for the priests, the H3972
Jos 21:33 The t *number of* towns of the Gershonite H3972
Jos 21:40 The t *number of* towns allotted to the H3972
1Sa 14:20 found the Philistines in t confusion, H1524+4394
2Ki 24:14 workers and artisans—a t of ten thousand. NDT
1Ch 6:60 The t *number of* towns distributed among H3972
1Ch 23: 3 the t number of men was thirty-eight H1653
2Ch 3:11 The **t wingspan** *of* the cherubim was H802+4053
2Ch 26:12 The t number of family leaders over the H3972
2Ch 35: 7 who were there a t of thirty H3972+4200+5031
Ne 7:72 **The t** given by the rest of the people was H8895
Job 20:26 t darkness lies in wait for his treasures. H3972
Jer 52:23 the t *number* of pomegranates above the H3972
Eze 48:13 Its t length will be 25,000 cubits and its H3972
Mal 4: 6 strike the land with **t destruction**. H3051
Ac 19:19 the t came to fifty thousand drachmas. NDT

TOTALED (2) [TOTAL]

Ne 11: 6 lived in Jerusalem t 468 men of standing. H3972
Ne 11:18 The Levites in the holy city t 284. H3972

TOTALLY (25) [TOTAL]

Nu 16:30 if the LORD brings about **something t new**, H1375
Nu 21: 2 our hands, *we will* **t destroy** their cities." H3049
Dt 7: 2 then *you* **must destroy** them **t**. H3049+3049
Jos 10: 1 Joshua had taken Ai and **t destroyed** it, H3049
Jos 10:28 the sword and **t destroyed** everyone in it. H3049
Jos 10:35 the sword and **t destroyed** everyone in it, H3049
Jos 10:37 *they* **t destroyed** it and everyone in it. H3049
Jos 10:39 Everyone in it *they* **t destroyed**. They left H3049
Jos 10:40 *He* **t destroyed** all who breathed, just as H3049
Jos 11:11 *They* **t destroyed** them, not sparing H3049
Jos 11:12 *He* **t destroyed** them, as Moses the H3049
Jos 11:20 so that *he might* **destroy** them **t** H3049
Jos 11:21 Joshua **t destroyed** them and their towns H3049
Jdg 1:17 in Zephath, and *they* **t destroyed** the city. H3049
1Sa 15: 3 Amalekites and **t destroy** all that belongs H3049
1Sa 15: 8 all his people *he* **t destroyed** with the H3049
1Sa 15: 9 was despised and weak *they* **t destroyed**. H3049
1Sa 15:15 your God, but *we* **t destroyed** the rest." H3049
2Ch 12:12 from him, and he was not t destroyed. H3986
Isa 2:18 the idols will **t** disappear. H4003
Isa 24: 3 laid waste and **t plundered**. H1024+1024
Isa 34: 2 *He will* **t destroy** them, he will give them H3049
Isa 34: 5 on Edom, the people I have **t destroyed**. H3051
Am 9: 8 Yet *I will* not **t destroy** the H9012+9012
Zec 11:17 withered, his right eye **t blinded**!" H3908+3908

TOTTER (1) [TOTTERING]

Jer 10: 4 it with hammer and nails so *it will* not t. H7048

TOTTERING (1) [TOTTER]

Ps 62: 3 me down—this leaning wall, this t fence? H1890

TOU (4)

2Sa 8: 9 When **T** king of Hamath heard that David H9497
2Sa 8:10 Hadadezer, who had been at war with **T**. H9497
1Ch 18: 9 When **T** king of Hamath heard that David H9495
1Ch 18:10 Hadadezer, who had been at war with **T**. H9495

TOUCH (40) [TOUCHED, TOUCHES, TOUCHING]

Ge 3: 3 the garden, and *you must* not **t** it, or you H5595
Ge 20: 6 That is why I did not let you **t** her. H5595
Ge 27:21 "Come near so *I can* **t** you, my son, H4630
Ex 12:13 plague *will* **t** you when I strike H2118+928
Ex 19:12 approach the mountain or **t** the foot of it. H5595
Lev 5: 2 *if they* unwittingly **t** anything ceremonially H5595
Lev 5: 3 *if they* **t** human uncleanness (anything H5595
Lev 11: 8 not eat their meat or **t** their carcasses; H5595
Lev 12: 4 *She must* not **t** anything sacred or go to H5595
Nu 4:15 But *they must* not **t** the holy things or they H5595
Nu 16:26 *Do* not **t** anything belonging to them, or H5595
Dt 14: 8 not to eat their meat or **t** their carcasses. H5595
Dt 28:56 not venture *to* **t** the ground *with* the sole H3657
Jos 9:19 God of Israel, and we cannot **t** them now. H5595
1Sa 24:12 but my hand *will* not **t** you. H2118+928
1Sa 24:13 deeds,' so my hand *will* not **t** you. H2118+928
2Sa 21:10 did not let the birds **t** them by day or the H5663
1Ch 16:22 "*Do* not **t** my anointed ones; do my H5595
Job 5:19 rescue you; in seven no harm *will* **t** you. H5595
Job 6: 7 I refuse to **t** it; such food makes me ill. H5595
Ps 105:15 "*Do* not **t** my anointed ones; do my H5595
Ps 144: 5 come down; **t** the mountains, so that H5595
Isa 28:15 sweeps by, *it* cannot **t** us, for we have H995
Isa 52:11 go out from there! **T** no unclean thing H5595
Jer 13: 1 your waist, but *do* not **let** it **t** water." H995+928
Jer 14:15 'No sword or famine *will* **t** this land. H2118+928
La 4:14 that no one dares *to* **t** their garments. H5595
La 4:15 Don't **t** us!" When they flee and H5595
Eze 9: 6 *do* not **t** anyone who has the mark. H5602
Mt 9:21 said to herself, "If *I* only **t** his cloak, I will *G721*
Mt 14:36 him to *let* the sick just **t** the edge of *G721*
Mk 3:10 diseases were pushing forward to **t** him. *G721*
Mk 5:28 she thought, "If *I* just **t** his clothes, I will be *G721*
Mk 6:56 him to let them **t** even the edge of his *G721*
Mk 8:22 a blind man and begged Jesus to **t** him. *G721*
Lk 6:19 the people all tried *to* **t** him, because *G721*
Lk 24:39 **T** me and see; a ghost does not have *G6027*
2Co 6:17 **T** no unclean thing, and I *G721*
Col 2:21 "Do not handle! Do not taste! *Do* not **t**!" *G2566*
Heb 11:28 of the firstborn *would* not **t** the firstborn of *G2566*

TOUCHED (60) [TOUCH]

Ge 27:22 his father Isaac, *who* **t** him and said, "The H5491
Ge 32:25 *he* **t** the socket of Jacob's hip so that his H5595
Ge 32:32 of Jacob's hip *was* **t** near the tendon. H5595
Ex 4:25 son's foreskin and **t** Moses' feet with it. H5595
Nu 19:18 sprinkle anyone *who has* **t** a human bone H5595
Nu 31:19 killed someone or **t** someone who was H5595
Jos 3:15 Jordan and their feet **t** the water's edge, H3188
Jos 16: 7 **t** Jericho and came out at the Jordan. H7003
Jos 19:11 west it ran to Maralah, **t** Dabbesheth, and H7003
Jos 19:22 The boundary **t** Tabor, Shahazumah and H7003
Jos 19:26 west the boundary **t** Carmel and Shihor H7003
Jos 19:27 **t** Zebulun and the Valley of Iphtah El H7003
Jos 19:34 *It* **t** Zebulun on the south, Asher on the H7003
Jdg 6:21 the angel of the LORD **t** the meat and the H5595
Jdg 13: 5 head *is* never **t** *to be* **t** *by* a razor H6590+6584
1Sa 10:26 by valiant men whose hearts God *had* **t**. H5595
1Ki 6:27 The wing of one cherub **t** one wall, while H5595
1Ki 6:27 the wing of the other **t** the other wall, H5595
1Ki 6:27 their wings **t** each other in the middle H5595
1Ki 19: 5 All at once an angel **t** him and said, "Get H5595
1Ki 19: 7 back a second time and **t** him and said, H5595
2Ki 13:21 When the body **t** Elisha's bones, the man H5595
2Ch 3:11 five cubits long and **t** the temple wall, H5595
2Ch 3:11 **t** the wing of the other cherub. H5595
2Ch 3:12 five cubits long and **t** the other temple H5595
2Ch 3:12 cubits long, **t** the wing of the first cherub. H1816
Est 5: 2 Esther approached and **t** the tip of the H5595
Isa 6: 7 With it *he* **t** my mouth and said, "See, this H5595
Isa 6: 7 this *has* **t** your lips; your guilt is H5595
Jer 1: 9 out his hand and **t** my mouth and said to H5595
Eze 1: 9 the wings of one **t** the wings of H2489
Da 4:11 large and strong and its top **t** the sky; A10413
Da 8:18 Then *he* **t** me and raised me to my feet. H5595
Da 10: 3 no meat or wine **t** my lips; and I used H995+448
Da 10:10 A hand **t** me and set me trembling on my H5595
Da 10:16 Then *one* who looked like a man **t** my lips H5595
Da 10:18 *the one* who looked like a man **t** me H5595
Mt 8: 3 Jesus reached out his hand and **t** the man *G721*
Mt 8:15 *He* **t** her hand and the fever left her, and *G721*
Mt 9:20 up behind him and **t** the edge of his cloak. *G721*
Mt 9:29 Then *he* **t** their eyes and said, "According *G721*
Mt 14:36 of his cloak, and all *who* **t** it were healed. *G721*
Mt 17: 7 But Jesus came and **t** them. "Get up," *G721*
Mt 20:34 had compassion on them and **t** their eyes. *G721*
Mk 1:41 He reached out his hand and **t** the man. "I *G721*
Mk 5:27 up behind him in the crowd and **t** his cloak, *G721*
Mk 5:30 the crowd and asked, "Who **t** my clothes?" *G721*
Mk 5:31 "and yet you can ask, 'Who **t** me? *G721*
Mk 6:56 of his cloak, and all *who* **t** it were healed. *G721*
Mk 7:33 Then he spit and **t** the man's tongue. *G721*

T

Lk 5:13 Jesus reached out his hand and t the man G721
Lk 7:14 Then he went up and t the bier they were G721
Lk 8:44 up behind him and t the edge of his cloak, G721
Lk 8:45 "Who t me?" Jesus asked. When they all G721
Lk 8:46 Jesus said, "Someone t me; I know that G721
Lk 8:47 she told why *she had* t him and how she G721
Lk 22:51 And *he* t the man's ear and healed him G721
Ac 19:12 aprons *that had* t him were G608+3836+5999
Heb 12:18 to a mountain *that can be* t and that is G6027
1Jn 1: 1 have looked at and our hands *have* t— G6027

TOUCHES (44) [TOUCH]

Ge 27:12 What if my father t me? I would appear to H5491
Ex 19:12 Whoever t the mountain is to be put to H5595
Ex 29:37 most holy, and whatever t it will be holy. H5595
Ex 30:29 and whatever t them will be holy. H5595
Lev 6:18 Whatever t them will become holy H5595
Lev 6:27 Whatever t any of the flesh will become H5595
Lev 7:19 " 'Meat that t anything ceremonially H5595
Lev 7:21 Anyone *who* t something unclean H5595
Lev 11:24 whoever t their carcasses will be unclean H5595
Lev 11:26 whoever t the carcass of any of them will H5595
Lev 11:27 whoever t their carcasses will be unclean H5595
Lev 11:31 Whoever t them when they are dead will H5595
Lev 11:36 but *anyone who* t one of these carcasses H5595
Lev 11:39 anyone *who* t its carcass will be unclean H5595
Lev 15: 5 Anyone who t his bed must wash their H5595
Lev 15: 7 " 'Whoever t the man who has a H5595
Lev 15:10 whoever t any of the things that were H5595
Lev 15:11 man with a discharge t without rinsing his H5595
Lev 15:12 'A clay pot that the man t must be broken, H5595
Lev 15:19 anyone who t her will be unclean till H5595
Lev 15:21 Anyone who t her bed will be unclean H5595
Lev 15:22 Anyone who t anything she sits on will be H5595
Lev 15:23 sitting on, when anyone t it, they will be H5595
Lev 15:24 her and her monthly flow t him, H2118+6584
Lev 15:27 Anyone who t them will be unclean; they H5595
Lev 22: 4 be unclean if he t something defiled by H5595
Lev 22: 5 if he t any crawling thing that makes H5595
Lev 22: 6 The one who t any such thing will be H5595
Nu 19:11 "Whoever t a human corpse will be H5595
Nu 19:16 out in the open who t someone who has H5595
Nu 19:16 anyone who t a human bone or a grave NDT
Nu 19:21 anyone *who* t the water of cleansing H5595
Nu 19:22 an unclean person t becomes unclean, H5595
Nu 19:22 anyone who t it becomes unclean till H5595
2Sa 23: 7 Whoever t thorns uses a tool of iron or the H5595
Job 20: 6 to the heavens and his head t the clouds, H5595
Ps 104:32 it trembles, *who* t the mountains, and H5595
Pr 6:29 no one who t her will go unpunished. H5595
Am 9: 5 Almighty—he t the earth and it melts H5595
Hag 2:12 that fold t some bread or stew H5595
Hag 2:13 with a dead body t one of these things, H5595
Zec 2: 8 whoever t you touches the apple of his H5595
Zec 2: 8 whoever touches you t the apple of his H5595
Heb 12:20 "If even an animal t the mountain, it must G2566

TOUCHING (5) [TOUCH]

Nu 19:13 purify themselves *after* t a human corpse, H5595
Eze 1:11 each wing t that of the creature on either H2489
Da 4:20 with its top t the sky, visible to A10413
Da 8: 5 the whole earth without t the ground. H5595
Lk 7:39 he would know who *is* t him and what kind G721

TOW (KJV) STRING, TINDER, WICK

TOWARD (227) [TO]

Ge 10:19 from Sidon t Gerar as far as H995+3870+2025
Ge 10:19 Gaza, and then t Sodom H3870+995+2025
Ge 10:30 from Mesha t Sephar, H995+3870+2025
Ge 12: 8 From there he went on t the hills east of H2025
Ge 12: 9 Abram set out and continued t the Negev. H2025
Ge 13:10 plain of the Jordan t Zoar was well H995+3870
Ge 13:11 plain of the Jordan and set out t the east. H4946
Ge 16:12 and he will live **in hostility** t all his H6584+7156
Ge 18:16 they looked down t Sodom, and H6584+7156
Ge 18:22 The men turned away and went t Sodom H2025
Ge 19:28 He looked down t Sodom and H6584+7156
Ge 19:28 t all the land of the plain H6584+7156
Ge 24:11 the town; it was t evening, the time the H4200
Ge 25:18 border of Egypt, as you go t Ashur. H2025
Ge 25:18 And *they* **lived in hostility** t H5877+6584+7156
Ge 31: 2 that Laban's attitude t him was not what it H6640
Ge 31: 5 father's attitude t me is not what it was H448
Ge 34:21 "These men are friendly t us," they said H907
Ge 48:13 Ephraim on his right t Israel's left hand H4946
Ge 48:13 Manasseh on his left t Israel's right hand, H4946
Ge 49:13 ships; his border will **extend** t Sidon. H6584
Ex 3:21 **favorably disposed** t this H2834+928+6524
Ex 9:22 out your hand t the sky so that hail H6584
Ex 9:23 Moses stretched out his staff t the sky, H6584
Ex 9:33 He spread out his hands t the LORD; the H448
Ex 10:21 "Stretch out your hand t the sky so that H6584
Ex 10:22 So Moses stretched out his hand t the sky H6584
Ex 11: 3 **favorably disposed** t the H2834+928+6524
Ex 12:36 **favorably disposed** t the H2834+928+6524
Ex 13:18 **led** the people **around** *by* the desert road *t* AIT
Ex 14:27 The Egyptians were fleeing t it, and the H7925
Ex 16:10 they looked t the desert, and there H448
Ex 25:20 are to face each other, looking t the cover. H448
Ex 27:13 On the east end, t the sunrise, the H2025
Ex 37: 9 faced each other, looking t the cover. H448
Ex 38:13 The east end, t the sunrise, was also fifty H2025
Lev 9:22 lifted his hands t the people and blessed H448
Lev 26:21 'If you remain hostile t me and refuse to H6640
Lev 26:23 correction but continue to be hostile t me, H6640
Lev 26:24 I myself will be hostile t you and will afflict H6640
Lev 26:27 to me but continue to be hostile t me, H6640
Lev 26:28 then in my anger I will be hostile t you H6640
Lev 26:40 their unfaithfulness and their hostility t me, H6640
Lev 26:41 made me hostile t them so that I sent H6640
Nu 2: 3 On the east, t the sunrise, the divisions of H2025
Nu 3:38 of the tabernacle, t the sunrise, in front H2025
Nu 6:26 LORD turn his face t you and give you peace H448
Nu 12:10 Aaron turned t her and saw that she had a H448
Nu 13:21 of Zin as far as Rehob, t Lebo Hamath. NDT
Nu 14:25 back tomorrow and **set out** *t* the desert along AIT
Nu 14:44 they went up t the highest point in the H448
Nu 16:42 Aaron and turned t the tent of meeting, H448
Nu 19: 4 it seven times t the front of the tent H448+5790
Nu 21:11 wilderness that faces Moab t the sunrise. H4946
Nu 21:33 turned and went up along the **road** *t* Bashan, AIT
Nu 24: 1 but turned his face t the wilderness. H448
Nu 34:15 Jordan across from Jericho, t the sunrise." H2025
Dt 1:19 from Horeb and went t the hill country of H2006
Dt 1:40 around and set out t the desert along the H2025
Dt 2: 1 back and set out t the wilderness along H2025
Dt 3: 1 turned and went up along the **road** *t* Bashan, AIT
Dt 11:30 westward, t the setting sun, near the great NDT
Dt 15: 7 not be hardhearted or tightfisted t them. H4946
Dt 15: 9 do not show ill will t the needy among your H928
Dt 15:11 you to be openhanded t your fellow H4200
Jos 1:15 gave you east of the Jordan t the sunrise." NDT
Jos 8:15 and they fled t the wilderness. H2006
Jos 8:18 "Hold out t Ai the javelin that is in your H448
Jos 8:18 So Joshua held out t the city the javelin H448
Jos 8:20 Israelites who *had been* **fleeing** *t* the AIT
Jos 11:17 Mount Halak, which **rises** *t* Seir, to Baal Gad AIT
Jos 12: 7 to Mount Halak, which rises t Seir. H2025
Jos 15: 9 the boundary headed t the spring of the H448
Jos 15: 9 of Mount Ephron and **went down** *t* Baalah AIT
Jos 15:11 slope of Ekron, turned t Shikkeron, passed H2025
Jos 15:21 Judah in the Negev t the boundary of H448
Jos 19:12 east from Sarid *t* the **sunrise** to the territory of AIT
Jos 19:13 it came out at Rimmon and **turned** *t* Neah. AIT
Jos 19:27 *It* then **turned** east *t* Beth Dagon, touched AIT
Jos 19:29 boundary then **turned back** *t* Ramah and AIT
Jos 19:29 **turned** *t* Hosah and came out at the AIT
Jdg 7:22 fled to Beth Shittah t Zererah as far as the H2025
Jdg 9:19 in good faith t Jerub-Baal and his H6640
Jdg 13:20 flame blazed up from the altar t heaven, H2025
Jdg 14: 5 suddenly a young lion **came** roaring t him. H7925
Jdg 15:14 the Philistines **came** t him shouting. H7925
Jdg 16:29 Then Samson **reached** t the two central H4369
Jdg 19:10 the man left and went t Jebus (that H6330+5790
Jdg 20:45 they turned and fled t the wilderness to H2025
1Sa 6: 9 to its own territory, t Beth Shemesh, then the NDT
1Sa 6:12 went straight up t Beth Shemesh, H6584+2006
1Sa 9:14 coming t them on his way up to the high H7925
1Sa 13:17 One turned t Ophrah in the vicinity H448+2006
1Sa 13:18 another t Beth Horon, and the third toward H2006
1Sa 13:18 the third t the borderland overlooking H2006
1Sa 14: 5 One cliff stood to the north t Mikmash, the H4578
1Sa 14: 5 Mikmash, the other to the south t Geba. H4578
1Sa 14: 8 we will cross over t them and let them see H448
1Sa 17:48 David **ran** quickly *t* the battle line to meet AIT
1Sa 20:12 If he is favorably disposed t you, will I not H448
1Sa 20:19 after tomorrow, **t evening**, go to the H3718+4394
1Sa 25: 8 *be* **favorable** t my men, H5162+2834+928+6524
1Sa 25:20 David and his men descending t her, H7925
2Sa 15: 6 behaved in this way t all the Israelites H4200
2Sa 15:23 moved on t the wilderness. H6584+7156+2006
2Sa 20:17 He went t her, and she asked, "Are you H448
2Sa 24: 6 on to Dan Jaan and around t Sidon. H448
2Sa 24: 7 Then *they* **went** *t* the fortress of Tyre and all AIT
2Sa 24:20 the king and his officials coming t him, H6584
1Ki 7:25 their hindquarters were t the center. H2025
1Ki 8:22 of Israel, **spread out** his hands *t* heaven AIT
1Ki 8:29 your eyes be open t this temple night and H448
1Ki 8:29 the prayer your servant prays t this place. H448
1Ki 8:30 people Israel when they pray t this place. H448
1Ki 8:35 when they pray t this place and give H448
1Ki 8:38 spreading out their hands t this temple— H448
1Ki 8:42 when they come and pray t this temple, H448
1Ki 8:44 they pray to the LORD t the city you have H2006
1Ki 8:48 pray to you t the land you gave their H2006
1Ki 8:48 t the city you have chosen and the temple I NDT
1Ki 8:54 kneeling with his hands **spread out** *t* heaven. AIT
1Ki 11:25 ruled in Aram and was hostile t Israel. H928
1Ki 13: 4 he stretched out t the man shriveled up, H6584
1Ki 18:43 "Go and look t the sea," he told his H2006
2Ki 5:21 When Naaman saw him running t him, he H339
2Ki 6:18 As the enemy came down t him, Elisha H448
2Ki 10:12 Jehu then set out and **went** *t* Samaria. AIT
2Ki 25: 4 They fled t the Arabah, H2006
1Ch 29: 7 They gave t the work on the temple of God H4200
2Ch 4: 4 their hindquarters were t the center. H2025
2Ch 6:13 Israel and spread out his hands t heaven. H2025
2Ch 6:20 your eyes be open t this temple day and H448
2Ch 6:20 the prayer your servant prays t this place. H448
2Ch 6:21 people Israel when they pray t this place. H448
2Ch 6:26 when they pray t this place and give H448
2Ch 6:29 spreading out their hands t this temple— H448
2Ch 6:32 when they come and pray t this temple, H448
2Ch 6:34 when they pray to you t this city you have H2006
2Ch 6:38 pray t the land you gave their H2006
2Ch 6:38 t the city you have chosen and toward the NDT
2Ch 6:38 you have chosen and t the temple I have H4200
2Ch 20:24 the desert and looked t the vast army, H448
Ezr 2:68 freewill offerings t the rebuilding of the H4200
Ezr 3:11 is good; his love t Israel endures forever." H6584
Ezr 8:15 them at the canal that flows t Ahava, H448
Ne 1: 7 We have acted very wickedly t you. H4200
Ne 2:13 the Valley Gate t the Jackal Well H448+7156
Ne 2:14 Then I moved on t the Fountain Gate and H448
Ne 3:26 the Water Gate t the east and the H4200
Ne 12:31 of the wall to the right, t the Dung Gate. H4200
Job 10:17 against me and increase your anger t me; H6643
Job 39:26 wisdom and spread its wings t the south? H4200
Ps 5: 7 in reverence I bow down t your holy temple. H448
Ps 25:10 loving and faithful t those who keep the H4200
Ps 28: 2 as I lift up my hands t your Most Holy Place. H448
Ps 74: 3 Turn your steps t these everlasting ruins H4200
Ps 85: 4 put away your displeasure t us. H6640
Ps 86:13 For great is your love t me; you have H6584
Ps 117: 2 For great is his love t us, and the H6584
Ps 119:36 Turn my heart t your statutes and not H448
Ps 119:36 toward your statutes and not t selfish gain. H448
Ps 138: 2 I will bow down t your holy temple and will H448
Pr 21: 1 that he channels t all who please him. H6584
Pr 24:11 hold back those staggering t slaughter. H4200
SS 7: 4 the tower of Lebanon looking t Damascus. H7156
Isa 8:22 Then they will look t the earth and see only H448
Isa 11:13 of Judah, nor Judah **hostile** *t* Ephraim. AIT
Isa 16: 8 once reached Jazer and **spread** *t* the desert. AIT
Jer 1:13 "It is **tilting** t us from the north. H7156
Jer 3:12 proclaim this message t the north: H2025
Jer 4:11 heights in the desert blows t my people, H2006
Jer 39: 4 the two walls, and headed t the Arabah. H2006
Jer 50: 5 the way to Zion and turn their faces t **it**. H2178
Jer 52: 7 They fled t the Arabah, H2006
Eze 1:23 wings were stretched out one t the other, H448
Eze 4: 3 you and the city and turn your face t it. H448
Eze 4: 7 Turn your face t the siege of Jerusalem H448
Eze 8: 5 said to me, "Son of man, look t the north." H2006
Eze 8:16 With their backs t the temple of the LORD H448
Eze 8:16 of the LORD and their faces t the east, H2025
Eze 17: 6 Its branches turned t him, but its roots H448
Eze 17: 7 now sent out its roots t him from the plot H6584
Eze 20:46 of man, set your face t the south; preach H2006
Eze 39:26 they showed t me when they lived in H928
Eze 41:19 of a human being t the palm tree on one H448
Eze 41:19 the face of a lion t the palm tree on the H448
Eze 47: 1 the threshold of the temple t the east H2025
Eze 47: 8 "This water flows t the eastern region and H448
Da 3:19 his attitude t them changed. A10542
Da 4:34 raised my eyes t heaven, and my sanity A10378
Da 6:10 where the windows opened t Jerusalem. A10458
Da 8: 4 the ram as it charged t the west and the H2025
Da 8: 6 It came t the two-horned ram I had seen H6330
Da 8: 8 horns grew up t the four winds of H4200
Da 8: 9 to the east and t the Beautiful Land. H448
Da 10:15 bowed with my face t the ground and was H2025
Da 11: 4 up and parceled out t the four winds of H4200
Da 11:19 he will turn back t the fortresses of his H4200
Da 12: 7 his right hand and his left hand t heaven, H448
Hos 3: 3 I will *behave the same way* t you. H448
Am 4: 3 you will be cast out t Harmon, H2025
Jnh 2: 4 I will look again t your holy temple. H448
Zec 6: 6 black horses is going t the north country, H448
Zec 6: 6 the one with the white horses t the west H448
Zec 6: 6 one with the dappled horses t the south." H448
Zec 6: 8 those going t the north country have given H448
Mt 14:29 walked on the water and came t Jesus. G4639
Lk 7:44 Then he turned t the woman and said to G4639
Lk 12:21 things for themselves but is not rich t God." G1650
Lk 12:38 in the middle of the night or t daybreak. G1877
Jn 1:29 John saw Jesus coming t him and said, G4639
Jn 4:30 out of the town and made their way t him. G4639
Jn 6: 5 up and saw a great crowd coming t him, G4639
Jn 17: 1 said this, he looked t heaven and prayed: G1650
Jn 20:16 She turned t him and cried out in Aramaic NDT
Ac 9:40 Turning t the dead woman, he said G4639
Ro 15: 5 same attitude of mind t each other that G1877
1Co 7:36 not be acting honorably t the virgin he is G2093
2Co 10: 1 with you, but "bold" t you when away! G1650
2Co 10: 2 as I expect to be t some people who think G2093
Php 3:13 is behind and **straining** t what is ahead, G2085
Php 3:14 I press on t the goal to win the prize for G2848
Col 4: 5 Be wise in the way you act t outsiders G4639
Titus 3: 2 always to be gentle t everyone. G4639
Heb 10:24 spur one another on *t* **love** and good deeds, AIT
1Pe 3:21 the pledge of a clear conscience t God. G1650
1Pe 5: 5 clothe yourselves with humility *t* **one another** AIT

TOWEL (2)

Jn 13: 4 wrapped a t around his waist. G3317
Jn 13: 5 drying them *with* the t that was wrapped G3317

TOWER (31) [TOWERED, TOWERING, TOWERS, WATCHTOWER, WATCHTOWERS]

Ge 11: 4 with a t that reaches to the heavens H4463
Ge 11: 5 to see the city and the t the people were H4463
Jdg 8: 9 I return in triumph, I will tear down this t." H4463
Jdg 8:17 pulled down the t *of* Peniel and killed H4463
Jdg 9:46 the citizens in the t *of* Shechem went into H4463
Jdg 9:49 So all the people in the t *of* Shechem H4463

Jdg 9:51 was a strong t, to which all the men H4463
Jdg 9:51 in and climbed up on the t roof. H4463
Jdg 9:52 Abimelek went to the t and attacked it. H4463
Jdg 9:52 the entrance to the t to set it on fire, H4463
2Ki 9:17 standing on the t in Jezreel saw Jehu's H4463
Ne 3: 1 building as far as the T of the Hundred H4463
Ne 3: 1 as far as the T of Hananel. H4463
Ne 3:11 another section and the T of the Ovens. H4463
Ne 3:25 the angle and the t projecting from the H4463
Ne 3:26 Gate toward the east and the projecting t. H4463
Ne 3:27 the great projecting t to the wall of Ophel. H4463
Ne 12:38 past the T of the Ovens to the Broad Wall, H4463
Ne 12:39 the T of Hananel and the Tower of the H4463
Ne 12:39 of Hananel and the T of the Hundred, H4463
Ps 61: 3 my refuge, a strong t against the foe. H4463
Pr 18:10 The name of the LORD is a fortified t; the H4463
SS 4: 4 Your neck is like the t of David, built with H4463
SS 7: 4 Your neck is like an ivory t. Your eyes are H4463
SS 7: 4 Your nose is like the t of Lebanon looking H4463
Isa 2:15 every lofty t and every fortified wall, H4463
Jer 31:38 me from the T of Hananel to the H4463
Eze 31:14 the waters are ever to t proudly on high, H1467
Zec 14:10 from the T of Hananel to the royal H4463
Lk 13: 4 who died when the t in Siloam fell on G4788
Lk 14:28 "Suppose one of you wants to build a t G4788

TOWERED (4) [TOWER]

Eze 19:11 It t high above the thick foliage H1467
Eze 31: 3 the forest; it t on high, its top above the H1468
Eze 31: 5 So it t higher than all the trees of the field H1467
Eze 31:10 great cedar t over the thick foliage, H1467+928+7757+2256+5989+7550

TOWERING (1) [TOWER]

Isa 2:14 all the t mountains and all the high H8123

TOWERS (19) [TOWER]

2Ch 14: 7 walls around them, with t, gates and bars. H4463
2Ch 26: 9 Uzziah built t in Jerusalem at the Corner H4463
2Ch 26:10 He also built t in the wilderness and dug H4463
2Ch 26:15 use on the t and on the corner H4463
2Ch 27: 4 forts and t in the wooded areas H4463
2Ch 32: 5 sections of the wall and building t on it. H4463
Ps 48:12 about Zion, go around her, count her t, H4463
SS 8: 9 is a wall, we will build t of silver on her. H3227
SS 8:10 my breasts are like t. Thus I have H4463
Isa 23:13 they raised up their siege t, they stripped H1032
Isa 29: 3 encircle you with t and set up my siege H5164
Isa 30:25 slaughter, when the t fall, streams of H4463
Isa 33:18 Where is the officer in charge of the t?" H4463
Jer 50:15 She surrenders, her t fall, her walls are torn H859
La 4:17 from our t we watched for a nation that H7610
Eze 26: 4 the walls of Tyre and pull down her t; H4463
Eze 26: 9 demolish your t with his weapons. H4463
Eze 27:11 men of Gammad were in your t. H4463
Zep 1:16 fortified cities and against the corner t. H1469

TOWING (1)

Jn 21: 8 followed in the boat, t the net full of fish G5359

TOWN (181) [HOMETOWN, TOWNS, TOWNSPEOPLE]

Ge 19:20 here is a t near enough to run to H6551
Ge 19:21 I will not overthrow the t you speak of. H6551
Ge 19:22 That is why the t was called Zoar.) H6551
Ge 24:10 made his way to the t of Nahor. H6551
Ge 24:11 kneel down near the well outside the t; H6551
Ge 26:33 the name of the t has been Beersheba. H6551
Lev 14:40 into an unclean place outside the t. H6551
Lev 14:41 into an unclean place outside the t. H6551
Lev 14:45 taken out of the t to an unclean place. H6551
Lev 14:53 live bird in the open fields outside the t. H6551
Lev 25:33 a house sold in any t they hold—and is to H6551
Nu 20:16 Kadesh, a t on the edge of your territory. H6551
Nu 22:36 him at the Moabite t on the Arnon border, H6551
Nu 35: 4 extend a thousand cubits from the t wall. H6551
Nu 35: 5 Outside the t, measure two thousand H6551
Nu 35: 5 on the north, with the t in the center. H6551
Dt 2:36 and from the t in the gorge, even H6551
Dt 2:36 as Gilead, not one t was too strong for us. H7953
Dt 13:13 have led the people of their t astray, H6551
Dt 13:15 put to the sword all who live in that t. H6551
Dt 13:16 all the plunder of the t into the middle H2023S
Dt 13:16 completely burn the t and all its plunder H6551
Dt 13:16 That t is to remain a ruin forever, never to NDT
Dt 16: 5 the Passover in any t the LORD your God H9133
Dt 16:18 your tribes in every t the LORD your God is H9133
Dt 19:12 the killer shall be sent for by the t elders H6551
Dt 21: 3 Then the elders of the t nearest the body H6551
Dt 21: 6 all the elders of the t nearest the body H6551
Dt 21:19 him to the elders at the gate of his t. H6551
Dt 21:21 all the men of his t are to stone him to H6551
Dt 22:15 shall bring to the t elders at the gate H6551
Dt 22:17 the cloth before the elders of the t, H6551
Dt 22:21 there the men of her t shall stone her to H6551
Dt 22:23 to meet in a t a virgin pledged to H6551
Dt 22:24 to the gate of that t and stone them to H6551
Dt 22:24 she was in a t and did not scream H6551
Dt 23:16 they like and in whatever t they choose. H9133
Dt 25: 7 go to the elders at the t gate and say, H9133
Dt 25: 8 the elders of his t shall summon him and H6551
Jos 3:16 at a t called Adam in the vicinity of H6551
Jos 13: 9 from the t in the middle of the gorge H6551
Jos 13:16 from the t in the middle of the gorge H6551
Jos 18: 9 on a scroll, t by town, in seven parts, NDT
Jos 18: 9 on a scroll, town by t, in seven parts, H6551
Jos 18:14 Kiriath Jearim), a t of the people of Judah. H6551
Jos 19:50 They gave him the t he asked for H6551
Jos 19:50 And he built up the t and settled there. H6551
Jos 20: 6 own home in the t from which they fled." H6551
Jdg 6:28 morning when the people of the t got up, H6551
Jdg 6:30 The people of the t demanded of Joash H6551
Jdg 8:14 officials of Sukkoth, the elders of the t. H2023S
Jdg 8:16 the elders of the t and taught the men of H6551
Jdg 8:17 of Peniel and killed the men of the t. H6551
Jdg 8:27 which he placed in Ophrah, his t. H6551
Jdg 12: 7 died and was buried in a t in Gilead. H6551
Jdg 14:18 seventh day the men of the t said to him, H6551
Jdg 17: 8 left that t in search of some other place to H6551
Ru 1:19 the whole t was stirred because of them H6551
Ru 2:18 She carried it back to t, and her H6551
Ru 3:11 All the people of my t know that you are a H9133
Ru 3:15 bundle on her. Then he went back to t. H6551
Ru 4: 1 went up to the t gate and sat down there H9133
Ru 4: 2 took ten of the elders of the t and said, H6551
1Sa 1: 3 man went up from his t to worship and H6551
1Sa 4:13 the man entered the t and told what had H6551
1Sa 4:13 had happened, the whole t sent up a cry. H6551
1Sa 6:21 Come down and take it up to your t." NDT
1Sa 8:22 "Everyone go back to your own t. H6551
1Sa 9: 6 in this t there is a man of God; he H6551
1Sa 9:10 set out for the t where the man of God H6551
1Sa 9:11 As they were going up the hill to the t H6551
1Sa 9:12 he has just come to our t today, for the H6551
1Sa 9:13 As soon as you enter the t, you will find H6551
1Sa 9:14 They went up to the t, and as they were H6551
1Sa 9:25 came down from the high place to the t, H6551
1Sa 9:27 were going down to the edge of the t, H6551
1Sa 10: 5 As you approach the t, you will meet a H6551
1Sa 16: 4 the elders of the t trembled when they H6551
1Sa 20:29 a sacrifice in the t and my brother has H6551
1Sa 20:40 boy and said, "Go, carry them back to t." H6551
1Sa 20:42 and Jonathan went back to the t. H6551
1Sa 22:19 to the sword Nob, the t of the priests, with H6551
1Sa 23: 7 by entering a t with gates and bars." H6551
1Sa 23:10 destroy the t on account of me. H6551
1Sa 28: 3 buried him in his own t of Ramah. H6551
2Sa 12: 1 "There were two men in a certain t, one H6551
2Sa 15: 2 call out to him, "What t are you from?" H6551
2Sa 19:37 may die in my own t near the tomb of my H6551
2Sa 24: 5 south of the t in the gorge, and H6551
1Ki 15:27 a Philistine t, while Nadab and all NDT
1Ki 16:15 encamped near Gibbethon, a Philistine t. H889S
1Ki 17:10 When he came to the t gate, a widow H6551
1Ki 22:36 "Every man to his t. Every man to his land!" H6551
2Ki 2:19 our lord, this t is well situated, as you can H6551
2Ki 2:23 boys came out of the t and jeered at him. H6551
2Ki 3:19 every fortified city and every major t. H6551
2Ch 14: 5 incense altars in every t in Judah, H6551
2Ch 20: 4 came from every t in Judah to seek him. H6551
2Ch 28:25 In every t in Judah he built high places to H6551
2Ch 30:10 couriers went from t to town in Ephraim H6551
2Ch 30:10 went from town to t in Ephraim and H6551
Ezr 2: 1 Jerusalem and Judah, each to their own t, H6551
Ezr 10:14 elders and judges of each t, H6551+2256+6551
Ne 7: 6 Jerusalem and Judah, each to his own t, H6551
Job 39: 7 It laughs at the commotion in the t; it H7953
Ecc 10:15 they do not know the way to t. H6551
Isa 22: 2 you t so full of commotion, you city of H7953
Isa 25: 2 the fortified t a ruin, the H7953
Jer 3:14 one from a t and two from a clan H6551
Jer 4:29 archers every t takes to flight. H6551
Jer 48: 8 The destroyer will come against every t H6551
Jer 48: 8 every town, and not a t will escape. H6551
Jer 49:25 been abandoned, the t in which I delight? H7953
Eze 39:16 near a t called Hamonah. And so they will H6551
Am 4: 6 in every city and lack of bread in every t, H5226
Am 4: 7 I sent rain on one t, but withheld it from H6551
Am 4: 8 staggered from t to town for water but H6551
Am 4: 8 from town to t for water but did not H6551
Am 5: 3 your t that marches out a hundred strong NDT
Mic 1:14 The t of Akzib will prove deceptive to the H1074
Hab 2:12 establishes a t by injustice! H7953
Mt 2:23 he went and lived in a t called Nazareth. G4484
Mt 5:14 A t built on a hill cannot be hidden. G4484
Mt 8:33 went into the t and reported all this G4484
Mt 8:34 Then the whole t went out to meet Jesus G4484
Mt 9: 1 crossed over and came to his own t. G4484
Mt 10: 5 Gentiles or enter any t of the Samaritans. G4484
Mt 10:11 Whatever t or village you enter, search G4484
Mt 10:14 leave that home or t and shake the dust G4484
Mt 10:15 on the day of judgment than for that t. G4484
Mt 13:57 honor except in his own t and in his own G4258
Mt 23:34 synagogues and pursue from t to town. G4484
Mt 23:34 synagogues and pursue from town to t. G4484
Mk 1:33 The whole t gathered at the door, G4484
Mk 1:45 no longer enter a t openly but stayed G4484
Mk 5:14 reported this in the t and countryside, G4484
Mk 6: 4 is not without honor except in his own t, G4258
Mk 6:10 a house, stay there until you leave that t. G1696S
Lk 1:26 angel Gabriel to Nazareth, a t in Galilee, G4484
Lk 1:39 hurried to a t in the hill country of G4484
Lk 2: 3 everyone went to their own t to register. G4484
Lk 2: 4 also went up from the t of Nazareth in G4484
Lk 2: 4 to Bethlehem the t of David, because he G4484
Lk 2:11 Today in the t of David a Savior has been G4484
Lk 2:39 to Galilee to their own t of Nazareth. G4484
Lk 4:29 drove him out of the t, and took him to G4484
Lk 4:29 brow of the hill on which the t was built, G4484
Lk 4:31 to Capernaum, a t in Galilee, and on G4484
Lk 7:11 Jesus went to a t called Nain, and his G4484
Lk 7:12 As he approached the t gate, a dead G4484
Lk 7:12 And a large crowd from the t was with her. G4484
Lk 7:37 A woman in that t who lived a sinful life G4484
Lk 8: 1 about from one t and village to another, G4484
Lk 8: 4 coming to Jesus from t after town, G2848+4484
Lk 8: 4 coming to Jesus from town after t, G2848+4484
Lk 8:27 by a demon-possessed man from the t. G4484
Lk 8:34 reported this in the t and countryside, G4484
Lk 8:39 told all over t how much Jesus had G4484
Lk 9: 4 you enter, stay there until you leave that t. G1696
Lk 9: 5 leave their t and shake the dust off your G4484
Lk 9:10 by themselves to a t called Bethsaida, G4484
Lk 10: 1 of him to every t and place where he G4484
Lk 10: 8 "When you enter a t and are welcomed G4484
Lk 10:10 But when you enter a t and are not G4484
Lk 10:11 the dust of your t we wipe from our feet G4484
Lk 10:12 on that day for Sodom than for that t. G4484
Lk 14:21 streets and alleys of the t and bring in the G4484
Lk 18: 2 "In a certain t there was a judge who G4484
Lk 18: 3 was a widow in that t who kept coming to G4484
Lk 23:51 He came from the Judean t of Arimathea G4484
Jn 1:44 Peter, was from the t of Bethsaida. G4484
Jn 4: 5 So he came to a t in Samaria called G4484
Jn 4: 8 disciples had gone into the t to buy food.) G4484
Jn 4:28 went back to the t and said to the people G4484
Jn 4:30 came out of the t and made their way G4484
Jn 4:39 Samaritans from that t believed in him G4484
Jn 7:42 from Bethlehem, the t where David lived?" G3267
Ac 16: 4 they traveled from t to town, G1388+3836+4484
Ac 16: 4 they traveled from town to t, G1388+3836+4484
Ac 27: 8 called Fair Havens, near the t of Lasea. G4484
Titus 1: 5 unfinished and appoint elders in every t, G4484

TOWNS (305) [TOWN]

Ge 35: 5 of God fell on the t all around them so H6551
Ex 20:10 any foreigner residing in your t. H9133
Lev 25:32 to redeem their houses in the Levitical t, H6551
Lev 25:33 the houses in the t of the Levites are their H6551
Lev 25:34 belonging to their t must not be sold; H6551
Nu 13:19 What kind of t do they live in? Are H6551
Nu 21: 3 completely destroyed them and their t; H6551
Nu 31:10 They burned all the t where the Midianites H6551
Nu 35: 2 to give the Levites t to live in from the H6551
Nu 35: 2 And give them pasturelands around the t H6551
Nu 35: 3 Then they will have t to live in and H6551
Nu 35: 4 around the t that you give the H6551
Nu 35: 5 have this area as pastureland for the t. H6551
Nu 35: 6 "Six of the t you give the Levites will be H6551
Nu 35: 6 In addition, give them forty-two other t. H6551
Nu 35: 7 all you must give the Levites forty-eight t, H6551
Nu 35: 8 The t you give the Levites from the land H6551
Nu 35: 8 Take many t from a tribe that has many H6551
Nu 35:11 select some t to be your cities of refuge, to H6551
Nu 35:13 These six t you give will be your cities of H6551
Nu 35:15 These six t will be a place of refuge for H6551
Dt 1:22 we are to take and the t we will come to." H6551
Dt 2:34 time we took all his t and completely H6551
Dt 2:35 plunder from the t we had captured we H6551
Dt 2:37 Jabbok nor that around the t in the hills. H6551
Dt 3:10 We took all the t on the plateau, and all H6551
Dt 3:10 Edrei, t of Og's kingdom in Bashan. H6551
Dt 3:12 hill country of Gilead, together with its t. H6551
Dt 3:19 may stay in the t I have given you, H6551
Dt 5:14 any foreigner residing in your t, so H9133
Dt 12:12 Levites from your t who have no allotment H9133
Dt 12:15 in any of your t and eat as much of the H9133
Dt 12:17 not eat in your own t the tithe of your H9133
Dt 12:18 the Levites from your t—and you are H9133
Dt 12:21 in your own t you may eat as much of H9133
Dt 13:12 about one of the t the LORD your God is H6551
Dt 14:21 it to the foreigner residing in any of your t, H9133
Dt 14:27 do not neglect the Levites living in your t, H9133
Dt 14:28 that year's produce and store it in your t, H9133
Dt 14:29 who live in your t may come and eat and H9133
Dt 15: 7 in any of the t of the land the LORD H9133
Dt 15:22 You are to eat it in your own t. Both the H9133
Dt 16:11 the Levites in your t, and the foreigners, H9133
Dt 16:14 the widows who live in your t. H9133
Dt 17: 2 you in one of the t the LORD gives you is H9133
Dt 18: 6 from one of your t anywhere in Israel H9133
Dt 19: 1 out and settled in their t and houses, H6551
Dt 21: 2 from the body to the neighboring t. H6551
Dt 24:14 a foreigner residing in one of your t. H9133
Dt 26:12 they may eat in your t and be satisfied. H9133
Dt 31:12 the foreigners residing in your t—so H9133
Jos 11:21 Joshua totally destroyed them and their t. H6551
Jos 13:10 all the t of Sihon king of the Amorites H6551
Jos 13:17 to Heshbon and all its t on the plateau H6551
Jos 13:21 all the t on the plateau and the entire H6551
Jos 13:23 These t and their villages were the H6551
Jos 13:25 all the t of Gilead and half the Ammonite H6551
Jos 13:28 These t and their villages were the H6551
Jos 13:30 the settlements of Jair in Bashan, sixty t, H6551
Jos 14: 4 no share of the land but only t to live in, H6551
Jos 15: 9 came out at the t of Mount Ephron and H6551
Jos 15:21 The southernmost t of the tribe of Judah H6551
Jos 15:32 a total of twenty-nine t and their villages. H6551

Jos 15:36 fourteen **t** and their villages. H6551
Jos 15:41 Makkedah—sixteen **t** and their villages. H6551
Jos 15:44 Mareshah—nine **t** and their villages. H6551
Jos 15:51 Giloh—eleven **t** and their villages. H6551
Jos 15:54 Zior—nine **t** and their villages. H6551
Jos 15:57 Timnah—ten **t** and their villages. H6551
Jos 15:59 Eltekon—six **t** and their villages. H6551
Jos 15:60 Rabbah—two **t** and their villages. H6551
Jos 15:62 Salt and En Gedi—six **t** and their villages. H6551
Jos 16: 9 also included all the **t** and their villages H6551
Jos 17: 9 There were **t** belonging to Ephraim lying H6551
Jos 17: 9 Ephraim lying among the **t** *of* Manasseh, H6551
Jos 17:12 were not able to occupy these **t**, H6551
Jos 18:21 according to its clans, had the following **t**: H6551
Jos 18:24 Geba—twelve **t** and their villages. H6551
Jos 18:28 Kiriath—fourteen **t** and their villages. H6551
Jos 19: 6 Sharuhen—thirteen **t** and their villages; H6551
Jos 19: 7 Ashan—four **t** and their villages— H6551
Jos 19: 8 villages around these **t** as far as Baalath H6551
Jos 19:15 There were twelve **t** and their villages. H6551
Jos 19:16 These **t** and their villages were the H6551
Jos 19:22 There were sixteen **t** and their villages. H6551
Jos 19:23 These **t** and their villages were the H6551
Jos 19:30 were twenty-two **t** and their villages. H6551
Jos 19:31 These **t** and their villages were the H6551
Jos 19:35 The fortified **t** were Ziddim, Zer H6551
Jos 19:38 There were nineteen **t** and their villages. H6551
Jos 19:39 These **t** and their villages were the H6551
Jos 19:48 These **t** and their villages were the H6551
Jos 21: 2 Moses that you give us **t** to live in, H6551
Jos 21: 3 the following **t** and pasturelands out H6551
Jos 21: 4 were allotted thirteen **t** from the tribes of H6551
Jos 21: 5 were allotted ten **t** from the clans of the H6551
Jos 21: 6 allotted thirteen **t** from the clans of the H6551
Jos 21: 7 received twelve **t** from the tribes of H6551
Jos 21: 8 to the Levites these **t** and their H6551
Jos 21: 9 they allotted the following **t** by name H6551
Jos 21:10 these **t** were assigned to the descendants of NDT
Jos 21:16 nine **t** from these two tribes. H6551
Jos 21:18 together with their pasturelands—four **t**. H6551
Jos 21:19 The total number of **t** *for* the priests, the H6551
Jos 21:20 Levites were allotted **t** from the tribe of H6551
Jos 21:22 together with their pasturelands—four **t**. H6551
Jos 21:24 together with their pasturelands—four **t**. H6551
Jos 21:25 together with their pasturelands—two **t**. H6551
Jos 21:26 All these ten **t** and their pasturelands H6551
Jos 21:27 together with their pasturelands—two **t**; H6551
Jos 21:29 together with their pasturelands—four **t**; H6551
Jos 21:31 together with their pasturelands—four **t**; H6551
Jos 21:32 together with their pasturelands—three **t**. H6551
Jos 21:33 The total number of **t** *of* the Gershonite H6551
Jos 21:35 together with their pasturelands—four **t**; H6551
Jos 21:37 together with their pasturelands—four **t**; H6551
Jos 21:39 with their pasturelands—four **t** in all. H6551
Jos 21:40 The total number of **t** allotted to the H6551
Jos 21:41 The **t** *of* the Levites in the territory held by H6551
Jos 21:42 **Each** of these **t** had pasturelands H6551+6551
Jos 21:42 surrounding it; this was true for all these **t**. H6551
Jdg 10: 4 They controlled thirty **t** in Gilead, which to H6551
Jdg 11:26 settlements and all the **t** along the Arnon. H6551
Jdg 11:33 He devastated twenty **t** from Aroer to the H6551
Jdg 20:14 From their **t** they came together at Gibeah H6551
Jdg 20:15 thousand swordsmen from their **t**, H6551
Jdg 20:42 came out of the **t** cut them down there H6551
Jdg 20:48 Benjamin and put all the **t** to the sword, H6551
Jdg 20:48 All the **t** they came across they set on fire. H6551
Jdg 21:23 rebuilt the **t** and settled in them. H6551
1Sa 6:18 number of Philistine **t** belonging to the H6551
1Sa 6:18 the fortified **t** with their country villages. H6551
1Sa 7:14 The **t** from Ekron to Gath that the H6551
1Sa 18: 6 out from all the **t** *of* Israel to meet King H6551
1Sa 27: 5 be assigned to me in one of the country **t**, H6551
1Sa 30:29 to those in the **t** *of* the Jerahmeelites and H6551
1Sa 31: 7 they abandoned their **t** and fled. H6551
2Sa 2: 1 "Shall I go up to one of the **t** *of* Judah?" H6551
2Sa 2: 3 they settled in Hebron and its **t**. H6551
2Sa 8: 8 Berothai, **t** *that belonged to* Hadadezer H6551
2Sa 12:31 David did this to all the Ammonite **t** H6551
2Sa 24: 7 of Tyre and all the **t** *of* the Hivites and H6551
1Ki 9:11 gave twenty **t** in Galilee to Hiram H6551
1Ki 9:12 from Tyre to see the **t** that Solomon had H6551
1Ki 9:13 "What kind of **t** are these you have given H6551
1Ki 9:19 store cities and the **t** *for* his chariots and H6551
1Ki 12:17 who were living in the **t** *of* Judah, H6551
1Ki 13:32 the high places in the **t** *of* Samaria will H6551
1Ki 15:20 of his forces against the **t** *of* Israel. H6551
2Ki 3:25 They destroyed the **t**, and each man threw H6551
2Ki 13:25 son of Hazael the **t** he had taken in battle H6551
2Ki 13:25 and so he recovered the Israelite **t**. H6551
2Ki 17: 6 the Habor River and in the **t** *of* the Medes. H6551
2Ki 17: 9 built themselves high places in all their **t**. H6551
2Ki 17:24 them in the **t** *of* Samaria to replace H6551
2Ki 17:24 They took over Samaria and lived in its **t**. H6551
2Ki 17:26 resettled in the **t** *of* Samaria do not know H6551
2Ki 17:29 own gods in the *several* **t** where they H6551
2Ki 18:11 on the Habor River and in **t** *of* the Medes. H6551
2Ki 23: 5 high places of the **t** *of* Judah and on H6551
2Ki 23: 8 the priests from the **t** *of* Judah and H6551
2Ki 23:19 had built in the **t** *of* Samaria and that had H6551
1Ch 2:22 who controlled twenty-three **t** in Gilead. H6551
1Ch 2:23 with its surrounding settlements—sixty **t**.) H6551
1Ch 4:31 These were their **t** until the reign of David. H6551
1Ch 4:32 Rimmon, Token and Ashan—five **t**— H6551
1Ch 4:33 villages around these **t** as far as Baalath. H6551
1Ch 6:60 The total number of **t** distributed among H6551
1Ch 6:61 were allotted ten **t** from the clans of half H6551
1Ch 6:62 were allotted thirteen **t** from the tribes of H6551
1Ch 6:63 were allotted twelve **t** from the tribes of H6551
1Ch 6:64 the Levites these **t** and their pasturelands H6551
1Ch 6:65 they allotted the previously named **t**. H6551
1Ch 6:66 given as their territory **t** from the tribe of H6551
1Ch 7:29 of Joseph son of Israel lived in these **t**. NDT
1Ch 9: 2 in their own **t** were some Israelites, H6551
1Ch 10: 7 they abandoned their **t** and fled. H6551
1Ch 13: 2 are with them in their **t** and pasturelands, H6551
1Ch 18: 8 **t** *that belonged to* Hadadezer H6551
1Ch 19: 7 mustered from their **t** and moved out for H6551
1Ch 20: 3 David did this to all the Ammonite **t** H6551
1Ch 27:25 districts, in the **t**, the villages and the H6551
2Ch 10:17 who were living in the **t** *of* Judah, H6551
2Ch 11: 5 built up **t** for defense in Judah: H6551
2Ch 13:19 took from him the **t** of Bethel, H6551
2Ch 14: 7 "Let us build up these **t**," he said to Judah H6551
2Ch 15: 8 from the **t** he had captured in H6551
2Ch 16: 4 of his forces against the **t** *of* Israel. H6551
2Ch 17: 2 in Judah and in the **t** *of* Ephraim that his H6551
2Ch 17: 7 Micaiah to teach in the **t** *of* Judah. H6551
2Ch 17: 9 around to all the **t** *of* Judah and taught H6551
2Ch 17:13 had large supplies in the **t** *of* Judah H6551
2Ch 23: 2 heads of Israelite families from all the **t**. H6551
2Ch 24: 5 "Go to the **t** *of* Judah and collect the H6551
2Ch 25:13 the war raided **t** *belonging to* Judah from H6551
2Ch 26: 6 He then rebuilt **t** near Ashdod and H6551
2Ch 27: 4 He built **t** in the hill country of Judah and H6551
2Ch 28:18 raided **t** *in* the foothills and *in* the Negev H6551
2Ch 31: 1 were there went out to the **t** *of* Judah, H6551
2Ch 31: 1 returned to their own **t** and to their own H6551
2Ch 31: 6 who lived in the **t** *of* Judah also brought a H6551
2Ch 31:15 him faithfully in the **t** *of* the priests, H6551
2Ch 31:19 around their **t** or in any other towns, H6551
2Ch 31:19 around their towns or in any other **t**, H6551
2Ch 34: 6 In the **t** *of* Manasseh, Ephraim and H6551
Ezr 2:59 following came up from the **t** of Tel Melah, NDT
Ezr 2:70 the temple servants settled in their own **t**, H6551
Ezr 2:70 the rest of the Israelites settled in their **t**. H6551
Ezr 3: 1 the Israelites had settled in their **t**, H6551
Ezr 10:14 let everyone in our **t** who has married a H6551
Ne 7:61 following came up from the **t** of Tel Melah, NDT
Ne 7:73 rest of the Israelites, settled in their own **t**. H6551
Ne 7:73 the Israelites had settled in their **t**, H6551
Ne 8:15 it throughout their **t** and in Jerusalem: H6551
Ne 10:37 the tithes in all the **t** *where* we work. H6551
Ne 11: 1 nine were to stay in their own **t**. H6551
Ne 11: 3 servants lived in the **t** *of* Judah, H6551
Ne 11: 3 on their own property in the *various* **t**, H6551
Ne 11:20 were in all the **t** *of* Judah, each on their H6551
Ne 12:44 the fields around the **t** they were to bring H6551
Job 15:28 will inhabit ruined **t** and houses where no H6551
Isa 40: 9 say to the **t** *of* Judah, "Here is your H6551
Isa 42:11 the wilderness and its **t** raise their voices; H6551
Isa 44:26 inhabited,' of the **t** *of* Judah, 'They shall H6551
Jer 1:15 walls and against all the **t** *of* Judah. H6551
Jer 2:15 his land; his **t** are burned and deserted. H6551
Jer 2:28 have as many gods as you have **t**. H6551
Jer 4: 7 Your **t** will lie in ruins without inhabitant H6551
Jer 4:26 all its **t** lay in ruins before the LORD H6551
Jer 4:29 All the **t** are deserted; no one lives in H6551
Jer 5: 6 in wait near their **t** to tear to pieces any H6551
Jer 7:17 are doing in the **t** *of* Judah and in the H6551
Jer 7:34 bridegroom in the **t** *of* Judah and the H6551
Jer 9:11 will lay waste the **t** *of* Judah so no one H6551
Jer 10:22 It will make the **t** *of* Judah desolate, H6551
Jer 11: 6 these words in the **t** *of* Judah and in the H6551
Jer 11:12 The **t** *of* Judah and the people of H6551
Jer 11:13 have as many gods as you have **t**; and the H6551
Jer 17:26 will come from the **t** *of* Judah and the H6551
Jer 20:16 that man be like the **t** the LORD overthrew H6551
Jer 22: 6 you like a wasteland, like **t** not inhabited. H6551
Jer 25:18 Jerusalem and the **t** *of* Judah, its kings H6551
Jer 26: 2 the people of the **t** *of* Judah who come to H6551
Jer 31:21 Return, Virgin Israel, return to your **t**. H6551
Jer 31:23 of Judah and in its **t** will once again use H6551
Jer 31:24 will live together in Judah and all its **t**— H6551
Jer 32:44 in the **t** *of* Judah and in the towns of the H6551
Jer 32:44 of Judah and in the **t** *of* the hill country, H6551
Jer 33:10 Yet in the **t** *of* Judah and the streets of H6551
Jer 33:12 in all its **t** there will again be pastures H6551
Jer 33:13 In the **t** *of* the hill country, of the western H6551
Jer 33:13 around Jerusalem and in the **t** *of* Judah, H6551
Jer 34: 1 Jerusalem and all its surrounding **t**, H6551
Jer 34:22 will lay waste the **t** *of* Judah so no one H6551
Jer 36: 6 people of Judah who come in from their **t**. H6551
Jer 36: 9 those who had come from the **t** *of* Judah. H6551
Jer 40: 5 has appointed over the **t** *of* Judah, H6551
Jer 40:10 and live in the **t** you have taken over." H6551
Jer 44: 2 on Jerusalem and on all the **t** *of* Judah. H6551
Jer 44: 6 it raged against the **t** *of* Judah and the H6551
Jer 44:17 officials did in the **t** *of* Judah and in the H6551
Jer 44:21 incense burned in the **t** *of* Judah and the H6551
Jer 47: 2 the **t** and those who live in them. H6551
Jer 48: 9 be laid waste; her **t** will become desolate H6551
Jer 48:15 Moab will be destroyed and her **t** invaded; H6551
Jer 48:24 Bozrah—to all the **t** *of* Moab, far and H6551
Jer 48:28 Abandon your **t** and dwell among the H6551
Jer 49: 1 Why do his people live in its **t**? H6551
Jer 49:13 all its **t** will be in ruins forever. H6551
Jer 49:18 along with their neighboring **t**," says the NDT
Jer 50:32 kindle a fire in her **t** that will consume all H6551
Jer 50:40 Gomorrah along with their neighboring **t**," NDT
Jer 51:43 Her **t** will be desolate, a dry and desert H6551
La 5:11 in Zion, and virgins in the **t** *of* Judah. H6551
Eze 6: 6 the **t** will be laid waste and the high H6551
Eze 12:20 The inhabited **t** will be laid waste and the H6551
Eze 19: 7 their strongholds and devastated their **t**. H6551
Eze 25: 9 beginning at its frontier **t**—Beth H6551
Eze 35: 4 I will turn your **t** into ruins and you will be H6551
Eze 35: 9 your **t** will not be inhabited. H6551
Eze 36: 4 ruins and the deserted **t** that have been H6551
Eze 36:10 The **t** will be inhabited and the ruins H6551
Eze 36:33 I will resettle your **t**, and the ruins will be H6551
Eze 39: 9 those who live in the **t** *of* Israel will go out H6551
Eze 45: 5 temple, as their possession for **t** to live in. H6551
Hos 8:14 built palaces; Judah has fortified many **t**. H6551
Hos 13:10 Where are your rulers in all your **t**, of H6551
Ob 20 Sepharad will possess the **t** *of* the Negev. H6551
Zec 1:12 from Jerusalem and from the **t** *of* Judah, H6551
Zec 1:17 'My **t** will again overflow with prosperity H6551
Zec 7: 7 its surrounding **t** were at rest and H6551
Mt 9:35 Jesus went through all the **t** and villages *G4484*
Mt 10:23 going through the **t** of Israel before the *G4484*
Mt 11: 1 to teach and preach in the **t** of Galilee. *G4484*
Mt 11:20 to denounce the **t** in which most of his *G4484*
Mt 14:13 crowds followed him on foot from the **t**. *G4484*
Mk 6:33 on foot from all the **t** and got there ahead *G4484*
Mk 6:56 into villages, **t** or countryside—they placed *G4484*
Lk 4:43 of the kingdom of God *to* the other **t** also, *G4484*
Lk 5:12 While Jesus was in one *of* the **t**, a man *G4484*
Lk 13:22 Jesus went through the **t** and villages, *G4484*
Ac 5:16 gathered also *from* the **t** around *G4484*
Ac 8:40 the gospel *in* all the **t** until he reached *G4484*
Ac 15:36 believers in all the **t** where we preached *G4484*
Jude 7 the surrounding **t** gave themselves up *G4484*

TOWNSPEOPLE (2) [TOWN]

Ge 24:13 daughters of the **t** are coming out to H408+6551
Jdg 6:27 he was afraid of his family and the **t**, H408+6551

TRACE (2) [TRACED, TRACING]

Da 2:35 swept them away without leaving a **t**. A10087
Heb 7: 6 however, *did* not **t** *his* **descent** from Levi *G1156*

TRACED (1) [TRACE]

Ro 9: 5 from them is **t** the human ancestry of NDT

TRACING (1) [TRACE]

Ro 11:33 his judgments, and his paths **beyond t out**! *G453*

TRACK (2) [TRACKED, TRACKLESS, TRACKS]

1Sa 23:23 *I will* **t** him **down** among all the clans of H2924
Job 14:16 count my steps but not **keep t** of my sin. H9068

TRACKED (1) [TRACK]

Ps 17:11 *They have* **t** me **down**, they now surround H892

TRACKLESS (2) [TRACK]

Job 12:24 makes them wander in a **t** waste. H4202+2006
Ps 107:40 made them wander in a **t** waste. H4202+2006

TRACKS (1) [TRACK]

SS 1: 8 follow the **t** *of* the sheep and graze your H6811

TRACONITIS (1)

Lk 3: 1 Philip tetrarch of Iturea and **T**, *G5551+6001*

TRACT (1) [TRACTS]

Jos 24:32 at Shechem in the **t** *of* land that Jacob H2754

TRACTS (1) [TRACT]

Jos 17: 5 consisted of ten **t of land** besides Gilead H824

TRADE (11) [TRADED, TRADERS, TRADES, TRADING]

Ge 34:10 Live in it, **t** *in* it, and acquire H6086
Ge 34:21 "Let them live in our land and **t** *in* it; the H6086
Ge 42:34 back to you, and *you can* **t** in the land. H6086
2Ch 20:37 wrecked and were not able to set sail to **t**. H9576
Isa 23:17 prostitution and *will* **ply her t** with all the H2388
Eze 27: 9 sailors came alongside to **t** *for* your wares. H6842
Eze 28:16 your widespread **t** you were filled with H8219
Eze 28:18 sins and dishonest **t** you have desecrated H8219
Zep 1:11 all **who t with** silver will be destroyed. H5744
Ac 19:27 not only that our **t** will lose its good name *G3538*
Rev 18:22 No worker *of* any **t** will ever be found in *G5492*

TRADED (8) [TRADE]

Eze 27:13 *they* **t** human beings and articles of H5989
Eze 27:15 " 'The men of Rhodes **t** *with* you, and H8217
Eze 27:17 " 'Judah and Israel **t with** you; they H8217
Eze 27:20 " 'Dedan **t** in saddle blankets *with* you. H8217
Eze 27:22 of Sheba and Raamah **t** *with* you; H8217
Eze 27:23 of Sheba, Ashur and Kilmad **t** *with* you. H8217
Eze 27:24 your marketplace they **t** *with* you beautiful H8217
Joel 3: 3 my people and **t** boys for prostitutes; H5989

TRADERS (6) [TRADE]

1Ki 10:15 from merchants and **t** and from all the H8217
2Ch 9:14 revenues brought in by merchants and **t**. H6086
Job 41: 6 Will **t** barter for it? Will they divide it up H2493
Isa 23: 8 whose **t** are renowned in the earth? H4048

Eze 17: 4 where he planted it in a city of t. H8217
1Ti 1:10 *for* **slave t** and liars and perjurers G435

TRADES (1) [TRADE]
Ac 19:25 along with the workers in **related** *t*, and said: AIT

TRADING (8) [TRADE]
1Ki 10:22 king had a **fleet of t ships** at sea H639+9576
1Ki 22:48 built a **fleet of t ships** to go to Ophir H641+9576
2Ch 9:21 had a **fleet of t ships** manned H641+2143+9576
2Ch 20:36 a **fleet of t ships**. H641+4200+2143+9576
Job 20:18 he will not enjoy the profit from his t. H9455
Pr 31:18 She sees that her t is profitable, and her H6087
Isa 2:16 every **t ship** and every stately H641+9576
Eze 28: 5 By your great skill in t you have increased H8219

TRADITION (9) [TRADITIONS]
Jdg 11:39 From this comes the Israelite t H2976
2Ch 35:25 These became a t in Israel and are H2976
Mt 15: 2 do your disciples break the t of the elders? G4142
Mt 15: 3 command of God for the sake of your t? G4142
Mt 15: 6 the word of God for the sake of your t. G4142
Mk 7: 3 washing, holding to the t of the elders. G4142
Mk 7: 5 according to the t of the elders instead G4142
Mk 7:13 the word of God *by* your t that you have G4142
Col 2: 8 depends on human t and the elemental G4142

TRADITIONS (6) [TRADITION]
Mic 6:16 Ahab's house; you have followed their t. H4600
Mk 7: 4 And they observe many other t, such as G4161
Mk 7: 8 of God and are holding on to human t." G4142
Mk 7: 9 of God in order to observe your own t! G4142
1Co 11: 2 holding to the t just as I passed them G4142
Gal 1:14 extremely zealous *for* the t of my fathers. G4142

TRAFFICK, TRAFFICKERS (KJV) MERCHANTS, TRADE, TRADERS, TRADING

TRAGEDY (1)
1Ki 17:20 *have you* **brought** t even on this widow I H8317

TRAIL (2)
Job 41:30 **leaving** a t in the mud like a threshing H8331
1Ti 5:24 of them; the sins of others **t behind** them. G2051

TRAIN (4) [TRAINED, TRAINING, TRAINS, WELL-TRAINED]
Isa 2: 4 nor *will they* t *for* war anymore. H4340
Isa 6: 1 the **t of** his **robe** filled the temple. H8767
Mic 4: 3 nor *will they* t *for* war anymore. H4340
1Ti 4: 7 wives' tales; rather, t yourself to be godly. G1214

TRAINED (12) [TRAIN]
Ge 14:14 he called out the 318 **t men** born in his H2849
1Ch 5:18 use a bow, and *who* **were** t *for* battle. H4340
1Ch 25: 7 all of *them* t and skilled *in* music for the H4340
2Ch 2:14 *He is* t to work in gold and silver, bronze H3359
2Ch 26:13 was an army of 307,500 *men* t *for* war, H6913
Da 1: 5 They *were* to *be* t for three years, and H1540
Hos 7:15 I t them and strengthened their arms, but H3579
Hos 10:11 Ephraim *is* a t heifer that loves to thresh H4340
Lk 6:40 everyone *who is* **fully** t will be like G2936
Ac 22: 3 Gamaliel and *was* thoroughly t in the law G4084
Heb 5:14 constant use *have* t themselves to G1214+2400
Heb 12:11 peace for those *who have been* t by it. G1214

TRAINING (4) [TRAIN]
1Co 9:25 competes in the games **goes into** strict t. G1603
Eph 6: 4 bring them up in the t and instruction of G4082
1Ti 4: 8 For physical t is of some value, but G1215
2Ti 3:16 correcting and t in righteousness, G4082

TRAINS (3) [TRAIN]
2Sa 22:35 *He* t my hands for battle; my arms can H4340
Ps 18:34 *He* t my hands for battle; my arms can H4340
Ps 144: 1 LORD my Rock, who t my hands for war, H4340

TRAITOR (4) [TREASON]
2Ki 17: 4 of Assyria discovered that Hoshea was a t, H8004
Isa 21: 2 The t betrays, the looter H953
Lk 6:16 Judas Iscariot, who became a t. G4595
Jn 18: 5 And Judas the t was standing there with G4140

TRAITORS (2) [TREASON]
Ps 59: 5 all the nations; show no mercy to wicked t. H953
Mic 2: 4 He assigns our fields to t.' " H8745

TRAMPLE (19) [TRAMPLED, TRAMPLING]
Job 39:15 that some wild animal *may* t them. H1889
Ps 7: 5 *let him* t my life to the ground and make H8252
Ps 44: 5 through your name *we* t our foes. H1008
Ps 60:12 and he *will* **t down** our enemies. H1008
Ps 91:13 *you will* t the great lion and the serpent. H8252
Ps 108:13 and he *will* **t down** our enemies. H1008
Isa 10: 6 and to t them **down** like mud in the H8492+5330
Isa 14:25 on my mountains *I will* t him **down.** H1008
Isa 26: 6 Feet t it **down**—the feet of the oppressed H8252
Jer 12:10 will ruin my vineyard and **t down** my field; H1008
Eze 26:11 hooves of his horses *will* t all your streets; H8252
Eze 34:18 *Must you* also t the rest of your pasture H8252
Joel 3:13 **t the grapes**, for the winepress is H8097
Am 2: 7 They t on the heads of the poor as on the H8635
Am 8: 4 *you who* t the needy and do away with H8635
Mal 4: 3 Then *you will* **t on** the wicked; they will be H6748
Mt 7: 6 If you do, *they may* t them under their feet G2922
Lk 10:19 given you authority *to* t on snakes and G4251
Rev 11: 2 *They will* **t on** the holy city for 42 months. G4251

TRAMPLED (32) [TRAMPLE]
2Sa 22:43 I pounded and t them like mud in the H8392
2Ki 7:17 the people t him in the gateway H8252
2Ki 7:20 for the people t him in the gateway H8252
2Ki 9:33 the horses as *they* t her **underfoot**. H8252
2Ki 14: 9 came along and t the thistle **underfoot**. H8252
2Ch 25:18 came along and t the thistle **underfoot**. H8252
Ps 18:42 *I* t them like mud in the streets. H8392
Isa 5: 5 I will break down its wall, and it will be t. H5330
Isa 14:19 Like a corpse **t underfoot**, H1008
Isa 16: 8 of the nations *have* **t down** the choicest H2150
Isa 25:10 Moab *will* **be** t in their land as straw is H1889
Isa 25:10 land as straw **is t down** in the manure. H1889
Isa 28: 3 Ephraim's drunkards, *will* **be** t underfoot. H8252
Isa 63: 3 *I* t them in my anger and trod them down H2005
Isa 63: 6 *I* t the nations in my anger; in my wrath I H1008
Isa 63:18 our enemies *have* **t down** your sanctuary H1008
Jer 51:33 is like a threshing floor at the time it *is* t; H2005
La 1:15 winepress the Lord *has* t Virgin Daughter H2005
La 3:16 teeth with gravel; *he has* t me in the dust. H4115
Eze 34:19 feed on **what** you have t and drink H5330+8079
Da 7: 7 its victims and t underfoot whatever was A10672
Da 7:19 its victims and t underfoot whatever was A10672
Da 8: 7 goat knocked it to the ground and t *on* it, H8252
Da 8:10 host down to the earth and t *on* them. H8252
Hos 5:11 is oppressed, t *in* judgment, intent on H8368
Mic 7:10 now she will be **t underfoot** like mire in H5330
Hab 3:15 *You* t the sea with your horses, churning H2005
Mt 5:13 except to be thrown out and t underfoot. G2922
Lk 8: 5 along the path; *it was* t on, and the birds G2922
Lk 21:24 Jerusalem will be **t on** by the Gentiles G4251
Heb 10:29 who *has* t the Son of God **underfoot**, G2922
Rev 14:20 *They were* t in the winepress outside the G4251

TRAMPLING (6) [TRAMPLE]
Isa 1:12 has asked this of you, this t *of* my courts? H8252
Isa 22: 5 has a day of tumult and t and terror in the H4431
Da 7:23 whole earth, t it **down** and crushing it. A10165
Da 8:13 sanctuary and the **t underfoot** of the LORD's H5330
Zec 10: 5 warriors in battle t their enemy into the H1008
Lk 12: 1 so that *they were* **t on** one another G2922

TRANCE (3)
Ac 10:10 meal was being prepared, he fell into a t. G1749
Ac 11: 5 Joppa praying, and in a t I saw a vision. G1749
Ac 22:17 was praying at the temple, I fell into a t G1749

TRANQUILLITY (1)
Ecc 4: 6 one handful with t than two handfuls with H5739

TRANS-EUPHRATES (17) [EUPHRATES]
Ezr 4:10 and elsewhere in T. A10526+10468+10191
Ezr 4:11 From your servants in T: A10526+10468+10191
Ezr 4:16 be left with nothing in T. A10526+10468+10002
Ezr 4:17 and elsewhere in T: A10526+10468+10191
Ezr 4:20 over the whole of T, A10526+10468+10191
Ezr 5: 3 governor of T, and A10526+10468+10191
Ezr 5: 6 governor of T, and A10526+10468+10191
Ezr 5: 6 the officials of T, sent to A10526+10468+10191
Ezr 6: 6 governor of T, and A10526+10468+10191
Ezr 6: 8 from the revenues of T A10526+10468+10191
Ezr 6:13 governor of T, and A10526+10468+10191
Ezr 7:21 treasurers of T are to A10526+10468+10191
Ezr 7:25 to all the people of T— A10526+10468+10191
Ezr 8:36 and to the governors of T, H6298+2021+5643
Ne 2: 7 letters to the governors of T, H6298+2021+5643
Ne 2: 9 governors of T and gave H6298+2021+5643
Ne 3: 7 of the governor of T. H6298+2021+5643

TRANSACTION (1) [TRANSACTIONS]
Jer 32:25 silver and **have the t witnessed.** H6386+6332

TRANSACTIONS (1) [TRANSACTION]
Ru 4: 7 was the **method of legalizing** t in Israel.) H9496

TRANSCENDS (1)
Php 4: 7 peace of God, which t all understanding G5660

TRANSFER (2) [TRANSFERRED]
Ru 4: 7 and **t of property** to become H9455+3972+1821
2Sa 3:10 t the kingdom from the house of Saul H6296

TRANSFERRED (1) [TRANSFER]
Ac 25: 3 favor to them, to *have* Paul t to Jerusalem G3569

TRANSFIGURED (2)
Mt 17: 2 There *he was* t before them. His face G3565
Mk 9: 2 There *he was* t before them. G3565

TRANSFORM (1) [TRANSFORMED]
Php 3:21 *will* t our lowly bodies so that they will be G3571

TRANSFORMED (3) [TRANSFORM]
Job 28: 5 which food comes, **is** t below as by fire; H2200
Ro 12: 2 but *be* t by the renewing of your mind. G3565
2Co 3:18 *are being* t into his image with G3565

TRANSGRESSED (2) [TRANSGRESSION]
Ps 17: 3 planned no evil; my mouth *has* not t. H6296
Da 9:11 All Israel *has* t your law and turned away H6296

TRANSGRESSION (11) [TRANSGRESSED, TRANSGRESSIONS, TRANSGRESSORS]
Ps 19:13 I will be blameless, innocent of great t. H7322
Isa 53: 8 the t *of* my people he was punished. H7322
Da 9:24 your people and your holy city to finish t, H7322
Mic 1: 5 All this is because of Jacob's t, because H7322
Mic 1: 5 What is Jacob's t? Is it not Samaria? H7322
Mic 3: 8 to declare to Jacob his t, to Israel his sin. H7322
Mic 6: 7 Shall I offer my firstborn for my t, the fruit H7322
Mic 7:18 sin and forgives the t of the remnant of H7322
Ro 4:15 And where there is no law there is no t. G4126
Ro 11:11 *because of* their t, salvation has G4183
Ro 11:12 But if their t means riches for the world G4183

TRANSGRESSIONS (15) [TRANSGRESSION]
Ps 32: 1 Blessed is the one whose t are forgiven H7322
Ps 32: 5 "I will confess my t to the LORD." And you H7322
Ps 39: 8 Save me from all my t; do not make me H7322
Ps 51: 1 to your great compassion blot out my t. H7322
Ps 51: 3 For I know my t, and my sin is always H7322
Ps 65: 3 overwhelmed by sins, you forgave our t. H7322
Ps 103:12 so far has he removed our t from us. H7322
Isa 43:25 am he who blots out your t, for my own H7322
Isa 50: 1 because of your t your mother was sent H7322
Isa 53: 5 But he was pierced for our t, he was H7322
Mic 1:13 the t *of* Israel were found in you. H7322
Ro 4: 7 "Blessed are those whose t are forgiven G490
Gal 3:19 was added because of t until the Seed to G4126
Eph 2: 1 you, you were dead *in* your t and sins, G4183
Eph 2: 5 Christ even when we were dead *in* t— G4183

TRANSGRESSORS (4) [TRANSGRESSION]
Ps 51:13 Then I will teach t your ways, so that H7321
Isa 53:12 unto death, and was numbered with the t. H7321
Isa 53:12 of many, and made intercession for the t. H7321
Lk 22:37 'And he was numbered with the t'; and I G491

TRANSITORY (2)
2Co 3: 7 because of its glory, t *though it was*, G2934
2Co 3:11 And if what *was* t came with glory, how G2934

TRANSLATE, TRANSLATED (KJV) BROUGHT, TAKEN, TRANSFER

TRANSLATED (2)
Ezr 4:18 us has been read and t in my presence. A10597
Jn 1:42 called Cephas" (which, *when* t, *is* Peter). G2257

TRANSPARENT (1)
Rev 21:21 of the city was of gold, as pure as t glass. G1420

TRANSPLANTED (1) [PLANT]
Ps 80: 8 *You* t a vine from Egypt; you drove out the H5825

TRANSPORT (1)
Ge 46: 5 the carts that Pharaoh had sent to t him. H5951

TRAP (25) [TRAPPED, TRAPS]
1Sa 28: 9 Why *have* you **set** a t for my life to bring H5943
Job 18: 9 A t seizes him by the heel; a snare holds H7062
Job 18:10 him on the ground; a t lies in his path. H4892
Job 40:24 it by the eyes, or t it and pierce its nose? H4613
Ps 31: 4 Keep me free from the t that is set for me H8407
Ps 69:22 may it become retribution and a t. H4613
Ps 119:85 The arrogant dig pits to *t* me, contrary to your AIT
Pr 20:25 It is a t to dedicate something rashly and H4613
Pr 28:10 an evil path will fall into their own t, H8819
Ecc 7:26 whose heart is a t and whose hands are H3052
Isa 8:14 of Jerusalem he will be a t and a snare. H7062
Jer 50:24 *I* **set** a t for you, Babylon, and you were H3704
Am 3: 5 swoop down to a t *on* the ground when H7062
Am 3: 5 Does a t spring up from the ground if it H7062
Ob 7 who eat your bread will set a t for you, H4650
Mt 22:15 out and laid plans to t him in his words. G4074
Mt 22:18 hypocrites, why *are you trying to* t me? G4279
Mk 12:15 "Why *are you trying to* t me?" he asked. G4279
Lk 20:26 They were unable *to* t him in what he had G2138
Lk 21:34 day will close on you suddenly like a t. G4075
Jn 8: 6 They were using this question *as a* t, in G4279
Ro 11: 9 "May their table become a snare and a t G2560
1Ti 3: 7 fall into disgrace and into the devil's t. G4075
1Ti 6: 9 temptation and a t and into many foolish G4075
2Ti 2:26 senses and escape from the t of the devil, G4075

TRAPPED (8) [TRAP]
Pr 6: 2 *you have* **been** t by what you said H3704
Pr 11: 6 the unfaithful **are** t by evil desires. H4334
Pr 12:13 Evildoers are t by their sinful talk, and so H4613
Ecc 9:12 so people **are** t by evil times that fall H3704
Isa 42:22 all of them t in pits or hidden away in H7072
Jer 8: 9 to shame; they will be dismayed and t. H4334
Eze 19: 4 about him, and *he* **was** t in their pit. H9530
Eze 19: 8 their net for him, and *he* **was** t in their pit. H9530

TRAPS (8) [TRAP]
Jos 23:13 they will become snares and t for you H4613
Jdg 2: 3 they will become t for you, and their H7397
Ps 38:12 Those who want to kill me **set** *their* **t** H5943
Ps 140: 5 net and have set t for me along my path. H4613
Ps 141: 9 Keep me safe from the t *set by* evildoers H4613
Jer 5:26 like those who set t to catch people. H5422
Jer 9: 8 in their hearts they set t *for* them. H744
La 4:20 our very life breath, was caught in their t. H8827

TRAVAIL, TRAVAILED, TRAVAILEST, TRAVAILETH, TRAVAILING (KJV) BIRTH, BURDEN, BUSINESS, CHILDBIRTH, HARDSHIP, HARDSHIPS, LABOR, MISFORTUNE, PAIN, PREGNANT, SUFFERED, SUFFERS, TASK, TOIL, TOILING

TRAVEL (9) [TRAVELED, TRAVELER, TRAVELERS, TRAVELING, TRAVELS]

Ex 13:21 so that they *could* t by day or night. H2143
Nu 20:17 *We will* t along the King's Highway and H2143
Nu 21:22 *We will* t along the King's Highway until H2143
2Ch 15: 5 it was not safe to t about, H3655+2256+995
Job 21:29 you never questioned *those who* t? H6296+2006
Pr 4:15 Avoid it, *do* not t on it; turn from it and go H6296
Eze 39:11 the valley of those *who* t east of the Sea. H6296
Mt 23:15 *You* t over land and sea to win a single G4310
Rev 18:17 and all who t by ship, the G2093+5536+4434

TRAVELED (37) [TRAVEL]

Ge 12: 6 Abram t through the land as far as the H6296
Ge 41:46 presence and t throughout Egypt. H6296
Ex 15:22 For three days they t in the desert without H2143
Nu 10:12 Sinai and t from place to place until the H5023
Nu 10:33 mountain of the LORD and t *for* three days. H2006
Nu 11:35 the people t *to* Hazeroth and stayed H5825
Nu 21: 4 *They* t from Mount Hor *along* the route to H5825
Nu 22: 1 Then the Israelites t to the plains of Moab H5825
Nu 33: 8 and when *they had* t for three days H2143+2006
Dt 2: 8 and t along the desert road of Moab. H6296
Dt 10: 6 The Israelites t from the wells of Bene H5825
Dt 10: 7 From there *they* t *to* Gudgodah and on to H5825
Jos 24:17 all the nations through which *we* t. H6296
Jdg 11:18 "Next *they* t through the wilderness H2143
2Sa 4: 7 *they* t all night by way of the Arabah. H2143
1Ki 19: 8 *he* t forty days and forty nights until he H2143
2Ki 5:19 After Naaman *had* t some distance, H2143
Isa 41: 3 by a path his feet *have* not t before. H995
Zec 7:14 that no *one* t through it. H6296+2256+8740
Mk 1:39 So *he* t throughout Galilee, preaching in G2262
Lk 2:44 their company, *they* t on for a day. G2262+3847
Lk 8: 1 Jesus t about from one town and village G1476
Lk 10:33 But a Samaritan, *as he* t, came where the G3841
Lk 17:11 Jesus t along the border between G1451
Ac 8:36 As *they* t along the road, they came to G4513
Ac 8:40 appeared at Azotus and t about G1451
Ac 9:32 *As* Peter t about the country, he went to G1451
Ac 11:19 Stephen was killed t as far as Phoenicia, G1451
Ac 13: 6 *They* t through the whole island until they G1451
Ac 13:31 was seen *by* those *who had* t with him G5262
Ac 15: 3 and *as they* t through Phoenicia and G1451
Ac 16: 4 As *they* t from town to town G1388+3836+4484
Ac 16: 6 his companions t throughout the region of G1451
Ac 16:12 From there we t to Philippi, a Roman colony NDT
Ac 18:23 and t from place to place throughout the G1451
Ac 20: 2 *He* t through that area, speaking many G1451
Ac 28:15 and *they* t as far as the Forum of Appius G2262

TRAVELER (5) [TRAVEL]

Jdg 19:17 he looked and saw the t in the city square, H782
2Sa 12: 4 "Now a t came to the rich man, but the H2144
2Sa 12: 4 a meal for the t who had come to him. H782
Job 31:32 my door was always open to the t— H782
Jer 14: 8 in the land, like a t who stays only a night? H782

TRAVELERS (4) [TRAVEL]

Jdg 5: 6 t took to winding paths. H2143+5986
Isa 33: 8 are deserted, no t are *on* the roads. H6296
Jer 9: 2 I had in the desert a lodging place for t, H782
Eze 39:11 It will block the way of t, because Gog H6296

TRAVELING (8) [TRAVEL]

Ex 14:19 who *had been* t in front of Israel's army H2143
Ex 17: 1 t from place to place as the LORD H5023
1Ki 18:27 he is deep in thought, or busy, or t. H2006
Job 6:19 the t merchants *of* Sheba look in hope. H2142
Isa 60:15 with no *one* t through, I will make H6296
Lk 14:25 Large crowds *were* t with Jesus, and G5233
Ac 9: 7 The men t with Saul stood there G5321
Ac 19:29 Paul's t companions from Macedonia G5292

TRAVELS (4) [TRAVEL]

Ex 40:36 In all the t *of* the Israelites, whenever the H5023
Ex 40:38 sight of all the Israelites during all their t. H5023
Jer 2: 6 a land where no one t and no one lives? H6296
Jer 51:43 no one lives, through which no one t. H6296

TRAYS (3)

Ex 25:38 Its wick trimmers and t are to be of pure H4746
Ex 37:23 as well as its wick trimmers and t, of pure H4746
Nu 4: 9 its wick trimmers and t, and all its jars H4746

TREACHEROUS (7) [TREASON]

Ps 25: 3 come on those *who are* t without cause. H953
Isa 21: 2 The t betray! With treachery H953
Isa 24:16 With treachery the t betray!" H953
Isa 48: 8 Well do I know how t *you are*; you H953+953
Hab 1:13 Why then do you tolerate the t? Why are H953
Zep 3: 4 are unprincipled; they are t people. H956
2Ti 3: 4 t, rash, conceited, lovers of pleasure rather G4595

TREACHEROUSLY (2) [TREASON]

Jdg 9:23 so that they acted t against Abimelek. H953
Ac 7:19 He dealt t with our people and oppressed G2947

TREACHERY (3) [TREASON]

2Ki 9:23 calling out to Ahaziah, "T, Ahaziah!" H5327
Isa 24:16 With t the treacherous betray! H954
Isa 59:13 rebellion and t against the LORD, turning H3950

TREAD (7) [TREADING, TREADS, TROD, TRODDEN]

Dt 33:29 and you *will* t on their heights. H2005
Job 24:11 the terraces; *they* t the winepresses H2005
Ps 91:13 *You will* t on the lion and the cobra; you H2005
Jer 25:30 He will shout like *those who* t the grapes H2005
Mic 7:19 *you will* t our sins underfoot and hurl all H3899
Na 3:14 Work the clay, t the mortar, repair the H8252
Hab 3:19 he enables me to t on the heights. H2005

TREADING (7) [TREAD]

Dt 25: 4 muzzle an ox while it *is* t out *the* grain. H1889
Ne 13:15 days I saw *people* in Judah t winepresses H2005
Isa 41:25 as if *he were* a potter t the clay. H8252
Isa 63: 2 like those of *one* t the winepress? H2005
Am 9:13 the planter by the *one* t grapes. H2005
1Co 9: 9 not muzzle an ox *while it is* t out the grain." G262
1Ti 5:18 not muzzle an ox *while it is* t out the grain," G262

TREADS (7) [TREAD]

Job 9: 8 out the heavens and t on the waves of the H2005
Isa 16:10 no *one* t out wine at the presses H2005
Isa 41:25 *He* t *on* rulers as if they were mortar, as if H995
Jer 48:33 presses; no *one* t them with shouts of joy. H2005
Am 4:13 t on the heights of the earth H2005
Mic 1: 3 he comes down and t on the heights of H2005
Rev 19:15 He t the winepress of the fury of the wrath G4251

TREASON (4) [TRAITOR, TRAITORS, TREACHEROUS, TREACHEROUSLY, TREACHERY]

2Ki 11:14 tore her robes and called out, "T! H8004
2Ki 11:14 her robes and called out, "Treason! T!" H8004
2Ch 23:13 Athaliah tore her robes and shouted, "T! H8004
2Ch 23:13 tore her robes and shouted, "Treason! T!" H8004

TREASURE (19) [TREASURED, TREASURER, TREASURERS, TREASURES, TREASURIES, TREASURY]

Ge 43:23 has given you t in your sacks; H4759
Job 3:21 who search for it more than for hidden t, H4759
Job 20:20 craving; he cannot save himself by his t. H2773
Pr 2: 4 silver and search for it as for hidden t, H4759
Pr 15: 6 house of the righteous contains great t, H2890
Ecc 2: 8 and the t *of* kings and provinces. H6035
Isa 33: 6 the fear of the LORD is the key to this t. H238
Isa 44: 9 the *things* they t are worthless. H2773
Eze 7:22 robbers will desecrate the *place* I t. H7621
Da 1: 2 put in the t house of his god. H238
Mt 6:21 For where your t is, there your heart will be G2565
Mt 13:44 of heaven is like t hidden in a field. G2565
Mt 19:21 the poor, and you will have t in heaven. G2565
Mk 10:21 the poor, and you will have t in heaven. G2565
Lk 12:33 wear out, a t in heaven that will never fail G2565
Lk 12:34 For where your t is, there your heart will be G2565
Lk 18:22 the poor, and you will have t in heaven. G2565
2Co 4: 7 But we have this t in jars of clay to show G2565
1Ti 6:19 In this way *they will* lay up t for themselves G631

TREASURED (10) [TREASURE]

Ex 19: 5 of all nations you will be my t possession. H6035
Dt 7: 6 earth to be his people, his t possession. H6035
Dt 14: 2 has chosen you to be his t possession. H6035
Dt 26:18 people, his t possession as he promised H6035
Job 23:12 *I have* t the words of his mouth more than H7621
Ps 135: 4 be his own, Israel to be his t possession. H6035
Isa 64:11 with fire, and all *that* we t lies in ruins. H4718
Mal 3:17 Almighty, "they will be my t possession. H6035
Lk 2:19 But Mary t up all these things and G5337
Lk 2:51 But his mother t all these things in her G1413

TREASURER (1) [TREASURE]

Ezr 1: 8 had them brought by Mithredath the t, H1601

TREASURERS (5) [TREASURE]

2Ki 12: 5 receive the money from one of the t, H4837
2Ki 12: 7 Take no more money from your t, but H4837
Ezr 7:21 decree that all the t of Trans-Euphrates A10139
Da 3: 2 advisers, t, judges, magistrates A10133
Da 3: 3 advisers, t, judges, magistrates A10133

TREASURES (44) [TREASURE]

Dt 33:19 on the t hidden *in* the sand. H3243+8561
1Ki 14:26 He carried off the t *of* the temple of the LORD H238
1Ki 14:26 of the LORD and the t *of* the royal palace. H238
2Ki 20:13 armory and everything found among his t. H238
2Ki 20:15 is nothing among my t that I did not show H238
2Ki 24:13 removed the t *from* the temple of the LORD H238
1Ch 29: 3 God I now give my personal t of gold and H6035
2Ch 12: 9 he carried off the t *of* the temple of the H238
2Ch 12: 9 of the LORD and the t *of* the royal palace. H238
2Ch 25:24 with the palace t and the hostages, H238
2Ch 36:18 the t *of* the LORD's temple and the H238
2Ch 36:18 LORD's temple and the t *of* the king and his H238
Job 20:26 total darkness lies in wait for his t. A fire H7621
Job 28:10 through the rock; their eyes see all its t. H3702
Pr 10: 2 Ill-gotten t have no lasting value, but H238
Pr 24: 4 rooms are filled with rare and beautiful t. H2104
Isa 2: 7 of silver and gold; there is no end to their t. H238
Isa 10:13 I plundered their t; like a mighty one I H6965
Isa 30: 6 their t on the humps of camels H238
Isa 39: 2 armory and everything found among his t. H238
Isa 39: 4 is nothing among my t that I did not show H238
Isa 45: 3 I will give you hidden t, riches stored in H238
Jer 15:13 "Your wealth and your t I will give as H238
Jer 17: 3 wealth and all your t I will give away as H238
Jer 20: 5 all the t *of* the kings of Judah. H238
Jer 50:37 A sword against her t! They will be H238
Jer 51:13 who live by many waters and are rich in t, H238
La 1: 7 remembers all the t that were hers in days H4719
La 1:10 The enemy laid hands on all her t; she H4718
La 1:11 they barter their t for food to keep H4718
Eze 22:25 take t and precious things and make H2890
Da 11:43 gain control of the t *of* gold and silver H4819
Hos 9: 6 Their t of silver will be taken over by briers H4718
Hos 13:15 will be plundered of all its t. H3998+2775
Joel 3: 5 carried off my finest t to your temples. H4718
Ob 6 will be ransacked, his hidden t pillaged! H5208
Mic 6:10 Am I still to forget your ill-gotten t, you H238
Na 2: 9 is endless, the wealth from all its t! H3998+2775
Mt 2:11 they opened their t and presented him G2565
Mt 6:19 "Do not store up for yourselves t on earth G2565
Mt 6:20 But store up for yourselves t in heaven G2565
Mt 13:52 out of his storeroom new *t* as well as old." AIT
Col 2: 3 are hidden all the t of wisdom and G2565
Heb 11:26 as of greater value *than* the t of Egypt, G2565

TREASURIES (20) [TREASURE]

1Ki 7:51 placed them in the t *of* the LORD's temple. H238
1Ki 15:18 that was left in the t *of* the LORD's temple H238
2Ki 12:18 the gold found in the t *of* the temple of the H238
2Ki 14:14 of the LORD and in the t *of* the royal palace. H238
2Ki 16: 8 the LORD and in the t *of* the royal palace H238
2Ki 18:15 of the LORD and in the t *of* the royal palace. H238
1Ch 9:26 the rooms and t *in* the house of God. H238
1Ch 26:20 in charge of the t *of* the house of God and H238
1Ch 26:20 house of God and the t *for* the dedicated H238
1Ch 26:22 were in charge of the t *of* the temple of the H238
1Ch 26:24 was the official in charge of the t. H238
1Ch 26:26 in charge of all the t *for* the things H238
1Ch 28:12 the t *of* the temple of God and for the H238
1Ch 28:12 of God and for the t *for* the dedicated H238
2Ch 5: 1 he placed them in the t *of* God's temple. H238
2Ch 8:15 in any matter, including that of the t. H238
2Ch 16: 2 gold out of the t *of* the LORD's temple H238
2Ch 32:27 he made t for his silver and gold and H238
Pr 8:21 those who love me and making their t full. H238
Eze 28: 4 amassed gold and silver in your t. H238

TREASURY (19) [TREASURE]

Jos 6:19 sacred to the LORD and must go into his t." H238
Jos 6:24 iron into the t *of* the LORD's house. H238
1Ch 29: 8 gave them to the t *of* the temple of the H238
Ezr 2:69 they gave to the t *for* this work 61,000 H238
Ezr 6: 1 in the archives stored in the t at Babylon. A10148
Ezr 6: 4 The costs are to be paid by the royal t. A10103
Ezr 6: 8 are to be fully paid out of the royal t, A10479
Ezr 7:20 you may provide from the royal t. A10103+10148
Ne 7:70 governor gave to the t 1,000 darics of gold, H238
Ne 7:71 families gave to the t *for* the work 20,000 H238
Ne 10:38 our God, to the storerooms of the t. H1074+238
Est 3: 9 to the king's administrators for the royal t." H1709
Est 4: 7 to pay into the royal t for the destruction H1709
Jer 38:11 went to a room under the t in the palace. H238
Mt 27: 6 "It is against the law to put this into the t G3168
Mk 12:41 putting their money into the temple t. G1126
Mk 12:43 put more into the t than all the others. G1126
Lk 21: 1 rich putting their gifts into the temple t. G1126
Ac 8:27 in charge of all the t of the Kandake G1125

TREAT (36) [TREATED, TREATING, TREATMENT, TREATMENTS, TREATS]

Ge 19: 9 the judge! *We'll* t you worse than them." H8317
Ge 30:20 time my husband *will* t me with honor, H2290
Ex 22:25 *do* not t it like a business deal H2118+4200
Lev 22: 2 his sons *to* t with respect the sacred H5692
Nu 10:29 Come with us and *we will* t you well, for H3512
Nu 11:15 If this is how you *are going to* t me, please H6913
Nu 14:11 *will* these people t me with contempt? H5540
Nu 16:14 *Do you want to* t these men like slaves H5941+6524
Nu 25:17 "T the Midianites as enemies and kill H7675
Dt 20:15 This is how *you are to* t all the cities that H6913
Dt 21:14 You must not sell her or t her as a slave H6683
Jos 2:14 *we will* t you kindly and faithfully when H6913
2Sa 19:43 Why then *do you* t us with contempt H7837
Job 6:26 and *t* my desperate words as wind? AIT
Ps 103:10 *he does* not t us as our sins deserve or H6913
Jer 3:19 " 'How gladly *would I* t you like my H8883
Jer 29:22 *'May* the LORD t you like Zedekiah and H8492
Jer 34:18 *I will* t *like* the calf they cut in two and H5989
Eze 15: 6 so *will I* t the people living in Jerusalem. H5989
Eze 35:11 *I will* t you in accordance with the anger H6913
Eze 35:15 became desolate, that is how *I will* t you. H6913
Da 1:13 t your servants in accordance with H6913
Hos 11: 8 How *can I* t you like Admah? How H5989
Na 3: 6 *I will* t you with contempt and make you H5571
Mt 18:17 t them as you would a pagan or a tax G1639
Mt 18:35 my heavenly Father *will* t each of you G4472

Jn 15:21 They will t you this way because of G4472+1650
Ro 14: 3 must not t with contempt the one G2024
Ro 14:10 Or why do you t them with contempt? G2024
1Co 12:23 less honorable we t with special honor. G4363
1Co 16:11 should t him with contempt. G2024
Gal 4:14 you did not t me with contempt or scorn. G2024
Eph 6: 9 masters, t your slaves in the same way. G4472
1Th 5:20 Do not t prophecies with contempt G2024
1Ti 5: 1 were your father. T younger men as brothers NDT
1Pe 3: 7 and t them with respect as the weaker G671

TREATED (38) [TREAT]

Ge 12:13 so that I will be t well for your sake and H3512
Ge 12:16 He t Abram well for her sake, and Abram H3512
Ge 26:29 harm you but always t you well and sent H6913
Ge 34:31 "Should he have t our sister like a H6913
Ge 39:19 "This is how your slave t me," he burned H6913
Ge 42:30 harshly to us and t us as though we were H5989
Ex 5:15 "Why have you t your servants this way H6913
Ex 18:11 this to those who had t Israel arrogantly." H2326
Lev 19:34 residing among you must be t as your H2118
Lev 25:40 They are to be t as hired workers or H3869
Lev 25:53 They are to be t as workers hired H2118+6640
Nu 14:23 No one who has t me with contempt will H5540
Nu 16:30 men have t the LORD with contempt." H5540
Nu 25:18 They t you as enemies when they H7675
Jdg 1:24 and we will see that you are t well." H6913+6640
Jdg 8: 1 Gideon, "Why have you t us like this? H6913
Jdg 9:16 Have you t him as he deserves H6913
1Sa 2:14 This is how they t all the Israelites who H6913
1Sa 24:17 "You have t me well, but I have treated H1694
1Sa 24:17 treated me well, but I have t you badly. H1694
1Sa 24:19 you well for the way you t me today. H6913
1Ki 1:21 my son Solomon will be t as criminals." H2118
1Ch 24:31 brother were t the same as those of H4200+6645
Ne 9:10 how arrogantly the Egyptians t them. H2326
La 2:20 Whom have you ever t like this H6618
Eze 7:19 and their gold will be t as a thing H2118+4200
Eze 22: 7 they have t father and mother with contempt H7837
Mt 21:36 the tenants t them the same way. G4472
Mk 12: 4 man on the head and t him shamefully. G869
Lk 2:48 "Son, why have you t us like this? G4472
Lk 6:23 that is how their ancestors t the prophets. G4472
Lk 6:26 is how their ancestors t the false prophets. G4472
Lk 20:11 they beat and t shamefully and sent away G869
1Co 4:11 we are in rags, we are brutally t, we are G3139
1Co 12:23 unpresentable are t with special modesty, G2400
1Th 2: 2 and been t outrageously in Philippi G5614
Heb 10:29 who has t as an unholy thing the blood of G2451
Heb 10:33 side by side with those who were so t. G418

TREATING (9) [TREAT]

Ge 18:25 t the righteous and the wicked alike. H2118
Ge 50:17 the wrongs they committed in t you so badly. AIT
Lev 22: 9 guilty and die for it t with contempt. H2725
Dt 24: 7 Israelite and t or selling them as a slave, H6683
1Sa 2:17 they were t the LORD's offering with contempt H5540
1Sa 25:39 cause against Nabal for t me with contempt. NDT
1Ki 8:32 the innocent by t them in accordance with H5989
2Ch 6:23 the innocent by t them in accordance with H5989
Heb 12: 7 as discipline; God is t you as his children. G4712

TREATMENT (4) [TREAT]

1Sa 20:34 at his father's shameful t of David. H4007
Isa 66: 4 also will choose harsh t for them and will H9500
1Co 12:24 our presentable parts need no special t. NDT
Col 2:23 false humility and their harsh t of the body, G910

TREATMENTS (3) [TREAT]

Est 2: 3 let beauty t be given to them. H9475
Est 2: 9 her with her beauty t and special food. H9475
Est 2:12 twelve months of beauty t prescribed for H5299

TREATS (3) [TREAT]

Job 39:16 She t her young harshly, as if they were H7998
Job 41:27 Iron it t like straw and bronze like rotten H3108
Pr 27:11 answer anyone who t me with contempt. H3070

TREATY (31)

Ge 21:27 to Abimelek, and the two men made a t. H1382
Ge 21:32 After the t had been made at Beersheba H1382
Ge 26:28 us and you. Let us make a t with you H1382
Ex 34:12 not to make a t with those who live H1382
Ex 34:15 not to make a t with those who live H1382
Dt 7: 2 Make no t with them, and show them no H1382
Dt 23: 6 a t of friendship with them H8934+2256+3208
Jos 9: 6 from a distant country; make a t with us." H1382
Jos 9: 7 so how can we make a t with you? H1382
Jos 9:11 "We are your servants; make a t with us." H1382
Jos 9:15 Then Joshua made a t of peace with them H1382
Jos 9:16 after they made the t with the Gibeonites, H1382
Jos 10: 1 of Gibeon had made a t of peace with H8966
Jos 11:19 not one city made a t of peace with the H8966
1Sa 11: 1 "Make a t with us, and we will H1382
1Sa 11: 2 "I will make a t with you only on the H4162
1Ki 5:12 Solomon, and the two of them made a t. H1382
1Ki 15:19 "Let there be a t between me and you," H1382
1Ki 15:19 Now break your t with Baasha king of H1382
1Ki 20:34 "On the basis of a t I will set you free." H1382
1Ki 20:34 So he made a t with him, and let him go. H1382
2Ch 16: 3 "Let there be a t between me and you," H1382
2Ch 16: 3 Now break your t with Baasha king of H1382
Ezr 9:12 a t of friendship with them H8934+2256+3208
Isa 33: 8 The t is broken, its witnesses are despised H1382
Eze 17:13 of the royal family and made a t with him, H1382
Eze 17:14 rise again, surviving only by keeping his t. H1382
Eze 17:15 Will he break the t and yet escape? H1382
Eze 17:16 oath he despised and whose t he broke. H1382
Hos 12: 1 He makes a t with Assyria and sends olive H1382
Am 1: 9 to Edom, disregarding a t of brotherhood, H1382

TREE (162) [TREES]

Ge 1:29 whole earth and every t that has fruit with H6770
Ge 2: 9 the garden were the t of life and the tree H6770
Ge 2: 9 tree of life and the t of the knowledge of H6770
Ge 2:16 are free to eat from any t in the garden; H6770
Ge 2:17 not eat from the t of the knowledge of H6770
Ge 3: 1 must not eat from any t in the garden'?" H6770
Ge 3: 3 eat fruit from the t that is in the middle H6770
Ge 3: 6 the fruit of the t was good for food and H6770
Ge 3:11 you eaten from the t that I commanded H6770
Ge 3:12 she gave me some fruit from the t, and I H6770
Ge 3:17 ate fruit from the t about which I H6770
Ge 3:22 take also from the t of life and eat, H6770
Ge 3:24 forth to guard the way to the t of life. H6770
Ge 12: 6 the site of the great t of Moreh at Shechem H471
Ge 18: 4 all wash your feet and rest under this t. H6770
Ge 18: 8 they ate, he stood near them under a t. H6770
Ge 21:33 Abraham planted a tamarisk t in Beersheba, H869
Ex 9:25 growing in the fields and stripped every t. H6770
Ex 10: 5 including every t that is growing in your H6770
Ex 10:15 green remained on t or plant in all the H6770
Lev 19:23 the land and plant any kind of fruit t, H6770
Dt 12: 2 on the hills and under every spreading t H6770
Dt 19: 5 as he swings his ax to fell a t, the H6770
Dt 22: 6 either in a t or on the ground, and H6770
Jos 19:33 from Heleph and the large t in Zaanannim, H471
Jdg 4:11 his tent by the great t in Zaanannim near H471
Jdg 9: 6 gathered beside the great t at the pillar in H471
Jdg 9: 8 They said to the olive t, 'Be our king.' H2339
Jdg 9: 9 "But the olive t answered, 'Should I give H2339
Jdg 9:10 the trees said to the fig t, 'Come and be H9300
Jdg 9:11 "But the fig t replied, 'Should I give up my H9300
Jdg 9:37 coming from the direction of the diviners' t." H471
1Sa 10: 3 there until you reach the great t of Tabor. H471
1Sa 14: 2 Gibeah under a pomegranate t in Migron. H8232
1Sa 22: 6 under the tamarisk t on the hill at Gibeah H869
1Sa 31:13 buried them under a tamarisk t at Jabesh, H869
2Sa 18: 9 Absalom's hair got caught in the t. H461
2Sa 18:10 "I just saw Absalom hanging in an oak t." H461
2Sa 18:14 while Absalom was still alive in the oak t. H461
1Ki 4:25 their own vine and under their own fig t. H9300
1Ki 13:14 him sitting under an oak t and asked, H461
1Ki 14:23 high hill and under every spreading t. H6770
2Ki 3:19 You will cut down every good t, stop up H6770
2Ki 3:25 all the springs and cut down every good t. H6770
2Ki 6: 5 As one of them was cutting down a t, the H7771
2Ki 16: 4 the hilltops and under every spreading t. H6770
2Ki 17:10 high hill and under every spreading t. H6770
2Ki 18:31 your own vine and fig t and drink water H9300
1Ch 10:12 their bones under the great t in Jabesh, H461
2Ch 3: 5 it with palm t and chain designs. H9474
2Ch 28: 4 the hilltops and under every spreading t. H6770
Ne 10:35 firstfruits of our crops and of every fruit t. H6770
Job 14: 7 "At least there is hope for a t: If it is cut H6770
Job 15:33 like an olive t shedding its blossoms. H2339
Job 19:10 I am gone; he uproots my hope like a t. H6770
Job 24:20 remembered but are broken like a t. H6770
Ps 1: 3 person is like a t planted by streams of H6770
Ps 37:35 man flourishing like a luxuriant native t, H8316
Ps 52: 8 But I am like an olive t flourishing in the H2339
Ps 92:12 The righteous will flourish like a palm t H9469
Pr 3:18 She is a t of life to those who take hold of H6770
Pr 11:30 The fruit of the righteous is a t of life, and H6770
Pr 13:12 but a longing fulfilled is a t of life. H6770
Pr 15: 4 The soothing tongue is a t of life, but a H6770
Pr 27:18 one who guards a fig t will eat its fruit, H9300
Ecc 11: 3 Whether a t falls to the south or to the H6770
Ecc 12: 5 when the almond t blossoms and the H9196
SS 2: 3 Like an apple t among the trees of the H9515
SS 2:13 The fig t forms its early fruit; the H9300
SS 4:14 with every kind of incense t, with myrrh H6770
SS 7: 8 "I will climb the palm t; I will take hold of H9469
SS 8: 5 Under the apple t I roused you; there your H9515
Isa 17: 6 remain, as when an olive t is beaten H2339
Isa 24:13 as when an olive t is beaten, or as H2339
Isa 34: 4 the vine, like shriveled figs from the fig t. H9300
Isa 36:16 your own vine and fig t and drink water H9300
Isa 56: 3 no eunuch complain, "I am only a dry t." H6770
Isa 57: 5 the oaks and under every spreading t; H6770
Isa 65:22 For as the days of a t, so will be the days H6770
Jer 1:11 "I see the branch of an almond t," I H9196
Jer 2:20 under every spreading t you lay down as a H6770
Jer 3: 6 every spreading t and has committed H6770
Jer 3:13 to foreign gods under every spreading t, H6770
Jer 8:13 There will be no figs on the t, and their H9300
Jer 10: 3 worthless; they cut a t out of the forest H6770
Jer 11:16 you a thriving olive t with fruit beautiful H2339
Jer 11:19 "Let us destroy the t and its fruit; let us cut H6770
Jer 17: 8 They will be like a t planted by the water H6770
Eze 6:13 every spreading t and every leafy oak— H6770
Eze 17:24 bring down the tall t and make the low H6770
Eze 17:24 the tall tree and make the low t grow tall. H6770
Eze 17:24 I dry up the green t and make the dry tree H6770
Eze 17:24 the green tree and make the dry t flourish. H6770
Eze 20:28 they saw any high hill or any leafy t, H6770
Eze 31: 8 no t in the garden of God could match its H6770
Eze 31:13 All the birds settled on the fallen t, and all NDT
Eze 40:22 its palm t decorations had the same H9474
Eze 40:26 it had palm t decorations on the faces of H9474
Eze 41:19 the face of a man toward the palm t on one side and H9474
Eze 41:19 of a lion toward the palm t on the other. H9474
Da 4:10 before me stood a t in the middle of the A10027
Da 4:11 The t grew large and strong and its top A10027
Da 4:14 'Cut down the t and trim off its branches A10027
Da 4:20 The t you saw, which grew large and A10027
Da 4:22 Majesty, you are that t! You have A10200S
Da 4:23 'Cut down the t and destroy it, but A10027
Da 4:26 the stump of the t with its roots means A10027
Hos 9:10 was like seeing the early fruit on the fig t. H9300
Hos 14: 6 His splendor will be like an olive t, his H2339
Joel 1:12 vine is dried up and the fig t is withered; H9300
Joel 1:12 the palm and the apple t—all the trees H9515
Joel 2:22 the fig t and the vine yield their riches. H9300
Mic 4: 4 their own vine and under their own fig t, H9300
Hab 3:17 Though the fig t does not bud and there H9300
Hag 2:19 the vine and the fig t, the pomegranate H9300
Hag 2:19 the olive t have not borne fruit. H6770
Zec 3:10 neighbor to sit under your vine and fig t, H9300
Mt 3:10 every t that does not produce good G1285
Mt 7:17 Likewise, every good t bears good fruit, G1285
Mt 7:17 good fruit, but a bad t bears bad fruit. G1285
Mt 7:18 A good t cannot bear bad fruit, and a bad G1285
Mt 7:18 and a bad t cannot bear good fruit. G1285
Mt 7:19 Every t that does not bear good fruit is cut G1285
Mt 12:33 "Make a t good and its fruit will be good G1285
Mt 12:33 make a t bad and its fruit will be bad G1285
Mt 12:33 be bad, for a t is recognized by its fruit. G1285
Mt 13:32 largest of garden plants and becomes a t, G1285
Mt 21:19 Seeing a fig t by the road, he went up to it G5190
Mt 21:19 Immediately the t withered. G5190
Mt 21:20 "How did the fig t wither so quickly?" G5190
Mt 21:21 can you do what was done to the fig t, G5190
Mt 24:32 "Now learn this lesson from the fig t: As G5190
Mk 11:13 Seeing in the distance a fig t in leaf, he G5190
Mk 11:14 Then he said to the t, "May no one ever G899S
Mk 11:20 they saw the fig t withered from the roots. G5190
Mk 11:21 The fig t you cursed has withered! G5190
Mk 13:28 "Now learn this lesson from the fig t: As G5190
Lk 3: 9 every t that does not produce good G1285
Lk 6:43 "No good t bears bad fruit, nor does a G1285
Lk 6:43 bad fruit, nor does a bad t bear good fruit. G1285
Lk 6:44 Each t is recognized by its own fruit G1285
Lk 13: 6 "A man had a fig t growing in his G5190
Lk 13: 7 fruit on this fig t and haven't found any G5190
Lk 13:19 It grew and became a t, and the birds G1285
Lk 17: 6 you can say to this mulberry t, 'Be G5189
Lk 19: 4 climbed a sycamore-fig t to see him, G5191
Lk 21:29 "Look at the fig t and all the trees. G5190
Lk 23:31 do these things when the t is green, G3833
Jn 1:48 were still under the fig t before Philip G5190
Jn 1:50 I told you I saw you under the fig t. G5190
Ro 11:24 cut out of an olive t that is wild by nature, G66
Ro 11:24 were grafted into a cultivated olive t, G2814
Ro 11:24 be grafted into their own olive t! G1777
Jas 3:12 sisters, can a fig t bear olives, or a G5190
Rev 2: 7 I will give the right to eat from the t of life, G3833
Rev 6:13 as figs drop from a fig t when shaken by a G3913
Rev 7: 1 on the land or on the sea or on any t. G1285
Rev 9: 4 the grass of the earth or any plant or t, G1285
Rev 22: 2 each side of the river stood the t of life, G3833
Rev 22: 2 And the leaves of the t are for the healing G3833
Rev 22:14 have the right to the t of life and may go G3833
Rev 22:19 any share in the t of life and in the Holy G3833

TREES (131) [TREE]

Ge 1:11 plants and t on the land that bear H6770
Ge 1:12 to their kinds and t bearing fruit with seed H6770
Ge 2: 9 God made all kinds of t grow out of the H6770
Ge 2: 9 t that were pleasing to the eye and good NDT
Ge 3: 2 may eat fruit from the t in the garden, H6770
Ge 3: 8 the LORD God among the t of the garden. H6770
Ge 13:18 to live near the great t of Mamre at Hebron H471
Ge 14:13 living near the great t of Mamre the H471
Ge 18: 1 near the great t of Mamre while he H471
Ge 23:17 all the t within the borders of the H6770
Ge 30:37 almond and plane t and made white H6895
Ex 10:15 in the fields and the fruit on the t. H6770
Ex 15:27 were twelve springs and seventy palm t, H9469
Lev 23:40 are to take branches from luxuriant t— H6770
Lev 23:40 willows and other leafy t—and rejoice H6770
Lev 26: 4 its crops and the t their fruit. H6770+2021+8441
Lev 26:20 will the t of your land yield their fruit. H6770
Lev 27:30 grain from the soil or fruit from the t, H6770
Nu 13:20 Are there t in it or not? Do your H6770
Nu 33: 9 were twelve springs and seventy palm t, H9469
Dt 8: 8 vines and fig t, pomegranates, H9300
Dt 11:30 near the great t of Moreh, in the H471
Dt 20:19 do not destroy its t by putting an ax to H6770
Dt 20:19 Are the t people, that you H6770+2021+8441
Dt 20:20 you may cut down t that you know are not H6770
Dt 20:20 know are not fruit t and use them to build H6770
Dt 24:20 When you beat the olives from your t, do H2339
Dt 28:40 You will have olive t throughout your H2339
Dt 28:42 take over all your t and the crops of your H6770

Jdg 9: 8 One day the **t** went out to anoint a king H6770
Jdg 9: 9 are honored, to hold sway over the **t**? H6770
Jdg 9:10 the **t** said to the fig tree, 'Come H6770
Jdg 9:11 good and sweet, to hold sway over the **t**? H6770
Jdg 9:12 "Then the **t** said to the vine, 'Come and H6770
Jdg 9:13 humans, to hold sway over the **t**? H6770
Jdg 9:14 "Finally all the **t** said to the thornbush H6770
Jdg 9:15 "The thornbush said to the **t**, 'If you really H6770
2Sa 5:23 attack them in front of the **poplar t**. H1132
2Sa 5:24 of marching in the tops of the **poplar t**, H1132
1Ki 6:29 cherubim, **palm t** and open flowers. H9474
1Ki 6:32 carved cherubim, **palm t** and open flowers H9474
1Ki 6:32 the cherubim and **palm t** with hammered H9474
1Ki 6:35 **palm t** and open flowers on them and H9474
1Ki 7:36 lions and **palm t** on the surfaces of the H9474
1Ki 10:27 as plentiful as **sycamore-fig t** in the H9204
2Ki 6: 4 to the Jordan and began to cut down **t**. H6770
2Ki 18:32 a land of **olive t** and honey. H2339+3658
1Ch 14:14 attack them in front of the **poplar t**. H1132
1Ch 14:15 of marching in the tops of the **poplar t**, H1132
1Ch 16:33 Let the **t** *of* the forest sing, let them sing H6770
1Ch 27:28 the olive and **sycamore-fig t** in the H9204
2Ch 1:15 as plentiful as **sycamore-fig t** in the H9204
2Ch 9:27 as plentiful as **sycamore-fig t** in the H9204
Ne 8:15 back branches from olive and wild olive **t**, H6770
Ne 8:15 palms and shade **t**, to make temporary H6770
Ne 9:25 olive groves and fruit **t** in abundance. H6770
Ne 10:37 the fruit of all our **t** and of our new wine H6770
Ps 74: 5 wielding axes to cut through a thicket of **t**. H6770
Ps 96:12 let all the **t** *of* the forest sing for joy. H6770
Ps 104:16 The **t** *of* the LORD are well watered, the H6770
Ps 105:33 their vines and **fig t** and shattered the H9300
Ps 105:33 trees and shattered the **t** *of* their country. H6770
Ps 148: 9 all hills, fruit **t** and all cedars, H6770
Ecc 2: 5 planted all kinds of fruit **t** in them. H6770
Ecc 2: 6 reservoirs to water groves of flourishing **t**. H6770
SS 2: 3 apple tree among the **t** *of* the forest is my H6770
SS 6:11 to the grove of **nut t** to look at the new H100
Isa 7: 2 as the **t** *of* the forest are shaken by the H6770
Isa 9:10 dressed stone; the **fig t** have been felled H9204
Isa 10:19 And the remaining **t** *of* his forests will be H6770
Isa 10:33 The **lofty t** will be felled, the tall H8123+7757
Isa 44: 4 meadow, like **poplar t** by flowing streams. H6857
Isa 44:14 He let it grow among the **t** *of* the forest, or H6770
Isa 44:23 you forests and all your **t**, for the LORD has H6770
Isa 55:12 all the **t** *of* the field will clap their H6770
Jer 5:17 herds, devour your vines and **fig t**. H9300
Jer 6: 6 "Cut down the **t** and build siege ramps H6785
Jer 7:20 on the **t** *of* the field and on the crops of H6770
Jer 17: 2 beside the spreading **t** and on the high H6770
Jer 46:22 her with axes, like men who cut down **t**. H6770
Eze 15: 2 of a branch from any of the **t** *in* the forest? H6770
Eze 15: 6 the vine among the **t** *of* the forest as fuel H6770
Eze 17:24 All the **t** *of* the forest will know that I the H6770
Eze 20:47 it will consume all your **t**, both green H6770
Eze 31: 4 sent their channels to all the **t** *of* the field. H6770
Eze 31: 5 towered higher than all the **t** *of* the field; H6770
Eze 31: 8 could the **plane t** compare with its H6895
Eze 31: 9 the envy of all the **t** *of* Eden in the garden H6770
Eze 31:14 Therefore no other **t** *by* the waters are ever H6770
Eze 31:14 No other **t** so well-watered are ever to reach NDT
Eze 31:15 all the **t** *of* the field withered away. H6770
Eze 31:16 Then all the **t** *of* Eden, the choicest and H6770
Eze 31:16 the well-watered **t**, were consoled in the NDT
Eze 31:18 " 'Which of the **t** *of* Eden can be H6770
Eze 31:18 down with the **t** *of* Eden to the earth H6770
Eze 34:27 The **t** will yield their fruit and H6770+2021+8441
Eze 36:30 the fruit of the **t** and the crops of the H6770
Eze 40:16 walls were decorated with **palm t**. H9474
Eze 40:31 outer court; **palm t** decorated its jambs H9474
Eze 40:34 **palm t** decorated the jambs on either side H9474
Eze 40:37 **palm t** decorated the jambs on either side H9474
Eze 41:18 were carved cherubim and **palm t**. H9474
Eze 41:18 **Palm t** alternated with cherubim H9474
Eze 41:20 cherubim and **palm t** were carved on the H9474
Eze 41:25 cherubim and **palm t** like those carved H9474
Eze 41:26 windows with **palm t** carved on each H9474
Eze 47: 7 a great number of **t** on each side of the H6770
Eze 47:12 Fruit **t** of all kinds will grow on both banks H6770
Hos 2:12 I will ruin her vines and her **fig t**, which H9300
Joel 1: 7 laid waste my vines and ruined my **fig t**. H9300
Joel 1:12 apple tree—all the **t** *of* the field—are H6770
Joel 1:19 have burned up all the **t** *of* the field. H6770
Joel 2:22 The **t** are bearing their fruit; the fig tree H6770
Am 4: 9 Locusts devoured your fig and **olive t**, yet H2339
Am 7:14 I also took care of **sycamore-fig t**. H9204
Na 3:12 fortresses are like **fig t** with their first ripe H9300
Zec 1: 8 standing among the **myrtle t** in a ravine. H2072
Zec 1:10 standing among the **myrtle t** explained, H2072
Zec 1:11 who was standing among the **myrtle t**, H2072
Zec 4: 3 Also there are two **olive t** by it, one on the H2339
Zec 4:11 are these two **olive t** on the right and H2339
Zec 11: 2 the cedar has fallen; the stately **t** are ruined! NDT
Mt 3:10 The ax is already at the root *of* the **t**, and *G1285*
Mt 21: 8 branches from the **t** and spread them on *G1285*
Mk 8:24 people; they look like **t** walking around." *G1285*
Lk 3: 9 The ax is already at the root *of* the **t**, and *G1285*
Lk 21:29 "Look at the fig tree and all the **t**. *G1285*
Jude 12 by the wind; autumn **t**, without fruit and *G1285*
Rev 7: 3 the sea or the **t** until we put a seal on *G1285*
Rev 8: 7 burned up, a third *of* the **t** were burned up *G1285*
Rev 11: 4 They are "the two **olive t**" and the two *G1777*

TREMBLE (43) [TREMBLED, TREMBLES, TREMBLING]

Ex 15:14 The nations will hear and **t**; anguish will H8074
Dt 2:25 of you and *will* **t** and be in anguish H8074
1Ch 16:30 **T** before him, all the earth! The world is H2655
Job 9: 6 from its place and **makes** its pillars **t**. H7145
Ps 4: 4 **T** and do not sin; when you are on your H8074
Ps 96: 9 of his holiness; **t** before him, all the earth H2655
Ps 99: 1 The LORD reigns, *let* the nations **t**; he sits H8074
Ps 114: 7 **T**, earth, at the presence of the Lord, at H2655
Ecc 12: 3 when the keepers of the house **t**, and the H2316
Isa 13:13 Therefore *I will* **make** the heavens **t**; and H8074
Isa 14:16 shook the earth and **made** kingdoms **t**, H8321
Isa 19: 1 The idols of Egypt **t** before him, and the H5675
Isa 21: 4 fear **makes** me **t**; the twilight I H1286
Isa 23:11 over the sea and **made** its kingdoms **t**. H8074
Isa 32:10 than a year you who feel secure *will* **t**; H8074
Isa 32:11 **T**, *you* complacent women; shudder, you H3006
Isa 41: 5 seen it and fear; the ends of the earth **t**. H3006
Isa 44: 8 *Do* not **t**, do not be afraid. Did I not H7064
Isa 64: 1 that the mountains *would* **t** before you! H2362
Isa 66: 2 contrite in spirit, and *who* **t** at my word. H3007
Isa 66: 5 word of the LORD, you who **t** at his word: H3007
Jer 5:22 "*Should you* not **t** in my presence H2655
Jer 23: 9 heart is broken within me; all my bones **t**. H8173
Jer 33: 9 will be in awe and *will* **t** at the abundant H8074
Jer 49:21 At the sound of their fall the earth *will* **t** H8321
Jer 50:46 of Babylon's capture the earth *will* **t**; H8321
Eze 7:27 the hands of the people of the land *will* **t**. H987
Eze 12:18 "Son of man, **t** as you eat your food, and H8323
Eze 26:10 Your walls *will* **t** at the noise of the H8321
Eze 26:15 *Will* not the coastlands **t** at the sound of H8321
Eze 26:18 Now the coastlands **t** on the day of your H3006
Eze 31:16 *I* **made** the nations **t** at the sound of its fall H8321
Eze 32:10 each of them *will* **t** every moment for his H3006
Eze 38:20 the face of the earth *will* **t** at my presence. H8321
Joel 2: 1 *Let* all who live in the land **t**, for the day H8074
Joel 2:10 the heavens **t**, the sun and moon H8321
Joel 3:16 the earth and the heavens *will* **t**. H8321
Am 3: 6 sounds in a city, *do* not the people **t**? H3006
Am 8: 8 "*Will* not the land **t** for this, and all who H8074
Na 2:10 give way, bodies **t**, every face grows pale H2714
Hab 2: 7 Will they not wake up and **make** you **t** H2316
Hab 3: 6 he looked, and **made** the nations **t**. H6001
Ro 11:20 stand by faith. Do not be arrogant, but **t**. *G5828*

TREMBLED (16) [TREMBLE]

Ge 27:33 Isaac **t violently** and said H3006+1524+6330+4394+3010
Ex 19:16 trumpet blast. Everyone in the camp **t**. H3006
Ex 19:18 the whole mountain **t** violently. H3006
Ex 20:18 the mountain in smoke, they **t** with fear. H5675
1Sa 16: 4 elders of the town **t** when they met him. H3006
1Sa 21: 1 Ahimelek **t** when he met him, and asked H3006
2Sa 22: 8 The earth **t** and quaked, the foundations H1723
2Sa 22: 8 *they* **t** because he was angry. H1723
Ezr 9: 4 Then everyone *who* **t** at the words of the H3007
Ps 18: 7 The earth **t** and quaked, and the H1723
Ps 18: 7 *they* **t** because he was angry. H1723
Ps 77:18 lit up the world; the earth **t** and quaked. H8074
Isa 64: 3 and the mountains **t** before you. H2362
Hos 13: 1 people **t**; he was exalted in H8417
Hab 3:16 decay crept into my bones, and my legs **t**. H8074
Ac 7:32 Moses **t with fear** and did not dare *G1958+1181*

TREMBLES (12) [TREMBLE]

Jdg 7: 3 'Anyone *who* **t** with fear may turn back H3007
Ps 97: 4 lights up the world; the earth sees and **t**. H2655
Ps 104:32 at the earth, and *it* **t**, who touches the H8283
Ps 119:120 My flesh **t** in fear of you; I stand in awe H6169
Ps 119:161 but my heart **t** at your word. H7064
Pr 28:14 is the one *who* always **t** before God, H7064
Pr 30:21 "Under three things the earth **t**, under four H8074
Isa 10:29 Ramah **t**; Gibeah of Saul flees. H3006
Jer 8:16 of their stallions the whole land **t**. H8321
Jer 10:10 is angry, the earth **t**; the nations cannot H8321
Jer 51:29 The land **t** and writhes, for the LORD's H8321
Na 1: 5 The earth **t** at his presence, the world H5951

TREMBLING (25) [TREMBLE]

Ge 42:28 sank and *they turned* to each other **t** and H3006
Ex 15:15 the leaders of Moab will be seized with **t** H8284
2Sa 22:46 *they* **come t** from their strongholds. H3004
Job 4:14 fear and **t** seized me and made all my H8285
Job 21: 6 I am terrified; **t** seizes my body. H7146
Ps 2:11 with fear and celebrate his rule with **t**. H8285
Ps 18:45 *they* **come t** from their strongholds. H3004
Ps 48: 6 **T** seized them there, pain like that of a H8285
Ps 55: 5 Fear and **t** have beset me; horror has H8284
Isa 33:14 in Zion are terrified; **t** grips the godless: H8285
Eze 26:16 sit on the ground, **t** every moment H3006
Da 10:10 touched me and **set** me **t** on my hands H5675
Da 10:11 And when he said this to me, I stood up **t**. H8283
Hos 3: 5 *They will* **come t** to the LORD and to his H7064
Hos 11:10 his children *will* **come t** from the west. H3006
Hos 11:11 *They will* come from Egypt, **t** like sparrows, H3006
Mic 7:17 *They will* **come t** out of their dens; they H8074
Mk 5:33 fell at his feet and, **t** with fear, told him *G5554*
Mk 16: 8 **T** and bewildered, the women *G2400+5571*
Lk 8:47 go unnoticed, came **t** and fell at his feet. *G5554*
Ac 16:29 in and fell **t** before Paul and *G1958+1181*
1Co 2: 3 to you in weakness with great fear and **t**. *G5571*
2Co 7:15 obedient, receiving him with fear and **t**. *G5571*
Php 2:12 to work out your salvation with fear and **t**, *G5571*
Heb 12:21 that Moses said, "I am **t** with fear. *G1769*

TREMENDOUS (1)

Rev 16:18 been on earth, so **t** was the quake. *G5496+3489*

TRENCH (4)

1Ki 18:32 he dug a **t** around it large enough to H9498
1Ki 18:35 around the altar and even filled the **t**. H9498
1Ki 18:38 and also licked up the water in the **t**. H9498
Da 9:25 It will be rebuilt with streets and a **t**, but H3022

TRESPASS (5) [TRESPASSES]

Ro 5:15 But the gift is not like the **t**. For if the *G4183*
Ro 5:15 if the many died *by* the **t** of the one man, *G4183*
Ro 5:17 *by* the **t** of the one man, death *G4183*
Ro 5:18 just as one **t** resulted in condemnation *G4183*
Ro 5:20 brought in so that the **t** might increase. *G4183*

TRESPASSES (1) [TRESPASS]

Ro 5:16 the gift followed many **t** and brought *G4183*

TRESSES (1)

SS 7: 5 tapestry; the king is held captive by its **t**. H8111

TRIAL (20) [TRIALS]

Nu 35:12 before they stand **t** before the assembly. H5477
Jos 20: 6 they have stood **t** before the assembly H5477
Jos 20: 9 of blood prior *to* **standing t** before the H6641
Ps 37:33 them be condemned when **brought to t**. H9149
Joel 3: 2 There *I will* **put** them **on t** for what they H9149
Mal 3: 5 "So I will come to **put** you **on t**. I will be H5477
Mk 13:11 Whenever you are arrested and **brought to t** *G72*
Ac 12: 4 bring him out for public **t** after the Passover. NDT
Ac 12: 6 night before Herod was to **bring** him **to t**, *G4575*
Ac 16:37 "They beat us publicly **without a t**, even *G185*
Ac 23: 6 *I* **stand on t** because of the hope of the *G3212*
Ac 24:21 of the dead *that I am* **on t** before you *G3212*
Ac 25: 9 to Jerusalem and **stand t** before me there *G3212*
Ac 25:20 to Jerusalem and **stand t** there on these *G3212*
Ac 26: 6 our ancestors *that I am* **on t** today. *G2705+3212*
Ac 27:24 You must **stand t before** Caesar; and God *G4225*
2Co 8: 2 In the midst of a very **severe t**, their *G1509+2568*
Gal 4:14 even though my illness was a **t** to you *G4280*
Jas 1:12 the one who perseveres *under* **t** because, *G4280*
Rev 3:10 you from the hour *of* **t** that is going to *G4280*

TRIALS (8) [TRIAL]

Dt 7:19 You saw with your own eyes the great **t** H4999
Dt 29: 3 With your own eyes you saw those great **t** H4999
Lk 22:28 are those who have stood by me in my **t**. *G4280*
1Th 3: 3 no one would be unsettled by these **t**. *G2568*
2Th 1: 4 the persecutions and **t** you are enduring. *G2568*
Jas 1: 2 whenever you face **t** of many kinds, *G4280*
1Pe 1: 6 have had to suffer grief in all kinds *of* **t**. *G4280*
2Pe 2: 9 to rescue the godly from **t** and to hold the *G4280*

TRIBAL (18) [TRIBE]

Ge 25:16 names of the twelve **t** rulers according to H569
Nu 4:18 "See that the Kohathite **t** clans are not H8657
Nu 7: 2 who were the **t** leaders in charge of H4751
Nu 25:15 a **t** chief of a Midianite family. H569
Nu 36: 4 will be taken from the **t** inheritance of our H4751
Nu 36: 6 as they marry within their father's **t** clan. H4751
Nu 36: 7 shall keep the **t** inheritance of their H4751
Nu 36: 8 must marry someone in her father's **t** clan, H4751
Dt 1:15 of fifties and of tens and as **t** officials. H8657
Jos 11:23 to Israel according to their **t** divisions. H8657
Jos 12: 7 of Israel according to their **t divisions**. H4713
Jos 14: 1 the heads of the **t** clans of Israel H4751
Jos 18:10 the Israelites according to their **t divisions**. H4713
Jos 19:51 the heads of the **t** clans of Israel H4751
Jos 21: 1 the heads of the other **t** families of Israel H4751
Eze 45: 7 border parallel to one of the **t** portions. NDT
Eze 48: 8 east to west will equal one of the **t** portions; NDT
Eze 48:21 the length of the **t** portions will belong to NDT

TRIBE (211) [HALF-TRIBE, TRIBAL, TRIBES]

Ex 2: 1 Now a man of the **t** *of* Levi married a H1074
Ex 31: 2 the son of Hur, of the **t** *of* Judah, H4751
Ex 31: 6 of Ahisamak, of the **t** *of* Dan, to help him. H4751
Ex 35:30 the son of Hur, of the **t** *of* Judah, H4751
Ex 35:34 of Ahisamak, of the **t** *of* Dan, the ability to H4751
Ex 38:22 the son of Hur, of the **t** *of* Judah, made H4751
Ex 38:23 Ahisamak, of the **t** *of* Dan—an engraver H4751
Nu 1: 4 One man from each **t**, each of them the H4751
Nu 1:21 number from the **t** *of* Reuben was 46,500. H4751
Nu 1:23 number from the **t** *of* Simeon was 59,300. H4751
Nu 1:25 number from the **t** *of* Gad was 45,650. H4751
Nu 1:27 number from the **t** *of* Judah was 74,600. H4751
Nu 1:29 The number from the **t** *of* Issachar was H4751
Nu 1:31 number from the **t** *of* Zebulun was 57,400 H4751
Nu 1:33 number from the **t** *of* Ephraim was 40,500 H4751
Nu 1:35 The number from the **t** *of* Manasseh was H4751
Nu 1:37 The number from the **t** *of* Benjamin was H4751
Nu 1:39 number from the **t** *of* Dan was 62,700. H4751
Nu 1:41 number from the **t** *of* Asher was 41,500. H4751
Nu 1:43 The number from the **t** *of* Naphtali was H4751
Nu 1:47 The ancestral **t** *of* the Levites, however H4751
Nu 1:49 must not count the **t** *of* Levi or include H4751
Nu 2: 5 The **t** *of* Issachar will camp next to them H4751
Nu 2: 7 The **t** *of* Zebulun will be next. The leader H4751
Nu 2:12 The **t** *of* Simeon will camp next to them H4751

Nu 2:14 The t of Gad will be next. The leader of H4751
Nu 2:20 The t of Manasseh will be next to them H4751
Nu 2:22 The t of Benjamin will be next. H4751
Nu 2:27 The t of Asher will camp next to them H4751
Nu 2:29 The t of Naphtali will be next. The leader H4751
Nu 3: 6 "Bring the t of Levi and present them to H4751
Nu 7:12 son of Amminadab of the t of Judah. H4751
Nu 10:15 was over the division of the t of Issachar, H4751
Nu 10:16 was over the division of the t of Zebulun. H4751
Nu 10:19 was over the division of the t of Simeon, H4751
Nu 10:20 was over the division of the t of Gad. H4751
Nu 10:23 over the division of the t of Manasseh, H4751
Nu 10:24 was over the division of the t of Benjamin. H4751
Nu 10:26 was over the division of the t of Asher, H4751
Nu 10:27 was over the division of the t of Naphtali. H4751
Nu 13: 2 From each ancestral t send one of its H4751
Nu 13: 4 from the t of Reuben, Shammua son of H4751
Nu 13: 5 from the t of Simeon, Shaphat son of Hori; H4751
Nu 13: 6 from the t of Judah, Caleb son of H4751
Nu 13: 7 from the t of Issachar, Igal son of Joseph; H4751
Nu 13: 8 from the t of Ephraim, Hoshea son of Nun; H4751
Nu 13: 9 from the t of Benjamin, Palti son of Raphu H4751
Nu 13:10 from the t of Zebulun, Gaddiel son of H4751
Nu 13:11 from the t of Manasseh (a tribe of Joseph), H4751
Nu 13:11 of Manasseh (a t of Joseph), Gaddi son H4751
Nu 13:12 from the t of Dan, Ammiel son of Gemalli; H4751
Nu 13:13 from the t of Asher, Sethur son of Michael; H4751
Nu 13:14 from the t of Naphtali, Nahbi son of H4751
Nu 13:15 from the t of Gad, Geuel son of Maki. H4751
Nu 17: 3 one staff for the head of each ancestral t. H1074
Nu 17: 8 which represented the t of Levi, had not H1074
Nu 18: 2 from your ancestral t to join you and assist H8657
Nu 24: 2 out and saw Israel encamped t by tribe, NDT
Nu 24: 2 out and saw Israel encamped tribe by t, H8657
Nu 26:55 according to the names for its ancestral t. H4751
Nu 31: 5 a thousand from each t, were supplied H4751
Nu 31: 6 a thousand from each t, along with H4751
Nu 34:14 because the families of the t of Reuben H4751
Nu 34:14 the t of Gad and the half-tribe of H4751
Nu 34:18 one leader from each t to help assign the H4751
Nu 34:19 son of Jephunneh, from the t of Judah; H4751
Nu 34:20 son of Ammihud, from the t of Simeon; H4751
Nu 34:21 son of Kislon, from the t of Benjamin; H4751
Nu 34:22 son of Jogli, the leader from the t of Dan; H4751
Nu 34:23 the leader from the t of Manasseh son of H4751
Nu 34:24 the leader from the t of Ephraim son of H4751
Nu 34:25 the leader from the t of Zebulun; H4751
Nu 34:26 the leader from the t of Issachar; H4751
Nu 34:27 Shelomi, the leader from the t of Asher; H4751
Nu 34:28 the leader from the t of Naphtali. H4751
Nu 35: 8 proportion to the inheritance of each t: H2257S
Nu 35: 8 Take many towns from a t that has many, H2257S
Nu 36: 3 added to that of the t they marry into. H4751
Nu 36: 4 added to that of the t into which they H4751
Nu 36: 5 "What the t of the descendants of Joseph H4751
Nu 36: 7 in Israel is to pass from one t to another, H4751
Nu 36: 8 in any Israelite t must marry someone in H4751
Nu 36: 9 may pass from one t to another, H4751
Nu 36: 9 each Israelite t is to keep the land it H4751
Nu 36:12 remained in their father's t and clan. H4751
Dt 1:23 twelve of you, one man from each t. H8657
Dt 10: 8 LORD set apart the t of Levi to carry the ark H8657
Dt 18: 1 the whole t of Levi—are to have H8657
Dt 29:18 clan or t among you today whose heart H8657
Jos 3:12 from the tribes of Israel, one from each t. H8657
Jos 4: 2 from among the people, one from each t, H8657
Jos 4: 4 from the Israelites, one from each t, H8657
Jos 7: 1 of Zerah, of the t of Judah, took some of H4751
Jos 7:14 the morning, present yourselves t by tribe. NDT
Jos 7:14 the morning, present yourselves tribe by t. H8657
Jos 7:14 The t the LORD chooses shall come forward H8657
Jos 7:18 of Zerah, of the t of Judah, was chosen. H4751
Jos 13: 7 nine tribes and half of the t of Manasseh." H8657
Jos 13:14 But to the t of Levi he gave no inheritance, H8657
Jos 13:15 what Moses had given to the t of Reuben, H4751
Jos 13:24 is what Moses had given to the t of Gad, H4751
Jos 13:33 But to the t of Levi, Moses had given no H8657
Jos 15: 1 The allotment for the t of Judah H4751
Jos 15:20 This is the inheritance of the t of Judah H4751
Jos 15:21 towns of the t of Judah in the Negev H4751
Jos 16: 8 inheritance of the t of the Ephraimites, H4751
Jos 17: 1 allotment for the t of Manasseh as H4751
Jos 17: 6 of the t of Manasseh received an H4985
Jos 18: 4 Appoint three men from each t. I will send H8657
Jos 18:11 came up for the t of Benjamin according H4751
Jos 18:21 The t of Benjamin, according to its clans H4751
Jos 19: 1 came out for the t of Simeon according to H4751
Jos 19: 8 the inheritance of the t of the Simeonites, H4751
Jos 19:23 were the inheritance of the t of Issachar, H4751
Jos 19:24 came out for the t of Asher according to H4751
Jos 19:31 were the inheritance of the t of Asher, H4751
Jos 19:39 were the inheritance of the t of Naphtali, H4751
Jos 19:40 lot came out for the t of Dan according to H4751
Jos 19:48 were the inheritance of the t of Dan, H4751
Jos 20: 8 on the plateau in the t of Reuben, H4751
Jos 20: 8 Ramoth in Gilead in the t of Gad, and H4751
Jos 20: 8 Golan in Bashan in the t of Manasseh. H4751
Jos 21:17 And from the t of Benjamin they gave H4751
Jos 21:20 were allotted towns from the t of Ephraim: H4751
Jos 21:23 Also from the t of Dan they received H4751
Jos 21:25 From half the t of Manasseh they received H4751
Jos 21:28 from the t of Issachar, Kishion, Daberath, H4751
Jos 21:30 from the t of Asher, Mishal, Abdon, H4751
Jos 21:32 from the t of Naphtali, Kedesh in Galilee H4751
Jos 21:34 from the t of Zebulun, Jokneam H4751
Jos 21:36 from the t of Reuben, Bezer, Jahaz, H4751
Jos 21:38 from the t of Gad, Ramoth in Gilead (a H4751
Jos 22: 7 the other half of the t Joshua gave land H2257S
Jdg 18: 1 in those days the t of the Danites was H8657
Jdg 18:19 that you serve a t and clan in Israel as H8657
Jdg 18:30 were priests for the t of Dan until the time H8657
Jdg 20:12 messengers throughout the t of Benjamin, H8657
Jdg 21: 3 Why should one t be missing from Israel H8657
Jdg 21: 6 Israelites grieved for the t of **Benjamin**, H1228
Jdg 21: 6 "Today one t is cut off from Israel," they H8657
Jdg 21:17 "so that a t of Israel will not be wiped out. H8657
1Sa 9:21 from the smallest t of Israel, and is not my H8657
1Sa 9:21 least of all the clans of the t of Benjamin? H8657
1Sa 10:20 the t of Benjamin was taken by lot. H8657
1Sa 10:21 he brought forward the t of Benjamin, H8657
2Sa 2: 4 anointed David king over the t of Judah. H1074
2Sa 2:10 The t of Judah, however, remained loyal H1074
2Sa 3:19 the whole t of Benjamin wanted to H1074
2Sa 4: 2 the Beerothite from the t of Benjamin— H1201
1Ki 7:14 a widow from the t of Naphtali and whose H4751
1Ki 8:16 chosen a city in any t of Israel to have a H8657
1Ki 11:13 will give him one t for the sake of David H8657
1Ki 11:32 all the tribes of Israel, he will have one t. H8657
1Ki 11:36 I will give one t to his son so that David H8657
1Ki 12:20 Only the t of Judah remained loyal to the H8657
1Ki 12:21 all Judah and the t of Benjamin— H8657
1Ki 15:27 of Ahijah from the t of Issachar plotted H1074
2Ki 17:18 Only the t of Judah was left, H8657
1Ch 4:18 His wife from the **t of Judah** gave birth to H3374
1Ch 6:60 And from the t of Benjamin they were H4751
1Ch 6:61 from the clans of half the t of Manasseh. H4751
1Ch 6:62 the part of the t of Manasseh that is in H4751
1Ch 6:66 their territory towns from the t of Ephraim. H4751
1Ch 6:70 And from half the t of Manasseh the H4751
1Ch 6:72 from the t of Issachar they received H4751
1Ch 6:74 from the t of Asher they received Mashal H4751
1Ch 6:76 from the t of Naphtali they received H4751
1Ch 6:77 From the t of Zebulun they received H4751
1Ch 6:78 from the t of Reuben across the Jordan H4751
1Ch 6:80 from the t of Gad they received H4751
1Ch 12: 2 relatives of Saul from the **t of Benjamin**): H1228
1Ch 12:19 Some of the **t of Manasseh** defected to H4985
1Ch 12:29 Benjamin, Saul's t—3,000, most of whom H278
1Ch 12:31 from half the t of Manasseh, designated H4751
1Ch 23:14 God were counted as part of the t of Levi. H8657
1Ch 27:20 of Azaziah; over half the t of Manasseh: H8657
1Ch 28: 4 from the t of Judah he chose my H1074
2Ch 6: 5 chosen a city in any t of Israel to have a H8657
2Ch 11:16 Those from every t of Israel who set their H8657
2Ch 19:11 the leader of the t of Judah, will be over H1074
Est 2: 5 of Susa a Jew of the **t of Benjamin**, H408+3549
Job 30:12 On my right the t attacks; they lay snares H7259
Ps 68:27 There is the little **t of Benjamin**, leading H1228
Ps 78:67 he did not choose the t of Ephraim; H8657
Ps 78:68 he chose the t of Judah, Mount Zion H8657
Eze 47:23 In whatever t a foreigner resides, there you H8657
Lk 2:36 the daughter of Penuel, of the t of Asher. G5876
Ac 13:21 son of Kish, of the t of Benjamin, who G5876
Ro 11: 1 of Abraham, from the t of Benjamin. G5876
Php 3: 5 people of Israel, of the t of Benjamin, G5876
Heb 7:13 things are said belonged to a different t, G5876
Heb 7:13 no one from **that** t has ever served G4005S
Heb 7:14 in regard to that t Moses said nothing G5876
Rev 5: 5 the Lion of the t of Judah, the Root G5876
Rev 5: 9 persons from every t and language and G5876
Rev 7: 5 From the t of Judah 12,000 were sealed G5876
Rev 7: 5 were sealed, from the t of Reuben 12,000 G5876
Rev 7: 5 12,000, from the t of Gad 12,000, G5876
Rev 7: 6 from the t of Asher 12,000, from the tribe G5876
Rev 7: 6 12,000, from the t of Naphtali 12,000 G5876
Rev 7: 6 12,000, from the t of Manasseh 12,000, G5876
Rev 7: 7 from the t of Simeon 12,000, from the G5876
Rev 7: 7 12,000, from the t of Levi 12,000, from G5876
Rev 7: 7 12,000, from the t of Issachar 12,000, G5876
Rev 7: 8 from the t of Zebulun 12,000, from the G5876
Rev 7: 8 12,000, from the t of Joseph 12,000, from G5876
Rev 7: 8 12,000, from the t of Benjamin 12,000. G5876
Rev 7: 9 from every nation, t, people and G5876
Rev 11: 9 from every people, t, language and G5876
Rev 13: 7 And it was given authority over every t G5876
Rev 14: 6 to every nation, t, language and people. G5876

TRIBES (118) [TRIBE]

Ge 25:18 in hostility toward all the **t related to** them. H278
Ge 49:16 his people as one of the t of Israel. H8657
Ge 49:28 All these are the twelve t of Israel, and H8657
Ex 24: 4 pillars representing the twelve t of Israel. H8657
Ex 28:21 seal with the name of one of the twelve t. H8657
Ex 39:14 seal with the name of one of the twelve t. H8657
Nu 1:16 the leaders of their ancestral t. H4751
Nu 10: 5 the t camping on the east are to set out. H4722
Nu 17: 2 the leader of each of their ancestral t. H1074
Nu 17: 6 the leader of each of their ancestral t, H1074
Nu 30: 1 Moses said to the heads of the t of Israel H4751
Nu 31: 4 thousand men from each of the t of Israel." H4751
Nu 32:28 to the family heads of the Israelite t. H4751
Nu 33:54 Distribute it according to your ancestral t. H4751
Nu 34:13 that it be given to the nine and a half t, H4751
Nu 34:15 These two and a half t have received their H4751
Nu 36: 3 they marry men from other Israelite t; H8657
Dt 1:13 respected men from each of your t, H8657
Dt 1:15 So I took the leading men of your t, wise H8657
Dt 5:23 the leaders of your t and your elders came H8657
Dt 12: 5 from among all your t to put his Name H8657
Dt 12:14 the LORD will choose in one of your t, H8657
Dt 16:18 each of your t in every town the LORD H8657
Dt 18: 5 out of all your t to stand and minister in H8657
Dt 27:12 these t shall stand on Mount Gerizim to NDT
Dt 27:13 And these t shall stand on Mount Ebal to NDT
Dt 29:21 out from all the t of Israel for disaster, H8657
Dt 31:28 the elders of your t and all your officials H8657
Dt 33: 5 assembled, along with the t of Israel. H8657
Jos 3:12 choose twelve men from the t of Israel H8657
Jos 4: 5 to the number of the t of the Israelites, H8657
Jos 4: 8 to the number of the t of the Israelites, H8657
Jos 7:16 Joshua had Israel come forward by t, H8657
Jos 12: 7 inheritance to the t of Israel according to H8657
Jos 13: 7 among the nine t and half of the tribe of H8657
Jos 14: 2 assigned by lot to the nine and a half t, H4751
Jos 14: 3 the two and a half t their inheritance east H4751
Jos 14: 4 descendants had become two t— H4751
Jos 17:17 But Joshua said to the t of Joseph—to H1074
Jos 18: 2 still seven Israelite t who had not yet H8657
Jos 18: 5 on the south and the t of Joseph in their H1074
Jos 18:11 lay between the t of Judah and Joseph: H1201
Jos 21: 4 thirteen towns from the t of Judah, H4751
Jos 21: 5 towns from the clans of the t of Ephraim, H4751
Jos 21: 6 towns from the clans of the t of Issachar, H4751
Jos 21: 7 twelve towns from the t of Reuben, H4751
Jos 21: 9 From the t of Judah and Simeon they H4751
Jos 21:16 nine towns from these two t. H8657
Jos 22:14 one from each of the t of Israel, each the H4751
Jos 23: 4 inheritance for your t all the land of the H8657
Jos 24: 1 assembled all the t of Israel at Shechem. H8657
Jdg 1:22 Now the t of Joseph attacked Bethel, and H1074
Jdg 1:35 the power of the t of Joseph increased, H1074
Jdg 18: 1 into an inheritance among the t of Israel. H8657
Jdg 20: 2 all the people of the t of Israel took their H8657
Jdg 20:10 of every hundred from all the t of Israel, H8657
Jdg 20:12 The t of Israel sent messengers H8657
Jdg 21: 5 "Who from all the t of Israel has failed to H8657
Jdg 21: 8 "Which one of the t of Israel failed to H8657
Jdg 21:15 LORD had made a gap in the t of Israel. H8657
Jdg 21:24 place and went home to their t and clans, H8657
1Sa 2:28 out of all the t of Israel to be my priest H8657
1Sa 10:19 before the LORD by your t and clans." H8657
1Sa 10:20 Samuel had all Israel come forward by t, H8657
1Sa 15:17 not become the head of the t of Israel? H8657
2Sa 5: 1 All the t of Israel came to David at H8657
2Sa 15: 2 "Your servant is from one of the t of Israel." H8657
2Sa 15:10 throughout the t of Israel to say, H8657
2Sa 19: 9 Throughout the t of Israel, all the people H8657
2Sa 19:20 first from the t of Joseph to come H3972+1074
2Sa 20:14 through all the t of Israel to Abel Beth H8657
2Sa 24: 2 "Go throughout the t of Israel from Dan to H8657
1Ki 8: 1 all the heads of the t and the chiefs of the H4751
1Ki 11:28 the whole labor force of the t of Joseph. H1074
1Ki 11:31 out of Solomon's hand and give you ten t. H8657
1Ki 11:32 I have chosen out of all the t of Israel, H8657
1Ki 11:35 from his son's hands and give you ten t. H8657
1Ki 14:21 chosen out of all the t of Israel in which to H8657
1Ki 18:31 one for each of the t descended from H8657
2Ki 21: 7 I have chosen out of all the t of Israel, H8657
1Ch 6:62 thirteen towns from the t of Issachar, H4751
1Ch 6:63 twelve towns from the t of Reuben, H4751
1Ch 6:65 From the t of Judah, Simeon and H4751
1Ch 27:16 The leaders of the t of Israel: over the H8657
1Ch 27:22 These were the leaders of the t of Israel. H8657
1Ch 28: 1 the officers over the t, the commanders of H8657
1Ch 29: 6 the officers of the t of Israel, the H8657
2Ch 5: 2 all the heads of the t and the chiefs of the H4751
2Ch 12:13 chosen out of all the t of Israel in which to H8657
2Ch 33: 7 I have chosen out of all the t of Israel, H8657
Ezr 6:17 one for each of the t of Israel. A10694
Ps 72: 9 May the **desert** t bow before him and his H7470
Ps 78:55 he settled the t of Israel in their homes. H8657
Ps 105:37 from among their t no one faltered. H8657
Ps 122: 4 That is where the t go up—the tribes of H8657
Ps 122: 4 tribes go up—the t of the LORD—to praise H8657
Isa 49: 6 to restore the t of Jacob and bring back H8657
Isa 63:17 servants, the t that are your inheritance. H8657
Eze 37:19 of the Israelite t associated with him H8657
Eze 45: 8 to possess the land according to their t. H8657
Eze 47:13 among the twelve t of Israel as their H8657
Eze 47:21 yourselves according to the t of Israel. H8657
Eze 47:22 an inheritance among the t of Israel. H8657
Eze 48: 1 "These are the t, listed by name: At the H8657
Eze 48:19 farm it will come from all the t of Israel. H8657
Eze 48:23 "As for the rest of the t: Benjamin will H8657
Eze 48:29 to allot as an inheritance to the t of Israel, H8657
Eze 48:31 the city will be named after the t of Israel. H8657
Hos 5: 9 Among the t of Israel I proclaim what is H8657
Am 5: 6 sweep through the t of Joseph like a fire; H1074
Zec 9: 1 people and all the t of Israel are on the H8657
Zec 10: 6 Judah and save the t of Joseph. H1074
Mt 19:28 thrones, judging the twelve t of Israel. G5876
Lk 22:30 on thrones, judging the twelve t of Israel. G5876
Ac 26: 7 the promise our **twelve** t are hoping to G1559
Jas 1: 1 To the twelve t scattered among the G5876
Rev 7: 4 144,000 from all the t of Israel. G5876
Rev 21:12 written the names of the twelve t of Israel. G5876

TRIBULATION (1)
Rev 7:14 they who have come out of the great **t**; G2568

TRIBUTARIES, TRIBUTARY (KJV) FORCED LABOR, FORCED LABORERS, SLAVE

TRIBUTE (27)
Nu 31:28 set apart as **t** for the LORD one out of every H4830
Nu 31:29 Take this **t** from their half share and give it NDT
Nu 31:37 of which the **t** for the LORD was 675; H4830
Nu 31:38 of which the **t** for the LORD was 72; H4830
Nu 31:39 of which the **t** for the LORD was 61; H4830
Nu 31:40 of whom the **t** for the LORD was 32. H4830
Nu 31:41 Moses gave the **t** to Eleazar the priest as H4830
Jdg 3:15 sent him with **t** to Eglon king of Moab. H4966
Jdg 3:17 He presented the **t** to Eglon king of Moab H4966
Jdg 3:18 After Ehud had presented the **t**, he sent on H4966
2Sa 8: 2 subject to David and brought him **t**. H4966
2Sa 8: 6 became subject to him and brought **t**. H4966
1Ki 4:21 countries brought **t** and were Solomon's H4966
2Ki 3: 4 *he had to* **pay** the king of Israel **a t** *of* **a** H8740
2Ki 17: 3 Shalmaneser's vassal and had paid him **t**. H4966
2Ki 17: 4 he no longer paid **t** to the king of H4966
1Ch 18: 2 became subject to him and brought him **t**. H4966
1Ch 18: 6 became subject to him and brought him **t**. H4966
2Ch 17:11 brought Jehoshaphat gifts and silver as **t**, H5362
2Ch 26: 8 The Ammonites brought **t** to Uzziah, and H4966
Ezr 4:13 no more taxes, **t** or duty will be paid A10107
Ezr 4:20 taxes, **t** and duty were paid to them. A10107
Ezr 7:24 **t** or duty on any of the priests A10107
Est 10: 1 King Xerxes imposed **t** throughout the H4989
Ps 72:10 of distant shores bring **t** to him. H4966
Isa 16: 1 Send lambs as **t** to the ruler of the land NDT
Hos 10: 6 carried to Assyria as **t** for the great king. H4966

TRICK (1) [TRICKERY, TRICKING]
1Th 2: 3 impure motives, nor are we trying to **t** you. G1515

TRICKERY (2) [TRICK]
Ac 13:10 You are full of all kinds of deceit and **t** G4816
2Co 12:16 crafty fellow that I am, I caught you *by* **t**! G1515

TRICKING (1) [TRICK]
Ge 27:12 I would appear *to be* **t** him and would H9506

TRICKLING (1)
Eze 47: 2 the water *was* **t** from the south side. H7096

TRIED (46) [TRY]
Ge 37:21 *he* **t** *to* **rescue** him from their hands. AIT
Ex 2:15 heard of this, *he* **t** to kill Moses, but H1335
Ex 8:18 the magicians **t** to produce gnats H6913+4027
Dt 4:34 *Has* any god *ever* **t** to take for himself one H5814
Dt 13: 5 prophet or dreamer *t* to **turn** you from the way AIT
Dt 13:10 because *they* **t** to turn you away from the H1335
1Sa 17:39 over the tunic and **t** walking around, H3283
1Sa 19:10 Saul **t** to pin him to the wall with his spear, H1335
2Sa 4: 8 your enemy, who **t to kill** you. H1335+5883
2Sa 21: 2 Israel and Judah *had* **t** to annihilate them H1335
1Ki 11:40 Solomon **t** to kill Jeroboam, but Jeroboam H1335
Ps 17: 4 Though people **t** to bribe me, I have kept NDT
Ps 73:16 When *I* **t** to understand all this, it troubled H3108
Ps 95: 9 tested me; *they* **t** me, though they had H1043
Ps 109: 7 When he **is t**, let him be found guilty, and H9149
Ecc 2: 3 *I* **t** cheering myself with wine H9365+928+4213
La 3:53 *They t to* **end** my life in a pit and threw AIT
Eze 24:13 Because *I t to* **cleanse** you but you would not AIT
Da 6: 4 the satraps **t** to find grounds for A10114
Jnh 4: 2 That is what *I t to* **forestall** by fleeing to AIT
Mt 3:14 But John *t to* **deter** him, saying, "I need to be AIT
Lk 4:42 *they t to* **keep** him from leaving them. AIT
Lk 5:18 man on a mat and **t** to take him into the G2426
Lk 6:19 the people all **t** to touch him, because G2426
Lk 9: 9 such things about?" And *he* **t** to see him. G2426
Lk 9:49 demons in your name and *we t to* **stop** him, AIT
Jn 5:18 this reason they **t** all the more **to** kill him; G2426
Jn 7:30 At this *they* **t to** seize him, but no one laid G2426
Jn 10:39 Again *they* **t** to seize him, but he escaped G2426
Jn 11: 8 while ago the Jews there **t to** stone you, G2426
Jn 19:12 From then on, Pilate **t** to set Jesus free G2426
Ac 7:26 *He t to* **reconcile** them by saying, 'Men, you AIT
Ac 9:26 to Jerusalem, *he* **t** to join the disciples G4279
Ac 9:29 the Hellenistic Jews, but they **t to** kill him. G2217
Ac 13: 8 opposed them and **t to** turn the proconsul G2426
Ac 16: 7 border of Mysia, *they* **t** to enter Bithynia G4279
Ac 19:13 out evil spirits **t** to invoke the name of G2217
Ac 24: 6 even **t** to desecrate the temple; so we G4279
Ac 25:10 Caesar's court, where I ought *to be* **t**. G3212
Ac 26:11 and *I t to* **force** them to blaspheme. AIT
Ac 26:21 me in the temple courts and **t to** kill me. G4281
Ac 28:23 the Prophets *he t to* **persuade** them about AIT
Gal 1:13 the church of God and *t to* **destroy** it. AIT
Gal 1:23 now preaching the faith *he* once *t to* **destroy**." AIT
Heb 3: 9 where your ancestors tested and **t** me G1508
Heb 11:29 but *when* the Egyptians **t** to do so G4278+3284

TRIES (3) [TRY]
Lk 17:33 Whoever **t** to keep their life will lose it G2426
2Ti 2: 4 rather *t to* **please** his commanding officer. AIT
Rev 11: 5 If anyone **t** to harm them, fire comes from G2527

TRIFLING (1)
Ne 9:32 *do* not *let* all this hardship *seem* **t** in your H5070

TRIM (2) [TRIMMED, TRIMMERS]
Dt 21:12 have her shave her head, **t** her nails H6913
Da 4:14 'Cut down the tree and **t off** its branches A10635

TRIMMED (6) [TRIM]
2Sa 19:24 care of his feet or **t** his mustache or H6913
1Ki 6:36 stone and one course of **t** cedar **beams**. H4164
1Ki 7: 2 cedar columns supporting **t** cedar **beams**. H4164
1Ki 7:12 stone and one course of **t** cedar **beams**, H4164
Eze 44:20 *they are to* **keep** *the* **hair** of their heads **t** H4080+4080
Mt 25: 7 all the virgins woke up and **t** their lamps. G3175

TRIMMERS (8) [TRIM]
Ex 25:38 Its **wick t** and trays are to be of pure gold. H4920
Ex 37:23 as well as its **wick t** and trays, of pure H4920
Nu 4: 9 with its lamps, its **wick t** and trays, and all H4920
1Ki 7:50 pure gold basins, **wick t**, sprinkling bowls, H4662
2Ki 12:13 silver basins, **wick t**, sprinkling bowls, H4662
2Ki 25:14 shovels, **wick t**, dishes and all the bronze H4662
2Ch 4:22 the pure gold **wick t**, sprinkling bowls H4662
Jer 52:18 the pots, shovels, **wick t**, sprinkling bowls H4662

TRIP (1)
Ps 140: 4 the violent, who devise ways to **t** my feet. H1890

TRIPOLIS (NIV84) ADMINISTRATORS

TRIUMPH (23) [TRIUMPHAL, TRIUMPHANT, TRIUMPHED, TRIUMPHING, TRIUMPHS]
Jdg 8: 9 "When I return in **t**, I will tear down this H8934
Jdg 11:31 me when I return in **t** from the Ammonites H8934
1Sa 26:25 will do great things and **surely t**." H3523+3523
Job 17: 4 therefore *you will* not **let** them **t**. H8123
Ps 9:19 *do* not *let* mortals **t**; let the nations H6451
Ps 13: 2 How long *will* my enemy **t** over me? H8123
Ps 25: 2 to shame, nor *let* my enemies **t** over me. H6636
Ps 41:11 for my enemy *does* not **t** over me. H8131
Ps 54: 7 my eyes have looked in **t** on my foes. NDT
Ps 60: 6 "*In* **t** I will parcel out Shechem and H6600
Ps 60: 8 toss my sandal; over Philistia *I* **shout in t**." H8131
Ps 108: 7 "*In* **t** I will parcel out Shechem and H6600
Ps 108: 9 toss my sandal; over Philistia *I* **shout in t**." H8131
Ps 112: 8 in the end they will look in **t** on their foes. NDT
Ps 118: 7 he is my helper. I **look** *in t* on my enemies. AIT
Pr 28:12 When the righteous **t**, there is great H6636
Isa 13: 3 out my wrath—those who rejoice in my **t**. H1452
Isa 42:13 the battle cry and *will* **t** over his enemies. H1504
Isa 58:14 and *I will* **cause** you **to ride in t** on the H8206
Jer 9: 3 it is not by truth that *they* **t** in the land. H1504
Jer 51:14 and *they will* **shout in t** over you. H6702+2116
Mic 5: 9 will be lifted up in **t** over your enemies, NDT
Rev 17:14 the Lamb *will* **t over** them because he G3771

TRIUMPHAL (2) [TRIUMPH]
Isa 60:11 nations—their kings **led in t procession**. H5627
2Co 2:14 **leads us as captives** in Christ's **t procession** G2581

TRIUMPHANT (1) [TRIUMPH]
Da 11:12 many thousands, yet *he will* not *remain* **t**. H6451

TRIUMPHED (5) [TRIUMPH]
Dt 32:27 say, 'Our hand *has* **t**; the LORD has not H8123
1Sa 17:50 So David **t** over the Philistine with a sling H2616
La 1: 9 on my affliction, for the enemy *has* **t**." H1540
Rev 5: 5 tribe of Judah, the Root of David, *has* **t**. G3771
Rev 12:11 They **t over** him by the blood of the Lamb G3771

TRIUMPHING (1) [TRIUMPH]
Col 2:15 of them, **t** over them by the cross. G2581

TRIUMPHS (1) [TRIUMPH]
Jas 2:13 been merciful. Mercy **t over** judgment. G2878

TRIVIAL (3)
1Ki 16:31 He not only **considered** *it* **t** to commit the H7837
Eze 8:17 *Is it a* **t** *matter* for the people of Judah to H7837
1Co 6: 2 are you not competent to judge **t** *cases*? G1788

TROAS (6)
Ac 16: 8 passed by Mysia and went down to **T**. G5590
Ac 16:11 From **T** we put out to sea and sailed G5590
Ac 20: 5 went on ahead and waited for us at **T**. G5590
Ac 20: 6 five days later joined the others at **T** G5590
2Co 2:12 Now when I went to **T** to preach the G5590
2Ti 4:13 bring the cloak that I left with Carpus at **T** G5590

TROD (2) [TREAD]
Job 22:15 to the old path that the wicked *have* **t**? H2005
Isa 63: 3 my anger and **t** them **down** in my wrath; H8252

TRODDEN (2) [TREAD]
Jdg 9:27 gathered the grapes and **t** them, H2005
Isa 63: 3 "*I have* **t** the winepress alone; from the H2005

TROOP (2) [TROOPS]
2Sa 22:30 With your help I can advance against a **t** H1522
Ps 18:29 With your help I can advance against a **t** H1522

TROOPS (77) [TROOP]
Ex 14: 9 horsemen and **t**—pursued the Israelites H2657
Jos 10: 5 up with all their **t** and took up positions H4722
Jos 11: 4 out with all their **t** and a large number of H4722
Jdg 4: 7 his chariots and his **t** to the Kishon River H2162
Jdg 4:16 all Sisera's **t** fell by the sword; not a H4722
Jdg 8: 5 Sukkoth, "Give my **t** some bread; they are H6639
Jdg 8: 6 Why should we give bread to your **t**?" H7372
Jdg 9:34 all his **t** set out by night and H6639
Jdg 9:35 as Abimelek and his **t** came out from their H6639
Jdg 11:20 He mustered all his **t** and encamped at H6639
Jdg 20:16 hundred select **t** who were left-handed H408
1Sa 13: 7 all the **t** with him were quaking with H6639
1Sa 14:24 So none of the **t** tasted food. H6639
1Sa 18: 5 This pleased all the **t**, and Saul's officers H6639
1Sa 18:13 David led the **t** in their campaigns. H6639
1Sa 26: 2 with his three thousand select Israelite **t**, to H408
2Sa 2:28 trumpet, and all the **t** came to a halt; they H6639
2Sa 10: 9 some of the **best** *t in* Israel and deployed AIT
2Sa 10:13 Then Joab and the **t** with him advanced H6639
2Sa 12:28 the rest of the **t** and besiege the city H6639
2Sa 16: 6 though all the **t** and the special guard H6639
2Sa 17: 8 he will not spend the night with the **t**. H6639
2Sa 17: 9 If he should attack **your t** first, whoever H2157S
2Sa 17: 9 among the **t** who follow Absalom. H6639
2Sa 18: 2 David sent out his **t**, a third under the H6639
2Sa 18: 2 The king told the **t**, "I myself will surely H6639
2Sa 18: 5 And all the **t** heard the king giving orders H6639
2Sa 18: 7 There Israel's **t** were routed by David's H6639
2Sa 18:16 trumpet, and the **t** stopped pursuing Israel H6639
2Sa 19: 2 because on that day the **t** heard it said H6639
2Sa 19:40 All the **t** *of* Judah and half the troops of H6639
2Sa 19:40 Judah and half the **t** *of* Israel had taken H6639
2Sa 20:12 saw that all the **t** came to a halt there H6639
2Sa 20:15 All the **t** with Joab came and besieged H6639
2Sa 23:10 The **t** returned to Eleazar, but only to strip H6639
2Sa 23:11 full of lentils, Israel's **t** fled from them. H6639
2Sa 24: 3 God multiply the **t** a hundred times over, H6639
2Ki 9:17 in Jezreel saw Jehu's **t** approaching, H9180
2Ki 9:17 he called out, "I see *some* **t** coming." H9180
2Ki 11:15 of a hundred, who were in charge of the **t**: H2657
1Ch 11:13 of barley, the **t** fled from the Philistines. H6639
1Ch 19: 7 as well as the king of Maakah with his **t** H6639
1Ch 19:10 selected some of the **best** *t* in Israel and AIT
1Ch 19:14 Then Joab and the **t** with him advanced H6639
1Ch 21: 2 to Joab and the commanders of the **t**, H6639
1Ch 21: 3 LORD multiply his **t** a hundred times over. H6639
2Ch 12: 3 the innumerable **t** of Libyans, H6639
2Ch 13: 3 eight hundred thousand able **t**. H1475+2657
2Ch 13:13 Jeroboam had sent **t** around to the rear, H4422
2Ch 13:17 Abijah and his **t** inflicted heavy losses on H6639
2Ch 17: 2 He stationed **t** in all the fortified cities of H2657
2Ch 23:14 who were in charge of the **t**, and said to H2657
2Ch 25: 7 these **t** *from* Israel must not march with H7372
2Ch 25: 9 talents I paid for these Israelite **t**? H1522
2Ch 25:10 dismissed the **t** who had come to him H1522
2Ch 25:13 Meanwhile the **t** that Amaziah had H1201+1522
Job 19:12 His **t** advance in force; they build a siege H1522
Job 29:25 I dwelt as a king among his **t**; I was like H1522
Ps 110: 3 Your **t** will be willing on your day of battle. H6639
SS 6: 4 Jerusalem, as majestic as **t with banners**. H1839
Jer 51:14 I will surely fill you with **t**, as with a swarm H132
Eze 12:14 his staff and all his **t**—and I will pursue H111
Eze 17:21 All his choice **t** will fall by the sword, and H111
Eze 38: 6 also Gomer with all its **t**, and Beth H111
Eze 38: 6 Togarmah from the far north with all its **t**— H111
Eze 38: 9 You and all your **t** and the many nations H111
Eze 38:22 on him and on his **t** and on the many H111
Eze 39: 4 you and all your **t** and the nations with you. H111
Da 11:15 even their best **t** will not have the strength H6639
Mic 5: 1 **Marshal** *your* **t** now, city of troops, for a H1518
Mic 5: 1 troops now, city of **t**, for a siege is laid H1522
Na 2: 5 Nineveh summons her **picked t**, yet they H129
Na 3:13 Look at your **t**—they are all weaklings H6639
Ac 21:31 the commander *of* the **Roman t** that the G5061
Ac 23:10 He ordered the **t** to go down and take him G5128
Ac 23:27 I came with my **t** and rescued him, for G5128
Rev 9:16 The number *of* the mounted **t** was twice G5128

TROPHIMUS (3)
Ac 20: 4 Tychicus and **T** from the province of G5576
Ac 21:29 had previously seen **T** the Ephesian in the G5576
2Ti 4:20 in Corinth, and I left **T** sick in Miletus. G5576

TROUBLE (121) [TROUBLED, TROUBLEMAKER, TROUBLEMAKERS, TROUBLER, TROUBLES, TROUBLESOME, TROUBLING]
Ge 34:30 "*You have* **brought t** *on* me by making me H6579
Ge 41:51 me forget all my **t** and all my father's H6662
Ge 43: 6 "Why *did you* **bring** *this* **t** on me by telling H8317
Ex 5:19 they were in **t** when they were told, H8273
Ex 5:22 why *have you* **brought t** on this people? H8317
Ex 5:23 *he has* **brought t** on this people H8317
Nu 11:11 "Why *have you* **brought** *this* **t** on your H8317
Nu 33:55 *They will* **give** you **t** in the land where you H7675
Jos 6:18 liable to destruction and **bring t** *on* it. H6579
Jos 7:25 "Why *have you* **brought** *this* **t** *on* us? H6579
Jos 7:25 The LORD *will* **bring t** *on* you today. H6579
Jdg 10:14 Let them save you when you are in **t**!" H7650
Jdg 11: 7 you come to me now, when you're *in* **t**?" H7639
1Sa 14:29 "My father *has* **made t** *for* the country. H6579
1Sa 20:19 place where you hid when this **t** began, H5126
1Sa 26:24 value my life and deliver me from all **t**." H7650
2Sa 4: 9 who has delivered me out of every **t**, H7650
1Ki 1:29 who has delivered me out of every **t**, H7650
1Ki 11:25 adding to the **t** caused by Hadad. H8288

1Ki 18:18 "*I have* not **made** t *for* Israel," Elijah H6579
1Ki 20: 7 "See how this man is looking for t! H8288
2Ki 4:13 '*You have* **gone to** all this t for us. H3006+3010
2Ki 14:10 Why ask for t and cause your own H8288
1Ch 2: 7 who **brought** t *on* Israel by violating the H6579
2Ch 25:19 Why ask for t and cause your own H8288
2Ch 28:20 but *he* **gave** him t instead of help. H7674
2Ch 28:22 In his time of t King Ahaz became even H7674
Ne 1: 3 the province are in great t and disgrace. H8288
Ne 2:17 I said to them, "You see the t we are in: H8288
Ne 4: 8 against Jerusalem and stir up t against it. H9360
Job 2:10 we accept good from God, and not t?" H8273
Job 3:10 the womb on me to hide t from my eyes. H6662
Job 4: 5 But now t comes to you, and you are NDT
Job 4: 8 plow evil and those who sow t reap it. H6662
Job 5: 6 nor does t sprout from the ground. H6662
Job 5: 7 Yet man is born to t as surely as sparks fly H6662
Job 11:16 You will surely forget your t, recalling it H6662
Job 14: 1 of woman, are of few days and full of t. H8075
Job 15:35 They conceive t and give birth to evil H6662
Job 19:28 since the root of the t lies in him, H1821
Job 30:25 Have I not wept for *those* **in** t? Has H7997+3427
Job 31:29 gloated over the t that came to him— H8273
Job 38:23 which I reserve for times of t, for days of H7639
Job 42:11 him over all the t the LORD had brought on H8288
Ps 7:14 with evil conceives t and gives birth to H6662
Ps 7:16 The t they *cause* recoils on them; their H6662
Ps 9: 9 the oppressed, a stronghold in times of t. H1314
Ps 10: 1 Why do you hide yourself in times of t? H1314
Ps 10: 7 t and evil are under his tongue. H6662
Ps 10:14 see the t of the afflicted; you H6662
Ps 22:11 t is near and there is no one to help. H7650
Ps 27: 5 For in the day of t he will keep me safe in H8288
Ps 32: 7 protect me from t and surround me with H7639
Ps 37:39 he is their stronghold in time of t. H7650
Ps 41: 1 the LORD delivers them in times of t. H8288
Ps 46: 1 strength, an ever-present help in t. H7650
Ps 50:15 call on me in the day of t; I will H7650
Ps 55: 2 My thoughts t *me* and I am distraught H8113
Ps 59:16 are my fortress, my refuge in times of t. H7639
Ps 66:14 my mouth spoke when I was in t. H7639
Ps 69:17 servant; answer me quickly, for I am in t. H7639
Ps 90:10 the best of them are but t and sorrow H6662
Ps 90:15 for as many years as we have seen t. H8288
Ps 91:15 I will be with him in t, I will deliver him H7650
Ps 94:13 you grant them relief from days of t, till a H8273
Ps 106:32 and t **came** to Moses because of them H8317
Ps 107: 6 Then they cried out to the LORD in their t H7639
Ps 107:13 Then they cried to the LORD in their t, and H7639
Ps 107:19 Then they cried to the LORD in their t, and H7639
Ps 107:28 Then they cried out to the LORD in their t H7639
Ps 119:143 **T** and distress have come upon me, but H7639
Ps 138: 7 Though I walk in the midst of t, you H7650
Ps 142: 2 him my complaint; before him I tell my t. H7650
Ps 143:11 in your righteousness, bring me out of t. H7650
Pr 1:27 when distress and t overwhelm you. H7442
Pr 5:14 I was soon in serious t in the assembly of H8273
Pr 11: 8 The righteous person is rescued from t H7650
Pr 12:13 sinful talk, and so the innocent escape t. H7650
Pr 12:21 the wicked have their fill of t. H8273
Pr 13:17 A wicked messenger falls into t, but a H8273
Pr 13:21 **T** pursues the sinner, but the righteous H8288
Pr 17:20 one whose tongue is perverse falls into t. H8288
Pr 19:23 then one rests content, untouched by t. H8273
Pr 24: 2 their lips talk about **making** t. H6662
Pr 24:10 If you falter in a time of t, how small is H7650
Pr 25:19 is reliance on the unfaithful in a time of t. H7650
Pr 28:14 whoever hardens their heart falls into t. H8288
Ecc 12: 1 before the days of t come and the years H8288
Isa 59: 4 they conceive t and give birth to evil. H6662
Jer 2:27 yet when they are in t, they say, H8288
Jer 2:28 if they can save you when you are in t! H8288
Jer 20:18 of the womb to see t and sorrow and to H6662
Jer 30: 7 It will be a time of t for Jacob, but he will H7650
Eze 32: 9 *I will* t the hearts of many peoples when I H4087
Da 9:25 with streets and a trench, but in times of t. H7441
Ob 12 boast so much in the day of their t. H7650
Ob 14 over their survivors in the day of their t. H7650
Jnh 1: 8 is responsible for making all this t for us? H8288
Na 1: 7 a refuge in times of t. He cares for those H7650
Na 1: 9 to an end; t will not come a second time. H7650
Zep 1:15 anguish, a day of t and ruin, a day of H8739
Zec 10:11 They will pass through the sea of t; the H7650
Mt 6:34 Each day has enough t of its own. *G2798*
Mt 13:21 When t or persecution comes because of *G2568*
Mt 28:14 we will satisfy him and keep you **out of** t." *G291*
Mk 4:17 When t or persecution comes because of *G2568*
Lk 7: 6 don't t *yourself*, for I do not deserve *G5035*
Jn 16:33 In this world you will have t. But take *G2568*
Ac 17: 6 "These men *who have* **caused** t all over the *G415*
Ro 2: 9 There will be t and distress for every *G2568*
Ro 8:35 Shall t or hardship or persecution or *G2568*
1Co 7:21 Don't *let* it t you—although if you can *G3508*
2Co 1: 4 comfort those in any t with the comfort we *G2568*
Gal 6:17 let no one cause me t, for I bear on my *G3160*
Php 1:17 that they can stir up t for me while I am in *G2568*
Php 3: 1 It is no t for me to write the same things *G3891*
2Th 1: 6 He will pay back t to those who trouble *G2568*
2Th 1: 6 will pay back trouble *to* those *who* t you *G2567*
1Ti 5:10 helping *those* **in** t and devoting herself to *G2567*
Heb 12:15 root grows up *to* **cause** t and defile many. *G1943*
Jas 5:13 *Is* anyone among you **in** t? Let them pray *G2802*

TROUBLED (23) [TROUBLE]

Ge 6: 6 on the earth, and his heart **was deeply** t. H6772
Ge 41: 8 In the morning his mind *was* t, so he sent H7192
Nu 11:10 angry, and Moses was t. H8273+928+6524
1Sa 1:15 "I am a woman who is **deeply** t. H7997+8120
Job 20: 2 "My t **thoughts** prompt me to answer H8546
Ps 38:18 I confess my iniquity; *I am* t by my sin. H1793
Ps 73:16 all this, it t me **deeply** H6662+928+6524
Ps 77: 4 my eyes from closing; *I was* too t to speak. H7192
Jer 49:23 t like the restless sea. H4202+3523+9200
Da 2: 1 his mind *was* t and he could not sleep. H7192
Da 7:15 *was* t in spirit, and the visions A10369
Da 7:28 *was* deeply t *by* my thoughts A10097
Mt 26:37 and he began to be sorrowful and t. *G86*
Mk 14:33 he began to be deeply distressed and t. *G86*
Lk 1:29 Mary *was* **greatly** t at his words and *G1410*
Lk 6:18 Those t by impure spirits were cured *G1943*
Lk 24:38 "Why are you t, and why do doubts *G5429*
Jn 11:33 he was deeply moved in spirit and t. *G5429*
Jn 12:27 "Now my soul *is* t, and what shall I say *G5429*
Jn 13:21 said this, Jesus *was* t in spirit and testified *G5429*
Jn 14: 1 "*Do* not *let* your hearts *be* t. You believe *G5429*
Jn 14:27 *Do* not *let* your hearts *be* t and do not be *G5429*
2Th 1: 7 give relief to you who *are* t, and to us *G2567*

TROUBLEMAKER (3) [TROUBLE]

2Sa 20: 1 Now a t named Sheba son of Bikri, H408+1175
Pr 6:12 A t and a villain, who goes about H132+1175
Ac 24: 5 "We have found this man to be a t *G3369*

TROUBLEMAKERS (2) [TROUBLE]

Dt 13:13 that t have arisen among you H408+1201+1175
1Sa 30:22 all the evil men and t among David's H1175

TROUBLER (1) [TROUBLE]

1Ki 18:17 said to him, "Is that you, you t *of* Israel?" H6579

TROUBLES (24) [TROUBLE]

Job 2:11 heard about all the t that had come upon H8288
Job 15:24 fill him with terror; t overwhelm him, like a NDT
Ps 25:17 Relieve the t *of* my heart and free me H7650
Ps 25:22 Deliver Israel, O God, from all their t! H7650
Ps 34: 6 heard him; he saved him out of all his t. H7650
Ps 34:17 he delivers them from all their t. H7650
Ps 34:19 The righteous person may have many t H8288
Ps 40:12 For t without number surround me; my H8288
Ps 54: 7 You have delivered me from all my t, and H7650
Ps 71:20 Though you have made me see t, many H7650
Ps 88: 3 am overwhelmed with t and my life draws H8288
Ecc 11:10 your heart and cast off the t of your body, H8288
Isa 22: 1 What t you now, that you have all gone H4200
Isa 46: 7 answer; it cannot save them from their t. H7650
Isa 65:16 For the past t will be forgotten and hidden H7650
Da 2: 3 have had a dream *that* t me and I want to H7192
Ac 7:10 rescued him from all his t. He gave *G2568*
1Co 7:28 who marry will face *many* t in this life, *G2568*
2Co 1: 4 who comforts us in all our t, so that we can *G2568*
2Co 1: 8 about the t we experienced in the *G2568*
2Co 4:17 light and momentary t are achieving for *G2568*
2Co 6: 4 in great endurance; in t, hardships and *G2568*
2Co 7: 4 in all our t my joy knows no bounds. *G2568*
Php 4:14 Yet it was good of you to share in my t. *G2568*

TROUBLESOME (1) [TROUBLE]

Ezr 4:15 a rebellious city, t *to* kings and provinces A10472

TROUBLING (4) [TROUBLE]

2Sa 14: 5 king asked her, "**What is** t you?" She said, H4537
2Ch 15: 6 because God *was* t them with every kind H2169
Est 4: 5 to find out what was t Mordecai and why. NDT
Ac 15:24 t your minds by what they said. *G412*

TROUGH (3) [TROUGHS]

Ge 24:20 So she quickly emptied her jar into the t H9216
Dt 28: 5 basket and your **kneading** t will be H5400
Dt 28:17 basket and your **kneading** t will be cursed. H5400

TROUGHS (5) [TROUGH]

Ge 30:38 branches in all the watering t, H8110+9216
Ge 30:41 the branches in the t in front of the H8110
Ex 2:16 water and fill the t to water their father's H8110
Ex 8: 3 into your ovens and **kneading** t. H5400
Ex 12:34 their shoulders in **kneading** t wrapped in H5400

TROUSERS (1)

Da 3:21 wearing their robes, t, turbans and other A10582

TRUDGE (1)

Isa 45:14 will be yours; *they will* t behind you H2143

TRUE (124) [TRUTH]

Nu 11:23 not what I say *will* **come** t *for* you. H7936
Nu 12: 7 But this is not t *of* my servant Moses; he is H4027
Dt 13:14 And if it is t and it has been proved that H622
Dt 17: 4 If it is t and it has been proved that this H622
Dt 18:22 of the LORD does not take place or **come** t, H995
Dt 22:20 the charge is t and no proof of the young H622
Jos 7:20 Achan replied, "It is t! I have sinned H593
Jos 21:42 this was t for all these towns. H4027
Jdg 13:17 may honor you when your word **comes** t?" H995
Ru 3:12 Although it is t that I am a H597
1Sa 9: 6 everything he says **comes** t. H995+995
1Ki 8:26 *let* your word that you promised your servant David my father **come** t H586
1Ki 10: 6 your achievements and your wisdom is t. H622
1Ki 13:32 of Samaria *will* **certainly come** t." H2118+2118
2Ki 9:12 "That's **not** t!" they said. "Tell us." Jehu H9214
2Ki 19:17 "It is t, LORD, that the Assyrian kings have H597
2Ch 6:17 *let* your word that you promised your servant David **come** t H586
2Ch 9: 5 your achievements and your wisdom is t. H622
2Ch 15: 3 For a long time Israel was without the t God, H622
Ne 6: 6 Geshem says it is t—that you and the NDT
Est 2:23 report was investigated and **found to be** t, H5162
Job 5:27 and it is t. So hear it and apply it H4027
Job 9: 2 I know that this is t. But how can mere H4027
Job 11: 6 of wisdom, for t **wisdom** has two sides. H9370
Job 19: 4 If it is t that I have gone astray, my error H597
Ps 31:23 The LORD preserves *those who* are t to him H573
Ps 33: 4 For the word of the LORD is **right and** t; H3838
Ps 78:20 **T**, he struck the rock, and water gushed H2176
Ps 105:19 till the word of the LORD **proved** him t. H7671
Ps 119:142 is everlasting and your law is t. H622
Ps 119:151 LORD, and all your commands are t. H622
Ps 119:160 All your words are t; all your righteous H622
Ps 144:15 Blessed is the people of whom *this* is t H3970
Pr 8: 7 My mouth speaks *what* is t, for my lips H622
Ecc 12:10 what he wrote was upright and t. H622
Isa 37:18 "It is t, LORD, that the Assyrian kings have H597
Isa 43: 9 so that others may hear and say, "It is t." H622
Isa 57:11 feared that *you have* **not** *been* t to me, H3941
Isa 63: 8 children *who will be* t to me"; and H4202+9213
Isa 65:16 in the land will do so by the one t God; H589
Isa 65:16 in the land will swear by the one t God. H589
Jer 10:10 But the LORD is the t God; he is the living H622
Jer 28: 9 by the LORD only if his prediction **comes** t." H995
Jer 37:14 "That's **not** t!" Jeremiah said. "I am not H9214
Jer 40:16 you are saying about Ishmael is **not** t." H9214
Jer 42: 5 "May the LORD be a t and faithful witness H622
Eze 16:45 You are a t daughter of your mother, who NDT
Eze 16:45 children; and you are a t sister of your sisters NDT
Eze 33:33 "When all this **comes** t—and it surely will— H995
Da 2:45 The dream is t and its interpretation is A10327
Da 3:14 said to them, "**Is it** t, Shadrach, A10190+10609
Da 8:26 mornings that has been given you is t, H622
Da 10: 1 Its message was t and it concerned a great H622
Am 2:11 Is this not t, people of Israel? H677
Am 7: 7 by a wall that had been built t **to plumb**, H643
Zec 7: 9 'Administer t justice; show mercy and H622
Zec 8:16 render t and sound judgment in your H622
Mal 2: 6 **T** instruction was in his mouth and nothing H622
Lk 1:20 which *will* **come** t at their appointed time." *G4444*
Lk 16:11 who will trust you with t riches? *G240*
Lk 24:34 saying, "**It is** t! The Lord has risen and *G3953*
Jn 1: 9 The t light that gives light to everyone was *G240*
Jn 4:18 What you have just said is *quite* t." *G239*
Jn 4:23 has now come when the t worshipers will *G240*
Jn 4:37 saying 'One sows and another reaps' is t. *G240*
Jn 5:31 I testify about myself, my testimony is not t. *G239*
Jn 5:32 I know that his testimony about me is t. *G239*
Jn 6:32 who gives you the t bread from heaven. *G240*
Jn 7:28 my own authority, but he who sent me is t. *G240*
Jn 8:16 my decisions are t, because I am not alone *G240*
Jn 8:17 that the testimony of two witnesses is t. *G239*
Jn 10:41 all that John said about this man was t." *G239*
Jn 15: 1 "I am the t vine, and my Father is the *G240*
Jn 17: 3 know you, the only t God, and Jesus Christ, *G240*
Jn 19:35 has given testimony, and his testimony is t. *G240*
Jn 21:24 We know that his testimony is t. *G239*
Ac 7: 1 asked Stephen, "Are these charges t?" *G4048*
Ac 10:34 "I now realize **how** t it is that God *G2093+237*
Ac 11:23 them all to remain t to the Lord with all *G4606*
Ac 14:22 encouraging them *to* **remain** t to the faith. *G1844*
Ac 17:11 every day to see if what Paul said was t. *G4048*
Ac 24: 9 asserting that these things were t. *G4048*
Ac 25:11 brought against me by these Jews are **not** *t*, AIT
Ac 26:25 "What I am saying is t and reasonable. *G237*
Ro 3: 4 Let God be t, and every human being a liar. *G239*
Ro 12: 1 to God—this is your t **and proper** worship. *G3358*
1Co 15:54 then the saying that is written *will* **come** t: *G1181*
2Co 7:14 But just as everything we said to you was t *G237*
2Co 7:14 you to Titus has proved to be t as well. *G237*
2Co 12:12 among you the marks *of* a *t* **apostle**, AIT
Eph 4:24 to be like God in t righteousness and *G237*
Php 1:15 **It is** t that some preach Christ out of envy *G2779*
Php 1:18 whether from false motives or t, Christ is *G237*
Php 4: 3 I ask you, my t companion, help *G1188*
Php 4: 8 whatever is t, whatever is noble, *G239*
Col 1: 5 already heard in the t message of the *G237*
1Th 1: 9 from idols to serve the living and t God, *G240*
1Ti 1: 2 To Timothy my t son in the faith: Grace *G1188*
1Ti 2: 7 a t and faithful teacher of the Gentiles *G4411*
1Ti 3:16 mystery *from which* t **godliness** *springs* is *G2354*
Titus 1: 4 To Titus, my t son in our common faith *G1188*
Titus 1:13 This saying is t. Therefore rebuke them *G239*
Heb 8: 2 the t tabernacle set up by the Lord *G240*
Heb 9:24 hands that was only a copy *of* the t *one*; *G240*
Heb 12: 8 legitimate, not *t* **sons and daughters** at all. AIT
1Pe 5:12 testifying that this is the t grace of God. *G239*
2Pe 2:10 This is **especially** *t* of those who follow the AIT
2Pe 2:22 Of them the proverbs are t: "A dog returns *G239*
1Jn 2: 8 is passing and the t light is already shining *G240*
1Jn 5:20 so that we may know him who is t. *G240*
1Jn 5:20 we are in him who is t by being in his Son *G240*

1Jn 5:20 He is the **t** God and eternal life. *G240*
3Jn 12 and you know that our testimony is **t**. *G239*
Rev 2:13 Yet *you* **remain t** to my name *G3195*
Rev 3: 7 are the words of him who is holy and **t**, *G240*
Rev 3:14 the faithful and **t** witness, the ruler of *G240*
Rev 6:10 holy and **t**, until you judge the *G240*
Rev 15: 3 Just and **t** are your ways, King of the *G240*
Rev 16: 7 Almighty, **t** and just are your judgments." *G240*
Rev 19: 2 **t** and just are his judgments. He has *G240*
Rev 19: 9 he added, "These are the **t** words of God." *G240*
Rev 19:11 whose rider is called Faithful and **T**. *G240*
Rev 21: 5 for these words are trustworthy and **t**." *G240*
Rev 22: 6 "These words are trustworthy and **t**. *G240*

TRULY (94) [TRUTH]

Ps 62: 1 **T** my soul finds rest in God; my salvation H421
Ps 62: 2 **T** he is my rock and my salvation; he is my H421
Ps 62: 6 **T** he is my rock and my salvation; he is my H421
Ps 116:16 **T** I am your servant, LORD; I serve you H3954
Pr 11:19 **T** the righteous attain life, but whoever H4026
Isa 10:20 them down but will **t** rely on the LORD, H928+622
Isa 45:15 **T** you are a God who has been hiding H434
Jer 28: 9 recognized as one **t** sent by the LORD H928+622
Mt 5:18 For **t** I tell you, until heaven and earth *G297*
Mt 5:26 **T** I tell you, you will not get out until you *G297*
Mt 6: 2 **T** I tell you, they have received their reward *G297*
Mt 6: 5 **T** I tell you, they have received their reward *G297*
Mt 6:16 **T** I tell you, they have received their reward *G297*
Mt 8:10 those following him, "**T** I tell you, I have *G297*
Mt 10:15 **T** I tell you, it will be more bearable for *G297*
Mt 10:23 **T** I tell you, you will not finish going *G297*
Mt 10:42 who is my disciple, **t** I tell you, that person *G297*
Mt 11:11 **T** I tell you, among those born of women *G297*
Mt 13:17 For **t** I tell you, many prophets and righteous *G297*
Mt 14:33 saying, "**T** you are the Son of God. *G242*
Mt 16:28 "**T** I tell you, some who are standing here *G297*
Mt 17:20 **T** I tell you, if you have faith as small as a *G297*
Mt 18: 3 "**T** I tell you, unless you change and *G297*
Mt 18:13 And if he finds it, **t** I tell you, he is happier *G297*
Mt 18:18 "**T** I tell you, whatever you bind on earth *G297*
Mt 18:19 **t** I tell you that if two of you on earth agree *G297*
Mt 19:23 said to his disciples, "**T** I tell you, it is hard *G297*
Mt 19:28 Jesus said to them, "**T** I tell you, at the *G297*
Mt 21:21 Jesus replied, "**T** I tell you, if you have faith *G297*
Mt 21:31 Jesus said to them, "**T** I tell you, the tax *G297*
Mt 23:36 **T** I tell you, all this will come on this *G297*
Mt 24: 2 "**T** I tell you, not one stone here will be left *G297*
Mt 24:34 **T** I tell you, this generation will certainly not *G297*
Mt 24:47 **T** I tell you, he will put him in charge of all *G297*
Mt 25:12 "But he replied, '**T** I tell you, I don't know *G297*
Mt 25:40 "The King will reply, '**T** I tell you, whatever *G297*
Mt 25:45 "He will reply, '**T** I tell you, whatever you *G297*
Mt 26:13 **T** I tell you, wherever this gospel is *G297*
Mt 26:21 he said, "**T** I tell you, one of you will betray *G297*
Mt 26:34 "**T** I tell you," Jesus answered, "this very *G297*
Mk 3:28 **T** I tell you, people can be forgiven all their *G297*
Mk 8:12 ask for a sign? **T** I tell you, no sign will *G297*
Mk 9: 1 he said to them, "**T** I tell you, some who *G297*
Mk 9:41 **T** I tell you, anyone who gives you a cup of *G297*
Mk 10:15 **T** I tell you, anyone who will not receive the *G297*
Mk 10:29 "**T** I tell you," Jesus replied, "no one who *G297*
Mk 11:23 "**T** I tell you, if anyone says to this mountain *G297*
Mk 12:43 Jesus said, "**T** I tell you, this poor widow *G297*
Mk 13:30 **T** I tell you, this generation will certainly not *G297*
Mk 14: 9 **T** I tell you, wherever the gospel is *G297*
Mk 14:18 he said, "**T** I tell you, one of you will betray *G297*
Mk 14:25 "**T** I tell you, I will not drink again from the *G297*
Mk 14:30 "**T** I tell you," Jesus answered, "today—yes *G297*
Lk 4:24 "**T** I tell you," he continued, "no prophet is *G297*
Lk 9:27 "**T** I tell you, some who are standing here *G242*
Lk 12:37 **T** I tell you, he will dress himself to serve *G297*
Lk 12:44 **T** I tell you, he will put him in charge of all *G242*
Lk 18:17 **T** I tell you, anyone who will not receive the *G297*
Lk 18:29 "**T** I tell you," Jesus said to them, "no one *G297*
Lk 21: 3 "**T** I tell you," he said, "this poor widow has *G242*
Lk 21:32 "**T** I tell you, this generation will certainly *G297*
Lk 23:43 Jesus answered him, "**T** I tell you, today *G297*
Jn 1:47 "Here **t** is an Israelite in whom there is no *G242*
Jn 1:51 He then added, "**Very t** I tell you, you *G297+297*
Jn 3: 3 Jesus replied, "**Very t** I tell you, no *G297+297*
Jn 3: 5 Jesus answered, "**Very t** I tell you, no *G297+297*
Jn 3:11 **Very t** I tell you, we speak of what we *G297+297*
Jn 5:19 "**Very t** I tell you, the Son can do *G297+297*
Jn 5:24 "**Very t** I tell you, whoever hears my *G297+297*
Jn 5:25 **Very t** I tell you, a time is coming and *G297+297*
Jn 6:26 Jesus answered, "**Very t** I tell you, you *G297+297*
Jn 6:32 said to them, "**Very t** I tell you, it is *G297+297*
Jn 6:47 **Very t** I tell you, the one who believes *G297+297*
Jn 6:53 said to them, "**Very t** I tell you, unless *G297+297*
Jn 8:34 Jesus replied, "**Very t** I tell you *G297+297*
Jn 8:51 **Very t** I tell you, whoever obeys my *G297+297*
Jn 8:58 "**Very t** I tell you," Jesus answered *G297+297*
Jn 10: 1 "**Very t** I tell you Pharisees, anyone *G297+297*
Jn 10: 7 said again, "**Very t** I tell you, I am *G297+297*
Jn 12:24 **Very t** I tell you, unless a kernel of *G297+297*
Jn 13:16 **Very t** I tell you, no servant is greater *G297+297*
Jn 13:20 **Very t** I tell you, whoever accepts *G297+297*
Jn 13:21 testified, "**Very t** I tell you, one of *G297+297*
Jn 13:38 **Very t** I tell you, before the rooster *G297+297*
Jn 14:12 **Very t** I tell you, whoever believes in *G297+297*
Jn 16: 7 But **very t** I tell you, it is for your good that *G237*
Jn 16:20 **Very t** I tell you, you will weep and *G297+297*
Jn 16:23 **Very t** I tell you, my Father will give *G297+297*
Jn 17:19 that they too may be **t** sanctified. *G1877+237*
Jn 21:18 **Very t** I tell you, when you were *G297+297*
Col 1: 6 you heard it and **t** understood God's *G1877+237*
1Ti 6:19 they may take hold of the life that is **t** life. *G3953*
Heb 7:26 Such a high priest **t** meets our need—one *G2779*
1Jn 2: 5 love for God is **t** made complete in them. *G242*

TRUMPET (66) [TRUMPETERS, TRUMPETS]

Ex 19:16 the mountain, and a very loud **t** blast. H8795
Ex 19:19 As the sound of the **t** grew louder and H8795
Ex 20:18 heard the **t** and saw the mountain in H8795
Lev 23:24 assembly commemorated with **t blasts**. H9558
Lev 25: 9 Then have the **t** sounded H8795+9558
Lev 25: 9 Atonement sound the **t** throughout your H8795
Nu 10: 5 When a **t blast** is sounded, the tribes H9558
Jos 6:16 when the priests sounded the **t** blast H8795
Jos 6:20 at the sound of the **t**, when the men H8795
Jdg 3:27 he blew a **t** in the hill country of Ephraim H8795
Jdg 6:34 Gideon, and he blew a **t**, summoning the H8795
1Sa 13: 3 Then Saul had the **t** blown throughout the H8795
2Sa 2:28 So Joab blew the **t**, and all the troops H8795
2Sa 18:16 Then Joab sounded the **t**, and the troops H8795
2Sa 20: 1 He sounded the **t** and shouted, "We have H8795
2Sa 20:22 So he sounded the **t**, and his men H8795
1Ki 1:34 Blow the **t** and shout, 'Long live King H8795
1Ki 1:39 they sounded the **t** and all the people H8795
1Ki 1:41 On hearing the sound of the **t**, Joab asked H8795
2Ki 9:13 Then they blew the **t** and shouted, "Jehu H8795
Ne 4:18 man who sounded the **t** stayed with me. H8795
Ne 4:20 Wherever you hear the sound of the **t**, join H8795
Job 39:24 it cannot stand still when the **t** sounds. H8795
Job 39:25 At the blast of the **t** it snorts, 'Aha!' It H8795
Ps 150: 3 Praise him with the sounding of the **t** H8795
Isa 18: 3 and when a **t** sounds, you will hear H8795
Isa 27:13 And in that day a great **t** will sound. Those H8795
Isa 58: 1 Raise your voice like a **t**. Declare to my H8795
Jer 4: 5 'Sound the **t** throughout the land H8795
Jer 4:19 For I have heard the sound of the **t**; I have H8795
Jer 4:21 standard and hear the sound of the **t**? H8795
Jer 6: 1 Sound the **t** in Tekoa! Raise the H8795
Jer 6:17 you and said, 'Listen to the sound of the **t**! H8795
Jer 42:14 see war or hear the **t** or be hungry for H8795
Jer 51:27 Blow the **t** among the nations H8795
Eze 7:14 " 'They have blown the **t**, they have made H9540
Eze 33: 3 land and blows the **t** to warn the people, H8795
Eze 33: 4 if anyone hears the **t** but does not heed H8795
Eze 33: 5 the sound of the **t** but did not heed the H8795
Eze 33: 6 does not blow the **t** to warn the people H8795
Hos 5: 8 "Sound the **t** in Gibeah, the horn in H8795
Hos 8: 1 "Put the **t** to your lips! An eagle is over H8795
Joel 2: 1 Blow the **t** in Zion; sound the alarm on my H8795
Joel 2:15 Blow the **t** in Zion, declare a holy fast, call H8795
Am 2: 2 amid war cries and the blast of the **t**. H8795
Am 3: 6 When a **t** sounds in a city, do not the H8795
Zep 1:16 a day of **t** and battle cry against the H8795
Zec 9:14 The Sovereign LORD will sound the **t**; he H8795
Mt 24:31 he will send his angels with a loud **t call**, *G4894*
1Co 14: 8 if the **t** does not sound a clear call *G4894*
1Co 15:52 in the twinkling of an eye, at the last **t**. *G4894*
1Co 15:52 For *the* **t** *will* **sound**, the dead will be *G4895*
1Th 4:16 the archangel and with the **t call** of God, *G4894*
Heb 12:19 to a **t** blast or to such a voice speaking *G4894*
Rev 1:10 I heard behind me a loud voice like a **t**, *G4894*
Rev 4: 1 first heard speaking to me like a **t** said, *G4894*
Rev 8: 7 The first angel **sounded** *his* **t**, and there *G4895*
Rev 8: 8 The second angel **sounded** *his* **t**, and *G4895*
Rev 8:10 The third angel **sounded** *his* **t**, and a *G4895*
Rev 8:12 The fourth angel **sounded** *his* **t**, and a *G4895*
Rev 8:13 because of the **t** blasts about to be *G4894*
Rev 9: 1 The fifth angel **sounded** *his* **t**, and I saw a *G4895*
Rev 9:13 The sixth angel **sounded** *his* **t**, and I *G4895*
Rev 9:14 It said to the sixth angel who had the **t** *G4894*
Rev 10: 7 the seventh angel is about to **sound** *his* **t**, *G4895*
Rev 11:15 The seventh angel **sounded** *his* **t**, and *G4895*

TRUMPETERS (4) [TRUMPET]

2Ki 11:14 officers and the **t** were beside the king H2956
2Ch 5:13 The **t** and musicians joined in unison to H2955
2Ch 23:13 officers and the **t** were beside the king H2956
Rev 18:22 pipers and **t**, will never be heard *G4896*

TRUMPETS (54) [TRUMPET]

Nu 10: 2 "Make two **t** *of* hammered silver, and use H2956
Nu 10: 7 the assembly, **blow** *the* **t**, but not with the H9546
Nu 10: 8 of Aaron, the priests, are to blow the **t**. H2956
Nu 10: 9 is oppressing you, sound a blast on the **t**. H2956
Nu 10:10 you are to sound the **t** over your burnt H2956
Nu 29: 1 It is a day for you to **sound the t**. H9558
Nu 31: 6 from the sanctuary and the **t** *for* signaling. H2956
Jos 6: 4 seven priests carry **t** *of* rams' horns in front H8795
Jos 6: 4 with the priests blowing the **t**. H8795
Jos 6: 5 them sound a long blast on the **t**, H7967+3413
Jos 6: 6 seven priests carry **t** in front of it." H8795+3413
Jos 6: 8 carrying the seven **t** before the LORD H8795+3413
Jos 6: 8 forward, blowing their **t**, and the ark of the H8795
Jos 6: 9 ahead of the priests who blew the **t**, H8795
Jos 6: 9 All this time the **t** were sounding. H8795
Jos 6:13 carrying the seven **t** went forward, H8795+3413
Jos 6:13 the ark of the LORD and blowing the **t**. H8795
Jos 6:13 ark of the LORD, while the **t** kept sounding. H8795
Jos 6:20 When the **t** sounded, the army shouted H8795
Jdg 7: 8 over the provisions and **t** *of* the others. H8795
Jdg 7:16 he placed **t** and empty jars in the hands H8795
Jdg 7:18 I and all who are with me blow our **t**, H8795
Jdg 7:19 They blew their **t** and broke the jars that H8795
Jdg 7:20 companies blew the **t** and smashed the H8795
Jdg 7:20 their right hands the **t** they were to blow, H8795
Jdg 7:22 When the three hundred **t** sounded, the H8795
2Sa 6:15 of the LORD with shouts and the sound of **t**. H8795
2Sa 15:10 "As soon as you hear the sound of the **t** H8795
2Ki 11:14 of the land were rejoicing and blowing **t**. H2956
2Ki 12:13 **t** or any other articles of gold or silver for H2956
1Ch 13: 8 with harps, lyres, timbrels, cymbals and **t**. H2956
1Ch 15:24 priests were to blow **t** before the ark of H2956
1Ch 15:28 with the sounding of rams' horns and **t** H2956
1Ch 16: 6 were to blow the **t** regularly before the ark H2956
1Ch 16:42 the sounding of the **t** and cymbals and H2956
2Ch 5:12 accompanied by 120 priests sounding **t**. H2956
2Ch 5:13 Accompanied by **t**, cymbals and other H2956
2Ch 7: 6 the priests **blew** *their* **t**, and all the H2955
2Ch 13:12 priests with their **t** will sound the battle H2956
2Ch 13:14 out to the LORD. The priests blew their **t** H2956
2Ch 15:14 with shouting and with **t** and horns. H2956
2Ch 20:28 of the LORD with harps and lyres and **t**. H2956
2Ch 23:13 of the land were rejoicing and blowing **t**, H2956
2Ch 29:26 instruments, and the priests with their **t**. H2956
2Ch 29:27 accompanied by **t** and the instruments of H2956
2Ch 29:28 the musicians played and the **t** sounded. H2956
Ezr 3:10 the priests in their vestments and with **t** H2956
Ne 12:35 as well as some priests with **t**, and also H2956
Ne 12:41 Zechariah and Hananiah with their **t**— H2956
Ps 47: 5 the LORD amid the sounding of **t**. H8795
Ps 98: 6 with **t** and the blast of the ram's horn H2956
Mt 6: 2 *do* not **announce** it **with t**, as the *G4895*
Rev 8: 2 and seven **t** were given to them. *G4894*
Rev 8: 6 who had the seven **t** prepared to sound *G4894*

TRUST (96) [ENTRUST, ENTRUSTED, TRUSTED, TRUSTEES, TRUSTFULLY, TRUSTING, TRUSTS, TRUSTWORTHY]

Ex 14:31 the LORD and **put** *their* **t** in him and in H586
Ex 19: 9 with you and *will* always **put** *their* **t** in you." H586
Nu 20:12 "Because *you did* not **t** in me enough to H586
Dt 1:32 you *did* not **t** in the LORD your God H586
Dt 9:23 *You did* not **t** him or obey him H586
Dt 28:52 fortified walls in which you **t** fall down. H1053
Jdg 11:20 *did* not **t** Israel to pass through his territory. H586
2Ki 17:14 who *did* not **t** in the LORD their God. H586
2Ki 18:30 *Do* not **let** Hezekiah **persuade** you **to t** in H1053
1Ch 9:22 to their positions of **t** by David and Samuel H575
Job 4:18 If God **places** no **t** in his servants, if he H586
Job 8:14 What they **t in** is fragile; what they rely on H4073
Job 15:15 If God **places** no **t** in his holy ones, if even H586
Job 31:24 "If I have put my **t** in gold or said to pure H4073
Job 39:12 *Can you* **t** it to haul in your grain and bring H586
Ps 4: 5 of the righteous and **t** in the LORD. H1053
Ps 9:10 Those who know your name **t** in you, for H1053
Ps 13: 5 But I **t** in your unfailing love; my heart H1053
Ps 20: 7 Some **t** in chariots and some in horses, but NDT
Ps 20: 7 we **t** in the name of the LORD our God. H2349
Ps 22: 4 In you our ancestors **put** *their* **t**; they H1053
Ps 22: 9 the womb; you **made** me **t** in you, even at H1053
Ps 24: 4 who *does* not **t** in an idol or swear H5951+5883
Ps 25: 1 In you, LORD my God, *I* **put** my **t**. H5951+5883
Ps 25: 2 *I* **t** in you; do not let me be put to shame H1053
Ps 31: 6 worthless idols; as for me, *I* **t** in the LORD. H1053
Ps 31:14 I **t** in you, LORD; I say, "You are my God H1053
Ps 33:21 hearts rejoice, for *we* **t** in his holy name. H1053
Ps 37: 3 **T** in the LORD and do good; dwell in the H1053
Ps 37: 5 to the LORD; **t** in him and he will do this: H1053
Ps 40: 3 fear the LORD and **put** *their* **t** in him. H1053
Ps 44: 6 *I* **put** no **t** in my bow, my sword does not H1053
Ps 49: 6 those *who* **t** in their wealth and boast of H1053
Ps 49:13 is the fate of those who **t** in themselves, H4073
Ps 52: 8 *I* **t** in God's unfailing love for ever and H1053
Ps 55:23 half their days. But as for me, *I* **t** in you. H1053
Ps 56: 3 When I am afraid, *I* **put** *my* **t** in you. H1053
Ps 56: 4 I praise—in God *I* **t** and am not afraid. H1053
Ps 56:11 in God *I* **t** and am not afraid. What can H1053
Ps 62: 8 **T** in him at all times, you people; pour H1053
Ps 62:10 *Do* not **t** in extortion or put vain hope in H1053
Ps 78: 7 would put their **t** in God and would not H4073
Ps 78:22 not believe in God or **t** in his deliverance. H1053
Ps 86: 4 servant, Lord, for *I* **put** my **t** in you. H5951+5883
Ps 91: 2 my fortress, my God, in whom *I* **t**. H1053
Ps 115: 8 like them, and so will all who **t** in them. H1053
Ps 115: 9 *All you* Israelites, **t** in the LORD—he is H1053
Ps 115:10 House of Aaron, **t** in the LORD—he is their H1053
Ps 115:11 *You* who fear him, **t** in the LORD—he is H1053
Ps 118: 8 refuge in the LORD than *to* **t** in humans. H1053
Ps 118: 9 refuge in the LORD than *to* **t** in princes. H1053
Ps 119:42 who taunts me, for *I* **t** in your word. H1053
Ps 119:66 good judgment, for *I* **t** your commands. H586
Ps 125: 1 Those *who* **t** in the LORD are like Mount H1053
Ps 135:18 like them, and so will all who **t** in them. H1053
Ps 143: 8 unfailing love, for *I have* **put** *my* **t** in you. H1053
Ps 146: 3 *Do* not **put** *your* **t** in princes, in human H1053
Pr 3: 5 **T** in the LORD with all your heart and lean H1053
Pr 11:28 *Those who* **t** in their riches will fall, but H1053
Pr 21:22 pull down the stronghold in which they **t**. H4440
Pr 22:19 So that your **t** may be in the LORD, I teach H4440
Pr 23: 4 to get rich; *do* **not t** your own cleverness. H2532
Pr 28:25 but *those who* **t** in the LORD will prosper. H1053

Pr 28:26 *Those who* **t** in themselves are fools, but H1053
Isa 8:17 *I will* **put** *my* **t** in him. H7747
Isa 12: 2 is my salvation; *I will* **t** and not be afraid. H1053
Isa 26: 3 are steadfast, because *they* **t** in you. H1053
Isa 26: 4 **T** in the LORD forever, for the LORD, H1053
Isa 30:15 in quietness and **t** is your strength, but H1057
Isa 31: 1 *who* **t** in the multitude of their chariots H1053
Isa 36:15 *Do* not **let** Hezekiah **persuade** you **to t** in H1053
Isa 42:17 But those *who* **t** in idols, who say to H1053
Isa 50:10 *Let* the one who walks in the dark, ... **t** H1053
Jer 2:37 the LORD has rejected *those* you **t**; you H4440
Jer 5:17 destroy the fortified cities in which you **t**. H1053
Jer 7: 4 *Do* not **t** in deceptive words and say, "This H1053
Jer 7:14 the temple you **t** in, the place I gave H1053
Jer 9: 4 your friends; *do* not **t** anyone in your clan. H1053
Jer 12: 6 *Do* not **t** them, though they speak well of H586
Jer 28:15 you *have* **persuaded** this nation **to t** in H1053
Jer 29:31 and *has* **persuaded** you **to t** in lies, H1053
Jer 39:18 your life, because *you* **t** in me, declares H1053
Jer 48: 7 Since you **t** in your deeds and riches, you H1053
Jer 49: 4 Ammon, you **t** in your riches and say H1053
Eze 33:13 then they **t** in their righteousness and H1053
Mic 7: 5 *Do* not **t** a neighbor; put no confidence in a H586
Na 1: 7 He cares for *those who* **t** in him, H2879
Zep 3: 2 *She does* not **t** in the LORD, she does not H1053
Zep 3:12 remnant of Israel *will* **t** in the name of the H2879
Lk 16:11 who *will* **t** you **with** true riches? *G4409*
Ac 14:23 to the Lord, in whom *they had* **put** *their* **t**. *G4409*
Ro 15:13 with all joy and peace as you **t** in him, *G4409*
1Co 4: 2 who have been **given a t** must prove *G3874*
1Co 9:17 simply discharging the **t** committed to me. *G3873*
2Co 13: 6 And *I* **t** that you will discover that we have *G1827*
Heb 2:13 again, "I *will* **put** *my* **t** in him." *G1639+4275*

TRUSTED (28) [TRUST]

1Sa 27:12 Achish **t** David and said to himself, "He has H586
2Ki 18: 5 Hezekiah **t** in the LORD, the God of Israel H1053
1Ch 5:20 their prayers, because *they* **t** in him. H1053
Job 12:20 the lips of **t advisers** and takes away the H586
Ps 5: 9 Not a *word* from their mouth *can* **be t** H3922
Ps 22: 4 their trust; *they* **t** and you delivered them. H1053
Ps 22: 5 in you *they* **t** and were not put to shame. H1053
Ps 26: 1 *I have* **t** in the LORD and have not faltered. H1053
Ps 41: 9 someone *I* **t**, one who shared my H1053
Ps 52: 7 his stronghold but **t** in his great wealth H1053
Ps 116:10 *I* **t** in the LORD when I said, "I am greatly H586
Pr 27: 6 Wounds from a friend *can* **be t**, but an H586
Isa 20: 5 Those who **t in** Cush and boasted in Egypt H4438
Isa 25: 9 this is our God; *we* **t** in him, and he saved H7747
Isa 25: 9 This is the LORD, *we* **t** in him; let us rejoice H7747
Isa 47:10 *You have* **t** in your wickedness and have H1053
Jer 13:25 have forgotten me and **t** in false gods. H1053
Jer 38:22 those **t friends** *of* yours. H408+8934
Jer 48:13 was ashamed when they **t** in Bethel. H4440
Eze 16:15 " 'But *you* **t** in your beauty and used your H1053
Da 3:28 *They* **t** in him and defied the king's A10665
Da 6:23 on him, because *he had* **t** in his God. A10041
Lk 11:22 in which the man **t** and divides up his *G4275*
Lk 16:10 "Whoever can be **t** with very little can also *G4412*
Lk 16:10 with very little can also be **t** with much, *G4412*
Ac 12:20 a **t personal servant** of the *G2093+3836+3131*
Titus 2:10 to show that they can be fully **t**, so *G4411*
Titus 3: 8 so that those *who have* **t** in God may be *G4409*

TRUSTEES (1) [TRUST]

Gal 4: 2 to guardians and **t** until the time set by *G3874*

TRUSTFULLY (1) [TRUST]

Pr 3:29 neighbor, who lives **t** near you. H4200+1055

TRUSTING (4) [TRUST]

Job 15:31 not deceive himself *by* **t** what is worthless, H586
Ps 112: 7 their hearts are steadfast, **t** in the LORD. H1053
Isa 2:22 **Stop t in** mere humans, who have H2532+4946
Jer 7: 8 you *are* **t** in deceptive words that are H1053

TRUSTS (16) [TRUST]

Ps 21: 7 For the king **t** in the LORD; through the H1053
Ps 22: 8 "*He* **t** in the LORD," they say, "let the LORD H1670
Ps 28: 7 my shield; my heart **t** in him, and he H1053
Ps 32:10 love surrounds the *one who* **t** in him. H1053
Ps 40: 4 is the one who **t** *in* the LORD, H8492+4440
Ps 84:12 Almighty, blessed is the one *who* **t** in you. H1053
Ps 86: 2 save your servant who **t** in you. H1053
Pr 16:20 blessed is the one *who* **t** in the LORD. H1053
Pr 29:25 but *whoever* **t** in the LORD is kept safe. H1053
Jer 17: 5 "Cursed is the one who **t** in man, who H1053
Jer 17: 7 "But blessed is the one who **t** in the LORD H1053
Hab 2:18 one who makes it **t** in his own creation; H1053
Mt 27:43 *He* **t** in God. Let God rescue him now if he *G4275*
Ro 4: 5 does not work but **t** God who justifies the *G4409*
1Co 13: 7 protects, always **t**, always hopes, always *G4409*
1Pe 2: 6 the *one who* **t** in him will never be *G4409*

TRUSTWORTHY (30) [TRUST]

Ex 18:21 fear God, **t** men who hate dishonest gain H622
2Sa 7:28 Your covenant is **t**, and you have promised H622
Ne 13:13 assistant, because they were considered **t**. H586
Ps 19: 7 The statutes of the LORD *are* **t**, making wise H586
Ps 111: 7 are faithful and just; all his precepts *are* **t**. H586
Ps 119:86 All your commands are **t**; help me, for I am H575
Ps 119:138 laid down are righteous; they are fully **t**. H575
Ps 145:13 The LORD *is* **t** in all he promises and faithful H586
Pr 8: 6 for I have **t things** to say; I open my H5592
Pr 11:13 a **t** *person* keeps a secret. H586+8120
Pr 12:22 but he delights in people who are **t**. H575
Pr 13:17 into trouble, but a **t** envoy brings healing. H574
Pr 25:13 at harvest time is a **t** messenger to the one H586
Da 2:45 dream is true and its interpretation *is* **t**." A10041
Da 6: 4 because he *was* **t** and neither corrupt A10041
Lk 16:11 if you have not been **t** in handling worldly *G4412*
Lk 16:12 you have not been **t** with someone else's *G4412*
Lk 19:17 you have been **t** in a very small matter *G4412*
Jn 8:26 But he who sent me is **t**, and what I have *G239*
1Co 7:25 as one who by the Lord's mercy is **t**. *G4412*
1Ti 1:12 that he considered me **t**, appointing me *G4412*
1Ti 1:15 Here is a **t** saying that deserves full *G4412*
1Ti 3: 1 Here is a **t** saying: Whoever aspires to be *G4412*
1Ti 3:11 talkers but temperate and **t** in everything. *G4412*
1Ti 4: 9 This is a **t** saying that deserves full *G4412*
2Ti 2:11 Here is a **t** saying: If we died with him, we *G4412*
Titus 1: 9 hold firmly to the **t** message as it has *G4412*
Titus 3: 8 This is a **t** saying. And I want you to stress *G4412*
Rev 21: 5 this down, for these words are **t** and true." *G4412*
Rev 22: 6 said to me, "These words are **t** and true. *G4412*

TRUTH (135) [TRUE, TRULY, TRUTHFUL, TRUTHFULLY, TRUTHFULNESS, TRUTHS]

Ge 42:16 be tested to see if you are telling the **t**. H622
1Ki 17:24 word of the LORD from your mouth is the **t**." H622
1Ki 22:16 me nothing but the **t** in the name of the H622
2Ch 18:15 me nothing but the **t** in the name of the H622
Job 42: 7 you have not spoken the **t** about me, H3922
Job 42: 8 You have not spoken the **t** about me, as H3922
Ps 15: 2 who speaks the **t** from their heart; H622
Ps 25: 5 Guide me in your **t** and teach me, for you H622
Ps 45: 4 ride forth victoriously in the cause of **t**, H622
Ps 52: 3 falsehood rather than speaking the **t**. H7406
Ps 119:43 Never take your word of **t** from my mouth H622
Ps 145:18 call on him, to all who call on him in **t**. H622
Pr 12:17 An honest witness tells the **t**, but a false H7406
Pr 22:21 you to be honest and to speak the **t**, H622
Pr 23:23 Buy the **t** and do not sell it—wisdom H622
Isa 45:19 the LORD, speak the **t**; I declare what is H7406
Isa 48: 1 of Israel—but not in **t** or righteousness— H622
Isa 59:14 at a distance; **t** has stumbled in the streets H622
Isa 59:15 **T** is nowhere to be found, and whoever H622
Jer 5: 1 person who deals honestly and seeks the **t**, H575
Jer 5: 3 do not your eyes look for **t**? You struck them H575
Jer 7:28 **T** has perished; it has vanished from their H575
Jer 9: 3 it is not by **t** that they triumph in the land. H575
Jer 9: 5 deceives friend, and no one speaks the **t**. H622
Jer 26:15 in **t** the LORD has sent me to you to H622
Da 8:12 and **t** was thrown to the ground. H622
Da 9:13 from our sins and giving attention to your **t**. H622
Da 10:21 tell you what is written in the Book of **T**. H622
Da 11: 2 I tell you the **t**: Three more kings will H622
Am 5:10 court and detest the one who tells the **t**. H9459
Zec 8:16 Speak the **t** to each other, and render true H622
Zec 8:19 Therefore love **t** and peace." H622
Mt 22:16 the way of God in accordance with the **t**. *G237*
Mk 5:33 trembling with fear, told him the whole **t**. *G237*
Mk 12:14 the way of God in accordance with the **t**. *G237*
Lk 20:21 the way of God in accordance with the **t**. *G237*
Jn 1:14 came from the Father, full of grace and **t**. *G237*
Jn 1:17 grace and **t** came through Jesus Christ. *G237*
Jn 3:21 whoever lives by the **t** comes into the light, *G237*
Jn 4:23 worship the Father in the Spirit and *in* **t**, *G237*
Jn 4:24 must worship in the Spirit and *in* **t**. *G237*
Jn 5:33 sent to John and he has testified *to* the **t**. *G237*
Jn 7:18 of the one who sent him is a man *of* **t**; *G239*
Jn 8:32 Then you will know the **t**, and the truth will *G237*
Jn 8:32 know the truth, and the **t** will set you free." *G237*
Jn 8:40 who has told you the **t** that I heard from *G237*
Jn 8:44 not holding to the **t**, for there is no truth in *G237*
Jn 8:44 holding to the truth, for there is no **t** in him. *G237*
Jn 8:45 Yet because I tell the **t**, you do not believe *G237*
Jn 8:46 If I am telling the **t**, why don't you believe *G237*
Jn 9:24 "Give **glory** to God **by telling the t**," they *G1518*
Jn 14: 6 "I am the way and the **t** and the life. *G237*
Jn 14:17 the Spirit *of* **t**. The world cannot accept him *G237*
Jn 15:26 the Spirit *of* **t** who goes out from the Father *G237*
Jn 16:13 when he, the Spirit *of* **t**, comes, he will *G237*
Jn 16:13 he will guide you into all the **t**. *G237*
Jn 17:17 Sanctify them by the **t**; your word is truth. *G237*
Jn 17:17 Sanctify them by the truth; your word is **t**. *G237*
Jn 18:23 if I spoke the **t**, why did you strike me?" *G2822*
Jn 18:37 came into the world is to testify *to* the **t**. *G237*
Jn 18:37 Everyone on the side of **t** listens to me." *G237*
Jn 18:38 "What is **t**?" retorted Pilate. With this he *G237*
Jn 19:35 He knows that he tells the **t**, and he *G239*
Ac 20:30 arise and **distort the t** in order to *G3281+1406*
Ac 21:24 will know there is **no** *t* in these reports about AIT
Ac 21:34 could not **get at** the **t** because of the *G1182+855*
Ac 24: 8 will be able *to* **learn the t** about all these *G2105*
Ac 28:25 Holy Spirit spoke **the t** to your ancestors *G2822*
Ro 1:18 who suppress the **t** by their wickedness, *G237*
Ro 1:25 They exchanged the **t** about God for a lie *G237*
Ro 2: 2 those who do such things is based on **t**. *G237*
Ro 2: 8 who reject the **t** and follow evil, *G237*
Ro 2:20 law the embodiment of knowledge and **t**— *G237*
Ro 9: 1 I speak the **t** in Christ—I am not lying, my *G237*
Ro 15: 8 a servant of the Jews on behalf of God's **t**, *G237*
1Co 5: 8 the unleavened bread of sincerity and **t**. *G237*
1Co 13: 6 not delight in evil but rejoices with the **t**. *G237*
2Co 4: 2 by setting forth the **t** plainly we commend *G237*
2Co 11:10 As surely as the **t** of Christ is in me, nobody *G237*
2Co 12: 6 because I would be speaking the **t**. *G237*
2Co 13: 8 For we cannot do anything against the **t**, but *G237*
2Co 13: 8 against the truth, but only for the **t**. *G237*
Gal 2: 5 so that the **t** of the gospel might be *G237*
Gal 2:14 not acting in line with the **t** of the gospel, *G237*
Gal 4:16 become your enemy *by* **telling** you **the t**? *G238*
Gal 5: 7 in on you to keep you from obeying the **t**? *G237*
Eph 1:13 in Christ when you heard the message *of* **t**, *G237*
Eph 4:15 **speaking the t** in love, we will grow *G238*
Eph 4:21 in accordance with the **t** that is in Jesus. *G237*
Eph 5: 9 in all goodness, righteousness and **t**) *G237*
Eph 6:14 with the belt of **t** buckled around your waist, *G237*
2Th 2:10 they refused to love the **t** and so be saved. *G237*
2Th 2:12 not believed the **t** but have delighted in *G237*
2Th 2:13 of the Spirit and through belief *in* the **t**. *G237*
1Ti 2: 4 saved and to come to a knowledge *of* the **t**. *G237*
1Ti 2: 7 I am telling the **t**, I am not lying— *G237*
1Ti 3:15 the pillar and foundation *of* the **t**. *G237*
1Ti 4: 3 by those who believe and who know the **t**. *G237*
1Ti 6: 5 have been robbed *of* the **t** and who think *G237*
2Ti 2:15 who correctly handles the word *of* **t**. *G237*
2Ti 2:18 who have departed from the **t**. They say that *G237*
2Ti 2:25 leading them to a knowledge *of* the **t**, *G237*
2Ti 3: 7 able to come to a knowledge *of* the **t**. *G237*
2Ti 3: 8 so also these teachers oppose the **t**. *G237*
2Ti 4: 4 ears away from the **t** and turn aside to *G237*
Titus 1: 1 their knowledge *of* the **t** that leads to *G237*
Titus 1:14 commands of those who reject the **t**. *G237*
Heb 10:26 we have received the knowledge *of* the **t**, *G237*
Jas 1:18 chose to give us birth through the word *of* **t**, *G237*
Jas 3:14 do not boast about it or deny the **t**. *G237*
Jas 5:19 wander from the **t** and someone should *G237*
1Pe 1:22 by obeying the **t** so that you have sincere *G237*
2Pe 1:12 firmly established in the **t** you now have. *G237*
2Pe 2: 2 will bring the way *of* **t** into disrepute. *G237*
1Jn 1: 6 darkness, we lie and do not live out the **t**. *G237*
1Jn 1: 8 we deceive ourselves and the **t** is not in us. *G237*
1Jn 2: 4 is a liar, and the **t** is not in that person. *G237*
1Jn 2: 8 command; its **t** is seen in him and in you *G239*
1Jn 2:20 the Holy One, and all of you know the **t**. NDT
1Jn 2:21 write to you because you do not know the **t**, *G237*
1Jn 2:21 it and because no lie comes from the **t**. *G237*
1Jn 3:18 words or speech but with actions and *in* **t**. *G237*
1Jn 3:19 that we belong to the **t** and how we set our *G237*
1Jn 4: 6 we recognize the Spirit *of* **t** and the spirit of *G237*
1Jn 5: 6 who testifies, because the Spirit is the **t**. *G237*
2Jn 1 whom I love in the **t**—and not I only, *G237*
2Jn 1 not I only, but also all who know the **t**— *G237*
2Jn 2 because of the **t**, which lives in us and will *G237*
2Jn 3 Father's Son, will be with us in **t** and love. *G237*
2Jn 4 find some of your children walking in the **t**, *G237*
3Jn 1 my dear friend Gaius, whom I love in the **t**. *G237*
3Jn 3 testified about your *faithfulness to* the **t**, *G237*
3Jn 4 hear that my children are walking in the **t**. *G237*
3Jn 8 so that we may work together *for* the **t**. *G237*
3Jn 12 of by everyone—and even by the **t** itself. *G237*

TRUTHFUL (6) [TRUTH]

Pr 12:19 **T** lips endure forever, but a lying tongue H622
Pr 14:25 A **t** witness saves lives, but a false witness H622
Pr 22:21 so that you bring back **t** reports to those you H622
Jer 4: 2 if in a **t**, just and righteous way you H622
Jn 3:33 has accepted it has certified that God is **t**. *G239*
2Co 6: 7 in **t** speech and in the power of God; with *G237*

TRUTHFULLY (1) [TRUTH]

Eph 4:25 off falsehood and speak **t** to your neighbor, *G237*

TRUTHFULNESS (1) [TRUTH]

Ro 3: 7 enhances God's **t** and so increases his *G237*

TRUTHS (3) [TRUTH]

1Ti 3: 9 keep hold of the **deep t** of the faith with a *G3696*
1Ti 4: 6 nourished *on* the **t** of the faith and of the *G3364*
Heb 5:12 you the **elementary t** of God's *G5122+3836+794*

TRY (22) [TRIED, TRIES, TRYING]

Nu 20:18 through here; if you **t**, we will march out NDT
Jdg 19:13 *let's t to* **reach** Gibeah or Ramah and spend AIT
1Sa 26:21 precious today, *I will* not *t to* **harm** you again. AIT
Job 17:10 all of you, **t again**! I will not find a H8740
Ps 26: 2 and **t** me, examine my heart and my H5814
Isa 7:13 not enough *to* **t** *the* **patience** *of* humans? H4206
Isa 7:13 *Will you* **t** *the* **patience** *of* my God also H4206
Isa 22: 4 *Do* not **t** to console me over the destruction H237
Jer 46:11 But you **t many** medicines in vain; there is H8049
Da 7:25 his holy people and **t** to change the set A10503
Da 11:26 the king's provisions *will t to* **destroy** him; AIT
Zec 12: 3 All *who t to* **move** it will injure themselves AIT
Mal 1: 8 *T* **offering** them to your governor AIT
Lk 12:58 **t hard** to be reconciled on the way *G1443+2238*
Lk 13:24 *will* **t** to enter and will not be able to. *G2426*
Lk 14:19 of oxen, and I'm on my way *to* **t** them **out**. *G1507*
Ac 15:10 why *do you t to* **test** God by putting on the AIT
1Co 10:33 even as I *t to* **please** everyone in every way AIT
1Co 14:12 **t** to excel in those that build up the church *G2426*
2Co 5:11 it is to fear the Lord, *we t to* **persuade** others. AIT
Titus 2: 9 in everything, *to* **t** to please them, not *G1639*
Heb 5:11 you because *you* **no longer t** to *G3821+1181*

TRYING (45) [TRY]
Nu 16:10 now *you are* **t to get** the priesthood H1335
Jdg 6:31 *Are you t to* **save** him? Whoever AIT
1Sa 20: 1 your father, that *he is* **t to kill** me?" H1335+5883
1Sa 22:23 wants to kill you *is* **t to kill** me too. H1335+5883
2Sa 14:16 of the man *who is t to* **cut off** both me and AIT
2Sa 16:11 own flesh and blood, *is* **t to kill** me. H1335+5883
2Sa 20:19 You *are* t to destroy a city that is a mother H1335
1Ki 19:10 one left, and now *they are* t to kill me too." H1335
1Ki 19:14 one left, and now *they are* t to kill me too." H1335
2Ki 5: 7 See how he *is* **t to pick a quarrel** with me!" H628
Ne 6: 9 They *were* all *t to* **frighten** us, thinking, AIT
Ne 6:14 the prophets have been *t to* **intimidate** me. AIT
Job 34: 9 'There is no profit in *t to* **please** God. AIT
Ps 54: 3 ruthless people *are* **t to kill** me H1335+5883
Ps 86:14 ruthless people are **t to kill** me H1335+5883
Isa 28: 9 "Who is it *he is t to* **teach**? To whom is he AIT
Da 2: 8 "I am certain that you *are t to* **gain** time AIT
Da 8:15 watching the vision and **t to** understand it, H1335
Mt 2:20 those *who were* **t to take** the child's *G2426*
Mt 22:18 "You hypocrites, why *are you t to* **trap** me? AIT
Mt 23:13 will you let those enter *who are* **t to**. *G1656*
Mk 12:15 "Why *are you t to* **trap** me?" he asked. AIT
Lk 19:47 among the people *were* t to kill him. *G2426*
Jn 5: 7 While *I am t to* **get in**, someone else goes AIT
Jn 7:19 keeps the law. Why *are you* t to kill me?" *G2426*
Jn 7:20 crowd answered. "Who *is* **t to** kill you?" *G2426*
Jn 7:25 "Isn't this the man *they are* **t to** kill? *G2426*
Ac 17:18 "What *is* this babbler **t** to say? *G2527*
Ac 18: 4 synagogue, *t to* **persuade** Jews and Greeks. AIT
Ac 21:31 *While they were* **t** to kill him, news *G2426*
Ro 11: 3 and *they are* **t to kill** me"? *G2426+3836+6034*
1Co 10:22 *Are we t to* **arouse** the Lord's **jealousy**? Are AIT
2Co 5:12 *We are* not *t to* **commend** ourselves to you AIT
2Co 10: 9 to seem to be **t to** frighten you with *G6055+323*
Gal 1: 7 into confusion and *are* t to pervert the *G2527*
Gal 1:10 *Am I* now *t to* **win** the **approval** of human AIT
Gal 1:10 Or *am I* **t** to please people? If I *G2426*
Gal 1:10 If *I were* still *t to* **please** people, I would not AIT
Gal 3: 3 *are you* now *t to* **finish** by means of the flesh? AIT
Gal 5: 4 *You* who *are t to be* **justified** by the law have AIT
Gal 6:12 means of the flesh *are t to* **compel** you to be AIT
1Th 2: 3 impure motives, nor are we **t to** trick you. *G1877*
1Th 2: 4 We are not **t to** please people but God *G6055*
1Pe 1:11 **t to find out** the time and circumstances to *G2236*
1Jn 2:26 you about those *who are t to* **lead** you **astray**. AIT

TRYPHENA (1)
Ro 16:12 Greet **T** and Tryphosa, those women who *G5586*

TRYPHOSA (1)
Ro 16:12 Greet Tryphena and **T**, those women who *G5589*

TUBAL (8)
Ge 10: 2 Javan, **T**, Meshek and Tiras. H9317
1Ch 1: 5 Javan, **T**, Meshek and Tiras. H9317
Isa 66:19 to **T** and Greece, and to the distant H9317
Eze 27:13 **T** and Meshek did business with you H9317
Eze 32:26 "Meshek and **T** are there, with all their H9317
Eze 38: 2 the chief prince of Meshek and **T** H9317
Eze 38: 3 Gog, chief prince of Meshek and **T**. H9317
Eze 39: 1 Gog, chief prince of Meshek and **T**. H9317

TUBAL-CAIN (1) [TUBAL-CAIN'S]
Ge 4:22 also had a son, **T**, who forged all kinds H9340

TUBAL-CAIN'S (1) [TUBAL-CAIN]
Ge 4:22 of bronze and iron. **T** sister was Naamah. H9340

TUBES (1)
Job 40:18 Its bones are **t** *of* bronze, its limbs like rods H692

TUCK (3) [TUCKED, TUCKING]
2Ki 4:29 "**T** your **cloak into** your **belt**, take H2520+5516
2Ki 9: 1 "**T** *your* **cloak into** your **belt**, take H2520+5516
Eze 5: 3 a few hairs and **t** them **away** in the folds H7443

TUCKED (1) [TUCK]
Ex 12:11 with your **cloak t into** your **belt**, H2520+5516

TUCKING (1) [TUCK]
1Ki 18:46 **t** his **cloak into** *his* **belt**, he ran H9113+5516

TUMBLES (1) [TUMBLING]
Ge 49:17 horse's heels so that its rider **t** backward. H5877

TUMBLEWEED (2) [WEED]
Ps 83:13 Make them like **t**, my God, like chaff H1650
Isa 17:13 like chaff on the hills, like **t** before a gale. H1650

TUMBLING (1) [TUMBLES]
Jdg 7:13 of barley bread **came t** into the Midianite H2200

TUMORS (8)
Dt 28:27 you with the boils of Egypt and with **t**, H6754
1Sa 5: 6 on them and afflicted them with **t**. H6754
1Sa 5: 9 both young and old, with an outbreak of **t**. H6754
1Sa 5:12 who did not die were afflicted with **t**, H6754
1Sa 6: 4 replied, "Five gold **t** and five gold rats H6754
1Sa 6: 5 Make models of the **t** and of the rats that H6754
1Sa 6:11 the gold rats and the models of the **t**. H3224
1Sa 6:17 These are the gold **t** the Philistines sent H3224

TUMULT (6)
1Sa 14:19 the **t** in the Philistine camp increased H2162
Isa 22: 2 of commotion, you city of **t** and revelry? H2159
Isa 22: 5 has a day of **t** and trampling and terror in H4539
Jer 25:31 The **t** will resound to the ends of the earth H8623
Eze 1:24 the Almighty, like the **t** of an army. H7754+2167
Am 2: 2 will go down in **great t** amid war cries H8623

TUNE (13) [TUNED]
Ps 9: T **To** *the t of* "The Death of the Son. AIT
Ps 22: T **To** *the t of* "The Doe of the Morning. AIT
Ps 45: T director of music. **To** *the t of* "Lilies." Of the AIT
Ps 56: T **To** *the t of* "A Dove on Distant Oaks. AIT
Ps 57: T To the **t** of "Do Not Destroy." Of NDT
Ps 58: T To the **t** of "Do Not Destroy." Of NDT
Ps 58: 5 that will not heed the **t** *of* the charmer H7754
Ps 59: T To the **t** of "Do Not Destroy." Of NDT
Ps 60: T **To** *the t of* "The Lily of the Covenant. AIT
Ps 69: T **To** *the t of* "Lilies." Of David AIT
Ps 75: T To the **t** of "Do Not Destroy." A NDT
Ps 80: T **To** *the t of* "The Lilies of the Covenant." AIT
1Co 14: 7 what **t** *is being* **played** unless *G884+2445+3068*

TUNED (1) [TUNE]
Job 30:31 My lyre is **t to** mourning, and my pipe to H4200

TUNIC (11) [TUNICS]
Ex 28: 4 a woven **t**, a turban and a sash. H4189
Ex 28:39 "Weave the **t** *of* fine linen and make the H4189
Ex 29: 5 the garments and dress Aaron with the **t**, H4189
Lev 8: 7 He put the **t** on Aaron, tied the sash H4189
Lev 16: 4 He is to put on the sacred linen **t**, with H4189
1Sa 17:38 Then Saul dressed David in his own **t**. H4496
1Sa 17:39 on his sword over the **t** and tried walking H4496
1Sa 18: 4 along with his **t**, and even his sword, H4496
2Sa 20: 8 Joab was wearing his **military t** H4496+4230
Ezr 9: 3 heard this, I tore my **t** and cloak, pulled H955
Ezr 9: 5 with my **t** and cloak torn, and H955

TUNICS (6) [TUNIC]
Ex 28:40 Make **t**, sashes and caps for Aaron's sons H4189
Ex 29: 8 Bring his sons and dress them in **t** H4189
Ex 39:27 they made **t** *of* fine linen—the work H4189
Ex 40:14 Bring his sons and dress them in **t**. H4189
Lev 8:13 sons forward, put **t** on them, tied sashes H4189
Lev 10: 5 still in their **t**, outside the camp, H4189

TUNNEL (2)
2Ki 20:20 the pool and the **t** by which he brought H9498
Job 28:10 *They* **t** through the rock; their eyes H1324+3284

TURBAN (15) [TURBANS]
Ex 28: 4 a woven tunic, a **t** and a sash. H5200
Ex 28:37 Fasten a blue cord to it to attach it to the **t** H5200
Ex 28:37 the turban; it is to be on the front of the **t**. H5200
Ex 28:39 of fine linen and make the **t** *of* fine linen. H5200
Ex 29: 6 Put the **t** on his head and attach the H5200
Ex 29: 6 attach the sacred emblem to the **t**. H5200
Ex 39:28 the **t** *of* fine linen, the linen caps and H5200
Ex 39:31 a blue cord to it to attach it to the **t**, H5200
Lev 8: 9 Then he placed the **t** on Aaron's head H5200
Lev 16: 4 sash around him and put on the linen **t**. H5200
Job 29:14 clothing; justice was my robe and my **t**. H7565
Eze 21:26 Take off the **t**, remove the crown. H5200
Eze 24:17 Keep your **t** fastened and your sandals on H6996
Zec 3: 5 "Put a clean **t** on his head." So H7565
Zec 3: 5 So they put a clean **t** on his head and H7565

TURBANS (4) [TURBAN]
Eze 23:15 their waists and flowing **t** on their heads; H3178
Eze 24:23 You will keep your **t** on your heads and H6996
Eze 44:18 are to wear linen **t** on their heads and H6996
Da 3:21 trousers, **t** and other clothes, were bound A10368

TURBULENT (1)
Ge 49: 4 **T** as the waters, you will no longer excel H7070

TURMOIL (8)
2Ch 15: 5 inhabitants of the lands were in great **t**. H4539
Job 3:17 There the wicked cease from **t**, and there H8075
Job 3:26 no quietness; I have no rest, but only **t**." H8075
Ps 65: 7 of their waves, and the **t** *of* the nations. H2162
Pr 15:16 fear of the LORD than great wealth with **t**. H4539
Isa 14: 3 your suffering and **t** and from the harsh H8075
Eze 22: 5 will mock you, you infamous city, full of **t**. H4539
Ac 17: 8 the city officials *were* **thrown into t**. *G5429*

TURN (326) [TURNED, TURNING, TURNS]
Ge 19: 2 "please **t aside** to your servant's house. H6073
Ge 24:49 tell me, so *I may know* which way *to* **t**." H7155
Ge 37:30 "The boy isn't there! Where *can* I **t** *now*?" H995
Ex 7:19 the reservoirs—and *they will* **t** to blood. H2118
Ex 14: 2 the Israelites *to* **t back** and encamp near H8740
Ex 23:27 *I will* **make** all your enemies **t** their H5989+448
Ex 32: 8 have been quick *to* **t away** from what I H6073
Ex 32:12 **T** from your fierce anger; relent and do H8740
Ex 34:22 Festival of Ingathering at the **t** *of* the year. H9543
Lev 19: 4 " '*Do* not **t** to idols or make metal gods H7155
Lev 19:29 the land *will* **t to prostitution** and be H2388
Lev 19:31 " '*Do* not **t** to mediums or seek out H7155
Lev 26:31 *I will* **t** your cities **into** ruins and lay waste H5989
Nu 6:26 the LORD **t** his face toward you and give H5951
Nu 14:25 **t back** tomorrow and set out toward the H7155
Nu 20:17 Highway and not **t** *to* the right or to the H5742
Nu 21:22 *We will* not **t aside** into any field or H5742
Nu 22:26 place where there was no room to **t**, H5742
Nu 25: 4 LORD's fierce anger *may* **t away** from Israel. H8740
Nu 32:15 If *you* **t away** from following him, he will H8740
Nu 34: 5 where it *will* **t**, join the Wadi of Egypt and H6015
Dt 1:40 **t around** and set out toward the desert H7155
Dt 2: 3 this hill country long enough; now **t** north. H7155
Dt 2:27 *we will* not **t aside** *to* the right or *to* the H6073
Dt 5:32 *do* not **t aside** *to* the right or to the left. H6073
Dt 7: 4 for *they will* **t** your children **away** from H6073
Dt 11:16 will be enticed *to* **t away** and worship H6073
Dt 11:28 LORD your God and **t** from the way that I H6073
Dt 13: 5 dreamer *tried* to **t** you from the way H5615
Dt 13:10 they tried to **t** you **away** from the LORD H5615
Dt 13:17 Then the LORD *will* **t** from his fierce anger H8740
Dt 17:11 *Do* not **t aside** from what they tell you, to H6073
Dt 17:20 fellow Israelites and **t** from the law to the H6073
Dt 23:14 anything indecent and **t** away from you. H8740
Dt 28:14 *Do* not **t aside** from any of the commands H6073
Dt 28:24 LORD *will* **t** the rain of your country **into** H5989
Dt 30:10 Book of the Law and **t** to the LORD your H8740
Dt 31:20 *they will* **t** to other gods and worship them H7155
Dt 31:29 utterly corrupt and *to* **t** from the way I have H6073
Jos 1: 7 *do* not **t** from it to the right or to the left H6073
Jos 7:12 *they* **t** their backs and run because they H7155
Jos 22:16 How could you **t away** from the LORD and H8740
Jos 22:23 our own altar to **t away** from the LORD and H8740
Jos 22:29 the LORD and **t away** from him today by H8740
Jos 23:12 "But if *you* **t away** and ally H8740+8740
Jos 24:20 *he will* **t** and bring disaster on you and H8740
Jdg 1: 3 We **in t** will go with you into yours." H1685
Jdg 7: 3 with fear *may* **t back** and leave Mount H8740
Jdg 7:22 **caused** the men throughout the camp **to t** H8492
Jdg 14:17 She **in t** explained the riddle to her H2256
Jdg 20:13 Now **t** those wicked men of Gibeah **over** to H5989
Ru 1:16 me to leave you or to **t back** from you. H8740
1Sa 6:12 *they did* not **t** *to* the right or *to* the left. H6073
1Sa 11:12 **T** these men **over** to us so that we may H5989
1Sa 12:20 this evil; yet *do* not **t away** from the LORD H6073
1Sa 12:21 *Do* not **t away** after useless idols. They can H6073
1Sa 22:17 "**T** and kill the priests of the LORD, because H6015
1Sa 22:18 "You **t** and strike down the priests. H6015
1Sa 29: 4 or *he will* **t against** us during H2118+4200+8477
1Sa 29: 7 Now **t back** and go in peace; do nothing to H8740
2Sa 1:22 the bow of Jonathan *did* not **t** back, the H6047
2Sa 2:21 "**T aside** to the right or to the left H5742
2Sa 14:19 no one can **t to the right** or to the left from H3554
2Sa 15:31 **t** Ahithophel's counsel **into foolishness**." H6118
2Sa 22:38 *I did* not **t back** till they were destroyed. H8740
2Sa 22:41 *You* **made** my enemies **t** their backs in H5989
1Ki 8:33 when *they* **t back** to you and give H8740
1Ki 8:35 to your name and **t** from their sin because H8740
1Ki 8:48 if *they* **t back** to you with all their H8740
1Ki 8:58 *May he* **t** our hearts to him, to walk in H5742
1Ki 9: 6 descendants **t away** from me and H8740+8740
1Ki 11: 2 because *they will* surely **t** your hearts after H5742
1Ki 12:15 this **t of events** was from the LORD H6016
1Ki 13:16 "I cannot **t back** and go with you H8740
1Ki 17: 3 **t** eastward and hide in the Kerith Ravine H7155
2Ki 3: 3 to commit; *he did* not **t away** from them. H6073
2Ki 10:29 he *did* not **t away** from the sins of H6073
2Ki 10:31 *He did* not **t away** from the sins of H6073
2Ki 13: 2 commit, and *he did* not **t away** from them. H6073
2Ki 13: 6 But *they did* not **t away** from the sins of the H6073
2Ki 13:11 of the LORD and *did* not **t away** from any of H6073
2Ki 14:24 of the LORD and *did* not **t away** from any of H6073
2Ki 15: 9 *He did* not **t away** from the sins of H6073
2Ki 15:18 entire reign *he did* not **t away** from the H6073
2Ki 15:24 *He did* not **t away** from the sins of H6073
2Ki 15:28 *He did* not **t away** from the sins of H6073
2Ki 17:13 prophets and seers: "**T** from your evil ways H8740
2Ki 17:22 Jeroboam and *did* not **t away** from them H6073
2Ki 23:26 the LORD *did* not **t away** from the heat of H8740
1Ch 12:23 Hebron to **t** Saul's kingdom **over** to him, H6015
2Ch 6:24 you and when *they* **t back** and give praise H8740
2Ch 6:26 to your name and **t** from their sin because H8740
2Ch 6:38 if *they* **t back** to you with all their H8740
2Ch 7:14 seek my face and **t** from their wicked H8740
2Ch 7:19 "But if you **t away** and forsake the decrees H8740
2Ch 10:15 people, for this **t of events** was from God H5813
2Ch 24:23 At the **t** *of* the year, the army of Aram H9543
2Ch 29:10 that his fierce anger *will* **t away** from us. H8740
2Ch 30: 8 that his fierce anger *will* **t away** from you. H8740
2Ch 30: 9 *He will* not **t** his face from you if you H6073
2Ch 35:22 *would* not **t away** from him H6015+7156
2Ch 36:13 his heart and *would* not **t** to the LORD, H8740
Ne 4: 4 **T** their insults **back** on their own heads H8740
Ne 4:12 "Wherever *you* **t**, they will attack us." H8740
Ne 9:26 them in order to **t** them **back** to you; H8740
Ne 9:29 them in order to **t** them **back** to your law, H8740
Ne 9:35 did not serve you or **t** from their evil ways. H8740
Est 2:12 a young woman's **t** came to go in to King H9366
Est 2:15 When the **t** came for Esther (the young H9366
Est 2:22 who **in t** reported it to the king H2256
Job 3: 4 That day—*may it* **t** to darkness; may God H2118
Job 5: 1 To which of the holy ones *will you* **t**? H7155
Job 6:18 Caravans **t aside** *from* their routes; they go H4369
Job 7: 4 and *I* **toss and t** until dawn. H8425+5611
Job 10: 8 *Will you* now **t** and destroy me? H6015
Job 10: 9 *Will you* now **t** me to dust **again**? H8740
Job 10:20 **T** away from me so I can have a H8883

Job 13: 9 Would it **t** out well if he examined you NDT
Job 13:16 this will **t** out for my deliverance, for NDT
Job 17:12 **t** night into day; in the face of the H8492
Job 20:14 his food *will* **t** sour in his stomach; it H2200
Job 30:21 *You* **t** on me ruthlessly; with the might of H2200
Job 33:17 to **t** them *from* wrongdoing and keep H6073
Job 33:30 to **t** them **back** from the pit, that the light H8740
Job 36:18 *do* not *let* a large bribe **t** you **aside**. H5742
Ps 4: 2 will you people **t** my glory **into** shame? H4200
Ps 6: 4 **T**, LORD, and deliver me; save me because H8740
Ps 6:10 *they will* **t back** and suddenly be put to H8740
Ps 9: 3 My enemies **t** back; they stumble and H8740
Ps 17: 6 **t** your **ear** to me and hear my prayer. H265
Ps 18:37 *I did* not **t back** till they were destroyed. H8740
Ps 18:40 *You* **made** my enemies **t** their backs in H5989
Ps 21:12 *You will* **make** them **t** their backs when H8883
Ps 22:27 the earth will remember and **t** to the LORD, H8740
Ps 25:16 **T** to me and be gracious to me, for I am H7155
Ps 27: 9 *do* not **t** your servant **away** in anger H5742
Ps 27:12 *Do* not **t** me **over** to the desire of my foes H5989
Ps 28: 1 are my Rock, *do* not **t** a **deaf ear** to me. H3087
Ps 31: 2 **T** your ear to me, come quickly to my H5742
Ps 34:14 **T** from evil and do good; seek peace and H6073
Ps 37: 8 Refrain from anger and **t** from wrath; do H6440
Ps 37:27 **T** from evil and do good; then you will H6073
Ps 40: 4 to *those who* **t aside** *to* false gods. H8454
Ps 49: 4 *I will* **t** my ear to a proverb; with the harp I H5742
Ps 51:13 so that sinners *will* **t back** to you. H8740
Ps 56: 9 Then my enemies *will* **t** back when I call H8740
Ps 64: 8 He will **t** their own tongues against them NDT
Ps 69:16 of your love; in your great mercy **t** to me. H7155
Ps 70: 3 *May* those who say to me, "Aha! Aha!" **t back** H8740
Ps 71: 2 deliver me; **t** your ear to me and save me. H5742
Ps 73:10 their people **t** to them and drink up H8740
Ps 74: 3 **T** your steps toward these everlasting H8123
Ps 78: 6 they **in t** would tell their children. H7756
Ps 80:18 Then *we will* not **t away** from you; revive H6047
Ps 81:14 their enemies and **t** my hand against their H8740
Ps 83: 1 *do* not **t** a **deaf ear**, do not stand H3087
Ps 85: 8 servants—but *let them* not **t** to folly. H8740
Ps 86:16 **T** to me and have mercy on me; show H7155
Ps 88: 2 come before you; **t** your ear to my cry. H5742
Ps 90: 3 *You* **t** people **back** to dust, saying, "Return H8740
Ps 102: 2 **T** your ear to me; when I call, answer me H5742
Ps 114: 5 Why, Jordan, *did you* **t** back? H6015
Ps 119:36 **T** my heart toward your statutes and not H5742
Ps 119:37 **T** my eyes **away** from worthless things H6296
Ps 119:51 unmercifully, but *I do* not **t** from your law. H5742
Ps 119:79 *May* those who fear you **t** to me, those H8740
Ps 119:132 **T** to me and have mercy on me, as you H7155
Ps 125: 5 But those *who* **t** *to* crooked ways the LORD H5742
Pr 1:26 I **in t** will laugh when disaster strikes you H1685
Pr 4: 5 not forget my words or **t** away from them. H5742
Pr 4:15 travel on it; **t** from it and go on your way. H8474
Pr 4:20 to what I say; **t** your ear to my words. H5742
Pr 4:27 *Do* not **t** *to* the right or the left; keep your H5742
Pr 5: 1 wisdom, **t** your ear to my words of insight H5742
Pr 5: 7 *do* not **t aside** from what I say. H6073
Pr 5:13 not obey my teachers or **t** my ear to my H5742
Pr 7:25 *Do* not *let* your heart **t** to her ways or stray H8474
Pr 17: 8 they think success will come at every **t**. H7155
Pr 22: 6 when they are old *they will* not **t** from it. H6073
Pr 22:17 attention and **t** your ear *to* the sayings of H5742
Pr 24:18 and **t** his wrath **away** from them. H8740
Pr 29: 8 stir up a city, but the wise **t away** anger. H8740
Pr 29:21 from youth will **t out** to be insolent. H344
SS 2:17 the shadows flee, **t**, my beloved, H6015
SS 6: 1 Which way *did* your beloved **t**, that we H7155
SS 6: 5 **T** your eyes from me; they overwhelm me H6015
Isa 1:25 *I will* **t** my hand against you; I will H8740
Isa 3:12 lead you astray; *they* **t** you *from* the path. H1182
Isa 6:10 with their hearts, and **t** and be healed." H8740
Isa 9:21 together they will **t** against Judah. NDT
Isa 14:23 "*I will* **t** her into a place for owls and into H8492
Isa 14:27 is stretched out, and who *can* **t** it **back**? H8740
Isa 17: 7 to their Maker and **t** their eyes to the Holy H8011
Isa 19:22 *They will* **t** to the LORD, and he will H8740
Isa 22: 4 Therefore I said, "**T** away from me; let me H9120
Isa 28: 6 strength to *those who* **t back** the battle at H8740
Isa 29:16 You **t** things **upside down**, as if the potter H2201
Isa 30:21 Whether *you* **t to the right** or to the left H3554
Isa 41:18 *I will* **t** the desert into pools of water, and H8492
Isa 42:15 *I will* **t** rivers into islands and dry up the H8492
Isa 42:16 *I will* **t** the darkness into light before them H8492
Isa 45:22 "**T** to me and be saved, all you ends of H7155
Isa 49:11 *I will* **t** all my mountains into roads, and H8492
Isa 50: 2 dry up the sea, *I* **t** rivers **into** a desert; their H8492
Isa 55: 7 *Let them* **t** to the LORD, and he will have H8740
Isa 56:11 they all **t** to their own way, they H7155
Isa 58: 7 not *to* **t away** from your own flesh and H6623
Jer 2:21 How then *did you* **t** against me **into** a H2200
Jer 3:19 'Father' and not **t away** from following me H8740
Jer 4:28 I have decided and *will* not **t back**. H8740
Jer 6: 8 I *will* **t away** from you and make your H3697
Jer 8: 5 Why does Jerusalem always **t away**? They H5412
Jer 12:10 *they will* **t** my pleasant field into a H5989
Jer 13:16 but *he will* **t** it to utter darkness and H8492
Jer 15:19 *Let* this people **t** to you, but you must not H8740
Jer 15:19 turn to you, but you *must* not **t** to them. H8740
Jer 17:13 *Those who* **t away** *from* you will be written H6073
Jer 18:11 So **t** from your evil ways, each one of you H8740
Jer 18:20 behalf to **t** your wrath **away** from them. H8740
Jer 21: 4 I *am about to* **t against** you the weapons H6015
Jer 23:20 of the LORD *will* not **t back** until he fully H8740
Jer 25: 5 They said, "**T** now, each of you, from your H8740
Jer 26: 3 will listen and each *will* **t** from their evil H8740
Jer 30:24 of the LORD *will* not **t back** until he fully H8740
Jer 31:13 *I will* **t** their mourning into gladness; I will H2200
Jer 31:39 to the hill of Gareb and then **t** to Goah. H6015
Jer 32:40 so that they *will* never **t away** from me. H6073
Jer 35:15 "Each of *you must* **t** from your wicked ways H8740
Jer 36: 3 *they will* each **t** from their wicked ways H8740
Jer 36: 7 the LORD and *will* each **t** from their wicked H8740
Jer 44: 5 they *did* not **t** from their wickedness or H8740
Jer 46:21 They too *will* **t** and flee together, they will H7155
Jer 47: 3 Parents *will* not **t to help** their children H7155
Jer 49: 8 **T** and flee, hide in deep caves, you who H7155
Jer 50: 5 the way to Zion and **t** their faces toward it. NDT
Eze 1: 9 *they did* not **t** as they moved. H6015
Eze 3:19 wicked person and *they do* not **t** from their H8740
Eze 4: 3 you and the city and **t** your face toward it. H3922
Eze 4: 7 **T** your face toward the siege of Jerusalem H3922
Eze 4: 8 ropes so that *you* cannot **t** from one side H2200
Eze 7:22 *I will* **t** my face away from the people, and H6015
Eze 10:11 the wheels *did* not **t about** as the H6015
Eze 13:22 the wicked not *to* **t** from their evil ways H8740
Eze 14: 6 **T** from your idols and renounce all your H8740
Eze 16:42 my jealous anger *will* **t away** from you; H6073
Eze 18:23 pleased when they **t** from their ways and H8740
Eze 18:28 have committed and **t away** from them, H8740
Eze 18:30 **T away** from all your offenses; then sin H8740
Eze 23:24 *I will* **t** you **over** to them for punishment H5989
Eze 25: 5 *I will* **t** Rabbah into a pasture for camels H5989
Eze 33: 9 the wicked person to **t** from their ways H8740
Eze 33:11 rather that they **t** from their ways and H8740
Eze 33:11 their ways and live. **T**! Turn from your evil H8740
Eze 33:11 **T** from your evil ways! Why will you H8740
Eze 33:14 but *they* then **t away** from their sin and H8740
Eze 35: 4 *I will* **t** your towns **into** ruins and you will H8492
Eze 38: 4 *I will* **t** you **around**, put hooks in your jaws H8740
Eze 38:12 loot and **t** my hand against the H8740
Eze 39: 2 *I will* **t** you **around** and drag you along. H8740
Da 9:16 **t away** your anger and your wrath from H8740
Da 11:18 Then *he will* **t** his attention to the H8740
Da 11:18 *will* **t** his insolence **back** on him. H8740
Da 11:19 *he will* **t back** toward the fortresses of his H8740
Da 11:30 Then *he will* **t back** and vent his fury H8740
Hos 2: 3 her like a desert, **t** her into a parched land H8883
Hos 3: 1 though they **t** to other gods and love the H7155
Hos 4:13 your daughters **t to prostitution** and your H2388
Hos 4:14 your daughters when *they* **t to prostitution**, H2388
Hos 7:14 new wine, but *they* **t away** from me. H6073
Hos 7:16 *They do* not **t** *to* the Most High; they are H8740
Hos 9:12 Woe to them when I **t away** from them! H6073
Hos 11: 7 My people are determined to **t from** me H5412
Joel 2:14 *He may* **t** and relent and leave behind a H8740
Am 1: 8 *I will* **t** my hand against Ekron, till the last H8740
Am 5: 7 There are those *who* **t** justice into H2200
Am 8: 3 "the songs in the temple *will* **t to wailing**. H3536
Am 8:10 *I will* **t** your religious festivals into H2200
Jnh 2: 8 worthless idols **t away from** God's love H6440
Jnh 3: 9 with compassion **t** from his fierce H8740
Mic 7:17 *they will* **t in fear** to the LORD our God and H7064
Hab 2:16 Now it is your **t**! Drink and let your NDT
Zep 1: 6 those *who* **t back** from following the LORD H6047
Zec 1: 4 '**T** from your evil ways and your evil H8740
Zec 13: 7 and *I will* **t** my hand against the little H8740
Mal 4: 6 *He will* **t** the hearts of the parents to their H8740
Mt 5:39 **t** to them the other cheek also. G5138
Mt 5:42 and *do* not **t away** from the one who wants G695
Mt 7: 6 their feet, and **t** and tear you to pieces. G5138
Mt 10:35 For I have come *to* **t** " 'a man against his G1495
Mt 13:15 understand with their hearts and **t**, and I G2188
Mt 15:36 to the disciples, and they in **t** to the people. NDT
Mt 24:10 many *will* **t away from the faith** and will G4997
Mk 4:12 otherwise they *might* **t** and be forgiven! G2188
Lk 1:17 *to* **t** the hearts of the parents to their G2188
Lk 6:29 on one cheek, **t** to them the other also. G4218
Lk 12:58 the judge **t** you **over** to the officer G4140
Jn 12:22 Andrew and Philip **in t** told Jesus. G2262
Jn 12:40 their hearts, nor **t**—and I would heal them G5138
Jn 16:20 You will grieve, but your grief *will* **t** to joy. G1181
Ac 3:19 and **t to** *God*, so that your sins may G2188
Ac 6: 3 *We will* **t** this responsibility **over to** them G2770
Ac 13: 8 them and tried to **t** the proconsul from the G1406
Ac 13:46 of eternal life, *we* now **t** to the Gentiles. G5138
Ac 14:15 telling you *to* **t** from these worthless G2188
Ac 20:21 must **t** to God **in repentance** and have G3567
Ac 21:21 among the Gentiles to **t away** from Moses, G686
Ac 26:18 open their eyes and **t** them from darkness G2188
Ac 26:20 should repent and **t** to God and G2188
Ac 28:27 understand with their hearts and **t**, and I G2188
Ro 11:26 *he will* **t** godlessness **away** from Jacob. G695
1Co 14:31 can all prophesy **in t** so that G2848+1651
1Co 15:23 But each in **t**: Christ, the firstfruits G2625+5413
2Co 7: 5 we were harassed at **every** *t*—conflicts on AIT
2Co 8:14 so that **in t** their plenty will supply what G2779
Php 1:19 has happened to me *will* **t out** for my G609
Col 4:16 that you **in t** read the letter from G2779
1Ti 6:20 **T away from** godless chatter and the G1762
2Ti 2:19 of the Lord *must* **t away** from wickedness G923
2Ti 4: 4 *They will* **t** their ears **away** from the truth G695
2Ti 4: 4 away from the truth and **t aside** to myths. G1762
Heb 12:25 if we **t away from** him who warns us from G695
Jas 3: 3 them obey us, *we can* **t** the whole animal. G3555
1Pe 3:11 *They must* **t from** evil and do good; they G1712
2Pe 2:21 it and then *to* **t** *their* **backs** on the sacred G5715
Rev 10: 9 *It will* **t** your stomach **sour**, but 'in your G4393
Rev 11: 6 they have power *to* **t** the waters into G5138

TURNED (263) [TURN]

Ge 9:23 faces were **t the other way** so that they H345
Ge 14: 7 Then *they* **t back** and went to En Mishpat H8740
Ge 18:22 The men **t** away and went toward Sodom H7155
Ge 41:13 And *things* **t out** exactly as he interpreted H2118
Ge 42:24 *He* **t away** from them and began to weep H6015
Ge 42:28 sank and *they t* to each other **trembling** and AIT
Ex 4: 4 snake and *it* **t** *back* **into** a staff in H2118+4200
Ex 7:23 he **t** and went into his palace H7155
Ex 10: 6 Then Moses **t** and left Pharaoh. H7155
Ex 14:21 a strong east wind and **t** it into dry land. H8492
Ex 32:15 Moses **t** and went down the mountain H7155
Lev 13: 3 hair in the sore *has* **t** white and the sore H2200
Lev 13: 4 deep and the hair in it *has* not **t** white, H2200
Lev 13:10 in the skin that *has* **t** the hair white and if H2200
Lev 13:13 Since it *has* all **t** white, they are H2200
Lev 13:17 if the sores *have* **t** white, the priest H2200
Lev 13:20 skin deep and the hair in it *has* **t** white, H2200
Lev 13:25 if the hair in it *has* **t** white, and it H2200
Nu 12:10 Aaron **t** toward her and saw that she had H7155
Nu 14:43 Because *you have* **t away** from the LORD H8740
Nu 16:42 Moses and Aaron and **t** toward the tent of H7155
Nu 20:21 their territory, Israel **t** away from them. H5742
Nu 21:33 Then *they* **t** and went up along the road H7155
Nu 22:23 in his hand, it **t** off the road into a field. H5742
Nu 22:33 donkey saw me and **t away** from me these H5742
Nu 22:33 If *it had* not **t away**, I would certainly have H5742
Nu 24: 1 **t** his face toward the wilderness. H8883
Nu 25:11 *has* **t** my anger **away** from the Israelites. H8740
Nu 33: 7 They left Etham, **t back** to Pi Hahiroth, to H8740
Dt 1:45 weeping and **t** a **deaf ear** to you. H4202+263
Dt 2: 1 Then *we* **t back** and set out toward the H7155
Dt 2: 8 *We* **t** from the Arabah road, which comes H7155
Dt 3: 1 Next *we* **t** and went up along the road H7155
Dt 9:12 *They have* **t away** quickly from what I H6073
Dt 9:15 So *I* **t** and went down from the mountain H7155
Dt 9:16 *You had* **t aside** quickly from the way that H6073
Dt 23: 5 not listen to Balaam but **t** the curse into a H2200
Dt 26:13 *I have* not **t aside** from your commands H6296
Jos 7:26 Then the LORD **t** from his fierce anger H8740
Jos 8:20 the wilderness *had* **t back** against their H2200
Jos 8:21 *they* **t around** and attacked the men of Ai. H8740
Jos 10:38 Israel with him **t around** and attacked H8740
Jos 11:10 that time Joshua **t back** and captured H8740
Jos 15: 7 the Valley of Achor and **t** north to Gilgal, H7155
Jos 15:11 slope of Ekron, **t** toward Shikkeron, passed H9305
Jos 18:14 the south the boundary **t** south along the H9305
Jos 19:12 *It* **t** east from Sarid toward the sunrise to H8740
Jos 19:13 came out at Rimmon and **t** *toward* Neah. H9305
Jos 19:27 *It* then **t** east *toward* Beth Dagon, touched H8740
Jos 19:29 boundary then **t back** *toward* Ramah and H8740
Jos 19:29 **t** *toward* Hosah and came out at the H8740
Jdg 2:17 *They* quickly **t** from the ways of their H6073
Jdg 6:14 The LORD **t** to him and said, "Go in the H7155
Jdg 14: 8 *he* **t aside** to look at the lion's carcass H6073
Jdg 18: 3 so *they* **t in** there and asked him H6073
Jdg 18:15 So *they* **t in** there and went to the house of H6073
Jdg 18:21 in front of them, *they* **t away** and left. H7155
Jdg 18:23 the Danites **t** and said to Micah H6015+7156
Jdg 18:26 him, **t around** and went back home. H7155
Jdg 20:40 the Benjamites **t** and saw the whole city H7155
Jdg 20:45 As *they* **t** and fled toward the wilderness to H7155
Jdg 20:47 But six hundred of them **t** and fled into the H7155
Ru 1:13 because the LORD's hand *has* **t** against me!" H3655
Ru 2: 3 **As it t out**, she was working in a H7936+5247
Ru 3: 8 startled the man; *he* **t**—and there was a H4369
1Sa 7: 2 all the people of Israel **t** back to the LORD. H5630
1Sa 8: 3 *They* **t aside** after dishonest gain and H5742
1Sa 9:20 And **to** whom is all the desire of Israel **t**, if H4200
1Sa 10: 9 As Saul **t** to leave Samuel, God H7155+8900
1Sa 13:17 One **t** toward Ophrah in the vicinity of H7155
1Sa 14:47 Wherever *he* **t**, he inflicted punishment H7155
1Sa 15:11 because he *has* **t** away from me and has H8740
1Sa 15:12 own honor and *has* **t** and gone on down H6015
1Sa 15:27 As Samuel **t** to leave, Saul caught hold of H6015
1Sa 17:30 *He* then **t** away to someone else and H6015
1Sa 17:35 When *it* **t** on me, I seized it by its hair H7756
1Sa 17:51 that their hero was dead, *they* **t and ran**. H5674
1Sa 22:18 So Doeg the Edomite **t** and struck them H6015
1Sa 25:12 David's men **t around** and went back H2200
2Sa 1: 7 When *he* **t** around and saw me, he called H7155
2Sa 19: 2 that day *was* **t into** mourning, H2118+4200
2Sa 22:23 *I have* not **t away** from his decrees. H6073
1Ki 6:34 each having two leaves that **t in sockets**. H1664
1Ki 8:14 the king **t around** and blessed them. H6015
1Ki 11: 4 his wives **t** his heart after other gods H5742
1Ki 11: 9 his heart *had* **t away** from the LORD, H5742
1Ki 14: 9 aroused my anger and **t** your back on me. H8959
1Ki 22:32 So *they* **t** to attack him, but when H6073
2Ki 2:24 *He* **t** around, looked at them and called H7155
2Ki 4:35 Elisha **t away** and walked back and forth H8740
2Ki 5:12 So *he* **t** and went off in a rage. H7155
2Ki 9:23 Joram **t about** and fled, calling out H2200+3338
2Ki 12:17 Then he **t** to attack Jerusalem H8492+7156
2Ki 19:25 that you *have* **t** fortified cities **into** piles of H8615

T

2Ki 20: 2 Hezekiah t his face to the wall and prayed H6015
2Ki 23:25 a king like him who t to the LORD as he did H8740
2Ki 24: 1 But then he t against Nebuchadnezzar H8740
1Ch 10:14 to death and t the kingdom over to David H6015
1Ch 21:20 threshing wheat, he t and saw the angel H8740
2Ch 6: 3 the king t around and blessed them. H6015
2Ch 11: 4 of the LORD and t back from marching H8740
2Ch 12:12 the LORD's anger t from him, and he was H8740
2Ch 13:14 Judah t and saw that they were being H7155
2Ch 15: 4 But in their distress they t to the LORD, the H8740
2Ch 18:31 So they t to attack him, but Jehoshaphat H6015
2Ch 19: 4 of Ephraim and t them back to the LORD, H8740
2Ch 20:10 so they t away from them and did not H6073
2Ch 25:27 time that Amaziah t away from following H6073
2Ch 29: 6 They t their faces away from the LORD's H6015
2Ch 29: 6 dwelling place and t their backs on him. H5989
Ezr 10:14 our God in this matter is t away from us." H8740
Ne 2:15 I t back and reentered through the Valley H8740
Ne 9:26 they t their backs on your law. H8959+339
Ne 9:29 Stubbornly they t their backs on you H5989
Ne 13: 2 however, t the curse into a blessing.) H2200
Est 9: 1 now the tables were t and the Jews H2200
Est 9:22 when their sorrow was t into joy and their H2200
Job 16:11 God has t me over to the ungodly and H6037
Job 19:19 detest me; those I love have t against me. H2200
Job 31: 7 if my steps have t from the path, if my H5742
Job 34:27 because they t from following him and H6073
Ps 14: 3 All have t away, all have become corrupt H6073
Ps 18:22 I have not t away from his decrees. H6073
Ps 22:14 My heart has t to wax; it has melted H2118
Ps 30:11 You t my wailing into dancing; you H2200
Ps 35: 4 may those who plot my ruin be t back in H6047
Ps 40: 1 the LORD; he t to me and heard my cry. H5742
Ps 40:14 may all who desire my ruin be t back in H6047
Ps 41: 9 shared my bread, has t against me. H1540+6811
Ps 44:18 Our hearts had not t back; our feet had H6047
Ps 53: 3 Everyone has t away, all have become H6047
Ps 66: 6 He t the sea into dry land, they passed H2200
Ps 70: 2 may all who desire my ruin be t back in H6047
Ps 78: 9 with bows, t back on the day of battle; H2200
Ps 78:30 But before they t from what they craved H2319
Ps 78:34 seek him; they eagerly t to him again. H8740
Ps 78:44 He t their river into blood; they could not H2200
Ps 85: 3 all your wrath and t from your fierce anger H8740
Ps 89:43 you have t back the edge of his sword H8740
Ps 105:25 whose hearts he t to hate his people, to H2200
Ps 105:29 He t their waters into blood, causing their H2200
Ps 105:32 He t their rain into hail, with lightning H5989
Ps 107:33 He t rivers into a desert, flowing springs H8492
Ps 107:35 He t the desert into pools of water and H8492
Ps 114: 3 sea looked and fled, the Jordan t back; H6015
Ps 114: 8 who t the rock into a pool, the hard rock H2200
Ps 116: 2 Because he t his ear to me, I will call on H5742
Ps 119:59 my ways and have t my steps to your H8740
Ps 119:157 but I have not t from your statutes. H5742
Ps 129: 5 May all who hate Zion be t back in shame H6047
Ecc 2:12 Then I t my thoughts to consider wisdom H7155
Ecc 7:25 So I t my mind to understand, to H6015
Isa 1: 4 One of Israel and t their backs on him. H2319
Isa 5:25 his anger is not t away, his hand is H8740
Isa 7:25 places where cattle are t loose and H5448
Isa 9:12 his anger is not t away, his hand is H8740
Isa 9:17 his anger is not t away, his hand is H8740
Isa 9:21 his anger is not t away, his hand is H8740
Isa 10: 4 his anger is not t away, his hand is H8740
Isa 12: 1 your anger has t away and you have H8740
Isa 23:13 its fortresses bare and t it into a ruin. H8492
Isa 29:17 will not Lebanon be t into a fertile field H8740
Isa 34: 9 Edom's streams will be t into pitch, her H2200
Isa 37:26 that you have t fortified cities into piles of H8615
Isa 38: 2 Hezekiah t his face to the wall and prayed H6015
Isa 42:17 our gods,' will be t back in utter shame. H6047
Isa 50: 5 not been rebellious, I have not t away. H6047
Isa 53: 6 each of us has t to our own way H7155
Isa 59: 8 They have t them into crooked roads; no H6835
Isa 63:10 So he t and became their enemy and he H2200
Jer 2:27 They have t their backs to me and not H7155
Jer 4: 8 anger of the LORD has not t away from us. H8740
Jer 5:23 they have t aside and gone away. H6073
Jer 6:12 Their houses will be t over to others H6015
Jer 8: 5 Why then have these people t away? Why H8740
Jer 23:22 my people and would have t them from H8740
Jer 30: 6 in labor, every face t deathly pale? H2200
Jer 32:33 They t their backs to me and not their H7155
Jer 34:16 But now you have t around and profaned H8740
Jer 39:14 They t him over to Gedaliah son of H5989
Jer 40: 5 before Jeremiah t to go, Nebuzaradan H8740
Jer 41:14 captive at Mizpah t and went over to H6015
Jer 49:24 she has t to flee and panic has gripped H7155
La 1:13 spread a net for my feet and t me back. H8740
La 3: 3 he has t his hand against me again and H2200
La 4: 6 in a moment without a hand t to help her. H2565
La 5: 2 inheritance has been t over to strangers, H2200
La 5:15 our hearts; our dancing has t to mourning. H2200
Eze 6: 9 which have t away from me, and H6073
Eze 17: 6 Its branches t toward him, but its roots H7155
Eze 21:16 then to the left, wherever your blade is t. H3585
Eze 23:17 by them, she t away from them in disgust. H3697
Eze 23:18 I t away from her in disgust, just as I H3697
Eze 23:18 just as I had t away from her sister. H5936
Eze 23:22 those you t away from in disgust, and I H5936
Eze 23:28 to those you t away from in disgust. H5936
Eze 23:35 have forgotten me and t your back on me, H8959
Eze 42:19 Then he t to the west side and measured H6015
Da 2: 5 your houses t into piles of rubble. A10682
Da 2:29 your mind t to things to come, and A10513
Da 3:29 their houses be t into piles of rubble A10702
Da 5: 6 His face t pale and he was so frightened A10731
Da 7:28 my face t pale, but I kept the A10731
Da 9: 3 So I t to the Lord God and pleaded H5989+7156
Da 9: 5 we have t away from your commands and H6073
Da 9:11 has transgressed your law and t away, H6073
Da 10: 8 my face t deathly pale and I was helpless. H2200
Hos 5: 3 you have now t to prostitution; Israel H2388
Hos 5:13 then Ephraim t to Assyria, and sent H2143
Hos 7: 8 nations; Ephraim is a flat loaf not t over. H2200
Hos 14: 4 for my anger has t away from them. H8740
Joel 2:31 The sun will be t to darkness and the H2200
Am 6:12 But you have t justice into poison and the H2200
Jnh 3:10 they did and how they t from their evil H8740
Zep 3:15 punishment, he has t back your enemy. H7155
Hag 1: 9 expected much, but see, it t out to be little. NDT
Zec 7:11 stubbornly they t their backs and covered H5989
Zec 8:10 since I had t everyone against their H8938
Mal 1: 3 and I have t his hill country into a H8492
Mal 2: 6 uprightness, and t many from sin. H8740
Mal 2: 8 But you have t from the way and by your H6073
Mal 3: 7 your ancestors you have t away from my H6073
Mt 9:22 Jesus t and saw her. "Take heart G5138
Mt 16:23 Jesus t and said to Peter, "Get behind me, G5138
Mk 5:30 He t around in the crowd and asked G2188
Mk 8:33 But when Jesus t and looked at his G2188
Lk 7:44 Then he t toward the woman and said to G5138
Lk 9:55 But Jesus t and rebuked them. G5138
Lk 10:23 Then he t to his disciples and said G5138
Lk 22:32 And when you have t back, strengthen G2188
Lk 22:61 The Lord t and looked straight at Peter G5138
Lk 23:28 Jesus t and said to them, "Daughters of G5138
Jn 2: 9 the water that had been t into wine. G1181
Jn 4:46 where he had t the water into wine. G4472
Jn 6:66 many of his disciples t back and no longer G599
Jn 9:17 Then they t again to the blind man G3306
Jn 13:18 bread has t against me. G2048+3836+4761+899
Jn 20:14 she t around and saw Jesus standing G5138
Jn 20:16 She t toward him and cried out in G5138
Jn 21:20 Peter t and saw that the disciple whom G2188
Ac 2:20 The sun will be t to darkness and the G3570
Ac 7:39 him and in their hearts t back to Egypt. G5138
Ac 7:42 But God t away from them and gave them G5138
Ac 9:35 Sharon saw him and t to the Lord. G2188
Ac 11:21 of people believed and t to the Lord. G2188
Ac 16:18 so annoyed that he t around and said to G2188
Ac 18:17 Then the crowd there t on Sosthenes the G2138
Ro 3:12 All have t away, they have together G1712
1Th 1: 9 They tell how you t to God from idols to G2188
1Th 3: 4 And it t out that way, as you G1181
1Ti 1: 6 from these and have t to meaningless talk G1762
1Ti 5:15 Some have in fact already t away to follow G1762
Heb 8: 9 covenant, and I t away from them, declares G288
Heb 11:34 whose weakness was t to strength; and G1540
Rev 1:12 I t around to see the voice that was G2188
Rev 1:12 And when I t I saw seven golden G2188
Rev 6:12 The sun t black like sackcloth made of G1181
Rev 6:12 of goat hair, the whole moon t blood red, G1181
Rev 8: 8 A third of the sea t into blood, G1181
Rev 8:11 A third of the waters t bitter, and G1181+1650
Rev 8:12 of the stars, so that a third of them t dark. G5029
Rev 10:10 when I had eaten it, my stomach t sour. G4393
Rev 16: 3 and it t into blood like that of a dead G1181

TURNING (33) [TURN]

Dt 31:18 of all their wickedness in t to other gods. H7155
Jos 22:18 And are you now t away from the LORD? H8740
Jos 23: 6 without t aside to the right or to the left. H6073
Jdg 8:20 T to Jether, his oldest son, he said, "Kill NDT
Jdg 11: 8 "Nevertheless, we are t to you now; come H8740
2Sa 2:19 t neither to the right nor to the left as he H5742
2Sa 22:22 LORD; I am not guilty of t from my God. H4946
1Ki 18:37 that you are t their hearts back again." H6015
2Ki 21:13 wiping it and t it upside down. H2200
2Ki 22: 2 not t aside to the right or to the left. H6073
2Ch 34: 2 not t aside to the right or to the left. H6073
Job 23:11 I have kept to his way without t aside. H5742
Job 36:21 Beware of t to evil, which you seem to H7155
Ps 18:21 LORD; I am not guilty of t from my God. H4946
Pr 2: 2 t your ear to wisdom and applying your H7992
Pr 13:14 t a person from the snares of death. H6073
Pr 13:19 to the soul, but fools detest t from evil. H6073
Pr 14:27 t a person from the snares of death. H6073
Isa 59:13 the LORD, t our backs on our God, inciting H6047
Eze 1:12 they would go, without t as they went. H6015
Eze 10:11 the head faced, without t as they went. H6015
Eze 29:16 a reminder of their sin in t to her for help. H7155
Da 9:13 of the LORD our God by t from our sins H8740
Hos 7:11 now calling to Egypt, now t to Assyria. H2143
Lk 7: 9 and t to the crowd following him G5138
Lk 14:25 with Jesus, and t to them he said: G5138
Jn 1:38 T around, Jesus saw them following and G5138
Jn 2:16 Stop t my Father's house into a market!" G4472
Ac 3:26 bless you by t each of you from your wicked G695
Ac 9:40 T toward the dead woman, he said G2188
Ac 15:19 difficult for the Gentiles who are t to God. G2188
Gal 1: 6 of Christ and are t to a different gospel— AIT
Gal 4: 9 how is it that you are t back to those weak G2188

TURNS (36) [TURN]

Lev 13:16 If the raw flesh changes and t white, they H2200
Lev 20: 6 against anyone who t to mediums and H7155
Dt 29:18 whose heart t away from the LORD our H7155
Dt 30:17 But if your heart t away and you are not H7155
2Sa 22:29 the LORD t my darkness into light. H5585
2Ki 11: 6 who take t guarding the temple H5005
Job 23: 9 not see him; when he t to the south, H6493
Ps 18:28 burning; my God t my darkness into light. H5585
Pr 15: 1 A gentle answer t away wrath, but a harsh H8740
Pr 26:14 As a door t on its hinges, so a sluggard H6015
Pr 26:14 on its hinges, so a sluggard t on his bed. NDT
Pr 28: 9 If anyone t a deaf ear to my instruction H6073
Ecc 1: 6 blows to the south and t to the north; H6015
Ecc 7: 7 Extortion t a wise person into a fool, and H2147
Isa 24:11 wine; all joy t to gloom, all joyful H6845
Isa 41: 2 He t them to dust with his sword, to H5989
Isa 44:25 of the wise and t it into nonsense, H6118
Jer 8: 4 When someone t away, do they not return H8740
Jer 17: 5 whose heart t away from the LORD. H6073
Jer 23:14 so that not one of them t from their H8740
Jer 48:39 How Moab t her back in shame H7155
La 1: 8 her naked; she herself groans and t away. H8740
Eze 3:20 when a righteous person t from their H8740
Eze 18:21 if a wicked person t away from all the sins H8740
Eze 18:24 if a righteous person t from their H8740
Eze 18:26 If a righteous person t from their H8740
Eze 18:27 if a wicked person t away from the H8740
Eze 33:18 If a righteous person t from their H8740
Eze 33:19 And if a wicked person t away from their H8740
Joel 2: 6 are in anguish; every face t pale. H6999+7695
Am 4:13 to mankind, who t dawn to darkness, and H6913
Am 5: 8 who t midnight into dawn and darkens H2200
Na 2: 8 they cry, but no one t back. H7155
2Co 3:16 But whenever anyone t to the Lord, the veil G2188
Heb 3:12 heart that t away from the living God. G923
Jas 5:20 Whoever t a sinner from the error of their G2188

TURQUOISE (7)

Ex 28:18 the second row shall be t, lapis lazuli and H5876
Ex 39:11 the second row was t, lapis lazuli and H5876
1Ch 29: 2 onyx for the settings, t, stones of various H7037
Isa 54:11 I will rebuild you with stones of t, your H7037
Eze 27:16 products; they exchanged t, purple fabric, H5876
Eze 28:13 onyx and jasper, lapis lazuli, t and beryl. H5876
Rev 21:20 the tenth t, the eleventh jacinth, G5995

TURTLE, TURTLEDOVE, TURTLEDOVES, TURTLES (KJV) DOVE, DOVES

TUSKS (1)

Eze 27:15 they paid you with ivory t and ebony. H7967

TUTORS (KJV) GUARDIANS

TWELFTH (24) [TWELVE]

Nu 7:78 On the t day Ahira son of Enan, the H9109+6925
1Ki 19:19 he himself was driving the t pair. H9109+6925
2Ki 8:25 In the t year of Joram son of Ahab H9109+6926
2Ki 17: 1 In the t year of Ahaz king of Judah H9109+6926
2Ki 25:27 twenty-seventh day of the t month. H9109+6925
1Ch 24:12 to Eliashib, the t to Jakim, H9109+6925
1Ch 25:19 the t to Hashabiah, his sons and H9109+6925
1Ch 27:15 The t, for the twelfth month, was H9109+6925
1Ch 27:15 twelfth, for the t month, was Heldai H9109+6925
2Ch 34: 3 In his t year he began to purge H9109+6926
Ezr 8:31 On the t day of the first month we H9109+6925
Est 3: 7 In the t year of King Xerxes, in the H9109+6926
Est 3: 7 And the lot fell on the t month, the H9109+6925
Est 3:13 the thirteenth day of the t month H9109+6925
Est 8:12 the thirteenth day of the t month, H9109+6925
Est 9: 1 the thirteenth day of the t month, H9109+6925
Jer 52:31 the twenty-fifth day of the t month, H9109+6925
Eze 26: 1 In the eleventh month of the t year H9109+6926
Eze 29: 1 in the tenth month on the t day H9109+6925
Eze 32: 1 In the t year, in the twelfth month H9109+6926
Eze 32: 1 in the t month on the first day H9109+6925
Eze 32:17 In the t year, on the fifteenth day of H9109+6926
Eze 33:21 In the t year of our exile, in the H9109+6926
Rev 21:20 the eleventh jacinth, and the t amethyst. G1558

TWELVE (146) [TWELFTH, 12, 12000, 144000]

Ge 14: 4 For t years they had been subject to H9109+6926
Ge 17:20 He will be the father of t rulers H9109+6925
Ge 25:16 are the names of the t tribal rulers H9109+6925
Ge 35:22 Jacob had t sons: H9109+6925
Ge 42:13 "Your servants were t brothers, the H9109+6925
Ge 42:32 We were t brothers, sons of one H9109+6925
Ge 49:28 All these are the t tribes of Israel H9109+6925
Ex 15:27 where there were t springs and H9109+6926
Ex 24: 4 mountain and set up t stone pillars H9109+6926
Ex 24: 4 representing the t tribes of Israel. H9109+6925
Ex 28:21 There are to be t stones, one for H9109+6926
Ex 28:21 the name of one of the t tribes. H9109+6925
Ex 39:14 There were t stones, one for each of H9109+6926
Ex 39:14 the name of one of the t tribes. H9109+6925
Lev 24: 5 flour and bake t loaves of bread, H9109+6926
Nu 1:44 Aaron and the t leaders of Israel H9109+6925
Nu 7: 3 LORD six covered carts and t oxen— H9109+6925
Nu 7:84 t silver plates, twelve silver H9109+6926
Nu 7:84 t silver sprinkling bowls and twelve H9109+6926
Nu 7:84 sprinkling bowls and t gold dishes. H9109+6926
Nu 7:86 The t gold dishes filled with H9109+6926

Nu 7:87 offering came to **t** young bulls, H9109+6925
Nu 7:87 **t** rams and twelve male lambs a H9109+6925
Nu 7:87 twelve rams and **t** male lambs a H9109+6925
Nu 7:87 **T** male goats were used for the sin H9109+6925
Nu 17: 2 and get **t** staffs from them, H9109+6925
Nu 17: 6 and their leaders gave him **t** staffs H9109+6925
Nu 29:17 the second day offer **t** young bulls, H9109+6925
Nu 31: 5 So **t** thousand men armed for battle, H9109+6925
Nu 33: 9 where there were **t** springs and H9109+6926
Dt 1:23 so I selected **t** of you, one man H9109+6925
Jos 3:12 choose **t** men from the tribes of H9109+6925
Jos 4: 2 "Choose **t** men from among the H9109+6925
Jos 4: 3 them to take up **t** stones from the H9109+6926
Jos 4: 4 called together the **t** men he had H9109+6925
Jos 4: 8 They took **t** stones from the middle H9109+6926
Jos 4: 9 Joshua set up the **t** stones that had H9109+6926
Jos 4:20 up at Gilgal the **t** stones they had H9109+6926
Jos 8:25 **T** thousand men and women fell H9109+6925
Jos 18:24 Geba—**t** towns and their villages. H9109+6926
Jos 19:15 There were **t** towns and their H9109+6926
Jos 21: 7 received **t** towns from the tribes of H9109+6926
Jos 21:40 the rest of the Levites, came to **t**. H9109+6926
Jdg 19:29 into **t** parts and sent them into all H9109+6925
Jdg 21:10 assembly sent **t** thousand fighting H9109+6925
2Sa 2:15 **t** men for Benjamin and H9109+6925
2Sa 2:15 son of Saul, and **t** for David. H9109+6925
2Sa 10: 6 and also **t** thousand men from Tob. H9109+6925
2Sa 17: 1 "I would choose **t** thousand men H9109+6925
1Ki 4: 7 Solomon had **t** district governors H9109+6925
1Ki 4:26 horses, and **t** thousand horses. H9109+6925
1Ki 7:15 cubits high and **t** cubits in H9109+6926
1Ki 7:25 The Sea stood on **t** bulls, three H9109+6925
1Ki 7:44 the Sea and the **t** bulls under it; H9109+6925
1Ki 10:20 **T** lions stood on the six steps, one H9109+6925
1Ki 10:26 chariots and **t** thousand horses, H9109+6925
1Ki 11:30 wearing and tore it into **t** pieces. H9109+6925
1Ki 16:23 and he reigned **t** years, six of them H9109+6926
1Ki 18:31 Elijah took **t** stones, one for each of H9109+6926
1Ki 19:19 was plowing with **t** yoke of oxen, H9109+6925
2Ki 3: 1 of Judah, and he reigned **t** years. H9109+6926
2Ki 21: 1 Manasseh was **t** years old when he H9109+6926
1Ch 6:63 were allotted **t** towns from the H9109+6926
2Ch 1:14 chariots and **t** thousand horses, H9109+6925
2Ch 4: 4 The Sea stood on **t** bulls, three H9109+6925
2Ch 4:15 the Sea and the **t** bulls under it; H9109+6925
2Ch 9:19 **T** lions stood on the six steps, one H9109+6925
2Ch 9:25 chariots, and **t** thousand horses H9109+6925
2Ch 12: 3 With **t hundred** chariots and H547+2256+4395
2Ch 33: 1 Manasseh was **t** years old when he H9109+6926
Ezr 6:17 all Israel, **t** male goats, one A10775+10573
Ezr 8:24 Then I set apart **t** of the leading H9109+6925
Ezr 8:35 **t** bulls for all Israel, ninety-six rams, H9109+6925
Ezr 8:35 as a sin offering, **t** male goats. H9109+6925
Ne 5:14 year—**t** years—neither I H9109+6926
Est 2:12 had to complete **t** months of H9109+6925
Ps 60: T and struck down **t** thousand H9109+6925
Jer 52:20 the Sea and the **t** bronze bulls H9109+6925
Jer 52:21 cubits high and **t** cubits in H9109+6926
Eze 40:49 and **t** cubits from front to back. H9109+6926
Eze 43:16 **t** cubits long and twelve cubits H9109+6926
Eze 43:16 cubits long and **t** cubits wide. H9109+6926
Eze 47:13 divide among the **t** tribes of Israel H9109+6925
Da 4:29 **T** months later, as the king was A10775+10573
Mt 9:20 to bleeding for **t** years came up behind *G1557*
Mt 10: 1 Jesus called his **t** disciples to him and *G1557*
Mt 10: 2 These are the names of the **t** apostles *G1557*
Mt 10: 5 These **t** Jesus sent out with the following *G1557*
Mt 11: 1 had finished instructing his **t** disciples, *G1557*
Mt 14:20 disciples picked up **t** basketfuls of broken *G1557*
Mt 19:28 followed me will also sit on **t** thrones, *G1557*
Mt 19:28 thrones, judging the **t** tribes of Israel. *G1557*
Mt 20:17 he took the **T** aside and said to them *G1557*
Mt 26:14 Then one *of* the **T**—the one called Judas *G1557*
Mt 26:20 was reclining at the table with the **T**. *G1557*
Mt 26:47 speaking, Judas, one *of* the **T**, arrived. *G1557*
Mt 26:53 my disposal more *than* **t** legions of angels *G1557*
Mk 3:14 He appointed **t** that they might be with *G1557*
Mk 3:16 These are the **t** he appointed: Simon (to *G1557*
Mk 4:10 the **T** and the others around him asked *G1557*
Mk 5:25 had been subject to bleeding for **t** years. *G1557*
Mk 5:42 walk around (she was **t** years old). *G1557*
Mk 6: 7 Calling the **T** to him, he began to send *G1557*
Mk 6:43 disciples picked up **t** basketfuls of broken *G1557*
Mk 8:19 pieces did you pick up?" "**T**," they replied. *G1557*
Mk 9:35 Jesus called the **T** and said, "Anyone who *G1557*
Mk 10:32 Again he took the **T** aside and told them *G1557*
Mk 11:11 he went out to Bethany with the **T**. *G1557*
Mk 14:10 Iscariot, one *of* the **T**, went to the chief *G1557*
Mk 14:17 evening came, Jesus arrived with the **T**. *G1557*
Mk 14:20 "It is one *of* the **T**," he replied, "one who *G1557*
Mk 14:43 speaking, Judas, one *of* the **T**, appeared. *G1557*
Lk 2:42 When he was **t** years old, they went up to *G1557*
Lk 6:13 his disciples to him and chose **t** of them, *G1557*
Lk 8: 1 kingdom of God. The **T** were with him, *G1557*
Lk 8:42 daughter, a girl *of* about **t**, was dying. *G1557*
Lk 8:43 had been subject to bleeding for **t** years, *G1557*
Lk 9: 1 When Jesus had called the **T** together, he *G1557*
Lk 9:12 the afternoon the **T** came to him and said *G1557*
Lk 9:17 disciples picked up **t** basketfuls of broken *G1557*
Lk 18:31 Jesus took the **T** aside and told them *G1557*
Lk 22: 3 called Iscariot, one of the **T**. *G1557*
Lk 22:30 on thrones, judging the **t** tribes of Israel. *G1557*
Lk 22:47 called Judas, one *of* the **T**, was leading *G1557*
Jn 6:13 them and filled **t** baskets with the pieces *G1557*
Jn 6:67 to leave too, do you?" Jesus asked the **T**. *G1557*
Jn 6:70 replied, "Have I not chosen you, the **T**? *G1557*
Jn 6:71 though one of the **T**, was later to betray *G1557*
Jn 11: 9 "Are there not **t** hours of daylight? *G1557*
Jn 20:24 one of the **T**, was not with the disciples *G1557*
Ac 6: 2 So the **T** gathered all the disciples *G1557*
Ac 7: 8 became the father of the **t** patriarchs. *G1557*
Ac 19: 7 There were about **t** men in all. *G1557*
Ac 24:11 that no more *than* **t** days ago I went up *G1557*
Ac 26: 7 the promise our **t tribes** are hoping to see *G1559*
1Co 15: 5 appeared to Cephas, and then *to* the **T**. *G1557*
Jas 1: 1 To the **t** tribes scattered among the *G1557*
Rev 12: 1 feet and a crown of **t** stars on her head. *G1557*
Rev 21:12 high wall with **t** gates, and with *G1557*
Rev 21:12 and with **t** angels at the gates. *G1557*
Rev 21:12 written the names of the **t** tribes of Israel. *G1557*
Rev 21:14 The wall of the city had **t** foundations, and *G1557*
Rev 21:14 the names of the **t** apostles of the Lamb. *G1557*
Rev 21:21 The **t** gates were twelve pearls, each gate *G1557*
Rev 21:21 The twelve gates were **t** pearls, each gate *G1557*
Rev 22: 2 tree of life, bearing **t** crops of fruit *G1557*

TWENTIETH (9) [TWENTY]

Nu 10:11 On the **t** day of the second month of the H6929
1Ki 15: 9 In the **t** year of Jeroboam king of Israel H6929
2Ki 15:30 him as king in the **t** year of Jotham son of H6929
1Ch 24:16 to Pethahiah, the **t** to Jehezkel, H6929
1Ch 25:27 the **t** to Eliathah, his sons and relatives 12 H6929
Ezr 10: 9 And on the **t** day of the ninth month, all H6929
Ne 1: 1 In the month of Kislev in the **t** year, while H6929
Ne 2: 1 month of Nisan in the **t** year of King H6929
Ne 5:14 from the **t** year of King Artaxerxes H6929

TWENTY (125) [TWENTIETH, 20]

Ge 6: 3 their days will be a hundred and **t** years." H6929
Ge 18:31 what if only **t** can be found there? H6929
Ge 18:31 "For the sake of **t**, I will not destroy it H6929
Ge 31:38 "I have been with you for **t** years now H6929
Ge 31:41 It was like this for the **t** years I was in your H6929
Ge 32:14 hundred female goats and **t** male goats, H6929
Ge 32:14 two hundred ewes and **t** rams, H6929
Ge 32:15 **t** female donkeys and ten male H6929
Ge 37:28 sold him for **t** shekels *of* silver to the H6929
Ex 26:18 Make **t** frames for the south side of the H6929
Ex 26:20 side of the tabernacle, make **t** frames H6929
Ex 27:10 with **t** posts and twenty bronze bases and H6929
Ex 27:10 with twenty posts and **t** bronze bases and H6929
Ex 27:11 with **t** posts and twenty bronze bases and H6929
Ex 27:11 twenty posts and **t** bronze bases and with H6929
Ex 27:16 provide a curtain **t** cubits long, of blue, H6929
Ex 30:13 sanctuary shekel, which weighs **t** gerahs. H6929
Ex 30:14 who cross over, those **t** years old or more H6929
Ex 36:23 They made **t** frames for the south side of H6929
Ex 36:25 of the tabernacle, they made **t** frames H6929
Ex 38:10 with **t** posts and twenty bronze bases, and H6929
Ex 38:10 with twenty posts and **t** bronze bases, and H6929
Ex 38:11 cubits long and had **t** posts and twenty H6929
Ex 38:11 had twenty posts and **t** bronze bases, H6929
Ex 38:18 It was **t** cubits long and, like the curtains H6929
Ex 38:26 to those counted, **t** years old or more, H6929
Lev 27: 3 between the ages of **t** and sixty at fifty H6929
Lev 27: 5 a person between the ages of five and **t**, H6929
Lev 27: 5 the value of a male at **t** shekels and of a H6929
Lev 27:25 sanctuary shekel, **t** gerahs to the shekel. H6929
Nu 1: 3 in Israel who are **t** years old or more and H6929
Nu 1:18 the men **t** years old or more were H6929
Nu 1:20 All the men **t** years old or more who were H6929
Nu 1:22 All the men **t** years old or more who were H6929
Nu 1:24 All the men **t** years old or more who were H6929
Nu 1:26 All the men **t** years old or more who were H6929
Nu 1:28 All the men **t** years old or more who were H6929
Nu 1:30 All the men **t** years old or more who were H6929
Nu 1:32 All the men **t** years old or more who were H6929
Nu 1:34 All the men **t** years old or more who were H6929
Nu 1:36 All the men **t** years old or more who were H6929
Nu 1:38 All the men **t** years old or more who were H6929
Nu 1:40 All the men **t** years old or more who were H6929
Nu 1:42 All the men **t** years old or more who were H6929
Nu 1:45 All the Israelites **t** years old or more who H6929
Nu 3:47 sanctuary shekel, which weighs **t** gerahs. H6929
Nu 7:86 dishes weighed a hundred and **t** shekels. H6929
Nu 11:19 or two days, or five, ten or **t** days, H6929
Nu 14:29 every one of you **t** years old or more who H6929
Nu 18:16 sanctuary shekel, which weighs **t** gerahs. H6929
Nu 26: 2 all those **t** years old or more who are able H6929
Nu 26: 4 a census of the men **t** years old or more, H6929
Nu 32:11 one of those who were **t** years old or more H6929
Dt 31: 2 now a hundred and **t** years old and I am H6929
Dt 34: 7 was a hundred and **t** years old when he H6929
Jdg 4: 3 cruelly oppressed the Israelites for **t** years, H6929
Jdg 8:10 a hundred and **t** thousand swordsmen H6929
Jdg 11:33 He devastated **t** towns from Aroer to the H6929
Jdg 15:20 led Israel for **t** years in the days of H6929
Jdg 16:31 He had led Israel **t** years. H6929
1Sa 7: 2 Kiriath Jearim a long time—**t** years in all. H6929
1Sa 14:14 killed some **t** men in an area of about H6929
2Sa 3:20 who had **t** men with him, came H6929
2Sa 8: 4 charioteers and **t** thousand foot soldiers. H6929
2Sa 9:10 Now Ziba had fifteen sons and **t** servants.) H6929
2Sa 10: 6 they hired **t** thousand Aramean foot H6929
2Sa 18: 7 that day were great—**t** thousand men. H6929
2Sa 19:17 his fifteen sons and **t** servants. H6929
2Sa 24: 8 at the end of nine months and **t** days. H6929
1Ki 4:23 **t** of pasture-fed cattle and a hundred H6929
1Ki 5:11 Solomon gave Hiram **t** thousand cors of H6929
1Ki 5:11 in addition to **t** thousand baths of pressed H6929
1Ki 6: 2 sixty cubits long, **t** wide and thirty high. H6929
1Ki 6: 3 the temple, that is **t** cubits, and projected H6929
1Ki 6:16 He partitioned off **t** cubits at the rear of the H6929
1Ki 6:20 The inner sanctuary was **t** cubits long H6929
1Ki 6:20 cubits long, **t** wide and twenty high. H6929
1Ki 6:20 cubits long, twenty wide and **t** high. H6929
1Ki 8:63 a hundred and **t** thousand sheep and H6929
1Ki 9:10 At the end of **t** years, during which H6929
1Ki 9:11 King Solomon gave **t** towns in Galilee to H6929
2Ki 4:42 the man of God **t** loaves of barley bread H6929
2Ki 15:27 Israel in Samaria, and he reigned **t** years. H6929
2Ki 16: 2 Ahaz was **t** years old when he became H6929
1Ch 18: 4 charioteers and **t** thousand foot soldiers. H6929
1Ch 23:24 the workers **t** years old or more who H6929
1Ch 23:27 counted from those **t** years old or more. H6929
1Ch 27:23 the number of the men **t** years old or less, H6929
2Ch 2:10 **t** thousand cors of ground wheat H6929
2Ch 2:10 of ground wheat, **t** thousand cors of barley H6929
2Ch 2:10 **t** thousand baths of wine and twenty H6929
2Ch 2:10 baths of wine and **t** thousand baths of H6929
2Ch 3: 3 was sixty cubits long and **t** cubits wide H6929
2Ch 3: 4 of the temple was **t** cubits long across the H6929
2Ch 3: 4 width of the building and **t** cubits high. H6929
2Ch 3: 8 **t** cubits long and twenty cubits wide. H6929
2Ch 3: 8 twenty cubits long and **t** cubits wide. H6929
2Ch 3:11 wingspan of the cherubim was **t** cubits. H6929
2Ch 3:13 of these cherubim extended **t** cubits. H6929
2Ch 4: 1 He made a bronze altar **t** cubits long H6929
2Ch 4: 1 **t** cubits wide and ten cubits high. H6929
2Ch 7: 5 a hundred and **t** thousand sheep and H6929
2Ch 8: 1 At the end of **t** years, during which H6929
2Ch 25: 5 then mustered those **t** years old or more H6929
2Ch 28: 1 Ahaz was **t** years old when he became H6929
2Ch 28: 6 a hundred and **t** thousand soldiers in H6929
2Ch 31:17 likewise to the Levites **t** years old or more, H6929
Ezr 3: 8 appointed Levites **t** years old and older to H6929
Eze 4:10 Weigh out **t** shekels of food to eat each H6929
Eze 40:49 The portico was **t** cubits wide, and twelve H6929
Eze 41: 2 it was forty cubits long and **t** cubits wide. H6929
Eze 41: 4 sanctuary; it was **t** cubits, and its width H6929
Eze 41: 4 its width was **t** cubits across the end H6929
Eze 41:10 priests' rooms was **t** cubits wide all H6929
Eze 42: 3 Both in the section **t** cubits from the inner H6929
Eze 45:12 The shekel is to consist of **t** gerahs. Twenty H6929
Eze 45:12 **T** shekels plus twenty-five shekels plus H6929
Jnh 4:11 a **hundred and t thousand** H8052+9109+6926
Hag 2:16 anyone came to a heap of **t** measures, H6929
Hag 2:16 to draw fifty measures, there were only **t**. H6929
Zec 5: 2 **t** cubits long and ten cubits wide. H6929
Lk 14:31 one coming against him with **t** thousand? *G1633*
Jn 2: 6 holding from **t** to thirty **gallons**. *G3583+1545*
Ac 1:15 a group numbering about a hundred and **t**) *G1633*
Ac 27:28 was **a hundred and t feet deep**. *G3976+1633*

TWENTY-EIGHT (4) [28]

Ex 26: 2 **t** cubits long and four cubits H9046+2256+6929
Ex 36: 9 **t** cubits long and four cubits H6929+2256+9046
2Ki 10:36 in Samaria was **t** years. H6929+2256+9046
2Ch 11:21 **t** sons and sixty daughters. H6929+2256+9046

TWENTY-FIFTH (3) [TWENTY-FIVE]

Ne 6:15 completed on the **t** of Elul, H6929+2256+2822
Jer 52:31 on the **t** day of the twelfth H6929+2256+2822
Eze 40: 1 In the **t** year of our exile, at H6929+2256+2822

TWENTY-FIRST (4) [TWENTY-ONE]

Ex 12:18 until the evening of the **t** day. H6929+2256+285
1Ch 24:17 the **t** to Jakin, the H285+2256+6929
1Ch 25:28 the **t** to Hothir, his sons and H285+2256+6929
Hag 2: 1 on the **t** day of the seventh H6929+2256+285

TWENTY-FIVE (23) [TWENTY-FIFTH]

Nu 8:24 Men **t** years old or more H6929+2256+2822
Jdg 20:46 On that day **t** thousand H6929+2256+2822
1Ki 22:42 in Jerusalem **t** years. H6929+2256+2822
2Ki 14: 2 He was **t** years old when he H6929+2256+2822
2Ki 15:33 He was **t** years old when he H6929+2256+2822
2Ki 18: 2 He was **t** years old when he H6929+2256+2822
2Ki 23:36 Jehoiakim was **t** years old H6929+2256+2822
2Ch 20:31 in Jerusalem **t** years. H6929+2256+2822
2Ch 25: 1 Amaziah was **t** years old H6929+2256+2822
2Ch 27: 1 Jotham was **t** years old H6929+2256+2822
2Ch 27: 8 He was **t** years old when he H6929+2256+2822
2Ch 29: 1 Hezekiah was **t** years old H6929+2256+2822
2Ch 36: 5 Jehoiakim was **t** years old H6929+2256+2822
Eze 8:16 the altar, were about **t** men. H6929+2256+2822
Eze 11: 1 of the gate were **t** men, H6929+2256+2822
Eze 40:13 distance was **t** cubits from H6929+2256+2822
Eze 40:21 long and **t** cubits wide. H6929+2256+2822
Eze 40:25 long and **t** cubits wide. H6929+2256+2822
Eze 40:29 long and **t** cubits wide. H6929+2256+2822
Eze 40:30 court were **t** cubits wide and H6929+2256+2822
Eze 40:33 long and **t** cubits wide. H6929+2256+2822
Eze 40:36 long and **t** cubits wide. H6929+2256+2822
Eze 45:12 shekels plus **t** shekels plus H6929+2256+2822

TWENTY-FOUR (11) [TWENTY-FOURTH]
Nu 7:88 offering came to **t** oxen, H6929+2256+752
2Sa 21:20 six toes on each foot—**t** in all. H6929+2256+752
1Ki 15:33 and he reigned **t** years. H6929+2256+752
1Ch 20: 6 six toes on each foot—**t** in all. H6929+2256+752
1Ch 23: 4 **t** thousand are to be in H6929+2256+752
Rev 4: 4 the throne were **t** other thrones, *G1633+5475*
Rev 4: 4 and seated on them were **t** elders. *G1633+5475*
Rev 4:10 the **t** elders fall down before him *G1633+5475*
Rev 5: 8 creatures and the **t** elders fell down *G1633+5475*
Rev 11:16 And the **t** elders, who were seated *G1633+5475*
Rev 19: 4 The **t** elders and the four living *G1633+5475*

TWENTY-FOURTH (9) [TWENTY-FOUR]
1Ch 24:18 and the **t** to Maaziah. H752+2256+6929
1Ch 25:31 the **t** to Romamti-Ezer, his H752+2256+6929
Ne 9: 1 On the **t** day of the same H6929+2256+752
Da 10: 4 On the **t** day of the first month H6929+2256+752
Hag 1:15 on the **t** day of the sixth month H6929+2256+752
Hag 2:10 On the **t** day of the ninth H6929+2256+752
Hag 2:18 from this **t** day of the ninth H6929+2256+752
Hag 2:20 time on the **t** day of the H6929+2256+752
Zec 1: 7 On the **t** day of the eleventh H6929+2256+752

TWENTY-NINE (5) [29]
Jos 15:32 a total of **t** towns and their H6929+2256+9596
2Ki 14: 2 in Jerusalem **t** years. H6929+2256+9596
2Ki 18: 2 in Jerusalem **t** years. H6929+2256+9596
2Ch 25: 1 in Jerusalem **t** years. H6929+2256+9596
2Ch 29: 1 in Jerusalem **t** years. H6929+2256+9596

TWENTY-ONE (4) [TWENTY-FIRST]
2Ki 24:18 Zedekiah was **t** years old H6929+2256+285
2Ch 36:11 Zedekiah was **t** years old H6929+2256+285
Jer 52: 1 Zedekiah was **t** years old H6929+2256+285
Da 10:13 kingdom resisted me **t** days. H6929+2256+285

TWENTY-SECOND (2) [TWENTY-TWO]
1Ch 24:17 to Jakin, the **t** to Gamul, H9109+2256+6929
1Ch 25:29 the **t** to Giddalti, his sons H9109+2256+6929

TWENTY-SEVEN (3) [TWENTY-SEVENTH]
Ge 23: 1 a hundred and **t** years old. H6929+2256+8679
1Ki 20:30 collapsed on **t** thousand of H6929+2256+8679
1Ch 26:32 had **t hundred** relatives H547+2256+8679+4395

TWENTY-SEVENTH (6) [TWENTY-SEVEN]
Ge 8:14 By the **t** day of the second H6929+2256+8679
1Ki 16:10 him in the **t** year of Asa king H6929+2256+8679
1Ki 16:15 In the **t** year of Asa king of H6929+2256+8679
2Ki 15: 1 In the **t** year of Jeroboam H6929+2256+8679
2Ki 25:27 did this on the **t** day of the H6929+2256+8679
Eze 29:17 In the **t** year, in the first H6929+2256+8679

TWENTY-SIX (2) [TWENTY-SIXTH]
Jdg 20:15 mobilized **t** thousand H6929+2256+9252
2Ch 35: 8 priests **t hundred** H547+2256+9252+4395

TWENTY-SIXTH (1) [TWENTY-SIX]
1Ki 16: 8 In the **t** year of Asa king of H6929+2256+9252

TWENTY-THIRD (7) [TWENTY-THREE]
2Ki 12: 6 But by the **t** year of King H6929+2256+8993
2Ki 13: 1 In the **t** year of Joash son of H6929+2256+8993
1Ch 24:18 the **t** to Delaiah and the H8993+2256+6929
1Ch 25:30 the **t** to Mahazioth, his sons H8993+2256+6929
2Ch 7:10 On the **t** day of the seventh H6929+2256+8993
Est 8: 9 on the **t** day of the third H8993+2256+6929
Jer 52:30 in his **t** year, 745 Jews taken H8993+2256+6929

TWENTY-THREE (7) [TWENTY-THIRD]
Nu 33:39 a hundred and **t** years old H6929+2256+8993
Jdg 10: 2 He led Israel **t** years; then he H6929+2256+8993
2Ki 23:31 Jehoahaz was **t** years old H6929+2256+8993
1Ch 2:22 who controlled **t** towns in H6929+2256+8993
2Ch 36: 2 Jehoahaz was **t** years old H8993+2256+6929
Jer 25: 3 *For* **t** years—from the H8993+2256+6929
1Co 10: 8 in one day **t** thousand of them *G1633+5552*

TWENTY-TWO (15) [TWENTY-SECOND, 22]
Jos 19:30 There were **t** towns and their H6929+2256+9109
Jdg 7: 3 So **t** thousand men left H6929+2256+9109
Jdg 10: 3 who led Israel **t** years. H6929+2256+9109
Jdg 20:21 and cut down **t** thousand H6929+2256+9109
2Sa 8: 5 struck down **t** thousand of H6929+2256+9109
1Ki 8:63 **t** thousand cattle and a H6929+2256+9109
1Ki 14:20 He reigned for **t** years and H6929+2256+9109
1Ki 16:29 Samaria over Israel **t** years. H6929+2256+9109
2Ki 8:26 Ahaziah was **t** years old H6929+2256+9109
2Ki 21:19 Amon was **t** years old when H6929+2256+9109
1Ch 18: 5 struck down **t** thousand of H6929+2256+9109
2Ch 7: 5 sacrifice of **t** thousand head H6929+2256+9109
2Ch 13:21 wives and had **t** sons and H6929+2256+9109
2Ch 22: 2 Ahaziah was **t** years old H6929+2256+9109
2Ch 33:21 Amon was **t** years old when H6929+2256+9109

TWICE (22) [TWO]
Ge 43:10 we could have gone and returned **t**." H7193
Ex 16: 5 that is to be **t as much** as they gather H5467
Ex 16:22 they gathered **t as much**—two omers for H5467
Nu 20:11 his arm and struck the rock **t** with his staff. H7193
Dt 15:18 has been worth **t as much** *as* that of a H5467
1Sa 18:11 But David eluded him **t**. H7193
1Sa 26: 8 thrust of the spear; *I* won't **strike** him **t**." H9101
1Ki 11: 9 God of Israel, who had appeared to him **t**. H7193
Ne 13:20 Once or **t** the merchants and sellers of all H9109
Job 33:29 things to a person—**t**, even three times— H7193
Job 40: 5 I have no answer—**t**, but I will say no H9109
Job 42:10 gave him **t** as much as he had H5467
Ecc 6: 6 a thousand years **t over** but fails to enjoy H7193
Eze 21:14 *Let* the sword **strike t**, even three H4100
Zec 9:12 that I will restore **t as much** to you. H5467
Mt 23:15 you make them **t as much** a child of hell *G1487*
Mk 14:30 before the rooster crows **t** you yourself will *G1489*
Mk 14:72 the rooster crows **t** you will disown me *G1489*
Lk 18:12 I fast **t** a week and give a tenth of all I get *G1489*
2Co 1:15 visit you first so that you might benefit **t**. *G1311*
Jude 12 without fruit and uprooted—**t** dead. *G1489*
Rev 9:16 troops was **t ten thousand** times ten *G1490*

TWIG (1) [TWIGS]
Hos 10: 7 swept away like a **t** on the surface of the H7913

TWIGS (4) [TWIG]
Isa 27:11 When its **t** are dry, they are broken off H7908
Isa 64: 2 As when fire sets **t** ablaze and causes H2173
Mt 24:32 As soon as its **t** get tender and its leaves *G3080*
Mk 13:28 As soon as its **t** get tender and its leaves *G3080*

TWILIGHT (14) [LIGHT]
Ex 12: 6 must slaughter them **at t**. H1068+2021+6847
Ex 16:12 them, '**At t** you will eat meat H1068+2021+6847
Ex 29:39 morning and the other **at t**. H1068+6847+2021
Ex 29:41 other lamb **at t** with the H1068+2021+6847
Ex 30: 8 the lamps **at t** so incense H1068+2021+6847
Lev 23: 5 Passover begins **at t** on the H1068+2021+6847
Nu 9: 3 **at t** on the fourteenth day of H1068+2021+6847
Nu 9: 5 Desert of Sinai **at t** on the H1068+2021+6847
Nu 9:11 of the second month **at t**. H1068+6847+2021
Nu 28: 4 morning and the other **at t**, H1068+2021+6847
Nu 28: 8 Offer the second lamb **at t** H1068+2021+6847
Pr 7: 9 at **t**, as the day was fading, as the dark of H5974
Isa 21: 4 the **t** I longed for has become a horror to H5974
Isa 59:10 At midday we stumble as if it were **t** H5974

TWIN (7) [TWINS]
Ge 25:24 give birth, there were **t** *boys* in her womb. H9339
Ge 38:27 give birth, there were **t** *boys* in her womb. H9339
SS 4: 2 Each **has** *its* **t**; not one of them H9298
SS 4: 5 like **t** fawns *of* a gazelle that browse H9339
SS 6: 6 Each **has** its **t**, not one of them H9298
SS 7: 3 like two fawns, like **t** fawns *of* a gazelle. H9339
Ac 28:11 *of* the **t gods Castor and Pollux**. *G1483*

TWINED (KJV) TWISTED

TWINKLING (1)
1Co 15:52 in a flash, in the **t** of an eye, at the last *G4846*

TWINS (1) [TWIN]
Ro 9:11 before *the t were* **born** or had done anything AIT

TWIST (1) [TWISTED, TWISTING, TWISTS]
Ps 56: 5 All day long *they* **t** my words; all their H6772

TWISTED (25) [TWIST]
Ex 26: 1 ten curtains of **finely t** linen and blue, H8813
Ex 26:31 purple and scarlet yarn and **finely t** linen H8813
Ex 26:36 scarlet yarn and **finely t** linen— H8813
Ex 27: 9 is to have curtains of **finely t** linen, H8813
Ex 27:16 scarlet yarn and **finely t** linen— H8813
Ex 27:18 with curtains of **finely t** linen five cubits H8813
Ex 28: 6 and of **finely t** linen—the work of H8813
Ex 28: 8 scarlet yarn, and with **finely t** linen. H8813
Ex 28:15 scarlet yarn, and of **finely t** linen. H8813
Ex 36: 8 ten curtains of **finely t** linen and blue, H8813
Ex 36:35 purple and scarlet yarn and **finely t** linen H8813
Ex 36:37 scarlet yarn and **finely t** linen— H8813
Ex 38: 9 long and had curtains of **finely t** linen, H8813
Ex 38:16 the courtyard were of **finely t** linen. H8813
Ex 38:18 scarlet yarn and **finely t** linen— H8813
Ex 39: 2 scarlet yarn, and of **finely t** linen. H8813
Ex 39: 5 and with **finely t** linen, as the LORD H8813
Ex 39: 8 scarlet yarn, and of **finely t** linen. H8813
Ex 39:24 scarlet yarn and **finely t** linen around the H8813
Ex 39:28 the undergarments of **finely t** linen. H8813
Ex 39:29 sash was made of **finely t** linen and blue, H8813
Eze 27:24 rugs with cords **t** and tightly knotted. H2502
Mt 27:29 then **t together** a crown of thorns and *G4428*
Mk 15:17 then **t together** a crown of thorns and set *G4428*
Jn 19: 2 The soldiers **t together** a crown of thorns *G4428*

TWISTING (1) [TWIST]
Pr 30:33 and as **t** the nose produces blood H4790

TWISTS (3) [TWIST]
Ex 23: 8 those who see and **t** the words of the H6156
Dt 16:19 eyes of the wise and **t** the words of the H6156
Ps 29: 9 The voice of the LORD **t** the oaks and strips H2655

TWO (626) [SECOND, TWICE, TWO-DRACHMA, TWO-HORNED, TWO-TENTHS, TWO-THIRDS]
Ge 1:16 God made **t** great lights—the greater light H9109
Ge 4:19 Lamech married **t** women, one named H9109
Ge 6:19 to bring into the ark **t** of all living H9109
Ge 6:20 **T** of every kind of bird, of every kind of H9109
Ge 9:22 naked and told his **t** brothers outside. H9109
Ge 10:25 **T** sons were born to Eber: One was H9109
Ge 11:10 *T* **years** after the flood, when Shem was 100 AIT
Ge 13:11 toward the east. The **t** men parted company: NDT
Ge 15:10 cut them in **t** and arranged the halves H9348
Ge 19: 1 The **t** angels arrived at Sodom in the H9109
Ge 19: 8 I have **t** daughters who have never slept H9109
Ge 19:12 The **t** men said to Lot, "Do you have anyone NDT
Ge 19:15 your wife and your **t** daughters who are H9109
Ge 19:16 his wife and of his **t** daughters and led H9109
Ge 19:30 Lot and his **t** daughters left Zoar and H9109
Ge 19:30 He and his **t** daughters lived in a cave H9109
Ge 21:27 Abimelek, and the **t** men made a treaty. H9109
Ge 21:31 because the **t** men swore an oath there. H9109
Ge 22: 3 He took with him **t** *of* his servants and his H9109
Ge 22: 6 As the **t** *of* them went on together H9109
Ge 22: 8 And the **t** *of* them went on together H9109
Ge 24:22 weighing a beka and **t** gold bracelets H9109
Ge 25:23 said to her, "**T** nations are in your womb H9109
Ge 25:23 **t** peoples from within you will be H9109
Ge 27: 9 flock and bring me **t** choice young goats, H9109
Ge 29:16 Now Laban had **t** daughters; the name of H9109
Ge 31:33 into the tent of the **t** female servants, H9109
Ge 31:37 let them judge between the **t** *of* us. H9109
Ge 31:41 years for your **t** daughters and six years H9109
Ge 32: 7 people who were with him into **t** groups, H9109
Ge 32:10 but now I have become **t** camps. H9109
Ge 32:14 *t* **hundred** female goats and twenty male AIT
Ge 32:14 *t* **hundred** ewes and twenty rams, AIT
Ge 32:22 night Jacob got up and took his **t** wives, H9109
Ge 32:22 his **t** female servants and his eleven sons H9109
Ge 33: 1 Rachel and the **t** female servants. H9109
Ge 34:25 were still in pain, **t** *of* Jacob's sons H9109
Ge 40: 2 Pharaoh was angry with his **t** officials, the H9109
Ge 40: 5 each *of* the **t** men—the cupbearer and the H9109
Ge 41: 1 When *t* **full years** had passed, Pharaoh had a AIT
Ge 41:32 given to Pharaoh *in t* **forms** is that the matter AIT
Ge 41:50 **t** sons were born to Joseph by Asenath H9109
Ge 44:27 'You know that my wife bore me **t** *sons*. H9109
Ge 45: 6 *For t* **years** now there has been famine in the AIT
Ge 46:27 With the **t** sons who had been born to H9109
Ge 48: 1 So he took his **t** sons Manasseh and H9109
Ge 48: 5 your **t** sons born to you in Egypt before I H9109
Ex 2:13 he went out and saw **t** Hebrews fighting. H9109
Ex 4: 9 do not believe these **t** signs or listen to H9109
Ex 16:22 twice as much—**t** omers for each person H9109
Ex 16:29 the sixth day he gives you bread *for t* **days**. AIT
Ex 18: 3 her **t** sons. One son was named H9109
Ex 18: 6 to you with your wife and her **t** sons." H9109
Ex 21:21 if the slave recovers after a day or **t**, H3427S
Ex 21:35 the **t** parties are to sell the live one and NDT
Ex 25:10 acacia wood—*t* and a half **cubits** long, AIT
Ex 25:12 with **t** rings on one side and two rings on H9109
Ex 25:12 rings on one side and **t** rings on the other. H9109
Ex 25:17 *t* and a half **cubits** long and a cubit and a half AIT
Ex 25:18 And make **t** cherubim out of hammered H9109
Ex 25:19 of one piece with the cover, at the **t** ends. H9109
Ex 25:22 the cover between the **t** cherubim that are H9109
Ex 25:23 of acacia wood—*t* **cubits** long, a cubit wide AIT
Ex 26:17 with **t** projections set parallel to each other H9109
Ex 26:19 to go under them—**t** bases for each frame H9109
Ex 26:21 forty silver bases—**t** under each frame. H9109
Ex 26:23 make **t** frames for the corners at the H9109
Ex 26:24 At these **t** corners they must be double H9109
Ex 26:25 sixteen silver bases—**t** under each frame. H9109
Ex 27: 7 so they will be on **t** sides of the altar H9109
Ex 28: 7 It is to have **t** shoulder pieces attached to H9109
Ex 28: 7 pieces attached to **t** *of* its corners, H9109
Ex 28: 9 "Take **t** onyx stones and engrave on them H9109
Ex 28:11 of Israel on the **t** stones the way a gem H9109
Ex 28:14 **t** braided chains of pure gold, like a H9109
Ex 28:23 Make **t** gold rings for it and fasten them to H9109
Ex 28:23 it and fasten them to **t** corners of the H9109
Ex 28:24 Fasten the **t** gold chains to the rings at the H9109
Ex 28:25 other ends of the chains to the **t** settings, H9109
Ex 28:26 Make **t** gold rings and attach them to the H9109
Ex 28:26 attach them to the other **t** corners of the H9109
Ex 28:27 Make **t** more gold rings and attach them to H9109
Ex 29: 1 a young bull and **t** rams without defect. H9109
Ex 29: 3 them along with the bull and the **t** rams. H9109
Ex 29:38 regularly each day: **t** lambs a year old. H9109
Ex 30: 2 a cubit wide, and *t* **cubits** high—its horns of AIT
Ex 30: 4 Make **t** gold rings for the altar below the H9109
Ex 30: 4 molding—**t** on each of the opposite sides H9109
Ex 31:18 he gave him the **t** tablets of the covenant H9109
Ex 32:15 the mountain with the **t** tablets of the H9109
Ex 34: 1 "Chisel out **t** stone tablets like the first H9109
Ex 34: 4 So Moses chiseled out **t** stone tablets like H9109
Ex 34: 4 he carried the **t** stone tablets in his H9109
Ex 34:29 Mount Sinai with the **t** tablets of the H9109
Ex 36:13 to fasten the *t sets of* **curtains** together so AIT
Ex 36:22 with **t** projections set parallel to each other H9109
Ex 36:24 to go under them—**t** bases for each frame H9109
Ex 36:26 forty silver bases—**t** under each frame. H9109
Ex 36:28 **t** frames were made for the corners of H9109
Ex 36:29 At these **t** corners the frames were double H9109
Ex 36:30 sixteen silver bases—**t** under each frame. H9109
Ex 37: 1 acacia wood—*t* and a half **cubits** long, AIT
Ex 37: 3 with **t** rings on one side and two rings on H9109
Ex 37: 3 rings on one side and **t** rings on the other. H9109
Ex 37: 6 *t* and a half **cubits** long and a cubit and a half AIT
Ex 37: 7 Then he made **t** cherubim out of H9109
Ex 37: 8 at the **t** ends he made them of one piece H9109

Ex 37:10 of acacia wood—*t* **cubits** long, a cubit wide AIT
Ex 37:25 long and a cubit wide and *t* **cubits** high— AIT
Ex 37:27 They made **t** gold rings below the molding H9109
Ex 37:27 molding—**t** on each of the opposite sides H9109
Ex 39: 4 which were attached to **t** *of* its corners, so H9109
Ex 39:16 They made **t** gold filigree settings and two H9109
Ex 39:16 two gold filigree settings and **t** gold rings, H9109
Ex 39:16 the rings to **t** *of* the corners of the H9109
Ex 39:17 They fastened the **t** gold chains to the H9109
Ex 39:18 other ends of the chains to the **t** settings, H9109
Ex 39:19 They made **t** gold rings and attached them H9109
Ex 39:19 them to the other **t** corners of the H9109
Ex 39:20 Then they made **t** more gold rings and H9109
Lev 5: 7 a lamb is to bring **t** doves or two young H9109
Lev 5: 7 bring two doves or **t** young pigeons to the H9109
Lev 5:11 they cannot afford **t** doves or two young H9109
Lev 5:11 afford two doves or **t** young pigeons, H9109
Lev 8: 2 the **t** rams and the basket containing H9109
Lev 12: 5 *for t* **weeks** the woman will be unclean AIT
Lev 12: 8 she is to bring **t** doves or two young H9109
Lev 12: 8 is to bring two doves or **t** young pigeons, H9109
Lev 14: 4 shall order that **t** live clean birds and H9109
Lev 14:10 they must bring **t** male lambs and one H9109
Lev 14:22 **t** doves or two young pigeons, such as H9109
Lev 14:22 two doves or **t** young pigeons, such as H9109
Lev 14:49 house he is to take **t** birds and some H9109
Lev 15:14 day he must take **t** doves or two young H9109
Lev 15:14 take two doves or **t** young pigeons and H9109
Lev 15:29 day she must take **t** doves or two young H9109
Lev 15:29 take two doves or **t** young pigeons and H9109
Lev 16: 1 the death of the **t** sons of Aaron who died H9109
Lev 16: 5 he is to take **t** male goats for a sin H9109
Lev 16: 7 Then he is to take the **t** goats and present H9109
Lev 16: 8 He is to cast lots for the **t** goats—one lot H9109
Lev 16:12 the LORD and **t handfuls** *of* finely H2908+4850
Lev 19:19 not plant your field with **t kinds** *of* seed. H3977
Lev 19:19 clothing woven of **t kinds** of material. H3977
Lev 23:17 bring **t** loaves made of two-tenths of an H9109
Lev 23:18 one young bull and **t** rams. H9109
Lev 23:19 male goat for a sin offering and **t** lambs, H9109
Lev 23:20 is to wave the **t** lambs before the LORD H9109
Lev 24: 6 Arrange them in **t** stacks, six in each stack H9109
Nu 6:10 day they must bring **t** doves or two young H9109
Nu 6:10 bring two doves or **t** young pigeons to the H9109
Nu 7: 3 from each leader and a cart from every **t**. H9109
Nu 7: 7 He gave **t** carts and four oxen to the H9109
Nu 7:17 **t** oxen, five rams, five male goats and H9109
Nu 7:23 **t** oxen, five rams, five male goats and H9109
Nu 7:29 **t** oxen, five rams, five male goats and H9109
Nu 7:35 **t** oxen, five rams, five male goats and H9109
Nu 7:41 **t** oxen, five rams, five male goats and H9109
Nu 7:47 **t** oxen, five rams, five male goats and H9109
Nu 7:53 **t** oxen, five rams, five male goats and H9109
Nu 7:59 **t** oxen, five rams, five male goats and H9109
Nu 7:65 **t** oxen, five rams, five male goats and H9109
Nu 7:71 **t** oxen, five rams, five male goats and H9109
Nu 7:77 **t** oxen, five rams, five male goats and H9109
Nu 7:83 **t** oxen, five rams, five male goats and H9109
Nu 7:85 dishes weighed *t* **thousand** four hundred AIT
Nu 7:89 from between the **t** cherubim above the H9109
Nu 9:22 over the tabernacle *for t* **days** or a month AIT
Nu 10: 2 "Make **t** trumpets of hammered silver, and H9109
Nu 11:19 not eat it for just one day, or *t* **days**, or five, AIT
Nu 11:26 However, **t** men, whose names were H9109
Nu 11:31 them up to *t* **cubits** deep all around the AIT
Nu 12: 5 When the **t** *of* them stepped forward H9109
Nu 13:23 **T** of them carried it on a pole between H9109
Nu 22:22 donkey, and his **t** servants were with him. H9109
Nu 23: 2 and **the t of them** offered a H1192+2256+1189S
Nu 28: 3 **t** lambs a year old without defect, as a H9109
Nu 28: 9 make an offering of **t** lambs a year old H9109
Nu 28:11 the LORD a burnt offering of **t** young bulls, H9109
Nu 28:19 of a burnt offering of **t** young bulls, H9109
Nu 28:27 Present a burnt offering of **t** young bulls H9109
Nu 29:13 **t** rams and fourteen male lambs a year H9109
Nu 29:14 with each of the **t** rams, two-tenths; H9109
Nu 29:17 **t** rams and fourteen male lambs a year H9109
Nu 29:20 **t** rams and fourteen male lambs a year H9109
Nu 29:23 **t** rams and fourteen male lambs a year H9109
Nu 29:26 **t** rams and fourteen male lambs a year H9109
Nu 29:29 **t** rams and fourteen male lambs a year H9109
Nu 29:32 **t** rams and fourteen male lambs a year H9109
Nu 34:15 These **t** and a half tribes have received H9109
Nu 35: 5 measure *t* **thousand** cubits on the east side AIT
Nu 35: 5 the east side, *t* **thousand** on the south side AIT
Nu 35: 5 *t* **thousand** on the west and two thousand on AIT
Nu 35: 5 on the west and *t* **thousand** on the north, AIT
Dt 1:16 case is between *t* **Israelites** or between an AIT
Dt 3: 8 we took from these **t** kings of the Amorites H9109
Dt 3:21 LORD your God has done to these **t** kings. H9109
Dt 4:13 then wrote them on **t** stone tablets. H9109
Dt 4:47 the **t** Amorite kings east of the Jordan. H9109
Dt 5:22 he wrote them on **t** stone tablets and H9109
Dt 9:10 The LORD gave me **t** stone tablets inscribed H9109
Dt 9:11 the LORD gave me the **t** stone tablets, the H9109
Dt 9:15 And the **t** tablets of the covenant were in H9109
Dt 9:17 So I took the **t** tablets and threw them out H9109
Dt 10: 1 "Chisel out **t** stone tablets like the first H9109
Dt 10: 3 wood and chiseled out **t** stone tablets like H9109
Dt 10: 3 mountain with the **t** tablets in my hands. H9109
Dt 17: 6 On the testimony of **t** or three witnesses a H9109
Dt 19:15 by the testimony of **t** or three witnesses. H9109
Dt 19:17 the **t** people involved in the dispute must H9109
Dt 21:15 If a man has **t** wives, and he loves one H9109
Dt 22: 9 Do not plant **t kinds** of seed in your H3977
Dt 25:11 If **t men** are fighting and H408+2256+278+3481
Dt 25:13 have **t differing weights** in your H74+2256+74
Dt 25:14 have **t differing measures** in H406+2256+406
Dt 32:30 a thousand, or **t** put ten thousand to flight H9109
Jos 2: 1 of Nun secretly sent **t** spies from Shittim. H9109
Jos 2: 4 had taken the **t** men and hidden them H9109
Jos 2:10 the **t** kings of the Amorites east of the H9109
Jos 2:23 Then the **t** men started back. They went H9109
Jos 3: 4 distance of about *t* **thousand** cubits between AIT
Jos 6:22 Joshua said to the **t** men who had spied H9109
Jos 7: 3 Send *t* or three **thousand** men to take it and AIT
Jos 7:21 *t* **hundred** shekels of silver and a bar of gold AIT
Jos 9:10 that he did to the **t** kings of the Amorites H9109
Jos 14: 3 Moses had granted the **t** and a half tribes H9109
Jos 14: 4 descendants had become **t** tribes— H9109
Jos 15:60 Rabbah—**t** towns and their villages. H9109
Jos 21:16 nine towns from these **t** tribes. H9109
Jos 21:25 together with their pasturelands—**t** towns. H9109
Jos 21:27 together with their pasturelands—**t** towns; H9109
Jos 24:12 out before you—also the **t** Amorite kings. H9109
Jdg 5:30 a woman or **t** for each man, colorful H8169S
Jdg 7:25 They also captured **t** *of* the Midianite H9109
Jdg 8:12 Zalmunna, the **t** kings of Midian, fled H9109
Jdg 9:44 Then **t** companies attacked those in the H9109
Jdg 11:37 "Give me **t** months to roam the hills and H9109
Jdg 11:38 And he let her go for **t** months. She and H9109
Jdg 11:39 After the **t** months, she returned to her H9109
Jdg 15:13 they bound him with **t** new ropes and led H9109
Jdg 16: 3 together with the **t** posts, and tore them H9109
Jdg 16:28 revenge on the Philistines for my **t** eyes." H9109
Jdg 16:29 reached toward the **t** central pillars on H9109
Jdg 17: 4 she took *t* **hundred** shekels of silver and gave AIT
Jdg 19: 3 had with him his servant and **t** donkeys. H7538
Jdg 19: 6 So the **t** *of* them sat down to eat and drink H9109
Jdg 19: 8 So the **t** *of* them ate together. H9109
Jdg 19:10 with his **t** saddled donkeys and his H7538
Jdg 20:45 as Gidom and struck down *t* **thousand** more. AIT
Ru 1: 1 together with his wife and **t** sons, went to H9109
Ru 1: 2 the names of his **t** sons were Mahlon and H9109
Ru 1: 3 and she was left with her **t** sons. H9109
Ru 1: 5 left without her **t** sons and her husband H9109
Ru 1: 7 With her **t** daughters-in-law she left the H9109
Ru 1: 8 Naomi said to her **t** daughters-in-law, H9109
Ru 1:19 So the **t** women went on until they came H9109
1Sa 1: 2 He had **t** wives; one was called Hannah H9109
1Sa 1: 3 Phinehas, the **t** sons of Eli, were H9109
1Sa 2:21 gave birth to three sons and **t** daughters. H9109
1Sa 2:34 " 'And what happens to your **t** sons H9109
1Sa 4: 4 And Eli's **t** sons, Hophni and Phinehas H9109
1Sa 4:11 captured, and Eli's **t** sons, Hophni and H9109
1Sa 4:17 Also your **t** sons, Hophni and Phinehas H9109
1Sa 6: 7 with **t** cows that have calved and have H9109
1Sa 6:10 They took **t** such cows and hitched them H9109
1Sa 10: 2 you will meet **t** men near Rachel's tomb H9109
1Sa 10: 4 greet you and offer you **t** loaves of bread, H9109
1Sa 11:11 so that no **t** of them were left together. H9109
1Sa 13: 2 *t* **thousand** were with him at Mikmash and in AIT
1Sa 15: 4 *t* **hundred** thousand foot soldiers and ten AIT
1Sa 18:27 went out and killed *t* **hundred** Philistines AIT
1Sa 23:18 The **t** *of* them made a covenant before the H9109
1Sa 25:13 while *t* **hundred** stayed with the supplies. AIT
1Sa 25:18 She took *t* **hundred** loaves of bread, two skins AIT
1Sa 25:18 loaves of bread, **t** skins of wine, five H9109
1Sa 25:18 of raisins and *t* **hundred** cakes of pressed AIT
1Sa 27: 3 with him, and David had his **t** wives: H9109
1Sa 28: 8 at night he and **t** men went to the H9109
1Sa 30: 5 David's **t** wives had been captured H9109
1Sa 30:10 *T* **hundred** of them were too exhausted to AIT
1Sa 30:12 cake of pressed figs and **t** cakes of raisins. H9109
1Sa 30:18 had taken, including his **t** wives. H9109
1Sa 30:21 came to the *t* **hundred** men who had been AIT
2Sa 1: 1 Amalekites and stayed in Ziklag **t** days. H9109
2Sa 2: 2 So David went up there with his **t** wives H9109
2Sa 2:10 king over Israel, and he reigned **t** years. H9109
2Sa 4: 2 Now Saul's son had **t** men who were H9109
2Sa 8: 2 Every **t** lengths of them were put to death H9109
2Sa 12: 1 "There were **t** men in a certain town H9109
2Sa 13:23 *T* **years** later, when Absalom's sheepshearers AIT
2Sa 14: 6 I your servant had **t** sons. They got into a H9109
2Sa 14:26 its weight was *t* **hundred** shekels by the AIT
2Sa 14:28 Absalom lived *t* **years** in Jerusalem without AIT
2Sa 15:11 *T* **hundred** men from Jerusalem had AIT
2Sa 15:27 You and Abiathar return with your **t** sons. H9109
2Sa 15:36 Their **t** sons, Ahimaaz son of Zadok and H9109
2Sa 16: 1 loaded with *t* **hundred** loaves of bread, AIT
2Sa 17:18 So the **t** *of* them left at once and went to H9109
2Sa 17:21 the **t** climbed out of the well and went to NDT
2Sa 21: 8 the **t** sons of Aiah's daughter Rizpah H9109
2Sa 23:20 struck down Moab's **t** mightiest warriors. H9109
1Ki 2: 5 what he did to the **t** commanders of H9109
1Ki 2:32 it he attacked **t** men and killed them H9109
1Ki 2:39 **t** *of* Shimei's slaves ran off to Achish son H9109
1Ki 3:16 Now **t** prostitutes came to the king and H9109
1Ki 3:18 was no one in the house but the **t** of us. H9109
1Ki 3:25 the living child in **t** and give half to one H9109
1Ki 3:26 I nor you shall have him. **Cut him in t**!" H1615
1Ki 5:12 the **t** *of* them made a treaty. H9109
1Ki 5:14 month in Lebanon and **t** months at home. H9109
1Ki 6:25 the **t** cherubim were identical in size H9109
1Ki 6:32 And on the **t** olive-wood doors he carved H9109
1Ki 6:34 He also made **t** doors out of juniper wood H9109
1Ki 6:34 each having **t** leaves that turned in H9109
1Ki 7:15 He cast **t** bronze pillars, each eighteen H9109
1Ki 7:16 He also made **t** capitals of cast bronze to H9109
1Ki 7:18 pomegranates in **t** rows encircling each H9109
1Ki 7:20 were the *t* **hundred** pomegranates in rows all AIT
1Ki 7:24 gourds were cast in **t** rows in one piece H9109
1Ki 7:26 like a lily blossom. It held *t* **thousand** baths. AIT
1Ki 7:41 the **t** pillars; the two bowl-shaped capitals H9109
1Ki 7:41 the **t** bowl-shaped capitals on top of the H9109
1Ki 7:41 the **t** *sets* of network decorating the two H9109
1Ki 7:41 decorating the **t** bowl-shaped capitals H9109
1Ki 7:42 pomegranates for the **t** *sets* of network H9109
1Ki 7:42 **t** rows of pomegranates for each network H9109
1Ki 8: 9 in the ark except the **t** stone tablets that H9109
1Ki 9:10 which Solomon built these **t** buildings— H9109
1Ki 10:16 Solomon made *t* **hundred** large shields of AIT
1Ki 11:29 The **t** *of* them were alone out in the H9109
1Ki 12:28 the king made **t** golden calves. H9109
1Ki 15:25 of Judah, and he reigned over Israel *t* **years**. AIT
1Ki 16: 8 of Israel, and he reigned in Tirzah *t* **years**. AIT
1Ki 16:21 people of Israel were split into **t** *factions*; H2942
1Ki 16:24 from Shemer for *t* **talents** *of* silver and built a AIT
1Ki 18: 4 prophets and hidden them in **t** caves, NDT
1Ki 18:13 a hundred of the LORD's prophets in **t** caves, NDT
1Ki 18:21 long will you waver between **t** opinions? H9109
1Ki 18:23 Get **t** bulls for us. Let Baal's prophets H9109
1Ki 18:32 it large enough to hold *t* **seahs** *of* seed. AIT
1Ki 20:27 opposite them like **t** small flocks of goats, H9109
1Ki 21:10 But seat **t** scoundrels opposite him and H9109
1Ki 21:13 Then **t** scoundrels came and sat opposite H9109
1Ki 22:51 of Judah, and he reigned over Israel *t* **years**. AIT
2Ki 1:14 consumed the first **t** captains and all their H9109
2Ki 2: 6 So the **t** *of* them walked on. H9109
2Ki 2: 8 the **t** *of* them crossed over on dry H9109
2Ki 2:11 appeared and separated the **t** *of* them, H9109
2Ki 2:12 took hold of his garment and tore it in **t**. H9109
2Ki 2:24 Then **t** bears came out of the woods and H9109
2Ki 4: 1 is coming to take my **t** boys as his slaves." H9109
2Ki 4:33 the door on the **t** *of* them and prayed to H9109
2Ki 5:22 '**T** young men from the company of the H9109
2Ki 5:22 a talent of silver and **t** sets of clothing. H9109
2Ki 5:23 all means, take *t* **talents**," said Naaman. AIT
2Ki 5:23 then tied up the *t* **talents** of silver in two AIT
2Ki 5:23 tied up the two talents of silver in **t** bags, H9109
2Ki 5:23 silver in two bags, with **t** sets of clothing. H9109
2Ki 5:23 He gave them to **t** *of* his servants, and H9109
2Ki 7: 1 sell for a shekel and *t* **seahs** of barley for a AIT
2Ki 7:14 So they selected **t** chariots with their H9109
2Ki 7:16 and *t* **seahs** *of* barley sold for a shekel AIT
2Ki 7:18 sell for a shekel and *t* **seahs** of barley for a AIT
2Ki 9:32 **T** or three eunuchs looked down at him H9109
2Ki 10: 4 said, "If **t** kings could not resist him H9109
2Ki 10: 8 "Put them in **t** piles at the entrance of the H9109
2Ki 11: 7 who are in the other **t** companies that H9109
2Ki 15:23 of Israel in Samaria, and he reigned *t* **years**. AIT
2Ki 17:16 made for themselves **t** idols cast in the H9109
2Ki 18:23 I will give you *t* **thousand** horses—if you can AIT
2Ki 21: 5 In the **t** courts of the temple of the LORD, he H9109
2Ki 21:19 and he reigned in Jerusalem **t** years. H9109
2Ki 23:12 had built in the **t** courts of the temple of H9109
2Ki 25: 4 the gate between the *t* **walls** near the king's AIT
2Ki 25:16 The bronze from the **t** pillars, the Sea H9109
1Ch 1:19 **T** sons were born to Eber: One was H9109
1Ch 4: 5 Ashhur the father of Tekoa had **t** wives H9109
1Ch 5:21 *t* **hundred** fifty thousand sheep and two AIT
1Ch 5:21 fifty thousand sheep and *t* **thousand** donkeys. AIT
1Ch 11:22 struck down Moab's **t** mightiest warriors. H9109
1Ch 26:17 on the south and **t at a time** at the H9109+9109
1Ch 26:18 four at the road and **t** at the court itself. H9109
2Ch 3:15 the front of the temple he made **t** pillars, H9109
2Ch 4: 3 bulls were cast in **t** rows in one piece with H9109
2Ch 4:12 the **t** pillars; the two bowl-shaped capitals H9109
2Ch 4:12 the **t** bowl-shaped capitals on top of the H9109
2Ch 4:12 the **t** *sets* of network decorating the two H9109
2Ch 4:12 decorating the **t** bowl-shaped capitals H9109
2Ch 4:13 pomegranates for the **t** *sets of* network H9109
2Ch 4:13 (**t** rows of pomegranates for each network H9109
2Ch 5:10 in the ark except the **t** tablets that Moses H9109
2Ch 8:10 **t hundred** and fifty officials supervising H4395
2Ch 9:15 Solomon made *t* **hundred** large shields of AIT
2Ch 14: 8 and *t* **hundred** and eighty thousand from AIT
2Ch 24: 3 Jehoiada chose **t** wives for him, and he H9109
2Ch 28: 8 were from Judah *t* **hundred** thousand wives, AIT
2Ch 29:32 a hundred rams and *t* **hundred** male lambs AIT
2Ch 33:21 and he reigned in Jerusalem **t** years. H9109
Ezr 6:17 a hundred bulls, *t* **hundred** rams, four AIT
Ezr 8:27 **t** fine articles of polished bronze H9109
Ezr 10:13 cannot be taken care of in a day or **t**, H9109
Ne 11:16 Jozabad, **t** of the heads of the Levites NDT
Ne 12:31 I also assigned **t** large choirs to give H9109
Ne 12:40 The **t** choirs that gave thanks then took H9109
Est 2:21 **t** of the king's officers who guarded the H9109
Est 2:23 the **t** officials were impaled on poles. H9109
Est 6: 2 **t** of the king's officers who guarded the H9109
Est 9:27 fail observe these **t** days every year, H9109
Job 11: 6 of wisdom, for true wisdom has **t sides**. H4101
Job 13:20 "Only grant me these **t** *things*, God, and H9109
Job 42: 7 "I am angry with you and your **t** friends H9109
Ps 62:11 God has spoken, **t** things I have heard: H9109
Pr 24:22 those **t** will send sudden destruction H9109

Pr 30: 7 "T *things* I ask of you, LORD; do not refuse H9109
Pr 30:15 "The leech has t daughters. 'Give! Give!' H9109
Ecc 4: 6 tranquillity than *t* **handfuls** with toil and AIT
Ecc 4: 9 T are better than one, because they have H9109
Ecc 4:11 if t lie down together, they will keep H9109
Ecc 4:12 overpowered, t can defend themselves. H9109
SS 4: 5 Your breasts are like t fawns, like twin H9109
SS 7: 3 Your breasts are like t fawns, like twin H9109
SS 8:12 and *t* **hundred** are for those who tend its fruit. AIT
Isa 6: 2 With t wings they covered their faces, with H9109
Isa 6: 2 their faces, with t they covered their feet H9109
Isa 6: 2 their feet, and with t they were flying. H9109
Isa 7: 4 because of these t smoldering stubs of H9109
Isa 7:16 the land of the t kings you dread will be H9109
Isa 7:21 will keep alive a young cow and t goats. H9109
Isa 17: 6 leaving t or three olives on the topmost H9109
Isa 22:11 between the *t* **walls** for the water of the AIT
Isa 36: 8 I will give you *t* **thousand** horses—if you can AIT
Jer 2:13 "My people have committed t sins: They H9109
Jer 3:14 one from a town and t from a clan—and H9109
Jer 24: 1 the LORD showed me t baskets of figs H9109
Jer 28: 3 Within *t* **years** I will bring back to this place AIT
Jer 28:11 off the neck of all the nations within *t* **years**. AIT
Jer 33:24 has rejected the t kingdoms he chose'? H9109
Jer 34:18 the calf they cut in t and then walked H9109
Jer 39: 4 through the gate between the *t* **walls**, and AIT
Jer 52: 7 the gate between the *t* **walls** near the king's AIT
Jer 52:20 The bronze from the t pillars, the Sea H9109
Eze 1:11 They each had t wings spreading out H9109
Eze 1:11 each had t other wings covering its H9109
Eze 1:23 each had t wings covering its body. H9109
Eze 18: 8 judges fairly between t **parties**. H408+4200+408
Eze 21:19 mark out t roads for the sword of the king H9109
Eze 21:21 at the junction of the t roads, to seek an H9109
Eze 23: 2 of man, there were t women, daughters of H9109
Eze 35:10 "These t nations and countries will be H9109
Eze 37:22 will never again be t nations or be H9109
Eze 37:22 two nations or be divided into t kingdoms. H9109
Eze 40: 9 deep and its jambs were t cubits thick. H9109
Eze 40:39 of the gateway were t tables on each side H9109
Eze 40:40 of the north gateway were t tables, H9109
Eze 40:40 the other side of the steps were t tables. H9109
Eze 40:44 the inner court, were t rooms, one at the H9109
Eze 41: 3 of the entrance; each was t cubits wide. H9109
Eze 41:18 with cherubim. Each cherub had t faces: H9109
Eze 41:22 altar three cubits high and t cubits square; H9109
Eze 41:24 Each door had t leaves—two hinged H9109
Eze 41:24 leaves—t hinged leaves for each door. H9109
Eze 43:14 goes around the altar it is t cubits high, H9109
Eze 45:15 from every flock of *t* **hundred** from the AIT
Eze 47:13 their inheritance, with *t* **portions** for Joseph. AIT
Da 7: 4 so that it stood on *t* **feet** like a human being, AIT
Da 8: 3 there before me was a ram with *t* **horns** AIT
Da 8: 7 striking the ram and shattering its t horns. H9109
Da 11:27 The t kings, with their hearts bent on evil H9109
Da 12: 5 there before me stood t others, one H9109
Hos 6: 2 After *t* **days** he will revive us; on the third day AIT
Am 1: 1 saw concerning Israel *t* **years** before the AIT
Am 3: 3 Do t walk together unless they have H9109
Am 3:12 lion's mouth only t leg bones or a piece H9109
Am 6: 2 Are they better off than your t kingdoms H465S
Zec 4: 3 Also there are t olive trees by it, one on H9109
Zec 4:11 "What are these t olive trees on the right H9109
Zec 4:12 "What are these t olive branches beside H9109
Zec 4:12 branches beside the t gold pipes that H9109
Zec 4:14 "These are the t who are anointed to H9109
Zec 5: 9 there before me were t women, with H9109
Zec 6: 1 coming out from between t mountains— H9109
Zec 6:13 And there will be harmony between the t H9109
Zec 11: 7 Then I took t staffs and called one Favor H9109
Zec 14: 4 Olives will be split in t from east to west, H2942
Mt 2:16 vicinity who were t **years old** and under, G1453
Mt 4:18 of Galilee, he saw t brothers, Simon G1545
Mt 4:21 from there, he saw t other brothers, James G1545
Mt 5:41 you to go one mile, go with them t miles. G1545
Mt 6:24 "No one can serve t masters. Either you G1545
Mt 8:28 t demon-possessed men coming from the G1545
Mt 9:27 on from there, t blind men followed him G1545
Mt 10:29 Are not t sparrows sold for a penny? Yet G1545
Mt 14:17 here only five loaves of bread and t fish," G1545
Mt 14:19 five loaves and the t fish and looking up G1545
Mt 18: 8 than to have t hands or two feet and G1545
Mt 18: 8 to have two hands or t feet and be thrown G1545
Mt 18: 9 eye than to have t eyes and be thrown G1545
Mt 18:15 just between **the t of you**. G5148+2779+899
Mt 18:16 take one or t *others* along, so that G1545
Mt 18:16 by the testimony *of* t or three witnesses. G1545
Mt 18:19 I tell you that if t of you on earth agree G1545
Mt 18:20 For where t or three gather in my name G1545
Mt 19: 5 and the t will become one flesh'? G1545
Mt 19: 6 So they are no longer t, but one flesh G1545
Mt 20:21 that one of these t sons of mine may sit at G1545
Mt 20:24 they were indignant with the t brothers. G1545
Mt 20:30 T blind men were sitting by the roadside G1545
Mt 21: 1 Mount of Olives, Jesus sent t disciples, G1545
Mt 21:28 There was a man who had t sons. G1545
Mt 21:31 "Which of the t did what his father G1545
Mt 22:40 hang on these t commandments. G1545
Mt 24:40 T *men* will be in the field; one will be G1545
Mt 24:41 T *women* will be grinding with a hand mill G1545
Mt 25:15 of gold, to another t bags, and to another G1545
Mt 25:17 the one with t bags of gold gained two G1545
Mt 25:17 one with two bags of gold gained t more. G1545
Mt 25:22 "The man with t bags of gold also came G1545
Mt 25:22 'you entrusted me *with* t bags of gold; see G1545
Mt 25:22 bags of gold; see, I have gained t more. G1545
Mt 26: 2 the Passover is t days away—and the Son G1545
Mt 26:37 He took Peter and the t sons of Zebedee G1545
Mt 26:60 came forward. Finally t came forward G1545
Mt 27:21 "Which of the t do you want me to G1545
Mt 27:38 T rebels were crucified with him, one on G1545
Mt 27:51 temple was torn in t from top to bottom. G1545
Mk 5:13 about t **thousand in number**, rushed G1493
Mk 6: 7 to send them out t by two and gave them G1545
Mk 6: 7 to send them out two *by* t and gave them G1545
Mk 6:38 found out, they said, "Five—and t fish." G1545
Mk 6:41 five loaves and the t fish and looking up G1545
Mk 6:41 He also divided the t fish among them all. G1545
Mk 9:43 maimed than with t hands to go into hell G1545
Mk 9:45 crippled than to have t feet and be thrown G1545
Mk 9:47 eye than to have t eyes and be thrown G1545
Mk 10: 8 the t will become one flesh.' So they G1545
Mk 10: 8 So they are no longer t, but one flesh. G1545
Mk 11: 1 of Olives, Jesus sent t of his disciples, G1545
Mk 12:42 came and put in t very small copper G1545
Mk 14: 1 Unleavened Bread were *only* t days away, G1545
Mk 14:13 So he sent t of his disciples, telling them G1545
Mk 15:27 They crucified t rebels with him, one on G1545
Mk 15:38 temple was torn in t from top to bottom. G1545
Mk 16:12 in a different form *to* t of them while they G1545
Lk 2:24 "a pair of doves or t young pigeons." G1545
Lk 3:11 "Anyone who has t shirts should share G1545
Lk 5: 2 He saw at the water's edge t boats, left G1545
Lk 7:18 about all these things. Calling t of them, G1545
Lk 7:41 "T *people* owed money to a certain G1545
Lk 9:13 have only five loaves of bread and t fish— G1545
Lk 9:16 five loaves and the t fish and looking up G1545
Lk 9:30 T men, Moses and Elijah, appeared in G1545
Lk 9:32 his glory and the t men standing with him G1545
Lk 10: 1 sent them t by two ahead of him G1545
Lk 10: 1 sent them two by t ahead of him to G1545
Lk 10:35 next day he took out t denarii and gave G1545
Lk 12: 6 Are not five sparrows sold for t pennies G1545
Lk 12:52 three against t and two against three. G1545
Lk 12:52 three against two and t against three. G1545
Lk 15:11 "There was a man who had t sons. G1545
Lk 16:13 "No one can serve t masters. Either you G1545
Lk 17:34 on that night t people will be in one bed G1545
Lk 17:35 T women will be grinding grain together G1545
Lk 18:10 "T men went up to the temple to pray, one G1545
Lk 19:29 of Olives, he sent t of his disciples, saying G1545
Lk 21: 2 a poor widow put in t very small copper G1545
Lk 22:38 "See, Lord, here are t swords. G1545
Lk 23:32 T other men, both criminals, were also G1545
Lk 23:45 the curtain of the temple was torn **in** t. G3545
Lk 24: 4 suddenly t men in clothes that gleamed G1545
Lk 24:13 Now that same day t of them were going G1545
Lk 24:35 Then **the** t told what had happened on the G899S
Jn 1:35 was there again with t of his disciples. G1545
Jn 1:37 When the t disciples heard him say this G1545
Jn 1:40 was one of the t who heard what John G1545
Jn 4:40 to stay with them, and he stayed t days. G1545
Jn 4:43 After the t days he left for Galilee. G1545
Jn 6: 9 five small barley loaves and t small fish, G1545
Jn 8:17 that the testimony of t witnesses is true. G1545
Jn 11: 6 he stayed where he was t *more* days, G1545
Jn 11:18 was **less than** t **miles** from G6055+5084+1278
Jn 19:18 and with him t others—one on each G1545
Jn 19:40 *the t of them* **wrapped** it, with the AIT
Jn 20:12 saw t angels in white, seated where G1545
Jn 21: 2 t other disciples were together. G1545
Ac 1:10 when suddenly t men dressed in white G1545
Ac 1:23 So they nominated t *men*: Joseph called G1545
Ac 1:24 Show us which of these t you have chosen G1545
Ac 7:26 Moses came upon t **Israelites** who were G899S
Ac 7:29 he settled as a foreigner and had t sons. G1545
Ac 9:38 they sent t men to him and urged him G1545
Ac 10: 7 Cornelius called t of his servants and a G1545
Ac 12: 6 Peter was sleeping between t soldiers G1545
Ac 12: 6 soldiers, bound with t chains, and sentries G1545
Ac 13: 4 *The t of* **them**, sent on their way by the Holy AIT
Ac 19:10 This went on for t years, so that all the G1545
Ac 19:22 He sent t of his helpers, Timothy and G1545
Ac 19:34 all shouted in unison for about t hours: G1545
Ac 21:33 ordered him to be bound with t chains. G1545
Ac 23:23 Then he called t of his centurions and G1545
Ac 23:23 ready a detachment of t **hundred** soldiers, G1357
Ac 23:23 horsemen and t **hundred** spearmen to go G1357
Ac 24:27 When t years had passed, Felix was G1454
Ac 28:30 *For* t whole **years** Paul stayed there in his G1454
1Co 6:16 it is said, "The t will become one flesh." G1545
1Co 14:27 speaks in a tongue, t—or at the most G1545
1Co 14:29 T or three prophets should speak, and the G1545
2Co 13: 1 by the testimony of t or three witnesses." G1545
Gal 4:22 For it is written that Abraham had t sons G1545
Gal 4:24 The women represent t covenants. G1545
Eph 2:14 who has made the t *groups* one and has G317
Eph 2:15 in himself one new humanity *out of* the t, G1545
Eph 5:31 his wife, and the t will become one flesh." G1545
Php 1:23 I am torn between the t: I desire to depart G1545
1Ti 5:19 it is brought by t or three witnesses. G1545
Heb 6:18 by t unchangeable things in which it is G1545
Heb 10:28 on the testimony of t or three witnesses. G1545
Heb 11:37 stoning; *they were* **sawed in** t; they were G4569
Rev 6: 6 "T **pounds** of wheat for a day's wages G5955
Rev 9:12 woe is past; t other woes are yet to come. G1545
Rev 11: 3 And I will appoint my t witnesses, and G1545
Rev 11: 4 They are "the t olive trees" and the two G1545
Rev 11: 4 olive trees" and the t lampstands, and G1545
Rev 11:10 because these t prophets had tormented G1545
Rev 12:14 woman was given the t wings of a great G1545
Rev 13:11 It had t horns like a lamb, but it spoke like G1545
Rev 19:20 The t of them were thrown alive into the G1545

TWO-DRACHMA (1) [DRACHMAS, TWO]

Mt 17:24 collectors *of* the t **temple tax** came to G1440

TWO-HORNED (2) [HORN, TWO]

Da 8: 6 toward the t ram I had seen H1251+2021+7967
Da 8:20 The t ram that you saw H1251+2021+7967

TWO-TENTHS (11) [TEN, TWO]

Lev 23:13 offering of t *of* an ephah of the H6928+9109
Lev 23:17 loaves made of t *of* an ephah of H6928+9109
Lev 24: 5 using t of an ephah for each loaf. H9109+6928
Nu 15: 6 grain offering of t of an ephah of H9109+6928
Nu 28: 9 grain offering of t of an ephah of H9109+6928
Nu 28:12 grain offering of t of an ephah of H9109+6928
Nu 28:20 mixed with oil; with the ram, t; H9109+6928
Nu 28:28 mixed with oil; with the ram, t; H9109+6928
Nu 29: 3 with olive oil; with the ram, t; H9109+6928
Nu 29: 9 mixed with oil; with the ram, t; H9109+6928
Nu 29:14 with each of the two rams, t; H9109+6928

TWO-THIRDS (2) [THREE, TWO]

1Sa 13:21 The price was **t of a shekel** for sharpening H7088
Zec 13: 8 "t will be struck down and perish H7023+9109

TWOEDGED (KJV) DOUBLE-EDGED

TYCHICUS (5)

Ac 20: 4 T and Trophimus from the province of G5608
Eph 6:21 T, the dear brother and faithful servant in G5608
Col 4: 7 T will tell you all the news about me. G5608
2Ti 4:12 I sent T to Ephesus. G5608
Titus 3:12 As soon as I send Artemas or T to you, do G5608

TYING (2) [TIE]

Pr 26: 8 Like t a stone in a sling is the giving of H7674
Mk 3:27 strong man's house without first t him **up**. G1313

TYPE (4)

Ex 25: 5 dyed red and **another** t *of* durable H9391S
Ex 35: 7 dyed red and **another** t *of* durable H9391S
1Ch 12:33 prepared for battle with **every** t *of* weapon, AIT
1Ch 12:37 armed with **every** *t of* weapon—120,000. AIT

TYRANNICAL (1) [TYRANNY]

Pr 28:16 A t ruler practices extortion, but H2894+9312

TYRANNUS (1)

Ac 19: 9 discussions daily in the lecture hall *of* T. G5598

TYRANNY (1) [TYRANNICAL]

Isa 54:14 T will be far from you; you will have H6945

TYRE (60) [TYRIANS]

Jos 19:29 Ramah and went to the fortified city of T, H7450
2Sa 5:11 Now Hiram king of T sent envoys to David, H7450
2Sa 24: 7 the fortress of T and all the towns of H7450
1Ki 5: 1 Hiram king of T heard that Solomon H7450
1Ki 7:13 Solomon sent to T and brought Huram, H7450
1Ki 7:14 whose father was from T and a skilled H7660
1Ki 9:11 towns in Galilee to Hiram king of T, H7450
1Ki 9:12 when Hiram went from T to see the towns H7450
1Ch 14: 1 Now Hiram king of T sent messengers to H7450
2Ch 2: 3 sent this message to Hiram king of T: H7450
2Ch 2:11 Hiram king of T replied by letter to H7450
2Ch 2:14 from Dan and whose father was **from** T. H7660
Ezr 3: 7 olive oil to the people of Sidon and T, H7660
Ne 13:16 **People from** T who lived in Jerusalem H7660
Ps 45:12 The city of T will come with a gift, people H7450
Ps 83: 7 Amalek, Philistia, with the people of T. H7450
Ps 87: 4 Philistia too, and T, along with Cush H7450
Isa 23: 1 A prophecy against T: Wail, you ships of H7450
Isa 23: 1 For T is destroyed and left without house NDT
Isa 23: 3 harvest of the Nile was the revenue of T, H2023S
Isa 23: 5 will be in anguish at the report from T. H7450
Isa 23: 8 Who planned this against T, the bestower H7450
Isa 23:15 At that time T will be forgotten for seventy H7450
Isa 23:15 it will happen to T as in the song of the H7450
Isa 23:17 seventy years, the LORD will deal with T. H7450
Jer 25:22 all the kings of T and Sidon; the kings of H7450
Jer 27: 3 T and Sidon through the envoys who have H7450
Jer 47: 4 all survivors who could help T and Sidon. H7450
Eze 26: 2 of man, because T has said of Jerusalem H7450
Eze 26: 3 I am against you, T, and I will bring many H7450
Eze 26: 4 destroy the walls of T and pull down her H7450
Eze 26: 7 to bring against T Nebuchadnezzar king H7450
Eze 26:15 "This is what the Sovereign LORD says to T H7450
Eze 27: 2 of man, take up a lament concerning T. H7450
Eze 27: 3 Say to T, situated at the gateway to the H7450
Eze 27: 3 " 'You say, T, "I am perfect in H7450
Eze 27: 8 your skilled men, T, were aboard as your H7450
Eze 27:32 "Who was ever silenced like T H7450
Eze 28: 2 say to the ruler of T, 'This is what the H7450
Eze 28:12 concerning the king of T and say to him: H7450
Eze 29:18 his army in a hard campaign against T; H7450

Eze 29:18 from the campaign he led against **T**. H7450
Hos 9:13 seen Ephraim, like **T**, planted in a H7450
Joel 3: 4 **T** and Sidon and all you regions of H7450
Am 1: 9 "For three sins of **T**, even for four, I will H7450
Am 1:10 fire on the walls of **T** that will consume H7450
Zec 9: 2 borders on it, and on **T** and Sidon, though H7450
Zec 9: 3 **T** has built herself a stronghold; she has H7450
Mt 11:21 you had been performed in **T** and Sidon, G5602
Mt 11:22 be more bearable *for* **T** and Sidon on the G5602
Mt 15:21 withdrew to the region *of* **T** and Sidon. G5602
Mk 3: 8 the Jordan and around **T** and Sidon. G5602
Mk 7:24 that place and went to the vicinity *of* **T**. G5602
Mk 7:31 left the vicinity *of* **T** and went through G5602
Lk 6:17 the coastal region around **T** and Sidon, G5602
Lk 10:13 you had been performed in **T** and Sidon, G5602
Lk 10:14 be more bearable *for* **T** and Sidon at the G5602
Ac 12:20 quarreling *with the* **people of T** and Sidon G5601
Ac 21: 3 We landed at **T**, where our ship was to G5602
Ac 21: 7 our voyage from **T** and landed at G5602

TYRIANS (1) [TYRE]
1Ch 22: 4 the Sidonians and **T** had brought large H7660

U

UCAL (NIV84) PREVAIL

UEL (1)
Ezr 10:34 descendants of Bani: Maadai, Amram, **U**, H198

UGLY (8)
Ge 41: 3 other cows, **u** and gaunt, came H8273+5260
Ge 41: 4 cows that were **u** and gaunt ate up H8273+5260
Ge 41:19 scrawny and very **u** and lean. H8273+9307
Ge 41:19 had never seen such **u** cows in all the H8278
Ge 41:20 **u** cows ate up the seven fat cows that H8273
Ge 41:21 done so; they looked just as **u** as before. H8273
Ge 41:27 **u** cows that came up afterward are seven H8273
Rev 16: 2 bowl on the land, and **u**, festering sores G2805

ULAI (2)
Da 8: 2 in the vision I was beside the **U** Canal. H217
Da 8:16 I heard a man's voice from the **U** calling, H217

ULAM (4)
1Ch 7:16 Sheresh, and his sons were **U** and Rakem. H220
1Ch 7:17 The son of **U**: Bedan. These were the sons H220
1Ch 8:39 **U** his firstborn, Jeush the second son and H220
1Ch 8:40 The sons of **U** were brave warriors who H220

ULLA (1)
1Ch 7:39 The sons of **U**: Arah, Hanniel and Rizia. H6587

UMMAH (1)
Jos 19:30 **U**, Aphek and Rehob. There were H6646

UNABLE (13)
Lev 25:35 poor and *are* **u to support** H4572+3338
Jdg 1:19 they were **u** to drive the people from H4202
Jdg 13: 2 a wife who was childless, **u** to give birth. H4202
Isa 46: 2 together; **u** to rescue the burden H4202+3523
Eze 3:26 you will be silent and **u** to rebuke them, H4202
Eze 17:14 would be brought low, **u** to rise again H1194
Da 6: 4 affairs, but *they were* **u** to do so. A10379+10321
Lk 1:22 signs to them but remained **u to speak**. G3273
Lk 1:36 was said to be **u to conceive** is in her sixth G5096
Lk 20:26 *They were* **u** to trap him in what he G4024+2710
Jn 8:43 Because *you are* **u** to hear what I G4024+1538
Jn 21: 6 *they were* **u** to haul the net in G4033+2710
Heb 4:15 a high priest *who is* **u** to empathize G3590+1538

UNAFRAID (1)
Ps 78:53 safely, so *they were* **u**; but the sea H4202+7064

UNANSWERED (2)
Job 11: 2 "*Are* all these words *to* **go u**? Is this H4202+6699
Ps 35:13 When my prayers **returned** to me **u** H8740+2668

UNAPPROACHABLE (1)
1Ti 6:16 alone is immortal and who lives in **u** light, G717

UNASHAMED (1)
1Jn 2:28 be confident and **u** before him at his G3590+159

UNAUTHORIZED (4)
Lev 10: 1 they offered **u** fire before the LORD H2424
Lev 22:13 No **u person**, however, may H2424
Nu 3: 4 made an offering with **u** fire before him in H2424
Nu 26:61 an offering before the LORD with **u** fire.) H2424

UNAVENGED (1)
Joel 3:21 Shall *I* **leave** their innocent blood **u**? No, H5927

UNAWARE (8)
Lev 4:13 community is **u** *of* the matter H6623+4946+6524
Lev 5: 2 and they *are* **u** that they have H6623+4946
Lev 5: 3 even though they *are* **u of** *it*, but H6623+4946
Lev 5: 4 even though they *are* **u of** *it*, but H6623+4946
Pr 28:22 to get rich and *are* **u** that poverty H4202+3359
Lk 2:43 in Jerusalem, but they *were* **u** of it. G4024+1182
Ro 1:13 I do not want you *to be* **u**, brothers and G51
2Co 2:11 For *we are* not **u** of his schemes. G51

UNAWARES (KJV) ACCIDENTALLY, DECEIVED, SECRETLY, SUDDENLY, SURPRISE, WITHOUT KNOWING

UNBELIEF (6) [UNBELIEVER, UNBELIEVERS, UNBELIEVING]
Mk 9:24 "I do believe; help me overcome my **u**!" G602
Ro 4:20 he did not waver *through* **u** regarding the G602
Ro 11:20 But they were broken off *because of* **u**, and G602
Ro 11:23 And if they do not persist *in* **u**, they will be G602
1Ti 1:13 mercy because I acted in ignorance and **u**. G602
Heb 3:19 were not able to enter, because of their **u**. G602

UNBELIEVER (5) [UNBELIEF]
1Co 7:15 But if the **u** leaves, let it be so. The brother G603
1Co 10:27 If an **u** invites you to a meal and you want G603
1Co 14:24 But if an **u** or an inquirer comes in while G603
2Co 6:15 a believer have in common with an **u**? G603
1Ti 5: 8 denied the faith and is worse *than* an **u**. G603

UNBELIEVERS (8) [UNBELIEF]
Lk 12:46 pieces and assign him a place with the **u**. G603
Ro 15:31 kept safe from the **u** in Judea and that the G578
1Co 6: 6 another to court—and this in front of **u**! G603
1Co 14:22 not for believers but *for* **u**; prophecy, G603
1Co 14:22 however, is not *for* **u** but for believers. G603
1Co 14:23 inquirers or **u** come in, will they not G603
2Co 4: 4 god of this age has blinded the minds *of* **u**, G603
2Co 6:14 Do not be yoked together *with* **u**. For what G603

UNBELIEVING (7) [UNBELIEF]
Mt 17:17 "You **u** and perverse generation," Jesus G603
Mk 9:19 "You **u** generation," Jesus replied, "how G603
Lk 9:41 "You **u** and perverse generation," Jesus G603
1Co 7:14 For the **u** husband has been sanctified G603
1Co 7:14 the **u** wife has been sanctified through G603
Heb 3:12 **u** heart that turns away from the living God. G602
Rev 21: 8 But the cowardly, the **u**, the vile, the G603

UNBLEMISHED (1)
Heb 9:14 the eternal Spirit offered himself **u** to God, G320

UNBORN (1) [BEAR]
Ps 22:31 declaring to a people **yet u**: H3528

UNBOUND (1)
Da 3:25 around in the fire, **u** and unharmed, and A10742

UNCEASING (2) [UNCEASINGLY]
Isa 14: 6 struck down peoples with **u** blows, H1194+6239
Ro 9: 2 great sorrow and **u** anguish in my heart. G89

UNCEASINGLY (1) [UNCEASING]
La 3:49 My eyes will flow **u**, without relief, H4202+1949

UNCERTAIN (1)
1Ti 6:17 in wealth, which is *so* **u**, but to put their G84

UNCHANGEABLE (1) [UNCHANGED]
Heb 6:18 by two **u** things in which it is impossible G292

UNCHANGED (5) [UNCHANGEABLE, UNCHANGING]
Lev 13: 5 sees that the sore *is* **u** and has not spread H6641
Lev 13:23 But if the spot *is* **u** and has not H6641+9393
Lev 13:28 the spot *is* **u** and has not spread in H6641+9393
Lev 13:37 the sore *is* **u** so far as the priest can see H6641
Jer 48:11 as she did, and her aroma *is* **u**. H4202+4614

UNCHANGING (1) [UNCHANGED]
Heb 6:17 to make the **u** *nature* of his purpose G292

UNCHECKED (1)
Am 1:11 continually and his fury **flamed u**, H9068+5905

UNCIRCUMCISED (38) [UNCIRCUMCISION]
Ge 17:14 Any **u** male, who has not been H6888
Ex 12:48 born in the land. No **u** *male* may eat it. H6888
Lev 26:41 then when their **u** hearts are humbled H6888
Jos 5: 7 They were still **u** because they had not H6888
Jdg 14: 3 Must you go to the **u** Philistines to get a H6888
Jdg 15:18 of thirst and fall into the hands of the **u**?" H6888
1Sa 14: 6 go over to the outpost of those **u** *men*. H6888
1Sa 17:26 Who is this **u** Philistine that he should H6888
1Sa 17:36 this **u** Philistine will be like one of them H6888
1Sa 31: 4 these **u** *fellows* will come and run me H6888
2Sa 1:20 lest the daughters of the **u** rejoice. H6888
1Ch 10: 4 these **u** *fellows* will come and abuse H6888
Isa 52: 1 The **u** and defiled will not enter you H6888
Jer 9:26 For all these nations are really **u**, and H6888
Jer 9:26 the whole house of Israel is **u** *in* heart." H6888
Eze 28:10 will die the death of the **u** at the hands of H6888
Eze 31:18 you will lie among the **u**, with those killed H6888
Eze 32:19 Go down and be laid among the **u**.' H6888
Eze 32:21 have come down and they lie with the **u**, H6888
Eze 32:24 living went down **u** to the earth below. H6888
Eze 32:25 All of them are **u**, killed by the sword H6888
Eze 32:26 All of them are **u**, killed by the sword H6888
Eze 32:28 will be broken and will lie among the **u** H6888
Eze 32:29 They lie with the **u**, with those who go H6888
Eze 32:30 They lie **u** with those killed by the sword H6888
Eze 32:32 all his hordes will be laid among the **u**, H6888
Eze 44: 7 brought foreigners **u** *in* heart and flesh H6888
Eze 44: 9 No foreigner **u** *in* heart and flesh is to H6888
Ac 7:51 Your hearts and ears are still **u**. You are G598
Ac 11: 3 the house of **u** men and ate with G213+2400
Ro 3:30 by faith and the **u** through that same faith. G213
Ro 4: 9 only for the circumcised, or also for the **u**? G213
Ro 4:11 he had by faith while he was still **u**. G1877+213
1Co 7:18 *He should* not *become* **u**. Was a G2177
1Co 7:18 Was a man **u** when he was called G1877+213
Gal 2: 7 the task of preaching the gospel *to* the **u**, G213
Eph 2:11 who are Gentiles by birth and called "**u**" G213
Col 3:11 Gentile or Jew, circumcised or **u**, barbarian, G213

UNCIRCUMCISION (4) [UNCIRCUMCISED]
1Co 7:19 Circumcision is nothing and **u** is nothing G213
Gal 5: 6 neither circumcision nor **u** has any value. G213
Gal 6:15 Neither circumcision nor **u** means anything G213
Col 2:13 dead in your sins and *in* the **u** of your flesh, G213

UNCLE (13) [UNCLE'S]
Ge 29:10 saw Rachel daughter of his **u** Laban, H562+278
Lev 10: 4 sons of Aaron's **u** Uzziel, and said to H1856
Lev 20:20 with his aunt, he has dishonored his **u**. H1856
Lev 25:49 An **u** or a cousin or any blood relative in H1856
1Sa 10:14 Now Saul's **u** asked him and his servant H1856
1Sa 10:15 Saul's **u** said, "Tell me what Samuel said H1856
1Sa 10:16 he did not tell his **u** what Samuel had H1856
1Sa 14:50 Abner son of Ner, and Ner was Saul's **u**. H1856
2Ki 24:17 Jehoiachin's **u**, king in his place and H1856
1Ch 27:32 Jonathan, David's **u**, was a counselor, H1856
2Ch 36:10 he made Jehoiachin's **u**, Zedekiah, H278
Est 2:15 the daughter of his **u** Abihail) to go to the H1856
Jer 32: 7 son of Shallum your **u** is going to come to H1856

UNCLE'S (1) [UNCLE]
Ge 29:10 of the well and watered his **u** sheep. H278+562

UNCLEAN (209) [UNCLEANNESS]
Ge 7: 2 one pair of every kind of **u** animal, H4202+3196
Ge 7: 8 Pairs of clean and **u** animals, of birds H401+3196
Lev 5: 2 touch anything **ceremonially u** H3238
Lev 5: 2 whether the carcass of an **u** animal, wild H3238
Lev 5: 2 of any **u** creature that moves along the H3238
Lev 5: 2 are unaware that they *have become* **u**, H3237
Lev 5: 3 anything that *would make them* **u**) even H3237
Lev 7:19 anything **ceremonially u** must not be H3238
Lev 7:20 But if anyone who is **u** eats any meat of H3240
Lev 7:21 Anyone who touches something **u** H3238
Lev 7:21 uncleanness or an **u** animal or any H3238
Lev 7:21 animal or any **u** creature that moves H3238
Lev 10:10 common, between the **u** and the clean, H3238
Lev 11: 4 divided hoof; it is **ceremonially u** for you. H3238
Lev 11: 5 not have a divided hoof; it is **u** for you. H3238
Lev 11: 6 not have a divided hoof; it is **u** for you. H3238
Lev 11: 7 does not chew the cud; it is **u** for you. H3238
Lev 11: 8 touch their carcasses; they are **u** for you. H3238
Lev 11:10 in the water—you are to regard as **u**. H9211
Lev 11:11 And since you are to regard them as **u** H9211
Lev 11:11 *you must* **regard** their carcasses **as u**. H9210
Lev 11:12 scales is to be regarded as **u** by you. H9211
Lev 11:13 the birds *you are to* **regard as u** and not H9210
Lev 11:13 unclean and not eat because they are **u**: H9211
Lev 11:20 all fours are to be regarded as **u** by you. H9211
Lev 11:23 that have four legs you are to regard as **u**. H9211
Lev 11:24 " '*You will* **make yourselves u** by these H3237
Lev 11:24 their carcasses *will be* **u** till evening. H3237
Lev 11:25 clothes, and *they will be* **u** till evening. H3237
Lev 11:26 that does not chew the cud is **u** for you; H3238
Lev 11:26 the carcass of any of them *will be* **u**. H3237
Lev 11:27 that walk on their paws are **u** for you; H3238
Lev 11:27 their carcasses *will be* **u** till evening. H3237
Lev 11:28 clothes, and *they will be* **u** till evening. H3237
Lev 11:28 These animals are **u** for you. H3238
Lev 11:29 along the ground, these are **u** for you: H3238
Lev 11:31 along the ground, these are **u** for you. H3238
Lev 11:31 when they are dead *will be* **u** till evening. H3237
Lev 11:32 whatever its use, *will be* **u**, whether it is H3237
Lev 11:32 Put it in water; *it will be* **u** till evening H3237
Lev 11:33 everything in it *will be* **u**, and you must H3237
Lev 11:34 contact with water from any such pot *is* **u**, H3237
Lev 11:34 liquid that is drunk from such a pot *is* **u**. H3237
Lev 11:35 one of their carcasses falls on *becomes* **u**; H3237
Lev 11:35 They are **u**, and you are to regard them as H3238
Lev 11:35 unclean, and you are to regard them as **u**. H3238
Lev 11:36 who touches one of these carcasses *is* **u**. H3237
Lev 11:38 a carcass falls on it, it is **u** for you. H3238
Lev 11:39 touches its carcass *will be* **u** till evening. H3237
Lev 11:40 clothes, and *they will be* **u** till evening. H3237
Lev 11:40 clothes, and *they will be* **u** till evening. H3237
Lev 11:41 along the ground is to be **regarded as u**; H9211
Lev 11:42 walks on all fours or on many feet; it is **u**. H9211
Lev 11:43 *Do* not **make yourselves u** by means of H3237
Lev 11:43 by means of them or **be made u** by them. H3237
Lev 11:44 *Do* not **make** yourselves **u** by any creature H3237
Lev 11:47 distinguish between the **u** and the clean, H3238
Lev 12: 2 to a son *will be* **ceremonially u** for seven H3237
Lev 12: 2 just as *she is* **u** during her monthly period. H3237
Lev 12: 5 two weeks the woman *will be* **u**, as H3237
Lev 13: 3 *he shall* **pronounce** them **ceremonially u**. H3237
Lev 13: 8 he *shall* **pronounce** them **u**; it is a H3237
Lev 13:11 the priest *shall* **pronounce** them **u**. H3237
Lev 13:11 isolate them, because they are already **u**. H3238
Lev 13:14 raw flesh appears on them, *they will be* **u**. H3237

U

Lev 13:15 the raw flesh, *he shall* **pronounce** them **u**. H3237
Lev 13:15 The raw flesh is **u**; they have a defiling H3238
Lev 13:20 the priest *shall* **pronounce** that person **u**. H3237
Lev 13:22 the priest *shall* **pronounce** them **u**; it is a H3237
Lev 13:25 The priest *shall* **pronounce** them **u**; it is a H3237
Lev 13:27 the priest *shall* **pronounce** him **u**; it is a H3237
Lev 13:30 the priest *shall* **pronounce** them **u**; it is a H3237
Lev 13:36 need to look for yellow hair; they are **u**. H3238
Lev 13:44 the man is diseased and is **u**. The priest H3238
Lev 13:44 priest *shall* **pronounce** him **u** H3237+3237
Lev 13:45 the lower part of their face and cry out, '**U**! H3238
Lev 13:45 of their face and cry out, 'Unclean! **U**!' H3238
Lev 13:46 have the disease they **remain u**. H3237+3238
Lev 13:51 a persistent defiling mold; the article is **u**. H3238
Lev 13:55 even though it has not spread, it is **u**. H3238
Lev 13:59 for pronouncing them clean or **u**. H3237
Lev 14:36 in the house *will be* **pronounced u**. H3237
Lev 14:40 thrown into an **u** place outside the H3238
Lev 14:41 off dumped into an **u** place outside the H3238
Lev 14:44 a persistent defiling mold; the house is **u**. H3238
Lev 14:45 taken out of the town to an **u** place. H3238
Lev 14:46 while it is closed up *will be* **u** till evening. H3237
Lev 14:57 determine when something is clean or **u**. H3238
Lev 15: 2 bodily discharge, such a discharge is **u**. H3238
Lev 15: 3 his body or is blocked, it will make him **u**. H3240
Lev 15: 4 man with a discharge lies on *will be* **u**, H3237
Lev 15: 4 anything he sits on *will be* **u**. H3237
Lev 15: 5 with water, and *they will be* **u** till evening. H3237
Lev 15: 6 with water, and *they will be* **u** till evening. H3237
Lev 15: 7 with water, and *they will be* **u** till evening. H3237
Lev 15: 8 with water, and *they will be* **u** till evening. H3237
Lev 15: 9 the man sits on when riding *will be* **u**, H3237
Lev 15:10 that were under him *will be* **u** till evening; H3237
Lev 15:10 with water, and *they will be* **u** till evening. H3237
Lev 15:11 with water, and *they will be* **u** till evening. H3237
Lev 15:16 with water, and *he will be* **u** till evening. H3237
Lev 15:17 with water, and *it will be* **u** till evening. H3237
Lev 15:18 with water, and *they will be* **u** till evening. H3237
Lev 15:19 who touches her *will be* **u** till evening. H3237
Lev 15:20 she lies on during her period *will be* **u**, H3237
Lev 15:20 anything she sits on *will be* **u**. H3237
Lev 15:21 Anyone who touches her bed will be **u**; they NDT
Lev 15:21 with water, and *they will be* **u** till evening. H3237
Lev 15:22 who touches anything she sits on will be **u**; NDT
Lev 15:22 with water, and *they will be* **u** till evening. H3237
Lev 15:23 touches it, *they will be* **u** till evening. H3237
Lev 15:24 touches him, *he will be* **u** for seven days H3237
Lev 15:24 seven days; any bed he lies on *will be* **u**. H3237
Lev 15:25 she will be **u** as long as she has the H3238
Lev 15:26 while her discharge continues will be **u**, H3240
Lev 15:26 anything she sits on will be **u**, as H3238
Lev 15:27 Anyone who touches them *will be* **u**; they H3237
Lev 15:27 with water, and *they will be* **u** till evening. H3237
Lev 15:31 separate from **things that make** them **u**, H3240
Lev 15:32 for *anyone made* **u** by an emission of H3237
Lev 15:33 with a *woman who is* **ceremonially u**. H3238
Lev 17:15 and *they will be* **ceremonially u** till H3237
Lev 20:25 between clean and **u** animals and H3238
Lev 20:25 animals and between **u** and clean birds. H3238
Lev 20:25 those that I have set apart as **u** for you. H3237
Lev 21: 1 *must* not **make himself ceremonially u** H3237
Lev 21: 3 husband—for her *he may* **make himself u**. H3237
Lev 21: 4 *He must* not **make himself u** for people H3237
Lev 21:11 *He must* not **make himself u**, even for his H3237
Lev 22: 3 is **ceremonially u** and yet comes H3240
Lev 22: 4 He will also be **u** if he touches something NDT
Lev 22: 5 any crawling thing that *makes* him **u**, H3237
Lev 22: 5 any person who *makes* him **u**, whatever H3237
Lev 22: 6 any such thing *will be* **u** till evening. H3237
Lev 22: 8 animals, and so *become* **u** through it. H3237
Lev 27:11 they vowed is a **ceremonially u** animal— H3238
Lev 27:27 If it is one of the **u** animals, it may be H3238
Nu 5: 2 who is **ceremonially u** because of a H3238
Nu 6: 7 *they must* not **make themselves ceremonially u** H3237
Nu 9: 6 they were **ceremonially u** on account of a H3238
Nu 9: 7 "We have become **u** because of a dead H3238
Nu 9:10 descendants are **u** because of a dead H3238
Nu 18:15 son and every firstborn male of **u** animals. H3238
Nu 19: 7 he *will be* **ceremonially u** till evening. H3237
Nu 19: 8 and *he* too *will be* **u** till evening. H3237
Nu 19:10 clothes, and *he* too *will be* **u** till evening. H3237
Nu 19:11 a human corpse *will be* **u** for seven days. H3237
Nu 19:13 on them, they are **u**; their uncleanness H3238
Nu 19:14 who is in it *will be* **u** for seven days, H3237
Nu 19:15 without a lid fastened on it will be **u**. H3238
Nu 19:16 bone or a grave, *will be* **u** for seven days. H3237
Nu 19:17 "For the **u** *person*, put some ashes from H3238
Nu 19:19 sprinkle those *who are* **u** on the third and H3238
Nu 19:20 But if those who *are* **u** do not purify H3237
Nu 19:20 been sprinkled on them, and they are **u**. H3238
Nu 19:21 water of cleansing *will be* **u** till evening. H3237
Nu 19:22 Anything that an **u** *person* touches H3238
Nu 19:22 an unclean person touches *becomes* **u**, H3237
Nu 19:22 who touches it *becomes* **u** till evening." H3237
Dt 12:15 Both the **ceremonially u** and the clean H3238
Dt 12:22 Both the **ceremonially u** and the clean H3238
Dt 14: 7 they are **ceremonially u** for you. H3238
Dt 14: 8 The pig is also **u**; although it has a H3238
Dt 14:10 scales you may not eat; for you it is **u**. H3238
Dt 14:19 All flying insects are **u** to you; do not eat H3238
Dt 15:22 Both the **ceremonially u** and the clean H3238
Dt 23:10 If one of your men is **u** because of a H4202+3196
Dt 26:14 have I removed any of it while I was **u**, H3238
Jdg 13: 4 drink and that you do not eat anything **u**. H3238
Jdg 13: 7 drink and do not eat anything **u**, H3240
Jdg 13:14 other fermented drink nor eat anything **u**. H3240
1Sa 20:26 to make him **ceremonially u**— H1194+3196
1Sa 20:26 unclean—surely he is **u**. H4202+3196
2Ch 23:19 that no *one who* was in any way **u** might H3238
2Ch 29:16 temple everything **u** that they found in the H3240
Ezr 2:62 were excluded from the priesthood *as* **u**. H1458
Ezr 6:21 from the **u practices** *of* their Gentile H3240
Ne 7:64 *were* excluded from the priesthood *as* **u**. H1458
Ecc 9: 2 the clean and the **u**, those who offer H3238
Isa 6: 5 For I am a man of **u** lips, and I live among H3238
Isa 6: 5 I live among a people of **u** lips, and H3238
Isa 35: 8 The **u** will not journey on it; wicked fools H3238
Isa 52:11 Touch no **u** *thing*! Come out from it H3238
Isa 64: 6 All of us have become like one *who* is **u** H3238
Isa 66:17 rats and other **u things**—they will meet H9211
Jer 13:27 How long *will you be* **u**?" H4202+3197
La 1: 8 has sinned greatly and so has become **u**. H5765
La 1:17 has become an **u thing** among them. H5614
La 4:15 You are **u**!" people cry to them H3238
Eze 7:19 their gold will be treated as a **thing u**. H5614
Eze 7:20 therefore I will make it a **thing u** for them. H5614
Eze 8:10 crawling things and **u** animals and all the H9211
Eze 22:10 when they are **ceremonially u**. H3238
Eze 22:26 difference between the **u** and the clean; H3238
Eze 44:23 distinguish between the **u** and the clean. H3238
Hos 9: 3 return to Egypt and eat **u** food in Assyria. H3238
Hos 9: 4 of mourners; all who eat them *will be* **u**. H3237
Mt 23:27 of the bones of the dead and everything **u**. *G174*
Ac 10:14 "I have never eaten anything impure or **u**." *G176*
Ac 10:28 that I should not call anyone impure or **u**. *G176*
Ac 11: 8 Nothing impure or **u** has ever entered my *G176*
Ro 14:14 the Lord Jesus, that nothing is **u** in itself. *G3123*
Ro 14:14 But if anyone regards something as **u** *G3123*
Ro 14:14 as unclean, then for that person it is **u**. *G3123*
1Co 7:14 Otherwise your children would be **u**, but as *G176*
2Co 6:17 Touch no **u** *thing*, and I will *G176*
Heb 9:13 *on* those *who are* **ceremonially u** sanctify *G3124*
Rev 18: 2 a haunt for every **u** bird, a haunt for every *G176*
Rev 18: 2 a haunt for every **u** and detestable animal. *G176*

UNCLEANNESS (18) [UNCLEAN]

Lev 5: 3 if they touch human **u** (anything that H3240
Lev 7:21 whether human **u** or an unclean animal H3240
Lev 14:19 the one to be cleansed from their **u**. H3240
Lev 15: 3 is how his discharge will bring about **u**: H3240
Lev 15:30 before the LORD for the **u** *of* her discharge. H3240
Lev 15:31 will not die in their **u** for defiling my H3240
Lev 16:16 because of the **u** and rebellion of the H3240
Lev 16:16 is among them in the midst of their **u**. H3240
Lev 16:19 consecrate it from the **u** *of* the Israelites. H3240
Lev 18:19 during the **u** *of* her monthly period. H3240
Lev 22: 5 him unclean, whatever the **u** may be. H3240
Nu 19:13 are unclean; their **u** remains on them. H3240
2Sa 11: 4 was purifying herself from her *monthly* **u**.) H3240
Eze 22:15 countries; and I will put an end to your **u**. H3240
Eze 36:17 a **woman's monthly u** in my H3240+2021+5614
Eze 36:29 I will save you from all your **u**. I will call H3240
Eze 39:24 according to their **u** and their offenses, H3240
Jn 18:28 to avoid **ceremonial u** they did not *G3620*

UNCLOTHED (1)

2Co 5: 4 we do not wish *to be* **u** but to be clothed *G1694*

UNCOMELY (KJV) LESS HONORABLE, NOT HONORABLY

UNCONCERNED (1)

Eze 16:49 overfed and **u**; they did not help H8932+9200

UNCORRUPTIBLE (KJV) IMMORTAL

UNCOVER (2) [UNCOVERED, UNCOVERS]

Ru 3: 4 Then go and **u** his feet and lie down H1655
Jer 49:10 strip Esau bare; *I will* **u** his hiding places H1655

UNCOVERED (12) [UNCOVER]

Ge 9:21 became drunk and *lay* **u** inside his tent. H1655
Ge 44:16 God *has* **u** your servants' guilt H5162
Lev 20:18 source of her flow, and she *has* also **u** it. H1655
Ru 3: 7 **u** his feet and lay down. H1655
Job 26: 6 before God; Destruction lies **u**. H401+4064
Isa 47: 3 will be exposed and your shame **u**. H8011
Isa 57: 8 Forsaking me, *you* **u** your bed, you H1655
Eze 16:57 before your wickedness **was u**. Even so H1655
Hab 3: 9 *You* **u** your bow, you called for H6423+6880
1Co 11: 5 prophesies *with* her head **u** dishonors *G184*
1Co 11:13 a woman to pray to God with her head **u**? *G184*
Heb 4:13 Everything is **u** and laid bare before the *G1218*

UNCOVERS (2) [UNCOVER]

Ex 21:33 "If anyone **u** a pit or digs one and fails to H7337
Isa 22: 6 charioteers and horses; Kir **u** the shield. H6867

UNCTION (KJV) ANOINTING

UNCUT (2)

Jos 8:31 Moses—an altar of **u** stones, on which no H8969
Job 8:12 While still growing and **u**, they H4202+7786

UNDEFILED (KJV) BLAMELESS, FAULTLESS, FLAWLESS, PERFECT, PURE, NEVER SPOIL

UNDENIABLE (1)

Ac 19:36 since these facts are **u**, you ought to calm *G394*

UNDEPENDABLE (1)

Job 6:15 But my brothers *are* as **u** as intermittent H953

UNDER (384)

Ge 1: 7 the water **u** the vault from the H4946+9393
Ge 1: 9 "Let the water **u** the sky be H4946+9393
Ge 4:11 Now you *are* **u a curse** and driven from the H826
Ge 6:17 to destroy all life **u** the heavens, H4946+9393
Ge 7:19 the high mountains **u** the entire heavens H9393
Ge 17:18 Ishmael might live **u** your **blessing**!" H4200+7156
Ge 18: 4 all wash your feet and rest **u** this tree. H9393
Ge 18: 8 they ate, he stood near them **u** a tree. H9393
Ge 19: 8 they have come **u** the protection of my H928
Ge 21:15 she put the boy **u** one of the bushes. H9393
Ge 24: 2 that he had, "Put your hand **u** my thigh. H9393
Ge 24: 9 servant put his hand **u** the thigh of his H9393
Ge 28:11 he put it **u** his **head** and lay down to H5265
Ge 28:18 he had placed **u** his **head** and set it up as H5265
Ge 30:29 how your livestock has fared **u** my **care**. H907
Ge 35: 4 Jacob buried them **u** the oak at Shechem. H9393
Ge 35: 8 died and was buried **u** the oak outside H9393
Ge 39:23 no attention to anything **u** Joseph's care, H928
Ge 41:35 store up the grain **u** the authority of H9393
Ge 47:29 put your hand **u** my thigh and promise H9393
Ge 48: 6 they will be reckoned **u** the names of their H6584
Ex 6: 6 will bring you out from **u** the yoke of the H9393
Ex 6: 7 brought you out from **u** the yoke of the H9393
Ex 17:12 a stone and put it **u** him and he sat on it. H9393
Ex 17:14 out the name of Amalek from **u** heaven." H9393
Ex 23: 5 who hates you fallen down **u** its load, H9393
Ex 24:10 **U** his feet was something like a pavement H9393
Ex 25:35 One bud shall be **u** the first pair of H9393
Ex 25:35 a second bud **u** the second pair, and a H9393
Ex 25:35 and a third bud **u** the third pair—six H9393
Ex 26:19 make forty silver bases to go **u** them H9393
Ex 26:19 each frame, one **u** each projection. H4200
Ex 26:21 forty silver bases—two **u** each frame. H9393
Ex 26:25 sixteen silver bases—two **u** each frame. H9393
Ex 27: 5 Put it **u** the ledge of the altar so that it is H9393
Ex 36:24 made forty silver bases to go **u** them— H9393
Ex 36:24 each frame, one **u** each projection. H4200
Ex 36:26 forty silver bases—two **u** each frame. H9393
Ex 36:30 sixteen silver bases—two **u** each frame. H9393
Ex 37:21 One bud was **u** the first pair of branches H9393
Ex 37:21 a second bud **u** the second pair, and a H9393
Ex 37:21 and a third bud **u** the third pair—six H9393
Ex 38: 4 network, to be **u** its ledge, halfway up H9393
Ex 38:21 command by the Levites **u** the direction of H928
Lev 15:10 things that were **u** him will be unclean H9393
Lev 27:32 animal that passes **u** the shepherd's rod H9393
Nu 1:52 them in their own camp **u** their standard. H6584
Nu 2: 2 each of them **u** their standard and H6584
Nu 2: 3 of Judah are to encamp **u** their standard. NDT
Nu 2:10 of the camp of Reuben **u** their standard. NDT
Nu 2:17 each in their own place **u** their standard. H4200
Nu 2:18 of the camp of Ephraim **u** their standard. NDT
Nu 2:25 of the camp of Dan **u** their standard. NDT
Nu 2:31 They will set out last, **u** their standards. H4200
Nu 2:34 the way they encamped **u** their standards, H4200
Nu 4:27 is to be done **u** the direction of Aaron H6584
Nu 4:28 Their duties are to be **u** the direction of H928
Nu 4:33 at the tent of meeting **u** the direction of H928
Nu 5:19 priest *shall* **put** the woman **u oath** and say H8678
Nu 5:21 priest is to put the woman **u** this curse— H928
Nu 6: 4 long as they remain **u** their **Nazirite vow**, H5694
Nu 6:18 it in the fire that is **u** the sacrifice of the H9393
Nu 7: 8 They were all **u** the direction of Ithamar H928
Nu 8:22 meeting **u** the **supervision** *of* Aaron H4200+7156
Nu 10:14 camp of Judah went first, **u** their standard. H4200
Nu 10:18 of Reuben went next, **u** their standard. H4200
Nu 10:22 of Ephraim went next, **u** their standard. H4200
Nu 10:25 the camp of Dan set out **u** their standard. H4200
Nu 16:31 the ground **u** them split apart H9393
Nu 19: 2 and that *has* never **been u** a yoke. H6584+6590
Nu 22:27 it lay down **u** Balaam, and he was H9393
Nu 30:10 vow or obligates herself by a pledge **u** oath H928
Nu 31:49 have counted the soldiers **u** our command, H928
Nu 33: 1 of Egypt by divisions **u** the leadership of H928
Dt 2:25 fear of you on all the nations **u** heaven. H9393
Dt 4:19 apportioned to all the nations **u** heaven. H9393
Dt 7:24 will wipe out their names from **u** heaven. H9393
Dt 9:14 blot out their name from **u** heaven. H9393
Dt 12: 2 on the hills and **u** every spreading tree H9393
Dt 21:23 who is hung on a pole is *u* God's **curse**. AIT
Dt 25:19 out the name of Amalek from **u** heaven. H9393
Dt 29:20 will blot out their names from **u** heaven. H9393
Dt 30: 4 to the **most distant land** *u* the heavens, AIT
Jos 2: 6 roof and hidden them **u** the stalks of flax H928
Jos 9:23 You *are* now **u a curse**: You will never be H826
Jos 18: 1 The country **was brought u** their **control**, H3899
Jos 24:26 set it up there **u** the oak near the holy H9393
Jdg 1: 7 cut off have picked up scraps **u** my table. H9393
Jdg 2:18 of their groaning **u** those who H4946+7156
Jdg 3:16 to his right thigh **u** his clothing. H4946+9393
Jdg 4: 5 She held court **u** the Palm of Deborah H9393
Jdg 4:10 men went up **u** his **command**. H928+8079

Jdg 5:15 sent **u** his **command** into the valley. H928+8079
Jdg 6:11 came and sat down **u** the oak in Ophrah H9393
Jdg 6:19 out and offered them to him **u** the oak. H9393
Jdg 9:29 If only this people were **u** my command H928
Jdg 9:31 **U cover** he sent messengers to H928+9564
Ru 2:12 **u** whose wings you have come to take H9393
1Sa 2:11 before the LORD **u** Eli the priest. H907+7156
1Sa 2:27 they were in Egypt **u** Pharaoh? H4200+1074
1Sa 3: 1 ministered before the LORD **u** Eli. H4200+7156
1Sa 14: 2 outskirts of Gibeah **u** a pomegranate tree H9393
1Sa 14:24 Saul *had* **bound** the people **u an oath,** H457
1Sa 14:28 **bound** the army **u a strict oath,** H8678+8678
1Sa 22: 6 **u** the tamarisk tree on the hill at Gibeah H9393
1Sa 31:13 buried them **u** a tamarisk tree at H9393
2Sa 10:10 the rest of the men **u** the command of H928
2Sa 11:16 So while Joab *had* the city **u siege,** he put H9068
2Sa 18: 2 his troops, a third **u** the command of Joab H928
2Sa 18: 2 a third **u** Joab's brother Abishai son H928+3338
2Sa 18: 2 and a third **u** Ittai the Gittite. H928+3338
2Sa 18: 9 as the mule went **u** the thick branches H9393
2Sa 20: 3 palace and put them in a house **u guard.** H5466
2Sa 20: 7 went out **u the command of** Abishai. H339
2Sa 22:10 came down; dark clouds were **u** his feet. H9393
2Sa 22:48 avenges me, who puts the nations **u** me, H9393
1Ki 4:25 everyone **u** their own vine and under their H9393
1Ki 4:25 their own vine and **u** their own fig tree. H9393
1Ki 5: 3 until the LORD put his enemies **u** his feet. H9393
1Ki 7:32 The four wheels were **u** the panels H4946+9393
1Ki 7:44 the Sea and the twelve bulls **u** it; H9393
1Ki 13:14 He found him sitting **u** an oak tree and H9393
1Ki 14:23 every high hill and **u** every spreading tree. H9393
1Ki 19: 4 sat down **u** it and prayed that he might H9393
1Ki 19: 5 Then he lay down **u** the bush and fell H9393
1Ki 20:14 'The **junior officers** *u* the provincial AIT
1Ki 20:15 the 232 **junior officers** *u* the provincial AIT
1Ki 20:17 The **junior officers** *u* the provincial AIT
1Ki 20:19 The **junior officers** *u* the provincial AIT
2Ki 6:30 they saw that, **u** his robes, he had H4946+1074
2Ki 9:13 spread them **u** him on the bare steps. H9393
2Ki 11: 4 with them and **put** them **u oath** at the H8678
2Ki 13: 3 time he kept them **u** the power of Hazael H928
2Ki 14:27 out the name of Israel from **u** heaven, H9393
2Ki 16: 4 on the hilltops and **u** every spreading tree. H9393
2Ki 17: 7 out of Egypt from **u** the power of Pharaoh H9393
2Ki 17:10 every high hill and **u** every spreading tree. H9393
2Ki 25: 2 The city was kept **u** siege until the eleventh H928
2Ki 25:10 Babylonian army **u** the commander of the H889
1Ch 10:12 they buried their bones **u** the great tree in H9393
1Ch 12:32 with all their relatives **u** their command; H6584
1Ch 17: 1 ark of the covenant of the LORD is **u** a tent." H9393
1Ch 19:11 the rest of the men **u** the command of H928
1Ch 23:24 they were registered **u** their names and H928
1Ch 23:32 **u** their relatives the descendants of Aaron NDT
1Ch 25: 2 sons of Asaph were **u** the supervision of H6584
1Ch 25: 2 who prophesied **u** the king's supervision. H6584
1Ch 25: 3 **u** the supervision of their father Jeduthun H6584
1Ch 25: 6 All these men were **u** the supervision of H6584
1Ch 25: 6 Heman were **u** the supervision of the H6584
2Ch 4:15 the Sea and the twelve bulls **u** it; H9393
2Ch 14: 5 the kingdom was at peace **u** him. H4200+7156
2Ch 17: 5 LORD established the kingdom **u** his control; H928
2Ch 24:13 and the repairs progressed **u** them. H928+3338
2Ch 26:11 Maaseiah the officer **u** the direction of H6584
2Ch 26:13 **U** their command was an army of 307,500 H6584
2Ch 28: 4 on the hilltops and **u** every spreading tree. H9393
2Ch 32:10 that you remain in Jerusalem **u** siege? H928
2Ch 34: 4 **U** his **direction** the altars of the H4200+7156
Ezr 4:14 since *we are* **u obligation** *to* the A10419+10420
Ezr 5: 8 making rapid progress **u** their direction. A10089
Ezr 5:16 present *it has been* **u construction** but is A10111
Ezr 6:14 to build and prosper **u** the preaching of A10089
Ezr 10: 5 **put** the leading priests and Levites and all Israel **u oath** H8678
Ne 3: 5 shoulders to the **work** *u* their supervisors. AIT
Ne 3: 7 places **u** the authority of the governor of H4200
Ne 3:17 made by the Levites **u** Rehum son of Bani. NDT
Ne 3:18 their fellow Levites **u** Binnui son of Henadad NDT
Ne 6:18 many in Judah were **u oath** to him, H1251+8652
Ne 11:23 The musicians were **u** the king's orders H6584
Ne 12:42 The choirs sang **u** the direction of Jezrahiah NDT
Est 2: 3 Let them be placed **u** the care of Hegai H448
Est 2: 8 of Susa and put **u** the care of Hegai. H448
Job 7:12 the deep, that you put me **u guard**? H5464+6584
Job 20:12 in his mouth and he hides it **u** his tongue, H9393
Job 26: 8 the clouds do not burst **u** their weight. H9393
Job 28:24 earth and sees everything **u** the heavens. H9393
Job 35: 9 "People cry out **u** a load of oppression H4946
Job 37:17 the land lies hushed **u** the south wind, H4946
Job 38:14 The earth takes shape like **clay** *u* a seal; its AIT
Job 40:21 **U** the lotus plants it lies, hidden among H9393
Job 41:11 Everything **u** heaven belongs to me H9393
Ps 8: 6 you put everything **u** their feet: H9393
Ps 10: 7 trouble and evil are **u** his tongue. H9393
Ps 10:10 they collapse; they fall **u** his strength. H928
Ps 18: 9 came down; dark clouds were **u** his feet. H9393
Ps 18:47 avenges me, who subdues nations **u** me, H9393
Ps 31:21 of his love when I was in a city **u siege.** H5189
Ps 37:18 spend their days **u** the LORD's **care,** H3359
Ps 42: 4 to the house of God **u** the protection of the H928
Ps 47: 3 He subdued nations **u** us, peoples under H9393
Ps 47: 3 nations under us, peoples **u** our feet. H9393
Ps 56:12 I am **u** vows to you, my God; I will present H6584
Ps 90: 9 All our days pass away **u** your wrath; we H928
Ps 91: 4 **u** his wings you will find refuge H9393
Ps 95: 7 people of his pasture, the flock **u** his **care.** H3338
Ps 144: 2 I take refuge, who subdues peoples **u** me. H9393
Pr 22:14 a *man who is* **u** the LORD's **wrath** falls into H2404
Pr 22:27 your very bed will be snatched from **u** you. H9393
Pr 29:24 *they are* **put u oath** and dare not H460+9048
Pr 30:21 "**U** three things the earth trembles, under H9393
Pr 30:21 earth trembles, **u** four it cannot bear up: H9393
Ecc 1: 3 their labors at which they toil **u** the sun? H9393
Ecc 1: 9 there is nothing new **u** the sun. H9393
Ecc 1:13 by wisdom all that is done **u** the heavens. H9393
Ecc 1:14 all the things that are done **u** the sun; H9393
Ecc 2: 3 people to do **u** the heavens during H9393
Ecc 2:11 the wind; nothing was gained **u** the sun. H9393
Ecc 2:17 work that is done **u** the sun was grievous H9393
Ecc 2:18 all the things I had toiled for **u** the sun, H9393
Ecc 2:19 have poured my effort and skill **u** the sun. H9393
Ecc 2:20 over all my toilsome labor **u** the sun. H9393
Ecc 2:22 striving with which they labor **u** the sun? H9393
Ecc 3: 1 a season for every activity **u** the heavens: H9393
Ecc 3:16 And I saw something else **u** the sun: In H9393
Ecc 4: 1 that was taking place **u** the sun: H9393
Ecc 4: 3 not seen the evil that is done **u** the sun. H9393
Ecc 4: 7 I saw something meaningless **u** the sun: H9393
Ecc 4:15 lived and walked **u** the sun followed the H9393
Ecc 5:13 I have seen a grievous evil **u** the sun H9393
Ecc 5:18 their toilsome labor **u** the sun during the H9393
Ecc 6: 1 I have seen another evil **u** the sun, and it H9393
Ecc 6:12 what will happen **u** the sun after they H9393
Ecc 7: 6 Like the crackling of thorns **u** the pot, so is H9393
Ecc 8: 9 my mind to everything done **u** the sun. H9393
Ecc 8:15 better for a person **u** the sun than to eat H9393
Ecc 8:15 of the life God has given them **u** the sun. H9393
Ecc 8:17 can comprehend what goes on **u** the sun. H9393
Ecc 9: 3 evil in everything that happens **u** the sun: H9393
Ecc 9: 6 a part in anything that happens **u** the sun. H9393
Ecc 9: 9 life that God has given you **u** the sun— H9393
Ecc 9: 9 life and in your toilsome labor **u** the sun. H9393
Ecc 9:11 I have seen something else **u** the sun H9393
Ecc 9:13 I also saw **u** the sun this example of H9393
Ecc 10: 5 There is an evil I have seen **u** the sun, the H9393
SS 2: 6 His left arm is **u** my head, and his right H9393
SS 4:11 milk and honey are **u** your tongue. H9393
SS 8: 3 His left arm is **u** my head and his right H9393
SS 8: 5 **U** the apple tree I roused you; there your H9393
Isa 1: 8 in a cucumber field, like a city **u siege.** H7443
Isa 10:16 **u** his pomp a fire will be kindled like a H9393
Isa 34:15 care for her young **u** the shadow of her H928
Isa 57: 5 among the oaks and **u** every spreading H9393
Isa 57: 5 in the ravines and **u** the overhanging H9393
Jer 2:20 every high hill and **u** every spreading tree H9393
Jer 3: 6 every high hill and **u** every spreading tree H9393
Jer 3:13 to foreign gods **u** every spreading tree, H9393
Jer 7:29 this **generation** *that* is *u* his wrath. AIT
Jer 10:11 from the earth and from **u** the heavens. A10757
Jer 10:17 to leave the land, you who live **u** siege. H928
Jer 27: 8 king of Babylon or bow its neck **u** his yoke, H928
Jer 27:11 will bow its neck **u** the yoke of the king of H928
Jer 27:12 "Bow your neck **u** the yoke of the king of H928
Jer 33:13 will again pass **u** the hand of the one H6584
Jer 38:11 went to a room **u** the treasury in the H9393
Jer 38:12 worn-out clothes **u** your arms to pad the H9393
Jer 52: 5 The city was kept **u** siege until the eleventh H928
Jer 52:14 **u** the commander of the imperial guard H907
Jer 52:20 the Sea and the twelve bronze bulls **u** it H9393
La 3:66 destroy them from **u** the heavens of the H9393
La 4:20 We thought that **u** his shadow we would H928
La 5:13 millstones; boys stagger **u** loads of wood. H928
Eze 1: 8 **U** their wings on their four sides H4946+9393
Eze 1:23 **U** the vault their wings were stretched out H9393
Eze 4: 3 It will be **u** siege, and you shall H928
Eze 6:13 **u** every spreading tree and every leafy oak H9393
Eze 10: 8 **U** the wings of the cherubim could be H9393
Eze 10:21 **u** their wings was what looked like H9393
Eze 17: 6 toward him, but its roots remained **u** it. H9393
Eze 17:13 a treaty with him, putting him **u** oath. H928
Eze 20:37 take note of you as you pass **u** my rod, H9393
Eze 31: 6 of the wild gave birth **u** its branches; H9393
Eze 31:12 the earth came out **from** *u* its shade and left AIT
Eze 32:27 their swords placed **u** their heads and their H9393
Eze 46:23 fire built all around **u** the ledge. H4946+9393
Eze 47: 1 coming out from **u** the threshold of the H9393
Eze 47: 1 coming down from **u** the south side of H9393
Da 4:12 **U** it the wild animals found shelter, and A10757
Da 4:14 animals flee from **u** it and the birds from A10757
Da 7:27 of all the kingdoms **u** heaven will be A10757
Da 9:12 **U** the whole heaven nothing has ever H9393
Hos 4:13 offerings on the hills, **u** oak, poplar and H9393
Hos 8:10 begin to waste away **u** the oppression of H4946
Mic 4: 4 Everyone will sit **u** their own vine and H9393
Mic 4: 4 their own vine and **u** their own fig tree, H9393
Zec 3:10 your neighbor to sit **u** your vine and fig H9393
Mal 1: 4 a people always **u the wrath** *of* the LORD. H2404
Mal 3: 9 You are **u** a curse—your whole nation H928
Mal 4: 3 they will be ashes **u** the soles of your feet H9393
Mt 2:16 its vicinity who were two years old and **u,** G3006
Mt 5:15 people light a lamp and put it **u** a bowl. G5679
Mt 7: 6 they may trample them **u** their feet, and G1877
Mt 8: 8 not deserve to have you come **u** my roof. G5679
Mt 8: 9 For I myself am a man **u** authority, with G5679
Mt 8: 9 man under authority, with soldiers **u** me. G5679
Mt 22:44 hand until I put your enemies **u** your feet." G5691
Mt 23:37 as a hen gathers her chicks **u** her wings G5679
Mt 26:63 "*I* **charge** you **u oath** by the living God: G2019
Mk 4:21 in a lamp to put it **u** a bowl or a bed? G5679
Mk 5:26 a great deal **u** *the care of* many doctors G5679
Mk 7:28 "even the dogs **u** the table eat the G5691
Mk 12:36 hand until I put your enemies **u** your feet." G5691
Mk 14:44 arrest him and lead him away **u guard.**" G857
Lk 7: 6 not deserve to have you come **u** my roof. G5679
Lk 7: 8 For I myself am a man **u** authority, with G5679
Lk 7: 8 man under authority, with soldiers **u** me. G5679
Lk 8:16 hides it in a clay jar or puts it **u** a bed. G5691
Lk 8:29 chained hand and foot and **kept u guard,** G5875
Lk 11:33 where it will be hidden, or **u** a bowl. G5679
Lk 12:50 what **constraint** *I am* **u** until it is G5309
Lk 13:34 as a hen gathers her chicks **u** her wings G5679
Lk 23: 7 that Jesus was **u** Herod's jurisdiction, G1666
Lk 23:40 "since you are **u** the same sentence? G1877
Jn 1:48 while you were still **u** the fig tree before G5679
Jn 1:50 I told you I saw you **u** the fig tree. G5691
Jn 13: 3 the Father had put all things **u** his power, G1650
Ac 2: 5 Jews from every nation **u** heaven. G5679
Ac 4:12 there is no other name **u** heaven given to G5679
Ac 7:45 our ancestors **u** Joshua brought it with G3552
Ac 10:38 all who *were* **u the power** of the devil, G2872
Ac 13:39 not able to obtain **u** the law of Moses. G1877
Ac 22: 3 I studied **u** Gamaliel and G4123+3836+4546
Ac 23:35 he ordered *that* Paul *be* **kept u guard** in G5875
Ac 24: 2 enjoyed a long period of peace **u** you, G1328
Ac 24:23 centurion *to* **keep** Paul **u guard** but to give G5498
Ac 27:17 ropes **u** the ship itself **to hold it together.** G5690
Ro 2:12 all who sin **u** the law will be judged G1877
Ro 3: 9 Gentiles alike are all **u the power of** sin. G5679
Ro 3:19 it says to those who are **u** the law, so that G1877
Ro 4:10 **U what circumstances** was it G4802+4036
Ro 6:14 because you are not **u** the law, but under G5679
Ro 6:14 you are not under the law, but **u** grace. G5679
Ro 6:15 because we are not **u** the law but under G5679
Ro 6:15 we are not under the law but **u** grace? G5679
Ro 16:20 peace will soon crush Satan **u** your feet. G5679
1Co 7:37 *who is* **u** no compulsion but has control G2400
1Co 9:20 To those **u** the law I became like one G5679
1Co 9:20 the law I became like one **u** the law G5679
1Co 9:20 though I myself am not **u** the law), so as to G5679
1Co 9:20 the law), so as to win those **u** the law. G5679
1Co 9:21 free from God's law but am **u** Christ's **law),** G1937
1Co 10: 1 ancestors were all **u** the cloud and that G5679
1Co 11:31 *we* would not **come u** *such* **judgment.** G3212
1Co 14:24 of sin and *are* **brought u judgment** by all, G373
1Co 15:25 he has put all his enemies **u** his feet. G5679
1Co 15:27 For he "*has* **put** everything **u** his feet." G5718
1Co 15:27 "everything" *has been* **put u** him, it is G5718
1Co 15:27 God himself, who **put** everything **u** Christ. G5718
1Co 15:28 subject to him *who* **put** everything **u** him, G5718
2Co 1: 8 *We were* **u** great **pressure,** far beyond our G976
2Co 9: 7 not reluctantly or **u** compulsion, for God G1666
2Co 11:12 order to **cut** the ground **from u** those who G1716
2Co 11:32 the governor *u* **King** Aretas had the city AIT
Gal 1: 8 let them be **u God's curse!** G353
Gal 1: 9 you accepted, let them be **u God's curse!** G353
Gal 3:10 rely on the works of the law are **u** a curse, G5679
Gal 3:22 locked up everything **u the control of** sin, G5679
Gal 3:23 we were held in custody **u** the law, locked G5679
Gal 3:25 has come, we are no longer **u** a guardian. G5679
Gal 4: 3 we were in slavery **u** the elemental G5679
Gal 4: 4 born of a woman, born **u** the law, G5679
Gal 4: 5 to redeem those **u** the law, that we might G5679
Gal 4:21 you who want to be **u** the law, are you not G5679
Gal 5:18 led by the Spirit, you are not **u** the law. G5679
Eph 1:10 all things in heaven and on earth **u** Christ. G1877
Eph 1:22 And God **placed** all things **u** his feet and G5718
Php 2:10 in heaven and on earth and **u the earth,** G2973
Php 3:21 him *to* **bring** everything **u** his **control,** G5718
Col 1:23 proclaimed to every creature **u** heaven, G5679
1Ti 3: 6 conceited and **fall u** the same judgment G1860
1Ti 6: 1 All who are **u** the yoke of slavery should G5679
Heb 2: 8 and **put** everything **u** their feet." In putting G5718
Heb 2: 8 In **putting** everything **u** them, God left G5718
Heb 9:15 the sins committed **u** the first covenant. G2093
Jas 1:12 is the one who perseveres *u* **trial** because, AIT
1Pe 2:19 if someone bears up *u* the **pain** of unjust AIT
1Pe 5: 2 of God's flock that is **u** your **care,** G1877
1Pe 5: 6 therefore, **u** God's mighty hand, that he G5679
1Jn 5:19 world *is* **u the control of** the evil G1877+3023
Rev 4: 8 with eyes all around, even **u** its wings. G2277
Rev 5: 3 on earth or **u** the earth could open G5691
Rev 5:13 on earth and **u** the earth and on the G5691
Rev 6: 9 I saw **u** the altar the souls of those who G5691
Rev 12: 1 with the moon **u** her feet and a crown of G5691

UNDERAGE (2) [AGE]

Gal 4: 1 I am saying is that as long as an heir is **u,** G3758
Gal 4: 3 when we were **u,** we were in slavery G3758

UNDERFOOT (13) [FOOT]

2Ki 9:33 the horses as *they* **trampled** her **u.** H8252
2Ki 14: 9 came along and **trampled** the thistle **u.** H8252
2Ch 25:18 came along and **trampled** the thistle **u.** H8252
Isa 14:19 Like a corpse **trampled u,** H1008
Isa 28: 3 drunkards, will be trampled **u.** H928+8079
La 3:34 To crush **u** all prisoners in the land, H9393+8079
Da 7: 7 and trampled **u** whatever was A10089+10655

Da 7:19 and trampled **u** whatever was A10089+10655
Da 8:13 the **trampling u** of the LORD's H5330
Mic 7:10 now she will be **trampled u** like mire in H5330
Mic 7:19 *you will* **tread** our sins **u** and hurl all our H3899
Mt 5:13 thrown out and trampled **u**. *G5679+3836+476S*
Heb 10:29 who *has* **trampled** the Son of God **u**, *G2922*

UNDERGARMENT (1) [GARMENT]

Jn 19:23 each of them, with the **u** remaining. *G5945*

UNDERGARMENTS (5) [GARMENT]

Ex 28:42 "Make linen **u** as a covering for the body H4829
Ex 39:28 caps and the **u** of finely twisted H4829+965
Lev 6:10 clothes, with linen **u** next to his body, and H4829
Lev 16: 4 with linen **u** next to his body; he is H4829
Eze 44:18 heads and linen **u** around their waists. H4829

UNDERGO (2) [UNDERGOES, UNDERGOING]

Ge 17:11 You *are to* **u circumcision**, H4576+906+1414+6889
Lk 12:50 But I have a baptism *to* **u**, and what *G966S*

UNDERGOES (1) [UNDERGO]

Heb 12: 8 everyone **u** discipline—then *G3581+1181*

UNDERGOING (1) [UNDERGO]

1Pe 5: 9 the world *is* **u** the same kind of *G2200*

UNDERGROWTH (2) [GROWTH]

Job 30: 7 among the bushes and huddled in the **u**. H3017
Isa 17: 9 like places abandoned to thickets and **u**. H580

UNDERLINGS (2)

2Ki 19: 6 with which the **u** *of* the king of Assyria H5853
Isa 37: 6 with which the **u** *of* the king of Assyria H5853

UNDERMINE (1)

Job 15: 4 But you even **u** piety and hinder devotion H7296

UNDERNEATH (3) [BENEATH]

Dt 33:27 and **u** are the everlasting arms. H4946+9393
Jos 7:21 ground inside my tent, with the silver **u**." H9393
Jos 7:22 hidden in his tent, with the silver **u**. H9393

UNDERSETTERS (KJV) HANDLES, SUPPORTS

UNDERSIDES (1)

Job 41:30 Its **u** are jagged potsherds, leaving a trail H9393

UNDERSTAND (124) [UNDERSTANDING, UNDERSTANDS, UNDERSTOOD]

Ge 11: 7 language so *they will* not **u** each other." H9048
Ge 42:23 did not realize that Joseph *could* **u** them, H9048
Dt 9: 6 **U**, then, that it is not because of your H3359
Dt 28:49 a nation whose language *you will* not **u**, H9048
Dt 32:29 were wise and *would* **u** this and discern H8505
1Sa 28: 1 "*You* **must u** that you and your men H3359+3359
2Sa 15:27 also said to Zadok the priest, "*Do* you **u**? H8011
2Ki 18:26 to your servants in Aramaic, since we **u** it. H9048
1Ch 28:19 and *he* **enabled** me **to u** all the details of H8505
Ne 8: 2 women and all who were able to **u**. H9048
Ne 8: 3 the men, women and others *who could* **u**. H1067
Ne 10:28 sons and daughters who are able *to* **u**— H1067
Job 26:14 Who then *can* **u** the thunder of his power?" H1067
Job 32: 9 not only the aged *who* **u** what is right. H1067
Job 36:29 *Who can* **u** how he spreads out the clouds H1067
Job 38: 4 foundation? Tell me, if *you* **u**. H3359+1069
Job 42: 3 Surely I spoke of things *I did* not **u**, things H1067
Ps 14: 2 all mankind to see if there are *any who* **u**, H8505
Ps 53: 2 all mankind to see if there are *any who* **u**, H8505
Ps 73:16 When I tried to **u** all this, it troubled me H3359
Ps 82: 5 know nothing, *they* **u** nothing. They walk H1067
Ps 92: 6 people do not know, fools *do* not **u**, H1067
Ps 119:27 **Cause** me **to u** the way of your precepts H1067
Ps 119:79 you turn to me, *those who* **u** your statutes. H3359
Ps 119:125 discernment that *I may* **u** your statutes. H3359
Pr 2: 5 then *you will* **u** the fear of the LORD and H1067
Pr 2: 9 Then *you will* **u** what is right and just and H1067
Pr 17:16 wisdom, when they are not **able to u** it? H4213
Pr 20:24 How then *can* anyone **u** their own way? H1067
Pr 28: 5 Evildoers *do* not **u** what is right, but those H1067
Pr 28: 5 those who seek the LORD **u** it fully. H1067
Pr 29:19 mere words; though *they* **u**, they will not H1067
Pr 30:18 too amazing for me, four *that I do* not **u**: H3359
Ecc 7:25 So I turned my mind to **u**, to investigate H3359
Ecc 7:25 scheme of things and to **u** the stupidity of H3359
Ecc 11: 5 so *you* cannot **u** the work of God H3359
Isa 1: 3 Israel does not know, my people *do* not **u**." H1067
Isa 6:10 hear with their ears, **u** with their hearts H1067
Isa 32: 4 The fearful heart will know and **u**, and the H1067
Isa 36:11 to your servants in Aramaic, since we **u** it. H9048
Isa 41:20 may consider and **u**, that the hand of the H8505
Isa 42:25 in flames, yet *they did* not **u**; it consumed H3359
Isa 43:10 know and believe me and **u** that I am he. H1067
Isa 44:18 They know nothing, *they* **u** nothing; their H1067
Isa 44:18 their minds closed so they cannot **u**. H8505
Isa 52:15 what they have not heard, *they will* **u**. H1067
Jer 5:15 do not know, whose speech *you do* not **u**. H9048
Jer 9:12 Who is wise enough *to* **u** this? Who has H1067
Jer 15:15 you **u**; remember me and care for H3359
Jer 17: 9 things and beyond cure. Who *can* **u** it? H3359
Jer 23:20 In days to come *you will* **u** it **clearly**. H1067+1069
Jer 30:24 In days to come *you will* **u** this. H1067
Jer 31:19 repented; after I *came to* **u**, I beat my H3359
Eze 3: 6 language, whose words *you* cannot **u**. H9048
Eze 12: 3 Perhaps *they will* **u**, though they are a H8011
Da 1: 4 informed, **quick to u**, and qualified H1067+4529
Da 1:17 And Daniel *could* **u** visions and dreams of H1067
Da 2:30 that *you may* **u** what went through A10313
Da 5:23 which cannot see or hear or **u**. A10313
Da 8:15 was watching the vision and trying to **u** it H1069
Da 8:17 "**u** that the vision concerns the time of the H1067
Da 9:23 consider the word and **u** the vision: H1067
Da 9:25 "Know and **u** this: From the time the word H8505
Da 12: 8 I heard, but *I did* not **u**. So I asked, "My H1067
Da 12:10 None of the wicked *will* **u**, but those who H1067
Da 12:10 those who are wise *will* **u**. H1067
Hos 14: 9 is discerning? *Let them* **u**. The ways of the H3359
Mic 4:12 of the LORD; *they do* not **u** his plan, that he H1067
Mt 13:13 though hearing, they do not hear or **u**. *G5317*
Mt 13:15 their ears, **u** with their hearts and turn *G5317*
Mt 13:19 about the kingdom and *does* not **u** it, *G5317*
Mt 15:10 the crowd to him and said, "Listen and **u**. *G5317*
Mt 16: 9 *Do you* still not **u**? Don't you remember *G3783*
Mt 16:11 How is it *you* don't **u** that I was not talking *G3783*
Mt 24:15 the prophet Daniel—*let* the reader **u**— *G3783*
Mt 24:43 But **u** this: If the owner of the house had *G1182*
Mk 4:13 said to them, "Don't *you* **u** this parable? *G3857*
Mk 4:13 How then *will you* **u** any parable? *G1182*
Mk 4:33 the word to them, as much as they could **u**. *G201*
Mk 7:14 "Listen to me, everyone, and **u** this. *G5317*
Mk 8:17 Do you still not see or **u**? Are your hearts *G5317*
Mk 8:21 He said to them, "*Do you* still not **u**?" *G5317*
Mk 9:32 But they *did* **not u** what he meant and were *G51*
Mk 13:14 not belong—*let* the reader **u**—then let *G3783*
Mk 14:68 "I don't know or **u** what you're talking *G2179*
Lk 2:50 But they *did* not **u** what he was saying to *G5317*
Lk 8:10 not see; though hearing, *they may* not **u**. *G5317*
Lk 9:45 But they *did* not **u** what this meant. It was *G51*
Lk 12:39 But **u** this: If the owner of the house had *G1182*
Lk 18:34 The disciples *did* not **u** any of this. *G5317*
Lk 24:45 their minds *so they could* **u** the Scriptures. *G5317*
Jn 3:10 "and *do you* not **u** these things? *G1182*
Jn 8:27 *They did* not **u** that he was telling them *G1182*
Jn 10: 6 the Pharisees *did* not **u** what he was *G1182*
Jn 10:38 you may know and **u** that the Father is in *G1182*
Jn 12:16 At first his disciples *did* not **u** all this. *G1182*
Jn 12:40 with their eyes, nor **u** with their hearts, nor *G3783*
Jn 13: 7 now what I am doing, but later *you will* **u**." *G1182*
Jn 13:12 "*Do you* **u** what I have done for you?" *G1182*
Jn 16:18 *We* don't **u** what he is saying. *G3857*
Jn 20: 9 *They* still *did* not **u** from Scripture that *G3857*
Ac 8:30 "*Do you* **u** what you are reading? *G1182*
Ac 22: 9 but *they did* not **u** the voice of him who *G201*
Ac 28:27 their ears, **u** with their hearts and turn *G5317*
Ro 7:15 *I do* not **u** what I do. For what I want to do *G1182*
Ro 10:19 *Did* Israel not **u**? First, Moses *G1182*
Ro 15:21 and those who have not heard *will* **u**." *G5317*
1Co 2:12 so that *we may* **u** what God has freely *G3857*
1Co 2:14 cannot **u** them because they are *G1182*
2Co 1:13 write you anything you cannot read or **u**. *G2105*
2Co 1:14 *you will come to* **u** fully that you can boast *G2105*
Gal 3: 7 **U**, then, that those who have faith are *G1182*
Eph 3: 4 you will be able *to* **u** my insight into the *G3783*
Eph 5:17 be foolish, but **u** what the Lord's will is. *G5317*
1Ti 6: 4 they are conceited and **u** nothing. *G2179*
Heb 5:11 clear to you because you no longer try to **u**. *G198*
Heb 11: 3 By faith *we* **u** that the universe was *G3783*
2Pe 1:20 *you must* **u** that no prophecy of Scripture *G1182*
2Pe 2:12 people blaspheme in matters *they do* **not u**. *G51*
2Pe 3: 3 *you must* **u** that in the last days scoffers *G1182*
2Pe 3: 9 keeping his promise, as some **u** slowness. *G2451*
2Pe 3:16 contain some things that are **hard to u**, *G1554*
Jude 10 people slander whatever *they do* not **u**, *G3857*
Jude 10 the very things *they do* **u** by instinct *G2179*

UNDERSTANDING (112) [UNDERSTAND]

Ex 31: 3 with wisdom, with **u**, with knowledge and H9312
Ex 35:31 with wisdom, with **u**, with knowledge and H9312
Dt 1:13 **u** and respected men from each of your H1067
Dt 4: 6 show your wisdom and **u** to the nations, H1069
Dt 4: 6 this great nation is a wise and **u** people." H1067
Dt 32:21 them angry by a nation that has **no u**. H5572
Jdg 13:18 do you ask my name? It is **beyond u**." H7100
1Ki 4:29 a breadth of **u** as measureless as the H4213
1Ki 7:14 with **u** and with knowledge to do all kinds H9312
1Ch 22:12 you discretion and **u** when he puts you in H1069
2Ch 30:22 who **showed** good **u** of the service H8505+8507
Job 8:10 they not bring forth words from their **u**? H4213
Job 12:12 Does not long life bring **u**? H9312
Job 12:13 power; counsel and **u** are his. H9312
Job 17: 4 You have closed their minds to **u** H8507
Job 20: 3 and my **u** inspires me to reply. H1069
Job 28:12 wisdom be found? Where does **u** dwell? H1069
Job 28:20 wisdom come from? Where does **u** dwell? H1069
Job 28:28 that is wisdom, and to shun evil is **u**." H1069
Job 32: 8 breath of the Almighty, *that* **gives** them **u**. H1067
Job 34:10 you men of **u**. Far be it from God to H4222
Job 34:16 "If you have **u**, hear this; listen to what I H1069
Job 34:34 "Men of **u** declare, wise men who hear H4222
Job 36:26 is God—beyond *our* **u**! The number of his H3359
Job 37: 5 he does great things beyond *our* **u**. H3359
Job 38:36 the ibis wisdom or gives the rooster **u**? H1069
Ps 32: 9 *which* **have** no **u** but must be controlled H1067
Ps 49: 3 the meditation of my heart will give you **u**. H9312
Ps 49:20 have wealth but lack **u** are like the beasts H1067
Ps 111:10 all who follow his precepts have good **u**. H8507
Ps 119:32 commands, for you have broadened my **u**. H4213
Ps 119:34 **Give me u**, so that I may keep your law H1067
Ps 119:73 **give** me **u** to learn your commands. H1067
Ps 119:100 *I* **have** more **u** than the elders, for I obey H1067
Ps 119:104 *I* **gain u** from your precepts; therefore I H1067
Ps 119:130 words gives light; *it* **gives u** *to* the simple. H1067
Ps 119:144 righteous; **give** me **u** that I may live. H1067
Ps 119:169 **give me u** according to your word. H1067
Ps 136: 5 who by his **u** made the heavens, His love H9312
Ps 147: 5 mighty in power; his **u** has no limit. H9312
Pr 1: 2 instruction; for **u** words of insight; H1067
Pr 1: 6 **u** proverbs and parables, the sayings H1067
Pr 2: 2 to wisdom and applying your heart to **u**— H9312
Pr 2: 3 you call out for insight and cry aloud for **u**, H9312
Pr 2: 6 from his mouth come knowledge and **u**. H9312
Pr 2:11 will protect you, and **u** will guard you. H9312
Pr 3: 5 all your heart and lean not on your own **u**; H1069
Pr 3:13 who find wisdom, those who gain **u**, H9312
Pr 3:19 by **u** he set the heavens in place H9312
Pr 3:21 do not let wisdom and **u** out of your sight NDT
Pr 4: 1 instruction; pay attention and gain **u**. H1069
Pr 4: 5 Get wisdom, get **u**; do not forget my H1069
Pr 4: 7 Though it cost all you have, get **u**. H1069
Pr 8: 1 Does not **u** raise her voice? H9312
Pr 9:10 knowledge of the Holy One is **u**. H1069
Pr 10:23 a person of **u** delights in wisdom. H9312
Pr 11:12 the one who has **u** holds their tongue. H9312
Pr 14:29 Whoever is patient has great **u**, but one H9312
Pr 15:21 whoever has **u** keeps a straight course. H9312
Pr 15:32 the one who heeds correction gains **u**. H4213
Pr 17:27 whoever has **u** is even-tempered. H9312
Pr 18: 2 find no pleasure in **u** but delight in airing H9312
Pr 19: 8 one who cherishes **u** will soon prosper. H9312
Pr 24: 3 and through **u** it is established; H9312
Pr 30: 2 not a man; I do not have human **u**. H1069
Ecc 1:17 Then I applied myself to the **u** *of* wisdom H3359
Isa 5:13 my people will go into exile for lack of **u**; H1981
Isa 6: 9 ever hearing, but never **u**; be ever seeing, H1067
Isa 10:13 by my wisdom, because *I* **have u**. H1067
Isa 11: 2 the Spirit of wisdom and of **u**, the Spirit of H1069
Isa 27:11 For this is a people without **u**; so their H1069
Isa 28:19 The **u** *of* this message will bring sheer H1067
Isa 29:24 who are wayward in spirit will gain **u**; H1069
Isa 40:14 knowledge, or showed him the path of **u**? H9312
Isa 40:28 weary, and his **u** no one can fathom. H9312
Isa 44:19 no one has the knowledge or **u** to say H9312
Isa 56:11 They are shepherds *who* lack **u**; they all H3359
Jer 3:15 who will lead you with knowledge and **u**. H8505
Jer 4:22 are senseless children; they **have** no **u**. H1067
Jer 9:24 that *they* **have** *the* **u** to know me, that I H8505
Jer 10:12 stretched out the heavens by his **u**. H9312
Jer 51:15 stretched out the heavens by his **u**. H9312
Eze 28: 4 By your wisdom and **u** you have gained H9312
Da 1:17 God gave knowledge and **u** of all kinds of H8505
Da 1:20 of wisdom and **u** about which the king H1069
Da 5:12 a keen mind and knowledge and **u**, A10684
Da 8:27 appalled by the vision; it was beyond **u**. H1067
Da 9:22 have now come to give you insight and **u**. H1069
Da 10: 1 The **u** *of* the message came to him in a H1067
Da 10:12 set your mind to **gain u** and to humble H1067
Hos 4:11 old wine and new wine take away their **u**. H4213
Hos 4:14 a people without **u** will come to ruin! H1067
Ob 8 *those of* **u** in the mountains of Esau? H9312
Mt 13:14 " 'You will be ever hearing but never **u** *G5317*
Mk 4:12 ever hearing but never **u**; otherwise *G5317*
Mk 12:33 with all your **u** and with all your strength *G5304*
Lk 2:47 was amazed at his **u** and his answers. *G5304*
Ac 28:26 "You will be ever hearing but never **u**; you *G5317*
Ro 1:31 they have **no u**, no fidelity, no love, no *G852*
Ro 10:19 make you angry by a nation that has **no u**." *G852*
Ro 13:11 And do this, **u** the present time: The hour *G3857*
1Co 14:15 I will also pray *with* my **u**; I will sing *G3808*
1Co 14:15 my spirit, but I will also sing *with* my **u**. *G3808*
2Co 6: 6 in purity, **u**, patience and kindness; in the *G1194*
Eph 1: 8 lavished on us. With all wisdom and **u**, *G5860*
Eph 4:18 are darkened *in* their **u** and separated *G1379*
Php 4: 7 which transcends all **u**, will guard your *G3808*
Col 1: 9 all the wisdom and **u** that the Spirit gives, *G5304*
Col 2: 2 may have the full riches *of* complete **u**, *G5304*
Phm 6 effective in **deepening** your **u** of every *G2106*
Jas 3:13 Who is wise and **u** among you? Let them *G2184*
1Jn 5:20 Son of God has come and has given us **u**, *G1379*

UNDERSTANDS (7) [UNDERSTAND]

Dt 29: 4 you a mind that **u** or eyes that see or H3359
1Ch 28: 9 every heart and **u** every desire and every H1067
Job 28:23 God **u** the way to it and he alone knows H1067
Isa 57: 1 no *one* **u** that the righteous are taken H1067
Mt 13:23 to someone who hears the word and **u** it. *G5317*
Ro 3:11 there is no one *who* **u**; there is no one *G5317*
1Co 14: 2 no one **u** them; they utter *G201*

UNDERSTOOD (18) [UNDERSTAND]

1Ch 12:32 men *who* **u** the times and knew H3359+1069
Ne 8: 8 so that the people **u** what was being read H1067
Ne 8:12 because *they* now **u** the words that had H1067
Est 1:13 spoke with the wise men *who* **u** the times H3359
Job 13: 1 seen all this, my ears have heard and **u** it. H1067
Ps 73:17 then *I* **u** their final destiny. H1067
Isa 40:21 *Have you* not **u** since the earth was H1067
Isa 48: 8 You have neither heard nor **u**; from of old H3359

Da 9: 2 **u** from the Scriptures, according to H1067
Mt 13:51 "*Have you* **u** all these things?" Jesus *G5317*
Mt 16:12 Then *they* **u** that he was not telling them *G5317*
Mt 17:13 Then the disciples **u** that he was talking to *G5317*
Mk 6:52 for *they had* not **u** about the loaves; their *G5317*
Jn 13:28 no one at the meal **u** why Jesus said this *G1182*
Ro 1:20 *being* **u** from what has been made *G3783*
1Co 2: 8 None of the rulers of this age **u** it, for if *G1182*
2Co 1:14 as *you have* **u** us in part, you will come to *G2105*
Col 1: 6 day you heard it and truly **u** God's grace. *G2105*

UNDERTAKEN (3) [UNDERTOOK]

1Ki 7:40 all the work *he had* **u** for King Solomon in H6913
2Ch 4:11 the work *he had* **u** for King Solomon H6913
Lk 1: 1 Many *have* **u** to draw up an account of the *G2217*

UNDERTAKES (1) [UNDERTOOK]

Jos 6:26 LORD is the one who **u** to rebuild this city, H7756

UNDERTOOK (4) [UNDERTAKEN, UNDERTAKES]

2Ki 18: 7 he was successful in whatever *he* **u**. H3655
2Ch 31:21 In everything that *he* **u** in the service of H2725
2Ch 32:30 He succeeded in everything he **u**. H5126
Ecc 2: 4 *I* **u great** projects: I built houses for myself H1540

UNDESERVED (1)

Pr 26: 2 an **u** curse does not come to rest. H2855

UNDESIRABLE (1)

Jos 24:15 But if serving the LORD seems **u** to you H8273

UNDETECTED (1)

Nu 5:13 from her husband and her impurity *is* **u** H6259

UNDIGNIFIED (1)

2Sa 6:22 *I will* **become** even more **u** than this, and I H7837

UNDISCIPLINED (1)

Pr 29:15 a child **left u** disgraces its mother. H8938

UNDISTURBED (2)

Job 12: 6 The tents of marauders *are* **u**, and those H8922
Isa 32:18 in secure homes, in **u** places of rest. H8633

UNDIVIDED (4)

1Ch 12:33 David with **u loyalty**— H4202+4213+2256+4213
Ps 86:11 faithfulness; give me an **u** heart, that I H3479
Eze 11:19 I will give them an **u** heart and put a new H285
1Co 7:35 live in a right way in **u** devotion to the Lord. *G597*

UNDOING (2) [UNDONE]

2Ch 22: 4 death they became his advisers, to his **u**. H5422
Pr 18: 7 The mouths of fools are their **u**, and their H4745

UNDONE (2) [UNDOING]

Jos 11:15 *he* **left** nothing **u** of all that the LORD H6073
Lk 11:42 the latter without **leaving** the former **u**. *G4223*

UNDOUBTEDLY (1)

1Co 14:10 **U** there are all sorts of languages in *G1623+5593*

UNDRESSED (KJV) UNTENDED

UNDULY (1)

Pr 11:24 another withholds **u**, but comes to H4946+3841

UNDYING (1)

Eph 6:24 love our Lord Jesus Christ with an **u** love. *G914*

UNEATEN (1)

Job 20:18 he toiled for he must give back **u**; H4202+1180

UNENDING (2)

Ps 21: 6 have granted him **u** blessings and H4200+6329
Jer 15:18 Why is my pain **u** and my wound grievous H5905

UNEQUALED (2)

Mt 24:21 **u** from the beginning of the *G3888+4024+1181*
Mk 13:19 of distress **u** from the *G3888+4024+1181+5525*

UNEXPECTED (1) [UNEXPECTEDLY]

Pr 25:23 wind that brings *u* **rain** is a sly tongue— AIT

UNEXPECTEDLY (1) [UNEXPECTED]

Ecc 9:12 by evil times that fall **u** upon them. H7328

UNFADING (1)

1Pe 3: 4 the **u** beauty of a gentle and quiet spirit *G915*

UNFAILING (42)

Ex 15:13 In your **u love** you will lead the people H2876
1Sa 20:14 But show me **u kindness** *like* the LORD's H2876
2Sa 22:51 he shows **u kindness** to his anointed H2876
Ps 6: 4 save me because of your **u love**. H2876
Ps 13: 5 But I trust in your **u love**; my heart rejoices H2876
Ps 18:50 victories; he shows **u love** to his anointed H2876
Ps 21: 7 through the **u love** *of* the Most High he H2876
Ps 26: 3 mindful of your **u love** and have lived in H2876
Ps 31:16 on your servant; save me in your **u love**. H2876
Ps 32:10 the LORD's **u love** surrounds the one H2876
Ps 33: 5 justice; the earth is full of his **u love**. H2876
Ps 33:18 on those whose hope is in his **u love**, H2876
Ps 33:22 May your **u love** be with us, LORD, even as H2876
Ps 36: 7 How priceless is your **u love**, O God H2876
Ps 44:26 help us; rescue us because of your **u love**. H2876
Ps 48: 9 we meditate on your **u love**. H2876
Ps 51: 1 according to your **u love**; according to your H2876
Ps 52: 8 I trust in God's **u love** for ever and ever. H2876
Ps 62:12 with you, Lord, is **u love**"; and, "You H2876
Ps 77: 8 Has his **u love** vanished forever? Has his H2876
Ps 85: 7 Show us your **u love**, LORD, and grant us H2876
Ps 90:14 Satisfy us in the morning with your **u love** H2876
Ps 94:18 is slipping," your **u love**, LORD, supported H2876
Ps 107: 8 the LORD for his **u love** and his wonderful H2876
Ps 107:15 the LORD for his **u love** and his wonderful H2876
Ps 107:21 the LORD for his **u love** and his wonderful H2876
Ps 107:31 the LORD for his **u love** and his wonderful H2876
Ps 109:26 save me according to your **u love**. H2876
Ps 119:41 May your **u love** come to me, LORD, your H2876
Ps 119:76 May your **u love** be my comfort, according H2876
Ps 119:88 In your **u love** preserve my life, that I may H2876
Ps 130: 7 with the LORD is **u love** and with him is full H2876
Ps 138: 2 your name for your **u love** and your H2876
Ps 143: 8 the morning bring me word of your **u love**, H2876
Ps 143:12 In your **u love**, silence my enemies H2876
Ps 147:11 fear him, who put their hope in his **u love**. H2876
Pr 19:22 What a person desires is **u love**; better to H2876
Pr 20: 6 Many claim to have **u love**, but a faithful H2876
Isa 54:10 my **u love** for you will not be shaken H2876
Jer 31: 3 I have drawn you with **u kindness**. H2876
La 3:32 show compassion, so great is his **u love**. H2876
Hos 10:12 reap the fruit of **u love**, and break up your H2876

UNFAIR (1)

Mt 20:13 one of them, '*I am* not *being* **u** to you, friend *G92*

UNFAITHFUL (63) [UNFAITHFULNESS]

Lev 5:15 "When anyone **is u** to the LORD by H5085+5086
Lev 6: 2 anyone sins and *is* **u** to the LORD by H5085+5086
Nu 5: 6 any way and so *is* **u** to the LORD is H5085+5086
Nu 5:12 wife goes astray and *is* **u** to him H5085+5086
Nu 5:27 impure and *been* **u** to her husband H5085+5086
Nu 31:16 the Israelites to *be* **u** to the LORD in the H5086
Dt 32:20 generation, children who are **u**. H4202+574
Jos 7: 1 the Israelites *were* **u** in regard to H5085+5086
Jos 22:20 *When* Achan son of Zerah *was* **u** in H5085+5086
Jos 22:31 because *you have* not *been* **u** to the LORD H5085
Jdg 19: 2 But she *was* **u** to him. She left him and H2388
1Ch 5:25 But *they were* **u** to the God of their H5085
1Ch 10:13 died because he was **u** to the LORD; H5085+5086
2Ch 12: 2 Because *they had been* **u** to the LORD H5085
2Ch 26:16 *He was* **u** to the LORD his God, and H5085
2Ch 26:18 for *you have been* **u**; and you will H5085
2Ch 28:19 Judah and *had been* **most u** to the H5085+5086
2Ch 28:22 Ahaz became even more **u** to the LORD. H5085
2Ch 29: 6 Our parents *were* **u**; they did evil in the H5085
2Ch 30: 7 Israelites, who *were* **u** to the LORD, the H5085
2Ch 36:14 *became* **more and more u**, H8049+5085+5086
Ezr 10: 2 "*We have been* **u** to our God by marrying H5085
Ezr 10:10 to them, "You *have been* **u**; you have H5085
Ne 1: 8 'If you *are* **u**, I will scatter you H5085
Ne 13:27 wickedness and *are being* **u** to our God by H5085
Job 31:28 for *I would have been* **u** to God on high. H3950
Ps 43: 1 my cause against an **u** nation. H4202+2883
Ps 73:27 you destroy all *who are* **u** to you. H2388
Pr 2:22 the land, and the **u** will be torn from it. H953
Pr 11: 3 the **u** are destroyed by their duplicity. H953
Pr 11: 6 but the **u** are trapped by evil desires. H953
Pr 13: 2 the **u** have an appetite for violence. H953
Pr 13:15 the way of the **u** leads to their H953
Pr 21:18 the righteous, and the **u** for the upright. H953
Pr 22:12 he frustrates the words of the **u**. H953
Pr 23:28 in wait and multiplies the **u** among men. H953
Pr 25:19 is reliance on the **u** in a time of trouble. H953
Jer 3: 7 she did not, and her **u** sister Judah saw it. H957
Jer 3: 8 Yet I saw that her **u** sister Judah had no H953
Jer 3:10 her **u** sister Judah did not return to me with H957
Jer 3:11 Israel is more righteous than **u** Judah. H953
Jer 3:20 But like a woman **u** to her husband, so you H953
Jer 3:20 so *you*, Israel, *have been* **u** to me, H953
Jer 5:11 of Judah *have been* **utterly u** to me," H953+953
Jer 9: 2 are all adulterers, a crowd of **u** *people*. H953
Jer 31:22 long will you wander, **u** Daughter Israel? H8745
Jer 49: 4 **U** Daughter Ammon, you trust in your H8745
Eze 14:13 against me by *being* **u** and I stretch H5085+5086
Eze 15: 8 because *they have been* **u**, H5085+5086
Eze 17:20 on him there because *he was* **u** to me. H5085
Eze 20:27 blasphemed me by *being* **u** to me: H5085+5086
Eze 39:23 their sin, because *they were* **u** to me. H5085
Hos 2: 5 Their mother *has been* **u** and has H2388
Hos 4:12 leads them astray; *they are* **u** to their God. H2388
Hos 5: 7 *They are* **u** to the LORD; they give birth to H953
Hos 6: 7 the covenant; *they were* **u** to me there. H953
Hos 9: 1 For *you have been* **u** to your God; you love H2388
Mal 2:10 of our ancestors *by being* **u** to one another? H953
Mal 2:11 Judah *has been* **u**. A detestable thing has H953
Mal 2:14 You *have been* **u** to her, though she is your H953
Mal 2:15 and *do not be* **u** to the wife of your youth. H953
Mal 2:16 So be on your guard, and *do not be* **u**. H953
Ro 3: 3 What if some *were* **u**? Will their *G601*

UNFAITHFULNESS (14) [UNFAITHFUL]

Lev 26:40 their **u** and their hostility toward me, H5086+5085
Nu 14:33 suffering for your **u**, until the last of your H2394
1Ch 9: 1 captive to Babylon because of their **u**. H5086
2Ch 29:19 Ahaz removed in his **u** while he was king. H5086
2Ch 33:19 as well as all his sins and **u**, and the sites H5086
Ezr 9: 2 officials have led the way in this **u**." H5086
Ezr 9: 4 around me because of this **u** *of* the exiles. H5086
Ezr 10: 6 to mourn over the **u** *of* the exiles. H5086
Eze 18:24 of the **u** *they are* **guilty of** and H5086+5085
Eze 39:26 all the **u** *they* **showed** toward me H5085+5086
Da 9: 7 us because of our **u** to you. H5085+5086
Hos 1: 2 wife this land *is* **guilty of u** to the LORD." H2388
Hos 2: 2 from her face and the **u** from between her H5538
Ro 3: 3 Will their **u** nullify God's faithfulness? *G602*

UNFAMILIAR (1)

Isa 42:16 along **u** paths I will guide them H4202+3359

UNFANNED (1)

Job 20:26 A fire **u** will consume him and H4202+5870

UNFAVORABLE (1)

Jer 42: 6 Whether it is favorable or **u**, we will obey H8273

UNFEELING (1)

Ps 119:70 Their hearts *are* callous and **u**, but I H3263

UNFEIGNED (KJV) SINCERE

UNFILLED (1)

Jer 14: 3 They return with their jars **u**; dismayed H8200

UNFINISHED (2)

Titus 1: 5 put in order what *was* **left** *u* and appoint AIT
Rev 3: 2 found your deeds **u** in the sight of *G4024+4444*

UNFIT (1)

Titus 1:16 disobedient and **u** for doing anything good. *G99*

UNFOLD (1) [UNFOLDING]

Ps 106:13 had done and did not wait for his plan to **u**. NDT

UNFOLDING (1) [UNFOLD]

Ps 119:130 The **u** *of* your words gives light; it gives H7340

UNFORGIVING (1)

2Ti 3: 3 without love, **u**, slanderous, without *G836*

UNFORMED (1)

Ps 139:16 Your eyes saw my **u body**; all the days H1677

UNFRIENDLY (1)

Pr 18: 1 An **u** *person* pursues selfish ends and H7233

UNFRUITFUL (3)

Mt 13:22 of wealth choke the word, making it **u**. *G182*
Mk 4:19 come in and choke the word, making it **u**. *G182*
1Co 14:14 a tongue, my spirit prays, but my mind is **u**. *G182*

UNFULFILLED (1)

Eze 19: 5 " 'When she saw *her* **hope u**, her H3498

UNFURLED (1)

Ps 60: 4 raised a banner to **be u** against the bow. H5824

UNGODLINESS (4) [UNGODLY]

Isa 32: 6 They practice **u** and spread error H2869
Jer 23:15 of Jerusalem **u** has spread throughout H2870
Titus 2:12 us to say "No" to **u** and worldly passions *G813*
Jude 15 acts *they have* **committed in** *their* **u**, *G814*

UNGODLY (19) [UNGODLINESS]

Job 16:11 me over to the **u** and thrown me into H6397
Job 17: 8 the innocent are aroused against the **u**. H2868
Ps 35:16 Like the **u** they maliciously mocked; they H2868
Pr 11:31 how much more the **u** and the sinner! H8401
Isa 9:17 everyone is **u** and wicked, every mouth H2868
Ro 4: 5 not work but trusts God who justifies the **u**, *G815*
Ro 5: 6 were still powerless, Christ died for the **u**. *G815*
1Co 6: 1 to take it before the **u** for judgment instead *G96*
1Ti 1: 9 rebels, the **u** and sinful, the unholy *G815*
2Ti 2:16 in it will become more and more **u**. *G813*
1Pe 4:18 what will become of the **u** and the sinner?" *G815*
2Pe 2: 5 when he brought the flood on its **u** *people*, *G815*
2Pe 2: 6 of what is going to happen *to* the **u**; *G815*
2Pe 3: 7 of judgment and destruction *of* the **u**. *G815+476*
Jude 4 They are **u** *people*, who pervert the grace *G815*
Jude 8 of their dreams these **u** people pollute their NDT
Jude 15 all of them of all the **u** acts they have *G813*
Jude 15 all the defiant words **u** sinners have spoken *G815*
Jude 18 scoffers who will follow their own **u** desires. *G813*

UNGRATEFUL (2)

Lk 6:35 because he is kind to the **u** and wicked. *G940*
2Ti 3: 2 disobedient to their parents, **u**, unholy, *G940*

UNHARMED (4)

1Sa 24:19 his enemy, does he let him get away **u**? H3208
2Sa 17: 3 the return of all; all the people will be **u**." H8934
Ps 55:18 He rescues me **u** from the battle H928+8934
Da 3:25 unbound and **u**, and the A10244+10379+10029

UNHEALTHY (3)

Mt 6:23 But if your eyes are **u**, your whole body *G4505*
Lk 11:34 But when they are **u**, your body also is full *G4505*
1Ti 6: 4 *They* **have an u interest** in controversies *G3796*

UNHEARD-OF (2)

Eze 7: 5 " 'Disaster! **U** disaster! See, it comes H285
Da 11:36 god and will say **u** *things* against the God H7098

UNHOLY (3)
1Ti 1: 9 sinful, the **u** and irreligious, for *G495*
2Ti 3: 2 disobedient to their parents, ungrateful, **u**, *G495*
Heb 10:29 has treated as an **u** *thing* the blood of the *G3123*

UNICORN, UNICORNS (KJV) WILD OX, WILD OXEN

UNIMPRESSIVE (1)
2Co 10:10 in person he is **u** and his speaking *G822*

UNINFORMED (3)
1Co 12: 1 sisters, I do not want you *to be* **u**. *G51*
2Co 1: 8 We do not want you *to be* **u**, brothers and *G51*
1Th 4:13 we do not want you *to be* **u** about those who *G51*

UNINHABITED (1)
Job 38:26 one lives, an **u** desert, H4202+132+928+2257

UNINTENTIONAL (1) [UNINTENTIONALLY]
Nu 15:26 the people were involved in the **u wrong**. H8705

UNINTENTIONALLY (17) [UNINTENTIONAL]
Lev 4: 2 anyone sins **u** and does what is H928+8705
Lev 4:13 community **sins u** and does what is H8706
Lev 4:22 a leader sins **u** and does what is H928+8705
Lev 4:27 community sins **u** and does what is H928+8705
Lev 5:15 LORD by sinning **u** in regard to any of H928+8705
Lev 5:18 the **wrong** *they have* **committed u**, H8705+8704
Nu 15:22 " 'Now if *you as a community* **u** fail to H8706
Nu 15:24 if this is done **u** without the H4200+8705
Nu 15:27 " 'But if just one person sins **u**, that H928+8705
Nu 15:28 the one who erred by sinning **u**, H928+8705
Nu 15:29 to everyone *who* **sins u**, H6913+928+8705
Nu 35:22 throws something at them **u** H928+4202+7402
Dt 4:42 flee if they *had* **u** killed a H928+1172+1981
Dt 19: 4 anyone who kills a neighbor **u**, H928+1172+1981
Jos 20: 3 and **u** may flee there H928+1172+1981
Jos 20: 5 their neighbor **u** and without H928+1172+1981
Eze 45:20 month for anyone *who* **sins u** or through H8706

UNION (2) [UNITE]
Zec 11: 7 called one Favor and the other **U**, H2482
Zec 11:14 Then I broke my second staff called **U** H2482

UNIQUE (2)
SS 6: 9 my perfect one, is **u**, the only daughter of H285
Zec 14: 7 It will be a **u** day—a day known only to the H285

UNISON (2) [UNITE]
2Ch 5:13 musicians joined **in u** to give praise H3869+285
Ac 19:34 all shouted **in u** for about *G5889+1181+1651*

UNIT (5) [UNITS]
Ex 26: 6 together so that the tabernacle is a **u**. H285
Ex 26:11 the loops to fasten the tent together as a **u**. H285
Ex 36:13 together so that the tabernacle was a **u**. H285
Ex 36:18 clasps to fasten the tent together as a **u**. H285
1Sa 17:18 ten cheeses to the commander of their **u**. H548

UNITE (3) [UNION, UNISON, UNITED, UNITES, UNITY]
Job 16:10 cheek in scorn and **u** together against me. H4848
Isa 14: 1 will join them and **u** with the descendants H6202
1Co 6:15 of Christ and **u** them with a *G4472+3517*

UNITED (13) [UNITE]
Ge 2:24 his father and mother and *is* **u** to his wife, H1815
Jdg 20:11 got together and **u** as one against the city H2492
Da 2:43 and will not remain **u**, A10158+10180+10554+10180
Mt 19: 5 father and mother and *be* **u** to his wife, *G3140*
Mk 10: 7 father and mother and *be* **u** to his wife, *G4681*
Ac 18:12 of Corinth made a **u** attack on Paul and *G3924*
Ro 6: 5 For if *we have been* **u with** him in a *G5242+1181*
Ro 6: 5 we will certainly also be **u** with him in a NDT
1Co 1:10 be perfectly **u** in mind and *G1877+3836+899*
1Co 6:17 But whoever *is* **u with** the Lord is one with *G3140*
Eph 5:31 father and mother and *be* **u to** his wife, *G4681*
Php 2: 1 encouragement from being **u with** Christ, *G1877*
Col 2: 2 be encouraged in heart and **u** in love, *G5204*

UNITES (1) [UNITE]
1Co 6:16 know that he *who* **u** *himself* **with** a *G3140*

UNITS (13) [UNIT]
Nu 10:25 as the rear guard for all the **u**, the H4722
Nu 31:48 officers who were over the **u** *of* the army— H548
1Sa 29: 2 with their **u of hundreds** and thousands, H4395
2Sa 18: 4 marched out in **u of hundreds** and of H4395
2Ki 11: 4 the commanders of **u of a hundred**, H4395
2Ki 11: 9 commanders of **u of a hundred** did just as H4395
2Ki 11:15 the commanders of **u of a hundred**, H4395
1Ch 12:20 leaders of **u of a thousand** in Manasseh. H547
1Ch 15:25 commanders of **u of a thousand** went to H547
2Ch 17:14 commanders of **u of 1,000**: Adnah the H547
2Ch 23: 1 with the commanders of **u of a hundred**: H4395
2Ch 23: 9 commanders of **u of a hundred** the spears H4395
2Ch 23:14 out the commanders of **u of a hundred**, H4395

UNITY (7) [UNITE]
2Ch 30:12 people to give them **u** of mind to carry out H285
Ps 133: 1 it is when God's people live **together in u**! H3480
Jn 17:23 so that they may be brought to complete **u**. *G1651*
Eph 1:10 *to* **bring u** to all things in heaven and on *G368*
Eph 4: 3 effort to keep the **u** of the Spirit through *G1942*
Eph 4:13 we all reach **u** in the faith and in the *G1942*
Col 3:14 which binds them all together *in* **perfect u**. *G5456*

UNIVERSE (4)
1Co 4: 9 been made a spectacle *to* the **whole u**, *G3180*
Eph 4:10 in order to fill the **whole u**. *G3836+4246*
Heb 1: 2 through whom also he made the **u**. *G172*
Heb 11: 3 understand that the **u** was formed at God's *G172*

UNJUST (19) [UNJUSTLY]
Job 6:29 do not be **u**; reconsider, for my H6406
Job 27: 7 like the wicked, my adversary like the **u**! H6405
Ps 82: 2 will you defend the **u** and show partiality H6404
Isa 10: 1 Woe to those who make **u** laws, to those H224
Jer 17:11 those who gain riches by **u** means. H4202+5477
Eze 18:25 *Is* my way **u**? Is it not H9419+4202
Eze 18:25 Is it not your ways *that are* **u**? H9419+4202
Eze 18:29 *Are* my ways **u**, people of H9419+4202
Eze 18:29 Is it not your ways *that are* **u**? H9419+4202
Eze 22:12 *You* extort **u gain** *from* your neighbors H1298
Eze 22:13 together at the **u gain** you have made H1299
Eze 22:27 and kill people to **make u gain**. H1298+1299
Eze 33:31 their hearts are greedy for **u gain**. H1299
Hab 2: 9 to him who builds his house by **u** gain, H8273
Lk 18: 6 Lord said, "Listen to what the **u** judge says. *G94*
Ro 3: 5 That God is **u** in bringing his wrath on us *G96*
Ro 9:14 What then shall we say? Is God **u**? Not at all! *G94*
Heb 6:10 God is not **u**; he will not forget your work *G96*
1Pe 2:19 up under the pain of **u** suffering because *G97*

UNJUSTLY (1) [UNJUST]
Jer 23:10 evil course and use their power **u**. H4202+4026

UNKEMPT (3)
Lev 10: 6 "*Do* not *let* your hair *become* **u** and do H7277
Lev 13:45 let their hair be **u**, cover the lower part of H7277
Lev 21:10 *must* not *let* his hair *become* **u** or tear his H7277

UNKNOWN (7)
Dt 28:36 you to a nation **u** *to* you or your H4202+3359
Ps 81: 5 I heard an **u** voice say: H4202+3359
Isa 48: 6 things, of hidden things **u** *to you*. H4202+3359
Da 11:38 a god **u** *to* his ancestors he will H4202+3359
Ac 17:23 this inscription: TO AN **U** GOD. So you are *G58*
2Co 6: 9 yet regarded as **u**; dying, and yet we *G51*
Gal 1:22 I was personally **u** to the churches of Judea *G51*

UNLAWFUL (4)
Mt 12: 2 are doing what *is* **u** on the Sabbath *G4024+2003*
Mk 2:24 doing what *is* **u** on the Sabbath *G4024+2003*
Lk 6: 2 you doing what *is* **u** on the *G4024+2003*
Ac 16:21 customs **u** for us Romans to *G4024+2003*

UNLEARNED (KJV) IGNORANT, INQUIRER, INQUIRERS, STUPID, UNSCHOOLED

UNLEASH (3) [UNLEASHED, UNLEASHES]
Job 40:11 **U** the fury of your wrath, look at all who H7046
Eze 7: 3 and *I will* **u** my anger against you. H8938
Eze 13:13 In my wrath *I will* **u** a violent wind, and in H1324

UNLEASHED (2) [UNLEASH]
Ex 15: 7 *You* **u** your burning anger; it consumed H8938
Ps 78:49 *He* **u** against them his hot anger, his H8938

UNLEASHES (1) [UNLEASH]
Job 37: 3 *He* **u** his lightning beneath the whole H9223

UNLEAVENED (30)
Ex 12:17 "Celebrate the **Festival of U Bread** H5174
Ex 12:20 you live, you must eat **u bread**." H5174
Ex 12:39 from Egypt, they baked loaves of **u bread**. H5174
Ex 13: 7 Eat **u bread** during those seven days H5174
Ex 23:15 "Celebrate the Festival of **U Bread**; for H5174
Ex 34:18 "Celebrate the Festival of **U Bread**. H5174
Lev 23: 6 the LORD's Festival of **U Bread** begins; H5174
Nu 6:17 the basket of **u bread** and is to sacrifice H5174
Nu 9:11 together with **u bread** and bitter herbs. H5174
Dt 16: 3 for seven days eat **u bread**, the bread H5174
Dt 16: 8 For six days eat **u bread** and on the H5174
Dt 16:16 at the Festival of **U Bread**, the Festival of H5174
Jos 5:11 of the land: **u bread** and roasted grain. H5174
Jdg 6:20 "Take the meat and the **u bread**, place H5174
Jdg 6:21 the meat and the **u bread** with the tip of H5174
2Ki 23: 9 they ate **u bread** with their fellow priests. H5174
2Ch 8:13 the Festival of **U Bread**, the Festival of H5174
2Ch 30:13 the Festival of **U Bread** in the second H5174
2Ch 30:21 the Festival of **U Bread** for seven days H5174
2Ch 35:17 the Festival of **U Bread** for seven days. H5174
Ezr 6:22 with joy the Festival of **U Bread**, H5174
Mt 26:17 On the first day *of* the **Festival of U Bread** *G109*
Mk 14: 1 the **Festival of U Bread** were only two *G109*
Mk 14:12 On the first day *of* the **Festival of U Bread** *G109*
Lk 22: 1 Now the Festival *of* **U Bread**, called the *G109*
Lk 22: 7 came the day *of* **U Bread** on which the *G109*
Ac 12: 3 happened during the **Festival of U Bread**. *G109*
Ac 20: 6 after the **Festival of U Bread**, *G2465+3836+109*
1Co 5: 7 so that you may be a new **u** batch—as you *G109*
1Co 5: 8 with the **u bread** of sincerity and truth. *G109*

UNLESS (63)
Ge 32:26 "I will not let you go **u** you bless me." H3954+561
Ge 42:15 not leave this place **u** your youngest H3954+561
Ge 43: 3 see my face again **u** your brother is with H1194
Ge 43: 5 see my face again **u** your brother is with H1194
Ge 44:23 '**U** your youngest brother comes H561+4202
Ge 44:26 see the man's face **u** our youngest brother H401
Ex 3:19 will not let you go **u** a mighty hand H4202
Ex 33:16 with your people **u** you go with us? H2022+4202
Lev 22: 6 the sacred offerings **u** he has bathed H3954+561
Dt 32:30 **u** their Rock had sold them H561+4202+3954
Dt 32:30 sold them, **u** the LORD had given them up? NDT
Jos 2:18 **u**, when we enter the land, you have tied H2180
Jos 2:18 **u** you have brought your father and NDT
Jos 7:12 be with you anymore **u** you destroy H561+4202
2Sa 3:13 my presence **u** you bring H3954+561+4200+7156
2Ki 4:24 don't slow down for me **u** I tell you." H3954+561
Est 2:14 return to the king **u** he was pleased H3954+561
Est 4:11 put to death **u** the king H4200+963+4946+889
Ps 94:17 **U** the LORD had given me help, I would H4295
Ps 127: 1 **U** the LORD builds the house, the H561+4202
Ps 127: 1 **U** the LORD watches over the city, the H561+4202
Isa 1: 9 **U** the LORD Almighty had left us some H4295
La 5:22 **u** you have utterly rejected us and H3954+561
Da 6: 5 this man Daniel **u** it has something to A10386
Am 3: 3 walk together **u** they have agreed H1194+561
Mt 5:20 I tell you that **u** your righteousness *G1569+3590*
Mt 12:29 off his possessions **u** he first ties up *G1569+3590*
Mt 18: 3 **u** you change and become like *G1569+3590*
Mt 18:35 treat each of you **u** you forgive your *G1569+3590*
Mt 26:42 cup to be taken away **u** I drink it, *G1569+3590*
Mk 7: 3 Jews do not eat **u** they give their *G1569+3590*
Mk 7: 4 they do not eat **u** they wash. *G1569+3590*
Lk 9:13 **u** we go and buy food for all this *G1623+3614*
Lk 13: 3 But **u** you repent, you too will all *G1569+3590*
Lk 13: 5 But **u** you repent, you too will all *G1569+3590*
Jn 3: 3 kingdom of God **u** they are born *G1569+3590*
Jn 3: 5 kingdom of God **u** they are born of *G1569+3590*
Jn 4:48 "**U** you people see signs and *G1569+3590*
Jn 6:44 can come to me **u** the Father who *G1569+3590*
Jn 6:53 **u** you eat the flesh of the Son of *G1569+3590*
Jn 6:65 can come to me **u** the Father has *G1569+3590*
Jn 10:37 Do not believe me **u** I do the works *G1623+4024*
Jn 12:24 **u** a kernel of wheat falls to the *G1569+3590*
Jn 13: 8 answered, "**U** I wash you, you *G1569+3590*
Jn 15: 4 you bear fruit **u** you remain in me. *G1569+3590*
Jn 16: 7 **U** I go away, the Advocate will not *G1569+3590*
Jn 20:25 "**U** I see the nail marks in his *G1569+3590*
Ac 8:31 "**u** someone explains it to me?" *G1569+3590*
Ac 15: 1 "**U** you are circumcised, according *G1569+3590*
Ac 24:21 **u** it was this one thing I shouted as I stood *G2445*
Ac 27:31 "**U** these men stay with the ship *G1569+3590*
Ro 9:29 "**U** the Lord Almighty had left us *G1623+3590*
Ro 10:15 can anyone preach **u** they are sent? *G1569+3590*
1Co 14: 5 **u** someone interprets *G1760+1623+3590*
1Co 14: 6 **u** I bring you some revelation or *G1569+3590*
1Co 14: 7 tune is being played **u** there is a *G1569+3590*
1Co 14: 9 **U** you speak intelligible words with *G1569+3590*
1Co 15:36 sow does not come to life **u** it dies. *G1569+3590*
2Co 13: 5 that Christ Jesus is in you—**u**, of course, *G1623*
1Ti 5: 9 on the list of widows **u** she is **over** sixty, *G1781*
1Ti 5:19 an elder **u** it is brought by *G1760+1623+3590*
Rev 2:22 **u** they repent of her ways. *G1569+3590*
Rev 13:17 not buy or sell **u** they had the mark, *G1623+3590*

UNLIKE (8)
2Ki 16: 2 **U** David his father, he did not do H4202+3869
2Ch 27: 2 **u** him he did not enter the temple of the NDT
2Ch 28: 1 **U** David his father, he did not do H4202+3869
2Ch 33:23 But **u** his father Manasseh, he did H4202+3869
Isa 7:17 of your father a time **u** any since Ephraim H4202
Eze 16:31 square, you were **u** a prostitute H4202+3869
2Co 2:17 **U** so many, we do not peddle the *G4024+6055*
Heb 7:27 **U** the other high priests, he does not need *G6061*

UNLOAD (1) [UNLOADED]
Ac 21: 3 where our ship was *to* **u** its cargo. *G711*

UNLOADED (1) [UNLOAD]
Ge 24:32 to the house, and the camels *were* **u**. H7337

UNLOCKED (1)
Jdg 3:25 of the room, they took a key and **u** them. H7337

UNLOVED (1)
Dt 21:17 the son of his **u** wife as the firstborn by H8533

UNMARKED (1)
Lk 11:44 because you are like **u** graves, which people *G83*

UNMARRIED (9)
Lev 21: 3 an **u** sister who is dependent on him H1435
Ru 1:13 *Would you* **remain u** for them? H6328+4200+1194+2118+4200+408
Eze 44:25 brother or **u** sister, then H4202+2118+4200+408
Ac 21: 9 He had four **u** daughters who prophesied. *G4221*
1Co 7: 8 Now *to* the **u** and the widows I say: It is *G23*
1Co 7: 8 It is good for them to stay **u**, as I do. NDT
1Co 7:11 she must remain **u** or else be reconciled to *G23*
1Co 7:32 An **u** *man* is concerned about the Lord's *G23*
1Co 7:34 An **u** woman or virgin is concerned about *G23*

UNMERCIFULLY (1)
Ps 119:51 The arrogant mock me **u**, but I do H6330+4394

UNMINDFUL (1)
Job 39:15 **u** that a foot may crush them, that some H8894

UNNATURAL (1)
Ro 1:26 natural sexual relations for **u** *ones.* *G4123+5882*

UNNI (3)
1Ch 15:18 Shemiramoth, Jehiel, **U**, Eliab, Benaiah H6716
1Ch 15:20 **U**, Eliab, Maaseiah and H6716
Ne 12: 9 Bakbukiah and **U**, their associates, stood H6716

UNNOTICED (3)
1Sa 24: 4 David crept up **u** and cut off a H928+2021+4319
Job 4:20 to pieces; **u**, they perish H4946+1172+8492
Lk 8:47 seeing that *she could* not **go u**, came *G3291*

UNOCCUPIED (1)
Mt 12:44 it finds the house **u**, swept clean and put *G5390*

UNPLOWED (5)
Ex 23:11 year *let* the land **lie u** and unused. H9023
Pr 13:23 An **u field** produces food for the poor, but H5776
Pr 21: 4 a proud heart—the **u field** *of* the wicked H5776
Jer 4: 3 "Break up your **u ground** and do not sow H5776
Hos 10:12 break up your **u ground**; for it is time H5776

UNPREPARED (1)
2Co 9: 4 come with me and find you **u**, *G564*

UNPRESENTABLE (1)
1Co 12:23 And the parts that are **u** are treated with *G860*

UNPRINCIPLED (1)
Zep 3: 4 Her prophets *are* **u**; they are treacherous H7069

UNPRODUCTIVE (4)
2Ki 2:19 the water is bad and the land *is* **u**. H8897
2Ki 2:21 will it cause death or **make** the land **u**. H8897
Titus 3:14 urgent needs and not live **u** lives. *G182*
2Pe 1: 8 ineffective and **u** in your knowledge of *G182*

UNPROFITABLE (2)
Isa 30: 6 humps of camels, to that **u** nation, H4202+3603
Titus 3: 9 the law, because these are **u** and useless. *G543*

UNPROTECTED (2)
Ge 42: 9 have come to see where our land is **u**." H6872
Ge 42:12 have come to see where our land is **u**." H6872

UNPUNISHED (19)
Ex 34: 7 Yet *he does* not **leave the guilty u** H5927+5927
Nu 14:18 Yet *he does* not **leave the guilty u** H5927+5927
Job 10:14 me and *would* not **let** my offense **go u**. H5927
Pr 6:29 no one who touches her *will* **go u**. H5927
Pr 11:21 The wicked *will* not **go u**, but those who H5927
Pr 16: 5 Be sure of this: *They will* not **go u**. H5927
Pr 17: 5 whoever gloats over disaster *will* not **go u**. H5927
Pr 19: 5 A false witness *will* not **go u**, and H5927
Pr 19: 9 A false witness *will* not **go u**, and H5927
Pr 28:20 one eager to get rich *will* not **go u**. H5927
Jer 25:29 Name, and *will* you **indeed go u**? H5927+5927
Jer 25:29 *You will* not **go u**, for I am calling down a H5927
Jer 30:11 *I will* not **let** you **go entirely u**." H5927+5927
Jer 46:28 *I will* not **let** you **go entirely u**." H5927+5927
Jer 49:12 must drink it, why *should* you **go u**? H5927+5927
Jer 49:12 *You will* not **go u**, but must H5927
Na 1: 3 the LORD *will* not **leave the guilty u**. H5927+5927
Zec 11: 5 buyers slaughter them and *go* **u**. H4202+870
Ro 3:25 **left** the sins committed beforehand **u**— *G4217*

UNQUENCHABLE (3)
Jer 17:27 I will kindle an **u** fire in the gates H4202+3882
Mt 3:12 barn and burning up the chaff with **u** fire." *G812*
Lk 3:17 he will burn up the chaff with **u** fire." *G812*

UNREASONABLE (1) [UNREASONING]
Ac 25:27 For I think it is **u** to send a prisoner on to *G263*

UNREASONING (1) [UNREASONABLE]
2Pe 2:12 They are like **u** animals, creatures of *G263*

UNRELENTING (1)
Job 6:10 my joy in **u** pain—that I had not H4202+2798

UNRELIABLE (2)
Ps 78:57 faithless, as **u** as a faulty bow. H2200
Pr 18:24 One who has *u* **friends** soon comes to ruin AIT

UNREPENTANT (1)
Ro 2: 5 of your stubbornness and your **u** heart, *G295*

UNREST (2)
Jer 50:34 but **u** to those who live in Babylon. H8074
Am 3: 9 see the great **u** within her and the H4539

UNRIGHTEOUS (5) [UNRIGHTEOUSNESS]
Isa 55: 7 their ways and the **u** their thoughts. H224+408
Zep 3: 5 does not fail, yet the **u** know no shame. H6405
Mt 5:45 sends rain on the righteous and the **u**. *G96*
1Pe 3:18 the righteous for the **u**, to bring you to God. *G96*
2Pe 2: 9 to hold the **u** for punishment on the *G96*

UNRIGHTEOUSNESS (3) [UNRIGHTEOUS]
Jer 22:13 to him who builds his palace by **u**, H4202+7406
Ro 3: 5 But if our **u** brings out God's righteousness *G94*
1Jn 1: 9 forgive us our sins and purify us from all **u**. *G94*

UNRIPE (1)
Job 15:33 will be like a vine stripped of its **u grapes**, H1235

UNROLLED (1) [UNROLLING]
Eze 2:10 which *he* **u** before me. On both sides of it H7298

UNROLLING (1) [UNROLLED]
Lk 4:17 was handed to him. **U** it, he found the *G408*

UNRULY (5)
Pr 7:11 She *is* **u** and defiant, her feet never stay H2159
Pr 9:13 Folly *is* an **u** woman; she is simple and H2159
Jer 31:18 'You disciplined me like an **u** calf H4202+4340
Eze 5: 7 You *have been* more **u** than the nations H2171
Hos 11:12 And Judah *is* **u** against God, even against H8113

UNSANDALED (1)
Dt 25:10 in Israel as The Family of the **U**. H2740+5837

UNSATISFIED (1)
2Sa 1:22 the sword of Saul did not return **u**. H8200

UNSAVOURY (KJV) SHREWD, TASTELESS

UNSCATHED (2)
Job 9: 4 Who has resisted him and *come out* **u**? H8966
Isa 41: 3 He pursues them and moves on **u**, by a H8934

UNSCHOOLED (1)
Ac 4:13 John and realized that they were **u**, *G63*

UNSEALED (3)
Ne 6: 5 message, and in his hand was an **u** letter H7337
Jer 32:11 conditions, as well as the **u** *copy*— H1655
Jer 32:14 the sealed and **u** *copies* of the deed of H1655

UNSEARCHABLE (3)
Pr 25: 3 is deep, so the hearts of kings are **u**. H401+2984
Jer 33: 3 you great and **u** *things* you do not know. H1290
Ro 11:33 How **u** his judgments, and his paths *G451*

UNSEEMLY (KJV) DISHONOR, SHAMEFUL

UNSEEN (4)
Mt 6: 6 pray to your Father, who is **u**. *G1877+3836+3220*
Mt 6:18 Father, who *is* **u**; and your *G1877+3836+3224*
2Co 4:18 on what *is* **u**, since what is *G3590+1063*
2Co 4:18 temporary, but what *is* **u** is eternal. *G3590+1063*

UNSETTLED (2)
1Th 3: 3 so that no one *would be* **u** by these trials *G4883*
2Th 2: 2 not to *become* easily **u** or alarmed by the *G4888*

UNSHARPENED (1)
Ecc 10:10 If the ax is dull and its edge **u** H4202+7837

UNSHEATHED (1)
Eze 21: 4 my sword *will be* **u** against H3655+4946+9509

UNSHRUNK (2)
Mt 9:16 one sews a patch of **u** cloth on an old *G47*
Mk 2:21 one sews a patch of **u** cloth on an old *G47*

UNSPEAKABLE (KJV) INDESCRIBABLE, INEXPRESSIBLE

UNSPIRITUAL (3)
Ro 7:14 is spiritual; but I am **u**, sold as a slave to *G4921*
Col 2:18 up with idle notions by their **u** mind. *G4922*
Jas 3:15 from heaven but is earthly, **u**, demonic. *G6035*

UNSTABLE (3)
Jas 1: 8 is double-minded and **u** in all they do. *G190*
2Pe 2:14 they seduce the **u**; they are experts *G6034+844*
2Pe 3:16 which ignorant and **u** *people* distort, as *G844*

UNSTOPPED (1)
Isa 35: 5 be opened and the ears of the deaf **u**. H7337

UNSTRUNG (1)
Job 30:11 Now that God *has* **u** my bow and afflicted H7337

UNSUCCESSFUL (1)
Dt 28:29 *You will be* **u** *in* everything you do H7503+4202

UNSUITABLE (1) [UNSUITED]
Ac 27:12 Since the harbor was **u** to winter in, the *G460*

UNSUITED (1) [UNSUITABLE]
Pr 17: 7 lips are **u** to a godless fool H4202+5534

UNSUSPECTING (4)
Ge 34:25 took their swords and attacked the **u** city H1055
Jdg 8:11 Jogbehah and attacked the **u** army. H1055
Jdg 18:10 you will find an **u** people and a spacious H1053
Eze 38:11 attack a peaceful and **u** people— H4200+1055

UNSWERVING (1) [UNSWERVINGLY]
1Ch 28: 7 kingdom forever if *he is* **u** in carrying out H2616

UNSWERVINGLY (1) [UNSWERVING]
Heb 10:23 Let us hold **u** to the hope we profess, for he *G195*

UNTENDED (2)
Lev 25: 5 itself or harvest the grapes of your **u vines**. H5687
Lev 25:11 what grows of itself or harvest the **u vines**. H5687

UNTHANKFUL (KJV) UNGRATEFUL

UNTHINKABLE (1)
Job 34:12 It is **u** that God would do wrong, that H597+4202

UNTIE (9) [UNTIED, UNTYING]
Isa 58: 6 of injustice and **u** the cords of the yoke, H6002
Mt 21: 2 **U** them and bring them to me. *G3395*
Mk 1: 7 I am not worthy to stoop down and **u**. *G3395*
Mk 11: 2 has ever ridden. **U** it and bring it here. *G3395*
Lk 3:16 of whose sandals I am not worthy *to* **u**. *G3395*
Lk 13:15 of you on the Sabbath **u** your ox or donkey *G3395*
Lk 19:30 has ever ridden. **U** it and bring it here. *G3395*
Jn 1:27 of whose sandals I am not worthy to **u**." *G3395*
Ac 13:25 me whose sandals I am not worthy *to* **u**. *G3395*

UNTIED (3) [UNTIE]
Job 39: 5 wild donkey go free? Who **u** its ropes? H7337
Mk 11: 4 the street, tied at a doorway. *As they* **u** it, *G3395*
Ac 27:40 at the same time **u** the ropes that held *G479*

UNTIL (422)
Ge 3:19 you will eat your food **u** you return to the H6330
Ge 8: 5 continued to recede **u** the tenth month, H6330
Ge 8: 7 back and forth **u** the water had dried H6330
Ge 13: 3 from place to place **u** he came to Bethel, H6330
Ge 19:22 I cannot do anything **u** you reach it." H6330
Ge 24:19 **u** they have had enough to drink." H6330+561
Ge 24:33 "I will not eat **u** I have told you what H6330+561
Ge 26:13 to grow **u** he became very H6330+3954
Ge 27:44 him for a while **u** your brother's fury H6330+889
Ge 28: 3 increase your numbers **u** you become a H2256
Ge 28:15 not leave you **u** I have done what I H6330+889
Ge 29: 8 "**u** all the flocks are gathered and H6330+889
Ge 33:14 children, **u** I come to my lord in Seir." H6330+889
Ge 34: 5 did nothing about it **u** they came home. H6330
Ge 37:35 continue to mourn *u I* **join** my son in the AIT
Ge 38:11 father's household **u** my son Shelah H6330
Ge 38:17 me something as a pledge **u** you send it?" H6330
Ge 39:16 cloak beside her **u** his master came home H6330
Ge 49:10 **u** he to whom it belongs shall H6330+3954
Ex 7:16 But **u** now you have not listened. H6330
Ex 10:15 They covered all the ground **u** it was black H2256
Ex 10:26 **u** we get there we will not know what H6330
Ex 12: 6 Take care of them **u** the fourteenth day of H6330
Ex 12:18 of the fourteenth day **u** the evening of the H6330
Ex 12:22 out of the door of your house **u** morning. H6330
Ex 15:16 as still as a stone—**u** your people pass by H6330
Ex 15:16 **u** the people you bought pass by. H6330
Ex 16:19 "No one is to keep any of it **u** morning." H6330
Ex 16:20 they kept part of it **u** morning, but it was H6330
Ex 16:23 whatever is left and keep it **u** morning. H6330
Ex 16:24 So they saved it **u** morning, as Moses H6330
Ex 16:35 **u** they came to a land that was settled H6330
Ex 16:35 they ate manna **u** they reached the border H6330
Ex 23:18 offerings must not be kept **u** morning. H6330
Ex 23:30 **u** you have increased enough to H6330+889
Ex 24:14 "Wait here for us **u** we come back to H6330+889
Ex 33: 8 watching Moses **u** he entered the tent. H6330
Ex 33:22 you with my hand **u** I have passed by. H6330
Ex 34:25 the Passover Festival remain **u** morning. H4200
Ex 34:34 he removed the veil **u** he came out. H6330
Ex 34:35 back over his face **u** he went in to speak H6330
Ex 40:37 they did not set out—**u** the day it lifted. H6330
Lev 8:33 **u** the days of your ordination are H6330
Lev 12: 4 go to the sanctuary **u** the days of her H6330
Lev 16:17 in the Most Holy Place **u** he comes out, H6330
Lev 19: 6 anything left over **u** the third day must be H6330
Lev 22: 4 sacred offerings **u** he is cleansed. H6330+889
Lev 23:14 **u** the very day you bring this offering to H6330
Lev 23:32 day of the month **u** the following evening H6330
Lev 24:12 put him in custody **u** the will of the LORD H4200
Lev 25:22 continue to eat from it **u** the harvest of the H6330
Lev 25:28 of the buyer **u** the Year of Jubilee. H6330
Lev 25:40 are to work for you **u** the Year of Jubilee. H6330
Lev 25:52 a few years remain **u** the Year of Jubilee, H6330
Lev 26: 5 Your threshing *will* **continue u** grape H5952
Lev 26: 5 grape harvest *will* **continue u** planting, H5952
Lev 27:18 of years that remain **u** the next Year of H6330
Nu 6: 5 They must be holy **u** the period of their H6330
Nu 9: 8 "Wait **u** I find out what the LORD H2256
Nu 10:12 from place to place **u** the cloud came to H2256
Nu 11:20 **u** it comes out of your nostrils and H6330+889
Nu 14:19 them from the time they left Egypt **u** now." H6330
Nu 14:33 **u** the last of your bodies lies in the H6330
Nu 20:17 right or to the left **u** we have passed H6330+889
Nu 21:22 King's Highway **u** we have passed H6330+889
Nu 32:13 **u** the whole generation of those who had H6330
Nu 32:17 the Israelites **u** we have H6330+889+561
Nu 32:18 return to our homes **u** each of the H6330
Nu 32:21 Jordan before the LORD **u** he has driven his H6330
Nu 35:25 must stay there **u** the death of the high H6330
Nu 35:28 the city of refuge **u** the death of the high H6330
Dt 1:31 all the way you went **u** you reached this H6330
Dt 2:14 left Kadesh Barnea **u** we crossed the H6330+889
Dt 2:15 was against them **u** he had completely H6330
Dt 2:29 **u** we cross the Jordan into the land H6330+889
Dt 3:20 **u** the LORD gives rest to your fellow H6330+889
Dt 7:20 hornet among them **u** even the survivors H6330
Dt 7:23 into great confusion **u** they are destroyed. H6330
Dt 9: 7 the day you left Egypt **u** you arrived here, H6330
Dt 11: 5 you in the wilderness **u** you arrived at this H6330

U

Dt 16: 4 evening of the first day remain **u** morning. H4200
Dt 20:20 to build siege works **u** the city at war with H6330
Dt 22: 2 with you and keep it **u** they come looking H6330
Dt 28:20 **u** you are destroyed and come to sudden H6330
Dt 28:21 you with diseases **u** he has destroyed you H6330
Dt 28:22 which will plague you **u** you perish. H6330
Dt 28:24 down from the skies **u** you are destroyed. H6330
Dt 28:45 you and overtake you **u** you are destroyed, H6330
Dt 28:48 yoke on your neck **u** he has destroyed you. H6330
Dt 28:51 crops of your land **u** you are destroyed. H6330
Dt 28:51 lambs of your flocks **u** you are ruined. H6330
Dt 28:52 throughout your land **u** the high fortified H6330
Dt 28:61 this Book of the Law, **u** you are destroyed. H6330
Dt 34: 8 **u** the time of weeping and mourning was H2256
Jos 1:15 **u** the LORD gives them rest, as he has H6330+889
Jos 1:15 **u** they too have taken possession of the NDT
Jos 2:16 yourselves there three days **u** they return, H6330
Jos 2:22 **u** the pursuers had searched all along the H6330
Jos 3:17 Israel passed by **u** the whole nation H6330+889
Jos 4:10 of the Jordan **u** everything the LORD H6330
Jos 4:23 Jordan before you **u** you had crossed over. H6330
Jos 4:23 it up before us **u** we had crossed over. H6330
Jos 5: 1 the Israelites **u** they had crossed over H6330
Jos 5: 6 forty years **u** all the men who were H6330
Jos 5: 8 they were in camp **u** they were healed. H6330
Jos 6:10 do not say a word **u** the day I tell you to H6330
Jos 7:13 against your enemies **u** you remove them. H6330
Jos 8: 6 They will pursue us **u** we have lured them H6330
Jos 8:26 out his javelin **u** he had destroyed H6330+889
Jos 8:29 Ai on a pole and left it there **u** evening. H6330
Jos 10:26 were left hanging on the poles **u** evening. H6330
Jos 10:33 his army—**u** no survivors were left. H6330
Jos 11: 8 on the east, **u** no survivors were left. H6330
Jos 11:14 they put to the sword **u** they completely H6330
Jos 20: 6 to stay in that city **u** they have stood trial H6330
Jos 20: 6 the assembly and **u** the death of the high H6330
Jos 23: 8 to the LORD your God, as you have **u** now. H6330
Jos 23:13 **u** you perish from this good land H6330
Jos 23:15 **u** the LORD your God has destroyed you H6330
Jdg 3:11 forty years, **u** Othniel son of Kenaz died. H2256
Jdg 4:24 king of Canaan **u** they destroyed him H6330+889
Jdg 5: 7 they held back **u** I, Deborah, H6330+8611
Jdg 5: 7 Deborah, arose, **u** I arose, a mother in H8611
Jdg 6:18 Please do not go away **u** I come back and H6330
Jdg 6:18 the LORD said, "I will wait **u** you return." H6330
Jdg 9:45 against the city **u** he had captured it and H2256
Jdg 13: 7 God from the womb **u** the day of his H6330
Jdg 13:15 like you to stay **u** we prepare a young H2256
Jdg 15: 7 I swear that I **won't** stop **u** I get my H3954+561
Jdg 16: 3 Samson lay there only **u** the middle of the H6330
Jdg 16:16 him day after day **u** he was sick to death H2256
Jdg 18:30 the tribe of Dan **u** the time of the H6330
Jdg 19:26 down at the door and lay there **u** daylight. H6330
Jdg 20:23 up and wept before the LORD **u** evening, H6330
Jdg 20:26 They fasted that day **u** evening and H6330
Jdg 21: 2 where they sat before God **u** evening H6330
Ru 1:13 would you wait **u** they grew up H6330+889
Ru 1:19 the two women went on **u** they came to H6330
Ru 2:17 So Ruth gleaned in the field **u** evening H6330
Ru 2:21 'Stay with my workers **u** they finish H6330+561
Ru 2:23 of Boaz to glean **u** the barley and wheat H6330
Ru 3: 3 know you are there **u** he has finished H6330
Ru 3:13 lives I will do it. Lie here **u** morning." H6330
Ru 3:14 So she lay at his feet **u** morning, but got H6330
Ru 3:18 **u** you find out what happens. H6330+889
Ru 3:18 man will not rest **u** the matter is H3954+561
1Sa 1:23 "Stay here **u** you have weaned him; only H6330
1Sa 1:23 nursed her son **u** she had weaned him H6330
1Sa 3:15 Samuel lay down **u** morning and then H6330
1Sa 8: 8 I brought them up out of Egypt **u** this day, H6330
1Sa 9:13 people will not begin eating **u** he comes, H6330
1Sa 10: 3 go on from there **u** you reach the great H2256
1Sa 10: 8 must wait seven days **u** I come to you H6330
1Sa 11:11 slaughtered them **u** the heat of the day. H6330
1Sa 12: 2 your leader from my youth **u** this day. H6330
1Sa 14: 9 'Wait there **u** we come to you,' we H6330
1Sa 15:18 war against them **u** you have wiped them H6330
1Sa 15:35 **U** the day Samuel died, he did not go to H6330
1Sa 16:11 him; we will not sit down **u** he arrives." H6330
1Sa 19:23 along prophesying **u** he came to Naioth. H6330
1Sa 20: 5 hide in the field **u** the evening of the H6330
1Sa 22: 3 and stay with you **u** I learn what God H6330+889
1Sa 25:36 So she told him nothing at all **u** daybreak H6330
1Sa 29: 3 from the day he left Saul **u** now, H6330
1Sa 29: 6 From the day you came to me **u** today, H6330
1Sa 29: 8 servant from the day I came to you **u** now? H6330
1Sa 30: 4 his men wept aloud **u** they had no H6330+889
1Sa 30:17 them from dusk **u** the evening of the H6330
2Sa 2:27 have continued pursuing them **u** morning." H4946
2Sa 15:24 offered sacrifices **u** all the people had H6330
2Sa 15:28 in the wilderness **u** word comes from you H6330
2Sa 17:13 to the valley **u** not so much as a H6330+889
2Sa 19:24 the day the king left **u** the day he returned H6330
2Sa 24:15 from that morning **u the end of** the time H6330
1Ki 3: 1 to the City of David **u** he finished building H6330
1Ki 5: 3 of the LORD his God **u** the LORD put his H6330
1Ki 10: 7 these things **u** I came and saw with H6330+889
1Ki 11:16 **u** they had destroyed all the men in Edom H6330
1Ki 11:40 stayed there **u** Solomon's death. H6330
1Ki 14:10 as one burns dung, **u** it is all gone. H6330
1Ki 17:14 oil will not run dry **u** the day the LORD H6330
1Ki 18:28 as was their custom, **u** their blood flowed. H6330

1Ki 18:29 prophesying **u the time for** the evening H6330
1Ki 19: 8 days and forty nights **u** he reached Horeb, H6330
1Ki 22:11 gore the Arameans **u** they are destroyed. H6330
1Ki 22:27 bread and water **u** I return safely. H6330
2Ki 2:17 But they persisted **u** he was too H6330
2Ki 3:24 rose up and fought them **u** they fled. H6330
2Ki 3:25 on every good field **u** it was covered. H2256
2Ki 4:20 the boy sat on her lap **u** noon, and then H6330
2Ki 7: 3 to each other, "Why stay here **u** we die? H6330
2Ki 7: 9 If we wait **u** daylight, punishment will H6330
2Ki 8: 6 from the day she left the country **u** now." H6330
2Ki 8:11 him with a fixed gaze **u** Hazael was H6330
2Ki 10: 8 at the entrance of the city gate **u** morning." H6330
2Ki 10:21 the temple of Baal **u** it was full from one H2256
2Ki 15: 5 the king with leprosy **u** the day he died, H6330
2Ki 17:20 **u** he thrust them from his presence. H6330+889
2Ki 17:23 **u** the LORD removed them from his H6330+889
2Ki 18:32 **u** I come and take you to a land like your H6330
2Ki 20:17 predecessors have stored up **u** this day, H6330
2Ki 21:15 ancestors came out of Egypt **u** this day." H6330
2Ki 25: 2 kept under siege **u** the eleventh year of H6330
1Ch 4:31 were their towns **u** the reign of David. H6330
1Ch 5:22 And they occupied the land **u** the exile. H6330
1Ch 6:32 **u** Solomon built the temple of the LORD in H6330
1Ch 12:22 to help David, **u** he had a great army H6330
1Ch 12:29 remained loyal to Saul's house **u** then; H6330
1Ch 28:20 you or forsake you **u** all the work for the H6330
2Ch 8:16 of the LORD was laid **u** its completion. H6330
2Ch 9: 6 what they said **u** I came and saw H6330+889
2Ch 15:19 was no more war **u** the thirty-fifth year H6330
2Ch 18:10 gore the Arameans **u** they are destroyed. H6330
2Ch 18:26 bread and water **u** I return safely. H6330
2Ch 18:34 chariot facing the Arameans **u** evening. H6330
2Ch 21:15 **u** the disease causes your bowels to come H6330
2Ch 24:10 dropping them into the chest **u** it was full. H6330
2Ch 26:15 greatly helped **u** he became H6330+3954
2Ch 26:21 Uzziah had leprosy **u** the day he died. H6330
2Ch 29:28 All this continued **u** the sacrifice of the H6330
2Ch 29:34 Levites helped them **u** the task was H6330
2Ch 29:34 task was finished and **u** other priests had H6330
2Ch 35:14 offerings and the fat portions **u** nightfall. H6330
2Ch 36:16 at his prophets **u** the wrath of the LORD H6330
2Ch 36:20 his successors **u** the kingdom of H6330
2Ch 36:21 **u** the seventy years were completed in H6330
Ezr 2:63 the most sacred food **u** there was a priest H6330
Ezr 4:21 this city will not be rebuilt **u** I so order. A10527
Ezr 4:24 came to a standstill **u** the second year of A10527
Ezr 5: 5 were not stopped **u** a report could go to A10527
Ezr 8:29 them carefully **u** you weigh them out H6330
Ezr 9: 4 I sat there appalled **u** the evening H6330
Ezr 9: 7 From the days of our ancestors **u** now, our H6330
Ezr 10:14 **u** the fierce anger of our God in this H6330
Ne 2: 7 me safe-conduct **u** I arrive in Judah? H6330+889
Ne 5:14 the land of Judah, **u** his thirty-second year H6330
Ne 7: 3 are not to be opened **u** the sun is hot. H6330
Ne 7:65 the most sacred food **u** there should be a H6330
Ne 8:17 the days of Joshua son of Nun **u** that day, H6330
Ne 9:32 the days of the kings of Assyria **u** today. H6330
Ne 13:19 shut and not opened **u** the Sabbath was H6330
Job 7: 4 drags on, and I toss and turn **u** dawn. H6330
Ps 57: 1 shadow of your wings **u** the disaster has H6330
Ps 104:23 out to their work, to their labor **u** evening. H6330
Ps 110: 1 at my right hand **u** I make your enemies a H6330
Pr 4:16 For they cannot rest **u** they do evil H561+4202
Pr 18:17 **u** someone comes forward and H2256
SS 2: 7 awaken love **u** it so desires. H6330+8611
SS 2:17 **U** the day breaks and the shadows H6330+8611
SS 3: 5 awaken love **u** it so desires. H6330+8611
SS 4: 6 **U** the day breaks and the shadows H6330+8611
SS 8: 4 awaken love **u** it so desires. H6330+8611
Isa 6:11 "**U** the cities lie ruined and H6330+889+561
Isa 6:11 **u** the houses are left deserted and the H2256
Isa 6:12 **u** the LORD has sent everyone far away H2256
Isa 26:20 a little while **u** his wrath has passed by H6330
Isa 36:17 **u** I come and take you to a land like your H6330
Isa 39: 6 predecessors have stored up **u** this day, H6330
Jer 2:25 Do not run **u** your feet are bare and your H4946
Jer 7:25 the time your ancestors left Egypt **u** now, H6330
Jer 7:32 the dead in Topheth **u** there is no more H4946
Jer 9:16 with the sword **u** I have made an end H6330
Jer 11: 7 your ancestors up from Egypt **u** today, H6330
Jer 19:11 the dead in Topheth **u** there is no more H4946
Jer 23:20 will not turn back **u** he fully accomplishes H6330
Jer 24:10 plague against them **u** they are destroyed H6330
Jer 25: 3 of Amon king of Judah **u** this very day— H6330
Jer 27: 7 son and his grandson **u** the time for his H6330
Jer 27: 8 the LORD, **u** I destroy it by his hand. H6330
Jer 27:22 they will remain **u** the day I come for H6330
Jer 30:24 will not turn back **u** he fully accomplishes H6330
Jer 32: 5 where he will remain **u** I deal with him H6330
Jer 32:31 From the day it was built **u** now, this city H6330
Jer 36:23 **u** the entire scroll was burned in the fire. H6330
Jer 37:21 the bakers each day **u** all the bread in the H6330
Jer 38:28 of the guard **u** the day Jerusalem was H6330
Jer 44:27 by sword and famine **u** they are all H6330
Jer 49:37 with the sword **u** I have made an end H6330
Jer 52: 5 kept under siege **u** the eleventh year of H6330
La 3:50 **u** the LORD looks down from heaven and H6330
Eze 4: 8 side to the other **u** you have finished the H6330
Eze 4:14 From my youth **u** now I have never eaten H6330
Eze 21:27 will not be restored **u** he to whom it H6330
Eze 24:13 not be clean again **u** my wrath against H6330

Eze 34:21 with your horns **u** you have driven H6330+889
Eze 39:15 a marker beside it **u** the gravediggers bury H6330
Eze 42:14 into the outer court **u** they leave behind H2256
Eze 46: 2 the gate will not be shut **u** evening. H6330
Eze 46:17 servant may keep it **u** the year of freedom; H6330
Da 1:21 Daniel remained there **u** the first year of H6330
Da 4:22 greatness has grown **u** it reaches the sky, A10221
Da 4:23 **u** seven times pass by for him. A10527+10168
Da 4:25 by for you **u** you acknowledge A10527+10168
Da 4:32 by for you **u** you acknowledge A10527+10168
Da 4:33 dew of heaven **u** his hair grew A10527+10168
Da 5:21 **u** he acknowledged that the A10527+10168
Da 6:14 made every effort **u** sundown to save A10527
Da 7: 4 I watched **u** its wings were torn A10527+10168
Da 7:11 I kept looking **u** the beast was A10527+10168
Da 7:22 **u** the Ancient of Days came and A10527+10168
Da 8:10 It grew **u** it reached the host of the H6330
Da 9:25 rebuild Jerusalem **u** the Anointed One, H6330
Da 9:26 War will continue **u** the end, and H6330
Da 9:27 **u** the end that is decreed is poured out on H6330
Da 10: 3 no lotions at all **u** the three weeks were H6330
Da 11:35 made spotless **u** the time of the end, H6330
Da 11:36 will be successful **u** the time of wrath is H6330
Da 12: 1 from the beginning of nations **u** then. H6330
Da 12: 4 words of the scroll **u** the time of the end. H6330
Da 12: 9 up and sealed **u** the time of the end. H6330
Hos 5:15 return to my lair **u** they have borne H6330+889
Hos 10:12 **u** he comes and showers his H6330
Joel 2:26 have plenty to eat, **u** you are full, and you H2256
Mic 5: 3 will be abandoned **u** the time when she H6330
Mic 7: 9 **u** he pleads my case and upholds H6330+889
Hag 2:19 **U** now, the vine and the fig tree, the H6330
Mt 1:25 their marriage **u** she gave birth to a *G2401+4005*
Mt 2: 9 went ahead of them **u** it stopped over the *G2401*
Mt 2:13 Stay there **u** I tell you, for Herod is *G2401+323*
Mt 2:15 where he stayed **u** the death of Herod *G2401*
Mt 5:18 **u** heaven and earth disappear *G2401+323*
Mt 5:18 from the Law **u** everything is *G2401+323*
Mt 5:26 will not get out **u** you have paid the *G2401+323*
Mt 10:11 and stay at their house **u** you leave. *G2401+323*
Mt 11:12 From the days of John the Baptist **u** now *G2401*
Mt 11:13 Prophets and the Law prophesied **u** John. *G2401*
Mt 13:30 Let both grow together **u** the harvest. *G2401*
Mt 13:33 pounds of flour **u** it worked all *G2401+4005*
Mt 17: 9 **u** the Son of Man has been raised *G2401+4005*
Mt 18:30 thrown into prison **u** he could pay the *G2401*
Mt 18:34 **u** he should pay back all he owed. *G2401+4005*
Mt 22:44 at my right hand **u** I put your *G2401+323*
Mt 23:39 you will not see me again **u** you say *G2401+323*
Mt 24:21 from the beginning of the world **u** now— *G2401*
Mt 24:34 not pass away **u** all these things *G2401+323*
Mt 24:39 what would happen **u** the flood came *G2401*
Mt 26:29 the vine from now on **u** that day when I *G2401*
Mt 27:45 From noon **u** three in the afternoon *G2401*
Mt 27:64 tomb to be made secure **u** the third day. *G2401*
Mk 6:10 stay there **u** you leave that town. *G2401+323*
Mk 9: 9 they had seen **u** the Son of *G1623+3590+4020*
Mk 12:36 at my right hand **u** I put your *G2401+323*
Mk 13:19 created the world, **u** now—and never to *G2401*
Mk 13:30 not pass away **u** all these things *G3588+4005*
Mk 14:25 fruit of the vine **u** that day when I drink *G2401*
Mk 15:33 over the whole land **u** three in the *G2401*
Lk 1:20 not able to speak **u** the day this happens, *G948*
Lk 1:80 in the wilderness **u** he appeared *G2401+2465*
Lk 2:37 then was a widow **u** she was eighty-four *G2401*
Lk 4:13 tempting, he left him **u** an opportune time. *G948*
Lk 9: 4 stay there **u** you leave that town. *G2779*
Lk 12:50 I am under **u** it is completed! *G2401+4015*
Lk 12:59 you will not get out **u** you have paid the *G2401*
Lk 13:21 pounds of flour **u** it worked all *G2401+4005*
Lk 13:35 you will not see me again **u** you say *G2401*
Lk 15: 4 go after the lost sheep **u** he finds it? *G2401*
Lk 15: 8 and search carefully **u** she finds it? *G2401+4005*
Lk 16:16 the Prophets were proclaimed **u** John. *G3588*
Lk 19:13 to work,' he said, '**u** I come back. *G1877+4005*
Lk 20:43 **u** I make your enemies a footstool *G2401+323*
Lk 21:24 on by the Gentiles **u** the times of the *G948+4005*
Lk 21:32 not pass away **u** all these things *G2401+323*
Lk 22:16 not eat it again **u** it finds *G2401+4015*
Lk 22:18 fruit of the vine **u** the kingdom of *G2401+4005*
Lk 23:44 over the whole land **u** three in the *G2401*
Lk 24:49 stay in the city **u** you have been *G2401+4005*
Jn 4:35 a saying, 'It's still four months **u** harvest'? *G2262*
Jn 7:14 **Not u** halfway through the festival did *G2453*
Jn 8: 9 the older ones first, **u** only Jesus was left *G2779*
Jn 9:18 his sight **u** they sent for the *G2401+4015*
Jn 16:24 **U** now you have not asked for anything in *G2401*
Jn 21:22 "If I want him to remain alive **u** I return *G2401*
Jn 21:23 "If I want him to remain alive **u** I return *G2401*
Ac 1: 2 **u** the day he was taken up to heaven, after *G948*
Ac 2:35 **u** I make your enemies a footstool *G2401+323*
Ac 3:21 must receive him **u** the time comes for God *G948*
Ac 4: 3 they put them in jail **u** the next day. *G1650*
Ac 7:45 remained in the land **u** the time of David, *G2401*
Ac 8:40 in all the towns **u** he reached Caesarea. *G2401*
Ac 13: 6 the whole island **u** they came to Paphos. *G948*
Ac 13:20 them judges **u the time of** Samuel the *G2401*
Ac 20: 7 the next day, kept on talking **u** midnight. *G3588*
Ac 20:11 After talking **u** daylight, he left. *G948*
Ac 22:22 The crowd listened to Paul **u** he said this *G948*
Ac 23:12 not to eat or drink **u** they had killed *G2401+4005*
Ac 23:14 to eat anything **u** we have killed *G2401+4005*

Ac 23:21 to eat or drink **u** they have killed G2401+4005
Ac 25:21 him held **u** I could send him G2401+4005
Ro 1:13 have been prevented from doing so **u** now) G948
Ro 11:25 hardening in part **u** the full number G948+4005
1Co 4:5 wait **u** the Lord comes. G2401+323
1Co 11:26 the Lord's death **u** he comes. G948+4005
1Co 15:25 For he must reign **u** he has put all his G948+4005
1Co 16:8 But I will stay on at Ephesus **u** Pentecost, G2401
Gal 3:19 transgressions **u** the Seed to whom G948+4005
Gal 3:23 locked up **u** the faith that was to come G1650
Gal 3:24 was our guardian **u** Christ came that we G1650
Gal 4:2 trustees **u** the time set by his G948
Gal 4:19 of childbirth **u** Christ is formed in G3588+4005
Eph 1:14 our inheritance **u** the redemption of those G1650
Eph 4:13 **u** we all reach unity in the faith and in the G3588
Php 1:5 in the gospel from the first day **u** now, G948
Php 1:6 it on to completion **u** the day of Christ G948
1Th 4:15 who are left **u** the coming of the Lord G1650
2Th 2:3 not come **u** the rebellion G1569+3590+4754
1Ti 4:13 **U** I come, devote yourself to the public G2401
1Ti 6:14 spot or blame **u** the appearing of our G3588
2Ti 1:12 what I have entrusted to him **u** that day. G1650
2Ti 1:17 he searched hard for me **u** he found me. G2779
Heb 1:13 at my right hand **u** I make your G2401+323
Heb 9:10 applying **u** the time of the new G3588
Jas 5:7 brothers and sisters, **u** the Lord's coming. G2401
1Pe 1:5 God's power **u** *the coming of* the G1650
2Pe 1:19 **u** the day dawns and the morning G2401+4005
Rev 2:25 on to what you have **u** I come. G948+4005+323
Rev 6:10 **u** you judge the inhabitants of the earth G4024
Rev 6:11 **u** the full number of their fellow servants G2401
Rev 7:3 the sea or the trees **u** we put a seal on the G948
Rev 15:8 enter the temple **u** the seven plagues of G948
Rev 17:17 royal authority, **u** God's words are fulfilled. G948
Rev 20:3 the nations anymore **u** the thousand years G948
Rev 20:5 did not come to life **u** the thousand years G948

UNTIMELY (KJV) STILLBORN

UNTIRING (1)
Ps 77:2 at night I stretched out **u** hands H4202+7028

UNTO (1)
Isa 53:12 because he poured out his life **u** death H4200

UNTOUCHED (2)
Job 28:4 cut a shaft, in places **u** by human feet; far H8894
Pr 19:23 one rests content, **u** *by* trouble. H1153+7212

UNTRAINED (1)
2Co 11:6 I may indeed be **u** as a speaker, but I do G2626

UNTRAVELED (1)
Jer 9:10 They are desolate and **u**, H4946+1172+408+6296

UNTRUE (1)
Jos 24:27 against you if *you are* **u** to your God." H3950

UNTYING (4) [UNTIE]
Mk 11:5 "What are you doing, **u** that colt? G3395
Lk 19:31 asks you, 'Why *are you* **u** it?' say, 'The G3395
Lk 19:33 *As* they *were* **u** the colt, its owners asked G3395
Lk 19:33 asked them, "Why *are you* **u** the colt?" G3395

UNUSED (1)
Ex 23:11 year let the land lie unplowed and **u**. H5759

UNUSUAL (3)
Lev 15:2 any man has an **u** bodily **discharge**, H2307
Ac 28:2 showed us **u** kindness. G4024+3836+5593
Ac 28:6 time and seeing nothing **u** happen to him, G876

UNVEILED (1)
2Co 3:18 *who with* **u** faces contemplate the Lord's G365

UNWALLED (3)
Nu 13:19 do they live in? Are they **u** or fortified? H4722
Dt 3:5 there were also a great many **u** villages. H7253
Eze 38:11 "I will invade a land of **u villages**; I will H7252

UNWARY (1)
Ps 116:6 The LORD protects the **u**; when I was H7343

UNWASHED (2)
Mt 15:20 eating with **u** hands does not defile G481
Mk 7:2 with hands that were defiled, that is, **u**. G481

UNWEIGHED (1)
1Ki 7:47 Solomon **left** all these things **u**, because H5663

UNWHOLESOME (1)
Eph 4:29 Do not let any **u** talk come out of your G4911

UNWILLING (11)
Ge 24:5 if the woman *is* **u** to come back with H14+4202
Ge 24:8 If the woman *is* **u** to come back with H14+4202
Dt 1:26 But *you were* **u** to go up; you rebelled H14+4202
Jdg 19:10 **u** to stay another night, the man H4202+14
1Sa 15:9 These *they were* **u** to destroy H14+4202
1Sa 22:17 king's officials *were* **u** to raise a hand H4202+14
2Ki 13:23 To this day *he has been* **u** to destroy H4202+14
Isa 30:9 children **u** to listen to the LORD's H4202+14
1Co 16:12 He was quite **u** to go now, but he G4024+2525
2Th 3:10 "The one *who is* **u** to work shall not G4024+2527
Rev 2:21 of her immorality, but *she is* **u**. G4024+2527

UNWISE (2)
Dt 32:6 the LORD, you foolish and **u** people? H4202+2682
Eph 5:15 how you live—not as **u** but as wise, G831

UNWITTINGLY (1)
Lev 5:2 if they **u** touch anything ceremonially NDT

UNWORTHY (4)
Ge 32:10 *I am* **u** of all the kindness and faithfulness H7781
Job 40:4 "*I am* **u**—how can I reply to you? I put my H7837
Lk 17:10 should say, 'We are **u** servants; we have G945
1Co 11:27 of the Lord **in an u manner** will be guilty G397

UNYIELDING (5)
Ex 7:14 "Pharaoh's heart is **u**; he refuses to let the H3878
Ex 9:7 Yet his heart *was* **u** and he would not let H3877
Pr 18:19 wronged is more **u** than a fortified city; NDT
SS 8:6 as death, its jealousy **u** as the grave. H7997
Eze 3:8 make you as **u** and hardened as H2617+7156

UP (1907) [UPPER, UPWARD]
Ge 2:5 the earth and no plant *had* yet **sprung u**, H7541
Ge 2:6 streams **came u** from the earth and H6590
Ge 2:21 then **closed u** the place *with* flesh. H6037
Ge 8:7 until the water *had* **dried u** from the earth. H3312
Ge 8:13 the water *had* **dried u** from the earth. H2990
Ge 13:1 So Abram **went u** from Egypt to the Negev H6590
Ge 14:8 out and **drew u** their battle **lines** in the H6885
Ge 15:5 "**Look u** at the sky and count the stars H5564
Ge 17:22 with Abraham, God **went u** from him. H6590
Ge 18:2 Abraham looked **u** and saw three men H5951
Ge 18:16 When the men **got u** to leave, they H7756
Ge 18:27 Then Abraham **spoke u** again: "Now that H6699
Ge 19:1 *he* **got u** to meet them and bowed down H7756
Ge 19:27 **Early** the next morning Abraham **got u** H8899
Ge 19:33 it when she lay down or when she **got u**. H7756
Ge 19:35 it when she lay down or when she **got u**. H7756
Ge 21:18 **Lift** the boy **u** and take him by the hand H5951
Ge 21:20 God was with the boy as *he* **grew u**. H1540
Ge 22:3 **Early** the next morning Abraham **got u** H8899
Ge 22:4 day Abraham looked **u** and saw the place H5951
Ge 22:7 Isaac **spoke u** and said to his father H606
Ge 22:13 Abraham looked **u** and there in a thicket H5951
Ge 24:16 filled her jar and **came u** again. H6590
Ge 24:54 When *they* **got u** the next morning, he H7756
Ge 24:63 as he looked **u**, he saw camels H5951
Ge 24:64 Rebekah also looked **u** and saw Isaac. H5951
Ge 25:27 The boys **grew u**, and Esau became a H1540
Ge 25:34 He ate and drank, and then **got u** and left. H7756
Ge 26:15 the Philistines **stopped u**, filling them H6258
Ge 26:18 Philistines *had* **stopped u** after Abraham H6258
Ge 26:23 From there *he* **went u** *to* Beersheba. H6590
Ge 27:19 Please sit **u** and eat some of my game, so H7756
Ge 27:31 *please* **sit u** and eat some of my game H7756
Ge 28:18 under his head and **set** it **u** *as* a pillar H8492
Ge 28:22 this stone that *I have* **set u** as a pillar will H8492
Ge 31:10 in which I looked **u** and saw that the male H5951
Ge 31:12 'Look **u** and see that all the male goats H5951
Ge 31:15 but *he has* **used u** what was paid for H430+430
Ge 31:23 seven days and **caught u** *with* him in the H1815
Ge 31:35 that I cannot **stand u** in your presence H7756
Ge 31:45 Jacob took a stone and **set** it **u** as a pillar. H8123
Ge 31:51 is this pillar *I have* **set u** between you H3721
Ge 32:22 That night Jacob **got u** and took his two H7756
Ge 33:1 Jacob looked **u** and there was Esau H5951
Ge 33:5 Then Esau looked **u** and saw the women H5951
Ge 33:20 There *he* **set u** an altar and called it El H5893
Ge 35:1 to Jacob, "**Go u** *to* Bethel and settle there H6590
Ge 35:3 Then come, *let us* **go u** *to* Bethel, where I H6590
Ge 35:13 Then God **went u** from him at the place H6590
Ge 35:14 Jacob **set u** a stone pillar at the place H5893
Ge 35:20 Over her tomb Jacob **set u** a pillar, and to H5893
Ge 37:25 they looked **u** and saw a caravan of H5951
Ge 37:26 we kill our brother and **cover u** his blood? H4059
Ge 37:28 pulled Joseph **u** out of the cistern and H6590
Ge 38:8 a brother-in-law *to* **raise u** offspring for H7756
Ge 38:11 household until my son Shelah **grows u**." H1540
Ge 38:12 from his grief, *he* **went u** to Timnah, to H6590
Ge 38:14 *though* Shelah *had* now **grown u**, she H1540
Ge 40:13 days Pharaoh *will* **lift u** your head and H5951
Ge 40:20 *He* **lifted u** the heads of the chief H5951
Ge 41:2 out of the river *there* **came u** seven cows, H6590
Ge 41:3 **came u** out of the Nile and stood beside H6590
Ge 41:4 were ugly and gaunt **ate u** the seven sleek, H430
Ge 41:4 fat cows. Then Pharaoh **woke u**. H3699
Ge 41:7 heads of grain **swallowed u** the seven H1180
Ge 41:7 Then Pharaoh **woke u**; it had been a H3699
Ge 41:18 out of the river *there* **came u** seven cows, H6590
Ge 41:19 seven other cows **came u**—scrawny and H6590
Ge 41:20 ugly cows **ate u** the seven fat cows that H430
Ge 41:20 ate up the seven fat cows that came **u** first. NDT
Ge 41:21 just as ugly as before. Then *I* **woke u**. H3699
Ge 41:24 heads of grain **swallowed u** the seven H1180
Ge 41:27 ugly cows that **came u** afterward are H6590
Ge 41:35 are coming and **store u** the grain under H7392
Ge 41:49 Joseph **stored u** huge quantities of grain H7392
Ge 43:19 So *they* **went u** to Joseph's steward and H5602
Ge 44:4 when *you* **catch u** *with* them, say to H5952
Ge 44:6 When *he* **caught u** *with* them, he H5952
Ge 44:18 Then Judah **went u** to him and said H5602
Ge 44:30 whose life *is* **closely bound u** with the H8003
Ge 45:25 So *they* **went u** out of Egypt and came to H6590
Ge 46:31 "*I will* **go u** and speak to Pharaoh and will H6590
Ge 48:2 rallied his strength and **sat u** on the bed. H3782
Ge 49:4 for *you* **went u** *onto* your father's bed H6590
Ge 49:33 to his sons, *he* **drew** his feet **u** into the bed H665
Ge 50:5 Now *let me* **go u** and bury my father H6590
Ge 50:6 Pharaoh said, "**Go u** and bury your father H6590
Ge 50:7 So Joseph **went u** to bury his father. H6590
Ge 50:9 horsemen also **went u** with him. H6590
Ge 50:24 to your aid and **take** you **u** out of this land H6590
Ge 50:25 then *you must* **carry** my bones **u** from H6590
Ex 2:11 after Moses *had* **grown u**, he went out to H1540
Ex 2:17 Moses **got u** and came to their rescue H7756
Ex 2:23 because of their slavery **went u** to God. H6590
Ex 3:2 the bush was on fire it *did* not **burn u**. H430
Ex 3:3 why the bush *does* not **burn u**. H1277
Ex 3:8 Egyptians and to **bring** them **u** out of that H6590
Ex 3:17 I have promised *to* **bring** you **u** out of your H6590
Ex 7:12 But Aaron's staff **swallowed u** their staffs. H1180
Ex 8:3 They will **come u** into your palace and H6590
Ex 8:4 The frogs *will* **come u** on you and your H6590
Ex 8:5 and **make** frogs **come u** on the land of H6590
Ex 8:6 the frogs **came u** and covered the H6590
Ex 8:7 *they* also **made** frogs **come u** on the land H6590
Ex 8:20 "**Get u early** in the morning and confront H8899
Ex 9:13 to Moses, "**Get u early** in the morning H8899
Ex 9:16 But *I have* **raised** you **u** for this very H6641
Ex 10:19 *which* **caught u** the locusts and carried H5951
Ex 12:30 all the Egyptians **got u** during the night, H7756
Ex 12:31 Moses and Aaron and said, "**U**! H7756
Ex 12:38 Many other people **went u** with them, and H6590
Ex 13:18 The Israelites **went u** out of Egypt ready H6590
Ex 13:19 then *you must* **carry** my bones **u** with H6590
Ex 14:10 the Israelites looked **u**, and there were H5951
Ex 15:8 blast of your nostrils the waters **piled u**. H6890
Ex 15:8 The surging waters **stood u** like a wall H5893
Ex 17:3 "Why *did you* **bring** us **u** out of Egypt to H6590
Ex 17:11 As long as Moses **held u** his hands, the H8123
Ex 17:12 Aaron and Hur **held** his hands **u**—one on H9461
Ex 17:16 hands were lifted **u** against the throne of NDT
Ex 19:3 Then Moses **went u** to God, and the LORD H6590
Ex 19:18 The smoke **billowed u** *from* it like smoke H6590
Ex 19:20 the top of the mountain. So Moses **went u** H6590
Ex 19:23 "The people cannot **come u** Mount Sinai H6590
Ex 19:24 "Go down and *bring* Aaron **u** with you. H6590
Ex 19:24 their way through to **come u** to the LORD, H6590
Ex 20:26 And *do* not **go u** to my altar on steps, or H6590
Ex 21:19 if the other *can* **get u** and walk around H7756
Ex 21:29 but *has* not **kept** it **penned u** and it H9068
Ex 21:36 the owner *did* not **keep** it **penned u** H9068
Ex 24:1 said to Moses, "**Come u** to the LORD, you H6590
Ex 24:2 And the people *may* not **come u** with him." H6590
Ex 24:4 *He* **got u early** the next morning and built H8899
Ex 24:4 the mountain and set **u** twelve stone pillars NDT
Ex 24:9 the seventy elders of Israel **went u** H6590
Ex 24:12 "**Come u** to me on the mountain and stay H6590
Ex 24:13 Moses **went u** on the mountain of H6590
Ex 24:15 When Moses **went u** on the mountain H6590
Ex 24:18 the cloud as *he* **went** on **u** the mountain. H6590
Ex 25:37 seven lamps and **set** them **u** *on* it so that H6590
Ex 26:30 "**Set u** the tabernacle according to the H7756
Ex 27:5 the altar so that it is halfway **u** the altar. H6330
Ex 29:34 till morning, **burn** it **u**. H8596+928+2021+836
Ex 32:1 Moses who **brought** us **u** out of Egypt, H6590
Ex 32:4 who **brought** you **u** out of Egypt. H6590
Ex 32:6 to eat and drink and **got u** to indulge in H7756
Ex 32:7 people, whom *you* **brought u** out of Egypt H6590
Ex 32:8 who **brought** you **u** out of Egypt. H6590
Ex 32:23 Moses who **brought** us **u** out of Egypt, H6590
Ex 32:30 But now *I will* **go u** to the LORD; perhaps I H6590
Ex 33:1 the people *you* **brought u** out of Egypt, H6590
Ex 33:1 and **go u** to the land I promised on oath H6590
Ex 33:3 Go **u** to the land flowing with milk and NDT
Ex 33:15 go with us, *do* not **send** us **u** from here. H6590
Ex 34:2 then **come u** on Mount Sinai. H6590
Ex 34:4 first ones and **went u** Mount Sinai early H6590
Ex 34:24 your land when you **go u** three times each H6590
Ex 38:4 to be under its ledge, halfway **u** the altar. H6330
Ex 40:2 "**Set u** the tabernacle, the tent of meeting H7756
Ex 40:4 in the lampstand and **set u** its lamps. H6590
Ex 40:8 **Set u** the courtyard around it and put the H8492
Ex 40:17 the tabernacle **was set u** on the first day H7756
Ex 40:18 When Moses **set u** the tabernacle, he put H7756
Ex 40:18 inserted the crossbars and **set u** the posts. H7756
Ex 40:25 and **set u** the lamps before the LORD, as H6590
Ex 40:28 Then *he* **put u** the curtain at the entrance H8492
Ex 40:33 Then Moses **set u** the courtyard around H7756
Ex 40:33 altar and **put u** the curtain at the H5989
Lev 5:1 because *they do* not **speak u** when they H5583
Lev 6:30 *it must* **be burned u**. H8596+928+2021+836
Lev 7:17 day *must* **be burned u**. H8596+928+2021+836
Lev 7:19 *it must* **be burned u**. H8596+928+2021+836
Lev 8:17 *he* **burned u** outside H8596+928+2021+836
Lev 8:32 Then **burn u** the rest of H8596+928+2021+836
Lev 9:11 hide *he* **burned u** H8596+928+2021+836
Lev 10:16 found that *it had* **been burned u**, H8596
Lev 11:25 Whoever **picks u** one of their carcasses H5951
Lev 11:28 Anyone *who* **picks u** their carcasses must H5951
Lev 11:35 an oven or cooking pot *must* **be broken u**. H5997
Lev 11:40 Anyone *who* **picks u** the carcass must H5951
Lev 11:45 who **brought** you **u** out of Egypt to be H6590
Lev 14:38 of the house and **close** it **u** for seven days. H6037
Lev 14:46 house while it *is* **closed u** will be unclean H6037

Lev 15:10 whoever **picks u** those things must wash H5951
Lev 16:27 *are to be* **burned u**. H8596+928+2021+836
Lev 19: 6 day *must* **be burned u**. H8596+928+2021+836
Lev 19:10 a second time or **pick u** the grapes that H4377
Lev 19:32 " '**Stand u** in the presence of the aged H7756
Lev 21: 8 because they **offer u** the food of your God. H7928
Lev 23:16 Count off fifty days **u to** the day after the H6330
Lev 25:50 sold themselves **u to** the Year of Jubilee. H6330
Lev 26: 1 not make idols or **set u** an image or a H7756
Lev 27:23 its value **u to** the Year of Jubilee H6330
Nu 1:51 whenever the tabernacle *is to be* **set u**, H2837
Nu 1:52 Israelites *are to* **set u** their **tents** by H2837
Nu 1:53 *are to* **set u** their **tents** around the H2837
Nu 7: 1 Moses finished **setting u** the tabernacle, H7756
Nu 8: 2 'When you **set u** the lamps, see H6590
Nu 8: 2 *see that* all seven **light u** the area in front H239
Nu 8: 3 *he* **set u** the lamps so that they faced H6590
Nu 9:15 the covenant law, *was* **set u**, the cloud H7756
Nu 10:21 tabernacle *was to be* **set u** before they H7756
Nu 10:35 the ark set out, Moses said, "**Rise u**, LORD! H7756
Nu 11:28 since youth, **spoke u** and said, "Moses, H6699
Nu 11:31 It scattered them **u to** two cubits deep all H3869
Nu 13:17 "**Go u** through the Negev and on into the H6590
Nu 13:21 So *they* **went u** and explored the land H6590
Nu 13:22 They **went u** through the Negev and came H6590
Nu 13:30 "*We* **should go u** and take H6590+6590
Nu 13:31 the men who *had* **gone u** with him said, H6590
Nu 14:13 power *you* **brought** these people **u** from H6590
Nu 14:40 "Now we *are ready to* **go u** to the land the H6590
Nu 14:42 *Do* not **go u**, because the LORD is not with H6590
Nu 14:44 their presumption *they* **went u** toward the H6590
Nu 16: 2 and **rose u** against Moses. With them H7756
Nu 16:13 that *you have* **brought** us **u** out of a H6590
Nu 16:25 Moses **got u** and went to Dathan and H7756
Nu 19: 9 who is clean *shall* **gather u** the ashes of H665
Nu 19:10 The *man who* **gathers u** the ashes of the H665
Nu 20: 5 Why *did you* **bring** us **u** out of Egypt to H6590
Nu 20:25 son Eleazar and **take** them **u** Mount Hor. H6590
Nu 20:27 *They* **went u** Mount Hor in the sight of the H6590
Nu 21: 5 "Why *have you* **brought** us **u** out of Egypt H6590
Nu 21: 8 "Make a snake and **put** it **u** on a pole H8492
Nu 21: 9 a bronze snake and **put** it **u** on a pole. H8492
Nu 21:17 sang this song: "**Spring u**, O well! Sing H6590
Nu 21:29 *He has* **given u** his sons as fugitives and H5989
Nu 21:33 they turned and **went u** *along* the road H6590
Nu 22: 4 "This horde *is* going to **lick u** everything H4308
Nu 22: 4 as an ox **licks u** the grass of the field." H4308
Nu 22:13 next morning Balaam **got u** and said to H7756
Nu 22:21 Balaam **got u** in the morning, saddled his H7756
Nu 22:41 Balak took Balaam **u** *to* Bamoth Baal, H6590
Nu 24:25 Then Balaam **got u** and returned home H7756
Nu 27:12 "**Go u** this mountain in the Abarim Range H6590
Nu 32: 9 After *they* **went u** to the Valley of Eshkol H6590
Nu 32:11 old or more *when* they **came u** out of H6590
Nu 32:16 Then *they* **came u** to him and said, "We H5602
Nu 32:34 The Gadites **built u** Dibon, Ataroth, Aroer, H1215
Nu 33:38 Aaron the priest **went u** Mount Hor, H6590
Dt 1:21 **Go u** and take possession of it as the LORD, H6590
Dt 1:24 They left and **went u** into the hill country H6590
Dt 1:26 But you were unwilling to **go u**; you H6590
Dt 1:28 the cities are large, with walls **u to** the sky. H928
Dt 1:41 We *will* **go u** and fight, as the LORD our H6590
Dt 1:41 thinking it easy to **go u** into the hill H6590
Dt 1:42 "Tell them, '*Do* not **go u** and fight H6590
Dt 1:43 arrogance *you* **marched u** into the hill H6590
Dt 2: 8 which comes **u** from Elath and Ezion Geber NDT
Dt 2:13 "Now **get u** and cross the Zered Valley." H7756
Dt 3: 1 we turned and **went u** *along* the road H6590
Dt 3:27 **Go u** *to* the top of Pisgah and look west H6590
Dt 4:19 And when you look **u** to the sky and see H5951
Dt 5: 5 of the fire and *did* not **go u** the mountain.) H6590
Dt 6: 7 when you lie down and when you **get u**. H7756
Dt 7:24 No one *will be able to* **stand u** against H3656
Dt 9: 1 large cities that have walls **u to** the sky. H928
Dt 9: 2 "Who *can* **stand u** against the Anakites?" H3656
Dt 9: 9 When I **went u** on the mountain to receive H6590
Dt 9:23 "**Go u** and take possession of the land I H6590
Dt 10: 1 the first ones and **come u** to me on the H6590
Dt 10: 3 and *I* **went u** on the mountain with the H6590
Dt 11: 6 all Israel and **swallowed** them **u** with their H1180
Dt 11:17 and *he will* **shut u** the heavens so that it H6806
Dt 11:19 when you lie down and when you **get u**. H7756
Dt 16:21 *Do* not **set u** any wooden Asherah pole H5749
Dt 18:15 The LORD your God *will* **raise u** for you a H7756
Dt 18:18 *I will* **raise u** for them a prophet like you H7756
Dt 19:14 boundary stone **set u** by your predecessors H1487
Dt 20: 1 your God, who **brought** you **u** out of Egypt H6590
Dt 20:10 When *you* **march u** to attack a city, make H7928
Dt 23:13 dig a hole and **cover u** your H2256+8740+4059
Dt 25: 9 brother's widow *shall* **go u** to him in the H5602
Dt 25: 9 the man who *will* not **build u** his brother's H1215
Dt 27: 2 **set u** some large stones and coat them H7756
Dt 27: 4 **set u** these stones on Mount Ebal H7756
Dt 27: 8 of this law on these stones you have set **u**." NDT
Dt 27:15 of skilled hands—and **sets** it **u** in secret." H8492
Dt 28: 7 the enemies who **rise u** against you will H7756
Dt 30:12 It is not **u** in heaven, so that you have to ask NDT
Dt 32: 8 *he* **set u** boundaries for the peoples H5893
Dt 32:11 like an eagle *that* **stirs u** its nest and H6424
Dt 32:30 unless the LORD *had* **given** them **u**? H6037
Dt 32:38 *Let them* **rise u** to help you! Let H7756
Dt 32:49 "**Go u** into the Abarim Range to Mount H6590
Jos 2: 5 *You may* **catch u** *with* them." H5952
Jos 2: 6 But she *had* **taken** them **u** to the roof and H6590
Jos 2: 8 down for the night, she **went u** on the roof H6590
Jos 2:10 how the LORD **dried u** the water of the H3312
Jos 3: 6 "**Take u** the ark of the covenant and pass H5951
Jos 3: 6 So *they* **took** it **u** and went ahead of them. H5951
Jos 3:13 will be cut off and **stand u** in a heap." H6641
Jos 3:16 *It* **piled u** in a heap a great distance away, H7756
Jos 4: 3 tell them *to* **take u** twelve stones from H5951
Jos 4: 5 Each of you *is to* **take u** a stone on his H8123
Jos 4: 9 Joshua **set u** the twelve stones that had H7756
Jos 4:16 the covenant law *to* **come u** out of the H6590
Jos 4:17 the priests, "**Come u** out of the Jordan." H6590
Jos 4:18 And the priests **came u** out of the river H6590
Jos 4:19 month the people **went u** from the Jordan H6590
Jos 4:20 And Joshua **set u** at Gilgal the twelve H7756
Jos 4:23 the LORD your God **dried u** the Jordan H3312
Jos 4:23 Red Sea when *he* **dried** it **u** before us H3312
Jos 5: 1 how the LORD *had* **dried u** the Jordan H3312
Jos 5: 7 So *he* **raised u** their sons in their place H7756
Jos 5:13 he looked **u** and saw a man standing in H5951
Jos 5:13 Joshua **went u** to him and asked, "Are H2143
Jos 6: 5 city will collapse and the army *will* **go u**, H6590
Jos 6: 6 "**Take u** the ark of the covenant of the H5951
Jos 6:12 Joshua **got u early** the next morning and H8899
Jos 6:12 the priests **took u** the ark of the LORD. H5951
Jos 6:15 *they* **got u** at daybreak and marched H8899
Jos 6:26 cost of his youngest *he will* **set u** its gates." H5893
Jos 7: 2 told them, "**Go u** and spy out the region." H6590
Jos 7: 2 So the men **went u** and spied out Ai. H6590
Jos 7: 3 all the army *will have to* **go u** *against* Ai. H6590
Jos 7: 4 So about three thousand **went u**; but they H6590
Jos 7:10 said to Joshua, "**Stand u**! What are you H7756
Jos 7:26 Over Achan *they* **heaped u** a large pile of H7756
Jos 8: 1 army with you, and **go u** and attack Ai. H6590
Jos 8: 7 you *are to* **rise u** from ambush and take H7756
Jos 8:11 was with him **marched u** and approached H6590
Jos 8:11 *They* **set u camp** north of Ai, with the H2837
Jos 8:13 So the soldiers **took u** *their* **positions**— H8492
Jos 8:20 the smoke of the city **rising u** into the sky, H6590
Jos 8:21 city and that smoke *was* **going u** *from* it, H6590
Jos 10: 4 "**Come u** and help me attack Gibeon," H6590
Jos 10: 5 They **moved u** with all their troops and H6590
Jos 10: 5 troops and **took u positions** against H2837
Jos 10: 6 **Come u** to us quickly and save us H6590
Jos 10: 7 So Joshua **marched u** from Gilgal with his H6590
Jos 10:10 along the road **going u** *to* Beth Horon H5090
Jos 10:18 "Roll large rocks **u to** the mouth of the cave, H448
Jos 10:31 *he* **took u positions** against it and H2837
Jos 10:33 king of Gezer *had* **come u** to help Lachish, H6590
Jos 10:34 *they* **took u positions** against it and H2837
Jos 10:36 all Israel with him **went u** from Eglon to H6590
Jos 13:27 the territory **u to** the end of the Sea of H6330
Jos 14: 8 Israelites who **went u** with me made the H6590
Jos 15: 3 it ran past Hezron **u** to Addar and curved H6590
Jos 15: 6 **went u** *to* Beth Hoglah and continued H6590
Jos 15: 7 The boundary then **went u** to Debir from H6590
Jos 15: 8 Then it **ran u** the Valley of Ben Hinnom H6590
Jos 16: 1 and **went u** from there through the desert H6590
Jos 17:15 **go u** into the forest and clear land for H6590
Jos 18: 1 at Shiloh and **set u** the tent of meeting H8905
Jos 18:11 The first lot **came u** for the tribe of H6590
Jos 19:10 The third lot **came u** for Zebulun H6590
Jos 19:12 went on to Daberath and **u** *to* Japhia. H6590
Jos 19:47 they **went u** and attacked Leshem H6590
Jos 19:50 And *he* **built u** the town and settled there H1215
Jos 22:17 **U to** this very day we have not cleansed H6330
Jos 24:17 who **brought** us and our parents **u** out of H6590
Jos 24:26 a large stone and **set** it **u** there under the H7756
Jos 24:32 the Israelites *had* **brought u** from Egypt, H6590
Jdg 1: 1 "Who of us *is to* **go u** first to fight against H6590
Jdg 1: 2 answered, "Judah *shall* **go** *u*; I have given AIT
Jdg 1: 3 "**Come u** with us into the territory allotted H6590
Jdg 1: 7 toes cut off *have* **picked u scraps** under my H4377
Jdg 1:16 **went u** from the City of Palms with the H6590
Jdg 2: 1 angel of the LORD **went u** from Gilgal to H6590
Jdg 2: 1 "*I* **brought** you **u** out of Egypt and led you H6590
Jdg 2:10 generation **grew u** who knew neither H7756
Jdg 2:16 Then the LORD **raised u** judges, who saved H7756
Jdg 2:18 Whenever the LORD **raised u** a judge for H7756
Jdg 2:19 *They* refused to **give u** their evil practices H5877
Jdg 3: 9 the LORD, he **raised u** for them a deliverer H7756
Jdg 4: 5 the Israelites **went u** to her to have H6590
Jdg 4: 6 Zebulun and **lead** them **u** to Mount Tabor H5432
Jdg 4:10 ten thousand men **went u** under his H6590
Jdg 4:10 Deborah also **went u** with him. H6590
Jdg 4:12 of Abinoam *had* **gone u** *to* Mount Tabor, H6590
Jdg 4:19 gave him a drink, and **covered** him **u**. H4059
Jdg 4:21 **picked u** a tent peg and a hammer and H4374
Jdg 5:12 '**Wake u**, wake up, Deborah! Wake up H6424
Jdg 5:12 'Wake up, **wake u**, Deborah! Wake up H6424
Jdg 5:12 **Wake u**, wake up, break out in H6424
Jdg 5:12 Wake up, **wake u**, break out in H6424
Jdg 6: 5 They **came u** with their livestock and their H6590
Jdg 6: 8 I **brought** you **u** out of Egypt, out of the H6590
Jdg 6:13 '*Did* not the LORD **bring** us **u** out of Egypt? H6590
Jdg 6:28 when the people of the town **got u**, H8899
Jdg 6:35 so that *they* too **went u** to meet them. H6590
Jdg 7: 9 said to Gideon, "**Get u**, go down against H7756
Jdg 7:15 the camp of Israel and called out, "**Get u**! H7756
Jdg 8: 4 exhausted yet *keeping u the* **pursuit**, came to AIT
Jdg 8: 8 From there *he* **went u** *to* Peniel and made H6590
Jdg 8:11 Gideon **went u** *by* the route of the nomads H6590
Jdg 8:33 *They* **set u** Baal-Berith as their god H8492
Jdg 9: 7 *he* **climbed u** on the top of Mount Gerizim H2143
Jdg 9: 9 tree answered, '*Should I* **give u** my oil, by H2532
Jdg 9:11 tree replied, '*Should I* **give u** my fruit, so H2532
Jdg 9:13 answered, '*Should I* **give u** my wine H2532
Jdg 9:23 God **stirred u** animosity between Abimelek H8938
Jdg 9:31 to Shechem and *are* **stirring u** the city H7443
Jdg 9:34 night and **took u concealed positions** near H741
Jdg 9:37 But Gaal **spoke u** again: "Look, people H1819
Jdg 9:48 he and all his men **went u** Mount Zalmon H6590
Jdg 9:51 themselves in and **climbed u** on the tower H6590
Jdg 11: 2 when they *were* **grown u**, they drove H1540
Jdg 11:13 "When Israel **came u** out of Egypt, they H6590
Jdg 11:16 But when they **came u** out of Egypt, Israel H6590
Jdg 12: 3 Now why *have you* **come u** today to fight H6590
Jdg 13: 8 to teach us how *to* **bring u** the boy who is H6913
Jdg 13:11 Manoah **got u** and followed his wife H7756
Jdg 13:20 As the flame **blazed u** from the altar H6590
Jdg 15: 5 *He* **burned u** the shocks and standing H1277
Jdg 15: 6 So the Philistines **went u** and burned her H6590
Jdg 15: 9 The Philistines **went u** and camped in H6590
Jdg 15:12 "We've come to **tie** you **u** and hand you H673
Jdg 15:13 "*We will* only **tie** you **u** and hand you H673+673
Jdg 15:13 new ropes and **led** him **u** from the rock. H6590
Jdg 15:19 Then God **opened u** the hollow place in H1324
Jdg 16: 3 Then *he* **got u** and took hold of the doors H7756
Jdg 16: 5 him so *we may* **tie** him **u** and subdue him. H673
Jdg 16: 6 how *you can* **be tied u** and subdued." H673
Jdg 16:14 his sleep and **pulled u** the pin and the H5825
Jdg 18:12 On their way *they* **set u camp** near Kiriath H2837
Jdg 18:30 There the Danites **set u** for themselves the H7756
Jdg 19: 5 the fourth day *they* **got u early** and he H8899
Jdg 19: 7 And when the man **got u** to go, his H7756
Jdg 19: 9 his servant, **got u** to leave, his H7756
Jdg 19: 9 **Early** tomorrow **morning** *you can* **get u** H8899
Jdg 19:27 When her master **got u** in the morning H7756
Jdg 19:28 He said to her, "**Get u**; let's go." But there H7756
Jdg 19:29 he took a knife and **cut u** his concubine H5983
Jdg 19:30 the day the Israelites **came u** out of Egypt. H6590
Jdg 19:30 We must do something! So **speak u**!" H1819
Jdg 20: 3 that the Israelites *had* **gone u** *to* Mizpah.) H6590
Jdg 20: 7 **speak u** and tell me what you have H2035
Jdg 20: 8 All the men **rose u** *together* as one H7756
Jdg 20: 9 We'll go **u** against it in the order decided by NDT
Jdg 20:18 The Israelites **went u** *to* Bethel and H6590
Jdg 20:18 "Who of us *is to* **go u** first to fight against H6590
Jdg 20:19 the Israelites **got u** and pitched camp H7756
Jdg 20:20 **took u** battle **positions** against them H6885
Jdg 20:22 again **took u** *their* **positions** where H6885
Jdg 20:23 The Israelites **went u** and wept before the H6590
Jdg 20:23 "Shall we **go u** again to fight against the H5602
Jdg 20:23 The LORD answered, "**Go u** against them." H6590
Jdg 20:26 the whole army, **went u** to Bethel, and H6590
Jdg 20:28 "Shall we **go u** again to fight against the H3655
Jdg 20:30 They **went u** against the Benjamites on H6590
Jdg 20:30 third day and **took u positions** against H6885
Jdg 20:33 places and **took u positions** at Baal Tamar H6885
Jdg 20:38 that they *should* **send u** a great cloud H6590
Jdg 20:40 city **going u** in smoke. H6590+2021+9028+2025
Ru 1:13 would you wait until *they* **grew u**? Would H1540
Ru 2: 2 to the fields and **pick u** the leftover grain H4377
Ru 2:15 As *she* **got u** to glean, Boaz gave orders to H7756
Ru 2:16 bundles and leave them for *her to* **pick u**, H4377
Ru 3:14 but **got u** before anyone could be H7756
Ru 4: 1 Meanwhile Boaz **went u** *to* the town gate H6590
Ru 4:11 who together **built u** the family of Israel. H1215
1Sa 1: 3 year this man **went u** from his town to H6590
1Sa 1: 7 Whenever Hannah **went u** to the house of H6590
1Sa 1: 9 drinking in Shiloh, Hannah **stood u**. H7756
1Sa 1:21 her husband Elkanah **went u** with all his H6590
1Sa 2: 6 he brings down to the grave and **raises u**. H6590
1Sa 2:14 the fork **brought u** the priest would H6590
1Sa 2:19 to him when she **went u** with her husband H6590
1Sa 2:21 the boy Samuel **grew u** in the presence of H1540
1Sa 2:28 to be my priest, to **go u** to my altar, to H6590
1Sa 2:35 *I will* **raise u** for myself a faithful priest H7756
1Sa 3: 6 And Samuel **got u** and went to Eli and H7756
1Sa 3: 8 And Samuel **got u** and went to Eli and H7756
1Sa 3:19 The LORD was with Samuel as he **grew u** H1540
1Sa 4:13 happened, the whole town **sent u a cry**. H2410
1Sa 5:12 the outcry of the city **went u** *to* heaven. H6590
1Sa 6: 7 their calves away and **pen** them **u**. H1074+2025
1Sa 6: 9 If *it* **goes u** to its own territory, toward Beth H6590
1Sa 6:10 cart and **penned u** their H3973+1074+928+2021
1Sa 6:12 Then the cows **went straight** *u* toward Beth AIT
1Sa 6:13 when they looked **u** and saw the ark H5951
1Sa 6:14 The people **chopped u** the wood of the H1324
1Sa 6:20 To whom *will* the ark **go u** from here?" H6590
1Sa 6:21 Come down and **take** it **u** to your town." H6590
1Sa 7: 1 Jearim came and **took u** the ark of the H6590
1Sa 7: 7 of the Philistines **came u** to attack them. H6590
1Sa 7:12 took a stone and **set** it **u** between Mizpah H8492
1Sa 8: 8 from the day *I* **brought** them **u** out of H6590
1Sa 9:11 As they *were* **going u** the hill to the town H6590
1Sa 9:13 find him before *he* **goes u** to the high H6590
1Sa 9:13 **Go u** now; you should find him about this H6590
1Sa 9:14 *They* **went u** *to* the town, and as they H6590
1Sa 9:14 toward them on *his* **way u** to the high H6590
1Sa 9:19 "**Go u** ahead of me *to* the high place, for H6590
1Sa 9:24 So the cook **took u** the thigh with what H8123
1Sa 10: 3 Three men **going u** to worship God at H6590

1Sa 10:18 'I **brought** Israel **u** out of Egypt, and I H6590
1Sa 11: 1 the Ammonite **went u** and besieged H6590
1Sa 12: 6 Aaron and **brought** your ancestors **u** out of H6590
1Sa 13: 5 *They* **went u** and camped at Mikmash H6590
1Sa 13: 9 And Saul **offered u** the burnt offering H6590
1Sa 13:15 left Gilgal and **went u** *to* Gibeah in H6590
1Sa 14: 9 stay where we are and not **go u** to them. H6590
1Sa 14:10 But if they say, '**Come u** to us,' we will H6590
1Sa 14:10 up to us,' *we will* **climb u**, because that H6590
1Sa 14:12 "**Come u** to us and we'll teach you a H6590
1Sa 14:12 armor-bearer, "**Climb u** after me; the LORD H6590
1Sa 14:13 Jonathan **climbed u**, using his hands and H6590
1Sa 14:21 Philistines and *had* **gone u** with them to H6590
1Sa 15: 2 waylaid them as they **came u** from Egypt. H6590
1Sa 15: 6 Israelites when they **came u** out of Egypt." H6590
1Sa 15:12 **Early** in the morning Samuel **got u** and H8899
1Sa 15:12 There *he has* **set u** a monument in his H5893
1Sa 15:34 Saul **went u** to his home in Gibeah of H6590
1Sa 16:23 David *would* **take u** his lyre and play. H4374
1Sa 17: 2 Elah and **drew u** their battle **line** to meet H6885
1Sa 17: 8 do you come out and **line u** *for* battle? H6885
1Sa 17:20 of a shepherd, **loaded u** and set out, as H5951
1Sa 17:21 Philistines *were* **drawing u** *their* lines H6885
1Sa 17:30 else and **brought u** the same matter H606
1Sa 19:15 "**Bring** him **u** to me in his bed so that I H6590
1Sa 20:30 Saul's anger **flared u** at Jonathan and he H3013
1Sa 20:34 Jonathan **got u** from the table in fierce H7756
1Sa 20:38 The boy **picked u** the arrow and returned H4377
1Sa 20:41 David **got u** from the south side of the H7756
1Sa 23: 8 And Saul **called u** all his forces for battle H9048
1Sa 23:19 The Ziphites **went u** to Saul at Gibeah H6590
1Sa 23:29 And David **went u** from there and lived in H6590
1Sa 24: 4 Then David **crept u** unnoticed and cut off H7756
1Sa 24:22 David and his men **went u** to the H6590
1Sa 25: 5 "**Go u** to Nabal at Carmel and greet him H6590
1Sa 25:13 four hundred men **went u** with David, H6590
1Sa 26:12 knew about it, nor *did anyone* **wake u**. H7810
1Sa 27: 1 Then Saul *will* **give u** searching for me H3286
1Sa 27: 8 David and his men **went u** and raided the H6590
1Sa 28: 4 came and **set u camp** at Shunem, H2837
1Sa 28: 4 all Israel and **set u camp** at Gilboa. H2837
1Sa 28: 8 "and **bring u** for me the one I name." H6590
1Sa 28:11 "Whom *shall I* **bring u** for you? H6590
1Sa 28:11 up for you?" "**Bring u** Samuel," he said. H6590
1Sa 28:13 a ghostly figure **coming u** out of the earth." H6590
1Sa 28:14 "An old man wearing a robe *is* **coming u**," H6590
1Sa 28:15 have you disturbed me by **bringing** me **u**?" H6590
1Sa 28:23 *He* **got u** from the ground and sat on the H7756
1Sa 28:25 That same night *they* **got u** and left. H7756
1Sa 29: 9 '*He must* not **go u** with us into battle. H6590
1Sa 29:10 Now **get u early**, along with your master's H8899
1Sa 29:11 his men **got u early** in the morning H8899
1Sa 29:11 the Philistines **went u** *to* Jezreel. H6590
2Sa 1:17 David **took u** this **lament** H7801+7806
2Sa 2: 1 "*Shall I* **go u** to one of the towns of Judah H6590
2Sa 2: 1 The LORD said, "**Go u**." David asked, H6590
2Sa 2: 2 So David **went u** there with his two wives H6590
2Sa 2:14 "*Let's have* some of the young men **get u** H7756
2Sa 2:15 So *they* **stood u** and were counted off H7756
2Sa 2:23 But Asahel refused to **give u** *the* **pursuit** H6073
2Sa 4: 4 His nurse **picked** him **u** and fled, but as H5951
2Sa 5: 9 David then **took u residence** in the fortress H3782
2Sa 5: 9 He **built u** the area around it, from the H1215
2Sa 5:17 they **went u** in full force to search for him H6590
2Sa 5:22 the Philistines **came u** and spread out in H6590
2Sa 5:23 answered, "*Do* not **go straight u**, but circle H6590
2Sa 6: 2 Baalah in Judah to **bring u** from there the H6590
2Sa 6:12 So David went *to* **bring u** the ark of God H6590
2Sa 6:15 all Israel *were* **bringing u** the ark of H6590
2Sa 7: 6 the day I **brought** the Israelites **u** out of H6590
2Sa 7:12 *I will* **raise u** your offspring to succeed you, H7756
2Sa 10: 8 out and **drew u** *in* battle formation *at* the H6885
2Sa 11: 2 evening David **got u** from his bed and H7756
2Sa 11:20 the king's anger *may* **flare u**, and he may H7756
2Sa 12: 3 and *it* **grew u** with him and his children. H1540
2Sa 12:17 beside him to **get** him **u** from the ground, H7756
2Sa 12:20 Then David **got u** from the ground. After H7756
2Sa 12:21 that the child is dead, *you* **get u** and eat!" H7756
2Sa 13:15 Amnon said to her, "**Get u** and get out!" H7756
2Sa 13:29 Then all the king's sons **got u**, mounted H7756
2Sa 13:31 The king **stood u**, tore his clothes and lay H7756
2Sa 13:34 watch looked **u** and saw many people H5951
2Sa 14: 7 the whole clan *has* **risen u** against your H7756
2Sa 15: 2 He *would* **get u early** and stand by the H8899
2Sa 15:30 But David *continued* **u** the Mount of H6590
2Sa 15:30 too and were weeping as *they* **went u**. H6590
2Sa 17:16 the people with him *will* **be swallowed u**. H1180
2Sa 18: 8 the forest **swallowed u** more men that H430
2Sa 18:17 in the forest and **piled u** a large heap of H5893
2Sa 18:24 the watchman **went u** to the roof of the H2143
2Sa 18:28 *He has* **delivered u** those who lifted their H6037
2Sa 18:31 the hand of all who **rose u** against you." H7756
2Sa 18:32 king and all who **rise u** to harm you be H7756
2Sa 18:33 *He* **went u** to the room over the gateway H6590
2Sa 19: 8 So the king **got u** and took his seat in the H7756
2Sa 19:34 that *I should* **go u** *to* Jerusalem with the H6590
2Sa 20:12 everyone who came **u to** Amasa stopped, H6584
2Sa 20:15 They built a siege ramp **u to** the city, and it H448
2Sa 20:19 Why *do you want to* **swallow u** the LORD's H1180
2Sa 20:20 "Far be it from me *to* **swallow u** or destroy! H1180
2Sa 20:21 *has* **lifted u** his hand against the king H5951
2Sa 21:13 been killed and exposed *were* **gathered u**. H665
2Sa 23: 7 *they* **are burned u** where H8596+928+2021+836+8596
2Sa 24:11 Before David **got u** the next morning, the H7756
2Sa 24:18 "**Go u** and build an altar to the LORD on H6590
2Sa 24:19 So David **went u**, as the LORD had H6590
2Sa 24:22 take whatever he wishes and **offer** it **u**. H6590
1Ki 1:35 Then *you are to* **go u** with him, and he is H6590
1Ki 1:40 And all the people **went u** after him H6590
1Ki 1:45 From there *they have* **gone u** cheering H6590
1Ki 2:19 Adonijah, the king **stood u** to meet her H7756
1Ki 2:34 son of Jehoiada **went u** and struck down H6590
1Ki 3:20 So *she* **got u** in the middle of the night H7756
1Ki 3:21 The next morning, *I* **got u** to nurse my son H7756
1Ki 6: 4 narrow windows **high u** in the temple H9209
1Ki 6: 8 a stairway *led* **u** to the middle level and H6590
1Ki 8: 1 to **bring u** the ark of the LORD's covenant H6590
1Ki 8: 3 had arrived, the priests **took u** the ark, H5951
1Ki 8: 4 and *they* **brought u** the ark of the LORD H6590
1Ki 8: 4 The priests and Levites **carried** them **u**, H6590
1Ki 8:35 the heavens *are* **shut u** and there is no H6806
1Ki 9:17 He built **u** Lower Beth Horon, NDT
1Ki 9:24 daughter *had* **come u** from the City of H6590
1Ki 11:14 Then the LORD **raised u** against Solomon H7756
1Ki 11:15 *who had* **gone u** to bury the dead H6590
1Ki 11:20 whom Tahpenes **brought u** in the royal H1694
1Ki 11:23 And God **raised u** against Solomon H7756
1Ki 12: 8 men who *had* **grown u** with him and H1540
1Ki 12:10 young men who *had* **grown u** with him H1540
1Ki 12:24 *Do* not **go u** to fight against your brothers H6590
1Ki 12:25 From there he went out and **built u** Peniel. H1215
1Ki 12:27 If these people **go u** to offer sacrifices at H6590
1Ki 12:28 is too much for you *to* **go u** to Jerusalem. H6590
1Ki 12:28 who **brought** you **u** out of Egypt. H6590
1Ki 12:29 One *he* **set u** in Bethel, and the other in H8492
1Ki 12:33 the Israelites and **went u** to the altar to H6590
1Ki 13: 4 stretched out toward the man **shriveled u**, H3312
1Ki 13:29 So the prophet **picked u** the body of the H5951
1Ki 14: 7 '*I* **raised** you **u** from among the people H8123
1Ki 14:10 *I will* **burn u** the house of Jeroboam as H1277
1Ki 14:14 "The LORD *will* **raise u** for himself a king H7756
1Ki 14:16 And *he will* **give** Israel **u** because of the H5989
1Ki 14:17 Jeroboam's wife **got u** and left and went H7756
1Ki 14:22 *they* **stirred u** his **jealous anger** more H7861
1Ki 14:23 They also **set u** for themselves high places, H1215
1Ki 15: 4 in Jerusalem by **raising u** a son to H7756
1Ki 15:17 king of Israel **went u** against Judah and H6590
1Ki 15:22 them King Asa **built u** Geba in Benjamin, H1215
1Ki 16: 2 "*I* **lifted** you **u** from the dust and appointed H8123
1Ki 16:32 *He* **set u** an altar for Baal in the temple of H7756
1Ki 16:34 and *he* **set u** its gates at the cost of his H5893
1Ki 17: 7 later the brook **dried u** because there had H3312
1Ki 17:14 jar of flour *will* not *be* **used u** and the jug H3983
1Ki 17:16 jar of flour *was* not **used u** and the jug of H3983
1Ki 17:23 Elijah **picked u** the child and carried him H4374
1Ki 18:38 of the LORD fell and **burned u** the sacrifice, H430
1Ki 18:38 also **licked u** the water in the trench. H4308
1Ki 18:43 And *he* **went u** and looked H6590
1Ki 18:44 '**Hitch u** your chariot and go down before H673
1Ki 19: 5 touched him and said, "**Get u** and eat." H7756
1Ki 19: 7 him and said, "**Get u** and eat, for the H7756
1Ki 19: 8 So *he* **got u** and ate and drank H7756
1Ki 19:19 Elijah **went u** to him and threw his cloak H6296
1Ki 20: 1 *he* **went u** and besieged Samaria and H6590
1Ki 20:26 the Arameans and **went u** to Aphek to H6590
1Ki 20:28 The man of God **came u** and told the king H5602
1Ki 20:33 sign and were quick *to* **pick u** his word. H2715
1Ki 20:33 Ahab **had** him **come u** into his chariot. H6590
1Ki 20:34 "*You may* **set u** your own market areas in H8492
1Ki 21: 7 king over Israel? **Get u** and eat! Cheer up. H7756
1Ki 21: 7 up and eat! **Cheer u**. I'll get you H3512+4213
1Ki 21:15 "**Get u** and take possession of the H7756
1Ki 21:16 he **got u** and went down to take H7756
1Ki 21:19 where dogs **licked u** Naboth's blood, H4379
1Ki 21:19 dogs *will* **lick u** your blood—yes, H4379
1Ki 22:24 son of Kenaanah **went u** and slapped H5602
1Ki 22:29 king of Judah **went u** *to* Ramoth Gilead. H6590
1Ki 22:35 the king was **propped u** in his chariot H6641
1Ki 22:38 and the dogs **licked u** his blood, as the H4379
2Ki 1: 3 "**Go u** and meet the messengers of the H6590
2Ki 1: 9 The captain **went u** to Elijah, who was H6590
2Ki 1:13 This third captain **went u** and fell on his H6590
2Ki 1:15 So Elijah **got u** and went down with him H7756
2Ki 2: 1 the LORD *was about to* **take** Elijah **u** to H6590
2Ki 2: 5 prophets at Jericho **went u** to Elisha and H5602
2Ki 2: 8 **rolled** it **u** and struck the water with it. H1676
2Ki 2:11 Elijah **went u** *to* heaven in a H6590
2Ki 2:13 Elisha then **picked u** Elijah's cloak that H8123
2Ki 2:16 of the LORD *has* **picked** him **u** and set him H5951
2Ki 2:23 From there Elisha **went u** *to* Bethel. As he H6590
2Ki 3:19 every good tree, **stop u** all the springs H6258
2Ki 3:21 bear arms **was called u** and stationed H7590
2Ki 3:22 When *they* **got u early** in the morning, the H8899
2Ki 3:24 the Israelites **rose u** and fought them until H7756
2Ki 3:25 *They* **stopped u** all the springs and cut H6258
2Ki 4:11 *he* **went u** to his room and lay down there. H6073
2Ki 4:20 the servant *had* **lifted** him **u** and carried H5951
2Ki 4:21 *She* **went u** and laid him on the bed of the H6590
2Ki 4:30 So *he* **got u** and followed her H7756
2Ki 4:39 *he* **cut** them **u** into the pot of stew H7114
2Ki 5:23 then **tied u** the two talents of silver in H7443
2Ki 6: 8 "I will **set u** my **camp** in such and such a H9381
2Ki 6:15 of the man of God **got u** and went out H7756
2Ki 6:24 entire army and **marched u** and laid siege H6590
2Ki 6:28 '**Give u** your son so we may eat him today, H5989
2Ki 6:29 '**Give u** your son so we may eat him H5989
2Ki 7: 5 At dusk *they* **got u** and went to the camp H7756
2Ki 7: 7 So *they* **got u** and fled in the dusk and H7756
2Ki 7:12 The king **got u** in the night and said to his H7756
2Ki 8: 7 man of God has come **all the way u** here," H6330
2Ki 8:20 Judah and **set u** its own **king**. H4887+4889
2Ki 8:21 he **rose u** and broke through by night H7756
2Ki 9: 6 Jehu **got u** and went into the house. H7756
2Ki 9:21 "**Hitch u** my chariot," Joram ordered. H673
2Ki 9:21 And when *it was* **hitched u**, Joram king of H673
2Ki 9:25 "**Pick** him **u** and throw him on the field H5951
2Ki 9:26 **pick** him **u** and throw him on that plot H5951
2Ki 9:27 *he* **fled u** the road to Beth Haggan. H5674
2Ki 9:27 chariot on the **way u** *to* Gur near Ibleam, H5090
2Ki 9:32 He looked **u** at the window and called out H5951
2Ki 10:15 Jehu **helped** him **u** into the chariot. H6590
2Ki 12:17 king of Aram **went u** and attacked Gath H6590
2Ki 13:21 man came to life and **stood u** on his feet. H7756
2Ki 15:14 of Gadi went from Tirzah **u** *to* Samaria. H6590
2Ki 16: 5 of Israel **marched u** to fight *against* H6590
2Ki 16: 7 **Come u** and save me out of the hand of H6590
2Ki 16:13 *He* **offered u** his burnt offering and grain H7787
2Ki 17: 3 king of Assyria **came u** to attack Hoshea, H6590
2Ki 17: 7 who *had* **brought** them **u** out of Egypt H6590
2Ki 17:10 *They* **set u** sacred stones and Asherah H5893
2Ki 17:29 and **set** them **u** in the shrines the people H5663
2Ki 17:36 who **brought** you **u** out of Egypt with H6590
2Ki 18: 4 for **u to** that time the Israelites had been H6330
2Ki 18:17 They came **u** *to* Jerusalem and stopped at H6590
2Ki 19:14 Then he **went u** *to* the temple of the LORD H6590
2Ki 19:24 of my feet *I have* **dried u** all the streams H2990
2Ki 19:26 on the roof, scorched before *it* **grows u**. H7850
2Ki 19:35 When *the people* **got u** the next morning H8899
2Ki 20: 5 day from now *you will* **go u** *to* the temple H6590
2Ki 20: 8 me and that *I will* **go u** *to* the temple of H6590
2Ki 20:17 predecessors *have* **stored u** until this day, H732
2Ki 22: 4 "**Go u** to Hilkiah the high priest and have H6590
2Ki 23: 2 He **went u** *to* the temple of the LORD with H6590
2Ki 23:29 king of Egypt **went u** to the Euphrates H6590
2Ki 24:11 Nebuchadnezzar *himself* **came u** to the city H995
2Ki 24:13 and **cut u** the gold articles that Solomon H7915
2Ki 25:13 The Babylonians **broke u** the bronze H8689
1Ch 5: 9 occupied the land **u to** the edge of the H6330
1Ch 5:26 the God of Israel **stirred u** the spirit of Pul H6424
1Ch 9:18 Gate on the east, **u to** the present time. H6330
1Ch 10:10 gods and **hung u** his head *in* the temple H9546
1Ch 11: 6 Joab son of Zeruiah **went u** first, and so H6590
1Ch 11: 7 David then **took u residence** in the fortress H3782
1Ch 11: 8 *He* **built u** the city around it, from the H1215
1Ch 13: 6 to **bring u** from there the ark of God the H6590
1Ch 14: 8 they **went u** in full force to search for him H6590
1Ch 14:11 So David and *his men* **went u** to Baal H6590
1Ch 15: 3 in Jerusalem to **bring u** the ark of the LORD H6590
1Ch 15:12 yourselves and **bring u** the ark of the LORD, H6590
1Ch 15:13 did not bring it **u** the first time that the LORD NDT
1Ch 15:14 in order to **bring u** the ark of the LORD, H6590
1Ch 15:25 a thousand went to **bring u** the ark of the H6590
1Ch 15:28 So all Israel **brought u** the ark of the H6590
1Ch 17: 5 the day *I* **brought** Israel **u** out of Egypt H6590
1Ch 17:11 *I will* **raise u** your offspring to succeed you, H7756
1Ch 18: 3 when he went to **set u** his monument at H5893
1Ch 19: 9 out and **drew u** *in* battle formation at the H6885
1Ch 21: 1 Satan **rose u** against Israel and incited H6641
1Ch 21:16 David looked **u** and saw the angel of the H5951
1Ch 21:18 Gad to tell David *to* **go u** and build an H6590
1Ch 21:19 So David **went u** in obedience to the word H6590
2Ch 1: 4 Now David *had* **brought u** the ark of God H6590
2Ch 1: 6 Solomon **went u** to the bronze altar before H6590
2Ch 2:16 You *can* then **take** them **u** *to* Jerusalem." H6590
2Ch 5: 2 to **bring u** the ark of the LORD's covenant H6590
2Ch 5: 4 had arrived, the Levites **took u** the ark, H5951
2Ch 5: 5 and *they* **brought u** the ark and the tent of H6590
2Ch 5: 5 The Levitical priests **carried** them **u**; H6590
2Ch 6:26 the heavens *are* **shut u** and there is no H6806
2Ch 7:13 "When *I* **shut u** the heavens so that there H6806
2Ch 8: 4 *He* also **built u** Tadmor in the desert and H1215
2Ch 8:11 **brought** Pharaoh's daughter **u** from H6590
2Ch 10: 8 men who *had* **grown u** with him and H1540
2Ch 10:10 young men who *had* **grown u** with him H1540
2Ch 11: 4 *Do* not **go u** to fight against your fellow H6590
2Ch 11: 5 in Jerusalem and **built u** towns for H1215
2Ch 13: 3 Jeroboam **drew u** *a* battle **line** against H6885
2Ch 14: 6 *He* **built u** the fortified cities of Judah H1215
2Ch 14: 7 "*Let us* **build u** these towns," he said to H1215
2Ch 14:10 and *they* **took u** battle **positions** in the H6885
2Ch 15: 7 be strong and *do* not **give u**, for H8332+3338
2Ch 15:16 **broke** it **u** and burned it in the Kidron H1990
2Ch 16: 1 king of Israel **went u** against Judah and H6590
2Ch 16: 6 With them *he* **built u** Geba and Mizpah. H1215
2Ch 18:23 son of Kenaanah **went u** and slapped H5602
2Ch 18:28 king of Judah **went u** to Ramoth Gilead. H6590
2Ch 18:34 of Israel **propped** *himself* **u** in his chariot H6641
2Ch 20: 5 Jehoshaphat **stood u** in the assembly H6641
2Ch 20:16 They *will be* **climbing u** by the Pass of Ziz H6590
2Ch 20:17 **Take u** *your* **positions**; stand firm and see H3656
2Ch 20:19 Korahites **stood u** and praised the H7756
2Ch 20:23 Moabites **rose u** against the men H6641
2Ch 21: 8 Judah and **set u** its own **king**. H4887+4889
2Ch 21: 9 *he* **rose u** and broke through by night. H7756
2Ch 25:14 *He* **set** them **u** as his own gods, bowed H6641

2Ch 28:14 So the soldiers gave u the prisoners and H6440
2Ch 28:24 the LORD's temple and set u altars at every H6913
2Ch 29:20 together and went u to the temple of the H6590
2Ch 30:16 Then they took u their regular H6641+6584
2Ch 33:19 high places and set u Asherah poles and H6641
2Ch 34:30 He went u to the temple of the LORD with H6590
2Ch 35:20 Necho king of Egypt went u to fight at H6590
2Ch 36:17 He brought u against them the king of the H6590
2Ch 36:23 Any of his people among you may go u H6590
Ezr 1: 3 among you may go u to Jerusalem in H6590
Ezr 1: 5 prepared to go u and build the house of H6590
Ezr 1:11 the exiles when they came u from H6590
Ezr 2: 1 the province who came u from the H6590
Ezr 2:59 The following came u from the towns of H6590
Ezr 4:12 the people who came u to us from you A10513
Ezr 7: 6 this Ezra came u from Babylon. He was a H6590
Ezr 7: 7 also came u to Jerusalem in the seventh H6590
Ezr 7:22 u to a hundred talents of silver, A10527
Ezr 7:28 leaders from Israel to go u with me. H6590
Ezr 8: 1 with them who came u with me from H6590
Ezr 9: 6 my God, to lift u my face to you, because H8123
Ezr 10: 4 Rise u; this matter is in your hands. H7756
Ezr 10: 5 So Ezra rose u and put the leading priests H7756
Ezr 10:10 Ezra the priest stood u and said to them, H7756
Ne 2:15 so I went u the valley by night, examining H6590
Ne 3:16 made repairs u to a point opposite the H6330
Ne 3:26 Ophel made repairs u to a point opposite H6330
Ne 4: 3 even a fox climbing u on it would break H6590
Ne 4: 5 Do not cover u their guilt or blot out their H4059
Ne 4: 8 Jerusalem and stir u trouble against it. H6913
Ne 4:14 I stood u and said to the nobles H7756
Ne 6: 1 though u to that time I had not set the H6330
Ne 6: 8 you are just making it u out of your head." H968
Ne 7: 6 the province who came u from the H6590
Ne 7:61 The following came u from the towns of H6590
Ne 8: 2 which was made u of men and women H4946
Ne 8: 5 as he opened it, the people all stood u. H6641
Ne 9: 5 "Stand u and praise the LORD your God H7756
Ne 9:18 your god, who brought you u out of Egypt H6590
Ne 10:38 are to bring a tenth of the tithes u to the H6590
Ne 12:23 descendants of Levi u to the time of H6330
Ne 12:31 I had the leaders of Judah go u on top of H6590
Ne 12:37 Gate they continued directly u the steps of H6590
Ne 13:18 Now you are stirring u more wrath against H3578
Est 2: 7 whom he had brought u because she had H587
Est 2:20 she had done when he was bringing her u. H594
Est 5: 3 Even u to half the kingdom, it will be H6330
Est 5: 6 Even u to half the kingdom, it will be H6330
Est 5:14 "Have a pole set u, reaching to H6913
Est 5:14 Haman, and he had the pole set u. H6913
Est 6: 4 on the pole he had set u for him. H3922
Est 7: 2 Even u to half the kingdom, it will be H6330
Est 7: 7 The king got u in a rage, left his wine and H7756
Est 7: 9 He had it set u for Mordecai, who spoke H6913
Est 7: 9 Mordecai, who spoke u to help the king." H1819
Est 7:10 on the pole he had set u for Mordecai. H3922
Est 8: 7 have impaled him on the pole he set u. NDT
Est 10: 3 his people and spoke u for the welfare of H1819
Job 1:16 the heavens and burned u the sheep and H1277
Job 1:20 Job got u and tore his robe and shaved H7756
Job 4:21 Are not the cords of their tent pulled u, so H5825
Job 5:18 wounds, but he also binds u; he injures, H2502
Job 7: 4 lie down I think, 'How long before I get u? H7756
Job 9:35 Then I would speak u without fear of him H1819
Job 11:15 free of fault, you will lift u your face; you H5951
Job 14: 2 They spring u like flowers and wither H3655
Job 14:11 the water of a lake dries u or a riverbed H261
Job 14:17 My offenses will be sealed u in a bag H3159
Job 15:16 corrupt, who drink u evil like water! H9272
Job 15:20 through all the years stored u for him. H7621
Job 16: 8 You have shriveled me u—and it has H7855
Job 16: 8 my gauntness rises u and testifies against H7756
Job 17: 3 will put u security for me? H9546+4200+3338
Job 18:16 His roots dry u below and his branches H3312
Job 20:15 God will make his stomach vomit them u. H3769
Job 20:27 his guilt; the earth will rise u against him. H7756
Job 21:19 'God stores u the punishment of the H7621
Job 22:22 his mouth and lay u his words in your H8492
Job 22:26 the Almighty and will lift u your face to H5951
Job 22:29 are brought low and you say, 'Lift them u! H1575
Job 24:14 the murderer rises u, kills the poor H7756
Job 24:24 brought low and gathered u like all others H7890
Job 26: 8 He wraps u the waters in his clouds, yet H7674
Job 26:12 By his power he churned u the sea; by his H8088
Job 27:16 Though he heaps u silver like dust and H7392
Job 27:17 what he lays u the righteous will wear H3922
Job 29:16 I took u the case of the stranger. H2983
Job 30:13 They break u my road; they succeed in H5995
Job 30:20 do not answer; I stand u, but you merely H6641
Job 30:22 You snatch me u and drive me before the H5951
Job 30:28 I stand u in the assembly and cry for help. H7756
Job 31:40 then let briers come u instead of wheat H3655
Job 33: 5 stand u and argue your case before me. H6885
Job 33:32 answer me; speak u, for I want to H1819
Job 34:24 the mighty and sets u others in their place H6641
Job 35: 5 Look u at the heavens and see; gaze at H5564
Job 36:27 "He draws u the drops of water, which H1758
Job 37:19 we cannot draw u our case because of our H6885
Job 37:20 Would anyone ask to be swallowed u? H1180
Job 38: 8 "Who shut u the sea behind doors when H6114
Job 38:33 Can you set u God's dominion over the H8492
Job 39:24 frenzied excitement it eats u the ground; H1686
Job 41: 6 Will they divide it u among the merchants H2936
Job 41:25 When it rises u, the mighty are terrified H8420
Job 41:31 caldron and stirs u the sea like a pot H8492
Ps 2: 2 kings of the earth rise u and the rulers H3656
Ps 2:12 his wrath can flare u in a moment. H1277
Ps 3: 1 How many rise u against me! H7756
Ps 7: 6 rise u against the rage of my enemies. H5951
Ps 9:13 Have mercy and lift me u from the gates H8123
Ps 10:12 Lift u your hand, O God. Do not H5951
Ps 16: 4 to such gods or take u their names on my H5951
Ps 17:10 They close u their callous hearts, and H6037
Ps 17:13 Rise u, LORD, confront them, bring them H7756
Ps 17:14 May what you have stored u for the H7621
Ps 20: 5 victory and lift u our banners in the name H1839
Ps 20: 8 fall, but we rise u and stand firm. H7756
Ps 21: 9 you will burn them u as in a blazing H4564
Ps 21: 9 The LORD will swallow them u in his wrath H1180
Ps 22:15 My mouth is dried u like a potsherd, and H3312
Ps 24: 7 Lift u your heads, you gates; be lifted up H5951
Ps 24: 7 you gates; be lifted u, you ancient doors H5951
Ps 24: 9 Lift u your heads, you gates; lift them up H5951
Ps 24: 9 you gates; lift them u, you ancient doors H5951
Ps 27:12 false witnesses rise u against me H7756
Ps 28: 2 as I lift u my hands toward your Most Holy H5951
Ps 28: 5 down and never build them u again. H1215
Ps 30: 3 You, LORD, brought me u from the realm of H6590
Ps 31:19 things that you have stored u for those H7621
Ps 32: 5 sin to you and did not cover u my iniquity. H4059
Ps 35: 2 Take u shield and armor; arise and come H2616
Ps 35:25 say, "We have swallowed him u." H1180
Ps 37:20 be consumed, they will go u in smoke. H3983
Ps 39: 6 heaping u wealth without knowing whose H7392
Ps 41: 8 he will never get u from the place where H7756
Ps 41:10 LORD; raise me u, that I may repay H7756
Ps 44:11 You gave us u to be devoured like sheep H5989
Ps 44:26 Rise u and help us; rescue us because of H7756
Ps 51:18 to build u the walls of Jerusalem. H1215
Ps 52: 5 He will snatch you u and pluck you from H3149
Ps 63: 4 in your name I will lift u my hands. H5951
Ps 66: 7 let not the rebellious rise u against him. H8123
Ps 69: 1 the waters have come u to my neck. H6330
Ps 69:15 me or the depths swallow me u or the pit H1180
Ps 71:20 of the earth you will again bring me u. H6590
Ps 73:10 turn to them and drink u waters in H5172
Ps 74: 4 they set u their standards as signs. H8492
Ps 74:15 It was you who opened u springs and H1324
Ps 74:15 you dried u the ever-flowing rivers. H3312
Ps 74:22 Rise u, O God, and defend your cause H7756
Ps 75: 4 to the wicked, 'Do not lift u your horns. H8123
Ps 75:10 the horns of the righteous will be lifted u." H8123
Ps 76: 9 rose u to judge, to save all the H7756
Ps 77:18 your lightning lit u the world; the earth H239
Ps 78:13 he made the water stand u like a wall. H5893
Ps 78:38 his anger and did not stir u his full wrath. H6424
Ps 78:60 the tent he had set u among humans. H8905
Ps 80:15 the son you have raised u for yourself. H599
Ps 80:17 son of man you have raised u for yourself. H599
Ps 81:10 your God, who brought you u out of Egypt. H6590
Ps 82: 8 Rise u, O God, judge the earth, for all the H7756
Ps 88:10 Do their spirits rise u and praise you? H7756
Ps 89: 9 when its waves mount u, you still them. H5951
Ps 89:19 I have raised u a young man from among H8123
Ps 90: 6 In the morning it springs u new, but by H7437
Ps 91:12 they will lift you u in their hands, so that H5951
Ps 92: 7 though the wicked spring u like grass and H7255
Ps 93: 3 The seas have lifted u, LORD, the seas H5951
Ps 93: 3 the seas have lifted u their voice H5951
Ps 93: 3 the seas have lifted u their pounding H5951
Ps 94: 2 Rise u, Judge of the earth; pay back to the H5951
Ps 94:16 Who will rise u for me against the wicked? H7756
Ps 97: 4 His lightning lights u the world; the earth H239
Ps 102:10 for you have taken me u and thrown me H5951
Ps 104:28 it to them, they gather it u; when you H4377
Ps 105:30 which went u into the bedrooms of their NDT
Ps 105:35 they ate u every green thing in their land H430
Ps 105:35 their land, ate u the produce of their soil. H430
Ps 106: 9 the Red Sea, and it dried u; he led them H2990
Ps 106:17 The earth opened u and swallowed H7337
Ps 106:30 But Phinehas stood u and intervened, and H6641
Ps 107:25 For he spoke and stirred u a tempest that H6641
Ps 107:26 They mounted u to the heavens and went H6590
Ps 110: 6 heaping u the dead and crushing the H4848
Ps 116:13 I will lift u the cup of salvation and call on H5951
Ps 118:27 the festal procession u to the horns of the H6330
Ps 121: 1 I lift u my eyes to the mountains—where H5951
Ps 122: 4 That is where the tribes go u—the tribes H6590
Ps 123: 1 I lift u my eyes to you, to you who sit H5951
Ps 127: 2 In vain you rise early and stay u late H3782
Ps 132:17 grow for David and set u a lamp for my H6885
Ps 134: 2 Lift u your hands in the sanctuary and H5951
Ps 139: 8 If I go u to the heavens, you are there; if I H6158
Ps 140: 2 in their hearts and stir u war every day. H1592
Ps 141: 2 may the lifting u of my hands be like the H5368
Ps 141: 7 "As one plows and breaks u the earth, so H1324
Ps 142: 1 I lift u my voice to the LORD for mercy. H2858
Ps 145:14 all who fall and lifts u all who are bowed H2422
Ps 146: 8 the LORD lifts u those who are bowed H2422
Ps 147: 2 The LORD builds u Jerusalem; he gathers H1215
Ps 147: 3 brokenhearted and binds u their wounds. H2502
Ps 147:18 melts them; he stirs u his breezes H5959
Ps 148:14 And he has raised u for his people a horn, H8123
Pr 2: 1 my words and store u my commands H7621
Pr 6: 1 if you have put u security for your H6842
Pr 6: 9 When will you get u from your sleep H7756
Pr 6:14 in his heart—he always stirs u conflict. H8938
Pr 6:19 lies and a person who stirs u conflict in H8938
Pr 7: 1 keep my words and store u my commands H7621
Pr 9: 1 her house; she has set u its seven pillars. H5893
Pr 10:12 Hatred stirs u conflict, but love covers over H6424
Pr 10:14 The wise store u knowledge, but the H7621
Pr 11:15 Whoever puts u security for a stranger will H6842
Pr 12:25 the heart, but a kind word cheers it u. H8523
Pr 13:22 a sinner's wealth is stored u for the H7621
Pr 15: 1 but a harsh word stirs u anger. H6590
Pr 15:18 A hot-tempered person stirs u conflict, but H1741
Pr 16:28 A perverse person stirs u conflict, and a H8938
Pr 17:18 in pledge and puts u security for a H6842+6859
Pr 17:22 a crushed spirit dries u the bones. H3312
Pr 20:16 of one who puts u security for a stranger H6842
Pr 20:17 one ends u with a mouth full of gravel. H339
Pr 21:20 The wise store u choice food H238+928+5659
Pr 21:22 who is wise can go u against the city of H6590
Pr 21:29 The wicked put u a bold front H6451+928+7156
Pr 22:15 Folly is bound u in the heart of a child H8003
Pr 22:23 the LORD will take u their case and will H8189
Pr 22:26 in pledge or puts u security for debts; H6842
Pr 22:28 boundary stone set u by your ancestors. H6913
Pr 23: 8 You will vomit u the little you have eaten H7794
Pr 23:11 he will take u their case against you. H8189
Pr 23:35 When will I wake u so I can find another H7810
Pr 24:31 thorns had come u everywhere, the H6590
Pr 25: 7 to say to you, "Come u here," than for him H6590
Pr 27:13 of one who puts u security for a stranger; H6842
Pr 28:25 The greedy stir u conflict, but those who H1741
Pr 29: 8 Mockers stir u a city, but the wise turn H7032
Pr 29:22 An angry person stirs u conflict, and a H1741
Pr 30: 4 Who has gone u to heaven and come H6590
Pr 30: 4 Whose hands have gathered u the wind H665
Pr 30: 4 Who has wrapped u the waters in a cloak? H7674
Pr 30:21 trembles, under four it cannot bear u: H5951
Pr 30:25 yet they store u their food in the summer; H3922
Pr 30:33 so stirring u anger produces strife. H4790
Pr 31: 8 Speak u for those who cannot H7337+7023
Pr 31: 9 Speak u and judge fairly; defend H7337+7023
Pr 31:15 She gets u while it is still night; she H7756
Ecc 2:26 gathering and storing u wealth to hand it H4043
Ecc 3: 6 a time to search and a time to give u, a time H6
Ecc 4:10 falls down, one can help the other u. H7756
Ecc 4:10 who falls and has no one to help them u. H7756
Ecc 8: 3 Do not stand u for a bad cause, for he will H6641
Ecc 12: 4 when people rise u at the sound of birds H7756
SS 3: 2 I will get u now and go about the city H7756
SS 3: 6 Who is this coming u from the wilderness H6590
SS 4: 2 just shorn, coming u from the washing. H6590
SS 4:12 You are a garden locked u, my sister, my H5835
SS 6: 6 flock of sheep coming u from the washing H6590
SS 7:13 old, that I have stored u for you, my H7621
SS 8: 5 Who is this coming u from the wilderness H6590
Isa 1: 2 "I reared children and brought them u H8123
Isa 1:17 Take u the cause of the fatherless; plead H9149
Isa 2: 3 let us go u to the mountain of the LORD H6590
Isa 2: 4 Nation will not take u sword against H5951
Isa 3: 5 The young will rise u against the old, the H8104
Isa 5: 2 He dug it u and cleared it of stones and H6466
Isa 5:11 who stay u late at night till they are H336
Isa 5:24 as tongues of fire lick u straw and as dry H430
Isa 5:26 He lifts u a banner for the distant nations H5951
Isa 7: 1 king of Israel marched u to fight against H6590
Isa 8: 8 through it and reaching u to the neck. H6330
Isa 8:16 Bind u this testimony of warning and seal H7674
Isa 8:16 of warning and seal u God's instruction H3159
Isa 10:15 rod were to wield the person who lifts it u, H8123
Isa 10:24 you with a rod and lift u a club against H5951
Isa 11: 1 A shoot will come u from the stump of H3655
Isa 11:15 The LORD will dry u the gulf of the H2990
Isa 11:15 He will break it u into seven streams so H5782
Isa 11:16 Israel when they came u from Egypt. H6590
Isa 13:17 I will stir u against them the Medes H6424
Isa 14: 4 you will take u this taunt against the king H5951
Isa 14:22 "I will rise u against them," declares the H7756
Isa 14:29 the root of that snake will spring u a viper, H3655
Isa 15: 2 Dibon goes u to its temple, to its high H6590
Isa 15: 5 They go u the hill to Luhith, weeping as H6590
Isa 15: 6 of Nimrim are dried u and the grass is H5457
Isa 15: 7 acquired and stored u they carry away H7213
Isa 16: 3 "Make u your mind," Moab says H995+6783
Isa 19: 2 "I will stir u Egyptian against Egyptian H6056
Isa 19: 5 The waters of the river will dry u, and the H5980
Isa 19: 6 streams of Egypt will dwindle and dry u. H2990
Isa 21: 5 Get u, you officers, oil the H7756
Isa 22: 1 that you have all gone u on the roofs, H6590
Isa 22: 6 Elam takes u the quiver, with her H5951
Isa 22: 9 you stored u water in the Lower Pool. H7695
Isa 22:18 He will roll you u tightly like H7571+7571+7572
Isa 23: 4 reared sons nor brought u daughters." H8123
Isa 23:12 "U, cross over to Cyprus; even there you H7756
Isa 23:13 creatures; they raised u their siege towers H7756
Isa 23:16 "Take u a harp, walk through the city, you H4374
Isa 23:18 LORD; they will not be stored u or hoarded. H732
Isa 24: 4 The earth dries u and withers, the world H62
Isa 24: 6 earth's inhabitants are burned u, H3081
Isa 24: 7 The new wine dries u and the vine withers H62
Isa 24:19 The earth is broken u, the earth is H8318+8318
Isa 24:22 they will be shut u in prison and be H6037

U

Isa 25: 8 *he will* **swallow u** death forever. H1180
Isa 26:19 *let* those who dwell in the dust **wake u** H7810
Isa 27:12 *will* **be gathered u** one by one. H4377
Isa 28:21 The LORD *will* **rise u** as he did at Mount H7756
Isa 28:24 *Does he keep on* **breaking u** and working H7337
Isa 29: 3 you with towers and **set u** my siege works H7756
Isa 30:18 therefore *he will* **rise u** to show you H8123
Isa 30:26 when the LORD **binds u** the bruises of his H2502
Isa 30:28 like a rushing torrent, **rising u** to the neck. H2936
Isa 30:29 playing pipes go **u** to the mountain of the H995
Isa 31: 2 *He will* **rise u** against that wicked nation H7756
Isa 32: 7 they **make u** evil schemes to destroy the H3619
Isa 32: 9 are so complacent, **rise u** and listen to me H7756
Isa 33: 3 when you **rise u**, the nations scatter. H8129
Isa 33: 9 The land **dries u** and wastes away, Lebanon H61
Isa 33:10 will I be exalted; now *will I* **be lifted u**. H5951
Isa 33:20 its stakes *will* never **be pulled u**, nor any H5825
Isa 34: 4 the heavens **rolled u** like a scroll; H1670
Isa 37:14 Then he **went u** *to* the temple of the LORD H6590
Isa 37:25 of my feet *I have* **dried u** all the streams H2990
Isa 37:27 on the roof, scorched before *it* **grows u**. H7850
Isa 37:36 When *the people* **got u** the next morning H8899
Isa 38:12 Like a weaver *I have* **rolled u** my life, and H7886
Isa 38:22 the sign that *I will* **go u** *to* the temple of H6590
Isa 39: 6 predecessors *have* **stored u** until this day, H732
Isa 40: 4 Every valley *shall* **be raised u**, every H5951
Isa 40: 9 news to Zion, **go u** on a high mountain. H6590
Isa 40: 9 to Jerusalem, **lift u** your voice with a shout H8123
Isa 40: 9 a shout, lift it **u**, do **not** be afraid; say to H440
Isa 40:20 a skilled worker to **set u** an idol that will H3922
Isa 40:26 **Lift u** your eyes and look to the heavens H5951
Isa 41: 2 "Who *has* **stirred u** one from the east H6424
Isa 41:16 the wind *will* **pick** them **u**, and a gale H5951
Isa 41:25 "*I have* **stirred u** one from the north, and H6424
Isa 42:13 like a warrior *he will* **stir u** his zeal; with a H6424
Isa 42:15 hills and **dry u** all their vegetation; H3312
Isa 42:15 rivers into islands and **dry u** the pools. H3312
Isa 43: 6 to the north, '**Give** them **u**!' and to the H5989
Isa 43:19 Now *it* **springs u**; do you not H7541
Isa 44: 4 *They will* **spring u** like grass in a meadow H7541
Isa 44: 9 **Those who** would **speak u for** them are H6332
Isa 44:27 and *I will* **dry u** your streams,' H3312
Isa 45: 8 open wide, *let* salvation **spring u**, let H7238
Isa 45:13 I *will* **raise u** Cyrus in my righteousness: H6424
Isa 46: 7 carry it; *they* **set** it **u** in its place, and H5663
Isa 47: 2 **Lift u** *your* skirts, bare your legs, and wade H3106
Isa 47:14 are like stubble; the fire *will* **burn** them **u**. H8596
Isa 48:13 I summon them, *they all* **stand u** together. H6641
Isa 49: 7 "Kings will see you and **stand u**, princes H7756
Isa 49:11 and my highways *will be* **raised u**. H8123
Isa 49:18 **Lift u** your eyes and look around; all your H5951
Isa 49:21 Who **brought** these **u**? I was left H1540
Isa 49:22 *I will* **lift u** my banner to the peoples H8123
Isa 50: 2 By a mere rebuke *I* **dry u** the sea, I turn H2990
Isa 50: 9 like a garment; the moths *will* **eat** them **u**. H430
Isa 51: 6 **Lift u** your eyes to the heavens, look at the H5951
Isa 51: 8 For the moth *will* **eat** them **u** like a garment H430
Isa 51:10 Was it not you who **dried u** the sea, the H2990
Isa 51:15 *who* **stirs u** the sea so that its waves roar— H8088
Isa 51:17 **Rise u**, Jerusalem, you who have drunk H7756
Isa 52: 2 Shake off your dust; **rise u**, sit enthroned H7756
Isa 52: 8 Your watchmen **lift u** their voices; together H5951
Isa 52:13 will be raised and **lifted u** and highly H5951
Isa 53: 2 *He* **grew u** before him like a tender shoot H6590
Isa 53: 4 Surely he **took u** our pain and bore our H5951
Isa 57: 7 there *you* **went u** to offer your sacrifices. H6590
Isa 57:14 it will be said: "**Build u**, build up, prepare H6148
Isa 57:14 "Build up, **build u**, prepare the road H6148
Isa 57:20 whose waves **cast u** mire and mud. H1764
Isa 58:12 ancient ruins and *will* **raise u** the age-old H7756
Isa 60: 4 "**Lift u** your eyes and look about you: All H5951
Isa 61: 1 He has sent me to **bind u** the H2502
Isa 61:11 the soil **makes** the sprout **come u** and a H3655
Isa 61:11 *will* **make** righteousness and praise **spring u** H7541
Isa 62:10 way for the people. **Build u**, build up the H6148
Isa 62:10 Build up, **build u** the highway H6148
Isa 63: 9 *he* **lifted** them **u** and carried them all the H5747
Isa 64: 6 filthy rags; we all **shrivel u** like a leaf, and H5570
Isa 66: 9 "*Do I* **close u** the womb when I bring to H6806
Jer 1:15 kings will come and **set u** their thrones in H5989
Jer 1:17 **Stand u** and say to them whatever I H7756
Jer 2: 6 who **brought** us **u** out of Egypt and led us H6590
Jer 3: 2 "Look **u** to the barren heights and see. H5951
Jer 3: 6 She *has* **gone u** on every high hill and H2143
Jer 4: 3 "**Break u** your unplowed ground and do H5774
Jer 4: 4 my wrath *will* **flare u** and burn like fire H3655
Jer 4:29 thickets; *some* **climb u** among the rocks. H6590
Jer 5: 1 "**Go u and down** the streets of Jerusalem H8763
Jer 6:22 great nation *is being* **stirred u** from the H6424
Jer 7:29 **take u** a lament on the barren heights H5951
Jer 7:30 *They have* **set u** their detestable idols in H8492
Jer 8: 2 *They will* not **be gathered u** or buried, but H665
Jer 8: 4 people fall down, *do they* not **get u**? H7756
Jer 9:10 mountains and take **u** a lament concerning NDT
Jer 10:17 **Gather u** your belongings to leave the land, H665
Jer 10:20 to pitch my tent or *to* **set u** my shelter. H7756
Jer 11: 7 the time I **brought** your ancestors **u** from H6590
Jer 11:13 the altars *you have* **set u** to burn H8492
Jer 13: 7 to Perath and **dug u** the belt and took H2916
Jer 13:19 The cities in the Negev *will* **be shut u** H6037
Jer 13:20 **Look u** and see those who are H5951+6524
Jer 13:26 I *will* **pull u** your skirts over your face that H3106
Jer 14: 2 and a cry **goes u** from Jerusalem. H6590
Jer 16:14 who **brought** the Israelites **u** out of Egypt H6590
Jer 16:15 who **brought** the Israelites **u** out of the H6590
Jer 18: 9 kingdom *is to be* **built u** and planted, H1215
Jer 18:15 them walk in byways, on roads not **built u**. H6148
Jer 20: 9 heart like a fire, a fire **shut u** in my bones. H6806
Jer 22: 7 and *they will* **cut u** your fine cedar beams H4162
Jer 22:20 "**Go u** *to* Lebanon and cry out, let your H6590
Jer 23: 5 "when *I will* **raise u** for David a righteous H7756
Jer 23: 7 who **brought** the Israelites **u** out of Egypt H6590
Jer 23: 8 who **brought** the descendants of Israel **u** H6590
Jer 24: 6 *I will* **build** them **u** and not tear them H1215
Jer 25:33 not be mourned or **gathered u** or buried, H665
Jer 26:10 *they* **went u** from the royal palace *to* the H6590
Jer 29:15 "The LORD *has* **raised u** prophets for us in H7756
Jer 30: 9 their king, whom *I will* **raise u** for them. H7756
Jer 31: 4 *I will* **build** you **u** again, and you, Virgin H1215
Jer 31: 4 Again *you will* **take u** your timbrels and H6335
Jer 31: 6 *let us* **go u** *to* Zion, to the LORD our H6590
Jer 31:21 "**Set u** road signs; put up guideposts H5893
Jer 31:21 up road signs; **put u** guideposts. H8492
Jer 31:35 *who* **stirs u** the sea so that its waves roar— H8088
Jer 32:24 the siege ramps *are* **built u** to take the city. H995
Jer 32:34 *They* **set u** their vile images in the house H8492
Jer 36:28 which Jehoiakim king of Judah **burned u**. H8596
Jer 38:13 and *they* **pulled** him **u** with the ropes and H5432
Jer 41: 2 who were with him **got u** and struck down H7756
Jer 41:12 *They* **caught u** *with* him near the great H5162
Jer 42:10 *I will* **build** you **u** and not tear you down H1215
Jer 46:11 "**Go u** *to* Gilead and get balm, Virgin H6590
Jer 46:16 They will say, '**Get u**, let us go back to our H7756
Jer 48: 5 *They* **go u** the hill to Luhith, weeping H6590
Jer 48:18 destroys Moab *will* **come u** against you H6590
Jer 48:34 even the waters of Nimrim are **dried u**. H5457
Jer 49:14 yourselves to attack it! **Rise u** for battle!" H7756
Jer 49:19 "Like a lion **coming u** from Jordan's H6590
Jer 50: 2 nations, **lift u** a banner and proclaim it H5951
Jer 50: 9 For I *will* **stir u** and bring against Babylon H6424
Jer 50: 9 *They will* **take u** *their* **positions** against H6885
Jer 50:14 "**Take u** *your* **positions** around Babylon H6885
Jer 50:26 granaries; **pile** her **u** like heaps of grain. H6148
Jer 50:32 fall and no *one will* **help** her **u**; H7756
Jer 50:38 on her waters! *They will* **dry u**. For it is a H3312
Jer 50:41 many kings *are* **being stirred u** from the H6424
Jer 50:44 Like a lion **coming u** from Jordan's H6590
Jer 51: 1 I *will* **stir u** the spirit of a destroyer against H6424
Jer 51:11 the arrows, **take u** the shields! The H4848
Jer 51:11 The LORD *has* **stirred u** the kings of the H6424
Jer 51:12 **Lift u** a banner against the walls of H5951
Jer 51:27 "**Lift u** a banner in the land! Blow the H5951
Jer 51:27 **send u** horses like a swarm of locusts. H6590
Jer 51:36 *I will* **dry u** her sea and make her springs H2990
Jer 52:17 The Babylonians **broke u** the bronze H8689
La 2: 2 pity the Lord *has* **swallowed u** all the H1180
La 2: 5 like an enemy; *he has* **swallowed u** Israel. H1180
La 2: 5 *He has* **swallowed u** all her palaces and H1180
La 2:16 say, "*We have* **swallowed** her **u**. H1180
La 2:19 **Lift u** your hands to him for the lives of H5951
La 3:41 *Let us* **lift u** our hearts and our hands to H5951
La 3:58 *You*, Lord, **took u** my case; you redeemed H8189
La 4: 5 Those **brought u** in royal purple now lie on H587
La 5:12 Princes *have* **been hung u** by their hands H9434
Eze 1:27 be his waist **u** he looked like H4200+5087+2025
Eze 2: 1 **stand u** on your feet and I will speak to H6641
Eze 3:12 Then the Spirit **lifted** me **u**, and I heard H5951
Eze 3:14 The Spirit then **lifted** me **u** and took me H5951
Eze 3:22 said to me, "**Get u** and go out to the plain H7756
Eze 3:23 So *I* **got u** and went out to the plain. H7756
Eze 4: 2 build a ramp **u to** it, set up camps H6584
Eze 4: 2 **set u** camps against it and put battering H5989
Eze 4: 8 *I will* **tie** you **u** *with* ropes so that you H5989
Eze 5: 1 take a set of scales and **divide u** the hair. H2745
Eze 5: 4 fire and **burn** them **u**. H8596+928+2021+836
Eze 8: 2 from there **u** his appearance H4200+5087+2025
Eze 8: 3 The Spirit **lifted** me **u** between earth and H5951
Eze 9: 3 the God of Israel **went u** from above the H6590
Eze 10: 7 *He* **took u** of it and put it into the H5951
Eze 11: 1 the Spirit **lifted** me **u** and brought me H5951
Eze 11:23 glory of the LORD **went u** from within the H6590
Eze 11:24 The Spirit **lifted** me **u** and brought me to H5951
Eze 11:24 the vision I had seen **went u** from me, H6590
Eze 13: 5 *You have* not **gone u** to the breaches in H6590
Eze 14: 3 these men *have* **set u** idols in their hearts H6590
Eze 14: 4 of the Israelites **set u** idols in their hearts H6590
Eze 14: 7 from me and **set u** idols in their hearts H6590
Eze 17: 9 many people to **pull** it **u** by the roots. H5951
Eze 17:24 *I* **dry u** the green tree and make the dry H3312
Eze 19: 1 "**Take u** a lament concerning the princes H5951
Eze 19: 3 *She* **brought u** one of her cubs, and he H6590
Eze 21:22 where he is to **set u** battering rams, to H8492
Eze 22:30 among them *who would* **build u** the wall H1553
Eze 23: 8 *She did* not **give u** the prostitution she H6440
Eze 23:22 I *will* **stir u** your lovers against you, those H6424
Eze 23:24 *they will* **take u positions** against you on H8492
Eze 24: 8 To **stir u** wrath and take revenge I put her H6590
Eze 25: 4 *They will* **set u** their camps and pitch their H3782
Eze 26: 3 like the sea **casting u** its waves. H6590
Eze 26: 8 *he will* **set u** siege works against you H5989
Eze 26: 8 build a ramp **u to** your walls and raise his H6584
Eze 26:17 Then *they will* **take u** a lament concerning H5951
Eze 27: 2 of man, **take u** a lament concerning Tyre. H5951
Eze 27:32 *they will* **take u a lament** concerning you: H7801
Eze 28:12 **take u** a lament concerning the king of H5951
Eze 29: 5 field and not be gathered or **picked u**. H7695
Eze 30:12 *I will* **dry u** the waters of the Nile H5989+3000
Eze 30:21 *It has* not **been bound u** to be healed H2502
Eze 32: 2 **take u** a lament concerning Pharaoh king H5951
Eze 32: 3 and *they will* **haul** you **u** in my net. H6590
Eze 34: 4 healed the sick or **bound u** the injured. H2502
Eze 34:16 *I will* **bind u** the injured and strengthen H2502
Eze 37:10 came to life and **stood u** on their feet— H6641
Eze 37:11 'Our bones *are* **dried u** and our hope is H3312
Eze 37:12 your graves and **bring** you **u** from them; H6590
Eze 37:13 your graves and **bring** you **u** from them. H6590
Eze 38: 9 the many nations with you *will* **go u**, H6590
Eze 39: 9 the weapons for fuel and **burn** them **u**— H5956
Eze 40:14 measurement was **u to** the portico facing H448
Eze 40:22 Seven steps **led u** to it, with its portico H6590
Eze 40:26 Seven steps **led u** *to* it, with its portico H6590
Eze 40:31 its jambs, and eight steps **led u** *to* it. H6590
Eze 40:34 on either side, and eight steps **led u** *to* it. H6590
Eze 40:37 on either side, and eight steps **led u** *to* it. H6590
Eze 41: 7 A stairway **went u** from the lowest floor to H6590
Eze 41:16 The floor, the wall **u to** the windows, and H6330
Eze 43: 5 Then the Spirit **lifted** me **u** and brought H5951
Eze 43:14 gutter on the ground **u to** the lower ledge H6330
Eze 45: 9 **Give u** your violence and oppression and H6073
Eze 47: 4 led me through **water** that was **u** *to* the waist. AIT
Da 2:21 he deposes kings and **raises u** others. A10624
Da 2:44 God of heaven *will* **set u** a kingdom that A10624
Da 3: 1 and **set** it **u** on the plain of Dura in the A10624
Da 3: 2 dedication of the image he *had* **set u**. A10624
Da 3: 3 that King Nebuchadnezzar *had* **set u**, A10624
Da 3: 5 that King Nebuchadnezzar *has* **set u**. A10624
Da 3: 7 that King Nebuchadnezzar *had* **set u**. A10624
Da 3:12 the image of gold *you have* **set u**." A10624
Da 3:14 worship the image of gold *I have* **set u**? A10624
Da 3:18 the image of gold *you have* **set u**." A10624
Da 3:20 soldiers in his army to **tie u** Shadrach, A10366
Da 3:22 killed the soldiers who **took u** Shadrach, A10513
Da 3:24 three men that we **tied u** and threw into A10366
Da 3:28 and *were willing to* **give u** their A10314
Da 5:23 *you have* **set** *yourself* **u** against the Lord A10659
Da 6:19 the king **got u** and hurried to the lions' A10624
Da 7: 2 of heaven **churning u** the great sea. A10137
Da 7: 3 from the others, **came u** out of the sea. A10513
Da 7: 5 *It* **was raised u** on one of its sides, and it A10624
Da 7: 5 was told, '**Get u** and eat your fill of flesh! A10624
Da 7: 8 a little one, *which* **came u** among them A10513
Da 7:20 about the other horn that **came u**, A10513
Da 8: 3 I looked **u**, and there before me was a ram H5951
Da 8: 3 longer than the other but **grew u** later. H6590
Da 8: 8 prominent horns **grew u** toward the four H6590
Da 8:11 *It* **set** *itself* **u to be as great** as the H1540
Da 8:26 you is true, but **seal u** the vision, for it H6258
Da 8:27 Then *I* **got u** and went about the king's H7756
Da 9:24 to **seal u** vision and prophecy and to H3159
Da 9:27 temple he will set **u** an abomination that NDT
Da 10: 5 I looked **u** and there before me was a man H5951
Da 10:11 to you, and **stand u**, for I H6641+6584+6642
Da 10:11 he said this to me, *I* **stood u** trembling. H6641
Da 11: 2 *he will* **stir u** everyone against the H6424
Da 11: 4 his empire *will* **be broken u** and parceled H8689
Da 11:15 will come and **build u** siege ramps and H9161
Da 11:25 a large army *he will* **stir u** his strength H6424
Da 11:31 armed forces *will* **rise u** to desecrate the H6641
Da 11:31 Then *they will* **set u** the abomination that H5989
Da 12: 4 **roll u** and seal the words of the scroll until H6258
Da 12: 9 the words *are* **rolled u** and sealed until H6258
Da 12:11 that causes desolation *is* **set u**, H5989
Hos 1:11 one leader and *will* **come u** out of the H6590
Hos 2:15 as in the day she **came u** out of Egypt. H6590
Hos 4: 3 Because of this the land **dries u**, and all who H62
Hos 4:15 go to Gilgal; *do* not **go u** to Beth Aven. H6590
Hos 6: 1 injured us but *he will* **bind u** our wounds. H2502
Hos 8: 4 They **set u kings** without my consent; they H4887
Hos 8: 7 yield grain, foreigners *would* **swallow** it **u**. H1180
Hos 8: 8 Israel **is swallowed u**; now she is among H1180
Hos 8: 9 For they *have* **gone u** *to* Assyria like a wild H6590
Hos 10: 4 therefore lawsuits **spring u** like poisonous H7255
Hos 10: 8 thistles *will* **grow u** and cover their H6590
Hos 10:11 and Jacob *must* **break u the ground**. H8440
Hos 10:12 and **break u** your unplowed ground H5774
Hos 11: 8 "How *can I* **give** you **u**, Ephraim? How can H5989
Hos 12:13 a prophet *to* **bring** Israel **u** from Egypt, H6590
Hos 13:12 The guilt of Ephraim *is* **stored u**, his sins H7674
Hos 13:15 his spring will fail and his well **dry u**. H2990
Joel 1: 5 **Wake u**, you drunkards, and weep! Wail H7810
Joel 1:10 the ground *is* **dried u**; the grain is H62
Joel 1:10 the new wine *is* **dried u**, the olive oil fails. H3312
Joel 1:12 The vine *is* **dried u** and the fig tree is H3312
Joel 1:12 all the trees of the field—*are* **dried u**. H3312
Joel 1:17 broken down, for the grain has **dried u**. H3312
Joel 1:19 flames *have* **burned u** all the trees of H4265
Joel 1:20 streams of water *have* **dried u** and fire has H3312
Joel 2: 5 like a mighty army **drawn u** *for* battle. H6885
Joel 2:20 And its stench *will* **go u**; its smell will H6590
Joel 3: 2 the nations and **divided u** my land. H2745
Am 1: 2 the pastures of the shepherds **dry u**, and the H62
Am 2:10 I **brought** you **u** out of Egypt and led you H6590
Am 2:11 "*I* also **raised u** prophets from among your H7756
Am 3: 1 the whole family *I* **brought u** out of Egypt: H6590
Am 3: 5 *Does* a trap **spring u** from the ground if it H6590
Am 3:10 "who **store u** in their fortresses what they H732

Book	Ref	Context	Number
Am	4: 7	had rain; another had none and **dried u**.	H3312
Am	5: 1	this lament I **take u** concerning you:	H5951
Am	5: 2	in her own land, with no *one to* **lift** her **u**."	H7756
Am	5:26	*You have* **lifted u** the shrine of your king	H5951
Am	6: 8	*I will* **deliver u** the city and everything in it.	H6037
Am	6:14	declares, "I *will* **stir u** a nation against you	H7756
Am	7: 1	just as the late crops *were* **coming u**.	H6590
Am	7: 4	*it* **dried u** the great deep and devoured the	H430
Am	7:17	land *will* **be** measured and **divided u**,	H2745
Am	8: 8	*it will* **be stirred u** and then sink like the	H1764
Am	9: 2	Though *they* **climb u** *to* the heavens	H6590
Am	9: 7	"*Did I* not **bring** Israel **u** from Egypt, the	H6590
Ob	21	Deliverers *will* **go u** on Mount Zion to	H6590
Jnh	1: 2	its wickedness *has* **come u** before me."	H6590
Jnh	1: 4	arose that the ship threatened to **break u**.	H8689
Jnh	1: 6	can you sleep? **Get u** and call on your god	H7756
Jnh	1:12	"**Pick** me **u** and throw me into the sea,"	H5951
Jnh	2: 6	But *you*, LORD my God, **brought** my life **u**	H6590
Jnh	3: 8	*Let* them **give u** their evil ways and	H8740+4946
Jnh	4: 6	plant and **made** it **grow u** over Jonah to	H6590
Jnh	4:10	*It* **sprang u** overnight and died overnight	H2118
Mic	2: 4	my people's possession *is* **divided u**.	H4614
Mic	2: 8	my people *have* **risen u** like an enemy.	H7756
Mic	2:10	**Get u**, go away! For this is not your resting	H7756
Mic	2:13	open the way *will* **go u** before them;	H6590
Mic	3: 3	*who* **chop** them **u** like meat for the pan	H7298
Mic	4: 2	*let us* **go u** to the mountain of the LORD	H6590
Mic	4: 3	Nation *will* not **take u** sword against	H5951
Mic	5: 9	Your hand *will be* **lifted u** in triumph over	H8123
Mic	6: 1	"**Stand u**, plead my case before the	H7756
Mic	6: 4	*I* **brought** you **u** out of Egypt and	H6590
Mic	6:14	*You will* **store u** but save nothing	H6047
Mic	7: 6	a daughter **rises u** against her mother	H7756
Na	1: 4	He rebukes the sea and **dries** it **u**; he	H3312
Na	2:13	"*I will* **burn u** your chariots in smoke, and	H1277
Hab	1: 6	I *am* **raising u** the Babylonians, that	H7756
Hab	1:13	while the wicked **swallow u** those more	H1180
Hab	1:15	wicked foe **pulls** all of them **u** with hooks,	H6590
Hab	1:15	in his net, *he* **gathers** them **u** in his dragnet	H665
Hab	2: 4	the enemy *is* **puffed u**; his desires	H6752
Hab	2: 6	" 'Woe to him *who* **piles u** stolen goods	H8049
Hab	2: 7	*Will they* not **wake u** and make you	H3699
Hab	2:19	to lifeless stone, '**Wake u**!' Can it give	H6424
Zep	1:10	LORD, "a cry will go **u** from the Fish Gate	NDT
Zep	3: 8	"for the day I *will* **stand u** to testify.	H7756
Hag	1: 8	**Go u** *into* the mountains and bring down	H6590
Hag	1:14	So the LORD **stirred u** the spirit of	H6424
Zec	1:18	Then I looked **u**, and there before me	H5951
Zec	1:21	of the nations who **lifted u** their horns	H5951
Zec	2: 1	Then I looked **u**, and there before me was	H5951
Zec	4: 1	talked with me returned and **woke** me **u**,	H6424
Zec	5: 5	"Look **u** and see what is appearing."	H5951
Zec	5: 9	Then I looked **u**—and there before me	H5951
Zec	5: 9	and *they* **lifted u** the basket between	H5951
Zec	6: 1	I looked **u** again, and there before me	H5951
Zec	9: 3	*she has* **heaped u** silver like dust	H7392
Zec	10:11	all the depths of the Nile *will* **dry u**.	H3312
Zec	11:16	For I *am going to* **raise u** a shepherd over	H7756
Zec	14: 1	*will* **be** plundered and **divided u** within	H2745
Zec	14:10	Jerusalem *will be* **raised u high** from the	H8027
Zec	14:16	Jerusalem *will* **go u** year after year to	H6590
Zec	14:17	of the earth *do* not **go u** to Jerusalem to	H6590
Zec	14:18	people *do* not **go u** and take part,	H6590
Zec	14:18	the nations that *do* not **go u** to celebrate	H6590
Zec	14:19	the nations that *do* not **go u** to celebrate	H6590
Mt	1:24	*When* Joseph **woke u**	*G1586+608+3836+5678*
Mt	2:13	"**Get u**," he said, "take the child and his	*G1586*
Mt	2:14	So he **got u**, took the child and his mother	*G1586*
Mt	2:20	said, "**Get u**, take the child and his	*G1586*
Mt	2:21	So he **got u**, took the child and his mother	*G1586*
Mt	3: 9	these stones God can **raise u** children	*G1586*
Mt	3:12	into the barn and **burning u** the chaff with	*G2876*
Mt	3:16	was baptized, *he* **went u** out of the water.	*G326*
Mt	4: 6	and *they will* **lift** you **u** in their hands	*G149*
Mt	5: 1	*he* **went u** on a mountainside and sat	*G326*
Mt	6:19	"*Do* not **store u** for yourselves treasures on	*G2564*
Mt	6:20	But **store u** for yourselves treasures in	*G2564*
Mt	7:12	this **sums u** the Law and the Prophets.	*G1639*
Mt	8:15	and *she* **got u** and began to wait on him.	*G1586*
Mt	8:17	"He **took u** our infirmities and bore our	*G3284*
Mt	8:24	a furious storm **came u** on the lake,	*G1181*
Mt	8:26	Then *he* **got u** and rebuked the winds	*G1586*
Mt	9: 5	are forgiven,' or to say, '**Get u** and walk'?	*G1586*
Mt	9: 6	paralyzed man, "**Get u**, take your mat	*G1586*
Mt	9: 7	Then the man **got u** and went home.	*G1586*
Mt	9: 9	and Matthew **got u** and followed him.	*G482*
Mt	9:19	Jesus **got u** and went with him, and so did	*G1586*
Mt	9:20	twelve years **came u** behind him and	*G4665*
Mt	9:25	took the girl by the hand, and *she* **got u**.	*G1586*
Mt	10:38	Whoever *does* not **take u** their cross and	*G3284*
Mt	12:29	unless *he* first **ties u** the strong man?	*G1313*
Mt	12:35	things out of the good **stored u** in him,	*G2565*
Mt	12:35	evil things out of the evil **stored u** in him.	*G2565*
Mt	12:41	men of Nineveh *will* **stand u** at the	*G482*
Mt	13: 4	the path, and the birds came and **ate** it **u**.	*G2983*
Mt	13: 5	*It* **sprang u** quickly, because the soil was	*G1984*
Mt	13: 6	But *when* the sun **came u**, the plants were	*G422*
Mt	13: 7	which **grew u** and choked the plants.	*G326*
Mt	13:28	'Do you want *us to* go and **pull** them **u**?	*G5198*
Mt	13:40	"As the weeds *are* **pulled u** and burned in	*G5198*
Mt	13:48	*the fishermen* **pulled** it **u** on the shore.	*G328*
Mt	14:19	the two fish and **looking u** to heaven,	*G329*
Mt	14:20	the disciples **picked u** twelve	*G149*
Mt	14:23	*he* **went u** on a mountainside by himself to	*G326*
Mt	15:13	not planted *will be* **pulled u by the roots**.	*G1748*
Mt	15:29	Then *he* **went u** on a mountainside and sat	*G326*
Mt	15:37	the disciples **picked u** seven basketfuls of	*G149*
Mt	16:24	deny themselves and **take u** their cross	*G149*
Mt	17: 1	and **led** them **u** a high mountain by	*G429*
Mt	17: 4	If you wish, *I will* **put u** three shelters	*G4472*
Mt	17: 7	touched them. "**Get u**," he said. "Don't	*G1586*
Mt	17: 8	*When* they **looked u**, they	*G2048+3836+4057*
Mt	17:17	How long *shall I* **put u with** you? Bring	*G462*
Mt	18:21	who sins against me? **U to** seven times?"	*G2401*
Mt	19:16	Just then a man **came u to** Jesus and	*G4665*
Mt	20:17	Now Jesus *was* **going u** to Jerusalem.	*G326*
Mt	20:18	"*We are* **going u** to Jerusalem, and the Son	*G326*
Mt	21:19	he went **u to** it but found nothing on it	*G2093*
Mt	22:24	the widow and **raise u** offspring for him.	*G482*
Mt	23: 4	*They* **tie u** heavy, cumbersome loads and	*G1297*
Mt	24: 1	away *when* his disciples **came u to** him to	*G4665*
Mt	24:38	**u to** the day Noah entered the ark;	*G948*
Mt	25: 7	all the virgins **woke u** and trimmed their	*G1586*
Mt	26:58	**right u to** the courtyard of the high priest.	*G2401*
Mt	26:62	the high priest **stood u** and said to Jesus,	*G482*
Mt	26:73	standing there **went u** to Peter and said,	*G4665*
Mt	27: 6	The chief priests **picked u** the coins and	*G3284*
Mt	27:35	*they* **divided u** his clothes by casting lots.	*G1374*
Mt	27:50	again in a loud voice, *he* **gave u** his spirit.	*G918*
Mk	1:10	Just as Jesus *was* **coming u** out of the water,	*G326*
Mk	1:31	took her hand and **helped** her **u**.	*G1586*
Mk	1:35	still dark, Jesus **got u**, left the house and	*G482*
Mk	2: 9	to say, '**Get u**, take your mat and walk'?	*G1586*
Mk	2:11	"I tell you, **get u**, take your mat and go	*G1586*
Mk	2:12	*He* **got u**, took his mat and walked out in	*G1586*
Mk	2:14	told him, and Levi **got u** and followed him.	*G482*
Mk	3: 3	"**Stand u** in front of everyone."	*G1586*
Mk	3:13	Jesus **went u** on a mountainside and	*G326*
Mk	3:27	man's house without first **tying** him **u**.	*G1313*
Mk	4: 4	the path, and the birds came and **ate** it **u**.	*G2983*
Mk	4: 5	*It* **sprang u** quickly, because the soil was	*G1984*
Mk	4: 6	But when the sun **came u**, the plants were	*G422*
Mk	4: 7	which **grew u** and choked the plants	*G326*
Mk	4: 8	*It* **came u**, grew and produced a crop, some	*G326*
Mk	4:27	whether he sleeps or **gets u**, the seed	*G1586*
Mk	4:37	A furious squall **came u**, and the waves	*G1181*
Mk	4:39	*He* **got u**, rebuked the wind and said to	*G1444*
Mk	5:27	*she* **came u** behind him in the crowd and	*G2262*
Mk	5:41	means "Little girl, I say to you, **get u**!"	*G1586*
Mk	5:42	the girl **stood u** and began to walk	*G482*
Mk	6:23	ask I will give you, **u to** half my kingdom."	*G2401*
Mk	6:41	the two fish and **looking u** to heaven,	*G329*
Mk	6:43	the disciples **picked u** twelve basketfuls	*G149*
Mk	6:46	*he* **went u** on a mountainside to pray.	*G599*
Mk	7:34	*He* **looked u** to heaven and with a deep	*G329*
Mk	8: 8	the disciples **picked u** seven basketfuls of	*G149*
Mk	8:19	many basketfuls of pieces *did you* **pick u**?"	*G149*
Mk	8:20	many basketfuls of pieces *did you* **pick u**?"	*G149*
Mk	8:24	*He* **looked u** and said, "I see people; they	*G329*
Mk	8:34	deny themselves and **take u** their cross	*G149*
Mk	9: 2	with him and **led** them **u** a high mountain,	*G429*
Mk	9: 5	*Let us* **put u** three shelters—one for you	*G4472*
Mk	9:19	How long *shall I* **put u with** you? Bring	*G462*
Mk	9:27	lifted him to his feet, and *he* **stood u**.	*G482*
Mk	10:17	a man **ran u to** him and fell on his knees	*G4708*
Mk	10:28	Then Peter **spoke u**, "We have left	*G3306*
Mk	10:32	They were on their way **u** to Jerusalem	*G326*
Mk	10:33	"*We are* **going u** to Jerusalem," he said	*G326*
Mk	10:49	So they called to the blind man, "**Cheer u**!	*G2510*
Mk	12:19	the widow and **raise u** offspring for his	*G1985*
Mk	14:57	Then some **stood u** and gave this false	*G482*
Mk	14:60	the high priest **stood u** before them and	*G482*
Mk	15: 8	The crowd **came u** and asked Pilate to do	*G326*
Mk	15:11	the chief priests **stirred u** the crowd to have	*G411*
Mk	15:24	**Dividing u** his clothes, they cast lots to	*G1374*
Mk	15:41	women who *had* **come u** with him to	*G5262*
Mk	16: 4	But *when they* **looked u**, they saw that the	*G329*
Mk	16:18	*they will* **pick u** snakes with their hands;	*G149*
Mk	16:19	*he was* **taken u** into heaven and he sat at	*G377*
Lk	1: 1	have undertaken *to* **draw u** an account of	*G421*
Lk	1:52	their thrones but *has* **lifted u** the humble.	*G5738*
Lk	1:60	his mother **spoke u** and said, "No! He is	*G646*
Lk	1:69	*He has* **raised u** a horn of salvation for us	*G1586*
Lk	2: 4	So Joseph also **went u** from the town of	*G326*
Lk	2:19	But Mary **treasured u** all these things and	*G5337*
Lk	2:38	**Coming u** to them at that very moment	*G2392*
Lk	2:42	twelve years old, they **went u** *to* the festival	*G326*
Lk	3: 8	these stones God can **raise u** children	*G1586*
Lk	3:17	but *he will* **burn u** the chaff with	*G2876*
Lk	3:20	*He* **locked** John **u** in prison.	*G2881*
Lk	4: 5	The devil **led** him **u** to a high place and	*G343*
Lk	4:11	*they will* **lift** you **u** in their hands, so that	*G149*
Lk	4:16	where he had been **brought u**, and on the	*G5555*
Lk	4:16	as was his custom. *He* **stood u** to read,	*G482*
Lk	4:20	Then *he* **rolled u** the scroll, gave it back to	*G4771*
Lk	4:29	*They* **got u**, drove him out of the town, and	*G482*
Lk	4:39	*She* **got u** at once and began to wait on	*G482*
Lk	5:11	So *they* **pulled** their boats **u** on shore, left	*G2864*
Lk	5:19	*they* **went u** on the roof and lowered him	*G326*
Lk	5:23	are forgiven,' or to say, '**Get u** and walk'?	*G1586*
Lk	5:24	"I tell you, **get u**, take your mat and go	*G1586*
Lk	5:25	Immediately *he* **stood u** in front of them	*G482*
Lk	5:28	Levi **got u**, left everything and followed	*G482*
Lk	6: 8	"**Get u** and stand in front of everyone."	*G1586*
Lk	6: 8	So *he* **got u** and stood there.	*G482*
Lk	6:45	out of the good **stored u** in his heart,	*G2565*
Lk	6:45	things out of the evil **stored u** in his heart.	*G2565*
Lk	7:14	Then *he* **went u** and touched the bier they	*G4665*
Lk	7:14	"Young man, I say to you, **get u**!"	*G1586*
Lk	7:15	The dead man **sat u** and began to talk, and	*G361*
Lk	8: 5	it was trampled on, and the birds **ate** it **u**.	*G2983*
Lk	8: 6	ground, and *when it* **came u**, the plants	*G5886*
Lk	8: 7	which **grew u with** it and choked the	*G5243*
Lk	8: 8	*It* **came u** and yielded a crop, a hundred	*G5886*
Lk	8:24	He **got u** and rebuked the wind and the	*G1444*
Lk	8:44	*She* **came u** behind him and touched the	*G4665*
Lk	8:54	by the hand and said, "My child, **get u**!"	*G1586*
Lk	8:55	at once *she* **stood u**. Then Jesus told	*G482*
Lk	9:16	the two fish and **looking u** to heaven,	*G329*
Lk	9:17	the disciples **picked u** twelve	*G149*
Lk	9:23	themselves and **take u** their cross daily	*G149*
Lk	9:28	with him and **went u** onto a mountain	*G326*
Lk	9:33	*Let us* **put u** three shelters—one for you	*G4472*
Lk	9:41	shall I stay with you and **put u with** you?	*G462*
Lk	9:51	him *to be* **taken u to heaven**,	*G378*
Lk	10:25	an expert in the law **stood u** to test Jesus.	*G482*
Lk	11: 7	I can't **get u** and give you anything	*G482*
Lk	11: 8	even though *he will* not **get u** and give you	*G482*
Lk	11: 8	audacity *he will surely* **get u** and give you	*G1586*
Lk	11:22	man trusted and **divides u** his plunder.	*G1344*
Lk	11:32	men of Nineveh *will* **stand u** at the	*G482*
Lk	12:19	have plenty of grain **laid u** for many years.	*G3023*
Lk	12:21	it will be *with* whoever **stores u** things	*G2564*
Lk	13: 7	Why *should it* **use u** the soil?'	*G2934*
Lk	13:11	bent over and could not **straighten u** at all.	*G376*
Lk	13:13	immediately *she* **straightened u** and	*G494*
Lk	13:25	owner of the house **gets u** and closes the	*G1586*
Lk	14:10	'Friend, **move u** to a better place.	*G4646*
Lk	14:33	of you who *do* not **give u** everything you	*G698*
Lk	15:20	So *he* **got u** and went to his father. "But	*G482*
Lk	16:23	he **looked u** and saw	*G2048+3836+4057*
Lk	17:24	flashes and **lights u** the sky from one	*G3290*
Lk	17:27	given in marriage **u to** the day Noah	*G948*
Lk	18: 1	they should always pray and not **give u**.	*G1591*
Lk	18:10	"Two men **went u** to the temple to pray	*G326*
Lk	18:13	not even **look u** to heaven,	*G3836+4057+2048*
Lk	18:31	told them, "*We are* **going u** to Jerusalem	*G326*
Lk	19: 5	the spot, *he* **looked u** and said to him	*G329*
Lk	19: 8	But Zacchaeus **stood u** and said to the	*G2705*
Lk	19:28	he went on ahead, **going u** to Jerusalem.	*G326*
Lk	20: 1	together with the elders, **came u** to him.	*G2392*
Lk	20:28	the widow and **raise u** offspring for his	*G1985*
Lk	21: 1	*As* Jesus **looked u**, he saw the rich putting	*G329*
Lk	21:14	But **make u** your **mind**	*G5502+1877+3836+2840*
Lk	21:28	take place, **stand u** and lift up your heads	*G376*
Lk	21:28	stand up and **lift u** your heads	*G2048*
Lk	22:46	"**Get u** and pray so that you will not fall	*G482*
Lk	22:47	he was still speaking a crowd **came u**,	*G2627*
Lk	23: 5	"*He* **stirs u** the people all over Judea by his	*G411*
Lk	23:34	And *they* **divided u** his clothes by casting	*G1374*
Lk	23:36	soldiers also **came u** and mocked him.	*G4665*
Lk	24:12	however, **got u** and ran to the tomb	*G482*
Lk	24:15	Jesus himself **came u** and walked along	*G1581*
Lk	24:33	*They* **got u** and returned at once to	*G482*
Lk	24:50	*he* **lifted u** his hands and blessed them.	*G2048*
Lk	24:51	he left them and *was* **taken u** into heaven.	*G429*
Jn	2:13	Passover, Jesus **went u** to Jerusalem.	*G326*
Jn	3:14	Just as Moses **lifted u** the snake in the	*G5738*
Jn	3:14	so the Son of Man must *be* **lifted u**,	*G5738*
Jn	4:14	a spring of water **welling u** to eternal life."	*G256*
Jn	5: 1	Jesus **went u** to Jerusalem for one of the	*G326*
Jn	5: 8	said to him, "**Get u**! Pick up your mat	*G1586*
Jn	5: 8	"Get up! **Pick u** your mat and walk."	*G149*
Jn	5: 9	*he* **picked u** his mat and walked.	*G149*
Jn	5:11	well said to me, '**Pick u** your mat and walk.	*G149*
Jn	5:12	fellow who told you *to* **pick** it **u** and walk?"	*G149*
Jn	6: 3	Then Jesus **went u** on a mountainside and	*G456*
Jn	6: 5	*When* Jesus **looked u** and	*G2048+3836+4057*
Jn	6: 8	Andrew, Simon Peter's brother, **spoke u**,	*G3306*
Jn	6:39	given me, but **raise** them **u** at the last day.	*G482*
Jn	6:40	and I *will* **raise** them **u** at the last day."	*G482*
Jn	6:44	I *will* **raise** them **u** at the last day.	*G482*
Jn	6:54	and I *will* **raise** them **u** at the last day.	*G482*
Jn	7: 8	I *am* not **going u** to this festival, because	*G326*
Jn	7:14	the festival *did* Jesus **go u** to the temple	*G326*
Jn	7:39	**U to that time** the Spirit had **not** been	*G4037*
Jn	8: 7	*he* **straightened u** and said to them	*G376*
Jn	8:10	Jesus **straightened u** and asked her	*G376*
Jn	8:28	"When *you have* **lifted u** the Son of Man	*G5738*
Jn	8:59	*they* **picked u** stones to stone him	*G149*
Jn	10:17	lay down my life—only to **take** it **u** again.	*G3284*
Jn	10:18	it down and authority *to* **take** it **u** again.	*G3284*
Jn	10:31	opponents **picked u** stones to stone	*G1002*
Jn	11:11	I am going there to **wake** him **u**.	*G2030*
Jn	11:29	*she* **got u** quickly and went to him.	*G1586*
Jn	11:31	how quickly she **got u** and went out,	*G482*
Jn	11:41	Then Jesus looked **u** and said, "Father,	*G539*
Jn	11:49	priest that year, **spoke u**, "You know	*G3306*
Jn	11:55	many **went u** from the country to Jerusalem	*G326*
Jn	12:20	among those *who* **went u** to worship at the	*G326*
Jn	12:32	when *I am* **lifted u** from the earth	*G5738*
Jn	12:34	The crowd **spoke u**, "We have heard from	*G646*
Jn	12:34	'The Son of Man must *be* **lifted u**'?	*G5738*
Jn	13: 4	so *he* **got u** from the meal, took off his	*G1586*
Jn	15: 6	such branches *are* **picked u**, thrown into	*G5251*
Jn	19: 3	went **u to** him again and again	*G4639*

U

Jn 19:30 he bowed his head and **gave u** his spirit. G4140
Ac 1: 2 the day *he was* **taken u** *to heaven* G377
Ac 1: 9 *he was* **taken u** before their very eyes G2048
Ac 1:10 They were **looking intently u** into the sky as G867
Ac 1:15 In those days Peter **stood u** among the G482
Ac 1:22 the time when Jesus *was* **taken u** from us. G377
Ac 2:14 Then Peter **stood u** with the Eleven G2705
Ac 3: 1 Peter and John *were* **going u** to the temple G326
Ac 3: 7 right hand, *he* **helped** him **u**, and G1586
Ac 3:22 Lord your God *will* **raise u** for you a prophet G482
Ac 3:26 *When* God **raised u** his servant, he sent him G482
Ac 4: 1 the Sadducees **came u** to Peter and John G2392
Ac 4:26 kings of the earth **rise u** and the rulers G4225
Ac 5: 6 came forward, **wrapped u** his body, and G5366
Ac 5:34 **stood u** in the Sanhedrin and ordered that G482
Ac 6:10 they could not **stand u against** the wisdom G468
Ac 6:12 So *they* **stirred u** the people and the G5167
Ac 7:21 took him and **brought** him **u** as her own G427
Ac 7:37 'God *will* **raise u** for you a prophet like me G482
Ac 7:43 *You have* **taken u** the tabernacle of Molek G377
Ac 7:55 looked **u to** heaven and saw the glory of G1650
Ac 8:30 Then Philip **ran u to** the chariot and heard G4708
Ac 8:31 invited Philip *to* **come u** and sit with him G326
Ac 8:39 When *they* **came u** out of the water, the G326
Ac 9: 6 "Now **get u** and go into the city, and you G482
Ac 9: 8 Saul **got u** from the ground, but when he G1586
Ac 9:18 *He* **got u** and was baptized, G482
Ac 9:34 heals you. **Get u** and roll up your mat." G482
Ac 9:34 Get up and **roll u** your **mat**." Immediately G5143
Ac 9:34 Immediately Aeneas **got u**. G482
Ac 9:40 the dead woman, he said, "Tabitha, **get u**." G482
Ac 9:40 her eyes, and seeing Peter *she* **sat u**. G361
Ac 10: 4 to the poor *have* **come u** as a memorial G326
Ac 10: 9 Peter **went u** on the roof to pray. G326
Ac 10:13 a voice told him, "**Get u**, Peter. Kill and eat G482
Ac 10:20 So **get u** and go downstairs. Do not hesitate G482
Ac 10:26 But Peter *made* him **get u**. "Stand up," G1586
Ac 10:26 "**Stand u**," he said, "I am only a man G482
Ac 11: 2 So when Peter **went u** to Jerusalem, the G326
Ac 11: 7 I heard a voice telling me, '**Get u**, Peter. G482
Ac 11:10 then *it was* all **pulled u** to heaven G413
Ac 11:28 **stood u** and through the Spirit predicted G482
Ac 12: 7 struck Peter on the side and **woke** him **u**. G1586
Ac 12: 7 woke him up. "Quick, **get u**!" he said, G482
Ac 13: 1 who had been **brought u with** Herod the G5343
Ac 13:16 **Standing u**, Paul motioned with his hand G482
Ac 13:33 their children, *by* **raising u** Jesus. G482
Ac 13:50 *They* **stirred u** persecution against Paul G2074
Ac 14: 2 refused to believe **stirred u** the other G2074
Ac 14:10 called out, "**Stand u** on your feet!" At G482
Ac 14:10 the man **jumped u** and began to walk. G256
Ac 14:20 *he* **got u** and went back into the city. G482
Ac 15: 2 *to* **go u** to Jerusalem to see the apostles G326
Ac 15: 5 party of the Pharisees **stood u** and said, G1985
Ac 15: 7 Peter **got u** and addressed them: G482
Ac 15:13 they finished, James **spoke u**. "Brothers," G646
Ac 16:18 *She* **kept** this **u** for many days. Finally Paul G4472
Ac 16:27 The jailer **woke u**, and when he G2031+1181
Ac 17: 5 so *they* **rounded u** some bad characters G4689
Ac 17:13 agitating the crowds and **stirring** them **u**. G5429
Ac 17:22 Paul then **stood u** in the meeting of the G2705
Ac 18:22 *he* **went u** *to Jerusalem* and greeted the G326
Ac 19:39 is anything further *you want to* **bring u**, G2118
Ac 20: 9 from the third story and *was* **picked u** dead. G149
Ac 20:32 which can **build** you **u** and give you an G3868
Ac 21:12 with Paul not *to* **go u** to Jerusalem. G326
Ac 21:14 be dissuaded, *we* **gave u** and said, "The G2483
Ac 21:15 we started **on** *our* **way u** to Jerusalem. G326
Ac 21:27 *They* **stirred u** the whole crowd and seized G5177
Ac 21:33 The commander **came u** and arrested him G1581
Ac 22: 3 Tarsus of Cilicia, but **brought u** in this city. G427
Ac 22:10 " '**Get u**,' the Lord said, 'and go into G482
Ac 22:16 **Get u**, be baptized and wash your sins G482
Ac 23: 9 who were Pharisees **stood u** and argued G482
Ac 24: 5 **stirring u** riots among the Jews all over G3075
Ac 24:11 twelve days ago I **went u** to Jerusalem to G326
Ac 24:12 or **stirring u** a crowd in the G2180+4472
Ac 25: 1 Festus **went u** from Caesarea to Jerusalem G326
Ac 25: 9 "Are you willing *to* **go u** to Jerusalem and G326
Ac 25:18 *When* his accusers **got u** to speak, they did G2705
Ac 26:16 'Now **get u** and stand on your feet. I have G482
Ac 27:20 we finally **gave u** all hope of being saved. G4311
Ac 27:21 Paul **stood u** before them and said: G2705
Ac 27:22 But now I urge you *to* **keep u** your **courage** G2313
Ac 27:25 So **keep u** *your* **courage**, men, for I have G2313
Ac 28: 6 expected him to **swell u** or suddenly fall G4399
Ac 28:13 The next day the south wind **came u**, and G2104
Ro 2: 5 *you are* **storing u** wrath against yourself G2564
Ro 8:22 of childbirth **right u to** the present time. G948
Ro 8:32 own Son, but **gave him u** for us all—how G4140
Ro 9:17 "*I* **raised** you **u** for this very purpose, that I G1995
Ro 10: 7 that is, *to* **bring** Christ **u** from the dead). G343
Ro 13: 9 *are* **summed u** in this one command: G368
Ro 13:11 come for you *to* **wake u** from your slumber G1586
Ro 14:13 **make u** *your* **mind** not to put any G3212
Ro 15: 2 neighbors for their good, to **build** them **u**. G3869
Ro 15:12 "The Root of Jesse *will* **spring u**, one who G1639
1Co 3:15 If it *is* **burned u**, the builder will suffer loss G2876
1Co 4: 6 Then *you will* not *be* **puffed u** in being a G5881
1Co 4:13 of the world—**right u to** this moment. G2401
1Co 7:37 *who has* **made u** his mind not to G3212
1Co 8: 1 But knowledge **puffs u** while love builds G5881
1Co 8: 1 knowledge puffs up while love **builds u**. G3868
1Co 9:12 *we* **put u with** anything rather than hinder G5095
1Co 10: 7 to eat and drink and **got u** to indulge in G482
1Co 12:14 so the body *is* not **made u of** one part G1639
1Co 14:12 to excel in those that **build u** the church. G3869
1Co 14:26 done so that the church may be **built u**. G3869
1Co 15:54 "Death *has been* **swallowed u** in victory." G2927
1Co 16: 2 your income, **saving** it **u**, so that when I G2564
2Co 2: 1 So *I* **made u** my **mind** that I would not G3212
2Co 5: 4 is mortal *may be* **swallowed u** by life. G2927
2Co 8: 2 extreme poverty **welled u** in rich G4355
2Co 10: 5 pretension *that* **sets** *itself* **u** against the G2048
2Co 10: 8 gave us for **building** you **u** rather than G3869
2Co 11: 1 I hope *you will* **put u with** me in a little G462
2Co 11: 1 Yes, *please* **put u with** me! G462
2Co 11: 4 accepted, *you* **put u with** it easily enough. G462
2Co 11:19 *You* gladly **put u with** fools since you are so G462
2Co 11:20 *you* even **put u with** anyone who enslaves G462
2Co 12: 2 years ago *was* **caught u** to the third G773
2Co 12: 4 *was* **caught u** to paradise and heard G773
2Co 12:14 should not have *to* **save u** for their parents G2564
2Co 13:10 the Lord gave me for **building** you **u**, G3869
Gal 1:17 *I did* not **go u** to Jerusalem to see those G456
Gal 1:18 *I* **went u** to Jerusalem to get acquainted G456
Gal 2: 1 fourteen years, *I* **went u** again to Jerusalem G326
Gal 3:22 But Scripture *has* **locked u** everything G5168
Gal 3:23 **locked u** until the faith that was to come G5168
Gal 6: 9 we will reap a harvest *if we do* not **give u**. G1725
Eph 2: 6 And God **raised** us **u with** Christ and G5283
Eph 4:12 so that the body of Christ may be **built u** G3869
Eph 4:16 grows and **builds** itself **u** in love, as each G3869
Eph 4:29 helpful for **building** others **u** according to G3869
Eph 5: 2 loved us and **gave** himself **u** for us as a G4140
Eph 5:14 "**Wake u**, sleeper, rise from the dead, and G1586
Eph 5:25 the church and **gave** himself **u** for her G4140
Eph 6: 4 **bring** them **u** in the training and G1763
Eph 6:16 to all this, **take u** the shield of faith G377
Php 1:17 supposing *that they can* **stir u** trouble for G1586
Php 2:30 risked his life to **make u for** the help you G405
Php 3:16 Only *let us* **live u** to what we have already G5123
Col 1: 5 from the hope **stored u** for you in heaven G641
Col 1:24 and *I* **fill u** in my flesh what is still lacking G499
Col 2: 7 rooted and **built u** in him, strengthened in G2224
Col 2:18 *they are* **puffed u** with idle notions by G5881
1Th 2: 5 did we put on a **mask to cover u** greed— G4733
1Th 2:16 they always **heap u** their sins **to the limit**. G405
1Th 4:17 are left *will be* **caught u** together with G773
1Th 5:11 one another and **build** each other **u**, G3868
2Th 2: 4 so that *he* **sets** himself **u** in God's temple G2767
1Ti 2: 8 **lifting u** holy hands without anger or G2048
1Ti 3:16 on in the world, *was* **taken u** in glory. G377
1Ti 5:10 such as **bringing u children**, showing G5452
1Ti 6:19 In this way *they will* **lay u treasure** for G631
2Ti 4: 3 when *people will* not **put u with** sound G462
Heb 1:12 *You will* **roll** them **u** like a robe; like a G1813
Heb 5: 7 he **offered u** prayers and petitions with G4712
Heb 8: 2 the true tabernacle **set u** *by* the Lord, not G4381
Heb 9: 2 A tabernacle *was* **set u**. In its first room G2941
Heb 10:25 not **giving u** meeting together, as some G1593
Heb 11:24 Moses, *when he had* **grown u** G3489+1181
Heb 12:15 no bitter root grows **u** to cause trouble and G539
Jas 4:10 before the Lord, and *he will* **lift** you **u**. G5738
Jas 5:15 person well; the Lord *will* **raise** them **u**. G1586
1Pe 2: 2 so that by it *you may* **grow u** in your G889
1Pe 2:19 if *someone* **bears u** under the G5722
1Pe 5: 6 that *he may* **lift** you **u** in due time. G5738
Jude 7 **gave** *themselves* **u to sexual immorality** G1745
Jude 13 waves of the sea, **foaming u** their shame G2072
Jude 20 *by* **building** yourselves **u** in your most holy G2224
Rev 3: 2 **Wake u**! Strengthen what remains G1181+1213
Rev 3: 3 But if *you do* not **wake u**, I will come like G1213
Rev 4: 1 a trumpet said, "**Come u** here, and I will G326
Rev 6:14 receded like a scroll *being* **rolled u**, G1813
Rev 7: 2 saw another angel **coming u** from the east, G326
Rev 8: 4 **went u** before God from the angel's hand. G326
Rev 8: 7 A third of the earth *was* **burned u**, a third G2876
Rev 8: 7 a third of the trees *were* **burned u**, and all G2876
Rev 8: 7 and all the green grass *was* **burned u**. G2876
Rev 10: 4 "**Seal u** what the seven thunders have G5381
Rev 11: 6 They have power *to* **shut u** the heavens so G3091
Rev 11: 7 the beast that **comes u** from the Abyss will G326
Rev 11:12 heaven saying to them, "**Come u** here." G326
Rev 11:12 And *they* **went u** to heaven in a cloud G326
Rev 12: 5 And her child *was* **snatched u** to God and G773
Rev 13:14 It ordered them *to* **set u** an image in G4472
Rev 16:12 its water *was* **dried u** to prepare the G3830
Rev 17: 8 yet will **come u** out of the Abyss and G326
Rev 18: 5 her sins *are* **piled u** to heaven, and G3140
Rev 18:21 a mighty angel **picked u** a boulder the size G149
Rev 19: 3 smoke from her **goes u** for ever and ever G326
Rev 20:13 The sea **gave u** the dead that were in it G1443
Rev 20:13 death and Hades **gave u** the dead that G1443
Rev 22:10 "*Do* not **seal u** the words of the prophecy G5381

UPBRAID, UPBRAIDED, UPBRAIDETH (KJV)
DENOUNCE, FINDING FAULT, REBUKED, TAUNTED

UPHARSIN (KJV) PARSIN

UPHAZ (2)
Jer 10: 9 is brought from Tarshish and gold from **U**. H233
Da 10: 5 a belt of fine gold from **U** around his waist. H233

UPHELD (4) [UPHOLD]
1Sa 25:39 who *has* **u** my cause against Nabal for H8189
2Ch 20:20 in the LORD your God and *you will* **be u**; H586
Ps 9: 4 For *you have* **u** my right and my cause H6913
Isa 46: 3 you whom I *have* **u** since your birth H6673

UPHOLD (17) [UPHELD, UPHOLDING, UPHOLDS]
Dt 27:26 is anyone who *does* not **u** the words of H7756
Dt 32:51 *you did* not **u** my **holiness** among H7727
1Sa 24:15 May he consider my cause and **u** it; may H8189
1Ki 8:45 prayer and their plea, and **u** their cause. H6913
1Ki 8:49 prayer and their plea, and **u** their cause. H6913
1Ki 8:59 that he *may* **u** the cause of his servant H6913
2Ch 6:35 prayer and their plea, and **u** their cause. H6913
2Ch 6:39 prayer and their pleas, and **u** their cause. H6913
2Ch 9: 8 Israel and his desire to **u** them forever, H6641
Ps 41:12 of my integrity *you* **u** me and set me in H9461
Ps 82: 3 **u the cause** *of* the poor and the H7405
Ps 119:117 **U** me, and I will be delivered; I will H6184
Isa 34: 8 a year of retribution, to **u** Zion's **cause**. H8189
Isa 41:10 *I will* **u** you with my righteous right hand. H9461
Isa 42: 1 my servant, whom *I* **u**, my chosen one in H9461
La 3:59 seen the wrong done to me. **U** my cause! H9149
Ro 3:31 Not at all! Rather, *we* **u** the law. G2705

UPHOLDING (1) [UPHOLD]
Isa 9: 7 establishing and **u** it with justice and H6184

UPHOLDS (8) [UPHOLD]
Ps 37:17 be broken, but the LORD **u** the righteous. H6164
Ps 37:24 not fall, for the LORD **u** him *with* his hand. H6164
Ps 63: 8 I cling to you; your right hand **u** me. H9461
Ps 140:12 the poor and **u** the cause of the needy. NDT
Ps 145:14 The LORD **u** all who fall and lifts up all H6164
Ps 146: 7 *He* **u** the cause of the oppressed and H6913
Am 5:10 who hate the *one who* **u justice** in court H3519
Mic 7: 9 until he pleads my case and **u** my cause. H6913

UPHOLSTERED (1)
SS 3:10 Its seat was **u** with purple, its interior inlaid NDT

UPLIFTED (13) [LIFT]
Ex 6: 8 to the land I **swore with u** hand to give to H5951
Nu 14:30 the land I **swore with u** hand to make H5951
Ne 9:15 of the land *you had* **sworn with u** hand to H5951
Ps 106:26 So *he* **swore** to them **with u** hand that he H5951
Isa 19:16 with fear at the **u** hand that the LORD H9485
Eze 20: 5 I **swore with u** hand to the descendants of H5951
Eze 20: 5 *With* **u** hand I said to them, "I am the H5951
Eze 20:15 Also **with u** hand I **swore** to them in the H5951
Eze 20:23 Also **with u** hand I **swore** to them in the H5951
Eze 20:42 the land I *had* **sworn with u** hand to give H5951
Eze 36: 7 I **swear with u** hand that the nations H5951
Eze 44:12 therefore I *have* **sworn with u** hand that H5951
Eze 47:14 Because I **swore with u** hand to give it to H5951

UPON (103) See Index of Articles Etc.

UPPER (44) [UP]
Ge 6:16 ark and make lower, middle and **u** *decks*. H8958
Dt 24: 6 not even the **u one**—as security for a debt H8207
Jos 15:19 Caleb gave her the **u** and lower springs. H6606
Jos 16: 5 Ataroth Addar in the east to **U** Beth Horon H6609
Jdg 1:15 Caleb gave her the **u** and lower springs. H6606
Jdg 3:20 alone in the **u room** *of* his palace and H6608
Jdg 3:23 the doors of the **u room** behind him and H6608
Jdg 3:24 found the doors of the **u room** locked. H6608
Jdg 9:53 a woman dropped an **u** millstone on his H8207
2Sa 11:21 a woman drop an **u** millstone on him H8207
1Ki 17:19 carried him to the **u room** where he was H6608
2Ki 1: 2 the lattice of his **u room** in Samaria and H6608
2Ki 15:35 Jotham rebuilt the **U** Gate of the temple H6609
2Ki 18:17 stopped at the aqueduct of the **U** Pool, H6609
2Ki 23:12 on the roof near the **u room** *of* Ahaz, H6608
1Ch 7:24 who built Lower and **U** Beth Horon as well H6609
1Ch 26:16 Gate on the **u** road fell to Shuppim H6590
1Ch 28:11 its storerooms, its **u parts**, its inner rooms H6608
2Ch 3: 9 He also overlaid the **u parts** with gold. H6608
2Ch 8: 5 He rebuilt **U** Beth Horon and Lower Beth H6609
2Ch 23:20 palace through the **U** Gate and seated H6609
2Ch 27: 3 Jotham rebuilt the **U** Gate of the temple of H6609
2Ch 32:30 who blocked the **u** outlet of the Gihon H6609
Ne 3:25 projecting from the **u** palace near the H6609
Est 9: 1 the Jews **got the u hand** over those H8948
Ps 104: 3 beams of his **u chambers** on their waters H6608
Ps 104:13 the mountains from his **u chambers**; H6608
Isa 7: 3 at the end of the aqueduct of the **U** Pool, H6609
Isa 11:11 Lower Egypt, from **U Egypt**, from Cush, H7356
Isa 36: 2 stopped at the aqueduct of the **U** Pool, H6609
Jer 20: 2 in the stocks at the **U** Gate of Benjamin at H6609
Jer 22:13 unrighteousness, his **u rooms** by injustice H6608
Jer 22:14 a great palace with spacious **u rooms**. H6608
Jer 36:10 which was in the **u** courtyard at the H6609
Jer 44: 1 and Memphis—and in **U Egypt**: H824+7356
Jer 44:15 the people living in Lower and **U** Egypt, H7356
Eze 9: 2 coming from the direction of the **u** gate, H6609
Eze 29:14 captivity and return them to **U Egypt**, H824+7356
Eze 30:14 I will lay waste **U Egypt**, set fire to Zoan H7356
Eze 42: 5 Now the **u** rooms were narrower, for the H6609
Eze 43:14 lower ledge to the **u** ledge that goes H1524
Eze 43:17 The **u** ledge also is square, fourteen cubits NDT
Eze 43:20 four corners of the **u** ledge and all around NDT
Eze 45:19 four corners of the **u** ledge of the altar and NDT

UPRAISED (6) [RISE]

Job 38:15 their light, and their **u** arm is broken. H8123
Isa 5:25 is not turned away, his hand *is* still **u**. H5742
Isa 9:12 is not turned away, his hand *is* still **u**. H5742
Isa 9:17 is not turned away, his hand *is* still **u**. H5742
Isa 9:21 is not turned away, his hand *is* still **u**. H5742
Isa 10: 4 is not turned away, his hand *is* still **u**. H5742

UPRIGHT (69) [UPRIGHTLY, UPRIGHTNESS, UPRIGHTS]

Ge 37: 7 suddenly my sheaf rose and **stood u**, H5893
Ex 26:15 "Make **u** frames of acacia wood for the H6641
Ex 36:20 They made **u** frames of acacia wood for H6641
Dt 32: 4 God who does no wrong, **u** and just is he. H7404
1Ki 2:32 were better men and more **u** than he. H7404
1Ki 3: 6 to you and righteous and **u** *in* heart. H3842
Job 1: 1 This man was blameless and **u**; he feared H3838
Job 1: 8 he is blameless and **u**, a man who fears H3838
Job 2: 3 he is blameless and **u**, a man who fears H3838
Job 4: 7 Where were the **u** ever destroyed? H3838
Job 8: 6 if you are pure and **u**, even now he will H3838
Job 17: 8 The **u** are appalled at this; the innocent H3838
Job 23: 7 There the **u** can establish their innocence H3838
Job 33: 3 My words come from an **u** heart; my lips H3841
Job 33:23 a thousand, sent to tell them how to be **u**, H3841
Ps 7:10 God Most High, who saves the **u** *in* heart. H3838
Ps 11: 2 shoot from the shadows at the **u** *in* heart. H3838
Ps 11: 7 he loves justice; the **u** will see his face. H3838
Ps 25: 8 Good and **u** is the LORD; therefore he H3838
Ps 32:11 all you *who* are **u** in heart! H3838
Ps 33: 1 it is fitting for the **u** to praise him. H3838
Ps 36:10 your righteousness to the **u** *in* heart. H3838
Ps 37:14 to slay *those* whose ways are **u**. H3838
Ps 37:37 observe the **u**; a future awaits those H3838
Ps 49:14 the **u** will prevail over them in the H3838
Ps 64:10 all the **u** *in* heart will glory in him! H3838
Ps 92:15 "The LORD is **u**; he is my Rock, H3838
Ps 94:15 all the **u** *in* heart will follow it. H3838
Ps 97:11 the righteous and joy on the **u** *in* heart. H3838
Ps 107:42 The **u** see and rejoice, but all the wicked H3838
Ps 111: 1 the council of the **u** and in the assembly. H3838
Ps 112: 2 the generation of the **u** will be blessed. H3838
Ps 112: 4 Even in darkness light dawns for the **u**, for H3838
Ps 119: 7 praise you with an **u** heart as I learn your H3841
Ps 125: 4 are good, to *those who* are **u** in heart. H3838
Ps 140:13 the **u** will live in your presence. H3838
Pr 2: 7 He holds success in store for the **u**, he is a H3838
Pr 2:21 For the **u** will live in the land, and the H3838
Pr 3:32 takes the **u** into his confidence. H3838
Pr 8: 9 they are **u** to those who have found H3838
Pr 11: 3 The integrity of the **u** guides them, but H3838
Pr 11: 6 The righteousness of the **u** delivers them H3838
Pr 11:11 the blessing of the **u** a city is exalted, H3838
Pr 12: 6 the speech of the **u** rescues them. H3838
Pr 14: 9 but goodwill is found among the **u**. H3838
Pr 14:11 the tent of the **u** will flourish. H3838
Pr 15: 7 The hearts of fools are not **u**. H4026
Pr 15: 8 the prayer of the **u** pleases him. H3838
Pr 15:19 but the path of the **u** is a highway. H3838
Pr 16:17 The highway of the **u** avoids evil; those H3838
Pr 20:11 so is their conduct really pure and **u**? H3838
Pr 21: 8 the conduct of the innocent is **u**. H2341
Pr 21:18 the righteous, and the unfaithful for the **u**. H3838
Pr 21:29 but the **u** give thought to their ways. H3838
Pr 28:10 Whoever leads the **u** along an evil path H3838
Pr 29:10 a person of integrity and seek to kill the **u**. H3838
Pr 29:27 dishonest; the wicked detest the **u**. H3838+2006
Ecc 7:28 I found one **u** man among a thousand NDT
Ecc 7:28 not one **u** woman among them all. NDT
Ecc 7:29 God created mankind **u**, but they have H3838
Ecc 12:10 and what he wrote was **u** and true. H3841
Isa 26: 7 the **U** *One*, make the way of the H3838
Mic 2: 7 do good to the one whose ways are **u**? H3838
Mic 7: 2 from the land; not one **u** person remains. H3838
Mic 7: 4 the most **u** worse than a thorn hedge. H3838
Hab 2: 4 his desires *are* not **u**—but the H3837
Lk 23:50 of the Council, a good and **u** man, G1465
Titus 1: 8 is self-controlled, **u**, holy and disciplined. G1465
Titus 2:12 **u** and godly lives in this present age G1469

UPRIGHTLY (2) [UPRIGHT]

Pr 14: 2 Whoever fears the LORD walks **u**, but H928+3841
Isa 57: 2 Those who walk **u** enter into peace; they H5791

UPRIGHTNESS (5) [UPRIGHT]

1Ki 9: 4 me faithfully with integrity of heart and **u**, H3841
Ps 25:21 May integrity and **u** protect me, because H3841
Ps 111: 8 ever, enacted in faithfulness and **u**. H3838
Isa 26:10 even in a land of **u** they go on doing evil H5791
Mal 2: 6 He walked with me in peace and **u**, and H4793

UPRIGHTS (3) [UPRIGHT]

1Ki 7:28 They had side panels attached to **u**. H8918
1Ki 7:29 On the panels between the **u** were lions H8918
1Ki 7:29 cherubim—and on the **u** as well. H8918

UPRISING (2) [RISE]

Mk 15: 7 who had committed murder in the **u**. G5087
Jn 18:40 Barabbas *had* **taken part in an u**. G1639+3334

UPRISINGS (1) [RISE]

Lk 21: 9 When you hear of wars and **u**, do not be G189

UPROAR (15)

1Sa 4: 6 Hearing the **u**, the Philistines asked, H7754+9558
1Sa 4:14 "What is the meaning of this **u**?" H7754+2162
Ps 46: 6 Nations *are* **in u**, kingdoms fall; he lifts H2159
Ps 74:23 adversaries, the **u** *of* your enemies, which H8623
Isa 13: 4 an **u** *among* the kingdoms, like H8623
Isa 25: 5 You silence the **u** *of* foreigners; as heat is H8623
Isa 33: 3 At the **u** *of* your army, the peoples flee H7754
Isa 66: 6 Hear that **u** from the city, hear that noise H8623
Mt 27:24 that instead an **u** was starting, he took G2573
Ac 16:20 and *are* **throwing** our city **into an u** G1752
Ac 19:29 the whole city *was* **in an u**. G4398+3836+5180
Ac 20: 1 When the **u** had ended, Paul sent for the G2573
Ac 21:31 the whole city of Jerusalem *was* **in an u**. G5177
Ac 21:34 not get at the truth because of the **u**, G2573
Ac 23: 9 There was a great **u**, and some of the G3199

UPROOT (16) [UPROOTED, UPROOTS]

1Ki 14:15 *He will* **u** Israel from this good land that H6004
2Ch 7:20 then *I will* **u** Israel from my land, which I H6004
Ps 52: 5 *he will* **u** you from the land of the living. H9245
Ps 59:11 In your might **u** them and bring them H5675
Ecc 3: 2 a time to plant and a time to **u**, H6827
Jer 1:10 kingdoms to **u** and tear down, H6004
Jer 12:14 I *will* **u** them from their lands and I will H6004
Jer 12:14 their lands and *I will* **u** the people of H6004
Jer 12:15 But after I **u** them, I will again have H6004
Jer 12:17 *I will* **completely u** and destroy it," H6004+6004
Jer 24: 6 I will plant them and not **u** them. H6004
Jer 31:28 I watched over them to **u** and tear down, H6004
Jer 42:10 I will plant you and not **u** you, for I have H6004
Jer 45: 4 I have built and **u** what I have planted, H6004
Mic 5:14 *I will* **u** from among you your Asherah H6004
Mt 13:29 *you may* **u** the wheat with them. G1748

UPROOTED (17) [UPROOT]

Dt 28:63 *You will* **be u** from the land you are H5815
Dt 29:28 wrath the LORD **u** them from their land H6004
Job 31: 8 I have sown, and *may* my crops **be u**. H9245
Job 31:12 Destruction; *it would have* **u** my harvest. H9245
Ps 9: 6 my enemies, *you have* **u** their cities; even H6004
Pr 10:30 The righteous *will* never **be u**, but the H4572
Pr 12: 3 the righteous cannot **be u**. H4572+9247
Jer 18: 7 that a nation or kingdom *is to be* **u**, H6004
Jer 31:40 The city *will* never again **be u** or H6004
Eze 17: 9 *Will* it not *be* **u** and stripped of its H5998+9247
Eze 19:12 But *it* **was u** in fury and thrown to the H6004
Da 7: 8 three of the first horns **were u** before it. A10566
Da 11: 4 because his empire *will* **be u** and given to H6004
Am 9:15 never again *to* **be u** from the land I have H6004
Zep 2: 4 Ashdod will be emptied and Ekron **u**. H6827
Lk 17: 6 '*Be* **u** and planted in the sea G1748
Jude 12 without fruit and **u**—twice dead. G1748

UPROOTS (1) [UPROOT]

Job 19:10 till I am gone; *he* **u** my hope like a tree. H5825

UPSET (2)

2Sa 11:25 'Don't *let* this **u** you; the H8317+928+6524
Lk 10:41 are worried and **u** about many things, G2571

UPSIDE (2)

2Ki 21:13 wiping it and turning it **u down**. H6584+7156
Isa 29:16 You **turn** things **u down**, as if the potter H2201

UPSTAIRS (8) [STAIRS]

Da 6:10 went home to his **u room** where the A10547
Mk 14:15 He will show you a large **room u**, furnished G333
Lk 22:12 He will show you a large **room u**, all G333
Ac 1:13 they went **u** to the **room** where they were G5673
Ac 9:37 was washed and placed in an **u room**. G5673
Ac 9:39 he arrived he was taken **u** to the **room**. G5673
Ac 20: 8 many lamps in the **u room** where we were G5673
Ac 20:11 Then *he* **went u** *again* and broke bread G326

UPSTREAM (1) [STREAM]

Jos 3:16 the water from **u** stopped H4200+5087+2025

UPWARD (11) [UP]

Ex 25:20 have their wings spread **u**, H4200+5087+2025
Ex 37: 9 had their wings spread **u**, H4200+5087+2025
Job 5: 7 is born to trouble as surely as sparks fly **u**. H1467
Pr 15:24 of life leads **u** for the H4200+5087+2025
Ecc 3:21 spirit rises **u** and if the spirit H4200+5087+2025
Isa 8:21 looking **u**, will curse H4200+5087+2025
Isa 9:18 so that *it* **rolls u** *in* a column of smoke. H60
Eze 1:11 wings spreading out **u**, H4946+4200+5087+2025
Eze 10:15 Then the cherubim **rose u**. These were H8250
Eze 41: 7 widened as one went **u**. H4200+5087+2025
Eze 43:15 four horns **project u** from the H4200+5087+2025

UR (5)

Ge 11:28 Haran died in **U** *of* the Chaldeans, in H243
Ge 11:31 they set out from **U** *of* the Chaldeans to go H243
Ge 15: 7 brought you out of **U** *of* the Chaldeans to H243
1Ch 11:35 son of Sakar the Hararite, Eliphal son of **U**, H244
Ne 9: 7 brought him out of **U** *of* the Chaldeans H243

URBANUS (1)

Ro 16: 9 Greet **U**, our co-worker in Christ, and my G4042

URGE (22) [URGED, URGENT, URGENTLY, URGING]

Ru 1:16 "Don't **u** me to leave you or to turn back H7003
Ac 27:22 But now *I* **u** you to keep up your courage G4147
Ac 27:34 Now *I* **u** you to take some food. You need G4151
Ro 12: 1 Therefore, *I* **u** you, brothers and sisters, in G4151
Ro 15:30 *I* **u** you, brothers and sisters, by our Lord G4151
Ro 16:17 *I* **u** you, brothers and sisters, to watch out G4151
1Co 4:16 Therefore *I* **u** you to imitate me. G4151
1Co 16:15 of the Lord's people. *I* **u** you, brothers G4151
2Co 2: 8 *I* **u** you, therefore, to reaffirm your love G4151
2Co 6: 1 God's co-workers *we* **u** you not to receive G4151
2Co 9: 5 thought it necessary *to* **u** the brothers to G4151
Eph 4: 1 *I* **u** you to live a life worthy of the calling G4151
1Th 4: 1 Now we ask you and **u** you in the Lord G4151
1Th 4:10 Yet *we* **u** you, brothers and sisters, to do G4151
1Th 5:14 And *we* **u** you, brothers and sisters, warn G4151
2Th 3:12 we command and **u** in the Lord Jesus G4151
1Ti 2: 1 *I* **u**, then, first of all, that petitions, prayers, G4151
Titus 2: 4 Then *they can* **u** the younger women to G5405
Heb 13:19 *I* particularly **u** you to pray so that I may be G4151
Heb 13:22 *I* **u** you to bear with my word of G4151
1Pe 2:11 Dear friends, *I* **u** you, as foreigners and G4151
Jude 3 to write and **u** you to contend for the G4151

URGED (27) [URGE]

Ge 19:15 coming of dawn, the angels **u** Lot, saying, H237
Ex 12:33 The Egyptians **u** the people to hurry and H2616
Jos 15:18 *she* **u** him to ask her father for a field. H6077
Jdg 1:14 *she* **u** him to ask her father for a field. H6077
1Sa 24:10 *Some* **u** me to kill you, but I spared you; H606
2Sa 3:35 all came and **u** David **to eat** something H1356
2Sa 13:25 Although Absalom **u** him, he still H7287
2Sa 13:27 But Absalom **u** him, so he sent with him H7287
1Ki 21:25 eyes of the LORD, **u on** *by* Jezebel his wife. H6077
2Ki 4: 8 was there, *who* **u** him to stay for a meal. H2616
2Ki 5:16 And even though Naaman **u** him, he H7210
2Ki 5:23 *He* **u** Gehazi to accept them, and then H7287
2Ch 18: 2 people with him and **u** him to attack H6077
Jer 36:25 Gemariah **u** the king not to burn H7003
Da 2:18 He **u** them to plead for mercy from the God NDT
Mt 15:23 So his disciples came to him and **u** him G2263
Lk 24:29 But *they* **u** him **strongly**, "Stay with us, for G4128
Jn 4:31 Meanwhile his disciples **u** him, "Rabbi G2263
Jn 4:40 came to him, *they* **u** him to stay with them G2263
Ac 9:38 they sent two men to him and **u** him G4151
Ac 13:43 with them and **u** them to continue in G4275
Ac 21: 4 the Spirit they **u** Paul not to go on to G3306
Ac 27:33 Just before dawn Paul **u** them all to eat G4151
1Co 16:12 *I* strongly **u** him to go to you with the G4151
2Co 8: 6 So we **u** Titus, just as he had earlier made G4151
2Co 12:18 *I* **u** Titus to go to you and I sent our brother G4151
1Ti 1: 3 As *I* **u** you when I went into Macedonia G4151

URGENT (4) [URGE]

Nu 22:37 "*Did I* not **send** you an **u** summons? H8938+8938
1Sa 21: 8 because the king's mission was **u**. H5722
Da 3:22 king's command *was* so **u** and the A10280
Titus 3:14 in order to provide for **u** needs and not live G338

URGENTLY (2) [URGE]

Jnh 3: 8 Let everyone call **u** on God. Let them H928+2622
2Co 8: 4 they **u** pleaded with us for G3552+4498+4155

URGING (3) [URGE]

Ru 1:18 to go with her, she stopped **u** her. H1819
1Sa 28:23 But his men joined the woman in **u** him H7287
1Th 2:12 comforting and **u** you to live lives worthy G3458

URI (8)

Ex 31: 2 I have chosen Bezalel son of **U**, the son of H247
Ex 35:30 the LORD has chosen Bezalel son of **U**, the H247
Ex 38:22 Bezalel son of **U**, the son of Hur, of the tribe H247
1Ki 4:19 Geber son of **U**—in Gilead (the country of H788
1Ch 2:20 Hur was the father of **U**, and Uri the father H247
1Ch 2:20 father of Uri, and **U** the father of Bezalel. H247
2Ch 1: 5 But the bronze altar that Bezalel son of **U** H247
Ezr 10:24 the gatekeepers: Shallum, Telem and **U**. H247

URIAH (34) [URIAH'S]

2Sa 11: 3 of Eliam and the wife of **U** the Hittite." H249
2Sa 11: 6 "Send me **U** the Hittite." And Joab H249
2Sa 11: 7 When **U** came to him, David asked him H249
2Sa 11: 8 Then David said to **U**, "Go down to your H249
2Sa 11: 8 So **U** left the palace, and a gift from the H249
2Sa 11: 9 But **U** slept at the entrance to the palace H249
2Sa 11:10 David was told, "**U** did not go home." H249
2Sa 11:10 So he asked **U**, "Haven't you just come H249
2Sa 11:11 **U** said to David, "The ark and Israel and H249
2Sa 11:12 So **U** remained in Jerusalem that day and H249
2Sa 11:13 But in the evening **U** went out to sleep on NDT
2Sa 11:14 wrote a letter to Joab and sent it with **U**. H249
2Sa 11:15 "Put **U** out in front where the fighting is H249
2Sa 11:16 he put **U** at a place where he knew the H249
2Sa 11:17 army fell; moreover, **U** the Hittite died. H249
2Sa 11:21 your servant **U** the Hittite is dead. H249
2Sa 11:24 your servant **U** the Hittite is dead. H249
2Sa 12: 9 You struck down **U** the Hittite with the H249
2Sa 12:10 took the wife of **U** the Hittite to be your H249
2Sa 23:39 **U** the Hittite. There were thirty-seven H249
1Ki 15: 5 his life—except in the case of **U** the Hittite. H249
2Ki 16:10 Damascus and sent to **U** the priest a sketch H249
2Ki 16:11 So **U** the priest built an altar in accordance H249
2Ki 16:15 then gave these orders to **U** the priest: H249
2Ki 16:16 And **U** the priest did just as King Ahaz had H249
1Ch 11:41 **U** the Hittite, Zabad son of Ahlai, H249

Ezr 8:33 into the hands of Meremoth son of U, H249
Ne 3: 4 Meremoth son of U, the son of Hakkoz H249
Ne 3:21 Meremoth son of U, the son of Hakkoz, H249
Ne 8: 4 Anaiah, U, Hilkiah and Maaseiah H249
Isa 8: 2 So I called in U the priest and Zechariah H249
Jer 26:20 U son of Shemaiah from Kiriath Jearim H250
Jer 26:21 But U heard of it and fled in fear to Egypt H250
Jer 26:23 They brought U out of Egypt and took him H250

URIAH'S (3) [URIAH]

2Sa 11:26 When U wife heard that her husband was H249
2Sa 12:15 struck the child that U wife had borne to H249
Mt 1: 6 whose mother had been U wife, G4043

URIAS, URIJAH (KJV) URIAH

URIEL (4)

1Ch 6:24 Tahath his son, U his son, Uzziah his son H248
1Ch 15: 5 of Kohath, U the leader and 120 relatives; H248
1Ch 15:11 Abiathar the priests, and U, Asaiah, H248
2Ch 13: 2 was Maakah, a daughter of U of Gibeah. H248

URIM (8)

Ex 28:30 Also put the U and the Thummim in the H242
Lev 8: 8 on him and put the U and Thummim in the H242
Nu 27:21 him by inquiring of the U before the LORD. H242
Dt 33: 8 "Your Thummim and U belong to your H242
1Sa 14:41 respond with U, but if the men of H242
1Sa 28: 6 answer him by dreams or U or prophets. H242
Ezr 2:63 ministering with the U and Thummim. H242
Ne 7:65 ministering with the U and Thummim. H242

URINE (4)

2Ki 18:27 own excrement and drink their own u?" H8875
Isa 36:12 own excrement and drink their own u?" H8875
Eze 7:17 will go limp; every leg will be wet with u. H4784
Eze 21: 7 faint and every leg will be wet with u. H4784

URUK (2)

Ge 10:10 were Babylon, U, Akkad and Kalneh, H804
Ezr 4: 9 people from Persia, U and Babylon, the A10074

US (1435) [WE] See Index of Articles Etc.

USE (89) [USED, USEFUL, USELESS, USES, USING]

Ex 5:12 over Egypt to gather stubble to u for straw. NDT
Ex 10:26 We have to u some of them in worshiping H4374
Ex 10:26 know what we are to u to worship the LORD." AIT
Ex 20:25 you will defile it if you u a tool on it. H5677
Ex 26: 6 fifty gold clasps and u them to fasten the H928
Ex 28: 5 Have them u gold, and blue, purple and H4374
Ex 30:16 the Israelites and u it for the service of H5989
Ex 30:26 Then u it to anoint the tent of meeting, the H928
Lev 11:32 whatever its u, will be unclean, H6913+4856
Lev 13:51 leather, whatever its u, it is a persistent H6913
Lev 19:35 "'Do not u dishonest standards when H6913
Lev 19:36 U honest scales and honest weights H2118+4200
Nu 3:26 ropes—and everything related to their u. H6275
Nu 3:31 and everything related to their u. H6275
Nu 3:36 everything related to their u, H6275
Nu 4:32 everything related to their u. H6275
Nu 10: 2 u them for calling the community H6913
Nu 19: 9 Israelite community for u in the water of H5466
Dt 14:26 U the silver to buy whatever you like: cattle AIT
Dt 20:14 And you may u the plunder the LORD your H430
Dt 20:20 fruit trees and u them to build siege works AIT
Dt 27: 5 Do not u any iron tool on them H5677
Dt 28:40 your country but you will not u the oil, H6057
Jdg 2:22 I will u them to test Israel and see whether H928
Jdg 18:31 They continued to u the idol Micah had H8492
Jdg 19:24 and you can u them and do to them H6700
1Sa 8:16 donkeys he will take for his own u. H6913+4856
2Sa 5: 8 Jebusites will have to u the water shaft to H928
2Sa 14: 2 clothes, and don't u any cosmetic lotions. H6057
1Ki 21: 2 have your vineyard to u for a vegetable H2118
2Ki 12: 5 then u it to repair whatever damage is found AIT
2Ki 16:15 But I will u the bronze altar for H2118+4200
2Ki 23:10 so no one could u it to sacrifice their son AIT
1Ch 5:18 sword, who could u a bow, and who H2005
1Ch 28:15 according to the u of each lampstand; H6275
2Ch 26:15 invented for u on the towers and on H2118
Job 19: 5 above me and u my humiliation against H3519S
Job 30: 2 Of what u was the strength of their H4200+4537
Ps 19: 3 no speech, they u no words; no sound is H401
Ps 50:19 You u your mouth for evil and harness H8938
Ps 102: 8 against me u my name as a curse. H8678+928
Ps 125: 3 righteous might u their hands to do evil. H8938
Pr 24:28 cause—would you u your lips to mislead? H928
Isa 7:20 In that day the Lord will u a razor hired from H928
Isa 28:28 one does not u horses to grind grain. H1990
Isa 32: 7 Scoundrels u wicked methods, they make up NDT
Isa 65:15 my chosen ones to u in their curses; H4200
Jer 2:22 soap and u an abundance of cleansing H8049
Jer 2:25 But you said, 'It's no u! I love foreign H3286
Jer 18:12 they will reply, 'It's no u. We will continue H3286
Jer 23:10 an evil course and u their power unjustly. NDT
Jer 29:22 who are in Babylon will u this curse: H4374
Jer 31:23 the people in the land of Judah and in its towns
will once again u H606
Eze 4: 9 storage jar and u them to make bread H6913
Eze 5: 1 a sharp sword and u it as a barber's razor H4374
Eze 23:43 'Now let them u her as a prostitute H2388+9373
Eze 39: 9 out and u the weapons for fuel and burn H1277
Eze 39: 9 seven years they will u them for fuel. H1277+836
Eze 39:10 they will u the weapons for fuel. H1277+836
Eze 45:10 You are to u accurate scales, an accurate H2118
Eze 48:15 will be for the common u of the city, for H2687
Am 2: 7 Father and son u the same girl and H2143+448
Am 6: 6 by the bowlful and u the finest lotions, H5417
Mic 6:15 you will press olives but not u the oil, you H6057
Mt 7: 2 with the measure you u, it will be G3582S
Mt 27: 7 they decided to u the money to buy the AIT
Mk 4:24 "With the measure you u, it will be G3582S
Mk 4:30 what parable shall we u to describe it? G5502
Lk 6:38 For with the measure you u, it will be G3582S
Lk 13: 7 Why should it u up the soil?' G2934
Lk 16: 9 u worldly wealth to gain friends for G1666
Jn 16:25 I will no longer u this kind of language G3281
Ac 5:26 They did not u force, because they feared G3552
Ro 9:21 special purposes and some for common u? G871
1Co 7:31 those who u the things of the world, as if G5968
1Co 9:12 But we did not u this right. G5968
1Co 9:18 so not make full u of my rights as a G2974
2Co 4: 2 ways; we do not u deception G4344+1877
2Co 13:10 I may not have to be harsh in my u of G5968
Gal 5:13 But do not u your freedom to indulge the NDT
Gal 6:11 what large letters I u as I write to you with NDT
Col 2:22 that are all destined to perish with u, G712
2Th 2: 9 He will u all sorts of displays of power G1877
1Ti 5:23 u a little wine because of your G5968
2Ti 2:20 special purposes and some for common u. G871
Heb 5:14 who by constant u have trained G2011
1Pe 2:16 but do not u your freedom as a cover-up G2400
1Pe 4:10 should u whatever gift you have received to serve G1354
2Jn 12 but I do not want to u paper and ink. G1328

USED (118) [USE]

Ge 11: 3 They u brick instead of stone, and tar for H2118
Ge 28:19 the city u to be called Luz. H4200+2021+8037
Ge 31:15 but he has u up what was paid for us. H430+430
Ge 40:13 just as you u to do when you were his H8037
Ge 41:36 to be u during the seven years of famine NDT
Ex 25:27 rim to hold the poles u in carrying the table. AIT
Ex 25:39 of pure gold is to be u for the lampstand H6913
Ex 27:19 All the other articles u in the service of the AIT
Ex 30: 4 to hold the poles u to carry it. H928
Ex 33: 7 Now Moses u to take a tent and pitch it AIT
Ex 36:13 fifty gold clasps and u them to fasten the H928
Ex 37:14 rim to hold the poles u in carrying the table. NDT
Ex 37:27 to hold the poles u to carry it. H928
Ex 38:21 of the materials u for the tabernacle, NDT
Ex 38:24 the wave offering u for all the work on H6913
Ex 38:27 talents of silver were u to cast the bases H2118
Ex 38:28 They u the 1,775 shekels to make the H6913
Ex 38:30 They u it to make the bases for the entrance H928
Ex 40:31 Aaron and his sons u it to wash their H4946
Lev 7:24 by wild animals may be u for any other H6913
Lev 16:10 the LORD to be u for making atonement by H6584
Lev 18: 3 in Egypt, where you u to live, and you must AIT
Nu 3:31 articles of the sanctuary u in ministering, H928
Nu 4: 9 all its jars for the olive oil u to supply it. H928
Nu 4:12 take all the articles u for ministering in the H928
Nu 4:14 on it all the utensils u for ministering at the H928
Nu 4:26 all the equipment u in the service of AIT
Nu 6: 5 no razor may be u on their head. H6296
Nu 7: 5 that they may be u in the work at the tent H6268
Nu 7:87 male goats were u for the sin offering. H4200
Dt 2:10 The Emites u to live there—a H4200+7156
Dt 2:12 Horites u to live in Seir, but the H4200+7156
Dt 2:20 Rephaites, who u to live there; but H4200+7156
Dt 3:13 in Bashan u to be known as a land of the AIT
Jos 8:31 on which no iron tool had been u. H5677
Jos 14:15 Hebron u to be called Kiriath Arba H4200+7156
Jdg 9: 4 Abimelek u it to hire reckless H928
Jdg 16:11 new ropes that have never been u, H6913+4856
Jdg 16:17 "No razor has ever been u on my head," H6590
Jdg 17: 4 silversmith, who u them to make the idol. H6913
Jdg 18:29 though the city u to be called H4200+2021+8037
1Sa 1:11 no razor will ever be u on his head." H6590
1Sa 9: 9 prophet of today u to be called a H4200+7156
1Sa 17:39 around, because he was not u to them. H5814
1Sa 17:39 to Saul, "because I am not u to them." H5814
2Sa 14:26 he u to cut his hair once a year because it H2118
2Sa 15:32 where people u to worship God, Hushai AIT
2Sa 20:18 "Long ago they u to say, 'Get your H1819+1819
1Ki 6: 7 only blocks dressed at the quarry were u H1215
1Ki 10:12 The king u the almugwood to make H6913
1Ki 17:14 jar of flour will not be u up and the jug of H3983
1Ki 17:16 jar of flour was not u up and the jug of H3983
2Ki 3:11 He u to pour water on the hands of Elijah." AIT
2Ki 10:27 and people have u it for a latrine to this H8492
2Ki 12:14 the workers, who u it to repair the temple. H928
2Ki 13:20 Moabite raiders u to enter the country every AIT
2Ki 21:13 the measuring line u against Samaria and AIT
2Ki 21:13 the plumb line u against the house of AIT
2Ki 25:14 the bronze articles u in the temple service. H928
1Ch 9:28 in charge of the articles u in the temple AIT
1Ch 18: 8 which Solomon u to make the bronze Sea H928
1Ch 23:26 any of the articles u in its service. H4200
1Ch 28:13 as for all the articles to be u in its service. AIT
1Ch 28:14 all the gold articles to be u in various kinds AIT
1Ch 28:14 all the silver articles to be u in various kinds AIT
2Ch 3: 6 And the gold he u was gold of Parvaim. NDT
2Ch 4: 6 In them the things to be u for the burnt AIT
2Ch 4: 6 the Sea was to be u by the priests for H4200
2Ch 7: 6 and which were u when he gave H928+3338
2Ch 9:11 The king u the algumwood to make steps H6913
2Ch 24: 7 temple of God and had u even its sacred H6913
Ne 13: 5 a large room formerly u to store the grain H2118
Job 1: 4 His sons u to hold feasts in their homes on AIT
Ps 42: 4 how I u to go to the house of God under the AIT
Pr 10: 7 name of the righteous is u in blessings, H4200
Ecc 8:10 those who u to come and go from the holy AIT
Isa 1:21 righteousness u to dwell in her—but now AIT
Isa 9: 5 Every warrior's boot u in battle and every NDT
Isa 44:15 It is u as fuel for burning; some of it he H4200
Isa 44:19 "Half of it I u for fuel; I even H8596+1198+836
Jer 23:38 You u the words, 'This is a message from H606
Jer 33: 4 been torn down to be u against the siege NDT
Jer 52:18 the bronze articles u in the temple service. H928
Jer 52:19 dishes and bowls u for drink offerings— H4984
Eze 7:20 beautiful jewelry and u it to make their H928
Eze 16:15 in your beauty and u your fame to H6584
Eze 19:14 is a lament and is to be u as a lament." H4200
Eze 45:15 These will be u for the grain offerings, NDT
Da 10: 3 and I u no lotions at all until the H6057+6057
Hos 2: 8 silver and gold—which they u for Baal. H6913
Hos 12:13 The LORD u a prophet to bring Israel up H928
Am 9:11 and will rebuild it as it u to be, H3427+6409
Mic 1: 7 wages of prostitutes they will again be u." H8740
Zec 9:15 like a bowl u for sprinkling the corners H4670
Mt 15: 5 might have been u to help their father or AIT
Mt 16:12 them to guard against the yeast u in bread, AIT
Mt 22:19 Show me the coin u for paying the tax." AIT
Mt 27:10 and they u them to buy the potter's field, as AIT
Mk 7:11 that what might have been u to help their AIT
Jn 2: 6 the kind u by the Jews for ceremonial G2848
Jn 5: 3 a great number of disabled people u to lie— AIT
Jn 9: 8 this the same man who u to sit and beg?" AIT
Jn 10: 6 Jesus u this figure of speech, but the G3306S
Jn 12: 6 he u to help himself to what was put into it. AIT
Ac 3:10 the same man who u to sit begging at the G1639
Ac 5:12 And all the believers u to meet together in AIT
Ro 6:17 to God that, though you u to be slaves to sin AIT
Ro 6:19 Just as you u to offer yourselves as slaves to AIT
Ro 7:13 it u what is good to bring about my death G1328
1Co 9:15 But I have not u any of these rights. And I G5968
Gal 2:12 from James, he u to eat with the Gentiles. AIT
Eph 2: 2 in which you u to live when you followed G4537
Php 2: 6 something to be u to his own advantage; G772
Col 3: 7 You u to walk in these ways, in the life G4537
1Th 2: 5 You know we never u flattery, nor G1877+1181
2Th 2: 5 I was with you I u to tell you these things? AIT
Heb 9:21 everything u in its ceremonies. AIT
1Pe 3: 5 put their hope in God u to adorn themselves. AIT

USEFUL (9) [USE]

Eze 15: 3 ever taken from it to make anything u? H4856
Eze 15: 4 chars the middle, is it then u for anything? H7503
Eze 15: 5 If it was not u for anything when it was H6913
Eze 15: 5 be made into something u when the fire H4856
Eph 4:28 doing something u with their own hands G19
2Ti 2:21 u to the Master and prepared to do any G2378
2Ti 3:16 is God-breathed and is u for teaching, G6068
Phm 11 now he has become u both to you and to G2378
Heb 6: 7 produces a crop u to those for whom it G2310

USELESS (17) [USE]

1Sa 12:21 Do not turn away after u idols. They can H9332
1Sa 12:21 can they rescue you, because they are u. H9332
1Sa 25:21 "It's been u—all my H4200+2021+9214
Job 15: 3 Would they argue with u words H4202+6122
Pr 1:17 How u to spread a net where every bird H2855
Pr 26: 7 Like the u legs of one who is lame is a H1927
Isa 30: 5 because of a people u to them, H4202+3603
Isa 30: 7 whose help is utterly u. H2039+2256+8198
Isa 59: 6 Their cobwebs are u for clothing; they H4202
Jer 13: 7 it was ruined and completely u. H4202+7503
Jer 13:10 will be like this belt—completely u! H4202+7503
Mal 1:10 you would not light u fires on my altar! H2855
1Co 15:14 our preaching is u and so is your faith. G3031
Titus 3: 9 because these are unprofitable and u. G3469
Phm 11 Formerly he was u to you, but now he has G947
Heb 7:18 is set aside because it was weak and u G543
Jas 2:20 evidence that faith without deeds is u? G734

USES (9) [USE]

Ge 44: 5 from and also u for divination? H5727+5727
1Sa 23:23 the hiding places he u and come back to H2461S
2Sa 23: 7 touches thorns u a tool of iron or the H4848
Pr 17:27 has knowledge u words with restraint, H3104
Isa 10:15 the saw boast against the one who u it? H5677
Eze 22: 6 Israel who are in you u his power to shed H4200
Hos 12: 7 The merchant u dishonest scales H928+3338
2Co 2:14 procession and u us to spread the aroma G1328
1Ti 1: 8 that the law is good if one u it properly. G5968

USHERS (1)

Pr 18:16 opens the way and u the giver into the H5697

USING (22) [USE]

Ge 42:23 since he was u an interpreter. H1068
Ex 30:32 not make any other oil u the same formula. H928
Lev 24: 5 u two-tenths of an ephah for each loaf. H2118
Nu 8:12 u one for a sin offering to the LORD and H6913
Jdg 6:26 U the wood of the Asherah pole that you H928
1Sa 14:13 climbed up, u his hands and feet H6584

1Ki 15:22 timber Baasha *had been* **u** there. H1215S
1Ch 25: 3 **u** the harp in thanking and praising the H928
2Ch 3: 3 cubits wide (**u** the cubit of the old standard). H928
2Ch 16: 6 stones and timber Baasha *had been* **u**. H1215S
Est 1:22 his own household, **u** his native tongue. H3869
Isa 22: 3 they have been captured **without** *u* the bow. AIT
Jer 21: 4 which you are **u** to fight the king of Babylon H928
Eze 4:12 of the people, **u** human excrement for fuel." H928
Mt 13:34 say anything to them **without** *u* a parable. AIT
Mk 4:34 say anything to them without **u** a parable. NDT
Jn 8: 6 *They were u* this **question** as a trap, in order AIT
Ac 7:25 that God was **u** him to rescue them *G1328+5931*
Ro 3: 5 (*I am* **u** a human argument. *G3306*
Ro 6:19 *I am* **u an example** from everyday life *G3306*
1Co 3:12 If anyone builds on this foundation *u* **gold** AIT
Rev 21:17 the wall **u** human measurement *G1639*

USUAL (6) [USUALLY]
1Sa 3: 2 barely see, was lying down in his **u** place. NDT
1Sa 17:23 from his lines and shouted his **u** defiance, H3869
1Sa 21: 5 **as u** whenever I set out. H3869+9453+8997
Da 3:19 heated seven times hotter than **u** A10255
Lk 22:39 went out **as u** to the Mount *G2848+3836+1621*
Ac 14: 1 Barnabas went **as u** into the *G2848+3836+899*

USUALLY (4) [USUAL]
1Sa 18:10 the lyre, **as** he **u did**. H3869+3427+928+3427
1Sa 23:22 out where David *u* **goes** and who has seen AIT
Eze 33:31 come to you, **as** they **u** do, and sit before H3869
Mk 15: 8 asked Pilate to do for them *what* he **u** did. *G2777*

USURY (NIV84) INTEREST

UTENSILS (13)
Ex 27: 3 Make all its **u** of bronze—its pots to H3998
Ex 30:28 the altar of burnt offering and all its **u**, and H3998
Ex 31: 9 the altar of burnt offering and all its **u**, the H3998
Ex 35:16 its poles and all its **u**; the bronze basin H3998
Ex 38: 3 They made all its **u** *of* bronze—its pots H3998
Ex 38:30 altar with its bronze grating and all its **u**, H3998
Ex 39:39 its poles and all its **u**; the basin with its H3998
Ex 40:10 the altar of burnt offering and all its **u**; H3998
Lev 8:11 the altar and all its **u** and the basin with H3998
Nu 4:14 place on it all the **u** used for ministering H3998
Nu 7: 1 consecrated the altar and all its **u**. H3998
2Ch 29:18 the altar of burnt offering with all its **u** H3998
Eze 40:42 were placed the **u** for slaughtering the H3998

UTHAI (2)
1Ch 9: 4 **U** son of Ammihud, the son of Omri, the H6433
Ezr 8:14 of Bigvai, **U** and Zakkur, and with H6433

UTMOST (4)
2Ki 19:23 the mountains, the **u heights** *of* Lebanon. H3752
Job 34:36 be tested to the **u** for answering like a H5905
Isa 14:13 on the **u heights** *of* Mount Zaphon. H3752
Isa 37:24 the mountains, the **u heights** *of* Lebanon. H3752

UTTER (32) [UTTERANCE, UTTERED, UTTERING, UTTERLY, UTTERS]
Nu 24:20 their end will be **u destruction**. H6330+7
Nu 30: 6 vow or after her lips **u** a rash promise by NDT
Dt 23:23 Whatever your lips **u** you must be sure to H4604
Jdg 17: 2 about which I heard you **u a curse**— H457
2Sa 12:14 *you have* **shown u contempt** *for* the H5540+5540
Job 3: 5 May gloom and **u darkness** claim it once H7516
Job 10:21 to the land of gloom and **u darkness**, H7516
Job 10:22 deepest night, of **u darkness** and disorder H7516
Job 12:22 brings **u darkness** into the light. H7516
Job 26: 4 Who has helped *you* **u** these words? And H5583
Job 27: 4 and my tongue *will* not **u** lies. H2047
Job 34:22 deep shadow, no **u darkness**, where H7516
Ps 31:11 I am the **u** contempt of my neighbors and H4394
Ps 37:30 The mouths of the righteous **u** wisdom H2047
Ps 59:12 For the curses and lies *they* **u**, H6218
Ps 78: 2 with a parable; *I will* **u** hidden things H5580
Ps 107:10 sat in darkness, in **u darkness**, prisoners H7516
Ps 107:14 darkness, the **u darkness**, and broke away H7516
Ps 115: 7 nor *can they* **u a sound** with their throats. H2047
Ecc 5: 2 in your heart to **u** anything before God. H3655
Isa 8:22 they will be thrust into **u darkness**. H696
Isa 42:17 will be turned back *in* **u shame**. H1017+1425
Isa 59: 4 empty arguments, *they* **u** lies; they H1819
Jer 2: 6 a land of drought and **u darkness**, a land H7516
Jer 13:16 will turn it to **u darkness** and change it to H7516
Jer 15:19 you may serve me; if *you* **u** worthy, not H3655
Eze 13: 9 see false visions and **u** lying **divinations**. H7876
Eze 14: 9 if the prophet is enticed *to* **u** a prophecy, H1819
Mt 13:35 *I will* **u** things hidden since the creation of *G2243*
Mk 3:28 all their sins and every slander *they* **u**, *G1059*
1Co 14: 2 *they* **u** mysteries by the Spirit. *G3281*
Rev 13: 5 given a mouth *to* **u** proud **words** and *G3281*

UTTERANCE (5) [UTTER]
2Sa 23: 1 "The **inspired u** *of* David son of Jesse, the H5536
2Sa 23: 1 the **u** *of* the man exalted by the Most H5536
Pr 30: 1 of Agur son of Jakeh—an **inspired u**. H5363
Pr 30: 1 This man's **u** to Ithiel: "I am H5536
Pr 31: 1 an **inspired u** his mother taught him. H5363

UTTERED (5) [UTTER]
Jos 10:21 and no one **u a word** against H3076+906+4383
Ps 89:34 my covenant or alter **what** my lips have **u**. H4604
Isa 45:23 my mouth *has* **u** in all integrity a H3655+4946
Jer 29:23 and in my name *they have* **u** lies H1819+1821
Eze 13: 7 false visions and **u** lying divinations when H606

UTTERING (1) [UTTER]
Isa 59:13 **u** lies our hearts have conceived. H2047

UTTERLY (21) [UTTER]
Dt 7:26 Regard it as vile and **u detest** it, for H9493+9493
Dt 31:29 *you are* **sure to become u corrupt** H8845+8845
Ps 38: 8 I am feeble and **u** crushed; I groan H6330+4394
Ps 39: 2 So *I remained* **u silent**, not even H519+1875
Ps 119: 8 your decrees; do not **u** forsake me. H6330+4394
Ecc 1: 2 "**U meaningless** H2039+2039
SS 8: 7 house for love, it *would be* **u scorned**. H996+996
Isa 6:12 far away and the land is **u** forsaken. H8045
Isa 30: 7 whose help is **u useless**. H2039+2256+8198
Isa 41:24 nothing and your works are **u** worthless; H4946
Isa 60:12 you will perish; it *will be* **u ruined**. H2990+2990
Jer 5:11 Judah *have been* **u unfaithful** to me," H953+953
La 5:22 unless *you have* **u rejected** us and H4415+4415
Eze 8: 6 the **u** detestable things the Israelites are H1524
Eze 20:13 and they **u** desecrated my Sabbaths. H4394
Ob 2 the nations; you will be **u** despised. H4394
Mic 2: 4 '*We are* **u ruined**; my people's H8720+8720
Hab 1: 5 and watch—and *be* **u amazed**. H9449+9449
Zep 2:13 Nineveh **u desolate** and dry as the H9039
Ac 2: 7 **U amazed**, they asked *G2014+2779+2513*
Ro 7:13 sin might become **u** sinful. *G2848+5651*

UTTERMOST (KJV) COMPLETELY, EDGE, EDGES, ENDS, EXTREME, FAR, FARTHEST, LAST, MOUTH, OUTSKIRTS, SOUTHERNMOST, TIP

UTTERS (1) [UTTER]
Ps 15: 3 whose tongue **u** no **slander**, who does no H8078

UZ (8)
Ge 10:23 The sons of Aram: **U**, Hul, Gether and H6419
Ge 22:21 **U** the firstborn, Buz his brother, Kemuel H6419
Ge 36:28 The sons of Dishan: **U** and Aran. H6419
1Ch 1:17 The sons of Aram: **U**, Hul, Gether and H6419
1Ch 1:42 The sons of Dishan: **U** and Aran. H6419
Job 1: 1 In the land of **U** there lived a man whose H6420
Jer 25:20 all the kings of **U**; all the kings of H824+6420
La 4:21 you who live in the land of **U**. H6420

UZAI (1)
Ne 3:25 Palal son of **U** worked opposite the H206

UZAL (2)

UZAL (NIV84) IZAL
Ge 10:27 Hadoram, **U**, Diklah, H207
1Ch 1:21 Hadoram, **U**, Diklah, H207

UZZA (5)
2Ki 21:18 in his palace garden, the garden of **U**. H6438
2Ki 21:26 buried in his tomb in the garden of **U**. H6438
1Ch 8: 7 who was the father of **U** and Ahihud. H6438
Ezr 2:49 **U**, Paseah, Besai, H6438
Ne 7:51 Gazzam, **U**, Paseah, H6438

UZZAH (9) [PEREZ UZZAH]
2Sa 6: 3 **U** and Ahio, sons of Abinadab, were H6438
2Sa 6: 6 **U** reached out and took hold of the ark of H6438
2Sa 6: 7 anger burned against **U** because of his H6446
2Sa 6: 8 LORD's wrath had broken out against **U**, H6446
1Ch 6:29 Libni his son, Shimei his son, **U** his son, H6446
1Ch 13: 7 on a new cart, with **U** and Ahio guiding it. H6438
1Ch 13: 9 **U** reached out his hand to steady the ark H6438
1Ch 13:10 The LORD's anger burned against **U**, and H6438
1Ch 13:11 LORD's wrath had broken out against **U**, H6438

UZZEN SHEERAH (1)
1Ch 7:24 Upper Beth Horon as well as **U**. H267

UZZI (12)
1Ch 6: 5 the father of Bukki, Bukki the father of **U**, H6454
1Ch 6: 6 **U** the father of Zerahiah, Zerahiah the H6454
1Ch 6:51 Bukki his son, **U** his son, Zerahiah his son, H6454
1Ch 7: 2 **U**, Rephaiah, Jeriel, Jahmai, Ibsam and H6454
1Ch 7: 3 The son of **U**: Izrahiah. The sons of H6454
1Ch 7: 7 **U**, Uzziel, Jerimoth and Iri, heads H6454
1Ch 9: 8 Jeroham; Elah son of **U**, the son of Mikri; H6454
Ezr 7: 4 Zerahiah, the son of **U**, the son of Bukki, H6454
Ne 11:22 Levites in Jerusalem was **U** son of Bani, H6454
Ne 11:22 **U** was one of Asaph's descendants, who NDT
Ne 12:19 of Joiarib's, Mattenai; of Jedaiah's, **U**; H6454
Ne 12:42 Shemaiah, Eleazar, **U**, Jehohanan H6454

UZZIA (1)
1Ch 11:44 **U** the Ashterathite, Shama and Jeiel the H6455

UZZIAH (29) [UZZIAH'S]
2Ki 15:13 in the thirty-ninth year of **U** king of Judah, H6459
2Ki 15:30 in the twentieth year of Jotham son of **U**. H6459
2Ki 15:32 Jotham son of **U** king of Judah began to H6460
2Ki 15:34 of the LORD, just as his father **U** had done. H6460
1Ch 6:24 Uriel his son, **U** his son and Shaul his son. H6459
1Ch 27:25 Jonathan son of **U** was in charge of the H6460
2Ch 26: 1 Then all the people of Judah took **U**, who H6460
2Ch 26: 3 **U** was sixteen years old when he became H6460
2Ch 26: 8 The Ammonites brought tribute to **U**, and H6460
2Ch 26: 9 **U** built towers in Jerusalem at the Corner H6460
2Ch 26:11 **U** had a well-trained army, ready to go H6460
2Ch 26:14 **U** provided shields, spears, helmets, coats H6460
2Ch 26:16 But after **U** became powerful, his pride H2257S
2Ch 26:18 They confronted King **U** and said, "It is not H6460
2Ch 26:18 is not right for you, **U**, to burn incense to H6460
2Ch 26:19 **U**, who had a censer in his hand ready to H6460
2Ch 26:21 King **U** had leprosy until the day he died H6460
2Ch 26:23 **U** rested with his ancestors and was buried H6460
2Ch 27: 2 just as his father **U** had done, but unlike H6460
Ezr 10:21 Shemaiah, Jehiel and **U**. H6459
Ne 11: 4 Athaiah son of **U**, the son of Zechariah H6459
Isa 1: 1 son of Amoz saw during the reigns of **U**, H6460
Isa 6: 1 In the year that King **U** died, I saw the H6460
Isa 7: 1 Jotham, the son of **U**, was king of Judah, H6460
Hos 1: 1 Hosea son of Beeri during the reigns of **U**, H6459
Am 1: 1 when **U** was king of Judah and Jeroboam H6459
Zec 14: 5 in the days of **U** king of Judah. H6459
Mt 1: 8 of Jehoram, Jehoram the father of **U**, *G3852*
Mt 1: 9 **U** the father of Jotham, Jotham the father *G3852*

UZZIAH'S (1) [UZZIAH]
2Ch 26:22 The other events of **U** reign, from H6460

UZZIEL (16) [UZZIELITES]
Ex 6:18 were Amram, Izhar, Hebron and **U**. H6457
Ex 6:22 The sons of **U** were Mishael, Elzaphan H6457
Lev 10: 4 sons of Aaron's uncle **U**, and said to them H6457
Nu 3:19 Amram, Izhar, Hebron and **U**. H6457
Nu 3:30 Kohathite clans was Elizaphan son of **U**. H6457
1Ch 4:42 Rephaiah and **U**, the sons of Ishi, H6457
1Ch 6: 2 Amram, Izhar, Hebron and **U**. H6457
1Ch 6:18 Amram, Izhar, Hebron and **U**. H6457
1Ch 7: 7 Uzzi, **U**, Jerimoth and Iri, heads of H6457
1Ch 15:10 from the descendants of **U**, Amminadab H6457
1Ch 23:12 Amram, Izhar, Hebron and **U**—four in all. H6457
1Ch 23:20 The sons of **U**: Micah the first and Ishiah H6457
1Ch 24:24 The son of **U**: Micah; from the sons of H6457
1Ch 25: 4 Bukkiah, Mattaniah, **U**, Shubael and H6457
2Ch 29:14 of Jeduthun, Shemaiah and **U**. H6457
Ne 3: 8 **U** son of Harhaiah, one of the goldsmiths H6457

UZZIELITES (2) [UZZIEL]
Nu 3:27 Hebronites and **U**; these were the H6458
1Ch 26:23 the Izharites, the Hebronites and the **U**: H6458

V

VAGABOND, VAGABONDS (KJV) WANDERER, WANDERING BEGGARS

VAIL, VAILS (KJV) CURTAIN, SHAWL, SHAWLS, SHEET, VEIL, VEILS

VAIN (37)
Lev 26:16 You will plant seed **in v**, because H4200+8198
Lev 26:20 Your strength will be spent **in v** H4200+8198
Job 3: 9 it wait for daylight **in v** and not see the first H401
Job 9:29 found guilty, why should I struggle **in v**? H2039
Job 24: 1 who know him look **in v** for such days? H4202
Job 39:16 cares not that her labor was **in v**, H4200+8198
Ps 2: 1 conspire and the peoples plot **in v**? H8198
Ps 33:17 A horse is a **v hope** for deliverance H9214
Ps 39: 6 like a mere phantom; **in v** they rush about H2039
Ps 62:10 in extortion or **put v hope** in stolen goods; H2038
Ps 73:13 Surely **in v** I have kept my heart pure and H8198
Ps 127: 1 builds the house, the builders labor **in v**. H8736
Ps 127: 1 over the city, the guards stand watch **in v**. H8736
Ps 127: 2 **In v** you rise early and stay up late, toiling H8736
Isa 45:19 to Jacob's descendants, 'Seek me **in v**. H9332
Isa 49: 4 "I have labored in **v**; I have spent my H8198
Isa 65:23 They will not labor **in v**, nor will H4200+8198
Jer 2:30 "**In v** I punished your people; H4200+2021+8736
Jer 4:30 You adorn yourself **in v**. H4200+2021+8736
Jer 6:29 but the refining goes on **in v**; H4200+2021+8736
Jer 46:11 you try many medicines **in v**; H4200+2021+8736
La 4:17 eyes failed, looking **in v** for help; from our H2039
Eze 6:10 I did not threaten **in v** to bring this H448+2855
Eze 7:25 terror comes, they will seek peace **in v**. H401
Zec 10: 2 that are false, they give comfort **in v**. H2039
Mt 15: 9 They worship me **in v**; their teachings are *G3472*
Mk 7: 7 They worship me **in v**; their teachings are *G3472*
Ac 4:25 nations rage and the peoples plot **in v**? *G3031*
1Co 15: 2 Otherwise, you have believed **in v**. *G1632*
1Co 15:58 that your labor in the Lord is not **in v**. *G3031*
2Co 6: 1 urge you not to receive God's grace in **v**. *G3031*
Gal 2: 2 had not been running my race in **v**. *G3031*
Gal 3: 4 Have you experienced so much **in v**—if it *G1632*
Gal 3: 4 so much in vain—if it really was **in v**? *G1632*
Php 2: 3 out of selfish ambition or **v conceit**. *G3029*
Php 2:16 of Christ that I did not run or labor in **v**. *G3031*
1Th 3: 5 that our labors might have been in **v**. *G3031*

VAIZATHA (1)
Est 9: 9 Parmashta, Arisai, Aridai and **V**, H2262

VALE (KJV) FOOTHILLS, VALLEY

VALIANT (11) [VALIANTLY]
Jdg 20:44 all of them **v fighters**. H408+2657

Jdg 20:46 all of them v **fighters**. H408+2657
1Sa 10:26 accompanied by v *men* whose hearts God H2657
1Sa 31:12 all their v men marched through the night H2657
2Sa 23:20 a v **fighter** from Kabzeel H1201+408+2657
2Ki 5: 1 He was a v **soldier**, but he had H1475+2657
1Ch 10:12 all their v men went and took the bodies H2657
1Ch 11:22 a v **fighter** from Kabzeel H1201+408+2657
2Ch 17:17 Eliada, a v **soldier**, with 200,000 H1475+2657
Ps 76: 5 The v lie plundered, they sleep their H52+4213
Jer 48:14 'We are warriors, men v in battle'? H2657

VALIANTLY (1) [VALIANT]
1Sa 14:48 He fought v and defeated the Amalekites H2657

VALID (3)
2Sa 15: 3 your claims are v and proper, but there H3202
Jn 8:13 your own witness; your testimony is not v." *G239*
Jn 8:14 my testimony is v, for I know where I *G239*

VALLEY (149) [VALLEYS]
Ge 14: 3 kings joined forces in the V *of* Siddim H6677
Ge 14: 3 Valley of Siddim (that is, the Dead Sea V). NDT
Ge 14: 8 up their battle lines in the V *of* Siddim H6677
Ge 14:10 Now the V *of* Siddim was full of tar pits H6677
Ge 14:17 out to meet him in the V *of* Shaveh H6677
Ge 14:17 Valley of Shaveh (that is, the King's V). H6677
Ge 26:17 there and encamped in the V *of* Gerar, H5707
Ge 26:19 servants dug in the v and discovered a H5707
Ge 37:14 he sent him off from the V *of* Hebron. H6677
Nu 13:23 When they reached the V *of* Eshkol, they H5707
Nu 13:24 was called the V *of* Eshkol because of H5707
Nu 21:12 moved on and camped in the Zered V. H5707
Nu 21:20 from Bamoth to the v in Moab where the H1628
Nu 32: 9 went up to the V *of* Eshkol and viewed H5707
Dt 1:24 came to the V *of* Eshkol and explored H5707
Dt 2:13 "Now get up and cross the Zered V." H5707
Dt 2:13 the Zered Valley." So we crossed the v. H5707
Dt 2:14 Barnea until we crossed the Zered V. H5707
Dt 3:29 So we stayed in the v near Beth Peor. H1628
Dt 4:46 were in the v near Beth Peor east of H1628
Dt 21: 4 lead it down to a v that has not been H5707
Dt 21: 4 There in the v they are to break the H5707
Dt 21: 6 heifer whose neck was broken in the v, H5707
Dt 34: 3 the whole region from the V *of* Jericho, H1326
Dt 34: 6 him in Moab, in the v opposite Beth Peor H1628
Jos 7:24 all that he had, to the V *of* Achor. H6677
Jos 7:26 has been called the V *of* Achor ever since. H6677
Jos 8:11 with the v between them and the city. H1628
Jos 8:13 That night Joshua went into the v. H6677
Jos 10:12 you, moon, over the V *of* Aijalon. H6677
Jos 11: 8 and to the V *of* Mizpah on the east H1326
Jos 11:17 to Baal Gad in the V *of* Lebanon below H1326
Jos 12: 7 Baal Gad in the V *of* Lebanon to Mount H1326
Jos 13:19 Zereth Shahar on the hill in the v, H6677
Jos 13:27 in the v, Beth Haram, Beth Nimrah H6677
Jos 15: 7 to Debir from the V *of* Achor and turned H6677
Jos 15: 8 Then it ran up the V *of* Ben Hinnom along H1628
Jos 15: 8 west of the Hinnom V at the northern end H1628
Jos 15: 8 at the northern end of the V *of* Rephaim. H6677
Jos 17:16 settlements and those in the V *of* Jezreel." H6677
Jos 18:16 of the hill facing the V *of* Ben Hinnom, H1628
Jos 18:16 Ben Hinnom, north of the V *of* Rephaim. H6677
Jos 18:16 down the Hinnom V along the southern H1628
Jos 19:14 ended at the V *of* Iphtah El. H1628
Jos 19:27 touched Zebulun and the V *of* Iphtah El H1628
Jdg 5:15 sent under his command into the v. H6677
Jdg 6:33 Jordan and camped in the V *of* Jezreel. H6677
Jdg 7: 1 north of them in the v near the hill of H6677
Jdg 7: 8 camp of Midian lay below him in the v. H6677
Jdg 7:12 eastern peoples had settled in the v, H6677
Jdg 16: 4 a woman in the V *of* Sorek whose name H5707
Jdg 18:28 The city was in a v near Beth Rehob. H6677
1Sa 6:13 were harvesting their wheat in the v, H6677
1Sa 13:18 overlooking the V *of* Zeboyim facing the H1628
1Sa 17: 2 camped in the V *of* Elah and drew up H6677
1Sa 17: 3 another, with the v between them. H1628
1Sa 17:19 all the men of Israel in the V *of* Elah, H6677
1Sa 21: 9 whom you killed in the V *of* Elah, is here; H6677
1Sa 30: 9 men with him came to the Besor V, H5707
1Sa 30:10 of them were too exhausted to cross the v, H5707
1Sa 30:21 who were left behind at the Besor V. H5707
1Sa 31: 7 Israelites along the v and those across the H6677
2Sa 5:18 spread out in the V *of* Rephaim; H6677
2Sa 5:22 up and spread out in the V *of* Rephaim; H6677
2Sa 8:13 thousand Edomites in the V *of* Salt. H1628
2Sa 15:23 The king also crossed the Kidron V, and H5707
2Sa 17:13 drag it down to the v until not so much as H5707
2Sa 18:18 it in the King's V as a monument to H6677
2Sa 23:13 was encamped in the V *of* Rephaim. H6677
1Ki 2:37 The day you leave and cross the Kidron V H5707
1Ki 15:13 cut it down and burned it in the Kidron V. H5707
1Ki 18:40 down to the Kishon V and slaughtered H5707
2Ki 2:16 down on some mountain or in some v." H1628
2Ki 3:16 I will fill this v with pools of water. H5707
2Ki 3:17 rain, yet this v will be filled with water H5707
2Ki 14: 7 Edomites in the V *of* Salt and captured H1628
2Ki 23: 4 fields of the Kidron V and took the ashes to NDT
2Ki 23: 6 LORD to the Kidron V outside Jerusalem H5707
2Ki 23:10 which was in the V *of* Ben Hinnom, so no H1628
2Ki 23:12 threw the rubble into the Kidron V. H5707
1Ch 4:39 to the east of the v in search of pasture H1628
1Ch 10: 7 Israelites in the v saw that the army had H6677
1Ch 11:15 was encamped in the V *of* Rephaim. H6677
1Ch 14: 9 had come and raided the V *of* Rephaim; H6677
1Ch 14:13 Once more the Philistines raided the v; H6677
1Ch 18:12 thousand Edomites in the V *of* Salt. H1628
2Ch 14:10 positions in the V *of* Zephathah near H1628
2Ch 15:16 broke it up and burned it in the Kidron V. H5707
2Ch 20:26 day they assembled in the V *of* Berakah, H6677
2Ch 20:26 it is called the V *of* Berakah to this day H6677
2Ch 25:11 strength and led his army to the V *of* Salt, H1628
2Ch 26: 9 at the V Gate and at the angle of the wall, H1628
2Ch 28: 3 sacrifices in the V *of* Ben Hinnom and H1628
2Ch 29:16 took it and carried it out to the Kidron V. H5707
2Ch 30:14 altars and threw them into the Kidron V. H5707
2Ch 33: 6 in the fire in the V *of* Ben Hinnom, H1628
2Ch 33:14 west of the Gihon spring in the v, as far as H5707
Ne 2:13 went out through the V Gate toward the H1628
Ne 2:15 so I went up the v by night, examining the H5707
Ne 2:15 back and reentered through the V Gate. H1628
Ne 3:13 The V Gate was repaired by Hanun and H1628
Ne 11:30 way from Beersheba to the V *of* Hinnom. H1628
Job 21:33 The soil in the v is sweet to them H5707
Ps 23: 4 Even though I walk through the darkest v H1628
Ps 60: T thousand Edomites in the V *of* Salt. H1628
Ps 60: 6 measure off the V *of* Sukkoth. H6677
Ps 84: 6 As they pass through the V *of* Baka, they H6677
Ps 108: 7 measure off the V *of* Sukkoth. H6677
Pr 30:17 will be pecked out by the ravens of the v H5707
SS 6:11 trees to look at the new growth in the v, H5707
Isa 17: 5 heads of grain in the V *of* Rephaim. H6677
Isa 22: 1 A prophecy against the V *of* Vision: What H1628
Isa 22: 5 trampling and terror in the V *of* Vision, H1628
Isa 28: 1 set on the head of a fertile v—to that city, H1628
Isa 28: 4 set on the head of a fertile v, will be like H1628
Isa 28:21 will rouse himself as in the V of Gibeon— H6677
Isa 40: 4 Every v shall be raised up, every mountain H1628
Isa 65:10 the V *of* Achor a resting place for H6677
Jer 2:23 See how you behaved in the v; consider H1628
Jer 7:31 of Topheth in the V *of* Ben Hinnom to H1628
Jer 7:32 call it Topheth or the V *of* Ben Hinnom, H1628
Jer 7:32 Ben Hinnom, but the V *of* Slaughter, for H1628
Jer 19: 2 go out to the V *of* Ben Hinnom, near H1628
Jer 19: 6 place Topheth or the V *of* Ben Hinnom, H1628
Jer 19: 6 of Ben Hinnom, but the V *of* Slaughter. H1628
Jer 21:13 who live above this v on the rocky plateau H6677
Jer 31:40 The whole v *where* dead bodies and H6677
Jer 31:40 out to the Kidron V on the east as far as H5707
Jer 32:35 places for Baal in the V *of* Ben Hinnom to H1628
Jer 48: 8 The v will be ruined and the plateau H6677
Eze 37: 1 the LORD and set me in the middle of a v; H1326
Eze 37: 2 a great many bones on the floor of the v, H1326
Eze 39:11 in the v *of* those who travel east of the H1628
Eze 39:11 So it will be called the V *of* Hamon Gog. H1628
Eze 39:15 bury it in the V *of* Hamon Gog, H1628
Hos 1: 5 will break Israel's bow in the V *of* Jezreel." H6677
Hos 2:15 will make the V *of* Achor a door of H6677
Joel 3: 2 bring them down to the V *of* Jehoshaphat. H6677
Joel 3:12 them advance into the V *of* Jehoshaphat, H6677
Joel 3:14 multitudes in the v *of* decision! H6677
Joel 3:14 of the LORD is near in the v *of* decision. H6677
Joel 3:18 house and will water the v *of* acacias. H5707
Am 1: 5 king who is in the V *of* Aven and the one H1326
Am 6:14 from Lebo Hamath to the v *of* the Arabah." H5707
Mic 1: 6 her stones into the v and lay bare her H1628
Zec 14: 4 to west, forming a great v, with half of the H1628
Zec 14: 5 You will flee by my mountain v, for it will H1628
Lk 3: 5 Every v shall be filled in, every mountain *G5754*
Jn 18: 1 his disciples and crossed the Kidron V. *G5929*

VALLEYS (26) [VALLEY]
Nu 14:25 the Canaanites are living in the v, H6677
Nu 24: 6 "Like v they spread out, like gardens H5707
Dt 8: 7 springs gushing out into the v and hills; H1326
Dt 11:11 of mountains and v that drinks rain from H1326
2Sa 22:16 The v *of* the sea were exposed and the H692
1Ki 18: 5 through the land to all the springs and v. H5707
1Ki 20:28 a god of the hills and not a god of the v, H6677
1Ch 12:15 they put to flight everyone living in the v, H6677
1Ch 27:29 Adlai was in charge of the herds in the v. H6677
Job 39:10 Will it till the v behind you? H6677
Ps 18:15 The v *of* the sea were exposed and the H692
Ps 65:13 with flocks and the v are mantled with H6677
Ps 104: 8 they went down into the v, to the place H1326
SS 2: 1 I am a rose of Sharon, a lily of the v. H6677
Isa 22: 7 Your choicest v are full of chariots, and H6677
Isa 41:18 barren heights, and springs within the v. H1326
Jer 49: 4 Why do you boast of your v, boast of your H6677
Jer 49: 4 of your valleys, boast of your v so fruitful? H6677
Eze 6: 3 mountains and hills, to the ravines and v: H1628
Eze 7:16 Like doves of the v, they will all moan H1628
Eze 31:12 fell on the mountains and in all the v; H1628
Eze 32: 5 fill the v with your remains. H1628
Eze 35: 8 your hills and in your v and in all your H1628
Eze 36: 4 to the ravines and v, to the desolate ruins H1628
Eze 36: 6 mountains and hills, to the ravines and v: H1628
Mic 1: 4 melt beneath him and the v split apart, H6677

VALOUR (KJV) ABLE, BRAVE, CAPABLE, FIGHTING, LEADING, MIGHTY, STANDING, STRONG, TROOPS, VALIANT, WARRIORS

VALUABLE (8) [VALUE]
2Ch 32:23 the LORD and v **gifts** for Hezekiah king H4458
Ezr 1: 6 with v **gifts**, in addition to all H4458
Pr 1:13 get all sorts of v **things** and fill our H2104+3701
Da 11: 8 images and their v articles of silver and H2775
Mt 6:26 *Are* you not much **more** v than they? *G1422*
Mt 12:12 How much **more** v *is* a person than a *G1422*
Lk 12:24 And how much more v you *are* than birds! *G1422*
Jas 5: 7 waits for the land to yield its v crop, *G5508*

VALUABLES (2) [VALUE]
2Ch 32:27 spices, shields and all kinds of v. H2775
Jer 20: 5 all its v and all the treasures of the kings H3702

VALUE (60) [VALUABLE, VALUABLES, VALUED]
Lev 5:15 defect and of the **proper** v *in* silver, H6886
Lev 5:16 penalty of a **fifth** *of* its *v* and give it all to the AIT
Lev 5:18 one without defect and of the **proper** v. H6886
Lev 6: 5 add a fifth of **the** v to it and give it all to H2257[S]
Lev 6: 6 one without defect and of the **proper** v. H6886
Lev 22:14 the offering and add a fifth of **the** v to it. H2257[S]
Lev 25:27 *they are to* **determine the** v *for* the years H3108
Lev 27: 2 to the LORD by giving the **equivalent** v, H6886
Lev 27: 3 set the v *of* a male between the ages of H6886
Lev 27: 4 a female, set her v at thirty shekels; H6886
Lev 27: 5 set the v *of* a male at twenty shekels and H6886
Lev 27: 6 set the v *of* a male at five shekels of silver H6886
Lev 27: 7 set the v *of* a male at fifteen shekels and H6886
Lev 27: 8 who *will* **set** *the* v according to what the H6885
Lev 27:12 Whatever v the priest then sets, that is H6886
Lev 27:13 the animal, a fifth must be added to its v. H6886
Lev 27:14 Whatever v the priest then **sets**, so it will H6885
Lev 27:15 they must add a fifth to its v, and H4084+6886
Lev 27:16 its v is to be set according to the amount H6886
Lev 27:17 Jubilee, the v that has been set remains. H6886
Lev 27:18 will determine the v according to the H4084
Lev 27:18 of Jubilee, and its **set** v will be reduced. H6886
Lev 27:19 they must add a fifth to its v, and H4084+6886
Lev 27:23 determine its v up to the Year of H4831+6886
Lev 27:23 the owner must pay its v on that day as H6886
Lev 27:25 Every v is to be set according to the H6886
Lev 27:27 it may be bought back at its **set** v, adding H6886
Lev 27:27 its set value, adding a fifth of **the** v to it. H2257[S]
Lev 27:27 not redeemed, it is to be sold at its **set** v. H6886
Lev 27:31 their tithe must add a fifth of **the** v to it. H2257[S]
Nu 5: 7 add a fifth of **the** v to it and give it all to H2257[S]
1Sa 26:24 so *may* the LORD v my life and H1540+928+6524
1Ki 10:21 considered of **little** v in Solomon's H4202+4399
1Ki 20: 6 everything you v and carry it away. H4718+6524
2Ch 9:20 considered of **little** v in Solomon's day H4399
2Ch 20:25 clothing and also articles of v— H2776
2Ch 21: 3 gifts of silver and gold and **articles of** v, H4458
2Ch 36:10 with articles of v *from* the temple of the H2775
2Ch 36:19 destroyed everything of v there. H4718
Job 15: 3 with speeches that **have** no v? H3603
Pr 10: 2 Ill-gotten treasures **have** no **lasting** v, but H3603
Pr 10:20 the heart of the wicked is **of little** v. H3869+5071
Pr 16:13 *they* v the one who speaks what is right. H170
Pr 31:11 confidence in her and lacks nothing of v. H8965
Eze 7:11 none of their wealth, nothing *of* v. H5625
Hab 2:18 "**Of** what v *is* an idol carved by a H3603
Mt 13:46 When he found one **of great** v, he went *G4501*
Lk 16:15 What people v **highly** is detestable in *G5734*
Ac 19:19 When they calculated the v of the scrolls *G5507*
Ro 2:25 Circumcision **has** v if you observe the law *G6067*
Ro 3: 1 or what v is there in circumcision? *G6066*
Gal 5: 2 Christ *will be* **of** no v to you at all. *G6067*
Gal 5: 6 circumcision nor uncircumcision **has** any v. *G2710*
Php 2: 3 in humility v others above yourselves, *G2451*
Col 2:23 they lack any v in restraining sensual *G5507*
1Ti 4: 8 For physical training is of some v, but *G6068*
1Ti 4: 8 godliness has v for all things, holding *G6068*
2Ti 2:14 it is of no v, and only ruins those *G5978*
Heb 4: 2 message they heard *was* **of** no v to them, *G6067*
Heb 11:26 the sake of Christ *as of* greater v than the *G4458*

VALUED (4) [VALUE]
1Sa 26:24 As surely as I v your life today H1540+928+6524
Ezr 8:27 20 bowls of gold v **at** 1,000 darics, and H4200
Zec 11:13 the handsome price at which they v *me*! H3700
Lk 7: 2 whom his master v **highly**, was sick *G1639+1952*

VANIAH (1)
Ezr 10:36 V, Meremoth, Eliashib, H2264

VANISH (12) [VANISHED, VANISHES]
Job 6:17 in the heat v from their channels. H1980
Ps 58: 7 *Let them* v like water that flows away H4416
Ps 102: 3 For my days v like smoke; my bones burn H3983
Ps 104:35 But *may* sinners v from the earth and the H9462
Isa 11:13 Ephraim's jealousy *will* v, and Judah's H6073
Isa 16: 4 the aggressor *will* v from the land. H9462
Isa 29:14 the intelligence of the intelligent *will* v." H6259
Isa 29:20 The ruthless *will* v, the mockers will H699
Isa 34:12 a kingdom, all her princes will v **away**. H700
Isa 51: 6 the heavens *will* v like smoke, the H4872
Jer 18:14 *Does* the snow of Lebanon *ever* v from its H6440
Jer 31:36 "Only if these decrees v from my sight," H4631

VANISHED (5) [VANISH]
Ps 12: 1 who are loyal *have* v from the human H7182
Ps 77: 8 *Has* his unfailing love v forever? Has his H699
Ecc 9: 6 hate and their jealousy *have* long since v; H6
Jer 7:28 has perished; *it has* v from their lips. H4162
Rev 18:14 All your luxury and splendor *have* v, never *G660*

VANISHES (3) [VANISH]

Job 7: 9 As a cloud v and is gone, so one who H3983
Job 30:15 as by the wind, my safety v like a cloud. H6296
Jas 4:14 that appears for a little while and then v. *G906*

VANITIES, VANITY (KJV) BREATH, CALAMITY, DECEIT, DELUSIONS, DESTRUCTION, DISHONEST, EMPTY, EVIL, FALSE, FALSEHOOD, FALSELY, FRUSTRATION, FUTILE, FUTILITY, IDOL, LIES, MALICIOUS, MEANINGLESS, NO MEANING, VAPOR, WORTHLESS (IDOLS, THINGS)

VAPOR (1)

Pr 21: 6 tongue is a fleeting v and a deadly snare. H2039

VAPOUR (KJV) BILLOWS, CLOUDS, MIST, STREAMS

VARIANCE (KJV) DISCORD, TURN

VARIED (1) [VARIOUS]

Eze 17: 3 full plumage *of* v colors came to Lebanon. H8391

VARIOUS (25) [VARIED]

Ge 1:11 with seed in it, according to their v **kinds**." H4786
Ge 7: 3 to keep their v **kinds** alive throughout the H2446
Jdg 2:12 worshiped v gods of the peoples H337
1Ch 18: 8 bronze Sea, the pillars and v bronze articles. NDT
1Ch 28:14 be used in v **kinds of service**, H6275+2256+6275
1Ch 28:14 be used in v **kinds of service**: H6275+2256+6275
1Ch 29: 2 stones of v **colors**, and all kinds of H8391
2Ch 8:14 by divisions for the v **gates**, H9133+2256+9133
2Ch 16:14 with spices and v blended perfumes, H2385
2Ch 31:16 to perform the daily duties of their v **tasks**, AIT
2Ch 32:28 he made stalls for v kinds of cattle H3972
Ne 11: 3 each on their own property in the v **towns**, AIT
Est 3:12 of the v **provinces** and the H4519+2256+4519
Est 3:12 the nobles of the v **peoples**. H6639+2256+6639
Eze 13:18 make veils of v lengths for their H3972
Mt 4:24 to him all who were ill with v diseases, *G4476*
Mt 24: 7 be famines and earthquakes **in** v places. *G2848*
Mk 1:34 Jesus healed many who had v diseases. *G4476*
Mk 13: 8 There will be earthquakes **in** v places *G2848*
Lk 4:40 to Jesus all who had v **kinds** of sickness, *G4476*
Lk 21:11 famines and pestilences **in** v places, and *G2848*
Heb 1: 1 the prophets at many times and **in** v **ways**, *G4502*
Heb 2: 4 by signs, wonders and v miracles, and by *G4476*
Heb 9:10 food and drink and v ceremonial *G1427*
1Pe 4:10 stewards of God's grace *in* its v **forms**. *G4476*

VASHTI (10)

Est 1: 9 Queen V also gave a banquet for the H2267
Est 1:11 to bring before him Queen V, wearing her H2267
Est 1:12 command, Queen V refused to come. H2267
Est 1:15 what must be done to Queen V? H2267
Est 1:16 the nobles, "Queen V has done wrong H2267
Est 1:17 commanded Queen V to be brought H2267
Est 1:19 that V is never again to enter the H2267
Est 2: 1 he remembered V and what she had H2267
Est 2: 4 pleases the king be queen instead of V." H2267
Est 2:17 head and made her queen instead of V. H2267

VASSAL (3) [VASSALS]

2Ki 16: 7 king of Assyria, "I am your servant and v. H1201
2Ki 17: 3 been Shalmaneser's v and had paid him H6269
2Ki 24: 1 Jehoiakim became his v for three years. H6269

VASSALS (2) [VASSAL]

2Sa 10:19 the kings who were v *of* Hadadezer saw H6269
1Ch 19:19 When the v *of* Hadadezer saw that they H6269

VAST (24)

Ge 2: 1 earth were completed in all their v **array**. H7372
Dt 1:19 through all that v and dreadful wilderness H1524
Dt 2: 7 your journey through this v wilderness. H1524
Dt 8:15 He led you through the v and dreadful H1524
1Ki 8:65 Israel with him—a v assembly, people H1524
1Ki 20:13 'Do you see this v army? I will give it H1524
1Ki 20:28 I will deliver this v army into your hands H1524
2Ch 7: 8 with him—a v assembly, people H1524+4394
2Ch 13: 8 You are indeed a v army and have with H8041
2Ch 14:11 name we have come against this v **army**. H2162
2Ch 20: 2 "A v army is coming against you from H8041
2Ch 20:12 no power to face this v army that is H8041
2Ch 20:15 discouraged because of this v army. H8041
2Ch 20:24 the desert and looked toward the v **army**, H2162
2Ch 32: 7 king of Assyria and the v army with him, H3972
Est 1: 4 he displayed the v wealth of his kingdom H3883
Est 1:20 is proclaimed throughout all his v realm, H8041
Est 5:11 boasted to them about his v wealth, H3883
Job 9: 4 his power is v. Who has resisted him H579
Job 38:18 the v **expanses** *of* the earth? H8144
Ps 104:25 There is the sea, v and spacious, teeming H1524
Ps 139:17 thoughts, God! How v *is* the sum of them! H6793
Eze 26:19 over you and its v waters cover you, H8041
Eze 37:10 up on their feet—a v army. H1524+4394+4394

VAT (1) [VATS]

Hag 2:16 anyone went to a **wine** v to draw fifty H3676

VATS (5) [VAT]

Ex 22:29 offerings from your granaries or your v. H1964
1Ch 27:27 the produce of the vineyards for the wine v. H238
Pr 3:10 your v will brim over with new wine. H3676
Joel 2:24 the v will overflow with new wine and oil. H3676
Joel 3:13 the winepress is full and the v overflow— H3676

VAULT (13) [VAULTED, VAULTS]

Ge 1: 6 "Let there be a v between the waters to H8385
Ge 1: 7 So God made the v and separated the H8385
Ge 1: 7 the water under the v from the water H8385
Ge 1: 8 God called the v "sky." And there was H8385
Ge 1:14 be lights in the v *of* the sky to separate H8385
Ge 1:15 them be lights in the v *of* the sky to give H8385
Ge 1:17 God set them in the v *of* the sky to give H8385
Ge 1:20 fly above the earth across the v *of* the sky." H8385
Eze 1:22 was what looked something like a v, H8385
Eze 1:23 Under the v their wings were stretched out H8385
Eze 1:25 voice from above the v over their heads as H8385
Eze 1:26 Above the v over their heads was what H8385
Eze 10: 1 lapis lazuli above the v that was over the H8385

VAULTED (2) [VAULT]

Job 22:14 see us as he goes about in the v heavens. H2553
Jer 37:16 was put into a v **cell** in a dungeon, H2844

VAULTS (1) [VAULT]

Dt 32:34 kept this in reserve and sealed it in my v? H238

VAUNT, VAUNTETH (KJV) BOAST

VAUNTS (1)

Job 15:25 his fist at God and v **himself** against the H1504

VEGETABLE (2) [VEGETABLES]

Dt 11:10 irrigated it by foot as in a v garden. H3763
1Ki 21: 2 have your vineyard to use for a v garden, H3763

VEGETABLES (4) [VEGETABLE]

Pr 15:17 a small serving of v with love than a H3763
Da 1:12 Give us nothing but v to eat and water to H2447
Da 1:16 were to drink and gave them v instead. H2448
Ro 14: 2 another, whose faith is weak, eats *only* v. *G3303*

VEGETATION (6)

Ge 1:11 "Let the land produce v: seed-bearing H2013
Ge 1:12 The land produced v: plants bearing seed H2013
Ge 19:25 in the cities—and also the v *in* the land. H7542
Dt 29:23 nothing sprouting, no v growing on it. H6912
Isa 15: 6 the v is gone and nothing green is left. H2013
Isa 42:15 mountains and hills and dry up all their v; H6912

VEHEMENTLY (1)

Lk 23:10 law were standing there, v accusing him. *G2364*

VEIL (16) [VEILED, VEILS]

Ge 24:65 So she took her v and covered herself. H7581
Ge 38:14 herself with a v to disguise herself, H7581
Ge 38:19 she took off her v and put on her widow's H7581
Ex 34:33 to them, he put a v over his face. H5003
Ex 34:34 he removed the v until he came out. H5003
Ex 34:35 Moses would put the v back over his face H5003
Job 22:14 Thick clouds v him, so he does not see us H6260
SS 4: 1 Your eyes behind your v are doves. H7539
SS 4: 3 temples behind your v are like the halves H7539
SS 6: 7 temples behind your v are like the halves H7539
Isa 47: 2 millstones and grind flour; take off your v. H7539
La 3:65 Put a v *over* their hearts, and may your H4485
2Co 3:13 who would put a v over his face to prevent *G2820*
2Co 3:14 this day the same v remains when the old *G2820*
2Co 3:15 Moses is read, a v covers their hearts. *G2820*
2Co 3:16 turns to the Lord, the v is taken away. *G2820*

VEILED (3) [VEIL]

SS 1: 7 I be like a v *woman* beside the flocks H6486
2Co 4: 3 And even if our gospel is v, it is veiled to *G2821*
2Co 4: 3 it is v to those who are perishing. *G2821*

VEILS (3) [VEIL]

Isa 3:19 the earrings and bracelets and v, H8304
Eze 13:18 their wrists and make v of various lengths H5029
Eze 13:21 I will tear off your v and save my people H5029

VENGEANCE (33) [AVENGE, AVENGED, AVENGER, AVENGES, AVENGING, REVENGE]

Ge 4:15 who kills Cain *will* **suffer** v seven times H5933
Nu 31: 2 "**Take** v on the Midianites *for* the H5933+5935
Nu 31: 3 they may carry out the LORD's v on them. H5935
Dt 32:41 *I will* **take** v on my adversaries and H8740+5934
Dt 32:43 *he will* **take** v on his enemies and H8740+5934
Ps 149: 7 to inflict v on the nations and punishment H5935
Isa 34: 8 For the LORD has a day of v, a year of H5934
Isa 35: 4 he will come with v; with divine H5934
Isa 47: 3 I will take v; I will spare no one. H5934
Isa 59:17 on the garments of v and wrapped H5934
Isa 61: 2 LORD's favor and the day of v of our God, H5934
Isa 63: 4 It was for me the day of v; the year for me H5934
Jer 11:20 let me see your v on them, for to you I H5935
Jer 20:12 let me see your v on them, for to you I H5935
Jer 46:10 Almighty—a day of v, for vengeance on H5935
Jer 46:10 a day of vengeance, for v on his foes. H5933
Jer 50:15 Since this is the v *of* the LORD, take H5935
Jer 50:15 of the LORD, **take** v on her; do to her as H5933
Jer 50:28 in Zion how the LORD our God has taken v, H5935
Jer 50:28 has taken vengeance, v *for* his temple. H5935
Jer 51: 6 It is time for the LORD's v; he will repay her H5935
Jer 51:11 The LORD will take v, vengeance for his H5935
Jer 51:11 LORD will take vengeance, v *for* his temple. H5935
La 3:60 You have seen the depth of their v, all H5935
Eze 16:38 bring on you the **blood** v *of* my wrath and H1947
Eze 25:14 I will take v on Edom by the hand of my H5935
Eze 25:14 they will know my v, declares the H5935
Eze 25:15 Philistines acted in v and took revenge H5935
Eze 25:17 I will carry out great v on them and punish H5935
Eze 25:17 that I am the LORD, when I take v on them. H5935
Mic 5:15 I will take v in anger and wrath on the H5934
Na 1: 2 the LORD **takes** v and is filled with wrath. H5933
Na 1: 2 The LORD **takes** v on his foes and vents his H5933

VENISON (KJV) GAME

VENOM (5) [VENOMOUS]

Dt 32:24 the v *of* vipers that glide in the dust. H2779
Dt 32:33 Their wine is the v *of* serpents, the deadly H2779
Job 20:14 it will become the v *of* serpents within H5355
Ps 58: 4 Their v is like the venom of a snake, like H2779
Ps 58: 4 Their venom is like the v *of* a snake, like H2779

VENOMOUS (4) [VENOM]

Nu 21: 6 Then the LORD sent v snakes among them H8597
Dt 8:15 with its v snakes and scorpions. H8597
Isa 14:29 its fruit will be a darting, v **serpent**. H8597
Jer 8:17 I will send v **snakes** among you H5729

VENT (6) [VENTS]

Job 15:13 so that *you* v your rage against God and H8740
Job 20:23 God *will* v his burning anger against him H8938
Pr 29:11 Fools **give** full v **to** their rage, but the wise H3655
Isa 1:24 *I will* v *my* **wrath** on my foes and avenge H5714
La 4:11 The LORD *has* **given full** v *to* his wrath; he H3983
Da 11:30 turn back and v *his* **fury** against the holy H2404

VENTS (1) [VENT]

Na 1: 2 on his foes and v *his* **wrath** against his H5757

VENTURE (4) [VENTURES]

Dt 28:56 gentle that *she would* not v to touch the H5814
Jer 5: 6 towns to tear to pieces any who v **out**, H3655
Ac 19:31 begging him not *to* v into the theater. *G1443*
Ro 15:18 *I will* not v to speak of anything except *G5528*

VENTURES (2) [VENTURE]

Job 4: 2 "If *someone* v a word with you, will you H5814
Ecc 11: 2 Invest in **seven** v, yes, in eight; you do not AIT

VERDANT (2)

SS 1:16 how charming! And our bed is v. H8316
Jer 50: 7 against the LORD, their v pasture, the LORD, H7406

VERDICT (6)

Dt 17: 9 them and they will give you the v. H1821+5477
1Ki 3:28 all Israel heard the v the king had given, H5477
2Ch 19: 6 is with you whenever you give a v. H1821+5477
Ps 51: 4 you are right in your v and justified when H1819
Da 4:17 the holy ones declare the v, so that the A10690
Jn 3:19 This is the v: Light has come into the world *G3213*

VERIFIED (1) [VERIFY]

Ge 42:20 that your words *may* **be** v and that you may H586

VERIFY (1) [VERIFIED]

Ac 24:11 You can *easily* v that no more than twelve *G2105*

VERILY (KJV) SAFE, SURELY, TRULY

VERITY (KJV) FAITHFUL

VERMILION (KJV) RED

VERMIN (2)

Mt 6:19 where moths and v destroy, and where *G1111*
Mt 6:20 where moths and v do not destroy, and *G1111*

VERSED (1)

Ezr 7: 6 He was a teacher **well** v in the Law of H4542

VERSES (1)

Ps 45: 1 noble theme as I recite my v for the king; H5126

VERY (340)

Ge 1:31 all that he had made, and it was v good. H4394
Ge 3:16 *I will* **make** your pains in childbearing v **severe** H8049+8049
Ge 4: 5 So Cain was v angry, and his face was H4394
Ge 7:13 On that v day Noah and his sons, Shem H6795
Ge 12:14 saw that Sarai was a v beautiful woman. H4394
Ge 13: 2 Abram had become v wealthy in livestock H4394
Ge 15: 1 I am your shield, your v great reward." H4394
Ge 17: 6 I will make you v fruitful; I will H4394+928+4394
Ge 17:23 On that v day Abraham took his son H6795
Ge 17:26 were both circumcised on that v day. H6795
Ge 18: 5 to your servant." "**V well**," they answered H4027
Ge 18:11 were already v **old**, H2418+995+928+2021+3427
Ge 19:20 me flee to it—it is v **small**, isn't it? Then my AIT
Ge 19:21 He said to him, "**V well**, I will grant this H2180
Ge 20: 8 had happened, they were v **much** afraid. H4394
Ge 21: 2 at the v time God had promised him. NDT
Ge 24: 1 Abraham *was* now v **old** H2416+995+928+2021+3427
Ge 24:16 The woman was v beautiful, a virgin; no H4394
Ge 26:13 to grow until he became v wealthy. H4394
Ge 30:15 "**V well**," Rachel said, "he can H4200+4027
Ge 37:13 send you to them." "**V well**," he replied. H2180

Ge 41:19 came up—scrawny and v ugly and lean. H4394
Ge 44:10 "**V well**, then," he said, "let it be as you H1685
Ge 50: 9 It was a v large company. H4394
Ex 8:28 but *you* **must** not go **v far**. H8178+8178
Ex 9:16 But I have raised you up for this v purpose H2296
Ex 10:19 changed the wind to a v strong west wind, H4394
Ex 12:17 because it was on this v day that I brought H6795
Ex 12:41 the 430 years, to the v day, all the LORD's H6795
Ex 12:51 And on that v day the LORD brought the H6795
Ex 19: 1 left Egypt—on that v day—they came to H2296
Ex 19:16 the mountain, and a v loud trumpet blast. H4394
Ex 33:17 "I will do the v thing you have asked H2296
Lev 19: 9 do not reap to the v edges of your field H3983
Lev 23:14 until the v day you bring this offering to H6795
Lev 23:22 do not reap to the v edges of your field H3983
Nu 12: 3 Now Moses was a v humble man, more H4394
Nu 13:28 the cities are fortified and v large. H4394
Nu 14:28 to you the **v thing** I heard you H3869+889+4027
Nu 16:15 Then Moses became v angry and said to H4394
Nu 22:22 But God *was* **v angry** when he went H3013+678
Nu 32: 1 who had v large herds and flocks H4394+6786
Dt 1:30 he did for you in Egypt, before your v eyes, NDT
Dt 2: 4 will be afraid of you, but be v careful. H4394
Dt 2:25 **This** v day I will begin to put the terror H2296
Dt 4:11 while it blazed with fire to the v heavens, H4213
Dt 4:15 Therefore watch yourselves v carefully, H4394
Dt 4:34 God did for you in Egypt before your v eyes? NDT
Dt 13: 6 If your **v own brother**, or H278+1201+562+3870
Dt 24: 8 be v careful to do exactly as the Levitical H4394
Dt 27: 8 And you shall write v clearly all the words H3512
Dt 30:14 the word is v near you; it is in your H4394
Jos 1: 7 "Be strong and v courageous. Be careful H4394
Jos 5:11 the Passover, that v day, they ate some of H6795
Jos 8: 4 Don't go v far from it. All of you H4394
Jos 9: 9 have come from a v distant country H4394
Jos 9:13 are worn out by the v long journey." H4394
Jos 10: 2 his people were v **much** alarmed at this, H4394
Jos 13: 1 "You *are now* **v old**, and H2416+995+928+2021+3427
Jos 13: 1 there are still v large areas of land to H4394
Jos 17:17 "You are numerous and v powerful. H1524
Jos 22: 3 time now—to **this** v day—you have not H2296
Jos 22: 5 But be v careful to keep the H4394
Jos 22:17 Up to **this** v day we have not cleansed H2296
Jos 23: 1 by then a v **old** *man*, H2416+995+928+2021+3427
Jos 23: 2 to them: "*I am* **v old**. H2416+995+928+2021+3427
Jos 23: 6 "Be v strong; be careful to obey all that is H4394
Jos 23:11 So be v careful to love the LORD your God. H4394
Jdg 2:20 the LORD *was* **v angry** with Israel and H3013+678
Jdg 3:17 Eglon king of Moab, who was a v fat man. H4394
Jdg 5:18 The people of Zebulun risked their v lives NDT
Jdg 9:30 son of Ebed said, he *was* **v angry**. H3013+678
Jdg 13: 6 looked like an angel of God, v awesome. H4394
Jdg 15:18 Because he was v thirsty, he cried out to H4394
Jdg 18: 9 the land, and it is v good. Aren't you H4394
Jdg 18:20 The priest *was* **v pleased**. He took H3512+4213
Ru 1:20 the Almighty has made my life v bitter. H4394
1Sa 2:17 the young men was v great in the LORD's H4394
1Sa 2:22 Now Eli, who was v old, heard about H4394
1Sa 4:10 The slaughter was v great; Israel lost thirty H4394
1Sa 4:16 the battle line; I fled from it **this** v day." H2021
1Sa 5:11 with panic; God's hand was v heavy on it. H4394
1Sa 16:21 Saul liked him **v much**, and David H4394
1Sa 17:12 time he *was* **v old**. H2416+995+928+2021+408
1Sa 17:46 **This** v day I will give the carcasses of the H2296
1Sa 18: 8 Saul was v angry; this refrain displeased H4394
1Sa 20: 3 father **knows v well** that I have H3359+3359
1Sa 20: 7 If he says, '**V well**,' then your servant is H3202
1Sa 21:12 to heart and was v **much** afraid of Achish H4394
1Sa 23:22 They tell me he *is* **v crafty**. H6891+6891
1Sa 25: 2 property there at Carmel, was v wealthy. H4394
1Sa 25:15 Yet these men were v good to us. They did H4394
1Sa 25:36 He was in high spirits and v drunk H6330+4394
1Sa 28: 2 replied, "**V well**, I will make you H4200+4027
2Sa 1:26 my brother; you were v dear to me. H4394
2Sa 2:17 The battle that day was v fierce H6330+4394
2Sa 3: 8 Abner was v angry because of what H4394
2Sa 3: 8 **This** v day I am loyal to the house of your H2021
2Sa 7:24 people Israel as **your v own** forever, H4200+3870
2Sa 11: 2 The woman was v beautiful, H4394
2Sa 12: 2 The rich man had a v large number of H4394
2Sa 12:11 Before your v eyes I will take your wives NDT
2Sa 13: 3 Jonadab was a v shrewd man. H4394
2Sa 13:36 and all his attendants wept v bitterly. H4394
2Sa 14:21 said to Joab, "**V well**, I will do it. H2180+5528
2Sa 19:32 Now Barzillai was v old, eighty years of H4394
2Sa 19:32 Mahanaim, for he was a v wealthy man. H4394
2Sa 24:10 I have done a v foolish thing." H4394
1Ki 1: 1 King David *was* **v old**, H2416+995+928+2021+3427
1Ki 1: 4 The woman was v beautiful; she H6330+4394
1Ki 1: 6 He was also v handsome and was born H4394
1Ki 1:30 surely carry out **this** v day what I swore to H2296
1Ki 2:18 "**V well**," Bathsheba replied, "I will speak H3202
1Ki 2:37 him a son to sit on his throne **this** v day. H2296
1Ki 4:29 Solomon wisdom and v great insight, H4394
1Ki 10: 2 at Jerusalem with a v great caravan— H4394
1Ki 16:16 king over Israel **that** v day there in the H2085
1Ki 19:10 "*I have been* **v zealous** for the LORD H7861+7861
1Ki 19:14 "*I have been* **v zealous** for the LORD H7861+7861
2Ki 6:12 the king of Israel the v words you speak in NDT
2Ki 17:18 So the LORD was v angry with Israel and H4394
2Ki 23:17 altar of Bethel the v things you have done H465
1Ch 17:22 people Israel **your v own** forever, H4200+3870
1Ch 21: 8 I have done a v foolish thing." H4394
1Ch 21:13 his mercy is v great; but do not let H4394
1Ch 23:17 Rehabiah were v numerous. H4200+5087+2025
1Ch 26: 6 because they were **v capable men**. H1475+2657
2Ch 9: 1 Arriving with a v great caravan—with H4394
2Ch 11:12 the cities, and made them v strong. H2221+4394
2Ch 20:19 of Israel, with a v loud voice. H4200+5087+2025
2Ch 21:15 You yourself will be v ill with a lingering H8041
2Ch 26: 8 had become v powerful. H6330+4200+5087+2025
2Ch 30:13 A v large crowd of people assembled in H4394
2Ch 32:27 Hezekiah had v great wealth and honor H4394
2Ch 32:29 God had given him v great riches. H4394
Ne 1: 7 *We have* **acted v wickedly** toward H2472+2472
Ne 2: 2 sadness of heart." I was v much afraid, H4394
Ne 2:10 they *were* v much **disturbed** that H8317+8288
Ne 4: 7 were being closed, they were v angry. H4394
Ne 5: 6 outcry and these charges, I was v angry. H4394
Ne 8:17 And their joy was v great. H4394
Est 1:18 **This** v day the Persian and Median women H2296
Job 1:12 said to Satan, "**V well, then**, everything he H2180
Job 2: 6 said to Satan, "**V well, then**, he is in your H2180
Job 10: 1 "I loathe my v life; therefore I will give free NDT
Job 32: 2 *became* **v angry** with Job for H3013+678
Job 33: 8 in my hearing—I heard the v words— H7754
Ps 38: 6 bowed down and brought v low; H6330+4394
Ps 75: 8 of the earth drink it down to its v dregs. NDT
Ps 77:16 writhed; the v depths were convulsed. H677
Ps 89:38 *you have been* **v angry** with your anointed H6297
Ps 102:14 your servants; her v dust moves them to pity. NDT
Ps 104: 1 LORD my God, you are v great; you are H4394
Ps 105:24 The LORD made his people v fruitful; he H4394
Ps 118:24 The LORD has done it this v day; let us H2021
Ps 119:112 your decrees **to the v end**. H4200+6409+6813
Ps 146: 4 on **that** v day their plans come to nothing. H2085
Pr 6:26 another man's wife preys on your v life. H3701
Pr 8:23 at the **v beginning**, when the world H8031
Pr 18: 7 their lips are a snare to **their** v lives. H2257
Pr 22:27 your v bed will be snatched from under you. NDT
Isa 10:25 **V soon** my anger against H6388+5071+4663
Isa 16:14 survivors will be **v few and feeble**." H5071+4663
Isa 24: 6 are burned up, and **v few** are left. H4663+632
Isa 25:12 them down to the ground, to the v dust. NDT
Isa 28:11 **V well then**, with foreign lips and strange H3954
Isa 29:17 **In a v short time**, will not H6388+5071+4663
Isa 47: 6 Even on the aged you laid a v heavy yoke. H4394
Isa 57: 9 you descended to the *v* **realm of the dead**! AIT
Isa 57:16 of me—the v **people** I have created. H5972s
Isa 65: 3 who continually provoke me to my v face, NDT
Jer 20:15 *who* **made** him **v glad** H8523+8523
Jer 24: 2 One basket had v good figs, like those that H4394
Jer 24: 2 the other basket had v bad figs, so bad H4394
Jer 24: 3 "The good ones are v good, but the bad H4394
Jer 25: 3 of Amon king of Judah until **this** v day— H2296
Jer 27:16 '**V soon** now the articles from the LORD's H4559
Jer 28:16 This v year you are going to die, because NDT
Jer 29:21 will put them to death before your v eyes. NDT
Jer 44:28 of Judah from Egypt will be **v few**. H5493+5031
La 4:20 LORD's anointed, our v life breath, was NDT
Eze 2: 3 been in revolt against me to this v day. H6795
Eze 4:15 "**V well**," he said, "I will let you bake your H8011
Eze 16:13 You became v beautiful and H928+4394+4394
Eze 16:34 You are the v **opposite**, for you give H2201
Eze 17:22 a shoot from the v **top** of a cedar and H8123
Eze 23:39 On the v day they sacrificed their children H2085
Eze 24: 2 this date, this v date, because the king H6795
Eze 24: 2 has laid siege to Jerusalem this v day. H6795
Eze 25:12 Judah and *became* **v guilty** by doing H870+870
Eze 37: 2 floor of the valley, bones that were v dry. H4394
Eze 40: 1 on that v day the hand of the LORD was on H6795
Eze 40: 2 Israel and set me on a v high mountain, H4394
Da 3:15 worship the image I made, v good. NDT
Da 5:30 That v night Belshazzar, king of the NDT
Da 7: 7 terrifying and frightening and v powerful. A10339
Da 8: 8 The goat became v great, but at the H6330+4394
Da 8:24 *He will become* **v strong**, but not by H6793+3946
Da 10:16 my lord, and *I* **feel v weak**. H4202+6806+3946
Da 11:25 with a large and v powerful army, H6330+4394
Hos 12: 8 "I am v rich; I have become H421
Joel 1:16 the food been cut off before our v eyes— NDT
Am 7:10 against you in the v heart of Israel. NDT
Jnh 2: 3 into the *v* **heart** *of* the seas, and the AIT
Jnh 3: 3 Now Nineveh was a v large city; it H4200+466
Jnh 4: 1 But to Jonah this seemed v wrong, and he H1524
Jnh 4: 6 Jonah was v happy about the plant. H1524
Mic 1: 9 It has reached the v gate of my people NDT
Zep 1: 4 the *v* **names** *of* the idolatrous priests AIT
Zep 3:20 I restore your fortunes before your v eyes," NDT
Zec 1: 2 "The LORD *was* **v angry** with your H7911+7912
Zec 1:14 'I am v jealous for Jerusalem and Zion H1524
Zec 1:15 I am v angry with the nations that feel H1524
Zec 7:12 So the LORD Almighty was v angry. H1524
Zec 8: 2 "I am v jealous for Zion; I am burning H1524
Zec 9: 2 Tyre and Sidon, though they are v skillful. H4394
Zec 14: 1 and divided up **within** your **v walls**. H928+7931
Mt 4: 8 devil took him to a v high mountain and *G3336*
Mt 10:30 And even **the** v hairs of your head are all *G3836*
Mt 21: 8 A v **large** crowd spread their cloaks on the *G4498*
Mt 26: 7 an alabaster jar of v **expensive** perfume, *G988*
Mt 26:22 They were v sad and began to say to him *G5379*
Mt 26:31 "**This** v night you will all fall away on *G4047*
Mt 26:34 Jesus answered, "**this** v night, before the *G4047*
Mt 28:15 among the Jews to **this** v **day**. *G4958+2465*
Mt 28:20 with you always, to the v **end** of the age." *G5333*
Mk 1:35 V early in the morning, while it was still *G3336*
Mk 6:35 they said, "and it's already v **late**. *G6052+4498*
Mk 9:35 who wants to be first must be the v last, *G4246*
Mk 12:42 came and put in two v **small copper coins**, *G3321*
Mk 14: 3 an alabaster jar of v **expensive** perfume, *G4500*
Mk 15: 1 **V early in the morning**, the chief *G2317+4745*
Mk 16: 2 V early on the first day of the week, just *G3336*
Mk 16: 4 the stone, which was v large, had been *G5379*
Lk 1: 7 they were both **v old**. *G4581+1877+3836+2465*
Lk 2:36 She was v old; she had lived with her *G4498*
Lk 2:38 Coming up to them *at* **that** v moment, she *G899*
Lk 7:21 At **that** v time Jesus cured many who had *G1697*
Lk 9:25 and yet lose or forfeit **their v self**? *G1571*
Lk 9:32 and his companions were v **sleepy**, *G976+5678*
Lk 12: 7 **the** *v* hairs of your head are all numbered. AIT
Lk 12:20 **This** v night your life will be demanded *G4047*
Lk 12:26 Since you cannot do this v **little** *thing*, why *G1788*
Lk 16:10 can be trusted with v **little** can also be *G1788*
Lk 16:10 is dishonest with v **little** will also be *G1788*
Lk 18:23 he became v **sad**, because he was *G4337*
Lk 18:23 very sad, because he was v wealthy. *G5379*
Lk 19:17 have been trustworthy in a v **small** *matter*, *G1788*
Lk 21: 2 widow put in two v **small copper coins**. *G3321*
Lk 24: 1 first day of the week, v early in the morning *G960*
Jn 1:51 He then added, "**V truly** I tell you, you *G297+297*
Jn 3: 3 Jesus replied, "**V truly** I tell you, no *G297+297*
Jn 3: 5 Jesus answered, "**V truly** I tell you, no *G297+297*
Jn 3:11 **V truly** I tell you, we speak of what we *G297+297*
Jn 5:17 Father is always at his work to **this v day**, *G785*
Jn 5:19 "**V truly** I tell you, the Son can do *G297+297*
Jn 5:24 "**V truly** I tell you, whoever hears my *G297+297*
Jn 5:25 **V truly** I tell you, a time is coming and *G297+297*
Jn 5:36 me to finish—the v works that I am doing *G899*
Jn 5:39 These are the v Scriptures that testify about NDT
Jn 6:26 answered, "**V truly** I tell you, you *G297+297*
Jn 6:32 said to them, "**V truly** I tell you, it is *G297+297*
Jn 6:47 **V truly** I tell you, the one who believes *G297+297*
Jn 6:53 said to them, "**V truly** I tell you, unless *G297+297*
Jn 8:34 Jesus replied, "**V truly** I tell you *G297+297*
Jn 8:51 **V truly** I tell you, whoever obeys my *G297+297*
Jn 8:58 "**V truly** I tell you," Jesus answered *G297+297*
Jn 10: 1 "**V truly** I tell you Pharisees, anyone *G297+297*
Jn 10: 7 said again, "**V truly** I tell you, I am *G297+297*
Jn 10:36 the Father **set apart as** *his* **v own** and sent *G39*
Jn 12:24 **V truly** I tell you, unless a kernel of *G297+297*
Jn 12:27 it was **for this v reason** I came to *G1328+4047*
Jn 12:48 the v words I have spoken will condemn *G1697*
Jn 13:16 **V truly** I tell you, no servant is greater *G297+297*
Jn 13:20 **V truly** I tell you, whoever accepts *G297+297*
Jn 13:21 testified, "**V truly** I tell you, one of *G297+297*
Jn 13:38 **V truly** I tell you, before the rooster *G297+297*
Jn 14:12 **V truly** I tell you, whoever believes in *G297+297*
Jn 16: 7 But **v truly** I tell you, it is for your good that *G237*
Jn 16:20 **V truly** I tell you, you will weep and *G297+297*
Jn 16:23 **V truly** I tell you, my Father will give *G297+297*
Jn 21:18 **V truly** I tell you, when you were *G297+297*
Ac 1: 9 he was taken up before **their** v eyes, and a *G899*
Ac 8:35 began with that v passage of Scripture *G4047*
Ac 15: 3 This news made all the believers v glad. *G3489*
Ac 17:22 I see that in every way you *are* **v religious**. *G1273*
Ac 17:23 you are ignorant *of the v* **thing** you worship— AIT
Ac 22: 2 to them in Aramaic, they became v quiet. *G3437*
Ac 22:13 And at **that** v moment I was able to see *G899*
Ac 25:10 to the Jews, as you yourself know **v well**. *G2822*
Ac 26:22 But God has helped me to this v day; so I *G3836*
Ac 27:14 **Before v long**, a wind of *G3552+4024+4498*
Ro 1:32 continue to do **these** *v things* but also AIT
Ro 3: 2 been entrusted with **the** v words of God. *G3836*
Ro 5: 7 **V rarely** will anyone die for a righteous *G3660*
Ro 7:10 I found that the v commandment that was *G4047*
Ro 9:17 "I raised you up for this v purpose, that I *G899*
Ro 9:26 "In **the** v place where it was said to them *G3836*
Ro 11: 8 that could not hear, to this **v day**." *G4958+2465*
Ro 14: 9 **For this v reason**, Christ died *G1650+4047+1142*
Ro 16: 6 Greet Mary, who worked v hard for you. *G4498*
Ro 16:12 who has worked v hard in the Lord. *G4498*
1Co 4: 3 **I care v little** if I am judged *G1650+1788+1639*
1Co 4:11 To **this** v hour we go hungry and thirsty, we *G785*
1Co 4:19 But I will come to you **v soon**, if the Lord *G5441*
1Co 6: 7 **The v fact that** you have lawsuits among *G4022*
1Co 11:14 Does not the v nature of things teach you *G899*
2Co 3:12 since we have such a hope, we are v bold. *G4498*
2Co 5: 5 has fashioned us for this v purpose is God, *G899*
2Co 8: 2 In the midst of a v severe trial, their *G4498*
2Co 12:15 So I will **v gladly** spend for you everything *G2452*
Gal 2:10 the v thing I had been eager to do all *G899*
Gal 3: 1 Before your *v* eyes Jesus Christ was clearly AIT
Eph 4:10 who descended is **the v one** who ascended *G899*
Eph 5:15 **Be v careful**, then, how you live— *G1063+209*
Eph 6:22 I am sending him to you for this v purpose *G899*
Php 2: 6 being in v **nature** God, did not *G3671*
Php 2: 7 by taking the v **nature** of a servant, *G3671*
1Th 4: 8 **the** *v* God who gives you his Holy Spirit. AIT
1Th 5: 2 you know **v well** that the day of the Lord *G209*
1Ti 1:16 But **for that v reason** I was shown *G1328+4047*
2Ti 1:18 You know **v well** in how many ways he *G1019*
2Ti 3: 9 But they will not get **v far** because *G2093+4498*
Titus 2:14 himself a people that are **his v own**, *G4342*
Phm 12 who is my **v heart**—back to you. *G5073*

V

Phm 16 He is v dear to me but even dearer to you *G3436*
Phm 19 to mention that you owe me **your v self**. *G4932*
Heb 3:14 our original conviction firmly to the v end. NDT
Heb 6:11 to show this same diligence to the v **end**, *G5465*
Heb 6:17 of his purpose v clear to the heirs of *G4358*
Jas 3: 4 are steered by a v **small** rudder wherever *G1788*
1Pe 4:11 do so as one who speaks the *v* **words** of God. AIT
2Pe 1: 4 he has given us his v **great** and precious *G3492*
2Pe 1: 5 **For this v reason**, make every effort *G899+4047*
Jude 3 although I was v eager to write to you *G4246*
Jude 8 In the v same way, on the strength of their *G3530*
Jude 10 and *the v* **things** they do understand by AIT
Rev 9:15 been kept ready for **this** *v* hour and day and AIT
Rev 11:13 At **that** v hour there was a severe *G1697*
Rev 21:11 was like that of a v **precious** jewel, *G5508*

VESSEL (2) [VESSELS]
Pr 25: 4 and a silversmith can produce a v; H3998
Isa 2:16 every trading ship and every stately v. H8500

VESSELS (3) [VESSEL]
Ex 7:19 in Egypt, even in **v of wood** and stone." H6770
Isa 22:24 all its lesser v, from the bowls to all H3998
Isa 66:20 of the LORD in ceremonially clean v. H3998

VESTMENTS (1)
Ezr 3:10 the priests *in their* v and with trumpets H4252

VESTURE (KJV) CLOAK, CLOTHES, CLOTHING, GARMENT, ROBE

VETERAN (1)
Eze 27: 9 **V** craftsmen of Byblos were on board as H2418

VEX, VEXATION, VEXATIONS, VEXED (KJV) AFFLICTED, AGONY, ANGUISH, BITTER, CHASING, CONFUSION, DISTRESS, ENEMIES, GRIEVED, INFLICTED, MISTREAT, MISTREATED, OPPRESSED, PERSECUTE, RIVAL, SHATTERED, SICK, TERRIFIES, TORMENT, TORMENTED, TROUBLE, TROUBLING, TURMOIL

VEXED (2)
Ps 78:41 to the test; *they* v the Holy One of Israel. H9345
Ps 112:10 The wicked will see and *be* v, they will H4087

VIAL, VIALS (KJV) FLASK, BOWL, BOWLS

VICINITY (15)
Dt 11:30 living in the Arabah **in the v of** Gilgal. H4578
Jos 3:16 a town called Adam in the v *of* Zarethan, H7396
Jos 15:46 all that were in the v *of* Ashdod, together H3338
Jdg 11:33 Aroer **to the v of** Minnith, H6330+995+3870
Jdg 20:43 them in the v *of* Gibeah on the east H5790
1Sa 5: 6 heavy on the people of Ashdod and its v; H1473
1Sa 13:17 turned toward Ophrah in the v *of* Shual, H824
2Ki 15:16 Tiphsah and everyone in the city and its v, H1473
1Ch 18: 3 king of Zobah, **in the v of** Hamath, when H2025
Mt 2:16 Bethlehem and its v who were two *G4246+3990*
Mt 15:22 woman from that v came to him, *G3990*
Mt 15:39 the boat and went to the v of Magadan. *G3990*
Mk 7:24 left that place and went to the v of Tyre. *G3990*
Mk 7:31 Then Jesus left the v of Tyre and went *G3990*
Lk 24:50 led them out **to the v of** Bethany, *G2401+4639*

VICIOUSLY (1)
Jdg 15: 8 *He* **attacked** them v and H5782+8797+6584+3751

VICTIM (5) [VICTIMS]
Ex 21:16 whether the v has been sold or is still in H2257S
Ex 21:18 with their fist and the v does not die but is NDT
Ex 21:19 see that the v is completely healed. NDT
Hos 6: 9 As marauders lie in ambush for a v, so do H408S
Mt 5:32 makes her the **v of adultery**, and anyone *G3658*

VICTIMS (11) [VICTIM]
Nu 23:24 its prey and drinks the blood of its v." H2728
Nu 31: 8 Among their v were Evi, Rekem, Zur, Hur H2728
Job 29:17 snatched the v from their teeth. H3272
Ps 10: 8 His eyes watch in secret for his v; H2724
Ps 10:10 His v are crushed, they collapse; they fall H2724
Ps 10:14 The v commit themselves to you; you are H2724
Pr 7:26 Many are the v she has brought down; her H2728
Eze 34:29 will no longer be v *of* famine in the land H665
Da 7: 7 devoured its v and trampled underfoot NDT
Da 7:19 devoured its v and trampled underfoot NDT
Na 3: 1 full of lies, full of plunder, never without v! H3272

VICTOR'S (2) [VICTORY]
2Ti 2: 5 *does* not **receive the v crown** except *G5110*
Rev 2:10 I will give you life as your v **crown**. *G5109*

VICTORIES (7) [VICTORY]
Jdg 5:11 They recite the v *of* the LORD, the victories H7407
Jdg 5:11 of the LORD, the v *of* his villagers in Israel. H7407
2Sa 22:51 "He gives his king great v; he shows H3802
Ps 18:50 He gives his king great v; he shows H3802
Ps 21: 1 How great is his joy in the v you give! H3802
Ps 21: 5 Through the v you gave, his glory is great H3802
Ps 44: 4 my God, who decrees v *for* Jacob. H3802

VICTORIOUS (18) [VICTORY]
1Ki 22:12 "Attack Ramoth Gilead and *be* v," they H7503
1Ki 22:15 "Attack and *be* v," he answered, "for the H7503
2Ch 13:18 the people of Judah *were* v because they H599
2Ch 18:11 "Attack Ramoth Gilead and *be* v," they H7503
2Ch 18:14 "Attack and *be* v," he answered, "for they H7503
Ps 20: 6 sanctuary with the v power of his right H3829
Da 11: 7 he will fight against them and *be* v. H2616
Zec 9: 9 righteous and v, lowly and riding on H3828
Rev 2: 7 *To the one who is* v, I will give the right to *G3771*
Rev 2:11 The *one who is* v will not be hurt at all by *G3771*
Rev 2:17 *To the one who is* v, I will give some of *G3771*
Rev 2:26 *To the one who is* v and does my will to *G3771*
Rev 3: 5 The *one who is* v will, like them, be *G3771*
Rev 3:12 The *one who is* v I will make a pillar in *G3771*
Rev 3:21 *To the one who is* v, I will give the right to *G3771*
Rev 3:21 just as I *was* v and sat down with my *G3771*
Rev 15: 2 those *who had been* v over the beast and *G3771*
Rev 21: 7 Those *who are* v will inherit all this, and I *G3771*

VICTORIOUSLY (1) [VICTORY]
Ps 45: 4 majesty ride forth v in the cause of truth, H7503

VICTORY (41) [VICTOR'S, VICTORIES, VICTORIOUS, VICTORIOUSLY]
Ex 32:18 "It is not the sound of v, it is not the H1476
Dt 20: 4 you against your enemies to *give you* v." H3828
Jdg 12: 3 LORD **gave** me the v *over* them H5989+928+3338
Jdg 15:18 "You have given your servant this great v. H9591
1Sa 19: 5 The LORD won a great v for all Israel, and H9591
2Sa 8: 6 The LORD **gave** David v wherever he went. H3828
2Sa 8:10 congratulate him on *his* v in battle over H5782
2Sa 8:14 The LORD **gave** David v wherever he went. H3828
2Sa 19: 2 the whole army the v that day was turned H9591
2Sa 23:10 The LORD brought about a great v that day H9591
2Sa 23:12 the LORD brought about a great v. H9591
2Ki 5: 1 him the LORD had given v to Aram. H9591
2Ki 13:17 "The LORD's arrow of v, the arrow of H9591
2Ki 13:17 of victory, the arrow of v over Aram!" H9591
2Ki 14:10 Glory in your v, but stay at home! Why NDT
1Ch 11:14 the LORD **brought about** a great v. H3828+9591
1Ch 18: 6 The LORD **gave** David v wherever he went H3828
1Ch 18:10 congratulate him on *his* v in battle over H5782
1Ch 18:13 The LORD **gave** David v wherever he went H3828
Ps 20: 5 joy over your v and lift up our banners H3802
Ps 20: 6 The LORD **gives** v *to* his anointed H3828
Ps 20: 9 **give** v *to* the king! Answer us when H3828
Ps 44: 3 nor *did* their arm **bring** them v; it was H3828
Ps 44: 6 my bow, my sword *does* not **bring** me v; H3828
Ps 44: 7 but *you* **give** us v over our enemies, you H3828
Ps 60:12 With God we will gain the v, and he will H2657
Ps 108:13 With God we will gain the v, and he will H2657
Ps 118:15 Shouts of joy and v resound in the tents of H3802
Ps 129: 2 but *they have* not **gained the** v over me. H3523
Ps 144:10 to the One who gives v to kings, who H9591
Ps 149: 4 his people; he crowns the humble with v. H3802
Pr 11:14 but v is won through many advisers. H9591
Pr 21:31 the day of battle, but v rests with the LORD. H9591
Pr 24: 6 and v is won through many advisers. H9591
Isa 63: 1 proclaiming v, mighty to save." H7407
Hab 3: 8 rode your horses and your chariots *to* v? H3802
Mt 12:20 till he has brought justice through to v. *G3777*
1Co 15:54 "Death has been swallowed up in v." *G3777*
1Co 15:55 O death, is your v? Where, O death, *G3777*
1Co 15:57 He gives us the v through our Lord Jesus *G3777*
1Jn 5: 4 This is the v that has overcome the world *G3772*

VICTUAL, VICTUALS (KJV) FOOD, GRAIN, PROVISIONS

VIEW (19) [VIEWED, VIEWPOINT, VIEWS]
Nu 23: 9 I see them, from the heights *I* v them. H8800
Nu 33: 3 out defiantly in **full v** *of* all the Egyptians, H6524
Dt 32:49 from Jericho, and v Canaan, the land I am H8011
2Sa 6:20 half-naked **in full v of** the slave H4200+6524
Ne 9:38 **"In v of** all this, we are making a binding H928
Ps 48:13 well her ramparts, v her citadels, that you H7170
Ps 68:24 *has* **come into** v, the procession of H8011
Pr 5:21 your ways are **in full v** *of* the LORD, H5790+6524
Pr 17:24 person keeps wisdom **in** v, H907+7156
Isa 5:19 it approach, *let it* **come into** v, so we may H995
Isa 33:17 in his beauty and v a land that stretches H8011
Isa 57: 6 grain offerings. **In v of** all this, should I H6584
Mk 2:12 mat and walked out **in full v of** them all. *G1869*
Ro 12: 1 sisters, **in v of** God's mercy, to offer *G1328*
2Co 5:16 regard no one **from** a worldly **point of v**. *G2848*
Gal 5:10 in the Lord that you *will* **take** no other v. *G5858*
Php 3:15 are mature *should* **take** such **a v of things**. *G5858*
2Ti 4: 1 in v of his appearing and his kingdom NDT
Rev 13:13 to the earth **in full v of** the people. *G1967*

VIEWED (2) [VIEW]
Nu 32: 9 up to the Valley of Eshkol and v the land, H8011
Ps 102:19 on high, from heaven *he* v the earth, H5564

VIEWPOINT (1) [VIEW]
1Jn 4: 5 therefore speak **from** *the v of* the world, AIT

VIEWS (2) [VIEW]
Job 28:24 he v the ends of the earth and sees H5564
Ac 28:22 But we want to hear what your v *are*, for *G5858*

VIGIL (3)
Ex 12:42 Because the LORD kept v that night to bring H9081
Ex 12:42 are to keep v to honor the LORD for H9081
Isa 65: 4 spend their nights **keeping secret** v; H5915

VIGILANT (KJV) SOBER, TEMPERATE

VIGOR (7) [VIGOROUS, VIGOROUSLY]
Job 5:26 You will come to the grave in **full** v, like H3995
Job 18: 7 The v *of* his step is weakened; his own H226
Job 20:11 The **youthful** v that fills his bones will lie H6596
Job 21:23 One person dies in full v, completely H6795
Job 30: 2 since their v had gone from them? H3995
Pr 31: 3 women, your v on those who ruin kings. H2006
Ecc 11:10 for youth and v are meaningless. H8841

VIGOROUS (3) [VIGOR]
Ex 1:19 they are v and give birth before the H2650
Jos 14:11 I'm just as v to go out to battle now as I H3946
Jdg 3:29 Moabites, all v and strong; not one H9045

VIGOROUSLY (6) [VIGOR]
Jdg 8: 1 And they challenged him v. H928+2622
Job 23: 6 Would he v oppose me? No H928+8044+3946
Pr 31:17 She sets about her work v; her arms H928+6437
Jer 50:34 *He will* v **defend** their cause so that H8189+8189
Ac 18:28 For he v refuted his Jewish opponents in *G2364*
Ac 23: 9 were Pharisees stood up and **argued** v. *G1372*

VILE (28) [VILEST]
Dt 7:26 **Regard** it **as** v and utterly detest it H9210+9210
Jdg 19:23 to them, "No, my friends, don't *be so* v. H8317
2Ki 23:13 Ashtoreth the v **goddess** *of* the Sidonians, H9199
2Ki 23:13 Chemosh the v **god** *of* Moab, and for H9199
Est 7: 6 This v Haman!" Then Haman H8273
Job 15:16 less mortals, *who are* v and corrupt, who H9493
Ps 12: 8 strut about when *what* is v is honored by H2359
Ps 14: 1 their deeds *are* v; there is no one H9493
Ps 15: 4 who despises a v *person* but honors those H4415
Ps 41: 8 "A v disease has afflicted him; he will H1175
Ps 53: 1 and *their* ways *are* v; there is no H9493
Ps 101: 3 look with approval on anything that is v. H1175
Jer 16:18 forms of their v **images** and have filled my H9199
Jer 32:34 They set up their v **images** in the house H9199
Eze 5:11 with all your v **images** and detestable H9199
Eze 7:20 They made it into v **images**; therefore I H9199
Eze 11:18 remove all its v **images** and detestable H9199
Eze 11:21 devoted to their v **images** and detestable H9199
Eze 16:52 Because your sins *were* more v than theirs, H9493
Eze 20: 7 get rid of the v **images** you have set your H9199
Eze 20: 8 not get rid of the v **images** they had set H9199
Eze 20:30 did and lust after their v **images**? H9199
Eze 37:23 their idols and v **images** or with any of H9199
Hos 9:10 idol and became as v as the thing they H9199
Na 1:14 I will prepare your grave, for *you are* v." H7837
Rev 21: 8 the unbelieving, the v, the murderers, the *G1009*
Rev 22:11 let the v *person* continue to be vile *G4865*
Rev 22:11 *let* the vile person continue *to be* v; let *G4862*

VILEST (1) [VILE]
1Ki 21:26 *He* **behaved in the v manner** by H9493+4394

VILLAGE (21) [VILLAGERS, VILLAGES]
Mt 10:11 Whatever town or v you enter, search there *G3267*
Mt 21: 2 to them, "Go to the v ahead of you, and *G3267*
Mk 6: 6 teaching **from v to village**. *G3836+3267+3241*
Mk 6: 6 teaching **from village to v**. *G3836+3267+3241*
Mk 8:23 by the hand and led him outside the v. *G3267*
Mk 8:26 saying, "Don't even go into the v." *G3267*
Mk 11: 2 to them, "Go to the v ahead of you, and *G3267*
Lk 5:17 come from every v of Galilee and from *G3267*
Lk 8: 1 about from one town and v to another, *G3267*
Lk 9: 6 and went **from v to village**, *G2848+3836+3267*
Lk 9: 6 and went **from village to v**, *G2848+3836+3267*
Lk 9:52 into a Samaritan v to get things ready *G3267*
Lk 9:56 he and his disciples went to another v. *G3267*
Lk 10:38 he came to a v where a woman named *G3267*
Lk 17:12 As he was going into a v, ten men who *G3267*
Lk 19:30 "Go to the v ahead of you, and as you *G3267*
Lk 24:13 them were going to a v called Emmaus, *G3267*
Lk 24:28 they approached the v to which they were *G3267*
Jn 11: 1 the v of Mary and her sister Martha. *G3267*
Jn 11:30 Now Jesus had not yet entered the v, but *G3267*
Jn 11:54 the wilderness, to a v called Ephraim *G4484*

VILLAGERS (2) [VILLAGE]
Jdg 5: 7 **V** in Israel would not fight; they held back H7251
Jdg 5:11 of the LORD, the victories of his v in Israel. H7251

VILLAGES (87) [VILLAGE]
Lev 25:31 But houses in v without walls around them H2958
Dt 2:23 the Avvites who lived in v as far as Gaza, H2958
Dt 3: 5 there were also a great many unwalled v. H6551
Jos 10:37 with its king, its v and everyone in it. H6551
Jos 10:39 its king and its v, and put them to the H6551
Jos 13:23 towns and their v were the inheritance H2958
Jos 13:28 towns and their v were the inheritance H2958
Jos 15:32 a total of twenty-nine towns and their v. H2958
Jos 15:36 fourteen towns and their v. H2958
Jos 15:41 Makkedah—sixteen towns and their v. H2958
Jos 15:44 Mareshah—nine towns and their v. H2958
Jos 15:45 with its surrounding settlements and v; H2958
Jos 15:46 vicinity of Ashdod, together with their v; H2958
Jos 15:47 its surrounding settlements and v; and H2958
Jos 15:47 its settlements and v, as far as the Wadi H2958
Jos 15:51 Giloh—eleven towns and their v. H2958
Jos 15:54 Hebron) and Zior—nine towns and their v. H2958
Jos 15:57 Timnah—ten towns and their v. H2958

Jos 15:59 Anoth and Eltekon—six towns and their v. H2958
Jos 15:60 Rabbah—two towns and their v. H2958
Jos 15:62 Salt and En Gedi—six towns and their v. H2958
Jos 16: 9 the towns and their v that were set aside H2958
Jos 18:24 Geba—twelve towns and their v. H2958
Jos 18:28 Kiriath—fourteen towns and their v. H2958
Jos 19: 6 Sharuhen—thirteen towns and their v; H2958
Jos 19: 7 Ashan—four towns and their v— H2958
Jos 19: 8 all the v around these towns as far as H2958
Jos 19:15 There were twelve towns and their v. H2958
Jos 19:16 towns and their v were the inheritance H2958
Jos 19:22 There were sixteen towns and their v. H2958
Jos 19:23 towns and their v were the inheritance H2958
Jos 19:30 There were twenty-two towns and their v. H2958
Jos 19:31 towns and their v were the inheritance H2958
Jos 19:38 There were nineteen towns and their v. H2958
Jos 19:39 towns and their v were the inheritance H2958
Jos 19:48 towns and their v were the inheritance H2958
Jos 21:12 the fields and v *around* the city they had H2958
1Sa 6:18 the fortified towns with their country v. H4108
1Ch 4:32 Their **surrounding** v were Etam, Ain H2958
1Ch 4:33 all the v around these towns as far as H2958
1Ch 5:16 in Bashan and its **outlying** v, and on all H1426
1Ch 6:56 But the fields and v *around* the city were H2958
1Ch 7:28 included Bethel and its **surrounding** v, H1426
1Ch 7:28 the east, Gezer and its v to the west, and H1426
1Ch 7:28 Shechem and its v all the way to H1426
1Ch 7:28 its villages all the way to Ayyah and its v. H1426
1Ch 7:29 Megiddo and Dor, together with their v. H1426
1Ch 8:12 built Ono and Lod with its **surrounding** v), H1426
1Ch 9:16 who lived in the v *of* the Netophathites. H2958
1Ch 9:22 were registered by genealogy in their v. H2958
1Ch 9:25 Levites in their v had to come from time H2958
1Ch 18: 1 Gath and its **surrounding** v from the H1426
1Ch 27:25 in the towns, the v and the watchtowers. H4107
2Ch 8: 2 Solomon rebuilt the v that Hiram had H6551
2Ch 13:19 Ephron, with their **surrounding** v. H1426
2Ch 14:14 They destroyed all the v around Gerar, for H6551
2Ch 14:14 They looted all these v, since there was H6551
2Ch 28:18 Gimzo, with their **surrounding** v. H1426
2Ch 32:29 He built v and acquired great numbers of H6551
Ne 6: 2 in one of the v on the plain of Ono." H4099
Ne 11:25 As for the v with their fields, some of the H2958
Ne 11:25 its settlements, in Jekabzeel and its v, H2958
Ne 11:30 Adullam and their v, in Lachish and its H2958
Ne 12:28 from the v *of* the Netophathites, H2958
Ne 12:29 musicians had built v for themselves H2958
Est 9:19 those living in v—observe the H6551+7252
Ps 10: 8 He lies in wait near the v; from ambush H2958
Ps 48:11 the v *of* Judah are glad because of your H1426
Ps 97: 8 rejoices and the v *of* Judah are glad H1426
SS 7:11 let us spend the night in the v. H4107
Jer 17:26 towns of Judah and the v around Jerusalem, NDT
Jer 19:15 city and all the v *around* it every disaster I H6551
Jer 32:44 of Benjamin, in the v around Jerusalem, in NDT
Jer 33:13 in the v around Jerusalem and in the towns NDT
Jer 49: 2 its **surrounding** v will be set on fire. H1426
Eze 30:18 and her v will go into captivity. H1426
Eze 38:11 "I will invade a land of **unwalled** v; I will H7252
Eze 38:13 of Tarshish and all her v will say to you, H4099
Mt 9:35 Jesus went through all the towns and v *G3267*
Mt 14:15 they can go to the v and buy themselves *G3267*
Mk 1:38 to the nearby v—so I can preach *G3268*
Mk 6:36 countryside and v and buy themselves *G3267*
Mk 6:56 he went—into v, towns or countryside *G3267*
Mk 8:27 went on to the v around Caesarea Philippi *G3267*
Lk 9:12 to the surrounding v and countryside and *G3267*
Lk 13:22 Then Jesus went through the towns and v *G3267*
Ac 8:25 the gospel *in* many Samaritan v. *G3267*

VILLAIN (1) [VILLAINS]

Pr 6:12 A troublemaker and a v, who goes H408+224

VILLAINS (1) [VILLAIN]

Ps 22:16 a pack of v encircles me; they H8317

VINDICATE (10) [VINDICATED, VINDICATES, VINDICATING, VINDICATION]

Dt 32:36 The LORD *will* v his people and relent H1906
1Sa 24:15 *may he* v me by delivering me from your H9149
Job 33:32 answer me; speak up, for I want *to* v you. H7405
Ps 7: 8 V me, LORD, according to my righteousness H9149
Ps 26: 1 V me, LORD, for I have led a blameless life; H9149
Ps 35:24 V me in your righteousness, LORD my God H9149
Ps 43: 1 V me, my God, and plead my cause H9149
Ps 54: 1 by your name; v me by your might. H1906
Ps 135:14 For the LORD *will* v his people and have H1906
Ps 138: 8 The LORD *will* v me; your love, LORD H1698

VINDICATED (9) [VINDICATE]

Ge 20:16 who are with you; *you* **are** completely v." H3519
Ge 30: 6 Rachel said, "God *has* v me; he has H1906
2Sa 18:19 king that the LORD *has* v him by delivering H9149
2Sa 18:31 The LORD *has* v you today by delivering H9149
Job 11: 2 to go unanswered? *Is* this talker *to be* v? H7405
Job 13:18 have prepared my case, I know I *will be* v. H7405
Ps 17:15 I will be v and will see your face H7406
Jer 51:10 " 'The LORD *has* v us; come, let us H3655+7407
1Ti 3:16 in the flesh, *was* v by the Spirit, was *G1467*

VINDICATES (2) [VINDICATE]

Ps 57: 2 out to God Most High, to God, *who* v me. H1698
Isa 50: 8 *He who* v me is near. Who then will bring H7405

VINDICATING (2) [VINDICATE]

1Ki 8:32 v the innocent by treating them in H7405
2Ch 6:23 v the innocent by treating them in H7405

VINDICATION (7) [VINDICATE]

Ps 17: 2 Let my v come from you; may your eyes H5477
Ps 24: 5 from the LORD and v from God their Savior. H7407
Ps 35:27 who delight in my v shout for joy and H7406
Ps 37: 6 the dawn, your v like the noonday sun. H5477
Isa 54:17 this is their v from me," declares the H7407
Isa 62: 1 till her v shines out like the dawn H7406
Isa 62: 2 The nations will see your v, and all kings H7406

VINE (48) [VINES, VINEYARD, VINEYARDS, VINTAGE]

Ge 40: 9 "In my dream I saw a v in front of me, H1728
Ge 40:10 on the v were three branches. As soon H1728
Ge 49:11 He will tether his donkey to a v, his colt to H1728
Ge 49:22 "Joseph is a **fruitful** v, a fruitful vine H1201+7238
Ge 49:22 a **fruitful** v near a spring H1201+7238
Dt 32:32 Their v comes from the vine of Sodom H1728
Dt 32:32 comes from the v *of* Sodom and from the H1728
Jdg 9:12 "Then the trees said to the v, 'Come and H1728
Jdg 9:13 "But the v answered, 'Should I give up my H1728
1Ki 4:25 under their own v and under their own fig H1728
2Ki 4:39 found a wild v and picked as many of H1728
2Ki 18:31 fruit from your own v and fig tree and H1728
Job 15:33 He will be like a v stripped of its unripe H1728
Ps 80: 8 You transplanted a v from Egypt; you H1728
Ps 80:14 from heaven and see! Watch over this v, H1728
Ps 80:16 Your v is cut down, it is burned with fire; at NDT
Ps 128: 3 will be like a fruitful v within your house; H1728
SS 7: 8 breasts be like clusters of grapes on the v, H1728
Isa 24: 7 The new wine dries up and the v withers H1728
Isa 34: 4 will fall like withered leaves from the v, H1728
Isa 36:16 fruit from your own v and fig tree and H1728
Jer 2:21 planted you like a **choice** v of sound and H8603
Jer 2:21 you turn against me into a corrupt, wild v? H1728
Jer 6: 9 the remnant of Israel as thoroughly as a v; H1728
Jer 8:13 There will be no grapes on the v. There H1728
Eze 15: 2 how is the wood of a v different from that H1728
Eze 15: 6 the wood of the v among the trees of H1728
Eze 17: 6 sprouted and became a low, spreading v. H1728
Eze 17: 6 So it became a v and produced branches H1728
Eze 17: 7 The v now sent out its roots toward him H1728
Eze 17: 8 bear fruit and become a splendid v. H1728
Eze 19:10 mother was like a v *in* your vineyard H1728
Hos 10: 1 Israel was a spreading v; he brought forth H1728
Hos 14: 7 they will blossom like the v—Israel's H1728
Joel 1:11 you v **growers**; grieve for the wheat H4144
Joel 1:12 The v is dried up and the fig tree is H1728
Joel 2:22 the fig tree and the v yield their riches. H1728
Mic 4: 4 sit under their own v and under their own H1728
Hag 2:19 Until now, the v and the fig tree, the H1728
Zec 3:10 neighbor to sit under your v and fig tree, H1728
Zec 8:12 will grow well, the v will yield its fruit H1728
Mt 26:29 from this fruit *of* the v from now on until *G306*
Mk 14:25 from the fruit *of* the v until that day when *G306*
Lk 22:18 from the fruit *of* the v until the kingdom *G306*
Jn 15: 1 "I am the true v, and my Father is the *G306*
Jn 15: 4 bear fruit by itself; it must remain in the v. *G306*
Jn 15: 5 "I am the v; you are the branches. If you *G306*
Rev 14:18 the clusters of grapes *from* the earth's v, *G306*

VINEDRESSERS (KJV) VINE GROWERS, WORK VINEYARDS

VINEGAR (9)

Nu 6: 3 must not drink v *made from* wine or other H2810
Ru 2:14 Have some bread and dip it in the **wine** v." H2810
Ps 69:21 in my food and gave me v for my thirst. H2810
Pr 10:26 As v to the teeth and smoke to the eyes H2810
Pr 25:20 a cold day, or like v poured on a wound H2810
Mt 27:48 He filled it *with* **wine** v, put it on a staff *G3954*
Mk 15:36 filled a sponge *with* **wine** v, put it on a *G3954*
Lk 23:36 mocked him. They offered him **wine** v *G3954*
Jn 19:29 A jar of **wine** v was there, so they soaked a *G3954*

VINES (24) [VINE]

Lev 25: 5 harvest the grapes of your **untended** v. H5687
Lev 25:11 grows of itself or harvest the **untended** v. H5687
Dt 8: 8 with wheat and barley, v and fig trees H1728
Dt 24:21 your vineyard, *do* not **go over the** v **again**. H6618
Ps 78:47 He destroyed their v with hail and their H1728
Ps 105:33 he struck down their v and fig trees and H1728
SS 2:13 the blossoming v spread their fragrance. H1728
SS 6:11 to see if the v had budded or the H1728
SS 7:12 the vineyards to see if the v have budded, H1728
Isa 5: 2 stones and planted it with the **choicest** v. H8603
Isa 5: 7 of Judah are the v he delighted in. H5750
Isa 7:23 there were a thousand v worth a thousand H1728
Isa 16: 8 of Heshbon wither, the v *of* Sibmah also. H1728
Isa 16: 8 have trampled down the **choicest** v, H8602
Isa 16: 9 as Jazer weeps, for the v *of* Sibmah. H1728
Isa 17:10 out the finest plants and plant imported v, H2367
Isa 32:12 the pleasant fields, for the fruitful v H1728
Jer 5:17 herds, devour your v and fig trees. H1728
Jer 48:32 you, as Jazer weeps, you v *of* Sibmah. H1728
Hos 2:12 I will ruin her v and her fig trees, which H1728
Joel 1: 7 It has laid waste my v and ruined my fig H1728
Na 2: 2 laid them waste and have ruined their v. H2367
Hab 3:17 not bud and there are no grapes on the v, H1728
Mal 3:11 the v in your fields will not drop their H1728

VINEYARD (69) [VINE]

Ge 9:20 a man of the soil, proceeded to plant a v. H4142
Ex 22: 5 in a field or v and lets them stray and H4142
Ex 22: 5 from the best of their own field or v. H4142
Ex 23:11 the same with your v and your olive grove. H4142
Lev 19:10 Do not go over your v a second time or H4142
Nu 20:17 We will not go through any field or v, or H4142
Nu 21:22 We will not turn aside into any field or v H4142
Dt 20: 6 Has anyone planted a v and not begun to H4142
Dt 22: 9 Do not plant two kinds of seed in your v; H4142
Dt 22: 9 also the fruit of the v will be defiled. H4142
Dt 23:24 If you enter your neighbor's v, you may H4142
Dt 24:21 When you harvest the grapes in your v, do H4142
Dt 28:30 You will plant a v, but you will not even H4142
1Ki 21: 1 involving a v belonging to Naboth H4142
1Ki 21: 1 **The** v was in Jezreel, close to the palace H889S
1Ki 21: 2 "Let me have your v to use for a vegetable H4142
1Ki 21: 2 In exchange I will give you a better v or, if H4142
1Ki 21: 6 Jezreelite, 'Sell me your v; or if you prefer, H4142
1Ki 21: 6 I will give you another v in its place.' H4142
1Ki 21: 6 But he said, 'I will not give you my v.' " H4142
1Ki 21: 7 I'll get you the v *of* Naboth the Jezreelite." H4142
1Ki 21:15 possession of the v *of* Naboth the H4142
1Ki 21:16 down to take possession of Naboth's v. H4142
1Ki 21:18 He is now in Naboth's v, where he has H4142
Pr 24:30 past the v *of* someone who has no sense H4142
Pr 31:16 out of her earnings she plants a v. H4142
SS 1: 6 the vineyards; my own v I had to neglect. H4142
SS 8:11 Solomon had a v in Baal Hamon; he let H4142
SS 8:11 Baal Hamon; he let out his v to tenants. H4142
SS 8:12 But my own v is mine to give; the H4142
Isa 1: 8 Daughter Zion is left like a shelter in a v H4142
Isa 3:14 "It is you who have ruined my v; the H4142
Isa 5: 1 sing for the one I love a song about his v: H4142
Isa 5: 1 My loved one had a v on a fertile hillside H4142
Isa 5: 3 of Judah, judge between me and my v. H4142
Isa 5: 4 been done for my v than I have done for H4142
Isa 5: 5 tell you what I am going to do to my v: H4142
Isa 5: 7 The v *of* the LORD Almighty is the nation H4142
Isa 5:10 A ten-acre v will produce only a bath of H4142
Isa 27: 2 In that day—"Sing about a fruitful v: H4142
Jer 12:10 will ruin my v and trample down my H4142
Eze 19:10 like a vine in your v planted by the water; H4142
Mic 7: 1 summer fruit at the gleaning of the v; H1292
Mt 20: 1 in the morning to hire workers for his v. *G308*
Mt 20: 2 the day and sent them into his v. *G308*
Mt 20: 4 'You also go and work in my v, and I will *G308*
Mt 20: 7 to them, 'You also go and work in my v.' *G308*
Mt 20: 8 the owner *of* the v said to his foreman *G308*
Mt 21:28 said, 'Son, go and work today in the v.' *G308*
Mt 21:33 There was a landowner who planted a v *G308*
Mt 21:33 Then he rented **the** v to some farmers *G899S*
Mt 21:39 threw him out of the v and killed him. *G308*
Mt 21:40 when the owner *of* the v comes, what will *G308*
Mt 21:41 "and he will rent the v to other tenants *G308*
Mk 12: 1 "A man planted a v. He put a wall around *G308*
Mk 12: 1 Then he rented **the** v to some farmers *G899S*
Mk 12: 2 collect from them some of the fruit *of* the v. *G308*
Mk 12: 8 killed him, and threw him out of the v. *G308*
Mk 12: 9 "What then will the owner *of* the v do? He *G308*
Mk 12: 9 kill those tenants and give the v to others. *G308*
Lk 13: 6 "A man had a fig tree growing in his v, and *G308*
Lk 13: 7 he said to the **man who took care of the** v, *G307*
Lk 20: 9 "A man planted a v, rented it to some *G308*
Lk 20:10 would give him some of the fruit *of* the v. *G308*
Lk 20:13 "Then the owner *of* the v said, 'What shall *G308*
Lk 20:15 they threw him out of the v and killed him. *G308*
Lk 20:15 then will the owner *of* the v do to them? *G308*
Lk 20:16 kill those tenants and give the v to others." *G308*
1Co 9: 7 Who plants a v and does not eat its grapes *G308*

VINEYARDS (54) [VINE]

Lev 25: 3 six years prune your v and gather their H4142
Lev 25: 4 Do not sow your fields or prune your v. H4142
Nu 16:14 given us an inheritance of fields and v. H4142
Nu 22:24 LORD stood in a narrow path through the v, H4142
Dt 6:11 v and olive groves you did not plant— H4142
Dt 28:39 You will plant v and cultivate them but you H4142
Jos 24:13 in them and eat from v and olive groves H4142
Jdg 14: 5 As they approached the v *of* Timnah H4142
Jdg 15: 5 together with the v and olive groves. H4142
Jdg 21:20 Benjamites, saying, "Go and hide in the v H4142
Jdg 21:21 rush from the v and each of you seize one H4142
1Sa 8:14 of your fields and v and olive groves and H4142
1Sa 22: 7 son of Jesse give all of you fields and v? H4142
2Ki 5:26 olive groves and v, or flocks and herds, H4142
2Ki 18:32 a land of bread and v, a land of olive H4142
2Ki 19:29 sow and reap, plant v and eat their fruit. H4142
2Ki 25:12 of the land to **work** *the* v and fields. H4144
1Ch 27:27 the Ramathite was in charge of the v. H4142
1Ch 27:27 of the produce of the v for the wine vats. H4142
2Ch 26:10 had people **working** his **fields and** v in the H4144
Ne 5: 3 our v and our homes to get grain during H4142
Ne 5: 4 to pay the king's tax on our fields and v. H4142
Ne 5: 5 our fields and our v belong to others." H4142
Ne 5:11 their fields, v, olive groves and houses, H4142
Ne 9:25 wells already dug, v, olive groves and fruit H4142
Job 24: 6 fields and glean in the v *of* the wicked. H4142
Job 24:18 is cursed, so that no one goes to the v. H4142
Ps 107:37 fields and planted v that yielded a fruitful H4142
Ecc 2: 4 I built houses for myself and planted v. H4142
SS 1: 6 with me and made me take care of the v; H4142

V

SS 1:14 of henna blossoms from the v *of* En Gedi. H4142
SS 2:15 the little foxes that ruin the v, our H4142
SS 2:15 the vineyards, our v that are in bloom. H4142
SS 7:12 Let us go early to the v to see if the vines H4142
Isa 16:10 no one sings or shouts in the v; no one H4142
Isa 36:17 new wine, a land of bread and v. H4142
Isa 37:30 sow and reap, plant v and eat their fruit. H4142
Isa 61: 5 foreigners will work your fields and v. H4144
Isa 65:21 they will plant v and eat their fruit. H4142
Jer 5:10 "Go through her v and ravage them, but H9224
Jer 31: 5 Again you will plant v on the hills of H4142
Jer 32:15 fields and v will again be bought in this H4142
Jer 35: 7 sow seed or plant v; you must never have H4142
Jer 35: 9 built houses to live in or had v, fields or H4142
Jer 39:10 at that time he gave them v and fields. H4142
Jer 52:16 of the land to **work** the v and fields. H4144
Eze 28:26 safety and will build houses and plant v; H4142
Hos 2:15 There I will give her back her v, and will H4142
Am 4: 9 "Many times I struck your gardens and v H4142
Am 5:11 though you have planted lush **v**, you will H4142
Am 5:17 There will be wailing in all the v, for I will H4142
Am 9:14 They will plant v and drink their wine H4142
Mic 1: 6 a heap of rubble, a place for planting v. H4142
Zep 1:13 though they plant v, they will not drink H4142

VINTAGE (1) [VINE]

1Sa 8:15 your grain and of your v and give it to his H4142

VIOL, VIOLS (KJV) HARPS, LYRES

VIOLATE (6) [VIOLATED, VIOLATES, VIOLATING, VIOLATION]

Lev 26:15 all my commands and so v my covenant, H7296
Jos 23:16 If you v the covenant of the LORD your God H6296
Ps 89:31 if *they* v my decrees and fail to keep my H2725
Ps 89:34 *I will* not v my covenant or alter what my H2725
Eze 22:10 in you are *those who* **v women** during H6700
Ac 23: 3 yet *you yourself* v **the law** by commanding *G4174*

VIOLATED (13) [VIOLATE]

Dt 22:24 the man because *he* v another man's wife H6700
Dt 22:29 marry the young woman, for *he has* v her. H6700
Jos 7:11 Israel has sinned; *they have* v my covenant H6296
Jos 7:15 *He has* v the covenant of the LORD and has H6296
Jdg 2:20 "Because this nation *has* v the covenant I H6296
1Sa 15:24 *I* v the LORD's command and your H6296
2Ki 18:12 their God, but *had* v his covenant—all H6296
Isa 13:16 houses will be looted and their wives v. H8711
Isa 24: 5 v the statutes and broken the everlasting H2736
Jer 34:18 Those who *have* v my covenant and have H6296
La 5:11 Women *have been* v in Zion, and virgins H6700
Da 11:32 will corrupt *those who have* v the H8399
Mal 2: 8 *you have* v the covenant with Levi, H8845

VIOLATES (2) [VIOLATE]

Ps 55:20 attacks his friends; *he* v his covenant. H2725
Eze 22:11 another v his sister, his own father's H6700

VIOLATING (1) [VIOLATE]

1Ch 2: 7 trouble on Israel *by* **v the ban** on taking H5085

VIOLATION (2) [VIOLATE]

Dt 17: 2 of the LORD your God in v *of* his covenant, H6296
Heb 2: 2 every v and disobedience received its *G4126*

VIOLENCE (51) [VIOLENT]

Ge 6:11 corrupt in God's sight and was full of v. H2805
Ge 6:13 the earth is filled with v because of them. H2805
Ge 49: 5 brothers—their swords are weapons of v. H2805
1Ch 12:17 enemies when my hands are free from v, H2805
Job 16:17 have been free of v and my prayer is pure. H2805
Job 19: 7 "Though I cry, 'V!' I get no response H2805
Ps 7: 9 Bring to an end the v *of* the wicked and H8273
Ps 7:16 their v comes down on their own heads. H2805
Ps 11: 5 those who love v, he hates with a H2805
Ps 55: 9 for I see v and strife in the city. H2805
Ps 58: 2 your hands mete out v on the earth. H2805
Ps 72:14 will rescue them from oppression and v, H2805
Ps 73: 6 necklace; they clothe themselves with v. H2805
Ps 74:20 because haunts of v fill the dark places of H2805
Pr 4:17 of wickedness and drink the wine of v. H2805
Pr 10: 6 v overwhelms the mouth of the wicked H2805
Pr 10:11 the mouth of the wicked conceals v. H2805
Pr 13: 2 the unfaithful have an appetite for v. H2805
Pr 21: 7 The v *of* the wicked will drag them away H8719
Pr 24: 2 their hearts plot v, and their lips talk H8719
Isa 42:25 on them his burning anger, the v *of* war. H6449
Isa 53: 9 though he had done no v, nor was any H2805
Isa 59: 6 and acts of v are in their hands. H2805
Isa 59: 7 **acts of** v mark their ways. H8719+2256+8691
Isa 60:18 No longer will v be heard in your land H2805
Jer 6: 7 V and destruction resound in her; her H2805
Jer 20: 8 I cry out proclaiming v and destruction. H2805
Jer 22: 3 Do no wrong or v *to* the foreigner, the H2803
Jer 51:35 May the v done to our flesh be on H2805
Jer 51:46 rumors of v in the land and of ruler H2805
Eze 7:11 V has arisen, a rod to punish the wicked H2805
Eze 7:23 full of bloodshed, and the city is full of v. H2805
Eze 8:17 fill the land with v and continually arouse H2805
Eze 12:19 in it because of the v *of* all who live there. H2805
Eze 22:26 Her priests **do** v *to* my law and profane my H2803
Eze 28:16 widespread trade you were filled with v, H2805
Eze 45: 9 Give up your v and oppression and do H2805
Hos 12: 1 wind all day and multiplies lies and v. H8719
Joel 3:19 because of v *done to* the people of Judah, H2805
Ob 10 Because of the v *against* your brother H2805
Jnh 3: 8 them give up their evil ways and their v. H2805
Hab 1: 2 Or cry out to you, "V!" but you do not save H2805
Hab 1: 3 Destruction and v are before me; there is H2805
Hab 1: 9 they all come intent on v. Their hordes H2805
Hab 2:17 The v you have done *to* Lebanon will H2805
Zep 1: 9 temple of their gods with v and deceit. H2805
Zep 3: 4 profane the sanctuary and **do** v *to* the law. H2803
Mal 2:16 "does v to the one he should protect," H2805
Mt 11:12 of heaven *has been* **subjected to** v, *G1041*
Ac 21:35 the v of the mob was so great he had to *G1040*
Rev 18:21 "*With* such v the great city of Babylon will *G3996*

VIOLENT (27) [VIOLENCE, VIOLENTLY]

2Sa 22: 3 my savior—from v *people* you save me. H2805
2Sa 22:49 my foes; from a v man you rescued me. H2805
Ps 17: 4 from the ways of the v through what your H7265
Ps 18:48 my foes; from a v man you rescued me. H2805
Ps 140: 1 evildoers; protect me from the v, H2805+408
Ps 140: 4 protect me from the v, who devise H2805+408
Ps 140:11 may disaster hunt down the v. H2805+408
Pr 3:31 Do not envy the v or choose any of H2805+408
Pr 16:29 A v person entices their neighbor and H2805
Eze 13:11 and v **winds** will burst forth. H8120+6194
Eze 13:13 In my wrath I will unleash a **v wind** H8120+6194
Eze 18:10 "Suppose he has a v son, who sheds H7265
Eze 28: 8 you will die a v death in the heart of H2728
Da 11:14 Those who are v *among* your own people H7265
Am 1:14 of battle, amid v **winds** on a stormy day. H6193
Jnh 1: 4 such a v storm arose that the ship H1524
Mic 6:12 Your rich people *are* v; your H2805+4848
Mt 8:28 They were so v that no one could pass *G5901*
Mt 11:12 and v *people* have been raiding it. *G1043*
Mt 28: 2 There was a v earthquake, for an angel of *G3489*
Ac 2: 2 the blowing of a v wind came from *G1042*
Ac 16:26 there was such a v earthquake that the *G3489*
Ac 23:10 The dispute became *so* v that the *G4498*
Ac 27:18 We took such a v battering from the storm *G5380*
1Ti 1:13 a persecutor and a v *man*, *G5616*
1Ti 3: 3 to drunkenness, not v but gentle, not *G4438*
Titus 1: 7 to drunkenness, not v, not pursuing *G4438*

VIOLENTLY (5) [VIOLENT]

Ge 27:33 Isaac **trembled** v and H3006+1524+6330+4394+3010
Ex 19:18 the whole mountain trembled v. H4394
Isa 24:19 split asunder, the earth **is** v **shaken**. H4572+4572
Mk 1:26 spirit **shook** the man v and came out *G5057*
Mk 9:26 shrieked, convulsed him v and came out. *G4498*

VIPER (4) [VIPER'S, VIPERS]

Ge 49:17 by the roadside, a v along the path, that H9159
Pr 23:32 it bites like a snake and poisons like a v. H7626
Isa 14:29 the root of that snake will spring up a v, H7625
Ac 28: 3 put it on the fire, a v, driven out by the *G2399*

VIPER'S (1) [VIPER]

Isa 11: 8 child will put its hand into the v nest. H7626

VIPERS (9) [VIPER]

Dt 32:24 the venom of v that glide in the dust. NDT
Ps 140: 3 serpent's; the poison of v is on their lips. H6582
Isa 59: 5 hatch the eggs of v and spin a spider's H7626
Jer 8:17 among you, v that cannot be charmed H7626
Mt 3: 7 "You brood *of* v! Who warned you *G2399*
Mt 12:34 You brood *of* v, how can you who are evil *G2399*
Mt 23:33 You brood *of* v! How will you *G2399*
Lk 3: 7 to be baptized by him, "You brood *of* v! *G2399*
Ro 3:13 "The poison *of* v is on their lips." *G835*

VIRGIN (41) [VIRGIN'S, VIRGINITY, VIRGINS]

Ge 24:16 was very beautiful, a v; no man had ever H1435
Ex 22:16 "If a man seduces a v who is not pledged H1435
Lev 21:13 'The woman he marries must **be a** v. H928+1436
Lev 21:14 only a v from his own people, H1435
Dt 22:15 elders at the gate **proof that** she was **a** v. H1436
Dt 22:17 'I did not find your daughter **to be a** v.' H1436
Dt 22:19 man has given an Israelite v a bad name. H1435
Dt 22:23 to meet in a town a v pledged to be H1435
Dt 22:28 happens to meet a v who is not pledged H1435
Jdg 11:39 And she *was a* v. From this H4202+3359+408
Jdg 19:24 here is my v daughter, and his H1435
Jdg 21:11 every woman *who is* **not a** v." H3359+5435+2351
2Sa 13: 2 She was a v, and it seemed impossible H1435
2Sa 13:18 kind of garment the v daughters of the H1435
1Ki 1: 2 us look for a young v to serve the king H1435
2Ki 19:21 " 'V Daughter Zion despises you and H1435
Ps 45:14 to the king; her v companions follow her H1435
Isa 7:14 The v will conceive and give birth to a son H6625
Isa 23:12 of your reveling, V Daughter Sidon, now H1435
Isa 37:22 "V Daughter Zion despises and mocks you H1435
Isa 47: 1 sit in the dust, V Daughter Babylon; sit on H1435
Jer 14:17 ceasing; for the V Daughter, my people, H1435
Jer 18:13 horrible thing has been done by V Israel. H1435
Jer 31: 4 you up again, and you, V Israel, will be H1435
Jer 31:21 Return, V Israel, return to your H1435
Jer 46:11 Gilead and get balm, V Daughter Egypt. H1435
La 1:15 the Lord has trampled V Daughter Judah. H1435
La 2:13 that I may comfort you, V Daughter Zion? H1435
Eze 23: 3 fondled and their v bosoms caressed. H1436
Eze 23: 8 caressed her v bosom and poured out H1435
Joel 1: 8 Mourn like a v in sackcloth grieving for H1435
Am 5: 2 "Fallen is V Israel, never to rise again H1435
Mt 1:23 "The v will conceive and give birth to a *G4221*
Lk 1:27 to a v pledged to be married to a man *G4221*
Lk 1:34 the angel, "since *I* **am a v**?" *G467+4024+1182*
1Co 7:28 not sinned; and if a v marries, she has not *G4221*
1Co 7:34 unmarried woman or v is concerned about *G4221*
1Co 7:36 honorably toward the v he is engaged to, *G4221*
1Co 7:37 made up his mind not to marry the v— *G4221*
1Co 7:38 he who marries the v does right, but he *G4221*
2Co 11: 2 I might present you *as* a pure v to him. *G4221*

VIRGIN'S (1) [VIRGIN]

Lk 1:27 The v name was Mary. *G4221*

VIRGINITY (3) [VIRGIN]

Dt 22:14 I did not find **proof of** her v," H1436
Dt 22:17 But here is the **proof of** my daughter's v." H1436
Dt 22:20 no **proof of** the young woman's v can H1436

VIRGINS (12) [VIRGIN]

Ex 22:17 he must still pay the bride-price for v. H1435
Est 2: 2 made for beautiful young v for the king. H1435
Est 2:17 approval more than any of the other v. H1435
Est 2:19 When the v were assembled a second H1435
SS 6: 8 concubines, and v beyond number; H6625
La 5:11 in Zion, and v in the towns of Judah. H1435
Eze 44:22 they may marry only v of Israelite descent H1435
Mt 25: 1 will be like ten v who took their lamps *G4221*
Mt 25: 7 "Then all the v woke up and trimmed *G4221*
Mt 25:10 **The** v who were ready went in with him *G3836S*
1Co 7:25 Now about v: I have no command from *G4221*
Rev 14: 4 with women, for they remained v. *G4221*

VIRTUE (KJV) EXCELLENT, GOODNESS, POWER

VIRTUES (1)

Col 3:14 And over all **these** *v* put on love, which binds AIT

VISAGE (KJV) APPEARANCE, ATTITUDE

VISIBLE (7)

Ge 8: 5 the tops of the mountains *became* v. H8011
Da 4:11 it was v to the ends of the earth. A10257
Da 4:20 touching the sky, v to the whole earth, A10257
Mt 24:27 comes from the east *is* v even in the west, *G5743*
Eph 5:13 exposed by the light *becomes* v— *G5746*
Col 1:16 heaven and on earth, v and invisible *G3971*
Heb 11: 3 is seen was not made out of *what was* v. *G5743*

VISION (71) [VISIONS]

Ge 15: 1 word of the LORD came to Abram in a v: H4690
Ge 46: 2 spoke to Israel in a v *at* night and said, H5261
Nu 24: 4 who sees a v *from* the Almighty H4690
Nu 24:16 who sees a v *from* the Almighty H4690
1Sa 3:15 He was afraid to tell Eli the v, H5261
2Ch 32:32 are written in the v *of* the prophet Isaiah H2606
Job 20: 8 be found, banished like a v *of* the night. H2612
Job 33:15 In a dream, in a v *of* the night, when H2612
Ps 89:19 Once you spoke in a v, to your faithful H2606
Isa 1: 1 The v concerning Judah and Jerusalem H2606
Isa 21: 2 A dire v has been shown to me: The H2607
Isa 22: 1 A prophecy against the Valley of V: What H2612
Isa 22: 5 trampling and terror in the Valley of V, H2612
Isa 29: 7 it is with a dream, with a v *in* the night— H2606
Isa 29:11 For you this whole v is nothing but words H2607
Eze 7:13 For the v concerning the whole crowd will H2606
Eze 7:26 will go searching for a v from the prophet, H2606
Eze 8: 4 as in the v I had seen in the plain. H5260
Eze 11:24 in Babylonia in the v given by the Spirit of H5260
Eze 11:24 Then the v I had seen went up from me H5260
Eze 12:22 days go by and every v comes to nothing'? H2606
Eze 12:23 are near when every v will be fulfilled. H2606
Eze 12:27 'The v he sees is for many years from now, H2606
Eze 43: 3 The v I saw was like the vision I had seen H5260
Eze 43: 3 I saw was like the v I had seen when he H5260
Da 2:19 mystery was revealed to Daniel in a v. A10256
Da 2:45 is the meaning of *the* v of the rock cut A10255
Da 7: 2 "In my v at night I looked, and there A10256
Da 7: 7 "After that, in my v *at* night I looked, and A10256
Da 7:13 "In my v *at* night I looked, and there A10256
Da 8: 1 had a v, after the one that had H2606
Da 8: 2 In my v I saw myself in the citadel of Susa H2606
Da 8: 2 in the v I was beside the Ulai Canal. H2606
Da 8:13 long will it take for the v to be fulfilled— H2606
Da 8:13 fulfilled—the v concerning the daily sacrifice NDT
Da 8:15 was watching the v and trying to H2606
Da 8:16 tell this man the meaning of the v." H5260
Da 8:17 that the v concerns the time of H2606
Da 8:19 because the v concerns the appointed time NDT
Da 8:26 "The v *of* the evenings and mornings that H5260
Da 8:26 but seal up the v, for it concerns the H2606
Da 8:27 I was appalled by the v; it was beyond H5260
Da 9:21 the man I had seen in the earlier v, came H2606
Da 9:23 consider the word and understand the v: H5260
Da 9:24 to seal up v and prophecy and to anoint H2606
Da 10: 1 of the message came to him in a v. H5260
Da 10: 7 was the only one who saw the v; those H5261
Da 10: 8 gazing at this great v; I had no strength H5261
Da 10:14 the v concerns a time yet to come. H2606
Da 10:16 overcome with anguish because of the v, H5261
Da 11:14 people will rebel in fulfillment of the v, H2606
Am 1: 1 **the** v *he* **saw** concerning Israel two years H2600

V

Ob 1 The v *of* Obadiah. This is what the H2606
Mic 1: 1 the v *he* **saw** concerning Samaria and H2600
Na 1: 1 The book of the v *of* Nahum the Elkoshite H2606
Zec 1: 8 During the night *I* **had a** v, and there H8011
Zec 13: 4 will be ashamed of their prophetic v. H2612
Lk 1:22 realized he had seen a v in the temple, *G3965*
Lk 24:23 told us that they had seen a v of angels, *G3965*
Ac 9:10 The Lord called to him in a v, "Ananias!" *G3969*
Ac 9:12 In a v he has seen a man named Ananias *G3969*
Ac 10: 3 about three in the afternoon he had a v. *G3969*
Ac 10:17 wondering about the meaning *of* the v, *G3969*
Ac 10:19 While Peter was still thinking about the v *G3969*
Ac 11: 5 Joppa praying, and in a trance I saw a v. *G3969*
Ac 12: 9 he thought he was seeing a v. *G3969*
Ac 16: 9 the night Paul had a v of a man of *G3969*
Ac 16:10 After Paul had seen the v, we got ready at *G3969*
Ac 18: 9 One night the Lord spoke to Paul in a v *G3969*
Ac 26:19 was not disobedient *to* the v from heaven. *G3965*
Rev 9:17 riders I saw in my v looked like this: *G3970*

VISIONS (37) [VISION]

Nu 12: 6 reveal myself to them in v, I speak to H5261
1Sa 3: 1 the LORD was rare; there were not many v. H2606
2Ch 9:29 the Shilonite and in the v *of* Iddo the seer H2608
Job 7:14 me with dreams and terrify me with v, H2612
Isa 28: 7 they stagger when **seeing** v, they stumble H8015
Isa 30:10 to the seers, "**See** no *more* v!" and to the H8011
Isa 30:10 "**Give** us no *more* v *of* what is right! H2600
Jer 14:14 They are prophesying to you false v H2606
Jer 23:16 They speak v *from* their own minds, not H2606
La 2: 9 prophets no longer find v from the LORD. H2606
La 2:14 *The* v of your prophets were false and H2600
Eze 1: 1 heavens were opened and I saw v *of* God. H5261
Eze 8: 3 heaven and in v *of* God he took me H5261
Eze 12:24 will be no more false v or flattering H2606
Eze 13: 6 *Their* v *are* false and their divinations a lie. H2600
Eze 13: 7 you not seen false v and uttered lying H4690
Eze 13: 8 Because of your false words and lying v, H2600
Eze 13: 9 prophets who **see** false v and utter lying H2600
Eze 13:16 and **saw** v *of* peace for her H2600+2606
Eze 13:23 therefore *you will* no longer **see** false v H2600
Eze 21:29 Despite false v concerning you and lying H2600
Eze 22:28 them by false v and lying divinations. H2600
Eze 40: 2 In v *of* God he took me to the land of H5261
Eze 43: 3 the city and like the v I had seen by the H5261
Da 1:17 could understand v and dreams of all H2606
Da 2:28 the v *that passed through* your mind A10256
Da 4: 5 and v *that passed through* my mind A10256
Da 4:10 These are the v I saw while lying in bed A10256
Da 4:13 "In the v I saw while lying in bed, A10256
Da 7: 1 and v *passed through* his mind as he A10256
Da 7:15 the v *that passed through* my mind A10256
Hos 12:10 gave them many v and told parables H2606
Joel 2:28 dreams, your young men will see v. H2612
Mic 3: 6 come over you, without v, and darkness, H2606
Zec 10: 2 deceitfully, diviners **see** v that lie; they tell H2600
Ac 2:17 your young men will see v, your old men *G3970*
2Co 12: 1 I will go on to v and revelations from the *G3965*

VISIT (24) [VISITED, VISITOR, VISITING, VISITS]

Ge 34: 1 went out to v the women of the land. H8011
Jdg 15: 1 took a young goat and *went to* v his wife. H7212
2Ch 22: 7 Through Ahaziah's v to Joram, God H995
Mt 25:36 I was in prison and you came **to** v me. AIT
Mt 25:39 we see you sick or in prison and go **to** *v* you? AIT
Jn 11:45 many of the Jews who had come **to** *v* Mary, AIT
Ac 7:12 *he* **sent** our forefathers **on** their first v. *G1990*
Ac 7:13 On their **second** *v*, Joseph told his brothers AIT
Ac 7:23 he decided *to* v his own people, the *G2170*
Ac 9:32 he went **to** *v* the Lord's people who lived in AIT
Ac 10:28 a Jew to associate with or v a Gentile. *G4665*
Ac 15:36 "Let us go back and v the believers in all *G2170*
Ac 19:21 he said, "I must v Rome also. *G3972*
Ro 15:23 longing for many years *to* v you, *G2262+4639*
Ro 15:28 I will go to Spain and v you **on the way**. *G1328*
1Co 16: 7 see you now and make *only* a **passing** v; *G4227*
2Co 1:15 I wanted *to* v you first so that you *G4639+2262*
2Co 1:16 I wanted *to* v you on my way to Macedonia *G1451*
2Co 2: 1 that I *would* not **make** another painful v to *G2262*
2Co 9: 5 urge the brothers to v you in advance and *G4601*
2Co 12:14 Now I am ready *to* v you for the *G2262+4639*
2Co 13: 1 This *will be my* third v to you. "Every *G2262*
1Th 2: 1 that our v to you was not without results. *G1658*
2Jn 12 I hope *to* v you and talk with you *G1181+4639*

VISITATION (KJV) COMING, FATE, JUDGMENT, PROVIDENCE, PUNISHED, PUNISHMENT, RECKONING, VISITS

VISITED (2) [VISIT]

Jn 4:46 Once more *he* v Cana in Galilee *G2262+1650*
Jn 19:39 the *man who* earlier *had* v Jesus at *G2262+4639*

VISITING (1) [VISIT]

Lk 24:18 "*Are* you the only *one* v Jerusalem who *G4228*

VISITORS (1) [VISIT]

Ac 2:10 parts of Libya near Cyrene; v from Rome *G2111*

VISITS (2) [VISIT]

Mic 7: 4 The day God v you has come, the day H7213
1Pe 2:12 deeds and glorify God on the day he v us. *G2175*

VOICE (190) [VOICES]

Ge 27:22 him and said, "The v is the voice of Jacob H7754
Ge 27:22 "The voice is the v *of* Jacob, but the H7754
Ex 19:19 spoke and the v of God answered him H7754
Ex 24: 3 they responded with one v, "Everything H7754
Nu 7:89 he heard the v speaking to him from H7754
Dt 4:12 saw no form; there was only a v. H7754
Dt 4:33 people heard the v *of* God speaking out H7754
Dt 4:36 he made you hear his v to discipline you. H7754
Dt 5:22 proclaimed in a loud v to your whole H7754
Dt 5:23 When you heard the v out of the darkness, H7754
Dt 5:24 we have heard his v from the fire. H7754
Dt 5:25 die if we hear the v *of* the LORD our God H7754
Dt 5:26 has ever heard the v *of* the living God H7754
Dt 18:16 "Let us not hear the v *of* the LORD our God H7754
Dt 26: 7 the LORD heard our v and saw our misery, H7754
Dt 27:14 to all the people of Israel in a loud v: H7754
Dt 30:20 listen to his v, and hold fast to him. H7754
Jdg 5:11 the v *of* the singers at the watering places. H7754
Jdg 18: 3 they recognized the v *of* the young Levite H7754
1Sa 1:13 lips were moving but her v was not heard. H7754
1Sa 24:16 Saul asked, "Is that your v, David my son?" H7754
1Sa 26:17 Saul recognized David's v and said, "Is H7754
1Sa 26:17 said, "Is that your v, David my son? H7754
1Sa 28:12 out at the top of her v and said to Saul, H7754
2Sa 22: 7 From his temple he heard my v; my cry H7754
2Sa 22:14 the v *of* the Most High resounded. H7754
1Ki 8:55 the whole assembly of Israel in a loud v, H7754
1Ki 19:13 Then a v said to him, "What are you H7754
2Ki 19:22 you raised your v and lifted your eyes H7754
2Ch 20:19 the God of Israel, with a very loud v. H7754
Ezr 10:12 whole assembly responded with a loud v: H7754
Job 4:16 before my eyes, and I heard a hushed v: H7754
Job 37: 2 Listen to the roar of his v, to the rumbling H7754
Job 37: 4 his roar; he thunders with his majestic v. H7754
Job 37: 4 When his v resounds, he holds nothing H7754
Job 37: 5 God's v thunders in marvelous ways; he H7754
Job 38:34 "Can you raise your v to the clouds and H7754
Job 40: 9 and can your v thunder like his? H7754
Ps 5: 3 you hear my v; in the morning I lay H7754
Ps 18: 6 From his temple he heard my v; my cry H7754
Ps 18:13 the v *of* the Most High resounded. H7754
Ps 19: 4 Yet their v goes out into all the earth H7754
Ps 27: 7 Hear my v when I call, LORD; be merciful H7754
Ps 29: 3 The v *of* the LORD is over the waters; the H7754
Ps 29: 4 The v *of* the LORD is powerful; the voice of H7754
Ps 29: 4 is powerful; the v *of* the LORD is majestic. H7754
Ps 29: 5 The v *of* the LORD breaks the cedars; the H7754
Ps 29: 7 The v *of* the LORD strikes with flashes of H7754
Ps 29: 8 The v *of* the LORD shakes the desert; the H7754
Ps 29: 9 The v *of* the LORD twists the oaks and H7754
Ps 46: 6 he lifts his v, the earth melts. H7754
Ps 55:17 I cry out in distress, and he hears my v. H7754
Ps 64: 1 my God, as I v my complaint; protect my H7754
Ps 68:33 heavens, who thunders with mighty v. H7754
Ps 81: 5 I heard an unknown v *say*: H8557
Ps 93: 3 the seas have lifted up their v; the seas H7754
Ps 95: 7 Today, if only you would hear his v, H7754
Ps 116: 1 he heard my v; he heard my cry for H7754
Ps 119:149 Hear my v in accordance with your love H7754
Ps 130: 2 hear my v. Let your ears be attentive H7754
Ps 142: 1 I lift up my v to the LORD for mercy. H7754
Pr 1:20 she raises her v in the public square H7754
Pr 8: 1 Does not understanding raise her v? H7754
Pr 8: 4 I call out; I raise my v to all mankind. H7754
SS 2:14 let me hear your v; for your voice is H7754
SS 2:14 your voice; for your v is sweet, and your H7754
SS 8:13 friends in attendance, let me hear your v! H7754
Isa 6: 8 Then I heard the v *of* the Lord saying H7754
Isa 28:23 Listen and hear my v; pay attention and H7754
Isa 29: 4 Your v will come ghostlike from the earth H7754
Isa 30:21 your ears will hear a v behind you, saying, H1821
Isa 30:30 to hear his majestic v and will make them H7754
Isa 30:31 The v *of* the LORD will shatter Assyria; H7754
Isa 37:23 you raised your v and lifted your eyes H7754
Isa 40: 3 A v *of* one calling: "In the wilderness H7754
Isa 40: 6 A v says, "Cry out." And I said, "What H7754
Isa 40: 9 lift up your v with a shout, lift it H7754
Isa 42: 2 cry out, or raise his v in the streets. H7754
Isa 58: 1 Raise your v like a trumpet H7754
Isa 58: 4 expect your v to be heard on high. H7754
Jer 4:15 A v is announcing from Dan, proclaiming H7754
Jer 22:20 cry out, let your v be heard in Bashan H7754
Jer 31:15 "A v is heard in Ramah, mourning and H7754
Jer 31:16 "Restrain your v from weeping and your H7754
Eze 1:24 like the v *of* the Almighty, like the H7754
Eze 1:25 Then there came a v from above the vault H7754
Eze 1:28 I heard the v *of* one speaking. H7754
Eze 9: 1 Then I heard him call out in a loud v H7754
Eze 10: 5 like the v *of* God Almighty when he H7754
Eze 11:13 I fell facedown and cried out in a loud v, H7754
Eze 27:30 They will raise their v and cry bitterly over H7754
Eze 33:32 songs with a beautiful v and plays an H7754
Eze 43: 2 His v was like the roar of rushing waters H7754
Da 4:14 He called in a **loud** *v*: 'Cut down the tree AIT
Da 4:31 were on his lips, a v came from heaven A10631
Da 6:20 he called to Daniel in an anguished v A10631
Da 8:16 And I heard a man's v from the Ulai H7754
Da 10: 6 his v like the sound of a multitude. H1821
Hag 1:12 people obeyed the v *of* the LORD their God H7754
Mt 2:18 "A v is heard in Ramah, weeping and *G5889*
Mt 3: 3 "A v of one calling in the wilderness *G5889*
Mt 3:17 And a v from heaven said, "This is my Son, *G5889*
Mt 12:19 no one will hear his v in the streets. *G5889*
Mt 17: 5 covered them, and a v from the cloud said *G5889*
Mt 27:46 the afternoon Jesus cried out *in* a loud v, *G5889*
Mt 27:50 Jesus had cried out again *in* a loud v, *G5889*
Mk 1: 3 "a v of one calling in the wilderness *G5889*
Mk 1:11 And a v came from heaven: "You are my *G5889*
Mk 5: 7 He shouted at the top of his v, "What do *G5889*
Mk 9: 7 and a v came from the cloud: *G5889*
Mk 15:34 the afternoon Jesus cried out *in* a loud v, *G5889*
Lk 1:42 *In* a loud v she exclaimed: "Blessed are *G3199*
Lk 3: 4 "A v of one calling in the wilderness *G5889*
Lk 3:22 And a v came from heaven *G5889*
Lk 4:33 He cried out at the top of his v, *G5889*
Lk 8:28 shouting at the top of his v, "What do you *G5889*
Lk 9:35 A v came from the cloud, saying, "This is *G5889*
Lk 9:36 When the v had spoken, they found that *G5889*
Lk 17:13 called out **in a loud** v, "Jesus *G149+5889*
Lk 17:15 came back, praising God in a loud v. *G5889*
Lk 23:46 Jesus called out *with* a loud v, "Father *G5889*
Jn 1:23 "I am the v of one calling in the *G5889*
Jn 3:29 of joy when he hears the bridegroom's v. *G5889*
Jn 5:25 dead will hear the v of the Son of God *G5889*
Jn 5:28 all who are in their graves will hear his v *G5889*
Jn 5:37 have never heard his v nor seen his form, *G5889*
Jn 7:37 Jesus stood and said **in a loud** v, "Let *G3189*
Jn 10: 3 him, and the sheep listen *to* his v. *G5889*
Jn 10: 4 follow him because they know his v. *G5889*
Jn 10: 5 they do not recognize a stranger's v." *G5889*
Jn 10:16 They too will listen *to* my v, and there *G5889*
Jn 10:27 My sheep listen *to* my v; I know them, and *G5889*
Jn 11:43 Jesus called *in* a loud v, "Lazarus, *G5889*
Jn 12:28 Then a v came from heaven, "I have *G5889*
Jn 12:30 Jesus said, "This v was for your benefit *G5889*
Ac 2:14 raised his v and addressed the crowd: *G5889*
Ac 9: 4 to the ground and heard a v say to him, *G5889*
Ac 10:13 Then a v told him, "Get up, Peter. Kill and *G5889*
Ac 10:15 The v spoke to him a second time, "Do *G5889*
Ac 11: 7 Then I heard a v telling me, 'Get up, Peter. *G5889*
Ac 11: 9 "The v spoke from heaven a second time *G5889*
Ac 12:14 When she recognized Peter's v, she was *G5889*
Ac 12:22 shouted, "This is the v of a god, not of a *G5889*
Ac 22: 7 to the ground and heard a v say to me, *G5889*
Ac 22: 9 did not understand the v of him who was *G5889*
Ac 26:14 I heard a v saying to me in Aramaic *G5889*
Ro 10:18 "Their v has gone out into all the earth *G5782*
Ro 15: 6 one mind and one v you may glorify the *G5125*
1Th 4:16 with the v of the archangel and with the *G5889*
Heb 3: 7 Holy Spirit says: "Today, if you hear his v, *G5889*
Heb 3:15 if you hear his v, do not harden your *G5889*
Heb 4: 7 if you hear his v, do not harden your *G5889*
Heb 12:19 blast or *to such a* v speaking words *G5889*
Heb 12:26 At that time his v shook the earth, but now *G5889*
2Pe 1:17 the Father when the v came to him from *G5889*
2Pe 1:18 ourselves heard this v that came from *G5889*
2Pe 2:16 spoke with a human v and restrained the *G5889*
Rev 1:10 heard behind me a loud v like a trumpet, *G5889*
Rev 1:12 around to see the v that was speaking to *G5889*
Rev 1:15 his v was like the sound of rushing *G5889*
Rev 3:20 If anyone hears my v and opens the door *G5889*
Rev 4: 1 And the v I had first heard speaking to me *G5889*
Rev 5: 2 a mighty angel proclaiming in a loud v, *G5889*
Rev 5:11 I looked and heard the v of many angels, *G5889*
Rev 5:12 *In* a loud v they were saying: "Worthy is *G5889*
Rev 6: 1 living creatures say *in* a v like thunder, *G5889*
Rev 6: 6 what sounded like a v among the four *G5889*
Rev 6: 7 I heard the v of the fourth living creature *G5889*
Rev 6:10 They called out *in* a loud v, "How long *G5889*
Rev 7: 2 He called out *in* a loud v to the four *G5889*
Rev 7:10 And they cried out in a loud v: "Salvation *G5889*
Rev 8:13 was flying in midair call out *in* a loud v: *G5889*
Rev 9:13 I heard a v coming from the four *G5889*
Rev 10: 4 but I heard a v from heaven say *G5889*
Rev 10: 8 Then the v that I had heard from heaven *G5889*
Rev 11:12 they heard a loud v from heaven saying to *G5889*
Rev 12:10 Then I heard a loud v in heaven say *G5889*
Rev 14: 7 He said in a loud v, "Fear God and give *G5889*
Rev 14: 9 angel followed them and said in a loud v: *G5889*
Rev 14:13 Then I heard a v from heaven say, "Write *G5889*
Rev 14:15 called in a loud v to him who was *G5889*
Rev 14:18 called *in* a loud v to him who had *G5889*
Rev 16: 1 Then I heard a loud v from the temple *G5889*
Rev 16:17 temple came a loud v from the throne, *G5889*
Rev 18: 2 With a mighty v he shouted: " 'Fallen *G5889*
Rev 18: 4 Then I heard another v from heaven say: *G5889*
Rev 18:23 The v of bridegroom and bride will never *G5889*
Rev 19: 5 Then a v came from the throne, saying *G5889*
Rev 19:17 who cried in a loud v to all the birds flying *G5889*
Rev 21: 3 And I heard a loud v from the throne *G5889*

VOICES (26) [VOICE]

Nu 14: 1 community raised their v and wept aloud. H7754
Jos 6:10 do not raise your v, do not say a word H7754
Jdg 21: 2 raising their v and weeping bitterly. H7754
2Sa 19:35 Can I still hear the v *of* male and female H7754
2Ch 5:13 singers raised their v in praise to the LORD H7754
Ne 9: 4 cried out with loud v to the LORD their God. H7754
Job 29:10 the v *of* the nobles were hushed, and H7754
Isa 6: 4 At the sound of their v the doorposts and H7924
Isa 15: 4 their v are heard all the way to Jahaz. H7754
Isa 24:14 They raise their v, they shout for joy; from H7754
Isa 42:11 Let the wilderness and its towns raise their v; NDT

Isa 52: 8 Your watchmen lift up their v; together H7754
Jer 7:34 gladness and to the v *of* bride and H7754
Jer 16: 9 gladness and to the v *of* bride and H7754
Jer 25:10 gladness, the v *of* bride and bridegroom H7754
Jer 33:11 gladness, the v *of* bride and bridegroom H7754
Jer 33:11 the v *of* those who bring thank H7754
Jer 51:55 the roar of their v will resound. H7754
Da 5:10 hearing the v *of* the king and his nobles A10418
Na 2:13 The v *of* your messengers will no longer H7754
Lk 19:37 to praise God *in* loud v for all the miracles *G5889*
Ac 4:24 they raised their v together in prayer to *G5889*
Ac 7:57 yelling at the top of their v, they all *G5889*
Ac 22:22 Then they raised their v and shouted, "Rid *G5889*
Rev 10: 3 the v of the seven thunders spoke. *G5889*
Rev 11:15 there were loud v in heaven, which *G5889*

VOID (KJV) BROKEN, DEPRIVE, EMPTY, NO, NOTHING, NULLIFIED, NULLIFIES, NULLIFY, PLUNDERED, RENOUNCED, RUIN, WITHOUT

VOLUME (KJV) SCROLL

VOLUNTARILY (4) [VOLUNTEER]

2Ki 12: 4 brought v to the temple H6590+6584+4213+408
2Ch 35: 8 also contributed v to the people and the H5607
1Co 9:17 If I preach v, I have a reward; if not *G1776*
1Co 9:17 I have a reward; if **not** v, I am simply *G220*

VOLUNTARY (1) [VOLUNTEER]

Phm 14 not seem forced but would be v. *G2848+1730*

VOLUNTEER (1) [VOLUNTARILY, VOLUNTARY, VOLUNTEERED, VOLUNTEERS]

Ezr 7:13 *who* v to go to Jerusalem with you A10461

VOLUNTEERED (3) [VOLUNTEER]

1Ch 12:38 fighting men *who* v **to serve** *in* the ranks. H6370
2Ch 17:16 who v **himself for** *the* **service** of the LORD H5605
Ne 11: 2 commended all who v to live in H5605

VOLUNTEERS (1) [VOLUNTEER]

Jdg 5: 9 with the **willing** v among the people. H5605

VOMIT (11) [VOMITED]

Lev 18:28 it *will* v you **out** as it vomited out the H7794
Lev 20:22 am bringing you to live *may* not v you **out**. H7794
Job 20:15 God *will* **make** his stomach v them **up**. H3769
Pr 23: 8 *You will* v **up** the little you have eaten H7794
Pr 25:16 enough—too much of it, and *you will* v. H7794
Pr 26:11 As a dog returns to its v, so fools repeat H7683
Isa 19:14 as a drunkard staggers around in his v. H7795
Isa 28: 8 are covered with v and there is not a spot H7795
Jer 25:27 get drunk and v, and fall to rise no H7794
Jer 48:26 Let Moab wallow in her v; let her be an H7795
2Pe 2:22 "A dog returns to its v," and, "A sow that *G2000*

VOMITED (3) [VOMIT]

Lev 18:25 and the land v **out** its inhabitants. H7794
Lev 18:28 vomit you out as *it* v **out** the nations that H7794
Jnh 2:10 the fish, and *it* v Jonah onto dry land. H7794

VOPHSI (1)

Nu 13:14 the tribe of Naphtali, Nahbi son of V; H2265

VOTE (1)

Ac 26:10 put to death, I cast my v against them. *G6029*

VOUCH (1)

Col 4:13 *I* v for him that he is working hard for you *G3455*

VOW (41) [VOWED, VOWS]

Ge 28:20 Then Jacob **made a** v, saying, "If H5623+5624
Ge 31:13 and where *you* **made a** v to me. H5623+5624
Lev 7:16 is the result of a v or is a freewill offering, H5624
Lev 22:18 either to fulfill a v or as a freewill offering, H5624
Lev 22:21 the LORD to **fulfill a special** v or as a H7098+5624
Lev 22:23 will not be accepted in fulfillment of a v. H5624
Lev 27: 2 **makes a special** v **to dedicate** a H7098+5624
Lev 27: 8 If anyone making the v is too poor to pay the NDT
Lev 27: 8 to what the *one* **making** *the* v can afford. H5623
Nu 6: 2 woman *wants* to **make a special** v, H5623+7098
Nu 6: 2 a v *of* dedication to the LORD as a Nazirite, H5624
Nu 6: 4 long as they remain **under** their **Nazirite** v, H5694
Nu 6: 5 the entire period of their **Nazirite** v, H5624+5694
Nu 15: 8 a **special** v or a fellowship H7098+5624
Nu 21: 2 Then Israel **made** *this* v to the LORD H5623+5624
Nu 29:39 'In addition to *what* you v and your H5624
Nu 30: 2 When a man **makes a** v to the LORD H5623+5624
Nu 30: 3 household **makes a** v to the LORD H5623+5624
Nu 30: 4 hears about her v or pledge but says H5624
Nu 30: 6 after she makes a v or after her lips utter a H5624
Nu 30: 8 he nullifies the v that obligates her or the H5624
Nu 30: 9 "Any v or obligation taken by a widow H5624
Nu 30:10 with her husband **makes a** v or obligates H5623
Nu 30:13 nullify any v she makes or any sworn H5624
Dt 23:18 house of the LORD your God to pay any v, H5624
Dt 23:21 If *you* **make a** v to the LORD your H5623+5624
Dt 23:22 But if you refrain from **making a** v, you H5623
Dt 23:23 because *you* **made** *your* v freely to the H5623
Jdg 11:30 And Jephthah **made a** v to the LORD H5623+5624
Jdg 11:35 I *have* **made a** v to the LORD that I H7198+7023
1Sa 1:11 And *she* **made a** v, saying, "LORD H5623+5624
1Sa 1:21 sacrifice to the LORD and to fulfill his v, H5624
2Sa 15: 7 and fulfill a v *I* **made** to the LORD. H5624+5623
2Sa 15: 8 at Geshur in Aram, *I* **made** *this* v: H5623+5624
Ps 132: 2 *he* **made a** v to the Mighty One of Jacob: H5623+5624
Ecc 5: 4 When *you* **make a** v to God, do not H5623+5624
Ecc 5: 4 He has no pleasure in fools; fulfill *your* v. H5623
Ecc 5: 5 It is better not *to* **make a** v than to make H5623
Ecc 5: 6 temple messenger, "**My** v was a mistake." H2085S
Ac 18:18 Cenchreae because of a v he had taken. *G2376*
Ac 21:23 are four men with us who have made a v. *G2376*

VOWED (9) [VOW]

Lev 23:38 whatever you have v and all the freewill H5624
Lev 27: 9 " 'If what they v is an animal that is NDT
Lev 27:11 If what they v is a ceremonially unclean NDT
Dt 12: 6 *what* you have v to give and your freewill H5624
Dt 12:11 possessions you *have* v to the LORD. H5623+5624
Dt 12:17 whatever you *have* v to give, or H5623+5624
Dt 12:26 things and whatever you have v to give, H5624
Jdg 11:39 and he did to her as he *had* v. H5623+5624
Jnh 2: 9 What *I have* v I will make good. H5623

VOWS (31) [VOW]

Nu 6:21 of the Nazirite who v offerings to the LORD H5623
Nu 6:21 must fulfill the v *they have* **made**, H5624+5623
Nu 15: 3 for **special** v or freewill offerings H7098+5624
Nu 30: 4 then all her v and every pledge by which H5624
Nu 30: 5 none of her v or the pledges by which she H5624
Nu 30: 7 then her v or the pledges by which she H5624
Nu 30:11 then all her v or the pledges by which she H5624
Nu 30:12 then none of the v or pledges that came H5624
Nu 30:14 he confirms all her v or the pledges H5624
2Ki 12: 4 received from **personal** v and the H5883+6886
Job 22:27 will hear you, and you will fulfill your v. H5624
Ps 22:25 those who fear you I will fulfill my v. H5624
Ps 50:14 fulfill your v to the Most High, H5624
Ps 56:12 I am under v *to* you, my God; I will H5624
Ps 61: 5 have heard my v; you have given me H5624
Ps 61: 8 your name and fulfill my v day after day. H5624
Ps 65: 1 in Zion; to you our v will be fulfilled. H5624
Ps 66:13 burnt offerings and fulfill my v to you— H5624
Ps 66:14 v my lips promised and my mouth spoke H889S
Ps 76:11 **Make** v to the LORD your God and fulfill H5623
Ps 116:14 I will fulfill my v to the LORD in the H5624
Ps 116:18 I will fulfill my v to the LORD in the H5624
Pr 7:14 "Today I fulfilled my v, and I have food H5624
Pr 20:25 rashly and only later to consider one's v. H5624
Isa 19:21 *they will* **make** v to the LORD and H5623+5624
Jer 44:25 carry out the v *we* **made** to burn H5623+5624
Jer 44:25 do what you promised! Keep your v! H5624
Jnh 1:16 to the LORD and **made** v to him. H5623+5624
Na 1:15 your festivals, Judah, and fulfill your v. H5624
Mal 1:14 male in his flock and v **to give** it, H5623
Mt 5:33 fulfill to the Lord the v you have made. *G3992*

VOYAGE (2)

Ac 21: 7 We continued our v from Tyre and landed *G4452*
Ac 27:10 I can see that our v is going to be *G4452*

VULGAR (1)

2Sa 6:20 girls of his servants as any v *fellow* would!" H8199

VULTURE (6) [VULTURES]

Lev 11:13 the eagle, the v, the black vulture, H7272
Lev 11:13 the eagle, the vulture, the **black** v, H6465
Dt 14:12 the eagle, the v, the black vulture, H7272
Dt 14:12 the eagle, the vulture, the **black** v, H6465
Job 15:23 He wanders about for food like a v; he H370
Mic 1:16 make yourself as bald as the v, for they H5979

VULTURES (3) [VULTURE]

Pr 30:17 the valley, will be eaten by the v. H1201+5979
Mt 24:28 there is a carcass, there the v will gather. *G108*
Lk 17:37 is a dead body, there the v will gather." *G108*

W

WADE (2)

Ps 68:23 that your feet *may* w in the blood of your H8175
Isa 47: 2 your legs, and **w through** the streams. H6296

WADI (10)

Ge 15:18 from the W *of* Egypt to the great river H5643
Nu 34: 5 join the W *of* Egypt and end at the H5707
Jos 15: 4 to Azmon and joined the **W** *of* Egypt, H5707
Jos 15:47 as far as the **W** *of* Egypt and the coastline H5707
1Ki 8:65 from Lebo Hamath to the **W** *of* Egypt. H5707
2Ki 24: 7 from the **W** *of* Egypt to the Euphrates H5707
2Ch 7: 8 from Lebo Hamath to the **W** *of* Egypt. H5707
Isa 27:12 the flowing Euphrates to the **W** *of* Egypt, H5707
Eze 47:19 then along the **W** *of Egypt* to the H5711
Eze 48:28 then along the **W** *of Egypt* to the H5711

WAFERS (1)

Ex 16:31 seed and tasted like w made with honey. H7613

WAG (1)

Jer 23:31 the prophets who w their own tongues H4374

WAGE (20) [WAGED, WAGES, WAGING]

Jos 9: 2 came together to **w war** against Joshua H4309
Jos 11:20 their hearts to **w** war *against* Israel, H7925
1Sa 15:18 **w war** against them until you have wiped H4309
2Ch 20: 1 of the Meunites came **to** *w* war against AIT
2Ch 22: 5 Ahab king of Israel **to w** war against Hazael AIT
2Ch 32: 2 that he intended to *w* **war** against Jerusalem, AIT
Pr 20:18 so if *you* **w** war, obtain guidance H6913
Pr 24: 6 Surely you need guidance *to* **w** war, and H6913
Isa 19:10 all the w earners will be sick at heart. H8512
Isa 41:12 Those who w war against you will be as NDT
Da 11:25 South *will* **w war** with a H1741+4200+2021+4878
Mic 3: 5 prepare to w war against anyone who NDT
Jn 4:36 who reaps draws a **w** and harvests a crop *G3635*
2Co 10: 3 *we do* not **w war** as the world does. *G5129*
1Pe 2:11 desires, which **w war** against your soul. *G5129*
Rev 12:17 woman and went off *to* **w** war against the *G4472*
Rev 13: 4 Who can **w war** against it?" *G4482*
Rev 13: 7 It was given power *to* **w** war against God's *G4472*
Rev 17:14 They *will* **w war** against the Lamb, but the *G4482*
Rev 19:19 gathered together *to* **w** war against the *G4472*

WAGED (6) [WAGE]

Jos 11:18 Joshua **w** war against all these kings for a H6913
1Ki 5: 3 **w against** my father David **from all sides**, H6015
1Ch 5:10 Saul's reign *they* **w** war against the H6913
1Ch 5:19 *They* **w** war against the Hagrites, Jetur H6913
2Ch 27: 5 Jotham **w war** against the king of the H4309
Ps 55:18 me unharmed from the battle **w** against me, NDT

WAGES (35) [WAGE]

Ge 29:15 Tell me what your **w** should be." H5382
Ge 30:28 He added, "Name your **w**, and I will pay H8510
Ge 30:32 speckled goat. They will be my **w**. H8510
Ge 30:33 you check on the **w** you *have paid* me. H8510
Ge 31: 7 cheated me by changing my **w** ten times. H5382
Ge 31: 8 'The speckled ones will be your **w**,' then H8510
Ge 31: 8 'The streaked ones will be your **w**,' then H8510
Ge 31:41 and you changed my **w** ten times. H5382
Lev 19:13 'Do not hold back the **w** *of* a hired worker H7190
Nu 18:31 it is your **w** for your work at the tent of H8510
Dt 24:15 Pay them their **w** each day before sunset H8510
1Ki 5: 6 pay you *for* your men whatever **w** you set. H8510
Pr 10:16 The **w** *of* the righteous is life, but the H7190
Pr 11:18 A wicked person earns deceptive **w**, but H7190
Pr 22: 4 its **w** are riches and honor and life. H6813
Hos 9: 1 you love the **w of a prostitute** at every H924
Mic 1: 7 gathered her gifts from the **w** *of* prostitutes, H924
Mic 1: 7 as the **w** *of* prostitutes they will again be H924
Hag 1: 6 You **earn w**, only to put them in a H8509+8509
Zec 8:10 time there were no **w** *for* people or hire H8510
Mal 3: 5 those who defraud laborers of their **w**, H8510
Mt 20: 8 'Call the workers and pay them their **w** *G3635*
Mk 6:37 take **more than half a year's w**! *G1324+1357*
Mk 14: 5 more than **a year's w** and the *G1324+5559*
Lk 10: 7 give you, for the worker deserves his **w**. *G3635*
Jn 6: 7 take **more than half a year's w** to *G1357+1324*
Jn 12: 5 **money** given to the poor? It was **worth a year's w** *G5559+1324*
Ro 4: 4 **w** are not credited as a gift but as an *G3635*
Ro 6:23 For the **w** of sin is death, but the gift of *G4072*
1Ti 5:18 and "The worker deserves his **w**. *G3635*
Jas 5: 4 The **w** you failed to pay the workers who *G3635*
2Pe 2:15 of Bezer, who loved the **w** of wickedness. *G3635*
Rev 6: 6 "Two pounds of wheat *for* **a day's w**, and *G1324*
Rev 6: 6 six pounds of barley *for* **a day's w** *G1324*
Rev 19:11 With justice he judges and **w war**. *G4482*

WAGING (3) [WAGE]

Jdg 11:27 are doing me wrong by **w war** against me. H4309
Da 7:21 this horn *was* **w** war against the holy A10522
Ro 7:23 **w war against** the law of my mind and *G529*

WAGON, WAGONS (KJV) CART, CARTS, CHARIOTS

WAGONS (3)

Isa 66:20 in chariots and **w**, and on mules and H7369
Eze 23:24 chariots and **w** and with a throng of H1649
Eze 26:10 **w** and chariots when he enters your gates H1649

WAHEB (NIV84) ZAHAB

WAIL (40) [WAILED, WAILING, WAILS]

Isa 13: 6 **W**, for the day of the LORD is near; it will H3536
Isa 14:31 **W**, *you* gate! Howl, you city! Melt away H3536
Isa 15: 3 roofs and in the public squares they all **w**, H3536
Isa 16: 7 Therefore the Moabites **w**, they wail H3536
Isa 16: 7 Moabites wail, they **w** together for Moab. H3536
Isa 22:12 called you on that day to weep and to **w** H5027
Isa 23: 1 **W**, *you* ships of Tarshish! For H3536
Isa 23: 6 over to Tarshish; **w**, you people of the H3536
Isa 23:14 **W**, *you* ships of Tarshish; your fortress is H3536
Isa 65:14 anguish of heart and **w** in brokenness of H3536
Jer 4: 8 lament and **w**, for the fierce anger H3536
Jer 9:10 I will weep and **w** for the mountains and H5631
Jer 9:18 come quickly and **w** over us till our H5951+5631
Jer 9:20 Teach your daughters how to **w**; teach H5631
Jer 14: 2 cities languish; *they* **w** for the land, and a H7722
Jer 25:34 Weep and **w**, *you* shepherds; roll in the H2410
Jer 47: 2 all who dwell in the land will **w** H3536
Jer 48:20 she is shattered. **W** and cry out H3536
Jer 48:31 Therefore *I* **w** over Moab, for all Moab I H3536
Jer 48:39 How *they* **w**! How Moab turns her H3536
Jer 49: 3 "**W**, Heshbon, for Ai is destroyed! Cry out H3536
Jer 51: 8 fall and be broken. **W** over her! Get balm H3536
Eze 21:12 Cry out and **w**, son of man, for it is against H3536

Eze 27:32 As they w and mourn over you, they will H5760
Eze 30: 2 " 'W and say, "Alas for that H3536
Eze 32:18 w for the hordes of Egypt and consign to H5629
Hos 7:14 me from their hearts but w on their beds. H3536
Joel 1: 5 W, all you drinkers of wine; wail because H3536
Joel 1: 5 drinkers of wine; w because of the new wine NDT
Joel 1:11 Despair, you farmers, w, you vine growers H3536
Joel 1:13 mourn; w, you who minister before H3536
Am 5:16 to weep and the mourners to w. H5027
Mic 1: 8 Because of this I will weep and w; I will H3536
Zep 1:11 W, you who live in the market district; all H3536
Zec 11: 2 W, *you* juniper, for the cedar has fallen H3536
Zec 11: 2 W, oaks of Bashan; the dense forest has H3536
Zec 11: 3 Listen to the w *of* the shepherds; their rich H3538
Mal 2:13 You weep and w because he no longer H651
Jas 4: 9 mourn and w. Change your G3081
Jas 5: 1 weep and w because of the misery that is G3909

WAILED (3) [WAIL]

Nu 11:18 The LORD heard you when *you* w, "If only H1134
Nu 11:20 is among you, and *have* w before him H1134
Lk 23:27 women who mourned and w for him. G2577

WAILING (24) [WAIL]

Ex 11: 6 There will be loud w throughout Egypt H7591
Ex 12:30 there was loud w in Egypt, for there H7591
Nu 11: 4 again the Israelites *started* w and said, H1134
Nu 11:10 of every family w at the entrance to H1134
Nu 11:13 these people? *They keep* w to me, 'Give H1134
2Sa 13:36 the king's sons came in, w loudly. H1134
Est 4: 1 into the city, w loudly and bitterly. H2410+2411
Est 4: 3 the Jews, with fasting, weeping and w. H5027
Job 30:31 mourning, and my pipe to the sound of w. H1134
Ps 30:11 You turned my w into dancing; you H5027
Isa 15: 8 of Moab; their w reaches as far as Eglaim H3538
Jer 6:26 mourn with bitter w as for an only son, for H5027
Jer 9:17 Call for the w *women* to come; send for H7801
Jer 9:19 The sound of w is heard from Zion: 'How H5631
Jer 20:16 May he hear w in the morning, a battle H2411
Jer 25:36 the w *of* the leaders of the flock H3538
Am 5:16 "There will be w in all the streets and H5027
Am 5:17 There will be w in all the vineyards, for I H5027
Am 8: 3 "the songs in the temple *will* **turn to w**. H3536
Zep 1:10 the Fish Gate, w from the New Quarter H3538
Mk 5:38 with people crying and w loudly. G226
Mk 5:39 to them, "Why all this commotion and w? G3081
Lk 8:52 all the people *were* w and mourning for G3081
Lk 8:52 "Stop w," Jesus said. "She is G3081

WAILS (1) [WAIL]

Isa 15: 2 Moab w over Nebo and Medeba. H3536

WAIST (24) [WAISTS]

Ex 28:42 reaching from the w to the thigh. H5516
2Sa 20: 8 strapped over it at his w was a belt with a H5516
1Ki 2: 5 the belt around his w and the sandals on H5516
1Ki 12:10 little finger is thicker than my father's w. H5516
2Ki 1: 8 hair and had a leather belt around his w." H5516
2Ch 10:10 little finger is thicker than my father's w. H5516
Job 12:18 kings and ties a loincloth around their w. H5516
Job 15:27 with fat and his w bulges with flesh, H4072
SS 7: 2 Your w is a mound of wheat encircled by H1061
Isa 5:27 not a belt is loosened at the w, not a H2743
Isa 11: 5 faithfulness the sash around his w. H2743
Jer 13: 1 buy a linen belt and put it around your w, H5516
Jer 13: 2 the LORD directed, and put it around my w. H5516
Jer 13: 4 bought and are wearing around your w, H5516
Jer 13:11 For as a belt is bound around the w, so I H5516
Jer 48:37 is slashed and every w is covered with H5516
Eze 1:27 appeared to be his w up he looked like H5516
Eze 8: 2 appeared to be his w down he was like H5516
Eze 47: 4 me through water that was up to the w. H5516
Da 10: 5 of fine gold from Uphaz around his w. H5516
Mt 3: 4 he had a leather belt around his w. G4019
Mk 1: 6 with a leather belt around his w, and he G4019
Jn 13: 4 **wrapped** a towel **around** his w. G1346
Eph 6:14 the belt of truth buckled around your w, G4019

WAISTBAND (8)

Ex 28: 8 Its skillfully woven w is to be like it—of H3109
Ex 28:27 the seam just above the w *of* the ephod. H3109
Ex 28:28 connecting it to the w, so that the H3109
Ex 29: 5 ephod on him by its skillfully woven w. H3109
Ex 39: 5 Its skillfully woven w was like it—of one H3109
Ex 39:20 the seam just above the w *of* the ephod. H3109
Ex 39:21 connecting it to the w so that the H3109
Lev 8: 7 fastened the ephod with a **decorative** w, H3109

WAISTS (4) [WAIST]

1Ki 20:31 around our w and ropes around our H5516
1Ki 20:32 around their w and ropes around their H5516
Eze 23:15 belts around their w and flowing turbans H5516
Eze 44:18 linen undergarments around their w. H5516

WAIT (89) [AWAIT, AWAITS, WAITED, WAITING, WAITS]

Ex 24:14 "W here for us until we come back to you. H3782
Lev 12: 4 Then the woman *must* w thirty-three days H3782
Lev 12: 5 Then *she must* w sixty-six days to be H3782
Nu 9: 8 "W until I find out what the LORD H6641
Dt 19:11 But if out of hate someone **lies in** w H741
Jos 8: 9 of ambush and **lay in** w between Bethel H3782
Jos 18: 3 "How long *will* you w before you begin to H8332
Jdg 6:18 the LORD said, "I *will* w until you return." H3782
Jdg 9:32 should come and **lie in** w in the fields. H741
Jdg 16: 2 the place and **lay in** w for him all night at H741
Jdg 19: 8 "Refresh yourself. W till afternoon!" So H4538
Ru 1:13 *would you* w until they grew up? Would H8432
Ru 3:18 Then Naomi said, "W, my daughter, until H3782
1Sa 10: 8 but *you must* w seven days until I come to H3498
1Sa 14: 9 say to us, 'W there until we come to you H1957
1Sa 20:10 trouble began, and w by the stone Ezel. H3782
1Sa 22: 8 has incited my servant to **lie in** w for me, H741
1Sa 22:13 rebelled against me and **lies in** w for me, H741
2Sa 15:28 I *will* w at the fords in the wilderness until H4538
2Sa 18:14 "I'm *not going to* w like this for you." H3498
2Sa 18:30 "Stand aside and w here." So he stepped H3656
2Ki 6:33 Why *should I* w for the LORD any longer?" H3498
2Ki 7: 9 If *we* w until daylight, punishment will H2675
Job 3: 9 *may it* w for daylight in vain and not see H7747
Job 14:14 my hard service *I will* **w for** my renewal to H3498
Job 20:26 total darkness **lies in** w for his treasures. H3243
Job 32:16 *Must I* w, now that they are silent, now H3498
Job 35:14 is before him and *you must* w for him, H2565
Job 38:40 crouch in their dens or lie in w in a thicket? H743
Ps 5: 3 requests before you and **w expectantly**. H7595
Ps 10: 8 He lies in w *near* the villages; from H4422
Ps 10: 9 in cover *he* **lies in** w. H741+928+2021+5041
Ps 10: 9 *He* **lies in** w to catch the helpless; he H741
Ps 27:14 **W** for the LORD; be strong and take heart H7747
Ps 27:14 strong and take heart and w for the LORD. H7747
Ps 33:20 We **w in hope** for the LORD; he is our help H2675
Ps 37: 7 before the LORD and **w patiently** for him; H2565
Ps 37:32 The wicked **lie in** w for the righteous H7595
Ps 38:15 *I* w for you; you will answer, Lord my H3498
Ps 59: 3 See how *they* **lie in** w for me! Fierce men H741
Ps 71:10 *those who* **w to kill** me conspire H9068+5883
Ps 106:13 he had done and *did* not w for his plan to H2675
Ps 119:84 **How long must** your servant w H3869+4537+3427
Ps 119:166 *I* w for your salvation, LORD, and I follow H8432
Ps 130: 5 *I* **w for** the LORD, my whole being waits H7747
Ps 130: 6 I w for the Lord more than watchmen wait NDT
Ps 130: 6 more than watchmen w for the morning, NDT
Ps 130: 6 more than watchmen w for the morning. NDT
Pr 1:11 *let's* **lie in** w for innocent blood H741
Pr 1:18 These men **lie in** w for their own blood H741
Pr 12: 6 The words of the wicked **lie in** w *for* blood H741
Pr 20:22 this wrong!" W for the LORD, and he H7747
Pr 23:28 Like a bandit she **lies in** w and multiplies H741
Isa 8:17 *I will* w for the LORD, who is hiding his face H2675
Isa 26: 8 way of your laws, *we* **w for** you; your name H7747
Isa 30:18 Blessed are all *who* w for him! H2675
Isa 51: 5 will look to me and **w in hope** for my arm. H3498
Isa 64: 4 acts on behalf of *those who* w for him. H2675
Jer 5: 6 a leopard *will* **lie in** w near their towns to H9193
Jer 5:26 are the wicked *who* **lie in** w like men who H8800
La 3:10 Like a bear **lying in** w, like a lion in hiding, H741
La 3:24 is my portion; therefore *I will* w for him." H3498
La 3:26 it is good to w quietly for the salvation of H3497
La 4:19 the mountains and **lay in** w for us in the H741
Eze 44:26 he is cleansed, *he must* w seven days. H6218
Hos 12: 6 justice, and w for your God always. H7747
Ob 14 *You should* not w at the crossroads to cut H6641
Mic 5: 7 which *do* not w for anyone or depend on H7747
Mic 7: 2 Everyone **lies in** w to shed blood; they hunt H741
Mic 7: 7 hope for the LORD, *I* w for God my Savior H3498
Hab 2: 3 Though it linger, w for it; it will certainly H2675
Hab 3:16 Yet *I will* **w patiently** for the day of H5663
Zep 3: 8 Therefore w for me," declares the LORD H2675
Mt 8:15 she got up and *began to* **w on** him. G1354
Mk 1:31 left her and *she began to* **w on** them. G1354
Lk 4:39 got up at once and *began to* **w on** them. G1354
Lk 12:37 the table and will come and **w on** them. G1354
Lk 17: 8 yourself ready and **w on** me while I eat G1354
Jn 18:16 Peter *had to* w outside at the door G2705
Ac 1: 4 but **w for** the gift my Father promised G4338
Ac 6: 2 the word of God *in order to* **w on** tables. G1354
Ro 8:23 groan inwardly *as we* **w eagerly** for our G587
Ro 8:25 we do not yet have, *we* **w for** it patiently. G587
1Co 1: 7 spiritual gift *as you* **eagerly w for** our Lord G587
1Co 4: 5 the appointed time; w until the Lord comes. NDT
1Th 1:10 and *to* **w for** his Son from heaven, whom he G388
Titus 2:13 *while we* **w for** the blessed hope—the G4657
Jude 21 in God's love *as you* **w for** the mercy of G4657
Rev 6:11 they were told to w a little longer, until G399

WAITED (16) [WAIT]

Ge 8:10 *He* w seven more days and again sent out H3498
Ge 8:12 *He* w seven more days and sent the dove H3498
Jdg 3:25 *They* w to the point of embarrassment, but H3498
Jdg 3:26 While they w, Ehud got away. He passed H4538
1Sa 13: 8 *He* w seven days, the time set by Samuel H3498
1Sa 25: 9 message in David's name. Then *they* w. H5663
1Ki 1: 4 she took care of the king and **w on** him H9250
Job 29:23 *They* w for me as for showers and drank in H3498
Job 32: 4 Now Elihu *had* w before speaking to Job H2675
Job 32:11 *I* w while you spoke, I listened to your H3498
Ps 40: 1 *I* **w patiently for** the LORD; he turned H7747+7747
Isa 38:13 *I* **w patiently** till dawn, but like a lion he H8750
La 2:16 This is the day *we have* **w for**; we have H7747
Jnh 4: 5 sat in its shade and w to see what would H6330
Ac 20: 5 went on ahead and w for us at Troas. G3531
1Pe 3:20 long ago when God w patiently in the days G587

WAITING (25) [WAIT]

Ex 5:20 found Moses and Aaron w to meet them, H5893
2Sa 16: 1 steward of Mephibosheth, w to meet him. NDT
1Ki 20:38 went and **stood** by the road w for the king. H6641
Job 7: 2 shadows, or a hired laborer w to be paid, H7747
Job 29:21 expectantly, **w in silence** for my counsel. H1957
Ps 119:95 The wicked *are* w to destroy me, but I will H7747
Pr 8:34 daily at my doors, w *at* my doorway. H9068
Jer 3: 2 By the roadside *you* **sat** w for lovers, sat H3782
Jer 20:10 All my friends *are* w *for* me to slip H9068
Mic 1:12 Maroth writhe in pain, w for relief, because NDT
Mk 15:43 who was himself w for the kingdom of G4657
Lk 1:21 the people were **w for** Zechariah and G4659
Lk 2:25 *He was* **w for** the consolation of Israel G4657
Lk 3:15 The people *were* **w expectantly** and were G4659
Lk 11:54 w to catch him in something he might say. G1910
Lk 12:36 like servants **w for** their master to return G4657
Lk 23:51 and *he* himself *was* **w for** the kingdom of G4657
Ac 17:16 *While* Paul *was* w for them in Athens, he G1683
Ac 22:16 And now what *are you* **w for**? Get up, be G3516
Ac 23:21 forty of them *are* **w in ambush** for him. G1910
Ac 23:21 **w for** your consent to their request. G4657
Ac 28: 6 but *after* w a long time and seeing G4659
Heb 6:15 And so *after* **w patiently**, Abraham G3428
Heb 9:28 bring salvation *to those who are* **w for** him. G587
Jas 5: 7 **patiently** w for the autumn and spring G3428

WAITS (6) [WAIT]

Ps 130: 5 my whole being w, and in his word I H7747
Da 12:12 Blessed is the *one who* **w for** and reaches H2675
Jn 3:29 the bridegroom w and listens for him, G2705
Ro 8:19 For the creation w in eager expectation G587
Heb 10:13 since that time *he* w for his enemies G1683
Jas 5: 7 See *how* the farmer **w for** the land to yield G1683

WAKE (17) [AWAKE, AWAKEN, AWAKENED, AWAKENS, AWAKES, AWOKE, WAKENS, WAKES, WOKE]

Jdg 5:12 **'W up**, wake up, Deborah! Wake up H6424
Jdg 5:12 'Wake up, **w up**, Deborah! Wake up H6424
Jdg 5:12 **W up**, wake up, break out in H6424
Jdg 5:12 Wake up, **w up**, break out in H6424
1Sa 26:12 knew about it, nor *did anyone* **w up**. H7810
Job 41:32 It leaves a glistening w behind it; one H5985
Ps 3: 5 down and sleep; *I* w again, because the H7810
Pr 23:35 When *will I* **w up** so I can find another H7810
Isa 26:19 *let* those who dwell in the dust **w up** and H7810
Joel 1: 5 **W up**, you drunkards, and weep! Wail, all H7810
Hab 2: 7 *Will they* not **w up** and make you tremble? H3699
Hab 2:19 to lifeless stone, **'W up!'** Can it give H6424
Jn 11:11 but I am going there to w him **up**. G2030
Ro 13:11 come for you *to* **w up** from your slumber, G1586
Eph 5:14 "**W up**, sleeper, rise from the dead, and G1586
Rev 3: 2 **W up**! Strengthen what remains G1181+1213
Rev 3: 3 But if *you do* not **w up**, I will come like a G1213

WAKENS (2) [WAKE]

Isa 50: 4 *He* w me morning by morning, wakens my H6424
Isa 50: 4 w my ear to listen like one being H6424

WAKES (1) [WAKE]

Ps 78:65 as a warrior **w from** *the* **stupor** of wine. H8130

WALK (133) [WALKED, WALKING, WALKS]

Ge 13:17 w through the length and breadth of the H2143
Ge 17: 1 w before me **faithfully** and be blameless. H2143
Ex 21:19 can get up and **w around** outside with a H2143
Lev 11:20 flying insects that w on all fours are to be H2143
Lev 11:21 flying insects that w on all fours that you H2143
Lev 11:27 Of all the animals that w on all fours H2143
Lev 11:27 those *that* w on their paws are unclean H2143
Lev 26:12 *I will* w among you and be your God, and H2143
Lev 26:13 yoke and **enabled** you to w with heads H2143
Nu 11:31 as far as a day's w in any direction. H2006
Dt 5:33 W in obedience to all that the LORD your H2143
Dt 6: 7 at home and when you w along the road, H2143
Dt 10:12 LORD your God, to w in obedience to him H2143
Dt 11:19 at home and when you w along the road, H2143
Dt 11:22 to w in obedience to him and to hold fast H2143
Dt 19: 9 your God and to w always in obedience H2143
Dt 26:17 God and that you *will* w in obedience to H2143
Dt 28: 9 LORD your God and w in obedience to him. H2143
Dt 30:16 LORD your God, to w in obedience to him H2143
Jos 22: 5 LORD your God, to w in obedience to him H2143
Jdg 2:22 the way of the LORD and w in it as their H2143
Jdg 5:10 blankets, and *you who* w along the road H2143
2Sa 3:31 on sackcloth and **w in mourning** in front H6199
1Ki 2: 3 W in obedience to him, and keep his H2143
1Ki 2: 4 if they w faithfully before me with all H2143
1Ki 3:14 And if *you* w in obedience to me and keep H2143
1Ki 8:25 they do to w before me **faithfully** as you H2143
1Ki 8:58 to w in obedience to him and keep the H2143
1Ki 9: 4 if *you* w before me **faithfully** with integrity H2143
1Ki 11:38 I command you and w in obedience to H2143
2Ki 21:22 and *did* not w in obedience to him. H2143
2Ch 6:16 in all they do to w before me according to H2143
2Ch 6:31 will fear you and w in obedience to you H2143
2Ch 7:17 if *you* w before me **faithfully** as David your H2143
Ne 5: 9 Shouldn't *you* w in the fear of our God to H2143
Ps 1: 1 is the one who *does* not w in step with H2143
Ps 15: 2 The *one whose* w *is* blameless, who does H2143
Ps 23: 4 Even though *I* w through the darkest H2143
Ps 48:12 **W about** Zion, go around her, count her H6015
Ps 56:13 that I *may* w before God in the light of life H2143
Ps 82: 5 *They* **w about** in darkness; all the H2143
Ps 84:11 from those *whose* w is blameless. H2143

Ps 89:15 *who* **w** in the light of your presence H2143
Ps 101: 6 the *one whose* **w** *is* H2143+928+2006
Ps 115: 7 but cannot **w**, nor can they utter a H2143
Ps 116: 9 that *I may* **w** before the LORD in the land of H2143
Ps 119: 1 who **w** according to the law of the LORD. H2143
Ps 119:45 *I will* **w about** in freedom, for I have H2143
Ps 128: 1 fear the LORD, who **w** in obedience to him. H2143
Ps 138: 7 Though *I* **w** in the midst of trouble, you H2143
Ps 142: 3 In the path where *I* **w** people have hidden H2143
Pr 2: 7 is a shield to *those whose* **w** is blameless, H2143
Pr 2:13 left the straight paths to **w** in dark ways, H2143
Pr 2:20 Thus *you will* **w** in the ways of the good H2143
Pr 4:12 When you **w**, your steps will not be H2143
Pr 4:14 path of the wicked or **w** in the way of H886
Pr 6:22 When you **w**, they will guide you; when H2143
Pr 6:28 Can a man **w** on hot coals without his feet H2143
Pr 8:20 *I* **w** in the way of righteousness, along the H2143
Pr 9: 6 you will live; **w** in the way of insight." H886
Pr 13:20 **W** with the wise and become wise, for a H2143
Pr 19: 1 the poor whose **w** is blameless than a H2143
Pr 28: 6 the poor *whose* **w** *is* blameless than H2143
Pr 28:18 The *one whose* **w** is blameless is kept H2143
Pr 28:26 but *those who* **w** in wisdom are kept safe. H2143
Ecc 10: 3 Even as fools **w** along the road, they lack H2143
Isa 2: 3 his ways, so that *we may* **w** in his paths." H2143
Isa 2: 5 of Jacob, *let us* **w** in the light of the LORD. H2143
Isa 23:16 **w through** the city, *you* forgotten prostitute H6015
Isa 30:21 saying, "This is the way; **w** in it. H2143
Isa 33:15 *Those who* **w** righteously and speak what H2143
Isa 35: 8 it will be for those *who* **w** *on* that Way. H2143
Isa 35: 9 But only the redeemed *will* **w** there, H2143
Isa 38:15 *I will* **w humbly** all my years because of H1844
Isa 40:31 grow weary, *they will* **w** and not be faint. H2143
Isa 42: 5 its people, and life to those *who* **w** on it: H2143
Isa 43: 2 When *you* **w** through the fire, you will not H2143
Isa 50:11 *go*, **w** in the light of your fires and of the H2143
Isa 51:23 'Fall prostrate that *we may* **w on** you. H6296
Isa 57: 2 *Those who* **w** uprightly enter into peace H2143
Isa 59: 9 brightness, but *we* **w** in deep shadows. H2143
Isa 65: 2 people, who **w** *in* ways not good H2143
Jer 6:16 the good way is, and **w** in it, and you will H2143
Jer 6:16 But you said, '*We will* not **w** in it.' H2143
Jer 6:25 not go out to the fields or **w** on the roads, H2143
Jer 7:23 **W** in obedience to all I command you H2143
Jer 10: 5 must be carried because *they* cannot **w**. H7575
Jer 18:15 They *made* them **w** in byways, on roads H2143
La 3: 2 me away and **made** me **w** *in* darkness H2143
La 4:18 so we *could* not **w** in our streets. H2143
Da 4:37 And those *who* **w** in pride he is able to A10207
Hos 11: 3 It was I *who* **taught** Ephraim to **w**, taking H8078
Hos 14: 9 are right; the righteous **w** in them, but the H2143
Am 3: 3 *Do* two **w** together unless they have H2143
Mic 2: 3 *You will* no longer **w** proudly, for it will be H2143
Mic 4: 2 his ways, so that *we may* **w** in his paths." H2143
Mic 4: 5 All the nations *may* **w** in the name of H2143
Mic 4: 5 we *will* **w** in the name of the LORD our H2143
Mic 6: 8 to love mercy and *to* **w** humbly with your H2143
Zec 3: 7 'If *you will* **w** in obedience to me and H2143
Mt 9: 5 are forgiven,' or to say, 'Get up and **w**'? *G4344*
Mt 11: 5 the lame **w**, those who have leprosy *G4344*
Mk 2: 9 to say, 'Get up, take your mat and **w**'? *G4344*
Mk 5:42 the girl stood up and *began to* **w around** *G4344*
Mk 12:38 They like *to* **w around** in flowing robes *G4344*
Lk 5:23 are forgiven,' or to say, 'Get up and **w**'? *G4344*
Lk 7:22 the lame **w**, those who have leprosy *G4344*
Lk 11:44 which people **w** over without knowing it." *G4344*
Lk 20:46 They like *to* **w around** in flowing robes *G4344*
Lk 24:17 you discussing together *as you* **w along**?" *G4344*
Jn 5: 8 Pick up your mat and **w**." *G4344*
Jn 5:11 well said to me, 'Pick up your mat and **w**. *G4344*
Jn 5:12 fellow who told you to pick it up and **w**?" *G4344*
Jn 8:12 follows me *will* never **w** in darkness, *G4344*
Jn 12:35 **W** while you have the light, before *G4344*
Ac 1:12 **a Sabbath day's w from** the city. *G1584+4879+2400+3847*
Ac 3: 6 the name of Jesus Christ of Nazareth, **w**." *G4344*
Ac 3: 8 He jumped to his feet and *began to* **w** *G4344*
Ac 3:12 godliness we had made this man **w**? *G4344*
Ac 14:10 the man jumped up and *began to* **w**. *G4344*
2Co 6:16 "I will live with them and **w among** them *G1853*
2Co 12:18 *Did* we not **w** in the same footsteps by the *G4344*
Gal 5:16 So I say, **w** by the Spirit, and you will not *G4344*
Eph 5: 2 **w** in the way of love, just as Christ *G4344*
Col 3: 7 You used to **w** in these ways, in the life *G4344*
1Jn 1: 6 with him and yet **w** in the darkness, *G4344*
1Jn 1: 7 But if *we* **w** in the light, as he is in the *G4344*
2Jn 6 that *we* **w** in obedience to his commands *G4344*
2Jn 6 his command is that *you* **w** in love. *G4344*
3Jn 3 telling how you *continue to* **w** in it. *G4344*
Rev 3: 4 *They will* **w** with me, dressed in white, for *G4344*
Rev 9:20 wood—idols that cannot see or hear or **w**. *G4344*
Rev 21:24 The nations *will* **w** by its light, and the *G4344*

WALKED (40) [WALK]

Ge 5:22 Enoch **w faithfully** with God 300 years H2143
Ge 5:24 Enoch **w faithfully** with God; then he was H2143
Ge 6: 9 of his time, and he **w faithfully** with God. H2143
Ge 9:23 then *they* **w** *in* backward and covered their H2143
Ge 18:16 Abraham **w along** with them to see H2143
Ge 24:40 before whom *I have* **w faithfully**, will send H2143
Ge 48:15 fathers Abraham and Isaac **w faithfully**, H2143
Ex 15:19 the Israelites **w** through the sea on dry H2143
Jos 14: 9 on which your feet *have* **w** will be your H2005
1Sa 19:23 and *he* **w along** prophesying until H2143+2143
2Sa 3:31 King David *himself* **w** behind the bier. H2143
2Sa 11: 2 from his bed and **w around** on the roof of H2143
1Ki 11:33 and *have* not **w** in obedience to me H2143
2Ki 2: 6 not leave you." So the two of them **w on**. H2143
2Ki 4:35 turned away and **w** back and forth in the H2143
2Ki 20: 3 how *I have* **w** before you faithfully and H2143
2Ch 27: 6 powerful because he **w** steadfastly before H2006
Est 2:11 Every day he **w back and forth** near the H2143
Job 29: 3 by his light *I* **w** *through* darkness! H2143
Job 31: 5 "If *I have* **w** with falsehood or my foot has H2143
Job 38:16 springs of the sea or **w** in the recesses of H2143
Ps 55:14 *as we* **w about** among the worshipers. H2143
Ecc 4:15 all who lived and **w** under the sun H2143
Isa 38: 3 how *I have* **w** before you faithfully and H2143
Isa 51:23 like the ground, like a street to *be* **w on**." H6296
Jer 34:18 cut in two and then **w** between its pieces. H6296
Jer 34:19 of the land who **w** between the pieces of H6296
Eze 28:14 *you* **w** among the fiery stones. H2143
Mal 2: 6 *He* **w** with me in peace and uprightness H2143
Mt 14:29 **w** on the water and came toward Jesus. *G4344*
Mk 1:16 *As* Jesus **w beside** the Sea of Galilee, he *G4135*
Mk 2:12 took his mat and **w out** in full view of *G2002*
Mk 2:14 *As he* **w along**, he saw Levi son of *G4135*
Mk 2:23 and *as* his disciples **w along**, they *G3847+4472*
Lk 4:30 But he **w right through** the *G1451+1328+3545*
Lk 24:15 himself came up and **w along with** them; *G5233*
Jn 5: 9 was cured; he picked up his mat and **w**. *G4344*
Ac 12:10 *When they had* **w the length** *of* one street, *G4601*
Ac 14: 8 that way from birth and *had* never **w**. *G4344*
Ac 17:23 For *as I* **w around** and looked carefully at *G1451*

WALKING (32) [WALK]

Ge 3: 8 the LORD God *as he was* **w** in the garden H2143
Ex 2: 5 her attendants *were* **w** along the H2143
Dt 8: 6 **w** in obedience to him and revering him. H2143
1Sa 17:39 sword over the tunic and tried **w around**, H2143
2Sa 6: 4 of God on it, and Ahio *was* **w** in front of it. H2143
1Ki 3: 3 his love for the LORD by **w** according to the H2143
1Ki 18: 7 As Obadiah was **w along** H928+2021+2006
2Ki 2:11 were **w along** and talking *together*, H2143+2143
2Ki 2:23 As he *was* **w** along the road, some boys H6590
Pr 7: 8 **w along** *in* the direction of her house H7575
Isa 3:16 haughty, **w along** with outstretched necks H2143
Isa 9: 2 The people **w** in darkness have seen a H2143
Isa 26: 8 **w** in the way of your laws, we wait for NDT
Da 3:25 I see four men **w around** in the fire A10207
Da 4:29 as the king was **w** on the roof of the A10207
Mt 4:18 *As* Jesus was **w** beside the Sea of Galilee, *G4344*
Mt 14:25 Jesus went out to them, **w** on the lake. *G4344*
Mt 14:26 When the disciples saw him **w** on the lake, *G4344*
Mt 15:31 the lame **w** and the blind seeing. *G4344*
Mt 24: 1 the temple and *was* **w away** when his *G4513*
Mk 6:48 dawn he went out to them, **w** on the lake. *G4344*
Mk 6:49 when they saw him **w** on the lake, they *G4344*
Mk 8:24 see people; they look like trees **w around**." *G4344*
Mk 11:27 and *while* Jesus *was* **w** in the temple *G4344*
Mk 16:12 to two of them *while they were* **w** in the *G4344*
Lk 9:57 *As* they *were* **w** along the road, a man *G4513*
Jn 6:19 the boat, **w** on the water; and *G4344*
Jn 10:23 Jesus *was* in the temple courts **w** in *G4344*
Ac 3: 8 the temple courts, **w** and jumping, and *G4344*
Ac 3: 9 the people saw him **w** and praising God, *G4344*
2Jn 4 find some of your children **w** in the truth, *G4344*
3Jn 4 than to hear *that* my children *are* **w** in the *G4344*

WALKS (12) [WALK]

Lev 11:42 moves on its belly or **w** on all fours or on H2143
Pr 10: 9 Whoever **w** in integrity walks securely, but H2143
Pr 10: 9 Whoever walks in integrity **w** securely, but H2143
Pr 14: 2 Whoever fears the LORD **w** uprightly, but H2143
Ecc 2:14 while the fool **w** in the darkness; but H2143
Isa 50:10 Let the *one* who **w** *in* the dark, who has H2143
Isa 59: 8 no one *who* **w** along them will know H2005
Jn 11: 9 Anyone *who* **w** in the daytime will not *G4344*
Jn 11:10 It is when a person **w** at night that they *G4344*
Jn 12:35 Whoever **w** in the dark does not know *G4344*
1Jn 2:11 darkness and **w around** in the darkness *G4344*
Rev 2: 1 in his right hand and **w** among the seven *G4344*

WALL (170) [WALLED, WALLS]

Ge 49:22 a spring, whose branches climb over a **w**. H8803
Ex 14:22 with a **w** *of* water on their right and on H2570
Ex 14:29 with a **w** *of* water on their right and on H2570
Ex 15: 8 The surging waters stood up like a **w**; the H5603
Lev 11:30 the **w lizard**, the skink and the H4321
Lev 14:37 to be deeper than the surface of the **w**, H7815
Nu 22:25 it pressed close to the **w**, crushing H7815
Nu 35: 4 a thousand cubits from the town **w**. H7815
Jos 2:15 house she lived in was part of the city **w**. H2570
Jos 6: 5 then the **w** *of* the city will collapse and H2570
Jos 6:20 a loud shout, the **w** collapsed; so H2570
1Sa 18:11 saying to himself, "I'll pin David to the **w**." H7815
1Sa 19:10 tried to pin him to the **w** with his spear, H7815
1Sa 19:10 him as Saul drove the spear into the **w**. H7815
1Sa 20:25 He sat in his customary place by the **w** H7815
1Sa 25:16 day they were a **w** around us the whole H2570
1Sa 31:10 fastened his body to the **w** *of* Beth Shan. H2570
1Sa 31:12 his sons from the **w** *of* Beth Shan and H2570
2Sa 11:20 know they would shoot arrows from the **w**? H2570
2Sa 11:21 an upper millstone on him from the **w**, H2570
2Sa 11:21 Why did you get so close to the **w**?' If he H2570
2Sa 11:24 shot arrows at your servants from the **w**, H2570
2Sa 18:24 up to the roof of the gateway by the **w**. H2570
2Sa 20:15 were battering the **w** to bring it down, H2570
2Sa 20:21 head will be thrown to you from the **w**." H2570
2Sa 22:30 a troop; with my God I can scale a **w**. H8803
1Ki 3: 1 of the LORD, and the **w** around Jerusalem. H2570
1Ki 6:27 The wing of one cherub touched one **w** H7815
1Ki 6:27 the wing of the other touched the other **w**, H7815
1Ki 7:12 was surrounded by a **w** of three courses of NDT
1Ki 9:15 the terraces, the **w** *of* Jerusalem, and H2570
1Ki 11:27 had filled in the **gap in the w** *of* the city of H7288
1Ki 20:30 where the **w** collapsed on twenty-seven H2570
1Ki 21:23 will devour Jezebel by the **w** *of* Jezreel. H2658
2Ki 3:27 offered him as a sacrifice on the **city w**. H2570
2Ki 6:26 king of Israel was passing by on the **w**, H2570
2Ki 6:30 As he went along the **w**, the people H2570
2Ki 9:33 blood spattered the **w** and the horses as H7815
2Ki 14:13 broke down the **w** *of* Jerusalem from H2570
2Ki 18:26 in the hearing of the people on the **w**." H2570
2Ki 18:27 not to the people sitting on the **w** H2570
2Ki 20: 2 his face to the **w** and prayed to the LORD H7815
2Ki 25: 4 Then the city **w** was broken through, and the NDT
1Ch 11: 8 from the terraces to the **surrounding** *w*, while AIT
2Ch 3:11 cubits long and touched the temple **w**, H7815
2Ch 3:12 long and touched the other temple **w**, H7815
2Ch 25:23 broke down the **w** *of* Jerusalem from H2570
2Ch 26: 9 the Valley Gate and at the **angle of the w**, H5243
2Ch 27: 3 work on the **w** *at* the hill of Ophel. H2570
2Ch 32: 5 sections of the **w** and building towers on H2570
2Ch 32: 5 He built another **w** outside that one and H2570
2Ch 32:18 people of Jerusalem who were on the **w**, H2570
2Ch 33:14 he rebuilt the outer **w** of the City of David, H2570
2Ch 36:19 broke down the **w** *of* Jerusalem; H2570
Ezr 9: 9 given us a **w of protection** in Judah and H1555
Ne 1: 3 The **w** *of* Jerusalem is broken down, and H2570
Ne 2: 8 for the city **w** and for the residence I H2570
Ne 2:15 up the valley by night, examining the **w**. H2570
Ne 2:17 let us rebuild the **w** *of* Jerusalem, and we H2570
Ne 3: 8 restored Jerusalem as far as the Broad **W**. H2570
Ne 3:13 cubits of the **w** as far as the Dung H2570
Ne 3:15 also repaired the **w** *of* the Pool of Siloam, H2570
Ne 3:19 to the armory as far as the angle of the **w**. NDT
Ne 3:27 great projecting tower to the **w** *of* Ophel. H2570
Ne 4: 1 heard that we were rebuilding the **w**, H2570
Ne 4: 2 *Will they* **restore** their **w**? Will they H6441
Ne 4: 3 on it would break down their **w** *of* stones!" H2570
Ne 4: 6 So we rebuilt the **w** till all of it reached H2570
Ne 4:10 rubble that we cannot rebuild the **w**." H2570
Ne 4:13 lowest points of the **w** at the exposed H2570
Ne 4:15 we all returned to the **w**, each to our own H2570
Ne 4:17 who were building the **w**. Those who H2570
Ne 4:19 separated from each other along the **w**. H2570
Ne 5:16 I devoted myself to the work on this **w**. H2570
Ne 6: 1 I had rebuilt the **w** and not a gap was left H2570
Ne 6: 6 therefore you are building the **w**. H2570
Ne 6:15 So the **w** was completed on the H2570
Ne 7: 1 After the **w** had been rebuilt and I had set H2570
Ne 12:27 At the dedication of the **w** *of* Jerusalem H2570
Ne 12:30 purified the people, the gates and the **w**. H2570
Ne 12:31 leaders of Judah go up on top of the **w**. H2570
Ne 12:31 to proceed on top of the **w** to the right, H2570
Ne 12:37 the ascent to the **w** and passed above the H2570
Ne 12:38 I followed them on top of the **w**, together H2570
Ne 12:38 the Tower of the Ovens to the Broad **W**, H2570
Ne 13:21 "Why do you spend the night by the **w**? H2570
Ps 18:29 a troop; with my God I can scale a **w**. H8803
Ps 62: 3 down—this leaning **w**, this tottering H7815
Ps 78:13 he made the water stand up like a **w**. H5603
Pr 1:21 on top of the **w** she cries out, at the city H2570
Pr 18:11 they imagine it a **w** too high to scale. H2570
Pr 24:31 with weeds, and the stone **w** was in ruins. H1555
Ecc 10: 8 breaks through a **w** may be bitten by a H1555
SS 2: 9 There he stands behind our **w**, gazing H4185
SS 8: 9 If she is a **w**, we will build towers of silver H2570
SS 8:10 I am a **w**, and my breasts are like towers H2570
Isa 2:15 every lofty tower and every fortified **w**, H2570
Isa 5: 5 I will break down its **w**, and it will be H1555
Isa 22:10 tore down houses to strengthen the **w**. H2570
Isa 25: 4 ruthless is like a storm driving against a **w** H7815
Isa 30:13 this sin will become for you like a high **w** H2570
Isa 36:11 in the hearing of the people on the **w**." H2570
Isa 36:12 not to the people sitting on the **w** H2570
Isa 38: 2 his face to the **w** and prayed to the LORD H7815
Isa 59:10 Like the blind we grope along the **w** H7815
Jer 1:18 pillar and a bronze **w** to stand against the H2570
Jer 15:20 I will make you a **w** to this people, H2570
Jer 15:20 this people, a fortified **w** of bronze; they will NDT
Jer 21: 4 who are outside the **w** besieging you. H2570
Jer 39: 2 the city **w** was broken through. NDT
Jer 51:44 And the **w** *of* Babylon will fall. H2570
Jer 51:58 "Babylon's thick **w** will be leveled and her H2570
Jer 52: 7 Then the city **w** was broken through, and the NDT
La 2: 8 to tear down the **w** *around* Daughter Zion. H2570
Eze 4: 3 place it as an iron **w** between you and the H7815
Eze 8: 7 I looked, and I saw a hole in the **w**. H7815
Eze 8: 8 "Son of man, now dig into the **w**. H7815
Eze 8: 8 So I dug into the **w** and saw a doorway H7815
Eze 12: 5 dig through the **w** and take your H7815
Eze 12: 7 I dug through the **w** with my hands. H7815
Eze 12:12 will be dug in the **w** for him to go through H7815
Eze 13: 5 to the breaches in the **w** to repair it for the H1555

Eze 13:10 because, when a **flimsy** w is built, they H2666
Eze 13:12 When the w collapses, will people not ask H7815
Eze 13:14 I will tear down the w you have covered H7815
Eze 13:15 my wrath against the w and against those H7815
Eze 13:15 "The w is gone and so are those who H7815
Eze 22:30 would build up the w and stand before H1555
Eze 23:14 She saw men portrayed on a w, figures of H7815
Eze 38:20 will crumble and every w will fall to the H2570
Eze 40: 5 I saw a w completely surrounding the H2570
Eze 40: 5 He measured the w; it was one H1230
Eze 40:12 of each alcove was a w one cubit high, H1473
Eze 40:13 from the **top of the** *rear* w *of* one alcove to H1511
Eze 40:40 By the outside w of the portico of the H4190
Eze 40:43 were attached to the w all around. H1074
Eze 41: 5 Then he measured the w *of* the temple; it H7815
Eze 41: 6 ledges all around the w of the temple to H7815
Eze 41: 6 not inserted into the w *of* the temple. H7815
Eze 41: 9 The outer w of the side rooms was five H7815
Eze 41:12 The w *of* the building was five cubits thick H7815
Eze 41:16 The floor, the w up to the windows, and the NDT
Eze 41:20 were carved on the w *of* the main hall. H7815
Eze 42: 1 opposite the **outer** w on the north H1230
Eze 42: 7 There was an outer w parallel to the H1555
Eze 42:10 the length of the w *of* the outer court, H1555
Eze 42:10 courtyard and opposite the **outer** w, H1230
Eze 42:12 the corresponding w extending eastward, H1556
Eze 42:20 It had a w around it, five hundred cubits H2570
Eze 43: 8 with only a w between me and them H7815
Da 5: 5 wrote on the plaster of the w, A10376
Hos 2: 6 *I will* w her **in** so that she cannot H1553+1555
Joel 2: 9 rush upon the city; they run along the w. H2570
Am 4: 3 go straight out through **breaches in the** w, H7288
Am 5:19 his hand on the w only to have a snake H7815
Am 7: 7 was standing by a w that had been built H2570
Na 2: 5 They dash to the **city** w; the protective H2570
Na 3: 8 river was her defense, the waters her w. H2570
Hab 2:11 The stones of the w will cry out, and the H7815
Zec 2: 5 And I myself will be a w *of* fire around it,' H2570
Mt 21:33 He put a w around it, dug a winepress in *G5850*
Mk 12: 1 He put a w around it, dug a pit for the *G5850*
Ac 9:25 in a basket through an opening *in* the w. *G5446*
Ac 23: 3 "God will strike you, *you* whitewashed w! *G5526*
2Co 11:33 a window in the w and slipped through *G5446*
Eph 2:14 the barrier, the **dividing** w of hostility, *G3546*
Rev 21:12 It had a great, high w with twelve gates *G5446*
Rev 21:14 The w of the city had twelve foundations *G5446*
Rev 21:17 The angel measured the w using human *G5446*
Rev 21:18 The w was made of jasper, and the city of *G5446*

WALLED (4) [WALL]

Lev 25:29 sells a house in a w city retains the right H2570
Lev 25:30 the house in the w city shall H4200+2257+2570
1Ki 4:13 its sixty large w cities with bronze H2570
La 3: 7 *He has* w me in so I cannot escape; he H1553

WALLOW (1) [WALLOWING]

Jer 48:26 *Let* Moab w in her vomit; let her be an H6216

WALLOWING (2) [WALLOW]

2Sa 20:12 Amasa **lay** w in his blood in the middle of H1670
2Pe 2:22 is washed returns to her w in the mud." *G3243*

WALLS (104) [WALL]

Lev 14:37 He is to examine the mold on the w, and H7815
Lev 14:39 If the mold has spread on the w, H7815
Lev 14:41 have all the inside w of the house scraped NDT
Lev 25:31 in villages without w around them are to H2570
Nu 22:24 the vineyards, with w on both sides. H1555
Dt 1:28 the cities are large, with w up to the sky. H1290
Dt 3: 5 fortified with high w and with gates and H2570
Dt 9: 1 with large cities that have w up to the sky. H1290
Dt 28:52 the high fortified w in which you trust fall H2570
1Ki 4:33 to the hyssop that grows out of w. H7815
1Ki 6: 4 narrow windows high up in the **temple** w. AIT
1Ki 6: 5 Against the w of the main hall and inner H7815
1Ki 6: 6 would be inserted into the temple w. H7815
1Ki 6:15 He lined its interior w with cedar boards H7815
1Ki 6:29 On the w all around the temple, in both H7815
2Ki 25: 4 gate between the *two* w near the king's H2570
2Ki 25:10 broke down the w around Jerusalem. H2570
1Ch 29: 4 the overlaying of the w *of* the buildings, H7815
2Ch 3: 7 w and doors of the temple with gold H7815
2Ch 3: 7 and he carved cherubim on the w. H7815
2Ch 8: 5 with w and with gates and bars H2570
2Ch 14: 7 to Judah, "and put w around them, with H2570
2Ch 26: 6 Philistines and broke down the w *of* Gath, H2570
2Ch 26:15 arrows and hurl large stones from the w. NDT
Ezr 4:12 are restoring the w and repairing the A10703
Ezr 4:13 if this city is built and its w are restored, A10703
Ezr 4:16 if this city is built and its w are restored, A10703
Ezr 5: 8 stones and placing the timbers in the w. A10376
Ne 2:13 examining the w *of* Jerusalem, which H2570
Ne 4: 7 to Jerusalem's w had gone ahead and H2570
Ps 51:18 to build up the w *of* Jerusalem. H2570
Ps 55:10 Day and night they prowl about on its w H2570
Ps 80:12 you broken down its w so that all who H1555
Ps 89:40 broken through all his w and reduced his H1556
Ps 122: 7 peace within your w and security within H2658
Ps 144:14 There will be no **breaching of** w, no going H7288
Pr 25:28 Like a city whose w are broken through is H2570
SS 5: 7 away my cloak, those watchmen of the w! H2570
Isa 22: 5 of battering down w and of crying out to H7815
Isa 22: 9 w of the City of David were **broken through** H1323
Isa 22:11 between the *two* w for the water of the H2570
Isa 25:12 your high fortified w and lay them low; H2570
Isa 26: 1 God makes salvation its w and ramparts. H2570
Isa 49:16 of my hands; your w are ever before me. H2570
Isa 54:12 and all your w of precious stones. H1473
Isa 56: 5 my temple and its w a memorial and a H2570
Isa 58:12 you will be called **Repairer of** Broken W H1553
Isa 60:10 "Foreigners will rebuild your w, and their H2570
Isa 60:18 you will call your w Salvation and your H2570
Isa 62: 6 I have posted watchmen on your w H2570
Jer 1:15 all her surrounding w and against all the H2570
Jer 39: 4 through the gate between the *two* w, and H2570
Jer 39: 8 broke down the w *of* Jerusalem. H2570
Jer 49: 3 rush here and there inside the w, for H1556
Jer 49:27 "I will set fire to the w *of* Damascus; it will H2570
Jer 50:15 her towers fall, her w are torn down. H2570
Jer 51:12 Lift up a banner against the w *of* Babylon H2570
Jer 52: 7 gate between the *two* w near the king's H2570
Jer 52:14 broke down all the w around Jerusalem. H2570
La 2: 7 He has given the w *of* her palaces into H2570
La 2: 8 He made ramparts and w lament H2570
La 2:18 You w *of* Daughter Zion, let your tears H2570
Eze 5:12 third will fall by the sword **outside** your w; H6017
Eze 8:10 all over the w all kinds of crawling H7815
Eze 26: 4 will destroy the w *of* Tyre and pull down H2570
Eze 26: 8 a ramp up to your w and raise his shields NDT
Eze 26: 9 rams against your w and demolish your H2570
Eze 26:10 Your w will tremble at the noise of the H2570
Eze 26:10 men enter a city whose w have been broken NDT
Eze 26:12 will break down your w and demolish your H2570
Eze 27:10 hung their shields and helmets on your w, NDT
Eze 27:11 Helek guarded your w on every side; H2570
Eze 27:11 They hung their shields around your w H2570
Eze 33:30 about you by the w and at the doors of H7815
Eze 38:11 them living without w and without gates H2570
Eze 40: 7 the projecting w between the alcoves NDT
Eze 40:10 the faces of the **projecting** w on each side H382
Eze 40:14 the faces of the **projecting** w all around the H382
Eze 40:16 The alcoves and the **projecting** w inside the H382
Eze 40:16 faces of the **projecting** w were decorated H382
Eze 40:21 its **projecting** w and its portico had the H382
Eze 40:26 the faces of the **projecting** w on each side. H382
Eze 40:29 its **projecting** w and its portico had the H382
Eze 40:33 its **projecting** w and its portico had the H382
Eze 40:36 its alcoves, its **projecting** w and its portico H382
Eze 40:48 cubits and its **projecting** w were three H4190
Eze 41: 2 the **projecting** w on each side *of* it H4190
Eze 41: 3 the projecting w on each side of it were NDT
Eze 41:13 building with its w were also a hundred H7815
Eze 41:17 on the w at regular intervals H7815
Eze 41:25 palm trees like those carved on the w, H7815
Joel 2: 7 like warriors; they scale w like soldiers. H2570
Am 1: 7 will send fire on the w *of* Gaza that will H2570
Am 1:10 will send fire on the w *of* Tyre that will H2570
Am 1:14 I will set fire to the w *of* Rabbah that will H2570
Am 9:11 I will repair its **broken** w and restore its H7288
Mic 7:11 The day for building your w will come, the H1555
Na 3:17 that settle in the w on a cold day— H1556
Zec 2: 4 will be a **city without** w because of the H7252
Zec 14: 1 and divided up **within** your **very** w. H928+7931
Lk 19:44 you and the children **within** your *w.* AIT
Heb 11:30 By faith the w of Jericho fell, after the *G5446*
Rev 21:15 to measure the city, its gates and its w. *G5446*
Rev 21:19 of the city w were decorated with *G5446*

WANDER (18) [WANDERED, WANDERER, WANDERERS, WANDERING, WANDERS]

Ge 20:13 And when God **had** me w from my father's H9494
Nu 32:13 Israel and *he* **made** them w in the H5675
2Sa 15:20 today *shall I* **make** you w **about** with us, H5675
2Ki 21: 8 **make** the feet of the Israelites w from H5653
Job 12:24 *he* **makes** them w in a trackless waste. H9494
Job 38:41 out to God and w **about** for lack of food? H9494
Ps 59:15 They w **about** for food and howl if not H5675
Ps 107:40 on nobles **made** them w in a trackless H9494
Pr 5: 6 her paths w **aimlessly**, but she does H5675
Pr 17:24 a fool's eyes w to the ends of the earth. NDT
Isa 63:17 *do you* **make** us w from your ways and H9494
Jer 14:10 "They greatly love to w; they do not H5675
Jer 31:22 How long *will you* w, unfaithful Daughter H2811
La 4:15 When they flee and w **about**, people H5675
Am 8:12 from sea to sea and w from north to east, H8763
Zec 10: 2 Therefore *the people* w like sheep H5825
Mt 18:13 about the ninety-nine that *did* not w **off**. *G4414*
Jas 5:19 if one of you *should* w from the truth and *G4414*

WANDERED (11) [WANDER]

Ge 21:14 went on her way and w in the Desert of H9494
1Ch 16:20 *they* w from nation to nation, from one H2143
Ps 105:13 *they* w from nation to nation, from one H2143
Ps 107: 4 *Some* w in desert wastelands, finding no H9494
Jer 50: 6 *They* w over mountain and hill and forgot H2143
Eze 34: 6 My sheep w over all the mountains and on H8706
Eze 44:10 went astray and who w from me after their H9494
Mt 18:12 hills and go to look for the *one that* w **off**? *G4414*
1Ti 6:10 *have* w from the faith and pierced *G675*
Heb 11:38 *They* w in deserts and mountains, living *G4414*
2Pe 2:15 straight way and w **off** to follow the way *G4414*

WANDERER (3) [WANDER]

Ge 4:12 You will be a restless w on the earth." H5653
Ge 4:14 I will be a restless w on the earth, and H5653
Isa 58: 7 to provide the poor w with shelter— H5291

WANDERERS (1) [WANDER]

Hos 9:17 they will be w among the nations. H5610

WANDERING (9) [WANDER]

Ge 37:15 a man found him w **around** in the fields H9494
Ex 14: 3 *are* w **around** the land **in confusion**, H1003
Ex 23: 4 across your enemy's ox or donkey w **off**, H9494
Dt 26: 5 "My father *was* a w Aramean, and he went H6
Ps 109:10 *May* his children *be* w beggars; may they H5675
La 1: 7 her affliction and w Jerusalem remembers H5291
La 3:19 I remember my affliction and my w, the H5291
Hos 8: 9 up to Assyria like a wild donkey w **alone**. H969
Jude 13 up their shame; w stars, for whom *G4417*

WANDERS (3) [WANDER]

Job 15:23 He w **about** for food like a vulture; he H5610
Job 18: 8 thrust him into a net; *he* w into its mesh. H2143
Mt 18:12 one of them w **away**, will he not *G4414*

WANE (1)

Isa 60:20 your moon *will* w no more; the LORD H665

WANT (194) [WANTED, WANTING, WANTS]

Ge 24: 3 *I* w you **to swear** by the LORD, the God of H8678
Ge 29:21 is completed, and *I* w *to* **make love to** her." AIT
Ge 42:36 is no more, and now *you* w *to* **take** Benjamin. AIT
Ex 16: 8 evening and **all** the bread you w in the H8425
Ex 16:23 So bake what *you* w *to* **bake** and boil what AIT
Ex 16:23 want to bake and boil what *you* w *to* **boil**. AIT
Ex 21: 5 wife and children and *do* not *w to* **go** free, AIT
Lev 26: 5 you will eat **all** the food you w and live in H8427
Nu 16:13 And now *you* also *w to* **lord it** over us! AIT
Nu 16:14 *Do you* w *to* **treat** these men **like slaves**? No, AIT
Nu 20:19 *We* only *w to* **pass through** on foot—nothing AIT
Dt 12:15 eat as much of the meat as you w, H205
Dt 12:20 then you may eat as much of it as you w. H205
Dt 12:21 you may eat as much of them as you w. H205
Dt 15:16 "*I* do not *w to* **leave** you," because AIT
Dt 23:24 you may eat **all** the grapes you w, but do H8427
Dt 25: 7 if a man *does* not w to marry his brother's H2911
Dt 25: 8 in saying, "*I do* not w to marry her," H2911
Jdg 9:15 'If you really *w to* **anoint** me king over you AIT
1Sa 2:16 then take whatever you w," the servant H203
1Sa 8:19 they said. "We w a king over us. H2118S
1Sa 12:12 we w a king to rule over us'—even NDT
1Sa 20: 4 "Whatever you w me to do, I'll do H606
1Sa 21: 9 If *you* w it, take it; there is no sword here H4374
2Sa 14:32 Now then, *I w to* **see** the king's face, and if I AIT
2Sa 18:22 Joab replied, "My son, why *do you w to* **go**? AIT
2Sa 18:23 "Come what may, *I w to* **run**." So Joab said, AIT
2Sa 20:19 Why *do you w to* **swallow up** the LORD's AIT
2Sa 21: 4 "What *do* you w me to do for you? H606
2Sa 24: 3 But why *does* my lord the king w to do H2911
1Ki 1:16 "What is it you w?" the king asked. H4200
1Ki 3: 5 "Ask for whatever you w me to give you." NDT
1Ki 5: 8 will do all you w in providing the H2914
1Ki 11:22 lacked here that you w to go back to your H1335
2Ki 3:13 of Israel, "Why do you w **to** involve me? H4200
2Ki 19: 7 I *will* **make** him w **to** return to H5989+8120+928
1Ch 21: 3 Why *does* my lord w **to do** this? Why H1335
2Ch 1: 7 "Ask for whatever you w me to give you." NDT
Ne 2: 4 "What is it you w?" Then I prayed to H1335
Job 24:16 *they* w nothing **to do with** the light. H3359
Job 30: 3 Haggard from w and hunger, they roamed H2895
Job 33:32 speak up, for *I* w to vindicate you. H2911
Job 37:20 Should he be told that *I w to* **speak**? Would AIT
Ps 38:12 *Those who* w **to kill** me set their H1335+5883
Ps 40:14 *May* all *who* w to take my life be put to H1335
Ps 63: 9 Those *who* w **to kill** me will be H1335+5883
Ps 70: 2 May *those who* w **to take** my life be put to H1335
Ps 71:13 may *those who* w to harm me be covered H1335
Isa 37: 7 I *will* **make** him w **to** return to H5989+928+8120
Jer 4:30 despise you; *they* w **to kill** you. H1335+5883
Jer 19: 7 hands of *those who* w **to kill** them, H1335+5883
Jer 21: 7 their enemies *who* w **to kill** them. H1335+5883
Jer 22:25 hands of *those who* w **to kill** you, H1335+5883
Jer 34:20 their enemies *who* w **to kill** them. H1335+5883
Jer 34:21 their enemies *who* w **to kill** them, H1335+5883
Jer 38:16 to those who w **to kill** you." H1335+906+5883
Jer 40: 4 but if you do **not** w to, then H8273+928+6524
Jer 42:22 in the place where *you* w to go to settle." H2911
Jer 44:30 of his enemies *who* w **to kill** him, H1335+5883
Jer 46:26 of *those who* w **to kill** them— H1335+5883
Jer 49:37 before *those who* w **to kill** them; H1335+5883
Eze 20:32 " 'You say, "*We* w *to* **be** like the nations, like AIT
Eze 36:32 *I* w you *to* **know** that I am not doing this for AIT
Da 2: 3 troubles me and I w to know what it means." NDT
Da 3:18 does not, we *w* you *to* **know**, Your Majesty, AIT
Mt 1:19 yet *did* not w to expose her to public *G2527*
Mt 8:29 **"What do you w with us** *G5515+5516+1609+2779+5148*
Mt 9: 6 But I w you to know that the Son of Man *G2671*
Mt 12:38 "Teacher, *we* w to see a sign from you." *G2527*
Mt 13:28 '*Do you* w us to go and pull them up? *G2527*
Mt 15:32 *I do* not w to send them away hungry, or *G2527*
Mt 19:17 If *you* w to enter life, keep the *G2527*
Mt 19:21 answered, "If *you* w to be perfect, go, *G2527*

W

Mt 20:14 *I* w to give the one who was hired last the *G2527*
Mt 20:15 right to do what *I* w with my own money? *G2527*
Mt 20:21 "What *is it you* w?" he asked. She said *G2527*
Mt 20:32 "What *do you* w me to do for you? *G2527*
Mt 20:33 they answered, "we w our sight." *G2671*
Mt 26:17 "Where *do you* w us to make preparations *G2527*
Mt 27:17 "Which one *do you* w me to release to *G2527*
Mt 27:21 of the two *do you* w me to release to *G2527*
Mk 1:24 "**What do** you w **with** us, Jesus of *G5515+5516*
Mk 2:10 But I w you to know that the Son of Man *G2671*
Mk 5: 7 "**What do** you w **with** me *G5515+5516*
Mk 6:22 "Ask me for anything *you* w, and I'll give *G2527*
Mk 6:25 "*I* w you to give me right now the head of *G2527*
Mk 6:26 dinner guests, *he did* not w to refuse her. *G2527*
Mk 7:24 a house and *did* not w anyone to know it; *G2527*
Mk 7:27 "First let the children **eat all** *they* w," *G5963*
Mk 9:30 Jesus *did* not w anyone to know where *G2527*
Mk 10:35 "*we* w you to do for us whatever we ask." *G2527*
Mk 10:36 "What *do you* w me to do for you?" he *G2527*
Mk 10:51 "What *do you* w me to do for you?" Jesus *G2527*
Mk 10:51 The blind man said, "Rabbi, I w to see." *G2671*
Mk 14: 7 you can help them any time *you* w. *G2527*
Mk 14:12 "Where *do you* w us to go and make *G2527*
Mk 15: 9 "*Do you* w me to release to you the king *G2527*
Lk 4: 6 and I can give it to anyone *I* w **to**. *G2527*
Lk 4:34 **What do** you w **with** us, Jesus of Nazareth *G5515*
Lk 5:24 But I w you to know that the Son of Man *G2671*
Lk 8:28 "**What do** you w **with** me *G5515+5516+2779*
Lk 9:54 *do you* w us to call fire down from heaven *G2527*
Lk 16:26 so that those *who* w to go from here to *G2527*
Lk 18:41 "What *do you* w me to do for you?" "Lord, *G2527*
Lk 18:41 "Lord, I w to see," he replied. *G2671*
Lk 19:14 '*We* don't w this man to be our king. *G2527*
Lk 19:27 of mine who *did* not w me to be king over *G2527*
Lk 22: 9 "Where *do you* w us to prepare for it?" *G2527*
Jn 1:38 following and asked, "What *do you* w?" *G2426*
Jn 4:27 one asked, "What *do you* w?" or "Why are *G2426*
Jn 5: 6 he asked him, "*Do you* w to get well?" *G2527*
Jn 6:67 "You *do* not w to leave too, do you?" *G2527*
Jn 7: 1 *He did* not w to go about in Judea *G2527*
Jn 8:44 you w **to** carry out your father's *G2527*
Jn 9:27 Why *do you* w to hear it again *G2527*
Jn 9:27 *Do you* w to become his disciples too?" *G2527*
Jn 17:24 *I* w those you have given me to be with *G2527*
Jn 18: 4 out and asked them, "Who is it *you* w?" *G2426*
Jn 18: 7 "Who is it *you* w?" "Jesus of *G2426*
Jn 18:39 *Do you* w me to release 'the king of the *G1089*
Jn 19:31 leaders did not w the bodies left on the NDT
Jn 21:18 lead you where *you do* not w to go." *G2527*
Jn 21:22 "If *I* w him to remain alive until I return *G2527*
Jn 21:23 "If *I* w him to remain alive until I return *G2527*
Ac 7:26 brothers; why *do you* w *to* **hurt** each other? AIT
Ac 13:22 he will do everything I w him to do. *G2525*
Ac 13:38 I w you *to* **know** that through Jesus the AIT
Ac 16:37 And now *do they* w *to* **get rid of** us quietly AIT
Ac 17:32 "*We* w *to* **hear** you again on this subject." AIT
Ac 19:39 If there is anything further *you* w *to* **bring up** AIT
Ac 23:19 asked, "What is it *you* w to tell me?" *G2400*
Ac 28:22 But *we* w to hear what your views are, for *G546*
Ac 28:28 "Therefore *I* w you *to* **know** that God's AIT
Ro 1:13 *I do* not w you to be unaware, brothers *G2527*
Ro 7:15 For what *I* w to do I do not do, but what I *G2527*
Ro 7:16 And if I do what *I do* not w to do, I agree *G2527*
Ro 7:19 For I do not do the good *I* w to do, but the *G2527*
Ro 7:19 but the evil *I do* not w to do—this I *G2527*
Ro 7:20 Now if I do what *I do* not w to do, it is no *G2527*
Ro 7:21 *Although* I w to do good, evil is right *G2527*
Ro 11:25 *I do* not w you to be ignorant of this *G2527*
Ro 13: 3 *Do you* w to be free from fear of the one *G2527*
Ro 16:19 but *I* w you to be wise about what is good, *G2527*
1Co 4: 8 Already *you* **have all** *you* w *G3170+1639*
1Co 7:28 troubles in this life, and I *w to* **spare** you this. AIT
1Co 10: 1 For *I do* not w you to be ignorant of the *G2527*
1Co 10:20 and *I do* not w you to be participants with *G2527*
1Co 10:27 invites you to a meal and *you* w to go, *G2527*
1Co 11: 3 But *I* w you to realize that the head of *G2527*
1Co 12: 1 *I do* not w you to be uninformed. *G2527*
1Co 12: 3 Therefore *I* w you *to* **know** that no one who is AIT
1Co 14:35 If *they* w to inquire about something, they *G2527*
1Co 15: 1 *I* w *to* **remind** you of the gospel I preached to AIT
1Co 16: 7 For *I do* not w to see you now and make *G2527*
2Co 1: 8 *We do* not w you to be uninformed *G2527*
2Co 8: 1 *we* w you *to* **know** about the grace that God AIT
2Co 8: 8 but *I* w *to* **test** the sincerity of your love by AIT
2Co 8:20 *We* w *to* **avoid** any criticism of the way we AIT
2Co 10: 9 I do not w **to** seem to be trying to frighten *G2671*
2Co 10:16 *For we* do not *w to* **boast** about work already AIT
2Co 11:12 from under those *who* w an opportunity to *G2527*
2Co 12:14 because what *I* w is not your possessions *G2426*
2Co 12:20 come I may not find you as *I* w you to be, *G2527*
2Co 12:20 you may not find me as *you* w me to be. *G2527*
Gal 1:11 *I* w you *to* **know**, brothers and sisters, that the AIT
Gal 4:17 What *they* w is to alienate you from us, so *G2527*
Gal 4:21 Tell me, you *who* w to be under the law *G2527*
Gal 5:17 so that you are not to do whatever *you* w. *G2527*
Gal 6:12 Those *who* w to impress people by means *G2527*
Gal 6:13 yet *they* w you to be circumcised that they *G2527*
Php 1:12 Now *I* w you to know, brothers and sisters *G1089*
Php 3:10 I w to know Christ—yes, to know the power NDT
Php 4:12 hungry, whether living in plenty or **in** w. *G5728*
Col 2: 1 *I* w you to know how hard I am *G2527*
1Th 4:13 *we do* not w you to be uninformed about *G2527*
1Ti 1: 7 *They* w to be teachers of the law, but they *G2527*
1Ti 2: 8 Therefore *I* w the men everywhere to pray *G1089*
1Ti 2: 9 I also w the women to dress modestly, with NDT
1Ti 5:11 their dedication to Christ, *they* w to marry. *G2527*
1Ti 6: 9 Those *who* w to get rich fall into *G1089*
2Ti 4: 3 *to* **say what** their **itching ears** w **to hear** *G3117+198*
Titus 3: 8 And *I* w you to stress these things, so that *G1089*
Phm 14 But *I did* not w to do anything without your *G2527*
Heb 6:11 *We* w each of you to show this same *G2121*
Heb 6:12 We do not w you to become lazy, but to *G2671*
Heb 13:23 I *w you to* **know** that our brother Timothy has AIT
Jas 2:20 *do you* w evidence that faith without *G2527*
Jas 4: 2 You covet but you cannot get what you w, NDT
2Pe 3: 2 I w you to recall the words spoken in the past NDT
2Jn 12 but *I do* not w to use paper and ink. *G1089*
3Jn 10 also stops those *who* w **to** do so and puts *G1089*
3Jn 13 but *I do* not w **to** do so with pen and ink. *G2527*
Jude 5 *I* w **to** remind you that the Lord at one *G1089*
Rev 11: 6 every kind of plague as often as *they* w. *G2527*

WANTED (56) [WANT]

Ex 4:19 those who w **to kill** you are H1335+906+5883
Ex 16: 3 pots of meat and ate **all** the food we w, H8427
Ru 2:14 She ate **all** *she* w and had some left over. H8425
2Sa 3:17 time *you have* w **to make** David H1335+4200
2Sa 3:19 tribe of Benjamin w **to do**. H3202+928+6524
1Ki 5:10 with all the cedar and juniper logs he w, H2914
1Ki 9:11 all the cedar and juniper and gold he w. H2914
1Ki 13:33 Anyone *who* w to become a priest he H2913
Est 2:13 Anything *she* w was given her to take with H606
Ps 35:25 not let them think, "Aha, **just what** we w!" H5883
Ps 71:24 for *those who* w to harm me have been H1335
Ecc 2: 3 *I w to* **see** what was good for people to do AIT
Jer 44:30 the enemy *who* w **to kill** him. H1335+5883
Jer 49: 9 they not steal only **as much as** they w? H1896
Da 5:19 Those the king w **to** put to death, he put A10605
Da 5:19 to death; those *he* w **to** spare, he spared A10605
Da 5:19 he spared; those *he* w **to** promote, he A10605
Da 5:19 those *he* w **to** humble, he humbled. A10605
Da 7:19 "Then *I* w to know the meaning of the A10605
Da 7:20 I also w to know about the ten horns on its NDT
Ob 5 they not steal only **as much as** they w? H1896
Jnh 4: 8 He w to die, and said, "It H8626+906+5883
Mt 14: 5 Herod w to kill John, but he was afraid of *G2527*
Mt 18:23 is like a king who w to settle accounts *G2527*
Mt 21:31 "Which of the two did what his father w?" *G2525*
Mk 3:13 called to him those he w, *G2527*
Mk 6:19 a grudge against John and w to kill him. *G2527*
Lk 10:24 prophets and kings w to see what you see *G2527*
Lk 10:29 But he w to justify himself, so he asked *G2527*
Lk 19: 3 *He* w to see who Jesus was, but because *G2426*
Jn 6:11 who were seated as much as *they* w. *G2527*
Jn 7:44 Some w to seize him, but no one laid a *G2527*
Jn 16:19 Jesus saw that *they* w to ask him about *G2527*
Jn 18:28 because *they w to be able to* **eat** the AIT
Jn 21:18 dressed yourself and went where *you* w; *G2527*
Ac 5:33 were furious and w to put them to death. *G1089*
Ac 10:10 became hungry and w something to eat, *G2527*
Ac 13: 7 Saul *because he* w **to** hear the word *G2118*
Ac 14:13 gates *because he* and the crowd w **to** *G2527*
Ac 15:37 Barnabas w to take John, also called Mark *G1089*
Ac 16: 3 Paul w to take him along on the journey *G2527*
Ac 18:27 *When* Apollos w to go to Achaia, the *G1089*
Ac 19:30 Paul w to appear before the crowd, but the *G1089*
Ac 22:30 The commander w to find out exactly why *G1089*
Ac 23:28 *I* w to know why they were accusing him *G1089*
Ac 24:27 but *because* Felix w to grant a favor to the *G2527*
Ac 27:38 *When they had* **eaten as much as** *they* w *G3170+5575*
Ac 27:43 But the centurion w to spare Paul's life *G1089*
Ac 28:18 They examined me and w to release me *G1089*
1Co 12:18 one of them, just as *he* w them to be. *G2527*
2Co 1:15 *I* w to visit you first so that you might *G1089*
2Co 1:16 I w to visit you on my way to Macedonia NDT
Gal 2: 2 I **w to be sure** I was **not** running *G3590+4803*
1Th 2:18 For *we* w to come to you—certainly I, Paul *G2527*
Heb 6:17 Because God w to make the unchanging *G1089*
Heb 12:17 *when he* w to inherit this blessing *G2527*

WANTING (10) [WANT]

Da 5:27 weighed on the scales and found **w**. A10276
Mt 12:46 brothers stood outside, w to speak to him. *G2426*
Mt 12:47 are standing outside, w to speak to you." *G2426*
Mk 15:15 W to satisfy the crowd, Pilate released *G1089*
Lk 8:20 are standing outside, w to see you." *G2527*
Lk 23: 8 a long time he had been w to see him. *G2527*
Lk 23:20 W to release Jesus, Pilate appealed to *G2527*
Ac 23:15 you on the pretext of w more accurate *G3516*
Ac 23:20 on the pretext of w more accurate *G3516*
2Pe 3: 9 with you, not w anyone to perish, but *G1089*

WANTON (1)

Na 3: 4 all because of the w **lust** *of* a prostitute H2393

WANTS (39) [WANT]

Ge 19: 9 a foreigner, and now *he w to* **play the judge**! AIT
Ge 43:18 He w to attack us and overpower us and NDT
Ex 12:48 among you *who w to* **celebrate** the LORD's AIT
Nu 6: 2 'If a man or woman *w* **to make a special vow** AIT
Ru 3:13 *he w to* **do** *his* **duty as** your **guardian-redeemer** AIT
1Sa 18:25 'The king w no other price for the bride H2914
1Sa 22:23 The man who **w to kill** you is trying H1335+5883
Jer 22:28 broken pot, an object no one w? H2914
Jer 48:38 broken Moab like a jar that no one w," H2914
Eze 46: 7 the lambs as much as he **w to give**, H5952+3338
Hos 8: 8 the nations like something no one w. H2914
Mt 5:40 And if anyone w to sue you and take your *G2527*
Mt 5:42 away from the *one who* w to borrow from *G2527*
Mt 16:24 "Whoever w to be my disciple must deny *G2527*
Mt 16:25 For whoever w to save their life will lose it *G2527*
Mt 20:26 whoever w to become great among you *G2527*
Mt 20:27 whoever w to be first must be your *G2527*
Mt 27:43 Let God rescue him now if *he* w him, for *G2527*
Mk 8:34 "Whoever w to be my disciple must deny *G2527*
Mk 8:35 For whoever w to save their life will lose it *G2527*
Mk 9:35 "Anyone *who* w to be first must be the *G2527*
Mk 10:43 whoever w to become great among you *G2527*
Mk 10:44 whoever w to be first must be slave of *G2527*
Lk 5:39 no one after drinking old wine w the new, *G2527*
Lk 9:23 "Whoever w to be my disciple must deny *G2527*
Lk 9:24 For whoever w to save their life will lose it *G2527*
Lk 12:47 do what the master w will be beaten with *G2525*
Lk 13:31 go somewhere else. Herod w to kill you." *G2527*
Lk 14:28 "Suppose one of you w to build a tower *G2527*
Jn 7: 4 No one *who* **w to** become a public figure *G2426*
Ro 9:18 has mercy on whom *he* w to have mercy, *G2527*
Ro 9:18 he hardens whom *he* w to harden. *G2527*
1Co 7:36 he ought to marry, he should do as *he* w. *G2527*
1Co 11:16 If anyone w to be contentious about this *G1506*
1Ti 2: 4 who w all people to be saved and to come *G2527*
2Ti 3:12 everyone who w to live a godly life in *G2527*
Jas 3: 4 small rudder wherever the pilot w to go. *G1089*
1Pe 5: 2 you are willing, **as** God w you to be; not *G2848*
Rev 11: 5 is how anyone *who* w to harm them must *G2527*

WAR (134) [WARFARE, WARHORSES, WARRIOR, WARRIOR'S, WARRIORS, WARS]

Ge 14: 2 kings **went to** w *against* Bera king H6913+4878
Ge 31:26 off my daughters like captives in w. H2995
Ex 1:10 numerous and, if w breaks out, will join H4878
Ex 13:17 "If they face w, they might change H4878
Ex 17:16 the LORD will be at w against the H4878
Ex 32:17 "There is the sound of w in the camp." H4878
Nu 31: 3 of your men to go to w against the H7372
Nu 32: 6 Israelites go to w while you sit here? H4878
Dt 2: 5 *Do* not **provoke** them **to** w, for I will not H1741
Dt 2: 9 the Moabites or provoke them to w, H4878
Dt 2:19 do not harass them or **provoke** them **to** w H1741
Dt 4:34 wonders, by w, by a mighty hand and H4878
Dt 20: 1 When you go to w against your enemies H4878
Dt 20:20 until the city **at** w with you falls. H6913+4878
Dt 21:10 When you go to w against your enemies H4878
Dt 24: 5 must not be sent to w or have any other H7372
Jos 4:13 the LORD to the plains of Jericho for w. H4878
Jos 6:10 the army, "*Do* not **give a** w **cry**, do not H8131
Jos 9: 2 came together to **wage** w against Joshua H4309
Jos 11:18 Joshua waged w against all these kings H4878
Jos 11:20 their hearts to wage w against Israel, H4878
Jos 11:23 Then the land had rest from w. H4878
Jos 14:15 Then the land had rest from w. H4878
Jos 22:12 at Shiloh to go to w against them. H7372
Jos 22:33 more about going to w against them to H7372
Jdg 3:10 he became Israel's judge and went to w. H4878
Jdg 5: 8 new leaders when w came to the city H4311
Jdg 11:27 doing me wrong by **waging** w against me. H4309
Jdg 21:22 did not get wives for them during the w. H4878
1Sa 8:12 to make weapons of w and equipment H4878
1Sa 14:52 there was bitter w with the Philistines, H4878
1Sa 15:18 **wage** w against them until you have H4309
1Sa 17: 1 their forces for w and assembled at Sokoh H4878
1Sa 17:13 oldest sons had followed Saul to the w: H4878
1Sa 17:20 to its battle positions, shouting the w **cry**. H4878
1Sa 19: 8 Once more w broke out, and David went H4878
2Sa 1:27 The weapons of w have perished!" H4878
2Sa 3: 1 The w between the house of Saul and the H4878
2Sa 3: 6 During the w between the house of Saul H4878
2Sa 8:10 who had been **at** w **with** Tou. H408+4878
2Sa 11: 1 at the time when kings **go off to** w, David H3655
2Sa 11: 7 soldiers were and how the w was going. H4878
1Ki 8:44 your people go to w against their H4878
1Ki 12:21 **to go to** w against Israel and to regain the H4309
1Ki 15: 6 There was w between Abijah and H4878
1Ki 15: 7 There was w between Abijah and H4878
1Ki 15:16 There was w between Asa and Baasha H4878
1Ki 15:32 There was w between Asa and Baasha H4878
1Ki 20:18 if they have come out for w, take them H4878
1Ki 22: 1 years there was no w between Aram and H4878
1Ki 22: 6 "Shall I go to w against Ramoth Gilead H4878
1Ki 22:15 shall we go to w against Ramoth Gilead H4878
2Ki 6: 8 the king of Aram was **at** w with Israel. H4309
2Ki 8:28 son of Ahab to w against Hazael king H4878
2Ki 13:12 including *his* w against Amaziah king of H4309
2Ki 14:15 including *his* w against Amaziah king of H4309
2Ki 18:20 have the counsel and the might for w— H4878
2Ki 24:16 strong and fit for w, and a thousand H4878
1Ch 5:10 reign they waged w against the Hagrites, H4878
1Ch 5:19 They waged w against the Hagrites, Jetur H4878
1Ch 7:11 17,200 fighting men ready to go out to w. H4878
1Ch 18:10 who had been **at** w **with** Tou. H408+4878
1Ch 20: 1 at the time when kings go off to w, Joab led NDT
1Ch 20: 4 of time, w broke out with the Philistines H4878
2Ch 6:34 your people go to w against their H4878
2Ch 11: 1 to **go to** w against Israel and to regain the H4309

W

2Ch 13: 2 There was w between Abijah and H4878
2Ch 14: 6 No one was at w with him during those H4878
2Ch 15:19 There was no more w until the thirty-fifth H4878
2Ch 16: 9 and from now on you will be at w. H4878
2Ch 17:10 so that *they did* not **go to** w against H4309
2Ch 18: 3 as your people; we will join you in the w." H4878
2Ch 18: 5 "Shall we go to w against Ramoth Gilead H4878
2Ch 18:14 shall we go to w against Ramoth Gilead H4878
2Ch 20: 1 came to wage w against Jehoshaphat. H4878
2Ch 22: 5 of Israel to wage w against Hazael king of H4878
2Ch 25:13 to take part in the w raided towns H4878
2Ch 26: 6 He went *to* w against the Philistines and H4309
2Ch 26:13 an army of 307,500 men trained for w, H4878
2Ch 27: 5 Jotham **waged** w against the king of the H4309
2Ch 28:12 those who were arriving from the w. H7372
2Ch 32: 2 he intended to *wage* w against Jerusalem H4878
2Ch 35:21 but the house with which I am **at** w. H4878
Job 38:23 times of trouble, for days of w and battle? H7930
Ps 27: 3 not fear; though w break out against me H4878
Ps 55:21 as butter, yet w is *in* his heart; his words H7930
Ps 68:30 Scatter the nations who delight in w. H7930
Ps 76: 3 the swords, the weapons of w. H4878
Ps 120: 7 but when I speak, they are for w. H4878
Ps 140: 2 in their hearts and stir up w every day. H4878
Ps 144: 1 who trains my hands for w, my fingers H7930
Pr 20:18 so if you wage w, obtain guidance. H4878
Pr 24: 6 Surely you need guidance to wage w, and H4878
Ecc 3: 8 a time for w and a time for peace. H4878
Ecc 8: 8 As no one is discharged in **time of** w, so H4878
Ecc 9:18 Wisdom is better than weapons of w, but H7930
Isa 2: 4 nor will they train for w anymore. H4878
Isa 8: 9 **Raise the** w **cry**, *you* nations, and be H8131
Isa 13: 4 LORD Almighty is mustering an army for w. H4878
Isa 36: 5 say you have counsel and might for w— H4878
Isa 41:12 Those who wage w *against* you will be as H4878
Isa 42:25 his burning anger, the violence of w. H4878
Jer 4:16 raising a w **cry** against the cities of Judah. H7754
Jer 21: 4 you the weapons of w that are in your H4878
Jer 28: 8 preceded you and me have prophesied w, H4878
Jer 42:14 we will not see w or hear the trumpet H4878
Jer 49:32 their large herds will be **spoils of** w. H8965
Jer 51:20 "You are my w **club**, my weapon for battle H5151
Eze 17:17 horde will be of no help to him in w, H4878
Eze 32:27 of the dead with their weapons of w— H4878
Eze 38: 8 invade a land that has recovered from w, H2995
Eze 39: 9 arrows, the w **clubs** and spears. H5234+3338
Da 7:21 this horn was waging w against the holy A10639
Da 9:26 W will continue until the end, and H4878
Da 10: 1 was true and it concerned a great w. H7372
Da 11:10 His sons *will* **prepare for** w and assemble H1741
Da 11:25 South *will* **wage** w with H1741+4200+2021+4878
Hos 10: 9 Will not w again overtake the evildoers in H4878
Joel 3: 9 Prepare for w! Rouse the warriors! H4878
Am 1:14 her fortresses amid w **cries** on the day of H9558
Am 2: 2 great tumult amid w **cries** and the blast of H9558
Mic 3: 5 prepare to wage w against anyone who H4878
Mic 4: 3 nor will they train for w anymore. H4878
Lk 14:31 is about to go to w against another king. *G4483*
Ro 7:23 **waging** w **against** the law of my mind and *G529*
2Co 10: 3 *we do* not **wage** w as the world does. *G5129*
1Pe 2:11 desires, which **wage** w against your soul. *G5129*
Rev 12: 7 Then w broke out in heaven. Michael *G4483*
Rev 12:17 went off to wage w against the rest of *G4483*
Rev 13: 4 Who can **wage** w against it?" *G4482*
Rev 13: 7 power to wage w against God's holy *G4483*
Rev 17:14 They *will* **wage** w against the Lamb, but *G4482*
Rev 19:11 With justice he judges and **wages** w. *G4482*
Rev 19:19 together to wage w against the rider on *G4483*

WARD (3)

2Sa 5: 6 the blind and the lame *can* w you **off**." H6073
Isa 47:11 you that you cannot w **off with a ransom**; H4105
La 2:14 not expose your sin to w **off** your captivity. H8740

WARDEN (3)

Ge 39:21 him favor in the eyes of the prison w. H8569
Ge 39:22 So the w put Joseph in charge of all those H8569
Ge 39:23 The w paid no attention to anything under H8569

WARDROBE (3)

2Ki 10:22 And Jehu said to the keeper of the w H4921
2Ki 22:14 the son of Harhas, keeper of the w. H955
2Ch 34:22 the son of Hasrah, keeper of the w. H955

WARES (9)

2Ki 8: 9 of all the **finest** w *of* Damascus. H3206
Eze 27: 9 came alongside to trade for your w. H5114
Eze 27:13 beings and articles of bronze for your w. H5114
Eze 27:17 olive oil and balm for your w. H5114
Eze 27:19 of wine from Izal in exchange for your w: H6442
Eze 27:25 of Tarshish serve as carriers for your w. H5114
Eze 27:27 merchandise and w, your mariners, H5114
Eze 27:33 great wealth and your w you enriched the H5114
Eze 27:34 your w and all your company have gone H5114

WARFARE (4) [WAR]

Jdg 3: 2 this only to teach w to the descendants of H4878
1Ki 14:30 was continual w between Rehoboam H4878
2Ch 12:15 was continual w *between* Rehoboam and H4878
Isa 27: 8 By w and exile you contend with her H6009

WARHORSES (3) [HORSE, WAR]

Eze 26:10 walls will tremble at the noise of the w, H7304
Hos 14: 3 cannot save us; we will not mount w. H6061
Zec 9:10 from Ephraim and the w from Jerusalem, H6061

WARM (11) [LUKEWARM, WARMED, WARMING, WARMLY, WARMS, WARMTH]

Jos 9:12 bread of ours was w when we packed it at H2768
1Ki 1: 1 he *could* not *keep* w even when they put H2801
1Ki 1: 2 him so that our lord the king *may keep* w." H2801
2Ki 4:34 out on him, the boy's body *grew* w. H2801
Job 39:14 the ground and **lets** them w in the sand, H2801
Ecc 4:11 if two lie down together, they will *keep* w. H2801
Ecc 4:11 But how *can* one *keep* w alone? H2801
Isa 44:16 says, "Ah! *I am* w; I see the fire." H2801
Hag 1: 6 on clothes, but *are* not w. You earn wages H2801
Jn 18:18 around a fire they had made *to keep* w. *G2548*
Jas 2:16 "Go in peace; *keep* w and well fed," *G2548*

WARMED (1) [WARM]

Mk 14:54 with the guards and w *himself* at the fire. *G2548*

WARMING (4) [WARM]

Job 31:20 not bless me for w them with the fleece H2801
Mk 14:67 When she saw Peter w *himself*, she *G2548*
Jn 18:18 also was standing with them, w *himself*. *G2548*
Jn 18:25 Peter was still standing there w *himself*. *G2548*

WARMLY (2) [WARM]

Ac 21:17 the brothers and sisters received us w. *G830*
1Co 16:19 Priscilla greet you w in the Lord, *G4498*

WARMS (2) [WARM]

Isa 44:15 some of it he takes and w *himself*, he H2801
Isa 44:16 *He* also w *himself* and says, "Ah H2801

WARMTH (2) [WARM]

Ps 19: 6 to the other; nothing is deprived of its w. H2780
Isa 47:14 These are not coals for w; this is not a fire H2801

WARN (24) [FOREWARNED, WARNED, WARNING, WARNINGS, WARNS]

Ex 19:21 "Go down and w the people so they do H6386
Nu 24:14 *let me* w you of what this people will do H3619
1Sa 8: 9 but w them **solemnly** and let them H6386+6386
1Ki 2:42 make you swear by the LORD and w you, H6386
2Ch 19:10 *you are to* w them not to sin against the H2302
Ps 81: 8 my people, and *I will* w you—if you H6386
Jer 42:19 Be sure of this: *I* w you today H6386
Eze 3:18 and *you do* not w them or speak out to H2302
Eze 3:19 But if you *do* w the wicked person and they H2302
Eze 3:20 Since *you did* not w them, they will die H2302
Eze 3:21 But if you *do* w the righteous person not to H2302
Eze 33: 3 blows the trumpet *to* w the people, H2302
Eze 33: 6 blow the trumpet *to* w the people and the H2302
Eze 33: 9 But if you *do* w the wicked person to turn H2302
Lk 16:28 Let *him* w them, so that they will not also *G1371*
Ac 4:17 *we must* w them to speak no longer to *G580*
1Co 4:14 not to shame you but *to* w you as my dear *G3805*
Gal 5:21 *I* w you, as I did before, that those who *G4625*
1Th 5:14 w those who are idle and disruptive *G3805*
2Th 3:15 w them as you would a fellow *G3805*
2Ti 2:14 W them before God against quarreling *G1371*
Titus 3:10 W a divisive person once, and then warn *G3804*
Titus 3:10 and then w them a second time. NDT
Rev 22:18 I w everyone who hears the words of the *G3455*

WARNED (40) [WARN]

Ge 43: 3 "The man w us **solemnly**, 'You will H6386+6386
Ex 19:23 because *you* yourself w us, 'Put H6386
Ex 21:29 the owner *has* **been** w but has not H6386
Nu 16:26 *He* w the assembly, "Move back from the H1819
1Sa 19: 2 w him, "My father Saul is looking for a H5583
1Sa 19:11 David's wife, w him, "If you don't run for H5583
2Sa 2:22 Again Abner w Asahel, "Stop chasing me H606
1Ki 13:26 as the word of the LORD *had* w him." H1819
2Ki 6:10 Time and again Elisha w the king, so that H2302
2Ki 17:13 The LORD w Israel and Judah through all H6386
2Ki 17:15 the statutes *he had* w them **to keep**. H6386
2Ki 17:23 as *he had* w through all his servants the H1819
Ne 9:26 who *had* w them in order to turn them H6386
Ne 9:29 "*You* w them in order to turn them back to H6386
Ne 9:30 By your Spirit *you* w them through your H6386
Ne 9:34 the statutes *you* w them **to keep**. H6386
Ne 13:15 Therefore *I* w them *against* selling food H6386
Ne 13:21 But *I* w them and said, "Why do you spend H6386
Ps 2:10 be wise; **be** w, *you* rulers of the earth. H3579
Ps 19:11 By them your servant **is** w; in keeping H2302
Ecc 12:12 **Be** w, my son, *of* anything in addition to H2302
Jer 11: 7 *I* w them again and again H6386+6386
Jer 18: 8 if that nation *I* w repents of its evil H1819
Jer 22:21 *I* w you when you felt secure, but you said, H1819
Mt 2:12 And *having been* w in a dream not to go *G5976*
Mt 2:22 *Having been* w in a dream, he withdrew *G5976*
Mt 3: 7 Who w you to flee from the coming wrath? *G5683*
Mt 9:30 Jesus w them **sternly**, "See that no one *G1839*
Mt 12:16 *He* w them not to tell others about him. *G2203*
Mk 8:15 "Be careful," Jesus w them. "Watch out *G1403*
Mk 8:30 Jesus w them not to tell anyone about *G2203*
Lk 3: 7 Who w you to flee from the coming wrath? *G5683*
Lk 9:21 Jesus **strictly** w them not to tell this *G2203+4133*
Jn 16: 4 will remember that I w you about them. *G3306*
Ac 2:40 With many other words *he* w them; and *G1371*
Ac 27: 9 the Day of Atonement. So Paul w them, *G4147*
1Th 4: 6 as we told you and w you before. *G1371*
Heb 8: 5 This is why Moses *was* w when he was *G5976*
Heb 11: 7 *when* w about things not yet seen *G5976*
Heb 12:25 they refused him *who* w them on earth, *G5976*

WARNING (26) [WARN]

Nu 26:10 And they served as a w **sign**. H5812
2Ki 10:24 had posted eighty men outside with *this* w: H606
Ecc 4:13 who no longer knows how to **heed a** w. H2302
Isa 8:11 w me not to follow the way of this people: H3579
Isa 8:16 Bind up this **testimony of** w and seal up H9496
Isa 8:20 God's instruction and the **testimony of** w. H9496
Jer 6: 8 **Take** w, Jerusalem, or I will turn away H3579
Jer 6:10 To whom can I speak and **give** w? Who H6386
Eze 3:17 word I speak and **give** them w from me. H2302
Eze 3:21 they will surely live because *they* **took** w H2302
Eze 5:15 a w and an object of horror to the nations H4592
Eze 23:48 that all women *may* **take** w and not H3579
Eze 33: 4 trumpet but *does* not **heed the** w and the H2302
Eze 33: 5 of the trumpet but *did* not **heed the** w, H2302
Eze 33: 5 If they *had* **heeded the** w, they would H2302
Eze 33: 7 word I speak and **give** them w from me. H2302
Jnh 3: 6 When Jonah's w reached the king of H1821
Mal 2: 1 "And now, you priests, this w is for you. H5184
Mal 2: 4 I have sent you this w so that my covenant H5184
Mk 1:43 sent him away at once *with a* **strong** w: *G1839*
Lk 10:11 town *we* **wipe from** our feet **as a** w to you. *G669*
Ac 13:51 they **shook** the dust **off** their feet **as a** w to *G1759*
Ac 20:31 I never stopped w each of you night and *G3805*
Ac 23:22 dismissed the young man *with this* w: *G4133*
2Co 13: 2 *I* **already gave** you a w when I was with *G4625*
1Ti 5:20 everyone, so that the others may take w. *G5832*

WARNINGS (2) [WARN]

Job 33:16 in their ears and terrify them with w, H4592
1Co 10:11 were written down as w for us, *G3804*

WARNS (2) [WARN]

Ac 20:23 city the Holy Spirit w me that prison and *G1371*
Heb 12:25 turn away from him who w us from heaven? NDT

WARP (KJV) WOVEN

WARPED (4)

Dt 32: 5 shame they are a w and crooked H6836
Pr 12: 8 and *one with* a w mind is despised. H6390
Php 2:15 without fault in a w and crooked *G5021*
Titus 3:11 be sure that such people *are* w and sinful; *G1750*

WARRANTED (1)

2Co 12: 6 will think **more** of me **than is** w by what I *G5642*

WARRIOR (27) [WAR]

Ge 10: 8 who became a **mighty** w on the earth. H1475
Ex 15: 3 The LORD is a w; the LORD is his name H408+4878
Jdg 6:12 he said, "The LORD is with you, mighty w." H1475
Jdg 11: 1 the Gileadite was a **mighty** w. H2657+1475
1Sa 16:18 He is a brave man and a w. H408+4878
1Sa 17:33 and he has been a w from his youth." H408+4878
1Ch 1:10 who became a **mighty** w on earth. H1475
1Ch 12: 4 Gibeonite, a **mighty** w among the Thirty H1475
1Ch 12:28 Zadok, a **brave** young w, with 22 H1475+2657
1Ch 27: 6 who was a **mighty** w *among* the Thirty H1475
1Ch 28: 3 because you are a w and have shed H408+4878
2Ch 28: 7 an Ephraimite w, killed Maaseiah H1475
Job 16:14 bursts upon me; he rushes at me like a w. H1475
Ps 33:16 no w escapes by his great strength. H1475
Ps 78:65 as a w wakes from the stupor of wine. H1475
Ps 89:19 "I have bestowed strength on a w; I have H1475
Ps 127: 4 in the hands of a w are children born in H1475
Ps 147:10 nor his delight in the legs of the w; H408
Pr 16:32 Better a patient person than a w, one with H1475
Isa 3: 2 the hero and the w, the judge and H408+4878
Isa 42:13 like a w he will stir up his zeal H408+4878
Jer 14: 9 by surprise, like a w powerless to save? H1475
Jer 20:11 But the LORD is with me like a mighty w; H1475
Jer 46:12 *One* w will stumble over another; both H1475
Am 2:14 strength, and the w will not save his life. H1475
Zep 1:14 the Mighty **W** shouts his battle cry. H1475
Zep 3:17 God is with you, the **Mighty W** who saves. H1475

WARRIOR'S (4) [WAR]

2Sa 18:11 you ten shekels of silver and a w **belt**." H2514
Ps 120: 4 He will punish you with a w sharp arrows H1475
Isa 9: 5 Every w boot used in battle and every H6008
Zec 9:13 Greece, and make you like a w sword. H1475

WARRIORS (63) [WAR]

1Sa 2: 4 "The bows of the w are broken, but those H1475
2Sa 20: 7 all the **mighty** w went out under the H1475
2Sa 23: 8 These are the names of David's **mighty** w H1475
2Sa 23: 9 As one of the three **mighty** w, he was with H1475
2Sa 23:13 of the thirty **chief** *w* came down to David AIT
2Sa 23:16 So the three **mighty** w broke through the H1475
2Sa 23:17 were the exploits of the three **mighty** w. H1475
2Sa 23:20 He struck down Moab's two **mightiest** w H738
2Sa 23:22 too was as famous as the three **mighty** w. H1475
1Ch 5:24 They were brave w, famous men, and H1475
1Ch 7:40 **brave** w and outstanding leaders. H1475+2657
1Ch 8:40 of Ulam were **brave** w who could H1475+2657
1Ch 11:10 were the chiefs of David's **mighty** w— H1475
1Ch 11:11 this is the list of David's **mighty** w H1475
1Ch 11:12 the Ahohite, one of the three **mighty** w. H1475
1Ch 11:19 were the exploits of the three **mighty** w. H1475

W

1Ch 11:22 He struck down Moab's two **mightiest w** H738
1Ch 11:24 too was as famous as the three **mighty w**. H1475
1Ch 11:26 The **mighty w** were: Asahel the H1475+2657
1Ch 12: 1 were among the w who helped him in H1475
1Ch 12: 8 They were **brave w**, ready for battle H1475+2657
1Ch 12:21 all of them were **brave w**, and H1475+2657
1Ch 12:25 from Simeon, w ready for battle H1475+2657
1Ch 12:30 from Ephraim, **brave w**, famous in H1475+2657
1Ch 28: 1 the w and all the brave fighting men. H1475
1Ch 29:24 All the officers and w, as well as all of H1475
Ps 76: 5 not one of the w can lift his hands. H408+2657
SS 3: 7 escorted by sixty w, the noblest of Israel, H1475
SS 4: 4 shields, all of them shields of w. H1475
Isa 3:25 will fall by the sword, your w in battle. H1476
Isa 9: 3 as *w* **rejoice** when dividing the plunder. AIT
Isa 10:16 send a wasting disease upon his **sturdy** *w*; AIT
Isa 13: 3 I have summoned my w to carry out my H1475
Isa 21:17 of the archers, the w *of* Kedar, will be few." H1475
Isa 49:24 Can plunder be taken from w, or captives H1475
Isa 49:25 captives will be taken from w, and H1475
Jer 5:16 an open grave; all of them are **mighty w**. H1475
Jer 46: 5 they are retreating, their w are defeated. H1475
Jer 46: 9 March on, you w—men of Cush and Put H1475
Jer 46:15 Why will your w be laid low? They cannot H52
Jer 48:14 can you say, 'We are w, men valiant in H1475
Jer 48:41 the hearts of Moab's w will be like the H1475
Jer 49:22 the hearts of Edom's w will be like the H1475
Jer 50: 9 will be like skilled w who do not return H1475
Jer 50:36 A sword against her w! They will be filled H1475
Jer 51:30 Babylon's w have stopped fighting; they H1475
Jer 51:56 against Babylon; her w will be captured H1475
Jer 51:57 governors, officers and w as well; they will H1475
La 1:15 "The Lord has rejected all the w in my midst H52
Eze 23: 5 lusted after her lovers, the Assyrians—w H7940
Eze 23:12 commanders, w in full dress H7940
Eze 32:27 But they do not lie with the fallen w of old H1475
Eze 32:27 though these w also had terrorized the H1475
Hos 10:13 your own strength and on your many w, H1475
Joel 2: 7 They charge like w; they scale walls like H1475
Joel 3: 9 Rouse the w! Let all the fighting H1475
Joel 3:11 assemble there. Bring down your w, LORD! H1475
Am 2:16 Even the bravest w will flee naked on that H1475
Ob 9 Your w, Teman, will be terrified, and H1475
Na 2: 3 are red; the w are clad in scarlet. H408+2657
Hab 3:14 his head when his w stormed out to H7250
Zec 10: 5 they will be like w in battle trampling H1475
Zec 10: 7 The Ephraimites will become like w, and H1475

WARS (12) [WAR]

Nu 21:14 is why the Book of the **W** *of* the LORD says: H4878
Jdg 3: 1 not experienced any of the w *in* Canaan H4878
1Ki 5: 3 that because of the w waged against my H4878
1Ki 14:19 Jeroboam's reign, *his* w and how he ruled H4309
1Ch 22: 8 much blood and have fought many w. H4878
2Ch 27: 7 including all his w and the other things H4878
Ps 46: 9 He makes w cease to the ends of the H4878
Mt 24: 6 You will hear *of* w and rumors of wars, but *G4483*
Mt 24: 6 You will hear of wars and rumors *of* w, but *G4483*
Mk 13: 7 When you hear *of* w and rumors of wars *G4483*
Mk 13: 7 When you hear of wars and rumors *of* w *G4483*
Lk 21: 9 When you hear *of* w and uprisings, do not *G4483*

WARTS (1) [WART]

Lev 22:22 or **anything with** w or festering or running H3301

WAS (4152) [BE] See Index of Articles Etc.

WASH (78) [WASHED, WASHERMAN'S, WASHING, WASHINGS, WHITEWASH, WHITEWASHED]

Ge 18: 4 then *you may all* w your feet and rest H8175
Ge 19: 2 *You can* w your feet and spend the night H8175
Ge 24:32 water for him and his men to w their feet. H8175
Ge 43:24 gave them water *to* w their feet and H8175
Ge 49:11 *he will* w his garments in wine H3891
Ex 19:10 tomorrow. *Have them* w their clothes H3891
Ex 29: 4 tent of meeting and w them with water. H8175
Ex 29:17 ram into pieces and w the internal organs H8175
Ex 30:19 his sons *are to* w their hands and H8175
Ex 30:20 *they shall* w *with* water so that they will H8175
Ex 30:21 *they shall* w their hands and feet so that H8175
Ex 40:12 tent of meeting and w them with water. H8175
Ex 40:31 his sons used it *to* w their hands and H8175
Lev 1: 9 *You are to* w the internal organs and the H8175
Lev 1:13 *You are to* w the internal organs and the H8175
Lev 6:27 *you must* w it in the sanctuary area. H3891
Lev 11:25 of their carcasses *must* w their clothes, H3891
Lev 11:28 up their carcasses *must* w their clothes, H3891
Lev 11:40 some of its carcass *must* w their clothes, H3891
Lev 11:40 picks up the carcass *must* w their clothes, H3891
Lev 13: 6 *They must* w their clothes, and they will H3891
Lev 13:34 *They must* w their clothes, and they will H3891
Lev 14: 8 to be cleansed *must* w their clothes, H3891
Lev 14: 9 *They must* w their clothes and bathe H3891
Lev 14:47 eats in the house *must* w their clothes. H3891
Lev 15: 5 touches his bed *must* w their clothes and H3891
Lev 15: 6 discharge sat on *must* w their clothes and H3891
Lev 15: 7 has a discharge *must* w their clothes and H3891
Lev 15: 8 *they must* w their clothes and bathe with H3891
Lev 15:10 up those things *must* w their clothes and H3891
Lev 15:11 hands with water *must* w their clothes H3891
Lev 15:13 *he must* w his clothes and bathe himself H3891
Lev 15:21 *they must* w their clothes and bathe with H3891
Lev 15:22 *they must* w their clothes and bathe with H3891
Lev 15:27 *they must* w their clothes and bathe with H3891
Lev 16:26 as a scapegoat *must* w his clothes and H3891
Lev 16:28 who burns them *must* w his clothes and H3891
Lev 17:15 by wild animals *must* w their clothes and H3891
Lev 17:16 But if *they do* not w their clothes and H3891
Nu 5:23 a scroll and then w them **off** into the bitter H4681
Nu 8: 7 their whole bodies and w their clothes. H3891
Nu 19: 7 the priest *must* w his clothes and bathe H3891
Nu 19: 8 who burns it *must* also w his clothes and H3891
Nu 19:10 of the heifer *must* also w his clothes, H3891
Nu 19:19 being cleansed *must* w their clothes and H3891
Nu 19:21 of cleansing *must* also w his clothes, H3891
Nu 31:24 On the seventh day w your clothes and you H3891
Dt 21: 6 nearest the body *shall* w their hands over H8175
Dt 23:11 as evening approaches *he is to* w *himself*, H8175
Ru 3: 3 **W**, put on perfume, and get dressed in H8175
1Sa 25:41 to serve you and w the feet of my lord's H8175
2Sa 11: 8 "Go down to your house and w your feet." H8175
2Ki 5:10 w *yourself* seven times in the Jordan H8175
2Ki 5:12 Couldn't *I* w in them and be cleansed?" H8175
2Ki 5:13 when he tells you, 'W and be cleansed'!" H8175
Job 14:19 away stones and torrents **w away** the soil, H8851
Ps 26: 6 *I* w my hands in innocence, and go about H8175
Ps 51: 2 **W away** all my iniquity and cleanse me H3891
Ps 51: 7 I will be clean; w me, and I will be H3891
Isa 1:16 **W** and make yourselves clean. Take your H8175
Isa 4: 4 The Lord *will* **w away** the filth of the H8175
Jer 2:22 Although *you* w *yourself* with soap and H3891
Jer 4:14 w the evil from your heart and be saved. H3891
Mt 6:17 put oil on your head and w your face, *G3782*
Mt 15: 2 *They* don't w their hands before they eat!" *G3782*
Mk 7: 4 marketplace they do not eat unless *they* w. *G966*
Lk 11:38 that Jesus *did* not first w before the meal. *G966*
Jn 9: 7 he told him, "w in the Pool of Siloam" *G3782*
Jn 9:11 He told me to go to Siloam and w. *G3782*
Jn 13: 5 a basin and began *to* w his disciples' feet *G3782*
Jn 13: 6 "Lord, *are* you *going to* w my feet? *G3782*
Jn 13: 8 said Peter, "*you shall* never w my feet." *G3782*
Jn 13: 8 answered, "Unless *I* w you, you have no *G3782*
Jn 13:10 have had a bath need only *to* w their feet; *G3782*
Jn 13:14 you also should w one another's feet. *G3782*
Ac 22:16 be baptized and w your sins **away**, calling *G666*
Jas 4: 8 **W** your hands, you sinners, and purify *G2751*
Rev 22:14 "Blessed are those *who* w their robes, that *G4459*

WASHBASIN (2)

Ps 60: 8 Moab is my w, on Edom I toss my H6105+8176
Ps 108: 9 Moab is my w, on Edom I toss my H6105+8176

WASHED (36) [WASH]

Ge 43:31 After *he had* w his face, he came out and H8175
Ex 19:14 and *they* w their clothes. H3891
Ex 40:32 *They* w whenever they entered the tent of H8175
Lev 8: 6 his sons forward and w them with water. H8175
Lev 8:21 *He* w the internal organs and the legs with H8175
Lev 9:14 *He* w the internal organs and the legs H8175
Lev 13:54 he shall order that the spoiled article *be* w. H3891
Lev 13:55 After the article *has* **been** w, the priest is H3891
Lev 13:56 has faded after the article *has* **been** w, H3891
Lev 13:58 article that *has been* w and is rid of the H3891
Lev 13:58 is rid of the mold, *must* **be** w again. H3891
Lev 15:17 has semen on it *must* **be** w with water, H3891
Nu 8:21 purified themselves and w their clothes. H3891
Jdg 19:21 After *they had* w their feet, they had H8175
2Sa 12:20 After *he had* w, put on lotions and H8175
2Sa 19:24 his mustache or w his clothes from the H3891
1Ki 22:38 *They* w the chariot at a pool in Samaria H8851
Job 9:30 Even if *I* w **myself** with soap and my H8175
Job 22:16 their foundations w **away** *by* a flood. H3668
Ps 73:13 my heart pure and *have* w my hands in H8175
SS 5: 3 *I have* w my feet—must I soil them again H8175
SS 5:12 the water streams, w in milk, mounted H8175
Eze 16: 4 nor **were** *you* w with water to make you H8175
Eze 16: 9 you with water and w the blood from you H8851
Eze 40:38 where the burnt offerings *were* w. H1866
Mt 27:24 he took water and w his hands in front of *G672*
Jn 9: 7 So the man went and w, and came home *G3782*
Jn 9:11 So I went and w, and then I could *G3782*
Jn 9:15 the man replied, "and *I* w, and now I see." *G3782*
Jn 13:14 Lord and Teacher, *have* w your feet, you *G3782*
Ac 9:37 her body *was* w and placed in an *G3374*
Ac 16:33 the jailer took them and w their wounds; *G3374*
1Co 6:11 But *you were* w, you were sanctified, you *G666*
Heb 10:22 and *having* our bodies w with pure *G3374*
2Pe 2:22 "A sow *that is* w returns to her wallowing *G3374*
Rev 7:14 *they have* w their robes and made them *G4459*

WASHERMAN'S (1) [WASH]

2Ki 18:17 Upper Pool, on the road to the **W** Field. H3891

WASHING (15) [WASH]

Ex 30:18 bronze basin, with its bronze stand, for w. H8175
Ex 40:30 the altar and put water in it for w, H8175
2Ch 4: 6 made ten basins for w and placed five on H8175
2Ch 4: 6 Sea was to be used by the priests for w. H8175
SS 4: 2 sheep just shorn, coming up from the w. H8177
SS 6: 6 a flock of sheep coming up from the w. H8177
Mk 7: 3 *they* **give** their hands **a** ceremonial w, *G3782*
Mk 7: 4 such as the w of cups, pitchers and *G968*
Lk 5: 2 by the fishermen, *who were* w their nets. *G4459*
Jn 2: 6 kind used by the Jews for **ceremonial** w, *G2752*
Jn 3:25 Jew over the matter of **ceremonial** w. *G2752*
Jn 13:12 When *he had finished* w their feet, he put *G3782*
Eph 5:26 cleansing her *by* the w with water through *G3373*
1Ti 5:10 hospitality, w the feet of the Lord's people *G3782*
Titus 3: 5 saved us through the w of rebirth and *G3373*

WASHINGS (1) [WASH]

Heb 9:10 food and drink and various **ceremonial** w— *G968*

WASN'T (5) [BE, NOT]

Ge 30:15 "**W** it **enough** *that* you took away my H5071
1Ki 3:21 I saw that *it* w the son I had borne." H2118+4202
Lk 14:30 began to build and w able to finish. *G4024*
Jn 12: 5 "Why w this perfume sold and the money *G4024*
Ac 5: 4 it was sold, w the money at your disposal? *G5639*

WASTE (70) [WASTED, WASTES, WASTING]

Lev 26:31 into ruins and **lay** w your sanctuaries, H9037
Lev 26:32 *I* myself *will* **lay** w the land, so that your H9037
Lev 26:33 Your land will be **laid** w, and your cities H9039
Lev 26:39 who are left *will* **w away** in the lands of H5245
Lev 26:39 of their ancestors' sins *they will* **w away**. H5245
Dt 29:23 land will be a **burning** w *of* salt and sulfur H8599
Dt 32:10 he found him, in a barren and howling w. H3810
Jdg 16:24 the *one who* **laid** w our land and H2990
2Ki 19:17 Assyrian kings *have* **laid** w these nations H2990
2Ki 22:19 would become a curse and *be* **laid** w— H9014
1Ch 20: 1 *He* **laid** w the land of the Ammonites H8845
Job 12:24 he makes them wander in a trackless w. H9332
Ps 107:34 fruitful land into a **salt** w, because of H4877
Ps 107:40 made them wander in a trackless w. H9332
Ps 112:10 they will gnash their teeth and **w away** H5022
Isa 1: 7 **laid** w as when overthrown by strangers. H9039
Isa 6:13 in the land, it will again be **laid** w. H1278
Isa 7:16 of the two kings you dread *will* **be laid** w. H6440
Isa 17: 4 will fade; the fat of his body *will* **w away**. H8135
Isa 24: 1 the LORD *is going to* **lay** w the earth and H1327
Isa 24: 3 earth *will* **be completely laid** w and H1327+1327
Isa 24:16 But I said, "I **w away**, I waste away! Woe H8140
Isa 24:16 "I waste away, I **w away**! Woe to me! H8140
Isa 37:18 Assyrian kings *have* **laid** w all these H2990
Isa 42:15 *I will* **lay** w the mountains and hills and H2990
Isa 49:17 and *those who* **laid** you w H2990+2256+2238
Isa 49:19 made desolate and your land laid w, H2233
Jer 2:15 They have laid w his land; his towns are H9014
Jer 4: 7 He has left his place to lay w your land H9014
Jer 9:11 I will lay w the towns of Judah so no H9039
Jer 9:12 been ruined and **laid** w like a desert that H5898
Jer 12:11 whole land *will* **be laid** w because there H9037
Jer 25:37 meadows **will be laid** w because of the H1959
Jer 32:43 'It is a **desolate** w, without people H9039
Jer 33:10 "It is a **desolate** w, without people H2992
Jer 34:22 And I will lay w the towns of Judah so no H9039
Jer 44:22 a desolate w without inhabitants, H9014
Jer 46:19 Memphis will be **laid** w and lie in ruins H9014
Jer 48: 9 Moab, for *she will be* **laid** w; her H5898+5898
Jer 50: 3 north will attack her and lay w her land. H9014
Jer 51:29 to lay w the land of Babylon so that no H9014
La 2: 6 *He has* **laid** w his dwelling like a garden H2803
La 4: 9 *they* w **away** for lack of food from the field. H2307
Eze 4:17 each other and *will* **w away** because of H5245
Eze 6: 6 the towns *will* be **laid** w and the high H2990
Eze 6: 6 your altars *will* be **laid** w and devastated, H2990
Eze 6:14 the land a desolate w from the desert to H5457
Eze 12:20 towns *will be* **laid** w and the land H2990
Eze 24:23 weep but *will* **w away** because of your H5245
Eze 25: 3 of Israel when *it* **was laid** w and over the H9037
Eze 25:13 I will lay it w, and from Teman to Dedan H2999
Eze 29:10 ruin and a desolate w from Migdol to H2997
Eze 30:12 of foreigners *I will* **lay** w the land and H9037
Eze 30:14 *I will* **lay** w Upper Egypt, set fire to Zoan H9037
Eze 33:28 I will make the land a desolate w, and her H5457
Eze 33:29 the land a desolate w because of all the H5457
Eze 35: 3 against you and make you a desolate w. H5457
Eze 35: 7 Seir a desolate w and cut off from it H9039
Eze 35:12 "*They have been* **laid** w and have been H9037
Eze 36:35 "This land that **was laid** w has become H9037
Hos 4: 3 all who live in it **w away**; the beasts of H581
Hos 5: 9 Ephraim will be **laid** w on the day of H9014
Hos 8:10 They will begin to **w away** under the H5071
Joel 1: 7 It has laid w my vines and ruined my fig H9014
Joel 2: 3 a desert w—nothing escapes them H9039
Joel 3:19 Edom a desert w, because of violence H9039
Na 2: 2 destroyers *have* **laid** them w and have H1327
Zep 3: 6 Their cities **are laid** w; they are deserted H7400
Mt 26: 8 were indignant. "Why this w?" they asked. *G724*
Mk 14: 4 to one another, "Why this w of perfume? *G724*

WASTED (7) [WASTE]

Ge 47:13 Egypt and Canaan w **away** because of the H3532
Ps 32: 3 my bones **w away** through my groaning H1162
Ps 106:43 on rebellion and *they* **w away** in their sin. H4812
Pr 23: 8 have eaten and *will have* w your H8845
La 2: 8 walls lament; together *they* **w away**. H581
Jn 6:12 that are left over. Let nothing *be* w." *G660*
Gal 4:11 that somehow I have w my efforts on you. *G1632*

WASTELAND (22) [LAND]

Nu 21:20 where the top of Pisgah overlooks the w. H3810
Nu 23:28 to the top of Peor, overlooking the w. H3810
2Sa 2:24 near Giah on the way to the w *of* Gibeon. H4497
Job 6:18 they go off into the w and perish. H9332
Job 24: 5 the w provides food for their children. H6858
Job 38:27 to satisfy a desolate w and make it sprout H5409
Job 39: 6 I gave it the w as its home, the salt flats H6858

Ps 78:40 the wilderness and grieved him in the **w**! H3810
Isa 5: 6 I will make it a **w**, neither pruned nor H1429
Isa 32:14 watchtower will become a **w** forever, H5118
Isa 41:19 I will set junipers in the **w**, the fir and the H6858
Isa 43:19 in the wilderness and streams in the **w**. H3810
Isa 43:20 in the wilderness and streams in the **w**, H3810
Isa 64:10 Your sacred cities have become a **w**; even H4497
Isa 64:10 even Zion is a **w**, Jerusalem a desolation. H4497
Jer 12:10 turn my pleasant field into a desolate **w**. H4497
Jer 12:11 It will be made a **w**, parched and H9039
Jer 22: 6 I will surely make you like a **w**, like towns H4497
Jer 25:11 whole country will become a desolate **w**, H9014
Eze 29: 9 Egypt will become a desolate **w**. H2999
Zep 2: 9 place of weeds and salt pits, a **w** forever. H9039
Mal 1: 3 his hill country into a **w** and left his H9039

WASTELANDS (4) [LAND]

Job 30: 3 the parched land in desolate **w** at night. H5409
Ps 107: 4 Some wandered in desert **w**, finding no H3810
Isa 51: 3 her **w** like the garden of the LORD. H6858
Jer 17: 6 That person will be like a bush in the **w** H6858

WASTES (4) [WASTE]

Job 13:28 "So man **w away** like something rotten H1162
Job 33:21 Their flesh **w away** to nothing, and their H3983
Isa 10:18 destroy, as *when* a sick person **w away**. H5022
Isa 33: 9 The land dries up and **w away**, Lebanon is H581

WASTING (8) [WASTE]

Lev 26:16 **w diseases** and fever that will destroy your H8831
Dt 28:22 The LORD will strike you with **w disease** H8831
Dt 32:24 I will send **w** famine against them H4642
Ps 106:15 but sent a **w disease** among them. H8137
Isa 10:16 will send a **w disease** upon his sturdy H8137
Eze 33:10 we *are* **w away** because of them. H5245
Lk 16: 1 was accused of **w** his possessions. G1399
2Co 4:16 Though outwardly we *are* **w away**, yet G1425

WATCH (87) [WATCHED, WATCHES, WATCHFUL, WATCHING, WATCHMAN, WATCHMEN]

Ge 21:16 she thought, "*I* cannot **w** the boy die." H8011
Ge 28:15 am with you and *will* **w over** you wherever H9068
Ge 28:20 be with me and *will* **w over** me on this H9068
Ge 31:49 "*May* the LORD **keep w** between you and H7595
Ex 14:24 the **last w of the night** the LORD H874+1332
Dt 4: 9 **w** yourselves closely so that you do H9068
Dt 4:15 Therefore **w** yourselves very **carefully**, H9068
Jdg 7:17 "**W** me," he told them. "Follow my lead H8011
Jdg 7:19 camp at the beginning of the middle **w**, H874
Jdg 21:21 **w**. When the young women of Shiloh H8011
Ru 2: 9 **W** the field where the men are H6524+928
1Sa 11:11 the **last w of the night** they H874+2021+1332
1Sa 17:28 you came down only to **w** the battle." H8011
1Sa 19:11 to David's house to **w** it and to kill him in H9068
2Sa 13: 5 in my sight so *I may* **w** her and then eat it H8011
2Sa 13:34 Now the man **standing w** looked up and H7595
1Ki 2: 4 'If your descendants **w** how they live, and H9068
2Ch 23: 4 the Sabbath are to **keep w** *at* the doors, H8788
Ne 11:19 associates, who **kept w** at the gates—172 H9068
Job 13:27 *you* **keep close w** *on* all my paths by H9068
Job 21:32 the grave, and **w** *is* **kept** over their tombs. H9193
Job 33:11 *he* **keeps close w** *on* all my paths. H9068
Job 39: 1 *Do you* **w** when the doe bears her fawn? H9068
Ps 10: 8 His **eyes** *w* in secret for his victims AIT
Ps 39: 1 "*I will* **w** my ways and keep my tongue H9068
Ps 56: 6 they lurk, *they* **w** my steps, hoping to take H9068
Ps 59: T Saul had sent men *to* **w** David's house in H9068
Ps 59: 9 You are my strength, *I* **w** for you; you, God, H9068
Ps 66: 7 his power, his eyes **w** the nations—let H7595
Ps 80:14 from heaven and see! **W over** this vine, H7212
Ps 90: 4 has just gone by, or like a **w** in the night. H874
Ps 121: 7 from all harm—*he will* **w over** your life; H9068
Ps 121: 8 the LORD *will* **w over** your coming and H9068
Ps 127: 1 over the city, the guards **stand w** in vain. H9193
Ps 141: 3 keep **w** over the door of my lips. H5917
Ps 142: 3 within me, it is you *who* **w over** my way. H3359
Pr 4: 6 love her, and *she will* **w over** you. H5915
Pr 6:22 you sleep, *they will* **w** over you; when H9068
Pr 15: 3 **keeping w** *on* the wicked and the good. H7595
Pr 22:12 eyes of the LORD **keep w over** knowledge, H5915
Isa 27: 3 the LORD, **w over** it; I water it continually H5915
Jer 24: 6 My eyes *will* **w over** them for their H8492+6584
Jer 31:10 gather them and *will* **w over** his flock like H9068
Jer 31:28 so *I will* **w** over them to build and to plant," H9193
Jer 48:19 Stand by the road and **w**, you who live in H7595
Eze 12: 3 daytime, as they **w**, set out and go H4200+6524
Eze 12: 4 while they **w**, bring out your H4200+6524
Eze 12: 5 While they **w**, dig through the wall H4200+6524
Da 7:11 "Then I continued *to* **w** because of the A10255
Mic 7: 7 But as for me, *I* **w in hope** for the LORD, H7595
Na 2: 1 Guard the fortress, **w** the road, brace H7595
Hab 1: 5 "Look at the nations and **w**—and be H5564
Hab 2: 1 I will stand at my **w** and station myself on H5466
Zec 9: 8 now I *am* **keeping w**. H8011+928+6524
Mt 7:15 "**W out** for false prophets. They come to G4668
Mt 24: 4 "**W out** that no one deceives you. G1063
Mt 24:42 "Therefore **keep w**, because you do not G1213
Mt 24:43 *he* would have **kept w** and would not G1213
Mt 25:13 "Therefore **keep w**, because you do not G1213
Mt 26:38 Stay here and **keep w** with me." G1213
Mt 26:40 you men **keep w** with me for one G1213
Mt 26:41 "**W** and pray so that you will not fall into G1213
Mt 27:36 sitting down, *they* **kept w over** him there. G5498
Mk 8:15 "**W out** for the yeast of the Pharisees and G1063
Mk 12:38 "**W out** for the teachers of the law. G1063
Mk 13: 5 "**W out** *that* no one deceives you. G1063
Mk 13:34 tells the one at the door to **keep w**. G1213
Mk 13:35 "Therefore **keep w** because you do not G1213
Mk 13:37 What I say to you, I say to everyone: '**W**!'" G1213
Mk 14:34 he said to them. "Stay here and **keep w**." G1213
Mk 14:37 Couldn't you **keep w** for one hour? G1213
Mk 14:38 **W** and pray so that you will not fall into G1213
Lk 2: 8 **keeping w over** their flocks at night. G5875+5871
Lk 12:15 said to them, "**W out**! Be on your guard G3972
Lk 17: 3 So **w** yourselves. "If your brother or sister G4668
Lk 20:20 **Keeping a close w on** him, they sent spies G4190
Lk 21: 8 "**W out** that you are not deceived G1063
Lk 21:36 *Be* always **on the w**, and pray that you may G70
Ac 9:24 night *they* **kept close w** on the city G4190
Ac 20:28 **Keep w over** yourselves and all the flock of G4668
Ro 16:17 *to* **w out** for those who cause divisions G5023
Gal 5:15 **w out** or you will be destroyed by each G1063
Gal 6: 1 But **w** yourselves, or you also may be G5023
Php 3: 2 **W out for** those dogs, those evildoers G1063
1Ti 4:16 **W** your life and doctrine **closely**. Persevere G2091
Heb 13:17 because they **keep w** over you as those who G70
2Jn 8 **W out** that you do not lose what we have G1063

WATCHED (31) [WATCH]

Ge 24:21 the man **w** her **closely** to learn whether H8617
Ex 2:11 people were and **w** them at their hard H8011
Ex 3:16 *I have* **w over** you **and** *have* **seen** H7212+7212
Dt 2: 7 *He has* **w over** your journey through this H3359
Dt 33: 9 but *he* **w over** your word and guarded your H9068
Jos 4:11 the other side while the people **w**. H4200+7156
Jdg 13:19 thing while Manoah and his wife **w**: H8011
1Sa 17:55 As Saul **w** David going out to meet the H8011
2Sa 6:16 Michal daughter of Saul **w** from a window. H9207
1Ch 15:29 Michal daughter of Saul **w** from a window. H9207
Job 10:12 in your providence **w over** my spirit. H9068
Job 29: 2 for the days when God **w over** me, H9068
Jer 31:28 Just as *I* **w** over them to uproot and tear H9193
La 4:17 from our towers *we* **w** for a nation that H7595
Eze 10: 2 And as I **w**, he went in. H4200+6524
Eze 10:19 While I **w**, the cherubim spread H4200+6524
Eze 12: 7 on my shoulders while they **w**. H4200+6524
Da 5: 5 The king **w** the hand as it wrote. A10255
Da 7: 4 I **w** until its wings were torn off and it A10255
Da 7:21 *As* I **w**, this horn was waging war against A10255
Da 8: 4 *I* **w** the ram as it charged toward the west H8011
Mt 26:16 From then on Judas **w for** an opportunity to G2426
Mk 3: 2 *so they* **w** him **closely** *to see* if he would G4190
Mk 12:41 were put and **w** the crowd putting G2555
Mk 14:11 So *he* **w for** an opportunity to hand him G2426
Lk 6: 7 so *they* **w** him **closely** *to see* if he would G4190
Lk 14: 1 Pharisee, he was *being* **carefully w**. G4190
Lk 22: 6 and **w for** an opportunity to hand Jesus G2426
Rev 6: 1 *I* **w** as the Lamb opened the first of the G3972
Rev 6:12 *I* **w** as he opened the sixth seal. There G3972
Rev 8:13 *As I* **w**, I heard an eagle that was flying in G3972

WATCHES (16) [WATCH]

Nu 19: 5 While he **w**, the heifer is to be burned—its H6524
Job 24:15 The eye of the adulterer **w** *for* dusk; he H9068
Ps 1: 6 For the LORD **w over** the way of the H3359
Ps 33:14 his dwelling place *he* **w** all who live on H8708
Ps 63: 6 I think of you through the **w of the night**. H874
Ps 119:148 eyes stay open through the **w of the night**, H874
Ps 121: 3 *he who* **w over** you will not slumber H9068
Ps 121: 4 *he who* **w over** Israel will neither slumber H9068
Ps 121: 5 The LORD **w over** you—the LORD is your H9068
Ps 127: 1 Unless the LORD **w over** the city, the guards H9068
Ps 145:20 The LORD **w over** all who love him, but all H9068
Ps 146: 9 The LORD **w over** the foreigner and H9068
Pr 31:27 *She* **w over** the affairs of her household H7595
Ecc 11: 4 *Whoever* **w** the wind will not plant H9068
La 2:19 as the **w of the night** begin; pour out H874
La 4:16 he no longer **w over** them. H5564

WATCHFUL (2) [WATCH]

Zec 12: 4 "*I will* **keep** a **w** eye over Judah, but I will H7219
Col 4: 2 to prayer, *being* **w** and thankful. G1213

WATCHING (29) [WATCH]

Ge 30:31 on tending your flocks and **w over** them: H9068
Ex 33: 8 **w** Moses until he entered the tent. H5564
Dt 28:32 wear out your eyes **w** for them day after H8011
Jdg 16:27 men and women **w** Samson perform. H8011
1Sa 4:13 the side of the road, **w**, because his heart H7595
1Sa 6: 9 but *keep* **w** it. If it goes up to its own H8011
1Sa 25:21 all *my* **w over** this fellow's property in the H9068
2Ki 2:15 prophets from Jericho, who *were* **w**, said, H8011
Ezr 5: 5 eye of their God was **w** over the elders of NDT
Job 10:14 *you would be* **w** me and would not let my H9068
Pr 8:34 who listen to me, **w** daily at my doors H9193
Jer 1:12 I *am* **w** to see that my word is fulfilled." H9193
Jer 7:11 But I *have been* **w**! declares the H8011
Jer 19:10 jar while those who go with you are **w**, H6524
Jer 43: 9 "While the Jews are **w**, take some large H6524
Jer 44:27 For I *am* **w** over them for harm, not for H9193
Eze 12: 4 while they are **w**, go out like those H4200+6524
Eze 12: 6 as they are **w** and carry them out H4200+6524
Eze 28:18 the ground in the sight of all *who were* **w**. H8011
Da 2:34 While you were **w**, a rock was cut out, but A10255
Da 8:15 *was* **w** the vision and trying to understand H8011
Zec 11:11 of the flock who *were* **w** me knew it was H9068
Mt 27:55 women were there, **w** from a distance. G2555
Mk 15:40 Some women were **w** from a distance G2555
Lk 12:37 master finds them **w** when he comes. G1213
Lk 23:35 The people stood **w**, and the rulers even G2555
Lk 23:49 stood at a distance, **w** these things. G3972
Jn 7:11 Jewish leaders *were* **w for** Jesus and G2426
1Pe 5: 2 your care, **w over** them—not because G2174

WATCHMAN (15) [WATCH]

2Sa 13:34 The **w** went and told the king, "I see men H7595
2Sa 18:24 the **w** went up to the roof of the gateway H7595
2Sa 18:25 The **w** called out to the king and reported H7595
2Sa 18:26 Then the **w** saw another runner, and he H7595
2Sa 18:27 The **w** said, "It seems to me that the first H7595
Job 27:18 a moth's cocoon, like a hut made by a **w**. H5915
Isa 21:11 to me from Seir, "**W**, what is left of the H9068
Isa 21:11 is left of the night? **W**, what is left of the H9068
Isa 21:12 The **w** replies, "Morning is coming, but H9068
Eze 3:17 I have made you a **w** for the people of H7595
Eze 33: 2 one of their men and make him their **w**, H7595
Eze 33: 6 But if the **w** sees the sword coming and H7595
Eze 33: 6 I will hold the **w** accountable for their H7595
Eze 33: 7 I have made you a **w** for the people of H7595
Hos 9: 8 with my God, *is* the **w** *over* Ephraim, yet H7595

WATCHMEN (12) [WATCH]

Ps 130: 6 the Lord more than **w** wait for the morning H9068
Ps 130: 6 more than **w** wait for the morning. H9068
SS 3: 3 The **w** found me as they made their H9068
SS 5: 7 The **w** found me as they made their H9068
SS 5: 7 took away my cloak, those **w** *of* the walls! H9068
Isa 52: 8 Your **w** lift up their voices; together they H7595
Isa 56:10 Israel's **w** are blind, they all lack H7595
Isa 62: 6 I have posted **w** on your walls, Jerusalem H9068
Jer 6:17 I appointed **w** over you and said, 'Listen H7595
Jer 31: 6 will be a day when **w** cry out on the hills H5915
Jer 51:12 station the **w**, prepare an ambush! H9068
Mic 7: 4 the day your **w** sound the alarm. H7595

WATCHTOWER (8) [TOWER]

2Ki 17: 9 From **w** to fortified city they built H4463+5915
2Ki 18: 8 From **w** to fortified city, he defeated H4463+5915
Isa 5: 2 He built a **w** in it and cut out a winepress H4463
Isa 21: 8 I stand on the **w**; every night I stay at H5205
Isa 32:14 citadel and **w** will become a wasteland H1044
Mic 4: 8 As for you, **w** *of* the flock, stronghold of H4463
Mt 21:33 dug a winepress in it and built a **w**. G4788
Mk 12: 1 dug a pit for the winepress and built a **w**. G4788

WATCHTOWERS (1) [TOWER]

1Ch 27:25 in the towns, the villages and the **w**. H4463

WATER (480) [WATER'S, WATERED, WATERFALLS, WATERING, WATERLESS, WATERS, WATERY, WELL-WATERED]

Ge 1: 6 the waters to separate **w** from water." H4784
Ge 1: 6 the waters to separate water from **w**." H4784
Ge 1: 7 separated the **w** under the vault from H4784
Ge 1: 7 water under the vault from the **w** above it. H4784
Ge 1: 9 "Let the **w** under the sky be gathered to H4784
Ge 1:20 "Let the **w** teem with living creatures H4784
Ge 1:21 with which the **w** teems and that moves H4784
Ge 1:22 in number and fill the **w** in the seas, H4784
Ge 7:18 the ark floated on the surface of the **w**. H4784
Ge 8: 3 The **w** receded steadily from the earth. H4784
Ge 8: 3 fifty days the **w** had gone down, H4784
Ge 8: 7 forth until the **w** had dried up from H4784
Ge 8: 8 dove to see if the **w** had receded from the H4784
Ge 8: 9 because there was **w** over all the surface H4784
Ge 8:11 Noah knew that the **w** had receded from H4784
Ge 8:13 the **w** had dried up from the earth. H4784
Ge 18: 4 Let a little **w** be brought, and then you H4784
Ge 21:14 food and a skin of **w** and gave them to H4784
Ge 21:15 When the **w** in the skin was gone, she put H4784
Ge 21:19 opened her eyes and she saw a well of **w**. H4784
Ge 21:19 filled the skin with **w** and gave the boy a H4784
Ge 21:25 about a well of **w** that Abimelek's H4784
Ge 24:11 the time the *women* go out to **draw w**. H8612
Ge 24:13 townspeople are coming out to draw **w**. H4784
Ge 24:14 and *I'll* **w** your camels too'—let her H9197
Ge 24:17 "Please give me a little **w** from your jar." H4784
Ge 24:19 she said, "*I'll* **draw w** for your camels too H8612
Ge 24:20 ran back to the well to **draw** *more* **w**, and H8612
Ge 24:32 **w** for him and his men to wash their H4784
Ge 24:43 comes out to **draw w** and I say to her, H8612
Ge 24:43 let me drink a little **w** from your jar," H4784
Ge 24:44 and *I'll* **draw w** for your camels too," H8612
Ge 24:45 She went down to the spring and **drew w** H8612
Ge 24:46 'Drink, and *I'll* **w** your camels too. H9197
Ge 26:19 discovered a well of fresh **w** there. H4784
Ge 26:20 those of Isaac and said, "The **w** is ours!" H4784
Ge 26:32 They said, "We've found **w**!" H4784
Ge 29: 3 from the well's mouth and **w** the sheep. H9197
Ge 29: 7 **W** the sheep and take them back to H9197
Ge 29: 8 Then *we will* **w** the sheep." H9197
Ge 37:24 cistern was empty; there was no **w** in it. H4784
Ge 43:24 gave them **w** to wash their feet and H4784
Ex 2:10 saying, "I drew him out of the **w**." H4784
Ex 2:16 they came *to* **draw w** and fill the H1926
Ex 2:16 fill the troughs to **w** their father's flock. H9197
Ex 2:19 *He* even **drew w** for us and watered H1926+1926

Ex 4: 9 take some w *from* the Nile and pour it on H4784
Ex 4: 9 The w you take from the river will become H4784
Ex 7:17 in my hand I will strike the w of the Nile, H4784
Ex 7:18 Egyptians will not be able to drink its w. H4784
Ex 7:20 his officials and struck the w of the Nile, H4784
Ex 7:20 all the w was changed into blood. H4784
Ex 7:21 that the Egyptians could not drink its w. H4784
Ex 7:24 dug along the Nile to get drinking w, H4784
Ex 7:24 they could not drink the w *of* the river. H4784
Ex 12: 9 Do not eat the meat raw or boiled in w H4784
Ex 14:16 over the sea to divide **the** w so that the H2084S
Ex 14:22 with a wall of w on their right and on their H4784
Ex 14:28 The w flowed back and covered the H4784
Ex 14:29 with a wall of w on their right and on their H4784
Ex 15:22 traveled in the desert without finding w. H4784
Ex 15:23 could not drink its w because it was bitter. H4784
Ex 15:25 He threw it into the w, and the water H4784
Ex 15:25 the water, and the w became fit to drink. H4784
Ex 15:27 and they camped there near the w. H4784
Ex 17: 1 there was no w for the people to drink. H4784
Ex 17: 2 with Moses and said, "Give us w to drink." H4784
Ex 17: 3 But the people were thirsty for w there H4784
Ex 17: 6 w will come out of it for the people to H4784
Ex 23:25 his blessing will be on your food and w. H4784
Ex 29: 4 tent of meeting and wash them with w. H4784
Ex 30:18 of meeting and the altar, and put w in it. H4784
Ex 30:19 to wash their hands and feet with w from it. NDT
Ex 30:20 they shall wash with w so that they will H4784
Ex 32:20 scattered it on the w and made the H4784
Ex 34:28 nights without eating bread or drinking w. H4784
Ex 40: 7 of meeting and the altar and put w in it. H4784
Ex 40:12 tent of meeting and wash them with w. H4784
Ex 40:30 the altar and put w in it for washing, H4784
Lev 1: 9 the internal organs and the legs with w, H4784
Lev 1:13 the internal organs and the legs with w, H4784
Lev 6:28 the pot is to be scoured and rinsed with w. H4784
Lev 8: 6 sons forward and washed them with w. H4784
Lev 8:21 the legs with w and burned the H4784
Lev 11: 9 living in the w of the seas and the H4784
Lev 11:10 all the other living creatures in the w— H4784
Lev 11:12 living in the w that does not have H4784
Lev 11:32 Put it in w; it will be unclean till evening H4784
Lev 11:34 into contact with w from any such pot is H4784
Lev 11:36 a cistern for collecting w remains clean H4784
Lev 11:38 But if w has been put on the seed and a H4784
Lev 11:46 moves about in the w and every creature H4784
Lev 14: 5 birds be killed over fresh w in a clay pot. H4784
Lev 14: 6 the bird that was killed over the fresh w. H4784
Lev 14: 8 shave off all their hair and bathe with w H4784
Lev 14: 9 clothes and bathe themselves with w, H4784
Lev 14:50 one of the birds over fresh w in a clay pot. H4784
Lev 14:51 blood of the dead bird and the fresh w, H4784
Lev 14:52 the bird's blood, the fresh w, the live bird, H4784
Lev 15: 5 must wash their clothes and bathe with w, H4784
Lev 15: 6 must wash their clothes and bathe with w, H4784
Lev 15: 7 must wash their clothes and bathe with w, H4784
Lev 15: 8 must wash their clothes and bathe with w, H4784
Lev 15:10 must wash their clothes and bathe with w, H4784
Lev 15:11 rinsing his hands with w must wash their H4784
Lev 15:11 must wash their clothes and bathe with w, H4784
Lev 15:12 any wooden article is to be rinsed with w. H4784
Lev 15:13 clothes and bathe himself with fresh w, H4784
Lev 15:16 he must bathe his whole body with w H4784
Lev 15:17 has semen on it must be washed with w, H4784
Lev 15:18 both of them must bathe with w, and they H4784
Lev 15:21 must wash their clothes and bathe with w, H4784
Lev 15:22 must wash their clothes and bathe with w, H4784
Lev 15:27 must wash their clothes and bathe with w, H4784
Lev 16: 4 bathe himself with w before he puts them H4784
Lev 16:24 bathe himself with w in the sanctuary H4784
Lev 16:26 his clothes and bathe himself with w; H4784
Lev 16:28 his clothes and bathe himself with w; H4784
Lev 17:15 must wash their clothes and bathe with w, H4784
Lev 22: 6 unless he has bathed himself with w. H4784
Nu 5:17 shall take some holy w in a clay jar and H4784
Nu 5:17 dust from the tabernacle floor into the w. H4784
Nu 5:18 holds the bitter w that brings a curse. H4784
Nu 5:19 may this bitter w that brings a curse not H4784
Nu 5:22 May this w that brings a curse enter your H4784
Nu 5:23 then wash them off into the bitter w. H4784
Nu 5:24 drink the bitter w that brings a curse, H4784
Nu 5:24 this w that brings a curse and causes H4784
Nu 5:26 he is to have the woman drink the w. H4784
Nu 5:27 is made to drink the w that brings a curse H4784
Nu 8: 7 Sprinkle the w *of* cleansing on them; then H4784
Nu 19: 7 his clothes and bathe himself with w. H4784
Nu 19: 8 also wash his clothes and bathe with w, H4784
Nu 19: 9 community for use in the w *of* cleansing; H4784
Nu 19:12 themselves with the w on the third day and NDT
Nu 19:13 Because the w *of* cleansing has not been H4784
Nu 19:17 into a jar and pour fresh w over them. H4784
Nu 19:18 dip it in the w and sprinkle the tent and H4784
Nu 19:19 must wash their clothes and bathe with w, H4784
Nu 19:20 The w *of* cleansing has not been H4784
Nu 19:21 who sprinkles the w *of* cleansing must H4784
Nu 19:21 who touches the w *of* cleansing will be H4784
Nu 20: 2 Now there was no w for the community H4784
Nu 20: 5 And there is no w to drink!" H4784
Nu 20: 8 before their eyes and it will pour out its w. H4784
Nu 20: 8 You will bring w out of the rock for the H4784
Nu 20:10 must we bring you w out of this rock?" H4784
Nu 20:11 W gushed out, and the community and H4784
Nu 20:17 field or vineyard, or drink w *from* any well. H4784
Nu 20:19 if we or our livestock drink any of your w, H4784
Nu 21: 5 There is no w! And we detest this H4784
Nu 21:16 people together and I will give them w." H4784
Nu 21:22 field or vineyard, or drink w *from* any well. H4784
Nu 24: 7 W will flow from their buckets; their seed H4784
Nu 24: 7 buckets; their seed will have abundant w. H4784
Nu 31:23 also be purified with the w *of* cleansing. H4784
Nu 31:23 withstand fire must be put through that w. H4784
Nu 33:14 where there was no w for the people to H4784
Dt 2: 6 the food you eat and the w you drink. H4784
Dt 2:28 Sell us food to eat and w to drink for their H4784
Dt 8:15 He brought you w out of hard rock. H4784
Dt 9: 9 I ate no bread and drank no w. H4784
Dt 9:18 I ate no bread and drank no w, because H4784
Dt 10: 7 on to Jotbathah, a land with streams of w. H4784
Dt 12:16 pour it out on the ground like w. H4784
Dt 12:24 pour it out on the ground like w. H4784
Dt 14: 9 Of all the creatures living in the w, you H4784
Dt 15:23 pour it out on the ground like w. H4784
Dt 23: 4 you with bread and w on your way when H4784
Dt 29:11 who chop your wood and carry your w. H4784
Jos 2:10 LORD dried up the w *of* the Red Sea for you H4784
Jos 3:16 the w from upstream stopped flowing. H4784
Jos 3:16 while the w flowing down to the Sea of the NDT
Jos 7: 5 people melted in fear and became like w. H4784
Jos 9:21 be woodcutters and w carriers in the H4784
Jos 9:23 as woodcutters and w carriers for the H4784
Jos 9:27 woodcutters and w carriers for the H4784
Jos 15:19 in the Negev, give me also springs of w." H4784
Jdg 1:15 in the Negev, give me also springs of w." H4784
Jdg 4:19 "Please give me some w." She opened a H4784
Jdg 5: 4 poured, the clouds poured down w. H4784
Jdg 5:25 He asked for w, and she gave him milk; in H4784
Jdg 6:38 wrung out the dew—a bowlful of w. H4784
Jdg 7: 4 Take them down to the w, and I will thin H4784
Jdg 7: 5 So Gideon took the men down to the w H4784
Jdg 7: 5 those who lap the w with their tongues as H4784
Jdg 15:19 place in Lehi, and w came out of it. H4784
Ru 2: 9 get a drink from the w jars the men have NDT
1Sa 7: 6 they drew w and poured it out before the H4784
1Sa 9:11 young women coming out to draw w, H4784
1Sa 25:11 Why should I take my bread and w, and H4784
1Sa 26:11 get the spear and w jug that are near his H4784
1Sa 26:12 took the spear and w jug near Saul's H4784
1Sa 26:16 the king's spear and w jug that were near H4784
1Sa 30:11 They gave him w to drink and food to eat H4784
1Sa 30:12 any food or drunk *any* w for three days H4784
2Sa 5: 8 will have to use the w **shaft** to reach those H7562
2Sa 12:27 against Rabbah and taken its w **supply**. H4784
2Sa 14:14 Like w spilled on the ground, which cannot H4784
2Sa 23:15 David longed for w and said, "Oh, that NDT
2Sa 23:15 get me a drink of w from the well near the H4784
2Sa 23:16 drew w from the well near the gate of H4784
1Ki 13: 8 would I eat bread or drink w here. H4784
1Ki 13: 9 eat bread or drink w or return by the way H4784
1Ki 13:16 I eat bread or drink w with you in this H4784
1Ki 13:17 eat bread or drink w there or return by the H4784
1Ki 13:18 so that he may eat bread and drink w. H4784
1Ki 13:22 ate bread and drank w in the place where H4784
1Ki 14:15 it will be like a reed swaying in the w. H4784
1Ki 17:10 you bring me a little w in a jar so I may H4784
1Ki 18: 4 had supplied them with food and w.) H4784
1Ki 18:13 supplied them with food and w. H4784
1Ki 18:33 four large jars with w and pour it on the H4784
1Ki 18:35 The w ran down around the altar and even H4784
1Ki 18:38 also licked up the w in the trench. H4784
1Ki 19: 6 baked over hot coals, and a jar of w. H4784
1Ki 22:27 bread and w until I return safely H4784
2Ki 2: 8 rolled it up and struck the w with it. H4784
2Ki 2: 8 The w divided to the right and to the left NDT
2Ki 2:14 fallen from Elijah and struck the w with it. H4784
2Ki 2:14 When he struck the w, it divided to the H4784
2Ki 2:19 the w is bad and the land is H4784
2Ki 2:21 'I have healed this w. Never again will it H4784
2Ki 2:22 And the w has remained pure to this day H4784
2Ki 3: 9 the army had no more w for themselves H4784
2Ki 3:11 He used to pour w on the hands of Elijah." H4784
2Ki 3:16 I will fill this valley with **pools of** w H1463+1463
2Ki 3:17 this valley will be filled with w, and H4784
2Ki 3:20 w flowing from the direction of Edom! H4784
2Ki 3:20 And the land was filled with w. H4784
2Ki 3:22 morning, the sun was shining on the w. H4784
2Ki 3:22 across the way, the w looked red—like H4784
2Ki 6: 5 the iron axhead fell into the w. H4784
2Ki 6:22 Set food and w before them so that they H4784
2Ki 8:15 soaked it in w and spread it over the H4784
2Ki 18:31 fig tree and drink w *from* your own cistern, H4784
2Ki 19:24 in foreign lands and drunk the w there. H4784
2Ki 20:20 by which he brought w into the city, H4784
1Ch 11:17 David longed for w and said, "Oh, that NDT
1Ch 11:17 get me a drink of w from the well near the H4784
1Ch 11:18 drew w from the well near the gate of H4784
2Ch 18:26 bread and w until I return safely H4784
2Ch 32: 3 blocking off the w *from* the springs H4784
2Ch 32: 4 of Assyria come and find plenty of w?" H4784
2Ch 32:30 channeled **the** w down to the west H4392S
Ezr 10: 6 he ate no food and drank no w, because H4784
Ne 3:26 point opposite the W Gate toward the H4784
Ne 4:23 his weapon, even when he went for w. H4784
Ne 8: 1 as one in the square before the W Gate. H4784
Ne 8: 3 square before the W Gate in the presence H4784
Ne 8:16 the square by the W Gate and the one by H4784
Ne 9:15 thirst you brought them w from the rock; H4784
Ne 9:20 you gave them w for their thirst. H4784
Ne 12:37 David's palace to the W Gate on the east. H4784
Ne 13: 2 with food and w but had hired Balaam to H4784
Job 3:24 my daily food; my groans pour out like w. H4784
Job 5:10 the earth; he sends w on the countryside. H4784
Job 6:19 The caravans of Tema look for w, the H4564S
Job 8:11 Can reeds thrive without w? H4784
Job 14: 9 at the scent of w it will bud and put H4784
Job 14:11 As the w of a lake dries up or a riverbed H4784
Job 14:19 as w wears away stones and torrents wash H4784
Job 15:16 vile and corrupt, who drink up evil like w! H4784
Job 22: 7 You gave no w to the weary and you H4784
Job 22:11 and why a flood of w covers you. H4784
Job 24:18 they are foam on the surface of the w; H4784
Job 29:19 My roots will reach to the w, and the dew H4784
Job 34: 7 anyone like Job, who drinks scorn like w? H4784
Job 36:27 "He draws up the drops of w, which distill H4784
Job 37:13 or to w his earth and show his love. NDT
Job 38:26 to w a land where no one lives, an H4763
Job 38:34 cover yourself with a flood of w? H4784
Job 38:37 can tip over the w **jars** *of* the heavens H5574
Ps 1: 3 is like a tree planted by streams of w, H4784
Ps 22:14 I am poured out like w, and all my bones H4784
Ps 42: 1 As the deer pants for streams of w, so my H4784
Ps 58: 7 Let them vanish like w that flows away H4784
Ps 63: 1 dry and parched land where there is no w. H4784
Ps 65: 9 You care for the land and w it; you enrich H8796
Ps 65: 9 God are filled with w to provide the H4784
Ps 66:12 we went through fire and w, but you H4784
Ps 77:17 The clouds poured down w, the heavens H4784
Ps 78:13 he made the w stand up like a wall. H4784
Ps 78:15 wilderness and **gave** them w as abundant H9197
Ps 78:16 rocky crag and made w flow down like H4784
Ps 78:20 struck the rock, and w gushed out, streams H4784
Ps 79: 3 out blood like w all around Jerusalem, H4784
Ps 104:10 He makes springs pour w into the ravines; it NDT
Ps 104:11 *They* **give** w *to* all the beasts of the field H9197
Ps 105:41 opened the rock, and w gushed out; it H4784
Ps 107:35 desert into pools of w and the parched H4784
Ps 109:18 it entered into his body like w, into his H4784
Ps 114: 8 the hard rock into springs of w. H4784
Pr 5:15 Drink w from your own cistern, running H4784
Pr 5:15 **running** w from your own well. H5689
Pr 5:16 your streams of w in the public squares? H4784
Pr 8:24 there were no springs overflowing with w; H4784
Pr 9:17 "Stolen w is sweet; food eaten in secret is H4784
Pr 21: 1 heart is a stream of w that he channels H4784
Pr 25:21 if he is thirsty, give him w to drink. H4784
Pr 25:25 Like cold w to a weary soul is good news H4784
Pr 27:19 As w reflects the face, so one's life H4784
Pr 30:16 which is never satisfied with w, and fire, H4784
Ecc 2: 6 I made reservoirs to w groves of flourishing H9197
Ecc 11: 3 If clouds are full of w, they pour rain on the NDT
SS 4:15 a well of flowing w streaming down from H4784
SS 5:12 His eyes are like doves by the w streams H4784
Isa 1:22 your choice wine is diluted with w. H4784
Isa 1:30 fading leaves, like a garden without w. H4784
Isa 3: 1 all supplies of food and all supplies of w, H4784
Isa 7:19 the thornbushes and at all the w **holes**. H5635
Isa 12: 3 With joy you will draw w from the wells of H4784
Isa 18: 2 by sea in papyrus boats over the w. H4784
Isa 19: 8 who throw nets on the w will pine away. H4784
Isa 21:14 bring w for the thirsty; you who live in H4784
Isa 22: 9 you stored up w *in* the Lower Pool. H4784
Isa 22:11 the two walls for the w *of* the Old Pool, H4784
Isa 27: 3 watch over it; *I* w it continually. H9197
Isa 28:17 and w will overflow your hiding place. H4784
Isa 30:14 a hearth or scooping w out of a cistern." H4784
Isa 30:20 bread of adversity and the w *of* affliction, H4784
Isa 30:25 streams of w will flow on every high H4784
Isa 32: 2 like streams of w in the desert and the H4784
Isa 32: 6 from the thirsty they withhold w. H5482
Isa 33:16 will be supplied, and w will not fail them. H4784
Isa 35: 6 W will gush forth in the wilderness and H4784
Isa 36:16 fig tree and drink w *from* your own cistern, H4784
Isa 37:25 in foreign lands and drunk the w there. H4784
Isa 41:17 "The poor and needy search for w, but H4784
Isa 41:18 I will turn the desert into pools of w, and H4784
Isa 43:20 because I provide w in the wilderness H4784
Isa 44: 3 For I will pour w on the thirsty land, and H4784
Isa 44:12 strength; he drinks no w and grows faint. H4784
Isa 48:21 he made w flow for them from the rock H4784
Isa 48:21 he split the rock and w gushed out. H4784
Isa 49:10 them and lead them beside springs of w. H4784
Isa 50: 2 their fish rot for lack of w and die of thirst. H4784
Isa 64: 2 sets twigs ablaze and causes w to boil, H4784
Jer 2:13 the spring of living w, and have dug their H4784
Jer 2:13 broken cisterns that cannot hold w. H4784
Jer 2:18 why go to Egypt to drink w *from* the Nile? H4784
Jer 2:18 to Assyria to drink w *from* the Euphrates? H4784
Jer 6: 7 As a well pours out its w, so she pours out H4784
Jer 8:14 perish and given us poisoned w to drink, H4784
Jer 9: 1 head were a **spring of** w and my eyes a H4784
Jer 9:15 eat bitter food and drink poisoned w. H4784
Jer 9:18 with tears and w streams from our H4784
Jer 13: 1 your waist, but do not let it touch w." H4784
Jer 14: 3 The nobles send their servants for w; they H4784
Jer 14: 3 they go to the cisterns but find no w. H4784
Jer 17: 8 a tree planted by the w that sends out its H4784
Jer 17:13 forsaken the LORD, the spring of living w. H4784

Jer 23:15 eat bitter food and drink poisoned w, H4784
Jer 31: 9 beside streams of w on a level path H4784
Jer 38: 6 the cistern; it had no w in it, only mud, H4784
La 2:19 out your heart like w in the presence of H4784
La 5: 4 We must buy the w we drink; our wood H4784
Eze 4:11 out a sixth of a hin of w and drink it at set H4784
Eze 4:16 in anxiety and drink rationed w in despair, H4784
Eze 4:17 food and w will be scarce. They will be H4784
Eze 12:18 shudder in fear as you drink your w. H4784
Eze 12:19 in anxiety and drink their w in despair, H4784
Eze 16: 4 you washed with w to make you clean, H4784
Eze 16: 9 'I bathed you with w and washed the H4784
Eze 17: 5 He planted it like a willow by abundant w, H4784
Eze 17: 7 stretched out its branches to him for w. H9197
Eze 17: 8 good soil by abundant w so that it would H4784
Eze 19:10 a vine in your vineyard planted by the w; H4784
Eze 19:10 full of branches because of abundant w. H4784
Eze 24: 3 cooking pot; put it on and pour w into it. H4784
Eze 32: 2 churning the w with your feet and H4784
Eze 34:18 Is it not enough for you to drink clear w H4784
Eze 36:25 I will sprinkle clean w on you, and you will H4784
Eze 47: 1 I saw w coming out from under the H4784
Eze 47: 1 The w was coming down from under the H4784
Eze 47: 2 the w was trickling from the south H4784
Eze 47: 3 led me through w that was ankle-deep H4784
Eze 47: 4 led me through w that was knee-deep H4784
Eze 47: 4 me through w that was *up to* the waist. H4784
Eze 47: 5 because the w had risen and was deep H4784
Eze 47: 8 "This w flows toward the eastern region H4784
Eze 47: 8 the sea, the salty w there becomes fresh. H4784
Eze 47: 9 because this w flows there and makes the H4784
Eze 47: 9 flows there and makes the salt w fresh; NDT
Eze 47:12 because the w from the sanctuary flows to H4784
Da 1:12 vegetables to eat and w to drink. H4784
Hos 2: 5 who give me my food and my w, my wool H4784
Hos 5:10 out my wrath on them like a flood of w. H4784
Hos 6: 3 like the spring rains *that* w the earth." H3722
Joel 1:20 the streams of w have dried up and fire H4784
Joel 3:18 all the ravines of Judah will run with w. H4784
Joel 3:18 the LORD's house and *will* w the valley of H9197
Am 4: 8 from town to town for w but did not get H4784
Am 8:11 not a famine of food or a thirst for w, but H4784
Mic 1: 4 the fire, like w rushing down a slope. H4784
Na 2: 8 is like a pool whose w is draining away. H4784
Na 3: 8 situated on the Nile, with w around her? H4784
Na 3:14 Draw w *for* the siege, strengthen your H4784
Hab 3:10 Torrents of w swept by; the deep roared H4784
Zec 14: 8 On that day living w will flow out from H4784
Mt 3:11 "I baptize you with w for repentance. G5623
Mt 3:16 was baptized, he went up out of the w. G5623
Mt 8:32 bank into the lake and died in the w. G5623
Mt 10:42 anyone **gives** even a cup of cold w **to** one G4540
Mt 14:28 replied, "tell me to come to you on the w." G5623
Mt 14:29 walked on the w and came toward Jesus. G5623
Mt 17:15 He often falls into the fire or into the w. G5623
Mt 27:24 he took w and washed his hands in front G5623
Mk 1: 8 I baptize you *with* w, but he will baptize G5623
Mk 1:10 Just as Jesus was coming up out of the w G5623
Mk 9:22 often thrown him into fire or w to kill him. G5623
Mk 9:41 gives you a cup *of* w in my name because G5623
Mk 14:13 a man carrying a jar *of* w will meet you. G5623
Lk 3:16 answered them all, "I baptize you *with* w. G5623
Lk 5: 4 "Put out into **deep** *w*, and let down the AIT
Lk 7:44 You did not give me *any* w for my feet G5623
Lk 8:25 He commands even the winds and the w G5623
Lk 13:15 from the stall and lead it out *to* **give** it w? G4540
Lk 16:24 tip of his finger *in* w and cool my tongue, G5623
Lk 22:10 a man carrying a jar *of* w will meet you. G5623
Jn 1:26 "I baptize with w," John replied, "but G5623
Jn 1:31 came baptizing with w was that he might G5623
Jn 1:33 who sent me to baptize with w told me, G5623
Jn 2: 6 Nearby stood six stone w **jars**, the kind G5620
Jn 2: 7 "Fill the jars *with* w"; so they filled them G5623
Jn 2: 9 banquet tasted the w that had been G5623
Jn 2: 9 the servants who had drawn the w knew. G5623
Jn 3: 5 unless they are born of w and the Spirit. G5623
Jn 3:23 because there was plenty *of* w, and G5623
Jn 4: 7 a Samaritan woman came to draw w, G5623
Jn 4:10 he would have given you living w. G5623
Jn 4:11 Where can you get this living w? G5623
Jn 4:13 who drinks this w will be thirsty again, G5623
Jn 4:14 whoever drinks the w I give them will G5623
Jn 4:14 the w I give them will become in them a G5623
Jn 4:14 in them a spring *of* w welling up to G5623
Jn 4:15 give me this w so that I won't get thirsty G5623
Jn 4:15 have to keep coming here *to* **draw** w." G533
Jn 4:28 leaving her w **jar**, the woman went G5620
Jn 4:46 where he had turned the w into wine. G5623
Jn 5: 7 me into the pool when the w is stirred. G5623
Jn 6:19 the boat, walking on the w; and they were G2498
Jn 7:38 rivers *of* living w will flow from within G5623
Jn 13: 5 he poured w into a basin and began to G5623
Jn 19:34 bringing a sudden flow of blood and w. G5623
Jn 21: 7 had taken it off) and jumped into the w. G2498
Ac 1: 5 For John baptized *with* w, but in a few G5623
Ac 8:36 they came to some w and the eunuch G5623
Ac 8:36 the eunuch said, "Look, here is w. G5623
Ac 8:38 went down into the w and Philip baptized G5623
Ac 8:39 When they came up out of the w, the G5623
Ac 10:47 in the way of their being baptized *with* w. G5623
Ac 11:16 'John baptized *with* w, but you will be G5623
Ac 27:28 found that the w was a hundred and NDT
Eph 5:26 by the washing *with* w through the word, G5623
1Ti 5:23 Stop **drinking only** w, and use a little wine G5621
Heb 9:19 together with w, scarlet wool and G5623
Heb 10:22 having our bodies washed *with* pure w. G5623
Jas 3:11 Can both **fresh** w and salt water flow from the AIT
Jas 3:11 fresh water and **salt** *w* flow from the same AIT
Jas 3:12 Neither can a salt spring produce fresh w. G5623
1Pe 3:20 eight in all, were saved through w, G5623
1Pe 3:21 and **this** *w* symbolizes baptism that now saves AIT
2Pe 2:17 are springs **without** w and mists driven G536
2Pe 3: 5 earth was formed out of w and by water. G5623
2Pe 3: 5 earth was formed out of water and by w. G5623
1Jn 5: 6 is the one who came by w and blood— G5623
1Jn 5: 6 He did not come by w only, but by water G5623
1Jn 5: 6 come by water only, but by w and blood. G5623
1Jn 5: 8 the Spirit, the w and the blood; and the G5623
Rev 7:17 'he will lead them to springs *of* living w. G5623
Rev 8:10 of the rivers and on the springs *of* w— G5623
Rev 12:15 mouth the serpent spewed w like a river, G5623
Rev 14: 7 the earth, the sea and the springs *of* w." G5623
Rev 16: 4 his bowl on the rivers and springs *of* w, G5623
Rev 16:12 its w was dried up to prepare the way G5623
Rev 21: 6 the thirsty I will give w without cost from NDT
Rev 21: 6 cost from the spring *of* the w of life. G5623
Rev 22: 1 showed me the river *of* the w of life, G5623
Rev 22:17 wishes take the free gift *of* the w of life. G5623

WATER'S (3) [WATER]

Jos 3:15 Jordan and their feet touched the w edge, H4784
Mk 4: 1 were along the shore at the w edge. G2498
Lk 5: 2 He saw at the w edge two boats, left there G3349

WATERED (10) [WATER]

Ge 2: 6 from the earth and w the whole surface of H9197
Ge 13:10 of the Jordan toward Zoar *was* **well** w, H5482
Ge 24:46 So I drank, and *she* w the camels also. H9197
Ge 29: 2 because the flocks *were* w from that well. H9197
Ge 29:10 of the well and w his uncle's sheep. H9197
Ex 2:17 came to their rescue and w their flock. H9197
Ex 2:19 He even drew water for us and w the flock." H9197
Dt 29:19 disaster on the w **land** as well as the dry. H8116
Ps 104:16 The trees of the LORD *are* **well** w, the H8425
1Co 3: 6 the seed, Apollos w it, but God has been G4540

WATERFALLS (1) [WATER]

Ps 42: 7 Deep calls to deep in the roar of your w H7562

WATERING (5) [WATER]

Ge 2:10 A river w the garden flowed from Eden H9197
Ge 30:38 the peeled branches in all the w troughs, H4784
Jdg 5:11 the voice of the singers at the w **places** H5393
Ps 72: 6 a mown field, like showers w the earth. H2449
Isa 55:10 to it without w the earth and making H8115

WATERLESS (2) [WATER]

Dt 8:15 that thirsty and w land, with its H401+4784
Zec 9:11 free your prisoners from the w pit. H401+4784

WATERPOT, WATERPOTS (KJV) (WATER) JAR, JARS

WATERS (164) [WATER]

Ge 1: 2 the Spirit of God was hovering over the w. H4784
Ge 1: 6 a vault between the w to separate water H4784
Ge 1:10 and the gathered w he called "seas." H4784
Ge 7: 7 the ark to escape the w *of* the flood. H4784
Ge 7:17 as the w increased they lifted the ark H4784
Ge 7:18 The w rose and increased greatly on the H4784
Ge 7:20 The w rose and covered the mountains to H4784
Ge 7:24 The w flooded the earth for a hundred H4784
Ge 8: 1 a wind over the earth, and the w receded. H4784
Ge 8: 5 The w continued to recede until the tenth H4784
Ge 9:11 all life be destroyed by the w *of* a flood; H4784
Ge 9:15 Never again will the w become a flood to H4784
Ge 49: 4 Turbulent as the w, you will no longer H4784
Ex 7:19 out your hand over the w *of* Egypt— H4784
Ex 8: 6 out his hand over the w *of* Egypt, H4784
Ex 14:21 it into dry land. The w were divided, H4784
Ex 14:26 the sea so that the w may flow back over H4784
Ex 15: 5 The **deep** w have covered them; they sank H9333
Ex 15: 8 By the blast of your nostrils the w piled up. H4784
Ex 15: 8 The surging w stood up like a wall; the NDT
Ex 15: 8 the **deep** w congealed in the heart of the H9333
Ex 15:10 They sank like lead in the mighty w. H4784
Ex 15:19 LORD brought the w *of* the sea back over H4784
Ex 20: 4 on the earth beneath or in the w below. H4784
Nu 20:13 These were the w *of* Meribah, where the H4784
Nu 20:24 my command at the w *of* Meribah. H4784
Nu 24: 6 by the LORD, like cedars beside the w. H4784
Nu 27:14 rebelled at the w in the Desert of Zin, H4784
Nu 27:14 These were the w *of* Meribah Kadesh, in H4784
Dt 4:18 the ground or any fish in the w below. H4784
Dt 5: 8 on the earth beneath or in the w below. H4784
Dt 11: 4 them with the w *of* the Red Sea as they H4784
Dt 32:51 Israelites at the w *of* Meribah Kadesh in H4784
Dt 33: 8 contended with him at the w *of* Meribah. H4784
Dt 33:13 with the **deep** w that lie below; H9333
Jos 3: 8 you reach the edge of the Jordan's w, H4784
Jos 3:13 its w flowing downstream will be cut off H4784
Jos 4: 7 the w *of* the Jordan were cut off. H4784
Jos 4:18 dry ground than the w *of* the Jordan H4784
Jos 11: 5 camp together at the W *of* Merom to fight H4784
Jos 11: 7 suddenly at the W *of* Merom and attacked H4784
Jos 15: 7 along to the w *of* En Shemesh and came H4784
Jos 15: 9 toward the spring of the w *of* Nephtoah, H4784
Jos 18:15 out at the spring of the w *of* Nephtoah. H4784
Jdg 5:19 At Taanach, by the w *of* Megiddo, they H4784
Jdg 7:24 seize the w of the Jordan ahead of H4784
Jdg 7:24 they seized the w of the Jordan as far H4784
2Sa 5:20 He said, "As w break out, the LORD has H4784
2Sa 22:17 hold of me; he drew me out of deep w. H4784
2Ki 5:12 Damascus, better than all the w *of* Israel? H4784
1Ch 14:11 He said, "As w break out, God has broken H4784
Ne 9:11 the depths, like a stone into mighty w. H4784
Job 11:16 trouble, recalling it only as w gone by. H4784
Job 12:15 If he holds back the w, there is drought; if H4784
Job 20:28 rushing w on the day of God's wrath. NDT
Job 26: 5 those beneath the w and all that live in H4784
Job 26: 8 He wraps up the w in his clouds, yet the H4784
Job 26:10 on the face of the w for a boundary H4784
Job 28:25 of the wind and measured out the w, H4784
Job 37:10 and the broad w become frozen. H4784
Job 38:30 when the w become hard as stone, when H4784
Ps 18:16 hold of me; he drew me out of deep w. H4784
Ps 23: 2 pastures, he leads me beside quiet w, H4784
Ps 24: 2 it on the seas and established it on the w. H5643
Ps 29: 3 The voice of the LORD is over the w; the H4784
Ps 29: 3 the LORD thunders over the mighty w. H4784
Ps 32: 6 rising of the mighty w will not reach them. H4784
Ps 33: 7 He gathers the w *of* the sea into jars; he H4784
Ps 46: 3 though its w roar and foam and the H4784
Ps 66: 6 they passed through the w on foot H5643
Ps 69: 1 for the w have come up to my neck. H4784
Ps 69: 2 I have come into the deep w; the floods H4784
Ps 69:14 those who hate me, from the deep w. H4784
Ps 73:10 to them and drink up w *in* abundance. H4784
Ps 74:13 broke the heads of the monster in the w. H4784
Ps 77:16 The w saw you, God, the waters saw you H4784
Ps 77:16 the w saw you and writhed; the very H4784
Ps 77:19 your way through the mighty w, though H4784
Ps 81: 7 I tested you at the w *of* Meribah. H4784
Ps 93: 4 Mightier than the thunder of the great w H4784
Ps 104: 3 beams of his upper chambers on their w. H4784
Ps 104: 6 the w stood above the mountains. H4784
Ps 104: 7 But at your rebuke the w fled, at the sound NDT
Ps 104:12 The birds of the sky nest by **the** w; they H2157
Ps 104:13 *He* w the mountains from his upper H9197
Ps 105:29 He turned their w into blood, causing H4784
Ps 106:11 The w covered their adversaries; not one H4784
Ps 106:32 By the w *of* Meribah they angered the H4784
Ps 107:23 they were merchants on the mighty w. H4784
Ps 124: 5 the raging w would have swept us away. H4784
Ps 136: 6 who spread out the earth upon the w, His H4784
Ps 144: 7 me and rescue me from the mighty w, H4784
Ps 147:18 he stirs up his breezes, and the w flow. H4784
Ps 148: 4 heavens and you w above the skies. H4784
Pr 8:29 its boundary so the w would not overstep H4784
Pr 18: 4 The words of the mouth are deep w, but H4784
Pr 20: 5 purposes of a person's heart are deep w, H4784
Pr 30: 4 Who has wrapped up the w in a cloak H4784
SS 8: 7 Many w cannot quench love; rivers cannot H4784
Isa 8: 6 the gently flowing w *of* Shiloah and H4784
Isa 10:26 he will raise his staff over the w, as H3542
Isa 11: 9 of the LORD as the w cover the sea. H4784
Isa 15: 6 The w *of* Nimrim are dried up and the H4784
Isa 15: 9 The w *of* Dimon are full of blood, but I H4784
Isa 17:12 they roar like the roaring of great w! H4784
Isa 17:13 peoples roar like the roar of surging w, H4784
Isa 19: 5 The w of the river will dry up, and the H4784
Isa 23: 3 On the great w came the grain of the H4784
Isa 40:12 has measured the w in the hollow of his H4784
Isa 43: 2 When you pass through the w, I will be H4784
Isa 43:16 the sea, a path through the mighty w, H4784
Isa 51:10 up the sea, the w *of* the great deep, who H4784
Isa 54: 9 I swore that the w *of* Noah would never H4784
Isa 55: 1 come to the w; and you who have no H4784
Isa 58:11 garden, like a spring whose w never fail. H4784
Isa 63:12 who divided the w before them, to gain H4784
Jer 10:13 he thunders, the w in the heavens roar H4784
Jer 18:14 Do its cool w from distant sources ever H4784
Jer 46: 7 rises like the Nile, like rivers of surging w? H4784
Jer 46: 8 rises like the Nile, like rivers of surging w. H4784
Jer 47: 2 "See how the w are rising in the north H4784
Jer 48:34 even the w *of* Nimrim are dried up. H4784
Jer 50:38 A drought on her w! They will dry up. H4784
Jer 51:13 You who live by many w and are rich in H4784
Jer 51:16 he thunders, the w in the heavens roar H4784
Jer 51:55 Waves of enemies will rage like great w H4784
La 3:54 the w closed over my head, and I thought H4784
Eze 1:24 like the roar of rushing w, like the voice of H4784
Eze 26:19 depths over you and its vast w cover you, H4784
Eze 27:34 by the sea in the depths of the w; H4784
Eze 30:12 I will dry up the **w of the Nile** and sell the H3284
Eze 31: 4 The w nourished it, deep springs made it H4784
Eze 31: 5 spreading because of abundant w. H4784
Eze 31: 7 its roots went down to abundant w. H4784
Eze 31:14 no other trees by the w are ever to tower H4784
Eze 31:15 its abundant w were restrained. H4784
Eze 32:13 from beside abundant w no longer to be H4784
Eze 32:14 Then I will let her w settle and make her H4784
Eze 43: 2 His voice was like the roar of rushing w H4784
Eze 47:19 Tamar as far as the w *of* Meribah Kadesh, H4784
Eze 48:28 from Tamar to the w *of* Meribah Kadesh, H4784
Da 12: 6 who was above the w *of* the river, "How H4784
Da 12: 7 who was above the w *of* the river, lifted H4784
Hos 10: 7 away like a twig on the surface of the w. H4784

Am 5: 8 who calls for the **w** *of* the sea and pours H4784
Am 9: 6 he calls for the **w** *of* the sea and pours H4784
Jnh 2: 5 The engulfing **w** threatened me, the deep H4784
Na 3: 8 river was her defense, the **w** her wall. H4784
Hab 2:14 glory of the LORD as the **w** cover the sea. H4784
Hab 3:15 with your horses, churning the great **w**. H4784
Lk 8:24 rebuked the wind and the raging **w**; *G5623*
Jn 6:18 wind was blowing and the **w** grew rough. *G2498*
1Co 3: 7 plants nor the *one who* **w** is anything, *G4540*
1Co 3: 8 plants and the *one who* **w** have one *G4540*
2Pe 3: 6 By these **w** also the world of that time was *G5623*
Rev 1:15 his voice was like the sound *of* rushing **w**. *G5623*
Rev 8:11 A third *of* the **w** turned bitter, and many *G5623*
Rev 8:11 people died from the **w** that had become *G5623*
Rev 11: 6 power to turn the **w** into blood and to *G5623*
Rev 14: 2 like the roar *of* rushing **w** and like a loud *G5623*
Rev 16: 5 I heard the angel *in charge of* the **w** say: *G5623*
Rev 17: 1 the great prostitute, who sits by many **w**. *G5623*
Rev 17:15 said to me, "The **w** you saw, where the *G5623*
Rev 19: 6 like the roar *of* rushing **w** and like loud *G4498*

WATERY (4) [WATER]

Ps 104: 6 it with the **w depths** as with a garment; H9333
Pr 3:20 his knowledge the **w depths** were divided, H9333
Pr 8:24 When there were no **w depths**, I was H9333
Isa 44:27 who says to the **w deep**, 'Be dry, and I will H7425

WAVE (37) [WAVED, WAVES, WAVY]

Ex 29:24 his sons and *have them* **w** them before H5677
Ex 29:24 them before the LORD as a **w offering**. H9485
Ex 29:26 **w** it before the LORD as a wave offering H5677
Ex 29:26 wave it before the LORD as a **w offering** H9485
Ex 35:22 their gold as a **w offering** to the LORD. H9485
Ex 38:24 gold from the **w offering** used for all the H9485
Ex 38:29 bronze from the **w offering** was 70 talents H9485
Lev 7:30 **w** the breast before the LORD as a H5677
Lev 7:30 the breast before the LORD as a **w offering**. H9485
Lev 8:27 them before the LORD as a **w offering**. H9485
Lev 8:29 waved it before the LORD as a **w offering**, H9485
Lev 9:21 right thigh before the LORD as a **w offering**, H9485
Lev 10:15 be waved before the LORD as a **w offering**. H9485
Lev 14:12 *he shall* **w** them before the LORD as a H5677
Lev 14:12 them before the LORD as a **w offering**. H9485
Lev 14:24 **w** them before the LORD as a wave H5677
Lev 14:24 them before the LORD as a **w offering**. H9485
Lev 23:11 *He is to* **w** the sheaf before the LORD so it H5677
Lev 23:11 the priest *is to* **w** it on the day after the H5677
Lev 23:12 On the day you **w** the sheaf, you must H5677
Lev 23:15 you brought the sheaf of the **w offering**, H9485
Lev 23:17 as a **w offering** of firstfruits to the LORD. H9485
Lev 23:20 The priest *is to* **w** the two lambs before the H5677
Lev 23:20 two lambs before the LORD as a **w offering**, H9485
Nu 5:25 **w** it before the LORD and bring it to the H5677
Nu 6:20 The priest *shall* then **w** these before the H5677
Nu 6:20 these before the LORD as a **w offering**; H9485
Nu 8:11 the LORD as a **w offering** from the Israelites H9485
Nu 8:13 present them as a **w offering** to the LORD. H9485
Nu 8:15 presented them as a **w offering**, H9485
Nu 8:21 them as a **w offering** before the LORD H9485
Nu 18:11 gifts of all the **w offerings** *of* the Israelites. H9485
Nu 18:18 the breast of the **w offering** and the right H9485
2Ki 5:11 **w** his hand over the spot and cure me of H5677
Job 10:17 forces come against me **w upon wave**. H2722
Job 10:17 forces come against me **wave upon w**. H2722
Jas 1: 6 the one who doubts is like a **w** of the sea, *G3114*

WAVED (10) [WAVE]

Ex 29:27 the breast that **was w** and the thigh H9485+5677
Lev 7:34 the breast that is **w** and the thigh that is H9485
Lev 8:27 and *they* **w** them before the LORD as a H5677
Lev 8:29 **w** it before the LORD as a wave H5677
Lev 9:21 Aaron **w** the breasts and the right thigh H5677
Lev 10:14 the breast that was **w** and the thigh that H9485
Lev 10:15 the breast that was **w** must be brought H9485
Lev 10:15 to *be* **w** before the LORD as a wave offering H5677
Lev 14:21 guilt offering to be **w** to make atonement H9485
Nu 6:20 the breast that was **w** and the thigh that H9485

WAVER (2)

1Ki 18:21 "How long *will* you **w** between two H7174
Ro 4:20 Yet *he did* not **w** through unbelief *G1359*

WAVES (29) [WAVE]

2Sa 22: 5 The **w** *of* death swirled about me; the H5403
Job 9: 8 heavens and treads on the **w** *of* the sea. H1195
Job 38:11 here is where your proud **w** halt'? H1644
Ps 42: 7 all your **w** and breakers have swept over H5403
Ps 65: 7 the roaring of their **w**, and the turmoil of H1644
Ps 88: 7 have overwhelmed me with all your **w**. H5403
Ps 89: 9 when its **w** mount up, you still H1644
Ps 93: 3 the seas have lifted up their **pounding w**. H1922
Ps 107:25 stirred up a tempest that lifted high the **w**. H1644
Ps 107:29 a whisper; the **w** *of* the sea were hushed. H1644
Isa 48:18 your well-being like the **w** *of* the sea. H1644
Isa 51:15 who stirs up the sea so that its **w** roar H1644
Isa 57:20 whose **w** cast up mire and mud. H4784
Jer 5:22 The **w** may roll, but they cannot prevail H1644
Jer 31:35 who stirs up the sea so that its **w** roar H1644
Jer 51:42 over Babylon; its roaring **w** will cover her. H1644
Jer 51:55 **W** *of* enemies will rage like great waters H1644
Eze 26: 3 against you, like the sea casting up its **w**. H1644
Jnh 2: 3 all your **w** and breakers swept over me. H1644
Hab 3:10 the deep roared and lifted its **w** on high. H3338
Mt 8:24 so that the **w** swept over the boat. *G3246*
Mt 8:26 got up and rebuked the winds and the **w**, *G2498*
Mt 8:27 Even the winds and the **w** obey him!" *G2498*
Mt 14:24 buffeted by the **w** because the wind was *G3246*
Mk 4:37 came up, and the **w** broke over the boat *G3246*
Mk 4:39 rebuked the wind and said *to* the **w** *G2498*
Mk 4:41 Even the wind and the **w** obey him!" *G2498*
Eph 4:14 **tossed back and forth by the w**, and *G3115*
Jude 13 They are wild **w** of the sea, foaming up *G3246*

WAVY (1) [WAVE]

SS 5:11 his hair is **w** and black as a raven. H9446

WAX (4)

Ps 22:14 My heart has turned to **w**; it has melted H1880
Ps 68: 2 like smoke—as **w** melts before the fire H1880
Ps 97: 5 mountains melt like **w** before the LORD, H1880
Mic 1: 4 split apart, like **w** before the fire, like H1880

WAY (592) [AWAY, BYWAYS, WAYS]

Ge 3:24 forth to guard the **w** *to* the tree of life. H2006
Ge 9:23 faces were **turned the other w** so that they H345
Ge 12:20 and *they* **sent** him **on** his **w**, with H8938+906
Ge 18: 5 can be refreshed and then **go on** *your* **w**— H6296
Ge 18:16 along with them to **see** them **on** their **w**. H8938
Ge 18:19 him to keep the **w** *of* the LORD by doing H2006
Ge 19: 2 then go on your **w** early in the H2006
Ge 19: 9 "Get out of our **w**," they replied. "This H2134
Ge 21:14 *She* **went on** *her* **w** and wandered in the H2143
Ge 24: 1 the LORD had blessed him in **every w**. H3972
Ge 24:10 Naharaim and **made** *his* **w** to the town of H2143
Ge 24:49 I may know **which w** to turn H6584+3545+196+6584+8520
Ge 24:50 say nothing to you **one w** or the other. H8273S
Ge 24:54 he said, "**Send** me **on** my **w** to my master." H8938
Ge 24:56 **Send** me **on** my **w** so I may go to my H8938
Ge 24:59 So *they* **sent** their sister Rebekah **on** her **w**, H8938
Ge 26:31 Then Isaac **sent** them **on** their **w**, and they H8938
Ge 27: 9 your father, **just the w** he likes it. H3869+889
Ge 27:14 **just the w** his father liked it. H3869+889
Ge 28: 5 Then Isaac **sent** Jacob **on** *his* **w**, and he H8938
Ge 30:25 "**Send** me **on** my **w** so I can go back to my H8938
Ge 30:26 I have served you, and *I will* **be on** *my* **w**. H2143
Ge 30:43 **In this w** the man grew exceedingly H2256
Ge 32: 1 Jacob also went on his **w**, and the angels H2006
Ge 33:12 "*Let us* **be on** *our* **w**; I'll H5825+2256+2143
Ge 33:16 day Esau started on his **w** back to Seir. H2006
Ge 35:19 died and was buried on the **w** to Ephrath H2006
Ge 37:25 and *they* **were on** *their* **w** to take them H2143
Ge 38:13 father-in-law **is on** *his* **w** to Timnah to H6590
Ge 41:43 people shouted before him, "**Make w**!" H91
Ge 44: 3 the men **were sent on** *their* **w** with their H8938
Ge 45:24 he said to them, "Don't quarrel on the **w**!" H2006
Ge 48: 7 of Canaan while we were still on the **w**, H2006
Ex 2:12 Looking **this w** and that and seeing no one AIT
Ex 3: 9 I have seen the **w** the Egyptians are H4316S
Ex 4:14 He *is* already **on** *his* **w** to meet you, and H3655
Ex 4:24 At a lodging place on the **w**, the LORD met H2006
Ex 5:15 have you treated your servants **this w**? H3907
Ex 13:21 guide them on their **w** and by night in a H2006
Ex 16: 4 **In this w** I will test them and see H4200+5100
Ex 18: 8 had met along the **w** and how the LORD H2006
Ex 18:20 show them the **w** they are to live and H2006
Ex 18:27 Moses **sent** his father-in-law **on** *his* **w**, H8938
Ex 19:21 so *they do* not **force** *their* **w through** to see H2238
Ex 19:24 people *must* not **force** *their* **w through** to H2238
Ex 23:20 guard you along the **w** and to bring you to H2006
Ex 23:28 and Hittites **out of** your **w**. H4946+4200+7156
Ex 26:17 all the frames of the tabernacle **in this w**. H4027
Ex 26:24 from the bottom **all the w to** the top and H6584
Ex 28:11 the two stones the **w** a gem cutter H5126
Ex 33: 3 people and I might destroy you on the **w**." H2006
Ex 36:22 all the frames of the tabernacle **in this w**. H4027
Ex 36:29 from the bottom **all the w to** the top and H448
Lev 4:20 **In this w** the priest will make atonement H2256
Lev 4:26 **In this w** the priest will make atonement H2256
Lev 4:31 **In this w** the priest will make atonement H2256
Lev 4:35 **In this w** the priest will make atonement H2256
Lev 5: 5 must confess in **what** *w* they have sinned. AIT
Lev 5:10 offering in the **prescribed w** and make H5477
Lev 5:13 **In this w** the priest will make atonement H2256
Lev 5:18 **In this w** the priest will make atonement H2256
Lev 6: 7 **In this w** the priest will make atonement H2256
Lev 9:16 offering and offered it in the **prescribed w**. H5477
Lev 12: 8 **In this w** the priest will make atonement H2256
Lev 14:31 **In this w** the priest will make atonement H2256
Lev 14:53 **In this w** he will make atonement for the H2256
Lev 15:15 **In this w** he will make atonement before H2256
Lev 15:30 **In this w** he will make atonement for her H2256
Lev 16:16 **In this w** he will make atonement for the H2256
Lev 19: 5 sacrifice it **in such a w that** it will be H4200
Lev 19:25 **In this w** your harvest will be increased H4200
Lev 22: 9 my service **in such a w that** they do not H2256
Lev 22:29 sacrifice it **in such a w that** it will be H4200
Nu 2:34 **that is the w** they encamped under their H4027
Nu 2:34 standards, and **that is the w** they set out H4027
Nu 5: 6 wrongs another in **any** *w* and so is unfaithful AIT
Nu 7:89 In this **w** the LORD spoke to him NDT
Nu 8:14 **In this w** you are to set the Levites apart H2256
Nu 14:45 beat them down **all the w to** Hormah. H6330
Nu 15:13 do these things **in this w** when they H3970
Nu 18:28 **In this w** you also will present an offering H4027
Nu 21: 4 But the people grew impatient on the **w**; H2006
Nu 21:30 has been destroyed **all the w to** Dibon. H6330
Nu 24:25 and Balak went his own **w**. H2006
Nu 28:24 **In this w** present the food offering every H3869
Dt 1:31 all the **w** you went until you reached this H2006
Dt 1:33 to show you the **w** you should go. H2006
Dt 1:44 you down from Seir **all the w to** Hormah. H6330
Dt 2: 1 long time *we* **made** *our* **w around** the hill H6015
Dt 2: 3 "You *have* **made** *your* **w around** this hill H6015
Dt 4: 7 gods near them the **w** the LORD our God is H3869
Dt 8: 2 God led you all the **w** in the wilderness H2006
Dt 9:16 aside quickly from the **w** that the LORD had H2006
Dt 10:11 "and lead the people on their **w**, so that H5023
Dt 11:28 turn from the **w** that I command you H2006
Dt 12: 4 not worship the LORD your God **in** their **w**. H4027
Dt 12:31 not worship the LORD your God **in** their **w**, H4027
Dt 13: 5 to turn you from the **w** the LORD your God H2006
Dt 16:17 in proportion to **the w** the LORD your God H889S
Dt 17:16 "You are not to go back that **w** again." H2006
Dt 23: 4 water on your **w** when you came out H2006
Dt 24: 9 to Miriam along the **w** after you came out H2006
Dt 25:17 to you along the **w** when you came out of H2006
Dt 29:16 through the countries **on the w** here. H6296
Dt 29:19 I **persist** in going my **own w**, H9244+4213
Dt 31:29 to turn from the **w** I have commanded you H2006
Dt 32: 6 Is **this** *the* **w** you repay the LORD, you foolish AIT
Jos 2: 5 I don't know **which w** they went. H625+2025
Jos 2:16 until they return, and then go on your **w**." H2006
Jos 3: 4 Then you will know which **w** to go, since H2006
Jos 3: 4 since you have never been this **w** before. H2006
Jos 5: 4 wilderness on the **w** after leaving Egypt. H2006
Jos 5: 7 they had not been circumcised on the **w**. H2006
Jos 9:22 'We live a **long w** from you,' while H8158+4394
Jos 10:10 cut them down **all the w to** Azekah and H6330
Jos 11: 8 pursued them **all the w to** Greater Sidon, H6330
Jos 18: 8 the men started **on** *their* **w** to map out the H2143
Jos 23:14 I am about to go the **w** *of* all the earth. H2006
Jdg 2:22 they will keep the **w** *of* the LORD and walk H2006
Jdg 2:28 *he* **sent on** their **w** those who had carried H8938
Jdg 6: 4 ruined the crops **all the w to** Gaza and did H6330
Jdg 9:40 chased him **all the w to** the entrance of H6330
Jdg 11:13 to the Jabbok, **all the w to** the Jordan. H6330
Jdg 17: 8 **On his w** he came to Micah's H6913+2006
Jdg 18: 7 they lived a **long w** from the Sidonians H8158
Jdg 18:12 **On** *their* **w** they set up camp near Kiriath H6590
Jdg 18:26 So the Danites went their **w**, and Micah H2006
Jdg 18:28 they lived a **long w** from Sidon and had H8158
Jdg 19: 9 you can get up and be on your **w** home." H2006
Jdg 19:18 "We *are* **on** our **w** from Bethlehem in H6296
Jdg 19:27 stepped out to continue on his **w**, H2006
Jdg 20:36 of Israel had given **w** before Benjamin, H5226
1Sa 1:18 Then she went her **w** and ate something H2006
1Sa 6: 6 Israelites out so *they could* **go on** *their* **w**? H2143
1Sa 6: 8 him as a guilt offering. Send it **on** its **w**, H2143
1Sa 6:12 **keeping** on the road and lowing **all the w** H2143+2143
1Sa 7:11 them along the **w** to a point below Beth Kar. NDT
1Sa 9: 6 Perhaps he will tell us what **w** to take." H2006
1Sa 9: 8 God so that he will tell us what **w** to take." H2006
1Sa 9:14 toward them **on** *his* **w up** *to* the high H6590
1Sa 9:19 morning *I will* **send** you **on** your **w** and H8938
1Sa 9:26 "Get ready, and *I will* **send** you **on** *your* **w**." H8938
1Sa 12:23 I will teach you the **w** that is good and H2006
1Sa 15: 7 Amalekites **all the w** from Havilah **to** Shur, H995
1Sa 16: 1 Fill your horn with oil and **be on** *your* **w**; H2143
1Sa 24: 3 He came to the sheep pens along the **w** H2006
1Sa 24: 7 And Saul left the cave and went his **w**. H2006
1Sa 24:19 reward you well for **the w** you treated me H889S
1Sa 26:25 So David went on his **w**, and Saul H2006
1Sa 28:22 have the strength to go on your **w**. H2006
1Sa 30: 2 carried them off as they went on their **w**. H2006
2Sa 2:24 near Giah on the **w** *to* the wasteland of H2006
2Sa 3:16 weeping behind her **all the w** to Bahurim. H2143
2Sa 4: 7 they traveled all night **by w of** the Arabah. H2006
2Sa 5:25 **all the w** from Gibeon **to** Gezer. H6330+995
2Sa 12:21 asked him, "Why are you acting this **w**? H1821
2Sa 13:30 While they were on their **w**, the report H2006
2Sa 15: 6 Absalom behaved in this **w** toward all the H1821
2Sa 18:23 Then Ahimaaz ran *by* **w** *of* the plain and H2006
2Sa 19:31 king and to **send** him **on** his **w** *from* there. H8938
2Sa 19:36 should the king reward me in this **w**? H1692S
2Sa 20: 2 by their king **all the w from** the Jordan to H4946
2Sa 22:31 "As for God, his **w** is perfect: The LORD's H2006
2Sa 22:33 me with strength and keeps my **w** secure. H2006
2Sa 22:37 my feet, so that my ankles *do* not **give w**. H5048
1Ki 2: 2 "I am about to go the **w** *of* all the earth," H2006
1Ki 5:10 **In this w** Hiram kept Solomon supplied H2256
1Ki 6:33 **In the same w**, for the entrance to the H4027
1Ki 7:37 This is the **w** he made the ten stands H3869
1Ki 8:23 continue wholeheartedly **in** your **w**. H4200+7156
1Ki 8:36 Teach them the right **w** to live, and send H2006
1Ki 11:29 the prophet of Shiloh met him on the **w**, H2006
1Ki 13: 9 drink water or return by the **w** you came. H2006
1Ki 13:10 not return by the **w** he had come to Bethel H2006
1Ki 13:12 father asked them, "Which **w** did he go?" H2006
1Ki 13:17 water there or return by the **w** you came. H2006
1Ki 13:24 As *he* **went on** *his* **w**, a lion met him on H2143
1Ki 18:46 of Ahab **all the w to** Jezreel. H6330+995+3870
1Ki 19:15 "Go back the **w** you came, and go to H2006
1Ki 22:24 "**Which w** did the spirit from the LORD H361+2296
2Ki 2: 1 Elisha **were on** *their* **w** from Gilgal. H2143
2Ki 3:22 To the Moabites **across the w**, the H4946+5584

2Ki 4: 9 who often comes our **w** is a holy man of NDT
2Ki 8: 7 man of God has come **all the w up** here," H6330
2Ki 9:27 chariot on the **w up** *to* Gur near Ibleam, H5090
2Ki 10:15 son of Rekab, *who was on his* **w** *to* **meet** him. AIT
2Ki 11:19 entering *by* **w** *of* the gate of the guards. H2006
2Ki 19:28 I will make you return by the **w** you came. H2006
2Ki 19:33 By the **w** that he came he will return; he H2006
1Ch 7:28 its villages **all the w to** Ayyah and its H6330
1Ch 14:16 **all the w** from Gibeon **to** Gezer. H6330
1Ch 15:13 about how to do it in the **prescribed w**." H5477
1Ch 23:31 number and in the **w prescribed** for them. H5477
2Ch 6:14 continue wholeheartedly **in** your **w**. H4200+7156
2Ch 6:27 Teach them the right **w** to live, and send H2006
2Ch 18:23 "**Which w** did the spirit H361+2296+2021+2006
2Ch 23:19 one who was in any **w** unclean might H1821
2Ch 29:25 lyres in the **w prescribed** *by* David and H5184
Ezr 7:27 house of the LORD in Jerusalem **in** this **w** H3869
Ezr 8:31 from enemies and bandits along the **w**. H2006
Ezr 9: 2 *have* **led the w** in this H3338+2118+8037
Ne 5:13 "**In this w** may God shake out of their H3970
Ne 9:12 them light on the **w** they were to take. H2006
Ne 9:19 night to shine on the **w** they were to take. H2006
Ne 11:30 living **all the w** from Beersheba **to** the H6330
Est 1:18 to all the king's nobles in the same **w**. NDT
Est 3: 6 Haman looked for a **w** to destroy all NDT
Est 9:27 **in the w** prescribed and at the time H3869
Job 3:23 is life given to a man whose **w** is hidden, H2006
Job 8:15 the web, but *it* **gives w**; they cling H4202+6641
Job 19: 8 He has blocked my **w** so I cannot pass; he H784
Job 22:21 in this **w** prosperity will come to you. NDT
Job 23:10 But he knows the **w** that I take; when he H2006
Job 23:11 I have kept to his **w** without turning aside. H2006
Job 28:23 God understands the **w** *to* it and he alone H2006
Job 29:25 I chose the **w** *for* them and sat as their H2006
Job 32: 3 they had found no **w** to **refute** Job, H5101
Job 33:14 speak—now **one w**, now another— H928+285
Job 36:31 **This is the w** he governs the nations H928+4392
Job 38:19 "What is the **w** to the abode of light? And H2006
Job 38:24 What is the **w** to the place where the H2006
Job 38:35 you send the lightning bolts **on** *their* **w**? H2143
Ps 1: 1 stand in the **w** *that* sinners *take* or sit in H2006
Ps 1: 6 LORD watches over the **w** *of* the righteous, H2006
Ps 1: 6 the **w** *of* the wicked leads to H2006
Ps 2:12 will be angry and your **w** will lead to your H2006
Ps 5: 8 make your **w** straight before me. H2006
Ps 18:30 As for God, his **w** is perfect: The LORD's H2006
Ps 18:32 me with strength and keeps my **w** secure. H2006
Ps 18:36 my feet, so that my ankles *do* not **give w**. H5048
Ps 25: 9 in what is right and teaches them his **w**. H2006
Ps 27:11 Teach me your **w**, LORD; lead me in a H2006
Ps 32: 8 teach you in the **w** you should go; H2006
Ps 37: 5 Commit your **w** to the LORD; trust in him H2006
Ps 37:34 Hope in the LORD and keep his **w**. He will H2006
Ps 46: 2 though the earth **give w** and the H4614
Ps 77:19 the sea, your **w** through the mighty waters H8666
Ps 85:13 him and prepares the **w** *for* his steps. H2006
Ps 86:11 Teach me your **w**, LORD, that I may rely on H2006
Ps 107: 4 finding no **w** *to* a city where they could H2006
Ps 107: 7 them by a straight **w** to a city where they H2006
Ps 109:24 My knees **give w** from fasting; my body is H4173
Ps 110: 7 He will drink from a brook along the **w** H2006
Ps 119:27 me to understand the **w** *of* your precepts, H2006
Ps 119:30 I have chosen the **w** *of* faithfulness; I have H2006
Ps 119:33 the **w** *of* your decrees, that I may H2006
Ps 139:24 See if there is any offensive **w** in me, and H2006
Ps 139:24 and lead me in the **w** everlasting. H2006
Ps 142: 3 within me, it is you who watch over my **w**. H5986
Ps 143: 8 Show me the **w** I should go, for to you I H2006
Pr 2: 8 protects the **w** *of* his faithful ones. H2006
Pr 3:23 Then you will go on your **w** in safety, and H2006
Pr 4:11 instruct you in the **w** *of* wisdom and lead H2006
Pr 4:14 the wicked or walk in the **w** *of* evildoers. H2006
Pr 4:15 travel on it; turn from it and **go on** *your* **w**. H6296
Pr 4:19 But the **w** *of* the wicked is like deep H2006
Pr 5: 6 She gives no thought to the **w** *of* life; her H784
Pr 6:23 correction and instruction are the **w** *to* life, H2006
Pr 8: 2 At the highest point along the **w**, where H2006
Pr 8:20 I walk in the **w** *of* righteousness, along the H784
Pr 9: 6 you will live; walk in the **w** *of* insight." H2006
Pr 9:15 who pass by, who go straight on their **w**, H784
Pr 10:17 heeds discipline shows the **w** to life, H784
Pr 10:29 The **w** *of* the LORD is a refuge for the H2006
Pr 12:15 The **w** *of* fools seems right to them, but H2006
Pr 12:26 the **w** *of* the wicked leads them astray. H2006
Pr 12:28 In the **w** *of* righteousness there is life H784
Pr 13:15 the **w** *of* the unfaithful leads to their H2006
Pr 14:12 There is a **w** that appears to be right, but H2006
Pr 15: 9 The LORD detests the **w** *of* the wicked, but H2006
Pr 15:19 The **w** *of* the sluggard is blocked with H2006
Pr 16: 7 the LORD takes pleasure in anyone's **w**, H2006
Pr 16:25 There is a **w** that appears to be right, but H2006
Pr 16:31 it is attained in the **w** *of* righteousness. H2006
Pr 18:16 A gift **opens the w** and ushers the giver H8143
Pr 19: 2 how much more *will* hasty feet **miss the w**! H2627
Pr 20:24 then can anyone understand their own **w**? H2006
Pr 21: 8 The **w** *of* the guilty is devious, but the H2006
Pr 22: 6 Start children off on the **w** they *should go* H2006
Pr 25:26 the righteous *who* **give w** to the wicked. H4572
Pr 30:19 the **w** *of* an eagle in the sky, the way of a H2006
Pr 30:19 in the sky, the **w** *of* a snake on a rock H2006
Pr 30:19 the **w** *of* a ship on the high seas H2006
Pr 30:19 the **w** *of* a man with a young woman. H2006

Pr 30:20 "This is the **w** *of* an adulterous woman H2006
Ecc 10:15 they do not know the **w** to town. H2143
SS 6: 1 **Which w** did your beloved turn, that H625+2025
Isa 8:11 me not to follow the **w** *of* this people: H2006
Isa 9: 1 the nations, *by* the **W** *of* the Sea, beyond H2006
Isa 15: 4 their voices are heard **all the w to** Jahaz. H6330
Isa 22:25 peg driven into the firm place *will* **give w**; H4631
Isa 26: 7 make the **w** *of* the righteous smooth. H5047
Isa 26: 8 walking in the **w** *of* your laws, we wait H784
Isa 28:26 instructs him and teaches him the **right w**. H5477
Isa 30:11 Leave this **w**, get off this path, and stop H2006
Isa 30:21 saying, "This is the **w**; walk in it. H2006
Isa 35: 3 steady the knees *that* **give w**; H4173
Isa 35: 8 it will be called the **W** *of* Holiness; it will H2006
Isa 35: 8 it will be for those who walk on that **W**. H2006
Isa 37:29 I will make you return by the **w** you came. H2006
Isa 37:34 By the **w** that he came he will return; he H2006
Isa 40: 3 the wilderness prepare the **w** *for* the LORD; H2006
Isa 40:14 and who taught him the right **w**? H784
Isa 40:27 "My **w** is hidden from the LORD; my H2006
Isa 43:16 he who made a **w** through the sea, H2006
Isa 43:19 I am making a **w** in the wilderness and H2006
Isa 48:17 who directs you in the **w** you should go. H2006
Isa 51: 5 my salvation is **on the w**, and my arm will H3655
Isa 53: 6 each of us has turned to our own **w**; and H2006
Isa 56:11 they all turn to their own **w**, they seek H2006
Isa 57:14 the obstacles out of the **w** *of* my people." H2006
Isa 58:13 not going your own **w** and not doing as H2006
Isa 59: 8 The **w** *of* peace they do not know; there is H2006
Isa 59:10 **feeling** *our* **w** like people without eyes. H1779
Isa 62:10 Prepare the **w** *for* the people. Build H2006
Jer 2:17 LORD your God when he led you in the **w**? H2006
Jer 4: 2 just and **righteous** *w* you swear, 'As AIT
Jer 5: 4 they do not know the **w** *of* the LORD, the H2006
Jer 5: 5 surely they know the **w** *of* the LORD, the H2006
Jer 5:31 authority, and my people love it **this w**. H4027
Jer 6:16 ask where the good **w** is, and walk in it, H2006
Jer 12: 1 Why does the **w** *of* the wicked prosper H2006
Jer 13: 9 '**In the same w** I will ruin the pride of H3970
Jer 21: 8 before you the **w** *of* life and the way of H2006
Jer 21: 8 you the way of life and the **w** *of* death. H2006
Jer 22:21 This has been your **w** from your youth H2006
Jer 28:11 '**In the same w** I will break the yoke of H3970
Jer 28:11 the prophet Jeremiah went on his **w**. H2006
Jer 39: 4 the city at night *by* **w** *of* the king's garden, H2006
Jer 41:17 near Bethlehem *on their* **w** to Egypt H2143
Jer 50: 5 They will ask the **w** to Zion and turn their H2006
La 2:15 All who pass your **w** clap their hands at H2006
La 3: 9 He has barred my **w** with blocks of stone H2006
Eze 4:13 "**In this w** the people of Israel will eat H3970
Eze 18:25 "Yet you say, 'The **w** *of* the Lord is not just. H2006
Eze 18:25 you Israelites: Is my **w** unjust? Is it not H2006
Eze 18:29 'The **w** *of* the Lord is not just. H2006
Eze 20:30 defile yourselves the **w** your ancestors did H2006
Eze 23:13 both of them went the same **w**. H2006
Eze 23:31 You have gone the **w** *of* your sister; so I H2006
Eze 32: 6 flowing blood **all the w to** the mountains, H448
Eze 33:17 people say, 'The **w** *of* the Lord is not just. H2006
Eze 33:17 But it is their **w** that is not just. H2006
Eze 33:20 'The **w** *of* the Lord is not just. H2006
Eze 39:11 It *will* **block the w** *of* travelers, because H2888
Eze 44: 3 He is to enter by **w** *of* the portico of the H2006
Eze 44: 3 of the gateway and go out the same **w**." H2006
Eze 44: 4 man brought me *by* **w** *of* the north gate to H2006
Eze 46: 8 he is to come out the same **w**. H2006
Da 1: 8 permission not to defile himself this **w**. NDT
Da 3:29 no other god can save **in** this **w**. A10341
Da 12: 9 He replied, "**Go** *your* **w**, Daniel, because H2143
Da 12:13 "As for you, **go** *your* **w** till the end. H2143
Hos 2: 6 wall her in so that she cannot find her **w**. H5986
Hos 3: 3 I will *behave the same w* **toward** you." AIT
Am 6:14 oppress you all the **w** from Lebo Hamath to NDT
Mic 2:13 who breaks open the **w** will go up before NDT
Na 1: 3 His **w** is in the whirlwind and the storm H2006
Na 2: 5 picked troops, yet they stumble on their **w**. H2142
Na 2:10 knees **give w**, bodies tremble, H7211
Mal 2: 8 turned from the **w** and by your teaching H2006
Mal 3: 1 who will prepare the **w** before me. H2006
Mt 2: 9 the king, *they* **went on** *their* **w**, and the *G4513*
Mt 3: 3 'Prepare the **w** for the Lord, make *G3847*
Mt 4:15 of Naphtali, the **W** of the Sea, beyond *G3847*
Mt 5:12 for **in the same w** they persecuted the *G4048*
Mt 5:16 **In the same w**, let your light shine before *G4048*
Mt 5:25 Do it while you are still together on the **w** *G3847*
Mt 7: 2 For in **the same w** you judge others, you *G3210S*
Mt 8:28 so violent that no one could pass that **w**. *G3847*
Mt 11:10 who will prepare your **w** before you. *G3847*
Mt 15:32 or they may collapse on the **w**. *G3847*
Mt 17:12 **In the same w** the Son of Man is going to *G4048*
Mt 18:14 **In the same w** your Father in heaven is not *G4048*
Mt 19: 8 But it was not **this w** from the beginning. *G4048*
Mt 19:12 there are eunuchs who were born **that w**, *G4048*
Mt 20:17 On the **w**, he took the Twelve aside and *G3847*
Mt 21:18 *as* Jesus *was* **on** *his* **w back** to the city *G2056*
Mt 21:32 you to show you the **w** of righteousness, *G3847*
Mt 21:36 the tenants treated them **the same w**. *G6058*
Mt 21:46 *They* **looked for a w** to arrest him, but they *G2426*
Mt 22:16 that you teach the **w** of God in accordance *G3847*
Mt 23:28 **In the same w**, on the outside you appear *G4048*
Mt 25:10 "But *while* they *were* **on** *their* **w** to buy the *G599*
Mt 26:54 fulfilled that say it must happen **in this w**?" *G4048*
Mt 27:41 **In the same w** the chief priests, the *G3931*

Mt 27:44 **In the same w** the rebels who were *G3836+899*
Mt 28:11 *While* the women *were* **on** *their* **w**, some *G4513*
Mk 1: 2 ahead of you, who will prepare your **w**"— *G3847*
Mk 1: 3 'Prepare the **w** for the Lord, make *G3847*
Mk 7: 9 "You have a **fine w** of setting aside the *G2822*
Mk 8: 3 they will collapse on the **w**, because *G3847*
Mk 8:27 On the **w** he asked them, "Who do *G3847*
Mk 9:34 quiet because on the **w** they had argued *G3847*
Mk 10:17 As Jesus started on his **w**, a man ran up *G3847*
Mk 10:32 They were on their **w** up to Jerusalem *G3847*
Mk 10:32 with Jesus **leading the w**, and the *G1639+4575*
Mk 11:18 this and began looking for a **w** to kill him, *G4802*
Mk 12:12 the elders **looked for a w** to arrest him *G2426*
Mk 12:14 you teach the **w** of God in accordance *G3847*
Mk 15:21 was passing by **on** *his* **w** *in* from the *G2262*
Mk 15:31 **In the same w** the chief priests and the *G3931*
Mk 16: 2 sunrise, *they were* **on** *their* **w** to the tomb *G2262*
Lk 1:76 before the Lord to prepare the **w** for him, *G3847*
Lk 3: 4 'Prepare the **w** for the Lord, make *G3847*
Lk 4:30 through the crowd and **went on** *his* **w**. *G4513*
Lk 5:19 could not find a **w** to do this because of *G4481*
Lk 7:27 who will prepare your **w** before you. *G3847*
Lk 7:29 **acknowledged** *that* God's *w was* **right** *G1467*
Lk 8:14 but *as they* **go on** *their* **w** they are choked *G4513*
Lk 8:42 As Jesus *was* **on** *his* **w**, the crowds almost *G5632*
Lk 10:38 Jesus and his disciples *were* **on** *their* **w**, *G4513*
Lk 12:58 try hard to be reconciled on the **w**, or your *G3847*
Lk 13: 2 other Galileans because they suffered **this** *w*? AIT
Lk 13:22 teaching as he made his **w** to Jerusalem. *G4512*
Lk 14: 4 he healed him and **sent** him **on** his **w**. *G668*
Lk 14:19 of oxen, and *I'm* **on** *my* **w** to try them out. *G4513*
Lk 14:32 other is still a **long w off** and will ask for *G4522*
Lk 14:33 **In the same w**, those of you who do not *G4048*
Lk 15: 7 I tell you that **in the same w** there will be *G4048*
Lk 15:10 **In the same w**, I tell you, there is rejoicing *G4048*
Lk 15:20 "But *while* he *was* still a long **w off**, his *G600*
Lk 16:16 everyone *is* **forcing** *their* **w** into it. *G1041*
Lk 17:11 Now on *his* **w** to Jerusalem, Jesus *G4513*
Lk 18:39 Those *who* **led the w** rebuked him and *G4575*
Lk 19: 4 to see him, since Jesus was coming **that** *w*. AIT
Lk 19:48 they could not find **any w** to do it, *G3836+5515*
Lk 20:19 chief priests **looked for a w** to arrest him *G2426*
Lk 20:21 teach the **w** of God in accordance *G3847*
Lk 20:31 and **in the same w** the seven died *G6058*
Lk 22: 2 were looking for **some w** to get rid of *G4802*
Lk 22:20 **In the same w**, after the supper he took *G6058*
Lk 23: 5 in Galilee and has come **all the w** here." *G2401*
Lk 23:26 *who was* **on** *his* **w** in from the country *G2262*
Lk 24:35 two told what had happened on the **w**, *G3847*
Jn 1:23 'Make straight the **w** for the Lord.' *G3847*
Jn 4:30 of the town and **made** *their* **w** toward him. *G2262*
Jn 4:51 *While* he *was* still **on the w**, his servants *G2849*
Jn 7: 1 there *were* **looking for a w** to kill him. *G2426*
Jn 7:46 "No one ever spoke **the w** this man does," *G4048*
Jn 8:37 Yet *you are* **looking for a w** to kill me *G2426*
Jn 8:40 *you are* **looking for a w** to kill me *G2426*
Jn 10: 1 climbs in **by some other w**, is a thief *G249*
Jn 12:12 that Jesus *was* **on** *his* **w** to Jerusalem. *G2262*
Jn 14: 4 You know the **w** to the place where I am *G3847*
Jn 14: 5 are going, so how can we know the **w**?" *G3847*
Jn 14: 6 "I am the **w** and the truth and the life. *G3847*
Jn 15:21 will treat you **this w** because of my *G4047+4246*
Jn 18:22 "Is **this the w** you answer the high priest?" *G4048*
Jn 21: 1 by the Sea of Galilee. It happened **this w**: *G4048*
Ac 1:11 back **in the same w** you *G4048+4005+5573*
Ac 7: 6 God spoke to him **in this w**: 'For four *G4048*
Ac 8:27 on his **w** he met an Ethiopian eunuch NDT
Ac 8:28 and **on** *his* **w home** was sitting in his *G5715*
Ac 8:36 What *can* **stand in the w** *of* my being *G3266*
Ac 8:39 him again, but went on his **w** rejoicing. *G3847*
Ac 9: 2 found any there who belonged to the **W**, *G3847*
Ac 10:47 no one can **stand in the w** *of* their being *G3266*
Ac 11:17 I to think *that* I could **stand in** God's **w**?" *G3266*
Ac 13: 4 of them, **sent on** *their* **w** by the Holy Spirit *G1734*
Ac 14: 8 He had been **that w** from birth and had *G6000S*
Ac 14:16 he let all nations go their own **w**. *G3847*
Ac 15: 3 The church **sent** them **on** *their* **w**, and as *G4636*
Ac 16:17 who are telling you the **w** to be saved." *G3847*
Ac 17:22 I see that in **every w** you are very religious. *G4246*
Ac 18:25 had been instructed *in* the **w** of the Lord, *G3847*
Ac 18:26 explained to him the **w** of God more *G3847*
Ac 19: 9 to believe and publicly maligned the **W**. *G3847*
Ac 19:20 **In this w** the word of the Lord spread *G4048*
Ac 19:23 arose a great disturbance about the **W**. *G3847*
Ac 21: 5 to leave, we left and **continued on** *our* **w**. *G4513*
Ac 21:11 '**In this w** the Jewish leaders in Jerusalem *G4048*
Ac 21:15 we started **on** *our* **w up** to Jerusalem. *G326*
Ac 22: 4 the followers *of* this **W** to their death, *G3847*
Ac 24: 3 Everywhere and *in every w*, most excellent AIT
Ac 24:14 of our ancestors as a follower of the **W**, *G3847*
Ac 24:22 who was well acquainted with the **W** *G3847*
Ac 25: 3 an ambush to kill him along the **w**. *G3847*
Ac 26: 4 all know the **w** I *have* **lived** ever since I *G1052*
Ac 27:15 so *we* **gave w** to it and were driven along. *G2113*
Ac 27:44 **In this w** everyone reached land safely. *G4048*
Ro 1:10 will *the w may be* **opened** *for me* to come *G2338*
Ro 1:27 **In the same w** the men also abandoned *G3931*
Ro 3: 2 Much in every **w**! First of all, the Jews have *G5573*
Ro 3:17 the **w** of peace they do not know. *G3847*
Ro 5:12 and **in this w** death came to all people *G4048*
Ro 6:11 **In the same w**, count yourselves dead to *G4048*
Ro 7: 6 that we serve in the **new w** of the Spirit, *G2786*

Ro 7: 6 not *in* the **old w** of the written code. G4095
Ro 8:26 **In the same w**, the Spirit helps us in our G6058
Ro 9:31 pursued the law *as the w of* **righteousness**, AIT
Ro 11:26 and **in this w** all Israel will be saved. As it G4048
Ro 14:13 *to* **put** any stumbling block or obstacle *in the w* AIT
Ro 14:18 who serves Christ in **this** *w* is pleasing to God AIT
Ro 15:19 Jerusalem **all the w** around **to** Illyricum, G3588
Ro 15:25 *I am* **on** *my* w to Jerusalem in the service G4513
Ro 15:28 I will go to Spain and **visit** you **on the w**. G1328
Ro 16: 2 her in the Lord **in a w worthy** of his people G547
Ro 16:17 put **obstacles in** your w that are G4998
1Co 1: 5 in him you have been enriched in **every** *w*— AIT
1Co 2:11 **In the same w** no one knows the thoughts G4048
1Co 4:17 remind you *of* my **w of life** in Christ Jesus G3847
1Co 5: 3 As one who is present with you **in this w**, G4048
1Co 6: 4 from those whose w of life is scorned in NDT
1Co 7: 4 **In the same w**, the husband does not G3931
1Co 7:35 you may live in a **right** *w* in undivided AIT
1Co 8:12 against them **in this w** and wound their G4048
1Co 9:14 **In the same w**, the Lord has commanded G4048
1Co 9:24 Run **in such a w** as to get the prize G4048
1Co 10:13 will also provide a **w out** so that you can G1676
1Co 10:33 even as I try to please everyone *in* **every** *w* AIT
1Co 11:25 **In the same w**, after supper he took the G6058
1Co 11:32 when we are judged in this w by the Lord NDT
1Co 12:31 I will show you the most excellent **w**. G3847
1Co 14: 1 Follow the *w of* **love** and eagerly desire gifts AIT
1Co 14:40 be done in a fitting and **orderly w**. G2848+5423
1Co 16:11 **Send** him **on** his w in peace so that he G4636
2Co 1:16 to visit you **on** my **w to** Macedonia and to G1650
2Co 1:16 then *to have* you **send** me **on** my w to G4636
2Co 5:16 we once regarded Christ **in this w**, G2848+4922S
2Co 6: 4 of God we commend ourselves in **every** *w*: AIT
2Co 7: 9 so were **not** harmed **in any w** by us. G3594
2Co 8:20 any criticism **of the w** we administer this G5679
2Co 9:11 be enriched in **every** *w* so that you can be AIT
2Co 11: 6 made this perfectly clear to you in **every** *w*. AIT
2Co 11: 9 myself from being a burden to you in **any** *w*, AIT
2Co 11:18 are boasting **in the w** the world does, G2848
Gal 1:13 have heard *of* my previous **w of life** in G419
Gal 5:12 *they would go the whole w and* **emasculate** *themselves* AIT
Gal 6: 2 and **in this w** you will fulfill the law of G4048
Eph 1:23 of him who fills everything in **every** *w*. AIT
Eph 4:20 however, is not **the w of life** you learned G4048S
Eph 4:22 with regard to your former **w of life**, to put G419
Eph 5: 2 walk **in the w of** love, just as Christ G1877
Eph 5:28 **In this same w**, husbands ought to love G4048
Eph 6: 9 treat your slaves *in* the **same** *w*. Do not AIT
Php 1: 7 is right for me to feel **this** *w* about all of you, AIT
Php 1:18 The important thing is that in every **w** G5573
Php 1:20 hope that I will in **no w** be ashamed, G4029
Php 1:28 being frightened **in any w** by those who G3594
Php 4: 1 stand firm in the Lord **in this w**, dear G4048
Col 1: 6 **In the same w**, the gospel is bearing fruit G2777
Col 1:10 worthy of the Lord and please him in **every** *w*: AIT
Col 4: 5 Be wise *in* **the w** *you* **act** toward outsiders G4344
1Th 2:16 **In this w** they always heap up their G1650+3836
1Th 2:18 again—but Satan **blocked** our **w**. G1601
1Th 3: 4 And it turned out **that w**, as you well know G2777
1Th 3: 5 was afraid that **in some w** the tempter G4803
1Th 3:11 Lord Jesus clear the **w** for us to come to G3847
1Th 4: 4 control your own body **in** *a* **w** that is holy AIT
2Th 2: 3 Don't let anyone deceive you in any **w**, for G5573
2Th 2: 7 to do so till he is taken out of **the w**. G3545
2Th 3:16 you peace at all times and in every **w**. G5573
1Ti 3: 8 **In the same w**, deacons are to be worthy G6058
1Ti 3:11 **In the same w**, the women are to be G6058
1Ti 5:25 **In the same w**, good deeds are obvious G6058
1Ti 6:19 In this w they will lay up treasure for NDT
2Ti 3: 6 kind who **worm their w into** homes and G1905
2Ti 3:10 my teaching, my **w of life**, my purpose, G73
Titus 2: 3 women to be reverent in the **w they live**, G2949
Titus 2:10 so that in **every** *w* they will make the AIT
Titus 3:13 *to* **help** Zenas the lawyer and Apollos **on** *their* **w** G4636
Heb 2:17 fully human in **every** *w*, in order that he AIT
Heb 4:15 have one who has been tempted in **every** *w*, AIT
Heb 5: 5 **In the same w**, Christ did not take on G4048
Heb 9: 8 by this that the **w** into the Most Holy Place G3847
Heb 9:21 **In the same w**, he sprinkled with the blood G3931
Heb 9:25 **the w** the high priest enters the Most Holy G6061
Heb 10:20 *by* a new and living **w** opened for us G3847
Heb 13: 7 the outcome *of* their **w of life** and imitate G419
Heb 13:18 desire to live honorably in **every** *w*. AIT
Jas 1:11 **In the same w**, the rich will fade away G4048
Jas 2:17 **In the same w**, faith by itself, if it is not G4048
Jas 2:25 **In the same w**, was not even Rahab the G3931
Jas 5:20 from the error *of* their **w** will save them G3847
1Pe 1:18 from the empty **w of life** handed down to G419
1Pe 3: 1 **in the same w** submit yourselves to your G3931
1Pe 3: 5 For **this is the w** the holy women of the G4048
1Pe 3: 6 do what is right and *do* not **give w to** fear. G5828
1Pe 3: 7 **in the same w** be considerate as you live G3931
1Pe 5: 5 **In the same w**, you who are younger G3931
2Pe 2: 2 will bring the **w** of truth into disrepute G3847
2Pe 2:15 left the straight **w** and wandered off to G3847
2Pe 2:15 off to follow the w of Balaam son of Bezer G3847
2Pe 2:21 not to have known the **w** of righteousness, G3847
2Pe 3:11 everything will be destroyed **in this w**, G4048
2Pe 3:16 He writes **the same w** in all his G6055+2779
3Jn 6 Please **send** them **on** their **w** in a G4472+4636
Jude 7 *In* a similar **w**, Sodom and Gomorrah and G5573
Jude 8 **In the** very **same w**, on the strength of G3931
Jude 11 They have taken the **w** of Cain; they have G3847
Rev 16:12 up to prepare the **w** for the kings from the G3847

WAYFARING (KJV) TRAVELER, TRAVELERS

WAYLAID (1)

1Sa 15: 2 when *they* **w** them as H8492+928+2021+2006

WAYS (213) [WAY]

Ge 6:12 people on earth had corrupted their **w**. H2006
Ex 33:13 teach me your **w** so I may know you and H2006
Lev 6: 4 sin in any of these **w** and realize their guilt, NDT
Lev 18:24 " 'Do not defile yourselves in any of **these** *w* AIT
Lev 25:54 someone is not redeemed in any of **these** *w*, AIT
Dt 18: 9 to imitate the **detestable w** *of* the nations H9359
Dt 32: 4 works are perfect, and all his **w** are just. H2006
Jdg 2:17 turned from the **w** *of* their ancestors, H2006
Jdg 2:19 people returned to **w** even more corrupt NDT
Jdg 2:19 up their evil practices and stubborn **w**. H2006
1Sa 8: 3 But his sons did not follow his **w**. H2006
1Sa 8: 5 your sons do not follow your **w**; now H2006
2Sa 14:14 he devises **w** so that a banished person H4742
2Sa 22:22 For I have kept the **w** *of* the LORD; I am not H2006
1Ki 13:33 Jeroboam did not change his evil **w**, but H2006
1Ki 15:26 following the **w** *of* his father and H2006
1Ki 15:34 following the **w** *of* Jeroboam and H2006
1Ki 16: 2 you followed the **w** *of* Jeroboam and H2006
1Ki 16:19 following the **w** *of* Jeroboam and H2006
1Ki 16:26 completely the **w** *of* Jeroboam son of H2006
1Ki 22:43 he followed the **w** *of* his father Asa and H2006
1Ki 22:52 he followed the **w** *of* his father and H2006
2Ki 8:18 He followed the **w** *of* the kings of Israel, as H2006
2Ki 8:27 He followed the **w** *of* the house of Ahab H2006
2Ki 16: 3 He followed the **w** *of* the kings of Israel H2006
2Ki 17:13 "Turn from your evil **w**. Observe my H2006
2Ki 21:21 He followed completely the **w** of his father, H2006
2Ki 22: 2 completely the **w** *of* his father David, H2006
2Ch 7:14 my face and turn from their wicked **w**, H2006
2Ch 11:17 following the **w** *of* David and Solomon H2006
2Ch 17: 3 he followed the **w** *of* his father David H2006
2Ch 17: 6 His heart was devoted to the **w** *of* the LORD H2006
2Ch 20:32 He followed the **w** *of* his father Asa and H2006
2Ch 20:35 king of Israel, whose **w** were wicked. H6913
2Ch 21: 6 He followed the **w** *of* the kings of Israel, as H2006
2Ch 21:12 have not followed the **w** *of* your father H2006
2Ch 21:13 have followed the **w** *of* the kings of Israel, H2006
2Ch 22: 3 too followed the **w** *of* the house of Ahab, H2006
2Ch 28: 2 He followed the **w** *of* the kings of Israel H2006
2Ch 28:26 other events of his reign and all his **w**, H2006
2Ch 34: 2 followed the **w** *of* his father David, H2006
Ne 9:35 did not serve you or turn from their evil **w**. H5095
Est 5:11 all **the w** the king had honored him H889S
Job 4: 6 your blameless **w** your hope? H2006
Job 13:15 I will surely defend my **w** to his face. H2006
Job 17: 9 the righteous will hold to their **w**, and H2006
Job 21:14 We have no desire to know your **w**. H2006
Job 22: 3 would he gain if your **w** were blameless? H2006
Job 22:28 be done, and light will shine on your **w**. H2006
Job 24:13 who do not know its **w** or stay in its paths. H2006
Job 24:23 of security, but his eyes are on their **w**. H2006
Job 27:11 **the w** of the Almighty I will not conceal. H889S
Job 31: 4 Does he not see my **w** and count my every H2006
Job 34:21 "His eyes are on the **w** *of* mortals; he sees H2006
Job 34:27 him and had no regard for any of his **w**. H2006
Job 36:23 Who has prescribed his **w** for him, or said H2006
Job 37: 5 God's voice thunders *in* **marvelous** *w*; he AIT
Ps 10: 5 His **w** are always prosperous; your laws H2006
Ps 17: 4 myself from the **w** *of* the violent through H784
Ps 18:21 For I have kept the **w** *of* the LORD; I am not H2006
Ps 25: 4 Show me your **w**, LORD, teach me your paths H784
Ps 25: 7 the sins of my youth and my **rebellious** *w*; AIT
Ps 25: 8 therefore he instructs sinners in his **w**. H2006
Ps 25:10 All the **w** *of* the LORD are loving and faithful H784
Ps 25:12 instruct them in the **w** they should choose. H2006
Ps 37: 7 not fret when people succeed in their **w**, H2006
Ps 37:14 to slay those whose **w** are upright. H2006
Ps 39: 1 "I will watch my **w** and keep my tongue H2006
Ps 51:13 Then I will teach transgressors your **w**, so H2006
Ps 53: 1 and their **w** are vile; there is no H6404
Ps 67: 2 so that your **w** may be known on earth H2006
Ps 77:13 Your **w**, God, are holy. What god is as H2006
Ps 81:13 if Israel would only follow my **w**, H2006
Ps 91:11 concerning you to guard you in all your **w**; H2006
Ps 95:10 go astray, and they have not known my **w**. H2006
Ps 103: 7 He made known his **w** to Moses, his H2006
Ps 107:17 their rebellious **w** and suffered affliction H2006
Ps 119: 1 Blessed are those whose **w** are blameless, H2006
Ps 119: 3 they do no wrong but follow his **w**. H2006
Ps 119: 5 that my **w** were steadfast in obeying your H2006
Ps 119:15 on your precepts and consider your **w**. H784
Ps 119:26 an account of my **w** and you answered me H2006
Ps 119:29 Keep me from deceitful **w**; be gracious to H2006
Ps 119:59 considered my **w** and have turned my H2006
Ps 119:168 statutes, for all my **w** are known to you. H2006
Ps 125: 5 those who turn to **crooked w** the LORD will H6824
Ps 138: 5 May they sing of the **w** *of* the LORD, for the H2006
Ps 139: 3 you are familiar with all my **w**. H2006
Ps 140: 4 the violent, who **devise w** to trip my feet. H3108
Ps 145:17 righteous in all his **w** and faithful in all he H2006
Ps 146: 9 he frustrates the **w** *of* the wicked. H2006
Pr 1:22 you who are simple love your **simple w**? H7344
Pr 1:31 the fruit of their **w** and be filled with the H2006
Pr 2:12 will save you from the **w** *of* wicked men, H2006
Pr 2:13 left the straight paths to walk in dark **w**, H2006
Pr 2:15 crooked and who are devious in their **w**. H5047
Pr 2:20 will walk in the **w** *of* the good and keep H2006
Pr 3: 6 in all your **w** submit to him, and he will H2006
Pr 3:17 Her **w** are pleasant ways, and all her H2006
Pr 3:17 Her ways are pleasant **w**, and all her H2006
Pr 3:31 envy the violent or choose any of their **w**. H2006
Pr 4:26 your feet and be steadfast in all your **w**. H2006
Pr 5:21 For your **w** are in full view of the LORD, H2006
Pr 6: 6 you sluggard; consider its **w** and be wise! H2006
Pr 7:25 your heart turn to her **w** or stray into her H2006
Pr 8:32 blessed are those who keep my **w**. H2006
Pr 9: 6 Leave your **simple w** and you will live H7344
Pr 11:20 delights in those whose **w** are blameless. H2006
Pr 14: 2 who despise him are devious in their **w**. H2006
Pr 14: 8 the prudent is to give thought to their **w**, H2006
Pr 14:14 faithless will be fully repaid for their **w**, H2006
Pr 16: 2 All a person's **w** seem pure to them, but H2006
Pr 16:17 who guard their **w** preserve their lives. H2006
Pr 19:16 shows contempt for their **w** will die. H2006
Pr 21: 2 A person may think their own **w** are right H2006
Pr 21:29 the upright give thought to their **w**. H2006
Pr 22:25 you may learn their **w** and get yourself H784
Pr 23:26 heart and let your eyes delight in my **w**, H2006
Pr 28: 6 than the rich whose **w** are perverse. H2006
Pr 28:18 the one whose **w** are perverse will fall H2006
Ecc 11: 9 Follow the **w** *of* your heart and whatever H2006
Isa 2: 3 He will teach us his **w**, so that we may H2006
Isa 42:16 lead the blind by **w** they have not known, H2006
Isa 42:24 For they would not follow his **w**; they did H2006
Isa 45:13 I will make all his **w** straight. He will H2006
Isa 55: 7 forsake their **w** and the unrighteous H2006
Isa 55: 8 neither are your **w** my ways," declares the H2006
Isa 55: 8 neither are your ways my **w**," declares the H2006
Isa 55: 9 so are my **w** higher than your ways and H2006
Isa 55: 9 higher than your **w** and my thoughts than H2006
Isa 57:17 yet they kept on in their willful **w**. H2006
Isa 57:18 I have seen their **w**, but I will heal them; H2006
Isa 58: 2 they seem eager to know my **w**, as if they H2006
Isa 59: 7 schemes; acts of violence mark their **w**. H5019
Isa 63:17 us wander from your **w** and harden our H2006
Isa 64: 5 gladly do right, who remember your **w**. H2006
Isa 65: 2 people, who walk in **w** not good, pursuing H2006
Isa 66: 3 They have chosen their own **w**, and they H2006
Jer 2:33 worst of women can learn from your **w**. H2006
Jer 2:36 you go about so much, changing your **w**? H2006
Jer 3:21 have perverted their **w** and have forgotten H2006
Jer 6:27 that you may observe and test their **w**. H2006
Jer 7: 3 Reform your **w** and your actions, and I will H2006
Jer 7: 5 really change your **w** and your actions H2006
Jer 10: 2 "Do not learn the **w** *of* the nations or be H2006
Jer 12:16 they learn well the **w** *of* my people and H2006
Jer 15: 7 they have not changed their **w**. H2006
Jer 16:17 My eyes are on all their **w**; they are not H2006
Jer 18:11 So turn from your evil **w**, each one of you H2006
Jer 18:11 and reform your **w** and your actions. H2006
Jer 18:15 which made them stumble in their **w**, in H2006
Jer 23:22 them from their evil **w** and from their evil H2006
Jer 25: 5 from your evil **w** and your evil practices H2006
Jer 26: 3 listen and each will turn from their evil **w**. H2006
Jer 26:13 Now reform your **w** and your actions and H2006
Jer 32:19 eyes are open to the **w** *of* all mankind; H2006
Jer 35:15 turn from your wicked **w** and reform your H2006
Jer 36: 3 they will each turn from their wicked **w** H2006
Jer 36: 7 will each turn from their wicked **w**, H2006
La 3:40 Let us examine our **w** and test them, and H2006
Eze 3:18 them from their evil **w** in order to save H2006
Eze 3:19 from their wickedness or from their evil **w**, H2006
Eze 13:22 turn from their evil **w** and so save their H2006
Eze 16:47 not only followed their **w** and copied their H2006
Eze 16:47 in all your **w** you soon became more H2006
Eze 16:61 will remember your **w** and be ashamed H2006
Eze 18:23 when they turn from their **w** and live? H2006
Eze 18:25 Is it not your **w** that are unjust? H2006
Eze 18:29 Are my **w** unjust, people of H2006
Eze 18:29 Is it not your **w** that are unjust? H2006
Eze 18:30 each of you according to your own **w**, H2006
Eze 20:44 according to your evil **w** and your corrupt H2006
Eze 28:15 blameless in your **w** from the day you H2006
Eze 33: 8 speak out to dissuade them from their **w**, H2006
Eze 33: 9 to turn from their **w** and they do not do so, H2006
Eze 33:11 rather that they turn from their **w** and live. H2006
Eze 33:11 Turn from your evil **w**! Why will you die, H2006
Eze 33:20 each of you according to your own **w**." H2006
Eze 36:31 remember your evil **w** and wicked deeds, H2006
Da 4:37 he does is right and all his **w** are just. A10068
Da 5:23 in his hand your life and all your **w**. A10068
Hos 4: 9 of them for their **w** and repay them for H2006
Hos 4:18 their rulers dearly love **shameful w**. H7830
Hos 12: 2 Jacob according to his **w** and repay him H2006
Hos 14: 9 The **w** *of* the LORD are right; the righteous H2006
Jnh 3: 8 give up their evil **w** and their violence. H2006
Jnh 3:10 did and how they turned from their evil **w**, H2006
Mic 2: 7 do good to the *one whose* **w** are upright? H2143
Mic 4: 2 He will teach us his **w**, so that we may H2006
Hag 1: 5 "Give careful thought to your **w**. H2006
Hag 1: 7 "Give careful thought to your **w**. H2006
Zec 1: 4 'Turn from your evil **w** and your evil H2006
Zec 1: 6 done to us what our **w** and practices H2006

Mal 2: 9 have not followed my **w** but have shown H2006
Lk 3: 5 become straight, the rough **w** smooth. *G3847*
Ac 3:26 turning each of you from your **wicked w.**" *G4504*
Ac 13:10 stop perverting the right **w** of the Lord? *G3847*
Ac 18:13 to worship God *in w* **contrary to** the law." AIT
Ac 28:10 They honored us *in* **many** *w*; and when we AIT
Ro 1:30 they invent *w of doing* **evil**; they disobey their AIT
Ro 3:16 ruin and misery mark their **w,** *G3847*
1Co 13:11 I put **the** *w* of childhood behind me. AIT
2Co 4: 2 we have renounced secret and **shameful** *w* AIT
2Co 8:22 proved to us in **many** *w* that he is zealous, AIT
Eph 2: 2 you followed the **w** of this world and of *G172*
Col 3: 7 You used to walk in **these w**, in the life *G4005S*
2Th 2:10 **all** *the w* that wickedness deceives those AIT
2Ti 1:18 know very well *in* **how many** *w* he helped me AIT
Heb 1: 1 prophets at many times and **in various w,** *G4502*
Heb 3:10 and they have not known my **w.** *G3847*
Jas 3: 2 We all stumble in **many** *w*. Anyone who is AIT
Rev 2:22 intensely, unless they repent of her **w.** *G2240*
Rev 15: 3 Just and true are your **w**, King of the *G3847*

WAYWARD (7) [WAYWARDNESS]

Ps 58: 3 from the womb *they are* **w**, spreading lies. H9494
Pr 2:16 from the **w** *woman* with her seductive H5799
Pr 5:20 Why embrace the bosom of a **w** *woman*? H5799
Pr 6:24 from the smooth talk of a **w** *woman*. H5799
Pr 7: 5 from the **w** *woman* with her seductive H5799
Pr 23:27 a deep pit, and a **w** *wife* is a narrow well. H5799
Isa 29:24 *Those who are* **w** *in* spirit will gain H9494

WAYWARDNESS (2) [WAYWARD]

Pr 1:32 For the **w** *of* the simple will kill them, and H5412
Hos 14: 4 "I will heal their **w** and love them freely H5412

WE (1891) [OUR, OURS, OURSELVES, US, WE'LL, WE'RE, WE'VE] See Index of Articles Etc.

WE'LL (13) [BE, WE]

Ge 19: 9 play the judge! *W* **treat** you **worse** than them." AIT
Ge 34:16 *W* **settle** among you and become one AIT
Ge 34:17 to be circumcised, *w* **take** our sister and go." AIT
Ge 37:20 Then *w* **see** what comes of his dreams." AIT
Jdg 8:25 answered, "*W be* **glad to give** them." So they AIT
Jdg 16: 2 the night, saying, "At dawn *w* **kill** him." AIT
Jdg 20: 9 But now this is what *w* **do** to Gibeah: We'll AIT
Jdg 20: 9 **W** go up against it in the order decided by NDT
Jdg 20:10 *W* **take** ten men out of every hundred from all AIT
1Sa 14:12 "Come up to us and *w* **teach** you a lesson." AIT
2Ki 6:28 eat him today, and tomorrow *w* **eat** my son. AIT
2Ki 7: 4 If we say, '*W* **go into** the city'—the famine is AIT
Jn 21: 3 told them, and they said, "**W** go with you." *G1609*

WE'RE (6) [BE, WE]

Ge 29: 4 "**W** from Harran," they replied. H636
Jdg 12: 1 *W going to* **burn down** your house over your AIT
1Sa 4: 8 **W** doomed! Who will deliver us from the H5646
2Ki 7: 9 to each other, "What **w** doing is not right. H636
Mt 8:25 "Lord, save us! *W going to* **drown**!" AIT
Lk 8:24 "Master, Master, *w going to* **drown**! AIT

WE'VE (3) [HAS, WE]

Ge 26:32 They said, "*W* **found** water!" AIT
Jdg 15:12 "*W* **come** to tie you up and hand you over to AIT
Lk 5: 5 *w* **worked hard** all night and haven't caught AIT

WEAK (63) [WEAKENED, WEAKENING, WEAKER, WEAKEST, WEAKLING, WEAKLINGS, WEAKNESS, WEAKNESSES]

Ge 27: 1 old and his eyes *were so* **w** that he could H3908
Ge 29:17 Leah had **w** eyes, but Rachel had a lovely H8205
Ge 30:42 if the animals *were* **w**, he would not H6494
Ge 30:42 So the **w** animals went to Laban and the H6488
Nu 13:18 the people who live there are strong or **w**, H8333
Dt 34: 7 his eyes *were* not **w** nor his strength H3908
Jdg 16: 7 I'll become as **w** as any other man." H2703
Jdg 16:11 I'll become as **w** as any other man." H2703
Jdg 16:13 I'll become as **w** as any other man." H2703
Jdg 16:17 I would become as **w** as any other man." H2703
1Sa 3: 2 eyes were becoming *so* **w** that he could H3910
1Sa 15: 9 that was despised and **w** they totally H5022
2Sa 3:39 anointed king, I am **w**, and these sons of H8205
2Sa 17: 2 him while he is weary and **w**. H8333+3338
2Ch 28:15 All *those who were* **w** they put on donkeys H4173
Ne 6: 9 "Their hands *will get* too **w** for the work H8332
Ps 6: 7 My eyes *grow* **w** with sorrow; they fail H6949
Ps 10: 2 the wicked man hunts down the **w**, H6714
Ps 31: 9 distress; my eyes *grow* **w** with sorrow, my H6949
Ps 31:10 of my affliction, and my bones *grow* **w**. H6949
Ps 34:10 The lions *may grow* **w** and hungry, but H8133
Ps 41: 1 are those who have regard for the **w**; H1924
Ps 72:13 will take pity on the **w** and the needy and H1924
Ps 82: 3 Defend the **w** and the fatherless; uphold H1924
Ps 82: 4 Rescue the **w** and the needy; deliver them H1924
Ps 102: T person *who has grown* **w** and pours out a H6494
Isa 14:10 "You also *have become* **w**, as we are; H2703
Isa 38:14 My eyes *grew* **w** as I looked to the H1937
Isa 40:29 increases the power of the **w**. H401+226
Eze 29:15 *I will* **make** it *so* **w** that it will never again H5070
Eze 34: 4 not strengthened the **w** or healed the sick H2703
Eze 34:16 bind up the injured and strengthen the **w**, H2703
Eze 34:21 butting all the **w** sheep with your horns H2703
Da 5: 6 that his legs *became* **w** and his knees A10742
Da 10:16 my lord, and *I* **feel very w**. H4202+6806+3946
Mt 26:41 The spirit is willing, but the flesh is **w**." *G822*
Mk 14:38 The spirit is willing, but the flesh is **w**." *G822*
Ac 20:35 this kind of hard work we must help the **w**, *G820*
Ro 14: 1 Accept the *one* whose faith *is* **w**, without *G820*
Ro 14: 2 another, whose faith *is* **w**, eats only *G820*
Ro 15: 1 with the failings *of* the **w** and not to please *G105*
1Co 1:27 God chose the **w** *things* of the world to *G822*
1Co 4:10 We are **w**, but you are strong *G822*
1Co 8: 7 since their conscience is **w**, it is defiled *G822*
1Co 8: 9 not become a stumbling block *to* the **w**. *G822*
1Co 8:10 if someone with a **w** conscience sees you, *G822*
1Co 8:11 So this **w** brother or sister, for whom Christ *G820*
1Co 8:12 in this way and wound their **w** conscience, *G820*
1Co 9:22 *To* the **w** I became weak, to win the weak. *G822*
1Co 9:22 To the weak I became **w**, to win the weak. *G822*
1Co 9:22 to win the **w**. I have become all *G822*
1Co 11:30 is why many among you are **w** and sick, *G822*
2Co 11:21 shame I admit that we *were too* **w** for that! *G820*
2Co 11:29 Who *is* **w**, and I do not feel weak? Who is *G820*
2Co 11:29 is weak, and *I do* not *feel* **w**? Who is led *G820*
2Co 12:10 For when *I am* **w**, then I am strong. *G820*
2Co 13: 3 He *is* not **w** in dealing with you, but is *G820*
2Co 13: 4 Likewise, we *are* **w** in him, yet by God's *G820*
2Co 13: 9 glad whenever we *are* **w** but you are strong *G820*
Gal 4: 9 back to those **w** and miserable forces? *G822*
1Th 5:14 disheartened, help the **w**, be patient with *G822*
Heb 7:18 is set aside because it was **w** and useless *G822*
Heb 12:12 strengthen your feeble arms and **w** knees. *G4168*

WEAKENED (2) [WEAK]

Job 18: 7 The vigor of his step *is* **w**; his own H7674
Ro 8: 3 to do because *it was* **w** by the flesh, *G820*

WEAKENING (1) [WEAK]

Ro 4:19 Without **w** in his faith, he faced the fact that *G820*

WEAKER (4) [WEAK]

2Sa 3: 1 of Saul **grew w and weaker**. H2143+2256+1924
2Sa 3: 1 of Saul **grew weaker and w**. H2143+2256+1924
1Co 12:22 body that seem to be **w** are indispensable, *G822*
1Pe 3: 7 with respect as the **w** partner and as heirs *G822*

WEAKEST (1) [WEAK]

Jdg 6:15 My clan is the **w** in Manasseh, and I am H1924

WEAKLING (1) [WEAK]

Joel 3:10 Let the **w** say, "I am strong!" H2766

WEAKLINGS (4) [WEAK]

Isa 19:16 Egyptians will become **w**. H3869+2021+851S
Jer 50:37 They will become **w**. A sword against her H851S
Jer 51:30 is exhausted; they have become **w**. H851S
Na 3:13 troops—they are all **w**. The gates of your H851S

WEAKNESS (11) [WEAK]

La 1: 6 in **w** they have fled before the H4202+3946
Ro 8:26 the same way, the Spirit helps us *in* our **w**. *G819*
1Co 1:25 the **w** of God is stronger than human *G822*
1Co 2: 3 I came to you in **w** with great fear and *G819*
1Co 15:43 it is sown in **w**, it is raised in power; *G819*
2Co 11:30 I will boast of the things that *show* my **w**. *G819*
2Co 12: 9 for my power is made perfect in **w**. *G819*
2Co 13: 4 he was crucified in **w**, yet he lives by God's *G819*
Heb 5: 2 since he himself is subject to **w**. *G819*
Heb 7:28 appoints as high priests men in all their **w**; *G819*
Heb 11:34 the sword; whose **w** was turned to strength *G819*

WEAKNESSES (4) [WEAK]

2Co 12: 5 not boast about myself, except about my **w**. *G819*
2Co 12: 9 I will boast all the more gladly about my **w**, *G819*
2Co 12:10 I delight in **w**, in insults, in hardships, *G819*
Heb 4:15 who is unable to empathize with our **w**, *G819*

WEALTH (118) [WEALTHY]

Ge 26:13 his **w** continued to grow until he H1541
Ge 31: 1 has gained all this **w** from what belonged H3883
Ge 31:16 Surely all the **w** that God took away from H6948
Ge 34:29 carried off all their **w** and all their women H2657
Dt 8:17 of my hands have produced this **w** for me." H2657
Dt 8:18 he who gives you the ability to produce **w**, H2657
Jos 22: 8 "Return to your homes with your great **w** H5794
1Sa 2: 7 The LORD sends poverty and **w**; he H6947
1Sa 17:25 king *will* **give** great **w** *to* the man H6947+6948
1Ki 3:11 this and not for long life or **w** for yourself, H6948
1Ki 3:13 not asked for—both **w** and honor—so that H6948
1Ki 10: 7 in wisdom and **w** you have far exceeded H3202
1Ch 29:12 **W** and honor come from you; you are the H6948
1Ch 29:28 having enjoyed long life, **w** and honor. H6948
2Ch 1:11 desire and you have not asked for **w**, H6948
2Ch 1:12 And I will also give you **w**, possessions H6948
2Ch 17: 5 so that he had great **w** and honor. H6948
2Ch 18: 1 Now Jehoshaphat had great **w** and honor H6948
2Ch 32:27 Hezekiah had very great **w** and honor H6948
Est 1: 4 displayed the vast **w** *of* his kingdom and H6948
Est 5:11 Haman boasted to them about his vast **w** H6948
Job 5: 5 and the thirsty pant after his **w**. H2657
Job 6:22 pay a ransom for me from your **w**, H3946
Job 15:29 longer be rich and his **w** will not endure, H2657
Job 20:10 his own hands must give back his **w**. H226
Job 22:20 are destroyed, and fire devours their **w**. H3856
Job 31:25 if I have rejoiced over my great **w**, the H2657
Job 36:19 Would your **w** or even all your mighty H8782
Ps 37:16 have than the **w** *of* many wicked; H2162
Ps 39: 6 **heaping up w** without knowing whose it H7392
Ps 39:11 you consume their **w** like a moth—surely H2773
Ps 45:12 people *of* **w** will seek your favor. H6938
Ps 49: 6 who trust in their **w** and boast of their H2657
Ps 49:10 also perish, leaving their **w** to others. H2657
Ps 49:12 despite their **w**, do not endure; they H3702
Ps 49:20 People who have **w** but lack H3702
Ps 52: 7 trusted in his great **w** and grew strong by H6948
Ps 73:12 free of care, they go on amassing **w**. H2657
Ps 112: 3 **W** and riches are in their houses, and H2104
Pr 3: 9 Honor the LORD with your **w**, with the H2104
Pr 5:10 feast on your **w** and your toil enrich H3946
Pr 6:31 though it costs him all the **w** *of* his house. H2104
Pr 8:18 honor, enduring **w** and prosperity. H2104
Pr 10: 4 poverty, but diligent hands **bring w**. H6947
Pr 10:15 The **w** *of* the rich is their fortified city, but H2104
Pr 10:22 The blessing of the LORD **brings w**, H6947
Pr 11: 4 **W** is worthless in the day of wrath, but H2104
Pr 11:16 but ruthless men gain only **w**. H6948
Pr 13: 7 pretends to be poor, yet has great **w**. H2104
Pr 13:22 a sinner's **w** is stored up for the H2657
Pr 14:24 The **w** *of* the wise is their crown, but the H6948
Pr 15:16 fear of the LORD than great **w** with turmoil. H238
Pr 18:11 The **w** *of* the rich is their fortified city; they H2104
Pr 19: 4 **W** attracts many friends, but even the H2104
Pr 19:14 Houses and **w** are inherited from parents H2104
Pr 22:16 poor to increase his **w** and one who gives NDT
Pr 28: 8 Whoever increases **w** by taking interest H2104
Pr 29: 3 companion of prostitutes squanders his **w**. H2104
Ecc 2:26 gathering and **storing up w** to hand it over H4043
Ecc 4: 8 his eyes were not content with his **w**. H6948
Ecc 5:10 whoever loves **w** is never satisfied with H2162
Ecc 5:13 **w** hoarded to the harm of its owners H6948
Ecc 5:14 **w** lost through some misfortune, so that H6948
Ecc 5:19 God gives someone **w** and possessions, H6948
Ecc 6: 2 God gives some people **w**, possessions H6948
Ecc 9:11 come to the wise or **w** to the brilliant or H6948
SS 8: 7 were to give all the **w** *of* one's house for H2104
Isa 8: 4 the **w** *of* Damascus and the plunder of H2657
Isa 10:14 my hand reached for the **w** *of* the nations; H2657
Isa 15: 7 So the **w** they have acquired and stored H3860
Isa 60: 5 the **w** *on* the seas will be brought to you H2162
Isa 60:11 may bring you the **w** *of* the nations— H2657
Isa 61: 6 You will feed on the **w** *of* nations, and in H2657
Isa 66:12 the **w** *of* nations like a flooding H3883
Jer 15:13 "Your **w** and your treasures I will give as H2657
Jer 17: 3 in the land and your **w** and all your H2657
Jer 20: 5 I will deliver all the **w** *of* this city into the H2890
Jer 48:36 The **w** they acquired is gone H3860
Eze 7:11 crowd—none of their **w**, nothing of value. H2155
Eze 7:21 I will give **their w** as plunder to H2257S
Eze 26:12 They will plunder your **w** and loot your H2657
Eze 27:12 you because of your great **w of goods**; H2104
Eze 27:18 your many products and great **w of goods**. H2104
Eze 27:27 Your **w**, merchandise and wares, your H2104
Eze 27:33 with your great **w** and your wares you H2104
Eze 28: 4 you have gained **w** for yourself and H2657
Eze 28: 5 skill in trading you have increased your **w**, H2657
Eze 28: 5 because of your **w** your heart has H2657
Eze 29:19 king of Babylon, and he will carry off its **w**. H2162
Eze 30: 4 her **w** will be carried away and her H2162
Da 11: 2 When he has gained power by his **w**, he H6948
Da 11:24 plunder, loot and **w** among his followers. H8214
Da 11:28 will return to his own country with great **w**, H8214
Hos 12: 8 With all my **w** they will not find in me any H3330
Ob 11 carried off his **w** and foreigners entered H2657
Ob 13 seize their **w** in the day of their H2657
Mic 4:13 their **w** to the Lord of all the earth. H2657
Na 2: 9 is endless, the **w** from all its treasures! H3883
Zep 1:13 Their **w** will be plundered, their houses H2657
Zec 14:14 The **w** *of* all the surrounding nations will H2657
Mt 13:22 the deceitfulness *of* **w** choke the word, *G4458*
Mt 19:22 went away sad, because he had great **w**. *G3228*
Mt 25:14 his servants and entrusted his **w** to them. *G5639*
Mk 4:19 the deceitfulness *of* **w** and the desires *G4458*
Mk 10:22 went away sad, because he had great **w**. *G3228*
Mk 12:44 They all gave out of their **w**; but she, out *G4355*
Lk 15:13 there squandered his **w** in wild living. *G4045*
Lk 16: 9 use worldly **w** to gain friends for *G3440*
Lk 16:11 been trustworthy in handling worldly **w**, *G3440*
Lk 21: 4 people gave their gifts out of their **w**; *G4355*
1Ti 6:17 to be arrogant nor to put their hope in **w**, *G4458*
Jas 5: 2 Your **w** has rotted, and moths have eaten *G4458*
Jas 5: 3 *You have* **hoarded w** in the last days. *G2564*
Rev 3:17 *I have* **acquired w** and do not need a *G4456*
Rev 5:12 to receive power and **w** and wisdom and *G4458*
Rev 18:15 things and **gained** *their* **w** from her will *G4456*
Rev 18:17 hour such great **w** has been brought to *G4458*
Rev 18:19 on the sea became rich through her **w**! *G5509*

WEALTHY (11) [WEALTH]

Ge 13: 2 Abram *had become* very **w** in livestock H3877
Ge 24:35 abundantly, and *he has become* **w**. H1540
Ge 26:13 to grow until *he became* very **w**. H1540
1Sa 25: 2 had property there at Carmel, was very **w**. H1524
2Sa 19:32 in Mahanaim, for he was a very **w** man. H1524
2Ki 15:20 Every **w** person had to contribute fifty H2657
Job 27:19 He lies down **w**, but will do so no more H6938
Hos 12: 8 "I am very rich; I have become **w**. H226
Hab 2: 6 goods and **makes** himself **w** by extortion! H3877
Lk 18:23 became very sad, because he was very **w**. *G4454*
Lk 19: 2 he was a chief tax collector and was **w**. *G4454*

WEANED (10)
Ge 21: 8 The child grew and **was** w, and on the H1694
Ge 21: 8 on the day Isaac **was** w Abraham held a H1694
1Sa 1:22 "After the boy **is** w, I will take him and H1694
1Sa 1:23 "Stay here until you *have* w him; only may H1694
1Sa 1:23 nursed her son until she *had* w him. H1694
1Sa 1:24 After he *was* w, she took the boy with her H1694
Ps 131: 2 I am like a w *child* with its mother H1694
Ps 131: 2 its mother; like a w *child* I am content. H1694
Isa 28: 9 To *children* w from their milk, to those just H1694
Hos 1: 8 After *she had* w Lo-Ruhamah, Gomer had H1694

WEAPON (16) [WEAPONS]
1Sa 21: 8 I haven't brought my sword or any *other* w, H3998
1Ki 20:35 "Strike me with your w," but he refused. NDT
2Ki 11: 8 the king, each of you with w in hand. H3998
2Ki 11:11 each with w in hand, stationed H3998
1Ch 12:33 battle with every type of w, H3998+4878
1Ch 12:37 armed with every type of w— H3998+7372+4878
2Ch 23: 7 around the king, each with w in hand. H3998
2Ch 23:10 each with his w in his hand, around H8939
Ne 4:17 with one hand and held a w in the other, H8939
Ne 4:23 each had his w, even when he went H8939
Job 20:24 Though he flees from an iron w, H5977
Isa 54:16 into flame and forges a w fit for its work. H3998
Isa 54:17 no w forged against you will prevail, and H3998
Jer 51:20 my war club, my w *for* battle—with you I H3998
Eze 9: 1 the city, each with a w in his hand." H3998+5424
Eze 9: 2 each with a deadly w in his hand. H3998

WEAPONS (28) [WEAPON]
Ge 49: 5 brothers—their swords are w *of* violence. H3998
Dt 1:41 So every one of you put on his w H3998+4878
1Sa 8:12 others to make w *of* war and equipment H3998
1Sa 17:54 he put the Philistine's w in his own tent. H3998
1Sa 20:40 Jonathan gave his w to the boy and said, H3998
2Sa 1:27 The w *of* war have perished!" H3998
2Sa 2:21 of the young men and strip him of his w." H2723
1Ki 10:25 w and spices, and horses and H5977
2Ki 10: 2 chariots and horses, a fortified city and w. H5977
2Ch 9:24 robes, w and spices, and horses and H5977
2Ch 32: 5 made large numbers of w and shields. H8939
Ps 7:13 He has prepared his deadly w; he makes H3998
Ps 76: 3 the shields and the swords, the w of war. NDT
Ecc 9:18 Wisdom is better than w *of* war, but one H3998
Isa 13: 5 the LORD and the w *of* his wrath—to H3998
Isa 22: 8 in that day to the w *in* the Palace of the H5977
Jer 21: 4 turn against you the w *of* war that are in H3998
Jer 22: 7 each man with his w, and they will cut up H3998
Jer 50:25 brought out the w *of* his wrath, H3998
Eze 23:24 They will come against you with w H2210
Eze 26: 9 demolish your towers with his w. H2995
Eze 32:27 realm of the dead with their w *of* war— H3998
Eze 39: 9 go out and use the w for fuel and burn H5977
Eze 39:10 because they will use the w for fuel. H5977
Jn 18: 3 were carrying torches, lanterns and w. G3960
2Co 6: 7 with w of righteousness in the right hand G3960
2Co 10: 4 The w we fight with are not the weapons G3960
2Co 10: 4 we fight with are not the w of the world. NDT

WEAR (44) [WEARING, WEARS, WORE, WORN, WORN-OUT]
Ge 28:20 will give me food to eat and clothes to w H4252
Ex 18:18 to you *will* **only** w *yourselves* **out**. H5570+5570
Ex 28:35 Aaron *must* w *it* when he ministers H2118+6584
Ex 28:43 his sons *must* w *them* whenever H2118+6584
Ex 29:30 in the Holy Place *is to* w them seven days. H4252
Lev 13:45 a defiling disease *must* w torn clothes, H2118
Lev 19:19 " '*Do* not w clothing woven of two kinds of H6590
Lev 21:10 has been ordained to w the priestly H4252
Dt 8: 4 Your clothes *did* not w **out** and your feet H1162
Dt 22: 5 A woman *must* not w men's H2118+6584
Dt 22: 5 clothing, nor a man w women's clothing H4252
Dt 22:11 *Do* not w **clothes** of wool and linen woven H4252
Dt 22:12 on the four corners of the cloak *you* w. H4059
Dt 28:32 you *will* w **out** your eyes watching for H3985
Dt 29: 5 your clothes *did* not w **out**, nor did the H1162
Jdg 8:24 of the Ishmaelites to w gold earrings.) H4200
1Sa 2:28 to w an ephod in my presence. H5951
1Ki 22:30 in disguise, but you w your royal robes." H4252
2Ch 18:29 in disguise, but you w your royal robes." H4252
Ne 9:21 their clothes *did* not w **out** nor did their H1162
Job 27:17 what he lays up the righteous *will* w, and H4252
Job 31:36 Surely *I would* w it on my shoulder, H5951
Ps 102:26 remain; they *will* all w **out** like a garment. H1162
Pr 23: 4 *Do* not w *yourself* **out** to get rich; do not H3333
Isa 15: 3 In the streets *they* w sackcloth; on the H2520
Isa 49:18 "*you will* w them all as ornaments H4252
Isa 50: 9 They *will* all w **out** like a garment; the H1162
Isa 51: 6 the earth *will* w **out** like a garment and its H1162
Jer 12:13 *they will* w **themselves out** but gain H2703
Eze 44:17 the inner court, *they are to* w linen clothes H4252
Eze 44:17 they *must* not w any woolen H6590+6584
Eze 44:18 *They are to* w linen turbans on their heads H2118
Eze 44:18 *They must* not w anything that makes H2520
Am 8:10 *I will* **make** all of you w H6590+6584+5516
Mt 6:25 or about your body, what *you will* w. G1907
Mt 6:31 shall we drink?' or 'What *shall we* w?' G4314
Mt 11: 8 those *who* w fine clothes are in kings' G5841
Mk 6: 9 W sandals but not an extra shirt. G5686
Lk 7:25 those who w expensive clothes and G1877
Lk 12:22 or about your body, what *you will* w. G1907
Lk 12:33 purses for yourselves *that will* not w **out**, G4096
Heb 1:11 remain; *they will* all w **out** like a garment. G4096
Rev 3:18 white clothes to w, so you can cover G4314
Rev 19: 8 bright and clean, was given her to w." G4314

WEARIED (6) [WEARY]
Isa 43:22 *you have* not w *yourselves* for me H3333
Isa 43:23 grain offerings nor w you with demands H3333
Isa 43:24 with your sins and w me with your H3333
Isa 57:10 *You* w *yourself* by such going about, but H3333
Mal 2:17 *You have* w the LORD with your words H3333
Mal 2:17 "How *have we* w him?" you ask. H3333

WEARIES (2) [WEARY]
Ecc 10:15 The toil of fools w them; they do not know H3333
Ecc 12:12 is no end, and much study w the body. H3331

WEARING (32) [WEAR]
Ge 37:23 of his robe—the ornate robe he was w— H6584
Ex 32: 2 your sons and your daughters are w H928+265
Dt 21:13 the clothes she was w when captured. H6584
Ru 3:15 me the shawl you are w and hold it out." H6584
1Sa 2:18 before the LORD—a boy w a linen ephod. H2520
1Sa 14: 3 whom was Ahijah, *who was* w an ephod. H5951
1Sa 18: 4 off the robe he was w and gave it to H6584
1Sa 28:14 "An old man w a robe is coming up," H6486
2Sa 6:14 W a linen ephod, David was dancing H2520
2Sa 13:18 She was w an ornate robe, for this was H6584
2Sa 13:19 head and tore the ornate robe she was w. H6584
2Sa 20: 8 Joab *was* w his military tunic, and H2520
1Ki 11:29 met him on the way, w a new cloak. H4059
1Ki 11:30 the new cloak he was w and tore it into H6584
1Ki 20:32 W sackcloth around their waists and ropes H2520
2Ki 19: 2 the leading priests, *all* w sackcloth, to the H4059
Ne 9: 1 fasting and w sackcloth and putting dust on H928
Est 1:11 him Queen Vashti, w her royal crown, in H928
Est 8:15 *he was* w royal garments of blue and white, H928
SS 3: 8 all of them w the sword, all experienced in H296
SS 3:11 Look on King Solomon w a crown, the H928
Isa 37: 2 the leading priests, *all* w sackcloth, to the H4059
Jer 13: 4 you bought and are w **around** your waist, H6584
Da 3:21 So these men, w their robes, trousers A10089
Mt 22:11 a man there *who was* not w wedding G1907
Mk 14:51 w **nothing** but a linen garment G4314+2093+1218
Jn 19: 5 When Jesus came out w the crown of G5841
Ac 12:21 day Herod, w his royal robes, sat G1907
Jas 2: 2 your meeting w **a gold ring** and fine G5993
Jas 2: 3 attention to the *man* w fine clothes and G5841
1Pe 3: 3 hairstyles and the w of gold jewelry or G4324
Rev 7: 9 *They were* w white robes and were G4314

WEARISOME (1) [WEARY]
Ecc 1: 8 All things are w, more than one can say H3335

WEARS (3) [WEAR]
Job 14:19 as water w **away** stones and torrents wash H8835
Ps 119:139 My zeal w me **out**, for my enemies ignore H7551
Isa 16:12 *she* only w **herself out**; when she H4206

WEARY (29) [WEARIED, WEARIES, WEARISOME]
Dt 25:18 When you were w and worn out, they met H6546
Dt 28:65 eyes w **with longing**, and a H4001
Jos 7: 3 to take it and *do* not w the whole army, H3333
2Sa 17: 2 I would attack him while he is w and weak. H3333
Job 3:17 turmoil, and there the w are at rest. H3329+3946
Job 22: 7 gave no water to the w and you withheld H6546
Job 31:16 poor or *let* the eyes of the widow **grow** w, H3983
Ps 68: 9 you refreshed your w inheritance. H4206
Ps 119:28 My soul *is* w with sorrow; strengthen me H1941
Pr 25:25 Like cold water to a w soul is good news H6546
Pr 30: 1 utterance to Ithiel: "*I am* w, God, but I can H4206
Isa 1:14 a burden to me; *I am* w *of* bearing them. H4206
Isa 28:12 is the resting place, let the w rest"; and, H6546
Isa 40:28 He will not grow tired or w, and his H3333
Isa 40:29 gives strength to the w and increases the H3617
Isa 40:30 Even youths grow tired and w, and young H3333
Isa 40:31 they will run and not *grow* w, they will H3333
Isa 46: 1 are burdensome, a burden for the w. H6546
Isa 50: 4 to know the word that sustains the w. H3617
Jer 9: 5 *they* w **themselves** *with* sinning. H4206
Jer 20: 9 up in my bones. *I am* w *of* holding it in H4206
Jer 31:25 I will refresh the w and satisfy the H5883+6546
La 5: 5 at our heels; *we are* w and find no rest. H3333
Zec 11: 8 flock detested me, and I **grew** w of them H7918
Mt 11:28 all you who *are* w and burdened, and G3159
Ac 24: 4 But in order not to w you further, I would G1601
Gal 6: 9 *Let us* not *become* w in doing good, for at G1591
Heb 12: 3 so that *you will* not *grow* w and lose heart. G2827
Rev 2: 3 my name, and *have* not *grown* w. G3159

WEASEL (1)
Lev 11:29 unclean for you: the w, the rat, any kind of H2700

WEATHER (1)
Mt 16: 2 you say, 'It will be **fair** w, for the sky is red G2304

WEAVE (2) [INTERWOVEN, WEAVER, WEAVER'S, WEAVERS, WEAVING, WOVE, WOVEN]
Ex 28:39 "W the tunic of fine linen and make the H8687
Jdg 16:13 "If *you* w the seven braids of my head into H755

WEAVER (3) [WEAVE]
Ex 39:22 entirely of blue cloth—the work of a w— H755
Ex 39:27 tunics of fine linen—the work of a w— H755
Isa 38:12 Like a w I have rolled up my life, and he H755

WEAVER'S (5) [WEAVE]
1Sa 17: 7 His spear shaft was like a w rod, and its iron H755
2Sa 21:19 who had a spear with a shaft like a w rod. H755
1Ch 11:23 had a spear like a w rod in his hand, H755
1Ch 20: 5 who had a spear with a shaft like a w rod. H755
Job 7: 6 "My days are swifter than a w **shuttle**, and H756

WEAVERS (2) [WEAVE]
Ex 35:35 fine linen, and w—all of them skilled H755
Isa 19: 9 despair, the w *of* fine linen will lose hope. H755

WEAVING (1) [WEAVE]
2Ki 23: 7 where women **did** w for Asherah. H755+1428

WEB (3) [COBWEBS]
Job 8:14 what they rely on is a spider's w. H1074
Job 8:15 They lean on the w, but it gives way; they H1074
Isa 59: 5 the eggs of vipers and spin a spider's w. H7770

WEDDING (18)
1Ki 9:16 then gave it as a w **gift** to his daughter, H8933
Ps 45: T the Sons of Korah. A maskil. A w song. H3353
Ps 78:63 their young women **had** no w **songs**; H2146
SS 3:11 mother crowned him on the day of his w, H3164
Jer 2:32 her jewelry, a bride her w **ornaments**? H8005
Mt 22: 2 who prepared a w **banquet** for his son. G1141
Mt 22: 4 Come to the w **banquet**.' G1141
Mt 22: 8 his servants, 'The w **banquet** is ready, but G1141
Mt 22:10 the w **hall** was filled with guests. G1141
Mt 22:11 there who was not wearing w clothes. G1141
Mt 22:12 did you get in here without w clothes, G1141
Mt 25:10 ready went in with him to the w **banquet**. G1141
Lk 12:36 their master to return from a w **banquet**, G1141
Lk 14: 8 "When someone invites you to a w **feast** G1141
Jn 2: 1 On the third day a w took place at Cana in G1141
Jn 2: 2 disciples had also been invited to the w. G1141
Rev 19: 7 For the w of the Lamb has come, and his G1141
Rev 19: 9 are invited to the w supper of the Lamb!" G1141

WEED (1) [SEAWEED, STINKWEED, TUMBLEWEED, WEEDS]
Mt 13:41 and *they will* w **out** of his kingdom G5198

WEEDS (11) [WEED]
Pr 24:31 the ground was covered with w, and the H3017
Hos 10: 4 spring up like **poisonous** w in a plowed H8032
Zep 2: 9 Gomorrah—a place of w and salt pits, H3017
Mt 13:25 came and sowed w among the wheat, G2429
Mt 13:26 formed heads, then the w also appeared. G2429
Mt 13:27 Where then did the w come from?' G2429
Mt 13:29 'because while you are pulling the w, you G2429
Mt 13:30 First collect the w and tie them in bundles G2429
Mt 13:36 to us the parable *of* the w in the field." G2429
Mt 13:38 The w are the people of the evil one, G2429
Mt 13:40 "As the w are pulled up and burned in G2429

WEEK (13) [WEEKS]
Ge 29:27 Finish this daughter's **bridal** w; then we H8651
Ge 29:28 He finished the w *with* Leah, and then H8651
Mt 28: 1 at dawn on the first day *of* the w, Mary G4879
Mk 16: 2 Very early on the first day *of* the w, just G4879
Mk 16: 9 Jesus rose early on the first day *of* the w, G4879
Lk 18:12 I fast twice a w and give a tenth of all I get G4879
Lk 24: 1 On the first day *of* the w, very early in the G4879
Jn 20: 1 Early on the first day *of* the w, while it was G4879
Jn 20:19 On the evening of that first day *of* the w G4879
Jn 20:26 **A** w **later** his disciples were G3552+2465+3893
Ac 20: 7 On the first day *of* the w we came G4879
Ac 28:14 invited us to spend a w with them. G2465+2231
1Co 16: 2 On the first day *of* every w, each one of G4879

WEEKS (11) [WEEK]
Ex 34:22 the Festival of W with the firstfruits of H8651
Lev 12: 5 *for two* w the woman will be unclean H8651
Lev 23:15 the wave offering, count off seven full w. H8701
Nu 28:26 of new grain during the **Festival of** W, H8651
Dt 16: 9 Count off seven w from the time you H8651
Dt 16:10 the Festival of W to the LORD your God by H8651
Dt 16:16 the Festival of W and the Festival of H8651
2Ch 8:13 the Festival of W and the Festival of H8651
Jer 5:24 who assures us of the regular w *of* harvest. H8651
Da 10: 2 Daniel, mourned *for* three w. H8651+3427
Da 10: 3 at all until the three w were over. H8651+3427

WEEP (48) [WEEPING, WEEPS, WEPT]
Ge 23: 2 to mourn for Sarah and to w *over* her. H1134
Ge 29:11 kissed Rachel and *began to* w aloud. H1134
Ge 42:24 turned away from them and *began to* w, H1134
Ge 43:30 hurried out and looked for a place to w. H1134
Jdg 11:37 to roam the hills and w with my friends, H1134
1Sa 30: 4 aloud until they had no strength left to w. H1134
2Sa 1:24 of Israel, w for Saul, who clothed H1134
2Ki 8:11 Then the man of God *began to* w. H1134
Ne 8: 9 Do not mourn or w." For all the people H1134
Job 2:12 *they began to* w aloud, and H1134
Job 27:15 and their widows *will* not w *for* them. H1134
Ps 69:10 When I w and fast, I must endure scorn; H1134
Ps 78:64 the sword, and their widows *could* not w. H1134
Ecc 3: 4 a time to w and a time to laugh, a time to H1134
Isa 15: 2 to its high places to w; Moab wails over H1140

W

Isa 16: 9 So *I* w, as Jazer weeps, *for* the vines of H1134
Isa 22: 4 "Turn away from me; let me **w** bitterly. H1140
Isa 22:12 called you on that day to w and to wail, to H1140
Isa 30:19 in Jerusalem, *you will* w no *more*. H1134+1134
Isa 33: 7 the streets; the envoys of peace w bitterly. H1134
Jer 9: 1 *I would* w day and night *for* the slain of H1134
Jer 9:10 *I will* w and wail for the mountains H5951+1140
Jer 13:17 I *will* w in secret because of your pride H1134
Jer 13:17 my eyes *will* **w bitterly**, overflowing H1963+1963
Jer 22:10 *Do* not w for the dead king or mourn his H1134
Jer 22:10 **w bitterly** for him who is exiled H1134+1134
Jer 25:34 **W** and wail, you shepherds; roll in the H3536
Jer 48:32 *I* w for you, as Jazer weeps, you vines of H1134
La 1:16 "This is why I w and my eyes overflow H1134
Eze 24:16 Yet do not lament or w or shed any tears. H1134
Eze 24:23 will not mourn or w but will waste away H1134
Eze 27:31 *They will* w over you with anguish of soul H1134
Joel 1: 5 you drunkards, and w! Wail, all you H1134
Joel 2:17 *Let* the priests, who minister ..., w H1134
Am 5:16 will be summoned to w and the mourners to H65
Mic 1: 8 Because of this *I will* w and wail; I will go H6199
Mic 1:10 not in Gath; w not **at all**. In Beth H1134+1134
Mal 2:13 *You* w and wail because he no longer H1140
Lk 6:21 Blessed are you who w now, for you will G3081
Lk 6:25 who laugh now, for you will mourn and **w**. G3081
Lk 23:28 of Jerusalem, *do* not w for me; weep for G3081
Lk 23:28 w for yourselves and for your children. G3081
Jn 16:20 you *will* w and mourn while the world G3081
Jas 5: 1 w and wail because of the misery that is G3081
Rev 5: 5 one of the elders said to me, "*Do* not w! G3081
Rev 18: 9 burning, *they will* w and mourn over her. G3081
Rev 18:11 of the earth *will* w and mourn over her G3081
Rev 18:15 at her torment. *They will* w and mourn G3081

WEEPING (57) [WEEP]

Ge 45:14 and Benjamin embraced him, w. H1134
Nu 25: 6 Israel while they *were* w at the entrance H1134
Dt 1:45 no attention to your w and turned a deaf H7754
Dt 34: 8 until the time of w and mourning was H1140
Jdg 20:26 there they sat w before the LORD. H1134
Jdg 21: 2 raising their voices and w bitterly. H1134+1140
1Sa 1: 8 say to her, "Hannah, why *are you* w? H1134
1Sa 1:10 prayed to the LORD, **w bitterly**. H1134+1134
1Sa 11: 5 Why *are they* w?" Then they H1134
2Sa 3:16 w behind her all the way to Bahurim. H1134
2Sa 13:19 went away, w **aloud** as she went. H2410
2Sa 15:30 Mount of Olives, w as he went; his head H1134
2Sa 15:30 heads too and *were* w as they went up. H1134
2Sa 19: 1 "The king *is* w and mourning for Absalom." H1134
2Ki 8:12 "Why *is* my lord w?" asked Hazael H1134
Ezr 3:13 of the shouts of joy from the sound of w, H1140
Ezr 10: 1 w and throwing himself down before the H1134
Ne 8: 9 all the people *had been* w as they H1134
Est 4: 3 the Jews, with fasting, w and wailing. H1140
Est 8: 3 with the king, falling at his feet and w. H1134
Job 16:16 My face is red with w, dark shadows ring H1140
Ps 6: 6 I flood my bed with w and drench my couch NDT
Ps 6: 8 who do evil, for the LORD has heard my w. H1140
Ps 30: 5 lasts a lifetime; w may stay for the night H1140
Ps 35:14 my head in grief as though w *for* my mother. H63
Ps 39:12 to my cry for help; do not be deaf to my w. H1965
Ps 126: 6 Those who go out w, carrying seed to sow, H1134
Isa 15: 3 squares they all wail, prostrate with w. H1140
Isa 15: 5 up the hill to Luhith, w as they go; on the H1140
Isa 65:19 the sound of w and of crying will be heard H1140
Jer 3:21 the w and pleading of the people of H1140
Jer 31: 9 They will come with w; they will pray as I H1140
Jer 31:15 mourning and great w, Rachel weeping H1140
Jer 31:15 Rachel w for her children and refusing to H1134
Jer 31:16 your voice from w and your eyes from H1140
Jer 41: 6 from Mizpah to meet them, w as he went. H1134
Jer 48: 5 to Luhith, **w bitterly** as they go; on H1140+1140
La 2:11 My eyes fail from w, I am in torment H1965
Joel 2:12 with fasting and w and mourning. H1140
Am 8:10 into mourning and all your singing into w. H7806
Zec 12:11 On that day the w in Jerusalem will be as H5027
Zec 12:11 be as great as the w *of* Hadad Rimmon in H5027
Mt 2:18 is heard in Ramah, w and great mourning G3088
Mt 2:18 Rachel w for her children and refusing to G3081
Mt 8:12 where there will be w and gnashing of G3088
Mt 13:42 where there will be w and gnashing of G3088
Mt 13:50 where there will be w and gnashing of G3088
Mt 22:13 where there will be w and gnashing of G3088
Mt 24:51 where there will be w and gnashing of G3088
Mt 25:30 where there will be w and gnashing of G3088
Mk 16:10 with him and who were mourning and w. G3081
Lk 7:38 As she stood behind him at his feet w, she G3081
Lk 13:28 "There will be w there, and gnashing of G3088
Jn 11:33 When Jesus saw her w, and the Jews who G3081
Jn 11:33 who had come along with her also w, G3081
Ac 21:13 "Why *are you* w and breaking my G4472+3081
Rev 18:19 and *with* w and mourning cry out: G3081

WEEPS (3) [WEEP]

Isa 16: 9 So I weep, as Jazer w, for the vines of H1140
Jer 48:32 you, as Jazer w, you vines of Sibmah. H1140
La 1: 2 **Bitterly** *she* w at night, tears are on H1134+1134

WEIGH (7) [OUTWEIGH, OUTWEIGHS, WEIGHED, WEIGHING, WEIGHS, WEIGHT, WEIGHTIER, WEIGHTS, WEIGHTY]

2Sa 14:26 too heavy for him—*he would* w it, and its H9202
Ezr 8:29 carefully until *you* w them **out** in the H9202
Job 31: 6 *let* God w me in honest scales and he will H9202
Isa 46: 6 from their bags and **w out** silver on the H9202
Eze 4:10 **W out** twenty shekels of food to eat each H5484
Eze 33:10 "Our offenses and sins **w** us **down**, and H6584
1Co 14:29 the others *should* **w carefully** what is said. G1359

WEIGHED (33) [WEIGH]

Ge 23:16 terms and **w out** for him the price H9202
Nu 7:85 Each silver plate w a hundred and thirty NDT
Nu 7:85 the silver dishes w two thousand four NDT
Nu 7:86 filled with incense w ten shekels each, NDT
Nu 7:86 the gold dishes w a hundred and twenty NDT
Nu 31:52 as a gift to the LORD w 16,750 shekels. H2118
1Sa 2: 3 God who knows, and by him deeds **are w**. H9419
1Sa 17: 7 its iron point w six hundred shekels. NDT
2Sa 12:30 It w a talent of gold, and it was set with H5486
2Sa 18:12 shekels *were* **w out** into my hands, H9202
2Sa 21:16 bronze spearhead w three hundred H5486
2Ki 25:16 of the LORD, was more than could be w. H5486
1Ch 22: 3 more bronze than could be w. H5486
1Ch 22:14 of bronze and iron too great to be w, H5486
2Ch 3: 9 The gold nails w fifty shekels. He also H5486
Ezr 8:25 and *I* **w out** to them the offering of silver H9202
Ezr 8:26 *I* **w out** to them 650 talents of silver, silver H9202
Ezr 8:30 that had been **w out** to be taken to the H5486
Ezr 8:33 *we* **w out** the silver and gold and the H9202
Job 6: 2 my anguish *could* **be w** and all my H9202+9202
Job 28:15 nor *can* its price **be w out** *in* silver. H9202
Ps 62: 9 If w on a balance, they are nothing H6590
Pr 16: 2 to them, but motives are w *by* the LORD. H9419
Ecc 8: 6 a person may be **w down** by misery. H8041
Isa 40:12 w the mountains on the scales and the H9202
Jer 6:11 and the old, *those* **w down** *with* years. H4849
Jer 32: 9 Hanamel and **w out** for him seventeen H9202
Jer 32:10 and **w out** the silver on the scales. H9202
Jer 52:20 of the LORD, was more than could be w. H5486
La 3: 7 escape; *he has* **w** me **down** *with* chains. H3877
Da 5:27 *You have* **been** w on the scales and A10769
Lk 21:34 your hearts *will be* **w down** with G976
Ac 27:13 so *they* **w anchor** and sailed along the G149

WEIGHING (43) [WEIGH]

Ge 24:22 a gold nose ring w a beka and two gold H5486
Ge 24:22 two gold bracelets w ten shekels. H5486
Nu 3:50 he collected silver w 1,365 shekels, NDT
Nu 7:13 one silver plate w a hundred and thirty H5486
Nu 7:13 one silver sprinkling bowl w seventy shekels, NDT
Nu 7:14 one gold dish w ten shekels, filled with NDT
Nu 7:19 one silver plate w a hundred and thirty H5486
Nu 7:19 one silver sprinkling bowl w seventy shekels, NDT
Nu 7:20 one gold dish w ten shekels, filled with NDT
Nu 7:25 one silver plate w a hundred and thirty H5486
Nu 7:25 one silver sprinkling bowl w seventy shekels, NDT
Nu 7:26 one gold dish w ten shekels, filled with NDT
Nu 7:31 one silver plate w a hundred and thirty H5486
Nu 7:31 one silver sprinkling bowl w seventy shekels, NDT
Nu 7:32 one gold dish w ten shekels, filled with NDT
Nu 7:37 one silver plate w a hundred and thirty H5486
Nu 7:37 one silver sprinkling bowl w seventy shekels, NDT
Nu 7:38 one gold dish w ten shekels, filled with NDT
Nu 7:43 one silver plate w a hundred and thirty H5486
Nu 7:43 one silver sprinkling bowl w seventy shekels, NDT
Nu 7:44 one gold dish w ten shekels, filled with NDT
Nu 7:49 one silver plate w a hundred and thirty H5486
Nu 7:49 one silver sprinkling bowl w seventy shekels, NDT
Nu 7:50 one gold dish w ten shekels, filled with NDT
Nu 7:55 one silver plate w a hundred and thirty H5486
Nu 7:55 one silver sprinkling bowl w seventy shekels, NDT
Nu 7:56 one gold dish w ten shekels, filled with NDT
Nu 7:61 one silver plate w a hundred and thirty H5486
Nu 7:61 one silver sprinkling bowl w seventy shekels, NDT
Nu 7:62 one gold dish w ten shekels, filled with NDT
Nu 7:67 one silver plate w a hundred and thirty H5486
Nu 7:67 one silver sprinkling bowl w seventy shekels, NDT
Nu 7:68 one gold dish w ten shekels, filled with NDT
Nu 7:73 one silver plate w a hundred and thirty H5486
Nu 7:73 one silver sprinkling bowl w seventy shekels, NDT
Nu 7:74 one gold dish w ten shekels, filled with NDT
Nu 7:79 one silver plate w a hundred and thirty H5486
Nu 7:79 one silver sprinkling bowl w seventy shekels, NDT
Nu 7:80 one gold dish w ten shekels, filled with NDT
Jos 7:21 of silver and a bar of gold w fifty shekels, H5486
1Sa 17: 5 armor of bronze w five thousand shekels H5486
Ezr 8:26 silver articles w 100 talents, 100 NDT
Rev 16:21 each w about **a hundred pounds**, fell on G5418

WEIGHS (9) [WEIGH]

Ex 30:13 sanctuary shekel, which w twenty gerahs. H9203
Nu 3:47 sanctuary shekel, which w twenty gerahs. NDT
Nu 18:16 sanctuary shekel, which w twenty gerahs. NDT
Pr 12:25 Anxiety **w down** the heart, but a kind word H8817
Pr 15:28 The heart of the righteous w its answers H2047
Pr 21: 2 ways are right, but the LORD w the heart. H9419
Pr 24:12 does not he *who* w the heart perceive it? H9419
Ecc 6: 1 the sun, and it **w heavily** on mankind: H8041
Isa 40:15 *he* w the islands as though they were fine H5747

WEIGHT (26) [WEIGH]

Ge 23:16 **according to the w current** among the H6296
Ge 43:21 his silver—**the exact w**—in the mouth of H5486
Lev 19:35 when measuring length, w or quantity. H5486
Lev 26:26 they will dole out the bread by w. H5486
Jdg 8:26 The w *of* the gold rings he asked for came H5486
2Sa 14:26 its w was two hundred shekels by the NDT
1Ki 7:47 the w *of* the bronze was not determined. H5486
1Ki 10:14 The w *of* the gold that Solomon received H5486
1Ch 20: 2 its w was found to be a talent of gold H5486
1Ch 28:14 He designated the w of gold for all the H5486
1Ch 28:14 the w of silver for all the silver articles H5486
1Ch 28:15 the w of gold for the gold lampstands and H5486
1Ch 28:15 with the w *for* each lampstand and its H5486
1Ch 28:15 the w of silver for each silver H5486
1Ch 28:16 the w of gold for each table for H5486
1Ch 28:16 the w of silver for the silver tables NDT
1Ch 28:17 the w of pure gold for the forks, sprinkling NDT
1Ch 28:17 pitchers; the w of gold for each gold dish H5486
1Ch 28:17 the w of silver for each silver dish; H5486
1Ch 28:18 the w of the refined gold for the altar H5486
2Ch 4:18 to so much that the w *of* the bronze could H5486
2Ch 9:13 The w *of* the gold that Solomon received H5486
Ezr 8:34 was accounted for by number and w, H5486
Ezr 8:34 the entire w was recorded at that H5486
Job 26: 8 the clouds do not burst under their w. NDT
La 4: 2 of Zion, once **worth their** w in gold, are H6131

WEIGHTIER (1) [WEIGH]

Jn 5:36 "I have testimony w than that of John. G3505

WEIGHTS (8) [WEIGH]

Lev 19:36 Use honest scales and honest w, an honest H74
Dt 25:13 not have **two differing** w in your H74+2256+74
Dt 25:15 have accurate and honest w and measures, H74
Pr 11: 1 but accurate w find favor with him. H74
Pr 16:11 all the w *in* the bag are of his making. H74
Pr 20:10 **Differing** w and differing H74+2256+74
Pr 20:23 The LORD detests **differing** w, and H74+2256+74
Mic 6:11 with dishonest scales, with a bag of false w? H74

WEIGHTY (1) [WEIGH]

2Co 10:10 "His letters are w and forceful, but in G987

WELCOME (17) [WELCOMED, WELCOMES]

Jdg 19:20 "You are w at my house," the old man H8934
Ps 5: 4 *with* you, evil people *are* not w. H1591
Mt 10:14 If anyone *will* not w you or listen to your G1312
Mk 6:11 And if any place *will* not w you or listen to G1312
Mk 9:37 welcomes me *does* not w me but the one G1312
Lk 9: 5 If people *do* not w you, leave their town G1312
Lk 9:53 but *the people there did* not w him G1312
Lk 16: 4 *people will* w me into their houses. G1312
Ac 18:27 wrote to the disciples there *to* w him. G622
Php 2:29 So then, w him in the Lord with great joy G4657
Col 4:10 about him; if he comes to you, w him.) G1312
Phm 17 w him as you would welcome me. G4689
Phm 17 a partner, welcome him as you would w me. NDT
2Pe 1:11 you will receive a rich w into the eternal G1658
2Jn 10 them into your house or w them. G5897+3306
3Jn 9 who loves to be first, *will* not w us. G2110
3Jn 10 he even refuses *to* w other believers. G2110

WELCOMED (18) [WELCOME]

Jdg 19: 3 her father saw him, he gladly w him. H7925
Lk 8:40 returned, a crowd w him, for they were all G622
Lk 9:11 *He* w them and spoke to them about the G622
Lk 10: 8 "When you enter a town and *are* w, eat G1312
Lk 10:10 But when you enter a town and *are* not w G1312
Lk 16: 9 you *will be* w into eternal dwellings. G1312
Lk 19: 6 he came down at once and w him gladly. G5685
Jn 4:45 arrived in Galilee, the Galileans w him. G1312
Ac 15: 4 *they were* w by the church and the G4138
Ac 17: 7 Jason *has* w them **into** his **house** G5685
Ac 28: 2 built a fire and w us all because it was G4689
Ac 28: 7 He w us to *his* **home** and showed us G346
Ac 28:30 rented house and w all who came to see G622
2Co 8:17 For Titus not only w our appeal, but he is G1312
Gal 4:14 *you* w me as if I were an angel of God G1312
1Th 1: 6 *for you* w the message in the midst of G1312
Heb 11:13 only saw them and w them from a distance G832
Heb 11:31 *because she* w the spies G1312+3552+1645

WELCOMES (17) [WELCOME]

Mt 10:40 "Anyone *who* w you welcomes me, and G1312
Mt 10:40 "Anyone who welcomes you w me, and G1312
Mt 10:40 anyone *who* w me welcomes the one G1312
Mt 10:40 who welcomes me w the one who sent G1312
Mt 10:41 Whoever w a prophet as a prophet will G1312
Mt 10:41 whoever w a righteous person as a G1312
Mt 18: 5 And whoever w one such child in my G1312
Mt 18: 5 one such child in my name w me. G1312
Mk 9:37 "Whoever w one of these little children in G1312
Mk 9:37 of these little children in my name w me; G1312
Mk 9:37 whoever w me does not welcome me G1312
Lk 9:48 "Whoever w this little child in my name G1312
Lk 9:48 this little child in my name w me; G1312
Lk 9:48 whoever w me welcomes the one G1312
Lk 9:48 welcomes me w the one who sent me G1312
Lk 15: 2 "This man w sinners and eats with them." G4657
2Jn 11 Anyone *who* w them shares in their G3306+5897

WELDING (1)

Isa 41: 7 One says of the w, "It is good." The H1817

WELFARE (4)

Ne 2:10 come to promote the w of the Israelites. H3208
Est 10: 3 spoke up for the w of all the Jews. H8934

Php 2:20 show genuine concern *for* your **w**. G3836+4309
1Ti 6: 2 are devoted to the w of their slaves. G2307

WELL (289) [GOOD, WELL'S, WELLED, WELLING, WELLS]

Ge 12:13 so that I *will be* **treated** w for your sake H3512
Ge 12:16 *He* **treated** Abram w for her sake, and H3512
Ge 13:10 of the Jordan toward Zoar *was* **w watered**, H5482
Ge 14: 7 **as w as** the Amorites who were H2256+1685
Ge 16:14 That is why the w was called Beer Lahai Roi; H931
Ge 18: 5 to your servant." **"Very w,"** they answered H4027
Ge 19:21 He said to him, "**Very w**, I will grant this H2180
Ge 21:19 opened her eyes and she saw a w *of* water. H931
Ge 21:25 to Abimelek about a w *of* water that H931
Ge 21:30 my hand as a witness that I dug this w." H931
Ge 24:11 down near the w outside the town; H931+4784
Ge 24:20 ran back to the w to draw more water, and H931
Ge 24:25 **as w as** room for you to spend the night." H1685
Ge 26:10 of the men **might w have** slept with H3869+5071
Ge 26:19 discovered a w *of* fresh water there. H931
Ge 26:20 So he named the w Esek, because they H931
Ge 26:21 Then they dug another w, but they H931
Ge 26:22 moved on from there and dug another w, H931
Ge 26:25 his tent, and there his servants dug a w. H931
Ge 26:29 always treated you w and sent you away H3202
Ge 26:32 told him about the w they had dug. H931
Ge 29: 2 There he saw a w in the open country, with H931
Ge 29: 2 the flocks were watered from that w. H931
Ge 29: 2 stone over the mouth of the w was large. H931
Ge 29: 3 stone to its place over the mouth of the w. H931
Ge 29: 6 Jacob asked them, "Is he w?" "Yes, he is," H8934
Ge 29: 8 been rolled away from the mouth of the w. H931
Ge 29:10 from the mouth of the w and watered his H931
Ge 30:15 "**Very w**," Rachel said, "he can H4200+4027
Ge 32: 7 the flocks and herds **and** camels **as w**. H2256
Ge 36: 6 **as w as** his livestock and all his other H2256
Ge 37:10 he told his father **as w as** his brothers, H2256
Ge 37:13 send you to them." "**Very w**," he replied. H2180
Ge 37:14 see if all is w *with* your brothers and H8934
Ge 40:14 But when *all* **goes** w with you, remember H3512
Ge 43:28 servant our father is still alive and w." H8934
Ge 44:10 "**Very w, then**," he said, "let it be as you H1685
Ge 47:19 before your eyes—we and our land **as w**? H1685
Ex 2:15 live in Midian, where he sat down by a w. H931
Ex 4:14 I know he *can* **speak** w. He is H1819+1819
Ex 4:18 Jethro said, "Go, and I **wish** you w." H4200+8934
Ex 11: 5 **and** all the firstborn of the cattle **as w**. H2256
Ex 12:29 **and** the firstborn of all the livestock **as w**. H2256
Ex 25:29 **as w as** its pitchers and bowls for the H2256
Ex 37:23 lamps, **as w as** its wick trimmers and trays H2256
Lev 4:11 all its flesh, **as w as** the head and legs H6584
Lev 21:22 food of his God, **as w as** the holy food; H2256
Lev 25: 7 **as w as** for your livestock and the wild H2256
Nu 3:37 **as w as** the posts of the surrounding H2256
Nu 4:32 **as w as** the posts of the surrounding H2256
Nu 10:29 Come with us and *we will* **treat** you w, for H3512
Nu 20:17 field or vineyard, or drink water from any w. H931
Nu 21:16 the w where the LORD said to Moses H931
Nu 21:17 "Spring up, O w! Sing about it, H931
Nu 21:18 about the w that the princes dug, that the H931
Nu 21:22 field or vineyard, or drink water from any w. H931
Nu 22:38 "W, I have come to you now," Balaam H2180
Nu 31:10 had settled, **as w as** all their camps. H2256
Nu 31:20 every garment **as w as** everything made of H2256
Nu 32:38 **as w as** Nebo and Baal Meon (these H2256
Dt 4:40 so that *it may* **go** w with you and your H3512
Dt 5:16 long and that *it may* **go** w with you in the H3512
Dt 5:29 so that *it might* **go** w with them and their H3512
Dt 6: 3 to obey so that *it may* **go** w with you and H3512
Dt 6:18 so that *it may* **go** w with you and you may H3512
Dt 7:18 **remember** w what the LORD your H2349+2349
Dt 8:16 so that in the end *it might* **go** w *with* you. H3512
Dt 12:25 so that *it may* **go** w with you and your H3512
Dt 12:28 so that *it may* always **go** w with you and H3512
Dt 15:16 you and your family and *is* **w off** with you, H3201
Dt 19:13 so that *it may* **go** w with you. H3201
Dt 22: 7 so that *it may* **go** w with you and you may H3512
Dt 29:19 on the watered land **as w as** the dry. H907
Jos 17:18 the forested hill country **as w**. Clear it H3954
Jdg 1:24 we will see that you are treated w. H2876
Ru 3: 1 you, where you *will be* **w provided for**. H3512
1Sa 16:17 someone who plays w and bring him to H3512
1Sa 16:18 He speaks w and is a fine-looking man H1067
1Sa 18: 5 all the troops, and Saul's officers **as w**. H1685
1Sa 18:30 and his name *became* **w known**. H3700+4394
1Sa 19: 4 Jonathan spoke w of David to Saul his H3202
1Sa 20: 3 father **knows very w** that I have H3359+3359
1Sa 20: 7 If he says, '**Very w**,' then your servant is H3202
1Sa 24:17 "You have treated me w, but I have H3208
1Sa 24:19 the LORD reward you w for the way you H3208
1Sa 25:13 they did, and David strapped his on **as w**. H1685
1Sa 28: 2 replied, "**Very w**, I will make you H4200+4027
2Sa 10: 6 **as w as** the king of Maakah with a H2256
2Sa 11:25 devours one **as w as** another. H2256+3869
2Sa 14: 7 then we will get rid of the heir **as w**. H1685
2Sa 14:21 said to Joab, "**Very w**, I will do it. H2180+5528
2Sa 17: 5 so we can hear what he has to say **as w**." H1685
2Sa 17:18 He had a w in his courtyard, and they H931
2Sa 17:19 the opening of the w and scattered grain H931
2Sa 17:21 climbed out of the w and went to inform H931
2Sa 18:28 Ahimaaz called out to the king, "**All is w**!" H8934
2Sa 23:15 from the w near the gate *of* Bethlehem!" H1014
2Sa 23:16 from the w near the gate *of* Bethlehem H1014
1Ki 2:18 "**Very w**," Bathsheba replied, "I will speak H3202
1Ki 2:22 *You might as w* **request** the kingdom for him AIT
1Ki 4:13 as w as the region of Argob in Bashan and NDT
1Ki 4:23 and goats, **as w as** deer H4200+963+4946
1Ki 5:16 **as w as** thirty-three hundred H4200+963+4946
1Ki 7:29 cherubim—and on the uprights **as w**. H4027
1Ki 8:18 '*You* **did** w to have it in your heart to build H3201
1Ki 9:19 **as w as** all his store cities and the towns H2256
1Ki 11:28 Solomon saw **how** w the young man H3954
2Ki 2:19 this town is w situated, as you can H3202
2Ki 10:11 house of Ahab, **as w as** all his chief men H2256
2Ki 10:14 slaughtered them by the w *of* Beth Eked— H1014
2Ki 10:30 "Because *you have* **done** w in H3201
2Ki 17: 8 **as w as** the practices that the kings of H2256
2Ki 25:24 king of Babylon, and *it will* **go** w with you." H3512
1Ch 2:23 as w as Kenath with its surrounding NDT
1Ch 7:24 Beth Horon **as w as** Uzzen Sheerah. H2256
1Ch 9:29 **as w as** the special flour and wine H2256
1Ch 11:17 from the w near the gate *of* Bethlehem!" H1014
1Ch 11:18 from the w near the gate *of* Bethlehem H1014
1Ch 19: 7 **as w as** the king of Maakah with his H2256
1Ch 22:15 **as w as** those skilled in every kind of work H2256
1Ch 23: 2 of Israel, **as w as** the priests and Levites. H2256
1Ch 25: 8 old alike, teacher **as w as** student, cast H6640
1Ch 28:13 **as w as** for all the articles to be used in its H2256
1Ch 29: 2 the wood, **as w as** onyx for the settings H2256
1Ch 29:24 **as w as** all of King David's sons H2256+1685
2Ch 6: 8 '*You* **did** w to have it in your heart to build H3201
2Ch 8: 6 **as w as** Baalath and all his store cities H2256
2Ch 9: 3 Solomon, **as w as** the palace he had built H2256
2Ch 19:11 may the LORD be with those who do w." H3202
2Ch 21: 3 of value, **as w as** fortified cities in Judah H6640
2Ch 28:18 Gederoth, **as w as** Soko, Timnah and H2256
2Ch 33:15 **as w as** all the altars he had built on the H2256
2Ch 33:19 **as w as** all his sins and unfaithfulness H2256
Ezr 3: 5 **as w as** those brought as freewill offerings H2256
Ezr 7: 6 He was a teacher **w versed** in the Law of H4542
Ezr 7:16 **as w as** the freewill offerings of the A10554
Ezr 8:28 "You **as w as** these articles are H2256
Ne 2:13 toward the Jackal W and the Dung Gate, H6524
Ne 5:17 **as w as** those who came to us from the H2256
Ne 12:22 Jaddua, **as w as** those of the priests H2256
Ne 12:35 **as w as** some priests with trumpets, and H2256
Ne 12:41 **as w as** the priests—Eliakim, Maaseiah H2256
Ne 13: 5 **as w as** the contributions for the priests. H2256
Job 1:12 to Satan, "**Very w, then**, everything he H2180
Job 2: 6 said to Satan, "**Very w, then**, he is in your H2180
Job 12: 3 But I have a mind **as w as** you; I am not H4017
Job 13: 9 Would it turn out w if he examined you H3202
Job 15:21 when all seems w, marauders attack H8934
Job 16:12 *All* was w with me, but he shattered me H8929
Job 21:24 **w nourished** in body, bones rich H4848+2692
Job 21:27 "I know **full** w what you are thinking, the H2176
Job 29:11 Whoever heard me **spoke** w **of** me, and H887
Ps 48:13 **consider** w her ramparts, view her H8883+4213
Ps 104:16 The trees of the LORD *are* **w watered**, the H8425
Ps 105:40 *he* **fed** them w *with* the bread of heaven. H8425
Ps 139:14 works are wonderful, I know that **full** w. H4394
Ps 141: 6 will learn that my words *were* w spoken. H5838
Pr 4:13 do not let it go; **guard** it w, for it is your H5915
Pr 5:15 running water from your own w. H931
Pr 23: 1 a ruler, **note** w what is before you H1067+1067
Pr 23:23 wisdom, instruction and insight **as w**. H2256
Pr 23:27 and a wayward wife is a narrow w. H931
Pr 24:25 But *it will* **go** w with those who convict the H5838
Pr 25:26 spring or a polluted w are the righteous H5227
Ecc 2: 8 a harem as w—the delights of a man's NDT
Ecc 7:14 made the one **as w as** the other. H4200+6645
Ecc 8:13 it will not go w with them, and their H3202
Ecc 11: 6 or whether both will do equally w. H3202
Ecc 12: 6 and the wheel broken at the w, H1014
SS 4:15 a w *of* flowing water streaming down from H931
Isa 3:10 Tell the righteous it will be w with them H3202
Isa 5: 2 in it and cut out a winepress **as w**. H1685
Isa 23:16 play the harp w, sing many a song, H3512
Isa 28:11 **Very w then**, with foreign lips and strange H3954
Isa 48: 8 **W** do I know how treacherous you are H3954
Jer 6: 7 As a w pours out its water, so she pours out H931
Jer 7:23 command you, that *it may* **go** w with you. H3512
Jer 12: 6 trust them, though they speak w of you. H3208
Jer 12:16 And if *they* **learn** w the ways of my H4340+4340
Jer 22:15 was right and just, so all went w with him. H3202
Jer 22:16 of the poor and needy, and so all went w. H3202
Jer 31:13 be glad, young men and old **as w**. H3481
Jer 32:11 conditions, **as w as** the unsealed copy H2256
Jer 32:39 me and that *all* will then go w for them H3202
Jer 38: 4 left in this city, **as w as** all the people, by H2256
Jer 38:20 Then *it will* **go** w with you, and your life H3512
Jer 40: 9 king of Babylon, and *it will* **go** w with you. H3512
Jer 41: 3 **as w as** the Babylonian soldiers who were H2256
Jer 42: 6 so that *it will* **go** w with us, for we H3512
Jer 44:17 of food and were **w off** and suffered no H3202
Jer 50:33 oppressed, and the people of Judah **as w**. H3481
Jer 51:57 officers and warriors **as w**; they will sleep H2256
La 3:20 *I* **w remember** them, and my soul is H2349+2349
Eze 4:15 "**Very w**," he said, "I will let you bake your H8011
Eze 16:37 those you loved **as w as** those you hated. H6584
Eze 18: 4 the parent **as w as** the child—both H3869
Eze 24:10 **Cook** the meat w, mixing in the spices H9462
Eze 24:25 their sons **and** daughters **as w**— H2256
Eze 30:22 the good arm **as w as** the broken one H2256
Eze 33:32 voice and plays an instrument w, H3512
Eze 40:19 on the east side **as w as** on the north. H2256
Eze 41:16 as w as the thresholds and the narrow NDT
Eze 45: 4 their houses **as w as** a holy place for H2256
Da 1: 4 of learning, **w informed**, quick to H3359+1981
Hos 13:15 his spring will fail and his w dry up. H5078
Zec 8:12 "The seed will **grow** w, the vine will yield H8934
Zec 12: 2 be besieged **as w as** Jerusalem. H2256+1685
Mt 3:17 whom I love; with him *I am* **w pleased**." G2305
Mt 5:40 take your shirt, hand over your coat **as w**. G2779
Mt 6:33 all these things *will be* **given** to you **as w**. G4707
Mt 13:52 his storeroom new treasures **as w as** old." G2779
Mt 15:31 the crippled **made** w, the lame walking G5618
Mt 17: 5 whom I love; with him *I am* **w pleased**. G2305
Mt 22:10 the bad **as w as** the good G5445+2779
Mt 25:21 master replied, '**W done**, good and G2292
Mt 25:23 master replied, '**W done**, good and G2292
Mt 25:27 **W then**, you should have put my money G4036
Mk 1:11 whom I love; with you *I am* **w pleased**." G2305
Mk 5:16 man—**and** told about the pigs **as w**. G2779
Mk 6:14 Jesus' name had become **w known**. G5745
Mk 7:37 "He has done everything w," they said G2822
Mk 8: 7 They had a few small fish **as w**; he gave G2779
Mk 12:32 "**W** said, teacher," the man replied. "You G2822
Mk 16:18 hands on sick people, and they will get w." G2822
Lk 1:18 old man and my wife *is* **w along** in years." G4581
Lk 3:22 whom I love; with you *I am* **w pleased**." G2305
Lk 4:22 All **spoke** w of him and were amazed at G3455
Lk 6:25 Woe to you who *are* **w fed** now, for you G1855
Lk 6:26 to you when everyone speaks w of you, G2822
Lk 6:48 could not shake it, because it was w built. G2822
Lk 7:10 to the house and found the servant w. G5617
Lk 12:31 these things *will be* **given** to you **as w**. G4707
Lk 14: 5 ox that falls into a w on the Sabbath day, G5853
Lk 17:19 "Rise and go; your faith *has* **made** you w." G5392
Lk 19:17 " '**W done**, my good servant!' his master G2301
Lk 20:39 of the law responded, "**W** said, teacher!" G2822
Jn 4: 6 Jacob's w was there, and Jesus, tired as G4380
Jn 4: 6 was from the journey, sat down by the w. G4380
Jn 4:11 nothing to draw with and the w is deep. G5853
Jn 4:12 who gave us the w and drank from it G5853
Jn 5: 6 he asked him, "Do you want to get w?" G5618
Jn 5:11 "The man who made me w said to me G5618
Jn 5:14 said to him, "See, you are w again. G5618
Jn 5:15 that it was Jesus who had made him w. G5618
Jn 12:10 priests made plans to kill Lazarus **as w**, G2779
Jn 13: 9 my feet but my hands and my head **as w**!" G2779
Jn 14: 7 know me, you will know my Father **as w**. G2779
Jn 15:23 Whoever hates me hates my Father **as w**. G2779
Jn 20: 7 **as w as** the cloth that had been wrapped G2779
Jn 21:25 Jesus did many other things **as w**. If every G2779
Ac 6: 9 Alexandria **as w as** the provinces of G2779
Ac 10:12 animals, **as w as** reptiles and birds. G2779
Ac 10:28 "You *are* **w aware** that it is against our G2179
Ac 15:29 You will do w to avoid these things G2292
Ac 16: 2 at Lystra and Iconium **spoke** w **of** him. G3455
Ac 17:17 **as w as** in the marketplace day by day G2779
Ac 24:22 who was w acquainted with the Way G209
Ac 25:10 to the Jews, as you yourself know **very** w. G2822
Ac 26: 3 you are w **acquainted** with all the G1195
1Co 4: 9 to angels **as w as** to human beings. G2779
1Co 11: 6 *she might* **as w have** *her* **hair cut off**; but AIT
1Co 14:17 You are giving thanks w **enough**, but no G2822
2Co 7:14 you to Titus has proved to be true **as w**. G2779
2Co 12:15 I have and **expend** *myself* **as w**. G1682
Eph 6: 3 "so that it may go w with you and that you G2292
Php 4:12 situation, whether w **fed** or hungry G5963
1Th 2: 8 only the gospel of God but our lives **as w**. G2779
1Th 3: 3 For you **know** *quite* w that we are destined AIT
1Th 3: 4 And it turned out that way, as *you* w **know**. AIT
1Th 5: 2 you know **very** w that the day of the Lord G209
2Th 1: 7 to you who are troubled, **and** to us **as w**. G3552
1Ti 1:18 recalling them you may fight the battle w, G2819
1Ti 3: 4 his own family w and see that his G2822
1Ti 3:12 his children and his household w. G2822
1Ti 3:13 who have served w gain an excellent G2822
1Ti 5:10 and *is* **w known** for her good deeds, such G3455
1Ti 5:17 of the church w are worthy of double G2822
2Ti 1:18 You know **very** w in how many ways he G1019
Heb 5: 3 **as w as** for the sins of the people. G2777
Heb 11: 4 *when* God **spoke** w of his offerings. G3455
Jas 2:16 keep warm and w **fed**," but does nothing G5963
Jas 5:15 in faith *will* **make** the sick person w; G5392
2Pe 1:17 whom I love; with him *I am* **w pleased**." G2305
2Pe 1:19 you will do w to pay attention to it G2822
1Jn 5: 1 who loves the father loves his child **as w**. G2779
3Jn 2 health and *that* all **may go** w with you, G2338
3Jn 2 even as your soul *is* **getting along** w. G2338
3Jn 12 Demetrius *is* **w spoken of** by everyone G3455
3Jn 12 We also **speak** w **of** him, and you know G3455

WELL'S (1) [WELL]

Ge 29: 3 away from the w mouth and water the H931

WELL-BEING (7)

Ezr 6:10 pray for the w *of* the king and his A10261
Job 33:26 he will restore them to **full** w. H7407
Ps 35:27 who delights in the w *of* his servant." H8934
Ps 119:122 Ensure your servant's w; do not let the H3202
Isa 48:18 your w like the waves of the sea. H7407
Isa 60:17 peace your governor and w your ruler. H7407
Jer 14:11 "Do not pray for the w of this people. H3208

WELL-BUILT (1) [BUILD]
Ge 39: 6 Now Joseph was **w** and handsome, H3637+9307

WELL-DRESSED (1) [DRESS]
Isa 3:24 a rope; instead of **w hair**, baldness H5126+5250

WELL-FED (2) [FEED]
Jer 5: 8 They are **w**, lusty stallions, each neighing H8889
Mal 4: 2 you will go out and frolic like **w** calves. H5272

WELL-INSTRUCTED (1) [INSTRUCT]
Isa 50: 4 Sovereign LORD has given me a **w** tongue, H4341

WELL-KNEADED (1) [KNEAD]
Lev 7:12 of the finest flour **w** and with oil mixed in. H8057

WELL-KNOWN (2) [KNOW]
Nu 16: 2 **w** community leaders who had been H408+9005
Mt 27:16 time they had a **w** prisoner whose name *G2168*

WELL-MIXED (1) [MIX]
Lev 6:21 bring it **w** and present the grain offering H8057

WELL-NOURISHED (1) [NOURISH]
Ne 9:25 They ate to the full and *were* **w**; they H9042

WELL-NURTURED (1)
Ps 144:12 sons in their youth will be like **w** plants, H1540

WELL-TO-DO (1)
2Ki 4: 8 And a **w** woman was there, who urged H1524

WELL-TRAINED (1) [TRAIN]
2Ch 26:11 Uzziah had a **w** army, ready to go H6913+4878

WELL-WATERED (6) [WATER]
Job 8:16 They are like a **w plant** in the sunshine H8183
Isa 58:11 You will be like a **w** garden, like a spring H8116
Jer 31:12 They will be like a **w** garden, and they H8116
Eze 31:14 No other trees *so* **w** are ever to H9272+4784
Eze 31:16 of Lebanon, the **w** trees, were H9272+4784
Eze 45:15 two hundred from the **w** pastures *of* Israel. H5482

WELLBELOVED (KJV) BELOVED, DEAR FRIEND, LOVE, LOVED ONE

WELLED (1) [WELL]
2Co 8: 2 extreme poverty **w up** in rich generosity. *G4355*

WELLING (1) [WELL]
Jn 4:14 them a spring of water **w up** to eternal life." *G256*

WELLPLEASING (KJV) PLEASING

WELLS (9) [WELL]
Ge 26:15 So all the **w** that his father's servants had H931
Ge 26:18 reopened the **w** that had been dug H931+4784
Dt 6:11 did not provide, **w** you did not dig, and H1014
Dt 10: 6 traveled from the **w** *of* Bene Jaakan to H931
2Ki 19:24 I *have* **dug w** in foreign lands and drunk H7769
Ne 9:25 kinds of good things, **w** already dug H1014
Isa 12: 3 will draw water from the **w** *of* salvation. H5078
Isa 37:25 I *have* **dug w** in foreign lands and drunk H7769
Zep 2: 6 pastures having **w** *for* shepherds and pens H1014

WELTS (1)
Isa 1: 6 only wounds and **w** and open sores, not H2467

WENT (1234) [GO]
Ge 4:16 So Cain **w out** from the LORD's presence H3655
Ge 6: 4 when the sons of God **w** to the daughters of H995
Ge 10:11 From that land *he* **w** *to* Assyria, where he H3655
Ge 12: 4 So Abram **w**, as the LORD had told him H2143
Ge 12: 4 LORD had told him; and Lot **w** with him. H2143
Ge 12: 8 From there *he* **w on** toward the hills east H6980
Ge 12:10 Abram **w down** to Egypt to live there H3718
Ge 13: 1 So Abram **w up** from Egypt to the Negev H6590
Ge 13: 1 everything he had, and Lot **w** with him. NDT
Ge 13: 3 From the Negev *he* **w** from place to place H2143
Ge 13:18 So Abram **w** to live near the great trees of H995
Ge 14: 2 kings **w to war** *against* Bera king H6913+4878
Ge 14: 5 allied with him **w out** and defeated the H995
Ge 14: 7 they turned back and **w** to En Mishpat H995
Ge 14:11 all their food; then *they* **w away**. H2143
Ge 14:14 household and **w in pursuit** as far as Dan. H8103
Ge 14:24 that belongs to the men who **w** with me— H2143
Ge 17:22 with Abraham, God **w up** from him. H6590
Ge 18:22 men turned away and **w** toward Sodom, H2143
Ge 19: 6 Lot **w** outside to meet them and shut the H3655
Ge 19:14 So Lot **w out** and spoke to his sons-in-law, H3655
Ge 19:33 the older daughter **w in** and slept with him. H995
Ge 19:35 younger daughter **w in** and slept with him H7756
Ge 21:14 *She* **w on** *her* **way** and wandered in the H2143
Ge 21:16 Then *she* **w off** and sat down about a H2143
Ge 21:19 So *she* **w** and filled the skin with water H2143
Ge 22: 6 As the two of them **w on** together, H2143
Ge 22: 8 And the two of them **w on** together. H2143
Ge 22:13 He **w over** and took the ram and sacrificed H2143
Ge 23: 2 Abraham **w** to mourn for Sarah and to H995
Ge 24:16 *She* **w down** to the spring, filled her jar H3718
Ge 24:30 *he* **w** *out* to the man and found him H995
Ge 24:32 So the man **w** to the house, and the H995
Ge 24:45 *She* **w down** to the spring and drew water H3718
Ge 24:61 the camels and **w** back with the man. H2143
Ge 24:63 He **w out** to the field one evening to H3655
Ge 25:22 So *she* **w** to inquire of the LORD. H2143
Ge 26: 1 Isaac **w** to Abimelek king of the H2143
Ge 26:23 From there *he* **w up** *to* Beersheba. H6590
Ge 26:31 on their way, and *they* **w** away peacefully. H2143
Ge 27:14 So *he* **w** and got them and brought them H2143
Ge 27:18 *He* **w** to his father and said, "My father." H995
Ge 27:22 Jacob **w close** to his father Isaac, who H5602
Ge 27:27 So *he* **w** to him and kissed him. H5602
Ge 28: 5 on his way, and *he* **w** to Paddan Aram, to H2143
Ge 28: 9 so he **w** to Ishmael and married Mahalath H2143
Ge 29:10 he **w over** and rolled the stone away from H5602
Ge 30:14 Reuben **w out** into the fields and found H2143
Ge 30:16 that evening, Leah **w out** to meet him. H3655
Ge 30:42 So the weak animals **w** to Laban and the H2118
Ge 31:33 So Laban **w** into Jacob's tent and into H995
Ge 32: 1 Jacob also **w** on his way, and the angels H2143
Ge 32: 6 they said, "*We* **w** to your brother Esau, and H995
Ge 32:21 So Jacob's gifts **w on** ahead of him, but he H6296
Ge 33: 3 *He* himself **w on** ahead and bowed down H6296
Ge 33:17 however, **w** to Sukkoth, where he built a H5825
Ge 34: 1 **w out** to visit the women of the land. H3655
Ge 34: 6 father Hamor **w out** to talk with Jacob. H3655
Ge 34:20 his son Shechem **w** to the gate of their H995
Ge 34:24 All the *men who* **w out** *of* the city gate H3655
Ge 35:13 Then God **w up** from him at the place H6590
Ge 35:22 Reuben **w in** and slept with his father's H2143
Ge 37:17 So Joseph **w** after his brothers and found H2143
Ge 37:30 *He* **w back** to his brothers and said, "The H8740
Ge 38: 1 his brothers and **w down** to stay with a H3718
Ge 38:11 So Tamar **w** to live in her father's H2143
Ge 38:12 from his grief, *he* **w up** to Timnah, to the H6590
Ge 38:12 his friend Hirah the Adullamite **w** with him. NDT
Ge 38:16 *he* **w over** to her by the roadside and said H5742
Ge 38:22 So *he* **w back** to Judah and said, "I didn't H8740
Ge 39:11 One day *he* **w** into the house to attend to H995
Ge 41:45 And Joseph **w** throughout the land of H3655
Ge 41:46 And Joseph **w out** from Pharaoh's H3655
Ge 42: 3 Joseph's brothers **w down** to buy grain H3718
Ge 42: 5 were among those *who* **w** to buy grain, H995
Ge 43:19 So *they* **w up** to Joseph's steward and H5602
Ge 43:30 *He* **w** into his private room and wept there H995
Ge 44:18 Then Judah **w up** to him and said H5602
Ge 44:24 When *we* **w back** to your servant my father H6590
Ge 44:28 One of them **w away** from me, and I said H3655
Ge 45:25 So *they* **w up** out of Egypt and came to H6590
Ge 46: 6 So Jacob and all his offspring **w** to Egypt H995
Ge 46: 8 Jacob and his descendants) who **w** to Egypt: H995
Ge 46:26 All those who **w** to Egypt with Jacob H995
Ge 46:27 Jacob's family, which **w** to Egypt, were H995
Ge 46:29 made ready and **w** to Goshen to meet his H6590
Ge 47: 1 Joseph **w** and told Pharaoh, "My father H995
Ge 47:10 Pharaoh and **w out** from his presence. H3655
Ge 49: 4 for *you* **w up** *onto* your father's bed H6590
Ge 50: 7 So Joseph **w up** to bury his father. H6590
Ge 50: 9 horsemen also **w up** with him. H6590
Ex 1: 1 sons of Israel who **w** to Egypt with Jacob, H995
Ex 2: 5 Pharaoh's daughter **w down** to the Nile to H3718
Ex 2: 8 So the girl **w** and got the baby's mother H2143
Ex 2:11 *he* **w out** to where his own people were H3655
Ex 2:13 The next day *he* **w out** and saw two H3655
Ex 2:15 fled from Pharaoh and **w** to live in Midian, NDT
Ex 2:23 help because of their slavery **w up** to God. H6590
Ex 4:18 Then Moses **w** back to Jethro his H2143
Ex 5: 1 Moses and Aaron **w** to Pharaoh and said, H995
Ex 5:10 the overseers **w out** and said to the H3655
Ex 5:15 Israelite overseers **w** and appealed to H995
Ex 5:23 Ever since *I* **w** to Pharaoh to speak in your H995
Ex 7:10 So Moses and Aaron **w** to Pharaoh and did H995
Ex 7:23 he turned and **w** into his palace, and H995
Ex 9:33 Moses left Pharaoh and **w** out of the city. NDT
Ex 10: 3 So Moses and Aaron **w** to Pharaoh and H995
Ex 12:38 Many other people **w up** with them, and H6590
Ex 13:18 The Israelites **w up** out of Egypt ready H6590
Ex 13:21 By day the LORD **w** ahead of them in a H2143
Ex 14:19 withdrew and **w** behind them. H2143
Ex 14:20 so neither **w near** the other all night long. H7928
Ex 14:22 the Israelites **w** through the sea on dry H995
Ex 14:27 at daybreak the sea **w back** to its place. H8740
Ex 14:29 But the Israelites **w** through the sea on dry H2143
Ex 15:19 chariots and horsemen **w** into the sea, the H995
Ex 15:22 the Red Sea and *they* **w** into the Desert of H3655
Ex 16:27 some of the people **w out** on the seventh H3655
Ex 17:10 Aaron and Hur **w** *to* the top of the hill. H6590
Ex 18: 7 So Moses **w out** to meet his father-in-law H3655
Ex 18: 7 each other and then **w** into the tent. H995
Ex 19: 3 Then Moses **w up** to God, and the LORD H6590
Ex 19: 7 So Moses **w back** and summoned the H995
Ex 19:20 the top of the mountain. So Moses **w up** H6590
Ex 19:25 So Moses **w down** to the people and told H3718
Ex 24: 3 When Moses **w** and told the people all the H995
Ex 24: 9 the seventy elders of Israel **w up** H6590
Ex 24:13 Moses **w up** on the mountain of God. H6590
Ex 24:15 When Moses **w up** on the mountain, the H6590
Ex 24:18 the cloud as *he* **w** on **up** the mountain. H6590
Ex 32:15 Moses turned and **w down** the mountain H3718
Ex 32:31 So Moses **w back** to the LORD and said H8740
Ex 33: 8 And whenever Moses **w out** to the tent, all H3655
Ex 33: 9 As Moses **w** into the tent, the pillar of cloud H995
Ex 34: 4 the first ones and **w up** Mount Sinai early H6590
Ex 34:35 over his face until he **w in** to speak with the H995
Lev 9:23 Moses and Aaron then **w** into the tent of H995
Lev 24:10 an Egyptian father **w out** among the H3655
Nu 10:14 The divisions of the camp of Judah **w** first H5825
Nu 10:18 divisions of the camp of Reuben **w** next, H5825
Nu 10:22 divisions of the camp of Ephraim **w** next, H5825
Nu 10:33 of the LORD **w** before them during H5825
Nu 11: 8 The people **w around** gathering it, and H8763
Nu 11:24 So Moses **w out** and told the people what H3655
Nu 11:31 Now a wind **w out** from the LORD and H5825
Nu 11:32 day the people **w out** and gathered quail H7756
Nu 12: 4 So the three of them **w out**. H3655
Nu 13:21 So *they* **w up** and explored the land from H6590
Nu 13:22 *They* **w up** through the Negev and came to H6590
Nu 13:27 "*We* **w** into the land to which you sent us H995
Nu 14:24 I will bring him into the land *he* **w** to, and H995
Nu 14:38 Of the men who **w** to explore the land H2143
Nu 14:44 their presumption *they* **w up** toward the H6590
Nu 16:25 Moses got up and **w** to Dathan and H2143
Nu 16:33 They **w down** alive into the realm of the H3718
Nu 16:43 Then Moses and Aaron **w** to the front of the H995
Nu 20: 6 Moses and Aaron **w** from the assembly to H995
Nu 20:15 Our ancestors **w down** into Egypt, and we H3718
Nu 20:27 *They* **w up** Mount Hor in the sight of the H6590
Nu 21:18 Then they **w** from the wilderness to NDT
Nu 21:28 "Fire **w out** from Heshbon, a blaze from H3655
Nu 21:33 they turned and **w up** *along* the road H6590
Nu 22:21 his donkey and **w** with the Moabite H2143
Nu 22:22 But God was very angry when he **w**, and H2143
Nu 22:35 So Balaam **w** with Balak's officials H2143
Nu 22:36 *he* **w out** to meet him at the Moabite H3655
Nu 22:39 Then Balaam **w** with Balak *to* Kiriath H2143
Nu 23: 3 Then *he* **w off** *to* a barren height H2143
Nu 23: 6 So *he* **w back** to him and found him H8740
Nu 23:17 So *he* **w** to him and found him standing H995
Nu 24:25 returned home, and Balak **w** his own way. H2143
Nu 31:13 of the community **w** to meet them outside H3655
Nu 31:48 commanders of hundreds—**w** to Moses H7928
Nu 32: 9 After *they* **w up** to the Valley of Eshkol H6590
Nu 32:39 of Makir son of Manasseh **w** to Gilead, H2143
Nu 33: 9 They left Marah and **w** to Elim, where there H995
Nu 33:38 Aaron the priest **w up** Mount Hor, H6590
Dt 1:19 **w** toward the hill country of the Amorites *through* H2143
Dt 1:24 They left and **w up** into the hill country H6590
Dt 1:31 all the way *you* **w** until you reached this H2143
Dt 1:33 who **w** ahead of you on your journey, in H2143
Dt 2: 8 So *we* **w on** past our relatives the H6296
Dt 3: 1 we turned and **w up** *along* the road H6590
Dt 9: 9 When I **w up** on the mountain to receive H6590
Dt 9:15 So I turned and **w down** from the H3718
Dt 10: 3 and *I* **w up** on the mountain with the two H6590
Dt 10:22 Your ancestors *who* **w down** into Egypt were AIT
Dt 26: 5 and *he* **w down** into Egypt with a few H3718
Dt 29:26 *They* **w off** and worshiped other gods and H2143
Dt 31: 1 Then Moses **w out** and spoke these words H2143
Jos 2: 1 So *they* **w** and entered the house of a H2143
Jos 2: 5 I don't know which way they **w**. Go after H2143
Jos 2: 8 down for the night, she **w up** on the roof H6590
Jos 2:22 *they* **w** into the hills and stayed there three H995
Jos 2:23 *They* **w down** out of the hills, forded the H3718
Jos 3: 1 set out from Shittim and **w** to the Jordan, H995
Jos 3: 2 days the officers **w** throughout the camp, H6296
Jos 3: 6 So they took it up and **w** ahead of them. H2143
Jos 3:14 the ark of the covenant **w** ahead of them. NDT
Jos 4:19 month the people **w up** from the Jordan H6590
Jos 5:13 Joshua **w up** to him and asked, "Are you H2143
Jos 6: 1 No *one* **w out** and no one came in H3655
Jos 6: 8 seven trumpets before the LORD **w forward**, H6296
Jos 6:13 carrying the seven trumpets **w forward**, H2143
Jos 6:13 The armed men **w** ahead of them and the H2143
Jos 6:23 had done the spying **w in** and brought out H995
Jos 7: 2 So the men **w up** and spied out Ai. H6590
Jos 7: 4 So about three thousand **w up**; but they H6590
Jos 8: 9 and *they* **w** to the place of ambush and H2143
Jos 8:13 That night Joshua **w** into the valley. H2143
Jos 8:17 the city open and **w in pursuit** *of* Israel. H8103
Jos 9: 4 *They* **w** as a delegation whose donkeys H2143
Jos 9: 6 Then *they* **w** to Joshua in the camp at H2143
Jos 10:36 all Israel with him **w up** from Eglon to H6590
Jos 11:21 At that time Joshua **w** and destroyed the H995
Jos 14: 8 Israelites who **w up** with me made the H6590
Jos 15: 3 on to Zin and **w over** to the south of H6590
Jos 15: 6 **w up** *to* Beth Hoglah and continued north H6590
Jos 15: 7 The boundary then **w up** to Debir from the H6590
Jos 15: 9 Ephron and **w down** *toward* Baalah H9305
Jos 15:11 It **w** to the northern slope of Ekron, turned H3655
Jos 16: 1 and **w up** from there through the desert H6590
Jos 16: 2 *It* **w on** from Bethel (that is, Luz), crossed H3655
Jos 16: 5 of their inheritance **w** from Ataroth Addar H2118
Jos 16: 7 Then *it* **w down** from Janoah to Ataroth H3718
Jos 16: 8 Tappuah the border **w** west to the Kanah H2143
Jos 17: 4 *They* **w** to Eleazar the priest, Joshua son of H7928
Jos 18: 9 So the men left and **w** through the land H6296
Jos 18:13 **w down** *to* Ataroth Addar on the hill H3718
Jos 18:16 The boundary **w down** to the foot of the H3718
Jos 18:17 then curved north, **w** *to* En Shemesh H3655
Jos 18:19 It then **w** to the northern slope of Beth H6296
Jos 19:10 of their inheritance **w** as far as Sarid. H2118
Jos 19:12 Kisloth Tabor and **w on** to Daberath and H3655
Jos 19:14 the boundary **w around** on the north to H6015
Jos 19:27 and **w** north to Beth Emek and Neiel NDT
Jos 19:28 It **w** to Abdon, Rehob, Hammon and Kanah NDT
Jos 19:29 toward Ramah and **w** to the fortified city NDT

Jos 19:33 Their boundary **w** from Heleph and the H2118
Jos 19:47 to them, they **w up** and attacked Leshem H6590
Jos 22: 6 them away, and *they* **w** to their homes. H2143
Jos 22:15 When *they* **w** to Gilead—to Reuben, Gad H995
Jos 24: 4 Jacob and his family **w down** *to* Egypt. H3718
Jdg 1: 3 So the Simeonites **w** with them. H2143
Jdg 1: 9 Judah **w down** to fight against the H3718
Jdg 1:16 **w up** from the City of Palms with the H6590
Jdg 1:17 the men of Judah **w** with the Simeonites H2143
Jdg 1:26 He then **w** *to* the land of the Hittites H2143
Jdg 2: 1 angel of the LORD **w up** from Gilgal to H6590
Jdg 2: 6 they **w** to take possession of the land H2143
Jdg 2:15 Whenever Israel **w out** to fight, the hand H3655
Jdg 3:10 he became Israel's judge and **w** to war. H3655
Jdg 3:19 near Gilgal *he* himself **w back** to Eglon H8740
Jdg 3:23 Then Ehud **w out** to the porch; he shut the H3655
Jdg 3:27 the Israelites **w down** with him from the H3718
Jdg 4: 5 the Israelites **w up** to her to have H6590
Jdg 4: 9 So Deborah **w** with Barak to Kedesh. H2143
Jdg 4:10 ten thousand men **w up** under his H6590
Jdg 4:10 Deborah also **w up** with him. H6590
Jdg 4:14 So Barak **w down** Mount Tabor, with ten H3718
Jdg 4:18 Jael **w out** to meet Sisera and said to him, H3655
Jdg 4:21 a hammer and **w** quietly to him while H995
Jdg 4:22 of Sisera, and Jael **w out** to meet him. H3655
Jdg 4:22 So *he* **w** in *with* her, and there lay Sisera H995
Jdg 5: 4 **w out** from Seir, when you marched H3655
Jdg 5:11 of the LORD **w down** to the city gates. H3718
Jdg 6:19 Gideon **w inside**, prepared a young goat H995
Jdg 6:35 so that *they* too **w up** to meet them. H6590
Jdg 7:11 Purah his servant **w down** to the outposts H3718
Jdg 8: 1 you call us when *you* **w** to fight Midian?" H2143
Jdg 8: 8 From there *he* **w up** *to* Peniel and made H6590
Jdg 8:11 Gideon **w up** *by* the route of the nomads H6590
Jdg 8:29 son of Joash **w back** home to live. H2143
Jdg 9: 1 son of Jerub-Baal **w** to his mother's H2143
Jdg 9: 5 *He* **w** *to* his father's home in Ophrah and on H995
Jdg 9: 8 One day the trees **w out** to anoint a H2143+2143
Jdg 9:42 people of Shechem **w out** *to* the fields, H3655
Jdg 9:46 tower of Shechem **w** into the stronghold H995
Jdg 9:48 he and all his men **w up** Mount Zalmon H6590
Jdg 9:50 Next Abimelek **w** to Thebez and besieged H2143
Jdg 9:52 Abimelek **w** to the tower and attacked it H995
Jdg 9:55 that Abimelek was dead, they **w** home. H2143
Jdg 11: 5 the elders of Gilead **w** to get Jephthah H2143
Jdg 11:11 So Jephthah **w** with the elders of Gilead H2143
Jdg 11:16 Israel **w** through the wilderness to the Red H2143
Jdg 11:32 Then Jephthah **w** over to fight the H6296
Jdg 11:38 She and her friends **w** into the hills and H2143
Jdg 13: 6 Then the woman **w** to her husband and H995
Jdg 14: 1 Samson **w down** to Timnah and saw there H3718
Jdg 14: 5 Samson **w down** to Timnah together with H3718
Jdg 14: 7 Then *he* **w down** and talked with the H3718
Jdg 14: 8 time later, when *he* **w back** to marry her H8740
Jdg 14: 9 his hands and ate as *he* **w along**. H2143+2143
Jdg 14:10 Now his father **w down** to see the woman H3718
Jdg 14:19 *He* **w down** *to* Ashkelon, struck down thirty H3718
Jdg 15: 1 took a young goat and *w to* **visit** his wife. AIT
Jdg 15: 4 So he **w out** and caught three hundred H2143
Jdg 15: 6 So the Philistines **w up** and burned her H6590
Jdg 15: 8 Then *he* **w down** and stayed in a cave in H3718
Jdg 15: 9 The Philistines **w up** and camped in H6590
Jdg 15:11 men from Judah **w down** to the cave in H3718
Jdg 16: 1 One day Samson **w** to Gaza, where he H2143
Jdg 16: 1 *He* **w in to spend the night with** her. H995+448
Jdg 16: 5 rulers of the Philistines **w** to her and said, H6590
Jdg 16:31 father's whole family **w down** to get him. H3718
Jdg 18:13 From there *they* **w on** *to* the hill country of H6296
Jdg 18:15 turned in there and **w** to the house of the H995
Jdg 18:17 spied out the land **w** inside and took the H995
Jdg 18:18 When the five men **w into** Micah's house H995
Jdg 18:20 the idol and **w** along with the people H995
Jdg 18:24 gods I made, and my priest, and **w away**. H2143
Jdg 18:26 So the Danites **w** their way, and Micah H2143
Jdg 18:26 him, turned around and **w back** home. H8740
Jdg 18:27 his priest, and **w on** to Laish, against a H995
Jdg 19: 2 She left him and **w** back to her parents' NDT
Jdg 19: 3 her husband **w** to her to persuade her to H2143
Jdg 19:10 the man left and **w** toward Jebus (that is, H995
Jdg 19:14 So *they* **w on**, and the sun set as they H6296
Jdg 19:15 *They* **w** and sat in the city square, but no H995
Jdg 19:23 of the house **w outside** and said to them, H3655
Jdg 19:26 the woman **w back** *to* the house where H995
Jdg 20:18 The Israelites **w up** *to* Bethel and inquired H6590
Jdg 20:20 The Israelites **w out** to fight the H3655
Jdg 20:23 The Israelites **w up** and wept before the H6590
Jdg 20:26 the whole army, **w up** to Bethel, and there H6590
Jdg 20:30 They **w up** against the Benjamites on the H6590
Jdg 20:48 The men of Israel **w back** to Benjamin H8740
Jdg 21: 2 The people **w** *to* Bethel, where they sat H995
Jdg 21:24 left that place and **w** home to their tribes H3655
Ru 1: 1 **w** to live for a while in the country of H2143
Ru 1: 2 And *they* **w** *to* Moab and lived there H995
Ru 1:19 So the two women **w on** until they came H2143
Ru 1:21 I **w away** full, but the LORD has brought me H2143
Ru 2: 3 So *she* **w out**, entered a field and began H2143
Ru 3: 6 So *she* **w down** *to* the threshing floor and H3718
Ru 3: 7 *he* **w over** to lie down at the far end of the H995
Ru 3:15 bundle on her. Then *he* **w back** *to* town. H995
Ru 4: 1 Meanwhile Boaz **w up** *to* the town gate H6590
Ru 4: 1 So *he* **w over** and sat down. H6073
1Sa 1: 3 after year this man **w up** from his town to H6590
1Sa 1: 7 This **w on** year after year. Whenever H6913
1Sa 1: 7 Whenever Hannah **w up** to the house of H6590
1Sa 1:18 Then she **w** her way and ate something H2143
1Sa 1:19 the LORD and then **w** back to their home at H995
1Sa 1:21 her husband Elkanah **w up** with all his H6590
1Sa 2:11 Then Elkanah **w** home to Ramah, but the H2143
1Sa 2:19 it to him when she **w up** with her husband H6590
1Sa 3: 5 lie down." So *he* **w** and lay down. H2143
1Sa 3: 6 And Samuel got up and **w** to Eli and said H2143
1Sa 3: 8 And Samuel got up and **w** to Eli and said H2143
1Sa 3: 9 So Samuel **w** and lay down in his place. H2143
1Sa 4: 1 Now the Israelites **w out** to fight against H3655
1Sa 4:12 the battle line and **w** *to* Shiloh with his H995
1Sa 4:19 *she* **w into labor** and gave birth H4156
1Sa 5:12 the outcry of the city **w up** *to* heaven. H6590
1Sa 6:12 Then the cows **w straight** *up* toward Beth H3837
1Sa 7:16 From year to year *he* **w** on a circuit from H2143
1Sa 7:17 But he always **w back** to Ramah, where his H9588
1Sa 9: 4 *They* **w on** into the district of Shaalim, but H6296
1Sa 9: 9 in Israel, if someone **w** to inquire of God H2143
1Sa 9:14 *They* **w up** *to* the town, and as they were H6590
1Sa 9:26 he and Samuel **w** outside together. H3655
1Sa 10:13 prophesying, *he* **w** *to* the high place. H995
1Sa 10:14 were not to be found, *we* **w** to Samuel." H995
1Sa 10:26 Saul also **w** to his home in Gibeah H2143
1Sa 11: 1 the Ammonite **w up** and besieged H6590
1Sa 11: 9 When the messengers **w** and reported this H995
1Sa 11:15 So all the people **w** *to* Gilgal and made H2143
1Sa 13: 5 *They* **w up** and camped at Mikmash, east H6590
1Sa 13:10 and Saul **w out** to greet him. H3655
1Sa 13:15 left Gilgal and **w up** *to* Gibeah in H6590
1Sa 13:17 Raiding parties **w out** from the Philistine H3655
1Sa 13:20 So all Israel **w down** *to* the Philistines to H3718
1Sa 14:20 all his men assembled and **w** to the battle. H995
1Sa 14:21 to their camp **w over** to the H2118+6017
1Sa 14:26 When they **w** into the woods, they saw the H995
1Sa 15: 5 Saul **w** to the city of Amalek and set an H995
1Sa 15:12 Samuel got up and **w to meet** Saul, H7925
1Sa 15:20 "*I* **w** on the mission the LORD assigned me H2143
1Sa 15:31 So Samuel **w back** with Saul, and Saul H8740
1Sa 15:34 Saul **w up** to his home in Gibeah of H6590
1Sa 16:13 Samuel then **w** to Ramah. H2143
1Sa 17: 7 His shield bearer **w** ahead of him. H2143
1Sa 17:15 David **w** back and **forth** from Saul to H2143
1Sa 17:35 *I* **w** after it, struck it and rescued the sheep H3655
1Sa 18:27 men with him and **w out** and killed two H2143
1Sa 19: 8 David **w out** and fought the H3655
1Sa 19:18 *he* **w** to Samuel at Ramah and told him all H995
1Sa 19:18 Then he and Samuel **w** to Naioth and H2143
1Sa 19:22 left for Ramah and **w** to the great cistern at H995
1Sa 19:23 So Saul **w** to Naioth at Ramah. But the H2143
1Sa 20: 1 Naioth at Ramah and **w** to Jonathan and H995
1Sa 20:11 into the field." So *they* **w** there together. H3655
1Sa 20:35 morning Jonathan **w out** *to* the field for H3655
1Sa 20:42 and Jonathan **w back** to the town. H995
1Sa 21: 1 David **w** to Nob, to Ahimelek the priest H995
1Sa 21:10 fled from Saul and **w** to Achish king of H995
1Sa 22: 1 heard about it, *they* **w down** to him there. H3718
1Sa 22: 3 From there David **w** *to* Mizpah in Moab H2143
1Sa 22: 5 So David left and **w** *to* the forest of Hereth. H995
1Sa 23: 5 So David and his men **w** *to* Keilah, fought H2143
1Sa 23:16 Saul's son Jonathan **w** to David at Horesh H2143
1Sa 23:18 Then Jonathan **w** home, but David H2143
1Sa 23:19 The Ziphites **w up** to Saul at Gibeah and H6590
1Sa 23:24 So they set out and **w** to Ziph ahead of H2143
1Sa 23:25 *he* **w down** *to* the rock and stayed in the H3718
1Sa 23:25 *he* **w** *into* the Desert of Maon **in pursuit** of H8103
1Sa 23:28 pursuit of David and **w** to meet the H2143
1Sa 23:29 And David **w up** from there and lived in H6590
1Sa 24: 3 was there, and Saul **w in** to relieve himself. H995
1Sa 24: 7 And Saul left the cave and **w** his way. H2143
1Sa 24: 8 Then David **w out** of the cave and called H3655
1Sa 24:22 David and his men **w up** to the stronghold H6590
1Sa 25:12 David's men turned around and **w back** H8740
1Sa 25:13 About four hundred men **w up** with David H6590
1Sa 25:36 When Abigail **w** to Nabal, he was in the H995
1Sa 25:40 His servants **w** to Carmel and said to H995
1Sa 25:42 **w** with David's messengers and became H2143
1Sa 26: 1 The Ziphites **w** to Saul at Gibeah and said H995
1Sa 26: 2 So Saul **w down** to the Desert of Ziph H3718
1Sa 26: 5 David set out and **w** to the place where H995
1Sa 26: 7 David and Abishai **w** to the army by night H995
1Sa 26:25 So David **w** on his way, and Saul H2143
1Sa 27: 2 with him left and **w over** to Achish son of H6296
1Sa 27: 8 David and his men **w up** and raided the H6590
1Sa 28: 8 at night he and two men **w** to the woman. H995
1Sa 29:11 the Philistines **w up** *to* Jezreel. H6590
1Sa 30: 2 carried them off as *they* **w** on their way. H2143
1Sa 30:24 as that of him *who* **w down** to the battle. H3718
1Sa 31:12 the wall of Beth Shan and **w** to Jabesh, H995
2Sa 2: 2 So David **w up** there with his two wives H6590
2Sa 2:12 left Mahanaim and **w** to Gibeon. NDT
2Sa 2:13 David's men **w out** and met them at H3655
2Sa 3:16 however, **w** with her, weeping behind her H2143
2Sa 3:16 "Go back home!" So *he* **w back**. H8740
2Sa 3:19 Then he **w** to Hebron to tell David H2143
2Sa 3:21 sent Abner away, and *he* **w** in peace. H2143
2Sa 3:24 So Joab **w** to the king and said, "What H995
2Sa 4: 6 They **w** into the inner part of the house as if H995
2Sa 5:17 they **w up** in full force to search for him H6590
2Sa 5:17 about it and **w down** to the stronghold H3718
2Sa 5:20 So David **w** to Baal Perazim, and there he H995
2Sa 6: 2 He and all his men **w** to Baalah in Judah H2143
2Sa 6:12 So David **w** to bring up the ark of God H2143
2Sa 6:19 And all the people **w** to their homes. H2143
2Sa 7:18 Then King David **w in** and sat before the H995
2Sa 7:23 on earth that God **w out** to redeem as a H2143
2Sa 8: 3 when he **w** to restore his monument at H2143
2Sa 8: 6 LORD gave David victory wherever *he* **w**. H2143
2Sa 8:14 LORD gave David victory wherever *he* **w**. H2143
2Sa 10:14 fled before Abishai and **w inside** the city. H995
2Sa 10:16 Euphrates River; *they* **w** *to* Helam, with H995
2Sa 10:17 crossed the Jordan and **w** *to* Helam. H995
2Sa 11: 4 Then *she* **w back** home. H8740
2Sa 11:13 the evening Uriah **w out** to sleep on his H3655
2Sa 12:20 *he* **w into** the house of the LORD and H995
2Sa 12:20 Then *he* **w** to his own house, and at his H995
2Sa 12:24 and *he* **w** to her and made love to her. H995
2Sa 12:29 the entire army and **w** to Rabbah, H2143
2Sa 13: 8 So Tamar **w** *to* the house of her brother H2143
2Sa 13:19 put her hands on her head and **w away**, H2143
2Sa 13:19 went away, weeping aloud *as she* **w**. H2143
2Sa 13:24 Absalom **w** to the king and said, "Your H995
2Sa 13:34 The watchman **w** and told the king, "I see H995
2Sa 13:37 Absalom fled and **w** to Talmai son of H2143
2Sa 13:38 After Absalom fled and **w** *to* Geshur, he H2143
2Sa 14: 4 the woman from Tekoa **w** to the king, H995
2Sa 14:23 Then Joab **w** to Geshur and brought H2143
2Sa 14:24 So Absalom **w** to his own house and did H6015
2Sa 14:33 So Joab **w** to the king and told him this H995
2Sa 15: 9 "Go in peace." So *he* **w** to Hebron. H2143
2Sa 15:11 invited as guests and **w** quite innocently, H2143
2Sa 15:30 of Olives, weeping as *he* **w**; his head was H6590
2Sa 15:30 too and were weeping as *they* **w up**. H6590
2Sa 16:13 cursing as *he* **w** and throwing stones at H2143
2Sa 16:16 confidant, **w** to Absalom and said to him H995
2Sa 17:18 left at once and **w** to the house of a man H995
2Sa 17:21 out of the well and **w** to inform King H2143
2Sa 17:24 David **w** to Mahanaim, and Absalom H995
2Sa 18: 9 and *as* the mule **w** under the thick H995
2Sa 18:24 the watchman **w up** to the roof of the H2143
2Sa 18:33 *He* **w up** to the room over the gateway H6590
2Sa 18:33 As he **w**, he said: "O my son H2143
2Sa 19: 5 Then Joab **w** into the house to the king H995
2Sa 19:15 king returned and **w** as far as the Jordan. H995
2Sa 19:24 grandson, also **w down** to meet the king. H3718
2Sa 20: 5 But when Amasa **w** to summon Judah, he H2143
2Sa 20: 7 mighty warriors **w out** under the command H3655
2Sa 20:13 everyone **w on** with Joab to pursue Sheba H6296
2Sa 20:17 *He* **w** toward her, and she asked, "Are you H7928
2Sa 20:22 Then the woman **w** to all the people with H995
2Sa 20:22 And Joab **w back** to the king in Jerusalem. H8740
2Sa 21:12 he **w** and took the bones of Saul and his H2143
2Sa 21:15 David **w down** with his men to fight H3718
2Sa 23:17 blood of men who **w** at the risk of their H2143
2Sa 23:20 He also **w down** into a pit on a snowy day H3718
2Sa 23:21 Benaiah **w** against him with a club. H3718
2Sa 24: 5 then **w** through Gad and on to Jazer. NDT
2Sa 24: 6 *They* **w** to Gilead and the region of Tahtim H995
2Sa 24: 7 Then *they* **w** *toward* the fortress of Tyre and H995
2Sa 24: 7 *they* **w on** to Beersheba in the Negev of H3655
2Sa 24:13 So Gad **w** to David and said to him, "Shall H995
2Sa 24:18 On that day Gad **w** to David and said to H995
2Sa 24:19 So David **w up**, as the LORD had H6590
2Sa 24:20 he **w out** and bowed down before the H3655
1Ki 1:15 So Bathsheba **w** to see the aged king in his H995
1Ki 1:23 So *he* **w** before the king and bowed with H995
1Ki 1:38 the Pelethites **w down** and had Solomon H3718
1Ki 1:40 And all the people **w up** after him, playing H6590
1Ki 1:50 **w** and took hold of the horns of the altar. H2143
1Ki 2: 8 curses on me the day I **w** *to* Mahanaim. H2143
1Ki 2:13 the son of Haggith, **w** to Bathsheba H995
1Ki 2:19 When Bathsheba **w** to King Solomon to H995
1Ki 2:34 son of Jehoiada **w up** and struck down H6590
1Ki 2:40 his donkey and **w** to Achish at Gath in H2143
1Ki 2:40 So Shimei **w away** and brought the slaves H2143
1Ki 2:46 and *he* **w out** and struck Shimei down H3655
1Ki 3: 4 The king **w** to Gibeon to offer sacrifices H2143
1Ki 8:66 They blessed the king and then **w** home H2143
1Ki 9:12 But when Hiram **w** from Tyre to see the H3655
1Ki 10:16 shekels of gold **w** into each shield. H6590
1Ki 11:18 They set out from Midian and **w** *to* Paran H995
1Ki 11:18 Paran with them, *they* **w** *to* Egypt, to H995
1Ki 11:24 their leader; *they* **w** *to* Damascus, where H2143
1Ki 12: 1 Rehoboam **w** *to* Shechem, for all Israel H2143
1Ki 12: 3 of Israel **w** *to* Rehoboam and said H995
1Ki 12: 5 So the people **w away**. H2143
1Ki 12:16 So the Israelites **w** home. H2143
1Ki 12:24 the word of the LORD and **w home** again, H2143
1Ki 12:25 From there *he* **w out** and built up Peniel. H3655
1Ki 12:30 the one at Bethel and **w** as far as Dan to NDT
1Ki 12:33 the Israelites and **w up** to the altar to H6590
1Ki 13:24 As *he* **w on** *his* **way**, a lion met him on the H2143
1Ki 13:25 and *they* **w** and reported it in the city where H995
1Ki 13:28 Then *he* **w out** and found the body lying H2143
1Ki 14: 4 what he said and **w** *to* Ahijah's house in H2143
1Ki 14:17 wife got up and left and **w** to Tirzah. H995
1Ki 14:28 Whenever the king **w** *to* the LORD's temple H995
1Ki 15:17 king of Israel **w up** against Judah and H6590
1Ki 16:18 *he* **w** into the citadel of the royal palace H995
1Ki 17: 5 *He* **w** to the Kerith Ravine, east of the H2143
1Ki 17:10 So *he* **w** to Zarephath. When he came to H2143
1Ki 17:15 *She* **w away** and did as Elijah had told H2143
1Ki 18: 2 So Elijah **w** to present himself to Ahab H2143

W

Book	Ref	Context	Number
1Ki	18:16	So Obadiah **w** to meet Ahab and told him	H2143
1Ki	18:16	told him, and Ahab **w** to meet Elijah.	H2143
1Ki	18:21	Elijah **w** before the people and said, "How	H5602
1Ki	18:42	So Ahab **w off** to eat and drink, but Elijah	H6590
1Ki	18:43	And *he* **w up** and looked	H6590
1Ki	19: 4	while *he* himself **w** a day's journey into	H2143
1Ki	19: 9	There *he* **w** into a cave and spent the night	H995
1Ki	19:13	over his face and **w out** and stood at the	H3655
1Ki	19:19	So Elijah **w** from there and found Elisha	H2143
1Ki	19:19	Elijah **w up** to him and threw his cloak	H6296
1Ki	19:21	So Elisha left him and **w back**. He took his	H8740
1Ki	20: 1	*he* **w up** and besieged Samaria and	H6590
1Ki	20:17	the provincial commanders **w out** first.	H3655
1Ki	20:26	the Arameans and **w up** to Aphek to fight	H6590
1Ki	20:32	*they* **w** to the king of Israel and said	H995
1Ki	20:36	And after the man **w** away, a lion found	H2143
1Ki	20:38	Then the prophet **w** and stood by the road	H2143
1Ki	20:39	"Your servant **w** into the thick of the battle,	H3655
1Ki	20:43	the king of Israel **w** to his palace in	H2143
1Ki	21: 4	So Ahab **w** home, sullen and angry	H995
1Ki	21:16	he got up and **w down** to take possession	H3718
1Ki	21:27	He lay in sackcloth and **w around** meekly.	H2143
1Ki	22: 2	king of Judah **w down** to see the king of	H3718
1Ki	22:24	son of Kenaanah **w up** and slapped	H5602
1Ki	22:24	the LORD go when he **w** from me to speak to	NDT
1Ki	22:29	king of Judah **w up** *to* Ramoth Gilead.	H6590
1Ki	22:30	Israel disguised himself and **w** into battle.	H995
2Ki	1: 4	You will certainly die!'" So Elijah **w**.	H2143
2Ki	1: 9	The captain **w up** to Elijah, who was	H6590
2Ki	1:13	This third captain **w up** and fell on his	H6590
2Ki	1:15	Elijah got up and **w down** with him to the	H3718
2Ki	2: 2	So *they* **w down** *to* Bethel.	H3718
2Ki	2: 4	I will not leave you." So *they* **w** *to* Jericho.	H995
2Ki	2: 5	prophets at Jericho **w up** to Elisha and	H5602
2Ki	2: 7	of the prophets **w** and stood at a distance	H2143
2Ki	2:11	Elijah **w up** *to* heaven in a whirlwind.	H6590
2Ki	2:13	from him and **w back** and stood on the	H8740
2Ki	2:15	And *they* **w** to meet him and bowed to the	H995
2Ki	2:21	Then *he* **w out** to the spring and threw the	H3655
2Ki	2:23	From there Elisha **w up** *to* Bethel. As he	H6590
2Ki	2:25	And *he* **w on** to Mount Carmel and from	H2143
2Ki	3:12	the king of Edom **w down** to him.	H3718
2Ki	4: 7	*She* **w** and told the man of God, and he	H995
2Ki	4: 8	One day Elisha **w** to Shunem. And a	H6296
2Ki	4:11	*he* **w up** to his room and lay down there.	H6073
2Ki	4:18	and one day *he* **w out** to his father	H3655
2Ki	4:21	*She* **w up** and laid him on the bed of the	H6590
2Ki	4:21	then shut the door and **w out**.	H3655
2Ki	4:31	Gehazi **w on** ahead and laid the staff on	H6296
2Ki	4:31	So Gehazi **w back** to meet Elisha and told	H8740
2Ki	4:33	*He* **w in**, shut the door on the two of them	H995
2Ki	4:37	Then she took her son and **w out**.	H3655
2Ki	4:39	One of them **w out** into the fields to	H3655
2Ki	5: 4	Naaman **w** to his master and told him what	H995
2Ki	5: 9	So Naaman **w** with his horses and chariots	H995
2Ki	5:11	But Naaman **w away** angry and said, "I	H2143
2Ki	5:12	So he turned and **w off** in a rage.	H2143
2Ki	5:13	Naaman's servants **w** to him and said	H5602
2Ki	5:14	So *he* **w down** and dipped himself in the	H3718
2Ki	5:15	his attendants **w back** to the man of God	H8740
2Ki	5:25	When he **w in** and stood before his master	H995
2Ki	5:27	Then Gehazi **w** from Elisha's presence	H3655
2Ki	6: 4	And *he* **w** with them. They went to the	H2143
2Ki	6: 4	*They* **w** to the Jordan and began to cut	H995
2Ki	6:14	*They* **w** by night and surrounded the city	H995
2Ki	6:15	of God got up and **w out** early the next	H3655
2Ki	6:30	As he **w** along the wall, the people	H6296
2Ki	7: 5	dusk they got up and **w** to the camp of the	H995
2Ki	7: 8	gold and clothes, and **w off** and hid them.	H2143
2Ki	7:10	So *they* **w** and called out to the city	H995
2Ki	7:10	"*We* **w** into the Aramean camp and no one	H995
2Ki	7:16	Then the people **w out** and plundered the	H3655
2Ki	8: 2	her family **w away** and stayed in the	H2143
2Ki	8: 3	the Philistines and **w** to appeal to the	H3655
2Ki	8: 7	Elisha **w** *to* Damascus, and Ben-Hadad	H995
2Ki	8: 9	Hazael **w** to meet Elisha, taking with him	H2143
2Ki	8: 9	*He* **w in** and stood before him, and said	H995
2Ki	8:21	So Jehoram **w** to Zair with all his chariots	H6296
2Ki	8:28	Ahaziah **w** with Joram son of Ahab to war	H2143
2Ki	8:29	king of Judah **w down** to Jezreel to see	H3718
2Ki	9: 4	the young prophet **w** *to* Ramoth Gilead.	H2143
2Ki	9: 6	Jehu got up and **w** into the house.	H995
2Ki	9:11	When Jehu **w out** to his fellow officers	H3655
2Ki	9:30	Then Jehu **w** to Jezreel. When Jezebel	H995
2Ki	9:34	Jehu **w in** and ate and drank. "Take care of	H995
2Ki	9:35	But when *they* **w out** to bury her, they	H2143
2Ki	9:36	*They* **w back** and told Jehu, who said	H8740
2Ki	10: 9	The next morning Jehu **w out**. He stood	H3655
2Ki	10:12	Jehu then set out and **w** *toward* Samaria	H2143
2Ki	10:23	son of Rekab **w into** the temple of Baal.	H995
2Ki	10:24	So *they* **w in** to make sacrifices and burnt	H995
2Ki	11:13	*she* **w** to the people at the temple of the	H995
2Ki	11:18	people of the land **w** *to* the temple of Baal	H995
2Ki	11:19	temple of the LORD and **w into** the palace,	H995
2Ki	12:17	king of Aram **w up** and attacked Gath	H6590
2Ki	13:14	king of Israel **w down** to see him and	H3718
2Ki	14:13	Then Jehoash **w** *to* Jerusalem and broke	H995
2Ki	15:14	Menahem son of Gadi **w** from Tirzah up to	H995
2Ki	16:10	Then King Ahaz **w** *to* Damascus to meet	H2143
2Ki	18:18	son of Asaph the recorder **w out** to them.	H3655
2Ki	18:37	son of Asaph the recorder **w** to Hezekiah,	H995
2Ki	19: 1	on sackcloth and **w into** the temple of the	H995
2Ki	19:14	Then he **w up** *to* the temple of the LORD	H6590
2Ki	19:35	angel of the LORD **w out** and put to death	H3655
2Ki	20: 1	Isaiah son of Amoz **w** to him and said,	H995
2Ki	20:14	Isaiah the prophet **w** to King Hezekiah	H995
2Ki	22: 9	Shaphan the secretary **w** to the king and	H995
2Ki	22:14	Shaphan and Asaiah **w** to speak to the	H2143
2Ki	23: 2	He **w up** *to* the temple of the LORD with the	H6590
2Ki	23:20	Then *he* **w back** *to* Jerusalem.	H8740
2Ki	23:29	king of Egypt **w up** to the Euphrates	H6590
2Ki	25:21	So Judah **w into captivity**, away from her	H1655
1Ch	4:39	and *they* **w** to the outskirts of Gedor to the	H2143
1Ch	7:21	when *they* **w down** to seize their livestock.	H3718
1Ch	10:12	their valiant men **w** and took the bodies	H7756
1Ch	11: 6	Joab son of Zeruiah **w up** first, and so he	H6590
1Ch	11:19	of these men who **w** at the risk of their	NDT
1Ch	11:22	He also **w down** into a pit on a snowy day	H3718
1Ch	11:23	Benaiah **w** against him with a club.	H3718
1Ch	12:17	David **w out** to meet them and said to	H3655
1Ch	12:19	to David when he **w** with the Philistines to	H995
1Ch	12:20	When David **w** to Ziklag, these were the	H2143
1Ch	13: 6	David and all Israel **w** to Baalah of Judah	H6590
1Ch	14: 8	they **w up** in full force to search for him	H6590
1Ch	14: 8	heard about it and **w out** to meet them.	H3655
1Ch	14:11	So David and *his men* **w up** to Baal	H6590
1Ch	15:25	units of a thousand **w** to bring up the ark	H2143
1Ch	17:16	Then King David **w in** and sat before the	H995
1Ch	17:21	on earth whose God **w out** to redeem a	H2143
1Ch	18: 3	when he **w** to set up his monument at the	H2143
1Ch	18: 6	LORD gave David victory wherever *he* **w**.	H2143
1Ch	18:13	LORD gave David victory wherever *he* **w**.	H2143
1Ch	19:15	his brother Abishai and **w** inside the city.	H995
1Ch	19:15	So Joab **w back** *to* Jerusalem.	H995
1Ch	20:	the Ammonites and **w** *to* Rabbah and	H995
1Ch	21: 4	so Joab left and **w** throughout Israel and	H2143
1Ch	21:11	So Gad **w** to David and said to him, "This	H995
1Ch	21:19	So David **w up** in obedience to the word	H6590
2Ch	1: 3	the whole assembly **w** to the high place	H2143
2Ch	1: 6	Solomon **w up** to the bronze altar before	H6590
2Ch	1:13	Then Solomon **w** *to* Jerusalem from the	H995
2Ch	8: 3	Solomon then **w** *to* Hamath Zobah and	H2143
2Ch	8:17	Then Solomon **w** to Ezion Geber and	H2143
2Ch	9:15	of hammered gold **w** into each shield.	H6590
2Ch	10: 1	Rehoboam **w** to Shechem, for all Israel	H2143
2Ch	10: 3	he and all Israel **w** to Rehoboam and said	H995
2Ch	10: 5	in three days." So the people **w away**.	H2143
2Ch	10:16	So all the Israelites **w** home.	H2143
2Ch	12:11	Whenever the king **w** *to* the LORD's temple	H995
2Ch	12:11	the guards **w** with him, bearing the	H995
2Ch	13: 3	Abijah **w into** battle with an army of four	H673
2Ch	14:10	Asa **w out** to meet him, and they took up	H3655
2Ch	15: 2	*He* **w out** to meet Asa and said to him	H3655
2Ch	16: 1	king of Israel **w up** against Judah and	H6590
2Ch	17: 9	*they* **w around** to all the towns of Judah	H6015
2Ch	18: 2	years later *he* **w down** to see Ahab in	H3718
2Ch	18:23	son of Kenaanah **w up** and slapped	H5602
2Ch	18:23	the LORD go when he **w** from me to speak to	NDT
2Ch	18:28	king of Judah **w up** to Ramoth Gilead.	H6590
2Ch	18:29	Israel disguised himself and **w** into battle.	H995
2Ch	19: 2	**w out** to meet him and said to the king	H3655
2Ch	19: 4	and *he* **w out** again among the people	H3655
2Ch	20:21	holiness as they **w out** at the head of the	H3655
2Ch	20:25	his men **w** to carry off their	H995
2Ch	20:28	*They* **entered** Jerusalem **and w** to the	H995
2Ch	21: 9	So Jehoram **w** there with his officers and	H6296
2Ch	22: 5	counsel when *he* **w** with Joram son of	H2143
2Ch	22: 6	king of Judah **w down** to Jezreel to see	H3718
2Ch	22: 7	*he* **w out** with Joram to meet Jehu son of	H3655
2Ch	22: 9	*He* then **w in search of** Ahaziah, and his	H1335
2Ch	23: 2	*They* **w throughout** Judah and gathered	H6015
2Ch	23:12	*she* **w** to them at the temple of the LORD.	H995
2Ch	23:17	All the people **w** *to* the temple of Baal and	H995
2Ch	23:20	*They* **w into** the palace through the Upper	H995
2Ch	26: 6	*He* **w** to war against the Philistines and	H3655
2Ch	28: 9	and *he* **w out** to meet the army when it	H3655
2Ch	29:15	*they* **w in** to purify the temple of the LORD	H995
2Ch	29:16	The priests **w** into the sanctuary of the LORD	H995
2Ch	29:18	Then *they* **w in** to King Hezekiah and	H995
2Ch	29:20	together and **w up** *to* the temple of the	H6590
2Ch	30: 6	couriers **w** throughout Israel and Judah	H2143
2Ch	30:10	The couriers **w** from town to town in	H6296
2Ch	30:11	humbled themselves and **w** to Jerusalem.	H995
2Ch	31: 1	who were there **w out** to the towns of	H3655
2Ch	31: 5	As soon as the order **w out**, the Israelites	H7287
2Ch	32:21	And when *he* **w into** the temple of his god	H995
2Ch	34: 7	Then *he* **w back** to Jerusalem.	H8740
2Ch	34: 9	*They* **w** to Hilkiah the high priest and gave	H995
2Ch	34:22	king had sent with him **w** to speak to the	H2143
2Ch	34:30	He **w up** *to* the temple of the LORD with the	H6590
2Ch	35:20	Necho king of Egypt **w up** to fight at	H6590
2Ch	35:22	God's command but **w** to fight him on the	H995
Ezr	4:23	*they* **w** immediately to the Jews in	A10016
Ezr	5: 3	their associates **w** to them and asked,	A10085
Ezr	5: 8	should know that *we* **w** to the district of	A10016
Ezr	10: 6	the house of God and **w** to the room of	H2143
Ne	2: 9	So *I* **w** to the governors of Trans-Euphrates	H995
Ne	2:11	*I* **w** to Jerusalem, and after staying there	H995
Ne	2:13	By night *I* **w out** through the Valley Gate	H3655
Ne	2:15	so *I* **w up** the valley by night, examining	H6590
Ne	3: 1	his fellow priests **w to work** and rebuilt the	H7756
Ne	4:23	had his weapon, even when he **w** for water.	NDT
Ne	6:10	One day I **w** *to* the house of Shemaiah son	H995
Ne	8:12	all the people **w away** to eat and drink,	H2143
Ne	8:16	So the people **w out** and brought back	H3655
Ne	9:24	Their children **w in** and took possession of	H995
Est	3:15	The couriers **w out**, spurred on by the	H3655
Est	4: 1	ashes, and **w out** into the city	H3655
Est	4: 2	But *he* **w** only as far as the king's gate	H995
Est	4: 6	So Hathak **w out** to Mordecai in the open	H3655
Est	4: 9	Hathak **w back** and reported to Esther what	H995
Est	4:17	So Mordecai **w away** and carried out all of	H6296
Est	5: 5	the king and Haman **w** to the banquet	H995
Est	5: 9	Haman **w out** that day happy and in high	H3655
Est	5:10	Haman restrained himself and **w** home.	H995
Est	7: 1	the king and Haman **w** to Queen Esther's	H995
Est	7: 7	left his wine and **w** out into the palace	NDT
Est	8:14	the royal horses, **w** out, spurred on by the	H987
Job	1:12	Then Satan **w out** from the presence of	H3655
Job	2: 7	So Satan **w out** from the presence of the	H3655
Job	29: 7	"When I **w** *to* the gate of the city and took	H3655
Ps	35:14	*I* **w about** mourning as though for my	H2143
Ps	66:12	our heads; *we* **w** through fire and water	H995
Ps	68: 7	**w out** before your people, when you	H3655
Ps	81: 5	When God **w out** against Egypt, he	H3655
Ps	104: 8	mountains, *they* **w down** *into* the valleys	H3718
Ps	105:30	which **w** up into the bedrooms of their rulers.	NDT
Ps	107:23	*Some* **w out** *on* the sea in ships; they	H3718
Ps	107:26	to the heavens and **w down** *to* the depths;	H3718
Ps	119:67	Before I was afflicted I **w astray**, but now I	H8704
Pr	24:30	I **w** past the field of a sluggard, past the	H6296
SS	6:11	*I* **w down** to the grove of nut trees to look	H3718
Isa	16: 8	shoots spread out and **w as far as** the sea.	H6296
Isa	36: 3	son of Asaph the recorder **w out** to him.	H3655
Isa	36:22	son of Asaph the recorder **w** to Hezekiah,	H995
Isa	37: 1	on sackcloth and **w into** the temple of the	H995
Isa	37:14	Then he **w up** *to* the temple of the LORD	H6590
Isa	37:36	angel of the LORD **w out** and put to death	H3655
Isa	38: 1	Isaiah son of Amoz **w** to him and said,	H995
Isa	38: 8	So the sunlight **w back** the ten steps it	H8740
Isa	39: 3	Isaiah the prophet **w** to King Hezekiah	H995
Isa	52: 4	first my people **w down** to Egypt to live;	H3718
Isa	57: 7	there *you* **w up** to offer your sacrifices.	H6590
Isa	57: 9	*You* **w** to Molek with olive oil and	H8801
Jer	1: 3	the people of Jerusalem **w into exile**.	H1655
Jer	3: 8	she also **w out** and committed adultery.	H2143
Jer	7:24	*They* **w** backward and not forward	H2118
Jer	13: 5	So *I* **w** and hid it at Perath, as the LORD told	H2143
Jer	13: 7	So *I* **w** to Perath and dug up the belt and	H2143
Jer	18: 3	So *I* **w down** to the potter's house, and I	H3718
Jer	22:15	was right and just, so all **w** well with him.	NDT
Jer	22:16	of the poor and needy, and so all **w** well.	NDT
Jer	26:10	*they* **w up** from the royal palace *to* the	H6590
Jer	28: 4	other exiles from Judah who **w** to Babylon,	H995
Jer	28:11	the prophet Jeremiah **w** on his way.	H2143
Jer	35: 3	So *I* **w** *to* **get** Jaazaniah son of Jeremiah, the	AIT
Jer	36:12	*he* **w down** to the secretary's room in the	H3718
Jer	36:14	Baruch son of Neriah **w** to them with the	H995
Jer	36:20	*they* **w** to the king in the courtyard and	H995
Jer	38: 8	Ebed-Melek **w out** of the palace and said	H3655
Jer	38:11	men with him and **w** to a room under the	H995
Jer	40: 6	So Jeremiah **w** to Gedaliah son of Ahikam	H995
Jer	41: 6	son of Nethaniah **w out** from Mizpah to	H3655
Jer	41: 6	to meet them, weeping *as he* **w**.	H2143+2143
Jer	41: 7	When they **w** into the city, Ishmael son of	H995
Jer	41:12	all their men and **w** to fight Ishmael son	H2143
Jer	41:14	Mizpah turned and **w over** to Johanan son	H2143
Jer	41:17	And *they* **w on**, stopping at Geruth	H2143
Jer	43: 7	to the LORD and **w** as far as Tahpanhes.	H995
Jer	51:59	when he **w** *to* Babylon with Zedekiah king	H2143
Jer	52:27	So Judah **w into captivity**, away from her	H1655
Eze	1: 9	Each one **w** straight ahead; they did not	H2143
Eze	1:12	Each one **w** straight ahead. Wherever the	H2143
Eze	1:12	they would go, without turning as they **w**.	H2143
Eze	1:17	not change direction as the creatures **w**.	H2143
Eze	3:14	and *I* **w** in bitterness and in the anger of	H2143
Eze	3:23	So I got up and **w out** to the plain.	H3655
Eze	8:10	So *I* **w in** and looked, and I saw portrayed	H995
Eze	9: 3	of the God of Israel **w up** from above the	H6590
Eze	9: 7	So *they* **w out** and began killing	H3655
Eze	10: 2	And as I watched, *he* **w in**.	H995
Eze	10: 3	side of the temple when the man **w in**,	H995
Eze	10: 6	the man **w in** and stood beside a wheel.	H995
Eze	10: 7	the man in linen, who took it and **w out**.	H3655
Eze	10:11	did not turn about as the cherubim **w**.	H2143
Eze	10:11	The cherubim **w** *in* whatever direction the	H2143
Eze	10:11	the head faced, without turning as they **w**.	H2143
Eze	10:19	ground, and as they **w**, the wheels went	H3655
Eze	10:19	as they went, the wheels **w** with them.	NDT
Eze	10:22	Each one **w** straight ahead.	H2143
Eze	11:23	The glory of the LORD **w up** from within	H6590
Eze	11:24	Then the vision I had seen **w up** from me,	H6590
Eze	16:16	You **w** to him, and he possessed your	H995
Eze	17:12	'The king of Babylon **w** *to* Jerusalem and	H995
Eze	23:13	both of them **w** the same way.	NDT
Eze	25: 3	people of Judah when *they* **w** into exile,	H2143
Eze	27:33	your merchandise **w out** on the seas,	H3655
Eze	31: 7	its roots **w** *down* to abundant waters.	H2118
Eze	32:24	of the living **w down** uncircumcised to	H3718
Eze	32:27	who **w down** *to* the realm of the dead	H3718
Eze	32:30	*they* **w down** with the slain in disgrace	H3718
Eze	36:20	And wherever *they* **w** among the nations	H995
Eze	39:23	people of Israel **w into exile** for their sin,	H1655
Eze	40: 6	Then *he* **w** to the east gate. He climbed its	H995
Eze	41: 3	Then *he* **w** into the inner sanctuary and	H995
Eze	41: 7	that the rooms widened as one **w** upward.	NDT

Eze 41: 7 A stairway w up from the lowest floor to H6590
Eze 44:10 " 'The Levites who w far from me when H8178
Eze 44:10 me when Israel w astray and who H9494
Eze 44:15 when the Israelites w astray from me, H9494
Eze 47: 3 As the man w eastward with a measuring H3655
Eze 48:11 Levites did when the Israelites w astray. H9494
Da 2:16 Daniel w in to the king and asked for A10549
Da 2:24 Then Daniel w to Arioch, whom the king A10549
Da 2:30 may understand what w through your mind. NDT
Da 6: 6 satraps w as a group to the king and A10656
Da 6:10 he w home to his upstairs room where A10549
Da 6:11 Then these men w as a group and found A10656
Da 6:12 So they w to the king and spoke to him A10638
Da 6:15 Then the men w as a group to King A10656
Da 8:27 Then I got up and w about the king's H6913
Da 9:23 a word w out, which I have come H3655
Hos 2:13 jewelry, and w after her lovers, but H2143
Hos 11: 2 the more they w away from me. H2143
Jnh 1: 3 He w down to Joppa, where he found a H3718
Jnh 1: 3 he w aboard and sailed for Tarshish H3718+928
Jnh 1: 6 The captain w to him and said, "How can H7928
Jnh 3: 3 the word of the LORD and w to Nineveh. H2143
Na 2:11 where the lion and lioness w, and the H2143
Na 3:10 she was taken captive and w into exile. H2143
Hab 3: 5 Plague w before him; pestilence followed H2143
Hag 2:16 When anyone w to a wine vat to draw fifty H995
Zec 1:15 they w too far with the punishment. H6468
Zec 6: 7 When the powerful horses w out, they H3655
Zec 6: 7 So they w throughout the earth H2143
Mt 2: 9 the king, they w on their way, and the star G4513
Mt 2: 9 when it rose w ahead of them until it G4575
Mt 2:21 his mother and w to the land of Israel G1656
Mt 2:23 and he w and lived in a town called G2262
Mt 3: 5 People w out to him from Jerusalem and G1744
Mt 3:16 was baptized, he w up out of the water. G326
Mt 4:13 Nazareth, he w and lived in Capernaum G2262
Mt 4:23 Jesus w throughout Galilee, teaching in G4310
Mt 5: 1 he w up on a mountainside and sat down. G326
Mt 8:25 The disciples w and woke him, saying G4665
Mt 8:32 So they came out and w into the pigs, and G599
Mt 8:33 w into the town and reported all this G599
Mt 8:34 Then the whole town w out to meet Jesus G2002
Mt 9: 7 Then the man got up and w home. G599
Mt 9: 9 As Jesus w on from there, he saw a man G4135
Mt 9:19 Jesus got up and w with him, and so did his G199
Mt 9:25 he w in and took the girl by the hand G1656
Mt 9:27 As Jesus w on from there, two blind men G4135
Mt 9:31 But they w out and spread the news about G2002
Mt 9:35 Jesus w through all the towns and villages AIT
Mt 11: 1 he w on from there to teach and preach in G3553
Mt 12: 1 At that time Jesus w through the G4513
Mt 12: 9 that place, he w into their synagogue G2262
Mt 12:14 But the Pharisees w out and plotted how G2002
Mt 13: 1 same day Jesus w out of the house and G2002
Mt 13: 3 "A farmer w out to sow his seed. G2002
Mt 13:25 weeds among the wheat, and w away. G599
Mt 13:36 he left the crowd and w into the house. G2262
Mt 13:44 then in his joy w and sold all he had G5632
Mt 13:46 he w away and sold everything he had G599
Mt 14:12 Then they w and told Jesus. G2262
Mt 14:23 he w up on a mountainside by himself to G326
Mt 14:25 Shortly before dawn Jesus w out to them G599
Mt 15:29 Jesus left there and w along the Sea of G2262
Mt 15:29 Then he w up on a mountainside and sat G326
Mt 15:39 got into the boat and w to the vicinity of G2262
Mt 16: 4 Jesus then left them and w away. G599
Mt 16: 5 When they w across the lake, the G2262
Mt 18:28 "But when that servant w out, he found G2002
Mt 18:30 he w off and had the man thrown into G599
Mt 18:31 were outraged and w and told their G2262
Mt 19: 1 he left Galilee and w into the region of G2262
Mt 19:15 his hands on them, he w on from there. G4513
Mt 19:22 heard this, he w away sad, because he G599
Mt 20: 1 like a landowner who w out early in the G2002
Mt 20: 3 in the morning he w out and saw others G2002
Mt 20: 5 So they w. "He went out again about noon G599
Mt 20: 5 "He w out again about noon and about G2002
Mt 20: 6 in the afternoon he w out and found still G2002
Mt 21: 6 The disciples w and did as Jesus had G4513
Mt 21: 9 The crowds that w ahead of him and those G4575
Mt 21:17 And he left them and w out of the city to G2002
Mt 21:19 he w up to it but found nothing on it G2262
Mt 21:28 He w to the first and said, 'Son, go and G4665
Mt 21:29 later he changed his mind and w. G599
Mt 21:30 "Then the father w to the other son and G4665
Mt 22: 5 "But they paid no attention and w off—one G599
Mt 22:10 So the servants w out into the streets and G2002
Mt 22:15 the Pharisees w out and laid plans to G4513
Mt 22:22 So they left him and w away. G599
Mt 25: 1 took their lamps and w out to meet the G2002
Mt 25:10 who were ready w in with him to the G1656
Mt 25:15 Then he w on his journey. G623
Mt 25:16 five bags of gold w at once and put his G4513
Mt 25:18 the man who had received one bag w off, G599
Mt 25:25 So I was afraid and w out and hid your gold G599
Mt 26:14 Judas Iscariot—w to the chief priests G4513
Mt 26:30 they w out to the Mount of Olives. G2002
Mt 26:36 Then Jesus w with his disciples to a place G2262
Mt 26:42 He w away a second time and prayed, "My G599
Mt 26:44 So he left them and w away once more G599
Mt 26:71 Then he w out to the gateway, where G2002
Mt 26:73 standing there w up to Peter and said, G4665
Mt 26:75 And he w outside and wept bitterly G2002
Mt 27: 5 Then he w away and hanged himself. G599
Mt 27:53 resurrection and w into the holy city and G1656
Mt 27:60 of the entrance to the tomb and w away. G599
Mt 27:62 priests and the Pharisees w to Pilate. G5251
Mt 27:66 So they w and made the tomb secure by G4513
Mt 28: 1 the other Mary w to look at the tomb. G2262
Mt 28:11 some of the guards w into the city and G2262
Mt 28:16 Then the eleven disciples w to Galilee, to G4513
Mk 1: 5 all the people of Jerusalem w out to him. G1744
Mk 1:14 was put in prison, Jesus w into Galilee G2262
Mk 1:21 They w to Capernaum, and when the G1660
Mk 1:21 Jesus w into the synagogue and began to G1656
Mk 1:29 they w with James and John to the home G2262
Mk 1:31 So he w to her, took her hand and helped G4665
Mk 1:35 left the house and w off to a solitary place G599
Mk 1:36 Simon and his companions w to look for him, AIT
Mk 1:45 Instead he w out and began to talk freely G2002
Mk 2:13 Once again Jesus w out beside the lake G2002
Mk 3: 1 Another time Jesus w into the synagogue G1656
Mk 3: 6 Then the Pharisees w out and began to G2002
Mk 3:13 Jesus w up on a mountainside and called G326
Mk 3:21 about this, they w to take charge of him G2002
Mk 4: 3 A farmer w out to sow his seed. G2002
Mk 5: 1 They w across the lake to the region of G2262
Mk 5:13 spirits came out and w into the pigs. G1656
Mk 5:14 and the people w out to see what had G2262
Mk 5:20 So the man w away and began to tell in the G599
Mk 5:24 So Jesus w with him. A large crowd G599
Mk 5:39 He w in and said to them, "Why all this G1656
Mk 5:40 with him, and w in where the child was. G1660
Mk 6: 1 Jesus left there and w to his hometown G2262
Mk 6: 6 Then Jesus w around teaching from village AIT
Mk 6:12 They w out and preached that people G2002
Mk 6:24 She w out and said to her mother, "What G2002
Mk 6:27 The man w, beheaded John G599
Mk 6:32 So they w away by themselves in a boat to G599
Mk 6:46 he w up on a mountainside to pray. G599
Mk 6:48 Shortly before dawn he w out to them G2262
Mk 6:56 And wherever he w—into villages, towns G1660
Mk 7:20 He w on: "What comes out of a person G3306
Mk 7:24 left that place and w to the vicinity of Tyre. G599
Mk 7:30 She w home and found her child lying on G599
Mk 7:31 the vicinity of Tyre and w through Sidon, G2262
Mk 8:10 with his disciples and w to the region of G2262
Mk 8:27 his disciples w on to the villages G2002
Mk 10: 1 left that place and w into the region of G2262
Mk 10:22 He w away sad, because he had great G599
Mk 11: 4 They w and found a colt outside in the G599
Mk 11: 9 Those who w ahead and those who G4575
Mk 11:11 Jerusalem and w into the temple courts. AIT
Mk 11:11 he w out to Bethany with the Twelve. G2002
Mk 11:13 he w to find out if it had any fruit. G2262
Mk 11:19 Jesus and his disciples w out of the city. G1744
Mk 11:20 the morning, as they w along, they saw G4182
Mk 12:12 of the crowd; so they left him and w away. G599
Mk 14:10 w to the chief priests to betray Jesus to G599
Mk 14:16 w into the city and found things just as G2262
Mk 14:26 they w out to the Mount of Olives. G2002
Mk 14:32 They w to a place called Gethsemane G2262
Mk 14:39 Once more he w away and prayed the G599
Mk 14:68 he said, and w out into the entryway. G2002
Mk 15:43 w boldly to Pilate and asked for Jesus' G1656
Mk 16: 8 the women w out and fled from the tomb. G2002
Mk 16:10 She w and told those who had been with G4513
Mk 16:20 Then the disciples w out and preached G2002
Lk 1:28 The angel w to her and said, "Greetings G1656
Lk 2: 3 And everyone w to their own town to G4513
Lk 2: 4 So Joseph also w up from the town of G326
Lk 2: 5 He w there to register with Mary, who was NDT
Lk 2:27 by the Spirit, he w into the temple courts. G2262
Lk 2:41 year Jesus' parents w to Jerusalem for the G4513
Lk 2:42 twelve years old, they w up to the festival G326
Lk 2:45 they w back to Jerusalem to look for him. G5715
Lk 2:51 Then he w down to Nazareth with them G2849
Lk 3: 3 He w into all the country around the G2262
Lk 4:16 He w to Nazareth, where he had been G2262
Lk 4:16 Sabbath day he w into the synagogue, G1656
Lk 4:30 right through the crowd and w on his way. G4513
Lk 4:31 Then he w down to Capernaum, a town in G2982
Lk 4:38 the synagogue and w to the home of G1656
Lk 4:42 daybreak, Jesus w out to a solitary place. G4513
Lk 5:19 they w up on the roof and lowered him on G326
Lk 5:25 been lying on and w home praising God. G599
Lk 5:27 Jesus w out and saw a tax collector by the G2002
Lk 6: 6 Sabbath he w into the synagogue and G1656
Lk 6:12 those days Jesus w out to a mountainside G2002
Lk 6:17 He w down with them and stood on a G2849
Lk 7: 6 So Jesus w with them. He was not far from G4513
Lk 7:11 afterward, Jesus w to a town called Nain G4513
Lk 7:11 a large crowd w along with him. G5233
Lk 7:13 his heart w out to her and he said G5072
Lk 7:14 Then he w up and touched the bier they G4665
Lk 7:31 Jesus w on to say, "To what, then, can I NDT
Lk 7:36 he w to the Pharisee's house and reclined G1656
Lk 8: 5 "A farmer w out to sow his seed. As he G2002
Lk 8:24 The disciples w and woke him, saying G4665
Lk 8:33 out of the man, they w into the pigs, and G1656
Lk 8:35 and the people w out to see what had G2002
Lk 8:39 So the man w away and told all over town G599
Lk 9: 6 So they set out and w from village to G1451
Lk 9:28 James with him and w up onto a mountain G326
Lk 9:52 who w into a Samaritan village to get G1656
Lk 9:56 Then he and his disciples w to another G4513
Lk 10:30 beat him and w away, leaving him half G599
Lk 10:34 He w to him and bandaged his wounds G4665
Lk 11:37 so he w in and reclined at the table. G1656
Lk 11:53 When Jesus w outside, the Pharisees G2002
Lk 13: 6 and he w to look for fruit on it but did not G2262
Lk 13:22 Then Jesus w through the towns and G1388
Lk 14: 1 when Jesus w to eat in the house of a G2262
Lk 15:15 So he w and hired himself out to a citizen G4513
Lk 15:20 So he got up and w to his father. "But G2262
Lk 15:28 So his father w out and pleaded with him. G2002
Lk 17:14 And as they w, they were cleansed. G5632
Lk 18:10 "Two men w up to the temple to pray, one G326
Lk 18:14 the other, w home justified before God. G2849
Lk 19:11 he w on to tell them a parable G4707
Lk 19:12 man of noble birth w to a distant country G4513
Lk 19:28 had said this, he w on ahead, going up to G4513
Lk 19:32 who were sent ahead w and found it just G599
Lk 19:36 As he w along, people spread their cloaks G4513
Lk 20: 9 He w on to tell the people this parable: "A G806
Lk 20: 9 some farmers and w away for a long time. G623
Lk 21:37 each evening he w out to spend the G2002
Lk 22: 4 And Judas w to the chief priests and the G599
Lk 22:39 Jesus w out as usual to the Mount of G2002
Lk 22:45 rose from prayer and w back to the G2262
Lk 22:62 And he w outside and wept bitterly. G2002
Lk 23:48 they beat their breasts and w away. G5715
Lk 23:56 Then they w home and prepared spices G5715
Lk 24: 1 they had prepared and w to the tomb. G2262
Lk 24:12 themselves, and he w away, wondering to G599
Lk 24:22 us. They w to the tomb early this morning G1181
Lk 24:24 of our companions w to the tomb and G599
Lk 24:29 So he w in to stay with them G1656
Jn 1:39 So they w and saw where he was staying G2262
Jn 2:12 After this he w down to Capernaum with G2849
Jn 2:13 Jewish Passover, Jesus w up to Jerusalem. G326
Jn 3:22 his disciples w out into the Judean G2262
Jn 4: 3 So he left Judea and w back once more to G599
Jn 4:28 the woman w back to the town and said to G599
Jn 4:47 he w to him and begged him to come and G599
Jn 5: 1 Jesus w up to Jerusalem for one of the G326
Jn 5:15 The man w away and told the Jewish G599
Jn 6: 3 Then Jesus w up on a mountainside and G456
Jn 6:16 his disciples w down to the lake, G2849
Jn 6:24 into the boats and w to Capernaum in G2262
Jn 6:65 He w on to say, "This is why I told you that no AIT
Jn 7: 1 After this, Jesus w around in Galilee. He did AIT
Jn 7:10 left for the festival, he w also, not publicly, G326
Jn 7:45 the temple guards w back to the chief G2262
Jn 7:53 Then they all w home, G4513
Jn 8: 1 Jesus w to the Mount of Olives. G4513
Jn 9: 1 As he w along, he saw a man blind from G4135
Jn 9: 7 So the man w and washed, and came G599
Jn 9:11 Siloam and wash. So I w and washed, and G599
Jn 10:40 Then Jesus w back across the Jordan to the G599
Jn 11:11 had said this, he w on to tell them, "Our AIT
Jn 11:20 was coming, she w out to meet him, but G5636
Jn 11:28 she w back and called her sister Mary aside G599
Jn 11:29 she got up quickly and w to him. G2262
Jn 11:31 noticed how quickly she got up and w out G2002
Jn 11:46 But some of them w to the Pharisees and G599
Jn 11:55 many w up from the country to Jerusalem G326
Jn 12:13 palm branches and w out to meet him, G2002
Jn 12:18 performed this sign, w out to meet him. G5636
Jn 12:20 among those who w up to worship at the G326
Jn 12:22 Philip w to tell Andrew; Andrew and Philip G2262
Jn 13:30 as Judas had taken the bread, he w out. G2002
Jn 16:16 Jesus w on to say, "In a little while you will NDT
Jn 18: 1 garden, and he and his disciples w into it. G1656
Jn 18: 4 to happen to him, w out and asked them G2002
Jn 18:15 he w with Jesus into the high priest's G5291
Jn 18:33 Pilate then w back inside the palace G1656
Jn 18:38 With this he w out again to the Jews G2002
Jn 19: 3 and w up to him again and again, saying G2262
Jn 19: 9 and he w back inside the palace. "Where G1656
Jn 19:17 cross, he w out to the place of the Skull G2002
Jn 20: 1 Mary Magdalene w to the tomb and saw G2262
Jn 20: 6 behind him and w straight into the tomb. G1656
Jn 20: 8 had reached the tomb first, also w inside. G1656
Jn 20:10 Then the disciples w back to where they G599
Jn 20:18 Mary Magdalene w to the disciples with G2262
Jn 21: 3 So they w out and got into the boat, but G2002
Jn 21:18 yourself and w where you wanted; G4344
Ac 1:13 they w upstairs to the room where they G326
Ac 3: 8 Then he w with them into the temple G1656
Ac 4:23 Peter and John w back to their own G2262
Ac 5:22 So they w back and reported, G418
Ac 5:26 the captain w with his officers and brought G599
Ac 7:15 Then Jacob w down to Egypt, where he G2849
Ac 7:24 so he w to his defense and avenged him G310
Ac 7:31 As he w over to get a closer look, he G4665
Ac 8: 4 preached the word wherever they w. G1451
Ac 8: 5 Philip w down to a city in Samaria and G2982
Ac 8:38 the eunuch w down into the water G2849
Ac 8:39 him again, but w on his way rejoicing. G4513
Ac 9: 1 Lord's disciples. He w to the high priest G4665
Ac 9:17 Then Ananias w to the house and entered G599
Ac 9:32 he w to visit the Lord's people who lived G2982
Ac 9:39 Peter w with them, and when he arrived G5302
Ac 10: 9 Peter w up on the roof to pray. G326
Ac 10:21 Peter w down and said to the men, "I'm G2849

Ac 10:23 of the believers from Joppa w along. G5302
Ac 10:27 Peter w inside and found a large G1656
Ac 10:38 how he w around doing good and G1451
Ac 11: 2 So when Peter w up to Jerusalem, the G326
Ac 11: 3 "You w into the house of uncircumcised G1656
Ac 11:12 These six brothers also w with me, and G2262
Ac 11:20 w to Antioch and began to speak to G2262
Ac 11:25 Then Barnabas w to Tarsus to look for G2002
Ac 12:10 them by itself, and they w through it. G2002
Ac 12:12 he w to the house of Mary the mother of G2262
Ac 12:19 Then Herod w from Judea to Caesarea G2982
Ac 13: 4 w down to Seleucia and sailed from there G2982
Ac 13:14 From Perga they w on to Pisidian Antioch G1451
Ac 13:51 as a warning to them and w to Iconium. G2262
Ac 14: 1 Barnabas w as usual into the Jewish G1656
Ac 14:20 he got up and w back into the city. G1656
Ac 14:25 the word in Perga, they w down to Attalia. G2849
Ac 15:24 heard that some w out from us without G2002
Ac 15:30 were sent off and w down to Antioch, G2982
Ac 15:41 He w through Syria and Cilicia G1451
Ac 16: 8 passed by Mysia and w down to Troas. G2849
Ac 16:11 the next day we w on to Neapolis. NDT
Ac 16:13 On the Sabbath we w outside the city G2002
Ac 16:40 out of the prison, they w to Lydia's house G1656
Ac 17: 2 his custom, Paul w into the synagogue G1656
Ac 17:10 they w to the Jewish synagogue. G583
Ac 17:13 God at Berea, some of them w there too G2262
Ac 18: 1 Paul left Athens and w to Corinth. G2262
Ac 18: 2 Jews to leave Rome. Paul w to see them, G4665
Ac 18: 7 and w next door to the house of G1656
Ac 18:19 He himself w into the synagogue and G1656
Ac 18:22 he w up to Jerusalem and greeted the G326
Ac 18:22 the church and then w down to Antioch. G2849
Ac 19:10 This w on for two years, so that all the G1181
Ac 19:13 Some Jews who w around driving out evil G4320
Ac 20: 5 These men w on ahead and waited for us G4601
Ac 20:10 Paul w down, threw himself on the young G2849
Ac 20:11 Then he w upstairs again and broke bread G326
Ac 20:13 We w on ahead to the ship and sailed G4601
Ac 20:14 we took him aboard and w on to Mitylene. G2262
Ac 21: 1 The next day we w to Rhodes and from G2262
Ac 21: 2 to Phoenicia, w on board and set sail. G2094
Ac 21: 6 to each other, we w aboard the ship, and G326
Ac 21:18 Paul and the rest of us w to see James, G1655
Ac 21:26 Then he w to the temple to give notice of G1655
Ac 22: 5 w there to bring these people as G4513
Ac 22:19 people know that I w from one synagogue G1639
Ac 22:26 he w to the commander and reported it. G4665
Ac 22:27 The commander w to Paul and asked G4665
Ac 23:14 They w to the chief priests and the elders G4665
Ac 23:16 he w into the barracks and told Paul. G1656
Ac 24: 1 priest Ananias w down to Caesarea with G2849
Ac 24:11 twelve days ago I w up to Jerusalem to G326
Ac 25: 1 Festus w up from Caesarea to Jerusalem G326
Ac 25: 6 with them, Festus w down to Caesarea. G2849
Ac 25:15 When I w to Jerusalem, the chief priests G1181
Ac 26:11 Many a time I w from one synagogue to NDT
Ac 28: 8 Paul w in to see him and, after prayer G1656
2Co 2:12 Now when I w to Troas to preach the G2262
2Co 2:13 goodbye to them and w on to Macedonia. G2002
Gal 1:17 apostles before I was, but I w into Arabia. G599
Gal 1:18 I w up to Jerusalem to get acquainted with G456
Gal 1:21 Then I w to Syria and Cilicia. G2262
Gal 2: 1 fourteen years, I w up again to Jerusalem G326
Gal 2: 2 I w in response to a revelation and G326
1Ti 1: 3 As I urged you when I w into Macedonia G4513
Heb 9:11 he w through the greater and more perfect AIT
Heb 11: 8 obeyed and w, even though he did not G2002
Heb 11:37 They w about in sheepskins and goatskins G4320
1Pe 3:19 he w and made proclamation to the G4513
1Jn 2:19 They w out from us, but they did not really G2002
3Jn 7 the sake of the Name that they w out, G2002
Rev 5: 7 He w and took the scroll from the right G2262
Rev 8: 4 w up before God from the angel's hand. G326
Rev 10: 9 So I w to the angel and asked him to give G599
Rev 11:12 And they w up to heaven in a cloud, while G326
Rev 12:17 at the woman and w off to wage war G599
Rev 16: 2 The first angel w and poured out his bowl G599

WEPT (52) [WEEP]

Ge 27:38 me too, my father!" Then Esau w aloud. H1134
Ge 33: 4 his neck and kissed him. And they w. H1134
Ge 37:35 son in the grave." So his father w for him. H1134
Ge 43:30 went into his private room and w there. H1134
Ge 45: 2 And he w so loudly that H1140+5989+906+7754+928
Ge 45:14 arms around his brother Benjamin and w, H1134
Ge 45:15 kissed all his brothers and w over them. H1134
Ge 46:29 around his father and w for a long time. H1134
Ge 50: 1 on his father and w over him and kissed H1134
Ge 50:17 their message came to him, Joseph w. H1134
Nu 14: 1 raised their voices and w aloud. H1134
Dt 1:45 You came back and w before the LORD, H1134
Jdg 2: 4 to all the Israelites, the people w aloud, H1134
Jdg 11:38 into the hills and w because she would H1134
Jdg 20:23 went up and w before the LORD until H1134
Ru 1: 9 kissed them goodbye and they w aloud H1134
Ru 1:14 At this they w aloud again. Then Orpah H1134
1Sa 1: 7 provoked her till she w and would not eat. H1134
1Sa 11: 4 terms to the people, they all w aloud. H1134
1Sa 20:41 they kissed each other and w together— H1134
1Sa 20:41 wept together—but David w the most. NDT
1Sa 24:16 David my son?" And he w aloud. H1134
1Sa 30: 4 So David and his men w aloud until they H1134
2Sa 1:12 They mourned and w and fasted till H1134
2Sa 3:32 the king w aloud at Abner's tomb. H1134
2Sa 3:32 at Abner's tomb. All the people w also. H1134
2Sa 3:34 And all the people w over him again. H1134
2Sa 12:21 you fasted and w, but now that the H1134
2Sa 12:22 the child was still alive, I fasted and w. H1134
2Sa 13:36 all his attendants w very bitterly. H1134+1140
2Sa 15:23 The whole countryside w aloud as all the H1134
2Sa 18:33 up to the room over the gateway and w. H1134
2Ki 13:14 went down to see him and w over him. H1134
2Ki 20: 3 And Hezekiah w bitterly. H1134+1140
2Ki 22:19 you tore your robes and w in my presence, H1134
2Ch 34:27 tore your robes and w in my presence, H1134
Ezr 3:12 w aloud when they saw the foundation of H1134
Ezr 10: 1 They too w bitterly. H1134+2221+1135
Ne 1: 4 I heard these things, I sat down and w. H1134
Job 30:25 Have I not w for those in trouble? Has not H1134
Ps 137: 1 we sat and w when we remembered H1134
Isa 38: 3 And Hezekiah w bitterly. H1134+1140
Hos 12: 4 he w and begged for his favor. H1134
Mt 26:75 And he went outside and w bitterly. G3081
Mk 14:72 And he broke down and w. G3081
Lk 19:41 Jerusalem and saw the city, he w over it G3081
Lk 22:62 And he went outside and w bitterly. G3081
Jn 11:35 Jesus w. G1233
Jn 20:11 As she w, she bent over to look into the G3081
Ac 20:37 They all w as they embraced G2653+3088+1181
Rev 5: 4 I w and wept because no one was G3081+4498
Rev 5: 4 I wept and w because no one was G3081+4498

WERE (2554) [BE] See Index of Articles Etc.

WEREN'T (3) [BE, NOT]

2Sa 1:14 "Why w you afraid to lift your hand to H4202
2Sa 19:43 W we the first to speak of bringing H2118+4202
Da 3:24 "W there three men that we tied up and A10379

WEST (95) [NORTHWEST, SOUTHWEST, WESTERN, WESTWARD]

Ge 12: 8 with Bethel on the w and Ai on the east. H3542
Ge 13:14 north and south, to the east and w. H3542+2025
Ge 28:14 will spread out to the w and to the east, H3542
Ex 10:19 changed the wind to a very strong w wind, H3542
Ex 26:22 that is, the w end of the tabernacle H3542+2025
Ex 26:27 five for the frames on the w, at the far H3542
Ex 27:12 "The w end of the courtyard shall be fifty H3542
Ex 36:27 that is, the w end of the tabernacle H3542+2025
Ex 36:32 five for the frames on the w, at the far H3542
Ex 38:12 The w end was fifty cubits wide and had H3542
Nu 2:18 On the w will be the divisions of the camp H3542
Nu 3:23 Gershonite clans were to camp on the w, H3542
Nu 34: 6 This will be your boundary on the w. H3542
Nu 35: 5 thousand on the w and two thousand on H3542
Dt 3:27 Pisgah and look w and north and H3542+2025
Jos 1: 4 Mediterranean Sea in the w. H4427+2021+9087
Jos 5: 1 Amorite kings w of the Jordan and H3542+2025
Jos 8: 9 Bethel and Ai, to the w of Ai—but Joshua H3542
Jos 8:12 Bethel and Ai, to the w of the city. H3542
Jos 8:13 of the city and the ambush to the w of it. H3542
Jos 9: 1 all the kings w of the Jordan heard H928+6298
Jos 11: 2 foothills and in Naphoth Dor on the w; H3542
Jos 11: 3 to the Canaanites in the east and w; to the H3542
Jos 12: 7 conquered on the w side of the Jordan, H3542
Jos 15: 8 top of the hill w of the Hinnom H3542+2025
Jos 15:46 w of Ekron, all that were in the vicinity of H3542
Jos 16: 8 the border went w to the Kanah H3542+2025
Jos 18:12 Jericho and headed w into the hill H3542+2025
Jos 18:15 at the outskirts of Kiriath Jearim on the w, H3542
Jos 19:11 Going w it ran to Maralah, touched H3542+2025
Jos 19:26 On the w the boundary touched Carmel H3542
Jos 19:34 boundary ran w through Aznoth H3542+2025
Jos 19:34 Asher on the w and the Jordan on the H3542
Jos 22: 7 gave land on the w side of the H3542+2025
Jos 23: 4 the Mediterranean Sea in the w. H4427+9087
Jdg 18:12 This is why the place w of Kiriath Jearim is H339
Jdg 20:33 out of its place on the w of Gibeah. H5115
2Sa 13:34 saw many people on the road w of him, H339
1Ki 4:24 all the kingdoms w of the Euphrates River, H6298
1Ki 7:25 three facing w, three facing south H3542+2025
1Ch 7:28 Gezer and its villages to the w, and H5115
1Ch 9:24 east, w, north and south H3542+2025
1Ch 12:15 in the valleys, to the east and to the w. H5115
1Ch 26:16 The lots for the W Gate and the H5115
1Ch 26:18 As for the court to the w, there were four at H5115
1Ch 26:30 in Israel w of the Jordan for all H4946+6298
2Ch 4: 4 three facing w, three facing south H3542+2025
2Ch 32:30 water down to the w side of the City of H5115
2Ch 33:14 w of the Gihon spring in the valley H5115+2025
Job 18:20 People of the w are appalled at his fate H340
Job 23: 8 not there; if I go to the w, I do not find him. H294
Ps 75: 6 from the east or the w or from the desert H5115
Ps 103:12 as far as the east is from the w, so far has H5115
Ps 107: 3 from east and w, from north and H5115
Isa 9:12 Philistines from the w have devoured Israel H294
Isa 11:14 down on the slopes of Philistia to the w; H3542
Isa 24:14 from the w they acclaim the LORD's H3542
Isa 43: 5 from the east and gather you from the w. H5115
Isa 49:12 some from the w, some from the H3542
Isa 59:19 From the w, people will fear the name of H5115
Eze 41:12 courtyard on the w side was seventy cubits H3542
Eze 42:19 he turned to the w side and measured; H3542
Eze 45: 7 westward from the w side and eastward H3542
Eze 47:20 "On the w side, the Mediterranean Sea H3542
Eze 48: 1 its border from the east side to the w side. H3542
Eze 48: 2 the territory of Dan from east to w. H3542+2025
Eze 48: 3 territory of Asher from east to w. H3542+2025
Eze 48: 4 territory of Naphtali from east to w. H3542+2025
Eze 48: 5 of Manasseh from east to w. H3542+2025
Eze 48: 6 territory of Ephraim from east to w. H3542+2025
Eze 48: 7 territory of Reuben from east to w. H3542+2025
Eze 48: 8 Judah from east to w will be the H3542+2025
Eze 48: 8 from east to w will equal one of H3542+2025
Eze 48:10 10,000 cubits wide on the w side, 10,000 H3542
Eze 48:16 cubits, and the w side 4,500 cubits. H3542+2025
Eze 48:17 on the east, and 250 cubits on the w. H3542
Eze 48:18 side and 10,000 cubits on the w side. H3542
Eze 48:23 from the east side to the w side. H3542+2025
Eze 48:24 of Benjamin from east to w. H3542+2025
Eze 48:25 territory of Simeon from east to w. H3542+2025
Eze 48:26 territory of Issachar from east to w. H3542+2025
Eze 48:27 territory of Zebulun from east to w. H3542+2025
Eze 48:34 "On the w side, which is 4,500 cubits long H3542
Da 8: 4 charged toward the w and the north and H3542
Da 8: 5 horn between its eyes came from the w, H5115
Hos 11:10 children will come trembling from the w. H3542
Zec 6: 6 the one with the white horses toward the w, H339
Zec 8: 7 the countries of the east and the w. H4427+9087
Zec 14: 4 Olives will be split in two from east to w, H3542
Zec 14: 8 Sea and half of it w to the Mediterranean H340
Mt 8:11 many will come from the east and the w, G1553
Mt 24:27 from the east is visible even in the w, G1553
Lk 12:54 "When you see a cloud rising in the w G1553
Lk 13:29 come from east and w and north and G1553
Rev 21:13 three on the south and three on the w. G1553

WESTERN (24) [WEST]

Nu 34: 6 " 'Your w boundary will be the coast of H3542
Dt 1: 7 in the w foothills, in the Negev H9169
Dt 3:17 Its w border was the Jordan in the H4667+2025S
Jos 9: 1 country, in the w foothills, and along the H9169
Jos 10:40 the w foothills and the mountain slopes H9169
Jos 11: 2 in the w foothills and in Naphoth Dor on H9169
Jos 11:16 of Goshen, the w foothills, the Arabah H9169
Jos 12: 8 hill country, the w foothills, the Arabah, H9169
Jos 15:12 The w boundary is the coastline of the H3542
Jos 15:33 In the w foothills: Eshtaol, Zorah, Ashnah, H9169
Jos 18:14 south along the w side and came out at H3542
Jos 18:14 people of Judah. This was the w side. H3542
Jdg 1: 9 country, the Negev and the w foothills. H9169
1Ch 27:28 sycamore-fig trees in the w foothills. H9169
Jer 17:26 territory of Benjamin and the w foothills, H9169
Jer 32:44 of the w foothills and of the Negev H9169
Jer 33:13 of the w foothills and of the Negev H9169
Eze 45: 7 lengthwise from the w to the eastern H3542
Eze 46:19 showed me a place at the w end. H3542+2025
Eze 47:20 This will be the w boundary. H3542
Eze 48:21 the 25,000 cubits to the w border. H3542+2025
Da 11:30 Ships of the w coastlands will oppose him H4183
Joel 2:20 the Dead Sea and its w ranks in the H6067
Zec 7: 7 Negev and the w foothills were settled? H9169

WESTWARD (5) [WEST]

Dt 11:30 across the Jordan, w, toward the H339+2006
Jos 15:10 Then it curved w from Baalah to H3542+2025
Jos 16: 3 descended w to the territory of the H3542+2025
Eze 45: 7 It will extend w from the west side H3542+2025
Eze 48:21 and w from the 25,000 cubits to H3542+2025

WET (5)

Job 31:38 me and all its furrows are w with tears, H1134
Eze 7:17 go limp; every leg will be w with urine. H2143
Eze 21: 7 faint and every leg will be w with urine. H2143
Lk 7:38 she began to w his feet with her tears. G1101
Lk 7:44 she w my feet with her tears and G1101

WHALE, WHALE'S, WHALES (KJV) HUGE FISH, CREATURES OF THE SEA, MONSTER (OF THE DEEP)

WHAT (2521) [SOMEWHAT, WHAT'S, WHATEVER]

Ge 2:19 to the man to see w he would name them H4537
Ge 3:13 to the woman, "W is this you have done?" H4537
Ge 4: 7 If you do w is right, will you not be H3512
Ge 4: 7 But if you do not do w is right, sin is H3512
Ge 4:10 The LORD said, "W have you done? Listen H4537
Ge 9:24 wine and found out w his youngest son H889
Ge 12:11 "I know w a beautiful woman you are. H3954
Ge 12:18 "W have you done to me? H4537
Ge 14:24 accept nothing but w my men have eaten H889
Ge 15: 2 w can you give me since I remain H4537
Ge 16: 2 Abram agreed to w Sarai said. H7754
Ge 18:17 I hide from Abraham w I am about to do? H889
Ge 18:19 way of the LORD by doing w is right and just, AIT
Ge 18:19 about for Abraham w he has promised him H889
Ge 18:21 see if w they have done is as bad as AIT
Ge 18:24 W if there are fifty righteous people in the H218
Ge 18:28 w if the number of the righteous is five less H218
Ge 18:29 "W if only forty are found there? H218
Ge 18:30 W if only thirty can be found there? H218
Ge 18:31 w if only twenty can be found there?" H218
Ge 18:32 more. W if only ten can be found there?" H218
Ge 19: 8 and you can do w you like with them. H3869
Ge 20: 9 in and said, "W have you done to us? H4537
Ge 20:10 "W was your reason for doing this? H4537

W

Ge 21: 1 did for Sarah **w** he had promised. H3869+889
Ge 21:17 "**W is the matter**, Hagar H4537+4200+3871
Ge 21:29 "**W is the meaning** *of* these seven H4537+2179
Ge 23:15 but **w** is that between you and me? H4537
Ge 24: 5 "**W if** the woman is unwilling to come back H218
Ge 24:30 heard Rebekah tell **w** the man said to her, H3907
Ge 24:33 eat until I have told you **w** I **have to say**." H1821
Ge 24:39 '**W if** the woman will not come back with H218
Ge 24:52 Abraham's servant heard **w** they **said**, H1821
Ge 25:32 "**W** *good* is the birthright to me?" H4200+4537
Ge 26:10 "**W** is this you have done to us? H4537
Ge 27: 8 listen carefully and do **w** I tell you: H889
Ge 27:12 **W if** my father touches me? I would appear H218
Ge 27:13 Just do **w** I say; go and get H928
Ge 27:37 So **w** can I possibly do for you H4537
Ge 27:42 was told **w** her older son Esau had **said**, H1821
Ge 27:43 my son, do **w** I **say**: Flee at once to H7754
Ge 27:45 with you and forgets **w** you did to him, H889
Ge 28:15 I have done **w** I have promised you." H889
Ge 29:15 Tell me **w** your wages should be. H4537
Ge 29:25 "**W** is this you have done to me? H4537
Ge 30:11 Then Leah said, "**W** good fortune!" So she H928
Ge 30:31 "**W** shall I give you?" he asked. "Don't H4537
Ge 31: 1 all this wealth from **w** belonged to our H889
Ge 31: 2 toward him was not **w** it had been. H3869
Ge 31: 5 attitude toward me is not **w** it was before, H3869
Ge 31:15 but he has used up **w** was **paid** *for* us. H4084
Ge 31:26 Laban said to Jacob, "**W** have you done? H4537
Ge 31:36 took Laban to task. "**W** is my crime?" H4537
Ge 31:37 **w** have you found that belongs to your H4537
Ge 31:43 Yet **w** can I do today about these H4537
Ge 32: 4 "**This is w** you are to say to my lord Esau H3907
Ge 32:13 and from **w** he had with him he H2021+995[S]
Ge 32:27 The man asked him, "**W** is your name?" H4537
Ge 33: 9 Keep **w** you have for yourself." H889
Ge 34: 7 as soon as they heard **w** had happened. NDT
Ge 34:19 lost no time in doing **w** they said H2021[S]
Ge 37: 8 because of his dream and **w** he had **said**. H1821
Ge 37:10 him and said, "**W** is this dream you had? H4537
Ge 37:15 asked him, "**W** are you looking for?" H4537
Ge 37:20 Then we'll see **w** comes of his dreams." H4537
Ge 37:26 "**W** will we gain if we kill our brother and H4537
Ge 38:10 **W** he did was wicked in the LORD's sight; so H889
Ge 38:16 "And **w** will you give me to sleep with you H4537
Ge 38:18 He said, "**W** pledge should I give you?" H4537
Ge 38:23 "Let her keep **w** she has, or we will NDT
Ge 40:12 "This is *w* it **means**," Joseph said to him AIT
Ge 40:18 "This is *w* it **means**," Joseph said. "The three AIT
Ge 41:25 revealed to Pharaoh **w** he is about to do. H889
Ge 41:28 has shown Pharaoh **w** he is about to do. H889
Ge 41:55 "Go to Joseph and do **w** he tells you." H889
Ge 42:28 "**W** is this that God has done to us?" H4537
Ge 44:15 said to them, "**W** is this you have done? H4537
Ge 44:16 "**W** can we say to my lord?" Judah replied. H4537
Ge 44:16 Judah replied. "**W** can we say? How can H4537
Ge 44:24 we told him **w** my lord had **said**. H1821
Ge 45: 9 '**This is w** your son Joseph says: H3907
Ge 45:23 And this is **w** he sent to his father: ten H3869
Ge 46:33 you in and asks, '**W** is your occupation? H4537
Ge 47: 3 the brothers, "**W** is your occupation?" H4537
Ge 49: 1 so I can tell you **w** will happen to you in H889
Ge 49:28 this is **w** their father said to them when H889
Ge 50:15 "**W if** Joseph holds a grudge against us H4273
Ge 50:17 '**This is w** you are to say to Joseph: I ask H3907
Ge 50:20 good to accomplish **w** is now being done, H3869
Ex 1:17 and did not do **w** the king of Egypt H3869+889
Ex 2: 4 a distance to see **w** would happen to him. H4537
Ex 2:14 "**W** I did must have become H2021+1821[S]
Ex 3:13 and they ask me, '**W** is his name? H4537
Ex 3:13 Then **w** shall I tell them?" H4537
Ex 3:14 **This is w** you are to say to the Israelites H3907
Ex 3:16 you and have seen **w** has been done to H2021
Ex 4: 1 "**W if** they do not believe me or listen to H2176
Ex 4: 2 LORD said to him, "**W** is that in your hand?" H4537
Ex 4:12 help you speak and will teach you **w** to say." H889
Ex 4:14 and he said, "**W about** your brother H2022+4202
Ex 4:15 of you speak and will teach you **w** to do. H889
Ex 4:22 say to Pharaoh, '**This is w** the LORD says: H3907
Ex 5: 1 said, "**This is w** the LORD, the God H3907
Ex 5:10 to the people, "**This is w** Pharaoh says: H3907
Ex 5:17 "Lazy, that's **w** you are—lazy! That is NDT
Ex 6: 1 "Now you will see **w** I will do to Pharaoh: H889
Ex 7:17 **This is w** the LORD says: By this you will H3907
Ex 8: 1 say to him, '**This is w** the LORD says: H3907
Ex 8:13 And the LORD did **w** Moses asked. H3869
Ex 8:20 say to him, '**This is w** the LORD says: H3907
Ex 8:31 the LORD did **w** Moses asked. The flies H3869
Ex 9: 1 say to him, '**This is w** the LORD, the H3907
Ex 9:13 say to him, '**This is w** the LORD, the H3907
Ex 10: 3 said to him, "**This is w** the LORD, the God H3907
Ex 10: 5 They will devour **w** little you have left H2021
Ex 10:11 since **that's** *w* you have been asking for." AIT
Ex 10:26 there we will not know **w** we are to use to H4537
Ex 11: 4 So Moses said, "**This is w** the LORD says H3907
Ex 12: 4 lamb needed **in accordance with** *w* each AIT
Ex 12:26 '**W** does this ceremony mean to you? H4537
Ex 12:28 Israelites did **just w** the LORD H3869+889+4027
Ex 12:36 and they **gave** them **w** they **asked for**; so H8626
Ex 12:50 did **just w** the LORD had H3869+889+4027
Ex 13: 8 'I do this because of **w** the LORD did for me H2296
Ex 13:14 your son asks you, '**W** does this **mean**? H4537
Ex 14: 5 about them and said, "**W** have we done? H4537
Ex 14:11 **W** have you done to us by bringing us out H4537
Ex 15:24 saying, "**W** are we to drink? H4537
Ex 15:26 your God and do **w** is right in his eyes H2021
Ex 16: 5 day they are to prepare **w** they bring in, H889
Ex 16:15 they said to each other, "**W** is it? H4943
Ex 16:15 For they did not know **w** it was. Moses H4537
Ex 16:16 This is **w** the LORD has commanded H2021+1821[S]
Ex 16:23 to them, "This is **w** the LORD commanded: H889
Ex 16:23 So bake **w** you want to bake and boil what H889
Ex 16:23 want to bake and boil **w** you want to boil. H889
Ex 16:32 "This is **w** the LORD has H2021+1821[S]
Ex 17: 4 "**W** am I to do with these people? H4537
Ex 18:14 "**W** is this you are doing for the people? H4537
Ex 18:17 "**W** you are doing is not good. H2021+1821[S]
Ex 19: 3 "**This is w** you are to say to the H3907
Ex 19: 3 of Jacob and **w** you are to tell the NDT
Ex 19: 4 'You yourselves have seen **w** I did to Egypt H889
Ex 19: 9 told the LORD **w** the people had **said**. H1821
Ex 22:27 neighbor has. **W** *else* can they sleep in H4537
Ex 23:11 and the wild animals may eat *w* is **left**. AIT
Ex 23:21 attention to him and listen to **w** he **says**. H7754
Ex 23:22 carefully to **w** he **says** and do all that I H7754
Ex 26:13 **w** is left will hang over the sides of the H2021
Ex 29: 1 "This is **w** you are to do to H2021+1821[S]
Ex 29:38 "This is **w** you are to offer on the altar H889
Ex 32: 1 we don't know **w** has happened to him." H4537
Ex 32: 4 He took **w** they handed him and made it into NDT
Ex 32: 8 turn away from **w** I commanded H2021+2006[S]
Ex 32:21 to Aaron, "**W** did these people do to you H4537
Ex 32:23 we don't know **w** has happened to him. H4537
Ex 32:27 said to them, "**This is w** the LORD, the God H3907
Ex 32:31 **w** a great sin these people have committed! NDT
Ex 32:35 a plague because of **w** they did with the H889
Ex 33: 5 I will decide **w** to do with you. H4537
Ex 33:16 **W** else will distinguish me and your people NDT
Ex 34:11 Obey **w** I command you today. I will drive H889
Ex 34:34 told the Israelites **w** he had been H889
Ex 35: 4 "This is **w** the LORD has H2021+1821[S]
Ex 35: 5 From **w** you have, take an offering for the NDT
Ex 35:25 her hands and brought **w** she had **spun**— H4757
Ex 36: 4 on the sanctuary left **w** they were doing H4856[S]
Ex 36: 7 because **w** they already had was H2021+4856[S]
Ex 40: 4 in the table and set out **w belongs** *on* it. H6886
Lev 3:14 From **w** you offer you are to present this H5647
Lev 4: 2 does **w** is forbidden in any of H889
Lev 4:13 does **w** is forbidden in any of H889
Lev 4:22 does **w** is forbidden in any of H889
Lev 4:27 does **w** is forbidden in any of H889
Lev 5: 5 must confess in **w** *way* they have sinned. H889
Lev 5:16 make restitution for **w** they have failed to H889
Lev 5:17 anyone sins and does **w** is forbidden in any H889
Lev 6: 4 they must return **w** they have stolen or H889
Lev 6: 4 by extortion, or **w** was entrusted to them H889
Lev 8: 5 "This is **w** the LORD has commanded to H1821[S]
Lev 8:34 **W** has been done today was H3869+889
Lev 8:35 seven days and do **w** the LORD **requires**, H5466
Lev 8:35 for **that is w** I have been commanded." H4027
Lev 9: 6 "This is **w** the LORD has H2021+1821[S]
Lev 10: 3 "This is **w** the LORD spoke of when he said: H889
Lev 17: 2 'This is **w** the LORD has H2021+1821[S]
Lev 19: 8 have desecrated **w** is **holy** *to* the LORD; H7731
Lev 20:12 **W** they have done is a perversion; their NDT
Lev 20:13 both of them have done **w** is **detestable**. H9359
Lev 25: 5 Do not reap **w grows of itself** or harvest the H6206
Lev 25:11 do not reap **w grows of itself** or harvest H6206
Lev 25:12 eat only **w is taken** directly from the fields. H9311
Lev 25:16 because *w is really being* **sold** to you is the AIT
Lev 25:20 "**W** will we eat in the seventh year if we H4537
Lev 25:25 is to come and redeem **w** they have **sold**. H4928
Lev 25:28 **w** was **sold** will remain in the possession H4928
Lev 27: 8 value according to **w** the one making the H889
Lev 27: 9 " 'If **w** they vowed is an animal that is NDT
Lev 27:11 If **w** they vowed is a ceremonially unclean NDT
Lev 27:12 value the priest then sets, that *is w it will* **be**. AIT
Nu 4:19 to each man his work and **w** he is **to carry**. H5362
Nu 4:49 was assigned his work and told **w to carry**. H5362
Nu 5:10 **w** they give to the priest will belong to H889
Nu 9: 8 until I find out **w** the LORD commands H4537
Nu 11:11 **W** have I done to displease you H4200+4537
Nu 11:23 see whether or not *w* I **say** will come true AIT
Nu 11:24 told the people **w** the LORD had **said**. H1821
Nu 13:18 See **w** the land is **like** and whether the H4537
Nu 13:19 **W** *kind of* land do they live in? Is it good H4537
Nu 13:19 **W** *kind of* towns do they live in H4537
Nu 14:34 your sins and **know w it is like** to have me H3359
Nu 15:34 it was not clear **w** should be done to him. H4537
Nu 20:14 "**This is w** your brother Israel says H3907
Nu 21:34 Do to him **w** you did to Sihon king of H3869+889
Nu 22: 7 Balaam, they told him **w** Balak had **said**. H1821
Nu 22:16 "**This is w** Balak son of Zippor says H3907
Nu 22:19 so that I can find out **w** else the LORD will H4537
Nu 22:20 but do only **w** I tell you. H2021+1821[S]
Nu 22:28 "**W** have I done to you to make you beat H4537
Nu 22:35 but speak only **w** I tell you. H2021+1821[S]
Nu 22:38 must speak only **w** God puts in my H2021+1821[S]
Nu 23:11 to Balaam, "**W** have you done to me? H4537
Nu 23:12 "Must I not speak **w** the LORD puts in my H889
Nu 23:17 Balak asked him, "**W** did the LORD say?" H4537
Nu 23:23 of Israel, 'See **w** God has done! H4537
Nu 24:13 and I must say only **w** the LORD says'? H889
Nu 24:14 let me warn you *of* **w** this people will do to H889
Nu 26:55 **W** each group inherits will be according to NDT
Nu 27: 7 "*W* Zelophehad's daughters *are* **saying** is AIT
Nu 29:39 " 'In addition to *w* you **vow** and your freewill AIT
Nu 30: 1 "This is **w** the LORD commands H2021+1821[S]
Nu 31:21 "This is **w is required** *by* the law that the H2978
Nu 32: 8 **This is w** your fathers did when I sent them H3907
Nu 32:24 your flocks, but do **w** you have promised." H2021
Nu 32:31 "Your servants will do **w** the LORD has said. H4027
Nu 33:56 I will do to you **w** I plan to do to H3869+889
Nu 36: 5 "**W** the tribe of the descendants of Joseph is NDT
Nu 36: 6 This is **w** the LORD commands for H2021+1821[S]
Dt 1:14 "**W** you propose to do is good." H2021+1821[S]
Dt 1:34 When the LORD heard **w** you **said** H7754+1821
Dt 3: 2 Do to him **w** you did to Sihon king of H3869+889
Dt 3:24 For **w** god is there in heaven or on earth H4769
Dt 4: 2 Do not add to **w** I command you H2021+1821[S]
Dt 4: 3 with your own eyes **w** the LORD did at Baal H889
Dt 4: 7 **W** other nation is so great as to have their H4769
Dt 4: 8 And **w** other nation is so great as to have H4769
Dt 5:26 For **w** mortal has ever heard the voice of H4769
Dt 5:28 "I have heard **w** this people said H7754+1821[S]
Dt 5:32 be careful to do **w** the LORD your God H3869+889
Dt 6:18 Do **w** is right and good in the LORD's sight, H2021[S]
Dt 6:20 "**W is the meaning of** the stipulations H4537
Dt 7: 5 **This is w** you are to do to them: Break H3907
Dt 7:18 remember well **w** the LORD your God did to H889
Dt 8: 2 you in order to know **w** was in your heart, H889
Dt 9: 5 to accomplish **w** he swore to your H2021+1821[S]
Dt 9:12 quickly from **w** I commanded H2021+2006[S]
Dt 9:18 doing **w** was evil in the LORD's sight and H2021[S]
Dt 10: 4 on these tablets **w** he had written before, H3869
Dt 10:12 **w** does the LORD your God ask of you but H4537
Dt 11: 4 **w** he did to the Egyptian army, to its horses H889
Dt 11: 5 children who saw **w** he did for you in the H889
Dt 11: 6 **w** he did to Dathan and Abiram, sons H889
Dt 12: 6 *w* you have **vowed** to give and your freewill AIT
Dt 12:25 you will be doing **w** is right in the eyes of H2021
Dt 12:28 you will be doing **w** is good and right in H2021
Dt 13:18 you today and doing **w** is right in his eyes. H2021
Dt 17:11 turn aside from **w** they tell you, H2021+1821[S]
Dt 18:16 this is **w** you asked of the LORD your God H889
Dt 18:17 The LORD said to me: "**W** they say is good. H889
Dt 18:22 If **w** a prophet proclaims in the name of the H889
Dt 21: 9 since you have done **w** is right in the eyes H2021
Dt 24: 8 carefully **w** I have commanded H3869+889
Dt 24: 9 Remember **w** the LORD your God did to H889
Dt 24:10 house to get *w* is **offered** *to* you **as a pledge**. AIT
Dt 24:20 Leave **w** remains for the foreigner, the NDT
Dt 24:21 Leave **w** remains for the foreigner, the NDT
Dt 25: 9 "**This is w** is done to the man who will not H3970
Dt 25:17 Remember **w** the Amalekites did to you H889
Dt 28:33 do not know will eat **w** your land and labor NDT
Dt 30:11 Now **w** I am H2021+5184+2021+2296[S]
Dt 31: 4 will do to them **w** he did to Sihon H3869+889
Dt 31:21 I know **w** they are disposed to do, even H889
Dt 31:29 his anger by **w** your hands have **made**." H5126
Dt 32:20 he said, "and see **w** their end will be; for H4537
Dt 32:21 made me jealous by **w** is no god and NDT
Dt 32:29 this and discern **w** their end will be! NDT
Dt 34: 9 to him and did **w** the LORD had H3869+889
Jos 2:10 of Egypt, and **w** you did to Sihon and Og H889
Jos 2:14 "If you don't tell **w** we are doing, we will H2296
Jos 2:20 But if you tell **w** we are doing, we will be H2296
Jos 4: 6 ask you, '**W** do these stones **mean**? H4537
Jos 4:21 their parents, '**W** do these stones **mean**? H4537
Jos 4:23 did to the Jordan **w** he had done to H3869+889
Jos 5:14 "**W** message does my Lord have for his H4537
Jos 7: 8 **W** can I say, now that Israel has been H4537
Jos 7: 9 **W** then will you do for your own great H4537
Jos 7:10 **W** are you doing down on your H4200+4537
Jos 7:13 tomorrow; for **this is w** the LORD, the H3907
Jos 7:19 Tell me **w** you have done; do not hide it H4537
Jos 7:20 the God of Israel. This is **w** I have done: H3869
Jos 8: 8 Do **w** the LORD has commanded H3869
Jos 8:31 built it according to **w** is written in the H2021
Jos 9: 3 of Gibeon heard **w** Joshua had done to H889
Jos 9:20 This is **w** we will do to them: We will let NDT
Jos 9:27 And that is **w** they are to this day. NDT
Jos 10:25 **This is w** the LORD will do to all the H3970
Jos 13:15 This is **w** Moses had given to the tribe of NDT
Jos 13:24 This is **w** Moses had given to the tribe of NDT
Jos 13:29 This is **w** Moses had given to the half-tribe NDT
Jos 14: 6 "You know **w** the LORD said to H2021+1821[S]
Jos 15:18 Caleb asked her, "**W** can I do for you?" H4537
Jos 22:24 '**W** do you have to do with the LORD H4537
Jos 22:30 heard **w** Reuben, Gad and H2021+1821[S]
Jos 24: 2 all the people, "**This is w** the LORD, the H3907
Jos 24: 5 I afflicted the Egyptians by **w** I did there, H889
Jos 24: 7 with your own eyes **w** I did to the Egyptians H889
Jdg 1: 7 me back for **w** I did to them." H3869+889+4027
Jdg 1:14 Caleb asked her, "**W** can I do for you?" H4537
Jdg 2:10 the LORD nor **w** he had done for H2021+5126[S]
Jdg 6: 8 who said, "**This is w** the LORD, the God of H3907
Jdg 6:38 And that *is w* **happened**. Gideon rose early AIT
Jdg 7:11 listen to **w** they are saying. Afterward H4537
Jdg 8: 2 "**W** have I accomplished compared to you H4537
Jdg 8: 3 **W** was I able to do compared to you?" H4537
Jdg 8:18 "**W** kind of men did you kill at Tabor?" H407
Jdg 9:30 of the city heard **w** Gaal son of Ebed **said**, H1821
Jdg 9:48 Do **w** you have seen me do! H4537
Jdg 11:12 "**W** do you have against me that you have H4537
Jdg 11:15 "**This is w** Jephthah says: Israel did H3907
Jdg 11:23 **w** right have you to take it over? NDT

Jdg 11:24 Will you not take **w** your god Chemosh H889
Jdg 13:12 **w** is to be the rule that governs the boy's H4537
Jdg 13:17 angel of the LORD, "**W** is your name, so H4769
Jdg 14: 6 his father nor his mother **w** he had done. H889
Jdg 14:18 said to him, "**W** is sweeter than honey? H4537
Jdg 14:18 **W** is stronger than a lion? H4537
Jdg 15:11 rulers over us? **W** have you done to us?" H4537
Jdg 15:11 did to them **w** they did to me." H3869+889+4027
Jdg 18: 3 **W** are you doing in this place H4537
Jdg 18: 4 told them **w** Micah had done H3869+2297+2256+3869+2296
Jdg 18:14 Now you know **w** to do." H4537
Jdg 18:18 the priest said to them, "**W** are you doing?" H4537
Jdg 18:24 went away. **W** else do I have? How H4537
Jdg 18:27 Then they took **w** Micah had made, and his H889
Jdg 20: 7 up and tell me **w** you have **decided to do**." H6783
Jdg 20: 9 But now this is **w** we'll do to H2021+1821S
Jdg 20:10 can give them **w** they **deserve for** this H3869
Jdg 20:12 "**W** *about* this awful crime that was H4537
Jdg 21:11 "**This is w** you are to do," they said H2021+1821S
Jdg 21:23 So **that is w** the Benjamites did. While H4027
Ru 2:11 been told all about **w** you have done for H889
Ru 2:12 the LORD repay you for **w** you have **done**. H7189
Ru 2:18 out and gave her **w** she had left over after H889
Ru 3: 4 He will tell you **w** to do." H889
Ru 3:18 my daughter, until you find out **w** happens. H375
1Sa 1:17 of Israel grant you **w** you have asked of H8924S
1Sa 1:23 "Do **w** seems best to you," her husband H2021
1Sa 1:27 LORD has granted me **w** I asked of him. H8629S
1Sa 2:27 said to him, "**This is w** the LORD says: H3907
1Sa 2:34 " 'And **w** happens to your two sons, Hophni H889
1Sa 2:35 will do according to **w** is in my heart and H889
1Sa 3:17 "**W** was it he said to you?" Eli asked. "Do H4537
1Sa 3:18 the LORD; let him do **w** is good in his eyes." H2021
1Sa 4:13 entered the town and told **w** had happened, NDT
1Sa 4:14 "**W is the meaning** *of* this uproar? H4537
1Sa 4:16 Eli asked, "**W** happened, my son?" H4537
1Sa 5: 7 people of Ashdod saw **w** was happening, H3954
1Sa 5: 8 "**W** shall we do with the ark of the god of H4537
1Sa 6: 2 "**W** shall we do with the ark of the LORD? H4537
1Sa 6: 4 "**W** guilt offering should we send to him?" H4537
1Sa 8: 9 let them know **w** the king who will reign NDT
1Sa 8:11 "**This is** *w* the king who will reign over you AIT
1Sa 9: 6 Perhaps he will tell us **w** way to take." H889
1Sa 9: 7 "If we go, **w** can we give the man? H4537
1Sa 9: 7 take to the man of God. **W** do we have?" H4537
1Sa 9: 8 God so that he will tell us **w** way to take." H5646S
1Sa 9:24 up the thigh with **w** was on it and set it H2021
1Sa 9:24 "Here is **w** has been kept for you. H2021
1Sa 10: 2 He is asking, "**W** shall I do about my son?" H4537
1Sa 10: 8 I come to you and tell you **w** you are to do." H889
1Sa 10:11 "**W** is this that has happened to the son H4537
1Sa 10:15 "Tell me **w** Samuel said to you. H4537
1Sa 10:16 not tell his uncle **w** Samuel had said H1821S
1Sa 10:18 said to them, "**This is w** the LORD, the God H3907
1Sa 11: 5 he asked, "**W is wrong** with everyone? H4537
1Sa 11: 5 to him **w** the men of Jabesh had **said**. H1821
1Sa 11: 7 "**This is w** will be done to the oxen of H3907
1Sa 12:17 And you will realize **w** an evil thing you H8041
1Sa 12:24 consider **w** great things he has done for H889
1Sa 13:11 "**W** have you done?" asked Samuel. H4537
1Sa 14:38 and let us find out **w** sin has been H928+4537
1Sa 14:40 "Do **w** seems best to you, H2021
1Sa 14:43 to Jonathan, "Tell me **w** you have done." H4537
1Sa 15: 2 **This is w** the LORD Almighty says: 'I will H3907
1Sa 15: 2 the Amalekites for **w** they did to Israel H889
1Sa 15:14 "**W** then is this bleating of sheep in my H4537
1Sa 15:14 **W** is this lowing of cattle that I hear?" NDT
1Sa 15:16 "Let me tell you **w** the LORD said to me last H889
1Sa 15:21 the best of **w** was devoted to God H2021
1Sa 16: 3 the sacrifice, and I will show you **w** to do. H889
1Sa 16: 4 Samuel did **w** the LORD said. When he H889
1Sa 17:26 "**W** will be done for the man who kills this H4537
1Sa 17:27 repeated to him **w** they had been saying H3869
1Sa 17:27 "**This is w** will be done for the man who H3907
1Sa 17:29 "Now **w** have I done?" said David. "Can't I H4537
1Sa 17:31 **W** David said was overheard and H2021+1821S
1Sa 18: 8 **W** more can he get but the kingdom?" NDT
1Sa 18:18 and **w** is my family or my clan in Israel H4769
1Sa 18:24 told him **w** David had H2021+1821+2021+465S
1Sa 19: 3 about you and will tell you **w** I find out." H4537
1Sa 19: 4 **w** he has **done** has benefited you H5126
1Sa 20: 1 to Jonathan and asked, "**W** have I done? H4537
1Sa 20: 1 "What have I done? **W** is my crime? How H4537
1Sa 20:32 he be put to death? **W** has he done?" H4537
1Sa 21: 3 Now then, **w** do you have on hand? Give H4537
1Sa 22: 3 you until I learn **w** God will do for me?" H4537
1Sa 25:17 Now think it over and see **w** you can do H4537
1Sa 25:24 hear **w** your servant has to **say**. H1821
1Sa 25:35 from her hand **w** she had brought him H889
1Sa 26:16 **W** you have done is not H2021+1821+2021+2296S
1Sa 26:18 **W** have I done, and what wrong am I H4537
1Sa 26:18 have I done, and **w** wrong am I guilty of? H4537
1Sa 27:11 on us and say, '**This is w** David did. H3907
1Sa 28: 2 will see for yourself **w** your servant can do." H889
1Sa 28: 9 "Surely you know **w** Saul has done. H889
1Sa 28:13 "Don't be afraid. **W** do you see?" The H4537
1Sa 28:14 "**W** does he look like?" he asked. "An old H4537
1Sa 28:15 So I have called on you to tell me **w** to do." H4537
1Sa 28:17 The LORD has done **w** he predicted H3869+889
1Sa 28:21 my hands and did **w** you told me to do. H1821S
1Sa 29: 3 "**W about** these Hebrews? H4537
1Sa 29: 8 "But **w** have I done?" asked David. "What H4537
1Sa 29: 8 "**W** have you found against your servant H4537
1Sa 30:23 not do that with **w** the LORD has given us H889
1Sa 30:24 Who will listen to **w** you **say**? The share of H1821
1Sa 31:11 Jabesh Gilead heard **w** the Philistines had H889
2Sa 1: 4 "**W** happened?" David asked. "Tell me." H4537
2Sa 1: 7 called out to me, and I said, '**W can** I **do**? H2180
2Sa 3: 8 very angry because of **w** Ish-Bosheth said H1821
2Sa 3: 9 not do for David **w** the LORD H3869+889
2Sa 3:24 to the king and said, "**W** have you done? H4537
2Sa 7: 5 servant David, '**This is w** the LORD says: H3907
2Sa 7: 8 '**This is w** the LORD Almighty says: H3907
2Sa 7:18 Sovereign LORD, and **w** is my family, that H4769
2Sa 7:20 "**W** more can David say to you? For you H4537
2Sa 8:15 doing **w** was just and right for all his people. NDT
2Sa 9: 8 down and said, "**W** is your servant, that H4537
2Sa 10:12 The LORD will do **w** is good in his sight." H2021
2Sa 12: 7 "You are the man! **This is w** the LORD, the H3907
2Sa 12: 9 of the LORD by doing **w** is evil in his eyes? H2021
2Sa 12:11 "**This is w** the LORD says: 'Out of your H3907
2Sa 13:13 **W about** me? Where could I get rid of my H2256
2Sa 13:13 **And w about** you? You H2256
2Sa 13:16 a greater wrong than **w** you have already H337S
2Sa 13:29 men did to Amnon **w** Absalom had H3869+889
2Sa 14: 5 asked her, "**W is troubling** you?" She said, H4537
2Sa 14:14 But that is not *w* God **desires**; rather, he AIT
2Sa 14:18 from me the answer to **w** I am going to ask H889
2Sa 15: 2 call out to him, "**W** town are you from?" H361
2Sa 16:10 "**W** does this have to do with you H4537
2Sa 16:20 "Give us your advice. **W** should we do?" H4537
2Sa 17: 5 so we can hear **w** he has to say as well." H4537
2Sa 17: 6 Should we do **w** he **says**? If not, H1821
2Sa 18:10 one of the men saw **w** had happened, NDT
2Sa 18:11 to the man who had told him this, "**W**! H2180
2Sa 18:21 tell the king **w** you have seen. H889
2Sa 18:22 to Joab, "**Come w may**, please let H2118+4537
2Sa 18:23 He said, "**Come w may**, I want to H2118+4537
2Sa 18:29 your servant, but I don't know **w** it was." H4537
2Sa 19:11 since **w** is being **said** throughout Israel H1821
2Sa 19:22 replied, "**W** does this have to do with you H4537
2Sa 19:22 **W** right do you have to interfere NDT
2Sa 19:28 So **w** right do I have to make any more H4537
2Sa 19:35 difference between **w** is enjoyable and what NDT
2Sa 19:35 between what is enjoyable and **w** is not? NDT
2Sa 19:35 your servant taste **w** he eats and drinks? H889
2Sa 20:17 "Listen to **w** your servant *has to* **say**." H1821
2Sa 21: 3 the Gibeonites, "**W** shall I do for you? H4537
2Sa 21: 4 "**W** do you want me to do for you?" H4537
2Sa 21:11 When David was told **w** Aiah's daughter H889
2Sa 24:10 "I have sinned greatly *in* **w** I have done. H889
2Sa 24:12 tell David, '**This is w** the LORD says: H3907
2Sa 24:17 are but sheep. **W** have they done? Let H4537
1Ki 1:14 in and add my word to **w** you have **said**." H1821
1Ki 1:16 before the king. "**W** is it you want?" the H4537
1Ki 1:30 out this very day **w** I swore to you by H3869+889
1Ki 2: 3 observe **w** the LORD your God **requires** H5466
1Ki 2: 5 you yourself know **w** Joab son of Zeruiah H889
1Ki 2: 5 **w** he did to the two commanders of Israel's H889
1Ki 2: 9 of wisdom; you will know **w** to do to him. H889
1Ki 2:38 answered the king, "**W** you **say** is good. H1821
1Ki 2:42 time you said to me, '**W** you **say** is good. H1821
1Ki 3:12 I will do **w** you have asked. I will give you H3869
1Ki 3:13 I will give you **w** you have not asked for H889
1Ki 8:15 hand has fulfilled **w** he promised with his H889
1Ki 8:32 down on their heads **w** they have **done**, H2006
1Ki 9:13 "**W** kind of towns are these you have given H4537
1Ki 10:13 besides **w** he had given her out of his royal H889
1Ki 11:22 "**W** have you lacked here that you want to H4537
1Ki 11:31 yourself, for **this is w** the LORD, the God H3907
1Ki 11:33 nor done **w** is right in my eyes, nor H2021
1Ki 11:38 to me and do **w** is right in my eyes by H2021
1Ki 12: 9 He asked them, "**W** is your advice? How H4537
1Ki 12:16 "**W** share do we have in David, what part H4537
1Ki 12:16 do we have in David, **w** part in Jesse's son? NDT
1Ki 12:24 '**This is w** the LORD says: Do not go up to H3907
1Ki 13: 2 **This is w** the LORD says: 'A son H3907
1Ki 13: 4 King Jeroboam heard **w** the man of God H1821S
1Ki 13:11 told their father **w** he had said to H2021+1821S
1Ki 13:21 from Judah, "**This is w** the LORD says: H3907
1Ki 14: 3 He will tell you **w** will happen to the boy." H4537
1Ki 14: 4 wife did **w** he said and went to H4027
1Ki 14: 7 tell Jeroboam that **this is w** the LORD, the H3907
1Ki 14: 8 doing only **w** was right in my eyes. H2021
1Ki 15: 5 For David had done **w** was right in the H2021
1Ki 15:11 Asa did **w** was right in the eyes of the H2021
1Ki 16: 5 **w** he did and his achievements H889
1Ki 16:27 **w** he did and the things he achieved H889
1Ki 17: 5 So he did **w** the LORD had told him. H3869
1Ki 17:13 bread for me from **w** you have and bring H9004S
1Ki 17:14 For **this is w** the LORD, the God of Israel H3907
1Ki 17:18 to Elijah, "**W** do you have against me H4537
1Ki 18: 9 "**W** have I done wrong," asked Obadiah H4537
1Ki 18:13 **w** I did while Jezebel was killing the H889
1Ki 18:24 all the people said, "**W** you say is good." H2021
1Ki 19: 9 "**W are you doing** here H4537+4200+3870
1Ki 19:13 "**W are you doing** here H4537+4200+3870
1Ki 19:20 Elijah replied. "**W** have I done to you?" H4537
1Ki 20: 2 saying, "**This is w** Ben-Hadad says: H3907
1Ki 20: 5 said, "**This is w** Ben-Hadad says: H3907
1Ki 20:13 announced, "**This is w** the LORD says: H3907
1Ki 20:14 prophet replied, "**This is w** the LORD says: H3907
1Ki 20:22 your position and see **w** must be done, H889
1Ki 20:28 king of Israel, "**This is w** the LORD says: H3907
1Ki 20:42 said to the king, "**This is w** the LORD says: H3907
1Ki 21:19 Say to him, '**This is w** the LORD says: H3907
1Ki 21:19 say to him, '**This is w** the LORD says: In H3907
1Ki 22:11 he declared, "**This is w** the LORD says: H3907
1Ki 22:14 I can tell him only **w** the LORD tells me." H889
1Ki 22:22 " '**By w means**?' the LORD asked. " 'I H928+4537
1Ki 22:27 '**This is w** the king says: Put this H3907
1Ki 22:43 he did **w** was right in the eyes of the LORD. H2021
2Ki 1: 4 Therefore **this is w** the LORD says: 'You H3907
2Ki 1: 6 you and tell him, "**This is w** the LORD says: H3907
2Ki 1: 7 "**W** kind of man was it who came to meet H4537
2Ki 1:11 "Man of God, **this is w** the king says H3907
2Ki 1:16 told the king, "**This is w** the LORD says: Is H3907
2Ki 1:18 Ahaziah's reign, and **w** he did, are they not H889
2Ki 2: 9 **w** can I do for you before I am taken from H4537
2Ki 2:21 saying, "**This is w** the LORD says: H3907
2Ki 3: 8 "**By w** route shall we attack?" he H361+2296
2Ki 3:10 "**W**!" exclaimed the king of Israel. "Has the H177
2Ki 3:16 he said, "**This is w** the LORD says: I will H3907
2Ki 3:17 For **this is w** the LORD says: You will see H3907
2Ki 4: 2 Tell me, **w** do you have in your house?" H4537
2Ki 4: 7 You and your sons can live on **w** is left." H2021
2Ki 4:13 trouble for us. Now **w** can be done for you H4537
2Ki 4:14 "**W** can be done for her?" Elisha asked H4537
2Ki 4:39 though no one knew **w** they were. NDT
2Ki 4:43 people to eat. For **this is w** the LORD says H3907
2Ki 5: 4 and told him **w** the girl H3869+2296+2256+3869+2296
2Ki 5:20 by not accepting from him **w** he brought. H889
2Ki 6:15 **W** shall we do?" the servant asked. H377
2Ki 7: 1 word of the LORD. **This is w** the LORD says H3907
2Ki 7: 9 to each other, "*W* we're **doing** is not right. AIT
2Ki 7:12 "I will tell you **w** the Arameans have done H889
2Ki 7:13 So let us send them to find out **w** happened." NDT
2Ki 7:14 "Go and find out **w** has happened. NDT
2Ki 7:20 And that is exactly *w* **happened** to him, for AIT
2Ki 8:14 "**W** did Elisha say to you? H4537
2Ki 9: 3 declare, '**This is w** the LORD says: H3907
2Ki 9: 6 declared, "**This is w** the LORD, the God H3907
2Ki 9:12 "**Here is w** he told me: H3869+2296+2256+3869+2296
2Ki 9:12 '**This is w** the LORD says: H3907
2Ki 9:18 Jehu and said, "**This is w** the king says: H3907
2Ki 9:18 "**W** do you have to do with peace? H4537
2Ki 9:19 to them he said, "**This is w** the king says: H3907
2Ki 9:19 "**W** do you have to do with peace? H4537
2Ki 9:27 king of Judah saw **w** had happened, NDT
2Ki 10:10 The LORD has done **w** he announced H889
2Ki 10:30 in accomplishing **w** is right in my eyes H2021
2Ki 11: 5 saying, "This is **w** you are to do: H2021+1821S
2Ki 12: 2 Joash did **w** was right in the eyes of the H2021
2Ki 14: 3 He did **w** was right in the eyes of the LORD H2021
2Ki 14: 6 in accordance with **w** is written in the H2021
2Ki 14:15 of Jehoash, **w** he did and his achievements H889
2Ki 15: 3 He did **w** was right in the eyes of the LORD H2021
2Ki 15:34 He did **w** was right in the eyes of the LORD H2021
2Ki 15:36 Jotham's reign, and **w** he did, are they not H889
2Ki 16: 2 he did not do **w** was right in the eyes of H2021
2Ki 16:19 reign of Ahaz, and **w** he did, are they not H889
2Ki 17:26 know **w** the god of that country **requires**. H5477
2Ki 17:26 the people do not know **w** he **requires**." H5477
2Ki 17:27 people **w** the god of the land **requires**." H5477
2Ki 18: 3 He did **w** was right in the eyes of the LORD H2021
2Ki 18:19 " '**This is w** the great king, the king of H3907
2Ki 18:19 On **w** are you basing this confidence of H4537
2Ki 18:29 **This is w** the king says: Do not let H3907
2Ki 18:31 **This is w** the king of Assyria says H3907
2Ki 18:37 told him **w** the field commander had **said**. H1821
2Ki 19: 3 They told him, "**This is w** Hezekiah says H3907
2Ki 19: 6 "Tell your master, '**This is w** the LORD says: H3907
2Ki 19: 6 Do not be afraid of **w** you have heard H889
2Ki 19:11 you have heard **w** the kings of Assyria H889
2Ki 19:20 "**This is w** the LORD, the God of Israel, says: H3907
2Ki 19:29 "This year you will eat **w grows by itself** H6206
2Ki 19:29 the second year **w springs from** *that*. H6084
2Ki 19:32 "Therefore **this is w** the LORD says H3907
2Ki 20: 1 to him and said, "**This is w** the LORD says: H3907
2Ki 20: 3 have done **w** is good in your eyes. H2021
2Ki 20: 5 of my people, '**This is w** the LORD, the God H3907
2Ki 20: 8 "**W** will be the sign that the LORD will heal H4537
2Ki 20: 9 LORD will do **w** he has promised: H2021+1821S
2Ki 20:14 asked, "**W** did those men say H4537
2Ki 20:15 "**W** did they see in your palace? H4537
2Ki 21:12 Therefore **this is w** the LORD, the God of H3907
2Ki 21:25 Amon's reign, and **w** he did, are they not H889
2Ki 22: 2 He did **w** was right in the eyes of the LORD H2021
2Ki 22:13 Judah about **w** is **written** *in* this book that H1821
2Ki 22:15 said to them, "**This is w** the LORD, the God H3907
2Ki 22:16 '**This is w** the LORD says: I am going to H3907
2Ki 22:18 the LORD, '**This is w** the LORD, the God of H3907
2Ki 22:19 LORD when you heard **w** I have spoken H889
2Ki 23:17 king asked, "**W** is that tombstone I see?" H4537
1Ch 10:11 Gilead heard **w** the Philistines had H3972S
1Ch 12:32 the times and knew **w** Israel should do— H4537
1Ch 16: 8 known among the nations **w** he has **done**. H6613
1Ch 17: 4 servant David, '**This is w** the LORD says: H3907
1Ch 17: 7 '**This is w** the LORD Almighty says: H3907
1Ch 17:16 LORD God, and **w** is my family, that you H4769
1Ch 17:18 "**W** more can David say to you for H4537
1Ch 18:14 doing *w* was **just** and right for all his people. AIT
1Ch 19:13 The LORD will do **w** is good in his sight." H2021

W

1Ch 21:10 tell David, '**This is w** the LORD says: H3907
1Ch 21:11 said to him, "**This is w** the LORD says: H3907
1Ch 21:17 are but sheep. **W** have they done? LORD H4537
1Ch 21:24 I will not take for the LORD **w** is yours, or H889
1Ch 29:14 have given you only **w** comes from your NDT
2Ch 6: 4 hands has fulfilled **w** he promised with his H889
2Ch 6:23 down on their heads **w** they have **done**, H2006
2Ch 8:14 because **this was w** David the man of God H4027
2Ch 9: 6 did not believe **w** they **said** until I came H1821
2Ch 10: 9 He asked them, "**W** is your advice? How H4537
2Ch 10:16 "**W** share do we have in David, what part H4537
2Ch 10:16 do we have in David, **w** part in Jesse's son? NDT
2Ch 11: 4 '**This is w** the LORD says: Do not go up to H3907
2Ch 12: 5 he said to them, "**This is w** the LORD says H3907
2Ch 13: 9 may become a priest of **w** are not gods. NDT
2Ch 13:22 Abijah's reign, **w** he **did** and what he said H2006
2Ch 13:22 what he did and **w** he **said**, are written in H1821
2Ch 14: 2 Asa did **w** was good and right in the eyes H2021
2Ch 18:10 he declared, "**This is w** the LORD says: H3907
2Ch 18:13 I can tell him only **w** my God says. H889
2Ch 18:20 " '**By w means**?' the LORD H928+4537
2Ch 18:26 '**This is w** the king says: Put this H3907
2Ch 19: 6 "Consider carefully **w** you do, because you H4537
2Ch 20:12 We do not know **w** to do, but our eyes are H4537
2Ch 20:15 **This is w** the LORD says to you H3907
2Ch 20:32 he did **w** was right in the eyes of the LORD. H2021
2Ch 20:37 the LORD will destroy **w** you have **made**." H5126
2Ch 21:12 "**This is w** the LORD, the God of your father H3907
2Ch 23: 4 Now this is **w** you are to do: H2021+1821S
2Ch 24: 2 Joash did **w** was right in the eyes of the H2021
2Ch 24:20 the people and said, "**This is w** God says: H3907
2Ch 25: 2 He did **w** was right in the eyes of the LORD H2021
2Ch 25: 4 in accordance with **w** is written in the Law, H2021
2Ch 25: 9 "But **w** about the hundred talents I paid H4537
2Ch 26: 4 He did **w** was right in the eyes of the LORD H2021
2Ch 27: 2 He did **w** was right in the eyes of the LORD H2021
2Ch 28: 1 he did not do **w** was right in the eyes of H2021
2Ch 29: 2 He did **w** was right in the eyes of the LORD H2021
2Ch 29:36 people rejoiced at **w** God had brought H2021
2Ch 30: 5 large numbers according to **w** was written. H2021
2Ch 30:12 **w** the king and his officials had **ordered**, H5184
2Ch 30:18 the Passover, contrary to **w** was written. H2021
2Ch 31:20 This is **w** Hezekiah did throughout Judah H3869
2Ch 31:20 doing **w** was good and right and faithful H2021
2Ch 32: 8 from **w** Hezekiah the king of Judah **said**. H1821
2Ch 32:10 "**This is w** Sennacherib king of Assyria H3907
2Ch 32:10 On **w** are you basing your confidence, that H4537
2Ch 32:13 "Do you not know **w** I and my H4537
2Ch 34: 2 He did **w** was right in the eyes of the LORD H2021
2Ch 34:21 Judah about **w** is **written** *in* this book that H1821
2Ch 34:23 said to them, "**This is w** the LORD, the God H3907
2Ch 34:24 '**This is w** the LORD says: I am going to H3907
2Ch 34:26 the LORD, '**This is w** the LORD, the God of H3907
2Ch 34:27 when you heard **w** he **spoke** against this H1821
2Ch 35: 6 doing **w** the LORD commanded through H3869
2Ch 35:21 saying, "**W** quarrel is there, king H4537
2Ch 35:22 not listen to **w** Necho had **said** at God's H1821
2Ch 35:26 in accordance with **w** is written in the Law H2021
2Ch 36:23 "**This is w** Cyrus king of Persia says: H3907
Ezr 1: 2 "**This is w** Cyrus king of Persia says: H3907
Ezr 3: 2 in accordance with **w** is written in the Law H2021
Ezr 3: 4 Then in accordance with **w** is written, they H2021
Ezr 5: 4 "**W** are the names of those who are A10426
Ezr 6: 8 I hereby decree **w** you are to do A10378+10408
Ezr 6:18 according to **w** is **written** *in* the Book of A10375
Ezr 8:17 I told them **w** to say to Iddo and his H1821S
Ezr 9:10 our God, **w** can we say after this? H4537
Ezr 9:13 "**W** has happened to us is a result of our H3972S
Ezr 10: 5 under oath to do **w** had been suggested. H3869
Ne 2: 4 king said to me, "**W** is it you want?" H6584+4537
Ne 2:12 had not told anyone **w** my God had put in H4537
Ne 2:16 know where I had gone or **w** I was doing, H4537
Ne 2:18 my God on me and **w** the king had said H1821S
Ne 2:19 "**W** is this you are doing? H4537
Ne 4: 2 he said, "**W** are those feeble Jews doing? H4537
Ne 4: 3 "**W** they are building—even a fox H889
Ne 5: 9 "**W** you are doing is not right. H2021+1821S
Ne 5:12 take an oath to do **w** they had promised. H3869
Ne 6: 8 "Nothing like **w** you are H2021+1821+2021+465S
Ne 6:14 my God, because of **w** they have done H465
Ne 6:19 good deeds and then telling him **w** I **said**. H1821
Ne 7: 5 This is **w** I found written there: NDT
Ne 8: 8 the people understood **w** was being read. H2021
Ne 9:28 they again did **w** was evil in your sight. NDT
Ne 13:14 do not blot out **w** I have so faithfully H889
Ne 13:17 "**W** is this wicked thing you are doing H4537
Est 1: 1 *This is w* **happened** during the time of Xerxes AIT
Est 1: 8 stewards to serve each man **w** he wished. H3869
Est 1:15 **w** must be done to Queen Vashti? H4537
Est 2: 1 Vashti and **w** she had done and what H889
Est 2: 1 she had done and **w** he had decreed about H889
Est 2:11 how Esther was and **w** was happening to H4537
Est 2:15 she asked for nothing other than **w** Hegai H889
Est 4: 5 him to find out **w** was troubling Mordecai H4537
Est 4: 9 reported to Esther **w** Mordecai had **said**. H1821
Est 5: 3 the king asked, "**W** is it, Queen Esther? H4537
Est 5: 3 Queen Esther? **W** is your request? Even up H4537
Est 5: 5 "so that we may do **w** Esther **asks**. H1821
Est 5: 6 asked Esther, "Now **w** is your petition? H4537
Est 5: 6 be given you. And **w** is your request? Even H4537
Est 6: 3 "**W** honor and recognition has Mordecai H4537
Est 6: 6 "**W** should be done for the man the king H4537
Est 6: 9 '**This is w** is done for the man the king H3970
Est 6:11 "**This is w** is done for the man the king H3970
Est 7: 2 "Queen Esther, **w** is your petition? H4537
Est 7: 2 will be given you. **W** is your request? Even H4537
Est 9: 5 they did **w** they pleased to those who H3869
Est 9:12 **W** have they done in the rest of the king's H4537
Est 9:12 Now **w** is your petition? It H4537
Est 9:12 It will be given you. **W** is your request? It H4537
Est 9:23 doing **w** Mordecai had written to them. H889
Est 9:26 because of **w** they had seen and H4537
Est 9:26 they had seen and **w** had happened to H4537
Job 2:10 In all this, Job did not sin in **w** he **said**. H8557
Job 3:25 **W** I feared has come upon me; what I H7065S
Job 3:25 **W** I dreaded has happened to me. H889
Job 4:16 I could not tell **w** it was. A form H5260S
Job 6: 8 that God would grant *w* I **hope** *for*, AIT
Job 6:11 "**W** strength do I have, that I should still H4537
Job 6:11 I should still hope? **W** prospects, that I H4537
Job 6:25 But **w** do your arguments prove H4537
Job 6:26 Do you mean to correct **w** I **say**, and treat H4863
Job 7:17 "**W** is mankind that you make so much of H4537
Job 7:20 If I have sinned, **w** have I done to you H4537
Job 8: 3 Does the Almighty pervert *w* is **right**? AIT
Job 8: 8 find out **w** their ancestors **learned**, H2984
Job 8:14 **W** they trust in is fragile; what they rely on H889
Job 8:14 is fragile; **w** they **rely on** is a spider's web. H4440
Job 9:12 Who can say to him, '**W** are you doing?' H4537
Job 10: 2 tell me **w** charges you have against H4537
Job 10:13 "But this is **w** you concealed in your heart NDT
Job 11: 8 than the heavens above—**w** can you do? H4537
Job 11: 8 than the depths below—**w** can you know? H4537
Job 12:14 **W** he tears down cannot be rebuilt; those NDT
Job 13: 2 **W** you know, I also know; I am not inferior H3869
Job 13:13 let me speak; then let come to me **w** may. H4537
Job 13:17 Listen carefully to **w** I **say**; let my words H4863
Job 14: 4 Who can bring *w* is **pure** from the impure AIT
Job 15: 9 **W** do you know that we do not know H4537
Job 15: 9 **W** insights do you have that we do not have NDT
Job 15:14 "**W** are mortals, that they could be pure H4537
Job 15:17 let me tell you **w** I have seen, H2296
Job 15:18 **w** the wise have declared, hiding nothing H889
Job 15:31 deceive himself by trusting **w** is worthless, H2021
Job 16: 3 **W** ails you that you keep on arguing? H4537
Job 20:18 **W** he **toiled for** he must give back H3334
Job 20:26 consume him and devour *w* is **left** in his tent. AIT
Job 21:15 **W** would we gain by praying to him H4537
Job 21:21 For **w** do they care about the families they H4537
Job 21:27 "I know full well **w** you are **thinking**, the H4742
Job 21:31 Who repays them for **w** they have done? H2085
Job 22: 3 **W** pleasure would it give the Almighty if NDT
Job 22: 3 **W** would he gain if your ways were NDT
Job 22:13 Yet you say, '**W** does God know? Does he H4537
Job 22:17 **W** can the Almighty do to us H4537
Job 22:28 **W** you decide on will be done, and light H608S
Job 23: 5 I would find out **w** he would answer me H4863S
Job 23: 5 and consider **w** he would say to me. H4537
Job 26: 3 **W** advice you have offered to one without H4537
Job 26: 3 And **w** great insight you have displayed NDT
Job 27: 8 For **w** hope have the godless when they H4537
Job 27:17 **w** he lays up the righteous will wear, and NDT
Job 30: 2 **Of w use** was the strength of their H4200+4537
Job 31: 2 For **w** is our lot from God above, our H4537
Job 31: 8 then may others eat **w** I have sown, and NDT
Job 31:14 **W** will I do when God confronts me? What H4537
Job 31:14 **W** will I answer when called to account? H4537
Job 32: 6 not daring to tell you **w** I **know**. H1976
Job 32: 9 not only the aged who understand *w* is **right**. AIT
Job 32:10 Listen to me; I too will tell you **w** I **know**. H1976
Job 32:17 will have my say; I too will tell **w** I **know**. H1976
Job 33: 3 my lips sincerely speak **w** I **know**. H1981
Job 33:27 I have perverted *w* is **right**, but I did not get AIT
Job 33:27 but I *did* not **get w** I **deserved**. H8750
Job 34: 4 Let us discern for ourselves *w* is **right**; let us AIT
Job 34: 4 let us learn together **w** is good. H4537
Job 34:11 He repays everyone for **w** they have **done** H7189
Job 34:11 brings on them **w** their conduct **deserves**. H3869
Job 34:16 hear this; listen to **w** I say. H7754S
Job 34:32 Teach me **w** I cannot see; if I have done NDT
Job 34:33 must decide, not I; so tell me **w** you know. H4537
Job 35: 3 Yet you ask him, '**W** profit is it to me, and H4537
Job 35: 3 it to me, and **w** do I gain by not sinning? H4537
Job 35: 6 sins are many, **w** does that do to him? H4537
Job 35: 7 If you are righteous, **w** do you give to him H4537
Job 35: 7 **w** does he receive from your hand? H4537
Job 36: 9 he tells them **w** they have **done**—that H7189
Job 37:19 "Tell us **w** we should say to him; we H4537
Job 38: 6 On **w** were its footings set, or who laid its H4537
Job 38:19 "**W** is the way to the abode of light H361+2296
Job 38:24 **W** is the way to the place where the H361+2296
Job 40:16 **W** strength it has in its loins, what power H2180
Job 40:16 its loins, **w** power in the muscles of its belly! NDT
Job 42: 9 Naamathite did **w** the LORD told H3869+889
Ps 8: 4 **w** is mankind that you are mindful of H4537
Ps 9:11 among the nations **w** he has **done**. H6613
Ps 11: 3 being destroyed, **w** can the righteous do?" H4537
Ps 12: 8 strut about when *w* is **vile** is honored by the AIT
Ps 15: 2 who does *w* is **righteous**, who speaks the AIT
Ps 17: 2 come from you; may your eyes see *w* is **right**. AIT
Ps 17: 4 through **w** your lips have **commanded**. AIT
Ps 17:14 May *w* you *have* **stored up** for the wicked fill AIT
Ps 25: 9 the humble in **w** is right and teaches H2021
Ps 28: 4 them for **w** their hands have **done** and H5126
Ps 28: 4 bring back on them **w** they **deserve**. H1691
Ps 28: 5 of the LORD and **w** his hands have **done**, H5126
Ps 30: 9 "**W** is gained if I am silenced, if I go H4537
Ps 35:25 let them think, "Aha, **just w** we **wanted**!" H5883
Ps 36: 4 a sinful course and do not reject *w* is **wrong**. AIT
Ps 37:30 wisdom, and their tongues speak *w* is **just**. AIT
Ps 38:20 though I seek only to do *w* is **good**. AIT
Ps 39: 7 "But now, Lord, **w** do I look for? My hope H4537
Ps 44: 1 have told us **w** you did in their days, H7189S
Ps 46: 8 Come and see **w** the LORD has **done**, the H5149
Ps 50:16 "**W right have you** to recite H4537+4200+3870
Ps 51: 4 I sinned and done **w** is evil in your sight; H2021
Ps 52: 9 For *w you have* **done** I will always praise you AIT
Ps 55: 3 because of **w** my enemy is **saying** H7754
Ps 56: 4 **W** can mere mortals do to me? H4537
Ps 56:11 am not afraid. **W** can man do to me? H4537
Ps 59: 7 See **w** they spew from their mouths—the NDT
Ps 62:12 everyone according to **w** they have **done**." H5126
Ps 64: 9 works of God and ponder **w** he has **done**. H5126
Ps 66: 5 Come and see **w** God has **done**, his H5149
Ps 66:16 let me tell you **w** he has done for me. H889
Ps 69: 4 I am forced to restore **w** I did not steal. H889
Ps 73:12 This is **w** the wicked are like—always free NDT
Ps 77:13 **W** god is as great as our God? H4769
Ps 78:11 They forgot **w** he had **done**, the wonders H6613
Ps 78:29 he had given them **w** they **craved**. H9294
Ps 78:30 But before they turned from **w** they craved NDT
Ps 85: 8 I will listen to **w** God the LORD says; he H4537
Ps 85:12 The LORD will indeed give **w** is good, and H2021
Ps 89:34 covenant or alter **w** my lips have **uttered**. H4604
Ps 89:47 For **w** futility you have created all H4537
Ps 92: 4 I sing for joy at **w** your hands have **done**. H5126
Ps 94: 2 pay back to the proud **w** they **deserve**. H1691
Ps 95: 9 tried me, though they had seen **w** I **did**. H7189
Ps 99: 4 in Jacob you have done *w* is **just** and **right**. AIT
Ps 101: 3 I hate *w* faithless people **do**; I will have no AIT
Ps 101: 4 I will have nothing to do with *w* is **evil**. AIT
Ps 105: 1 known among the nations **w** he has **done**. H6613
Ps 105:19 till **w** he **foretold** came to pass, till the H1821
Ps 105:44 they fell heir to **w** others had **toiled for**— H6662
Ps 106: 3 who act justly, who always do *w* is **right**. AIT
Ps 106:13 soon forgot **w** he had **done** and did not H5126
Ps 106:15 So he gave them **w** they **asked for**, but H8629
Ps 106:39 They defiled themselves by **w** they **did**; by H5126
Ps 116:12 **W** shall I return to the LORD for all his H4537
Ps 118: 6 **W** can mere mortals do to me? H4537
Ps 118:17 will proclaim **w** the LORD has **done**. H5126
Ps 119:68 are good, and *w you* **do** *is* **good**; teach me AIT
Ps 119:121 I have done *w* is **righteous** and just; do not AIT
Ps 120: 3 **W** will he do to you, and what more H4537
Ps 120: 3 he do to you, and **w** more besides, you H4537
Ps 137: 7 **w** the Edomites did on the day Jerusalem NDT
Ps 137: 8 repays you **according to w** you have H1691S
Ps 138: 4 when they hear **w** you have **decreed**. H609+7023
Ps 141: 4 my heart be drawn to **w** is evil so that I H1821S
Ps 143: 5 consider **w** your hands have **done**. H5126
Ps 144: 3 **w** are human beings that you care for H4537
Pr 1: 3 behavior, *doing w* is **right** and just and fair AIT
Pr 2: 9 will understand *w* is **right** and just and fair— AIT
Pr 4:10 accept **w** I **say**, and the years of H609
Pr 4:19 they do not know **w** makes them H928+4537
Pr 4:20 pay attention to **w** I **say**; turn your ear to H1821
Pr 5: 7 do not turn aside from **w** I **say**. H609+7023
Pr 6: 2 have been trapped by **w** you **said**, H609+7023
Pr 7:24 listen to me; pay attention to **w** I **say**. H609+7023
Pr 8: 6 I open my lips to speak *w* is **right**. AIT
Pr 8: 7 My mouth speaks *w* is **true**, for my lips detest AIT
Pr 8:19 fine gold; *w* I **yield** surpasses choice silver. AIT
Pr 10:24 *W* the wicked **dread** will overtake them; what AIT
Pr 10:24 *w* the righteous **desire** will be granted. AIT
Pr 10:32 The lips of the righteous know *w* **finds favor** AIT
Pr 10:32 the mouth of the wicked only *w* is **perverse**. AIT
Pr 13: 5 The righteous hate **w** is false, but the H1821S
Pr 14:22 But those who plan *w* is **good** find love and AIT
Pr 16:13 they value the one who speaks **w** is **right**. H3838
Pr 18:22 finds a wife finds *w* is **good** and receives AIT
Pr 19:17 he will reward them for **w** they have **done**. H1691
Pr 19:22 *W* a person **desires** is unfailing love; better AIT
Pr 21: 3 To do *w* is **right** and just is more acceptable AIT
Pr 21: 7 them away, for they refuse to do *w* is **right**. AIT
Pr 22:17 of the wise; apply your heart to **w** I **teach**, H1981
Pr 23: 1 with a ruler, note well **w** is before you, H889
Pr 23:16 will rejoice when your lips speak *w* is **right**. AIT
Pr 24:12 everyone according to **w** they have **done**? H7189
Pr 24:22 who knows **w** calamities they can bring? NDT
Pr 24:29 I'll pay them back for **w** they did. H3869
Pr 24:32 I applied my heart to **w** I observed and NDT
Pr 24:32 learned a lesson from **w** I saw: NDT
Pr 25: 7 **W** you have seen with your eyes H889
Pr 25: 8 **w** will you do in the end if your H4537
Pr 27: 1 you do not know **w** a day may bring. H4537
Pr 27: 7 to the hungry even *w* is **bitter** tastes sweet. AIT
Pr 28: 5 Evildoers do not understand **w** is **right**, but H5477
Pr 30: 4 **W** is his name, and what is the name of H4537
Pr 30: 4 his name, and **w** is the name of his son? H4537
Pr 31: 5 they drink and forget *w has* **been decreed**, AIT
Ecc 1: 3 **W** do people gain from all their labors at H4537
Ecc 1: 9 **W** has been will be again, what has been H4537
Ecc 1: 9 **w** has been done will be done again H4537
Ecc 1:13 **W** a heavy burden God has laid on H2085
Ecc 1:15 *W* **is crooked** cannot be straightened; what is AIT
Ecc 1:15 straightened; *w* is **lacking** cannot be counted. AIT

Ecc 2: 1 test you with pleasure to find out *w* is **good**." AIT
Ecc 2: 2 And **w** does pleasure accomplish? H4537
Ecc 2: 3 I wanted to see **w** was good for H361+2296
Ecc 2:11 hands had done and **w** I had toiled to H6662S
Ecc 2:12 **W more** can the king's successor H3954+4537
Ecc 2:12 successor do than **w** has already been H889
Ecc 2:15 **W** then do I gain by being wise?" H4200+4537
Ecc 2:22 **W** do people get for all the toil and H4537
Ecc 3: 9 **W** do workers gain from their toil? H4537
Ecc 3:11 one can fathom **w** God has done H2021+5126S
Ecc 3:15 and **w** will be has been before H889
Ecc 3:22 can bring them to see **w** will happen after H4537
Ecc 5: 6 God be angry at **w** you **say** and destroy H7754
Ecc 5:11 And **w** benefit are they to the owners H4537
Ecc 5:16 so they depart, and **w** do they gain, since H4537
Ecc 5:18 This is **w** I have observed to be good: that H889
Ecc 6: 8 **W** advantage have the wise over fools H4537
Ecc 6: 8 **W** do the poor gain by knowing how to H4537
Ecc 6: 9 Better **w** the eye **sees** than the roving of H5260
Ecc 6:10 **w** humanity is has been known H889
Ecc 6:12 For who knows **w** is good for a person in H4537
Ecc 6:12 Who can tell them **w** will happen under H4537
Ecc 7:13 Consider **w** God has **done**: Who can H5126
Ecc 7:13 Who can straighten **w** he has made H889
Ecc 7:20 no one who does *w* is **right** and never sins. AIT
Ecc 7:27 the Teacher, "this is **w** I have discovered: NDT
Ecc 8: 4 who can say to him, "**W** are you doing?" H4537
Ecc 8: 7 can tell someone else **w** is to come? H3869+889
Ecc 8:14 who get **w** the wicked **deserve**, H3869+5126
Ecc 8:14 who get **w** the righteous **deserve**. H3869+5126
Ecc 8:17 can comprehend **w** goes on under H2021+5126S
Ecc 9: 1 the wise and **w** they **do** are in God's H6271
Ecc 9: 7 God has already approved **w** you **do**. H5126
Ecc 10:14 No one knows **w** is coming—who can tell H4537
Ecc 10:14 can tell someone else **w** will happen after H889
Ecc 10:20 a bird on the wing may report **w** you **say**. H1821
Ecc 11: 2 you do not know **w** disaster may come H4537
Ecc 12:10 **w** he wrote was upright and true. H1821S
SS 5: 8 you find my beloved, **w** will you tell him? H4537
SS 8: 8 **W** shall we do for our sister on the day H4537
Isa 1:11 your sacrifices—**w** are they to me?" H4200+4537
Isa 2: 1 This is **w** Isaiah son of Amoz saw H889
Isa 2: 8 their hands, to **w** their fingers have made. H889
Isa 3:11 be paid back for **w** their hands have **done**. H1691
Isa 3:15 **W** do you mean by crushing my people H4537
Isa 5: 4 **W** more could have been done for my H4537
Isa 5: 5 Now I will tell you **w** I am going to do to H889
Isa 7: 7 Yet **this is w** the Sovereign LORD says: " 'It H3907
Isa 8:11 **This is w** the LORD says to me with his H3907
Isa 8:12 do not fear *w* they **fear**, and do not dread it. AIT
Isa 10: 3 **W** will you do on the day of reckoning H4537
Isa 10: 7 But this is not **w** he intends, this is not H4027
Isa 10: 7 intends, this is not **w** he has in mind; his H4027
Isa 10:24 Therefore **this is w** the Lord, the LORD H3907
Isa 11: 3 will not judge by **w** he **sees** *with* his eyes, H5260
Isa 11: 3 decide by **w** he **hears** *with* his ears; H5461
Isa 12: 4 known among the nations **w** he has **done**, H6613
Isa 14:32 **W** answer shall be given to the envoys of H4537
Isa 18: 4 **This is w** the LORD says to me: "I will H3907
Isa 19:12 and make known **w** the LORD Almighty H4537
Isa 19:17 because of **w** the LORD Almighty is planning H889
Isa 20: 6 'See **w** has **happened** *to* those we relied H3907
Isa 21: 3 I am staggered by *w* I **hear**, I am bewildered AIT
Isa 21: 3 by what I hear, I am bewildered by *w* I **see**. AIT
Isa 21: 6 **This is w** the Lord says to me: "Go, post a H3907
Isa 21: 6 a lookout and have him report **w** he sees. H889
Isa 21:10 I tell you **w** I have heard from the LORD H889
Isa 21:11 "Watchman, **w** is left of the night? H4537
Isa 21:11 Watchman, **w** is left of the night?" H4537
Isa 21:16 **This is w** the Lord says to me: "Within one H3907
Isa 22: 1 **W** troubles you now, that you have all H4537
Isa 22:15 **This is w** the Lord, the LORD Almighty, says: H3907
Isa 22:16 **W are you doing** here and H4537+4200+3870
Isa 22:22 of David; **w** he opens no one can shut NDT
Isa 22:22 can shut, and **w** he shuts no one can open. NDT
Isa 28:16 So **this is w** the Sovereign LORD says: "See H3907
Isa 28:23 my voice; pay attention and hear **w** I **say**. H614
Isa 29:16 Shall *w* is **formed** say to the one who formed AIT
Isa 29:22 Therefore **this is w** the LORD, who H3907
Isa 30:10 "Give us no more visions of *w* is **right**! AIT
Isa 30:12 Therefore **this is w** the Holy One of Israel H3907
Isa 30:15 **This is w** the Sovereign LORD, the Holy H3907
Isa 31: 4 **This is w** the LORD says to me: "As a lion H3907
Isa 32: 9 who feel secure, hear **w** I **have to say**! H614
Isa 33:13 are far away, hear **w** I have done; you who H889
Isa 33:15 who walk righteously and speak *w* is **right**, AIT
Isa 36: 4 " '**This is w** the great king, the king of H3907
Isa 36: 4 On **w** are you basing this confidence of H4537
Isa 36:14 **This is w** the king says: Do not let H3907
Isa 36:16 **This is w** the king of Assyria says H3907
Isa 36:22 told him **w** the field commander had **said**. H1821
Isa 37: 3 They told him, "**This is w** Hezekiah says H3907
Isa 37: 6 "Tell your master, '**This is w** the LORD says: H3907
Isa 37: 6 Do not be afraid of **w** you have heard H889
Isa 37:11 you have heard **w** the kings of Assyria H889
Isa 37:21 "**This is w** the LORD, the God of Israel, says: H3907
Isa 37:30 "This year you will eat **w grows by itself** H6206
Isa 37:30 the second year **w springs from** *that*. H8826
Isa 37:33 "Therefore **this is w** the LORD says H3907
Isa 38: 1 to him and said, "**This is w** the LORD says: H3907
Isa 38: 3 have done **w** is good in your eyes. H2021
Isa 38: 5 tell Hezekiah, '**This is w** the LORD, the God H3907
Isa 38: 7 LORD will do **w** he has H2021+1821+2021+2296S
Isa 38:15 But **w** can I say? He has spoken to me H4537
Isa 38:22 "**W** will be the sign that I will go up to the H4537
Isa 39: 2 showed them **w** was in his storehouses NDT
Isa 39: 3 asked, "**W** did those men say H4537
Isa 39: 4 "**W** did they see in your palace? H4537
Isa 40: 6 And I said, "**W** shall I cry?" "All H4537
Isa 40:18 To **w** image will you liken him H4537
Isa 41:22 "Tell us, you idols, **w** is going to happen H889
Isa 41:22 Tell us **w** the former things were, so that H4537
Isa 41:23 tell us **w** the future holds, so we may H2021
Isa 42: 5 **This is w** God the LORD says—the Creator H3907
Isa 43: 1 But now, **this is w** the LORD says—he who H3907
Isa 43:14 **This is w** the LORD says—your Redeemer H3907
Isa 43:16 **This is w** the LORD says—he who made a H3907
Isa 44: 2 **This is w** the LORD says—he who made H3907
Isa 44: 6 "**This is w** the LORD says—Israel's King H3907
Isa 44: 7 out before me **w** has **happened** since I H2023S
Isa 44: 7 ancient people, and *w is yet to* **come**—yes, AIT
Isa 44: 7 yes, let them foretell **w** will come. H889
Isa 44:19 I make a detestable thing from *w* is **left**? AIT
Isa 44:24 "**This is w** the LORD says—your Redeemer H3907
Isa 45: 1 "**This is w** the LORD says to his anointed, to H3907
Isa 45: 9 clay say to the potter, '**W** are you making? H4537
Isa 45:10 says to a father, '**W** have you begotten? H4537
Isa 45:10 a mother, '**W** have you brought to birth? H4537
Isa 45:11 "**This is w** the LORD says—the Holy One of H3907
Isa 45:14 **This is w** the LORD says: "The products of H3907
Isa 45:18 For **this is w** the LORD says—he who H3907
Isa 45:19 the LORD, speak the truth; I declare *w* is **right**. AIT
Isa 45:21 Declare **w** is to be, present it—let them NDT
Isa 46:10 from ancient times, **w** is still to come. H889
Isa 46:11 **W** I have said, that I will bring about; what I NDT
Isa 46:11 I will bring about; **w** I have planned, that I NDT
Isa 47: 7 these things or reflect on **w might happen**. H344
Isa 47:13 them save you from **w** is coming upon you. H889
Isa 48:17 **This is w** the LORD says—your Redeemer H3907
Isa 48:17 who teaches you *w is* **best** for you, who AIT
Isa 49: 4 Yet *w* is **due** me is in the LORD's hand, and AIT
Isa 49: 7 **This is w** the LORD says—the Redeemer H3907
Isa 49: 8 **This is w** the LORD says: "In the time of my H3907
Isa 49:22 **This is w** the Sovereign LORD says: "See, H3907
Isa 49:25 But **this is w** the LORD says: "Yes, captives H3907
Isa 50: 1 **This is w** the LORD says: "Where is your H3907
Isa 50:11 **This is w** you shall receive from my hand H2296
Isa 51: 7 you who know *w* is **right**, you people who AIT
Isa 51:22 **This is w** your Sovereign LORD says, your H3907
Isa 52: 3 For **this is w** the LORD says: "You were sold H3907
Isa 52: 4 For **this is w** the Sovereign LORD says: "At H3907
Isa 52: 5 "And now **w** do I have here?" declares the H4537
Isa 52:15 For **w** they were not told, they will see, and H889
Isa 52:15 they will see, and **w** they have not heard H889
Isa 55: 2 Why spend money on *w* is not **bread**, and AIT
Isa 55: 2 and your labor on *w* does not **satisfy**? AIT
Isa 55: 2 listen to me, and eat *w* is **good**, and you will AIT
Isa 55:11 will accomplish **w** I desire and achieve H889
Isa 56: 1 **This is w** the LORD says: "Maintain justice H3907
Isa 56: 1 "Maintain justice and do *w* is **right**, for my AIT
Isa 56: 4 For **this is w** the LORD says: "To the H3907
Isa 56: 4 who choose **w** pleases me and hold fast to H889
Isa 57:15 For **this is w** the high and exalted One H3907
Isa 58: 2 a nation that does *w* is **right** and has not AIT
Isa 58: 5 Is that **w** you call a fast, a day acceptable to NDT
Isa 59: 6 cover themselves with **w** they **make**. H5126
Isa 59:18 According to **w** they have **done**, so will he H1692
Isa 65: 8 **This is w** the LORD says: "As when juice is H3907
Isa 65:12 in my sight and chose **w** displeases me." H889
Isa 65:13 Therefore **this is w** the Sovereign LORD H3907
Isa 65:18 glad and rejoice forever in **w** I will create, H889
Isa 66: 1 **This is w** the LORD says: "Heaven is my H3907
Isa 66: 4 them and will bring on them *w* they **dread**. AIT
Isa 66: 4 in my sight and chose **w** displeases me." H889
Isa 66:12 For **this is w** the LORD says: "I will extend H3907
Isa 66:18 of **w** they have **planned** and done, H4742
Jer 1:11 LORD came to me: "**W** do you see H4537
Jer 1:13 came to me again: "**W** do you see?" H4537
Jer 1:16 in worshiping **w** their hands have **made**. H5126
Jer 2: 2 Jerusalem: "**This is w** the LORD says: " 'I H3907
Jer 2: 5 **This is w** the LORD says: "What fault did H3907
Jer 2: 5 "**W** fault did your ancestors find in me H4537
Jer 2:23 in the valley; consider **w** you have done. H4537
Jer 3: 6 "Have you seen **w** faithless Israel has done H889
Jer 4: 3 **This is w** the LORD says to the people of H3907
Jer 4:27 **This is w** the LORD says: "The whole land H3907
Jer 4:30 **W** are you doing, you devastated one H4537
Jer 5:13 in them; so let **w** they say be done to them." NDT
Jer 5:14 Therefore **this is w** the LORD God Almighty H3907
Jer 5:31 But **w** will you do in the end? H4537
Jer 6: 6 **This is w** the LORD Almighty says: "Cut H3907
Jer 6: 9 **This is w** the LORD Almighty says: "Let H3907
Jer 6:16 **This is w** the LORD says: "Stand at the H3907
Jer 6:18 witnesses, observe **w** will happen to them. H889
Jer 6:20 **W do I care about** incense H4200+4537+2296+4200+3276
Jer 6:21 Therefore **this is w** the LORD says: "I will H3907
Jer 6:22 **This is w** the LORD says: "Look, an army is H3907
Jer 7: 3 **This is w** the LORD Almighty, the God of H3907
Jer 7:12 see **w** I did to it because of the H889
Jer 7:14 **w** I did to Shiloh I will now do to the H3869+889
Jer 7:17 Do you not see **w** they are doing in the H4537
Jer 7:20 " 'Therefore **this is w** the Sovereign LORD H3907
Jer 7:21 " '**This is w** the LORD Almighty, the God of H3907
Jer 8: 4 "Say to them, '**This is w** the LORD says: H3907
Jer 8: 6 attentively, but they do not say *w* is **right**. AIT
Jer 8: 6 their wickedness, saying, "**W** have I done?" H4537
Jer 8: 9 the LORD, **w kind** *of* wisdom do they have? H4537
Jer 8:13 **W** I have given them will be taken from NDT
Jer 9: 7 Therefore **this is w** the LORD Almighty says H3907
Jer 9: 7 for **w else** can I do because of the sin of my H375
Jer 9:15 Therefore **this is w** the LORD Almighty, the H3907
Jer 9:17 **This is w** the LORD Almighty says H3907
Jer 9:22 "**This is w** the LORD declares: " 'Dead H3907
Jer 9:23 **This is w** the LORD says: "Let not the wise H3907
Jer 10: 1 Hear **w** the LORD says to you H2021+1821S
Jer 10: 2 **This is w** the LORD says: "Do not learn the H3907
Jer 10: 9 **W** the craftsman and goldsmith have **made** H5126
Jer 10:18 For **this is w** the LORD says: "At this time I H3907
Jer 11: 3 Tell them that **this is w** the LORD, the God H3907
Jer 11:11 Therefore **this is w** the LORD says: 'I will H3907
Jer 11:15 "**W** is my beloved **doing** in my H4537+4200
Jer 11:18 time he showed me **w** they were **doing**. H5095
Jer 11:21 Therefore **this is w** the LORD says about the H3907
Jer 11:22 therefore **this is w** the LORD Almighty says H3907
Jer 12: 4 "He will not see **w happens** *to* us. H344
Jer 12:14 **This is w** the LORD says: "As for all my H3907
Jer 13: 1 **This is w** the LORD said to me: "Go and H3907
Jer 13: 9 "**This is w** the LORD says: 'In the same way H3907
Jer 13:12 "Say to them: '**This is w** the LORD, the God H3907
Jer 13:13 then tell them, '**This is w** the LORD says: H3907
Jer 13:21 **W** will you say when the LORD sets over H4537
Jer 14:10 **This is w** the LORD says about this people H3907
Jer 14:15 Therefore **this is w** the LORD says about the H3907
Jer 15: 2 tell them, '**This is w** the LORD says: H3907
Jer 15: 4 of the earth because of **w** Manasseh son of H889
Jer 15:19 Therefore **this is w** the LORD says: "If you H3907
Jer 16: 3 For **this is w** the LORD says about the sons H3907
Jer 16: 5 For **this is w** the LORD says: "Do not enter H3907
Jer 16: 9 For **this is w** the LORD Almighty, the God H3907
Jer 16:10 **W** wrong have we done H4537
Jer 16:10 **W** sin have we committed against the H4537
Jer 17: 5 **This is w** the LORD says: "Cursed is the one H3907
Jer 17:10 according to **w** their deeds **deserve**." H7262
Jer 17:16 **W passes** my lips is open before you H4604
Jer 17:19 **This is w** the LORD said to me: "Go and H3907
Jer 17:21 **This is w** the LORD says: Be careful not to H3907
Jer 18:11 in Jerusalem, '**This is w** the LORD says: H3907
Jer 18:13 Therefore **this is w** the LORD says: "Inquire H3907
Jer 18:19 LORD; hear **w** my accusers are **saying**! H7754
Jer 19: 1 **This is w** the LORD says: "Go and buy a H3907
Jer 19: 3 **This is w** the LORD Almighty, the God of H3907
Jer 19:11 them, '**This is w** the LORD Almighty says: H3907
Jer 19:12 **This is w** I will do to this place and to H4027
Jer 19:15 "**This is w** the LORD Almighty, the God of H3907
Jer 20: 4 For **this is w** the LORD says: 'I will make H3907
Jer 21: 4 '**This is w** the LORD, the God of Israel, says H3907
Jer 21: 8 tell the people, '**This is w** the LORD says: H3907
Jer 21:12 **This is w** the LORD says to you, house of H3907
Jer 22: 1 **This is w** the LORD says: "Go down to the H3907
Jer 22: 3 **This is w** the LORD says: Do what is just H3907
Jer 22: 3 Do *w* is **just** and right. Rescue AIT
Jer 22: 6 For **this is w** the LORD says about the H3907
Jer 22:11 For **this is w** the LORD says about Shallum H3907
Jer 22:15 He did *w* was **right** and just, so all went well AIT
Jer 22:16 Is that not **w** it means to know me? NDT
Jer 22:18 Therefore **this is w** the LORD says about H3907
Jer 22:30 **This is w** the LORD says: "Record this man H3907
Jer 23: 2 Therefore **this is w** the LORD, the God of H3907
Jer 23: 5 reign wisely and do *w* is **just** and right in the AIT
Jer 23:15 Therefore **this is w** the LORD Almighty says H3907
Jer 23:16 **This is w** the LORD Almighty says: "Do not H3907
Jer 23:16 "Do not listen to **w** the prophets are H1821S
Jer 23:25 "I have heard **w** the prophets say who H889
Jer 23:28 For **w** has straw to do with grain? H4537
Jer 23:33 ask you, '**W** is the message from the LORD? H4537
Jer 23:33 say to them, '**W** message? I will H4537
Jer 23:35 **This is w** each of you keeps saying to your H3907
Jer 23:35 other Israelites: '**W** is the LORD's answer?' H4537
Jer 23:35 answer?' or '**W** has the LORD spoken H4537
Jer 23:37 **This is w** you keep saying to a prophet H3907
Jer 23:37 '**W** is the LORD's answer to you H4537
Jer 23:37 answer to you?' or '**W** has the LORD spoken H4537
Jer 23:38 from the LORD,' **this is w** the LORD says: H3907
Jer 24: 3 the LORD asked me, "**W** do you see H4537
Jer 24: 5 "**This is w** the LORD, the God of Israel, says H3907
Jer 25: 6 my anger with **w** your hands have **made**. H5126
Jer 25: 7 my anger with **w** your hands have **made**, H5126
Jer 25:15 **This is w** the LORD, the God of Israel, said H3907
Jer 25:27 tell them, '**This is w** the LORD Almighty H3907
Jer 25:28 '**This is w** the LORD Almighty says: H3907
Jer 25:32 **This is w** the LORD Almighty says: "Look H3907
Jer 26: 2 "**This is w** the LORD says: Stand in the H3907
Jer 26: 4 Say to them, '**This is w** the LORD says: If H3907
Jer 26:18 '**This is w** the LORD Almighty says: H3907
Jer 27: 2 **This is w** the LORD said to me: "Make a H3907
Jer 27: 4 say, '**This is w** the LORD Almighty H3907
Jer 27:16 all these people, "**This is w** the LORD says: H3907
Jer 27:19 For **this is w** the LORD Almighty says about H3907
Jer 27:21 **this is w** the LORD Almighty, the God of H3907
Jer 28: 2 "**This is w** the LORD Almighty, the God of H3907
Jer 28: 7 listen to **w** I have to say H2021+1821+2021+2296S
Jer 28:11 all the people, "**This is w** the LORD says: H3907
Jer 28:13 tell Hananiah, '**This is w** the LORD says: H3907
Jer 28:14 **This is w** the LORD Almighty, the God of H3907
Jer 28:16 Therefore **this is w** the LORD says: 'I am H3907

Jer 29: 4 **This is w** the LORD Almighty, the God of H3907
Jer 29: 5 plant gardens and eat *w* they **produce**. AIT
Jer 29: 8 **this is w** the LORD Almighty, the God H3907
Jer 29:10 **This is w** the LORD says: "When seventy H3907
Jer 29:16 but **this is w** the LORD says about the king H3907
Jer 29:17 **this is w** the LORD Almighty says: "I H3907
Jer 29:21 **This is w** the LORD Almighty, the God of H3907
Jer 29:25 "**This is w** the LORD Almighty, the God of H3907
Jer 29:28 plant gardens and eat *w* they **produce**. AIT
Jer 29:31 '**This is w** the LORD says about Shemaiah H3907
Jer 29:32 **this is w** the LORD says: I will surely punish H3907
Jer 30: 2 "**This is w** the LORD, the God of Israel, says H3907
Jer 30: 5 "**This is w** the LORD says: " 'Cries of fear H3907
Jer 30:12 "**This is w** the LORD says: " 'Your wound H3907
Jer 30:18 "**This is w** the LORD says: " 'I will restore H3907
Jer 31: 2 **This is w** the LORD says: "The people who H3907
Jer 31: 7 **This is w** the LORD says: "Sing with joy H3907
Jer 31:15 **This is w** the LORD says: "A voice is heard H3907
Jer 31:16 **This is w** the LORD says: "Restrain your H3907
Jer 31:23 **This is w** the LORD Almighty, the God of H3907
Jer 31:35 **This is w** the LORD says, he who appoints H3907
Jer 31:37 **This is w** the LORD says: "Only if the H3907
Jer 32: 3 You say, '**This is w** the LORD says: H3907
Jer 32:14 '**This is w** the LORD Almighty, the God of H3907
Jer 32:15 For **this is w** the LORD Almighty, the God H3907
Jer 32:23 they did not do **w** you commanded them H3972S
Jer 32:24 **W** you said has happened, as you now see. H889
Jer 32:28 Therefore **this is w** the LORD says: I am H3907
Jer 32:30 my anger with **w** their hands have **made**, H5126
Jer 32:36 of Babylon'; but **this is w** the LORD, the H3907
Jer 32:42 "**This is w** the LORD says: As I have brought H3907
Jer 33: 2 "**This is w** the LORD says, he who made the H3907
Jer 33: 4 For **this is w** the LORD, the God of Israel H3907
Jer 33:10 "**This is w** the LORD says: 'You say about H3907
Jer 33:12 "**This is w** the LORD Almighty says: 'In this H3907
Jer 33:15 he will do *w* is **just** and right in the land. AIT
Jer 33:17 For **this is w** the LORD says: 'David will H3907
Jer 33:20 "**This is w** the LORD says: 'If you can break H3907
Jer 33:25 **This is w** the LORD says: 'If I have not made H3907
Jer 34: 2 "**This is w** the LORD, the God of Israel, says H3907
Jer 34: 2 tell him, '**This is w** the LORD says: H3907
Jer 34: 4 **This is w** the LORD says concerning you H3907
Jer 34:13 "**This is w** the LORD, the God of Israel, says H3907
Jer 34:15 you repented and did *w* is **right** in my sight: AIT
Jer 34:17 "Therefore **this is w** the LORD says: You H3907
Jer 35:13 "**This is w** the LORD Almighty, the God of H3907
Jer 35:17 "Therefore **this is w** the LORD God H3907
Jer 35:18 Rekabites, "**This is w** the LORD Almighty H3907
Jer 35:19 Therefore **this is w** the LORD Almighty, the H3907
Jer 36:29 king of Judah, '**This is w** the LORD says: H3907
Jer 36:30 Therefore **this is w** the LORD says about H3907
Jer 37: 7 "**This is w** the LORD, the God of Israel, says H3907
Jer 37: 9 "**This is w** the LORD says: Do not deceive H3907
Jer 37:18 "**W** crime have I committed against you H4537
Jer 38: 1 Malkijah heard **w** Jeremiah was H2021+1821S
Jer 38: 2 "**This is w** the LORD says: 'Whoever stays H3907
Jer 38: 3 And **this is w** the LORD says: 'This city H3907
Jer 38:17 "**This is w** the LORD God Almighty H3907
Jer 38:20 "Obey the LORD by doing **w** I tell you. H889
Jer 38:21 this is **w** the LORD has revealed to H2021+1821S
Jer 38:25 'Tell us **w** you said to the king and what H4537
Jer 38:25 to the king and **w** the king said to you H4537
Jer 39:16 the Cushite, '**This is w** the LORD Almighty H3907
Jer 40:16 *W* you *are* **saying** about Ishmael is not true." AIT
Jer 42: 3 should go and **w** we should do." H2021+1821S
Jer 42: 9 He said to them, "**This is w** the LORD, the H3907
Jer 42:15 **This is w** the LORD Almighty, the God of H3907
Jer 42:18 **This is w** the LORD Almighty, the God of H3907
Jer 43:10 say to them, '**This is w** the LORD Almighty H3907
Jer 44: 2 "**This is w** the LORD Almighty, the God of H3907
Jer 44: 7 "Now **this is w** the LORD God Almighty, H3907
Jer 44: 8 my anger with **w** your hands have **made**, H5126
Jer 44:11 "Therefore **this is w** the LORD Almighty, H3907
Jer 44:25 **This is w** the LORD Almighty, the God of H3907
Jer 44:25 your wives have done **w** you said you would NDT
Jer 44:25 do **w** you **promised**! Keep your H5624
Jer 44:30 **This is w** the LORD says: 'I am going to H3907
Jer 45: 2 "**This is w** the LORD, the God of Israel, says H3907
Jer 45: 4 me to say to you, '**This is w** the LORD says: H3907
Jer 45: 4 I will overthrow **w** I have built and uproot H889
Jer 45: 4 I have built and uproot **w** I have planted, H889
Jer 46: 5 **W** do I see? They are terrified, they are H4508
Jer 47: 2 **This is w** the LORD says: "See how the H3907
Jer 48: 1 **This is w** the LORD Almighty, the God of H3907
Jer 48:19 escaping, ask them, '**W** has happened? H4537
Jer 48:40 **This is w** the LORD says: "Look! An eagle H3907
Jer 49: 1 the Ammonites: **This is w** the LORD says H3907
Jer 49: 7 **This is w** the LORD Almighty says H3907
Jer 49:12 **This is w** the LORD says: "If those who do H3907
Jer 49:19 And **w** shepherd can stand against me?" H4769
Jer 49:20 hear **w** the LORD has planned against Edom, H889
Jer 49:20 **w** he has purposed against those who live H889
Jer 49:28 Babylon attacked: **This is w** the LORD says H3907
Jer 49:35 **This is w** the LORD Almighty says: "See, H3907
Jer 50:18 Therefore **this is w** the LORD Almighty, H3907
Jer 50:33 **This is w** the LORD Almighty says: "The H3907
Jer 50:44 And **w** shepherd can stand against H4769+2296
Jer 50:45 hear **w** the LORD has planned against H889
Jer 50:45 **w** he has purposed against the land of the H889
Jer 51: 1 **This is w** the LORD says: "See, I will stir up H3907
Jer 51: 6 he will repay her **w** she **deserves**. H1691
Jer 51:10 tell in Zion **w** the LORD our God has **done**. H5126
Jer 51:33 **This is w** the LORD Almighty, the God of H3907
Jer 51:36 Therefore **this is w** the LORD says: "See, H3907
Jer 51:44 make him spew out **w** he has **swallowed**. H1183
Jer 51:58 **This is w** the LORD Almighty says H3907
La 1:21 they rejoice at **w** you have done. NDT
La 2:13 **W** can I say for you? With what can I H4537
La 2:13 With **w** can I compare you, Daughter H4537
La 2:13 To **w** can I liken you, that I may comfort H4537
La 2:17 The LORD has done **w** he planned; he has H889
La 3:17 of peace; I have forgotten **w** prosperity is. NDT
La 3:51 **W** I **see** brings grief to my soul because of H6524
La 3:62 *w* my enemies **whisper** and mutter against AIT
La 3:64 Pay them back **w** they **deserve**, LORD, for H1691
La 3:64 for **w** their hands have **done**. H5126
La 5: 1 Remember, LORD, **w** has happened to us H4537
Eze 1: 5 in the fire was *w* **looked like** four living AIT
Eze 1:22 was *w* **looked something like** a vault, AIT
Eze 1:26 over their heads was **w** looked like a throne NDT
Eze 1:27 I saw that from *w* **appeared** to be his waist up AIT
Eze 2: 4 '**This is w** the Sovereign LORD says. H3907
Eze 2: 6 not be afraid of **w** they **say** or be terrified H1821
Eze 2: 8 son of man, listen to **w** I say to you. Do not H889
Eze 2: 8 open your mouth and eat **w** I give you." H889
Eze 3: 1 "Son of man, eat **w** is before you, eat this H889
Eze 3:11 '**This is w** the Sovereign LORD says H3907
Eze 3:27 '**This is w** the Sovereign LORD says. H3907
Eze 5: 5 "**This is w** the Sovereign LORD says: This H3907
Eze 5: 7 "Therefore **this is w** the Sovereign LORD H3907
Eze 5: 8 "Therefore **this is w** the Sovereign LORD H3907
Eze 5: 9 I will do to you **w** I have never done H889+4017
Eze 6: 3 **This is w** the Sovereign LORD says to the H3907
Eze 6: 6 and **w** you have **made** wiped out. H5126
Eze 6:11 " '**This is w** the Sovereign LORD says: H3907
Eze 7: 2 **this is w** the Sovereign LORD says to the H3907
Eze 7: 5 "**This is w** the Sovereign LORD says: H3907
Eze 8: 2 From *w* **appeared** to be his waist down he AIT
Eze 8: 3 He stretched out *w* **looked like** a hand and AIT
Eze 8: 6 of man, do you see **w** they are doing—the H4537
Eze 8:12 have you seen **w** the elders of Israel are H889
Eze 9:10 on their own heads **w** they have **done**." H2006
Eze 10: 8 could be seen *w* **looked like** human hands.) AIT
Eze 10:21 their wings was *w* **looked like** human hands. AIT
Eze 11: 5 told me to say: "**This is w** the LORD says H3907
Eze 11: 5 **That is w** you are saying, you leaders in H4027
Eze 11: 5 I know **w is going through** your mind. H5091
Eze 11: 7 "Therefore **this is w** the Sovereign LORD H3907
Eze 11: 8 the sword is **w** I will bring against you NDT
Eze 11:16 '**This is w** the Sovereign LORD says H3907
Eze 11:17 '**This is w** the Sovereign LORD says H3907
Eze 11:21 on their own heads **w** they have **done**, H2006
Eze 12: 9 people, ask you, '**W** are you doing? H4537
Eze 12:10 '**This is w** the Sovereign LORD says: H3907
Eze 12:19 '**This is w** the Sovereign LORD says about H3907
Eze 12:22 **w** is this proverb you have in the land of H4537
Eze 12:23 '**This is w** the Sovereign LORD says: H3907
Eze 12:25 But I the LORD will speak **w** I will, and it H889
Eze 12:28 '**This is w** the Sovereign LORD says: H3907
Eze 13: 3 **This is w** the Sovereign LORD says: Woe to H3907
Eze 13: 8 " 'Therefore **this is w** the Sovereign LORD H3907
Eze 13:13 " 'Therefore **this is w** the Sovereign LORD H3907
Eze 13:18 '**This is w** the Sovereign LORD says: H3907
Eze 13:20 " 'Therefore **this is w** the Sovereign LORD H3907
Eze 14: 4 '**This is w** the Sovereign LORD says: H3907
Eze 14: 6 '**This is w** the Sovereign LORD says: H3907
Eze 14:21 "For **this is w** the Sovereign LORD says H3907
Eze 15: 6 "Therefore **this is w** the Sovereign LORD H3907
Eze 16: 3 '**This is w** the Sovereign LORD says to H3907
Eze 16:19 *That is w* **happened**, declares the Sovereign AIT
Eze 16:36 **This is w** the Sovereign LORD says: H3907
Eze 16:43 down on your head **w** you have **done**, H2006
Eze 16:48 daughters never did **w** you and your H3869+889
Eze 16:55 will return to *w* they were **before**; and you AIT
Eze 16:55 daughters will return to *w* you were **before**. AIT
Eze 16:59 " '**This is w** the Sovereign LORD says: H3907
Eze 17: 3 '**This is w** the Sovereign LORD says: H3907
Eze 17: 9 '**This is w** the Sovereign LORD says: H3907
Eze 17:12 'Do you not know **w** these things **mean**? H4537
Eze 17:19 " 'Therefore **this is w** the Sovereign LORD H3907
Eze 17:22 " '**This is w** the Sovereign LORD says: H3907
Eze 18: 2 "**W do you people mean** by H4537+4200+4013
Eze 18: 5 righteous man who does *w* is **just** and right. AIT
Eze 18: 7 returns **w** he **took in pledge** *for* a loan. H2481
Eze 18:12 He does not return **w** he **took in pledge** H2478
Eze 18:18 brother and did **w** was wrong among his H889
Eze 18:19 the son has done *w* is **just** and right and has AIT
Eze 18:21 all my decrees and does *w* is **just** and right, AIT
Eze 18:27 have committed and does *w* is **just** and right, AIT
Eze 19: 2 " '**W** a lioness was your mother among H4537
Eze 20: 3 '**This is w** the Sovereign LORD says: H3907
Eze 20: 5 '**This is w** the Sovereign LORD says H3907
Eze 20:14 sake of my name I did **w** would keep it from NDT
Eze 20:22 sake of my name I did **w** would keep it from NDT
Eze 20:27 '**This is w** the Sovereign LORD says: H3907
Eze 20:29 **W** is this high place you go to H4537
Eze 20:30 '**This is w** the Sovereign LORD says H3907
Eze 20:32 But **w** you have in mind will never happen H2021
Eze 20:39 of Israel, **this is w** the Sovereign LORD says: H3907
Eze 20:47 **This is w** the Sovereign LORD says H3907
Eze 21: 3 '**This is w** the LORD says: H3907
Eze 21: 9 prophesy and say, '**This is w** the Lord says: H3907
Eze 21:13 And **w** if even the scepter, which the H4537
Eze 21:24 "Therefore **this is w** the Sovereign LORD H3907
Eze 21:26 **this is w** the Sovereign LORD says: Take off H3907
Eze 21:28 '**This is w** the Sovereign LORD says about H3907
Eze 22: 3 '**This is w** the Sovereign LORD says H3907
Eze 22:19 **this is w** the Sovereign LORD says: H3907
Eze 22:28 '**This is w** the Sovereign LORD says' H3907
Eze 23:22 **this is w** the Sovereign LORD says: H3907
Eze 23:28 "For **this is w** the Sovereign LORD says: H3907
Eze 23:32 "**This is w** the Sovereign LORD says: "You H3907
Eze 23:35 "Therefore **this is w** the Sovereign LORD H3907
Eze 23:39 **That is w** they did in my house. H3907
Eze 23:46 "**This is w** the Sovereign LORD says: Bring H3907
Eze 24: 3 '**This is w** the Sovereign LORD says H3907
Eze 24: 6 " 'For **this is w** the Sovereign LORD says: H3907
Eze 24: 9 " 'Therefore **this is w** the Sovereign LORD H3907
Eze 24:19 "Won't you tell us **w** these things have to H4537
Eze 24:21 '**This is w** the Sovereign LORD says: H3907
Eze 25: 3 **This is w** the Sovereign LORD says H3907
Eze 25: 6 For **this is w** the Sovereign LORD says H3907
Eze 25: 8 "**This is w** the Sovereign LORD says H3907
Eze 25:12 "**This is w** the Sovereign LORD says H3907
Eze 25:13 therefore **this is w** the Sovereign LORD says H3907
Eze 25:15 "**This is w** the Sovereign LORD says H3907
Eze 25:16 therefore **this is w** the Sovereign LORD says H3907
Eze 26: 3 therefore **this is w** the Sovereign LORD says H3907
Eze 26: 7 "For **this is w** the Sovereign LORD says H3907
Eze 26:15 "**This is w** the Sovereign LORD says to Tyre H3907
Eze 26:19 "**This is w** the Sovereign LORD says: When H3907
Eze 27: 3 '**This is w** the Sovereign LORD says: H3907
Eze 28: 2 '**This is w** the Sovereign LORD says: H3907
Eze 28: 6 " 'Therefore **this is w** the Sovereign LORD H3907
Eze 28:12 '**This is w** the Sovereign LORD says H3907
Eze 28:22 '**This is w** the Sovereign LORD says H3907
Eze 28:25 " '**This is w** the Sovereign LORD says H3907
Eze 29: 3 '**This is w** the Sovereign LORD says H3907
Eze 29: 8 " 'Therefore **this is w** the Sovereign LORD H3907
Eze 29:13 " 'Yet **this is w** the Sovereign LORD says: H3907
Eze 29:19 **this is w** the Sovereign LORD says: H3907
Eze 30: 2 '**This is w** the Sovereign LORD says H3907
Eze 30: 6 " '**This is w** the LORD says: " 'The allies of H3907
Eze 30:10 " '**This is w** the Sovereign LORD says: " 'I H3907
Eze 30:13 " '**This is w** the Sovereign LORD says: " 'I H3907
Eze 30:22 **this is w** the Sovereign LORD says: H3907
Eze 31:10 " 'Therefore **this is w** the Sovereign LORD H3907
Eze 31:15 " '**This is w** the Sovereign LORD says: On H3907
Eze 32: 3 " '**This is w** the Sovereign LORD says: H3907
Eze 32:11 " 'For **this is w** the Sovereign LORD says: H3907
Eze 33:10 to the Israelites, '**This is w** you are saying: H4027
Eze 33:14 from their sin and do *w* is **just** and right— AIT
Eze 33:15 back **w** they **took in pledge for a loan**, H2478
Eze 33:15 return **w** they have **stolen**, follow the H1611
Eze 33:16 They have done *w* is **just** and right; they will AIT
Eze 33:19 their wickedness and does *w* is **just** and right, AIT
Eze 33:25 '**This is w** the Sovereign LORD says: H3907
Eze 33:27 '**This is w** the Sovereign LORD says H3907
Eze 34: 2 '**This is w** the Sovereign LORD says H3907
Eze 34:10 **This is w** the Sovereign LORD says: I am H3907
Eze 34:11 " 'For **this is w** the Sovereign LORD says: H3907
Eze 34:17 flock, **this is w** the Sovereign LORD says: H3907
Eze 34:19 feed on **w** you have **trampled** and H5330+8079
Eze 34:19 drink **w** you have **muddied** *with* your H5343
Eze 34:20 " 'Therefore **this is w** the Sovereign LORD H3907
Eze 35: 3 '**This is w** the Sovereign LORD says H3907
Eze 35:14 **This is w** the Sovereign LORD says: While H3907
Eze 36: 2 **This is w** the Sovereign LORD says: The H3907
Eze 36: 3 '**This is w** the Sovereign LORD says: H3907
Eze 36: 4 **This is w** the Sovereign LORD says to the H3907
Eze 36: 5 **this is w** the Sovereign LORD says: In my H3907
Eze 36: 6 '**This is w** the Sovereign LORD says H3907
Eze 36: 7 **this is w** the Sovereign LORD says: H3907
Eze 36:13 " '**This is w** the Sovereign LORD says H3907
Eze 36:22 '**This is w** the Sovereign LORD says: H3907
Eze 36:33 " '**This is w** the Sovereign LORD says: On H3907
Eze 36:36 the LORD have rebuilt **w** was destroyed H2021
Eze 36:36 have replanted **w** was desolate. H2021
Eze 36:37 "**This is w** the Sovereign LORD says: Once H3907
Eze 37: 5 **This is w** the Sovereign LORD says to these H3907
Eze 37: 9 '**This is w** the Sovereign LORD says: H3907
Eze 37:12 '**This is w** the Sovereign LORD says H3907
Eze 37:18 'Won't you tell us **w** you mean by this? H4537
Eze 37:19 '**This is w** the Sovereign LORD says: H3907
Eze 37:21 '**This is w** the Sovereign LORD says: H3907
Eze 38: 3 '**This is w** the Sovereign LORD says H3907
Eze 38:10 " '**This is w** the Sovereign LORD says: On H3907
Eze 38:14 '**This is w** the Sovereign LORD says H3907
Eze 38:17 " '**This is w** the Sovereign LORD says: You H3907
Eze 38:18 *This is w will* **happen** in that day: When Gog AIT
Eze 39: 1 '**This is w** the Sovereign LORD says H3907
Eze 39:17 of man, **this is w** the Sovereign LORD says: H3907
Eze 39:25 "Therefore **this is w** the Sovereign LORD H3907
Eze 42:15 finished measuring **w** was inside the temple NDT
Eze 43:18 of man, **this is w** the Sovereign LORD says: H3907
Eze 44: 6 '**This is w** the Sovereign LORD says: H3907
Eze 44: 9 **This is w** the Sovereign LORD says: No H3907
Eze 45: 9 " '**This is w** the Sovereign LORD says: You H3907
Eze 45: 9 oppression and do *w* is **just** and right. AIT
Eze 45:18 " '**This is w** the Sovereign LORD says: In H3907
Eze 46: 1 " '**This is w** the Sovereign LORD says: The H3907
Eze 46:16 " '**This is w** the Sovereign LORD says: If H3907
Eze 47:13 **This is w** the Sovereign LORD says: "These H3907
Eze 48:18 **W** remains of the area, bordering on the H2021
Eze 48:21 "**W** remains on both sides of the area H2021
Da 1:13 your servants in accordance with **w** you see." H889

Da 2: 2 astrologers to tell him w he had **dreamed**. AIT
Da 2: 3 me and I want to **know w** it **means**." H3359
Da 2: 5 astrologers, "This is w I have firmly decided: NDT
Da 2: 5 If you do not tell me w my dream was and NDT
Da 2: 8 realize that this is w I have firmly decided: NDT
Da 2:10 on earth who can do w the king **asks**! A10418
Da 2:11 W the king asks is too difficult A10418+10002S
Da 2:22 he knows w lies in darkness, and A10408
Da 2:23 made known to me w we asked of you, A10168
Da 2:25 who can tell the king w his dream **means**." AIT
Da 2:26 you able to tell me w I saw in my dream A10168
Da 2:28 Nebuchadnezzar w will happen in days A10408
Da 2:29 showed you w is going to happen. A10408
Da 2:30 you may understand w went through your NDT
Da 2:45 has shown the king w will take place in A10408
Da 3: 4 this is w you are commanded to do: NDT
Da 3:15 Then w god will be able to rescue you A10426
Da 4:18 tell me w it **means**, for none of the AIT
Da 4:27 Renounce your sins by doing w is **right**, and AIT
Da 4:31 from heaven, "This is w is decreed for you NDT
Da 4:33 Immediately w had been **said** about A10418
Da 4:35 say to him: "W have you done?" A10408
Da 5: 7 tells me w it **means** will be clothed in AIT
Da 5: 8 read the writing or tell the king w it **meant**. AIT
Da 5:12 he will tell you w the writing **means**. AIT
Da 5:15 to read this writing and tell me w it **means**, AIT
Da 5:16 can read this writing and tell him w it **means**, AIT
Da 5:17 writing for the king and tell him w it **means**. AIT
Da 5:26 "Here is w these **words** mean: Mene: God AIT
Da 8:19 am going to tell you w will happen later in H889
Da 9:12 ever been done like w has been done to H889
Da 10:14 to explain to you w will happen to your H889
Da 10:21 first I will tell you w is written in the Book H2021
Da 11:24 them and will achieve w neither his fathers H889
Da 11:29 will be different from w it was before. NDT
Da 11:36 for w *has* **been determined** must take place. AIT
Da 12: 8 w will the outcome of all this be? H4537
Hos 5: 9 the tribes of Israel I proclaim w *is* **certain**. AIT
Hos 6: 4 "W can I do with you, Ephraim? What can H4537
Hos 6: 4 W can I do with you, Judah H4537
Hos 8: 3 But Israel has rejected w is good; an enemy NDT
Hos 9: 5 W will you do on the day of your H4537
Hos 9:14 Give them, LORD—w will you give them H4537
Hos 10: 3 if we had a king, w could he do for us?" H4537
Hos 14: 3 gods' to w our own hands have **made**, H5126
Hos 14: 8 Ephraim, w more have I to do with idols? H4537
Joel 1: 4 W the locust swarm has **left** the great locusts AIT
Joel 1: 4 w the great locusts have **left** the young AIT
Joel 1: 4 w the young locusts have **left** other locusts AIT
Joel 3: 2 put them on trial for w they did to my NDT
Joel 3: 4 "Now w have you against me, Tyre and H4537
Joel 3: 4 on your own heads w you have **done**. H1691
Joel 3: 7 on your own heads w you have **done**. H1691
Am 1: 3 **This is** w the LORD says: "For three sins of H3907
Am 1: 6 **This is** w the LORD says: "For three sins of H3907
Am 1: 9 **This is** w the LORD says: "For three sins of H3907
Am 1:11 **This is** w the LORD says: "For three sins of H3907
Am 1:13 **This is** w the LORD says: "For three sins of H3907
Am 2: 1 **This is** w the LORD says: "For three sins of H3907
Am 2: 4 **This is** w the LORD says: "For three sins of H3907
Am 2: 6 **This is** w the LORD says: "For three sins of H3907
Am 3:10 fortresses w they have **plundered** and looted." AIT
Am 3:11 Therefore **this is** w the Sovereign LORD H3907
Am 3:12 **This is** w the LORD says: "As a shepherd H3907
Am 4: 5 you Israelites, for this is w you love to do," H4027
Am 4:12 "Therefore **this is** w I will do to you, Israel H3907
Am 5: 3 **This is** w the Sovereign LORD says to Israel H3907
Am 5: 4 **This is** w the LORD says to Israel: "Seek me H3907
Am 5:16 Therefore **this is** w the Lord, the LORD God H3907
Am 7: 1 **This is** w the Sovereign LORD showed me H3907
Am 7: 4 **This is** w the Sovereign LORD showed me H3907
Am 7: 7 **This is** w he showed me: The Lord was H3907
Am 7: 8 LORD asked me, "W do you see, Amos?" H4537
Am 7:11 For **this is** w Amos is saying: " 'Jeroboam H3907
Am 7:17 "Therefore **this is** w the LORD says: " 'Your H3907
Am 8: 1 **This is** w the Sovereign LORD showed me H3907
Am 8: 2 "W do you see, Amos?" he asked. "A H4537
Ob 1 **This is** w the Sovereign LORD says about H3907
Ob 5 in the night—oh, w a disaster awaits you!— H375
Jnh 1: 8 trouble for us? W kind of work do you do H4537
Jnh 1: 8 do you come from? W is your country H4537
Jnh 1: 8 is your country? From w people are you?" H2296
Jnh 1:10 them and they asked, "W have you done?" H4537
Jnh 1:11 "W should we do to you to make the sea H4537
Jnh 2: 9 W I have vowed I will make good H889
Jnh 3:10 When God saw w they **did** and how they H5126
Jnh 4: 2 to the LORD, "Isn't this w I **said**, LORD, H1821
Jnh 4: 2 **That is** w I tried to forestall by H4027+6584
Jnh 4: 5 waited to see w would happen to the H4537
Mic 1: 5 W is Jacob's transgression H4769
Mic 1: 5 Is it not Samaria? W is Judah's high place H4769
Mic 3: 5 **This is** w the LORD says: "As for the H3907
Mic 6: 1 Listen to w the LORD says: "Stand up, plead H889
Mic 6: 1 let the hills hear w you **have to say**. H7754
Mic 6: 3 "My people, w have I done to you? How H4537
Mic 6: 5 remember w Balak king of Moab plotted H4537
Mic 6: 5 Moab plotted and w Balaam son of Beor H4537
Mic 6: 6 With w shall I come before the LORD and H4537
Mic 6: 8 O mortal, w is good. And what H4537
Mic 6: 8 And w does the LORD require of you H4537
Mic 6:14 because w you save I will give to the sword. H889
Mic 7: 1 W **misery** is mine! I am like one who H518
Mic 7: 3 the powerful dictate w they desire—they all NDT
Na 1:12 **This is** w the LORD says: "Although they H3907
Hab 2: 1 I will look to see w he will say to me, and H4537
Hab 2: 1 w answer I am to give to this H4537
Hab 2:18 "Of w value is an idol carved by a H4537
Zep 2: 3 of the land, you who do w he commands. H889
Zep 2:10 This is w they will get in return for their NDT
Zep 2:15 W a ruin she has become, a lair for wild H375
Hag 1: 2 **This is** w the LORD Almighty says: "These H3907
Hag 1: 5 Now **this is** w the LORD Almighty says H3907
Hag 1: 7 **This is** w the LORD Almighty says: "Give H3907
Hag 1: 9 out to be little. W you brought home, I blew NDT
Hag 2: 5 'This is w I covenanted with you when you H889
Hag 2: 6 "**This is** w the LORD Almighty says: 'In a H3907
Hag 2: 7 and w is **desired** *by* all nations will come AIT
Hag 2:11 "**This is** w the LORD Almighty says: 'Ask H3907
Hag 2:11 'Ask the priests w the law says: NDT
Zec 1: 3 **This is** w the LORD Almighty says H3907
Zec 1: 4 **This is** w the LORD Almighty says H3907
Zec 1: 6 to us w our ways and practices **deserve**, H3869
Zec 1: 9 I asked, "W are these, my lord?" The H4537
Zec 1: 9 me answered, "I will show you w they are." H4537
Zec 1:14 **This is** w the LORD Almighty says H3907
Zec 1:16 "Therefore **this is** w the LORD says: 'I will H3907
Zec 1:17 **This is** w the LORD Almighty says H3907
Zec 1:19 who was speaking to me, "W are these?" H4537
Zec 1:21 "W are these coming to do?" He H4537
Zec 2: 8 For **this is** w the LORD Almighty says: H3907
Zec 3: 7 "**This is** w the LORD Almighty says: 'If H3907
Zec 4: 2 He asked me, "W do you see?" I answered H4537
Zec 4: 4 talked with me, "W are these, my lord?" H4537
Zec 4: 5 answered, "Do you not know w these are?" H4537
Zec 4: 7 "W are you, mighty mountain? Before H4769
Zec 4:11 "W are these two olive trees on the right H4537
Zec 4:12 "W are these two olive branches beside H4537
Zec 4:13 replied, "Do you not know w these are?" H4537
Zec 5: 2 He asked me, "W do you see?" I H4537
Zec 5: 3 for according to w it says on one side NDT
Zec 5: 3 according to w it says on the other NDT
Zec 5: 5 "Look up and see w is appearing." H4537
Zec 5: 6 I asked, "W is it?" He replied, "It is a H4537
Zec 6: 4 speaking to me, "W are these, my lord?" H4537
Zec 6:12 Tell him **this is** w the LORD Almighty says H3907
Zec 7: 9 "**This is** w the LORD Almighty said H3907
Zec 8: 2 **This is** w the LORD Almighty says: "I am H3907
Zec 8: 3 **This is** w the LORD says: "I will return to H3907
Zec 8: 4 **This is** w the LORD Almighty says: "Once H3907
Zec 8: 6 **This is** w the LORD Almighty says: "It may H3907
Zec 8: 7 **This is** w the LORD Almighty says: "I will H3907
Zec 8: 9 **This is** w the LORD Almighty says: "Now H3907
Zec 8: 9 is also w the prophets **said** who H4946+7023
Zec 8:14 **This is** w the LORD Almighty says: "Just H3907
Zec 8:19 **This is** w the LORD Almighty says: "The H3907
Zec 8:20 **This is** w the LORD Almighty says: "Many H3907
Zec 8:23 **This is** w the LORD Almighty says: "In H3907
Zec 11: 4 **This is** w the LORD my God says H3907
Zec 13: 6 'W are these wounds on your body?' H4537
Mal 1: 4 But **this is** w the LORD Almighty says H3907
Mal 1:13 And you say, 'W a burden!' and you sniff H4537
Mal 2:15 And w does the one God seek H4537
Mal 3:13 you ask, 'W have we said against you?' H4537
Mal 3:14 W do we gain by carrying out his H4537
Mt 1:20 because w is conceived in her is from the G3836
Mt 1:22 took place to fulfill w the Lord had said G3836
Mt 1:24 he did w the angel of the Lord had G6055
Mt 2: 5 "for **this is** w the prophet has written: G4048
Mt 2:15 And so was fulfilled w the Lord had said G3836
Mt 2:17 Then w was said through the prophet G3836
Mt 2:23 So was fulfilled w was said through the G3836
Mt 4:14 to fulfill w was said through the prophet G3836
Mt 5:46 who love you, w reward will you get? G5515
Mt 5:47 w are you doing more than others? G5515
Mt 6: 3 your left hand know w your right hand is G5515
Mt 6: 4 your Father, who sees w is done in secret NDT
Mt 6: 6 your Father, who sees w is done in secret NDT
Mt 6: 8 your Father knows w you need before you G4005
Mt 6:18 your Father, who sees w is done in secret NDT
Mt 6:25 about your life, w you will eat or drink G5515
Mt 6:25 or about your body, w you will wear. G5515
Mt 6:31 not worry, saying, 'W shall we eat?' G5515+5516
Mt 6:31 or 'W shall we drink?' G5515+5516
Mt 6:31 or 'W shall we wear?' G5515+5516
Mt 7: 6 "Do not give dogs w is sacred; do not G3836
Mt 7:12 do to others w you would have G4012+1569
Mt 8:17 This was to fulfill w was spoken through G3836
Mt 8:27 asked, "W **kind of** *man* is this? G4534
Mt 8:29 "**W do you want with us** G5515+5516+1609+2779+5148
Mt 8:33 including w **had happened** to the G3836
Mt 9:13 But go and learn w this means: 'I desire G5515
Mt 10:19 do not worry about w to say or how to say G5515
Mt 10:19 At that time you will be given w to say, G5515
Mt 10:27 W I tell you in the dark, speak in the G4005
Mt 10:27 in the daylight; w is whispered in your ear G4005
Mt 11: 4 report to John w you hear and see: G4005
Mt 11: 7 "W did you go out into the G5515+5516
Mt 11: 8 w did you go out to see? A man G5515
Mt 11: 9 Then w did you go out to see? A prophet G5515
Mt 11:16 "*To* w can I compare this generation G5515
Mt 11:26 for this is w you were pleased to do. NDT
Mt 12: 2 disciples are doing w is unlawful on the G4005
Mt 12: 3 "Haven't you read w David did when he G5515
Mt 12: 7 If you had known w these words mean, 'I G5515
Mt 12:17 This was to fulfill w was spoken through G3836
Mt 12:34 For the mouth speaks w the heart is full of. G3836
Mt 13: 8 a hundred, sixty or thirty times w was sown. NDT
Mt 13:12 even w they have will be taken from them. G4005
Mt 13:17 longed to see w you see but did not G4005
Mt 13:17 to hear w you hear but did not hear it. G4005
Mt 13:18 **Listen** then *to* w the parable of the sower *means* AIT
Mt 13:19 snatches away w was sown in their G3836
Mt 13:23 a hundred, sixty or thirty times w was sown." NDT
Mt 13:35 So was fulfilled w was spoken through the G3836
Mt 14:13 When Jesus heard w had happened, he NDT
Mt 15: 5 declares that w might have been used G4005
Mt 15:11 W goes into someone's mouth does not G3836
Mt 15:11 but w comes out of their mouth G3836
Mt 15:11 out of their mouth, that *is* w **defiles** them." AIT
Mt 15:20 These are w defile a person; but eating G3836
Mt 16:15 "But w about you?" he asked. "Who do you NDT
Mt 16:26 W good will it be for someone to gain the G5515
Mt 16:26 Or w can anyone give in exchange for G5515
Mt 16:27 person according to w they have done. G3836
Mt 17: 9 "Don't tell anyone w you have seen, until G3836
Mt 17:25 first to speak. "W do you think G5515+5516
Mt 18:12 "W do you think? If a man owns a G5515
Mt 18:28 'Pay back w you owe me!' he G1623+5516
Mt 18:31 the other servants saw w had happened, G3836
Mt 19: 6 Therefore w God has joined together, let G4005
Mt 19:16 w good thing must I do to get eternal life?" G5515
Mt 19:17 "Why do you ask me about w is good?" G3836
Mt 19:20 the young man said. "W do I still lack?" G5515
Mt 19:27 to follow you! W then will there be for us?" G5515
Mt 20:15 have the right to do w I want with my own G4005
Mt 20:21 "W is it you want?" he asked. G5515+5516
Mt 20:22 "You don't know w you are asking," Jesus G5515
Mt 20:32 "W do you want me to do for you?" G5515+5516
Mt 21: 4 took place to fulfill w was spoken through G3836
Mt 21:16 "Do you hear w these children are saying?" G5515
Mt 21:21 not only can you do w was done to the fig G3836
Mt 21:23 "By w authority are you doing these things G4481
Mt 21:24 I will tell you by w authority I am doing G4481
Mt 21:27 will I tell you by w authority I am doing G4481
Mt 21:28 "W do you think? There was a man who G5515
Mt 21:31 of the two did w his father wanted?" G3836
Mt 21:40 w will he do to those tenants? G5515
Mt 22:17 Tell us then, w is your opinion? Is it right G5515
Mt 22:21 "So give back to Caesar w is Caesar's, and G3836
Mt 22:21 what is Caesar's, and to God w is God's." G3836
Mt 22:31 have you not read w God said to you, G3836
Mt 22:42 "W do you think about the Messiah? G5515+5516
Mt 23: 3 But do not do w they do, for they do not G3836
Mt 23: 3 for they do not practice w they preach. NDT
Mt 23:32 w your ancestors **started**! G3836+3586S
Mt 24: 3 w will be the sign of your coming and G5515
Mt 24:39 knew nothing about w would happen until NDT
Mt 24:42 you do not know *on* w day your Lord will G4481
Mt 24:43 house had known *at* w time of night the G4481
Mt 25:25 See, here is w belongs to you.' G3836
Mt 25:29 even w they have will be taken from them. G4005
Mt 26:13 w she has done will also be told G4005
Mt 26:15 "W are you willing to give me if I G5515+5516
Mt 26:50 Jesus replied, "Do w you came for G2093+4005
Mt 26:62 W is this testimony that these men are G5515
Mt 26:66 W do you think?" "He is worthy of death," G5515
Mt 26:70 "I don't know w you're talking about," G5515
Mt 27: 4 innocent blood." "W is that to us?" G5515+5516
Mt 27: 9 Then w was spoken by Jeremiah the G3836
Mt 27:22 "W shall I do, then, with Jesus who G5515+5516
Mt 27:23 W crime has he committed? G5515+5516
Mk 1:24 "**W do** you **want with** us, Jesus of G5515+5516
Mk 1:27 they asked each other, "W is this? G5515+5516
Mk 2: 8 in his spirit that **this was** w they were G4048
Mk 2:24 why are they doing w is unlawful on the G4005
Mk 2:25 you never read w David did when he G5515
Mk 4:20 some a hundred times w was sown. NDT
Mk 4:24 "Consider carefully w you hear," he G5515
Mk 4:25 even w they have will be taken from them." G4005
Mk 4:26 "**This is** w the kingdom of God is like. G4048
Mk 4:30 "W shall we say the kingdom of God is G4802
Mk 4:30 w parable shall we use to describe it? G5515
Mk 5: 7 "**W do** you **want with** me G5515+5516
Mk 5: 9 Jesus asked him, "W is your name?" G5515+5516
Mk 5:14 people went out to see w had happened. G5515
Mk 5:16 it told the people w had happened to the G4802
Mk 5:33 woman, knowing w had happened to her G4005
Mk 5:36 Overhearing w they said, Jesus G3836+3364S
Mk 6: 2 W are these remarkable miracles he is NDT
Mk 6:24 to her mother, "W shall I ask for?" G5515+5516
Mk 7:11 declares that w might have been G4005+1569
Mk 7:15 it is w comes out of a person that defiles G3836
Mk 7:20 "W comes out of a person is what defiles G3836
Mk 7:20 comes out of a person is w defiles them. G1697
Mk 8:29 "But w about you?" he asked. "Who do you NDT
Mk 8:36 W good is it for someone to gain the G5515
Mk 8:37 Or w can anyone give in exchange for their G5515
Mk 9: 6 He did not know w to say, they were so G5515
Mk 9: 9 not to tell anyone w they had seen until G4005
Mk 9:10 discussing w "rising from the dead G5515
Mk 9:16 "W are you arguing with them G5515+5516
Mk 9:32 did not understand w he meant and were G3836
Mk 9:33 "W were you arguing about on the G5515+5516
Mk 10: 3 "W did Moses command you?" G5515+5516

Book	Ref	Context	Number
Mk	10: 9	Therefore **w** God has joined together, let	*G4005*
Mk	10:17	"**w** must I do to inherit eternal life?	*G5515*
Mk	10:32	told them **w** was going to happen	*G3836*
Mk	10:36	"**W** do you want me to do for you?"	*G5515+5516*
Mk	10:38	"You don't know **w** you are asking," Jesus	*G5515*
Mk	10:51	"**W** do you want me to do for you?"	*G5515+5516*
Mk	11: 5	there asked, "**W** are you doing	*G5515+5516*
Mk	11:23	believes that **w** they say will happen,	*G4005*
Mk	11:28	By **w** authority are you doing these things?	*G4481*
Mk	11:29	I will tell you by **w** authority I am doing	*G4481*
Mk	11:33	will I tell you by **w** authority I am doing	*G4481*
Mk	12: 9	"**W** then will the owner of the vineyard do	*G5515*
Mk	12:17	"Give back to Caesar **w** is Caesar's and to	*G3836*
Mk	12:17	what is Caesar's and to God **w** is God's."	*G3836*
Mk	13: 1	**W massive** stones! What	*G4534*
Mk	13: 1	**W magnificent** buildings!"	*G4534*
Mk	13: 4	And **w** will be the sign that they are all	*G5515*
Mk	13:11	do not worry beforehand about **w** to say.	*G5515*
Mk	13:37	**W** I say to you, I say to everyone: 'Watch!'	*G4005*
Mk	14: 8	She did **w** she could. She poured perfume	*G4005*
Mk	14: 9	**w** she has done will also be told	*G4005*
Mk	14:36	Yet not **w** I will, but what you	*G5515*
Mk	14:36	Yet not what I will, but **w** you will."	*G5515*
Mk	14:40	They did not know **w** to say to him.	*G5515*
Mk	14:60	**W** is this testimony that these men are	*G5515*
Mk	14:64	the blasphemy. **W** do you think?" They	*G5515*
Mk	14:68	know or understand **w** you're talking	*G5515*
Mk	15: 8	asked Pilate to do for them *w* he **usually** did.	AIT
Mk	15:12	"**W** shall I do, then, with the one	*G5515+5516*
Mk	15:14	**W** crime has he committed?	*G5515+5516*
Mk	15:24	they cast lots to see **w** each would get.	*G5515*
Lk	1:29	wondered **w kind of** greeting this	*G4534*
Lk	1:62	to find out **w** he would like to name the	*G5515*
Lk	1:66	"**W** then is this child going to be?"	*G5515+5516*
Lk	2:17	word concerning **w** had been told them	*G3836*
Lk	2:18	it were amazed at **w** the shepherds said	*G3836*
Lk	2:24	in keeping with **w** is said in the Law of the	*G3836*
Lk	2:27	Jesus to do for him **w** the custom of the Law	NDT
Lk	2:33	mother marveled at **w** was said about him	*G3836*
Lk	2:50	not understand **w** he was saying	*G3836+4839*^S
Lk	3:10	"**W** should we do then?" the crowd	*G5515+5516*
Lk	3:12	they asked, "**w** should we do?"	*G5515*
Lk	3:14	asked him, "And **w** should we do?"	*G5515+5516*
Lk	4:23	in your hometown **w** we have heard that	*G4012*
Lk	4:34	**W do** you **want with** us, Jesus of Nazareth	*G5515*
Lk	4:36	to each other, "**W** words these are!	*G5515+5516*
Lk	5:22	Jesus knew **w** they were thinking and	*G3836*
Lk	5:25	took **w** he had been lying on and went	*G4005*
Lk	6: 2	"Why are you doing **w** is unlawful on the	*G4005*
Lk	6: 3	you never read **w** David did when he	*G4005*
Lk	6: 4	he ate **w** is lawful only for priests to eat.	*G4005*
Lk	6: 8	But Jesus knew **w** they were thinking and	*G3836*
Lk	6:11	with one another **w** they might do to	*G5515*
Lk	6:30	if anyone takes **w** belongs to you, do	*G3836*
Lk	6:32	who love you, **w** credit is that to you?	*G4481*
Lk	6:33	are good to you, **w** credit is that to you?	*G4481*
Lk	6:34	expect repayment, **w** credit is that to you?	*G4481*
Lk	6:45	For the mouth speaks **w** the heart is **full of**.	*G4354*
Lk	6:46	'Lord, Lord,' and do not do **w** I say?	*G4005*
Lk	6:47	practice, I will show you **w** they are like.	*G5515*
Lk	7:22	report to John **w** you have seen and	*G4005*
Lk	7:24	"**W** did you go out into the	*G5515+5516*
Lk	7:25	**w** did you go out to see? A man	*G5515*
Lk	7:26	But **w** did you go out to see? A prophet	*G5515*
Lk	7:31	went on to say, "*To* **w**, then, can I	*G5515*
Lk	7:31	of this generation? **W** are they like?	*G5515*
Lk	7:39	him and **w kind of** woman she is—	*G4534*
Lk	8: 9	disciples asked him **w** this parable meant.	*G5515*
Lk	8:18	even **w** they think they have will be taken	*G4005*
Lk	8:28	"**W do you want with** me	*G5515+5516+2779*
Lk	8:30	Jesus asked him, "**W** is your name?"	*G5515+5516*
Lk	8:34	tending the pigs saw **w** had happened,	*G3836*
Lk	8:35	people went out to see **w** had happened.	*G3836*
Lk	8:56	them not to tell anyone **w** had happened.	*G3836*
Lk	9:10	they reported to Jesus **w** they had done.	*G4012*
Lk	9:20	"But **w** about you?" he asked. "Who do you	NDT
Lk	9:25	**W** good is it for someone to gain the	*G5515*
Lk	9:33	He did not know **w** he was saying.)	*G4005*
Lk	9:36	tell anyone at that time **w** they had seen.	*G4005*
Lk	9:44	"Listen carefully *to* **w** I am about to tell	*G4047*
Lk	9:45	But they did not understand **w** this meant	*G3836*
Lk	10: 8	are welcomed, eat **w** is offered to you.	*G3836*
Lk	10:21	for **this** *is w* you were pleased to do.	AIT
Lk	10:23	"Blessed are the eyes that see **w** you see.	*G4005*
Lk	10:24	kings wanted to see **w** you see but did not	*G4005*
Lk	10:24	to hear **w** you hear but did not hear it."	*G4005*
Lk	10:25	"**w** must I do to inherit eternal life?	*G5515*
Lk	10:26	"**W** is written in the Law?" he replied	*G5515*
Lk	10:39	at the Lord's feet listening to **w** he said.	*G3836*
Lk	10:42	Mary has chosen **w** is better, and it will	*G3535*^S
Lk	11:41	But now *as for* **w** is inside you—be	*G3836*
Lk	11:48	that you approve of **w** your ancestors did;	*G3836*
Lk	12: 3	**W** you have said in the dark will be heard	*G4012*
Lk	12: 3	**w** you have whispered in the ear in	*G4005*
Lk	12:11	will defend yourselves or **w** you will say,	*G5515*
Lk	12:12	teach you at that time **w** you should say."	*G4005*
Lk	12:17	thought to himself, '**W** shall I do?	*G5515+5516*
Lk	12:18	"Then he said, 'This is **w** I'll do. I will tear	NDT
Lk	12:20	Then who will get **w** you have prepared	*G4005*
Lk	12:22	about your life, **w** you will eat; or about	*G5515*
Lk	12:22	or about your body, **w** you will wear.	*G5515*
Lk	12:29	set your heart on **w** you will eat or drink	*G5515*
Lk	12:39	house had known *at* **w** hour the thief was	*G4481*
Lk	12:47	ready or does not do **w** the master wants	*G3836*
Lk	12:50	**w** constraint I am under until it is	*G4802*
Lk	12:57	don't you judge for yourselves **w** is right?	*G3836*
Lk	13:16	on the Sabbath day from **w** bound her?"	*G3836*
Lk	13:18	"**W** is the kingdom of God like?	*G5515*
Lk	13:18	**W** shall I compare it *to*?	*G5515*
Lk	13:20	**W** shall I compare the kingdom of God *to*?	*G5515*
Lk	14:22	'**w** you ordered has been done	*G4005*
Lk	15:26	asked him **w** was going on.	*G5515+323+4047*
Lk	16: 2	'**W** is this I hear about you?	*G5515+5516*
Lk	16: 3	said to himself, '**W** shall I do now?	*G5515+5516*
Lk	16: 4	I know **w** I'll do so that, when I lose my job	*G5515*
Lk	16:15	**W** people value highly is detestable in	*G3836*
Lk	16:21	longing to eat **w** fell from the rich	*G3836*
Lk	17: 9	because he did **w** he was told to do?	*G3836*
Lk	18: 2	feared God nor **cared w** people **thought**.	*G1956*
Lk	18: 4	I don't fear God or **care w** people **think**,	*G1956*
Lk	18: 6	"Listen *to* **w** the unjust judge says.	*G5515*
Lk	18:18	**w** must I do to inherit eternal life?	*G5515*
Lk	18:27	"**W** is impossible with man is possible	*G3836*
Lk	18:34	they did not know **w** he was talking about.	*G3836*
Lk	18:36	going by, he asked **w** was happening.	*G5515*
Lk	18:41	"**W** do you want me to do for you?"	*G5515+5516*
Lk	19:15	order to find out **w** they had gained with	*G5515*
Lk	19:21	You take out **w** you did not put in and	*G4005*
Lk	19:21	not put in and reap **w** you did not sow.	*G4005*
Lk	19:22	hard man, taking out **w** I did not put in	*G4005*
Lk	19:22	not put in, and reaping **w** I did not sow?	*G4005*
Lk	19:26	even **w** they have will be taken away.	*G4005*
Lk	19:42	known on this day **w** would bring you	*G3836*
Lk	20: 2	"Tell us by **w** authority you are doing these	*G4481*
Lk	20: 8	will I tell you by **w** authority I am doing	*G4481*
Lk	20:13	of the vineyard said, '**W** shall I do?	*G5515+5516*
Lk	20:15	"**W** then will the owner of the vineyard do	*G5515*
Lk	20:17	"Then **w** is the meaning of that	*G5515+5516*
Lk	20:21	know that you speak and teach **w is right**,	*G3987*
Lk	20:25	"Then give back to Caesar **w** is Caesar's	*G3836*
Lk	20:25	what is Caesar's, and to God **w** is God's."	*G3836*
Lk	20:26	to trap him *in* **w** he had **said** there in	*G4839*
Lk	21: 6	"*As for* **w** you see here, the time will come	*G4047*
Lk	21: 7	And **w** will be the sign that they are about	*G5515*
Lk	21:26	apprehensive *of* **w** is coming on the world,	*G3836*
Lk	22:37	**w** is written about me is reaching its	*G3836*
Lk	22:49	followers saw **w** was going to happen,	*G3836*
Lk	22:60	I don't know **w** you're talking about!"	*G4005*
Lk	23: 8	From **w** he had heard about him, he	*G3836*
Lk	23:22	**W** crime has this man committed	*G5515+5516*
Lk	23:31	is green, **w** will happen when it is dry?"	*G5515*
Lk	23:34	they do not know **w** they are doing."	*G5515*
Lk	23:41	we are getting **w** our deeds deserve.	*G4005*
Lk	23:47	centurion, seeing **w** had happened	*G3836*
Lk	23:48	to witness this sight saw **w** took place,	*G3836*
Lk	24:12	wondering to himself **w** had happened.	*G3836*
Lk	24:17	"**W** are you discussing together as you	*G5515*
Lk	24:19	"**W** *things*?" he asked. "About Jesus of	*G4481*
Lk	24:21	And **w is more**, it is the third	*G5250+4246+4047*
Lk	24:27	*he* **explained** to them **w was said** in all	*G1450*
Lk	24:35	the two told **w had happened** on the way,	*G3836*
Lk	24:44	"This is **w** I told you while I was still with	*G4005*
Lk	24:46	He told them, "**This is w** is written: The	*G4048*
Lk	24:49	I am going to send you **w** my Father has	*G3836*
Jn	1:22	**W** do you say about yourself?	*G5515*
Jn	1:38	and asked, "**W** do you want?	*G5515+5516*
Jn	1:40	who heard **w** John *had* **said** and who	*G4123*^S
Jn	2:11	**W** Jesus did here in Cana of Galilee was	*G4047*
Jn	2:18	"**W** sign can you show us to prove	*G5515+5516*
Jn	2:22	his disciples recalled **w** he had said.	*G4047*
Jn	2:25	he knew **w** was in each person.	*G5515*
Jn	3:11	tell you, we speak of **w** we know, and we	*G4005*
Jn	3:11	we testify to **w** we have seen, but still	*G4005*
Jn	3:21	seen plainly that **w** they have done has	*G3836*
Jn	3:27	can receive only *w* **is given** them from	AIT
Jn	3:32	He testifies *to* **w** he has seen and heard	*G4005*
Jn	4:18	**W** you have just said is quite true.	*G4047*
Jn	4:22	Samaritans worship **w** you do not know;	*G4005*
Jn	4:22	not know; we worship **w** we do know, for	*G4005*
Jn	4:27	But no one asked, "**W** do you want?"	*G5515+5516*
Jn	4:38	I sent you to reap **w** you have not worked	*G4005*
Jn	4:42	longer believe just because of **w** you said;	*G3836*
Jn	5:19	he can do only **w** he sees his Father doing	*G5516*
Jn	5:29	those who have done **w** is good will rise to	*G3836*
Jn	5:29	those who have done **w** is evil will rise to	*G3836*
Jn	5:47	But since you do not believe **w** he wrote	*G3836*
Jn	5:47	how are you going to believe **w** I say?"	*G3836*
Jn	6: 6	had in mind **w** he was going to do.	*G5515*
Jn	6:28	"**W** must we do to do the works	*G5515+5516*
Jn	6:30	"**W** sign then will you give that we may	*G5515*
Jn	6:30	see it and believe you? **W** will you do?	*G5515*
Jn	6:62	Then **w if** you see the Son of Man ascend	*G1569*
Jn	7:36	**W** did he mean when he said, 'You will	*G5515*
Jn	7:51	him to find out **w** he has been doing?"	*G5515*
Jn	8: 5	stone such women. Now **w** do you say?"	*G5515*
Jn	8:25	"**Just w** I have been telling you	*G4005+5516*
Jn	8:26	**w** I have heard from him I tell the	*G4005*
Jn	8:28	my own but speak **just w** the Father has	*G2777*
Jn	8:29	me alone, for I always do **w** pleases him."	*G3836*
Jn	8:38	I am telling you **w** I have seen in the	*G4005*
Jn	8:38	you are doing **w** you have heard from	*G4005*
Jn	8:39	"then you would do **w** Abraham did.	*G3836*
Jn	8:43	Because you are unable to hear **w** I say.	*G3836*
Jn	8:47	belongs to God hears **w** God says.	*G3836*
Jn	9:17	"**W** have you to say about him?	*G5515+5516*
Jn	9:26	asked him, "**W** did he do to you?	*G5515+5516*
Jn	9:40	heard him say this and asked, "**W**?	*G3590*^S
Jn	10: 6	did not understand **w** he was telling them	*G5515*
Jn	10:36	**w** about the one whom the Father set apart	NDT
Jn	11:45	and had seen **w** Jesus did, believed	*G4005*
Jn	11:46	told them **w** Jesus had done.	*G4005*
Jn	11:47	"**W** are we accomplishing?	*G5515+5516*
Jn	11:56	one another, "**W** do you think?	*G5515+5516*
Jn	12: 6	used to help himself to **w** was put into it.	*G3836*
Jn	12:27	my soul is troubled, and **w** shall I say?	*G5515*
Jn	12:50	whatever I say is **just w** the Father has told	*G2777*
Jn	13: 7	"You do not realize now **w** I am doing	*G4005*
Jn	13:12	"Do you understand **w** I have done for you	*G5515*
Jn	13:13	'Lord,' and rightly so, for *that is w I* **am**.	AIT
Jn	13:27	Jesus told him, "**W** you are about to do	*G4005*
Jn	13:29	telling him to buy **w** was needed for the	*G4005*
Jn	14:31	Father and do exactly **w** my Father has	*G4048*
Jn	15:14	You are my friends if you do **w** I command.	*G4005*
Jn	15:20	Remember **w** I told you: 'A servant	*G3836+3364*^S
Jn	15:25	this is to fulfill **w** is written in their	*G3836+3364*^S
Jn	16:13	he will speak only **w** he hears, and he will	*G4012*
Jn	16:13	he will tell you **w** is yet to come.	*G3836*
Jn	16:14	that he will receive **w** he will make known to	NDT
Jn	16:15	will receive from me **w** he will make known	NDT
Jn	16:17	"**W** does he mean by saying	*G5515+5516*
Jn	16:18	"**W** does he mean by 'a little while'?	*G5515*
Jn	16:18	We don't understand **w** he is saying."	*G5515*
Jn	16:19	one another **w I meant** when I	*G4309+4047*^S
Jn	18:21	Surely they know **w** I said."	*G4005*
Jn	18:23	Jesus replied, "testify as to **w** is wrong.	*G3836*
Jn	18:29	"**W** charges are you bringing against this	*G5515*
Jn	18:32	place to fulfill **w** Jesus had said	*G3836+3364*^S
Jn	18:35	you over to me. **W** is it you have done?"	*G5515*
Jn	18:38	"**W** is truth?" retorted Pilate.	*G5515+5516*
Jn	19:22	Pilate answered, "**W** I have written, I have	*G4005*
Jn	19:24	So this is **w** the soldiers did.	NDT
Jn	21:21	he asked, "Lord, **w** *about* him?"	*G5515+5516*
Jn	21:22	alive until I return, **w** is that to you?	*G5515*
Jn	21:23	alive until I return, **w** is that to you?"	*G5515*
Ac	2: 3	They saw **w seemed to be** tongues of fire	*G6059*
Ac	2:12	one another, "**W** does this mean?"	*G5515+5516*
Ac	2:14	this to you; listen carefully to **w** I say.	*G3836*
Ac	2:16	this is **w** was spoken by the prophet Joel:	*G3836*
Ac	2:31	**Seeing w was to come**, he spoke of the	*G4632*
Ac	2:33	has poured out **w** you now see and	*G4005*
Ac	2:37	apostles, "Brothers, **w** shall we do?"	*G5515+5516*
Ac	3: 6	I do not have, but **w** I do have I give you.	*G4005*
Ac	3:10	amazement at **w** had happened to	*G3836*
Ac	3:18	is how God fulfilled **w** he had foretold	*G4005*
Ac	4: 7	"By **w** power or what name did you do this	*G4481*
Ac	4: 7	"By what power or **w** name did you do this	*G4481*
Ac	4:16	"**W** are we going to do with these	*G5515+5516*
Ac	4:20	help speaking *about* **w** we have seen	*G4005*
Ac	4:21	were praising God for **w** had happened.	*G3836*
Ac	4:28	They did **w** your power and will had	*G4012*
Ac	5: 4	**W** made you think of doing such a	*G5515+4022*
Ac	5: 5	fear seized all who heard **w** had happened.	NDT
Ac	5: 7	came in, not knowing **w** had happened.	*G3836*
Ac	5:24	at a loss, wondering **w** this might lead to.	*G5515*
Ac	5:35	consider carefully **w** you intend to do to	*G5515*
Ac	7:40	we don't know **w** has happened to him!	*G5515*
Ac	7:41	it and reveled in **w** their own hands had	*G3836*
Ac	7:42	This agrees with *w is* **written** in the book of	AIT
Ac	7:49	**W kind of** house will you build for me	*G4481*
Ac	8: 6	they all paid close attention to **w** he said.	*G3836*
Ac	8:30	"Do you understand **w** you are reading?"	*G4005*
Ac	8:36	**W** can stand in the way of my being	*G5515*
Ac	9: 6	and you will be told **w** you must do."	*G4005+5515*
Ac	10: 1	a centurion in **w** was known as the Italian	*G3836*
Ac	10: 4	at him in fear. "**W** is it, Lord?" he	*G5515+5516*
Ac	10:22	so that he could hear *w* you have *to* **say**."	AIT
Ac	10:35	one who fears him and does **w is right**.	*G1466*
Ac	10:37	You know **w** has happened	*G3836+4839*^S
Ac	11:16	I remembered **w** the Lord had	*G3836+4839*^S
Ac	11:23	he arrived and saw **w** the grace of God had	NDT
Ac	12: 9	idea that **w** the angel was **doing** was	*G1328*
Ac	12:18	the soldiers as to **w** had become of Peter.	*G5515*
Ac	13: 8	the sorcerer (for **that is w** his name means	*G4048*
Ac	13:12	When the proconsul saw **w** had happened,	*G3836*
Ac	13:32	**W** God promised our ancestors	*G3836*
Ac	13:40	Take care that **w** the prophets have said	*G3836*
Ac	13:45	to contradict **w** Paul was saying and	*G3836*
Ac	13:47	For **this is w** the Lord has commanded us:	*G4048*
Ac	14:11	When the crowd saw **w** Paul had done	*G4005*
Ac	15:24	troubling your minds *by* **w** they **said**.	*G3364*
Ac	15:27	by word of mouth **w** we are writing.	*G3836*
Ac	16:30	asked, "Sirs, **w** must I do to be saved?"	*G5515*
Ac	17:11	every day to see if **w Paul said** was true.	*G4047*^S
Ac	17:18	"**W** is this babbler trying to	*G5515+5516+323*
Ac	17:19	"May we know **w** this new teaching is that	*G5515*
Ac	17:20	we would like to know **w** they mean."	*G5515*
Ac	17:23	this is **w** I am going to proclaim to you.	NDT
Ac	19: 3	"Then **w** baptism did you receive?	*G5515*
Ac	19:18	openly confessed **w** they had done.	*G3836*
Ac	19:40	rioting because of **w happened** today.	*G3836*^S
Ac	20:22	not knowing **w** will happen to me there.	*G3836*
Ac	20:38	**W** grieved them most was his statement that	NDT
Ac	21:19	in detail **w** God had done among	*G4005*
Ac	21:22	**W shall we do**? They will	*G5515+4036+1639*
Ac	21:23	so do **w** we tell you. There are four men	*G4005*
Ac	21:33	asked who he was and **w** he had done.	*G5515*

W

Ac 22:10 “‘**W** shall I do, Lord?’ I asked. G5515+5516
Ac 22:15 to all people *of* **w** you have seen and G4005
Ac 22:16 And now **w** are you waiting for? Get up, G5515
Ac 22:26 “**W** are you going to do? G5515+5516
Ac 23: 9 “**W if** a spirit or an angel has spoken to G1623
Ac 23:19 asked, “**W** is it you want to tell me?” G5515+5516
Ac 23:34 letter and asked **w** province he was from G4481
Ac 24:20 here should state **w** crime they found in G5515
Ac 26: 6 of my hope in **w** God has promised our G3836
Ac 26:10 And that is *just* **w** I did in Jerusalem. G4005
Ac 26:16 as a witness *of* **w** you have seen and G4005
Ac 26:22 nothing beyond **w** the prophets and G4005
Ac 26:25 “**W** I am saying is true and reasonable G4839S
Ac 26:29 to me today may become **w** I am, G5525+3961
Ac 27:11 instead of listening to **w** Paul said G3836
Ac 28:22 But we want to hear **w** your **views** are, for G4005
Ac 28:24 Some were convinced by **w** he said, but G3836
Ro 1:19 since **w** may be known about God is plain G3836
Ro 1:20 being understood *from* **w** has been made G3836
Ro 1:28 so that they do **w** ought not to be done. G3836
Ro 2: 6 person according to **w** they have done.” G3836
Ro 2:18 will and approve of **w** is superior because G3836
Ro 3: 1 **W** advantage, then, is there in being a G5515
Ro 3: 1 or **w** value is there in circumcision? G5515
Ro 3: 3 **W** if some were unfaithful? Will their G5515
Ro 3: 5 more clearly, **w** shall we say? G5515
Ro 3: 9 **W** shall we conclude then? Do we have G5515
Ro 3:27 Because of **w** law? The law that G4481
Ro 4: 1 **W** then shall we say that Abraham, our G5515
Ro 4: 3 **W** does Scripture say? “Abraham believed G5515
Ro 4:10 **Under w circumstances** was it G4802+4036
Ro 4:21 God had power to do **w** he had promised. G4005
Ro 6: 1 **W** shall we say, then? Shall we go on G5515
Ro 6:15 **W** then? Shall we sin because we are not G5515
Ro 6:21 **W** benefit did you reap at that time from G5515
Ro 7: 6 But now, by dying to **w** once bound us, we G4005
Ro 7: 7 **W** shall we say, then? Is the law sinful G5515
Ro 7: 7 not have known **w** sin was had it not G3836
Ro 7: 7 not have known **w** coveting really was G3836
Ro 7:13 it used **w** is good to bring about my death, G3836
Ro 7:15 I do not understand **w** I do. For what I want G4005
Ro 7:15 For **w** I want to do I do not do, but what I G4005
Ro 7:15 I want to do I do not do, but **w** I hate I do. G4005
Ro 7:16 And if I do **w** I do not want to do, I agree G4005
Ro 7:18 For I have the desire to do **w** is good, but I G3836
Ro 7:20 Now if I do **w** I do not want to do, it is no G4005
Ro 7:24 **W** a wretched man I am! Who will rescue NDT
Ro 8: 3 For **w** the law was powerless to do G3836
Ro 8: 5 their minds set on **w** the flesh **desires**; G3836S
Ro 8: 5 their minds set on **w** the Spirit **desires**. G3836S
Ro 8:24 Who hopes for **w** they already have? G4005
Ro 8:25 But if we hope for **w** we do not yet have G4005
Ro 8:26 We do not know **w** we ought to pray *for* G5515
Ro 8:31 **W**, then, shall we say in response to G5515
Ro 9:14 **W** then shall we say? Is God unjust? Not G5515
Ro 9:20 “Shall **w** is formed say to the one who G3836
Ro 9:22 **W** if God, although choosing to show his NDT
Ro 9:23 **W if** he did this to make the riches of his G2779
Ro 9:30 **W** then shall we say? That the Gentiles G5515
Ro 10: 8 But **w** does it say? “The word is near you; G5515
Ro 11: 2 Don’t you know **w** Scripture says in the G5515
Ro 11: 4 And **w** was God’s answer to him? “I have G5515
Ro 11: 7 **W** then? What the people of Israel G5515+5516
Ro 11: 7 **W** the people of Israel sought so G4005
Ro 11:15 **w** will their acceptance be but life from G5515
Ro 12: 2 able to test and approve **w** God’s will is— G5515
Ro 12: 9 must be sincere. Hate **w** is evil; cling to G3836
Ro 12: 9 Hate what is evil; cling to **w** is good. G3836
Ro 12:17 Be careful to do *w* is **right** in the eyes of AIT
Ro 13: 2 is rebelling against **w** God has instituted, G3836
Ro 13: 3 Then do **w** is right and you will be G3836
Ro 13: 7 Give to everyone **w** you owe them: If you G3836
Ro 14:15 sister is distressed because of **w** you **eat**, G1109
Ro 14:16 do not let **w** you know is good be G3836
Ro 14:19 every effort to do **w** leads to peace and to G3836
Ro 14:22 not condemn himself by **w** he approves. G4005
Ro 15:18 of anything except **w** Christ has G4005
Ro 15:18 to obey God *by* **w** I have **said** and done— G3364
Ro 16:19 I want you to be wise about **w** is good, G3836
Ro 16:19 is good, and innocent about **w** is evil. G3836
1Co 1:10 *of you* **agree** *with one another* **in w** *you* **say** G3836+899+3306
1Co 1:12 **W** I mean is this: One of you says, “I follow NDT
1Co 1:21 the foolishness of **w** was preached to save G3836
1Co 1:26 think of **w** you were when you were called. G3836
1Co 2: 9 “**W** no eye has seen, what no ear has G4005
1Co 2: 9 no eye has seen, **w** no ear has heard, and NDT
1Co 2: 9 **w** no human mind has conceived NDT
1Co 2:12 **W** we have received is not the spirit of the NDT
1Co 2:12 we may understand **w** God has freely G3836
1Co 2:13 This is **w** we speak, not in words taught us NDT
1Co 3: 5 **W**, after all, is Apollos? And what G5515+5516
1Co 3: 5 is Apollos? And **w** is Paul? Only G5515
1Co 3:13 their work will be **shown for w it is** G5745
1Co 3:14 If **w** has been built survives G5516+3836+2240
1Co 4: 5 will bring to light **w** is hidden in darkness G3836
1Co 4: 6 “Do not go beyond **w** is written. G4005
1Co 4: 7 **W** do you have that you did not receive G5515
1Co 4:17 which agrees with **w** I teach everywhere in NDT
1Co 4:19 are talking, but **w** power they have. G3836
1Co 4:21 **W** do you prefer? Shall I come to you with G5515
1Co 5:12 **W** *business* is it of mine to judge those G5515
1Co 6:11 And that *is* **w** some of *you* **were**. But you AIT
1Co 7:19 Keeping God’s commands is **w counts**. G247S
1Co 7:29 **W** I mean, brothers and sisters, is that the G4047
1Co 8:10 be emboldened to eat **w** is sacrificed to G3836
1Co 8:13 if **w** I **eat** causes my brother or sister to fall G1109
1Co 9:13 at the altar share in **w** is offered on the altar NDT
1Co 9:18 **W** then is my reward? Just this: that in G5515
1Co 10:13 you except **w is common to mankind**. G474
1Co 10:13 you be tempted beyond **w** you can bear. G4005
1Co 10:15 people; judge for yourselves **w** I say. G4005
1Co 11:22 who have nothing? **W** shall I say to you G5515
1Co 11:23 from the Lord **w** I also passed on to G4005
1Co 13:10 **w** is in part disappears. G3836
1Co 14: 6 speak in tongues, **w** good will I be to you G5515
1Co 14: 7 will anyone know **w** tune is being played G3836
1Co 14: 9 how will anyone know **w** you are saying? G3836
1Co 14:11 the meaning of **w** someone is saying, G3836
1Co 14:13 pray that they may interpret **w** they say. NDT
1Co 14:15 So **w** shall I do? I will pray with my spirit G5515
1Co 14:16 since they do not know **w** you are saying? G5515
1Co 14:26 **W** then shall we say, brothers and sisters G5515
1Co 14:29 the others should weigh carefully **w** is said. NDT
1Co 14:37 acknowledge that **w** I am writing to you G4005
1Co 15: 3 For **w** I received I passed on to you as of G4005
1Co 15:10 But by the grace of God I am **w** I am, and G4005
1Co 15:11 it is I or they, **this is w** we preach, and this G4048
1Co 15:11 we preach, and **this is w** you believed. G4048
1Co 15:29 **w** will those do who are baptized for the G5515
1Co 15:32 than human hopes, **w** have I gained? G5515
1Co 15:35 *With* **w kind** *of* body will they come?” G4481
1Co 15:36 **W** you sow does not come to life unless it G4005
1Co 16: 1 Do **w** I told the Galatian churches to do. G6061
1Co 16:17 they have supplied **w** was lacking from G3836
2Co 1:22 *as* a **deposit, guaranteeing w is to come**. G775
2Co 2:10 And **w** I have forgiven—if there was G4005
2Co 3:10 For **w** was glorious has no glory now in G3836
2Co 3:11 And if **w** was transitory came with glory G3836
2Co 3:13 seeing the end of **w** was passing away. G3836
2Co 4: 5 For **w** we preach is not ourselves, but Jesus NDT
2Co 4:18 So we fix our eyes not on **w** is seen, but on G3836
2Co 4:18 what is seen, but on **w** is unseen, since G3836
2Co 4:18 is unseen, since **w** is seen is temporary G3836
2Co 4:18 is temporary, but **w** is unseen is eternal. G3836
2Co 5: 4 so that **w** is mortal may be swallowed up G3836
2Co 5: 5 *as* a **deposit, guaranteeing w is to come**. G775
2Co 5:10 each of us *may* **receive w is due** us for the G3152
2Co 5:11 we know **w** it is to fear the Lord, we G3836
2Co 5:11 *W we are is* **plain** to God, and I hope it is AIT
2Co 5:12 who take pride in **w is seen** rather than in G4725
2Co 5:12 what is seen rather than in **w** is in the heart. NDT
2Co 6:14 For **w** do righteousness and wickedness G5515
2Co 6:14 Or **w** fellowship can light have with G5515
2Co 6:15 **W** harmony is there between Christ and G5515
2Co 6:15 Or **w** does a believer have in common G5515
2Co 6:16 **W** agreement is there between the temple G5515
2Co 7:11 See **w** this godly sorrow has produced in G4531
2Co 7:11 **w** earnestness, what eagerness to clear NDT
2Co 7:11 **w** eagerness to clear yourselves G247
2Co 7:11 to clear yourselves, **w** indignation, what G247
2Co 7:11 what indignation, **w** alarm, what longing G247
2Co 7:11 what alarm, **w** longing, what concern G247
2Co 7:11 what longing, **w** concern, what readiness to G247
2Co 7:11 concern, **w** readiness to see justice done. G247
2Co 8:10 is my judgment *about* **w** is best for you in G4047
2Co 8:12 acceptable **according to w** one has, G2771+1569
2Co 8:12 not **according to w** one does not have. G2771
2Co 8:14 time your plenty will supply **w** they need, G3836
2Co 8:14 turn their plenty will supply **w** you need. G3836
2Co 8:19 **W is more**, he was G4024+3667+1254+247+2779
2Co 8:21 For we are taking pains to do **w** is right, not NDT
2Co 9: 7 of you should give **w** you have decided in G2777
2Co 10:11 should realize that **w** we are in our letters G3888
2Co 11: 9 from Macedonia supplied **w** I needed. G3836
2Co 11:12 I will keep on doing **w** I am doing in order G4005
2Co 11:15 Their end will be **w** their actions **deserve**. G2848
2Co 12: 6 of me than is warranted *by* **w** I do or say, G4005
2Co 12:14 because **w** I want is not your possessions NDT
2Co 13: 7 so that you will do **w** is right even though G3836
Gal 1: 9 you a gospel other than **w** you accepted, G4005
Gal 1:20 you before God that **w** I am writing you is G4005
Gal 2:18 If I rebuild **w** I destroyed, then I really G4005
Gal 3: 2 of the law, or by believing **w** you **heard**? G198
Gal 3: 5 the law, or by your believing **w** you **heard**? G198
Gal 3:17 **W** I mean is this: The law, introduced 430 NDT
Gal 3:22 so that **w** was promised, being G3836
Gal 4: 1 *W I am* **saying** is that as long as an heir is AIT
Gal 4:17 **W** they want is to alienate you from us, so NDT
Gal 4:21 law, *are you* not **aware of w** the law **says**? G201
Gal 4:30 But **w** does Scripture say? “Get rid of the G5515
Gal 5:17 the flesh desires **w** is contrary to the Spirit NDT
Gal 5:17 the Spirit **w** is contrary to the flesh. NDT
Gal 6: 7 A man reaps **w** he sows. G4005+1569
Gal 6:11 See **w large** letters I use as I write to you G4383
Gal 6:15 anything; **w counts** is the new creation. G247
Eph 4: 9 (**W** does “he ascended” mean except that G5515
Eph 4:29 only **w** is helpful for building others G5516
Eph 5:10 find out **w** pleases the Lord. G5515
Eph 5:12 even to mention **w** the disobedient do in G3836
Eph 5:17 understand **w** the Lord’s will is. G5515
Eph 6:21 may know how I am and **w** I am doing. G5515
Php 1:10 be able to discern **w** is best and may be G3836
Php 1:12 that **w has happened to** me has G3836+2848
Php 1:18 But **w does it matter**? The important G5515+5516
Php 1:19 of Jesus Christ **w** has **happened** to me will G4047
Php 1:22 labor for me. Yet **w** shall I choose? I do G5515
Php 3: 8 **W is more**, I consider G247+3529+2779
Php 3:13 Forgetting **w** is behind and straining G3836
Php 3:13 behind and straining toward **w** is ahead, G3836
Php 3:16 Only let us live up to **w** we have already G4005
Php 4:12 I know **w** it is to be in need, and I know what NDT
Php 4:12 in need, and I know **w** it is to have plenty. NDT
Php 4:17 **w** I desire is that more be credited to your NDT
Col 1:24 Now I rejoice in **w** I am suffering for you G3836
Col 1:24 I fill up in my flesh **w** is still lacking in G3836
Col 2:16 let anyone judge you by *w* you **eat** or drink, AIT
Col 2:18 into great detail *about* **w** they have seen; G4005
Col 4: 1 provide your slaves *with* **w** is right and fair, G3836
1Th 1: 9 themselves report **w kind** *of* reception you G3961
1Th 2:19 For **w** is our hope, our joy, or the crown in G5515
1Th 3:10 you again and supply **w** is lacking in your G3836
1Th 4: 2 For you know **w** instructions we gave you G5515
1Th 5:15 always strive to do **w** is good for each G3836
1Th 5:21 test them all; hold on to **w** is good, G3836
2Th 2: 6 And now you know **w** is holding him back G3836
2Th 3:13 sisters, never tire *of* **doing w is good**. G2818
1Ti 1: 7 they do not know **w** they are talking G4005
1Ti 1: 7 are talking about or **w** they so confidently G5515
1Ti 6:20 guard **w** has been entrusted to your care. G3836
1Ti 6:20 the opposing ideas of **w** is falsely called G3836
2Ti 1:12 he is able to guard **w** I have entrusted to G3836
2Ti 1:13 **W** you heard from me, keep as the G4005
2Ti 2: 7 Reflect on **w** I am saying, for the Lord will G4005
2Ti 3:11 **w kinds** *of things* happened to me in G3888
2Ti 3:14 continue in **w** you have learned and have G4005
2Ti 4: 3 *to* **say w** their **itching ears want to hear** G3117+198
2Ti 4:14 Lord will repay him for **w** he has done. G3836
Titus 1: 5 might put in order **w** was left unfinished G3836
Titus 1: 8 one who **loves w is good**, who is G5787
Titus 2: 1 must teach **w** is appropriate to sound G4005
Titus 2: 3 to much wine, but to **teach w is good**. G2815
Titus 2: 7 set them an example by doing **w** is good. NDT
Titus 2:14 that are his very own, eager to do **w** is good. NDT
Titus 3: 8 to devote themselves to doing **w** is good. NDT
Titus 3:14 to devote themselves to doing *w* is **good**, AIT
Phm 8 order you to do **w** you ought to do, G3836
Heb 2: 1 therefore, *to* **w** we have heard, so that we G3836
Heb 2: 6 “**W** is mankind that you are G5515+5516
Heb 2:10 their salvation perfect through *w* he **suffered**. AIT
Heb 3: 5 bearing witness to **w** would be spoken by G3836
Heb 3: 9 though for forty years they saw **w** I **did**. G2240
Heb 5: 8 he learned obedience from **w** he suffered G4005
Heb 6:11 so that **w** you hope for may be fully G3836
Heb 6:12 patience inherit **w** has been promised. G3836
Heb 6:15 Abraham received **w** was promised. G3836
Heb 6:16 the oath confirms **w** is said and puts an NDT
Heb 6:17 very clear to the heirs of **w** was promised, G3836
Heb 7:15 And **w** we have said is even more clear if NDT
Heb 8: 1 the main point of **w** we are saying is this G3836
Heb 8: 5 is a copy and shadow of **w** is in heaven. G3836
Heb 8:13 **w** is obsolete and outdated will soon G3836
Heb 10:36 you will receive **w** he has promised. G3836
Heb 11: 1 is confidence *in w* we **hope for** and AIT
Heb 11: 1 assurance *about* **w** we do not see. G4547S
Heb 11: 2 This is **w** the ancients were commended for. NDT
Heb 11: 3 so that **w** is seen was not made out of G3836
Heb 11: 3 is seen was not made out of *w was* **visible**. AIT
Heb 11:32 And **w** more shall I say? I do not have G5515
Heb 11:33 and gained **w** was promised; who NDT
Heb 11:39 of them received **w** had been promised, G3836
Heb 12: 7 For **w** children are not disciplined by their G5515
Heb 12:17 he could not change **w** he had done. NDT
Heb 12:20 they could not bear **w** was commanded: G3836
Heb 12:27 the removing of **w** can be shaken— G3836
Heb 12:27 so that **w** cannot be shaken may remain. G3836
Heb 13: 5 money and be content with **w** you have, G3836
Heb 13: 6 **W** can mere mortals do to me? G5515
Heb 13:21 may he work in us **w** is pleasing to him, G3836
Jas 1:22 so deceive yourselves. Do **w** it says. NDT
Jas 1:23 word but does not do **w** it says is like NDT
Jas 1:24 forgets **w** *he* **looks like**. G3961+1639
Jas 1:25 not forgetting **w** they have heard, but NDT
Jas 1:25 they will be blessed in **w** they do. G3836
Jas 2:14 **W** good is it, my brothers and sisters, if G5515
Jas 2:16 about their physical needs, **w** good is it? G5515
Jas 2:21 righteous for *w* he **did** when he offered his AIT
Jas 2:22 his faith was made complete by **w** he did. G3836
Jas 2:24 righteous by **w** they **do** and not by faith G2240
Jas 2:25 righteous for **w** she **did** when she gave G2240
Jas 3: 2 is never at fault in **w** they **say** is perfect, G3364
Jas 3: 5 Consider **w a great** forest is set on fire by G2462
Jas 4: 1 **W causes** fights and quarrels among you G4470
Jas 4: 2 You covet but you cannot get **w** you want, NDT
Jas 4: 3 that you may spend **w** you get on your NDT
Jas 4:14 do not even know **w** will happen G3836
Jas 4:14 happen tomorrow. **W** is your life? You are G4481
Jas 5:11 have seen **w** the Lord finally brought G3836
1Pe 2: 8 which is also **w** they were destined for. NDT
1Pe 3: 6 her daughters *if you* **do** *w is* **right** and do not AIT
1Pe 3:14 But even if you should suffer for **w is right** G1466
1Pe 4: 3 in the past doing **w** pagans choose to do G3836
1Pe 4:17 **w** will the outcome be for those who do G5515
1Pe 4:18 **w** will become of the ungodly and the G4544
2Pe 2: 6 an example *of w* is **going to happen** to the AIT

2Pe 3:11 w **kind of** *people* ought you to be? *G4534*
1Jn 1: 3 We proclaim to you w we have seen and *G4005*
1Jn 2: 4 does not do w he **commands** is a liar *G1953*
1Jn 2:24 see that w you have heard from the *G4005*
1Jn 2:25 And this is w he promised us—eternal life. *G4005*
1Jn 2:29 everyone who does w is right has been *G3836*
1Jn 3: 1 See w **great** love the Father has lavished *G4534*
1Jn 3: 1 And that is w we are! The reason NDT
1Jn 3: 2 w we will be has not yet been made *G5515*
1Jn 3: 7 The one who does w is right is righteous *G3836*
1Jn 3: 8 The one who does w is sinful is of the *G3836*
1Jn 3:10 who does not do w **is right** is not God's *G1466*
1Jn 3:16 This is how we know w love is: Jesus *G3836*
1Jn 3:22 his commands and do w pleases him. *G3836*
1Jn 5:15 that we have w we asked of him. *G3836+161S*
2Jn 8 you do not lose w we have worked for, *G4005*
3Jn 5 are faithful in w you are doing for *G4005+1569*
3Jn 10 I will call attention to w he is doing *G3836*
3Jn 11 do not imitate w is evil but what is good. *G3836*
3Jn 11 do not imitate what is evil but w is good. *G3836*
3Jn 11 Anyone *who* **does** *w is* **good** is from God AIT
3Jn 11 Anyone *who* **does** *w is* **evil** has not seen God. AIT
Jude 17 remember w the apostles of our *G3836+4839S*
Rev 1: 1 show his servants w must soon take place *G4005*
Rev 1: 3 hear it and take to heart w is written in it, *G3836*
Rev 1:11 "Write on a scroll w you see and send it *G4005*
Rev 1:19 therefore, w you have seen, what is now *G4005*
Rev 1:19 w is now and what will take place later. *G4005*
Rev 1:19 what is now and w will take place later. *G4005*
Rev 2: 7 let them hear w the Spirit says to the *G5515*
Rev 2:10 Do not be afraid *of* w you are about to *G4005*
Rev 2:11 let them hear w the Spirit says to the *G5515*
Rev 2:17 let them hear w the Spirit says to the *G5515*
Rev 2:25 except to hold on to w you have until I *G4005*
Rev 2:29 let them hear w the Spirit says to the *G5515*
Rev 3: 2 Strengthen w remains and is about to die *G3836*
Rev 3: 3 therefore, w you have received and heard *G4802*
Rev 3: 3 you will not know at w time I will come to *G4481*
Rev 3: 6 let them hear w the Spirit says to the *G5515*
Rev 3: 7 W he opens no one can shut, and what he NDT
Rev 3: 7 can shut, and w he shuts no one can open. NDT
Rev 3:11 Hold on to w you have, so that no one *G4005*
Rev 3:13 let them hear w the Spirit says to the *G5515*
Rev 3:22 let them hear w the Spirit says to the *G5515*
Rev 4: 1 I will show you w must take place *G4005*
Rev 4: 6 the throne there was w looked like a sea of NDT
Rev 6: 6 Then I heard w sounded like a voice among NDT
Rev 10: 4 "Seal up w the seven thunders have said *G4005*
Rev 15: 2 And I saw w looked like a sea of glass NDT
Rev 16:11 refused to repent of w they had done. *G3836*
Rev 18: 6 pay her back double for w she has done. *G3836*
Rev 19: 1 After this I heard w sounded like the roar of NDT
Rev 19: 6 Then I heard w sounded like a great NDT
Rev 20:12 judged according to w they had done as *G3836*
Rev 20:13 judged according to w they had done. *G3836*
Rev 21:27 anyone who does *w is* **shameful** or deceitful, AIT
Rev 22:12 person according to w they have done. *G3836*

WHAT'S (7) [WHAT]

Ge 33: 8 "**W the meaning of** all these flocks H4769+4200
Jdg 18:23 "**W the matter** with you that you called H4537
Jdg 18:24 can you ask, '**W the matter** with you?' " H4537
1Sa 4: 6 "W all this shouting in the Hebrew camp?" H4537
1Ki 1:41 "**W the meaning of** all the noise in the H4508
2Ki 6:28 asked her, "**W the matter**?" She answered H4537
Mk 6: 2 "W this wisdom that has been given him *G5515*

WHATEVER (182) [WHAT]

Ge 2:19 and w the man called each living H3972+889
Ge 16: 6 "Do with her w you think best." Then H2021
Ge 21:12 Listen to w Sarah tells you, because H3972+889
Ge 31:16 So do w God has told you. H3972+889
Ge 31:39 from me for *w* **was stolen** *by* day or night. AIT
Ge 34:11 in your eyes, and I will give you w you ask. H889
Ge 34:12 you like, and I'll pay w you ask me. H3869+889
Ge 39:23 Joseph and gave him success in w he did. H889
Ex 16:23 Save w is left and keep it until morning H3972
Ex 21:22 must be fined w the woman's H3869+889
Ex 21:30 payment of w is demanded. H3869+3972+889
Ex 27:19 of the tabernacle, w their function H3972
Ex 28:38 Israelites consecrate, w their gifts may be. H3972
Ex 29:37 most holy, and w touches it will be holy. H3972
Ex 30:29 and w touches them will be holy. H3972
Lev 6: 5 w it was they swore falsely about H3972+889
Lev 6:18 W touches them will become holy H3972+889
Lev 6:27 W touches any of the flesh will H3972+889
Lev 11:32 that article, w its use, will be unclean H889
Lev 13:51 the leather, w its use, it is a H3972+889
Lev 13:57 w has the mold must be burned. H889
Lev 16:16 of the Israelites, w their sins have been. H3972
Lev 22: 5 him unclean, w the uncleanness may be. H3972
Lev 23:38 to your gifts and w you have vowed and H3972
Lev 25: 6 W the land yields during the sabbath year NDT
Lev 25: 7 W the land produces may be eaten H3972
Lev 27:12 W value the priest then sets, that is what H3972
Lev 27:14 W value the priest then sets, so it H3869+889
Nu 6:21 in addition to w *else* they can afford. H889
Nu 10:32 will share with you w good things the LORD H889
Nu 11:8 *w is* **set aside** *from* the gifts of all the wave AIT
Nu 18:19 W is set aside from the holy offerings the H3972
Nu 22:17 you handsomely and do w you say. H3972+889
Nu 22:38 "But I can't say w I *please*. I must speak H4399
Nu 23: 3 W he reveals to me I will tell you." H4537+1821
Nu 23:26 tell you I must do w the LORD says?" H3972+889
Nu 31:23 And w cannot withstand fire must be H3972+889
Nu 33:54 W falls to them by lot will be theirs H889
Dt 5:27 Then tell us w the LORD our God tells H3972+889
Dt 12:17 flocks, or w you have vowed to give H3972
Dt 12:26 things and w you have vowed to give H889
Dt 14:26 Use the silver to buy w you like H3972+889
Dt 15: 8 freely lend them w they need. H1896
Dt 17:11 Act according to w they teach you H2021+9368S
Dt 23:16 they like and in w town they choose. H285S
Dt 23:23 W your lips utter you must be sure to H3869+889
Jos 1:16 "W you have commanded us we will H3972+889
Jos 1:18 obey it, w you may command them H3972+889
Jos 7:12 unless you destroy w among you is H2021
Jos 9:25 Do to us w seems good and right to you." H3869
Jdg 10:15 Do with us w you think best, but H3869+3972
Jdg 11:24 w the LORD our God has given us H3972+889
Jdg 11:31 w comes out of the door of my H2021+3655S
Jdg 18:10 a land that lacks **nothing** w." H401+3972+1821
Jdg 19:20 "Let me supply w you need. Only don't H3972
Jdg 19:24 can use them and do to them w you wish. H2021
Ru 3: 5 "I will do w you say," Ruth answered. H3972+889
1Sa 2:14 W the fork brought up the priest H3972+889
1Sa 2:16 and then take w you want," the H3869+889
1Sa 10: 7 are fulfilled, do w your hand finds to do H889
1Sa 11:10 and you can do to us w you like." H3869+3972
1Sa 14:36 of them alive." "Do w seems best to you," H3972
1Sa 18: 5 W *mission* Saul sent him on, David H3972+889
1Sa 20: 4 said to David, "W you want me to do, I'll H4537
1Sa 21: 3 five loaves of bread, or w you can find." H2021
1Sa 25: 8 your son David w you can find for them H889
2Sa 7: 3 to the king, "W you have in mind H3972+889
2Sa 9:11 will do w my lord the H3869+3972+889+4027
2Sa 15:15 are ready to do w our lord the H3869+3972+889
2Sa 15:26 let him do to me w seems good to H3869+889
2Sa 18: 4 answered, "I will do w seems best to you." H889
2Sa 19:18 household over and to do w he wished. H2021
2Sa 19:27 is like an angel of God; so do w you wish. H2021
2Sa 19:37 my lord the king. Do for him w you wish." H889
2Sa 19:38 with me, and I will do for him w you wish. H2021
2Sa 24:22 lord the king take w he wishes and offer H2021
1Ki 3: 5 "Ask for w you want me to give you." H4537
1Ki 5: 6 your men w wages you set H3869+3972+889
1Ki 8:37 w disaster or disease may come H3972
1Ki 8:43 Do w the foreigner asks of H3869+3972+889
1Ki 9:19 —w he desired to build in Jerusalem H889
1Ki 11:38 If you do w I command you and walk H3972+889
1Ki 21: 2 if you prefer, I will pay you *w* it is **worth**." AIT
2Ki 10: 5 anyone as king; you do w you think best." H2021
2Ki 12: 5 use it to repair w damage is found H3972+889
2Ki 18: 7 he was successful in w he undertook. H3972+889
2Ki 18:14 and I will pay w you demand of me." H889
1Ch 17: 2 to David, "W you have in mind H3972+889
1Ch 21:23 Let my lord the king do w pleases him H2021
2Ch 1: 7 "Ask for w you want me to give you." H4537
2Ch 6:28 w disaster or disease may come H3972
2Ch 6:33 Do w the foreigner asks of H3869+3972+889
2Ch 8: 6 —w he desired to build in Jerusalem H3972
Ezr 6: 9 W is needed—young bulls, rams, male A10408
Ezr 7:18 may then do w seems best with A10408+10168
Ezr 7:21 with diligence w Ezra the priest, A10353+10168
Ezr 7:23 W the God of heaven has A10353+10168
Job 23:13 can oppose him? He does w he pleases. NDT
Job 37:12 earth to do w he commands them. H3972+889
Ps 1: 3 not wither—w they do prospers. H3972+889
Ps 115: 3 in heaven; he does w pleases him. H3972+889
Ps 135: 6 The LORD does w pleases him, in the H3972+889
Pr 16: 3 Commit to the LORD w you **do**, and he will H5126
Ecc 3:15 W is has already been, and what will be H4537
Ecc 6:10 W exists has already been named, and H4537
Ecc 7:24 W exists is far off and most H4537+8611
Ecc 8: 3 for he will do w he pleases. H3972+889
Ecc 9:10 W your hand finds to do, do it with H3972+889
Ecc 11: 9 the ways of your heart and *w* your eyes **see**, AIT
Jer 1: 7 you to and say w I command you. H3972+889
Jer 1:17 and say to them w I command you. H3972+889
Jer 26:14 do with me w you think is good and right. H3869
Jer 39:12 him but do for him w he asks." H3869+889+4027
Eze 10:11 The cherubim went in w direction the head H889
Eze 12:25 I will fulfill *w I* **say**, declares the AIT
Eze 12:28 delayed any longer; w I say will be fulfilled H889
Eze 24: 6 piece **in w order** it H4202+5877+1598+6584
Eze 47:23 In w tribe a foreigner resides, there you H2021
Da 7: 7 its victims and trampled underfoot *w* was **left**. AIT
Da 7:19 its victims and trampled underfoot *w* was **left**. AIT
Da 8:24 devastation and will succeed in w he does. NDT
Na 1: 9 W they plot against the LORD he will bring H4537
Hag 2:14 'W they do and whatever they offer there H3972
Hag 2:14 'Whatever they do and w they offer there is H889
Mt 10:11 W town or village you enter *G4005+1254+323*
Mt 14: 7 an oath to give her w she asked. *G4005+1569*
Mt 15:17 you see that w enters the mouth *G4246+3836*
Mt 16:19 w you bind on earth will be bound *G4005+1569*
Mt 16:19 and w you loose on earth will be *G4005+1569*
Mt 18:18 w you bind on earth will be bound *G4012+1569*
Mt 18:18 and w you loose on earth will be *G4012+1569*
Mt 20: 4 and I will pay you w is right. *G4005+1569*
Mt 21:22 will receive w you ask for in *G4246+4012+323*
Mt 25:40 w you did for one of the least of *G2093+4012*
Mt 25:45 w you did not do for one of the *G2093+4012*
Mk 4:22 For w is hidden is meant to be disclosed *G1569*
Mk 4:22 and *w* **is** concealed is meant to be brought AIT
Mk 6:23 "W you ask I will give *G4005+323+5516+1569*
Mk 10:35 "we want you to do for us w we ask." *G4005+1569*
Mk 11:24 I tell you, w you ask for in prayer *G4246+4012*
Mk 13:11 Just say w is given you at the time *G4005+1569*
Lk 9: 4 W house you enter, stay there until *G4005+323*
Lk 10: 7 eating and drinking w they give you, for *G3836*
Jn 2: 5 "Do w he tells you. *G4005+3836+5516+323*
Jn 5:19 because w the Father does the Son *G4005+323*
Jn 11:22 now God will give you w you ask." *G4012+323*
Jn 12:50 So w I say is just what the Father has told *G4005*
Jn 14:13 And I will do w you ask in my *G4005+5516+323*
Jn 15: 7 in you, ask w you wish, and it *G4005+1569*
Jn 15:16 and so that w you ask in my *G4005+5516+323*
Jn 16:23 will give you w you ask in my name. *G323+5516*
Ac 18:17 Gallio showed **no** concern w. *G4029*
Ro 2: 1 for at w *point* you judge another *G4005*
Ro 3:19 Now we know that w the law says, it says *G4012*
Ro 13: 9 and w other command there may be, are *G5516*
Ro 14:22 So w you believe about these things keep *G4005*
1Co 7:17 as a believer *in* w *situation* the Lord has *G6055*
1Co 10:27 eat w is put before you without raising *G4246*
1Co 10:31 So whether you eat or drink or w you do *G5516*
2Co 11:21 W anyone else dares to *G1877+4005+1254+323*
Gal 2: 6 w they were makes no difference to *G5516+3961*
Gal 5:17 that you are not to do w you want. *G4005+1569*
Eph 6: 8 each one for w good they do, *G1569+5516*
Php 1:27 **W happens**, conduct yourselves in a *G3667*
Php 3: 7 But w were gains to me I now consider *G4015*
Php 4: 8 brothers and sisters, w is true, whatever is *G4012*
Php 4: 8 whatever is true, w is noble, whatever is *G4012*
Php 4: 8 whatever is noble, w is right, whatever is *G4012*
Php 4: 8 whatever is right, w is pure, whatever is *G4012*
Php 4: 8 whatever is pure, w is lovely, whatever is *G4012*
Php 4: 8 whatever is lovely, w is admirable—if *G4012*
Php 4: 9 W you have learned or received or heard *G4005*
Php 4:11 to be content w *the circumstances*. *G4005*
Col 3: 5 w belongs to your earthly nature: *G3836*
Col 3:17 And w you do, whether *G4246+4005+5516+1569*
Col 3:23 W you do, work at it with all your *G4005+1569*
1Ti 1:10 *for* w else is contrary to the sound *G5516*
Titus 3: 1 be obedient, to be ready to do w is good, *G4246*
1Pe 4:10 Each of you should use w gift you have *G2777*
2Pe 2:19 are slaves to w has mastered them *G4005*
1Jn 5:15 he hears us—w we ask—we know *G4005+1569*
Jude 10 these people slander w they do not *G4012*

WHEAT (46)

Ge 30:14 During w harvest, Reuben went out into H2636
Ex 9:32 The w and spelt, however, were not H2636
Ex 29: 2 And from the finest w flour make round H2636
Ex 34:22 Weeks with the firstfruits of the w harvest, H2636
Dt 8: 8 a land with w and barley, vines and fig H2636
Dt 32:14 of Bashan and the finest kernels of w. H2636
Jdg 6:11 Gideon was threshing w in a winepress to H2636
Jdg 15: 1 at the time of w harvest, Samson took H2636
Ru 2:23 until the barley and w harvests were H2636
1Sa 6:13 were harvesting their w in the valley, H2636
1Sa 12:17 Is it not w harvest now? I will call on the H2636
2Sa 4: 6 part of the house as if to get *some* w, H2636
2Sa 17:28 They also brought w and barley, flour H2636
1Ki 5:11 twenty thousand cors of w as food for his H2636
1Ch 21:20 While Araunah was threshing w, he H2636
1Ch 21:23 and the w for the grain offering. H2636
2Ch 2:10 twenty thousand cors of ground w, twenty H2636
2Ch 2:15 his servants the w and barley and the H2636
2Ch 27: 5 ten thousand cors of w and ten thousand H2636
Ezr 6: 9 to the God of heaven, and w, salt, A10272
Ezr 7:22 a hundred cors of w, a hundred baths of A10272
Job 31:40 come up instead of w and stinkweed H2636
Ps 81:16 But you would be fed with the finest of w H2636
Ps 147:14 satisfies you with the finest of w. H2636
SS 7: 2 waist is a mound of w encircled by lilies. H2636
Isa 28:25 Does he not plant w in its place, barley in H2636
Jer 12:13 They will sow w but reap thorns; they will H2636
Jer 41: 8 We have w and barley, olive oil and H2636
Eze 4: 9 "Take w and barley, beans and lentils H2636
Eze 27:17 they exchanged w *from* Minnith and H2636
Eze 45:13 from each homer of w and a sixth of an H2636
Joel 1:11 grieve for the w and the barley, because H2636
Am 8: 5 Sabbath be ended that we may market w?" H1339
Am 8: 6 selling even the sweepings with the w. H1339
Mt 3:12 gathering his w into the barn and burning *G4992*
Mt 13:25 came and sowed weeds among the w, *G4992*
Mt 13:26 When the w sprouted and formed heads *G5965*
Mt 13:29 you may uproot the w with them. *G4992*
Mt 13:30 then gather the w and bring it into my *G4992*
Lk 3:17 floor and to gather the w into his barn, *G4992*
Lk 16: 7 " 'A thousand bushels *of* w,' he replied *G4992*
Lk 22:31 Satan has asked to sift all of you as w. *G4992*
Jn 12:24 unless a kernel *of* w falls to the ground *G4992*
1Co 15:37 perhaps *of* w or of something else. *G4992*
Rev 6: 6 "Two pounds *of* w for a day's wages *G4992*
Rev 18:13 of fine flour and w; cattle and sheep; *G4992*

WHEEL (13) [WHEELS]

1Ki 7:32 The diameter of each w was a cubit and a H236
1Ki 22:34 "**W around** and get me out of the H2200+3338
2Ch 18:33 "**W around** and get me out of the H2200+3338
Pr 20:26 he drives the *threshing* w over them. H236
Ecc 12: 6 the spring, and the w broken at the well, H1649
Isa 28:27 is the w *of* a cart rolled over cumin H236

W

Jer 18: 3 and I saw him working at the **w**. H78
Eze 1:15 I saw a **w** on the ground beside each H236
Eze 1:16 to be made like a **w** intersecting a wheel. H236
Eze 1:16 to be made like a wheel intersecting a **w**. H236
Eze 10: 6 the man went in and stood beside a **w**. H236
Eze 10:10 each was like a **w** intersecting a wheel. H236
Eze 10:10 each was like a wheel intersecting a **w**. H236

WHEELS (32) [WHEEL]

Ex 14:25 He jammed the **w** *of* their chariots so that H236
1Ki 7:30 stand had four bronze **w** with bronze axles, H236
1Ki 7:32 The four **w** were under the panels, and the H236
1Ki 7:32 the axles of the **w** were attached to the H236
1Ki 7:33 The **w** were made like chariot wheels; the H236
1Ki 7:33 The wheels were made like chariot **w**; the H236
Isa 5:28 like flint, their **chariot** **w** like a whirlwind. H1649
Isa 28:28 The **w** *of* a threshing cart may be rolled H1651
Jer 47: 3 enemy chariots and the rumble of their **w**. H1649
Eze 1:16 was the appearance and structure of the **w**: H236
Eze 1:17 the **w** did not change direction as the NDT
Eze 1:19 the **w** beside them moved H236
Eze 1:19 rose from the ground, the **w** also rose. H236
Eze 1:20 and the **w** would rise along with them H236
Eze 1:20 spirit of the living creatures was in the **w**. H236
Eze 1:21 the ground, the **w** rose along with them H236
Eze 1:21 spirit of the living creatures was in the **w**. H236
Eze 3:13 other and the sound of the **w** beside them, H236
Eze 10: 2 "Go in among the **w** beneath the H1649
Eze 10: 6 "Take fire from among the **w**, from among H1649
Eze 10: 9 I saw beside the cherubim four **w**, one H236
Eze 10: 9 of the cherubim; the **w** sparkled like topaz. H236
Eze 10:11 the **w** did not turn about as the cherubim NDT
Eze 10:12 full of eyes, as were their four **w**. H236
Eze 10:13 I heard the **w** being called "the whirling H236
Eze 10:13 the wheels being called "the **whirling** **w**." H1649
Eze 10:16 the **w** beside them moved H236
Eze 10:16 the ground, the **w** did not leave their side. H236
Eze 10:19 as they went, the **w** went with them. H236
Eze 11:22 cherubim, with the **w** beside them, spread H236
Da 7: 9 with fire, and its **w** were all ablaze. A10143
Na 3: 2 the clatter of **w**, galloping horses and H236

WHELP, WHELPS (KJV) BEASTS, CUB, CUBS

WHEN (2814) [WHENEVER] See Index of Articles Etc.

WHENEVER (71) [WHEN]

Ge 9:14 **W** I bring clouds over the earth and the H928
Ge 9:16 **W** the rainbow appears in the clouds, H2256
Ge 30:33 **w** you check on the wages you have paid H3954
Ge 30:41 **W** the stronger females were in heat H928+3972
Ge 38: 9 so **w** he slept with his brother's wife H561
Ex 17:11 **w** he lowered his hands H3869+889
Ex 18:16 **W** they have a dispute, it is brought to me H3954
Ex 28:29 "**W** Aaron enters the Holy Place, he will H928
Ex 28:30 be over Aaron's heart **w** he enters the H928
Ex 28:43 sons must wear them **w** they enter the tent H928
Ex 30:20 **W** they enter the tent of meeting, they shall H928
Ex 33: 8 And **w** Moses went out to the tent, all the H3869
Ex 33:10 **W** the people saw the pillar of cloud H2256
Ex 34:34 But **w** he entered the LORD's presence to H928
Ex 40:32 They washed **w** they entered the tent of H928
Ex 40:36 **w** the cloud lifted from above the H928
Lev 10: 9 fermented drink **w** you go into the tent H928
Lev 13:14 But **w** raw flesh appears on them H928+3427
Lev 16: 2 is not to come **w** he chooses H928+3972+6961
Nu 1:51 **W** the tabernacle is to move, the Levites are H928
Nu 1:51 and **w** the tabernacle is to be set up H928
Nu 9:17 **W** the cloud lifted from above the H4200+7023
Nu 9:21 by day or by night, **w** the cloud lifted, they H2256
Nu 10:35 **W** the ark set out, Moses said, "Rise up H2256
Nu 10:36 **W** it came to rest, he said, "Return, LORD, to H928
Nu 15:14 **w** a foreigner or anyone else living H3954
Dt 4: 7 God is near us **w** we pray to him? H928+3972
Jdg 2:15 **W** Israel went out to fight, the H928+3972+889
Jdg 2:18 **W** the LORD raised up a judge for them, he H3954
Jdg 6: 3 **W** the Israelites planted their crops, the H561
Jdg 12: 5 Ephraim, and **w** a survivor of Ephraim said H3954
Ru 2: 9 And *w you are* **thirsty**, go and get a drink AIT
1Sa 1: 4 **W** the day came for Elkanah to sacrifice H2256
1Sa 1: 7 **W** Hannah went up to the house of H4946+1896
1Sa 2:13 **w** any of the people offered a sacrifice NDT
1Sa 14:52 **and** **w** Saul saw a mighty or brave man H2256
1Sa 16:23 **W** the spirit from God came on Saul, David H928
1Sa 17:24 **W** the Israelites saw the man, they all fled H928
1Sa 21: 5 been kept from us, as usual **w** I set out. H928
1Sa 23:20 come down **w** it pleases you to do so H3972
1Sa 27: 9 **W** David attacked an area, he did not H2256
2Sa 14:26 **W** he cut the hair of his head—he used to H928
2Sa 15: 2 **W** anyone came with a complaint to be H2256
2Sa 15: 5 **w** anyone approached him to bow down H928
1Ki 8:52 you listen to them **w** they cry out to H928+3972
1Ki 14:28 **W** the king went to the LORD's H4946+1896
1Ki 18:10 And **w** a nation or kingdom claimed you NDT
2Ki 4: 8 So **w** he came by, he stopped there H4946+1896
2Ki 4:10 Then he can stay there **w** he comes to us." H928
2Ki 12:10 **W** they saw that there was a large amount H3869
1Ch 23:31 **w** burnt offerings were H4200+3972
2Ch 12:11 **W** the king went to the LORD's H4946+1896
2Ch 19: 6 who is with you **w** you give a verdict. H928
2Ch 24:11 **W** the chest was brought in by the H928+6961
Ps 78:34 **W** God slew them, they would seek him H561
Jer 20: 8 **W** I speak, I cry out H3954+4946+1896
Jer 36:23 **W** Jehudi had read three or four columns H3869
Jer 48:27 head in scorn **w** you speak of her? H4946+1896
Hos 6:11 "**W** I would restore the fortunes of my H928
Hos 7: 1 **w** I would heal Israel, the sins of Ephraim H3869
Mk 3:11 **W** the impure spirits saw him, they fell *G4020*
Mk 6:10 **W** you enter a house, stay there *G3963+1569*
Mk 9:18 **W** it seizes him, it throws him to the *G3963+1569*
Mk 13:11 **W** you are arrested and brought to trial, do *G4020*
1Co 11:25 do this, **w** you drink it, in *G4006+1569*
1Co 11:26 For **w** you eat this bread and drink *G4006+1569*
2Co 3:16 But **w** anyone turns to the Lord, the *G2471+1569*
2Co 13: 9 We are glad **w** we are weak but you are *G4020*
Eph 6:19 also for me, that **w** I speak, words may be *G1877*
Jas 1: 2 **w** you face trials of many kinds, *G4020*
Rev 4: 9 **W** the living creatures give glory, honor *G4020*

WHERE (701) [ELSEWHERE, SOMEWHERE, WHEREVER]

Ge 2:11 entire land of Havilah, **w** there is gold. H9004
Ge 3: 9 LORD God called to the man, "**W** are you?" H361
Ge 4: 9 LORD said to Cain, "**W** is your brother Abel?" H361
Ge 10:11 land he went to Assyria, **w** he built Nineveh NDT
Ge 10:30 The **region** **w** they **lived** stretched from H4632
Ge 13: 3 Bethel and Ai **w** his tent had been H9004
Ge 13: 4 **w** he had first built an altar. There H9004
Ge 13:14 "Look around from **w** you are, to H2021+5226S
Ge 13:18 of Mamre at Hebron, **w** he pitched his tents. NDT
Ge 16: 8 slave of Sarai, **w** have you come from, and H361
Ge 16: 8 come from, and **w** are you going?" H625+2025
Ge 17: 8 Canaan, **w** you now reside as a foreigner H824S
Ge 18: 9 "**W** is your wife Sarah?" they asked him H372
Ge 19: 5 "**W** are the men who came to you tonight? H372
Ge 19:27 to the place **w** he had stood before H9004
Ge 19:29 that overthrew the cities **w** Lot had lived. H889
Ge 21:23 me and the country **w** you now reside as a H889
Ge 22: 7 "but **w** is the lamb for the burnt offering?" H372
Ge 26: 2 to Egypt; live in the land **w** I tell you to live. H889
Ge 26:17 in the Valley of Gerar, **w** he settled. H9004
Ge 28: 4 possession of the **land** *w* you now reside as a AIT
Ge 29: 4 shepherds, "My brothers, **w** are you from?" H402
Ge 31: 4 to come out to the fields **w** his flocks were. NDT
Ge 31:13 **w** you anointed a pillar and where you H9004
Ge 31:13 a pillar and **w** you made a vow to me. H9004
Ge 32:17 belong to, and **w** are you going, and H625+2025
Ge 33:17 **w** he built a place for himself and made NDT
Ge 33:19 the plot of ground **w** he pitched his tent. H9004
Ge 34:27 looted the city **w** their sister had been H889
Ge 35: 3 up to Bethel, **w** I will build an altar to God H9004
Ge 35:13 from him at the place **w** he had talked with H889
Ge 35:14 pillar at the place **w** God had talked with H889
Ge 35:15 called the place **w** God had talked with H9004
Ge 35:27 **w** Abraham and Isaac had stayed. H9004
Ge 36: 7 the **land** *w* they were staying could not AIT
Ge 37: 1 Jacob lived in the **land** *w* his father had AIT
Ge 37:16 Can you tell me **w** they are grazing their H407
Ge 37:30 boy isn't there! **W** can I turn now?" H625+2025
Ge 38:21 "**W** is the shrine prostitute who was beside H372
Ge 39:20 the place **w** the king's prisoners were H889
Ge 40: 3 in the same prison **w** Joseph was H9004
Ge 42: 7 harshly to them. "**W** do you come from?" H402
Ge 42: 9 You have come to see **w** our land is NDT
Ge 42:12 "You have come to see **w** our land is NDT
Ge 42:27 the **place** **w** **they stopped for the night** H4869
Ge 43:21 the **place** **w** **we stopped for the night** we H4869
Ge 47:30 of Egypt and bury me **w** they are buried." H928
Ex 2:11 he went out to *w* his own people were and AIT
Ex 2:15 to live in Midian, **w** he sat down by a well. NDT
Ex 2:20 "And **w** is he?" Reuel asked his daughters H361
Ex 3: 5 the place **w** you are standing is holy H889
Ex 6: 4 of Canaan, **w** they **resided** as foreigners. H4472
Ex 8:22 the land of Goshen, **w** my people live; no H889
Ex 9:26 the land of Goshen, **w** the Israelites were. H889
Ex 10:23 had light in the **places** **w** they **lived**. H4632
Ex 12: 7 of the houses **w** they eat the lambs. H889
Ex 12:13 a sign for you on the houses **w** you are, H9004
Ex 15:27 **w** there were twelve springs and seventy H9004
Ex 16:29 Everyone is to stay **w** they are on the H9393
Ex 18: 5 **w** he was camped near the mountain of H9004
Ex 20:21 the thick darkness **w** God was. H9004
Ex 25:26 to the four corners, **w** the four legs are. H889
Ex 30: 6 law—**w** I will meet with you. H9004+2025
Ex 30:36 of meeting, **w** I will meet with you. H9004+2025
Ex 33:21 is a place near me **w** you may stand on a NDT
Ex 34:12 those who live in the land **w** you are going, H889
Ex 37:13 to the four corners, **w** the four legs were. H889
Lev 1:16 down east of the altar **w** the ashes are. H5226S
Lev 4:12 **w** the ashes are **thrown**, and burn it H9162
Lev 4:24 it at the place **w** the burnt offering is H889
Lev 4:33 offering at the place **w** the burnt offering is H889
Lev 7: 2 in the place **w** the burnt offering is H889
Lev 13:19 in the place **w** the boil was, a white NDT
Lev 13:20 disease that has broken out **w** the boil was. H928
Lev 14:13 in the sanctuary area **w** the sin offering H889
Lev 18: 3 as they do in Egypt, **w** you used to live, and H889
Lev 18: 3 of Canaan, **w** I am bringing you. H9004+2025
Lev 20:22 so that the land **w** I am bringing H9004+2025
Lev 21:11 not enter a place **w** there is a dead body. NDT
Nu 5: 3 defile their camp, **w** I dwell among them." H889
Nu 10:31 You know **w** we should camp in the NDT
Nu 11:13 **W** can I get meat for all these H4946+402
Nu 13:22 came to Hebron, **w** Ahiman, Sheshai and H9004
Nu 17: 4 covenant law, **w** I meet with you. H9004+2025
Nu 18: 4 no one else may come near **w** you are. NDT
Nu 20:13 **w** the Israelites quarreled with the LORD H889
Nu 20:13 with the LORD and **w** he was proved holy NDT
Nu 21:16 the well **w** the LORD said to Moses H889
Nu 21:20 to the valley in Moab **w** the top of Pisgah NDT
Nu 22:26 in a narrow place **w** there was no room to H889
Nu 23:13 me to another place **w** you can see them; H889
Nu 31:10 burned all the towns **w** the Midianites had H928
Nu 33: 9 **w** there were twelve springs and H928+396S
Nu 33:14 **w** there was no water for the people to H9004
Nu 33:38 **w** he died on the first day of the fifth H9004
Nu 33:55 give you trouble in the land **w** you will live. H889
Nu 34: 5 **w** it will turn, join the Wadi of Egypt and H6801S
Nu 35:33 " 'Do not pollute the land **w** you are H889
Nu 35:34 not defile the land **w** you live and where I H889
Nu 35:34 the land where you live and **w** I dwell, H889
Dt 1:28 **W** can we go? Our brothers have H625+2025
Dt 3:21 the kingdoms over there **w** you are going. H889
Dt 8: 9 a land **w** bread will not be scarce and you H889
Dt 8: 9 a land **w** the rocks are iron and you can dig H889
Dt 11:10 **w** you planted your seed and irrigated it by H889
Dt 11:24 Every place **w** you set your foot will be yours: H889
Dt 12: 2 **w** the nations you are dispossessing H9004
Dt 12:21 If the place **w** the LORD your God chooses to H889
Dt 14:24 because the place **w** the LORD will choose H9004
Dt 18: 6 towns anywhere in Israel **w** he is living, H9004
Dt 21: 4 plowed or planted and **w** there is a flowing NDT
Dt 23:12 outside the camp **w** you can go to H9004+2025
Dt 28:37 all the peoples **w** the LORD will H9004+2025
Dt 30: 3 all the nations **w** he scattered you. H9004+2025
Dt 31:14 tent of meeting, **w** I will commission him." NDT
Dt 32:37 "Now **w** are their gods, the rock they took H361
Dt 33:28 new wine, **w** the heavens drop dew. NDT
Dt 34: 6 to this day no one knows **w** his grave is. NDT
Jos 1: 3 give you every place **w** you set your foot, H889
Jos 2: 4 I did not know **w** they had come from. H402
Jos 3: 1 **w** they camped before crossing over. H9004
Jos 4: 3 from **right** **w** the priests are standing H2296
Jos 4: 3 them down at the place **w** you stay tonight." H889
Jos 4: 8 to their camp, **w** they put them down. H9004
Jos 4: 9 the Jordan at the spot **w** the priests who NDT
Jos 5: 8 they remained **w** they were in camp until H9393
Jos 5:15 the place **w** you are standing is holy." H889
Jos 8:24 in the wilderness **w** they had chased them, H889
Jos 9: 8 "Who are you and **w** do you come from?" H402
Jos 10:27 them into the cave **w** they had been H9004
Jos 22:19 **w** the LORD's tabernacle stands H9004
Jos 22:33 the country **w** the Reubenites and H889
Jdg 1:26 **w** he built a city and called it Luz NDT
Jdg 5:27 he sank, he fell; **w** he sank, there he H928+889
Jdg 6:11 **w** his son Gideon was threshing wheat in a NDT
Jdg 6:13 **W** are all his wonders that our ancestors H372
Jdg 9:38 Zebul said to him, "**W** is your big talk now H372
Jdg 11: 3 **w** a gang of scoundrels gathered around NDT
Jdg 13: 6 I didn't ask him **w** he came from, and he H361
Jdg 16: 1 went to Gaza, **w** he saw a prostitute. H9004
Jdg 16:26 "Put me **w** I can feel the pillars that support NDT
Jdg 17: 9 Micah asked him, "**W** are you from?" H402
Jdg 18: 1 a place of their own **w** they might settle, NDT
Jdg 18: 2 house of Micah, **w** they spent the night. H9004
Jdg 18: 7 **w** they saw that the people were living in NDT
Jdg 19:17 old man asked, "**W** are you going? H625+2025
Jdg 19:17 are you going? **W** did you come from?" H402
Jdg 19:18 the hill country of Ephraim **w** I live. H4946+9004
Jdg 19:26 back to the house **w** her master was H9004
Jdg 20:22 their positions **w** they had H928+2021+5226S
Jdg 20:47 **w** they stayed four months. H928+6152+8234S
Jdg 21: 2 **w** they sat before God until evening H9004
Ru 1: 7 she left the place **w** she had been H9004+2025
Ru 1:16 **W** you go I will go, and where you stay I H889
Ru 1:16 you go I will go, and **w** you stay I will stay. H889
Ru 1:17 **W** you die I will die, and there I will be H889
Ru 2: 9 Watch the field **w** the men are harvesting H889
Ru 2:19 asked her, "**W** did you glean today? H407
Ru 2:19 you glean today? **W** did you work H625+2025
Ru 3: 1 you, **w** you will be well provided for. H889
Ru 3: 4 lies down, note the place **w** he is lying. H9004
1Sa 1: 3 at Shiloh, **w** Hophni and Phinehas H9004
1Sa 3: 3 house of the LORD, **w** the ark of God was. H9004
1Sa 7:17 back to Ramah, **w** his home was, and H9004
1Sa 9:10 out for the town **w** the man of God was. H9004
1Sa 9:18 please tell me **w** the seer's house H361+2296
1Sa 10: 5 **w** there is a Philistine outpost. H9004
1Sa 10:14 him and his servant, "**W** have you been?" H625
1Sa 14: 9 we will stay **w** we are and not go up to H9393
1Sa 19: 3 with my father in the field **w** you are. H9004
1Sa 19:22 And he asked, "**W** are Samuel and David?" H407
1Sa 20:19 go to the place **w** you hid when this H9004
1Sa 20:37 came to the place **w** Jonathan's arrow had H889
1Sa 23:22 Find out **w** David usually goes and who H5226S
1Sa 25:11 give it to men coming from who knows **w**?" H361
1Sa 26: 5 went to the place **w** Saul had camped. H9004
1Sa 26: 5 He saw **w** Saul and Abner son of H2021+5226S
1Sa 26:16 **W** are the king's spear and water jug that H361
1Sa 27:10 "**W** did you go raiding today? H625
1Sa 30: 9 the Besor Valley, **w** some stayed behind. H2256
1Sa 30:13 do you belong to? **W** do you come from?" H361
1Sa 30:31 the other places **w** he and his men had H9004
1Sa 31:12 went to Jabesh, **w** they burned them. H9004
2Sa 1: 3 "**W** have you come from?" David asked him H361
2Sa 1:13 brought him the report, "**W** are you from?" H361
2Sa 2: 1 David asked, "**W** shall I go?" "To H625+2025

2Sa 2:23 he came to the place w Asahel had fallen H9004
2Sa 9: 4 "W is he?" the king asked. Ziba answered H407
2Sa 11:15 "Put Uriah out in front w the fighting is NDT
2Sa 11:16 put Uriah at a place w he knew the H9004
2Sa 13:13 W could I get rid of my disgrace H625+2025
2Sa 15:20 **do not know** w I **am going** H2143+6584+889+2143
2Sa 15:32 summit, w people used to worship God H9004
2Sa 16: 3 then asked, "W is your master's grandson?" H372
2Sa 17:20 "W are Ahimaaz and Jonathan? H372
2Sa 19:17 to the Jordan, w the king was. H4200+7156S
2Sa 21:12 w the Philistines had hung them after H9004
2Sa 23: 7 of a spear; they are burned up w they lie." H928
2Sa 23:11 together at a place w there was a field H9004
1Ki 1:15 w Abishag the Shunammite was attending NDT
1Ki 7: 7 Hall of Justice, w he was to judge, and H9004
1Ki 8: 9 w the LORD made a covenant with the H889
1Ki 8:47 of heart in the land w they are held H9004
1Ki 8:54 w he had been kneeling with his hands NDT
1Ki 11:24 w they settled and took control. H928+2023S
1Ki 11:36 the city w I chose to put my Name. H9004
1Ki 12: 2 w he had fled from King Solomon) H889
1Ki 13:22 water in the place w he told you not to eat H889
1Ki 13:25 it in the city w the old prophet lived. H889
1Ki 13:31 bury me in the grave w the man of God is H889
1Ki 17:19 him to the upper room w he was staying, H9004
1Ki 18:10 a nation or kingdom w my master has not H9004
1Ki 18:12 I don't know w the Spirit of the LORD may H889
1Ki 20:30 w the wall collapsed on twenty-seven NDT
1Ki 21:18 w he has gone to take possession of it. H9004
1Ki 21:19 In the place w dogs licked up Naboth's H889
1Ki 22:38 a pool in Samaria (w the prostitutes bathed), NDT
2Ki 2: 7 facing the place w Elijah and Elisha had NDT
2Ki 2:14 the water with it. "W now is the LORD, the H372
2Ki 5:25 asked him, "W have you been H4946+402
2Ki 6: 1 the place w we meet with you is too small H9004
2Ki 6: 2 w each of us can get a pole H4946+9004
2Ki 6: 6 man of God asked, "W did it fall?" H625+2025
2Ki 6:13 find out w he is," the king ordered H378
2Ki 6:27 help you, w can I get help for you? H4946+402
2Ki 11:16 as she reached the **place** *w* the horses enter AIT
2Ki 14: 6 the Law of Moses w the LORD commanded: H889
2Ki 17:29 gods in the several towns w they settled, H9004
2Ki 18:34 W are the gods of Hamath and Arpad H372
2Ki 18:34 W are the gods of Sepharvaim, Hena and H372
2Ki 19:13 W is the king of Hamath or the king of H361
2Ki 19:13 W are the kings of Lair, Sepharvaim, Hena NDT
2Ki 19:27 " 'But I know *w* you **are** and when you come AIT
2Ki 20:14 those men say, and w did they come from?" H402
2Ki 23: 7 the quarters w women did weaving for H9004
2Ki 23: 8 w the priests had burned incense. H9004+2025
2Ki 25: 6 w sentence was pronounced on him. NDT
1Ch 3: 4 w he reigned seven years and six months. H9004
1Ch 5:26 the river of Gozan, w they are to this day. NDT
1Ch 11:13 At a place w there was a field full of barley NDT
2Ch 3: 1 w the LORD had appeared to his father H889
2Ch 5:10 w the LORD made a covenant with the H889
2Ch 6:37 of heart in the land w they are held H9004
2Ch 6:38 land of their captivity w they were taken, H889
2Ch 10: 2 w he had fled from King Solomon) H889
2Ch 20:26 of Berakah, w they praised the LORD. H9004
2Ch 25: 4 Book of Moses, w the LORD commanded: H889
2Ch 25:11 w he killed ten thousand men of Seir. NDT
2Ch 32:33 was buried on the **hill** *w* the tombs of David's AIT
2Ch 33:19 the sites w he built high places and H889
2Ch 35:24 brought him to Jerusalem, w he died. NDT
Ezr 1: 4 And in any locality w survivors may now H9004
Ezr 8:32 in Jerusalem, w we rested three days. H9004
Ne 2: 3 sad when the city w my ancestors are H1074S
Ne 2: 5 to the city in Judah w my ancestors are NDT
Ne 2:16 did not know w I had gone or what I H625+2025
Ne 9: 3 They stood w they were and read H6584+6642S
Ne 10:37 collect the tithes in all the **towns** *w* we work. AIT
Ne 10:39 w the articles for the sanctuary and for the H9004
Ne 12:27 sought out from w they **lived** and were H5226
Est 7: 5 W is he—the man who has dared to do H361
Est 7: 8 falling on the couch w Esther was reclining. H889
Job 1: 7 said to Satan, "W have you come from?" H402
Job 2: 2 said to Satan, "W have you come from?" H361
Job 4: 7 W were the upright ever destroyed? H407
Job 6:24 be quiet; show me w I have been wrong. H4537
Job 8:11 Can papyrus grow tall w there is no marsh H928
Job 10:22 disorder, w even the light is like darkness." NDT
Job 15:28 towns and houses w no one lives, H4200+4564S
Job 17:15 w then is my hope—who can see any H372
Job 18:19 his people, no survivor w once he lived. H928
Job 20: 7 who have seen him will say, 'W is he? H361
Job 21:28 You say, 'W now is the house of the great H372
Job 21:28 of the great, the tents w the wicked lived? NDT
Job 23: 3 If only I knew w to find him; if only I could NDT
Job 28: 1 silver and a place w gold is refined. NDT
Job 28:12 But w can wisdom be found? Where H4946+402
Job 28:12 W does understanding dwell? H361+2296
Job 28:20 W then does wisdom come from? Where H402
Job 28:20 W does understanding dwell? H361+2296
Job 28:23 way to it and he alone knows w it **dwells**, H5226
Job 34:22 no utter darkness, w evildoers can hide. H9004
Job 34:26 wickedness w everyone can see H928+5226S
Job 35:10 But no one says, 'W is God my Maker, who H372
Job 38: 4 "W were you when I laid the earth's H407
Job 38:11 no farther; here is w your proud waves halt'? NDT
Job 38:19 And w does darkness reside? H361+2296
Job 38:24 is the way to the place w the lightning is NDT
Job 38:24 the place w the east winds are scattered NDT
Job 38:26 to water a land w no one lives, an NDT
Job 39:30 feast on blood, and w the slain are H928+889
Job 40:12 crush the wicked w they **stand**. H9393
Ps 26: 8 I love the house w you **live**, the place H5061
Ps 26: 8 you live, the place w your glory **dwells**. H5438
Ps 41: 8 will never get up from the place w he lies." H889
Ps 42: 3 say to me all day long, "W is your God?" H372
Ps 42:10 saying to me all day long, "W is your God?" H372
Ps 43: 3 holy mountain, to the **place** w you **dwell**. H5438
Ps 46: 4 the holy place w the Most High **dwells**. H5438
Ps 50: 1 from the rising of the sun to w it **sets**. H4427
Ps 53: 5 with dread, w there was nothing to dread. NDT
Ps 63: 1 a dry and parched land w there is no water. NDT
Ps 65: 8 your wonders; w morning **dawns**, where H4604
Ps 65: 8 morning dawns, w evening fades, you NDT
Ps 68:16 at the mountain w God chooses to reign NDT
Ps 68:16 w the LORD himself will dwell forever? NDT
Ps 69: 2 in the miry depths, w there is no foothold. NDT
Ps 74: 2 Mount Zion, w you dwelt. H928+2257S
Ps 74: 4 roared in the **place** w you **met** with us; H4595
Ps 74: 8 every **place** w God was **worshiped** in the H4595
Ps 79:10 should the nations say, "W is their God?" H372
Ps 84: 3 nest for herself, w she may have her young H889
Ps 89:49 w is your former great love, which in H372
Ps 95: 9 w your ancestors tested me; they tried me H889
Ps 107: 4 no way to a city w they could **settle**. H4632
Ps 107: 7 a straight way to a city w they could **settle**. H4632
Ps 107:36 they founded a **city** *w* they could settle. AIT
Ps 113: 3 the rising of the sun to the **place** w it **sets**, H4427
Ps 115: 2 Why do the nations say, "W is their God?" H372
Ps 121: 1 mountains—w does my help come from? H402
Ps 122: 4 That is w the tribes go up—the tribes of H9004
Ps 139: 7 W can I go from your Spirit? Where H625+2025
Ps 139: 7 W can I flee from your presence H625+2025
Ps 142: 3 In the path w I walk people have hidden H2306
Pr 1:17 to spread a net w every bird can see it! H928
Pr 8: 2 point along the way, w the paths meet, she NDT
Pr 13:10 W there is strife, there is pride, but wisdom H928
Pr 14: 4 W there are no oxen, the manger is empty H928
Pr 29:18 W there is no revelation, people cast off H928
Pr 31:23 w he takes his seat among the elders of H928
Ecc 1: 5 sun sets, and hurries back to w it rises. H5226S
Ecc 8:10 receive praise in the city w they did this. H889
Ecc 9:10 realm of the dead, w you are going H9004+2025
Ecc 11: 3 in the place w it falls, there it will H8611
SS 1: 7 w you graze your flock and where you rest H377
SS 1: 7 graze your flock and w you rest your sheep H377
SS 6: 1 W has your beloved gone, most H625+2025
Isa 7:23 in every place w there were a thousand H9004
Isa 7:25 **places** w cattle are **turned loose** and H5448
Isa 7:25 cattle are turned loose and w sheep **run**. H5330
Isa 10: 3 W will you leave your riches H625+2025
Isa 19:12 W are your wise men now? Let them show H361
Isa 29: 1 Ariel, Ariel, the **city** *w* David settled! AIT
Isa 33:18 the former terror: "W is that chief officer H372
Isa 33:18 W is the one who took the revenue H372
Isa 33:18 W is the officer in charge of the towers?" H372
Isa 35: 7 In the haunts w jackals once **lay**, grass H8070
Isa 36:19 W are the gods of Hamath and Arpad H372
Isa 36:19 W are the gods of Sepharvaim H372
Isa 37:13 W is the king of Hamath or the king of H372
Isa 37:13 W are the kings of Lair, Sepharvaim, Hena NDT
Isa 37:28 "But I know *w* you **are** and when you come AIT
Isa 39: 3 those men say, and w did they come from?" H402
Isa 42:11 let the settlements w Kedar lives rejoice. NDT
Isa 49:21 but these—w have they come **from**? H407
Isa 50: 1 "W is your mother's certificate of H361+2296
Isa 51:13 For w is the wrath of the oppressor? H372
Isa 63:11 w is he who brought them through the sea H372
Isa 63:11 W is he who set his Holy Spirit among H372
Isa 63:15 W are your zeal and your might H372
Isa 64:11 w our ancestors praised you H889
Isa 66: 1 W is the house you will build for me H361+2296
Isa 66: 1 W will my resting place be H361+2296
Jer 2: 6 They did not ask, 'W is the LORD, who H372
Jer 2: 6 a land w no one travels and no one lives? H9004
Jer 2: 8 priests did not ask, 'W is the LORD?' Those H372
Jer 2:28 W then are the gods you made for H372
Jer 3: 2 Is there *any place* w you have not been H407
Jer 6:16 ancient paths, ask w the good way is H361+2296
Jer 7:12 to the place in Shiloh w I first made a H9004
Jer 13: 7 it from the place w I had hidden it, H9004+2025
Jer 13:20 W is the flock that was entrusted to you H372
Jer 15: 2 if they ask you, 'W shall we go?' tell H625+2025
Jer 16: 5 "Do not enter a **house** *w there* is a funeral AIT
Jer 16: 8 do not enter a **house** *w there* is feasting AIT
Jer 16:15 the countries w he had banished H9004+2025
Jer 17: 6 of the desert, in a salt land w no one lives. NDT
Jer 17:15 saying to me, "W is the word of the LORD? H372
Jer 19:13 all the houses w they burned incense on H889
Jer 19:14 w the LORD had sent him to prophesy H9004
Jer 22:12 will die in the place w they have led him H9004
Jer 22:26 country, w neither of you was born H9004
Jer 23: 3 of all the countries w I have driven them H9004
Jer 23: 3 w they will be fruitful and increase in NDT
Jer 23: 8 all the countries w he had banished them H9004
Jer 29:14 nations and places w I have banished you H9004
Jer 29:18 among all the nations w I drive them. H9004
Jer 31: 9 on a level path w they will not H928+2023S
Jer 31:40 The whole **valley** *w* dead bodies and ashes AIT
Jer 32: 5 w he will remain until I deal with him H9004
Jer 32:29 with the houses w the people aroused my H889
Jer 32:37 from all the lands w I banish them in my H9004
Jer 34:16 slaves you had set free to go w they wished. NDT
Jer 35: 7 long time in the land w you are nomads. H9004
Jer 36:12 w all the officials were sitting: H9004
Jer 36:19 Don't let anyone know w you are." H407
Jer 37:16 a dungeon, w he remained a long time. H9004
Jer 37:17 to the palace, w he asked him privately NDT
Jer 37:19 W are your prophets who prophesied to you, H372
Jer 38: 9 w he will starve to death when there is no H9393
Jer 39: 5 w he pronounced sentence on him. NDT
Jer 40:12 from all the countries w they had been H9004
Jer 41: 9 Now the cistern w he threw all the bodies H9004
Jer 42: 3 will tell us w we should go and H2021+2006S
Jer 42:14 w we will not see war or hear the trumpet H889
Jer 42:22 plague in the place w you want to go to H9004
Jer 43: 5 from all the nations w they had been H9004
Jer 44: 8 gods in Egypt, w you have come to live? H9004
Jer 49:36 not be a nation w Elam's exiles do not H9004
Jer 51:37 of horror and scorn, a place w no one lives. NDT
Jer 51:43 desert land, a land w no one lives H928+2177S
Jer 52: 9 w he pronounced sentence on him. NDT
Jer 52:11 w he put him in prison till the day of his NDT
La 2:12 to their mothers, "W is bread and wine?" H372
Eze 3:12 rose from the **place** w it was **standing**. H5226
Eze 3:15 And **there**, *w* they were living, I sat among AIT
Eze 4:13 among the nations w I will drive them." H9004
Eze 6: 9 Then in the nations w they have been H9004
Eze 6:13 places w they offered fragrant incense to H9004
Eze 8: 3 w the idol that provokes to jealousy stood. H9004
Eze 9: 3 above the cherubim, w it had been, and H889
Eze 11:16 them in the countries w they have gone. H9004
Eze 11:17 from the countries w you have been H889
Eze 12: 3 set out and go from w you are to another H5226S
Eze 12:16 so that in the nations w they go they may H9004
Eze 13:12 "W is the whitewash you covered it with?" H372
Eze 16:16 w you carried on your prostitution. H6584+2157S
Eze 17: 4 w he planted it in a city of traders. NDT
Eze 17: 7 him from the **plot** *w* it was planted and AIT
Eze 17:10 strikes it—wither away in the **plot** *w* it grew? AIT
Eze 20:34 you from the countries w you have been H889
Eze 20:38 bring them out of the **land** *w* they are living, AIT
Eze 20:41 you from the countries w you have been H889
Eze 21:19 Make a signpost w the road branches off to H928
Eze 21:22 Jerusalem, w he is to set up battering rams NDT
Eze 21:30 In the place w you were created, in the H889
Eze 24: 7 it on the ground, w the dust would cover it. NDT
Eze 28:25 Israel from the nations w they have been H889
Eze 29:13 from the nations w they were H9004+2025
Eze 34:12 from all the places w they were scattered H9004
Eze 36:21 the nations w they had gone. H9004+2025
Eze 36:22 among the nations w you have gone. H9004
Eze 37:21 out of the nations w they have gone. H9004
Eze 37:25 the land w your ancestors lived. H889
Eze 40:38 w the burnt offerings were washed. H9004
Eze 42:13 w the priests who approach the LORD will H9004
Eze 43: 7 This is w I will live among the Israelites H9004
Eze 44:19 outer court w the people H2021+2958+2021+2667S
Eze 46:20 "This is the place w the priests are to cook H9004
Eze 46:24 are the kitchens w those who minister at H9004
Eze 47: 8 into the Arabah, w it enters the Dead Sea. NDT
Eze 47: 9 so w the river flows everything will H9004+2025
Da 6:10 to his upstairs room w the windows opened NDT
Da 8:17 he came near the **place** w I was **standing**, H6642
Da 9: 7 in all the countries w you have scattered H9004
Hos 1:10 In the place w it was said to them, 'You are H889
Hos 4:13 terebinth, w the shade is pleasant. H3954
Hos 13:10 W is your king, that he may save you H180+686
Hos 13:10 W are your rulers in all your towns, of whom NDT
Hos 13:14 them from death. W, O death, are your H180
Hos 13:14 are your plagues? W, O grave, is your H180
Joel 2:17 say among the peoples, 'W is their God? H372
Jnh 1: 3 w he found a ship bound for that port. NDT
Jnh 1: 5 w he lay down and fell into a deep sleep. NDT
Jnh 1: 8 of work do you do? W do you come from H402
Mic 1:13 You are w the sin of Daughter Zion began NDT
Mic 7:10 who said to me, "W is the LORD your God?" H361
Na 2:11 W now is the lions' den, the place where H372
Na 2:11 the **place** w they **fed** their young H5337
Na 2:11 their young, w the lion and lioness went H9004
Na 3: 7 W can I find anyone to comfort you?" H4946+402
Na 3:17 they fly away, and no one knows w. H5226+361
Hab 3: 4 from his hand, w his power was hidden. H9004
Zep 3:19 honor in every **land** *w* they have suffered AIT
Zec 1: 5 W are your ancestors now? And the H372
Zec 2: 2 I asked, "W are you going?" He H625+2025
Zec 5:10 "W are they taking the basket?" H625+2025
Zec 7:14 all the nations, w they were strangers. H889
Mal 1: 6 If I am a father, w is the honor due me? If I H372
Mal 1: 6 If I am a master, w is the respect due me?" H372
Mal 1:11 from w the sun **rises** to where it sets. H4667
Mal 1:11 from where the sun rises to w it **sets**. H4427
Mal 2:17 with them" or "W is the God of justice?" H372
Mt 2: 2 "W is the one who has been born king of *G4544*
Mt 2: 4 he asked them w the Messiah was to be *G4544*
Mt 2: 9 it stopped over **the place** w the child was. *G4023*
Mt 2:15 w he stayed until the death of Herod. *G1695*
Mt 3: 7 Sadducees coming **to** w he was baptizing, *G2093*
Mt 6:19 on earth, w moths and vermin destroy *G3963*
Mt 6:19 destroy, and w thieves break in and steal. *G3963*
Mt 6:20 w moths and vermin do not destroy *G3963*

Mt 6:20 w thieves do not break in and steal. G3963
Mt 6:21 For w your treasure is, there your heart will G3963
Mt 8:12 w there will be weeping and gnashing of G1695
Mt 13: 5 rocky places, w it did not have much soil. G3963
Mt 13: 8 fell on good soil, w it produced a crop—a NDT
Mt 13:27 W then did the weeds come from?' G4470
Mt 13:42 w there will be weeping and gnashing of G1695
Mt 13:50 w there will be weeping and gnashing of G1695
Mt 13:54 "W did this man get this wisdom and G4470
Mt 13:56 W then did this man get all these things?" G4470
Mt 15:33 "W could we get enough bread in this G4470
Mt 18:20 For w two or three gather in my name G4023
Mt 21:17 the city to Bethany, w he spent the night. G1695
Mt 21:25 baptism—w did it come from? Was it from G4470
Mt 22:13 w there will be weeping and gnashing of G1695
Mt 24:51 w there will be weeping and gnashing of G1695
Mt 25:24 harvesting w you have not sown and G3963
Mt 25:24 sown and gathering w you have not G3854
Mt 25:26 knew that I harvest w I have not sown G3963
Mt 25:26 not sown and gather w I have not G3854
Mt 25:30 w there will be weeping and gnashing of G1695
Mt 26:17 "W do you want us to make preparations G4544
Mt 26:57 w the teachers of the law and the elders G3963
Mt 26:71 w another servant girl saw him and said to NDT
Mt 28: 6 Come and see the place w he lay. G3963
Mt 28:16 to the mountain w Jesus had told them to G4023
Mk 1:35 went off to a solitary place, w he prayed. G2795
Mk 4: 5 rocky places, w it did not have much soil. G3963
Mk 4:15 seed along the path, w the word is sown. G3963
Mk 5:40 with him, and went in w the child was. G3963
Mk 6: 2 "W did this man get these things? G4470
Mk 8: 4 "But w in this remote place can anyone G4470
Mk 9: 2 up a high mountain, w they were all alone. NDT
Mk 9:30 did not want anyone to know w they were, NDT
Mk 9:43 to go into hell, w the fire never goes out. NDT
Mk 9:48 w " 'the worms that eat them do not die G3963
Mk 12:41 the place w the offerings were put and G1126
Mk 13:14 standing w it does not belong— G3963
Mk 14:12 "W do you want us to go and make G4544
Mk 14:14 W is my guest room, where I may eat the G4544
Mk 14:14 w I may eat the Passover with my G3963
Mk 15:47 the mother of Joseph saw w he was laid. G4544
Mk 16: 6 See the place w they laid him. G3963
Lk 1:40 w she entered Zechariah's home and NDT
Lk 4: 2 w for forty days he was tempted by the devil NDT
Lk 4:16 to Nazareth, w he had been brought up G4023
Lk 4:17 he found the place w it is written: G4023
Lk 4:42 him and when they came to w he was, G2401
Lk 8:25 "W is your faith?" he asked his disciples G4544
Lk 10: 1 town and place w he was about to go. G4023
Lk 10:33 as he traveled, came w the man was; and G2848
Lk 10:38 came to a village w a woman named NDT
Lk 11:33 puts it in a place *w it will be* hidden, AIT
Lk 12:33 w no thief comes near and no moth G3963
Lk 12:34 For w your treasure is, there your heart will G3963
Lk 13:25 'I don't know you or w you come from. G4470
Lk 13:27 'I don't know you or w you come from. G4470
Lk 16:23 In Hades, w he was in torment, he looked up NDT
Lk 17:17 all ten cleansed? W are the other nine? G4544
Lk 17:37 "W, Lord?" they asked. He replied G4544
Lk 17:37 He replied, "W there is a dead body G3963
Lk 19:37 near the place w the road goes down the G2853
Lk 20: 7 answered, "We don't know w it was from." G4470
Lk 22: 9 "W do you want us to prepare for it?" G4544
Lk 22:11 W is the guest room, where I may eat the G4544
Lk 22:11 w I may eat the Passover with my G3963
Jn 1:28 side of the Jordan, w John was baptizing. G3963
Jn 1:38 means "Teacher"), "w are you staying?" G4544
Jn 1:39 So they went and saw w he was staying G4544
Jn 2: 9 He did not realize w it had come from G4470
Jn 3: 8 cannot tell w it comes from or where it is G4470
Jn 3: 8 tell where it comes from or w it is going. G4544
Jn 3:22 w he spent some time with them G1695
Jn 4:11 W can you get this living water G4470
Jn 4:20 claim that the place w we must worship is G3963
Jn 4:46 w he had turned the water into wine. G3963
Jn 6: 5 "W shall we buy bread for these people G4470
Jn 6:17 w they got into a boat and set off across the NDT
Jn 6:21 the shore w they were heading G1650+4005
Jn 6:23 near the place w the people had eaten G3963
Jn 6:62 Son of Man ascend *to* w he was before! G3963
Jn 7:11 watching for Jesus and asking, "W is he?" G4544
Jn 7:27 But we know w this man is from; when the G4470
Jn 7:27 no one will know w he is from. G4470
Jn 7:28 you know me, and you know w I am from. G4470
Jn 7:34 not find me; and w I am, you cannot G3963
Jn 7:35 "W does this man intend to go that we G4544
Jn 7:35 Will he go w our people live scattered G1650
Jn 7:36 not find me,' and 'W I am, you cannot G3963
Jn 7:42 from Bethlehem, the town w David lived?" G3963
Jn 8: 2 w all the people gathered around him NDT
Jn 8:10 up and asked her, "Woman, w are they? G4544
Jn 8:14 I know w I came from and where I am G4470
Jn 8:14 where I came from and w I am going. G4544
Jn 8:14 have no idea w I come from or where I G4470
Jn 8:14 idea where I come from or w I am going. G4544
Jn 8:19 they asked him, "W is your father?" "You G4544
Jn 8:20 near the place w the offerings were put. G1126
Jn 8:21 die in your sin. W I go, you cannot come G3963
Jn 8:22 Is that why he says, 'W I go, you cannot G3963
Jn 9:12 "W is this man?" they asked him. "I don't G4544
Jn 9:29 we don't even know w he comes from." G4470
Jn 9:30 You don't know w he comes from, yet he G4470
Jn 10:40 Jordan to the place w John had been G3963
Jn 11: 6 he stayed w he was two G1877+4005+5536
Jn 11:30 still at the place w Martha had met him. G3963
Jn 11:32 Mary reached the place w Jesus was and G3963
Jn 11:34 "W have you laid him?" he asked. "Come G4544
Jn 11:54 Ephraim, w he stayed with his disciples. G2795
Jn 11:57 who found out w Jesus was should G4544
Jn 12: 1 came to Bethany, w Lazarus lived, whom G3963
Jn 12:26 must follow me; and w I am, my servant G3963
Jn 12:35 the dark does not know w they are going. G4544
Jn 13:33 so I tell you now: W I am going, you G3963
Jn 13:36 Peter asked him, "Lord, w are you going?" G4544
Jn 13:36 Jesus replied, "W I am going, you cannot G3963
Jn 14: 3 be with me that you also may be w I am. G3963
Jn 14: 4 know the way *to the place* w I am going." G3963
Jn 14: 5 we don't know w you are going, so G4544
Jn 16: 5 None of you asks me, 'W are you going?' G4544
Jn 16:10 to the Father, w you can see me no longer; NDT
Jn 17:24 you have given me to be with me w I am, G3963
Jn 18:20 the temple, w all the Jews come together. G3963
Jn 19: 9 "W do you come from?" he asked G4470
Jn 19:20 the place w Jesus was crucified was G3963
Jn 19:41 At the place w Jesus was crucified, there G3963
Jn 20: 2 we don't know w they have put him!" G4544
Jn 20:10 went back to w they were staying. G899S
Jn 20:12 in white, seated w Jesus' body had been G3963
Jn 20:13 "and I don't know w they have put him." G4544
Jn 20:15 him away, tell me w you have put him G4544
Jn 20:25 put my finger w the nails G1650+3836+5596S
Jn 21:18 dressed yourself and went w you wanted; G3963
Jn 21:18 you and lead you w you do not want to go G3963
Ac 1:13 upstairs to the room w they were staying. G4023
Ac 1:25 left to go w he belongs." G1650+3836+5536
Ac 2: 2 the whole house w they were sitting. G4023
Ac 3: 2 w he was put every day to beg from those G4005
Ac 4:31 the place w they were meeting was G1877+4005
Ac 7: 4 him to this land w you are now G1650+4005
Ac 7:15 down to Egypt, w he and our ancestors died. NDT
Ac 7:29 w he settled as a foreigner and had two G4023
Ac 7:33 the place w you are standing is G2093+4005
Ac 7:49 Or w will my resting place be G5515
Ac 10:17 Cornelius found out w Simon's house was NDT
Ac 11: 5 four corners, and it came down to w I was. G948
Ac 11:11 at the house w I was staying. G1877+4005
Ac 12:12 w many people had gathered and were G4023
Ac 13:13 w John left them to return to Jerusalem. NDT
Ac 14: 7 w they continued to preach the gospel. G2795
Ac 14:26 w they had been committed to the grace G3854
Ac 15:30 w they gathered the church together and NDT
Ac 15:35 w they and many others taught and NDT
Ac 15:36 in all the towns w we preached the G1877+4005
Ac 16: 1 w a disciple named Timothy lived G1695
Ac 16:13 w we expected to find a place of prayer. G4023
Ac 16:40 w they met with the brothers and sisters NDT
Ac 17: 1 w there was a Jewish synagogue. G3963
Ac 17:19 of the Areopagus, w they said to him, "May NDT
Ac 18:19 at Ephesus, w Paul left Priscilla and Aquila. NDT
Ac 20: 3 w he stayed three months. Because some NDT
Ac 20: 6 others at Troas, w we stayed seven days. G3963
Ac 20: 8 in the upstairs room w we were meeting. G4023
Ac 20:13 w we were going to take Paul aboard. G1696
Ac 21: 3 w our ship was to unload its cargo. G1698
Ac 21: 7 w we greeted the brothers and sisters and NDT
Ac 21:16 of Mnason, w we were to stay. G4123+4005
Ac 25: 2 w the chief priests and the Jewish leaders NDT
Ac 25:10 Caesar's court, w I ought to be tried. G4023
Ac 27:39 w they decided to run the ship G1650+4005
Ac 28:23 numbers to the place w he was staying. G3825
Ro 3:27 W, then, is boasting? It is excluded G4544
Ro 4:15 And w there is no law there is no G4023
Ro 5:13 against anyone's account *w there* is no law. AIT
Ro 5:20 But w sin increased, grace increased all G4023
Ro 9:26 "In the very place w it was said to them G4023
Ro 15:20 preach the gospel w Christ was not known G3963
1Co 1:20 W is the wise person? Where is the G4544
1Co 1:20 W is the teacher of the law G4544
1Co 1:20 W is the philosopher of this age G4544
1Co 12:17 w would the sense of hearing be? G4544
1Co 12:17 w would the sense of smell be? G4544
1Co 12:19 were all one part, w would the body be? G4544
1Co 13: 8 But w there are prophecies, they will G1664
1Co 13: 8 they will cease; w there are tongues, they G1664
1Co 13: 8 they will be stilled; w there is knowledge G1664
1Co 15:55 "W, O death, is your victory? Where, G4544
1Co 15:55 is your victory? W, O death, is your sting?" G4544
2Co 3:17 is the Spirit, and w the Spirit of the Lord is G4023
Gal 4:15 W, then, is your blessing of me now? I can G4544
Col 3: 1 on things above, w Christ is, seated at G4023
Heb 2: 6 But there is a place w someone has G4543
Heb 3: 9 w your ancestors tested and tried me G4023
Heb 6:20 w our forerunner, Jesus, has entered on G3963
Heb 10:18 And w these have been forgiven, sacrifice G3963
Heb 11: 8 though he did not know w he was going. G4544
Jas 3:16 For w you have envy and selfish ambition G3963
2Pe 3: 4 will say, "W is this 'coming' he promised? G4544
2Pe 3:13 new earth, w righteousness dwells. G1877+4005
1Jn 2:11 They do not know w they are going G4544
Rev 2:13 I know w you live—where Satan has his G4544
Rev 2:13 where you live—w Satan has his throne. G3963
Rev 2:13 put to death in your city—w Satan lives. G3963
Rev 7:13 who are they, and w did they come from?" G4470
Rev 11: 8 Egypt—w also their Lord was crucified. G3963
Rev 12: 6 w she might be taken care of for 1,260 G1695
Rev 12:14 w she would be taken care of for a time G3963
Rev 17:15 "The waters you saw, w the prostitute sits G4023
Rev 18:19 w all who had ships on the sea G1877+4005
Rev 20:10 w the beast and the false prophet had G3963

WHEREVER (67) [WHERE]

Ge 20:15 "My land is before you; live w you like." H928
Ge 28:15 will watch over you w you go, H928+3972+889
Ge 30:30 has blessed you w I have been. H4200+8079
Ge 35: 3 with me w I have gone." H2021+928+889+2006
Ex 5:11 get your own straw w you can find it, H4946+889
Ex 12:20 W you live, you must eat H928+3972
Ex 20:24 W I cause my name to be honored H928+3972+2021+5226+889
Lev 3:17 the generations to come, w you live: H928+3972
Lev 7:26 And w you live, you must not eat the H928+3972
Lev 23: 3 not to do any work; w you live, it is a H928+3972
Lev 23:14 the generations to come, w you live. H928+3972
Lev 23:17 From *w* you live, bring two loaves made of AIT
Lev 23:21 the generations to come, w you live. H928+3972
Lev 23:31 the generations to come, w you live. H928+3972
Nu 9:17 set out; w the cloud settled H928+5226+889
Nu 35:29 the generations to come, w you live. H928+3972
Dt 11:25 fear of you on the whole land, w you go. H889
Dt 21:14 pleased with her, let her go w she wishes. H4200
Dt 23:16 among you w they like H928+2021+5226+889
Dt 30: 1 them to heart w the LORD your H889+9004+2025
Jos 1: 7 may be successful w you go. H928+3972+889
Jos 1: 9 God will be with you w you go." H928+3972+889
Jos 1:16 and w you send us we will go. H448+3972+889
1Sa 14:47 W he turned, he inflicted H928+3972+889
2Sa 7: 7 W I have moved with all the H928+3972+889
2Sa 7: 9 with you w you have gone H928+3972+889
2Sa 8: 6 gave David victory w he went. H928+3972+889
2Sa 8:14 gave David victory w he went. H928+3972+889
2Sa 15:21 w my lord the king may be H928+5226+889
2Sa 17:12 attack him w he may be H928+285+2021+5226+889
1Ki 2: 3 in all you do and w you go H3972+889+9004
1Ki 8:44 w you send them H928+2021+2006+889
2Ki 8: 1 family and stay for a while w you can, H928+889
2Ki 11: 8 close to the king w he goes." H928+3655+2256+928+995
1Ch 17: 6 W I have moved with all the H928+3972+889
1Ch 17: 8 with you w you have gone H928+3972+889
1Ch 18: 6 gave David victory w he went. H928+3972+889
1Ch 18:13 gave David victory w he went. H928+3972+889
2Ch 6:34 w you send them H928+2021+2006+889
2Ch 23: 7 close to the king w he goes." H928+995+2256+928+3655
Ne 4:12 times over, "W you turn H4946+3972+2021+5226
Ne 4:20 W you hear the sound of the H928+5226+889
Ps 119:54 are the theme of my song w I lodge. H928
Jer 8: 3 W I banish them, all the H928+3972+2021+5226
Jer 24: 9 w I banish them. H928+3972+2021+5226+889
Jer 40: 4 lies before you; go w you please." H9004+2025
Jer 45: 5 but w you go I will let H6584+3972+2021+5226+889
Eze 1:12 W the spirit would go, they would H9004+2025
Eze 1:20 W the spirit would go, they would go, and H9004
Eze 6: 6 W you live, the towns will be laid H928+3972
Eze 6:14 the desert to Diblah—w they live. H928+3972
Eze 21:16 to the left, w your blade is turned. H625+2025
Eze 36:20 And w they went among the nations they H889
Eze 47: 9 will live w the river flows. H448+3972+889
Da 2:38 W they live, he has A10089+10353+10168
Mt 8:19 I will follow you w you go. G3963+1569
Mt 24:28 W there is a carcass, there the G3963+1569
Mt 26:13 w this gospel is preached G3963+1569
Mk 6:55 the sick on mats to w they heard he was. G3963
Mk 6:56 And w he went—into villages, towns G3963+323
Mk 14: 9 w the gospel is preached G3963+1569
Lk 9:57 him, "I will follow you w you go." G3963+1569
Jn 3: 8 The wind blows w it pleases. You hear its G3963
Ac 8: 4 scattered preached the word *w they* went. AIT
1Co 16: 6 can help me on my journey, w I go. G4023+1569
Jas 3: 4 a very small rudder w the pilot wants to G3963
Rev 14: 4 They follow the Lamb w he goes G3963+323

WHET (KJV) SHARPEN, UNSHARPENED

WHETHER (121)

Ge 17:13 *W* born in your household or bought with AIT
Ge 24:21 her closely to learn w or not the LORD had H2022
Ge 27:21 to know w you really are my son Esau H2022
Ge 31:32 see for yourself w there is anything of H4537
Ge 37:32 Examine it to see w it is your son's H561+4202
Ge 42:33 is how I will know w you are honest men: H3954
Ex 12:19 And anyone, w foreigner or native-born H928
Ex 13: 2 belongs to me, w human or animal." H928
Ex 16: 4 them and see w they will H2022+561+4202
Ex 21:16 w the victim has been sold or is still in the H2256
Ex 22: 4 possession—w ox or donkey or sheep H4946
Ex 22: 8 must determine w the owner of the H561+4202
Ex 34:19 males of your livestock, w from herd or flock. NDT
Lev 3: 1 from the herd, w male or female, you H561
Lev 5: 2 (w the carcass of an unclean animal H196
Lev 5: 4 to do anything, w good or evil (in any H196
Lev 7:10 offering, w mixed with olive oil or dry H2256
Lev 7:21 w human uncleanness or an unclean H196
Lev 11:10 w among all the swarming things or H2256

W

Lev 11:32 **w** it is made of wood, cloth, hide **or** H196
Lev 11:42 **w** it moves on its belly **or** walks on all H2256
Lev 15: 3 **W** it continues flowing from his body **or** is H196
Lev 15:23 **W** it is the bed or anything she was sitting H561
Lev 16:29 **w** native-born **or** a foreigner residing H2256
Lev 17:15 " '**A**nyone, **w** native-born or foreigner, who H928
Lev 18: 9 **w** she was born in the same home **or** H196
Lev 22:18 **w** an Israelite **or** a foreigner residing in H2256
Lev 24:16 **W** foreigner **or** native-born, when they H3869
Lev 27:26 belongs to the LORD; **w** an ox or a sheep, it H561
Lev 27:28 **w** a human being or an animal or family H4946
Lev 27:30 **w** grain from the soil or fruit from the trees H4946
Nu 3:13 firstborn in Israel, **w** human or animal. H4946
Nu 4:27 **w** carrying or doing other work H4200
Nu 8:17 male in Israel, **w** human or animal, is mine H928
Nu 9:21 **W** by day or by night, whenever the cloud H196
Nu 9:22 **W** the cloud stayed over the tabernacle H196
Nu 11:23 Now you will see **w** or not what I say will H2022
Nu 13:18 the land is like and **w** the people who live H2022
Nu 15: 3 to the LORD—**w** burnt offerings **or** sacrifices H196
Nu 15:29 **w** a native-born Israelite **or** a foreigner H2021
Nu 15:30 sins defiantly, **w** native-born **or** foreigner H2256
Nu 18: 9 offerings, **w** grain **or** sin or guilt offerings H2256
Nu 31:28 of every five hundred, **w** people, cattle, H4946
Nu 31:30 one out of every fifty, **w** people, cattle, H4946
Dt 1:16 **w** the case is between two Israelites **or** H2256
Dt 4:16 **w** formed like a man **or** a woman, H196
Dt 8: 2 **w** or not you would keep his commands. H2022
Dt 13: 3 you to find out **w** you love him with all H2022
Dt 13: 7 around you, **w** near **or** far, from one end H196
Dt 17: 8 you to judge—**w** bloodshed, lawsuits H1068
Dt 23:19 **w** on money or food or anything else that NDT
Dt 24:14 **w** that worker is a fellow Israelite **or** a H196
Jos 24:15 **w** the gods your ancestors served beyond H561
Jdg 2:22 test Israel and see **w** they will keep the H2022
Jdg 3: 4 Israelites to see **w** they would obey the H2022
Jdg 18: 5 of God to learn **w** our journey will be H2022
Ru 3:10 run after the younger men, **w** rich or poor. H561
1Sa 14: 6 LORD from saving, **w** by many **or** by few." H196
2Sa 15:21 the king may be, **w** it means life or death H561
1Ki 16:11 spare a single male, **w** relative or friend. H2256
2Ki 14:26 in Israel, **w** slave or free, was H2256+700
2Ch 15:13 to be put to death, **w** small or great, man H4946
2Ch 19:10 **w** bloodshed or other concerns of the law H1068
2Ch 20: 9 **w** the sword of judgment, **or** plague or H2256
Est 3: 4 about it to see **w** Mordecai's behavior H2022
Job 31:13 of my servants, **w** male **or** female, when H2256
Ps 58: 9 of the thorns—**w** they be green or dry H4017
Ecc 2:19 And who knows **w** that person will be wise H2022
Ecc 5:12 a laborer is sweet, **w** they eat little or much H561
Ecc 9: 1 no one knows **w** love or hate awaits H1685
Ecc 11: 3 **W** a tree falls to the south or to the north H561
Ecc 11: 6 which will succeed, **w** this or that, or H2022
Ecc 11: 6 this or that, or **w** both will do equally well. H561
Ecc 12:14 every hidden thing, **w** it is good or evil. H561
Isa 7:11 **w** in the deepest depths **or** in the highest H196
Isa 30:21 **W** you turn to the right or to the left, your H3954
Isa 41:23 Do something, **w** good or bad, so that we H677
Jer 24: 8 **w** they remain in this land **or** live in Egypt. H2256
Jer 42: 6 **W** it is favorable or unfavorable, we will H561
Eze 2: 5 And **w** they listen or fail to listen—for they H561
Eze 2: 7 words to them, **w** they listen or fail to listen H561
Eze 3:11 LORD says,' **w** they listen or fail to listen." H561
Eze 44:31 not eat anything, **w** bird or animal, found H4946
Eze 46:12 **w** a burnt offering **or** fellowship offerings H4946
Mk 4:27 Night and day, **w** he sleeps **or** gets up, the *G2779*
Mk 13:35 will come back—**w** in the evening, or *G2445*
Lk 14:31 down and consider **w** he is able with ten *G1623*
Jn 7:17 of God will find out **w** my teaching comes *G4538*
Jn 7:17 comes from God or **w** I speak on my own. NDT
Jn 9:25 replied, "**W** he is a sinner **or not**, I don't *G1623*
Ac 9: 2 to the Way, **w** men or women, he *G5445*
Ro 6:16 the one you obey—**w** you are slaves to sin *G2486*
Ro 14: 8 **w** we live or die, we belong to *G1569+5445*
1Co 3:22 **w** Paul or Apollos or Cephas or the world *G1664*
1Co 7:16 wife, **w** you will save your husband? *G1623*
1Co 7:16 husband, **w** you will save your wife? *G1623*
1Co 8: 5 so-called gods, **w** in heaven or on earth *G1664*
1Co 10:31 So **w** you eat or drink or whatever you do *G1664*
1Co 10:32 anyone to stumble, **w** Jews, Greeks or the *G2779*
1Co 12:13 as to form one body—**w** Jews or Gentiles *G1664*
1Co 15:11 **W**, then, it is I or they, this is what we *G1664*
2Co 5: 9 **w** we are at home in the body or away *G1664*
2Co 5:10 done while in the body, **w** good or bad. *G1664*
2Co 12: 2 **W** it was in the body or out of the body I *G1664*
2Co 12: 3 **w** in the body or apart from the body I do *G1664*
2Co 13: 5 yourselves to see **w** you are in the faith; *G1623*
Eph 6: 8 good they do, **w** they are slave or free. *G1664*
Php 1: 7 **w** I am in chains **or** defending and *G2779*
Php 1:18 in every way, **w** from false motives or true *G1664*
Php 1:20 exalted in my body, **w** by life or by death. *G1664*
Php 1:27 **w** I come and see you or only hear about *G1664*
Php 4:12 every situation, **w** well fed or hungry *G2779*
Php 4:12 hungry, **w** living in plenty or in want. *G2779*
Col 1:16 **w** thrones or powers or rulers or *G1664*
Col 1:20 **w** things on earth or things in heaven *G1664*
Col 3:17 whatever you do, *w* in word **or** deed, do it all AIT
1Th 5:10 us so that, **w** we are awake or asleep *G1664*
2Th 2: 2 **w** by a prophecy or by word of mouth or by *G3612*
2Th 2:15 on to you, **w** by word of mouth or by letter. *G1664*
1Pe 2:13 **w** to the emperor, as the supreme *G1664*
1Jn 4: 1 test the spirits to see **w** they are from God, *G1623*

WHICH (696) [WHAT] See Index of Articles Etc.

WHILE (436) [MEANWHILE]

Ge 2:21 a deep sleep; and **w** he was sleeping, he H2256
Ge 4: 8 **W** they were in the field, Cain attacked his H928
Ge 11:28 **W** his father Terah was **still alive** H6584+7156
Ge 12:10 to Egypt to **live** there **for a w** because the H1591
Ge 13: 6 not support them **w** they stayed together, H4200
Ge 13:12 **w** Lot lived among the cities of the plain H2256
Ge 18: 1 great trees of Mamre **w** he was sitting at H2256
Ge 18: 8 **W** they ate, he stood near them under a H2256
Ge 20: 1 **For a w** *he* **stayed** in Gerar, H1591
Ge 21:21 **W** he was living in the Desert of Paran, his H2256
Ge 22: 5 here with the donkey **w** I and the boy go H2256
Ge 25: 6 But **w** he was still living, he gave gifts to the H928
Ge 25:27 **w** Jacob was content to stay at home H2256
Ge 26: 3 **Stay** in this land **for a w**, and I will be with H1591
Ge 27:11 Esau is a hairy man **w** I have smooth skin. H2256
Ge 27:44 Stay with him **for a w** until your H3427+285
Ge 29: 9 **W** he was **still** talking with them, Rachel H6388
Ge 30:36 **w** Jacob continued to tend the rest of H2256
Ge 33:14 **w** I move along slowly at the pace of the H2256
Ge 34:25 days later, **w** all of them were still in pain H928
Ge 35:16 **W** they were still some distance from H2256
Ge 35:22 **W** Israel was living in that region, Reuben H928
Ge 36:24 springs in the desert **w** he was grazing the H928
Ge 37: 7 **w** your sheaves gathered around mine H2256
Ge 39: 7 and **after a w** his H339+2021+1821+2021+465
Ge 39:20 **But w** Joseph was there in the prison H2256
Ge 42:19 **w** the rest of you go and take grain back H2256
Ge 47: 4 "We have come to **live** here **for a w** H1591
Ge 48: 7 the land of Canaan **w** we were still on the H928
Ex 16:10 **W** Aaron was speaking to the whole H3869
Ex 18:14 **w** all these people stand around you from H2256
Ex 20:21 **w** Moses approached the thick darkness H2256
Ex 22:10 injured or is taken away **w** no *one is* **looking**, AIT
Ex 22:14 is injured or dies **w** the owner **is not** present, AIT
Ex 33: 9 entrance, **w** the LORD spoke with Moses. H2256
Lev 14:46 into the house **w** it is closed up H3972+3427
Lev 15:26 on **w** her discharge **continues** will H3972+3427
Lev 18:18 relations with her **w** your wife is living. H928
Lev 25:22 **W** you plant during the eighth year, you H2256
Lev 26:43 will enjoy its sabbaths **w** it lies desolate H928
Nu 5:18 **w** he himself holds the bitter water that H2256
Nu 5:19 impure **w married to** your husband H9393
Nu 5:20 gone astray **w married to** your husband H9393
Nu 5:29 herself impure **w married to** her husband, H9393
Nu 11:33 But **w** the meat was **still** between their H6388
Nu 15:32 **W** the Israelites were in the wilderness, H2256
Nu 18:21 the work they do **w** serving at the tent of NDT
Nu 19: 5 **W** he watches, the heifer is to be burned— H4200
Nu 23: 3 here beside your offering **w** I go aside. H2256
Nu 23:15 your offering **w** I meet with him over H2256
Nu 25: 1 **W** Israel was staying in Shittim, the men H2256
Nu 25: 6 assembly of Israel **w** they were weeping H2256
Nu 32: 6 fellow Israelites go to war **w** you sit here? H2256
Dt 4:11 foot of the mountain **w** it blazed with fire H2256
Dt 5:23 **w** the mountain was ablaze with fire H2256
Dt 9:15 from the mountain **w** it was ablaze with H2256
Dt 22:21 by being promiscuous **w** still in her father's NDT
Dt 25: 4 Do not muzzle an ox **w** it is treading out H928
Dt 26:14 of the sacred portion **w** I was in mourning, H928
Dt 26:14 have I removed any of it **w** I was unclean, H928
Dt 31:27 against the LORD **w** I am still alive and with H928
Dt 32:42 with blood, **w** my sword devours flesh: H2256
Jos 3:16 **w** the water flowing down to the Sea of H2256
Jos 3:17 **w** all Israel passed by until the whole H2256
Jos 4:11 to the other side **w** the people watched. NDT
Jos 5:10 *w* **camped** at Gilgal on the plains of Jericho AIT
Jos 6:13 of the LORD, **w** the trumpets kept sounding. H2256
Jos 9:22 from you,' **w** actually you live near us? H2256
Jos 14:10 **w** Israel moved about in the wilderness. H889
Jdg 3:20 then approached him **w** he was sitting H2256
Jdg 3:26 **W** they waited, Ehud got away. H6330
Jdg 4:21 went quietly to him **w** he lay fast asleep, H2256
Jdg 7: 3 men left, **w** ten thousand remained. H2256
Jdg 7:21 **W** each man held his position around the H2256
Jdg 9:27 **W** they were eating and drinking, they H2256
Jdg 13: 9 again to the woman **w** she was out in the H2256
Jdg 13:19 an amazing thing **w** Manoah and his wife H2256
Jdg 13:25 began to stir him **w** he was in Mahaneh NDT
Jdg 16:13 So *w he was* **sleeping**, Delilah took the AIT
Jdg 16:25 **W** they were in high spirits, they shouted H3869
Jdg 16:30 many more when he died than **w** he lived. H928
Jdg 18:17 the household gods **w** the priest and the H2256
Jdg 19:22 *W* they *were* **enjoying** themselves, some of AIT
Jdg 20:32 **W** the Benjamites were saying, "We are H2256
Jdg 21:23 **W** the young women were dancing, each H4946
Ru 1: 1 went to **live for a w** in the country of Moab H1591
1Sa 2:13 fork in his hand **w** the meat was being H3869
1Sa 7:10 **W** Samuel was sacrificing the burnt H2256
1Sa 9:27 "but you stay here **for a w**, so H3869+2021+3427
1Sa 13:16 **w** the Philistines camped at Mikmash. H2256
1Sa 14:19 **W** Saul was talking to the priest, the H6330
1Sa 18:10 in his house, **w** David was playing the lyre H2256
1Sa 19: 9 **W** David was playing the lyre, H2256
1Sa 21:13 **w** he was in their hands he acted like a NDT
1Sa 23:15 **W** David was at Horesh in the Desert of H2256
1Sa 25: 4 **W** David was in the wilderness, he heard H2256
1Sa 25:13 **w** two hundred stayed with the supplies. H2256
1Sa 28: 4 **w** Saul gathered all Israel and set up H2256
2Sa 3: 1 **w** the house of Saul grew weaker and H2256
2Sa 3:35 David to eat something **w** it was still day; H928
2Sa 4: 5 in the heat of the day **w** he was taking his H2256
2Sa 4: 7 into the house **w** he was lying on the H2256
2Sa 5: 2 In the past, **w** Saul was king over us, you H928
2Sa 6:15 **w** he and all Israel were bringing up the H2256
2Sa 7: 2 **w** the ark of God remains in a tent." H2256
2Sa 10: 8 **w** the Arameans of Zobah and Rehob H2256
2Sa 11:16 So **w** Joab had the city under siege, he put H928
2Sa 12:18 they thought, "**W** the child was still living H928
2Sa 12:21 **W** the child was alive, you fasted H928+6288
2Sa 12:22 He answered, "**W** the child was still alive, H928
2Sa 13:30 **W** they were on their way, the report H2256
2Sa 15: 8 **W** your servant was living at Geshur in H928
2Sa 15:12 **W** Absalom was offering sacrifices, he also H928
2Sa 16:13 along the road **w** Shimei was going along H2256
2Sa 17: 2 I would attack him **w** he is weary and weak H2256
2Sa 18: 4 beside the gate **w** all his men marched H2256
2Sa 18: 9 **w** the mule he was riding kept on going. H2256
2Sa 18:14 heart **w** Absalom was **still** alive in the H6388
2Sa 18:24 **W** David was sitting between the inner H2256
2Sa 20: 8 **W** they were at the great rock in Gibeon NDT
2Sa 20:15 **W** they were battering the wall to bring it H2256
2Sa 23:13 **w** a band of Philistines was encamped in H2256
2Sa 24:13 from your enemies **w** they pursue you? H2256
1Ki 1:14 **W** you are **still** there talking to the king, H6388
1Ki 1:22 **W** she was **still** speaking with the king H6388
1Ki 3:17 I had a baby **w** she was there with me. NDT
1Ki 3:20 my son from my side **w** I your servant was H2256
1Ki 3:23 your son is dead,' **w** that one says, 'No! H2256
1Ki 6: 7 at the temple site **w** it was being built. H928
1Ki 6:27 **w** the wing of the other touched the other H2256
1Ki 8:14 **W** the whole assembly of Israel was H2256
1Ki 11:21 **W** he was in Egypt, Hadad heard that H2256
1Ki 13:20 **W** they were sitting at the table, the word H2256
1Ki 15:27 **w** Nadab and all Israel were besieging it. H2256
1Ki 18: 4 **W** Jezebel was killing off the LORD's H928
1Ki 18:13 what I did **w** Jezebel was killing the H928
1Ki 19: 4 **w** he himself went a day's journey into the H2256
1Ki 20:12 heard this message **w** he and the kings H3869
1Ki 20:16 set out at noon **w** Ben-Hadad and the H2256
1Ki 20:27 **w** the Arameans covered the countryside. H2256
1Ki 20:40 **W** your servant was busy here and there H2256
2Ki 3:15 **W** the harpist was playing, the hand of H3869
2Ki 4:38 **W** the company of the prophets was H2256
2Ki 6:33 **W** he was **still** talking to them, the H6388
2Ki 8: 1 your family and **stay for a w** wherever you H1591
2Ki 11: 3 the LORD for six years **w** Athaliah ruled the H2256
2Ki 13:21 Once *w* some Israelites *were* **burying** a man AIT
2Ki 17:41 **Even w** these people were worshiping the H2256
2Ki 19:37 *w* he *was* **worshiping** in the temple of his AIT
2Ki 23:29 **W** Josiah was king, Pharaoh Necho H928+3427
2Ki 24:11 came up to the city **w** his officers were H2256
1Ch 11: 2 In the past, even **w** Saul was king, you were H928
1Ch 11: 8 **w** Joab restored the rest of the city. H2256
1Ch 11:15 **w** a band of Philistines was encamped in H2256
1Ch 12: 1 **w** he was banished from the presence of H6388
1Ch 17: 1 **w** the ark of the covenant of the LORD is H2256
1Ch 19: 7 **w** the Ammonites were mustered from H2256
1Ch 19: 9 **w** the kings who had come were by H2256
1Ch 21:20 **W** Araunah was threshing wheat, he H2256
2Ch 3:11 the temple wall, **w** its other wing, also H2256
2Ch 6: 3 **W** the whole assembly of Israel was H2256
2Ch 13:13 so that *w he* **was** in front of Judah the AIT
2Ch 22: 8 **W** Jehu was executing judgment on the H3869
2Ch 22: 9 his men captured him **w** he was hiding in H2256
2Ch 22:12 of God for six years **w** Athaliah ruled the H2256
2Ch 25:16 **W** he was *still* speaking, the king said to H928
2Ch 26:19 **W** he was raging at the priests in their H928
2Ch 28:18 **w** the Philistines had raided towns in the H2256
2Ch 29:19 in his unfaithfulness **w** he was king. H928
2Ch 29:28 **w** the musicians played and the trumpets H2256
2Ch 30:21 **w** the Levites and priests praised the LORD H2256
2Ch 34: 3 of his reign, **w** he was **still** young, he H6388
2Ch 34:14 **W** they were bringing out the money that H928
2Ch 35:11 **w** the Levites skinned the animals. H2256
Ezr 3:12 being laid, **w** many others shouted for joy. H2256
Ezr 10: 1 **W** Ezra was praying and confessing H3869
Ezr 10: 6 **W** he was there, he ate no food and drank NDT
Ne 1: 1 **w** I was in the citadel of Susa, H2256
Ne 4:16 **w** the other half were equipped with H2256
Ne 6: 3 the work stop **w** I leave it and go H3869+889
Ne 7: 3 **W** the gatekeepers are still on duty, have H6330
Ne 8: 7 the people in the Law **w** the people were H2256
Ne 9:33 acted faithfully, **w** we acted wickedly. H2256
Ne 9:35 Even **w** they were in their kingdom, enjoying NDT
Ne 11: 1 **w** the remaining nine were to stay in their H2256
Ne 11: 4 **w** other people from both Judah and H2256
Ne 13: 6 But **w** all this was going on, I was not in H928
Est 6:14 **W** they were **still** talking with him, the H6388
Est 7: 8 molest the queen **w** she is with me in the NDT
Job 1:16 **W** he was **still** speaking, another H6388
Job 1:17 **W** he was **still** speaking, another H6388
Job 1:18 **W** he was **still** speaking, yet another H6330
Job 8:12 **W still** growing and uncut, they wither H6388
Job 10: 3 **w** you smile on the plans of the wicked? H2256
Job 21: 3 Bear with me **w** I speak, and after I have H2256
Job 24:24 *For a* **little w** they are exalted, and then H5071
Job 32:11 I waited **w** you spoke, I listened to your H4200
Job 32:11 **w** you were searching for words H6330
Job 38: 7 **w** the morning stars sang together and all H928
Ps 7: 7 **w** you sit enthroned over them on high. H2256
Ps 32: 6 pray to you **w** you may be found; H4200+6961

Ps 37:10 A little w, and the wicked will be H6388+5071
Ps 39: 1 on my mouth w in the presence of H928+6388
Ps 39: 3 W I meditated, the fire burned; then I H928
Ps 41: 6 falsely, w his heart gathers slander; then AIT
Ps 42: 3 night, w people say to me all day long H928
Ps 49:18 Though w they live they count themselves H928
Ps 63:11 w the mouths of liars will be silenced. H3954
Ps 68:13 Even w you sleep among the sheep pens H561
Ps 68:23 w the tongues of your dogs have their share." NDT
Ps 78:30 even w the food was still in their mouths, H6388
Ps 109:28 W they curse, may you bless; may those who AIT
Ps 119:17 Be good to your servant w I live, that I may AIT
Ps 137: 4 the songs of the LORD w in a foreign land? NDT
Ps 141:10 into their own nets, w I pass by in safety. H6330
Pr 31:15 She gets up w it is still night; she provides H928
Ecc 2:14 w the fool walks in the darkness H2256
Ecc 3:12 to be happy and to do good w they live. H928
Ecc 7:28 w I was still searching but not finding—I H6388
Ecc 9: 3 there is madness in their hearts w they live, H928
Ecc 10: 6 positions, w the rich occupy the low ones. H2256
Ecc 10: 7 w princes go on foot like slaves. H2256
Ecc 11: 9 are young, be happy w you are young, and H928
SS 1:12 W the king was at his table, my H6330+8611
Isa 22: 3 having fled w the enemy was still far away. NDT
Isa 26:20 a little w until his wrath H5071+8092
Isa 37:38 w he was worshiping in the temple of his AIT
Isa 55: 6 Seek the LORD w he may be found; call on H928
Isa 55: 6 he may be found; call on him w he is near. H928
Isa 63:18 For a little w your people possessed your H5203
Isa 65:24 w they are still speaking I will hear. H6388
Jer 7:13 W you were doing all these things H3610
Jer 15: 9 Her sun will set w it is still day; she will be H928
Jer 19:10 "Then break the jar w those who go with H4200
Jer 33: 1 W Jeremiah was still confined in the H6388
Jer 34: 1 W Nebuchadnezzar king of Babylon and H2256
Jer 34: 7 w the army of the king of Babylon was H2256
Jer 36: 4 w Jeremiah dictated all the words the NDT
Jer 38: 7 W the king was sitting in the Benjamin H2256
Jer 39:15 W Jeremiah had been confined in the H928
Jer 41: 1 W they were eating together there, H2256
Jer 43: 9 "W the Jews are watching, take some H4200
Jer 51:39 But w they are aroused, I will set out a H928
La 1:19 perished in the city w they searched for H3954
La 3:27 a man to bear the yoke w he is young. H928
Eze 1: 1 w I was among the exiles by the Kebar H2256
Eze 8: 1 w I was sitting in my house and the elders of AIT
Eze 9: 8 W they were killing and I was left alone, H3869
Eze 10:19 W I watched, the cherubim spread their NDT
Eze 11:16 yet for a little w I have been a sanctuary H5071
Eze 12: 4 During the daytime, w they watch, bring out NDT
Eze 12: 4 Then in the evening, w they are watching NDT
Eze 12: 5 W they watch, dig through the wall and take NDT
Eze 12: 7 them on my shoulders w they watched. NDT
Eze 23: 5 in prostitution w she was still mine; NDT
Eze 35:14 W the whole earth rejoices, I will make H3869
Eze 42: 8 W the row of rooms on the side next to the H3954
Eze 43: 6 W the man was standing beside me, H2256
Eze 44: 7 my temple w you offered me food, H928
Eze 44:17 any woolen garment w ministering at the H928
Da 2:34 W you were watching, a rock was A10527+10168
Da 2:49 w Daniel himself remained at the royal A10221
Da 4:10 These are the visions I saw w lying in bed: NDT
Da 4:13 "In the visions I saw w lying in bed, I looked, NDT
Da 4:23 the field, w its roots remain in the ground. NDT
Da 5: 2 W Belshazzar was drinking his wine, he A10089
Da 7: 8 "W I was thinking about the horns, there AIT
Da 8:15 W I, Daniel, was watching the vision and H928
Da 8:18 W he was speaking to me, I was in a deep H928
Da 9:20 W I was speaking and praying, confessing H6388
Da 9:21 w I was still in prayer, Gabriel, the man I H6388
Da 10:15 W he was saying this to me, I bowed with H928
Ob 11 you stood aloof w strangers carried H928+3427
Hab 1:13 Why are you silent w the wicked swallow H928
Hag 1: 4 houses, w this house remains a ruin?" H2256
Hag 1: 9 w each of you is busy with your own H2256
Hag 2: 6 'In a little w I will once more shake the H5071
Zec 2: 3 W the angel who was speaking to me H2180
Zec 3: 5 w the angel of the LORD stood by. H2256
Zec 14:12 Their flesh will rot w they are still H2256
Mt 5:25 Do it w you are still together on the G2401+4015
Mt 9:10 W Jesus was having dinner at Matthew's AIT
Mt 9:15 mourn w he is with them? G2093+4012
Mt 9:18 W he was saying this, a synagogue leader AIT
Mt 9:32 W they were going out, a man who was AIT
Mt 12:46 W Jesus was still talking to the crowd, his AIT
Mt 13: 2 w all the people stood on the shore. AIT
Mt 13:25 But w everyone was sleeping, his G1877+3836
Mt 13:29 'because w you are pulling the weeds AIT
Mt 14:22 w he dismissed the crowd. G2401+4005
Mt 17: 5 W he was still speaking, a bright cloud AIT
Mt 21: 8 w others cut branches from the trees and AIT
Mt 21:23 w he was teaching, the chief priests and AIT
Mt 22:41 W the Pharisees were gathered together AIT
Mt 25:10 "But w they were on their way to buy the oil AIT
Mt 26: 6 W Jesus was in Bethany in the home of AIT
Mt 26:21 And w they were eating, he said, "Truly I tell AIT
Mt 26:26 W they were eating, Jesus took bread, and AIT
Mt 26:36 "Sit here w I go over there and pray G2401+4005
Mt 26:47 W he was still speaking, Judas, one of G2285
Mt 26:73 After a little w, those standing there went up AIT
Mt 27:19 W Pilate was sitting on the judge's seat, his AIT
Mt 27:63 remember that w he was still alive that AIT
Mt 28:11 W the women were on their way, some of AIT
Mt 28:13 night and stole him away w we were asleep. AIT
Mk 1:35 the morning, w it was still dark, Jesus got G1939
Mk 2:15 W Jesus was having dinner at Levi's house AIT
Mk 2:19 bridegroom fast w he is with them? G1877+4005
Mk 4: 1 w all the people were along the shore at G2779
Mk 5:21 gathered around him w he was by the lake. AIT
Mk 5:35 W Jesus was still speaking, some people AIT
Mk 6:45 to Bethsaida, w he dismissed the crowd. G2401
Mk 10:32 w those who followed were afraid. G1254
Mk 11: 8 w others spread branches they had cut in G1254
Mk 11:27 and w Jesus was walking in the temple AIT
Mk 12:35 W Jesus was teaching in the temple courts AIT
Mk 14: 3 W he was in Bethany, reclining at the table AIT
Mk 14:18 W they were reclining at the table eating, he AIT
Mk 14:22 W they were eating, Jesus took bread, and AIT
Mk 14:32 said to his disciples, "Sit here w I pray." G2401
Mk 14:66 W Peter was below in the courtyard, one of AIT
Mk 14:70 After a little w, those standing near said to AIT
Mk 16:12 to two of them w they were walking in the AIT
Lk 2: 2 place w Quirinius was governor of Syria.) AIT
Lk 2: 6 W they were there, the time came G1877+3836
Lk 2:43 w his parents were returning home G1877+3836
Lk 5:12 W Jesus was in one of the towns, G1877+3836
Lk 5:34 bridegroom fast w he is with them? G1877+4005
Lk 8: 4 W a large crowd was gathering and people AIT
Lk 8:13 They believe for a w, but in the time of G2789
Lk 8:49 W Jesus was still speaking, someone came AIT
Lk 9:34 W he was speaking, a cloud appeared and AIT
Lk 9:42 Even w the boy was coming, the demon AIT
Lk 9:43 W everyone was marveling at all that Jesus AIT
Lk 14:32 a delegation w the other is still a long way AIT
Lk 15:20 "But w he was still a long way off, his father AIT
Lk 16:25 w Lazarus received bad things G2779
Lk 17: 8 ready and wait on me w I eat and drink; G2401
Lk 19:11 W they were listening to this, he went on to AIT
Lk 20:45 W all the people were listening, Jesus said AIT
Lk 22:47 W he was still speaking a crowd came up AIT
Lk 24: 4 W they were wondering about this G1877+3836
Lk 24: 6 told you, w he was still with you in Galilee: AIT
Lk 24:32 burning within us w he talked with us on G6055
Lk 24:36 W they were still talking about this, Jesus AIT
Lk 24:41 And w they still did not believe it because of AIT
Lk 24:44 "This is what I told you w I was still with you: AIT
Lk 24:51 W he was blessing them, he left G1877+3836
Jn 1:48 "I saw you w you were still under the fig tree AIT
Jn 2:23 Now w he was in Jerusalem at the G6055
Jn 4:51 W he was still on the way, his servants met AIT
Jn 5: 7 W I am trying to get in, someone G1877+4005
Jn 6:59 He said this w teaching in the synagogue in AIT
Jn 8:20 spoke these words w teaching in the temple AIT
Jn 9: 5 W I am in the world, I am the light of the G4020
Jn 11: 8 "a short w ago the Jews there tried to G3814
Jn 12: 2 w Lazarus was among those reclining at G1254
Jn 12:25 w anyone who hates their life in this G2779
Jn 12:35 to have the light just a little w longer. G5989
Jn 12:35 Walk w you have the light, before G6055
Jn 12:36 Believe in the light w you have the light G6055
Jn 14:25 "All this I have spoken w still with you. AIT
Jn 15: 2 w every branch that does bear fruit he G2779
Jn 16:16 "In a little w you will see me no more G3625
Jn 16:16 then after a little w you will see me." G3625
Jn 16:17 'In a little w you will see me no more G3625
Jn 16:17 then after a little w you will see me G3625
Jn 16:18 "What does he mean by 'a little w'? G3625
Jn 16:19 'In a little w you will see me no more G3625
Jn 16:19 then after a little w you will see me'? G3625
Jn 16:20 will weep and mourn w the world rejoices. AIT
Jn 17:12 W I was with them, I protected them and G4021
Jn 17:13 I say these things w I am still in the world, AIT
Jn 20: 1 first day of the week, w it was still dark, Mary AIT
Ac 1: 4 occasion, w he was eating with them, he AIT
Ac 3:11 W the man held on to Peter and John, all AIT
Ac 4: 1 John w they were speaking to the AIT
Ac 5:34 that the men be put outside for a little w. G1099
Ac 7: 2 father Abraham w he was still in AIT
Ac 7:59 W they were stoning him, Stephen prayed AIT
Ac 9:39 Dorcas had made w she was still with them. AIT
Ac 10:10 and w the meal was being prepared, he AIT
Ac 10:17 W Peter was wondering about the G6055
Ac 10:19 W Peter was still thinking about the vision AIT
Ac 10:27 W talking with him, Peter went inside and AIT
Ac 10:44 W Peter was still speaking these words, the AIT
Ac 13: 2 W they were worshiping the Lord and fasting AIT
Ac 17:16 W Paul was waiting for them in Athens, he AIT
Ac 18:12 W Gallio was proconsul of Achaia, the Jews AIT
Ac 19: 1 W Apollos was at Corinth, Paul G1877+3836
Ac 19:22 w he stayed in the province of Asia a little AIT
Ac 21:31 W they were trying to kill him, news reached AIT
Ac 23:32 on with him, w they returned to the barracks. AIT
Ro 4:11 that he had by faith w he was still NDT
Ro 5: 8 love for us in this: W we were still sinners AIT
Ro 5:10 w we were God's enemies, we were AIT
Ro 7: 3 another man w her husband is still alive, AIT
Ro 15:24 to see you w passing through and to have AIT
Ro 15:24 after I have enjoyed your company for a w. G3538
1Co 2: 2 to know nothing w I was with you except NDT
1Co 8: 1 But knowledge puffs up w love builds up. G1254
1Co 9: 9 muzzle an ox w it is treading out the grain." AIT
1Co 12:24 w our presentable parts need no special AIT
1Co 14:24 inquirer comes in w everyone is prophesying, AIT
1Co 16: 6 Perhaps I will stay with you for a w, or G4169
1Co 16:10 that he has nothing to fear w he is with you, AIT
2Co 5: 4 For w we are in this tent, we groan and are AIT
2Co 5:10 is due us for the things done w in the body, AIT
2Co 7: 8 my letter hurt you, but only for a little w— G6052
2Co 8:13 might be relieved w you are hard pressed, NDT
2Co 13: 2 I now repeat it w absent: On my return I will AIT
Eph 4:26 let the sun go down w you are still angry, G2093
Php 1:17 can stir up trouble for me w I am in chains. NDT
1Th 2: 9 to anyone w we preached the gospel of AIT
1Th 5: 3 W people are saying, "Peace and safety," G4020
1Ti 5: 6 lives for pleasure is dead even w she lives. AIT
1Ti 5:18 muzzle an ox w it is treading out the grain," AIT
1Ti 6:13 who w testifying before Pontius Pilate made AIT
2Ti 3:13 w evildoers and impostors will go from bad to AIT
Titus 2:13 w we wait for the blessed hope—the AIT
Phm 10 who became my son w I was in chains. NDT
Phm 13 place in helping me w I am in chains for the NDT
Phm 15 from you for a little w was that you might G6052
Heb 2: 9 made lower than the angels for a little w, AIT
Heb 9:17 never takes effect w the one who made it G4021
Heb 10:37 "In just a little w, he who G2285+4012+4012
Heb 12:10 us for a little w as they thought best; G2465
Jas 1:11 rich will fade away even w they go about G1877
Jas 4:14 appears for a little w and then vanishes G3900
1Pe 1: 6 though now for a little w you may have G3900
1Pe 3:20 the days of Noah w the ark was being built. AIT
1Pe 5:10 after you have suffered a little w, will G3900
2Pe 2:13 in their pleasures w they feast with you. AIT
2Pe 2:19 w they themselves are slaves of depravity AIT
Rev 11:12 in a cloud, w their enemies looked on. G2779
Rev 17:10 he must remain for only a little w. AIT

WHIP (3) [WHIPS]
Pr 26: 3 A w for the horse, a bridle for the donkey H8765
Isa 10:26 LORD Almighty will lash them with a w, H8765
Jn 2:15 So he made a w out of cords, and drove G5848

WHIPS (6) [WHIP]
Jos 23:13 w on your backs and thorns in your eyes H8849
1Ki 12:11 My father scourged you with w; I will H8765
1Ki 12:14 My father scourged you with w; I will H8765
2Ch 10:11 My father scourged you with w; I will H8765
2Ch 10:14 My father scourged you with w; I will H8765
Na 3: 2 The crack of w, the clatter of wheels H8765

WHIRLING (1)
Eze 10:13 the wheels being called "the w wheels." H1649

WHIRLWIND (13) [WIND]
2Ki 2: 1 about to take Elijah up to heaven in a w, H6194
2Ki 2:11 Elijah went up to heaven in a w. H6194
Ps 77:18 Your thunder was heard in the w, your H1649
Pr 1:27 when disaster sweeps over you like a w H6070
Isa 5:28 like flint, their chariot wheels like a w. H6070
Isa 40:24 a w sweeps them away like chaff. H6194
Isa 66:15 his chariots are like a w; he will bring H6070
Jer 4:13 his chariots come like a w, his horses are H6070
Jer 23:19 a w swirling down on the heads of the H6193
Hos 4:19 A w will sweep them away, and their H8120
Hos 8: 7 "They sow the wind and reap the w. H6070
Na 1: 3 His way is in the w and the storm, and H6070
Zec 7:14 'I scattered them with a w among all the H6192

WHIRLWINDS (1) [WIND]
Isa 21: 1 Like w sweeping through the southland H6070

WHIRRING (1)
Isa 18: 1 Woe to the land of w wings along the H7527

WHISPER (9) [WHISPERED, WHISPERING]
1Ki 19:12 And after the fire came a gentle w. H7754+1960
Job 4:12 brought to me, my ears caught a w of it. H9066
Job 26:14 his works; how faint the w we hear of him! H1821
Ps 41: 7 All my enemies w together against me H4317
Ps 107:29 He stilled the storm to a w; the waves of H1960
Isa 8:19 spiritists, who w and mutter, should H7627
Isa 26:16 they could barely w a prayer. H4318+7440
Isa 29: 4 out of the dust your speech will w. H7627
La 3:62 what my enemies w and mutter against H8557

WHISPERED (2) [WHISPER]
Mt 10:27 in the daylight; what is w in your ear G2018
Lk 12: 3 what you have w in the ear in the G3281

WHISPERING (5) [WHISPER]
2Sa 12:19 his attendants were w among themselves, H4317
Ps 31:13 For I hear many w, "Terror on every side!" H1804
Jer 20:10 I hear many w, "Terror on every side H1804
Jn 7:12 there was widespread w about him. G1198
Jn 7:32 heard the crowd w such things about him. G1197

WHISTLE (1) [WHISTLES, WHISTLING]
Isa 7:18 that day the LORD will w for flies from the H9239

WHISTLES (1) [WHISTLE]
Isa 5:26 he w for those at the ends of the earth. H9239

WHISTLING (1) [WHISTLE]
Jdg 5:16 sheep pens to hear the w for the flocks? H9241

WHIT (KJV) EVERYTHING, NOT IN THE LEAST, WHOLE

WHITE (62) [REDDISH-WHITE, WHITER]
Ge 30:35 all that had w on them) and all the H4237

Ge 30:37 trees and made **w** stripes on them by H4237
Ge 30:37 exposing the **w** inner *wood* of the H4237
Ex 4: 6 leprous—it had become as **w as snow**. H8920
Ex 16:31 It was **w** like coriander seed and tasted H4237
Lev 11:18 the **w owl**, the desert owl, the osprey, H9492
Lev 13: 3 the sore has turned **w** and the sore H4237
Lev 13: 4 spot on the skin is **w** but does not appear H4237
Lev 13: 4 deep and the hair in it has not turned **w**, H4237
Lev 13:10 if there is a **w** swelling in the skin H4237
Lev 13:10 has turned the hair **w** and if there is raw H4237
Lev 13:13 Since it has all turned **w**, they are clean. H4237
Lev 13:16 If the raw flesh changes and turns **w**, they H4237
Lev 13:17 if the sores have turned **w**, the priest H4237
Lev 13:19 a **w** swelling or reddish-white spot H4237
Lev 13:20 skin deep and the hair in it has turned **w**, H4237
Lev 13:21 there is no **w** hair in it and it is not more H4237
Lev 13:24 a reddish-white or **w** spot appears in the H4237
Lev 13:25 if the hair in it has turned **w**, and it H4237
Lev 13:26 it and there is no **w** hair in the spot and if H4237
Lev 13:38 a man or woman has **w** spots on the skin, H4237
Lev 13:39 if the spots are dull **w**, it is a H4237
Nu 12:10 was leprous—it became as **w as snow**. H8920
Dt 14:16 the little owl, the great owl, the **w owl**, H9492
Jdg 5:10 "You who ride on **w** donkeys, sitting on H7467
2Ki 5:27 was leprous—it had become as **w** as snow. NDT
Est 1: 6 had hangings of **w** and blue linen, H2580
Est 1: 6 with cords of **w linen** and purple material H1009
Est 8:15 wearing royal garments of blue and **w**, H2580
Job 41:32 one would think the deep had **w hair**. H8484
Ecc 9: 8 Always be clothed in **w**, and always anoint H4237
Isa 1:18 like scarlet, *they shall be* as **w** as snow H4235
Da 7: 9 His clothing was as **w** as snow; the hair A10254
Da 7: 9 the hair of his head was **w** like wool. A10490
Joel 1: 7 thrown it away, **leaving** their branches **w**. H4235
Zec 1: 8 him were red, brown and **w** horses. H4237
Zec 6: 3 the third **w**, and the fourth dappled—all of H4237
Zec 6: 6 the one with the **w** horses toward the west H4237
Mt 5:36 cannot make even one hair **w** or black. *G3328*
Mt 17: 2 his clothes became as **w** as the light. *G3328*
Mt 28: 3 his clothes were **w** as snow. *G3328*
Mk 9: 3 His clothes became dazzling **w**, whiter *G3328*
Mk 16: 5 man dressed in a **w** robe sitting on the *G3328*
Jn 20:12 saw two angels in **w**, seated where *G3328*
Ac 1:10 two men dressed in **w** stood beside them. *G3328*
Rev 1:14 The hair on his head was **w** like wool, as *G3328*
Rev 1:14 white like wool, as **w** as snow, and his *G3328*
Rev 2:17 give that person a **w** stone with a new *G3328*
Rev 3: 4 with me, dressed in **w**, for they are worthy. *G3328*
Rev 3: 5 victorious will, like them, be dressed in **w**. *G3328*
Rev 3:18 become rich; and **w** clothes to wear, so *G3328*
Rev 4: 4 were dressed in **w** and had crowns of *G3328*
Rev 6: 2 there before me was a **w** horse! *G3328*
Rev 6:11 Then each of them was given a **w** robe *G3328*
Rev 7: 9 They were wearing **w** robes and were *G3328*
Rev 7:13 "These in **w** robes—who are they, *G3328*
Rev 7:14 robes and **made** them **w** in the blood *G3326*
Rev 14:14 there before me was a **w** cloud, and *G3328*
Rev 19:11 open and there before me was a **w** horse, *G3328*
Rev 19:14 riding on **w** horses and dressed in fine *G3328*
Rev 19:14 dressed in fine linen, **w** and clean. *G3328*
Rev 20:11 Then I saw a great **w** throne and him who *G3328*

WHITER (4) [WHITE]

Ge 49:12 darker than wine, his teeth **w** than milk. H4237
Ps 51: 7 wash me, and *I will be* **w** than snow. H4235
La 4: 7 were brighter than snow and **w** than milk, H7458
Mk 9: 3 **w** than anyone in the world could bleach NDT

WHITEWASH (6) [WASH]

Eze 13:10 a flimsy wall is built, they cover it with **w**, H9521
Eze 13:11 who cover it with **w** that it is going to H9521
Eze 13:12 "Where is the **w** you covered it with?" H3225
Eze 13:14 have covered with **w** and will level it to H9521
Eze 13:15 against those who covered it with **w**. H9521
Eze 22:28 Her prophets **w** these deeds for H3212+9521

WHITEWASHED (3) [WASH]

Eze 13:15 wall is gone and so are those *who* **w** it, H3212
Mt 23:27 You are like **w** tombs, which look *G3154*
Ac 23: 3 "God will strike you, you **w** wall! *G3154*

WHO (5087) [WHOEVER, WHOM, WHOSE] See Index of Articles Etc.

WHOEVER (305) [WHO]

Ge 4:14 on the earth, and **w** finds me will kill me." H3972
Ge 9: 6 "***W*** **sheds** human blood, by humans shall AIT
Ge 12: 3 who bless you, and *w* **curses** you I will curse AIT
Ge 44:10 **W** is found to have it will become my slave; H889
Ex 12:15 **w** eats anything with yeast in it from H3972
Ex 19:12 **W** touches the mountain is to be put to H3972
Ex 22: 1 "**W** steals an ox or a sheep and slaughters H408
Ex 22:20 "*W* **sacrifices** to any god other than the LORD AIT
Ex 30:33 **W** makes perfume like it and puts it H408+889
Ex 30:38 **W** makes incense like it to enjoy its H408+889
Ex 31:15 **W** does any work on the Sabbath day is to H3972
Ex 32:24 So I told them, '**W** has any gold jewelry H4769
Ex 32:26 the camp and said, "**W** is for the LORD H4769
Ex 32:33 "**W** has sinned against me I will blot out H4769
Ex 35: 2 **W** does any work on it is to be put to H3972
Lev 11:24 **w** touches their carcasses will be unclean H3972
Lev 11:25 **W** picks up one of their carcasses must H3972
Lev 11:26 **w** touches the carcass of any of them will H3972
Lev 11:27 **w** touches their carcasses will be unclean H3972
Lev 11:31 **W** touches them when they are dead will H3972
Lev 15: 6 **W** sits on anything that the man with a H2021
Lev 15: 7 " '**W** touches the man who has a H2021
Lev 15:10 **w** touches any of the things that were H3972
Lev 15:10 **w** picks up those things must wash their H2021
Lev 19: 8 *W* **eats** it will be held responsible because AIT
Lev 24:21 *W* **kills** an animal must make restitution, but AIT
Lev 24:21 but *w* **kills** a human being is to be put to AIT
Lev 27:31 **W** would redeem any of their tithe must H408
Nu 19:11 "**W** touches a human corpse will be H2021
Nu 22: 6 For I know that **w** you bless is blessed, and H889
Nu 22: 6 bless is blessed, and **w** you curse is cursed." H889
Jos 1:18 **W** rebels against your word and H3972+408+889
Jos 7:15 **W** is caught with the devoted things shall H2021
Jdg 6:31 **W** fights for him shall be put to death by H889
Jdg 10:18 "**W** will take the lead in H4769+2021+408
2Sa 17: 9 your troops first, **w** hears about it will say H2021
2Sa 20:11 and said, "**W** favors Joab, and H4769+889
2Sa 20:11 favors Joab, and **w** is for David, let H4769+889
2Sa 23: 7 **W** touches thorns uses a tool of iron or the H408
1Ch 11: 6 "**W** leads the attack on the Jebusites will H3972
2Ch 13: 9 **W** comes to consecrate himself with a H3972
Ezr 7:26 **W** does not obey the law of your A10353+10168
Job 29:11 **W** heard me spoke well of me, and those H265S
Ps 7:14 *W is* **pregnant** *with* evil conceives trouble AIT
Ps 7:15 *W* **digs** a hole and scoops it out falls into the AIT
Ps 15: 5 *W* **does** these things will never be shaken. AIT
Ps 34:12 **W** of you loves life and H4769+2021+408
Ps 91: 1 *W* **dwells** in the shelter of the Most High will AIT
Ps 101: 5 *W* **slanders** their neighbor in secret, I will put AIT
Ps 101: 5 **w** has haughty eyes and a proud heart NDT
Pr 1:33 but **w listens** to me will live in safety and be AIT
Pr 6:32 has no sense; **w** does so destroys himself. H2085
Pr 9: 7 *W* **corrects** a mocker invites insults; whoever AIT
Pr 9: 7 *w* **rebukes** the wicked incurs abuse. AIT
Pr 10: 9 **W** walks in integrity walks securely, but H2021
Pr 10: 9 but *w* **takes crooked** paths will be found out. AIT
Pr 10:10 *W* **winks maliciously** causes grief, and a AIT
Pr 10:17 *W* **heeds** discipline shows the way to life, but AIT
Pr 10:17 but **w ignores** correction leads others astray. AIT
Pr 10:18 *W* **conceals** hatred with lying lips and AIT
Pr 11:12 *W* **derides** their neighbor has no sense, but AIT
Pr 11:15 *W* **puts up security** *for* a stranger will surely AIT
Pr 11:15 but **w refuses** to shake hands in pledge is AIT
Pr 11:19 attain life, but *w* **pursues** evil finds death. AIT
Pr 11:25 *w* **refreshes** others will be refreshed. AIT
Pr 11:27 *W* **seeks** good finds favor, but evil comes to AIT
Pr 11:29 *W* **brings ruin** *on* their family will inherit AIT
Pr 12: 1 *W* **loves** discipline loves knowledge, but AIT
Pr 12: 1 knowledge, but *w* **hates** correction is stupid. AIT
Pr 13:11 but **w gathers** money little by little makes it AIT
Pr 13:13 *W* **scorns** instruction will pay for it, but AIT
Pr 13:13 but *w* **respects** a command is rewarded. AIT
Pr 13:18 *W* **disregards** discipline comes to poverty AIT
Pr 13:18 but **w heeds** correction is honored. AIT
Pr 13:24 *W* **spares** the rod hates their children, but the AIT
Pr 14: 2 *W* **fears** the LORD walks uprightly, but those AIT
Pr 14:26 *W* **fears** the LORD has a secure fortress, and AIT
Pr 14:29 *W* is **patient** has great understanding, but AIT
Pr 14:31 *W* **oppresses** the poor shows contempt for AIT
Pr 14:31 but *w is* **kind** *to* the needy honors God. AIT
Pr 15: 5 but **w heeds** correction shows prudence. AIT
Pr 15:21 but **w** *has* understanding keeps a straight H408
Pr 15:31 *W* **heeds** life-giving correction will be at AIT
Pr 16:20 *W* **gives heed** to instruction prospers, and AIT
Pr 16:30 *W* **winks** *with* their eye is plotting perversity AIT
Pr 16:30 perversity; *w* **purses** their lips is bent on evil. AIT
Pr 17: 5 *W* **mocks** the poor shows contempt for their AIT
Pr 17: 5 *w* **gloats** over disaster will not go unpunished AIT
Pr 17: 9 *W would* **foster** love covers over an offense AIT
Pr 17: 9 but *w* **repeats** the matter separates close AIT
Pr 17:19 *W* **loves** a quarrel loves sin; whoever builds a AIT
Pr 17:19 **w builds** a **high** gate invites destruction. AIT
Pr 17:27 and **w** *has* understanding is H408S
Pr 19: 5 and *w* **pours out** lies will not go free. AIT
Pr 19: 9 unpunished, and *w* **pours out** lies will perish. AIT
Pr 19:16 *W* **keeps** commandments keeps their life, but AIT
Pr 19:16 but **w shows contempt** *for* their ways will die. AIT
Pr 19:17 *W is* **kind** *to* the poor lends to the LORD, and AIT
Pr 19:26 *W* **robs** their father and drives out their AIT
Pr 20: 1 **w** is led astray by them is not wise. H3972
Pr 21:13 *W* **shuts** their ears to the cry of the poor will AIT
Pr 21:16 **W** strays from the path of prudence comes H132
Pr 21:17 **W** loves pleasure will become poor H408S
Pr 21:17 *w* **loves** wine and olive oil will never be rich. AIT
Pr 21:21 *W* **pursues** righteousness and love finds life AIT
Pr 22: 8 *W* **sows** injustice reaps calamity, and the rod AIT
Pr 24: 8 *W* **plots** evil will be known as a schemer. AIT
Pr 24:24 *W* **says** to the guilty, "You are innocent," AIT
Pr 26:27 *W* **digs** a pit will fall into it; if someone rolls AIT
Pr 27:18 and *w* **protects** their master will be honored. AIT
Pr 28: 8 *W* **increases** wealth by taking interest or AIT
Pr 28:10 *W* **leads** the upright along an evil path will AIT
Pr 28:13 *W* **conceals** their sins does not prosper, but AIT
Pr 28:14 but *w* **hardens** their heart falls into trouble. AIT
Pr 28:23 *W* **rebukes** a person will in the end gain AIT
Pr 28:24 *W* **robs** their father or mother and says, "It's AIT
Pr 29: 1 **W** remains stiff-necked after many rebukes H408
Pr 29:25 but *w* **trusts** in the LORD is kept safe. AIT
Ecc 5:10 *W* **loves** money never has enough; whoever AIT
Ecc 5:10 **w** loves wealth is never satisfied with their H4769
Ecc 7:18 *W* **fears** God will avoid all extremes. AIT
Ecc 8: 5 *W* **obeys** his command will come to no harm AIT
Ecc 10: 8 *W* **digs** a pit may fall into it; whoever breaks AIT
Ecc 10: 8 *w* **breaks through** a wall may be bitten by a AIT
Ecc 10: 9 *W* **quarries** stones may be injured by them AIT
Ecc 10: 9 *w* **splits** logs may be endangered by them. AIT
Ecc 11: 4 *W* **watches** the wind will not plant; whoever AIT
Ecc 11: 4 not plant; *w* **looks** at the clouds will not reap. AIT
Isa 13:15 **W** is captured will be thrust through; all H3972
Isa 24:18 **W** flees at the sound of terror will fall into H2021
Isa 24:18 **w** climbs out of the pit will be caught in a H2021
Isa 41:24 worthless; *w* **chooses** you is detestable. AIT
Isa 54:15 **w** attacks you will surrender to you. H4769
Isa 57:13 But **w** takes refuge in me will inherit the H2021
Isa 59: 5 **W** eats their eggs will die, and when one H2021
Isa 59:15 be found, and *w* **shuns** evil becomes a prey. AIT
Isa 65:16 **W** invokes a blessing in the land will do so H889
Isa 65:16 **w** takes an oath in the land will swear by H2021
Isa 66: 3 But *w* **sacrifices** a bull is like one who kills a AIT
Isa 66: 3 and *w* **offers** a lamb is like one who breaks a AIT
Isa 66: 3 *w* **makes** a grain **offering** is like one who AIT
Isa 66: 3 and *w* **burns memorial** incense is like one AIT
Jer 21: 9 **W** stays in this city will die by the sword H2021
Jer 21: 9 But **w** goes out and surrenders to the H2021
Jer 31:30 own sin; **w** eats sour grapes H3972+2021+132
Jer 38: 2 '**W** stays in this city will die by the sword H2021
Jer 38: 2 **w** goes over to the Babylonians will H2021
Jer 48:44 "**W** flees from the terror will fall into a pit H2021
Jer 48:44 **w** climbs out of the pit will be caught in a H2021
Jer 50: 7 **W** found them devoured them; their H3972
Eze 3:27 **W** will listen let them listen, and H2021
Eze 3:27 and **w** will refuse let them refuse H2021
Eze 46: 9 **w** enters by the north gate to worship is to H2021
Eze 46: 9 **w** enters by the south gate is to go H2021
Da 3: 6 **W** does not fall down and A10426+10168
Da 3:11 that **w** does not fall down A10426+10168
Da 5: 7 "**W** reads this writing A10353+10050+10168
Zec 2: 8 **w** touches you touches the apple of H2021S
Mal 2:12 **w he may be**, may the H6424+2256+6699
Mt 5:19 **w** practices and teaches these *G4005+323*
Mt 10:32 "**W** acknowledges me before *G4246+4015*
Mt 10:33 But **w** disowns me before others, *G4015+323*
Mt 10:38 **W** does not take up their cross and follow *G4005*
Mt 10:39 **W** finds their life will lose it, and whoever *G3836*
Mt 10:39 **w** loses their life for my sake will find *G3836*
Mt 10:41 **W** welcomes a prophet as a prophet will *G3836*
Mt 10:41 **w** welcomes a righteous person as a *G3836*
Mt 11:11 **w** is least in the kingdom of heaven is *G3836*
Mt 11:15 **W** has ears, let them hear. *G3836*
Mt 12:30 "**W** is not with me is against me, and *G3836*
Mt 12:30 **w** does not gather with me scatters. *G3836*
Mt 12:50 For **w** does the will of my Father in *G4015+323*
Mt 13: 9 **W** has ears, let them hear. *G3836*
Mt 13:12 **W** has will be given more, and they will *G4015*
Mt 13:12 **W** does not have, even what they have *G4015*
Mt 13:43 of their Father. **W** has ears, let them hear. *G3836*
Mt 16:24 "**W** wants to be my disciple must deny *G5516*
Mt 16:25 For **w** wants to save their life will *G4005+1569*
Mt 16:25 **w** loses their life for me will find *G4005+323*
Mt 18: 4 **w** takes the lowly position of this child is *G4015*
Mt 18: 5 And **w** welcomes one such child in *G4005+1569*
Mt 20:26 **w** wants to become great among *G4005+1569*
Mt 20:27 **w** wants to be first must be your *G4005+323*
Mt 25:29 For **w** has will be given more, and they will *G4246*
Mt 25:29 **W** does not have, even what they have *G3836*
Mk 3:29 **w** blasphemes against the Holy *G4005+323*
Mk 3:35 **W** does God's will is my brother and *G4005+323*
Mk 4: 9 Then Jesus said, "**W** has ears to hear, let *G4005*
Mk 4:25 **W** has will be given more; whoever does *G4005*
Mk 4:25 be given more; **w** does not have, even *G4005*
Mk 8:34 "**W** wants to be my disciple must deny *G5516*
Mk 8:35 For **w** wants to save their life will *G4005+1569*
Mk 8:35 **w** loses their life for me and for *G4005+323*
Mk 9:37 "**W** welcomes one of these little *G4005+323*
Mk 9:37 and **w** welcomes me does not *G4005+323*
Mk 9:40 **w** is not against us is for us. *G4005*
Mk 10:43 **w** wants to become great among *G4005+323*
Mk 10:44 **w** wants to be first must be slave *G4005+323*
Mk 16:16 **W** believes and is baptized will be saved *G3836*
Mk 16:16 **w** does not believe will be *G3836*
Lk 7:47 But **w** has been forgiven little loves little." *G4005*
Lk 8: 8 he called out, "**W** has ears to hear, let *G3836*
Lk 8:18 **W** has will be given more; whoever *G4005+323*
Lk 8:18 be given more; **w** does not have *G4005+323*
Lk 9:23 "**W** wants to be my disciple must deny *G5516*
Lk 9:24 For **w** wants to save their life will lose *G4005+323*
Lk 9:24 **w** loses their life for me will save *G4005+323*
Lk 9:26 **W** is ashamed of me and my words *G4005+323*
Lk 9:48 "**W** welcomes this little child in my *G4005+1569*
Lk 9:48 and **w** welcomes me welcomes the *G4005+323*
Lk 9:50 "for **w** is not against you is for you. *G4005*
Lk 10:16 "**W** listens to you listens to me; whoever *G3836*
Lk 10:16 you listens to me; **w** rejects you rejects me *G3836*
Lk 10:16 **w** rejects me rejects him who sent me." *G3836*
Lk 11:23 "**W** is not with me is against me, and *G3836*
Lk 11:23 **w** does not gather with me scatters. *G3836*
Lk 12: 8 **w** publicly acknowledges me *G4246+4005+323*
Lk 12: 9 But **w** disowns me before others will be *G3836*
Lk 12:21 how it will be with **w** stores up things for *G3836*
Lk 14:27 And **w** does not carry their cross and follow *G4015*
Lk 14:35 it is thrown out. "**W** has ears to hear, let *G3836*
Lk 16:10 "**W** can be trusted with very little can also *G3836*

Lk 16:10 w is dishonest with very little will also *G3836*
Lk 17:33 W tries to keep their life will lose it *G4005+1569*
Lk 17:33 and w loses their life will preserve it. *G4005+323*
Jn 3:16 that w believes in him shall not perish *G4246*
Jn 3:18 W believes in him is not condemned, but *G3836*
Jn 3:18 w does not believe stands *G3836*
Jn 3:21 But w lives by the truth comes into the *G3836*
Jn 3:33 W has accepted it has certified that God is *G3836*
Jn 3:36 W believes in the Son has eternal life, but *G3836*
Jn 3:36 but w rejects the Son will not see life *G3836*
Jn 4:14 w drinks the water I give them *G4005+323*
Jn 5:23 W does not honor the Son does not honor *G3836*
Jn 5:24 w hears my word and believes him who *G3836*
Jn 6:35 W comes to me will never go hungry, and *G3836*
Jn 6:35 w believes in me will never be thirsty. *G3836*
Jn 6:37 w comes to me I will never drive *G3836*
Jn 6:51 W eats this bread will live forever *G1569+5516*
Jn 6:54 W eats my flesh and drinks my blood has *G3836*
Jn 6:56 W eats my flesh and drinks my blood *G3836*
Jn 6:58 w feeds on this bread will live forever." *G3836*
Jn 7:18 W speaks on their own does so to gain *G3836*
Jn 7:38 W believes in me, as Scripture has said *G3836*
Jn 8:12 W follows me will never walk in darkness *G3836*
Jn 8:47 W belongs to God hears what God says *G3836*
Jn 8:51 w obeys my word will never see *G1569+5516*
Jn 8:52 you say that w obeys your word *G1569+5516*
Jn 10: 9 w enters through me will be saved. *G1569+5516*
Jn 11:26 w lives by believing in me will never *G4246*
Jn 12:26 W serves me must follow me; and *G1569+5516*
Jn 12:35 W walks in the dark does not know where *G3836*
Jn 12:44 "W believes in me does not believe in *G3836*
Jn 13:20 w accepts anyone I send accepts me *G3836*
Jn 13:20 w accepts me accepts the one who *G3836*
Jn 14:12 w believes in me will do the works I have *G3836*
Jn 14:21 W has my commands and keeps them is *G3836*
Jn 15:23 W hates me hates my Father as well. *G3836*
Ro 13: 2 w rebels against the authority is rebelling *G3836*
Ro 13: 8 w loves others has fulfilled the law. *G3836*
Ro 14: 6 W regards one day as special does so to *G3836*
Ro 14: 6 W eats meat does so to the Lord, for they *G3836*
Ro 14: 6 w abstains does so to the Lord and *G3836*
Ro 14:23 But w has doubts is condemned if they eat, *G3836*
1Co 6:17 But w is united with the Lord is one with *G3836*
1Co 6:18 outside the body, but w sins sexually, sins *G3836*
1Co 8: 3 But w loves God is known by God. *G5516*
1Co 9:10 because w plows and threshes should be *G3836*
1Co 11:27 w eats the bread or drinks the cup of *G4005+323*
2Co 9: 6 W sows sparingly will also reap sparingly *G3836*
2Co 9: 6 w sows generously will also reap *G3836*
Gal 5:10 into confusion, w that may be, will *G4015+1569*
Gal 6: 8 W sows to please their flesh, from the *G3836*
Gal 6: 8 destruction; w sows to please the Spirit *G3836*
1Ti 3: 1 W aspires to be an overseer desires a *G5516*
Jas 1:25 But w looks intently into the perfect law *G3836*
Jas 2:10 For w keeps the whole law and yet *G4015*
Jas 5:20 W turns a sinner from the error of their *G3836*
1Pe 3:10 "W would love life and see good days *G3836*
1Pe 4: 1 because w suffers in the body is done *G3836*
2Pe 1: 9 But w does not have them is nearsighted *G4005*
1Jn 2: 4 W says, "I know him," but does not do *G3836*
1Jn 2: 6 W claims to live in him must live as Jesus *G3836*
1Jn 2:17 w does the will of God lives forever. *G3836*
1Jn 2:22 It is w denies that Jesus is the Christ *G3836*
1Jn 2:23 w acknowledges the Son has the Father *G3836*
1Jn 4: 6 from God, and w knows God listens to us *G3836*
1Jn 4: 6 w is not from God does not listen to *G4005*
1Jn 4: 8 W does not love does not know God *G3836*
1Jn 4:16 W lives in love lives in God, and God in *G3836*
1Jn 4:20 W claims to love God yet hates a *G1569+5516*
1Jn 4:20 For w does not love their brother and *G3836*
1Jn 5:10 W believes in the Son of God accepts this *G3836*
1Jn 5:10 W does not believe God has made him *G3836*
1Jn 5:12 W has the Son has life; whoever does not *G3836*
1Jn 5:12 w does not have the Son of God does not *G3836*
2Jn 9 w continues in the teaching has both the *G3836*
Rev 2: 7 W has ears, let them hear what the Spirit *G3836*
Rev 2:11 W has ears, let them hear what the Spirit *G3836*
Rev 2:17 W has ears, let them hear what the Spirit *G3836*
Rev 2:29 W has ears, let them hear what the Spirit *G3836*
Rev 3: 6 W has ears, let them hear what the Spirit *G3836*
Rev 3:13 W has ears, let them hear what the Spirit *G3836*
Rev 3:22 W has ears, let them hear what the Spirit *G3836*
Rev 13: 9 W has ears, let them hear. *G5516*

WHOLE (391) [WHOLLY, WHOLEHEARTED, WHOLEHEARTEDLY]

Ge 1:29 on the face of the w earth and every tree H3972
Ge 2: 6 watered the w surface of the ground H3972
Ge 7: 1 you and your w family, because I H3972
Ge 9:19 who were scattered over the w earth. H3972
Ge 11: 1 Now the w world had one language and H3972
Ge 11: 4 be scattered over the face of the w earth." H3972
Ge 11: 9 confused the language of the w world. H3972
Ge 11: 9 them over the face of the w earth. H3972
Ge 13: 9 Is not the w land before you? Let's part H3972
Ge 13:10 saw that the w plain of the Jordan H3972
Ge 13:11 himself the w plain of the Jordan H3972
Ge 14: 7 they conquered the w territory of the H3972
Ge 17: 8 The w land of Canaan, where you now H3972
Ge 18:26 I will spare the w place for their sake." H3972
Ge 18:28 Will you destroy the w city for lack of five H3972
Ge 25:25 his w *body* was like a hairy garment H3972
Ge 29:14 had stayed with him for a w **month**, H2544+3427
Ge 41:41 put you in charge of the w land of Egypt." H3972
Ge 41:43 put him in charge of the w land of Egypt. H3972
Ge 41:54 in the w land of Egypt there was food. H3972
Ge 41:56 the famine had spread over the w country, H3972
Ge 47:13 in the w region because the famine was H3972
Ex 8: 2 send a plague of frogs on your w country. H3972
Ex 9: 9 fine dust over the w land of Egypt, H3972
Ex 12: 3 Tell the w community of Israel that on the H3972
Ex 12: 4 If any household is too small for a *w* **lamb** AIT
Ex 12:47 The w community of Israel must celebrate H3972
Ex 16: 1 The w Israelite community set out from H3972
Ex 16: 2 In the desert the w community grumbled H3972
Ex 16:10 speaking to the w Israelite community H3972
Ex 17: 1 The w Israelite community set out from H3972
Ex 19: 5 Although the w earth is mine, H3972
Ex 19:18 the w mountain trembled violently. H3972
Ex 22: 6 of grain or standing grain or the *w* **field**, AIT
Ex 35: 1 assembled the w Israelite community H3972
Ex 35: 4 Moses said to the w Israelite community H3972
Ex 35:20 Then the w Israelite community withdrew H3972
Lev 4:13 " 'If the w Israelite community sins H3972
Lev 8:21 water and burned the w ram on the altar. H3972
Lev 10: 6 LORD will be angry with the w community. H3972
Lev 13:13 if the disease has covered their w body, H3972
Lev 15:16 he must bathe his w body with water, and H3972
Lev 16:17 household and the w community of Israel. H3972
Nu 1: 2 a census of the w Israelite community H3972
Nu 1:18 they called the w community together H3972
Nu 3: 7 him and for the w community at the H3972
Nu 8: 7 them shave their w bodies and wash their H3972
Nu 8: 9 assemble the w Israelite community. H3972
Nu 8:20 Aaron and the w Israelite community did H3972
Nu 10: 3 the w community is to assemble before H3972
Nu 11:20 for a w month—until it comes out of H3427
Nu 11:21 will give them meat to eat for a w month! H3427
Nu 13:26 Aaron and the w Israelite community H3972
Nu 13:26 to them and to the w assembly and H3972
Nu 14: 2 and the w assembly said to them H3972
Nu 14: 5 in front of the w Israelite assembly H3972
Nu 14:10 But the w assembly talked about stoning H3972
Nu 14:21 as the glory of the LORD fills the w earth, H3972
Nu 14:35 these things to this w wicked community, H3972
Nu 14:36 made the w community grumble H3972
Nu 15:24 then the w community is to offer a young H3972
Nu 15:25 atonement for the w Israelite community, H3972
Nu 15:26 The w Israelite community and the H3972
Nu 15:33 to Moses and Aaron and the w assembly, H3972
Nu 15:35 The w assembly must stone him outside H3972
Nu 16: 3 The w community is holy, every one of H3972
Nu 16:41 The next day the w Israelite community H3972
Nu 20: 1 the first month the w Israelite community H3972
Nu 20:22 The w Israelite community set out from H3972
Nu 20:27 Hor in the sight of the w community. H3972
Nu 20:29 when the w community learned that H3972
Nu 21:33 of Bashan and his w army marched out to H3972
Nu 21:34 along with his w army and his land. H3972
Nu 21:35 together with his sons and his w army H3972
Nu 25: 6 of Moses and the w assembly of Israel H3972
Nu 26: 2 a census of the w Israelite community H3972
Nu 27: 2 the leaders and the w assembly at the H3972
Nu 27:20 authority so the w Israelite community H3972
Nu 27:22 Eleazar the priest and the w assembly. H3972
Nu 32:13 until the w generation of those who had H3972
Nu 32:33 the w land with its cities and the territory NDT
Dt 2:33 together with his sons and his w army. H3972
Dt 3: 1 of Bashan with his w army marched out to H3972
Dt 3: 2 along with his w army and his land. H3972
Dt 3: 4 take from them—the w region of Argob H3972
Dt 3:13 The w region of Argob in Bashan used to H3972
Dt 3:14 took the w region of Argob as far as the H3972
Dt 5:22 a loud voice to your w assembly there on H3972
Dt 6:22 Egypt and Pharaoh and his w household. H3972
Dt 11: 3 king of Egypt and to his w country; H3972
Dt 11:25 the terror and fear of you on the w land, H3972
Dt 13:16 plunder as a w **burnt offering** to the LORD H4003
Dt 18: 1 the w tribe of Levi—are to have no H3972
Dt 19: 8 gives you the w land he promised H3972
Dt 29:23 The w land will be a burning waste of salt H3972
Dt 31:30 in the hearing of the w assembly of Israel: H3972
Dt 33:10 you and w **burnt offerings** on your altar H4003
Dt 34: 1 There the LORD showed him the w land H3972
Dt 34: 3 Negev and the w **region** *from* the Valley H3971
Dt 34:11 to all his officials and to his w land. H3972
Jos 2: 3 they have come to spy out the w land." H3972
Jos 2:24 surely given the w land into our hands; H3972
Jos 3:17 passed by until the w nation had H3972
Jos 4: 1 When the w nation had finished crossing H3972
Jos 5: 8 And after the w nation had been H3972
Jos 6: 5 have the w army give a loud shout H3972
Jos 6:24 Then they burned the w city and everything NDT
Jos 7: 3 to take it and do not weary the w army, H3972
Jos 8: 1 Take the w army with you, and go up and H3972
Jos 8: 3 So Joshua and the w army moved out to H3972
Jos 8:35 did not read to the w assembly of Israel, H3972
Jos 9:18 The w assembly grumbled against the H3972
Jos 9:21 carriers in the service of the w assembly." H3972
Jos 9:24 to give you the w land and to wipe out H3972
Jos 10:21 The w army then returned safely to Joshua H3972
Jos 10:40 So Joshua subdued the w region H3972
Jos 10:41 Gaza and from the w region of Goshen to H3972
Jos 11: 7 So Joshua and his w army came against H3972
Jos 11:16 all the Negev, the w region of Goshen H3972
Jos 13: 9 included the w plateau of Medeba as H3972
Jos 13:12 the w kingdom of Og in Bashan H3972
Jos 13:16 and the w plateau past Medeba H3972
Jos 18: 1 The w assembly of the Israelites gathered H3972
Jos 22:12 the w assembly of Israel gathered at H3972
Jos 22:16 "The w assembly of the LORD says: 'How H3972
Jos 22:18 be angry with the w community of Israel. H3972
Jos 22:20 wrath come on the w community of Israel? H3972
Jdg 1:25 spared the man and his w family. H3972
Jdg 2:10 After that w generation had been H3972
Jdg 7:14 Midianites and the w camp into his hands H3972
Jdg 9:29 say to Abimelek, 'Call out your w army! H8049
Jdg 11:21 gave Sihon and his w army into Israel's H3972
Jdg 14:17 She cried the w seven days of the feast. NDT
Jdg 16:31 his father's w family went down to H3972
Jdg 20:26 the Israelites, the w army, went up to H3972
Jdg 20:37 spread out and put the w city to the sword. H3972
Jdg 20:40 turned and saw the w city going up in H4003
Jdg 21:13 Then the w assembly sent an offer of H3972
Ru 1:19 the w town was stirred because of them H3972
1Sa 1:28 For his w life he will be given over to the H3972
1Sa 4:13 had happened, the w town sent up a cry. H3972
1Sa 7: 9 sacrificed it as a w burnt offering to the H4003
1Sa 9:20 if not to you and your w family line?" H3972
1Sa 13:19 could be found in the w land of Israel, H3972
1Sa 14:15 Then panic struck the w army—those in H3972
1Sa 17:46 the w world will know that there is a H3972
1Sa 19: 7 David and told him the w conversation. H3972
1Sa 20: 6 is being made there for his w clan. H3972
1Sa 22:15 knows nothing at all about this w affair." H3972
1Sa 22:16 Ahimelek, you and your w family. H3972
1Sa 22:22 responsible for the death of your w family. H3972
1Sa 25: 7 the w time they were at Carmel H3972
1Sa 25:15 the w time we were out in the fields H3972
1Sa 25:16 wall around us the w time we were H3972
1Sa 25:17 over our master and his w household. H3972
2Sa 2:30 Abner and assembled the w army. H3972
2Sa 3:19 that Israel and the w tribe of Benjamin H3972
2Sa 3:29 on the head of Joab and on his w family! H3972
2Sa 6:19 each person in the w crowd of Israelites, H3972
2Sa 11: 1 the king's men and the w Israelite army. H3972
2Sa 14: 7 Now the w clan has risen up against your H3972
2Sa 15:23 The w countryside wept aloud as all the H3972
2Sa 18: 8 battle spread out over the w countryside, H3972
2Sa 19: 2 And for the w army the victory that day H3972
1Ki 2:31 clear me and my w **family** of the guilt H3+1074
1Ki 6:22 So he overlaid the w interior with gold. H3972
1Ki 8:14 While the w assembly of Israel was H3972
1Ki 8:22 LORD in front of the w assembly of Israel, H3972
1Ki 8:55 blessed the w assembly of Israel in H3972
1Ki 10:24 The w world sought audience with H3972
1Ki 11:13 Yet I will not tear the w kingdom from him H3972
1Ki 11:28 him in charge of the w labor force of the H3972
1Ki 11:34 I will not take the w kingdom out of H3972
1Ki 12: 3 he and the w assembly of Israel went H3972
1Ki 15:29 to reign, he killed Jeroboam's w family. H3972
1Ki 16:11 he killed off Baasha's w family. H3972
1Ki 16:12 So Zimri destroyed the w family of Baasha H3972
2Ki 7:15 they found the w road strewn with the H3972
2Ki 9: 8 The w house of Ahab will perish. I will cut H3972
2Ki 11: 1 proceeded to destroy the w royal family. H3972
2Ki 21: 8 will keep the w Law that my servant H3972
2Ki 25: 1 against Jerusalem with his w army. H3972
2Ki 25: 4 the w army fled at night through the H3972
2Ki 25:10 The w Babylonian army under the H3972
1Ch 11:10 support to extend it over **the w land,** H3776S
1Ch 13: 2 He then said to the w assembly of Israel H3972
1Ch 13: 4 The w assembly agreed to do this H3972
1Ch 28: 4 chose me from my w family to be king H3972
1Ch 29: 1 Then King David said to the w assembly H3972
1Ch 29:10 LORD in the presence of the w assembly, H3972
1Ch 29:20 Then David said to the w assembly H3972
2Ch 1: 3 Solomon and the w assembly went to H3972
2Ch 6: 3 While the w assembly of Israel was H3972
2Ch 6:12 LORD in front of the w assembly of Israel H3972
2Ch 6:13 down before the w assembly of Israel H3972
2Ch 15: 8 idols from the w land of Judah and H3972
2Ch 22:10 to destroy the w royal family of the H3972
2Ch 23: 3 the w assembly made a covenant with the H3972
2Ch 29:28 The w assembly bowed in worship, while H3972
2Ch 30: 2 officials and the w assembly in Jerusalem H3972
2Ch 30: 4 both to the king and to the w assembly. H3972
2Ch 30:23 The w assembly then agreed to celebrate H3972
2Ch 31:18 daughters of the w community listed in H3972
Ezr 2:64 The w company numbered 42,360, H3972
Ezr 4:20 ruling over the w *of* Trans-Euphrates, A10353
Ezr 10:12 The w assembly responded with a loud H3972
Ezr 10:14 Let our officials act for the w assembly H3972
Ne 5:13 At this the w assembly said, "Amen," H3972
Ne 7:66 The w company numbered 42,360, H3972
Ne 8:17 The w company that had returned from H3972
Est 3: 6 throughout the w kingdom of Xerxes. H3972
Job 17: 7 with grief; my w frame is but a shadow. H3972
Job 34:13 Who put him in charge of the w world? H3972
Job 37: 3 beneath the w heaven and sends it H3972
Job 37:12 face of the w **earth** to do whatever H9315+824
Ps 35:10 My w being will exclaim, "Who is like you, H3972
Ps 48: 2 the joy of the w earth, like the heights H3972
Ps 51:19 in burnt offerings **offered** w; then bulls H4003
Ps 63: 1 thirst for you, my w **being** longs for you, in H1414
Ps 65: 8 The w **earth** is filled with awe at H3782+7921

Ps 72:19 may the w earth be filled with his glory. H3972
Ps 90: 2 you brought forth the w **world**, H824+2256+9315
Ps 110: 6 crushing the rulers of the w earth. H8041
Ps 130: 5 the LORD, my w **being** waits, and in his H5883
Pr 1:12 like the grave, and w, like those who go H9459
Pr 4:22 find them and health to one's w body. H3972
Pr 8:31 in his w **world** and delighting H9315+824
Isa 1: 5 Your w head is injured, your whole heart H3972
Isa 1: 5 head is injured, your w heart afflicted. H3972
Isa 6: 3 Almighty; the w earth is full of his glory." H3972
Isa 10:23 the destruction decreed upon the w land. H3972
Isa 13: 5 of his wrath—to destroy the w country. H3972
Isa 14:26 is the plan determined for the w world; H3972
Isa 28:22 destruction decreed against the w land. H3972
Isa 29:11 For you this w vision is nothing but words H3972
Isa 31: 4 though a w **band** *of* shepherds is H4850
Jer 1:18 bronze wall to stand against the w land— H3972
Jer 4:20 follows disaster; the w land lies in ruins. H3972
Jer 4:27 "The w land will be ruined, though I will H3972
Jer 8:16 of their stallions the w land trembles. H3972
Jer 9:26 even the w house of Israel is H3972
Jer 12:11 the w land will be laid waste because H3972
Jer 15:10 a man with whom the w land strives and H3972
Jer 25:11 This w country will become a desolate H3972
Jer 31:40 The w valley where dead bodies and H3972
Jer 35: 3 his sons—the w family of the Rekabites. H3972
Jer 39: 1 Jerusalem with his w army and laid siege H3972
Jer 40: 4 the w country lies before you; go H3972
Jer 44:28 Then the w remnant of Judah who came H3972
Jer 50:23 shattered is the hammer of the w earth! H3972
Jer 51: 7 LORD's hand; she made the w earth drunk. H3972
Jer 51:25 you who destroy the w earth," declares H3972
Jer 51:41 captured, the boast of the w earth seized! H3972
Jer 51:47 her w land will be disgraced and her slain H3972
Jer 52: 4 against Jerusalem with his w army. H3972
Jer 52: 7 was broken through, and the w army fled. H3972
Jer 52:14 The w Babylonian army, under the H3972
La 2:15 of beauty, the joy of the w earth? H3972
Eze 7:12 for my wrath is on the w crowd. H3972
Eze 7:13 vision concerning the w crowd will not be H3972
Eze 7:14 for my wrath is on the w crowd. H3972
Eze 15: 5 not useful for anything when it was w, H9459
Eze 32:22 "Assyria is there with her w army; she is H3972
Eze 34: 6 They were scattered over the w earth, and H3972
Eze 35:14 While the w earth rejoices, I will make H3972
Eze 38: 4 bring you out with your w army— H3972
Eze 41:19 were carved all around the w temple. H3972
Eze 43:11 its w design and all its regulations and H3972
Da 1:20 enchanters in his w kingdom. H3972
Da 2:35 a huge mountain and filled the w earth. A10353
Da 2:39 one of bronze, will rule over the w earth. A10353
Da 4:20 touching the sky, visible to the w earth, A10353
Da 6: 3 planned to set him over the w kingdom. A10353
Da 7:23 kingdoms and will devour the w earth, A10353
Da 8: 5 crossing the w earth without touching the H3972
Da 9:12 Under the w heaven nothing has ever H3972
Am 1: 6 she took captive w communities and sold H8969
Am 1: 9 Because she sold w communities of H8969
Am 3: 1 against the w family I brought up out of H3972
Am 8: 8 The w land will rise like the Nile; it will H3972
Am 9: 5 in it mourn; the w land rises like the Nile H3972
Hab 1: 6 who sweep across the w earth to seize H5303
Zep 1:18 of his jealousy the w earth will be H3972
Zep 3: 8 The w world will be consumed by the fire H3972
Hag 1:12 the w remnant of the people obeyed H3972
Hag 1:14 the spirit of the w remnant of the people H3972
Zec 1:11 earth and found the w world at rest and in H3972
Zec 5: 3 curse that is going out over the w land; H3972
Zec 6: 5 in the presence of the Lord of the w world. H3972
Zec 13: 8 In the w land," declares the LORD H3972
Zec 14: 9 The LORD will be king over the w earth. H3972
Zec 14:10 The w land, from Geba to Rimmon, south H3972
Mal 3: 9 a curse—your w nation—because you H3972
Mal 3:10 Bring the w tithe into the storehouse, that H3972
Mt 3: 5 all Judea and the w region of the Jordan. *G4246*
Mt 5:29 body than for your w body to be thrown *G3910*
Mt 5:30 body than for your w body to go into hell. *G3910*
Mt 6:22 healthy, your w body will be full of light. *G3910*
Mt 6:23 your w body will be full of darkness. *G3910*
Mt 8:32 the w herd rushed down the steep *G4246*
Mt 8:34 Then the w town went out to meet Jesus *G4246*
Mt 16:26 it be for someone to gain the w world, *G3910*
Mt 21:10 the w city was stirred and asked *G4246*
Mt 24:14 be preached in the w world as a *G3910*
Mt 26:59 chief priests and the w Sanhedrin were *G3910*
Mt 27:27 gathered the w company of soldiers *G3910*
Mk 1: 5 The w Judean countryside and all the *G4246*
Mk 1:28 quickly over the w region of Galilee *G4116+3910*
Mk 1:33 The w town gathered at the door, *G4246*
Mk 5:33 trembling with fear, told him the w truth. *G4246*
Mk 6:55 ran throughout that w region and carried *G3910*
Mk 8:36 is it for someone to gain the w world, *G3910*
Mk 11:18 because the w crowd was amazed at his *G4246*
Mk 14:55 chief priests and the w Sanhedrin were *G3910*
Mk 15: 1 teachers of the law and the w Sanhedrin, *G3910*
Mk 15:16 called together the w company of soldiers *G3910*
Mk 15:33 came over the w land until three in *G3910*
Lk 4:14 him spread through the w countryside. *G3910*
Lk 9:25 is it for someone to gain the w world, *G3910*
Lk 11:34 healthy, your w body also is full of light. *G3910*
Lk 11:36 Therefore, if your w body is full of light *G3910*
Lk 15:14 was a severe famine **in** that w country, *G2848*
Lk 19:37 the w crowd of disciples began joyfully to *G570*
Lk 21:35 those who live on the face *of* the w earth. *G4246*
Lk 23: 1 Then the w assembly rose and led him off *G570*
Lk 23:18 But the w **crowd** shouted, "Away with this *G4101*
Lk 23:44 came over the w land until three in *G3910*
Jn 4:53 So he and his w household believed. *G3910*
Jn 7:23 healing a man's w *body* on the Sabbath? *G3910*
Jn 11:50 the people than that the w nation perish." *G3910*
Jn 12:19 Look how the *w* **world** has gone after him!" AIT
Jn 13:10 to wash their feet; their w *body* is clean. *G3910*
Jn 21:25 that even the w world would not have *G899*
Ac 1:21 been with us the w time the Lord Jesus *G4246*
Ac 2: 2 filled the w house where they were *G3910*
Ac 5:11 Great fear seized the w church and all who *G3910*
Ac 6: 5 This proposal pleased the w group. *G4246*
Ac 7:14 sent for his father Jacob and his w family, *G4246*
Ac 11: 4 beginning, Peter told them **the w story**: *G2759*
Ac 11:26 So for a w year Barnabas and Saul met *G3910*
Ac 13: 6 traveled through the w island until they *G3910*
Ac 13:44 Sabbath almost the w city gathered to *G4246*
Ac 13:49 of the Lord spread through the w region. *G3910*
Ac 15:12 The w assembly became silent as they *G4246*
Ac 15:22 elders, with the w church, decided to *G3910*
Ac 16:34 believe in God—he and his w **household**. *G4109*
Ac 17:26 they should inhabit the w earth; *G4246+4725*
Ac 19:26 in practically the w province of Asia. *G4246*
Ac 19:29 Soon **the** *w* city was in an uproar. The people AIT
Ac 20:18 how I lived the w time I was with you, *G4246*
Ac 20:27 to proclaim to you the w will of God. *G4246*
Ac 21:27 They stirred up the w crowd and seized *G4246*
Ac 21:30 The w city was aroused, and the people *G3910*
Ac 21:31 troops that the w city of Jerusalem was *G3910*
Ac 25:24 The w Jewish community has petitioned *G570*
Ac 28:30 For two w years Paul stayed there in his *G3910*
Ro 3:19 be silenced and the w world held *G4246*
Ro 8:22 We know that the w creation has been *G4246*
Ro 11:16 then the *w* **batch** is holy; if the root is AIT
Ro 16:23 hospitality I and the w church here enjoy, *G3910*
1Co 4: 9 been made a spectacle *to* the w **universe**, *G3180*
1Co 5: 6 little yeast leavens the w batch of dough? *G3910*
1Co 12:17 If the w body were an eye, where would *G3910*
1Co 12:17 If the w body were an ear, where would *G3910*
1Co 14:23 So if the w church comes together and *G3910*
Gal 4: 1 a slave, although he owns *the* w *estate*. *G4246*
Gal 5: 3 that he is obligated to obey the w law. *G3910*
Gal 5: 9 yeast works through the w batch of dough." *G3910*
Gal 5:12 *they would go the w way and* **emasculate** *themselves* AIT
Eph 2:21 In him the w building is joined together *G4246*
Eph 4:10 in order to fill **the w universe**.) *G3836+4246*
Eph 4:13 attaining to the w measure of the fullness *G2461*
Eph 4:16 From him the w body, joined and held *G4246*
Php 1:13 throughout the w palace guard and to *G3910*
Col 1: 6 growing throughout the w world— *G4246*
Col 2:11 Your w **self** ruled by the flesh was put off *G5393*
Col 2:19 from whom the w body, supported and *G4246*
1Th 5:23 May your w spirit, soul and body be kept *G3908*
Titus 1:11 they are disrupting households by *G3910*
Jas 2:10 whoever keeps the w law and yet *G3910*
Jas 3: 2 able to keep their w body in check. *G3910*
Jas 3: 3 them obey us, we can turn the w animal. *G3910*
Jas 3: 6 It corrupts the w body, sets the whole *G3910*
Jas 3: 6 sets the *w* **course** of one's life on fire AIT
1Jn 2: 2 ours but also for the sins of the w world. *G3910*
1Jn 5:19 that the w world is under the control *G3910*
Rev 3:10 going to come on the w world to test the *G3910*
Rev 6:12 of goat hair, the w moon turned blood red *G3910*
Rev 12: 9 Satan, who leads the w world astray. *G3910*
Rev 13: 3 The w world was filled with wonder and *G3910*
Rev 16:14 they go out to the kings of the w world, *G3910*

WHOLEHEARTED (4) [HEART, WHOLE]

2Ki 20: 3 and with w **devotion** and have H4222+8969
1Ch 28: 9 him with w **devotion** and with a H4213+8969
1Ch 29:19 Solomon the w **devotion** to keep H4222+8969
Isa 38: 3 and with w **devotion** and have H4213+8969

WHOLEHEARTEDLY (16) [HEART, WHOLE]

Nu 14:24 has a different spirit and follows me w, H4848
Nu 32:11 'Because *they have* not followed me w H4848
Nu 32:12 son of Nun, for *they* followed the LORD w. H4848
Dt 1:36 feet on, because *he* followed the LORD w." H4848
Jos 14: 8 however, followed the LORD my God w. H4848
Jos 14: 9 *you have* followed the LORD my God w. H4848
Jos 14:14 he followed the LORD, the God of Israel, w. H4848
1Ki 8:23 who continue w in your way. H928+3972+4213
1Ch 29: 9 freely and w to the LORD. H928+4213+8969
2Ch 6:14 who continue w in your way. H928+3972+4213
2Ch 15:15 because they had sworn it w. H928+3972+4222
2Ch 19: 9 faithfully and w in the fear of H928+4222+8969
2Ch 25: 2 eyes of the LORD, but not w. H928+4222+8969
2Ch 31:21 his God and worked w. H928+3972+4222
Ps 119:80 May I w follow your decrees, that I H4213+9459
Eph 6: 7 Serve w, as if you were serving the *G3552+2334*

WHOLESOME (1)

2Pe 3: 1 reminders to stimulate you to w thinking. *G1637*

WHOLLY (3) [WHOLE]

Nu 3: 9 *who are to* **be given** w to him. H5989+5989
Nu 8:16 *who are to* **be given** w to me. H5989+5989
1Ti 4:15 these matters; **give yourself** w to them, so *G3509*

WHOM (393) [WHO] See Index of Articles Etc.

WHORE, WHORE'S, WHORES (KJV) ADULTEROUS, PROMISCUOUS, PROSTITUTE, PROSTITUTES, PROSTITUTION, UNFAITHFUL

WHOREDOM, WHOREDOMS (KJV) ADULTERY, FAVORS, IDOLATRY, IMMORALITY, LUST, PROMISCUITY, PROSTITUTING, PROSTITUTION, UNFAITHFULNESS

WHOREMONGER, WHOREMONGERS (KJV) (SEXUALLY) IMMORAL

WHOSE (289) [WHO] See Index of Articles Etc.

WHY (562)

Ge 2:24 **That is** w a man leaves his father H6584+4027
Ge 4: 6 said to Cain, "W are you angry? H4200+4537
Ge 4: 6 W is your face downcast H4200+4537
Ge 10: 9 before the LORD; **that is** w it is said H6584+4027
Ge 11: 9 **That is** w it was called Babel H6584+4027
Ge 12:18 "W didn't you tell me she was your H4200+4537
Ge 12:19 W did you say, 'She is my sister,' so H4200+4537
Ge 16:14 **That is** w the well was called Beer H6584+4027
Ge 18:13 "W did Sarah laugh and say H4200+4537
Ge 19:22 **That is** w the town was called Zoar.) H6584+4027
Ge 20: 6 **That is** w I did not let you touch her H6584+4027
Ge 24:31 "W are you standing out here H4200+4537
Ge 25:22 "W is this happening to H561+4027+4200+4537
Ge 25:30 **That is** w he was also called Edom. H6584+4027
Ge 26: 9 is really your wife! W did you say, 'She is H375
Ge 26:27 asked them, "W have you come to me H4508
Ge 27:45 W should I lose both of you in one H4537+4200
Ge 29:25 W have you deceived me? H4200+4537
Ge 31:27 W did you run off secretly and H4200+4537
Ge 31:27 W didn't you tell me, so I could send you NDT
Ge 31:30 But w did you steal my gods? H4200+4537
Ge 31:48 " **That is** w it was called Galeed H6584+4027
Ge 32:29 replied, "W do you ask my name?" H4200+4537
Ge 33:15 "**But** w do that?" Jacob H4200+4537
Ge 33:17 **That is** w the place is called H6584+4027
Ge 40: 7 "W do you look so sad today? H4508
Ge 42: 1 "W do you just keep looking at H4200+4537
Ge 42:21 **that's** w this distress has come on H6584+4027
Ge 43: 6 "W did you bring this trouble on H4200+4537
Ge 44: 4 'W have you repaid good with evil? H4200+4537
Ge 44: 7 "W does my lord say such things? H4200+4537
Ge 44: 8 So w would we steal silver or gold from H375
Ge 47:15 W should we die before your eyes H4200+4537
Ge 47:19 W should we perish before your H4200+4537
Ge 47:22 **That is** w they did not sell their H6584+4027
Ge 50:11 **That is** w that place near the H6584+4027
Ex 1:18 asked them, "W have you done this? H4508
Ex 1:18 you done this? W have you let the boys live?" NDT
Ex 2:13 "W are you hitting your fellow H4200+4537
Ex 2:18 "W have you returned so early today?" H4508
Ex 2:20 "W did you leave him H4200+4537
Ex 3: 3 sight—w the bush does not burn up." H4508
Ex 5: 4 w are you taking the people away H4200+4537
Ex 5: 8 lazy; **that is** w they are crying out H6584+4027
Ex 5:14 "W haven't you met your quota of bricks H4508
Ex 5:15 "W have you treated your servants H4200+4537
Ex 5:17 **That is** w you keep saying, 'Let us H6584+4027
Ex 5:22 returned to the LORD and said, "W, Lord, NDT
Ex 5:22 w have you brought trouble on this H4200+4537
Ex 5:22 this people? Is this w you sent me? H4200+4537
Ex 6:12 listen to me, w would Pharaoh listen to me H375
Ex 6:30 w would Pharaoh listen to me?" H375
Ex 13:15 **This is** w I sacrifice to the LORD the H6584+4027
Ex 14:15 to Moses, "W are you crying out to me? H4537
Ex 15:23 **That is** w the place is called Marah.) H6584+4027
Ex 16:29 **that is** w on the sixth day he gives H6584+4027
Ex 17: 2 replied, "W do you quarrel with me? H4537
Ex 17: 2 W do you put the LORD to the test? H4537
Ex 17: 3 "W did you bring us up out of H4200+4537
Ex 18:14 W do you alone sit as judge, while all H4508
Ex 32:11 "w should your anger burn against H4200+4537
Ex 32:12 W should the Egyptians say, 'It was H4200+4537
Lev 10:17 "W didn't you eat the sin offering in the H4508
Lev 17:14 **That is** w I have said to the Israelites H2256
Nu 9: 7 w should we be kept from H4200+4537
Nu 11:11 "W have you brought this trouble H4200+4537
Nu 11:12 W do you tell me to carry them in my H3954
Nu 11:20 "W did we ever leave Egypt? H4200+4537
Nu 12: 8 W then were you not afraid to speak H4508
Nu 14: 3 W is the LORD bringing us to this H4200+4537
Nu 14:41 "W are you disobeying the LORD's H4200+4537
Nu 16: 3 W then do you set yourselves above the H4508
Nu 18:24 **That is** w I said concerning them H6584+4027
Nu 20: 4 W did you bring the LORD's H4200+4537
Nu 20: 5 W did you bring us up out of Egypt H4200+4537
Nu 21: 5 "W have you brought us up out of H4200+4537
Nu 21:14 **That is** w the Book of the Wars of H6584+4027
Nu 21:27 **That is** w the poets say: "Come to H6584+4027
Nu 22:32 "W have you beaten your donkey H6584+4537
Nu 22:37 W didn't you come to me H4200+4537
Nu 27: 4 W should our father's name H4200+4537
Nu 32: 7 W do you discourage the Israelites H4200+4537
Dt 5:25 But now, w should we die? This H4200+4537
Dt 10: 9 **That is** w the Levites have no share H6584+4027
Dt 15:15 **That is** w I give you this command H6584+4027

Dt 19: 7 **This is w** I command you to set H6584+4027
Dt 24:18 **That is w** I command you to do this. H6584+4027
Dt 24:22 **That is w** I command you to do this. H6584+4027
Dt 29:24 "W has the LORD done this to this H6584+4537
Dt 29:24 this to this land? W this fierce, burning H4537
Jos 5: 4 Now this is w he did so: All those who H1821
Jos 7: 7 w did you ever bring this people H4200+4537
Jos 7:12 **That is w** the Israelites cannot stand H2256
Jos 7:25 "W have you brought this trouble on us? H4537
Jos 9:22 "W did you deceive us by saying H4200+4537
Jos 9:24 because of you, **and that is w** we did this. H2256
Jos 17:14 "W have you given us only one allotment H4508
Jos 22:26 "**That is w** we said, 'Let us get ready and H2256
Jdg 2: 2 disobeyed me. W have you done this H4537
Jdg 5:16 W did you stay among the sheep H4200+4537
Jdg 5:17 w did he linger by the ships? H4200+4537
Jdg 5:28 'W is his chariot so long in coming? H4508
Jdg 5:28 W is the clatter of his chariots delayed H4508
Jdg 6:13 w has all this happened to us? H4200+4537
Jdg 8: 1 Gideon, "W have you treated us like this? H4537
Jdg 8: 1 W didn't you call us when you went to fight NDT
Jdg 8: 6 W should we give bread to your troops?" H3954
Jdg 8:15 W should we give bread to your H3954
Jdg 9:28 w should we Shechemites be subject H4769
Jdg 9:28 W should we serve Abimelek H4508
Jdg 11: 7 W do you come to me now, when you're H4508
Jdg 11:26 W didn't you retake them during that time H4508
Jdg 12: 1 "W did you go to fight the Ammonites H4508
Jdg 12: 3 Now w have you come up today to H4200+4537
Jdg 13:18 replied, "W do you ask my name? H4200+4537
Jdg 14:16 he replied, "so *w should I* **explain** it to you?" AIT
Jdg 15:10 "W have you come to fight us?" H4200+4537
Jdg 18: 3 doing in this place? W are you here?" H4537
Jdg 18:12 **This is w** the place west of Kiriath H6584+4027
Jdg 21: 3 "w has this happened to Israel? H4200+4537
Jdg 21: 3 W should one tribe be missing from Israel NDT
Ru 1:11 W would you come with me H4200+4537
Ru 1:21 me back empty. W call me Naomi H4200+4537
Ru 2:10 "W have I found such favor in your eyes H4508
1Sa 1: 8 "Hannah, w are you weeping? H4200+4537
1Sa 1: 8 are you weeping? W don't you eat H4200+4537
1Sa 1: 8 W are you downhearted H4200+4537
1Sa 2:23 "W do you do such things? H4200+4537
1Sa 2:29 W do you scorn my sacrifice and H4200+4537
1Sa 2:29 W do you honor your sons more than me by NDT
1Sa 4: 3 "W did the LORD bring defeat on us H4200+4537
1Sa 5: 5 **That is w** to this day neither the H6584+4027
1Sa 6: 3 you will know w his hand has not H4200+4537
1Sa 6: 6 W do you harden your hearts as the H4200+4537
1Sa 9:21 W do you say such a thing to me?" H4200+4537
1Sa 11: 5 with everyone? W are they weeping?" H3954
1Sa 14:28 **That is w** the men are faint. H2256
1Sa 14:41 "W have you not answered your H4200+4537
1Sa 15:19 W did you not obey the LORD? Why H4200+4537
1Sa 15:19 W did you pounce on the plunder and do NDT
1Sa 17: 8 "W do you come out and line up H4200+4537
1Sa 17:28 "W have you come down here? H4200+4537
1Sa 19: 5 W then would you do wrong to an H4200+4537
1Sa 19:17 "W did you deceive me like this H4200+4537
1Sa 19:17 me get away. W should I kill you H4200+4537
1Sa 19:24 **This is w** people say, "Is Saul also H6584+4027
1Sa 20: 2 W would he hide this from me H4508
1Sa 20: 8 W hand me over to your father?" H4200+4537
1Sa 20:27 "W hasn't the son of Jesse come to the H4508
1Sa 20:29 **That is w** he has not come to the H6584+4027
1Sa 20:32 "W should he be put to death H4200+4537
1Sa 21: 1 met him, and asked, "W are you alone? H4508
1Sa 21: 1 "Why are you alone? W is no one with you?" NDT
1Sa 21:14 He is insane! W bring him to me? H4200+4537
1Sa 22: 8 **Is that w** you have all conspired against H3954
1Sa 22:13 "W have you conspired against me, H4200+4537
1Sa 23:28 **That is w** they call this place Sela H6584+4027
1Sa 24: 9 "W do you listen when men say H4200+4537
1Sa 25:11 W should I take my bread and water, and NDT
1Sa 26:15 W didn't you guard your lord the H4200+4537
1Sa 26:18 "W is my lord pursuing his servant? H4200+4537
1Sa 27: 5 W should your servant live in the H4200+4537
1Sa 28: 9 W have you set a trap for my life to H4200+4537
1Sa 28:12 "W have you deceived me? H4200+4537
1Sa 28:15 "W have you disturbed me by H4200+4537
1Sa 28:16 "W do you consult me H4200+4537
1Sa 29: 8 W can't I go and fight against the H3954
2Sa 1:14 "W weren't you afraid to lift your hand to H375
2Sa 2:22 W should I strike you down H4200+4537
2Sa 3: 7 "W did you sleep with my father's H4508
2Sa 3:24 came to you. W did you let him go H4200+4537
2Sa 5: 8 **That is w** they say, "The 'blind H6584+4027
2Sa 7: 7 "W have you not built me a house H4200+4537
2Sa 11:10 W didn't you go home? H4508
2Sa 11:20 'W did you get so close to the city to fight? H4508
2Sa 11:21 W did you get so close to the wall H4200+4537
2Sa 12: 9 W did you despise the word of the LORD by H4508
2Sa 12:21 asked him, "W are you acting this way? H4537
2Sa 12:23 is dead, w should I go on fasting? H4200+4537
2Sa 13: 4 He asked Amnon, "W do you, the king's H4508
2Sa 13:26 "W should he go with you? H4200+4537
2Sa 14:13 "W then have you devised a thing H4200+4537
2Sa 14:31 "W have your servants set my field H4200+4537
2Sa 14:32 "W have I come from Geshur? H4200+4537
2Sa 15:19 "W should you come along with us H4200+4537
2Sa 16: 2 asked Ziba, "W have you brought these?" H4537
2Sa 16: 9 "W should this dead dog curse my H4200+4537
2Sa 16:10 who can ask, 'W do you do this? H4508
2Sa 16:17 friend, w didn't you go with him?" H4200+4537
2Sa 18:11 W didn't you strike him to the ground H4508
2Sa 18:22 "My son, w do you want to go? H4200+4537
2Sa 19:10 So w do you say nothing about H4200+4537
2Sa 19:11 'W should you be the last to bring H4200+4537
2Sa 19:12 So w should you be the last to H4200+4537
2Sa 19:25 "W didn't you go with me H4200+4537
2Sa 19:29 The king said to him, "W say more? H4200+4537
2Sa 19:35 W should your servant be an H4200+4537
2Sa 19:36 w should the king reward me in H4200+4537
2Sa 19:41 saying to him, "W did our brothers H4508
2Sa 19:42 W are you angry about it H4200+4537
2Sa 19:43 W then do you treat us with contempt H4508
2Sa 20:19 W do you want to swallow up the H4200+4537
2Sa 24: 3 But w does my lord the king want H4200+4537
2Sa 24:21 "W has my lord the king come to his H4508
1Ki 1: 6 by asking, "W do you behave as you do?" H4508
1Ki 1:13 W then has Adonijah become king H4508
1Ki 2:22 "W do you request Abishag the H4200+4537
1Ki 2:43 W then did you not keep your oath to the H4508
1Ki 9: 8 'W has the LORD done such a thing H6584+4537
1Ki 9: 9 **that is w** the LORD brought all this H6584+4027
1Ki 14: 6 of Jeroboam. W this pretense? H4200+4537
1Ki 20:23 **That is w** they were too strong for H6584+4027
1Ki 21: 5 in and asked him, "W are you so sullen? H4537
1Ki 21: 5 "Why are you so sullen? W won't you eat?" NDT
2Ki 1: 5 he asked them, "W have you come back?" H4537
2Ki 3:13 of Israel, "W do you want to involve me? H4537
2Ki 4:23 "W go to him today?" he asked. "It's not H4508
2Ki 4:27 hidden it from me and has not told me w." NDT
2Ki 5: 7 W does this fellow send someone to me H3954
2Ki 5: 8 "W have you torn your robes H4200+4537
2Ki 6:33 W should I wait for the LORD any longer?" H4537
2Ki 7: 3 to each other, "W stay here until we die? H4537
2Ki 8:12 "W is my lord weeping?" asked Hazael H4508
2Ki 9:11 W did this maniac come to you? H4508
2Ki 12: 7 "W aren't you repairing the damage done H4508
2Ki 14:10 W ask for trouble and cause your H4200+4537
1Ch 17: 6 "W have you not built me a house H4200+4537
1Ch 21: 3 W does my lord want to do this H4200+4537
1Ch 21: 3 W should he bring guilt on Israel?" H4200+4537
2Ch 7:21 'W has the LORD done such a thing H928+4537
2Ch 7:22 **that is w** he brought all this disaster H6584+4027
2Ch 20:26 **This is w** it is called the Valley of H6584+4027
2Ch 24: 6 "W haven't you required the Levites to H4508
2Ch 24:20 "W do you disobey the LORD's H4537+4200
2Ch 25:15 "W do you consult this people's H4200+4537
2Ch 25:16 W be struck down?" So the H4200+4537
2Ch 25:19 W ask for trouble and cause your H4200+4537
2Ch 29: 9 **This is w** our fathers have fallen by the H2180
2Ch 29: 9 by the sword and w our sons and H6584+2296
2Ch 32: 4 "W should the kings of Assyria H4200+4537
Ezr 4:15 **That is w** this city was destroyed. A10542+10180
Ezr 4:22 W let this threat grow, to the A10378+10408
Ezr 7:23 W should his wrath fall on the A10378+10408
Ne 2: 2 "W does your face look so sad when you H4508
Ne 2: 3 W should my face not look sad when the H4508
Ne 6: 3 W should the work stop while I H4200+4537
Ne 13:11 "W is the house of God neglected?" H4508
Ne 13:21 "W do you spend the night by the wall? H4508
Est 3: 3 "W do you disobey the king's command?" H4508
Est 4: 5 was troubling Mordecai and w. H6584+4537
Est 9:19 **That is w** rural Jews—those living H6584+4027
Job 3:11 "W did I not perish at birth, and H4200+4537
Job 3:12 W were there knees to receive me and H4508
Job 3:16 Or w was I not hidden away in the ground NDT
Job 3:20 "W is light given to those in misery, H4200+4537
Job 3:23 W is life given to a man whose way is NDT
Job 7:20 W have you made me your target H4200+4537
Job 7:21 W do you not pardon my offenses and H4537
Job 9:22 is all the same; **that is w** I say, 'He H6584+4027
Job 9:29 w should I struggle in vain? H4200+4537
Job 10:18 "W then did you bring me out of H4200+4537
Job 13:14 W do I put myself in jeopardy and H6584+4537
Job 13:24 W do you hide your face and H4200+4537
Job 15:12 W has your heart carried you away, and H4537
Job 15:12 you away, and w do your eyes flash, H4537
Job 18: 3 W are we regarded as cattle and H4508
Job 19:22 W do you pursue me as God does H4200+4537
Job 21: 4 W should I not be impatient? H4508
Job 21: 7 W do the wicked live on, growing old H4508
Job 22:10 **That is w** snares are all around you, H6584+4027
Job 22:10 all around you, w sudden peril terrifies you, NDT
Job 22:11 w it is so dark you cannot see, and why a NDT
Job 22:11 and w a flood of water covers you. NDT
Job 23:15 **That is w** I am terrified before him H6584+4027
Job 24: 1 "W does the Almighty not set times for H4508
Job 24: 1 W must those who know him look in vain NDT
Job 27:12 W then this meaningless talk H4200+4537
Job 32: 6 you are old; **that is w** I was fearful H6584+4027
Job 33:13 W do you complain to him that he H4508
Ps 2: 1 W do the nations conspire and the H4200+4537
Ps 10: 1 W, LORD, do you stand far off? Why H4200+4537
Ps 10: 1 *W do you* **hide** *yourself* in times of trouble AIT
Ps 10:13 W does the wicked man revile God H6584+4537
Ps 10:13 W does he say to himself, "He won't call NDT
Ps 22: 1 my God, w have you forsaken me? H4200+4537
Ps 22: 1 W are you so far from saving me, so far from NDT
Ps 42: 5 W, my soul, are you downcast? Why so H4537
Ps 42: 5 you downcast? W so disturbed within me NDT
Ps 42: 9 "W have you forgotten me? H4200+4537
Ps 42: 9 W must I go about mourning H4200+4537
Ps 42:11 W, my soul, are you downcast? Why so H4537
Ps 42:11 you downcast? W so disturbed within me H4537
Ps 43: 2 W have you rejected me H4200+4537
Ps 43: 2 W must I go about mourning H4200+4537
Ps 43: 5 W, my soul, are you downcast? Why so H4537
Ps 43: 5 you downcast? W so disturbed within me H4537
Ps 44:23 W do you sleep? Rouse H4200+4537
Ps 44:24 W do you hide your face and forget H4200+4537
Ps 49: 5 W should I fear when evil days H4200+4537
Ps 52: 1 W do you boast of evil, you mighty hero H4537
Ps 52: 1 W do you boast all day long, you who are a NDT
Ps 68:16 w gaze in envy, you rugged H4200+4537
Ps 74: 1 w have you rejected us forever? H4200+4537
Ps 74: 1 W does your anger smolder against the NDT
Ps 74:11 W do you hold back your hand H4200+4537
Ps 79:10 W should the nations say, "Where H4200+4537
Ps 80:12 W have you broken down its walls H4200+4537
Ps 88:14 W, LORD, do you reject me and hide H4200+4537
Ps 114: 5 W was it, sea, that you fled? Why, Jordan H4537
Ps 114: 5 that you fled? W, Jordan, did you turn NDT
Ps 114: 6 W, mountains, did you leap like rams, you NDT
Ps 115: 2 W do the nations say, "Where is H4200+4537
Pr 5:20 W, my son, be intoxicated with H4200+4537
Pr 5:20 W embrace the bosom of a wayward NDT
Pr 17:16 W should fools have money H4200+4537+2296
Ecc 4: 8 "and w am I depriving myself of enjoyment?" NDT
Ecc 5: 6 W should God be angry at what H4200+4537
Ecc 7:10 "W were the old days better than these?" H4537
Ecc 7:16 be overwise—w destroy yourself? H4200+4537
Ecc 7:17 be a fool—w die before your time? H4200+4537
SS 1: 7 W should I be like a veiled H8611+4200+4537
SS 6:13 W would you gaze on the Shulammite as H4537
Isa 1: 5 W should you be beaten anymore H6584+4537
Isa 1: 5 W do you persist in rebellion NDT
Isa 2:22 W hold them in esteem? H928+4537
Isa 5: 4 good grapes, w did it yield only bad? H4508
Isa 8:19 W consult the dead on behalf of the living NDT
Isa 40:27 W do you complain, Jacob? Why H4200+4537
Isa 40:27 W do you say, Israel, "My way is hidden NDT
Isa 50: 2 When I came, w was there no one? When H4508
Isa 50: 2 w was there no one to answer? NDT
Isa 55: 2 W spend money on what is not H4200+4537
Isa 58: 3 'W have we fasted,' they say, 'and H4200+4537
Isa 58: 3 W have we humbled ourselves, and you NDT
Isa 63: 2 W are your garments red, like those of H4508
Isa 63:17 W, LORD, do you make us wander H4200+4537
Jer 2:14 W then has he become plunder H4508
Jer 2:18 Now w go to Egypt to drink water from the H4537
Jer 2:18 And w go to Assyria to drink water from H4537
Jer 2:29 "W do you bring charges against H4200+4537
Jer 2:31 W do my people say, 'We are free to H4508
Jer 2:36 W do you go about so much, changing H4537
Jer 4:30 W dress yourself in scarlet and put on H3954
Jer 4:30 W highlight your eyes with makeup H3954
Jer 5: 7 "W should I forgive you? Your H361+4200+2296
Jer 5:19 'W has the LORD our God done all H9393+4537
Jer 8: 5 W then have these people turned away H4508
Jer 8: 5 W does Jerusalem always turn away NDT
Jer 8:14 W are we sitting here? Gather H6584+4537
Jer 8:19 "W have they aroused my anger with their H4508
Jer 8:22 W then is there no healing for the wound H4508
Jer 9:12 W has the land been ruined and H6584+4537
Jer 12: 1 W does the way of the wicked prosper H4508
Jer 12: 1 W do all the faithless live at ease NDT
Jer 13:22 yourself, "W has this happened to me?" H4508
Jer 14: 8 w are you like a stranger in the H4200+4537
Jer 14: 9 W are you like a man taken by H4200+4537
Jer 14:19 W have you afflicted us so that we cannot H4508
Jer 15:18 W is my pain unending and my H4200+4537
Jer 16:10 'W has the LORD decreed such a H6584+4537
Jer 20:18 W did I ever come out of the womb H4200+4537
Jer 22: 8 'W has the LORD done such a thing H6584+4537
Jer 22:28 W will he and his children be hurled out H4508
Jer 26: 9 W do you prophesy in the LORD's name H4508
Jer 27:13 W will you and your people die by H4200+4537
Jer 27:17 W should this city become a ruin H4200+4537
Jer 29:27 So w have you not reprimanded H4200+4537
Jer 30: 6 Then w do I see every strong man with his H4508
Jer 30:15 W do you cry out over your wound, your H4537
Jer 32: 3 "W do you prophesy as you do? H4508
Jer 36:29 "W did you write on it that the king of H4508
Jer 40:15 W should he take your life and H4200+4537
Jer 44: 7 W bring such great disaster on H4200+4537
Jer 44: 8 W arouse my anger with what your hands NDT
Jer 46:15 W will your warriors be laid low? They H4508
Jer 49: 1 W then has Molek taken possession of H4508
Jer 49: 1 W do his people live in its towns NDT
Jer 49: 4 W do you boast of your valleys, boast of H4537
Jer 49:12 must drink it, w should you go unpunished? NDT
Jer 49:25 W has the city of renown not been H375
La 1:16 "**This is w** I weep and my eyes H6584+465
La 3:39 W should the living complain when H4537
La 5:20 W do you always forget us? Why H4200+4537
La 5:20 W do you forsake us so long NDT
Eze 18:19 'W does the son not share the guilt of his H4508
Eze 18:31 and a new spirit. W will you die H4200+4537
Eze 21: 7 they ask you, 'W are you groaning? H6584+4537
Eze 24:19 to do with us? W are you acting like this?" H3954
Eze 33:11 your evil ways! W will you die H4200+4537
Eze 40: 4 for **that is w** you have been brought H4200+5100
Da 1:10 W should he see you looking H4200+4537

Da	2:15	"W did the king issue such a	A10542+10408
Da	10:20	"Do you know w I have come to	H4200+4537
Joel	2:17	W should they say among the	H4200+4537
Am	5:18	W do you long for the day of the	H4200+4537
Mic	4: 9	W do you now cry aloud—have	H4200+4537
Hab	1: 3	W do you make me look at	H4200+4537
Hab	1: 3	W do you tolerate wrongdoing	NDT
Hab	1:13	W then do you tolerate the	H4200+4537
Hab	1:13	W are you silent while the wicked swallow	NDT
Hag	1: 9	I blew away. W?" declares the LORD	H3610+4537
Mal	2:10	W do we profane the covenant of our	H4508
Mal	2:14	You ask, "W?" It is because the LORD	H6584+4537
Mt	6:28	"And w do you worry about clothes? See	*G5515*
Mt	7: 3	"W do you look at the speck of sawdust in	*G5515*
Mt	8:26	of little faith, w are you so afraid?"	*G5515+5516*
Mt	9: 4	"W do you entertain evil thoughts in your	*G2672*
Mt	9:11	"W does your teacher eat with tax	*G1328+5515*
Mt	13:10	"W do you speak to the people in	*G1328+5515*
Mt	13:13	**This is w** I speak to them in	*G1328+4047*
Mt	14: 2	**That is w** miraculous powers are at	*G1328+4047*
Mt	14:31	he said, "w did you doubt?"	*G1650+5515*
Mt	15: 2	"W do your disciples break the	*G1328+5515*
Mt	15: 3	"And w do you break the command	*G1328+5515*
Mt	16: 8	w are you talking among	*G5515+5516*
Mt	17:10	"W then do the teachers of the law	*G5515+5516*
Mt	17:19	asked, "W couldn't we drive it out?"	*G1328+5515*
Mt	19: 7	"W then," they asked, "did Moses	*G5515+5516*
Mt	19:17	"W do you ask me about what is	*G5515+5516*
Mt	20: 6	'W have you been standing here	*G5515+5516*
Mt	21:25	'Then w didn't you believe him?	*G1328+5515*
Mt	22:18	w are you trying to trap me?	*G5515+5516*
Mt	26: 8	were indignant. "W this waste?"	*G1650+5515*
Mt	26:10	"W are you bothering this woman?	*G5515+5516*
Mt	26:65	W do we need any more witnesses	*G5515*
Mt	27: 8	**That is w** it has been called the Field of	*G1475*
Mt	27:23	"W? What crime has he committed?"	*G1142*
Mt	27:46	my God, w have you forsaken me?	*G2672*
Mk	1:38	**That is w** I have come."	*G1650+4047*
Mk	2: 7	"W does this fellow talk like that	*G5515+5516*
Mk	2: 8	"W are you thinking these things?	*G5515+5516*
Mk	2:16	"W does he eat with tax collectors and	*G4022*
Mk	2:24	w are they doing what is unlawful on the	*G5515*
Mk	4:40	his disciples, "W are you so afraid?	*G5515+5516*
Mk	5:35	"W bother the teacher anymore?	*G5515*
Mk	5:39	"W all this commotion and wailing	*G5515+5516*
Mk	6:14	and **that is w** miraculous powers	*G1328+4047*
Mk	7: 5	"W don't your disciples live	*G1328+5515*
Mk	8:12	"W does this generation ask for a	*G5515+5516*
Mk	8:17	"W are you talking about having	*G5515+5516*
Mk	9:11	"W do the teachers of the law say that	*G4022*
Mk	9:12	W then is it written that the Son of Man	*G4802*
Mk	9:28	him privately, "W couldn't we drive it out?"	*G4022*
Mk	10:18	"W do you call me good?" Jesus	*G5515+5516*
Mk	11: 3	asks you, 'W are you doing this?	*G5515+5516*
Mk	11:31	'Then w didn't you believe him?	*G1328+5515*
Mk	12:15	"W are you trying to trap me?	*G5515+5516*
Mk	12:35	"W do the teachers of the law say that the	*G4802*
Mk	14: 4	another, "W this waste of perfume?	*G1650+5515*
Mk	14: 6	"W are you bothering her	*G5515*
Mk	14:63	"W do we need any more	*G5515+5516*
Mk	15:14	"W? What crime has he committed?"	*G1142*
Mk	15:34	my God, w have you forsaken me?"	*G1650+5515*
Lk	1:21	Zechariah and **wondering** w he stayed so	*G2513*
Lk	1:43	But w am I so favored, that the mother of	*G4470*
Lk	2:48	w have you treated us like this?	*G5515*
Lk	2:49	"W were you searching for me?"	*G5515+5516*
Lk	4:43	because **that is w** I was sent.	*G2093+4047*
Lk	5:22	"W are you thinking these things in	*G5515+5516*
Lk	5:30	"W do you eat and drink with tax	*G1328+5515*
Lk	6: 2	"W are you doing what is unlawful	*G5515+5516*
Lk	6:41	"W do you look at the speck of sawdust in	*G5515*
Lk	6:46	"W do you call me, 'Lord, Lord,' and do	*G5515*
Lk	7: 7	**That is w** I did not even consider myself	*G1475*
Lk	8:47	she told w she had touched	*G1328+4005+162*
Lk	12:26	little thing, w do you worry about the rest?	*G5515*
Lk	12:57	"W don't you judge for yourselves what is	*G5515*
Lk	13: 7	W should it use up the soil	*G2672*
Lk	18:19	"W do you call me good?" Jesus	*G5515+5516*
Lk	19:23	W then didn't you put my money on	*G1328+5515*
Lk	19:31	asks you, 'W are you untying it?'	*G1328+5515*
Lk	19:33	"W are you untying the colt?"	*G5515+5516*
Lk	20: 5	'W didn't you believe him?	*G1328+5515*
Lk	20:41	"W is it said that the Messiah is the son	*G4802*
Lk	22:46	"W are you sleeping?" he asked	*G5515+5516*
Lk	22:71	"W do we need any more	*G5515+5516*
Lk	23:22	he spoke to them: "W? What crime has	*G1142*
Lk	24: 5	"W do you look for the living	*G5515+5516*
Lk	24:38	He said to them, "W are you troubled, and	*G5515*
Lk	24:38	and w do doubts rise in your minds	*G1328+5515*
Jn	1:25	"W then do you baptize if you are	*G5515+5516*
Jn	2: 4	**w do** you **involve** me?	*G5515+5516+2779*
Jn	4:27	"W are you talking with her?	*G5515+5516*
Jn	6:65	"**This is w** I told you that no one	*G1328+4047*
Jn	7:19	W are you trying to kill me?	*G5515*
Jn	7:23	*w are you* **angry** with me for healing a man's	AIT
Jn	7:45	"W didn't you bring him in?	*G1328+5515*
Jn	8:22	**Is that w** he says, 'Where I go, you cannot	*G4022*
Jn	8:43	W is my language not clear to you	*G1328+5515*
Jn	8:46	the truth, w don't you believe me?	*G1328+5515*
Jn	9:23	**That was w** his parents said, "He is	*G1328+4047*
Jn	9:27	W do you want to hear it again	*G5515*
Jn	10:20	raving mad. W listen to him?"	*G5515*
Jn	10:36	W then do you accuse me of blasphemy	NDT
Jn	12: 5	"W wasn't this perfume sold and	*G1328+5515*
Jn	13:11	and **that was w** he said not every	*G1328+4047*
Jn	13:28	meal understood w Jesus said this	*G4639+5515*
Jn	13:37	w can't I follow you now?	*G1328+5515*
Jn	14:22	w do you intend to show yourself to us	*G5515*
Jn	15:19	**That is w** the world hates you.	*G1328+4047*
Jn	16:15	**That is w** I said the Spirit will	*G1328+4047*
Jn	18:21	W question me? Ask those who heard me	*G5515*
Jn	18:23	if I spoke the truth, w did you strike me?"	*G5515*
Jn	20:13	asked her, "Woman, w are you crying?"	*G5515*
Jn	20:15	asked her, "Woman, w are you crying	*G5515*
Ac	1:11	"w do you stand here looking into the sky?	*G5515*
Ac	3:12	Israelites, w does this surprise you?	*G5515*
Ac	3:12	W do you stare at us as if by our own	*G5515*
Ac	4:25	" 'W do the nations rage and the peoples	*G2672*
Ac	7:26	w do you want to hurt each other?	*G2672*
Ac	9: 4	"Saul, Saul, w do you persecute me?"	*G5515*
Ac	10:21	W have you come?	*G5515+3836+162*
Ac	10:29	May I ask w you sent for me?"	*G5515+3364*
Ac	14:15	"Friends, w are you doing this? We too are	*G5515*
Ac	15:10	w do you try to test God by putting on the	*G5515*
Ac	19:32	not even know w they were there.	*G5515+1915*
Ac	21:13	"W are you weeping and breaking	*G5515+5516*
Ac	22: 7	Saul! W do you persecute me	*G5515*
Ac	22:24	to find out w the people were	*G1328+4005+162*
Ac	22:30	to find out exactly w Paul was being	*G5515*
Ac	23:28	to know w they were	*G3836+162+1328+4005*
Ac	26: 8	W should any of you consider it incredible	*G5515*
Ac	26:14	Saul, w do you persecute me?	*G5515*
Ac	26:21	**That is w** some Jews seized me in	*G1915+4047*
Ro	1:15	**That is w** I am so eager to preach the	*G4048*
Ro	3: 7	w am I still condemned as a sinner?"	*G5515*
Ro	3: 8	W not say—as some slanderously claim that	NDT
Ro	4:22	**This is w** "it was credited to him as	*G1475*
Ro	9:19	"Then w does God still blame us	*G5515+5516*
Ro	9:20	'W did you make me like this?	*G5515+5516*
Ro	9:32	W not? Because they	*G1328+5515+5516*
Ro	13: 6	**This is** also w you pay taxes	*G1328+4047+1142*
Ro	14:10	w do you judge your brother or sister?	*G5515*
Ro	14:10	Or w do you treat them with contempt	*G5515*
Ro	15:22	**This is w** I have often been hindered from	*G1475*
1Co	4: 7	w do you boast as though you did not?	*G5515*
1Co	6: 7	W not rather be wronged	*G1328+5515*
1Co	6: 7	W not rather be cheated?	*G1328+5515*
1Co	10:29	For w is my freedom being judged by	*G2672*
1Co	10:30	w am I denounced because of something	*G5515*
1Co	11:30	**That is w** many among you are	*G1328+4047*
1Co	15:29	w are people baptized for them?	*G5515*
1Co	15:30	w do we endanger ourselves every	*G5515+5516*
2Co	11:11	W? Because I do not love	*G1328+5515+5516*
2Co	12:10	**That is w**, for Christ's sake, I delight in	*G1475*
2Co	13:10	**This is w** I write these things when I	*G1328+4047*
Gal	3:19	W, then, was the law given at all? It was	*G5515*
Gal	5:11	w am I still being persecuted?	*G5515*
Eph	4: 8	**This is w** it says: "When he ascended on	*G1475*
Eph	5:14	**This is w** it is said: "Wake up, sleeper, rise	*G1475*
Col	2:20	forces of this world, w, as though you still	*G5515*
1Ti	4:10	**That is w** we labor and strive	*G1650+4047*
2Ti	1:12	**That is w** I am suffering as I	*G1328+4005+162*
Heb	3:10	**That is w** I was angry with that generation;	*G1475*
Heb	5: 3	**This is w** he has to offer sacrifices	*G1328+899*
Heb	7:11	w was there still need for another priest to	*G5515*
Heb	8: 5	**This is w** Moses was warned when he was	*G2777*
Heb	9:18	**This is w** even the first covenant was not	*G3854*
Jas	4: 6	us more grace. **That is w** Scripture says	*G1475*
Jas	4:14	W, you do not even know what will happen	NDT
1Jn	3:12	And w did he murder him	*G5920+5515*
Rev	17: 7	said to me: "W are you astonished	*G1328+5515*

WICK (11)

Ex	25:38	Its **w trimmers** and trays are to be of pure	H4920
Ex	37:23	as well as its **w trimmers** and trays, of	H4920
Nu	4: 9	its lamps, its **w trimmers** and trays, and all	H4920
1Ki	7:50	gold basins, **w trimmers**, sprinkling bowls	H4662
2Ki	12:13	silver basins, **w trimmers**, sprinkling bowls	H4662
2Ki	25:14	shovels, **w trimmers**, dishes and all the	H4662
2Ch	4:22	the pure gold **w trimmers**, sprinkling	H4662
Isa	42: 3	a smoldering w he will not snuff out.	H7325
Isa	43:17	extinguished, snuffed out like a w:	H7325
Jer	52:18	shovels, **w trimmers**, sprinkling	H4662
Mt	12:20	a smoldering w he will not snuff out	*G3351*

WICKED (372) [OVERWICKED, WICKEDLY, WICKEDNESS]

Ge	13:13	of Sodom were w and were sinning	H8273
Ge	18:23	you sweep away the righteous with the w?	H8401
Ge	18:25	to kill the righteous with the w, treating	H8401
Ge	18:25	treating the righteous and the w alike.	H8401
Ge	19: 7	my friends. Don't **do** *this* **w thing.**	H8317
Ge	38: 7	Judah's firstborn, was w in the LORD's sight	H8273
Ge	38:10	What he did *was* w in the LORD's sight; so	H8317
Ge	39: 9	could I do such a **w thing** and sin against	H8288
Ge	44: 5	*This is a* w *thing* you have done	H8317
Lev	20:14	both a woman and her mother, it is w.	H2365
Nu	14:27	"How long will this w community grumble	H8273
Nu	14:35	these things to this whole w community,	H8273
Nu	16:26	back from the tents of these w men!	H8401
Dt	15: 9	Be careful not to harbor this w thought	H1175
Jdg	19:22	some of the w men of the city	H1201+1175
Jdg	20:13	Now turn those w men of Gibeah	H1201+1175
1Sa	1:16	Do not take your servant for a w woman;	H1175
1Sa	2: 9	the w will be silenced in the place of	H8401
1Sa	2:23	the people about these w deeds of yours.	H8273
1Sa	15:18	completely destroy those **w people**,	H2629
1Sa	17:28	you are and how w your heart is;	H8278
1Sa	25:17	He is such a w man that no one can talk	H1175
1Sa	25:25	attention, my lord, to that w man Nabal.	H1175
2Sa	3:34	You fell as one falls before the w."	H1201+6406
2Sa	4:11	when w men have killed an innocent man	H8401
2Sa	7:10	W people will not oppress them anymore	H6406
2Sa	13:12	be done in Israel! Don't do this **w thing.**	H5576
2Sa	13:13	would be like one of the **w fools** in Israel.	H5572
2Ki	17:11	They did w things that aroused the LORD's	H8273
1Ch	2: 3	Judah's firstborn, was w in the LORD's sight	H8273
1Ch	17: 9	W people will not oppress them anymore	H6406
2Ch	7:14	seek my face and turn from their w ways,	H8273
2Ch	19: 2	you help the w and love those who	H8401
2Ch	20:35	king of Israel, whose ways *were* w.	H8399
2Ch	24: 7	the sons of that w *woman* Athaliah had	H5360
Ezr	4:12	are rebuilding that rebellious and w city.	A10090
Ne	13:17	"What is this w thing you are doing	H8273
Job	3:17	There the w cease from turmoil, and there	H8401
Job	8:22	the tents of the w will be no more.	H8401
Job	9:22	destroys both the blameless and the w.	H8401
Job	9:24	When a land falls into the hands of the w,	H8401
Job	10: 3	while you smile on the plans of the w?	H8401
Job	11:20	But the eyes of the w will fail, and escape	H8401
Job	15:20	All his days the w *man* suffers torment	H8401
Job	16:11	thrown me into the clutches of the w.	H8401
Job	18: 5	"The lamp of a w *man* is snuffed out; the	H8401
Job	20: 5	that the mirth of the w is brief, the joy of	H8401
Job	20:29	Such is the fate God allots the w, the	H8401
Job	21: 7	Why do the w live on, growing old and	H8401
Job	21:16	so I stand aloof from the plans of the w.	H8401
Job	21:17	often is the lamp of the w snuffed out?	H8401
Job	21:19	punishment of the w for their children.	H2257S
Job	21:19	Let him repay **the w**, so that they	H2257S
Job	21:28	of the great, the tents where the w lived?	H8401
Job	21:30	that the w are spared from the day of	H8273
Job	22:15	to the old path that the w have trod?	H224+5493
Job	22:18	so I stand aloof from the plans of the w.	H8401
Job	24: 6	fields and glean in the vineyards of the w.	H8401
Job	24:20	the w are no longer remembered but are	H6406
Job	27: 4	my lips will not say **anything** w, and my	H6406
Job	27: 7	"May my enemy be like the w, my	H8401
Job	27:13	"Here is the fate God allots to the w, the	H8401
Job	29:17	broke the fangs of the w and snatched the	H6405
Job	31: 3	Is it not ruin for the w, disaster for those	H6405
Job	31:11	For that would have been w, a sin to be	H2365
Job	34: 8	evildoers; he associates with the w.	H8400+408
Job	34:18	are worthless,' and to nobles, 'You are w,'	H8401
Job	34:36	to the utmost for answering like a w man!	H224
Job	35:12	cry out because of the arrogance of the w.	H8273
Job	36: 6	does not keep the w alive but gives the	H8401
Job	36:17	are laden with the judgment due the w;	H8401
Job	38:13	by the edges and shake the w out of it?	H8401
Job	38:15	The w are denied their light, and their	H8401
Job	40:12	crush the w where they stand.	H8401
Ps	1: 1	in step with the w or stand in the way	H8401
Ps	1: 4	Not so the w! They are like chaff that the	H8401
Ps	1: 5	Therefore the w will not stand in the	H8401
Ps	1: 6	the way of the w leads to destruction.	H8401
Ps	3: 7	on the jaw; break the teeth of the w.	H8401
Ps	7: 9	the violence of the w and make the	H8401
Ps	9: 5	rebuked the nations and destroyed the w;	H8401
Ps	9:16	the w are ensnared by the work of their	H8401
Ps	9:17	The w go down to the realm of the dead	H8401
Ps	10: 2	his arrogance the w *man* hunts down the	H8401
Ps	10: 4	In his pride the w *man* does not seek him	H8401
Ps	10:13	Why does the w *man* revile God? Why	H8401
Ps	10:15	Break the arm of the w *man*; call the	H8401
Ps	11: 2	For look, the w bend their bows; they set	H8401
Ps	11: 5	the righteous, but the w, those who love	H8401
Ps	11: 6	On the w he will rain fiery coals and	H8401
Ps	12: 7	will protect us forever from the w,	H1887+2306S
Ps	17: 9	from the w who are out to destroy me	H8401
Ps	17:13	with your sword rescue me from the w.	H8401
Ps	17:14	have stored up for the w fill their bellies;	NDT
Ps	21:11	evil against you and devise **w schemes**,	H4659
Ps	26: 5	of evildoers and refuse to sit with the w.	H8401
Ps	26:10	in whose hands are **w schemes**, whose	H2365
Ps	27: 2	When the w advance against me to	H8317
Ps	28: 3	Do not drag me away with the w, with	H8401
Ps	31:17	let the w be put to shame and be	H8401
Ps	32:10	Many are the woes of the w, but the	H8401
Ps	34:21	Evil will slay the w; the foes of the	H8401
Ps	36: 1	heart concerning the sinfulness of the w:	H8401
Ps	36: 3	words of their mouths are w and deceitful;	H224
Ps	36:11	nor the hand of the w drive me away.	H8401
Ps	37: 7	when they carry out their **w schemes**.	H4659
Ps	37:10	little while, and the w will be no more	H8401
Ps	37:12	The w plot against the righteous and	H8401
Ps	37:13	the Lord laughs at **the w**, for he	H2257S
Ps	37:14	The w draw the sword and bend the bow	H8401
Ps	37:16	have than the wealth of many w;	H8401
Ps	37:17	the power of the w will be broken, but	H8401
Ps	37:20	But the w will perish: Though the LORD's	H8401
Ps	37:21	The w borrow and do not repay, but the	H8401
Ps	37:28	the offspring of the w will perish.	H8401
Ps	37:32	The w lie in wait for the righteous, intent	H8401
Ps	37:33	in the power of the w or let them be	H2257
Ps	37:34	the land; when the w are destroyed, you	H8401
Ps	37:35	I have seen a w and ruthless man	H8401

W

Ps 37:38 there will be no future for the **w**. H8401
Ps 37:40 delivers them from the **w** and saves them, H8401
Ps 39: 1 my mouth while in the presence of the **w**." H8401
Ps 43: 1 me from those who are deceitful and **w**. H6406
Ps 49: 5 when **w** deceivers surround me— H6411
Ps 50:16 But to the **w** *person*, God says: "What H8401
Ps 55: 3 because of the threats of the **w**; for they H8401
Ps 55: 9 confuse the **w**, confound their words NDT
Ps 55:23 will bring down **the w** into the pit of H4392S
Ps 58: 3 Even from birth the **w** go astray; from the H8401
Ps 58: 9 green or dry—**the w** will be swept away. H5647S
Ps 58:10 they dip their feet in the blood of the **w**. H8401
Ps 59: 5 all the nations; show no mercy to **w** traitors. H224
Ps 64: 2 Hide me from the conspiracy of the **w** H8317
Ps 68: 2 the fire, may the **w** perish before God. H8401
Ps 71: 4 from the hand of the **w**, from the grasp of H8401
Ps 73: 3 when I saw the prosperity of the **w**. H8401
Ps 73:12 This is what the **w** are like—always free H8401
Ps 75: 4 no more,' and to the **w**, 'Do not lift up H8401
Ps 75: 8 all the **w** *of* the earth drink it down to H8401
Ps 75:10 "I will cut off the horns of all the **w**, but H8401
Ps 82: 2 the unjust and show partiality to the **w**? H8401
Ps 82: 4 deliver them from the hand of the **w**. H8401
Ps 84:10 my God than dwell in the tents of the **w**. H8400
Ps 89:22 of him; the **w** will not oppress him. H1201+6406
Ps 91: 8 eyes and see the punishment of the **w**. H8401
Ps 92: 7 that though the **w** spring up like grass H8401
Ps 92:11 my ears have heard the rout of my **w** foes. H8317
Ps 94: 3 will the **w**, how long will the wicked H8401
Ps 94: 3 how long will the **w** be jubilant? H8401
Ps 94:13 days of trouble, till a pit is dug for the **w**. H8401
Ps 94:16 Who will rise up for me against the **w** H8317
Ps 94:21 The **w** band together against the righteous NDT
Ps 97:10 delivers them from the hand of the **w**. H8401
Ps 101: 8 I will put to silence all the **w** *in* the land; H8401
Ps 104:35 from the earth and the **w** be no more. H8401
Ps 106:18 their followers; a flame consumed the **w**. H8401
Ps 106:29 the LORD's anger by their **w deeds**, H5095
Ps 107:42 but all the **w** shut their mouths. H6406
Ps 109: 2 for *people who* are **w** and deceitful have H8401
Ps 112:10 The **w** will see and be vexed, they will H8401
Ps 112:10 the longings of the **w** will come to H8401
Ps 119:53 Indignation grips me because of the **w** H8401
Ps 119:61 Though the **w** bind me with ropes, I will H8401
Ps 119:95 The **w** are waiting to destroy me, but I will H8401
Ps 119:110 The **w** have set a snare for me, but I have H8401
Ps 119:119 All the **w** *of* the earth you discard like H8401
Ps 119:150 Those who devise **w schemes** are near H2365
Ps 119:155 Salvation is far from the **w**, for they do H8401
Ps 125: 3 The scepter of the **w** will not remain over H8400
Ps 129: 4 has cut me free from the cords of the **w**." H8401
Ps 139:19 would slay the **w**! Away from me, H8401
Ps 140: 4 from the hands of the **w**; protect me from H8401
Ps 140: 8 Do not grant the **w** their desires, LORD; do H8401
Ps 141: 4 that I take part in **w** deeds along with H8400
Ps 141: 6 the **w** will learn that my words were NDT
Ps 141:10 Let the **w** fall into their own nets, while I H8401
Ps 145:20 love him, but all the **w** he will destroy. H8401
Ps 146: 9 he frustrates the ways of the **w**. H8401
Ps 147: 6 the humble but casts the **w** to the ground. H8401
Pr 2:12 will save you from the ways of **w** *men*, H8273
Pr 2:22 the **w** will be cut off from the land H8401
Pr 3:25 of the ruin that overtakes the **w**, H8401
Pr 3:33 The LORD's curse is on the house of the **w** H8401
Pr 4:14 on the path of the **w** or walk in the way of H8401
Pr 4:19 But the way of the **w** is like deep darkness; H8401
Pr 5:22 The evil deeds of the **w** ensnare them H8401
Pr 6:18 a heart that devises **w** schemes, feet that H224
Pr 9: 7 whoever rebukes the **w** incurs abuse. H8401
Pr 10: 3 he thwarts the craving of the **w**. H8401
Pr 10: 6 violence overwhelms the mouth of the **w**. H8401
Pr 10: 7 blessings, but the name of the **w** will rot. H8401
Pr 10:11 the mouth of the **w** conceals violence. H8401
Pr 10:16 the earnings of the **w** are sin and death. H8401
Pr 10:20 the heart of the **w** is of little value. H8401
Pr 10:23 A fool finds pleasure in **w** schemes, but a H2365
Pr 10:24 What the **w** dread will overtake them H8401
Pr 10:25 has swept by, the **w** are gone, but the H8401
Pr 10:27 but the years of the **w** are cut short. H8401
Pr 10:28 the hopes of the **w** come to nothing. H8401
Pr 10:30 the **w** will not remain in the land. H8401
Pr 10:32 the mouth of the **w** only what is H8401
Pr 11: 5 the **w** are brought down by their own H8401
Pr 11: 8 from trouble, and it falls on the **w** instead. H8401
Pr 11:10 city rejoices; when the **w** perish, there are H8401
Pr 11:11 by the mouth of the **w** it is destroyed. H8401
Pr 11:18 A **w** *person* earns deceptive wages, but H8401
Pr 11:21 The **w** will not go unpunished, but those H8273
Pr 11:23 but the hope of the **w** only in wrath. H8401
Pr 12: 2 condemns those who devise **w schemes**. H4659
Pr 12: 5 but the advice of the **w** is deceitful. H8401
Pr 12: 6 The words of the **w** lie in wait for blood H8401
Pr 12: 7 The **w** are overthrown and are no more H8401
Pr 12:10 the kindest acts of the **w** are cruel. H8401
Pr 12:12 The **w** desire the stronghold of evildoers H8401
Pr 12:21 the **w** have their fill of trouble. H8401
Pr 12:26 the way of the **w** leads them astray. H8401
Pr 13: 5 the **w** make themselves a stench and H8401
Pr 13: 9 the lamp of the **w** is snuffed out. H8401
Pr 13:17 A **w** messenger falls into trouble, but a H8401
Pr 13:25 the stomach of the **w** goes hungry. H8401
Pr 14:11 The house of the **w** will be destroyed, but H8401
Pr 14:19 the **w** at the gates of the righteous. H8401
Pr 14:32 calamity comes, the **w** are brought down H8401
Pr 15: 3 keeping watch on the **w** and the good. H8273
Pr 15: 6 the income of the **w** brings ruin. H8401
Pr 15: 8 The LORD detests the sacrifice of the **w**, H8401
Pr 15: 9 The LORD detests the way of the **w**, but he H8401
Pr 15:26 The LORD detests the thoughts of the **w** H8273
Pr 15:28 the mouth of the **w** gushes evil. H8401
Pr 15:29 The LORD is far from the **w**, but he hears H8401
Pr 16: 4 even the **w** for a day of disaster. H8401
Pr 17: 4 A **w** *person* listens to deceitful lips; a liar H8317
Pr 17:23 The **w** accept bribes in secret to pervert H8401
Pr 18: 5 to be partial to the **w** and so deprive the H8401
Pr 19:28 the mouth of the **w** gulps down evil. H8401
Pr 20:26 A wise king winnows out the **w**; he drives H8401
Pr 21: 4 the unplowed field of the **w**—produce sin. H8401
Pr 21: 7 violence of the **w** will drag them away H8401
Pr 21:10 The **w** crave evil; their neighbors H8401+5883
Pr 21:12 of the house of the **w** and brings the H8401
Pr 21:12 of the wicked and brings the **w** to ruin. H8401
Pr 21:18 The **w** become a ransom for the righteous, H8401
Pr 21:27 The sacrifice of the **w** is detestable—how H8401
Pr 21:29 The **w** put up a bold front, but the H8401+408
Pr 22: 5 In the paths of the **w** are snares and H6836
Pr 24: 1 Do not envy the **w**, do not desire H8288+408
Pr 24:16 the **w** stumble when calamity strikes. H8401
Pr 24:19 of evildoers or be envious of the **w**, H8401
Pr 24:20 the lamp of the **w** will be snuffed out. H8401
Pr 25: 5 remove **w** *officials* from the king's H8401
Pr 25:26 are the righteous who give way to the **w**. H8401
Pr 28: 1 The **w** flee though no one pursues, but H8401
Pr 28: 4 who forsake instruction praise the **w**, H8401
Pr 28:12 when the **w** rise to power, people H8401
Pr 28:15 a charging bear is a **w** ruler over a H8401
Pr 28:28 When the **w** rise to power, people go into H8401
Pr 28:28 into hiding; but when **the w** perish, the H4392S
Pr 29: 2 when the **w** rule, the people H8401
Pr 29: 7 the poor, but the **w** have no such concern. H8401
Pr 29:12 listens to lies, all his officials become **w**. H8401
Pr 29:16 When the **w** thrive, so does sin, but the H8401
Pr 29:27 the dishonest; the **w** detest the upright. H8401
Ecc 3:17 judgment both the righteous and the **w**, H8401
Ecc 7:15 the **w** living long in their wickedness. H8401
Ecc 8:10 Then too, I saw the **w** buried—those who H8401
Ecc 8:12 Although a **w** *person* who commits a H2627
Ecc 8:13 Yet because the **w** do not fear God, it will H8401
Ecc 8:14 the righteous who get what the **w** deserve, H8401
Ecc 8:14 the **w** who get what the righteous H8401
Ecc 9: 2 the righteous and the **w**, the good and the H8401
Ecc 10:13 at the end they are **w** madness— H8273
Isa 3:11 Woe to the **w**! Disaster is upon them H8401
Isa 9:17 everyone is ungodly and **w**, every H8317
Isa 11: 4 the breath of his lips he will slay the **w**. H8401
Isa 13:11 the world for its evil, the **w** for their sins. H8401
Isa 14: 5 The LORD has broken the rod of the **w**, the H8401
Isa 14:20 the offspring of the **w** never be mentioned H8317
Isa 26:10 But when grace is shown to the **w**, they do H8401
Isa 31: 2 He will rise up against that **w** nation H8317
Isa 32: 7 Scoundrels use **w** methods, they make up H8273
Isa 35: 8 **w fools** will not go about on it. H211
Isa 48:22 is no peace," says the LORD, "for the **w**." H8401
Isa 53: 9 He was assigned a grave with the **w**, and H8401
Isa 55: 7 Let the **w** forsake their ways and the H8401
Isa 57:20 But the **w** are like the tossing sea, which H8401
Isa 57:21 is no peace," says my God, "for the **w**." H8401
Isa 58: 4 in striking each other with **w** fists. H8400
Isa 59: 3 and your tongue mutters **w** *things*. H6406
Jer 4:14 How long will you harbor **w** thoughts? H224
Jer 5:26 my people are the **w** who lie in wait like H8401
Jer 6:29 goes on in vain; the **w** are not purged out. H8273
Jer 12: 1 Why does the way of the **w** prosper? Why H8401
Jer 12: 4 Because those who live in it are **w**, the H8288
Jer 12:14 "As for all my **w** neighbors who seize the H8273
Jer 13:10 These **w** people, who refuse to listen to H8273
Jer 15:21 the hands of the **w** and deliver you from H8273
Jer 20:13 life of the needy from the hands of the **w**. H8317
Jer 23:19 swirling down on the heads of the **w**. H8401
Jer 25:31 all mankind and put the **w** to the sword,' H8401
Jer 30:23 swirling down on the heads of the **w**. H8401
Jer 35:15 must turn from your **w** ways and reform H8288
Jer 36: 3 they will each turn from their **w** ways; then H8288
Jer 36: 7 LORD and will each turn from their **w** ways, H8288
Jer 44:22 no longer endure your **w** actions and the H8278
Eze 3:18 When I say to a **w** *person*, 'You will surely H8401
Eze 3:18 that **w** *person* will die for their sin H8401
Eze 3:19 you do warn the **w** *person* and they do not H8401
Eze 6:11 because of all the **w** and detestable H8288
Eze 7:11 has arisen, a rod to punish the **w**. H8400
Eze 7:21 as loot to the **w** *of* the earth, H8401
Eze 7:24 I will bring the *most* **w** *of* nations to take H8273
Eze 8: 9 "Go in and see the **w** and detestable H8273
Eze 11: 2 evil and giving **w** advice in this city. H8273
Eze 13:22 you encouraged the **w** not to turn from H8401
Eze 14: 3 their hearts and put **w** stumbling blocks H6411
Eze 14: 4 hearts and put a **w** stumbling block before H6411
Eze 14: 7 hearts and put a **w** stumbling block before H6411
Eze 18:20 the wickedness of the **w** will be charged H8401
Eze 18:21 "But if a **w** *person* turns away from all the H8401
Eze 18:23 I take any pleasure in the death of the **w**? H8401
Eze 18:24 detestable things the **w** *person* does, H8401
Eze 18:27 But if a **w** *person* turns away from the H8401
Eze 21: 3 off from you both the righteous and the **w**. H8401
Eze 21: 4 going to cut off the righteous and the **w**, H8401
Eze 21:25 " 'You profane and **w** prince of Israel H8401
Eze 21:29 on the necks of the **w** who are to be slain, H8401
Eze 33: 8 When I say to the **w**, 'You wicked person H8401
Eze 33: 8 the wicked, 'You **w** *person*, you will surely H8401
Eze 33: 8 that **w** *person* will die for their sin H8401
Eze 33: 9 if you do warn the **w** *person* to turn from H8401
Eze 33:11 I take no pleasure in the death of the **w** H8401
Eze 33:12 And if someone who is **w** repents, that H8401
Eze 33:14 And if I say to a **w** *person*, 'You will surely H8401
Eze 33:19 And if a **w** *person* turns away from their H8401
Eze 36:31 your evil ways and **w** deeds, H4202+3202
Da 2: 9 to tell me misleading and **w** things, A10705
Da 8:23 when rebels have become completely **w**, NDT
Da 9: 5 *We have been* **w** and have rebelled; we H8399
Da 12:10 the **w** will continue to be wicked. H8401
Da 12:10 the wicked *will continue to be* **w**. H8399
Da 12:10 None of the **w** will understand, but those H8401
Hos 6: 9 to Shechem, carrying out their **w schemes**. H2365
Hos 12:11 Is Gilead **w**? Its people are worthless! Do H224
Mic 6:10 treasures, you **w** house, and the short H8401
Na 1:11 evil against the LORD and devises **w** plans. H1175
Na 1:15 No more will the **w** invade you; they will H1175
Hab 1: 4 The **w** hem in the righteous, so that H8401
Hab 1:13 you silent while the **w** swallow up those H8401
Hab 1:15 The **w** foe pulls all of them up with hooks NDT
Zep 1: 3 the idols that cause the **w** to stumble." H8401
Mal 1: 4 They will be called the **W** Land, a people H8402
Mal 3:18 between the righteous and the **w**, H8401
Mal 4: 3 Then you will trample on the **w**; they will H8401
Mt 12:39 "A **w** and adulterous generation asks for a *G4505*
Mt 12:45 it seven other spirits **more w** than itself, *G4505*
Mt 12:45 is how it will be with this **w** generation." *G4505*
Mt 13:49 separate the **w** from the righteous *G4505*
Mt 16: 4 A **w** and adulterous generation looks for a *G4505*
Mt 18:32 'You **w** servant,' he said, 'I canceled all *G4505*
Mt 24:48 that servant is **w** and says to himself, *G2805*
Mt 25:26 master replied, '*You* **w**, lazy servant! So *G4505*
Lk 6:35 he is kind to the ungrateful and **w**. *G4505*
Lk 11:26 seven other spirits **more w** than itself, *G4505*
Lk 11:29 Jesus said, "This is a **w** generation. *G4505*
Lk 19:22 you by your own words, *you* **w** servant! *G4505*
Ac 2:23 with the help *of* **w** *men*, put him to death *G491*
Ac 3:26 by turning each of you from your **w ways**." *G4504*
Ac 24:15 resurrection of both the righteous and the **w**. *G96*
1Co 5:13 "Expel the **w** *person* from among you." *G4505*
2Th 3: 2 may be delivered from **w** and evil people, *G876*
2Jn 11 welcomes them shares in their **w** work. *G4505*
Rev 2: 2 I know that you cannot tolerate **w** *people* *G2805*

WICKEDLY (9) [WICKED]

1Ki 8:47 we have done wrong, *we have* **acted w**'; H8399
2Ch 6:37 we have done wrong and **acted w**'; H8399
2Ch 22: 3 his mother encouraged him to **act w**. H8399
Ne 1: 7 *We have* **acted very w** toward you H2472+2472
Ne 9:33 have acted faithfully, while we **acted w**. H8399
Job 13: 7 Will you speak **w** on God's behalf? Will H6406
Ps 106: 6 we have done wrong and **acted w**. H8399
Jer 16:12 have behaved more **w** than your ancestors H8317
Jer 38: 9 these men *have* **acted w** in all they have H8317

WICKEDNESS (109) [WICKED]

Ge 6: 5 saw how great the **w** *of* the human race H8288
Ex 34: 7 forgiving **w**, rebellion and sin. H6411
Ex 34: 9 people, forgive our **w** and our sin, and H6411
Lev 16:21 over it all the **w** and rebellion of the H6411
Lev 18:17 they are her close relatives. That is **w**. H2365
Lev 19:29 turn to prostitution and be filled with **w**. H2365
Lev 20:14 the fire, so that no **w** will be among you. H2365
Dt 9: 4 on account of the **w** *of* these nations that H8402
Dt 9: 5 on account of the **w** *of* these nations H8402
Dt 9:27 of this people, their **w** and their sin. H8400
Dt 31:18 because of all their **w** in turning to other H8288
Jdg 9:56 Thus God repaid the **w** that Abimelek had H8288
Jdg 9:57 the people of Shechem pay for all their **w**. H8288
2Ch 28:19 for *he had* **promoted w** in Judah and had H7277
Ne 13:27 doing all this terrible **w** and are being H8288
Job 6:30 Is there any **w** on my lips? Can my mouth H6406
Job 22: 5 Is not your **w** great? Are not your sins H8288
Job 22:23 If you remove **w** far from your tent H6406
Job 34:26 them for their **w** where everyone can see H8401
Job 35: 8 Your **w** only affects humans like yourself H8400
Job 35:15 he does not take the least notice of **w**. H7317
Ps 5: 4 you are not a God who is pleased with **w**; H8400
Ps 10:15 to account for his **w** that would not H8400
Ps 45: 7 You love righteousness and hate **w** H8400
Ps 56: 7 Because of their **w** do not let them escape H224
Ps 92:15 he is my Rock, and there is no **w** in him." H6406
Ps 94:23 their sins and destroy them for their **w**; H8288
Ps 107:34 because of the **w** *of* those who lived there. H8288
Pr 4:17 eat the bread of **w** and drink the wine of H8400
Pr 8: 7 speaks what is true, for my lips detest **w**. H8400
Pr 11: 5 wicked are brought down by their own **w**. H8402
Pr 12: 3 No one can be established through **w**, but H8400
Pr 13: 6 of integrity, but **w** overthrows the sinner. H8402
Pr 18: 3 When **w** comes, so does contempt, and H8401
Pr 26:26 their **w** will be exposed in the H8288
Ecc 3:16 place of judgment—**w** was there, in the H8400
Ecc 3:16 in the place of justice—**w** was there. H8400
Ecc 7:15 the wicked living long in their **w**. H8288
Ecc 7:25 the stupidity of **w** and the madness of H8400
Ecc 8: 8 so **w** will not release those who practice it. H8400

W

Isa 5:18 cords of deceit, and **w** as with cart ropes, H2632
Isa 9:18 Surely **w** burns like a fire; it consumes H8402
Isa 47:10 You have trusted in your **w** and have said H8288
Jer 1:16 because of their **w** in forsaking me, H8288
Jer 2:19 Your **w** will punish you; your backsliding H8288
Jer 3: 2 the land with your prostitution and **w**. H8288
Jer 6: 7 out its water, so she pours out her **w**. H8288
Jer 7:12 to it because of the **w** *of* my people Israel. H8288
Jer 8: 6 None of them repent of their **w**, saying H8288
Jer 11:15 When you engage in your **w**, then you H8288
Jer 14:10 now remember their **w** and punish them H6411
Jer 14:20 We acknowledge our **w**, LORD, and the H8400
Jer 16:18 them double for their **w** and their sin, H6411
Jer 22:22 disgraced because of all your **w**. H8288
Jer 23:11 even in my temple I find their **w**, H8288
Jer 23:14 so that not one of them turns from their **w**. H8288
Jer 31:34 I will forgive their **w** and will remember H6411
Jer 33: 5 my face from this city because of all its **w**. H8288
Jer 36: 3 then I will forgive their **w** and their sin." H6411
Jer 36:31 his children and his attendants for their **w**; H6411
Jer 44: 5 not turn from their **w** or stop burning H8288
Jer 44: 9 forgotten the **w** committed *by* your H8288
Jer 44: 9 the **w** committed *by* you and your H8288
La 1:22 "Let all their **w** come before you; deal H8288
La 4:22 Daughter Edom, and expose your **w**. H2633
Eze 3:19 do not turn from their **w** or from their evil H8400
Eze 5: 6 Yet in her **w** she has rebelled against my H8402
Eze 16:23 In addition to all your other **w**, H8288
Eze 16:57 before your **w** was uncovered. Even so, H8288
Eze 18:20 the **w** *of* the wicked will be charged H8402
Eze 18:27 away from the **w** they have committed H8402
Eze 28:15 you were created till **w** was found in you. H6406
Eze 31:11 him to deal with according to its **w**. H8400
Eze 33:12 that person's former **w** will not bring H8402
Eze 33:19 away from their **w** and does what is just H8402
Da 4:27 your **w** by being kind to the A10532
Da 9:24 to atone for **w**, to bring in H6411
Hos 4: 8 the sins of my people and relish their **w**. H6411
Hos 7: 3 "They delight the king with their **w**, the H8288
Hos 8:13 will remember their **w** and punish their H6411
Hos 9: 9 remember their **w** and punish them for H6411
Hos 9:15 "Because of all their **w** in Gilgal, I hated H8288
Hos 10: 8 The high places of **w** will be destroyed—it H224
Hos 10:13 But you have planted **w**, you have reaped H8400
Hos 10:15 Bethel, because your **w is great**. H8288+8288
Joel 3:13 the vats overflow—so great is their **w**!" H8288
Jnh 1: 2 because its **w** has come up before me." H8288
Mic 3:10 with bloodshed, and Jerusalem with **w**. H6406
Hab 3:13 You crushed the leader of the land of **w** H8401
Zec 5: 8 He said, "This is **w**," and he pushed her H8402
Mt 23:28 the inside you are full of hypocrisy and **w**. *G490*
Mt 24:12 Because of the increase *of* **w**, the love of *G490*
Lk 11:39 inside you are full of greed and **w**. *G4504*
Ac 1:18 With the payment he *received for* his **w** *G94*
Ac 8:22 Repent of this **w** and pray to the Lord in *G2798*
Ro 1:18 all the godlessness and **w** of people, *G94*
Ro 1:18 who suppress the truth by their **w**, *G94*
Ro 1:29 They have become filled with every kind *of* **w**, *G94*
Ro 6:13 part of yourself to sin as an instrument *of* **w**, *G94*
Ro 6:19 and *to* **ever-increasing w**, *G490+1650+490*
1Co 5: 8 old bread leavened with malice and **w**, *G4504*
2Co 6:14 do righteousness and **w** have in common? *G490*
2Th 2:10 all the ways that **w** deceives those who *G94*
2Th 2:12 believed the truth but have delighted in **w**. *G94*
2Ti 2:19 name of the Lord must turn away from **w**." *G94*
Titus 2:14 us to redeem us from all **w** and to purify *G490*
Heb 1: 9 You have loved righteousness and hated **w**; *G490*
Heb 8:12 I will forgive their **w** and will remember their *G94*
2Pe 2:15 son of Bezer, who loved the wages *of* **w**. *G94*

WIDE (106) [WIDELY, WIDENED, WIDER, WIDTH]

Ge 6:15 fifty cubits **w** and thirty cubits high. H8145
Ex 25:10 a cubit and a half **w**, and a cubit and a H8145
Ex 25:17 half cubits long and a cubit and a half **w**. H8145
Ex 25:23 a cubit **w** and a cubit and a half high. H8145
Ex 25:25 it a rim a **handbreadth** *w* and put a gold AIT
Ex 26: 2 twenty-eight cubits long and four cubits **w**. H8145
Ex 26: 8 thirty cubits long and four cubits **w**. H8145
Ex 26:16 ten cubits long and a cubit and a half **w**, H8145
Ex 27: 1 five cubits long and five cubits **w**. H8145
Ex 27:12 shall be fifty cubits **w** and have curtains, H8145
Ex 27:13 the courtyard shall also be fifty cubits **w**. H8145
Ex 27:18 a hundred cubits long and fifty cubits **w**, H8145
Ex 28:16 a span long and a span **w**—and folded H8145
Ex 30: 2 a cubit long and a cubit **w**, and two cubits H8145
Ex 36: 9 twenty-eight cubits long and four cubits **w**. H8145
Ex 36:15 thirty cubits long and four cubits **w**. H8145
Ex 36:21 ten cubits long and a cubit and a half **w**, H8145
Ex 37: 1 a cubit and a half **w**, and a cubit and a H8145
Ex 37: 6 half cubits long and a cubit and a half **w**. H8145
Ex 37:10 a cubit **w** and a cubit and a half high. H8145
Ex 37:12 a rim a handbreadth **w** and put a gold NDT
Ex 37:25 long and a cubit **w** and two cubits high— H8145
Ex 38: 1 five cubits long and five cubits **w**. H8145
Ex 38:12 west end was fifty cubits **w** and had curtains, NDT
Ex 38:13 toward the sunrise, was also fifty cubits **w**. NDT
Ex 39: 9 a span long and a span **w**—and folded H8145
Dt 3:11 than nine cubits long and four cubits **w**. H8145
1Sa 26:13 there was a **w** space between them. H8041
1Ki 6: 2 sixty cubits long, twenty **w** and thirty high. H8145
1Ki 6: 6 The lowest floor was five cubits **w**, the H8145
1Ki 6:20 cubits long, twenty **w** and twenty high. H8145
1Ki 7: 2 cubits long, fifty **w** and thirty high, with H8145
1Ki 7: 6 a colonnade fifty cubits long and thirty **w**. H8145
1Ki 7:27 four cubits long, four **w** and three high. H8145
1Ch 13: 2 let us send word **far and w** to the rest of H7287
2Ch 3: 3 was sixty cubits long and twenty cubits **w** H8145
2Ch 3: 8 twenty cubits long and twenty cubits **w**. H8145
2Ch 4: 1 twenty cubits **w** and ten cubits high. H8145
2Ch 6:13 five cubits **w** and three cubits high H8145
2Ch 26:15 fame spread **far and w**, H6330+4200+4946+8158
Ezr 6: 3 to be sixty cubits high and sixty cubits **w**, A10603
Ps 22:13 prey **open** their mouths **w** against me H7198
Ps 81:10 **Open w** your mouth and I will fill it H8143
Isa 5:14 jaws, opening **w** its mouth H4200+1172+2976
Isa 18: 2 people feared **far and w**, H4946+2085+2256+2134
Isa 18: 7 people feared **far and w**, H4946+2085+2256+2134
Isa 30:33 Its fire pit has been made deep and **w** H8143
Isa 45: 8 *Let* the earth **open w**, let salvation spring H7337
Isa 54: 2 **stretch** your tent curtains **w**, do not H5742
Isa 57: 8 you climbed into it and **opened** it **w**; you H8143
La 2:16 enemies **open** their mouths **w** against you H7198
La 3:46 enemies *have* **opened** their mouths **w** H7198
Eze 40: 7 guards were one rod long and one rod **w**, H8145
Eze 40:18 gateways and was as **w** as they were long; NDT
Eze 40:21 fifty cubits long and twenty-five cubits **w**. H8145
Eze 40:25 fifty cubits long and twenty-five cubits **w**. H8145
Eze 40:29 fifty cubits long and twenty-five cubits **w**. H8145
Eze 40:30 twenty-five cubits **w** and five cubits deep.) H802
Eze 40:33 fifty cubits long and twenty-five cubits **w**. H8145
Eze 40:36 fifty cubits long and twenty-five cubits **w**. H8145
Eze 40:42 a cubit and a half **w** and a cubit high. H8145
Eze 40:47 cubits long and a hundred cubits **w**. H8145
Eze 40:48 they were five cubits **w** on either side. NDT
Eze 40:48 walls were three cubits **w** on either side. NDT
Eze 40:49 The portico was twenty cubits **w**, and twelve H802
Eze 41: 2 The entrance was ten cubits **w**, and the H8145
Eze 41: 2 walls on each side of it were five cubits **w**. NDT
Eze 41: 2 was forty cubits long and twenty cubits **w**. H8145
Eze 41: 3 of the entrance; each was two cubits **w**. NDT
Eze 41: 3 The entrance was six cubits **w**, and the NDT
Eze 41: 3 on each side of it were seven cubits **w**. H8145
Eze 41: 5 around the temple was four cubits **w**. H8145
Eze 41:10 was twenty cubits **w** all around the temple H8145
Eze 41:11 open area was five cubits **w** all around. H8145
Eze 41:12 on the west side was seventy cubits **w**. H8145
Eze 42: 2 a hundred cubits long and fifty cubits **w**. H8145
Eze 42: 4 ten cubits **w** and a hundred cubits H8145
Eze 42:20 cubits long and five hundred cubits **w**, H8145
Eze 43:13 Its gutter is a cubit deep and a cubit **w** H8145
Eze 43:14 cubits high, and the ledge is a cubit **w**. H8145
Eze 43:14 and that ledge is also a cubit **w**. H8145
Eze 43:16 twelve cubits long and twelve cubits **w**. H8145
Eze 43:17 cubits long and fourteen cubits **w**. H8145
Eze 45: 1 25,000 cubits long and 20,000 cubits **w** H8145
Eze 45: 3 25,000 cubits long and 10,000 cubits **w**. H8145
Eze 45: 5 10,000 cubits **w** will belong to the H8145
Eze 45: 6 an area 5,000 cubits **w** and 25,000 cubits H8145
Eze 46:22 forty cubits long and thirty cubits **w**; each H8145
Eze 48: 8 It will be 25,000 cubits **w**, and its length H8145
Eze 48: 9 25,000 cubits long and 10,000 cubits **w**. H8145
Eze 48:10 10,000 cubits **w** on the west side H8145
Eze 48:10 10,000 cubits **w** on the east side and H8145
Eze 48:13 25,000 cubits long and 10,000 cubits **w**. H8145
Eze 48:15 5,000 cubits **w** and 25,000 cubits long H8145
Da 3: 1 sixty cubits high and six cubits **w**, and set A10603
Mic 4: 3 strong nations **far and w**. H6330+8158
Na 3:13 of your land *are* **w open** to your H7337+7337
Zec 2: 2 to find out how **w** and how long it is." H8145
Zec 5: 2 twenty cubits long and ten cubits **w**." H8145
Mt 7:13 For **w** is the gate and broad is the road *G4426*
Mt 23: 5 *They* **make** their phylacteries **w** and the *G4425*
2Co 6:11 and **opened w** our hearts to you. *G4425*
2Co 6:13 to my children—**open w** your hearts also. *G4425*
Eph 3:18 to grasp how **w** and long and high and *G4424*
Rev 21:16 laid out like a square, as long as it was **w**. *G4424*
Rev 21:16 in length, and as **w** and high as it is long. *G4424*

WIDELY (3) [WIDE]

Ne 4:19 we are **w** separated from each other H8158
Mt 28:15 story *has been* **w circulated** among the *G1424*
Ac 19:20 word of the Lord **spread w** and grew in *G889*

WIDENED (1) [WIDE]

Eze 41: 7 so that the rooms **w** as one went upward. H8145

WIDER (2) [WIDE]

Job 11: 9 longer than the earth and **w** than the sea. H8146
Eze 41: 7 around the temple *were* **w** at each H8143

WIDESPREAD (2) [SPREAD]

Eze 28:16 Through your **w** trade you were filled with H8044
Jn 7:12 crowds there was **w** whispering about him *G4498*

WIDOW (58) [WIDOW'S, WIDOWHOOD, WIDOWS, WIDOWS']

Ge 38:11 "Live *as* a **w** in your father's household H530
Ex 22:22 take advantage of the **w** or the fatherless. H530
Lev 21:14 He must not marry a **w**, a divorced woman H530
Lev 22:13 daughter becomes a **w** or is divorced, H530
Nu 30: 9 obligation taken by a **w** or divorced woman H530
Dt 10:18 the cause of the fatherless and the **w**, H530
Dt 24:17 take the cloak of the **w** as a pledge. H530
Dt 24:19 the fatherless and the **w**, so that the LORD H530
Dt 24:20 the foreigner, the fatherless and the **w**. H530
Dt 24:21 the foreigner, the fatherless and the **w**. H530
Dt 25: 5 his **w** must not marry outside the H851+4637
Dt 25: 9 his **brother's w** shall go up to him in the H3304
Dt 26:12 the fatherless and the **w**, so that they may H530
Dt 26:13 the fatherless and the **w**, according to all H530
Dt 27:19 from the foreigner, the fatherless or the **w**." H530
Ru 4: 5 the dead man's **w**, in order to maintain H851
Ru 4:10 Ruth the Moabite, Mahlon's **w**, as my wife, H851
1Sa 27: 3 Abigail of Carmel, the **w** *of* Nabal. H851
1Sa 30: 5 Abigail, the **w** *of* Nabal of Carmel. H851
2Sa 2: 2 Abigail, the **w** *of* Nabal of Carmel. H851
2Sa 3: 3 son of Abigail the **w** *of* Nabal of Carmel; H851
2Sa 14: 5 She said, "I am a **w**; my husband is dead. H530
1Ki 7:14 whose mother was a **w** from the tribe of H530
1Ki 11:26 his mother was a **w** named Zeruah. H530
1Ki 17: 9 I have directed a **w** there to supply you with H530
1Ki 17:10 town gate, a **w** was there gathering sticks. H530
1Ki 17:20 tragedy even on this **w** I am staying with, H530
Job 24:21 to the **w** they show no kindness. H530
Job 31:16 poor or let the eyes of the **w** grow weary, H530
Job 31:18 from my birth I guided the **w**— H5626S
Ps 94: 6 They slay the **w** and the foreigner; they H530
Ps 109: 9 his children be fatherless and his wife a **w**. H530
Ps 146: 9 sustains the fatherless and the **w**, H530
Isa 1:17 of the fatherless; plead the case of the **w**. H530
Isa 47: 8 I will never be a **w** or suffer the loss of H530
Jer 7: 6 the fatherless or the **w** and do not shed H530
Jer 22: 3 the fatherless or the **w**, and do not shed H530
La 1: 1 How like a **w** is she, who once was great H530
Eze 22: 7 mistreated the fatherless and the **w**. H530
Zec 7:10 Do not oppress the **w** or the fatherless, the H530
Mt 22:24 must marry the **w** and raise up offspring *G1222*
Mk 12:19 man must marry the **w** and raise up *G1222*
Mk 12:21 The second one married **the w**, but he *G899S*
Mk 12:42 But a poor **w** came and put in two very *G5939*
Mk 12:43 this poor **w** has put more into the treasury *G5939*
Lk 2:37 then was a **w** until she was *G5939*
Lk 4:26 to a **w** in Zarephath in the *G1222+5939*
Lk 7:12 only son of his mother, and she was a **w**. *G5939*
Lk 18: 3 And there was a **w** in that town who kept *G5939*
Lk 18: 5 because this **w** keeps bothering me, *G5939*
Lk 20:28 man must marry the **w** and raise up *G1222*
Lk 21: 2 He also saw a poor **w** put in two very small *G5939*
Lk 21: 3 "this poor **w** has put in more than all the *G5939*
1Ti 5: 4 But if a **w** has children or grandchildren *G5939*
1Ti 5: 5 The **w** who is really in need and left all *G5939*
1Ti 5: 6 But the **w** who lives for pleasure is dead NDT
1Ti 5: 9 No **w** may be put on the list of widows *G5939*
Rev 18: 7 I am not a **w**; I will never mourn *G5939*

WIDOW'S (6) [WIDOW]

Ge 38:14 she took off her **w** clothes, covered herself H531
Ge 38:19 off her veil and put on her **w** clothes again. H531
Job 24: 3 donkey and take the **w** ox in pledge. H530
Job 29:13 dying blessed me; I made the **w** heart sing. H530
Pr 15:25 he sets the **w** boundary stones in place. H530
Isa 1:23 the **w** case does not come before them. H530

WIDOWHOOD (2) [WIDOW]

Isa 47: 9 loss of children and **w**. They will come H529
Isa 54: 4 remember no more the reproach of your **w**. H531

WIDOWS (31) [WIDOW]

Ex 22:24 your wives will become **w** and your children H530
Dt 14:29 fatherless and the **w** who live in your towns H530
Dt 16:11 the fatherless and the **w** living among you. H530
Dt 16:14 fatherless and the **w** who live in your towns H530
2Sa 20: 3 till the day of their death, living as **w**. H531
Job 22: 9 And you sent **w** away empty-handed and H530
Job 27:15 and their **w** will not weep for them. H530
Ps 68: 5 a defender of **w**, is God in his holy H530
Ps 78:64 to the sword, and their **w** could not weep. H530
Isa 9:17 will he pity the fatherless and **w**, for H530
Isa 10: 2 making **w** their prey and robbing the H530
Jer 15: 8 I will make their **w** more numerous than H530
Jer 18:21 Let their wives be made childless and **w** H530
Jer 49:11 Your **w** too can depend on me H530
La 5: 3 become fatherless, our mothers are **w**. H530
Eze 22:25 things and make many **w** within her. H530
Eze 44:22 They must not marry **w** or divorced women H530
Eze 44:22 virgins of Israelite descent or **w** of priests. H530
Mal 3: 5 who oppress the **w** and the fatherless H530
Lk 4:25 that there were many **w** in Israel in *G5939*
Ac 6: 1 Jews because their **w** were being *G5939*
Ac 9:39 All the **w** stood around him, crying and *G5939*
Ac 9:41 especially the **w**, and presented her to *G5939*
1Co 7: 8 Now to the unmarried and the **w** I say: It *G5939*
1Ti 5: 3 recognition *to* those **w** who are really in *G5939*
1Ti 5: 9 be put on the list of **w** unless she is over NDT
1Ti 5:11 As for younger **w**, do not put them on *G5939*
1Ti 5:14 So I counsel younger **w** to marry, to have NDT
1Ti 5:16 who is a believer has **w** in her care, *G5939*
1Ti 5:16 church can help those **w** who are really in *G5939*
Jas 1:27 after orphans and **w** in their distress and *G5939*

WIDOWS' (2) [WIDOW]

Mk 12:40 They devour **w** houses and for a show make *G5939*
Lk 20:47 They devour **w** houses and for a show make *G5939*

WIDTH (13) [WIDE]

1Ki 6: 3 the temple extended the **w** *of* the temple, H8145
1Ki 6:31 one fifth of the **w** of the sanctuary. H382+4647S
1Ki 6:33 that were **one fourth** *of the* **w** *of* the hall. AIT

2Ch 3: 4 long across the w *of* the building and H8145
2Ch 3: 8 corresponding to the w *of* the temple— H8145
Eze 40:11 he measured the w *of* the entrance of H8145
Eze 40:20 the length and w *of* the north gate, H8145
Eze 40:48 The w *of* the entrance was fourteen cubits H8145
Eze 41: 1 the w *of* the jambs was six cubits on each H8145
Eze 41: 4 its w was twenty cubits across the end H8145
Eze 41:14 The w *of* the temple courtyard on the east H8145
Eze 42:11 they had the same length and w, with H8145
Eze 48:13 be 25,000 cubits and its w 10,000 cubits. H8145

WIELD (2) [WIELDED, WIELDING]

Pr 22: 8 the **rod** they *w in* fury will be broken. AIT
Isa 10:15 As if a rod *were to* w the person who lifts H5677

WIELDED (1) [WIELD]

2Sa 7:14 I will punish him with a **rod** *w by* men, with AIT

WIELDING (1) [WIELD]

Ps 74: 5 like *men* w axes to cut H995+4200+5087+2025

WIFE (335) [WIFE'S, WIVES, WIVES']

Ge 2:24 father and mother and is united to his w, H851
Ge 2:25 Adam and his w were both naked, and H851
Ge 3: 8 the man and his w heard the sound of H851
Ge 3:17 you listened to your w and ate fruit from H851
Ge 3:20 Adam named his w Eve, because she H851
Ge 3:21 skin for Adam and his w and clothed them. H851
Ge 4: 1 Adam made love to his w Eve, and she H851
Ge 4:17 Cain made love to his w, and she became H851
Ge 4:25 Adam made love to his w again, and she H851
Ge 6:18 your sons and your w and your sons' wives H851
Ge 7: 7 his sons and his w and his sons' wives H851
Ge 7:13 together with his w and the wives of his H851
Ge 8:16 you and your w and your sons and their H851
Ge 8:18 his sons and his w and his sons' wives. H851
Ge 11:29 The name of Abram's w was Sarai, and the H851
Ge 11:29 the name of Nahor's w was Milkah H851
Ge 11:31 the w *of* his son Abram, and H851
Ge 12: 5 He took his w Sarai, his nephew Lot, all the H851
Ge 12:11 he said to his w Sarai, "I know what a H851
Ge 12:12 see you, they will say, 'This is his w. H851
Ge 12:17 his household because of Abram's w Sarai. H851
Ge 12:18 "Why didn't you tell me she was your w? H851
Ge 12:19 is my sister,' so that I took her to be my w? H851
Ge 12:19 Now then, here is your w. Take her and go!" H851
Ge 12:20 his way, with his w and everything he had. H851
Ge 13: 1 with his w and everything he had H851
Ge 16: 1 Now Sarai, Abram's w, had borne him no H851
Ge 16: 3 Sarai his w took her Egyptian slave Hagar H851
Ge 16: 3 gave her to her husband to be his w. H851
Ge 17:15 "As for Sarai your w, you are no longer to H851
Ge 17:19 but your w Sarah will bear you a son H851
Ge 18: 9 "Where is your w Sarah?" they asked him H851
Ge 18:10 and Sarah your w will have a son. H851
Ge 19:15 Take your w and your two daughters who H851
Ge 19:16 the hands of his w and of his two H851
Ge 19:26 But Lot's w looked back, and she became a H851
Ge 20: 2 there Abraham said of his w Sarah H851
Ge 20: 7 Now return the man's w, for he is a prophet H851
Ge 20:11 they will kill me because of my w. H851
Ge 20:12 not of my mother; and she became my w. H851
Ge 20:14 he returned Sarah his w to him. H851
Ge 20:17 his w and his female slaves so they could H851
Ge 20:18 conceiving because of Abraham's w Sarah. H851
Ge 21:21 his mother got a w for him from Egypt. H851
Ge 23: 3 from beside his **dead** *w* and spoke to the AIT
Ge 23:19 Abraham buried his w Sarah in the cave in H851
Ge 24: 3 you will not get a w for my son from the H851
Ge 24: 4 own relatives and get a w for my son Isaac." H851
Ge 24: 7 that you can get a w for my son from there H851
Ge 24:15 who was the w *of* Abraham's brother Nahor H851
Ge 24:36 My master's w Sarah has borne him a son H851
Ge 24:37 'You must not get a w for my son from the H851
Ge 24:38 to my own clan, and get a w for my son. H851
Ge 24:40 so that you can get a w for my son from my H851
Ge 24:51 let her become the w of your master's son, H851
Ge 24:67 So she became his w, and he loved her H851
Ge 25: 1 Abraham had taken another w, whose H851
Ge 25:10 Abraham was buried with his w Sarah. H851
Ge 25:21 Isaac prayed to the LORD on behalf of his w H851
Ge 25:21 his w Rebekah became pregnant. H851
Ge 26: 7 men of that place asked him about his w, H851
Ge 26: 7 because he was afraid to say, "She is my w." H851
Ge 26: 8 saw Isaac caressing his w Rebekah. H851
Ge 26: 9 Isaac and said, "She is really your w! H851
Ge 26:10 the men might well have slept with your w, H851
Ge 26:11 harms this man or his w shall surely be put H851
Ge 27:46 If Jacob takes a w from among the women H851
Ge 28: 2 Take a w for yourself there, from among H851
Ge 28: 6 to Paddan Aram to take a w from there, H851
Ge 29:21 "Give me my w. My time is H851
Ge 29:28 gave him his daughter Rachel to be his w. H851
Ge 30: 4 So she gave him her servant Bilhah as a w H851
Ge 30: 9 Zilpah and gave her to Jacob as a w. H851
Ge 34: 4 father Hamor, "Get me this girl as my w." H851
Ge 34: 8 Please give her to him as his w. H851
Ge 34:12 Only give me the young woman as my w." H851
Ge 36:10 the son of Esau's w Adah, and Reuel, H851
Ge 36:10 Reuel, the son of Esau's w Basemath. H851
Ge 36:12 These were grandsons of Esau's w Adah. H851
Ge 36:13 were grandsons of Esau's w Basemath. H851
Ge 36:14 The sons of Esau's w Oholibamah H851
Ge 36:17 they were grandsons of Esau's w Basemath. H851
Ge 36:18 The sons of Esau's w Oholibamah: Chiefs H851
Ge 36:18 from Esau's w Oholibamah daughter H851
Ge 38: 6 Judah got a w for Er, his firstborn, and her H851
Ge 38: 8 with your brother's w and fulfill your duty H851
Ge 38: 9 so whenever he slept with his brother's w H851
Ge 38:12 After a long time Judah's w, the daughter H851
Ge 38:14 she had not been given to him as his w. H851
Ge 39: 7 a while his master's w took notice of H851
Ge 39: 9 me except you, because you are his w. H851
Ge 39:19 his master heard the story his w told him, H851
Ge 41:45 of Potiphera, priest of On, to be his w. H851
Ge 44:27 'You know that my w bore me two sons. H851
Ge 46:19 The sons of Jacob's w Rachel: Joseph and H851
Ge 49:31 Abraham and his w Sarah were buried, H851
Ge 49:31 there Isaac and his w Rebekah were buried, H851
Ex 4:20 So Moses took his w and sons, put them on H851
Ex 18: 2 After Moses had sent away his w Zipporah H851
Ex 18: 5 together with Moses' sons and w, came to H851
Ex 18: 6 to you with your w and her two sons." H851
Ex 20:17 You shall not covet your neighbor's w, or H851
Ex 21: 3 if he has a w when he comes, she is H851
Ex 21: 4 master gives him a w and she bears him H851
Ex 21: 5 my master and my w and children and do H851
Ex 22:16 pay the bride-price, and she shall be his w. H851
Lev 18: 8 have sexual relations with your father's w; H851
Lev 18:11 with the daughter of your father's w, H851
Lev 18:14 by approaching his w to have sexual H851
Lev 18:15 She is your son's w; do not have relations H851
Lev 18:16 have sexual relations with your brother's w; H851
Lev 18:18 wife's sister as a **rival** w and have sexual H7675
Lev 18:18 relations with her while **your** w is living. H2023S
Lev 18:20 with your neighbor's w and defile yourself H851
Lev 20:10 commits adultery with another man's w— H851
Lev 20:10 with the w *of* his neighbor—both H851
Lev 20:11 has sexual relations with his father's w, H851
Lev 20:21 " 'If a man marries his brother's w, it is an H851
Nu 5:12 'If a man's w goes astray and is unfaithful H851
Nu 5:14 he suspects his w and she is impure— H851
Nu 5:15 then he is to take his w to the priest. H851
Nu 5:30 over a man because he suspects his w. H851
Nu 12: 1 against Moses because of his Cushite w, H851
Nu 26:59 the name of Amram's w was Jochebed, H851
Nu 30:16 relationships between a man and his w, H851
Dt 5:21 "You shall not covet your neighbor's w. H851
Dt 13: 6 son or daughter, or the w you love, or your H851
Dt 21:11 you may take her as your w. H851
Dt 21:13 be her husband and she shall be your w. H851
Dt 21:15 is the son of the w he does not love, NDT
Dt 21:16 to the son of the w he loves in preference to NDT
Dt 21:16 firstborn, the son of the w he does not love. NDT
Dt 21:17 the son of his unloved w as the firstborn by NDT
Dt 22:13 If a man takes a w and, after sleeping with H851
Dt 22:19 She shall continue to be his w; he must not H851
Dt 22:22 sleeping with another man's w, H851+1249
Dt 22:24 man because he violated another man's w. H851
Dt 22:30 A man is not to marry his father's w; he H851
Dt 24: 2 house she becomes the w of another man, NDT
Dt 24: 5 bring happiness to the w he has married. H851
Dt 25: 7 does not want to marry his **brother's** w, H3304
Dt 25:11 fighting and the w *of* one of them comes H851
Dt 27:20 is anyone who sleeps with his father's w, H851
Dt 28:54 his own brother or the w he loves or his H851
Jdg 4: 4 a prophet, the w *of* Lappidoth, was leading H851
Jdg 4:17 the tent of Jael, the w *of* Heber the Kenite H851
Jdg 4:21 But Jael, Heber's w, picked up a tent peg H851
Jdg 5:24 women be Jael, the w *of* Heber the Kenite H851
Jdg 11: 2 Gilead's w also bore him sons, and when H851
Jdg 13: 2 of the Danites, had a w who was childless H851
Jdg 13:11 Manoah got up and followed his w. H851
Jdg 13:11 "Are you the man who talked to my w?" H851
Jdg 13:13 "Your w must do all that I have told her. H851
Jdg 13:19 thing while Manoah and his w watched: H851
Jdg 13:20 Manoah and his w fell with their faces to H851
Jdg 13:21 show himself again to Manoah and his w, H851
Jdg 13:22 he said to his w. "We have seen God!" H851
Jdg 13:23 But his w answered, "If the LORD had meant H851
Jdg 14: 2 in Timnah; now get her for me as my w." H851
Jdg 14: 3 to the uncircumcised Philistines to get a w?" H851
Jdg 14:15 they said to Samson's w, "Coax your H851
Jdg 14:16 Then Samson's w threw herself on him H851
Jdg 14:20 And Samson's w was given to one of his H851
Jdg 15: 1 took a young goat and went to visit his w. H851
Jdg 15: 6 because his w was given to his companion." H851
Jdg 21:18 be anyone who gives a w to a Benjamite. H851
Jdg 21:21 of you seize one of them to be your w. H851
Jdg 21:23 caught one and carried her off to be his w. H851
Ru 1: 1 together with his w and two sons, went to H851
Ru 4:10 as my w, in order to maintain H851
Ru 4:13 So Boaz took Ruth and she became his w H851
1Sa 1: 4 of the meat to his w Peninnah and to all H851
1Sa 1:19 Elkanah made love to his w Hannah, and H851
1Sa 2:20 Eli would bless Elkanah and his w, saying H851
1Sa 4:19 daughter-in-law, the w *of* Phinehas, was H851
1Sa 19:11 But Michal, David's w, warned him, "If you H851
1Sa 25:14 told Abigail, Nabal's w, "David sent H851
1Sa 25:37 was sober, his w told him all these things H851
1Sa 25:39 asking her to **become** his w. H4374+4200+851
1Sa 25:40 sent us to you to take you to become his w." H851
1Sa 25:42 David's messengers and became his w. H851
1Sa 25:44 David's w, to Paltiel son of Laish H851
1Sa 30:22 man may take his w and children and go." H851
2Sa 3: 5 Ithream the son of David's w Eglah. H851
2Sa 3:14 "Give me my w Michal, whom I H851
2Sa 11: 3 of Eliam and the w *of* Uriah the Hittite." H851
2Sa 11:11 to eat and drink and make love to my w? H851
2Sa 11:26 When Uriah's w heard that her husband H851
2Sa 11:27 she became his w and bore him a son. H851
2Sa 12: 9 the sword and took his w to be your own. H851
2Sa 12:10 me and took the w *of* Uriah the Hittite to H851
2Sa 12:15 child that Uriah's w had borne to David, H851
2Sa 12:24 Then David comforted his w Bathsheba H851
2Sa 17:19 His w took a covering and spread it out over H851
1Ki 2:17 me Abishag the Shunammite as my w." H851
1Ki 9:16 wedding gift to his daughter, Solomon's w. H851
1Ki 11:19 that he gave him a sister of his own w, H851
1Ki 14: 2 Jeroboam said to his w, "Go, disguise H851
1Ki 14: 2 won't be recognized as the w *of* Jeroboam. H851
1Ki 14: 4 So Jeroboam's w did what he said and H851
1Ki 14: 5 "Jeroboam's w is coming to ask you about H851
1Ki 14: 6 he said, "Come in, w *of* Jeroboam. H851
1Ki 14:17 Then Jeroboam's w got up and left and H851
1Ki 21: 5 His w Jezebel came in and asked him H851
1Ki 21: 7 Jezebel his w said, "Is this how you act as H851
1Ki 21:25 of the LORD, urged on by Jezebel his w. H851
2Ki 4: 1 The w of a man from the company of the H851
2Ki 5: 2 from Israel, and she served Naaman's w. H851
2Ki 22:14 who was the w *of* Shallum son of Tikvah H851
1Ch 2:18 of Hezron had children by his w Azubah H851
1Ch 2:24 Abijah the w *of* Hezron bore him Ashhur H851
1Ch 2:26 Jerahmeel had another w, whose name H851
1Ch 2:29 Abishur's w was named Abihail, who bore H851
1Ch 3: 3 the sixth, Ithream, by his w Eglah. H851
1Ch 4:18 His w *from* the tribe of Judah gave birth to H851
1Ch 4:19 The sons of Hodiah's w, the sister of H851
1Ch 7:15 Makir took a w from among the Huppites H851
1Ch 7:16 Makir's w Maakah gave birth to a son and H851
1Ch 7:23 Then he made love to his w again, and H851
1Ch 8: 9 By his w Hodesh he had Jobab, Zibia H851
2Ch 8:11 "My w must not live in the palace of David H851
2Ch 22:11 of King Jehoram and w *of* the priest H851
2Ch 34:22 who was the w *of* Shallum son of Tokhath H851
Est 5:10 together his friends and Zeresh, his w, H851
Est 5:14 His w Zeresh and all his friends said to him H851
Est 6:13 told Zeresh his w and all his friends H851
Est 6:13 His advisers and his w Zeresh said to him H851
Job 2: 9 His w said to him, "Are you still H851
Job 19:17 My breath is offensive to my w; I am H851
Job 31:10 then may my w grind another man's grain H851
Ps 109: 9 children be fatherless and his w a widow. H851
Ps 128: 3 Your w will be like a fruitful vine within H851
Pr 5:18 may you rejoice in the w *of* your youth. H851
Pr 5:20 be intoxicated with **another** *man's w*? AIT
Pr 6:24 keeping you from your neighbor's w, from H851
Pr 6:26 another man's w preys on your very life. H851
Pr 6:29 So is he who sleeps with another man's w H851
Pr 12: 4 A w *of* noble character is her husband's H851
Pr 12: 4 a disgraceful w is like decay in his NDT
Pr 18:22 He who finds a w finds what is good and H851
Pr 19:13 a quarrelsome w is like the constant H851
Pr 19:14 parents, but a prudent w is from the LORD. H851
Pr 21: 9 than share a house with a quarrelsome w. H851
Pr 21:19 than with a quarrelsome and nagging w. H851
Pr 23:27 deep pit, and a **wayward** *w* is a narrow well. AIT
Pr 25:24 than share a house with a quarrelsome w. H851
Pr 27:15 A quarrelsome w is like the dripping of a H851
Pr 31:10 A w *of* noble character who can find? She H851
Ecc 9: 9 Enjoy life with your w, whom you love, all H851
Isa 54: 6 back as if you were a w deserted and H851
Isa 54: 6 in spirit—a w *who married* young, only to H851
Jer 3: 1 a man divorces his w and she leaves him H851
Jer 5: 8 each neighing for another man's w. H851
Jer 6:11 both husband and w will be caught in it H851
Eze 16:32 " 'You adulterous w! You prefer strangers to H851
Eze 18: 6 defile his neighbor's w or have sexual H851
Eze 18:11 He defiles his neighbor's w. H851
Eze 18:15 He does not defile his neighbor's w. H851
Eze 22:11 a detestable offense with his neighbor's w, H851
Eze 24:18 morning, and in the evening my w died. H851
Eze 33:26 each of you defiles his neighbor's w. H851
Hos 1: 2 for *like an* **adulterous** *w* this land is guilty of AIT
Hos 2: 2 for she is not my w, and I am not her H851
Hos 3: 1 show your love to your w again, though she H851
Hos 12:12 Israel served to get a w, and to pay for her H851
Am 7:17 " 'Your w will become a prostitute in the H851
Mal 2:14 between you and the w *of* your youth. H851
Mal 2:14 the w *of* your marriage covenant. H851
Mal 2:15 do not be unfaithful to the w *of* your youth. H851
Mal 2:16 "The man who hates and divorces his w," NDT
Mt 1: 6 whose mother had been Uriah's w, *G3836*
Mt 1:20 be afraid to take Mary home *as* your w, *G1222*
Mt 1:24 him and took Mary home *as* his w. *G1222*
Mt 5:31 who divorces his w must give her a *G1222*
Mt 5:32 I tell you that anyone who divorces his w, *G1222*
Mt 14: 3 of Herodias, his brother Philip's w, *G1222*
Mt 18:25 that he and his w and his children and *G1222*
Mt 19: 3 a man to divorce his w for any and every *G1222*
Mt 19: 5 father and mother and be united *to* his w, *G1222*
Mt 19: 7 that a man give his w a certificate of divorce NDT
Mt 19: 9 I tell you that anyone who divorces his w *G1222*
Mt 19:10 the situation between a husband and w, *G1222*
Mt 19:29 father or mother or w or children or fields *G1222*
Mt 22:25 no children, he left his w to his brother. *G1222*
Mt 22:28 whose w will she be of the seven *G1222*

Mt 27:19 his **w** sent him this message: *G1222*
Mk 6:17 his brother Philip's **w**, whom he had *G1222*
Mk 6:18 lawful for you to have your brother's **w**." *G1222*
Mk 10: 2 "Is it lawful for a man to divorce his **w**?" *G1222*
Mk 10: 7 father and mother and be united to his **w**, *G1222*
Mk 10:11 who divorces his **w** and marries another *G1222*
Mk 12:19 dies and leaves a **w** but no children, *G1222*
Mk 12:23 At the resurrection whose **w** will she be *G1222*
Lk 1: 5 his **w** Elizabeth was also a descendant of *G1222*
Lk 1:13 Your **w** Elizabeth will bear you a son, and *G1222*
Lk 1:18 am an old man and my **w** is well along in *G1222*
Lk 1:24 After this his **w** Elizabeth became *G1222*
Lk 3:19 his brother's **w**, and all the other evil *G1222*
Lk 8: 3 Joanna the **w** of Chuza, the manager of *G1222*
Lk 14:26 father and mother, **w** and children *G1222*
Lk 16:18 who divorces his **w** and marries another *G1222*
Lk 17:32 Remember Lot's **w**! *G1222*
Lk 18:29 who has left home or **w** or brothers or *G1222*
Lk 20:28 dies and leaves a **w** but no children, *G1222*
Lk 20:33 at the resurrection whose **w** will she be *G1222*
Jn 19:25 Mary **the w** of Clopas, and Mary *G3836*
Ac 5: 1 together with his **w** Sapphira, also sold a *G1222*
Ac 5: 7 About three hours later his **w** came in, not *G1222*
Ac 18: 2 come from Italy with his **w** Priscilla, *G1222*
Ac 24:24 days later Felix came with his **w** Drusilla, *G1222*
1Co 5: 1 A man is sleeping with his father's **w**. *G1222*
1Co 7: 2 have sexual relations with his own **w**, *G1222*
1Co 7: 3 should fulfill his marital duty *to* his **w**, *G1222*
1Co 7: 3 and likewise the **w** to her husband. *G1222*
1Co 7: 4 The **w** does not have authority over her *G1222*
1Co 7: 4 over his own body but yields it to his **w**. *G1222*
1Co 7:10 A **w** must not separate from her husband. *G1222*
1Co 7:11 And a husband must not divorce his **w**. *G1222*
1Co 7:12 If any brother has a **w** who is not a *G1222*
1Co 7:14 has been sanctified through his **w**, *G1222*
1Co 7:14 the unbelieving **w** has been sanctified *G1222*
1Co 7:16 How do you know, **w**, whether you will *G1222*
1Co 7:16 husband, whether you will save your **w**? *G1222*
1Co 7:27 such a commitment? Do not look for a **w**. *G1222*
1Co 7:33 of this world—how he can please his **w**— *G1222*
1Co 9: 5 right to take a believing **w** along with us, *G1222*
Eph 5:23 is the head *of* the **w** as Christ is the *G1222*
Eph 5:28 He who loves his **w** loves himself. *G1222*
Eph 5:31 father and mother and be united to his **w**, *G1222*
Eph 5:33 also must love his **w** as he loves himself, *G1222*
Eph 5:33 the **w** must respect her husband. *G1222*
1Ti 3: 2 reproach, **faithful to his w** *G1651+1222+467*
1Ti 3:12 must be **faithful to his w** and *G1651+1222+467*
Titus 1: 6 **faithful to his w**, a man *G1651+1222+467*
Rev 21: 9 show you the bride, the **w** of the Lamb." *G1222*

WIFE'S (10) [WIFE]

Ge 36:39 his **w** name was Mehetabel daughter H851
Lev 18:18 " 'Do not take your **w** sister as a rival wife H851
Jdg 15: 1 "I'm going to my **w** room." But her father H851
Ru 1: 2 was Elimelek, his **w** name was Naomi, and H851
1Sa 14:50 His **w** name was Ahinoam daughter of H851
1Sa 25: 3 was Nabal and his **w** name was Abigail. H851
1Ch 1:50 his **w** name was Mehetabel daughter H851
1Ch 8:29 lived in Gibeon. His **w** name was Maakah, H851
1Ch 9:35 lived in Gibeon. His **w** name was Maakah, H851
Ac 5: 2 With his **w** full knowledge he kept back *G1222*

WILD (119) [WILDER, WILDERNESS, WILDS]

Ge 1:24 the ground, and the **w** animals, each H824
Ge 1:25 God made the **w** animals according to their H824
Ge 1:26 over the livestock and all the **w** animals H824
Ge 2:19 the ground all the **w** animals and all the H8441
Ge 2:20 the birds in the sky and all the **w** animals. H8441
Ge 3: 1 than any of the **w** animals the LORD God H8441
Ge 3:14 you above all livestock and all **w** animals! H8441
Ge 7:14 with them every **w animal** according to its H2651
Ge 7:21 livestock, **w animals**, all the creatures that H2651
Ge 8: 1 Noah and all the **w animals** and the H2651
Ge 9:10 the livestock and all the **w** animals, all H824
Ge 16:12 He will be a **w donkey** of a man; his hand H7230
Ge 25:28 who had a taste for **w game**, loved Esau, H7473
Ge 27: 3 country to hunt *some* **w game** for me. H7473
Ge 31:39 not bring you **animals torn by w beasts**; H3274
Ex 22:13 *it* **was torn to pieces by a w animal**, H3271+3271
Ex 22:31 an animal torn by **w** beasts; H928+2021+8441
Ex 23:11 and the **w** animals may eat what is left. H8441
Ex 23:29 desolate and the **w** animals too H8441
Ex 32:25 the people *were* **running w** and that H7277
Lev 5: 2 of an unclean **animal**, **w** or domestic, H2651
Lev 7:24 dead or **torn by w animals** may be used H3274
Lev 17:15 dead or **torn by w animals** must wash H3274
Lev 22: 8 found dead or **torn by w animals**, H3274
Lev 25: 7 livestock and the **w animals** in your land. H2651
Lev 26: 6 I will remove **w** beasts from the land, and H8273
Lev 26:22 I will send **w** animals against you, and H8441
Nu 23:22 of Egypt; they have the strength of a **w ox**. H8028
Nu 24: 8 of Egypt; they have the strength of a **w ox**. H8028
Dt 7:22 the **w** animals will multiply around you. H8441
Dt 14: 5 the roe deer, the **w goat**, the ibex, the H735
Dt 28:26 all the birds and the **w animals**, H989+824
Dt 32:24 send against them the fangs of **w beasts**, H989
Dt 33:17 his horns are the horns of a **w ox**. H8028
1Sa 17:44 your flesh to the birds and the **w** animals!" H8441
1Sa 17:46 army to the birds and the **w** animals, H824
1Sa 24: 2 his men near the Crags of the **W Goats**. H3604
2Sa 2:18 fleet-footed as a **w** gazelle. H928+2021+8441
2Sa 17: 8 fierce as a **w** bear robbed of H928+2021+8441
2Sa 21:10 them by day or the **w** animals by night. H8441
2Ki 4:39 herbs and found a **w** vine and picked as H8441
2Ki 14: 9 Then a **w** beast in Lebanon came along H8441
2Ch 25:18 Then a **w** beast in Lebanon came along H8441
Ne 8:15 branches from olive and **w olive** trees, H9043
Job 5:22 and need not fear the **w** animals. H824
Job 5:23 the **w** animals will be at peace with H8441
Job 6: 5 Does a **w donkey** bray when it has grass H7230
Job 11:12 wise than a **w donkey's** colt can be born H7230
Job 24: 5 Like **w donkeys** in the desert, the poor go H7230
Job 39: 5 "Who let the **w donkey** go free? Who H7230
Job 39: 9 "Will the **w ox** consent to serve you? Will H8028
Job 39:15 that some **w** animal may trample them. H8441
Job 40:20 all the **w** animals play nearby. H8441
Ps 8: 7 herds, and the animals of the **w**, H8442
Ps 22:21 save me from the horns of the **w oxen**. H8028
Ps 29: 6 leap like a calf, Sirion like a young **w ox**. H8028
Ps 74:19 over the life of your dove to **w beasts**; H2651
Ps 79: 2 your own people for the animals of the **w**. H824
Ps 92:10 have exalted my horn like that of a **w ox**; H8028
Ps 104:11 the **w donkeys** quench their thirst. H7230
Ps 104:18 high mountains belong to the **w goats**; H3604
Ps 148:10 **w animals** and all cattle, small creatures H2651
Isa 13:21 there the **w goats** will leap about. H8538
Isa 18: 6 birds of prey and to the **w** animals; H824
Isa 18: 6 them all summer, the **w** animals all winter. H824
Isa 34: 7 And the **w oxen** will fall with them, the H8028
Isa 34:14 and **w goats** will bleat to each other H8538
Isa 43:20 The **w** animals honor me, the jackals and H8441
Jer 2:21 turn against me into a corrupt, **w** vine? H5799
Jer 2:24 a **w donkey** accustomed to the desert H7241
Jer 7:33 food for the birds and the **w** animals, H824
Jer 12: 9 Go and gather all the **w** beasts; bring H8441
Jer 14: 6 **W donkeys** stand on the barren heights H7230
Jer 15: 3 the birds and the **w** animals to devour and H824
Jer 16: 4 food for the birds and the **w** animals." H824
Jer 19: 7 as food to the birds and the **w** animals. H824
Jer 27: 6 I will make even the **w** animals subject to H8441
Jer 28:14 even give him control over the **w** animals. H8441
Jer 34:20 food for the birds and the **w** animals. H824
Eze 4:14 found dead or **torn by w animals**. H3274
Eze 5:17 send famine and **w** beasts against you, H8273
Eze 14:15 "Or if I send **w** beasts through that country H8273
Eze 14:21 famine and **w** beasts and plague— H8273
Eze 31: 6 the animals of the **w** gave birth under its H8441
Eze 31:13 all the **w** animals lived among its H8441
Eze 32: 4 the animals of the **w** gorge themselves on H824
Eze 33:27 will give to the **w animals** to be devoured, H2651
Eze 34: 5 they became food for all the **w** animals. H8441
Eze 34: 8 has become food for all the **w** animals, H8441
Eze 34:28 nations, nor will **w** animals devour them. H824
Eze 39: 4 of carrion birds and to the **w** animals. H8441
Eze 39:17 every kind of bird and all the **w** animals: H8441
Eze 44:31 animal, found dead or **torn by w animals**. H3274
Da 4:12 Under it the **w** animals found shelter A10119
Da 4:21 giving shelter to the **w** animals, and A10119
Da 4:23 let him live with the **w** animals, until A10119
Da 4:25 people and will live with the **w** animals; A10119
Da 4:32 people and will live with the **w** animals; A10119
Da 5:21 lived with the **w donkeys** and ate grass A10570
Hos 2:12 and **w** animals will devour them. H8441
Hos 8: 9 Assyria like a **w donkey** wandering alone. H7230
Hos 13: 8 a **w** animal will tear them apart. H8441
Joel 1:20 Even the **w** animals pant for you; the H8441
Joel 2:22 Do not be afraid, you **w** animals, for the H8442
Zep 2:15 ruin she has become, a lair for **w beasts**! H2651
Mt 3: 4 His food was locusts and **w** honey. *G67*
Mk 1: 6 his waist, and he ate locusts and **w** honey. *G67*
Mk 1:13 He was with the **w animals**, and angels *G2563*
Lk 12:27 "Consider how the **w flowers** grow. *G3211*
Lk 15:13 there squandered his wealth in **w** living. *G862*
Ac 11: 6 of the earth, **w beasts**, reptiles and birds. *G2563*
Ro 11:17 though a **w olive shoot**, have been *G66*
Ro 11:24 cut out of an **olive tree that is w** by nature, *G66*
1Co 15:32 If *I* **fought w beasts** in Ephesus with no *G2562*
Titus 1: 6 to the charge of being **w** and disobedient. *G861*
Jas 1:10 they will pass away like a **w flower**. *G470+5965*
1Pe 4: 4 in their reckless, **w living**, and they heap *G861*
Jude 13 They are **w** waves of the sea, foaming up *G67*
Rev 6: 8 plague, and by the **w beasts** of the earth. *G2563*

WILDER (1) [WILD]

Jnh 1:13 the sea **grew even w** than H6192+2143+2256

WILDERNESS (165) [WILD]

Ge 37:22 Throw him into this cistern here in the **w** H4497
Ex 3: 1 the far side of the **w** and came to Horeb, H4497
Ex 3:18 journey into the **w** to offer sacrifices to the H4497
Ex 4:27 to Aaron, "Go into the **w** to meet Moses." H4497
Ex 5: 1 they may hold a festival to me in the **w**. H4497
Ex 5: 3 journey into the **w** to offer sacrifices to the H4497
Ex 7:16 so that they may worship me in the **w**. H4497
Ex 8:27 journey into the **w** to offer sacrifices to the H4497
Ex 8:28 sacrifices to the LORD your God in the **w**, H4497
Ex 16:32 you to eat in the **w** when I brought you H4497
Ex 18: 5 came to him in the **w**, where he was H4497
Lev 16:10 by sending it into the **w** as a scapegoat. H4497
Lev 16:21 goat away into the **w** in the care of H4497
Lev 16:22 the man shall release it in the **w**. H4497
Nu 10:31 know where we should camp in the **w**, H4497
Nu 14: 2 only we had died in Egypt! Or in this **w**! H4497
Nu 14:16 on oath, so he slaughtered them in the **w**. H4497
Nu 14:22 in Egypt and in the **w** but who disobeyed H4497
Nu 14:29 In this **w** your bodies will fall—every one H4497
Nu 14:32 as for you, your bodies will fall in this **w**. H4497
Nu 14:33 until the last of your bodies lies in the **w**. H4497
Nu 14:35 They will meet their end in this **w**; here H4497
Nu 15:32 While the Israelites were in the **w**, a man H4497
Nu 16:13 with milk and honey to kill us in the **w**? H4497
Nu 20: 4 bring the LORD's community into this **w**, H4497
Nu 21: 5 us up out of Egypt to die in the **w**? H4497
Nu 21:11 in the **w** that faces Moab toward the H4497
Nu 21:13 which is in the **w** extending into Amorite H4497
Nu 21:18 Then they went from the **w** to Mattanah, H4497
Nu 21:23 marched out into the **w** against Israel. H4497
Nu 24: 1 but turned his face toward the **w**. H4497
Nu 26:65 Israelites they would surely die in the **w**, H4497
Nu 27: 3 "Our father died in the **w**. He was not H4497
Nu 32:13 made them wander in the **w** forty years, H4497
Nu 32:15 will again leave all this people in the **w**, H4497
Dt 1: 1 to all Israel in the **w** east of the Jordan— H4497
Dt 1:19 vast and dreadful **w** that you have seen, H4497
Dt 1:31 in the **w**. There you saw how the LORD H4497
Dt 2: 1 set out toward the **w** along the route to H4497
Dt 2: 7 over your journey through this vast **w**. H4497
Dt 4:43 Bezer in the **w** plateau, for the Reubenites H4497
Dt 8: 2 you all the way in the **w** these forty years, H4497
Dt 8:15 led you through the vast and dreadful **w**, H4497
Dt 8:16 He gave you manna to eat in the **w** H4497
Dt 9: 7 the anger of the LORD your God in the **w**. H4497
Dt 9:28 them out to put them to death in the **w**. H4497
Dt 11: 5 he did for you in the **w** until you arrived at H4497
Dt 29: 5 forty years that I led you through the **w**, H4497
Jos 5: 4 died in the **w** on the way after leaving H4497
Jos 5: 5 people born in the **w** during the journey H4497
Jos 5: 6 moved about in the **w** forty years until all H4497
Jos 8:15 before them, and they fled toward the **w**. H4497
Jos 8:20 fleeing toward the **w** had turned back H4497
Jos 8:24 fields and in the **w** where they had H4497
Jos 12: 8 mountain slopes, the **w** and the Negev. H4497
Jos 14:10 while Israel moved about in the **w**. H4497
Jos 15:61 In the **w**: Beth Arabah, Middin, Sekakah, H4497
Jos 18:12 coming out at the **w** *of* Beth Aven. H4497
Jos 20: 8 Bezer in the **w** on the plateau in the H4497
Jos 24: 7 Then you lived in the **w** for a long time. H4497
Jdg 11:16 went through the **w** to the Red Sea and H4497
Jdg 11:18 "Next they traveled through the **w**, skirted H4497
Jdg 20:42 the Israelites in the direction of the **w**, H4497
Jdg 20:45 fled toward the **w** to the rock of H4497
Jdg 20:47 fled into the **w** to the rock of Rimmon, H4497
1Sa 4: 8 with all kinds of plagues in the **w**. H4497
1Sa 13:18 the Valley of Zeboyim facing the **w**. H4497
1Sa 17:28 did you leave those few sheep in the **w**? H4497
1Sa 23:14 David stayed in the **w** strongholds and in H4497
1Sa 25: 4 While David was in the **w**, he heard that H4497
1Sa 25:14 messengers from the **w** to give our master H4497
1Sa 25:21 property in the **w** so that nothing of his H4497
1Sa 26: 3 Jeshimon, but David stayed in the **w**. H4497
2Sa 15:23 all the people moved on toward the **w**. H4497
2Sa 15:28 at the fords in the **w** until word comes H4497
2Sa 16: 2 those who become exhausted in the **w**." H4497
2Sa 17:16 not spend the night at the fords in the **w**; H4497
2Sa 17:29 hungry and thirsty in the **w**. H4497
1Ki 19: 4 himself went a day's journey into the **w**. H4497
1Ch 6:78 of Jericho they received Bezer in the **w**, H4497
1Ch 12: 8 to David at his stronghold in the **w**. H4497
1Ch 21:29 which Moses had made in the **w**, and the H4497
2Ch 1: 3 the LORD's servant had made in the **w**. H4497
2Ch 24: 9 of God had required of Israel in the **w**. H4497
2Ch 26:10 built towers in the **w** and dug many H4497
Ne 9:19 you did not abandon them in the **w**. H4497
Ne 9:21 forty years you sustained them in the **w**; H4497
Ps 65:12 The grasslands of the **w** overflow; the hills H4497
Ps 68: 7 when you marched through the **w**, H3810
Ps 78:15 the rocks in the **w** and gave them water as H4497
Ps 78:17 rebelling in the **w** against the Most High. H7480
Ps 78:19 "Can God really spread a table in the **w**? H4497
Ps 78:40 against him in the **w** and grieved him in H4497
Ps 78:52 he led them like sheep through the **w**. H4497
Ps 95: 8 as you did that day at Massah in the **w**, H4497
Ps 106:14 craving; in the **w** they put God to the test. H3810
Ps 106:26 that he would make them fall in the **w**, H4497
Ps 136:16 to him who led his people through the **w** H4497
SS 3: 6 coming up from the **w** like a column of H4497
SS 8: 5 coming up from the **w** leaning on her H4497
Isa 14:17 the man who made the world a **w**, who H4497
Isa 27:10 forsaken like the **w**; there the calves graze H4497
Isa 35: 1 be glad; the **w** will rejoice and blossom. H6858
Isa 35: 6 will gush forth in the **w** and streams in the H4497
Isa 40: 3 "In the **w** prepare the way for the LORD H4497
Isa 42:11 Let the **w** and its towns raise their voices H4497
Isa 43:19 making a way in the **w** and streams in the H4497
Isa 43:20 provide water in the **w** and streams in the H4497
Jer 2: 2 loved me and followed me through the **w**, H4497
Jer 2: 6 of Egypt and led us through the **barren w**, H4497
Jer 9:10 up a lament concerning the **w** grasslands. H4497
Jer 9:26 all who live in the **w** in distant places. H4497
Jer 23:10 the pastures in the **w** are withered. H4497
Jer 25:24 of the foreign people who live in the **w**; H4497
Jer 31: 2 survive the sword will find favor in the **w**; H4497
Jer 50:12 the least of the nations—a **w**, a dry land, H4497
Eze 20:10 out of Egypt and brought them into the **w**. H4497
Eze 20:13 of Israel rebelled against me in the **w**. H4497

W

Eze 20:13 wrath on them and destroy them in the **w**. H4497
Eze 20:15 swore to them in the **w** that I would not H4497
Eze 20:17 them or put an end to them in the **w**. H4497
Eze 20:18 I said to their children in the **w**, "Do not H4497
Eze 20:21 spend my anger against them in the **w**. H4497
Eze 20:23 swore to them in the **w** that I would H4497
Eze 20:35 bring you into the **w** *of* the nations and H4497
Eze 20:36 ancestors in the **w** *of* the land of Egypt, H4497
Eze 34:25 they may live in the **w** and sleep in the H4497
Hos 2:14 lead her into the **w** and speak tenderly to H4497
Hos 13: 5 I cared for you in the **w**, in the land of H4497
Joel 1:19 the pastures in the **w** and flames have H4497
Joel 1:20 fire has devoured the pastures in the **w**. H4497
Joel 2:22 pastures in the **w** are becoming green. H4497
Am 2:10 forty years in the **w** to give you the land H4497
Am 5:25 offerings forty years in the **w**, H4497
Mt 3: 1 Baptist came, preaching in the **w** of Judea *G2245*
Mt 3: 3 "A voice of one calling in the **w**, 'Prepare *G2245*
Mt 4: 1 the Spirit into the **w** to be tempted by the *G2245*
Mt 11: 7 "What did you go out into the **w** to see? *G2245*
Mt 24:26 out in the **w**,' do not go out; or, *G2245*
Mk 1: 3 "a voice of one calling in the **w**, 'Prepare *G2245*
Mk 1: 4 so John the Baptist appeared in the **w**, *G2245*
Mk 1:12 At once the Spirit sent him out into the **w**, *G2245*
Mk 1:13 he was in the **w** forty days, being *G2245*
Lk 1:80 he lived in the **w** until he appeared *G2245*
Lk 3: 2 came to John son of Zechariah in the **w**. *G2245*
Lk 3: 4 "A voice of one calling in the **w**, 'Prepare *G2245*
Lk 4: 1 was led by the Spirit into the **w**, *G2245*
Lk 7:24 "What did you go out into the **w** to see? *G2245*
Jn 1:23 "I am the voice of one calling in the **w** *G2245*
Jn 3:14 Just as Moses lifted up the snake in the **w** *G2245*
Jn 6:31 Our ancestors ate the manna in the **w**; as *G2245*
Jn 6:49 Your ancestors ate the manna in the **w**, yet *G2245*
Jn 11:54 he withdrew to a region near the **w**, *G2245*
Ac 7:36 at the Red Sea and for forty years in the **w**. *G2245*
Ac 7:38 He was in the assembly in the **w**, with the *G2245*
Ac 7:42 offerings forty years in the **w**, *G2245*
Ac 7:44 of the covenant law with them in the **w**. *G2245*
Ac 13:18 years he endured their conduct in the **w**; *G2245*
Ac 21:38 terrorists out into the **w** some time ago?" *G2245*
1Co 10: 5 their bodies were scattered in the **w**. *G2245*
Heb 3: 8 during the time of testing in the **w**, *G2245*
Heb 3:17 whose bodies perished in the **w**? *G2245*
Rev 12: 6 fled into the **w** to a place prepared *G2245*
Rev 12:14 fly to the place prepared for her in the **w**, *G2245*
Rev 17: 3 carried me away in the Spirit into a **w**. *G2245*

WILDS (1) [WILD]

Job 39: 4 young thrive and grow strong in the **w**; H1340

WILL (171 of 10122) [FREEWILL, WILLFUL, WILLFULLY, WILLING, WILLINGLY, WILLINGNESS, WILLS, WON'T]

See Index of Articles Etc. for an Exhaustive Index

Ge 15: 2 and the **one who w inherit** my H1201+5479
Ge 23:13 in their hearing, "Listen to me, if you **w**. H4273
Ge 24:42 Abraham, if you **w**, please grant success H3780
Ge 24:49 Now if you **w** show kindness and H3780
Ge 27:33 and indeed *he* **w** be blessed! H2118
Ge 27:46 my **life w not be worth living**." H2644+4200+4537
Ge 43: 4 If you **w** send our brother along with us H3780
Ge 43: 5 But if you **w not** send him, we will not go H401
Ge 45: 6 next five years **there w be no** plowing and H401
Ex 9: 9 festering boils **w** break out on people H2118
Ex 18:15 the people come to me to **seek** God's **w**. H2011
Lev 24:12 until the **w** *of* the LORD should H6584+7023
Dt 10:10 *It was* not his **w** to destroy you. H14
Dt 11:17 the heavens so that *it* **w** not rain and the H2118
Dt 15: 9 that you *do* not **show ill w** toward H8317+6524
Dt 25: 7 *He* **w** not fulfill the duty of a brother-in-law H14
Dt 28:26 and **there w be no** one to frighten them H401
Dt 28:34 The sights you see **w** drive you mad. H2118
Dt 28:66 You **w** live in constant suspense, filled H2118
Dt 33:21 he carried out the LORD's **righteous w**, and H7407
Jdg 6:36 "If you **w** save Israel by my hand as you H3780
Ru 4:15 *He* **w** renew your life and sustain you in H2118
1Sa 2:25 for *it was* the LORD's **w** to put them to H2911
1Sa 23:11 And the LORD said, "*He* **w**." H3718S
1Sa 23:12 And the LORD said, "*They* **w**." H6037S
1Sa 25:28 no wrongdoing **w be found** in you as long H5162
2Sa 5:24 because **that w mean** the LORD has gone H255
2Sa 7:21 of your word and according to your **w**, H4213
2Sa 15:14 none of us **w** escape from Absalom. H2118
2Ki 2:10 it will be yours—otherwise, *it* **w** not." H2118+401
2Ki 6: 3 your servants?" "I **w**," Elisha replied. H2143S
1Ch 13: 2 you and if it is the **w** *of* the LORD our God, H4946
1Ch 14:15 **because that w mean** God has gone out H3954
1Ch 17:19 of your servant and according to your **w**, H4213
Ezr 4:16 you **w be left with** nothing in A10029+10378
Ezr 7:18 in accordance with the **w** *of* your God. A10668
Ezr 10:11 the God of your ancestors, and do his **w**. H8356
Job 5: 1 "Call **if you w**, but who will answer you H5528
Ps 40: 8 I desire to do your **w**, my God; your law is H8356
Ps 103:21 you his servants who do his **w**. H8356
Ps 143:10 Teach me to do your **w**, for you are my H8356
Ps 144:14 **There w be no** breaching of walls, no H401
Isa 5:24 so their roots **w** decay and their flowers H2118
Isa 8: 8 Its outspread wings **w** cover the breadth of H2118
Isa 9: 7 government and peace **there w be no** end. H401
Isa 29: 2 besiege Ariel; *she* **w** mourn and lament H2118
Isa 30:29 And you **w** sing as on the night you H2118
Isa 34:12 a kingdom, all her princes **w** vanish away. H2118
Isa 47:12 Perhaps *you* **w** succeed, perhaps you will H3523
Isa 53:10 Yet *it was* the LORD's **w** to crush him and H2911
Isa 53:10 the **w** *of* the LORD will prosper in his H2914
Jer 7:33 and **there w be no** one to frighten them H401
Jer 8:13 **There w be no** grapes on the vine H401
Jer 8:13 **There w be no** figs on the tree, and their H401
Jer 13:19 and **there w be no** one to open them. H401
Jer 14:16 **There w be no** one to bury them, their H401
Jer 25:37 meadows **w be laid waste** because of the H1959
Jer 29: 7 because if it prospers, you too **w** prosper." H2118
Jer 30: 7 **No other w be** like it. H4946+401
Jer 31: 6 **There w be** a day when watchmen cry out H3780
Jer 42:17 not *one* of them **w** survive or escape the H2118
Jer 44:14 to live in Egypt **w** escape or survive to H2118
Jer 50:20 but **there w be none**, and for the sins H401
Jer 51: 2 *they* **w** oppose her on every side in the H2118
Eze 12:25 But I the LORD will speak what *I* **w** H1819+1821S
Eze 18:13 such a man live? *He* **w** not! Because he H2649S
Eze 33:33 comes true—and *it* surely **w**—then they H995S
Da 11:42 over many countries; Egypt **w** not escape. H2118
Mic 5:12 witchcraft and you **w** no longer cast spells. H2118
Zec 2: 9 them so that their slaves **w** plunder them. H2118
Mt 6:10 kingdom come, your **w** be done, on earth *G2525*
Mt 7:21 one who does the **w** of my Father who is *G2525*
Mt 12:50 For whoever does the **w** of my Father in *G2525*
Mt 21:29 " '*I* **w** not,' he answered, but later he *G2527*
Mt 24: 6 *You* **w** hear of wars and rumors of wars *G3516*
Mt 26:33 fall away on account of you, I never **w**." *G4997S*
Mt 26:39 Yet not as I **w**, but as you will." *G2527*
Mt 26:42 unless I drink it, may your **w** be done." *G2525*
Mk 3:35 Whoever does God's **w** is my brother and *G2525*
Mk 13:13 Everyone **w** hate you because of me, but *G1639*
Mk 14:36 Yet not what I **w**, but what you will." *G2527*
Mk 16: 3 "Who **w roll** the stone **away** from the *G653*
Lk 1:33 his kingdom **w** never end. *G1639*
Lk 5: 5 because you say so, **I w let down** the nets." *G5899*
Lk 12:47 knows the master's **w** and does not get *G2525*
Lk 13:25 *you* **w** stand outside knocking and pleading *G806*
Lk 13:26 "Then *you* **w** say, 'We ate and drank with *G806*
Lk 14: 9 *you* **w** have to take the least important *G806*
Lk 14:29 everyone who sees it **w** ridicule you, *G806*
Lk 22:42 from me; yet not my **w**, but yours be done." *G2525*
Lk 23:25 and surrendered Jesus *to* their **w**. *G2525*
Lk 23:30 Then " '*they* **w** say to the mountains, "Fall *G806*
Jn 1:13 of human decision or a husband's **w** *G2525*
Jn 4:34 "is to do the **w** of him who sent me and to *G2525*
Jn 6:38 heaven not to do my **w** but to do the will *G2525*
Jn 6:38 will but to do the **w** of him who sent me. *G2525*
Jn 6:39 And this is the **w** of him who sent me, that *G2525*
Jn 6:40 For my Father's **w** is that everyone who *G2525*
Jn 7: 6 is not yet here; for you any time **w** do. *G1639*
Jn 7:17 chooses to do the **w** of God will find out *G2525*
Jn 7:35 *W he* go where our people live scattered *G3516*
Jn 9:31 to the godly person who does his **w**. *G2525*
Jn 11: 4 "This sickness **w** not end in death. *G1639*
Ac 4:28 what your power and **w** had decided *G1087*
Ac 17:31 has set a day when *he* **w** judge the world *G3516*
Ac 18:15 I **w** not be a judge of such things. *G1089*
Ac 18:21 "I will come back *if it is* God's **w**. *G2527*
Ac 19:27 **w** be robbed of her divine majesty." *G3516*
Ac 20:27 to proclaim to you the whole **w** of God. *G1087*
Ac 21:14 gave up and said, "The Lord's **w** be done." *G2525*
Ac 22:14 chosen you to know his **w** and to see the *G2525*
Ac 23: 3 Paul said to him, "God **w** strike you, you *G3516*
Ac 24:15 that there **w** be a resurrection of both the *G3516*
Ro 1:10 now at last by God's **w** the way may be *G2525*
Ro 2:18 if you know his **w** and approve of what is *G2525*
Ro 4:24 to whom God **w** credit righteousness *G3516*
Ro 8:13 to the flesh, *you* **w** die; but if by the *G3516*
Ro 8:18 with the glory *that* **w** *be* revealed in us. *G3516*
Ro 8:20 but **by the w of** the one who subjected it *G1328*
Ro 8:27 people **in accordance with the w of** God. *G2848*
Ro 9:19 For who is able to resist his **w**?" *G1088*
Ro 11:23 unbelief, **they w be grafted in**, for God is *G1596*
Ro 12: 2 to test and approve what God's **w** is— *G2525*
Ro 15:32 with joy, by God's **w**, and in your company *G2525*
1Co 1: 1 apostle of Christ Jesus by the **w** of God, *G2525*
1Co 7:37 has control over his own **w**, *G2525*
1Co 9:25 They do it to get a crown **that w not last** *G5778*
1Co 9:25 we do it to get a crown **that w last forever**. *G915*
2Co 1: 1 an apostle of Christ Jesus by the **w** of God, *G2525*
2Co 8: 5 and then by the **w** of God also to us. *G2525*
Gal 1: 4 according to the **w** of our God and Father, *G2525*
Eph 1: 1 an apostle of Christ Jesus by the **w** of God, *G2525*
Eph 1: 5 in accordance with his pleasure and **w**— *G2525*
Eph 1: 9 to us the mystery *of* his **w** according to his *G2525*
Eph 1:11 in conformity with the purpose *of* his **w**, *G2525*
Eph 5:17 understand what the Lord's **w** is. *G2525*
Eph 6: 6 doing the **w** of God from your heart. *G2525*
Php 2:13 who works in you *to* **w** and to act in order *G2527*
Col 1: 1 an apostle of Christ Jesus by the **w** of God, *G2525*
Col 1: 9 the knowledge *of* his **w** through all the *G2525*
Col 4:12 you may stand firm in all the **w** of God, *G2525*
1Th 4: 3 It is God's **w** that you should be sanctified: *G2525*
1Th 5:18 this is God's **w** for you in Christ Jesus. *G2525*
2Ti 1: 1 an apostle of Christ Jesus by the **w** of God, *G2525*
2Ti 2:26 who has taken them captive to do his **w**. *G2525*
2Ti 4: 1 who **w** judge the living and the dead *G3516*
Heb 1:14 to serve those *who* **w** inherit salvation? *G3516*
Heb 2: 4 Holy Spirit distributed according to his **w**. *G2526*
Heb 9:16 In the case of a **w**, it is necessary to prove *G1347*
Heb 9:17 because a **w** is in force only when *G1347*
Heb 10: 7 I have come to do your **w**, my God. *G2525*
Heb 10: 9 "Here I am, I have come to do your **w**." *G2525*
Heb 10:10 And by that **w**, we have been made holy *G2525*
Heb 10:27 raging fire that **w** consume the enemies *G3516*
Heb 10:36 that when you have done the **w** of God, *G2525*
Heb 13:21 you with everything good for doing his **w**, *G2525*
Jas 4:15 "If *it is* the Lord's **w**, we will live *G2527*
1Pe 2:15 For it is God's **w** that by doing good you *G2525*
1Pe 3:17 is better, if *it is* God's **w**, to suffer *G2527+2525*
1Pe 4: 2 desires, but rather *for* the **w** of God. *G2525*
1Pe 4:19 according to God's **w** should commit *G2525*
2Pe 1:12 So *I* **w** always remind you of these things *G3516*
2Pe 1:21 never had its origin *in* the human **w**, *G2525*
1Jn 2:17 whoever does the **w** of God lives forever *G2525*
1Jn 5:14 that if we ask anything according to his **w** *G2525*
Rev 1:19 what is now and what **w** take place later. *G3516*
Rev 2:10 the devil **w** put some of you in prison to *G3516*
Rev 2:26 is victorious and does my **w** to the end, *G2240*
Rev 4:11 by your **w** they were created and have *G2525*
Rev 12: 5 who "**w** rule all the nations with an iron *G3516*
Rev 17: 8 and **yet w** come up out of the Abyss and *G3516*

WILLFUL (3) [WILL]

Ps 19:13 Keep your servant also from **w sins**; may H2294
Isa 10:12 the **w pride** *of* his heart and H7262+1542
Isa 57:17 in anger, yet they kept on in their **w** ways. H4213

WILLFULLY (1) [WILL]

Ps 78:18 They **w** put God to the test by H928+4222

WILLING (56) [WILL]

Ge 23: 8 "If you are **w** to let me bury my dead H5883
Ex 10:27 and *he was* not **w** to let them go. H14
Ex 35: 5 Everyone who is **w** is to bring to the H5618+4213
Ex 35:21 everyone who *was* **w** and whose H5605+8120
Ex 35:22 All who were **w**, men and women H5618+4213
Ex 35:26 women who *were* **w** and had the H5951+4213
Ex 35:29 and women who *were* **w** brought to H5605+4213
Ex 36: 2 and who *was* **w** to come and do H5951+4213
Dt 29:20 The LORD *will* never *be* **w** to forgive them; H14
Jdg 5: 9 with the **w volunteers** among the people. H5605
Ru 3:13 But if *he is* not **w**, as surely as the LORD H2911
2Sa 6:10 He *was* not **w** to take the ark of the LORD to H14
2Ki 8:19 the LORD *was* not **w** to destroy Judah. H14
2Ki 24: 4 and the LORD *was* not **w** to forgive. H14
1Ch 19:19 So the Arameans *were* not **w** to help the H14
1Ch 28: 9 devotion and with a **w** mind, H2913
1Ch 28:21 every **w** *person* skilled in any craft will H5618
1Ch 29: 5 who *is* **w** to consecrate themselves to the H5605
1Ch 29: 9 at the **w response** *of* their leaders, H5605
2Ch 21: 7 the LORD *was* not **w** to destroy the house of H14
2Ch 29:31 all whose hearts were **w** brought burnt H5618
Job 6: 9 that God *would be* **w** to crush me, to let H3283
Ps 51:12 of your salvation and grant me a **w** spirit, H5618
Ps 110: 3 Your troops will be **w** on your day of battle H5607
Ps 119:108 the **w** praise *of* my mouth, and teach H5607
Pr 11:26 God's blessing on the *one who is* **w** *to* **sell**. AIT
Pr 19:18 *do* not **be a w party** to their death. H5951+5883
Isa 1:19 If *you are* **w** and obedient, you will eat the H14
Eze 3: 7 people of Israel *are* not **w** to listen to you H14
Eze 3: 7 you because they *are* not **w** to listen to me, H14
Da 3:28 command and *were* **w** *to* **give up** their lives AIT
Mt 8: 2 if *you are* **w**, you can make me *G2527*
Mt 8: 3 touched the man. "*I am* **w**," he said. "Be *G2527*
Mt 11:14 And if *you are* **w** to accept it, he is the *G2527*
Mt 18:14 in heaven is not **w** that any of these *G2525*
Mt 23: 4 but *they* themselves *are* not **w** to lift a *G2527*
Mt 23:37 under her wings, and *you were* not **w**. *G2527*
Mt 26:15 "What *are you* **w** to give me if I deliver *G2527*
Mt 26:41 The spirit is **w**, but the flesh is weak." *G4609*
Mk 1:40 his knees, "If *you are* **w**, you can make me *G2527*
Mk 1:41 touched the man. "*I am* **w**," he said. "Be *G2527*
Mk 14:38 The spirit is **w**, but the flesh is weak." *G4609*
Lk 5:12 if *you are* **w**, you can make me *G2527*
Lk 5:13 touched the man. "*I am* **w**," he said. "Be *G2527*
Lk 13:34 under her wings, and *you were* not **w**. *G2527*
Lk 22:42 if *you are* **w**, take this cup from me *G1089*
Jn 6:21 Then *they were* **w** to take him into the *G2527*
Ac 25: 9 "*Are you* **w** to go up to Jerusalem and *G2527*
Ac 25:20 so I asked if *he would be* **w** to go to *G1089*
Ac 26: 5 can testify, if *they are* **w**, that I conformed *G2527*
Ro 12:16 but *be* **w** *to* **associate with** people of low AIT
1Co 4:19 if the Lord *is* **w**, and then I will find *G2527*
1Co 7:12 a believer and she *is* **w** to live with him, *G5306*
1Co 7:13 not a believer and he *is* **w** to live with her, *G5306*
1Ti 6:18 to be generous and **w to share**. *G3127*
1Pe 5: 2 because you are **w**, as God wants you *G1731*

WILLINGLY (5) [WILL]

Jdg 5: 2 when the people **w offer themselves** H5605
1Ch 29: 6 in charge of the king's work **gave w**. H5605
1Ch 29:17 these things I *have* **given w** and with H5605
1Ch 29:17 **w** your people who are here *have* **given** to H5605
La 3:33 For he does not **w** bring affliction H4946+4213

WILLINGNESS (2) [WILL]

2Co 8:11 so that your eager **w** to do it may be *G2527*
2Co 8:12 For if the **w** is there, the gift is acceptable *G4608*

WILLOW (1) [WILLOWS]

Eze 17: 5 He planted it like a **w** by abundant water, H7628

WILLOWS (1) [WILLOW]

WILLOWS (KJV) POPLAR, POPLARS
Lev 23:40 from palms, **w** and other leafy trees H6857+5707

WILLS (1) [WILL]
Dt 21:16 when he **w** his property *to* his sons, he H5706

WILY (1)
Job 5:13 the schemes of the **w** are swept away. H7349

WIN (13) [WINNING, WINS, WON]
Pr 3: 4 Then *you will* **w** favor and a good name H5162
Mt 23:15 over land and sea *to* **w** a single convert, *G4472*
Lk 21:19 Stand firm, and *you will* **w** life. *G3227*
1Co 9:19 to everyone, to **w** as many as possible. *G3045*
1Co 9:20 Jews I became like a Jew, to **w** the Jews. *G3045*
1Co 9:20 the law), so as to **w** those under the law. *G3045*
1Co 9:21 so as to **w** those not having the law. *G3045*
1Co 9:22 the weak I became weak, to **w** the weak. *G3045*
Gal 1:10 *Am I* now *trying to* **w** *the* **approval** of *G4275*
Gal 4:17 *Those people are* **zealous** *to* **w** you *over*, but AIT
Eph 6: 6 not only to **w** their **favor** when their eye *G473*
Php 3:14 on toward the goal **to** **w** the prize for which AIT
1Th 4:12 daily life may **w** **the respect** of outsiders *G2361*

WIND (123) [WINDBLOWN, WINDING, WINDS, WINDSTORM, WOUND]
Ge 8: 1 and he sent a **w** over the earth, and H8120
Ge 41: 6 thin and scorched by the **east w**. H7708
Ge 41:23 thin and scorched by the **east w**. H7708
Ge 41:27 heads of grain scorched by the **east w**: H7708
Ex 10:13 LORD made an east **w** blow across the land H8120
Ex 10:13 By morning the **w** had brought the locusts; H8120
Ex 10:19 the LORD changed the **w** to a very strong west NDT
Ex 10:19 changed the wind to a very strong west **w**, H8120
Ex 14:21 with a strong east **w** and turned it into dry H8120
Nu 11:31 Now a **w** went out from the LORD and H8120
2Sa 22:11 he soared on the wings of the **w**. H8120
1Ki 18:45 black with clouds, the **w** rose, a heavy rain H8120
1Ki 19:11 great and powerful **w** tore the mountains H8120
1Ki 19:11 the LORD, but the LORD was not in the **w**. H8120
1Ki 19:11 After the **w** there was an earthquake, but H8120
2Ki 3:17 You will see neither **w** nor rain, yet this H8120
Job 1:19 suddenly a mighty **w** swept in from the H8120
Job 6:26 and treat my desperate words as **w**? H8120
Job 8: 2 Your words are a blustering **w**. H8120
Job 15: 2 fill their belly with the **hot east w**? H7708
Job 21:18 often are they like straw before the **w**, H8120
Job 27:21 The **east w** carries him off, and he is gone H7708
Job 28:25 the force of the **w** and measured out the H8120
Job 30:15 my dignity is driven away as by the **w**, my H8120
Job 30:22 snatch me up and drive me before the **w**; H8120
Job 37:17 the land lies hushed under the **south w**, H1999
Job 37:21 the skies after the **w** has swept them H8120
Ps 1: 4 They are like chaff that the **w** blows away. H8120
Ps 11: 6 a scorching **w** will be their lot. H8120
Ps 18:10 he soared on the wings of the **w**. H8120
Ps 35: 5 May they be like chaff before the **w**, with H8120
Ps 48: 7 ships of Tarshish shattered by an east **w**. H8120
Ps 78:26 He let loose the **east w** from the heavens H7708
Ps 78:26 by his power made the **south w** blow. H9402
Ps 83:13 my God, like chaff before the **w**. H8120
Ps 103:16 the **w** blows over it and it is gone, and its H8120
Ps 104: 3 chariot and rides on the wings of the **w**. H8120
Ps 135: 7 brings out the **w** from his storehouses H8120
Pr 11:29 ruin on their family will inherit *only* **w**, H8120
Pr 25:14 Like clouds and **w** without rain is one who H8120
Pr 25:23 Like a north **w** that brings unexpected rain H8120
Pr 27:16 like restraining the **w** or grasping oil with H8120
Pr 30: 4 Whose hands have gathered up the **w** H8120
Ecc 1: 6 The **w** blows to the south and turns to the H8120
Ecc 1:14 are meaningless, a chasing after the **w**. H8120
Ecc 1:17 that this, too, is a chasing after the **w**. H8120
Ecc 2:11 a chasing after the **w**; nothing was gained H8120
Ecc 2:17 it is meaningless, a chasing after the **w**. H8120
Ecc 2:26 too is meaningless, a chasing after the **w**. H8120
Ecc 4: 4 too is meaningless, a chasing after the **w**. H8120
Ecc 4: 6 handfuls with toil and chasing after the **w**. H8120
Ecc 4:16 too is meaningless, a chasing after the **w**. H8120
Ecc 5:16 do they gain, since they toil for the **w**? H8120
Ecc 6: 9 too is meaningless, a chasing after the **w**. H8120
Ecc 8: 8 no one has power over the **w** to contain it, H8120
Ecc 11: 4 Whoever watches the **w** will not plant H8120
Ecc 11: 5 As you do not know the path of the **w**, or H8120
SS 4:16 **north** **w**, and come, south wind H7600
SS 4:16 and come, **south** **w**! Blow on my H9402
Isa 7: 2 trees of the forest are shaken by the **w**. H8120
Isa 11:15 with a scorching **w** he will sweep his hand H8120
Isa 17:13 driven before the **w** like chaff on the hills H8120
Isa 24:20 it sways like a hut in the **w**; so heavy upon it NDT
Isa 26:18 writhed in labor, but we gave birth to **w**. H8120
Isa 27: 8 her out, as on a day the **east** **w** blows. H7708
Isa 28: 2 Like a hailstorm and a destructive **w**, like H8551
Isa 32: 2 a shelter from the **w** and a refuge from H8120
Isa 41:16 will winnow them, the **w** will pick them up H8120
Isa 41:29 their images are but **w** and confusion. H8120
Isa 57:13 The **w** will carry all of them off, a mere H8120
Isa 64: 6 like the **w** our sins sweep us away. H8120
Jer 2:24 sniffing the **w** in her craving—in H8120
Jer 4:11 "A scorching **w** *from* the barren heights in H8120
Jer 4:12 a **w** too strong for that comes from me H8120
Jer 5:13 prophets are but **w** and the word is not H8120
Jer 10:13 brings out the **w** from his storehouses H8120
Jer 13:24 you like chaff driven by the desert **w**. H8120
Jer 18:17 Like a **w** *from* the east, I will scatter them H8120
Jer 22:22 The **w** will drive all your shepherds away H8120
Jer 30:23 a driving **w** swirling down on the heads of H6193
Jer 51:16 brings out the **w** from his storehouses H8120
Eze 5: 2 And scatter a third to the **w**. For I will H8120
Eze 13:13 my wrath I will unleash a **violent w**, H8120+6194
Eze 17:10 completely when the east **w** strikes it— H8120
Eze 19:12 The east **w** made it shrivel, it was stripped H8120
Eze 27:26 But the east **w** will break you to pieces far H8120
Da 2:35 The **w** swept them away without leaving A10658
Hos 8: 7 "They sow the **w** and reap the whirlwind H8120
Hos 12: 1 Ephraim feeds on the **w**; he pursues the H8120
Hos 12: 1 he pursues the **east** **w** all day and H7708
Hos 13:15 An east **w** *from* the LORD will come H8120
Am 4:13 who creates the **w**, and who reveals his H8120
Jnh 1: 4 Then the LORD sent a great **w** on the sea H8120
Jnh 4: 8 God provided a scorching east **w**, and the H8120
Hab 1: 9 advance like a **desert** **w** and gather H7708
Hab 1:11 they sweep past like the **w** and go on— H8120
Zec 5: 9 two women, with the **w** in their wings! H8120
Mt 11: 7 A reed swayed by the **w**? *G449*
Mt 14:24 by the waves because the **w** was against it. *G449*
Mt 14:30 But when he saw the **w**, he was afraid and *G449*
Mt 14:32 climbed into the boat, the **w** died down. *G449*
Mk 4:39 rebuked the **w** and said to the waves *G449*
Mk 4:39 Then the **w** died down and it was *G449*
Mk 4:41 Even the **w** and the waves obey him!" *G449*
Mk 6:48 the oars, because the **w** was against them. *G449*
Mk 6:51 the boat with them, and the **w** died down. *G449*
Lk 7:24 A reed swayed by the **w**? *G449*
Lk 8:24 up and rebuked the **w** and the raging *G449*
Lk 12:55 And when the **south** **w** blows, you say, 'It's *G3803*
Jn 3: 8 The **w** blows wherever it pleases. You hear *G4460*
Jn 6:18 A strong **w** was blowing and the waters *G449*
Ac 2: 2 like the blowing *of* a violent **w** came from *G4466*
Ac 27: 7 When the **w** did not allow us to hold our *G449*
Ac 27:13 When a gentle **south** **w** began to blow *G3803*
Ac 27:14 Before very long, a **w** of hurricane force *G449*
Ac 27:15 the storm and could not head into the **w**; *G449*
Ac 27:40 the foresail *to* the **w** and made for the *G4463*
Ac 28:13 The next day the **south** **w** came up, and *G3803*
Eph 4:14 here and there *by* every **w** of teaching and *G449*
Jas 1: 6 of the sea, **blown** and tossed **by the w**. *G448*
Jude 12 blown along by the **w**; autumn trees, *G449*
Rev 6:13 from a fig tree when shaken by a strong **w**. *G449*
Rev 7: 1 earth to prevent any **w** from blowing on the *G449*

WINDBLOWN (5) [WIND, BLOW]
Lev 26:36 that the sound of a **w** leaf will put them to H5622
Job 13:25 Will you torment a **w** leaf? Will you chase H5622
Ps 18:42 beat them as fine as **w** dust; H6584+7156+8120
Isa 41: 2 with his sword, to **w** chaff with his bow. H5622
Zep 2: 2 effect and that day passes like **w chaff**, H5161

WINDING (1) [WIND]
Jdg 5: 6 abandoned; travelers took to **w** paths. H6824

WINDOW (16) [WINDOWS]
Ge 8: 6 Noah opened a **w** he had made *in* the ark H2707
Ge 26: 8 looked down from a **w** and saw Isaac H2707
Jos 2:15 let them down by a rope through the **w**, H2707
Jos 2:18 scarlet cord in the **w** through which you let H2707
Jos 2:21 And she tied the scarlet cord in the **w**. H2707
Jdg 5:28 "Through the **w** peered Sisera's mother H2707
1Sa 19:12 So Michal let David down through a **w** H2707
2Sa 6:16 daughter of Saul watched from a **w**. H2707
2Ki 9:30 arranged her hair and looked out of a **w**. H2707
2Ki 9:32 He looked up at the **w** and called out H2707
2Ki 13:17 "Open the east **w**," he said, and he H2707
1Ch 15:29 daughter of Saul watched from a **w**. H2707
Pr 7: 6 At the **w** *of* my house I looked down H2707
Hos 13: 3 like smoke escaping through a **w**. H748
Ac 20: 9 Seated in a **w** was a young man named *G2600*
2Co 11:33 in a basket from a **w** in the wall and *G2600*

WINDOWS (13) [WINDOW]
1Ki 6: 4 He made narrow **w** high up in the temple H2707
1Ki 7: 4 Its **w** were **placed high** in sets of three H9209
Ecc 12: 3 those looking through the **w** grow dim H748
SS 2: 9 gazing through the **w**, peering through H2707
Jer 9:21 in through our **w** and has entered our H2707
Jer 22:14 So he makes large **w** in it, panels it with H2707
Eze 41:16 the narrow **w** and galleries around H2707
Eze 41:16 the wall up to the **w**, and the windows H2707
Eze 41:16 to the windows, and the **w** were covered. H2707
Eze 41:26 portico were narrow **w** with palm trees H2707
Da 6:10 room where the **w** opened toward A10348
Joel 2: 9 like thieves they enter through the **w**. H2707
Zep 2:14 Their hooting will echo through the **w** H2707

WINDS (30) [WIND]
Ge 2:11 it **w through** the entire land of Havilah H6015
Ge 2:13 it **w through** the entire land of Cush. H6015
Job 37: 9 its chamber, the cold from the **driving** **w**. H4668
Job 38:24 place where the **east** **w** are scattered over H7708
Ps 104: 4 He makes **w** his messengers, flames of H8120
Ps 148: 8 clouds, stormy **w** that do his bidding, H8120
Jer 49:32 I will scatter to the **w** those who are in H8120
Jer 49:36 against Elam the four **w** from the four H8120
Jer 49:36 I will scatter them to the four **w**, and there H8120
Eze 5:10 will scatter all your survivors to the **w**. H8120
Eze 5:12 will scatter to the **w** and pursue with H8120
Eze 12:14 I will scatter to the **w** all those around him H8120
Eze 13:11 and **violent** **w** will burst forth. H8120+6194
Eze 17:21 the survivors will be scattered to the **w**. H8120
Eze 37: 9 from the four **w** and breathe into these H8120
Da 7: 2 me were the four **w** *of* heaven churning A10658
Da 8: 8 grew up toward the four **w** *of* heaven. H8120
Da 11: 4 parceled out toward the four **w** *of* heaven. H8120
Am 1:14 of battle, amid **violent** **w** on a stormy day. H6193
Zec 2: 6 scattered you to the four **w** *of* heaven," H8120
Mt 7:25 the **w** blew and beat against that *G449*
Mt 7:27 the **w** blew and beat against that *G449*
Mt 8:26 got up and rebuked the **w** and the waves, *G449*
Mt 8:27 Even the **w** and the waves obey him!" *G449*
Mt 24:31 they will gather his elect from the four **w**, *G449*
Mk 13:27 gather his elect from the four **w**, *G449*
Lk 8:25 He commands even the **w** and the water *G449*
Ac 27: 4 of Cyprus because the **w** were against us. *G449*
Jas 3: 4 are so large and are driven by strong **w**, *G449*
Rev 7: 1 holding back the four **w** of the earth to *G449*

WINDSTORM (2) [STORM, WIND]
Isa 29: 6 with **w** and tempest and flames of a H6070
Eze 1: 4 and I saw a **w** coming out of the H8120+6194

WINE (236) [WINES]
Ge 9:21 When he drank some of its **w**, he became H3516
Ge 9:24 awoke from his **w** and found out what H3516
Ge 14:18 king of Salem brought out bread and **w**. H3516
Ge 19:32 our father to drink **w** and then sleep with H3516
Ge 19:33 That night they got their father to drink **w** H3516
Ge 19:34 Let's get him to drink **w** again tonight H3516
Ge 19:35 got their father to drink **w** that night also, H3516
Ge 27:25 he brought *some* **w** and he drank. H3516
Ge 27:28 an abundance of grain and **new w**. H9408
Ge 27:37 sustained him with grain and **new w**. H9408
Ge 49:11 he will wash his garments in **w**, his robes H3516
Ge 49:12 His eyes will be darker than **w**, his teeth H3516
Ex 29:40 a quarter of a hin of **w** as a drink offering. H3516
Lev 10: 9 sons are not to drink **w** or other fermented H3516
Lev 23:13 its drink offering of a quarter of a hin of **w**. H3516
Nu 6: 3 must abstain from **w** and other fermented H3516
Nu 6: 3 vinegar made from **w** or other fermented H3516
Nu 6:20 After that, the Nazirite may drink **w**. H3516
Nu 15: 5 a quarter of a hin of **w** as a drink offering. H3516
Nu 15: 7 a third of a hin of **w** as a drink offering. H3516
Nu 15:10 bring half a hin of **w** as a drink offering. H3516
Nu 18:12 all the finest **new w** and grain they H9408
Nu 28:14 is to be a drink offering of half a hin of **w**; H3516
Dt 7:13 your grain, **new w** and olive oil—the H9408
Dt 11:14 gather in your grain, **new w** and olive oil. H9408
Dt 12:17 of your grain and **new w** and olive oil, H9408
Dt 14:23 of your grain, **new w** and olive oil, and H9408
Dt 14:26 **w** or other fermented drink, or H3516
Dt 18: 4 of your grain, **new w** and olive oil, and H9408
Dt 28:39 will not drink the **w** or gather the grapes, H3516
Dt 28:51 leave you no grain, **new w** or olive oil, nor H9408
Dt 29: 6 bread and drank no **w** or other fermented H3516
Dt 32:33 Their **w** is the venom of serpents, the H3516
Dt 32:38 drank the **w** *of* their drink offerings? H3516
Dt 33:28 secure in a land of grain and **new w**, H9408
Jdg 9:13 'Should I give up my **w**, which cheers both H9408
Jdg 13: 4 it that you drink no **w** or other fermented H3516
Jdg 13: 7 drink no **w** or other fermented drink and H3516
Jdg 13:14 drink any **w** or other fermented drink H3516
Jdg 19:19 bread and **w** for ourselves your H3516
Ru 2:14 some bread and dip it in the **w vinegar**." H2810
1Sa 1:14 going to stay drunk? Put away your **w**." H3516
1Sa 1:15 I have not been drinking **w** or beer; I was H3516
1Sa 1:24 an ephah of flour and a skin of **w**, and H3516
1Sa 10: 3 loaves of bread, and another a skin of **w**. H3516
1Sa 16:20 a skin of **w** and a young goat and sent H3516
1Sa 25:18 two skins of **w**, five dressed sheep, H3516
2Sa 13:28 spirits from drinking **w** and I say to you, H3516
2Sa 16: 1 a hundred cakes of figs and a skin of **w**. H3516
2Sa 16: 2 the **w** is to refresh those who become H3516
2Ki 18:32 a land of grain and **new w**, a land of H9408
1Ch 9:29 as well as the special flour and **w**, and H3516
1Ch 12:40 raisin cakes, **w**, olive oil, cattle and H3516
1Ch 27:27 produce of the vineyards for the **w** vats. H3516
2Ch 2:10 thousand baths of **w** and twenty thousand H3516
2Ch 2:15 the olive oil and **w** he promised, H3516
2Ch 11:11 with supplies of food, olive oil and **w**. H3516
2Ch 31: 5 of their grain, **new w**, olive oil and honey H9408
2Ch 32:28 harvest of grain, **new w** and olive oil; and H9408
Ezr 6: 9 **w** and olive oil, as requested by the A10271
Ezr 7:22 a hundred baths of **w**, a hundred baths A10271
Ne 2: 1 Artaxerxes, when **w** was brought for him H3516
Ne 2: 1 I took the **w** and gave it to the king. H3516
Ne 5:11 of the money, grain, **new w** and olive oil." H9408
Ne 5:15 from them in addition to food and **w**. H3516
Ne 5:18 days an abundant supply of **w** of all kinds. H3516
Ne 10:37 our trees and of our **new w** and olive oil. H9408
Ne 10:39 **new w** and olive oil to the storerooms H9408
Ne 13: 5 **new w** and olive oil prescribed for the H9408
Ne 13:12 **new w** and olive oil into the storerooms. H9408
Ne 13:15 it on donkeys, together with **w**, grapes, H3516
Est 1: 7 **W** *was* **served** in goblets of gold, each one H9197
Est 1: 7 and the royal **w** was abundant, in H3516
Est 1: 8 all the **w stewards** to serve each H8042+1074
Est 1:10 King Xerxes was in high spirits from **w**, H3516

Est 5: 6 As they were drinking **w**, the king again H3516
Est 7: 2 they were drinking **w** on the second day, H3516
Est 7: 7 left his **w** and went out into the palace H3516
Job 1:13 feasting and drinking **w** at the oldest H3516
Job 1:18 feasting and drinking **w** at the oldest H3516
Job 32:19 inside I am like bottled-up **w**, like new H3516
Ps 4: 7 joy when their grain and **new w** abound. H9408
Ps 60: 3 you have given us **w** that makes us H3516
Ps 75: 8 a cup full of foaming **w** mixed with spices; H3516
Ps 78:65 as a warrior wakes from the stupor of **w**. H3516
Ps 104:15 **w** that gladdens human hearts, oil to H3516
Pr 3:10 your vats will brim over with **new w**. H9408
Pr 4:17 of wickedness and drink the **w** *of* violence. H3516
Pr 9: 2 has prepared her meat and mixed her **w**; H3516
Pr 9: 5 eat my food and drink the **w** I have mixed. H3516
Pr 20: 1 **W** is a mocker and beer a brawler H3516
Pr 21:17 whoever loves **w** and olive oil will never H3516
Pr 23:20 who drink too much **w** or gorge H3516
Pr 23:30 Those who linger over **w**, who go to H3516
Pr 23:30 who go to sample **bowls of mixed w**. H4932
Pr 23:31 Do not gaze at **w** when it is red, when it H3516
Pr 31: 4 it is not for kings to drink **w**, not for rulers H3516
Pr 31: 6 perishing, **w** for those who are in anguish! H3516
Ecc 2: 3 I tried cheering myself with **w**, and H3516
Ecc 9: 7 drink your **w** with a joyful heart, for H3516
Ecc 10:19 made for laughter, **w** makes life merry H3516
SS 1: 2 your love is more delightful than **w**. H3516
SS 1: 4 we will praise your love more than **w**. H3516
SS 4:10 much more pleasing is your love than **w**, H3516
SS 5: 1 I have drunk my **w** and my milk. H3516
SS 7: 2 goblet that never lacks **blended w**. H4641
SS 7: 9 your mouth like the best **w**. May the H3516
SS 7: 9 May the **w** go straight to my beloved NDT
SS 8: 2 I would give you spiced **w** to drink, the H3516
Isa 1:22 your **choice w** is diluted with water. H6011
Isa 5:10 vineyard will produce only a bath of **w**; NDT
Isa 5:11 late at night till they are inflamed with **w**. H3516
Isa 5:12 pipes and timbrels and **w**, but they have H3516
Isa 5:22 heroes at drinking **w** and champions at H3516
Isa 16:10 no one treads out **w** at the presses, for I H3516
Isa 22:13 eating of meat and drinking of **w**! H3516
Isa 24: 7 The **new w** dries up and the vine withers H9408
Isa 24: 9 No longer do they drink **w** with a song H3516
Isa 24:11 In the streets they cry out for **w**; all joy H3516
Isa 25: 6 a banquet of **aged w**—the best of meats H9069
Isa 28: 1 that city, the pride of those laid low by **w**! H3516
Isa 28: 7 also stagger from **w** and reel from beer: H3516
Isa 28: 7 from beer and are befuddled with **w**; H3516
Isa 29: 9 but not from **w**, stagger, but not H3516
Isa 36:17 a land of grain and **new w**, a land of H9408
Isa 49:26 be drunk on their own blood, as with **w**. H6747
Isa 51:21 afflicted one, made drunk, but not with **w**. H3516
Isa 55: 1 buy **w** and milk without money and H3516
Isa 56:12 "let me get **w**! Let us drink our fill H3516
Isa 62: 8 drink the **new w** for which you have H9408
Isa 65:11 fill **bowls of mixed w** for Destiny, H4932
Jer 13:12 Every wineskin should be filled with **w**.' H3516
Jer 13:12 every wineskin should be filled with **w**? H3516
Jer 23: 9 like a strong man overcome by **w** H3516
Jer 25:15 cup filled with the **w** of my wrath and H3516
Jer 31:12 the grain, the **new w** and the olive oil, the H9408
Jer 35: 2 of the LORD and give them **w** to drink." H3516
Jer 35: 5 I set bowls full of **w** and some cups before H3516
Jer 35: 5 said to them, "Drink *some* **w**. H3516
Jer 35: 6 "We do not drink **w**, because our H3516
Jer 35: 6 your descendants must ever drink **w**. H3516
Jer 35: 8 our sons and daughters have ever drunk **w** H3516
Jer 35:14 not to drink **w** and this command has H3516
Jer 35:14 To this day they do not drink **w**, because NDT
Jer 40:10 you are to harvest the **w**, summer fruit H3516
Jer 40:12 an abundance of **w** and summer fruit. H3516
Jer 48:11 rest from youth, like **w** left on its dregs, not NDT
Jer 48:33 stopped the flow of **w** from the presses; H3516
Jer 51: 7 The nations drank her **w**; therefore they H3516
La 2:12 to their mothers, "Where is bread and **w**?" H3516
Eze 27:18 They offered **w** *from* Helbon, wool from H3516
Eze 27:19 casks of **w** from Izal in exchange for H3516
Eze 44:21 No priest is to drink **w** when he enters the H3516
Da 1: 5 amount of food and **w** from the king's H3516
Da 1: 8 defile himself with the royal food and **w**, H3516
Da 1:16 choice food and the **w** they were to drink H3516
Da 5: 1 of his nobles and drank **w** with them. A10271
Da 5: 2 While Belshazzar was drinking his **w**, he A10271
Da 5: 4 As they drank the **w**, they praised the A10271
Da 5:23 your concubines drank **w** from them. A10271
Da 10: 3 no meat or **w** touched my lips; and I H3516
Hos 2: 8 her the grain, the **new w** and oil, who H9408
Hos 2: 9 it ripens, and my **new w** when it is ready. H9408
Hos 2:22 to the grain, the **new w** and the olive oil H9408
Hos 4:11 **old w** and new wine take away their H3516
Hos 4:11 old wine and **new w** take away their H9408
Hos 7: 5 king the princes become inflamed with **w**, H3516
Hos 7:14 to their gods for grain and **new w**, H9408
Hos 9: 2 feed the people; the **new w** will fail them. H9408
Hos 9: 4 will not pour out **w offerings** to the LORD, H3516
Hos 14: 7 fame will be like the **w** *of* Lebanon. H3516
Joel 1: 5 all you drinkers of **w**; wail because of the H3516
Joel 1: 5 wail because of the **new w**, for it has H6747
Joel 1:10 is destroyed, the **new w** is dried up, the H9408
Joel 2:19 sending you grain, **new w** and olive oil H9408
Joel 2:24 the vats will overflow with **new w** and oil. H9408
Joel 3: 3 prostitutes; they sold girls for **w** to drink. H3516
Joel 3:18 that day the mountains will drip **new w**, H6747
Am 2: 8 of their god they drink **w** *taken as* fines. H3516
Am 2:12 the Nazirites drink **w** and commanded the H3516
Am 5:11 lush vineyards, you will not drink their **w**. H3516
Am 6: 6 You drink **w** by the bowlful and use the H3516
Am 9:13 **New w** will drip from the mountains and H6747
Am 9:14 will plant vineyards and drink their **w**; H3516
Mic 2:11 prophesy for you plenty of **w** and beer, H3516
Mic 6:15 you will crush grapes but not drink the **w**. H3516
Na 1:10 among thorns and drunk from their **w**; H6011
Hab 2: 5 indeed, **w** betrays him; he is arrogant H3516
Zep 1:12 who are like **w** left on its dregs, who NDT
Zep 1:13 plant vineyards, they will not drink the **w**." H3516
Hag 1:11 on the grain, the **new w**, the olive oil and H9408
Hag 2:12 bread or stew, some **w**, olive oil or other H3516
Hag 2:16 When anyone went to a **w vat** to draw fifty H3676
Zec 9:15 They will drink and roar as with **w**; they H3516
Zec 9:17 men thrive, and **new w** the young women. H9408
Zec 10: 7 their hearts will be glad as with **w**. H3516
Mt 9:17 do people pour new **w** into old wineskins. G3885
Mt 9:17 the **w** will run out and the wineskins will G3885
Mt 9:17 they pour new **w** into new wineskins G3885
Mt 27:34 There they offered Jesus **w** to drink, mixed G3885
Mt 27:48 He filled it *with* **w vinegar**, put it on a staff G3954
Mk 2:22 no one pours new **w** into old wineskins. G3885
Mk 2:22 Otherwise, the **w** will burst the skins, and G3885
Mk 2:22 both the **w** and the wineskins will be G3885
Mk 2:22 they pour new **w** into new wineskins." G3885
Mk 15:23 Then they offered him **w** mixed with myrrh G3885
Mk 15:36 filled a sponge *with* **w vinegar**, put it on a G3954
Lk 1:15 He is never to take **w** or other fermented G3885
Lk 5:37 no one pours new **w** into old wineskins. G3885
Lk 5:37 Otherwise, the new **w** will burst the skins G3885
Lk 5:37 **the w** will run out and the wineskins will G899S
Lk 5:38 new **w** must be poured into new G3885
Lk 5:39 no one after drinking **old** *w* wants the new, AIT
Lk 7:33 came neither eating bread nor drinking **w**, G3885
Lk 10:34 his wounds, pouring on oil and **w**. G3885
Lk 23:36 They offered him **w vinegar** G3954
Jn 2: 3 When the **w** was gone, Jesus' mother said G3885
Jn 2: 3 said to him, "They have no more **w**." G3885
Jn 2: 9 the water that had been turned into **w**. G3885
Jn 2:10 brings out the choice **w** first and then the G3885
Jn 2:10 then the cheaper **w** after the guests NDT
Jn 4:46 where he had turned the water into **w**. G3885
Jn 19:29 A jar of **w vinegar** was there, so they G3954
Ac 2:13 said, "They have had too much **w**. G1183
Ro 14:21 to eat meat or drink **w** or to do anything G3885
Eph 5:18 Do not get drunk *on* **w**, which leads to G3885
1Ti 3: 8 not indulging in much **w**, and not G3885
1Ti 5:23 use a little **w** because of your G3885
Titus 2: 3 to be slanderers or addicted to much **w**, G3885
Rev 6: 6 do not damage the oil and the **w**! G3885
Rev 14: 8 drink the maddening **w** of her adulteries." G3885
Rev 14:10 will drink the **w** of God's fury, which G3885
Rev 16:19 her the cup *filled with* the **w** of the fury of G3885
Rev 17: 2 intoxicated with the **w** of her adulteries." G3885
Rev 18: 3 drunk the maddening **w** of her adulteries. G3885
Rev 18:13 frankincense, *of* **w** and olive oil, of G3885

WINEBIBBER, WINEBIBBERS (KJV) DRINK TOO MUCH, DRUNKARD

WINEFAT (KJV) WINEPRESS

WINEPRESS (17) [WINEPRESSES]

Nu 18:27 the threshing floor or juice from the **w**. H3676
Nu 18:30 the product of the threshing floor or the **w**. H3676
Dt 15:14 your flock, your threshing floor and your **w**. H3676
Dt 16:13 of your threshing floor and your **w**. H3676
Jdg 6:11 threshing wheat in a **w** to keep it from the H1780
Jdg 7:25 rock of Oreb, and Zeeb at the **w** *of* Zeeb. H3676
2Ki 6:27 From the threshing floor? From the **w**?" H3676
Isa 5: 2 a watchtower in it and cut out a **w** as well. H3676
Isa 63: 2 like those of one treading the **w**? H1780
Isa 63: 3 "I have trodden the **w** alone; from the H7053
La 1:15 In his **w** the Lord has trampled Virgin H1780
Joel 3:13 the **w** is full and the vats overflow H1780
Mt 21:33 dug a **w** in it and built a watchtower. G3332
Mk 12: 1 dug a **pit for the w** and built a watchtower. G5700
Rev 14:19 them into the great **w** of God's wrath. G3332
Rev 14:20 were trampled *in* the **w** outside the city G3332
Rev 19:15 He treads the **w** of the fury of the G3332+3885

WINEPRESSES (4) [WINEPRESS]

Ne 13:15 in Judah treading **w** on the Sabbath and H1780
Job 24:11 terraces; they tread the **w**, yet suffer thirst. H3676
Hos 9: 2 Threshing floors and **w** will not feed the H3676
Zec 14:10 from the Tower of Hananel to the royal **w**, H3676

WINES (1) [WINE]

Isa 25: 6 the best of meats and the finest of **w**. H9069

WINESKIN (4) [WINESKINS]

Ps 119:83 Though I am like a **w** in the smoke, I do H5532
Jer 13:12 Every **w** should be filled with wine.' H5574
Jer 13:12 we know that every **w** should be filled H5574
Hab 2:15 pouring it from the **w** till they are drunk H2827

WINESKINS (12) [WINESKIN]

Jos 9: 4 with worn-out sacks and old **w**, H5532+3516
Jos 9:13 And these **w** that we filled were H5532+3516
Job 32:19 bottled-up wine, like new **w** ready to burst. H199
Mt 9:17 do people pour new wine into old **w**. G829
Mt 9:17 wine will run out and the **w** will be ruined. G829
Mt 9:17 they pour new wine into new **w**, and both G829
Mk 2:22 And no one pours new wine into old **w** G829
Mk 2:22 both the wine and the **w** will be ruined. G829
Mk 2:22 they pour new wine into new **w**." G829
Lk 5:37 And no one pours new wine into old **w** G829
Lk 5:37 wine will run out and the **w** will be ruined. G829
Lk 5:38 new wine must be poured into new **w**. G829

WING (15) [WINGED, WINGS, WINGSPAN]

1Ki 6:24 One **w** *of* the first cherub was five cubits H4053
1Ki 6:24 and the other **w** five cubits—ten H4053
1Ki 6:24 cubits—ten cubits from **w** tip to wing tip. H4053
1Ki 6:24 cubits—ten cubits from wing tip to **w** tip. H4053
1Ki 6:27 The **w** *of* one cherub touched one wall H4053
1Ki 6:27 while the **w** *of* the other touched the other H4053
2Ch 3:11 One **w** *of* the first cherub was five cubits H4053
2Ch 3:11 while its other **w**, also five cubits H4053
2Ch 3:11 touched the **w** *of* the other cherub. H4053
2Ch 3:12 Similarly one **w** *of* the second cherub was H4053
2Ch 3:12 and its other **w**, also five cubits long, H4053
2Ch 3:12 touched the **w** *of* the first cherub. H4053
Ecc 10:20 and a **bird on the w** may report H1251+4053
Isa 10:14 not one flapped a **w**, or opened its mouth H4053
Eze 1:11 each **w** touching that of the creature on NDT

WINGED (2) [WING]

Ge 1:21 every **w** bird according to its kind. H4053
Dt 14:20 But any **w creature** that is clean you may H6416

WINGS (73) [WING]

Ge 7:14 according to its kind, everything with **w**. H4053
Ex 19: 4 you on eagles' **w** and brought you to H4053
Ex 25:20 are to have their **w** spread upward, H4053
Ex 37: 9 The cherubim had their **w** spread upward H4053
Lev 1:17 He shall tear it open by the **w**, not dividing H4053
Dt 32:11 that spreads its **w** to catch them and H4053
Ru 2:12 under whose **w** you have come to take H4053
2Sa 22:11 flew; he soared on the **w** *of* the wind. H4053
1Ki 6:27 of the temple, with their **w** spread out. H4053
1Ki 6:27 their **w** touched each other in the H4053
1Ki 8: 6 put it beneath the **w** *of* the cherubim. H4053
1Ki 8: 7 spread their **w** over the place of the H4053
1Ch 28:18 that spread their **w** and overshadow the ark NDT
2Ch 3:13 The **w** *of* these cherubim extended twenty H4053
2Ch 5: 7 put it beneath the **w** *of* the cherubim. H4053
2Ch 5: 8 spread their **w** over the place of the H4053
Job 39:13 "The **w** *of* the ostrich flap joyfully, though H4053
Job 39:13 with the **w** and feathers *of* the stork. H89
Job 39:26 spread its **w** toward the south? H4053
Ps 17: 8 hide me in the shadow of your **w** H4053
Ps 18:10 flew; he soared on the **w** *of* the wind. H4053
Ps 36: 7 take refuge in the shadow of your **w**. H4053
Ps 55: 6 that I had the **w** of a dove! I would fly H88
Ps 57: 1 in the shadow of your **w** until the disaster H4053
Ps 61: 4 take refuge in the shelter of your **w**. H4053
Ps 63: 7 my help, I sing in the shadow of your **w**. H4053
Ps 68:13 the **w** *of* my dove are sheathed with silver H4053
Ps 91: 4 under his **w** you will find refuge H4053
Ps 104: 3 his chariot and rides on the **w** *of* the wind. H4053
Ps 139: 9 If I rise on the **w** *of* the dawn, if I settle on H4053
Pr 23: 5 will surely sprout **w** and fly off to the sky H4053
Isa 6: 2 him were seraphim, each with six **w**: H4053
Isa 6: 2 With two **w** they covered their faces, with NDT
Isa 8: 8 Its outspread **w** will cover the breadth of H4053
Isa 18: 1 the land of whirring **w** along the rivers of H4053
Isa 34:15 her young under the shadow of her **w**; NDT
Isa 40:31 They will soar on **w** like eagles; they will run H88
Jer 48:40 spreading its **w** over Moab. H4053
Jer 49:22 swoop down, spreading its **w** over Bozrah. H4053
Eze 1: 6 each of them had four faces and four **w**. H4053
Eze 1: 8 Under their **w** on their four sides they had H4053
Eze 1: 8 All four of them had faces and **w**, H4053
Eze 1: 9 the **w** *of* one touched the wings of H4053
Eze 1: 9 the wings of one touched the **w** of another. NDT
Eze 1:11 They each had two **w** spreading out H4053
Eze 1:11 each had two other **w** covering its body. NDT
Eze 1:23 Under the vault their **w** were stretched out H4053
Eze 1:23 each had two **w** covering its body. NDT
Eze 1:24 I heard the sound of their **w**, like the roar H4053
Eze 1:24 they stood still, they lowered their **w**. H4053
Eze 1:25 their heads as they stood with lowered **w**. H4053
Eze 3:13 was the sound of the **w** *of* the living H4053
Eze 10: 5 The sound of the **w** *of* the cherubim could H4053
Eze 10: 8 Under the **w** of the cherubim could be H4053
Eze 10:12 their hands and their **w**, were completely H4053
Eze 10:16 cherubim spread their **w** to rise from the H4053
Eze 10:19 spread their **w** and rose from the H4053
Eze 10:21 Each had four faces and four **w**, and under H4053
Eze 10:21 under their **w** was what looked like H4053
Eze 11:22 spread their **w**, and the glory of the H4053
Eze 17: 3 A great eagle with powerful **w**, long H4053
Eze 17: 7 eagle with powerful **w** and full plumage. H4053
Da 7: 4 like a lion, and it had the **w** of an eagle. A10149
Da 7: 4 I watched until its **w** were torn off and it A10149
Da 7: 6 its back it had four **w** like those of a bird. A10149
Zec 5: 9 two women, with the wind in their **w**! H4053
Zec 5: 9 They had **w** like those of a stork, and they H4053
Mt 23:37 as a hen gathers her chicks under her **w** G4763
Lk 13:34 as a hen gathers her chicks under her **w** G4763
Rev 4: 8 creatures had six **w** and was covered with G4763

Rev 4: 8 with eyes all around, even under its w. NDT
Rev 9: 9 the sound *of* their w was like the *G4763*
Rev 12:14 was given the two w of a great eagle, *G4763*

WINGSPAN (1) [WING]
2Ch 3:11 The **total** w *of* the cherubim was H802+4053

WINK (1) [WINKS]
Ps 35:19 *do* not *let* those who hate me without reason **maliciously** w H7975

WINKS (3) [WINK]
Pr 6:13 *who* w **maliciously** with his eye, signals H7975
Pr 10:10 *Whoever* w **maliciously** causes H7975+6524
Pr 16:30 *Whoever* w *with* their eye is plotting H6781

WINNING (2) [WIN]
Ex 17:11 the Israelites *were* w, but whenever he H1504
Ex 17:11 his hands, the Amalekites *were* w. H1504

WINNOW (4) [WINNOWING, WINNOWS]
Isa 41:16 *You will* w them, the wind will pick them H2430
Jer 4:11 my people, but not to w or cleanse; H2430
Jer 15: 7 *I will* w them with a winnowing fork at the H2430
Jer 51: 2 to Babylon *to* w her and to devastate H2430

WINNOWING (4) [WINNOW]
Ru 3: 2 Tonight he *will be* w barley *on* the H2430
Jer 15: 7 them with a w **fork** at the city gates H4665
Mt 3:12 His w **fork** is in his hand, and he will clear *G4768*
Lk 3:17 His w **fork** is in his hand to clear his *G4768*

WINNOWS (2) [WINNOW]
Pr 20: 8 to judge, he w **out** all evil with his eyes. H2430
Pr 20:26 A wise king w **out** the wicked; he drives H2430

WINS (1) [WIN]
Pr 13:15 Good judgment w favor, but the way of H5989

WINTER (16) [WINTERED]
Ge 8:22 summer and w, day and night will H3074
Ps 74:17 the earth; you made both summer and w. H3074
SS 2:11 The w is past; the rains are over and gone H6255
Isa 18: 6 them all summer, the wild animals **all** w. H3069
Jer 36:22 the king was sitting in the w apartment, H3074
Hos 6: 3 he will come to us like the w **rains**, like H1773
Am 3:15 will tear down the w house along with the H3074
Zec 14: 8 Mediterranean Sea, in summer and in w. H3074
Mt 24:20 not take place *in* w or on the Sabbath. *G5930*
Mk 13:18 Pray that this will not take place *in* w, *G5930*
Jn 10:22 of Dedication at Jerusalem. It was w, *G5930*
Ac 27:12 Since the harbor was unsuitable to w **in** *G4200*
Ac 27:12 hoping to reach Phoenix and w there. *G4199*
1Co 16: 6 a while, or even **spend the** w, so that you *G4199*
2Ti 4:21 Do your best to get here before w. Eubulus *G5930*
Titus 3:12 because I have decided *to* w there. *G4199*

WINTERED (1) [WINTER]
Ac 28:11 to sea in a ship *that had* w in the island— *G4199*

WIPE (21) [WIPED, WIPES, WIPING]
Ge 6: 7 "*I will* w from the face of the earth the H4681
Ge 7: 4 and *I will* w from the face of the earth H4681
Ex 23:23 Jebusites, and *I will* w them **out**. H3948
Ex 32:12 mountains and to w them off the face of H3983
Dt 7:24 and *you will* w **out** their names from under H6
Dt 12: 3 of their gods and w **out** their names from H6
Jos 7: 9 surround us and w **out** our name from the H4162
Jos 9:24 whole land and to w **out** all its H9012
1Sa 24:21 descendants or w **out** my name from my H9012
1Ki 16: 3 So I *am about to* w **out** Baasha and his H1277
1Ki 21:21 *I will* w **out** your descendants and cut off H1277
2Ki 21:13 *I will* w **out** Jerusalem as one wipes a H4681
Isa 14:22 *I will* w **out** Babylon's name and survivors H4162
Isa 25: 8 Sovereign LORD *will* w **away** the tears from H4681
Jer 36:29 this land and w from it both man and H8697
Eze 25: 7 *I will* w you **out** from among the nations H4162
Eze 25:16 and *I will* w **out** the Kerethites and destroy H4162
Eze 30:15 of Egypt, and w **out** the hordes of Thebes. H4162
Lk 10:11 town *we* w **from** our feet **as a warning** to *G669*
Rev 7:17 'And God *will* w **away** every tear from *G1981*
Rev 21: 4 '*He will* w every tear from their eyes. *G1981*

WIPED (15) [WIPE]
Ge 7:23 thing on the face of the earth *was* w **out**; H4681
Ge 7:23 the birds *were* w from the earth. H4681
Ex 9:15 a plague *that would have* w *you* off the H3948
Jdg 21:17 "so that a tribe of Israel *will* not **be** w **out**. H4681
1Sa 15:18 against them until you *have* w them **out**. H3983
Ps 119:87 *They* almost w me from the earth, but I H3983
Pr 6:33 and his shame *will* never **be** w **away**. H4681
Isa 26:14 them to ruin; *you* w **out** all memory of them. H6
Eze 6: 6 and what you have made w **out**. H4681
Zep 1:11 all your merchants *will* **be** w **out**, all who H1950
Lk 7:38 Then *she* w them with her hair, kissed *G1726*
Lk 7:44 with her tears and w them with her hair. *G1726*
Jn 11: 2 on the Lord and w his feet with her hair.) *G1726*
Jn 12: 3 it on Jesus' feet and w his feet with her *G1726*
Ac 3:19 so that your sins *may be* w **out**, that times *G1981*

WIPES (2) [WIPE]
2Ki 21:13 I will wipe out Jerusalem as *one* w a dish H4681
Pr 30:20 She eats and w her mouth and says, 'I've H4681

WIPING (1) [WIPE]
2Ki 21:13 w it and turning it upside down. H4681

WISDOM (218) [WISE]
Ge 3: 6 also desirable for **gaining** w, she took H8505
Ex 28: 3 I have given w in such matters H8120+2683
Ex 31: 3 Spirit of God, with w, with understanding, H2683
Ex 35:31 Spirit of God, with w, with understanding, H2683
Dt 4: 6 this will show your w and understanding H2683
Dt 34: 9 with the spirit of w because Moses had H2683
2Sa 14:20 My lord has w like that of an angel of God H2682
1Ki 2: 6 Deal with him according to your w, but do H2683
1Ki 2: 9 You are a man of w; you will know what H2682
1Ki 3:28 saw that he had w *from* God to administer H2683
1Ki 4:29 God gave Solomon w and very great H2683
1Ki 4:30 Solomon's w was greater than the wisdom H2683
1Ki 4:30 greater than the w *of* all the people of H2683
1Ki 4:30 and greater than all the w *of* Egypt. H2683
1Ki 4:34 people came to listen to Solomon's w, H2683
1Ki 4:34 of the world, who had heard of his w. H2683
1Ki 5:12 The LORD gave Solomon w, just as he had H2683
1Ki 7:14 Huram was filled with w, with H2683
1Ki 10: 4 Sheba saw all the w *of* Solomon and the H2683
1Ki 10: 6 your achievements and your w is true. H2683
1Ki 10: 7 in w and wealth you have far exceeded H2683
1Ki 10: 8 stand before you and hear your w! H2683
1Ki 10:23 greater in riches and w than all the other H2683
1Ki 10:24 Solomon to hear the w God had put in his H2683
1Ki 11:41 all he did and the w he displayed—are H2683
2Ch 1:10 Give me w and knowledge, that I may H2683
2Ch 1:11 a long life but for w and knowledge to H2683
2Ch 1:12 therefore w and knowledge will be given H2683
2Ch 9: 3 queen of Sheba saw the w *of* Solomon, H2683
2Ch 9: 5 your achievements and your w is true. H2683
2Ch 9: 6 half the greatness of your w was told me; H2683
2Ch 9: 7 stand before you and hear your w! H2683
2Ch 9:22 greater in riches and w than all the other H2683
2Ch 9:23 Solomon to hear the w God had put in his H2683
Ezr 7:25 in accordance with the w *of* your God A10266
Job 4:21 tent pulled up, so that they die without w? H2683
Job 9: 4 His w is profound, his power is vast. H2682
Job 11: 6 disclose to you the secrets of w, for H2683
Job 11: 6 of wisdom, for **true** w has two sides. H9370
Job 12: 2 who matter, and w will die with you! H2683
Job 12:12 Is not w found among the aged? Does not H2683
Job 12:13 "To God belong w and power; counsel H2683
Job 13: 5 For you, that would be w. H2683
Job 15: 8 Do you have a monopoly on w? H2683
Job 26: 3 advice you have offered to one without w! H2683
Job 26:12 the sea; by his w he cut Rahab to pieces. H9312
Job 28:12 But where can w be found? Where does H2683
Job 28:18 mention; the price of w is beyond rubies. H2683
Job 28:20 Where then does w come from? Where H2683
Job 28:27 then he looked at w and appraised it; he H2023S
Job 28:28 of the Lord—that is w, and to shun evil is H2683
Job 32: 7 advanced years should teach w. H2683
Job 32:13 'We have found w; let God, not a man H2683
Job 33:33 be silent, and I will teach you w. H2683
Job 38:36 Who gives the ibis w or gives the rooster H2683
Job 38:37 Who has the w to count the clouds? Who H2683
Job 39:17 not endow her with w or give her a share H2683
Job 39:26 take flight by your w and spread its wings H1069
Ps 37:30 The mouths of the righteous utter w, and H2683
Ps 49: 3 My mouth will speak *words of* w; the H2684
Ps 51: 6 you taught me w in that secret place. H2683
Ps 90:12 our days, that we may gain a heart of w. H2683
Ps 104:24 In w you made them all; the earth is full H2683
Ps 105:22 as he pleased and **teach** his elders w. H2681
Ps 111:10 The fear of the LORD is the beginning of w H2683
Pr 1: 2 gaining w and instruction; for H2683
Pr 1: 7 fools despise w and instruction. H2683
Pr 1:20 Out in the open w calls aloud, she raises H2684
Pr 2: 2 turning your ear to w and applying your H2683
Pr 2: 6 For the LORD gives w; from his mouth H2683
Pr 2:10 For w will enter your heart, and H2683
Pr 2:12 W will save you from the ways of wicked NDT
Pr 2:16 W will save you also from the adulterous NDT
Pr 3:13 Blessed are those who find w, those who H2683
Pr 3:19 By w the LORD laid the earth's foundations H2683
Pr 3:21 do not let w and understanding out of your NDT
Pr 4: 5 Get w, get understanding; do not forget H2683
Pr 4: 6 Do not forsake w, and she will protect H2023S
Pr 4: 7 The beginning of w is this: Get wisdom H2683
Pr 4: 7 wisdom is this: Get w. Though it cost all H2683
Pr 4:11 you in the way of w and lead you along H2683
Pr 5: 1 pay attention to my w, turn your ear to my H2683
Pr 7: 4 Say to w, "You are my sister," and to H2683
Pr 8: 1 Does not w call out? Does not H2683
Pr 8:11 w is more precious than rubies, and H2683
Pr 8:12 w, dwell together with prudence; H2683
Pr 9: 1 W has built her house; she has set up its H2684
Pr 9:10 The fear of the LORD is the beginning of w H2683
Pr 9:11 For through w your days will be many H2023S
Pr 9:12 If you are wise, *your* w will reward you; if H2681
Pr 10:13 W is found on the lips of the discerning H2683
Pr 10:23 a person of understanding delights in w. H2683
Pr 10:31 of the righteous comes the fruit of w, H2683
Pr 11: 2 disgrace, but with humility comes w. H2683
Pr 13:10 w is found in those who take advice. H2683
Pr 14: 6 The mocker seeks w and finds none, but H2683
Pr 14: 8 The w *of* the prudent is to give thought to H2683
Pr 14:33 W reposes in the heart of the discerning H2683
Pr 16:16 How much better to get w than gold, to H2683
Pr 17:16 fools have money in hand to buy w, H2683
Pr 17:24 A discerning person keeps w in view, but H2683
Pr 18: 4 the fountain of w is a rushing stream. H2683
Pr 19: 8 The one who gets w loves life; the one H4213
Pr 19:11 A person's w yields patience; it is to one's H8507
Pr 21:11 punished, the simple *gain* w; by paying H2681
Pr 21:30 There is no w, no insight, no plan that H2683
Pr 23:23 do not sell it—w, instruction and H2683
Pr 24: 3 By w a house is built, and through H2683
Pr 24: 7 W is too high for fools; in the assembly at H2684
Pr 24:14 Know also that w is like honey for you: If H2683
Pr 28:26 those who walk in w are kept safe. H2683
Pr 29: 3 A man who loves w brings joy to his H2683
Pr 29:15 A rod and a reprimand impart w, but a H2683
Pr 30: 3 I have not learned w, nor have I attained H2683
Pr 31:26 She speaks with w, and faithful instruction H2683
Ecc 1:13 to explore by w all that is done under H2683
Ecc 1:16 I have increased in w more than anyone H2683
Ecc 1:16 experienced much of w and knowledge." H2683
Ecc 1:17 applied myself to the understanding of w, H2683
Ecc 1:18 For with much w comes much sorrow; the H2683
Ecc 2: 3 my mind still guiding me with w. H2683
Ecc 2: 9 In all this my w stayed with me. H2683
Ecc 2:12 Then I turned my thoughts to consider w H2683
Ecc 2:13 I saw that w is better than folly, just as H2683
Ecc 2:21 For a person may labor with w, knowledge H2683
Ecc 2:26 God gives w, knowledge and H2683
Ecc 7:11 W, like an inheritance, is a good thing H2683
Ecc 7:12 W is a shelter as money is a shelter, but H2683
Ecc 7:12 W preserves those who have it H2683
Ecc 7:19 W makes one wise person more powerful H2683
Ecc 7:23 All this I tested by w and I said, "I am H2683
Ecc 7:25 to search out w and the scheme of H2683
Ecc 8: 1 A person's w brightens their face and H2683
Ecc 8:16 my mind to know w and to observe the H2683
Ecc 9:10 planning nor knowledge nor w. H2683
Ecc 9:13 sun this example of w that greatly H2683
Ecc 9:15 wise, and he saved the city by his w. H2683
Ecc 9:16 So I said, "W is better than strength." H2683
Ecc 9:16 But the poor man's w is despised, and H2683
Ecc 9:18 W is better than weapons of war, but one H2683
Ecc 10: 1 so a little folly outweighs w and honor. H2683
Isa 10:13 done this, and by my w, because I have H2683
Isa 11: 2 the Spirit of w and of understanding H2683
Isa 28:29 is wonderful, whose w is magnificent. H9370
Isa 29:14 wonder; the w *of* the wise will perish H2683
Isa 33: 6 store of salvation and w and knowledge; H2683
Isa 47:10 Your w and knowledge mislead you H2683
Jer 8: 9 of the LORD, what kind of w do they have? H2683
Jer 9:23 wise boast of their w or the strong boast H2683
Jer 10:12 the world by his w and stretched out the H2683
Jer 49: 7 "Is there no longer w in Teman? Has H2683
Jer 49: 7 from the prudent? Has their w decayed? H2683
Jer 51:15 the world by his w and stretched out the H2683
Eze 28: 4 By your w and understanding you have H2683
Eze 28: 7 your beauty and w and pierce your H2683
Eze 28:12 perfection, full of w and perfect in beauty. H2683
Eze 28:17 you corrupted your w because of your H2683
Da 1:20 In every matter of w and understanding H2683
Da 2:14 Daniel spoke to him with w and tact. A10539
Da 2:20 ever and ever; w and power are his. A10266
Da 2:21 He gives w to the wise and knowledge A10266
Da 2:23 You have given me w and power, you A10266
Da 2:30 I have greater w than anyone else alive A10266
Da 5:11 intelligence and w like that of the A10266
Da 5:14 intelligence and outstanding w. A10266
Hos 13:13 he is a child without w; when the time H2682
Mic 6: 9 to fear your name is w—"Heed the H9370
Mt 11:19 But w is proved right by her deeds." *G5053*
Mt 12:42 of the earth to listen *to* Solomon's w, *G5053*
Mt 13:54 this man get this w and these miraculous *G5053*
Mk 6: 2 "What's this w that has been given him *G5053*
Lk 1:17 disobedient to the w of the righteous— *G5860*
Lk 2:40 he was filled with w, and the grace of *G5053*
Lk 2:52 And Jesus grew in w and stature, and in *G5053*
Lk 7:35 But w is proved right by all her children." *G5053*
Lk 11:31 of the earth to listen to Solomon's w; *G5053*
Lk 11:49 God in his w said, 'I will send *G5053*
Lk 21:15 give you words and w that none of your *G5053*
Ac 6: 3 are known to be full of the Spirit and w. *G5053*
Ac 6:10 up against the w the Spirit gave him *G5053*
Ac 7:10 He gave Joseph w and enabled him to *G5053*
Ac 7:22 was educated *in* all the w of the *G5053*
Ro 11:33 of the riches *of* the w and knowledge of *G5053*
1Co 1:17 gospel—not with w and eloquence, lest *G5053*
1Co 1:19 "I will destroy the w of the wise; the *G5053*
1Co 1:20 not God made foolish the w of the world? *G5053*
1Co 1:21 For since in the w of God the world *G5053*
1Co 1:21 the world through its w did not know him, *G5053*
1Co 1:22 Jews demand signs and Greeks look for w, *G5053*
1Co 1:24 Christ the power of God and the w of God. *G5053*
1Co 1:25 foolishness of God is wiser than human w, NDT
1Co 1:30 who has become for us w from God—that *G5053*
1Co 2: 1 eloquence or *human* w as I proclaimed *G5053*
1Co 2: 5 that your faith might not rest on human w, *G5053*
1Co 2: 6 speak a message of w among the mature *G5053*
1Co 2: 6 not the w of this age or of the rulers of *G5053*
1Co 2: 7 we declare God's w, a mystery that has *G5053*
1Co 2:13 words taught us *by* human w but in words *G5053*
1Co 3:19 For the w of this world is foolishness in *G5053*
1Co 12: 8 given through the Spirit a message *of* w, *G5053*

W

2Co 1:12 not on worldly w but on God's grace. G5053
Eph 1: 8 With all w and understanding, G5053
Eph 1:17 give you the Spirit *of* w and revelation, G5053
Eph 3:10 the manifold w of God should be made G5053
Col 1: 9 will through all the w and understanding G5053
Col 1:28 teaching everyone with all w, G5053
Col 2: 3 all the treasures *of* w and knowledge. G5053
Col 2:23 indeed have an appearance *of* w, G5053
Col 3:16 one another with all w through psalms, G5053
Jas 1: 5 If any of you lacks w, you should ask God G5053
Jas 3:13 done in the humility *that comes from* w. G5053
Jas 3:15 Such "w" does not come down from G5053
Jas 3:17 But the w that comes from heaven is first G5053
2Pe 3:15 wrote you with the w that God gave him. G5053
Rev 5:12 wealth and w and strength and G5053
Rev 7:12 glory and w and thanks and honor G5053
Rev 13:18 This calls for w. Let the person who has G5053
Rev 17: 9 "This calls for a mind with w. The seven G5053

WISDOM'S (2) [WISE]

Pr 15:33 **W** instruction is to fear the LORD, and H2683
Pr 29:18 blessed is the one who heeds w instruction. NDT

WISE (181) [OVERWISE, WISELY, WISDOM, WISDOM'S, WISER, WISEST]

Ge 41: 8 all the magicians and w *men of* Egypt. H2682
Ge 41:33 a discerning and w man and put him in H2682
Ge 41:39 is no one so discerning and w as you. H2682
Ex 7:11 then summoned the w *men* and sorcerers, H2682
Dt 1:13 Choose *some* w, understanding and H2682
Dt 1:15 men of your tribes, w and respected men H2682
Dt 4: 6 great nation is a w and understanding H2682
Dt 16:19 the eyes of the w and twists the words H2682
Dt 32:29 If only *they were* w and would understand H2681
2Sa 14: 2 Tekoa and had a w woman brought from H2682
2Sa 20:16 a w woman called from the city, "Listen H2682
2Sa 20:22 went to all the people with her **w advice,** H2683
1Ki 3:12 I will give you a w and discerning heart H2682
1Ki 5: 7 he has given David a w son to rule over H2682
1Ch 26:14 his son Zechariah, a w counselor, and the H8507
2Ch 2:12 He has given King David a w son H2682
Est 1:13 he spoke with the w *men* who understood H2682
Job 5:13 He catches the w in their craftiness, and H2682
Job 11:12 the witless *can* no more **become** w than a H4220
Job 15: 2 "Would a w *person* answer with empty H2682
Job 15:18 what the w have declared, hiding nothing H2682
Job 17:10 I will not find a w *man* among you. H2682
Job 22: 2 Can even a w *person* benefit him? H8505
Job 32: 9 It is not only the old *who are* w, not only H2681
Job 34: 2 my words, you w *men*; listen to me, you H2682
Job 34:34 declare, w men who hear me say to me H2682
Job 37:24 he not have regard for all the w *in* heart?" H2682
Ps 2:10 Therefore, *you* kings, *be* w; be warned H8505
Ps 19: 7 are trustworthy, **making** w the simple. H2681
Ps 49:10 For all can see that the w die, that the H2682
Ps 94: 8 you fools, when *will you become* w? H8505
Ps 107:43 Let the one who is w heed these things H2682
Pr 1: 5 let the w listen and add to their learning H2682
Pr 1: 6 the sayings and riddles of the w. H2682
Pr 3: 7 Do not be w in your own eyes; fear the H2682
Pr 3:35 The w inherit honor, but fools get only H2682
Pr 6: 6 you sluggard; consider its ways and *be* w! H2681
Pr 8:33 Listen to my instruction and *be* w; do not H2681
Pr 9: 8 rebuke the w and they will love you. H2682
Pr 9: 9 Instruct the w and they will be wiser still H2682
Pr 9:12 If *you are* w, your wisdom will reward you H2681
Pr 10: 1 A w son brings joy to his father, but a H2682
Pr 10: 8 The w *in* heart accept commands, but a H2682
Pr 10:14 The w store up knowledge, but the mouth H2682
Pr 11:29 the fool will be servant to the w. H2682+4213
Pr 11:30 and the *one who* is w saves lives. H2682
Pr 12:15 right to them, but the w listen to advice. H2682
Pr 12:18 the tongue of the w brings healing. H2682
Pr 13: 1 A w son heeds his father's instruction, but H2682
Pr 13:14 The teaching of the w is a fountain of life H2682
Pr 13:20 Walk with the w and become wise, for a H2682
Pr 13:20 Walk with the wise and *become* w, for a H2681
Pr 14: 1 The w woman builds her house, but with H2682
Pr 14: 3 but the lips of the w protect them. H2682
Pr 14:16 The w fear the LORD and shun evil, but a H2682
Pr 14:24 The wealth of the w is their crown, but the H2682
Pr 14:35 A king delights in a w servant, but a H8505
Pr 15: 2 The tongue of the w adorns knowledge H2682
Pr 15: 7 The lips of the w spread knowledge, but H2682
Pr 15:12 resent correction, so they avoid the w. H2682
Pr 15:20 A w son brings joy to his father, but a H2682
Pr 15:31 correction will be at home among the w. H2682
Pr 16:14 of death, but the w will appease it. H2682+408
Pr 16:21 The w *in* heart are called discerning, and H2682
Pr 16:23 The hearts of the w make their mouths H2682
Pr 17:28 fools are thought w if they keep silent, H2682
Pr 18:15 the ears of the w seek it out. H2682
Pr 19:20 end *you will be* **counted among the w.** H2681
Pr 20: 1 whoever is led astray by them *is* not w. H2681
Pr 20:26 A w king winnows out the wicked; he H2682
Pr 21:11 attention to the w they get knowledge. H2682
Pr 21:20 The w store up choice food and olive oil H2682
Pr 21:22 *One who* is w can go up against the city H2682
Pr 22:17 turn your ear to the sayings of the w; H2682
Pr 23:15 if your heart *is* w, then my heart will H2681
Pr 23:19 my son, and *be* w, and set your heart on H2681
Pr 23:24 man who fathers a w son rejoices in him H2682
Pr 24: 5 The w prevail through great power, and H2682
Pr 24:23 These also are sayings of the w: To show H2682
Pr 25:12 is the rebuke of a w *judge* to a listening H2682
Pr 26: 5 his folly, or he will be w in his own eyes. H2682
Pr 26:12 Do you see a person w in their own eyes H2682
Pr 27:11 *Be* w, my son, and bring joy to my heart H2681
Pr 28:11 The rich are w in their own eyes; one who H2682
Pr 29: 8 stir up a city, but the w turn away anger. H2682
Pr 29: 9 If a w person goes to court with a fool, the H2682
Pr 29:11 but the w bring calm in the end. H2682
Pr 30:24 are small, yet they *are* **extremely** w: H2681+2682
Ecc 2:14 The w have eyes in their heads, while the H2682
Ecc 2:15 What then do I gain *by being* w?" I said H2681
Ecc 2:16 For the w, like the fool, will not be long H2682
Ecc 2:16 Like the fool, the w too must die! H2682
Ecc 2:19 whether that person will be w or foolish? H2682
Ecc 4:13 Better a poor but w youth than an old H2682
Ecc 6: 8 What advantage have the w over fools H2682
Ecc 7: 4 The heart of the w is in the house of H2682
Ecc 7: 5 the rebuke of a w *person* than to listen to H2682
Ecc 7: 7 Extortion turns a w *person* into a fool, and H2682
Ecc 7:10 For it is not w to ask such questions H2683
Ecc 7:19 makes one w *person* more powerful H2682
Ecc 7:23 "*I am determined to be* w"—but H2681
Ecc 8: 1 Who is like the w? Who knows the H2682
Ecc 8: 5 the w heart will know the proper time H2682
Ecc 8:17 Even if the w claim they know, they H2682
Ecc 9: 1 righteous and the w and what they do are H2682
Ecc 9:11 does food come to the w or wealth to the H2682
Ecc 9:15 there lived in that city a man poor but w, H2682
Ecc 9:17 quiet words of the w are more to be H2682
Ecc 10: 2 The heart of the w inclines to the right H2682
Ecc 10:12 from the mouth of the w are gracious, H2682
Ecc 12: 9 Not only was the Teacher w, but he also H2682
Ecc 12:11 The words of the w are like goads, their H2682
Isa 5:21 Woe to *those who* are w in their own eyes H2682
Isa 19:11 the w counselors of Pharaoh give H2682
Isa 19:11 "I am one of the w *men*, a disciple of the H2682
Isa 19:12 Where are your w *men* now? Let them H2682
Isa 29:14 the wisdom of the w will perish, the H2682
Isa 31: 2 Yet he too is w and can bring disaster; he H2682
Isa 44:25 the learning of the w and turns it into H2682
Jer 8: 8 you say, "We are w, for we have the law H2682
Jer 8: 9 The w will be put to shame; they will be H2682
Jer 9:12 Who is w *enough* to understand this H2682
Jer 9:23 "Let not the w boast of their wisdom or H2682
Jer 10: 7 Among all the w *leaders of* the nations H2682
Jer 18:18 will counsel from the w, nor the word H2682
Jer 50:35 against her officials and w *men*! H2682
Jer 51:57 I will make her officials and w *men* drunk H2682
Eze 28: 2 though you think you are as w as a god. H4213
Eze 28: 6 " 'Because you think you are w, as wise as a NDT
Eze 28: 6 you think you are wise, as w as a god, H4213
Da 2:12 execution of all the w *men of* Babylon. A10265
Da 2:13 was issued to put the w *men* to death, A10265
Da 2:14 to put to death the w *men of* Babylon, A10265
Da 2:18 with the rest of the w *men of* Babylon. A10265
Da 2:21 gives wisdom to the w and knowledge to A10265
Da 2:24 to execute the w *men of* Babylon, A10265
Da 2:24 "Do not execute the w *men of* Babylon. A10265
Da 2:27 Daniel replied, "No w *man*, enchanter A10265
Da 2:48 placed him in charge of all its w *men*. A10265
Da 4: 6 that all the w *men of* Babylon be A10265
Da 4:18 none of the w *men* in my kingdom can A10265
Da 5: 7 Then he said to these w *men of* Babylon, A10265
Da 5: 8 Then all the king's w *men* came in, but A10265
Da 5:15 The w *men* and enchanters were brought A10265
Da 11:33 "Those *who are* w will instruct many H8505
Da 11:35 Some of the w will stumble, so that they H8505
Da 12: 3 Those *who are* w will shine like the H8505
Da 12:10 those *who are* w will understand. H8505
Hos 14: 9 Who is w? Let them realize these things H2682
Ob 8 "will I not destroy the w *men* of Edom H2682
Mt 7:24 practice is like a w man who built his G5861
Mt 11:25 these things from the w and learned, G5055
Mt 24:45 "Who then is the faithful and w servant G5861
Mt 25: 2 Five of them were foolish and five were w. G5861
Mt 25: 4 The w *ones*, however, took oil in jars G5861
Mt 25: 8 The foolish ones said *to* the w, 'Give us G5861
Lk 10:21 these things from the w and learned, G5055
Lk 12:42 "Who then is the faithful and w manager G5861
Ac 15:38 Paul *did* not **think it** w to take him G546
Ro 1:14 both *to* the w and the foolish. G5055
Ro 1:22 Although they claimed to be w, they G5055
Ro 16:19 I want you to be w about what is good, G5055
Ro 16:27 to the only w God be glory forever through G5055
1Co 1:19 "I will destroy the wisdom *of* the w; the G5055
1Co 1:20 Where is the w *person*? Where is the G5055
1Co 1:26 many of you were w by human standards; G5055
1Co 1:27 things of the world to shame the w; G5055
1Co 2: 4 were not with w and persuasive words, G5053
1Co 3:10 I laid a foundation as a w builder, and G5055
1Co 3:18 of you think you are w by the standards of G5055
1Co 3:18 so that you may become w. G5055
1Co 3:19 "He catches the w in their craftiness"; G5055
1Co 3:20 that the thoughts *of* the w are futile." G5055
1Co 4:10 fools for Christ, but you are *so* w in Christ! G5861
1Co 6: 5 nobody among you w enough to judge a G5055
2Co 10:12 with themselves, *they are* not w. G5317
2Co 11:19 put up with fools since you are *so* w! G5861
Eph 5:15 how you live—not as unwise but as w, G5055
Col 4: 5 Be w in the way you act toward outsiders G5053
2Ti 3:15 are able *to* **make** you w for salvation G5054
Jas 3:13 Who is w and understanding among you G5055

WISELY (5) [WISE]

2Ch 11:23 *He* **acted** w, dispersing some of his sons H1067
Ps 36: 3 deceitful; they fail to **act** w or do good. H8505
Isa 52:13 my servant *will* **act** w; he will be H8505
Jer 23: 5 King who will reign w and do what is just H8505
Mk 12:34 When Jesus saw that he had answered w G3807

WISER (8) [WISE]

1Ki 4:31 *He was* w than anyone else, including H2681
1Ki 4:31 Ethan the Ezrahite—w than Heman, Kalkol NDT
Job 35:11 the earth and **makes** us w than the birds H2681
Ps 119:98 with me and **make** me w than my H2681
Pr 9: 9 Instruct the wise and *they will be* w still H2681
Pr 26:16 A sluggard is w in his own eyes than H2682
Eze 28: 3 Are you w than Daniel? Is no secret H2682
1Co 1:25 of God is w than human wisdom, G5055

WISEST (1) [WISE]

Jdg 5:29 The w *of* her ladies answer her; indeed H2682

WISH (24) [WISHED, WISHES, WISHING]

Ex 4:18 "Go, and I w you **well.**" H4200+8934
Nu 11:29 **I w** *that* all the LORD's people were H5989+4769
Dt 14:26 other fermented drink, or anything you w. H8626
Jdg 19:24 do to them whatever you w. H3202+928+6524
1Sa 24: 4 you to deal with as you w. H3512+928+6524
2Sa 19:27 so do whatever you w. H3202+928+6524
2Sa 19:37 Do for him whatever you w." H3202+928+6524
2Sa 19:38 do for him whatever you w. H3202+928+6524
1Ki 5: 9 you are to grant my w by providing food H2914
Job 10:18 *I w I had* **died** before any eye saw me. AIT
Job 11: 5 **Oh, how I w** that God would speak H4769+5989
Jnh 4: 9 "And I'm so angry I w I were dead." NDT
Mt 17: 4 If *you* w, I will put up three shelters—one G2527
Lk 12:49 how *I* w it were already kindled! G2527
Jn 15: 7 ask whatever *you* w, and it will be G2527
Ro 9: 3 For *I could* w that I myself were cursed G2377
1Co 4: 8 **How I w that** you really had begun to G4054
1Co 7: 7 *I* w that all of you were as I am. But each G2527
2Co 5: 4 because *we do* not w to be unclothed G2527
Gal 4: 9 *Do you* w to be enslaved by them all over G2527
Gal 4:20 *how I* w I could be with you now and G2527
Gal 5:12 **I w** they would go the whole way and G4054
Phm 20 I do w, brother, that I may have some G3721
Rev 3:15 hot. *I* w you were either one or the other! G4054

WISHED (6) [WISH]

2Sa 19:18 and to do whatever he w. H3202+928+6524
Est 1: 8 stewards to serve each man what he w. H8356
Job 9: 3 Though *they* w to dispute with him, they H2911
Jer 34:16 you had set free to go where they w. H5883
Mt 17:12 have done to him everything *they* w. G2527
Mk 9:13 they have done to him everything *they* w, G2527

WISHES (11) [WISH]

Lev 27:13 If the owner *w to* **redeem** the animal, a fifth AIT
Lev 27:15 who dedicates their house *w to* **redeem** it, AIT
Lev 27:19 one who dedicates the field *w to* **redeem** it, AIT
Dt 21:14 with her, let her go wherever she w. H5883
2Sa 24:22 whatever he w and offer it up. H3202+928+6524
Da 4:17 them to anyone he w and sets over them A10605
Da 4:25 earth and gives them to anyone *he* w. A10605
Da 4:32 earth and gives them to anyone *he* w." A10605
Da 5:21 earth and sets over them anyone *he* w. A10605
1Co 7:39 she is free to marry anyone *she* w, but he G2527
Rev 22:17 let the *one who* w take the free gift of G2527

WISHING (1) [WISH]

Ac 25: 9 w to do the Jews a favor, said to G2527

WIST (KJV) AWARE, IDEA, KNOW, REALIZE

WIT (KJV) KNOW, LEARN, SEE

WITCH (KJV) SORCERESS, WITCHCRAFT

WITCHCRAFT (6) [BEWITCHED]

Dt 18:10 interprets omens, **engages in** w, H4175
2Ki 9:22 the idolatry and w *of* your mother Jezebel H4176
2Ch 33: 6 practiced divination and w, sought omens H5727
Mic 5:12 I will destroy your w and you will no H4176
Na 3: 4 by her prostitution and peoples by her w. H4176
Gal 5:20 idolatry and w; hatred, discord, jealousy G5758

WITH (5964) See Index of Articles Etc.

WITHDRAW (12) [WITHDRAWN, WITHDRAWS, WITHDREW]

Lev 26:25 When *you* w into your cities, I will send a H665
1Sa 14:19 So Saul said to the priest, "W your hand." H665
2Sa 11:15 Then w from him so he will be struck H8740
2Sa 20:21 over this one man, and *I'll* w from the city." H2143
2Sa 24:16 W your hand." The angel of the H8332
1Ki 15:19 king of Israel so *he will* w from me." H6590
2Ki 18:14 W from me, and I will pay whatever you H8740
1Ch 21:15 W your hand." The angel of the H8332
2Ch 16: 3 king of Israel so *he will* w from me." H6590
Job 13:21 W your hand **far** from me, and stop H8178
Jer 21: 2 as in times past so that *he will* w from us." H6590
Ac 4:15 they ordered them *to* w from the Sanhedrin G599

WITHDRAWN (5) [WITHDRAW]

Jer 16: 5 because *I have* w my blessing, my H665
Jer 34:21 king of Babylon, which *has* w from you. H6590
Jer 37:11 Babylonian army *had* w from Jerusalem H6590
La 2: 3 *He has* w his right hand at the H8740+294
Hos 5: 6 not find him; *he has* w *himself* from them. H2740

WITHDRAWS (1) [WITHDRAW]

2Sa 17:13 If *he* w into a city, then all Israel will bring H665

WITHDREW (31) [WITHDRAW]

Ex 14:19 of Israel's army, w and went behind them. H5825
Ex 35:20 Israelite community w from Moses' H3655
1Sa 14:46 Philistines, and they w to their own land. H2143
1Ki 8:10 When the priests w from the Holy Place H3655
1Ki 15:21 stopped building Ramah and w to Tirzah. H3782
1Ki 16:17 Israelites with him w from Gibbethon and H6590
2Ki 3:27 *they* w and returned to their own land. H5825
2Ki 12:18 of Aram, *who* then w from Jerusalem. H6590
2Ki 15:20 the king of Assyria w and stayed in the H8740
2Ki 19: 8 *he* w and found the king fighting against H8740
2Ki 19:36 king of Assyria broke camp and w. H2143
2Ch 5:11 The priests then w from the Holy Place H3655
2Ch 24:25 When the Arameans w, they left H2143+4946
2Ch 32:21 So *he* w to his own land in disgrace H8740
Ezr 10: 6 Then Ezra w from before the house of God H7756
Job 34:14 his intention and *he* w his spirit and breath H665
Isa 37: 8 *he* w and found the king fighting against H8740
Isa 37:37 king of Assyria broke camp and w. H2143
Jer 37: 5 about them, *they* w from Jerusalem. H6590
Mt 2:22 in a dream, *he* w to the district of Galilee, *G432*
Mt 4:12 had been put in prison, *he* w to Galilee. *G432*
Mt 12:15 Aware of this, Jesus w from that place. *G432*
Mt 14:13 *he* w by boat privately to a solitary place. *G432*
Mt 15:21 Jesus w to the region of Tyre and Sidon. *G432*
Mk 3: 7 Jesus w with his disciples to the lake, and *G432*
Lk 5:16 But Jesus *often* w to lonely places *G1639+5723*
Lk 9:10 with him and *they* w by themselves to *G5723*
Lk 22:41 He w about a stone's throw beyond them *G685*
Jn 6:15 by force, w again to a mountain by himself. *G432*
Jn 11:54 Instead *he* w to a region near the *G599*
Ac 22:29 about to interrogate him w immediately. *G923*

WITHER (20) [WITHERED, WITHERS]

Job 8:12 *they* w more quickly than grass. H3312
Job 14: 2 They spring up like flowers and **w away** H4908
Job 15:30 darkness; a flame *will* w his shoots, and H3312
Job 15:32 Before his time *he will* w, and his H4908
Job 18:16 dry up below and his branches w above. H4908
Ps 1: 3 in season and whose leaf *does* not w— H5570
Ps 37: 2 like the grass *they will* soon w, like H4908
Ps 37:19 In times of disaster *they will* not w; in H3312
Ps 102:11 the evening shadow; I **w away** like grass. H3312
Isa 16: 8 The fields of Heshbon w, the vines of H581
Isa 19: 6 The reeds and rushes *will* w, H7857
Isa 40:24 than he blows on them and *they* w, and a H3312
Jer 8:13 figs on the tree, and their leaves *will* w. H5570
Eze 17: 9 All its new growth *will* w. It will not take a H3312
Eze 17:10 *Will it* not w **completely** when the H3312+3312
Eze 17:10 it—**w away** in the plot where it grew? H3312
Eze 47:12 Their leaves *will* not w, nor will their fruit H5570
Na 1: 4 Bashan and Carmel w and the blossoms of H581
Zec 9: 5 and Ekron too, for her hope *will* w. H3312
Mt 21:20 "How *did* the fig tree w so quickly? *G3830*

WITHERED (20) [WITHER]

Ge 41:23 w and thin and scorched by the east wind. H7568
Ps 90: 6 up new, but by evening it is dry and w. H3312
Ps 102: 4 My heart is blighted and w like grass; H3312
Isa 15: 6 of Nimrim are dried up and the grass *is* w; H3312
Isa 34: 4 host will fall like w leaves from the vine, H5570
Jer 12: 4 parched and the grass in every field *be* w? H3312
Jer 23:10 the pastures in the wilderness *are* w. H3312
Eze 19:12 its strong branches w and fire consumed H3312
Eze 31:15 all the trees of the field w **away**. H6634
Hos 9:16 blighted, their root *is* w, they yield no fruit H3312
Joel 1:12 The vine is dried up and the fig tree *is* w H581
Joel 1:12 Surely the people's joy *is* w **away**. H3312
Jnh 4: 7 which chewed the plant so that *it* w. H3312
Zec 11:17 *May* his arm *be* **completely** w, his H3312+3312
Mt 13: 6 and *they* w because they had no root. *G3830*
Mt 21:19 bear fruit again!" Immediately the tree w. *G3830*
Mk 4: 6 and *they* w because they had no root. *G3830*
Mk 11:20 they saw the fig tree w from the roots. *G3830*
Mk 11:21 The fig tree you cursed *has* w!" *G3830*
Lk 8: 6 the plants w because they had no *G3830*

WITHERS (13) [WITHER]

Job 8:19 Surely its life w **away**, and from the soil H5376
Ps 129: 6 on the roof, which w before it can grow; H3312
Isa 24: 4 The earth dries up and w, the world H5570
Isa 24: 4 the world languishes and w, the heavens H5570
Isa 24: 7 The new wine dries up and the vine w; all H581
Isa 33: 9 Lebanon is ashamed and w; Sharon is H7857
Isa 40: 7 The grass w and the flowers fall, because H3312
Isa 40: 8 The grass w and the flowers fall, but the H3312
Eze 17: 9 stripped of its fruit so that *it* w? H3312
Am 1: 2 and the top of Carmel w. H3312
Jn 15: 6 like a branch that is thrown away and w; *G3830*
Jas 1:11 rises with scorching heat and w the plant; *G3830*
1Pe 1:24 the field; the grass w and the flowers fall, *G3830*

WITHHELD (14) [WITHHOLD]

Ge 22:12 because *you have* not w from me your son H3104
Ge 22:16 have done this and *have* not w your son, H3104
Ge 39: 9 My master *has* w nothing from me except H3104
Job 22: 7 to the weary and *you* w food from the H4979
Ps 21: 2 desire and *have* not w the request of H4979
Ps 66:20 rejected my prayer or w his love from me! NDT
Ps 77: 9 *Has he* in anger w his compassion?" H7890
Isa 63:15 tenderness and compassion **are** w from us. H706
Jer 3: 3 Therefore the showers *have* **been** w, and H4979
Eze 20:22 But *I* w my hand, and for the sake of my H8740
Joel 1:13 drink offerings *are* w from the house of H4979
Am 4: 7 "I also w rain from you when the harvest H4979
Am 4: 7 one town, but w it from another. H4202+4763S
Hag 1:10 you the heavens *have* w their dew and H3973

WITHHOLD (10) [WITHHELD, WITHHOLDING, WITHHOLDS]

Ne 9:20 *You did* not w your manna from their H4979
Ps 40:11 *Do* not w your mercy from me, LORD; may H3973
Ps 84:11 no good thing *does he* w from those H4979
Pr 3:27 *Do* not w good from those to whom it is H4979
Pr 23:13 *Do* not w discipline from a child; if you H4979
Isa 10: 2 rights and w justice *from* the oppressed of H1608
Isa 32: 6 empty and *from* the thirsty *they* w water. H2893
La 2: 8 line and *did* not w his hand from H8740
Zec 1:12 how long will you w mercy from H4202
Lk 6:29 your coat, *do* not w your shirt from them. *G3266*

WITHHOLDING (2) [WITHHOLD]

2Co 6:12 *We are* not w our affection from you, but *G5102*
2Co 6:12 from you, but *you are* w yours from us. *G5102*

WITHHOLDS (5) [WITHHOLD]

Dt 27:19 "Cursed is *anyone who* w justice from the H5742
Job 6:14 "Anyone *who* w kindness *from* a friend H4415
Pr 11:24 gains even more; *another* w unduly, but H3104
Eze 18: 8 *He* w his hand from doing wrong and H8740
Eze 18:17 *He* w his hand from mistreating the poor H8740

WITHIN (107) [IN]

Ge 10: 5 territories by their clans w their nations, H928
Ge 10:32 to their lines of descent, w their nations. H928
Ge 23:17 all the trees w the borders of the field H928
Ge 25:22 The babies jostled each other w her H928+7931
Ge 25:23 two peoples from w you will be H5055
Ge 33:18 and camped w **sight of** the city. H907+7156
Ge 40:13 W three days Pharaoh will lift up H928+6388
Ge 40:19 W three days Pharaoh will lift off H928+6388
Ex 3: 2 to him in flames of fire from w a bush. H9348
Ex 3: 4 God called to him from w the bush H9348
Ex 13: 7 yeast be seen anywhere w your borders. H928
Ex 24:16 LORD called to Moses from w the cloud. H9348
Nu 36: 6 long as they marry w their father's tribal H4200
Nu 36:12 They married w the clans of the H4946
Jos 16: 9 the Ephraimites w the inheritance of H928+9348
Jos 17:11 W Issachar and Asher, Manasseh also had H928
Jos 19: 1 inheritance lay w the territory of H928+9348
Jos 19: 9 their inheritance w the territory of H928+9348
Jdg 14:12 me the answer *w* the seven **days** *of* the feast, AIT
Jdg 17: 7 who had been living w the clan of Judah, H4946
2Sa 20: 4 men of Judah to come to me *w* three **days**, AIT
1Ki 6:16 to ceiling to form w the temple an inner H4946
1Ki 6:19 inner sanctuary w the temple to set H928+9348
1Ki 9:18 Tadmor in the desert, w his land, H928
2Ki 7:11 and it was reported w the palace. H7163
Ezr 10: 8 who failed to appear w three days would H4200
Ezr 10: 9 W the three days, all the men of Judah H4200
Job 19:27 How my heart yearns w me! H928+2668
Job 20:14 the venom of serpents w him. H928+7931
Job 27: 3 as long as I have life w me, the breath of H928
Job 31:15 the same one form us both w our mothers? H928
Job 32:18 and the spirit w me compels me; H1061
Ps 22:14 to wax; it has melted w me. H928+9348+5055
Ps 39: 3 my heart grew hot w me. While I H928+7931
Ps 40: 8 my God; your law is w my heart." H928+9348
Ps 40:12 hairs of my head, and my heart **fails** *w* me. AIT
Ps 42: 5 Why so disturbed w me? Put your hope in H6584
Ps 42: 6 My soul is downcast w me; therefore I will H6584
Ps 42:11 Why so disturbed w me? Put your hope in H6584
Ps 43: 5 Why so disturbed w me? Put your hope in H6584
Ps 45:13 All glorious is the princess w her **chamber**; H7163
Ps 46: 5 God is w her, she will not fall; God H928+7931
Ps 48: 9 W your temple, O God, we meditate H928+7931
Ps 51:10 and renew a steadfast spirit w me. H928+7931
Ps 55: 4 My heart is in anguish w me; the H928+7931
Ps 55:10 its walls; malice and abuse are w it. H928+7931
Ps 94:19 When anxiety was great w me, your H928+7931
Ps 109:22 and my heart is wounded w me. H928+7931
Ps 122: 7 May there be peace w your walls and H928
Ps 122: 7 your walls and security w your citadels." H928
Ps 122: 8 friends, I will say, "Peace be w you. H928
Ps 128: 3 be like a fruitful vine w your house; H928+3752
Ps 142: 3 When my spirit grows faint w me, it is you H6584
Ps 143: 4 So my spirit grows faint w me; my heart H6584
Ps 143: 4 my heart w me is dismayed. H928+9348
Ps 147:13 and blesses your people w you. H928+7931
Pr 2: 1 words and store up my commands w you, H907
Pr 4:21 your sight, keep them w your heart; H928+9348
Pr 7: 1 words and store up my commands w you. H907
Ecc 4:14 have been born in poverty w his kingdom. H928
Isa 7: 8 W sixty-five years Ephraim will be H928+6388
Isa 13: 9 desolate and destroy the sinners w it. H4946
Isa 16:14 "W three years, as a servant bound by H928
Isa 21:16 "W one year, as a servant bound by H928+6388
Isa 41:18 heights, and springs w the valleys. H928+9348
Isa 56: 5 to them I will give w my temple and its H928
Isa 60:18 ruin or destruction w your borders, but H928
Jer 4:19 My heart pounds w me, I cannot keep H4200
Jer 8:18 in sorrow, my heart is faint w me. H6584
Jer 23: 9 My heart is broken w me; all my H928+7931
Jer 28: 3 W two years I will bring back to this H928+6388
Jer 28:11 neck of all the nations w two years. H928+6388
Jer 51:47 her slain will all lie fallen w her. H928+9348
La 1:20 I am in torment w, and in my heart I H928+7931
La 2:11 I am in torment w; my heart is poured out H5055
La 3:20 and my soul is downcast w me. H6584
La 4:13 who shed w her the blood of the H928+7931
Eze 11:23 LORD went up from w the city and stopped H9348
Eze 22:25 of her princes w her like a roaring H928+9348
Eze 22:25 and make many widows w her. H928+9348
Eze 22:27 Her officials w her are like wolves H928+7931
Eze 28:22 on you and w you am proved to be H928
Eze 28:23 The slain will fall w you, with the H928+9348
Eze 30: 6 to Aswan they will fall by the sword w her, H928
Eze 32:21 From w the realm of the dead the mighty H9348
Eze 40:44 the inner gate, w the inner court, were H928
Hos 11: 8 My heart is changed w me; all my H6584
Am 3: 9 see the great unrest w her and the H928+9348
Zep 3: 3 Her officials w her are roaring lions H928+7931
Zep 3: 5 The LORD w her is righteous; he does H928+7931
Zep 3:12 But I will leave w you the meek and H928+7931
Zec 2: 5 the LORD, 'and I will be its glory w. H928+9348
Zec 12: 1 forms the human spirit w a person, H928+7931
Zec 14: 1 and divided up w your **very walls**. H928+7931
Mt 6:23 If then the light w you is darkness, how *G1877*
Mk 7:21 For it is **from** w, out of a person's heart *G2277*
Lk 11:35 that the light w you is not darkness. *G1877*
Lk 19:44 you and the children w your *walls*. *G1877*
Lk 24:32 our hearts burning w us while he talked *G1877*
Jn 7:38 of living water will flow from w them." *G3120*
Jn 17:13 have the full measure of my joy w them. *G1877*
Ro 7:23 a prisoner of the law of sin at work w me. *G1877*
1Co 2:11 thoughts except their own spirit w them? *G1877*
2Co 7: 5 conflicts on the outside, fears w. *G2277*
Eph 3:20 to his power that is at work w us, *G1877*
Jas 4: 1 desires that battle w you? *G1877+3836+3517*
Rev 11:19 w his temple was seen the ark of his *G1877*

WITHOUT (370)

Ge 19: 3 baking **bread w yeast**, and they ate. H5174
Ge 24:21 **W saying a word**, the man watched her H3087
Ge 41:44 w your word no one will lift hand or H1187
Ex 12: 5 choose must be year-old males w **defect**, H9459
Ex 12: 8 bitter herbs, and **bread made w yeast**. H5174
Ex 12:15 days you are to eat **bread made w yeast**. H5174
Ex 12:18 you are to eat **bread made w yeast**, H5174
Ex 12:30 there was not a house w someone dead. H401
Ex 12:39 The dough was w yeast because they had H4202
Ex 13: 6 days eat **bread made w yeast** and on the H5174
Ex 15:22 traveled in the desert w finding water. H4202
Ex 21: 2 he shall go free, w **paying anything**. H2855
Ex 21:11 to go free, w **any payment** of money. H2855+401
Ex 23:15 seven days eat **bread made w yeast** H5174
Ex 29: 1 Take a young bull and two rams w **defect**. H9459
Ex 29: 2 wheat flour make round loaves w **yeast**, H5174
Ex 29: 2 thick loaves w **yeast** and with olive oil H5174
Ex 29: 2 thin loaves w **yeast** and brushed with H5174
Ex 29:23 From the basket of **bread made w yeast** H5174
Ex 34:18 For seven days eat **bread made w yeast** H5174
Ex 34:28 days and forty nights w eating bread or H4202
Lev 1: 3 the herd, you are to offer a male w **defect**. H9459
Lev 1:10 you are to offer a male w **defect**. H9459
Lev 2: 4 thick loaves made w **yeast** and with olive H5174
Lev 2: 4 thin loaves made w **yeast** and brushed H5174
Lev 2: 5 finest flour mixed with oil, and w **yeast**. H5174
Lev 2:11 bring to the LORD must be made w yeast, H4202
Lev 3: 1 before the LORD an animal w **defect**. H9459
Lev 3: 6 are to offer a male or female w **defect**. H9459
Lev 4: 3 LORD a young bull w **defect** as a sin H9459
Lev 4:23 as his offering a male goat w **defect**. H9459
Lev 4:28 they committed a female goat w **defect**. H9459
Lev 4:32 they are to bring a female w **defect**. H9459
Lev 5:15 one w **defect** and of the proper value in H9459
Lev 5:18 one w **defect** and of the proper value. H9459
Lev 6: 6 one w **defect** and of the proper value. H9459
Lev 6:16 it is to be eaten w **yeast** in the sanctuary H5174
Lev 7:12 thick loaves **made w yeast** and with olive H5174
Lev 7:12 thin loaves **made w yeast** and brushed H5174
Lev 8: 2 basket containing **bread made w yeast**, H5174
Lev 8:26 from the basket of **bread made w yeast**, H5174
Lev 9: 2 burnt offering, *both* w **defect**, and present H9459
Lev 9: 3 both a year old and w **defect**—for a burnt H9459
Lev 10:12 offerings **prepared w yeast** and presented H5174
Lev 14:10 a year old, each w **defect**, along with H9459
Lev 15:11 a discharge touches w rinsing his hands H4202
Lev 22:19 present a male w **defect** from the cattle, H9459
Lev 22:21 it must be w **defect** or blemish to be H9459
Lev 23: 6 days you must eat **bread made w yeast**. H5174
Lev 23:12 to the LORD a lamb a year old w **defect**, H9459
Lev 23:18 each a year old and w **defect**, one young H9459
Lev 25:31 houses in villages w walls around them are H401
Lev 26:43 its sabbaths while it lies desolate w them. H4946
Nu 6:14 a year-old male lamb w **defect** for a burnt H9459

W

Nu	6:14	year-old ewe lamb **w defect** for a sin	H9459
Nu	6:14	a ram **w defect** for a fellowship offering,	H9459
Nu	6:15	**bread** *made with* the finest flour and **w yeast**	H5174
Nu	6:19	loaf from the basket, both **made w yeast**.	H5174
Nu	15:24	**w** the community **being aware** *of* it,	H4946+6524
Nu	19:2	you a red heifer **w defect** or blemish and	H9459
Nu	19:15	every open container **w** a lid fastened on it	H401
Nu	27:17	will not be like sheep **w** a shepherd."	H401
Nu	28:3	two lambs a year old **w defect**, as a	H9459
Nu	28:9	offering of two lambs a year old **w defect**,	H9459
Nu	28:11	male lambs a year old, *all* **w defect**.	H9459
Nu	28:17	seven days eat **bread made w yeast**.	H5174
Nu	28:19	male lambs a year old, *all* **w defect**.	H9459
Nu	28:31	Be sure the animals are **w defect**.	H9459
Nu	29:2	male lambs a year old, *all* **w defect**.	H9459
Nu	29:8	male lambs a year old, *all* **w defect**.	H9459
Nu	29:13	male lambs a year old, *all* **w defect**.	H9459
Nu	29:17	male lambs a year old, *all* **w defect**.	H9459
Nu	29:20	male lambs a year old, *all* **w defect**.	H9459
Nu	29:23	male lambs a year old, *all* **w defect**.	H9459
Nu	29:26	male lambs a year old, *all* **w defect**.	H9459
Nu	29:29	male lambs a year old, *all* **w defect**.	H9459
Nu	29:32	male lambs a year old, *all* **w defect**.	H9459
Nu	29:36	male lambs a year old, *all* **w defect**.	H9459
Nu	35:22	" 'But if **w** enmity someone suddenly	H928+4202
Nu	35:23	**w** seeing them, drops on them a	H928+4202
Nu	35:27	may kill the accused **w** being guilty of	H401
Dt	4:42	killed a neighbor **w** malice aforethought.	H4202
Dt	7:14	will any of your livestock be **w young**.	H6829
Dt	15:10	to them and do so **w** a grudging heart;	H4202
Dt	19:4	unintentionally, **w** malice aforethought.	H4202
Dt	19:6	it to his neighbor **w** malice aforethought.	H4202
Dt	25:5	together and one of them dies **w** a son,	H401
Dt	28:50	fierce-looking nation **w** respect for the old	H4202
Dt	32:28	They are a nation **w** sense, there is no	H6
Jos	2:22	the road and returned **w** finding them.	H4202
Jos	11:20	exterminating them **w** mercy, as the LORD	H1194
Jos	20:5	**w** malice aforethought	H4202
Jos	23:6	**w** turning aside to the right or to the left.	H1194
Jdg	6:19	an ephah of flour he made **bread w yeast**.	H5174
Jdg	12:1	fight the Ammonites **w** calling us to go	H4202
Ru	1:5	Naomi was left **w** her two sons and	H4946
Ru	4:14	who this day *has* not **left** you **w a**	H8697
1Sa	6:3	do not send it back to him **w a gift**; by all	H8200
1Sa	17:50	**w** a sword in his hand he struck down the	H401
1Sa	20:2	great or small, **w** letting me know.	H4202
1Sa	28:24	kneaded it and baked **bread w yeast**.	H5174
2Sa	3:29	*May* Joab's family never **be w**	H4162+4946
2Sa	14:9	let the king and his throne be **w guilt**."	H5929
2Sa	14:28	years in Jerusalem **w** seeing the king's	H4202
2Sa	17:16	wilderness; **cross over w fail**, or the	H6296+6296
2Sa	20:10	on the ground. **W** being stabbed again	H4202
1Ki	1:27	the king has done **w** letting his servants	H4202
1Ki	2:32	because **w** my father David knowing it he	H4202
1Ki	22:13	other prophets **w exception** are	H285+7023
1Ki	22:17	on the hills like sheep **w** a shepherd,	H401
2Ki	18:25	this place **w** word from the LORD	H4946+1187
1Ch	2:30	Seled died **w** children.	H4202
1Ch	2:32	Jonathan. Jether died **w** children.	H4202
1Ch	23:22	Eleazar died **w** having sons: he had only	H4202
1Ch	23:29	the thin loaves **made w yeast**, the baking	H5174
1Ch	29:15	days on earth are like a shadow, **w** hope.	H401
2Ch	15:3	time Israel was **w** the true God,	H4200+4202
2Ch	15:3	**w** a priest to teach and without the	H4200+4202
2Ch	15:3	a priest to teach and **w** the law.	H4200+4202
2Ch	18:12	other prophets **w exception** are	H285+7023
2Ch	18:16	on the hills like sheep **w** a shepherd,	H401
Ezr	6:9	must be given them daily **w** fail,	A10379
Ezr	7:22	baths of olive oil, and salt **w** limit.	A10379
Est	4:11	in the inner court **w** being summoned the	H4202
Est	9:27	join them should **w** fail observe these	H4202
Job	2:3	me against him to ruin him **w any reason**."	H2855
Job	4:21	pulled up, so that they die **w** wisdom?	H4202
Job	5:4	from safety, crushed in court **w** a defender.	H401
Job	6:6	Is tasteless food eaten **w** salt, or is	H4946+1172
Job	7:6	they come to an end **w** hope.	H928+700
Job	8:11	Can reeds thrive **w** water?	H1172
Job	9:5	He moves mountains **w** their knowing it	H4202
Job	9:25	a runner; they fly away **w** a glimpse of joy.	H4202
Job	9:35	Then I would speak up **w** fear of him, but	H4202
Job	11:15	your face; you will stand firm and **w** fear.	H4202
Job	16:13	**W** pity, he pierces my kidneys and spills	H4202
Job	23:11	I have kept to his way **w** turning aside.	H4202
Job	26:3	advice you have offered to one **w** wisdom!	H4202
Job	27:22	itself against him **w** mercy as he flees	H4202
Job	31:19	lack of clothing, or the needy **w** garments,	H401
Job	31:39	devoured its yield **w** payment or broken	H1172
Job	34:20	the mighty are removed **w** human hand.	H4202
Job	34:24	**W** inquiry he shatters the mighty and sets	H4202
Job	34:35	'Job speaks **w** knowledge; his words	H4202+928
Job	35:16	**w** knowledge he multiplies words."	H928+1172
Job	36:12	by the sword and die **w** knowledge.	H3869+1172
Job	38:2	my plans with words **w** knowledge?	H1172
Job	41:33	is its equal—a creature **w** fear.	H4200+1172
Job	42:3	this that obscures my plans **w** knowledge?	H1172
Ps	7:4	ally with evil or **w cause** have robbed my	H8200
Ps	15:5	lends money to the poor **w** interest;	H928+4202
Ps	25:3	on those who are treacherous **w cause**.	H8200
Ps	35:7	their net for me **w cause** and without	H2855
Ps	35:7	cause and **w cause** dug a pit for me	H2855
Ps	35:15	gathered against me **w** my knowledge.	H4202
Ps	35:15	They slandered me **w** ceasing.	H4202
Ps	35:19	over me who are my enemies **w cause**;	H9214
Ps	35:19	who hate me **w reason** maliciously wink	H2855
Ps	38:19	Many have become my enemies **w cause**	H2855
Ps	38:19	who hate me **w reason** are numerous.	H9214
Ps	39:6	heaping up wealth **w** knowing whose it	H4202
Ps	40:12	For troubles **w** number surround me	H6330+401
Ps	54:3	to kill me—people **w** regard for God.	H4202
Ps	64:4	the innocent; they shoot suddenly, **w** fear.	H4202
Ps	69:4	who hate me **w reason** outnumber the	H2855
Ps	69:4	many are my enemies **w cause**, those	H9214
Ps	88:4	down to the pit; I am like one **w** strength.	H401
Ps	105:34	the locusts came, grasshoppers **w** number;	H401
Ps	109:3	surround me; they attack me **w cause**.	H2855
Ps	119:78	put to shame for wronging me **w cause**;	H9214
Ps	119:86	for I am being persecuted **w cause**.	H9214
Ps	119:161	Rulers persecute me **w cause**, but my	H2855
Pr	1:33	in safety and be at ease, **w** fear of harm."	H4946
Pr	6:15	he will suddenly be destroyed—**w** remedy.	H401
Pr	6:27	scoop fire into his lap **w** his clothes being	H4202
Pr	6:28	man walk on hot coals **w** his feet being	H4202
Pr	10:22	brings wealth, **w** painful toil for it.	H4202+3578
Pr	14:28	**w** subjects a prince is ruined.	H928+700
Pr	19:2	Desire **w** knowledge is not good	H928+4202
Pr	20:9	my heart pure; I am clean and **w** sin"?	H4946
Pr	21:26	but the righteous give **w** sparing.	H4202
Pr	24:28	testify against your neighbor **w cause**—	H2855
Pr	25:14	Like clouds and wind **w** rain is one who	H401
Pr	26:20	**W** wood a fire goes out; without a	H928+700
Pr	26:20	**w** a gossip a quarrel dies down.	H928+401
Pr	29:1	will suddenly be destroyed—**w** remedy.	H401
Ecc	2:25	**w** him, who can eat or find	H2575+4946
Ecc	6:4	It comes **w meaning**, it	H928+2021+2039
Isa	1:30	leaves, like a garden **w** water.	H401+4200
Isa	5:9	the fine mansions left **w** occupants.	H4946+401
Isa	6:11	cities lie ruined and **w** inhabitant,	H4946+401
Isa	13:14	gazelle, like sheep **w** a shepherd, they will	H401
Isa	22:3	they have been captured **w** *using* the bow.	H4946
Isa	23:1	is destroyed and left **w** house or harbor.	H4946
Isa	27:11	For this is a people **w** understanding; so	H4202
Isa	28:8	with vomit and there is not a spot **w** filth.	H1172
Isa	30:2	who go down to Egypt **w** consulting me	H4202
Isa	36:10	and destroy this land **w** the LORD?	H4946+1187
Isa	47:1	sit on the ground **w** a throne, queen city of	H401
Isa	52:3	and **w** money you will be redeemed."	H4202+928
Isa	55:1	wine and milk **w** money and without	H928+4202
Isa	55:1	and milk without money and **w** cost.	H928+4202
Isa	55:10	not return to it **w** watering the earth	H3954+561
Isa	56:2	who keeps the Sabbath **w** desecrating it	H4946
Isa	56:6	keep the Sabbath **w** desecrating it and	H4946
Isa	59:10	feeling our way like people **w** eyes.	H401
Jer	2:32	people have forgotten me, days **w** number.	H401
Jer	4:6	Flee for safety **w** delay! For I am	H440
Jer	4:7	towns will lie in ruins **w** inhabitant.	H4946+401
Jer	10:14	Everyone is senseless and **w** knowledge	H4946
Jer	14:17	with tears night and day **w** ceasing;	H440
Jer	15:13	give as plunder, **w** charge, because	H928+4202
Jer	20:16	like the towns the LORD overthrew **w** pity.	H4202
Jer	32:43	**w** people or animals	H4946+401
Jer	33:10	**w** people or animals.	H4946+401
Jer	33:12	desolate and **w** people or animals	H4946+401
Jer	44:7	so leave yourselves **w** a remnant?	H1194
Jer	44:22	and a desolate waste **w** inhabitants,	H4946+401
Jer	46:5	They flee in haste **w** looking back, and	H4202
Jer	46:19	waste and lie in ruins **w** inhabitant.	H4946+401
Jer	50:42	spears; they are cruel and **w** mercy.	H4202
Jer	51:17	"Everyone is senseless and **w** knowledge	H4946
La	2:2	**W** pity the Lord has swallowed up all the	H4202
La	2:17	He has overthrown you **w** pity, he has let	H4202
La	2:21	you have slaughtered them **w** pity.	H4202
La	3:11	mangled me and left me **w help**.	H9037
La	3:43	pursued us; you have slain **w** pity.	H4202
La	3:49	eyes will flow unceasingly, **w** relief,	H4946+401
La	3:52	were my enemies **w cause** hunted me like	H2855
La	4:6	in a moment **w** a hand turned to help	H4202
Eze	1:12	they would go, **w** turning as they went.	H4202
Eze	9:5	city and kill, **w** showing pity or compassion.	H440
Eze	10:11	the head faced, **w** turning as they went.	H4202
Eze	12:25	and it shall be fulfilled **w** delay.	H4202
Eze	14:23	that I have done nothing in it **w cause**,	H2855
Eze	35:13	me and spoke against me **w restraint**,	H6984
Eze	38:11	all of them living **w** walls and without	H928+401
Eze	38:11	living without walls and **w** gates and bars.	H401
Eze	43:22	offer a male goat **w defect** for a sin	H9459
Eze	43:23	a ram from the flock, both **w defect**.	H9459
Eze	43:25	a ram from the flock, *both* **w defect**.	H9459
Eze	45:18	take a young bull **w defect** and purify the	H9459
Eze	45:21	which you shall eat **bread made w yeast**.	H5174
Eze	45:23	seven rams **w defect** as a burnt	H9459
Eze	46:4	six male lambs and a ram, *all* **w defect**.	H9459
Eze	46:6	six lambs and a ram, *all* **w defect**.	H9459
Eze	46:13	a year-old lamb **w defect** for a burnt	H9459
Da	1:4	young men **w** any physical defect	H401
Da	2:35	swept them away **w** leaving a trace.	A10379
Da	6:18	spent the night **w eating** and without	A10297
Da	6:18	without eating and **w** any entertainment	A10379
Da	8:5	the whole earth **w** touching the ground.	H401
Da	11:14	in fulfillment of the vision, but **w success**.	H4173
Hos	3:4	will live many days **w** king or prince,	H401
Hos	3:4	king or prince, **w** sacrifice or sacred stones	H401
Hos	3:4	sacred stones, **w** ephod or household gods.	H401
Hos	4:14	a people **w** understanding will come to	H4202
Hos	8:4	They set up kings **w** my consent; they	H4202
Hos	8:4	they choose princes **w** my approval.	H4202
Hos	13:13	he is a child **w** wisdom; when the	H4202
Joel	1:6	a mighty army **w** number; it has the	H401
Joel	2:8	through defenses **w** breaking ranks.	H4202
Am	3:7	LORD does nothing **w** revealing his	H3954+561
Am	5:20	pitch-dark, **w** a ray of brightness?	H4202
Mic	2:8	robe from those who pass by **w a care**,	H1055
Mic	3:6	will come over you, **w** visions, and	H4946
Mic	3:6	and darkness, **w** divination.	H4946
Na	3:1	full of lies, full of plunder, never **w** victims!	H4631
Na	3:3	piles of dead, bodies **w** number, people	H401
Hab	1:17	destroying nations **w** mercy?	H4202
Zec	2:4	will be **a city w walls** because of the	H7252
Mt	9:36	helpless, like sheep **w** a shepherd.	*G3590+2400*
Mt	13:34	say anything to them **w** *using* a parable.	*G6006*
Mt	13:57	"A prophet is not **w honor** except in his	*G872*
Mt	22:12	you get in here **w** wedding clothes,	*G3590+2400*
Mt	22:24	us that if a man dies **w** having children,	*G3590*
Mt	23:23	the latter, **w** neglecting the former.	*G3590*
Mk	1:20	**W delay** he called them, and they left	*G2317*
Mk	3:27	man's house **w** first tying him up	*G1569+3590*
Mk	4:34	say anything to them **w** using a parable.	*G6006*
Mk	6:4	"A prophet is not **w honor** except in his	*G872*
Mk	6:34	they were like sheep **w** a shepherd.	*G3590+2400*
Mk	12:20	married and died **w** leaving any children	*G4024*
Lk	1:74	to enable us to serve him **w fear**	*G925*
Lk	4:35	them all and came out **w** injuring him.	*G3594*
Lk	6:35	to them **w** expecting to get **anything** back.	*G3594*
Lk	6:49	a house on the ground **w** a foundation.	*G6006*
Lk	11:42	practiced the latter **w** leaving the former	*G3590*
Lk	11:44	which people walk over **w** knowing it."	*G4024*
Lk	22:35	"When I sent you **w** purse, bag or sandals,	*G868*
Jn	1:3	**w** him nothing was made that has been	*G6006*
Jn	3:34	God gives the Spirit **w** limit.	*G4024+1666*
Jn	7:15	get such learning **w** having been taught?"	*G3590*
Jn	7:51	condemn a man **w** first hearing	*G1569+3590*
Jn	8:7	any one of you who is **w sin** be the first to	*G387*
Jn	15:25	'They hated me **w reason**.'	*G1562*
Jn	16:29	speaking clearly and **w** figures of speech.	*G4029*
Ac	10:29	sent for, I came **w raising any objection**.	*G395*
Ac	12:11	"Now I know **w a doubt** that the Lord has	*G242*
Ac	12:14	overjoyed she ran back **w** opening it and	*G4024*
Ac	14:17	Yet he has not left himself **w testimony**: He	*G282*
Ac	15:24	went out from us **w** our authorization and	*G4024*
Ac	16:37	"They beat us publicly **w a trial**, even	*G185*
Ac	25:27	a prisoner on to Rome **w** specifying the	*G3590*
Ac	27:21	After they had gone a long time **w food**	*G826*
Ac	27:33	suspense and have gone **w food**—	*G827*
Ac	28:31	with all boldness and **w hindrance**!	*G219*
Ro	1:20	been made, so that people are **w excuse**.	*G406*
Ro	4:19	**W weakening** in his faith, he faced the	*G3590*
Ro	10:14	how can they hear **w** someone preaching	*G6006*
Ro	14:1	**w** quarreling over disputable matters.	*G3590*
1Co	2:14	The person **w the Spirit** does not accept	*G6035*
1Co	4:8	to reign—and that **w** us! How I wish that	*G6006*
1Co	10:25	in the meat market **w** raising questions of	*G3594*
1Co	10:27	is put before you **w** raising questions of	*G3594*
1Co	11:29	who eat and drink **w** discerning the body	*G3590*
1Co	14:10	the world, yet none of them is **w meaning**.	*G936*
1Co	15:10	and his grace to me was not **w effect**.	*G3031*
2Co	11:27	toiled and have often **gone w sleep**;	*G71*
2Co	11:27	thirst and have often **gone w food**;	*G3763*
Gal	6:4	**w** comparing themselves to someone else	*G4024*
Eph	2:12	**w** hope and without God in the	*G3590+2400*
Eph	2:12	without hope and **w God** in the world.	*G117*
Eph	5:27	**w** stain or wrinkle or any other	*G3590+2400*
Php	1:14	all the more to proclaim the gospel **w fear**.	*G925*
Php	1:28	**w** being frightened in any way by those	*G3590*
Php	2:14	Do everything **w** grumbling or arguing,	*G6006*
Php	2:15	"children of God **w fault** in a warped and	*G320*
Col	1:22	**w blemish** and free from accusation	*G320*
1Th	2:1	that our visit to you was not **w results**.	*G3031*
2Th	3:8	did we eat anyone's food **w paying** for it.	*G1562*
1Ti	2:8	lifting up holy hands **w** anger or disputing.	*G6006*
1Ti	5:21	to keep these instructions **w** partiality, and	*G6006*
1Ti	6:14	keep this command **w spot** or blame until	*G834*
2Ti	3:3	**w love**, unforgiving, slanderous, without	*G845*
2Ti	3:3	slanderous, **w self-control**, brutal, not	*G203*
Phm	14	not want to do anything **w** your consent,	*G6006*
Heb	7:3	**W father** or mother, without genealogy	*G574*
[Heb	7:3	**W** father or **mother**, without genealogy	*G298*]
Heb	7:3	father or mother, **w genealogy**, without	*G37*
Heb	7:3	**w** beginning of days or end of life	*G3612*
Heb	7:7	And **w** doubt the lesser is blessed	*G6006+4246*
Heb	7:20	And it was not **w** an oath! Others became	*G6006*
Heb	7:20	Others became priests **w** any oath,	*G6006*
Heb	9:7	once a year, and never **w** blood, which he	*G6006*
Heb	9:18	covenant was not put into effect **w** blood.	*G6006*
Heb	9:22	**w** the shedding of blood there is no	*G6006*
Heb	10:28	the law of Moses died **w** mercy on the	*G6006*
Heb	11:6	And **w** faith it is impossible to please God	*G6006*
Heb	12:14	**w** holiness no one will see the Lord.	*G6006*
Heb	13:2	shown hospitality to angels **w knowing it**.	*G3291*
Jas	1:5	gives generously to all **w** finding fault,	*G3590*
Jas	2:13	because judgment **w mercy** will be shown	*G447*
Jas	2:15	a sister is **w clothes** and daily food.	*G1218*
Jas	2:18	Show me your faith **w** deeds, and I will	*G6006*
Jas	2:20	evidence that faith **w** deeds is useless?	*G6006*
Jas	2:26	As the body **w** the spirit is dead, so faith	*G6006*
Jas	2:26	spirit is dead, so faith **w** deeds is dead.	*G6006*
Jas	4:5	Scripture says **w reason** that he jealously	*G3036*

1Pe 1:19 of Christ, a lamb w **blemish** or defect. *G320*
1Pe 3: 1 they may be won over w words by the *G459*
1Pe 4: 9 hospitality to one another w grumbling. *G459*
2Pe 2:16 an animal w **speech**—who spoke with *G936*
2Pe 2:17 are springs w **water** and mists driven *G536*
1Jn 1: 8 If we claim to be w sin, we deceive *G4024*
Jude 12 eating with you w **the slightest qualm** *G925*
Jude 12 They are clouds w **rain**, blown along by the *G536*
Jude 12 autumn trees, w **fruit** and uprooted—twice *G182*
Jude 24 glorious presence w **fault** and with great *G320*
Rev 8:12 A third of the day was w light, and also a *G3590*
Rev 21: 6 I will give water w **cost** from the spring of *G1562*

WITHS (KJV) BOWSTRINGS

WITHSTAND (9) [WITHSTOOD]

Nu 31:23 else that *can* w fire must be put H995+928
Nu 31:23 whatever cannot w fire must be put H995+928
Jos 10: 8 of them *will be able to* w you." H6641+928+7156
Jos 23: 9 one *has been able to* w you. H6641+928+7156
2Ch 20: 6 your hand, and no one *can* w you. H3656+6640
Ps 147:17 Who *can* w his icy blast H6641+4200+7156
La 1:14 me into the hands of those I cannot w. H7756
Na 1: 6 Who *can* w his indignation H6641+4200+7156
Rev 6:17 their wrath has come, and who can w it?" *G2705*

WITHSTOOD (1) [WITHSTAND]

Jos 21:44 one of their enemies w them; H6641+928+7156

WITLESS (1) [WITS']

Job 11:12 But the w can no more become wise H408+5554

WITNESS (67) [EYEWITNESSES, WITNESSED, WITNESSES]

Ge 21:30 from my hand as a w that I dug this well." H6338
Ge 31:44 and let it serve as a w between us." H6332
Ge 31:48 "This heap is a w between you and me H6332
Ge 31:50 that God is a w between you and me." H6332
Ge 31:52 This heap is a w, and this pillar is a H6332
Ge 31:52 this pillar is a w, that I will not go H6338
Ex 23: 1 a guilty person by being a malicious w. H6332
Nu 5:13 since there is no w against her and she H6332
Nu 35:30 to death on the testimony of only one w. H6332
Dt 17: 6 to death on the testimony of only one w. H6332
Dt 19:15 One w is not enough to convict anyone H6332
Dt 19:16 If a malicious w takes the stand to accuse H6332
Dt 19:18 if the w proves to be a liar H6332
Dt 19:19 then do to **the false** w as that witness H2257S
Dt 19:19 false witness as that w intended to do to the NDT
Dt 31:19 so that it may be a w for me against them. H6332
Dt 31:26 There it will remain as a w against you. H6332
Jos 22:27 it is to be a w between us and you and H6332
Jos 22:28 sacrifices, but as a w between us and you. H6332
Jos 22:34 altar this name: A W Between Us—that H6332
Jos 24:27 "This stone will be a w against us. It has H6338
Jos 24:27 It will be a w against you if you are untrue H6338
Jdg 11:10 "The LORD is our w; we will certainly H9048+1068
1Sa 6:18 ark of the LORD is a w to this day in the H6332
1Sa 12: 5 "The LORD is w against you, and H6332
1Sa 12: 5 also his anointed is w this day, that H6332
1Sa 12: 5 "He is w," they said. H6332
1Sa 20:23 the LORD is w between you and me forever." NDT
1Sa 20:42 'The LORD is w between you and me NDT
Job 16: 8 it has become a w; my gauntness H6332
Job 16:19 Even now my w is in heaven; my advocate H6332
Ps 89:37 like the moon, the faithful w in the sky." H6332
Pr 6:19 a false w who pours out lies and a person H6332
Pr 12:17 An honest w tells the truth, but a false H7032
Pr 12:17 tells the truth, but a false w tells lies. H6332
Pr 14: 5 An honest w does not deceive, but a false H6332
Pr 14: 5 not deceive, but a false w pours out lies. H6332
Pr 14:25 A truthful w saves lives, but a false H6332
Pr 14:25 saves lives, but a false w is deceitful. H7032
Pr 19: 5 A false w will not go unpunished, and H6332
Pr 19: 9 A false w will not go unpunished, and H6332
Pr 19:28 A corrupt w mocks at justice, and the H6332
Pr 21:28 A false w will perish, but a careful listener H6332
Isa 19:20 will be a sign and w to the LORD Almighty H6332
Isa 30: 8 days to come it may be an everlasting w. H6332
Isa 55: 4 I have made him a w *to* the peoples, H6332
Jer 29:23 I know it and am a w to it," declares the H6332
Jer 42: 5 a true and faithful w against us if we do H6332
Mic 1: 2 Sovereign LORD may bear w against you, H6332
Mal 2:14 the LORD *is the* w between you and H6386
Lk 23:48 who had gathered to w this sight saw what NDT
Jn 1: 7 He came as a w to testify concerning that *G3456*
Jn 1: 8 he came only as a w to the light. *G3455*
Jn 8:13 you are, *appearing* as your own w; your *G3455*
Jn 8:18 myself; my *other* w *is* the Father, who *G3455*
Ac 1:22 of these must become a w with us of his *G3459*
Ac 22:15 You will be his w to all people of what you *G3459*
Ac 26:16 as a servant and *as* a w of what you have *G3459*
Ro 1: 9 is my w how constantly I remember you *G3459*
Ro 2:15 their consciences **also bearing** w, and *G5210*
2Co 1:23 I call God *as* my w—and I stake my life on *G3459*
1Th 2: 5 a mask to cover up greed—God is our w. *G3459*
Heb 3: 5 bearing w to what would be spoken by *G3457*
1Pe 5: 1 a fellow elder and a w of Christ's *G3459*
Rev 1: 5 who is the faithful w, the firstborn from *G3459*
Rev 2:13 Antipas, my faithful w, who was put to *G3459*
Rev 3:14 the faithful and true w, the ruler of God's *G3459*

WITNESSED (5) [WITNESS]

Jer 32:10 the deed, **had** it w, and weighed H6386+6332
Jer 32:25 silver and **have the transaction** w. H6386+6332
Jer 32:44 sealed and w in the territory of H6386+6332
Ac 28:23 *He* w to them from morning till evening *G1371*
1Ti 2: 6 This has now been w *to* at the proper *G3457*

WITNESSES (48) [WITNESS]

Nu 35:30 as a murderer only on the testimony of w. H6332
Dt 4:26 *I* **call** the heavens and the earth **as** w H6386
Dt 17: 6 of two or three w a person is to be put to H6332
Dt 17: 7 The hands of the w must be the first in H6332
Dt 19:15 by the testimony of two or three w. H6332
Dt 30:19 day *I* **call** the heavens and the earth **as** w H6386
Jos 24:22 "You are w against yourselves that you H6332
Jos 24:22 "Yes, we are w," they replied. H6332
Ru 4: 9 "Today you are w that I have bought from H6332
Ru 4:10 from his hometown. Today you are w!" H6332
Ru 4:11 the people at the gate said, "We are w. H6332
Job 10:17 You bring new w against me and increase H6332
Ps 27:12 of my foes, for false w rise up against me H6332
Ps 35:11 Ruthless w come forward; they question H6332
Isa 8: 2 *I* **called in** Uriah the priest and Zechariah son of Jeberekiah **as** reliable w H6386+6332
Isa 33: 8 is broken, its w are despised, no one H6332
Isa 43: 9 them bring in their w to prove they were H6332
Isa 43:10 "You are my w," declares the LORD, "and H6332
Isa 43:12 You are my w," declares the LORD, "that I H6332
Isa 44: 8 You are my w. Is there any God H6332
Jer 6:18 nations; you who are w, observe what will H6338
Jer 32:12 of the w who had signed the H6332
Mt 10:18 kings as w to them and to the *G3457*
Mt 18:16 by the testimony of two or three w. *G3459*
Mt 26:60 though many **false** w came forward. *G6020*
Mt 26:65 Why do we need any more w? Look, *G3459*
Mk 13: 9 before governors and kings as w to them. *G3457*
Mk 14:63 "Why do we need any more w?" he asked *G3459*
Lk 24:48 You are w of these things. *G3459*
Jn 8:17 written that the testimony *of* two w is true. *G476*
Ac 1: 8 you will be my w in Jerusalem, and *G3459*
Ac 2:32 this Jesus to life, and we are all w of it. *G3459*
Ac 3:15 him from the dead. We are w of this. *G3459*
Ac 5:32 We are w of these things, and so is the *G3459*
Ac 6:13 They produced false w, who testified *G3459*
Ac 7:58 the w laid their coats at the feet of a *G3459*
Ac 10:39 "We are w of everything he did in the *G3459*
Ac 10:41 but *by* w whom God had already chosen— *G3459*
Ac 13:31 They are now his w to our people. *G3459*
1Co 15:15 are then found to be **false** w about God, *G6020*
2Co 13: 1 by the testimony *of* two or three w. *G3459*
1Th 2:10 You are w, and so is God, of how holy *G3459*
1Ti 5:19 unless it is brought by two or three w. *G3459*
1Ti 6:12 confession in the presence of many w. *G3459*
2Ti 2: 2 the presence of many w entrust to reliable *G3459*
Heb 10:28 mercy on the **testimony of** two or three w. *G3459*
Heb 12: 1 surrounded by such a great cloud *of* w, *G3459*
Rev 11: 3 And I will appoint my two w, and they will *G3459*

WITS' (1) [WITLESS]

Ps 107:27 they *were* **at** their w **end**. H3972+2683+1182

WIVES (112) [WIFE]

Ge 4:23 Lamech said to his w, "Adah and Zillah H851
Ge 4:23 listen to me; w *of* Lamech, hear my words H851
Ge 6:18 your wife and your sons' w with you. H851
Ge 7: 7 his wife and his sons' w entered the ark to H851
Ge 7:13 with his wife and the w *of* his three sons, H851
Ge 8:16 your wife and your sons and their w. H851
Ge 8:18 with his sons and his wife and his sons' w. H851
Ge 28: 9 in addition to the w he already had. H851
Ge 30:26 Give me my w and children, for whom I H851
Ge 31:17 put his children and his w on camels, H851
Ge 31:50 if you take any w besides my daughters, H851
Ge 32:22 That night Jacob got up and took his two w, H851
Ge 36: 2 Esau took his w from the women of Canaan H851
Ge 36: 6 Esau took his w and sons and daughters H851
Ge 37: 2 his father's w, and he brought their H851
Ge 45:19 from Egypt for your children and your w, H851
Ge 46: 5 their children and their w in the carts that H851
Ge 46:26 not counting his sons' w—numbered H851
Ex 22:24 your w will become widows and your H851
Ex 32: 2 "Take off the gold earrings that your w H851
Ex 34:16 *you* **choose** some of their daughters **as** w H4374
Nu 14: 3 Our w and children will be taken as H851
Nu 16:27 come out and were standing with their w, H851
Nu 32:26 Our children and w, our flocks and herds H851
Dt 3:19 However, your w, your children and your H851
Dt 17:17 He must not take many w, or his heart will H851
Dt 21:15 If a man has two w, and he loves one but H851
Dt 29:11 together with your children and your w, and H851
Jos 1:14 Your w, your children and your livestock H851
Jdg 8:30 sons of his own, for he had many w. H851
Jdg 12: 9 *he* **brought in** thirty young women **as** w H995
Jdg 21: 7 "How can we provide w for those who are H851
Jdg 21:16 shall we provide w for the men who are H851
Jdg 21:18 We can't give them our daughters as w H851
Jdg 21:22 we did not get w *for* them during the war. H851
1Sa 1: 2 He had two w; one was called Hannah H851
1Sa 25:43 of Jezreel, and they both were his w. H851
1Sa 27: 3 family with him, and David had his two w: H851
1Sa 30: 3 by fire and their w and sons and daughters H851
1Sa 30: 5 David's two w had been captured H851
1Sa 30:18 Amalekites had taken, including his two w. H851
2Sa 2: 2 So David went up there with his two w H851
2Sa 5:13 took more concubines and w in Jerusalem, H851
2Sa 12: 8 and your master's w into your arms. H851
2Sa 12:11 I will take your w and give them to one H851
2Sa 12:11 he will sleep with your w in broad daylight. H851
2Sa 19: 5 the lives of your w and concubines. H851
1Ki 11: 3 He had seven hundred w of royal birth and H851
1Ki 11: 3 concubines, and his w led him astray. H851
1Ki 11: 4 his w turned his heart after other gods H851
1Ki 11: 8 He did the same for all his foreign w, who H851
1Ki 20: 3 the best of your w and children are H851
1Ki 20: 5 silver and gold, your w and your children. H851
1Ki 20: 7 When he sent for my w and my children H851
2Ki 24:15 king's mother, his w, his officials and the H851
1Ch 4: 5 Ashhur the father of Tekoa had two w H851
1Ch 4:17 One of Mered's w gave birth to Miriam NDT
1Ch 7: 4 for they had many w and children. H851
1Ch 8: 8 he had divorced his w Hushim and Baara. H851
1Ch 14: 3 David took more w and became the father H851
2Ch 11:21 than any of his other w and concubines. H851
2Ch 11:21 he had eighteen w and sixty concubines H851
2Ch 11:23 provisions and took many w for them. H851
2Ch 13:21 He married fourteen w and had twenty-two H851
2Ch 20:13 with their w and children and little ones H851
2Ch 21:14 your w and everything that is yours H851
2Ch 21:17 together with his sons and w. H851
2Ch 24: 3 Jehoiada chose two w for him, and he had H851
2Ch 28: 8 were from Judah two hundred thousand w, H851
2Ch 29: 9 daughters and our w are in captivity. H851
2Ch 31:18 all the little ones, the w, and the sons and H851
Ezr 9: 2 *They have* **taken** some of their daughters **as** w H5951
Ezr 10:11 around you and from your foreign w." H851
Ezr 10:19 their hands in pledge to put away their w, H851
Ezr 10:44 some of them had children by these w. H851
Ne 4:14 your daughters, your w and your homes." H851
Ne 5: 1 the men and their w raised a great outcry H851
Ne 10:28 together with their w and all their sons H851
Isa 13:16 houses will be looted and their w violated. H851
Jer 6:12 together with their fields and their w, when H851
Jer 8:10 I will give their w to other men and their H851
Jer 14:16 to bury them, their w, their sons and their H851
Jer 18:21 Let their w be made childless and widows H851
Jer 29: 6 find w for your sons and give your H851
Jer 29:23 committed adultery with their neighbors' w, H851
Jer 35: 8 Neither we nor our w nor our sons and H851
Jer 38:23 "All your w and children will be brought H851
Jer 44: 9 by you and your w in the land of Judah H851
Jer 44:15 who knew that their w were burning H851
Jer 44:25 You and your w have done what you said H851
Da 5: 2 his w and his concubines might drink A10699
Da 5: 3 his w and his concubines drank from A10699
Da 5:23 your w and your concubines drank wine A10699
Da 6:24 along with their w and children. A10493
Zec 12:12 clan by itself, with their w by themselves: NDT
Zec 12:12 the clan of the house of David and their w H851
Zec 12:12 clan of the house of Nathan and their w, H851
Zec 12:13 the clan of the house of Levi and their w H851
Zec 12:13 their wives, the clan of Shimei and their w, H851
Zec 12:14 all the rest of the clans and their w. H851
Mt 19: 8 you to divorce your w because your hearts *G1222*
Ac 21: 5 All of them, including w and children *G1222*
1Co 7:29 on those who have w should live as if *G1222*
Eph 5:22 W, submit yourselves to your own *G1222*
Eph 5:24 so also w should submit to their husbands *G1222*
Eph 5:25 Husbands, love your w, just as Christ *G1222*
Eph 5:28 ought to love their w as their own bodies. *G1222*
Col 3:18 W, submit yourselves to your husbands *G1222*
Col 3:19 love your w and do not be harsh with *G1222*
1Pe 3: 1 W, in the same way submit yourselves to *G1222*
1Pe 3: 1 without words by the behavior *of* their w, *G1222*
1Pe 3: 7 be considerate as you live with your w, *G1221*

WIVES' (1) [WIFE]

1Ti 4: 7 to do with godless myths and old w tales; *G1221*

WIZARD, WIZARDS (KJV) SPIRITIST, SPIRITISTS

WOE (104) [WOES]

Nu 21:29 W to you, Moab! You are destroyed H208
Job 10:15 If I am guilty—w to me! Even if I am H518
Ps 120: 5 W to me that I dwell in Meshek, that I live H210
Pr 23:29 Who has w? Who has sorrow? Who has H208
Ecc 10:16 W to the land whose king was a servant H365
Isa 1: 4 W *to* the sinful nation, a people whose H2098
Isa 3: 9 they do not hide it. W to them! They have H208
Isa 3:11 W to the wicked! Disaster is upon them H208
Isa 5: 8 W *to* you who add house to house and H2098
Isa 5:11 W to those who rise early in the morning H2098
Isa 5:18 W *to* those who draw sin along with cords H2098
Isa 5:20 W *to* those who call evil good and good H2098
Isa 5:21 W *to* those who are wise in their own H2098
Isa 5:22 W *to* those who are heroes at drinking H2098
Isa 6: 5 "W to me!" I cried. "I am ruined! For I am a H208
Isa 10: 1 W *to* those who make unjust laws, to H2098
Isa 10: 5 "W *to* the Assyrian, the rod of my anger H2098
Isa 17:12 W *to* the many nations that rage—they H2098
Isa 17:12 W *to* the peoples who roar—they roar like NDT
Isa 18: 1 W *to* the land of whirring wings along the H2098
Isa 24:16 W to me! The treacherous H208
Isa 28: 1 W *to* that wreath, the pride of Ephraim's H2098
Isa 29: 1 W *to* you, Ariel, Ariel, the city where H2098

W

Isa 29:15 **W** *to* those who go to great depths to H2098
Isa 30: 1 "**W** *to* the obstinate children," declares H2098
Isa 31: 1 **W** *to* those who go down to Egypt for help H2098
Isa 33: 1 **W** *to* you, destroyer, you who have not H2098
Isa 33: 1 **W** to you, betrayer, you who have not been NDT
Isa 45: 9 "**W** *to* those who quarrel with their Maker H2098
Isa 45:10 **W** *to* the one who says to a father, 'What H2098
Jer 4:13 **W** to us! We are ruined H208
Jer 10:19 **W** to me because of my injury! My wound H208
Jer 13:27 in the fields. **W** to you, Jerusalem H208
Jer 22:13 "**W** *to* him who builds his palace by H2098
Jer 23: 1 "**W** *to* the shepherds who are destroying H2098
Jer 45: 3 You said, '**W** to me! The LORD has added H208
Jer 48: 1 "**W** to Nebo, for it will be ruined H2098
Jer 48:46 **W** to you, Moab! The people of Chemosh H208
Jer 50:27 to the slaughter! **W** to them! For their day H2098
La 5:16 fallen from our head. **W** to us, for we have H208
Eze 2:10 words of lament and mourning and **w**. H2113
Eze 13: 3 **W** to the foolish prophets who follow their H2098
Eze 13:18 **W** to the women who sew magic charms H2098
Eze 16:23 " '**W**! Woe to you, declares the Sovereign H208
Eze 16:23 **W** to you, declares the Sovereign H208
Eze 24: 6 " '**W** *to* the city of bloodshed, to the pot H208
Eze 24: 9 " '**W** *to* the city of bloodshed H208
Eze 34: 2 **W** *to* you shepherds of Israel who only H2098
Hos 7:13 **W** to them, because they have strayed from H208
Hos 9:12 **W** to them when I turn away from them! H208
Am 5:18 **W** to you who long for the day of the LORD H2098
Am 6: 1 **W** to you who are complacent in Zion H2098
Mic 2: 1 **W** to those who plan iniquity, to those H2098
Na 3: 1 **W** to the city of blood, full of lies, full of H2098
Hab 2: 6 " '**W** to him who piles up stolen goods H2098
Hab 2: 9 "**W** to him who builds his house by unjust H2098
Hab 2:12 "**W** to him who builds a city with H2098
Hab 2:15 "**W** to him who gives drink to his H2098
Hab 2:19 **W** to him who says to wood, 'Come to life! H2098
Zep 2: 5 **W** to you who live by the sea, you H2098
Zep 3: 1 **W** to the city of oppressors, rebellious H2098
Zec 11:17 "**W** to the worthless shepherd, who H2098
Mt 11:21 "**W** to you, Chorazin! Woe to you *G4026*
Mt 11:21 **W** to you, Bethsaida! For if the *G4026*
Mt 18: 7 **W** to the world because of the things that *G4026*
Mt 18: 7 **w** to the person through whom they *G4026*
Mt 23:13 "**W** to you, teachers of the law and *G4026*
Mt 23:15 "**W** to you, teachers of the law and *G4026*
Mt 23:16 "**W** to you, blind guides! You say, 'If *G4026*
Mt 23:23 "**W** to you, teachers of the law and *G4026*
Mt 23:25 "**W** to you, teachers of the law and *G4026*
Mt 23:27 "**W** to you, teachers of the law and *G4026*
Mt 23:29 "**W** to you, teachers of the law and *G4026*
Mt 26:24 But **w** to that man who betrays the Son of *G4026*
Mk 14:21 But **w** to that man who betrays the Son of *G4026*
Lk 6:24 "But **w** to you who are rich, for you have *G4026*
Lk 6:25 **W** to you who are well fed now, for you *G4026*
Lk 6:25 **W** to you who laugh now, for you will *G4026*
Lk 6:26 **W** to you when everyone speaks well of *G4026*
Lk 10:13 "**W** to you, Chorazin! Woe to you *G4026*
Lk 10:13 **W** to you, Bethsaida! For if the *G4026*
Lk 11:42 "**W** to you Pharisees, because you give *G4026*
Lk 11:43 "**W** to you Pharisees, because you love *G4026*
Lk 11:44 "**W** to you, because you are like *G4026*
Lk 11:46 experts in the law, **w** to you, because you *G4026*
Lk 11:47 "**W** to you, because you build tombs for *G4026*
Lk 11:52 "**W** to you experts in the law, because you *G4026*
Lk 17: 1 **w** to anyone through whom they come *G4026*
Lk 22:22 But **w** to that man who betrays him!" *G4026*
1Co 9:16 **W** to me if I do not preach the gospel *G4026*
Jude 11 **W** to them! They have taken the way of *G4026*
Rev 8:13 midair call out in a loud voice: "**W**! Woe! *G4026*
Rev 8:13 **W**! Woe to the inhabitants of the *G4026*
Rev 8:13 **W** to the inhabitants of the earth *G4026*
Rev 9:12 The first **w** is past; two other woes are *G4026*
Rev 11:14 The second **w** has passed; the third woe *G4026*
Rev 11:14 has passed; the third **w** is coming soon. *G4026*
Rev 12:12 But **w** to the earth and the sea, because *G4026*
Rev 18:10 stand far off and cry: " '**W**! Woe to you, *G4026*
Rev 18:10 **W** to you, great city, you mighty city of *G4026*
Rev 18:16 " '**W**! Woe to you, great city *G4026*
Rev 18:16 **W** to you, great city, dressed in fine linen *G4026*
Rev 18:19 mourning cry out: " '**W**! Woe to you, *G4026*
Rev 18:19 **W** to you, great city, where all who had *G4026*

WOES (2) [WOE]

Ps 32:10 Many are the **w** of the wicked, but the H4799
Rev 9:12 woe is past; two other **w** are yet to come. *G4026*

WOKE (11) [WAKE]

Ge 41: 4 fat cows. Then Pharaoh **w up**. H3699
Ge 41: 7 Then Pharaoh **w up**; it had been a H3699
Ge 41:21 just as ugly as before. Then *I* **w up**. H3699
Zec 4: 1 talked with me returned and **w** me **up**, H6424
Mt 1:24 *When* Joseph **w up**, he *G1586+608+3836+5678*
Mt 8:25 The disciples went and **w** him, saying *G1586*
Mt 25: 7 all the virgins **w up** and trimmed their *G1586*
Mk 4:38 The disciples **w** him and said to him *G1586*
Lk 8:24 The disciples went and **w** him, saying *G1444*
Ac 12: 7 He struck Peter on the side and **w** him **up** *G1586*
Ac 16:27 The jailer **w up**, and when he saw *G2031+1181*

WOLF (6) [WOLVES]

Ge 49:27 "Benjamin is a ravenous **w**; in the H2269
Isa 11: 6 The **w** will live with the lamb, the leopard H2269
Isa 65:25 The **w** and the lamb will feed together H2269
Jer 5: 6 a **w** *from* the desert will ravage them H2269
Jn 10:12 So when he sees the **w** coming, he *G3380*
Jn 10:12 Then the **w** attacks the flock and scatters it *G3380*

WOLVES (7) [WOLF]

Eze 22:27 within her are like **w** tearing their prey; H2269
Hab 1: 8 than leopards, fiercer than **w** *at* dusk. H2269
Zep 3: 3 her rulers are evening **w**, who leave H2269
Mt 7:15 inwardly they are ferocious **w**. *G3380*
Mt 10:16 am sending you out like sheep among **w**. *G3380*
Lk 10: 3 am sending you out like lambs among **w**. *G3380*
Ac 20:29 savage **w** will come in among you and *G3380*

WOMAN (388) [WOMAN'S, WOMEN, WOMEN'S]

Ge 2:22 the LORD God made a **w** from the rib he had H851
Ge 2:23 she shall be called '**w**,' for she was taken H851
Ge 3: 1 He said to the **w**, "Did God really say, 'You H851
Ge 3: 2 The **w** said to the serpent, "We may eat H851
Ge 3: 4 certainly die," the serpent said to the **w**. H851
Ge 3: 6 When the **w** saw that the fruit of the tree H851
Ge 3:12 man said, "The **w** you put here with me H851
Ge 3:13 Then the LORD God said to the **w**, "What is H851
Ge 3:13 The **w** said, "The serpent deceived me H851
Ge 3:15 I will put enmity between you and the **w**, H851
Ge 3:16 To the **w** he said, "I will make your pains in H851
Ge 12:11 "I know what a beautiful **w** you are. H851
Ge 12:14 saw that Sarai was a very beautiful **w**. H851
Ge 20: 3 as dead because of the **w** you have taken; H851
Ge 20: 3 woman you have taken; she *is a* **married** *w*." AIT
Ge 21:10 "Get rid of that **slave w** and her son, for H563
Ge 21:12 distressed about the boy and your **slave w**. H563
Ge 24: 5 "What if the **w** is unwilling to come back H851
Ge 24: 8 If the **w** is unwilling to come back with you H851
Ge 24:14 May it be that when I say to a **young w** H5855
Ge 24:16 The **w** was very beautiful, a virgin; no man H5855
Ge 24:28 The **young w** ran and told her mother's H5855
Ge 24:39 'What if the **w** will not come back with me? H851
Ge 24:43 If a **young w** comes out to draw water H6625
Ge 24:55 "Let the **young w** remain with us ten days H5855
Ge 24:57 "Let's call the **young w** and ask her about H5855
Ge 28: 1 "Do not marry a Canaanite **w**. H1426
Ge 28: 6 "Do not marry a Canaanite **w**," H1426
Ge 34: 3 he loved the **young w** and spoke tenderly H5855
Ge 34:12 Only give me the **young w** as my wife." H5855
Ge 38:20 in order to get his pledge back from the **w**, H851
Ge 46:10 Zohar and Shaul the son of a **Canaanite** *w*. AIT
Ex 2: 1 of the tribe of Levi married a Levite **w**, H1426
Ex 2: 9 So the **w** took the baby and nursed him H851
Ex 3:22 *Every* **w** is to ask her neighbor and any H851
Ex 3:22 neighbor and *any w* **living** *in* her house for AIT
Ex 6:15 Zohar and Shaul the son of a **Canaanite** *w*. AIT
Ex 21: 4 the **w** and her children shall belong to her H851
Ex 21:10 If he marries **another** *w*, he must not deprive AIT
Ex 21:22 hit a pregnant **w** and she gives birth H851
Ex 21:28 "If a bull gores a man or **w** to death, the H851
Ex 21:29 kept it penned up and it kills a man or **w**, H851
Ex 35:25 Every skilled **w** spun with her hands and H851
Ex 36: 6 "No man or **w** is to make anything else as H851
Lev 12: 2 'A **w** who becomes pregnant and gives H851
Lev 12: 4 Then the **w** must wait thirty-three days to be NDT
Lev 12: 5 two weeks the **w** will be unclean, as NDT
Lev 12: 7 the *w who* **gives birth** to a boy or a girl AIT
Lev 13:29 "If a man or **w** has a sore on their head H851
Lev 13:33 then *the man or w must* **shave themselves** AIT
Lev 13:38 "When a man or **w** has white spots on the H851
Lev 15:18 sexual relations with a **w** and there is an H851
Lev 15:19 " 'When a **w** has her regular flow of blood H851
Lev 15:25 " 'When a **w** has a discharge of blood for H851
Lev 15:33 a *w* in her **monthly period**, for a man or a AIT
Lev 15:33 a man or a **w** with a discharge, and H5922
Lev 15:33 with a *w who is* **ceremonially unclean**. AIT
Lev 18:17 relations with both a **w** and her daughter. H851
Lev 18:19 " 'Do not approach a **w** to have sexual H851
Lev 18:22 relations with a man as one does with a **w**; H851
Lev 18:23 A **w** must not present herself to an animal H851
Lev 20:11 Both **the man and the w** are to be put to H2157S
Lev 20:13 relations with a man as one does with a **w**, H851
Lev 20:14 'If a man marries both a **w** and her mother, H851
Lev 20:16 " 'If a **w** approaches an animal to have H851
Lev 20:16 kill both the **w** and the animal. H851
Lev 20:18 relations with a **w** during her monthly H851
Lev 20:27 " 'A man or **w** who is a medium or spiritist H851
Lev 21:13 " 'The **w** he marries must be a virgin. H851
Lev 21:14 marry a widow, a **divorced** *w*, or a woman AIT
Lev 21:14 or a *w* **defiled** *by* prostitution, but AIT
Lev 24:11 of the Israelite **w** blasphemed the Name H851
Nu 3:12 the first male offspring of every Israelite **w**. NDT
Nu 5: 6 'Any man or **w** who wrongs another in any H851
Nu 5:18 priest has had the **w** stand before the LORD, H851
Nu 5:19 priest shall put the **w** under oath and say to H851
Nu 5:21 the priest is to put the **w** under this curse— H851
Nu 5:22 " 'Then the **w** is to say, "Amen. So be H851
Nu 5:24 He shall make the **w** drink the bitter water H851
Nu 5:26 he is to have the **w** drink the water. H851
Nu 5:28 the **w** has not made herself impure H851
Nu 5:29 of jealousy when a **w** goes astray and H851
Nu 5:31 the **w** will bear the consequences of H851
Nu 6: 2 'If a man or **w** wants to make a special vow, H851
Nu 8:16 first male offspring from every Israelite **w**. H8167
Nu 25: 6 into the camp a **Midianite** *w* right before the AIT
Nu 25:14 killed with the **Midianite** *w* was Zimri son of AIT
Nu 25:15 of the Midianite **w** who was put to death H851
Nu 25:18 the *w who* **was killed** when the plague came AIT
Nu 30: 3 "When a young **w** still living in her father's H851
Nu 30: 9 by a widow or **divorced** *w* will be binding on AIT
Nu 30:10 "If a **w** living with her husband makes a vow NDT
Nu 31:17 And kill every **w** who has slept with a man, H851
Dt 4:16 whether formed like a man or a **w**, H5922
Dt 17: 2 If a man or **w** living among you in one of H851
Dt 17: 5 take the man or **w** who has done this evil H851
Dt 20: 7 pledged to a **w** and not married her H851
Dt 21:11 captives a beautiful **w** and are attracted to H851
Dt 22: 5 A **w** must not wear men's clothing, nor a H851
Dt 22:14 "I married this **w**, but when I approached H851
Dt 22:22 who slept with her and the **w** must die. H851
Dt 22:24 the **young w** because she was in a town H5855
Dt 22:25 to meet a **young w** pledged to be H5855
Dt 22:26 Do nothing to the **w**; she has committed H5855
Dt 22:27 the man found **the young w** out in the H2023S
Dt 22:27 though the betrothed **w** screamed H5855
Dt 22:29 He must marry the young **w**, for he has NDT
Dt 23:17 No Israelite man or **w** is to become a H1426
Dt 24: 1 If a man marries a **w** who becomes H851
Dt 28:30 You will be pledged to be married to a **w** H851
Dt 28:56 most gentle and **sensitive** *w* among you— AIT
Dt 29:18 Make sure there is no man or **w**, clan or H851
Jos 2: 4 But the **w** had taken the two men and H851
Jdg 4: 9 will deliver Sisera into the hands of a **w**." H851
Jdg 5:30 a **w** or two for each man, colorful H8167
Jdg 9:53 a **w** dropped an upper millstone on his H851
Jdg 9:54 so that they can't say, 'A **w** killed him. H851
Jdg 11: 2 "because you are the son of another **w**." H851
Jdg 13: 6 Then the **w** went to her husband and told H851
Jdg 13: 9 came again to the **w** while she was out in H851
Jdg 13:10 The **w** hurried to tell her husband, "He's H851
Jdg 13:24 The **w** gave birth to a boy and named him H851
Jdg 14: 1 saw there a young Philistine **w**. H851
Jdg 14: 2 "I have seen a Philistine **w** in Timnah; now H851
Jdg 14: 3 there an acceptable **w** among your H851
Jdg 14: 7 Then he went down and talked with the **w** H851
Jdg 14:10 Now his father went down to see the **w** H851
Jdg 16: 4 fell in love with a **w** in the Valley of Sorek H851
Jdg 19:19 the **w** and the young man with us. H563
Jdg 19:26 At daybreak the **w** went back to the house H851
Jdg 20: 4 the husband of the murdered **w**, said, H851
Jdg 21:11 every male and every **w** who is not a virgin." H851
Ru 2: 5 "Who does that **young w** belong to?" H5855
Ru 3: 8 there was a **w** lying at his feet! H851
Ru 3:11 know that you are a **w** *of* noble character. H851
Ru 3:14 one must know that a **w** came to the H851
Ru 4:11 the LORD make the **w** who is coming into H851
Ru 4:12 the LORD gives you by this **young w**, H5855
1Sa 1:15 "I am a **w** who is deeply troubled. H851
1Sa 1:16 Do not take your servant for a wicked **w**; H1426
1Sa 1:23 So the **w** stayed at home and nursed her H851
1Sa 1:26 I am the **w** who stood here beside you H851
1Sa 2:20 you children by this **w** to take the place of H851
1Sa 20:30 "You son of a **perverse** and rebellious *w*! AIT
1Sa 25: 3 She was an intelligent and beautiful **w**, but H851
1Sa 27: 9 he did not leave a man or **w** alive, but took H851
1Sa 27:11 not leave a man or **w** alive to be brought to H851
1Sa 28: 7 "Find me a **w** who is a medium, so I H851
1Sa 28: 8 at night he and two men went to the **w**. H851
1Sa 28: 9 But the **w** said to him, "Surely you know H851
1Sa 28:11 Then the **w** asked, "Whom shall I bring up H851
1Sa 28:12 When the **w** saw Samuel, she cried out at H851
1Sa 28:13 The **w** said, "I see a ghostly figure coming H851
1Sa 28:21 When the **w** came to Saul and saw that he H851
1Sa 28:23 But his men joined the **w** in urging him H851
1Sa 28:24 The **w** had a fattened calf at the house H851
2Sa 3: 8 accuse me of an offense involving this **w**! H851
2Sa 11: 2 From the roof he saw a **w** bathing. H851
2Sa 11: 2 woman bathing. The **w** was very beautiful, H851
2Sa 11: 5 The **w** conceived and sent word to David H851
2Sa 11:21 Didn't a **w** drop an upper millstone on him H851
2Sa 13:17 "Get **this** *w* out of my sight and bolt the door AIT
2Sa 13:20 her brother Absalom's house, a **desolate** *w*. AIT
2Sa 14: 2 had a wise **w** brought from there. H851
2Sa 14: 2 Act like a **w** who has spent many days H851
2Sa 14: 4 When the **w** from Tekoa went to the king H851
2Sa 14: 8 The king said to the **w**, "Go home, and I H851
2Sa 14: 9 But the **w** from Tekoa said to him, "Let my H851
2Sa 14:12 Then the **w** said, "Let your servant speak a H851
2Sa 14:13 The **w** said, "Why then have you devised a H851
2Sa 14:18 Then the king said to the **w**, "Don't keep H851
2Sa 14:18 "Let my lord the king speak," the **w** said. H851
2Sa 14:19 The **w** answered, "As surely as you live H851
2Sa 14:27 was Tamar, and she became a beautiful **w**. H851
2Sa 17:20 men came to the **w** at the house, H851
2Sa 17:20 The **w** answered them, "They crossed over H851
2Sa 20:16 a wise **w** called from the city, "Listen! H851
2Sa 20:21 The **w** said to Joab, "His head will be H851
2Sa 20:22 Then the **w** went to all the people with her H851
1Ki 1: 3 a beautiful **young w** and found H5855
1Ki 1: 4 The **w** was very beautiful; she took care of H5855
1Ki 3:17 This **w** and I live in the same house, and I H851
1Ki 3:18 my child was born, this **w** also had a baby. H851
1Ki 3:22 The other **w** said, "No! The living one is my H851
1Ki 3:26 The **w** whose son was alive was deeply H851
1Ki 3:27 "Give the living baby to **the first w**. H2023S
1Ki 17:15 Elijah and for **the w** and her family. H2085S
1Ki 17:17 the son of the **w** who owned the house H851
1Ki 17:24 Then the **w** said to Elijah, "Now I know that H851

W

2Ki 4: 8 And a well-to-do **w** was there, who urged H851
2Ki 4:17 But the **w** became pregnant, and the next H851
2Ki 6:26 by on the wall, a **w** cried to him, "Help me, H851
2Ki 6:28 She answered, "This **w** said to me, 'Give H851
2Ki 8: 1 Elisha had said to the **w** whose son he had H851
2Ki 8: 2 The **w** proceeded to do as the man of God H851
2Ki 8: 5 the **w** whose son Elisha had brought back H851
2Ki 8: 5 "This is the **w**, my lord the king, H851
2Ki 8: 6 The king asked the **w** about it, and she told H851
2Ki 9:34 "Take care of that **cursed** *w*," he said, "and AIT
1Ch 2: 3 three were born to him by a **Canaanite** *w*, AIT
1Ch 16: 3 cake of raisins to each Israelite man and **w**. H851
2Ch 15:13 to death, whether small or great, man or **w**. H851
2Ch 24: 7 the sons of that **wicked** *w* Athaliah had AIT
2Ch 24:26 son of Shimeath an **Ammonite** *w*, and AIT
2Ch 24:26 Jehozabad, son of Shimrith a **Moabite** *w*. AIT
Ezr 10:14 married a foreign **w** come at a set time, H851
Est 2: 4 Then let the **young w** who pleases the H5855
Est 2: 7 This **young w**, who was also known as H5855
Est 2:15 (**the young w** Mordecai had adopted H889S
Est 4:11 that for any man or **w** who approaches the H851
Job 2:10 "You are talking like a **foolish** *w*. Shall we AIT
Job 14: 1 "Mortals, born of **w**, are of few days and H851
Job 15:14 or those born of **w**, that they could be H851
Job 24:21 They prey on the barren and **childless** *w*, AIT
Job 25: 4 How can one born of **w** be pure? H851
Job 31: 1 my eyes not to look lustfully at a **young w**. H1435
Job 31: 9 "If my heart has been enticed by a **w**, or if I H851
Ps 48: 6 them there, pain like that of a *w* **in labor**. AIT
Ps 113: 9 He settles the **childless** *w* in her home as a AIT
Pr 2:16 will save you also from the **adulterous** *w*, AIT
Pr 2:16 the **wayward** *w* with her seductive words, AIT
Pr 5: 3 For the lips of the **adulterous** *w* drip honey AIT
Pr 5:20 Why embrace the bosom of a **wayward** *w*? AIT
Pr 6:24 from the smooth talk of a **wayward** *w*. AIT
Pr 7: 5 They will keep you from the **adulterous** *w* AIT
Pr 7: 5 the **wayward** *w* with her seductive words. AIT
Pr 7:10 Then out came a **w** to meet him, dressed H851
Pr 9:13 Folly is an unruly **w**; she is simple and H851
Pr 11:16 A kindhearted **w** gains honor, but ruthless H851
Pr 11:22 snout is a beautiful **w** who shows no H851
Pr 14: 1 The wise **w** builds her house, but with her H851
Pr 22:14 The mouth of an **adulterous** *w* is a deep pit AIT
Pr 23:27 an **adulterous** *w* is a deep pit, and a AIT
Pr 30:19 the way of a man with a **young w**. H6625
Pr 30:20 "This is the way of an **adulterous** *w*: She eats AIT
Pr 30:23 a **contemptible** *w* who gets married, and a AIT
Pr 31:30 a **w** who fears the LORD is to be praised. H851
Ecc 7:26 bitter than death the **w** who is a snare, H851
Ecc 7:28 not one upright **w** among them all. H851
SS 1: 7 should I be like a **veiled** *w* beside the flocks AIT
Isa 13: 8 grip them; they will writhe like a *w* **in labor**. AIT
Isa 21: 3 like those of a *w* **in labor**; I am staggered by AIT
Isa 26:17 As a **pregnant** *w* about to give birth writhes AIT
Isa 42:14 But now, like a *w* **in childbirth**, I cry out, AIT
Isa 54: 1 **barren** *w*, you who never bore a child AIT
Isa 54: 1 children of the **desolate** *w* than of her who AIT
Isa 62: 5 As a young man marries a **young w**, so H1435
Jer 2:32 Does a **young w** forget her jewelry, H1435
Jer 3:20 But like a **w** unfaithful to her husband, so H851
Jer 4:31 I hear a cry as of a *w* **in labor**, a groan as of AIT
Jer 6:24 has gripped us, pain like that of a *w* **in labor**. AIT
Jer 13:21 not pain grip you like that of a **w** in labor? H851
Jer 22:23 upon you, pain like that of a *w* **in labor**! AIT
Jer 30: 6 his hands on his stomach like a *w* **in labor**, AIT
Jer 31:22 on earth—the **w** will return to the man." H5922
Jer 48:19 Ask the man fleeing and the *w* **escaping**, ask AIT
Jer 48:41 will be like the heart of a **w** in labor. H851
Jer 49:22 will be like the heart of a **w** in labor. H851
Jer 49:24 seized her, pain like that of a *w* **in labor**. AIT
Jer 50:43 gripped him, pain like that of a *w* **in labor**. AIT
Jer 51:22 with you I shatter man and **w**, with you I H851
Jer 51:22 you I shatter young man and **young w**, H1435
Eze 18: 6 sexual relations with a **w** during her period. H851
Eze 23:42 the wrists of **the w and her sister** and H2177S
Hos 1: 2 marry a promiscuous **w** and have children H851
Hos 13:13 Pains as of a *w* **in childbirth** come to him, AIT
Mic 4: 9 that pain seizes you like that of a *w* **in labor**? AIT
Mic 4:10 like a *w* **in labor**, for now you must AIT
Mic 7: 5 Even with the *w who* **lies** *in* your embrace AIT
Zec 5: 7 was raised, and there in the basket sat a **w**! H851
Mt 5:28 who looks at a **w** lustfully has already G1222
Mt 5:32 who marries a **divorced** *w* commits adultery. AIT
Mt 9:20 Just then a **w** who had been subject to G1222
Mt 9:22 And the **w** was healed at that moment. G1222
Mt 13:33 is like yeast that a **w** took and mixed into G1222
Mt 15:22 A Canaanite **w** from that vicinity came to G1222
Mt 15:25 The *w* **came** and knelt before him. "Lord AIT
Mt 15:28 Jesus said to her, "**W**, you have great G1222
Mt 19: 9 marries **another** *w* commits adultery. AIT
Mt 22:27 the **w** died. G1222
Mt 26: 7 a **w** came to him with an alabaster jar of G1222
Mt 26:10 to them, "Why are you bothering this **w**? G1222
Mk 5:25 And a **w** was there who had been subject G1222
Mk 5:33 Then the **w**, knowing what had happened G1222
Mk 7:25 a **w** whose little daughter was possessed G1222
Mk 7:26 The **w** was a Greek, born in Syrian G1222
Mk 10:11 wife and marries **another** *w* commits adultery AIT
Mk 12:22 Last of all, the **w** died too. G1222
Mk 14: 3 a **w** came with an alabaster jar of very G1222
Lk 7:37 A **w** in that town who lived a sinful life G1222
Lk 7:39 touching him and what kind of **w** she is— G1222
Lk 7:44 turned toward the **w** and said to Simon, G1222
Lk 7:44 said to Simon, "Do you see this **w**? G1222
Lk 7:45 not give me a kiss, but **this** *w*, from the time I AIT
Lk 7:50 Jesus said to the **w**, "Your faith has saved G1222
Lk 8:43 And a **w** was there who had been subject G1222
Lk 8:47 Then the **w**, seeing that she could not go G1222
Lk 10:38 a village where a **w** named Martha G1222
Lk 11:27 these things, a **w** in the crowd called out G1222
Lk 13:11 a **w** was there who had been crippled G1222
Lk 13:12 said to her, "**W**, you are set free from G1222
Lk 13:16 Then should not **this** *w*, a daughter of AIT
Lk 13:21 It is like yeast that a **w** took and mixed into G1222
Lk 15: 8 "Or suppose a **w** has ten silver coins and G1222
Lk 16:18 wife and marries **another** *w* commits adultery AIT
Lk 16:18 marries a **divorced w** commits G668+608+467
Lk 20:29 first one married a **w** and died childless. G1222
Lk 20:32 the **w** died too. G1222
Lk 22:57 But he denied it. "**W**, I don't know him," G1222
Jn 2: 4 "**W**, why do you involve me?" Jesus G1222
Jn 4: 7 When a Samaritan **w** came to draw water G1222
Jn 4: 9 The Samaritan **w** said to him, "You are a G1222
Jn 4: 9 "You are a Jew and I am a Samaritan **w**. G1222
Jn 4:11 the **w** said, "you have nothing to draw G1222
Jn 4:15 The **w** said to him, "Sir, give me this G1222
Jn 4:19 the **w** said, "I can see that you are a G1222
Jn 4:21 "**W**," Jesus replied, "believe me, a time is G1222
Jn 4:25 The **w** said, "I know that Messiah" (called G1222
Jn 4:27 surprised to find him talking with a **w**. G1222
Jn 4:28 the **w** went back to the town and said to G1222
Jn 4:42 They said *to* the **w**, "We no longer G1222
Jn 8: 3 brought in a **w** caught in adultery. G1222
Jn 8: 4 this **w** was caught in the act of adultery. G1222
Jn 8: 9 was left, with the **w** still standing there. G1222
Jn 8:10 up and asked her, "**W**, where are they? G1222
Jn 16:21 A **w** giving birth to a child has pain G1222
Jn 19:26 he said to her, "**W**, here is your son," G1222
Jn 20:13 They asked her, "**W**, why are you crying?" G1222
Jn 20:15 He asked her, "**W**, why are you crying G1222
Ac 9:40 Turning toward the **dead** *w*, he said AIT
Ac 16:14 of those listening was a **w** from the city of G1222
Ac 17:34 Areopagus, also a **w** named Damaris G1222
Ro 7: 2 by law a married **w** is bound to her G1222
Ro 16:12 *another w* **who** has worked very hard in the AIT
1Co 7: 1 not to have sexual relations *with* **a w**." G1222
1Co 7: 2 own wife, and **each** *w* with her own husband. AIT
1Co 7:13 And if a **w** has a husband who is not a G1222
1Co 7:27 Are you pledged *to* a **w**? Do not seek to be G1222
1Co 7:34 An unmarried **w** or virgin is concerned G1222
1Co 7:34 But a **married** *w* is concerned about the AIT
1Co 7:39 A **w** is bound to her husband as long as G1222
1Co 11: 3 the head *of* the **w** is man, and the G1222
1Co 11: 5 But every **w** who prays or prophesies with G1222
1Co 11: 6 For if a **w** does not cover her head, she G1222
1Co 11: 6 if it is a disgrace *for* a **w** to have her hair G1222
1Co 11: 7 glory of God; but **w** is the glory of man. G1222
1Co 11: 8 For man did not come from **w**, but woman G1222
1Co 11: 8 not come from woman, but **w** from man; G1222
1Co 11: 9 neither was man created for **w**, but woman G1222
1Co 11: 9 man created for woman, but **w** for man. G1222
1Co 11:10 this reason that a **w** ought to have G1222
1Co 11:11 in the Lord **w** is not independent of man G1222
1Co 11:11 of man, nor is man independent of **w**. G1222
1Co 11:12 For as **w** came from man, so also man is G1222
1Co 11:12 came from man, so also man is born of **w**. G1222
1Co 11:13 Is it proper *for* a **w** to pray to God with her G1222
1Co 11:15 that if a **w** has long hair, it is her glory G1222
1Co 14:35 it is disgraceful *for* a **w** to speak in the G1222
Gal 4: 4 his Son, born of a **w**, born under the law, G1222
Gal 4:22 one by the **slave w** and the other by the G4087
Gal 4:22 the slave woman and the other by the **free** *w*. AIT
Gal 4:23 His son by the **slave w** was born according G4087
Gal 4:23 his son by the **free** *w* was born as the AIT
Gal 4:27 "Be glad, **barren** *w*, you who never bore a AIT
Gal 4:27 the children *of* the **desolate** *w* than of her AIT
Gal 4:30 "Get rid of the **slave w** and her son, for G4087
Gal 4:31 we are not children *of* the **slave w**, but of G4087
Gal 4:31 of the slave woman, but *of* the **free** *w*. AIT
1Th 5: 3 as labor pains *on* a **pregnant** *w*, and they will AIT
1Ti 2:11 A **w** should learn in quietness and full G1222
1Ti 2:12 I do not permit a **w** to teach or to assume G1222
1Ti 2:14 it was the **w** who was deceived and G1222
1Ti 5:16 If any *w who is a* **believer** has widows in her AIT
Rev 2:20 You tolerate that **w** Jezebel, who calls G1222
Rev 12: 1 a **w** clothed with the sun, with the moon G1222
Rev 12: 4 in front of the **w** who was about to give G1222
Rev 12: 6 The **w** fled into the wilderness to a place G1222
Rev 12:13 he pursued the **w** who had given birth to G1222
Rev 12:14 The **w** was given the two wings of a great G1222
Rev 12:15 to overtake the **w** and sweep her away G1222
Rev 12:16 earth helped the **w** by opening its mouth G1222
Rev 12:17 was enraged at the **w** and went off to G1222
Rev 17: 3 There I saw a **w** sitting on a scarlet beast G1222
Rev 17: 4 The **w** was dressed in purple and scarlet G1222
Rev 17: 6 I saw that the **w** was drunk with the blood G1222
Rev 17: 7 you the mystery *of* the **w** and of the beast G1222
Rev 17: 9 heads are seven hills on which the **w** sits. G1222
Rev 17:18 The **w** you saw is the great city that rules G1222

WOMAN'S (18) [WOMAN]

Ge 21:10 that **w** son will never share in the H563
Ex 21:22 fined whatever the **w** husband demands H851
Nu 25: 8 the Israelite man and into the **w** stomach. H851
Dt 22:15 then the **young w** father and mother shall H5855
Dt 22:19 give them to the **young w** father, H5855
Dt 22:20 proof of the **young w** virginity can H4200+5855
Jdg 19: 4 father-in-law, the **w** father, prevailed on H5855
Jdg 19: 5 the **w** father said to his son-in-law H5855
Jdg 19: 6 Afterward the **w** father said, "Please stay H5855
Jdg 19: 8 he rose to go, the **w** father said, "Refresh H5855
Jdg 19: 9 his father-in-law, the **w** father, said, "Now H5855
1Ki 3:19 the night this **w** son died because she H851
2Ki 6:30 When the king heard the **w** words, he tore H851
Est 2:12 Before a **young w** turn came to go in to H5855
Eze 36:17 a **w monthly uncleanness** in H3240+2021+5614
Jn 4:39 in him because of the **w** testimony, G1222
Gal 4:30 the **slave w** son will never share in the G4087
Gal 4:30 share in the inheritance with the **free** *w* son." AIT

WOMB (62) [WOMBS]

Ge 25:23 "Two nations are in your **w**, and two H1061
Ge 25:24 give birth, there were twin boys in her **w**. H1061
Ge 38:27 give birth, there were twin boys in her **w**. H1061
Ge 49:25 blessings of the breast and **w**. H8167
Ex 13: 2 offspring of every **w** among the Israelites H8167
Ex 13:12 to the LORD the first offspring of every **w**. H8167
Ex 13:15 offspring of every **w** and redeem each of H8167
Ex 34:19 first offspring of every **w** belongs to me, H8167
Nu 5:21 when he makes your **w** miscarry and your H3751
Nu 5:22 abdomen swells or your **w** miscarries." H3751
Nu 5:27 will swell and her **w** will miscarry, H3751
Nu 12:12 from its mother's **w** with its flesh half H8167
Nu 18:15 The first offspring of every **w**, both human H8167
Dt 7:13 He will bless the fruit of your **w**, the crops H1061
Dt 28: 4 The fruit of your **w** will be blessed, and H1061
Dt 28:11 in the fruit of your **w**, the young of your H1061
Dt 28:18 The fruit of your **w** will be cursed, and the H1061
Dt 28:53 you will eat the fruit of the **w**, the flesh of H1061
Dt 28:57 from her **w** and the children H1068+8079
Dt 30: 9 of your hands and in the fruit of your **w**, H1061
Jdg 13: 5 a Nazirite, dedicated to God from the **w**. H1061
Jdg 13: 7 of God from the **w** until the day of his H1061
Jdg 16:17 dedicated to God from my mother's **w**. H1061
1Sa 1: 5 loved her, and the LORD had closed her **w**. H8167
1Sa 1: 6 Because the LORD had closed Hannah's **w** H8167
Job 1:21 "Naked I came from my mother's **w**, and H1061
Job 3:10 the doors of the **w** on me to hide trouble H1061
Job 3:11 at birth, and die as I came from the **w**? H1061
Job 10:18 "Why then did you bring me out of the **w** H8167
Job 10:19 carried straight from the **w** to the grave! H1061
Job 15:35 give birth to evil; their **w** fashions deceit." H1061
Job 24:20 The **w** forgets them, the worm feasts on H8167
Job 31:15 he who made me in the **w** make them? H1061
Job 38: 8 doors when it burst forth from the **w**, H8167
Job 38:29 From whose **w** comes the ice? Who gives H1061
Ps 22: 9 Yet you brought me out of the **w**; you H1061
Ps 22:10 from my mother's **w** you have been my H1061
Ps 51: 6 Yet you desired faithfulness even in the **w**; H3219
Ps 58: 3 go astray; from the **w** they are wayward H1061
Ps 71: 6 you brought me forth from my mother's **w**. H5055
Ps 110: 3 to you like dew from the morning's **w**. H8167
Ps 139:13 you knit me together in my mother's **w**. H1061
Pr 30:16 the barren **w**, land, which is never H8167
Pr 31: 2 Listen, son of my **w**! Listen, my son, H1061
Ecc 5:15 comes naked from their mother's **w**, H1061
Ecc 11: 5 how the body is formed in a mother's **w**, H1061
Isa 44: 2 who formed you in the **w**, and who will H1061
Isa 44:24 your Redeemer, who formed you in the **w**: H1061
Isa 49: 1 from my mother's **w** he has spoken my H5055
Isa 49: 5 formed me in the **w** to be his servant to H1061
Isa 66: 9 "Do I close up the **w** when I bring to delivery NDT
Jer 1: 5 "Before I formed you in the **w** I knew you H1061
Jer 20:17 For he did not kill me in the **w**, with my H8167
Jer 20:17 as my grave, her **w** enlarged forever. H8167
Jer 20:18 ever come out of the **w** to see trouble H8167
Hos 12: 3 In the **w** he grasped his brother's heel; as H1061
Hos 13:13 the sense to come out of the **w**. H5402+1201
Lk 1:41 the baby leaped in her **w**, and Elizabeth G3120
Lk 1:44 my ears, the baby in my **w** leaped for joy. G3120
Jn 3: 4 time into their mother's **w** to be born!" G3120
Ro 4:19 and that Sarah's **w** was also dead. G3616
Gal 1:15 from my mother's **w** and called me by his G3120

WOMBS (2) [WOMB]

Hos 9:14 Give them **w** that miscarry and breasts H8167
Lk 23:29 the **w** that never bore and the breasts that G3120

WOMEN (248) [WOMAN]

Ge 4:19 Lamech married two **w**, one named Adah H851
Ge 14:16 together with the **w** and the other people. H851
Ge 20:18 *had* **kept all the w** in Abimelek's household **from conceiving** H6806+1237+8167+6806
Ge 24:11 the time the *w* go out *to* **draw water**. AIT
Ge 27:46 with living because of these Hittite **w**. H1426
Ge 27:46 a wife from among the **w** *of* this land, H1426
Ge 27:46 this land, from Hittite **w** like these, my life H1426
Ge 28: 8 the Canaanite **w** were to his father Isaac; H1426
Ge 30:13 The **w** will call me happy. H1426
Ge 31:43 "The **w** are my daughters H1426
Ge 33: 5 looked up and saw the **w** and children. H851
Ge 34: 1 went out to visit the **w** *of* the land. H1426
Ge 34:29 their wealth and all their **w** and children, H851
Ge 36: 2 Esau took his wives from the **w** *of* Canaan H1426
Ex 1:16 are helping the **Hebrew** *w* during childbirth AIT
Ex 1:19 "**Hebrew** *w* are not like Egyptian women AIT

Ex 1:19 "Hebrew women are not like Egyptian w H851
Ex 2: 7 one of the Hebrew w to nurse the baby H851
Ex 10:10 along with your w and children! H3251
Ex 10:24 your w and children may go with you H3251
Ex 11: 2 people that men and w alike are to ask H851
Ex 12:37 men on foot, besides w and children. H3251
Ex 15:20 her hand, and all the w followed her, with H851
Ex 35:22 were willing, men and w alike, came and H851
Ex 35:26 And all the w who were willing and had the H851
Ex 35:29 the Israelite men and w who were willing H851
Ex 38: 8 mirrors of the w who served at the entrance AIT
Lev 21: 7 " 'They must not marry w defiled by H851
Lev 26:26 ten w will be able to bake your bread in H851
Nu 25: 1 in sexual immorality with Moabite w, H1426
Nu 31: 9 the Midianite w and children and took H851
Nu 31:15 "Have you allowed all the w to live?" H5922
Nu 31:35 32,000 w who had never slept with a H851
Nu 32:16 livestock and cities for our w and children. H3251
Nu 32:17 Meanwhile our w and children will live in H3251
Nu 32:24 Build cities for your w and children, and H3251
Dt 2:34 destroyed them—men, w and children. H851
Dt 3: 6 destroying every city—men, w and children. H851
Dt 7:14 none of your men or w will be childless, nor AIT
Dt 15:12 Hebrew men or w—sell themselves to H6303
Dt 20:14 As for the w, the children, the livestock and H851
Dt 31:12 w and children, and the foreigners H851
Dt 32:25 The young men and young w will perish H1435
Jos 6:21 thing in it—men and w, young and old, H851
Jos 8:25 Twelve thousand men and w fell that day H851
Jos 8:35 including the w and children, and the H851
Jdg 5:24 "Most blessed of w be Jael, the wife of H851
Jdg 5:24 most blessed of tent-dwelling w. H851
Jdg 9:49 about a thousand men and w, also died. H851
Jdg 9:51 to which all the men and w—all the H851
Jdg 11:40 that each year the young w of Israel go out H1426
Jdg 12: 9 he brought in thirty young w as wives from H1426
Jdg 16:27 the temple was crowded with men and w; H851
Jdg 16:27 thousand men and w watching Samson H851
Jdg 21:10 living there, including the w and children. H851
Jdg 21:12 four hundred young w who had never H1435
Jdg 21:14 were given the w of Jabesh Gilead who H851
Jdg 21:16 "With the w of Benjamin destroyed H851
Jdg 21:21 When the young w of Shiloh come out to H1426
Jdg 21:23 While the young w were dancing, each man AIT
Ru 1: 4 They married Moabite w, one named Orpah AIT
Ru 1:19 So the two w went on until they came to H2157S
Ru 1:19 of them, and the w exclaimed, "Can this be AIT
Ru 2: 8 Stay here with the w who work for me. H5855
Ru 2: 9 harvesting, and follow along after the w. H2177S
Ru 2:22 to go with the w who work for him H5855
Ru 2:23 stayed close to the w of Boaz to glean H5855
Ru 3: 2 with whose w you have worked, is H5855
Ru 4:14 The w said to Naomi: "Praise be to the LORD, H851
Ru 4:17 The w living there said, "Naomi has a son!" AIT
1Sa 2:22 they slept with the w who served at the H851
1Sa 4:20 was dying, the w attending her said, "Don't AIT
1Sa 9:11 they met some young w coming out to H5855
1Sa 15: 3 put to death men and w, children and H851
1Sa 15:33 "As your sword has made w childless, so H851
1Sa 15:33 so will your mother be childless among w." H851
1Sa 18: 6 the w came out from all the towns of Israel H851
1Sa 21: 4 the men have kept themselves from w." H851
1Sa 21: 5 "Indeed w have been kept from us H851
1Sa 22:19 with its men and w, its children and infants H851
1Sa 30: 2 taken captive the w and everyone else in H851
2Sa 1:26 wonderful, more wonderful than that of w. H851
2Sa 6:19 whole crowd of Israelites, both men and w. H851
1Ki 11: 1 loved many foreign w besides Pharaoh's H851
2Ki 8:12 to the ground, and rip open their pregnant w." AIT
2Ki 15:16 Tiphsah and ripped open all the pregnant w. AIT
2Ki 23: 7 the quarters where w did weaving for H851
2Ch 28:10 to make the men and w of Judah and H9148
2Ch 36:17 did not spare young men or young w H1435
Ezr 10: 1 w and children—gathered around him H851
Ezr 10: 2 by marrying foreign w from the peoples H851
Ezr 10: 3 send away all these w and their children, H851
Ezr 10:10 you have married foreign w, adding to H851
Ezr 10:17 all the men who had married foreign w. H851
Ezr 10:18 the following had married foreign w: H851
Ezr 10:44 All these had married foreign w, and some H851
Ne 8: 2 made up of men and w and all who were H851
Ne 8: 3 w and others who could understand. H851
Ne 12:43 The w and children also rejoiced H851
Ne 13:23 of Judah who had married w from Ashdod, H851
Ne 13:26 even he was led into sin by foreign w. H851
Ne 13:27 to our God by marrying foreign w? H851
Est 1: 9 a banquet for the w in the royal palace of H851
Est 1:17 conduct will become known to all the w, H851
Est 1:18 Median w of the nobility who have H8576
Est 1:20 all the w will respect their husbands H851
Est 2: 3 beautiful young w into the harem H1435+5855
Est 2: 3 who is in charge of the w; and let beauty H851
Est 2: 8 many young w were brought to the citadel H5855
Est 2:12 of beauty treatments prescribed for the w, H851
Est 2:17 to Esther more than to any of the other w, H851
Est 3:13 young and old, w and children—on a single H851
Est 8:11 attack them and their w and children, H851
Job 41: 5 on a leash for the young w in your house? H5855
Job 42:15 were there found w as beautiful as Job's H851
Ps 45: 9 of kings are among your honored w; AIT
Ps 68:11 the w who proclaim it are a mighty AIT
Ps 68:12 in haste; the w at home divide the plunder. AIT
Ps 68:25 with them are the young w playing the H6625
Ps 78:63 their young w had no wedding songs; H1435
Ps 148:12 young men and w, old men and children. H1435
Pr 31: 3 Do not spend your strength on w, your vigor H851
Pr 31:29 "Many w do noble things, but you surpass H1426
SS 1: 3 No wonder the young w love you! H6625
SS 1: 8 most beautiful of w, follow the tracks of H851
SS 2: 2 thorns is my darling among the young w. H1426
SS 5: 9 better than others, most beautiful of w? H851
SS 6: 1 your beloved gone, most beautiful of w? H851
SS 6: 9 The young w saw her and called her H1426
Isa 3:12 oppress my people, w rule over them. H851
Isa 3:16 The LORD says, "The w of Zion are haughty H1426
Isa 3:17 bring sores on the heads of the w of Zion; H1426
Isa 4: 1 In that day seven w will take hold of one H851
Isa 4: 4 will wash away the filth of the w of Zion; H1426
Isa 16: 2 so are the w of Moab at the fords of the H1426
Isa 27:11 are broken off and w come and make fires H851
Isa 32: 9 You w who are so complacent, rise up and H851
Isa 32:11 Tremble, you complacent w; shudder, you AIT
Jer 2:33 Even the worst of w can learn from your ways AIT
Jer 7:18 the w knead the dough and make H851
Jer 9:17 Call for the wailing w to come; send for the AIT
Jer 9:20 you w, hear the word of the LORD H851
Jer 16: 3 land and about the w who are their H3528S
Jer 31: 8 expectant mothers and w in labor; a great AIT
Jer 31:13 Then young w will dance and be glad H1435
Jer 38:22 All the w left in the palace of the king of H851
Jer 38:22 Those w will say to you: " 'They AIT
Jer 40: 7 w and children who were the poorest in the H851
Jer 41:16 the soldiers, w, children and court officials H851
Jer 43: 6 the men, the w, the children and the king's H851
Jer 44: 7 by cutting off from Judah the men and w, H851
Jer 44:15 along with all the w who were present—a H851
Jer 44:19 The w added, "When we burned incense to NDT
Jer 44:20 both men and w, who were answering H851
Jer 44:24 including the w, "Hear the word of H851
La 1: 4 her young w grieve, and she H1435
La 1:18 young men and young w have gone into H1435
La 2:10 The young w of Jerusalem have bowed H1435
La 2:20 Should w eat their offspring, the children H851
La 2:21 young men and young w have fallen by H1435
La 3:51 to my soul because of all the w of my city. H1426
La 4:10 hands compassionate w have cooked their H851
La 5:11 W have been violated in Zion, and virgins H851
Eze 8:14 of the LORD, and I saw w sitting there H851
Eze 9: 6 the young men and w, the mothers and H1435
Eze 13:18 Woe to the w who sew magic charms on all AIT
Eze 16:38 of w who commit adultery and who shed AIT
Eze 16:41 punishment on you in the sight of many w. H851
Eze 22:10 in you are those who violate w during H6700
Eze 23: 2 there were two w, daughters of the H851
Eze 23:10 She became a byword among w, and H851
Eze 23:44 so they slept with those lewd w, Oholah H851
Eze 23:45 of w who commit adultery and shed AIT
Eze 23:48 that all w may take warning and not H851
Eze 44:22 They must not marry widows or divorced w AIT
Da 11:37 of his ancestors or for the one desired by w, H851
Hos 13:16 the ground, their pregnant w ripped open." H2230
Joel 2:29 both men and w, I will pour out my H9148
Am 1:11 sword and slaughtered the w of the land, H8171
Am 1:13 ripped open the pregnant w of Gilead in H2226
Am 4: 1 you w who oppress the poor and crush the AIT
Am 8:13 day "the lovely young w and strong young H1435
Mic 2: 9 You drive the w of my people from their H851
Zec 5: 9 there before me were two w, with the H851
Zec 8: 4 "Once again men and w of ripe old age H2418
Zec 9:17 men thrive, and new wine the young w. H1435
Zec 14: 2 the houses ransacked, and the w raped. H851
Mal 2:11 by marrying w who worship a foreign god. H1426
Mt 11:11 among those born of w there has not G1222
Mt 14:21 thousand men, besides w and children. G1222
Mt 15:38 thousand men, besides w and children. G1222
Mt 24:19 be in those days for pregnant w and nursing AIT
Mt 24:41 Two w will be grinding with a hand mill; one AIT
Mt 27:55 Many w were there, watching from a G1222
Mt 28: 5 The angel said to the w, "Do not be G1222
Mt 28: 8 So the w hurried away from the tomb, afraid NDT
Mt 28:11 While the w were on their way, some of G899S
Mk 13:17 be in those days for pregnant w and nursing AIT
Mk 15:40 Some w were watching from a distance G1222
Mk 15:41 In Galilee these w had followed him and AIT
Mk 15:41 Many other w who had come up with him to AIT
Mk 16: 8 the w went out and fled from the tomb. G899S
Lk 1:42 "Blessed are you among w, and blessed G1222
Lk 7:28 among those born of w there is no one G1222
Lk 8: 2 also some w who had been cured of G1222
Lk 8: 3 These w were helping to support them out of AIT
Lk 12:45 both men and w, and to eat and drink G4087
Lk 17:35 Two w will be grinding grain together; one AIT
Lk 21:23 be in those days for pregnant w and nursing AIT
Lk 23:27 including w who mourned and wailed G1222
Lk 23:29 'Blessed are the childless w, the wombs G5096
Lk 23:49 including the w who had followed him G1222
Lk 23:55 The w who had come with Jesus from G1222
Lk 24: 1 the w took the spices they had prepared NDT
Lk 24: 5 In their fright the w bowed down with their NDT
Lk 24:11 But they did not believe the w, because G899S
Lk 24:22 some of our w amazed us. They went G1222
Lk 24:24 tomb and found it just as the w had said, G1222
Jn 8: 5 Law Moses commanded us to stone such w. AIT
Ac 1:14 along with the w and Mary the mother of G1222
Ac 2:18 servants, both men and w, I will pour out G1527
Ac 5:14 more men and w believed in the Lord G1222
Ac 8: 3 off both men and w and put them in G1222
Ac 8:12 they were baptized, both men and w. G1222
Ac 9: 2 whether men or w, he might take them G1222
Ac 13:50 the God-fearing w of high standing and G1222
Ac 16:13 began to speak to the w who had G1222
Ac 17: 4 Greeks and quite a few prominent w. G1222
Ac 17:12 prominent Greek w and many Greek men G1222
Ac 22: 4 both men and w and throwing them into G1222
Ro 1:26 Even their w exchanged natural sexual G2559
Ro 1:27 relations with w and were inflamed G2559
Ro 16:12 those w who work hard in the Lord. AIT
1Co 14:34 W should remain silent in the churches G1222
Gal 4:24 The w represent two covenants G4047S
Php 4: 3 help these w since they have contended at AIT
1Ti 2: 9 I also want the w to dress modestly, with G1222
1Ti 2:10 appropriate for w who profess to worship G1222
1Ti 2:15 But w will be saved through childbearing— NDT
1Ti 3:11 the w are to be worthy of respect G1222
1Ti 5: 2 older w as mothers, and younger women as AIT
1Ti 5: 2 as mothers, and younger w as sisters, with AIT
2Ti 3: 6 homes and gain control over gullible w, G1220
Titus 2: 3 teach the older w to be reverent in the way AIT
Titus 2: 4 they can urge the younger w to love their AIT
Heb 11:35 W received back their dead, raised to life G1222
1Pe 3: 5 is the way the holy w of the past who put G1222
Rev 14: 4 who did not defile themselves with w, G1222

WOMEN'S (2) [WOMAN]

Dt 22: 5 a man wear w clothing, for the LORD H851
Rev 9: 8 Their hair was like w hair, and their teeth G1222

WOMENSERVANTS (KJV) FEMALE SERVANTS, FEMALE SLAVES

WON (13) [WIN]

Ge 30: 8 struggle with my sister, and I have w." H3523
1Sa 19: 5 The LORD w a great victory for all Israel H6913
2Sa 19:14 He w over the hearts of the men of Judah H5742
Est 2: 9 him and w his favor. H5951+4200+7156
Est 2:15 And Esther w the favor of H5951+928+6524
Est 2:17 and she w his favor and H5951+4200+7156
Ps 44: 3 not by their sword that they w the land, H3769
Pr 11:14 but victory is w through many advisers. NDT
Pr 24: 6 and victory is w through many advisers. NDT
Mt 18:15 they listen to you, you have w them over. G3045
Ac 14:19 Iconium and w the crowd over. G4275
Ac 14:21 city and w a large number of disciples. G3411
1Pe 3: 1 they may be w over without words by the G3045

WON'T (24) [NOT, WILL]

Ge 34:23 W their livestock, their property and all H4202
Jdg 4: 8 but if you don't go with me, I w go." H4202
Jdg 15: 7 I swear that I w stop until I get my H3954+561
Jdg 15:12 "Swear to me that you w kill me H7153
Jdg 16:15 'I love you,' when you w confide in me? H401
Jdg 19:12 We w go into any city whose people are H4202
1Sa 2:15 he w accept boiled meat from you H4202
1Sa 26: 8 thrust of the spear; I w strike him twice." H4202
2Sa 13: 4 after morning? W you tell me?" Amnon H4202
2Sa 15:35 W the priests Zadok and Abiathar be there H4202
2Sa 18: 3 are forced to flee, they w care about us. H4202
2Sa 18: 3 half of us die, they w care; but you are H4202
1Ki 14: 2 so you w be recognized as the wife of H4202
1Ki 21: 5 "Why are you so sullen? Why w you eat?" H401
2Ki 6: 3 "W you please come with your servants?" AIT
Ps 10:13 say to himself, "He w call me to account"? H4202
Eze 24:19 "W you tell us what these things have to H4202
Eze 37:18 'W you tell us what you mean by this? H4202
Lk 14:28 W you first sit down and estimate the cost G4049
Lk 14:31 W he first sit down and consider whether G4049
Lk 17: 8 W he rather say, 'Prepare my supper, get G4049
Lk 18: 5 so that she w eventually come and attack G3590
Jn 4:15 this water so that I w get thirsty and have G3590
1Co 8:10 w that person be emboldened to eat what G4049

WONDER (12) [WONDERED, WONDERFUL, WONDERFULLY, WONDERING, WONDERS]

Dt 13: 1 you and announces to you a sign or w, H4603
Dt 13: 2 if the sign or w spoken of takes place H4603
Dt 28:46 will be a sign and a w to you and your H4603
Job 6: 3 no w my words have been H6584+4027
SS 1: 3 No w the young women love you H6584+4027
Isa 29:14 these people with w upon wonder; H7098
Isa 29:14 these people with wonder upon w; H7099
Mk 9:15 they were overwhelmed with w and ran to G1701
Ac 3:10 were filled with w and amazement at G2502
Ac 13:41 you scoffers, w and perish, for I am going G2513
2Co 11:14 And no w, for Satan himself masquerades G2512
Rev 13: 3 whole world was filled with w and G2513

WONDERED (2) [WONDER]

Lk 1:29 at his words and w what kind of greeting G1368
Lk 1:66 heard this w about it, G5502+1877+3836+2840

WONDERFUL (26) [WONDER]

2Sa 1:26 Your love for me was w, more wonderful H7098
2Sa 1:26 was wonderful, more w than that of women. NDT
1Ch 16: 9 sing praise to him; tell of all his w acts. H7098
Job 42: 3 understand, things too w for me to know. H7098
Ps 9: 1 all my heart; I will tell of all your w deeds. H7098
Ps 26: 7 praise and telling of all your w deeds. H7098

W

Ps 75: 1 people tell of your *deeds*. H7098
Ps 105: 2 sing praise to him; tell of all his **w** *acts*. H7098
Ps 107: 8 love and his **w** *deeds* for mankind, H7098
Ps 107:15 love and his **w** *deeds* for mankind, H7098
Ps 107:21 love and his **w** *deeds* for mankind. H7098
Ps 107:24 of the LORD, his **w** *deeds* in the deep. H7098
Ps 107:31 love and his **w** *deeds* for mankind. H7098
Ps 119:18 eyes that I may see **w** *things* in your law. H7098
Ps 119:27 that I may meditate on your **w deeds**. H7098
Ps 119:129 Your statutes are **w**; therefore I obey them. H7099
Ps 131: 1 with great matters or *things* too **w** for me. H7098
Ps 139: 6 Such knowledge is too **w** for me, too lofty H7100
Ps 139:14 your works **are w**, I know that full H7098
Ps 145: 5 I will meditate on your **w** *works*. H7098
Isa 9: 6 And he will be called **W** Counselor H7099
Isa 25: 1 faithfulness you have done **w things**, H7099
Isa 28:29 whose plan *is* **w**, whose wisdom is H7098
Mt 21:15 the law saw the **w** *things* he did and the *G2514*
Lk 13:17 with all the **w** *things* he was doing. *G1902*
1Pe 2: 9 called you out of darkness into his **w** light. *G2515*

WONDERFULLY (1) [WONDER]

Ps 139:14 you because *I* **am** fearfully and **w made**; H7098

WONDERING (6) [WONDER]

Lk 1:21 Zechariah and **w why** he stayed so *G2513*
Lk 3:15 expectantly and *were* all **w** in their hearts *G1368*
Lk 24: 4 While they *were* **w** about this, suddenly two *G679*
Lk 24:12 **w** to himself what had happened. *G2513*
Ac 5:24 were at a loss, **w** what this might lead to. NDT
Ac 10:17 Peter *was* **w** about the *G1877+1571+1389*

WONDERS (65) [WONDER]

Ex 3:20 Egyptians with all the **w** that I will perform H7098
Ex 4:21 Pharaoh all the **w** I have given you the H4603
Ex 7: 3 I multiply my signs and **w** in Egypt, H4603
Ex 11: 9 so that my **w** may be multiplied in Egypt." H4603
Ex 11:10 performed all these **w** before Pharaoh, H4603
Ex 15:11 in holiness, awesome in glory, working **w**? H7099
Ex 34:10 people I will do **w** never before done in H7098
Dt 4:34 by signs and **w**, by war, by a mighty H4603
Dt 6:22 our eyes the LORD sent signs and **w**— H4603
Dt 7:19 the signs and **w**, the mighty hand and H4603
Dt 10:21 those great and **awesome w** you saw with H3707
Dt 26: 8 with great terror and with signs and **w**. H4603
Dt 29: 3 great trials, those signs and great **w**. H4603
Dt 34:11 all those signs and **w** the LORD sent him to H4603
Jdg 6:13 Where are all his **w** that our ancestors H7098
2Sa 7:23 great and **awesome w** by driving out H3707
1Ch 16:12 Remember the **w** he has done, his H7098
1Ch 17:21 great and **awesome w** by driving out H3707
Ne 9:10 You sent signs and **w** against Pharaoh H4603
Job 5: 9 He performs **w** that cannot be fathomed H1524
Job 9:10 He performs **w** that cannot be fathomed H1524
Job 37:14 Job; stop and consider God's **w**. H7098
Job 37:16 *those* **w** *of* him who has perfect H5140
Ps 17: 7 **Show** me *the* **w** *of* your great love, you H7098
Ps 31:21 for *he* **showed** me the **w** *of* his love when H7098
Ps 40: 5 my God, are the **w** you have done, the H7098
Ps 65: 8 whole earth is filled with awe at your **w**; H253
Ps 78: 4 his power, and the **w** he has done. H7098
Ps 78:11 he had done, the **w** he had shown them. H7098
Ps 78:32 in spite of his **w**, they did not believe. H7098
Ps 78:43 in Egypt, his **w** in the region of Zoan. H4603
Ps 88:10 Do you show your **w** to the dead? Do their H7099
Ps 88:12 Are your **w** known in the place of darkness H7099
Ps 89: 5 The heavens praise your **w**, LORD, your H7099
Ps 105: 5 Remember the **w** he has done, his H7098
Ps 105:27 among them, his **w** in the land of Ham. H4603
Ps 111: 4 He has caused his **w** to be remembered H7098
Ps 135: 9 He sent his signs and **w** into your midst H4603
Ps 136: 4 to him who alone does great **w**, His love H7098
Jer 21: 2 the LORD will perform **w** for us as in times H7098
Jer 32:20 performed signs and **w** in Egypt and have H4603
Jer 32:21 Israel out of Egypt with signs and **w**, H4603
Da 4: 2 signs and **w** that the Most High A10763
Da 4: 3 great are his signs, how mighty his **w**! A10763
Da 6:27 signs and **w** in the heavens and A10763
Joel 2:26 who has worked **w** for you; never H7098
Joel 2:30 I will show **w** in the heavens and on the H4603
Mic 7:15 out of Egypt, I will show them my **w**." H7098
Mt 24:24 perform great signs and **w** to deceive, *G5469*
Mk 13:22 perform signs and **w** to deceive, *G5469*
Jn 4:48 "Unless you people see signs and **w**," *G5469*
Ac 2:11 them declaring the **w** of God in our own *G3483*
Ac 2:19 I will show **w** in the heavens above and *G5469*
Ac 2:22 to you by miracles, **w** and signs, which *G5469*
Ac 2:43 filled with awe *at* the many **w** and signs *G5469*
Ac 4:30 perform signs and **w** through the name of *G5469*
Ac 5:12 many signs and **w** among the people. *G5469*
Ac 6: 8 performed great **w** and signs among the *G5469*
Ac 7:36 performed **w** and signs in Egypt, *G5469*
Ac 14: 3 by enabling them to perform signs and **w**. *G5469*
Ac 15:12 the signs and **w** God had done among *G5469*
Ro 15:19 by the power of signs and **w**, through the *G5469*
2Co 12:12 apostle, including signs, **w** and miracles. *G5469*
2Th 2: 9 through signs and **w** that serve the lie, *G5469*
Heb 2: 4 to it by signs, **w** and various miracles, and *G5469*

WONT (KJV) CUSTOM, EXPECTED, HABIT, USED TO, USUAL

WOOD (121) [BRUSHWOOD, OLIVE-WOOD, WOODCUTTERS, WOODED, WOODEN, WOODPILE, WOODS, WOODSMEN, WOODWORK]

Ge 6:14 So make yourself an ark of cypress **w** H6770
Ge 22: 3 When he had cut *enough* **w** *for* the burnt H6770
Ge 22: 6 Abraham took the **w** *for* the burnt offering H6770
Ge 22: 7 "The fire and **w** are here," Isaac said, "but H6770
Ge 22: 9 an altar there and arranged the **w** on it. H6770
Ge 22: 9 laid him on the altar, on top of the **w**. H6770
Ge 30:37 exposing the **white** inner *w* of the branches AIT
Ex 7:19 in Egypt, even in **vessels of w** and stone." H6770
Ex 15:25 the LORD showed him a **piece of w**. H6770
Ex 25: 5 another type of durable leather; acacia **w**; H6770
Ex 25:10 "Have them make an ark of acacia **w** H6770
Ex 25:13 make poles of acacia **w** and overlay them H6770
Ex 25:23 "Make a table of acacia **w**—two cubits H6770
Ex 25:28 Make the poles of acacia **w**, overlay them H6770
Ex 26:15 frames of acacia **w** for the tabernacle. H6770
Ex 26:26 "Also make crossbars of acacia **w**: five H6770
Ex 26:32 on four posts of **acacia w** overlaid with H8847
Ex 26:37 five posts of **acacia w** overlaid with H8847
Ex 27: 1 "Build an altar of acacia **w**, three cubits H6770
Ex 27: 6 Make poles of acacia **w** for the altar and H6770
Ex 30: 1 an altar of acacia **w** for burning incense. H6770
Ex 30: 5 the poles of acacia **w** and overlay them H6770
Ex 31: 5 to work in **w**, and to engage in all H6770
Ex 35: 7 type of durable leather; acacia **w**; H6770
Ex 35:24 who had acacia **w** for any part of the H6770
Ex 35:33 to work in **w** and to engage in all kinds of H6770
Ex 36:20 frames of acacia **w** for the tabernacle. H6770
Ex 36:31 They also made crossbars of acacia **w** H6770
Ex 36:36 made four posts of **acacia w** for it and H8847
Ex 37: 1 Bezalel made the ark of acacia **w**—two H6770
Ex 37: 4 poles of acacia **w** and overlaid them H6770
Ex 37:10 They made the table of acacia **w**—two H6770
Ex 37:15 were made of acacia **w** and were overlaid H6770
Ex 37:25 made the altar of incense out of acacia **w**. H6770
Ex 37:28 the poles of acacia **w** and overlaid them H6770
Ex 38: 1 the altar of burnt offering of acacia **w**, H6770
Ex 38: 6 the poles of acacia **w** and overlaid them H6770
Lev 1: 7 fire on the altar and arrange **w** on the fire. H6770
Lev 1: 8 on the **w** that is burning on the altar. H6770
Lev 1:12 on the **w** that is burning on the altar. H6770
Lev 1:17 shall burn it on the **w** that is burning on H6770
Lev 3: 5 offering that is lying on the burning **w**; H6770
Lev 4:12 burn it there in a **w** fire on the ash heap. H6770
Lev 11:32 unclean, whether it is made of **w**, cloth, H6770
Lev 14: 4 two live clean birds and *some* cedar **w**, H6770
Lev 14: 6 together with the cedar **w**, the scarlet yarn H6770
Lev 14:49 he is to take two birds and *some* cedar **w**, H6770
Lev 14:51 Then he is to take the cedar **w**, the hyssop H6770
Lev 14:52 live bird, the cedar **w**, the hyssop and the H6770
Nu 15:32 found gathering **w** on the Sabbath day. H6770
Nu 15:33 found him gathering **w** brought him to H6770
Nu 19: 6 The priest is to take *some* cedar **w**, hyssop H6770
Nu 31:20 made of leather, goat hair or **w**. H6770
Dt 4:28 worship man-made gods of **w** and stone, H6770
Dt 10: 3 ark out of acacia **w** and chiseled out two H6770
Dt 19: 5 into the forest with his neighbor to cut **w**, H6770
Dt 28:36 worship other gods, gods of **w** and stone. H6770
Dt 28:64 other gods—gods of **w** and stone, which H6770
Dt 29:11 camps who chop your **w** and carry your H6770
Dt 29:17 images and idols of **w** and stone, H6770
Jdg 6:26 Using the **w** *of* the Asherah pole that you H6770
1Sa 6:14 people chopped up the **w** *of* the cart and H6770
2Sa 24:22 threshing sledges and ox yokes for the **w**. H6770
1Ki 6:23 made a pair of cherubim *out of* olive **w**, H6770
1Ki 6:31 he made doors *out of* olive **w** that were H6770
1Ki 6:33 doorframes *out of* olive **w** that were one H6770
1Ki 6:34 He also made two doors *out of* juniper **w** H6770
1Ki 18:23 put it on the **w** but not set fire to it. H6770
1Ki 18:23 put it on the **w** but not set fire to it H6770
1Ki 18:33 He arranged the **w**, cut the bull into pieces H6770
1Ki 18:33 the bull into pieces and laid it on the **w**. H6770
1Ki 18:33 pour it on the offering and on the **w**." H6770
1Ki 18:38 up the sacrifice, the **w**, the stones and the H6770
2Ki 19:18 they were not gods but only **w** and stone, H6770
1Ch 21:23 the threshing sledges for the **w**, and the H6770
1Ch 22:14 great to be weighed, and **w** and stone. H6770
1Ch 29: 2 iron for the iron and **w** for the wood, as H6770
1Ch 29: 2 iron for the iron and wood for the **w**, as H6770
2Ch 2:14 iron, stone and **w**, and with purple H6770
Ne 10:34 a contribution of **w** to burn on the altar H6770
Ne 13:31 contributions of **w** at designated times, H6770
Job 41:27 treats like straw and bronze like rotten **w**. H6770
Pr 26:20 Without **w** a fire goes out; without a H6770
Pr 26:21 As charcoal to embers and as **w** to fire, so H6770
SS 3: 9 carriage; he made it of **w** *from* Lebanon. H6770
Isa 10:15 a club brandish the one who is not **w**! H6770
Isa 30:33 with an abundance of fire and **w**; the H6770
Isa 37:19 they were not gods but only **w** and stone, H6770
Isa 40:20 such an offering selects **w** that will not rot; H6770
Isa 44:16 Half of **the w** he burns in the fire; over it H2257S
Isa 44:19 Shall I bow down to a block of **w**?" H6770
Isa 45:20 are those who carry about idols of **w**, H6770
Isa 60:17 Instead of **w** I will bring you bronze, and H6770
Jer 2:27 They say to **w**, 'You are my father,' and to H6770
Jer 3: 9 committed adultery with stone and **w**. H6770
Jer 5:14 fire and these people the **w** it consumes. H6770
Jer 7:18 The children gather **w**, the fathers light the H6770
La 5: 4 our **w** can be had only at a price. H6770
La 5:13 millstones; boys stagger under **loads of w**. H6770
Eze 15: 2 how is the **w** *of* a vine different from that H6770
Eze 15: 3 Is **w** ever taken from it to make anything H6770
Eze 15: 6 I have given the **w** *of* the vine among the H6770
Eze 20:32 of the world, who serve **w** and stone." H6770
Eze 24: 5 **Pile w** beneath it *for* the bones; bring it to H1883
Eze 24: 9 of bloodshed! I, too, will pile the **w** high. H4509
Eze 24:10 So heap on the **w** and kindle the fire H6770
Eze 27: 6 of **cypress w** from the coasts of Cyprus H9309
Eze 37:16 of man, take a **stick of w** and write on it H6770
Eze 37:16 Then take another **stick of w**, and write H6770
Eze 37:19 I will make them into a single **stick of w** H6770
Eze 39:10 not need to gather **w** from the fields or cut H6770
Eze 41:16 the threshold was covered with **w**. H6770
Eze 41:22 corners, its base and its sides were of **w**. H6770
Da 5: 4 silver, of bronze, iron, **w** and stone. A10058
Da 5:23 **w** and stone, which cannot see or A10058
Hab 2:19 Woe to him who says to **w**, 'Come to life!' H6770
1Co 3:12 silver, costly stones, **w**, hay or straw, *G3833*
2Ti 2:20 but also **of w** and clay; some are *G3832*
Rev 9:20 stone and **w**—idols that cannot *G3832*
Rev 18:12 every sort *of* citron **w**, and articles of *G3833*
Rev 18:12 every kind made of ivory, costly **w**, bronze, *G3833*

WOODCUTTERS (3) [WOOD]

Jos 9:21 let them be **w** and water H2634+6770
Jos 9:23 from service as **w** and water carriers H2634+6770
Jos 9:27 the Gibeonites **w** and water carriers H2634+6770

WOODED (1) [WOOD]

2Ch 27: 4 forts and towers in the **w areas**. H3091

WOODEN (11) [WOOD]

Lev 15:12 any **w** article is to be rinsed with H6770
Nu 35:18 if anyone is holding a **w** object and strikes H6770
Dt 10: 1 me on the mountain. Also make a **w** ark. H6770
Dt 16:21 Do not set up any **w** Asherah pole beside H6770
Ne 8: 4 Law stood on a high **w** platform built for H6770
Isa 48: 5 my **w** image and metal god ordained them. NDT
Jer 10: 8 they are taught by worthless **w** idols. H6770
Jer 28:13 You have broken a **w** yoke, but in its place H6770
Eze 41:22 There was a **w** altar three cubits high and H6770
Eze 41:25 there was a **w** overhang on the front H6770
Hos 4:12 My people consult a **w idol**, and a H6770

WOODPILE (1) [WOOD]

Zec 12: 6 the clans of Judah like a firepot in a **w**, H6770

WOODS (3) [WOOD]

1Sa 14:25 The entire army entered the **w**, and there H3623
1Sa 14:26 When they went into the **w**, they saw the H3623
2Ki 2:24 came out of the **w** and mauled forty-two H3623

WOODSMEN (1) [WOOD, MAN]

2Ch 2:10 your servants, the **w** who cut the timber H2634

WOODWORK (1) [WOOD]

Hab 2:11 and the beams of the **w** will echo it. H6770

WOOF (KJV) KNITTED

WOOING (1)

Job 36:16 "*He is* **w** you from the jaws of distress to a H6077

WOOL (18) [WOOLEN]

Lev 13:48 woven or knitted material of linen or **w**, H7547
Lev 13:52 woven or knitted material of **w** or linen, H7547
Nu 19: 6 hyssop and **scarlet w** and throw H9357+9106
Dt 18: 4 the first **w from** *the* **shearing** *of* your sheep H1600
Dt 22:11 Do not wear clothes of **w** and linen woven H7547
Jdg 6:37 I will place a **w** fleece on the threshing H7547
2Ki 3: 4 lambs and the **w** of a hundred thousand H7547
Ps 147:16 spreads the snow like **w** and scatters the H7547
Pr 31:13 She selects **w** and flax and works with H7547
Isa 1:18 are red as crimson, they shall be like **w**. H7547
Isa 51: 8 the worm will devour them like **w**. H7547
Eze 27:18 offered wine from Helbon, **w** *from* Zahar H7547
Eze 34: 3 yourselves with the **w** and slaughter the H7547
Da 7: 9 the hair of his head was white like **w**. A10556
Hos 2: 5 my water, my **w** and my linen, my H7547
Hos 2: 9 I will take back my **w** and my linen H7547
Heb 9:19 scarlet **w** and branches of hyssop *G2250*
Rev 1:14 The hair on his head was white like **w**, as *G2250*

WOOLEN (3) [WOOL]

Lev 13:47 a defiling mold—any **w** or linen clothing, H7547
Lev 13:59 defiling molds in **w** or linen clothing, H7547
Eze 44:17 must not wear any **w garment** while H7547

WORD (572) [BYWORD, WORDLESS, WORDS]

Ge 15: 1 the **w** *of* the LORD came to Abram in a H1821
Ge 15: 4 Then the **w** *of* the LORD came to him: "This H1821
Ge 24:21 **Without saying a w**, the man watched her H3087
Ge 27:45 *I'll* **send w** *for* you to come back from H8938
Ge 31: 4 So Jacob **sent w** to Rachel H8938+2256+7924
Ge 37: 4 him and could not **speak** a kind *w to* him. AIT
Ge 37:14 with the flocks, and bring **w** back to me." H1821
Ge 41:44 without your **w** no one will lift hand or NDT
Ge 44:18 my lord, let me speak a **w** to my lord. H1821
Ge 50:16 So *they* **sent w** to Joseph, saying, "Your H7422
Ex 9:20 who feared the **w** *of* the LORD hurried to H1821
Ex 9:21 who ignored the **w** *of* the LORD left their H1821
Ex 18: 6 Jethro *had* **sent w** to him, "I, your H606
Ex 36: 6 they sent this **w** throughout the camp: H7754

Nu 3:16 he was commanded by the **w** *of* the LORD. H7023
Nu 3:51 he was commanded by the **w** *of* the LORD. H7023
Nu 15:31 despised the LORD's **w** and broken his H1821
Nu 23: 5 The LORD put a **w** in Balaam's mouth and H1821
Nu 23: 5 "Go back to Balak and **give** him this **w**." H1819
Nu 23:16 Balaam and put a **w** in his mouth and H1821
Nu 23:16 "Go back to Balak and **give** him this **w**." H1819
Nu 30: 2 he must not break his **w** but must do H1821
Dt 5: 5 you to declare to you the **w** *of* the LORD, H1821
Dt 8: 3 on every **w that comes from** the mouth H4604
Dt 30:14 the **w** is very near you; it is in your H1821
Dt 33: 9 he watched over your **w** and guarded your H614
Jos 1:18 rebels against your **w** and does not obey H7023
Jos 6:10 do not say a **w** until the day I tell you to H1821
Jos 8:35 There was not a **w** of all that Moses had H1821
Jos 10: 6 Gibeonites then sent **w** to Joshua in the H606
Jos 10:21 no one **uttered a w** against H3076+906+4383
Jos 11: 1 *he* **sent w** to Jobab king of Madon H8938
Jdg 11:36 "*you have* **given** your **w** to the H7198+906+7023
Jdg 12: 6 he could not pronounce the **w** correctly, NDT
Jdg 13:17 may honor you when your **w** comes true?" H1821
Jdg 16:18 she sent **w** to the rulers of the Philistines H7924
Jdg 18:19 **Don't say a w.** H8492+3338+6584+7023
1Sa 1:23 only may the LORD make good his **w**." H1821
1Sa 3: 1 In those days the **w** *of* the LORD was rare H1821
1Sa 3: 7 The **w** *of* the LORD had not yet been H1821
1Sa 3:21 himself to Samuel through his **w**. H1821
1Sa 4: 1 And Samuel's **w** came to all Israel. H1821
1Sa 14:39 But not one of them **said a w**. H6699
1Sa 15:10 Then the **w** *of* the LORD came to Samuel: H1821
1Sa 15:23 you have rejected the **w** *of* the LORD, H1821
1Sa 15:26 You have rejected the **w** *of* the LORD, and H1821
1Sa 16:22 Then Saul **sent w** to Jesse, saying, "Allow H8938
1Sa 19:19 **W came** to Saul: "David is in Naioth at H5583
1Sa 20:12 *will I* not **send** you **w** and let you know? H8938
1Sa 25:12 When they arrived, they reported every **w**. H1821
1Sa 25:39 Then David **sent w** to Abigail, asking her H8938
2Sa 3:11 did not dare to say another **w** to Abner, H1821
2Sa 7: 4 But that night the **w** *of* the LORD came to H1821
2Sa 7:21 For the sake of your **w** and according to H1821
2Sa 11: 5 and **sent w** to David, H8938+2256+5583
2Sa 11: 6 So David **sent** *this* **w** to Joab: "Send me H8938
2Sa 12: 9 you despise the **w** *of* the LORD by doing H1821
2Sa 12:25 *he* **sent w** through Nathan the prophet to H8938
2Sa 13: 7 David sent **w** to Tamar at the palace: "Go H606
2Sa 13:22 And Absalom never **said a w** to Amnon H1819
2Sa 14:12 servant speak a **w** to my lord the king." H1821
2Sa 14:17 'May the **w** *of* my lord the king secure my H1821
2Sa 14:32 *I* **sent w** to you and said, 'Come H8938
2Sa 15:28 the wilderness until **w** comes from you to H1821
2Sa 19:14 *They* **sent w** to the king, "Return, you and H8938
2Sa 22:31 The LORD's **w** is flawless; he shields all who H614
2Sa 23: 2 through me; his **w** was on my tongue. H4863
2Sa 24: 4 The king's **w**, however, overruled Joab H1821
2Sa 24:11 the **w** *of* the LORD had come to Gad the H1821
1Ki 1:14 come in and **add** *my* **w to** what you have H4848
1Ki 2:27 fulfilling the **w** the LORD had spoken at H1821
1Ki 5: 8 So Hiram sent **w** to Solomon: "I have H606
1Ki 6:11 The **w** *of* the LORD came to Solomon: H1821
1Ki 8:26 let your **w** that you promised your servant H1821
1Ki 8:56 Not one **w** has failed of all the good H1821
1Ki 12:15 to fulfill the **w** the LORD had spoken to H1821
1Ki 12:22 But this **w** *of* God came to Shemaiah the H1821
1Ki 12:24 they obeyed the **w** *of* the LORD and went H1821
1Ki 13: 1 By the **w** *of* the LORD a man of God came H1821
1Ki 13: 2 By the **w** *of* the LORD he cried out against H1821
1Ki 13: 5 by the man of God by the **w** *of* the LORD. H1821
1Ki 13: 9 I was commanded by the **w** *of* the LORD H1821
1Ki 13:17 I have been told by the **w** *of* the LORD: H1821
1Ki 13:18 an angel said to me by the **w** *of* the LORD: H1821
1Ki 13:20 the **w** *of* the LORD came to the old prophet H1821
1Ki 13:21 have defied the **w** *of* the LORD and have H7023
1Ki 13:26 man of God who defied the **w** *of* the LORD. H7023
1Ki 13:26 as the **w** *of* the LORD had warned him." H1821
1Ki 13:32 he declared by the **w** *of* the LORD against H1821
1Ki 15:29 according to the **w** *of* the LORD given H1821
1Ki 16: 1 Then the **w** *of* the LORD came to Jehu son H1821
1Ki 16: 7 the **w** *of* the LORD came through the H1821
1Ki 16:12 accordance with the **w** *of* the LORD spoken H1821
1Ki 16:34 with the **w** *of* the LORD spoken by H1821
1Ki 17: 1 rain in the next few years except at my **w**." H1821
1Ki 17: 2 Then the **w** *of* the LORD came to Elijah: H1821
1Ki 17: 8 Then the **w** *of* the LORD came to him: H1821
1Ki 17:16 keeping with the **w** *of* the LORD spoken by H1821
1Ki 17:24 God and that the **w** *of* the LORD from your H1821
1Ki 18: 1 the **w** *of* the LORD came to Elijah: H1821
1Ki 18:20 So Ahab **sent w** throughout all Israel and H8938
1Ki 18:31 to whom the **w** *of* the LORD had come H1821
1Ki 19: 9 And the **w** *of* the LORD came to him H1821
1Ki 20:33 sign and were quick to pick up his **w**. H2023S
1Ki 20:35 By the **w** *of* the LORD one of the company H1821
1Ki 21:14 Then they sent **w** to Jezebel: "Naboth has H606
1Ki 21:17 Then the **w** *of* the LORD came to Elijah the H1821
1Ki 21:28 Then the **w** *of* the LORD came to Elijah the H1821
1Ki 22:13 Let your **w** agree with theirs, and speak H1821
1Ki 22:19 "Therefore hear the **w** *of* the LORD: H1821
1Ki 22:38 as the **w** *of* the LORD had declared. H1821
2Ki 1:17 according to the **w** *of* the LORD that Elijah H1821
2Ki 2:22 according to the **w** Elisha had spoken. H1821
2Ki 3:12 "The **w** *of* the LORD is with him. H1821
2Ki 4:44 left over, according to the **w** *of* the LORD. H1821
2Ki 6: 9 The man of God sent **w** to the king of Israel H606
2Ki 7: 1 replied, "Hear the **w** *of* the LORD. This is H1821
2Ki 9:26 in accordance with the **w** *of* the LORD." H1821
2Ki 9:36 "This is the **w** *of* the LORD that he spoke H1821
2Ki 10:10 that not a **w** the LORD has spoken against H1821
2Ki 10:17 according to the **w** *of* the LORD spoken to H1821
2Ki 10:21 Then he **sent w** throughout Israel, and all H8938
2Ki 14:25 in accordance with the **w** *of* the LORD, the H1821
2Ki 15:12 So the **w** *of* the LORD spoken to Jehu was H1821
2Ki 18:25 destroy this place without **w** from the LORD? NDT
2Ki 18:28 Hebrew, "Hear the **w** *of* the great king H1821
2Ki 19: 9 sent messengers to Hezekiah *with this* **w**: H606
2Ki 19:21 This is the **w** that the LORD has spoken H1821
2Ki 20: 4 the **w** *of* the LORD came to him: H1821
2Ki 20:16 said to Hezekiah, "Hear the **w** *of* the LORD: H1821
2Ki 20:19 "The **w** *of* the LORD you have spoken is H1821
2Ki 23:16 accordance with the **w** *of* the LORD H1821
2Ki 24: 2 accordance with the **w** *of* the LORD H1821
1Ch 10:13 did not keep the **w** *of* the LORD and even H1821
1Ch 13: 2 *let us* **send w** far and wide to the rest of H8938
1Ch 15:15 in accordance with the **w** *of* the LORD. H1821
1Ch 17: 3 But that night the **w** *of* God came to H1821
1Ch 21: 4 The king's **w**, however, overruled Joab; so H1821
1Ch 21:19 obedience to the **w** that Gad had spoken H1821
1Ch 22: 8 But this **w** *of* the LORD came to me: 'You H1821
2Ch 6:17 let your **w** that you promised your servant H1821
2Ch 10:15 to fulfill the **w** the LORD had spoken to H1821
2Ch 11: 2 But this **w** *of* the LORD came to Shemaiah H1821
2Ch 12: 7 this **w** *of* the LORD came to Shemaiah: H1821
2Ch 18:12 Let your **w** agree with theirs, and speak H1821
2Ch 18:18 "Therefore hear the **w** *of* the LORD: H1821
2Ch 29:15 had ordered, following the **w** *of* the LORD. H1821
2Ch 30: 1 Hezekiah **sent w** to all Israel and Judah H8938
2Ch 30:12 had ordered, following the **w** *of* the LORD. H1821
2Ch 34:21 before us have not kept the **w** *of* the LORD; H1821
2Ch 36:12 who **spoke the w** *of* the LORD. H4946+7023
2Ch 36:15 **sent w** to them through his messengers H8938
2Ch 36:21 fulfillment of the **w** *of* the LORD spoken by H1821
2Ch 36:22 order to fulfill the **w** *of* the LORD spoken by H1821
Ezr 1: 1 order to fulfill the **w** *of* the LORD spoken by H1821
Ne 6: 1 When **w came** to Sanballat, Tobiah H9048
Ne 8:15 should proclaim this **w** and spread it H7754
Est 7: 8 As soon as the **w** left the king's mouth H1821
Est 9:26 days were called Purim, from the **w** pur.) H9005
Job 2:13 No one said a **w** to him, because they H1821
Job 4: 2 "If someone ventures a **w** with you, will H1821
Job 4:12 "A **w** was secretly brought to me, my ears H1821
Ps 5: 9 Not a *w* from their mouth *can* **be trusted** AIT
Ps 18:30 The LORD's **w** is flawless; he shields all H614
Ps 33: 4 For the **w** *of* the LORD is right and true; he H1821
Ps 33: 6 By the **w** *of* the LORD the heavens were H1821
Ps 52: 4 You love every harmful **w**, you deceitful H1821
Ps 56: 4 whose **w** I praise—in God I trust H1821
Ps 56:10 whose **w** I praise, in the LORD H1821
Ps 56:10 I praise, in the LORD, whose **w** I praise— H1821
Ps 68:11 The Lord announces the **w**, and the women H608
Ps 103:20 ones who do his bidding, who obey his **w**. H1821
Ps 105:19 till the **w** *of* the LORD proved him true. H614
Ps 107:20 He sent out his **w** and healed them; he H1821
Ps 119: 9 By living according to your **w**. H1821
Ps 119:11 I have hidden your **w** in my heart that I H614
Ps 119:16 in your decrees; I will not neglect your **w**. H1821
Ps 119:17 while I live, that I may obey your **w**. H1821
Ps 119:25 preserve my life according to your **w**. H1821
Ps 119:28 strengthen me according to your **w**. H1821
Ps 119:37 preserve my life according to your **w**. H1821
Ps 119:42 who taunts me, for I trust in your **w**. H1821
Ps 119:43 Never take your **w** *of* truth from my mouth H1821
Ps 119:49 Remember your **w** to your servant, for you H1821
Ps 119:65 good to your servant according to your **w**, H1821
Ps 119:67 I went astray, but now I obey your **w**. H614
Ps 119:74 see me, for I have put my hope in your **w**. H1821
Ps 119:81 I have put my hope in your **w**. H1821
Ps 119:89 Your **w**, LORD, is eternal; it stands firm in H1821
Ps 119:101 evil path so that I might obey your **w**. H1821
Ps 119:105 Your **w** is a lamp for my feet, a light on H1821
Ps 119:107 my life, LORD, according to your **w**. H1821
Ps 119:114 my shield; I have put my hope in your **w**. H1821
Ps 119:133 Direct my footsteps according to your **w**; H614
Ps 119:147 for help; I have put my hope in your **w**. H1821
Ps 119:158 with loathing, for they do not obey your **w**. H614
Ps 119:161 but my heart trembles at your **w**. H1821
Ps 119:169 me understanding according to your **w**. H1821
Ps 119:172 May my tongue sing of your **w**, for all H614
Ps 130: 5 being waits, and in his **w** I put my hope. H1821
Ps 139: 4 Before a **w** is on my tongue you, LORD H4863
Ps 143: 8 *Let* the morning **bring** me **w** *of* your H9048
Ps 147:15 command to the earth; his **w** runs swiftly. H1821
Ps 147:18 He sends his **w** and melts them; he stirs H1821
Ps 147:19 He has revealed his **w** to Jacob, his laws H1821
Pr 12:25 down the heart, but a kind **w** cheers it up. H1821
Pr 15: 1 away wrath, but a harsh **w** stirs up anger. H1821
Pr 15:23 apt reply—and how good is a timely **w**! H1821
Pr 30: 5 "Every **w** *of* God is flawless; he is a shield H614
Ecc 7:21 not pay attention to every **w** people say, H1821
Ecc 8: 4 Since a king's **w** is supreme, who can say H1821
Isa 1:10 Hear the **w** *of* the LORD, you rulers of H1821
Isa 2: 3 the **w** *of* the LORD from Jerusalem. H1821
Isa 5:24 spurned the **w** *of* the Holy One of H614
Isa 8:20 does not speak according to this **w**, H1821
Isa 16:13 This is the **w** the LORD has already spoken H1821
Isa 23: 1 the land of Cyprus **w** *has* **come** to them. H1655
Isa 23: 5 When **w** comes to Egypt, they will be in H9051
Isa 24: 3 The LORD has spoken this **w**. H1821
Isa 28:13 the **w** *of* the LORD to them will become: H1821
Isa 28:14 Therefore hear the **w** *of* the LORD, you H1821
Isa 29:21 those who with a **w** make someone out to H1821
Isa 37: 9 sent messengers to Hezekiah *with this* **w**: H606
Isa 37:22 this is the **w** the LORD has spoken against H1821
Isa 38: 4 Then the **w** *of* the LORD came to Isaiah: H1821
Isa 39: 5 "Hear the **w** *of* the LORD Almighty: H1821
Isa 39: 8 "The **w** *of* the LORD you have spoken is H1821
Isa 40: 8 but the **w** *of* our God endures forever." H1821
Isa 45:23 in all integrity a **w** that will not be revoked H1821
Isa 50: 4 to know the **w** that sustains the weary. H1821
Isa 50:10 the LORD and obeys the **w** *of* his servant? H7754
Isa 55:11 so is my **w** that goes out from my mouth H1821
Isa 66: 2 in spirit, and who tremble at my **w**. H1821
Isa 66: 5 Hear the **w** *of* the LORD, you who tremble H1821
Isa 66: 5 of the LORD, you who tremble at his **w**: H1821
Jer 1: 2 The **w** *of* the LORD came to him in the H1821
Jer 1: 4 The **w** *of* the LORD came to me, saying, H1821
Jer 1:11 The **w** *of* the LORD came to me: "What do H1821
Jer 1:12 am watching to see that my **w** is fulfilled." H1821
Jer 1:13 The **w** *of* the LORD came to me again H1821
Jer 2: 1 The **w** *of* the LORD came to me: H1821
Jer 2: 4 Hear the **w** *of* the LORD, you descendants H1821
Jer 2:31 generation, consider the **w** *of* the LORD: H1821
Jer 5:13 are but wind and the **w** is not in them; H1825
Jer 6:10 The **w** *of* the LORD is offensive to them H1821
Jer 7: 1 This is the **w** that came to Jeremiah from H1821
Jer 7: 2 " 'Hear the **w** *of* the LORD, all you people H1821
Jer 8: 9 Since they have rejected the **w** *of* the LORD, H1821
Jer 9:20 you women, hear the **w** *of* the LORD; open H1821
Jer 11: 1 This is the **w** that came to Jeremiah from H1821
Jer 13: 3 Then the **w** *of* the LORD came to me a H1821
Jer 13: 8 Then the **w** *of* the LORD came to me: H1821
Jer 14: 1 This is the **w** *of* the LORD that came to H1821
Jer 14:17 "Speak this **w** to them: " 'Let my eyes H1821
Jer 16: 1 Then the **w** *of* the LORD came to me: H1821
Jer 17:15 "Where is the **w** *of* the LORD? H1821
Jer 17:20 to them, 'Hear the **w** *of* the LORD, you H1821
Jer 18: 1 This is the **w** that came to Jeremiah from H1821
Jer 18: 5 Then the **w** *of* the LORD came to me. H1821
Jer 18:18 the wise, nor the **w** from the prophets. H1821
Jer 19: 3 'Hear the **w** *of* the LORD, you kings H1821
Jer 20: 8 So the **w** *of* the LORD has brought me H1821
Jer 20: 9 will not mention **his w** or speak anymore H5647S
Jer 20: 9 his **w** is in my heart like a fire, a fire shut NDT
Jer 21: 1 The **w** came to Jeremiah from the LORD H1821
Jer 21:11 house of Judah, 'Hear the **w** *of* the LORD. H1821
Jer 22: 2 'Hear the **w** *of* the LORD to you, king of H1821
Jer 22:29 land, land, hear the **w** *of* the LORD! H1821
Jer 23:18 council of the LORD to see or to hear his **w**? H1821
Jer 23:18 Who has listened and heard his **w**? H1821
Jer 23:28 the one who has my **w** speak it faithfully. H1821
Jer 23:29 "Is not my **w** like fire," declares the LORD H1821
Jer 23:36 because each one's **w** becomes their own H1821
Jer 24: 4 Then the **w** *of* the LORD came to me: H1821
Jer 25: 1 The **w** came to Jeremiah concerning all H1821
Jer 25: 3 the **w** *of* the LORD has come to me and I H1821
Jer 26: 1 king of Judah, this **w** came from the LORD: H1821
Jer 26: 2 I command you; do not omit a **w**. H1821
Jer 27: 1 this **w** came to Jeremiah from the LORD: H1821
Jer 27: 3 Then **send w** to the kings of Edom, Moab H8938
Jer 27:18 are prophets and have the **w** *of* the LORD, H1821
Jer 28:12 the **w** *of* the LORD came to Jeremiah: H1821
Jer 29:20 Therefore, hear the **w** *of* the LORD, all you H1821
Jer 29:30 Then the **w** *of* the LORD came to Jeremiah: H1821
Jer 30: 1 This is the **w** that came to Jeremiah from H1821
Jer 31:10 "Hear the **w** *of* the LORD, you nations H1821
Jer 32: 1 This is the **w** that came to Jeremiah from H1821
Jer 32: 6 "The **w** *of* the LORD came to me: H1821
Jer 32: 8 "I knew that this was the **w** *of* the LORD; H1821
Jer 32:26 Then the **w** *of* the LORD came to Jeremiah: H1821
Jer 33: 1 the **w** *of* the LORD came to him a second H1821
Jer 33:19 The **w** *of* the LORD came to Jeremiah: H1821
Jer 33:23 The **w** *of* the LORD came to Jeremiah: H1821
Jer 34: 1 this **w** came to Jeremiah from the LORD: H1821
Jer 34: 8 The **w** came to Jeremiah from the LORD H1821
Jer 34:12 Then the **w** *of* the LORD came to Jeremiah: H1821
Jer 35: 1 This is the **w** that came to Jeremiah from H1821
Jer 35:12 Then the **w** *of* the LORD came to Jeremiah H1821
Jer 36: 1 this **w** came to Jeremiah from the LORD: H1821
Jer 36:27 the **w** *of* the LORD came to Jeremiah: H1821
Jer 37: 6 Then the **w** *of* the LORD came to Jeremiah H1821
Jer 37:17 privately, "Is there any **w** from the LORD?" H1821
Jer 39:15 the guard, the **w** *of* the LORD came to him: H1821
Jer 40: 1 The **w** came to Jeremiah from the LORD H1821
Jer 42: 7 Ten days later the **w** *of* the LORD came to H1821
Jer 42:15 then hear the **w** *of* the LORD, you remnant H1821
Jer 43: 8 In Tahpanhes the **w** *of* the LORD came to H1821
Jer 44: 1 This **w** came to Jeremiah concerning all H1821
Jer 44:24 women, "Hear the **w** *of* the LORD, all you H1821
Jer 44:26 But hear the **w** *of* the LORD, all you Jews H1821
Jer 44:28 in Egypt will know whose **w** will stand— H1821
Jer 46: 1 This is the **w** *of* the LORD that came to H1821
Jer 47: 1 This is the **w** *of* the LORD that came to H1821
Jer 49:34 This is the **w** *of* the LORD that came to H1821
Jer 50: 1 This is the **w** the LORD spoke through H1821
La 2:17 he has fulfilled his **w**, which he decreed H614
Eze 1: 3 the **w** *of* the LORD came to Ezekiel the H1821
Eze 3:16 of seven days the **w** *of* the LORD came to H1821
Eze 3:17 so hear the **w** I speak and give them H1821
Eze 6: 1 The **w** *of* the LORD came to me: H1821

Eze 6: 3 hear the w *of* the Sovereign LORD. H1821
Eze 7: 1 The w *of* the LORD came to me: H1821
Eze 9:11 the writing kit at his side brought back w, H1821
Eze 11:14 The w *of* the LORD came to me: H1821
Eze 12: 1 The w *of* the LORD came to me: H1821
Eze 12: 8 In the morning the w *of* the LORD came to H1821
Eze 12:17 The w *of* the LORD came to me: H1821
Eze 12:21 The w *of* the LORD came to me: H1821
Eze 12:26 The w *of* the LORD came to me: H1821
Eze 13: 1 The w *of* the LORD came to me: H1821
Eze 13: 2 imagination: 'Hear the w *of* the LORD! H1821
Eze 14: 2 Then the w *of* the LORD came to me: H1821
Eze 14:12 The w *of* the LORD came to me: H1821
Eze 15: 1 The w *of* the LORD came to me: H1821
Eze 16: 1 The w *of* the LORD came to me: H1821
Eze 16:35 you prostitute, hear the w *of* the LORD! H1821
Eze 17: 1 The w *of* the LORD came to me: H1821
Eze 17:11 Then the w *of* the LORD came to me: H1821
Eze 18: 1 The w *of* the LORD came to me: H1821
Eze 20: 2 Then the w *of* the LORD came to me: H1821
Eze 20:45 The w *of* the LORD came to me: H1821
Eze 20:47 'Hear the w *of* the LORD. This is H1821
Eze 21: 1 The w *of* the LORD came to me: H1821
Eze 21: 8 The w *of* the LORD came to me: H1821
Eze 21:18 The w *of* the LORD came to me: H1821
Eze 22: 1 The w *of* the LORD came to me: H1821
Eze 22:17 Then the w *of* the LORD came to me: H1821
Eze 22:23 Again the w *of* the LORD came to me: H1821
Eze 23: 1 The w *of* the LORD came to me: H1821
Eze 24: 1 tenth day, the w *of* the LORD came to me: H1821
Eze 24:15 The w *of* the LORD came to me: H1821
Eze 24:20 to them, "The w *of* the LORD came to me: H1821
Eze 25: 1 The w *of* the LORD came to me: H1821
Eze 25: 3 'Hear the w *of* the Sovereign LORD. H1821
Eze 26: 1 the month, the w *of* the LORD came to me: H1821
Eze 27: 1 The w *of* the LORD came to me: H1821
Eze 28: 1 The w *of* the LORD came to me: H1821
Eze 28:11 The w *of* the LORD came to me: H1821
Eze 28:20 The w *of* the LORD came to me: H1821
Eze 29: 1 twelfth day, the w *of* the LORD came to me: H1821
Eze 29:17 first day, the w *of* the LORD came to me: H1821
Eze 30: 1 The w *of* the LORD came to me: H1821
Eze 30:20 the w *of* the LORD came to me: H1821
Eze 31: 1 first day, the w *of* the LORD came to me: H1821
Eze 32: 1 first day, the w *of* the LORD came to me: H1821
Eze 32:17 the month, the w *of* the LORD came to me: H1821
Eze 33: 1 The w *of* the LORD came to me: H1821
Eze 33: 7 so hear the w I speak and give them H1821
Eze 33:23 Then the w *of* the LORD came to me: H1821
Eze 34: 1 The w *of* the LORD came to me: H1821
Eze 34: 7 you shepherds, hear the w *of* the LORD: H1821
Eze 34: 9 you shepherds, hear the w *of* the LORD: H1821
Eze 35: 1 The w *of* the LORD came to me: H1821
Eze 36: 1 of Israel, hear the w *of* the LORD. H1821
Eze 36: 4 hear the w *of* the Sovereign LORD: H1821
Eze 36:16 Again the w *of* the LORD came to me: H1821
Eze 37: 4 'Dry bones, hear the w *of* the LORD! H1821
Eze 37:15 The w *of* the LORD came to me: H1821
Eze 38: 1 The w *of* the LORD came to me: H1821
Da 9: 2 according to the w *of* the LORD given to H1821
Da 9:23 you began to pray, a w went out, which I H1821
Da 9:23 consider the w and understand the vision: H1821
Da 9:25 From the time the w goes out to restore H1821
Hos 1: 1 The w *of* the LORD that came to Hosea son H1821
Hos 4: 1 Hear the w *of* the LORD, you Israelites H1821
Joel 1: 1 The w *of* the LORD that came to Joel son H1821
Am 3: 1 Hear this w, people of Israel, the word the H1821
Am 3: 1 **the** w the LORD has spoken against you H889S
Am 4: 1 Hear this w, you cows of Bashan on H1821
Am 5: 1 Hear this w, Israel, this lament I take up H1821
Am 7:16 Now then, hear the w *of* the LORD. You say H1821
Am 8:12 searching for the w *of* the LORD, but they H1821
Jnh 1: 1 The w *of* the LORD came to Jonah son of H1821
Jnh 3: 1 Then the w *of* the LORD came to Jonah a H1821
Jnh 3: 3 Jonah obeyed the w *of* the LORD and went H1821
Mic 1: 1 The w *of* the LORD that came to Micah of H1821
Mic 4: 2 the w *of* the LORD from Jerusalem. H1821
Zep 1: 1 The w *of* the LORD that came to Zephaniah H1821
Zep 2: 5 people; the w *of* the LORD is against you H1821
Hag 1: 1 the w *of* the LORD came through the H1821
Hag 1: 3 Then the w *of* the LORD came through the H1821
Hag 2: 1 the w *of* the LORD came through the H1821
Hag 2:10 the w *of* the LORD came to the prophet H1821
Hag 2:20 The w *of* the LORD came to Haggai a H1821
Zec 1: 1 the w *of* the LORD came to the prophet H1821
Zec 1: 7 the w *of* the LORD came to the prophet H1821
Zec 1:14 was speaking to me said, "Proclaim this w: H606
Zec 4: 6 "This is the w *of* the LORD to Zerubbabel: H1821
Zec 4: 8 Then the w *of* the LORD came to me: H1821
Zec 6: 9 The w *of* the LORD came to me: H1821
Zec 7: 1 the w *of* the LORD came to Zechariah on H1821
Zec 7: 4 Then **the** w *of* the LORD Almighty came to H1821
Zec 7: 8 And the w *of* the LORD came again to H1821
Zec 8: 1 The w *of* the LORD Almighty came to me. H1821
Zec 8:18 The w *of* the LORD Almighty came to me. H1821
Zec 9: 1 The w *of* the LORD is against the land of H1821
Zec 11:11 me knew it was the w *of* the LORD. H1821
Zec 12: 1 The w *of* the LORD concerning Israel H1821
Mal 1: 1 The w *of* the LORD to Israel through H1821
Mt 4: 4 on every w that comes from the mouth G4839
Mt 8: 8 But just say the w, and my servant will be G3364
Mt 8:16 out the spirits *with a* w and healed all the G3364
Mt 12:32 who speaks a w against the Son of G3364
Mt 12:36 every empty w they have spoken. G4839
Mt 13:20 who hears the w and at once receives G3364
Mt 13:21 persecution comes because of the w, G3364
Mt 13:22 refers to someone who hears the w, G3364
Mt 13:22 the deceitfulness of wealth choke the w, G3364
Mt 13:23 who hears the w and understands it. G3364
Mt 14:35 *they* **sent** w to all the surrounding country. G690
Mt 15: 6 Thus you nullify the w of God for the sake G3364
Mt 15:23 Jesus did not answer a w. So his disciples G3364
Mt 19:11 "Not everyone can accept this w, but only G3364
Mt 22:46 No one could say a w in reply, and from G3364
Mt 26:75 remembered the w Jesus had spoken: G4839
Mk 2: 2 the door, and he preached the w to them. G3364
Mk 4:14 The farmer sows the w. G3364
Mk 4:15 along the path, where the w is sown. G3364
Mk 4:15 takes away the w that was sown in G3364
Mk 4:16 hear the w and at once receive it with joy. G3364
Mk 4:17 persecution comes because of the w, G3364
Mk 4:18 seed sown among thorns, hear the w; G3364
Mk 4:19 other things come in and choke the w, G3364
Mk 4:20 sown on good soil, hear the w, accept it, G3364
Mk 4:33 parables Jesus spoke the w to them, G3364
Mk 7:13 Thus you nullify the w of God by your G3364
Mk 14:72 remembered the w Jesus had spoken to G4839
Mk 16:20 confirmed his w by the signs that G3364
Lk 1: 2 were eyewitnesses and servants *of* the w. G3364
Lk 1:37 For no w from God will ever fail. G4839
Lk 1:38 "May your w to me be fulfilled. G4839
Lk 2:17 they spread the w concerning what had G4839
Lk 3: 2 the w of God came to John son of G4839
Lk 5: 1 around him and listening to the w of God. G3364
Lk 7: 7 But say the w, and my servant will be G3364
Lk 8:11 of the parable: The seed is the w of God. G3364
Lk 8:12 takes away the w from their hearts, G3364
Lk 8:13 who receive the w with joy when they G3364
Lk 8:15 good heart, who hear the w, retain it, G3364
Lk 8:21 those who hear God's w and put it into G3364
Lk 11:28 those who hear the w of God and obey it." G3364
Lk 12:10 who speaks a w against the Son of G3364
Lk 22:61 remembered the w the Lord had spoken G4839
Lk 24:19 powerful in w and deed before God and G3364
Jn 1: 1 In the beginning was the **W**, and the G3364
Jn 1: 1 the Word, and the **W** was with God, and G3364
Jn 1: 1 Word was with God, and the **W** was God. G3364
Jn 1:14 The **W** became flesh and made his G3364
Jn 4:50 man **took** Jesus **at** *his* w and G4409+3836+3364
Jn 5:24 whoever hears my w and believes him G3364
Jn 5:38 does his w dwell in you, for you do not G3364
Jn 7:26 publicly, and they are **not** saying *a w* to him. AIT
Jn 8:37 because you have no room for my w. G3364
Jn 8:51 whoever obeys my w will never see death." G3364
Jn 8:52 whoever obeys your w will never taste G3364
Jn 8:55 but I do know him and obey his w. G3364
Jn 9: 7 Pool of Siloam" (**this** w means "Sent") G4005S
Jn 10:35 to whom the w of God came—and G3364
Jn 11: 3 So the sisters sent w to Jesus, "Lord, the G3306
Jn 12:17 from the dead *continued to* **spread the** w. G3455
Jn 12:38 was to fulfill the w of Isaiah the prophet: G3364
Jn 15: 3 because of the w I have spoken to you G3364
Jn 17: 6 them to me and they have obeyed your w. G3364
Jn 17:14 given them your w and the world has G3364
Jn 17:17 Sanctify them by the truth; your w is truth. G3364
Ac 4:29 to speak your w with great boldness. G3364
Ac 4:31 Holy Spirit and spoke the w of God boldly. G3364
Ac 6: 2 the ministry of the w of God in order to G3364
Ac 6: 4 to prayer and the ministry *of* the w." G3364
Ac 6: 7 So the w of God spread. The number of G3364
Ac 8: 4 preached the w wherever they went. G3364
Ac 8:14 that Samaria had accepted the w of God, G3364
Ac 8:25 further proclaimed the w of the Lord and G3364
Ac 11: 1 Gentiles also had received the w of God. G3364
Ac 11:19 spreading the w only among Jews. G3364
Ac 12:24 But the w of God continued to spread G3364
Ac 13: 5 they proclaimed the w of God in the G3364
Ac 13: 7 because he wanted to hear the w of God. G3364
Ac 13:15 the leaders of the synagogue **sent** *w* to them AIT
Ac 13:15 if you have a w of exhortation for the G3364
Ac 13:44 city gathered to hear the w of the Lord. G3364
Ac 13:46 had to speak the w of God to you first. G3364
Ac 13:48 were glad and honored the w of the Lord; G3364
Ac 13:49 The w of the Lord spread through the G3364
Ac 14:25 when they had preached the w in Perga, G3364
Ac 15:27 to confirm by **w of mouth** what we are G3364
Ac 15:35 taught and preached the w of the Lord. G3364
Ac 15:36 we preached the w of the Lord and see G3364
Ac 16: 6 from preaching the w in the province of G3364
Ac 16:32 Then they spoke the w of the Lord to him G3364
Ac 17:13 was preaching the w of God at Berea, G3364
Ac 18:11 a half, teaching them the w of God. G3364
Ac 19:10 province of Asia heard the w of the Lord. G3364
Ac 19:20 In this way the w of the Lord spread widely G3364
Ac 20:32 you to God and *to* the w of his grace, G3364
Ro 9: 6 It is not as though God's w had failed. G3364
Ro 10: 8 "The w is near you; it is in your mouth G4839
Ro 10:17 is heard through the w about Christ. G4839
1Co 14: 6 prophecy or **w of instruction**? G1439
1Co 14:26 a hymn, or a **w of instruction**, a revelation, G1439
1Co 14:36 Or did the w of God originate with you? Or G3364
1Co 15: 2 you hold firmly *to* the w I preached to you G3364
2Co 2:17 we do not peddle the w of God for profit. G3364
2Co 4: 2 deception, nor do we distort the w of God. G3364
Gal 6: 6 instruction *in* the w should share all G3364
Eph 5:26 by the washing with water through the w, G4839
Eph 6:17 sword of the Spirit, which is the w of God. G4839
Php 2:16 as you hold firmly *to* the w of life. G3364
Col 1:25 to present to you the w of God in its G3364
Col 3:17 whether in w or deed, do it all in G3364
1Th 2:13 when you received the w of God, which G3364
1Th 2:13 you accepted it not *as* a human w, but as G3364
1Th 2:13 as it actually is, the w of God, which is G3364
1Th 4:15 According to the Lord's w, we tell you that G3364
2Th 2: 2 a prophecy or by **w of mouth** or by letter— G3364
2Th 2:15 whether by **w of mouth** or by letter. G3364
2Th 2:17 strengthen you in every good deed and w. G3364
1Ti 4: 5 consecrated by the w of God and prayer. G3364
2Ti 2: 9 But God's w is not chained. G3364
2Ti 2:15 who correctly handles the w of truth. G3364
2Ti 4: 2 Preach the w; be prepared in season and G3364
Titus 2: 5 so that no one will malign the w of God. G3364
Heb 1: 3 sustaining all things *by* his powerful w. G4839
Heb 4:12 For the w of God is alive and active G3364
Heb 5:12 truths of God's w all over again. G3359
Heb 6: 5 the goodness *of* the w of God and the G4839
Heb 12: 5 forgotten this *w of* **encouragement** that AIT
Heb 12:19 that no further w be spoken to them, G3364
Heb 12:24 blood *that* **speaks a** better w than the G3281
Heb 13: 7 leaders, who spoke the w of God to you. G3364
Heb 13:22 urge you to bear with my w of exhortation, G3364
Jas 1:18 to give us birth *through* the w of truth, G3364
Jas 1:21 humbly accept the w planted in you, G3364
Jas 1:22 Do not merely listen *to* the w, and so G3364
Jas 1:23 who listens *to* the w but does not do G3364
1Pe 1:23 through the living and enduring w of God. G3364
1Pe 1:25 the w of the Lord endures forever. G4839
1Pe 1:25 And this is the w that was preached to G4839
1Pe 3: 1 if any of them do not believe the w, they G3364
2Pe 3: 5 that long ago *by* God's w the heavens G3364
2Pe 3: 7 *By* the same w the present heavens and G3364
1Jn 1: 1 this we proclaim concerning the **W** of life. G3364
1Jn 1:10 him out to be a liar and his w is not in us. G3364
1Jn 2: 5 But if anyone obeys his w, love for God is G3364
1Jn 2:14 are strong, and the w of God lives in you G3364
Rev 1: 2 the w of God and the testimony of Jesus G3364
Rev 1: 9 Patmos because of the w of God and the G3364
Rev 3: 8 you have kept my w and have not denied G3364
Rev 6: 9 slain because of the w of God and the G3364
Rev 12:11 the Lamb and by the w of their testimony; G3364
Rev 19:13 in blood, and his name is the **W** of God. G3364
Rev 20: 4 about Jesus and because of the w of God. G3364

WORDLESS (1) [WORD]

Ro 8:26 himself intercedes for us through w groans. G227

WORDS (421) [WORD]

Ge 4:23 listen to me; wives of Lamech, hear my w. H614
Ge 27:34 When Esau heard his father's w, he burst H1821
Ge 42:16 so that your w may be tested to see if you H1821
Ge 42:20 so that your w may be verified and that H1821
Ge 44: 6 with them, he repeated these w to them. H1821
Ex 4:15 speak to him and put w in his mouth; H1821
Ex 19: 6 These are the w you are to speak to the H1821
Ex 19: 7 before them all the w the LORD had H1821
Ex 20: 1 And God spoke all these w: H1821
Ex 23: 8 who see and twists the w *of* the innocent. H1821
Ex 24: 3 told the people all the LORD's w and laws, H1821
Ex 24: 8 with you in accordance with all these w." H1821
Ex 33: 4 the people heard these distressing w, H1821
Ex 34: 1 write on them the w that were on the first H1821
Ex 34:27 "Write down these w, for in accordance H1821
Ex 34:27 accordance with these w I have made a H1821
Ex 34:28 on the tablets the w *of* the covenant— H1821
Nu 12: 6 "Listen to my w: "When there is a H1821
Nu 24: 4 prophecy of one who hears the w *of* God, H609
Nu 24:16 prophecy of one who hears the w *of* God, H609
Dt 1: 1 These are the w Moses spoke to all Israel H1821
Dt 4:10 before me to hear my w so that they may H1821
Dt 4:12 heard the sound of w but saw no form; H1821
Dt 4:36 you heard his w from out of the fire. H1821
Dt 10: 2 on the tablets the w that were on the first H1821
Dt 11:18 Fix these w *of* mine in your hearts and H1821
Dt 13: 3 must not listen to the w *of* that prophet H1821
Dt 16:19 the wise and twists the w *of* the innocent. H1821
Dt 17:19 carefully all the w *of* this law and these H1821
Dt 18:18 I will put my w in his mouth. H1821
Dt 18:19 does not listen to my w that the prophet H1821
Dt 27: 3 on them all the w *of* this law when you H1821
Dt 27: 8 very clearly all the w *of* this law on these H1821
Dt 27:26 does not uphold the w *of* this law by H1821
Dt 28:58 not carefully follow all the w *of* this law, H1821
Dt 29:19 a person hears the w *of* this oath and they H1821
Dt 29:29 that we may follow all the w *of* this law. H1821
Dt 31: 1 went out and spoke these w to all Israel: H1821
Dt 31:12 follow carefully all the w *of* this law. H1821
Dt 31:24 writing in a book the w *of* this law from H1821
Dt 31:28 I can speak these w in their hearing and H1821
Dt 31:30 And Moses recited the w *of* this song from H1821
Dt 32: 1 hear, you earth, the w *of* my mouth. H609
Dt 32: 2 fall like rain and my w descend like dew, H614
Dt 32:44 spoke all the w *of* this song in the H1821
Dt 32:45 finished reciting all these w to all Israel, H1821
Dt 32:46 "Take to heart all the w I have solemnly H1821
Dt 32:46 to obey carefully all the w *of* this law. H1821
Dt 32:47 They are not just idle w for you—they are H1821

Jos 3: 9 listen to the w of the LORD your God. H1821
Jos 8:34 Joshua read all the w of the law—the H1821
Jos 24:27 It has heard all the w the LORD has said to H609
Jdg 11:11 he repeated all his w before the LORD in H1821
Jdg 13:12 "When your w are fulfilled, what H1821
1Sa 3:19 let none of Samuel's w fall to the ground. H1821
1Sa 8:10 Samuel told all the w of the LORD to the H1821
1Sa 11: 6 When Saul heard their w, the Spirit of H1821
1Sa 17:11 On hearing the Philistine's w, Saul and all H1821
1Sa 18:23 They repeated these w to David. H1821
1Sa 21:12 David took these w to heart and was very H1821
1Sa 24: 7 With these w David sharply rebuked his H1821
1Sa 25:35 I have heard your w and granted your H7754
1Sa 26:19 my lord the king listen to his servant's w. H1821
1Sa 28:20 filled with fear because of Samuel's w. H1821
2Sa 7:17 to David all the w of this entire revelation H1821
2Sa 14: 3 go to the king and speak these w to him." H1821
2Sa 14: 3 And Joab put the w in her mouth. H1821
2Sa 14:19 who put all these w into the mouth of H1821
2Sa 22: 1 to the LORD the w of this song when the H1821
2Sa 23: 1 These are the last w of David: "The H1821
1Ki 8:59 And may these w of mine, which I have H1821
1Ki 21:27 When Ahab heard these w, he tore his H1821
1Ki 22:28 he added, "Mark my w, all you people H9048
2Ki 6:12 king of Israel the very w you speak in your H1821
2Ki 6:30 When the king heard the woman's w, he H1821
2Ki 18:20 but you speak only empty w. H1821+8557
2Ki 19: 4 will hear all the w of the field commander H1821
2Ki 19: 4 rebuke him for the w the LORD your God H1821
2Ki 19: 6 those w with which the underlings of the H1821
2Ki 19:16 listen to the w Sennacherib has sent to H1821
2Ki 22:11 the king heard the w of the Book of the H1821
2Ki 22:13 us have not obeyed the w of this book; H1821
2Ki 22:18 says concerning the w you heard: H1821
2Ki 23: 2 their hearing all the w of the Book of the H1821
2Ki 23: 3 thus confirming the w of the covenant H1821
1Ch 17:15 to David all the w of this entire revelation H1821
2Ch 11: 4 So they obeyed the w of the LORD and H1821
2Ch 15: 8 Asa heard these w and the prophecy of H1821
2Ch 18:27 he added, "Mark my w, all you people H9048
2Ch 29:30 the LORD with the w of David and of Asaph H1821
2Ch 32: 6 gate and encouraged them with these w: H606
2Ch 33:18 to his God and the w the seers spoke to H1821
2Ch 34:19 When the king heard the w of the Law, he H1821
2Ch 34:26 says concerning the w you heard: H1821
2Ch 34:30 their hearing all the w of the Book of the H1821
2Ch 34:31 to obey the w of the covenant written H1821
2Ch 36:16 despised his w and scoffed at his H1821
Ezr 9: 4 trembled at the w of the God of Israel H1821
Ne 1: 1 The w of Nehemiah son of Hakaliah: In H1821
Ne 8: 9 as they listened to the w of the Law. H1821
Ne 8:12 understood the w that had been made H1821
Ne 8:13 to give attention to the w of the Law. H1821
Est 4:12 When Esther's w were reported to H1821
Est 9:30 kingdom—w of goodwill and assurance H1821
Job 4: 4 Your w have supported those who H4863
Job 6: 3 no wonder my w have been impetuous. H1821
Job 6:10 I had not denied the w of the Holy One. H609
Job 6:25 How painful are honest w! But what do H609
Job 6:26 and treat my desperate w as wind? H609
Job 8: 2 Your w are a blustering wind. H609+7023
Job 8:10 they not bring forth w from their H4863
Job 9:14 How can I find w to argue with him? H1821
Job 11: 2 "Are all these w to go unanswered? Is this H1821
Job 12:11 the ear test w as the tongue tastes H4863
Job 13:17 to what I say; let my w ring in your ears. H289
Job 15: 3 Would they argue with useless w, with H1821
Job 15:11 enough for you, w spoken gently to you? H1821
Job 15:13 God and pour out such w from your mouth H4863
Job 19: 2 will you torment me and crush me with w? H4863
Job 19:23 that my w were recorded, that they H4863
Job 21: 2 "Listen carefully to my w; let this be the H4863
Job 22:22 his mouth and lay up his w in your heart. H609
Job 23:12 have treasured the w of his mouth more H609
Job 24:25 me false and reduce my w to nothing?" H4863
Job 26: 4 Who has helped you utter these w? And H4863
Job 29:22 no more; my w fell gently on their ears. H4863
Job 29:23 drank in my w as the spring rain. NDT
Job 31:40 The w of Job are ended. H1821
Job 32:11 while you were searching for w, H4863
Job 32:14 Job has not marshaled his w against me, H4863
Job 32:15 have no more to say; w have failed them. H4863
Job 32:18 For I am full of w, and the spirit within me H4863
Job 33: 1 listen to my w; pay attention to H4863
Job 33: 2 my w are on the tip of my tongue. H1819
Job 33: 3 My w come from an upright heart; my lips H609
Job 33: 8 said in my hearing—I heard the very w— H4863
Job 33:13 to him that he responds to no one's w? H1821
Job 34: 2 "Hear my w, you wise men; listen to me H4863
Job 34: 3 For the ear tests w as the tongue tastes H4863
Job 34:35 without knowledge; his w lack insight. H1821
Job 34:37 us and multiplies his w against God." H609
Job 35:16 without knowledge he multiplies w." H4863
Job 36: 4 Be assured that my w are not false; one H4863
Job 38: 2 my plans with w without knowledge? H4863
Job 41: 3 Will it speak to you with gentle w? H1819
Ps 5: 1 Listen to my w, LORD, consider my lament. H609
Ps 12: 6 And the w of the LORD are flawless, like H614
Ps 18: T to the LORD the w of this song when the H1821
Ps 19: 3 speech, they use no w; no sound is heard H1821
Ps 19: 4 the earth, their w to the ends of the world. H4863
Ps 19:14 May these w of my mouth and this H609
Ps 36: 3 The w of their mouths are wicked and H1821
Ps 49: 3 My mouth will speak w of wisdom; the AIT
Ps 50:17 my instruction and cast my w behind you. H1821
Ps 54: 2 O God; listen to the w of my mouth. H609
Ps 55: 9 confound their w, for I see violence H4383
Ps 55:21 his w are more soothing than oil H1821
Ps 56: 5 All day long they twist my w; all their H1821
Ps 59: 7 the w from their lips are sharp as swords NDT
Ps 59:12 mouths, for the w of their lips, let them H1821
Ps 64: 3 aim cruel w like deadly arrows. H1821
Ps 78: 1 my teaching; listen to the w of my mouth. H609
Ps 94: 4 They pour out arrogant w; all the H1819
Ps 105:28 had they not rebelled against his w? H1821
Ps 106:33 and rash w came from Moses' lips. H1051
Ps 109: 3 With w of hatred they surround me; they H1821
Ps 119:57 I have promised to obey your w. H1821
Ps 119:103 How sweet are your w to my taste, sweeter H614
Ps 119:130 The unfolding of your w gives light; it H1821
Ps 119:139 me out, for my enemies ignore your w. H1821
Ps 119:160 All your w are true; all your righteous H1821
Ps 141: 6 will learn that my w were well spoken. H609
Pr 1: 2 instruction; for understanding w of insight; H609
Pr 2: 1 if you accept my w and store up my H609
Pr 2:12 from men whose w are perverse, H1819
Pr 2:16 the wayward woman with her seductive w, H609
Pr 4: 4 "Take hold of my w with all your heart H1821
Pr 4: 5 do not forget my w or turn away from H609+7023
Pr 4:20 to what I say; turn your ear to my w. H609
Pr 5: 1 wisdom, turn your ear to my w of insight, H9312
Pr 6: 2 you said, ensnared by the w of your mouth. H609
Pr 7: 1 keep my w and store up my commands H609
Pr 7: 5 the wayward woman with her seductive w. H609
Pr 7:21 With persuasive w she led him astray; she H4375
Pr 8: 8 All the w of my mouth are just; none of H609
Pr 10:19 Sin is not ended by multiplying w, but the H1821
Pr 12: 6 The w of the wicked lie in wait for blood H1821
Pr 12:18 The w of the reckless pierce like swords H1051
Pr 15:26 gracious w are pure in his sight. H609
Pr 16:21 gracious w promote instruction. H8557
Pr 16:24 Gracious w are a honeycomb, sweet to the H609
Pr 17:27 who has knowledge uses w with restraint, H609
Pr 18: 4 The w of the mouth are deep waters, but H1821
Pr 18: 8 The w of a gossip are like choice morsels H1821
Pr 19:27 you will stray from the w of knowledge. H609
Pr 22:12 he frustrates the w of the unfaithful. H1821
Pr 23: 9 to fools, for they will scorn your prudent w. H4863
Pr 23:12 your ears to w of knowledge. H609
Pr 26:22 The w of a gossip are like choice morsels H1821
Pr 29:19 Servants cannot be corrected by mere w H1821
Pr 30: 6 Do not add to his w, or he will rebuke you H1821
Ecc 1: 1 The w of the Teacher, son of David, king H1821
Ecc 5: 2 you are on earth, so let your w be few. H1821
Ecc 5: 3 many w mark the speech of a fool. H1821
Ecc 5: 7 dreaming and many w are meaningless. H1821
Ecc 6:11 The more the w, the less the meaning H1821
Ecc 9:16 his w are no longer heeded. H1821
Ecc 9:17 The quiet w of the wise are more to be H1821
Ecc 10:12 W from the mouth of the wise are H1821
Ecc 10:13 At the beginning their w are folly H1821+7023
Ecc 10:14 fools multiply w. No one knows what H1821
Ecc 10:20 because a bird in the sky may carry your w, H7754
Ecc 12:10 Teacher searched to find just the right w, H1821
Ecc 12:11 The w of the wise are like goads, their H1821
Isa 3: 8 their w and deeds are against the LORD H4383
Isa 29:11 vision is nothing but w sealed in a scroll. H1821
Isa 29:18 day the deaf will hear the w of the scroll, H1821
Isa 31: 2 disaster; he does not take back his w. H1821
Isa 36: 5 but you speak only empty w. H1821+8557
Isa 36:13 Hebrew, "Hear the w of the great king H1821
Isa 37: 4 God will hear the w of the field H1821
Isa 37: 4 rebuke him for the w the LORD your God H1821
Isa 37: 6 those w with which the underlings of the H1821
Isa 37:17 listen to all the w Sennacherib has sent to H1821
Isa 41:26 foretold it, no one heard any w from you. H609
Isa 44:26 who carries out the w of his servants and H1821
Isa 51:16 I have put my w in your mouth and H1821
Isa 58:13 doing as you please or speaking idle w, H1821
Isa 59:21 my w that I have put in your mouth H1821
Jer 1: 1 The w of Jeremiah son of Hilkiah, one of H1821
Jer 1: 9 "I have put my w in your mouth. H1821
Jer 5:14 the people have spoken these w, H1821
Jer 5:14 I will make my w in your mouth a fire and H1821
Jer 6:19 not listened to my w and have rejected H1821
Jer 7: 4 Do not trust in deceptive w and say, "This H1821
Jer 7: 8 trusting in deceptive w that are worthless. H1821
Jer 9:20 open your ears to the w of his mouth. H1821
Jer 11: 6 "Proclaim all these w in the towns of H1821
Jer 11:10 ancestors, who refused to listen to my w. H1821
Jer 13:10 who refuse to listen to my w, who follow H1821
Jer 15:16 When your w came, I ate them; they were H1821
Jer 15:19 not worthless, w, you will be my NDT
Jer 19: 2 There proclaim the w I tell you, H1821
Jer 19:15 stiff-necked and would not listen to my w. H1821
Jer 23: 9 because of the LORD and his holy w. H1821
Jer 23:22 have proclaimed my w to my people and H1821
Jer 23:30 from one another w supposedly from me. H1821
Jer 23:36 So you distort the w of the living God, the H1821
Jer 23:38 You used the w, 'This is a message from H1821
Jer 25: 8 "Because you have not listened to my w, H1821
Jer 25:30 prophesy all these w against them and H1821
Jer 26: 5 do not listen to the w of my servants the H1821
Jer 26: 7 speak these w in the house of the H1821
Jer 26:15 you to speak all these w in your hearing." H1821
Jer 26:21 all his officers and officials heard his w, H1821
Jer 27:14 Do not listen to the w of the prophets who H1821
Jer 28: 6 the LORD fulfill the w you have prophesied H1821
Jer 29:19 For they have not listened to my w," H1821
Jer 29:19 "w that I sent to them again and again by NDT
Jer 30: 2 in a book all the w I have spoken to you. H1821
Jer 30: 4 These are the w the LORD spoke H1821
Jer 31:23 in its towns will once again use these w: H1821
Jer 35:13 you not learn a lesson and obey my w? H1821
Jer 36: 2 write on it all the w I have spoken to you H1821
Jer 36: 4 dictated all the w the LORD had spoken to H1821
Jer 36: 6 from the scroll the w of the LORD that you H1821
Jer 36: 8 temple he read the w of the LORD from the H1821
Jer 36:10 LORD's temple the w of Jeremiah from the H1821
Jer 36:11 heard all the w of the LORD from the scroll H1821
Jer 36:16 When they heard all these w, they looked H1821
Jer 36:16 "We must report all these w to the king." H1821
Jer 36:18 "he dictated all these w to me, and I H1821
Jer 36:24 who heard all these w showed no fear, H1821
Jer 36:27 scroll containing the w that Baruch had H1821
Jer 36:28 write on it all the w that were on the first H1821
Jer 36:32 wrote on it all the w of the scroll that H1821
Jer 36:32 And many similar w were added to them. H1821
Jer 37: 2 attention to the w the LORD had spoken H1821
Jer 39:16 am about to fulfill my w against this city— H1821
Jer 39:16 against this city—w concerning disaster NDT
Jer 43: 1 the people all the w of the LORD their God H1821
Jer 45: 1 on a scroll the w Jeremiah the prophet H1821
Jer 51:61 see that you read all these w aloud. H1821
Jer 51:64 The w of Jeremiah end here. H1821
Eze 2: 6 do not be afraid of them or their w. H1821
Eze 2: 7 You must speak my w to them, whether H1821
Eze 2:10 of it were written w of lament and H4180
Eze 3: 4 people of Israel and speak my w to them. H1821
Eze 3: 6 whose w you cannot understand. H1821
Eze 3:10 take to heart all the w I speak to you. H1821
Eze 12:28 None of my w will be delayed any longer H1821
Eze 13: 6 and expect him to fulfill their w. H1821
Eze 13: 8 Because of your false w and lying visions H1819
Eze 33:31 sit before you to hear your w, but they H1821
Eze 33:32 they hear your w but do not put them H1821
Da 4:31 Even as the w were on his lips, a voice A10418
Da 5:26 "Here is what these w mean: Mene: God A10418
Da 7:11 of the boastful w the horn was speaking. A10418
Da 9:12 have fulfilled the w spoken against us H1821
Da 10:11 carefully the w I am about to speak to H1821
Da 10:12 before your God, your w were heard, and I H1821
Da 12: 4 roll up and seal the w of the scroll until H1821
Da 12: 9 because the w are rolled up and sealed H1821
Hos 6: 5 I killed you with the w of my mouth—then H609
Hos 7:16 by the sword because of their insolent w. H4383
Hos 14: 2 Take w with you and return to the LORD H1821
Am 1: 1 The w of Amos, one of the shepherds of H1821
Am 7:10 The land cannot bear all his w. H1821
Am 8:11 a famine of hearing the w of the LORD. H1821
Mic 2: 7 "Do not my w do good to the one whose H1821
Mic 7: 5 in your embrace guard the w of your lips. H7339
Zec 1: 6 But did not my w and my decrees, which I H1821
Zec 1:13 kind and comforting w to the angel who H1821
Zec 7: 7 Are these not the w the LORD proclaimed H1821
Zec 7:12 to the law or to the w that the LORD H1821
Zec 8: 9 "Now hear these w, 'Let your hands be H1821
Mal 2:17 You have wearied the LORD with your w H1821
Mt 6: 7 will be heard because of their many w. G4494
Mt 7:24 who hears these w of mine and puts them G3364
Mt 7:26 who hears these w of mine and does not G3364
Mt 10:14 will not welcome you or listen to your w, G3364
Mt 12: 7 If you had known what these w mean, 'I AIT
Mt 12:37 For by your w you will be acquitted, and by G3364
Mt 12:37 by your w you will be condemned. G3364
Mt 22:15 out and laid plans to trap him in his w. G3364
Mt 24:35 but my w will never pass away. G3364
Mk 8:38 of me and my w in this adulterous G3364
Mk 10:24 The disciples were amazed at his w. G3364
Mk 12:13 Herodians to Jesus to catch him in his w. G3364
Mk 13:31 but my w will never pass away. G3364
Lk 1:20 because you did not believe my w, which G3364
Lk 1:29 troubled at his w and wondered what kind G3364
Lk 3: 4 written in the book of the w of Isaiah the G3364
Lk 3:18 And with many other w John exhorted the AIT
Lk 4:22 at the gracious w that came from his G3364
Lk 4:32 his teaching, because his w had authority. G3364
Lk 4:36 said to each other, "What w these are! G3364
Lk 6:47 to me and hears my w and puts them into G3364
Lk 6:49 the one who hears my w and does not put NDT
Lk 7:29 collectors, when they heard Jesus' w AIT
Lk 9:26 Whoever is ashamed of me and my w, the G3364
Lk 19:22 'I will judge you by your own w, you G5125
Lk 19:48 because all the people hung on his w. G201
Lk 21:15 For I will give you w and wisdom that none G5125
Lk 21:33 but my w will never pass away. G3364
Lk 24: 8 Then they remembered his w. G4839
Lk 24:11 because their w seemed to them like G4839
Jn 1:23 John replied in the w of Isaiah the G2777+3306
Jn 2:22 scripture and the w that Jesus had spoken G3364
Jn 3:34 whom God has sent speaks the w of God, G4839
Jn 4:41 And because of his w many more became G3364
Jn 6:63 The w I have spoken to you—they are full G4839
Jn 6:68 You have the w of eternal life. G4839
Jn 7:40 On hearing his w, some of the people G3364
Jn 8:20 He spoke these w while teaching in the G4839

Jn 10:19 who heard these w were again divided. G3364
Jn 12:47 "If anyone hears my w but does not keep G4839
Jn 12:48 rejects me and does not accept my w; G4839
Jn 12:48 the very w I have spoken will condemn G3364
Jn 14:10 The w I say to you I do not speak on my G4839
Jn 14:24 These w you hear are not my own; they G3364
Jn 15: 7 remain in me and my w remain in you, G4839
Jn 17: 8 For I gave them the w you gave me and G4839
Jn 18: 9 so that the w he had spoken would G3364
Ac 2:40 *With* many other w he warned them; and G3364
Ac 6:11 speak blasphemous w against Moses G4839
Ac 7:35 same Moses they had rejected *with the* w, G3306
Ac 7:38 he received living w to pass on to us. G3359
Ac 10:44 While Peter was still speaking these w G4839
Ac 13:27 they fulfilled the w of the prophets that G5889
Ac 14:18 Even with these w, they had difficulty G3306
Ac 15:15 The w of the prophets are in agreement G3364
Ac 18:15 questions about w and names and your G3364
Ac 20: 2 speaking many w of encouragement to G3364
Ac 20:35 remembering the w the Lord Jesus G3364
Ac 22:14 One and to hear w from his mouth. G5889
Ro 3: 2 been entrusted with the very w of God. G3359
Ro 4:23 The w "it was credited to him" were written NDT
Ro 9: 8 **In other** w, it is not the children by G4047+1639
Ro 10:18 the earth, their w to the ends of the world." G4839
1Co 2: 4 were not with wise and persuasive w, G3364
1Co 2:13 not in w taught us by human wisdom but G3364
1Co 2:13 human wisdom but in w taught by the Spirit, NDT
1Co 2:13 spiritual realities *with* **Spirit-taught** *w*. AIT
1Co 14: 9 you speak intelligible w with your tongue, G3364
1Co 14:19 five intelligible w to instruct others than G3364
1Co 14:19 others than ten thousand w in a tongue. G3364
Gal 5: 2 **Mark my** w! I, Paul, tell you that if you let G2623
Eph 5: 6 Let no one deceive you *with* empty w, for G3364
Eph 6:19 w may be given me so that I will G3364
1Th 1: 5 you not simply with w but also with power G3364
1Th 4:18 encourage one another with these w. G3364
1Ti 6: 4 and **quarrels about** w that result in G3363
2Ti 2:14 before God against **quarreling about** w; G3362
Heb 4: 4 spoken about the seventh day **in these** w: G4048
Heb 12:19 to such a voice *speaking* w that those who G4839
Heb 12:27 The *w* "once more" indicate the removing of AIT
1Pe 3: 1 be won over without w by the behavior of G3364
1Pe 4:11 so as one who speaks the *very* w of God. G3359
2Pe 2:18 For *they* **mouth** empty, boastful w and, by G5779
2Pe 3: 2 you to recall the w spoken in the past by G4839
1Jn 3:18 let us not love *with* w or speech but with G3364
Jude 15 defiant w ungodly sinners *have* **spoken** G3281
Rev 1: 3 who reads aloud the w of this prophecy, G3364
Rev 2: 1 These *are the* w *of him* who holds the G3306
Rev 2: 8 These *are the* w *of him* who is the First G3306
Rev 2:12 These *are the* w *of him* who has the sharp G3306
Rev 2:18 These *are the* w *of* the Son of God, whose G3306
Rev 3: 1 These *are the* w *of him* who holds the G3306
Rev 3: 7 These *are the* w *of him* who is holy and G3306
Rev 3:14 These *are the* w *of* the Amen, the faithful G3306
Rev 13: 5 given a mouth *to* **utter** proud w and G3281
Rev 17:17 royal authority, until God's w are fulfilled. G3364
Rev 19: 9 he added, "These are the true w of God." G3364
Rev 21: 5 these w are trustworthy and true. G3364
Rev 22: 6 "These w are trustworthy and true. G3364
Rev 22: 7 the one who keeps the w of the prophecy G3364
Rev 22: 9 with all who keep the w of this scroll. G3364
Rev 22:10 "Do not seal up the w of the prophecy of G3364
Rev 22:18 who hears the w of the prophecy of G3364
Rev 22:19 And if anyone takes w away from this G3364

WORE (11) [WEAR]

Jos 9: 5 sandals on their feet and w old clothes. H6584
1Sa 17: 5 on his head and w a coat of scale armor H4229
1Sa 17: 6 on his legs he w bronze greaves, and a NDT
1Sa 22:18 eighty-five men *who* w the linen ephod. H5951
2Sa 13:18 the virgin daughters of the king w. H4252
1Ch 15:27 David also w a linen ephod. H6584
Ne 4:18 each of the builders w his sword at his side H673
Ps 109:18 *He* w cursing as his garment; it entered H4252
Mk 1: 6 John w **clothing** made of camel's G1639+1907
Rev 9: 7 On their heads they w something like NDT
Rev 15: 6 shining linen and w golden sashes G4322

WORK (379) [CO-WORKER, CO-WORKERS, HARDWORKING, METALWORKER, WORKED, WORKER, WORKERS, WORKING, WORKMAN'S, WORKS]

Ge 2: 2 had finished the w he had been doing; H4856
Ge 2: 2 the seventh day he rested from all his w. H4856
Ge 2: 3 rested from all the w of creating that he H4856
Ge 2: 5 there was no one to w the ground, H6268
Ge 2:15 Garden of Eden to w it and take care of H6268
Ge 3:23 Garden of Eden to w the ground from H6268
Ge 4:12 When *you* w the ground, it will no longer H6268
Ge 29:15 of mine, *should you* w **for** me for nothing? H6268
Ge 29:18 "*I'll* w **for** you seven years in return for H6268
Ge 29:27 in return for another seven years of w." H6275
Ge 30:26 You know how much w I've done for you." H6275
Ex 1:14 with all kinds of w in the fields; H6275
Ex 5: 4 from their labor? Get back to your w!" H6026
Ex 5: 9 Make the w harder for the people so that H6275
Ex 5:11 but your w will not be reduced at all. H6275
Ex 5:13 "Complete the w *required of* you for each H5126
Ex 5:18 Now get *to* w. You will not be given any H6268
Ex 12:16 Do no w at all on these days, except to H4856
Ex 18:18 The w is too heavy for you; you cannot H1821
Ex 20: 9 Six days you shall labor and do all your w, H4856
Ex 20:10 On it you shall not do any w, neither you H4856
Ex 23:12 "Six days do your w, but on the seventh H5126
Ex 23:12 on the seventh day **do not** w, so that H8697
Ex 26:36 twisted linen—the w *of* an embroiderer. H5126
Ex 27:16 twisted linen—the w *of* an embroiderer H5126
Ex 28: 6 twisted linen—the w *of* skilled hands. H5126
Ex 28:15 making decisions—the w *of* skilled hands. H5126
Ex 28:39 The sash is to be the w *of* an embroiderer. H5126
Ex 30:25 a fragrant blend, the w *of* a perfumer. H5126
Ex 30:35 blend of incense, the w *of* a perfumer. H5126
Ex 31: 4 to make artistic designs for w in gold H6913
Ex 31: 5 set stones, to w *in* wood, and to H3098
Ex 31:14 those who do any w on that day must be H4856
Ex 31:15 For six days w is to be done, but the H4856
Ex 31:15 Whoever does any w on the Sabbath day H4856
Ex 32:16 The tablets were the w *of* God; the writing H5126
Ex 34:10 will see how awesome is the w that I, H5126
Ex 35: 2 For six days, w is to be done, but the H4856
Ex 35: 2 Whoever does any w on it is to be put to H4856
Ex 35:21 to the LORD for the w *on* the tent of H4856
Ex 35:24 wood for any part of the w brought it. H6275
Ex 35:29 offerings for all the w the LORD through H4856
Ex 35:32 to make artistic designs for w in gold H6913
Ex 35:33 to w *in* wood and to engage in all kinds H3098
Ex 35:35 with skill to do all kinds of w *as* engravers, H4856
Ex 36: 1 to carry out all the w *of* constructing the H4856
Ex 36: 1 the sanctuary *are to* **do** *the* w just as the H6913
Ex 36: 2 who was willing to come and do the w. H4856
Ex 36: 3 to carry out the w *of* constructing the H4856
Ex 36: 4 were doing all the w *on* the sanctuary left H4856
Ex 36: 5 doing the w the LORD commanded H4856
Ex 36: 7 was more than enough to do all the w. H4856
Ex 36:37 twisted linen—the w *of* an embroiderer; H5126
Ex 37:29 fragrant incense—the w *of* a perfumer. H5126
Ex 38:18 twisted linen—the w *of* an embroiderer. H5126
Ex 38:24 used for all the w *on* the sanctuary was 29 H4856
Ex 39: 3 fine linen—the w *of* skilled hands. H5126
Ex 39: 8 breastpiece—the w *of* a skilled craftsman. H5126
Ex 39:22 of blue cloth—the w *of* a weaver— H5126
Ex 39:27 tunics of fine linen—the w *of* a weaver— H5126
Ex 39:29 scarlet yarn—the w *of* an embroiderer—as H5126
Ex 39:32 So all the w *on* the tabernacle, the tent of H6275
Ex 39:42 had done all the w just as the LORD had H6275
Ex 39:43 Moses inspected the w and saw that they H4856
Ex 40:33 And so Moses finished the w. H4856
Lev 16:29 must deny yourselves and not do any w— H4856
Lev 23: 3 are six days when *you may* w, H6913+4856
Lev 23: 3 You are not to do any w; wherever you H4856
Lev 23: 7 assembly and do no **regular** w. H4856+6275
Lev 23: 8 assembly and do no **regular** w. H4856+6275
Lev 23:21 assembly and do no **regular** w. H4856+6275
Lev 23:25 Do no **regular** w, but present a food H4856+6275
Lev 23:28 Do not do any w on that day, because it is H4856
Lev 23:30 anyone who does any w on that day. H4856
Lev 23:31 You shall do no w at all. This is to be a H4856
Lev 23:35 sacred assembly; do no **regular** w. H4856+6275
Lev 23:36 special assembly; do no **regular** w. H4856+6275
Lev 25:39 *do* not **make** them w as slaves. H6268
Lev 25:40 *they are* to w for you until the Year of H6268
Nu 3: 7 meeting by doing the w *of* the tabernacle. H6275
Nu 3: 8 by doing the w *of* the tabernacle. H6275
Nu 4: 3 come to serve in the w at the tent of H4856
Nu 4: 4 "This is the w *of* the Kohathites at the tent H6275
Nu 4:19 to each man his w and what he is to H6275
Nu 4:23 to serve in the w at the tent of H6268+6275
Nu 4:24 clans in their carrying and their *other* w: H6268
Nu 4:27 whether carrying or **doing** other w, is to be H6275
Nu 4:30 to serve in the w *at* the tent of H6268+6275
Nu 4:33 clans as they w at the tent of meeting H6275
Nu 4:35 came to serve in the w at the tent of H6275
Nu 4:39 came to serve in the w at the tent of H6275
Nu 4:43 came to serve in the w at the tent of H6275
Nu 4:47 who came to do the w *of* serving and H6275
Nu 4:49 each was assigned his w and told what to H6275
Nu 7: 5 may be used in the w *at* the tent of H6275
Nu 7: 5 to the Levites as each man's w requires." H6275
Nu 7: 7 to the Gershonites, as their w required, H6275
Nu 7: 8 oxen to the Merarites, as their w required. H6275
Nu 8:11 they may be ready to do the w *of* the LORD. H6275
Nu 8:15 are to come to **do** *their* w at the tent of H6268
Nu 8:19 the w at the tent of meeting *on behalf of* H6275
Nu 8:22 came to do their w at the tent of meeting H6275
Nu 8:24 to take part in the w *at* the tent of H6275
Nu 8:25 their regular service and w no longer. H6268
Nu 8:26 they themselves must not do the w. H6275
Nu 16: 9 himself to do the w *at* the LORD's H6275
Nu 18: 4 of meeting—all the w *at* the tent—and no H6275
Nu 18: 6 the LORD to do the w *at* the tent of H6275
Nu 18:21 in return for the w they do while serving at H6275
Nu 18:23 who are to do the w *at* the tent of H6275
Nu 18:31 your wages for your w at the tent of H6275
Nu 28:18 assembly and do no **regular** w. H4856+6275
Nu 28:25 assembly and do no **regular** w. H4856+6275
Nu 28:26 assembly and do no **regular** w. H4856+6275
Nu 29: 1 assembly and do no **regular** w. H4856+6275
Nu 29: 7 You must deny yourselves and do no w. H4856
Nu 29:12 assembly and do no **regular** w. H4856+6275
Nu 29:35 assembly and do no **regular** w. H4856+6275
Dt 2: 7 blessed you in all the w *of* your hands. H5126
Dt 5:13 Six days you shall labor and do all your w, H4856
Dt 5:14 On it you shall not do any w, neither you H4856
Dt 14:29 you in all the w *of* your hands. H5126+6913
Dt 15:10 you in all your w and in everything you H5126
Dt 15:19 *Do* not **put** the firstborn of your cows **to** w H6268
Dt 16: 8 to the LORD your God and do no w. H4856
Dt 16:15 harvest and in all the w *of* your hands, H5126
Dt 20:11 to forced labor and *shall* w **for** you. H6268
Dt 24:19 may bless you in all the w *of* your hands. H5126
Dt 27:15 to the LORD, the w *of* skilled hands—and H5126
Dt 28:12 to bless all the w *of* your hands. H5126
Dt 30: 9 in all the w *of* your hands and in H5126
Dt 33:11 be pleased with the w *of* his hands. H7189
Jdg 13:12 the rule that governs the boy's life and w?" H5126
Jdg 19:16 came in from his w in the fields. H5126
Ru 2: 8 Stay here with the **women who** w *for* me. H5855
Ru 2:19 Where *did you* w? Blessed be the H6913
Ru 2:22 to go with the **women who** w *for* him H5855
2Sa 12:31 and *he* **made** them w at brickmaking. H6268
1Ki 5: 6 My men *will* w with yours, and I will pay H2118
1Ki 7:14 knowledge to do all kinds of bronze w. H4856
1Ki 7:14 did all the w *assigned to* him. H4856
1Ki 7:22 And so the w *on* the pillars was H4856
1Ki 7:29 bulls were wreaths of hammered w. H5126
1Ki 7:40 finished all the w he had undertaken for H4856
1Ki 7:49 the gold **floral** w and lamps and tongs H7258
1Ki 7:51 When all the w King Solomon had done H4856
1Ki 9:23 officials supervising those who did the w. H4856
1Ki 11:28 saw how well the young man did his w, H4856
2Ki 12:11 to supervise the w on the temple. H4856
2Ki 22: 5 to supervise the w on the temple. H4856
2Ki 25:12 of the land to w *the* **vineyards** and fields. H4144
1Ch 9:33 were responsible for the w day and night. H4856
1Ch 22:15 as well as those skilled in every kind of w H4856
1Ch 22:16 Now begin *the* w, and the LORD be with H6913
1Ch 23: 4 be in charge of the w *of* the temple of the H4856
1Ch 26: 8 men with the strength to do the w— H6275
1Ch 26:30 Jordan for all the w *of* the LORD and for H4856
1Ch 28:10 the sanctuary. Be strong and **do** *the* w." H6913
1Ch 28:13 for all the w *of* serving in the temple H4856
1Ch 28:20 "Be strong and courageous, and **do** *the* w. H6913
1Ch 28:20 you until all the w *for* the service of the H4856
1Ch 28:21 ready for all the w *on* the temple of God, H6275
1Ch 28:21 in any craft will help you in all the w. H4856
1Ch 29: 2 of my God—gold for the **gold** *w*, silver for AIT
1Ch 29: 5 the **gold** *w* and the silver work, and for all AIT
1Ch 29: 5 the gold work and the **silver** *w*, and for all AIT
1Ch 29: 5 for all the w to be done by the H4856
1Ch 29: 6 in charge of the king's w gave willingly. H4856
1Ch 29: 7 gave toward the w *on* the temple of God H6275
2Ch 2: 7 a man skilled to w in gold and silver H6913
2Ch 2: 7 to w in Judah and Jerusalem with my skilled NDT
2Ch 2: 8 My servants will w with yours NDT
2Ch 2:14 He is trained to w in gold and silver H6913
2Ch 2:14 He will w with your skilled workers and NDT
2Ch 4:11 Huram finished the w he had undertaken H4856
2Ch 4:21 the gold **floral** w and lamps and tongs H7258
2Ch 5: 1 When all the w Solomon had done for H4856
2Ch 8: 9 not make slaves of the Israelites for his w; H4856
2Ch 8:16 All Solomon's w was carried out, from the H4856
2Ch 15: 7 not give up, for your w will be rewarded." H7190
2Ch 16: 5 building Ramah and abandoned his w. H4856
2Ch 24:12 who carried out the w required for the H4856
2Ch 24:13 The men in charge of the w were diligent H4856
2Ch 27: 3 the LORD and **did** extensive w on the wall H1215
2Ch 29:12 Then these Levites **set to** w: from the H7756
2Ch 32:19 of the world—the w *of* human hands. H5126
2Ch 34:10 to supervise the w on the LORD's temple. H4856
Ezr 2:69 treasury for this w 61,000 darics of gold H4856
Ezr 3: 8 the captivity to Jerusalem) began the w. NDT
Ezr 4: 5 They bribed officials to w against them and NDT
Ezr 4:21 issue an order to these men to **stop** w, A10098
Ezr 4:24 Thus the w on the house of God in A10525
Ezr 5: 2 of Jozadak **set to** w to A10624+10221+10742
Ezr 5: 8 The w is being carried on with diligence A10525
Ezr 6: 7 interfere with the w *on* this temple of A10525
Ezr 6: 8 Trans-Euphrates, so that the w will not stop. NDT
Ezr 6:22 them in the w *on* the house of God, H4856
Ne 2:16 any others who would be doing the w. H4856
Ne 2:18 So they began this **good** w. H3208
Ne 3: 1 fellow priests **went to** w and rebuilt the H7756
Ne 3: 5 shoulders to the w *under* their supervisors. H6275
Ne 4:11 will kill them and put an end to the w." H4856
Ne 4:15 returned to the wall, each to our own w. H4856
Ne 4:16 half of my men did the w, while the other H4856
Ne 4:17 materials did their w with one hand and H4856
Ne 4:19 "The w is extensive and spread out H4856
Ne 4:21 So we continued the w with half the men H4856
Ne 5:16 I devoted myself to the w *on* this wall. H4856
Ne 5:16 my men were assembled there for the w; H4856
Ne 6: 3 Why should the w stop while I leave it H4856
Ne 6: 9 "Their hands will get too weak for the w H4856
Ne 6:16 realized that this w had been done with H4856
Ne 7:70 of the families contributed to the w. H4856
Ne 7:71 the treasury for the w 20,000 darics of H4856
Ne 10:37 the tithes in all the towns where we w. H6275
Ne 11:12 who carried on w for the temple—822 H4856
Ne 11:16 of the outside w of the house of God; H4856
Job 1:10 You have blessed the w *of* his hands, so H5126
Job 10: 3 to spurn the w *of* your hands, while H3330
Job 23: 9 When he *is* **at** w in the north, I do not see H6913
Job 34:19 for they are all the w *of* his hands? H5126
Job 36:24 Remember to extol his w, which people H7189

Job 37: 7 that everyone he has made may know his w, NDT
Job 39:11 Will you leave your **heavy** w to it? H3330
Ps 8: 3 your heavens, the w *of* your fingers, the H5126
Ps 9:16 are ensnared by the w *of* their hands. H7189
Ps 19: 1 the skies proclaim the w *of* his hands. H5126
Ps 28: 4 them for their deeds and for their evil w; H5095
Ps 55:11 Destructive forces are at w in the city; NDT
Ps 90:17 establish the w *of* our hands for us H5126
Ps 90:17 us—yes, establish the w *of* our hands. H5126
Ps 102:25 the heavens are the w *of* your hands. H5126
Ps 104:13 the land is satisfied by the fruit of his w. H5126
Ps 104:23 Then people go out to their w, to their H7189
Pr 12:11 *Those who* w their land will have H6268
Pr 12:14 the w *of* their hands brings them H1691
Pr 14:23 All **hard** w brings a profit, but mere talk H6776
Pr 18: 9 who is slack in his w is brother to one who H4856
Pr 21:25 because his hands refuse to w. H6913
Pr 22:29 Do you see someone skilled in their w H4856
Pr 24:27 Put your outdoor w in order and get your H4856
Pr 28:19 *Those who* w their land will have H6268
Pr 31:17 *She* **sets about** her w vigorously H5516+2520
Ecc 2:17 because the w that is done under the sun H5126
Ecc 2:23 All their days their w is grief and pain H6721
Ecc 3:22 better for a person than to enjoy their w, H5126
Ecc 5: 6 you say and destroy the w *of* your hands? H5126
Ecc 11: 5 so you cannot understand the w *of* God H5126
SS 7: 1 are like jewels, the w *of* an artist's hands. H5126
Isa 1:31 will become tinder and his w a spark; H7189
Isa 2: 8 they bow down to the w *of* their hands, to H5126
Isa 5:12 no respect for the w *of* his hands. H5126
Isa 5:19 let him hasten his w so we may see it. H5126
Isa 10:12 has finished all his w against Mount Zion H5126
Isa 17: 8 to the altars, the w *of* their hands, and H5126
Isa 19: 9 *Those who* w *with* combed flax will H6268
Isa 28:21 of Gibeon—to do his w, his strange work, H5126
Isa 28:21 his strange w, and perform his task H5126
Isa 29:15 who do their w in darkness and think H5126
Isa 29:23 their children, the w *of* my hands, they H5126
Isa 30:24 oxen and donkeys *that* w the soil will eat H6268
Isa 45: 9 Does your w say, 'The potter has no H7189
Isa 45:11 give me orders about the w *of* my hands? H7189
Isa 54:16 flame and forges a weapon fit for its w. H5126
Isa 60:21 I have planted, the w *of* my hands, for the H5126
Isa 61: 5 foreigners will w your **fields** and vineyards. H438
Isa 64: 8 the potter; we are all the w *of* your hand. H5126
Isa 65:22 ones will long enjoy the w *of* their hands. H5126
Jer 17:22 your houses or do any w on the Sabbath, H4856
Jer 17:24 day holy by not doing any w on it, H4856
Jer 22:13 making his own people w for nothing, not H6268
Jer 25:14 to their deeds and the w *of* their hands." H5126
Jer 31:16 from tears, for your w will be rewarded," H7190
Jer 48:10 anyone who is lax in doing the LORD's w! H4856
Jer 50:25 LORD Almighty has w to do in the land of H4856
Jer 52:16 of the land to w the **vineyards** and fields. H4144
La 4: 2 as pots of clay, the w *of* a potter's hands! H5126
Eze 27:16 purple fabric, **embroidered** w, fine linen H8391
Eze 27:24 **embroidered** w and multicolored rugs H8391
Eze 44:14 temple for all the w that is to be done in H6275
Hos 13: 2 images, all of them the w *of* craftsmen. H5126
Jnh 1: 8 What *kind of* w do you do? Where H4856
Mic 5:13 longer bow down to the w *of* your hands. H5126
Na 3:14 **W** the clay, tread the mortar, repair the H995
Hag 1:14 came and began to w on the house of the H4856
Hag 2: 4 of the land,' declares the LORD, 'and w. H6913
Hag 2:17 I struck all the w *of* your hands with blight H5126
Mt 14: 2 is why miraculous powers *are* **at** w in him." *G1919*
Mt 20: 4 'You also go and w in my vineyard, and I NDT
Mt 20: 7 to them, 'You also go and w in my vineyard. NDT
Mt 20:12 the burden of the w and the heat of the day NDT
Mt 20:13 Didn't you agree to w for a denarius? NDT
Mt 21:28 go and w today in the vineyard. *G2237*
Mt 25:16 once and **put** his money **to** w and gained *G2237*
Mk 6:14 is why miraculous powers *are* **at** w in him." *G1919*
Lk 10:40 sister has left me *to* **do** *the* w by myself? *G1354*
Lk 13:14 to the people, "There are six days for w. *G2237*
Lk 19:13 '**Put** this money **to** w,' he said, 'until I *G4549*
Jn 4:34 of him who sent me and to finish his w. *G2240*
Jn 4:38 Others *have* **done the hard** w, and you *G3159*
Jn 5:17 "My Father *is always* **at** *his* w to this very *G2237*
Jn 6:27 *Do* not w for food that spoils, but for food *G2237*
Jn 6:29 Jesus answered, "The w of God is this: to *G2240*
Jn 9: 4 Night is coming, when no one can w. *G2237*
Jn 10:33 "We are not stoning you for any good w," *G2819*
Jn 14:10 living in me, who is doing his w. *G2240*
Jn 17: 4 by finishing the w you gave me to do. *G2240*
Ac 4:33 grace *was* so powerfully **at** w in them *G1639*
Ac 13: 2 Saul for the w to which I have called *G2240*
Ac 13:25 As John was completing his w, he said *G1536*
Ac 14:26 grace of God for the w they had now *G2240*
Ac 15:38 had not continued with them in the w. *G2240*
Ac 20:35 by this kind of **hard** w we must help the *G3159*
Ro 4: 5 *to the one who does* not w but trusts God *G2237*
Ro 7: 5 aroused by the law *were* **at** w in us, *G1919*
Ro 7:21 So I find this law at w: Although I want to NDT
Ro 7:23 I see another law at w in me, waging NDT
Ro 7:23 prisoner of the law of sin **at** w within me. *G1639*
Ro 14:20 Do not destroy the w of God for the sake of *G2240*
Ro 15:23 no more place for me to w in these regions, NDT
Ro 16:12 those *women who* w **hard** in the Lord. *G3159*
1Co 3:13 their w will be shown for what it is *G2240*
1Co 3:13 will test the quality of each person's w. *G2240*
1Co 4:12 *We* w **hard** with our own hands *G3159+2237*
1Co 9: 1 Are you not the **result of** my w in the Lord? *G2240*
1Co 9: 6 who lack the right *to* not w **for a living**? *G2237*
1Co 12: 6 in everyone it is the same God **at** w. *G1919*
1Co 12:11 All these *are the* w of one and the same *G1919*
1Co 12:29 Are all teachers? Do all w **miracles**? *G1539*
1Co 15:58 give yourselves fully to the w of the Lord, *G2240*
1Co 16: 9 a great door *for* **effective** w has opened to *G1921*
1Co 16:10 he is carrying on the w of the Lord, just *G2240*
1Co 16:16 everyone who **joins in the** w and labors at *G5300*
2Co 1:24 but *we* w **with** you for your joy *G5301+1639*
2Co 4:12 So then, death *is* **at** w in us, but life is at *G1919*
2Co 4:12 death is at work in us, but life is at w in you. NDT
2Co 6: 5 riots; in **hard** w, sleepless nights and *G3160*
2Co 8:11 Now finish the w, so that your eager *G4472*
2Co 9: 8 you will abound in every good w. *G2240*
2Co 10:15 limits by boasting *of* w done by others. *G3160*
2Co 10:16 boast about w **already done** in someone *G2289*
Gal 2: 8 who *was* **at** w in Peter as an apostle to *G1919*
Gal 2: 8 *was* also **at** w in me as an apostle to the *G1919*
Gal 3: 5 you his Spirit and w miracles among you *G1919*
Eph 2: 2 the spirit who *is* now **at** w in those who *G1919*
Eph 3:20 to his power that *is* **at** w within us, *G1919*
Eph 4:16 as each part **does** its w. *G1918+1877+3586*
Eph 4:28 no longer, but *must* w, doing something *G3159*
Php 1: 6 he who began a good w in you will carry *G2240*
Php 2:12 *continue to* w **out** your salvation with fear *G2981*
Php 2:22 served with me in the w **of the gospel**. *G2295*
Php 2:30 because he almost died for the w of Christ *G2240*
Col 1:10 bearing fruit in every good w, growing in *G2240*
Col 3:23 w *at* it with all your heart *G2237*
1Th 1: 3 God and Father your w produced by faith, *G2240*
1Th 2:13 which *is* indeed **at** w in you who believe. *G1919*
1Th 4:11 your own business and w with your hands, *G2237*
1Th 5:12 those *who* w **hard** among you, *G3159*
1Th 5:13 highest regard in love because of their w. *G2240*
2Th 2: 7 power of lawlessness *is* already **at** w; *G1919*
2Th 2:13 saved through the **sanctifying** w of the Spirit *G40*
2Th 3:10 one who is unwilling *to* w shall not eat." *G2237*
1Ti 1: 4 rather than advancing God's w— *G3873*
1Ti 5:17 especially those *whose* w is preaching *G3159*
2Ti 2:21 Master and prepared to do any good w. *G2240*
2Ti 3:17 be thoroughly equipped for every good w. *G2240*
2Ti 4: 5 hardship, do the w of an evangelist *G2240*
Heb 1:10 the heavens are the w of your hands. *G2240*
Heb 6:10 will not forget your w and the love you *G2240*
Heb 13:17 Do this so that *their* w *will be* a joy, not a *G4472*
Heb 13:21 and *may he* w in us what is pleasing to *G4472*
Jas 1: 4 finish its w so that you may be *G2240*
1Pe 1: 2 through the **sanctifying** w of the Spirit, to *G40*
1Pe 1:17 who judges each person's w impartially, *G2240*
1Jn 3: 8 appeared was to destroy the devil's w. *G2240*
2Jn 11 welcomes them shares in their wicked w. *G2240*
3Jn 8 so that *we may* w **together** for the *G5301+1181*
Rev 2: 2 your **hard** w and your perseverance. *G3160*
Rev 9:20 still did not repent of the w of their hands; *G2240*

WORKED (38) [WORK]

Ge 4: 2 Now Abel kept flocks, and Cain w the soil. H6268
Ge 29:30 And *he* w for Laban another seven years. H6268
Ge 30:29 "You know how *I have* w **for** you and how H6268
Ge 31: 6 You know that *I've* w **for** your father with H6268
Ge 31:41 *I* w **for** you fourteen years for your two H6268
Ex 1:13 w them ruthlessly. H6268
Ex 1:14 labor the Egyptians w them ruthlessly. H6268
Ex 39: 3 cut strands to *be* w into the blue, H6913
Dt 21: 3 a heifer that *has* never **been** w and has H6268
Ru 2:19 name of the man *I* w with today is Boaz," H6913
Ru 3: 2 with whose women *you have* w, is a H2118S
2Ki 12:11 it they paid those *who* w on the temple of H6913
1Ch 4:23 they stayed there and w for the king. H4856
2Ch 3:14 fine linen, with cherubim w into it. H6590
2Ch 25:20 God so w that he might deliver them H4946
2Ch 31:21 he sought his God and w wholeheartedly. H6913
2Ch 32: 5 Then *he* w **hard** repairing all the broken H2616
Ne 3:25 Palal son of Uzai w opposite the angle NDT
Ne 4: 6 the people w with all their heart. H6913
Ne 4:18 wore his sword at his side as *he* w. H1215
Est 10: 3 because *he* w **for** the good of his people H2011
Ps 98: 1 his holy arm *have* w **salvation** for him. H3828
Eze 23:29 take away everything you have w *for*. H3330
Joel 2:26 your God, who *has* w wonders for you H6913
Mt 13:33 of flour until *it* w all **through the dough**." *G2435*
Mt 20:12 who were hired last w only one hour, *G4472*
Mk 16:20 the Lord w **with** them and confirmed *G5300*
Lk 5: 5 *we've* w **hard** all night and haven't caught *G3159*
Lk 13:21 of flour until *it* w all **through the dough**." *G2435*
Jn 4:38 I sent you to reap what you *have* not w **for** *G3159*
Ac 18: 3 as they were, he stayed and w with them. *G2237*
Ro 16: 6 Greet Mary, who w very **hard** for you. *G3159*
Ro 16:12 woman who *has* w very **hard** in the Lord. *G3159*
1Co 15:10 *I* w harder than all of them—yet not I *G3159*
2Co 11:23 I have w much harder, been in prison *G3160*
1Th 2: 9 *we* w night and day in order not to be a *G2237*
2Th 3: 8 On the contrary, *we* w night and day *G2237*
2Jn 8 that you do not lose what *we have* w **for**, *G2237*

WORKER (17) [WORK]

Ex 12:45 resident or a **hired** w may not eat it. H8502
Ex 26: 1 cherubim woven into them by a **skilled** w. H3110
Ex 26:31 with cherubim woven into it by a **skilled** w. H3110
Ex 36:35 with cherubim woven into it by a **skilled** w. H3110
Lev 19:13 back the wages of a **hired** w overnight. H8502
Lev 22:10 the guest of a priest or his **hired** w eat it. H8502
Lev 25: 6 the **hired** w and temporary resident H8502
Lev 25:50 the rate paid to a **hired** w for that number H8502
Dt 24:14 advantage of a **hired** w who is poor and H8502
Dt 24:14 whether that w is a fellow Israelite or a NDT
Isa 40:20 look for a skilled w to set up an idol that H3093
Mt 10:10 a staff, for the w is worth his keep. *G2239*
Lk 10: 7 give you, for the w deserves his wages. *G2239*
1Ti 5:18 and "The w deserves his wages. *G2239*
2Ti 2:15 a w who does not need to be ashamed *G2239*
Phm 1 Philemon our dear friend and **fellow** w— *G5301*
Rev 18:22 No w of any trade will ever be found in *G5493*

WORKERS (49) [WORK]

Ex 28: 3 Tell all the **skilled** w to whom I H2682+4213
Ex 31: 6 ability to all the **skilled** w to make H2682+4213
Ex 35:35 all of them **skilled** w and designers. H6913+4856
Ex 36: 4 So all the **skilled** w who were doing all the H2682
Ex 36: 8 skilled among the w made the H6913+4856
Lev 25:40 are to be treated as **hired** w or temporary H8502
Lev 25:53 to be treated as w **hired** *from* year to year; H8502
Ru 2:21 'Stay with my w until they finish H5853
1Ki 5:16 and directed the w. H6913+928+2021+4856
1Ki 5:18 Hiram and w **from Byblos** cut and H1490
2Ki 12:14 it was paid to the w, who used it to H6913+4856
2Ki 12:15 they gave the money to pay the w, H6913+4856
2Ki 22: 5 men pay the w who repair the H6913+4856
2Ki 22: 9 it to the w and supervisors at H6913+4856
2Ki 24:14 all the **skilled** w and artisans—a H3093
2Ki 24:16 a thousand **skilled** w and artisans. H3093
1Ch 4:14 this because its people were **skilled** w. H3093
1Ch 4:21 of the linen w at Beth Ashbea, H1074+6275
1Ch 22:15 You have many w: stonecutters H6913+4856
1Ch 23:24 the w twenty years old or more who H6913+4856
1Ch 27:26 charge of the w who farmed H6913+4856+8441
2Ch 2: 7 Judah and Jerusalem with my **skilled** w, H2682
2Ch 2:14 work with your **skilled** w and with those of H2682
2Ch 24:12 also w *in* iron and bronze to repair H3093
2Ch 34:10 These men paid the w who repaired and H6913
2Ch 34:12 The w labored faithfully. Over them H408+6913
2Ch 34:13 all the w from job to job. H6913+4856
2Ch 34:17 it to the supervisors and w. H6913+4856
Ezr 7:24 servants or other w *at* this house of God. A10586
Ne 4:22 us as guards by night and as w by day." H4856
Ecc 3: 9 What do w gain from their toil? H6913
Isa 19:10 The w **in cloth** will be dejected, and all H9271
Isa 58: 3 do as you please and exploit all your w. H6774
Jer 10: 9 in blue and purple—all made by **skilled** *w*. AIT
Jer 24: 1 the **skilled** w and the artisans of Judah H3093
Jer 29: 2 the **skilled** w and the artisans had gone H3093
Eze 48:18 will supply food for the w *of* the city. H6268
Eze 48:19 The w *from* the city who farm it will come H6268
Mt 9:37 "The harvest is plentiful but the w are few. *G2239*
Mt 9:38 to send out w into his harvest field." *G2239*
Mt 20: 1 in the morning to hire w for his vineyard. *G2239*
Mt 20: 8 'Call the w and pay them their wages *G2239*
Mt 20: 9 "**The** w **who were hired** about five in the *G3836S*
Lk 10: 2 harvest is plentiful, but the w are few. *G2239*
Lk 10: 2 to send out w into his harvest field. *G2239*
Ac 19:25 along with the w in related trades, and *G2239*
2Co 11:13 apostles, deceitful w, masquerading as *G2239*
Phm 24 Demas and Luke, my **fellow** w. *G5301*
Jas 5: 4 failed to pay the w who mowed your *G2239*

WORKING (20) [WORK]

Ex 5: 5 you are stopping them from w. H6026
Ex 5: 9 people so that *they keep* w and pay no H6913
Ex 15:11 holiness, awesome in glory, w wonders? H6913
Ru 2: 3 she was w in a field belonging to Boaz NDT
Ru 2:19 the one at whose place *she had been* w. H6913
2Ch 2:18 foremen over them to **keep** the people w. H6268
2Ch 26:10 people w his **fields and vineyards** in the H4144
Ezr 3: 9 in supervising *those* w *on* the house of H6913
Ne 10:31 year we will forgo w the land and will NDT
Ecc 9:10 there is neither w nor planning nor H5126
Isa 28:24 he keep on breaking up and w the soil? H8440
Jer 18: 3 and I saw him w at the wheel. H6913+4856
Eze 46: 1 facing east is to be shut on the six w days, H5126
Jn 5:17 his work to this very day, and I too *am* w." *G2237*
1Co 12: 6 There are different kinds *of* w, but in all of *G1920*
Eph 3: 7 given me through the w of his power. *G1918*
Col 2:12 him through your faith *in* the w of God, *G1918*
Col 3:23 with all your heart, as w for the Lord, not NDT
Col 4:13 him that he is w hard for you and for *G4506*
Jas 2:22 his faith and his actions *were* w **together**, *G5300*

WORKMAN'S (1) [WORK, MAN]

Jdg 5:26 her right hand for the w hammer. H6664

WORKS (87) [WORK]

Dt 3:24 can do the deeds and **mighty** w you do? H1476
Dt 20:20 use them to build **siege** w until the city at H5189
Dt 32: 4 He is the Rock, his w are perfect, and all H7189
2Ki 25: 1 the city and built **siege** w all around it. H1911
Job 26:14 these are but the outer fringe of his w; H2006
Job 40:19 It ranks first among the w *of* God, yet its H2006
Ps 8: 6 them rulers over the w *of* your hands; H5126
Ps 64: 9 will proclaim the w *of* God and ponder H7189
Ps 77:12 consider all your w and meditate on all H7189
Ps 92: 5 How great are your w, LORD, how profound H5126
Ps 103: 6 The LORD w righteousness and justice for H6913
Ps 103:22 all his w everywhere in his dominion. H5126
Ps 104:24 How many are your w, LORD! In wisdom H5126

Ps 104:31 may the LORD rejoice in his w— H5126
Ps 107:22 tell of his w with songs of joy. H5126
Ps 107:24 They saw the w *of* the LORD, his wonderful H5126
Ps 111: 2 Great are the w *of* the LORD; they are H5126
Ps 111: 6 has shown his people the power of his w, H5126
Ps 111: 7 The w *of* his hands are faithful and just H5126
Ps 138: 8 do not abandon the w *of* your hands. H5126
Ps 139:14 your w are wonderful, I know H5126
Ps 143: 5 meditate on all your w and consider what H7189
Ps 145: 4 generation commends your w to another; H5126
Ps 145: 5 I will meditate on your **wonderful** *w*. AIT
Ps 145: 6 tell of the power of your **awesome** w— H3707
Ps 145:10 All your w praise you, LORD; your faithful H5126
Pr 8:22 LORD brought me forth as the first of his w, H2006
Pr 16: 4 The LORD w **out** everything to its proper H7188
Pr 16:26 The appetite of laborers w for them; their H6661
Pr 26:28 and a flattering mouth w ruin. H6913
Pr 31:13 wool and flax and w with eager hands. H6913
Pr 31:31 let her w bring her praise at the city H5126
Ecc 9:14 it and built huge **siege** w against it. H5189
Isa 29: 3 set up my **siege** w against you. H5193
Isa 41:24 nothing and your w are utterly worthless H7189
Isa 44:12 takes a tool and w with it in the coals; H7188
Isa 57:12 expose your righteousness and your w, H5126
Jer 11:15 *as* she, with many others, w **out** her H6913
Jer 52: 4 the city and built **siege** w all around it. H1911
Eze 4: 2 Erect **siege** w against it, build a ramp up H1911
Eze 17:17 are built and **siege** w erected to destroy H1911
Eze 21:22 to build a ramp and to erect **siege** w. H1911
Eze 26: 8 he will set up **siege** w against you, build H1911
Jn 5:20 will show him even greater w than these, *G2240*
Jn 5:36 For the w that the Father has given me to *G2240*
Jn 5:36 me to finish—the very w that I am doing *G2240*
Jn 6:28 must we do to do the w God requires?" *G2240*
Jn 7: 3 disciples there may see the w you do. *G2240*
Jn 7: 7 me because I testify that its w are evil. *G2240*
Jn 8:41 You are doing the w of your own father." *G2240*
Jn 9: 3 happened so that the w of God might be *G2240*
Jn 9: 4 we must do the w of him who sent me. *G2240*
Jn 10:25 The w I do in my Father's name testify *G2240*
Jn 10:32 shown you many good w from the Father. *G2240*
Jn 10:37 me unless I do the w of my Father. *G2240*
Jn 10:38 believe the w, that you may know *G2240*
Jn 14:11 on the evidence of the w themselves. *G2240*
Jn 14:12 in me will do the w I have been doing, *G2240*
Jn 15:24 done among them the w no one else did, *G2240*
Ro 3:20 in God's sight by the w of the law; *G2240*
Ro 3:27 The law that *requires* w? No, *G2240*
Ro 3:28 by faith apart from the w of the law. *G2240*
Ro 4: 2 Abraham was justified by w, he had *G2240*
Ro 4: 4 Now *to* the *one who* w, wages are not *G2237*
Ro 4: 6 God credits righteousness apart from w: *G2240*
Ro 8:28 in all things God w for the good of those *G5300*
Ro 9:12 not by w but by him who calls—she was *G2240*
Ro 9:32 it not by faith but as if it were by w. *G2240*
Ro 11: 6 then it cannot be based on w; if it were, *G2240*
Ro 16:23 who is the city's **director of public** w, and *G3874*
Gal 2:16 person is not justified by the w of the law, *G2240*
Gal 2:16 faith in Christ and not by the w of the law, *G2240*
Gal 2:16 because by the w of the law no one will *G2240*
Gal 3: 2 you receive the Spirit by the w of the law, *G2240*
Gal 3: 5 miracles among you by the w of the law, *G2240*
Gal 3:10 all who rely on the w of the law are under *G2240*
Gal 5: 9 "A little yeast w **through** the whole batch *G2435*
Eph 1:11 the plan of him *who* w **out** everything in *G1919*
Eph 2: 9 not by w, so that no one can boast. *G2240*
Eph 2:10 created in Christ Jesus to do good w *G2240*
Eph 4:12 to equip his people for w of service, so *G2240*
Php 2:13 it is God who w **in** you to will and to act *G1919*
Col 1:29 the energy Christ so powerfully w **in** me. *G1919*
2Th 2: 9 will be in accordance with *how* Satan w. *G1918*
Heb 4: 3 And yet his w have been finished since *G2240*
Heb 4: 4 the seventh day God rested from all his w." *G2240*
Heb 4:10 enters God's rest also rests from their w, *G2240*

WORLD (259) [WORLD'S, WORLDLY]

Ge 11: 1 Now the whole w had one language and a H824
Ge 11: 9 confused the language of the whole w. H824
Ge 41:57 And all the w came to Egypt to buy grain H824
Ex 34:10 before done in any nation in all the w. H824
1Sa 2: 8 are the LORD's; on them he has set the w. H9315
1Sa 17:46 the whole w will know that there is a H824
1Ki 4:34 sent by all the kings of the w, who had H824
1Ki 8:53 all the nations of the w to be your own H824
1Ki 10:24 The whole w sought audience with H824
2Ki 5:15 is no God in all the w except in Israel. H824
1Ch 16:30 The w is firmly established; it cannot be H9315
2Ch 32:19 the gods of the other peoples of the w— H824
Job 18:18 of darkness and is banished from the w. H9315
Job 34:13 Who put him in charge of the whole w? H9315
Ps 9: 8 He rules the w in righteousness and H9315
Ps 17:14 from those of this w whose reward is in H2698
Ps 19: 4 their words to the ends of the w. H9315
Ps 24: 1 everything in it, the w, and all who live in H9315
Ps 33: 8 let all the people of the w revere him. H9315
Ps 49: 1 you peoples; listen, all who live in this w, H2698
Ps 50:12 not tell you, for the w is mine, and all that H9315
Ps 77:18 your lightning lit up the w; the earth H9315
Ps 89:11 you founded the w and all that is in it. H9315
Ps 90: 2 brought forth the **whole** w, H824+2256+9315
Ps 93: 1 indeed, the w is established, firm and H9315
Ps 96:10 The w is firmly established, it cannot be H9315
Ps 96:13 He will judge the w in righteousness and H9315
Ps 97: 4 His lightning lights up the w; the earth H9315
Ps 98: 7 everything in it, the w, and all who live in H9315
Ps 98: 9 He will judge the w in righteousness and H9315
Pr 8:23 very beginning, when the w came to be. H824
Pr 8:26 before he made the w or its fields or any of H824
Pr 8:31 in his **whole** w and delighting H9315+824
Isa 12: 5 let this be known to all the w. H824
Isa 13:11 I will punish the w for its evil, the wicked H9315
Isa 14: 9 all those who were leaders in the w; it H824
Isa 14:17 the man who made the w a wilderness H9315
Isa 14:26 is the plan determined for the whole w; H824
Isa 18: 3 All you people of the w, you who live on H9315
Isa 24: 4 withers, the w languishes and withers H9315
Isa 26: 9 the people of the w learn righteousness. H9315
Isa 26:18 the people of the w have not come to life H9315
Isa 27: 6 blossom and fill all the w with fruit. H9315
Isa 34: 1 all that is in it, the w, and all that comes H9315
Isa 38:11 be with those who now dwell in **this** w. H2698
Isa 40:23 reduces the rulers of this w to nothing. H824
Jer 10:12 he founded the w by his wisdom and H9315
Jer 51:15 he founded the w by his wisdom and H9315
La 4:12 did any of the peoples of the w, that H9315
Eze 20:32 like the peoples of the w, who serve wood H824
Na 1: 5 his presence, the w and all who live in it. H9315
Zep 3: 8 The whole w will be consumed by the fire H824
Zec 1:11 found the whole w at rest and in H824
Zec 6: 5 in the presence of the Lord of the whole w. H824
Mt 4: 8 all the kingdoms *of* the w and their *G3180*
Mt 5:14 "You are the light *of* the w. A town built *G3180*
Mt 13:35 things hidden since the creation *of* the w." *G3180*
Mt 13:38 The field is the w, and the good seed *G3180*
Mt 16:26 it be for someone to gain the whole w, *G3180*
Mt 18: 7 Woe *to* the w because of the things that *G3180*
Mt 24:14 in the whole w as a testimony to all *G3876*
Mt 24:21 from the beginning *of* the w until now— *G3180*
Mt 25:34 you since the creation *of* the w. *G3180*
Mt 26:13 this gospel is preached throughout the w, *G3180*
Mk 8:36 is it for someone to gain the whole w, *G3180*
Mk 9: 3 than anyone in the w could bleach them. *G1178*
Mk 13:19 when God created the w, until now— *G3232*
Mk 14: 9 the gospel is preached throughout the w, *G3180*
Mk 16:15 "Go into all the w and preach the gospel *G3180*
Lk 2: 1 should be taken *of* the entire **Roman** w. *G3876*
Lk 4: 5 in an instant all the kingdoms **of the** w. *G3876*
Lk 9:25 is it for someone to gain the whole w, *G3180*
Lk 11:50 been shed since the beginning *of* the w, *G3180*
Lk 12:30 For the pagan w runs after all such things *G3180*
Lk 16: 8 For the people *of* this w are more shrewd in *G172*
Lk 21:26 apprehensive of what is coming on the w *G3876*
Jn 1: 9 light to everyone was coming into the w. *G3180*
Jn 1:10 He was in the w, and though the world *G3180*
Jn 1:10 though the w was made through him *G3180*
Jn 1:10 through him, the w did not recognize him. *G3180*
Jn 1:29 who takes away the sin *of* the w! *G3180*
Jn 3:16 God so loved the w that he gave his one *G3180*
Jn 3:17 his Son into the w to condemn the world, *G3180*
Jn 3:17 his Son into the world to condemn the w, *G3180*
Jn 3:17 the world, but to save the w through him. *G3180*
Jn 3:19 Light has come into the w, but people *G3180*
Jn 4:42 that this man really is the Savior *of* the w." *G3180*
Jn 6:14 is the Prophet who is to come into the w." *G3180*
Jn 6:33 down from heaven and gives life *to* the w." *G3180*
Jn 6:51 which I will give for the life *of* the w." *G3180*
Jn 7: 4 these things, show yourself *to* the w." *G3180*
Jn 7: 7 The w cannot hate you, but it hates me *G3180*
Jn 8:12 people, he said, "I am the light *of* the w. *G3180*
Jn 8:23 You are of this w; I am not of this *G3180*
Jn 8:23 You are of this world; I am not of this w. *G3180*
Jn 8:26 what I have heard from him I tell the w." *G3180*
Jn 9: 5 While I am in the w, I am the light of the *G3180*
Jn 9: 5 I am in the world, I am the light *of* the w." *G3180*
Jn 9:39 "For judgment I have come into this w, so *G3180*
Jn 10:36 apart as his very own and sent into the w? *G3180*
Jn 11:27 Son of God, who is to come into the w." *G3180*
Jn 12:19 Look how the *whole* w has gone after him!" *G3180*
Jn 12:25 their life in this w will keep it for eternal *G3180*
Jn 12:31 Now is the time for judgment *on* this w *G3180*
Jn 12:31 now the prince *of* this w will be driven out. *G3180*
Jn 12:46 I have come into the w as a light, so that *G3180*
Jn 12:47 For I did not come to judge the w, but to *G3180*
Jn 12:47 to judge the world, but to save the w. *G3180*
Jn 13: 1 him to leave this w and go to the Father. *G3180*
Jn 13: 1 Having loved his own who were in the w *G3180*
Jn 14:17 The w cannot accept him, because it *G3180*
Jn 14:19 the w will not see me anymore *G3180*
Jn 14:22 to show yourself to us and not *to* the w?" *G3180*
Jn 14:27 I do not give to you as the w gives. Do not *G3180*
Jn 14:30 for the prince *of* this w is coming. *G3180*
Jn 14:31 he comes so that the w may learn that I *G3180*
Jn 15:18 "If the w hates you, keep in mind that it *G3180*
Jn 15:19 If you belonged to the w, it would love you *G3180*
Jn 15:19 you do not belong to the w, but I have *G3180*
Jn 15:19 but I have chosen you out of the w. *G3180*
Jn 15:19 That is why the w hates you. *G3180*
Jn 16: 8 he will prove the w to be in the wrong *G3180*
Jn 16:11 because the prince *of* this w now stands *G3180*
Jn 16:20 weep and mourn while the w rejoices. *G3180*
Jn 16:21 of her joy that a child is born into the w. *G3180*
Jn 16:28 I came from the Father and entered the w *G3180*
Jn 16:28 now I am leaving the w and going back to *G3180*
Jn 16:33 In this w you will have trouble *G3180*
Jn 16:33 But take heart! I have overcome the w." *G3180*
Jn 17: 5 glory I had with you before the w began. *G3180*
Jn 17: 6 to those whom you gave me out of the w. *G3180*
Jn 17: 9 I am not praying for the w, but for those *G3180*
Jn 17:11 I will remain in the w no longer, but they *G3180*
Jn 17:11 they are still in the w, and I am *G3180*
Jn 17:13 I say these things while I am still in the w, *G3180*
Jn 17:14 your word and the w has hated them, *G3180*
Jn 17:14 they are not of the w any more than I am *G3180*
Jn 17:14 of the world any more than I am of the w. *G3180*
Jn 17:15 them out of the w but that you protect *G3180*
Jn 17:16 They are not of the w, even as I am not of *G3180*
Jn 17:18 As you sent me into the w, I have sent *G3180*
Jn 17:18 the world, I have sent them into the w. *G3180*
Jn 17:21 in us so that the w may believe that you *G3180*
Jn 17:23 Then the w will know that you sent me *G3180*
Jn 17:24 loved me before the creation *of* the w. *G3180*
Jn 17:25 though the w does not know you, *G3180*
Jn 18:20 "I have spoken openly *to* the w," Jesus *G3180*
Jn 18:36 "My kingdom is not of this w. If it were, *G3180*
Jn 18:37 came into the w is to testify to the *G3180*
Jn 21:25 even the whole w would not have room *G3180*
Ac 11:28 would spread over the entire **Roman** w. *G3876*
Ac 17: 6 trouble **all over** the w have now come *G3876*
Ac 17:24 God who made the w and everything in it *G3180*
Ac 17:31 he will judge the w with justice by the *G3876*
Ac 19:27 the province of Asia and the w, *G3876*
Ac 19:35 doesn't all the w know that the city of *G476*
Ac 24: 5 up riots among the Jews all over the w. *G3876*
Ro 1: 8 your faith is being reported all over the w. *G3180*
Ro 1:20 since the creation *of* the w God's invisible *G3180*
Ro 3: 6 that were so, how could God judge the w? *G3180*
Ro 3:19 the whole w held accountable to *G3180*
Ro 4:13 promise that he would be heir *of* the w, *G3180*
Ro 5:12 as sin entered the w through one man, *G3180*
Ro 5:13 sin was in the w before the law was given, *G3180*
Ro 10:18 their words to the ends *of* the w. *G3876*
Ro 11:12 their transgression means riches *for* the w, *G3180*
Ro 11:15 rejection brought reconciliation *to* the w, *G3180*
Ro 12: 2 Do not conform to the pattern *of* this w, but *G172*
1Co 1:20 God made foolish the wisdom *of* the w? *G3180*
1Co 1:21 wisdom of God the w through its wisdom *G3180*
1Co 1:27 foolish things *of* the w to shame the wise *G3180*
1Co 1:27 the weak things *of* the w to shame the *G3180*
1Co 1:28 the lowly things *of* this w and the *G3180*
1Co 2:12 we have received is not the spirit *of* the w, *G3180*
1Co 3:19 For the wisdom *of* this w is foolishness in *G3180*
1Co 3:22 Cephas or the w or life or death or the *G3180*
1Co 4:13 the garbage *of* the w—right up to this *G4246*
1Co 5:10 the people *of* this w who are immoral, *G3180*
1Co 5:10 that case you would have to leave this w. *G3180*
1Co 6: 2 that the Lord's people will judge the w? *G3180*
1Co 6: 2 And if you are to judge the w, are you not *G3180*
1Co 7:31 those who use the **things of the** w, as if *G3180*
1Co 7:31 For this w in its present form is passing *G3180*
1Co 7:33 is concerned about the affairs *of* this w— *G3180*
1Co 7:34 is concerned about the affairs *of* this w— *G3180*
1Co 8: 4 that "An idol is nothing at all in the w" *G3180*
1Co 11:32 will not be finally condemned with the w. *G3180*
1Co 14:10 there are all sorts of languages in the w, *G3180*
2Co 1:12 we have conducted ourselves in the w, *G3180*
2Co 5:19 was reconciling the w to himself in Christ, *G3180*
2Co 10: 2 that we live by the standards of **this** w. *G4922*
2Co 10: 3 For though we live in **the** w, we do not *G4922*
2Co 10: 3 we do not wage war as **the** w does. *G4922*
2Co 10: 4 fight with are not the weapons **of the** w. *G4920*
2Co 11:18 many are boasting in the way **the** w does, *G4922*
Gal 4: 3 the elemental spiritual forces *of* the w. *G3180*
Gal 6:14 through which the w has been crucified to *G3180*
Gal 6:14 has been crucified to me, and I *to* the w. *G3180*
Eph 1: 4 the creation *of* the w to be holy and *G3180*
Eph 2: 2 the ways *of* this w and of the ruler *G3180*
Eph 2:12 without hope and without God in the w. *G3180*
Eph 6:12 against the **powers of** this dark w and *G3179*
Col 1: 6 growing throughout the whole w— *G3180*
Col 2: 8 spiritual forces *of* this w rather than on *G3180*
Col 2:20 to the elemental spiritual forces *of* this w, *G3180*
Col 2:20 as though you still belonged to the w, do *G3180*
1Ti 1:15 Jesus came into the w to save sinners— *G3180*
1Ti 3:16 was believed on in the w, was taken up in *G3180*
1Ti 6: 7 For we brought nothing into the w, and we *G3180*
1Ti 6:17 rich in this present w not to be arrogant *G172*
2Ti 4:10 because he loved this w, has deserted me *G172*
Heb 1: 6 when God brings his firstborn into the w *G3876*
Heb 2: 5 that he has subjected the w to come, *G3876*
Heb 4: 3 been finished since the creation *of* the w. *G3180*
Heb 9:26 many times since the creation *of* the w. *G3180*
Heb 10: 5 when Christ came into the w, he said: *G3180*
Heb 11: 7 he condemned the w and became heir of *G3180*
Heb 11:38 the w was not worthy of them. *G3180*
Jas 1:27 oneself from being polluted by the w. *G3180*
Jas 2: 5 are poor *in the eyes of* the w to be rich *G3180*
Jas 3: 6 a w of evil among the parts of the body. *G3180*
Jas 4: 4 that friendship *with* the w means enmity *G3180*
Jas 4: 4 to be a friend *of* the w becomes an *G3180*
1Pe 1:20 was chosen before the creation *of* the w, *G3180*
1Pe 5: 9 throughout the w is undergoing the same *G3180*
2Pe 1: 4 the corruption in the w caused by evil *G3180*
2Pe 2: 5 spare the ancient w when he brought the *G3180*
2Pe 2:20 the corruption *of* the w by knowing our *G3180*
2Pe 3: 6 these waters also the w of that time was *G3180*
1Jn 2: 2 ours but also for the sins *of* the whole w. *G3180*

1Jn 2:15 Do not love the **w** or anything in the world *G3180*
1Jn 2:15 not love the world or anything in the **w**. *G3180*
1Jn 2:15 If anyone loves the **w**, love for the Father *G3180*
1Jn 2:16 For everything in the **w**—the lust of the *G3180*
1Jn 2:16 comes not from the Father but from the **w**. *G3180*
1Jn 2:17 The **w** and its desires pass away, but *G3180*
1Jn 3: 1 The reason the **w** does not know us is that *G3180*
1Jn 3:13 my brothers and sisters, if the **w** hates you. *G3180*
1Jn 4: 1 false prophets have gone out into the **w**. *G3180*
1Jn 4: 3 coming and even now is already in the **w**. *G3180*
1Jn 4: 4 is greater than the one who is in the **w**. *G3180*
1Jn 4: 5 They are from the **w** and therefore speak *G3180*
1Jn 4: 5 speak from the viewpoint of the **w**, *G3180*
1Jn 4: 5 of the world, and the **w** listens to them. *G3180*
1Jn 4: 9 only Son into the **w** that we might live *G3180*
1Jn 4:14 has sent his Son to be the Savior *of* the **w**. *G3180*
1Jn 4:17 In this **w** we are like Jesus. *G3180*
1Jn 5: 4 everyone born of God overcomes the **w** *G3180*
1Jn 5: 4 is the victory that has overcome the **w**, *G3180*
1Jn 5: 5 Who is it that overcomes the **w**? Only the *G3180*
1Jn 5:19 that the whole **w** is under the control *G3180*
2Jn 7 in the flesh, have gone out into the **w**. *G3180*
Rev 3:10 to come on the whole **w** to test the *G3876*
Rev 11:15 "The kingdom *of* the **w** has become the *G3180*
Rev 12: 9 Satan, who leads the whole **w** astray. *G3876*
Rev 13: 3 The whole **w** was filled with wonder and *G1178*
Rev 13: 8 who was slain from the creation *of* the **w**. *G3180*
Rev 16:14 they go out to the kings *of* the whole **w**, *G3876*
Rev 17: 8 from the creation *of* the **w** will be *G3180*

WORLD'S (2) [WORLD]
Jn 11: 9 not stumble, for they see by this **w** light. *G3180*
Rev 18:23 merchants were the **w** important people. *G1178*

WORLDLY (10) [WORLD]
Lk 16: 9 use **w** wealth to gain friends for yourselves *G94*
Lk 16:11 not been trustworthy in handling **w** wealth, *G96*
1Co 3: 1 the Spirit but as **people who are** *still* **w**— *G4921*
1Co 3: 3 You are still **w**. For since there is jealousy *G4920*
1Co 3: 3 quarreling among you, are you not **w**? *G4920*
2Co 1:12 relying not on **w** wisdom but on God's *G4920*
2Co 1:17 I make my plans in a **w** manner so that in *G4922*
2Co 5:16 we regard no one from a **w** point of view. *G4922*
2Co 7:10 no regret, but **w** sorrow brings death. *G3180*
Titus 2:12 to ungodliness and **w** passions, and to *G3176*

WORM (8) [WORMS]
Job 17:14 and to the **w**, 'My mother' or 'My H8231
Job 24:20 forgets them, the **w** feasts on them; the H8231
Job 25: 6 a human being, who is only a **w**! H9357
Ps 22: 6 But I am a **w** and not a man, scorned by H9357
Isa 41:14 Do not be afraid, you **w** Jacob, little Israel, H9357
Isa 51: 8 the **w** will devour them like wool. H6182
Jnh 4: 7 at dawn the next day God provided a **w**, H9357
2Ti 3: 6 the kind who **w their way into** homes and *G1905*

WORMS (7) [WORM]
Dt 28:39 the grapes, because **w** will eat them. H9357
Job 7: 5 My body is clothed with **w** and scabs, my H8231
Job 21:26 lie in the dust, and **w** cover them both. H8231
Isa 14:11 spread out beneath you and **w** cover you. H9357
Isa 66:24 the **w** *that eat* them will not die H9357
Mk 9:48 where " 'the **w** *that eat* them do not die *G5038*
Ac 12:23 and he was **eaten by w** and died. *G5037*

WORMWOOD (1)
Rev 8:11 the name of the star is **W**. A third of the *G952*

WORN (20) [WEAR]
Ge 18:12 "After I *am* **w out** and my lord is old H1162
Ex 35:19 the woven garments **w** for ministering in the NDT
Ex 39:26 the hem of the robe to be **w** for ministering, NDT
Ex 39:41 the woven garments **w** for ministering in NDT
Dt 21: 3 worked and *has* never **w** a yoke H5432+928
Dt 25:18 When you were weary and **w out**, they met H3335
Jos 9: 5 They put **w** and patched sandals on their H1165
Jos 9:13 sandals *are* **w out** by the very long H1162
Jdg 8: 5 some bread; they are **w out**, and I am still H6546
Jdg 8:26 purple garments **w** *by* the kings of Midian H6584
Est 6: 8 royal robe the king *has* **w** and a horse the H4252
Job 16: 7 *you have* **w** me **out**; you have H4206
Ps 6: 6 *I am* **w out** from my groaning. All night H3333
Ps 69: 3 *I am* **w out** calling for help; my throat is H3333
Isa 47:13 you have received *has only* **w** *you* **out**! H4206
Jer 12: 5 men on foot and *they have* **w** you **out**, H4206
Jer 45: 3 *I am* **w out** with groaning and find no rest. H3333
Eze 23:43 I said about the *one* **w out** *by* adultery, H1165
Da 8:27 Daniel, *was* **w out**. I lay exhausted for H2118
Lk 8:27 a long time *this man had* not **w** clothes *G1907*

WORN-OUT (3) [WEAR]
Jos 9: 4 were loaded with **w** sacks and old H1165
Jer 38:11 some old rags and **w** clothes from there H1170
Jer 38:12 these old rags and **w** clothes under your NDT

WORRIED (3) [WORRY]
1Sa 10: 2 thinking about them and *is* **w** about you. H1793
Lk 10:41 "*you are* **w** and upset about many things, *G3534*
1Co 7:36 If anyone *is* **w** that he might not be acting *G3787*

WORRIES (4) [WORRY]
Jer 17: 8 *It* **has** no **w** in a year of drought and never H1793
Mt 13:22 the **w** of this life and the deceitfulness *G3533*
Mk 4:19 the **w** of this life, the deceitfulness of *G3533*
Lk 8:14 on their way they are choked by life's **w**, *G3533*

WORRY (13) [WORRIED, WORRIES, WORRYING]
1Sa 9:20 *do* not **w** about them H8492+906+4213
Mt 6:25 I tell you, *do* not **w about** your life, what *G3534*
Mt 6:28 "And why *do you* **w** about clothes? See *G3534*
Mt 6:31 So *do* not **w**, saying, 'What shall we eat?' *G3534*
Mt 6:34 Therefore *do* not **w** about tomorrow, for *G3534*
Mt 6:34 tomorrow, for tomorrow *will* **w about** itself. *G3534*
Mt 10:19 *do* not **w about** what to say or how to say *G3534*
Mk 13:11 *do* not **w beforehand about** what to say. *G4628*
Lk 12:11 *do* not **w about** how you will defend *G3534*
Lk 12:22 I tell you, *do* not **w about** your life, what *G3534*
Lk 12:26 little thing, why *do you* **w** about the rest? *G3534*
Lk 12:29 you will eat or drink; *do* not **w about** it. *G3577*
Lk 21:14 mind not *to* **w beforehand** how you will *G4627*

WORRYING (3) [WORRY]
1Sa 9: 5 about the donkeys and *start* **w** about us." H1793
Mt 6:27 Can any one of you *by* **w** add a single hour *G3534*
Lk 12:25 Who of you *by* **w** can add a single hour to *G3534*

WORSE (22) [WORST]
Ge 19: 9 the judge! *We'll* **treat** you **w** than them." H8317
Ex 11: 6 **w** *than* there has ever been or ever H4202+4017
2Sa 19: 7 This will be **w** for you than all the H8273
1Ki 17:17 He **grew w and worse** H2118+2716+2617+4394
1Ki 17:17 He **grew worse and w** H2118+2716+2617+4394
Pr 17: 7 **how much w** lying lips to a ruler! H677+3954
Pr 19:10 **how much w** for a slave to rule over H677+3954
Eze 14:21 **How much w** will it be when I send H677+3954
Da 1:10 he see you **looking w** than the other H2407
Mic 7: 4 the most upright **w than** a thorn hedge. H4946
Mt 9:16 from the garment, making the tear **w**. *G5937*
Mt 12:45 condition of that person is **w** than the first. *G5937*
Mt 27:64 This last deception will be **w** than the first." *G5937*
Mk 2:21 away from the old, making the tear **w**. *G5937*
Mk 5:26 instead of getting better she grew **w**. *G5937*
Lk 11:26 condition of that person is **w** than the first." *G5937*
Lk 13: 2 Galileans were *w* sinners **than** all the other AIT
Jn 5:14 something **w** may happen to you. *G5937*
1Co 8: 8 near to God; *we are* no **w** if we do not eat *G5728*
1Ti 5: 8 the faith and is **w** than an unbeliever. *G5937*
2Ti 3:13 impostors will go *from bad* to **w**, *G5937*
2Pe 2:20 they are **w off** at the end than they were *G5937*

WORSHIP (162) [WORSHIPED, WORSHIPER, WORSHIPERS, WORSHIPING, WORSHIPS]
Ge 22: 5 *We will* **w** and then we will come back to H2556
Ex 3:12 *you will* **w** God on this mountain. H6268
Ex 4:23 "Let my son go, so *he may* **w** me. H6268
Ex 7:16 so that *they may* **w** me in the wilderness. H6268
Ex 8: 1 my people go, so that *they may* **w** me. H6268
Ex 8:20 my people go, so that *they may* **w** me. H6268
Ex 9: 1 my people go, so that *they may* **w** me." H6268
Ex 9:13 Let my people go, so that *they may* **w** me, H6268
Ex 10: 3 my people go, so that *they may* **w** me. H6268
Ex 10: 7 so that *they may* **w** the LORD their God. H6268
Ex 10: 8 "Go, **w** the LORD your God, H6268
Ex 10:11 Have only the men go and **w** the LORD H6268
Ex 10:24 Moses and said, "Go, **w** the LORD. H6268
Ex 10:26 know what *we are to use to* **w** the LORD." H6268
Ex 12:31 **w** the LORD as you have requested H6268
Ex 20: 5 shall not bow down to them or **w** them; H6268
Ex 23:24 before their gods or **w** them or follow their H6268
Ex 23:25 **W** the LORD your God, and his blessing H6268
Ex 23:33 because the **w** *of* their gods will certainly H6268
Ex 24: 1 *You are to* **w** at a distance, H2556
Ex 34:14 *Do* not **w** any other god, for the LORD H2556
Dt 4:28 There *you will* **w** man-made gods of wood H6268
Dt 5: 9 shall not bow down to them or **w** them; H6268
Dt 8:19 other gods and **w** and bow down to them, H6268
Dt 11:16 to turn away and **w** other gods and bow H6268
Dt 12: 2 you are dispossessing **w** their gods. H6268
Dt 12: 4 *You must* not **w** the LORD your God in their H6913
Dt 12:31 *You must* not **w** the LORD your God in their H6913
Dt 13: 2 have not known) "and *let us* **w** them," H6268
Dt 13: 6 "Let us go and **w** other gods" (gods that H6268
Dt 13:13 "Let us go and **w** other gods" (gods you H6268
Dt 28:36 There *you will* **w** other gods, gods of H6268
Dt 28:64 There *you will* **w** other gods—gods of H6268
Dt 29:18 our God to go and **w** the gods of those H6268
Dt 30:17 to bow down to other gods and **w** them, H6268
Dt 31:20 they will turn to other gods and **w** them H6268
Jos 22:27 that we *will* **w** the LORD at his H6268+6275
Jdg 6:10 *do* not **w** the gods of the Amorites H3707
1Sa 1: 3 up from his town to **w** and sacrifice to the H2556
1Sa 10: 3 Three men going up **to** *w* God at Bethel will AIT
1Sa 15:25 back with me, so that *I may* **w** the LORD." H2556
1Sa 15:30 so that *I may* **w** the LORD your God. H2556
2Sa 15: 8 to Jerusalem, *I will* **w** the LORD in Hebron. H6268
2Sa 15:32 where *people used to* **w** God, Hushai H2556
1Ki 1:47 And the king **bowed in w** on his bed H2556
1Ki 9: 6 go off to serve other gods and **w** them, H2556
1Ki 12:30 people came to **w** the one at H4200+7156
1Ki 12:30 went as far as Dan to **w** the other. H4200+7156
1Ki 15:13 a repulsive image **for** the *w of* Asherah. AIT
1Ki 16:31 began to serve Baal and **w** him. H2556
2Ki 10:28 So Jehu destroyed **Baal w** in Israel. H1251
2Ki 10:29 the **w** of the golden calves at Bethel and NDT
2Ki 17:25 lived there, *they did* not **w** the LORD; so he H3707
2Ki 17:28 taught them how *to* **w** the LORD. H3707
2Ki 17:34 They neither **w** the LORD nor adhere to the H3710
2Ki 17:35 "*Do* not **w** any other gods or bow down to H3707
2Ki 17:36 outstretched arm, is the one *you must* **w**. H3707
2Ki 17:37 he wrote for you. *Do* not **w** other gods. H3707
2Ki 17:38 made with you, and *do* not **w** other gods. H3707
2Ki 17:39 **w** the LORD your God; it is he who H3707
2Ki 18:22 "*You must* **w** before this altar in H2556
1Ch 16:29 **W** the LORD in the splendor of his holiness. H2556
2Ch 7:19 go off to serve other gods and **w** them, H2556
2Ch 15:16 a repulsive image **for** the *w of* Asherah. AIT
2Ch 20:18 Jerusalem fell down in **w** before the LORD. H2556
2Ch 29:28 The whole assembly **bowed in w**, while H2556
2Ch 32:12 '*You must* **w** before one altar and burn H2556
Ezr 7:19 to you for **w** *in* the temple of your A10587
Ne 9: 6 the multitudes of heaven **w** you. H2556
Job 1:20 Then he fell to the ground *in* **w** H2556
Ps 22:29 All the rich of the earth will feast and **w** H2556
Ps 29: 2 **w** the LORD in the splendor of his holiness. H2556
Ps 81: 9 *you shall* not **w** any god other than me. H2556
Ps 86: 9 have made will come and **w** before you, H2556
Ps 95: 6 let us bow down *in* **w**, let us kneel before H2556
Ps 96: 9 **W** the LORD in the splendor of his holiness; H2556
Ps 97: 7 All *who* **w** images are put to shame H6268
Ps 97: 7 who boast in idols—**w** him, all *you* gods! H2556
Ps 99: 5 the LORD our God and **w** at his footstool; H2556
Ps 99: 9 LORD our God and **w** at his holy mountain H2556
Ps 100: 2 **W** the LORD with gladness; come before H6268
Ps 102:22 the kingdoms assemble to **w** the LORD. H6268
Ps 132: 7 dwelling place, *let us* **w** at his footstool H2556
Isa 2:20 idols of gold, which they made to **w**. H2556
Isa 19:21 *They will* **w** *with* sacrifices and grain H6268
Isa 19:23 Egyptians and Assyrians *will* **w** together. H6268
Isa 27:13 Egypt will come and **w** the LORD on the H2556
Isa 29:13 Their **w** *of* me is based on merely human H3707
Isa 36: 7 Jerusalem, "*You must* **w** before this altar"? H2556
Isa 46: 6 into a god, and they bow down and **w** it. H2556
Jer 7: 2 come through these gates to **w** the LORD. H2556
Jer 13:10 go after other gods to serve and **w** them, H2556
Jer 23:27 ancestors forgot my name through **Baal w**. H1251
Jer 25: 6 follow other gods to serve and **w** them; H2556
Jer 26: 2 Judah who come to **w** *in* the house of the H2556
Eze 46: 2 *He is to* **bow down in w** at the threshold H2556
Eze 46: 3 of the land *are to* **w** in the presence H2556
Eze 46: 9 by the north gate to **w** is to go out the H2556
Da 3: 5 must fall down and **w** the image of gold A10504
Da 3: 6 not fall down and **w** will immediately be A10504
Da 3:10 must fall down and **w** the image of gold, A10504
Da 3:11 not fall down and **w** will be thrown into A10504
Da 3:12 serve your gods nor **w** the image of gold A10504
Da 3:14 serve my gods or **w** the image of gold I A10504
Da 3:15 to fall down and **w** the image I made, A10504
Da 3:15 But if *you do* not **w** it, you will be thrown A10504
Da 3:18 serve your gods or **w** the image of gold A10504
Da 3:28 than serve or **w** any god except their A10504
Da 7:27 all rulers *will* **w** and obey him. A10586
Hos 13: 1 But he became guilty of **Baal w** and died. H1251
Jnh 1: 9 "I am a Hebrew and I **w** the LORD, the God H3707
Zep 1: 4 every remnant of **Baal w** in this place, H1251
Zep 1: 5 *who* **bow down** on the roofs **to w** the H2556
Zec 14:16 will go up year after year to **w** the King, H2556
Zec 14:17 do not go up to Jerusalem to **w** the King, H2556
Mal 2:11 by marrying **women who w** a foreign god. H1426
Mt 2: 2 when it rose and have come *to* **w** him." *G4686*
Mt 2: 8 so that I too may go and **w** him. *G4686*
Mt 4: 9 he said, "if *you will* bow down and **w** me." *G4686*
Mt 4:10 For it is written: '**W** the Lord your God, *G4686*
Mt 15: 9 *They* **w** me in vain; their teachings are *G4936*
Mk 7: 7 *They* **w** me in vain; their teachings are *G4936*
Lk 4: 7 If you **w** me, it will all be yours." *G4686*
Lk 4: 8 '**W** the Lord your God and serve him only *G4686*
Jn 4:20 place where we must **w** is in Jerusalem." *G4686*
Jn 4:21 is coming when *you will* **w** the Father *G4686*
Jn 4:22 You Samaritans **w** what you do not know *G4686*
Jn 4:22 you do not know; we **w** what we do know *G4686*
Jn 4:23 true worshipers *will* **w** the Father in the *G4686*
Jn 4:24 his worshipers must **w** in the Spirit and in *G4686*
Jn 12:20 those who went up to **w** at the festival. *G4686*
Ac 7: 7 out of that country and **w** me in this place. *G3302*
Ac 7:42 gave them over *to* the **w** of the sun, *G3302*
Ac 7:43 god Rephan, the idols you made *to* **w**. *G4686*
Ac 8:27 This man had gone to Jerusalem *to* **w**, *G4686*
Ac 13:16 Israelites and you *Gentiles who* **w** God, *G5828*
Ac 17:23 looked carefully at your **objects of w**, *G4934*
Ac 17:23 you are ignorant of the very thing *you* **w**— *G2355*
Ac 18:13 the people *to* **w** God in ways contrary *G4936*
Ac 24:11 days ago I went up to Jerusalem *to* **w**. *G4686*
Ac 24:14 I admit that *I* **w** the God of our ancestors *G3302*
Ro 9: 4 the law, the **temple w** and the promises. *G3301*
Ro 12: 1 to God—this is your true and proper **w**. *G3301*
1Co 14:25 So they will fall down and **w** God *G4686*
Col 2:18 humility and the **w** of angels disqualify *G2579*
Col 2:23 with their **self-imposed w**, their false *G1615*
1Ti 2:10 women who profess *to* **w God**. *G2537*
Heb 1: 6 he says, "*Let* all God's angels **w** him." *G4686*
Heb 9: 1 had regulations *for* **w** and also an earthly *G3301*
Heb 10: 1 make perfect those *who* **draw near to w**. *G4665*
Heb 12:28 so **w** God acceptably with reverence *G3302*
Rev 4:10 on the throne and **w** him who lives for *G4686*
Rev 13: 8 inhabitants of the earth *will* **w** the beast— *G4686*
Rev 13:12 earth and its inhabitants **w** the first beast, *G4686*
Rev 13:15 all who refused *to* **w** the image to be *G4686*

W

Rev 14: 7 **W** him who made the heavens, the earth *G4686*
Rev 14:11 night for those *who* **w** the beast and its *G4686*
Rev 15: 4 All nations will come and **w** before you *G4686*
Rev 19:10 At this I fell at his feet *to* **w** him. But he *G4686*
Rev 19:10 testimony of Jesus. **W** God! For it is the *G4686*
Rev 22: 8 I fell down *to* **w** at the feet of the angel *G4686*
Rev 22: 9 keep the words of this scroll. **W** God!" *G4686*

WORSHIPED (64) [WORSHIP]

Ge 24:26 the man bowed down and **w** the LORD, H2556
Ge 24:48 I bowed down and **w** the LORD. H2556
Ge 47:31 Israel **w** *as he* **leaned** on the top of H2556
Ex 4:31 their misery, they bowed down and **w**. H2556
Ex 12:27 Then the people bowed down and **w**. H2556
Ex 33:10 they all stood and **w**, each at the entrance H2556
Ex 34: 8 bowed to the ground at once and **w**. H2556
Dt 17: 3 to my command *has* **w** other gods, H6268
Dt 29:26 They went off and **w** other gods and H6268
Jos 24: 2 the Euphrates River and **w** other gods. H6268
Jos 24:14 gods your ancestors **w** beyond the H6268
Jdg 2:12 They followed and **w** various gods of the H2556
Jdg 2:17 themselves to other gods and **w** them. H2556
Jdg 7:15 its interpretation, *he* **bowed down and w**. H2556
1Sa 1:19 they arose and **w** before the LORD and H2556
1Sa 1:28 And *he* **w** the LORD there. H2556
1Sa 15:31 went back with Saul, and Saul **w** the LORD. H2556
2Sa 12:20 he went into the house of the LORD and **w**. H2556
1Ki 11:33 have forsaken me and **w** Ashtoreth the H2556
1Ki 18:12 I your servant *have* **w** the LORD since my H3707
1Ki 22:53 He served and **w** Baal and aroused the H2556
2Ki 17: 7 Pharaoh king of Egypt. *They* **w** other gods H3707
2Ki 17:12 *They* **w** idols, though the LORD had said H6268
2Ki 17:16 to all the starry hosts, and *they* **w** Baal. H6268
2Ki 17:32 *They* **w** the LORD, but they also appointed H3710
2Ki 17:33 *They* **w** the LORD, but they also served their H3710
2Ki 21: 3 down to all the starry hosts and **w** them. H6268
2Ki 21:21 worshiping the idols his father *had* **w**, and H6268
2Ch 7: 3 and *they* **w** and gave thanks to the LORD H2556
2Ch 24:18 **w** Asherah poles and idols. H6268
2Ch 29:29 present with him knelt down and **w**. H2556
2Ch 29:30 with gladness and bowed down and **w**. H2556
2Ch 33: 3 down to all the starry hosts and **w** them. H6268
2Ch 33:22 Amon **w** and offered sacrifices to all the H6268
Ne 8: 6 bowed down and **w** the LORD with their H2556
Ps 74: 8 every **place where** God was **w** in the land H4595
Ps 106:19 they made a calf and **w** an idol cast from H2556
Ps 106:36 *They* **w** their idols, which became a snare H6268
Jer 8: 2 they have followed and consulted and **w**. H2556
Jer 16:11 other gods and served and **w** them. H2556
Jer 22: 9 their God and *have* **w** and served other H2556
Da 3: 7 fell down and **w** the image of gold that A10504
Da 7:14 peoples of every language **w** him. A10586
Mt 2:11 and they bowed down and **w** him. *G4686*
Mt 14:33 Then those who were in the boat **w** him *G4686*
Mt 28: 9 came to him, clasped his feet and **w** him. *G4686*
Mt 28:17 When they saw him, *they* **w** him; but some *G4686*
Lk 2:37 never left the temple but **w** night and day, *G3302*
Lk 24:52 Then they **w** him and returned to *G4686*
Jn 4:20 Our ancestors **w** on this mountain, but you *G4686*
Jn 9:38 "Lord, I believe," and *he* **w** him. *G4686*
Ac 19:27 who *is* **w** throughout the province of Asia *G4936*
Ro 1:25 **w** and served created things rather *G4933*
2Th 2: 4 over everything that is called God or is **w**, *G4934*
Heb 11:21 **w** as he leaned on the top of his staff. *G4686*
Rev 5:14 "Amen," and the elders fell down and **w**. *G4686*
Rev 7:11 their faces before the throne and **w** God, *G4686*
Rev 11:16 fell on their faces and **w** God, *G4686*
Rev 13: 4 *People* **w** the dragon because he had *G4686*
Rev 13: 4 and *they* also **w** the beast and asked *G4686*
Rev 16: 2 the mark of the beast and **w** its image. *G4686*
Rev 19: 4 four living creatures fell down and **w** God, *G4686*
Rev 19:20 the mark of the beast and **w** its image. *G4686*
Rev 20: 4 They *had* not **w** the beast or its image *G4686*

WORSHIPER (3) [WORSHIP]

Ac 16:14 She was a **w** of God. The Lord *G4936*
Ac 18: 7 to the house of Titius Justus, a **w** of God. *G4936*
Heb 9: 9 not able to clear the conscience *of* the **w**. *G3302*

WORSHIPERS (9) [WORSHIP]

Ps 55:14 as we walked about among the **w**. H8094
Ps 109:30 in the **great** *throng of* **w** I will praise him. AIT
Zep 3:10 From beyond the rivers of Cush my **w**, my H6985
Lk 1:10 all the **assembled w** were *G4436+3836+3295*
Jn 4:23 come when the true **w** will worship the *G4687*
Jn 4:23 they are the kind of **w** the Father seeks. *G4686*
Jn 4:24 his **w** must worship in the Spirit and *G4686*
Heb 10: 2 For the **w** would have been cleansed once *G3302*
Rev 11: 1 temple of God and the altar, with its **w**. *G4686*

WORSHIPING (18) [WORSHIP]

Ex 10:26 use some of them in **w** the LORD our God, H6268
Dt 4:19 down to them and **w** things the LORD your H6268
Dt 12:31 their way, because in **w** their gods, they do NDT
Dt 20:18 detestable things they do in **w** their gods, NDT
Jdg 2:19 other gods and serving and **w** them. H2556
Jdg 8:27 Israel prostituted themselves *by* **w** it there, H339
1Ki 9: 9 embraced other gods, **w** and serving them H2556
2Ki 17:41 Even while these people were **w** the LORD H3710
2Ki 19:37 *while* he *was* **w** in the temple of his god H2556
2Ki 21:21 **w** the idols his father had worshiped H6268
2Ch 7:22 embraced other gods, **w** and serving them H2556
2Ch 28: 2 Israel and also made idols for **w** the Baals. NDT
Ne 9: 3 in confession and *in* **w** the LORD their God. H2556
Isa 37:38 *while* he *was* **w** in the temple of his god H2556
Jer 1:16 to other gods and *in* **w** what their hands H2556
Jer 44: 3 burning incense to and **w** other gods that H6268
Ac 13: 2 *While* they *were* **w** the Lord and fasting *G3310*
Rev 9:20 *they did* not stop **w** demons, and *G4686*

WORSHIPS (4) [WORSHIP]

Isa 44:15 But he also fashions a god and **w** it; he H2556
Isa 44:17 his idol; he bows down to it and **w**. H2556
Isa 66: 3 incense is like *one who* **w** an idol. H1385
Rev 14: 9 "If anyone **w** the beast and its image and *G4686*

WORST (6) [WORSE]

Ex 9:18 I will send the **w** hailstorm that has H3878+4394
Ex 9:24 It was the **w** storm in all the land of H3878+4394
Ps 41: 7 they imagine the **w** for me, saying, H8288
Jer 2:33 Even the **w** *of women* can learn from your H8273
1Ti 1:15 to save sinners—of whom I am the **w**. *G4755*
1Ti 1:16 so that in me, the **w** of sinners, Christ *G4755*

WORTH (19) [WORTHLESS, WORTHWHILE, WORTHY]

Ge 23:15 the land is **w** four hundred shekels of silver NDT
Ge 27:46 my **life will not be w living**." H2644+4200+4537
Dt 15:18 been **w** twice as much as that *of* a hired H8510
2Sa 18: 3 but you are **w** ten thousand *of* us. H4017
1Ki 21: 2 you prefer, I will pay you *whatever* it is **w**." H4697
Job 28:13 No mortal comprehends its **w**; it cannot H6886
Pr 31:10 She is **w** far more than rubies H4836
Isa 7:23 were a thousand vines **w** a thousand silver H928
La 4: 2 of Zion, once **w their weight** in gold, are H6131
Mt 10:10 a staff, for the worker is **w** his keep. *G545*
Mt 10:31 you *are* **w more** than many sparrows. *G1422*
Mk 12:42 small copper coins, **w** only a few cents. *G1639*
Lk 12: 7 *you are* **w more than** many sparrows. *G1422*
Jn 12: 5 **money** given to the poor? It was **w a year's wages** *G5559+1324*
Ac 20:24 I consider my life **w** nothing to me; my *G5508*
Ro 8:18 sufferings are not **w** comparing with the *G545*
Php 3: 8 because of the **surpassing w** of knowing *G5660*
1Pe 1: 7 of your faith—*of* **greater w** than gold *G4501*
1Pe 3: 4 which is *of* **great w** in God's sight. *G4500*

WORTHLESS (43) [WORTH]

Ge 41:27 so are the seven **w** heads of grain H8199
Dt 32:21 god and angered me with their **w idols**. H2039
1Ki 16:13 the God of Israel, by their **w idols**. H2039
1Ki 16:26 the God of Israel, by their **w idols**. H2039
2Ki 17:15 They followed **w idols** and themselves H2039
2Ki 17:15 idols and *themselves became* **w**. H2038
2Ch 13: 7 Some **w** scoundrels gathered around him H8199
Job 13: 4 me with lies; you are **w** physicians, all of H496
Job 15:31 not deceive himself by trusting what is **w**, H8736
Job 34:18 says to kings, 'You are **w**,' and to nobles, H1175
Ps 31: 6 I hate those who cling to **w idols** H2039+8736
Ps 60:11 against the enemy, for human help is **w**. H8736
Ps 108:12 against the enemy, for human help is **w**. H8736
Ps 119:37 Turn my eyes away from **w things** H8736
Pr 11: 4 Wealth *is* **w** in the day of wrath H4202+3603
Isa 1:13 I cannot bear your **w** assemblies. H224
Isa 40:17 regarded by him as **w** and less than H9332
Isa 41:24 than nothing and your works are utterly **w**; H703
Isa 44: 9 and the things they treasure *are* **w**. H1153+3603
Jer 2: 5 They followed **w idols** and became H2039
Jer 2: 5 idols and *became* **w** *themselves*. H2038
Jer 2: 8 by Baal, following **w idols**. H4202+3603
Jer 2:11 their glorious God for **w idols**. H4202+3603
Jer 7: 8 in deceptive words *that are* **w**. H3603+1194
Jer 8:19 their images, with their **w** foreign **idols**?" H2039
Jer 10: 3 For the practices of the peoples are **w** H2039
Jer 10: 8 they are taught by **w** wooden **idols**. H2039
Jer 10:15 They are **w**, the objects of mockery; when H2039
Jer 14:22 Do any of the **w idols** *of* the nations bring H2039
Jer 15:19 you utter worthy, not **w**, words, you will be H2361
Jer 16:19 **w idols** that did them no good. H2039
Jer 18:15 they burn incense to **w idols**, which made H8736
Jer 51:18 They are **w**, the objects of mockery; when H2039
La 2:14 visions of your prophets were false and **w**; H9522
Hos 12:11 Its people are **w**! Do they sacrifice H8736
Jnh 2: 8 "Those who cling to **w** idols turn away H2039
Zec 11:17 "Woe to the **w** shepherd, who deserts the H496
Mt 25:30 And throw that **w** servant outside, into the *G945*
Ac 14:15 turn from these **w** *things* to the living God, *G3469*
Ro 3:12 *they have* together *become* **w**; there *G946*
Ro 4:14 faith means nothing and the promise *is* **w**, *G2934*
Heb 6: 8 thorns and thistles is **w** and is in danger of *G99*
Jas 1:26 themselves, and their religion is **w**. *G3469*

WORTHWHILE (1) [WORTH]

Ro 1:28 just as *they did* not **think it w** to retain the *G1507*

WORTHY (49) [WORTH]

2Sa 22: 4 to the LORD, *who is* **w of praise**, and have H2146
1Ki 1:42 A **w** man like you must be bringing good H2657
1Ki 1:52 "If he shows himself to be **w**, not a H1201+2657
2Ki 10: 3 the best and most **w** of your master's sons H3838
1Ch 16:25 For great is the LORD and most **w of praise** H2146
Job 28:18 Coral and jasper *are* not **w of mention** H2349
Ps 18: 3 to the LORD, *who is* **w of praise**, and I have H2146
Ps 48: 1 and most **w of praise**, in the city of H2146
Ps 96: 4 For great is the LORD and most **w of praise** H2146
Ps 145: 3 Great is the LORD and most **w of praise**; H2146
Jer 15:19 serve me; if you utter **w**, not worthless, H3701
Mt 3:11 whose sandals I am not **w** to carry. *G2653*
Mt 10:11 there for some **w** *person* and stay at their *G545*
Mt 10:37 mother more than me is not **w** of me; *G545*
Mt 10:37 daughter more than me is not **w** of me. *G545*
Mt 10:38 their cross and follow me is not **w** of me. *G545*
Mt 26:66 "He is **w** of death," they *G1944*
Mk 1: 7 sandals I am not **w** to stoop down and *G2653*
Mk 14:64 They all condemned him as **w** of death. *G1944*
Lk 3:16 of whose sandals I am not **w** to untie. *G2653*
Lk 7: 7 is why *I did* not even **consider** myself **w** to *G546*
Lk 15:19 I am no longer **w** to be called your son *G545*
Lk 15:21 I am no longer **w** to be called your son *G545*
Lk 20:35 But those *who are* **considered w** of taking *G2921*
Jn 1:27 of whose sandals I am not **w** to untie." *G545*
Ac 5:41 because *they had been* **counted w** of *G2921*
Ac 13:25 me whose sandals I am not **w** to untie. *G545*
Ac 13:46 do not consider yourselves **w** of eternal life, *G545*
Ro 16: 2 her in the Lord **in a way w** of his people *G547*
Eph 4: 1 you to live a life **w of** the calling you have *G547*
Php 1:27 yourselves **in a manner w** of the gospel of *G547*
Col 1:10 you may live a life **w** of the Lord and *G547*
1Th 2:12 urging you to live lives **w** of God, *G547*
2Th 1: 5 a result you *will be* **counted w** of the *G2921*
2Th 1:11 that our God *may* **make** you **w** of his calling *G546*
1Ti 3: 4 must do so **in a manner w of** full respect *G3552*
1Ti 3: 8 deacons are to be **w of respect**, sincere, *G4948*
1Ti 3:11 the women are to be **w of respect**, not *G4948*
1Ti 5:17 of the church well *are* **w** of double honor, *G546*
1Ti 6: 1 consider their masters **w** of full respect, *G545*
Titus 2: 2 to be temperate, **w of respect** *G4948*
Heb 3: 3 Jesus *has been* **found w** of greater honor *G546*
Heb 11:38 the world was not **w** of them. *G545*
Rev 3: 4 with me, dressed in white, for they are **w**. *G545*
Rev 4:11 "You are **w**, our Lord and God, to receive *G545*
Rev 5: 2 "Who is **w** to break the seals and open the *G545*
Rev 5: 4 was found who was **w** to open the scroll *G545*
Rev 5: 9 "You are **w** to take the scroll and to open *G545*
Rev 5:12 "**W** is the Lamb, who was slain, to receive *G545*

WOT, WOTTETH (KJV) CONCERN, KNOW

WOULD (686) [WOULDN'T]

Ge 2:19 to the man to see what *he* **w name** them; AIT
Ge 3:20 because she **w become** the mother of all the AIT
Ge 4:15 so that no one who found him *w* **kill** him. AIT
Ge 9:23 other way so that *they w* not **see** their father AIT
Ge 21: 7 "Who *w have* **said** to Abraham that Sarah AIT
Ge 21: 7 to Abraham that Sarah *w* **nurse** children? AIT
Ge 26:10 and *you w have* **brought** guilt upon us." AIT
Ge 27:12 *I w* **appear** to be tricking him and would AIT
Ge 27:12 tricking him and **w bring down** a curse on AIT
Ge 29: 3 the shepherds *w* **roll** the stone away from the AIT
Ge 29: 3 Then *they w* **return** the stone to its place over AIT
Ge 30:38 so that they **w** be directly in front of the NDT
Ge 30:41 Jacob *w* **place** the branches in the troughs in AIT
Ge 30:41 animals so they *w* **mate** near the branches, AIT
Ge 30:42 were weak, *he w* not **place** them there. AIT
Ge 31:31 I thought you **w** take your daughters H7153
Ge 31:42 *you w* surely *have* **sent** me **away** AIT
Ge 34:14 not circumcised. That **w** be a disgrace to us. NDT
Ge 38: 9 But Onan knew that the child *w* not **be** his; AIT
Ge 42:21 but *we w* not **listen**; that's why this AIT
Ge 43: 7 How were we to know *he w* **say**, 'Bring your AIT
Ge 44: 8 So why *w we* **steal** silver or gold from your AIT
Ge 44:34 me see the misery that *w* **come on** my father." AIT
Ex 2: 4 at a distance to see what *w* **happen** to him. AIT
Ex 6:12 why *w* Pharaoh **listen** *to* me, since I AIT
Ex 6:30 faltering lips, why *w* Pharaoh **listen** to me?" AIT
Ex 7:13 became hard and *he w* not **listen** to them, AIT
Ex 7:22 *he w* not **listen** to Moses and Aaron AIT
Ex 8:15 his heart and *w* not **listen** to Moses and AIT
Ex 8:19 heart was hard and *he w* not **listen**, AIT
Ex 8:26 "That *w* not *be* **right**. The sacrifices AIT
Ex 8:26 the LORD our God **w** be detestable to the NDT
Ex 8:32 his heart and *w* not **let** the people **go**. AIT
Ex 9: 7 unyielding and *he w* not **let** the people **go**. AIT
Ex 9:12 heart and *he w* not **listen** to Moses and AIT
Ex 9:15 a plague *that w have* **wiped** *you* off the earth AIT
Ex 9:35 was hard and *he w* not **let** the Israelites **go**, AIT
Ex 10:20 and *he w* not **let** the Israelites **go**. AIT
Ex 11:10 and *he w* not **let** the Israelites **go** out of his AIT
Ex 14:12 It **w** have been better for us to serve the NDT
Ex 23:29 because the land *w* **become** desolate and AIT
Ex 33: 7 inquiring of the LORD *w* **go** to the tent of AIT
Ex 33: 9 pillar of cloud *w* **come down** and stay at the AIT
Ex 33:11 The LORD *w* **speak** to Moses face to face, as AIT
Ex 33:11 Then Moses *w* **return** to the camp, but his AIT
Ex 34:35 Then Moses *w* **put** the veil **back** over his face AIT
Ex 38: 7 the rings so they **w** be on the sides of the NDT
Ex 39:21 breastpiece *w* not **swing out** from the ephod AIT
Ex 39:23 around this opening, so that *it w* not **tear**. AIT
Ex 40:36 from above the tabernacle, *they w* **set out**; AIT
Lev 5: 3 anything that *w make them* **unclean**) even AIT
Lev 10:19 *W* the LORD *have been* **pleased** if I had eaten AIT
Lev 18: 8 father's wife; that **w** dishonor your father. NDT
Lev 18:10 daughter's daughter; that **w** dishonor you. NDT
Lev 18:16 brother's wife; that **w** dishonor your brother. NDT
Lev 20:19 for *that w* **dishonor** a close relative AIT
Lev 20:19 both of you *w be* **held responsible**. AIT
Lev 25:35 help them as you **w** a foreigner and stranger NDT
Lev 26:13 so that you *w* no longer **be** slaves to the AIT
Lev 27:31 Whoever *w* **redeem** any of their tithe must AIT

Nu 9:20 at the LORD's command *they w* **encamp**, and AIT
Nu 9:20 then at his command *they w* **set out**. AIT
Nu 9:22 the Israelites *w* **remain in camp** and not set AIT
Nu 9:22 not set out; but when it lifted, *they w* **set out**. AIT
Nu 11:22 *W* they **have enough** if flocks and herds were AIT
Nu 11:22 *W* they **have enough** if all the fish in the sea AIT
Nu 11:29 that the LORD *w* **put** his Spirit on them!" AIT
Nu 12:14 *w she* not *have* **been in disgrace** for seven AIT
Nu 14:31 children that you said *w be* **taken** as plunder, AIT
Nu 16:40 or *he w* **become** like Korah and his followers. AIT
Nu 21:23 But Sihon *w* not **let** Israel pass through his AIT
Nu 22:29 a sword in my hand, *I w* **kill** you right now." AIT
Nu 22:33 *I w* certainly *have* **killed** you by now AIT
Nu 22:33 killed you by now, but *I w have* **spared** it." AIT
Nu 24:11 I said *I w* **reward** you **handsomely**, but the AIT
Nu 26:65 those Israelites *they w* **surely die** in the AIT
Nu 32:16 "*We w like* to **build** pens here for our AIT
Dt 1: 8 the LORD swore *he w* **give** to your fathers— AIT
Dt 1:39 little ones that you said *w* **be** taken captive, AIT
Dt 1:43 I told you, but *you w* not **listen**. You rebelled AIT
Dt 3:26 was angry with me and *w* not **listen** to me. AIT
Dt 4:21 swore that *I w* not **cross** the Jordan and enter AIT
Dt 5:29 that their hearts *w be* **inclined** to fear me AIT
Dt 8: 2 whether or not *you w* **keep** his commands. AIT
Dt 9:25 because the LORD had said *he w* **destroy** you. AIT
Dt 12:20 meat and say, "*I w* **like** some meat," then AIT
Dt 12:22 Eat them as you **w** gazelle or deer. H430S
Dt 17: 1 flaw in it, for that **w** be detestable to him. NDT
Dt 23: 5 the LORD your God **w** not listen to Balaam H14
Dt 24: 4 That **w** be detestable in the eyes of the LORD. NDT
Dt 24: 6 *w be* **taking** a person's livelihood **as security**. AIT
Dt 28:56 gentle that *she w* not **venture** to touch the AIT
Dt 32:26 I said *I w* **scatter** them and erase their name AIT
Dt 32:29 were wise and *w* **understand** this and discern AIT
Jos 5: 6 to them that they *w* not **see** the land he had AIT
Jos 9:27 of the LORD at the place the LORD *w* **choose**. AIT
Jos 24:10 But *I w* not listen to Balaam, so he blessed H14
Jdg 2:17 Yet *they w* not **listen** to their judges but AIT
Jdg 3: 4 to see whether *they w* **obey** the LORD's AIT
Jdg 5: 7 Villagers in Israel **w not** *fight*; they held H2532
Jdg 7: 2 or Israel *w* boast **against** me, 'My own AIT
Jdg 8:19 if you had spared their lives, *I w* not **kill** you." AIT
Jdg 9:29 Then *I w* **get rid of** him. I would AIT
Jdg 9:29 *I w* **say** to Abimelek, 'Call out your whole AIT
Jdg 11:17 but the king of Edom *w* not **listen**. AIT
Jdg 11:38 hills and wept because she **w** never marry. NDT
Jdg 13:15 "*We w like* you to **stay** until we prepare a AIT
Jdg 13:23 *he w* not *have* **accepted** a burnt offering AIT
Jdg 14:18 my heifer, *you w* not *have* **solved** my riddle." AIT
Jdg 15: 1 But her father *w* not **let** him go in. AIT
Jdg 16:17 my strength *w* **leave** me, and I would AIT
Jdg 16:17 *I w* **become** as weak as any other man." AIT
Jdg 19:25 But the men **w** not listen to him. So the man H14
Jdg 20:13 But the Benjamites **w** not listen to their H14
Jdg 20:39 then the Israelites *w* **counterattack**. AIT
Ru 1: 7 the road that *w* **take** them **back** to the land of AIT
Ru 1:11 Why *w you* **come** with me? Am I AIT
Ru 1:13 *w you* **wait** until they grew up? Would you AIT
Ru 1:13 *W you* **remain unmarried** for them AIT
1Sa 1: 4 *he w* **give** portions of the meat to his wife AIT
1Sa 1: 7 provoked her till she wept and *w* not **eat**. AIT
1Sa 1: 8 Her husband Elkanah *w* **say** to her, "Hannah AIT
1Sa 2:13 the priest's servant *w* **come** with a AIT
1Sa 2:14 and *w* **plunge** the fork into the pan or kettle AIT
1Sa 2:14 fork brought up the priest *w* **take** for himself. AIT
1Sa 2:15 the priest's servant *w* **come** and say to the AIT
1Sa 2:16 the servant *w* **answer**, "No, hand it AIT
1Sa 2:20 Eli *w* **bless** Elkanah and his wife, saying AIT
1Sa 2:20 gave to the LORD." Then *they w* **go** home. AIT
1Sa 2:30 of your family *w* **minister** before me forever. AIT
1Sa 3:13 I told him that *I w* **judge** his family forever AIT
1Sa 9: 9 went to inquire of God, *they w* **say**, "Come, AIT
1Sa 9:18 "*W you* please **tell** me where the seer's AIT
1Sa 13:13 he *w have* **established** your kingdom over AIT
1Sa 14:30 How much better it **w** have been if the men NDT
1Sa 14:30 *W* not the slaughter of the Philistines
have been even **greater** AIT
1Sa 16:23 on Saul, David *w* **take up** his lyre and play. AIT
1Sa 16:23 Then **relief** *w* **come** to Saul; he would feel AIT
1Sa 16:23 come to Saul; he *w* **feel better**, and the evil AIT
1Sa 16:23 feel better, and the evil spirit *w* **leave** him. AIT
1Sa 19: 5 Why then *w you* **do wrong** to an innocent AIT
1Sa 20: 2 Why *w* he **hide** this from me? It AIT
1Sa 22: 3 "*W you let* my father and mother **come** and AIT
1Sa 22:22 was there, I knew *he w* **be sure to tell** Saul. AIT
1Sa 25:34 to Nabal *w have* **been left alive** by daybreak." AIT
1Sa 26:23 but *I* **w** not lay a hand on the LORD's H14
1Sa 27:10 David *w* **say**, "Against the Negev of Judah AIT
1Sa 29: 6 I **w** be pleased to have you serve with NDT
1Sa 31: 4 armor-bearer was terrified and **w** not **do** it; H14
2Sa 2:21 But Asahel **w** not stop chasing him H14
2Sa 2:27 the men *w have* **continued** pursuing them AIT
2Sa 6:20 servants as any vulgar fellow **w**!" H1655+1655S
2Sa 11:20 you know *they w* **shoot arrows** from the wall? AIT
2Sa 12: 8 too little, *I w have* **given** you **even more**. AIT
2Sa 12:17 and *he w* not **eat** any food with them. AIT
2Sa 13: 5 '**I w like** my sister Tamar to come and give H5528
2Sa 13: 6 "**I w like** my sister Tamar to come and H5528
2Sa 13:13 You **w** be like one of the wicked fools in AIT
2Sa 13:16 "Sending me away **w** be a greater wrong NDT
2Sa 13:25 should not go; *we w* only *be a* **burden** to you." AIT
2Sa 14: 7 *They w* **put out** the only burning coal I have AIT
2Sa 14:26 too heavy for him—*he w* **weigh** it, and its AIT
2Sa 14:32 It **w** be better for me if I were still there!" NDT
2Sa 15: 2 He *w* **get up early** and stand by the side of AIT
2Sa 15: 2 decision, Absalom *w* **call out** to him, "What AIT
2Sa 15: 2 *He w* **answer**, "Your servant is from one of AIT
2Sa 15: 3 Then Absalom *w* **say** to him, "Look, your AIT
2Sa 15: 4 And Absalom *w* **add**, "If only I were AIT
2Sa 15: 4 to me and *I w* **see that** they **receive justice**." AIT
2Sa 15: 5 Absalom *w* **reach out** his hand, take AIT
2Sa 17: 1 "*I w* **choose** twelve thousand men and set AIT
2Sa 17: 2 *I w* **attack** him while he is weary and weak. AIT
2Sa 17: 2 *I w* **strike** him **with terror**, and then all the AIT
2Sa 17: 2 *I w* **strike down** only the king AIT
2Sa 18: 3 *It w* **be** better now for you to give us support AIT
2Sa 18:11 Then I **w** have had to give you ten shekels NDT
2Sa 18:12 *I w* not **lay** a hand on the king's son. AIT
2Sa 18:13 you *w have* **kept** *your* **distance** *from* me." AIT
2Sa 19: 6 I see that you **w** be pleased if Absalom NDT
2Sa 21:16 with a new sword, said *he w* **kill** David. AIT
2Sa 23: 5 surely *he w* not *have* **made** with me an AIT
2Sa 23: 5 surely *he w* not **bring to fruition** my salvation AIT
2Sa 23:15 that someone *w* **get** me **a drink** *of* water from AIT
2Sa 23:17 And David **w** not drink it. Such were H14
1Ki 6: 6 so that nothing *w be* **inserted** into the temple AIT
1Ki 8:12 LORD has said that *he w* **dwell** in a dark cloud; AIT
1Ki 12: 6 "How *w* you **advise** me to answer these AIT
1Ki 13: 8 your possessions, *I w* not **go** with you, nor AIT
1Ki 13: 8 nor *w I* **eat** bread or drink water here. AIT
1Ki 14: 2 the one who told me I **w** be king over this NDT
1Ki 17:10 "*W you* **bring** me a little water in a jar so I AIT
2Ki 3:14 of Judah, *I w* not **pay any attention** to you. AIT
2Ki 5: 3 "If only my master **w** see the prophet who is NDT
2Ki 5: 3 *He w* **cure** him of his leprosy. AIT
2Ki 5:11 thought that *he w* **surely come out** to me AIT
2Ki 5:13 do some great thing, *w you* not *have* **done** it? AIT
2Ki 6:22 "*W* you **kill** those you have captured with AIT
2Ki 8:14 "He told me that *you w* **certainly recover**." AIT
2Ki 11:17 people that *they w* **be** the LORD's people. AIT
2Ki 12: 8 agreed that *they w* not **collect** any more AIT
2Ki 12: 8 people and that they *w* not **repair** the temple AIT
2Ki 13:19 then *you w have* **defeated** Aram and AIT
2Ki 14:11 however, *w* not **listen**, so Jehoash king of AIT
2Ki 14:27 had not said he *w* **blot out** the name of Israel AIT
2Ki 17:14 But *they w* not **listen** and were as stiff-necked AIT
2Ki 17:40 They *w* not **listen**, however, but persisted in AIT
2Ki 22:19 that they *w* **become** a curse and be laid waste AIT
1Ch 4:10 that *you w* **bless** me and enlarge my territory! AIT
1Ch 9:27 *They w* **spend the night** stationed around the AIT
1Ch 10: 4 armor-bearer was terrified and **w** not do it; H14
1Ch 11:17 that someone *w* **get** me **a drink** *of* water from AIT
1Ch 11:19 lives to bring it back, David **w** not drink it. H14
1Ch 22:11 of the LORD your God, as he said you **w**. NDT
2Ch 6: 1 LORD has said that he *w* **dwell** in a dark cloud; AIT
2Ch 6:20 which you said *you w* **put** your Name there. AIT
2Ch 10: 6 "How *w* you **advise** me to answer these AIT
2Ch 15:13 All who *w* not **seek** the LORD, the God of, AIT
2Ch 20:10 whose territory *you w* not **allow** Israel to AIT
2Ch 23:16 people and the king *w* **be** the LORD's people. AIT
2Ch 24:11 of the chief priest *w* **come** and empty the AIT
2Ch 24:19 they testified against them, *they w* not **listen**. AIT
2Ch 25:20 however, *w* not **listen**, for God so worked that AIT
2Ch 31:16 all who *w* **enter** the temple of the LORD to AIT
2Ch 35:22 however, *w* not **turn away** from him, but AIT
2Ch 35:22 *He w* not **listen** to what Necho had said at AIT
2Ch 36:13 his heart and *w* not **turn** to the LORD, AIT
Ezr 3: 7 so that they *w* **bring** cedar logs by sea from AIT
Ezr 9:14 *W you* not *be* **angry** enough with us to AIT
Ezr 10: 8 within three days *w* **forfeit** all his property, AIT
Ezr 10: 8 and *w* himself *be* **expelled** from the AIT
Ne 2:16 any others *who w be* **doing** the work. AIT
Ne 3: 5 their nobles *w* not **put** their shoulders to AIT
Ne 4: 3 climbing up on it *w* **break down** their wall of AIT
Ne 6:13 me so that *I w* **commit a sin** by doing this, AIT
Ne 6:13 then they *w* **give** me a bad name to AIT
Est 1:17 be brought before him, but *she w* not **come**. AIT
Est 2:13 And this is how she *w* **go** to the king AIT
Est 2:14 In the evening she *w* **go** there and in the AIT
Est 2:14 *She w* not **return** to the king unless he was AIT
Est 3: 2 But Mordecai *w* not **kneel down** or pay him AIT
Est 3: 4 whether Mordecai's behavior *w be* **tolerated**, AIT
Est 3: 5 that Mordecai *w* not **kneel down** or pay him AIT
Est 3:14 nationality so they *w* **be** ready for that day. AIT
Est 4: 4 of his sackcloth, but *he w* not **accept** them. AIT
Est 6: 6 there that the king *w* **rather** honor than me?" AIT
Est 7: 4 *I w have* **kept** *quiet*, because no AIT
Est 7: 4 no such distress *w* **justify** disturbing the king." AIT
Est 8:13 so that the Jews *w* **be** ready on that day to AIT
Job 1: 4 and *they w* **invite** their three sisters to eat AIT
Job 1: 5 Job *w* **make arrangements** *for* them to be AIT
Job 1: 5 *he w* **sacrifice** a burnt offering *for* each of AIT
Job 3:13 For now *I w be* **lying down** in peace; I would AIT
Job 3:13 down in peace; *I w be* **asleep** and at rest AIT
Job 5: 8 if I were you, *I w* **appeal** to God; I would lay AIT
Job 5: 8 appeal to God; *I w* **lay** my cause before him. AIT
Job 6: 3 *It w* surely **outweigh** the sand of the seas AIT
Job 6: 8 my request, that God *w* **grant** what I hope for, AIT
Job 6: 9 that God *w be* **willing** to crush me, to let AIT
Job 6:10 Then I *w* still **have** this consolation—my joy AIT
Job 6:27 *You w* even **cast** lots for the fatherless and AIT
Job 6:28 so kind as to look at me. *W I* **lie** to your face? AIT
Job 7:16 I despise my life; *I w* not **live** forever. Let me AIT
Job 9:16 I do not believe *he w* **give** me **a hearing**. AIT
Job 9:17 He *w* **crush** me with a storm and multiply my AIT
Job 9:18 *He w* not **let** me catch my breath but would AIT
Job 9:18 my breath but *w* **overwhelm** me *with* misery. AIT
Job 9:20 innocent, my mouth *w* **condemn** me; if I were AIT
Job 9:20 if I were blameless, *it w* **pronounce** me **guilty**. AIT
Job 9:31 *you w* **plunge** me into a slime pit so that AIT
Job 9:31 pit so that even my clothes *w* **detest** me. AIT
Job 9:34 so that his terror *w* **frighten** me no more. AIT
Job 9:35 Then *I w* **speak up** without fear of him, but AIT
Job 10:14 *you w be* **watching** me and would not let my AIT
Job 10:14 me and *w* not **let** my offense **go unpunished**. AIT
Job 11: 5 how I wish that God *w* **speak**, that he would AIT
Job 11: 5 that *he w* **open** his lips against you AIT
Job 13: 5 If only *you w be* **altogether silent**! For you AIT
Job 13: 5 altogether silent! For you, *that w* **be** wisdom. AIT
Job 13: 9 **W** it turn out well if he examined you NDT
Job 13:10 *He w* **surely call** you **to account** if you AIT
Job 13:11 *W* not his splendor **terrify** you? Would not AIT
Job 13:11 *W* not the dread of him **fall** on you? AIT
Job 13:16 no godless person *w dare* **come** before him! AIT
Job 14:13 "If only *you w* **hide** me in the grave and AIT
Job 14:13 If only *you w* **set** me a time and then AIT
Job 15: 2 "*W* a wise person **answer** *with* empty notions AIT
Job 15: 3 *W* they **argue** with useless words, with AIT
Job 16: 5 But my mouth *w* **encourage** you; comfort AIT
Job 16: 5 comfort from my lips *w* **bring** you **relief**. AIT
Job 19: 5 If indeed *you w* **exalt** *yourselves* above me AIT
Job 21:15 What *w we* **gain** by praying to him AIT
Job 21:27 the schemes by which *you w* **wrong** me. AIT
Job 22: 3 What pleasure **w** it give the Almighty if you NDT
Job 22: 3 What **w** he gain if your ways were NDT
Job 23: 4 *I w* **state** my case before him and fill my AIT
Job 23: 5 *I w* **find out** what he would answer me, and AIT
Job 23: 5 I would find out what *he w* **answer** me, and AIT
Job 23: 5 and consider what *he w* **say** to me. AIT
Job 23: 6 *W he* vigorously **oppose** me? No, he would AIT
Job 23: 6 he *w* not **press charges** against me. AIT
Job 23: 7 there *I w be* **delivered** forever from my AIT
Job 30: 1 whose fathers *I w have* **disdained** to put with AIT
Job 31:11 For that **w** have been wicked, a sin to be NDT
Job 31:12 Destruction; *it w have* **uprooted** my harvest. AIT
Job 31:18 from my youth I reared them as a father **w**, NDT
Job 31:28 then these also **w** be sins to be judged, for I NDT
Job 31:28 for *I w have been* **unfaithful** to God on high. AIT
Job 31:34 that I kept silent and *w* not **go** outside— AIT
Job 31:36 Surely *I w* **wear** it on my shoulder, I would AIT
Job 31:36 it on my shoulder, *I w* **put** it **on** like a crown. AIT
Job 31:37 *I w* **give** him an account of my every step; AIT
Job 31:37 every step; *I w* **present** it *to* him as to a ruler.) AIT
Job 32:22 in flattery, my Maker *w* soon **take** me **away**. AIT
Job 34:12 It is unthinkable that God *w* **do wrong**, that AIT
Job 34:12 do wrong, that the Almighty *w* **pervert** justice. AIT
Job 34:15 all humanity *w* **perish** together and mankind AIT
Job 34:15 together and mankind *w* **return** to the dust. AIT
Job 35: 4 "I *w like to* **reply** *to* you and to your friends AIT
Job 36:19 *W* your wealth or ... mighty efforts **sustain** AIT
Job 36:19 sustain you so you **w** not be in distress? NDT
Job 37:20 *W* anyone **ask** to be swallowed up AIT
Job 40: 8 "*W you* **discredit** my justice? Would you AIT
Job 40: 8 *W you* **condemn** me to justify yourself? AIT
Job 41:32 one *w* **think** the deep had white hair. AIT
Ps 10:15 *that w* not otherwise *be* **found out**. AIT
Ps 14: 7 that salvation for Israel **w** come out of Zion! NDT
Ps 38:12 *those who* **w** harm me talk of my ruin H2011
Ps 39: 9 I was silent; *I w* not **open** my mouth, for you AIT
Ps 40: 5 your deeds, *they w be* too **many** to declare. AIT
Ps 44:21 *w* not God *have* **discovered** it, since he knows AIT
Ps 50:12 If I were hungry *I w* not **tell** you, for the world AIT
Ps 51:16 in sacrifice, or *I w* **bring** it; you do not take AIT
Ps 53: 6 that salvation for Israel **w** come out of Zion! NDT
Ps 55: 6 wings of a dove! *I w* **fly away** and be at rest. AIT
Ps 55: 7 *I w* flee **far away** and stay in the desert; AIT
Ps 55: 8 *I w* **hurry** *to* my place of shelter, far from the AIT
Ps 62: 3 *W* all of you **throw** me **down**—this leaning AIT
Ps 66:18 sin in my heart, the Lord *w* not *have* **listened**; AIT
Ps 73:11 They say, "How *w* God **know**? Does the Most AIT
Ps 73:15 out like that, *I w have* **betrayed** your children. AIT
Ps 77: 2 untiring hands, and I **w not** be comforted. H4412
Ps 78: 6 so the next generation *w* **know** them, even AIT
Ps 78: 6 be born, and *they* in turn *w* **tell** their children. AIT
Ps 78: 7 Then *they w* **put** their trust in God and would AIT
Ps 78: 7 trust in God and *w* not **forget** his deeds but AIT
Ps 78: 7 forget his deeds but *w* **keep** his commands. AIT
Ps 78: 8 *They w* not *be* like their ancestors—a AIT
Ps 78:34 God slew them, *they w* **seek** him; they AIT
Ps 78:36 But then *they w* **flatter** him with their mouths AIT
Ps 81: 8 warn you—*if you w only* **listen** to me, Israel! AIT
Ps 81:11 "But my people *w* not **listen** to me; Israel AIT
Ps 81:11 not listen to me; Israel *w* not **submit** to me. AIT
Ps 81:13 "If my people *w only* **listen** to me, if Israel AIT
Ps 81:13 listen to me, if Israel *w only* **follow** my ways, AIT
Ps 81:14 how quickly *I w* **subdue** their enemies and AIT
Ps 81:15 who hate the LORD *w* **cringe** before him, AIT
Ps 81:15 and their punishment *w* **last** forever. AIT
Ps 81:16 But you *w be* **fed** with the finest of wheat AIT
Ps 81:16 with honey from the rock *I w* **satisfy** you." AIT
Ps 84:10 *I* **w rather be** a doorkeeper in the house of H1047
Ps 94:17 I *w* soon *have* **dwelt** in the silence of death. AIT
Ps 95: 7 Today, if only *you w* **hear** his voice, AIT
Ps 106:23 So he said *he w* **destroy** them—had not AIT
Ps 106:26 hand that he *w* **make** them **fall** in the AIT
Ps 109:31 their lives from *those who w* **condemn** them. AIT

Ps 119: 6 Then *I w* not *be* **put to shame** when I AIT
Ps 119:92 *I w have* **perished** in my affliction. AIT
Ps 124: 3 *they w have* **swallowed** us alive when their AIT
Ps 124: 4 the flood *w have* **engulfed** us, the torrent AIT
Ps 124: 4 the torrent *w have* **swept** over us, AIT
Ps 124: 5 the raging waters *w have* **swept** us **away**. AIT
Ps 139:18 *they w* **outnumber** the grains of sand AIT
Ps 139:19 If only *you*, God, *w* **slay** the wicked! Away AIT
Pr 1:30 Since *they w* not **accept** my advice and AIT
Pr 5:13 *I w* not **obey** my teachers or turn my ear to my AIT
Pr 8:29 so the waters *w* not **overstep** his command, AIT
Pr 17: 9 *Whoever w* **foster** love covers over an offense, AIT
Pr 22: 5 but *those who w* **preserve** their life stay far AIT
Pr 24:28 *w you* use your lips *to* **mislead**? AIT
SS 3: 4 I held him and *w* not **let** him **go** till I had AIT
SS 6:13 Why *w you* **gaze** on the Shulammite as on AIT
SS 8: 1 I found you outside, *I w* **kiss** you, and no one AIT
SS 8: 1 I would kiss you, and no *one w* **despise** me. AIT
SS 8: 2 *I w* **lead** you and bring you to my mother's AIT
SS 8: 2 *I w* **give** you spiced wine **to drink**, the nectar AIT
SS 8: 7 one's house for love, it *w be* **utterly scorned**. AIT
Isa 1: 9 survivors, *we w have* **become** like Sodom, we AIT
Isa 1: 9 like Sodom, *we w have* **been like** Gomorrah. AIT
Isa 14:17 its cities and *w* not *let* his captives **go** home?" AIT
Isa 16:14 a servant bound by contract **w** count them, NDT
Isa 21:12 If *you w* **ask**, then ask; and come back yet AIT
Isa 21:16 as a servant bound by contract **w** count it, all NDT
Isa 27: 4 *I w* **march** against them in battle; I would set AIT
Isa 27: 4 them in battle; *I w* **set** them all **on fire**. AIT
Isa 28:12 the place of repose"—but *they* **w** not listen. H14
Isa 30:15 is your strength, but *you* **w have** none of it. H14
Isa 42:24 For *they* **w** not follow his ways; they did not H14
Isa 44: 9 Those who **w** speak up for them are blind NDT
Isa 48:18 your peace *w have* **been** like a river, your AIT
Isa 48:19 Your descendants *w have* **been** like the sand AIT
Isa 48:19 their name *w* never **be blotted out** nor AIT
Isa 54: 9 of Noah *w* never again **cover** the earth. AIT
Isa 57:10 going about, but *you w* not **say**, 'It is AIT
Isa 57:16 then they *w* **faint away** because of me AIT
Isa 64: 1 that *you w* **rend** the heavens and come down, AIT
Isa 64: 1 that the mountains *w* **tremble** before you! AIT
Jer 3: 1 *W* not the land *be* **completely defiled**? But AIT
Jer 3: 1 many lovers—**w** you now **return** to me?" AIT
Jer 3: 7 had done all this *she w* **return** to me but she AIT
Jer 3:19 " 'How gladly *w I* **treat** you like my children AIT
Jer 3:19 I thought *you w* **call** me 'Father' and not turn AIT
Jer 9: 1 *I w* **weep** day and night *for* the slain of my AIT
Jer 12: 1 Yet *I w* **speak** with you about your justice AIT
Jer 15: 1 my heart **w** not go out to this people. NDT
Jer 17:23 stiff-necked and *w* not **listen** or respond to AIT
Jer 19:15 stiff-necked and *w* not **listen** *to* my words. AIT
Jer 22:24 ring on my right hand, *I w* still **pull** you **off**. AIT
Jer 23:22 *they w have* **proclaimed** my words *to* my AIT
Jer 23:22 my people and *w have* **turned** them from AIT
Jer 30:14 you as an enemy **w** and punished you as NDT
Jer 30:14 would and punished you as **w** the cruel, NDT
Jer 32:33 they *w* not **listen** or respond to discipline. AIT
Jer 34:10 agreed that they *w* **free** their male and AIT
Jer 36:25 to burn the scroll, he *w* not **listen** to them. AIT
Jer 36:29 king of Babylon *w* **certainly come** and destroy AIT
Jer 37:10 *they w* **come out** and burn this city down." AIT
Jer 37:14 But Irijah *w* not **listen** to him; instead, he AIT
Jer 38:15 did give you counsel, *you w* not **listen** to me." AIT
Jer 40: 3 it about; he has done just as he said he **w**. NDT
Jer 44:17 will certainly do everything we said we **w**: NDT
Jer 44:25 what you said you **w** do when you promised, NDT
Jer 49: 9 came to you, *w they* not **leave** a few grapes? AIT
Jer 49: 9 *w they* not **steal** only as much as they wanted AIT
Jer 51: 9 " '*We w have* **healed** Babylon, but she AIT
Jer 51:60 all the disasters that *w* come upon Babylon— AIT
La 3:30 him offer his cheek to *one who w* **strike** him, AIT
La 3:36 of justice—*w* not the Lord **see** such things? AIT
La 4:20 under his shadow *we w* **live** among the AIT
Eze 1:12 Wherever the spirit *w* **go**, they would go AIT
Eze 1:12 spirit would go, *they w* **go**, without turning as AIT
Eze 1:17 *they w* **go** in any one of the four directions AIT
Eze 1:20 Wherever the spirit *w* **go**, they would go, and AIT
Eze 1:20 spirit would go, *they w* **go**, and the wheels AIT
Eze 1:20 and the wheels *w* **rise** along with them AIT
Eze 3: 6 you to them, they *w have* **listened** to you. AIT
Eze 4:12 Eat the food as you **w** a loaf of barley bread NDT
Eze 10:11 *they w* **go** in any one of the four directions AIT
Eze 14:16 They alone *w* **be saved**, but the land would AIT
Eze 14:16 would be saved, but the land *w* **be** desolate. AIT
Eze 14:18 sons or daughters. They alone *w be* **saved**. AIT
Eze 14:20 They *w* **save** only themselves by their AIT
Eze 16:56 You **w** not even mention your sister Sodom NDT
Eze 17: 8 water so that *it w* **produce** branches, AIT
Eze 17:14 so that the kingdom *w* **be** brought low AIT
Eze 20: 6 to them that *I w* **bring** them **out** of Egypt into AIT
Eze 20: 8 rebelled against me and **w** not listen to me; H14
Eze 20: 8 So I said *I w* **pour out** my wrath on them AIT
Eze 20:12 so they *w* **know** that I the LORD made them AIT
Eze 20:13 So I said *I w* **pour out** my wrath on them AIT
Eze 20:14 of my name I did what **w** keep it from being NDT
Eze 20:15 wilderness that I *w* not **bring** them into the AIT
Eze 20:21 So I said *I w* **pour out** my wrath on them AIT
Eze 20:22 of my name I did what **w** keep it from being NDT
Eze 20:23 wilderness that I *w* **disperse** them among the AIT
Eze 20:26 horror so *they w* **know** that I am the LORD. AIT
Eze 22:30 among them *who w* **build up** the wall and AIT
Eze 22:30 of the land so I *w* not *have to* **destroy** it, AIT
Eze 24: 7 it on the ground, where the dust *w* **cover** it. AIT
Eze 24: 8 on the bare rock, so that it *w* not **be covered**. AIT
Eze 24:13 you but *you w* not *be* **cleansed** from your AIT
Eze 33: 5 the warning, *they w have* **saved** themselves. AIT
Eze 38:17 years that I *w* **bring** you against them. AIT
Da 1:10 The king **w** then have my head because of NDT
Da 6:12 Majesty, *w* **be thrown** into the lions' den?" AIT
Da 9: 2 desolation of Jerusalem *w* **last** seventy years. AIT
Hos 6:11 "Whenever I *w* **restore** the fortunes of my AIT
Hos 7: 1 whenever I *w* **heal** Israel, the sins of Ephraim AIT
Hos 8: 7 it to yield grain, foreigners *w* **swallow** it **up**. AIT
Ob 5 *w they* not **steal** only as much as they wanted AIT
Ob 5 came to you, *w they* not **leave** a few grapes? AIT
Jnh 4: 5 waited to see what *w* **happen** to the city. AIT
Jnh 4: 8 "It **w** be better for me to die than to live." NDT
Mic 2:11 *that w* **be** just the prophet for this people! AIT
Hab 1: 5 in your days that *you w* not **believe**, AIT
Zep 3: 7 Then her place of refuge *w* not **be destroyed**, AIT
Zec 1: 4 But *they w* not **listen** or pay attention to me AIT
Zec 7:12 flint and *w* not **listen** *to* the law or *to* the AIT
Zec 7:13 they called, *I w* not **listen**,' says the LORD AIT
Mal 1: 8 *W he be* **pleased with** you? Would AIT
Mal 1: 8 *W he* **accept** you?" says the AIT
Mal 1:10 that one of you *w* **shut** the temple doors AIT
Mal 1:10 so that *you w* not **light** useless **fires** *on* my AIT
Mt 2:23 prophets, that *he w be* **called** a Nazarene. AIT
Mt 7:12 do to others what *you* **w** have them do to *G2527*
Mt 8:13 Let it be done just as you believed it **w**." NDT
Mt 11:21 they **w have** repented long ago in sackcloth *G323*
Mt 11:23 in Sodom, it **w have** remained to this day. *G323*
Mt 12: 7 you **w** not **have** condemned the innocent. *G323*
Mt 13:15 with their hearts and turn, and *I w* **heal** them. AIT
Mt 18: 6 *it w be* **better** for them to have a large AIT
Mt 18:17 treat them **as** you *w* a pagan or a tax AIT
Mt 23:30 we **w** not **have** taken part with them in *G323*
Mt 24:22 cut short, no one **w** survive, but for the *G323*
Mt 24:39 nothing about what **w** happen until the NDT
Mt 24:43 he **w have** kept watch and would not have *G323*
Mt 24:43 kept watch and **w** not **have** let his house be *G323*
Mt 25:27 when I returned I **w have** received it back *G323*
Mt 26:24 *It w* **be** better for him if he had not been born AIT
Mt 26:25 Then Judas, the *one who w* **betray** him, said AIT
Mt 26:54 how then *w* the Scriptures *be* **fulfilled** that AIT
Mk 1:34 but *he w* not **let** the demons speak because AIT
Mk 3: 2 closely to see if *he w* **heal** him on the AIT
Mk 5: 5 in the hills *he* **w** cry out and cut *G1639*
Mk 6:37 "That **w** take more than half a year's wages! NDT
Mk 9:42 *it w* **be** better for them if a large millstone AIT
Mk 11:16 and *w* not **allow** anyone to carry merchandise AIT
Mk 13:20 not cut short those days, no one **w** survive. *G323*
Mk 14:21 It **w** be better for him if he had not been NDT
Mk 15:24 they cast lots to see what each *w* **get**. AIT
Lk 1:45 that the Lord *w* **fulfill** his promises to her!" AIT
Lk 1:62 to find out what he **w** like to name the *G323*
Lk 2:26 Holy Spirit *that he w* not **die** before he had AIT
Lk 4:41 them and *w* not **allow** them to speak, AIT
Lk 6: 7 closely to see if *he w* **heal** on the Sabbath. AIT
Lk 6:31 Do to others as *you* **w** have them do to you *G2527*
Lk 7:39 he **w** know who is touching him and what *G323*
Lk 9:46 as to which of them *w* **be** the greatest. AIT
Lk 10:13 Sidon, they **w have** repented long ago *G323*
Lk 12:39 he **w** not **have** let his house be broken into. *G323*
Lk 17: 2 *It w be* **better** for them to be thrown into the AIT
Lk 17:20 Pharisees when the kingdom of God *w* **come**, AIT
Lk 18:13 *He* **w** not even look up to heaven, but *G2527*
Lk 19:42 on this day what **w** bring you peace— NDT
Lk 20:10 the tenants so *they w* **give** him some of the AIT
Lk 22:23 which of them it might be who **w** do this. *G3516*
Lk 22:68 if I asked you, *you w* not **answer**. AIT
Jn 2:24 But Jesus *w* not **entrust** himself to them, for AIT
Jn 4:10 you **w have** asked him and he would have *G323*
Jn 4:10 asked him and he **w have** given you living *G323*
Jn 5:46 believed Moses, you **w** believe me, for he *G323*
Jn 6: 7 "It **w** take more than half a year's wages to NDT
Jn 6:64 did not believe and who **w** betray him. *G1639*
Jn 7:13 But no one *w* **say** anything publicly about him AIT
Jn 8:19 you knew me, you **w** know my Father also." *G323*
Jn 8:24 I told you that *you w* **die** in your sins; if you AIT
Jn 8:39 "then *you w* **do** what Abraham did. AIT
Jn 8:42 were your Father, you **w** love me, for I have *G323*
Jn 8:55 If I said I did not, *I w* **be** a liar like you, but I AIT
Jn 9:22 Jesus was the Messiah *w* **be** put out of the AIT
Jn 9:41 you were blind, you **w** not be guilty of sin *G323*
Jn 11:21 been here, my brother **w** not **have** died. *G323*
Jn 11:32 been here, my brother **w** not **have** died." *G323*
Jn 11:51 that Jesus **w** die for the Jewish *G3516*
Jn 12:21 they said, "*we w* **like** to see Jesus." AIT
Jn 12:37 presence, *they still w* not **believe** in him. AIT
Jn 12:40 their hearts, nor turn—and *I w* **heal** them." AIT
Jn 12:42 *they w* not **openly acknowledge** *their* **faith** AIT
Jn 12:42 their faith for fear *they w* **be** put out of the AIT
Jn 14: 2 **w** I have told you that I am going there to *G323*
Jn 14:28 you **w** be glad that I am going to the Father *G323*
Jn 15:19 to the world, it **w** love you as its own. *G323*
Jn 15:22 to them, *they w* not **be guilty of sin**; but now AIT
Jn 15:24 no one else did, *they w* not *be* **guilty of sin**. AIT
Jn 17:12 to destruction so that Scripture *w* **be fulfilled**. AIT
Jn 18: 9 that the words he had spoken *w be* **fulfilled**: AIT
Jn 18:14 leaders that *it w be* **good** if one man died AIT
Jn 18:30 "we **w** not **have** handed him over to you." *G323*
Jn 18:36 my servants **w** fight to prevent my arrest by *G323*
Jn 19:11 "*You w* **have** no power over me if it were not AIT
Jn 19:28 so that Scripture *w be* **fulfilled**, Jesus AIT
Jn 19:36 happened so that the scripture *w be* **fulfilled**: AIT
Jn 21:19 kind of death by which Peter *w* **glorify** God. AIT
Jn 21:23 the believers that this disciple *w* not **die**. AIT
Jn 21:23 But Jesus did not say that *he w* not **die**; he AIT
Jn 21:25 whole world *w* not **have room** for the books AIT
Jn 21:25 have room for the books that *w be* **written**. AIT
Ac 2:30 him on oath *that he w* **place** one of his AIT
Ac 3:18 prophets, saying that his Messiah *w* **suffer**. AIT
Ac 5:26 they feared that the people *w* **stone** them. AIT
Ac 6: 2 "*It w* not **be** right for us to neglect the AIT
Ac 7: 5 descendants after him *w* **possess** the land, AIT
Ac 7:19 out their newborn babies so that *they w* **die**. AIT
Ac 7:25 his own people *w* **realize** that God was using AIT
Ac 11:28 that a severe famine **w** spread over the *G3516*
Ac 12:11 Jewish people were **hoping w happen**." *G4660*
Ac 13:41 in your days that *you w* never **believe**, AIT
Ac 16: 7 the Spirit of Jesus *w* not **allow** them to. AIT
Ac 17:20 and *we w* **like** to know what they mean." AIT
Ac 17:27 God did this *so that they w* **seek** him and AIT
Ac 18:14 it **w** be reasonable for me to listen to you. *G323*
Ac 19:13 *They w* **say**, "In the name of the Jesus whom AIT
Ac 19:30 the crowd, but the disciples *w* not **let** him. AIT
Ac 19:40 In that case *we w* not *be* **able** to account AIT
Ac 20:20 anything that *w be* **helpful** to you but have AIT
Ac 20:38 his statement that *they* **w** never see his *G3516*
Ac 21:14 *When* he *w* not *be* **dissuaded**, we gave up AIT
Ac 21:26 days of purification **w** end and the offering NDT
Ac 21:26 the offering *w be* **made** for each of them AIT
Ac 23:10 was afraid Paul *w be* **torn to pieces** by them. AIT
Ac 24: 4 *I w* **request** *that* you be kind enough to hear AIT
Ac 24:26 he was hoping that Paul *w* **offer** him a bribe, AIT
Ac 25:20 so I asked if *he w be* **willing** to go to AIT
Ac 25:22 to Festus, "*I w* **like** to hear this man myself." AIT
Ac 26:22 the prophets and Moses said **w** happen— *G3516*
Ac 26:23 that the Messiah **w** suffer and, as the first to NDT
Ac 26:23 **w** bring the message of light to his own *G3516*
Ac 27: 1 When it was decided *that* we *w* **sail** for Italy AIT
Ac 27:17 were afraid *they w* **run aground** on the AIT
Ac 27:21 then *you w have* **spared** *yourselves* this AIT
Ac 27:29 Fearing that *we w be* **dashed** against the AIT
Ac 27:41 The bow stuck fast and *w* **not move**, and the AIT
Ac 28:24 by what he said, but others *w* **not believe**. AIT
Ac 28:27 with their hearts and turn, and *I w* **heal** them. AIT
Ro 4:13 the promise *that he w* **be** heir of the world, AIT
Ro 7: 7 *I w* not *have* **known** what sin was had it not AIT
Ro 7: 7 For *I w* not *have* **known** what coveting really AIT
Ro 9:29 we **w have** become like Sodom *G323*
Ro 9:29 we **w have** been like Gomorrah. *G323*
Ro 11: 6 if it were, grace *w* no longer **be** grace. AIT
Ro 15:20 so that *I w* not *be* **building** on someone AIT
1Co 2: 8 they **w** not **have** crucified the Lord of glory. *G323*
1Co 5:10 In that case *you w* **have to** leave this world. AIT
1Co 7:14 Otherwise your children *w* **be** unclean, but as AIT
1Co 7:32 *I w* **like** you to be free from concern. AIT
1Co 9:15 I *w* rather **die** than allow anyone to AIT
1Co 11:31 we **w** not come under such judgment. *G323*
1Co 12:15 *it w* not for that reason stop **being** part of the AIT
1Co 12:16 *it w* not for that reason stop **being** part of the AIT
1Co 12:17 where **w** the sense of hearing be? NDT
1Co 12:17 where **w** the sense of smell be? NDT
1Co 12:19 were all one part, where **w** the body be? NDT
1Co 14: 5 *I w* **like** every one of you to speak in tongues AIT
1Co 14: 5 I **w** rather have you prophesy. *G2671*
1Co 14:19 But in the church *I* **w rather** speak five *G2527*
2Co 2: 1 that I *w* not **make** another painful visit to you. AIT
2Co 2: 3 so that when I came *I w* not **be** distressed by AIT
2Co 2: 3 in all of you, that you *w* all **share** my joy. AIT
2Co 2: 9 see if you *w* stand the test and **be** obedient AIT
2Co 3:13 who *w* **put** a veil over his face to prevent the AIT
2Co 5: 8 and *w* **prefer** to be away from the body and AIT
2Co 7: 3 in our hearts that *we w* **live** or die **with** you. AIT
2Co 9: 3 that you may be ready, as I said you **w** be. NDT
2Co 9: 4 *we w* **be ashamed** *of* having been so confident. AIT
2Co 10:14 **as** *w be the case* if we had not come to you AIT
2Co 11:16 **then** tolerate me just as you **w** a fool *G2829*
2Co 11:17 boasting I am not **talking** as the Lord **w**, *G2848*
2Co 12: 6 choose to boast, *I w* not **be** a fool, because I AIT
2Co 12: 6 be a fool, because *I w be* **speaking** the truth. AIT
Gal 1:10 I **w** not be a servant of Christ. *G323*
Gal 2:18 then I **really w** be a lawbreaker. *G5319*
Gal 3: 2 *I w* **like** to learn just one thing from you: Did AIT
Gal 3: 8 foresaw that God *w* **justify** the Gentiles by AIT
Gal 3:21 righteousness **w** certainly **have** come by the *G323*
Gal 3:23 the faith that was to come *w be* **revealed**. AIT
Gal 4:15 *you w have* **torn out** your eyes and given AIT
Gal 5:12 *they w go the whole way and* **emasculate** *themselves* AIT
Eph 6: 5 sincerity of heart, just as you **w** obey Christ. NDT
1Th 3: 3 so that no one *w be* **unsettled** by these trials AIT
1Th 3: 4 kept telling you that *we* **w** be persecuted. *G3516*
2Th 3: 8 so that *we w* not *be a* **burden** to any of you. AIT
2Th 3:15 warn them as you **w** a fellow believer. NDT
1Ti 1:16 as an example *for* those *who* **w** believe in *G3516*
Phm 13 I *w have* **liked** to keep him with me so that he AIT
Phm 14 any favor you do *w* not **seem** forced but AIT
Phm 14 would not seem forced but **w** be voluntary. NDT
Phm 17 welcome him as you **w** welcome me. NDT
Heb 3: 5 *to* what *w be* **spoken** by God *in the future*. AIT
Heb 3:18 God swear *that they w* never **enter** his rest if AIT
Heb 4: 8 God **w** not **have** spoken later about another *G323*
Heb 8: 4 If he were on earth, he **w** not be a priest, for *G323*

Heb 8: 7 no place w have been sought for another. G323
Heb 9:26 Otherwise Christ *w have* **had to** suffer many AIT
Heb 10: 2 w they not **have** stopped being offered? G323
Heb 10: 2 worshipers *w have been* **cleansed** once for AIT
Heb 10: 2 and w no longer *have* **felt** guilty for their sins. AIT
Heb 11: 8 to go to a place *he* w **later** receive as his AIT
Heb 11:15 they w **have** had opportunity to return. G323
Heb 11:28 of the firstborn *w* not **touch** the firstborn of AIT
Heb 11:40 together with us *w they be* **made perfect**. AIT
Heb 13:17 a burden, for that w be of no benefit to you. NDT
Jas 5:17 He prayed earnestly that *it w* not **rain**, and it AIT
1Pe 1:11 the Messiah and the glories that w follow. NDT
1Pe 3:10 "Whoever w love life and see good days G2527
2Pe 2:21 *It* w *have* **been** better for them not to have AIT
1Jn 2:19 they w **have** remained with us G323
Rev 12:14 where *she* w *be* **taken care of** for a time AIT

WOULDN'T (6) [NOT, WOULD]

Ge 38:26 since I w give her to my son Shelah." H4202
Ge 42:22 But you w listen! Now we must H4202
Nu 14: 3 W it be better for us to go back to Egypt?" H4202
Jdg 12: 3 When I saw that you w help, I took my life H401
1Sa 20: 9 was determined to harm you, w I tell you?" H4202
2Sa 12:18 he w listen to us when we spoke to him. H4202

WOUND (21) [WIND, WINDING, WINDS, WOUNDED, WOUNDING, WOUNDS]

Ex 21:25 burn for burn, w for wound, bruise for H7206
Ex 21:25 burn, wound for w, bruise for bruise. H7206
1Ki 22:35 The blood from his w ran onto the floor of H4804
Job 34: 6 guiltless, his arrow inflicts an **incurable** w. H631
Ps 69:26 persecute those you w and talk about the H5782
Pr 25:20 like vinegar poured on a w, is one who H6003
Jer 6:14 They dress the w *of* my people as though H8691
Jer 8:11 They dress the w *of* my people as though H8691
Jer 8:22 is there no **healing for** the w *of* my people? H776
Jer 10:19 My w is incurable! Yet I said H4804
Jer 14:17 has suffered a grievous w, a crushing H8691
Jer 15:18 pain unending and my w grievous and H4804
Jer 30:12 " 'Your w is incurable, your injury beyond H8691
Jer 30:15 Why do you cry out over your w, your pain H8691
La 2:13 Your w is as deep as the sea H8691
Da 6:23 from the den, no w was found on him A10244
Na 3:19 can heal you; your w is fatal. All who hear H4804
1Co 8:12 them in this way and w their weak G5597
Rev 13: 3 the beast seemed *to have* **had** a fatal w, G5377
Rev 13: 3 but the fatal w had been healed. G4435
Rev 13:12 whose fatal w had been healed. G4435

WOUNDED (23) [WOUND]

Dt 32:39 I bring to life, *I have* w and I will heal H4730
1Sa 31: 3 archers overtook him, they w *him* critically. H2655
1Ki 20:37 So the man struck him and w him. H7205
1Ki 22:34 get me out of the fighting. *I've* **been** w." H2703
2Ki 8:28 Ramoth Gilead. The Arameans w Joram; H5782
2Ki 8:29 son of Ahab, because he *had been* w. H2703
2Ki 9:27 They w him in his chariot on the way up to NDT
1Ch 10: 3 the archers overtook him, they w *him*. H2655
2Ch 18:33 get me out of the fighting. *I've* **been** w." H2703
2Ch 22: 5 Ramoth Gilead. The Arameans w Joram; H5782
2Ch 22: 6 son of Ahab because he *had been* w. H2703
2Ch 24:25 withdrew, they left Joash severely w. H4708
2Ch 35:23 his officers, "Take me away; *I am* badly w." H2703
Job 24:12 the souls of the w cry out for help. H2728
Ps 109:22 needy, and my heart *is* w within me. H2726
Jer 37:10 you and only w men were left in their H1991
Jer 51: 4 slain in Babylon, **fatally** w in her streets. H1991
Jer 51:52 throughout her land the w will groan. H2728
La 2:12 they faint like the w in the streets of the H2728
Eze 26:15 when the w groan and the slaughter takes H2728
Eze 30:24 groan before him like a **mortally** w **man**. H2728
Lk 20:12 and they w him and threw him out. G5547
Rev 13:14 beast who *was* w by the G2400+3836+4435

WOUNDING (1) [WOUND]

Ge 4:23 I have killed a man for w me, a young H7206

WOUNDS (25) [WOUND]

2Ki 8:29 to recover from the w the Arameans had H4804
2Ki 9:15 to recover from the w the Arameans had H4804
2Ch 22: 6 to recover from the w they had inflicted on H4804
Job 5:18 For he w, but he also binds up; he injures H3872
Job 9:17 a storm and multiply my w for no reason. H7206
Ps 38: 5 My w fester and are loathsome because H2467
Ps 38:11 companions avoid me because of my w; H5596
Ps 147: 3 the brokenhearted and binds up their w. H6780
Pr 20:30 Blows and w scrub away evil, and H7206
Pr 26:10 Like an archer *who* w at random is one H2726
Pr 27: 6 W *from* a friend can be trusted, but an H7206
Isa 1: 6 only w and welts and open sores H7206
Isa 30:26 his people and heals the w he inflicted. H4731
Isa 53: 5 was on him, and by his w we are healed. H2467
Jer 6: 7 her sickness and w are ever before me. H4804
Jer 19: 8 will scoff because of all its w. H4804
Jer 30:17 will restore you to health and heal your w, H4804
Jer 49:17 will scoff because of all its w. H4804
Jer 50:13 they will scoff because of all her w. H4804
Hos 6: 1 he has injured us but he will bind up our w. NDT
Zec 13: 6 'What are these w on your body?' H4804
Zec 13: 6 'The w *I* **was given** at the house of my H5782
Lk 10:34 He went to him and bandaged his w G5546
Ac 16:33 the jailer took them and washed their w; G4435
1Pe 2:24 "*by* his w you have been healed. G3698

WOVE (1) [WEAVE]

Jdg 16:13 braids of his head, w them into the fabric H755

WOVEN (27) [WEAVE]

Ex 26: 1 with cherubim w *into* them *by* a skilled H5126
Ex 26:31 with cherubim w *into* it *by* a skilled worker. H5126
Ex 28: 4 an ephod, a robe, a w tunic, a turban H9587
Ex 28: 8 Its **skillfully** w waistband is to be like it— H682
Ex 28:32 There shall be a w edge like a collar H5126+755
Ex 29: 5 ephod on him by its skillfully w waistband. NDT
Ex 31:10 also the w garments, both the sacred H8573
Ex 35:19 the w garments worn for ministering in the H8573
Ex 36: 8 cherubim w *into* them *by* expert hands H5126
Ex 36:35 with cherubim w *into* it *by* a skilled worker. H5126
Ex 39: 1 scarlet yarn they made w garments for H8573
Ex 39: 5 Its **skillfully** w waistband was like it—of one H682
Ex 39:41 the w garments worn for ministering H8573
Lev 13:48 any w or knitted material of linen or wool H9274
Lev 13:49 the leather, the w or knitted material, or H9274
Lev 13:51 in the fabric, the w or knitted material, or H9274
Lev 13:52 the w or knitted material of wool or linen H9274
Lev 13:53 in the fabric, the w or knitted material, or H9274
Lev 13:56 the leather, or the w or knitted material. H9274
Lev 13:57 in the fabric, in the w or knitted material H9274
Lev 13:58 Any fabric, w or knitted material, or any H9274
Lev 13:59 linen clothing, w or knitted material, or H9274
Lev 19:19 wear clothing w of two kinds of **material**. H9122
Dt 22:11 clothes of wool and linen w together. H9122
Ps 139:15 *when I* **was** w **together** in the depths of H8387
La 1:14 by his hands *they were* w **together**. H8571
Jn 19:23 w *in one piece* from top to bottom. G5733

WRAP (5) [WRAPPED, WRAPS]

Nu 4:10 Then *they are to* w it and all its H5989
Nu 4:12 in the sanctuary, w them in a blue cloth H5989
Isa 28:20 the blanket too narrow *to* w **around** *you*. H4043
Isa 32:11 clothes and w yourselves **in rags**. H2520+6584
Ac 12: 8 "W your cloak **around** you and follow me," G4314

WRAPPED (21) [WRAP]

Ex 12:34 in kneading troughs w in clothing. H7674
1Sa 21: 9 it *is* w in a cloth behind the ephod. H4286
Job 38: 9 its garment and w it in thick darkness, H3157
Ps 109:19 May it be like a cloak w about him, like a H6486
Ps 109:29 with disgrace and w *in* shame as in a H6486
Pr 30: 4 Who *has* w **up** the waters in a cloak H7674
Isa 59:17 vengeance and w **himself** *in* zeal as in a H6486
Eze 16: 4 you rubbed with salt or w **in cloths**. H3156+3156
Jnh 2: 5 seaweed *was* w **around** my head. H2502
Mt 27:59 took the body, w it in a clean linen cloth G1962
Mk 15:46 took down the body, w it **in** the linen, and G1912
Lk 2: 7 *She* w him **in cloths** and placed him in a G5058
Lk 2:12 will find a baby w **in cloths** and lying in a G5058
Lk 23:53 w it **in** linen cloth and placed it in a tomb G1962
Jn 11:44 his hands and feet w with strips of linen G1313
Jn 13: 4 clothing, and w a towel **around** his **waist**. G1346
Jn 13: 5 with the towel that was w **around** him. G1346
Jn 19:40 Jesus' body, *the two of them* w it, with the G1313
Jn 20: 7 that had been w **around** Jesus' head. G1962
Jn 21: 7 *he* w his outer garment **around** him (for G1346
Ac 5: 6 men came forward, w **up** his body, and G5366

WRAPS (2) [WRAP]

Job 26: 8 *He* w **up** the waters in his clouds, yet the H7674
Ps 104: 2 The LORD w **himself** *in* light as with a H6486

WRATH (188)

Nu 1:53 law so that my w will not fall on the H7912
Nu 16:46 W has come out from the LORD; the H7912
Nu 18: 5 so that my w will not fall on the Israelites H7912
Dt 9: 8 At Horeb *you* **aroused** the LORD's w so that H7911
Dt 9:19 I feared the anger and w of the LORD, for H2779
Dt 29:20 his w and zeal will burn against them. H678
Dt 29:28 anger and in great w the LORD uprooted H7912
Dt 32:22 For a fire will be kindled by my w, one that H678
Jos 9:20 so that God's w will not fall on us for H7912
Jos 22:20 did not w come on the whole community H7912
1Sa 28:18 carry out his fierce w against the H678
2Sa 6: 8 because the LORD's w had broken out H7288
1Ch 13:11 because the LORD's w had broken out H7288
1Ch 27:24 God's w came on Israel on account of this H7912
2Ch 12: 7 My w will not be poured out on Jerusalem H2779
2Ch 19: 2 the w of the LORD is on you. H7912
2Ch 19:10 otherwise his w will come on you and H7912
2Ch 32:25 therefore the LORD's w was on him and on H7912
2Ch 32:26 the LORD's w did not come on them H7912
2Ch 36:16 prophets until the w *of* the LORD was H2779
Ezr 7:23 Why should his w fall on the realm of A10634
Ne 13:18 are stirring up more w against Israel by H3019
Job 19:29 w will bring punishment by the sword H2779
Job 20:28 rushing waters on the day of God's w. H678
Job 21:20 drink the cup of the w *of* the Almighty. H2779
Job 21:30 that they are delivered from the day of w? H6301
Job 40:11 Unleash the fury of your w, look at all who H678
Ps 2: 5 in his anger and terrifies them in his w, H3019
Ps 2:12 his w can flare up in a moment. H678
Ps 6: 1 in your anger or discipline me in your w. H2779
Ps 7:11 a God *who* **displays** his w every day. H2404
Ps 21: 9 The LORD will swallow them up in his w H678
Ps 37: 8 Refrain from anger and turn from w; do H2779
Ps 38: 1 in your anger or discipline me in your w. H2779
Ps 38: 3 Because of your w there is no health in H2405
Ps 59:13 consume them in your w, consume them H2779
Ps 69:24 Pour out your w on them; let your fierce H2405
Ps 76:10 Surely your w *against* mankind brings you H2779
Ps 76:10 the survivors of your w are restrained. H2779
Ps 78:21 and his w rose against Israel, H678
Ps 78:38 his anger and did not stir up his full w. H2779
Ps 78:49 his hot anger, his w, indignation and H6301
Ps 79: 6 Pour out your w on the nations that do not H2779
Ps 85: 3 set aside all your w and turned from your H6301
Ps 88: 7 Your w lies heavily on me; you have H2779
Ps 88:16 Your w has swept over me; your terrors H3019
Ps 89:46 How long will your w burn like fire? H2779
Ps 90: 9 All our days pass away under your w; we H6301
Ps 90:11 Your w is as great as the fear that is your H6301
Ps 102:10 because of your **great** w, for H2405+2256+7912
Ps 106:23 him to keep his w from destroying them. H2779
Ps 110: 5 he will crush kings on the day of his w. H678
Pr 11: 4 Wealth is worthless in the day of w, but H6301
Pr 11:23 the hope of the wicked only in w. H6301
Pr 15: 1 A gentle answer turns away w, but a H2779
Pr 16:14 A king's w is a messenger of death, but H2779
Pr 20: 2 A king's w strikes terror like the roar of a H399
Pr 21:14 concealed in the cloak pacifies great w. H2779
Pr 22:14 a *man who is* **under** the LORD's w falls into H2404
Pr 24:18 disapprove and turn his w away from them. H678
Isa 1:24 *I will* **vent** *my* w on my foes and avenge H5714
Isa 9:19 By the w *of* the LORD Almighty the land H6301
Isa 10: 5 in whose hand is the club of my w! H2405
Isa 10:25 you will end and my w will be directed to H678
Isa 13: 3 summoned my warriors to carry out my w— H678
Isa 13: 5 the LORD and the weapons of his w—to H2405
Isa 13: 9 a cruel day, with w and fierce anger—to H6301
Isa 13:13 its place at the w *of* the LORD Almighty, H6301
Isa 26:20 a little while until his w has passed by. H2405
Isa 30:27 his lips are full of w, and his tongue is a H2405
Isa 34: 2 all nations; his w is on all their armies. H2779
Isa 48: 9 For my own name's sake I delay my w; for H678
Isa 51:13 day because of the w *of* the oppressor, H2779
Isa 51:13 For where is the w *of* the oppressor? H2779
Isa 51:17 the hand of the LORD the cup of his w, H2779
Isa 51:20 They are filled with the w *of* the LORD, H2779
Isa 51:22 the goblet of my w, you will never drink H2779
Isa 59:18 so will he repay w to his enemies and H2779
Isa 63: 3 in my anger and trod them down in my w; H2779
Isa 63: 5 me, and my own w sustained me. H2779
Isa 63: 6 in my w I made them drunk and poured H2779
Jer 3: 5 Will your w continue forever?' NDT
Jer 4: 4 my w will flare up and burn like fire H2779
Jer 6:11 But I am full of the w *of* the LORD, and I H2779
Jer 7:20 My anger and my w will be poured out on H2779
Jer 7:29 this generation that is under his w. H6301
Jer 10:10 the nations cannot endure his w. H2405
Jer 10:25 Pour out your w on the nations that do not H2779
Jer 18:20 behalf to turn your w away from them. H2779
Jer 21: 5 arm in furious anger and in great w. H7912
Jer 21:12 my w will break out and burn like fire H2779
Jer 23:19 the storm of the LORD will burst out in w, H2779
Jer 25:15 with the wine of my w and make all the H2779
Jer 30:23 the storm of the LORD will burst out in w, H2779
Jer 32:31 my anger and w that I must remove H2779
Jer 32:37 them in my furious anger and great w; H7912
Jer 33: 5 the people I will slay in my anger and w. H2779
Jer 36: 7 the anger and w pronounced against H2779
Jer 42:18 'As my anger and w have been poured H2779
Jer 42:18 so will my w be poured out on you when H2779
Jer 50:25 brought out the weapons of his w, H2405
La 2: 2 in his w he has torn down the strongholds H6301
La 2: 4 has poured out his w like fire on the tent H2779
La 3: 1 seen affliction by the rod of the LORD's w. H6301
La 4:11 The LORD has given full vent to his w; he H2779
Eze 5:13 will cease and my w against them will H2779
Eze 5:13 And when I have spent my w on them H2779
Eze 5:15 you in anger and in w and with stinging H2779
Eze 6:12 So will I pour out my w on them. H2779
Eze 7: 8 to pour out my w on you and spend my H2779
Eze 7:12 for my w is on the whole crowd. H3019
Eze 7:14 for my w is on the whole crowd. H3019
Eze 7:19 to deliver them in the day of the LORD's w. H6301
Eze 9: 8 this outpouring of your w on Jerusalem?" H2779
Eze 13:13 In my w I will unleash a violent wind, and H2779
Eze 13:15 I will pour out my w against the wall and H2779
Eze 14:19 land and pour out my w on it through H2779
Eze 16:38 vengeance of my w and jealous anger. H2779
Eze 16:42 Then my w against you will subside and H2779
Eze 20: 8 would pour out my w on them and spend H2779
Eze 20:13 would pour out my w on them and destroy H2779
Eze 20:21 would pour out my w on them and spend H2779
Eze 20:33 outstretched arm and with outpoured w. H2779
Eze 20:34 outstretched arm and with outpoured w. H2779
Eze 21:17 hands together, and my w will subside. H2779
Eze 21:31 I will pour out my w on you and breathe H2405
Eze 22:20 in my anger and my w and put you inside H2779
Eze 22:21 I will blow on you with my fiery w, H6301
Eze 22:22 I the LORD have poured out my w on you. H2779
Eze 22:24 cleansed or rained on in the day of w. H2405
Eze 22:31 I will pour out my w on them and H2405
Eze 24: 8 To stir up w and take revenge I put her H2779
Eze 24:13 clean again until my w against you has H2779
Eze 25:14 in accordance with my anger and my w; H2779
Eze 25:17 on them and punish them in my w. H2779
Eze 30:15 I will pour out my w on Pelusium, the H2779
Eze 36: 6 I speak in my jealous w because you have H2779

Eze 36:18 So I poured out my w on them because H2779
Eze 38:19 In my zeal and fiery w I declare that at that H6301
Da 8:19 what will happen later in the time of w, H2405
Da 9:16 your anger and your w from Jerusalem, H2779
Da 11:36 until the time of w is completed, H2405
Hos 5:10 I will pour out my w on them like a flood H6301
Hos 13:11 you a king, and in my w I took him away. H6301
Mic 5:15 in anger and w on the nations that H2779
Mic 7: 9 I will bear the LORD's w, until he pleads H2408
Na 1: 2 LORD takes vengeance and is filled with w. H2779
Na 1: 2 on his foes and **vents** *his* w against his H5757
Na 1: 6 His w is poured out like fire; the rocks are H2779
Hab 3: 2 make them known; in w remember mercy. H8075
Hab 3: 8 Was your w against the streams? Did H678
Hab 3:12 In w you strode through the earth and in H2405
Zep 1:15 That day will be a day of w—a day of H6301
Zep 1:18 to save them on the day of the LORD's w." H6301
Zep 2: 2 the day of the LORD's w comes upon you. H678
Zep 3: 8 to pour out my w on them— H2405
Mal 1: 4 a people always **under the w** *of* the LORD. H2404
Mt 3: 7 warned you to flee from the coming w? *G3973*
Lk 3: 7 warned you to flee from the coming w? *G3973*
Lk 21:23 in the land and w against this people. *G3973*
Jn 3:36 not see life, for God's w remains on them. *G3973*
Ro 1:18 The w of God is being revealed from *G3973*
Ro 2: 5 you are storing up w against yourself for *G3973*
Ro 2: 5 against yourself for the day *of* God's w, *G3973*
Ro 2: 8 follow evil, there will be w and anger. *G3973*
Ro 3: 5 God is unjust in bringing his w on us? *G3973*
Ro 4:15 because the law brings w. And where *G3973*
Ro 5: 9 we be saved from God's w through him! *G3973*
Ro 9:22 to show his w and make his power *G3973*
Ro 9:22 with great patience the objects *of* his w— *G3973*
Ro 12:19 leave room *for* God's w, for it is *G3973*
Ro 13: 4 agents of w to bring punishment on the *G3973*
Eph 2: 3 we were by nature deserving of w. *G3973*
Eph 5: 6 such things God's w comes on those who *G3973*
Col 3: 6 Because of these, the w of God is coming. *G3973*
1Th 1:10 who rescues us from the coming w. *G3973*
1Th 2:16 The w of God has come upon them at last *G3973*
1Th 5: 9 appoint us to suffer w but to receive *G3973*
Rev 6:16 the throne and from the w of the Lamb! *G3973*
Rev 6:17 For the great day *of* their w has come, and *G3973*
Rev 11:18 nations were angry, and your w has come. *G3973*
Rev 14:10 poured full strength into the cup *of* his w. *G3973*
Rev 14:19 them into the great winepress *of* God's w. *G2596*
Rev 15: 1 because with them God's w is completed. *G2596*
Rev 15: 7 golden bowls filled with the w of God, *G2596*
Rev 16: 1 the seven bowls *of* God's w on the earth." *G2596*
Rev 16:19 filled with the wine of the fury *of* his w. *G3973*
Rev 19:15 of the fury *of* the w of God Almighty. *G3973*

WREAK (1)
Isa 54:16 have created the destroyer to w **havoc**; H2472

WREATH (3) [WREATHS]
Isa 28: 1 Woe to that w, the pride of Ephraim's H6498
Isa 28: 3 That w, the pride of Ephraim's drunkards H6498
Isa 28: 5 a beautiful w for the remnant of his H6498

WREATHS (4) [WREATH]
1Ki 7:29 bulls were w *of* hammered work. H4324
1Ki 7:30 four supports, cast with w on each side. H4324
1Ki 7:36 every available space, with w all around. H4324
Ac 14:13 brought bulls and w to the city gates *G5098*

WRECKED (2) [SHIPWRECK, SHIPWRECKED]
1Ki 22:48 set sail—they **were** w at Ezion Geber. H8689
2Ch 20:37 The ships **were** w and were not able to H8689

WRENCHED (2)
Ge 32:25 hip so that his hip *was* w as he wrestled H3697
Eze 29: 7 you broke and their backs *were* w. H5048

WREST (KJV) DENY, DISTORT, PERVERT, SIDING, TWIST

WRESTLE (1) [WRESTLED, WRESTLING]
Ps 13: 2 How long *must I* w *with* my thoughts and H8883

WRESTLED (2) [WRESTLE]
Ge 32:24 and a man w with him till daybreak. H84
Ge 32:25 his hip was wrenched as he w with the man. H84

WRESTLING (1) [WRESTLE]
Col 4:12 *He is* always w in prayer for you, that you *G76*

WRETCHED (5) [WRETCHES]
Pr 15:15 All the days of the oppressed are w, but H8273
Hab 3:14 to devour the w who were in hiding. H6714
Mt 21:41 "He will bring those wretches to a w end," *G2809*
Ro 7:24 What a w man I am! Who will rescue me *G5417*
Rev 3:17 But you do not realize that you are w *G5417*

WRETCHES (1) [WRETCHED]
Mt 21:41 "He will bring those w to a wretched end," *G2805*

WRING (2)
Lev 1:15 w **off** the head and burn it on the altar H4916
Lev 5: 8 *He is to* w its head from its neck, not H4916

WRINKLE (1)
Eph 5:27 without stain or w or any other blemish *G4869*

WRIST (2) [WRISTS]
Ge 38:28 thread and tied it on his w and said, H3338
Ge 38:30 who had the scarlet thread on his w H3338

WRISTS (4) [WRIST]
Jer 40: 4 am freeing you from the chains on your w. H3338
Eze 13:18 on all their w and make veils of H723+3338
Eze 23:42 bracelets on the w *of* the woman and her H3338
Ac 12: 7 he said, and the chains fell off Peter's w. *G5931*

WRITE (83) [WRITER, WRITES, WRITING, WRITINGS, WRITTEN, WROTE]
Ex 17:14 "W this on a scroll as something to be H4180
Ex 34: 1 and *I will* w on them the words that were H4180
Ex 34:27 said to Moses, "**W down** these words, for H4180
Nu 5:23 " 'The priest *is to* w these curses on a H4180
Nu 17: 2 **W** the name of each man on his staff H4180
Nu 17: 3 On the staff of Levi w Aaron's name, for H4180
Dt 6: 9 **W** them on the doorframes of your houses H4180
Dt 10: 2 *I will* w on the tablets the words that were H4180
Dt 11:20 **W** them on the doorframes of your houses H4180
Dt 17:18 *he is to* w for himself on a scroll a copy of H4180
Dt 27: 3 **W** on them all the words of this law when H4180
Dt 27: 8 And *you shall* w very clearly all the words H4180
Dt 31:19 "Now **w down** this song and teach it to H4180
Jos 18: 4 of the land and *to* **w a description** *of* it, H4180
Jos 18: 8 of the land and **w a description** *of* it. H4180
Ezr 5:10 so that *we could* **w down** the names of A10374
Est 8: 8 Now w another decree in the king's name H4180
Job 13:26 For *you* **w down** bitter things against me H4180
Ps 87: 6 The LORD *will* w in the register of the H6218
Pr 3: 3 w them on the tablet of your heart. H4180
Pr 7: 3 w them on the tablet of your heart. H4180
Isa 8: 1 a large scroll and w on it with an ordinary H4180
Isa 10:19 so few that a child *could* w them **down**. H4180
Isa 30: 8 Go now, w it on a tablet for them, inscribe H4180
Isa 44: 5 still others *will* w *on* their hand, 'The H4180
Jer 30: 2 'W in a book all the words I have spoken H4180
Jer 31:33 in their minds and w it on their hearts. H4180
Jer 36: 2 "Take a scroll and w on it all the words I H4180
Jer 36:17 "Tell us, how *did you come to* w all this? H4180
Jer 36:28 another scroll and w on it all the words H4180
Jer 36:29 "Why *did you* w on it that the king of H4180
Eze 37:16 take a stick of wood and w on it H4180
Eze 37:16 stick of wood, and w on it, 'Belonging to H4180
Eze 43:11 **W** these **down** before them so that they H4180
Hab 2: 2 "**W down** the revelation and make it plain H4180
Mk 10: 4 permitted a man *to* w a certificate of *G1211*
Lk 1: 3 decided *to* w **an** orderly **account** for you, *G1211*
Jn 8: 6 bent down and *started to* w on the ground *G2863*
Jn 19:21 to Pilate, "*Do* not w 'The King of the Jews *G1211*
Ac 15:20 Instead *we should* w to them, telling them *G2182*
Ac 25:26 nothing definite *to* w to His Majesty about *G1211*
Ac 25:26 investigation I may have something *to* w. *G1211*
1Co 16:21 w this greeting in my own hand. NDT
2Co 1:13 For *we do* not w you anything you cannot *G1211*
2Co 9: 1 is no need for me *to* w to you about this *G1211*
2Co 13:10 This is why *I* w these things when I am *G1211*
Gal 6:11 letters I use *as I* w to you with my own *G1211*
Php 3: 1 no trouble for me *to* w the same things to *G1211*
Col 4:18 w this greeting in my own hand NDT
1Th 4: 9 one another we do not need *to* w to you, *G1211*
1Th 5: 1 dates we do not need *to* w to you, *G1211*
2Th 3:17 w this greeting in my own hand, which NDT
2Th 3:17 mark in all my letters. This is how *I* w. *G1211*
Phm 21 of your obedience, *I* w to you, knowing *G1211*
Heb 8:10 in their minds and w them **on** their hearts. *G2108*
Heb 10:16 and *I will* w them **on** their minds. *G2108*
1Jn 1: 4 We w this to make our joy complete. *G1211*
1Jn 2: 1 *I* w this to you so that you will not sin. *G1211*
1Jn 2:14 *I* w to you, dear children, because you *G1211*
1Jn 2:14 *I* w to you, fathers, because you know him *G1211*
1Jn 2:14 *I* w to you, young men, because you are *G1211*
1Jn 2:21 *I do* not w to you because you do not know *G1211*
1Jn 5:13 *I* w these things to you who believe in the *G1211*
2Jn 12 I have much *to* w to you, but I do not want *G1211*
3Jn 13 I have much *to* w you, but I do not want to *G1211*
Jude 3 I was very eager *to* w to you about the *G1211*
Jude 3 I felt compelled *to* w and urge you to *G1211*
Rev 1:11 "W on a scroll what you see and send it *G1211*
Rev 1:19 "W, therefore, what you have seen, what *G1211*
Rev 2: 1 "To the angel of the church in Ephesus w *G1211*
Rev 2: 8 "To the angel of the church in Smyrna w *G1211*
Rev 2:12 the angel of the church in Pergamum w: *G1211*
Rev 2:18 "To the angel of the church in Thyatira w *G1211*
Rev 3: 1 "To the angel of the church in Sardis w *G1211*
Rev 3: 7 the angel of the church in Philadelphia w: *G1211*
Rev 3:12 *I will* w on them the name of my God *G1211*
Rev 3:12 I will also w on them my new name. NDT
Rev 3:14 "To the angel of the church in Laodicea w: *G1211*
Rev 10: 4 I was about to w; but I heard a voice *G1211*
Rev 10: 4 thunders have said and *do* not w it **down**." *G1211*
Rev 14:13 I heard a voice from heaven say, "**W** this: *G1211*
Rev 19: 9 angel said to me, "**W** this: Blessed are *G1211*
Rev 21: 5 Then he said, "**W** this **down**, for these *G1211*

WRITER (1) [WRITE]
Ps 45: 1 my tongue is the pen of a skillful w. H6221

WRITES (4) [WRITE]
Dt 24: 1 and *he* w her a certificate of divorce H4180
Dt 24: 3 dislikes her and w her a certificate of H4180
Ro 10: 5 Moses w this about the righteousness that *G1211*
2Pe 3:16 He w the same way in all his letters NDT

WRITHE (6) [WRITHED, WRITHES]
Isa 13: 8 *they will* w like a woman in labor. H2655
Jer 4:19 *I* **w in pain**. Oh, the agony of H2655
Eze 30:16 to Egypt; Pelusium *will* **w in agony**. H2655+2655
Mic 1:12 Those who live in Maroth **w in pain** H2655
Mic 4:10 **W** in agony, Daughter Zion, like a woman H2655
Zec 9: 5 Gaza *will* **w in agony**, and Ekron H2655+4394

WRITHED (3) [WRITHE]
Ps 77:16 the waters saw you and w; the very depths H2655
Isa 26:18 with child, *we* **w in labor**, but we gave H2655
Hab 3:10 the mountains saw you and w. Torrents of H2655

WRITHES (2) [WRITHE]
Isa 26:17 about to give birth w and cries out in her H2655
Jer 51:29 The land trembles and w, for the LORD's H2655

WRITING (38) [WRITE]
Ex 32:16 work of God; the w was the writing of God H4844
Ex 32:16 the writing was the w *of* God, engraved H4844
Dt 31:24 Moses finished w in a book the words H4180
1Ch 28:19 "I have in w as a result of the LORD's hand H4181
2Ch 36:22 his realm and also to put it in w: H4844
Ezr 1: 1 his realm and also to put it in w: H4844
Ne 9:38 agreement, **putting** it **in** w, and our H4180
Job 31:35 *let* my accuser **put** *his* indictment **in** w. H4180
Isa 38: 9 A w of Hezekiah king of Judah after his H4844
Eze 9: 2 in linen who had a w kit at his side. H6221
Eze 9: 3 in linen who had the w kit at his side H6221
Eze 9:11 in linen with the w **kit** at his side brought H7879
Da 5: 7 reads this w and tells me what A10375
Da 5: 8 could not read the w or tell the king A10375
Da 5:12 he will tell you what the w means. NDT
Da 5:15 me to read this w and tell me what it A10375
Da 5:16 If you can read this w and tell me what it A10375
Da 5:17 I will read the w for the king and tell him A10375
Da 6: 8 decree and **put** it **in** w so that it A10673+10375
Da 6: 9 King Darius **put** the decree **in** w. A10673+10375
Da 6:13 Majesty, or to the decree *you* **put in** w. A10673
Lk 1:63 He asked for a w **tablet**, and to everyone's *G4400*
Ac 15:27 confirm by word of mouth what we are w. *G899S*
1Co 4:14 *I am* w this not to shame you but to warn *G1211*
1Co 5:11 But now *I am* w to you that you must not *G1211*
1Co 9:15 And *I am* not w this in the hope that you *G1211*
1Co 14:37 that what *I am* w to you is the Lord's *G1211*
Gal 1:20 before God that what *I am* w you is no lie. *G1211*
1Ti 3:14 *I am* w you these instructions so that *G1211*
Phm 19 *am* w this with my own hand. I will *G1211*
1Jn 2: 7 *I am* not w you a new command but an *G1211*
1Jn 2: 8 Yet *I am* w you a new command; its truth *G1211*
1Jn 2:12 *I am* w to you, dear children, because *G1211*
1Jn 2:13 *I am* w to you, fathers, because you know *G1211*
1Jn 2:13 *I am* w to you, young men, because you *G1211*
1Jn 2:26 *I am* w these things to you about those *G1211*
2Jn 5 *I am* not w you a new command but one *G1211*
Rev 5: 1 throne a scroll *with* w on both sides and *G1211*

WRITINGS (2) [WRITE]
Mt 26:56 taken place that the w of the prophets *G1210*
Ro 16:26 the prophetic w by the command of the *G1210*

WRITTEN (254) [WRITE]
Ge 5: 1 This is the w account of Adam's family H6219
Ex 24:12 law and commandments *I have* w for their H4180
Ex 32:32 then blot me out of the book *you have* w." H4180
Dt 10: 4 on these tablets what he had w before, H4844
Dt 28:58 of this law, which *are* w in this book, and H4180
Dt 29:20 All the curses w in this book will fall on H4180
Dt 29:21 of the covenant w in this Book of the H4180
Dt 29:27 brought on it all the curses w in this book. H4180
Dt 30:10 decrees that *are* w in this Book of the H4180
Jos 1: 8 may be careful to do everything w in it. H4180
Jos 8:31 according to what *is* w in the Book of the H4180
Jos 8:34 just as it *is* w in the Book of the Law. H4180
Jos 10:13 enemies, as it *is* w in the Book of Jashar. H4180
Jos 18: 6 After you *have* w **descriptions** *of* the seven H4180
Jos 23: 6 to obey all that *is* w in the Book of the H4180
2Sa 1:18 of the bow (*it is* w in the Book of Jashar): H4180
1Ki 2: 3 regulations, as w in the Law of Moses. H4180
1Ki 11:41 *are* they not w in the book of the annals of H4180
1Ki 14:19 *are* w in the book of the annals of the H4180
1Ki 14:29 *are* they not w in the book of the annals H4180
1Ki 15: 7 *are* they not w in the book of the annals H4180
1Ki 15:23 *are* they not w in the book of the annals H4180
1Ki 15:31 *are* they not w in the book of the annals H4180
1Ki 16: 5 *are* they not w in the book of the annals H4180
1Ki 16:14 *are* they not w in the book of the annals H4180
1Ki 16:20 *are* they not w in the book of the annals H4180
1Ki 16:27 *are* they not w in the book of the annals H4180
1Ki 21:11 directed in the letters she *had* w to them. H4180
1Ki 22:39 *are* they not w in the book of the annals H4180
1Ki 22:45 *are* they not w in the book of the annals H4180
2Ki 1:18 *are* they not w in the book of the annals H4180
2Ki 8:23 *are* they not w in the book of the annals H4180
2Ki 10:34 *are* they not w in the book of the annals H4180
2Ki 12:19 *are* they not w in the book of the annals H4180
2Ki 13: 8 *are* they not w in the book of the annals H4180
2Ki 13:12 *are* they not w in the book of the annals H4180
2Ki 14: 6 with what *is* w in the Book of the H4180
2Ki 14:15 *are* they not w in the book of the annals H4180

2Ki 14:18 are they not w in the book of the annals H4180
2Ki 14:28 are they not w in the book of the annals H4180
2Ki 15: 6 are they not w in the book of the annals H4180
2Ki 15:11 Zechariah's reign are w in the book of the H4180
2Ki 15:15 are w in the book of the annals of the H4180
2Ki 15:21 are they not w in the book of the annals H4180
2Ki 15:26 are w in the book of the annals of the H4180
2Ki 15:31 are they not w in the book of the annals H4180
2Ki 15:36 are they not w in the book of the annals H4180
2Ki 16:19 are they not w in the book of the annals H4180
2Ki 20:20 are they not w in the book of the annals H4180
2Ki 21:17 are they not w in the book of the annals H4180
2Ki 21:25 are they not w in the book of the annals H4180
2Ki 22:13 Judah about **what** is w *in* this book that H1821
2Ki 22:13 with all that *is* w there concerning us." H4180
2Ki 22:16 to everything w *in* the book the king of H1821
2Ki 23: 3 the words of the covenant w in this book. H4180
2Ki 23:21 as *it is* w in this Book of the Covenant." H4180
2Ki 23:24 of the law w in the book that H4180
2Ki 23:28 are they not w in the book of the annals H4180
2Ki 24: 5 are they not w in the book of the annals H4180
1Ch 16:40 with everything w in the Law of the LORD, H4180
1Ch 29:29 they *are* w in the records of Samuel the H4180
2Ch 9:29 are they not w in the records of Nathan H4180
2Ch 12:15 are they not w in the records of Shemaiah H4180
2Ch 13:22 are w in the annotations of the prophet H4180
2Ch 16:11 are w in the book of the kings of Judah H4180
2Ch 20:34 are w in the annals of Jehu son of Hanani H4180
2Ch 23:18 of the LORD as w in the Law of Moses, H4180
2Ch 24:27 the temple of God *are* w in the H4180
2Ch 25: 4 in accordance with what *is* w in the Law, H4180
2Ch 25:26 are they not w in the book of the kings of H4180
2Ch 27: 7 are w in the book of the kings of Israel H4180
2Ch 28:26 are w in the book of the kings of Judah H4180
2Ch 30: 5 large numbers according to what *was* w. H4180
2Ch 30:18 ate the Passover, contrary to what *was* w. H4180
2Ch 31: 3 festivals as w in the Law of the LORD H4180
2Ch 32:32 acts of devotion *are* w in the vision of the H4180
2Ch 33:18 are w in the annals of the kings of Israel. NDT
2Ch 33:19 all these *are* w in the records of the seers. H4180
2Ch 34:21 Judah about **what** is w *in* this book that H1821
2Ch 34:21 accordance with all that *is* w in this book." H4180
2Ch 34:24 all the curses w in the book that has been H4180
2Ch 34:31 the words of the covenant w in this book. H4180
2Ch 35: 4 to the **instructions** w *by* David king of H4181
2Ch 35:12 the LORD, as *it is* w in the Book of Moses. H4180
2Ch 35:25 in Israel and *are* w in the Laments. H4180
2Ch 35:26 with what *is* w in the Law of the H4180
2Ch 35:27 are w in the book of the kings of Israel H4180
2Ch 36: 8 are w in the book of the kings of Israel H4180
Ezr 3: 2 with what *is* w in the Law of Moses H4180
Ezr 3: 4 Then in accordance with what *is* w, they H4180
Ezr 4: 7 The letter *was* w in Aramaic script and in H4180
Ezr 5: 5 go to Darius and his **reply** be received. A10496
Ezr 6: 2 province of Media, and this **was** w on it: A10374
Ezr 6:18 according to **what** is w *in* the Book of A10375
Ne 6: 6 in which *was* w: "It is reported among the H4180
Ne 7: 5 This is what I found w there: H4180
Ne 8:14 They found w in the Law, which the LORD H4180
Ne 8:15 to make temporary shelters"—as *it is* w. H4180
Ne 10:34 of the LORD our God, as *it is* w in the Law. H4180
Ne 10:36 "As it *is* also w in the Law, we will bring H4180
Ne 13: 1 there it was found w that no Ammonite H4180
Est 1:19 royal decree and *let it* **be** w in the laws of H4180
Est 3:12 *These* **were** w in the name of King Xerxes H4180
Est 8: 5 *let an* **order be** w overruling the H4180
Est 8: 8 no document w in the king's name and H4180
Est 8: 9 These orders were w in the script of each NDT
Est 9:23 doing what Mordecai *had* w to them. H4180
Est 9:25 he issued w orders that the evil scheme H6219
Est 9:26 Because of everything w *in* this letter and H1821
Est 9:32 and *it* **was** w **down** in the records. H4180
Est 10: 2 are they not w in the book of the annals H4180
Job 19:23 recorded, that *they* **were** w on a scroll, H2980
Ps 40: 7 come—*it is* w about me in the scroll. H4180
Ps 102:18 *Let* this **be** w for a future generation, that H4180
Ps 139:16 ordained for me **were** w in your book H4180
Ps 149: 9 carry out the sentence w against them— H4180
Pr 22:20 *Have I* not w thirty sayings for you, sayings H4180
Isa 65: 6 *it stands* w before me: I will not H4180
Jer 17:13 turn away from you *will* **be** w in the dust H4180
Jer 25:13 all that *are* w in this book and prophesied H4180
Jer 36:27 words that Baruch *had* w at Jeremiah's H4180
Jer 51:60 Jeremiah *had* w on a scroll *about* all the H4180
Eze 2:10 both sides of it *were* w words of lament H4180
Eze 37:20 before their eyes the sticks *you have* w on H4180
Da 5:25 "This is the inscription that **was** w: MENE, A10673
Da 9:11 sworn judgments w in the Law of Moses H4180
Da 9:13 Just as *it is* w in the Law of Moses, all this H4180
Da 10:21 I will tell you what *is* w in the Book of H8398
Da 12: 1 whose name is found w in the book— H4180
Mal 3:16 of remembrance **was** w in his presence H4180
Mt 2: 5 "for this is what the prophet *has* w: G1211
Mt 4: 4 Jesus answered, "*It is* w: 'Man shall not G1211
Mt 4: 6 yourself down. For *it is* w: " 'He will G1211
Mt 4: 7 answered him, "*It is* also w: 'Do not put G1211
Mt 4:10 For *it is* w: 'Worship the Lord your G1211
Mt 11:10 This is the one about whom *it is* w: " 'I will G1211
Mt 21:13 "*It is* w," he said to them, " 'My house will G1211
Mt 26:24 of Man will go just as *it is* w about him. G1211
Mt 26:31 all fall away on account of me, for *it is* w: G1211
Mt 27:37 they placed the w charge against him: G1211
Mk 1: 2 as *it is* w in Isaiah the prophet: "I will send G1211
Mk 7: 6 about you hypocrites; as *it is* w: G1211
Mk 9:12 Why then *is it* w that the Son of Man must G1211
Mk 9:13 they wished, just as *it is* w about him." G1211
Mk 11:17 as he taught them, he said, "*Is it* not w: G1211
Mk 14:21 of Man will go just as *it is* w about him. G1211
Mk 14:27 all fall away," Jesus told them, "for *it is* w: G1211
Mk 15:26 The w **notice** of the charge against him G2107
Lk 2:23 as *it is* w in the Law of the Lord, "Every G1211
Lk 3: 4 As *it is* w in the book of the words of G1211
Lk 4: 4 Jesus answered, "*It is* w: 'Man shall not G1211
Lk 4: 8 Jesus answered, "*It is* w: 'Worship the G1211
Lk 4:10 For *it is* w: " 'He will command his angels G1211
Lk 4:17 he found the place where it is w: G1211
Lk 7:27 This is the one about whom *it is* w: " 'I will G1211
Lk 10:20 rejoice that your names *are* w in heaven." G1582
Lk 10:26 "What *is* w in the Law?" he replied. "How G1211
Lk 18:31 everything that *is* w by the prophets G1211
Lk 19:46 "*It is* w," he said to them, " 'My house will G1211
Lk 20:17 what is the meaning of that which *is* w: G1211
Lk 21:22 in fulfillment of all that *has been* w. G1211
Lk 22:37 It *is* w: 'And he was numbered with the G1211
Lk 22:37 what is w about me is reaching its NDT
Lk 23:38 There was a w **notice** above him, which G2107
Lk 24:44 be fulfilled that *is* w about me in the Law G1211
Lk 24:46 "This is what *is* w: The Messiah will G1211
Jn 2:17 His disciples remembered that it is w G1211
Jn 6:31 the manna in the wilderness; as it is w: G1211
Jn 6:45 It is w in the Prophets: 'They will all be G1211
Jn 8:17 In your own Law *it is* w that the testimony G1211
Jn 10:34 "Is it not w in your Law, 'I have said G1211
Jn 12:14 a young donkey and sat on it, as it is w: G1211
Jn 12:16 things had been w about him and that G1211
Jn 15:25 But this is to fulfill what *is* w in their Law G1211
Jn 19:20 the sign was w in Aramaic, Latin and G1211
Jn 19:22 answered, "What *I have* w, I have written." G1211
Jn 19:22 answered, "What I have written, *I have* w." G1211
Jn 20:31 But these *are* w that you may believe that G1211
Jn 21:25 If every one of them *were* w **down**, G1211
Jn 21:25 have room for the books that *would be* w. G1211
Ac 1:20 said Peter, "*it is* w in the Book of Psalms: G1211
Ac 7:42 This agrees with *what is* w in the book of G1211
Ac 13:29 had carried out all that *was* w about him, G1211
Ac 13:33 As *it is* w in the second Psalm G1211
Ac 15:15 are in agreement with this, as *it is* w: G1211
Ac 21:25 we *have* w to them our decision that they G2182
Ac 23: 5 that he was the high priest; for *it is* w: G1211
Ac 24:14 the Law and that *is* w in the Prophets, G1211
Ro 1:17 is by faith from first to last, just as *it is* w: G1211
Ro 2:15 of the law are w on their hearts, G1209
Ro 2:24 As *it is* w: "God's name is blasphemed G1211
Ro 2:27 you have the w **code** and circumcision, G1207
Ro 2:29 the heart, by the Spirit, not *by* the w **code**. G1207
Ro 3: 4 As *it is* w: "So that you may G1211
Ro 3:10 As *it is* w: "There is no one righteous, not G1211
Ro 4:17 As *it is* w: "I have made you a father of G1211
Ro 4:23 credited to him" *were* w not for him alone G1211
Ro 7: 6 not in the old way *of* the w **code**. G1207
Ro 8:36 As *it is* w: "For your sake we face death all G1211
Ro 9:13 Just as *it is* w: "Jacob I loved, but Esau I G1211
Ro 9:33 As *it is* w: "See, I lay in Zion a stone that G1211
Ro 10:15 they are sent? As *it is* w: "How beautiful G1211
Ro 11: 8 as *it is* w: "God gave them a spirit of G1211
Ro 11:26 will be saved. As *it is* w: "The deliverer G1211
Ro 12:19 leave room for God's wrath, for *it is* w: G1211
Ro 14:11 *It is* w: " 'As surely as I live,' says the Lord G1211
Ro 15: 3 did not please himself but, as *it is* w: G1211
Ro 15: 4 that *was* w **in the past** was written to G4592
Ro 15: 4 was written in the past *was* w to teach us, G1211
Ro 15: 9 his mercy. As *it is* w: "Therefore I will G1211
Ro 15:15 Yet *I have* w you quite boldly on some G1211
Ro 15:21 as *it is* w: "Those who were not G1211
1Co 1:19 For *it is* w: "I will destroy the wisdom of G1211
1Co 1:31 Therefore, as *it is* w: "Let the one who G1211
1Co 2: 9 However, as *it is* w: "What no eye has G1211
1Co 3:19 in God's sight. As *it is* w: "He catches the G1211
1Co 4: 6 the saying, "Do not go beyond what *is* w." G1211
1Co 9: 9 For *it is* w in the Law of Moses: "Do not G1211
1Co 9:10 *this was* w for us, because whoever G1211
1Co 10: 7 as some of them were; as *it is* w: G1211
1Co 10:11 examples and *were* w **down** as warnings G1211
1Co 14:21 In the Law *it is* w: "With other tongues G1211
1Co 15:45 So *it is* w: "The first man Adam became a G1211
1Co 15:54 then the saying that *is* w will come true: G1211
2Co 3: 2 are our letter, w on our hearts, known G1582
2Co 3: 3 w not with ink but with the Spirit of the G1582
2Co 4:13 *It is* w: "I believed; therefore I have G1211
2Co 8:15 as *it is* w: "The one who gathered much G1211
2Co 9: 9 As *it is* w: "They have freely scattered their G1211
Gal 3:10 of the law are under a curse, as *it is* w: G1211
Gal 3:10 to do everything w in the Book of the Law." G1211
Gal 3:13 law by becoming a curse for us, for *it is* w: G1211
Gal 4:22 For *it is* w that Abraham had two sons, one G1211
Gal 4:27 For *it is* w: "Be glad, barren woman, you G1211
Eph 3: 3 by revelation, as *I have* **already** w briefly. G4592
Heb 10: 7 'Here I am—*it is* w about me in the scroll G1211
Heb 12:23 firstborn, *whose names are* w in heaven. G616
Heb 13:22 in fact *I have* w to you quite briefly. G2182
1Pe 1:16 for *it is* w: "Be holy, because I am holy." G1211
1Pe 5:12 a faithful brother, *I have* w to you briefly G1211
2Pe 3: 1 *I have* w both of them as reminders to G1211
Jude 4 condemnation *was* w **about** long ago G4592
Rev 1: 3 hear it and take to heart what *is* w in it, G1211
Rev 2:17 a white stone with a new name w on it, G1211
Rev 13: 8 whose names *have* not *been* w in the G1211
Rev 14: 1 his Father's name w on their foreheads. G1211
Rev 17: 5 The name w on her forehead was a G1211
Rev 17: 8 whose names *have* not *been* w in the G1211
Rev 19:12 He has a name w on him that no one G1211
Rev 19:16 on his thigh he has this name w: G1211
Rev 20:15 name was not found w in the book of life G1211
Rev 21:12 **On** the gates *were* w the names of the G2108
Rev 21:27 those whose names *are* w in the Lamb's G1211
Rev 22: 7 the words of the prophecy *w in* this **scroll**." AIT

WRONG (99) [WRONGDOER, WRONGDOERS, WRONGDOING, WRONGDOINGS, WRONGED, WRONGING, WRONGS]

Ge 16: 5 are responsible for the w I am *suffering*. H2805
Ex 2:13 He asked the **one in the w**, "Why are you H8401
Ex 9:27 and I and my people are **in the w**. H8401
Ex 23: 2 "Do not follow the crowd in *doing* w H8288
Lev 5:18 w *they have* **committed unintentionally** H8705+8704
Nu 5: 7 full restitution for the w they have *done*, H871
Nu 5: 8 to whom restitution can be made for the w, H871
Nu 15:25 the LORD for their w a food offering and a H8705
Nu 15:26 were involved in the **unintentional** w. H8705
Dt 32: 4 A faithful God who does no w, upright H6404
Jdg 11:27 you are doing me w by waging war H8288
1Sa 11: 5 he asked, "**What is** w with everyone? H4537
1Sa 19: 4 "*Let* not the king **do** w to his servant David H2627
1Sa 19: 5 Why then *would you* **do** w to an innocent H2627
1Sa 25:39 his servant from doing w and has brought H8288
1Sa 26:18 have I done, and what w am I guilty of? H8288
1Sa 26:21 acted like a fool and *have been* terribly w." H8706
2Sa 7:14 When he **does** w, I will punish him with a H6390
2Sa 13:16 would be a greater w than what you have H8288
2Sa 19:19 how your servant **did** w on the day my lord H6390
2Sa 24:17 I, the shepherd, *have* **done** w. H6390
1Ki 2:44 your heart all the w you did to my father H8288
1Ki 3: 9 to distinguish between right and w. H8273
1Ki 8:47 have sinned, *we have* **done** w, we have H6390
1Ki 18: 9 "What *have I* **done** w," asked Obadiah H2627
2Ki 18:14 "*I have* **done** w. Withdraw H2627
1Ch 21:17 have sinned and **done** w. These are but H8317
2Ch 6:37 *we have* **done** w and acted wickedly' H6390
Est 1:16 "Queen Vashti *has* **done** w, not only H6390
Job 6:24 be quiet; show me where *I have been* w. H8706
Job 21:27 the schemes by which *you would* w me. H2803
Job 31: 3 the wicked, disaster for those who do w? H224
Job 32:12 But not *one* of you *has* **proved** Job w H3519
Job 33: 9 I have done no w; I am clean and free H7322
Job 34:10 God to do evil, from the Almighty to do w. H6404
Job 34:12 It is unthinkable that God *would* **do** w H8399
Job 34:32 if I have done w, I will not do so H6404
Job 36:23 or said to him, 'You have done w'? H6406
Ps 5: 5 in your presence. You hate all who do w; H224
Ps 15: 3 who does no w to a neighbor, and H8288
Ps 36: 4 sinful course and do not reject *what is* w. H8273
Ps 37: 1 are evil or be envious of those who do w; H6406
Ps 59: 4 I have done no w, yet they are ready to H6411
Ps 106: 6 *we have* **done** w and acted wickedly. H6390
Ps 119: 3 they do no w but follow his ways. H6406
Ps 119:104 precepts; therefore I hate every w path. H9214
Ps 119:128 your precepts right, I hate every w path. H9214
Pr 2:14 who delight in doing w and rejoice in the H8273
Pr 20:22 "I'll pay you back for this w!" Wait for the H8273
Pr 28:21 a person *will* **do** w for a piece of bread H7321
Pr 28:24 says, "It's not w," is partner to one H7322
Pr 30:20 her mouth and says, 'I've done nothing w.' H224
Ecc 5: 1 of fools, who do not know that they do w. H8273
Ecc 8:11 hearts are filled with schemes to do w. H8273
Isa 1:16 evil deeds out of my sight; stop **doing** w. H8317
Isa 7:15 to reject the w and choose the right H8273
Isa 7:16 to reject the w and choose the right H8273
Jer 16:10 What w have we done? What H6411
Jer 22: 3 **Do** no w or violence to the foreigner, the H3561
Jer 51:24 Babylonia for all the w they have done in H8288
La 3:59 you have seen the w **done** *to* me. Uphold H6432
Eze 18: 8 his hand from **doing** w and judges fairly H6404
Eze 18:18 did what was w among his people H4202+3202
Da 6:22 Nor have I ever done any w before you A10242
Da 9: 5 we have sinned and **done** w. We have H6390
Da 9:15 we have sinned, *we have* **done** w. H8399
Jnh 4: 1 But to Jonah *this* **seemed** very w H8317+8288
Zep 3: 5 within her is righteous; he does no w. H6406
Zep 3:13 They will do no w; they will tell no lies. H6406
Mal 1: 8 blind animals for sacrifice, is that not w? H8273
Mal 1: 8 lame or diseased animals, is that not w? H8273
Lk 23:41 But this man has done nothing w." G876
Jn 16: 8 *he will* **prove** the world **to be in the** w G1794
Jn 18:23 "If I said *something* w," Jesus replied G2809
Jn 18:23 Jesus replied, "testify as to what is w. G2805
Ac 23: 9 "We find nothing w with this man," they G2805
Ac 25: 5 if the man has done anything w, they G876
Ac 25: 8 "*I have* **done** nothing w against the Jewish G279
Ac 25:10 *I have* not **done** any w to the Jews, as you G92
Ro 13: 3 who do right, but *for* those who do w. G2805
Ro 13: 4 But if you do w, be afraid, for rulers do not G2805
Ro 14:20 it is w for a person to eat anything G2805
1Co 6: 8 you yourselves cheat and **do** w, and you do G691
2Co 7:12 account of the *one who* **did** the w nor on G92
2Co 12:13 never a burden to you? Forgive me this w! G94

W

2Co 13: 7 to God that you will not do anything w— G2805
Gal 4:12 I became like you. *You* **did** me no w. G92
Col 3:25 Anyone *who* **does** w will be repaid for their G92
1Th 4: 6 this matter no *one should* w or take G5648
1Th 5:15 sure that nobody pays back w for wrong, G2805
1Th 5:15 sure that nobody pays back wrong for w, G2805
Phm 18 If *he has* **done** you any w or owes you G92
Heb 8: 7 if there had been **nothing** w *with* that first G289
Jas 4: 3 because you ask **with** w **motives**, that you G2809
1Pe 2:12 though they accuse you of **doing** w, they G2804
1Pe 2:14 him to punish **those who do** w and to G2804
1Pe 2:20 a beating *for* **doing** w and endure it? G279
Rev 22:11 Let the *one who* **does** w continue to do G92
Rev 22:11 *Let* the one who does wrong continue *to* **do** w G92

WRONGDOER (2) [WRONG]

Nu 5: 8 with which atonement is made for **the** w. H2257S
Ro 13: 4 to bring punishment *on* the w. G2805+4556

WRONGDOERS (2) [WRONG]

Ps 37:28 W will be completely destroyed; the H6405
1Co 6: 9 Or do you not know that w will not inherit the G96

WRONGDOING (17) [WRONG]

Lev 5:19 *they have been* **guilty of** w against H870+870
Nu 5:15 reminder-offering to draw attention to w. H6411
Nu 5:31 The husband will be innocent of any w H6411
Nu 30:15 he must bear the consequences of her w." H6411
1Sa 24:11 indicate that I am **guilty of** w or rebellion. H8288
1Sa 25:28 no w will be found in you as long as H8288
1Sa 25:39 has brought Nabal's w down on his own H8288
1Ki 2:44 Now the LORD will repay you for your w. H8288
Job 1:22 Job did not sin by charging God with w. H9524
Job 24:12 But God charges no one with w. H9524
Job 33:17 to turn them from w and keep them from H5126
Pr 16:12 Kings detest w, for a throne is H6913+8400
Isa 61: 8 love justice; I hate robbery and w. H6406
Hab 1: 3 Why do you tolerate w? Destruction and H6662
Hab 1:13 to look on evil; you cannot tolerate w. H6662
2Pe 2:16 he was rebuked *for* his w by a donkey— G4175
1Jn 5:17 All w is sin, and there is sin that does not G94

WRONGDOINGS (1) [WRONG]

Jer 5:25 Your w have kept these away; your sins H6411

WRONGED (12) [WRONG]

Ge 20: 9 How *have I* w you that you have brought H2627
Ge 31:36 "How have I w you that you hunt me H2633
Nu 5: 7 it and give it all to the person *they have* w. H870
Nu 16:15 from them, nor *have I* w any of them." H8317
Jdg 11:27 I *have* not w you, but you are doing me H2627
1Sa 19: 4 *he has* not w you, and what H2627
1Sa 20: 1 How have I w your father, that he is trying H2633
1Sa 24:11 *I have* not w you, but you are hunting me H2627
Job 19: 6 know that God *has* w me and drawn his H6430
Pr 18:19 A brother w is more unyielding than a H7321
1Co 6: 7 Why not rather *be* w? Why not rather be G92
2Co 7: 2 *We have* w no one, we have corrupted no G92

WRONGING (1) [WRONG]

Ps 119:78 be put to shame for w me without cause; H6430

WRONGS (11) [WRONG]

Ge 50:15 pays us back for all the w we did to him?" H8288
Ge 50:17 the sins and the w they committed in H2633
Nu 5: 6 man or woman *who* w another in H6913+2633
1Sa 24:12 *may* the LORD **avenge** the w you have *done to* H5933
1Ki 8:31 "When anyone w their neighbor and is H2627
2Ch 6:22 "When anyone w their neighbor and is H2627
Job 13:23 How many w and sins have I committed H6411
Pr 10:12 stirs up conflict, but love covers over all w. H7322
Zep 3:11 shame for all the w you *have* done to me, H7321
1Co 13: 5 easily angered, it keeps no record *of* w. G2805
Col 3:25 who does wrong will be repaid *for* their w, G92

WROTE (62) [WRITE]

Ex 24: 4 Moses then w **down** everything the LORD H4180
Ex 34:28 And *he* w on the tablets the words of the H4180
Dt 4:13 to follow and then w them on two stone H4180
Dt 5:22 Then *he* w them on two stone tablets H4180
Dt 10: 4 The LORD w on these tablets what he had H4180
Dt 31: 9 So Moses w **down** this law and gave it to H4180
Dt 31:22 So Moses w **down** this song that day and H4180
Jos 8:32 Joshua w on stones a copy of the law of H4180
Jos 18: 9 *They* w its **description** on a scroll, town by H4180
Jdg 8:14 the young man w **down** for him the H4180
1Sa 10:25 *He* w them **down** on a scroll and H4180
2Sa 11:14 the morning David w a letter to Joab and H4180
2Sa 11:15 In it *he* w, "Put Uriah out in front where H4180
1Ki 21: 8 So *she* w letters in Ahab's name, placed H4180
1Ki 21: 9 In those letters *she* w: "Proclaim a day of H4180
2Ki 10: 1 So Jehu w letters and sent them to H4180
2Ki 10: 6 Then Jehu w them a second letter, saying, H4180
2Ki 17:37 the laws and commands *he* w for you. H4180
2Ch 30: 1 Judah and also w letters to Ephraim H4180
2Ch 32:17 The king also w letters ridiculing the LORD H4180
Ezr 4: 7 of his associates w a letter to Artaxerxes H4180
Ezr 4: 8 Shimshai the secretary w a letter against A10374
Est 3:12 *They* w **out** in the script of each province H4180
Est 8: 5 devised and w to destroy the Jews in all H4180
Est 8: 9 *They* w **out** all Mordecai's orders to the H4180
Est 8:10 Mordecai w in the name of King Xerxes H4180
Est 9:22 He w them to observe the days as days of NDT
Est 9:29 w with full authority to confirm this second H4180
Ecc 12:10 what *he* w was upright and true. H4180
Jer 36: 4 Baruch w them on the scroll. H4180
Jer 36: 6 words of the LORD that *you* w as I dictated. H4180
Jer 36:18 and I w them in ink on the scroll. H4180
Jer 36:32 Baruch w on it all the words of the scroll H4180
Jer 45: 1 Baruch son of Neriah w on a scroll the H4180
Da 5: 5 hand appeared and w on the plaster of A10374
Da 5: 5 The king watched the hand as *it* w. A10374
Da 5:24 he sent the hand that w the inscription. A10673
Da 6:25 Then King Darius w to all the nations A10374
Da 7: 1 *He* w **down** the substance of his dream. A10374
Hos 8:12 *I* w for them the many things of my law H4180
Mk 10: 5 were hard that Moses w you this law," G1211
Mk 12:19 "Moses w for us that if a man's brother G1211
Lk 1:63 to everyone's astonishment *he* w G1211
Lk 20:28 "Moses w for us that if a man's brother G1211
Jn 1:45 found the one Moses w **about** in the Law, G1211
Jn 1:45 about whom the prophets also w NDT
Jn 5:46 you would believe me, for he w about me. G1211
Jn 5:47 But since you do not believe what he w G1207
Jn 8: 8 he stooped down and w on the ground. G1211
Jn 21:24 to these things and who w them **down**. G1211
Ac 1: 1 *I* w about all that Jesus began to do and G4472
Ac 18:27 encouraged him and w to the disciples G1211
Ac 23:25 *He* w a letter as follows: G1211
Ro 16:22 who w **down** this letter, greet you G1211
1Co 5: 9 *I* w to you in my letter not to associate G1211
1Co 7: 1 Now for the matters *you* w about: "It is G1211
2Co 2: 3 *I* w as I did, so that when I came I would G1211
2Co 2: 4 For *I* w you out of great distress and G1211
2Co 2: 9 Another reason *I* w you was to see if you G1211
2Co 7:12 So even though *I* w to you, it was neither G1211
2Pe 3:15 brother Paul also w you with the wisdom G1211
3Jn 9 *I* w to the church, but Diotrephes, who G1211

WROUGHT (1)

Eze 27:19 your wares: w iron, cassia and calamus H6936

WRUNG (1)

Jdg 6:38 squeezed the fleece and w **out** the dew— H5172

X

XERXES (29) [XERXES']

Ezr 4: 6 At the beginning of the reign of X, they H347
Est 1: 1 is what happened during the time of X, H347
Est 1: 1 the X who ruled over 127 provinces H347
Est 1: 2 At that time King X reigned from his royal H347
Est 1: 9 the women in the royal palace of King X. H347
Est 1:10 when King X was in high spirits from wine H347
Est 1:15 the command of King X that the eunuchs H347
Est 1:16 the peoples of all the provinces of King X. H347
Est 1:17 'King X commanded Queen Vashti to be H347
Est 1:19 again to enter the presence of King X. H347
Est 2:12 woman's turn came to go in to King X, H347
Est 2:16 She was taken to King X in the royal H347
Est 2:21 angry and conspired to assassinate King X. H347
Est 3: 1 King X honored Haman son of H347
Est 3: 6 throughout the whole kingdom of X. H347
Est 3: 7 In the twelfth year of King X, in the first H347
Est 3: 8 Then Haman said to King X, "There is a H347
Est 3:12 name of King X *himself* and sealed with H347
Est 6: 2 who had conspired to assassinate King X. H347
Est 7: 5 King X asked Queen Esther, "Who is he H347
Est 8: 1 That same day King X gave Queen Esther H347
Est 8: 7 King X replied to Queen Esther and to H347
Est 8:10 Mordecai wrote in the name of King X H347
Est 8:12 the provinces of King X was the thirteenth H347
Est 9: 2 all the provinces of King X to attack those H347
Est 9:20 Jews throughout the provinces of King X, H347
Est 10: 1 King X imposed tribute throughout the H347
Est 10: 3 the Jew was second in rank to King X, H347
Da 9: 1 In the first year of Darius son of X (a Mede H347

XERXES' (2) [XERXES]

Est 2: 1 Later when King X fury had subsided, he H347
Est 9:30 Jews in the 127 provinces of X kingdom— H347

Y

YAHWEH See LORD*, LORD'S*

YARDS (1)

Jn 21: 8 far from shore, about **a hundred** y. G4388+1357

YARN (34)

Ex 25: 4 purple and **scarlet** y and fine linen H9357+9106
Ex 26: 1 purple and **scarlet** y, with cherubim H9357+9106
Ex 26:31 purple and **scarlet** y and finely H9357+9106
Ex 26:36 purple and **scarlet** y and finely H9357+9106
Ex 27:16 purple and **scarlet** y and finely H9357+9106
Ex 28: 5 purple and **scarlet** y, and fine linen H9357+9106
Ex 28: 6 purple and **scarlet** y, and of finely H9357+9106
Ex 28: 8 purple and **scarlet** y, and with H9357+9106
Ex 28:15 purple and **scarlet** y, and of finely H9357+9106
Ex 28:33 purple and **scarlet** y around the H9357+9106
Ex 35: 6 purple and **scarlet** y and fine linen H9357+9106
Ex 35:23 purple or **scarlet** y or fine linen H9357+9106
Ex 35:25 purple or **scarlet** y or fine linen. H9357+9106
Ex 35:35 purple and **scarlet** y and fine linen H9357+9106
Ex 36: 8 purple and **scarlet** y, with cherubim H9357+9106
Ex 36:35 purple and **scarlet** y and finely H9357+9106
Ex 36:37 purple and **scarlet** y and finely H9357+9106
Ex 38:18 purple and **scarlet** y and finely H9357+9106
Ex 38:23 purple and **scarlet** y and fine linen.) H9357+9106
Ex 39: 1 purple and **scarlet** y they made H9357+9106
Ex 39: 2 purple and **scarlet** y, and of finely H9357+9106
Ex 39: 3 purple and **scarlet** y and fine linen H9357+9106
Ex 39: 5 purple and **scarlet** y, and with H9357+9106
Ex 39: 8 purple and **scarlet** y, and of finely H9357+9106
Ex 39:24 purple and **scarlet** y and finely H9357+9106
Ex 39:29 purple and **scarlet** y—the work of H9357+9106
Lev 14: 4 **scarlet** y and hyssop be brought H9357+9106
Lev 14: 6 the **scarlet** y and the hyssop H9357+9106
Lev 14:49 cedar wood, **scarlet** y and hyssop. H9357+9106
Lev 14:51 the **scarlet** y and the live bird H9357+9106
Lev 14:52 the hyssop and the **scarlet** y. H9357+9106
2Ch 2: 7 crimson and **blue** y, and experienced H9418
2Ch 2:14 purple and **blue** and crimson y and fine H9418
2Ch 3:14 of **blue**, purple and crimson y and fine H9418

YAUDI (NIV84) JUDAH

YEA (KJV) EVEN, REALLY, SURELY, YES

YEAR (352) [YEAR-OLD, YEAR'S, YEARLING, YEARLY, YEARS]

Ge 7:11 In the six hundredth y of Noah's life, on H9102
Ge 8:13 month of Noah's six hundred and first y, H9102
Ge 14: 4 in the thirteenth y they rebelled. H9102
Ge 14: 5 In the fourteenth y, Kedorlaomer and the H9102
Ge 17:21 Sarah will bear to you by this time next y." H9102
Ge 18:10 surely return to you about this time **next** y, H2645
Ge 18:14 return to you at the appointed time **next** y, H2645
Ge 26:12 land and the same y reaped a H9102
Ge 47:17 them through that y with food in H9102
Ge 47:18 When that y was over, they came to him H9102
Ge 47:18 came to him the following y and said, H9102
Ex 12: 2 the first month, the first month of your y. H9102
Ex 13:10 at the appointed time y after year. H3427
Ex 13:10 at the appointed time year after y. H3427
Ex 21: 2 But in the seventh y, he shall go free NDT
Ex 23:11 during the seventh y let the land lie NDT
Ex 23:14 "Three times a y you are to celebrate a H9102
Ex 23:16 Festival of Ingathering at the end of the y, H9102
Ex 23:17 "Three times a y all the men are to H9102
Ex 23:29 But I will not drive them out in a single y H9102
Ex 29:38 regularly each day: two lambs a y old. H9102
Ex 30:10 Once a y Aaron shall make atonement on H9102
Ex 34:22 Festival of Ingathering at the turn of the y. H9102
Ex 34:23 Three times a y all your men are to appear H9102
Ex 34:24 up three times each y to appear before H9102
Ex 40:17 first day of the first month in the second y. H9102
Lev 9: 3 a lamb—both a y old and without defect H9102
Lev 14:10 male lambs and one ewe lamb a y old, H9102
Lev 16:34 is to be made once a y for all the sins of H9102
Lev 19:24 In the fourth y all its fruit will be holy, an H9102
Lev 19:25 But in the fifth y you may eat its fruit. H9102
Lev 23:12 to the LORD a lamb a y old without defect, H9102
Lev 23:18 each a y old and without defect H9102
Lev 23:19 two lambs, each a y old, for a fellowship H9102
Lev 23:41 festival to the LORD for seven days each y. H9102
Lev 25: 4 But in the seventh y the land is to have a H9102
Lev 25: 4 year the land is to have a y of sabbath rest, NDT
Lev 25: 5 The land is to have a y *of* rest. H9102
Lev 25: 6 during the sabbath y will be food for you— NDT
Lev 25:10 the fiftieth y and proclaim liberty H9102
Lev 25:11 The fiftieth y shall be a jubilee for you; do H9102
Lev 25:13 " 'In this Y *of* Jubilee everyone is to return H9102
Lev 25:20 eat in the seventh y if we do not plant H9102
Lev 25:21 a blessing in the sixth y that the land will H9102
Lev 25:22 While you plant during the eighth y, you H9102
Lev 25:22 it until the harvest of the ninth y comes in. H9102
Lev 25:28 of the buyer until the Y *of* Jubilee. H9102
Lev 25:29 right of redemption a full y after its sale. H9102
Lev 25:30 not redeemed before a full y has passed, H9102
Lev 25:40 are to work for you until the Y *of* Jubilee. H9102
Lev 25:50 the time from the y they sold themselves H9102
Lev 25:50 sold themselves up to the Y *of* Jubilee. H9102
Lev 25:52 a few years remain until the Y *of* Jubilee, H9102
Lev 25:53 be treated as workers hired from y to year; H9102
Lev 25:53 be treated as workers hired from year to y; H9102
Lev 25:54 are to be released in the Y *of* Jubilee, H9102
Lev 27:17 dedicate a field during the Y *of* Jubilee, H9102
Lev 27:18 that remain until the next Y *of* Jubilee, H9102
Lev 27:23 determine its value up to the Y *of* Jubilee, H9102
Lev 27:24 In the Y *of* Jubilee the field will revert to H9102
Nu 1: 1 month of the second y after the Israelites H9102
Nu 7:15 one male lamb a y old for a burnt H9102
Nu 7:17 five male lambs a y old to be sacrificed H9102
Nu 7:21 one male lamb a y old for a burnt H9102
Nu 7:23 five male lambs a y old to be sacrificed H9102
Nu 7:27 one male lamb a y old for a burnt H9102
Nu 7:29 five male lambs a y old to be sacrificed H9102
Nu 7:33 one male lamb a y old for a burnt H9102
Nu 7:35 five male lambs a y old to be sacrificed H9102
Nu 7:39 one male lamb a y old for a burnt H9102

Nu 7:41 five male lambs a y old to be sacrificed H9102
Nu 7:45 one male lamb a y old for a burnt H9102
Nu 7:47 five male lambs a y old to be sacrificed H9102
Nu 7:51 one male lamb a y old for a burnt H9102
Nu 7:53 five male lambs a y old to be sacrificed H9102
Nu 7:57 one male lamb a y old for a burnt H9102
Nu 7:59 five male lambs a y old to be sacrificed H9102
Nu 7:63 one male lamb a y old for a burnt H9102
Nu 7:65 five male lambs a y old to be sacrificed H9102
Nu 7:69 one male lamb a y old for a burnt H9102
Nu 7:71 five male lambs a y old to be sacrificed H9102
Nu 7:75 one male lamb a y old for a burnt H9102
Nu 7:77 five male lambs a y old to be sacrificed H9102
Nu 7:81 one male lamb a y old for a burnt H9102
Nu 7:83 five male lambs a y old to be sacrificed H9102
Nu 7:87 rams and twelve male lambs a y old, H9102
Nu 7:88 male goats and sixty male lambs a y old. H9102
Nu 9: 1 month of the second y after they came out H9102
Nu 9:22 tabernacle for two days or a month or a y, H3427
Nu 10:11 day of the second month of the second y, H9102
Nu 14:34 one y for each of the forty days you H9102
Nu 28: 3 two lambs a y old without defect, as a H9102
Nu 28: 9 of two lambs a y old without defect, H9102
Nu 28:11 one ram and seven male lambs a y old H9102
Nu 28:14 be made at each new moon during the y. H9102
Nu 28:19 one ram and seven male lambs a y old H9102
Nu 28:27 seven male lambs a y old as an aroma H9102
Nu 29: 2 one ram and seven male lambs a y old H9102
Nu 29: 8 one ram and seven male lambs a y old H9102
Nu 29:13 rams and fourteen male lambs a y old, H9102
Nu 29:17 rams and fourteen male lambs a y old, H9102
Nu 29:20 rams and fourteen male lambs a y old, H9102
Nu 29:23 rams and fourteen male lambs a y old, H9102
Nu 29:26 rams and fourteen male lambs a y old, H9102
Nu 29:29 rams and fourteen male lambs a y old, H9102
Nu 29:32 rams and fourteen male lambs a y old, H9102
Nu 29:36 one ram and seven male lambs a y old H9102
Nu 33:38 month of the fortieth y after the Israelites H9102
Nu 36: 4 When the **Y of Jubilee** for the Israelites H3413
Dt 1: 3 In the fortieth y, on the first day of the H9102
Dt 11:12 it from the beginning of the y to its end. H9102
Dt 14:22 all that your fields produce **each** y. H9102+9102
Dt 15: 9 "The seventh y, the year for canceling H9102
Dt 15: 9 seventh year, the y *for* canceling debts, is H9102
Dt 15:12 in the seventh y you must let them go free H9102
Dt 15:20 **Each** y you and your family are H9102+928+9102
Dt 16:16 Three times a y all your men must appear H9102
Dt 24: 5 *For* one y he is to be free to stay at home H9102
Dt 26:12 a tenth of all your produce in the third y, H9102
Dt 26:12 the third year, the y *of* the tithe, you shall H9102
Dt 31:10 seven years, in the y *for* canceling debts H9102
Jos 5:12 that y they ate the produce of Canaan. H9102
Jdg 10: 8 who that y shattered and crushed them H9102
Jdg 11:40 that **each** y the young H4946+3427+3427+2025
Jdg 17:10 you ten shekels of silver a y, H4200+2021+3427
1Sa 1: 3 **Y** after year this man went up from his H3427
1Sa 1: 3 Year after y this man went up from his H3427
1Sa 1: 7 This went on y after year. Whenever H9102
1Sa 1: 7 This went on year after y. Whenever H9102
1Sa 2:19 **Each** y his mother made H4946+3427+3427+2025
1Sa 7:16 From y to year he went on a circuit from H9102
1Sa 7:16 From year to y he went on a circuit from H9102
1Sa 27: 7 in Philistine territory a y and four months. H3427
1Sa 29: 3 been with me for **over a** y, H2296+3427+196+2296+9102
2Sa 14:26 cut his hair **once a** y because H4946+7891+3427+4200+2021+3427
1Ki 4: 7 provide supplies for one month in the y. H9102
1Ki 5:11 continued to do this for Hiram y after year. H9102
1Ki 5:11 continued to do this for Hiram year after y. H9102
1Ki 6: 1 eightieth y after the Israelites H9102
1Ki 6: 1 in the fourth y of Solomon's reign over H9102
1Ki 6:37 of the LORD was laid in the fourth y, H9102
1Ki 6:38 In the eleventh y in the month of Bul, the H9102
1Ki 9:25 Three times a y Solomon sacrificed burnt H9102
1Ki 10:25 **Y** after year, everyone who came brought a H9102
1Ki 10:25 Year after y, everyone who came brought a H9102
1Ki 14:25 In the fifth y of King Rehoboam, Shishak H9102
1Ki 15: 1 In the eighteenth y of the reign of H9102
1Ki 15: 9 In the twentieth y of Jeroboam king of H9102
1Ki 15:25 in the second y of Asa king of Judah H9102
1Ki 15:28 Nadab in the third y of Asa king of Judah H9102
1Ki 15:33 In the third y of Asa king of Judah H9102
1Ki 16: 8 In the twenty-sixth y of Asa king of Judah H9102
1Ki 16:10 the twenty-seventh y of Asa king of Judah H9102
1Ki 16:15 the twenty-seventh y of Asa king of Judah H9102
1Ki 16:23 In the thirty-first y of Asa king of Judah H9102
1Ki 16:29 In the thirty-eighth y of Asa king of Judah H9102
1Ki 18: 1 in the third y, the word of the LORD H9102
1Ki 22: 2 But in the third y Jehoshaphat king of H9102
1Ki 22:41 Judah in the fourth y of Ahab king of H9102
1Ki 22:51 in the seventeenth y of Jehoshaphat king H9102
2Ki 1:17 as king in the second y of Jehoram son of H9102
2Ki 3: 1 in the eighteenth y of Jehoshaphat king H9102
2Ki 4:16 "About this time **next** y," Elisha said H6961+2645
2Ki 4:17 and the **next** y about that same H6961+2645
2Ki 8:16 In the fifth y of Joram son of Ahab king of H9102
2Ki 8:25 In the twelfth y of Joram son of Ahab king H9102
2Ki 8:26 and he reigned in Jerusalem one y. H9102
2Ki 9:29 In the eleventh y of Joram son of Ahab H9102
2Ki 11: 4 In the seventh y Jehoiada sent for the H9102
2Ki 12: 1 In the seventh y of Jehu, Joash became H9102
2Ki 12: 6 But by the twenty-third y of King Joash the H9102
2Ki 13: 1 In the twenty-third y of Joash son of H9102
2Ki 13:10 In the thirty-seventh y of Joash king of H9102
2Ki 14: 1 In the second y of Jehoash son of H9102
2Ki 14:23 In the fifteenth y of Amaziah son of Joash H9102
2Ki 15: 1 the twenty-seventh y of Jeroboam king of H9102
2Ki 15: 8 In the thirty-eighth y of Azariah king of H9102
2Ki 15:13 in the thirty-ninth y of Uzziah king of H9102
2Ki 15:17 In the thirty-ninth y of Azariah king of H9102
2Ki 15:23 In the fiftieth y of Azariah king of Judah H9102
2Ki 15:27 In the fifty-second y of Azariah king of H9102
2Ki 15:30 king in the twentieth y of Jotham son of H9102
2Ki 15:32 In the second y of Pekah son of Remaliah H9102
2Ki 16: 1 In the seventeenth y of Pekah son of H9102
2Ki 17: 1 In the twelfth y of Ahaz king of Judah H9102
2Ki 17: 4 king of Assyria, as he had done y by year. H9102
2Ki 17: 4 king of Assyria, as he had done year by y. H9102
2Ki 17: 6 In the ninth y of Hoshea, the king of H9102
2Ki 18: 1 In the third y of Hoshea son of Elah king H9102
2Ki 18: 9 In King Hezekiah's fourth y, which was H9102
2Ki 18: 9 was the seventh y of Hoshea son of Elah H9102
2Ki 18:10 was captured in Hezekiah's sixth y, H9102
2Ki 18:10 which was the ninth y of Hoshea king of H9102
2Ki 18:13 In the fourteenth y of King Hezekiah's H9102
2Ki 19:29 "This y you will eat what grows by itself H9102
2Ki 19:29 the second y what springs from that. H9102
2Ki 19:29 But in the third y sow and reap, plant H9102
2Ki 22: 3 In the eighteenth y of his reign, King H9102
2Ki 23:23 But in the eighteenth y of King Josiah, this H9102
2Ki 24:12 In the eighth y of the reign of the king of H9102
2Ki 25: 1 So in the ninth y of Zedekiah's reign, on H9102
2Ki 25: 2 until the eleventh y of King Zedekiah. H9102
2Ki 25: 8 in the nineteenth y of Nebuchadnezzar H9102
2Ki 25:27 In the thirty-seventh y of the exile of H9102
2Ki 25:27 in the y Awel-Marduk became king of H9102
1Ch 26:31 In the fortieth y of David's reign a search H9102
1Ch 27: 1 on duty month by month throughout the y. H9102
2Ch 3: 2 second month in the fourth y of his reign. H9102
2Ch 9:24 **Y** after year, everyone who came H1821+9102
2Ch 9:24 Year after y, everyone who came brought H9102
2Ch 12: 2 in the fifth y of King Rehoboam. H9102
2Ch 13: 1 In the eighteenth y of the reign of H9102
2Ch 15:10 month of the fifteenth y of Asa's reign. H9102
2Ch 15:19 war until the thirty-fifth y of Asa's reign. H9102
2Ch 16: 1 In the thirty-sixth y of Asa's reign Baasha H9102
2Ch 16:12 In the thirty-ninth y of his reign Asa was H9102
2Ch 16:13 in the forty-first y *of* his reign Asa died H9102
2Ch 17: 7 In the third y of his reign he sent his H9102
2Ch 21:19 at the end of the second y, his bowels H3427
2Ch 22: 2 and he reigned in Jerusalem one y. H9102
2Ch 23: 1 In the seventh y Jehoiada showed his H9102
2Ch 24:23 At the turn of the y, the army of Aram H9102
2Ch 27: 5 That y the Ammonites paid him a H9102
2Ch 29: 3 In the first month of the first y of his reign H9102
2Ch 34: 3 In the eighth y *of* his reign, while he was H9102
2Ch 34: 3 In his twelfth y he began to purge Judah H9102
2Ch 34: 8 In the eighteenth y *of* Josiah's reign, to H9102
2Ch 35:19 in the eighteenth y of Josiah's reign. H9102
2Ch 36:22 In the first y of Cyrus king of Persia, in H9102
Ezr 1: 1 In the first y of Cyrus king of Persia, in H9102
Ezr 3: 8 month of the second y after their arrival at H9102
Ezr 4:24 until the second y of the reign of Darius A10732
Ezr 5:13 in the first y of Cyrus king of Babylon A10732
Ezr 6: 3 In the first y of King Cyrus, the king A10732
Ezr 6:15 in the sixth y of the reign of King Darius. A10732
Ezr 7: 7 in the seventh y of King Artaxerxes. H9102
Ezr 7: 8 fifth month of the seventh y of the king. H9102
Ne 1: 1 In the month of Kislev in the twentieth y H9102
Ne 2: 1 in the twentieth y of King Artaxerxes, H9102
Ne 5:14 from the twentieth y of King Artaxerxes H9102
Ne 5:14 until his thirty-second y—twelve years— H9102
Ne 10:31 Every seventh y we will forgo working the H9102
Ne 10:32 of a shekel each y for the service of the H9102
Ne 10:34 at set times **each** y a H9102+928+9102
Ne 10:35 of the LORD **each** y the H9102+928+9102
Ne 13: 6 in the thirty-second y of Artaxerxes king of H9102
Est 1: 3 in the third y of his reign he gave a H9102
Est 2:16 of Tebeth, in the seventh y of his reign. H9102
Est 3: 7 In the twelfth y of King Xerxes, in the first H9102
Est 9:27 fail observe these two days every y, H9102
Job 3: 6 the days of the y nor be entered in any H9102
Ps 65:11 You crown the y with your bounty, and H9102
Isa 6: 1 In the y *that* King Uzziah died, I saw the H9102
Isa 14:28 prophecy came in the y King Ahaz died: H9102
Isa 20: 1 In the y that the supreme commander H9102
Isa 21:16 "Within *one* y, as a servant bound by H9102
Isa 29: 1 Add y to year and let your cycle of H9102
Isa 29: 1 Add year to y and let your cycle of H9102
Isa 32:10 In little more than a y you who feel secure H9102
Isa 34: 8 a day of vengeance, a y *of* retribution, to H9102
Isa 36: 1 In the fourteenth y of King Hezekiah's H9102
Isa 37:30 "This y you will eat what grows by itself H9102
Isa 37:30 the second y what springs from that. H9102
Isa 37:30 But in the third y sow and reap, plant H9102
Isa 61: 2 to proclaim the y *of* the LORD's favor and H9102
Isa 63: 4 the y *for* me to redeem had come. H9102
Jer 1: 2 him in the thirteenth y of the reign of H9102
Jer 1: 3 of the eleventh y of Zedekiah son of H9102
Jer 11:23 of Anathoth in the y *of* their punishment." H9102
Jer 17: 8 has no worries in a y *of* drought and never H9102
Jer 23:12 on them in the y they are punished," H9102
Jer 25: 1 Judah in the fourth y of Jehoiakim son of H9102
Jer 25: 1 which was the first y of Nebuchadnezzar H9102
Jer 25: 3 from the thirteenth y of Josiah son of H9102
Jer 28: 1 In the fifth month of that same y, the H9102
Jer 28: 1 same year, the fourth y, early in the reign H9102
Jer 28:16 This very y you are going to die, because H9102
Jer 28:17 In the seventh month of that same y H9102
Jer 32: 1 the LORD in the tenth y of Zedekiah king H9102
Jer 32: 1 was the eighteenth y of Nebuchadnezzar. H9102
Jer 34:14 'Every seventh y each of you must free any H9102
Jer 36: 1 In the fourth y of Jehoiakim son of Josiah H9102
Jer 36: 9 month of the fifth y of Jehoiakim son of H9102
Jer 39: 1 In the ninth y of Zedekiah king of Judah H9102
Jer 39: 2 fourth month of Zedekiah's eleventh y, H9102
Jer 45: 1 in the fourth y of Jehoiakim son of H9102
Jer 46: 2 in the fourth y of Jehoiakim son of H9102
Jer 48:44 bring on Moab the y *of* her punishment," H9102
Jer 51:46 one rumor comes this y, another the next, H9102
Jer 51:59 king of Judah in the fourth y of his reign. H9102
Jer 52: 4 So in the ninth y of Zedekiah's reign, on H9102
Jer 52: 5 until the eleventh y of King Zedekiah. H9102
Jer 52:12 in the nineteenth y of Nebuchadnezzar H9102
Jer 52:28 in the seventh y, 3,023 Jews; H9102
Jer 52:29 in Nebuchadnezzar's eighteenth y, 832 H9102
Jer 52:30 in his twenty-third y, 745 Jews taken into H9102
Jer 52:31 In the thirty-seventh y of the exile of H9102
Jer 52:31 in the y Awel-Marduk became king of H9102
Eze 1: 1 In my thirtieth y, in the fourth month on H9102
Eze 1: 2 it was the fifth y of the exile of King H9102
Eze 4: 6 assigned you 40 days, a day for each y. H9102
Eze 8: 1 In the sixth y, in the sixth month on the H9102
Eze 20: 1 In the seventh y, in the fifth month on the H9102
Eze 24: 1 In the ninth y, in the tenth month on the H9102
Eze 26: 1 In the eleventh month of the twelfth y, on H9102
Eze 29: 1 In the tenth y, in the tenth month on the H9102
Eze 29:17 In the twenty-seventh y, in the first month H9102
Eze 30:20 In the eleventh y, in the first month on the H9102
Eze 31: 1 In the eleventh y, in the third month on H9102
Eze 32: 1 In the twelfth y, in the twelfth month on H9102
Eze 32:17 In the twelfth y, on the fifteenth day of the H9102
Eze 33:21 In the twelfth y of our exile, in the tenth H9102
Eze 40: 1 In the twenty-fifth y of our exile, at the H9102
Eze 40: 1 at the beginning of the y, on the tenth of H9102
Eze 40: 1 in the fourteenth y after the fall of the city H9102
Eze 46:17 servant may keep it until the y *of* freedom; H9102
Da 1: 1 In the third y of the reign of Jehoiakim H9102
Da 1:21 there until the first y of King Cyrus. H9102
Da 2: 1 In the second y of his reign H9102
Da 7: 1 In the first y of Belshazzar king of A10732
Da 8: 1 In the third y of King Belshazzar's reign, H9102
Da 9: 1 In the first y of Darius son of Xerxes (a H9102
Da 9: 2 in the first y *of* his reign, I, Daniel H9102
Da 10: 1 In the third y of Cyrus king of Persia, H9102
Da 11: 1 And in the first y of Darius the Mede, H9102
Mic 6: 6 with burnt offerings, with calves a y old? H9102
Hag 1: 1 In the second y of King Darius, on the first H9102
Hag 1:15 In the second y of King Darius, H9102
Hag 2:10 in the second y of Darius, the word H9102
Zec 1: 1 eighth month of the second y of Darius, H9102
Zec 1: 7 in the second y of Darius, the word H9102
Zec 7: 1 In the fourth y of King Darius, the word of H9102
Zec 14:16 Jerusalem will go up y after year to H9102
Zec 14:16 will go up year after y to worship the King, H9102
Lk 2:41 Every y Jesus' parents went to Jerusalem *G2291*
Lk 3: 1 In the fifteenth y of the reign of Tiberius *G2291*
Lk 4:19 to proclaim the y of the Lord's favor." *G1929*
Lk 13: 8 'leave it alone *for* one more y, and I'll dig *G2291*
Lk 13: 9 If it bears fruit **next** y, fine! If not, then cut it AIT
Jn 11:49 who was high priest that y, spoke up, *G1929*
Jn 11:51 as high priest that y he prophesied that *G1929*
Jn 18:13 of Caiaphas, the high priest that y. *G1929*
Ac 11:26 So *for* a whole y Barnabas and Saul met *G1929*
Ac 18:11 Paul stayed in Corinth *for* a y and a half, *G1929*
[Ac 18:11 stayed in Corinth *for* a y and a **half**, *G3604+1971*]
2Co 8:10 **Last** y you were the first not only to give *G4373*
2Co 9: 2 them that since **last** y you in Achaia were *G4373*
Heb 9: 7 that only once a y, and never without *G1929*
Heb 9:25 Most Holy Place every y with blood that is *G1929*
Heb 10: 1 repeated endlessly y **after year**, *G2848+1929*
Heb 10: 1 repeated endlessly **year after** y, *G2848+1929*
Jas 4:13 that city, spend a y there, carry on *G1929*
Rev 9:15 day and month and y were released to kill *G1929*

YEAR'S (6) [YEAR]

Lev 26:10 be eating **last** y **harvest** when you H3824+3823
Dt 14:28 all the tithes of that y produce and store it H9102
Mk 6:37 take **more than half a** y **wages!** *G1324+1357*
Mk 14: 5 more than **a** y **wages** and the *G1324+5559*
Jn 6: 7 take **more than half a** y **wages** to *G1357+1324*
Jn 12: 5 **money** given to the poor? It was **worth a** y **wages** *G5559+1324*

YEAR-OLD (7) [YEAR]

Ex 12: 5 choose must be y males without H1201+9102
Lev 12: 6 of meeting a y lamb for a burnt H1201+9102
Nu 6:12 and must bring a y male lamb as a H1201+9102
Nu 6:14 a y male lamb without defect for a H1201+9102
Nu 6:14 a y ewe lamb without defect for a H1426+9102
Nu 15:27 must bring a y *female* goat for a H1426+9102
Eze 46:13 are to provide a y lamb without H1201+9102

YEARLING (1) [YEAR]

Isa 11: 6 the calf and the lion and the y together H5309

YEARLY (3) [YEAR]

1Ki 10:14 received y was 666 talents, H928+9102+285
2Ch 9:13 received y was 666 talents, H928+9102+285
Hos 2:11 her y **festivals**, her New Moons, her H2504

YEARNS (4)

Job 19:27 How my heart y within me! H3983
Ps 84: 2 My soul y, even faints, for the courts of the H4083
Isa 26: 9 My soul y **for** you in the night; in the H203
Jer 31:20 Therefore my heart y for him; I have great H2159

YEARS (496) [YEAR]

Ge 1:14 to mark sacred times, and days and y, H9102
Ge 5: 3 When Adam had lived 130 y, he had a H9102
Ge 5: 4 Adam lived 800 y and had other sons H9102
Ge 5: 5 Adam lived a total of 930 y, and then he H9102
Ge 5: 6 When Seth had lived 105 y, he became H9102
Ge 5: 7 Seth lived 807 y and had other sons and H9102
Ge 5: 8 Seth lived a total of 912 y, and then he H9102
Ge 5: 9 When Enosh had lived 90 y, he became H9102
Ge 5:10 Enosh lived 815 y and had other sons H9102
Ge 5:11 Enosh lived a total of 905 y, and then he H9102
Ge 5:12 When Kenan had lived 70 y, he became H9102
Ge 5:13 Kenan lived 840 y and had other sons H9102
Ge 5:14 Kenan lived a total of 910 y, and then he H9102
Ge 5:15 When Mahalalel had lived 65 y, he H9102
Ge 5:16 Mahalalel lived 830 y and had other sons H9102
Ge 5:17 Mahalalel lived a total of 895 y, and then H9102
Ge 5:18 When Jared had lived 162 y, he became H9102
Ge 5:19 Jared lived 800 y and had other sons and H9102
Ge 5:20 Jared lived a total of 962 y, and then he H9102
Ge 5:21 When Enoch had lived 65 y, he became H9102
Ge 5:22 with God 300 y and had other sons and H9102
Ge 5:23 Altogether, Enoch lived a total of 365 y. H9102
Ge 5:25 When Methuselah had lived 187 y, he H9102
Ge 5:26 lived 782 y and had other sons H9102
Ge 5:27 Methuselah lived a total of 969 y, and H9102
Ge 5:28 When Lamech had lived 182 y, he had a H9102
Ge 5:30 Lamech lived 595 y and had other sons H9102
Ge 5:31 Lamech lived a total of 777 y, and then H9102
Ge 5:32 After Noah was 500 y old, he became the H9102
Ge 6: 3 their days will be a hundred and twenty y." H9102
Ge 7: 6 Noah was six hundred y old when the H9102
Ge 9:28 After the flood Noah lived 350 y. H9102
Ge 9:29 Noah lived a total of 950 y, and then he H9102
Ge 11:10 *Two* y after the flood, when Shem was H9102
Ge 11:10 when Shem was 100 y old, he became H9102
Ge 11:11 Shem lived 500 y and had other sons H9102
Ge 11:12 When Arphaxad had lived 35 y, he H9102
Ge 11:13 Arphaxad lived 403 y and had other sons H9102
Ge 11:14 When Shelah had lived 30 y, he became H9102
Ge 11:15 Shelah lived 403 y and had other sons H9102
Ge 11:16 When Eber had lived 34 y, he became H9102
Ge 11:17 Eber lived 430 y and had other sons and H9102
Ge 11:18 When Peleg had lived 30 y, he became H9102
Ge 11:19 Peleg lived 209 y and had other sons H9102
Ge 11:20 When Reu had lived 32 y, he became the H9102
Ge 11:21 Reu lived 207 y and had other sons and H9102
Ge 11:22 When Serug had lived 30 y, he became H9102
Ge 11:23 Serug lived 200 y and had other sons H9102
Ge 11:24 When Nahor had lived 29 y, he became H9102
Ge 11:25 Nahor lived 119 y and had other sons H9102
Ge 11:26 After Terah had lived 70 y, he became H9102
Ge 11:32 Terah lived 205 y, and he died in Harran. H9102
Ge 12: 4 was seventy-five y old when he set out H9102
Ge 14: 4 For twelve y they had been subject to H9102
Ge 15: 9 a ram, each **three y old**, along with a H8992
Ge 15:13 certain that *for* four hundred y your H9102
Ge 16: 3 Abram had been living in Canaan ten y, H9102
Ge 16:16 was eighty-six y old when Hagar bore H9102
Ge 17: 1 When Abram was ninety-nine y old, the H9102
Ge 17:17 a son be born to a man a hundred y old? H9102
Ge 17:24 was ninety-nine y old when he was H9102
Ge 21: 5 was a hundred y old when his son H9102
Ge 23: 1 to be a hundred and twenty-seven y *old*. H9102
Ge 25: 7 lived a hundred and seventy-five y. H9102
Ge 25: 8 an old man and full of y; and he was NDT
Ge 25:17 lived a hundred and thirty-seven y. H9102
Ge 25:20 Isaac was forty y old when he married H9102
Ge 25:26 Isaac was sixty y old when Rebekah gave H9102
Ge 26:34 When Esau was forty y old, he married H9102
Ge 29:18 "I'll work for you seven y in return for H9102
Ge 29:20 So Jacob served seven y to get Rachel, but H9102
Ge 29:27 in return for another seven y *of* work." H9102
Ge 29:30 And he worked for Laban another seven y. H9102
Ge 31:38 "I have been with you for twenty y now H9102
Ge 31:41 this for the twenty y I was in your H9102
Ge 31:41 you fourteen y for your two daughters H9102
Ge 31:41 two daughters and six y for your flocks, H9102
Ge 35:28 Isaac lived a hundred and eighty y. H9102
Ge 35:29 gathered to his people, old and full of y. H3427
Ge 41: 1 When *two* **full** y had passed H9102+3427
Ge 41:26 The seven good cows are seven y, and the H9102
Ge 41:26 seven good heads of grain are seven y; H9102
Ge 41:27 cows that came up afterward are seven y, H9102
Ge 41:27 They are seven y *of* famine. H9102
Ge 41:29 Seven y *of* great abundance are coming H9102
Ge 41:30 seven y *of* famine will follow them H9102
Ge 41:34 of Egypt during the seven y *of* abundance. H9102
Ge 41:35 food of these good y that are coming and H9102
Ge 41:36 during the seven y *of* famine that will H9102
Ge 41:46 Joseph was thirty y old when he entered H9102
Ge 41:47 During the seven y *of* abundance the land H9102
Ge 41:48 in those seven y of abundance in Egypt H9102
Ge 41:50 Before the y *of* famine came, two sons H9102
Ge 41:53 The seven y *of* abundance in Egypt came H9102
Ge 41:54 the seven y *of* famine began, just as H9102
Ge 45: 6 *For two* y now there has been famine in H9102
Ge 45: 6 and *for* the next five y there will be no H9102
Ge 45:11 because five y *of* famine are still to come. H9102
Ge 47: 9 "The y *of* my pilgrimage are a H3427+9102
Ge 47: 9 My y have been few and difficult H3427+9102
Ge 47: 9 do not equal the y of the H3427+9102
Ge 47:28 Jacob lived in Egypt seventeen y, and the H9102
Ge 47:28 and the y *of* his life were a H3427+9102
Ge 50:22 He lived a hundred and ten y H9102
Ex 6:16 Kohath and Merari. Levi lived 137 y. H9102
Ex 6:18 Hebron and Uzziel. Kohath lived 133 y. H9102
Ex 6:20 Aaron and Moses. Amram lived 137 y. H9102
Ex 7: 7 Moses was eighty y old and Aaron H9102
Ex 12:40 Israelite people lived in Egypt was 430 y. H9102
Ex 12:41 At the end of the 430 y, to the very day, all H9102
Ex 16:35 The Israelites ate manna forty y, until they H9102
Ex 21: 2 servant, he is to serve you *for* six y. H9102
Ex 23:10 "*For* six y you are to sow your fields and H9102
Ex 30:14 those twenty y old or more, are to H9102
Ex 38:26 counted, twenty y old or more, a total H9102
Lev 19:23 *For* three y you are to consider it forbidden H9102
Lev 25: 3 *For* six y sow your fields, and for six years H9102
Lev 25: 3 and *for* six y prune your vineyards and H9102
Lev 25: 8 " 'Count off seven sabbath y—seven times H9102
Lev 25: 8 seven times seven y—so that the seven H9102
Lev 25: 8 the seven sabbath y amount to a period H9102
Lev 25: 8 years amount to a period of forty-nine y. H9102
Lev 25:15 of the number of y since the Jubilee. H9102
Lev 25:15 of the number of y *left for* harvesting crops H9102
Lev 25:16 When the y are many, you are to increase H9102
Lev 25:16 and when the y are few, you are to H9102
Lev 25:21 that the land will yield enough for three y. H9102
Lev 25:27 the value for the y *since* they sold it and H9102
Lev 25:50 to a hired worker for that number of y. H9102
Lev 25:51 If many y remain, they must pay for their H9102
Lev 25:52 If only a few y remain until the Year of H9102
Lev 26:34 will enjoy its sabbath y all the time that it NDT
Lev 27: 6 a person between one month and five y, H9102
Lev 27: 7 a person sixty y old or more, set the H9102
Lev 27:18 to the number of y that remain until the H9102
Nu 1: 3 who are twenty y old or more and able H9102
Nu 1:18 the men twenty y old or more were H9102
Nu 1:20 All the men twenty y old or more who H9102
Nu 1:22 All the men twenty y old or more who H9102
Nu 1:24 All the men twenty y old or more who H9102
Nu 1:26 All the men twenty y old or more who H9102
Nu 1:28 All the men twenty y old or more who H9102
Nu 1:30 All the men twenty y old or more who H9102
Nu 1:32 All the men twenty y old or more who H9102
Nu 1:34 All the men twenty y old or more who H9102
Nu 1:36 All the men twenty y old or more who H9102
Nu 1:38 All the men twenty y old or more who H9102
Nu 1:40 All the men twenty y old or more who H9102
Nu 1:42 All the men twenty y old or more who H9102
Nu 1:45 Israelites twenty y old or more who were H9102
Nu 4: 3 from thirty to fifty y of age who come to H9102
Nu 4:23 from thirty to fifty y of age who come to H9102
Nu 4:30 from thirty to fifty y of age who come to H9102
Nu 4:35 from thirty to fifty y of age who came to H9102
Nu 4:39 from thirty to fifty y of age who came to H9102
Nu 4:43 from thirty to fifty y of age who came to H9102
Nu 4:47 from thirty to fifty y of age who came to do H9102
Nu 8:24 Men twenty-five y old or more shall come H9102
Nu 13:22 been built seven y before Zoan in Egypt H9102
Nu 14:29 one of you twenty y old or more who was H9102
Nu 14:33 children will be shepherds here *for* forty y, H9102
Nu 14:34 *For* forty y—one year for each of the forty H9102
Nu 20:15 into Egypt, and we lived there many y. H3427
Nu 26: 2 all those twenty y old or more who are H9102
Nu 26: 4 a census of the men twenty y old or more, H9102
Nu 32:11 who were twenty y old or more when they H9102
Nu 32:13 them wander in the wilderness forty y, H9102
Nu 33:39 twenty-three y old when he died on H9102
Dt 2: 7 These forty y the LORD your God has been H9102
Dt 2:14 Thirty-eight y passed from the time we H9102
Dt 8: 2 all the way in the wilderness these forty y, H9102
Dt 8: 4 feet did not swell *during* these forty y. H9102
Dt 14:28 At the end of every three y, bring all the H9102
Dt 15: 1 end of every seven y you must cancel H9102
Dt 15:12 sell themselves to you and serve you six y H9102
Dt 15:18 to you these six y has been worth twice as H9102
Dt 29: 5 "*During* the forty y that I led you through H9102
Dt 30:20 will give you **many** y in the land he H802+3427
Dt 31: 2 a hundred and twenty y old and I am no H9102
Dt 31:10 "At the end of every seven y, in the year H9102
Dt 34: 7 hundred and twenty y old when he died, H9102
Jos 5: 6 the wilderness forty y until all the men H9102
Jos 14: 7 I was forty y old when Moses the servant of H9102
Jos 14:10 kept me alive *for* forty-five y since the H9102
Jos 14:10 So here I am today, eighty-five y old! H9102
Jdg 3: 8 the Israelites were subject *for* eight y. H9102
Jdg 3:11 So the land had peace *for* forty y, until H9102
Jdg 3:14 to Eglon king of Moab *for* eighteen y. H9102
Jdg 3:30 the land had peace *for* eighty y. H9102
Jdg 4: 3 oppressed the Israelites *for* twenty y, H9102
Jdg 5:31 Then the land had peace forty y. H9102
Jdg 6: 1 and *for* seven y he gave them into the H9102
Jdg 6:25 your father's herd, the one seven y old. H9102
Jdg 8:28 lifetime, the land had peace forty y. H9102
Jdg 9:22 Abimelek had governed Israel three y, H9102
Jdg 10: 2 He led Israel twenty-three y; then he died H9102
Jdg 10: 3 of Gilead, who led Israel twenty-two y. H9102
Jdg 10: 8 *For* eighteen y they oppressed all the H9102
Jdg 11:26 *For* three hundred y Israel occupied H9102
Jdg 12: 7 Jephthah led Israel six y. Then Jephthah H9102
Jdg 12: 9 outside his clan. Ibzan led Israel seven y. H9102
Jdg 12:11 Elon the Zebulunite led Israel ten y. H9102
Jdg 12:14 on seventy donkeys. He led Israel eight y. H9102
Jdg 13: 1 into the hands of the Philistines *for* forty y. H9102
Jdg 15:20 led Israel *for* twenty y in the days of H9102
Jdg 16:31 He had led Israel twenty y. H9102
Ru 1: 4 After they had lived there about ten y, H9102
1Sa 4:15 was ninety-eight y old and whose eyes H9102
1Sa 4:18 he was heavy. He had led Israel forty y. H9102
1Sa 7: 2 Jearim a long time—twenty y in all. H9102
1Sa 13: 1 Saul was thirty y old when he became H9102
1Sa 13: 1 he reigned over Israel forty- two y. H9102
2Sa 2:10 of Saul was forty y old when he became H9102
2Sa 2:10 king over Israel, and he reigned two y. H9102
2Sa 2:11 over Judah was seven y and six months. H9102
2Sa 4: 4 He was five y old when the news about H9102
2Sa 5: 4 David was thirty y old when he became H9102
2Sa 5: 4 he became king, and he reigned forty y. H9102
2Sa 5: 5 over Judah seven y and six months, H9102
2Sa 5: 5 over all Israel and Judah thirty-three y. H9102
2Sa 13:23 *Two* y later, when Absalom's H9102+3427
2Sa 13:38 went to Geshur, he stayed there three y. H9102
2Sa 14:28 Absalom lived *two* y in Jerusalem H9102+3427
2Sa 15: 7 At the end of four y, Absalom said to the H9102
2Sa 19:32 was very old, eighty y of age. He had H9102
2Sa 19:34 "How many more y will I live, that I H9102
2Sa 19:35 I am now eighty y old. Can I tell the H9102
2Sa 21: 1 famine *for* three **successive** y; H9102+339+9102
2Sa 24:13 come on you three y of famine in your H9102
1Ki 2:11 He had reigned forty y over Israel—seven H9102
1Ki 2:11 seven y in Hebron and thirty-three in H9102
1Ki 2:39 But three y later, two of Shimei's slaves H9102
1Ki 6:38 He had spent seven y building it. H9102
1Ki 7: 1 It took Solomon thirteen y, however, to H9102
1Ki 9:10 At the end of twenty y, during which H9102
1Ki 10:22 Once every three y it returned, carrying H9102
1Ki 11:42 in Jerusalem over all Israel forty y. H9102
1Ki 14:20 He reigned *for* twenty-two y and then H9102
1Ki 14:21 He was forty-one y old when he became H9102
1Ki 14:21 he reigned seventeen y in Jerusalem H9102
1Ki 15: 2 he reigned in Jerusalem three y. H9102
1Ki 15:10 he reigned in Jerusalem forty-one y. H9102
1Ki 15:25 and he reigned over Israel *two* y. H9102
1Ki 15:33 in Tirzah, and he reigned twenty-four y. H9102
1Ki 16: 8 of Israel, and he reigned in Tirzah *two* y. H9102
1Ki 16:23 he reigned twelve y, six of them in H9102
1Ki 16:29 in Samaria over Israel twenty-two y. H9102
1Ki 17: 1 dew nor rain *in* the next few y except at H9102
1Ki 22: 1 *For* three y there was no war between H9102
1Ki 22:42 was thirty-five y old when he became king H9102
1Ki 22:42 he reigned in Jerusalem twenty-five y. H9102
1Ki 22:51 and he reigned over Israel *two* y. H9102
2Ki 3: 1 king of Judah, and he reigned twelve y. H9102
2Ki 8: 1 a famine in the land that will last seven y." H9102
2Ki 8: 2 in the land of the Philistines seven y. H9102
2Ki 8: 3 end of the seven y she came back from H9102
2Ki 8:17 He was thirty-two y old when he became H9102
2Ki 8:17 he reigned in Jerusalem eight y. H9102
2Ki 8:26 was twenty-two y old when he became H9102
2Ki 10:36 over Israel in Samaria was twenty-eight y. H9102
2Ki 11: 3 temple of the LORD *for* six y while Athaliah H9102
2Ki 11:21 Joash was seven y old when he began to H9102
2Ki 12: 1 and he reigned in Jerusalem forty y. H9102
2Ki 12: 2 of the LORD all the y Jehoiada the priest H3427
2Ki 13: 1 in Samaria, and he reigned seventeen y. H9102
2Ki 13:10 in Samaria, and he reigned sixteen y. H9102
2Ki 14: 2 He was twenty-five y old when he became H9102
2Ki 14: 2 he reigned in Jerusalem twenty-nine y. H9102
2Ki 14:17 of Judah lived *for* fifteen y after the death H9102
2Ki 14:21 who was sixteen y old, and made him H9102
2Ki 14:23 in Samaria, and he reigned forty-one y. H9102
2Ki 15: 2 He was sixteen y old when he became H9102
2Ki 15: 2 he reigned in Jerusalem fifty-two y. H9102
2Ki 15:17 and he reigned in Samaria ten y. H9102
2Ki 15:23 Israel in Samaria, and he reigned *two* y. H9102
2Ki 15:27 in Samaria, and he reigned twenty y. H9102
2Ki 15:33 He was twenty-five y old when he became H9102
2Ki 15:33 he reigned in Jerusalem sixteen y. H9102
2Ki 16: 2 Ahaz was twenty y old when he became H9102
2Ki 16: 2 he reigned in Jerusalem sixteen y. H9102
2Ki 17: 1 Israel in Samaria, and he reigned nine y. H9102
2Ki 17: 5 Samaria and laid siege to it *for* three y. H9102
2Ki 18: 2 He was twenty-five y old when he became H9102
2Ki 18: 2 he reigned in Jerusalem twenty-nine y. H9102
2Ki 18:10 At the end of three y the Assyrians took it H9102
2Ki 20: 6 I will add fifteen y to your life. And I will H9102
2Ki 21: 1 was twelve y old when he became H9102
2Ki 21: 1 he reigned in Jerusalem fifty-five y. H9102
2Ki 21:19 was twenty-two y old when he became H9102
2Ki 21:19 and he reigned in Jerusalem two y. H9102
2Ki 22: 1 Josiah was eight y old when he became H9102
2Ki 22: 1 he reigned in Jerusalem thirty-one y. H9102
2Ki 23:31 was twenty-three y old when he became H9102
2Ki 23:36 was twenty-five y old when he became H9102

2Ki 23:36 he reigned in Jerusalem eleven y. H9102
2Ki 24: 1 Jehoiakim became his vassal *for* three y. H9102
2Ki 24: 8 was eighteen y old when he became king H9102
2Ki 24:18 was twenty-one y old when he became H9102
2Ki 24:18 he reigned in Jerusalem eleven y. H9102
1Ch 2:21 when he was sixty y old, married the H9102
1Ch 3: 4 where he reigned seven y and six months. H9102
1Ch 3: 4 David reigned in Jerusalem thirty-three y, H9102
1Ch 21:12 three y of famine, three months of being H9102
1Ch 23: 1 When David was old and full of y, he H3427
1Ch 23: 3 The Levites thirty y old or more were H9102
1Ch 23:24 the workers twenty y old or more who H9102
1Ch 23:27 counted from those twenty y old or more. H9102
1Ch 27:23 number of the men twenty y old or less, H9102
1Ch 29:27 He ruled over Israel forty y—seven in H9102
2Ch 8: 1 At the end of twenty y, during which H9102
2Ch 9:21 Once every three y it returned, carrying H9102
2Ch 9:30 in Jerusalem over all Israel forty y. H9102
2Ch 11:17 Rehoboam son of Solomon three y, H9102
2Ch 12:13 He was forty-one y old when he became H9102
2Ch 12:13 he reigned seventeen y in Jerusalem H9102
2Ch 13: 2 he reigned in Jerusalem three y. H9102
2Ch 14: 1 days the country was at peace *for* ten y. H9102
2Ch 14: 6 one was at war with him during those y, H9102
2Ch 18: 2 **Some y later** he went down H4200+7891+9102
2Ch 20:31 He was thirty-five y old when he became H9102
2Ch 20:31 he reigned in Jerusalem twenty-five y. H9102
2Ch 21: 5 was thirty-two y old when he became H9102
2Ch 21: 5 he reigned in Jerusalem eight y. H9102
2Ch 21:20 was thirty-two y old when he became NDT
2Ch 21:20 he reigned in Jerusalem eight y. H9102
2Ch 22: 2 was twenty-two y old when he became H9102
2Ch 22:12 the temple of God *for* six y while Athaliah H9102
2Ch 24: 1 Joash was seven y old when he became H9102
2Ch 24: 1 and he reigned in Jerusalem forty y. H9102
2Ch 24: 2 of the LORD all the y *of* Jehoiada the priest H3427
2Ch 24:15 Now Jehoiada was old and full of y, and H3427
2Ch 25: 1 was twenty-five y old when he became H9102
2Ch 25: 1 he reigned in Jerusalem twenty-nine y. H9102
2Ch 25: 5 those twenty y old or more and found H9102
2Ch 25:25 of Judah lived *for* fifteen y after the death H9102
2Ch 26: 1 who was sixteen y old, and made him H9102
2Ch 26: 3 was sixteen y old when he became H9102
2Ch 26: 3 he reigned in Jerusalem fifty-two y. H9102
2Ch 27: 1 was twenty-five y old when he became H9102
2Ch 27: 1 he reigned in Jerusalem sixteen y. H9102
2Ch 27: 5 amount also in the second and third y. H9102
2Ch 27: 8 He was twenty-five y old when he became H9102
2Ch 27: 8 he reigned in Jerusalem sixteen y. H9102
2Ch 28: 1 Ahaz was twenty y old when he became H9102
2Ch 28: 1 he reigned in Jerusalem sixteen y. H9102
2Ch 29: 1 was twenty-five y old when he became H9102
2Ch 29: 1 he reigned in Jerusalem twenty-nine y. H9102
2Ch 31:16 to the males three y old or more whose H9102
2Ch 31:17 to the Levites twenty y old or more, H9102
2Ch 33: 1 was twelve y old when he became H9102
2Ch 33: 1 he reigned in Jerusalem fifty-five y. H9102
2Ch 33:21 was twenty-two y old when he became H9102
2Ch 33:21 and he reigned in Jerusalem two y. H9102
2Ch 34: 1 Josiah was eight y old when he became H9102
2Ch 34: 1 he reigned in Jerusalem thirty-one y. H9102
2Ch 36: 2 was twenty-three y old when he became H9102
2Ch 36: 5 was twenty-five y old when he became H9102
2Ch 36: 5 he reigned in Jerusalem eleven y. H9102
2Ch 36: 9 was eighteen y old when he became king H9102
2Ch 36:11 was twenty-one y old when he became H9102
2Ch 36:11 he reigned in Jerusalem eleven y. H9102
2Ch 36:21 until the seventy y were completed in H9102
Ezr 3: 8 Levites twenty y old and older to H9102
Ezr 5:11 the temple that was built many y ago, A10732
Ne 5:14 twelve y—neither I nor my brothers H9102
Ne 9:21 *For* forty y you sustained them in the H9102
Ne 9:30 *For* many y you were patient with them. H9102
Job 10: 5 of a mortal or your y like those of a strong H9102
Job 15:20 man through all the y stored up for him. H9102
Job 16:22 "Only a few y will pass before I take the H9102
Job 21:13 They spend their y in prosperity and go H3427
Job 32: 6 "I am young in y, and you are old; that is H3427
Job 32: 7 advanced y should teach wisdom. H9102
Job 36:11 in prosperity and their y in contentment. H9102
Job 36:26 The number of his y is past finding out. H9102
Job 38:21 You have lived so many y! H3427
Job 42:16 Job lived a hundred and forty y; he saw H9102
Job 42:17 And so Job died, an old man and full of y. H3427
Ps 31:10 by anguish and my y by groaning; H9102
Ps 39: 5 the **span of** my y is as nothing before you. H2698
Ps 61: 6 the king's life, his y for many generations. H9102
Ps 77: 5 about the former days, the y *of* long ago; H9102
Ps 77:10 the y *when* the Most High stretched out H9102
Ps 78:33 their days in futility and their y in terror. H9102
Ps 90: 4 A thousand y in your sight are like a day H9102
Ps 90: 9 your wrath; we finish our y with a moan. H9102
Ps 90:10 Our days may come to seventy y, or eighty, H9102
Ps 90:15 *for* as many y as we have seen trouble. H9102
Ps 95:10 *For* forty y I was angry with that generation H9102
Ps 102:24 your y go on through all generations. H9102
Ps 102:27 the same, and your y will never end. H9102
Pr 3: 2 your life **many** y and bring H3427+2256+9102
Pr 4:10 and the y *of* your life will be many. H9102
Pr 9:11 be many, and y will be added to your life. H9102
Pr 10:27 but the y *of* the wicked are cut short. H9102
Ecc 6: 3 have a hundred children and live many y; H9102
Ecc 6: 6 he lives a thousand y twice over but fails H9102
Ecc 11: 8 However many y anyone may live, let H9102
Ecc 12: 1 come and the y approach when you H9102
Isa 7: 8 Within sixty-five y Ephraim will be too H9102
Isa 16:14 "Within three y, as a servant bound by H9102
Isa 20: 3 gone stripped and barefoot *for* three y, H9102
Isa 23:15 time Tyre will be forgotten *for* seventy y, H9102
Isa 23:15 But at the end of these seventy y, it will H9102
Isa 23:17 At the end of seventy y, the LORD will deal H9102
Isa 38: 5 your tears; I will add fifteen y to your life. H9102
Isa 38:10 death and be robbed of the rest of my y?" H9102
Isa 38:15 walk humbly all my y because of this H9102
Isa 65:20 an old man who does not live out his y H3427
Jer 6:11 the old, those weighed down with y. H3427
Jer 25: 3 For twenty-three y—from the thirteenth H9102
Jer 25:11 will serve the king of Babylon seventy y. H9102
Jer 25:12 "But when the seventy y are fulfilled, I will H9102
Jer 28: 3 Within *two* y I will bring back to this H9102+3427
Jer 28:11 neck of all the nations within *two* y. H9102+3427
Jer 29:10 "When seventy y are completed for H9102
Jer 34:14 After they have served you six y, you must H9102
Jer 52: 1 was twenty-one y old when he became H9102
Jer 52: 1 he reigned in Jerusalem eleven y. H9102
Eze 4: 5 same number of days as the y *of* their sin. H9102
Eze 12:27 vision he sees is for many y from now, H3427
Eze 22: 4 a close, and the end of your y has come. H9102
Eze 29:11 no one will live there *for* forty y. H9102
Eze 29:12 lie desolate forty y among ruined cities. H9102
Eze 29:13 At the end of forty y I will gather the H9102
Eze 38: 8 In future y you will invade a land that has H9102
Eze 38:17 they prophesied *for* y that I would bring H9102
Eze 39: 9 *For* seven y they will use them for fuel. H9102
Da 1: 5 They were to be trained *for* three y, and H9102
Da 9: 2 of Jerusalem would last seventy y. H9102
Da 11: 6 After *some* y, they will become allies. H9102
Da 11: 8 *For some* y he will leave the king of the H9102
Da 11:13 and after *several* y, he will H2021+6961+9102
Da 11:20 In a few y, however, he will be destroyed H3427
Joel 2:25 repay you for the y the locusts have eaten H9102
Am 1: 1 saw concerning Israel *two* y before the H9102
Am 2:10 led you forty y in the wilderness to H9102
Am 4: 4 every morning, your tithes every three y. H3427
Am 5:25 offerings forty y in the wilderness, H9102
Zec 1:12 have been angry with these seventy y?" H9102
Zec 7: 3 fifth month, as I have done for so many y?" H9102
Zec 7: 5 seventh months for the past seventy y, H9102
Mal 3: 4 as in days gone by, as in former y. H9102
Mt 2:16 its vicinity who were **two y old** and under, G1453
Mt 9:20 to bleeding *for* twelve y came up behind G2291
Mk 5:25 had been subject to bleeding *for* twelve y. G2291
Mk 5:42 she was twelve y *old*). At this they were G2291
Lk 1:18 old man and my wife is well along in y." G2465
Lk 2:36 her husband seven y after her marriage, G2291
Lk 2:42 When he was twelve y *old*, they went up G2291
Lk 3:23 was about thirty y *old* when he began his G2291
Lk 4:25 for **three and a half** y G2291+5552+2779+3604+1971
Lk 8:43 had been subject to bleeding for twelve y, G2291
Lk 12:19 have plenty of grain laid up for many y. G2291
Lk 13: 7 'For three y now I've been coming to look G2291
Lk 13:11 been crippled by a spirit *for* eighteen y. G2291
Lk 13:16 Satan has kept bound for eighteen *long* y, G2291
Lk 15:29 All these y I've been slaving for you and G2291
Jn 2:20 has taken forty-six y to build this temple, G2291
Jn 5: 5 had been an invalid *for* thirty-eight y. G2291
Jn 8:57 "You are not yet fifty y *old*," they said to G2291
Ac 4:22 miraculously healed was over forty y *old*. G2291
Ac 7: 6 'For four hundred y your descendants will G2291
Ac 7:23 "When Moses was **forty** y old, he decided G5478
Ac 7:30 "After forty y had passed, an angel G2291
Ac 7:36 the Red Sea and *for* forty y in the G2291
Ac 7:42 offerings forty y in the wilderness, G2291
Ac 9:33 had been bedridden for eight y. G2291
Ac 13:18 *for* about **forty** y he endured their G5478+5989
Ac 13:20 All this took about 450 y. "After this, God G2291
Ac 13:21 of the tribe of Benjamin, who ruled forty y. G2291
Ac 19:10 This went on for two y, so that all the Jews G2291
Ac 20:31 Remember that *for* **three** y I never stopped G5562
Ac 24:10 that for a number *of* y you have been a G2291
Ac 24:17 "After an absence of several y, I came to G2291
Ac 24:27 When **two** y had passed, Felix was G1454
Ac 28:30 *For* **two** whole y Paul stayed there in his G1454
Ro 4:19 since he was about **a hundred y old**—and G1670
Ro 15:23 have been longing for many y to visit you, G2291
2Co 12: 2 Christ who fourteen y ago was caught up G2291
Gal 1:18 Then after three y, I went up to Jerusalem G2291
Gal 2: 1 Then after fourteen y, I went up again to G2291
Gal 3:17 introduced 430 y later, does not set G2291
Gal 4:10 days and months and seasons and y! G1929
Heb 1:12 the same, and your y will never end." G2291
Heb 3: 9 though *for* forty y they saw what I did. G2291
Heb 3:17 And with whom was he angry *for* forty y G2291
Jas 5:17 not rain on the land *for* three and a half y. G1929
[Jas 5:17 on the land *for* three and a **half** y. G3604+1971]
2Pe 3: 8 With the Lord a day is like a thousand y G2291
2Pe 3: 8 and a thousand y are like a day. G2291
Rev 20: 2 Satan, and bound him *for* a thousand y. G2291
Rev 20: 3 until the thousand y were ended. G2291
Rev 20: 4 life and reigned with Christ a thousand y. G2291
Rev 20: 5 to life until the thousand y were ended.) G2291
Rev 20: 6 will reign with him *for* a thousand y. G2291
Rev 20: 7 When the thousand y are over, Satan will G2291

YEAST (57)

Ge 19: 3 baking **bread without** y, and they H5174
Ex 12: 8 bitter herbs, and **bread made without** y. H5174
Ex 12:15 days you are to eat **bread made without** y. H5174
Ex 12:15 first day remove the y from your houses, H8419
Ex 12:15 eats **anything with** y **in it** from the H2809
Ex 12:18 you are to eat **bread made without** y, H5174
Ex 12:19 For seven days no y is to be found in your H8419
Ex 12:19 who eats **anything with** y **in it** must be cut H4721
Ex 12:20 Eat nothing **made with** y. Wherever you H4721
Ex 12:34 took their dough before *the* y *was* **added**, H2806
Ex 12:39 The dough *was* without y because they H2806
Ex 13: 3 a mighty hand. Eat nothing **containing** y. H2809
Ex 13: 6 days eat **bread made without** y and on H5174
Ex 13: 7 nothing **with** y **in it** is to be seen among H2809
Ex 13: 7 shall *any* y be seen anywhere within H8419
Ex 23:15 seven days eat **bread made without** y H5174
Ex 23:18 to me along with **anything containing** y. H2809
Ex 29: 2 wheat flour make round loaves **without** y, H5174
Ex 29: 2 thick loaves **without** y and with olive oil H5174
Ex 29: 2 thin loaves **without** y and brushed H5174
Ex 29:23 From the basket of **bread made without** y H5174
Ex 34:18 For seven days eat **bread made without** y H5174
Ex 34:25 to me along with **anything containing** y, H2809
Lev 2: 4 loaves made **without** y and with olive H5174
Lev 2: 4 thin loaves made **without** y and brushed H5174
Lev 2: 5 finest flour mixed with oil, and **without** y. H5174
Lev 2:11 bring to the LORD must be made without y, H2809
Lev 2:11 are not to burn any y or honey in a food H8419
Lev 6:16 it is to be eaten **without** y in the sanctuary H5174
Lev 6:17 It must not be baked with y; I have given it H2809
Lev 7:12 thick loaves **made without** y and with H5174
Lev 7:12 thin loaves **made without** y and brushed H5174
Lev 7:13 with thick loaves of bread **made with** y. H2809
Lev 8: 2 basket containing **bread made without** y, H5174
Lev 8:26 from the basket of **bread made without** y, H5174
Lev 10:12 offerings **prepared without** y and H5174
Lev 23: 6 days you must eat **bread made without** y. H5174
Lev 23:17 baked with y, as a wave offering of H2809
Nu 6:15 **bread** *made with* the finest flour and **without** y H5174
Nu 6:19 from the basket, both **made without** y. H5174
Nu 28:17 seven days eat **bread made without** y. H5174
Dt 16: 3 Do not eat it with **bread made with** y, but H2809
Dt 16: 4 Let no y be found in your possession in all H8419
Jdg 6:19 ephah of flour he made **bread without** y. H5174
1Sa 28:24 kneaded it and baked **bread without** y. H5174
1Ch 23:29 the thin loaves **made without** y, the H5174
Eze 45:21 you shall eat **bread made without** y. H5174
Mt 13:33 of heaven is like y that a woman took G2434
Mt 16: 6 guard against the y of the Pharisees and G2434
Mt 16:11 guard against the y of the Pharisees and G2434
Mt 16:12 to guard against the y used in bread, G2434
Mk 8:15 "Watch out for the y of the Pharisees and G2434
Lk 12: 1 your guard against the y of the Pharisees, G2434
Lk 13:21 It is like y that a woman took and mixed G2434
1Co 5: 6 you know that a little y leavens the whole G2434
1Co 5: 7 Get rid of the old y, so that you may be a G2434
Gal 5: 9 "A little y works through the whole batch G2434

YELLING (1) [YELL]

Ac 7:57 their ears and, y at the top of their voices G3189

YELLOW (4)

Lev 13:30 skin deep and the hair in it is y and thin, H7411
Lev 13:32 there is no y hair in it and it does H7411
Lev 13:36 he does not need to look for y hair; they H7411
Rev 9:17 were fiery red, dark blue, and y **as sulfur**. G2523

YES (94)

Ge 17:19 "**Y, but** your wife Sarah will bear you a son H66
Ge 18:15 But he said, "Y, you did laugh." H4202+3954
Ge 20: 6 him in the dream, "Y, I know you did this H1685
Ge 22: 7 "Y, my son?" Abraham H2180
Ge 27:18 "Y, my son," he answered H2180
Ge 29: 5 Nahor's grandson?" "Y, we know him," NDT
Ge 29: 6 "Y, he is," they said, "and here comes H8934S
Ex 2: 8 "Y, go," she answered. So the girl went NDT
Jos 2: 4 She said, "Y, the men came to me, but I H4026
Jos 24:22 to serve the LORD." "Y, we are witnesses," NDT
Jdg 5:15 were with Deborah; y, Issachar was with H4027
1Sa 10:22 And the LORD said, "Y, he has hidden H2180
1Sa 16: 5 Samuel replied, "Y, in peace; I have come NDT
1Sa 22:12 son of Ahitub." "Y, my lord," he answered H2180
1Sa 26:17 David replied, "Y it is, my lord the NDT
2Sa 12:19 he asked. "Y," they replied, "he is NDT
2Sa 14:19 **Y**, it was your servant Joab who instructed H3954
1Ki 2:13 He answered, "Y, peacefully." NDT
1Ki 2:22 he is my older brother—y, for him and H2256
1Ki 18: 8 "Y," he replied. "Go tell your master H638S
1Ki 20:33 to pick up his word. "Y, your brother NDT
1Ki 21:19 dogs will lick up your blood—y, yours! H1685
2Ki 2: 3 from you today?" "Y, I know," Elisha H1685
2Ki 2: 5 from you today?" "Y, I know," he replied H1685
2Ki 7:13 Israelites left here—y, they will only be H2180
Ps 62: 5 Y, my soul, find rest in God; my hope H421
Ps 77:11 deeds of the LORD; y, I will remember your H3954
Ps 90:17 of our hands for us—y, establish the work H2256
Ps 128: 4 **Y**, this will be the blessing for the H2180+3954
Ecc 11: 2 Invest in seven ventures, y, in eight; H2256+1685
Isa 26: 8 **Y**, LORD, walking in the way of your laws, H677
Isa 27: 5 make peace with me, y, let them make NDT

Isa 32:13 thorns and briers—y, mourn for all H3954
Isa 43:13 Y, and from ancient days I am he. No one NDT
Isa 44: 7 what is yet to come—y, let them foretell H2256
Isa 48: 7 So you cannot say, 'Y, I knew of them.' H2180
Isa 48:15 have spoken; y, I have called him. H677
Isa 49:25 "Y, captives will be taken from warriors H1685
Isa 52: 6 know that it is I who foretold it. Y, it is I." H2180
Isa 57: 6 Y, to them you have poured out drink H1685
Isa 63: 7 has done for us—y, the many good H2256
Jer 3:22 "Y, we will come to you, for you are the H2180
Jer 16:20 make their own gods? Y, but they are not NDT
Jer 23:31 Y," declares the LORD, "I am against the H2180
Jer 27:21 y, this is what the LORD Almighty, the God H3954
Jer 29: 8 Y, this is what the LORD Almighty, the God H3954
Jer 29:17 y, this is what the LORD Almighty says: NDT
Jer 36:18 "Y," Baruch replied, "he dictated all these NDT
Jer 37:17 "Y," Jeremiah replied, "you will be H3780
Eze 36:10 many people to live on you—y, all of Israel. NDT
Da 7:18 possess it forever—y, for ever and ever. A10221
Hag 2:13 "Y," the priests replied, "it becomes defiled NDT
Mal 2: 2 Y, I have already cursed them H2256+1685
Mt 5:37 need to say is **simply** 'Y' or 'No'; *G3721+3721*
Mt 9:28 able to do this?" "Y, Lord," they replied. *G3721*
Mt 11: 9 Y, I tell you, and more than a *G3721*
Mt 11:26 Y, Father, for this is what you were pleased *G3721*
Mt 13:51 Jesus asked. "Y," they replied. *G3721*
Mt 15:27 "Y it is, Lord," she said. "Even the dogs *G3721*
Mt 17:25 "Y, he does," he replied. When Peter *G3721*
Mt 21:16 "Y," replied Jesus, "have you never read *G3721*
Mk 14:30 "today—y, **tonight**—before *G4047+3836+3816*
Lk 7:26 Y, I tell you, and more than a *G3721*
Lk 10:21 Y, Father, for this is what you were *G3721*
Lk 11:51 Y, I tell you, this generation will be held *G3721*
Lk 12: 5 throw you into hell. Y, I tell you, fear him. *G3721*
Lk 14:26 and sisters—y, even their own life *G2285+5445*
Lk 22:37 Y, what is written about me is reaching its *G1142*
Jn 5:20 Y, and he will show him even greater works NDT
Jn 7:28 cried out, "Y, you know **me**, and you know *G2743*
Jn 11:27 "Y, Lord," she replied, "I believe that you *G3721*
Jn 21:15 "Y, Lord," he said, "you know that I love *G3721*
Jn 21:16 He answered, "Y, Lord, you know that I *G3721*
Ac 5: 8 got for the land?" "Y," she said, "that is *G3721*
Ac 9:10 "Y, Lord," he answered. *G2627+1609*
Ac 22:27 a Roman citizen?" "Y, I am," he answered *G3721*
Ro 3:29 God of Gentiles too? Y, of Gentiles too, *G3721*
1Co 1:16 Y, I also baptized the household of *G1254*
1Co 9:10 Y, this was written for us, because *G1142*
1Co 15:31 y, **just as surely as** I boast about you in *G3755*
2Co 1:17 so that in the same breath I say both "Y, *G3721*
2Co 1:17 same breath I say both "Yes, y" and "No, *G3721*
2Co 1:18 our message to you is not "Y" and "No." *G3721*
2Co 1:19 Silas and Timothy—was not "Y" and "No," *G3721*
2Co 1:19 but in him it has always been "Y. *G3721*
2Co 1:20 God has made, they are "Y" in Christ. *G3721*
2Co 11: 1 foolishness. Y, please put up with *G247+2779*
Php 1:18 of this I rejoice. Y, and I will continue to *G247*
Php 3:10 want to know Christ—y, to know the power *G2779*
Php 4: 3 Y, and I ask you, my true companion, help *G3721*
Jas 5:12 All you need to say is a *simple* "Y" or "No." *G3721*
Rev 14:13 "Y," says the Spirit, "they will rest from *G3721*
Rev 16: 7 "Y, Lord God Almighty, true and just are *G3721*
Rev 22:20 these things says, "Y, I am coming soon." *G3721*

YESTERDAY (8)

Ex 5:14 you met your quota of bricks y or today, H9453
1Sa 20:27 Jesse come to the meal, either y or today?" H9453
2Sa 15:20 You came only y. And today shall I make H9453
2Ki 9:26 'Y I saw the blood of Naboth and the blood H621
Job 8: 9 we were born only y and know nothing, H9453
Jn 4:52 they said to him, "Y, at one in the *G2396*
Ac 7:28 of killing me as you killed the Egyptian y? *G2396*
Heb 13: 8 Christ is the same y and today and forever *G2396*

YESTERNIGHT (KJV) LAST NIGHT

YET (407)

Ge 2: 5 Now **no** shrub had y appeared on the H3270
Ge 2: 5 earth and **no** plant had y sprung up H3972+3270
Ge 15:16 Amorites has not y reached its full H6330+2178
Ge 21: 7 Y I have borne him a son in his old age." H3954
Ge 31: 7 y your father has cheated me by changing H2256
Ge 31:43 Y what can I do today about these H2256
Ge 32:30 face to face, **and** y my life was spared." H2256
Ex 5:16 are given no straw, y we are told, 'Make H2256
Ex 5:18 y you must produce your full quota of H2256
Ex 7:13 Y Pharaoh's heart became hard and he H2256
Ex 9: 7 Y his heart was unyielding and he would H2256
Ex 10: 7 Do you **not** y realize that Egypt is ruined?" H3270
Ex 10:23 Y all the Israelites had light in the places H2256
Ex 21:36 y the owner did not keep it penned up H2256
Ex 34: 7 Y he does not leave the guilty H2256
Lev 19:20 Y they are not to be put to death, because NDT
Lev 21:23 y because of his defect, he must not go H421
Lev 22: 3 unclean **and** y comes near the H2256
Lev 22:13 is divorced, y has no children, and H2256
Lev 26:44 Y in spite of this, when they are in H2256+677
Nu 11:26 Y the Spirit **also** rested on them, and they H2256
Nu 14:18 Y he does not leave the guilty H2256
Nu 24:22 y you Kenites will be destroyed H3954+561
Dt 1:39 who do not y know good from bad H2021+3427
Dt 10:15 Y the LORD set his affection on your H8370
Dt 12: 9 since you have not y reached the H6964+6330
Dt 20: 5 a new house and not *y begun to* **live in** it? AIT
Dt 29: 5 Y the LORD says, "During the forty years H2256
Dt 34: 7 y his eyes were not weak nor his strength NDT
Jos 3:15 Y as soon as the priests who carried the H2256
Jos 11:13 Y Israel did not burn any of the cities built H8370
Jos 17:12 Y the Manassites were not able to occupy H2256
Jos 18: 2 tribes who *had* not *y* **received** their AIT
Jdg 2: 2 Y you have disobeyed me H2256
Jdg 2:17 Y they would not listen to their H2256+1685
Jdg 8: 4 exhausted y keeping up the pursuit H2256
Jdg 18: 1 had not y come into an inheritance H6330+2021+3427+2021+2085
1Sa 3: 3 The lamp of God had **not** y gone out, and H3270
1Sa 3: 7 Now Samuel did **not** y know the LORD: H3270
1Sa 3: 7 of the LORD had **not** y been revealed to H3270
1Sa 10:22 of the LORD, "Has the man come here y?" H6388
1Sa 12:20 this evil; y do not turn away from the LORD H421
1Sa 12:25 Y if you persist in doing evil, both you and H2256
1Sa 14:26 y no one put his hand to his mouth H2256
1Sa 20: 3 Y as surely as the LORD lives and as you H219
1Sa 22:17 he was fleeing, y they did not tell me." H2256
1Sa 25:15 Y these men were very good to us. H2256
2Sa 3: 8 Y now you accuse me of an offense H2256
1Ki 3: 2 had not y been built for H6330+2021+3427+2021+2156
1Ki 8:28 Y give attention to your servant's prayer H2256
1Ki 11:13 Y I will not tear the whole kingdom from H8370
1Ki 18:12 Y I your servant have worshiped the LORD H2256
1Ki 19:18 Y I reserve seven thousand in Israel—all H2256
1Ki 22: 3 Gilead belongs to us **and** y we are doing H2256
2Ki 2:10 "**y if** you see me when I am taken from you H561
2Ki 3:17 y this valley will be filled with water H2256
2Ki 10:31 Y Jehu was not careful to keep the law of H2256
2Ki 14: 6 Y he did not put the children of the H2256
1Ch 28: 4 "Y the LORD, the God of Israel, chose me H2256
2Ch 6:19 Y, LORD my God, give attention to your H2256
2Ch 13: 6 Y Jeroboam son of Nebat, an official of H2256
2Ch 16: 8 Y when you relied on the LORD, he H2256
2Ch 25: 4 Y he did not put their children to death H2256
2Ch 30:18 themselves, y they ate the Passover H3954
Ezr 3: 6 **the foundation** of the LORD's temple *had* not *y* **been laid** AIT
Ezr 5:16 been under construction but is **not** y finished." AIT
Ezr 9:13 deeds and our great guilt, and y, our God, H3954
Ne 2:16 because as y I had said nothing to the H4027
Ne 5: 5 y we have to subject our sons and H2256
Ne 7: 4 and the houses had **not** y been rebuilt. AIT
Ne 9:30 Y they paid no attention, so you gave H2256
Est 3: 6 Y having learned who Mordecai's people H3954
Job 1:18 y another messenger came and said H2256
Job 4:10 y the teeth of the great lions are broken. H2256
Job 5: 7 Y man is born to trouble as surely as H3954
Job 8:21 He will y fill your mouth with laughter H6330
Job 11:13 "**Y if** you devote your heart to him and H561
Job 13:15 Though he slay me, y will I hope in him; NDT
Job 14: 9 y at the scent of water it will bud and put NDT
Job 16: 6 "**Y if** I speak, my pain is not relieved; and if H561
Job 16:17 y my hands have been free of violence H6584
Job 17:11 Y the desires of my heart NDT
Job 19:26 destroyed, y in my flesh I will see God; H2256
Job 20:14 y his food will turn sour in his stomach; it NDT
Job 21:14 Y they say to God, 'Leave us alone! We H2256
Job 21:17 "Y how often is the lamp of the wicked NDT
Job 22:13 Y you say, 'What does God know? Does H2256
Job 22:18 Y it was he who filled their houses with H2256
Job 23:17 Y I am not silenced by the darkness, by H3954
Job 24:11 they tread the winepresses, y suffer thirst. H2256
Job 24:18 "Y they are foam on the surface of the water; NDT
Job 26: 8 y the clouds do not burst under their H2256
Job 30:26 Y when I hoped for good, evil came H3954
Job 32: 3 to refute Job, **and** y had condemned him. H2256
Job 33:10 Y God has found fault with me; he H2176
Job 33:23 Y **if** there is an angel at their side, H561
Job 34:29 Y he is over individual and nation alike, H2256
Job 35: 3 Y you ask him, 'What profit is it to me H3954
Job 39:18 Y when she spreads her feathers to run H3869
Job 40:19 y its Maker can approach it with his sword. NDT
Ps 19: 4 Y their voice goes out into all the earth NDT
Ps 22: 3 Y you are enthroned as the Holy One; you H2256
Ps 22: 9 Y you brought me out of the womb; you H3954
Ps 22:31 declaring to a people y **unborn**: H3528
Ps 31:22 Y you heard my cry for mercy when I called H434
Ps 35:13 Y when they were ill, I put on sackcloth H2256
Ps 37:25 y I have never seen the righteous forsaken H2256
Ps 42: 5 for I will y praise him, my Savior H6388
Ps 42:11 for I will y praise him, my Savior H6388
Ps 43: 5 for I will y praise him, my Savior H6388
Ps 44:22 Y for your sake we face death all day long; H3954
Ps 51: 6 Y you desired faithfulness even in the H2176
Ps 55:21 is smooth as butter, y war is in his heart H2256
Ps 55:21 than oil, y they are drawn swords. H2256
Ps 59: 4 no wrong, y they are ready to attack me. NDT
Ps 73:23 Y I am always with you; you hold me by H2256
Ps 78: 6 even the children *y to* **be born**, and they in AIT
Ps 78:23 Y he gave a command to the skies above H2256
Ps 78:38 Y he was merciful; he forgave their H2256
Ps 90: 5 Y you sweep people away in the sleep of NDT
Ps 90:10 y the best of them are but trouble and H2256
Ps 102:18 that a people **not** y **created** may praise H1343
Ps 106: 8 Y he saved them for his name's sake, to H2256
Ps 106:44 Y he took note of their distress when he H2256
Ps 119:151 Y you are near, LORD, and all your NDT
Pr 6: 8 y it stores its provisions in summer and NDT
Pr 6:31 Y if he is caught, he must pay sevenfold H2256
Pr 11:24 person gives freely, y gains even more H2256
Pr 12: 9 to be a nobody **and** y have a servant than H2256
Pr 13: 7 to be rich, y has nothing; another H2256
Pr 13: 7 pretends to be poor, y has great wealth. H2256
Pr 14:16 a fool is hotheaded **and** y feels secure. H2256
Pr 19: 3 y their heart rages against the LORD. H2256
Pr 28:21 y a person will do wrong for a piece of H2256
Pr 30:12 in their own eyes **and** y are not cleansed H2256
Pr 30:24 earth are small, y they are extremely wise: H2256
Pr 30:25 y they store up their food in the summer; H2256
Pr 30:26 y they make their home in the crags H2256
Pr 30:27 no king, y they advance together in ranks H2256
Pr 30:28 the hand, y it is found in kings' palaces. H2256
Ecc 1: 7 flow into the sea, y the sea is never full. H2256
Ecc 1:11 even those y to come will not be H340
Ecc 2:11 Y when I surveyed all that my hands had H2256
Ecc 2:19 Y they will have control over all the fruit of H2256
Ecc 3:11 y no one can fathom what H4946+1172+889
Ecc 4: 8 y his eyes were not content with his H1685
Ecc 6: 3 many years; y no matter how long he lives H2256
Ecc 6: 7 y their appetite is never satisfied. H2256+1685
Ecc 8:13 Y because the wicked do not fear God, it H2256
SS 1: 5 Dark am I, y lovely, daughters of H2256
SS 8: 8 little sister, and her breasts are **not** *y* grown. AIT
Isa 5:25 Y for all this, his anger is not turned away NDT
Isa 7: 7 Y this is what the Sovereign LORD says: NDT
Isa 9:12 Y for all this, his anger is not turned away NDT
Isa 9:17 Y for all this, his anger is not turned away NDT
Isa 9:21 Y for all this, his anger is not turned away NDT
Isa 10: 4 Y for all this, his anger is not turned away NDT
Isa 17: 6 Y some gleanings will remain, as when H2256
Isa 17:11 y the harvest will be as nothing in the day of NDT
Isa 21:12 then ask; and come back y again. NDT
Isa 23:18 Y her profit and her earnings will be set H2256
Isa 29: 2 Y I will besiege Ariel; she will mourn and H2256
Isa 30:18 Y the LORD longs to be gracious to H4200+4027
Isa 31: 2 Y he too is wise and can bring disaster H2256
Isa 42:25 them in flames, y they did not understand H2256
Isa 43:22 "Y you have not called on me, Jacob, you H2256
Isa 44: 7 ancient people, and *what is y to* **come**—yes, AIT
Isa 49: 4 Y what is due me is in the LORD's hand, and H434
Isa 49:20 bereavement will y say in your hearing, H6388
Isa 53: 4 y we considered him punished by God H2256
Isa 53: 7 afflicted, y he did not open his mouth H2256
Isa 53: 8 Y who of his generation protested H2256
Isa 53:10 Y it was the LORD's will to crush him and H2256
Isa 54:10 y my unfailing love for you will not be H2256
Isa 57:17 y they kept on in their willful ways. H2256
Isa 58: 3 "Y on the day of your fasting, you do as H2176
Isa 63:10 Y they rebelled and grieved his Holy Spirit H2256
Isa 64: 8 Y you, LORD, are our Father. We are H2256+6964
Isa 66: 5 Y they will be put to shame. H2256
Isa 66: 8 Y no sooner is Zion in labor than she H3954
Jer 2:11 (Y they are not gods at all. H2256
Jer 2:27 not their faces; y when they are in trouble H2256
Jer 2:32 Y my people have forgotten me, days H2256
Jer 2:34 them breaking in. Y in spite of all this H3954
Jer 3: 3 Y you have the brazen look of a prostitute H2256
Jer 3: 8 Y I saw that her unfaithful sister Judah H2256
Jer 5: 7 y they committed adultery and thronged H2256
Jer 5:18 "Y even in those days," declares the LORD H2256
Jer 10:19 Y I said to myself, "This is my sickness H2256
Jer 12: 1 Y I would speak with you about your justice: H421
Jer 12: 3 Y you know me, LORD; you see me and test H2256
Jer 14:15 did not send them, y they are saying, 'No H2256
Jer 15:10 lent nor borrowed, y everyone curses me. NDT
Jer 17:23 Y they did not listen or pay attention; they H2256
Jer 18:15 Y my people have forgotten me; they burn H3954
Jer 18:20 Y they have dug a pit for me H3954
Jer 23:21 y they have run with their message H2256
Jer 23:21 speak to them, y they have prophesied. H2256
Jer 23:31 wag their own tongues **and** y declare, H2256
Jer 23:32 y I did not send or appoint them. H2256
Jer 28:15 y you have persuaded this nation to trust H2256
Jer 33:10 Y in the towns of Judah and the streets of NDT
Jer 34: 4 " 'Y hear the LORD's promise to you H421
Jer 35:14 again, y you have not obeyed me. H2256
Jer 37: 4 for he had **not** *y* been put in prison. AIT
Jer 48:47 "Y I will restore the fortunes of Moab in H2256
Jer 49: 6 "Y afterward, I will restore the fortunes of H2256
Jer 49:39 "Y I will restore the fortunes of Elam in H2256
Jer 50:34 Y their Redeemer is strong; the LORD NDT
La 1:18 y I rebelled against his command. H3954
La 3:21 Y this I call to mind and therefore I have NDT
La 3:29 his face in the dust—there **may** y be hope. H218
Eze 5: 6 Y in her wickedness she has rebelled H2256
Eze 11:16 y for a little while I have been a sanctuary H2256
Eze 14:22 Y there will be some survivors—sons and H2256
Eze 15: 7 out of the fire, the fire *will y* **consume** them. AIT
Eze 16: 7 hair had grown, y you were stark naked. H2256
Eze 16:60 Y I will remember the covenant I made H2256
Eze 17:15 Will he break the treaty **and** y escape? H2256
Eze 17:18 his hand in pledge **and** y did all these H2256
Eze 18:19 "Y you ask, 'Why does the son not share H2256
Eze 18:25 "Y you say, 'The way of the Lord is not just H2256
Eze 18:29 Y the Israelites say, 'The way of the Lord is H2256
Eze 20:13 " 'Y the people of Israel rebelled against H2256
Eze 20:17 Y I looked on them with pity and did not H2256
Eze 20:38 y they will not enter the land of Israel. H2256
Eze 23:11 y in her lust and prostitution she was H2256
Eze 23:19 Y she became more and more H2256

Eze 24:16 **Y** do not lament or weep or shed any H2256
Eze 29:13 " '**Y** this is what the Sovereign LORD says H3954
Eze 29:18 **Y** he and his army got no reward from the H2256
Eze 31:18 **Y** you, too, will be brought down with the H2256
Eze 33:17 "**Y** your people say, 'The way of the Lord H2256
Eze 33:20 **Y** you Israelites say, 'The way of the Lord H2256
Eze 33:24 only one man, **y** he possessed the land. H2256
Eze 36:20 people, **and y** they had to leave his land. H2256
Da 2:41 **y** it will have some of the strength of iron A10221
Da 8:25 **Y** he will be destroyed, but not by human NDT
Da 9:13 **y** we have not sought the favor of the LORD H2256
Da 9:14 he does; **y** we have not obeyed him. H2256
Da 10:14 the vision concerns a time **y to come**." H6388
Da 11:12 **y** he will not remain triumphant. H2256
Da 11:20 be destroyed, **y** not in anger or in battle. H2256
Da 11:45 **Y** he will come to his end, and no one H2256
Hos 1:7 **Y** I will show love to Judah; and I will save H2256
Hos 1:10 "**Y** the Israelites will be like the sand on H2256
Hos 9:8 Ephraim, **y** snares await him on all his paths NDT
Am 2:9 "**Y** I destroyed the Amorites before them H2256
Am 4:4 go to Gilgal and sin **y more**. H8049
Am 4:6 **y** you have not returned to me, H2256
Am 4:8 to drink, **y** you have not returned to me," H2256
Am 4:9 olive trees, **y** you have not returned to me," H2256
Am 4:10 **y** you have not returned to me, H2256
Am 4:11 the fire, **y** you have not returned to me," H2256
Am 9:8 **Y** I will not totally destroy the H700+3954
Jnh 2:4 **y** I will look again toward your holy temple. H421
Jnh 3:9 God may **y** relent and with compassion turn NDT
Mic 3:11 **Y** they look for the LORD's support and say H2256
Na 2:5 picked troops, **y** they stumble on their way. NDT
Na 3:10 **Y** she was taken captive and went into H1685
Hab 3:16 **Y** I will wait patiently for the day of H889
Hab 3:18 **y** I will rejoice in the LORD, I will be joyful H2256
Zep 3:5 **y** the unrighteous know no shame. H2256
Hag 1:2 'The time *has* not *y* **come** to rebuild the AIT
Hag 2:17 hail, **y** you did not return to me H2256
Hag 2:19 Is there **y** any seed left in the barn? Until H6388
Zec 8:20 the inhabitants of many cities will **y** come, H6388
Zec 10:9 **y** in distant lands they will remember me. H2256
Zec 13:8 perish; **y** one-third will be left in it. H2256
Mal 1:2 declares the LORD. "**Y** I have loved Jacob, H2256
Mal 3:8 mortal rob God? **Y** you rob me. "But you H3954
Mal 3:13 "**Y** you ask, 'What have we said against H2256
Mt 1:19 **and y** did not want to expose her to public *G2779*
Mt 6:26 **and y** your heavenly Father feeds them. *G2779*
Mt 6:29 **Y** I tell you that not even Solomon in all *G1254*
Mt 7:25 against that house; **y** it did not fall *G2779*
Mt 10:29 **Y** not one of them will fall to the ground *G2779*
Mt 11:11 **y** whoever is least in the kingdom of *G1254*
Mt 12:5 the Sabbath **and y** are innocent? *G2779*
Mt 13:32 smallest of all seeds, **y** when it grows, it is *G1254*
Mt 16:26 gain the whole world, **y** forfeit their soul? *G1254*
Mt 26:39 be taken from me. **Y** not as I will, but as *G4440*
Mt 28:8 from the tomb, afraid **y** filled with joy, and *G2779*
Mk 1:45 **Y** the people still came to him from *G2779*
Mk 4:32 **Y** when planted, it grows and becomes the *G2779*
Mk 5:26 **y** instead of getting better she grew *G247+3437*
Mk 5:31 answered, "**and y** you can ask, 'Who *G2779*
Mk 6:20 puzzled; **y** he liked to listen to him. *G2779*
Mk 7:24 **y** he could not keep his presence secret. *G2779*
Mk 8:36 gain the whole world, **y** forfeit their soul? *G2779*
Mk 14:36 this cup from me. **Y** not what I will, but *G247*
Mk 14:59 **Y** even then their testimony did not agree. *G2779*
Lk 4:26 **Y** Elijah was not sent to any of them, but *G2779*
Lk 4:27 prophet, **y** not one of them was cleansed *G2779*
Lk 5:15 **Y** the news about him spread all the more *G1254*
Lk 7:28 **y** the one who is least in the kingdom of *G1254*
Lk 9:25 **and y** lose or forfeit their very self? *G1254*
Lk 10:11 as a warning to you. **Y** be sure of this: The *G4440*
Lk 11:8 **y** because of your shameless audacity he *G1145*
Lk 12:6 **Y** not one of them is forgotten by God. *G2779*
Lk 12:24 no storeroom or barn; **y** God feeds them. *G2779*
Lk 12:27 **Y** I tell you, not even Solomon in all his *G1254*
Lk 15:29 **Y** you never gave me **even** a young goat *G2779*
Lk 18:5 **y** because this widow keeps bothering me *G1145*
Lk 19:48 **Y** they could not find any way to do it *G2779*
Lk 22:42 this cup from me; **y** not my will, but yours *G4440*
Lk 23:53 in which no one had **y** been laid. *G4024+4037*
Jn 1:12 **Y** to all who did receive him, to those who *G1254*
Jn 2:4 Jesus replied. "My hour has **not y** come." *G4037*
Jn 4:23 **Y** a time is coming and has now come *G247*
Jn 5:40 **y** you refuse to come to me to have life. *G2779*
Jn 6:17 and Jesus had **not y** joined them. *G4037*
Jn 6:49 the manna in the wilderness, **y** they died. *G2779*
Jn 6:64 **Y** there are some of you who do not believe." *G247*
Jn 6:70 the Twelve? **Y** one of you is a devil!" *G2779*
Jn 7:6 "My time is **not y** here; for you any *G4037*
Jn 7:8 because my time has **not y** fully come." *G4037*
Jn 7:19 **Y** not one of you keeps the law *G2779*
Jn 7:22 **Y**, because Moses gave you circumcision NDT
Jn 7:30 on him, because his hour had **not y** come. *G4037*
Jn 7:39 since Jesus had **not y** been glorified. *G4031*
Jn 8:20 **Y** no one seized him, because his hour *G2779*
Jn 8:20 because his hour had **not y** come. *G4037*
Jn 8:37 **Y** you are looking for a way to kill me *G247*
Jn 8:45 **Y** because I tell the truth, you do not *G1254*
Jn 8:52 **y** you say that whoever obeys your word *G2779*
Jn 8:57 "You are **not y** fifty years old," they said to *G4037*
Jn 9:30 he comes from, **y** he opened my eyes. *G2779*
Jn 11:8 to stone you, **and y** you are going back?" *G2779*
Jn 11:30 Now Jesus had **not y** entered the village *G4037*
Jn 12:42 **Y** at the same time many even among the *G3530*
Jn 15:24 **and y** they have hated both me and my *G2779*
Jn 16:13 and he will tell you what *is y to* **come**. AIT
Jn 16:32 **Y** I am not alone, for my Father is with me. *G2779*
Jn 20:17 I have **not y** ascended to the Father. *G4037*
Jn 20:29 who have not seen **and y** have believed." *G2779*
Ac 2:34 ascend to heaven, **and y** he said, " 'The *G1254*
Ac 5:28 "**Y** you have filled Jerusalem with *G2779+2627*
Ac 8:16 the Holy Spirit had **not y** come on any of *G4031*
Ac 9:22 **Y** Saul grew more and more powerful and *G1254*
Ac 13:27 **y** in condemning him they fulfilled the *G2779*
Ac 14:17 **Y** he has not left himself without testimony *G2792*
Ac 23:3 **y** you yourself violate the law by *G2779*
Ro 2:3 judgment on them **and y** do the same *G2779*
Ro 2:27 physically and *y* **obeys** the law will condemn AIT
Ro 4:20 **Y** he did not waver through unbelief *G1254*
Ro 8:25 But if we hope for what *we* **do not y have** *G1063*
Ro 9:11 **Y**, before the twins were born or had done *G1142*
Ro 15:15 **Y** I have written you quite boldly on some *G1254*
1Co 3:2 solid food, for you were **not y** ready for it. *G4037*
1Co 3:15 will suffer loss **but y** will be saved— *G1254*
1Co 8:2 know something do **not y** know as they *G4037*
1Co 8:6 **y** for us there is but one God, the Father *G247*
1Co 12:31 And **y** I will show you the most excellent *G2285*
1Co 14:10 **y** none of them is without meaning. *G2779*
1Co 15:10 than all of them—**y** not I, but the grace of *G1254*
2Co 4:16 **y** inwardly we are being renewed day by *G247*
2Co 6:8 genuine, **y** regarded as impostors; *G2779*
2Co 6:9 **y** regarded as unknown; dying, and *G2779*
2Co 6:9 unknown; dying, and **y** we live on; beaten *G2627*
2Co 6:9 we live on; beaten, **and y** not killed; *G2779*
2Co 6:10 sorrowful, **y** always rejoicing; poor, yet *G1254*
2Co 6:10 rejoicing; poor, **y** making many rich *G1254*
2Co 6:10 nothing, **and y** possessing everything. *G2779*
2Co 7:9 **y** now I am happy, not because you were NDT
2Co 8:9 he was rich, **y** for your sake he became poor NDT
2Co 12:16 **Y**, crafty fellow that I am, I caught you by *G247*
2Co 13:4 in weakness, **y** he lives by God's power. *G247*
2Co 13:4 **y** by God's power we will live with him in *G247*
Gal 2:3 **Y** not even Titus, who was with me, was *G247*
Gal 2:14 **y** you live like a Gentile and not like a Jew. NDT
Gal 6:13 **y** they want you to be circumcised that they *G247*
Php 1:22 labor for me. **Y** what shall I choose? *G2779*
Php 3:13 I do **not** consider myself **y** to have taken *G4037*
Php 4:14 **Y** it was good of you to share in my *G4440*
1Th 4:10 **Y** we urge you, brothers and sisters, to do *G1254*
2Th 3:15 **Y** do not regard them as an enemy, but *G2779*
2Ti 1:12 **Y** this is no cause for shame, because I *G247*
2Ti 3:11 **Y** the Lord rescued me from all of them. *G2779*
Phm 9 *y I* prefer *to* **appeal** to you on the basis of love AIT
Heb 2:8 **Y** at present we do not see everything *G1254*
Heb 4:3 **And y** his works have been finished since *G2792*
Heb 4:15 every way, just as we are—**y** he did not sin. NDT
Heb 7:6 *y he* **collected a tenth** from Abraham and AIT
Heb 9:8 Holy Place had **not y** been disclosed as *G3609*
Heb 11:7 when warned about things **not y** seen, in *G3596*
Heb 11:39 **y** none of them received what had been NDT
Heb 12:4 you have **not y** resisted to the point of *G4037*
Jas 1:26 and *y do* not **keep a tight rein on** their AIT
Jas 2:10 the whole law **and y** stumbles at just *G1254*
2Pe 2:11 **y even** angels, although they are stronger *G3963*
1Jn 1:6 fellowship with him **and y** walk in the *G2779*
1Jn 2:8 **Y** I am writing you a new command; its *G4099*
1Jn 3:2 we will be has **not y** been made known. *G4037*
1Jn 4:20 claims to love God **y** hates a brother or *G2779*
Jude 10 **Y** these people slander whatever they do *G1254*
Rev 2:4 **Y** I hold this against you: You have *G247*
Rev 2:9 afflictions and your poverty—**y** you are rich! *G247*
Rev 2:13 **Y** you remain true to my name *G2779*
Rev 3:4 **Y** you have a few people in Sardis who *G247*
Rev 3:8 **y** you have kept my word and have not *G2779*
Rev 9:12 two other woes are **y** to come. *G2285*
Rev 13:14 who was wounded by the sword and *y* **lived**. AIT
Rev 17:8 and **y will** come up out of the Abyss and *G3516*
Rev 17:8 it once was, now is not, and *y will* **come**. AIT
Rev 17:10 the other has **not y** come; but when he *G4037*
Rev 17:12 ten kings who have **not y** received a *G4037*

YIELD (25) [YIELDED, YIELDING, YIELDS]

Ge 4:12 *it will* no longer **y** its crops for you. H5989
Lev 25:19 Then the land *will* **y** its fruit, and you will H5989
Lev 25:21 year that the land *will* **y** enough for three H6913
Lev 26:4 the ground *will* **y** its crops and the H5989
Lev 26:20 because your soil *will* not **y** its crops, nor H5989
Lev 26:20 nor *will* the trees of your land **y** their fruit. H5989
Dt 11:17 not rain and the ground *will* **y** no produce, H5989
Dt 13:8 *do* not **y** to them or listen to them. H14
Dt 33:14 forth and the finest the moon can **y**; H1765
Jos 24:23 are among you and **y** your hearts to the H5742
Job 31:39 I have devoured its **y** without payment H3946
Ps 85:12 is good, and our land *will* **y** its harvest. H5989
Pr 8:19 fine gold; *what* I **y** surpasses choice silver. H9311
Isa 5:4 good grapes, why *did it* **y** only bad? H6913
Isa 5:10 a homer of seed *will* **y** only an ephah of H6913
Isa 42:8 *I will* not **y** my glory to another or my H5989
Isa 48:11 *I will* not **y** my glory to another. H5989
Eze 34:27 The trees *will* **y** their fruit and the ground H5989
Eze 34:27 their fruit and the ground *will* **y** its crops; H5989
Eze 36:37 Once again *I will* **y to** Israel's **plea** and do H2011
Hos 8:7 Were it to **y** grain, foreigners would H6913
Hos 9:16 their root is withered, *they* **y** no fruit. H6913
Joel 2:22 the fig tree and the vine **y** their riches. H5989
Zec 8:12 grow well, the vine *will* **y** its fruit, the H5989
Jas 5:7 waits for the land to **y** its valuable crop, NDT

YIELDED (4) [YIELD]

Ps 107:37 planted vineyards *that* **y** a fruitful harvest; H6913
Isa 5:2 of good grapes, but *it* **y** only bad fruit. H6913
Lk 8:8 It came up and **y** a crop, a hundred times *G4472*
Lk 12:16 a certain rich man **y an abundant harvest**. *G2369*

YIELDING (3) [YIELD]

SS 5:13 cheeks are like beds of spice **y** perfume. H1540
Mt 13:23 who produces a crop, **y** a hundred, sixty *G4472*
Rev 22:2 twelve crops of fruit, **y** its fruit every month. *G625*

YIELDS (9) [YIELD]

Lev 25:6 Whatever the land **y** during the sabbath year NDT
Ps 1:3 which **y** its fruit in season and whose leaf H5989
Ps 67:6 The land **y** its harvest; God, our God H5989
Pr 3:14 than silver and **y** better **returns** than gold. H9311
Pr 14:24 is their crown, but the folly of fools **y** folly. NDT
Pr 19:11 A person's wisdom **y patience**; it is to H799+678
Isa 55:10 so that *it* **y** seed for the sower and bread H5989
1Co 7:4 over her own body but **y** it to her husband. NDT
1Co 7:4 over his own body but **y** it to his wife. NDT

YOKE (60) [YOKED, YOKES]

Ge 27:40 you will throw his **y** from off your neck." H6585
Ex 6:6 you out from under the **y** *of* the Egyptians. H6026
Ex 6:7 you out from under the **y** *of* the Egyptians. H6026
Lev 26:13 the bars of your **y** and enabled you to H6585
Nu 19:2 that has never been under a **y**. H6585
Dt 21:3 been worked and has never worn a **y** H6585
Dt 28:48 He will put an iron **y** on your neck until he H6585
1Ki 12:4 "Your father put a heavy **y** *on* us, but now H6585
1Ki 12:4 harsh labor and the heavy **y** he put on us, H6585
1Ki 12:9 'Lighten the **y** your father put on us'?" H6585
1Ki 12:10 'Your father put a heavy **y** *on* us, but make H6585
1Ki 12:10 a heavy yoke on us, but make our **y** lighter. NDT
1Ki 12:11 My father laid on you a heavy **y**; I will H6585
1Ki 12:14 "My father made your **y** heavy; I will make H6585
1Ki 19:19 He was plowing with twelve **y of oxen** H7538
1Ki 19:21 He took his **y** *of* oxen and slaughtered H7538
2Ch 10:4 "Your father put a heavy **y** *on* us, but now H6585
2Ch 10:4 harsh labor and the heavy **y** he put on us, H6585
2Ch 10:9 'Lighten the **y** your father put on us'?" H6585
2Ch 10:10 'Your father put a heavy **y** *on* us, but make H6585
2Ch 10:10 a heavy yoke on us, but make our **y** lighter. NDT
2Ch 10:11 My father laid on you a heavy **y**; I will H6585
2Ch 10:14 "My father made your **y** heavy; I will make H6585
Job 1:3 five hundred **y** *of* oxen and five hundred H7538
Job 42:12 a thousand **y** *of* oxen and a thousand H7538
Isa 9:4 have shattered the **y** *that* burdens them, H6585
Isa 10:27 your shoulders, their **y** from your neck; the H6585
Isa 10:27 the **y** will be broken because you have H6585
Isa 14:25 His **y** will be taken from my people, and H6585
Isa 47:6 Even on the aged you laid a very heavy **y**. H6585
Isa 58:6 of injustice and untie the cords of the **y**, H4574
Isa 58:6 set the oppressed free and break every **y**? H4574
Isa 58:9 "If you do away with the **y** of oppression H4574
Jer 2:20 ago you broke off your **y** and tore off your H6585
Jer 5:5 had broken off the **y** and torn off the H6585
Jer 27:2 "Make a **y** *out of* **straps** and crossbars and H4593
Jer 27:8 of Babylon or bow its neck under his **y**, H6585
Jer 27:11 its neck under the **y** *of* the king of Babylon H6585
Jer 27:12 your neck under the **y** *of* the king of H6585
Jer 28:2 'I will break the **y** *of* the king of Babylon. H6585
Jer 28:4 I will break the **y** *of* the king of Babylon. H6585
Jer 28:10 Hananiah took the **y** off the neck of the H4574
Jer 28:11 I will break the **y** *of* Nebuchadnezzar king H6585
Jer 28:12 had broken the **y** off the neck of the H4574
Jer 28:13 You have broken a wooden **y**, but in its H4574
Jer 28:13 in its place you will get a **y** *of* iron. H4574
Jer 28:14 I will put an iron **y** on the necks of all H6585
Jer 30:8 'I will break the **y** off their necks and will H6585
La 1:14 "My sins have been bound into a **y**; by his H6585
La 3:27 a man to bear the **y** while he is young. H6585
Eze 30:18 at Tahpanhes when I break the **y** *of* Egypt; H4574
Eze 34:27 the bars of their **y** and rescue them from H6585
Hos 10:11 to thresh; so I *will* **put a y** on her fair neck. H6296
Na 1:13 I will break their **y** from your neck and H4573
Mt 11:29 Take my **y** upon you and learn from me *G2433*
Mt 11:30 For my **y** is easy and my burden is light." *G2433*
Lk 14:19 'I have just bought five **y** of oxen, and I'm *G2414*
Ac 15:10 necks of Gentiles a **y** that neither we nor *G2433*
Gal 5:1 be burdened again *by* a **y** of slavery. *G2433*
1Ti 6:1 All who are under the **y** of slavery should *G2433*

YOKED (6) [YOKE]

Nu 25:3 So Israel **y themselves** to the Baal of Peor H7537
Nu 25:5 *those of* your people who *have* **y themselves** H7537
Dt 22:10 plow with an ox and a donkey **y** together. NDT
1Sa 6:7 calved and *have* never *been* **y**. H6590+6585
Ps 106:28 *They* **y themselves** to the Baal of Peor H7537
2Co 6:14 Do not be **y together** with unbelievers. *G2282*

YOKEFELLOW (NIV84) COMPANION

YOKES (1) [YOKE]

2Sa 24:22 threshing sledges and ox **y** for the wood. H3998

YONDER (KJV) SOME DISTANCE AWAY, THERE

YOU (13983) [YOU'LL, YOU'RE, YOU'VE, YOUR, YOURS, YOURSELF, YOURSELVES] See Index of Articles Etc.

YOU'LL (1) [BE, YOU]

1Sa 19:11 your life tonight, tomorrow y be killed." H911

YOU'RE (9) [BE, YOU]

Jdg 4:22 "I will show you the man y looking for." H911
Jdg 11: 7 you come to me now, when y in trouble?" H4013
1Sa 26:15 David said, "Y a man, aren't you? And who H911
Mt 26:70 "I don't know what *y* **talking about**," he said. AIT
Mk 14:68 know or understand what y talking about," *G5148*
Mk 14:71 "I don't know this man *y* **talking about**." AIT
Lk 22:60 I don't know what *y* **talking about**! AIT
Ac 10:21 said to the men, "I'm the one *y* **looking for**. AIT
Ac 12:15 "*Y* **out of** *your* **mind**," they told her. AIT

YOU'VE (4) [HAVE, YOU]

Ge 31:26 *Y* **deceived** me, and you've carried off my AIT
Ge 31:26 and *y* **carried off** my daughters like captives AIT
Jdg 14:16 *Y* **given** my people a riddle, but you haven't AIT
Jdg 15: 7 said to them, "Since *y* **acted** like this, I swear AIT

YOUNG (335) [YOUNGER, YOUNGEST, YOUTH, YOUTHFUL, YOUTHS]

Ge 4:23 wounding me, a y **man** for injuring me. H3529
Ge 15: 9 along with a dove and a y **pigeon**. H1578
Ge 19: 4 of Sodom—both y and old—surrounded H5853
Ge 19:11 the door of the house, y and old, with H7785
Ge 24:14 May it be that when I say to a y **woman** H5855
Ge 24:28 The y **woman** ran and told her mother's H5855
Ge 24:43 If a y **woman** comes out to draw water H6625
Ge 24:55 "Let the y **woman** remain with us ten days H5855
Ge 24:57 "Let's call the y **woman** and ask her about H5855
Ge 27: 9 and bring me two choice y **goats**, H6436+1531
Ge 30:39 And they **bore** y that were streaked or H3528
Ge 30:40 set apart the y **of the flock** by themselves, H4166
Ge 31: 8 then all the flocks gave birth to **speckled** *y* AIT
Ge 31: 8 then all the flocks bore **streaked** *y*. AIT
Ge 32:15 thirty female camels with their y, forty cows H1201
Ge 33:13 ewes and cows *that are* **nursing** *their* y. H6402
Ge 34: 3 he loved the y **woman** and spoke tenderly H5855
Ge 34:12 Only give me the y **woman** as my wife." H5855
Ge 34:19 The y **man**, who was the most honored of H5853
Ge 37: 2 Joseph, a y **man** of seventeen, was H5853
Ge 38:17 send you a y **goat** from my flock," H1531+6436
Ge 38:20 Judah sent the y **goat** by his friend H1531+6436
Ge 38:23 I did send her this y **goat**, but you didn't H1531
Ge 41:12 Now a y Hebrew was there with us, H5853
Ge 44:20 there is a y son born to him in his old H7783
Ex 10: 9 "We will go with our y and our old, with H5853
Ex 23:19 "Do not cook a y **goat** in its mother's milk. H1531
Ex 24: 5 Then he sent y Israelite **men**, and they H5853
Ex 24: 5 sacrificed y **bulls** as fellowship H7228
Ex 29: 1 Take a y bull and two rams without defect. H1201
Ex 33:11 his y aide Joshua son of Nun did not H5853
Ex 34:26 "Do not cook a y **goat** in its mother's milk." H1531
Lev 1: 5 are to slaughter the y bull before the LORD, H1201
Lev 1:14 you are to offer a dove or a y pigeon. H1201
Lev 4: 3 bring to the LORD a y bull without defect H1201
Lev 4:14 assembly must bring a y bull as a sin H1201
Lev 5: 7 two doves or two y pigeons to the LORD as H1201
Lev 5:11 cannot afford two doves or two y pigeons, H1201
Lev 12: 6 offering and a y pigeon or a dove for H1201
Lev 12: 8 she is to bring two doves or two y pigeons, H1201
Lev 14:22 two doves or two y pigeons, such as H1201
Lev 14:30 shall sacrifice the doves or the y pigeons, H1201
Lev 15:14 two doves or two y pigeons and come H1201
Lev 15:29 take two doves or two y pigeons and bring H1201
Lev 16: 3 He must first bring a y bull for a sin H1201
Lev 22:28 cow or a sheep and its y on the same day. H1201
Lev 23:18 without defect, one y bull and two rams. H1201
Nu 6:10 two doves or two y pigeons to the priest H1201
Nu 7:15 one y bull, one ram and one male lamb a H1201
Nu 7:21 one y bull, one ram and one male lamb a H1201
Nu 7:27 one y bull, one ram and one male lamb a H1201
Nu 7:33 one y bull, one ram and one male lamb a H1201
Nu 7:39 one y bull, one ram and one male lamb a H1201
Nu 7:45 one y bull, one ram and one male lamb a H1201
Nu 7:51 one y bull, one ram and one male lamb a H1201
Nu 7:57 one y bull, one ram and one male lamb a H1201
Nu 7:63 one y bull, one ram and one male lamb a H1201
Nu 7:69 one y bull, one ram and one male lamb a H1201
Nu 7:75 one y bull, one ram and one male lamb a H1201
Nu 7:81 one y bull, one ram and one male lamb a H1201
Nu 7:87 the burnt offering came to twelve y **bulls**, H7228
Nu 8: 8 Have them take a y bull with its grain H1201
Nu 8: 8 are to take a second y bull for a sin H1201
Nu 11:27 A y **man** ran and told Moses, "Eldad and H5853
Nu 15: 8 " 'When you prepare a y bull as a burnt H1201
Nu 15:11 each lamb or y **goat**, is to be H6436
Nu 15:24 community is to offer a y bull for a burnt H1201
Nu 28:11 to the LORD a burnt offering of two y bulls, H1201
Nu 28:19 of a burnt offering of two y bulls, H1201
Nu 28:27 Present a burnt offering of two y bulls, one H1201
Nu 29: 2 offer a burnt offering of one y bull, one H1201
Nu 29: 8 to the LORD a burnt offering of one y bull, H1201
Nu 29:13 of a burnt offering of thirteen y bulls, H1201
Nu 29:17 " 'On the second day offer twelve y bulls H1201
Nu 30: 3 "When a y woman still living in her H5830
Nu 30:16 a father and his y daughter still living at H5830
Dt 7:14 will any of your livestock be **without** y. H6829
Dt 14:21 Do not cook a y **goat** in its mother's milk. H1531
Dt 22: 6 mother is sitting on the y or on the eggs, H711
Dt 22: 6 do not take the mother with the y. H1201
Dt 22: 7 You may take the y, but be sure to let the H1201
Dt 22:15 then the y **woman's** father and mother H5855
Dt 22:19 give them to the y **woman's** father, H5855
Dt 22:20 proof of the y **woman's** virginity can H4200+5855
Dt 22:24 the y **woman** because she was in a town H5855
Dt 22:25 to meet a y **woman** pledged to be H5855
Dt 22:27 the man found **the y woman** out in the H2023S
Dt 22:29 He must marry the y woman, for he has NDT
Dt 28: 4 of your land and the y *of* your livestock— H7262
Dt 28:11 the y *of* your livestock and the crops of H7262
Dt 28:50 without respect for the old or pity for the y. H5853
Dt 28:51 They will devour the y *of* your livestock H7262
Dt 30: 9 the y *of* your livestock and the crops of H7262
Dt 32:11 that stirs up its nest and hovers over its y, H1578
Dt 32:25 The y **men** and young women will perish H1033
Dt 32:25 The young men and y **women** will perish H1435
Jos 6:21 men and women, y and old, cattle H5853
Jos 6:23 So the y **men** who had done the spying H5853
Jdg 6:19 prepared a y **goat**, and from an H1531+6436
Jdg 8:14 He caught a y **man** of Sukkoth and H5853
Jdg 8:14 the y man wrote down for him the NDT
Jdg 11:40 each year the y **women** *of* Israel go out H1426
Jdg 12: 9 brought in thirty y **women** as wives from H1426
Jdg 13:15 until we prepare a y **goat** for you." H1531+6436
Jdg 13:19 Then Manoah took a y **goat** H1531+6436
Jdg 14: 1 saw there a y Philistine woman. H1426
Jdg 14: 5 suddenly a y **lion** came roaring H4097+787
Jdg 14: 6 hands as he might have torn a y **goat**. H1531
Jdg 14:10 held a feast, as was customary for y **men**. H1033
Jdg 15: 1 Samson took a y **goat** and went to H1531+6436
Jdg 17: 7 A y Levite from Bethlehem in Judah, who H5853
Jdg 17:11 the y **man** became like one of his H5853
Jdg 17:12 the y **man** became his priest and H5853
Jdg 18: 3 they recognized the voice of the y Levite H5853
Jdg 18:15 to the house of the y Levite at Micah's H5853
Jdg 19:19 the woman and the y **man** with us. H5853
Jdg 20:15 to seven hundred **able** y men from those H1047
Jdg 20:34 of Israel's **able** y men made a frontal H1047
Jdg 21:12 four hundred y women who had never H5855
Jdg 21:21 When the y **women** *of* Shiloh come out to H1426
Jdg 21:23 While the *y women* were **dancing**, each man AIT
Ru 2: 5 "Who does that y **woman** belong to?" H5855
Ru 4:12 the LORD gives you by this y **woman**, H5855
1Sa 1:24 the boy with her, y as he was, along with H5853
1Sa 2:17 This sin of the y **men** was very great in the H5853
1Sa 5: 9 people of the city, both y and old, with an H7785
1Sa 9: 2 as handsome a y **man** as could be found H1033
1Sa 9:11 they met *some* y **women** coming out to H5855
1Sa 10: 3 One will be carrying three y **goats** H1531
1Sa 14: 1 son of Saul said to his y armor-bearer, H5853
1Sa 14: 6 Jonathan said to his y armor-bearer H5853
1Sa 16:20 of wine and a y **goat** and sent H1531+6436
1Sa 17:33 you are only a y **man**, and he has been a H5853
1Sa 17:55 "Abner, whose son is that y **man**? H5853
1Sa 17:56 "Find out whose son this y **man** is. H6624
1Sa 17:58 son are you, y **man**?" Saul asked him. H5853
1Sa 24: 2 took three thousand **able** y men from all H1047
1Sa 25: 5 So he sent ten y **men** and said to them H5853
1Sa 26:22 "Let one of your y **men** come over and get H5853
1Sa 30: 2 everyone else in it, both y and old. H7785
1Sa 30:17 four hundred y men who rode off on H5853
1Sa 30:19 y or old, boy or girl, plunder or anything H7785
2Sa 1: 5 David said to the y man who brought him H5853
2Sa 1: 6 the y **man** said, "and there H5853
2Sa 1:13 David said to the y **man** who brought him H5853
2Sa 2:14 "Let's have *some* of the y **men** get up H5853
2Sa 2:21 take on one of the y **men** and strip him of H5853
2Sa 6: 1 together all the **able** y *men* of Israel— H1047
2Sa 9:12 Mephibosheth had a y son named Mika H7783
2Sa 14:21 bring back the y **man** Absalom." H5853
2Sa 17:18 But a y **man** saw them and told Absalom H5853
2Sa 18: 5 gentle with the y **man** Absalom for my H5853
2Sa 18:12 'Protect the y **man** Absalom for my sake. H5853
2Sa 18:29 king asked, "Is the y **man** Absalom safe?" H5853
2Sa 18:32 the Cushite, "Is the y **man** Absalom safe?" H5853
2Sa 18:32 rise up to harm you be like that y **man**." H5853
1Ki 1: 2 "Let us look for a y virgin to serve the king H5855
1Ki 1: 3 a beautiful y **woman** and found H5855
1Ki 11:28 saw how well the y **man** did his work, H5853
1Ki 12: 8 consulted the y **men** who had grown up H3529
1Ki 12:10 The y **men** who had grown up with him H3529
1Ki 12:14 the advice of the y **men** and said, H3529
1Ki 12:21 eighty thousand **able** y **men**— H1033
2Ki 3:21 man, y **and old**, who could H2256+5087+2025
2Ki 5: 2 had taken captive a y girl from Israel, H7783
2Ki 5:14 became clean like that of a y boy. H7785
2Ki 5:22 'Two y **men** from the company of the H5853
2Ki 8:12 kill their y **men** with the sword H1033
2Ki 9: 4 So the y prophet went to Ramoth Gilead. H5853
1Ch 12:28 Zadok, a brave y warrior, with 22 H5853
1Ch 22: 5 "My son Solomon is y and inexperienced H5853
1Ch 25: 8 Y and old alike, teacher as well as student, H7785
1Ch 26:13 to their families, y and old alike. H7785
1Ch 29: 1 God has chosen, is y and inexperienced. H5853
2Ch 10: 8 consulted the y **men** who had grown up H3529
2Ch 10:10 The y **men** who had grown up with him H3529
2Ch 10:14 the advice of the y **men** and said, H3529
2Ch 11: 1 eighty thousand **able** y **men**— H1033
2Ch 13: 7 when he was y and indecisive and H5853
2Ch 13: 9 himself with a y bull and seven rams may H1201
2Ch 31:15 to their divisions, old and y alike. H7783
2Ch 34: 3 while he was still y, he began to seek the H5853
2Ch 36:17 who killed their y **men** with the sword in H1033
2Ch 36:17 did not spare y **men** or young women, H1033
2Ch 36:17 did not spare young men or y **women**, H1435
Ezr 6: 9 is needed—y bulls, rams, male A10120
Est 2: 2 made for beautiful y virgins for the king. H5855
Est 2: 3 beautiful y **women** into the harem H1435+5855
Est 2: 4 Then let the y **woman** who pleases the H5855
Est 2: 7 This y **woman**, who was also known as H5855
Est 2: 8 many y **women** were brought to the H5855
Est 2:12 Before a y **woman's** turn came to go in to H5855
Est 2:15 (**the y woman** Mordecai had adopted H889S
Est 3:13 all the Jews—y and old, women and H5853
Job 29: 8 the y **men** saw me and stepped aside H5853
Job 30: 9 "And now *those* y **men** mock me in song; H4392S
Job 31: 1 eyes not to look lustfully at a y **woman**. H1435
Job 32: 6 "I am y in years, and you are old; that is H7582
Job 38:41 the raven when its y cry out to God and H3529
Job 39: 3 They crouch down and bring forth their y H3529
Job 39: 4 Their y thrive and grow strong in the wilds; H1201
Job 39:16 She treats her y harshly, as if they were H1201
Job 39:30 Its y **ones** feast on blood, and where the H711
Job 41: 5 a leash for the y **women** in your house? H5855
Ps 29: 6 leap like a calf, Sirion like a y wild ox. H1201
Ps 37:25 I was y and now I am old, yet I have never H5853
Ps 68:25 with them are the y **women** playing the H6625
Ps 78:31 cutting down the y **men** *of* Israel. H1033
Ps 78:63 Fire consumed their y **men**, and their H1033
Ps 78:63 their y **women** had no wedding songs H1435
Ps 84: 3 where she may have her y—a place near H711
Ps 89:19 I have raised up a y **man** from among the H1033
Ps 110: 3 your y *men* will come to you like dew from H3531
Ps 119: 9 How can a y **person** stay on the path of H5853
Ps 147: 9 cattle and for the y ravens when they call. H1201
Ps 148:12 y **men** and women, old men and children. H1033
Pr 1: 4 knowledge and discretion to the y— H5853
Pr 7: 7 I noticed among the y **men**, a youth who H1201
Pr 20:29 The glory of y **men** is their strength, gray H1033
Pr 30:19 the way of a man with a y **woman**. H6625
Ecc 11: 9 You *who are* y, be happy while you are H1033
Ecc 11: 9 be happy while you are y, and let your H3531
SS 1: 3 No wonder the y **women** love you! H6625
SS 1: 8 graze your y **goats** by the tents of the H1537
SS 2: 2 thorns is my darling among the y **women**. H1426
SS 2: 3 forest is my beloved among the y **men**. H1201
SS 2: 9 beloved is like a gazelle or a y **stag**. H6762+385
SS 2:17 like a y **stag** on the rugged H6762+385
SS 6: 9 The y **women** saw her and called her H1426
SS 8:14 gazelle or like a y **stag** on the H6762+385
Isa 3: 5 The y will rise up against the old, the H5853
Isa 5:29 they roar like y **lions**; they growl as they H4097
Isa 7:21 keep alive a y **cow** and two goats. H6320+1330
Isa 9:17 Lord will take no pleasure in the y **men**, H1033
Isa 11: 7 the bear, their y will lie down together H3529
Isa 11: 8 the y **child** will put its hand into the H1694
Isa 13:18 Their bows will strike down the y **men** H5853
Isa 20: 4 Cushite exiles, y and old, with H5853
Isa 31: 8 the sword and their y **men** will be put to H1033
Isa 33: 4 is harvested as by y **locusts**; like a swarm H2885
Isa 34:15 and **care for** *her* y under the shadow of H1842
Isa 40:11 he gently leads *those that* **have** y. H6402
Isa 40:30 weary, and y **men** stumble and fall; H1033
Isa 54: 6 a wife who married y, only to be rejected," H5830
Isa 60: 6 your land, y **camels** *of* Midian and Ephah. H1145
Isa 62: 5 As a y **man** marries a young woman, so H1033
Isa 62: 5 As a young man marries a y **woman**, so H1435
Jer 1: 6 "I do not know how to speak; I am **too** y." H5853
Jer 1: 7 LORD said to me, "Do not say, 'I am **too** y. H5853
Jer 2:32 Does a y **woman** forget her jewelry, H1435
Jer 6:11 street and on the y **men** gathered H1033
Jer 9:21 the streets and the y **men** from the public H1033
Jer 11:22 Their y **men** will die by the sword, their H1033
Jer 15: 8 against the mothers of their y **men**; H1033
Jer 18:21 their y **men** slain by the sword in battle. H1033
Jer 31:12 the olive oil, the y *of* the flocks and herds. H1201
Jer 31:13 Then y **women** will dance and be glad H1435
Jer 31:13 be glad, y **men** and old as well. H1033
Jer 48:15 her finest y **men** will go down in the H1033
Jer 49:20 The y *of* the flock will be dragged away H7582
Jer 49:26 her y **men** will fall in the streets H1033
Jer 50:27 Kill all her y **bulls**; let them go down to H7228
Jer 50:30 her y **men** will fall in the streets H1033
Jer 50:45 The y *of* the flock will be dragged away H7582
Jer 51: 3 Do not spare her y **men**; completely H1033
Jer 51:22 you I shatter y **man** and young woman, H1033
Jer 51:22 you I shatter young man and y **woman**, H1435
Jer 51:38 Her people all roar like y **lions**, they growl H4097
La 1: 4 her y **women** grieve, and she H1435
La 1:15 an army against me to crush my y **men**. H1033
La 1:18 My y **men** and young women have gone H1033
La 1:18 young men and y **women** have gone into H1435
La 2:10 The y **women** *of* Jerusalem have bowed H1435
La 2:21 "**Y** and old lie together in the dust of the H5853
La 2:21 my y **men** and young women have fallen H1033
La 2:21 young men and y **women** have fallen by H1435
La 3:27 a man to bear the yoke while he is y. H5830
La 4: 3 jackals offer their breasts to nurse their y, H1594
La 5:13 **Y men** toil at the millstones; boys stagger H1033
La 5:14 the y **men** have stopped their music. H1033
Eze 9: 6 the old men, the y **men** and women, H1033

[Eze 9: 6 the old men, the y men and **women**, H1435]
Eze 23: 6 all of them handsome **y men**, and H1033
Eze 23:12 mounted horsemen, all handsome **y men**. H1033
Eze 23:21 was caressed and your y breasts fondled. H5830
Eze 23:23 with them, handsome **y men**, all of them H1033
Eze 30:17 The **y men** *of* Heliopolis and Bubastis will H1033
Eze 43:19 You are to give a **y** bull as a sin offering to H1201
Eze 43:23 you are to offer a **y** bull and a ram from H1201
Eze 43:25 also to provide a **y** bull and a ram from H1201
Eze 45:18 day you are to take a **y** bull without defect H1201
Eze 46: 6 of the New Moon he is to offer a **y** bull, H1201
Da 1: 4 **y men** without any physical defect H3529
Da 1:10 worse than the other **y men** your age? H3529
Da 1:13 with that of the **y men** who eat the royal H3529
Da 1:15 than any of the **y men** who ate the royal H3529
Da 1:17 To these four **y men** God gave knowledge H3529
Hos 14: 6 his **y shoots** will grow. His splendor will H3438
Joel 1: 4 locusts have left the **y locusts** have eaten; H3540
Joel 1: 4 what the **y locusts** have left other locusts H3540
Joel 2:25 the great locust and the **y locust**, the other H3540
Joel 2:28 dreams, your **y men** will see visions. H1033
Am 4:10 I killed your **y men** with the sword, along H1033
Am 8:13 day "the lovely **y women** and strong H1435
Am 8:13 young women and **strong y men** will faint H1033
Mic 5: 8 like a **y lion** among flocks of sheep H4097
Na 2:11 the place where they fed their **y**, where H4097
Na 2:13 the sword will devour your **y lions**. H4097
Zec 2: 4 tell that **y man**, 'Jerusalem will be a H5853
Zec 9:17 Grain will make the **y men** thrive, and H1033
Zec 9:17 men thrive, and new wine the **y women**. H1435
Zec 11:16 the lost, or seek the **y**, or heal the injured, H5853
Mt 19:20 I have kept," the **y man** said. "What do I *G3734*
Mt 19:22 When the **y man** heard this, he went *G3734*
Mk 14:51 A **y man**, wearing nothing but a linen *G3734*
Mk 16: 5 they saw a **y man** dressed in a white robe *G3734*
Lk 2:24 "a pair of doves or two **y** pigeons." *G3801*
Lk 7:14 He said, "**Y man**, I say to you, get up!" *G3734*
Lk 15:29 never gave me even a **y goat** so I could *G2253*
Jn 12:14 Jesus found a **y donkey** and sat on it, as it *G3942*
Ac 2:17 will prophesy, your **y men** will see visions *G3734*
Ac 5: 6 Then some **y** *men* came forward, wrapped *G3742*
Ac 5:10 Then the **y men** came in and, finding her *G3734*
Ac 7:58 coats at the feet *of* a **y man** named Saul. *G3733*
Ac 20: 9 a window was a **y man** named Eutychus, *G3733*
Ac 20:10 himself on the **y man** and put his arms *G899S*
Ac 20:12 people took the **y** *man* home alive and *G4090*
Ac 23:17 "Take this **y man** to the commander *G3733*
Ac 23:18 me to bring this **y man** to you because he *G3734*
Ac 23:19 commander took the **y man** by the hand, *G899S*
Ac 23:22 dismissed the **y man** with this warning: *G3734*
1Th 2: 7 we were like **y children** among you. *G3758*
1Ti 4:12 look down on you because you are **y**, *G3744*
Titus 2: 6 encourage the **y** *men* to be self-controlled *G3742*
1Jn 2:13 writing to you, **y men**, because you have *G3734*
1Jn 2:14 I write to you, **y men**, because you are *G3734*

YOUNGER (32) [YOUNG]

Ge 19:31 One day the older daughter said to the **y** H7582
Ge 19:34 next day the older daughter said to the **y**, H7582
Ge 19:35 the **y** *daughter* went in and slept with H7582
Ge 19:38 The **y** *daughter* also had a son, and she H7582
Ge 25:23 the other, and the older will serve the **y**." H7582
Ge 27:15 and put them on her **y** son Jacob. H7783
Ge 27:42 she sent for her **y** son Jacob and said to H7783
Ge 29:16 and the name of the **y** was Rachel. H7783
Ge 29:18 years in return for your **y** daughter Rachel." H7783
Ge 29:26 here to give the **y** *daughter* in marriage H7582
Ge 29:27 then we will give you **the y one** also, in H2296S
Ge 48:14 though he was the **y**, and crossing his H7582
Ge 48:19 his **y** brother will be greater than he H7785
Jdg 1:13 son of Kenaz, Caleb's **y** brother, took it; H7785
Jdg 3: 9 of Kenaz, Caleb's **y** brother, who saved H7785
Jdg 15: 2 Isn't her **y** sister more attractive H7783
Ru 3:10 You have not run after the **y men**, whether H1033
1Sa 14:49 was Merab, and that of the **y** was Michal. H7783
Job 30: 1 mock me, *men* **y** than I H7582+4200+3427
Eze 16:46 daughters; and your **y** sister, who lived to H7783
Eze 16:61 are older than you and those *who are* **y**. H7783
Mk 15:40 the mother of James the **y** and of Joseph, *G3625*
Lk 15:12 The **y** *one* said to his father, 'Father, give *G3742*
Lk 15:13 the **y** son got together all he had *G3742*
Jn 21:18 when you were **y** you dressed yourself *G3742*
Ro 9:12 she was told, "The older will serve the **y**." *G1781*
1Ti 5: 1 were your father. Treat **y** *men* as brothers, *G3742*
1Ti 5: 2 as mothers, and **y** *women* as sisters, with *G3742*
1Ti 5:11 *As for* **y** widows, do not put them on such *G3742*
1Ti 5:14 So I counsel **y** widows to marry, to have *G3742*
Titus 2: 4 they can urge the **y** *women* to love their *G3742*
1Pe 5: 5 you who are **y**, submit yourselves to *G3742*

YOUNGEST (22) [YOUNG]

Ge 9:24 found out what his **y** son had done to him H7783
Ge 42:13 The **y** is now with our father, and one is H7785
Ge 42:15 place unless your **y** brother comes here. H7785
Ge 42:20 But you must bring your **y** brother to me, H7785
Ge 42:32 the **y** is now with our father in H7785
Ge 42:34 But bring your **y** brother to me so I will H7785
Ge 43:29 "Is this your **y** brother, the one you H7785
Ge 43:33 from the firstborn to the **y**; and they H7582
Ge 44: 2 in the mouth of the **y** *one's* sack, along H7785
Ge 44:12 with the oldest and ending with the **y**. H7785
Ge 44:23 'Unless your **y** brother comes down with H7785
Ge 44:26 Only if our **y** brother is with us will we go H7785
Ge 44:26 man's face unless our **y** brother is with us. H7785
Jos 6:26 at the cost of his **y** he will set up its gates." H7582
Jdg 9: 5 But Jotham, the **y** son of Jerub-Baal H7785
1Sa 16:11 "There is still the **y**," Jesse answered H7785
1Sa 17:14 David was the **y**. The three oldest followed H7783
1Ki 16:34 up its gates at the cost of his **y** *son* Segub, H7582
1Ch 24:31 were treated the same as those of the **y**. H7783
2Ch 21:17 son was left to him except Ahaziah, the **y**. H7785
2Ch 22: 1 Ahaziah, Jehoram's **y** son, king in his H7785
Lk 22:26 greatest among you should be like the **y**, *G3742*

YOUR (6686) [YOU] See Index of Articles Etc.

YOURS (86) [YOU] See Index of Articles Etc.

YOURSELF (187) [SELF, YOU] See Index of Articles Etc.

YOURSELVES (219) [SELF, YOU] See Index of Articles Etc.

YOUTH (54) [YOUNG]

Lev 22:13 live in her father's household as in her **y**, H5830
Nu 11:28 who had been Moses' aide since **y**, spoke H1036
1Sa 12: 2 been your leader from my **y** until this day. H5830
1Sa 17:33 he has been a warrior from his **y**. H5830
2Sa 19: 7 have come on you from your **y** till now." H5830
1Ki 18:12 have worshiped the LORD since my **y**. H5830
Job 13:26 me and make me reap the sins of my **y**. H5830
Job 31:18 from my **y** I reared them as a father H5830
Job 33:25 be restored as in the days of their **y**'— H6596
Job 36:14 They die in their **y**, among male H5854
Ps 25: 7 the sins of my **y** and my rebellious ways; H5830
Ps 71: 5 Sovereign LORD, my confidence since my **y**. H5830
Ps 71:17 Since my **y**, God, you have taught me H5830
Ps 88:15 From my **y** I have suffered and been close H5854
Ps 89:45 You have cut short the days of his **y**; you H6596
Ps 103: 5 things so that your **y** is renewed like the H5830
Ps 127: 4 of a warrior are children born in one's **y**. H5830
Ps 129: 1 have greatly oppressed me from my **y**," H5830
Ps 129: 2 have greatly oppressed me from my **y**, H5830
Ps 144:12 Then our sons in their **y** will be like H5830
Pr 2:17 left the partner of her **y** and ignored the H5830
Pr 5:18 may you rejoice in the wife of your **y**. H5830
Pr 7: 7 the young men, a **y** who had no sense. H5853
Pr 29:21 pampered from **y** will turn out to be H5854
Ecc 4:13 Better a poor but wise **y** than an old but H3529
Ecc 4:14 The **y** may have come from prison to the NDT
Ecc 4:15 walked under the sun followed the **y**, H3529
Ecc 11: 9 heart give you joy in the days of your **y**. H1035
Ecc 11:10 for **y** and vigor are meaningless. H3531
Ecc 12: 1 your Creator in the days of your **y**, H1035
Isa 54: 4 the shame of your **y** and remember no H6596
Jer 2: 2 " 'I remember the devotion of your **y**, how H5830
Jer 3: 4 'My Father, my friend from my **y**, H5830
Jer 3:24 From our **y** shameful gods have consumed H5830
Jer 3:25 from our **y** till this day we have not H5830
Jer 22:21 This has been your way from your **y**; you H5830
Jer 31:19 because I bore the disgrace of my **y**. H5830
Jer 32:30 nothing but evil in my sight from their **y**; H5831
Jer 48:11 "Moab has been at rest from **y**, like wine H5830
Jer 51:22 with you I shatter old man and **y**, with you H5853
Eze 4:14 From my **y** until now I have never eaten H5830
Eze 16:22 you did not remember the days of your **y**, H5830
Eze 16:43 the days of your **y** but enraged me with all H5830
Eze 16:60 I made with you in the days of your **y**, H5830
Eze 23: 3 engaging in prostitution from their **y**. H5830
Eze 23: 8 when during her **y** men slept with her H5830
Eze 23:19 as she recalled the days of her **y**, H5830
Eze 23:21 So you longed for the lewdness of your **y** H5830
Hos 2:15 she will respond as in the days of her **y**, H5830
Joel 1: 8 grieving for the betrothed of her **y**. H5830
Zec 13: 5 land has been my livelihood since my **y**. H5830
Mal 2:14 between you and the wife of your **y**. H5830
Mal 2:15 do not be unfaithful to the wife of your **y**. H5830
2Ti 2:22 Flee the evil desires **of y** and pursue *G3754*

YOUTHFUL (1) [YOUNG]

Job 20:11 The **y vigor** that fills his bones will lie with H6596

YOUTHS (4) [YOUNG]

Isa 3: 4 "I will make *mere* **y** their officials; children H5853
Isa 3: 5 **Y** oppress my people, women rule over H6620
Isa 40:30 Even **y** grow tired and weary, and young H5853
Am 2:11 children and Nazirites from among your **y**. H1033

Z

ZAANAN (1)

Mic 1:11 Those who live in **Z** will not come out H7367

ZAANANNIM (2)

Jos 19:33 went from Heleph and the large tree in **Z**, H7588
Jdg 4:11 tent by the great tree in **Z** near Kedesh. H7588

ZAAVAN (2)

Ge 36:27 The sons of Ezer: Bilhan, **Z** and Akan. H2401
1Ch 1:42 Bilhan, **Z** and Akan. The sons of H2401

ZABAD (8)

1Ch 2:36 father of Nathan, Nathan the father of **Z**, H2274
1Ch 2:37 **Z** the father of Ephlal, Ephlal the father of H2274
1Ch 7:21 **Z** his son and Shuthelah his son. H2274
1Ch 11:41 Uriah the Hittite, **Z** son of Ahlai, H2274
2Ch 24:26 Those who conspired against him were **Z** H2274
Ezr 10:27 Mattaniah, Jeremoth, **Z** and Aziza. H2274
Ezr 10:33 Mattattah, **Z**, Eliphelet, Jeremai, H2274
Ezr 10:43 Matthithiah, **Z**, Zebina, Jaddai, Joel H2274

ZABBAI (2)

Ezr 10:28 Jehohanan, Hananiah, **Z** and Athlai. H2287
Ne 3:20 Baruch son of **Z** zealously repaired H2287

ZABDI (3)

1Ch 8:19 Zikri, **Z**, H2275
1Ch 27:27 **Z** the Shiphmite was in charge of the H2275
Ne 11:17 of Mika, the son of **Z**, the son of Asaph, H2275

ZABDIEL (2)

1Ch 27: 2 the first month, was Jashobeam son of **Z**. H2276
Ne 11:14 chief officer was **Z** son of Haggedolim. H2276

ZABUD (1)

1Ki 4: 5 district governors; **Z** son of Nathan—a H2280

ZABULON (KJV) ZEBULUN

ZACCAI (NIV84) ZAKKAI

ZACCHAEUS (3)

Lk 19: 2 A man was there by the name of **Z**; he *G2405*
Lk 19: 5 up and said to him, "**Z**, come down *G2405*
Lk 19: 8 But **Z** stood up and said to the Lord, "Look, *G2405*

ZACCUR (NIV84) ZAKKUR

ZACHARIAH, ZACHARIAS (KJV) ZECHARIAH

ZADOK (53) [ZADOKITES]

2Sa 8:17 **Z** son of Ahitub and Ahimelek son of H7401
2Sa 15:24 **Z** was there, too, and all the Levites who H7401
2Sa 15:25 Then the king said to **Z**, "Take the ark of H7401
2Sa 15:27 The king also said to **Z** the priest, "Do you H7401
2Sa 15:29 So **Z** and Abiathar took the ark of God H7401
2Sa 15:35 Won't the priests **Z** and Abiathar be there H7401
2Sa 15:36 Ahimaaz son of **Z** and Jonathan son of H7401
2Sa 17:15 Hushai told **Z** and Abiathar, the priests H7401
2Sa 18:19 Now Ahimaaz son of **Z** said, "Let me run H7401
2Sa 18:22 Ahimaaz son of **Z** again said to Joab H7401
2Sa 18:27 the first one runs like Ahimaaz son of **Z**." H7401
2Sa 19:11 sent this message to **Z** and Abiathar, H7401
2Sa 20:25 was secretary; **Z** and Abiathar were priests H7401
1Ki 1: 8 But **Z** the priest, Benaiah son of Jehoiada H7401
1Ki 1:26 me your servant, and **Z** the priest, and H7401
1Ki 1:32 David said, "Call in **Z** the priest, Nathan H7401
1Ki 1:34 There have **Z** the priest and Nathan the H7401
1Ki 1:38 So **Z** the priest, Nathan the prophet H7401
1Ki 1:39 **Z** the priest took the horn of oil from the H7401
1Ki 1:44 The king has sent with him **Z** the priest H7401
1Ki 1:45 **Z** the priest and Nathan the prophet H7401
1Ki 2:35 replaced Abiathar with **Z** the priest. H7401
1Ki 4: 2 Azariah son of **Z**—the priest; H7401
1Ki 4: 4 commander in chief; **Z** and Abiathar H7401
2Ki 15:33 name was Jerusha daughter of **Z**. H7401
1Ch 6: 8 Ahitub the father of **Z**, Zadok the father of H7401
1Ch 6: 8 father of Zadok, **Z** the father of Ahimaaz H7401
1Ch 6:12 Ahitub the father of **Z**, Zadok the father of H7401
1Ch 6:12 father of Zadok, **Z** the father of Shallum H7401
1Ch 6:53 **Z** his son and Ahimaaz his son. H7401
1Ch 9:11 the son of **Z**, the son of Meraioth, H7401
1Ch 12:28 **Z**, a brave young warrior, with 22 H7401
1Ch 15:11 David summoned **Z** and Abiathar the H7401
1Ch 16:39 David left **Z** the priest and his fellow H7401
1Ch 18:16 **Z** son of Ahitub and Ahimelek son of H7401
1Ch 24: 3 With the help of **Z** a descendant of H7401
1Ch 24: 6 **Z** the priest, Ahimelek son of Abiathar H7401
1Ch 24:31 in the presence of King David and of **Z** H7401
1Ch 27:17 Hashabiah son of Kemuel; over Aaron: **Z**; H7401
1Ch 29:22 the LORD to be ruler and **Z** to be priest. H7401
2Ch 27: 1 name was Jerusha daughter of **Z**. H7401
2Ch 31:10 from the family of **Z**, answered, H7401
Ezr 7: 2 Shallum, the son of **Z**, the son of Ahitub, H7401
Ne 3: 4 next to him **Z** son of Baana also H7401
Ne 3:29 **Z** son of Immer made repairs opposite his H7401
Ne 10:21 Meshezabel, **Z**, Jaddua, H7401
Ne 11:11 the son of **Z**, the son of Meraioth, H7401
Ne 13:13 Shelemiah the priest, **Z** the scribe, and a H7401
Eze 40:46 These are the sons of **Z**, who are the only H7401
Eze 43:19 to the Levitical priests of the family of **Z**, H7401
Eze 44:15 descendants of **Z** and who guarded my H7401
Mt 1:14 Azor the father of **Z**, Zadok the father of *G4882*
Mt 1:14 the father of Zadok, **Z** the father of Akim *G4882*

ZADOKITES (1) [ZADOK]

Eze 48:11 priests, the **Z**, who were faithful in H1201+7401

ZAHAB (1)

Nu 21:14 **Z** in Suphah and the ravines, the Arnon H2298.5

ZAHAM (1)

2Ch 11:19 bore him sons: Jeush, Shemariah and **Z**. H2300

ZAHAR (1)

Eze 27:18 offered wine from Helbon, wool from **Z** H7466

ZAIR (1)
2Ki 8:21 So Jehoram went to Z with all his chariots H7583

ZAKKAI (2)
Ezr 2: 9 of Z 760 H2347
Ne 7:14 of Z 760 H2347

ZAKKUR (10)
Nu 13: 4 the tribe of Reuben, Shammua son of Z; H2346
1Ch 4:26 his son, Z his son and Shimei his son. H2346
1Ch 24:27 from Jaaziah: Beno, Shoham, Z and Ibri. H2346
1Ch 25: 2 the sons of Asaph: Z, Joseph, Nethaniah H2346
1Ch 25:10 the third to Z, his sons and relatives 12 H2346
Ezr 8:14 of Bigvai, Uthai and Z, and with them 70 H2346
Ne 3: 2 Z son of Imri built next to them. H2346
Ne 10:12 Z, Sherebiah, Shebaniah, H2346
Ne 12:35 Micaiah, the son of Z, the son of Asaph, H2346
Ne 13:13 storerooms and made Hanan son of Z, H2346

ZALAPH (1)
Ne 3:30 the sixth son of Z, repaired another H7523

ZALMON (3)
Jdg 9:48 he and all his men went up Mount Z. H7515
2Sa 23:28 Z the Ahohite, Maharai the Netophathite, H7514
Ps 68:14 it was like snow fallen on *Mount* Z. H7515

ZALMONAH (2)
Nu 33:41 They left Mount Hor and camped at Z. H7517
Nu 33:42 They left Z and camped at Punon. H7517

ZALMUNNA (10)
Jdg 8: 5 I am still pursuing Zebah and Z, the H7518
Jdg 8: 6 hands of Zebah and Z in your possession? H7518
Jdg 8: 7 has given Zebah and Z into my hand, H7518
Jdg 8:10 Now Zebah and Z were in Karkor with a H7518
Jdg 8:12 Zebah and Z, the two kings of Midian, fled H7518
Jdg 8:15 "Here are Zebah and Z, about whom you H7518
Jdg 8:15 hands of Zebah and Z in your possession? H7518
Jdg 8:18 Then he asked Zebah and Z, "What kind H7518
Jdg 8:21 Zebah and Z said, "Come, do it yourself H7518
Ps 83:11 all their princes like Zebah and Z, H7518

ZAMZUMMITES (1)
Dt 2:20 but the Ammonites called them Z. H2368

ZANOAH (5)
Jos 15:34 Z, En Gannim, Tappuah, Enam, H2391
Jos 15:56 Jezreel, Jokdeam, Z, H2391
1Ch 4:18 of Soko, and Jekuthiel the father of Z.) H2392
Ne 3:13 repaired by Hanun and the residents of Z. H2391
Ne 11:30 Z, Adullam and their villages, in Lachish H2391

ZAPHENATH-PANEAH (1)
Ge 41:45 gave Joseph the name Z and gave him H7624

ZAPHON (4)
Jos 13:27 Sukkoth and Z with the rest of the realm H7601
Jdg 12: 1 called out, and they crossed over to Z. H7601
Ps 48: 2 like the heights of Z is Mount Zion, the H7601
Isa 14:13 on the utmost heights of Mount Z. H7601

ZARA, ZARAH (KJV) ZERAH

ZAREPHATH (4)
1Ki 17: 9 "Go at once to Z in the region of Sidon H7673
1Ki 17:10 So he went to Z. When he came to the H7673
Ob 20 Canaan will possess the land as far as Z; H7673
Lk 4:26 to a widow in Z in the region of Sidon. G4919

ZARETHAN (4)
Jos 3:16 at a town called Adam in the vicinity of Z H7681
1Ki 4:12 all of Beth Shan next to Z below Jezreel, H7681
1Ki 7:46 of the Jordan between Sukkoth and Z. H7681
2Ch 4:17 of the Jordan between Sukkoth and Z. H7649

ZATTU (5)
Ezr 2: 8 of Z 945 H2456
Ezr 8: 5 of the descendants of Z, Shekaniah son of H2456
Ezr 10:27 From the descendants of Z: Elioenai H2456
Ne 7:13 of Z 845 H2456
Ne 10:14 Pahath-Moab, Elam, Z, Bani, H2456

ZAZA (1)
1Ch 2:33 Peleth and Z. These were the H2321

ZEAL (21) [ZEALOUS, ZEALOUSLY]
Nu 25:11 I did not put an end to them in my z. H7863
Dt 29:20 his wrath and z will burn against them. H7863
2Sa 21: 2 Saul in his z for Israel and Judah had H7861
2Ki 10:16 "Come with me and see my z for the LORD." H7863
2Ki 19:31 "The z *of* the LORD Almighty will H7863
Ps 69: 9 for z *for* your house consumes me, and H7863
Ps 119:139 My z wears me out, for my enemies H7863
Isa 9: 7 The z *of* the LORD Almighty will H7863
Isa 26:11 Let them see your z *for* your people and H7863
Isa 37:32 The z *of* the LORD Almighty will H7863
Isa 42:13 like a warrior he will stir up his z; with a H7863
Isa 59:17 wrapped himself in z as in a cloak. H7863
Isa 63:15 Where are your z and your might? Your H7863
Eze 5:13 know that I the LORD have spoken in my z. H7863
Eze 36: 5 In my burning z I have spoken against the H7863
Eze 38:19 In my z and fiery wrath I declare that at H7863
Jn 2:17 "Z for your house will consume me." G2419
Ro 10: 2 but their z is not based on knowledge. NDT
Ro 12:11 Never be lacking *in* z, but keep your G5082
Gal 4:17 from us, so that *you may* have z for them. G2420
Php 3: 6 as for z, persecuting the church; as for G2419

ZEALOT (4)
Mt 10: 4 Simon the Z and Judas Iscariot, who G2831
Mk 3:18 of Alphaeus, Thaddaeus, Simon the Z G2831
Lk 6:15 Alphaeus, Simon who was called the Z, G2421
Ac 1:13 James son of Alphaeus and Simon the Z G2421

ZEALOUS (13) [ZEAL]
Nu 25:11 Since he *was* as z *for* my *honor* among H7861
Nu 25:13 because *he was* z for the honor of his God H7861
1Ki 19:10 "*I have been* very z for the LORD H7861+7861
1Ki 19:14 "*I have been* very z for the LORD H7861+7861
Pr 23:17 always be z for the fear of the LORD. NDT
Eze 39:25 of Israel, and *I will be* z for my holy name. H7861
Ac 21:20 all of them are z for the law. G2421
Ac 22: 3 I was just as z for God as any of you are G2421
Ro 10: 2 testify about them that they are z for God, G2419
2Co 8:22 proved to us in many ways that he is z, G5080
Gal 1:14 was extremely z for the traditions of G2421
Gal 4:17 *Those people are* z *to win* you *over*, but G2420
Gal 4:18 It is fine *to be* z, provided the purpose is G2420

ZEALOUSLY (1) [ZEAL]
Ne 3:20 Baruch son of Zabbai z repaired another H3013

ZEBADIAH (9)
1Ch 8:15 Z, Arad, Eder, H2277
1Ch 8:17 Z, Meshullam, Hizki, Heber, H2277
1Ch 12: 7 Joelah and Z the sons of Jeroham H2278
1Ch 26: 2 Jediael the second, Z the third, Jathniel H2278
1Ch 27: 7 of Joab; his son Z was his successor. H2277
2Ch 17: 8 Shemaiah, Nethaniah, Z, Asahel H2278
2Ch 19:11 the LORD, and Z son of Ishmael, the H2278
Ezr 8: 8 of Shephatiah, Z son of Michael, and with H2277
Ezr 10:20 descendants of Immer: Hanani and Z. H2277

ZEBAH (10)
Jdg 8: 5 I am still pursuing Z and Zalmunna H2286
Jdg 8: 6 have the hands of Z and Zalmunna in H2286
Jdg 8: 7 the LORD has given Z and Zalmunna into H2286
Jdg 8:10 Now Z and Zalmunna were in Karkor with H2286
Jdg 8:12 Z and Zalmunna, the two kings of Midian H2286
Jdg 8:15 Sukkoth, "Here are Z and Zalmunna H2286
Jdg 8:15 have the hands of Z and Zalmunna in H2286
Jdg 8:18 Then he asked Z and Zalmunna, "What H2286
Jdg 8:21 Z and Zalmunna said, "Come, do it H2286
Ps 83:11 all their princes like Z and Zalmunna, H2286

ZEBEDEE (10) [ZEBEDEE'S]
Mt 4:21 James son *of* Z and his brother John. G2411
Mt 4:21 They were in a boat with their father Z G2411
Mt 10: 2 Andrew; James son *of* Z, and his brother G2411
Mt 26:37 the two sons *of* Z along with him, G2411
Mk 1:19 he saw James son *of* Z and his brother G2411
Mk 1:20 they left their father Z in the boat with the G2411
Mk 3:17 James son *of* Z and his brother John (to G2411
Mk 10:35 John, the sons *of* Z, came to him. G2411
Lk 5:10 John, the sons *of* Z, Simon's partners. G2411
Jn 21: 2 in Galilee, the sons *of* Z, and two other G2411

ZEBEDEE'S (2) [ZEBEDEE]
Mt 20:20 Then the mother of Z sons came to Jesus G2411
Mt 27:56 Joseph, and the mother of Z sons. G2411

ZEBIDAH (1)
2Ki 23:36 mother's name was Z daughter of H2288

ZEBINA (1)
Ezr 10:43 Mattithiah, Zabad, Z, Jaddai, Joel and H2289

ZEBOIIM (NIV84) ZEBOYIM

ZEBOIM (1)
Ne 11:34 in Hadid, Z and Neballat, H7391

ZEBOYIM (6)
Ge 10:19 Gomorrah, Admah and Z, as far as Lasha. H7375
Ge 14: 2 Shemeber king of Z, and the king of Bela H7375
Ge 14: 8 the king of Z and the king of Bela H7375
Dt 29:23 Gomorrah, Admah and Z, which the LORD H7375
1Sa 13:18 the Valley of Z facing the wilderness. H7391
Hos 11: 8 How can I make you like Z? My heart is H7375

ZEBUL (6)
Jdg 9:28 Jerub-Baal's son, and isn't Z his deputy? H2291
Jdg 9:30 When Z the governor of the city heard H2291
Jdg 9:36 When Gaal saw them, he said to Z, "Look, H2291
Jdg 9:36 Z replied, "You mistake the shadows of H2291
Jdg 9:38 Then Z said to him, "Where is your big H2291
Jdg 9:41 Z drove Gaal and his clan out of H2291

ZEBULUN (50) [ZEBULUNITE]
Ge 30:20 So she named him Z. H2282
Ge 35:23 Simeon, Levi, Judah, Issachar and Z. H2282
Ge 46:14 The sons of Z: Sered, Elon and Jahleel. H2282
Ge 49:13 "Z will live by the seashore and become a H2282
Ex 1: 3 Issachar, Z and Benjamin; H2282
Nu 1: 9 from Z, Eliab son of Helon; H2282
Nu 1:30 From the descendants of Z: All the men H2282
Nu 1:31 number from the tribe of Z was 57,400. H2282
Nu 2: 7 The tribe of Z will be next. The leader of H2282
Nu 2: 7 of the people of Z is Eliab son of Helon. H2282
Nu 7:24 the leader of the people of Z, brought his H2282
Nu 10:16 over the division of the tribe of Z. H1201+2282
Nu 13:10 from the tribe of Z, Gaddiel son of Sodi; H2282
Nu 26:26 The descendants of Z by their clans were H2282
Nu 26:27 These were the clans of Z; those H2283
Nu 34:25 the leader from the tribe of Z; H1201+2282
Dt 27:13 Asher, Z, Dan and Naphtali. H2282
Dt 33:18 About Z he said: "Rejoice, Zebulun, in H2282
Dt 33:18 "Rejoice, Z, in your going out, and you H2282
Jos 19:10 lot came up for Z according to its H1201+2282
Jos 19:16 villages were the inheritance of Z, H1201+2282
Jos 19:27 touched Z and the Valley of Iphtah El H2282
Jos 19:34 It touched Z on the south, Asher on the H2282
Jos 21: 7 from the tribes of Reuben, Gad and Z. H2282
Jos 21:34 from the tribe of Z, Jokneam, Kartah, H2282
Jdg 1:30 Neither did Z drive out the Canaanites H2282
Jdg 1:30 Z did subject them to forced labor. NDT
Jdg 4: 6 of Naphtali and Z and lead them H1201+2282
Jdg 4:10 There Barak summoned Z and Naphtali H2282
Jdg 5:14 from Z those who bear a commander's H2282
Jdg 5:18 The people of Z risked their very lives; so H2282
Jdg 6:35 also into Asher, Z and Naphtali, so H2282
Jdg 12:12 was buried in Aijalon in the land of Z. H2282
1Ch 2: 1 Reuben, Simeon, Levi, Judah, Issachar, Z, H2282
1Ch 6:63 from the tribes of Reuben, Gad and Z. H2282
1Ch 6:77 From the tribe of Z they received Jokneam, H2282
1Ch 12:33 from Z, experienced soldiers prepared H2282
1Ch 12:40 Z and Naphtali came bringing food on H2282
1Ch 27:19 over Z: Ishmaiah son of Obadiah; over H2282
2Ch 30:10 as far as Z, but people scorned H2282
2Ch 30:11 Manasseh and Z humbled themselves H2282
2Ch 30:18 Issachar and Z had not purified H2282
Ps 68:27 there the princes of Z and of Naphtali. H2282
Isa 9: 1 he humbled the land of Z and the land of H2282
Eze 48:26 "Z will have one portion; it will border the H2282
Eze 48:27 border the territory of Z from east to west. H2282
Eze 48:33 the gate of Issachar and the gate of Z. H2282
Mt 4:13 the lake in the area *of* Z and Naphtali— G2404
Mt 4:15 "Land *of* Z and land of Naphtali, the Way G2404
Rev 7: 8 from the tribe *of* Z 12,000, from the tribe G2404

ZEBULUNITE (1) [ZEBULUN]
Jdg 12:11 After him, Elon the Z led Israel ten years. H2283

ZECHARIAH (53) [ZECHARIAH'S]
2Ki 14:29 And Z his son succeeded him as king H2357
2Ki 15: 8 Z son of Jeroboam became king of Israel H2358
2Ki 15:10 son of Jabesh conspired against Z. H2257S
2Ki 18: 2 mother's name was Abijah daughter of Z. H2357
1Ch 5: 7 genealogical records: Jeiel the chief, Z, H2358
1Ch 9:21 Z son of Meshelemiah was the H2357
1Ch 9:37 Ahio, Z and Mikloth. H2357
1Ch 15:18 Z, Jaaziel, Shemiramoth, Jehiel, Unni H2358
1Ch 15:20 Z, Jaaziel, Shemiramoth, Jehiel, Unni H2357
1Ch 15:24 Amasai, Z, Benaiah and Eliezer the H2358
1Ch 16: 5 next to him in rank were Z, then H2357
1Ch 24:25 Ishiah; from the sons of Ishiah: Z. H2358
1Ch 26: 2 Z the firstborn, Jediael the second H2358
1Ch 26:11 Tabaliah the third and Z the fourth. H2358
1Ch 26:14 Then lots were cast for his son Z, a wise H2358
1Ch 27:21 Iddo son of Z; over Benjamin H2358
2Ch 17: 7 Obadiah, Z, Nethanel and Micaiah to H2357
2Ch 20:14 of the LORD came on Jahaziel son of Z, H2358
2Ch 21: 2 Azariah, Jehiel, Z, Azariahu, Michael H2358
2Ch 24:20 of God came on Z son of Jehoiada the H2357
2Ch 26: 5 He sought God during the days of Z, who H2358
2Ch 29: 1 mother's name was Abijah daughter of Z. H2358
2Ch 29:13 descendants of Asaph, Z and Mattaniah; H2358
2Ch 34:12 from Merari, and Z and Meshullam H2357
2Ch 35: 8 Hilkiah, Z and Jehiel, the officials in H2358
Ezr 5: 1 Haggai the prophet and Z the prophet, A10230
Ezr 6:14 preaching of Haggai the prophet and Z, A10230
Ezr 8: 3 of Parosh, Z, and with him were H2357
Ezr 8:11 of Bebai, Z son of Bebai, and H2357
Ezr 8:16 Nathan, Z and Meshullam, who were H2357
Ezr 10:26 Mattaniah, Z, Jehiel, Abdi, Jeremoth and H2357
Ne 8: 4 Hashbaddanah, Z and Meshullam. H2357
Ne 11: 4 the son of Z, the son of Amariah, H2357
Ne 11: 5 of Joiarib, the son of Z, a descendant of H2357
Ne 11:12 of Amzi, the son of Z, the son of Pashhur, H2357
Ne 12:16 of Iddo's, Z; of Ginnethon's, Meshullam; H2357
Ne 12:35 trumpets, and also Z son of Jonathan, the H2357
Ne 12:41 Z and Hananiah with their trumpets H2357
Isa 8: 2 the priest and Z son of Jeberekiah as H2358
Zec 1: 1 came to the prophet Z son of Berekiah, H2357
Zec 1: 7 came to the prophet Z son of Berekiah, H2357
Zec 7: 1 of the LORD came to Z on the fourth day of H2357
Zec 7: 8 And the word of the LORD came again to Z: H2357
Mt 23:35 Abel to the blood *of* Z son of Berekiah, G2408
Lk 1: 5 king of Judea there was a priest named Z, G2408
Lk 1:12 When Z saw him, he was startled and was G2408
Lk 1:13 "Do not be afraid, Z; your prayer has been G2408
Lk 1:18 Z asked the angel, "How can I be sure of G2408
Lk 1:21 were waiting for Z and wondering why he G2408
Lk 1:59 going to name him after his father Z, G2408
Lk 1:67 His father Z was filled with the Holy Spirit G2408
Lk 3: 2 came to John son *of* Z in the wilderness. G2408
Lk 11:51 from the blood of Abel to the blood *of* Z G2408

ZECHARIAH'S (4) [ZECHARIAH]
2Ki 15:11 The other events of **Z** reign are written in H2357
2Ch 24:22 the kindness **Z** father Jehoiada had H2257S
Lk 1: 8 Once when **Z** division was on duty and he *G899S*
Lk 1:40 where she entered **Z** home and greeted *G2408*

ZEDAD (2)
Nu 34: 8 Then the boundary will go to **Z**, H7398
Eze 47:15 the Hethlon road past Lebo Hamath to **Z**, H7398

ZEDEKIAH (60) [ZEDEKIAH'S]
1Ki 22:11 Now **Z** son of Kenaanah had made iron H7408
1Ki 22:24 Then **Z** son of Kenaanah went up and H7409
2Ki 24:17 in his place and changed his name to **Z**. H7409
2Ki 24:18 **Z** was twenty-one years old when he H7409
2Ki 24:20 Now **Z** rebelled against the king of H7409
2Ki 25: 2 siege until the eleventh year of King **Z**. H7409
2Ki 25: 7 They killed the sons of **Z** before his eyes H7409
1Ch 3:15 the second son, **Z** the third, Shallum the H7409
1Ch 3:16 of Jehoiakim: Jehoiachin his son, and **Z**. H7408
2Ch 18:10 Now **Z** son of Kenaanah had made iron H7409
2Ch 18:23 Then **Z** son of Kenaanah went up and H7409
2Ch 36:10 Jehoiachin's uncle, **Z**, king over Judah H7409
2Ch 36:11 **Z** was twenty-one years old when he H7409
Ne 10: 1 the governor, the son of Hakaliah. **Z**, H7408
Jer 1: 3 the eleventh year of **Z** son of Josiah king H7409
Jer 21: 1 the LORD when King **Z** sent to him Pashhur H7409
Jer 21: 3 But Jeremiah answered them, "Tell **Z**, H7409
Jer 21: 7 the LORD, I will give **Z** king of Judah, his H7409
Jer 24: 8 'so will I deal with **Z** king of Judah, his H7409
Jer 27: 1 in the reign of **Z** son of Josiah king of H7409
Jer 27: 3 come to Jerusalem to **Z** king of Judah. H7409
Jer 27:12 the same message to **Z** king of Judah. H7408
Jer 28: 1 early in the reign of **Z** king of Judah, the H7408
Jer 29: 3 whom **Z** king of Judah sent to King H7408
Jer 29:21 son of Kolaiah and **Z** son of Maaseiah, H7409
Jer 29:22 'May the LORD treat you like **Z** and Ahab H7409
Jer 32: 1 LORD in the tenth year of **Z** king of Judah, H7409
Jer 32: 3 Now **Z** king of Judah had imprisoned him H7409
Jer 32: 4 **Z** king of Judah will not escape the H7409
Jer 32: 5 He will take **Z** to Babylon, where he will H7409
Jer 34: 2 Go to **Z** king of Judah and tell him, 'This H7409
Jer 34: 4 LORD's promise to you, **Z** king of Judah. H7409
Jer 34: 6 prophet told all this to **Z** king of Judah, H7409
Jer 34: 8 LORD after King **Z** had made a covenant H7409
Jer 34:21 "I will deliver **Z** king of Judah and his H7409
Jer 36:12 son of Shaphan, **Z** son of Hananiah, and H7409
Jer 37: 1 **Z** son of Josiah was made king of Judah H7409
Jer 37: 3 King **Z**, however, sent Jehukal son of H7409
Jer 37:17 Then King **Z** sent for him and had him H7409
Jer 37:18 Then Jeremiah said to King **Z**, "What H7409
Jer 37:21 King **Z** then gave orders for Jeremiah to H7409
Jer 38: 5 your hands," King **Z** answered. "The king H7409
Jer 38:14 Then King **Z** sent for Jeremiah the H7409
Jer 38:15 Jeremiah said to **Z**, "If I give you an H7409
Jer 38:16 But King **Z** swore this oath secretly to H7409
Jer 38:17 Then Jeremiah said to **Z**, "This is what H7409
Jer 38:19 King **Z** said to Jeremiah, "I am afraid of H7409
Jer 38:24 Then **Z** said to Jeremiah, "Do not let H7409
Jer 39: 1 In the ninth year of **Z** king of Judah, in the H7409
Jer 39: 4 When **Z** king of Judah and all the soldiers H7409
Jer 39: 5 them and overtook **Z** in the plains of H7409
Jer 39: 6 the sons of **Z** before his eyes and H7409
Jer 44:30 just as I gave **Z** king of Judah into the H7409
Jer 49:34 early in the reign of **Z** king of Judah: H7408
Jer 51:59 to Babylon with **Z** king of Judah in the H7409
Jer 52: 1 **Z** was twenty-one years old when he H7409
Jer 52: 3 Now **Z** rebelled against the king of H7409
Jer 52: 5 siege until the eleventh year of King **Z**. H7409
Jer 52: 8 army pursued King **Z** and overtook him in H7409
Jer 52:10 killed the sons of **Z** before his eyes; H7409

ZEDEKIAH'S (5) [ZEDEKIAH]
2Ki 25: 1 So in the ninth year of **Z** reign, on the H2257S
Jer 39: 2 fourth month of **Z** eleventh year, H4200+7409
Jer 39: 7 Then he put out **Z** eyes and bound him H7409
Jer 52: 4 So in the ninth year of **Z** reign, on the H2257S
Jer 52:11 Then he put out **Z** eyes, bound him with H7409

ZEEB (6)
Jdg 7:25 two of the Midianite leaders, Oreb and **Z**. H2270
Jdg 7:25 of Oreb, and **Z** at the winepress of Zeeb. H2270
Jdg 7:25 of Oreb, and the heads of **Z**. at the winepress of Z. H2270
Jdg 7:25 the heads of Oreb and **Z** to Gideon, H2270
Jdg 8: 3 God gave Oreb and **Z**, the Midianite H2270
Ps 83:11 Make their nobles like Oreb and **Z**, all H2270

ZEKER (1)
1Ch 8:31 Gedor, Ahio, **Z** H2353

ZELA (1)
2Sa 21:14 father Kish, at **Z** in Benjamin, and did H7522

ZELAH (1)
Jos 18:28 **Z**, Haeleph, the Jebusite city (that is H7522

ZELEK (2)
2Sa 23:37 **Z** the Ammonite, Naharai the Beerothite H7530
1Ch 11:39 **Z** the Ammonite, Naharai the Berothite H7530

ZELOPHEHAD (5) [ZELOPHEHAD'S]
Nu 26:33 (**Z** son of Hepher had no sons; he had H7524
Nu 27: 1 The daughters of **Z** son of Hepher, the H7524
Nu 36: 2 of our brother **Z** to his daughters. H7524
Jos 17: 3 Now **Z** son of Hepher, the son of Gilead H7524
1Ch 7:15 Another descendant was named **Z**, who H7524

ZELOPHEHAD'S (4) [ZELOPHEHAD]
Nu 27: 7 "What **Z** daughters are saying is right. H7524
Nu 36: 6 what the LORD commands for **Z** daughters: H7524
Nu 36:10 So **Z** daughters did as the LORD H7524
Nu 36:11 **Z** daughters—Mahlah, Tirzah, Hoglah H7524

ZELZAH (1)
1Sa 10: 2 at **Z** on the border of Benjamin. H7525

ZEMARAIM (2)
Jos 18:22 Beth Arabah, **Z**, Bethel, H7549
2Ch 13: 4 Abijah stood on Mount **Z**, in the hill H7549

ZEMARITES (2)
Ge 10:18 Arvadites, **Z** and Hamathites. Later the H7548
1Ch 1:16 Arvadites, **Z** and Hamathites. H7548

ZEMIRAH (1)
1Ch 7: 8 **Z**, Joash, Eliezer, Elioenai, Omri H2371

ZENAN (1)
Jos 15:37 **Z**, Hadashah, Migdal Gad, H7569

ZENAS (1)
Titus 3:13 you can to help **Z** the lawyer and Apollos *G2424*

ZEPHANIAH (11)
2Ki 25:18 **Z** the priest next in rank and the three H7623
1Ch 6:36 the son of Azariah, the son of **Z**, H7622
Jer 21: 1 the priest **Z** son of Maaseiah. H7622
Jer 29:25 to the priest **Z** son of Maaseiah, and to H7622
Jer 29:25 to all the other priests. You said to **Z**, NDT
Jer 29:29 **Z** the priest, however, read the letter to H7622
Jer 37: 3 with the priest **Z** son of Maaseiah to H7623
Jer 52:24 **Z** the priest next in rank and the three H7622
Zep 1: 1 of the LORD that came to **Z** son of Cushi, H7622
Zec 6:10 same day to the house of Josiah son of **Z**. H7622
Zec 6:14 Hen son of **Z** as a memorial in the H7622

ZEPHATH (1)
Jdg 1:17 attacked the Canaanites living in **Z**, H7634

ZEPHATHAH (1)
2Ch 14:10 in the Valley of **Z** near Mareshah. H7635

ZEPHO (3)
Ge 36:11 Teman, Omar, **Z**, Gatam and Kenaz. H7598
Ge 36:15 Chiefs Teman, Omar, **Z**, Kenaz, H7598
1Ch 1:36 Teman, Omar, **Z**, Gatam and Kenaz; by H7598

ZEPHON (2) [BAAL ZEPHON, ZEPHONITE]
Ge 46:16 **Z**, Haggi, Shuni, Ezbon, Eri, Arodi and H7602
Nu 26:15 through **Z**, the Zephonite clan; through H7602

ZEPHONITE (1) [ZEPHON]
Nu 26:15 Zephon, the **Z** clan; through Haggi H7604

ZER (1)
Jos 19:35 fortified towns were Ziddim, **Z**, Hammath, H7643

ZERAH (21) [ZERAHITE, ZERAHITES]
Ge 36:13 Nahath, **Z**, Shammah and H2438
Ge 36:17 Chiefs Nahath, **Z**, Shammah and Mizzah H2438
Ge 36:33 Jobab son of **Z** from Bozrah succeeded H2438
Ge 38:30 came out. And he was named **Z**. H2438
Ge 46:12 Shelah, Perez and **Z** (but Er and Onan H2438
Nu 26:13 through **Z**, the Zerahite clan; through H2438
Nu 26:20 through **Z**, the Zerahite clan. H2438
Jos 7: 1 of Zimri, the son of **Z**, of the tribe of H2438
Jos 7:18 of Zimri, the son of **Z**, of the tribe of H2438
Jos 7:24 all Israel, took Achan son of **Z**, the silver, H2438
Jos 22:20 When Achan son of **Z** was unfaithful in H2438
1Ch 1:37 Nahath, **Z**, Shammah and H2438
1Ch 1:44 Jobab son of **Z** from Bozrah succeeded H2438
1Ch 2: 4 Tamar bore Perez and **Z** to Judah. H2438
1Ch 2: 6 The sons of **Z**: Zimri, Ethan, Heman H2438
1Ch 4:24 Nemuel, Jamin, Jarib, **Z** and Shaul; H2438
1Ch 6:21 his son, **Z** his son and Jeatherai his son. H2438
1Ch 6:41 of Ethni, the son of **Z**, the son of Adaiah, H2438
2Ch 14: 9 **Z** the Cushite marched out against them H2438
Ne 11:24 one of the descendants of **Z** son of Judah H2438
Mt 1: 3 Judah the father of Perez and **Z**, whose *G2406*

ZERAHIAH (5)
1Ch 6: 6 Uzzi the father of **Z**, Zerahiah the father of H2440
1Ch 6: 6 of Zerahiah, **Z** the father of Meraioth H2440
1Ch 6:51 Bukki his son, Uzzi his son, **Z** his son, H2440
Ezr 7: 4 the son of **Z**, the son of Uzzi, the son of H2440
Ezr 8: 4 Eliehoenai son of **Z**, and with him 200 H2440

ZERAHITE (4) [ZERAH]
Nu 26:13 through Zerah, the **Z** clan; through Shaul H2439
Nu 26:20 Perezite clan; through Zerah, the **Z** clan. H2439
1Ch 27:11 was Sibbekai the Hushathite, a **Z**. H2439
1Ch 27:13 was Maharai the Netophathite, a **Z**. H2439

ZERAHITES (3) [ZERAH]
Jos 7:17 came forward, and the **Z** were chosen. H2439
Jos 7:17 He had the clan of the **Z** come forward by H2439
1Ch 9: 6 Of the **Z**: Jeuel. The people from H1201+2438

ZERED (3)
Nu 21:12 moved on and camped in the **Z** Valley. H2429
Dt 2:13 "Now get up and cross the **Z** Valley." H2429
Dt 2:14 Barnea until we crossed the **Z** Valley. H2429

ZEREDAH (1)
1Ki 11:26 an Ephraimite from **Z**, and his mother was H7649

ZERERAH (1)
Jdg 7:22 Beth Shittah toward **Z** as far as the border H7678

ZERESH (4)
Est 5:10 Calling together his friends and **Z**, his H2454
Est 5:14 His wife **Z** and all his friends said to him H2454
Est 6:13 told **Z** his wife and all his friends H2454
Est 6:13 His advisers and his wife **Z** said to him H2454

ZERETH (1) [ZERETH SHAHAR]
1Ch 4: 7 The sons of Helah: **Z**, Zohar, Ethnan, H7679

ZERETH SHAHAR (1) [ZERETH]
Jos 13:19 Sibmah, **Z** on the hill in the valley H7680

ZERI (1)
1Ch 25: 3 Gedaliah, **Z**, Jeshaiah, Shimei H7662

ZEROR (1)
1Sa 9: 1 of Abiel, the son of **Z**, the son of Bekorath H7657

ZERUAH (1)
1Ki 11:26 his mother was a widow named **Z**. H7654

ZERUBBABEL (25)
1Ch 3:19 sons of Pedaiah: **Z** and Shimei. The sons H2428
1Ch 3:19 The sons of **Z**: Meshullam and H2428
Ezr 2: 2 in company with **Z**, Joshua, Nehemiah H2428
Ezr 3: 2 fellow priests and **Z** son of Shealtiel and H2428
Ezr 3: 8 of God in Jerusalem, **Z** son of Shealtiel H2428
Ezr 4: 2 they came to **Z** and to the heads of the H2428
Ezr 4: 3 But **Z**, Joshua and the rest of the heads of H2428
Ezr 5: 2 Then **Z** son of Shealtiel and Joshua son A10239
Ne 7: 7 in company with **Z**, Joshua, Nehemiah H2428
Ne 12: 1 who returned with **Z** son of Shealtiel and H2428
Ne 12:47 So in the days of **Z** and of Nehemiah, all H2428
Hag 1: 1 the prophet Haggai to **Z** son of Shealtiel, H2428
Hag 1:12 Then **Z** son of Shealtiel, Joshua son of H2428
Hag 1:14 stirred up the spirit of **Z** son of Shealtiel, H2428
Hag 2: 2 "Speak to **Z** son of Shealtiel, governor of H2428
Hag 2: 4 But now be strong, **Z**,' declares the LORD H2428
Hag 2:21 "Tell **Z** governor of Judah that I am going H2428
Hag 2:23 take you, my servant **Z** son of Shealtiel,' H2428
Zec 4: 6 "This is the word of the LORD to **Z**: H2428
Zec 4: 7 Before **Z** you will become level ground H2428
Zec 4: 9 "The hands of **Z** have laid the foundation H2428
Zec 4:10 the chosen capstone in the hand of **Z**?" H2428
Mt 1:12 of Shealtiel, Shealtiel the father of **Z**, *G2431*
Mt 1:13 **Z** the father of Abihud, Abihud the father *G2431*
Lk 3:27 son of Rhesa, the son *of* **Z**, the son of *G2431*

ZERUIAH (25) [ZERUIAH'S]
1Sa 26: 6 the Hittite and Abishai son of **Z**, H7653
2Sa 2:13 Joab son of **Z** and David's men went out H7653
2Sa 2:18 The three sons of **Z** were there: Joab H7653
2Sa 3:39 these sons of **Z** are too strong for me. H7653
2Sa 8:16 Joab son of **Z** was over the army H7653
2Sa 14: 1 Joab son of **Z** knew that the king's heart H7653
2Sa 16: 9 Then Abishai son of **Z** said to the king H7653
2Sa 16:10 this have to do with you, you sons of **Z**? H7653
2Sa 17:25 sister of **Z** the mother of Joab. H7653
2Sa 18: 2 under Joab's brother Abishai son of **Z**, H7653
2Sa 19:21 Then Abishai son of **Z** said, "Shouldn't H7653
2Sa 19:22 this have to do with you, you sons of **Z**? H7653
2Sa 21:17 But Abishai son of **Z** came to David's H7653
2Sa 23:18 of Joab son of **Z** was chief of the Three H7653
2Sa 23:37 the armor-bearer of Joab son of **Z**. H7653
1Ki 1: 7 with Joab son of **Z** and with Abiathar the H7653
1Ki 2: 5 know what Joab son of **Z** did to me— H7653
1Ki 2:22 Abiathar the priest and Joab son of **Z**!" H7653
1Ch 2:16 Their sisters were **Z** and Abigail H7653
1Ch 11: 6 Joab son of **Z** went up first, and so he H7653
1Ch 11:39 the armor-bearer of Joab son of **Z**, H7653
1Ch 18:12 Abishai son of **Z** struck down eighteen H7653
1Ch 18:15 Joab son of **Z** was over the army H7653
1Ch 26:28 Abner son of Ner and Joab son of **Z**, and H7653
1Ch 27:24 Joab son of **Z** began to count the men H7653

ZERUIAH'S (1) [ZERUIAH]
1Ch 2:16 **Z** three sons were Abishai, Joab and H7653

ZETHAM (2)
1Ch 23: 8 Jehiel the first, **Z** and Joel—three in all. H2457
1Ch 26:22 the sons of Jehieli, **Z** and his brother Joel H2457

ZETHAN (1)
1Ch 7:10 Kenaanah, **Z**, Tarshish and H2340

ZETHAR (1)
Est 1:10 Abagtha, **Z** and Karkas— H2458

ZEUS (2)
Ac 14:12 Barnabas they called **Z**, and Paul they *G2416*
Ac 14:13 The priest *of* **Z**, whose temple was just *G2416*

ZIA (1)

1Ch 5:13 Jakan, **Z** and Eber—seven in H2333

ZIBA (16) [ZIBA'S]

2Sa 9: 2 a servant of Saul's household named **Z**. H7471
2Sa 9: 2 the king said to him, "Are you **Z**? H7471
2Sa 9: 3 **Z** answered the king, "There is still a son H7471
2Sa 9: 4 **Z** answered, "He is at the house of Makir H7471
2Sa 9: 9 Then the king summoned **Z**, Saul's H7471
2Sa 9:10 Now **Z** had fifteen sons and twenty H7471
2Sa 9:11 Then **Z** said to the king, "Your servant will H7471
2Sa 16: 1 the summit, there was **Z**, the steward of H7471
2Sa 16: 2 The king asked **Z**, "Why have you brought H7471
2Sa 16: 2 **Z** answered, "The donkeys are for the H7471
2Sa 16: 3 **Z** said to him, "He is staying in H7471
2Sa 16: 4 Then the king said to **Z**, "All that H7471
2Sa 16: 4 "I humbly bow," **Z** said. "May I find favor H7471
2Sa 19:17 along with **Z**, the steward of Saul's H7471
2Sa 19:26 But **Z** my servant betrayed me NDT
2Sa 19:29 I order you and **Z** to divide the land." H7471

ZIBA'S (1) [ZIBA]

2Sa 9:12 all the members of **Z** household were H7471

ZIBEON (8)

Ge 36: 2 granddaughter of **Z** the Hivite— H7390
Ge 36:14 of Anah and granddaughter of **Z**, H7390
Ge 36:20 in the region: Lotan, Shobal, **Z**, Anah, H7390
Ge 36:24 The sons of **Z**: Aiah and Anah. This is the H7390
Ge 36:24 was grazing the donkeys of his father **Z**. H7390
Ge 36:29 the Horite chiefs: Lotan, Shobal, **Z**, Anah, H7390
1Ch 1:38 Shobal, **Z**, Anah, Dishon, Ezer and H7390
1Ch 1:40 The sons of **Z**: Aiah and Anah. H7390

ZIBIA (1)

1Ch 8: 9 his wife Hodesh he had Jobab, **Z**, Mesha, H7384

ZIBIAH (2)

2Ki 12: 1 His mother's name was **Z**; she was from H7385
2Ch 24: 1 His mother's name was **Z**; she was from H7385

ZICRI (NIV84) ZIKRI

ZIDDIM (1)

Jos 19:35 The fortified towns were **Z**, Zer, Hammath, H7403

ZIDON, ZIDONIANS (KJV) SIDON, SIDONIANS

ZIF (KJV) ZIV

ZIHA (3)

Ezr 2:43 the descendants of **Z**, Hasupha, Tabbaoth H7484
Ne 7:46 the descendants of **Z**, Hasupha, Tabbaoth H7484
Ne 11:21 **Z** and Gishpa were in charge of them. H7484

ZIKLAG (15)

Jos 15:31 **Z**, Madmannah, Sansannah, H7637
Jos 19: 5 **Z**, Beth Markaboth, Hazar Susah, H7637
1Sa 27: 6 So on that day Achish gave him **Z**, and it H7637
1Sa 30: 1 his men reached **Z** on the third day. H7637
1Sa 30: 1 Amalekites had raided the Negev and **Z**. H7637
1Sa 30: 1 They had attacked **Z** and burned it, H7637
1Sa 30: 3 David and his men reached **Z**, H2021+6551S
1Sa 30:14 the Negev of Caleb. And we burned **Z**." H7637
1Sa 30:26 When David reached **Z**, he sent some of H7637
2Sa 1: 1 the Amalekites and stayed in **Z** two days. H7637
2Sa 4:10 I seized him and put him to death in **Z**. H7637
1Ch 4:30 Bethuel, Hormah, **Z**, H7637
1Ch 12: 1 were the men who came to David at **Z**, H7637
1Ch 12:20 When David went to **Z**, these were the H7637
Ne 11:28 in **Z**, in Mekonah and its settlements, H7637

ZIKRI (12)

Ex 6:21 sons of Izhar were Korah, Nepheg and **Z**. H2356
1Ch 8:19 **Z**, Zabdi, H2356
1Ch 8:23 **Z**, Hanan, H2356
1Ch 8:27 Elijah and **Z** were the sons of Jeroham. H2356
1Ch 9:15 of Mika, the son of **Z**, the son of Asaph; H2356
1Ch 26:25 his son, **Z** his son and Shelomith his son. H2356
1Ch 27:16 Eliezer son of **Z**; over the Simeonites H2356
2Ch 17:16 Amasiah son of **Z**, who volunteered H2356
2Ch 23: 1 son of Adaiah, and Elishaphat son of **Z**. H2356
2Ch 28: 7 **Z**, an Ephraimite warrior, killed Maaseiah H2356
Ne 11: 9 Joel son of **Z** was their chief officer, and H2356
Ne 12:17 of Abijah's, **Z**; of Miniamin's and of H2356

ZILLAH (3)

Ge 4:19 one named Adah and the other **Z**. H7500
Ge 4:22 **Z** also had a son, Tubal-Cain, who forged H7500
Ge 4:23 to his wives, "Adah and **Z**, listen to me; H7500

ZILLETHAI (2)

1Ch 8:20 Elienai, **Z**, Eliel, H7531
1Ch 12:20 Jozabad, Elihu and **Z**, leaders of units of H7531

ZILPAH (7)

Ge 29:24 gave his servant **Z** to his daughter as her H2364
Ge 30: 9 she took her servant **Z** and gave her to H2364
Ge 30:10 Leah's servant **Z** bore Jacob a son. H2364
Ge 30:12 Leah's servant **Z** bore Jacob a second son. H2364
Ge 35:26 The sons of Leah's servant **Z**: Gad and H2364
Ge 37: 2 the sons of Bilhah and the sons of **Z**, his H2364
Ge 46:18 were the children born to Jacob by **Z**, H2364

ZIMMAH (3)

1Ch 6:20 Libni his son, Jahath his son, **Z** his son, H2366
1Ch 6:42 of Ethan, the son of **Z**, the son of Shimei, H2366
2Ch 29:12 Joah son of **Z** and Eden son of Joah; H2366

ZIMRAN (2)

Ge 25: 2 She bore him **Z**, Jokshan, Medan, Midian H2383
1Ch 1:32 **Z**, Jokshan, Medan, Midian, Ishbak and H2383

ZIMRI (17) [ZIMRI'S]

Nu 25:14 the Midianite woman was **Z** son of Salu, H2381
Jos 7: 1 of Karmi, the son of **Z**, the son of Zerah, H2381
Jos 7:17 forward by families, and **Z** was chosen. H2381
Jos 7:18 of Karmi, the son of **Z**, the son of Zerah, H2381
1Ki 16: 9 **Z**, one of his officials, who had command H2381
1Ki 16:10 **Z** came in, struck him down and killed him H2381
1Ki 16:12 So **Z** destroyed the whole family of Baasha H2381
1Ki 16:15 of Judah, **Z** reigned in Tirzah seven days. H2381
1Ki 16:16 camp heard that **Z** had plotted against H2381
1Ki 16:18 When **Z** saw that the city was taken, he H2381
2Ki 9:31 come in peace, you **Z**, you murderer of H2381
1Ch 2: 6 **Z**, Ethan, Heman, Kalkol and Darda—five H2381
1Ch 8:36 Azmaveth and **Z**, and Zimri was the H2381
1Ch 8:36 Zimri, and **Z** was the father of Moza. H2381
1Ch 9:42 Azmaveth and **Z**, and Zimri was the H2381
1Ch 9:42 Zimri, and **Z** was the father of Moza. H2381
Jer 25:25 all the kings of **Z**, Elam and Media; H2382

ZIMRI'S (1) [ZIMRI]

1Ki 16:20 As for the other events of **Z** reign, and the H2381

ZIN (10)

Nu 13:21 land from the Desert of **Z** as far as Rehob, H7554
Nu 20: 1 community arrived at the Desert of **Z**, H7554
Nu 27:14 rebelled at the waters in the Desert of **Z**, H7554
Nu 27:14 of Meribah Kadesh, in the Desert of **Z**.) H7554
Nu 33:36 camped at Kadesh, in the Desert of **Z**. H7554
Nu 34: 3 of the Desert of **Z** along the border of H7554
Nu 34: 4 continue on to **Z** and go south of Kadesh H7554
Dt 32:51 in the Desert of **Z** and because you did H7554
Jos 15: 1 to the Desert of **Z** in the extreme south. H7554
Jos 15: 3 continued on to **Z** and went over to the H7554

ZION (163) [ZION'S]

2Sa 5: 7 David captured the fortress of **Z**—which is H7482
1Ki 8: 1 up the ark of the LORD's covenant from **Z**, H7482
2Ki 19:21 " 'Virgin Daughter **Z** despises you and H7482
2Ki 19:31 out of Mount **Z** a band of survivors. H7482
1Ch 11: 5 David captured the fortress of **Z**—which is H7482
2Ch 5: 2 up the ark of the LORD's covenant from **Z**, H7482
Ps 2: 6 "I have installed my king on **Z**, my holy H7482
Ps 9:11 enthroned in **Z**; proclaim among the H7482
Ps 9:14 your praises in the gates of Daughter **Z**, H7482
Ps 14: 7 salvation for Israel would come out of **Z**! H7482
Ps 20: 2 sanctuary and grant you support from **Z**. H7482
Ps 48: 2 like the heights of Zaphon is Mount **Z**, the H7482
Ps 48:11 Mount **Z** rejoices, the villages of Judah H7482
Ps 48:12 Walk about **Z**, go around her, count her H7482
Ps 50: 2 From **Z**, perfect in beauty, God shines H7482
Ps 51:18 May it please you to prosper **Z**, to build H7482
Ps 53: 6 salvation for Israel would come out of **Z**! H7482
Ps 65: 1 our God, in **Z**; to you our vows will be H7482
Ps 69:35 God will save **Z** and rebuild the cities H7482
Ps 74: 2 redeemed—Mount **Z**, where you dwelt. H7482
Ps 76: 2 tent is in Salem, his dwelling place in **Z**. H7482
Ps 78:68 tribe of Judah, Mount **Z**, which he loved. H7482
Ps 84: 7 till each appears before God in **Z**. H7482
Ps 87: 2 loves the gates of **Z** more than all the H7482
Ps 87: 4 and will say, 'This one was born **in Z**. H9004S
Ps 87: 5 Indeed, of **Z** it will be said, "This one H7482
Ps 87: 6 "This one was born **in Z**." H9004S
Ps 97: 8 **Z** hears and rejoices and the villages of H7482
Ps 99: 2 Great is the LORD in **Z**; he is exalted over H7482
Ps 102:13 You will arise and have compassion on **Z** H7482
Ps 102:16 the LORD will rebuild **Z** and appear in his H7482
Ps 102:21 will be declared in **Z** and his praise in H7482
Ps 110: 2 will extend your mighty scepter from **Z**, H7482
Ps 125: 1 who trust in the LORD are like Mount **Z**, H7482
Ps 126: 1 When the LORD restored the fortunes of **Z** H7482
Ps 128: 5 May the LORD bless you from **Z**; may you H7482
Ps 129: 5 May all who hate **Z** be turned back in H7482
Ps 132:13 For the LORD has chosen **Z**, he has desired H7482
Ps 133: 3 dew of Hermon were falling on Mount **Z**. H7482
Ps 134: 3 May the LORD bless you from **Z**, he who is H7482
Ps 135:21 Praise be to the LORD from **Z**, to him who H7482
Ps 137: 1 we sat and wept when we remembered **Z**. H7482
Ps 137: 3 they said, "Sing us one of the songs of **Z**!" H7482
Ps 146:10 your God, O **Z**, for all generations. H7482
Ps 147:12 the LORD, Jerusalem; praise your God, **Z**. H7482
Ps 149: 2 let the people of **Z** be glad in their King. H7482
SS 3:11 you daughters of **Z**. Look on King H7482
Isa 1: 8 Daughter **Z** is left like a shelter in a H7482
Isa 1:27 **Z** will be delivered with justice, her H7482
Isa 2: 3 The law will go out from **Z**, the word of H7482
Isa 3:16 "The women of **Z** are haughty H7482
Isa 3:17 sores on the heads of the women of **Z**; H7482
Isa 3:26 The gates of **Z** will lament and mourn H2023S
Isa 4: 3 Those who are left in **Z**, who remain in H7482
Isa 4: 4 wash away the filth of the women of **Z**; H7482
Isa 4: 5 over all of Mount **Z** and over those who H7482
Isa 8:18 LORD Almighty, who dwells on Mount **Z**. H7482
Isa 10:12 his work against Mount **Z** and Jerusalem, H7482
Isa 10:24 "My people who live in **Z**, do not be H7482
Isa 10:32 their fist at the mount of Daughter **Z**, H7482
Isa 12: 6 joy, people of **Z**, for great is the Holy H7482
Isa 14:32 "The LORD has established **Z**, and in her H7482
Isa 16: 1 the desert, to the mount of Daughter **Z**. H7482
Isa 18: 7 the gifts will be brought to Mount **Z**, the H7482
Isa 24:23 will reign on Mount **Z** and in Jerusalem, H7482
Isa 28:16 I lay a stone in **Z**, a tested stone, H7482
Isa 29: 8 all the nations that fight against Mount **Z**. H7482
Isa 30:19 People of **Z**, who live in Jerusalem, you H7482
Isa 31: 4 do battle on Mount **Z** and on its heights. H7482
Isa 31: 9 whose fire is in **Z**, whose furnace is in H7482
Isa 33: 5 he will fill **Z** with his justice and H7482
Isa 33:14 The sinners in **Z** are terrified; trembling H7482
Isa 33:20 Look on **Z**, the city of our festivals; your H7482
Isa 33:24 No one living in **Z** will say, "I am ill"; and NDT
Isa 35:10 They will enter **Z** with singing; everlasting H7482
Isa 37:22 "Virgin Daughter **Z** despises and mocks H7482
Isa 37:32 out of Mount **Z** a band of survivors. H7482
Isa 40: 9 You who bring good news to **Z**, go up on H7482
Isa 41:27 I was the first to tell **Z**, 'Look, here they H7482
Isa 46:13 I will grant salvation to **Z**, my splendor to H7482
Isa 49:14 But **Z** said, "The LORD has forsaken me H7482
Isa 51: 3 will surely comfort **Z** and will look with H7482
Isa 51:11 They will enter **Z** with singing; everlasting H7482
Isa 51:16 who say to **Z**, 'You are my people. H7482
Isa 52: 1 awake, **Z**, clothe yourself with H7482
Isa 52: 2 on your neck, Daughter **Z**, now a captive. H7482
Isa 52: 7 salvation, who say to **Z**, "Your God reigns!" H7482
Isa 52: 8 When the LORD returns to **Z**, they will see H7482
Isa 59:20 "The Redeemer will come to **Z**, to those H7482
Isa 60:14 of the LORD, **Z** *of* the Holy One of Israel. H7482
Isa 61: 3 provide for those who grieve in **Z**—to H7482
Isa 62:11 "Say to Daughter **Z**, 'See, your Savior H7482
Isa 64:10 a wasteland; even **Z** is a wasteland H7482
Isa 66: 8 Yet no sooner is **Z** in labor than she gives H7482
Jer 3:14 two from a clan—and bring you to **Z**. H7482
Jer 4: 6 Raise the signal to go to **Z**! Flee for safety H7482
Jer 4:31 the cry of Daughter **Z** gasping for breath H7482
Jer 6: 2 I will destroy Daughter **Z**, so beautiful H7482
Jer 6:23 formation to attack you, Daughter **Z**." H7482
Jer 8:19 "Is the LORD not in **Z**? Is her King no H7482
Jer 9:19 The sound of wailing is heard from **Z** H7482
Jer 14:19 Do you despise **Z**? Why have you afflicted H7482
Jer 26:18 " '**Z** will be plowed like a field, Jerusalem H7482
Jer 30:17 an outcast, **Z** for whom no one cares. H7482
Jer 31: 6 let us go up to **Z**, to the LORD our God. H7482
Jer 31:12 shout for joy on the heights of **Z**; H7482
Jer 50: 5 will ask the way to **Z** and turn their faces H7482
Jer 50:28 declaring in **Z** how the LORD our God H7482
Jer 51:10 let us tell in **Z** what the LORD our God has H7482
Jer 51:24 all the wrong they have done in **Z**, H7482
Jer 51:35 be on Babylon," say the inhabitants of **Z**. H7482
La 1: 4 The roads to **Z** mourn, for no one comes H7482
La 1: 6 splendor has departed from Daughter **Z**. H7482
La 1:17 **Z** stretches out her hands, but there is no H7482
La 2: 1 has covered Daughter **Z** with the cloud of H7482
La 2: 4 wrath like fire on the tent of Daughter **Z**. H7482
La 2: 6 The LORD has made **Z** forget her H7482
La 2: 8 to tear down the wall around Daughter **Z**. H7482
La 2:10 elders of Daughter **Z** sit on the ground in H7482
La 2:13 that I may comfort you, Virgin Daughter **Z**? H7482
La 2:18 You walls of Daughter **Z**, let your tears H7482
La 4: 2 How the precious children of **Z**, once H7482
La 4:11 He kindled a fire in **Z** that consumed her H7482
La 4:22 will end, Daughter **Z**; he will not prolong H7482
La 5:11 Women have been violated in **Z**, and H7482
La 5:18 Mount **Z**, which lies desolate, with H7482
Joel 2: 1 Blow the trumpet in **Z**; sound the alarm H7482
Joel 2:15 Blow the trumpet in **Z**, declare a holy fast H7482
Joel 2:23 Be glad, people of **Z**, rejoice in the LORD H7482
Joel 2:32 on Mount **Z** and in Jerusalem there H7482
Joel 3:16 LORD will roar from **Z** and thunder from H7482
Joel 3:17 LORD your God, dwell in **Z**, my holy hill. H7482
Joel 3:21 I will not." The LORD dwells in **Z**! H7482
Am 1: 2 "The LORD roars from **Z** and thunders from H7482
Am 6: 1 Woe to you who are complacent in **Z**, and H7482
Ob 17 But on Mount **Z** will be deliverance; it will H7482
Ob 21 will go up on Mount **Z** to govern the H7482
Mic 1:13 are where the sin of Daughter **Z** began, H7482
Mic 3:10 who build **Z** with bloodshed, and H7482
Mic 3:12 **Z** will be plowed like a field H7482
Mic 4: 2 The law will go out from **Z**, the word of H7482
Mic 4: 7 over them in Mount **Z** from that day and H7482
Mic 4: 8 stronghold of Daughter **Z**, the former H7482
Mic 4:10 in agony, Daughter **Z**, like a woman in H7482
Mic 4:11 her be defiled, let our eyes gloat over **Z**!" H7482
Mic 4:13 thresh, Daughter **Z**, for I will give you H7482
Zep 3:14 Daughter **Z**; shout aloud, Israel! Be H7482
Zep 3:16 "Do not fear, **Z**; do not let your hands H7482
Zec 1:14 'I am very jealous for Jerusalem and **Z**, H7482
Zec 1:17 will again comfort **Z** and choose H7482
Zec 2: 7 **Z**! Escape, you who live in H7482
Zec 2:10 be glad, Daughter **Z**. For I am coming, H7482
Zec 8: 2 "I am very jealous for **Z**; I am burning with H7482
Zec 8: 3 "I will return to **Z** and dwell in Jerusalem H7482
Zec 9: 9 Daughter **Z**! Shout, Daughter H7482
Zec 9:13 will rouse your sons, **Z**, against your sons, H7482
Mt 21: 5 "Say to Daughter **Z**, 'See, your king comes *G4994*
Jn 12:15 be afraid, Daughter **Z**; see, your king is *G4994*
Ro 9:33 I lay in **Z** a stone that causes people to *G4994*
Ro 11:26 "The deliverer will come from **Z**; he will *G4994*

Z

Heb 12:22 But you have come to Mount **Z**, to the city *G4994*
1Pe 2: 6 I lay a stone in **Z**, a chosen and precious *G4994*
Rev 14: 1 standing on Mount **Z**, and with him *G4994*

ZION'S (2) [ZION]
Isa 34: 8 a year of retribution, to uphold **Z** cause. H7482
Isa 62: 1 For **Z** sake I will not keep silent, for H7482

ZIOR (1)
Jos 15:54 Hebron) and **Z**—nine towns and their H7486

ZIPH (9) [ZIPHITES]
Jos 15:24 **Z**, Telem, Bealoth, H2334
Jos 15:55 Carmel, **Z**, Juttah, H2334
1Sa 23:14 in the hills of the Desert of **Z**. H2334
1Sa 23:15 David was at Horesh in the Desert of **Z**, H2334
1Sa 23:24 they set out and went to **Z** ahead of Saul. H2334
1Sa 26: 2 So Saul went down to the Desert of **Z** H2334
1Ch 2:42 who was the father of **Z**, and his son H2335
1Ch 4:16 sons of Jehallelel: **Z**, Ziphah, Tiria and H2335
2Ch 11: 8 Mareshah, **Z**, H2334

ZIPHAH (1)
1Ch 4:16 Ziph, **Z**, Tiria and Asarel. H2336

ZIPHITES (3) [ZIPH]
1Sa 23:19 The **Z** went up to Saul at Gibeah and said H2337
1Sa 26: 1 The **Z** went to Saul at Gibeah and said H2337
Ps 54: T When the **Z** had gone to Saul and said H2337

ZIPHRON (1)
Nu 34: 9 continue to **Z** and end at Hazar Enan. H2412

ZIPPOR (7)
Nu 22: 2 Now Balak son of **Z** saw all that Israel had H7607
Nu 22: 4 So Balak son of **Z**, who was king of Moab H7607
Nu 22:10 "Balak son of **Z**, king of Moab, H7607
Nu 22:16 "This is what Balak son of **Z** says: Do not H7607
Nu 23:18 and listen; hear me, son of **Z**. H7607
Jos 24: 9 When Balak son of **Z**, the king of Moab H7607
Jdg 11:25 Are you any better than Balak son of **Z** H7607

ZIPPORAH (4)
Ex 2:21 gave his daughter **Z** to Moses in marriage H7631
Ex 2:22 **Z** gave birth to a son, and Moses named him NDT
Ex 4:25 But **Z** took a flint knife, cut off her son's H7631
Ex 18: 2 After Moses had sent away his wife **Z**, his H7631

ZITHER (4)
Da 3: 5 the sound of the horn, flute, **z**, lyre, harp, A10630
Da 3: 7 of the horn, flute, **z**, lyre, harp and all A10630
Da 3:10 the sound of the horn, flute, **z**, lyre, harp, A10630
Da 3:15 the sound of the horn, flute, **z**, lyre, harp, A10630

ZIV (2)
1Ki 6: 1 in the month of **Z**, the second month, H2304
1Ki 6:37 laid in the fourth year, in the month of **Z**. H2304

ZIZ (1)
2Ch 20:16 They will be climbing up by the Pass of **Z** H7489

ZIZA (4)
1Ch 4:37 **Z** son of Shiphi, the son of Allon, the H2330
1Ch 23:10 Jahath, **Z**, Jeush and Beriah H2330
1Ch 23:11 Jahath was the first and **Z** the second, but H2331
2Ch 11:20 bore him Abijah, Attai, **Z** and Shelomith. H2330

ZOAN (7)
Nu 13:22 been built seven years before **Z** *in* Egypt.) H7586
Ps 78:12 in the land of Egypt, in the region of **Z**. H7586
Ps 78:43 in Egypt, his wonders in the region of **Z**. H7586
Isa 19:11 The officials of **Z** are nothing but fools H7586
Isa 19:13 The officials of **Z** have become fools, the H7586
Isa 30: 4 have officials in **Z** and their envoys have H7586
Eze 30:14 set fire to **Z** and inflict punishment on H7586

ZOAR (10) [BELA]
Ge 13:10 of the Jordan toward **Z** was well watered, H7593
Ge 14: 2 Zeboyim, and the king of Bela (that is, **Z**). H7593
Ge 14: 8 **Z**) marched out and drew up their H7593
Ge 19:22 That is why the town was called **Z**.) H7593
Ge 19:23 By the time Lot reached **Z**, the sun had H7593
Ge 19:30 his two daughters left **Z** and settled in the H7593
Ge 19:30 mountains, for he was afraid to stay in **Z**. H7593
Dt 34: 3 of Jericho, the City of Palms, as far as **Z**. H7593
Isa 15: 5 her fugitives flee as far as **Z**, as far as H7593
Jer 48:34 from **Z** as far as Horonaim and Eglath H7593

ZOBAH (12) [ARAM ZOBAH, HAMATH ZOBAH, ZOBAH'S]
1Sa 14:47 the kings of **Z**, and the Philistines. H7420
2Sa 8: 3 son of Rehob, king of **Z**, when he went to H7420
2Sa 8: 5 came to help Hadadezer king of **Z**, H7420
2Sa 8:12 from Hadadezer son of Rehob, king of **Z**. H7420
2Sa 10: 6 foot soldiers from Beth Rehob and **Z**, H7419
2Sa 10: 8 the Arameans of **Z** and Rehob and the H7419
2Sa 23:36 Igal son of Nathan from **Z**, the son of H7420
1Ki 11:23 fled from his master, Hadadezer king of **Z**. H7420
1Ch 18: 3 David defeated Hadadezer king of **Z**, in H7420
1Ch 18: 5 came to help Hadadezer king of **Z**, H7420
1Ch 18: 9 the entire army of Hadadezer king of **Z**, H7420
1Ch 19: 6 Aram Naharaim, Aram Maakah and **Z**. H7420

ZOBAH'S (1) [ZOBAH]
1Ki 11:24 When David destroyed **Z** army, Rezon NDT

ZOHAR (5)
Ge 23: 8 with Ephron son of **Z** on my behalf H7468
Ge 25: 9 in the field of Ephron son of **Z** the Hittite, H7468
Ge 46:10 **Z** and Shaul the son of a Canaanite H7468
Ex 6:15 **Z** and Shaul the son of a Canaanite H7468
1Ch 4: 7 The sons of Helah: Zereth, **Z**, Ethnan, H7468

ZOHELETH (1)
1Ki 1: 9 calves at the Stone of **Z** near En Rogel. H2325

ZOHETH (1)
1Ch 4:20 descendants of Ishi: **Z** and Ben-Zoheth. H2311

ZOPHAH (2)
1Ch 7:35 his brother Helem: **Z**, Imna, Shelesh and H7432
1Ch 7:36 The sons of **Z**: Suah, Harnepher, Shual H7432

ZOPHAI (1)
1Ch 6:26 Elkanah his son, **Z** his son, Nahath his H7433

ZOPHAR (4)
Job 2:11 Bildad the Shuhite and **Z** the Naamathite H7436
Job 11: 1 Then **Z** the Naamathite replied: H7436
Job 20: 1 Then **Z** the Naamathite replied: H7436
Job 42: 9 the Shuhite and **Z** the Naamathite did H7436

ZOPHIM (1)
Nu 23:14 him to the field of **Z** on the top of Pisgah, H7614

ZORAH (10)
Jos 15:33 the western foothills: Eshtaol, **Z**, Ashnah, H7666
Jos 19:41 **Z**, Eshtaol, Ir Shemesh H7666
Jdg 13: 2 A certain man of **Z**, named Manoah, from H7666
Jdg 13:25 in Mahaneh Dan, between **Z** and Eshtaol. H7666
Jdg 16:31 buried him between **Z** and Eshtaol in the H7666
Jdg 18: 2 leading men from **Z** and Eshtaol to spy H7666
Jdg 18: 8 When they returned to **Z** and Eshtaol H7666
Jdg 18:11 battle, set out from **Z** and Eshtaol. H7666
2Ch 11:10 **Z**, Aijalon and Hebron. These were H7666
Ne 11:29 in En Rimmon, in **Z**, in Jarmuth, H7666

ZORATHITES (2)
1Ch 2:53 these descended the **Z** and Eshtaolites. H7670
1Ch 4: 2 These were the clans of the **Z**. H7670

ZORITES (1)
1Ch 2:54 Beth Joab, half the Manahathites, the **Z**, H7668

ZOROBABEL (KJV) ZERUBBABEL

ZUAR (5)
Nu 1: 8 from Issachar, Nethanel son of **Z**; H7428
Nu 2: 5 people of Issachar is Nethanel son of **Z**. H7428
Nu 7:18 On the second day Nethanel son of **Z**, the H7428
Nu 7:23 was the offering of Nethanel son of **Z**. H7428
Nu 10:15 Nethanel son of **Z** was over the division of H7428

ZUPH (3) [ZUPHITE]
1Sa 1: 1 son of Tohu, the son of **Z**, an Ephraimite. H7431
1Sa 9: 5 When they reached the district of **Z**, Saul H7431
1Ch 6:35 the son of **Z**, the son of Elkanah, the son H7431

ZUPHITE (1) [ZUPH]
1Sa 1: 1 a **Z** from the hill country of Ephraim H7434

ZUR (5) [BETH ZUR]
Nu 25:15 was put to death was Kozbi daughter of **Z**, H7448
Nu 31: 8 were Evi, Rekem, **Z**, Hur and Reba—the H7448
Jos 13:21 Rekem, **Z**, Hur and Reba—princes H7448
1Ch 8:30 son was Abdon, followed by **Z**, Kish, H7448
1Ch 9:36 son was Abdon, followed by **Z**, Kish, H7448

ZURIEL (1)
Nu 3:35 the Merarite clans was **Z** son of Abihail; H7452

ZURISHADDAI (5)
Nu 1: 6 from Simeon, Shelumiel son of **Z**; H7453
Nu 2:12 people of Simeon is Shelumiel son of **Z**. H7453
Nu 7:36 On the fifth day Shelumiel son of **Z**, the H7453
Nu 7:41 was the offering of Shelumiel son of **Z**. H7453
Nu 10:19 Shelumiel son of **Z** was over the division H7453

ZUZITES (1)
Ge 14: 5 Karnaim, the **Z** in Ham, the Emites in H2309

NUMERALS

12 (24) [TWELVE]
1Ch 25: 9 sons and relatives **12** the second to H9109+6925
1Ch 25: 9 him and his relatives and sons **12** H9109+6925
1Ch 25:10 to Zakkur, his sons and relatives **12** H9109+6925
1Ch 25:11 his sons and relatives **12** H9109+6925
1Ch 25:12 his sons and relatives **12** H9109+6925
1Ch 25:13 Bukkiah, his sons and relatives **12** H9109+6925
1Ch 25:14 his sons and relatives **12** H9109+6925
1Ch 25:15 Jeshaiah, his sons and relatives **12** H9109+6925
1Ch 25:16 his sons and relatives **12** H9109+6925
1Ch 25:17 Shimei, his sons and relatives **12** H9109+6925
1Ch 25:18 to Azarel, his sons and relatives **12** H9109+6925
1Ch 25:19 his sons and relatives **12** H9109+6925
1Ch 25:20 Shubael, his sons and relatives **12** H9109+6925
1Ch 25:21 his sons and relatives **12** H9109+6925
1Ch 25:22 Jerimoth, his sons and relatives **12** H9109+6925
1Ch 25:23 his sons and relatives **12** H9109+6925
1Ch 25:24 his sons and relatives **12** H9109+6925
1Ch 25:25 Hanani, his sons and relatives **12** H9109+6925
1Ch 25:26 Mallothi, his sons and relatives **12** H9109+6925
1Ch 25:27 Eliathah, his sons and relatives **12** H9109+6925
1Ch 25:28 to Hothir, his sons and relatives **12** H9109+6925
1Ch 25:29 Giddalti, his sons and relatives **12** H9109+6925
1Ch 25:30 his sons and relatives **12** H9109+6925
1Ch 25:31 his sons and relatives **12**. H9109+6925

13 (1) [THIRTEEN]
1Ch 26:11 relatives of Hosah were **13** in all. H8993+6925

18 (2) [EIGHTEEN]
1Ch 26: 9 who were able men—**18** in all. H9046+6925
Ezr 8:18 sons and brothers, **18** in all; H9046+6925

20 (2) [TWENTY]
Ezr 8:19 his brothers and nephews, **20** *in all*. H6929
Ezr 8:27 **20** bowls of gold valued at 1,000 darics H6929

22 (1) [TWENTY-TWO]
1Ch 12:28 with **22** officers from his H6929+2256+9109

28 (1) [TWENTY-EIGHT]
Ezr 8:11 and with him **28** men; H6929+2256+9046

29 (3) [TWENTY-NINE]
Ge 11:24 Nahor had lived **29** years, H9596+2256+6929
Ex 38:24 was **29** talents and H9596+2256+6929
Ezr 1: 9 dishes 1,000 silver pans **29** H9596+2256+6929

30 (5) [THIRTY]
Ge 11:14 When Shelah had lived **30** years, he H8993
Ge 11:18 When Peleg had lived **30** years, he H8993
Ge 11:22 When Serug had lived **30** years, he H8993
Ezr 1: 9 gold dishes **30** silver dishes 1,000 silver H8993
Ezr 1:10 gold bowls **30** matching silver bowls 410 H8993

32 (3) [THIRTY-TWO]
Ge 11:20 Reu had lived **32** years, H9109+2256+8993
Nu 31:40 tribute for the LORD was **32**. H9109+2256+8993
1Ki 20:16 and the **32** kings allied with H8993+2256+9109

34 (1)
Ge 11:16 Eber had lived **34** years, H752+2256+8993

35 (1) [THIRTY-FIVE]
Ge 11:12 had lived **35** years, H2822+2256+8993

40 (1) [FORTY]
Eze 4: 6 I have assigned you **40** days, a day for H752

42 (3) [FORTY-TWO]
Ezr 2:24 of Azmaveth **42** H752+2256+9109
Ne 7:28 of Beth Azmaveth **42** H752+2256+9109
Rev 11: 2 the holy city for **42** months. *G5477+2779+1545*

50 (3) [FIFTY]
Ezr 8: 6 son of Jonathan, and with him **50** men; H2822
Ne 7:70 **50** bowls and 530 garments for priests. H2822
Eze 45: 2 with **50** cubits around it for open land. H2822

52 (2) [FIFTY-TWO]
Ezr 2:29 of Nebo **52** H2822+2256+9109
Ne 7:33 of the other Nebo **52** H2822+2256+9109

56 (1)
Ezr 2:22 of Netophah **56** H2822+2256+9252

60 (1) [SIXTY]
Ezr 8:13 Shemaiah, and with them **60** men; H9252

61 (1)
Nu 31:39 tribute for the LORD was **61**; H285+2256+9252

62 (1) [SIXTY-TWO]
1Ch 26: 8 of Obed-Edom, **62** in all. H9252+2256+9109

65 (2) [SIXTY-FIVE]
Ge 5:15 had lived **65** years, H2822+2256+9252
Ge 5:21 Enoch had lived **65** years, H2822+2256+9252

67 (1)
Ne 7:72 of silver and **67** garments H9252+2256+8679

70 (5) [SEVENTY]
Ge 5:12 When Kenan had lived **70** years, he H8679
Ge 11:26 After Terah had lived **70** years, he H8679
Ex 38:29 wave offering was **70** talents and 2,400 H8679
Ezr 8: 7 son of Athaliah, and with him **70** men; H8679
Ezr 8:14 Uthai and Zakkur, and with them **70** men. H8679

72 (1) [SEVENTY-TWO]
Nu 31:38 tribute for the LORD was **72**; H9109+2256+8679

74 (2)
Ezr 2:40 of the line of Hodaviah) **74** H8679+2256+752
Ne 7:43 the line of Hodaviah) **74** H8679+2256+752

80 (2) [EIGHTY]
1Ch 15: 9 Hebron, Eliel the leader and **80** relatives; H9046
Ezr 8: 8 son of Michael, and with him **80** men; H9046

90 (1) [NINETY]
Ge 5: 9 When Enosh had lived **90** years, he H9596

95 (2)
Ezr 2:20 of Gibbar **95** H9596+2256+2822
Ne 7:25 of Gibeon **95** H9596+2256+2822

98 (2) [NINETY-EIGHT]
Ezr 2:16 Ater (through Hezekiah) **98** H9596+2256+9046
Ne 7:21 Ater (through Hezekiah) **98** H9596+2256+9046

100 (8) [HUNDRED]
Ge 11:10 when Shem was **100** years old, he H4395
Ex 38:25 in the census was **100** talents and 1,775 H4395
Ex 38:27 The **100** talents of silver were used to cast H4395
Ex 38:27 curtain—**100** bases from the 100 talents H4395
Ex 38:27 100 bases from the **100** talents, one talent H4395
Ezr 2:69 minas of silver and **100** priestly garments. H4395
Ezr 8:26 silver articles weighing **100** talents, 100 H4395
Ezr 8:26 100 talents, **100** talents of gold, H4395

105 (1)
Ge 5: 6 Seth had lived **105** years, H2822+2256+4395

110 (1)
Ezr 8:12 and with him **110** men; H4395+2256+6927

112 (3)
1Ch 15:10 and **112** relatives. H4395+2256+9109+6925
Ezr 2:18 of Jorah **112** H4395+2256+9109+6925
Ne 7:24 of Hariph **112** H4395+9109+6925

119 (1)
Ge 11:25 lived **119** years and H9596+6926+2256+4395

120 (6)
1Ki 9:14 to the king **120** talents of H4395+2256+6929
1Ki 10:10 gave the king **120** talents of H4395+2256+6929
1Ch 15: 5 leader and **120** relatives; H4395+2256+6929
2Ch 5:12 accompanied by **120** priests H4395+2256+6929
2Ch 9: 9 gave the king **120** talents of H4395+2256+6929
Da 6: 1 appoint **120** satraps to H10395+10221+10574

122 (2)
Ezr 2:27 of Mikmash **122** H4395+6929+2256+9109
Ne 7:31 of Mikmash **122** H4395+2256+6929+2256+9109

123 (2)
Ezr 2:21 men of Bethlehem **123** H4395+6929+2256+8993
Ne 7:32 of Bethel and Ai **123** H4395+6929+2256+8993

127 (3)
Est 1: 1 ruled over **127** provinces H8679+2256+6929+2256+4395
Est 8: 9 of the **127** provinces H8679+2256+6929+2256+4395
Est 9:30 in the **127** provinces H8679+2256+6929+2256+4395

128 (4)
Ezr 2:23 of Anathoth **128** H4395+6929+2256+9046
Ezr 2:41 of Asaph **128** H4395+6929+2256+9046
Ne 7:27 of Anathoth **128** H4395+6929+2256+9046
Ne 11:14 men of standing—**128**. H4395+6929+2256+9046

130 (2)
Ge 5: 3 Adam had lived **130** years, H8993,+2256+4395
1Ch 15: 7 leader and **130** relatives; H4395+2256+8993

133 (1)
Ex 6:18 Kohath lived **133** years. H8993+2256+8993+2256+4395

137 (2)
Ex 6:16 Levi lived **137** years. H8679+2256+8993+2256+4395
Ex 6:20 Amram lived **137** years. H8679+2256+8993+2256+4395

138 (1)
Ne 7:45 Hatita and Shobai **138** H4395+8993+2256+9046

139 (1)
Ezr 2:42 Hatita and Shobai **139** H4395+8993+2256+9596

144 (1)
Rev 21:17 and it was **144** cubits thick. *G1669+5477+5475*

148 (1)
Ne 7:44 of Asaph **148** H4395+752+2256+9046

150 (2)
1Ch 8:40 and grandsons—**150** in all. H4395+2256+2822
Ezr 8: 3 were registered **150** men; H4395+2256+2822

153 (1)
Jn 21:11 large fish, **153**, but even *G1669+4299+5552*

156 (1)
Ezr 2:30 of Magbish **156** H4395+2822+2256+9252

160 (1)
Ezr 8:10 and with him **160** men; H4395+2256+9252

162 (1)
Ge 5:18 had lived **162** years, H9109+2256+9252+2256+4395

172 (1)
Ne 11:19 at the gates—**172** men. H4395+8679+2256+9109

180 (1)
Est 1: 4 For a full **180** days he H9046+2256+4395

182 (1)
Ge 5:28 had lived **182** years, H9109+2256+9046+2256+4395

187 (1)
Ge 5:25 had lived **187** years, H8679+2256+9046+2256+4395

188 (1)
Ne 7:26 and Netophah **188** H4395+9046+2256+9046

200 (5)
Ge 11:23 Serug lived **200** years and had other sons H4395
1Ch 12:32 Israel should do—**200** chiefs, with all H4395
1Ch 15: 8 Shemaiah the leader and **200** relatives; H4395
Ezr 2:65 they also had **200** male and female H4395
Ezr 8: 4 son of Zerahiah, and with him **200** men; H4395

205 (1)
Ge 11:32 Terah lived **205** years, and H2822+2256+4395

207 (1)
Ge 11:21 Reu lived **207** years and had H8679+2256+4395

209 (1)
Ge 11:19 Peleg lived **209** years and H9596+2256+4395

212 (1)
1Ch 9:22 numbered **212**. H4395+2256+9109+6925

218 (1)
Ezr 8: 9 and with him **218** men; H4395+2256+9046+6925

220 (2)
1Ch 15: 6 leader and **220** relatives; H4395+2256+6929
Ezr 8:20 also brought **220** of the H4395+2256+6929

223 (2)
Ezr 2:19 of Hashum **223** H4395+6929+2256+8993
Ezr 2:28 of Bethel and Ai **223** H4395+6929+2256+8993

232 (1)
1Ki 20:15 the **232** junior H4395+9109+2256+8993

242 (1)
Ne 11:13 of families—**242** men H4395+752+2256+9109

245 (3)
Ezr 2:66 736 horses, **245** mules, H4395+752+2256+2822
Ne 7:67 also had **245** male and H4395+2256+752+2256+2822
Ne 7:68 736 horses, **245** mules, H4395+752+2256+2822

250 (10)
Ex 30:23 that is, **250** shekels) of H2822+2256+4395
Ex 30:23 **250** shekels of fragrant H2822+2256+4395
Nu 16: 2 them were **250** Israelite H2822+2256+4395
Nu 16:17 in it—**250** censers in all H2822+2256+4395
Nu 16:35 the **250** men who were H2822+2256+4395
Nu 26:10 fire devoured the **250** men. H2822+2256+4395
Eze 48:17 city will be **250** cubits on the H2822+2256+4395
Eze 48:17 **250** cubits on the south H2822+2256+4395
Eze 48:17 **250** cubits on the east H2822+2256+4395
Eze 48:17 and **250** cubits on the west. H2822+2256+4395

273 (1)
Nu 3:46 redeem the **273** firstborn H8993+2256+8679+2256+4395

276 (1)
Ac 27:37 there were **276** of us on *G1357+1573+1971*

284 (1)
Ne 11:18 the holy city totaled **284**. H4395+9046+2256+752

288 (1)
1Ch 25: 7 they numbered **288**. H4395+9046+2256+9046

300 (2)
Ge 5:22 with God **300** years and had other H8993+4395
Ezr 8: 5 Jahaziel, and with him **300** men; H8993+4395

318 (1)
Ge 14:14 out the **318** trained men H9046+6925+2256+8993+4395

320 (2)
Ezr 2:32 of Harim **320** H8993+4395+2256+6929
Ne 7:35 of Harim **320** H8993+4395+2256+6929

323 (1)
Ezr 2:17 of Bezai **323** H4395,+8993+6929+2256+8993

324 (1)
Ne 7:23 of Bezai **324** H8993+4395+6929+2256+752

328 (1)
Ne 7:22 of Hashum **328** H8993+4395+6929+2256+9046

345 (2)
Ezr 2:34 of Jericho **345** H8993+4395+752+2256+2822
Ne 7:36 of Jericho **345** H8993+4395+752+2256+2822

350 (1)
Ge 9:28 Noah lived **350** years. H8993+4395+2256+2822

365 (1)
Ge 5:23 a total of **365** years. H2822+2256+9252+2256+8993+4395

372 (2)
Ezr 2: 4 of Shephatiah **372** H8993+4395+8679+2256+9109
Ne 7: 9 of Shephatiah **372** H8993+4395+8679+2256+9109

390 (2)
Eze 4: 5 So for **390** days you will H8993+4395+2256+9596
Eze 4: 9 during the **390** days you H8993+4395+2256+9596

392 (2)
Ezr 2:58 of Solomon **392** H8993+4395+9596+2256+9109
Ne 7:60 of Solomon **392** H8993+4395+9596+2256+9109

403 (2)
Ge 11:13 lived **403** years and had H8993+2256+752+4395
Ge 11:15 lived **403** years and H8993+2256+752+4395

410 (1)
Ezr 1:10 silver bowls **410** other H752+4395+2256+6927

420 (1)
1Ki 9:28 back **420** talents of H752+4395+2256+6929

430 (4)
Ge 11:17 Eber lived **430** years and H8993+2256+752+4395
Ex 12:40 in Egypt was **430** years. H8993+2256+752+4395
Ex 12:41 end of the **430** years, H8993+2256+752+4395
Gal 3:17 introduced **430** years later *G5484+2779+5558*

435 (2)
Ezr 2:67 **435** camels and 6,720 H752+4395+8993+2256+2822
Ne 7:69 **435** camels and 6,720 H752+4395+8993+2256+2822

450 (1)
Ac 13:20 All this took about **450** years *G5484+2779+4299*

454 (1)
Ezr 2:15 of Adin **454** H752+4395+2822+2256+752

468 (1)
Ne 11: 6 totaled **468** men H752+4395+9252+2256+9046

500 (5)
Ge 5:32 After Noah was **500** years old, he H2822+4395
Ge 11:11 Shem lived **500** years and had H2822+4395
Ex 30:23 **500** shekels of liquid myrrh, half as H2822+4395
Ex 30:24 **500** shekels of cassia—all H2822+4395
Eze 45: 2 a section **500** cubits square is to be H2822+4395

530 (1)
Ne 7:70 bowls and **530** garments H2822+4395+2256+8993

550 (1)
1Ki 9:23 **550** officials supervising H2822+2256+2822+4395

595 (1)
Ge 5:30 lived **595** years and H2822+2256+9596+2256+2822+4395

621 (2)
Ezr 2:26 of Ramah and Geba **621** H9252+4395+6929+2256+285
Ne 7:30 of Ramah and Geba **621** H9252+4395+6929+2256+285

623 (1)
Ezr 2:11 of Bebai **623** H9252+4395+6929+2256+8993

628 (1)
Ne 7:16 of Bebai **628** H9252+4395+6929+2256+9046

642 (2)
Ezr 2:10 of Bani **642** H9252+4395+752+2256+9109
Ne 7:62 Tobiah and Nekoda **642** H9252+4395+2256+752+2256+9109

648 (1)
Ne 7:15 of Binnui **648** H9252+4395+752+2256+9046

650 (1)
Ezr 8:26 to them **650** talents of H9252+4395+2256+2822

652 (2)
Ezr 2:60 Tobiah and Nekoda **652** H9252+4395+2822+2256+9109
Ne 7:10 of Arah **652** H9252+4395+2822+2256+9109

655 (1)
Ne 7:20 of Adin **655** H9252+4395+2822+2256+2822

666 (4)
1Ki 10:14 yearly was **666** talents, H9252+4395+9252+2256+9252
2Ch 9:13 yearly was **666** talents, H9252+4395+2256+9252+2256+9252
Ezr 2:13 of Adonikam **666** H9252+4395+9252+2256+9252
Rev 13:18 That number is **666**. *G1980+2008+1971*

667 (1)
Ne 7:18 of Adonikam **667** H9252+4395+9252+2256+8679

675 (1)
Nu 31:37 for the LORD was **675**; H9252+4395+2822+2256+8679

690 (1)
1Ch 9:6 Judah numbered **690**. H9252+4395+2256+9596

721 (1)
Ne 7:37 Hadid and Ono **721** H8679+4395+2256+6929+2256+285

725 (1)
Ezr 2:33 Hadid and Ono **725** H8679+4395+6929+2256+2822

730 (1)
Ex 38:24 talents and **730** shekels, H8679+4395+2256+8993

736 (2)
Ezr 2:66 They had **736** horses H8679+4395+8993+2256+9252
Ne 7:68 There were **736** horses H8679+4395+8993+2256+9252

743 (2)
Ezr 2:25 and Beeroth **743** H8679+4395+2256+752+2256+8993
Ne 7:29 and Beeroth **743** H8679+4395+752+2256+8993

745 (1)
Jer 52:30 **745** Jews taken into exile H8679+4395+752+2256+2822

760 (2)
Ezr 2:9 of Zakkai **760** H8679+4395+2256+9252
Ne 7:14 of Zakkai **760** H8679+4395+2256+9252

775 (1)
Ezr 2:5 of Arah **775** H8679+4395+2822+2256+8679

777 (1)
Ge 5:31 a total of **777** years, H8679+2256+8679+2256+8679+4395

782 (1)
Ge 5:26 lived **782** years and had H9109+2256+9046+2256+8679+4395

800 (2)
Ge 5:4 Adam lived **800** years and had H9046+4395
Ge 5:19 Jared lived **800** years and had H9046+4395

807 (1)
Ge 5:7 Seth lived **807** years H8679+2256+9046+4395

815 (1)
Ge 5:10 lived **815** years and H2822+6926+2256+9046+4395

822 (1)
Ne 11:12 the temple—**822** men H9046+4395+6929+2256+9109

830 (1)
Ge 5:16 lived **830** years and had H8993+2256+9046+4395

832 (1)
Jer 52:29 **832** people from H9046+4395+8993+2256+9109

840 (1)
Ge 5:13 lived **840** years and H752+2256+9046+4395

845 (1)
Ne 7:13 of Zattu **845** H9046+4395+2256+2822+752

895 (1)
Ge 5:17 a total of **895** years, H2822+2256+9596+2256+9046+4395

905 (1)
Ge 5:11 a total of **905** years, H2822+2256+9596+4395

910 (1)
Ge 5:14 a total of **910** years, H6924+2256+9596+4395

912 (1)
Ge 5:8 a total of **912** years, H9109+6926+2256+9596+4395

928 (1)
Ne 11:8 and Sallai—**928** men. H9596+4395+6929+2256+9046

930 (1)
Ge 5:5 a total of **930** years, H9596+4395+2256+8993

945 (1)
Ezr 2:8 of Zattu **945** H9596+4395+2256+752+2256+2822

950 (1)
Ge 9:29 a total of **950** years, H9596+4395+2256+2822

956 (1)
1Ch 9:9 numbered **956**. H9596+4395+2256+2822+2256+9252

962 (1)
Ge 5:20 a total of **962** years, H9109+2256+9252+2256+9596+4395

969 (1)
Ge 5:27 a total of **969** years, H9596+2256+9252+2256+9596+4395

973 (2)
Ezr 2:36 family of Jeshua) **973** H9596+4395+8679+2256+8993
Ne 7:39 family of Jeshua) **973** H9596+4395+8679+2256+8993

1,000 (6) [THOUSAND]
1Ch 12:34 from Naphtali—**1,000** officers, together H547
2Ch 17:14 commanders of **units of 1,000**: Adnah the H547
Ezr 1:9 dishes 30 silver dishes **1,000** silver pans 29 H547
Ezr 1:10 silver bowls 410 other articles **1,000** H547
Ezr 8:27 20 bowls of gold valued at **1,000** darics H547
Ne 7:70 gave to the treasury **1,000** darics of gold, H547

1,017 (2)
Ezr 2:39 of Harim **1,017** H547+2256+8679+6925
Ne 7:42 of Harim **1,017** H547+8679+6925

1,052 (2)
Ezr 2:37 of Immer **1,052** H547+2822+2256+9109
Ne 7:40 of Immer **1,052** H547+2822+2256+9109

1,222 (1)
Ezr 2:12 of Azgad **1,222** H547+4395+6929+2256+9109

1,247 (2)
Ezr 2:38 of Pashhur **1,247** H547+4395+752+2256+8679
Ne 7:41 of Pashhur **1,247** H547+4395+752+2256+8679

1,254 (4)
Ezr 2:7 of Elam **1,254** H547+4395+2822+2256+752
Ezr 2:31 the other Elam **1,254** H547+4395+2256+752+2822
Ne 7:12 of Elam **1,254** H547+4395+2822+2256+752
Ne 7:34 the other Elam **1,254** H547+4395+2822+2256+752

1,260 (2)
Rev 11:3 will prophesy for **1,260** days, *G5943+1357+2008*
Rev 12:6 taken care of for **1,260** days. *G5943+1357+2008*

1,290 (1)
Da 12:11 there will be **1,290** days. H547+4395+2256+9596

1,335 (1)
Da 12:12 end of the **1,335** days. H547+8993+4395+8993+2256+2822

1,365 (1)
Nu 3:50 weighing **1,365** shekels H2822+2256+9252+2256+8993+4395+2256+547

1,600 (1)
Rev 14:20 a distance of **1,600** stadia. *G5943+1980*

1,760 (1)
1Ch 9:13 numbered **1,760**. H547+2256+8679+4395+2256+9252

1,775 (2)
Ex 38:25 and **1,775** shekels, H547+2256+8679+4395+2256+2822+2256+8679
Ex 38:28 used the **1,775** shekels H547+2256+8679+4395+2256+2822+2256+8679

2,000 (1)
Ne 7:72 **2,000** minas of silver and 67 garments H547

2,056 (1)
Ezr 2:14 of Bigvai **2,056** H547+2822+2256+9252

2,067 (1)
Ne 7:19 of Bigvai **2,067** H547+9252+2256+8679

2,172 (2)
Ezr 2:3 of Parosh **2,172** H547+4395+8679+2256+9109
Ne 7:8 of Parosh **2,172** H547+4395+2256+8679+2256+9109

2,200 (1)
Ne 7:71 of gold and **2,200** minas of H547+2256+4395

2,300 (1)
Da 8:14 will take **2,300** evenings H547+2256+8993+4395

2,322 (1)
Ne 7:17 of Azgad **2,322** H547+8993+4395+6929+2256+9109

2,400 (1)
Ex 38:29 and **2,400** shekels. H547+2256+752+4395

2,600 (1)
2Ch 26:12 fighting men was **2,600**. H547+2256+9252+4395

2,630 (1)
Nu 4:40 families, were **2,630**. H547+2256+9252+4395+2256+8993

2,750 (1)
Nu 4:36 by clans, were **2,750**. H547+8679+4395+2256+2822

2,812 (1)
Ezr 2:6 Jeshua and Joab) **2,812** H547+9046+4395+2256+9109+6925

2,818 (1)
Ne 7:11 Jeshua and Joab) **2,818** H547+2256+9046+4395+9046+6925

3,000 (1)
1Ch 12:29 Saul's tribe—**3,000**, most of whom H8993+547

3,023 (1)
Jer 52:28 **3,023** Jews; H8993+547+2256+6929+2256+8993

3,200 (1)
Nu 4:44 their clans, were **3,200**. H8993+547+2256+4395

3,600 (2)
2Ch 2:2 hills and **3,600** as H8993+547+2256+9252+4395
2Ch 2:18 with **3,600** foremen H8993+547+2256+9252+4395

3,630 (1)
Ezr 2:35 of Senaah **3,630** H8993+547+2256+9252+4395+2256+8993

3,700 (1)
1Ch 12:27 Aaron, with **3,700** men, H8993+547+2256+8679+4395

3,930 (1)
Ne 7:38 of Senaah **3,930** H8993+547+9596+4395+2256+8993

4,500 (8)
Eze 48:16 north side **4,500** cubits, H2822+4395+2256+752+547
Eze 48:16 south side **4,500** cubits, H2822+4395+2256+752+547
Eze 48:16 east side **4,500** cubits, H2822+4395+2256+752+547
Eze 48:16 west side **4,500** cubits. H2822+4395+2256+752+547
Eze 48:30 which is **4,500** cubits H2822+4395+2256+752+547
Eze 48:32 which is **4,500** cubits H2822+4395+2256+752+547
Eze 48:33 measures **4,500** cubits, H2822+4395+2256+752+547
Eze 48:34 which is **4,500** cubits H2822+4395+2256+752+547

4,600 (2)
1Ch 12:26 from Levi—**4,600**, H752+547+2256+9252+4395
Jer 52:30 were **4,600** people H752+547+2256+9252+4395

5,000 (3)
Ezr 2:69 **5,000** minas of silver and 100 H2822+547
Eze 45:6 an area **5,000** cubits wide and H2822+547
Eze 48:15 **5,000** cubits wide and 25,000 cubits H2822+547

5,400 (1)
Ezr 1:11 there were **5,400** articles H2822+547+2256+752+4395

6,200 (1)
Nu 3:34 counted was **6,200**. H9252+547+2256+4395

6,720 (2)
Ezr 2:67 and **6,720** donkeys. H9252+547+8679+4395+2256+6929
Ne 7:69 and **6,720** donkeys. H9252+547+8679+4395+2256+6929

6,800 (1)
1Ch 12:24 **6,800** armed for battle H9252+547+2256+9046+4395

7,000 (1)
1Ki 20:15 rest of the Israelites, **7,000** in all. H8679+547

7,100 (1)
1Ch 12:25 ready for battle—**7,100**; H8679+547+2256+4395

7,337 (2)
Ezr 2:65 their **7,337** male and H8679+547+8993+4395+8993+2256+8679

Ne 7:67 their **7,337** male and H8679+547+8993+4395+8993+2256+8679

7,500 (1)
Nu 3:22 counted was **7,500**. H8679+547+2256+2822+4395

8,580 (1)
Nu 4:48 numbered **8,580**. H9046+547+2256+2822+4395+2256+9046

8,600 (1)
Nu 3:28 old or more was **8,600**. H9046+547+2256+9252+4395

10,000 (9)
Eze 45: 3 cubits long and **10,000** cubits wide. H6930+547
Eze 45: 5 cubits long and **10,000** cubits wide H6930+547
Eze 48: 9 cubits long and **10,000** cubits wide. H6930+547
Eze 48:10 **10,000** cubits wide on the west side H6930+547
Eze 48:10 **10,000** cubits wide on the east side H6930+547
Eze 48:13 cubits long and **10,000** cubits wide. H6930+547
Eze 48:13 cubits and its width **10,000** cubits. H6930+547
Eze 48:18 will be **10,000** cubits on the east H6930+547
Eze 48:18 east side and **10,000** cubits on the H6930+547

12,000 (13)
Rev 7: 5 tribe of Judah **12,000** were sealed, *G1557+5942*
Rev 7: 5 from the tribe of Reuben **12,000** *G1557+5942*
Rev 7: 5 from the tribe of Gad **12,000**, *G1557+5942*
Rev 7: 6 from the tribe of Asher **12,000** *G1557+5942*
Rev 7: 6 from the tribe of Naphtali **12,000** *G1557+5942*
Rev 7: 6 from the tribe of Manasseh **12,000** *G1557+5942*
Rev 7: 7 from the tribe of Simeon **12,000** *G1557+5942*
Rev 7: 7 from the tribe of Levi **12,000**, from *G1557+5942*
Rev 7: 7 from the tribe of Issachar **12,000**, *G1557+5942*
Rev 7: 8 from the tribe of Zebulun **12,000** *G1557+5942*
Rev 7: 8 from the tribe of Joseph **12,000** *G1557+5942*
Rev 7: 8 from the tribe of Benjamin **12,000**. *G1557+5942*
Rev 21:16 found it to be **12,000** stadia in *G1557+5942*

14,700 (1)
Nu 16:49 But **14,700** people died H752+6925+547+2256+8679+4395

16,000 (2)
Nu 31:40 **16,000** people, of whom the H9252+6925+547
Nu 31:46 and **16,000** people. H9252+6925+547

16,750 (1)
Nu 31:52 weighed **16,750** shekels H9252+6925+547+8679+4395+2256+2822

17,200 (1)
1Ch 7:11 were **17,200** fighting men H8679+6925+547+2256+4395

18,000 (2)
1Ch 12:31 make David king—**18,000**; H9046+6925+547
Eze 48:35 around will be **18,000** cubits. H9046+6925+547

20,000 (3)
Ne 7:71 the work **20,000** darics of gold H9109+8052
Ne 7:72 people was **20,000** darics of gold H9109+8052
Eze 45: 1 cubits long and **20,000** cubits wide; H6929+547

20,200 (1)
1Ch 7: 9 and **20,200** fighting H6929+547+2256+4395

20,800 (1)
1Ch 12:30 in their own clans—**20,800**; H6929+547+2256+9046+4395

22,000 (1)
Nu 3:39 more, was **22,000**. H9109+2256+6929+547

22,034 (1)
1Ch 7: 7 listed **22,034** fighting men. H6929+2256+9109+547+2256+8993+2256+752

22,200 (1)
Nu 26:14 numbered were **22,200**. H9109+2256+6929+547+2256+4395

22,273 (1)
Nu 3:43 by name, was **22,273**. H9109+2256+6929+547+8993+2256+8679+2256+4395

22,600 (1)
1Ch 7: 2 numbered **22,600** H6929+2256+9109+547+2256+9252+4395

23,000 (1)
Nu 26:62 more numbered **23,000**. H8993+2256+6929+547

24,000 (14)
Nu 25: 9 numbered **24,000**. H752+2256+6929+547
1Ch 27: 1 of **24,000** men. H6929+2256+752+547
1Ch 27: 2 were **24,000** men in his H6929+2256+752+547
1Ch 27: 4 were **24,000** men in his H6929+2256+752+547
1Ch 27: 5 were **24,000** men in his H6929+2256+752+547
1Ch 27: 7 were **24,000** men in his H6929+2256+752+547
1Ch 27: 8 were **24,000** men in his H6929+2256+752+547
1Ch 27: 9 were **24,000** men in his H6929+2256+752+547
1Ch 27:10 were **24,000** men in his H6929+2256+752+547
1Ch 27:11 were **24,000** men in his H6929+2256+752+547
1Ch 27:12 were **24,000** men in his H6929+2256+752+547
1Ch 27:13 were **24,000** men in his H6929+2256+752+547
1Ch 27:14 were **24,000** men in his H6929+2256+752+547
1Ch 27:15 were **24,000** men in his H6929+2256+752+547

25,000 (14)
Eze 45: 1 **25,000** cubits long and H2822+2256+6929+547
Eze 45: 3 a section **25,000** cubits H2822+2256+6929+547
Eze 45: 5 An area **25,000** cubits H2822+2256+6929+547
Eze 45: 6 wide and **25,000** cubits H2822+2256+6929+547
Eze 48: 8 It will be **25,000** cubits H2822+2256+6929+547
Eze 48: 9 will be **25,000** cubits H2822+2256+6929+547
Eze 48:10 It will be **25,000** cubits H2822+2256+6929+547
Eze 48:10 side and **25,000** cubits H2822+2256+6929+547
Eze 48:13 allotment **25,000** cubits H2822+2256+6929+547
Eze 48:13 will be **25,000** cubits H2822+2256+6929+547
Eze 48:15 wide and **25,000** cubits H2822+2256+6929+547
Eze 48:20 **25,000** cubits on each H2822+2256+6929+547
Eze 48:21 from the **25,000** cubits H2822+2256+6929+547
Eze 48:21 from the **25,000** cubits H2822+2256+6929+547

25,100 (1)
Jdg 20:35 struck down **25,100** H6929+2256+2822+547+2256+4395

26,000 (1)
1Ch 7:40 genealogy, was **26,000**. H6929+2256+9252+547

28,600 (1)
1Ch 12:35 for battle—**28,600**; H6929+2256+9046+547+2256+9252+4395

30,500 (2)
Nu 31:39 **30,500** donkeys, H8993+547+2256+2822+4395
Nu 31:45 **30,500** donkeys H8993+547+2256+2822+4395

32,000 (1)
Nu 31:35 and **32,000** women who H9109+2256+8993+547

32,200 (2)
Nu 1:35 Manasseh was **32,200**. H9109+2256+8993+547+2256+4395
Nu 2:21 numbers **32,200**. H9109+2256+8993+547+2256+4395

32,500 (1)
Nu 26:37 numbered were **32,500**. H9109+2256+8993+547+2256+2822+4395

35,400 (2)
Nu 1:37 Benjamin was **35,400** H2822+2256+8993+547+2256+752+4395
Nu 2:23 numbers **35,400**. H2822+2256+8993+547+2256+752+4395

36,000 (3)
Nu 31:38 **36,000** cattle, of which H9252+2256+8993+547
Nu 31:44 **36,000** cattle, H9252+2256+8993+547
1Ch 7: 4 they had **36,000** men H8993+2256+9252+547

37,000 (1)
1Ch 12:34 with **37,000** men H8993+2256+8679+547

40,000 (1)
1Ch 12:36 soldiers prepared for battle—**40,000**; H752+547

40,500 (3)
Nu 1:33 of Ephraim was **40,500**. H752+547+2256+2822+4395
Nu 2:19 numbers **40,500**. H752+547+2256+2822+4395
Nu 26:18 numbered were **40,500**. H752+547+2256+2822+4395

41,500 (2)
Nu 1:41 of Asher was **41,500** H285+2256+752+547+2256+2822+4395
Nu 2:28 numbers **41,500** H285+2256+752+547+2256+2822+4395

42,360 (2)
Ezr 2:64 numbered **42,360**, H752+8052+547+8993+4395+9252
Ne 7:66 numbered **42,360**, H752+8052+547+8993+4395+2256+9252

43,730 (1)
Nu 26: 7 numbered were **43,730**. H8993+2256+752+547+2256+8679+4395+2256+8993

44,760 (1)
1Ch 5:18 had **44,760** men ready H752+2256+752+547+2256+8679+4395+2256+9252

45,400 (1)
Nu 26:50 numbered were **45,400**. H2822+2256+752+547+2256+752+4395

45,600 (1)
Nu 26:41 numbered were **45,600** H2822+2256+752+547+2256+9252+4395

45,650 (2)
Nu 1:25 tribe of Gad was **45,650**. H2822+2256+752+547+2256+9252+4395+2256+2822
Nu 2:15 numbers **45,650**. H2822+2256+752+547+2256+9252+4395+2256+2822

46,500 (2)
Nu 1:21 of Reuben was **46,500**. H9252+2256+752+547+2256+2822+4395
Nu 2:11 numbers **46,500**. H9252+2256+752+547+2256+2822+4395

50,000 (1)
1Ch 12:33 with undivided loyalty—**50,000**; H2822+547

52,700 (1)
Nu 26:34 numbered were **52,700**. H9109+2256+2822+547+2256+8679+4395

53,400 (3)
Nu 1:43 of Naphtali was **53,400**. H8993+2256+2822+547+2256+752+4395
Nu 2:30 numbers **53,400**. H8993+2256+2822+547+2256+752+4395
Nu 26:47 numbered were **53,400**. H8993+2256+2822+547+2256+752+4395

54,400 (2)
Nu 1:29 of Issachar was **54,400**. H752+2256+2822+547+2256+752+4395
Nu 2: 6 numbers **54,400**. H752+2256+2822+547+2256+752+4395

57,400 (2)
Nu 1:31 of Zebulun was **57,400**. H8679+2256+2822+547+2256+752+4395
Nu 2: 8 numbers **57,400**. H8679+2256+2822+547+2256+752+4395

59,300 (2)
Nu 1:23 of Simeon was **59,300**. H9596+2256+2822+547+2256+8993+4395
Nu 2:13 numbers **59,300**. H9596+2256+2822+547+2256+8993+4395

60,500 (1)
Nu 26:27 numbered were **60,500**. H9252+547+2256+2822+4395

61,000 (2)
Nu 31:34 **61,000** donkeys H285+2256+9252+547
Ezr 2:69 work **61,000** darics of H9252+8052+2256+547

62,700 (2)
Nu 1:39 tribe of Dan was **62,700**. H9109+2256+9252+547+2256+8679+4395
Nu 2:26 numbers **62,700**. H9109+2256+9252+547+2256+8679+4395

64,300 (1)
Nu 26:25 numbered were **64,300**. H752+2256+9252+547+2256+8993+4395

64,400 (1)
Nu 26:43 numbered were **64,400**. H752+2256+9252+547+2256+752+4395

70,000 (2)
2Ch 2: 2 He conscripted **70,000** men as H8679+547
2Ch 2:18 He assigned **70,000** of them to be H8679+547

72,000 (1)
Nu 31:33 **72,000** cattle, H9109+2256+8679+547

74,600 (2)
Nu 1:27 of Judah was **74,600**. H752+2256+8679+547+2256+9252+4395
Nu 2: 4 numbers **74,600**. H752+2256+8679+547+2256+9252+4395

76,500 (1)
Nu 26:22 numbered were **76,500**. H9252+2256+8679+547+2256+2822+4395

80,000 (2)
2Ch 2: 2 carriers and **80,000** as stonecutters H9046+547
2Ch 2:18 be carriers and **80,000** to be H9046+547

87,000 (1)
1Ch 7: 5 were **87,000** in all. H9046+2256+8679+547

108,100 (1)
Nu 2:24 number **108,100**. H4395+547+2256+9046+547+2256+4395

120,000 (1)
1Ch 12:37 of weapon—**120,000**. H4395+2256+6929+547

144,000 (3)
Rev 7: 4 **144,000** from all the *G1669+5477+5475+5942*
Rev 14: 1 him **144,000** who had *G1669+5477+5475+5942*
Rev 14: 3 the **144,000** who had *G1669+5477+5475+5942*

151,450 (1)
Nu 2:16 number **151,450**. H4395+547+2256+285+2256+2822+547+2256+752+4395+2256+2822

153,600 (1)
2Ch 2:17 found to be **153,600**. H4395+2256+2822+547+2256+8993+547+2256+9252+4395

157,600 (1)
Nu 2:31 of Dan number **157,600**. H4395+547+2256+8679+2256+2822+547+2256+9252+4395

180,000 (1)
2Ch 17:18 with **180,000** men H4395+2256+9046+547

186,400 (1)
Nu 2: 9 number **186,400**. H4395+547+2256+9046+547+2256+9252+547+2256+752+4395

200,000 (2)
2Ch 17:16 service of the LORD, with **200,000**. H4395+547
2Ch 17:17 with **200,000** men armed with bows H4395+547

280,000 (1)
2Ch 17:15 with **280,000**; H4395+2256+9046+547

300,000 (1)
2Ch 17:14 with **300,000** fighting men; H8993+4395+547

307,500 (1)
2Ch 26:13 an army of **307,500** men H8993+4395+547+2256+8679+547+2256+2822+4395

337,500 (2)
Nu 31:36 **337,500** sheep, H8993+4395+547+2256+8993+547+2256+8679+547+2256+2822+4395
Nu 31:43 **337,500** sheep, H8993+4395+547+2256+8993+547+8679+547+2256+2822+4395

601,730 (1)
Nu 26:51 of Israel was **601,730**. H9252+4395+547+2256+547+8679+4395+2256+8993

603,550 (3)
Ex 38:26 a total of **603,550** men. H9252+4395+547+2256+8993+547+2256+2822+4395+2256+2822
Nu 1:46 number was **603,550**. H9252+4395+547+2256+8993+547+2256+2822+4395+2256+2822
Nu 2:32 number **603,550**. H9252+4395+547+2256+8993+547+2256+2822+4395+2256+2822

675,000 (1)
Nu 31:32 was **675,000** sheep, H9252+4395+547+2256+8679+547+2256+2822+547

INDEX OF ARTICLES, CONJUNCTIONS, PARTICLES, PREPOSITIONS, AND PRONOUNS

A (9013)

Ge 1:6; **2:**7,7,8,10,18,21,22,24; **3:**24; **4:**1,11,12,14,15,17,22,23,23,25,26; **5:**3,5,8,11,14,17,20,23,27,28,31; **6:**3,9,16,16; **7:**2,2,20,24; **8:**1,6,7,8,11; **9:**11,11,12,15,20,20,23,29; **10:**8,9,9; **11:**1,2,4,4,4; **12:**2,2,10,10,11,14; **14:**13,13,20,23,23; **15:**1,3,4,9,9,9,9,9,12,12,13,15,17,17,18; **16:**2,7,11,12,12,15; **17:**5,8,12,16,17,17,17,17,19,20,27; **18:**4,7,7,8,10,13,14,18,25; **19:**3,8,9,20,26,28,30,37,38; **20:**1,3,3,5,6,7,16; **21:**2,5,7,8,13,14,16,18,19,19,21,23,25,27,30,33,34; **22:**2,2,12,13,13,13,15,20; **23:**1,4,4,6,9,20; **24:**3,4,7,14,14,16,17,18,19,21,22,22,29,31,36,37,38,40,40,43,43,45; **25:**7,8,17,25,27,27,28; **26:**1,3,8,8,12,19,25,28,28,30,35; **27:**11,12,12,27,34,41,44,46; **28:**1,2,3,4,6,6,11,12,12,18,20,22,22; **29:**2,9,12,12,14,15,17,20,22,32,33,34,35; **30:**3,4,5,6,7,8,9,10,12,17,19,20,21,23,36; **31:**10,13,13,24,28,44,44,45,45,46,48,50,52,52,54,54; **32:**13,18,24; **33:**17,19; **34:**7,14,14,14,31; **35:**11,11,14,14,20,28; **36:**6,12; **37:**2,2,4,5,15,20,22,25,31; **38:**1,2,3,4,6,8,11,12,14,15,17,17,23,24,25,28; **39:**7,9; **40:**5,5,9,15,16,16,19,20; **41:**1,5,5,7,11,11,12,12,15,15,22,33,34,42,43; **42:**7; **43:**2,11,11,11,12,16,30; **44:**5,15,17,18,19,19,20,25; **45:**7,7; **46:**2,3,10,29; **47:**4,9,22,24,26,26,28; **48:**4,7,19,19; **49:**9,9,9,11,13,14,17,17,19,20,21,22,22,22,22,27,30; **50:**3,9,10,11,13,15,22,26,26; **Ex 1:**8,16,16; **2:**1,1,2,2,3,4,11,15,16,22,22,22; **3:**2,8,8,17,18,19; **4:**2,3,4,20,24,25,25; **5:**1,3,21; **6:**8,15; **7:**9,9,10,12,15; **8:**2,23,27,31; **9:**3,4,5,8,10,15,19,24; **10:**7,9,14,19,19,26; **11:**7,7; **12:**3,4,9,13,14,14,14,16,17,22,24,30,45,45,48; **13:**3,5,6,9,9,13,14,16,16,21,21; **14:**21,22,29; **15:**3,5,8,16,20,25,25; **16:**13,23,23,25,33,35; **17:**12,14; **18:**3,3,12,12,16; **19:**6,6,9,13,13,16,16,18; **20:**5,6,10,18,21,25; **21:**2,3,4,7,7,9,12,12,13,18,19,20,20,21,22,26,27,28,28,29,31,32,33,33; **22:**1,2,2,5,6,7,9,9,9,10,10,13,16,16,18,21,25,26; **23:**1,1,2,3,3,7,8,8,9,14,14,17,18,19,26,29,32,33; **24:**1,10,14,17; **25:**8,10,10,10,10,10,11,17,17,17,23,23,23,23,24,25,25,25,31,35,35,39; **26:**1,6,11,13,14,14,16,16,24,31,31,36; **27:**2,4,4,4,9,9,11,16,18,21; **28:**4,4,4,4,4,11,11,12,14,15,16,16,21,22,29,32,32,36,36,37,42,43; **29:**1,3,9,14,18,18,18,24,25,25,26,31,36,36,38,40,40,40,40,40,40,41,41; **30:**2,2,3,9,10,12,12,13,15,16,18,20,21,24,25,25,25,33,35,35; **31:**13,15,16,17; **32:**4,4,5,8,9,10,11,25,27,30,31,35; **33:**3,5,5,7,11,21,21,22; **34:**9,10,12,12,14,15,20,23,25,26,27,33; **35:**2,3,22; **36:**13,18,19,19,21,21,29,35,37; **37:**1,1,1,1,1,2,6,6,6,10,10,10,11,12,12,12,21,21,25,25,26,29; **38:**2,4,4,9,11,26,26; **39:**6,8,9,9,14,15,22,23,23,27,30,31; **40:**15; **Lev 1:**3,3,9,9,10,10,13,13,14,14,14,17,17; **2:**1,2,2,2,3,4,5,6,7,9,10,11,12,14,15,16; **3:**1,3,5,6,6,7,9,11,12,16,16,17; **4:**3,3,10,12,12,14,14,22,23,24,28,32,32,33; **5:**1,6,6,6,7,7,7,7,9,10,11,11,11,12,12,12,15,15,15,16,16,18,18,19; **6:**2,5,6,6,11,15,20,20,21,23,27,28,29; **7:**5,5,6,8,9,9,14,16,16,25,29,30,32; **8:**7,21,21,21,27,28,28,29; **9:**2,2,3,3,3,3,3,3,4,4,4,8,15,17,21; **10:**9,14,15; **11:**3,4,4,5,6,7,26,33,34,36,36,37,38; **12:**2,2,5,6,6,6,6,6,6,7,7,8,8,8; **13:**2,2,2,2,2,3,6,8,9,10,11,15,18,19,20,22,23,24,24,25,25,27,28,28,29,29,30,38,39,40,41,42,42,43,45,47,49,51,57; **14:**5,10,10,12,12,21,21,21,21,22,22,24,31,31,32,34,34,35,44,50,54,55,56,56,56; **15:**2,4,6,7,11,12,13,15,15,16,18,18,19,24,25,25,25,25,30,30,32,32,33,33,33,33,33,33; **16:**3,3,3,3,5,5,5,9,10,12,22,26,29,29,31,31,34,34; **17:**3,3,7,8,11; **18:**17,18,19,22,22,23,23; **19:**5,5,10,13,14,17,18,20,20,21,21,29,33; **20:**10,11,12,12,13,13,13,14,14,15,16,17,17,18,18,19,20,21,24,25,27,27; **21:**1,2,9,9,11,11,13,14,14,14,14,17,19,20,20,21; **22:**4,4,4,4,9,10,10,11,11,12,12,13,13,14,14,18,18,18,18,18,19,20,21,21,21,22,23,23,23,25,27,27,27,27,28,28,29,29; **23:**3,3,3,7,8,8,10,12,12,12,13,13,13,13,14,17,18,18,18,19,19,19,20,20,21,21,24,24,25,27,27,31,32,35,36,36,39,39,41,41; **24:**3,7,7,8,9,10,11,17,21; **25:**2,4,4,5,8,10,11,12,21,24,29,29,29,30,33,35,37,47,47,49,50,51,52; **26:**1,1,8,8,25,36; **27:**2,2,3,4,5,5,5,6,6,6,7,7,7,10,10,10,10,11,13,15,16,17,18,19,21,22,26,27,28,28,30,31,33; **Nu 1:**2; **3:**15,22,28,34,39,40,40,43; **4:**2,6,6,7,8,9,10,10,11,12,12,13,14,20,22; **5:**2,2,2,7,9,12,15,15,15,17,18,19,20,21,22,23,24,24,26,26,27,27,29,30; **6:**2,2,2,2,6,11,11,12,12,14,14,14,14,14,14,15,17,19,20; **7:**3,13,13,15,15,16,17,17,19,19,21,21,22,23,23,25,25,27,27,28,29,29,31,31,33,33,34,35,35,37,37,39,39,40,41,41,43,43,45,45,46,47,47,49,49,51,51,52,53,53,55,55,57,57,58,59,59,61,61,63,63,64,65,65,67,67,69,69,70,71,71,73,73,75,75,76,77,77,79,79,81,81,82,83,83,85,86,87,88; **8:**8,8,8,11,12,12,13,15,21; **9:**6,7,10,10,13,14,19,20,22,22; **10:**5,6,8,9,10,33; **11:**8,8,8,12,20,21,27,31,31,33; **12:**1,3,5,6,10,12; **13:**11,23,23,23,32; **14:**4,8,12,12,14,14,24,36,37; **15:**2,4,4,4,4,5,5,5,6,6,6,6,7,7,7,8,8,8,8,9,9,10,10,10,13,14,14,15,19,20,22,24,24,24,24,25,25,27,27,29,29,32,38; **16:**3,13,14,15,29,38,40; **17:**10; **18:**6,7,16,17,17,17,17,23,26; **19:**2,2,2,9,9,10,11,13,14,14,15,16,16,16,16,17,18,18,18,18,21; **20:**16,20; **21:**8,8,9,9,9,28; **22:**5,6,11,11,12,17,23,23,24,26,29,29,32; **23:**2,2,3,4,4,5,9,10,14,14,16,19,20,22,24,24,30,30; **24:**4,6,8,9,9,16,17,17,19,21; **25:**6,7,13,13,14,15,15,18,18; **26:**2,4,10,46,54,54,54,54,59,62; **27:**8,17,18; **28:**3,3,5,5,5,5,6,6,7,7,8,9,9,11,11,12,12,13,13,13,13,13,14,14,14,14,14,14,15,17,18,19,19,19,20,22,25,26,27,27,28; **29:**1,1,2,2,3,5,6,7,8,8,9,11,12,12,13,13,13,14,16,17,19,20,22,23,25,26,28,29,31,32,34,35,36,36,36,38; **30:**2,2,2,3,3,3,6,6,9,10,10,10,16,16; **31:**4,5,6,16,17,18,35,52,54; **32:**14,41; **33:**39,54,54,54,54; **34:**7,10,13,15; **35:**4,6,8,11,15,16,16,17,17,17,18,18,18,21,23,30,30,31,31,32,32; **Dt 1:**9,11,16,22,25,31,33,44,45; **2:**1,9,10,19,20,21; **3:**5,13,14; **4:**6,12,16,16,24,24,25,27,31,34,42,42; **5:**2,9,10,14,15,22,24; **6:**3,10,15,21; **7:**6,8,9,16,21,26; **8:**5,7,7,8,9,9; **9:**3,6,13,14,16,21,26; **10:**1,7; **11:**9,10,11,12,26,26; **12:**11; **13:**1,1,16,16; **14:**2,6,7,7,8,21,21,22,23; **15:**2,3,10,18,18,21; **16:**2,6,10,11,16,17,19,19,22; **17:**1,2,6,14,15,15,18,18,20; **18:**3,3,6,11,15,18,20,20,21,22,22; **19:**3,4,4,5,5,6,11,15,16,16,18,18,18; **20:**5,6,7,10,15,19,19; **21:**1,3,3,4,4,11,13,14,15,17,18,20,20,22,22,23; **22:**5,5,6,6,7,8,8,10,13,13,14,15,17,19,19,22,23,23,23,24,25,25,26,28,28,30; **23:**2,4,5,6,10,12,13,15,17,18,18,19,20,20,21,22,25; **24:**1,1,1,3,5,6,6,6,7,7,10,10,13,14,14,14,17,19,20; **25:**1,5,5,7,7; **26:**2,2,5,5,5,8,9,12,15,19; **27:**3,14,15,25; **28:**8,25,29,30,30,30,32,33,36,37,37,46,46,49,49,50,65,68; **29:**4,12,12,19,19,23; **31:**2,15,19,24,26; **32:**4,5,10,10,20,21,21,22,28,30,52; **33:**17,17,20,22,28,29; **34:**7; **Jos 2:**1,9,12,15,19; **3:**4,13,16,16,16; **4:**5,6,7; **5:**6,13,13; **6:**5,5,10,10,20,23; **7:**3,21,21,26; **8:**14,17,28,28,29,29,32,35; **9:**4,4,6,6,7,9,11,15,22,23; **10:**1,13,14,14,14,20,21; **11:**4,4,18,19; **12:**7; **14:**2,3,7; **15:**13,18,19,32; **17:**14; **18:**4,4,7,8,8,9,14; **20:**3,4; **21:**13,21,27,32,38; **22:**3,8,14,17,25,27,28,34; **23:**1,1,10; **24:**7,9,13,19,19,25,26,27,27,29,32; **Jdg 1:**14,15,24,26; **2:**2,8,18; **3:**9,15,15,16,16,17,19,20,25,27; **4:**4,9,16,18,19,19,21,21; **5:**7,8,14,25,30; **6:**4,8,11,17,19,19,19,26,26,31,34,37,38; **7:**5,13,13,13,13,20; **8:**10,10,14,16,18,20,25,25,27,31,32; **9:**8,18,27,37,44,49,51,53,54; **10:**1; **11:**1,1,3,30,31,35,39; **12:**2,5,7; **13:**2,2,3,5,5,5,6,7,7,15,16,19,19,23,24; **14:**1,2,3,5,6,8,10,12,16,18; **15:**1,3,4,8,15,15,15,16,16,16; **16:**1,4,9,9,10,13,15,17,23; **17:**1,2,4,5,7,9,9,10; **18:**1,7,10,10,19,19,27,28,28; **19:**1,1,1,18,29,30; **20:**10,10,10,16,16,34,37,38; **21:**1,5,11,12,15,17,18,18; **Ru 1:**1,1,1,12; **2:**1,1,3,3,7,9,9,10,11; **3:**1,2,8,9,11,12,14; **4:**13,14,17; **1Sa 1:**1,1,5,11,11,15,16,20,24,24; **2:**3,8,13,13,18,18,19,27,34,35,36,36; **3:**8,20; **4:**5,7,12,13,20; **5:**9; **6:**3,3,7,8,8,14,14,17,18; **7:**2,9,9,10,11,12,16; **8:**5,6,10,15,17,19,20,22; **9:**1,1,2,2,2,6,8,8,9,12,16,21,21,27,27; **10:**1,3,5,5,6,10,12,12,19,23,25; **11:**1,2,7,15; **12:**1,2,3,12,13,17,19; **13:**2,13,14,19,21,21,21,22,22,23; **14:**2,3,4,12,15,28,29,33,39,43,45,52; **15:**12,18,29; **16:**2,12,18,18,18,18,20,20,20; **17:**4,4,5,5,6,7,8,8,10,20,33,33,34,34,34,38,38,42,43,46,49,50,50,50,52; **18:**3,5,9,10,13,17,21,21,23,23,25; **19:**1,2,5,12,13,20,21; **20:**3,8,16,20,21,29,30,35; **21:**2,2,8,8,9,13; **22:**8,13,17; **23:**7,17,18,27; **24:**3,4,5,6,14,14,19; **25:**2,2,3,8,16,17,18,20,28,29,36,36,37,42; **26:**9,11,12,13,15,20,20,21,23; **27:**5,7,9,11; **28:**7,7,8,9,13,14,24; **29:**3; **30:**11,12,25,26; **31:**13; **2Sa 1:**2,13,19; **2:**18,25,25,28; **3:**1,7,8,14,20,21,22,22,29,29,38,38; **4:**4; **5:**3,11; **6:**3,13,13,14,16,19,19,19; **7:**2,2,5,6,6,7,10,10,11,13,14,19,23,23,27; **8:**2,4,4,8; **9:**2,3,8,12; **10:**2,6; **11:**2,8,10,11,14,16,18,21,27; **12:**1,2,3,4,4,6,24,30,30; **13:**2,3,12,16,20,22,25; **14:**2,2,5,6,12,13,14,25,26,27,27,29; **15:**1,2,2,4,7,13,19,33; **16:**1,1,1,1,1,5,8,22; **17:**8,9,9,10,10,13,13,16,17,18,18,18,19; **18:**2,2,2,9,11,12,12,17,17,18,18,21,22,24,27; **19:**7,17,28,32,36,43; **20:**1,1,3,8,8,12,12,12,15,16,19,19,21; **21:**1,2,9,10,15,16,19,19,19,20; **22:**20,30,30,34,35,37,49; **23:**4,7,7,8,10,11,11,12,13,15,20,20,20,20,21,21,21; **24:**1,3,3,9,10,15; **1Ki 1:**2,3,3,42,48,52; **2:**1,2,4,9,19,24,36,38; **3:**2,4,5,6,7,8,9,12,14,15,15,17,18,24,24; **4:**5,23,29,32; **5:**3,5,7,12,14,17; **6:**5,8,23; **7:**2,3,6,6,8,12,14,14,17,23,24,26,26,26,30,31,31,31,32,32,35,35; **8:**9,12,13,13,16,16,17,18,21,25,38,41,47,55,63,63,65; **9:**2,5,7,8,8,13,16,25; **10:**2,18,19,19,22,25,29,29,29; **11:**7,7,17,18,19,20,24,26,28,29,36,38; **12:**4,7,7,10,11,21,30,32,33; **13:**1,2,3,7,7,11,18,24,33; **14:**3,14,15; **15:**4,4,13,19,19,27; **16:**11,15,24; **17:**9,10,10,10,10,11,12,12,12,12,12,12,13,24; **18:**1,3,4,10,10,13,27,32,34,41,44,44,45; **19:**2,4,4,6,7,9,11,12,12,13; **20:**10,13,28,28,29,33,34,34,36,36,39,39,42; **21:**1,2,2,9,9,12,12,19; **22:**7,8,17,21,22,23,36,38,47,48; **2Ki 1:**6,8,8,9,9,10,12,13; **2:**1,7,9,10,11,11,20,24; **3:**4,4,4,9,15,25,27; **4:**1,2,3,6,8,8,9,10,10,10,10,10,13,16,17,19,22,28,38,39,42,43; **5:**1,1,2,5,7,8,10,12,14,15,16,17,22; **6:**2,2,5,6,8,14,23,25,25,25,25,26,32; **7:**1,1,1,6,9,10,16,16,16,18,18,18; **8:**1,1,8,9,11,13,13,15,18,19,26; **9:**1,5,17,19,20,30,34; **10:**2,6,10,18,19,27; **11:**2,4,4,5,6,6,9,12,15,17,17; **12:**9,9,10; **13:**3,5,15,21,21; **14:**9,9,9,9,13; **15:**5,19; **16:**8,10,17; **17:**4,21,35; **18:**17,21,23,32,32,32,32; **19:**3,7,9,20,30,31,31,32,35; **20:**7,10,12,14; **21:**13; **22:**10,19; **23:**25,30,33,33,33; **24:**14,16; **25:**17,28,30; **1Ch 1:**10; **2:**3; **4:**33; **5:**2,6,18; **6:**57,67; **7:**15,16,23; **9:**4,14,31; **10:**13; **11:**3,11,13,13,14,15,17,22,22,22,22,23,23,23; **12:**4,4,14,14,14,20,22,28; **13:**7; **14:**1; **15:**1,1,16,25,27,27,29; **16:**3,3,3,15,17; **17:**1,1,4,5,6,9,9,10,12,21,21,25; **18:**4,4,8; **19:**2,6; **20:**2,2,5,5,5,6; **21:**1,3,5,8,14,16,24; **22:**3,6,7,8,9,9,10,14,14; **24:**3,3,4,6; **26:**14,17,17,17,17,24,31; **27:**3,6,11,12,13,18,32,32,32; **28:**2,2,3,3,9,10,19; **29:**7,15,16,21,21,21,22,28; **2Ch 1:**4,6,9,11,17,17,17; **2:**1,1,3,4,4,6,6,6,7,12,12,12,13,17; **3:**10,15,16; **4:**1,2,3,5,5,5,8; **5:**10; **6:**1,2,2,5,5,7,8,13,16,29,32,36,37; **7:**5,5,8,12,13,18,20,21,21; **9:**1,17,18,18,21,24; **10:**4,7,10,11; **11:**1; **13:**2,3,5,8,9,9; **14:**13,13; **15:**3,3,12,16; **16:**3,8,9,12,14,14; **17:**17; **18:**6,7,16,20,21,22; **19:**6; **20:**2,3,8,14,19,25,36; **21:**6,7,12,14,15,17; **22:**2,9,11; **23:**1,1,3,4,5,5,9,11,14,16; **24:**8,9,11,11,15,24,24,26; **25:**6,6,7,10,12,15,18,18,18,18,23; **26:**11,13,19,21,23; **27:**5; **28:**6,8,9,9; **29:**10,21,24,32; **30:**5,13,24,24,24; **31:**5,5,6,6,12; **32:**4,7,24; **33:**11; **34:**18; **35:**5,7,18,25; **36:**3,3,3,4,22,23; **Ezr 1:**1,2; **2:**61,61,63; **3:**11; **4:**1,3,7,8,11,15,15,15,15,19,19,19,24; **5:**1,5,6,11,13,14,17,17; **6:**2,3,3,11,11,12,14,17,17; **7:**6,11,11,11,22,22,22,22; **8:**18,20,21,21,28,35,35; **9:**8,8,8,8,9,11,12,13,13,15; **10:**1,3,7,12,13,14,14,19,19; **Ne 1:**9; **2:**6,8,12; **3:**9,12,13,16,16,19,26; **4:**2,3,4,9,17; **5:**1,7,13,15,17; **6:**1,3,7,11,13,13; **7:**2,63,63,65; **8:**4,11; **9:**3,8,10,11,12,12,17,17,18,31,38; **10:**29,32,32,34,37,38,38; **11:**4,5; **13:**2,2,5,7,13; **Est 1:**3,4,5,6,9,19; **2:**2,5,7,7,12,17,18,18,19; **3:**1,4,6,7,8,9,13,14; **4:**8,14; **5:**4,14,14; **6:**8,8,8; **7:**5,7,9,9; **8:**13,15,15,15,16; **9:**17,18,19,19,22; **10:**2; **Job 1:**1,3,5,5,8,10,12,14,19; **2:**3,4,8,10,12,13; **3:**3,5,16,23; **4:**2,12,12,15,16,16,17,17,19; **5:**2,3,4,23; **6:**5,14,22; **7:**2,2,6,7,9,20; **8:**2,9,14,16,17,17; **9:**3,16,17,19,19,23,24,25,25,31,32; **10:**4,5,5,16,20; **11:**10,12,20; **12:**3,4,4,18,24; **13:**9,25,28; **14:**5,6,7,9,10,11,11,13,17,18,18,19; **15:**2,8,23,24,26,30,33; **16:**8,14,21,21,22; **17:**6,6,7,10; **18:**5,8,9,9,10,10; **19:**10,12,15,15,23; **20:**3,5,8,8,24,26,28; **21:**4,11,18,33; **22:**2,2,8,11,16; **24:**9,14,20,23,24; **25:**4,6,6,6,6; **26:**10; **27:**13,18,18,18,20,20; **28:**1,1,4,22,26,26; **29:**16,25; **30:**8,9,14,15,24,24,29,29; **31:**1,1,9,11,12,13,18,27,30,36,37; **32:**8,13; **33:**6,15,15,19,23,23,24,25,29; **34:**6,36; **35:**9; **36:**2,16,18,22; **37:**6,18; **38:**3,5,14,14,25,25,26,27,28,34,40; **39:**7,10,15,17,19,20,28,28; **40:**7,17,23; **41:**1,1,2,2,5,5,5,8,11,20,24,29,29,30,30,31,31,32,33; **42:**8,11,11,12,12,16; **Ps 1:**3; **2:**9,12; **3:**T,3; **4:**T; **5:**T,4,9,12; **6:**T; **7:**T,T,2,11,11,15; **8:**T,2,5; **9:**T,9,9; **10:**9; **11:**1,5,6; **12:**T,6; **13:**T; **15:**T,3,4,5; **16:**T,6; **17:**T,12,12; **18:**19,29,29,33,34,36,48; **19:**T,4,5,5; **20:**T; **21:**T,3,9; **22:**T,6,6,15,16,31; **23:**T,5; **24:**T,4,4; **26:**1,11; **27:**5,11; **28:**1,8; **29:**T,6,6; **30:**T,T,5,5; **31:**T,2,8,21; **32:**T; **33:**3,17,17; **35:**7; **36:**1,4; **37:**10,26,35,35,37; **38:**T,T,4; **39:**T,1,5,5,6,11,11,12,12; **40:**T,2,2,3,3; **41:**T,8; **42:**T,8; **44:**T,12,13,14,19,20; **45:**T,T,1,1,6,12; **46:**T,4; **47:**T,7; **48:**T,T,6; **49:**T,4,7,8; **50:**T,3,3,5,6,9,10,18; **51:**T,10,10,12,17,17; **52:**T,1,2; **53:**T; **54:**T,6; **55:**T,6,12,13; **56:**T,T; **57:**T,6,6; **58:**T,4,4,8,8,11; **59:**T; **60:**T,4; **61:**3; **62:**T,9,9,9,9; **63:**T,1; **64:**T,6; **65:**T,T; **66:**T,T,12; **67:**T,T; **68:**T,T,5,5,6,11,20; **69:**8,8,22,22,31; **70:**T; **71:**7; **72:**6; **73:**T,20,22; **74:**T,5; **75:**T,T,8; **76:**T,T; **77:**T,20; **78:**T,2,8,13,16,19,23,39,49,50,52,57,65; **79:**T; **80:**T,1,8; **81:**4,5,7; **82:**T; **83:**T,T,1,4,14; **84:**T,3,3,3,6,10,10,11; **85:**T; **86:**T,15,17; **87:**T,T; **88:**T,T,T,17; **89:**T,3,19,19,19,45; **90:**T,4,4,4,9,12; **91:**7,12; **92:**T,T,10,12,12; **94:**1,13,16,20,20; **95:**10; **96:**1; **98:**T,1; **99:**8; **100:**T; **101:**T,2,2,5; **102:**T,T,6,7,7,8,18,18,26; **103:**13,15; **104:**2,2,6,9,18; **105:**8,10,17,17,23,39,39,39,41; **106:**9,15,18,19,20,29,36; **107:**4,7,7,25,29,33,34,36,37,40; **108:**T,T; **109:**T,4,9,11,16,17,19,19,23,29; **110:**T,1,4,7; **113:**9; **114:**1,8; **115:**7; **116:**11,17; **118:**5; **119:**9,19,63,83,96,105,105,110,164,176; **120:**T,4; **121:**T; **122:**T,3; **123:**T,2; **124:**T,7; **125:**T; **126:**T; **127:**T,3,3,4; **128:**T,3; **129:**T,7; **130:**T,3; **131:**T,2,2; **132:**T,2,5,5,11,17,17,18; **133:**T; **134:**T; **136:**12; **137:**4; **139:**T,4; **140:**T,3,5; **141:**T,3,5,5; **142:**T,T,3; **143:**T,6; **144:**4,4,9,12; **145:**T; **148:**6,14; **149:**1,6; **Pr 1:**9,9,17,27,27; **2:**7; **3:**4,12,18; **4:**1,3,9,9; **5:**4,8,19,19,20; **6:**1,5,5,10,10,10,11,12,12,12,17,18,19,19,23,23,24,26,26,27,28,30,32,34,35; **7:**7,10,10,13,19,22,22,23,23,26,27; **8:**21; **9:**7,12,14; **10:**1,1,5,5,8,10,11,13,14,18,23,23,29,31; **11:**11,13,13,13,13,14,15,16,18,18,22,22,22,25,28,30; **12:**4,4,8,8,9,9,17,19,19,23,25; **13:**1,1,4,5,8,12,12,13,14,14,17,17,19,20,22,22; **14:**3,5,7,12,16,17,21,23,25,25,26,26,27,27,28,28,28,30,34,35,35,35; **15:**1,1,4,4,5,5,13,14,15,16,17,17,18,18,19,20,20,21,23,23,30; **16:**2,4,8,10,12,14,14,15,15,18,18,22,24,25,27,27,28,28,29,29,31,32,32,32; **17:**1,1,2,2,4,4,4,6,7,7,8,8,10,10,10,10,12,12,14,14,14,17,17,17,18,19,19,21,21,21,22,22,24,24,25,26; **18:**4,6,7,8,10,11,12,14,16,17,19,19,19,20,22,24,24; **19:**1,3,5,6,9,10,10,11,12,12,13,13,13,13,14,18,19,21,22,22,24,25,26,28; **20:**1,1,2,2,5,6,8,15,16,17,19,19,24,25,26,28; **21:**1,2,4,6,6,6,6,9,9,9,11,14,14,18,19,19,25,28,28,29; **22:**1,11,11,13,14,14,15,24; **23:**1,2,5,6,13,18,24,24,24,27,27,27,28,32,32; **24:**3,8,9,10,14,15,26,30,32,33,33,33,34; **25:**2,2,4,4,6,11,12,12,13,13,15,15,15,18,18,18,18,19,19,19,20,20,20,20,23,23,23,24,24,24,25,25,26,26,28,28; **26:**1,2,2,3,3,3,4,5,6,6,7,7,8,8,8,9,9,9,9,10,11,12,12,13,13,13,14,14,15,16,17,17,18,20,20,20,21,22,23,27,27,28,28; **27:**1,3,3,6,8,9,10,10,10,13,14,15,15,15,18,22,22,22,24,26; **28:**1,2,2,3,3,7,7,9,10,15,15,15,15,16,16,20,21,21,23,23; **29:**3,3,4,4,8,9,9,10,12,14,15,15,15,20,21,22,23,25,26; **30:**2,2,4,5,6,10,17,19,19,19,19,19,22,22,23,23,28,30,31,31,31; **31:**10,16,16,30; **Ecc 1:**13,14,17;

2:8,8,11,17,21,21,24,26; **3:**1,1,2,2,2,2,3,3,3,3,4,4,4,4,5,5,5,5,6,6,6,6,7,7,7,7,8,8,8,8,17,17,22; **4:**4,8,8,9,12,13,13,16; **5:**3,3,4,5,6,8,8,12,13,16,18,19; **6:**2,3,3,3,6,9,12,12; **7:**1,2,2,3,5,7,7,7,8,11,12,12,17,19,26,26,28; **8:**1,3,3,4,6,6,9,9,11,12,12,12,13,15; **9:**2,4,4,6,7,12,12,14,14,14,15,17; **10:**1,1,4,5,8,8,8,11,16,17,19,20,20; **11:**1,3,5; **SS 1:**7,9,13,14; **2:**1,1,2,9,9,17,17; **3:**6,11; **4:**1,2,3,3,4,5,12,12,12,15,15; **5:**11; **6:**5,6,7; **7:**2,2,3; **8:**1,6,6,6,8,9,9,10,11,11,14,14; **Isa 1:**4,4,8,8,8,8,8,14,21,30,31; **2:**12,22; **3:**6,6,24,24,24; **4:**4,4,5,5,5,6,6; **5:**1,1,1,2,2,2,6,10,10,10,23,26,27,27,28; **6:**1,5,5,6,13; **7:**8,11,14,14,17,20,21,21,23,23; **8:**1,3,12,14,14,14,14,14,19; **9:**2,2,6,6,8,14,18,18; **10:**6,6,13,14,14,15,15,16,16,16,17,17,17,18,19,21,21,22,24,24,26; **11:**1,1,6,10,11,12,15,16; **13:**1,2,2,4,4,8,9,14,14; **14:**17,19,19,21,23,29,29,31,31; **15:**1,1,1,9; **16:**3,5,5,11,14; **17:**1,1,1,13; **18:**2,2,3,3,4,5,7,7; **19:**1,1,4,4,11,14,14,19,20,20,22,23,24; **20:**3; **21:**1,1,2,3,4,6,9,9,9,11,13,16; **22:**1,5,5,11,16,18,18,18,21,23,23,23; **23:**1,10,13,13,15,16,16; **24:**6,9,18,18,20,20,22; **25:**2,2,2,4,4,4,4,4,4,5,6,6; **26:**1,10,16,17,20; **27:**2,8,11,13; **28:**1,2,2,2,2,4,5,5,6,6,8,10,10,10,10,13,13,13,13,15,15,16,16,16,24,27,27,27,27,28; **29:**6,7,7,8,8,10,11,17,17,17,21; **30:**5,6,6,8,8,13,14,14,14,17,17,17,17,17,18,21,22,27,28,28,29,33; **31:**4,4,4,8; **32:**1,2,2,2,2,10,13,14,14,15,15; **33:**4,6,11,17,20,20,21; **34:**4,6,6,8,8,12,13,13; **35:**6,7,8; **36:**2,6,8,17,17,17; **37:**3,7,9,21,31,32,32,33,36; **38:**9,12,12,13,14,14,21; **39:**1,3; **40:**3,3,4,6,9,9,10,11,12,12,15,15,19,19,20,20,22,22,24; **41:**3,15,16,25,27; **42:**3,3,6,6,10,13,13,13,14,14,22; **43:**16,16,17,19,19; **44:**4,10,12,13,13,13,14,14,15,15,17,19,19,20,20,20,22; **45:**4,10,10,13,15,19,21,21,23; **46:**1,6,6,11,11,11; **47:**1,6,8,9,9,11,11,11,14; **48:**8,18; **49:**2,2,6,6,8,15,18; **50:**2,2,4,9; **51:**4,6,8,10,20,23; **52:**2; **53:**2,2,3,7,7,9,12; **54:**1,1,6,6,7,8,8,16; **55:**4,4; **56:**3,5,5,7; **57:**3,4,7,8,13,15; **58:**1,2,5,5,5,5,11,11,11,13; **59:**4,5,14,15,17,19; **60:**22,22; **61:**3,3,3,3,7,7,9,10,10,10,10,11; **62:**1,2,3,3,5,5,5,10; **63:**13,14,18; **64:**6,10,10,10; **65:**1,3,5,8,8,10,10,11,16,17,18,18,20,20,20,20,22,23; **66:**3,3,3,3,3,7,8,8,8,8,12,12,13,15,19; **Jer 1:**5,13,18,18; **2:**2,2,6,6,6,7,11,14,14,20,21,21,23,24,26,30,31,31,32,32; **3:**1,1,2,3,14,14,18,19,20,21,23; **4:**2,7,7,11,12,13,15,16,16,16,17,20,26,31,31,31; **5:**6,6,6,9,14,15,15,19,22,29,30; **6:**7,9,20,22,24,25,27; **7:**11,12,29; **8:**6,15,19; **9:**1,1,2,2,3,4,4,8,9,10,11,11,12,20; **10:**3,3,5,5,14,22,22; **11:**5,9,11,16,16,19,23; **12:**1,6,8,9,10,11; **13:**1,2,3,4,11,21,23; **14:**2,8,8,8,9,9,17,17,18,19; **15:**7,8,10,11,12,14,14,18,18,20,20; **16:**5,5,7,7,7,8,10,13; **17:**1,4,6,6,8,8,11,12,17,21,22; **18:**7,9,11,11,13,17,20,22,22; **19:**1,1,3,4; **20:**4,9,9,11,15,15,16; **21:**5,6,14; **22:**5,6,8,14,15,19,23,24,28,28,30; **23:**5,5,9,9,14,19,23,23,25,25,28,29,29,33,33,34,34,34,36,37,38,38,38; **24:**7,9,9,9; **25:**11,18,18,29,32,38; **26:**2,6,18,18,18,19,23; **27:**2,4,17; **28:**13,13; **29:**11,18,23,26,27,28; **30:**2,6,6,7,10,23; **31:**6,8,9,10,12,15,22,31,32,36; **32:**14,14,21,22,35,43; **33:**1,10,15,17,18,21,24; **34:**5,5,8,9,13,15; **35:**7,13,19; **36:**2,6,9,22,23,26; **37:**15,16,16,16,21; **38:**7,9,11; **39:**3,3,13,13; **40:**5,11,16; **41:**7,8; **42:**2,5,18,18,20; **43:**12; **44:**7,8,12,12,14,15,22,22; **45:**1; **46:**10,17,20,20,22,27; **48:**6,8,10,10,28,28,36,36,38,41,42,44,44,45,45; **49:**2,9,13,13,14,19,19,22,24,30,31,31,33,33,36; **50:**2,3,11,12,12,12,17,24,32,35,36,36,37,37,38,38,41,43,44,44; **51:**1,7,12,14,17,25,26,26,27,27,27,33,34,37,37,37,39,43,43,50,54,56,56,60,63; **52:**22,23,32,34; **La 1:**1,1,13,14; **2:**3,4,6,7,8,18,22; **3:**10,10,27,44,52,53,65; **4:**2,6,6,8,11,17; **5:**4; **Eze 1:**4,7,10,10,15,16,16,22,25,26,26,26,28,28; **2:**3,5,5,6,9,9; **3:**5,9,12,13,17,18,20,20,26,27; **4:**1,2,3,6,9,11,11,12; **5:**1,1,1,2,2,2,3,4,4,12,12,12,14,14,15,15,15; **6:**3,14; **7:**11,19,20,26; **8:**2,2,3,7,8,11,11,17; **9:**1,1,2,2,2,4; **10:**1,3,6,10,10,14,14,14; **11:**3,11,13,16,16,19,19; **12:**2,2,3,6,11,12,16; **13:**6,10,13,19; **14:**4,4,7,7,8,9,13,17,19; **15:**2,2; **16:**3,7,8,11,12,12,13,15,24,24,29,30,31,40,41,45,45,45; **17:**2,3,3,4,4,5,6,6,8,9,13,13,15,22,22,22,22,23; **18:**5,6,7,8,10,13,13,14,16,16,21,24,26,27,31,31; **19:**1,2,3,3,5,6,6,9,10,11,13,14,14,14; **20:**6,6,12,15,20,33,34; **21:**9,9,14,14,19,22,23,27,27,27,28,28; **22:**4,4,11,12,18,20,20,22,24,25,25; **23:**7,10,14,19,24,27,32,41,42,43,44,46; **24:**3,5,24,26,27; **25:**4,5,5,10; **26:**4,5,7,8,10,14,14,17,17,19,21; **27:**2,5,5,32,36; **28:**2,2,2,2,2,6,8,9,9,9,12,14,17,18,19,23; **29:**6,8,9,10,10,14,16,16,18,20,21; **30:**3,3,4,13,21,21,24; **31:**3,14; **32:**2,2,2,3,7,25; **33:**2,7,13,14,15,18,19,21,27,28,29,32,33; **34:**8,12,12,14,14,25,26,29; **35:**3,7; **36:**17,26,26,26; **37:**1,2,7,7,10,16,19,26; **38:**4,8,9,9,11,11,15,15,16,19,21; **39:**11,13,14,15,15,16; **40:**2,2,3,3,3,5,5,5,12,17,19,23,23,27,27,38,38,42,42,42,42,42,43,47,47,49; **41:**7,8,13,13,14,15,19,19,21,22,25; **42:**2,4,8,11,12,20; **43:**8,13,13,13,13,13,14,14,17,17,17,19,19,22,22,23,23,24,25,25,25,25; **44:**25,25,27,30; **45:**1,1,2,3,4,4,11,11,11,11,13,13,14,14,14,18,21,22,22,23,23,23,24,24; **46:**4,5,6,6,7,7,11,11,11,12,12,13,13,14,14,14,14,14,15,16,17,19,23; **47:**3,3,5,5,7,20,23; **48:**8,12,12,20,20; **Da 1:**5; **2:**3,10,15,19,25,28,31,34,35,35,35,39,40,41,43,44,45,45,47,48; **3:**6,10,11,15,25,27; **4:**5,10,13,13,14,16,19,23,23,31,33; **5:**1,1,5,7,11,12,16,29; **6:**6,10,11,12,13,15,17,26; **7:**1,4,4,4,5,5,6,6,7,8,8,8,10,12,13,20,23,25,25; **8:**1,3,5,5,13,15,16,18,23,23; **9:**1,15,15,23,25,26,27; **10:**1,1,1,5,5,6,9,10,14,16,18; **11:**2,3,10,11,11,13,15,17,18,20,20,21,22,23,24,25,25,33,34,38,38,39,39,40,40,44; **12:**1,7,7; **Hos 1:**2,3,6; **2:**3,3,12,15,18; **3:**2,2,3; **4:**1,4,4,12,12,12,14,16,16,19; **5:**1,1,4,10,12,14,14; **6:**8,9,10,11; **7:**6,8,11,16; **8:**6,9; **9:**1,7,7,11,13; **10:**1,3,4,7,11,11; **11:**1,4,6,9,10; **12:**1,2,3,11,12,13,13; **13:**3,3,7,7,8,8,8,10,11,13,13; **14:**5,5,6,8; **Joel 1:**6,6,6,6,8,14,14; **2:**2,2,2,3,3,5,5,5,14,15,15,17,20; **3:**8,16,16,18,19; **Am 1:**9,11,14; **2:**6,13; **3:**4,5,5,5,6,6,6,12,12,12,12,12; **4:**5,11; **5:**3,3,3,6,9,11,11,19,19,19,19,20,21,24,24; **6:**3,14; **7:**7,7,8,8,10,10,14,14,14,17,17; **8:**1,2,6,10,11,11,11,11; **9:**9,9; **Ob** 1,5,5,7,18,18; **Jnh 1:**3,4,4,5,9,16,17; **3:**1,3,4,5; **4:**2,2,5,5,6,7,8,11; **Mic 1:**4,6,6,8,15; **2:**3,8,11,12,12; **3:**11,11,12,12,12; **4:**7,9,10; **5:**1,1,3,8,8; **6:**2,2,6,11; **7:**4,4,5,5,6,6,6,6,14,17,18; **Na 1:**1,2,7,9,14; **2:**8; **3:**4,6,15,17; **Hab 1:**7,7,9; **2:**2,12,12,18; **3:**1,19; **Zep 1:**7,10,10,15,15,15,15,15,16,18; **2:**9,9,15,15; **3:**13,18; **Hag 1:**4,4,6,9,11; **2:**6,13,13,16,16,20; **Zec 1:**8,8,8,8,15; **2:**1,1,4,5; **3:**2,5,5,7,9; **4:**2,2; **5:**1,2,6,7,9,11; **6:**11,13,14; **7:**14; **8:**13,13; **9:**1,3,6,7,9,9,9,13,15,16,16; **10:**2,3; **11:**15,16; **12:**1,1,2,4,6,6,6,10,10; **13:**1,4,5,5; **14:**1,3,4,7,7,15,21; **Mal 1:**1,3,4,6,6,6,6,13,14,14; **2:**2,5,7,11,11; **3:**2,2,3,8,9,12,16,17; **4:**1,1,1; **Mt 1:**20,21,23,25; **2:**6,12,13,18,19,22,23,23; **3:**3,4,16,17; **4:**6,8,16,16,18,21; **5:**1,14,14,15,15,18,22,22,28,31,32; **6:**27; **7:**4,9,10,10,14,17,18,18,24,26,27; **8:**2,4,5,9,14,16,19,24,30; **9:**1,2,2,9,12,16,18,20,32,36; **10:**10,21,24,29,34,35,35,35,36,41,41,41,41,41,41,42; **11:**7,8,9,9,17,18,19,19,19; **12:**10,10,10,11,11,12,12,15,20,20,22,29,32,33,33,33,35,38,39,39,40,43; **13:**2,3,8,8,21,23,23,24,31,31,32,33,34,44,44,45,47,52,52,57; **14:**5,8,11,13,14,15,23,24,26; **15:**14,18,20,22,23,29,33,34; **16:**1,4,4,23; **17:**1,5,5,14,20,27; **18:**2,6,12,12,17,17,23,24,28; **19:**3,5,7,7,10,16,24,24,29; **20:**1,2,9,10,13,20,28,29; **21:**2,5,5,5,8,13,13,19,26,28,33,33,33,33,33,35,41,43,46,46; **22:**2,2,11,16,19,23,24,46; **23:**4,15,15,23,24,24,37; **24:**14,28,31,41,48,50,51; **25:**5,14,14,18,19,21,23,24,32,35,38,43,44; **26:**5,7,9,10,18,27,30,36,39,42,47,48,55,58,69,73,74; **27:**7,14,15,16,19,19,28,29,29,32,33,46,48,48,50,55,57,57,59,60,65,66; **28:**2,12,12; **Mk 1:**3,4,6,10,11,16,19,19,23,26,27,30,35,40,43,44,45,45; **2:**1,3,13,17,21; **3:**1,1,2,7,9,13,20,20,24,25,27,32,34; **4:**1,3,8,8,17,20,20,21,21,21,26,31,34,37,38; **5:**2,3,6,11,21,24,25,26,38; **6:**4,5,8,10,11,15,19,20,21,25,28,29,31,31,32,32,34,34,35,37,46,49; **7:**3,9,15,15,18,20,21,23,24,25,26,29,32,34; **8:**3,7,11,12,22; **9:**2,7,7,14,17,17,20,25,26,36,39,41,42; **10:**2,4,4,7,15,17,20,25,25,30,45,46,46; **11:**2,4,4,13,17,17,18,32; **12:**1,1,1,1,1,2,6,12,14,15,18,19,19,28,40,42,42; **13:**12,34; **14:**3,5,6,13,13,15,23,26,32,35,43,44,48,51,51,54,70,70; **15:**6,7,17,17,19,21,34,36,36,37,40,43,46,46; **16:**5,5,12; **Lk 1:**5,5,13,14,17,22,26,27,27,27,31,34,36,39,42,57,63,69,76; **2:**1,1,5,7,7,11,12,12,12,13,24,24,25,32,34,35,36,37,44; **3:**3,4,22,22; **4:**5,11,25,25,26,31,33,33,38,42; **5:**3,4,6,8,12,14,18,18,19,27,29,29,31,36,36; **6:**6,7,12,16,17,17,17,38,39,43,45,48,48,48,49,49,49; **7:**2,8,11,11,12,12,12,16,24,25,26,26,32,33,34,34,34,37,37,39,39,41,45; **8:**4,5,8,8,13,15,15,16,16,16,16,22,23,27,27,27,32,40,41,41,42,43; **9:**5,10,12,28,29,34,35,37,38,39,42,47,52,57,62; **10:**4,5,8,10,11,30,31,32,33,36,38,38,39; **11:**1,5,6,6,11,11,12,14,16,17,21,24,27,29,29,30,33,33,33,36,37,42; **12:**1,10,14,16,25,33,36,45,46,46,50,54; **13:**6,6,10,11,11,16,19,19,19,21,23,34; **14:**1,2,5,5,8,8,10,12,13,16,16,18,24,26,28,31,32,32; **15:**4,8,8,11,13,14,15,20,22,23,29; **16:**1,7,17,18,19,20,26; **17:**2,4,6,7,12,12,13,15,16,37; **18:**1,2,2,3,10,10,12,12,13,13,17,18,21,25,25,35; **19:**2,2,4,7,9,11,12,12,14,17,20,21,22,30,46,46; **20:**3,6,9,9,9,10,12,19,20,24,27,28,28,29,43,47; **21:**2,18,27,34; **22:**10,10,12,24,29,36,36,36,41,47,48,52,53,54,55,56,58,59; **23:**2,4,6,8,8,27,38,46,47,49,50,50,50,53; **24:**13,19,23,37,39,42; **Jn 1:**6,7,8,13,30,32; **2:**1,12,15,16; **3:**1,1,1,2,4,25,27; **4:**5,7,7,9,9,9,10,14,19,21,23,27,29,35,36,36,44,46; **5:**2,3,6,9,25,28,35,35; **6:**2,3,5,7,7,9,15,17,18,60,70; **7:**1,4,12,18,22,23,23,26,30,33,37,44,49,51,52; **8:**3,6,6,7,9,34,35,35,37,40,40,44,44,48,49,55; **9:**1,14,16,17,24,24,25,32; **10:**1,1,5,5,13,21,21,21,33,41; **11:**1,8,10,38,38,39,43,44,47,54,54; **12:**2,3,5,6,9,14,15,21,24,24,28,35,46,48; **13:**4,5,10,16,22,33,34; **14:**2,3,9; **15:**6,15,20; **16:**2,16,16,17,17,18,19,19,21,21,21,25,32; **18:**1,3,10,18,26,27,30,35,37,37,38; **19:**2,2,4,6,7,11,12,13,19,29,29,29,31,34,34,38,39,41,41; **20:**26; **21:**8,9; **Ac 1:**3,5,9,12,15,15,18,22; **2:**2,2,6,22,30,35; **3:**2,14,22; **4:**9,16,36,37; **5:**1,1,4,15,24,30,34,34,34,37; **6:**5,5,7,8; **7:**6,9,11,16,18,29,30,31,37,41,46,47,52,58; **8:**1,5,9,11,22,32,32; **9:**3,4,10,10,11,12,12,23,25,26,31,33,36,43; **10:**1,1,3,4,5,7,10,11,13,15,22,22,26,27,28,28,30,32,39,48; **11:**5,5,5,7,9,14,21,24,24,26,28; **12:**7,9,11,13,19,20,21,22,22; **13:**6,10,11,15,21,22,28,29,39,47,51; **14:**1,5,8,21,27,28; **15:**7,10,14,39; **16:**1,1,1,3,9,9,12,13,14,14,14,15,16,16,16,26,34,37; **17:**1,4,4,5,5,12,12,18,19,31,34,34,34; **18:**2,2,3,7,9,11,11,12,14,15,18,24,24,24,24,27; **19:**2,4,14,16,19,22,23,24,24,25,31,33,34,38,39; **20:**9,9,9,16; **21:**2,7,10,10,16,23,38,39,39; **22:**3,6,7,12,12,17,25,26,27,28,28,29; **23:**6,7,9,9,12,14,23,25,27,30; **24:**1,2,5,5,10,10,12,14,14,15,26,27; **25:**3,9,13,14,14,19,20,26,27; **26:**4,5,5,11,13,14,16,16,18,26,28,28; **27:**1,2,2,8,12,13,14,16,18,21,28,28,34,39,39,41; **28:**2,3,3,4,6,6,11,14,16,23; **Ro 1:**1,3,13,17,23,25,28; **2:**3,14,17,19,19,20,27,28,28,29,29,29; **3:**1,4,5,7,25,28; **4:**4,11,11,17,19; **5:**7,7,14,14; **6:**4,5,5; **7:**2,14,23,24,25,25; **8:**3; **9:**9,20,30,33,33; **10:**19,19,21; **11:**1,5,8,9,9,9,9,17,24,25,30,31; **12:**1; **13:**5,10; **14:**13,17,20; **15:**8,16,24,26; **16:**1,2,13,16; **1Co 1:**23; **2:**4,6,7,11,15; **3:**10,10,14; **4:**2,6,9,20,21,21; **5:**1,1,6,7,11,11; **6:**1,4,5,15,16,18,20; **7:**1,1,5,6,6,10,11,12,12,13,13,13,17,18,18,21,22,23,25,26,27,27,27,28,33,34,35,39; **8:**7,9,10; **9:**5,6,7,7,7,11,17,18,19,20,24,24,25,25,26,27; **10:**13,16,16,21,27; **11:**6,6,6,7,10,13,14,14,15,15,18,21,30; **12:**8,8,12,15,27; **13:**1,1,2,11,11,11,11,11,12,12; **14:**2,4,7,8,11,11,13,14,19,22,26,26,26,26,27,27,30,33,35,37,40; **15:**21,21,37,38,44,44,44,44,45,45,51,52; **16:**2,6,7,9,20; **2Co 1:**10,17,22; **2:**12,16; **3:**3,6,12,13,15; **5:**1,5,16; **6:**13,15,18; **7:**3,8; **8:**2,6; **9:**5,7; **10:**13; **11:**1,2,2,4,4,4,6,7,9,9,16,16,16,17,21,25,25,33,33; **12:**2,5,6,7,7,11,12,13,14,16; **13:**2,12; **Gal 1:**1,6,8,9,10; **2:**2,3,5,14,14,14,16,18; **3:**10,13,13,15,18,19,20,21,25; **4:**1,4,7,14,23,27,27; **5:**1,7,9; **6:**1,7,9; **Eph 1:**13,14; **2:**21,22; **3:**7; **4:**1,1,27; **5:**2,3,5,13,27,31,32; **6:**2; **Php 1:**6,13,27,28; **2:**7,8,8,15,17,22; **3:**1,5,5,8,9,15,17,20; **4:**18; **Col 1:**7,10,23; **2:**11,15,16,16,16,17,18; **3:**13,24; **4:**1,3,7,7,11,12; **1Th 1:**7; **2:**5,7,9,11,13,17; **4:**4,6,7,8,11,16; **5:**2,3,4,8,8,26; **2Th 1:**5; **2:**2,11; **3:**8,9,15; **1Ti 1:**5,5,5,13,13,13,15,19; **2:**4,6,7,7,11,12,12,14; **3:**1,1,3,4,6,7,9,12; **4:**2,6,9; **5:**4,11,16,23; **6:**5,9,10,19; **2Ti 1:**3,9,11,11; **2:**3,4,6,9,11,15,20,22,25; **3:**5,7,12; **4:**3,6,14; **Titus 1:**1,6; **2:**14; **3:**8,10,10; **Phm** 1,9,15,16,16,16,16,16,17,22; **Heb 1:**8,11,12,12,13; **2:**3,6,6,7,9,17; **3:**3,5,12; **4:**7,7,9,14,15; **5:**5,6; **6:**7,20; **7:**2,3,4,5,6,13,16,16,17,19,21,21,22,24,26; **8:**1,2,4,5,5,8; **9:**2,3,7,10,11,13,15,15,16,17,24,24,28; **10:**1,5,20,21,22,22,27,31,32,37; **11:**4,8,9,9,13,14,16,16,16,17,19; **12:**1,5,10,11,16,18,19,19,24,24,28,29; **13:**11,15,17,17,18; **Jas 1:**1,6,8,10,18,23,26; **2:**2,2,2,3,11,15,15,24,25; **3:**4,5,5,5,6,6,8,12,12,12,18; **4:**4,11,13,14,14; **5:**12,16,17,17,20,20; **1Pe 1:**3,6,17,19; **2:**5,5,6,6,8,8,9,9,9,10,16,20; **3:**4,9,16,20,21; **4:**2,8,15,15,16; **5:**1,1,8,10,12,14; **2Pe 1:**1,1,3,11,19,19; **2:**5,7,16,16,17,22,22; **3:**8,8,8,8,10,10,13,13; **1Jn 1:**10; **2:**4,7,8,9,11,22; **3:**15,15,17; **4:**20,20; **5:**10,16,16; **2Jn** 5; **3Jn** 6; **Jude** 1,1,4,7; **Rev 1:**6,10,10,11,13,13,13,15,16; **2:**9,14,17,17,20,22; **3:**1,3,4,12,17; **4:**1,1,2,3,6,7,7,7,7; **5:**1,2,2,6,8,9,10,12; **6:**1,2,2,2,2,4,4,5,5,6,6,6,8,8,10,11,11,12,13,13,14; **7:**2,3,9,10; **8:**3,7,7,8,8,9,9,10,10,10,11,12,12,12,12,12,12,13; **9:**1,2,5,13,15,18; **10:**1,1,2,3,3,4; **11:**1,1,9,11,12,12,13,13,19; **12:**1,1,1,4,5,5,6,10,14,14,14,15; **13:**1,1,2,2,2,2,3,5,11,11,11,16,18; **14:**2,2,3,7,8,9,9,13,14,14,14,14,15,17,18,20; **15:**2; **16:**1,3,15,17,18,21; **17:**3,3,3,4,5,9,10,12; **18:**2,2,2,2,2,6,7,18,21,21,21,22,23; **19:**1,5,6,10,11,12,13,15,17; **20:**1,2,3,4,6,11; **21:**1,1,2,3,10,11,11,12,15,16,21,22; **22:**5,9

AM (1130)

See select index of "I AM" in the Main Concordance.

Ge 4:9; **6:**13,13,17; **9:**12; **13:**17; **15:**1,7; **16:**5; **17:**1; **18:**12,13,17,27; **20:**16; **22:**1,11; **23:**4; **24:**3,13,24,34,43; **25:**32; **26:**24,24; **27:**1,2,19,24,32; **28:**13,15,20; **29:**33; **30:**2,13; **31:**11,13; **32:**5,10,11,20; **34:**12; **35:**11; **37:**13; **38:**25; **39:**9; **41:**9,44; **43:**14,14; **45:**3,4,12; **46:**2,3,30; **48:**4,21; **49:**29; **50:**5,19,24; **Ex 3:**4,6,7,10,11,14,14,14; **4:**10; **6:**2,6,7,8,29; **7:**5,17; **8:**22; **10:**2; **12:**12; **14:**4,18; **15:**26; **16:**12; **17:**4; **18:**6; **19:**9; **20:**2,5; **22:**27; **23:**20; **29:**46,46; **31:**13; **33:**17; **34:**10; **Lev 11:**44,44,45,45; **14:**34; **18:**2,3,4,5,6,21,24,30; **19:**2,3,4,10,12,14,16,18,25,28,30,31,32,34,36,37; **20:**7,8,22,23,24,26; **21:**8,12,15,23; **22:**2,3,8,9,16,30,31,32,33; **23:**10,22,43; **24:**22; **25:**2,17,38,55; **26:**1,2,13,44,45; **Nu 3:**13,41,45; **10:**10,30; **11:**21; **13:**2; **15:**2,18,41,41; **18:**7,20; **22:**30,37; **24:**14; **25:**11,12; **Dt 4:**1,8,40; **5:**6,9,31; **8:**1,11; **10:**13; **11:**8,13,22,26,27,32; **12:**28; **13:**18; **15:**5; **28:**15; **29:**6,14; **30:**8,11; **31:**2,2,27; **32:**39,49,52; **Jos 1:**2; **3:**7; **14:**10,11; **23:**2,14; **Jdg 6:**10,14,15; **7:**9; **8:**5; **9:**2; **11:**35; **13:**11; **18:**4; **19:**18; **Ru 1:**11,12; **3:**9,12; **4:**4; **1Sa 1:**15,26; **3:**4,5,6,8,11,16; **9:**19,21; **12:**2,7; **14:**7; **15:**1; **16:**1,22; **17:**8,39,43,58; **18:**18; **20:**5,8; **21:**2,15; **22:**22; **23:**4; **24:**11; **25:**41,41; **26:**18; **28:**15; **30:**13; **2Sa 1:**13; **3:**8,8,39,39; **7:**2,18; **11:**5; **12:**11; **14:**5,18,32; **15:**20,26,26; **19:**22,26,35; **20:**17; **22:**22; **24:**12,14; **1Ki 2:**2; **3:**7; **11:**31; **13:**14,18; **14:**10; **15:**19; **16:**3; **17:**12,20; **18:**22,36; **19:**4,10,14; **20:**6,13,28; **21:**21; **22:**4; **2Ki 1:**10,12; **2:**9,10; **3:**7; **5:**6,7; **10:**15,15,19,24; **16:**7; **21:**12; **22:**16,20; **1Ch 12:**17; **17:**1,16; **21:**10,13; **29:**14; **2Ch 2:**4,5,6,13; **16:**3; **18:**3; **34:**24,28; **35:**21,21,23; **Ezr 9:**6; **Ne 6:**3; **Job 1:**15,16,17,19; **7:**12; **9:**21,29; **10:**7,15,15,15; **11:**4; **12:**3; **13:**2; **19:**10,17,20; **20:**2; **21:**6; **23:**15,17; **30:**19; **31:**6; **32:**6,18,19; **33:**2,6,6,9,9; **34:**5,6,6,6,31; **35:**2; **40:**4; **42:**7; **Ps 6:**2,6; **18:**21; **22:**6,14; **25:**16; **30:**9; **31:**9,11,12,22; **35:**3; **37:**25; **38:**6,8,13,17,18; **39:**10,13; **40:**7,17; **46:**10; **50:**7; **52:**8; **55:**2; **56:**3,4,11,12; **57:**4,4; **69:**3,4,8,12,17,19; **70:**5; **71:**9,18; **73:**23; **81:**10; **86:**1,2,7; **88:**3,4,4,5,8,15; **102:**2,5,6; **109:**4,22,23,25; **116:**10,16; **119:**19,25,63,83,86,94,125,141; **120:**7; **131:**2,2; **139:**14,18; **142:**6; **143:**12; **Pr 20:**9; **30:**1,2; **Ecc 4:**8,8; **7:**23; **SS 1:**5,6,6; **2:**1,5,16; **5:**8; **6:**3; **8:**10; **Isa 1:**14,15; **5:**5; **6:**5,5,8; **8:**18; **19:**11; **21:**3,3; **27:**4; **33:**24; **38:**14,19; **41:**4,10,10,13; **42:**8; **43:**3,5,10,11,12,13,15,19,19,25; **44:**6,6,16,24; **45:**3,5,6,18,22; **46:**4,4,9,9,13; **47:**7,8,10; **48:**12,12,12,16,17; **49:**5,23,26; **51:**12,15; **56:**3; **58:**9; **60:**16,22; **65:**1,1,5; **66:**18; **Jer 1:**6,7,8,12,15,19; **2:**23,35; **3:**12,14; **4:**6,31; **5:**15; **6:**11,19; **7:**19; **8:**21; **9:**24; **13:**13; **15:**6,20; **18:**11; **19:**3,15; **20:**7,9; **21:**4,8,13; **23:**9,23,30,31,32; **24:**7; **25:**29,29; **26:**14; **28:**16; **29:**23; **30:**11; **31:**9; **32:**3,27,28; **34:**2,22; **35:**17; **36:**5,5; **37:**14; **38:**14,19; **39:**16; **40:**4; **42:**11; **44:**11,27,30; **45:**3; **46:**25,28; **50:**31; **51:**25; **La 1:**11,20,20,20; **2:**11; **3:**1; **Eze 2:**3,4; **3:**3; **4:**16; **5:**8; **6:**3,7,10,13,14; **7:**4,8,27; **11:**10,12; **12:**11,15,16,20,23; **13:**8,9,14,20,21,23; **14:**8; **15:**7; **16:**30,37,62; **18:**23; **20:**5,7,19,20,26,31,38,42,44,47; **21:**3,4; **22:**16,26; **23:**28,49; **24:**16,21,24,27; **25:**4,5,7,11,16,17; **26:**3,6,7; **27:**3; **28:**2,7,9,22,22,22,23,24,26; **29:**3,6,9,10,16,19,21; **30:**8,19,22,25,26; **32:**15; **33:**29; **34:**10,27,30,31; **35:**3,4,9,15; **36:**9,11,22,23,23,32,38; **37:**6,12,13,19; **38:**3,16,23; **39:**1,6,7,17,19,22,28; **40:**4; **44:**28; **Da 1:**10; **2:**8; **8:**19; **10:**11,16; **Hos 1:**9; **2:**2,14; **5:**12; **11:**9; **12:**8; **14:**8; **Joel 2:**19,27,27; **3:**7,10; **Am 7:**8; **Jnh 1:**9; **Mic 2:**3; **3:**8; **6:**10; **7:**1; **Na 2:**13; **3:**5; **Hab 1:**5,6; **2:**1; **Zep 2:**15; **Hag 1:**13; **2:**4,21; **Zec 1:**14,15; **2:**10; **3:**8; **8:**2,2,21; **9:**8; **10:**6; **11:**5,16; **12:**2; **13:**5,5; **Mal 1:**6,6,10,14; **Mt 3:**11,17; **8:**3,9; **9:**28; **10:**16; **11:**29; **16:**15; **17:**5; **18:**20; **20:**13,15,22; **21:**24,27; **22:**32; **23:**34; **24:**5; **26:**18,55,61; **27:**24,43; **28:**20; **Mk 1:**7,11,41; **8:**27,29; **10:**38,39; **11:**29,33; **12:**26; **13:**6; **14:**48,62; **Lk 1:**18,19,34,38,43; **3:**16,22; **5:**8,13; **7:**8; **9:**18,20,44; **10:**3; **12:**50; **15:**17,19,21; **16:**24; **18:**11; **19:**22; **20:**8; **21:**8; **22:**27,33,52,58,70; **24:**49; **Jn 1:**20,21,23,27; **3:**28,28; **4:**9,26; **5:**7,17,36; **6:**35,41,48,51; **7:**8,28,28,29,33,33,34,36; **8:**12,14,14,16,18,21,23,23,24,28,38,46,49,50,58; **9:**5,5,9; **10:**7,9,11,14,36; **11:**11,15,25; **12:**26,32; **13:**7,13,18,19,19,19,33,36; **14:**2,3,4,6,10,11,12,20,20,28,28,28; **15:**1,5; **16:**5,7,10,17,26,28,32; **17:**9,11,13,13,14,16,21,24; **18:**5,6,8,17,25,35,37; **19:**4,28; **20:**17,21; **Ac 7:**32; **9:**5; **10:**26; **13:**25,25,25,41; **17:**3,23; **18:**6,10; **20:**22,26; **21:**13,39; **22:**3,8,27; **23:**6; **24:**21; **25:**4,10,11; **26:**6,15,17,22,25,25,26,29; **28:**20; **Ro 1:**14,15,16; **3:**5,7; **6:**19; **7:**1,14,24,25; **8:**38; **9:**1; **11:**1,3,13,13; **14:**14; **15:**14,25; **1Co 4:**3,14; **5:**3,3,4,11; **7:**7,35; **9:**1,1,2,15,16,17,19,20,21,21; **10:**29,30,33; **12:**15,16; **13:**1,2,12; **14:**11,37; **15:**9,10,10; **16:**10,11; **2Co 7:**4,9,16; **8:**8; **9:**3; **10:**1; **11:**2,3,5,12,17,21,22,22,22,23,23,31; **12:**10,10,11,11,14,16,20,21; **13:**10; **Gal 1:**6,10,10,20; **4:**1,18,19,20; **5:**10,11,11; **Eph 3:**8; **5:**32; **6:**20,21,21,22; **Php 1:**7,13,16,17,22,23; **2:**17,17,24,28; **4:**11,11,18; **Col 1:**24; **2:**1,5,5; **4:**3,8; **1Ti 1:**15,18; **2:**7,7; **3:**14,15; **2Ti 1:**5,5,12,12,12; **2:**7,9; **4:**6; **Phm** 12,13,19; **Heb 2:**13; **10:**7,9; **12:**21; **1Pe 1:**16; **2Pe 1:**17; **1Jn 2:**7,8,12,13,13,26; **5:**16; **2Jn** 5; **Rev 1:**8,17,18,18; **2:**23; **3:**11,16,17,20; **18:**7; **19:**10; **21:**5,6; **22:**7,8,9,12,13,16,20

AN (1100)

Ge 4:3,4; **6:**13,14,16; **8:**20; **9:**5,5,5; **12:**7,8; **13:**4,18; **14:**22; **16:**1; **17:**7,8,13,19; **20:**4; **21:**20,31; **22:**9; **24:**9,37; **25:**8,33; **26:**25,31; **27:**2,28; **31:**53; **33:**20; **34:**7,15; **35:**1,3,7; **37:**3; **39:**1; **41:**53; **42:**22,23; **43:**16; **44:**20; **48:**4; **50:**5,25; **Ex 2:**11,19; **6:**6; **9:**19; **10:**13; **13:**19; **16:**16,32,33,36,36; **17:**15; **20:**4,24,25; **21:**6,26,27,33; **22:**1,9,10,11,14,19,31; **23:**7,20,22; **24:**4; **25:**2,10,17; **26:**36; **27:**1,16; **28:**4,32,39; **29:**40; **30:**1,13,14; **32:**4,5,8; **33:**2; **35:**5,5,21,24,24; **36:**6,6,37; **38:**18,23,23; **39:**23,29,30; **Lev 1:**2,2,9,13,17; **2:**2,4,9,12; **3:**1,1,5,6; **4:**31; **5:**2,4,11,11,16; **6:**15,20,21; **7:**9,12,13,14,21,24,25; **8:**28; **9:**4; **11:**35,39; **14:**10,21,40,41,45; **15:**2,16,18,32; **17:**3,4,6; **18:**23,23; **19:**24,36,36; **20:**15,16,21,24; **21:**3; **22:**4,18,23,24; **23:**13,16,17,18; **24:**5,10,10,10,21; **25:**49; **26:**1; **27:**9,9,9,11,26,26,28; **Nu 3:**4; **5:**15,15; **7:**3; **10:**9; **11:**12; **15:**3,4,4,6,7,9,10,13,14,19,20,24; **16:**14,21,45; **17:**10; **18:**17,19,24,28; **19:**22; **20:**16; **22:**4,37; **25:**6,11; **26:**53,61; **27:**7; **28:**2,5,8,9,9,12,12,13,20,24,26,27,28; **29:**2,3,8,9,13,14,36; **30:**2; **31:**50; **34:**2,13,17; **35:**16,23; **36:**2; **Dt 1:**16; **4:**16,16,23,34; **5:**8,15; **9:**12,16; **12:**10; **13:**11; **15:**17,21; **16:**2,8; **17:**1,15; **19:**3,20; **20:**1,10,16,19; **21:**8,23; **22:**10,19,21; **23:**7,7; **24:**4; **25:**4,19; **26:**1,8; **27:**5,5,15,25; **28:**37,48,49,65; **29:**8,12; **32:**11; **Jos 6:**7; **7:**15; **8:**2,4,14,30,31; **9:**18; **10:**2,9; **11:**23; **12:**7; **13:**6,7; **14:**1,3; **17:**4,4,6,14; **19:**49; **22:**10,16,19,26,29; **23:**4; **24:**20; **Jdg 3:**31; **4:**17; **6:**19,24; **8:**24,27; **9:**43,48,53; **11:**34; **12:**5; **13:**6,19; **14:**3,4; **17:**3,5; **18:**1,10,14,14; **19:**16,24; **20:**29; **21:**1,4,7,13; **Ru 2:**17; **1Sa 1:**1,24; **2:**28; **4:**18; **5:**9; **7:**17; **12:**17; **14:**3,14,14,24,35; **15:**5; **16:**14,15; **17:**12; **18:**10; **19:**5,9,13; **20:**3,6,36; **25:**3; **26:**19; **27:**9; **28:**14; **29:**3,9; **30:**11,13,13; **2Sa 1:**8,13; **3:**8,12,13,27,35; **4:**11,12; **11:**21; **13:**3,18; **14:**8,17,20; **15:**19; **17:**8,25; **18:**10; **19:**27,35; **23:**5; **24:**18,21,25; **1Ki 1:**29; **3:**1,25; **6:**16; **7:**6,31; **8:**31,33,36,37; **9:**7; **11:**14,26; **13:**1,14,18; **14:**5,21,31; **15:**22; **16:**32,33; **18:**32; **19:**5,11; **20:**25,30; **21:**1; **22:**25; **2Ki 3:**11,18; **6:**15; **8:**6; **9:**2; **10:**20; **12:**15; **16:**10,11; **17:**16; **19:**32; **21:**3; **23:**11; **25:**8,24; **1Ch 2:**34; **11:**23; **16:**17,29; **21:**15,18,22,26; **27:**10,14; **28:**8; **2Ch 6:**22,24,27; **7:**9,20; **12:**13; **13:**3,6; **14:**8,9; **15:**14; **18:**24; **20:**11,35,37; **21:**18; **24:**26; **25:**16; **26:**13; **28:**7; **29:**8; **30:**7; **32:**21; **36:**13; **Ezr 4:**6,19,21; **6:**1; **9:**12; **Ne 4:**11; **5:**12,18; **6:**5; **8:**18; **9:**18,31; **10:**29; **13:**25; **Est 7:**6; **8:**3,5; **9:**14; **Job 3:**16; **6:**5; **7:**6,19; **15:**33; **18:**21; **19:**24; **20:**16,24; **21:**21; **22:**8; **28:**3; **31:**37; **33:**3,23; **34:**6,20; **38:**26; **40:**9,15; **41:**4; **42:**15,17; **Ps 5:**9; **7:**9; **15:**4; **24:**4; **27:**3; **31:**11; **43:**1; **46:**1; **48:**7; **52:**8; **55:**12; **66:**15; **69:**31; **78:**55; **80:**6; **81:**4,5; **83:**5; **86:**11; **89:**44; **96:**8; **102:**T,6; **105:**10; **106:**19,20; **109:**6,23,25; **119:**7,26,106; **132:**2,11; **135:**12,12; **136:**21,22; **145:**13; **Pr 3:**22; **6:**11,15; **7:**22,23; **9:**13; **12:**16,17; **13:**2,22,23; **14:**4,5; **15:**23; **16:**10; **17:**9; **18:**1; **19:**11; **20:**16,21; **22:**14,28; **23:**5,10,27; **24:**26,34; **25:**12,12; **26:**2,10,23; **27:**2,6,13; **28:**10; **29:**22,26; **30:**1,17,19,20; **31:**1; **Ecc 4:**13; **7:**11; **8:**2; **10:**5; **SS 2:**3; **4:**13; **7:**1,4; **Isa 1:**30; **5:**10; **8:**1; **10:**7,34; **13:**4,4,11; **14:**4; **16:**4,10; **17:**6; **18:**2,7; **19:**19; **21:**1,2,16; **23:**11; **24:**13; **27:**10; **28:**15,15; **29:**2,5,20; **30:**1,8,13,33; **33:**23; **37:**33; **38:**12,13; **40:**19,20,20; **44:**10,12,13,15; **45:**17; **53:**10; **55:**3,13; **56:**5; **59:**5; **61:**8; **65:**2,16,20,20; **66:**3,20; **Jer 1:**11,18; **2:**22; **3:**18; **4:**20; **5:**15,16,22; **6:**22,26; **7:**34; **9:**16; **13:**23; **16:**9; **17:**1,27; **18:**16; **19:**8; **21:**5; **22:**28; **23:**10; **24:**9,9; **25:**9,9,18; **28:**14; **29:**18; **30:**14,17; **31:**3,18; **32:**21,40; **38:**7,15; **40:**9,12; **42:**18,18; **44:**8,12,12; **47:**2; **48:**2,26,35,39,39,40; **49:**13,14,17,19,22,37; **50:**5,9,41,44; **51:**12,34,37; **La 1:**15,17; **2:**4,5,7; **5:**10; **Eze 1:**4,10,10,24; **4:**3,3; **5:**2,15; **7:**24,26; **10:**14; **11:**19; **12:**23; **14:**8; **16:**3,10,45,60; **17:**2; **20:**17,33,34; **21:**21; **22:**4,15; **23:**41,48; **26:**13; **30:**10,12,13,18; **33:**28,32; **35:**5; **37:**26; **38:**10; **42:**4,7,9; **45:**1,5,6,10,10,13,13,24,24; **46:**5,11,11,14; **47:**22,

AND (29510)

20,24,24,24,25,26,28,30,32,33,33; **7:**2,3,5,6,6,7,7,7,8,12,13,13,14,14,18,19,22,22,24,25,25,26,27,27,27,29; **8:**2,2,3,4,7,8,9,9,9,9,10,11,11,11,12,13,15,15,15,16,17,19,20,21,22,23,25,26,26,26,27,27,32,32,32,33,34; **9:**1,5,6,7,8,9,9,10,10,10,11,13,14,14,17,17,18,18,18,18,19,19,20,22,22,23,23,25,25,28,29,30,31,32,33,33,35,35,35,36; **10:**1,1,1,2,2,3,3,3,4,11,14,15,16,17,18,18,21,21,25,28,30,38,39,40,41,42; **11:**1,4,4,5,9,12,13,14,16,17,17,18,19,19,19,19,21,21,22,23,25,25,25,27,27,28,28,29,29,29,30; **12:**1,1,3,4,4,5,10,11,11,13,14,15,18,20,22,22,22,23,25,25,27,29,30,31,31,33,33,35,37,38,39,40,40,41,41,42,42,43,44,45,45,45,45,46,47,48,49,50,50; **13:**1,2,4,4,6,7,10,12,15,15,15,16,17,17,19,19,20,22,23,25,25,26,27,28,30,30,31,32,32,33,36,36,38,39,39,40,41,41,42,44,44,44,46,47,48,49,50,50,54,54,55,55,57,57,58; **14:**2,3,3,6,9,10,11,12,12,12,14,14,15,15,15,17,19,19,19,19,20,20,21,22,24,26,29,30,31,32,35,36,36; **15:**1,1,3,4,4,10,10,12,17,18,21,22,23,25,26,28,29,29,30,30,30,31,31,32,32,34,36,36,36,36,37,38,39; **16:**1,1,3,3,4,4,6,7,9,10,11,12,14,17,18,18,18,19,21,21,21,21,22,23,24,24,27; **17:**1,1,2,3,4,5,7,11,12,14,15,17,18,18,19,20,23,23,24,24,25,27,27,27,27; **18:**1,2,3,3,5,6,8,8,9,9,9,12,12,13,15,17,18,21,25,25,25,26,27,28,29,29,30,31,31; **19:**1,2,3,4,5,5,5,5,7,9,10,12,13,14,16,19,19,21,21,25,26,29,29,30; **20:**2,3,4,4,5,5,6,7,8,8,9,12,12,14,16,17,18,18,19,19,19,20,21,25,25,27,28,29,30,31,32,34,34; **21:**1,2,2,3,5,5,6,7,7,8,9,10,10,12,12,12,14,14,15,15,16,17,17,21,21,23,23,23,25,28,28,29,30,31,32,32,32,32,33,33,35,36,38,39,39,41,42,43,45; **22:**4,4,4,5,6,7,7,9,10,10,13,13,13,15,16,20,20,21,22,24,25,25,26,32,37,37,38,39,40,46; **23:**1,2,4,5,6,7,8,9,9,12,13,15,15,15,20,21,21,22,22,23,23,23,25,25,25,26,26,27,27,28,29,29,30,32,34,34,34,34,35,35,37,37; **24:**1,3,3,5,6,7,7,9,9,10,10,11,11,14,14,19,21,24,24,24,29,29,30,30,31,31,32,35,38,38,39,39,40,41,43,45,48,49,49,49,50,51,51; **25:**1,2,5,5,7,9,9,10,14,15,16,16,18,19,21,21,23,23,24,25,25,26,28,29,30,30,31,32,33,35,35,35,36,36,36,37,37,38,38,39,40,41,42,42,43,43,43,43,44; **26:**2,3,4,4,9,15,17,18,19,21,22,26,26,26,27,31,35,36,36,37,37,37,38,39,40,41,42,44,44,45,45,47,47,49,50,51,53,55,55,56,57,58,59,61,61,62,64,65,67,68,69,71,73,74,75,75; **27:**1,2,3,3,5,5,6,10,11,12,20,20,24,25,26,27,28,29,29,29,30,30,30,31,32,36,38,40,40,41,42,48,48,50,52,53,53,54,54,54,56,56,58,60,60,61,62,64,64,66,66; **28:**1,2,2,3,4,6,7,7,8,9,10,11,12,13,14,15,15,18,18,19,19,19,20,20; **Mk 1:**4,5,6,6,7,7,9,10,11,13,13,15,16,17,18,19,20,20,21,21,26,27,27,29,29,30,31,31,32,34,35,36,37,39,40,41,42,44,45; **2:**2,4,8,9,11,12,12,13,14,14,15,15,16,16,18,18,18,20,22,22,22,23,25,25,26,26; **3:**1,5,5,6,7,8,8,8,11,13,13,14,15,17,19,20,20,22,23,26,26,28,31,32,32,33,34,34,35,35; **4:**1,2,4,4,6,7,8,10,12,12,15,16,19,19,20,22,24,27,27,32,37,38,39,39,41,41; **5:**3,4,4,5,5,5,6,10,10,13,13,13,14,14,14,15,15,16,19,20,20,22,23,23,24,25,26,27,29,30,31,33,33,34,37,38,39,39,40,40,40,41,42,43; **6:**1,2,3,3,3,4,5,7,11,11,12,13,13,14,15,17,17,19,20,20,21,21,22,22,22,23,24,26,28,28,29,29,30,30,31,31,33,33,34,35,36,36,37,37,38,38,40,41,41,41,42,43,43,45,47,50,50,51,53,55,56,56; **7:**1,2,3,4,4,5,8,9,10,10,13,14,14,17,19,22,23,24,24,25,27,30,30,31,31,32,32,33,34,35,37; **8:**1,2,6,6,6,7,8,10,11,12,13,15,16,18,18,20,22,22,23,23,24,25,27,28,31,31,31,31,32,32,33,34,34,34,35,38,38; **9:**1,2,2,4,4,5,7,7,11,12,12,13,14,15,18,20,22,25,25,26,27,27,30,31,32,35,35,37,38,42,45,45,47,47,48,50; **10:**1,1,1,2,4,6,7,7,8,11,12,12,14,16,16,17,19,21,21,21,23,26,27,29,30,30,31,32,32,33,33,33,34,34,35,37,39,41,42,42,44,45,46,48,49,50,52; **11:**1,1,2,2,3,4,6,7,9,11,14,15,15,15,16,17,18,18,19,21,23,24,25,27,27,28,29,31; **12:**1,1,3,4,5,7,8,8,9,9,11,12,12,13,14,15,16,16,17,17,19,19,20,26,28,30,30,30,32,33,33,33,34,38,39,39,40,41,42; **13:**3,4,6,7,8,8,9,9,10,11,12,12,17,19,22,22,22,24,25,26,27,27,28,31,34,34; **14:**1,1,1,1,3,5,5,7,11,12,13,15,16,19,22,22,23,23,27,31,32,33,33,33,34,35,37,38,39,41,43,43,44,45,46,47,48,49,50,53,53,54,55,57,58,60,61,62,62,65,65,65,68,71,72,72; **15:**1,1,5,8,15,16,17,18,19,19,20,20,21,21,24,27,29,29,30,31,32,34,36,39,40,40,41,43,46,47; **16:**1,3,5,7,8,8,10,10,10,11,13,14,15,16,17,18,18,19,20,20,20; **Lk 1:**2,6,7,8,9,10,12,13,14,14,15,17,17,17,18,19,19,20,20,21,24,25,28,29,31,31,32,33,35,36,39,40,41,42,46,47,55,56,58,58,59,60,63,64,64,65,67,68,71,72,74,75,76,79,80,80,80; **2:**3,4,5,7,7,8,9,9,12,13,14,15,15,16,16,16,18,19,20,20,22,24,25,25,28,32,33,34,34,34,35,37,37,37,38,39,40,40,40,44,46,47,48,51,52,52,52,52; **3:**1,1,2,5,6,8,9,9,11,14,14,15,16,17,18,18,19,21,22,22; **4:**1,2,5,6,6,6,8,9,14,15,16,17,18,20,22,23,25,25,27,29,30,31,35,36,36,36,37,38,38,39,39,39,40,41,42,44; **5:**1,3,3,4,5,7,7,7,8,9,10,10,11,12,13,13,14,15,16,17,17,17,17,17,18,19,21,22,23,24,25,26,26,27,28,28,29,29,30,30,30,33,33,33,36,37,37,39; **6:**1,1,3,4,4,6,6,7,8,8,8,10,10,11,11,12,13,16,17,17,17,17,18,19,19,22,22,23,25,30,33,34,35,35,35,37,37,37,38,38,41,42,45,46,47,47,48,49,49; **7:**2,3,3,5,7,8,8,8,9,10,11,11,12,12,13,14,14,15,15,16,17,21,21,22,22,22,25,26,30,32,32,32,33,34,34,34,36,38,39,41,44,44; **8:**1,2,2,3,4,5,6,7,8,12,12,12,14,14,15,15,16,17,19,20,21,21,22,23,24,24,24,25,25,25,28,29,29,29,29,31,32,33,33,34,34,35,35,35,37,39,39,41,43,44,44,45,47,47,50,51,51,51,52,54,55; **9:**1,1,2,2,5,6,6,7,8,9,10,11,11,11,12,12,12,13,13,15,16,16,16,17,17,18,19,22,22,22,22,22,23,23,25,26,26,26,28,28,29,30,32,32,33,34,34,36,36,39,39,41,41,42,43,45,47,48,49,52,54,55,56,58,59,60,61,62; **10:**1,1,4,7,8,9,10,10,13,13,14,15,17,19,19,21,21,21,22,22,23,24,24,27,27,27,27,28,29,30,31,32,33,34,34,34,35,35,37,37,38,40,41,42; **11:**4,5,5,6,7,7,7,7,8,8,9,9,9,10,14,17,17,22,22,23,24,25,26,26,26,26,27,28,31,31,32,32,33,36,37,39,39,41,42,42,43,46,46,47,48,49,51,52,53,53; **12:**3,4,10,11,16,18,18,19,19,23,24,28,29,30,31,33,33,35,36,37,37,42,45,45,45,45,45,46,46,47,48,48,49,50,52,53,53,54,55,55,56,58,58; **13:**6,7,8,8,11,11,12,13,13,14,15,19,19,19,21,22,24,25,25,26,26,28,28,29,29,29,29,30,31,31,32,32,32,33,33,34,34; **14:**3,4,6,9,11,12,14,16,18,18,19,21,21,21,21,21,23,23,25,26,26,26,26,27,27,28,29,30,31,32; **15:**1,2,2,4,4,5,6,6,6,8,8,9,9,9,13,14,15,17,18,18,18,20,20,20,21,22,22,23,23,24,24,25,26,27,27,28,28,29,31,32,32,32; **16:**2,3,6,6,7,7,10,12,13,13,13,14,16,16,17,18,18,19,19,21,21,22,22,23,24,24,25,26,26,29,31; **17:**3,4,6,6,7,8,8,8,11,13,14,16,16,19,24,25,27,27,28,28,28,29,29,33,34,35; **18:**1,3,5,6,7,7,8,9,10,11,12,13,14,16,16,20,22,22,24,30,31,31,32,33,34,39,40,43; **19:**1,2,4,5,6,7,8,8,8,10,11,12,13,14,15,16,18,20,21,22,24,27,29,30,30,32,35,38,41,42,43,43,44,47; **20:**1,1,5,9,10,11,11,12,12,14,14,15,16,16,17,19,20,21,21,23,24,25,26,28,28,29,31,31,34,35,36,37,37,40,46,46,46,47; **21:**5,7,8,9,10,11,11,11,12,12,12,12,13,15,16,16,16,19,21,23,23,24,25,25,25,27,28,29,30,33,34,34,36,36,37,38; **22:**2,2,4,4,4,5,6,8,8,11,13,14,15,17,17,19,19,19,25,26,29,30,30,32,33,36,36,36,37,37,39,41,43,44,44,45,46,47,50,51,51,52,52,53,54,55,55,56,58,61,62,62,63,64,65,66,66,68; **23:**1,2,2,4,5,10,11,11,12,13,14,14,16,19,22,23,25,25,26,26,27,28,28,29,30,34,35,36,37,39,44,45,47,48,50,51,51,53,54,55,55,56,56; **24:**1,7,9,10,12,12,15,15,19,19,20,20,21,23,24,25,26,27,27,30,31,31,32,33,33,34,34,35,36,37,38,39,39,39,40,41,41,43,43,44,46,47,50,51,52,53; **Jn 1:**1,4,5,10,14,14,14,17,18,18,19,29,32,33,33,34,38,39,39,39,40,41,42,42,44,45,45,46,51,51; **2:**2,2,8,9,10,10,11,12,12,14,14,15,15,15,19,20,22,23; **3:**2,5,10,11,12,16,18,20,22,22,23,23,25,26,26,29,29,29,31,32,35; **4:**1,3,6,9,10,10,11,12,12,15,16,18,23,23,24,24,27,28,30,34,35,36,36,37,38,40,41,42,46,47,47,48,50,53; **5:**2,6,8,9,10,11,12,14,15,17,20,20,21,24,24,25,25,27,29,29,30,32,33,35,35,37,43; **6:**2,3,5,9,10,11,13,15,17,17,18,19,21,22,24,26,30,33,35,36,37,39,40,40,42,44,45,50,53,54,54,55,56,56,57,58,63,64,66,69; **7:**3,11,14,15,21,26,28,29,32,33,34,35,36,37,37,37,42,45,50,52; **8:**2,3,4,6,7,8,10,11,14,21,21,26,28,32,33,38,44,44,48,49,50,52,53,55,56,57; **9:**6,7,7,8,8,11,11,11,11,14,15,15,18,20,27,28,34,35,38,39,40; **10:**1,3,3,4,8,9,9,10,10,10,12,12,12,13,14,15,15,16,16,18,20,23,27,28,30,35,36,38,38,41,42; **11:**1,2,5,5,7,8,15,19,19,25,26,28,28,29,31,32,32,33,33,34,41,44,44,44,45,46,47,48,48,48,52,52,56,57; **12:**3,3,5,9,11,13,14,16,17,22,24,26,27,28,29,32,36,38,40,40,41,48; **13:**1,2,3,3,4,5,9,10,11,12,13,13,14,20,21,24,30,31,32,33; **14:**3,3,3,6,6,7,8,10,11,12,13,14,16,16,16,17,20,20,21,21,21,22,23,23,26,27,28,31; **15:**1,5,6,6,7,7,10,11,16,16,16,22,24,24,27; **16:**8,8,11,13,16,17,17,19,20,22,22,24,24,27,28,29,30,32; **17:**1,3,5,6,8,8,10,10,11,12,14,21,21,23,24,25,25,26,26; **18:**1,1,1,3,3,3,4,5,6,10,12,13,15,16,18,18,19,27,28,29,31,33,35,37,38; **19:**1,2,3,3,3,4,5,6,6,7,9,13,18,18,19,20,20,24,25,26,27,28,28,29,30,30,31,31,32,32,33,34,35,35,37,38,39,41,42; **20:**1,2,2,2,3,4,5,6,8,12,12,13,14,15,16,17,17,17,18,19,19,20,22,22,25,25,26,26,26,27,27,28,29,31; **21:**2,3,3,6,7,9,11,12,13,13,18,18,20,20,24; **Ac 1:**1,3,3,6,8,8,8,8,9,13,13,13,13,13,14,14,15,16,16,17,18,20,23,26; **2:**2,3,4,9,9,9,10,10,11,11,12,13,14,14,17,18,18,19,19,19,20,20,21,22,23,23,26,29,29,30,32,33,33,34,36,37,37,38,38,39,40,41,42,42,43,44,45,46,46,47,47; **3:**1,3,7,7,8,8,8,9,10,10,11,11,13,13,14,14,16,16,19,20,25,25; **4:**1,1,1,3,3,5,6,6,7,7,8,9,10,13,13,15,15,16,18,19,20,23,23,23,24,24,24,25,25,26,26,27,27,28,29,30,30,31,31,32,33,35,35,37,37; **5:**2,3,4,5,5,6,6,8,9,10,10,10,11,12,12,14,14,14,15,15,16,16,17,18,19,20,21,21,21,22,24,25,26,27,28,29,31,31,32,33,34,36,36,37,37,40,40,42,42; **6:**2,3,3,4,4,5,5,6,7,8,8,9,9,11,11,12,12,12,13,14,15; **7:**2,3,3,4,5,6,6,7,7,8,8,8,10,10,10,11,11,13,14,15,16,19,20,21,21,22,22,24,27,27,29,32,32,34,35,35,36,36,36,38,38,39,41,42,42,42,43,46,49,51,52,52,54,55,55,56,57,58,60; **8:**1,1,1,2,3,3,5,6,7,9,10,10,10,12,12,13,13,13,14,17,17,19,22,23,25,25,27,28,29,30,31,32,35,36,38,38,38,39,40; **9:**2,4,6,6,9,11,12,13,14,15,15,17,17,18,18,19,21,21,22,22,24,25,27,27,27,28,29,30,31,31,31,33,34,35,35,36,37,37,37,38,39,39,39,40,41,41,42; **10:**2,2,2,3,4,7,8,9,10,10,11,12,13,16,17,20,21,22,23,24,24,25,27,31,31,33,35,38,38,38,39,40,41,42,42,46; **11:**1,3,3,5,5,6,6,7,10,12,13,14,18,19,20,20,21,21,22,23,23,24,24,26,26,26,28,29,30; **12:**6,7,7,7,8,8,8,10,10,10,11,11,11,12,13,14,16,16,17,17,17,19,19,19,20,20,21,23,23,24,25; **13:**1,1,2,2,3,3,4,6,7,8,9,10,10,11,11,13,14,15,15,16,16,19,21,24,26,27,29,31,34,36,41,42,43,43,43,45,46,46,48,48,50,50,50,51,52,52; **14:**1,1,2,3,3,5,5,6,6,6,8,10,10,12,13,13,14,14,15,15,15,17,17,19,19,19,20,20,21,21,22,23,23,23,25,27,27,28; **15:**1,2,2,2,2,3,3,4,4,5,5,6,7,7,9,12,12,16,16,20,21,21,22,22,22,22,23,23,24,24,25,25,27,28,29,30,30,31,32,32,35,35,35,36,36,38,39,40,41; **16:**1,2,4,5,6,6,8,9,9,11,11,12,12,13,15,15,15,17,18,19,19,20,20,22,22,22,23,24,25,25,26,27,27,29,29,30,31,31,32,33,33,34,34,36,37,37,37,38,38,39,40,40,40; **17:**1,1,2,3,3,4,4,4,5,5,6,7,8,9,9,10,11,12,13,14,15,15,17,18,18,19,19,21,21,22,23,23,24,24,25,25,25,26,26,27,27,28,29,34,34; **18:**1,3,3,4,5,6,6,7,8,8,8,10,10,11,12,15,15,17,17,18,18,18,19,19,22,22,23,23,25,25,26,26,27,27; **19:**1,2,6,6,8,9,9,10,12,12,12,15,16,16,17,17,18,19,20,21,22,25,26,26,26,26,27,27,28,29,29,33,35,35,36,36,38,38; **20:**1,1,2,4,4,4,5,6,7,9,9,10,11,11,12,13,14,15,15,19,19,20,21,21,22,23,24,28,29,30,31,31,32,32,34,36,37; **21:**1,1,2,3,4,5,5,5,6,7,7,7,8,11,11,11,12,13,14,16,16,17,18,18,19,20,24,25,26,26,27,28,28,28,28,29,30,30,32,32,32,33,33,33,34,34,38,40; **22:**1,3,4,4,5,5,7,10,12,13,13,14,14,15,16,16,17,18,19,20,20,22,23,23,24,26,27,30,30,30; **23:**1,6,7,7,8,9,9,10,10,11,12,14,14,15,16,17,18,19,23,23,27,27,31,33,34; **24:**1,1,2,3,6,13,14,15,15,16,17,19,23,24,25,25,26; **25:**2,4,5,6,9,13,15,15,16,17,19,20,23,23,23,24,24,26; **26:**1,3,3,4,5,6,7,10,10,11,12,13,14,16,16,16,17,18,18,18,20,20,20,20,21,22,22,22,23,23,25,26,30,30,30; **27:**1,2,3,4,5,6,7,8,9,10,10,10,11,12,12,13,15,15,17,20,21,21,23,24,24,28,28,28,29,31,32,33,35,35,36,40,40,41,41,41,42,43,43; **28:**2,2,3,5,6,6,7,8,8,8,9,10,11,12,13,13,14,14,15,15,15,17,18,20,21,23,23,23,25,26,27,27,27,28,30,31,31; **Ro 1:**4,5,6,7,7,7,10,12,13,14,14,18,20,21,23,23,23,23,25,25,27,27,29,29,30; **2:**3,4,5,7,8,8,8,9,10,12,15,15,17,18,20,27,27,28,29; **3:**4,4,7,9,14,16,17,19,21,22,23,24,26,30; **4:**3,11,12,13,14,15,16,17,18,19,20,25; **5:**2,4,5,12,12,15,16,16,17,18; **6:**13,18,19,22,22; **7:**1,3,4,6,9,11,12,12,16,23; **8:**2,3,6,9,11,12,15,17,21,21,27,28,29,30,34; **9:**2,3,4,5,9,15,17,18,21,22,25,26,28,33,33; **10:**1,1,3,8,9,10,10,10,12,12,14,14,15,17,20,21; **11:**3,3,4,6,8,9,9,9,10,12,14,17,17,20,22,23,24,25,26,27,29,33,33,36,36; **12:**1,1,1,2,2,4,5,14; **13:**2,3,9,11,12,13,13,13,14; **14:**3,4,6,6,7,8,9,9,17,17,18,19,22,23; **15:**1,4,5,6,6,9,11,12,13,14,14,18,19,21,23,24,26,27,28,28,30,30,31,32; **16:**2,3,7,7,9,12,13,14,14,15,15,15,17,17,18,19,21,23,23,26; **1Co 1:**1,2,2,3,3,5,10,10,10,11,14,17,22,23,24,24,25,26,28,28,30; **2:**1,1,2,3,4,4,7,9,14; **3:**1,3,4,5,8,8,10,13,16,17,20,23,23; **4:**1,5,6,6,7,8,11,19,21; **5:**1,2,2,4,4,8,8,10; **6:**2,6,8,8,8,11,11,13,13,13,14,15; **7:**2,3,5,8,11,12,13,13,14,19,24,28,28,29,34,34,36,36,37,40; **8:**4,5,6,6,7,8,12; **9:**4,5,5,6,7,7,10,13,15,18,19,27; **10:**1,1,2,4,4,7,7,8,9,10,10,11,13,16,20,21,21,26,27,28; **11:**2,3,3,7,18,21,22,24,24,26,27,28,29,29,30,30,33,34; **12:**1,2,3,6,10,11,11,13,16,21,23,23,27,28,28,31; **13:**2,2,2,3,9,13,13; **14:**1,3,6,6,11,20,21,23,23,24,25,26,27,28,28,29,30,31,39,39,40; **15:**1,1,5,5,6,8,9,10,11,14,14,17,24,30,32,34,38,39,40,40,41,41,46,48,49,50,52,53,54,56,58; **16:**3,7,9,15,15,16,16,17,18,19,19,20; **2Co 1:**1,2,2,3,3,6,7,8,10,12,12,13,16,16,17,18,19,19,19,20,21,22,23; **2:**4,4,7,9,10,12,13,14,15,16; **3:**2,11,17,18; **4:**2,3,5,7,13,14,15,17; **5:**4,6,8,8,11,14,15,15,18,19; **6:**2,4,5,5,6,6,7,7,8,8,9,9,10,11,14,15,16,16,16,16,17,17,18,18,18; **7:**1,7,9,10,14,15,15; **8:**1,1,2,3,5,5,7,10,15,17,18,19,22,23,23,24; **9:**2,2,4,5,6,8,10,10,10,11,13,13,14; **10:**1,5,5,6,10,10,12; **11:**3,4,9,9,9,12,14,23,23,25,26,27,27,27,27,29,29,31,33; **12:**1,3,4,12,14,15,18,19,20,20,21,21,21; **13:**6,9,11,11,11,14,14; **Gal 1:**1,2,2,3,3,4,5,6,7,11,13,14,15,18,21,24; **2:**2,2,4,9,9,9,12,14,15,16,20,20; **3:**5,6,8,15,16,16,16,17,19,28,29; **4:**2,7,9,10,10,10,12,14,15,18,20,22,24,25,26,27,28,30,31; **5:**1,11,12,13,15,16,17,19,20,21,21,23,24,26; **6:**1,2,14,16,18; **Eph 1:**2,2,3,4,5,8,10,13,15,17,19,20,21,21,21,22,22; **2:**1,2,3,3,6,6,8,11,12,12,14,15,16,17,17,19,19,20,21,22; **3:**5,6,9,10,12,12,15,17,17,18,18,18,19,21,21; **4:**2,4,6,6,6,8,11,13,13,14,14,14,14,14,16,16,17,18,19,21,24,24,25,27,30,31,31,32; **5:**2,2,5,9,10,13,14,19,19,25,27,27,29,31,31,31,32,33; **6:**2,3,4,5,5,9,9,9,10,12,13,15,15,17,18,18,18,21,21,22,23,23,23; **Php 1:**1,1,2,2,7,7,9,9,9,10,10,11,12,13,14,14,14,15,18,18,19,20,21,23,25,25,27,28,30; **2:**1,2,8,9,10,10,11,12,13,15,15,16,17,17,18,24,25,26,27,27,28,29; **3:**1,1,3,9,10,11,13,13,15,17,17,18,19,20; **4:**1,1,1,2,3,3,6,7,7,8,9,12,12,15,18,19,20,20,21; **Col 1:**1,2,2,4,5,5,6,6,8,9,10,11,12,13,16,16,16,17,18,18,20,21,21,22,23,23,23,24,26,28; **2:**1,1,2,3,5,5,7,7,8,8,10,10,13,14,15,15,18,19,19,22,23; **3:**3,5,8,10,11,12,12,13,14,15,16,16,17,19,22,22,22,25; **4:**1,2,3,7,8,9,11,12,12,13,13,14,15,15,15,16; **1Th 1:**1,1,1,2,3,3,4,5,6,7,7,8,9,10; **2:**1,2,9,9,9,10,10,12,12,13,14,15,15,15,17,18,20; **3:**2,2,4,5,6,6,6,7,7,10,10,11,11,12,12,13,13; **4:**1,1,1,4,6,6,10,10,10,11,11,12,13,14,14,16,16,17,17; **5:**1,1,3,3,4,5,6,7,8,8,11,12,12,14,14,14,15,23,23,24,25,27; **2Th 1:**1,2,2,3,3,3,3,4,4,5,7,7,8,9,9,10,11,11,12,12; **2:**1,1,3,4,6,8,8,9,10,10,12,13,13,15,15,16,16,16,17,17; **3:**1,1,2,2,3,3,4,5,6,6,6,8,8,11,12,12,13,13,16; **1Ti 1:**1,2,2,4,5,5,6,9,9,9,10,10,10,13,13,13,14,16,17,17,19,19,20; **2:**1,2,2,2,3,4,5,5,7,7,7,7,9,11,14,14,15; **3:**4,4,6,7,8,10,11,12,12,13,15; **4:**1,1,3,3,4,5,6,6,7,8,10,10,11,12,13,16,16; **5:**2,4,4,5,5,5,5,8,8,10,10,13,13,14,16,17,18,21,21,21,22,23,23,25; **6:**1,2,2,3,3,4,4,5,5,7,8,9,9,9,9,10,11,11,13,15,15,16,16,18,18,20,21; **2Ti 1:**2,2,3,5,5,7,9,9,10,10,11,11,11,12,13,15,16; **2:**4,14,15,16,17,18,19,20,20,20,21,22,22,23,24,26,26; **3:**6,6,8,11,13,13,14,15,16,16; **4:**1,1,1,2,2,2,4,6,8,10,10,11,13,17,17,17,18,18,19,19,20,21,21,21; **Titus 1:**1,1,3,4,4,5,6,6,8,9,10,11,14,15,15,16; **2:**2,2,4,5,5,8,10,12,12,12,13,14,15; **3:**1,2,2,3,3,3,4,5,8,8,9,9,9,9,10,11,13,13,14; **Phm 1:**1,2,2,3,3,5,7,8,9,11,16,22,24,24; **Heb 1:**1,2,3,5,6,7,8,9,10,12; **2:**2,2,4,4,7,8,9,10,10,11,11,12,13,13,13,14,15,17,17; **3:**1,1,6,6,9,10,12,16,17,18; **4:**3,5,6,12,12,12,12,13,16; **5:**1,1,2,4,6,7,7,7,9,10; **6:**1,1,2,3,5,6,6,7,8,8,10,10,12,14,15,16,16,19; **7:**1,1,2,6,7,11,13,14,15,18,19,20,21,27; **8:**2,3,3,5,8,8,9,10,10,12,13,13; **9:**1,2,4,4,7,7,7,9,10,10,11,12,13,13,19,19,19,21,22,25,27,28; **10:**2,4,5,6,8,8,10,11,11,13,16,17,18,19,20,21,22,22,24,24,25,27,29,30,33,34,34,37,38,38,39,39; **11:**1,4,6,6,7,8,9,10,11,12,12,13,13,17,19,20,21,22,23,28,32,32,32,32,33,34,34,34,36,36,36,37,37,38,38; **12:**1,1,2,2,3,5,5,6,8,8,9,9,11,12,14,15,15,18,18,24,28,28; **13:**1,3,3,4,4,5,7,8,8,12,16,16,17,18,21,21,22,24; **Jas 1:**1,2,4,5,6,6,8,11,11,14,15,16,17,19,19,21,21,22,24,24,25,26,26,27,27,27,27; **2:**1,2,2,3,4,5,5,9,10,12,14,15,16,18,19,22,22,23,23,23,24,25; **3:**4,6,7,7,9,9,10,10,11,11,13,14,16,16,17,17; **4:**1,2,7,8,8,9,9,10,11,11,12,12,13,14,15,17; **5:**1,2,3,5,6,7,7,8,9,11,12,14,15,16,16,17,17,18,18,19,19,20; **1Pe 1:**1,2,2,3,4,7,8,8,8,10,11,11,13,21,21,21,23,24,24,25; **2:**1,1,4,6,6,8,8,11,12,14,18,20,20,22,24,25; **3:**2,3,4,6,6,7,7,8,10,10,11,11,12,15,19,21,22,22; **4:**3,4,5,7,11,11,14,17,18,18,19; **5:**1,4,8,10,10,10,11,12,13; **2Pe 1:**1,1,2,2,3,4,5,6,6,6,7,7,8,9,10,10,10,11,11,12,15,17,19,19; **2:**2,3,5,6,6,7,8,9,10,10,11,12,12,13,15,16,17,18,20,20,20,21,22; **3:**2,2,3,5,5,6,7,7,8,10,10,11,12,12,13,14,16,17,18,18,18; **1Jn 1:**1,2,2,2,3,3,3,5,6,6,7,8,9,9,9,10; **2:**4,4,8,8,10,10,11,14,14,16,17,18,20,21,22,24,25,27,27,28,28; **3:**1,2,5,10,10,12,12,13,15,16,16,17,18,19,20,22,22,23,23,24,24; **4:**3,4,5,5,6,6,7,9,10,12,13,14,14,15,16,16,16,20,21,21; **5:**1,2,3,6,6,6,8,8,11,11,15,16,17,18,19,20,20,20; **2Jn 1:**1,2,3,3,3,5,6,7,9,9,10,12,12; **3Jn** 2,3,5,10,12,12,13,14; **Jude** 1,1,2,3,4,4,6,7,7,7,8,10,12,15,15,16,16,19,20,24,24,25,25; **Rev 1:**2,3,3,4,4,4,4,5,5,5,6,6,6,6,6,7,7,8,8,8,9,9,9,9,10,11,11,12,13,13,14,15,16,17,17,18,18,18,19,20,20; **2:**1,2,2,3,3,5,5,8,8,9,9,10,10,14,16,18,19,19,19,20,22,23,23,24,26,27; **3:**1,2,3,3,3,5,7,7,8,9,9,12,12,14,17,17,18,18,19,19,20,20,20,20,21; **4:**1,1,1,2,3,3,4,4,5,6,6,8,8,8,8,9,9,9,10,10,10,11,11,11,11,11; **5:**1,2,2,4,5,6,6,7,8,8,8,9,9,9,9,9,9,10,10,11,11,11,11,12,12,12,12,12,13,13,13,13,13,13,13,13,13,13,14,14; **6:**2,2,2,4,5,6,6,6,8,8,8,8,9,10,10,11,11,13,14,14,15,15,15,16,16,16,17; **7:**2,9,9,9,9,10,10,11,11,11,12,12,12,12,12,12,13,14,14,15,15,15,17; **8:**2,2,3,5,5,5,7,7,7,7,8,9,10,10,11,12,12,12; **9:**1,2,3,3,5,7,8,9,9,10,11,13,15,15,15,16,17,17,17,18,19,20,20; **10:**1,2,3,4,4,5,6,6,6,6,6,6,8,9,9,10,11; **11:**1,1,3,3,4,4,5,6,6,7,7,8,9,9,9,10,11,11,11,12,13,13,13,15,15,15,15,16,16,17,17,18,18,18,18,18,19,19,19; **12:**1,2,3,3,4,5,5,7,7,7,8,9,10,10,10,10,10,11,12,12,14,15,16,17,17; **13:**1,1,1,2,2,2,3,4,4,5,5,6,6,6,7,7,7,10,12,12,13,14,15,16,16,16; **14:**1,1,1,2,2,3,3,3,4,4,6,6,7,7,8,9,9,9,10,11,11,12,14,14,15,15,16,17,18,18,19,20; **15:**1,2,2,2,2,3,3,3,3,4,4,5,5,6,7,8,8,8; **16:**2,2,2,3,3,4,4,5,6,6,7,7,8,9,9,10,11,11,12,13,14,15,15,17,18,19,19,20,21; **17:**1,2,3,3,4,4,4,4,5,7,7,8,8,8,11,11,13,13,14,14,14,15,16,16,16; **18:**1,2,2,3,5,7,7,8,9,9,10,11,12,12,12,12,13,13,13,13,13,13,14,15,15,16,16,16,17,17,19,19,20,21,21,22,22,23,24; **19:**1,1,2,3,3,4,4,4,5,6,7,7,8,9,10,10,11,11,11,12,13,14,14,16,16,17,18,18,18,18,19,19,19,20,20,21; **20:**1,1,2,3,3,4,4,4,4,6,6,6,8,8,8,8,9,9,10,10,10,10,11,11,11,12,12,12,13,13,13,14; **21:**1,1,1,3,3,3,3,5,6,6,7,7,8,9,10,10,11,12,13,14,15,16,16,16,17,18,20,22,23,24,26; **22:**1,2,3,3,4,5,5,6,8,8,8,9,9,11,12,13,13,13,14,15,15,16,16,17,17,17,19,19

ARE (4117)

Ge 2:12,16; **3:**9,14,19; **4:**6,11,14; **6:**3,15,19,21; **9:**2; **10:**20,31,32; **12:**11,13; **13:**8,14; **16:**5,8,11,13; **17:**10,11,12,15; **18:**24,29; **19:**5,13,15; **20:**3,16,16; **22:**7; **23:**6,8; **24:**13,23,31,31,47; **25:**13,16,23; **26:**29; **27:**21,22,24,32,41; **28:**13; **29:**4,8,14,15; **31:**12,43,43,43,49; **32:**4,6,17,18,18,19; **33:**5,5,13,13,13; **34:**21,22,30; **36:**10; **37:**13,15,16; **38:**25; **39:**9; **40:**12,18; **41:**25,26,26,27,27,27,29,35,40; **42:**9,11,11,14,16,16,16,19,21,31,31,33,34,38; **43:**16; **44:**16,18; **45:**11,19; **46:**8,30,32,34; **47:**1,3,8,9,30; **48:**5,8,9; **49:**3,5,5,9,26,28; **50:**11,17,18; **Ex 1:**1,16,19,19; **2:**13,14; **3:**5,9,14,18; **4:**18,19,25; **5:**4,5,5,7,8,8,16,16,16,17,19; **6:**5; **7:**2; **8:**26; **9:**27; **10:**9,10,26; **11:**2; **12:**4,4,7,8,11,13,14,15,18,42,43; **13:**4,5,12; **14:**2,3,15; **15:**4,24; **16:**4,5,7,8,8,26,29; **17:**4; **18:**14,17,20,20; **19:**3,3,6,6,13; **21:**1,1,13,21,22,23,35; **22:**7,9,31; **23:**10,14,17; **24:**1,14; **25:**2,3,3,15,15,20,20,22,26,27,32,33,34,38; **26:**2,8; **27:**2,7,14,15,17,19,21; **28:**3,4,4,4,21,28,34; **29:**1,28,32,33,33,38; **30:**14,15,15,19,32; **31:**11,16; **32:**2,4,8,9,22; **33:**3,5,13,16; **34:**12,23; **35:**1,10,10; **36:**1,5; **38:**21; **Lev 1:**3,4,5,6,7,9,10,11,12,13,14,16; **2:**1,11,12; **3:**1,2,3,5,6,7,9,12,14; **4:**12,15,29,32,33; **5:**2,2,3,4,5,8,11,12,15,17,18; **6:**9,14,14,16,20,25; **7:**1,11,12,13,14,30,30,32,37; **8:**31,33; **10:**9; **11:**2,4,8,10,11,13,13,13,20,21,23,27,28,29,31,31,34,35,35,37,39,42,46; **12:**4,6,7; **13:**11,13,35,36,37,39,39,59; **14:**2,2,13,21,32,42,54,57; **15:**32; **16:**4,27; **17:**5; **18:**17; **19:**20,23; **20:**2,10,11,12,13,16,17,18,26,27; **21:**6,7; **22:**7,9,11,24,25; **23:**2,2,3,3,4,4,20,21,24,32,37,37,38,40,42; **24:**9,14,16,22; **25:**15,15,16,16,16,27,31,31,33,35,40,40,41,42,44,50,52,53,54,55; **26:**3,34,36,39,41,44,46; **27:**29,34; **Nu 1:**3,3,5,5,50,50,51,52,53,53; **2:**2,3,32; **3:**7,8,9,9,12,13,13,40,45; **4:**5,6,7,8,9,10,11,12,13,14,14,15,15,15,18,19,25,26,27,28,31; **6:**8,11,13,14,18,20,23; **8:**8,10,10,12,14,15,16,16,26; **9:**10,10,10,11,11; **10:**3,4,5,6,8,10,29; **11:**15,16,27,29; **13:**4,16,18,19,20,28,28,31,31,32; **14:**14,25,40,41; **15:**21,38; **16:**6,10,16,17,37; **17:**12,12,13; **18:**1,1,3,3,4,4,5,9,16,17,18,23; **19:**13,13,19,19,20,20; **20:**16; **21:**29; **22:**6,9,12,34; **24:**4,5,16; **26:**2,63; **27:**7; **28:**3,31; **29:**6,6; **30:**16; **31:**26,30; **32:**4,14,21; **33:**1; **34:**17,17,19,29; **35:**8,31,31; **36:**13; **Dt 1:**1,9,10,22,28,28,28; **2:**4,6,18; **3:**21,27; **4:**4,5,14,14,20,22,26,30,45; **5:**3,22,31; **6:**1,1,6,11,25; **7:**1,5,6,12,17,17,23,25; **8:**9,10,12; **9:**1,2,5,6,13,29; **10:**2,5,19,19; **11:**8,10,11,12,21,29,29,30,31,31; **12:**1,2,5,8,11,18,18,29; **13:**16,17; **14:**1,2,4,7,8,19,21; **15:**5,11,20,22; **17:**8,16; **18:**1,4; **19:**9,17; **20:**2,3,15,15,19,20; **21:**4,11,14,21; **22:**28; **23:**7,9,20; **24:**11,15,15,16,19; **25:**1,5,11; **26:**18,18; **28:**10,20,21,24,45,51,51,58,61,63; **29:**1,10,12,15,15; **30:**10,16,17,17,18; **31:**13,16,16,21,27,29; **32:**4,4,5,5,17,20,20,21,28,32,37,47,47,47; **33:**3,17,17,17,27,29; **Jos 1:**14; **2:**9,14,19,20,24; **3:**3; **4:**3,7,9; **5:**13,15; **6:**17,17,19; **7:**10,13,21; **8:**4,6,7; **9:**8,8,11,13,13,23,

AS (4068)

AT (2255)

BE (5152)

BEEN (918)

BUT (3962)

BY (2348)

FOR (7336)

FROM (5029)

28; 19:1,16,16,17,18; 20:1,1,10,10,10,13,14,15,15,17,25,31,32,33,38,40; 21:3,5,6,8,19,21; Ru 1:1,2,6,16,22; 2:1,3,4,6,7,8,9,16; 4:3,5,9,10,10; 1Sa 1:1,1,3; 2:8,8,10,15,23,30,33; 3:12,17,17,18,20; 4:3,3,8,12,16,16,21,22; 5:1; 6:3,5,20; 7:8,14,14,14,16,16; 8:8,18; 9:16,16,21,24,25,27; 10:3,4,5,18; 11:5; 12:2,3,4,10,11,20,23; 13:2,17; 14:6,30,31,48; 15:1,2,4,6,7,11,15,21,28; 16:13,14,14,15,16,23; 17:4,12,15,18,23,23,24,25,26,33,34,35,37,37,40,51,53,57; 18:2,6,9,10,12,13; 19:9; 20:1,2,15,15,34,41; 21:4,5,6,10; 22:3; 23:13,13,26,29; 24:1,2,13,15,21; 25:10,11,14,26,26,29,33,33,34,35,39,44; 26:19,20,24; 27:8; 28:3,9,15,16,23; 29:3,6,8; 30:13,16,17,25,26; 31:12; 2Sa 1:1,2,3,3,4,13,22,22; 2:4; 3:10,10,15,18,18,22,26; 4:2,4,11; 5:9,25; 6:2,3,12,16,21; 7:1,6,6,8,8,9,11,15,15,15,23,23; 8:1,8,11,12,13; 9:3,5,5; 10:6,6,14,16; 11:2,2,4,8,10,15,20,21,24; 12:3,4,7,10,17,20,30,30; 13:5,6,10,13,28; 14:2,4,9,11,14,16,16,18,19,25,32; 15:2,2,11,12,14,18,19,28; 16:5,5; 17:11,27,27,27,29; 18:3,13,13,19,31; 19:3,7,9,9,9,16,20,24,25,28,31,31,38; 20:2,6,7,12,13,16,20,20,21,21,21,22; 21:4,10,10,12,12,13,20; 22:1,1,3,4,7,9,9,14,16,17,18,18,22,23,24,44,46,49,49; 23:4,11,15,16,17,20,21,24,26,27,29,30,36; 24:2,13,15,15; 1Ki 1:20,39,45,53; 2:7,8,15,27,40,41; 3:20,28; 4:12,21,24,25,33,34; 5:3,9,13,17,18; 6:3,8,15,16,24; 7:7,9,9,14,23,34; 8:1,8,8,10,30,32,34,35,36,39,41,43,45,49,53,54,65; 9:6,7,12,20,24; 10:11,11,15,15,28,28,28,29; 11:2,9,11,13,14,18,18,23,26,35; 12:2,2,15,25,31; 13:1,4,12,14,21,26,33,34; 14:7,8,10,15; 15:12,13,17,19,22,27; 16:2,17,24; 17:1,4,6,13,19,23,24; 18:19,26,31,44; 19:16,19; 20:17,24,34,41; 21:21; 22:3,24,24,35,43; 2Ki 1:2,10,10,12,12,14; 2:1,3,5,7,9,10,13,14,15,23,25; 3:3,6,20; 4:1,27,42,42; 5:2,2,4,15,20,20,21,22,22,24,26,27; 6:23,27,27,33; 7:8; 8:3,6,6,8,9,29; 9:1,2,8,15; 10:21,29,31,33; 11:2,2,11,19; 12:1,4,5,7,8,15,16,18; 13:2,5,6,11,14,14,23,25,25; 14:2,13,24,25,25,27; 15:2,9,14,16,18,20,24,28; 16:11,12,14,14,17,17; 17:7,9,13,18,20,21,21,22,23,23,24,27,28,30,30,30,33,39; 18:8,14,14,17,25,29,31,31,33,34,35,35; 19:14,19,29; 20:5,6,8,14,14,14; 21:8,15,16,19; 22:1,4,10; 23:2,4,6,8,8,11,12,16,17,18,26,27,30,31,35,36; 24:3,7,7,8,13,13,15,18,20; 25:5,16,21,26,27; 1Ch 1:12,44,45,47,48; 2:53,55; 4:10,10,18,22; 5:2,8,23; 6:33,44,54,60,61,62,62,63,65,66,70,71,72,74,76,77,78,80; 7:15; 9:3,3,3,6,9,19,25,33; 11:8,13,17,18,22,23,26,28,28,31,32; 12:1,2,7,16,17,24,25,26,28,29,30,31,32,33,34,35,36,37,37,40; 13:5,5,6,7; 14:16; 15:5,6,7,8,9,10,17,17,25,29; 16:20,20,35,36; 17:5,5,5,7,7,8,13,13,21,21; 18:1,8,11; 19:6,7,16; 20:2,2,6; 21:2,26; 22:2,9; 23:27; 24:4,4,6,6,20,20,21,22,22,24,25,27,28,29; 25:2,3,4; 26:1,23,29,29,30; 27:15; 28:4,4,4; 29:10,12,14,14,16,29; 2Ch 1:4,13,13,16,16,16,17; 2:8,14,14,16; 4:2; 5:2,9,9,9,11; 6:21,23,25,26,27,30,32,33,35,39; 7:1,8,14,14,20; 8:7,11,15,16; 9:10,26,28,28,29; 10:2,2,15; 11:4,13,16; 12:3,12,15; 13:19; 14:8,8; 15:8,8,9,9,11,16,17; 16:1,3,6,7,9,11,12,12; 17:6,14,17; 18:23,23,31; 19:4,10; 20:2,2,4,4,10,10,10,19,23,23,32,34; 21:12; 22:6,11,11; 23:2,10,20; 24:1,5,6; 25:1,6,7,10,13,14,15,23,26,27,27; 26:3,15,21,22; 28:8,8,12,15,21,21,21,24,26; 29:5,6,10,12,12,12,13,13,14,14; 30:5,6,6,6,8,9,10,11,18,25,25; 31:3,10; 32:3,8,11,13,14,14,15,15,17,17,22,22,23; 33:15; 34:9,9,12,12,13,18,30,33; 35:7,22,27; 36:7,10,18,20; Ezr 1:7,11; 2:1,59,59,61,62; 3:7,8,13; 4:9,11,12; 5:14,14,16; 6:5,6,8,11,21,21; 7:6,9,16,20,28; 8:1,18,19,22,31,31,35; 9:1,3,5,7,11; 10:2,6,8,11,11,14,16,18,19,20,21,22,24,24,25,26,27,28,29,30,31,33,34,38,43; Ne 1:2,9; 3:7,15,19,20,21,22,24,25,27; 4:2,5,16,19,21; 5:12,14,15,17; 6:17; 7:6,61,61,63,64; 8:3,8,15,15,17,17,18,18; 9:2,3,5,13,15,15,20,27,27,28,32,35; 10:28,31,38; 11:4,4,7,10,15,30,31; 12:27,28,28,29,29,44; 13:3,16,21,23,28; Est 1:1,2,5,7,10,20; 2:6,9,13; 3:8,10; 4:14; 7:8; 8:2,9; 9:16,22,26; Job 1:7,7,12,16,19,21; 2:2,2,7,7,10,11,12; 3:10,11,17,19; 4:2; 5:4,5,6,6,15,15,19,20,20,21; 6:13,14,17,18,22,23,23; 7:19; 8:10,18,19; 9:6,34; 10:7,19,20; 13:20,21; 14:4,6,12,18; 15:13,18; 16:5; 18:4,14,17,18,18; 19:9,13,13; 20:4,18,20,24; 21:9,16,30,30; 22:6,7,18,22,23; 23:7,12; 24:4,9,12; 26:4; 27:13,22; 28:2,2,4,4,5,6,20,21,21; 29:9,17; 30:2,3,5; 31:2,2,7,18,18,20,22,23; 33:3,9,17,17,18,18,24,28,30; 34:10,10,27,30,30; 35:7,9; 36:3,16,16,20,25,29; 37:1,2,7,9,9; 38:8,29,29; 39:22,25,29,29; 41:19,20,20,21; Ps 3:T,4,8; 4:1; 5:9; 6:5,6,8; 7:1; 9:13; 10:8,16; 11:2; 12:1,5,7; 13:1; 14:2; 15:2; 16:2; 17:1,2,4,7,9,9,13,14,14; 18:T,T,3,6,8,8,13,15,16,17,17,21,22,23,43,45,48,48; 19:3,10,13; 20:2,2,6; 21:10,10; 22:1,1,10,10,11,19,20,20,21,21,24,25; 24:5,5; 25:6,15,17,22; 27:4,9; 30:3,3; 31:4,11,15,15,20,20,22; 32:7; 33:13,14,19; 34:4,13,13,14,16,17,19; 35:10,10,17,17,22; 36:1,8; 37:8,8,27,39,40; 38:9,10,21; 39:1,8,10,13; 40:10,11; 41:3,8,13; 42:6,6; 43:1; 44:12,18; 45:8; 49:14,15; 50:1,2,9,9; 51:2,5,9,11,11,14; 52:5,5; 53:2; 54:7; 55:8,18,19; 56:13,13; 57:T,3; 58:3,3; 59:1,2,2,7,7; 60:6; 61:2; 62:1,4,5; 64:1,2,2,4; 66:9,20; 68:10,17,18,18,20,20,22,22,31; 69:5,14,14,14,17; 71:4,4,6,6,12,20; 72:8,8,13,14,15; 73:5,7,27; 74:9,11,12; 75:6,6; 76:8; 77:4; 78:2,4,14,26,30,42,44,50,65,65,70,71; 79:13; 80:8,13,13,14,18; 81:6,6,16; 82:4; 84:7,11; 85:3,11,11; 86:13,13; 88:5,8,14,15,18; 89:19,33; 90:2; 91:3,3; 93:2; 94:12,13; 97:10; 99:7; 101:4,8; 102:2,19,19; 103:4,12,12,17; 104:13,14,21,35; 105:13,13,37; 106:10,10,19,23,33,47,48; 107:2,3,3,3,6,13,19,20; 108:7; 109:10,13,15,17,24,31; 110:2,3,7; 113:3,7,7; 114:1; 116:8,8,8,16; 118:26; 119:10,13,19,21,22,29,37,43,51,72,87,101,102,104,110,115,118,134,136,150,152,155,157; 120:2,2; 121:1,2,7; 123:4,4; 124:7; 127:3,3; 128:5; 129:1,2,4; 130:8; 134:3; 135:7,7,21; 136:11,21; 138:6; 139:2,7,7,15,19; 140:1,1,4,4; 141:6,9,9; 142:6,7; 143:7,9; 144:7,7,7,10,11; 148:1,7; Pr 2:6,12,12,16,16,22,22; 3:26,27; 4:5,15,23,24,27; 5:7,8,15,15; 6:5,5,9,24,24; 7:5,5,14,16; 8:35; 9:3; 10:2,31; 11:4,8; 12:2,14; 13:2,14,19; 14:4,7,27; 15:24,29; 16:1,33; 18:20,22; 19:14,14,27; 21:10,16,23; 22:5,6,27; 23:13,14; 24:13,18,32; 25:4,5,25; 27:6,7,8,9,22,25; 28:8; 29:21,26; 30:8,14,14; 31:14; Ecc 1:3,7; 2:24; 3:5,9,11,14,20; 4:4,14; 5:9,9,15,15; 8:10; 10:5,12; 11:10; 12:7; SS 1:14; 3:6,6,9; 4:1,2,8,8,8,8,15; 6:5,5,6; 8:5; Isa 1:6,15; 2:3,3,6,10,19,21; 3:1,12,14; 4:4,6,6; 6:6; 7:17,18,18,20; 8:17,18; 9:7,12,12,14; 10:2,3,27,27; 11:1,1,11,11,11,11,11,11,11,11,12,16,16; 12:3; 13:5,5,6,13; 14:3,3,9,12,25,25,29,31; 16:1,2,4,4,5,10; 17:3,3; 18:4,7,7; 19:23; 20:2,2,6; 21:1,1,10,10,11,15,15,15,15; 22:4,19,19,24; 23:1,5; 24:11,14,16; 25:4,4,8,8; 27:12; 28:7,7,7,7,9,9,29; 29:4,4,9,9,13,15; 30:14,23,27; 31:1; 32:2,2,6,15; 33:15,15; 34:4,4,6,10,17; 36:2,16,16,18,19,20,20; 37:14,20,30; 38:6,12,12,17; 39:3,3,3; 40:2,21,27; 41:2,4,9,9,25,25,26,26; 42:5,7,7,10,11; 43:5,5,6,6,11,13; 44:6,17,19; 45:5,6,19,20,21,21; 46:6,7,7,10,10,11,11,12; 47:13,14; 48:1,6,8,8,9,16,19,20,21; 49:1,12,12,12,12,17,21,24,24,25,25; 50:6,11; 51:1,1,4,17,22; 52:2,11,11; 53:3,8; 54:8,14,17; 55:10,11; 56:2,3; 57:1; 58:7,13,13; 59:2,2,9,19,19,21,21; 60:4,6,9; 61:1; 63:1,1,3,15,15,15,16,17,19; 64:7; 65:9,9,14,16; 66:6,20,23,23; Jer 1:13,14; 2:5,18,18,33; 3:4,14,14,18,19,24,25; 4:6,8,11,12,14,15,15,16; 5:6,6; 6:1,8,13,20,20,22,22; 7:1,15,25,28; 8:1,10,13,16,19; 9:2,3,18,19,21,21; 10:9,9,11,11,13,13,20,22; 11:1,7,7,19; 12:2,12,14,14; 13:7,14,18,18,20; 14:2; 15:1,12,21,21; 16:5,16,17,17,19; 17:5,5,12,13,16,18,18,26,26,26; 18:1,4,11,14,14,17,18,18,20,22,23; 19:1,14; 20:3,13; 21:1,2,12; 22:3,8,11,20,21; 23:14,15,16,16,22,22,30,30,33,34,36,38,38,38; 24:1,5,5,8,10; 25:3,5,10,15,17,28,30,30,32,32,33; 26:1,3,10,20; 27:1,10,16,16,20; 28:1,3,4,6,8,16; 29:1,1,2,4,14,14,14,20,22,27; 30:1,3,10,19,21; 31:8,8,11,16,16,16,23,34,36,38,39; 32:1,9,30,31,31,37,40; 33:5,7,8,15; 34:1,3,8,21; 35:1,15; 36:1,2,3,6,6,7,8,9,10,10,11,13,14,21,29; 37:5,11,17,21; 38:10,11,14,18,23,25; 40:1,1,4,12; 41:5,6,15,16,16; 42:1,4,8,11; 43:5; 44:5,7,12,12,26,28; 46:16,20,27; 47:4; 48:3,10,11,11,12,18,33,33,34,34,44,45,45; 49:5,7,14,16,19,19,31,32,36; 50:3,9,9,16,26,28,39,41,41,44,44; 51:6,16,16,26,45,54,54; 52:1,3,8,20,27,29,31; La 1:6,13; 2:1,8,9,11,19; 3:11,13,18,38,48,50,55,66; 4:9,17; 5:8,10,14,15,16,19; Eze 1:19,21,25,27,27; 3:12,17,18,19,19,20; 4:8,14; 5:4; 6:9,14; 7:22,26; 8:2,2,6; 9:2,3; 10:2,4,6,6,16,18,19; 11:15,17,17,19,23,24; 12:3,16,27; 13:20,21,22,23; 14:6,7,8,9,11; 15:2,2,3,3; 16:9,33,37,42; 17:7,22,22; 18:8,8,17,17,21,23,24,26,27,28,30; 19:8,14; 20:9,14,22,34,34,41,41,47; 21:3,3,4,5,14,19; 22:12,12; 23:3,17,18,18,22,22,28,40,42,42; 24:13,16; 25:7,7,13; 26:7,16; 27:5,5,6,6,7,7,17,18,18,19; 28:3,15,16,16,18,25; 29:4,10,13,14,18; 30:6,9,22; 31:12; 32:13,21; 33:7,8,9,11,11,14,18,19,21,30; 34:10,10,12,13,13,27; 35:7; 36:3,24,25,25,26,29,33; 37:9,12,13,21,23; 38:6,8,8,8,12,15; 39:2,3,3,10,10,17,18,22,23,24,27,27,29; 40:13,13,15,19,23,27,49; 41:7,11,20; 42:3,5,5,9,20; 43:2,6,9,14,14,15,23,25,27; 44:10,10,15; 45:7,7,7,13,13,14,15,15; 46:2,16,17,18; 47:1,1,2,10,12,15,17,19; 48:1,2,3,4,5,6,7,8,8,12,19,19,21,21,23,24,25,26,27,28,35; Da 1:2,3,5,6; 2:6,18,25; 3:15,17,17; 4:3,12,13,14,14,16,23,25,31,31,32,33,34; 5:2,2,3,3,13,20,21,23,23; 6:13,20,23,27; 7:3,4,7,10,17,19,23,24,24; 8:4,5,7,11,16,22; 9:2,5,13,16,25; 10:5; 11:7,26,29,41,44; 12:1,11; Hos 2:2,2,12,17,18; 4:6; 5:3,6; 7:4,13,14,14; 8:6; 9:6,12; 10:5; 11:2,7,10,11,11; 12:13; 13:2,3,14,14,15,15; 14:4,8; Joel 1:5,9,13,15,16; 2:7,13,20; 3:6,11,16,16; Am 1:2,2; 2:11,11; 3:5,12,12; 4:7,7,8,11; 5:19; 6:2,14; 7:11,15,17; 8:12,12; 9:2,2,3,7,7,7,8,13,13,14,15; Ob 1,4,18,19,19,20; Jnh 1:3,3,8,8,10; 2:1,2,4,6,8,9; 3:5,6,9,10; 4:2,11; Mic 1:2,3,7,12,16; 2:3,4,8,8,9,9; 3:2,2,4,7; 4:2,2,7; 5:2,2,6,7,10,13,14; 6:4,5; 7:2,12,12,12,12; Na 1:10,11,13; 2:9; 3:7,11; Hab 1:8,12; 2:15,16; 3:3,3,4,13; Zep 1:2,6,10,10,10; 3:10,11,18; Hag 2:15,18,18,19; Zec 1:4,12,12; 2:6,13; 3:2; 4:1; 6:1,5,10,10,12; 8:7,23; 9:7,7,10,10,10,10,11; 10:4,4,4,4,10,10; 11:6; 13:1,2,2; 14:2,4,5,8,10,10,10,16; Mal 1:9,10,11,13; 2:3,6,7,8,12,13; 3:7,11; Mt 1:17,17,17,20,21; 2:1,7,16; 3:5,7,13,17; 4:4,10,17,21,25; 5:18,37,42,42; 6:1,13; 7:5,16,16,23; 8:1,11,28,30; 9:9,15,16,27; 10:27; 11:1,12,25,29; 12:9,15,38,42; 13:12,27,49,53; 14:2,13,24; 15:1,8,18,22,27; 16:1,21; 17:5,9,20,25,25,25,26; 18:35; 19:8,15; 20:23; 21:8,11,16,25,25,25,43; 22:46; 23:34,35; 24:10,21,27,29,31,31,32; 25:28,29,32,32,41; 26:16,27,29,29,39,47,64; 27:32,40,42,45,51,55,55,57,64; 28:2,7,8; Mk 1:9,11,45; 2:20,21; 3:7,8,9,22; 4:25; 5:2,6,29,30,34,35; 6:14,16,33; 7:1,4,6,18,21,23,33; 8:11; 9:7,9,10,21; 11:14,20,30,31; 12:2,34,34; 13:19,25,27,27,28; 14:23,25,35,36,43; 15:21,21,30,32,38,40,45; 16:3,8; Lk 1:2,3,7,48,50,52,71,71,74,78; 2:4; 3:7,22; 4:9,22,38,42; 5:3,3,8,10,17,17,35,36; 6:17,17,17,19,29,34,42,44,44; 7:6,12,45; 8:1,2,4,12,18,26,27,35,38,46,49; 9:6,7,35,37,45,54; 10:7,11,18,21,30,42; 11:16,31,51; 12:3,20,36,48,48,52; 13:12,15,16,25,27,27,29; 14:2; 16:21,26,26,30,31; 17:7,24,29; 18:34; 19:24,42; 20:4,5,7,35; 21:11,26; 22:18,42,43,45,45,69,71; 23:8,26,26,49,51,55; 24:2,9,13,16,31,46,49; Jn 1:6,14,32,44,46; 2:6,9,15,22; 3:2,8,13,27,31,31,31,31; 4:6,12,22,39,47,54; 5:24,41,44,44; 6:23,31,32,32,33,38,41,42,45,46,50,51,58,64,66; 7:16,17,22,22,27,27,28,29,38,41,42,42,52; 8:14,14,23,23,25,26,38,40,42,44,59; 9:1,16,29,30,33; 10:5,18,18,32; 11:1,18,37,53,55; 12:1,9,17,17,21,27,28,32,34,36,43; 13:3,4; 14:7; 15:5,15,26,26,27; 16:4,14,15,27,28,30; 17:7,8,15; 18:3,28,36; 19:9,11,12,23,27; 20:1,7,9,9; 21:2,8,14; Ac 1:9,11,12,12,22,22; 2:2,5,10,24,24,33,40; 3:2,2,5,15,19,22,23,26; 4:10,15,17,34,34,36; 5:16,30,39,42; 6:3,5,9; 7:10,16,37,42,45; 8:3,26,33; 9:3,8,11,14,18; 10:22,23,35,40,41; 11:4,5,9,11,20,27; 12:11,11,19,25; 13:4,8,13,14,15,23,29,30,31,34,37,39,50; 14:8,15,17,18,19,26; 15:1,7,14,18,20,20,20,20,21,24,29,29,29,29; 16:4,6,11,12,14,39; 17:2,3,5,26,27,31; 18:2,5,6,21,23,23,28; 19:25,29,35; 20:4,4,4,4,6,9,15,17,18,20,30; 21:1,1,7,10,16,16,21,25,25,25,27,30,30,39; 22:5,6,14,19; 23:6,10,34,34; 24:19; 25:1,7; 26:4,11,13,17,17,18,18,19,23; 27:2,2,4,14,18,21,29,30,30,34,42,43; 28:4,4,8,13,21,21,23,23,23; Ro 1:4,5,7,7,13,17,18,20; 2:12,12,29,29; 3:21,28; 4:6,24; 5:9,14; 6:4,7,9,13,17,18,19,20,21,22; 7:2,3,4,6,8,9,24; 8:2,11,11,21,35,39; 9:3,5,6,24,24; 10:7,9,17; 11:1,15,17,26,26,36; 13:3,11; 14:23,23; 15:19,22,31; 16:2,17,26; 1Co 1:3,11,30; 2:12,14; 4:5,6,7; 5:13; 6:4,14,18,19; 7:7,10,25,27,29,32; 8:6; 9:11,12,13,14,21; 10:4,6,14; 11:8,8,12,12,23,28; 15:12,15,20,41; 16:17; 2Co 1:2,4,10,16; 2:17; 3:1,3,5,13,18; 4:7,7,14; 5:1,6,8,9,16,16,18; 6:12,12,17; 7:1; 11:3,4,4,8,8,9,9,12,24,26,26,26,26,26,33; 12:1,3,7,8; Gal 1:1,1,3,4,8,12,12,15; 2:12,12; 3:2,13,15; 4:1,17,24; 5:4,4,7,8; 6:8,8,17; Eph 1:2,20; 2:8,12,12; 3:15; 4:16,18; 5:14,19,19; 6:6,15,23; Php 1:2,5,18; 2:1,1,17; 3:9,9,11,20; 4:9,15,18; Col 1:2,5,7,13,18,21,22,23; 2:5,12,19; 3:8,16,24; 4:16; 1Th 1:8,9,10,10,10; 2:3,6,6,13,14,14,16,17; 3:6; 4:16; 2Th 1:2,7,9,9; 2:2; 3:2,3,6,6; 1Ti 1:2,5,6; 3:16; 4:3; 5:13; 6:10,11,20,21; 2Ti 1:2,13,18; 2:8,8,18,19,21,26; 3:11,13,14,15; 4:4,17,18; Titus 1:4; 2:10,14; Phm 3,15,20; Heb 3:12; 4:4,10,10,13; 5:1,7,8,14; 6:1; 7:1,5,5,5,6,6,13,14,23,26; 8:9,11; 9:14,15; 10:22; 11:5,12,13,19,22; 12:3,25,25; 13:5,10,20,24; Jas 1:7,17,17,27; 3:11,13,15,17; 4:1,7; 5:19,20,20; 1Pe 1:3,12,18,18,21,22; 2:11; 3:3,10,10,11,21; 2Pe 1:8,9,17,17,18,21; 2:9,11,18; 3:17; 1Jn 1:1,5,7,9; 2:13,14,16,16,19,20,21,24,27; 3:8,11,14,22; 4:1,2,3,4,5,5,6,6,7; 5:21; 2Jn 3,3,5,6; 3Jn 7,11; Jude 14,23,24; Rev 1:1,4,4,5,5,5; 2:5,7,27; 3:5,10,12,18; 4:5; 5:7,9; 6:4,13,14,16,16; 7:1,2,4,5,5,5,6,6,6,7,7,7,8,8,8,9,13,17; 8:4,5,10,11; 9:1,2,2,2,13; 10:1,4,8,10; 11:5,7,9,11,12; 12:11,15; 13:8,13; 14:2,3,4,13,13,13,18,18; 15:8,8; 16:1,12,17,21; 17:8; 18:1,3,4,6,14,15,17; 19:3,5; 20:3,7,9,11; 21:2,3,4,6,10; 22:1,19,19

HAD (2808)

See select index of "HAD" in the Main Concordance.

Ge 1:31; 2:2,2,3,5,5,5,8,8,19,22; 3:1,23; 4:22,26; 5:3,3,4,6,7,9,10,12,13,15,16,18,19,21,22,25,26,28,28,30; 6:4,5,6,10,12,12; 7:9,14,16,22; 8:2,2,3,6,7,8,11,13; 9:24; 10:1; 11:1,11,12,13,14,15,16,17,18,19,20,21,22,23,24,25,26; 12:1,4,5,5,7,20; 13:1,2,3,4,5,14; 14:13,14; 15:17,17; 16:1,1,3,15; 17:22; 18:8,33; 19:4,17,23,27,29,37,38; 20:4,8,13,18; 21:1,1,2,9,25,32; 22:3,3,9,24; 23:10,16,18; 24:1,2,11,15,16,19,19,21,22,29,30,30,48,52,66; 25:1,10,28; 26:8,14,15,18,18,18,26,32; 27:15,17,30,41,42; 28:6,6,7,7,9,11,12,18; 29:12,14,16,17,17; 30:8,9,30,35; 31:2,10,18,19,21,22,25,32,34,42,54; 32:10,13,23; 34:1,5,7,7,7,13,27; 35:4,13,14,15,16,22,27; 36:6,12; 37:1,3,5,6,8,9,9,10,12; 38:12,14,14,15,30; 39:1,1,5,6,13,13; 40:4,5,5,8,16,16,22; 41:1,1,5,7,11,11,14,15,19,21,43,54,56; 42:24,29; 43:2,2,6,10,25,26,31,33; 44:4,24; 45:4,16,21,27,27; 46:5,6,12,18,25,27,29; 47:22; 49:33; 50:4,12,13,14; Ex 1:7; 2:11,16; 3:4; 4:6,19,28,28,30,31; 5:13,14; 7:13,20,22; 8:12,15,19; 9:7,12,24,28,31,34,35; 10:13,14,23; 11:1,9; 12:36,39,39,50; 13:19,19; 14:5,6,19,25,28; 16:1,3,18; 17:10; 18:1,1,2,6,8,8,8,9,11; 19:7,9,14; 21:29,36; 24:4; 32:14,20,25,35; 33:5; 34:4,29,32,34; 35:23,24,25,26,29; 36:2,3,7; 37:9; 38:9,11,12,17,26; 39:42,42,43,43; 40:35; Lev 10:16,19; 19:20; 21:10; 23:43; Nu 1:17,48; 3:4; 5:4,18,19; 7:11; 8:4; 11:3,4,18,24,24,26,28,34; 12:1,10,14; 13:22,31,32; 14:2,6,36; 16:2,19,27,39,39,47,49,50; 17:8,8; 20:3,29; 21:26,26,32; 22:2,7,29,33; 23:30; 26:33,33,46,65; 27:4,11,22; 31:10,21,35,53; 32:1,9,13; 33:4,4,8; Dt 1:3,4,4; 2:1,14,14,15,16,22,30,35; 3:6; 4:25,42,42; 8:3,16; 9:9,16,16,16,16,18,21,25,28; 10:4,4,5,10; 25:18; 29:1,26; 32:17,30,30; 34:5,9,9; Jos 2:4,4,6,6,7,17,22,23; 3:17; 4:1,4,8,9,9,10,10,11,12,14,18,20,23,23,23; 5:1,1,1,5,5,6,6,6,6,6,7,8; 6:8,10,11,22,23,25; 7:7,16,17,18,24,25; 8:12,14,20,20,20,21,24,24,24,26,27,31,31,33,35; 9:3,18,24; 10:1,1,1,1,16,17,24,24,27,28,30,32,33,35,39,40; 11:9,10,12,20,23,23; 12:1; 13:1,8,8,8,12,12,15,21,22,24,29,32,33; 14:2,3,3,4,5,15; 17:1,3,8,11; 18:2,21; 19:49,50; 21:3,8,12,42,43,44; 22:7,9,11,30; 23:1,1; 24:31,31,32,33; Jdg 1:19,20; 2:4,6,7,7,10,10,12,15,17,23; 3:1,2,2,4,11,16,18,18,24,30; 4:3,3,11,12; 5:31; 7:12,13,19; 8:8,10,19,28,30,30,33,34,35; 9:22,24,27,35,45,47,51,51,56; 10:4; 11:34,39; 12:4,9,14; 13:2,23; 14:6,9,18,19,20; 16:8,18,20,22,31; 17:5,6,7; 18:1,1,4,7,14,17,22,27,28,31; 19:1,2,3,21,21; 20:3,22,30,36,36,37,38,39,41; 21:1,5,8,12,14,15,25; Ru 1:4,6,7,12; 2:1,14,17,18,18,18,19; 3:7,16; 4:1; 1Sa 1:2,2,2,5,6,9,23,25; 2:5,12; 3:3,7; 4:6,13,15,18,19; 5:1,4,9,11; 6:1,19; 7:6,7,14; 9:2,15; 10:11,16,16,20,26; 11:5,9; 13:3,13,19,22,22,23; 14:3,21,21,22,24,27,27,30,31,35,47,48; 15:35; 16:8,9,10,12,12,14; 17:5,12,13,20,25,27; 18:1,6,10,12,14,24; 19:1,18,18; 20:9,17,35,37,41; 21:6; 22:6,21; 23:6,7,13,15; 25:2,2,21,34,35,43,44; 26:3,4,5,5,12; 27:3,3,4,8; 28:3,3,20,24; 30:1,1,2,4,5,12,16,18,19,21,31; 31:7,7,11; 2Sa 1:10,12,16; 2:4,8,23,27,31; 3:6,7,7,15,20,22,22,23,23,23,30,37; 4:1,2,4,7; 5:3,8,12,12,17,18; 6:8,13,17,18,23; 7:1; 8:9,10,11,11; 9:5,10,12; 10:6,15,16,19; 11:16,22,27,27; 12:2,3,3,4,4,6,8,15,15,20; 13:3,10,15,22,24,29,34; 14:2,6; 15:11,11,18,24,31; 16:1,1; 17:14,18,21,22,23,25,25; 18:10,11,11,13,18,33; 19:8,15,24,32,40; 20:3,3,5,13; 21:2,2,8,8,11,12,12,13,19; 23:21; 24:8,10,11,19; 1Ki 1:4,6,38; 2:11,19,27,28,29,41,41; 3:2,10,15,17,18,21,28,28; 4:7,7,15,24,26,34; 5:1,1,12,15; 6:38; 7:5,8,28,30,30,31,34,40,46,51,51; 8:3,5,9,17,54,54,66; 9:1,1,1,2,11,12,14,16,16,24,24,25; 10:2,4,13,19,19,20,22,24,26; 11:2,3,4,6,9,9,10,15,15,16,17,23,27,27; 12:1,2,6,8,10,12,15,20,24,32,32,33; 13:10,11,11,12,13,20,21,23,23,26,26,28; 14:5,18,21,22,24,26; 15:3,3,5,5,11,12,13,15,22,26,30,30,34; 16:7,9,13,13,16,19,19,26; 17:5,7,15; 18:3,4,4,5,26,30,31,40; 19:1,1,4; 20:17,33,42; 21:4,11,15; 22:3,11,13,31,38,53; 2Ki 1:2,8,8,17,17; 2:7,9,13,14,22; 3:2,2,3,4,9,21,21,26; 4:17,20,44; 5:1,1,2,2,4,8,13,14,19,27; 6:15,18,23,29,30; 7:6,8,15,16,17,17,18,19,19; 8:1,1,4,5,5,18,19,27,29,29; 9:14,15,15,16,21,27,29; 10:16,24,25,29,30,31; 11:4,10,15,20; 12:6,10,11,18; 13:2,5,6,7,7,11,14,16,23,25; 14:3,5,24,26,27,28; 15:3,5,9,9,18,20,24,28,34; 16:3,11,16,18; 17:3,3,4,4,7,7,8,8,11,11,12,15,15,15,19,23,28,29,33; 18:3,4,4,6,12,12,16,36,37; 19:8; 20:4,8,11,12; 21:2,3,3,4,7,7,9,16,20,21,24; 23:2,8,11,12,12,13,15,16,18,19,19,19,22,24,26,32,37; 24:3,4,7,9,13,13,19; 25:1,11,16,21,22,23; 1Ch 2:4,18,26,34,34; 4:5,9,18,27,40,43; 5:9,18,25; 6:49; 7:4,4,15,23; 8:8,9,11,38,40; 9:19,22,25,27,27,44; 10:7,7,11; 11:3,3,6,10,23; 12:22,23,29,39; 13:10,11,14; 14:2,2,8,9,12; 15:1,3,15,26; 16:1,2,40; 18:9,10,11,11; 19:6,9,16,16,19; 20:5; 21:19,28,29; 22:4,7; 23:17,22,25; 24:2,19,28; 26:2,4,5,6,9,10,10,12,12,32; 27:23; 28:2,12; 29:8,9,25; 2Ch 1:3,4,4,4,5,12,14; 2:17; 3:1; 4:11,17; 5:1,1,4,6,10,11; 6:7,13,13; 7:6,7,9,10,11,11,11; 8:2,4,8,11,12,14; 9:1,3,9,11,12,18,19,21,23,25; 10:1,2,6,8,10,12,15; 11:14,15,21; 12:1,2,5,9,13,14; 13:13,21; 14:8,14; 15:8,9,9,11,15,16,18; 16:6,14; 17:2,5,13; 18:1,10,12,30; 20:24,27,29,30,33; 21:3,3,6,7,7,10,11,11,11,19; 22:1,4,6,6,7,8; 23:8,9,14,18,18,21; 24:3,7,7,9,14,16,22,24,24; 25:3,10,13,13,24; 26:4,8,10,10,11,19,20,20,21,21,23; 27:2; 28:3,6,17,18,19,19,19,23; 29:2,15,15,24,34,34,34,36; 30:3,3,3,5,12,17,17,18,25,25,26; 31:1,1,10; 32:1,2,27,29,31; 33:2,3,4,7,7,9,15,22,22,25; 34:4,9,9,11,13,14,14,22,30,32,33; 35:3,10,16,18,18,20,22; 36:13,14,15; Ezr 1:5,7,7,8; 2:1,61,65,66; 3:1,6,8,12; 4:20; 5:14,14; 6:13,20,21,21,22; 7:6,6,9,10,11; 8:20,22,25,30,35; 9:1; 10:5,9,17,18,44,44; Ne 1:2; 2:1,9,10,12,12,13,13,16,16,18; 4:7,15,23; 5:4,12,13; 6:1,1,12,12,12,13,16,18; 7:1,1,4,5,6,63,67,73; 8:1,9,12,14,17,17; 9:2,15,26; 11:16; 12:29,30,31,43,46; 13:2,2,4,5,6,7,10,10,23; Est 1:6,14; 2:1,1,1,6,7,7,7,7,7,8,8,10,10,12,15,20,20,20; 3:2,4; 4:1,7,7,8,9; 5:5,11,11,14; 6:2,2,4,4,13,14; 7:4,7,9,10; 8:1,2,3,17; 9:1,3,18,23,23,24,24,25,26,26,31,31; 10:2; Job 1:2,3,5; 2:11; 3:15; 6:10,20; 10:18,19,19; 28:17; 29:12,22; 30:2; 31:13,21,25,32,35; 32:3,3,4,5; 34:27; 41:32; 42:5,7,10,10,11,11,12,13; Ps 44:17,17,18,18,20; 49:11; 51:T; 52:T; 54:T; 55:6; 56:T; 57:T; 59:T; 66:18; 73:2,2,15; 78:11,11,29,54,60,63; 94:17; 95:9; 105:26,28,38,44; 106:13,21,23,34; 119:92; 124:1,2; Pr 6:26; 7:7; 24:31; Ecc 2:7,11,11,18; 4:2,8; SS 1:6; 3:4,4; 5:6; 6:11; 8:11; Isa 1:9; 5:1; 6:6; 36:21,22; 37:8; 38:8,21,22; 39:1; 48:18; 53:2,9; 63:4; Jer 2:21; 3:7,8; 4:25; 5:5; 9:2; 11:8,19,19; 13:7; 15:17; 16:15; 18:8,10; 19:14; 20:2; 23:8,22,25,25; 24:2,2; 26:8,23; 28:12; 29:1,2; 31:26; 32:3,8,10,12,16,22; 34:8,11,16; 35:9; 36:4,9,13,23,26,27,32; 37:2,4,5,11,15,15,17; 38:6,7,14,27,27; 39:9,11,14,15; 40:1,1,7,7,7,11,11,12; 41:1,2,5,9,9,10,11,13,14,16,16,16,16,18,18; 43:1,1,5,5,6; 44:17,18; 51:60,60; 52:2,6,15,20,27; La 1:10; 3:18; 4:18; 5:4; Eze 1:6,8,8,10,10,10,11,11,23; 3:6,23; 8:4,11; 9:2,3,3; 10:14,15,20,21,22,22; 11:24,25; 13:22; 16:5,7,7,14; 17:8,18; 20:6,8,9,14,15,22,24,24,28,42; 23:17,18,41; 24:18; 31:17; 32:23,24,25,27,32; 33:5,21; 36:18,18,20,21,21; 38:8,8; 40:10,10,17,21,22,24,25,26,27,28,29,29,32,33,33,35,36; 41:8,18,21,23,24,26; 42:6,6,9,11,15,20; 43:3,3; 47:5; Da 1:9,11; 2:1,2,3,14,24; 3:2,3,7,27; 4:5,18,33; 5:2,3,23; 6:10,10,23,24; 7:1,4,5,6,6,7,7,8,12,20; 8:1,1,6; 9:21; 10:8; Hos 1:8,8; 10:3,5; Am 4:7,7; 7:1,2,7; Ob 16; Jnh 1:5,10; 3:10; 4:5; Hag 1:12; Zec 1:8; 5:9; 6:2; 7:2,12; 8:10,14; 10:6; 11:10; Mt 1:6,19,20,22,24; 2:4,7,9,9,13,15,16,16; 3:4; 4:5,12; 7:25,28,29; 8:5,33; 9:8,20,25,28,33,36; 11:1,20,21,23; 12:7; 13:6,44,46,53; 14:3,4,10,13,14,23,34; 15:36,39; 18:25,30,31,31,33,33; 19:1,15,22; 20:34; 21:6,28; 22:3,25,34; 23:30; 24:22,43; 25:16,18,20,24; 26:1,19,24,26,27,30,48,57,57,75; 27:3,16,17,18,26,31,35,50,52,54,55,57,60; 28:11,12,16; Mk 1:19,22,34; 2:1; 3:10; 4:6; 5:4,8,14,15,16,16,18,19,20,21,25,26,26,26,30,32,33; 6:14,17,17,17,18,30,34,44,52,53; 7:1,17; 8:1,6,7,9,14,14,23; 9:9,9,28,34; 10:22; 11:6,8,13; 12:6,12,28,34,44; 13:20; 14:16,21,22,23,26,44,72; 15:7,10,15,20,41,41,44; 16:4,9,10,11,14,14,19; Lk 1:22,58; 2:15,17,17,20,20,21,26,26,36,39,49; 3:19; 4:9,13,16,32,40; 5:4,6,9,17,25; 6:18; 7:1,10,21,29,30,39,42,43; 8:2,2,6,27,27,29,29,29,29,30,34,35,35,36,36,38,39,43,47,47,56; 9:1,7,8,8,10,36,36,47; 10:13,37,39,40; 11:14,37; 12:1,39; 13:1,6,11,14; 14:6,17; 15:11,13,14,32; 16:8; 17:12; 18:28; 19:15,15,28,32,37,42; 20:19,26; 21:4; 22:7,13,52,55,55,61; 23:8,8,12,19,25,46,47,48,49,51,53,55; 24:1,12,

14,21,23,24,35,40,50; Jn 1:24,40,40; 2:2,9,9,9,10,21,22,22; 4:1,4,5,8,18,44,45,45,45,46,47,53; 5:5,6,10,13,13,15; 6:2,6,12,12,13,17,19,22,22,22,22,23,23,26,64; 7:9,10,30,39,39,50; 8:20,31; 9:8,13,14,15,18,18,22,24,35; 10:40; 11:11,13,17,19,21,28,30,30,31,32,33,43,45,45,46,57; 12:1,9,12,16,16,18,18,29,29,36,37; 13:1,2,3,3,10,12,21,29,30; 15:22,24; 17:5; 18:1,2,9,10,14,16,18,26,32,40; 19:1,19,28,30,32,39,41; 20:1,7,8,9,12,18; 21:7,15,20,20; Ac 1:2,16; 2:13,30,44,45; 3:10,12,13,18; 4:7,13,14,21,23,28,32,35; 5:5,7,21,40,41; 7:5,16,17,29,30,35,41,44,44,44,60; 8:4,9,11,14,16,16,25,27; 9:23,27,27,27,33,39; 10:3,7,8,24,41,45,45; 11:1,11,13,15,16,18,19,23; 12:2,9,10,12,12,17,18,19,20,25; 13:1,3,12,29,31,36,46; 14:8,8,9,11,18,20,23,25,26,26,27,27; 15:3,4,12,33,38,38,39; 16:9,10,10,13,16,23,27,34; 17:1,3; 18:2,2,18,18,25,27; 19:9,12,16,18,19,21,41; 20:1,3,13,16,36; 21:1,9,10,19,29,29,33,35; 22:11,28,29,30; 23:12,27,29; 24:27; 25:7,12,16,18,19,25; 26:32; 27:5,7,9,9,21,38; 28:9,11,15,17,25; Ro 1:13; 2:25; 3:25; 4:2,11,12,18,21,21; 7:7,7; 9:6,11,29; 15:5; 1Co 2:8; 4:8,15; 11:24; 2Co 1:9; 2:3,12,13; 5:21; 7:5,7,14; 8:6; 9:5; 10:14; 11:32; Gal 2:2,4,7,7,10; 3:19,21; 4:4,22; Php 1:30; 2:27; 4:10; 1Th 2:2; 3:5; Titus 3:5; Heb 1:3; 2:17; 4:2,6,8; 7:6; 8:7; 9:1,4,4,6,7,8,19,26; 10:12,32,34; 11:5,11,15,15,15,17,18,24,30,39,40; 12:9,17; 1Pe 1:6,14; 2:10; 2Pe 1:21; 1Jn 2:7,19; 2Jn 5; Rev 2:4; 4:1,3,4,7,8; 5:6,6,8,8; 6:9,9,11; 7:2; 8:3,6,11; 9:1,9,10,10,11,14,15; 10:5,8,10; 11:10; 12:13,13,16; 13:1,2,3,3,4,11,12,17; 14:1,3,6,17,18,18; 15:2; 16:2,9,11; 17:1,3; 18:1,19; 19:20,20,20; 20:4,4,4,4,10,12,13; 21:1,9,12,14,15; 22:8,8

HAS (2328)

See select index of "HAS" in the Main Concordance.

Ge 1:29,30; 3:22; 4:25; 5:29; 6:17; 9:4,6; 15:16; 16:2,11; 17:14,14; 18:19,21; 19:13,19; 21:6,17,26; 22:20; 24:27,27,35,35,35,36,36,44,51,56; 26:22,33; 27:27,36; 29:8,32; 30:2,6,6,18,20,23,27,29,30,30; 31:1,1,5,7,7,9,9,12,15,15,16,32,42; 33:5,11; 34:8,21; 35:3; 37:33,33; 38:23; 39:8,9,14; 41:25,28,32,39,51,52; 42:21,28,28; 43:23; 44:16,28; 45:6,9; 48:2,9,11,15,16; Ex 3:9,13,14,15,16,18; 4:5; 5:3,23; 7:16; 9:18,19; 11:6; 15:1,2,4,21; 16:7,8,9,15,16,29,32; 19:8; 20:20; 21:3,8,8,8,16,29,29,29; 22:8,19,27; 24:3,7,8; 32:1,23,24,29,33; 35:1,4,10,30,31,34,35; 36:1,1; Lev 4:3,23; 6:10; 7:18; 8:5,34; 9:6,7; 10:6,11,15; 11:3,7,34,38; 13:2,3,4,5,6,6,8,9,10,13,13,18,20,20,21,23,24,25,25,26,28,28,29,32,34,36,37,38,39,40,41,41,42,51,52,53,55,55,55,55,56,56,57,58; 14:32,37,39,44,48,48; 15:2,7,16,17,18,19,24,25,25,25,33; 16:20; 17:2; 19:20,22; 20:3,11,11,12,13,15,17,18,18,18,20,20,21,24; 21:3,10,10,12,17,18,20,20,21,21; 22:4,4,6,13; 24:20; 25:30; 27:17; Nu 5:2,8,13,13,18,19,27,28; 6:19; 10:29; 12:2; 14:23,24,29,35; 15:28; 16:9,10,28,29,46,46; 19:2,2,13,16,16,18,18,18,20; 20:5; 21:29,30; 22:5,11,13; 23:8,8,20,23; 24:11,16; 25:11; 27:9,10; 30:5,12; 31:17,18,19; 32:7,18,19,21,31; 34:13; 35:6,8,8,11,15,32,33; Dt 1:10,11,21; 2:7,7,7,30; 3:18,20,21; 4:19,23,32,32,33,34; 5:12,15,16,24,26,32,33; 6:17,20,25; 7:2,6; 8:10; 9:3,4,4; 10:22; 11:7,29; 12:1,7,20,21; 13:14,14; 14:2,6,8,9; 15:2,6,14,18,21,21; 16:10,17; 17:1,3,4,4,4,5,16; 18:5,8,14,21,22,22; 19:1; 20:5,6,7,17; 21:3,3,4,5,13,15,17,18; 22:17,19,21,25,26,29; 23:1,15; 24:4,5,5; 26:11,18,19,19; 27:21; 28:21,48,53,55; 29:4,22,24; 31:2; 32:21,27,27; 34:10,12; Jos 1:15; 2:9,9,24; 5:9; 6:16; 7:8,11,15,15,26; 8:8; 10:4,14,19; 14:10,14; 17:14; 18:3; 22:4,22,25; 23:3,9,9,13,14,14,14,15,15,15,15,16; 24:20,27,27; Jdg 1:7; 2:20,20; 3:28; 4:14,14; 6:13,13,30; 7:2,14,15; 8:7; 11:23,24,36; 16:17,18,23,24; 17:13; 18:4,6,10,14; 19:18,30; 21:3,5; Ru 1:13,20,21,21,21; 2:7,20; 3:3; 4:3,4,14,15,17; 1Sa 1:27; 2:5,5,8,8; 4:7,7,17,17,21,22,22; 6:3,4,9; 7:12; 9:12,16,24; 10:1,2,11,22,22,24; 11:13; 12:13,24; 13:4,4,14; 14:10,12,17,29,33,38,45; 15:11,11,12,12,12,23,26,28,28,33; 16:8,9,10; 17:33,34,36,36; 18:7; 19:4,4,4; 20:3,13,15,22,29,29,32; 21:11; 22:8,13; 23:7,7,10,11,22; 24:14; 25:21,24,26,27,30,30,31,32,34,39,39,39,40; 26:8,19,20; 27:6,12; 28:9,9,15,16,17,17,18,21; 29:3,5; 30:23,23; 2Sa 3:29,38; 4:8,9; 5:20,24; 6:12,12,20; 7:27; 12:13; 13:20,24,30,32,35; 14:2,7,13,20,22,22,30; 15:4; 16:8,8,11; 17:5,6,7,9,15,21; 18:19,28,31; 19:9,10,11,27,30; 20:17,21; 22:21,21,25,36; 24:21; 1Ki 1:11,13,18,19,19,19,25,25,27,29,43,44,46,48; 2:15,15,24,24,38; 5:4,7; 8:12,15,20,41,56,56; 9:8; 10:9,9,12; 12:19; 13:3,26,26; 14:11,13,16,16; 18:10,22; 21:10,13,14,18,29,29; 22:23,23,28; 2Ki 1:14; 2:2,4,6,16,22; 3:7,10; 4:2,14,27,27,31; 7:6,14; 8:1,4,7,9,10,13,22; 9:18,20; 10:10,10; 13:23; 14:7; 17:26; 18:33,35; 19:4,4,16,21,28; 20:9; 21:11,11,11; 22:4,10,13,16; 1Ch 14:11,15; 16:8,12; 17:25; 22:18,18; 23:25,25; 28:5,5,10; 29:1; 2Ch 2:11,12; 6:1,4,10,32; 7:21; 8:11; 9:8,8; 10:19; 13:5; 14:7; 16:7; 18:22,22,27; 21:10; 24:20; 25:8,16; 29:8,8,11; 30:8; 31:10; 32:14,15; 34:16,18,21,24; 35:21; 36:23,23; Ezr 1:2,2; 4:18,19,19,20; 5:16; 6:12; 7:23,27,28; 9:6,7,8,9,9,9,9,13; 10:14; Ne 2:5; 9:32,33; Est 1:15,16; 4:11; 5:12; 6:3,3,8,8,13; 7:5; Job 1:10,11,12,15,16,17,19,21; 2:4; 3:23,24,25,25; 4:7; 6:5,5,13; 9:4; 11:6,6; 12:6,9; 14:6,13; 15:12; 16:8,11,12; 17:6; 18:17,19; 19:6,8,8,9,13,21,26; 20:4,19,19,23; 23:10,14,16,16; 26:4; 27:2,2; 28:7,22; 30:11,25; 31:5,7,9,31; 32:12,12,14; 33:4,10,28; 34:23; 36:4,23,25; 37:7,16,21; 38:37; 40:16; 41:11,15,26; 42:7,8; Ps 4:3; 6:8,9; 7:13; 9:6,6,7,11; 13:6; 17:3; 18:20,20,24,35; 19:4; 22:14,14,24,24,24,31; 24:4; 28:6; 38:2,4,10; 39:9; 41:8,9; 45:2,7; 46:8,8; 47:5; 48:3; 52:T; 53:3; 55:5; 57:1; 58:4; 60:6; 62:11; 64:9; 66:5,9,16,19,19,20; 68:17,24; 69:20,20; 71:11; 73:25; 74:3,18; 77:8,8,9,9; 78:4; 80:15; 83:8; 84:3; 87:1; 88:16; 89:41,50; 90:4; 94:22; 98:1,2,3; 101:5; 102:T,13; 103:12,13,13,19; 104:17; 105:1,5; 108:7; 109:11; 110:4; 111:4,6; 115:16; 116:7; 118:14,15,16,17,18,18,22,23,24,27; 119:56; 124:6,7; 126:2,3; 129:4; 132:13,13; 135:4; 145:9,9; 147:5,19,20; 148:14; 150:6; Pr 2:17; 6:7,32; 7:19,26; 9:1,1,2,2,3; 10:13,25; 11:12,12; 13:7,7; 14:26,29; 15:15,21,21; 17:18,27,27; 18:21,24; 20:5,12; 23:24,29,29,29,29,29,29; 24:20,30; 28:2,23; 30:4,4,4,15; 31:5,11,21; Ecc 1:8,9,9,13,16; 2:12,21; 3:10,11,11,11,15,15; 4:3,3,10; 5:4,10,18; 6:5,10,10; 7:13,13,14; 8:8,8,15,17; 9:4,7,9; 12:13; SS 2:12; 4:2; 6:1,2,6; 8:2; Isa 1:2,12,20,21,22; 2:12; 5:9; 6:7,12; 7:2; 8:6,18; 9:2,8,11,11; 10:7,9,12,22; 12:1,2,4,5; 14:4,4,5,11,24,27,32; 16:13; 19:12,14; 20:3,6; 21:2,4,9,9,17; 22:5,14,25; 23:1,4,11,11; 24:3,8; 25:8; 26:20; 27:7,7,11; 28:2,22,25; 29:10,10,10; 30:33,33,33; 34:5,6,8,16; 35:10; 37:4,4,17,22,29; 38:7,8,12,12,15,15; 40:2,2,2,5,12,12,21; 41:2,4,20,20; 44:7,19,23,23; 45:9,15,23; 47:13; 48:14,16,20; 49:1,5,7,10,14,14,15; 50:4,5,10; 51:11; 52:4,9,9; 53:1,1,6,6,11; 54:1,10; 55:5; 58:2,14; 59:14; 60:1,9; 61:1,1,9,10; 62:8,11; 63:7,7; 64:4,4,4,11; 66:2,8,8; Jer 2:10,11,14,30,37; 3:6,6,6; 4:7,7,7,8,17; 5:19,30; 6:24,25,30; 7:11,28,28,28,29; 8:8,14,15,20; 9:12,12,21,21,21; 11:17; 12:8,9; 13:15,22; 14:17,19; 16:10; 17:8; 18:13,13; 20:8; 21:12; 22:3,8,11,21; 23:15,18,18,28,28,28,35,37; 25:3,4,34; 26:11,13,15,16; 27:13; 28:15; 29:15,26,28,31,31,32; 30:15; 32:24,31,43; 33:24; 34:16,21; 35:14; 37:7; 38:16,21; 40:3,3,5,14; 42:19; 43:2; 44:23; 45:3,4; 46:10,17; 47:4,7,7; 48:8,11,11,19,21,26,32,39,45; 49:1,1,1,7,7,20,20,24,24,24,25,30,30,31; 50:14,15,25,25,27,28,29,29,31,43,43,45,45; 51:10,10,11,13,14,34,34,34,34,34,44; La 1:1,3,5,6,8,8,9,14,14,15,15,15,16,17,17; 2:1,1,1,2,2,2,3,3,3,4,4,4,5,5,5,6,6,6,6,7,7,9,17,17,17,17,17,22; 3:1,2,3,4,4,5,6,7,7,9,9,15,16,16,28,37; 4:1,8,8,11,11,16; 5:1,2,15,16; Eze 2:3,5; 4:14; 5:6,6,6; 7:2,6,6,6,7,7,10,10,10,11,12,12,19; 8:12; 9:6,9; 13:6; 15:5; 17:10; 18:10,11,13,14,19,19,24; 21:25,25,29,29; 22:4,24,28; 24:2,12,12,13,14,24; 25:8; 26:2; 28:5; 30:21; 33:13,16,21,24,30,33; 34:8,8; 36:23,35; 38:8; 44:2; 46:12; Da 1:10; 2:10,27,28,30,37,38,38,45; 3:5,10,28; 4:2,22,24,31; 5:11,26; 6:5,20,27; 8:26; 9:11,12,12,13; 11:2,4,21,36; 12:1,7; Hos 2:5,5,8; 4:1; 5:6; 6:1,1; 8:3,6,7,9,14,14; 11:12; 12:2,14; 14:4; Joel 1:2,4,5,6,6,7,7,16,17,19,20; 2:20,21,23,26,32; 3:8; Am 3:1,4,4,5,6,8,8; 4:2; 6:8,11; 8:7; Ob 3,18; Jnh 1:2,12; Mic 1:9,9,12; 4:4,9,12; 6:2,8; 7:4; Na 1:11,14; 3:13,19; Hab 2:13; Zep 1:7,7,7; 2:15; 3:15,15; Hag 1:2; Zec 1:6,10; 2:8,9,11,13; 3:2; 4:9; 6:15; 9:3,3; 11:2,2; 13:5; Mal 1:14; 2:11,11,11,15; 3:17; Mt 2:2,5; 3:2; 4:16,17; 5:23,28,31; 6:34; 8:20; 9:6,18,22,33; 10:7,25; 11:11,12,15,18; 12:11,20,28; 13:9,11,12,15,43,52; 14:2; 15:13; 17:9,12,15; 19:6,11,29; 20:7; 21:42,42; 23:35; 24:45; 25:28,29; 26:10,13,23,45,56,65; 27:8,23,64; 28:6,7,15,18; Mk 1:15,15; 2:10; 3:26,30; 4:9,11,23,25,29; 5:19,19,34; 6:2,14,16; 7:29,37; 9:1,13,17,21,22; 10:9,29,52; 11:2,21; 12:10,11,43; 13:20,20; 14:6,9,41; 15:14; 16:6; Lk 1:13,25,25,45,48,49,51,51,52,52,53,53,54,61,68,69; 2:11,15,15; 3:11,11,11; 4:6,18,18; 5:24; 7:5,16,16,33,45,46,47,47,50; 8:8,10,18,39,46,48; 9:19,58; 10:9,11,40,42; 11:6,20,50; 12:5,5,32,48,48; 13:16; 14:5,22,35; 15:4,8,27,27,27,30; 16:26; 17:7,18,19; 18:29,42; 19:7,9,16,18,24,25,26,26,30; 20:17; 21:3,22; 22:22,31; 23:5,15,15,22,41; 24:6,34,34,49; Jn 1:3,5,15,18,18,30; 2:4,20; 3:2,13,19,21,32,33,33,34,35,36; 4:23,44; 5:22,24,24,25,26,26,27,33,36,36,37; 6:27,29,32,39,45,46,46,47,54,65; 7:8,19,38,47,51; 8:10,28,29,35,40; 9:32; 10:4,29; 11:11,39; 12:19,23,38,38,40,50; 13:18; 14:2,9,9,21,30,31; 15:9,13; 16:21,21,32; 17:1,10,12,14; 18:11; 19:35; 20:21; Ac 1:7,11; 2:32,33,33,36; 3:13,16,20; 4:11; 5:3,32; 7:40,50; 9:12,13,14,17; 10:15,28,31,33,37; 11:8,9,18; 12:11; 13:23,26,33,34,47; 14:17,17; 15:14,21; 17:7,31,31,31; 19:26; 20:24,28; 21:28; 22:14; 23:9,17,18; 24:2; 25:5,11,24; 26:6,22,26; 27:24; 28:4,21,27,28; Ro 1:19,20; 2:25; 3:21; 5:5,5; 6:7,7,9,17; 7:1,3; 8:2,22,33; 9:18; 10:16,18,19; 11:11,25,25,32,34,34,35; 12:3,4; 13:1,2,8,11; 14:3,23; 15:8,18,20; 16:2,10,12,13,19; 1Co 1:9,20,24,30; 2:7,9,9,9,9,10,12,16; 3:5,6,10,14; 4:1,9; 5:2,3,7; 6:1; 7:7,7,7,12,13,14,14,15,17,17,28,37,37,37; 9:14; 10:11,13,28; 11:14,15; 12:12,18,24,28; 14:26,36; 15:12,13,14,16,17,20,24,25,27,27,28,38,41,54,54; 16:9,10,12; 2Co 1:10,19,20; 2:5,5,5; 3:6,10,14; 4:4; 5:5,5,17,17,19; 6:16; 7:11,13,14; 8:1,12,22; 9:2,14; 10:13; Gal 3:1,15,22,25; 4:7,27; 5:1,6,11; 6:14; Eph 1:3,6,18; 2:14,14; 3:5; 4:7,28; 5:5; Php 1:12,12,13,19,29; 2:22,22; 3:14; Col 1:6,6,12,13,22,23,26,27; 2:14; 3:13; 4:16; 1Th 1:4,8; 2:16; 3:6,6,6; 2Th 2:2; 3:2; 1Ti 1:12; 2:6; 4:8; 5:4,8,9,16; 6:16,20; 2Ti 1:9,10,10,10,15; 2:18,26; 4:10,10,10,14; Titus 1:3,9,12; 2:11; Phm 7,11,18; Heb 1:2,4,9; 2:5,6,13; 3:3,3,12,15; 4:3,4,14,15; 5:3; 6:12,20,20; 7:13,16,21,22,24,28; 8:6,13; 9:15,17,20,26; 10:14,29,29,29,36; 11:16; 12:26; 13:5,23; Jas 1:12,15; 2:5,13,14; 4:5; 5:2; 1Pe 1:3; 2:7; 3:22; 4:12; 2Pe 1:3,4,14; 2:3,3,19; 3:4; 1Jn 1:2; 2:11,23,23,27,29; 3:1,2,6,8,15,17,17; 4:2,7,12,13,14,16,18,21; 5:4,9,10,10,11,12,12,20,20; 2Jn 4,9; 3Jn 11; Jude 6,13; Rev 1:5,6; 2:7,11,12,13,17,29; 3:6,13,22; 5:5; 6:17; 11:2,14,15,18,18; 12:10,12; 13:9,18; 14:7,10,15; 16:18,18; 17:7,10,17; 18:2,5,6,6,10,17,19,20; 19:2,2,7,7,12,16; 20:6; 21:4

HAVE (4448)

See select index of "HAVE" in the Main Concordance.

Ge 3:11,13,14; 4:1,7,10,23; 6:7,7; 7:1,4,15; 8:21; 9:13,17; 11:6; 12:18; 13:8; 14:22,24,24; 15:3; 16:8,13; 17:5,20; 18:3,5,10,12,13,14,19,21,27,31; 19:5,8,8,8,12,19; 20:3,5,6,9,9,9,9,17; 21:7,7,23,29; 22:12,16,16,18; 24:14,14,14,19,25,31,33,33,40,42; 25:30; 26:10,10,10,16,27; 27:11,19,37,37,37,38; 28:15,15,22; 29:25,25,34; 30:8,8,16,20,26,27,27,29,30,33,34; 31:12,14,26,28,29,30,36,37,37,38,38,38,42,43,51; 32:4,4,5,10,10,12,28,28; 33:9,9,10,10,11; 34:30,31; 35:2,3,17; 37:17; 38:24,29; 40:15; 41:15; 42:2,9,10,12,36; 43:7,10,21,22; 44:4,5,9,10,15,16,17,19,20,28; 45:1,10,13; 46:30,31,32,34; 47:1,4,4,5,9,23,25,29; 49:6; 50:4; Ex 1:9,18,18; 2:14,18,20,22; 3:7,7,8,9,12,12,16,16,17; 4:10,10,21; 5:15,21,21,22,23; 6:5,5; 7:1,16; 9:8,15,15,16,19,27,28,28,29; 10:1,5,6,11,11,16,25,26; 12:31,32,39,44,44,48; 14:5,5,5,11,12; 15:5,13; 16:3,12,16,18,18; 18:3,16,22,22; 19:4,10; 20:3,19,22,22; 22:3,15; 23:7,13,20,30; 24:12; 25:8,10,20; 27:9,11,12,17; 28:1,3,5,7; 29:24,35; 31:2,3,6,6,6; 32:7,8,8,8,8,9,29,30,31,31,32; 33:12,12,12,12,17,19,19,19,19,22; 34:9,27; 35:5; Lev 4:28,35; 5:1,2,5,6,10,13,16,18,19; 6:4,17; 7:33,34,34; 8:35; 10:13,14,18,19,19; 11:4,4,5,6,9,10,12,21,23,26; 13:7,15,17,46; 14:3,35,41,43; 16:16; 17:4,11,14; 18:6,7,8,9,10,11,12,13,14,15,15,16,17,17,18,19,20,22,23,23; 19:8,10,30; 20:9,12,13,16,17,19,25,26; 22:25; 23:24,38,39; 24:22; 25:4,5,9,25,32,48; 26:2,10,35,35; 27:20,22; Nu 3:12; 4:15,16; 5:7,7,7,16,19,20,20,26,28,30; 6:21; 8:7,8,13,15,16,18,19; 9:2,7,14; 11:6,11,11,15,16,17,20,20,22,22; 12:11,14; 14:11,14,14,15,17,19,20,27,31,34,35,40,43; 15:15,25,31,39; 16:3,5,7,11,13,15,15,30,38,41; 18:6,8,9,20,20,24; 19:20; 20:14,17; 21:5,22,30,30,34; 22:5,20,28,29,30,30,32,32,33,33,34,38; 23:4,4,11,11,20,22; 24:7,8,10; 25:5,13; 27:11,12,13,19; 31:15,49,50; 32:4,5,11,17,24; 33:53; 34:2,14,15; 35:3,5,29; Dt 1:6,8,15,19,20,28,41; 2:3,5,7,9,19,22,24,31; 3:2,19,19,20,20,21,24; 4:5,7,8,9,25,25,30,33; 5:7,24,24,26,28; 7:2,20; 8:10,13,17; 9:1,2,7,12,12,12,13,23,24,24; 10:9; 11:8,10,28,31; 12:6,7,9,11,12,17,21,26,29,30; 13:2,6,13,13,13,17; 14:7,7,10,24,27,29; 15:2; 16:13; 17:14; 18:1,2,20; 19:1,15; 20:9; 21:8,9,9,12,14; 22:3,7; 23:13; 24:5,8; 25:1,2,13,14,15; 26:1,1,3,10,12,13,13,13,13,14,14,14,14,14,15,17; 27:2,3,4,8,9,12; 28:20,33,40,41,54,64; 29:2,22; 30:1,3,4,12,13,19; 31:5,17,19,20,27,29,29; 32:34,39,46,50; 33:9; 34:4; Jos 1:9,15,16; 2:2,3,10,12,18,18; 3:4; 5:9,14,14; 6:2,4,5,6; 7:3,11,11,11,11,11,12,19,20,20,25; 8:1,6,8,8; 9:6,9,9,19; 10:6,8; 13:6; 14:9,9; 15:19; 17:14,16,17,18; 18:6,7; 20:6; 22:2,2,3,3,17,23,24,25,27,31,31; 23:3,4,8,15; 24:22; Jdg 1:2,7,15; 2:2,2,3; 3:19,20; 4:5; 6:10,14,17,22,36; 7:2; 8:1,2,6,15,22,24; 9:2,16,16,16,18,18,18,19,19,20,31,48; 10:10,13,14,15; 11:12,12,23,27,35,35,36; 12:3; 13:5,7,13,14,22,23; 14:2,6,18; 15:3,10,10,11,16,16,18; 16:7,10,11,13,15,17; 17:2; 18:9,24; 19:18,19,22; 20:7; 21:7,17,18; Ru 1:8,11,12; 2:9,9,10,11,12,12,13,13,14; 3:2,10; 4:9,10,11; 1Sa 1:15,16,17,23; 2:36; 4:9,16,20; 5:8,10; 6:7,7,21; 7:6; 8:5,7,7,8,18; 9:7,7,8,12,16,20,24; 10:2,14,19,19; 12:1,1,2,2,3,3,3,3,3,3,4,4,5,10,10,13,19,20; 13:11,12,13,13,13,14,20; 14:7,24,30,30,33,41,43; 15:11,13,18,23,24,26,30; 16:1,1,2,5,7,11,18; 17:8,28,29,45; 18:8,21,25; 20:1,1,3,8,26,29,30,42; 21:2,3,4,4,5,8,15; 22:8,13,17; 24:10,11,12,17,17,18; 25:11,31,34,35; 26:16,18,19,19,19,21,21,21; 27:5; 28:9,12,15,15,22; 29:3,6,6,6,8,8,9,9,10; 2Sa 1:3,3,10,19,21,25,27,27; 2:6,7,14,27; 3:17,24,33; 4:3,11; 5:8; 7:3,6,6,7,7,9,9,9,10,11,18,19,21,22,24,24,25,27,28,29; 9:9; 10:5; 11:19; 12:8,13,14,27; 13:16,35; 14:7,13,15,15,31,32; 16:2,8,8,10,21; 17:15,29; 18:11,13,18,21,22,25; 19:5,5,6,7,20,20,22,22,26,28,42,42,43,43,43; 20:1; 21:4,4,5,5; 22:4,22,23,24,24,44,44; 23:5; 24:10,10,10,17,17,17; 1Ki 1:11,14,24,33,34,35,44,45,45,47; 2:4,8,14,16,20; 3:6,6,6,7,8,11,11,12,12,13,13,26; 5:6,8; 8:13,16,16,16,18,20,20,21,24,24,24,25,25,27,32,33,33,35,35,43,44,44,47,47,47,47,48,48,50,50,59; 9:3,3,3,3,5,6,7,7,9,9,13,13; 10:7; 11:11,13,22,32,32,33,33,34,36; 12:10,16; 13:17,21,21; 14:6,8,9,9,9; 17:4,9,10,12,13,13,18,20; 18:5,9,12,18,18,18,18,36; 19:4,10,10,14,14,18,18,20; 20:4,18,18,31,36,40,42; 21:2,10,19,20,20,20,22,22,29; 22:17; 2Ki 1:5,13,14,16,16; 2:10,16,21; 3:14,23; 4:2,13,13,43; 5:8,8,13,18,22,25; 6:22; 7:12,12,13; 9:5,18,19,22,31; 10:2,2,8,13,27,30,30; 13:19,19; 14:10; 16:6; 17:27,38; 18:14,20,25,27,34; 19:6,6,7,11,11,15,17,18,20,22,22,23,23,23,23,23,24,24,25,25,25; 20:3,3,5,10,17,19; 21:7,15,15; 22:4,4,5,5,6,8,9,9,13,13,13,17,17,19,19; 23:17; 1Ch 4:27,43; 12:17,17; 15:12; 17:2,5,5,6,6,8,8,8,9,10,16,17,17,19,20,22,23,25,26,27,27; 19:5; 21:8,8,17,17,22; 22:8,8,8,9,11,13,14,15; 23:5,11; 28:3,6,19; 29:2,3,14,16,17,17,17,19; 2Ch 1:8,8,9,11,11,11,12; 6:2,5,5,5,6,6,8,10,10,11,15,15,15,16,16,18,23,24,24,26,26,33,34,34,37,37,37,38,38,39; 7:12,12,16,18,19,20,20,22,22; 9:6; 10:10,16; 12:5,7; 13:8,10,11; 14:7,11; 16:9; 18:16; 19:3,3; 20:8,8,12,17,20,20,37,37; 21:12,13,13,13; 24:20; 25:16,16,16,19; 26:18,18; 28:9,11,23; 29:9,18,19,31; 30:6; 31:10; 32:13; 33:7; 34:15,17,17,21,21,21,25,25,27; Ezr 4:2,3,12; 6:12; 7:15,24; 9:1,2,2,2,7,10,11,13,13; 10:2,10,10,13; Ne 1:3,6,7,7,9; 2:3,7,8,17,20; 4:5,22; 5:4,5,5,8,19; 6:7,14,14; 7:3; 8:10; 9:8,33,33,37; 10:34; 13:14; Est 1:15,18; 4:11,14; 5:4,14,14; 6:8,10,10; 7:3,4,4; 8:7,7; 9:12,12,21; Job 1:5,7,8,10,10; 2:2,3; 3:26,26; 4:3,3,4,4,8; 5:3,16,23,27; 6:3,8,10,11,12,13,21,22,24; 7:1,3,3,16,20,20,20,20; 9:21; 10:2,4,20; 12:3,4,5; 13:1,1,18,23; 14:5,5,15; 15:3,8,9,9,17,18; 16:2,7,7,8,15,17; 17:4,7,11; 19:3,4,14,14,19,20,21,21; 20:7,20; 21:3,14,29,29,31; 22:15; 23:11,11,12,12; 24:2,7,19,22; 26:2,2,3,3; 27:3,8,12,14; 30:1,9,25,29; 31:5,7,7,8,9,11,12,13,16,17,19,21,24,25,26,28,29,30,31,33,39; 32:13,15,15,17; 33:8,9,24,27,27,32; 34:11,16,32; 36:9,9,17,23,24; 37:24; 38:12,16,17,17,18,21,22,28; 40:5,9; 42:5,7,8; Ps 2:6,7; 4:1; 5:10; 6:2; 7:3,4,4,15; 8:1,2,3,5; 9:4,5,5,6,10,13,15,15,15; 12:1; 13:2,4; 14:3,3; 16:2,6,6; 17:3,4,4,5,5,11,14; 18:3,21,22,23,23,43,43; 19:3; 21:2,2,5,6; 22:1,10; 26:1,1,1,3,3; 27:9; 28:4,5,5; 31:1,8,8,12,17,19; 32:9; 34:19; 35:21,22,25; 36:1; 37:16,25,35; 38:2,14,19; 39:5; 40:5,6,7,12; 41:1,4,4,10; 42:3,7,9; 43:2; 44:1,1,9,10,11,13,14,21; 45:2; 48:8,8; 49:19,20; 50:9,16; 51:1,4,8; 52:9; 53:3; 54:7,7; 55:4,5,19; 56:13; 57:1,1,6; 59:4; 60:1,1,2,3,3,4,10; 61:3,5,5; 62:11,12; 63:2; 64:6; 65:9; 66:18; 68:23,28; 69:1,2; 71:1,5,6,7,14,17,19,20,23,24; 72:12; 73:4,7,13,13,14,15,25,28; 74:1,18,20; 78:3,3; 79:1,1,1,2,3,7,12; 80:5,5,6,12,15,17; 81:9; 84:3; 86:3,9,13,14,16,17; 88:6,7,8,8,15,15,16,17,18; 89:2,3,3,15,19,19,20,20,34,35,38,38,38,39,39,40,41,42,42,43,43,44,45,45,47,51,51; 90:1,8,13,15,15; 92:4,10,10,11,11; 93:3,3,3; 94:17; 95:10; 98:1,3; 99:4,4; 101:3,4; 102:7,10,13; 106:6,6; 108:11; 109:2,2,27; 111:10; 112:7,8,9; 115:5,6,7; 116:8,16; 118:21; 119:4,11,30,30,32,43,45,49,53,57,58,59,59,69,74,75,81,87,92,93,94,99,100,101,102,102,106,107,110,110,114,117,121,132,138,140,143,147,153,157,165,173,176,176; 120:6; 123:3,3,3,4; 124:3,4,4,5,7,7; 129:1,2,2,3; 131:2; 132:14; 135:14,16,17; 137:8; 138:2,4; 139:1,22; 140:5,5,5; 141:7,9; 142:3,4; 143:5,8; Pr 2:13; 3:25,28,30; 4:7; 6:1,1,2,3; 7:14,15,16,17; 8:6,9,14,14; 9:4,5,16; 10:2; 12:9,9,11,11,20,21; 13:2; 14:20; 17:16,21; 19:17,19; 20:6,9,13; 22:2,11,18,20; 23:8,8; 24:5,12,29; 25:7; 27:27; 28:19,19; 29:7,13; 30:2,3,3,4,9,27; 31:31; Ecc 1:14,16,16; 2:14,16,16,19,19; 3:10,19,19; 4:1,1,9,14,14; 5:13,14,18; 6:1,3,8; 7:12,15,22,27,29,29; 9:5,6,6,11; 10:5,7; SS 3:3; 4:9,9; 5:1,1,1,1,3,3; 7:12,12,13; 8:8,10; Isa 1:2,4,4,9,9,11,11,14,29,29; 2:6,8,22; 3:6,7,7,9,11,14; 5:4,4,12,12,24; 6:5; 7:5; 8:20; 9:2,3,4,10,10,12,13,13; 10:13,13,27; 12:1; 13:3,3,17,18; 14:1,8,10,10,12,12,20,24,24; 15:7; 16:6,8,9,10; 17:8,8,10,10; 19:13,13; 21:6,10; 22:1,3,3,11; 23:2,4,4,7,10,13; 24:5; 25:1,2,4; 26:1,12,12,13,15,15,15,15,18,18; 28:15,15,15; 29:13,20; 30:4,4,12,15; 31:6,7; 32:9; 33:1,1,13; 34:5,12; 36:5,10,12,18,19,20; 37:6,6,7,11,11,16,18,19,21,23,23,24,24,24,24,24,25,25,26,26,26; 38:3,3,5,12,17; 39:6,8; 40:11,21,21,28; 41:3,5,8,9,9,25; 42:6,9,14,14,16,20,22,22,24; 43:1,1,8,8,10,12,22,22,23,23,24,24; 44:1,2,21,22,22; 45:5,8,10,10,19,19,23,24; 46:3,3,4,11,11; 47:10,10,12,13,15; 48:6,7,8,8,10,10,12,15,15,16,18,19; 49:4,4,6,13,15,16,21; 50:5,5,7,11; 51:7,16,17,17,19,20,22; 52:5,5,15; 53:6; 54:8,9,14,16; 55:1,4,7; 56:11; 57:6,7,8,11,11,11,11,16,18; 58:3,3,3,3,5,6; 59:2,2,3,8,13,18,21; 60:15,21; 61:4; 62:6,8; 63:3,18,19,19; 64:6,7,7,10; 65:2; 66:3,5,18,19; Jer 1:9,12,16,18; 2:11,13,13,13,15,15,15,16,17,19,23,23,27,28,28,29,31,32,35; 3:1,2,2,3,3,3,4,6,13,13,13,16,20,21,21,24,25,25; 4:4,10,10,18,19,19,22,28,28; 5:7,11,12,14,19,21,21,23,23,25,25,27,28,28; 6:15,19,19,24,27; 7:9,11,30,30,30,31; 8:2,2,5,6,6,8,9,9,12,13,14,16,19; 9:5,10,13,13,14,14,16,16,24; 10:9,14,25,25; 11:10,10,10,13,13,13,17,20; 12:2,2,4,5,5,6,6,15; 13:11,22,25,25,27; 14:7,7,14,18,19,19,20; 15:5,6,7,10; 16:2,5,10,10,12,13,18,18; 17:4,13,16,16; 18:15,20,22,22; 19:4,4,4,5; 20:6,12; 21:10,12; 22:9,9,12,15,15,19,21; 23:2,2,2,3,14,17,21,21,22,22,25; 25:3,3,4,6,7,7,7,8,13,35; 26:3,4,5,5,11,12; 27:3,15,18; 28:6,7,8,13,15,16; 29:6,6,7,8,9,11,14,19,19,20,23,23,23,27,32; 30:2,10,14,14,15,18; 31:3,3,18,18,20,29,37; 32:17,20,20,25,30,30,30,32,32,42,42; 33:4,8,17,18,21,24,25,26; 34:14,14,16,16,17,17,18,18; 35:7,8,8,10,10,11,14,14,15,15,16,16,18,18,18,19; 36:2,14,30,31; 37:18,18; 38:9,9,9,19,22; 40:10; 41:8; 42:4,4,10,10,12,18,21,21; 43:10; 44:3,8,8,9,10,10,14,16,18,18,23,23,23,25; 45:4,4; 46:27; 48:29,33,38; 49:14,16,23,24,37; 50:6,6,10,17,21; 51:5,7,9,17,24,30,30,49,50,51,51,62; La 1:2,2,3,5,5,6,8,14,14,18,20,21,21,21,21,22; 2:7,9,10,10,16,16,16,20,20,21,21,21; 3:17,17,21,37,42,42,43,43,44,45,46,47,59,60,61,64; 4:3,10; 5:3,11,12,14,16,22; Eze 2:3; 3:6,17,19,21; 4:5,6,6,8,14,14; 5:5,7,7,7,9,11,13,13,15,17; 6:6,9,9,9,9,9; 7:14,14; 8:12,17; 9:10,11; 11:6,7,12,12,15,16,16,17,21; 12:2,6,11,22; 13:3,5,7,7,14,19,19,19,19; 14:3,5,9,22,22,23; 15:6,7,8; 16:43,48,50,51,51,51,52,52,54,59,63; 17:21,24; 18:6,21,22,22,24,26,27,28,31; 20:3,7,32,34,41,43,43,48; 21:5,15,17,23,24,24,32; 22:4,4,4,4,4,7,7,8,12,13,13,14,16,18,19,22,30,31; 23:29,30,31,34,35,37,38; 24:14,14,19,22; 25:6; 26:2,5,10,14; 27:34,36; 28:4,5,10,18,19,24,25; 29:6,20; 30:12,21; 32:9,21,22; 33:5,7,13,15,16,29,29; 34:4,4,4,15,19,19,21,24; 35:10,12,12,12,12; 36:2,4,5,6,22,22,23,36,36,36; 37:14,14,20,21,24; 38:13,13; 39:5,8,25,27,27; 40:4; 43:11,23; 44:12,19,28; 45:7,9; 47:22; 48:1,2,3,4,5,6,7,13,16,23,24,25,26,27; Da 1:10; 2:3,5,5,8,9,23,23,23,25,30,41; 3:12,12,14,18; 4:22,30,35; 5:7,11,12,14,14,16,16,22,23,27; 6:7,22,22; 8:22,23; 9:5,5,5,5,6,7,8,9,10,11,11,12,13,14,15,15,16,22,23,26,26; 10:11,12,14,19,20; 11:4,15,16,32; Hos 1:2; 4:6,6,10,10; 5:1,3,15; 6:7,10; 7:13,13; 8:1,9,10,11; 9:1,9,13,17; 10:3,9,9,13,13,13,13; 12:8,9; 13:4,13,14,16; 14:1,3,8; Joel 1:4,4,4,4,4,17,18,19,20; 2:4,25,26; 3:4,4,4,7; Am 2:4,4,4; 3:2,3,10; 4:6,8,9,10,11; 5:3,3,6,11,11,15,19,22,26; 6:12; 8:7; 9:15; Ob 1,15; Jnh 1:10,14; 2:4,9; 4:10,11; Mic 2:5,

8; 3:4,5; 4:6,9; 5:15; 6:1,3,3,13,16,16; 7:2,8,9,19; Na 1:12,12,14; 2:2,2; 3:16; Hab 1:12,12,14,14; 2:8,8,8,10,17,17,17; 3:2; Zep 1:17; 2:8; 3:6,6,8,11,19; Hag 1:6,6,6,10; 2:19,23; Zec 1:11,12,21; 2:6,8; 3:4,7,9; 4:9; 6:8,10; 7:3; 8:13,15,23; 10:6; 11:6; 12:10; 13:3; 14:16,17,18; Mal 1:2,2,2,3,3,4,6,7; 2:2,2,4,8,8,8,9,9,9,10,14,17,17; 3:3,7,7,13,13,14; Mt 2:2; 3:9; 4:16; 5:17,17,21,26,27,33,33,38,43; 6:1,2,5,12,16; 7:12; 8:8,10,20,20,29; 9:13,27; 10:8,8,21,34,35; 11:5,12,21,23,25,27; 12:7,18,36,36; 13:5,12,12,12,15,21,51; 14:4,17; 15:5,22,28,32,32,32,34; 16:23,27; 17:9,12,15,20,20; 18:6,8,9,15,33; 19:12,20,21,27,28; 20:6,12,12,15,23,30,31; 21:16,16,21,42; 22:4,4,4,31; 23:8,9,10,15,23,23,30,37; 24:25,34,43,43; 25:20,21,22,23,24,24,26,26,27,27,29,29,29; 26:9,11,11,25,32,35,55,64,65; 27:1,4,4,11,19,19,20,46; 28:7,20; Mk 1:24,38; 2:12,17,19,25; 3:9,15; 4:5,17,25,25,40; 6:17,18,31,38,39; 7:8,9,11,13; 8:2,2,2,3,5,16,18,33; 9:13,45,47,50; 10:20,21,21,28,40,47,48; 11:17,22,24; 12:26,39; 13:12,23,30; 14:5,7,7,28,31,48,64; 15:2,11,34; Lk 1:1,1,3,4,19,30,36,57; 2:29,30,31,48,48; 3:8; 4:23,34; 5:26,32,36; 6:3,24,31; 7:4,6,9,22,22,36,40,43,47; 8:13,18,18; 9:13,14,35,58,58; 10:13,19,21,22,28,35; 11:5,6,42,52,52,52; 12:3,3,17,19,20,24,37,39,49,50,59; 13:34; 14:8,9,18,19,28,33; 15:6,9,17,18,21,23,31; 16:11,12,24,28,29; 17:6,10,10,13; 18:13,21,22,22,28,38,39; 19:8,12,17,20,23,26,46; 20:46; 21:32; 22:15,28,32,32,36,36,52,71; 23:2,3,14,14,22,22; 24:18,25,26,39,39,41,49; Jn 1:14,16,34,41,45; 2:3,10,10; 3:11,12,15,16,18,21; 4:10,10,11,15,17,17,18,18,18,32,33,35,38,38,38,42; 5:7,26,29,29,33,36,37,39,40,42,43; 6:7,10,36,38,40,53,63,68,69,70; 7:26,48; 8:6,12,14,25,26,26,28,33,37,38,38,41,42,42,57; 9:17,27,37,39; 10:8,8,10,10,10,16,18,32,34; 11:10,21,32,34,37,41; 12:8,8,28,34,35,35,36,46,48,49; 13:8,10,12,14,15,15,18,26,34; 14:2,7,9,12,25,26,29; 15:3,9,10,11,12,15,15,19,22,24,24,27; 16:1,3,4,6,12,24,25,27,27,30,33,33,33,33; 17:2,3,4,6,6,7,9,10,10,13,14,18,21,22,23,23,24,24,25,26,26; 18:9,20,30,31,35; 19:7,10,11,15,22,22,31,37; 20:2,2,13,13,15,15,17,18,25,29,29,29,29,31; 21:10,12,25; Ac 1:4,11,21,24; 2:13,28; 3:6,6,24,24; 4:16,20; 5:3,3,4,28; 6:11,14; 7:34,34,34,43,52,53,53; 8:21,24; 9:13; 10:4,14,20,21,22,22,47,47; 11:12; 13:2,15,22,28,33,40,47; 14:11; 15:10,24,26; 16:36; 17:6,6,28,28; 18:10; 19:2,21,37,37,38; 20:20,20,21,21,25,27,33,34; 21:20,21,22,23,24,25; 22:10,15; 23:1,11,14,14,20,21,21,22; 24:2,5,10,15,15,19; 25:3,8,10,12,16,16,26,26,26; 26:1,4,5,11,16,16,32; 27:21,21,25,33,33; 28:17,20,21,21,27; Ro 1:13,13,13,20,29,31; 2:1,6,14,14,20,25,27; 3:2,9,9,12,12,23,26; 4:9,11,16,17; 5:1,1,2,9,11; 6:2,5,13,17,18,18,22,22; 7:6,7,7,18; 8:5,5,9,12,23,24,25,28; 9:2,9,15,15,15,15,18,21,29,29,30,31; 10:14,14,21; 11:3,4,4,17,17,30,31,32; 12:4,6; 13:1; 15:3,4,15,18,19,21,22,23,24,24,27,28,28,28; 16:7,17; 1Co 1:5,11; 2:8,12,16; 3:8; 4:2,6,7,8,8,8,9,13,15,17,18,19; 5:2,2,3,10; 6:4,7,7,9,12,12,19; 7:1,2,4,4,25,28,29,40; 9:1,4,5,11,12,12,15,17,19,22,27; 10:21,23,23; 11:6,6,10,16,17,19,19,22,22,30; 12:25,30; 13:1,2,2,2,3; 14:5; 15:1,2,6,15,18,19,20,32,39,39,49; 16:2,15,17; 2Co 1:10,12,12,14,16; 2:2,3,10,10; 3:4,12; 4:1,2,7,13,13; 5:1; 6:11,14,14,15; 7:1,2,2,2,3,3,4,11,14,16; 8:7,10,12,15,15,16; 9:2,7,9,13; 10:2,4; 11:6,6,9,23,26,26,27,27,27,27,27; 12:11,11,14,15,16,19,19,19,21,21,21; 13:6,7,7,10; Gal 1:9,13; 2:4,16,20; 3:4,7,21,27; 4:11,15,15,16,17; 5:4,4,10,24; 6:10; Eph 1:7,16; 2:5,8,13,18; 3:2,3,18; 4:1,19,28; 5:11; 6:13; Php 1:7,14,20,30; 2:1,5,12,20,28; 3:4,4,4,8,12,12,13,16,17,18; 4:3,9,11,12,12,18,18,18; Col 1:4,4,5,9,11,14,16,18,19,23,25; 2:1,2,10,18,19,22,23; 3:1,9,10; 4:1,10,11,17; 1Th 2:6; 3:5,6,9; 4:9,13,14,15; 5:27; 2Th 1:3,10; 2:12,12; 3:4,9; 1Ti 1:6,6,19,19,20; 3:7,13; 4:2,6,7,10; 5:12,14,15; 6:2,4,5,8,10,21,21; 2Ti 1:9,12,12; 2:2,18,23; 3:5,14,14,15; 4:7,7,7,8; Titus 2:8; 3:8,10,12,13; Phm 7,13,15,20; Heb 1:5,9; 2:1,14; 3:10,14; 4:1,2,3,3,8,14,15,15; 5:5,11,14; 6:4,4,4,5,6,9,10,10,18,19; 7:11,15,23; 8:1,3,7; 9:26; 10:2,2,2,7,9,10,18,19,21,26,36,39; 11:15,32; 12:4,5,9,11,18,22,22,23; 13:2,5,10,10,14,17,18,22; Jas 1:25; 2:4,6,11,14,18,18; 3:7,9,16; 4:2,2; 5:2,3,4,5,5,6,11,11,11,15; 1Pe 1:2,6,7,8,12,12,22,22,23; 2:3,10,24,25; 3:15; 4:3,5,10; 5:10,12; 2Pe 1:1,9,9,12,19; 2:13,15,20,21,21,21; 3:1,17; 1Jn 1:1,1,1,1,2,3,3,5,6,7,10; 2:1,3,7,7,12,13,14,18,18,19,20,24; 3:3,9,14,21; 4:1,3,4,14,17,20,20; 5:10,12,12,13,14,15; 2Jn 5,6,7,8,9,12; 3Jn 4,6,13; Jude 1,4,11,11,11,15,15,19; Rev 1:19; 2:2,2,3,3,3,4,5,6,14,15,20,21,24,25,27; 3:1,2,3,4,4,8,8,8,8,9,10,11,17; 4:11; 5:10; 7:14,14; 9:4; 10:4; 11:6,6,7,17,17; 12:10; 13:3,8; 15:4; 16:6,6; 17:8,10,12,13; 18:3,14,24; 22:12,14,16

HE (8526)

Ge 1:4,5,10,16,27,27,31; 2:2,2,3,3,8,8,19,19,21,21,22,22; 3:1,6,8,10,11,15,16,16,17,22,23,24,24; 4:5,9,17,20,21,26; 5:1,2,2,3,3,5,6,7,8,9,10,11,12,13,14,15,16,17,18,19,20,21,22,24,25,26,27,28,29,29,31,32; 6:6,9; 8:1,6,8,9,10,12,20; 9:21,21,25,25,26,29; 10:9,11,11; 11:10,11,12,13,14,15,16,17,18,19,20,21,22,23,24,25,26,32; 12:4,5,7,8,8,11,11,16,18,20; 13:1,3,3,4,18,18; 14:12,14,15,16,18,19; 15:5,5,6,7,10; 16:4,8,12,12; 17:14,17,20,22,24; 18:1,2,2,3,6,7,8,8,9,15,19,19,28,29,29,30,30,31,32,32,33; 19:1,1,2,3,3,9,13,14,14,16,21,25,27,28,28,29,29,30,30,33,35,37,38; 20:1,4,5,5,7,7,8,13,14,16; 21:1,1,13,14,17,20,20,21,30,33; 22:1,1,3,3,3,5,6,9,10,11,12,13,13; 23:3,8,9,10,11,13,16; 24:2,2,7,10,11,12,15,23,29,30,30,31,33,34,35,35,36,36,40,52,53,54,54,56,62,63,63,63,65,66,67,67; 25:5,6,6,8,17,17,20,26,30,30,33,34; 26:7,7,7,13,14,17,18,20,21,22,22,23,25,33,34; 27:1,1,1,9,10,10,14,18,18,20,23,23,24,24,25,25,25,25,27,27,31,31,32,33,34,35,36,36,36,36,41; 28:1,4,5,6,6,9,9,11,11,11,12,12,13,16,17,18,19; 29:2,5,6,6,7,9,10,12,12,13,13,23,28,30,31,33,34; 30:6,14,15,16,22,28,31,35,35,36,38,40,42; 31:5,8,8,12,15,15,15,18,18,20,21,21,23,33,33,33,35,36,42,46,49,54,55; 32:2,2,4,6,8,11,13,13,13,16,17,18,19,20,20,21,23,23,25,25,25,27,29,29,31,31; 33:1,2,3,3,4,5,8,17,18,19,19,20; 34:2,3,5,19,31; 35:7,7,7,10,13,14,14,29; 36:6,24; 37:2,3,3,5,6,8,9,9,9,10,13,14,14,16,18,21,21,23,27,29,30,33,35,35; 38:2,9,9,10,11,11,12,15,16,17,18,18,20,21,22,26,29,29,30; 39:2,2,3,4,4,5,5,6,6,6,8,8,8,8,10,11,12,13,14,15,15,18,19,21,22,23; 40:4,6,7,9,16,20,20,21,21,22,23; 41:1,5,8,10,12,13,14,14,14,16,25,28,42,43,43,46,48,49,52,55; 42:1,2,4,7,7,7,9,12,17,21,21,23,24,24,27,28,38; 43:7,7,14,16,18,23,23,27,27,27,29,29,29,30,31,31; 44:2,6,6,9,10,20,22,28,31; 45:1,1,2,4,8,14,15,21,22,22,23,24,24,26,26,27; 46:1,1,2,3,29; 47:2,14,17,17,22,29,30,31,31; 48:1,3,8,10,14,14,15,16,17,17,19,19,19,20,20; 49:9,10,11,11,15,15,19,20,27,27,28,29,33; 50:6,12,16,21,22,24,26; Ex 1:9,21; 2:2,6,10,11,11,12,13,13,15,15,18,19,20,24; 3:1,4,6,6,20; 4:2,3,6,7,7,14,14,14,14,16,16,20,21,23,27,28,30; 5:3,23; 6:1,1,13,29; 7:4,13,14,15,20,22,23; 8:12,15,19,20,27,29; 9:7,12,27,33,34,34,35; 10:8,20,27; 11:1,1,1,10; 12:23,23,25,27,48; 13:5,11,19; 14:4,6,7,8,25; 15:1,1,2,2,4,21,21,25,26; 16:7,8,8,9,23,29; 17:7,11,12,16; 18:4,4,5,10,11,14,24,25; 19:14,15,24; 20:11; 21:2,2,3,3,3,3,6,6,8,8,8,9,9,10,10,11; 22:16,17; 23:21,21,22; 24:4,5,6,7,14,18,18; 28:3,29,30,35,35,35,35,38; 29:21; 30:7,8,8,12; 31:17,18; 32:4,5,11,12,14,17,19,20,20,21,26,27,29; 33:8,20; 34:4,6,7,7,9,28,29,29,31,32,33,34,34,34,34,34,35; 35:31,34,35; 37:2,3,4,5,6,7,8,8; 40:13,18,19,20,21,24,28,29,30; Lev 1:1,16,17; 2:9; 4:3,3,4,4,6,7,8,9,12,17,18,18,19,20,21,21,22,23,23,24,26,26,26; 5:8; 6:11,20; 7:38; 8:7,7,7,8,9,11,12,13,14,15,15,15,17,18,20,21,22,24,25,26,26,27,30; 9:2,9,9,10,11,12,12,13,14,15,15,16,17,18,18,22; 10:3,16,20; 12:7; 13:3,5,5,8,11,13,15,36,36,41,41,42,51,52,54,54,56; 14:6,7,7,12,13,25,28,28,30,36,37,40,41,48,49,50,51,52,53,53; 15:4,13,13,13,14,15,16,16,24,24,30; 16:2,2,2,3,4,4,4,4,5,7,8,11,12,13,13,14,14,15,15,15,16,16,17,18,18,19,20,21,21,23,23,23,24,24,25,26,28,32; 19:22; 20:3,11,14,15,17,18,20,21; 21:3,4,11,11,12,13,14,15,21,21,22,23; 22:4,4,4,4,5,6,6,7,7,8; 23:11; Nu 1:1,19; 3:16,32,50,51; 4:16,19,32; 5:14,14,15,15,15,17,18,18,21,24,26,30; 6:17; 7:1,1,7,8,19,89; 8:3; 9:1; 10:30,36; 11:1,2,11,24,25,33; 12:1,2,5,6,7,8,9,11; 13:17; 14:8,16,16,18,18,24,43; 16:4,5,5,5,5,10,26,31,39,40,48; 19:5,7,7,8,10,18,19; 20:9,10,13,16,24,26; 21:1,23,23,23,29; 22:22,25,27,30,31,31,36,41; 23:3,3,6,7,12,14,14,17,18,19,19,19,19,20; 24:1,3,10,15,17,21,23; 25:7,8,11,13,13; 26:33; 27:3,3,4,9,10,11,21,21,22,23; 30:2,2,5,8,8,12,14,14,14,15,15,15; 31:15; 32:10,13,15,21,29; 33:38,39; 36:2; Dt 1:4,8,11,27,30,34,36,36,36,38,45; 2:7,15,22,30; 3:20,28; 4:10,13,13,21,23,31,31,36,36,37,37; 5:5,22,22; 6:10,15,17,23,23,25; 7:8,8,9,10,10,12,13,13,13,15,15,24; 8:3,10,15,15,16,18,18; 9:3,3,5,8,19,23,25,28,28,28; 10:4,4,15,18,21,21; 11:3,3,4,4,5,6,17,25; 12:10,20; 13:17,17; 14:23; 15:4,6,16,17,20; 16:1,6,11,16; 17:15,17,17,18,18,19,19,20; 18:2,6,7,8,8,18; 19:1,5,6,6,8,8; 20:3,5,6,7; 21:15,15,16,16,16,16,17,17,20,20; 22:16,17,19,19,23,24,29,29,29,29,29,30; 23:10,11,11,14; 24:1,1,3,5,5,5; 25:7,8,19; 26:5,9,18,19,19,19,19; 27:20; 28:8,9,11,21,45,48,48,54,55,55,55,60; 29:1,13,13,13,25,25,26,27; 30:3,5,5,9,20,20; 31:3,4,4,6,8,11,25; 32:4,4,6,7,8,8,10,10,10,13,13,19,20,36,37,39,43,43,46; 33:2,2,2,5,7,7,8,9,9,9,10,10,12,12,13,17,17,18,20,20,21,21,22,23,23,24,27,29; 34:6,7; Jos 1:13,15,17; 2:1; 3:10; 4:4,21,23,23,24; 5:4,6,7,13,14; 6:7,11,26,26; 7:15,17,24; 8:3,10,14,14,19,26,29,31,33; 9:9,10,27; 10:1,2,4,18,24,28,28,28,28,30,30,30,31,32,32,40,40; 11:1,9,11,12,15,17,20,23; 12:2,3,5; 13:8,12,14,14,32,33; 14:10,10,12,14; 15:15; 18:10; 19:50,50; 21:43,44; 22:4,7,18,20,22; 23:5,10,15,15,15,16,16; 24:1,7,7,9,10,17,18,19,19,19,20,20,25,26,27; Jdg 1:7,25,26,26; 2:10,14,15,18,21,23; 3:2,4,8,9,10,15,16,17,18,19,20,23,24,24,25,26,27,27,28,31; 4:3,18,19,20,21,21,22; 5:17,25,27,27,27,27,27,27,27; 6:1,8,12,19,19,22,27,27,30,30,31,34,35,38; 7:4,4,11,13,15,15,16,17; 8:2,5,8,9,12,14,16,17,18,20,20,24,26,27,30,30,31,35; 9:3,5,7,16,18,21,21,28,30,31,36,43,43,43,45,45,48,48,48,48,52,54,54; 10:1,2,2,3,4,5,7,7,16; 11:11,17,20,25,29,29,33,34,35,35,38,38,39,39; 12:5,6,6,9,9,9,14,14; 13:5,6,6,6,7,11,11,11,18,22,23,24,25; 14:2,2,6,6,6,6,7,7,8,8,8,9,9,9,9,9,9,14,16,17,19,19; 15:1,2,4,4,5,8,8,10,11,14,15,17,17,18,18,19; 16:1,1,3,3,4,9,11,12,13,13,14,16,17,17,18,18,20,20,25,30,30,30,30,31; 17:3,4,5,8,9; 18:4,4,20,24; 19:3,3,4,5,7,8,13,17,18,21,28,29,29; Ru 2:14,20,20,21; 3:2,3,4,4,4,7,8,9,10,13,13,14,15,15,15,17; 4:1,1,3,4,8,13,14,15,17; 1Sa 1:2,4,5,5,22,24,24,28,28; 2:6,7,7,8,8,8,9,10,15,23; 3:2,5,5,9,13,13,15,17,17,18,19,19,21; 4:3,13,15,16,18,18,18,18,18; 5:6,9; 6:5; 7:3,8,9,12,16,17,17,17; 8:1,6,11,11,12,13,14,15,16,17,21; 9:2,4,4,6,6,6,8,8,12,12,13,13,13,16,17,26; 10:2,10,10,13,14,16,16,21,21,22,23,23,25; 11:5,6,7; 12:5,9,11,24; 13:1,1,2,8,9,10,13; 14:1,3,27,27,33,34,35,39,45,45,45,47,47,47,48,52; 15:6,8,8,11,11,12,12,18,23,29,29,29,32,35,35; 16:2,4,5,11,11,11,12,12,16,18,18,23; 17:5,6,9,12,20,23,25,25,26,28,30,33,36,38,39,39,39,40,42,42,42,43,44,47,49,49,50,51,51,51,54,55; 18:1,3,4,8,8,10,10,11,13,14,14,15,15,16,20,21,26,29; 19:4,4,5,5,7,8,9,12,14,17,17,18,18,20,21,22,22,23,23,24,24,24; 20:1,2,3,3,7,7,7,12,13,17,17,25,26,26,29,29,30,31,32,32,34,34,35,36,36,38; 21:1,7,11,13,13,13,14; 22:2,4,7,7,8,10,12,13,13,17,18,19,21,22; 23:2,5,6,7,9,11,13,15,17,22,23,23,25,25; 24:1,3,4,6,6,9,10,15,15,16,17,19; 25:2,2,3,4,5,14,17,21,25,29,30,36,36,37,38,39,39; 26:3,4,5,10,10,10,14,18,19; 27:4,9,9,11,11,11,12,12; 28:5,6,8,8,9,11,14,14,14,15,17,20,21,23,23,23; 29:3,3,4,4,4,4,9; 30:8,12,12,13,15,16,20,21,23,26,31; 31:5; 2Sa 1:2,2,3,4,7,7,8,9,10,10,13,15,15,18; 2:1,5,9,10,10,19,19,20,23,23; 3:8,11,16,19,21,22,23,23,24,25,27,28,30; 4:1,4,4,5,7,10; 5:4,4,5,5,9,10,13,20,20,23,25; 6:2,7,10,10,12,13,15,18,18,19,21; 7:2,13,14,14,18; 8:1,2,3,4,6,6,10,11,11,12,13,14,14; 9:2,3,4,4,6,6,13,13; 10:5,9,10,17,18,18; 11:2,4,10,13,13,15,15,16,16,19,20,21,21,22,22; 12:1,1,3,3,4,6,6,11,15,16,17,17,18,18,19,19,19,20,20,20,20,22,23,23,24,25,31,31; 13:2,4,9,11,13,14,14,14,15,15,16,17,20,21,22,22,23,25,26,27,36,38,39; 14:2,7,11,12,13,14,15,20,22,22,24,24,26,26,26,29,29,30,30,31,33; 15:2,2,6,9,12,14,16,25,26,30,30; 16:1,3,3,5,5,6,7,10,13,14,21,22; 17:2,5,6,8,9,9,12,12,13,18,23,23,23; 18:9,9,9,10,14,18,18,23,24,24,25,25,26,26,27,28,28,30,33,33,33; 19:9,9,14,18,18,21,24,24,25,26,27,32,32,35; 20:1,3,3,3,5,6,8,12,12,17,17,17,22; 21:1,9,12,15,16,17,20,21; 22:2,3,7,8,10,11,11,12,15,15,17,17,18,20,20,20,21,31,34,34,35,42,48,51,51; 23:3,4,5,5,8,8,9,12,16,16,17,18,18,18,19,19,19,20,20,21,21,22,23,23; 24:1,10,10,17,20,22; 1Ki 1:1,5,6,9,10,13,17,19,19,23,24,25,25,26,30,33,35,37,42,51,51,52,52; 2:1,2,5,5,5,8,11,13,14,15,17,17,19,22,24,24,25,25,28,30,31,32,32,32,34,40,46,46; 3:1,1,3,6,15,15,15,21,25,28; 4:11,15,19,24,31,32,33,33; 5:1,1,3,5,7,7,10,12,14; 6:1,4,5,6,9,10,15,16,19,20,20,21,22,22,23,27,28,29,30,31,32,33,34,35,36,38; 7:2,6,7,7,7,8,8,14,15,16,18,18,21,21,23,27,36,37,38,39,39,40,40,51,51; 8:12,15,15,15,19,20,21,21,54,54,55,56,56,57,57,58,58,59,64,66; 9:1,2,11,12,13,13,16,16,17,19,19,24,25; 10:4,5,9,13,17,26,26; 11:3,5,6,8,10,19,21,26,27,28,30,31,32,41,41,43; 12:2,2,2,3,4,6,9,14,21,25,28,29,32,32,32,32,32,33,33,33; 13:2,2,4,4,4,10,10,11,12,13,13,14,14,18,18,21,22,24,26,28,30,31,32,33; 14:3,4,5,6,13,13,15,15,16,19,20,21,21,21,26,26,29; 15:2,3,7,10,12,13,14,15,15,18,19,19,20,21,23,23,25,26,27,29,29,29,30,31,33,34; 16:5,7,7,7,8,10,11,11,11,14,18,18,19,20,23,24,26,27,27,29,31,31,32,32,34,34; 17:5,5,6,10,10,10,11,17,19,19,20,21,22,23; 18:8,10,12,12,14,17,17,24,27,27,27,27,30,32,32,33,33,34,34,39,39,43,43,43,46; 19:1,3,3,4,4,4,4,5,6,6,8,8,8,9,10,13,14,19,19,20,21,21,21; 20:1,2,7,9,12,12,14,15,18,25,31,32,32,34,35,38,39,42; 21:4,6,6,10,15,15,16,18,18,20,21,26,27,27,29; 22:4,8,8,11,15,15,18,22,24,24,28,33,35,39,39,39,42,42,43,43,45,46,51,52,52,53; 2Ki 1:2,5,6,8,9,13,16,17,18; 2:4,5,6,12,14,14,14,14,17,17,18,20,21,23,24,25; 3:1,2,2,3,3,3,4,7,7,8,8,11,16,18,26,27; 4:1,6,7,8,8,10,10,11,12,12,15,18,19,20,23,25,30,33,34,34,36,36,38,39,39,41,44; 5:1,1,1,3,6,7,7,8,8,11,12,13,14,15,16,18,20,21,21,23,23,24,24,25; 6:2,4,5,6,7,8,10,11,13,13,14,17,17,18,19,21,22,23,23,28,30,30,30,31,32,33; 7:14,17,17,20; 8:1,6,8,9,10,11,12,14,15,15,17,17,17,18,18,18,19,21,23,26,26,27,27,29; 9:5,5,5,5,10,11,12,16,17,18,19,19,20,20,20,22,24,27,27,32,34,36; 10:1,8,9,10,13,14,14,15,15,15,16,17,17,21,22,25,29,29,31,31,34; 11:2,3,4,4,5,8,10,12,17,19,21; 12:1,9,17,18,18,19,21; 13:1,2,2,2,3,4,6,8,10,11,11,11,12,14,14,15,16,16,17,17,17,18,18,23,25,25; 14:2,2,2,3,3,5,6,7,11,14,14,15,19,20,22,23,24,24,25,27,27,28,28; 15:2,2,2,3,5,5,6,8,9,9,9,10,13,14,15,16,17,18,18,18,21,23,24,24,25,26,27,28,28,28,29,30,31,33,33,33,34,36; 16:2,2,2,3,4,9,10,12,13,14,17,18,19; 17:1,2,4,4,4,6,15,15,20,20,21,23,25,26,26,34,35,37,39; 18:2,2,2,3,4,4,6,6,7,7,7,8,16,22,29,30,32,32; 19:1,2,4,7,8,9,10,14,32,32,33,33,33,36,37; 20:7,9,12,19,20,20; 21:1,1,2,3,3,3,4,5,6,6,7,7,11,16,16,17,17,19,19,20,21,22,25,26; 22:1,1,2,3,8,11,12; 23:2,2,4,5,6,6,7,8,10,11,12,12,15,15,16,16,18,19,20,24,25,28,31,31,32,33,33,34,34,35,35,36,36,37; 24:1,3,4,5,8,8,9,12,14,15,17,18,18,19,20; 25:1,6,6,9,9,19,19,22,24,27,27,28,30; 1Ch 2:4,21,21,34; 3:4; 5:1,1,1,20,26; 6:10; 7:23,23; 8:8,9,11; 10:5,13,13; 11:3,6,8,11,11,13,18,18,19,20,20,20,21,21,22,22,23,23,24,25,25; 12:1,18,19,19,19,22; 13:2,10,10,10,13,13,14; 14:11,11; 15:1,3,4,12,22; 16:2,3,4,8,12,12,14,15,15,16,16,17,21,21,25,33,34,38,40; 17:1,12,13,16; 18:1,3,4,6,6,10,11,11,13,13; 19:5,10,11,17,17,18; 20:1,2,6,7; 21:3,7,20,21,26,27,28,30; 22:2,3,4,6,10,10,11,12,18,18,18; 23:1,2,13,22; 26:10; 27:3,5; 28:4,4,4,5,6,7,9,9,12,13,14,18,19,20; 29:23,27,28; 2Ch 1:4,4,13,14,14; 2:2,11,12,14,14,14,15,18; 3:2,4,5,6,6,7,7,8,8,9,10,14,15,16,16,17,17; 4:1,2,6,7,8,8,9,10,11; 5:1,1,13; 6:1,4,4,4,9,10,11,13,13,14; 7:3,6,7,7,10,11,22; 8:4,4,5,6,6,11,11,12,14,14; 9:3,4,8,12,16,25,26,31; 10:2,2,2,3,4,6,9,14; 11:1,11,12,15,15,20,21,23,23; 12:1,1,4,5,9,9,12,13,13,13,14,14; 13:2,7,12,13,20,21,22,22; 14:3,4,5,6,7,7; 15:2,2,2,4,8,8,8,8,9,15,17,18,18; 16:3,3,5,6,8,10,10,12,14; 17:2,3,3,5,6,7,12,13,19; 18:1,2,7,7,10,14,14,17,21,23,23,27,32,34; 19:4,5,6,9; 20:3,14,15,31,31,31,32,32,36; 21:3,3,4,5,5,6,6,6,7,9,11,19,20,20,20; 22:2,2,3,4,5,5,6,6,7,8,8,9,9,9,9,12; 23:1,7,9,10,16,19,20; 24:1,1,3,5,15,16,16,17,20,20,22,25; 25:1,1,2,3,4,5,6,11,14,14,15,16,17,20,21,24,27,28; 26:2,3,3,4,5,5,6,6,8,9,10,10,10,10,15,15,15,16,19,20,20,21,21,23; 27:1,1,2,2,4,6,7,8,8,8; 28:1,1,1,2,3,4,5,9,9,9,19,20,23,23,24,25,27; 29:1,1,2,3,4,8,19,25; 30:6,7,8,9; 31:4,21,21,21; 32:1,2,3,5,5,5,6,9,11,21,21,22,23,24,25,27,28,28,29,30,30,33; 33:1,1,2,3,3,3,4,5,6,6,7,7,12,13,13,14,14,14,15,15,15,16,19,19,21,21,22,23; 34:1,1,2,3,3,3,4,4,5,5,7,7,8,15,19,20,27,30,30,32,33,33; 35:2,3,21,22,23,24,24; 36:2,2,5,5,5,8,9,9,9,10,11,11,12,13,13,14,15,17,18,20,23; Ezr 1:2; 3:11; 5:12,14,14,15; 6:22; 7:6,6,9,9; 8:23,31; 9:9,9,9; 10:6,6,6; Ne 2:8; 3:14,15,15; 4:1,1,2,18,23; 6:10,12,13,18; 7:2; 8:3,3,5,5; 13:4,5,26,26; Est 1:3,4,8,10,13,15,22; 2:1,1,4,7,9,9,11,14,17,18,20; 3:4,4,4,5,6; 4:1,2,4,8,8,13; 5:2,2,9,9,9,11,14; 6:1,4,7,11; 7:5,5,8,9,10; 8:1,2,3,5,5,7,15; 9:4,20,22,25,25; 10:3; Job 1:1,2,3,3,5,8,10,11,11,12,16,17,18,20; 2:3,3,4,5,6,8,10,10; 3:2; 4:18; 5:9,10,10,11,12,13,15,15,18,18,18,19,20; 7:10; 8:4,6,21; 9:5,6,7,7,8,9,10,11,11,12,16,16,17,18,19,22,23,24,24,32; 11:5,10,11,11,11; 12:4,14,14,15,15,17,18,19,20,21,22,23,23,24,24,25; 13:9,10,15; 14:5,6,10,12; 15:22,22,23,23,25,28,29,30,31,32,33; 16:12,12,12,13,14,14,21; 18:8,12,14,17,18,19,19; 19:8,8,9,10,10,11,13,16,25; 20:7,7,8,12,13,15,15,16,17,18,18,18,19,19,19,20,20,23,24,25; 21:22; 22:3,4,13,14,14,18,27,29,30; 23:5,5,6,6,8,9,9,10,10,13,13,13,14,14; 24:15,15,23; 25:2; 26:7,7,8,9,10,12,12; 27:16,17,18,19,19,21,22; 28:23,24,25,26,27,27,28; 30:18,19,24; 31:4,6,15; 32:1,3,4,5; 33:10,11,11,13,16,24,26; 34:8,8,9,11,11,14,18,21,24,25,25,26,28,29,29,29,37,37; 35:7,11,12,14,15,16; 36:5,6,7,7,9,10,13,15,15,16,27,29,29,30,31,32; 37:3,4,4,5,6,7,7,11,11,12,13,20,22,23,24; 38:1; 42:7,10,12,13,14,16; Ps 2:5,7,12; 3:T,4; 7:T,12,12,12,13,13; 9:7,8,11,12,12; 10:2,3,3,5,6,6,8,8,9,9,9,11,11,13,13; 11:4,5,6,7; 13:6; 18:T,T,6,7,9,10,10,11,14,14,16,16,17,19,19,19,20,30,33,33,34,41,47,50,50; 20:2,3,4,6; 21:4,7; 22:8,8,24,24,28,31; 23:2,2,3,3; 24:2,10,10; 25:8,9,12,14,15; 27:5,5; 28:5,6,7; 29:6; 31:21,23; 33:4,4,7,7,9,9,10,12,14,15,20; 34:T,T,4,4,6,7,17,20; 37:4,5,6,13,22,24,24,34,36,36,39,40; 40:1,2,2,3; 41:2,5,6,6,8,8; 44:21; 45:11; 46:6,8,9,9,9,10; 47:3,4,4,9; 48:3,14; 49:15; 50:4,4,6; 52:5,5; 55:17,18,19,20,22,22; 57:T,3; 60:T,12; 61:7; 62:2,2,6,6,7; 63:T; 64:8,9; 66:6,7,9,16; 68:6; 72:2,4,4,5,6,8,12,13,14,15; 74:12; 75:7,7,8; 76:3,12,12; 77:7,9; 78:4,5,5,11,11,12,13,13,14,15,16,20,20,20,21,23,24,24,25,26,27,28,29,31,33,38,38,38,39,42,43,44,45,46,47,48,49,50,50,51,52,52,53,54,55,55,59,59,60,60,61,62,62,66,66,67,67,68,68,69,69,70,71,72; 81:5; 82:1; 84:11; 85:8; 87:1; 89:7,26,41; 91:2,3,4,11,14,14,15; 92:15; 93:1; 94:9,9,10,10,11,14,23; 95:5,7; 96:4,10,13,13,13; 97:10; 98:1,3,9,9; 99:1,2,3,4,5,6,7,7; 100:3; 102:17,17,19,23,23; 103:7,9,9,10,12,14,14; 104:2,3,4,5,10,13,14,16,19,32; 105:1,5,5,7,8,8,9,9,10,14,14,16,17,19,21,21,22,24,25,26,26,28,29,31,32,33,34,36,37,39,40,40,41,42,43,44; 106:1,8,9,9,10,10,13,15,23,23,26,26,41,43,44,44,45,45,46; 107:1,2,3,6,7,9,12,13,14,16,19,20,20,25,28,29,30,33,35,36,38,38,40,41; 108:13; 109:7,11,15,16,17,17,18,31; 110:5,6,7,7; 111:4,5,5,6,9,9; 113:7,8,9; 115:3,9,10,11,12,12,13,16; 116:1,1,2,6; 118:1,5,7,14,18,26,27,29; 120:1,3,4; 121:3,3,4,7; 123:2; 127:2,2; 129:4; 130:8; 132:2,2,11,13; 134:3; 135:7,7,8,9,10,12; 136:1,23,25; 138:6,6; 142:T; 143:3,3; 144:2; 145:9,9,13,13,17,19,19,20; 146:6,6,7,9; 147:2,3,4,8,8,9,13,14,15,16,17,18,18,19,20; 148:6,6,14; 149:4; Pr 2:7,7,8; 3:6,12,12,19,33,34; 4:4,4; 5:21; 6:14,15,29,30,30,31,31,34,34,35,35; 7:8,19,20,22; 8:26,27,27,28,29,29; 10:3,5,5; 11:20; 12:2,22; 15:9,25,29; 16:3,7; 18:22; 19:17,24; 20:8,22,26; 21:1,26; 22:12; 23:7,7,11; 24:12,12,12; 25:13,21; 26:5,15; 30:5,6; 31:23,28; Ecc 2:26; 3:11,11; 4:8,8,14; 5:4; 6:3,3,3,6; 7:13; 8:3,3; 9:15; 12:9,9,10; SS 2:8,9,16; 3:9,10; 5:6,6,16; 6:3; 8:11; Isa 2:3,4,19,21; 3:7,13; 4:4; 5:2,2,2,7,7,25,26,26; 6:6,7,9,11; 7:15,15,17; 8:13,13,14,14,14; 9:1,1,6,7,17; 10:7,7,8,12,13,26,26,26,34; 11:3,3,3,3,4,4,4,4,12,12,15,15; 12:2,4,5; 14:1; 17:13; 18:5; 19:20,20,22,22; 20:2,2; 21:6,7,9; 22:18,21,22,22,23; 23:11,12; 24:1; 25:7,8,8,9,12,12; 26:5,5,5; 27:1,7,8,9; 28:2,6,9,9,12,21,21,24,24,25,25,25; 29:10,10; 30:18,19,19,19,23,26,28,28,31,32; 31:2,2,2,5,5; 33:5,5,6,22; 34:2,2,17; 35:4,4; 36:7,14,15,18; 37:1,2,4,7,8,9,9,10,14,33,33,34,34,34,37,38; 38:7,12,13,15,15,21; 39:1,8; 40:10,11,11,11,15,22,22,23,24,26,28,29; 41:2,2,3,4,25,25,25,26; 42:1,2,3,3,3,4,4,13,13,25; 43:1,1,10,13,16,25; 44:2,12,12,12,12,13,13,14,14,15,15,15,15,16,16,16,16,17,17,17,20,23,28,28; 45:13,18,18,18,18,18,18; 46:4,4; 48:12,15,21,21,21; 49:1,2,2,2,3,5,6,10; 50:4,8; 51:2,3,12; 52:9,13,15; 53:2,2,3,3,4,5,5,7,7,7,7,8,8,8,9,9,10,11,11,11,12,12,12; 54:5; 55:5,6,6,7,7; 56:8; 57:15; 58:9,11; 59:2,16,16,17,17,18,18,19; 60:9; 61:1,10; 62:7; 63:7,7,8,8,9,9,9,10,10,11,11; 65:15; 66:15; Jer 2:14,17,26,35; 3:1; 4:7,13; 5:12; 10:10,10,12,13,13,13,14,16,16; 11:16,18; 12:4; 13:16,16; 14:10; 16:15; 18:4,6,18; 20:2,10,13,16,17; 21:2,7,7,10; 22:10,11,12,12,14,14,15,16,19,28; 23:6,8,20; 25:17,30,30,31,38; 26:11,13,16,18,19,19,20,24; 27:20; 28:6,11; 29:3,21,28,32,32,32; 30:7,21,21,24; 31:10,35; 32:3,5,5; 33:2,15,24; 34:1,2,3; 35:18; 36:8,12,13,18,25,30; 37:1,2,4,13,14,16,17; 38:1,4,4,5,9,10,11,27; 39:5,7,10,12,14; 40:1,2,3,3,3,9,15; 41:6,6,6,8,9,9,16; 42:8,9,12,20,21; 43:10,11,12,12,12,13; 46:17; 47:7; 49:10,20,30; 50:34,34,45; 51:6,15,15,16,16,16,17,19,19,34,34,34,44,55,56,59,61; 52:1,1,2,3,9,9,9,10,11,11,13,13,25,25,31,32,34; La 1:13,13,13,14,15; 2:1,1,2,2,3,3,3,4,4,4,5,5,5,6,6,6,7,8,8,9,17,17,17,17,17,17; 3:2,3,4,5,6,7,7,8,9,9,11,12,13,15,16,16,27,32,32,33; 4:11,11,16,22,22; Eze 1:27,27; 2:1,2,3,10; 3:1,2,3,4,10,22,24; 4:15,16; 8:2,3,3,5,6,7,8,9,12,13,14,15,16,17; 9:5,7,9; 10:2,5,7; 11:5; 12:12,12,13,13,13,27,27; 16:16; 17:4,4,5,5,13,13,15,15,15,16,16,16,18,18,18,20,20; 18:6,6,7,7,7,8,8,9,9,10,11,11,12,12,12,12,12,12,13,13,13,13,14,14,15,15,16,16,17,17,17,17,18,19;

HER (1667)

HERSELF (45)

HIM (4822)

11:13,19,20,22; 12:1,3,8,11,12,16; 13:3,7,10,11,19, 20; 14:1,5,6,6,7,10; 15:2,2,2,2,4,9,9; 16:7,9,10,14, 14; 17:1,3,11; 18:2,2,2,7,12,13,14,15,20,21,25,26, 31,31,31,32; 19:2; 20:4,21,30,36; 21:1,7,9,17; 22:3, 6,9,9,11,11,11; 23:11,11,11,11,20; 24:3,6,19,21,21, 22,25,25,26,27,27; 25:7,10,15,16,23,27,27,27; 26:1, 5,5,7,17,20,20,20,23; 27:2,5,5,9; 28:5,5,5,20,20,21, 23,27; 29:6,6,11,11,11,29; 30:9; 31:15; 32:3,6,7,7,8, 15,17,21,24,24,25,25,29,31,31,31,33,33; 33:11,11, 13,13,18,20,24,24; 34:9,16,22; 35:20,21,22,22,22, 24,24,24,24; 36:1,3,4,6,6,6,8,8,10,10,13,20,23; Ezr 1:2; 4:2,11; 5:7,15; 7:6,6,9; 8:3,4,5,6,7,8,9,10, 11,12,21,22,22,33; 10:1; Ne 1:5,11; 2:1,5,6,7; 3:4,4, 10,16,17,17,18,19,20,21,22,24,25,29,30,31; 6:8,12, 12,18,19; 8:4,5; 9:7,7,8; 13:5,26,26,28; Est 1:10,11, 17,19; 2:9; 3:1,1,2,2,4,5; 4:4,5,7,7,8,8,8,10; 5:4,11, 11,14; 6:1,3,4,5,6,9,9,11,11,13,13,13,14; 7:9; 8:2,3, 4,7; Job 1:8,10; 2:1,3,3,3,9,11,11,11,12,12,13,13; 5:8; 7:10; 8:4; 9:3,3,4,11,11,12,12,14,14,15,16,19, 32,35; 11:10,13,13; 12:16; 13:7,8,9,11,15,16; 14:6, 6; 15:20,21,24,24,26,30,31; 18:6,7,8,9,9,10,11,12, 12,17; 19:16,27,28,28; 20:7,9,9,9,11,14,16,21,22, 22,23,23,24,25,26,27; 21:15,15,19; 22:2,14,21,27; 23:3,4,7,8,9,9,13,15,15; 24:1; 26:14; 27:15,20,20, 21,21,22,23; 30:13; 31:29,37,37; 32:3,13,14; 33:13, 26; 34:13,13,23,27,28,29,29; 35:3,6,6,7,14,14,14; 36:11,22,23,23,30; 37:16,18,19,24; 40:2,2,2; 42:10, 11,11,11,11,11; Ps 2:12; 3:2; 4:3; 7:5; 10:4,5; 13:4; 16:8; 18:T,6,11,23,30; 20:6; 21:2,3,4,5,6,6; 22:8,8, 8,8,23,23,23,24,26,27,29,30; 24:6; 25:14; 27:4; 28:7,7; 31:23; 32:10; 33:1,2,3,8,18,21; 34:T,5,6,6,7, 8,9,19,22; 35:25; 37:5,7,23,24,36,40; 40:3; 41:8; 42:5,11; 43:5; 45:11; 47:7; 50:3,3,18; 51:T; 52:T; 56:T; 59:T; 61:7; 62:1,5,8,8; 63:11; 64:10,10; 66:6, 7,17; 67:7; 68:1,4,4,33; 69:30,34; 71:11,11,11,11; 72:9,10,10,11,11,15,15,15,17,17; 78:8,17,34,34,36, 36,37,40,40,58,70,71; 81:15; 85:9,13; 89:7,20,21, 21,22,22,23,24,27,28,28,33,41,43,45; 91:14,14,15, 15,15,15,16,16; 92:15; 95:2,2,4; 96:6,9; 97:2,3,7; 98:1; 100:2,4; 103:11,13,17; 104:34; 105:2,2,19,20, 20,21; 106:23,31; 107:32,32; 109:7,7,12,17,17,19, 19,30; 111:5,10; 115:3,11; 116:2; 117:1; 119:2; 127:3; 128:1; 130:7; 135:1,6,20,21; 136:4,10,13,16, 17; 141:5; 142:2,2; 145:18,18,19,20; 147:1,11; 148:1,2,2,3,3,4; 149:3; 150:1,2,2,3,3,4,4,5,5; Pr 3:6; 6:15,16,31; 7:10,13,21,21,23; 11:1; 14:2, 15:8; 17:25; 20:2,23; 21:1,25; 23:24; 25:7,7,13,21, 21; 26:4; 30:5; 31:1,12; Ecc 2:25,26; 3:14; 8:4,12; 12:6; SS 1:2; 2:4; 3:1,1,2,2,4,4,4,11; 5:4,6,6,6,8,8; 6:1; Isa 1:4; 5:19; 6:2; 7:4,14; 8:3,17; 9:13; 10:6,6, 20; 11:2,10; 14:25,27; 19:1; 20:2; 21:6,7; 22:21,21, 21,23,24; 25:9,9; 28:26,26; 30:18; 36:3,6,21,22; 37:3,4,7,7,9,22,38,38; 38:1; 40:10,10,14,14,14,14, 17,17,18; 41:2,2,2; 42:1; 44:7,7,20; 45:1,1,24,24, 25; 48:5,15; 49:5,7; 50:8; 51:2,2,2; 52:14,15; 53:2, 2,2,3,4,4,5,6,10,10,12; 55:4,6; 56:6; 59:16,16; 62:7, 11,11; 64:4; Jer 1:2; 2:15; 3:1; 4:2,2; 8:14; 10:25; 11:19; 17:7; 18:3,4,18; 19:14; 20:3,3,10,10,10,10, 15; 21:1; 22:10,12,13,15,18,18; 26:8,8,19,21,23,23; 27:6,7,7,11,12; 28:14,14; 29:31; 30:10,21; 31:20, 20,20,20; 32:3,4,4,5,9; 33:1; 34:2; 36:4,8,15,20,21, 22,31; 37:13,14,14,15,17,17,17; 38:6,8,9,11,13,13, 14,27,27,27; 39:5,5,5,7,7,9,12,12,12,12,14,14,15; 40:1,2,3,5,5,5,6,7,14; 41:2,7,11,12,13,13,16; 42:2, 8,11; 43:1; 44:20,23,30,30; 46:27; 49:8; 50:43; 51:3,44,44; 52:8,8,9,11,11,11,31,32,32,32; La 2:19; 3:24,25,25,28,28,29,30,30,30; Eze 1:3,27,28; 2:2; 9:1,4,5; 12:12,13,13,14; 13:6; 14:9,9,10; 16:16; 17:6,7,7,12,13,13,15,16,17,19,20,20,20; 19:4,4,5,8, 8,9,9,9; 21:23,27; 24:27; 28:12; 29:2,3,20; 30:24; 31:11; 32:2,32; 33:2; 37:16,16,19; 38:2,22,22,22; 40:46; 46:12; Da 2:2,14,16,22,24,24,46,46,48,48, 48; 3:16,28; 4:8,8,15,15,16,16,19,23,23,23,34,35; 5:11,11,13,17,19,19; 6:3,4,12,14,15,16,18,23; 7:10, 10,10,14,16,27; 8:13; 9:3,4,9,14,27; 10:1,9,9; 11:1, 16,17,17,18,22,23,25,26,30,32,39,40,40,44,45; 12:7,7; Hos 1:2,3,4,9; 4:17; 5:6; 6:3; 7:6,10,10; 8:3; 9:4,8,17; 11:1; 12:2,4,4,4,13,14,14; 13:11,13; 14:2, 8,8; Am 2:3; 5:19; Ob 18,18; Jnh 1:6,8,11,15,16; Mic 1:4; 6:6; 7:9; Na 1:5,6,7; Hab 2:5,6,6,9,12,15, 19,20; 3:5,13; Zep 1:6; 2:11; 3:9; Hag 1:12; Zec 1:8; 2:3,4; 3:1,4,5; 4:12; 6:12; 8:22; 10:4,4,4; 12:10,10; 14:5; Mal 2:5,5,12,15,17; 3:17; 4:4; Mt 1:20,21,23, 24,25; 2:2,3,8,8,11,11,13; 3:3,5,6,14,16,17; 4:3,5,5, 7,8,8,10,10,11,11,20,22,24,24,25; 5:1; 6:8; 7:9,10, 11; 8:1,2,4,5,7,7,10,15,16,18,19,21,22,23,25,27,28, 34,34; 9:2,9,9,10,14,18,19,20,24,27,28,31; 10:1,4; 11:3,27; 12:2,10,15,16,18,22,22,35,35,38,46,47,48; 13:2,10,27,28,36,57; 14:2,3,3,4,13,15,22,26,31,33, 35,36; 15:10,12,22,23,23,25,30,32; 16:1,1,22,22; 17:1,5,5,10,12,12,14,16,16,23,26; 18:2,24,24,26, 27,27,28,28,28,29,34; 19:2,3,3,10,13,27; 20:18,19, 20,29,34; 21:9,14,16,23,25,32,32,38,39,39,39,41, 46; 22:13,13,15,16,19,22,23,24,35,43,45,46; 24:1,3, 44,46,47,50,51,51; 25:6,10,28,31,32,37; 26:4,7,15, 15,16,18,22,24,24,25,37,47,48,49,50,52,56,57,58, 59,63,67,67,69,71; 27:2,2,2,3,9,11,13,18,19,19,22, 23,26,27,28,28,29,29,30,30,31,31,31,31,32,35,36, 37,38,39,41,42,42,43,43,44,44,49,49,54,58; 28:4,7, 9,9,13,14,17,17; Mk 1:3,5,5,10,12,13,18,20,25,26, 27,28,36,37,40,40,42,43,45; 2:3,4,13,14,14,15,15, 16,19,24; 3:2,2,8,9,9,10,11,11,12,13,13,14,19,21, 23,27,31,32,32,34; 4:1,10,10,36,36,38,38,41; 5:2,3, 4,6,8,9,18,19,20,21,23,24,24,27,30,33,36,37,40,40; 6:2,2,3,7,14,17,19,20,20,20,30,35,37,45,49,50,56; 7:14,17,25,32,32,33,34; 8:1,11,11,22,23,23,26,30, 32,32,34; 9:2,7,11,13,13,15,17,18,18,20,22,22,25, 25,26,27,27,28,31,32,38,39; 10:1,2,13,17,17,21,21, 32,33,33,34,34,34,34,35,48,48,49,51; 11:14,18,18, 27,31; 12:3,3,3,4,6,7,8,8,8,12,12,13,14,17,18,26, 28,32,33,34,34,37,37,43; 13:1,3,36; 14:1,11,11,12, 13,19,21,21,33,35,40,43,44,44,45,46,50,51,54,55, 56,57,58,61,64,65,65,65,65,65,67,69,72; 15:1,1,3,4, 10,13,14,15,17,17,18,19,19,19,20,20,20,20,21,23, 24,25,26,27,29,31,32,32,36,36,41,41,44; 16:6,7,10, 11,14; Lk 1:11,12,13,13,19,31,32,50,59,66,74,75, 76; 2:5,7,7,17,21,22,22,25,26,27,28,33,40,44,45,45, 46,47,48,48; 3:4,7,14,22; 4:3,5,5,6,8,9,9,13,14,15, 17,20,22,29,29,29,35,35,37,42,42; 5:1,3,11,12,13, 14,15,15,18,18,19,27,28,33; 6:7,13,18,19,19; 7:3,3, 4,6,9,9,11,14,15,18,36,38,39,39,40,41,42,42; 8:1,9, 19,19,20,24,25,29,30,30,38,38,39,40,40,41,42,44, 47,51,53; 9:9,10,11,12,18,28,32,33,35,37,39,39,39, 39,42,42,45,47,47,49,50,51,52,53,57,60; 10:1,16, 22,30,30,30,32,32,33,33,34,34,34,35,37,37,38,40; 11:1,5,6,11,12,13,16,22,37,37,39,45,53,53,54; 12:5, 5,13,20,36,40,44,46,46,46; 13:15,23,31; 14:2,4,4, 15,31; 15:15,16,18,20,20,20,20,21,22,26,27,28,30; 16:2,2,6,7,22,24,28,31; 17:12,16,19; 18:3,7,15,16, 18,22,24,28,32,32,32,33,33,37,39,39,40,40,42; 19:4,5,6,9,14,14,24,47; 20:1,5,10,10,10,12,12,13, 14,14,15,15,19,20,20,21,26,38,40,44; 21:38; 22:5, 10,21,22,39,43,43,47,48,51,52,54,54,54,56,56,56, 57,58,59,61,63,64,65; 23:1,2,7,8,8,8,9,9,10,11,11, 11,14,14,15,16,16,21,21,22,22,22,26,26,26,27,27, 32,33,35,35,36,36,38,39,40,43,49,49; 24:16,18,20, 20,29,31,42,52; Jn 1:3,3,4,7,10,10,11,12,15,18,19, 21,25,29,31,32,33,37,39,41,42,42,43,45,47; 2:3,11, 18; 3:2,15,16,17,18,26,26,28,29; 4:9,10,15,27,30, 31,33,34,39,40,40,45,47,47,48,51,52,52,53; 5:6,6,8, 12,14,14,15,16,18,20,20,23,24,27,30,43; 6:2,5,6,7, 15,21,25,25,27,28,30,38,39,40,41,45,64,66,68,71; 7:1,3,5,12,13,18,18,26,28,29,29,30,30,31,32,32,35, 39,44,44,45,48,51; 8:2,6,7,13,19,20,26,29,30,31,33, 44,48,55,55,55,57,59; 9:2,3,4,7,8,9,12,15,17,21,23, 26,28,34,35,35,36,37,38,40,40; 10:3,4,5,20,24,31, 39,41; 11:11,15,16,20,29,30,32,34,36,44,45,48,48, 57; 12:2,4,9,11,11,13,16,16,17,17,18,19,29,37,41, 42; 13:1,5,6,11,16,23,24,25,27,27,28,29,31,32,32, 36; 14:5,7,7,17,17,17,17; 16:5,7,19; 17:2,2; 18:2,4, 12,13,22,24,25,26,26,30,31,31,33,38,40; 19:1,2,3,3, 4,4,6,6,6,6,9,15,15,15,16,18,18; 20:2,6,13,15,15, 15,16,25,28,29; 21:7,7,12,17,17,19,21,21,22,23; Ac 1:6,6,9,11; 2:22,23,23,24,24,24,25,30; 3:4,7,7,9, 10,10,13,13,13,15,16,16,21,23,26; 4:19; 5:6,6,30, 31,32,36,37; 6:10,12,14; 7:4,5,5,5,6,8,9,9,10,10,10, 21,21,24,25,33,35,35,38,39,39,40,47,52,54,57,58,58, 59; 8:1,2,10,11,31,35,38,39; 9:2,3,4,8,10,11,12,16, 21,23,24,25,25,26,27,27,27,29,30,30,34,35,38,38, 39,39; 10:3,4,7,13,15,19,22,25,26,27,35,38,39,39, 40,40,41,43,43; 11:2,26,26; 12:4,4,4,4,5,6,7,8,8,9, 10,12,16,17,19,19,20,23; 13:11,11,22,22,27,28,29, 29,29,30,31,34,39,45; 14:9,19,20; 15:38; 16:2,3,3, 9,32; 17:15,15,18,19,19,19,27,27,27,28,31; 18:12, 17,20,26,26,26,27,27; 19:4,9,12,30,31,31,33; 20:3, 10,14,37,37,38; 21:11,27,29,30,31,33,33,36; 22:2,9, 13,20,22,24,25,25,29,30,30; 23:2,3,9,10,10,15,15, 17,18,19,20,21,21,27,27,27,28,28,29,30,30,31,32,33; 24:6,8,8,10,23,24,26,26,26; 25:2,3,5,6,7,7,15,18, 19,21,21,22,24,25,26,26,27; 26:26,30; 27:3; 28:4,6, 6,8,8,8,16,30; Ro 1:5,21,21; 4:3,9,18,22,23,23,24; 5:9,10; 6:4,5,5,6,8,9,13; 7:2,4; 8:11,15,28,32,32,37; 9:12,33; 10:9,11,12; 11:4,36,36,36,36; 12:20,20; 15:11,12,13,21; 16:25; 1Co 1:5,21,29,30; 2:2,9,16; 6:17; 7:12,13; 11:14; 15:15,23,27,28,28; 16:11,11, 11,12; 2Co 1:10,19,20; 2:6,7,8,14; 5:9,15,21,21; 7:7,14,15; 8:18; 11:2; 12:18; 13:4,4; Gal 1:1,16,18; 2:11,13; 3:6; Eph 1:4,7,11,11,13,17,20,22,23; 2:6, 18,21,22; 3:12,12,20,21; 4:15,16,21; 6:9,22; Php 1:29,29; 2:9,9,20,23,27,27,28,28,29,29; 3:9,10, 21; 4:13; Col 1:10,16,16,16,17,19,20; 2:6,7,11,12, 12,12; 3:4,17; 4:8,10,10,13; 1Th 4:14; 5:10; 2Th 1:12; 2:1,6; 1Ti 1:16; 3:4; 5:1; 6:16; 2Ti 1:12; 2:11,11,12,12; 4:1,14,15,18; Titus 1:16; Phm 12, 13,15,17; Heb 1:6; 2:3,6,13,14; 3:2; 4:13; 5:5,7,9; 6:6,10,13; 7:1,2,4,6,8,21,25; 9:28; 10:30; 11:5,6,6, 9,11,17,18,23,27; 12:2,3,25,25,25; 13:13,21,23; Jas 1:12; 2:5,7,23; 1Pe 1:8,8,8,8,21,21,21; 2:4,4,6, 9,14,23,23; 3:6,22; 4:5,11; 5:7,9,11; 2Pe 1:3,17,17, 18; 3:14,15,18; 1Jn 1:5,5,6,10; 2:3,4,5,6,8,13,14, 27,27,28,28,29; 3:1,2,2,3,5,6,6,6,12,15,22,22,24; 4:9,13; 5:10,15,20,20; 3Jn 12; Jude 9,15,24; Rev 1:1,4,5,6,7,7,7,17; 2:1,8,12; 3:1,7; 4:9,10,10; 5:1,7,13; 6:4,8,16; 7:15; 10:6,9; 12:9,11; 14:1,7,7, 15,18; 16:9; 17:14; 19:5,7,10,12,14; 20:1,3,3,3,6, 11; 22:3

HIMSELF (346)

Ge 8:9; 13:11; 17:17; 22:6,8; 27:41,42; 30:36,40; 32:21; 33:3,17; 35:7; 39:6,8; 43:31,32; 44:18; 45:1, 1; 50:1; Ex 11:3; 21:8; Lev 7:8; 9:8; 15:13; 16:4, 6,11,17,24,24,24,26,28; 21:1,3,4,4,11; 22:6; 26:46; Nu 5:18; 16:9,10; 19:7; 30:2; 31:53; 32:42; Dt 3:22; 4:34; 17:16,18,20; 23:11; 31:3,8; 33:21; Jos 11:20; 22:23; 23:5; 24:17; Jdg 3:19,24; 6:31; 13:21; 16:29; 1Sa 2:14; 3:21; 10:22; 18:1,3,11,17; 19:22; 20:3, 17; 23:7; 24:3,8; 25:31; 26:10; 27:1,12; 28:8,14; 2Sa 3:31; 6:20; 7:11,23,23; 13:2; 14:13; 15:1; 16:14; 17:23; 18:18,18; 1Ki 1:5,52; 12:26; 14:14; 17:21; 18:2; 19:4,19; 20:38; 21:25,29,29; 22:30; 2Ki 1:2; 4:34; 5:14,20; 12:18; 18:25; 24:11; 1Ch 15:1; 17:21; 2Ch 1:1; 2:1,12; 12:12,13; 13:9; 16:14; 17:1, 16; 18:1,29,34; 21:4; 26:20; 32:1,12; 33:12,19,23; 35:22; 36:12; Ezr 7:10; 10:1,8; Est 3:12; 5:10; 6:6; Job 1:12; 2:1,8; 8:6; 15:25,31; 20:20; 32:2; Ps 4:3; 10:6,11,13; 48:3; 49:15; 68:16; 87:5; 104:2; 130:8; Pr 6:32; Ecc 5:9; SS 3:9; Isa 7:14; 12:2; 19:21; 26:4; 28:21; 36:10; 38:11,15; 44:15,16,20; 45:15; 49:5; 59:17; 63:10,12; Jer 30:21; 49:10; 51:14; La 4:16; Eze 44:3,25,25,27; 45:22; Da 1:8,8; 2:49; 6:3; 8:25; 11:16,36,37; Hos 5:6; 10:1; Am 6:8; 8:7; Jnh 3:6; 4:5; Hab 2:5,6; Zec 2:13; Mt 12:26; 14:23; 24:48; 27:5,42,57; Mk 3:26; 5:5; 6:17; 12:36,37; 14:54,67; 15:31,43; Lk 3:23; 7:39; 10:29; 11:18; 12:17,37,45; 15:15; 16:3; 17:16; 18:4,11; 19:12; 20:42; 23:35,51; 24:12,15,27,36; Jn 1:8,18; 2:24; 4:12,44; 5:18,19, 26,26,37; 6:15; 8:22,41,59; 9:9,21; 12:6,36; 13:32; 16:27; 18:18,25; Ac 1:3; 7:35; 8:13,34; 12:11; 14:17; 16:27; 17:25; 18:5,19; 20:10,35; 21:26; 22:29; 28:16; Ro 8:16,26; 14:22; 15:3; 1Co 6:15, 16; 14:28; 15:27,28; 2Co 4:14; 5:18,19; 8:19; 10:13, 18; 11:14; Gal 1:4; 2:12,20; 4:14; 5:3; Eph 2:14,15, 20; 4:11; 5:2,25,27,28,33; Php 2:7,8,22; Col 1:20; 1Th 3:11; 4:16; 5:23; 2Th 2:4,4,4,16; 3:16; 1Ti 2:6; 2Ti 2:13; Titus 2:14,14; Heb 2:18; 5:2,4,5; 6:13; 7:27; 9:7,14,25,26; Jas 1:24; 1Pe 2:23,24; 5:10; Jude 9; Rev 19:12; 21:3

HIS (6189)

Ge 1:27; 2:2,7,24,24,25; 3:8,15,20,21,22; 4:1,2,4,4, 5,5,8,8,17,17,21,23,25; 5:3,3; 6:6,9,9; 7:7,7,7,13, 13,13; 8:9,18,18,18,21; 9:1,8,21,22,22,24,24,25; 10:10,15,25,25; 11:28,28,31,31,31,31; 12:5,5,8,11, 12,15,17,20,20,20; 13:1,3,12,18; 14:12,14,14,15,16, 16; 16:3,3,12,12; 17:14,19,20,23,23,23,23,25,26, 27; 18:1,2,19,19; 19:1,3,14,14,14,16,16,16,30,30; 20:2,8,14,17,17; 21:2,4,5,7,11,21,22,32; 22:3,3,3,5, 6,7,9,10,10,13,19,21,24; 23:3,6,9,10,10,18,19; 24:2, 7,9,9,10,10,10,20,21,27,30,32,40,48,59,67,67,67; 25:6,6,8,8,9,10,11,17,17,18,21,21,21,25,26,26,33, 34; 26:7,8,11,13,15,15,18,18,25,25,26,26; 27:1,1,5, 10,11,13,14,14,16,16,18,19,20,22,23,23,26,27,30, 30,31,32,34,34,37,37,38,39,40,41; 28:5,7,8,11,16, 18; 29:1,6,10,10,13,13,20,23,24,24,28,28,29,29,30, 30; 30:14,35; 31:4,17,17,18,18,19,23,25,25,46,53, 54,55,55; 32:1,3,13,16,16,22,22,22,23,25,31; 33:1, 3,4,4,14,16,17,19; 34:3,4,5,5,5,8,8,13,18,19,20,24, 26; 35:2,7,18,21,22,27,29,29,29; 36:2,6,6,6,6,6,24, 32,35,39,39; 37:1,2,2,3,3,4,5,8,8,9,10,10,10,11,11, 12,17,20,21,22,23,23,26,26,27,28,29,30,34,34,35, 35; 38:1,6,9,9,9,9,11,11,12,12,12,13,13,14,16,20, 20,28,28,29,29,30,30; 39:2,3,4,4,4,4,5,7,9,11,12,12, 13,15,16,16,18,19,19; 40:2,7,9,11,13,13,20,20,21, 22; 41:8,8,10,12,14,37,42,42,42,43,45,51; 42:1,7,8, 9,21,22,25,27,27,27,27,28,35,37,38; 43:7,8,9,16,18, 21,21,29,29,30,30,31; 44:1,1,2,4,11,14,19,20,20,20, 20,22,22,33; 45:1,1,3,3,3,4,8,14,14,15,15,16,23,23, 24; 46:1,1,6,7,7,7,8,15,15,18,25,26,26,29,29,29,29, 31,31; 47:2,7,10,11,11,12,12,12,28,29,31; 48:1,2,9, 10,10,12,13,13,14,14,14,17,17,17,18,19,19,19; 49:1,10,10,11,11,11,11,12,12,13,15,15,15,16,24,24, 26,31,31,33,33,33,33; 50:1,2,2,7,7,8,8,10,14,14,14, 18,22,24; Ex 1:1,6,9,22; 2:4,7,11,11,20,21,24; 3:1, 6,13; 4:4,6,6,7,7,7,14,15,18,20,20,21; 5:21; 6:1,11, 20; 7:2,10,10,12,20,20,23; 8:6,15,17,24,29,29,31, 31,32; 9:7,23,33,34; 10:1,1,13,22; 11:10; 12:3,30, 48; 13:9,16; 14:4,5,6,6,17,17,17,18,18,21,27,31; 15:3,4,26,26,26; 17:11,11,12,12; 18:1,2,2,7,8,13, 14,20,24,27,27,27; 20:7,17,17; 21:4,6,6,6,7,9,30; 22:16; 23:25; 24:10,11,13; 27:21; 28:1,3,4,12,29, 30,41,43,43; 29:4,6,7,8,9,9,10,15,19,20,21,21,21, 24,27,28,29,32,35,44; 30:12,19,21,30; 31:10; 32:11, 14,15,19,19,27,27; 33:11; 34:4,5,29,29,30,33,35,35; 35:19; 39:27,41; 40:12,14,31; Lev 2:3,10; 4:4,6,17, 22,22,23,24,25,30,34; 6:9,10,10,16,18,20,25; 7:31, 33,34,35; 8:2,6,14,15,18,22,23,23,27,29,30,30,30, 30,31,31,36; 9:1,9,9,12,18,22; 10:1,6,12; 13:2,40, 41,41,42,42,43,44; 14:15,16,16,16,17,18,26,27,27, 28,29; 15:3,3,5,11,13,13,13,15,16; 16:4,6,6,11,11, 11,14,14,17,19,24,26,28,32; 17:2; 18:14; 19:22; 20:2,3,3,4,5,10,11,11,12,17,17,17,17,20,20,21,21; 21:1,2,2,2,10,10,10,10,11,12,12,14,15,15,17,21,22, 23,24; 22:2,7,10,11,11,18; 24:9,11,14; Nu 1:4,44; 2:4,6,8,11,13,15,19,21,23,26,28,30; 3:9,10,38,48, 51; 4:5,15,19,19,27,49; 5:14,15,30; 6:23,25,26; 7:11,12,13,18,24,25,30,31,36,37,42,43,48,49,54,55, 60,61,66,67,72,73,78,79; 8:13,19,22; 9:18,20,23; 11:1,29; 12:1; 14:24; 15:31; 16:5,17,18,19,40; 17:2, 9; 19:3,4,7,8,10,21; 20:11,11,24,25,26,26,28; 21:23, 23,24,26,29,29,33,34,34,35,35,35; 22:5,18,21,22, 22,23,27,31,36; 23:6,7,16,17,18,19; 24:1,3,10,13, 15,18,20,21,23,25; 25:7,13,13; 27:3,4,8,8,9,9,10, 10,11,11,11,21,21,23; 30:2,16,16; 32:13,21; 36:2; Dt 1:31,36,36,41; 2:5,24,30,30,31,31,32,33,33,34; 3:1,2,2,3,4,11; 4:13,20,25,36,36,36,37,37,40,47; 5:11,21,21,24,24,24; 6:2,13,15,22; 7:6,6,7,9,9,12; 8:2,5,11,11,11,18; 9:18; 10:6,8,10,15,20; 11:1,1,1,1, 2,2,2,3; 12:5,5,11,21; 13:4,17,18,18; 14:2,23,24; 15:17; 16:2,6,11; 17:2,17,18,19,19,20,20,20; 18:7, 7,18; 19:5,5,5,5,6; 20:8; 21:16,16,16,17,17,18,19, 19,21; 22:19,30,30; 24:1,2,3; 25:2,5,6,7,7,8,9,9,9,9, 10,11; 26:2,17,18,18,18,19; 27:10,20,20,22,22,22,23; 28:1,9,12,15,54,54,55; 29:2,2,13,20; 30:8,10,16,20; 31:29; 32:4,4,5,9,9,10,19,36,36,43,43,43,43,50; 33:1,2,6,7,7,7,7,7,9,9,9,11,11,11,12,13,16,17,21,23, 24,26; 34:6,7,7,9,11,11; Jos 4:5,14; 5:13,14; 6:19,26,26,27; 7:6,18,22,24,24,24,26; 8:1,1,1,3,10, 18,26; 9:24; 10:2,7,33; 11:7,15; 14:13; 15:17; 21:12; 22:5,20,27,29; 24:4,10,30,33; Jdg 1:6,13,25; 2:9, 14; 3:16,16,19,20,20,21,21,22; 4:2,7,7,10,11,13,13, 15,15,21,22; 5:11,15,17,22,26,26,28,28; 6:11,13,21, 27,27,31; 7:1,11,13,14,14,21; 8:4,20,20,21,25,27, 27,30,31,32; 9:1,1,4,5,5,16,17,18,18,19,19,21,24, 26,28,31,33,34,35,41,43,45,48,48,53,53,54,54,56, 56; 11:1,3,3,11,20,20,21,23,32,34,34,35; 12:9,9,9,9; 13:6,7,11,19,20,21,22,23; 14:2,3,3,4,5,6,6,6,9,9,10, 11,19,20; 15:1,6,6,14,14,19; 16:3,5,9,12,13,14,19, 19,20,21,22,26,29,29,30,31,31,31; 17:2,2,3,4,5,5,8, 11,12,12; 18:4,27,30; 19:3,4,5,7,9,9,9,10,10,11,12, 16,21,21,24,25,27,27,28,29; 20:8; 21:1,23,24; Ru 1:1,2,2,6; 2:5,15,20; 3:4,7,8,13,14; 4:5,7,8,10, 10,10,10,13; 1Sa 1:3,4,9,11,11,19,21,21,23,28; 2:9, 10,10,13,19,20,22,25,35; 3:2,9,12,13,13,18,21; 4:10,12,12,13,13,18,18,19; 5:3,3,4,4,4,7; 6:3,5,9; 7:1,15,17; 8:1,2,2,3,3,9,11,11,11,12,12,12,14,15,16, 17; 9:3,7,10,14,22,25; 10:1,10,14,16,26; 11:5,11; 12:3,5,14,15,15,22,22,22; 13:14,14,16,22,22; 14:1, 1,6,7,12,12,13,13,13,14,17,20,26,26,27,27,27,27, 27,34,45,49,50,52; 15:1,8,12,27,29,29,34; 16:1,5,7, 7,10,13,16,17,20,21,21,23; 17:4,5,6,6,7,7,15,16,17, 22,22,23,23,25,25,33,34,38,38,39,40,40,40,40,40, 41,43,49,49,50,51,54; 18:2,4,4,4,4,7,7,10,10,22,22, 22,25,27,27,28,29,29,30; 19:1,4,4,5,5,9,9,9,10,10, 15,18,24; 20:6,6,7,17,25,27,32,33,33,34,35,38,40, 41; 21:11,11,13,14; 22:1,1,6,6,6,11,15,17; 23:5,8,8, 13,14,15,24,25,26,26,26,28; 24:2,3,5,6,7,7,8,19,22, 22; 25:1,3,3,3,13,13,14,17,20,21,24,25,31,37,37, 39,39,39,40,40,42,43,44; 26:2,3,7,7,10,11,16,18,19, 25; 27:1,3,3,3,8,11,12; 28:3,5,7,14,18,20,23,25; 29:2,4,5,5,11; 30:1,3,4,6,6,18,20,21,22,26,31; 31:2, 2,4,4,4,5,6,6,6,7,8,9,9,12,13; 2Sa 1:2,2,4,5,6,10, 10,12,15,17; 2:2,3,16,16,21,23,23,29,32,32; 3:2, 3,6,8,12,20,27,29,29,30,38,39; 4:4,4,5,6,7,7,8,9,10, 11,11,11,12; 5:6,12,12,21; 6:2,7,11,14,20,20,21; 7:1,1,12,13,14,25; 8:3,4,10,10,15; 9:9,11; 10:1,2,2, 2,10,12; 11:2,9,9,13,13,27,27; 12:3,3,3,3,4,9,9,17, 19,20,20,20,21,24,30,31; 13:2,8,10,17,18,22,24,25, 28,31,31,32,36,37; 14:7,7,7,11,13,15,16,22,22,24, 24,25,25,25,26,26,27,30,33; 15:5,12,14,16,18,22, 25,30,32,32; 16:5,9,11,12,12,13,18,22; 17:8,12,18, 19,23,23,23,23,23,23,29; 18:2,4,9,14,18,19,28; 19:2,4,8,11,11,17,19,24,24,24,31,32,39,41,41; 20:1, 3,8,8,9,10,10,10,12,21,21,22,22; 21:1,2,4,6,12, 13,14,15,22; 22:1,7,7,9,9,10,12,13,15,16,23,23,25, 31,51,51,51; 23:2,8,10,10,12,18,21,21,23; 24:14,16, 20,20,21,25; 1Ki 1:2,6,9,10,15,21,23,27,37,46,47, 47,51,52; 2:1,3,3,4,5,5,6,9,10,12,12,19,19,22,23, 33,33,33,33,34,40,40; 3:1,1,3,3,6,15,27,27; 4:2,10, 13,21,27,31,32,34; 5:1,1,3,3,3,11; 7:1,51; 8:1,11,15, 15,17,22,28,54,56,56,59,59,61,61,66,66; 9:15,16, 18,19,19,19,22,22,22,22,27; 10:1,5,5,5,13,24; 11:3,4,4,4,4,4,6,8,9,17,19,21,23,26,27,28,34,35,36, 43,43,43; 12:6,6,18,33; 13:4,12,13,19,23,24,24,26, 27,29,30,31,31,33; 14:2,4,4,8,18,19,20,20,21,21,22, 31,31,31; 15:2,3,3,3,3,4,5,8,8,10,11,12,13,14,15,18, 18,20,23,23,23,24,24,24,26,26,29; 16:3,5,6,6,7,7,9, 9,13,28,28,34,34; 17:19,23; 18:3,42,42,43,46,46; 19:3,3,6,13,13,19,20,21,21; 20:1,8,11,12,20,20,31, 33,33,35,38,38,39,41,42,42,43; 21:4,5,7,8,19,25,27, 29,29,29; 22:3,9,19,19,19,20,22,31,34,34,34,35,35, 36,36,38,40,40,42,43,45,46,50,50,50,52,53; 2Ki 1:2,8,9,10,11,12,13,13; 2:8,12; 3:2,2,27; 4:1,1, 11,12,18,19,19,19,20,25,27,32,35,37,38,39,43; 5:1, 3,4,6,7,7,8,9,11,11,14,15,23,25,26,27; 6:7,8,10,11, 12,17,24,30,30,30,31,32,32; 7:12,13,17; 8:14,16,19, 19,21,21,21,24,24,26,29; 9:2,3,11,16,21,24,24,24, 25,25,26,27,28,28,28,36; 10:3,10,11,11,11,15,16, 19,19,24,31,34,35,35; 11:2,3,9,19; 12:1,18,20,21, 21; 13:3,8,9,9,12,12,13,16,21,23,23,24,25; 14:2,3, 3,5,5,12,15,15,16,16,20,21,22,25,28,29,29; 15:2,3, 7,7,9,18,19,19,22,22,25,33,34,38,38,38; 16:2,2,3, 13,13,13,15,20,20; 17:13,15,17,18,20,23,23; 18:2,3, 12,17,17,17,33,35; 19:1,4,7,19,37,37,37; 20:2,13, 13,13,13,13,20,21,21; 21:1,3,6,6,7,10,11,18,18,18, 19,20,21,21,22,23,24,24,26,26; 22:1,2,3,11; 23:3,3, 3,18,18,25,25,25,26,26,30,30,30,31,32,34,36,37; 24:1,2,3,6,6,7,7,8,9,11,12,12,12,12,15,15,17,17,18, 20; 25:1,5,7,7,29,29; 1Ch 1:13,19,19,46,50,50; 2:13,18,25,35,35,42,42; 3:3,9,9,10,10,10,11,11,11, 12,12,12,13,13,13,14,14,16,17,22; 4:9,9,10,18,25, 25,26,26,26,27; 5:1,1,1,2,4,4,4,5,5,5,6; 6:20,20,20, 21,21,21,21,22,22,22,23,23,23,24,24,24,24,26,26, 26,27,27,27,27,29,29,29,30,30,30,39,44,49,50,50, 50,51,51,51,52,52,52,53,53; 7:14,14,15,16,16,18, 20,20,20,20,21,21,22,22,23,24,24,25,25,25,26,26, 26,27,27,35; 8:1,8,9,10,29,30,37,37,37,39,39; 9:5, 19,19,35,36,43,43,43; 10:2,2,4,4,4,5,6,6,7,8,9,9,10, 10,12; 11:10,11,20,23,23,25,45; 12:8,16,18,19,19, 21,28; 13:1,9,10,14,14; 14:2,2,11; 15:17,22; 16:7,8, 9,10,11,11,12,13,13,14,15,23,24,24,27,29,29,34,37, 38,39,41,43; 17:1,11,12,13,14,23; 18:3,4,10,10,14; 19:1,2,2,2,3,7,11,13,15,17,17; 20:3,8; 21:3,13,16, 20,21,27; 22:5,6,9,9,9,10,10,17,18; 23:1,13,13,25; 24:21; 25:3,4,9,9,10,11,12,13,14,15,16,17,18,19, 20,21,22,23,24,25,26,27,28,29,30,31; 26:7,10,14, 15,22,25,25,25,25,25,25,26,28,29,30; 27:2,4,4,5,6, 6,7,7,7,8,9,10,11,12,13,14,15; 28:1,2,6,7,11,12,20; 29:23,28,30; 2Ch 1:1,1,8; 2:11,15,17; 3:1,2; 5:1,13; 6:4,4,7,12,13,19; 7:3,6,10,11; 8:1,6,6,6,9,9,9,9,14, 18; 9:4,4,8,8,23,31,31,31; 10:6,6,18; 11:12,14,15, 21,22,23; 12:13,13,14,16,16; 13:2,5,6,12,17; 14:1, 1,1,2,4,11,13,13; 15:9,16,17,18; 16:2,4,5,12,12,12, 12,13,13,14; 17:1,2,3,4,4,5,6,7,7; 18:8,18,18,18,19, 21,30,33,34; 19:1,10; 20:18,20,21,21,25,30,31,32; 21:1,1,3,4,4,7,9,9,9,10,17,19,19,19,19; 22:1,2,3,4, 4,4,6,9,9,11; 23:1,8,10,10,11,13; 24:1,16,22,25,25, 27,27; 25:1,3,3,11,11,14,17,22,28; 26:1,2,3,4,8,10, 13,15,16,16,16,19,19,20,21,23,23; 27:1,2,6,7,9,9; 28:1,3,5,5,13,22,23,25,26,26,27,27; 29:1,2,3,10,19, 25,30,36; 30:2,6,8,8,9,12,27; 31:3,8,8,10,12,13,20, 21; 32:3,9,9,14,15,16,17,21,21,21,21,26,27,27,31, 32,33,33; 33:3,6,6,7,10,11,12,12,12,13,13,13,18,18, 19,19,19,20,20,20,22,23,23,24,25,25; 34:2,3,3,3,4, 8,19,31,31,31,31; 35:3,4,8,9,23,24,24,24,26; 36:1, 5,7,8,12,13,13,15,15,15,16,16,18,20,20,23; Ezr 1:1, 3,7; 3:2,2,9,9,11; 4:7; 5:5,17; 6:10,12; 7:6,9,9,14, 15,23,23,28,28; 8:17,19,22,25,25; 9:8; 10:8,11,18; Ne 1:5,5; 2:1,5,20; 3:1,10,12,17,23,28,29,30; 4:2,3, 18,18,22,23; 5:14; 6:5,5,10,11,18,19; 7:6; 8:4,4; 9:8,8,10,10,32; 11:8,13,14,17; 12:8,36,45; 13:6,26,

30; **Est 1:**2,3,3,4,4,20,21,22,22; **2:**3,7,9,15,16,17,18; **3:**10,10,12; **4:**1,4; **5:**1,2,9,10,10,11,11,14,14; **6:**1,3,5,12,13,13,13,13; **7:**7,7,7; **8:**2,3,7,8; **9:**4,25,25; **10:**2,3,3; **Job 1:**4,10,10,10,20,20; **2:**3,4,5,6,7,7,9,13; **3:**1,1; **4:**9,17,18,18; **5:**3,4,5,5,18; **6:**9; **7:**10,10; **9:**4,4,5,13,13,34; **11:**5; **12:**6,10,13,16; **13:**11,15; **14:**5,6,10; **15:**15,15,20,21,25,27,27,29,29,30,32,32; **16:**9,9,9,12,13; **18:**5,6,7,7,8,10,11,13,13,14,15,15,16,16,19,20; **19:**6,11,11,12; **20:**6,7,9,10,10,10,11,12,12,13,14,14,15,18,20,20,21,22,23,23,23,25,25,26,26,27,28; **21:**17; **22:**22,22; **23:**2,3,11,11,12,12,14; **24:**15,22,23; **25:**3,3,5; **26:**8,9,11,12,12,13,13,14,14; **27:**1,14,14,17,19,21,23; **29:**1,3,3,25; **30:**18,24; **31:**23,35; **32:**1,5,12,14; **33:**10; **34:**6,14,14,19,21,27,29,35,37,37,37; **35:**15,16; **36:**5,7,22,23,24,26,29,30,32,33; **37:**2,2,3,4,4,4,7,11,12,13,13,15,23; **40:**9,19; **42:**8,10,10,11,11,16; **Ps 1:**2; **2:**2,5,5,11,12,12; **3:**T,4; **4:**3; **7:**11,12,12,13,13,17; **9:**7,16; **10:**2,3,4,4,5,5,7,7,8,8,9,10,10,11,15,16; **11:**4,4,4,7; **14:**1,7; **18:**T,6,6,8,8,9,11,11,12,14,22,22,24,30,50,50,50; **19:**1,5,5; **20:**6,6,6; **21:**1,2,2,3,5,9,9; **22:**24,24,31; **23:**3; **24:**3; **25:**8,9,10,14; **27:**4,5,5,6,8; **28:**5,8,8; **29:**2,2,9,11,11; **30:**4,4,5,5; **31:**21,23; **33:**5,6,11,12,14,16,16,18,21; **34:**1,3,6,9,15,20,22; **35:**9,27; **37:**24,28,34; **41:**5,6; **42:**8,8; **46:**6; **47:**8; **48:**1; **50:**4,6; **52:**7,7; **53:**1,6; **55:**20,20,21,21,21; **57:**3,3; **60:**6; **61:**6; **64:**7; **66:**2,2,5,7,7,8,17,20; **67:**1; **68:**1,1,4,4,5,17,21,35; **69:**33,36,36; **72:**7,9,14,17,19,19; **76:**1,2,2,5; **77:**7,8,8,9,10; **78:**4,7,7,10,20,21,21,22,26,32,37,38,38,42,43,43,49,49,50,52,54,54,56,58,61,61,62,62,66,69,70,71,71; **79:**7; **85:**8,8,9,9,13; **87:**1; **89:**23,23,24,25,25,29,29,30,36,36,39,40,40,41,42,42,43,44,44,45; **91:**4,4,4,11; **94:**14,14; **95:**4,5,5,7,7,7; **96:**2,2,3,3,6,8,8,9,13; **97:**2,3,4,6,6,10,12; **98:**1,1,2,2,3,3; **99:**5,6,6,7,9; **100:**3,3,3,4,4,4,5,5; **102:**16,19,21; **103:**1,2,7,7,9,11,13,17,18,18,19,19,20,20,20,21,21,21,22,22; **104:**3,3,4,4,13,13,31; **105:**1,2,3,4,4,5,6,6,7,8,18,18,21,22,22,24,25,25,26,27,27,28,42,42,43,43,45,45; **106:**1,2,8,8,12,12,13,23,23,24,40,40,45,45; **107:**1,8,8,15,15,20,21,21,22,24,31,31; **108:**7; **109:**6,7,8,8,9,9,10,11,12,13,14,14,18,18,18; **110:**4,5,7; **111:**3,3,4,5,6,6,7,7,9,9,9,10; **112:**1; **113:**1,4,8; **114:**2; **115:**12; **116:**2,12,14,15,18; **117:**2; **118:**1,2,3,4,27,29; **119:**2,3; **123:**2; **125:**2; **129:**7,7; **130:**5; **132:**1,7,7,13,18,18; **133:**2,3; **135:**3,4,4,7,9,9,12,14,14; **136:**1,2,3,4,5,5,6,7,8,9,10,11,12,13,14,15,15,16,16,17,18,19,20,21,22,22,23,24,25,26; **144:**10; **145:**3,17,21; **147:**5,10,10,11,15,15,17,17,18,18,19,19,20; **148:**2,2,5,8,13,13,14,14,14; **149:**1,1,3,4,5,9; **150:**1,1,2,2; **Pr 2:**6,8; **3:**11,20,32; **6:**13,13,13,14,27,27,28,30,31,33,33; **7:**20,23,23; **8:**22,22,29,30,30,31; **10:**1,1; **12:**4; **13:**1; **14:**35; **15:**20,20,26; **16:**10,11,15; **17:**25; **18:**9; **19:**12,24,24; **20:**8,8,28; **21:**24,25; **22:**16; **23:**3,6,7; **24:**18; **25:**5,6,7,13,22; **26:**4,5,5,14,15,15,16; **28:**7; **29:**3,3,12,14; **30:**4,4,6; **31:**1,23; **Ecc 4:**8,8,8,14; **6:**3,6; **8:**5,9; **9:**15,16; **12:**13; **SS 1:**2,4,12; **2:**3,3,4,6,6,16; **3:**8,8,11,11,11; **4:**16; **5:**4,6,11,11,12,13,13,14,14,15,15,16; **6:**2; **7:**10; **8:**3,3,10,11; **Isa 1:**31; **2:**3,3,10,19,21; **3:**6,6,8,13,14; **5:**1,12,16,16,19,25,25,25,25; **6:**1,3,6; **7:**2; **8:**7,11,17; **9:**6,7,7,12,12,17,17,21,21; **10:**4,4,7,12,12,12,16,16,17,17,18,19,26; **11:**1,3,3,4,4,5,5,10,11,11,15,16; **12:**4,4; **13:**5,13; **14:**4,17,18,21,25,25,27,32; **17:**4; **19:**14; **22:**22,23,24; **23:**11; **24:**2; **25:**8,9; **26:**20,21; **27:**1,1,8,9; **28:**1,4,5,9,21,21,21,21,26; **30:**26,27,27,28,30,30,31,32,32; **31:**2,3; **32:**16; **33:**5,17; **34:**2,16,16,17; **36:**2; **37:**1,4,7,20,38,38,38; **38:**2,9; **39:**1,2,2,2,2,2; **40:**10,10,11,11,11,12,12,13,26,28; **41:**2,2,2,3; **42:**2,4,10,12,13,13,21,21,24,24,25; **44:**12,12,16,16,16,17,23,26,26; **45:**1,13; **47:**4; **48:**2,14,14,15,16,20; **49:**2,2,5,13,13; **50:**10; **51:**15,17,22; **52:**9,10,14,14; **53:**2,5,7,7,8,9,9,10,10,10,10,11,12; **54:**5; **56:**3,6; **59:**1,2,16,16,17,17,18,18,19; **60:**2; **61:**3,10,10; **62:**5,8,8,11,11; **63:**1,1,7,9,9,10,11,11,11,11,12; **65:**15,20; **66:**5,6,14,14,14,15,15,15,16; **Jer 1:**9; **2:**3,15,15; **3:**1; **4:**7,7,13,13,26; **6:**3; **7:**29; **9:**20; **10:**3,10,12,12,12,13,14,16,16,25; **11:**19; **13:**23; **18:**4; **20:**9,9,9; **21:**7; **22:**7,10,10,11,13,13,13,18,28,30,30; **23:**6,9,18,18,20; **24:**8; **25:**4,12,19,19,19,30,30,38; **26:**19,21,21,23; **27:**7,7,7,8,8,12; **28:**9,11; **29:**32; **30:**6,6,18,24; **31:**10,35; **32:**4; **33:**2,11,21,26; **34:**1,3,3,21; **35:**3,3,14,18; **36:**14,24,30,31,31; **37:**2,12; **38:**27; **39:**1,6,14,14; **41:**9,15; **42:**11; **43:**10,10,12; **44:**23,23,23,30; **46:**10,17,26; **48:**7; **49:**1,3,10,10,10; **50:**16,18,25,25,28,34,43; **51:**3,3,11,11,12,12,15,15,15,16,17,19,19,31,34,59; **52:**1,3,4,8,10,11,30,33,33,34; **La 1:**12,14,15,17,17,18; **2:**1,1,1,2,3,4,4,4,6,6,6,7,7,8,17; **3:**3,12,12,13,22,29,30,32; **4:**11,11,20; **Eze 1:**27; **8:**2,2,11,12; **9:**1,2,2,3,11; **10:**7; **12:**12,12,12,14,14; **16:**15; **17:**14,15,17,18,21; **18:**6,7,8,11,13,13,14,15,16,17,17,18,18,18,18,19; **19:**7,9; **21:**21,22; **22:**6,11,11,11,11; **26:**8,9,9,10,11; **29:**18,18,19,20,20; **30:**11,22,22,24; **31:**2,18; **32:**10,31,31,32; **33:**26; **34:**12; **36:**20; **38:**21,22; **39:**11; **40:**3; **43:**2,2; **44:**25; **45:**8; **46:**2,2,12,12,16,16,16,17,17,17,17,18,18; **47:**3; **Da 1:**2,2,2,3,18,20; **2:**1,1,7,13,17,17,18,20,24,25; **3:**19,20,24,24,28,28; **4:**3,3,3,3,16,19,31,33,33,33,34,34,35,37; **5:**1,2,2,2,2,2,3,3,3,6,6,6,7,9,9,10,20,20,20,21,22,23,23,29; **6:**3,4,5,10,10,10,12,17,17,18,22,22,23,26,26; **7:**1,1,9,9,9,9,13,14,14,25,25,26,27; **8:**11,22,24,25; **9:**2,4,4,10,20; **10:**5,6,6,6,6,6; **11:**2,4,4,4,5,5,6,7,9,10,10,17,17,18,18,18,19,20,24,24,24,25,26,28,28,28,30,31,37,38,41,42,45,45; **12:**7,7; **Hos 3:**5; **5:**13,13; **6:**2; **7:**9,9,10; **9:**8,8; **10:**1,1,1,12; **11:**10; **12:**2,2,3,4,5,14,14,14,14; **13:**12,15,15,15,15; **14:**5,6,6,6,7; **Joel 2:**11,11,11,16,18,18; **3:**16; **Am 1:**11,11,11,13,15; **2:**4,14,15,15; **3:**7,7; **4:**2,13,13; **5:**8,19,19; **6:**8; **7:**7,10; **9:**6,6; **Ob** 6,11,11,12,17; **Jnh 1:**5; **2:**1; **3:**6,6,7,9; **4:**6,6; **Mic 1:**2,3; **3:**4,8,8; **4:**2,2,12; **5:**3,4,4,4; **6:**2; **7:**6,6,9,18; **Na 1:**2,2,2,3,3,5,6,6,6,8; **2:**12,12,12,12; **Hab 1:**15,15,16,16,16,17; **2:**4,4,9,9,15,18,20; **3:**3,3,4,4,4,5,14,14,14; **Zep 1:**14,18; **2:**13; **3:**5,17; **Hag 2:**22; **Zec 2:**1,8,12,13; **3:**1,4,5,5; **4:**9; **6:**12,13,13; **7:**12; **8:**23; **9:**10,14,16,16,16; **10:**3,12; **11:**17,17,17,17; **14:**4,9; **Mal 1:**3,3,6,6,14; **2:**6,6,7,16; **3:**1,2,14,16,16,17; **Mt 1:**2,11,18,21,24; **2:**2,11,13,14,20,21,22; **3:**4,4,12,12,12,12; **4:**6,18,21; **5:**1,28,31,32,35,45; **6:**29,33,33; **7:**24,26,28; **8:**3,3,13,20,23; **9:**1,10,11,19,20,21,37,38; **10:**1,2,2,10,21,24,25,35,36; **11:**1,2,20; **12:**1,3,4,19,21,26,29,29,46,49; **13:**3,24,25,31,36,41,41,44,52,54,55,55,56,57,57; **14:**2,3,9,9,11,12,31,36; **15:**23,30,32,33; **16:**13,20,21,24,27,27,28; **17:**2,2,24; **18:**23,25,25,26,28,29,29,34; **19:**3,5,5,7,9,13,15,23,28; **20:**1,2,8,28,29; **21:**18,29,31,34,34,35,37,38,41; **22:**2,3,5,5,6,7,8,15,24,25,25,33,45; **23:**1; **24:**1,1,31,31,43,45,47,49; **25:**14,14,15,15,16,18,21,23,26,31,31,33,33,34,41,41; **26:**1,7,23,26,36,39,40,51,51,65,67; **27:**19,24,25,29,29,31,35,37,38,38,50,55,60,64; **28:**3,3,7,8,9,13; **Mk 1:**6,7,16,19,22,36,40,41; **2:**8,12,15,16,23,25,26; **3:**5,7,9,17,20,21,21,26; **4:**2,3,34,35,40; **5:**4,6,7,15,22,27,28,31,33; **6:**1,1,3,4,4,4,5,8,17,21,21,22,26,26,28,29,35,41,45,56; **7:**2,17,24,25,32,33,35; **8:**1,4,6,10,23,25,25,25,27,33,34,38; **9:**3,18,27,28,31,36; **10:**1,2,7,7,11,13,16,16,17,17,23,24,45,46,50,50,52; **11:**1,14,18,19; **12:**13,19,37,43; **13:**1,12,27,27,34,34; **14:**3,13,22,32,37,47,47,52,63; **15:**20,21,24,27,27,37,41; **16:**7,20; **Lk 1:**5,14,23,24,25,29,32,33,45,48,49,50,51,54,55,59,60,62,63,64,64,67,68,69,70,72,77; **2:**14,28,34,43,47,47,48,48,51; **3:**1,17,17,17,17,19,19,23; **4:**10,16,22,24,30,32,32,33,40; **5:**9,12,13,19,27,29,30; **6:**1,3,4,10,13,14,17,20,45,45; **7:**2,3,11,12,13,15,16,38,38; **8:**5,9,22,25,28,28,29,35,41,42,42,44,47; **9:**14,18,26,29,29,31,32,32,42,43,56,58; **10:**2,7,23,30,34,34,38; **11:**1,1,18,21,21,22,49; **12:**1,22,27,31,39,42,44; **13:**6,13,17,19,22; **14:**2,4,12,17,21,21,23; **15:**5,6,12,12,13,15,16,17,20,20,20,20,22,22,22,28,29; **16:**1,1,5,18,20,21,23,24; **17:**1,11,22,24; **18:**1,7,13,15,43; **19:**13,14,17,19,22,24,29,48; **20:**26,28,44,45; **21:**5; **22:**14,39,44,50,71; **23:**5,11,26,33,33,34,46,55; **24:**8,23,26,40,47,50; **Jn 1:**11,11,12,14,14,16,35,41; **2:**2,5,11,11,12,12,17,21,22,23; **3:**16,17,22,32,35; **4:**2,5,8,12,12,24,27,31,33,34,41,44,47,50,51,51,52,53; **5:**9,17,17,18,19,28,32,35,37,37,38,43; **6:**3,8,12,16,22,24,27,52,53,60,61,66; **7:**5,10,30,40; **8:**6,20,27,44,55; **9:**2,2,3,8,15,18,21,22,23,27,31; **10:**3,3,4,4,4,11,31,36; **11:**2,7,12,13,13,17,32,44,44,51,53,54; **12:**3,4,12,16,50; **13:**1,3,4,4,5,12,12,16,22; **14:**10; **15:**10,15,20; **16:**13,17; **18:**1,1,2,10,19,19,25; **19:**2,17,23,25,25,26,27,30,30,33,35,36; **20:**20,25,25,26,30,31; **21:**1,7,14,24; **Ac 1:**3,7,14,18,18,18,20,20,22; **2:**14,29,30,30,31,41; **3:**5,8,13,18,21,26; **4:**26; **5:**1,2,6,7,10,17,21,26,31,36,37,40; **6:**15; **7:**4,5,5,8,10,10,13,14,14,17,20,23,24,25,60; **8:**11,27,28,28,32,33,33,33,39; **9:**3,8,12,12,17,19,25,27,40; **10:**2,7,7,22,23,24,25,43; **11:**13; **12:**11,15,17,21,21; **13:**8,13,16,19,25,31,36,36,36; **14:**3; **15:**14; **16:**3,6,27,32,33,34,34; **17:**1,2,7,28; **18:**2,6,8,18,28; **19:**6,22,38; **20:**10,28,32,38,38; **21:**11,19,32; **22:**14,14,15,16; **23:**15,23,26,30; **24:**2,23,23,24; **25:**8,12,18,21,25,26; **26:**1,1,23,26; **27:**3,3,34; **28:**3,4,7,8,8,30; **Ro 1:**2,3,3,4,5,7,9,20; **2:**4,5,18; **3:**5,7,24,25,25,25,26; **4:**13,19,19,20; **5:**8,9,10,10; **6:**3,5,5; **8:**3,11,17,17,28,29,32; **9:**7,19,22,22,22,23,23,28; **11:**1,2,22,29,33,33,34; **12:**2,20; **15:**9,10; **16:**2,13,15,21,23; **1Co 1:**2,4,9; **2:**10; **3:**5; **5:**1,5; **6:**14; **7:**2,3,3,4,4,11,14,33,34,36,37,37,37; **9:**7; **11:**4,4,7; **15:**10,25,25,27; **16:**11; **2Co 1:**1,22,22; **2:**11; **3:**13,18; **4:**6,11; **5:**20; **7:**7,13,15; **8:**9,17,18,22; **9:**15; **10:**10,10; **11:**15,33; **Gal 1:**15,16; **2:**11,13; **3:**5,16,18; **4:**2,4,6,6,7,23,23; **Eph 1:**4,5,6,7,9,9,11,12,14,18,18,19,20,22,23; **2:**4,7,7,15,15,19,22; **3:**7,10,11,16,16,20; **4:**8,12; **5:**23,28,30,31,31,33; **6:**10; **Php 2:**1,6,13,22,30; **3:**3,10,10,10,21,21; **4:**19; **Col 1:**9,11,12,19,20,22,24; **4:**10; **1Th 1:**10; **2:**2,11,12; **3:**13; **4:**8; **2Th 1:**7,9,10,11,11; **2:**8,8,16; **1Ti 1:**12,16; **3:**2,4,4,5,12,12,12; **5:**18; **6:**15; **2Ti 1:**8,9; **2:**4,19,26; **4:**1,1,8,18; **Titus 1:**3,6; **2:**14; **3:**5,7; **Phm** 5; **Heb 1:**2,3,3,5,6,7,7; **2:**4,14; **3:**6,7,15,18; **4:**1,3,4,7,10; **5:**3,7; **6:**10,13,17; **7:**6,10,16,21,27; **9:**12,25; **10:**11,13,13,20,30; **11:**4,7,7,8,9,17,21,22,22,26; **12:**5,6,7,10,16,26; **13:**12,15,21; **Jas 1:**23; **2:**21,22,22,22; **1Pe 1:**2,3,13; **2:**9,21,22,24,24; **3:**12; **4:**1,13; **5:**10; **2Pe 1:**3,3,4,16; **2:**8,16; **3:**9,13,16,16; **1Jn 1:**3,7,10; **2:**3,5,12,27,28; **3:**12,12,12,16,19,22,23,23; **4:**9,9,10,12,13,14; **5:**1,2,3,3,9,10,11,14,20; **2Jn** 6,6; **Jude** 5,14,24; **Rev 1:**1,1,1,4,5,6,13,13,14,14,15,15,16,16,16,17,17; **2:**1,13; **3:**5,21; **6:**5; **7:**15,15; **8:**7,8,10,12; **9:**1,13; **10:**1,1,1,2,2,2,5,7,7; **11:**15,15,19,19; **12:**5,7,7,9,10,12,15,16; **13:**2,2,6,6; **14:**1,1,7,10,12,14,14,16,19; **15:**8; **16:**2,3,4,8,10,12,17,19; **17:**11,14,17; **18:**1; **19:**2,2,5,7,10,12,12,13,15,16,16,19; **20:**1,7,11; **21:**3; **22:**3,4,4,6,6

I (8795)

See select index of "I AM" in the Main Concordance.

Ge 1:29,30; **2:**18; **3:**10,10,10,10,11,12,13,15,16,17; **4:**1,9,9,13,14,14,23; **6:**7,7,7,7,13,13,17,18; **7:**1,4,4,4; **8:**21,21,21; **9:**3,3,5,5,5,9,11,12,13,14,15,16,17; **12:**1,2,2,2,3,3,7,11,13,19; **13:**15,16,17; **14:**22,23,23,24; **15:**1,2,7,8,8,14,18; **16:**2,5,5,10,13; **17:**1,2,5,6,6,7,8,8,16,16,19,20,20,20,20,21; **18:**3,10,12,12,13,13,14,15,17,17,19,21,21,26,26,27,27,28,28,29,30,30,31,31,32; **19:**8,19,21,21,22,34; **20:**5,6,6,6,9,11,13,16; **21:**7,13,16,18,23,24,26,26,30; **22:**1,2,5,11,12,16,17; **23:**4,4,11,11,11,13,13; **24:**3,3,5,7,13,14,14,14,24,31,33,33,33,34,37,39,40,42,42,42,43,43,45,45,46,47,47,48,48,49,56,58; **25:**32; **26:**2,3,3,3,4,5,9,9,24,24,24; **27:**1,2,4,4,4,6,7,7,8,9,11,12,13,19,19,21,24,25,32,33,33,37,37,37,41,43,45; **28:**13,13,15,15,15,15,15,16,20,21,22,22; **29:**19,21,25,25,33,34,35; **30:**2,3,8,8,13,16,20,25,26,26,27,27,28,29,30,30,30,31,31; **31:**3,5,10,10,11,11,12,13,27,29,31,31,35,36,38,38,39,39,41,41,43,44,51,52; **32:**4,5,5,5,9,10,10,10,10,11,11,12,20,20,20,26,30; **33:**8,9,10,11,11,13,14,14; **34:**11,12,30; **35:**3,3,11,12,12,12; **37:**6,9,10,13,17,30,35,35; **38:**18,22,23,25,26,26; **39:**9,9,14,18; **40:**9,11,15,15,16; **41:**9,13,15,15,16,17,19,21,22,24,28,40,41,44; **42:**2,14,18,22,33,34,34,37,37; **43:**9,9,9,14,14,23; **44:**21,28,28,30,32,32,32,34; **45:**3,4,11,12,18,28,28; **46:**2,3,3,4,4,30,30,31; **47:**16,23,29,30,30; **48:**4,4,4,5,7,7,9,11,19,19,21,22,22; **49:**1,7,18,29,31; **50:**4,5,5,5,17,19,21,24; **Ex 2:**7,9,10,14,22; **3:**3,4,6,7,7,7,8,9,10,11,11,12,12,13,13,14,14,14,16,17,19,20,20,21; **4:**10,10,11,12,14,15,18,21,21,23,23; **5:**2,2,2,10,23; **6:**1,2,3,3,4,5,5,6,6,6,6,7,7,7,8,8,8,8,12,29,29,30; **7:**1,2,3,3,4,4,5,5,17,17; **8:**2,8,9,21,22,22,23,28,29,29; **9:**14,15,16,16,18,27,27,28,29,29,30; **10:**1,1,2,2,2,4,10,16,29; **11:**1,4,8; **12:**12,12,12,13,13,13,17; **13:**8,8,15; **14:**4,4,4,17,17,18,18; **15:**1,2,2,9,9,9,9,9,26,26,26; **16:**4,4,12,12,32,32; **17:**4,6,9,14; **18:**3,6,11,16,19; **19:**4,4,9; **20:**2,5,22,24,24; **21:**5,13; **22:**23,24,27,27; **23:**7,13,15,20,20,22,22,23,25,26,27,27,28,29,30,31,31; **24:**12,12; **25:**8,9,16,21,22; **28:**3; **29:**35,42,43,44,45,46,46,46; **30:**6,36; **31:**2,3,6,6,6,11,13; **32:**8,9,10,10,13,13,13,18,24,24,30,30,33,34,34; **33:**1,1,2,3,3,5,5,5,12,13,14,17,17,17,19,19,19,19,19,19,22,22,23; **34:**1,9,10,10,10,11,11,18,24,27; **Lev 6:**17; **7:**34; **8:**31,35; **10:**3,3,13,18,19; **11:**44,44,45,45; **14:**34,34,35; **16:**2; **17:**10,10,11,12,14; **18:**2,3,4,5,6,21,24,25,30; **19:**2,3,4,10,12,14,16,18,25,28,30,31,32,34,36,37; **20:**3,5,6,6,7,8,22,23,23,24,24,24,25,26,26; **21:**8,8,12,15,23; **22:**2,3,8,9,16,30,31,32,32,33; **23:**10,22,30,43,43,43; **24:**22; **25:**2,17,21,38,42,55,55; **26:**1,2,4,6,6,9,9,11,11,12,13,13,16,16,17,18,19,21,22,24,25,25,26,28,28,30,30,31,31,32,33,36,41,42,42,44,44,45,45,45; **Nu 3:**12,13,13,13,41,45; **5:**3; **6:**27; **8:**16,17,17,18,19; **9:**8; **10:**10,29,30,30; **11:**11,12,12,13,14,15,17,17,21,21,23,29; **12:**6,6,8,11; **13:**2; **14:**11,12,12,20,21,22,23,24,27,28,28,28,30,31,35,35; **15:**2,18,41,41; **16:**15,15,21,45; **17:**4,5,5; **18:**6,7,8,8,11,12,19,20,21,24,24,26; **20:**12,24; **21:**16,34; **22:**6,6,8,11,17,18,19,20,28,29,29,30,30,32,33,33,34,34,34,35,37,37,38,38,38,38; **23:**3,3,4,4,8,8,9,9,9,11,12,15,20,20,26,26; **24:**10,11,11,12,13,13,14,17,17; **25:**11,11,12; **27:**12; **32:**8,11; **33:**53,56,56; **35:**34,34; **Dt 1:**8,9,12,13,15,16,17,18,20,23,29,35,36,39,42,43; **2:**5,5,9,9,19,19,24,25,26,31; **3:**2,12,13,15,16,18,19,19,20,21,23; **4:**1,2,2,5,8,21,22,22,26,40; **5:**1,5,6,9,28,31,31; **6:**2,6; **7:**11; **8:**1,11,19; **9:**9,9,9,12,13,14,14,15,16,16,17,18,18,19,20,21,21,23,24,25,26; **10:**2,3,3,5,5,10,10,11,13; **11:**8,13,14,15,22,26,27,28,32; **12:**11,14,20,21,28,32; **13:**18; **15:**5,11,15,16; **18:**18,18,18,19,20; **19:**7,9; **22:**14,14,14,16,17; **24:**8,18,22; **25:**8; **26:**3,3,10,13,13,13,14,14,14,14,14,14,14; **27:**1,4,10; **28:**1,13,14,15,68; **29:**5,6,6,14,19,19; **30:**1,2,8,11,15,16,18,19,19; **31:**2,2,5,14,16,17,17,18,20,20,21,21,21,23,23,27,27,27,28,29,29; **32:**1,3,20,21,21,23,24,24,26,26,27,34,35,39,39,39,39,39,40,40,41,41,42,46,49,52; **33:**9; **34:**4,4,4,4; **Jos 1:**2,3,3,5,5,5,6,9; **2:**4,5,9,12; **3:**7,7,7; **5:**9,14; **6:**2,10; **7:**8,11,12,20,20,21,21; **8:**1,5,18; **10:**8; **11:**6; **13:**6,6; **14:**7,7,8,10,11,11,12; **15:**16,18; **18:**4,6,8; **20:**2; **22:**2; **23:**2,4,4,14; **24:**3,3,4,4,5,5,5,5,6,7,8,8,8,10,10,11,12,13; **Jdg 1:**2,7,12,14; **2:**1,1,1,1,3,3,20,21,22; **3:**19,20; **4:**7,8,8,9,22; **5:**3,3,3,7,7; **6:**8,9,9,9,10,10,14,15,15,16,17,18,18,22,37,37; **7:**2,4,4,4,7,9,13,17,17,18; **8:**2,3,5,7,9,9,19,23,24; **9:**2,9,11,13,29,29; **10:**12,13; **11:**9,27,31,31,35,35,35,37; **12:**2,2,3,3; **13:**6,8,11,13,14,16; **14:**2,12,16,16; **15:**2,2,3,3,7,7,7,11,16,16,18; **16:**15,17,17,26,26; **17:**2,2,2,3,3,13; **18:**4,24,24; **19:**18,18,18,24; **20:**4,6,28; **Ru 1:**11,12,12,12,16,16,17,17,21; **2:**2,9,10,13,13,19; **3:**1,5,9,11,12,12,13; **4:**4,4,4,4,4,6,6,6,9,10; **1Sa 1:**8,11,15,15,15,16,20,22,26,27,27,28; **2:**1,23,24,27,28,28,29,30,30,31,33,33,35,35,36; **3:**4,5,5,6,6,8,11,12,12,13,13,14,16; **4:**16,16; **7:**5; **8:**8; **9:**8,8,16,16,17,19,19,21,23,23,24,24,26,27; **10:**2,8,8,18,18; **11:**2,2; **12:**1,2,2,3,3,3,3,3,3,3,3,7,17,23,23; **13:**11,12,12,12; **14:**7,24,29,37,40,43,43; **15:**1,2,6,11,11,13,14,20,20,20,24,24,24,24,25,25,26,30,30; **16:**1,1,1,2,2,3,3,5,7,18,22; **17:**8,9,10,28,29,29,35,35,39,39,43,45,46,55,58; **18:**17,17,18,18,21; **19:**3,3,15,17; **20:**1,1,3,5,8,9,9,12,12,12,13,14,14,20,20,21,21,22,23,29,30,36; **21:**2,2,4,5,8,15; **22:**3,9,15,22,22; **23:**2,4,17,23,23; **24:**4,6,10,10,10,11,11,11,17,17,20; **25:**7,11,11,22,25,35,41; **26:**8,11,18,18,21,21,21,23,24; **27:**1,1,1,5,5; **28:**2,7,8,11,13,15,15,21,23; **29:**3,6,6,8,8,8,9; **30:**8,8,13,13,15; **2Sa 1:**3,6,7,7,8,10,10,10,13,16,26; **2:**1,1,6,22,22; **3:**8,8,8,9,12,13,13,14,18,28,35,39,39; **4:**10,10,11; **5:**19,19; **6:**21,22,22,22; **7:**2,6,6,6,7,7,7,8,9,9,9,10,11,11,12,12,13,14,14,15,15,18,27; **9:**1,3,7,7,9; **10:**2,11; **11:**5,11,11,12; **12:**7,7,8,8,8,11,11,12,13,22,22,23,23,23,27,28; **13:**5,5,6,6,10,13,28,28,34; **14:**5,6,7,8,15,15,18,21,32,32,32,32,32,32; **15:**4,4,7,8,8,20,20,20,25,26,26,28,34,34,34; **16:**4,4,18,18,19,19,19,19; **17:**1,2,2,2,11,15; **18:**2,4,10,11,12,13,18,23,29,29,33; **19:**6,7,20,20,20,22,22,26,26,26,26,28,29,33,34,34,35,35,35,37,38,38; **20:**16,17; **21:**3,3,6; **22:**3,4,7,7,22,22,23,24,30,30,38,38,39,41,43,43,44,50,50; **24:**2,10,10,10,10,12,13,14,17,17,21,24,24; **1Ki 1:**5,14,21,30,30,35; **2:**2,7,8,8,8,14,16,18,20,20,26,30,42,42,43; **3:**7,12,12,13,14,17,17,20,21,21,21,21,26; **5:**5,5,6,8,9,9; **6:**12,12,13; **8:**13,16,16,16,20,20,20,21,27,43,44,48,59; **9:**3,3,4,5,5,5,6,7,7,7; **10:**6,7,7,7; **11:**11,11,12,12,13,13,21,31,32,33,34,34,34,35,36,36,37,38,38,38,38,39; **12:**11,11,14,14; **13:**7,8,8,9,14,16,16,17,18,31; **14:**2,6,7,8,10,10,10; **15:**19; **16:**2,3,3; **17:**1,4,9,10,12,12,20,24; **18:**1,9,12,12,12,12,13,13,15,15,18,22,23,24,36; **19:**2,4,4,10,10,14,14,18,20,20; **20:**4,4,5,6,7,9,13,13,28,28,34,34,42; **21:**2,2,3,4,6,6,6,20,21,21,22,29,29; **22:**4,6,6,8,14,16,17,18,19,21,22,27,30; **2Ki 1:**2,10,12; **2:**2,3,4,5,6,9,9,10,18,21; **3:**7,7,14,14,14,16; **4:**2,9,13,22,24,28,28,30,43; **5:**5,6,7,7,11,12,15,16,16,18,18,20; **6:**3,8,13,19,21,21,27,29,33; **7:**12; **8:**8,9,12; **9:**3,5,6,7,8,9,12,17,25,26,26; **10:**9,15,15,19,24,30; **16:**7,15; **17:**13,13,38; **18:**14,14,21,23,25,32; **19:**7,7,20,23,23,23,24,24,25,25,25,27,28,28,34; **20:**3,5,5,6,6,6,8,15; **21:**4,7,7,8,8,8,12,13,13,14; **22:**8,16,19,19,20,20; **23:**17,27,27,27,27,27; **1Ch 4:**9,10; **11:**19,19; **12:**17; **13:**12; **14:**10,10; **15:**12; **16:**18; **17:**1,5,5,5,6,6,6,7,8,8,8,9,10,10,10,11,11,12,13,13,13,14,16,17; **19:**2,12; **21:**2,8,8,8,10,12,13,17,17,22,23,23,24,24; **22:**5,7,9,9,10,10,14; **23:**5; **28:**2,2,6,6,7,8,19; **29:**2,3,3,14,17,17,17,19; **2Ch 1:**10,11,12; **2:**4,5,6,8,9,10,13; **6:**2,5,5,5,6,6,10,10,10,11,18,33,34,38; **7:**12,13,14,14,16,17,18,18,18,19,20,20,20,20; **9:**5,6,6,6; **10:**11,11,14,14; **12:**5,7; **16:**3; **18:**3,5,7,13,14,15,16,17,18,20,21,26,29; **25:**9,16; **28:**23; **29:**10; **32:**13; **33:**7,7,8,8,8; **34:**15,24,27,28,28; **35:**21,21,23; **Ezr 4:**19,21; **6:**8,11,12; **7:**13,21,28; **8:**15,15,15,16,17,17,21,22,24,25,26,28; **9:**3,3,4,5,6; **Ne 1:**1,2,4,4,4,5,6,8,9,9,11; **2:**1,1,2,3,4,5,5,6,7,7,7,8,8,9,11,12,12,12,13,14,15,15,16,16,16,17,18,20; **4:**13,14,14,19,22,23; **5:**6,6,7,7,7,9,10,12,13,14,14,15,16,18,19; **6:**1,1,3,3,3,4,8,9,10,11,11,12,13,19; **7:**1,2,3,5,5; **12:**31,31,38,40; **13:**6,6,6,7,8,9,9,10,11,11,13,14,15,15,17,19,19,21,21,22,23,25,25,25,28,30,31; **Est 3:**9; **4:**11,16,16,16,16; **5:**4,8,8,13; **7:**3,4,4; **8:**6,6,7; **Job 1:**15,16,17,19,21,21; **3:**11,11,12,13,13,16,25,25,26,26; **4:**8,16,16; **5:**3,8,8,8; **6:**7,8,8,10,10,11,11,11,12,13,22,24,24,26,28; **7:**3,4,4,4,4,8,11,11,11,12,13,15,16,16,20,20,20,21,21; **8:**18; **9:**2,11,11,14,14,15,15,15,16,16,20,20,21,21,21,22,27,27,27,28,28,29,29,30,32,35,35; **10:**1,1,2,7,13,14,15,15,15,15,16,18,18,19,20,21; **11:**4,5; **12:**3,3,4,4; **13:**2,2,3,14,15,15,17,18,18,18,19,20,22,23; **14:**14,15; **15:**17,17; **16:**2,4,4,6,6,15,22; **17:**10,13,13,14; **19:**4,7,7,7,8,10,16,16,17,18,19,20,20,25,26,27,27; **20:**2,3; **21:**3,3,4,6,6,16,27; **22:**18; **23:**3,3,4,5,7,8,8,8,9,9,10,10,11,12,12,15,15,15,17; **27:**3,5,5,5,6,6,11,11; **29:**2,3,4,7,12,13,14,15,16,16,17,18,18,22,24,25,25,25; **30:**1,1,9,19,20,20,23,25,26,26,28,28,29; **31:**1,5,6,8,9,13,14,14,16,17,18,18,19,21,21,23,23,24,25,26,28,29,30,33,34,34,35,35,36,36,37,37,39; **32:**6,6,6,7,10,10,10,11,11,12,14,16,17,17,17,18,19,20,20,21,21,22; **33:**1,2,3,6,6,8,9,9,9,12,24,27,27,27,27,28,31,32,33; **34:**5,6,6,6,16,31,32,32,32,33; **35:**2,3,4; **36:**2,3,3; **37:**20; **38:**3,4,9,10,11,23; **39:**6; **40:**4,4,4,5,5,5,7,14,15; **41:**11,12; **42:**2,3,3,4,4,6,7,8; **Ps 2:**6,7,7,8; **3:**4,5,5,6; **4:**1,3,8; **5:**2,3,7,7; **6:**2,6,6; **7:**1,3,4,17,17; **8:**3; **9:**1,1,2,2,14; **11:**1; **12:**5,5; **13:**2,3,4,4,5,6; **16:**1,2,2,3,4,6,7,8,8; **17:**3,4,6,15,15,15; **18:**1,2,3,3,6,6,21,21,22,23,29,29,37,37,38,40,42,42,43,49,49; **19:**13; **20:**6; **22:**2,2,6,10,14,22,22,25; **23:**1,4,4,6; **25:**1,2,16,20; **26:**1,1,3,4,4,5,6,8,11,12; **27:**1,1,3,4,4,4,6,6,7,8,13,13; **28:**1,1,2,2,7; **30:**1,2,6,6,6,7,8,8,9,9,12; **31:**1,5,6,6,7,9,11,12,12,12,13,14,14,17,21,22,22,22; **32:**3,5,5,5,8,8; **34:**1,2,4,11; **35:**3,11,13,14,14,15,18,18; **36:**1; **37:**25,25,25,35,36; **38:**6,6,8,8,13,14,15,16,17,18,18,20; **39:**1,1,1,2,3,3,7,9,9,10,12,13,13; **40:**1,5,7,7,7,8,9,9,10,10,10,12,17; **41:**4,4,9,10,11; **42:**2,4,4,4,5,6,9,9,11; **43:**2,4,4,5; **44:**6,15; **45:**1,17; **46:**10,10,10; **49:**4,4,5; **50:**7,7,7,8,9,11,12,12,13,15,21,21,21,22,23; **51:**3,4,5,7,7,13,16; **52:**8,8,9,9; **54:**6,6; **55:**2,6,6,6,7,8,9,12,12,14,16,17,23; **56:**3,3,4,4,9,9,10,10,11,12,12,13; **57:**1,1,2,4,4,6,7,8,9,9; **59:**4,9,10,16,16,17,17; **60:**6,8,8; **61:**2,2,2,4,8; **62:**2,6,11; **63:**1,1,2,4,4,4,5,6,6,7,8; **64:**1; **66:**13,14,15,15,17,18; **68:**22,22; **69:**2,2,3,4,4,7,8,10,10,11,12,13,17,19,20,20,30; **70:**5; **71:**1,3,6,6,7,9,14,14,15,16,16,17,18,18,22,22,23,23; **73:**2,3,3,13,14,15,15,16,17,17,22,22,23,25,25,28,28; **75:**2,2,3,4,9,9,10; **77:**1,1,2,2,2,2,3,3,3,4,5,6,10,10,11,11,12; **78:**2,2; **81:**5,6,7,7,7,8,10,10,12,14,16; **82:**6; **84:**10; **85:**8; **86:**1,2,3,4,7,7,11,11,12,12,16; **87:**4; **88:**1,3,4,4,5,8,9,9,13,15,15; **89:**1,1,2,3,3,4,19,19,20,20,23,25,27,28,29,32,33,33,34,35,35,50; **91:**2,2,14,14,15,15,15,16; **92:**4; **94:**17,18,22; **95:**9,10,10,11; **101:**1,1,2,2,3,3,3,4,5,5,8,8; **102:**2,2,4,5,6,7,7,9,11,24; **104:**33,33,33,34; **105:**11; **106:**5,5; **108:**1,2,3,3,7,9,9; **109:**1,4,22,23,23,25,30,30; **110:**1; **111:**1; **116:**1,2,2,3,4,6,9,10,10,10,11,12,13,14,16,16,17,18; **118:**5,6,7,10,11,12,13,17,19,21,28,28; **119:**6,6,7,7,8,10,11,11,13,14,15,16,16,17,17,18,19,22,25,26,27,30,30,31,32,33,34,35,39,40,42,42,43,44,45,45,46,47,47,48,48,48,51,52,52,54,55,55,56,57,58,59,60,61,62,63,66,67,67,67,69,70,71,74,75,77,78,80,80,81,82,83,83,86,87,88,92,93,94,94,95,96,97,97,99,99,100,100,101,101,102,104,104,106,106,107,109,109,110,113,113,114,115,116,117,117,119,120,121,125,125,127,128,128,129,131,134,141,141,144,145,145,146,146,147,147,148,152,153,157,158,159,162,163,163,164,166,166,167,167,168,173,174,175,176,176; **120:**1,5,5,6,7,7; **121:**1; **122:**1,8,9; **123:**1; **130:**1,5,5,6; **131:**1,2,2,2; **132:**3,4,5,11,12,14,14,15,15,16,17,18; **135:**5; **137:**5,6,6; **138:**1,1,2,3,7; **139:**2,2,7,7,8,8,9,9,11,14,14,14,15,15,18,18,18,21,22,22; **140:**6,12; **141:**1,1,4,8,10; **142:**1,1,2,2,3,4,5,5,6,7; **143:**5,5,6,6,7,8,8,8,9,12; **144:**2,9,9; **145:**1,1,2,5,6; **146:**2,2,2; **Pr 1:**23,23,24,24,26,26,28; **4:**2,3,10,11,20; **5:**7,12,13,14; **7:**6,7,7,14,14,15,15,16,17,24; **8:**4,4,6,6,12,12,13,14,14,17,19,20,23,24,25,27,30,30; **9:**5; **20:**9,9; **22:**17,19,20; **23:**35,35,35; **24:**30,32,32,32; **26:**19; **27:**11; **30:**1,1,2,2,3,3,7,7,9,9,18; **Ecc 1:**12,13,14,16,16,16,17,17; **2:**1,1,2,3,3,4,4,5,6,7,7,8,8,9,10,10,11,11,12,13,14,15,15,15,17,18,18,18,19,24; **3:**10,12,14,16,17,18,

I'LL (38)

I'M (25)

IN (11336)

IS (7121)

ISN'T (33)

IT (5230)

IT'S (19)

ITS (1101)

ITSELF (53)

MAY (1262)

ME (4036)

MY (4637)

MYSELF (155)

NOT (5859)

O (67)

OF (24887)

OH (34)

ON (4894)

For "ON" as a proper name, see the Main Concordance.

OUR (1217)

9,9,9,9,25,26,26; 12:27; 17:3,9; 34:9,9; Lev 25:20; Nu 10:31; 11:6; 13:33; 14:3; 20:3,4,15,15,16,19; 21:2; 27:3,4,4; 31:49; 32:5,16,16,17,18,19,25,26,26,27; 36:2,3,4; Dt 1:6,19,20,25,28,28,41; 2:1,8,29,33,36,37; 3:3,3; 4:7; 5:2,3,24,25,27,27; 6:4,20,22,23,24,25,25; 18:16; 21:7,7; 26:3,7,7,7,15; 29:15,18,29,29; 31:17; 32:3,27,31,31; Jos 2:11,14,19,24; 5:13; 7:9; 9:11,11,13,19,24; 17:4; 18:6; 21:2; 22:19,23,27,28,28,29; 24:17,17,17,17,18,24; Jdg 6:13; 7:18; 9:8,10,12,14; 10:10; 11:2,6,10,19,24; 13:23; 14:3,15; 16:23,23,23,24,24,24,24,24; 18:5,19; 19:18,19; 20:23,28; 21:7,18; Ru 2:20,20; 3:9,12; 4:3; 1Sa 2:2; 4:3; 5:7,10,11; 7:8; 8:20; 9:7,12; 12:10,19; 14:6,10,10; 16:16; 17:9,47; 20:29; 24:15; 25:14,16,17; 29:4; 30:23; 2Sa 7:22; 10:12,12; 15:15; 18:12; 19:9,41,43; 22:32; 1Ki 1:2,11,43,47; 8:21,40,53,57,57,58,58,59,61,65; 12:10; 18:5; 20:31,31; 2Ki 2:19; 4:9; 18:22; 19:19; 1Ch 12:17,19; 13:2,2,3; 15:13; 16:14,35; 17:20; 19:13,13; 28:2,8; 29:10,13,15,15,16,18; 2Ch 2:4,5; 6:31; 10:10; 13:10,11,12; 14:7,11,11; 19:7; 20:6,7,9,12,12; 28:13,13; 29:6,6,9,9,9; 32:8,8,11; Ezr 4:3; 5:12; 7:27; 8:17,18,21,21,21,22,23,23,25,30,31,33; 9:6,6,6,7,7,7,7,7,8,8,8,8,9,9,9,10,13,13,13,13,15; 10:2,3,3,14,14,14; Ne 4:4,9,11,15,15,20,23; 5:2,3,3,3,4,5,5,5,5,5,5,8,9,9; 6:1,16,16; 8:10; 9:9,16,32,32,32,32,34,34,34,34,36,37,37,37,38,38,38; 10:29,30,30,32,33,34,34,34,35,36,36,36,36,36,37,37,37,37,37,37,38,39; 13:2,4,18,27; Job 8:9; 15:10; 22:20; 28:22; 31:2,2,15; 36:26; 37:5,19,19,23; Ps 8:1,9; 12:4,4; 18:31; 20:5,5,7; 22:4; 33:20,20,21,22; 35:21; 40:3; 44:1,1,2,2,5,5,7,7,8,9,10,13,18,18,20,20,24,25; 46:1,7,11; 47:3,4,6; 48:1,8,14,14; 50:3; 59:11; 60:10,12; 62:8; 65:1,1,3,5; 66:8,9,9,11,12; 67:6; 68:19,19,20,28; 77:13; 78:3,5; 79:4,9,9,10,12; 80:6,6; 81:1,3; 84:9; 85:4,9,12; 89:17,18,18; 90:1,8,8,9,9,10,10,12,14,17,17,17; 92:13; 94:23; 95:1,6,7; 98:3; 99:5,8,9,9; 103:10,10,12; 105:7; 106:6,7,47; 108:11,13; 113:5; 115:3; 116:5; 118:23; 122:2,9; 123:2,2; 124:1,2,8; 126:2,2,4; 135:2,5; 136:23,24; 137:2,3,3; 141:7; 144:12,12,13,13,13,14,14; 147:1,5,7; Pr 1:13; Ecc 1:10; SS 1:16,17,17; 2:9,12,15; 7:13; 8:8; Isa 1:10; 3:6; 4:1,1,1; 25:9; 26:8,13; 28:15,15; 33:2,2,20,21,22,22,22; 35:2; 36:7; 37:20; 38:20; 40:3,8; 42:17; 47:4; 52:10; 53:1,4,4,5,5,6; 55:7; 56:12; 59:10,12,12,12,12,13,13,13; 61:2,6; 63:16,16,16,17,18; 64:6,6,7,8,9,11,11; Jer 3:22,23,24,24,25,25,25,25,25,25; 4:10; 5:19,24; 6:24; 8:14; 9:18,18,19,19,19,21,21; 11:21; 14:7,20,20,22,22; 16:10,19; 17:12; 18:12,12,18; 20:10; 21:13; 23:6,36; 26:16; 31:6; 33:16; 35:6,8,8,8,10; 37:3; 42:2,6,6,20; 43:2; 44:17,17,17,19; 46:16,16; 50:28; 51:9,10,34,35,35,51; La 3:40,41,41,46; 4:17,17,18,18,18,18,19,20; 5:1,2,2,3,4,5,7,9,9,10,15,15,16,17,17,21; Eze 11:3,15; 33:10,21,24; 36:2; 37:11,11; 40:1; Da 1:13; 9:6,6,6,7,8,8,8,9,10,12,13,13,14,15,16,16,17,18; Hos 6:1; 7:5; 8:2; 14:2,2,3,3; Joel 1:16,16; Am 6:13; Mic 2:4; 4:5,11; 5:5,5,5,6,6; 7:17,19,19,20; Hab 3:2,2; Zec 1:6; 9:7; 13:9; Mal 2:10; Mt 3:9; 6:9,11,12,12; 8:17,17; 20:33; 21:42; 23:30; 25:8; 27:25; Mk 11:10; 12:11,29; Lk 1:55,71,72,73,74,75,78,79; 3:8; 7:5,5; 10:11; 11:3,4; 13:26; 17:5,10; 19:14; 22:49; 23:2,41; 24:20,22,24,32; Jn 3:11; 4:12,20; 6:31; 7:35,51; 8:39,53; 9:20; 11:11,48,48; 12:38; 14:23; Ac 1:17,17; 2:8,11,39; 3:12,13; 4:25; 5:30; 6:4; 7:2,11,12,15,17,19,19,38,39,44,45; 10:28; 13:17,31,32; 15:10,11,24,25,26; 16:20; 17:20,28; 19:27,37; 20:21; 21:3,5,7,15,21,25,28,28; 22:3,14; 24:14; 26:5,6,7; 27:7,10,10; 28:17,17,21; Ro 1:4,7; 3:5,20; 4:1,12,17,24,25,25; 5:1,3,5,11,21; 6:6,23; 7:25; 8:16,18,23,23,26,27,39; 9:10; 10:16; 13:11; 15:2,6,30; 16:1,9,18,20,23; 1Co 1:1,2,3,6,7,8,9,10,30; 2:7; 4:12; 5:3,4,7; 6:11; 9:1; 10:1,6; 12:24; 15:3,14,31,57; 16:12; 2Co 1:1,2,3,4,5,7,7,7,8,10,11,12,12,12,18,22; 3:2,2,3,5; 4:3,6,10,10,11,17,18; 5:2,4,9,13,13; 6:3,11,12; 7:3,4,13,14; 8:5,9,13,17,19,22,23,24; 9:3; 10:11,11,13,14,15,15,15; 12:18; 13:4,9; Gal 1:3,4,4; 2:4,16; 3:24; 4:6,26; 6:14,18; Eph 1:2,3,12,14,17; 2:3,14; 3:11; 5:20; 6:12,24; Php 1:2; 3:20,21; 4:20; Col 1:1,2,3,7,7; 2:13,14; 4:3,8,9,14; 1Th 1:2,3,3,5; 2:1,2,4,5,6,8,9,17,18,19,19,19,20; 3:2,5,7,9,11,11,13,13; 5:9,23,28; 2Th 1:1,8,10,11,12,12; 2:1,1,14,14,16,16; 3:7,14,18; 1Ti 1:1,1,2,12,14; 2:3; 4:10; 6:1,3,14,17; 2Ti 1:2,8,10; 4:15; Titus 1:3,4,4; 2:10,13; 3:4,6,14; Phm 1,1,2,2,3; Heb 1:1; 3:1,6,14; 4:15,16; 6:20,20; 7:14,26; 9:14; 10:22,22; 12:2,10,29; 13:9,20,23; Jas 1:27; 2:1,21; 3:9; 1Pe 1:3; 2:24; 2Pe 1:1,2,3,8,11,14,16; 2:20; 3:2,4,15,15,18; 1Jn 1:1,1,3,4,9,9; 2:2; 3:5,16,16,19,20,20,21; 4:10; 5:4; 2Jn 12; 3Jn 12; Jude 4,4,17,21,25,25; Rev 1:5; 4:11; 5:10; 6:10; 7:3,10,12; 11:15; 12:10,10,10; 19:1,5,6

OURS (18)

Ge 26:20; 34:21,23; Dt 21:20; Jos 9:12; 22:24,25,27; Ru 3:2; 2Ch 14:7; Eze 35:10; Mk 12:7; Lk 20:14; 1Co 1:2; 1Th 3:12; 2Pe 1:1; 1Jn 2:2; Rev 1:9

OURSELVES (48)

Ge 11:4,4; 34:16; 43:7; 44:16; Nu 31:50; 32:17; Dt 2:35; 3:7; Jos 22:17; Jdg 19:19; 2Sa 19:42; 2Ki 7:9; Ezr 8:21; Job 34:4; Pr 7:18; Isa 7:6; 58:3; Jer 26:19; Da 3:16; Jn 4:42; Ac 21:1; Ro 8:23; 14:7,7,12; 15:1; 1Co 11:31; 15:30; 2Co 1:4,9,12; 3:1,5,5; 4:2,5,5; 5:12; 6:4; 7:1; 10:12; 12:19; Gal 2:17; 1Th 3:1; 2Th 3:9; 2Pe 1:18; 1Jn 1:8

OUT (2440)

Ge 2:9,19,22,23; 3:22,24; 4:8,10,16,22; 6:14; 7:23; 8:7,8,9,10,12,16,17,18,19; 9:10,18,24; 10:5,32; 11:31; 12:4,5,9; 13:11; 14:5,8,14,17,18; 15:7,14; 18:12; 19:5,8,9,10,12,14,14,16,17,24,29; 22:3,10,11; 23:16; 24:7,10,11,13,15,22,29,30,31,43,45,53,63; 25:25,26; 27:3,9,34; 28:10,14; 30:14,16; 31:4,33; 34:1,6,24,28; 35:5,14; 37:7,28; 38:24,25,28,28,29,29,30; 39:12,13,15,18; 40:14,17; 41:2,3,13,18,46; 43:23,30,31; 44:15; 45:1,25; 46:1; 47:10,30; 48:14; 50:24; Ex 1:10; 2:10,11,13,23; 3:7,8,10,11,12,17,20; 4:4,4,6,7; 5:8,10; 6:1,6,7,11,13,26,27; 7:2,4,5,5,15,19; 8:5,6,12,16,17; 9:9,10,15,19,22,23,29,29,33,33; 10:11,12,13,21,22,28; 11:1,10; 12:17,22,39,42,51; 13:3,3,3,8,9,14,14,16,18; 14:8,10,11,15,16,21,26,27; 15:12,25; 16:1,1,3,4,6,27,29,32; 17:1,3,4,5,6,9,14; 18:1,7,18; 19:2,5,17,22,24; 20:2,2; 21:27; 22:6,23,27; 23:15,23,28,29,30,31; 24:13; 25:11,18,29,31,36; 27:8; 28:28,35; 29:12,46; 32:1,4,7,8,11,12,19,23,24,25,32,33; 33:1,2,8; 34:1,4,11,18,24,34,34; 36:1,3; 37:2,7,16,17,22,25; 38:7; 39:3,21,30; 40:4,23,36,37; Lev 1:15; 2:9,13; 4:7,18,25,30,34; 5:9; 6:12,13; 8:15; 9:9,23,24; 10:2; 11:45; 13:12,20,25,39,42,45,56; 14:38,40,43,45; 16:17,18,24; 17:13; 18:24,25,28,28; 19:31,36; 20:22,23; 22:33; 23:43; 24:8,10,10; 25:38,42,55; 26:10,13,14,15,26,33,45; 27:33; Nu 1:1; 2:9,16,17,17,24,31,34; 9:1,8,17,18,19,20,21,21,22,22,23; 10:2,5,6,6,7,12,13,17,21,25,28,29,33,34,35; 11:2,20,24,26,31,32,32; 12:4,4,13; 13:3; 14:25,40; 15:41; 16:13,22,27,35,39,46; 17:9; 19:16; 20:5,8,8,10,11,16,16,18,20,22; 21:5,11,13,23,28,32,33; 22:5,6,11,19,36; 23:22; 24:2,6,8,17,17,19; 26:4,11; 27:17,17,21; 28:7; 31:3,28,30,47; 32:11,21,23,39; 33:1,3,3,38,52,55; 35:21; Dt 1:19,22,27,33,40,44; 2:1,12,21,22,23,24,32; 3:1,16; 4:12,15,20,20,33,34,36,37,38,45,46; 5:4,6,6,15,22,23,26; 6:12,12,19,21,23; 7:1,6,8,17,19,22,24; 8:4,7,9,14,14,15; 9:3,4,4,5,10,12,14,17,23,26,28,29; 10:1,3,3,4; 11:23; 12:3,16,24,29; 13:3,5,10,10; 14:2; 15:23; 16:1; 18:5,12; 19:1,11; 20:1; 21:2; 22:25,27; 23:4; 24:9,11; 25:4,6,11,17,18,19; 26:7,8; 27:26; 28:6,19,32; 29:5,7,20,21,25; 31:1; 32:39; 33:18,21,22,27; Jos 2:2,3,3,6,7,7,10,23; 3:1,3,10; 4:16,17,18,20; 5:4,5; 6:1,22,22,23,23; 7:2,2,9,23; 8:3,3,5,14,18,18,22,26; 9:13,17,24; 10:22,23; 11:4; 13:6,10,13; 14:11,11,12; 15:7,9,14; 16:7; 17:13,18; 18:4,8,12,14,15,19,20; 19:1,13,17,24,29,32,34,40; 21:3,4; 22:3; 23:5,5,9,13; 24:5,6,10,12,17,18; Jdg 1:21,23,24,27,28,29,30,31,32,33,35; 2:1,3,12,15,16,18,21,23; 3:9,15,22,23; 4:18,22; 5:4,12,28; 6:6,7,8,8,9,13,14,19,20,30,38; 7:4,15,21,23,24; 8:5,25; 9:8,15,20,20,27,29,33,34,35,35,38,39,41,42,43; 10:10,14; 11:13,16,23,31,34,40; 12:1,2; 13:9; 14:9,14,14; 15:4,9,18,19; 16:20,21,25,25; 18:2,11,14,17,23; 19:22,24,27,28,30; 20:10,20,21,25,31,33,37,42; 21:17,21; Ru 1:7; 2:3,3,16,18; 3:15,18; 1Sa 1:15,16; 2:5,28; 3:3,12; 4:1; 5:10; 6:6; 7:3,6,8,9,11; 8:8,18,20; 9:10,11; 10:2,18,19,23; 11:2,7; 12:6,8,10; 13:10,14,17,23; 14:11,26,27,34,38; 15:6,11,11,13,18; 17:4,8,20,20,23,25,25,33,49,55,56; 18:6,27,27,30; 19:3,3,8,8; 20:11,12,17,35,37; 21:5; 23:15,22,23,24; 24:2,8,8,14,21; 25:15; 26:4,5,14,20; 27:1; 28:12,13,17,18; 30:21,22; 2Sa 1:7; 2:13,23,26; 3:25; 4:5,9; 5:18,20,20,22,24; 6:6,8,20; 7:6,23,23; 10:3,7,8; 11:1,3,13,15,17,22,23; 12:11,31; 13:9,15,17,18; 14:7; 15:2,5,16,17; 16:5,5,7,7; 17:1,19,21,21,22,23; 18:2,2,3,4,6,8,12,24,25,28; 19:7,7,15,19; 20:7,7,8,10; 21:10,17; 22:7,9,13,17,20; 23:16; 24:12,16,20; 1Ki 1:29,30; 2:30,34,46; 3:7,26; 4:33; 6:1,23,27,31,33,34; 8:9,16,21,22,38,51,51,52,53,53,54; 9:9; 10:13; 11:12,18,29,29,31,32,34; 12:18,25,28; 13:2,3,4,4,4,5,21,28; 14:21,24; 16:3,20; 17:20,21,21; 19:11,13,21; 20:16,17,18,18,19,27,33,39; 21:10,21,26; 22:22,25,32,34; 2Ki 2:3,12,21,23,23,23,24; 3:6,9; 4:1,18,21,25,34,35,37,39,40,40; 5:2,11; 6:5,7,7,13,15; 7:10,12,13,14,16; 9:11,15,17,19,21,23,30,32,35; 10:9,12,22,25,26; 11:12,14,15; 14:27; 15:16; 16:3,6,7,13; 17:7,8,11,36; 18:12,18,28,31; 19:9,14,31,31,35; 21:2,7,13,13,15; 22:9; 23:29; 24:7; 25:7; 1Ch 4:10; 5:20; 7:11; 8:13; 9:28,32; 11:18; 12:17; 13:9,11; 14:8,11,11,15,15; 15:13; 16:35; 17:5,21,21; 19:3,7,8,9; 20:1,3,4; 21:10; 23:29,32; 28:7; 2Ch 2:4; 5:10; 6:5,12,13,29; 7:11,22; 8:16; 10:18; 12:7,13; 13:9,11,14; 14:9,10; 15:2; 16:2,14; 18:24,31,33; 19:2,4; 20:7,9,11,17,20,21; 21:15,19; 22:7; 23:11,14,14; 24:12; 26:11,19,20; 28:3,9; 29:7,16,16,18; 30:12; 31:1,5; 32:18,20; 33:2,7,15; 34:14,17,21,25; 35:16,20,24; Ezr 1:7,8; 4:4; 6:8,12,13; 8:25,26,29,30,31,33; 9:5; Ne 2:12,13; 3:17; 4:5,10,19,21; 5:13,13,13,15; 6:8; 8:1,15,16; 9:4,7,18,21,27,28; 10:32,33; 11:1; 12:27; 13:8,14,25; Est 2:11,22; 3:12,15; 4:1,5,6,17; 5:2,9; 7:7; 8:9,14; 9:1,13,28; Job 1:11,12; 2:5,7,11; 3:24; 7:11; 8:8; 9:3,4,8; 10:1,6,10,18; 11:13; 13:9,16; 15:13; 16:7,20; 17:13; 18:5,6; 20:15,25,25; 21:17; 23:5,14; 24:12; 26:7,10; 27:21,23; 28:3,15,25; 29:6; 30:8,20; 31:38; 33:21,23; 35:9,12; 36:26,29; 37:9,18,22; 38:1,13,14,32,41; 40:6; 41:18,19; Ps 3:4; 6:6; 7:15; 9:5; 10:15; 14:7; 16:4; 17:9; 18:8,12,16,19; 19:4,5; 22:2,5,9,14,14; 27:3; 30:1; 31:17; 34:6,16,17; 37:7; 40:2,2; 41:6; 42:4; 44:2,9,20; 51:1,9; 53:6; 55:17,23; 57:2; 58:2,6; 60:6,10; 62:8; 66:17; 68:6,7; 69:3,16,24,28; 72:12; 73:15; 75:8; 77:1,1,2,10; 78:16,20,21,52,55; 79:3,6; 80:8; 81:5,7,10; 84:2; 88:1,9; 89:26; 94:4; 102:T,26; 104:2,23; 105:37,39,41,43; 106:29,45; 107:6,14,20,23,28,28,41; 108:7,11; 109:13,14,15,21; 114:1; 119:45,48,94,139,146,155; 126:6; 130:1; 135:7; 136:6,11; 138:7; 139:3; 140:5; 142:2; 143:6,11; 149:9; Pr 1:20,21,23,24; 2:3; 3:21; 4:21; 6:19; 7:10,15; 8:1,4,27,29; 9:3,15; 10:9; 12:23; 13:9; 14:3,5; 16:4; 17:14; 18:15; 19:5,9,26; 20:5,8,20,26; 21:13; 22:10,10; 23:4; 24:20; 25:2,27; 26:20; 29:21; 30:17; 31:16,18; Ecc 2:1; 7:25; 8:11,17; 12:9; SS 1:3; 3:11; 7:13; 8:11; Isa 1:15,16; 2:3; 3:7; 5:2; 7:3; 10:23,30; 11:11; 13:3; 14:11,19,22,26,27; 15:4,4,5; 16:8,10,12; 17:10,11; 19:20; 22:5,12,16; 23:11; 24:11,18; 25:11,11; 26:14,17,21; 27:8; 28:20,27; 29:4,4,18,21; 30:1,14,24; 31:3; 34:1,3,11; 36:3,13,16; 37:9,14,32,32,36; 40:6,22,22,26; 42:2,3,5,5,13,14,25; 43:8,13,17,17,25; 44:3,7,13,24,24,26; 45:12; 46:6,6,7; 47:13; 48:13,14,19,20,21; 49:9; 50:6,9; 51:4,6,13,22; 52:11,11; 53:2,12; 54:3; 55:11,12; 57:4,6,13,14; 58:2; 62:1; 65:2,14,14,20; 66:24; Jer 1:9,14; 2:6; 3:8; 4:1,7,7,31; 5:6; 6:1,7,7,11,12,25,29; 7:18,20,22; 10:3,12,13,18,25; 11:4,4,11,12,15; 12:5,13; 14:16,16; 15:1,6; 16:13,14,15,15; 17:8,19,22; 18:23; 19:2,13; 20:8,18; 21:9,12; 22:4,20,20,28; 23:3,7,8,8,19,39; 26:23; 27:2; 30:7,10,15,23; 31:4,6,32,37,40; 32:9,10,21,29; 34:7,13,13; 35:16; 36:30; 37:5,7,10; 38:8,10,13,22,23; 39:7,14; 41:6,10; 42:18,18; 44:6,17,18,19,19,25,25; 45:3; 46:3,27; 47:2; 48:4,12,20,31,44,45; 49:2,2,3; 50:8,25; 51:12,15,16,25,34,39,44,45,48; 52:11; La 1:17; 2:4,8,11,18,19,19; 3:8,8; 4:11; Eze 1:4,11,13,22,23; 2:9; 3:18,22,23,25; 4:10,11; 6:6,11,12,14; 7:8; 8:3; 9:1,7,8; 10:7,7; 11:7,9,13; 12:3,4,4,5,6,7,7; 13:2,15,17; 14:9,13,19,22; 15:7; 16:5,27,36; 17:6,7,7; 20:6,6,8,9,10,13,14,21,22,28,38,41; 21:12,19,20,31,31; 22:22,31; 23:8,43; 24:6; 25:7,7,13,16,16,17; 26:5; 27:26,26,28,33; 28:18; 29:4; 30:9,9,15,15; 31:12; 32:7; 33:8,27; 34:13; 35:3; 36:18,24; 37:1,21; 38:4,8; 39:9,14,14,17,29; 42:15; 44:3,8,19; 46:2,8,9,9,9,10,10,12,12,18; 47:1,2; Da 2:14,34,45; 3:26,26; 4:36; 6:23; 7:3,10; 8:9,27; 9:11,15,23,25,27; 11:4,11,20,40,44; Hos 1:11; 2:10,15; 5:1,10; 6:9; 7:14; 8:2,5; 9:4,13,15; 11:1,9; 12:9; 13:4,13; Joel 1:14; 2:28,29; 3:7,18; Am 2:10; 3:1; 4:3,3; 5:3,3,8; 6:10; 7:2,5,12; 9:6; Jnh 1:5,7,14; 4:5; Mic 1:11; 2:1,13; 3:4; 4:2,10; 5:2; 6:4; 7:9,15,17; Na 1:6; Hab 1:2; 2:11; 3:13,14; Zep 1:4,11,17; 2:13; 3:8; Hag 1:9; 2:5; Zec 1:16; 2:2; 4:7,12; 5:3,4; 6:1,5,7,12; 12:1,9,10; 14:3,8; Mal 3:10,14; 4:2; Mt 2:6,7,15; 3:5,9,16; 4:19; 5:13,26,29; 7:4,5,15,22; 8:3,16,31,32,34; 9:17,27,31,32,33,34,38; 10:1,5,8,16; 11:7,8,9,16; 12:11, 13, 13, 14, 19, 20, 24, 26, 27, 27, 28, 35, 35, 43; 13:1,3,41,41,52; 14:25,26,29,30,31; 15:11,17,18,19,22,23; 17:18,19,27; 18:9,15,28; 20:1,3,5,6; 21:12,17,39; 22:10,15; 23:24; 24:4,17,26,26,32; 25:1,6,6,8,25; 26:15,28,30,51,55,69,71; 27:18,32,46,50,53,60; 28:14; Mk 1:5,10,12,17,23,25,26,34,39,41,45; 2:12,13; 3:5,5,6,11,14,15,21,22,23; 4:1,3,22; 5:2,5,8,10,13,14,30,40; 6:7,12,13,24,38,48,49,54; 7:15,19,20,21,26; 8:15; 9:18,25,26,28,29,38,43,47; 11:11,13,15,19; 12:8,38,44,44; 13:5,15,28; 14:24,26,48,68; 15:10,18,20,34,46; 16:8,9,17,20; Lk 1:22,62; 2:8; 3:7,8; 4:29,33,35,35,36,41,42; 5:3,4,13,27,36,37; 6:10,12,42,42,45,45; 7:12,13,24,25,26,32; 8:2,3,5,8,17,22,28,29,33,35,35,38,46; 9:1,2,6,38,40,49,51; 10:2,3,35; 11:14,15,18,19,19,20,24,27; 12:15,33,59; 13:15,28,32; 14:5,19,21,23,35; 15:15,18,28; 16:17; 17:13; 18:7,38; 19:8,15,21,22,40,45; 20:12,15; 21:4,4,8,21,37; 22:20,39; 23:32,46; 24:50; Jn 1:15,16; 2:8,10,15,16; 3:22; 4:30,44; 5:29; 7:17,28,51,52; 8:44; 9:22,34,35; 10:3,4,9,28,29; 11:20,31,43,44,57; 12:9,13,18,31,42,44; 13:30; 15:19,26; 16:2; 17:6,15; 18:4,29,38; 19:4,4,5,13,17; 20:2,16,27; 21:3,3,5,18; Ac 1:18; 2:17,18,33; 3:19; 4:30; 5:6,9,10,19; 7:7,19,36,40,45,58,60; 8:1,7,27,39; 9:1,40; 10:17,18,23,45; 11:19; 12:4,9,15,17; 13:17,29; 14:6,10,14; 15:24; 16:11,18,30,37,40; 17:5,26,27; 18:6,23; 19:13,13,16; 20:1; 21:1,4,5,38; 22:24,25,30; 23:6,7,30,31; 26:24; 27:2,4,43; 28:1,3,11; Ro 3:5; 5:5; 7:18; 9:21,27,28; 10:18,21; 11:24,33; 16:17; 1Co 4:19; 5:2; 9:9; 10:13; 14:23; 2Co 2:4; 4:6; 5:13; 6:17; 7:1; 9:14; 11:23; 12:2; Gal 4:6,15; 5:15; Eph 1:11; 2:15; 3:16; 4:29; 5:4,10,21; Php 1:15,15,16,17,19; 2:3,12,17,21; 3:2; 4:15; Col 1:23; 1Th 1:8; 2:15,17; 3:4,5; 2Th 1:9; 2:7; 1Ti 1:14; 4:6; 5:18,21; 6:7; 2Ti 2:22; 4:2,6; Titus 3:6; Heb 1:11; 3:16; 8:9; 11:3; 12:1; Jas 3:10; 5:4; 1Pe 1:11,17; 2:9; 2Pe 3:5; 1Jn 1:6,10; 2:19; 4:1,18; 5:2,10; 2Jn 7,8; 3Jn 7,10; Jude 5; Rev 1:16; 3:5,12,16; 5:6; 6:2,4,10; 7:2,10,14; 8:13; 9:3,17,18; 12:2,4,7,14,16; 13:1,11; 14:15,17,20; 15:6; 16:1,2,2,3,4,8,10,12,13,13,13,14,17,17; 17:8; 18:4,16,19; 19:15,21; 20:1,8; 21:2,10,16

SHALL (482)

Ge 2:23; 9:6; 15:5; 16:11; 17:10; 18:17; 24:5; 26:11; 30:31; 31:32; 41:40; 45:10; 49:10,10; Ex 2:7; 3:13,15; 4:15; 12:14,22; 13:7; 19:13; 20:3,4,5,7,9,10,13,14,15,16,17,17; 21:2,4,4,6; 22:13,13,16; 25:35,36; 26:24; 27:9,11,12,13,18; 28:17,18,19,20,32; 29:9,10,15,19; 30:10,20,21,29,36; 34:21,21; 35:2; Lev 1:5,8,11,12,15,15,17,17; 2:2,8,9,16; 3:2,8,11,13,16; 4:5,7,7,8,10,15,17,18,19,21,25,26,31,31,34,35,35; 5:6,8,10,12; 6:10,10,16,22,23,26; 7:3,5,16,31,33; 12:7; 13:3,6,8,11,13,15,17,20,22,23,25,27,28,30,34,37,44,54; 14:4,5,7,11,12,15,18,19,25,29,30,38,39,48,50,52; 16:9,10,11,14,15,15,18,18,19,20,21,22,24,24,25; 17:4; 19:6; 23:31; 25:10,11,30; Nu 1:51; 4:27; 5:16,17,18,19,24; 6:20; 8:24; 15:4,15; 18:10; 19:9; 35:19,19,21; 36:7; Dt 1:35,37; 5:7,8,9,11,13,14,17,18,19,20,21,21; 12:7,7; 14:26; 15:2,2; 16:18; 18:1,2; 19:12; 20:2,3,5,8,9,11,11; 21:2,3,5,6,7,13,19,20; 22:15,17,18,19,19,21,21,24,25,29; 25:2,5,6,7,8,9,10,12,19; 26:4,5,11,12; 27:8,12,13,14,15,16,17,18,19,20,21,22,23,24,25,26; 31:2,11; Jos 6:17; 7:14,14,14,15; 8:2; Jdg 1:2; 2:2,2; 6:31; 7:4,4,4,4; 20:18,23,28; 21:16; 1Sa 5:8; 6:2; 10:2; 11:12; 14:37; 23:2; 28:11; 30:8; 2Sa 2:1,1; 5:19; 15:20; 19:23,38; 21:3,3; 24:13; 1Ki 1:13,17,24,30; 2:24; 3:26; 8:25,29; 9:5; 18:31; 22:6,6,15; 2Ki 3:8; 6:15,21,21; 17:12,36; 20:9,9; 23:27; 1Ch 14:10; 2Ch 6:16; 7:18; 18:5,5,14,14; 23:3; 25:4; Ezr 9:14; Job 2:10; 33:28; 38:3; 40:7; 42:4; Ps 27:1,1; 81:9,9; 95:11; 101:4; 116:12; SS 8:8; Isa 1:18,18; 6:8; 10:11; 14:32; 29:16; 40:4,4,6; 44:19,19,26,26; 50:11; Jer 15:2; Eze 3:27; 4:3; 12:25; 17:16,18; 21:7,10,27; 38:19; 45:21; 46:12,12,13,15; Da 6:7; Hos 13:4; Joel 3:21; Mic 6:6,6,7,11; Mt 4:4; 5:21,27; 6:31,31,31; 8:7; 16:22; 17:17,17; 18:21; 19:18,18,18,18; 27:22; Mk 4:30,30; 6:24; 9:19,19; 10:19,19,19,19,19; 15:12; Lk 3:5,5; 4:4; 9:41; 12:17; 13:18,20; 16:3; 18:20,20,20,20; 20:13; Jn 3:16; 6:5,39,40,68; 8:33; 10:16,28; 12:27; 13:8; 18:11; 19:15; Ac 2:37; 21:22; 22:10; Ro 3:5,9; 4:1,18; 5:9,10; 6:1,1,14,15; 7:7,7; 8:31,35,35; 9:14,20,30; 13:9,9,9,9; 1Co 4:21,21; 6:15; 11:22,22; 13:12,12; 14:15,26; 15:49; Php 1:22; 2Th 3:10; Heb 2:3; 3:11; 4:3,5; 11:32; Jas 2:11,11; 1Jn 3:2,2; Rev 1:7

SHE (1007)

Ge 2:23,23; 3:6,6,12,20; 4:1,1,2,17,25; 11:29,30; 12:15,18,19; 16:1,2,4,4,4,4,5,5,5,6,8,13,13,15; 17:16; 18:12,15; 19:26,33,33,35,35,37,38; 20:2,3,5,5,12,12; 21:7,10,14,15,16,16,16,16,19,19; 22:20; 23:2; 24:14,15,16,18,19,19,20,24,25,44,45,46,46,47,58,64,65,67; 25:2,21,22,22; 26:7,7,7,9,9; 27:14,15,16,17,17,42; 29:9,12,32,32,33,33,33,33,34,34,34,35,35,35,35,35; 30:1,1,1,3,3,4,5,6,8,9,9,11,13,15,16,17,18,20,21,23,24; 35:17,18,18,18; 36:14; 38:3,4,5,5,14,14,14,15,15,16,16,17,18,18,19,19,23,24,25,25,25,25,26,28,29; 39:10,12,13,14,14,16,17; Ex 2:2,2,2,3,3,3,5,6,6,6,8,10,10; 4:25,26; 6:23,25; 21:3,4,7,8,11,22; 22:16; 35:25; Lev 12:2,4,5,5,6,7,8,8,8; 15:20,20,22,23,25,25,26,26,28,28,28,29; 18:7,9,11,12,13,14,15; 19:20; 20:18; 21:3,9,9; 22:12,13,13; Nu 5:13,14,14,27,27,27,28; 12:10,14,14,15; 26:59; 30:4,5,6,6,6,7,8,11,13; Dt 21:13,13,13,14; 22:15,19,21,21,24,26; 24:2,2,4; 25:6,7,11; 28:56,56,57,57; Jos 2:4,6,6,8,15,15,16,21,21,21; 6:17,25,25; 15:18,18,18,19; Jdg 1:14,14,14,15; 4:5,6,18,19,21,22; 5:25,25,26,26,26,28,29; 11:34,36,37,38,38,39,39; 13:9,14,14; 14:17,17,17; 16:8,9,12,14,15,16,18,19,20; 17:3,4; 19:2,2,2,3; 20:5; Ru 1:3,6,7,7,9,18,20; 2:3,3,6,7,7,10,10,13,14,14,14,15,17,17,18,18,18,18,19,19,20,23; 3:6,9,14,15,16; 4:13,13; 1Sa 1:7,11,12,13,18,18,20,22,23,24,26; 2:5,5,19,20,21; 4:19,19,20,20,21,22; 18:19,21; 25:3,18,19,19,20,20,23,24,35,36,41; 28:12,14,21,24,24,25; 2Sa 4:4; 6:16,16; 11:3,4,4,4,26,27; 12:24; 13:2,8,9,10,11,12,14,16,18,19,19,19; 14:4,4,5,11,27; 20:17,17,18; 21:8,8,10; 1Ki 1:2,4,17,22,28; 2:14,16,19,20,21; 3:17,19,20,20,27; 10:1,2,2,5,6,10,13,13; 14:5,5,17,21,31; 15:13; 17:11,12,15,18; 21:8,9,11,15; 2Ki 4:2,5,5,6,7,9,12,13,14,15,16,17,21,22,23,24,25,26,27,27,27,28,36,37,37; 5:2,3; 6:28,29; 8:2,3,6,6; 9:30,31,34; 11:1,2,13,14,15,16,16; 12:1; 14:2; 15:2; 21:19; 22:1,14,15; 23:31,36; 24:8,18; 1Ch 2:21,26,35,49; 7:14,23; 15:29,29; 2Ch 9:1,1,1,4,5,9,12,12,12; 11:19; 12:13; 15:16; 22:10,11,11; 23:12,13,15; 24:1; 25:1; 26:3; 34:22,23; Ne 6:14; Est 1:11,15,17,19; 2:1,7,9,12,13,13,14,14,15,16,17,20,20; 4:4,4,10; 5:12,12; 7:8; 8:3,4,5; Job 39:14,16,16,18,18; Ps 45:14; 46:5; 84:3; Pr 1:20,21,21; 2:17; 3:14,15,18; 4:6,6,8,8,9; 5:4,6,6; 7:11,12,13,13,21,21,26; 8:2,3; 9:1,2,2,3,3,4,13,14,16; 14:33; 23:22,25,28; 30:20; 31:10,12,13,14,15,15,16,16,17,18,19,20,21,22,22,24,25,25,26,27; Ecc 7:26; SS 8:2,5,8,9,9; Isa 1:21; 3:26; 8:3; 13:20; 16:12,12; 19:14; 21:2; 23:3,17; 27:7; 29:2,2; 34:13,15; 40:2; 49:15,15; 51:18,18; 66:7,7,7,8; Jer 3:1,6,7,7,7,8,9; 4:17; 6:7; 11:15; 12:8; 15:9; 46:8; 48:9,11,11,11,20,26,27,39,42; 49:24; 50:9,12,12,13,14,15,15,29,29; 51:6,7,8,9; 52:1; La 1:1,1,2,3,3,4,8,9,10; Eze 5:6,6; 16:49; 19:2,3,5,5; 23:5,5,7,7,8,8,9,10,11,12,13,14,14,16,16,17,17,18,19,19,19,20,43; 24:7,7,7; 26:2,5,5; 30:18; 32:22; Da 5:10; 11:6,6; Hos 1:3,8; 2:2,3,5,6,7,7,7,8,12,13,13,13,15,15; 3:1; 8:8; Am 1:3,6,9; Mic 1:7; 5:3; 7:10,10; Na 2:10; 3:10; Zep 2:15,15; 3:2,2,2,2; Zec 9:3,4; Mal 2:14; Mt 1:18,21,25; 8:15; 9:18,21,25; 12:42; 14:7,8; 15:23,25,27; 20:21; 22:28; 26:7,10,12,12,13,69; Mk 1:31; 5:23,26,26,26,27,27,28,29,29,42; 6:19,22,24,24,28; 7:25,26,28,30; 10:12,12; 12:23,44,44; 14:3,6,8,8,8,9,67,67,67,69; 16:10,11; Lk 1:25,36,40,42,45,57; 2:7,7,36,36,37,37,38; 4:39; 7:12,37,38,38,38,39,39,44,46; 8:44,47,47,47,47,50,52,53,55; 10:39,40; 11:31; 13:11,13; 15:8,8,9,9; 18:5,5; 20:33; 21:4,4; 22:56; Jn 4:17; 8:11; 11:20,27,28,28,28,29,31,31,32; 12:3,7; 16:21; 18:17; 20:2,11,11,13,14,14,15,16,18; Ac 5:8,10; 9:36,37,39,40,40; 12:14,14,14,15; 16:14,15,15,15,15,16,16,17,18; Ro 7:2,3,3,3,3; 9:12; 16:2,2; 1Co 7:11,11,12,13,28,34,39,39,40,40,40; 11:6,6; Gal 4:25,26; 1Ti 2:12; 5:6,9,16; Heb 11:11,31; Jas 2:25,25; 1Pe 5:13; Rev 2:20,21; 12:2,2,5,6,14,14; 17:4,7; 18:2,6,6,7,7,8,19,20

SO (3102)

For "SO" as a proper name, see the Main Concordance.

Ge 1:7,7,9,11,15,21,24,26,27,30; 2:2,20,21; 3:7,10,14,23; 4:5,15,15,16; 6:7,13,14; 8:9,17,18; 9:17,23; 11:4,7,8; 12:4,7,13,18,19; 13:1,6,8,11,16,18; 14:23; 15:3,5,9; 16:2,3,6,10,15; 17:16; 18:5,6,12,15,19,19,20,20,27,31; 19:3,5,11,13,14,29,34,35,36; 20:4,6,17; 21:12,19,27,31; 22:14; 23:4,9,13,17,20; 24:7,9,20,32,34,40,46,49,55,56,58,59,61,65,67; 25:22,25,26,33,34; 26:6,9,11,14,15,17,20,21,28; 27:1,4,7,9,10,14,19,20,21,23,25,27,31,37; 28:1,4,9,21; 29:12,20,22,25,28,33,34,35; 30:1,3,4,8,11,13,16,16,18,20,25,38,41,42; 31:4,9,16,21,27,32,33,35,45,46,53;

32:2,21,24,25,30; 33:1,14,16; 34:5,20,23; 35:2,4,5, 8,10,19; 36:8; 37:14,17,23,28,35; 38:7,9,10,11,18, 22,28,29; 39:2,6,22; 40:7,7,9,21; 41:8,14,21,27,31, 36,38,39,41,49; 42:2,5,6,16,20,34; 43:2,8,14,15,19, 21,34; 44:8,21,30; 45:1,2,4,8,12,21,25; 46:1,6; 47:4,11,17,19,20,23,26; 48:1,7,9,10,17,20; 49:1,7, 7,17; 50:2,7,12,16,17,21,26; Ex 1:7,11,12,20; 2:8,9, 18,25; 3:3,8,10,20,21,22; 4:4,5,6,7,17,20,21,23,23, 26,27; 5:1,9,12; 7:10,16,21; 8:1,6,10,20,22; 9:1,4, 10,13,14,22,23,29,35; 10:1,3,3,5,7,12,13,21,22; 11:4,9; 12:34,36; 13:18,21; 14:4,6,8,16,17,20,25, 26; 15:24; 16:6,20,23,24,30,32,33,34; 17:2,6,10,12, 13; 18:7,23; 19:7,8,9,20,21,25; 20:12,20; 22:6,31; 23:12,12; 25:37; 26:6,13,25; 27:2,5,7,20; 28:1,3,4, 7,28,30,32,35,38,41,43; 29:1,29,44,46; 30:8,20,21, 29,30; 31:13; 32:1,3,6,10,24,25,26,31; 33:6,13; 34:4,31; 36:1,4,6,13,30,33; 38:2,7,17; 39:4,21,23, 32,43; 40:13,15,17,33,38; Lev 1:3; 8:10,15,30,35, 36; 9:6,8; 10:2,5,7,10,11,13; 13:12,37; 14:36; 15:31; 16:4,13; 17:5; 18:25; 19:12,17; 20:14,22; 21:4,15, 23,24; 22:2,8,16; 23:11,39,43,44; 24:2,11; 25:8,33, 35,36; 26:13,15,17,22,32,36,37,41,44; 27:14,28; Nu 1:19,53; 2:34; 3:4,16,42,49; 4:19,46; 5:3,4,6,13, 22,22; 6:27; 7:6; 8:3,3,7,11,19; 9:4,5,6; 10:33; 11:3, 17,24,25; 12:4,11,13,15; 13:3,21; 14:16,28,36; 15:36,39; 16:15,18,21,27,39,45,47; 17:6,10; 18:5; 20:8,9; 21:3,7,9,31,35; 22:3,4,8,14,19,25,31,35; 23:6,14,17; 25:3,4,5; 26:3; 27:5,17,18,20; 31:3,3,5, 16,31,50; 32:2,40; 35:12,15,20,21,32; 36:3,8,10; Dt 1:10,15,19,23,27,41,43,46; 2:8,13; 3:3,8,14,29; 4:1,5,7,8,9,10,16,32,35,40; 5:14,16,29,31,32,33; 6:2,2,3,18,24; 8:1,5,16,18,20; 9:8,14,15,17,18; 10:3,11; 11:8,9,13,14,17,21; 12:10,25,28; 14:23,24, 29,29; 15:9,10; 16:3,20; 17:19; 18:14,22; 19:3,10, 10,13; 20:8; 22:7,8; 23:14,20; 24:13,19; 25:6,15; 26:8,12; 28:56,63; 29:6,9,27; 30:6,12,12,13,13,14, 19; 31:9,12,14,19,22,28; 32:46; 33:28; 34:9; Jos 1:5, 8,10,17; 2:1,3,7,9,15,16,21; 3:6,7,14,16; 4:4,8,17, 24,24; 5:3,4,7,9,15; 6:6,11,14,18,20,23,27; 7:1,2,4, 22; 8:3,6,13,18,22,28; 9:7,17,20,21,24,26; 10:3,7, 10,13,20,23,24,40; 11:7,15,16,20,23; 13:13; 14:5,9, 10,14; 15:17,19; 16:4; 17:2,4,15; 18:3,9,16; 19:9, 51; 20:3,7; 21:3,8,13,43; 22:9,13,25; 23:11,15; 24:10,13; Jdg 1:3,13,15,25,30; 3:8,10,11,28; 4:2,9, 14,18,22; 5:18,28,31; 6:2,6,20,24,27,32,35,40; 7:3, 5,8,11,24; 8:9,21,21,25; 9:7,11,19,23,34,39,43,49, 49,54,54; 10:13; 11:3,6,11,17; 13:1,12,17; 14:6,16, 17; 15:2,4,6,13,19; 16:2,5,6,9,12,13,17,18,19,25, 26; 17:4,11; 18:2,2,3,7,15,26; 19:4,6,7,8,14,21,22, 23,25,30; 20:4,11,13,31,34,42; 21:10,14,17,20,23; Ru 1:1,17,19,22; 2:3,8,17,23; 3:6,14,15; 4:1,2,4,4, 8,10,13; 1Sa 1:15,20,23,28; 2:3,23,31,36; 3:2,5,9,9, 17,18; 4:3,4,10,15; 5:8,8,10,11; 6:6,10; 7:1,3,4,13; 8:4,6,8; 9:4,8,10,24,27,27; 10:12,19,22; 11:2,3,11, 12,15; 12:9,11,18,19; 13:4,9,12,20,22; 14:11,12,19, 23,24,27,34,37,43,44,45; 15:1,4,6,6,24,25,30,31, 33; 16:11,12,13,17,20; 17:39,50; 18:5,13,19,21,21, 21,26,27; 19:7,12,15,17,20,23; 20:2,5,11,13,14,16, 24; 21:5,6,13,15; 22:4,5,13,18; 23:5,13,20,24; 24:2, 13,22; 25:5,13,21,22,36; 26:2,7,12,24,25; 27:2,6, 12; 28:7,8,15,22; 29:6,11; 30:4; 31:4,6; 2Sa 1:10, 15; 2:2,15,16,23,28; 3:8,9,15,16,21,21,24,35,37; 4:12; 5:19,20,20,23,25; 6:12; 7:10,26,27; 8:2; 9:5, 10,11; 10:2,4,9,14,19; 11:6,8,10,12,15,16,20,21,21; 12:29; 13:2,4,5,6,6,8,9,10,18,27,29; 14:2,7,11,14, 14,24,25,29,30,32,33; 15:6,9,12,17,22,29,31,37; 16:13,17,19,22; 17:5,11,13,15,15,18,20,22,23; 18:4, 14,20,23,30; 19:8,10,12,13,14,23,26,27,28,39,43; 20:2,7,16,22; 21:1,3,5,6,17; 22:37; 23:16,18; 24:2, 2,4,13,15,19,21,24; 1Ki 1:2,2,5,15,23,28,36,37,38, 40; 2:2,3,12,17,21,23,25,27,30,31,34,40; 3:9,11,12, 13,20,22,24; 4:1; 5:6,6,8,14; 6:6,9,14,22; 7:22,40, 47; 8:5,8,16,29,40,43,60,63,65; 9:25; 10:10,12; 11:6,11,19,25,36; 12:3,5,15,16,19,24,33; 13:4,6,10, 13,15,18,19,27,29; 14:2,4,6,15,27; 15:19; 16:3,12, 13,18,22,26; 17:5,10,10,15; 18:2,5,6,16,20,25,26, 28,37,42,44; 19:2,2,8,19,21; 20:9,10,12,15,25,34, 36,37; 21:4,5,8,11,13,20; 22:4,6,9,23,29,30,32,37; 2Ki 1:2,4,13,15,17; 2:2,3,4,5,6,17,20; 3:6,9,12,21; 4:8,12,15,22,25,30,31; 5:5,6,9,12,14,15,21; 6:10, 10,13,17,18,20,22,23,23,25,28,29,29,31; 7:4,6,7,10, 12,13,14,15,16; 8:15,21,29; 9:4,14,19,33,37; 10:1, 5,11,14,15,15,20,22,24,25,28; 11:2,16; 13:3,5,15, 21,25; 14:11; 15:12,20,25; 16:11; 17:4,18,23,25,28; 18:10,14,15; 19:9,19,36; 20:7; 21:9,16,16; 22:20; 23:10,18,27,33,35; 25:1,3,21,29; 1Ch 2:3; 4:10,27; 5:1,26; 6:57,64; 10:4,6,14; 11:6,7,18,20; 12:18; 13:5,10; 14:10,11,11,14,16,17; 15:14,17,25,28; 17:9,24,25; 19:2,4,10,15,19; 21:2,2,4,7,11,14,15, 19,22,25; 22:2,5,12,19; 23:11,32; 24:2; 28:8; 29:20, 23; 2Ch 1:5; 4:11,18; 5:6,9; 6:5,31,33; 7:5,8,13,16; 8:16; 10:3,5,15,16,19; 11:4,12; 12:8,10; 13:13,17; 14:7; 15:15; 16:3,10; 17:5,10; 18:5,8,22,28,29,31; 20:10,25,25,31; 21:9,14; 22:1,6,9,11; 23:15,19; 24:25; 25:10,12,16,20,21; 26:15,20; 28:14,15,23; 29:10,22,26,30,31,34,35,36; 30:7,8,23; 31:4,21; 32:1,17,21,22; 33:9,11,13; 34:5,28; 35:14,16,21,24; Ezr 2:62; 3:7,13; 4:15,21,21; 5:10,16; 6:8,10,14,21, 22; 8:16,17,21,23,32,33; 9:8; 10:4,5,13,16; Ne 2:2, 2,5,6,7,8,9,15,18; 4:6,10,21,22; 5:7,9,13; 6:3,7,13, 15; 7:5,64; 8:2,8,16; 9:11,27,28,30,36; 11:30; 12:40, 47; 13:11,14,18,19,30; Est 1:17,21; 2:10,17; 3:10, 14; 4:6,17; 5:2,5,5; 6:1,7,11; 7:1,10; 8:13; 9:14,23, 29; Job 1:10; 2:7; 4:21; 5:12,16,17,27; 6:28; 7:3,9, 15,17,17; 8:7,13; 9:31,34; 10:20; 13:19,28; 14:6,12, 19; 15:13; 19:8; 21:16,19,34; 22:11,14,18; 24:18,19, 25; 27:19; 31:27,34,34; 32:1,6; 33:20; 34:10,28,32, 33; 35:5,16; 36:19; 37:7; 38:21; 41:16; 42:8,9,17; Ps 1:4; 10:18; 18:36,38; 22:1,1; 39:2; 42:1,5,11; 43:5; 48:8; 49:9; 51:4,13; 65:9; 66:3; 67:2,7; 69:23; 75:5; 78:6,33,53,54; 80:12; 81:12; 83:4,15,16; 91:12; 95:11; 102:21,24; 103:5,11,12,13; 106:15,23, 26; 107:12; 110:7; 115:8; 119:34,38,71,101; 123:2; 125:2; 130:4; 135:18; 138:2; 141:4,7; 143:4; 144:5; 145:12; Pr 4:2; 6:3,29,32; 7:15; 8:29; 10:26; 12:13; 15:12; 17:14; 18:3,5; 20:4,11,18,19; 21:27; 22:19, 21; 23:35; 25:3; 26:11,14,21; 27:17,19; 29:16; 30:9, 13,13,33; Ecc 2:17,20; 3:14,18,19,22; 5:2,11,14,15, 16; 6:2; 7:6,25; 8:8,8,15; 9:1,2,2,12,16; 10:1; 11:5, 10; SS 2:7; 3:2,5; 5:9; 8:4; Isa 2:3,9; 5:15,19,19,24; 6:13; 7:2; 8:2; 9:14,18; 10:14,14,19,27; 11:15; 14:24,24; 15:7; 16:2,9; 19:21; 20:2,4; 22:2,18; 23:16; 24:13,20; 25:5; 26:17; 27:3,11; 28:13,13,16, 28; 29:8; 30:14; 31:4,6; 32:9; 37:20,37; 38:8; 41:7, 10,20,22,23,23,26,26; 42:25; 43:9,10,28; 44:18,18; 45:1,3,6; 48:5,7,9; 51:10,15; 52:14,15; 53:7; 54:9; 55:9,10,11; 57:10,11; 59:2,9,14,16,18; 60:11; 61:7, 11; 62:5,5; 63:5,8,10,17; 65:8,16,22; 66:2,4,13,22; Jer 2:5,26,36; 3:9,20; 4:8; 5:5,13,19; 6:2,5,7,8,10, 15; 7:16,32; 8:12; 9:2,11; 10:4,18,21; 11:8; 13:2,5, 7,11; 14:10,19; 15:6; 16:13; 18:3,4,6,11,18,21; 19:6, 9; 20:8,11; 21:2; 22:14,15,16; 23:7,14,24,36; 24:2, 3,8,8; 25:2,17; 26:19,24; 27:9; 28:6; 29:6,17,27; 30:10,14,14,22; 31:17,28,35; 32:9,14,23,31,35,39, 40,42; 33:20,24; 34:5,10,17,22; 35:3,11; 36:4,6,14, 15,32; 37:21; 38:6,11,12,27; 39:13,14; 40:6; 41:8; 42:6,8,12,13,18,22; 43:3,4,7,12; 44:7,29; 48:11,36; 49:4,10,10,18; 50:10,34,39,40; 51:29,39,62,64; 52:4,6,27,33; La 1:1,8,21; 2:22; 3:7,18,32,44; 4:14, 18; 5:20; Eze 1:28; 3:2,3,17,23,25,26; 4:5,8,14; 6:6, 12; 8:5,8,10; 9:6,7,10; 12:6,7,11,12,16; 13:5,14,15, 15,22; 14:15; 15:6; 16:13,27,34,52,54,57,62; 17:6, 8,9,14; 19:9; 20:8,12,13,21,25,26,36; 21:14,15; 22:20,22,26,30,31; 23:21,27,31,32,44,48; 24:8,10, 11,18,20,27; 25:10,12; 26:10; 28:14,16,17,18; 29:15; 30:19,21; 31:5,14; 33:7,9,19,22,28; 34:5,8, 10,12,25; 36:3,5,18,30,38; 37:7,10,17; 38:16,23; 39:11,16,23; 40:41; 41:6,7; 42:6,20; 43:8,11,20; 44:19,30; 45:20; 46:15,18; 47:9; 48:22; Da 1:14,16, 19; 2:2,6,9,12,13,16,18,30,40,41,42,43; 3:3,13,21, 22,22,26; 4:6,17,19; 5:2,3,6,9,10,13; 6:2,3,4,6,8,9, 12,16,17,28; 7:4,16; 9:3; 10:8,20; 11:35; 12:8; Hos 1:3; 2:6,10,18; 3:2; 4:5; 6:9; 9:7,7; 10:5,11,14, 15; 13:7,11; Joel 3:13; Am 2:7; 3:3,12; 7:2,3,5,6; 9:1,12; Ob 12,16; Jnh 1:6,8,10,11; 3:9; 4:7,8,9; Mic 4:2; Hab 1:4,15; 2:2,15; Hag 1:8,14; 2:14; Zec 1:13,21; 2:9; 3:5; 4:6,14; 6:7; 7:3,12,13,14; 8:9, 13,15; 11:1,7,11,12,13; 12:7,8; Mal 1:10; 2:4,9,15, 16; 3:5,6,10; Mt 2:8,14,15,21,23; 3:15; 4:6; 6:2,4, 18,31; 7:12; 8:24,26,28,32; 9:6,19; 10:26,31; 12:13, 22,27,31,40; 13:32,35,40; 14:6,15; 15:16,23; 17:20, 27; 18:16; 19:6; 20:5,10,16,26; 21:20,27,39; 22:9, 10,21,22; 23:3,31,35; 24:15,26,27,33,37,44,46; 25:17,25,26,27,28; 26:15,19,25,41,44,59,64; 27:2, 5,7,11,17,64,66; 28:4,8,15; Mk 1:4,27,31,38,39; 2:10,19,28; 3:2,10,20,23; 4:1,7,12,37,40; 5:20,23, 24; 6:19,27,31,32,34,35,36,40; 7:5,18,36; 8:6; 9:6, 20,26; 10:8,43,49; 11:25,33; 12:8,12; 13:23,29; 14:11,13,16,38,55; 15:1,2,4,29,42,45,46; 16:1; Lk 1:4,21,35,43; 2:4,16,35; 3:23; 4:11,39; 5:5,6,7, 7,10,11,15,24,33; 6:7,8,10; 7:6,22,37,42; 8:10,12, 16,22,23,37,39; 9:6,12,15,39,45; 10:29,32; 11:9,19, 30,33,37,48; 12:1,36,43; 13:7,14; 14:4,9,10,12,20, 23; 15:12,15,20,24,26,28,29; 16:2,4,5,9,11,24,26, 28; 17:3,10,26; 18:5; 19:4,6,13,23; 20:7,10,15,20, 21; 21:13,31; 22:13,30,46; 23:3,3,24; 24:29,45; Jn 1:7,39; 2:7,8,15; 3:8,14,16,21; 4:3,5,15,36,40, 53; 5:10,12,16,20,21,26; 6:9,13,30,57; 7:3,18,23; 8:28,36,52,53; 9:3,7,11,16,36,39; 10:12; 11:3,4,6, 14,15,41,53,57; 12:10,19,34,36,37,40,46,50; 13:4, 13,19,27,33,34; 14:2,5,13,29,31; 15:2,9,11,16,16; 16:1,4,19,22,33; 17:11,12,13,21,23; 18:3,9,25,29; 19:16,24,28,29,35,36; 20:2,3,25; 21:3,11,11; Ac 1:19,23,26; 3:5,19; 4:4,6,15,33; 5:3,15,22,32; 6:2,7,12; 7:4,10,19,24; 8:8,19,24,27,31,32; 9:2,8, 17,28,38; 10:20,22,29,33,48; 11:2,17,18,26; 12:5,8, 14,15; 13:3,34,35,51; 14:1,3; 15:2,25,30; 16:3,5,8, 18; 17:5,17,23,27; 18:11,16; 19:3,9,10,12; 20:31; 21:23,24,35; 22:30; 23:10,11,18,24,28,31; 24:6,10, 16,26; 25:20,26; 26:1,3,11,18,19,22; 27:3,9,13,15, 17,25,32; 28:14,19; Ro 1:11,13,15,20,28,28; 2:3,26; 3:4,6,7,19,26; 4:11,16,18,18; 5:3,11,18,19,20,21, 21; 6:1,6,12,19; 7:3,4,5,6,12,13,21,25; 8:3,7,15,23; 10:4; 11:5,7,10,11,16,19,25,31,32; 12:5; 13:2,12; 14:6,6,6,8,9,12,22; 15:4,6,8,13,16,19,20,24,28,32; 16:19,26; 1Co 1:8,15,29; 2:1,5,12,16; 3:7,18,21; 4:6,8,10; 5:4,5,7; 7:5,5,15,21,38; 8:4,7,11,13; 9:10, 18,20,21,22,27; 10:12,13,31,33; 11:12,20,27,32,33, 34; 12:12,13,14,25; 14:5,9,12,15,23,25,26,31; 15:14,22,28,42,45,48,48,49; 16:2,6,11,19; 2Co 1:4, 5,7,8,12,15,17,20; 2:1,3,5,7,13,17; 3:7; 4:4,10,11, 12,15,18; 5:4,9,10,12,16,16,21; 6:3; 7:7,9,12,14; 8:6,9,10,11,14,22,24; 9:4,5,8,11; 10:8,16; 11:2,8,9, 16,19,22,22,22; 12:6,9,15; 13:7,7; Gal 1:6,9,16; 2:5,13,16,19; 3:3,4,5,6,9,14,15,22,24,26; 4:3,7,15, 17,18; 5:16,17; Eph 1:17; 2:9; 3:17; 4:11,12,17,19; 5:24; 6:3,11,13,19,21; Php 1:10,16,20,26; 2:15,18, 28,29; 3:11,21; Col 1:10,11,18,28,29; 2:2,4,6; 4:3,6; 1Th 1:7; 2:8,8,10,16; 3:1,3,13; 4:10,12,12,13,14, 17; 5:4,6,10; 2Th 1:3,12; 2:4,6,7,10,11,12,15; 3:8; 1Ti 1:3,7,16,18,19; 3:4,7,14; 4:15; 5:4,7,14,16,20; 6:1,17,19,21; 2Ti 1:4,8; 3:8,17; 4:17,21; Titus 1:9, 13; 2:5,8,10; 3:7,8; Phm 13,14,17,24; Heb 1:4; 2:1, 3,9,11,14; 3:7,11,13,19; 4:3,11,16; 6:3,11,15,18; 8:3; 9:13,14,28; 10:33,35,36; 11:3,5,12,19,28,29, 35,40; 12:1,3,13,21,27,28; 13:2,6,9,12,17,19; Jas 1:4,21,22; 2:26; 3:4; 4:2,2; 5:16; 1Pe 1:7,15,21, 22; 2:2,24; 3:1,7,9,16; 4:6,7,11,11,11,13,19; 5:13; 2Pe 1:4,12; 2:9; 3:14,17; 1Jn 1:3; 2:1,28; 3:5; 4:11, 16,17; 5:13,20; 2Jn 12; 3Jn 8,10,10,13; Rev 1:7; 2:14,22; 3:11,16,18,18,18,19; 8:12; 10:9; 11:6; 12:4,11,14; 13:15,17; 14:16; 16:15,18,21; 18:4,4; 19:18

THAT (5820)

Ge 1:4,10,11,12,18,21,21,24,25,25,26,26,28,29,30, 30,31; 2:3,9,12,19,24; 3:3,5,6,11,11; 4:15,26; 6:2,5, 6,7,7,17,20,21; 7:5,8,11,13,14,15,21,21,22,23; 8:1, 11,13,17,17,19,19; 9:2,3,4,10,10,23; 10:9,11; 11:4, 4,9; 12:6,13,14,19; 13:6,7,10,15,16; 14:2,3,7,8,14, 17,23,23,24; 15:8,13,13,18; 16:5,7,10,14; 17:16,23, 26; 18:5,8,13,19,19,21,21,27,31; 19:3,5,11,13,22, 29,33,35; 20:6,7,8,9,9; 21:7,9,10,10,12,22,23,25, 30,31; 22:12,14,16; 23:2,11,15; 24:2,3,6,7,14,14,14, 24,40,56,65; 25:30,30; 26:7,12,14,15,18,21,24,28, 29,32; 27:1,4,7,10,19,25,27,31,33; 28:4,6,6,7,19, 21,22,22; 29:2,12,19,31,33; 30:1,3,9,15,16,16,27, 33,33,35,35,35,38,39,40; 31:1,2,5,6,10,12,12,16,22, 32,32,35,36,37,37,48,50,52,52; 32:2,5,8,22,25,25; 33:10,11,13,13,13,15,16,17; 34:2,5,7,14,15,22; 35:5,6,7,19,20,22,27; 36:1,8,19; 37:4,19,20,29; 38:1,5,9,14,16; 39:2,3,3,5,13,17,22; 40:6,16,21; 41:4,15,20,21,27,31,32,35,36,36,49; 42:1,2,2,4,16, 20,20,23,28,29,34; 43:8,12,14,18,25,32; 44:7,15,27, 31,34; 45:2,5,12,16; 46:1,5,30; 47:14,17,18,18,19, 19,22,23,26,26,29; 48:7,20; 49:17,17,21; 50:3,11, 11,15; Ex 1:6,7,16,22; 2:2,12,23; 3:2,4,8,11,12,19, 20,20,21; 4:2,5,5,21,21,26,31; 5:1,2,6,8,9,17; 6:7; 7:5,15,16,17,17,21; 8:1,9,9,10,15,20,22,22,22,26, 26,29; 9:1,4,4,7,11,13,14,15,16,16,18,19,22,29,30, 34; 10:1,2,2,2,3,5,5,7,7,12,13,13,15,21,21; 11:1,2, 7,8,9; 12:3,8,12,16,17,23,25,42,51; 13:8,9,16,17, 21; 14:4,5,8,11,16,17,18,21,25,26,28,30; 15:23; 16:4,5,6,7,8,12,13,29,29,34,35; 17:12,14; 18:11,14, 22; 19:1,9,11,12; 20:11,12,17,20,22; 21:14,19,36; 22:6,11,27; 23:12,12,15,22; 24:8; 25:21,22,37,40; 26:6,12,14,22,24; 27:2,5,20,21; 28:3,28,32,35,38, 43; 29:27,27,27,29,32,46,46; 30:6,6,20,21,23; 31:13,14; 32:1,2,10,10,12,18,21,25,25,28; 33:13, 16; 34:1,10,18,29,35; 35:12,14; 36:13,19,27,33; 38:2,26; 39:21,23,43; 40:15; Lev 1:3,8,12,17; 3:3,5, 9,14; 4:7,8,12,18; 5:2,2,2,3,5; 6:3,6,7,10,11; 7:3,19, 21,34,34,35,36; 8:25,35; 9:6,7,15; 10:10,14,14,15, 15,16; 11:2,3,3,4,9,10,12,20,21,21,21,23,26,26,27, 27,29,31,32,34,34,35,37,39,41,42,44,46,46,47,47; 13:2,3,5,8,10,20,20,25,27,36,39,47,52,54,58; 14:4, 5,6,7,19,34,35,36,37,40,41; 15:6,10,12,17,25,28, 31; 16:2,13,18; 17:4,5,11,13,14; 18:8,10,16,17,22, 23,24,28,30; 19:5,10,16; 20:4,14,19,22,25,25; 21:15; 22:3,3,5,7,9,19,23,29,30; 23:6,21,28,29,30, 43; 24:2,3; 25:8,21,24,29,33,36,50,52,53; 26:13,16, 17,22,32,34,35,36,41,46; 27:6,9,11,12,17,18,23,28, 32; Nu 1:53; 2:34,34; 4:6,7,8,9,11,12,15,18,19,25, 26; 5:8,13,18,19,22,22,24,24,26,27; 6:4,9,11,18,18, 19,20,20,20; 7:5; 8:2,3,11,19,22; 9:6,6,16; 11:3,11, 16,17,17,25,29,29,32; 12:10,14,16; 13:24; 14:1,8, 14,14,14,14,31,45; 15:27,28,39; 16:5,9,11,11,13,28, 28,30,30,40; 17:8,10; 18:5,9,9,13,14,15,24,24,26; 19:2,2,7,14,19,22; 20:4,8,14,29; 21:1,7,11,14,15, 18,18,27; 22:2,4,6,11,19,20,36; 23:19,19,24; 24:1; 25:4,18; 26:55; 27:11; 28:2,8; 29:40; 30:8,12; 31:2, 3,16,21,23,23,26,32,42,52; 32:1,10,23; 33:40; 34:2, 13; 35:4,8,8,12,15,16,17,18,20,21,21,21,23; 36:3,4, 8; Dt 1:1,3,9,10,16,18,19,19,25,39; 2:14,20,34,37; 3:4,4,8,12,12,14,17,18,20,20,21,21,23,25,26,28; 4:1,2,5,9,10,14,14,16,17,18,21,22,23,26,26,35,35, 39,40,40,48; 5:3,5,14,15,15,16,16,21,24,27,29,29, 31,33,33,33; 6:1,2,2,2,3,3,6,12,18,24,25; 7:8,9,16; 8:1,3,3,5,11,11,15,16,19; 9:1,3,4,5,6,6,8,9,14,16, 16,20,21,21,26,29; 10:1,2,8,9,11,13; 11:2,6,7,8,8,9, 11,14,17,21,21,27,28,32; 12:1,5,10,25,28,32; 13:3, 5,5,6,13,14,15,16,18; 14:6,6,7,7,9,10,20,22,23,24, 28,29,29; 15:9,15,15,18; 16:3,12,20; 17:1,1,4,5,7,8, 9,16,18,19; 18:1,19,22,22; 19:3,5,10,10,13,19; 20:8, 12,15,16,19,20; 21:3,4,17,23; 22:7,8,15,24,26; 23:14,19,20; 24:4,6,13,14,18,18,19,22,22; 25:3,6, 10,15; 26:2,3,10,12,17,17,17,17,18,18,19,19; 27:1, 10; 28:7,10,13,33,35,55,56,60,67,67; 29:2,4,4,4,5, 6,6,9,13,18,22,27,29; 30:5,6,10,12,13,18,19,19,20; 31:5,7,17,17,18,19,22,28,29; 32:11,11,17,21,22,24, 39,46,48,50; 33:1,4,13; 34:12; Jos 1:7,8,13,14,15; 2:7,9,9,9,12,13,13,23; 3:7,10,10,16; 4:7,9,14,24,24, 24; 5:2,5,6,11,12; 6:15,15,17,18,26; 7:8,12,15,24, 26; 8:2,9,11,13,14,18,18,21,21,22,25,26,35,35; 9:9, 10,13,16,20,24,27,27; 10:1,1,17,28,30,35; 11:10,11, 14,15,20,21; 12:3,7; 13:2,6,8,12,21,29; 14:9,9,12, 12,12; 15:8,9,10,13,25,46,49,54,60; 16:2,9; 17:1, 12; 18:3,13,14,20,28; 19:51; 20:3,4,6,6,7; 21:2,11; 22:2,4,4,5,11,17,24,26,27,27,29,31,34; 23:4,6,7,12, 13,14; 24:13,17,22,23,25,32; Jdg 1:5,9,24,27; 2:5, 10; 3:8,10,28,29,30; 4:1,4,12,23; 5:1; 6:6,11,13,17, 21,22,25,26,32,35,37,38,40; 7:1,7,9,13,19; 8:7,10, 24,26,35; 9:7,17,23,24,38,45,47,54,55,56; 10:8; 11:12,21,26,35,36,40; 12:3,6; 13:4,4,12,13,14,16, 17,21; 14:4,4,6,9; 15:2,7,11,12; 16:3,7,8,11,18,20, 26,26; 17:2,2,8,13; 18:7,10,10,14,19,23,26; 19:7, 10,16; 20:3,12,13,21,26,31,34,35,36,38,41,46; 21:5, 8,9,14,17,19,23,24,24; Ru 1:6,7,9,18; 2:5,10,20; 3:10,11,12,14; 4:3,4,9,10,12; 1Sa 2:9,13,29,30,31, 33; 3:2,8,11,12,13,20; 4:3,5,6,12,15,19,19; 5:5,9; 6:5,7,9,9,9,15,16; 7:6,7,8,10,10,14; 8:7,18,18,21; 9:8,19,24,27; 10:5,9,11,16,18; 11:2,11,12,12; 12:5, 11,12,18,19,23,23; 13:6,6,11,11,11; 14:3,4,7,10,10, 14,18,22,23,24,27,27,28,31,33,34,37,49; 15:3,6,9,9, 11,11,14,25,29,30,35; 16:13; 17:26,42,43,46,47,47, 51,55; 18:2,5,9,17,18,21,21,27,28,28; 19:8,10,15, 17,18,24,24; 20:1,3,7,9,12,14,26,29,30,33,34; 21:5, 6,7,9,10,15; 22:6,8,8,13,15,18,21,22; 23:7,9,10,13, 15,28; 24:6,11,11,16,20,20,21; 25:4,6,7,17,21,25, 36,39; 26:3,4,11,11,16,17; 27:4,5,6,12; 28:1,16,20, 20,21,25; 29:4,9; 30:15,23,23,24,25; 31:5,6,7,7; 2Sa 1:5,10,10,18,26; 2:4,16,17,20,26,29; 3:19,21, 21,21,23,23,23,37,37,38; 4:1,10; 5:8,8,12,17,20,24; 6:8,9,17; 7:4,10,11,18,23,26,29; 8:7,8,9; 9:7,8,9,10; 10:6,9,14,15,19; 11:12,21,26; 12:4,6,15,18,19,21, 23; 13:2,20,32,33; 14:1,7,11,14,14,20,20,22; 15:4, 22; 16:4,12,21,23,23; 17:10,10,13,14,23; 18:7,8,19, 22,27,32; 19:2,2,3,6,6,7,7,14,20,22,30,34,37; 20:12, 12,18,19,21; 21:3,5,14,17,18; 22:37; 23:4,10,14,15; 24:2,15,18,21,24; 1Ki 1:2,11,24,24,40,51; 2:3,4,5, 29,31,41,42; 3:3,4,4,10,12,13,21,23,28; 4:27,33; 5:1,3,6,6,14; 6:2,3,6,22,31,33,34; 7:3,6,31,45,48; 8:5,5,8,9,12,16,21,26,28,29,40,43,43,51,59,60,60, 60,64,64,65; 9:9,12; 10:2,12,14; 11:19,21,21,21,22, 29,36,37; 12:16,20; 13:3,4,6,11,11,18,34; 14:1,7,15, 15; 15:15,18,29; 16:3,13,16,16,18,26,32; 17:12,24, 24; 18:9,17,36,36,37,37; 19:2,4,8; 20:13,20,23,28, 31,40; 21:3,10,15,15,16,22,22; 22:3,18,20,33,35, 49; 2Ki 1:3,6,8,16,17; 2:3,5,13,14; 3:2,6,21,26; 4:1, 9,17,38; 5:6,6,8,8,11,14,15; 6:9,10,17,22,25,30; 7:6,13,13,20; 8:1,6,10,13,14,15; 9:20,21,25,26,34, 36,37; 10:10,19,23,36; 11:1,5,7,10,10,17; 12:4,8,8, 9,10,10; 14:10; 15:16; 16:6,11,14,17,18; 17:4,8,9, 11,13,13,26,34; 18:4,12,15,20,21,27; 19:4,4,4,8,9, 12,17,19,19,21,25,29,33,35; 20:8,8,9,12,13,13,15, 17; 21:8,9,12,16,16,16; 22:4,9,13,13,13,19; 23:7,11, 13,15,16,17,19,19,24,26,33; 24:10,13,20; 25:3,13, 15,23; 1Ch 1:27; 4:10,10; 5:9,23,26; 6:49,49,62; 10:5,7,7; 11:4,16,17,19; 13:6,11,12; 14:2,2,8,11,15; 15:13,22; 16:1,7,32,35; 17:3,9,10,16,24,24,25,27; 18:8,9; 19:6,10,15,16,19; 20:4; 21:2,19,22,24,28, 28,29; 22:12,13,19,19; 23:5,24; 27:1,1; 28:8,12,18, 18; 29:14,16,17,22,30; 2Ch 1:5,7,10; 2:8,16; 4:16, 18,18,19; 5:6,6,9,10; 6:1,5,11,17,19,31,33,33; 7:8, 13,16,22; 8:2,12,15; 9:13; 10:16; 12:3,7,8,15; 13:5, 8,13,14,17,18; 14:13; 15:8,9,11,18; 16:7,10,14; 17:2,5,10; 18:17,19,32; 19:10; 20:2,9,12,24,25; 21:14; 22:10; 23:9,9,16,19; 24:7,9,9,11; 25:5,9,12, 13,16,19,19,20,24,27; 26:15,18,20,23; 27:5; 28:9, 16,21; 29:10,16,19,35; 30:6,7,8; 31:5,21; 32:1,2,2, 4,5,10,14,31,31; 33:9,13; 34:4,9,11,14,14,16,17,21, 21,21,24,25; 35:3,16,17; 36:8; Ezr 2:59,61; 3:5,7; 4:1,12,12,13,15,15,15,16,19,21; 5:3,6,8,10,11,11, 16; 6:6,8,10,11,22; 7:13,15,20,21,24; 8:15,17,20,21, 25,30,34; 9:12; 10:23; Ne 1:2; 2:5,7,10; 3:8; 4:1,7,7, 10,15,15,16,22; 5:15; 6:1,1,6,12,12,13,16; 7:61,63; 8:8,12,14,15,17,17; 9:6,6,11,13,13,23,28,32,33; 12:40,43,44; 13:1,1,10,10,15,18,19,21,26,27; Est 1:2,15,19,22; 3:1,5,7,14; 4:1,7,11,11,13,14; 5:2, 5,9,9,13; 6:1,2,6,13; 7:7; 8:1,5,13,13; 9:11,14,19, 24,25,25,27; Job 1:10; 2:11; 3:3,4,6,7,8,12,21; 4:21; 5:9,9,12,24,25; 6:8,8,9,10,11,11,13,15,17; 7:7,8,12,15,17,17,18; 8:18; 9:2,10,10,22,31,32,32, 34; 10:6,7,7,9,13; 11:5,5,14; 12:9; 13:5,18; 15:3,9, 9,13,14,14; 16:3; 19:4,6,23,23,24,25,25,29; 20:3,5, 9,11; 21:15,19,30,30; 22:4,10,15; 23:10,15,17; 24:18; 26:2,5; 28:7,28; 30:11; 31:6,11,12,21,27,29, 34,35; 32:5,6,8,16,16; 33:13,20,24,26,30; 34:12,12, 23,28,36; 35:6,6,14,14,15; 36:2,4,9,18; 37:2,4,7,20; 38:2,13; 39:15,15,16; 40:14; 41:11,16,26,34,34; 42:2,3; Ps 1:1,3,4; 4:3; 5:11; 8:4,4,8; 9:14,17; 10:15,18; 14:7; 17:3; 18:36,38; 22:13; 24:7,9; 27:4; 30:12; 31:4,19,19; 34:8; 37:16; 39:13; 41:10,11; 44:3; 46:10; 48:6,13; 49:9,10,10,12,20; 50:4,12; 51:6,13; 53:6; 55:6; 56:9,13; 58:4,4,5,7,8,8; 59:13; 60:3,5; 61:2; 66:3; 67:2,7; 68:18,23; 69:34; 73:15; 78:35,35,39,39,45,45,69; 79:6,6,10; 80:3,7,12,19; 83:4,16,18,18; 85:6,9; 86:11,11,17; 87:5; 89:2,2,11, 36; 90:4,11,12,14; 91:5,6,6,12; 92:7,10; 94:11,20; 95:8,10; 96:11; 100:3; 101:3,6; 102:18; 103:5,14; 104:15,15,16; 105:45; 106:5,5,26,47; 107:25,37; 108:6; 109:15,27,27; 114:5; 116:9; 119:4,5,11,13, 17,18,27,33,34,38,48,55,71,75,75,77,80,88,101, 106,115,125,134,144,148,152,175; 120:5,5; 122:3, 4; 130:4; 135:3,5,5; 138:2; 139:14; 140:12; 141:4,5, 5,6; 142:7; 144:3,3,5; 145:12; 146:4; 148:6,8; 150:6; Pr 3:25; 5:2; 6:16,17,18,18; 8:15; 9:18,18; 12:28; 14:12; 16:25,29; 18:13; 19:18,21; 20:12,12, 15,27; 21:1,30; 22:19,21; 23:3; 24:14,27; 25:23,27; 27:8; 28:3,22; 29:26; 30:15,15,17,17,18,18,29,29; 31:18,31; Ecc 1:13,14,17; 2:1,11,13,14,17,19; 3:12, 13,14,14,18,18,19,22,22; 4:1,2,3,4,15; 5:1,14,15, 18; 6:2,3,5,11; 7:22; 8:12,14,16,17; 9:1,3,5,6,9,12, 13,15,15; 10:5; 11:6,9; SS 2:15,15; 4:5,16; 5:9; 6:1, 10,13; 7:2,7,13; Isa 1:1,29; 2:3,11,12,17,20; 3:7,18; 4:1,2; 5:29,30; 6:1; 7:18,20,21,23; 8:14,14; 9:4,7, 18; 10:19,20,27; 11:10,11,15,16; 12:1,4,4; 13:1,4; 14:8,29,29,29,32; 17:4,7,9,12; 18:7; 19:14,16,16, 18,19,21,23,24; 20:1,2,6; 22:1,8,9,12,20,25; 23:11, 13,15,16; 24:20,21; 25:7,7,9; 26:1,2,2,12; 27:1,2,3, 12,13; 28:1,1,3,4,5,10,10,13,13,13; 29:7,7,8,18; 30:1,6,8,13,14,23,23,24,28; 31:2,7; 32:17; 33:11, 17,18,20; 34:1,1,16; 35:3,8; 36:5,6,12; 37:4,4,4,8,9, 12,18,20,20,26,30,34; 38:7,17,22; 39:1,2,4,6; 40:2, 2,2,11,14,20,20; 41:20,20,20,22,23,23; 42:5,7,8,10; 43:9,10,10,12,21; 44:11,13,28; 45:1,3,3,6,20,23; 46:1,5,7,10,11,11; 47:11,15,15; 48:5; 49:6,23,26; 50:4; 51:9,10,12,13,13,15,17,22,22,23; 52:6,6,14; 53:2,5; 54:9,17; 55:3,10,11,13; 56:5; 57:1,11,11; 58:2,5; 59:2,15,16,16,19,21; 60:8,11,12,16; 61:4,9; 62:2; 63:5,14,17; 64:1,1,3,11; 65:1,5; 66:5,6,6,19, 22,24,24; Jer 1:12,13; 2:5,13,24,37; 3:7,8,17; 4:9, 11,12; 5:7; 6:24,27; 7:1,8,14,23,28,29,30; 8:1,17; 9:1,2,2,3,12,16,24,24; 10:18,23,25; 11:1,3,8,13,18, 19,19; 12:9; 13:12,20,21,22,26; 14:1,19; 15:10,14, 18,19; 16:16,19,21; 17:6,8,11,27; 18:1,7,8,9,20; 19:3,4; 20:16; 21:2,4,7,14; 22:5,16,23; 23:14,24,29, 38,40; 24:2,7; 25:13,13,29,33; 26:9,15,19; 27:5,8, 10,11,13,18,19,21; 28:1,3,17; 29:1,6,17,19; 30:1,7, 8,15; 31:1,21,33,35; 32:1,8,20,31,34,35,39,39,40;

33:4,9,10,15,20,24; 34:7,10,15; 35:1,4; 36:6,27,28, 29,29,32; 37:10,18; 38:7,25; 39:10,16,17; 40:7,11, 14; 42:3,6,12,20; 44:3,4,15,17,19,26,29,29,29; 46:1, 7,10; 47:1; 48:2,20,27,28,38,41; 49:10,13,22,24,26, 31,34; 50:4,5,8,17,20,30,32,34,38,43; 51:29,31,39, 48,60,60,61,62; 52:3,6,17,19; La 1:6,7,12,12,17; 2:3,13,15; 3:18,38,44; 4:6,11,12,14,17,20; 5:21; Eze 1:11,26,27,27; 2:3,5,8; 3:18,20,25,26; 4:8; 5:13; 6:6,7,10,13,14; 7:4,9,11,13,27; 8:2,3,6,6,13, 15; 9:4; 10:1,7,14,20; 11:1,5,10,12; 12:6,9,12,15, 16,16,20; 13:5,9,11,14,14,20,21,23; 14:8,9,15,15, 17,19,23; 15:2,7; 16:8,19,28,54,62; 17:8,9,14,21, 24; 18:9,21,24,25,28,29; 20:6,6,12,15,20,20,23,25, 26,26,28,38,42,44,48; 21:5,7,15,24; 22:3,16,22,24, 26,26; 23:3,13,20,38,39,41,43,48,49; 24:8,11,24,26, 27,27; 25:5,7,9,10,11,17; 26:2,6,10; 28:22,23,24, 26; 29:6,9,15,16,21,21; 30:2,8,9,19,21,25,26; 32:15, 31; 33:6,8,11,12,12,13,13,15,15,16,17,28,29,30,33; 34:10,25,27,30,30; 35:4,9,12,15,15; 36:3,4,5,7,11, 22,23,30,32,35,35,36,36,38; 37:2,6,9,13,14,16,17, 28; 38:8,10,14,16,16,17,17,18,19,19,20,23; 39:6,7, 11,14,22,22,23,28; 40:1,2,4,17; 41:6,7,8,22; 42:12, 14; 43:10,11,13,14,14,14,15; 44:12,14,18,19,30; 45:22; 46:3,18; 47:3,4,4,5,5,13; 48:22,35; Da 1:5, 13; 2:3,8,8,9,12,16,18,28,30,30,35,38,41,44,45,46; 3:3,5,7,10,11,14,18,22,24,27,29; 4:2,5,5,6,9,16,17, 17,18,22,25,26,26,27,32,34,36; 5:2,2,3,6,11,14,14, 16,21,24,25,30; 6:2,3,7,7,8,10,12,15,15,17,26; 7:4, 6,6,7,8,14,14,15,17,19,20,20,20,20,23; 8:1,13,17, 20,22,22,22,26; 9:2,15,18,27,27; 10:2,7,12; 11:31, 35; 12:1,1,11,11; Hos 1:1,5,6; 2:6,8,16,18,18,18,21; 6:2,3,4; 7:2; 8:6,14; 9:10,14,14; 10:11,14,15; 13:3, 10; 14:2; Joel 1:1,15; 2:5,11,25,27,27,27; 3:1,6,17, 18; Am 1:4,7,10,12,14; 2:2,5,16; 5:3,3,14,18; 6:14; 7:7; 8:3,5,5,9,10,13; 9:1,11,12,12; Ob 8; Jnh 1:3,4, 6,12,12; 3:9; 4:2,2,7,8; Mic 1:1,2; 2:4,11; 3:4,9; 4:2, 6,7,9,9,12; 5:10,15; 6:5; 7:1,12,17; Na 1:14; 2:7; 3:17; Hab 1:1,4,5,6,14; 2:2,13,13,15,18,18; Zep 1:1,3,9,10,12,15,17; 2:2,7,15; 3:9,11,16,19,20, 20; Hag 1:8; 2:12,21,23; Zec 1:15,19,21,21; 2:4,8,9, 9,11,11; 3:9,10; 4:9,10,12; 5:3,4; 6:15; 7:5,12,14; 8:6,9,10,23; 9:12,16; 10:2,2; 11:1,11; 12:2,3,4,6,7, 7,8,8,9,9,11; 13:1,2,4; 14:4,6,8,9,12,13,16,18,19, 20,21; Mal 1:7,8,8,10,10; 2:4,4; 3:10,10; 4:1,5; Mt 2:8,16,22,23; 3:9,10,16; 4:4,6,12,17; 5:16,17, 20,20,21,22,23,27,28,32,33,38,43,45,46,47; 6:4,18, 18,23,29,30,32; 7:13,14,19,22,25,27; 8:4,9,11,13, 24,28,28; 9:6,14,22,26,28,30,31,34; 10:14,15,19,26, 26,34,42; 11:21,23,24,25; 12:1,5,6,9,15,22,24,28, 36,45,45; 13:1,2,30,32,33,41,44,47; 14:1,2,7,9,20, 23,35; 15:5,5,11,12,13,17,18,21,22,27,28,37; 16:11, 12,18,20,21,21,21; 17:10,13,18,27; 18:1,7,10,10,12, 13,13,14,16,19,25,25,28,31,32; 19:4,7,9,12; 20:21, 25,30; 21:3,9,9,26,43,46; 22:4,16,16,23,24,34,43, 46; 23:16,17,18,19,31,35; 24:4,6,10,15,20,23,27,32, 33,36,39,46,48,50; 25:1,24,26,27,30; 26:24,29,41, 51,54,55,55,56,59,62; 27:3,4,8,16,18,19,24,24,51, 54,58,60,63,63,64; 28:4,5,11; Mk 1:9,27,32,38,44, 44; 2:1,2,7,8,10,18,20; 3:10,14,14,20,24,25; 4:1,1, 7,12,15,32,35,37; 5:23,29,30; 6:2,10,11,12,14,31, 36,37,37,47,55; 7:2,2,11,11,11,13,13,15,18,18,21, 24; 8:8,15,31,31; 9:1,11,12,17,25,26,30,48; 10:1,5, 42,47; 11:5,23,24,25,32; 12:5,14,19,28,32,34,35; 13:4,5,14,18,21,24,26,28,29,32,33; 14:21,25,35,38, 48,55,60,67; 15:10,16,32,42,44,45; 16:1,4,11,11,20; Lk 1:1,4,39,43,45,58,61; 2:1,2,10,15,26,34,35,38; 3:8,9; 4:11,22,23,25,43; 5:6,7,14,15,24; 6:23,23,26, 32,33,33,34,48,49; 7:7,8,21,29,37,37,39; 8:10,12, 14,16,17,17,23,46,47,53; 9:4,7,7,8,8,17,19,36,36, 39,43,45; 10:12,12,13,20,20,21,23,24,40,40; 11:14, 18,26,33,35,38,48,50; 12:1,2,2,4,12,28,30,33,33,36, 43,46,56; 13:1,2,21,31,32; 14:5,10,23; 15:7,13,14, 15,16; 16:4,9,16,25,26,28; 17:1,8,20,31,34; 18:1,3, 5,5,8,11,14,31; 19:4,11,22,23,26; 20:6,11,17,18,20, 21,21,28,37,41; 21:7,8,15,20,22,27,30,31,34,36,36, 36; 22:10,22,26,30,32,34,37,40,46,52,70; 23:7,7,12, 23,29,29; 24:4,13,14,18,21,23,25,44; Jn 1:3,4,7,7, 9,11,31,34,39,41,50; 2:9,17,22; 3:2,15,16,16,20,21, 21,26,28,29,33; 4:1,1,10,15,19,20,25,32,36,39,42, 44,45,47,51,53; 5:6,13,15,20,23,32,34,34,35,36,36, 36,36,39,39,42,44; 6:1,10,12,15,22,22,22,22,24,27, 27,30,33,39,40,41,50,51,58,61,65,69; 7:3,7,23,25, 26,35,39,42,49,52; 8:17,22,24,24,27,28,28,33,37, 40,47,48,52,52; 9:2,3,9,18,19,22,22,23,29,30,31,35, 36,39,41; 10:10,16,17,38,38,41,42; 11:4,6,10,15,16, 17,20,22,27,40,41,42,42,42,49,50,50,50,51,51,52, 53,57,57; 12:7,9,12,12,16,16,17,18,29,34,36,46,47, 49,50; 13:1,3,3,5,5,11,13,14,15,17,19,19,35; 14:2,2, 3,8,10,10,11,13,20,20,28,29,31,31; 15:2,2,2,6,8,11, 11,15,16,16,16,18,19; 16:1,4,4,7,14,15,15,19,21,23, 26,26,27,30,30,30,33; 17:1,2,3,7,8,8,11,12,12,13, 15,15,19,21,21,21,22,22,23,23,25,26,26; 18:4,8,9, 13,14,27,34,37; 19:4,7,21,24,24,27,28,28,30,33,35, 35,36; 20:1,7,9,14,18,19,22,31,31,31; 21:3,4,15,16, 17,20,22,23,23,23,24,25,25; Ac 1:1,3,19,19; 2:3,8, 29,30,30,31,41; 3:14,16,16,17,18,19,19,20; 4:10,13, 13,23,32,34; 5:3,3,8,10,15,26,26,31,34,42; 6:14,15; 7:5,5,7,12,16,19,20,25,25,41,46,53; 8:1,8,9,14,15, 18,19,22,23,24,26,29,35; 9:2,17,20,22,26,27,37,38, 39; 10:8,15,22,28,28,34,37,42,43,45,48; 11:1,9,17, 18,19,28; 12:1,3,9,11,15,19; 13:8,10,17,26,27,29, 34,38,40,41,47; 14:1,8,9,10,21,27; 15:7,7,8,10,11, 17,19,24,39; 16:3,3,10,12,18,18,19,26,33,36,38; 17:3,7,13,16,19,22,26,27,29,33; 18:5,28; 19:2,4,10, 12,12,16,23,25,26,27,27,35,40; 20:2,15,20,20,21, 23,23,25,26,29,31,34,35,38; 21:21,22,24,24,25,29, 31,34,36; 22:10,13,19,24,24,29; 23:3,5,6,8,8,10,22, 24,27,29,29,34,35; 24:4,9,10,11,14,14,14,15,21,26; 25:6,15,16,24,26; 26:5,6,7,8,9,9,10,11,18,20,21,23, 26,28,29,31; 27:1,10,12,18,25,28,29,32,40; 28:1,7, 11,15,20,22,28; Ro 1:5,10,11,12,12,13,13,15,16,17, 20,28,32; 2:2,4,15,19,22; 3:4,5,6,8,8,9,19,19,24,27, 27,28,30; 4:1,9,11,11,12,13,13,13,16,17,19,19,21; 5:3,15,17,20,21; 6:1,3,4,6,6,6,8,9,12,16,17,17,21, 22; 7:1,1,2,3,4,4,5,6,10,10,13,13,13,14,16,18,18, 20,24; 8:4,15,16,17,18,18,21,22,24,28,29,34,38,39; 9:3,7,10,11,17,17,30,30,33,33; 10:1,2,4,5,6,6,7,8,8, 9,10,10,19; 11:8,8,14,19,22,24,25,31,32,35; 13:1,1; 14:9,14,14,20,21,23; 15:4,4,5,6,8,8,9,13,14,16,20, 23,28,29,31,31,32; 16:5,17,26,26; 1Co 1:8,10,10, 10,11,14,15,16,28,28,29,30,30; 2:5,7,7,12,14; 3:16, 16,17,17,18,20; 4:2,4,5,6,7,8,8,8,9; 5:1,1,5,6,7,10, 11; 6:2,3,5,7,9,11,15,16,19; 7:5,5,7,7,26,29,35,36, 40; 8:1,4,4,7,9,10,13; 9:9,13,13,14,15,18,22,23,24, 25,25,27; 10:1,1,4,4,12,13,16,19,19,33; 11:3,10,14, 15,18,30,32,34; 12:2,3,9,15,16,22,23,23,24,25,25; 13:2,3; 14:5,7,12,13,18,23,26,31,37; 15:3,4,4,5,6, 10,12,12,15,15,27,27,28,37,42,46,50,54,58; 16:2,6, 10,11,15,19,22; 2Co 1:4,7,8,9,10,12,13,14,15,17, 23,23,24; 2:1,3,3,7,11,12,16,16; 3:3,5,7,7,9,9,11; 4:4,4,7,10,11,13,14,15,15,17; 5:1,4,6,10,12,14,15, 19,21; 6:3; 7:1,3,3,7,8,10,12,15; 8:1,3,7,9,9,11,13, 13,14,22,24; 9:2,3,3,8,8,11,12,13; 10:2,2,5,7,7,11, 13,15,16; 11:2,3,16,21,21,30,31; 12:3,4,5,9,10,13, 16,16,19,20,20,21; 13:3,5,6,6,7,7,7,7,9,10; Gal 1:6, 11,16,20,22; 2:2,5,7,9,10,13,14,14,16,16,17,17,19; 3:7,8,14,14,15,21,22,23,24,25; 4:1,5,9,9,11,13,15, 17,22,26,29; 5:1,2,3,6,8,10,10,11,17,21; 6:1,13; Eph 1:8,12,17,17,18,18,19,21; 2:7,9,11,12,12; 3:2, 3,6,10,11,16,17,17,19,19,20; 4:9,12,15,17,18,20,21, 28,29; 5:13; 6:3,3,8,9,11,13,15,19,19,20,21,22,22; Php 1:6,9,10,11,12,13,15,16,17,18,19,20,20,24,25, 26,27,28,28,28,30; 2:9,10,11,15,16,19,22,24,28; 3:8,9,9,9,12,12,15,21,21; 4:10,17,17,18; Col 1:5,6, 9,10,11,18,23,23,26,28; 2:2,2,2,4,8,17,22; 3:24; 4:1,3,3,4,6,8,8,9,12,13,16,16,17; 1Th 1:4; 2:1,11, 16; 3:3,3,4,4,5,5,6,6,10,13; 4:3,3,4,4,6,12,12,13,14, 14,15,17; 5:2,4,10,15; 2Th 1:5,11,11,12; 2:2,3,4,4, 5,6,9,10,11,12,14; 3:1,2,4,8,11,14; 1Ti 1:3,8,9,11, 12,14,15,16,16,18; 2:1,2; 3:4,7,14; 4:1,6,9,10,15; 5:7,16,20,25; 6:1,4,5,8,9,19,19; 2Ti 1:1,4,12,12,12, 14,15,18,18; 2:1,10,10,18,25,26; 3:17; 4:8,13,17; Titus 1:1,5,9,11,13; 2:5,8,8,10,10,11,14; 3:7,8,10, 11,13; Phm 2,6,10,13,14,15,19,20,21; Heb 2:1,5,6, 6,8,9,10,14,14,17,17; 3:10,10,12,12,13,18,19; 4:1, 3,6,11,11,16; 6:1,7,7,8,9,11,18; 7:5,9,11,13,14,14; 8:5,5,7,10; 9:4,7,8,9,11,11,11,13,14,14,15,15,22,24, 25,27; 10:1,10,13,16,20,22,27,29,34,36; 11:3,3,5,6, 6,7,13,14,18,19,28,35,40; 12:1,1,3,5,10,13,15,15, 16,18,18,19,19,21,24,25,26,27,27,28; 13:14,15,17, 17,18,19,20,23; Jas 1:3,4,7,12,12,18,20,21,25,27; 2:12,19,19,20,22,23,24; 3:1,13,17; 4:1,3,4,5,6,13, 14,15; 5:1,16,17,19; 1Pe 1:4,5,7,10,11,12,12,13,18, 18,22,22,25; 2:2,3,3,8,8,9,12,15,21,24; 3:1,4,7,9, 15,16,21; 4:4,6,7,11,12,13,16,16; 5:2,4,6,9,12; 2Pe 1:4,9,14,15,18,20; 2:8,21,22; 3:3,5,6,12,15,15, 16,17; 1Jn 1:1,3; 2:1,3,4,18,19,22,24,27,28,29,29; 3:1,1,1,2,5,5,14,15,17,19,20,24; 4:2,2,3,9,10,10,13, 14,15,17; 5:1,2,4,5,5,7,13,13,14,15,15,16,16,16,16, 17,18,19,19,20,20; 2Jn 5,6,6,8,8,12; 3Jn 2,2,4,6,7, 8,10,12; Jude 3,5; Rev 1:2,9,12,20; 2:2,2,14,17,19, 20,23,27,28; 3:5,5,8,8,9,10,11,15,17,20; 4:3; 5:13; 7:9; 8:11,12,13; 9:1,3,5,11,13,18,20; 10:6,6,6,8,8; 11:6,7,13; 12:4,9,12,13,14,16; 13:2,15,17,18; 14:2; 15:5; 16:3,13,14,16; 17:3,6,18; 18:4,4; 19:10,12,18; 20:2,3,13,13; 21:11; 22:6,9,14,18,19

THE (55924)

Ge 1:1,1,1,2,2,2,2,2,4,4,4,5,5,5,6,7,7,7,7,8,8,9,9, 10,10,11,11,12,13,14,14,14,14,15,15,15,16,16,16, 16,16,17,17,17,18,18,19,20,20,20,20,21,21,21,22, 22,22,22,23,24,24,24,24,24,25,25,25,25,26,26,26, 26,26,26,26,26,27,28,28,28,28,28,28,29,29,30,30, 30,30,30,30,30,31; 2:1,1,2,2,2,3,3,4,4,4,4,4,4,5,5,5, 5,6,6,6,7,7,7,7,7,8,8,8,9,9,9,9,9,9,9,9,10,11,11,11, 11,12,13,13,13,13,14,14,14,14,14,14,15,15,15,16, 16,16,17,17,18,18,19,19,19,19,19,19,19,20,20,20, 20,20,21,21,21,21,22,22,22,22,23; 3:1,1,1,1,1,2,2, 2,2,3,3,4,4,6,6,6,7,8,8,8,8,8,8,8,8,9,9,10,11, 12,12,12,13,13,13,13,14,14,14,15,16,17,17,17,18, 18,19,19,20,20,21,22,22,22,23,23,23,24,24,24,24, 24; 4:1,1,2,3,3,3,3,4,4,6,8,8,9,10,10,11,12,12,13, 14,14,15,15,16,16,18,18,18,19,20,21,26,26; 5:1,1,6, 7,9,10,12,13,15,16,18,19,21,22,25,26,29,29,29,32; 6:1,2,2,3,4,4,4,4,4,5,5,5,5,5,5,6,6,7,7,7,7,7,7,7,7, 8,8,9,9,11,12,12,13,13,15,16,16,16,17,17,17,18,19, 20; 7:1,1,3,4,4,4,5,6,6,7,7,7,8,9,10,10,10,11,11,11, 11,11,11,11,12,13,13,14,15,15,16,16,17,17,17,17, 17,18,18,18,18,18,19,19,19,20,20,21,21,22,23,23, 23,23,23,23,23,24,24; 8:1,1,1,1,1,2,2,2,2,2,2,3,3,3, 3,3,4,4,4,4,5,5,5,5,5,5,6,7,7,8,8,8,9,9,9,9,9,9,10,10, 11,11,11,11,12,13,13,13,13,13,13,13,13,14,14,14, 16,17,17,17,17,17,19,19,19,19,19,20,20,21,21,21, 21,22; 9:1,2,2,2,2,2,2,2,2,3,5,6,7,10,10,10,10,11, 11,12,12,13,13,13,13,14,14,14,15,16,16,16,16,17, 17,17,18,18,18,19,19,19,20,22,23,25,26,26,26,27, 27,28; 10:1,1,2,3,4,4,4,5,6,7,7,8,8,9,9,10,12,13,13, 14,15,15,18,19,20,21,21,22,23,24,24,25,26,30,30, 31,32,32,32,32; 11:1,4,4,4,5,5,5,6,6,8,8,8,9,9,9,9, 9,9,10,10,10,11,12,13,14,15,16,17,18,19,20,21,22, 23,24,25,26,27,27,27,28,28,29,29,29,29,31,31; 12:1,1,4,5,5,5,6,6,6,6,6,7,7,8,8,8,8,8,8,9,10,10,12, 14,17; 13:1,3,3,4,4,6,7,7,9,9,9,9,9,10,10,10,10,10, 10,11,11,11,11,12,12,12,13,13,14,14,14,15,16,16, 16,17,17,18,18; 14:1,2,3,3,4,5,5,5,5,5,6,6,6,7,7,7,8, 8,8,8,8,8,10,10,10,10,10,11,11,13,13,13,14,15,16, 16,16,17,17,17,17,21,21,21,22,22,23,24,24; 15:1,1, 2,4,4,5,5,6,7,7,9,10,10,11,12,13,14,16,16,16,17,17, 18,18,18,18,19,19; 16:2,5,5,7,7,7,7,7,9,9,10,11,11, 11,13,13,13,14,15,15; 17:1,4,7,7,8,9,10,11,11,12, 14,16,17,20; 18:1,1,1,1,1,2,2,6,6,7,8,9,10,10,11,13, 14,14,16,17,19,19,19,20,20,21,22,22,23,23,24,24, 24,24,25,25,25,25,25,25,26,26,26,27,28,28,28,29, 30,31,31,32,32,33; 19:1,1,1,1,1,2,2,2,2,4,4,4,5,6,8, 9,9,10,10,10,11,11,11,11,12,12,13,13,14,14,15,15, 15,16,16,16,16,17,17,19,21,22,23,23,23,24,24,24, 25,25,25,25,27,27,27,28,28,28,29,29,29,29,30,31, 31,31,31,33,34,34,34,35,37,37,37,38,38,38; 20:1,1, 3,6,7,8,12,16,18,18; 21:1,1,2,3,3,8,8,9,9,10,11,12, 13,13,14,14,14,15,15,15,15,16,17,17,17,17,18,18, 19,19,20,20,21,22,23,23,27,28,29,31,32,32,32,32, 33,33,33,34,34; 22:2,3,3,3,4,4,4,5,5,6,6,6,6,6,7,7,7, 8,8,8,9,9,9,9,10,11,11,12,13,14,14,14,15,15,16,17, 17,17,17,17,21,21,23; 23:2,3,5,6,7,7,7,9,9,9,10,10, 10,10,11,11,11,12,12,13,13,15,16,16,16,16,16,17, 17,17,17,17,18,18,18,18,19,19,19,20,20,20; 24:1,2, 2,3,3,3,3,3,5,5,5,7,7,8,9,9,10,10,11,11,11,11,11,13, 13,14,15,15,16,16,17,18,20,20,21,21,22,22,23,24, 24,25,26,26,27,27,27,27,27,28,29,29,30,30,30,30, 30,30,31,31,31,32,32,32,32,35,37,37,39,40,42,42, 44,44,45,46,47,47,47,48,48,48,48,48,50,50,51,51, 52,52,53,54,54,54,55,56,57,60,61,61,61,62,63,65, 65,65,66,67; 25:3,3,3,3,3,4,6,6,6,9,9,9,10,10,12,12, 12,13,13,13,13,16,16,16,18,18,18,19,19,19,20,20, 21,21,22,22,23,23,23,23,24,25,27,27,27,29,32; 26:1,1,1,2,2,3,4,4,7,7,8,10,11,12,12,13,14,15,15, 15,17,18,18,18,18,19,20,20,20,22,22,24,24,24,24, 25,25,26,28,29,31,31,32,33,33,34,34; 27:2,3,4,5,7, 7,9,9,13,14,15,15,16,16,17,17,20,22,22,22,22,27, 27,27,27,29,36,39,39,40,41,41,46; 28:2,2,4,4,4,5,5, 5,8,9,9,11,11,11,12,12,13,13,13,13,13,14,14,14,14, 14,14,16,17,17,18,18,19,21; 29:1,1,2,2,2,2,2,3,3,3, 3,3,3,3,3,4,6,7,7,7,8,8,8,8,8,10,10,10,13,16,16,16, 16,22,22,26,26,27,28,31,32,33,35; 30:2,13,14,16, 24,27,30,30,33,33,35,35,35,35,36,37,37,37,38,38, 38,38,39,40,40,40,40,41,41,41,41,41,42,42,42,43; 31:3,3,4,5,8,8,8,8,10,10,11,11,12,12,13,14,16,18, 18,20,21,21,22,23,24,25,27,29,29,32,32,33,33,34, 34,35,37,39,40,40,40,41,42,42,42,42,43,43,43,43, 46,49,53,53,53,53,53,54,54,55; 32:1,2,3,3,6,7,7,8, 10,11,11,12,12,13,16,16,17,17,19,19,19,19,19,21, 21,22,22,23,25,25,25,26,27,28,30,31,32,32,32,32, 32,32; 33:1,1,2,2,3,5,5,6,8,10,11,13,13,13,14,14,14, 14,15,17,18,18,19,19,19; 34:1,1,1,2,2,3,5,7,10,12, 12,12,12,19,19,20,20,21,22,22,24,24,24,25,26,27, 27,27,28,28,29,30,30; 35:2,3,4,4,4,5,5,6,6,7,8,12, 13,14,15,17,19,23,23,24,25,26,26; 36:1,1,2,2,2,5,6, 6,7,8,9,9,9,9,9,10,10,10,11,13,14,15,15,15,16,17, 17,18,18,19,20,20,20,22,23,24,24,24,24,24,25,26, 27,28,29,30,30,31,34,34,35,37,39,40,43,43,43,43, 43; 37:1,1,2,2,2,2,5,7,8,9,10,11,13,14,14,15,17,18, 22,23,24,24,27,28,28,28,29,30,31,31,32,35,36,36, 36; 38:2,7,7,9,9,10,10,12,12,12,14,14,16,18,20,20, 20,21,21,21,22,25,27,28,30; 39:1,1,1,2,2,3,3,5,5,5, 5,5,5,5,5,6,8,11,11,12,13,15,18,19,20,20,20,21,21, 21,22,22,23,23; 40:1,1,1,1,2,2,3,3,3,3,4,4,5,5,5,5,5, 6,9,10,11,11,12,15,15,16,17,17,17,18,19,20,20,20, 20,20,21,21,22,23; 41:1,2,2,3,3,4,4,6,7,7,8,8,9,10, 10,10,10,11,12,12,12,13,14,16,17,17,18,18,19,20, 20,23,24,24,24,25,25,26,26,26,27,27,27,29,30,30, 30,31,31,31,32,32,32,33,34,34,34,35,35,35,35,36, 36,36,36,37,38,40,41,43,45,45,46,47,47,48,48,48, 48,49,49,50,52,52,53,54,54,54,55,55,55,56,56,56, 56,56,57,57; 42:4,5,6,6,6,6,7,11,13,13,13,16,16,18, 19,22,27,27,27,29,30,30,30,32,33,33,34,35,38,38, 38; 43:1,1,2,3,5,6,7,8,9,11,11,11,12,12,12,13,14,15, 15,15,16,17,17,18,18,18,19,19,20,21,21,21,21,23, 24,24,26,26,26,29,30,31,32,32,33,33,33,33; 44:1,1, 1,2,2,2,2,3,4,5,8,8,8,9,10,11,12,12,12,12,13,14,14, 16,16,17,17,17,20,22,26,29,30,30,31,31,31,32,32, 33,33,34,34; 45:2,4,6,6,10,13,16,17,18,18,18,18,20, 21,23,24,25,27,27; 46:1,3,5,6,8,8,8,9,10,10,11,12, 12,12,13,14,15,16,17,17,18,19,21,22,23,24,25,27, 27,28,31,32,34,34; 47:1,3,4,6,6,6,9,9,9,11,11,11,12, 13,13,13,14,14,15,15,18,18,19,20,20,20,20,21,21, 22,22,22,23,23,24,24,24,25,26,26,26,27,27,28,29, 31; 48:2,3,6,6,7,7,7,8,9,12,14,14,15,15,16,16,16, 18,21,22,22; 49:3,4,8,9,10,10,10,10,11,11,13,14,15, 16,17,17,17,24,24,24,24,25,25,25,25,26,26,26,26, 26,26,26,27,27,27,27,28,28,29,29,29,30,30,30,30, 32,32,32,33; 50:2,2,3,3,4,5,5,7,7,8,10,10,11,11,11, 11,11,13,13,13,13,13,14,15,17,17,17,17,17,19,20, 23,23,24,25,26; Ex 1:1,1,5,7,7,9,10,12,12,12,12,14, 14,15,15,16,16,16,17,17,17,18,18,18,19,19,20,20, 21,22; 2:1,3,3,3,3,5,5,5,5,6,6,7,7,8,8,9,9,10,10,12, 12,13,13,13,14,14,16,18,19,19,21,23,23,25; 3:1,1,1, 1,1,1,2,2,2,3,4,4,5,6,6,6,6,7,7,8,8,8,8,9,9,9,9,10,11, 12,12,13,13,14,15,15,15,15,15,15,15,16,16,16,16, 17,17,18,18,18,18,18,18,18,18,19,20,20,21,22; 4:1, 2,3,3,3,4,4,4,5,5,5,5,5,5,6,6,7,8,8,8,9,9,9,9,9,10,10, 11,11,14,14,16,17,19,20,21,21,21,21,22,24,24,26, 27,27,27,28,28,29,29,30,30,30,31; 5:1,1,1,2,2,3,3, 3,3,3,4,4,5,5,6,6,7,8,8,9,9,10,10,10,12,13,13,14,15, 16,17,19,19,21,22; 6:1,2,3,4,5,5,5,6,6,6,6,7,7,7,8,8, 9,10,11,12,12,13,13,13,14,14,14,14,15,15,15,16,16, 17,18,19,19,21,22,24,24,25,25,25,26,26,27,27,28, 29,30; 7:1,2,4,5,5,5,6,8,10,11,11,13,14,14,15,15,15, 15,15,16,16,16,16,17,17,17,17,17,18,18,18,18,19, 19,19,19,19,20,20,20,20,20,21,21,21,21,22,22,22, 24,24,24,24,25,25; 8:1,1,3,3,4,5,5,5,6,6,6,7,7,7,8,8, 8,9,9,9,9,10,11,11,12,12,13,13,13,13,13,14,15,16, 16,16,16,16,17,17,17,17,17,18,18,19,19,19,20,20, 20,20,21,21,21,22,22,24,24,24,24,25,26,26,26,27, 27,28,28,29,29,29,29,30,31,31,32; 9:1,1,1,1,3,3,3, 4,4,4,5,5,5,6,6,6,6,6,7,7,7,8,8,8,9,9,10,11,11,11,12, 12,13,13,13,13,13,14,14,15,16,18,18,19,19,19,20, 20,21,21,21,22,22,22,23,23,23,23,23,24,24,25,25, 26,26,26,27,27,27,28,29,29,29,29,29,30,31,31,31, 32,33,33,33,33,33,34,35,35; 10:1,1,2,2,3,3,3,5,5,5, 6,6,7,7,8,9,10,11,11,12,12,12,12,13,13,13,13,14,15, 15,15,15,15,15,16,17,18,19,19,19,19,20,20,21,21, 22,23,23,24,25,26,26,27,28; 11:1,2,3,3,3,3,4,5,5,5, 5,5,5,7,7,8,9,10,10; 12:1,2,2,3,3,4,4,5,5,5,6,6,6,6,7, 7,7,7,7,8,8,9,9,11,12,12,13,13,13,14,14,15,15,15, 15,16,16,17,17,18,18,18,18,18,19,21,21,21,22,22, 22,22,22,22,23,23,23,23,23,23,23,25,25,27,27,27, 27,27,27,28,28,29,29,29,29,29,29,29,29,29,30,30, 31,31,31,33,33,33,34,34,35,35,36,36,36,36,37,39, 39,39,40,40,41,41,41,41,42,42,42,42,43,43,43,46, 46,46,46,47,48,48,48,49,49,49,50,50,51,51; 13:1,2, 2,3,3,3,3,4,5,5,5,5,6,6,8,9,9,10,11,11,11,12,12,12, 12,14,14,15,15,15,15,16,17,17,17,18,18,18,18,19, 19,20,20,21,22,22,22; 14:1,2,2,2,3,3,3,4,4,4,5,5,5, 7,7,8,8,8,9,9,9,10,10,10,11,12,12,12,13,13,13,13, 14,15,15,16,16,16,16,17,17,18,18,19,19,20,20,20, 20,20,20,21,21,21,21,22,22,23,23,24,24,24,24,24, 25,25,25,25,26,26,26,26,27,27,27,27,27,28,28,28, 28,28,29,29,30,30,30,30,30,31,31,31,31,31,31; 15:1,1,1,1,2,3,3,4,4,4,5,5,6,7,8,8,8,8,8,8,9,9,10,10, 11,12,13,14,14,15,15,15,16,16,17,17,17,18,19,19, 19,19,19,19,20,20,21,21,22,22,22,23,24,25,25,25, 25,25,25,26,26,26,26,27; 16:1,1,1,1,2,2,3,3,3,4,4,5, 5,6,6,6,7,7,7,8,8,8,8,8,9,9,10,10,10,10,10,11,12,12, 12,12,13,13,13,14,14,14,15,15,15,16,17,18,18,18, 21,22,22,22,23,23,25,25,26,26,27,27,28,29,29,29, 29,30,30,31,31,32,32,32,32,33,33,34,34,34,34,35, 35; 17:1,1,1,1,2,2,3,4,5,5,5,5,5,6,6,6,6,6,7,7,7,7,8, 8,9,9,9,10,10,10,11,11,12,13,13,14,14,15,16,16,16, 16; 18:1,1,4,4,5,5,7,8,8,8,8,8,9,9,9,9,10,10,10,10, 10,10,11,12,12,13,13,14,14,15,16,18,19,20,21,22, 22,23,25,26,26,26; 19:1,1,1,1,2,2,2,3,3,3,3,5,6,6,7, 7,7,7,8,8,8,9,9,9,9,10,10,11,11,11,11,12,12,12,12, 12,13,13,14,14,15,15,16,16,16,16,17,17,17,17,18, 18,18,19,19,19,20,20,20,20,21,21,21,22,22,22,23, 23,23,24,24,24,24,25; 20:2,2,4,4,4,5,5,5,5,5,7,7,7, 8,10,10,11,11,11,11,11,11,11,12,12,18,18,18,18,20, 20,21,21,22,22; 21:1,2,4,4,5,6,6,6,8,9,10,16,16,18, 19,19,19,19,19,19,20,21,21,22,22,22,26,26,26,27, 27,27,28,28,28,29,29,29,29,30,30,31,32,32,32,32, 32,34,34,34,34,34,35,35,35,35,36,36,36,36,36; 22:1,1,2,3,4,5,5,6,6,6,7,7,8,8,8,8,8,8,8,9,9,9,9,11, 11,11,11,11,11,12,12,12,13,13,13,14,15,15,15,15, 15,15,15,16,17,20,22,22,24,27,28,29,30,30,31,31; 23:2,2,5,7,8,8,10,11,11,11,11,11,12,12,12,13,15,15, 15,16,16,16,16,16,16,16,17,17,18,18,19,19,19,19, 20,20,23,23,25,28,28,29,29,30,31,31,31,31,31,31, 33; 24:1,1,1,2,2,2,3,3,3,4,4,4,4,4,5,6,6,6,7,7,7,7,8, 8,8,8,8,9,10,10,11,12,12,12,12,13,14,15,15,16,16, 16,16,16,16,16,17,17,17,17,18,18,18; 25:1,2,2,3,6, 6,6,7,9,12,14,14,14,14,15,15,16,16,16,18,18,19,19, 19,19,19,20,20,20,20,21,21,21,21,21,22,22,22,22, 22,25,26,26,26,27,27,27,27,28,28,29,30,30,32,32, 32,33,33,33,34,35,35,35,35,36,36,37,39,40,40; 26:1,2,2,3,3,3,4,4,4,4,4,5,5,5,6,6,7,7,8,9,9,9,9,9,10, 10,10,10,10,11,11,12,12,12,12,12,13,13,13,14,14, 15,17,17,18,18,20,20,20,22,22,22,23,23,24,24,24, 26,26,27,27,27,27,27,28,28,28,29,29,29,30,30,30, 33,33,33,33,33,33,33,33,34,34,34,34,35,35,35,35, 35,35,36,36,36; 27:2,2,2,2,3,4,4,5,5,5,6,7,7,7,8,8,9, 9,10,11,11,12,12,13,13,13,14,15,16,16,16,17,17,18, 19,19,19,19,19,20,20,20,21,21,21,21,21,21,21,21; 28:1,3,4,6,6,8,9,9,10,10,10,11,11,11,11,11,12,12, 12,12,12,14,14,15,15,17,18,19,20,21,21,21,21,22, 23,24,24,24,24,25,25,25,25,25,25,26,26,26,26,27, 27,27,27,27,27,27,28,28,28,28,28,28,29,29,29, 29,29,30,30,30,30,30,30,30,30,31,31,32,33,33,34, 34,34,34,35,35,35,35,36,37,37,37,38,38,38,38,39, 39,39,39,42,42,42,43,43,43; 29:2,3,3,4,4,5,5,5,5,5, 5,5,6,6,6,7,9,10,10,10,11,11,11,12,12,12,12,12,12, 13,13,13,13,13,13,14,14,15,16,16,16,17,17,17,17, 17,18,18,18,18,19,20,20,20,20,20,21,21,22,22, 22,22,22,22,22,22,22,22,23,23,24,24,25,25,25,25, 26,26,26,27,27,27,28,28,28,28,28,30,30,30,31,31, 31,32,32,32,32,32,32,34,34,36,37,37,38,39,39,40, 40,41,41,41,41,42,42,42,42,43,43,44,44,45,46,46; 30:3,3,3,4,4,4,4,5,6,6,6,6,6,6,7,7,8,8,8,10,10,10, 10,11,12,12,12,13,13,14,15,15,15,15,16,16,16,16, 16,16,17,18,18,20,20,20,21,22,23,24,25,25,26,26, 26,27,27,27,28,28,31,31,32,34,35,36,36,36,37; 31:1,2,2,3,6,6,7,7,7,7,7,7,8,8,8,9,9,10,10,10,10,11, 11,12,13,13,13,14,15,15,15,16,16,16,17,17,17,17, 17,18,18,18,18,18; 32:1,1,2,3,4,5,5,6,6,7,8,9,11,11, 12,12,12,12,13,13,14,14,15,15,15,16,16,16,16,16, 17,17,17,17,18,18,18,19,19,19,19,19,19,20,20,20, 20,20,24,24,25,26,26,26,26,27,27,27,27,28,28,29, 30,30,30,31,32,33,34,34,34,35,35,35; 33:1,1,1,2,3, 3,4,5,5,6,7,7,7,7,7,8,8,8,8,9,9,9,9,10,10,10,10,10, 11,11,11,12,14,16,16,16,17,17,19,19,21,22; 34:1,1, 1,1,2,2,3,3,3,4,4,4,4,5,5,5,6,6,6,7,7,7,7,7,8,9,10,10, 10,10,10,11,12,14,15,16,18,18,18,19,19,20,21,21, 22,22,22,22,22,22,23,23,24,25,25,25,26,26,26,26, 27,28,28,28,28,28,29,29,29,30,31,31,32,32,32,34, 34,34,35,35; 35:1,1,1,2,2,3,4,4,5,5,8,8,8,9,10,11, 12,12,12,13,13,13,14,14,15,15,15,15,15,15,15,16, 16,17,17,17,17,17,18,18,18,19,19,19,19,19,20,21, 21,21,21,22,23,24,24,26,26,26,27,27,28,28,28,29, 29,29,29,30,30,30,30,31,34,34; 36:1,1,1,1,1,2,2,3, 3,3,3,3,4,4,4,5,5,5,6,6,6,7,8,8,9,9,10,10,10,11,11, 11,11,11,12,12,12,13,13,14,14,15,16,16,17,17,17, 17,17,18,19,19,20,22,22,23,23,25,25,25,27,27,27, 28,28,28,29,29,29,29,31,31,32,32,32,32,32,33,33, 33,34,34,34,35,37,37,37,38,38; 37:1,3,5,5,5,5,6,7, 7,8,8,8,8,9,9,9,9,10,12,13,13,13,14,14,14,14,15,15, 16,16,16,17,18,18,18,19,19,19,20,21,21,21,21,22, 22,22,24,25,26,26,26,27,27,27,28,29,29,29; 38:1,2, 2,2,2,4,4,5,5,5,6,7,7,7,7,8,8,8,8,8,9,9,10,11,11,12, 12,13,13,14,15,15,15,16,16,17,17,17,17,17,17,18, 18,18,18,18,18,20,20,20,21,21,21,21,21,21,21,21, 22,22,22,23,24,24,24,24,24,24,25,25,25,25,26,27, 27,27,27,27,28,28,28,28,28,29,29,30,30,30,30,31,

THEIR (4400)

THEIRS (23)

THEM (5584)

THEMSELVES (316)

THEN (2968)

THERE (1894)

THESE (1112)

17; 8:2,4; 9:4,5; 10:4; 11:7,18,22,23,30; 12:1,28,30; 14:4,12; 15:5,18; 16:12,22; 17:19; 18:12,12; 19:3,5,9,11; 20:14; 25:16; 26:16; 27:1,4,8,12,13; 28:2,15,45; 29:1; 30:1,7; 31:1,3,16,17,28; 32:45; 33:16; Jos 1:2,6; 4:6,7,21; 5:7; 8:4; 9:1,13; 10:24,24,42; 11:5,10,12,14,18; 12:1,8,8; 13:23,28; 14:1; 15:12; 17:2,12; 18:20; 19:8,16,23,31,39,48,51; 20:4,9; 21:8,10,16,26,42,42; 23:3,7,12,13; 24:26,29; Jdg 1:30; 2:4,16; 3:1; 9:25,38; 13:23; 18:2,14; 20:16; Ru 3:17; 4:4; 1Sa 2:23; 4:8; 6:17; 10:7,9; 11:4,12; 12:3; 15:9; 16:10,11; 17:17,18,39; 18:23,26; 21:12; 23:2; 24:7; 25:10,15,37; 27:1,8; 29:3; 31:4; 2Sa 3:5,39; 5:14; 6:22; 7:28; 8:11; 14:3,19; 16:2,18; 21:22; 23:1,8; 24:17; 1Ki 4:2,8,21; 7:9,45,47; 8:8,54,59; 9:10,13,20,21; 10:7; 12:6,7,9,10,27; 14:27; 18:36,37; 21:27; 22:11,17,23; 2Ki 1:13; 4:38; 6:20; 7:13; 10:7,9; 16:15; 17:41; 18:27,35; 19:17; 21:11; 22:5,12; 23:16; 24:3; 1Ch 1:23,29,31,33,43,54; 2:1,3,18,23,33,50,53,55; 3:1,4,5,5,9; 4:2,3,4,6,12,18,22,31,33,33,42; 5:14,17,24; 6:17,19,31,50,54,64; 7:8,11,17,29,33,40; 8:6,10,28,38,38,40; 9:9,18,34,44,44; 10:4; 11:10,19; 12:1,14,20,23,38; 14:4; 17:19,26; 18:11,11; 20:8; 21:17; 23:4,9,10,24; 24:1,30; 25:5,6; 26:8,12,19; 27:22,31; 29:2,17,18; 2Ch 3:13; 4:18; 5:9; 8:7,8,18; 10:6,7,9; 11:10; 12:10; 14:7,8,14; 15:8; 17:19; 18:10,16,22; 19:9; 20:36; 21:2; 25:7,9; 29:12,21; 31:12,13,18; 32:6,14; 33:19; 34:4,10,20; 35:25; Ezr 1:11; 2:1,62; 4:15,21; 5:15; 6:8; 7:1; 8:1,28; 9:1; 10:3,44,44; Ne 1:4; 5:6,18,19; 6:6; 7:6,64; 10:8,29; 11:3; 12:1,7,12; 13:26; Est 1:5; 2:3; 3:1,12; 8:9; 9:20,26,27,28,28,28,31,32; Job 11:2; 12:3,9; 13:20; 16:2; 18:2; 26:4,14; 31:28; 32:1; 33:29; 42:7; Ps 14:4; 15:5; 19:14; 35:17; 42:4; 50:21; 53:4; 74:3; 107:43; Pr 1:18; 24:23; 25:1; Ecc 7:10,15; 11:9; Isa 7:4; 23:15; 28:7; 29:13,14; 30:9; 34:16; 36:12,20; 37:18; 40:26; 42:16; 44:21; 45:7; 47:7,9,14,15; 48:5,6,14; 49:21,21,21; 51:19; 56:7; 60:8; 66:2,2; Jer 5:4,10,14,14,23,25; 7:2,10,13; 8:5; 9:24,26; 10:11,16; 11:6; 13:10; 16:10; 17:20; 20:1; 22:2,4,5; 23:21,26,32,33; 24:5; 25:11,30; 26:7,10,15; 27:16; 28:14; 30:4,15; 31:23,36; 32:13,14; 33:24; 34:7; 35:7,16; 36:16,16,18,24; 38:4,9,12; 39:11; 43:10; 51:19,27,61; La 5:17; Eze 5:4; 10:15,20; 11:2; 14:3,14,16,18; 16:5,30,43,51; 17:12,18; 18:10,13; 22:28; 23:27; 24:4,19; 32:27; 35:10; 36:20,22; 37:3,4,5,9,11; 40:46; 42:11,14; 43:11,13,18,27; 45:15; 46:24; 47:13; 48:1,16,21,29,30; Da 1:2,17; 2:28; 3:13,21,23; 4:10; 5:7,26; 6:5,6,11; 7:16; 12:6,7; Hos 8:11; 13:2; 14:9; Am 9:12; Mic 2:6; Hag 1:2; 2:13; Zec 1:9,12,19,19,21,21,21; 3:7; 4:4,5,11,12,13,14; 6:4,5; 7:7; 8:9,12,16; 13:6; Mt 3:9; 4:3; 5:19,19; 6:29,32,33; 7:24,26,28; 10:2,5,42; 11:25; 12:7; 13:34,51,53,54,56; 15:8,18,20,32; 18:6,10,14; 19:1,14,20; 20:12,21,23; 21:16,23,24,27; 22:40; 24:2,8,33,34; 25:40,45; 26:1,62; Mk 2:8; 3:16; 6:2,2,8; 7:6,23; 8:2; 9:37,42; 10:14,20,40; 11:28,29,33; 12:31,40; 13:2,4,8,29,30; 14:60; 15:41; 16:13,17; Lk 1:25,65; 2:19,51; 3:8; 4:36; 5:22; 7:18; 8:3; 10:21,36; 11:27,45; 12:27,31; 13:2; 15:29; 17:2; 18:16,21; 20:2,8,47; 21:4,7,9,28,31,32; 23:31,49; 24:9,15,18,26,48; Jn 2:16; 3:10; 5:16,20,39; 6:5; 7:4; 8:20; 10:19,21,32; 12:16,16; 13:17; 14:12,24; 16:6,33; 17:13; 18:8; 19:36; 20:18,31; 21:15,24; Ac 1:22,24; 2:7,15; 3:24; 4:13,16; 5:11,32,35,38,39; 6:6; 7:1,50; 10:44; 11:12; 13:42; 14:15,18; 15:17,29; 16:17,20,24; 17:6; 19:36,37; 20:5,34; 21:24,24; 22:5,19; 23:8; 24:8,9,15,20; 25:9,11,20; 26:7,12,26,29; 27:31; 28:15; Ro 1:32; 8:31,37; 10:5; 11:24; 12:4; 14:22; 15:23; 1Co 2:10; 4:6,19; 9:15; 10:6,11; 12:11; 13:13,13; 2Co 7:1; 8:24; 12:7; 13:10; Gal 3:12; 4:24; Eph 5:3; Php 4:3; Col 2:17,22; 3:6,7,8,14; 4:11; 1Th 3:3; 4:18; 2Th 2:5; 1Ti 1:6; 3:14; 4:6,11,15; 5:4,7,21; 6:2; 2Ti 2:14; 3:8; Titus 2:15; 3:8,8,9; Heb 1:2; 4:4; 7:13; 9:5,23,23; 10:18; 11:13,39; 1Pe 1:7,12,20; 2Pe 1:4,8,10,12,15; 2:3,12,17; 3:6,16; 1Jn 2:26; 5:13; Jude 6,8,10,12,16,19; Rev 2:1,8,12,18; 3:1,7,14; 4:5; 7:13,14; 9:20; 11:10; 14:4; 16:5,9; 18:15; 19:9,20; 21:5; 22:6,8,20

THEY (7211)

Ge 1:26,29; 2:4,24,25; 3:7,7,7,8; 4:8; 5:2; 6:2,2,3,4; 7:14,17,19; 8:17; 9:2,23,23; 10:30; 11:2,3,3,4,6,6,7,8,31,31,31; 12:5,5,5,5,12,12,15,20; 13:6,6; 14:4,4,7,7,11,12; 15:13,14,14; 16:10; 17:13; 18:5,8,9,16,21; 19:2,3,3,4,5,8,9,9,11,11,17,33,35; 20:8,11,17; 22:9,19; 24:19,41,52,54,57,58,59,60; 25:18,25; 26:20,21,21,28,30,31,32,32,35; 29:3,4,5,6,8,20; 30:32,38,38,39,39,41; 31:43,46,46,54,54; 32:6,18,18; 33:4,5,7,13; 34:5,7,7,13,14,19,21,21,22,23,26,28,29,30,31; 35:4,4,5,16,16; 36:7,16,17,43; 37:4,5,8,16,17,18,18,19,23,24,25,25,25,31,32; 38:21; 40:4,6,8; 41:2,18,21,21,21,27,35; 42:6,7,8,10,13,20,21,23,26,27,28,29,29,29,35,35,35; 43:2,2,7,15,16,18,18,19,20,25,25,25,26,26,26,27,28,28,32,33,34; 44:1,4,7,13,13,14; 45:3,4,24,25,26,27; 46:6,28,32,32,32; 47:1,3,4,9,14,17,18,22,22,25,27,30; 48:6,6,9,16,16; 49:6,6,23; 50:10,10,11,13,15,16,17,18,26; Ex 1:7,10,11,11,12,12,14,17,19; 2:16,19; 3:13; 4:1,5,8,8,9,31,31,31; 5:1,3,8,8,9,14,19,19,20,20,21; 6:4,9,27; 7:7,16,19,24; 8:1,3,7,11,14,17,18,20,26; 9:1,10,13,19,32; 10:3,5,5,6,6,7,14,15,15,23; 12:4,7,7,8,33,36,36,36,39,39; 13:17,17,20,21; 14:2,9,10,11,17,25; 15:5,10,16,22,22,23,23,27,27; 16:1,4,5,5,5,10,15,15,16,17,18,18,20,21,22,24,27,29,32,35,35,35; 17:1,2,3,3,4,7,12; 18:7,8,13,16,20,20,22,22,26,26,26; 19:1,2,2,13,13,14,17,21; 20:18,18; 21:13,21; 22:3,3,4,5,7,8,14,23,27,27; 23:33; 24:3,5,7,11,11; 25:15,37; 26:24; 27:7; 28:1,3,4,4,4,30,38,41,43,43; 29:1,29,33,33,46; 30:20,20,20,20,21,21,29,30; 31:10,11; 32:1,4,4,6,8,8,9,15,23,24,31,35; 33:4,10; 34:12,15,15,16,30,35; 35:19,22,28; 36:3,4,6,7,10,11,12,13,14,16,17,18,19,20,22,23,25,27,31,33,34,34,35,36,36,37,38,38; 37:10,11,12,13,16,17,17,23,24,25,26,27,28,29; 38:1,2,2,3,4,5,6,7,7,7,8,9,28,30; 39:1,1,2,3,4,6,7,8,8,10,13,15,16,17,19,20,21,22,24,25,27,30,31,33,43; 40:15,32,32,36,37; Lev 2:1,12; 4:13,14,20,27,28,28,28,29,31,31,32,33,35,35,35; 5:1,1,1,1,2,2,2,2,2,3,3,3,4,4,5,5,5,6,6,8,10,10,11,11,11,12,13,13,15,16,16,16,17,17,18,18,18,19; 6:2,3,3,4,4,4,4,5,5,5,6,7,7,16; 7:7,12,12,13,14,15,16,20,30,30,35,36; 8:27; 9:5,13,20,23,23,24; 10:1,2,5,7,14,19; 11:8,13,25,28,31,35,37,40,40; 13:2,6,6,7,7,9,11,13,14,15,16,17,19,34,34,35,36,37,39,46,46,46,46; 14:2,3,8,8,8,9,9,9,9,10,20,21,21,22,23,42; 15:5,6,7,8,8,10,11,18,21,21,22,22,23,27,27,31; 16:1; 17:4,5,5,7,7,15,15,16,16; 18:3,3,17; 19:8,8,20; 20:4,9,12,13,14,16,17,17,20,20,21,23; 21:6,6,6,7,8; 22:2,7,9,11,25,25; 23:18,20; 24:11,12,16,16,23; 25:15,25,26,27,27,27,27,28,28,31,31,32,33,35,36,40,40,41,41,42,45,48,48,49,49,50,50,51,52,53,53,54,55; 26:7,22,26,36,36,37,39,40,41,43,43,44; 27:9,10,10,11,15,17,18,19,20,20,22,29; Nu 1:16,18,50,50; 2:9,16,17,17,24,31,34,34; 3:4,4,7,8,9,13,31,35,38; 4:6,7,8,9,10,11,12,13,14,14,15,15,19,19,20,25,27,31,33,49; 5:3,4,4,7,7,7,7,10; 6:3,3,4,4,5,5,7,8,9,10,11,11,12,12,13,14,18,20,21,21,21,27; 7:3,3,5,8,9,9; 8:3,7,11,15,16,19,22,25,26,26; 9:1,5,6,6,10,11,11,12,12,12,13,13,18,18,20,20,21,21,22,23,23,23; 10:10,13,21,28,33,34; 11:8,13,16,17,22,22,25,26,26,32,34; 12:2; 13:19,19,19,21,22,23,23,25,26,26,27,31,32,32,32; 14:4,11,12,14,14,19,35,35,39,40,44; 15:13,14,25,25,31,31,34; 16:3,12,16,27,30,33,33,33,38,41,45; 17:9,10; 18:3,3,3,4,9,12,13,16,17,21,22,23,23,24; 19:9,12,12,12,12,13,13,13,13,19,20,20,20; 20:1,3,8,20,27; 21:3,4,5,6,9,11,12,13,16,18,33,35,35; 22:5,6,7,7,12,16; 23:22,24; 24:6,8,8,8,9,24,24; 25:6,18,18; 26:9,10,19,61,62,62,63,64,65; 27:1,21; 29:6; 31:3,7,8,10,11,16; 32:2,5,9,9,11,11,12,16,30,30,38,38,40; 33:1,3,6,7,8,8,8,9,9,10,11,12,13,14,15,16,17,18,19,20,21,22,23,24,25,26,27,28,29,30,31,32,33,34,35,36,37,41,42,43,44,45,46,47,48,49,55; 35:3,3,5,12,12,20,21,23,25,26,28,31; 36:2,3,3,4,6,6,6,12; Dt 1:24,25,28,39,39,44; 2:4,11,12,21,22,25; 3:20; 4:10,10,42,42,45,46,47; 5:28; 7:4,23; 9:12,13,14,29; 10:5,7,8,11; 11:4; 12:8,30,31,31; 13:10; 14:7,7,7,21,27; 15:2,2,8,9; 16:18; 17:9,10,10,11,11,11; 18:1,2,17; 19:15; 20:9,11,12,12,18,18; 21:4,7,18,20; 22:2,2,3,19,28; 23:4,4,16,16; 24:13,15,15; 25:1,18,18; 26:12; 28:7,10,41,44,44,45,46,51,51,52,52,60; 29:19,19,26,26; 31:12,16,16,17,17,20,20,21; 32:5,5,7,15,15,16,17,17,20,21,28,29,37,47,47; 33:3,11,19,19; Jos 1:15,16; 2:1,3,4,5,5,16,21,22,22,23,24; 3:1,6,7; 4:8,8,8,9,14,14,18,20; 5:1,1,6,6,6,7,7,8,8,8,11,12,12; 6:14,14,15,15,20,21,23,24,24; 7:3,3,4,5,9,11,11,11,11,11,12,12,21,22,23,25,25,26; 8:5,6,6,6,6,9,11,15,16,17,19,20,21,22,23,24,29,31; 9:2,4,4,5,6,8,9,13,16,16,21,24,26,27; 10:5,11,23,24,24,26,27,27,27,34,35,35,37,37,37,39,39,39,39,39; 11:4,8,11,11,14,14; 12:1; 13:13; 16:10; 17:4,13,18; 18:4,9; 19:9,47,47,49,50,51; 20:4,4,6,6,6,6,7,8; 21:9,11,12,13,17,21,23,25,43; 22:6,9,10,11,14,15,15,28,30,33,33; 23:13; 24:1,7,8,22,30; Jdg 1:4,5,6,7,8,10,11,17,19,19,19,23,24,25,28,32,35; 2:3,5,5,6,9,12,12,12,13,14,15,17,17,19,22; 3:4,4,6,7,9,12,13,19,24,25,25,25,26,28,28,29; 4:3,12,24; 5:7,11,19,19,20,23,30; 6:4,5,5,6,13,29,29,29,32,35; 7:11,19,19,20,20,21,23,24,25,25,25; 8:1,5,8,18,25,25,33,35; 9:3,3,4,8,23,27,27,27,27,40,47,49,51,54,55; 10:4,6,8,16; 11:2,2,2,6,13,16,17,18,18,21; 12:1,1,6,6; 14:4,5,9,11,13,14,15; 15:6,10,11,12,13,13; 16:2,2,12,21,24,25,25,25,25,31; 17:6; 18:1,1,2,2,2,3,3,3,5,7,7,7,8,9,12,13,15,19,21,22,23,26,27,27,28,29,31; 19:5,11,14,14,15,15,21,21,22,22,25,25; 20:5,6,10,14,18,22,23,23,25,26,26,28,30,30,31,36,36,36,38,39,41,42,42,43,45,45,47,48,48,48; 21:2,3,5,6,8,8,9,9,11,12,12,17,20,23,25; Ru 1:2,2,4,4,9,13,14,19,19; 2:4,21; 4:2,17; 1Sa 1:9,19,25; 2:12,14,17,20,22,27,34,35; 4:4,6,7,8,9; 5:1,2,3,4,7,8,8,8,9,10,10,11; 6:3,4,6,6,10,10,11,12,13,13,19,21; 7:1,6,6,6,6,7,8,10,13; 8:2,3,5,6,7,7,8,8,11,19; 9:4,4,4,5,9,10,11,11,11,12,14,14,20,25,26,27; 10:2,4,5,11,14,21,22,23,27; 11:4,5,5,7,9,9,10,11,15; 12:4,5,8,9,10,21,21,21; 13:5,6,15; 14:9,10,11,17,20,22,26,26,26,30,31,32,32,36,40,46; 15:2,2,2,6,9,9,15; 16:4,4,6; 17:1,19,22,24,27,27,51,53; 18:7,7,8,20,23,27,30; 19:8,20,20,21,21,22; 20:11,41; 21:11; 22:1,4,11,17,17,17; 23:12,22,24,28; 25:1,7,8,9,9,12,12,13,15,16,43; 26:12,12,19,19; 27:11; 28:7,25,25; 29:5; 30:1,2,2,3,4,11,11,16,16,19,21,21,22; 31:2,3,7,8,9,9,10,12,12,13,13; 2Sa 1:12,12,23,23,23,23; 2:3,4,15,16,24,25,28,28,29,32; 3:21,26,32,35; 4:2,5,6,6,7,7,7,7,8,12,12,12; 5:3,6,8,11,17; 6:3,6,17; 7:10,10; 9:2; 10:5,6,6,13,14,15,15,16,18,19,19; 11:1,20; 12:18,19,20,24; 13:30,32; 14:6,7,7,10; 15:4,11,17,24,30; 16:22; 17:8,17,17,18,20,20,20,21,21,28,29; 18:3,3,17; 19:3,8,14,14,17,18; 20:3,7,8,15,15,18,22; 21:5,9,12,12,14,22; 22:8,19,38,39,39,42,45,45,46,46; 23:7,7,9; 24:4,5,6,7,7,8,8,13,17; 1Ki 1:1,3,7,25,32,38,39,41,44,45,53; 2:4,4,7; 3:22,24,28,28; 4:20,20,20,27,28; 5:14,17; 6:10; 7:5,28,37; 8:4,5,8,9,25,30,31,32,33,33,35,39,40,40,42,42,44,46,47,47,48,50,51,52,65,66; 9:9,13,22,23,28,28; 10:11,29,29; 11:2,2,16,18,18,24,24,33,41; 12:3,7,7,16,20,24,27,27,31; 13:11,13,20,25,27,30; 14:15,18,22,22,23,28,29; 15:7,22,23,31; 16:5,13,14,16,20,26,27; 18:6,6,10,26,26,26,26,26,28,29,30,34,34,39,40; 19:10,14,21; 20:6,9,12,16,18,18,23,23,25,27,29,32,33; 21:12,13,14; 22:6,11,12,32,32,37,38,39,45,48,48; 2Ki 1:6,8,18; 2:2,4,9,11,15,16,17,17,18,20,23; 3:22,23,24,25,25,26,27; 4:5,39,40,40,40,43,44; 5:23,24; 6:4,14,20,20,20,20,22,23,23,30; 7:3,4,4,5,5,6,7,7,8,8,9,10,10,12,12,12,13,14,15,15; 8:23; 9:12,13,13,21,27,33,33,35,35,36; 10:4,7,8,13,14,20,21,24,25,26,27,34; 11:12,16,17,18,19; 12:8,8,10,11,11,12,15,15,15,19; 13:5,5,6,6,8,12,21,21; 14:15,18,19,19,28; 15:6,16,21,31,36; 16:5,19; 17:7,9,10,11,11,12,14,15,15,15,15,16,16,16,17,17,19,21,23,24,25,25,25,29,32,32,33,33,33,34,34,40,41; 18:12,12,17,18,34; 19:3,18,18,26,37; 20:7,14,14,15,15,18,20; 21:8,9,14,15,16,17,24,25; 22:7,7,13,17,19,20; 23:9,11,18,28; 24:5; 25:4,7,7,13,14,23; 1Ch 4:23,23,28,33,39,40,41,41,43,43; 5:8,9,10,10,16,19,20,20,20,21,21,22,23,24,25,26; 6:32,32,54,55,60,65,67,71,72,74,76,77,78,80; 7:4,4,21; 8:28,32,40; 9:1,13,22,23,27,27,27,28,28,28,33,34,38; 10:2,3,7,8,9,10,12,12; 11:3,10,14,14,19; 12:1,2,2,8,8,15,15,19,21,21,38; 13:7,9; 14:8,16; 16:1,1,5,19,20; 17:9,9; 18:2; 19:5,6,7,11,14,15,16,16,17,18,19,19; 20:8; 21:3,17; 23:11,24,29,30,30,31; 24:2,4,5,19,31; 25:5,7; 26:6,8,22,27; 29:7,9,20,20,21,22,22,29; 2Ch 1:17,17; 2:17; 3:13; 4:21; 5:5,6,9,10,12; 6:16,21,22,23,24,24,26,30,31,31,32,34,36,37,37,38,38; 7:3,3,9,9,22; 8:9,10,15,18; 9:6,10,29; 10:3,7,7,16; 11:4,17; 12:2,7,7,8,8,11,15; 13:11,11,14,14,18; 14:7,10,13,13,14,14,15,15; 15:4,9,10,11,11,12,14,15,15; 16:4,6,14,14,14; 17:9,9,10; 18:5,10,11,14,31,31,32; 19:8; 20:4,8,10,10,11,16,20,20,21,22,22,23,23,24,25,25,26,26,28,29; 21:17,19; 22:4,6,9,9; 23:2,2,6,6,11,11,15,15,17,20; 24:9,11,11,12,13,14,14,18,19,19,21,21,23,25,25; 25:10,13,20,26,27,27; 26:18,20,20; 28:8,8,13,15,15,15,15,18,23,23; 29:6,6,7,7,15,15,16,16,17,17,17,18,19,21,22,22,22,23,30; 30:3,5,14,15,16,18,19,22,23; 31:1,1,4,5,6,7,8,12,16,17,18,18; 32:3,4,4,18,19,19; 33:8,9,10,25; 34:9,10,11,14,17,21,25,28,33; 35:12,12,13,14,24; 36:16,19,19,20; Ezr 1:11; 2:1,59,62,65,66,68,69; 3:3,4,5,6,7,7,8,11,12; 4:2,5,6,11,12,23; 5:4,5,7,11; 6:1,5,10,11,14,17,18,22; 8:17,18,20,36; 9:2,11; 10:1,5,16,17,19,19; Ne 1:3,10; 2:7,10,18,18,19,19; 3:1,1,3,6,8,13,13; 4:2,2,2,2,2,3,5,7,8,11,12,22; 5:8,8,12,12,13; 6:2,4,9,10,13,14,16,19; 7:6,61,64,67; 8:1,6,8,9,12,14,15,18; 9:2,3,3,4,11,12,16,16,17,17,18,18,19,21,22,24,25,25,25,25,26,26,26,26,27,27,28,28,28,28,29,29,29,30,34,35,35,36,37,37; 10:38; 11:30; 12:26,27,30,37,39,43,44,45,47; 13:2,3,13,13,15,21,29; Est 1:17; 3:4,4,8,12,14; 4:11; 5:6; 6:14; 7:2,8,10; 8:7,9; 9:5,5,7,10,12,14,15,15,16,17,18,23,26,27,31; 10:2; Job 1:4,15,17,19; 2:11,12,12,12,12,13,13; 3:18,22; 4:9,9,20,20,21; 5:14; 6:18,20,20,20; 7:6; 8:10,10,12,14,14,15,15,16; 9:3,3,25,26; 11:8,8; 12:7,7,15,25; 14:2,2,14,20,21,21,22; 15:3,14,14,35; 16:10; 19:12,15,18,23,24; 21:8,11,12,12,13,14,18,19,21,21,26,30,31,32; 22:16,17; 24:2,2,3,4,6,7,7,8,10,10,11,11,16,16,17,18,21,21,22,22,24,24,24,24; 27:8,10,10; 28:3,4,4,10,11; 29:22,23,24; 30:1,3,4,5,5,6,7,8,10,10,11,12,12,13,13,13,14,14; 31:13; 32:3,4,15,16,16; 33:15,22,26,27; 34:11,19,20,20,23,25,27,28; 35:9; 36:9,9,11,11,12,12,13,14; 37:8,12; 38:35,40; 39:2,2,3,4,13,16; 40:12; 41:6,17,17,23,25; 42:11; Ps 1:3,4; 5:9,10; 6:7,10; 7:2,15,16; 9:3,15,15,20; 10:10,10; 11:2; 12:2; 14:1,4,4,5; 16:3; 17:10,11,11,12; 18:7,18,37,38,38,41,44,44,45,45; 19:2,2,3,3,10,10,13; 20:8; 21:11,11; 22:4,5,5,7,8,16,18,31; 23:4; 24:5; 25:6,12,13,19; 28:4,5; 31:13,18; 32:9; 33:15; 35:5,7,8,8,11,12,13,15,15,16,16,20,21,27; 36:2,3,4,4,8; 37:2,2,7,10,19,19,20,20,26,40; 38:12; 39:6; 40:5,12; 41:2,7; 44:3; 45:15; 48:4,5,5; 49:9,11,12,14,17,17,18,18,19; 52:6; 53:1,4,4,5; 55:3,10,19,21; 56:1,5,6,6,6,8; 57:6,6,6; 58:3,7,8,9,10,10; 59:3,4,6,7,7,12,13,14,15; 62:4,4,4,4,9,9,12; 63:9,10; 64:3,4,4,5,5,5,6,7,9; 65:13; 66:4,4,6; 68:3; 69:21,23,26,28; 71:11; 72:17; 73:4,5,5,6,8,8,11,12,19,20; 74:4,5,6,7,7,8,8; 76:5; 78:6,7,8,10,11,17,18,18,19,19,22,25,29,29,29,30,30,32,32,34,34,35,36,37,39,40,41,41,42,44,53,56,56,57,58,58; 79:1,1,2,3,7,12; 82:5,5; 83:3,3,4,5,5,16,17,17; 84:4,6,6,7; 86:9,14; 87:7,7; 88:17,17; 89:16,16,31,51; 90:5,10; 91:12; 92:7,12,13,14,14; 94:2,4,5,5,6,6,7,11; 95:9,9,10,10,11; 99:6,7; 101:6; 102:26,26,26; 103:15; 104:7, 8, 8, 9, 9, 11, 12, 22, 22, 28, 28, 29, 29, 30, 32; 105:12,13,18,27,28,35,38,40,44,45; 106:7,7,7,12,13,14,14,15,16,19,20,21,24,24,25,28,29,32,33,34,35,36,37,38,38,39,39,39,43,43; 107:4,5,6,7,11,12,13,18,19,23,24,26,27,27,28,30,36,36,37,39; 109:2,3,3,4,5,10,25,25,28; 111:2,8; 112:6,7,8,8,9,10; 115:5,6,7,7; 118:11,12,12; 119:3,24,74,87,111,138,150,155,158; 120:7; 124:3; 127:5,5; 129:1,2,2,6; 135:16,17; 137:3,7; 138:4,5; 139:18,20; 140:3,5,10; 141:7,9; 142:6; 144:4,5; 145:4,5,6,7,11; 146:4; 147:9,20; 148:5; Pr 1:9,11,16,18,28,28,29,30,31; 3:2,22,30; 4:16,16,16,16,17,19,22; 5:23; 6:22,22,22; 7:5; 8:9; 9:8,8,9,9,18; 11:26; 15:12,22; 16:5,13; 17:8,16,28,28; 18:8,11,20; 19:7,17,25; 20:4; 21:7,11,22; 22:6,6,6,8,9,22,29,29; 23:5,5,9,13,35,35; 24:7,12,16,17,22,29,29; 25:17; 26:22,24; 28:11; 29:17,17,19,19,24; 30:10,15,24,25,26,27; 31:5; Ecc 1:3,7; 2:19,21,21,22; 3:12,18,18; 4:1,1,9,11; 5:1,11,12,14,15,15,15,16,16,16,17,20; 6:2,12,12; 7:29; 8:10,17,17; 9:1,3,3,5,5,6; 10:3,3,13,15; 11:3; 12:3; SS 1:4; 3:3; 5:7,7,7,7; 6:5; Isa 1:2,4,4,11,14,18,18,18,23,23; 2:4,4,6,6,8,12,20,21; 3:9,9,9,10,11,12; 5:11,12,12,24,26,29,29,29,30; 6:2,2,2,3,10,13; 7:1,19,22,25; 8:12,15,15,20,21,21,21,22,22; 9:3,13,19,20,20,21; 10:28,28,28,29,32,32; 11:9,14,14,14,16; 13:5,8,8,14,14,18,18; 14:2,7,10,10,16,21; 15:3,3,5,5,5,7,7; 16:7; 17:8,8,9,12,12,13,14; 18:6; 19:3,14,16,20,21,21,21,22; 21:5,5,5,5,15; 22:2,3; 23:5,10,13,13,18; 24:5,9,11,14,14,14,22,22; 25:9,11; 26:3,10,10,11,14,14,16,16; 27:10,10,11; 28:4,7,7,7,12,13,13,13; 29:11,12,13,23,23,23; 30:4,10; 31:8; 32:6,6,6,7,8; 33:12,16; 34:17; 35:2,9,10; 36:19; 37:3,19,19,27,38; 38:19; 39:3,3,4,4,7; 40:15,15,17,20,24,24,24,24,31,31,31; 41:5,6,25,27,29; 42:9,16,22,22,24,24,25,25; 43:2,9,14,17,21; 44:4,9,9,11,18,18,18,18,26; 45:14,14,14,16,24; 46:2,2,6,6,7,7; 47:9,14,14,15; 48:3,5,7,13,21; 49:9,10,12,21,22,23,23,26; 50:9; 51:11,14,14,20,20; 52:6,8,8,15,15,15,15; 56:10,10,10,10,10,11,11,11,11,11; 57:2,2,6,12,16,17; 58:2,2,2,2,3; 59:4,4,4,5,6,6,7,7,8,8,18,19; 60:7,11,21,21; 61:3,4,4,9; 62:4,6,12; 63:8,10,13,14,19; 65:7,17,21,21,22,23,23,23,23,24,24,25; 66:2,3,3,4,4,5,6,17,17,18,18,19,20,20,24,24; Jer 1:15,19; 2:5,5,6,11,13,15,15,24,26,27,27,27,27,28,30; 3:17,17,18,21; 4:2,17,22,22,22,22,22,24,30; 5:2,2,3,3,3,4,4,5,5,7,8,12,12,13,17,17,17,22,22,22,23,24,27,28,28,28; 6:3,10,10,14,14,15,15,15,15,15,19,23,23,23,23,23,28,28,28,30; 7:17,18,19,19,24,24,24,26,26,27,27,30,31,32; 8:2,2,2,2,4,4,5,5,6,9,9,9,11,11,12,12,12,12,12,12,16,17,19; 9:2,3,3,3,3,5,5,6,8,8,10,13,13,14,14,16,24; 10:3,4,4,5,5,5,5,8,8,14,15,15,18,21,25,25; 11:8,8,8,10,10,11,11,12,12,14,18,19; 12:2,2,5,6,6,6,10,13,13,13,16,16,16; 13:11,12; 14:2,3,3,3,10,10,12,12,14,15,16,16,18; 15:2,7,16,20; 16:4,4,4,6,10,11,16,16,17,18,20,21; 17:6,6,8,11,13,15,23,23,25; 18:12,15,15,18,20,22; 19:4,4,4,4,5,9,11,13,15; 20:5,11; 21:1,6,9; 22:7,9,12,18,18,28; 23:3,4,8,8,12,12,12,13,14,14,14,16,16,17,17,21,21,22,22,25,27,27,32,32; 24:2,3,7,7,8,8,10; 25:5,14,16,16,18,28,33; 26:3,3,10,23; 27:10,14,15,16,18,22,22; 28:14; 29:5,6,9,17,19,23,23,23,28; 30:9,14,19,19; 31:1,9,9,9,11,12,12,12,12,15,16,32,33,34,34,37; 32:14,23,23,23,29,32,32,33,33,34,35,35,38,39,40; 33:5,7,8,9,11,24; 34:5,10,10,11,11,14,16,18,18,22; 35:6,14,14,15,17,17; 36:3,7,15,16,16,17,20,20,24,31; 37:5,8,9,10,15,15; 38:2,2,6,6,7,9,9,13,18,19,20,22,25,27; 39:4,4,5,14,16; 40:8,12,12,12; 41:1,7,12,12,13,17,18; 42:5; 43:3,5,6,6,7; 44:2,3,3,3,5,5,6,10,10,12,12,12,12,14,27; 46:5,5,5,6,15,16,16,16,17,21,21,22,23,23,23; 47:2,2; 48:5,5,12,12,13,32,33,36,39; 49:9,9,9,23,23; 50:5,5,6,7,9,13,19,36,36,37,37,38,42,42,42,42,42; 51:2,4,7,14,17,18,18,24,28,30,30,38,39,39,57; 52:4,7,7,17,18; La 1:2,6,8,11,11,14,14,19,19,21,21; 2:7,8,10,12,12,14,14,15,16,20; 3:14, 23, 53, 63, 64; 4:8, 8, 9, 14, 14, 14, 15, 15, 19; Eze 1:8,9,9,11,12,12,16,17,17,20,21,21,24,24,25; 2:3,5,5,5,6,6,7,7; 3:6,7,8,9,11,15,19,19,20,20,21,21,21,25,26,27; 4:17; 5:13,17; 6:9,9,9,10,11,13,13,14,14; 7:14,14,16,18,19,20,20,22,25,26,27; 8:6,9,12,16,17,17,18; 9:2,6,7,8,9,10; 10:11,11,11,17,17,19,19,20; 11:3,15,16,18,20,20,21; 12:2,2,3,3,3,4,4,5,6,7,11,15,16,16,16,19,23; 13:6,9,9,10,10,21; 14:10,11,11,14,15,16,16,18,18,20,20,22; 15:3,7,8; 16:37,39,39,40,41,47,49,50,51,52,55; 17:23; 18:21,21,22,22,22,23,24,24,24,24,26,26,26,27,27,28,28,28; 19:4,8,9,9; 20:1,8,8,8,8,9,12,13,13,16,20,21,21,21,24,25,26,28,28,38,38,49; 21:7,12; 22:7,7,10,18,25,26,26,26,27,28,29,31; 23:3,4,10,17,24,24,24,25,25,25,26,29,29,37,37,37,37,38,38,39,39,39,40,40,42,44,44,45,47; 24:27; 25:3,4,4,11,13,14,14,17; 26:4,6,10,12,12,16,17; 27:5,5,6,6,10,11,11,12,13,15,16,17,18,21,22,24,30,30,31,31,32,32; 28:7,8,13,24,25,25,26,26,26; 29:7,7,9,13,14,16,21; 30:6,7,8,11,19,25,26; 31:14,17; 32:3,12,15,16,16,20,21,21,24,25,25,26,27,29,29,30,30; 33:5,5,5,9,9,11,12,13,13,13,13,14,15,15,15,15,16,16,18,19,29,29,31,31,32,33; 34:5,5,5,6,12,14,14,22,25,27,28,28,29,30,30; 35:12,15; 36:3,5,5,8,11,12,17,18,18,19,20,20,20,21,35,38; 37:9,10,11,17,19,21,22,23,23,24,24,25,25,27; 38:8,17,23; 39:6,9,10,10,10,14,14,14,15,16,18,23,23,26,26,26,28; 40:18,24,48; 41:19; 42:6,11,13,14,14,14,14,14; 43:7,8,8,10,11,11,11,26,26; 44:11,11,12,12,13,13,15,16,16,17,17,17,18,18,19,19,19,20,20,22,22,23,24,24,29; 46:9,10,10; 47:11,12,22; 48:14; Da 1:5,5,15,16,19; 2:2,7,11,38; 3:3,7,9,12,24,27,28; 4:7; 5:3,4,4,8,15; 6:4,4,12,13,16,22,24; 7:22; 8:25; 10:7; 11:6,31,33,34,34,35; Hos 1:10,11; 2:4,8,21,22,23; 3:1,5; 4:2,7,7,8,10,10,10,12,13,14,14,18; 5:4,6,6,7,7,7,15,15; 6:7,7,9; 7:1,2,2,3,4,6,7,12,13,13,13,14,14,14,15,16,16,16; 8:4,4,4,5,6,7,9,10,10,12,13,13,13; 9:3,4,6,9,10,10,10,12,16,16,17,17; 10:2,3,4,8; 11:2,2,2,2,3,5,5,7,10,11; 12:8,11; 13:2,2,2,2,3,6,6,6,6,16,16; 14:7,7; Joel 1:18; 2:4,4,5,7,7,7,8,8,9,9,9,9,17; 3:2,2,3,3,8,19; Am 2:4,4,6,7,8,8,9; 3:3,10,10; 6:2,9; 7:2; 8:7,12,14; 9:2,2,3,3,4,12,14,14,14; Ob 5,5,5,16,16,18,19; Jnh 1:5,7,8,10,10,11,13,14,15,16; 3:10,10; Mic 1:7,16; 2:1,2,2,2,4,13; 3:4,4,5,5,7,11; 4:3,3,11,12,12; 5:1,4,6; 7:2,3,3,16,17,17,17; Na 1:9,10,10,12,12,15; 2:3,4,4,5,5,8,11; 3:12,13,15,16,16,17; Hab 1:7,7,8,9,10,10,10,11; 2:7,15; Zep 1:13,13,13,13,17,17; 2:7,7,10; 3:4,6,7,7,13,13,13,16,19; Hag 1:14; 2:14,14; Zec 1:4,5,6,9,10,11,15; 3:5; 4:10; 5:9,9,10; 6:7,7; 7:11,11,12,13,13,14,14,14; 8:8; 9:2,15,15,15,16,17; 10:2,2,5,5,5,6,8,9,9,9,11,12; 11:6,12,13; 12:6,10,10,10; 13:2,3,4,6,9,9,9; 14:12,13,17,18; Mal 1:4,4; 3:15,15,17; 4:3; Mt 1:18,23; 2:5,9,9,9,10,10,11,11,11,12,13,18; 3:6; 4:6,18,18,20,21,22; 5:4,5,6,7,8,9,12,15,16; 6:2,5,5,7,7,14,16,16,16,26,26,28; 7:6,15,15; 8:28,29,32,34,34; 9:8,8,11,15,17,17,24,28,31,32,36; 10:19; 11:16,18,19,20,21; 12:2,10,14,22,24,27,36,41,45; 13:6,6,12,12,13,13,15,15,15,16,16,21,21,21,41,42,48,51,54,54,57; 14:5,12,15,16,17,20,26,26,32,34,34,35; 15:2,2,6,9,12,14,31,31,32,32,34,36,37; 16:5,7,12,14,27,28; 17:6,8,8,9,12,12,14,16,22,23; 18:7,15,16,17,17,19,31; 19:3,6,7,25; 20:5,7,10,11,11,12,18,22,23,24,30,30,31,33,34; 21:1,7,15,16,20,20,23,25,26,27,31,35,37,38,39,41,45,46,46; 22:3,5,10,16,16,16,19,21,22,22,22,24,30,33,42; 23:3,3,3,3,4,4,5,5,6,7,25; 24:3,30,31,39; 25:5,9,10,11,29,29,44,46; 26:4,5,

THIS (3729)

THOSE (1488)

TO (21090)

8,11,13,14,15,17,20,20,20,21; **27:**1,3,3,4,5,9,9,11,
26,26,36; **28:**1,2,7,8,11,12,17,18,19,20,22,25; **29:**1,
3,3,4,4,5,10,14,16,17,19,19; **30:**1,6,8,9,9,10,11,12,
13,14,16,18,20,21,21; **31:**1,2,2,4,7,11,11,14,14,14,
15,16,16,16,17,17,18; **32:**1,2,6,10,12,13,17,18,18,
19,24,24,25,27,29,30; **33:**1,2,2,3,6,8,8,9,10,11,12,
12,14,20,21,22,23,24,25,25,27,27,27,28,30,31,31,
32; **34:**1,2,2,18,18,20; **35:**1,5,6,12,12; **36:**1,4,4,4,6,
6,10,12,13,15,16,19,20,22,22,27,27,32,37; **37:**4,4,4,
5,5,6,6,7,9,9,9,10,11,12,12,12,15,16,16,16,19,19,
19,21,24,25; **38:**1,8,8,13,13,13,13,13,13,14,16,20;
39:4,4,10,12,17,17,23,23,24,26,28; **40:**2,4,4,4,6,7,
13,13,14,15,19,22,23,23,24,26,27,31,32,34,35,37,
43,45,46,46,48,49; **41:**1,4,6,7,11,16,17,20,22; **42:**1,
7,8,11,12,13,14,14,19,20; **43:**1,3,6,8,10,11,11,14,
14,18,19,19,19,20,21,22,22,23,24,24,24,25,25,26,
27; **44:**1,2,2,2,3,3,4,5,5,5,5,6,7,8,9,13,13,14,14,15,
15,15,15,16,16,16,17,18,19,19,20,21,23,23,24,24,
24,24,27,27,28,28,29,29,30,30; **45:**1,1,2,4,5,5,6,6,
7,7,8,8,10,11,11,12,13,14,15,15,16,16,17,17,18,19,
20,20,21,22,23,23,24,25; **46:**1,1,2,2,2,3,4,4,5,5,6,7,
7,8,8,9,9,9,9,9,10,11,12,12,13,13,14,14,14,16,16,
16,17,17,17,18,19,19,20,20,20,21,21,24,24; **47:**1,1,
2,4,5,6,8,10,12,14,14,14,15,15,17,17,18,19,20,21,
21,22,22,22,23; **48:**1,1,1,2,3,4,5,6,7,8,8,8,9,9,12,
14,21,21,21,21,22,22,23,24,25,26,27,28,28,29,29;
Da 1:1,2,3,4,4,4,5,5,7,7,7,7,8,8,9,9,11,12,12,14,16,
17,18,18,19; **2:**2,3,3,5,8,9,11,13,13,13,13,13,14,14,
14,15,16,17,17,18,19,20,21,21,23,23,24,24,24,24,
25,26,27,28,29,29,29,30,35,36,39,40,44,44,45,46,
47,47; **3:**2,2,4,9,12,14,15,15,16,16,17,18,20,24,28,
28; **4:**1,2,3,6,11,17,19,19,20,21,22,25,26,26,27,27,
28,32,34,35,36,36,37; **5:**2,7,11,12,12,13,15,16,16,
17,19,19,19,19,19,19,23,26,28; **6:**1,1,2,3,4,4,5,6,7,
7,10,10,12,12,12,12,13,13,13,14,14,15,15,15,16,18,
18,19,20,20,23,25; **7:**4,6,11,12,19,20,25,27,28; **8:**1,
7,7,9,9,10,11,12,12,13,13,14,15,17,18,18,18,19,25;
9:2,2,3,4,6,6,6,7,11,12,13,14,15,16,20,21,22,22,23,
23,24,24,24,24,24,24,24,25,26,27; **10:**1,1,9,9,11,11,
11,11,12,12,12,13,14,14,14,14,15,16,16,19,20,20;
11:1,4,4,6,6,7,8,9,15,15,16,16,17,17,18,18,19,20,
23,23,25,26,27,27,28,28,30,31,38,44,45; **12:**2,2,3,4,
6,10,13; **Hos 1:**1,2,2,2,4,4,6,6,6,7,10; **2:**4,7,9,13,14,
14,19,21,21,22,22,23,23; **3:**1,1,1,3,5,5; **4:**1,10,11,
12,12,13,13,14,14,15,15,17; **5:**3,4,4,6,7,7,12,12,13,
13,13,13,14,14,14,14,15; **6:**1,1,3,3,7,9,10; **7:**10,11,
11,13,13,13,14,14,16; **8:**1,2,4,7,9,9,10,13,13; **9:**1,3,
4,4,10,10,12,13; **10:**6,8,8,10,11,12,14,15; **11:**2,2,3,
4,4,4,5,5,6,7; **12:**1,2,2,2,6,7,10,12,12,12,13; **13:**7,
13,13,16; **14:**1,2,2,3,5,8; **Joel 1:**1,3,3,3,14,14,19;
2:2,12,13,13,19,19,19,26,31,31; **3:**2,2,3,5,6,7,7,8,8,
12,19; **Am 1:**5,6,9,13,14; **2:**1,7,10,12; **3:**3,5,6,7,9,9,
10,14; **4:**1,4,4,5,6,8,8,8,9,10,10,11,12,12,12,13,13;
5:2,2,3,4,5,5,5,6,7,9,16,16,18,19,19,21,23; **6:**1,1,1,
2,2,2,7,10,10,10,14; **7:**7,10,12,12,15,15; **8:**2,3,12,
12,14; **9:**2,2,3,4,7,11,15; **Ob** 1,1,3,3,5,5,7,14,15,21;
Jnh 1:1,2,3,3,4,5,5,6,7,7,11,11,13,13,14,16,16,17;
2:1,2,2,6,7,7,8,9; **3:**1,2,2,3,3,5; **4:**1,2,2,2,2,3,3,4,5,
5,6,6,8,8,8,9,9; **Mic 1:**1,7,9,9,12,13,14,14,15; **2:**1,1,
1,4,5,7; **3:**4,5,5,5,8,8,8; **4:**1,2,2,6,8,8,10,10,12,13,
13,13; **5:**3,4,13; **6:**1,1,3,4,5,8,8,8,9,9,10,13,13,14,
16,16; **7:**1,2,10,12,12,12,12,17,18,20,20,20; **Na 1:**3,
9,14; **2:**5,11; **3:**1,7,10,13,18,18; **Hab 1:**2,5,6,7,8,12,
12,13,16,16,17; **2:**1,1,1,1,5,6,9,9,12,15,15,16,17,
19,19,19,19; **3:**8,13,13,13,14,14,16,19; **Zep 1:**1,3,5,
18; **2:**5,7,11,11,15; **3:**1,2,4,7,8,8,8,8,9,11,11,16;
Hag 1:1,1,2,4,5,6,7,9,13,14; **2:**2,2,2,3,3,10,15,16,
16,16,17,18,20,21; **Zec 1:**1,3,3,4,4,6,6,7,10,11,13,
14,16,19,21,21,21; **2:**2,2,3,3,4,6,11; **3:**1,2,4,4,6,7,8,
8,10; **4:**2,6,6,7,8,9,14; **5:**3,3,3,5,5,10,11,11; **6:**4,7,8,
9,10,14,15,15; **7:**1,2,4,8,9,11,12,12; **8:**1,3,6,6,8,8,
12,14,15,15,16,16,17,18,21,21,22,22,22; **9:**1,6,7,8,
9,10,10,10,12,12; **10:**1,1,5,10; **11:**3,3,13,13,13,15,
16,17; **12:**2,3,9; **13:**1,1,3,3,4,7; **14:**2,2,4,5,7,8,8,10,
10,10,10,16,16,17,17,18,19,20,21,21; **Mal 1:**1,3,8,
9,9,11,11,14,14,14; **2:**2,2,5,7,8,9,10,12,14,15,15,16;
3:1,4,5,5,7,7,7,10,14,15; **4:**1,5,6,6; **Mt 1:**11,12,17,
17,17,17,18,18,18,19,19,19,19,20,20,21,21,22,23,
25; **2:**1,2,4,8,8,11,12,12,12,13,13,13,13,16,18,19,
20,20,21,22,22; **3:**5,7,7,7,9,11,13,13,14,14,14,15,
15; **4:**1,3,3,5,7,8,10,12,14,17,19,24; **5:**1,2,13,15,17,
17,17,21,21,22,22,22,24,25,25,25,29,29,29,30,30,
30,33,33,37,39,40,41,42,42,45; **6:**1,1,2,2,3,5,5,6,
16,18,18,24,27,33; **7:**2,3,4,5,6,6,7,7,8,11,11,11,12,
12,13,14,15,21,22; **8:**4,4,4,5,7,8,9,10,11,13,15,16,
17,18,18,19,20,21,25,29,32,33,34,34; **9:**1,2,2,3,5,5,
6,6,6,8,13,20,21,28,28,29,29,32,37,38; **10:**1,1,1,6,
9,13,14,17,18,18,19,19,19,21,21,22,23,25,29,34,34,
34,35,42; **11:**1,3,3,4,5,7,7,7,8,9,12,14,14,16,16,20,
21,21,23,23,23,25,26,27,27,27,28; **12:**1,2,4,10,10,
11,12,13,16,17,18,20,25,32,36,38,38,42,42,44,46,
46,46,47,47,48,49; **13:**3,10,10,11,11,13,17,17,18,
20,22,23,27,28,30,34,34,36,36,52,54,57; **14:**2,4,4,5,
7,11,11,13,15,15,16,16,18,19,19,19,19,22,23,25,27,
28,28,30,35,35,36; **15:**1,4,4,5,5,6,10,12,15,21,22,
23,24,26,26,28,30,32,32,32,33,35,36,36,39; **16:**1,1,
3,5,6,11,12,13,17,20,21,21,21,21,22,22,23,23,24,
24,25,26,27,27; **17:**4,4,5,6,11,12,12,13,14,16,17,19,
20,20,22,22,23,24,25,26,27,27; **18:**1,2,6,6,6,7,7,7,
8,8,8,9,9,9,12,15,17,17,17,17,21,21,23,24,25,25,28,
29,32,34,34; **19:**1,3,3,3,5,8,10,10,11,12,13,13,14,
14,16,16,17,21,21,23,23,24,24,27,28; **20:**1,2,7,8,8,
10,11,12,13,13,14,15,17,17,18,18,18,19,19,19,20,
22,22,23,23,23,23,26,27,28,28,28,31,32; **21:**1,2,2,2,
3,4,5,5,7,9,13,14,15,17,18,19,19,21,21,23,28,30,31,
32,32,33,33,33,34,34,36,37,38,40,41,41,42,43,44,
46; **22:**1,3,3,3,3,3,4,5,5,8,8,9,9,11,15,16,16,17,17,
18,21,21,21,23,25,26,26,28,31,43,44,46; **23:**1,1,3,4,
4,5,7,7,8,10,13,13,15,15,16,23,25,27,28,29,33,34,
35,37,37,38; **24:**1,1,1,3,6,6,9,9,13,14,16,17,18,21,
23,24,31,38,45,48,49,49,51; **25:**1,6,8,9,10,10,14,15,
15,15,15,16,25,28,34,35,35,36,37,39,41,42,42,46,
46; **26:**1,2,4,7,9,10,10,12,14,15,15,16,17,17,17,18,
18,22,22,24,26,27,30,35,36,36,37,38,38,39,40,42,
45,45,49,52,55,55,57,58,58,59,61,62,62,63,64,68,
69,71,71,73,74,74; **27:**1,2,3,4,6,7,7,8,10,14,14,15,
17,17,18,19,20,20,21,21,26,26,31,32,33,34,34,40,
48,48,49,51,52,53,55,58,58,60,62,64; **28:**1,2,5,8,9,
10,10,10,11,13,14,15,16,16,16,18,18,20,20; **Mk 1:**5,
7,17,21,21,24,27,29,31,31,32,35,36,38,40,44,44,44,
45,45; **2:**2,3,4,5,6,8,9,9,9,10,10,10,13,13,17,17,23,
24,26,26,27; **3:**2,2,3,4,4,4,4,5,6,7,8,9,9,10,12,13,
13,14,15,15,16,17,20,21,23,23,23,31; **4:**1,3,9,11,11,
13,21,21,22,22,23,24,29,30,33,34,35,35,38,39,40;
5:1,2,4,8,10,12,14,15,16,17,17,18,19,20,21,25,32,
33,34,38,39,41,41,42,43,43,43; **6:**1,2,4,6,7,7,11,17,
18,18,19,19,20,20,20,22,22,23,24,25,25,26,27,28,
28,30,31,31,31,32,35,36,36,37,37,37,37,37,39,41,
41,41,41,45,46,48,48,50,55,56; **7:**3,5,8,9,10,10,11,
11,14,14,24,24,26,27,27,31,32,32,34,34,35,36; **8:**1,
1,2,4,6,6,6,6,7,10,11,11,12,13,14,18,18,21,22,22,
27,30,31,32,34,34,35,36; **9:**1,5,5,6,7,9,10,12,13,14,
15,18,18,19,20,22,25,27,30,31,31,32,33,35,36,38,
41,42,43,43,43,45,45,45,47,47,47; **10:**1,2,4,7,13,13,
14,14,14,17,17,21,23,23,24,25,25,26,28,30,30,32,
32,32,33,33,33,33,35,35,36,39,40,40,40,43,44,45,
45,45,46,47,48,49,50,50,51,51; **11:**1,2,2,6,7,11,13,
14,16,18,21,23,27,28; **12:**1,1,1,1,2,2,4,6,7,9,12,13,
13,14,14,14,14,15,17,17,17,18,23,26,33,33,34,36,
37,38,43,44; **13:**1,4,5,7,9,9,10,11,11,12,12,13,14,
15,16,19,21,22,27,34,37,37; **14:**1,4,5,6,8,10,10,10,
11,11,11,12,12,12,14,19,21,22,23,24,26,31,32,32,
33,34,34,35,37,37,40,40,41,45,48,53,55,60,65,69,
70,71,71,72; **15:**1,4,6,8,9,9,10,11,15,15,15,18,18,
19,20,21,22,24,29,36,36,36,38,41,43,44,45; **16:**1,2,
8,9,12,13,14,14,15,15,19; **Lk 1:**1,2,3,5,7,9,9,11,13,
13,14,15,16,17,17,17,17,19,19,19,19,20,22,22,22,
26,27,27,27,28,30,31,31,35,36,36,36,38,39,43,45,
50,50,54,55,57,57,59,59,60,61,62,62,62,63,64,66,
68,68,72,72,72,73,74,74,74,76,77,78,79,79,80; **2:**3,
3,4,4,4,5,5,5,6,7,9,10,11,12,14,14,15,15,18,21,22,
22,22,23,23,24,26,27,32,34,34,34,38,38,38,38,39,
39,41,42,42,45,45,46,48,49,50,51,51; **3:**2,7,7,7,8,8,
12,13,16,17,17,18,19,20; **4:**3,3,5,6,6,6,6,9,10,12,
14,16,16,17,18,18,18,18,19,20,21,23,23,26,26,29,
29,31,34,36,36,38,38,39,40,41,42,42,42,43; **5:**1,3,3,
4,6,7,7,10,12,14,14,15,15,16,17,18,18,19,21,23,23,
24,24,24,26,27,30,30,32,32,33,36; **6:**1,4,4,5,7,7,8,
9,9,9,9,9,10,11,11,12,12,12,13,18,18,19,24,25,25,
26,27,27,29,30,30,31,31,32,33,33,33,34,34,34,34,
35,35,35,35,38,38,41,42,42,42,47; **7:**1,2,3,3,4,4,6,
6,6,7,7,8,9,10,11,13,14,15,15,16,19,19,19,20,20,20,
20,21,22,22,22,24,24,24,25,26,31,31,32,36,36,38,
39,40,41,42,44,48,49,50; **8:**1,3,4,5,8,10,10,19,19,
20,22,22,24,26,29,31,31,32,35,35,37,38,41,41,43,
48,50,55,55,56; **9:**1,1,2,2,6,8,9,10,10,11,12,12,13,
14,16,16,16,16,19,21,21,22,23,23,24,25,28,31,31,
33,33,35,36,38,40,42,42,43,44,44,44,45,46,48,49,
51,51,52,54,54,56,57,58,59,60,61,62; **10:**1,1,2,5,6,
7,8,9,11,13,13,15,15,16,16,17,19,19,20,21,21,22,
22,22,23,24,24,25,25,29,30,31,32,34,34,35,36,38,
38,39,40,40,40,40; **11:**1,1,2,5,5,6,6,9,9,9,10,13,13,
13,17,24,30,30,31,31,35,37,39,41,42,43,44,46,46,
47,51,52,52,53,53,54; **12:**1,1,5,13,13,15,17,17,19,
20,22,25,31,32,33,36,37,41,41,42,45,45,45,46,49,
50,51,54,54,55,56,56,58,58,58,58; **13:**6,7,7,12,14,
15,18,20,22,23,23,24,24,24,31,31,31,34,34,35;
14:1,3,6,8,9,9,10,10,12,15,17,18,19,21,23,23,25,
26,28,28,28,29,30,30,31,31,31,35; **15:**1,7,12,14,15,
15,15,16,17,17,17,18,18,19,20,20,21,21,22,24,28,
32; **16:**3,3,3,9,13,15,17,17,21,22,24,24,26,26,26,27,
28,29,30,31,31; **17:**1,1,1,1,2,2,2,4,5,6,7,7,9,10,11,
14,18,18,19,22,22,24,27,31,33; **18:**1,3,4,6,7,9,10,
10,13,15,15,16,16,16,18,22,22,24,25,25,28,28,29,
30,30,31,32,39,40,40,41,41,42; **19:**3,4,5,7,7,8,8,9,
9,10,10,11,11,11,12,12,12,13,14,14,15,15,24,24,26,
27,28,29,30,35,37,39,44,44,45,46,47,48; **20:**1,9,9,
10,15,16,18,19,20,20,20,22,22,23,25,25,25,26,27,
33,35,38,40,41,42,45,46,46; **21:**4,5,7,10,12,13,14,
15,16,21,24,28,36,36,36,37,38; **22:**2,4,5,6,6,7,8,9,
10,11,15,15,19,21,22,23,24,24,25,26,31,33,33,33,
36,39,40,43,44,45,47,49,52,61,65; **23:**1,2,2,2,4,7,8,
8,11,14,14,15,15,18,20,20,22,24,25,28,30,30,32,33,
48,51,52,54,56; **24:**1,5,5,7,9,9,10,11,12,12,13,20,
20,21,22,24,25,25,26,27,28,29,30,30,32,33,34,36,
38,41,44,47,49,50,52; **Jn 1:**7,8,9,11,12,12,12,19,20,
22,22,27,31,33,41,42,43,43; **2:**2,3,5,6,7,7,8,10,12,
13,16,18,18,18,20,20,24; **3:**2,4,6,6,11,12,17,17,26,
26,26,27,29,31,32; **4:**3,4,5,5,7,7,8,9,11,14,15,15,15,
17,25,26,27,28,28,32,32,33,34,34,38,40,40,42,47,
47,47,52,52,53,54; **5:**1,3,6,7,7,8,10,10,11,12,14,14,
16,17,17,18,21,21,22,24,26,27,29,29,30,33,33,35,
36,40,40,40,47; **6:**1,5,5,6,6,7,7,11,12,12,14,14,15,
15,16,20,21,24,27,28,29,31,32,33,35,37,37,38,38,
40,41,44,45,52,52,53,61,62,63,65,65,67,68,69,69,
71; **7:**1,1,3,3,4,4,8,8,14,14,17,18,19,20,21,25,25,
26,30,32,33,35,35,37,39,39,44,45,50,51; **8:**1,2,4,5,
6,6,7,7,9,12,21,26,31,31,34,35,37,40,42,43,43,44,
44,44,47,47,57,59; **9:**8,11,11,13,17,17,24,26,27,27,
29,31,31,34; **10:**3,8,10,10,16,17,18,18,20,27,29,31,
32,33,35,39,40,41; **11:**3,7,7,8,11,11,15,16,19,19,20,
21,23,25,27,29,31,31,38,44,45,46,52,53,54,54,55,
56; **12:**1,4,5,6,6,9,10,11,12,13,16,17,18,19,20,21,
21,22,23,24,27,29,32,33,33,35,38,38,47,47,49,50,
50; **13:**1,1,1,2,3,5,6,6,6,10,11,12,18,18,21,22,23,24,
26,26,27,28,29,29,29; **14:**2,3,4,5,6,10,12,16,18,21,
22,22,22,23,24,26,27,28,28,30; **15:**3,8,8,13,15,19,
19,22,25,26; **16:**2,5,7,7,8,10,12,12,13,14,15,15,16,
17,17,19,19,20,21,28,30,32; **17:**2,4,6,6,10,11,12,13,
23,24,24,26,26; **18:**3,4,4,6,13,15,16,16,16,18,20,23,
24,27,28,28,28,28,29,30,31,32,32,34,35,36,37,37,
37,38,39,39,39; **19:**3,4,4,4,5,7,7,10,10,10,10,11,11,
12,12,14,16,16,17,19,21,21,23,24,26,27,29,31,31,
33; **20:**1,2,9,10,11,16,17,17,17,17,17,18,18,25,27,
28; **21:**1,3,5,6,7,10,12,13,14,15,17,18,19,19,20,22,
22,23,23,24; **Ac 1:**1,1,2,2,3,3,6,6,7,7,8,12,13,16,20,
21,22,25,25,26,26; **2:**3,3,4,11,14,14,20,20,22,22,23,
23,23,24,27,28,29,31,31,32,33,34,34,37,37,41,42,
42,42,42,45,45,46,47; **3:**1,2,2,3,5,8,8,10,10,11,11,
12,13,13,14,19,21,22,23,25,26,26; **4:**1,1,4,7,8,9,9,
12,15,16,17,17,17,18,19,19,19,21,23,23,24,27,29,
30,33,33,34,35; **5:**3,4,4,4,9,9,12,14,21,21,24,27,27,
28,28,31,31,32,33,33,35,35,36,36,36,39,40,42; **6:**2,
2,3,3,4,5,6,7,9,11,14; **7:**2,2,2,3,4,5,6,10,15,16,17,
17,18,18,19,23,24,25,26,26,29,30,31,32,33,34,34,
35,35,38,38,38,39,39,40,41,42,43,44,55,58; **8:**3,3,5,
6,14,22,23,24,24,25,26,26,26,27,27,29,30,31,31,32,
36,38; **9:**1,2,2,2,4,4,10,11,12,13,14,15,15,15,15,17,
17,20,21,21,23,24,26,26,27,27,29,30,30,32,34,35,
38,39,41,41; **10:**2,2,3,4,5,5,7,8,9,10,11,15,16,19,20,
21,22,22,22,22,23,28,28,31,32,33,33,33,33,34,36,
40,42,42,42,48; **11:**2,5,10,11,12,13,15,17,18,18,20,
20,20,21,22,23,23,24,25,25,26,27,29,30; **12:**1,1,2,3,
4,4,5,6,6,8,10,10,11,12,13,17,18,19,21,23,24; **13:**2,
4,4,6,7,8,11,11,11,13,13,13,14,15,16,19,22,23,24,
25,26,28,31,31,34,34,38,38,39,40,41,42,43,43,44,
45,46,46,46,47,51,51; **14:**2,3,5,6,6,7,9,9,10,11,13,
13,13,15,15,18,21,22,22,22,23,25,26,26,27; **15:**1,1,
2,2,2,4,4,5,5,6,8,8,10,10,12,13,14,14,19,20,20,22,
22,23,25,25,27,28,28,28,29,29,29,30,32,33,33,36,
37,38,40; **16:**1,1,3,4,4,7,7,7,8,9,10,10,10,11,11,12,
13,13,13,13,14,14,15,16,17,18,18,19,21,22,23,25,
25,27,30,32,32,34,35,37,37,38,39,39,40; **17:**1,3,3,5,
5,5,10,10,11,14,15,15,16,17,18,18,18,19,19,20,20,
21,23,23,23,30,31,32; **18:**1,2,2,4,5,5,6,6,7,9,10,12,
13,13,14,14,14,14,20,22,22,23,24,26,26,26,27,27,
27,27,27; **19:**4,9,12,13,13,17,19,21,21,22,30,31,33,
33,33,36,39,40; **20:**2,3,3,7,7,7,9,13,13,14,15,16,16,
16,17,18,20,20,20,21,21,22,22,24,24,24,26,27,27,
30,32,32,35,35,38; **21:**1,1,1,1,2,3,3,3,4,4,5,5,6,11,
11,12,12,13,13,15,16,16,18,20,21,21,21,24,25,25,
26,26,31,32,33,35,37,37,39,40,40; **22:**1,2,4,5,5,5,5,
7,7,9,10,12,13,14,14,14,15,17,18,19,19,21,21,22,
22,24,25,25,25,26,26,27,28,29,30,30; **23:**1,1,2,3,3,
3,9,10,10,12,14,14,15,15,17,17,18,18,18,18,19,20,
20,21,21,21,22,23,23,24,26,27,28,28,29,30,30,30,
30,32,33,33; **24:**1,4,4,5,6,8,10,11,11,13,16,17,17,
17,19,23,23,23,24,25,27,27; **25:**1,3,3,3,3,6,9,9,9,9,
10,10,11,11,11,11,12,12,13,13,15,16,16,17,18,20,
20, 20, 21, 21, 22, 22, 24, 25, 25, 25, 26, 26, 26, 27, 27;
26:1,1,2,3,3,5,7,9,9,10,11,11,11,11,12,14,14,14,16,
16,17,18,18,18,19,20,20,20,20,21,22,22,23,23,23,
26,28,28,29,29,31,32,32; **27:**1,1,2,2,3,3,3,4,4,7,7,8,
10,10,10,11,12,12,13,15,16,16,17,18,21,22,23,30,
30,31,33,34,34,35,35,39,40,41,42,42,43,43,43,44;
28:4,4,6,6,7,7,8,10,11,14,14,15,16,16,16,17,17,18,
19, 19, 19, 20, 22, 23, 23, 23, 23, 25, 25, 26, 28, 28, 30;
Ro 1:1,3,5,5,6,6,7,7,7,10,10,11,11,11,13,13,13,14,
14,15,15,16,16,16,17,19,19,21,22,23,24,26,28,28,
28,32; **2:**4,4,6,7; **3:**15,19,19,21,22,25,25,26,26; **4:**1,
2,3,4,5,6,9,11,16,16,16,17,18,20,21,22,23,24,25,25;
5:5,5,7,10,12,13,14,14,15,21; **6:**2,6,10,10,11,11,13,
13,13,13,16,16,16,16,16,17,17,17,17,18,19,19,19,
19,19,20,22; **7:**1,2,2,4,4,4,6,9,10,11,13,13,14,15,16,
18,19,19,20,21,24,25,25,25; **8:**3,3,4,4,5,7,7,9,10,11,
12,12,12,13,13,15,19,20,21,22,23,26,28,29,29,31,
34,36,39; **9:**4,15,17,18,18,19,19,20,20,20,21,22,23,
23,26,33,33; **10:**1,3,3,6,7,11,14,18,20,21; **11:**2,3,4,
4,8,11,11,11,13,13,14,15,18,18,22,22,23,24,25,30,
31,32,35,36; **12:**1,1,2,2,3,3,5,6,6,8,8,8,9,10,16,17,
19,20; **13:**1,3,4,5,5,6,7,8,10,11,14; **14:**2,4,4,4,6,6,6,
6,6,8,9,12,13,18,19,19,19,20,20,21,21,21; **15:**1,1,2,
4,7,7,8,12,14,15,16,16,16,17,18,18,19,20,22,23,23,
24,24,24,24,25,26,27,27,27,27,28,29,30,30,31,32;
16:1, 2, 2, 4, 5, 10, 10, 13, 17, 17, 19, 21, 25, 25, 26, 27;
1Co 1:1,2,2,2,3,7,8,10,17,17,18,18,21,23,23,24,27,
27,28; **2:**1,1,2,3,6,10,15,16; **3:**5,5,8,13; **4:**1,5,6,8,8,
9,9,9,9,9,11,13,14,14,16,17,18,19,21; **5:**5,9,9,10,11,
11,12,12; **6:**1,2,2,5,5,6,8,12,12; **7:**1,3,3,4,4,5,8,8,9,
9,10,11,12,12,13,15,17,22,24,26,27,27,28,30,32,34,
34,35,35,36,36,37,39,39,39; **8:**1,2,4,7,7,8,9,10,10,
13,13; **9:**2,2,3,4,5,6,10,15,16,16,17,19,19,19,20,20,
20,20,21,21,22,22,22,24,25,25,27,27; **10:**1,6,7,7,11,
13, 15, 19, 20, 20, 20, 22, 23, 23, 27, 27, 28, 29, 32, 33;
11:2,2,3,6,7,10,13,13,14,15,16,18,19,19,22,22,23,
28,31,33; **12:**1,2,3,7,8,8,9,9,10,10,10,10,10,11,13,
13,15,16,18,21,21,22,24; **13:**3,3,12; **14:**2,2,3,5,6,6,
11,11,12,16,19,20,21,21,28,28,30,32,34,35,35,37,
39; **15:**1,1,2,2,3,3,4,5,5,6,7,7,8,8,9,10,15,19,23,24,
26,28,34,34,36,38,50,57,58; **16:**1,2,3,3,4,5,7,7,9,
10,10,11,12,12,12,15,16,16,16,24; **2Co 1:**1,2,3,8,8,
10,11,14,15,16,16,16,16,16,16,17,18,20,22,23,23;
2:1,2,4,4,5,5,7,8,9,10,12,12,13,13,14,14,15,16,16,
16; **3:**1,1,5,13,14,15,16; **4:**2,3,6,7,11,14,15,15; **5:**2,
4,4,5,8,9,11,11,11,11,12,12,12,18,19,19,20,21; **6:**1,
11,11,13,18; **7:**3,4,9,10,11,11,11,12,12,13,13,14,14,
14,14; **8:**1,4,5,5,6,6,8,10,10,10,11,11,12,12,16,17,
18,19,19,19,19,20,21,22,23; **9:**1,1,1,2,2,2,2,4,5,5,7,
8,9,10,11,12,14,15; **10:**1,1,2,2,4,5,5,6,7,7,9,9,9,10,
12,13,13,14,15,16; **11:**2,2,2,3,4,5,6,7,7,7,8,9,9,9,
12,12,21,21,21,23,23,31,32; **12:**1,1,2,4,4,6,7,7,8,9,
11, 11, 11, 13, 13, 14, 14, 14, 16, 17, 18, 18, 19, 20, 20;
13:1,4,5,7,7,10; **Gal 1:**2,3,4,4,5,6,6,7,8,9,10,10,10,
11,13,16,16,17,17,17,18,18,21,22,23; **2:**1,2,2,2,3,4,
4,5,6,6,7,7,8,8,9,9,9,10,10,11,11,12,12,12,14,14,17,
19; **3:**2,3,6,8,10,14,14,15,16,16,16,16,18,19,19,21,
22,23,29,29; **4:**2,5,5,8,9,9,13,14,15,17,17,18,18,21,
23,24,25,29; **5:**2,3,3,4,7,10,13,13,17,17,17,24; **6:**4,
8, 8, 10, 10, 10, 11, 12, 12, 12, 12, 13, 14, 14, 16, 16;
Eph 1:1,2,3,4,5,6,9,9,10,10,10,11,12,14,18,21,22;
2:2,7,10,10,12,15,16,16,16,17,17,18,21,22; **3:**2,3,4,
5,5,8,8,9,9,10,11,13,18,19,19,20,20,20,21; **4:**1,3,4,
7,8,9,10,12,13,15,18,19,19,22,22,23,24,24,25,28,
29,32; **5:**2,11,12,18,19,19,20,21,22,22,24,24,26,27,
27,28,31; **6:**6,13,13,16,22,23,24; **Php 1:**1,2,6,7,10,
11,12,12,12,13,14,18,19,21,21,21,22,23,28,29,29,
29; **2:**4,4,6,6,8,9,11,12,13,13,13,16,16,19,19,23,25,
25,25,27,28,30; **3:**1,1,4,5,7,10,10,11,12,13,14,15,
16,21; **4:**2, 5, 6, 10, 11, 12, 12, 14, 17, 18, 19, 20, 22;
Col 1:2,2,6,9,11,12,12,19,20,20,22,23,24,25,25,26,
27,27,29; **2:**1,5,6,8,10,14,16,17,19,20,20,20,22,22;
3:5,5,7,9,15,16,17,18,22; **4:**2,6,8,10,11,15,15,16,
17; **1Th 1:**1,1,5,7,8,9,9,10; **2:**1,2,3,4,4,5,8,9,9,9,12,
15,16,16,16,17,18,18; **3:**1,2,5,6,6,6,11,11; **4:**1,1,1,
4,7,7,9,9,9,10,11,11,13,15,17; **5:**1,1,5,5,8,9,9,12,
15,21,27,27; **2Th 1:**1,2,3,6,7,7,10,10,10,11,12; **2:**1,
2,3,4,5,7,10,13,13,14,15,15; **3:**4,6,6,7,8,9,9,9,10,
12; **1Ti 1:**2,3,4,4,6,7,10,11,11,12,15,17,19,19,20,
20,20; **2:**4,4,4,6,8,9,10,12,12; **3:**1,2,2,2,3,5,8,11,12,
14,14,15; **4:**3,3,3,4,6,7,7,8,13,13,13,15; **5:**3,4,4,5,5,
7,9,10,11,11,13,13,14,14,14,14,15,16,20,21,21; **6:**2,
2,2,3,3,5,9,12,13,14,16,17,17,17,18,18,18,18,20;
2Ti 1:2,4,6,9,10,12,12,14,16; **2:**2,2,4,5,6,9,15,15,
15,21,21,23,24,24,25,26,26; **3:**2,5,7,7,9,11,12,13,
15; **4:**3,3,3,4,8,8,8,9,9,10,10,10,11,12,16,18,18,21;
Titus 1:1,1,3,3,4,6,6,7,9,11,14,14,15,15,16; **2:**1,2,3,
3,3,3,4,5,5,5,5,5,6,8,9,9,9,9,9,9,10,10,11,12,12,12,
14,14,14; **3:**1,1,1,1,1,2,2,2,8,8,8,10,12,12,12,12,13,
14,14,14; **Phm** 1,2,2,3,8,8,9,9,10,11,11,11,12,13,
14,16,16,18,19,21,22,22,22; **Heb 1:**1,2,4,4,5,13,14;
2:1,3,4,4,5,5,8,8,10,11,12,17,17,18; **3:**2,5,6,12,14,
14,18,18,19; **4:**1,2,2,6,6,11,12,13,14,15,16; **5:**1,1,1,
2,2,3,5,7,10,11,11,11,11,12,12,14; **6:**1,1,6,6,6,6,7,9,
10,11,11,12,12,13,13,16,17,17,18,18; **7:**5,8,11,11,
13,14,16,19,21,25,25,25,27; **8:**3,3,3,5,5,5,6,6,9,9,
11,11; **9:**6,9,11,14,14,15,16,19,20,23,24,25,26,26,
27,27,28,28,28,28; **10:**1,4,7,9,9,13,15,19,22,22,23,
29,30,31,33,36,39,39; **11:**6,6,7,8,8,10,11,15,16,17,
18,20,24,25,25,26,29,32,34,35,35,37; **12:**4,9,14,14,
15,15,17,18,18,19,19,19,20,22,22,22,23,23,23,24,
24,25; **13:**2,2,2,3,6,7,9,9,10,12,13,14,15,16,16,17,
17,18,19,19,21,21,22,22,23,23; **Jas 1:**1,5,5,7,9,12,
15,15,18,19,19,19,22,23,27,27; **2:**3,3,5,5,7,12,13,
14,16,23,25; **3:**2,3,4; **4:**4,5,6,7,8,8,9,9,12,12,13,15,
17; **5:**4,7,12,14,16; **1Pe 1:**1,2,2,2,3,5,6,10,10,11,11,
12,12,12,13,13,14,18,25; **2:**4,4,5,5,6,7,7,8,11,13,13,
14,14,14,17,18,18,18,20,21,23,24,25; **3:**1,5,5,6,9,
12,13,13,15,15,15,17,18,18,18,19,20,22; **4:**3,5,5,5,
6,6,6,6,6,9,10,11,12,12,17,18,19,19,19; **5:**1,1,2,2,3,
3,5,5,8,10,11,12,14; **2Pe 1:**1,5,5,5,6,6,6,7,7,10,13,
14,15,15,17,19,19,19; **2:**4,4,6,6,6,9,9,10,12,13,15,
18,19,21,21,21,21,22,22; **3:**1,1,1,2,9,9,9,11,11,12,
13,14,14,16,16,18; **1Jn 1:**2,2,2,3,4,5,6,8,10; **2:**1,3,
6,9,10,12,13,13,14,14,14,19,19,19,21,26,26,27; **3:**6,
8,9,12,14,16,19,23,23; **4:**1,5,6,6,11,14,18,20; **5:**3,
10,13,14,16,16,16,16,17,18; **2Jn** 1,1,4,6,10,12,12,
12,12,12; **3Jn** 1,3,3,4,5,8,8,9,9,10,10,10,13,13,14,
14,14; **Jude** 1,3,3,3,3,3,5,7,9,11,15,15,18,21,21,22,
23,24,24,24,25; **Rev 1:**1,1,2,3,4,4,4,5,6,6,6,8,11,11,
12,12,13; **2:**1,2,5,7,7,7,8,8,10,10,10,11,12,13,13,14,
14,14,14,15,16,17,17,17,18,20,21,23,24,24,24,25,
25,26,26,27,29; **3:**1,2,3,6,7,9,10,10,10,11,13,14,16,
18,18,18,21,21,22; **4:**1,8,9,11; **5:**2,4,5,5,9,9,10,10,
12,13,13; **6:**4,4,4,8,11,13,16; **7:**1,2,2,10,10,12,17;
8:2,3,6,13,13; **9:**1,1,4,5,5,6,10,12,14,15; **10:**4,5,7,7,
8,9,9,9; **11:**2,5,5,6,6,6,12,12,13,17,17; **12:**2,4,4,5,5,
5,6,9,11,12,12,13,13,14,15,17; **13:**3,4,5,5,6,6,7,7,
10,10,13,13,14,14,15,15,15,15,16; **14:**4,6,6,6,12,15,
15,18; **15:**4,7; **16:**1,6,8,9,11,12,14,14,15,16; **17:**1,6,
7,7,8,11,11,13,15,16,17,17,17; **18:**5,6,10,14,16,17,
19,19,21; **19:**1,8,9,9,10,10,10,10,15,17,19; **20:**1,3,
4,4,5,8,8,12,13; **21:**6,6,8,9,10,15,16,23; **22:**6,6,8,8,
9,11,11,11,11,12,12,14,16,18,18,20

UPON (103)

Ge 9:7; **20:**9; **24:**60; **26:**10; **34:**27; **41:**36;
Lev 22:16; **Nu 35:**19; **Dt 24:**4; **32:**35; **Jdg 14:**6,
19; **15:**14; **16:**9,12,14,20; **Ru 1:**21; **1Sa 10:**6,10;
11:6; **16:**13; **2Sa 16:**12; **2Ki 10:**15; **2Ch 14:**9; **20:**9;
Job 2:11; **3:**25; **5:**14; **10:**17; **16:**14; **20:**22; **21:**17;
27:9; **Ps 27:**5; **44:**17; **60:**1; **69:**27; **119:**143; **132:**6;
136:6; **139:**5; **Ecc 9:**12; **11:**2; **Isa 3:**9,11; **8:**11;
10:16,23; **15:**9,9,9; **24:**20; **26:**9; **29:**14; **30:**1; **47:**9,
11,11,11,13; **51:**19; **60:**1,2; **66:**7; **Jer 6:**26; **22:**23;
44:23; **46:**21; **51:**60; **Eze 4:**4; **5:**16; **7:**2,3,7,7,26,
26; **14:**13; **20:**35; **28:**23; **30:**4; **36:**29; **37:**6; **Da 7:**10;
Joel 2:9; **Ob** 15; **Jnh 1:**12; **Mic 3:**11; **Zep 2:**2,2; **3:**7;
Mt 11:29; **12:**28; **23:**35; **Lk 11:**20; **19:**43; **Ac 7:**26;
Php 2:27; **1Th 2:**16; **Heb 12:**22; **Jude** 14; **Rev 5:**11

US (1435)

Ge 1:26; **3:**22; **5:**29; **11:**4,7; **19:**5,13,31; **20:**9; **23:**6,
6,6; **24:**23,33,55,65; **26:**10,10,16,16,22,28,28,28,
29; **31:**15,15,15,16,37,44,50,53; **32:**18,20; **33:**12;
34:9,9,10,14,15,21,22,23,23; **35:**3; **37:**8,8; **39:**14,
14,17; **41:**11,12,12,13; **42:**2,21,21,28,30,30,33;
43:2,3,4,5,7,7,18,18,18,21,21,22; **44:**9,26,26,27,30;
47:15,19,19; **50:**15,15; **Ex 1:**9,10; **2:**14,19,19; **3:**18,
18; **5:**3,3,3,8,17,21,21; **8:**26,27; **10:**7,25,26; **13:**14,
15,16; **14:**11,11,11,12,12,12; **16:**3,7,8; **17:**2,3,3,7;
19:23; **20:**19,19; **24:**14; **32:**1,1,1,23,23,23; **33:**15,
15,16; **34:**9,9; **Nu 10:**29,31,32,32; **11:**13; **12:**2,11;
13:27; **14:**3,3,3,8,8,8,9; **16:**13,13,13,14,14,34; **20:**5,
14,15,16,17; **21:**5,7,22; **22:**4,14; **27:**4; **31:**50; **32:**5,
19; **36:**3; **Dt 1:**6,19,20,22,22,25,25,27,27,27,27,41;
2:27,28,28,29,29,30,32,33,36,36; **3:**1; **4:**7; **5:**2,3,3,
24,25,27; **6:**21,23,23,23,24,25; **9:**28; **13:**2,2,6,13;
17:14,14,14; **18:**16; **21:**20; **26:**3,6,6,6,8,9,9,15; **29:**7,
15,29; **30:**12,13; **31:**17,17; **33:**4; **Jos 1:**16,16; **2:**9,
13,14,17,17,18,20,24; **4:**23; **5:**6,13; **7:**7,7,9,25; **8:**5,

WAS (4152)

WE (1891)

WERE (2554)

WHEN (2814)

WHICH (696)

WHO (5087)

12; 2:1,12,18; 3:4,25; 4:9,11,12; 1Th 1:10; 2:4,10,12,13,15; 3:2; 4:5,6,8,8,13,13,14,15,15,15,17; 5:6,7,7,12,12,12,14,24; 2Th 1:6,7,8,10; 2:7,10,12,16; 3:6,10,14; 1Ti 1:9,12,16; 2:4,6,10,14; 3:13; 4:3,3,10,10; 5:3,5,6,8,13,16,16,17,20; 6:1,2,5,5,9,13,13,16,16,17,17; 2Ti 1:10,14; 2:2,5,14,15,15,16,18,19,19,21,22,26; 3:6,6,8,12; 4:1,8; Titus 1:2,8,8,9,14,15; 2:8,14; 3:8,15; Phm 10,12; Heb 1:14; 2:3,9,11,11,14,15,18; 3:1,2,16,16,17,18; 4:2,3,6,10,14,15,15; 5:2,7,9,13,14; 6:4,4,4,5,6,12,18; 7:5,6,8,8,9,16,25,26,28; 8:1,2,4; 9:13,14,15,16,17,28; 10:1,14,23,28,29,29,29,30,33,37,38,39,39; 11:5,6,6,9,11,11,14,17,27,31,33,33,34,35; 12:3,9,11,16,19,25,25,25; 13:3,7,9,10,17,20; Jas 1:5,6,12,12,17,23,23,26; 2:5,5,6,6,7,11,12,13; 3:1,2,9,13,18; 4:4,11,12,12,13; 5:4,6,10,11; 1Pe 1:2,5,10,12,15,17,21; 2:6,7,7,9,14,14,14,18,18,23; 3:5,6,12,13,15,16,20,22; 4:5,6,11,17,19; 5:1,5,10,13,14; 2Pe 1:1,3; 2:1,7,10,15,16,18,18; 1Jn 2:9,10,11,13,14,22,23,26,29; 3:3,4,6,6,7,8,9,10,10,10,10,12,14,15,24; 4:4,4,7,18,21; 5:1,1,5,5,6,6,13,18,20,20; 2Jn 1,7,9,11,13; 3Jn 9,10,11,11; Jude 1,1,4,5,6,7,12,18,19,19,22,24; Rev 1:2,3,3,4,4,4,5,5,7,8,8,8; 2:1,2,7,8,8,9,11,12,13,14,14,15,17,17,20,22,23,24,26; 3:1,4,5,7,7,9,9,12,21; 4:3,8,9,9,10,10; 5:1,2,4,7,12,13; 6:9,16,17; 7:2,4,10,13,14,15; 8:2,3,6; 9:4,14,14,15,20; 10:6,6,8; 11:5,10,11,16,17,17,18,18; 12:4,5,9,10,12,13,17; 13:4,4,6,8,14,15,18; 14:1,3,4,6,7,11,11,12,13,15,16,18,18; 15:2,4,7; 16:2,5,5,9,15; 17:1,1,6,11,12,12; 18:8,9,15,17,17,19,24; 19:2,4,5,9,10,10,17,20,20; 20:2,4,4,6,10,11; 21:5,7,8,9,15,27; 22:6,7,8,8,9,11,11,14,15,15,17,17,17,18,20

WHOM (393)

Ge 10:14; 14:13; 17:21; 21:9; 22:2; 24:3,40,47; 25:12; 30:26; 36:14; 41:38; 46:18,25; 48:15; 49:10; Ex 1:8; 6:5,26; 22:9; 28:3; 32:7,11,13; 33:12,19,19; 36:1,2; Lev 17:7; 25:27,42,53,55; 26:45; 27:24; Nu 5:8; 23:8,8; 27:18; 31:40; 33:4; Dt 9:12; 21:8; 24:11; 31:4; 34:10; Jos 2:10; 12:1; 24:15; Jdg 2:14; 3:8; 8:15,31; 20:16; Ru 4:12; 1Sa 6:20; 9:20; 12:3,3; 14:3; 17:28,45; 21:9; 24:14; 28:11; 2Sa 3:14; 7:7,15,23; 9:1,3; 14:7; 16:19,21; 19:10; 21:8,8; 22:3; 23:8,18; 1Ki 5:5; 7:8; 8:51; 9:21; 11:20,34; 14:13; 17:1; 18:15,31; 22:7,8; 2Ki 3:11,14; 5:16; 8:5; 12:15; 17:11,34; 18:20; 19:4,22; 1Ch 1:12; 4:18; 5:6,25; 11:11,20; 12:29; 17:6,21; 29:1; 2Ch 1:11; 2:7; 8:8; 18:6,7; 22:7; 23:18; Ezr 2:1; 4:10; 5:14; Ne 1:10; 7:6; Est 2:7; 6:13; 10:2; Job 3:23; 5:17; 15:19; 25:3; Ps 16:3; 18:2; 27:1,1; 47:4; 55:14; 59:10,17; 71:23; 73:25; 74:2; 88:5; 91:2; 94:22; 105:26; 106:38; 109:1; 144:2,15; Pr 3:27; Ecc 4:8; 9:9; SS 1:7; Isa 6:8; 10:3; 19:17; 23:2; 28:9,12; 36:5; 37:4,23; 40:14,18,25; 41:8; 42:1,1,24; 43:7,7,10; 44:1,2; 46:3,5,5; 48:12; 49:3; 53:1,3; 57:4,11; Jer 6:10; 11:12; 15:10; 20:6; 24:5; 25:15,17; 26:5; 29:3,20,22; 30:9,17; 31:20; 40:5; 41:2,10,16,18; 42:6,9,11; 43:6; 52:25; La 2:20; Eze 2:4; 16:20,37; 20:9; 21:27; 23:9,37; Da 1:11; 2:24; 3:12; 5:12; 6:2,16,20; Hos 13:10; Joel 2:32; Am 6:1; Mic 1:16; Zec 1:4; 13:3; Mal 3:1; Mt 3:17; 11:10,27; 12:18,18,27; 17:5,25; 18:7; 19:11; 20:23; 21:44; 23:35; 24:45; Mk 1:11; 3:16; 6:16,17; 9:7,36; 10:40; 12:6; 13:20; 15:6; 16:9; Lk 2:14; 3:22; 6:13,14,34; 7:2,27; 8:2,35,38; 9:35; 10:22; 11:19,49; 12:5,42,43; 13:16; 17:1; 19:15; 20:13,18; Jn 1:33,45,47; 3:34; 5:21,45; 6:68; 7:39; 8:54; 10:35,36; 12:1,9,38; 13:23,26; 14:26; 15:26; 17:3,6; 19:26; 21:7,20; Ac 2:36,39; 3:16; 4:10,10,27,36; 5:30,32; 7:18; 8:19; 9:5; 10:41,42; 13:37; 14:23; 15:4; 19:13; 20:25; 22:8; 25:14; 26:15; 27:23,23; Ro 1:9; 4:6,17,24; 5:2,11; 8:33; 9:15,15,18,18,23,24; 10:14; 11:2; 14:15; 1Co 1:24; 3:5; 4:17; 6:19; 8:6,6,6,6,11; 10:11; 15:6; 2Co 2:2; 10:18; Gal 1:5; 3:19; 4:19; Eph 3:15; 4:30; Php 2:25; 4:1; Col 1:14; 2:3,19; 1Th 1:10; 2Th 2:8; 1Ti 1:15,20; 6:16; 2Ti 1:3,12; 3:14; Titus 3:6; Heb 1:2,2; 2:10,10; 3:1,17,18; 4:13; 6:7; 7:13; 13:21; Jas 2:7; 1Pe 5:12; 2Pe 1:17; 1Jn 4:20,20; 2Jn 1; 3Jn 1; Jude 13; Rev 3:19

WHOSE (289)

Ge 10:21; 22:24; 24:23,37,47; 25:1; 38:25; 44:30; 49:22; Ex 1:15; 25:2; 34:14; 35:21; Lev 6:30; 16:9,27; 22:24; 27:24; Nu 1:17; 11:26; 24:3,4,15,16; 26:10,33; Dt 19:1; 21:6; 28:49; 29:18; Jos 9:4; 12:1; 17:3; 24:15; Jdg 5:14; 6:10; 13:5; 16:4; 19:12; Ru 2:1,2,12,19; 3:2; 1Sa 1:1; 3:2; 4:15; 9:1; 10:26; 12:3,3,3; 17:55,56,58; 2Sa 3:12; 16:8; 17:10; 21:16; 1Ki 1:5; 3:26; 7:14,14; 13:11; 19:18,18; 2Ki 7:2,17; 8:1,5; 18:22; 1Ch 1:43; 2:17,26; 4:41; 17:21; 2Ch 2:14,14; 16:9; 20:10,35; 29:31; 31:16; Ezr 1:5; 7:15; 8:13; Job 1:1; 3:23; 4:19; 12:5; 17:6; 26:4; 30:1; 38:29; Ps 1:2,3; 15:2,3; 17:14; 18:27; 26:10,10; 32:1,1,2,2; 33:12,18; 37:14; 38:14; 39:6; 46:4; 56:4,10,10; 57:4,4; 68:34,34; 78:8,8; 83:18; 84:5,5,11; 95:10; 101:6; 105:25; 119:1; 127:5; 144:8,8,11,11,15; 146:5,5; Pr 2:7,12,15; 11:20,20; 17:20,20; 19:1,1; 25:28; 28:6,6,18,18; 30:4,13,13,14,14; Ecc 7:26,26; 10:16,16,17,17; Isa 1:4; 10:5,10; 18:2,7; 23:7,8,8; 26:3; 28:29,29; 30:7; 31:9,9; 33:16,19,19; 36:7; 45:1; 57:8,15,20; 58:11; 65:4; Jer 5:15,15; 17:5,7; 32:18; 37:13; 44:28; 46:18; 48:15; 51:57; La 3:25; Eze 3:6; 11:21; 17:16,16; 20:9,14,22; 21:25,25,29,29; 23:20,20; 24:6; 26:10; 38:8; 40:2,3; 42:2; Da 12:1; Hos 7:4; Joel 3:19; Am 5:27; Mic 2:7; 5:2; Na 2:8; Hab 1:11; Zec 6:12; Mt 1:3,5,5,6; 3:11; 22:20,20,28,42; 24:46; 26:3; 27:16; Mk 1:7; 7:25; 12:16,16,23; Lk 3:16; 6:6; 12:37,38; 13:1; 16:1; 20:24,33; Jn 1:6,27; 4:46; 6:42; 11:2; 18:26; Ac 10:6; 13:25; 14:13; 16:1,1; Ro 4:7,7,8; 14:1,2; 16:10,23; 1Co 6:4; Php 3:8; 4:3; 1Ti 4:2; 5:17; Titus 1:6; Heb 3:17; 11:10,34; 12:23; 1Jn 5:16; Jude 4; Rev 2:18,18; 9:11; 13:8,12; 17:8; 19:11; 20:15; 21:27

WILL (10122)

See select index of "WILL" in the Main Concordance.

Ge 1:29; 2:17,18; 3:3,4,5,5,14,14,15,15,15,16,16,16,16,17,18,18,19,19; 4:7,12,12,14,14,14,15; 5:29; 6:3,3,7,17,18,18,20; 7:4,4; 8:21,21,22; 9:2,3,5,5,5,11,11,13,15,15,16,25; 11:4,6,7; 12:1,2,2,2,2,3,3,3,7,12,12,12,13,13; 13:15,16; 14:23,23,24; 15:2,3,4,4,8,13,13,14,14,15,16; 16:10,10,11,12,12,12; 17:2,2,4,5,5,6,6,6,7,8,8,11,14,15,16,16,16,16,16,17,17,19,19,19,20,20,20,20,20,21,21; 18:10,10,12,13,14,14,18,18,19,19,21,21,23,24,25,26,28,28,29,30,31,32; 19:2,15,17,19,20,21,21; 20:4,7,7,7,11; 21:6,10,12,13,18,23; 22:2,5,5,8,14,14,17,17,18; 23:6,9,13,13; 24:3,4,7,7,8,14,33,39,40,41,41,42,49,58,58; 25:23,23,23; 26:3,3,3,3,4,4,4,22,24,24,29; 27:33,39,40,40,40,41,46; 28:13,14,14,14,15,15,15,20,20,20,21,22,22; 29:8,27,32,34,35; 30:13,15,20,26,28,31,31,32,33,33; 31:3,8,8,52,52; 32:9,11,12,12,20,20,26,28; 33:13; 34:11,15,16,17,22,23,30; 35:3,10,10,11,11,12; 37:8,10,26,35; 38:16,17,23; 40:13,13,19,19; 41:16,30,30,30,31,31,32,36,40,44; 42:15,15,16,18,33,34,34,37,38,38; 43:3,4,4,5,5,5,8,9,9,14; 44:9,9,10,10,17,22,23,26,29,31,31,32; 45:6,11,11,18,20,28; 46:3,4,4,4,31,31,34; 47:16,19,25,29,30; 48:4,4,5,5,6,6,19,19,19,19,20,21; 49:1,4,7,8,8,8,10,11,11,12,13,13,15,16,17,19,19,20,20; 50:5,21,24,25; Ex 1:10,10; 2:9; 3:3,12,12,12,18,19,20,20,20,21,21,22,22; 4:9,12,12,14,15,15,16,16,21,21,23; 5:2,10,11,18; 6:1,1,1,1,6,6,6,7,7,7,8,8,12; 7:1,3,4,4,4,5,9,17,17,17,18,18,18,19,19; 8:2,3,3,4,8,10,11,11,16,21,21,21,22,22,22,23,23,26,28,29,29; 9:3,4,4,5,9,9,14,17,18,19,19,22,28,29,29,29; 10:3,4,5,5,6,7,8,9,14,26,28,29; 11:1,1,1,4,5,6,6,7,7,8,8,9; 12:4,12,12,13,13,13,23,23,23,25,33; 13:9,16,19; 14:3,4,4,4,4,13,13,13,14,17,17,17,18; 15:1,2,2,9,9,9,9,9,9,13,13,14,14,15,15,15,16,16,17,26; 16:4,4,4,6,7,8,12,12,12,25,26,28; 17:6,6,9,14,16; 18:15,18,19,22,22,23,23; 19:5,6,8,9,9,11,22,24; 20:7,19,19,20,24,25; 21:6,13,19,28; 22:11,15,23,24,24,24,27; 23:7,21,22,22,23,23,25,25,26,26,27,27,28,29,30,31,31,31,33,33; 24:3,7,7,12; 25:8,9,16,21,22; 26:13,13,25,33; 27:7; 28:28,29,30,32,35,35,38,38,38,38,43; 29:21,26,29,37,37,42,43,43,44,44,45,46; 30:6,8,12,16,20,21,25,29,29,36; 31:13,17; 32:1,5,10,13,13,13,23,30,33,34,34; 33:1,2,3,5,12,14,14,16,16,17,19,19,19,19,19,19,22,23,23; 34:1,10,10,10,11,12,15,15,16,24,24; 40:9,10,15,15; Lev 1:3,4; 3:4,10,15; 4:9,20,20,26,26,31,31,35,35; 5:1,10,13,13,13,16,16,17,18,18; 6:7,7,18,27; 7:18,18,18; 8:33,35; 9:4; 10:3,3,6,6,7,9,15; 11:24,24,25,26,27,28,31,32,32,32,33,39,40,40; 12:2,5,7,8,8; 13:6,14,17,34,58; 14:8,9,20,31,36,46,53,53; 15:3,3,4,4,5,6,7,8,9,10,10,11,13,15,16,17,18,19,19,20,20,21,21,22,22,23,24,24,25,26,26,27,27,28,30,31; 16:2,2,13,13,16,22,30,30; 17:5,10,10,15,15,16; 18:5,28; 19:5,7,8,17,22,24,25,29,31; 20:3,3,5,5,6,6,9,11,12,13,14,16,17,20,20,21,24,24,27; 21:15; 22:2,4,6,7,20,23,25,27,29; 23:11,18,30,43; 24:12,15; 25:6,18,19,19,20,21,21,22,22,28,28,41,45; 26:4,4,5,5,5,6,6,6,6,6,7,7,8,8,8,9,9,10,10,11,11,12,12,14,16,16,16,16,16,17,17,17,17,18,18,19,20,20,20,21,22,22,22,24,24,25,25,25,26,26,26,26,28,28,29,30,30,31,31,32,32,33,33,33,33,34,34,35,36,36,36,36,37,37,38,38,39,39,40,42,42,43,43,43,44,45; 27:8,12,12,14,14,15,18,18,19,21,21,23,24,32; Nu 1:53; 2:5,7,9,10,12,14,16,17,17,18,20,22,24,25,27,29,31; 4:15,20; 5:3,9,10,24,27,27,27,27,27,28,28,31,31; 6:27,27; 8:7,14,19; 9:13; 10:6,9,10,29,29,30,32; 11:17,17,17,17,18,18,18,19,21,23,23; 14:3,8,8,9,11,11,12,12,13,14,15,23,23,24,24,27,28,29,30,31,32,33,34,35,35,35,41,42,43,43,43; 15:10,16,25,26,28,39,39,40,40; 16:5,5,5,7,12,14,22,26,28,30; 17:5,5,10,10,12,13; 18:3,5,13,20,20,22,22,23,24,27,28,30,32,32,32; 19:7,8,10,10,11,12,12,14,15,16,19,21; 20:8,8,12,17,17,18,19,19,24,24,26,26; 21:2,2,7,16,22,22; 22:6,8,11,17,19,34; 23:3,3,13,23,27; 24:7,7,7,7,14,17,17,17,18,18,18,19,20,22,24,24,24; 25:13; 26:55; 27:13,17,17,20,21,21,21; 30:4,5,5,7,8,9,11,12,12; 31:2,23,24; 32:11,15,15,17,17,18,19,20,20,22,23,23,25,26,27,31,32,32; 33:54,55,55,55,56; 34:2,3,3,4,5,6,6,8,9,11,12,12; 35:2,3,4,5,6,12,13,15; 36:3,3,4,4,8; Dt 1:13,17,22,30,36,36,38,38,39,39,39,41,42,42; 2:4,5,9,19,25,25,25,27,27; 3:21,22,28,28,28; 4:6,6,22,22,26,26,26,27,27,27,28,29,30,31; 5:11,25,25,27,33; 6:15,15,25; 7:4,4,4,10,10,12,13,13,14,14,14,15,15,15,16,19,20,22,22,22,23,24,24,24,24,25,26; 8:9,9,14,14,19,20; 9:3,3,3,5,14,28; 10:2,10; 11:14,15,15,16,17,17,17,17,17,23,23,24,24,25,25; 12:5,10,10,10,11,14,18,25,26,28,29,30; 13:11,11,17,17,17,17; 14:23,24,25; 15:4,6,6,6,6,6,9,9,10,11,17,18,20; 16:2,6,7,11,15,15,15,16; 17:8,9,10,13,13,17,20; 18:6,12,14,15,16,18,18,18,19; 19:10,10,20,20; 20:1,8,18,18; 21:8,9,18,20,21; 22:9,16; 23:14,21,21,22; 24:13,13,15,16; 25:1,3,6,7,9; 26:2,17,17,17,19,19; 28:1,2,3,4,5,6,7,7,7,8,8,9,10,10,11,12,12,12,13,13,15,16,17,18,19,20,21,22,22,23,24,24,25,25,25,26,26,27,28,29,29,29,30,30,30,30,30,30,31,31,31,31,31,31,32,32,33,33,34,35,36,36,37,37,38,38,38,39,39,39,40,40,40,41,41,41,42,43,43,44,44,44,44,45,45,46,48,48,49,49,51,51,52,52,53,53,54,55,55,55,56,57,59,60,60,61,62,63,63,64,64,65,65,66,67,67,67,68,68,68; 29:19,19,20,20,20,20,21,22,23,23,24,25; 30:3,4,5,5,5,6,7,8,9,9,12,13,16,16,18,18,20; 31:3,3,3,3,4,5,6,8,8,11,14,16,16,17,17,17,17,17,18,20,21,21,23,23,26,27,29,29; 32:1,3,7,7,20,20,21,21,22,22,23,24,24,25,25,25,29,35,35,36,37,39,41,42,43,43,47,50,52,52; 33:17,19,19,21,23,25,25,27,28,28,29,29; 34:4,4; Jos 1:3,4,5,5,5,6,8,9,11,13,16,16,17,18; 2:12,13,13,14,16,17,19,19,19,20; 3:4,5,7,10,10,11,13; 6:5,5,18,18,26,26; 7:3,9,9,9,12,25; 8:5,5,6,6,7,18; 9:20,20,20,23; 10:8,25; 11:6; 13:6; 14:9,12; 15:16; 17:17,18; 18:3,4,4,6,8; 22:18,27,27,28; 23:5,5,5,13,13,15,16,16; 24:15,15,18,19,20,21,24,27,27; Jdg 1:3,12,24; 2:1,3,3,3,21,22,22; 4:7,8,9,9,9,22; 5:3,3; 6:16,16,18,36,37,37,37; 7:4,7,11; 8:7,9,23,23,23; 10:13,18,18; 11:8,9,10,24,24,31,31,37; 13:5,5,7,7,16; 14:12,15; 15:3,13,13; 16:5; 17:3,13; 18:5,10,25; 19:12,24; 20:8,8,28; 21:1,17,22,22; Ru 1:9,10,16,16,16,17,17; 2:22; 3:1,2,4,5,11,13,18; 4:4,4,4,4,10,15; 1Sa 1:11,11,11,22,22,28; 2:9,9,10,10,10,10,25,25,30,30,31,31,32,32,32,33,33,34,34,35,35,35,35,36; 3:11,12,14; 4:8,9; 5:11; 6:3,3,5,9,20; 7:3,5; 8:9,9,11,11,11,11,12,13,14,15,16,17,17,18,18,20; 9:5,6,8,8,13,13,13,16,16,17,19,19,26; 10:2,2,3,3,3,4,4,5,5,5,6,6,6,8; 11:1,2,3,7,9,10,13; 12:3,10,15,17,17,19,22,23,25; 13:12,14,19; 14:6,8,9,10,10,37,40,45; 15:2,26,33; 16:1,2,3,11,16,16; 17:9,9,25,25,25,26,27,32,36,37,46,46,46,47,47; 18:17,17,21; 19:3,3,6; 20:3,10,12,12,18,18,20,21,31; 22:3,7,7,16,23; 23:11,11,11,12,12,17,17,17,20,23,23; 24:4,10,12,13,20,20,21; 25:8,28,28,29,29,31; 26:6,10,10,10,10,21,25; 27:1,1,1,12; 28:1,2,2,10,19,19,19,23; 29:4; 30:8,8,15,15,22,24,24; 31:4; 2Sa 2:6,26; 3:12,13,18; 5:2,2,6,8,8,19,19,24; 6:21,22,22,22; 7:9,10,10,10,11,11,12,12,13,13,14,14,14,15,16,16,21,26,26,26,27,29; 9:7,7,7,10,11; 10:2,11,12; 11:11,12,15; 12:10,11,11,12,14,23,23,28,28; 13:13,24; 14:7,8,10,11,11,15,15,16,21; 15:8,14,14,21,25,28,33,34,34; 16:3,12,18,18,19,21,21; 17:2,3,3,8,9,10,12,12,12,13,13,16; 18:2,4,22; 19:7,7,26,26,33,34,36,38,38; 20:6,6,21; 21:3,6,17,17; 22:50,50; 24:24; 1Ki 1:5,13,14,17,20,21,24,30,30,51,52,52; 2:4,8,9,17,18,20,26,30,32,37,37,38,42,42,44,45,45; 3:12,12,12,12,13,13,14; 5:5,5,6,6,8,9,9,9; 6:12,13,13; 8:19,27,29,40,42; 9:3,5,7,7,7,8,8,8,9; 11:2,11,12,12,13,13,32,33,34,35,36,37,37,37,38,38,38,39; 12:4,7,7,11,11,14,14,26,27,27; 13:2,2,2,3,3,7,22,32; 14:3,3,5,10,10,11,11,12,13,13,14,14,15,15,15,16; 15:19; 16:3,4,4; 17:1,4,14,14; 18:1,5,12,14,15,21,23,24,37; 19:17,17,20; 20:6,9,13,13,14,14,14,14,22,23,25,28,28,31,34,34,36,39; 21:2,2,4,6,6,19,21,22,23,24,24,29,29; 22:4,6,11,12,15,20,21,22,22,25,30; 2Ki 1:2,4,4,6,6,16,16; 2:2,4,6,10,10,21; 3:7,7,16,17,17,17,18,19,19; 4:16,30,43; 5:5,8,10,10,16,17,17,20,27; 6:3,8,19; 7:1,2,2,4,4,9,12,12,12,13,13,18,19,19; 8:1,8,9,10,10,12,12,13; 9:7,8,8,9,10,10,26,36,37,37; 10:5,5,6,10,18,19,24,30; 13:17,19; 14:6; 15:12; 16:15; 17:39; 18:14,23,27,30,30,31,32; 19:4,4,7,7,10,11,28,28,29,29,30,31,31,32,32,33,33,34; 20:1,5,5,6,6,6,8,8,8,9,17,17,17,18,18,18,19; 21:4,7,8,8,8,12,13,13,14,14; 22:17,17,20,20,20; 23:27,27; 25:24; 1Ch 4:10; 10:4; 11:2,2,5,6; 12:18,19; 13:2; 14:10,10,15; 16:18,18; 17:8,9,9,9,10,10,11,11,12,12,13,13,13,14,14,19,24,24,24,24,25,27; 19:2,12,13; 21:23,23,24; 22:5,9,9,9,9,9,10,10,10,10,13,19; 28:6,6,7,9,9,20,21,21; 2Ch 1:12,12,12; 2:5,8,10,12,14,16,16; 6:9,18,31; 7:14,14,14,14,15,16,18,20,20,20,21,21,22; 10:4,7,7,11,11,14,14; 12:7,7,7,8; 13:12,12; 15:2,2,7; 16:3,9; 18:3,3,5,10,11,14,19,20,21,21,24,29; 19:10,10,11,11,11; 20:9,9,9,12,16,16,17,17,17,20,20,37; 21:15; 24:20; 25:4,8; 26:18; 28:13,23,23; 29:10; 30:8,9,9,9; 32:11,15,17; 33:4,7,8,8; 34:25,25,28,28,28; 35:21; Ezr 4:3,13,13,15,16,21; 6:8; 7:18; 10:4,11; Ne 1:8,9; 2:6,6,7,8,8,17,20,20; 4:2,2,2,11,11,12,20; 5:12,12,12; 6:7,9,9,11; 9:29; 10:31,31,31,36,37,37,39; 13:21; Est 1:17,17,18,18,20; 3:9; 4:13,14,14,16,16; 5:3,6,6,8,8; 6:13; 7:2,2,8; 9:12,12; Job 1:11,21; 2:4,5; 4:2; 5:1,1,1,19,19,20,21,22,23,23,24,24,25,25,26; 6:24; 7:7,8,8,8,10,10,11,11,11,13,13,19,21,21,21; 8:2,5,6,7,7,10,10,21,22,22; 9:27,27,28; 10:1,8,9; 11:3,3,15,15,16,17,17,18,18,19,19,20,20,20; 12:2,7,7,8; 13:7,7,8,8,15,15,16,18,19,20,22,25,25; 14:3,7,7,9,12,14,14,15,15,15,16,17,17; 15:17,28,29,29,29,30,30,30,31,32,32,33,34,34; 16:3,22; 17:3,4,5,9,9,10,16,16; 18:2; 19:2,22,25,26,27,28,29,29; 20:7,7,9,9,11,14,14,15,15,16,16,17,18,20,21,22,22,23,25,26,27,27,28; 21:19; 22:15,21,23,25,26,26,27,27,27,28,28,29,30,30; 23:10; 24:15; 27:4,4,5,5,6,6,10,10,11,11,14,15,15,17,17,19; 29:18,19,19,20,20; 30:23; 31:6,14,14; 32:10,14,17,17,21,21; 33:26,26,27,31,33; 34:17,31,32; 35:14; 36:2,3,11,12; 38:3; 39:9,9,10,11,11; 40:2,5,7,14; 41:3,3,4,6,6,8,12; 42:4,4,8,8; Ps 1:5; 2:7,8,9,9,12,12; 3:2,6; 4:2,2,6,8; 6:10,10; 7:2,12,12,17,17; 9:1,1,2,2,18,18; 10:6,6,11,16,18; 11:6,6,7; 12:4,4,5,5,7,7; 13:1,1,2,3,4,4,6; 15:5; 16:4,4,7,8,9,10,10,11; 17:3,6,15,15,15; 18:49,49; 19:13; 21:7,8,8,9,9,9,10,12,13; 22:22,22,25,26,26,27,27,29,29,30,30,31; 23:4,6,6; 24:5; 25:3,3,12,13,13,15; 26:12; 27:2,3,3,5,5,6,6,6,8,10,13; 28:1,5; 30:1,6,9,9,12; 31:7; 32:5,6,7,8,8,9; 34:1,1,2,11,20,21,21,22,22; 35:9,10,17,18,18,28; 37:2,2,4,5,6,9,9,10,10,11,15,15,17,18,19,19,20,20,20,22,22,24,26,27,28,28,28,29,33,34,34,38,38; 38:15; 39:1,1,6; 40:3,8; 41:5,8; 42:5,6,11; 43:4,4,5; 44:8; 45:6,6,12,12,16,16,17,17; 46:2,5,5,10,10; 48:14; 49:3,3,4,4,11,14,14,14,15,15,17,17,19,19; 50:3,7,7,15,15,22,23; 51:7,7,13,13,14,15,17,19,19; 52:5,5,5,6,6,9,9; 54:6,6; 55:19,22,22,23,23; 56:9,9,12; 57:1,7,8,9,9; 58:5,9,10,11; 59:10,10,11,13,16,16; 60:6,9,9,12,12; 61:8; 62:2,3,6; 63:3,4,4,5,5,9,9,10,11,11,11; 64:5,7,7,8,8,9,9,10,10; 65:1,2; 66:13,15,15; 67:7; 68:16,21,22,22,29,31,31; 69:30,31,32,35,35,36,36; 71:6,11,14,14,15,16,16,20,20,21,22,22,23,24; 72:12,13,14,17,17; 73:20,24,27,28; 74:8,9,10,10; 75:9,9,10,10; 77:7,7,10,11,11,12; 78:2,2,4,4; 79:5,5,13,13; 80:4,18,18; 81:8,10; 82:2,7,7; 83:16; 85:5,5,6,8,12,12; 86:9,9,12,12; 87:4,4,5,5,6,7; 89:1,1,2,4,21,21,22,22,23,24,24,25,26,27,28,28,29,32,33,33,34,35,36,37,46,46; 90:13; 91:1,2,3,4,4,4,5,7,8,10,10,11,12,12,13,13,14,14,15,15,15,15,16; 92:7,9,9,12,12,13,14,14; 94:3,3,8,14,14,15,15,16,16,23,23; 96:10,13; 98:9; 101:1,1,2,2,2,3,3,4,5,5,6,6,7,7,8,8; 102:13,15,15,16,17,17,21,26,26,26,26,27,28,28; 103:9,9,21; 104:9,33,33; 105:11,11; 108:1,2,3,3,7,10,10,13,13; 109:30,30; 110:2,3,3,4,5,6,7,7; 111:1; 112:2,2,5,6,6,7,8,8,9,10,10,10; 115:8,8,12,12,12,13; 116:2,13,14,17,18; 118:6,17,17,19,21,28,28; 119:7,8,16,23,44,45,46,46,60,61,78, 82, 84, 93, 95, 106, 109, 116, 117, 117, 145, 146; 120:3,4; 121:3,3,4,6,7,7,8; 122:8,9; 125:3,5; 126:5,6; 127:5; 128:2,2,3,3,4; 130:8; 132:3,4,11,11,12,14,15,15,16,16,17,18,18; 135:14,18,18; 138:1,1,2,2,8; 139:10,10,11,12,12; 140:13,13; 141:5,5,6,6,7; 142:7; 143:7,10; 144:9,9,12,12,13,13,14,14; 145:1,1,2,5,6,20,21; 146:2,2; 148:6; Pr 1:13,14,22,22,23,23,26,26,28,28,28,28,31,32,32,33; 2:5,9,10,10,11,11,12,16,20,21,21,22,22; 3:2,4,6,8,10,10,18,22,23,23,24,24,26,26; 4:4,6,6,8,8,9,10,12,12; 5:11,12,23; 6:9,9,11,15,15,22,22,22,29,33,34,35,35; 7:2,5,20,23; 9:6,8,8,9,9,11,11,12,12; 10:7,9,24,24,30,30,31; 11:15,21,21,25,25,28,28,29,29; 12:11,24; 13:3,13; 14:7,11,11,14,19,26; 15:10,27,31; 16:3,5,14; 17:2,2,5,8,11,13; 18:21; 19:2,5,5,8,9,9,16,17,19,20,24,25,25,27; 20:13,13,20,21,22; 21:7,13,17,17,25,28,28; 22:6,8,9,11,15,23,23,27,29,29; 23:5,8,8,9,11,13,15,16,18,33,33,34,35,35; 24:8,12,14,18,20,22,24,25,25,34; 25:5,8,10,16,17,22,22; 26:4,5,26,27,27; 27:14,18,18,22,26,27; 28:8,10,10,16,17,18,19,19,20,20,21,23,25,27; 29:1,14,16,17,17,19,21,25; 30:6,10,10,17,17; Ecc 1:9,9,11; 2:1,15,16,19,19; 3:14,14,15,15,17,17,22; 4:11; 6:12; 7:18,26,26; 8:3,5,5,8,12,13,13,15; 9:5,6,12; 10:10,14; 11:3,4,4,6,6,8,9; 12:1,14; SS 1:4,11; 3:2,2; 4:6; 5:8; 7:8,8,12; 8:9,9; Isa 1:19,20,24,25,25,26,26,27,28,28,29,29,30,31,31; 2:2,2,2,3,3,3,4,4,4,4,4,9,11,11,12,17,17,18,19,20,21; 3:4,4,5,5,6,7,10,10,11,17,17,18,24,25,26,26; 4:1,1,2,2,3,4,4,5,5,6; 5:1,5,5,5,5,5,6,6,6,9,10,10,13,13,13,14,15,16,16,17,17,24,30,30; 6:8,13,13; 7:7,7,8,9,12,12,13,14,14,14,15,16,17,17,18,19,20,21,22,22,23,24,24,25,25; 8:4,7,8,10,10,14,14,14,15,15,15,17,17,21,21,21,22,22; 9:1,1,5,5,6,6,7,7,7,8,9,10,10,14,17,17,19,19,19,20,20,20,21,21; 10:3,3,3,4,12,12,16,16,17,17,18,19,20,20,21,21,22,23,25,25,26,26,27,27,29,32,32,33,33,33,34,34; 11:1,1,2,3,3,4,4,4,4,5,6,6,6,7,7,7,8,8,9,9,10,10,10,11,12,12,13,13,13,14,14,14,14,15,15,15,16; 12:1,1,2,3,4; 13:6,7,7,8,8,8,8,10,10,10,11,11,11,12,13,13,14,14,15,15,16,16,17,18,18,18,19,20,20,20,21,21,21,21,22,22; 14:1,1,1,1,2,2,2,4,10,10,13,13,13,14,14,20,22,22,23,23,24,24,25,25,25,29,29,30,30,30,30,32; 15:9; 16:4,4,4,5,5,14,14; 17:1,1,2,2,3,3,4,4,5,6,7,8,8,9,9,11; 18:3,3,4,4,5,6,6,7,7; 19:2,2,3,3,3,4,4,5,5,6,6,6,7,7,8,8,9,9,10,10,16,16,17,17,18,18,19,20,20,20,21,21,21,21,22,22,22,22,23,23,23,24,25; 20:4,5,6; 21:2,16,17; 22:14,18,18,18,19,19,20,21,21,22,23,23,24,25,25,25,25; 23:5,12,15,15,16,17,17,17,18,18,18; 24:1,2,3,13,18,18,21,22,22,23,23; 25:1,2,3,3,6,7,8,8,8,9,10,10,11,11,12,12; 26:1,3,19,19,19,21,21; 27:1,1,6,6,9,9,9,12,12,13,13; 28:2,3,4,5,6,11,13,13,13,16,17,17,17,18,18,18,19,19,19,21,21,22; 29:2,2,2,3,3,4,4,4,4,5,6,7,8,11,12,14,14,14,15,17,18,18,19,19,20,20,20,22,22,23,23,23,24,24; 30:3,3,5,13,14,14,16,16,16,16,17,17,18,19,19,19,20,20,21,22,22,23,23,23,24,25,26,26,29,29,30,30,31,31,32; 31:2,3,3,3,4,5,5,5,5,7,8,8,8,8,9,9; 32:1,1,2,3,3,4,4,5,10,10,10,14,14,16,17,17,18,20; 33:1,1,5,6,10,10,10,12,12,16,16,16,16,17,18,19,20,20,20,21,21,21,21,22,23,23,24,24; 34:2,2,3,3,3,4,4,7,7,7,9,9,10,10,10,10,11,11,11,12,12,13,13,14,14,14,15,15,15,16,16,16,17; 35:1,1,2,2,2,2,4,4,4,5,6,6,7,7,8,8,8,8,8,9,9,9,10,10,10,10,10; 36:8,12,15,15,16,18; 37:4,4,7,7,10,11,29,29,30,30,31,32,32,33,33,34,34,35; 38:1,5,6,6,7,8,11,11,15,20,20,21,22,22; 39:6,6,6,7,7,7,8; 40:5,5,18,18,20,20,25,28,31,31,31,31; 41:7,10,10,11,11,12,12,13,14,15,15,16,16,16,16,17,17,18,18,19,19,23; 42:1,1,2,3,3,3,4,4,6,6,6,8,13,13,13,13,15,15,16,16,16,16,16,17,23; 43:2,2,2,2,4,5,6,10,14; 44:2,3,3,4,5,5,5,5,7,11,11,21,26,27,28,28; 45:1,2,2,2,3,5,13,13,13,14,14,14,14,16,16,17,17,23,23,23,24,24,25,25; 46:4,4,4,4,5,5,10,10,11,11,13,13; 47:1,3,3,3,5,8,9,9,11,11,11,11,12,12,14; 48:6,6,11,14,14,15,15; 49:3,6,7,7,8,8,8,8,9,10,10,10,11,11,12,13,15,18,18,19,19,20,21,22,22,22,23,23,23,23,23,25,25,25,26,26,26; 50:7,7,8,9,9,9,11; 51:3,3,3,3,4,4,5,5,6,6,6,6,8,8,8,11,11,11,11,11,14,14,14,22,23; 52:1,3,6,6,8,10,10,12,12,12,13,13,15,15,15,15; 53:10,10,10,10,11,11,11,12,12; 54:3,3,4,4,4,6,7,8,10,11,12,13,13,14,14,14,14,14,15,15,17,17; 55:2,3,5,5,7,7,11,11,12,12,12,13,13,13,13; 56:1,3,5,5,5,7,7,7,8,12; 57:12,12,13,13,13,14,16,16,18,18,19; 58:8,8,8,8,9,9,9,9,10,10,11,11,11,11,12,12,12,14,14; 59:2,5,8,18,18,19,19,19,20,21,21; 60:3,5,5,5,5,6,6,7,7,7,7,10,10,10,11,11,12,12,12,13,13,14,14,14,15,16,16,17,17,17,18,18,19,19,19,19,20,20,20,20,21,21,22,22; 61:3,4,4,5,5,6,6,6,6,7,7,7,7,8,9,9,11; 62:1,1,2,2,2,3,4,4,4,4,5,5,6,8,8,9,9,12,12; 63:7,8; 64:12,12; 65:6,6,6,7,8,8,9,9,9,9,10,12,12,13,13,13,13,13,13,14,14,15,15,15,16,16,16,17,17,17,18,18,19,19,20,20,20,21,21,22,22,22,23,23,23,24,24,25,25,25,25; 66:1,1,4,4,5,11,11,12,12,13,13,14,14,14,14,15,16,16,17,18,19,19,19,20,20,21,22,22,23,24,24,24,24; Jer 1:8,14,15,15,16,17,19,19,19; 2:9,19,19,20,24,31,35,36,37,37; 3:5,5,12,12,14,15,15,16,16,16,16,17,17,17,18,18,22,22; 4:1,2,2,4,7,9,9,9,10,11,14,27,27,28,28,28; 5:1,5,6,

WITH (5964)

YOU (13983)

24,24,25,26,26,27,34,34,35,35,35,36,36,36,37,37, 37,38,38,38,39,39,40,40,41,42,42,43,43,43,44, 44,45,45,45; 26:2,10,11,11,11,13,15,15,17,17,21, 21,22,25,25,27,29,31,32,33,34,34,35,35,39,40, 41,45,50,53,55,55,62,62,63,63,64,64,65,66,68, 69,73,73,75; 27:11,11,13,13,17,17,21,21,40,40,46, 65; 28:5,7,7,7,13,14,20,20; Mk 1:2,8,8,11,11,17,24, 24,24,37,40,40,44; 2:8,10,11,25; 3:11,28,32; 4:11, 13,13,21,21,24,24,24,38,40,40; 5:7,8,19,19,31,31, 31,34,41; 6:10,10,11,11,18,22,22,23,23,25,37,38; 7:6,8,9,11,12,13,13,13,18,18,29; 8:5,12,17,17,18, 18,19,20,21,23,29,29,29,33; 9:1,5,13,16,17,19,19, 19,22,23,25,25,33,41,41,41,43,43,45,45,47,47,50; 10:3,5,15,18,19,19,19,19,19,21,21,21,28,29,35, 36,36,38,38,38,39,42,43,43,49,51,51,52; 11:2,2,2,3, 3,5,14,17,21,23,24,24,24,25,25,25,28,28,29,29,31, 33; 12:10,14,14,14,14,15,24,24,26,27,32,34,43; 13:2,5,7,9,9,9,11,11,11,13,14,21,23,28,29,29,30,33, 35,36,37; 14:6,7,7,7,7,7,9,12,12,13,15,18,18,19,25, 27,28,30,30,31,31,36,36,37,37,38,41,48,49,49,60, 60,61,62,64,64,67,70,70,72; 15:2,2,4,4,9,9,12,29, 34; 16:6,7,7,7; Lk 1:3,4,4,13,13,14,19,19,20,20,28, 28,30,31,31,35,35,42,42,76,76; 2:10,11,12,12,29, 29,31,48,48,49,49; 3:7,7,8,13,16,16,22,22; 4:3,6,7, 9,10,10,11,11,23,23,23,24,25,34,34,34,41; 5:5,10, 12,12,22,24,24,30,34; 6:2,3,9,20,21,21,21,21,22,22, 22,22,24,24,25,25,25,25,26,26,27,27,28,28,29,30, 30,31,31,32,32,32,33,33,33,34,34,34,35,37,37,37, 38,38,38,41,42,42,42,42,46,47; 7:4,6,7,9,14,19,20, 20,22,24,25,26,26,27,27,28,32,32,32,33,34,40,43, 44,44,45,46,47,50; 8:10,18,20,28,28,39,45,48; 9:4, 4,5,13,20,20,27,33,38,41,41,41,44,48,50,50,54,57, 57,60,61; 10:3,5,6,7,8,8,9,10,11,12,13,13,13,14,15, 15,15,16,16,19,19,20,21,21,21,23,24,24,24,26,28, 28,35,35,36,40,41; 11:2,5,5,7,8,8,8,8,9,9,9,9,11,13, 13,18,20,27,27,35,36,39,39,40,41,41,42,42,42,42, 43,43,44,44,45,45,46,46,46,46,47,47,48,48,48,51, 52,52,52,52; 12:3,3,4,5,5,5,5,7,8,11,11,11,12,12,14, 19,20,20,20,22,22,24,25,26,26,27,28,28,29,30, 31,32,37,40,40,41,44,51,51,54,54,55,56,56,57,58, 58,58,58,59,59,59; 13:2,3,3,3,4,5,5,5,12,15,15,24, 25,25,25,26,26,26,27,27,27,28,28,31,34,34,34,35, 35,35,35; 14:5,5,8,8,9,9,9,10,10,10,12,12,12,12,13, 14,14,14,22,24,28,28,28,29,29,33,33; 15:4,7,10,18, 21,29,29,30,31; 16:2,2,5,7,9,9,11,11,12,12,13,13, 13,15,25,25,26,26,27; 17:3,4,4,4,6,6,6,7,8,10,10, 10,19,22,22,23,34; 18:8,11,14,17,19,20,20,20,20, 20,22,22,22,28,29,41,41,42; 19:17,19,21,21,21,21, 21,22,22,22,22,23,26,30,30,30,31,31,33,40,42,42, 42,43,43,43,43,44,44,44,44,46; 20:2,2,3,5,8,21,21; 21:3,6,8,9,12,12,12,12,13,14,15,16,16,17,19,20, 20,30,31,31,32,34,36,36; 22:9,10,10,12,15,16,17, 18,19,20,26,26,27,28,29,30,31,32,32,33,34,34,34, 35,35,36,36,37,40,42,46,46,48,52,53,53,58,61,64, 67,67,67,68,68,70,70; 23:3,3,14,15,29,37,39,40,40, 42,43,43; 24:5,6,6,17,17,18,25,36,38,39,41,44,44, 48,49,49; Jn 1:21,21,21,22,22,25,25,26,26,33,38, 38,39,42,42,48,48,48,48,49,49,50,50,50,50,51,51; 2:4,5,10,18,20; 3:2,2,3,5,7,7,8,8,10,10,11,11,12,12, 12,26,26,28; 4:7,9,9,10,10,10,10,11,11,12,17,17,17, 18,18,18,19,20,21,22,22,26,26,27,27,32,35,35,38,38, 38,42,48,48; 5:6,10,12,14,14,19,20,24,25,33,34,35, 37,38,38,39,39,39,40,42,42,43,43,44,44,45,46,46, 47,47; 6:25,26,26,26,26,27,30,30,32,32,32,36, 36,36,47,53,53,53,53,61,62,63,64,65,67,67,68,69, 70,70; 7:3,4,6,7,8,19,19,19,20,20,21,22,22,23,28, 28,28,33,34,34,34,36,36,36,45,47,47,52,52; 8:5,7, 10,11,13,14,15,19,19,19,21,21,21,22,23,23,24,24, 24,24,25,25,26,28,28,31,31,32,32,33,34,36,36,37, 37,37,38,38,38,39,39,40,40,41,42,43,43,44,44,45, 46,46,47,47,48,49,51,52,52,53,53,53,54,55,55,57, 57,58; 9:17,19,26,27,27,27,27,28,30,34,34,35,37, 37,41,41,41,41; 10:1,7,24,24,25,25,26,26,32,32,33, 33,34,36,38,38; 11:3,8,8,15,21,22,22,26,27,28,32, 34,40,40,40,41,41,42,42,49,50,50,56; 12:8,8,8,24, 34,35,35,35,36,36; 13:6,7,7,8,8,8,10,10,12,12,13, 14,15,15,15,16,17,17,17,18,19,19,20,21,21,27,33, 33,33,33,34,34,34,35,35,36,36,36,37,37,38,38,38; 14:1,2,2,3,3,3,4,5,7,7,7,9,9,9,10,10,12,13,14,15,16, 16,16,17,17,17,18,18,19,19,20,20,20,22,24,25,26, 26,26,27,27,27,28,28,28,28,29,29,30; 15:3,3,4,4,4, 5,5,5,5,5,6,6,7,7,7,7,8,9,10,10,11,11,12,14,14,15, 15,15,16,16,16,16,16,16,18,19,19,19,19,19,20,20, 21,26,27,27; 16:1,1,2,2,4,4,4,4,4,5,5,6,7,7,7,10,12, 12,13,13,14,15,16,16,17,17,19,19,19,20,20,20,22, 22,22,23,23,23,23,24,24,25,26,26,27,27,29,30,30,30, 30,31,32,32,33,33,33; 17:1,2,2,3,3,4,4,5,6,6,6,7,7, 8,8,8,9,10,11,11,12,13,15,15,18,21,21,21,22,23,23, 23,24,24,24,25,25,25,26,26,26; 18:4,7,8,8,9,17,17, 22,23,25,25,26,29,30,33,34,36,35,37,37,39,39; 19:4,4,6,9,10,10,10,10,11,11,11,12,12,35; 20:13,15, 15,15,15,19,21,21,23,23,26,29,29,31,31; 21:3,5,6, 10,12,15,15,15,16,16,16,17,17,17,17,17,18,18,18, 18,18,18,18,18,18,20,22,22,23; Ac 1:4,5,6,7,8,8,8, 11,11,11,24,24; 2:14,14,15,22,22,22,23,23,27,27, 28,28,29,33,36,38,38,39; 3:6,12,12,13,13,14,14,15, 16,16,17,20,22,22,22,25,26,26,26; 4:7,10,10,10,11, 19,19,24,25,27; 5:3,3,4,4,4,8,9,9,25,28,28,30,35, 38,39,39; 6:3; 7:3,4,26,26,27,28,28,33,34,35,37,42, 43,43,43,49,51,51,51,52,53; 8:20,20,20,21,22,23, 24,30,30; 9:4,5,5,6,6,17,17,17,34; 10:19,21,22,22, 28,29,33,33,33,36,37; 11:3,14,14,16; 12:8; 13:10, 10,10,11,11,15,16,25,25,26,32,33,34,35,38,38,39, 40,41,41,41,46,46,47,47; 14:15,15,15,15,17,17; 15:1,1,7,7,10,24,25,28,29,29; 16:15,17,18,31,31, 36,36; 17:3,19,20,22,23,23,23,32; 18:10,10,14,14; 19:2,2,3,13,15,25,26,36,37,39; 20:18,18,20,20,20, 25,26,26,27,28,29,31,32,32,32,34,35; 21:13,20,21, 22,23,24,24,37,37,38; 22:3,7,8,8,10,10,14,15,15,16, 19,21,25,26,27; 23:3,3,3,3,4,11,11,15,15,18,18,19, 20,22,30,30; 24:2,4,4,8,10,11,13,19,21,25,25; 25:9, 10,12,12,22,24,26,26; 26:1,2,3,3,8,14,14,15,15,16, 16,16,17,17,24,24,27,27,28,28,29; 27:21,21,22,22, 24,24,24,31,33,33,34,34,34; 28:20,20,21,21,26,26, 28; Ro 1:6,7,8,9,10,11,11,11,12,13,13,13,15; 2:1,1, 1,1,1,3,3,3,4,4,5,17,17,17,18,18,19,19,20,21,21,21, 21,22,22,22,22,23,23,24,25,25,25,25,27,27; 3:4,4, 4; 4:17; 5:6; 6:3,12,14,16,16,16,16,16,17,17,18,19, 20,20,21,21,22,22; 7:1,4,4,7; 8:2,9,9,10,11,11,13, 13,13,13,15,15,15,15; 9:17,17,19,20,20,26; 10:8,9, 9,10,10,19,19; 11:2,13,17,18,18,18,19,20,21,22,22, 22,24,25,25,30,31; 12:1,2,3,3,3,14,18,20; 13:3,3,4, 6,7,7,9,9,9,9,11; 14:4,10,10,10,15,15,16,22; 15:3,5, 6,7,8,9,10,11,13,13,13,14,15,15,22,23,24,24,28,29, 30,32,33; 16:1,2,2,6,17,17,19,19,20,21,22,23,23, 25; 1Co 1:3,4,4,5,6,7,7,8,8,9,10,10,10,10,10,11,12, 13,13,14,15,26,26,26,30; 2:1,1,2,3; 3:1,2,2,2,3,3,3, 3,4,5,9,16,16,17,18,18,18,18,23; 4:1,3,6,6,7,7,7,7, 7,7,8,8,8,8,8,8,10,10,10,14,14,15,15,16,17,17,18, 18,19,21,21; 5:1,2,2,2,3,3,4,4,6,7,7,9,10,11,11,12,13; 6:1,1,2,2,2,3,4,4,5,5,7,7,7,8,8,9,11,11,11,11,12,13, 15,16,19,19,19,19,20; 7:1,5,5,7,7,16,16,16,16,21, 21,21,21,23,27,27,28,28,28,32,35,35; 8:10,12,12; 9:1,2,2,11,11,12,13,15,24; 10:1,12,12,12,13,13,13, 13,13,20,21,21,23,27,27,27,28,28,31,31; 11:2,2,3, 14,17,18,18,19,19,20,20,21,21,22,22,22,23,24, 25,26,26,30,30,33,33,34; 12:1,2,2,2,3,21,21,27,27, 31; 14:5,5,6,6,6,9,9,9,9,12,12,16,16,17,18,23,25, 26,26,31,36,36,37; 15:1,1,1,1,2,2,2,2,3,11,12,17,31, 34,36,37,37,50,51,58,58; 16:2,3,5,6,6,7,7,10,12,15, 15,17,19,19,20,23,24; 2Co 1:2,6,7,7,7,8,11,12,13, 13,14,14,14,14,15,15,16,16,16,18,19,21,23,24,24; 2:1,2,2,3,3,4,4,4,4,5,7,8,9,9,10; 3:1,1,2,3,3; 4:12, 14; 5:12,12,12,13,20; 6:1,2,2,2,11,11,12,12,17,18, 18; 7:3,3,3,4,4,7,8,8,9,9,9,11,11,12,12,12,13,14,14, 14,14,15,15,16; 8:1,7,7,7,8,9,9,10,10,13,14,16,17, 22,23,24; 9:1,2,3,3,3,4,4,5,5,7,7,8,8,8,11,11,12,13, 14,14,14; 10:1,1,1,2,7,8,8,9,13,14,14,15,16; 11:1,2, 2,4,4,4,4,4,4,6,7,7,8,9,9,11,16,16,19,19,20,20,20, 20,20; 12:9,11,11,12,13,13,14,14,14,15,15,15,16, 16,17,17,18,18,19,19,20,20,20,20,21; 13:1,2,2,3,3, 3,4,5,5,5,5,6,7,7,9,9,10,10,11,14; Gal 1:3,6,6,7,8,9, 9,11,13,20,20; 2:5,14,14,14; 3:1,1,2,2,2,3,3,4,5,5,5, 8,26,27,28,29,29; 4:6,7,7,7,8,8,9,9,9,9,10,11,11,12, 12,12,13,13,14,14,14,15,15,16,17,17,17,18,19,20, 20,21,21,27,27,28; 5:2,2,2,4,4,7,7,7,8,10,10,13,15, 15,16,17,17,18,18,21; 6:1,1,2,11,12,13; Eph 1:2,13, 13,13,13,16,16,17,17,18,18; 2:1,1,2,2,5,8,11,12,13, 17,19,22; 3:1,2,2,4,13,13,16,17,19; 4:1,1,4,4,17,17, 20,21,22,25,26,30,32; 5:3,5,6,8,8,14,15,22,33; 6:3, 3,5,6,7,8,9,11,13,13,16,21,21,22,22,22; Php 1:2,3, 4,6,7,7,7,8,10,12,24,25,26,27,27,27,28,28,29,30, 30; 2:1,4,12,13,15,15,16,17,18,19,19,22,25,25,26, 26,28,28,30; 3:1,1,15,15,17,18,18; 4:1,3,9,9,10,10, 10,14,15,16,16,18,22; Col 1:2,3,4,5,5,6,6,6,7,9,9,9, 10,11,12,21,22,22,23,23,24,25,27; 2:1,1,4,4,5,5,5,6, 7,8,10,11,11,11,12,13,13,16,16,18,20,20,20; 3:1,3,4,7, 7,8,9,13,13,15,16,16,17,22,23,24,24,24; 4:1,1,5,6, 7,8,8,9,9,10,10,10,12,12,12,13,16,16,17,17,18; 1Th 1:1,2,2,4,5,5,5,6,6,7,8,9,9; 2:1,1,2,2,3,5,6,7,8, 8,8,9,9,10,10,11,11,12,12,13,13,13,13,14,14,17,17, 18,19,20; 3:2,3,4,4,4,5,6,6,6,6,7,8,9,9,10,10,11,12,13; 4:1,1,1,1,2,2,3,3,4,6,6,8,9,9,10,10,11,11,12,13,13, 15; 5:1,2,4,4,5,11,12,12,12,12,14,18,23,24,27,28; 2Th 1:2,3,3,4,5,5,6,7,10,10,10,11,11,12,12; 2:1,3,5, 5,5,6,13,13,14,14,15,17; 3:1,3,3,4,6,6,7,7,7,8,9,10, 10,11,13,15,16,16,18; 1Ti 1:3,3,18,18,18; 3:14,14, 15; 4:6,6,6,12,12,14,14,16; 5:20,21; 6:2,11,12, 12,13,21; 2Ti 1:3,4,5,6,6,13,14,15,18; 2:1,2,7,23; 3:10,14,14,14,15,15; 4:1,5,11,13,15,21,22; Titus 1:5,5,5; 2:1,8,15,15; 3:8,11,12,13,15,15; Phm 3,4,7,8,8,9,10,11,11,12,14,15,15,16,17,17,18, 18,19,20,21,21,22,23; Heb 1:5,9,9,9,10,11,12,12; 2:6,6,7,7; 3:7,8,12,13,15,15; 4:1,7; 5:5,6,11,11,12, 12,12,12; 6:10,10,11,11,12,14,14; 7:17,21; 8:5,5; 9:20; 10:5,5,6,8,8,25,29,32,32,33,33,34,34,34,36, 36,36; 12:3,4,5,5,5,7,8,8,17,18,22,22,23,25; 13:3,3, 5,5,5,7,17,17,19,19,21,22,22,23,23,24,25; Jas 1:2, 3,4,5,5,5,6,6,21,21; 2:3,3,3,4,6,6,6,7,8,8,9,9,11,11, 11,11,16,18,18,19,20,20,22,24; 3:1,1,13,14,16,16; 4:1,1,2,2,2,2,2,2,2,2,3,3,3,3,3,4,4,5,7,8,8,8,10,11, 11,12,12,13,14,14,15,16; 5:1,1,3,3,4,4,5,5,6,6,8,9, 11,11,12,12,13,14,16,19; 1Pe 1:4,6,6,8,8,8,8,9,10, 12,12,12,13,14,14,15,15,17,18,18,18,21,22,22,23, 25; 2:2,3,4,5,7,9,9,9,10,10,10,10,11,12,15,20,20,20, 21,21,21,21,24,25,25; 3:6,6,7,7,8,9,9,13,13,14,14, 15,15,18,21,21; 4:3,4,4,7,10,10,12,12,12,13,13,14, 14,14,15,16,16; 5:1,2,2,2,3,4,5,5,6,7,9,10,10,10,10, 12,12,13,13,14; 2Pe 1:4,8,8,10,10,11,12,12,12,15, 16,19,20; 2:1,3,13; 3:1,1,2,3,9,11,11,12,14,15,17, 17; 1Jn 1:2,3,3,5; 2:1,1,7,7,7,8,8,12,13,13,13,13, 14,14,14,14,14,14,14,18,20,20,21,21,21,24,24, 24,24,26,26,27,27,27,27,27,27,29,29; 3:5,7,11, 13,15; 4:2,3,4,4; 5:13,13,13,16,16,16; 2Jn 5,6,6,8,8, 10,12,12,12; 3Jn 2,2,3,5,5,5,12,13,14,14; Jude 3,3, 4,5,5,9,12,18,19,20,21,21,24,24; Rev 1:4,11,19,20; 2:2,2,3,4,4,4,5,5,5,5,6,6,9,10,10,10,10,10,10,13,13, 13,14,14,15,16,19,19,20,20,23,24,24,24,25; 3:1,1,3, 3,3,3,4,8,8,9,10,10,11,15,15,15,16,16,17,17,17,18, 18,18,18; 4:1,11,11; 5:9,9,9,10; 6:10; 7:14; 10:11; 11:17,17; 12:12,12,12; 15:4,4,4; 16:5,6; 17:1,7,7, 8,12,15,16,18; 18:4,4,10,10,14,14,16,19,20,20,20, 22,22,22,22,23; 19:5,5,10,18; 21:9; 22:9,16

YOUR (6686)

Ge 3:5,14,14,15,15,15,16,16,16,17,17,19,19; 4:6,7,9, 10,11,11,14; 6:18,18,18; 7:1; 8:16,16; 9:2,5,9; 12:1, 1,1,2,7,13,18,19; 13:8,15,16,16; 14:20,20; 15:1,1,4, 4,4,5,13,15,16,18; 16:5,6,6,9,10,11; 17:2,5,7,7,7,8, 9,10,12,12,13,13,13,15,18,19; 18:3,3,4,5,5,9,10; 19:2,2,2,15,15,17,19,19; 20:10,13,16; 21:12,12,13; 22:2,2,12,12,16,16,17,17,18,20; 23:6,6,11,15; 24:2, 5,7,14,14,14,17,19,23,40,43,44,46,51,60; 25:23,31; 26:3,3,4,4,9,10,24,24; 27:3,3,6,6,9,10,19,19,20,25, 29,29,31,32,32,35,35,39,40,40,42,44,45; 28:2,2,3,4, 13,13,14,14; 29:15,18; 30:14,15,27,28,29,31,32; 31:3,3,5,6,7,8,8,9,13,29,30,31,32,35,37,37,38,38, 41,41,41,52; 32:4,5,6,9,9,10,12,18,20,27,28,29; 33:5,8,10,10; 34:8,9,11,15,16; 35:1,2,10,10,11,12; 37:7,10,10,13,14,32; 38:8,8,8,11,13,18,18,24; 39:19; 40:8,13,13,19,19,19; 41:40,44; 42:10,11,13, 15,16,16,16,19,19,20,20,33,33,34,34; 43:3,5,7,7,11, 12,13,14,20,23,23,23,23,27,28,29; 44:7,8,9,16,17, 18,18,21,23,23,24,27,30,31,32,33; 45:4,7,9,10,10, 11,17,17,18,18,19,19,19,20; 46:3,4,33,34; 47:3,3,4, 4,5,5,6,6,15,16,16,16,19,23,24,24,29,29; 48:1,2,4, 4,5,11,11,18,20,21,22; 49:2,4,8,8,8,8,18,25,26; 50:4,6,16,17,17,18,21,24,25; Ex 2:13; 3:5,6,13,15, 16,17,22; 4:2,4,6,6,7,10,10,13,14,16,17,23; 5:4,11, 11,14,15,16,16,16,18,23,23; 6:7,7; 7:1,1,2,9,15,19, 19; 8:2,3,3,3,3,3,3,4,4,5,5,8,9,9,9,11,11,11,16,21, 21,21,23,25,28; 9:3,3,3,14,14,15,19,22,30; 10:2,4, 5,6,6,6,6,8,10,12,16,17,21,24,24; 12:2,11,11,11,11, 11,11,15,17,19,21,22,23,24,26,32; 13:5,7,8,9,9,9, 11,12,13,14,16,16,19; 14:16,16,26; 15:6,6,7,7,8,10, 12,12,13,13,13,16,16,17,17,17,26; 16:7,8,9,12,16; 17:5; 18:6,6,22; 20:2,5,7,9,10,10,10,10,10,12,12, 12,16,17,17,17,24,24,24,26; 22:24,24,26,27,28,29, 29,29,30,30; 23:4,6,10,11,11,11,12,12,12,13,13,16, 16,19,19,21,22,25,25,26,27,28,31,31,33; 28:1,2,4, 41; 29:12,26; 30:15,16; 32:2,2,2,4,7,8,11,11,12,12, 13,13,13,13,29,30; 33:1,5,13,13,15,16,16,18,19; 34:9,9,10,16,16,19,20,23,24,24,24,26,26; 35:2,3; Lev 1:2,4,4; 2:5,7,13,13,13,13; 3:1,2,2,8,12,13; 7:32; 8:33,33; 9:2,2,7,7; 10:4,6,6,6,9,13,13,14,14, 14,14,15; 11:44,45; 14:34; 16:2,30; 18:2,4,7,7,7,8, 8,9,9,9,10,10,11,11,11,12,12,13,13,14,14,15,15,16, 16,18,18,20,21,21,30; 19:2,3,3,4,5,9,9,9,10,10,12, 13,14,15,16,16,17,17,18,18,19,25,25,27,27,28,29, 31,32,33,34,34,36; 20:7,19,19,24; 21:8,17; 22:3,19, 20,24,25,25,29,33; 23:11,14,22,22,22,22,28,32,38, 40,43,43; 24:22; 25:3,3,4,4,5,6,7,7,9,10,10,14,15, 17,17,19,25,35,36,38,38,39,43,44,45,45,46,46,47, 55; 26:1,1,5,5,6,7,8,9,12,13,13,16,16,17,18,19, 20,20,20,21,21,22,22,24,25,26,26,28,29,29,30, 30,30,30,31,31,31,32,33,33,34,37,38; Nu 5:19,20, 20,21,21,21,22,22,22; 9:10; 10:9,9,9,10,10,10,10, 10,35,35; 11:11,15,20; 13:20; 14:13,14,19,29,30,31, 32,33,33,33,34,42; 15:20,21,38,39,40,41,41,41; 16:6,10,11,16,17,46; 18:1,1,1,2,2,2,6,7,8,8,8,9,11, 11,11,13,19,19,19,20,20,26,27,31,31,31; 20:8,14, 16,17,17,19; 21:22,22,34; 22:13,30,32,32; 23:3,15; 24:5,5,14,21,21; 25:5; 27:13,13,18,20; 29:39,39,39; 31:2,3,19,24,49; 32:4,5,5,6,8,14,22,22,23,24,24,25, 27,31; 33:54,54,55,55; 34:3,6,6,7,9,10,12; 35:11, 13; Dt 1:8,10,10,11,12,12,12,13,15,16,16,21,21,26, 27,30,30,31,32,33,35,38,39,42,43,45; 2:3,4,5,7,7,7, 7,24,27,30,30; 3:2,18,18,19,19,19,20,20,21,21,22, 24,24,24,27; 4:1,2,3,3,4,6,9,9,9,10,19,21,21,23,23, 24,25,29,29,29,30,31,31,32,34,34,37,38,40,40; 5:1, 6,9,11,12,13,14,14,14,14,14,14,14,15,15,15,16, 16,16,20,21,21,21,21,22,23,23,32,33,33; 6:1,2,2,3, 5,5,5,5,6,7,8,8,9,9,10,10,13,13,15,16,17,18,19,20; 7:1,2,3,3,4,6,6,8,9,12,12,13,13,13,13,13,13,14, 14,16,18,19,19,19,20,21,22,23,24,25,26; 8:1,2,2,3, 4,4,5,5,6,7,10,11,13,13,14,14,16,18,19,20; 9:3,4, 5,5,5,5,6,6,7,12,16,17,23,26,26,27,29,29,29,29; 10:9,12,12,12,12,13,14,15,16,17,20,20,21,21,22, 22; 11:1,2,2,5,7,9,10,12,12,13,13,14,14,15,18, 18,18,19,20,20,21,21,22,24,24,25,27,28,29,31; 12:1,4,5,5,6,6,6,6,7,7,7,7,9,10,11,11,11,11,12,12, 12,12,13,14,15,15,15,17,17,17,17,18,18,18,18, 18,18,19,19,20,20,21,21,25,26,27,27,27,28,28,29, 31; 13:3,3,3,4,5,5,6,6,6,6,9,10,12,16,17,17,17,18; 14:1,1,2,21,21,22,23,23,23,23,24,24,25,25,26,26, 27,28,29,29,29; 15:3,4,4,5,6,7,7,9,10,10,10,11, 12,14,14,14,14,16,16,17,17,18,18,19,19,19,19, 20,20,21,22; 16:1,2,2,3,3,4,4,5,6,7,7,8,10,10,11,11, 11,11,13,13,14,14,14,14,15,15,15,15,16,16,17, 18,18,20,21,22; 17:1,2,4,5,8,8,12,14,15,15; 18:4,4, 5,5,6,9,12,13,14,15,15,16; 19:1,2,3,8,8,8,9,10,10, 10,14,14,14; 20:1,1,3,4,4,13,13,14,14,16,17,18; 21:1,2,5,8,8,10,10,10,11,12,13,13,23; 22:1,4,5,8,8, 9,17; 23:4,5,5,9,10,13,13,14,14,14,14,18,18,20,20, 21,21,23,23,23,23,24,24,25,25; 24:4,9,10,12,13,13, 14,18,19,19,20,21; 25:3,13,13,14,15,16,18,19; 26:1,2,2,3,4,4,5,10,11,11,12,12,13,13,15,15,16,16, 16,17,19; 27:2,3,3,5,6,6,7,9,10; 28:1,1,2,4,4,4,4,4, 5,5,8,8,8,9,11,11,11,11,12,12,13,15,17,17,18,18,18, 18,20,23,24,25,26,31,31,31,31,31,32,32,33,33,35, 35,35,36,40,42,42,45,46,47,48,51,51,51,51,52,52, 53,53,55,55,57,57,58,59,62,64,65,66,67,67,68; 29:2,3,5,5,6,10,10,10,11,11,11,11,11,12,13,13,22; 30:1,2,2,2,2,3,3,4,5,5,6,6,6,6,6,7,7,9,9,9,9,9,9,10, 10,10,10,11,14,14,16,16,17,19,20,20,20; 31:3,6,11, 12,12,13,14,16,26,28,28,29; 32:6,6,7,7,7,46,47,50, 50; 33:3,3,8,8,9,9,10,10,10,18,18,25,25,25,27,27, 29,29,29; 34:4,4; Jos 1:3,4,5,8,9,11,11,11,13,14,14, 14,14,14,15,15,17,18; 2:3,11,14,16,18,18,18,18,19; 3:3,3,9; 4:5,6,21,23,23,24; 5:15; 6:2,10,18,22; 7:8, 9,10,13; 8:1,7,7,18,18; 9:8,9,9,11,11,24,24,25; 10:6, 8,19,19,19,24; 14:9,9,9; 18:3; 22:3,3,4,4,5,5,5,8,8, 8,8,24,25,27; 23:3,3,3,4,5,5,5,8,10,11,13,13,13,13, 14,14,15,15,16; 24:2,3,6,7,8,11,12,14,15,19,19,23, 27; Jdg 2:1; 3:19,28,28; 4:7,14; 5:10,12,31; 6:9,10, 17,25,25,26,30; 7:7,9,10,15; 8:3,6,6,7,15,15,22,22, 24; 9:2,19,29,32,38,54; 11:9,17,19,24,36,36; 12:1, 1; 13:8,12,13,16,17,17; 14:3,13,15,15; 15:2,18; 16:6,15; 17:10,10; 18:6,10,23,25,25; 19:9,19,22; 20:28; 21:21,22,22; Ru 1:8,8,10,11,15,16,16; 2:10, 11,11,11,11,13,13,13,13; 3:3,9,9,13,17; 4:4,11,12,15, 15,15; 1Sa 1:11,11,14,16,18,18; 2:1,3,27,28,28,29, 30,31,31,32,33,33,33,34,36; 3:9,10; 4:17; 6:4,5,5,6, 21; 7:3; 8:5,5,11,13,14,15,15,16,16,17,22; 9:19,19, 20,26; 10:2,7,19,19,19; 12:2,2,6,7,8,11,12,14,15, 16,19,19,20,24,25; 13:13,13,14; 14:19,28,34,41; 15:15,17,21,24,28,30,33,33; 16:1,1,19; 17:9,17,18, 28,32,34,36,44,46,55,58; 19:2,11; 20:1,3,3,6,7,8,8, 10,15,18,29,30,31,42; 22:14,14,14,15,15,16,22; 23:4,10,11,11,20,20,21; 24:4,4,10,11,11,15,16,18, 20; 25:6,7,8,8,8,13,24,24,25,26,26,26,27,28,28,29, 29,29,31,31,33,35,35,41; 26:8,8,15,15,16,16,17,22, 24; 27:5,5; 28:1,2,16,17,17,19,21,22,22; 29:8,10; 31:4; 2Sa 1:14,16,16,16,19,21,24,25,26; 2:5,7,22, 26; 3:8,17,21,25,31,34,34; 4:8,11; 5:1,19; 6:21; 7:9, 9,11,12,12,12,12,16,16,16,19,19,20,21,21,21,23,23, 24,24,25,26,26,26,27,27,28,28,29,29,29,29; 9:2,6,7, 7,8,9,10,10,10,10,11; 10:3,5; 11:8,8,21,24,24; 12:8, 8,8,9,10,10,11,11,11,11,13; 13:5,7,10,20,20,24,35; 14:4,6,7,8,11,12,15,17,17,19,19,20,22,22,31; 15:2, 3,8,15,19,20,21,27,27,34,34,34,34; 16:3,4,8,17,17, 19,20,21,21; 17:6,8,8,9,10; 18:13,28,29; 19:5,5,5,5, 7,7,14,19,20,26,27,28,28,35,35,36,37,37; 20:6,17, 18; 22:28,30,36,36,50; 24:3,10,13,13,13,16,17,21, 23,23; 1Ki 1:12,12,13,13,17,17,17,19,24,26,26,30, 33,47,53; 2:3,4,6,7,7,21,26,37,37,38,39,43,44,44; 3:6,7,8,9,9,11,13,14,20,23,23; 5:5,5,6; 6:12; 8:18, 19,19,23,23,23,24,24,24,24,25,25,26,26,28,28,28, 29,29,30,30,30,31,32,33,33,34,35,35,35,36,36,38, 39,41,41,42,42,42,43,43,43,43,44,44,48,49,50,51, 51,52,52,52,53,53,61; 9:4,5,5,6; 10:6,6,8,8,8,9; 11:2,11,11,12,12,12,22,37; 12:4,7,9,9,10,14,16,16, 24,28; 13:6,8,18,21,22,22; 14:9,12; 15:19,19; 16:3; 17:12,13,19,23,24; 18:8,9,10,12,18,24,25,31,36,36, 44; 19:2,10,10,14,14,14; 20:3,3,5,5,5,6,6,9,13, 22,28,31,32,33,34,34,35,39,39,40,40,42,42; 21:2,6, 19,21,22; 22:4,4,13,30; 2Ki 1:10,12,13; 2:3,5,9,16, 16; 3:7,7,13,13,17,17,18; 4:1,2,2,3,4,7,7,13,16,16, 26,26,29,29,29,36; 5:8,10,15,17,17,18,18,25,27; 6:3,12,22,28,29; 7:2,19; 8:1,9,13; 9:1,1,7,22,31; 10:2,3,3,5,6,15,24,24,30; 11:8; 12:7; 13:16; 14:9, 10,10; 15:12; 16:7; 17:13,13,39,39; 18:26,27,31,31, 32; 19:4,4,6,16,20,22,22,23,28,28,28; 20:1,3,5,5,5, 6,15,17,17,18,18; 22:9,19,19,20,20; 23:21; 1Ch 4:10; 10:4; 11:1,2; 12:18; 14:10; 15:12; 16:35, 35; 17:8,8,10,11,11,11,11,13,17,17,18,18,19,19,21, 21,22,22,23,24,24,25,25,26,26,27,27; 19:3,5; 21:8,11, 12,15,17,17,22; 22:11,12,18,19,19; 28:6,8,8,9,21; 29:12,13,14,15,16,16,17,18,19,20; 2Ch 1:9,11,11; 2:8,10,14,14; 6:8,9,9,14,14,14,15,15,15,16,16, 17,17,19,19,19,20,20,20,21,21,21,22,23,24,24,25, 26,26,27,27,27,29,30,32,32,32,33,33,33,33,34, 34,38,39,39,40,40,41,41,41,41,41,42,42; 7:12,17, 18,18; 9:5,6,7,7,7,8,8,8; 10:4,7,9,9,10,14,16,16; 11:4; 13:8,9,12; 14:11; 15:7; 16:3,3,7,7,8; 18:3,12, 14,29; 19:3,10,10; 20:6,7,8,9,9,17,20; 21:12,12, 13,13,14,14,14,15; 24:5; 25:7,15,18,19; 28:9,9,10, 10,11; 29:5,8; 30:7,7,8,8,9,9,9; 32:10,14,15; 33:8; 34:16,27,27,28,28; 35:3,3,4,5,6; Ezr 4:2,11,15; 5:10; 7:14,14,17,18,18,19,20,25,25,26; 8:28; 9:11, 12,12,12,14,15; 10:4,11,11; Ne 1:6,6,6,6,7,8,9,10, 10,10,10,11,11,11,11,11; 2:2,5,6; 4:5,14,14,14,14, 14; 5:7,8; 6:8; 8:9,10; 9:5,5,8,14,14,16,18,19,20,20, 25,26,26,27,28,28,29,29,29,30,30,31,32,32,34,34, 35; 13:18,22,22,25; Est 3:8; 4:14,14; 5:3,6,6; 6:13; 7:2,2,3; 9:12,12; Job 1:11,11,12,17,18; 2:5,5,6,9; 4:4,6,6,6,6; 5:24,24,25,25; 6:22,25,27,28; 7:20; 8:2, 4,4,6,6,6,7; 10:3,5,5,7,8,12,13,13,16,17,17; 11:3,4,6,13,13,14,14,15,16,18,19; 13:12,12,17,21, 21,24,24; 14:3,13,15; 15:5,5,6,6,10,12,12,13,13; 16:3; 18:3,4,4; 21:5,5,14,34,34; 22:3,4,5,5,6,22,23, 24,24,25,26,27,28,30; 26:4; 30:21; 32:11,14; 33:5, 34:33; 35:4,6,7,8,8,14; 36:16,19,19; 37:17; 38:11, 34; 39:9,11,12,26,27; 40:9,11,14; 41:4,5; 42:7,8; Ps 2:7,8,8,12,12; 3:8,8; 4:4,4,6; 5:5,7,7,7,8,8,11,11, 12; 6:1,1,4,5; 7:6; 8:1,1,2,3,3,6,9; 9:1,2,10,14,14, 19; 10:5,12; 11:1; 13:1,5,5; 15:1,1; 16:10,11,11; 17:2,4,5,6,7,7,8,8,13,14,15,15; 18:15,15,29,35,35, 35,49; 19:11,13,14; 20:3,3,4,4,5,5; 21:1,6,8,8,8,8, 13,13; 22:22,26; 23:4,4,6; 24:6,7,9; 25:4,4,5,6,7,11; 26:3,3,6,7,7,8; 27:8,9,9,11; 28:2,9,9; 30:7,9,12; 31:1,2,3,5,7,15,16,16,16,20,20,22; 32:4; 33:22; 34:13,13; 35:3,24,28,28; 36:5,5,6,6,7,7,8,8,9,10,10; 37:4,5,6,6; 38:1,1,2,2,3; 39:10,10; 40:5,8,8,9,10,10, 10,10,10,11,11,11,16; 41:12; 42:3,5,7,7,10,11; 43:3, 3,5; 44:2,3,3,3,5,8,12,17,18,22,24,26; 45:2,3,3,4,4, 5,5,6,6,7,7,8,9,9,10,10,11,11,12,16,16,17; 47:1; 48:9,9,10,10,10,11; 50:7,8,8,9,9,14,16,18,19,19,20, 20; 51:1,1,4,4,9,11,11,12,13,14,15,19; 52:2,5,9,9,9; 54:1,1,5,6; 55:22; 56:7,8,8; 57:1,5,10,10,11; 58:2,2, 9; 59:11,13,16,16; 60:3,5; 61:4,4,5,7,8; 62:8,10,10; 63:2,2,3,4,7,8; 65:4,4,4,6,8,11,11; 66:3,3,3,4,13; 67:2,2; 68:7,9,10,10,23,23,23,24,28,28,29,35; 69:7, 9,13,13,13,16,16,17,17,24,24,27,29,32; 70:4; 71:2, 2,8,8,15,15,16,16,17,18,18,19,22,24; 72:1,1,2,2; 73:15,24,28; 74:1,1,2,3,4,7,7,10,11,11,11,13,18,19, 19,20,21,22,23,23; 75:1,1,4,5; 76:6,10,10,11; 77:11, 12,12,13,14,15,15,17,18,18,19,19,19,20; 79:1,1,2,2, 5,6,6,8,9,9,10,11,13,13,13; 80:2,3,4,4,7,15,16,16, 16,17,17,18,19; 81:7,10,10; 82:8; 83:2,2,3,15,15, 16; 84:1,3,4,9,10; 85:1,2,3,3,4,5,6,7,7; 86:2,4,9,11, 11,11,12,13,16,16,17; 88:2,5,7,7,10,11,11,12,12,14, 15,16,16; 89:1,2,2,4,4,5,5,8,10,10,12,13,13,13,14, 15,16,16,17,19,38,39,46,49,49,50,51,51; 90:4,7,7,8, 9,11,11,11,13,14,16,16,16; 91:4,7,7,8,9,10,11,12; 92:1,2,2,4,4,5,5,9,9; 93:2,5,5; 94:5,5,12,18,19; 95:8,9; 97:8; 99:3; 101:1; 102:2,2,10,12,14,15,24, 25,27,28,28; 103:3,3,4,5,5; 104:7,7,24,24,28,29,30; 106:4,5,5,5,7,7,47,47; 108:4,4,5,6; 109:21,21,26, 27,28; 110:1,1,2,2,3,3,3,5; 115:1,1,14; 116:7,16,19;

YOURS (86)

YOURSELF (187)

YOURSELVES (219)

BIBLICAL LANGUAGE DICTIONARY-INDEXES

FEATURES OF THE HEBREW TO ENGLISH DICTIONARY-INDEX

G/K NUMBER
Matches the number at the end of context lines; Hebrew G/K numbers start with "H" (see pages xii, xv, xvi).

LEXICAL FORM and TRANSLITERATION
See the table of transliteration and pronunciation below.

PART OF SPEECH
The part of speech is abbreviated (see the table of abbreviations below).

FREQUENCY COUNT
Indicates the total in the NIV Hebrew text; if a Hebrew word is not in the NIV Hebrew text, it is noted by "Not used in the NIVEBC" (see page xvii).

H29 אֲבִידָן ***'ªbîdān***, n.pr.m. [5] [√ 3 + 1906]. ← **RELATED WORDS LIST** Hebrew words related by common elements are listed by one- to four-digit G/K number; Aramaic by five-digits (see page xvii).

Abidan, "*[my] father is judge*":– ← **DEFINITION and ETYMOLOGY** Words are defined, often with expanded explanations. If a proper name, the possible definition (etymology) is given in italics (see page xvi).

Abidan (5) ← **NIV WORD and FREQUENCY COUNT** Following the symbol :– NIV words are listed according to their exact textual spelling and are organized according to frequency (see page xvi).

he[S] (2), him[S] (1), his[S] (1) ← **RAISED LETTER "S"** Indicates "substitution" translation (see pages xiv, xvi).

members of family (1 [+1074]) ← **MULTIPLE WORDS / MULTIPLE NUMBERS** More than one NIV word and/or more than one G/K number indicate multiple-word translations (see pages xi, xiii, xvi).

NDT (2) ← **NDT (NOT DIRECTLY TRANSLATED)** Always the final entry, this indicates the number of times the Hebrew word was not translated in the NIV for stylistic reasons (see pages xiv, xvi).

TABLE OF SIMPLIFIED TRANSLITERATION AND PRONUNCIATION

Consonants

Hebrew	Translit.	Sound
א	'	[no sound]
בּ, ב	*b*	boy
גּ, ג	*g*	girl
דּ, ד	*d*	dog
ה	*h*	hot
ו	*w*	vote
ז	*z*	zip
ח	*ḥ*	Ba*ch*
ט	*ṭ*	tip
י	*y*	yes
כּ, כ, ך	*k*	kit
ל	*l*	let
מ, ם	*m*	mother
נ, ן	*n*	not
ס	*s*	sip
ע	'	[no sound]
פּ, פ, ף	*p*	pet
צ, ץ	*ṣ*	si*ts*
ק	*q*	tor*q*ue
ר	*r*	rot
שׂ	*ś*	sip
שׁ	*š*	*sh*ip
תּ, ת	*t*	tip

Vowels

Hebrew	Translit.	Sound
ָה	*â*	f*a*ther
ָ	*ā*	f*a*ther
ַ	*a*	f*a*ther
ֲ	*ª*	b*a*ton
וּ	*û*	t*u*ne
ֻ	*u*	s*u*re
ֵי	*ê*	th*ey*
ֵ	*ē*	th*ey*
ֶ	*e*	g*e*t
ְ if (vocal)	*ᵉ*	s*e*lect
ֱ	*ᵉ*	s*e*lect
ִי	*î*	mach*i*ne
ִ	*i*	p*i*n
וֹ	*ô*	ph*o*ne
ֹ	*ō*	ph*o*ne
ָ	*o*	ph*o*ne
ֳ	*ᵒ*	m*o*tel

TABLE OF HEBREW DICTIONARY ABBREVIATIONS

&	and
+	plus: in combination with
?	uncertain
[]	uncertain part of speech
→	see these related words
√	see this organizing word
1	first person
2	second person
3	third person
a.	adjective
abst.	abstract
adv.	adverb
art.	article
c.	conjunction
col.	collective
com.	common gender
demo.	demonstrative
den.	denominative
du.	dual number
emph.	emphatic
excl.	exclamation
f.	feminine
fig.	figurative(ly)
g.	gentilic
indecl.	indeclinable
indef.	indefinite
inf.	infinitive
intens.	intensive
inter.	interrogative
interj.	interjection
l.	loanword
loc.	location
m.	masculine
n.	noun
neg.	negative
num.	numeral
ord.	ordinal
p.	pronoun
pl.	plural
poss.	possibly
pp.	preposition
pr.	proper [noun]
pref.	prefix
prob.	probably
pt.	particle
ptcp.	participle
rel.	relative
s.	singular
subst.	substantive
suf.	suffix
temp.	temporal
tt.	technical term in Psalm title
v.	verb
var.	variant
vbl.	verbal

Hebrew Verbal Stems

[H]	Hiphil
[Ho]	Hophal
[Hotpaal]	Hotpaal
[Hotpael]	Hotpael
[Hsh]	Histaphel
[Ht]	Hitpael
[Htpal]	Hitpalpel
[Htpalpal]	Hitpalpal
[Htpo]	Hitpoel
[Htpoal]	Hitpoal
[Htpol]	Hitpolel
[Htpolal]	Hitpolal
[N]	Niphal
[P]	Piel
[Pilal]	Pilal
[Pilel]	Pilel
[Pilpal]	Pilpal
[Pil]	Pilpel
[Po]	Poel
[Poal]	Poal
[Poalal]	Poalal
[Pol]	Polel
[Polal]	Polal
[Pu]	Pual
[Pualal]	Pualal
[Pul]	Pulal
[Pulpal]	Pulpal
[Q]	Qal
[Qp]	Qal passive

HEBREW TO ENGLISH DICTIONARY-INDEX

H1 **א** **'**, letter. Not used in NIVEBC [cf. 66; 10001]. letter of the Hebrew alphabet

H2 **אָ-** **-ā'**, p.suf.3.f.sg. [1] [cf. 2023]. she, her:– NDT (1)

H3 **אָב** **'āb**, n.m. [1211] [→ 10003; *also used with compound proper names*]. father, grandfather, forefather, ancestor; (pl.) ancestors (of both genders); by extension: originator, founder (of a city or profession); a title of respect referring to humans or god. The "house of a father" is a subdivision of a clan:– father (527), ancestors (270), father's (100), families (57 [+1074]), families (35), parents (33), family (32 [+1074]), fathers (32), family (16), predecessors (13), ancestral (10), them[S] (9 [+2257]), forefather (8), ancestor (5), father's (4 [+4200]), parent (4), parents (3 [+2256, 562]), ancestors (2 [+3]), ancestor's (2), clans (2), forefathers (2 [+3]), grandfather's (2), he[S] (2 [+3870]), him[S] (2 [+2257]), those who have gone before (2), ancestors (1 [+8037]), before[S] (1), clan (1 [+5476]), clan (1 [+5476, 1074]), clans (1 [+1074]), family line (1 [+1074]), family possessions (1), fatherless (1 [+3846, 2256, 401]), forefather's (1), grandfather (1), group (1 [+2755, 1074]), he[S] (1 [+2023]), he[S] (1 [+3276]), him[S] (1 [+3276]), him[S] (1 [+2023]), his[S] (1 [+2257]), members of family (1 [+1074]), members of family (1 [+1074, 2256, 1074]), parent's (1), people (1), priestly[S] (1), them[S] (1 [+3870]), them[S] (1 [+4013]), they[S] (1 [+4013]), who have gone before (1 [+1887]), whole family (1 [+1074]), NDT (11)

H4 **אֵב** **'ēb**, n.[m.] [2] [cf. 817; 10004]. new (plant) growth, shoot:– growing (1), new growth (1)

H5 **אֲבַגְתָא** **'ᵃbagtā'**, n.pr.m. [1] Abagtha:– Abagtha (1)

H6 **אָבַד** **'ābad**, v. [184] [→ 7, 8, 9, 10, 11, 12, 13; 10005]. [Q] perish, [P, H] destroy, demolish, annihilate; "to destroy the heart" means "to lose courage":– perish (43), destroy (28), destroyed (16), lost (9), perished (9), destruction (5), gone (5), perishing (4), ruined (4), annihilate (3), come to nothing (3), perishes (3), cease (2), certainly be destroyed (2 [+6]), comes to nothing (2), destroy completely (2 [+6]), destroys (2), lose (2), perish (2 [+6]), surely be destroyed (2 [+6]), wipe out (2), annihilated (1), banish (1), be destroyed (1), broken (1), brought ruin (1), come to ruin (1), corrupts (1), dead (1), demolish (1), destroying (1), die (1), died (1), dying (1), elude (1), expelled (1), exterminate (1), give up (1), have no (1 [+4946]), have nowhere (1 [+4946]), kill (1), lead to destruction (1), leads to destruction (1), lost (1 [+8]), not escape (1 [+4960]), ruin (1), silence (1), squanders (1), swept (1), vanished (1), wandering (1), wiped out (1), without (1), NDT (2)

H7 **אֹבֵד** **'ōbēd**, n.[m.] [2] [√ 6]. ruin:– ruin (1), utter destruction (1 [+6330])

H8 **אֲבֵדָה** **'ᵃbēdâ**, n.f. [4] [√ 6]. lost item:– lost property (2), lost (1), lost (1 [+6])

H9 **אֲבַדֹּה** **'ᵃbaddōh**, n.f. [1] [→ 11; cf. 6]. destruction; this can refer to the nether world of the dead, with a focus that this is the place of decay:– Destruction (1)

H10 **אֲבַדּוֹ** **'ᵃbaddô**, n.f. Not used in NIVEBC [√ 6]. destruction

H11 **אֲבַדּוֹן** **'ᵃbaddôn**, n.f. [5] [√ 9; cf. 6]. destruction; some translate as a proper noun, the Place of Destruction (the realm of the dead); see also 9:– Destruction (5)

H12 **אַבְדָן** **'abdān**, n.[m.] [1] [√ 6]. destruction:– destroying (1)

H13 **אָבְדַן** **'obdān**, n.[m.] [1] [√ 6]. destruction:– destruction (1)

H14 **אָבָה** **'ābâ**, v. [53] [→ 16, 20?, 22?, 36?, 1066?; cf. 3277, 9289?]. [Q] to be willing, consent, yield; with the negative, to be unwilling, refuse:– would (12), refused (11 [+4202]), willing (10), unwilling (8 [+4202]), accept (2), refuse (2 [+4202]), will (2), agree to demands (1), consent (1), submit (1), would do (1), would have (1), yield (1)

H15 **אֵבֶה** **'ēbeh**, n.[m.] [1] papyrus or reed (boat):– papyrus (1)

H16 **אֲבוֹי** **'ᵃbôy**, interj. [1] [√ 14]. sorrow (uneasiness); some parse as an interjection: woe!:– sorrow (1)

H17 **אֵבוּס** **'ēbûs**, n.m. [3] [√ 80]. manger:– manger (3)

H18 **אִבְחָה** **'ibḥâ**, n.f. Not used in NIVEBC [cf. 3181]. slaughter

H19 **אֲבַטִּיחַ** **'ᵃbaṭṭîaḥ**, n.[m.] [1] [√ 1053]. melon:– melons (1)

H20 **אָבִי¹** **'ābî[1]**, interj. [1] [√ 14?]. Oh, that!:– Oh that (1)

H21 **אָבִי²** **'ābî[2]**, n.pr.m. Not used in NIVEBC [cf. 2671]. Abi, "*[my] father*"

H22 **אָבִי³** **'ābî[3]**, v. Not used in NIVEBC [√ 14?]. see 995

H23 **אֲבִי** **'ᵃbî**, n.pr.m. [1] [√ 31]. Abijah, Abiezrite, "*[my] father is* Yahweh, Abi [my] father":– Abijah (1)

H24 **אֲבִיאֵל** **'ᵃbî'ēl**, n.pr.m. [3] [√ 446 + 3]. Abiel, "*[my] father is God [El]*":– Abiel (3)

H25 **אֲבִיאָסָף** **'ᵃbî'āsāp**, n.pr.m. [1] [√ 47; cf. 3 + 3758]. Abiasaph, "*[my] father has gathered*":– Abiasaph (1)

H26 **אָבִיב** **'ābîb**, n.m. [8] [cf. 9425]. (month of) Abib, the first month of the Canaanite calendar equal to Nisan (March-April); head (of grain), already ripe but still soft:– Aviv (5), headed (1), heads (1), that[S] (1)

H27 **אֲבִיבַעַל** **'ᵃbîba'al**, n.pr.m. Not used in NIVEBC [√ 3 + 1251]. Abi-Baal

H28 **אֲבִיגַיִל** **'ᵃbîgayil**, n.pr.f. [16] [√ 3 + 1635?]. Abigail, "*[my] father rejoices* or *father [cause] of joy*":– Abigail (16)

H29 **אֲבִידָן** **'ᵃbîdān**, n.pr.m. [5] [√ 3 + 1906]. Abidan, "*[my] father is judge*":– Abidan (5)

H30 **אֲבִידָע** **'ᵃbîdā'**, n.pr.m. [2] [√ 3 + 3359]. Abida, "*[my] father knows*":– Abida (2)

H31 **אֲבִיָּה** **'ᵃbiyyâ**, n.pr.m. & f. [29] [→ 23, 32; cf. 3 + 3378]. Abijah, "*[my] father is Yahweh*":– Abijah (26), Abijah's (3)

H32 **אֲבִיָּהוּ** **'ᵃbiyyāhû**, n.pr.m. & f. [2] [√ 31; cf. 3 + 3378]. Abijah, "*[my] father is Yahweh*":– Abijah (2)

H33 **אֲבִיהוּא** **'ᵃbîhû'**, n.pr.m. [12] [√ 3 + 2085]. Abihu, "*he is [my] father*":– Abihu (12)

H34 **אֲבִיהוּד** **'ᵃbîhûd**, n.pr.m. [1] [√ 3 + 2086]. Abihud, "*[my] father has majesty*":– Abihud (1)

H35 **אֲבִיהַיִל** **'ᵃbîhayil**, n.pr.m. [2] [√ 3 + 2657]. Abihail, "*[my] father has strength/wealth* or *cause of strength/wealth*":– Abihail (2)

H36 **אֶבְיוֹן** **'ebyôn**, a. [61] [√ 14?]. poor, needy, often as a class of persons with physical needs, of low status and little political power, with an associative meaning of oppression and misery:– needy (46), poor (13), needy (1 [+132]), them[S] (1 [+2021, 278])

H37 **אֲבִיּוֹנָה** **'ᵃbiyyônâ**, n.f. [1] caper berry (that stimulates desire):– desire (1)

H38 **אֲבִיחַיִל** **'ᵃbîḥayil**, n.pr.m. [4] [√ 3 + 2657]. Abihail, "*[my] father has strength/wealth* or *cause of strength/wealth*":– Abihail (4)

H39 **אֲבִיטוּב** **'ᵃbîṭûb**, n.pr.m. [1] [√ 3 + 3202]. Abitub, "*[my] father is good*":– Abitub (1)

H40 **אֲבִיטַל** **'ᵃbîṭāl**, n.pr.f. [2] [√ 3 + 3228]. Abital, "*[my] father is [the] night dew*":– Abital (2)

H41 **אֲבִיָּם** **'ᵃbiyyām**, n.pr.m. Not used in NIVEBC [√ 3 + 3542]. Abiyam, "*[my] father is Yam [the sea]*"

H42 **אֲבִימָאֵל** **'ᵃbîmā'ēl**, n.pr.m. [2] [√ 3 + 446]. Abimael, "*[my] father is God [El]*":– Abimael (2)

H43 **אֲבִימֶלֶךְ** **'ᵃbîmelek**, n.pr.m. [66] [√ 3 + 4889]. Abimelech, "*[my] father is king* or *[my] father is Molech*":– Abimelek (60), Abimelek's (2), he[S] (2), him[S] (1), his[S] (1)

H44 **אֲבִינָדָב** **'ᵃbînādāb**, n.pr.m. [12] [√ 3 + 5605]. Abinadab, "*[my] father is generous* or *[my] father is Nadab*":– Abinadab (9), Abinadab's (2), NDT (1)

H45 **אֲבִינֹעַם** **'ᵃbînō'am**, n.pr.m. [4] [√ 3 + 5840]. Abinoam, "*[my] father is graciousness*":– Abinoam (4)

H46 **אֲבִינֵר** **'ᵃbînēr**, n.pr.m. [1] [√ 3 + 5944; cf. 79]. Abner, "*[my] father is Ner [a lamp]*":– Abner (1)

H47 **אֶבְיָסָף** **'ebyāsāp**, n.pr.m. [3] [→ 25; cf. 3 + 3758]. Ebiasaph, "*[my] father has gathered*":– Ebiasaph (3)

H48 **אֲבִיעֶזֶר** **'ᵃbî'ezer**, n.pr.m. [7] [→ 49; cf. 3 + 6469]. Abiezer, "*[my] father is help*":– Abiezer (6), Abiezrites (1)

H49 **אֲבִי עֶזְרִי** **'ᵃbî 'ezrî**, a.g. [3] [√ 48]. Abiezrite, "*of Abiezer*":– Abiezrites (2), Abiezrite (1)

H50 **אֲבִי־עַלְבוֹן** **'ᵃbî-'albôn**, n.pr.m. [1] [√ 3 + 6588]. Abi-Albon, "*[my] father is Albon*":– Abi-Albon (1)

H51 **אָבִיר** **'ābîr**, a. [6] [→ 52, 87, 88, 89]. mighty, powerful; (as a divine title) the Mighty One:– Mighty One (6)

H52 **אַבִּיר** **'abbîr**, a. [17] [√ 51]. mighty, powerful; this can refer to strong animals, social leaders, and angelic beings:– mighty (4), bulls (2), stallions (2), warriors (2), angels (1), chief (1), great (1), steeds (1), strong (1), stubborn-hearted (1 [+4213]), valiant (1 [+4213])

H53 **אֲבִירָם** **'ᵃbîrām**, n.pr.m. [11] [√ 3 + 8123; cf. 92]. Abiram, "*[my] father is exalted*":– Abiram (11)

H54 **אֲבִישַׁג** **'ᵃbîšag**, n.pr.f. [5] [√ 3 + 8704]. Abishag, "*[my] father strays*":– Abishag (5)

H55 **אֲבִישׁוּעַ** **'ᵃbîšûa'**, n.pr.m. [5] [√ 3 + 8781]. Abishua, "*[my] father is salvation*":– Abishua (5)

H56 **אֲבִישׁוּר** **'ᵃbîšûr**, n.pr.m. [2] [√ 3 + 8802]. Abishur, "*[my] father is a wall*":– Abishur (1), Abishur's (1)

H57 **אֲבִישַׁי** **'ᵃbîšay**, n.pr.m. [19] [cf. 93]. Abishai, "*[my] father is Jesse* or *father exists*":– Abishai (19)

H58 **אֲבִישָׁלוֹם** **'ᵃbîšālôm**, n.pr.m. [2] [√ 3 + 8934]. Abishalom, "*[my] father is peace*":– Abishalom (2)

H59 **אֶבְיָתָר** **'ebyātār**, n.pr.m. [30] [√ 3 + 3855]. Abiathar, "*[my] father gives abundance* or *the father is preeminent*":– Abiathar (27), Abiathar's (1), he[S] (1), them[S] (1 [+7401, 2256])

H60 **אָבַךְ** **'ābak**, v. [1] [cf. 2200]. [Ht] to roll upward, to be borne along:– rolls upward (1)

H61 **אָבַל¹** **'ābal[1]**, v. [31] [→ 63, 65]. [Q, Ht] to mourn, lament, grieve, [H] cause to mourn; mourning can be the emotion or attitude of sorrow, as well as the active observation of mourning rites and ceremonies; see also 63:– mourn (12), mourned (9), mourning (2), dries up (1), grieve (1), grieving (1), in mourning (1), lament (1), made lament (1), mourns (1), pretend in mourning (1)

H62 **אָבַל²** **'ābal[2]**, v. [8] [Q] to dry up, lie parched:– dries up (3), parched (3), dried up (1), dry up (1)

H63 **אָבֵל¹** **'ābēl[1]**, a. [8] [√ 61]. mourning, grieving, weeping:– mourn (3), mourners (2), grief (1), grieve (1), weeping (1)

H64 **אָבֵל²** **'ābēl[2]**, n.pr.loc. [1] [→ 67-3673; cf. 3297]. Abel, "*meadow*":– Abel (1)

H65 **אֵבֶל** **'ēbel**, n.m. [24] [√ 61]. ceremony of mourning, period of mourning; a mourning ceremony was a ritual for burial of the dead, with distinctive clothing, music, behaviors, and a set time period for the ritual, generally a longer period for more important people:– mourning (15), mourn (2), ceremony of mourning (1), moan (1), mourn (1 [+6913]), period of mourning (1), sorrow (1), time of mourning (1), weep (1)

H66 **אֲבָל** **'ᵃbāl**, adv. [11] [√ 1153 + 1]. but; however, surely, indeed:– but (3), however (2), not at all (1), now (1), surely (1), yes but (1), NDT (2)

H67 **אֻבָל** **'ubāl**, n.[m.] [3] [√ 64]. canal:– canal (3)

H68 **אָבֵל בֵּית מַעֲכָה** **'ābēl bêt ma'ᵃkâ**, n.pr.loc. [4] [√ 64 + 1074 + 5081]. Abel Beth Maacah, "*meadow of the house of Maacah [oppression]*":– Abel Beth Maakah (4)

H69 אָבֵל הַשִּׁטִּים ***'ābēl haššiṭṭîm***, n.pr.loc. [1] [√ 64 + 2243]. Abel Shittim, "*meadow of the acacia trees*":– Abel Shittim (1)

H70 אָבֵל כְּרָמִים ***'ābēl kᵉrāmîm***, n.pr.loc. [1] [√ 64 + 4148]. Abel Keramim, "*meadow of vineyards*":– Abel Keramim (1)

H71 אָבֵל מְחוֹלָה ***'ābēl mᵉḥôlâ***, n.pr.loc. [3] [√ 64 + 4703; cf. 4716?]. Abel Meholah, "*meadow of the round dance*":– Abel Meholah (3)

H72 אָבֵל מַיִם ***'ābēl mayim***, n.pr.loc. [1] [√ 64 + 4784]. Abel Maim, "*meadow of waters*":– Abel Maim (1)

H73 אָבֵל מִצְרַיִם ***'ābēl miṣrayim***, n.pr.loc. [1] [√ 64 + 5213]. Abel Mizraim, "*meadow of Egypt* or *mourning of Egypt*":– Abel Mizraim (1)

H74 אֶבֶן ***'eben***, n.f. [273] [→ 75, 78?; 10006]. stone, rock, natural or shaped, sometimes of specific size for use in a balance scale; a "precious stone" is a gem or jewel; by extension: hailstone. Rock is a title of God, with a focus of strength and stability, a place of refuge:– stone (92), stones (88), rock (8), rocks (7), stone (5 [+8083, 928, 2021]), weights (5), gems (4), stoned (4 [+8083]), hailstones (3 [+453]), slingstones (3 [+7845]), stone (3 [+6232, 928, 2021]), blocks (2), differing weights (2 [+2256, 74]), hail (2 [+1352]), lapis lazuli (2 [+6209]), onyx (2 [+8732]), ore (2), some[S] (2), stoned (2 [+6232, 928, 2021]), another[S] (1), blocks of stone (1), capstone (1), capstone (1 [+8036]), charm (1 [+2834]), cornerstone (1 [+7157]), cover (1), differing weights (1 [+74, 2256]), differing weights (1 [+74, 2256]), fieldstones (1 [+8969]), gem (1), hailstones (1), jewels (1), limestone (1 [+1732]), marble (1 [+8880]), masons (1 [+3093]), plumb line (1), sling stones (1 [+928, 2021]), sparkling jewels (1 [+734]), standard (1), stone (1 [+8083]), stonecutters (1 [+2935]), stoned (1 [+8083, 928, 2021]), stoned to death (1 [+8083]), stonemasons (1 [+3093, 7815]), stoning (1 [+8083, 928, 2021]), them[S] (1), them[S] (1 [+9109, 2021]), these[S] (1 [+2021]), topaz (1 [+9577]), two differing weights (1 [+2256, 74]), two differing weights (1 [+74, 2256]), NDT (3)

H75 אֶבֶן הָעֵזֶר ***'eben hā'ēzer***, n.pr.loc. [3] [√ 74 + 6469]. Ebenezer, "*stone of help*":– Ebenezer (3)

H76 אֲבָנָה ***'ᵃbānâ***, n.pr.loc. [1] [cf. 592]. Abana:– Abana (1)

H77 אַבְנֵט ***'abnēṭ***, n.[m.] [9] (linen) sash, wrapped around the waist:– sash (6), sashes (3)

H78 אָבְנַיִם ***'obnayim***, n.[m.] [2] [√ 74?]. potter's wheel; delivery stool:– delivery stool (1), wheel (1)

H79 אַבְנֵר ***'abnēr***, n.pr.m. [62] [√ 3 + 5944; cf. 46]. Abner, "*[my] father is Ner [a lamp]*":– Abner (55), Abner's (3), him[S] (2), he[S] (1), NDT (1)

H80 אָבַס ***'ābas***, v. [2] [→ 17, 4393]. [Qp] to be fattened:– choice (1), fattened (1)

H81 אֲבַעְבֻּעֹת ***'ᵃba'bu'ōt***, n.f.pl. [2] [√ 5580]. festers, blisters:– festering (2)

H82 אֶבֶץ ***'ebeṣ***, n.pr.loc. [1] [→ 83]. Ebez:– Ebez (1)

H83 אִבְצָן ***'ibṣān***, n.pr.m. [2] [√ 82]. Ibzan, "*swift*":– Ibzan (2)

H84 אָבַק ***'ābaq***, v.den. [2] [cf. 3909?]. [N] to wrestle (with):– wrestled (2)

H85 אָבָק ***'ābāq***, n.m. [6] [→ 86]. fine dust, powder:– dust (4), fine dust (1), powder (1)

H86 אֲבָקָה ***'ᵃbāqâ***, n.f. [1] [√ 85]. spice (scented powders):– spices (1)

H87 אָבַר ***'ābar***, v.den. [1] [√ 88; cf. 51]. [H] to take flight, soar upward:– take flight (1)

H88 אֵבֶר ***'ēber***, n.[m.] [3] [→ 87, 89; cf. 51]. feather, wing; other sources: the strong joint of the body to the wing, "pinion," with the associative meaning of strength that can bring freedom:– wings (2), feathers (1)

H89 אֶבְרָה ***'ebrâ***, n.f. [4] [√ 88; cf. 51]. feather, pinion, wing; in some contexts may have the associative meaning of protection:– feathers (2), aloft (1 [+6584]), wings (1)

H90 אַבְרָהָם ***'abrāhām***, n.pr.m. [175] [cf. 92]. Abraham, "*father of many*":– Abraham (153), Abraham's (11), he[S] (6), him[S] (2), his[S] (1), his[S] (1 [+4200]), NDT (1)

H91 אַבְרֵךְ ***'abrēk***, l.excl. [1] Make way!; others: Kneel down! or Watch out!:– Make way (1)

H92 אַבְרָם ***'abrām***, n.pr.m. [61] [√ 3 + 8123; cf. 53, 90]. Abram, "*exalted father*":– Abram (50), Abram's (5), him[S] (3), he[S] (1), his[S] (1), NDT (1)

H93 אַבְשַׁי ***'abšay***, n.pr.m. [6] [cf. 57]. Abishai, "*[my] father is Jesse* or *father exists*":– Abishai (6)

H94 אַבְשָׁלוֹם ***'abšālôm***, n.pr.m. [109] [√ 3 + 8934]. Absalom, "*father is peace*":– Absalom (88), Absalom's (10), he[S] (6), him[S] (2), Absalom's (1 [+4200]), NDT (2)

H95 אֹבֹת ***'ōbōt***, n.pr.loc. [4] [√ 3277?]. Oboth, "*fathers*":– Oboth (4)

H96 אָגֵא ***'āgē'***, n.pr.m. [1] Agee, "[poss.] *fugitive*":– Agee (1)

H97 אֲגַג ***'ᵃgag***, n.pr.m. [8] [→ 98?]. Agag, "[poss.] *violent*":– Agag (7), NDT (1)

H98 אֲגָגִי ***'ᵃgāgî***, a.g. [5] [√ 97?]. Agagite, "*of Agag*":– Agagite (5)

H99 אֲגֻדָּה ***'ᵃguddâ***, n.f. [4] bunch, bundle; group, band; cord, bands; foundation, structure:– bunch (1), cords (1), foundation (1), group (1)

H100 אֱגוֹז ***'ᵉgôz***, n.[m.] [1] nut tree:– nut trees (1)

H101 אָגוּר ***'āgûr***, n.pr.m. [1] [√ 112]. Agur, "*gatherer* [or poss.] *wage earner*":– Agur (1)

H102 אֲגוֹרָה ***'ᵃgôrâ***, n.f. [1] [→ 115]. fee, payment, a piece of precious metal used as a medium of exchange (but not a minted coin):– piece (1)

H103 אֶגֶל ***'ēgel***, n.[m.] [1] [→ 104]. drop (of dew):– drops (1)

H104 אֶגְלַיִם ***'eglayim***, n.pr.loc. [1] [√ 103]. Eglaim:– Eglaim (1)

H105 אָגַם ***'āgam***, v. [Q] to be hot

H106 אֲגַם¹ ***'ᵃgam¹***, n.[m.] [9] [→ 109]. swamp, pond, marsh (with reeds):– pools (3), ponds (2), marshes (1), pool (1), pool (1 [+4784]), swampland (1 [+4784])

H107 אֲגַם² ***'ᵃgam²***, n.[m.] Not used in NIVEBC. outwork (of a fort)

H108 אָגֵם ***'āgēm***, a. [1] [cf. 6327]. sick, grieved:– sick (1)

H109 אַגְמוֹן ***'agmôn***, n.[m.] [5] [√ 106]. reed; cord (made of reeds):– reed (3), cord (1), reeds (1)

H110 אַגָּן ***'aggān***, n.[m.] [3] (large and deep) bowl, goblet:– bowls (2), goblet (1)

H111 אֲגַף ***'ᵃgap***, n.[m.] [7] [√ 1727]. troop, band:– troops (7)

H112 אָגַר ***'āgar***, v. [3] [→ 101]. [Q] to gather (in):– gather grapes (1), gathers (1), gathers crops (1)

H113 אֲגַרְטָל ***'ᵃgarṭāl***, n.m. [2] dish; in context made of precious metals:– dishes (2)

H114 אֶגְרֹף ***'egrōp***, n.[m.] [2] [√ 1759?]. fist (the hand clenched to strike):– fist (1), fists (1)

H115 אִגֶּרֶת ***'iggeret***, n.f. [10] [√ 102; 10007]. letter, document:– letters (6), letter (4)

H116 אֵד ***'ēd***, n.m. [2] stream, fresh water that moves from a higher to lower place; in some contexts this may be an artesian spring:– streams (2)

H117 אָדַב ***'ādab***, v. Not used in NIVEBC [→ 118]. [H] to grieve

H118 אַדְבְּאֵל ***'adbᵉ'ēl***, n.pr.m. [2] [√ 117 + 446]. Adbeel, "*[the] grief of God [El]*":– Adbeel (2)

H119 אֲדַד ***'ᵃdad***, n.pr.m. [1] [√ 2060]. Hadad, "*sharp*":– Hadad (1)

H120 אִדּוֹ ***'iddô***, n.pr.m. [2] Iddo, "[prob.] *Yahweh has adorned*":– Iddo (2)

H121 אֱדוֹם ***'ᵉdôm***, n.pr.m. [104] [→ 122, 6273; cf. 131]. Edom, referring to a person and his ancestral territory S.E. of the Dead Sea, "*red*":– Edom (80), Edom (10 [+824]), Edomites (10), Edom's (2), Edomites (1 [+1201]), NDT (1)

H122 אֲדוֹמִי ***'ᵃdômî***, a.g. [12] [√ 121; cf. 131]. Edomite, "*of Edom*":– Edomite (8), Edomites (4)

H123 אָדוֹן ***'ādôn***, n.m. [332] [→ 151, 152, 153, 154, 155, 156, 157]. lord, master, supervisor, one who has authority over another; husband; owner; the Lord, (with Yahweh [3378]) Sovereign. "Lord of lords" means the highest power or authority; see also 151:– lord (175), master (91), master's (27), lords (5), lord's (4 [+4200]), you[S] (4 [+3276]), lord's (3), masters (3), sovereign (2), commander (1), fellow officers (1 [+6269]), gods (1), her[S] (1 [+851, 2257]), him[S] (1 [+3276]), husbands (1), owner (1), owners (1), sir (1), supervisors (1), the Lord (1), your[S] (1 [+3276]), NDT (6)

H124 אַדּוֹן ***'addôn***, n.pr.loc. [1] [cf. 150]. Addon:– Addon (1)

H125 אֲדוֹנִיָּה ***'ᵃdôniyyâ***, n.pr.m. Not used in NIVEBC [→ 3207]. Adonijah, "*of the compound Tob-Adonijah*"

H126 אֲדוֹרַיִם ***'ᵃdôrayim***, n.pr.m. [1] [√ 1884?]. Adoraim, "[poss.] *pair of knolls*":– Adoraim (1)

H127 אֲדוֹרָם ***'ᵃdôrām***, n.pr.m. Not used in NIVEBC [√ 157]. Adoram

H128 אֹדוֹת ***'ōdôt***, n.f. [11] on account of, because of, for the reason that:– because of (4 [+6584]), about (3 [+6584]), concerned (1), for sake (1 [+6584]), NDT (2)

H129 אַדִּיר ***'addîr***, a. [28] [√ 158]. mighty, noble, majestic, splendid; (n.) any powerful or awesome person: noble, believer, elite soldier; (as a divine title) the Mighty One, with a focus on the power and splendor of God:– nobles (7), mighty (6), leaders (3), majestic (3), mighty one (3), leader (1), mightier (1), noble (1), picked troops (1), splendid (1), stately (1)

H130 אֲדַלְיָא ***'ᵃdalyā'***, n.pr.m. [1] Adalia, "[poss.] *honorable*":– Adalia (1)

H131 אָדֵם ***'ādēm***, v. [10] [→ 121, 122, 132, 133?, 134, 135, 136, 137, 138, 139, 140, 141, 143, 145, 147]. [Q] be ruddy; [Pu] be dyed red:– dyed red (6), red (3), ruddy (1)

H132 אָדָם¹ ***'ādām¹***, n.m. [547] [√ 131]. man, human being; humankind, people, often in contrast to animals; "son of man" means a human being (Nu 23:19), but often assumes messianic significance (Ps 8):– man (141), people (80), human (42), one (25), person (22), mankind (21), anyone (13), mankind (13 [+1201]), humans (12), human being (10), mortals (7), people (7 [+1201]), human beings (6), them[S] (5), those[S] (5), everyone (4), men (4), mortal (4), people (4 [+1201, 2021]), someone (4), everyone (3 [+3972, 2021]), human (3 [+1201]), human beings (3 [+1201]), human race (3), human race (3 [+1201]), person's (3), anyone (2 [+3972, 2021]), body (2), else[S] (2), everyone (2 [+3972]), everyone (2 [+3972]), human (2 [+5883]), human (2 [+1201, 2021]), human being (2 [+1201]), humanity (2), man (2 [+1201]), man-eater (2 [+430]), men (2 [+1201]), mortals (2 [+1201]), one (2 [+1201]), Adam (1), all (1 [+1201]), all mankind (1 [+1201]), all people (1 [+1201, 2021]), another (1), another[S] (1 [+2021]), anyone else's (1), arrogant (1 [+1471]), charioteers (1 [+8207]), commanders (1 [+5817]), dead bodies (1 [+5577]), deserted (1 [+4946, 401]), every (1), everyone (1 [+408]), everyone on earth (1 [+1201]), everyone's (1 [+3972, 2021]), evildoers (1 [+8273]), fellow man (1), fools (1 [+4067]), giver[S] (1), godless (1 [+2868]), he[S] (1), human beings (1 [+5883]), human beings (1 [+1201, 2021]), human hands (1 [+1201]), humanity (1 [+1201]), humans (1 [+1201, 2021]), individual (1), life (1), living (1 [+2645]), low (1 [+1201]), lowborn (1 [+1201]), man-made (1 [+5126, 3338]), mankind (1 [+1201, 2021]), man's (1), man's (1 [+1201, 2021]), natural (1 [+3869, 3972, 2021]), needy (1 [+36]), nobody (1 [+4202]), others[S] (1), people (1 [+5883]), people's (1 [+4200]), people's (1 [+4946, 1201]), people's (1 [+1201, 2021]), person (1 [+1201]), prudent (1 [+6874]), rabble (1 [+8044]), reflects (1 [+4200, 2021]), ruler[S] (1), someone (1 [+3972, 2021]), son (1), successor (1 [+8611, 995, 339]), their[S] (1), them[S] (1 [+2021]), they[S] (1), those[S] (1 [+2021]), troops (1), troublemaker (1 [+1175]), uninhabited (1 [+4202, 928, 2257]), we[S] (1 [+2021]), whoever (1), whoever (1 [+3972, 2021]), NDT (10)

H133 אָדָם² ***'ādām²***, n.m. Not used in NIVEBC [√ 131?]. leather

H134 אָדָם³ ***'ādām³***, n.pr.m. [11] [→ 142; cf. 131]. Adam, "*[red] earth* or *[ruddy] skin color*":– Adam (10), Adam's (1)

H135 אָדָם⁴ ***'ādām⁴***, n.m. [1] [√ 131]. ground:– hunt[S] (1)

H136 אָדָם⁵ ***'ādām⁵***, n.pr.loc. [2] [√ 131]. Adam, "*[red] earth*":– Adam (2)

H137 אָדֹם ***'ādōm***, a. [9] [→ 147; cf. 131]. red; ruddy (skin):– red (7), ruddy (1), NDT (1)

H138 אֹדֶם ***'ōdem***, n.[f.] [3] [√ 131]. ruby:– carnelian (3)

H139 אֱדֹם ***'ᵉdōm***, n.[m.] Not used in NIVEBC [→ 6273; cf. 131]. Edom

H140 אֲדַמְדָּם ***'ᵃdamdām***, a. [6] [√ 131]. reddish, reddish-white:– reddish-white (4 [+4237]), reddish (2)

H141 אֲדָמָה¹ ***'ᵃdāmâ¹***, n.f. [226] [√ 131]. earth, the entire surface of the place where humans dwell, as well as smaller regions: land; with a focus on the elements of the earth: ground, soil, dust. A "man of the soil" is a farmer; "fruit of the soil" are crops:– land (121), ground (43), earth (28), soil (11), dust (4), lands (3), clay (2), country (2), crops (2), fields (2), native land (2), below (1 [+6584, 2021]), crops (1 [+7262, 2021]), farmer (1 [+408, 6268]), her[S] (1 [+3776]), home (1), homeland (1)

H142 אֲדָמָה² ***'ᵃdāmâ²***, n.pr.loc. [1] [√ 134; cf. 131]. Adamah, "*[red] earth*":– Adamah (1)

H143 אֲדָמָה³ ***'ᵃdāmâ³***, n.f. Not used in NIVEBC [√ 131]. [red] blood

H144 אַדְמָה ***'admâ***, n.pr.loc. [5] Admah, "*[red] earth*":– Admah (5)

H145 אַדְמוֹנִי ***'admônî***, a. [3] [√ 131]. red; ruddy (skin):– glowing with health (2), red (1)

H146 אֲדָמִי הַנֶּקֶב ***'ᵃdāmî hanneqeb***, n.pr.loc. [1] [√ 131 + 2186]. Adami Nekeb, "*ground of piercing*":– Adami Nekeb (1)

H147 אֲדֻמִּים ***'ᵃdummîm***, n.pr.loc. [2] [√ 137; cf. 131]. Adummim, "*red [streaks]*":– Adummim (2)

H148 אַדְמָתָא ***'admātā'***, n.pr.m. [1] Admatha, "*unrestrained*":– Admatha (1)

H149 אֶדֶן ***'eden***, n.m. [53] base, footing, pedestal:– bases (41), base (2), footings (1), those[S] (1), NDT (8)

H150 אַדָּן ***'addān***, n.pr.loc. [1] [cf. 124]. Addon:– Addon (1)

H151 אֲדֹנָי ***'ᵃdōnāy***, n.[pr.]m. [441] [√ 123]. the Lord, (with Yahweh [3378]) Sovereign, a title of the one true God, with a focus on his majesty and authority; see also 123:– sovereign (291), the Lord (91), Lord (56), the Lord's (3)

H152 אֲדֹנִי בֶזֶק ***'ᵃdōnî bezeq***, n.pr.m. [3] [√ 123 + 1028]. Adoni-Bezek, "*lord of Bezek*":– Adoni-Bezek (3)

H153 אֲדֹנִיָּה ***'ᵃdōniyyâ***, n.pr.m. [7] [→ 154; cf. 123 + 3378]. Adonijah, "*[my] lord is Yahweh*":– Adonijah (7)

H154 אֲדֹנִיָּהוּ ***'ᵃdōniyyāhû***, n.pr.m. [19] [√ 153; cf. 123 + 3378]. Adonijah, "*[my] lord is Yahweh*":– Adonijah (17), Adonijah's (1 [+4200]), NDT (1)

H155 אֲדֹנִי־צֶדֶק ***'adōnî-ṣedeq***, n.pr.m. [2] [√ 123 + 7406]. Adoni-Zedek, *"[my] lord is righteousness"*:– Adoni-Zedek (2)

H156 אֲדֹנִיקָם ***'adōnîqām***, n.pr.m. [3] [√ 123 + 7756]. Adonikam, *"[my] lord arises"*:– Adonikam (3)

H157 אֲדֹנִירָם ***'adōnîrām***, n.pr.m. [4] [→ 127, 164; cf. 123 + 8123]. Adoniram, *"[my] lord is exalted"*:– Adoniram (4)

H158 אָדַר ***'ādar***, v. [3] [→ 129, 159, 160, 168]. [N] to prove oneself majestic, powerful; [H] to make glorious, make powerful:– majestic (2), glorious (1)

H159 אֶדֶר ***'eder***, n.[m.] [2] [√ 158]. splendor, handsomeness, of obvious quality:– handsome (1), rich (1)

H160 אֲדָר ***'adār***, n.pr.[m.] [8] [√ 158; 10009]. Adar, "[poss.] *dark, clouded*":– Adar (8)

H161 1אַדָּר ***'addār[1]***, n.pr.m. [1] Addar, *"glorious"*:– Addar (1)

H162 2אַדָּר ***'addār[2]***, n.pr.loc. [1] [→ 2960, 6501]. Addar, *"glorious"*:– Addar (1)

H163 אֲדַרְכֹּנִים ***'adarkōnîm***, n.[m.pl.?] [2] [√ 2007]. darics, Persian gold coins:– darics (2)

H164 אֲדֹרָם ***'adōrām***, n.pr.m. Not used in NIVEBC [√ 157]. Adoram

H165 1אַדְרַמֶּלֶךְ ***'adrammelek[1]***, n.pr.[m.] [1] [→ 166]. Adrammelech (pagan god), *"nobility of Molech [king]"*:– Adrammelek (1)

H166 2אַדְרַמֶּלֶךְ ***'adrammelek[2]***, n.pr.m. [2] [√ 165]. Adrammelech, *"nobility of Molech [king]"*:– Adrammelek (2)

H167 אֶדְרֶעִי ***'edre'î***, n.pr.loc. [8] Edrei, *"strong"*:– Edrei (8)

H168 אַדֶּרֶת ***'adderet***, n.f. [12] [√ 158]. cloak, royal robe, (hairy) garment:– cloak (5), robe (2), garment (1), prophet's garment (1), rich pastures (1), royal robes (1), splendid (1)

H169 אָדַשׁ ***'ādaš***, v. Not used in NIVEBC [cf. 1889]. see 1889

H170 אָהַב ***'āhab***, v. [215] [→ 171, 172, 173, 174?, 175]. [Q] to love, like, be a friend; [N] to be loved; [P] be a lover, an ally; love can refer to friendship, familial love, romantic love, or covenant loyalty:– love (93), loves (38), loved (31), lovers (12), friends (8), friend (5), allies (4), in love with (3), fell in love with (2), liked (2), long for (2), adore (1), attracted to (1), both[S] (1 [+2021, 2256, 2021, 8533]), chosen ally (1), dearly (1), desires (1), like (1), likes (1), on friendly terms (1), resent (1 [+4202]), show love (1), showed love (1), value (1), was loved (1), were loved (1)

H171 אֹהַב ***'ōhab***, n.[m.] [2] [√ 170]. love; something loved:– love (1), thing loved (1)

H172 אַהַב ***'ahab***, n.[m.] [2] [√ 170]. lover (negative); loving, charming (positive):– lovers (1), loving (1)

H173 1אַהֲבָה ***'ahabâ[1]***, n.f. [33] [√ 170]. love; friendship, familial love, romantic love, or covenant loyalty:– love (27), friendship (2), loved (2), that[S] (1), NDT (1)

H174 2אַהֲבָה ***'ahabâ[2]***, n.f. Not used in NIVEBC [cf. 170?]. leather

H175 אֲהַבְהָבַי ***'ahabhābay***, n.m. Not used in NIVEBC [√ 170]. ardor of love

H176 אֹהַד ***'ōhad***, n.pr.m. [2] Ohad:– Ohad (2)

H177 אֲהָהּ ***'ahāh***, interj. [15] Ah!, Oh!, Alas!; an exclamation of emphasis, surprise, or sorrow:– alas (8), oh no (3), ah (1), not so (1), what (1), NDT (1)

H178 אַהֲוָא ***'ahawā'***, n.pr.loc. [3] Ahava:– Ahava (3)

H179 אֵהוּד ***'ēhûd***, n.pr.m. [9] [cf. 287?]. Ehud, *"united"*:– Ehud (8), NDT (1)

H180 אֱהִי ***'ehî***, adv. [3] Where?:– where (2), where (1 [+686])

H181 אֶהְיֶה ***'ehyeh***, v. (used as n.pr.) Not used in NIVEBC [√ 2118]. I am, I will be (self-designation of God)

H182 1אָהַל ***'āhal[1]***, v.den. [3] [√ 185]. [Q, P] to pitch a tent:– pitched tents (2), pitch tents (1)

H183 2אָהַל ***'āhal[2]***, v. [1] [√ 2145]. [H] to be bright:– bright (1)

H184 אָהָל ***'āhāl***, n.m. Ahal

H185 1אֹהֶל ***'ōhel[1]***, n.m. [344] [→ 182, 186, 188; *also used with compound proper names*]. tent, tent-dwelling; by extension: home, dwelling place, a permanent dwelling; family group. "The Tent of Meeting" was the worship tent built before the Temple:– tent (262), tents (45), home (10), homes (9), dwellings (3), its[S] (3 [+2021]), house (2), another[S] (1), broke camp (1 [+5825, 4946]), camps (1), home (1 [+2257]), house (1 [+1074]), household (1), nomads (1 [+8905, 928]), tent site (1), tent-dwelling (1 [+928, 2021]), NDT (1)

H186 2אֹהֶל ***'ōhel[2]***, n.pr.m. [1] [√ 185]. Ohel, *"tent"*:– Ohel (1)

H187 אֵהֶל ***'ēhel***, pr.pl.m. & f. Not used in NIVEBC [√ 447]. these, those

H188 אָהֳלָה ***'oholâ***, n.pr.f. [5] [→ 191, 192; cf. 185]. Oholah, *"she who has a tent"*:– Oholah (5)

H189 אֲהָלוֹת ***'ahālôt***, n.[m.] [2] [cf. 193, 194]. aloes; an aromatic wood from India:– aloes (2)

H190 אָהֳלִיאָב ***'oholî'āb***, n.pr.m. [5] [√ 185 + 3]. Oholiab, *"tent of [my] father"*:– Oholiab (5)

H191 אָהֳלִיבָה ***'oholîbâ***, n.pr.f. [6] [√ 188 + 928 + 2023]. Oholibah, *"my tent is in her"*:– Oholibah (6)

H192 אָהֳלִיבָמָה ***'oholîbāmâ***, n.pr.m. & f. [8] [√ 185 + 1195?]. Oholibamah, *"[my] tent is a high place"*:– Oholibamah (8)

H193 1אֲהָלִים ***'ahālîm[1]***, n.[m.] [2] [cf. 189, 194]. aloes:– aloes (2)

H194 2אֲהָלִים ***'ahālîm[2]***, n.[m.] Not used in NIVEBC [cf. 189, 193]. ice plant

H195 אַהֲרֹן ***'aharôn***, n.pr.m. [346] Aaron:– Aaron (300), Aaron's (31), he[S] (5), his[S] (3), Aaronic (1 [+1201]), Aaron's (1 [+4200]), family of Aaron (1), him[S] (1), NDT (3)

H196 אוֹ ***'ô***, c. [321] [→ 218?]. or, or if, whether:– or (240), whether or (12), and (4), either or (4), if (3), whether (3), also (1), at all (1 [+7785, 1524]), if (1 [+4537]), no matter (1), nor (1), or else (1), or so (1), over a year (1 [+2296, 3427, 2296, 9102]), rather than (1), when (1), which way (1 [+6584, 3545, 6584, 8520]), NDT (44)

H197 אַו ***'aw***, n.m. [1] [√ 203]. crave:– crave (1)

H198 אוּאֵל ***'û'ēl***, n.pr.m. [1] [√ 203? + 446]. Uel, "[poss.] *will of God [El]*":– Uel (1)

H199 1אוֹב ***'ōb[1]***, n.m. [1] [cf. 200?]. wineskin, bag, a leather bag of goatskin turned inside out to hold fluids:– wineskins (1)

H200 2אוֹב ***'ōb[2]***, n.m. [16] [cf. 199?]. medium, spiritist, one who communicates with and conjures ghosts or spirits:– mediums (9), medium (2), ghostlike (1 [+3869]), medium (1 [+1266]), medium (1 [+8626]), one[S] (1 [+1266]), spirit (1)

H201 אוֹבִיל ***'ôbîl***, n.pr.m. [1] [√ 3297]. Obil, *"camel driver"*:– Obil (1)

H202 אוּד ***'ûd***, n.m. [3] [→ 369]. burning stick:– burning stick (2), firewood (1)

H203 1אָוָה ***'āwâ[1]***, v. [26] [→ 197, 205, 2094, 4397, 9294; *also used with compound proper names*]. [P, Ht] to crave, desire, yearn for, long for:– crave (5), desired (3), desire (2), desires (2), longed for (2), appetite (1 [+5883]), crave other food (1 [+9294]), craved other food (1), craves for more (1 [+9294]), enthralled (1), gave in to craving (1 [+9294]), like (1), long for (1), pleases (1), set desire on (1), want (1), yearns for (1)

H204 2אָוָה ***'āwâ[2]***, v. [1] [→ 253?; cf. 9292, 9295, 9344]. [Ht] to run a line, measure:– run a line (1)

H205 אַוָּה ***'awwâ***, n.f. [7] [→ 2094; cf. 203]. wanting, craving; earnestness:– want (3), craving (1 [+5883]), earnestness (1 [+5883]), please (1), pleases (1)

H206 אוּזַי ***'ûzay***, n.pr.m. [1] Uzai, *"Yahweh has given ear, listened"*:– Uzai (1)

H207 אוּזָל ***'ûzāl***, n.pr.loc. [& m.] [2] [poss. related to 374.5] Uzal, a person and a place:– Uzal (2)

H208 אוֹי ***'ôy***, interj. [24] [→ 210]. Woe! Alas!:– woe (18), alas (4), doomed (1), oh no (1)

H209 אֱוִי ***'ewî***, n.pr.m. [2] Evi, *"desire"*:– Evi (2)

H210 אוֹיָה ***'ôyâ***, interj. [1] [√ 208]. Woe!, Alas!:– Woe (1)

H211 1אֱוִיל ***'ewîl[1]***, a. [25] [→ 216, 222; cf. 3282]. foolish; (n.) a fool:– fool (11), fools (11), fool's (2), wicked fools (1)

H212 2אֱוִיל ***'ewîl[2]***, n.m. Not used in NIVEBC [cf. 380?, 446?]. citizenry (of the land)

H213 אֱוִיל מְרֹדַךְ ***'ewîl merōdak***, n.pr.m. [2] Evil-Merodach, *"worshiper of Marduk[s]"*; [corrupted to read] *fool of blessing"*:– Awel-Marduk (2)

H214 1אוּל ***'ûl[1]***, n.[m.] [1] [√ 380?]. belly, sometimes referring to the whole body:– bodies (1)

H215 2אוּל ***'ûl[2]***, n.[m.] Not used in NIVEBC [√ 380; cf. 3283]. leading man, noble

H216 אֱוִלִי ***'ewilî***, a. [1] [√ 211]. foolish, without understanding:– foolish (1)

H217 1אוּלַי ***'ûlay[1]***, n.pr.loc. [2] Ulai:– Ulai (2)

H218 2אוּלַי ***'ûlay[2]***, adv. [45] [√ 196? + 4202?]. what if, perhaps, maybe; this is in an expression of hope, pleading, or fear:– perhaps (25), what if (9), it may be (3), maybe (3), but (1), but perhaps (1), if not (1), may yet (1), were it to (1)

H219 1אוּלָם ***'ûlām[1]***, adv. [19] but, however, on the other hand, nevertheless:– but (5 [+2256]), but (2), though (2), but if (1), but now (1), however (1 [+2256]), if (1), nevertheless (1), nevertheless (1 [+2256]), now (1), otherwise (1), yet (1), NDT (1)

H220 2אוּלָם ***'ûlām[2]***, n.pr.m. [4] Ulam, *"first, leader"*:– Ulam (4)

H221 3אוּלָם ***'ûlām[3]***, n.m. Not used in NIVEBC [√ 395]. portico; hall; colonnade

H222 אִוֶּלֶת ***'iwwelet***, n.f. [25] [√ 211]. foolishness, folly; in some contexts this may refer to thoughtless speech:– folly (22), foolish (2), sinful folly (1)

H223 אוֹמָר ***'ômār***, n.pr.m. [3] [√ 606]. Omar, *"speaker"*:– Omar (3)

H224 1אָוֶן ***'āwen[1]***, n.m. [77] [→ 1077, 1204, 9303?]. evil, wickedness, iniquity; evildoer; an unfavorable circumstance: calamity, trouble, injustice; this can also refer to idols, with a focus that they are morally evil:– evil (19), evildoers (16), wicked (6), sin (3), wrong (3), calamity (2), wickedness (2), deceitful (1), deceitfully (1), disaster (1), distress (1), evildoer (1 [+7188]), evildoers (1 [+7188]), false (1), hardship (1), harm (1), idol (1), iniquity (1), injustice (1), malice (1), malicious (1), misfortune (1), nothing (1), punishment (1), sins (1), slander (1), sorrow (1), suffering (1), unjust (1), unrighteous (1 [+408]), villain (1 [+408]), wicked (1 [+5493]), worthless (1)

H225 2אָוֶן ***'āwen[2]***, n.pr.loc. [2] Heliopolis; (Valley of) Aven, *"evil power, wickedness"*:– Aven (1), Heliopolis (1)

H226 1אוֹן ***'ôn[1]***, n.m. [12] [→ 227, 229, 231, 232]. power, strength, vigor, manhood; wealth:– power (3), manhood (2), man (1), sign of strength (1), strength (1), vigor (1), weak (1 [+401]), wealth (1), wealthy (1)

H227 2אוֹן ***'ôn[2]***, n.pr.m. [1] [√ 231; cf. 226]. On, *"Sun [god] city"*:– On (1)

H228 3אוֹן ***'ôn[3]***, n.pr.loc. [3] On, *"Sun [god] city"*:– On (3)

H229 אוֹנוֹ ***'ônô***, n.pr.loc. [5] [√ 226]. Ono, *"strong"*:– Ono (5)

H230 אוֹנִי ***'ônî***, n.pr.m. [1] [√ 627]. mourning:– mourners (1)

H231 אוֹנָם ***'ônām***, n.pr.m. [4] [√ 227; cf. 226]. Onam, *"intense, strong"*:– Onam (4)

H232 אוֹנָן ***'ônān***, n.pr.m. [8] [√ 226]. Onan, *"powerful, intense"*:– Onan (7), NDT (1)

H233 אוּפָז ***'ûpāz***, n.pr.loc. [2] Uphaz:– Uphaz (2)

H234 1אוֹפִיר ***'ôpîr[1]***, n.pr.loc. [12] [→ 235; cf. 709]. Ophir:– Ophir (10), gold of Ophir (1), there[S] (1)

H235 2אוֹפִיר ***'ôpîr[2]***, n.pr.m. [1] [√ 234; cf. 709]. Ophir:– Ophir (1)

H236 אוֹפָן ***'ôpan***, n.m. [34] [cf. 698?]. wheel (of a vehicle):– wheels (23), wheel (9), NDT (2)

H237 אוּץ ***'ûṣ***, v. [10] [Q] to be in haste, be eager; to press (for an answer); to be small, narrow; [H] to urge, insist upon:– delayed (1 [+4202]), eager (1), haste (1), hasty (1), in haste (1), pressing (1), run (1), small (1), try (1), urged (1)

H238 אוֹצָר ***'ôṣār***, n.m. [79] [√ 732]. treasury, storehouse, storeroom, storage vault:– treasures (22), treasuries (20), storehouses (9), treasury (7), riches (2), storehouse (2), supplies (2), treasure (2), arsenal (1), fortune (1), put in charge of the storerooms (1 [+732, 6584]), store up (1 [+928, 5659]), storehouse (1 [+1074]), storerooms (1), storerooms (1 [+5969, 4200]), treasury (1 [+1074]), vats (1), vaults (1), wealth (1), NDT (2)

H239 1אוֹר ***'ôr[1]***, v. [43] [→ 240, 241, 244, 245, 246, 247, 251?, 797, 4401, 4402?; *also used with compound proper names*]. [Q] to shine, be bright; [H] to give light, make shine, brighten; [N] to be resplendent with light, shine on; the fig. extension "to make the face shine" is to establish favorable circumstance, peace and relief from trouble:– give light (6), make shine (6), shine (6), light (3), brightened (2), gives light (2), brightens (1), dawned (1), daybreak (1), give light (1 [+240]), gives sight (1), giving light (1), keep burning (1), leaves glistening (1), light fires (1), light up (1), lights up (1), lit up (1), look with favor (1 [+7156]), made light shine (1), make fires (1), radiant (1), radiant with light (1), shining ever brighter (1 [+2143, 2256])

H240 2אוֹר ***'ôr[2]***, n.m. [122] [→ 245, 246; cf. 239]. light, contrasted with darkness; by extension: brightness; lightning; daylight, sunshine; the fig. extension "light of the face" is a positive, happy attitude, resulting from relief from trouble:– light (82), lightning (6), sun (5), daylight (3), daybreak (2 [+2021, 1332]), shine (2), shining (2), brightens (1), broad daylight (1 [+3427]), dawn (1), dawn (1 [+2021, 1332]), dawn (1 [+1332, 2021]), daybreak (1), daybreak (1 [+1332, 2021]), daylight (1 [+2021, 1332]), give light (1 [+239]), glint (1), lamp (1), light of day (1), lights (1), new day (1), shine (1 [+2118]), sunlight (1), sunlight (1 [+2780]), sunrise (1), sunshine (1), NDT (1)

H241 1אוּר ***'ûr[1]***, n.m. [6] [→ 797; cf. 239]. light; east [the region of light], the direction of the sunrise:– fire (3), burn (1 [+1277, 928, 2021]), east (1), light (1)

H242 2אוּר ***'ûr[2]***, n.m. [8] [cf. 239?]. Urim, devices used by the high priest to make God's will known, possibly related to radiating or reflecting light:– Urim (8)

H243 3אוּר ***'ûr[3]***, n.pr.loc. [4] Ur:– Ur (4)

H244 4אוּר ***'ûr[4]***, n.pr.m. [1] [√ 239]. Ur, *"flame, light"*:– Ur (1)

H245 1אוֹרָה ***'ôrâ[1]***, n.f. [3] [√ 240; cf. 239]. light, morning light; happiness, serenity, cheerfulness:– light (1), morning (1), time of happiness (1)

H246 2אוֹרָה ***'ôrâ[2]***, n.f. [1] [√ 240; cf. 239]. herb, mallow; a tasty, edible plant:– herbs (1)

H247 אוּרִי ***'ûrî***, n.pr.m. [7] [√ 239]. Uri, "*Yahweh is [my] flame, light*":– Uri (7)

H248 אוּרִיאֵל ***'ûrî'ēl***, n.pr.m. [4] [√ 239 + 446]. Uriel, "*God [El] is [my] flame, light*":– Uriel (4)

H249 אוּרִיָּה ***'ûriyyâ***, n.pr.m. [36] [→ 250; cf. 239 + 3378]. Uriah, "*Yahweh is [my] flame, light*":– Uriah (30), Uriah's (2), him[S] (2), NDT (2)

H250 אוּרִיָּהוּ ***'ûriyyāhû***, n.pr.m. [3] [√ 249; cf. 239 + 3378]. Uriah, "*Yahweh is [my] flame, light*":– Uriah (3)

H251 אוּרִים ***'ûrîm***, n.m.[pl.] Not used in NIVEBC [√ 239? *or* 768? *or* 826?]. Urim, see 242

H252 אוּת ***'ût***, v. [4] [N] to consent, agree:– agree (1), agree to terms (1), agreed (1), enter into an agreement (1)

H253 [1]אוֹת ***'ôt[1]***, n.m. & f. [78] [√ 204?; 10084]. sign, mark, symbol, a signal or event that communicates; a supernatural event or miracle as a sign from God:– sign (39), signs (30), symbols (2), accounts (1), banners (1), example (1), mark (1), signs (1 [+1821]), standards (1), wonders (1)

H254 [2]אוֹת ***'ôt[2]***, pt. Not used in NIVEBC [√ 906]. see 906

H255 אָז ***'āz***, adv. [140] [→ 259, 4403; 10008]. then, at that time, meanwhile:– then (60), at that time (11), and (5), long ago (5 [+4946]), now (2), since (2 [+4946]), so (2), time (2), about this time (1), after (1), already (1), already (1 [+4946]), and (1 [+2256]), distant past (1), ever since (1 [+4946]), ever since (1 [+4946]), from (1 [+4946]), in this manner (1), meanwhile (1), now (1 [+4946]), of old (1), old (1), once (1), past (1), that will mean (1), thus (1), when (1), when (1 [+4946]), NDT (31)

H256 אֶזְבַּי ***'ezbāy***, n.pr.m. [1] [√ 257?]. Ezbai:– Ezbai (1)

H257 אֵזוֹב ***'ēzôb***, n.m. [10] [→ 256?]. hyssop:– hyssop (10)

H258 אֵזוֹר ***'ēzôr***, n.m. [14] [→ 273]. garments that are wrapped: belt, sash, loincloth:– belt (9), belt (1 [+5516]), belts (1 [+2513]), it[S] (1 [+2021]), loincloth (1), sash (1)

H259 אֲזַי ***'ᵃzay***, adv. [3] [√ 255]. (if not ...) then:– NDT (3)

H260 אַזְכָּרָה ***'azkārâ***, n.f. [7] [√ 2349]. memorial offering, memorial portion; the portion of the meal burnt as a token of honor to the Lord:– memorial portion (6), memorial offering (1)

H261 אָזַל ***'āzal***, v. [5] [√ 10016]. [Q] to go about, go away; disappear:– gone (2), dries up (1), go about (1), goes off (1)

H262 אֶזֶל ***'ezel***, n.pr.loc. [1] Ezel:– Ezel (1)

H263 [1]אָזַן ***'āzan[1]***, v.den. [41] [√ 265]. [H] to listen, pay attention, give ear:– listen (20), hear (11), pay attention (3), ear perceived (1), give a hearing (1 [+7754]), hear (1 [+7754]), listened (1), paid attention (1), pays attention (1), turned a deaf ear (1 [+4202])

H264 [2]אָזַן ***'āzan[2]***, v. [1] [P] to ponder, give serious thought, an extension of weighing and testing on scales:– pondered (1)

H265 אֹזֶן ***'ōzen***, n.f. [187] [→ 263, 269, 270, 271; cf. 266?]. ear: the organ for hearing; by extension: listening, and hence, responding, obeying. "To be in the ear" shows close proximity; "to reveal to the ear" means "to inform":– ears (58), ear (28), hearing (24), to (19 [+928]), pay attention (6 [+5742]), give ear (4 [+5742]), heard (3 [+928]), before (2 [+928]), let know (2 [+1655, 906]), listen closely (2 [+9048, 928]), revealed (2 [+1655]), tells (2 [+1655, 906]), they[S] (2), bring to attention (1 [+1655]), earlobe (1), hear (1 [+5742]), heard (1), heard (1 [+606, 928]), heeds (1 [+9048]), in person (1 [+928]), letting know (1 [+1655, 906]), listen (1 [+5742]), listen (1 [+7992]), listen carefully (1 [+928, 9048]), listened (1 [+928]), listened attentively to (1 [+448]), make sure hears (1 [+8492, 928]), makes listen (1 [+1655]), news (1 [+2245]), paid any attention (1 [+5742, 4200, 9048]), paid attention (1 [+5742]), pay careful attention (1 [+8011, 2256, 5742]), revealed (1 [+1655, 906]), speaks (1 [+1655]), tell (1 [+1819, 928]), tell (1 [+1655, 906]), tell (1 [+6218, 928]), told (1 [+1819, 928]), turn ear (1), wearing (1 [+928]), whoever[S] (1), NDT (5)

H266 אָזֵן ***'āzēn***, n.[m.] [1] [cf. 265?]. equipment, tools, specifically a digging tool:– equipment (1)

H267 אֻזֵּן שֶׁאֱרָה ***'uzzēn še'ᵉrâ***, n.pr.loc. [1] [cf. 8641]. Uzzen Sheerah, "[perhaps] *ear of Sheerah*":– Uzzen Sheerah (1)

H268 אַזְנוֹת תָּבוֹר ***'aznôt tābôr***, n.pr.loc. [1] [cf. 9314]. Aznoth Tabor, "[poss.] *peaks of Tabor*":– Aznoth Tabor (1)

H269 [1]אָזְנִי ***'oznî[1]***, n.pr.m. [1] [→ 270; cf. 265]. Ozni, "*my ear, my hearing*":– Ozni (1)

H270 [2]אָזְנִי ***'oznî[2]***, a.g. [1] [√ 269; cf. 265]. Oznite, "*belonging to Ozni*":– Oznite (1)

H271 אֲזַנְיָה ***'ᵃzanyâ***, n.pr.m. [1] [√ 265 + 3378]. Azaniah, "*Yahweh has listened*":– Azaniah (1)

H272 אֲזִקִּים ***'ᵃziqqîm***, n.[m.] [2] [cf. 2414]. chains, which in context refer to manacles or wrist cuffs:– chains (2)

H273 אָזַר ***'āzar***, v. [17] [√ 258]. [Q] to gird up, belt on; [P] to gird someone; [N, Ht] to gird oneself; the action of wrapping a belt or sash around the waist; by extension "to take action" of various kinds: working, providing, going to battle:– armed (4), arms (2), brace (2 [+2743]), prepare for battle (2), armed yourself (1), binds (1), clothed (1), get ready (1 [+5516]), provide (1), strengthen (1), NDT (1)

H274 אֶזְרוֹעַ ***'ezrôa'***, n.f. [2] [cf. 2432; 10013]. arm, with the associative meaning of power and potency:– arm (1), it[S] (1 [+3276])

H275 אֶזְרָח ***'ezrāḥ***, n.m. [17] [√ 2436]. native-born:– native-born (13), born (1), native (1), native-born (1 [+824]), native-born (1 [+2021, 824])

H276 אֶזְרָחִי ***'ezrāḥî***, a.g. [3] [√ 2438; cf. 2436]. Ezrahite, "*of Ezrah*":– Ezrahite (3)

H277 [1]אָח ***'āḥ[1]***, interj. [2] Alas!, Oh!:– alas (1), look (1)

H278 [2]אָח ***'āḥ[2]***, n.m. [633] [→ 288, 295, 306; 10017; *also used with compound proper names*]. brother; by extension: family, kinsman, relative (of either gender); a term of endearment; anyone of the same race or large social group: countryman; associate. "Each to his brother" is usually translated "to each other" or "one to another.":– brother (187), brothers (127), relatives (80), fellow Israelites (37), fellow (22), associates (17), other[S] (17), people (15), brother's (14), another[S] (9), fellow Levites (9), fellow Israelite (7), family (6), relative (6), clan (3), related to (3), they[S] (3 [+3870]), companions (2), cousins (2), families (2), fellow Danites (2), fellow Israelite's (2), fellow Jews (2), friends (2), nephew (2 [+1201]), others[S] (2), them[S] (2), them[S] (2 [+2257]), they[S] (2), God's people (1), Israelite (1), Israelites (1), allies (1), among yourselves (1 [+408, 448]), anyone among people (1 [+8276, 2256]), anyone else[S] (1), associate (1), brotherhood (1), brothers (1 [+562]), brothers and sisters (1), camp[S] (1), close relatives (1 [+408]), community (1), each (1 [+408, 2257]), equally (1 [+408, 3869, 2257]), equally among them (1 [+408, 3869, 2257]), fellow citizens (1), in clan (1), its owner[S] (1), other Israelites (1), other party[S] (1), own people (1 [+8276]), people from Benjamin (1 [+2157]), people from Judah (1 [+2157]), priests[S] (1 [+2157]), relative's (1), them[S] (1 [+4013]), them[S] (1 [+2021, 36]), tribe (1), tribes related to (1), two men (1 [+408, 2256, 3481]), uncle (1), uncle (1 [+562]), uncle's (1 [+562]), very own brother (1 [+1201, 562, 3870]), NDT (11)

H279 אָח ***'aḥ***, n.f. [2] firepot:– firepot (2)

H280 אֹחַ ***'ōaḥ***, n.[m.] [1] a howling animal: jackal, hyena, eagle owl:– jackals (1)

H281 אַחְאָב ***'aḥ'āb***, n.pr.m. [92] [√ 278 + 3]. Ahab, "*brother of father*":– Ahab (79), Ahab's (7), he[S] (3), he[S] (1 [+1201, 6687]), NDT (2)

H282 אֶחָב ***'eḥāb***, n.pr.m. [1] [√ 278 + 3]. Ahab, "*brother of father*":– Ahab (1)

H283 אַחְבָּן ***'aḥbān***, n.pr.m. [1] Ahban, "*brother of intelligent one*":– Ahban (1)

H284 אָחַד ***'āḥad***, v. Not used in NIVEBC [cf. 2523]. see 2523

H285 אֶחָד ***'eḥād***, a.num. [965] [→ 287; cf. 2522; 10248]. one; a certain one; first:– one (462), a (71), each (58), first (38), same (32), other[S] (27), any (17), single (13), another[S] (12), eleven (6 [+6926]), once (6), one (6 [+408]), the (6), certain (5), an (4), eleventh (4 [+6926]), forty-one (4 [+752, 2256]), only (4), together (4 [+448, 285]), twenty-one (4 [+6929, 2256]), unit (4), any (3 [+3972]), eleven (3 [+6925]), man[S] (3), next (3), once (3 [+7193]), one and the same (3), some (3), thirty-one (3 [+8993, 2256]), 41,500 (2 [+2256, 752, 547, 2256, 2822, 4395]), 621 (2 [+9252, 4395, 6929, 2256]), agree (2 [+2118, 3869]), alike (2), all (2), another (2), anyone (2), common (2), identical (2), leaving none alive (2 [+3869, 408]), numbered (2 [+3869]), second (2), the other[S] (2), together (2 [+285, 448]), twenty-first (2 [+6929, 2256]), twenty-first (2 [+2256, 6929]), unique (2), yearly (2 [+928, 9102]), 151,450 (1 [+4395, 547, 2256, 2822, 547, 752, 4395, 2822, 2256, 2256, 2256]), 61 (1 [+2256, 9252]), 61,000 (1 [+2256, 9252, 547]), 721 (1 [+8679, 4395, 2256, 6929, 2256]), all (1 [+928]), all the same (1), alone (1 [+928]), annual (1 [+928, 2021, 9102]), appointed (1), back and forth (1 [+2178, 2256, 285, 2178]), back and forth (1 [+285, 2178, 2256, 2178]), daily (1 [+4200, 3427]), did the same[S] (1 [+2489, 448, 285]), did the same[S] (1 [+2489, 285, 448]), each one (1), either (1), equally (1 [+3869]), fellow[S] (1), few (1), for a while (1 [+3427]), forty-first (1 [+752, 2256]), in unison (1 [+3869]), joined together (1 [+6641, 3869]), none (1 [+4202]), of one mind (1 [+3869, 408]), once for all (1), one way (1 [+928]), one-tenth (1 [+6928]), only a few (1), other (1), over here (1 [+4200, 6298]), over there (1 [+4200, 6298]), same one (1), share (1 [+2118, 4200]), shoulder to shoulder (1 [+8900]), singleness (1), some other[S] (1), someone (1), someone (1 [+2021, 6639]), the[S] (1), third[S] (1), thirty-first (1 [+8993, 2256]), time and again (1 [+4202, 2256, 4202, 9109]), together (1 [+3869]), undivided (1), unheard-of (1), unity (1), whatever[S] (1), wherever (1 [+928, 2021, 5226, 889]), whose[S] (1 [+2021, 2021, 9108]), without exception (1 [+7023]), without exception[S] (1 [+7023]), NDT (66)

H286 אָחוּ ***'āḥû***, n.m.col. [3] reeds:– reeds (3)

H287 אֵהוּד ***'ēḥûd***, n.pr.m. [1] [√ 285; cf. 179?]. Ehud, "*united*":– Ehud (1)

H288 [1]אַחֲוָה ***'aḥᵃwâ[1]***, n.f. [1] [√ 278]. brotherhood, community:– family bond (1)

H289 [2]אַחֲוָה ***'aḥᵃwâ[2]***, n.f. [1] [√ 2555]. what is said, declaration:– words (1)

H290 אָחוּז ***'āḥûz***, n.m. *or* v.ptcp. Not used in NIVEBC [√ 296]. see 296

H291 אֲחוֹחַ ***'ᵃḥôaḥ***, n.pr.m. [1] [→ 292]. Ahoah, "*brotherly*":– Ahoah (1)

H292 אֲחוֹחִי ***'ᵃḥôḥî***, a.g. [5] [√ 291]. Ahohite:– Ahohite (4), Ahohite (1 [+1201])

H293 אֲחוּמַי ***'ᵃḥûmay***, n.pr.m. [1] Ahumai:– Ahumai (1)

H294 אָחוֹר ***'āḥôr***, subst. [41] [→ 345; cf. 336]. back (of the body), rear, hindquarters; backward, from behind; west, as a compass point, because east (the direction of the sunrise) is the direction of orientation:– back (14), away (2), backs (2), backward (2), behind (2), hindquarters (2), rear (2), west (2), backsliding (1), backward (1 [+4200]), behind (1 [+4946]), deserted (1 [+6047]), end (1), future (1), is driven back (1 [+6047]), made retreat (1 [+8740]), on both sides (1 [+7156, 2256]), overthrows (1 [+8740]), retreating (1 [+6047]), time to come (1), withdrawn (1 [+8740])

H295 אָחוֹת ***'āḥôt***, n.f. [113] [√ 278]. sister, by extension: half-sister, any female blood-relative; a term of endearment. "Each to her sister" is a marker of reciprocal reference: one to another:– sister (88), sisters (11), other[S] (4), sister's (4), together (2 [+851, 448]), another[S] (1), NDT (3)

H296 [1]אָחַז ***'āḥaz[1]***, v. [64] [→ 290, 297, 298, 299, 303, 304;; *also used with compound proper names*]. [Q] grasp, seize, hold; [Qp] to be fastened; [N] to be caught, acquire:– seized (9), grip (4), seizes (3), caught (2), grips (2), hold (2), seize (2), supports (2), take (2), took (2), took hold (2), accept possession (1), acquire property (1), acquired (1), acquired property (1), are caught (1), are taken (1), bar (1), being taken (1), catch (1), clinging (1), closely followed (1), did so[S] (1), embracing (1), fastened (1), grasp (1), grasping (1), grasps (1), handle (1), held (1), hold fast (1), hold out (1), in (1), inserted (1), kept from closing (1 [+9073]), share (1), steady (1), take hold (1), take on (1), wearing (1), NDT (3)

H297 [2]אָחַז ***'āḥaz[2]***, v. [3] [√ 296]. [Q] to attach, cover, panel; [Ho] be attached; [P] to cover:– attached to (1), covers (1), was attached (1)

H298 אָחָז ***'āḥāz***, n.pr.m. [42] [√ 301; cf. 296]. Ahaz, "*he has grasped*":– Ahaz (41), NDT (1)

H299 אֲחֻזָּה ***'ᵃḥuzzâ***, n.f. [66] [√ 296]. property, possession:– property (28), possession (14), land (4 [+824]), possess (4), family land (3 [+8441]), place (2), site (2), family property (1), hold (1), hold as a possession (1), lands (1), occupied (1), property (1 [+824]), territory (1), that[S] (1), NDT (1)

H300 אַחְזַי ***'aḥzay***, n.pr.m. [1] [√ 301; cf. 296 + 3378]. Ahzai, "*Yahweh has grasped*":– Ahzai (1)

H301 אֲחַזְיָה ***'ᵃḥazyâ***, n.pr.m. [7] [→ 298, 300, 302, 304; cf. 296 + 3378]. Ahaziah, "*Yahweh has upheld*":– Ahaziah (7)

H302 אֲחַזְיָהוּ ***'ᵃḥazyāhû***, n.pr.m. [31] [√ 301; cf. 296 + 3378]. Ahaziah, "*Yahweh has upheld*":– Ahaziah (27), Ahaziah's (4)

H303 אֲחֻזָּם ***'ᵃḥuzzām***, n.pr.m. [1] [√ 296]. Ahuzzam, "*possessor*":– Ahuzzam (1)

H304 אֲחֻזַּת ***'ᵃḥuzzat***, n.pr.m. [1] [√ 301; cf. 296]. Ahuzzath, "*possession*":– Ahuzzath (1)

H305 אֵחִי ***'ēḥî***, n.pr.m. [1] [√ 325]. Ehi, "*my brother [is exalted]*":– Ehi (1)

H306 אֲחִי ***'ᵃḥî***, n.pr.m. [2] [√ 278]. Ahi, "*my brother*, [poss.] *Yahweh is [my] brother*":– Ahi (2)

H307 אֲחִיאָם ***'ᵃḥî'ām***, n.pr.m. [2] [√ 278 + 4392?]. Ahiam, "*brother of mother*":– Ahiam (2)

H308 אֲחִיָּה ***'ᵃḥiyyâ***, n.pr.m. [18] [√ 278 + 3378]. Ahijah, "*[my] brother is Yahweh*":– Ahijah (16), Ahiah (1), Ahijah's (1)

H309 אֲחִיָּהוּ ***'ᵃḥiyyāhû***, n.pr.m. [5] [√ 278 + 3378]. Ahijah, "*[my] brother is Yahweh*":– Ahijah (5)

H310 אֲחִיהוּד ***'ᵃḥîhûd***, n.pr.m. [1] [√ 278 + 2086]. Ahihud, "*[my] brother has majesty*":– Ahihud (1)

H311 אַחְיוֹ ***'aḥyô***, n.pr.m. [6] [√ 278 + 3378]. Ahio, "*[my] brother is Yahweh*":– Ahio (6)

H312 אֲחִיחֻד ***'ᵃḥîḥud***, n.pr.m. [1] [√ 278 + 2086]. Ahihud, "*[my] brother has majesty*":– Ahihud (1)

H313 אֲחִיטוּב ***'ᵃḥîṭûb***, n.pr.m. [15] [√ 278 + 3202]. Ahitub, "*[my] brother is goodness*":– Ahitub (15)

H314 אֲחִילוּד ***'ᵃḥîlûd***, n.pr.m. [5] [√ 278 + 3528?]. Ahilud, "*[my] brother is born*":– Ahilud (5)

H315 אֲחִימוֹת ***'ᵃḥîmôt***, n.pr.m. [1] [√ 278 + 4637]. Ahimoth, "*[my] brother is my support* [or poss.] *[my] brother is Mot*":– Ahimoth (1)

H316 אֲחִימֶלֶךְ ***'ᵃḥîmelek***, n.pr.m. [18] [√ 278 + 4889]. Ahimelech, "*[my] brother is king*":– Ahimelek (18)

H317 אֲחִימָן ***'ᵃḥîman***, n.pr.m. [4] [√ 278 + ?]. Ahiman, "[poss.] *[my] brother is a gift*":– Ahiman (4)

H318 אֲחִימַעַץ **'aḥîma'aṣ**, n.pr.m. [15] [√ 278 + 5106]. Ahimaaz, *"[my] brother is fury"*:– Ahimaaz (15)

H319 אַחְיָן **'aḥyān**, n.pr.m. [1] [√ 278 + 5527?]. Ahian, *"little brother"*:– Ahian (1)

H320 אֲחִינָדָב **'aḥînādāb**, n.pr.m. [1] [√ 278 + 5605]. Ahinadab, *"[my] brother is willing"*:– Ahinadab (1)

H321 אֲחִינֹעַם **'aḥînō'am**, n.pr.f. [7] [√ 278 + 5840]. Ahinoam, *"[my] brother is pleasant"*:– Ahinoam (7)

H322 אֲחִיסָמָךְ **'aḥîsāmāk**, n.pr.m. [3] [√ 278 + 6164]. Ahisamach, *"[my] brother is a support"*:– Ahisamak (3)

H323 אֲחִיעֶזֶר **'aḥî'ezer**, n.pr.m. [6] [√ 278 + 6469]. Ahiezer, *"[my] brother is a help"*:– Ahiezer (6)

H324 אֲחִיקָם **'aḥîqām**, n.pr.m. [20] [√ 278 + 7756]. Ahikam, *"[my] brother stands"*:– Ahikam (20)

H325 אֲחִירָם **'aḥîrām**, n.pr.m. [1] [→ 305, 326, 2586, 2587, 2670, 2671; cf. 278 + 8123]. Ahiram, *"[my] brother is exalted"*:– Ahiram (1)

H326 אֲחִירָמִי **'aḥîrāmî**, a.g. [1] [√ 325; cf. 278 + 8123]. Ahiramite, *"of Ahiram"*:– Ahiramite (1)

H327 אֲחִירַע **'aḥîra'**, n.pr.m. [5] [√ 278 + 8275 *or* 8276 *or* 8277]. Ahira, *"[my] brother is my friend* or *my brother is evil"*:– Ahira (5)

H328 אֲחִישַׁחַר **'aḥîšāḥar**, n.pr.m. [1] [√ 278 + 8837]. Ahishahar, *"[my] brother was born at early dawn"*:– Ahishahar (1)

H329 אֲחִישָׁר **'aḥîšār**, n.pr.m. [1] Ahishar, *"[my] brother is upright* or *[my] brother has sung"*:– Ahishar (1)

H330 אֲחִיתֹפֶל **'aḥîtōpel**, n.pr.m. [20] [√ 278 + 9523?]. Ahithophel, "[poss.] *[my] brother is in the desert* or *[my] brother is foolishness"*:– Ahithophel (17), Ahithophel's (3)

H331 אַחְלָב **'aḥlāb**, n.pr.loc. [1] Ahlab, *"fat, fruitful, healthy"*:– Ahlab (1)

H332 אַחֲלַי **'aḥalay**, subst. [2] Oh that!; If only!:– if only (1), oh that (1)

H333 אַחְלָי **'aḥlāy**, n.pr. [2] [√ 278 + 446]. Ahlai, *"Alas! I wish that!"*:– Ahlai (2)

H334 אַחְלָמָה **'aḥlāmâ**, n.f. [2] amethyst (exact identification uncertain):– amethyst (2)

H335 אֲחַסְבַּי **'aḥasbay**, n.pr.m. [1] [√ 2879 + 928? + 3378?]. Ahasbai, *"I seek refuge in Yahweh"*:– Ahasbai (1)

H336 אָחַר **'āḥar**, v. [17] [→ 294, 339, 340, 343, 344, 345, 4737, 4740; cf. 3508]. [Q] to remain, stay on; [P] to detain, delay, slow down; [H] to take longer (than a set time), come late:– delay (5), delayed (2), slow (2), detain (1), hold back (1), late (1), linger (1), lost time (1), remained (1), stay up late (1), took longer (1)

H337 [1]אַחֵר **'aḥēr[1]**, a. [165] [→ 338]. other, another, different; next, additional, more, extra:– other (84), another (37), others (12), else (4), next (4), another (3 [+6388]), different (2), more (2), more (2 [+6388]), someone else's (2), additional (1), another's (1), changed (1 [+2200]), new (1), second (1), set farther back (1 [+2958, 2021]), someone else (1), strange (1), swords[S] (1), various (1), what[S] (1), NDT (2)

H338 [2]אַחֵר **'aḥēr[2]**, n.pr.m. [1] [√ 337]. Aher, *"another, substitute"*:– Aher (1)

H339 אַחַר **'aḥar**, subst. & adv. & pp. [713] [→ 343; cf. 336; 10021]. (temporal) after, afterward, later, some time later; (spatial) back, behind, following:– after (203), behind (38), followed (27 [+2143]), follow (20 [+2143]), next to (17), with (16), afterward (15 [+4027]), to (13), from (12 [+4946]), follow (11), following (11), after that (10), followed (10), then (10), behind (9 [+4946]), in the course of time (8 [+4027]), afterward (7), pursue (7), back (6), followed (6 [+995]), following (6 [+2143]), pursuing (6), some time later (6 [+2021, 1821, 2021, 465]), of (5), since (5), now (4), some time later (4), tending (4), after (3 [+4027]), later (3), later (3 [+4027]), succeed (3), west (3), after this (2), against (2), around (2), away from (2 [+4946]), back (2 [+4946]), beyond (2), chasing (2), finished (2), flee (2), follow (2 [+2118]), followers (2), follows (2 [+995]), in addition to (2), join (2), loyal to (2), on (2), outlived (2 [+799, 3427]), pursue (2 [+8938]), pursuing (2 [+4946]), rear (2), then (2 [+4027]), after (1 [+4946]), after a while (1 [+2021, 1821, 2021, 465]), after the time of (1), again (1), at (1), back (1 [+7155]), back to (1), backs (1), butt (1), calling to arms (1 [+2410]), chasing (1 [+1944]), descendants (1), deserted (1 [+6590, 4946]), devoted to (1 [+2143]), ends up (1), ever (1), far side (1), follow (1 [+6296]), follow (1 [+995]), follow (1 [+1815]), follow (1 [+3655]), follow (1 [+7756]), follow (1 [+7756, 4946]), followed (1 [+3655]), followed (1 [+7756]), followed in (1 [+995]), followers (1 [+2143]), followers (1 [+2021, 6639, 889]), follows (1), follows (1 [+4027]), for (1), from then on (1 [+4946, 4027]), future (1), gave support (1 [+6468]), go over the branches a second time (1 [+6994]), greedy (1 [+2143]), how long (1 [+5503, 6388]), imitated (1), in (1), in hot pursuit (1), in the course of time (1 [+4946, 4027]), last of all (1), later (1 [+2296]), later (1 [+4946, 4027]), later (1 [+2021, 1821, 2021, 465]), lead on (1 [+3870]), lead to do the same[S] (1 [+2388, 466, 2177]), leave behind (1), led (1 [+2143]), left (1 [+4946]), left behind (1), lust after (1 [+2388]), lusted after (1 [+2388]), next (1), next after (1), next in line (1), only then (1 [+4027]), over (1), pursue (1 [+2143]), pursue (1 [+3655]), pursued (1 [+2143]), pursuing (1 [+2143]), right behind (1), runs after for favors (1 [+2388]), since (1 [+889]), some time after (1), succeeded (1), successive years (1 [+9102, 9102]), successor (1), successor (1 [+132, 8611, 995]), supported (1), supported (1 [+2118]), then (1 [+2256]), those[S] (1 [+2021, 6639, 889]), to (1 [+4946]), toward (1), turned (1 [+8959]), under the command of (1), westward (1 [+2006]), when (1), worshiping (1), NDT (79)

H340 אַחֲרוֹן **'aḥarôn**, a.f. [51] [√ 336]. (temporal) next, later, last, end; (spatial) at the back, behind, west, as a compass point, because east (the direction of the sunrise) is the direction of orientation:– last (11), end (10), next (4), Mediterranean[S] (3), then (3), future (2), later (2), rear (2), second (2), to come (2), west (2), end (1 [+2118, 928, 2021]), follow (1), he[S] (1 [+2021, 408, 2021]), later (1 [+928, 2021]), present (1), this[S] (1), time (1), yet (1)

H341 אֲחַרְחַ **'aḥraḥ**, n.pr.m. [1] Aharah, *"brother of Rah"*:– Aharah (1)

H342 אֲחַרְחֵל **'aḥarḥēl**, n.pr.m. [1] Aharhel, *"brother of Rachel"*:– Aharhel (1)

H343 אַחֲרַי **'aḥaray**, a. [1] [√ 339; cf. 336]. in the end, afterward:– in the end (1)

H344 אַחֲרִית **'aḥarît**, n.f. [61] [√ 336; 10022]. (spatial) the far side, the other side; (temporal) at the last, at the end, (in days) to come:– end (19), to come (8), future (6), last (4), descendants (3), future hope (3), left (3), end of life (1), far side (1), final destiny (1), final end (1), final outcome (1), future (1 [+3427]), later (1), later in time (1 [+928]), latter part (1), latter part of life (1), least (1), outcome (1), turn out (1), what happens (1), what might happen (1)

H345 אֲחֹרַנִּית **'aḥōrannît**, adv. [7] [→ 294; cf. 336]. backwardly, by turning around, in turning back:– back (2), backward (2), go back (1 [+8740]), gone down (1 [+3718]), turned the other way (1)

H346 אֲחַשְׁדַּרְפָּן **'aḥašdarpān**, n.m.pl. [4] [√ 10026]. satraps, an administrative governor of a Persian province:– satraps (4)

H347 אֲחַשְׁוֵרוֹשׁ **'aḥašwērôš**, n.pr.m. [31] [cf. 348]. Ahaseurus, Xerxes:– Xerxes (31)

H348 אֲחַשְׁרֹשׁ **'aḥašērōš**, n.pr.m. Not used in NIVEBC [cf. 347]. see 347

H349 אֲחַשְׁתָּרִי **'aḥaštārî**, n.pr.m. *or* a.g. Not used in NIVEBC [→ 2028]. Ahashtari

H350 אֲחַשְׁתְּרָן **'aḥašterān**, a. [2] royal, belonging to the king and used in the king's service:– for king (1), royal (1)

H351 [1]אַט **'aṭ[1]**, subst. [5] (adv.) gently, meekly, slowly:– gently (2 [+4200]), gentle (1), meekly (1), slowly (1 [+4200])

H352 [2]אַט **'aṭ[2]**, v. Not used in NIVEBC [cf. 5742]. see 5742

H353 [1]אָטָד **'āṭād[1]**, n.m. [4] [→ 354]. thornbush:– thornbush (3), thorns (1)

H354 [2]אָטָד **'āṭād[2]**, n.pr.loc. [2] [√ 353]. Atad, *"of the thorns [?]"*:– Atad (2)

H355 אֵטוּן **'ēṭûn**, n.[m.] [1] linen, possibly red in color:– linens (1)

H356 אִטִּים **'iṭṭîm**, n.m. [1] spirits of the dead:– spirits of the dead (1)

H357 אָטַם **'āṭam**, v. [8] [Q] to stop up (one's ears); to hold (one's tongue); [Qp] to be narrow:– narrow (4), hold (1), shuts (1), stop (1), stopped (1)

H358 אָטַר **'āṭar**, v. [1] [→ 359, 360]. [Q] to close:– close (1)

H359 אָטֵר **'āṭēr**, n.pr.m. [5] [√ 358]. Ater, "[poss.] *crippled one, left-handed one,* or *Etir"*:– Ater (5)

H360 אִטֵּר **'iṭṭēr**, a. [2] [√ 358]. hindered on the right hand, (thus) left-handed; other sources: ambidextrous:– left-handed (2 [+3338, 3545])

H361 אֵי **'ê**, adv.inter. [38] [→ 372, 377, 378, 379, 402, 407, 686?]. where?, which way?:– where (17), where (5 [+2296]), what (3), where (3 [+2296]), which (2 [+2296]), by what (1 [+2296]), no more (1), what (1 [+2296]), where (1 [+5226]), which way (1 [+2296]), which way (1 [+2296, 2021, 2006]), why (1 [+4200, 2296]), NDT (1)

H362 [1]אִי **'î[1]**, n.m. & f. [36] [cf. 363?]. island; coastland; distant shores:– islands (15), coastlands (8), coasts (5), island (2), coast (1), distant (1 [+3972]), distant shores (1), distant shores (1 [+3542]), maritime (1), shores (1)

H363 [2]אִי **'î[2]**, n.m. [3] [cf. 362?]. hyena, jackals; some understand this to be a spirit or demon:– hyenas (3)

H364 [3]אִי **'î[3]**, adv. [1] [→ 374?, 376, 388]. not:– not (1)

H365 [4]אִי **'î[4]**, interj. [2] Woe!:– pity (1), woe (1)

H366 אָיַב **'āyab**, v. [1] [→ 367, 368, 373]. [Q] to be an enemy, be hostile towards:– enemy (1)

H367 אֹיֵב **'ōyēb**, n.m. *or* v.ptcp. [282] [√ 366]. enemy, foe:– enemies (192), enemy (68), foes (11), foe (3), enemy's (1), opponents (1), their[S] (1 [+3870]), their own[S] (1 [+2021]), whom[S] (1), NDT (3)

H368 אֵיבָה **'êbâ**, n.f. [5] [√ 366]. hostility, enmity:– enmity (3), hostility (2)

H369 אֵיד **'êd**, n.m. [25] [√ 202]. disaster, calamity, destruction:– disaster (16), calamity (3), destruction (3), fall (1), ruin (1), siege ramps (1 [+784])

H370 [1]אַיָּה **'ayyâ[1]**, n.f. [4] [→ 371]. black kite; falcon; vulture:– black kite (2), falcon's (1), vulture (1)

H371 [2]אַיָּה **'ayyâ[2]**, n.pr.m. [6] [√ 370]. Aiah, *"black kite"*:– Aiah (4), Aiah's (2)

H372 אַיֵּה **'ayyēh**, adv.inter. [44] [√ 361]. Where?:– where (43), NDT (1)

H373 אִיּוֹב **'iyyôb**, n.pr.m. [58] [√ 366]. Job, *"where is my father,* [or perhaps] *Where is my father, O God?"*:– Job (50), Job's (5), he[S] (2), NDT (1)

H374 אִיזֶבֶל **'îzebel**, n.pr.f. [22] [√ 364? + 2292?]. Jezebel, "[poss.] *unhusbanded, unexalted"*:– Jezebel (18), Jezebel's (3), she[S] (1)

H374.5 אִיזָל **'îzāl**, n.pr.loc. [1] [poss. related to 207]. Izal. Conjectured in Eze 27:19:– Izal (1)

H375 אֵיךְ **'êk**, adv.inter. & excl. [61] [cf. 2120]. How? Why?; How! Also!:– how (48), why (6), what (3), how gladly (1), too (1), what else (1), NDT (1)

H376 אִיכָבוֹד, אִי-כָבוֹד **'îkābôd, 'î-kābôd**, n.pr.m. [2] [√ 364 + 3883]. Ichabod, *"where is the glory?"*:– Ichabod (1), Ichabod's (1)

H377 אֵיכָה **'êkâ**, adv.inter. & excl. [17] [√ 361]. how?, where?; how! (in lament):– how (12), where (2), but how (1), see how (1), what (1)

H378 אֵיכֹה **'êkōh**, adv.inter. & excl. [1] [√ 361]. Where?:– where (1)

H379 אֵיכָכָה **'êkākâ**, adv.inter. [4] [√ 361]. How?:– how (2), NDT (2)

H380 [1]אַיִל **'ayil[1]**, n.m. [162] [→ 214?, 215, 381, 382?, 383, 385, 442, 463, 464, 471, 473, 475]. ram, a male sheep generally more aggressive and protective of the flock; by extension: leading man, ruler:– ram (88), rams (62), its[S] (4 [+2021]), it[S] (2 [+2021]), leaders (1), leading men (1), prominent people (1), ruler (1), rulers (1), NDT (1)

H381 [2]אַיִל **'ayil[2]**, n.m. [5] [→ 390, 391, 392, 393?, 396, 397?, 443, 461, 462, 471, 473, 474, 935; cf. 380]. oaks; or any large, mighty tree without reference to a specific species:– oaks (4), sacred oaks (1)

H382 [3]אַיִל **'ayil[3]**, n.[m.] [19] [→ 444; cf. 380?]. projecting wall; jamb:– jambs (9), projecting walls (9), widths[S] (1 [+4647])

H383 [4]אַיִל **'ayil[4]**, n.m. Not used in NIVEBC [√ 380]. leader, chief

H384 אֱיָל **'eyāl**, n.m. [1] [→ 394; cf. 380]. strength:– strength (1)

H385 אַיָּל **'ayyāl**, n.[m.] & f. [12] [→ 387, 389; cf. 380]. deer, young stag:– deer (9), young stag (3 [+6762])

H386 אֵיל פָּארָן **'êl pā'rān**, n.pr.loc. [1] [√ 381 + 7000]. El Paran, *"tree of Paran"*:– El Paran (1)

H387 אַיָּלָה **'ayyālâ**, n.f. [10] [√ 385]. deer, doe:– doe (5), deer (3), does (2)

H388 אִילוֹ **'îlô**, interj. Not used in NIVEBC [√ 364]. woe!, alas!

H389 אַיָּלוֹן **'ayyālôn**, n.pr.loc. [10] [√ 385]. Aijalon, *"place of the deer"*:– Aijalon (10)

H390 [1]אֵילוֹן **'êlôn[1]**, n.pr.m. [4] [√ 381; cf. 380]. Elon, *"species of a mighty tree"*:– Elon (4)

H391 [2]אֵילוֹן **'êlôn[2]**, n.pr.loc. [1] [→ 381; cf. 380]. Elon, *"species of a mighty tree"*:– Elon (1)

H392 אֵילוֹן בֵּית חָנָן **'êlôn bêt ḥānān**, n.pr.loc. [1] [√ 381 + 1074 + 2860]. Elon Bethhanan, *"tree of Bethhanan"*:– Elon Bethhanan (1)

H393 אֵילוֹת **'êlôt**, n.pr.loc. [4] [√ 381?]. Elath, *"grove of large trees"*:– Elath (3), NDT (1)

H394 אֱיָלוּת **'eyālût**, n.m. [1] [√ 384; cf. 380]. Strength, Power, a title of the one true God, with a focus that he is potent to help:– strength (1)

H395 אֵילָם **'êlām**, n.m. [52] [→ 221]. portico, porch, hall:– portico (45), hall (3), colonnade (1 [+6647]), porticoes (1), NDT (2)

H396 אֵילִם **'êlim**, n.pr.loc. [6] [√ 381; cf. 380]. Elim, *"big trees"*:– Elim (5), where[S] (1 [+928])

H397 אֵילַת **'êlat**, n.pr.loc. [4] [√ 381?]. Elath, *"grove of large trees"*:– Elath (4)

H398 אָיֹם **'āyōm**, a. [3] [√ 399]. fearful; majestic, with an implication that this majesty instills awe that borders on fear:– majestic (2), feared (1)

H399 אֵימָה **'êmâ**, n.f. [17] [→ 398, 400; 10028]. terror, dread, fear:– terror (7), terrors (4), fear (2), dreadful (1), fearsome (1), great fear (1), wrath (1)

H400 אֵימִים **'êmîm**, n.pr.m.pl. [3] [√ 399]. Emites, *"frightening beings"*:– Emites (3)

HEBREW INDEX

H401 [1]אַיִן ***'ayin***[1], subst.neg. [789] [cf. 403]. there is no, not, none, without:– no (209), there is no (101), not (92), nothing (30), there was no (29), without (29), is not (20), none (11), cannot (9), there will be no (9), without (9 [+4946]), gone (8), never (7), be no more (6), lack (6), are no more (5), beyond (5), don't (5), is no more (5), neither (5), be no (4), is no (4), is there no (4), nor (4 [+2256]), there is none (4), there is nothing (4), there was none (4), there were no (4), were not (4), it is not (3), no (3 [+4946]), nothing (3 [+3972]), there is no (3 [+1172]), there is not (3), was not (3), are not (2), in vain (2), is that not (2), is there no longer (2), isn't (2), lacks (2), none (2 [+408]), nothing (2 [+1821]), nothing (2 [+4399]), senseless (2 [+4213]), there are no (2), there is nothing (2 [+4399]), there was not (2), there was nothing (2), was no more (2), was there no (2), waterless (2 [+4784]), without (2 [+928]), won't (2), all alone (1 [+9108]), allowed (1 [+646]), am no more (1), any[S] (1), aren't (1), bare (1 [+4399, 928]), be nothing (1 [+1194]), before (1 [+3954]), boundless (1 [+7897]), cannot (1 [+3946]), countless (1 [+5031]), deserted (1 [+3782]), deserted (1 [+4946, 3782]), deserted (1 [+4946, 132]), disappeared (1), empty (1 [+4946, 3782]), endless (1 [+7891]), endless (1 [+7897]), fatherless (1 [+3846, 2256, 3]), found[S] (1 [+4946]), free from (1), gone from (1 [+907]), have no (1), incomprehensible (1 [+1069]), incurable (1 [+5340]), innumerable (1 [+5031]), is never (1), is nothing (1), isn't there (1), it isn't (1), it was impossible (1), it was not (1), it's not (1), kept secret (1 [+5583]), lack (1 [+928]), lack (1 [+4200]), loses (1), more (1 [+4200]), more than (1 [+4200]), naught (1), nearly (1 [+3869]), neither (1 [+4946]), never (1 [+4200, 6409]), no one (1), no other will be (1 [+4946]), none (1 [+4946]), nor (1 [+677]), nor (1 [+2256, 4946]), nor (1 [+2256, 1685]), nothing at all (1 [+2256, 700]), nothing whatever (1 [+3972, 1821]), or (1), or (1 [+2256]), or (1 [+2256, 561]), powerless (1 [+3946]), powerless (1 [+4200, 445]), powerless (1 [+4200, 445, 3338]), regardless (1 [+4200, 9068]), so[S] (1), surely (1 [+561]), than (1), there is neither (1), there is no (1 [+3972]), there is no (1 [+4946]), there is nothing (1 [+3972]), there were no (1 [+1172]), there were not (1), there will be none (1), these are not (1), too (1), unclean (1 [+3196]), uncovered (1 [+4064]), unless (1), unsearchable (1 [+2984]), use no (1), was no (1), weak (1 [+226]), will (1 [+2118]), will not (1), without (1 [+4200]), without (1 [+6330]), without any payment (1 [+2855]), wouldn't (1), NDT (14)

H402 [2]אַיִן ***'ayin***[2], adv. [17] [→ 4406; cf. 361]. where (from)?:– where (12), where (3 [+4946]), where (2 [+4946])

H403 אִין ***'în***, subst.neg. [1] [cf. 401]. there is not:– Don't (1)

H404 אִיעֶזֶר ***'î'ezer***, n.pr.m. [1] [→ 405; cf. 3 + 3276 + 6469]. Iezer, "*my [father] is help*":– Iezer (1)

H405 אִיעֶזְרִי ***'î'ezrî***, a.g. [1] [√ 404]. Iezerite, "*of Iezer*":– Iezerite (1)

H406 אֵיפָה ***'êpâ***, n.f. [40] ephah (dry measure, about three-fifths of a bushel (22 liters); also a large basket of unspecified measure; "ephah and ephah" means "two differing measures," as a measure that is not standardized:– ephah (29), basket (5), differing measures (1 [+2256, 406]), differing measures (1 [+406, 2256]), measure (1), measures (1), two differing measures (1 [+2256, 406]), two differing measures (1 [+406, 2256])

H407 אֵיפֹה ***'êpōh***, adv. [10] [√ 361 + 7024]. where?:– where (8), what (1), where from (1)

H408 [1]אִישׁ ***'îš***[1], n.m. [2187] [→ 413, 843, 851; *also used with compound proper names*]. man, sometimes in contrast to woman, human, sometimes in contrast to animal (without gender distinction); by extension: husband, in contrast to wife; (p.) each, every, someone, a certain one, anyone, whoever. This word is often used in phrases meaning "one of a kind," so a "man of war" is a soldier; a "man of bow" is an archer, etc.:– man (420), men (387), each (155), one (127), people (70), husband (65), anyone (52), person (34), Israelites (30 [+3776]), someone (27), everyone (26), those[S] (23), them[S] (15), man's (14), every (13), soldiers (12 [+4878]), they[S] (12), some[S] (10), any (9), everyone (9 [+3972]), human (9), they[S] (9 [+2021]), those[S] (9 [+2021]), he[S] (7 [+2021]), all (6), any (6 [+408]), one (6 [+285]), person's (6), warrior (6 [+4878]), he[S] (5), humans (5), none (5 [+4202]), swordsmen (5 [+8990, 2995]), whoever (5), Israelite (4 [+3776]), Israelite (4 [+4946, 1074, 3776]), anyone (4 [+4769, 2021]), anyone (4 [+408]), army (4 [+4878]), each (4 [+408]), husbands (4), male (4), neighbor (4), successor (4), them[S] (4 [+2021]), violent (4 [+2805]), another (3), anyone (3 [+2021]), anyone's (3), father (3), foot soldiers (3 [+8081]), him[S] (3 [+2021]), others (3), the[S] (3), they (3), who (3), who[S] (3), you[S] (3), Egyptian (2 [+5212]), Israelite (2 [+4946, 1201, 3776]), any (2 [+3972]), any man (2 [+408]), anyone (2 [+3972, 2021]), at war with (2 [+4878]), champion (2 [+2021, 1227]), deceitful (2 [+5327]), everyone (2 [+2021]), evildoers (2 [+8273]), fellow (2), forces (2), him[S] (2 [+2021, 2085, 2021]), human being (2), inhabitants (2), leaving none alive (2 [+3869, 285]), merchants (2 [+9365]), mortals (2), mourners[S] (2), none (2 [+401]), one's (2), prophet[S] (2), servants (2), their[S] (2), them[S] (2 [+2021, 2085, 2021]), townspeople (2 [+6551]), troops (2), valiant fighter (2 [+1201, 2657]), valiant fighters (2 [+2657]), warriors (2 [+2657]), whoever (2 [+889]), whoever (2 [+4769, 2021]), whoever[S] (2), Benjamin (1 [+1201, 3549]), Benjamite (1 [+1228]), Benjamite (1 [+3549]), Benjamites (1 [+1228]), Benjamites (1 [+4946, 1228]), Boaz[S] (1 [+2021]), Ephraimites (1 [+713]), Gibeonites (1 [+1500]), Gileadites (1 [+1680]), Hebrew (1 [+6303]), Hebrews (1 [+6303]), Israel (1 [+3776]), Israelite (1 [+2021, 3778]), Israelite[S] (1), Israelites[S] (1), Moabites (1 [+4566]), Ninevites (1 [+5770]), accuser (1 [+8190]), all (1 [+3972, 2021]), all[S] (1), allies (1 [+1382]), among yourselves (1 [+448, 278]), anyone (1 [+1201]), anyone (1 [+3972]), archers (1 [+4619, 928, 2021, 8008]), army (1), bloodthirsty (1 [+1947]), brother (1), captive (1), careful listener (1 [+9048]), census (1 [+6296]), champions (1 [+2657]), child (1), close friend (1 [+8934]), close relatives (1 [+278]), conscripts (1), counselor (1 [+6783]), counselors (1 [+6783]), creature[S] (1), cubs (1), descendant (1), descendant (1 [+4946, 2446]), deserted (1 [+4946, 1172]), deserve to (1), deserved (1), devout (1 [+2876]), each (1 [+278, 2257]), eloquent (1 [+1821]), enemies (1 [+5194]), equally (1 [+3869, 278, 2257]), equally among them (1 [+3869, 278, 2257]), everyone (1 [+132]), everyone (1 [+3972, 2021]), everyone's (1 [+928]), exiles (1 [+1460]), experienced fighter (1 [+4878]), experienced fighting men (1 [+4878, 1475, 2657]), family (1), famous (1 [+9005]), farmer (1 [+6268, 141]), fit for battle (1 [+4878]), followers (1 [+889, 2143, 6640]), fool (1 [+4067]), foreigner (1 [+1731]), friend (1), friends (1 [+8934]), from[S] (1), gang (1), give in marriage (1 [+5989, 4200]), good (1 [+3202]), great soldiers (1 [+4878]), guards (1 [+5464]), have[S] (1), he[S] (1 [+2021, 5283]), he[S] (1 [+2021, 2021, 340]), he[S] (1 [+2021, 2021, 8886, 6640]), high (1 [+1201]), highborn (1 [+1201]), himself[S] (1 [+2021]), his[S] (1 [+2021]), human beings (1), hunter (1 [+7473]), husband's (1), in the prime of life (1), judges[S] (1), kings[S] (1), leaders (1 [+8031]), leaders[S] (1), liar (1 [+3942]), man (1 [+2256, 408]), man (1 [+408, 2256]), maniac (1 [+8713]), mankind (1), mankind (1 [+1414]), man's body (1), marries (1 [+2118, 4200]), marries (1 [+2118, 4200, 2118]), marry (1 [+2118, 4200]), me[S] (1), members (1), men (1 [+8081]), men's (1), messengers (1), mockers (1 [+4371]), more[S] (1), mortal (1), murderer (1 [+1947]), murderer (1 [+2021, 1947]), neighbor's (1), none[S] (1), of one mind (1 [+3869, 285]), officials (1), officials (1 [+6269]), one (1 [+2424]), one[S] (1), one and all (1), one party[S] (1), opponent (1), oppressor (1 [+9412]), other[S] (1), owner[S] (1), people (1 [+1201]), ready for battle (1 [+7372, 4200, 2021, 4878]), remain unmarried (1 [+6328, 4200, 1194, 2118, 4200]), rich (1 [+6938]), sailors (1 [+641]), scoffers (1 [+4371]), scoundrel (1 [+1175]), scoundrel (1 [+2021, 1175]), servant (1), slanderers (1 [+4383]), slanderers (1 [+8215]), slept with (1 [+3359, 4200, 5435]), soldier (1 [+7372]), soldiers (1 [+7372]), soldiers (1 [+1505, 4878]), some (1), some of them[S] (1), son (1), son (1 [+2446]), spies (1 [+8078]), steward[S] (1), steward[S] (1 [+2021, 889, 6584, 1074]), stingy (1 [+8273, 6524]), strangers (1 [+5799]), strongest defenders (1 [+2657]), successor[S] (1), talker (1 [+8557]), tall (1 [+4500]), tend livestock (1 [+5238, 2118]), tended livestock (1 [+5238, 2118]), the parties (1 [+2256, 8276, 2084]), their[S] (1 [+3373]), their[S] (1 [+2021]), them (1), them[S] (1 [+3316]), they[S] (1 [+3315]), they[S] (1 [+7159]), they[S] (1 [+2021, 2085, 2021]), this[S] (1), those (1), those who[S] (1 [+2021]), together (1 [+907, 8276, 2084]), tribe of Benjamin (1 [+3549]), troublemaker (1 [+1175]), troublemakers (1 [+1201, 1175]), trusted friends (1 [+8934]), two men (1 [+2256, 278, 3481]), two parties (1 [+4200, 408]), two parties (1 [+408, 4200]), unmarried (1 [+4202, 2118, 4200]), unrighteous (1 [+224]), untraveled (1 [+4946, 1172, 6296]), very old (1 [+2416, 995, 928, 2021]), victim[S] (1), villain (1 [+224]), virgin (1 [+4202, 3359]), voluntarily (1 [+6590, 6584, 4213]), warrior (1), well-known (1 [+9005]), who (1 [+4769, 2021]), who (1 [+2021, 6504]), whoever (1 [+3972, 889]), wicked (1 [+8288]), wicked (1 [+8400]), wicked (1 [+8401]), wise (1 [+2682]), witless (1 [+5554]), workers (1 [+6913]), your[S] (1), NDT (248)

H409 [2]אִשׁ ***'îš***[2], subst. Not used in NIVEBC [√ 3780]. there is

H410 אִישׁ־בֹּשֶׁת ***'îš-bōšet***, n.pr.m. [11] [√ 408 + 1425]. Ish-Bosheth, "*man of shame*":– Ish-Bosheth (11)

H411 אִישׁ־טוֹב ***'îš-ṭôb***, n.pr.m. Not used in NIVEBC [√ 408 + 3202]. Ish-Tob, "*man from Tob*"

H412 אִישְׁהוֹד ***'îšhôd***, n.pr.m. [1] [√ 408 + 2086]. Ishhod, "*man of grandeur*":– Ishhod (1)

H413 אִישׁוֹן ***'îšôn***, n.[m.] [4] [√ 408]. pupil, the black center of the eyeball, formally, "the little man (of the eye)," often translated as "the apple of the eye," an idiom of care and love:– apple (2), apple (1 [+1426]), dark (1 [+696])

H414 אִישַׁי ***'îšay***, n.pr.m. [1] [√ 3805]. Jesse:– Jesse (1)

H415 אִיתוֹן ***'îtôn***, n.m. [1] [√ 910; cf. 3289]. entrance:– entrance (1)

H416 אִיתַי ***'îtay***, n.pr.m. [1] [cf. 417, 915]. Ithai:– Ithai (1)

H417 אִיתִיאֵל ***'îtî'ēl***, n.pr.m. [2] [cf. 416]. Ithiel, "*God [El] is with me*":– Ithiel (2)

H418 אִיתָמָר ***'îtāmār***, n.pr.m. [21] Ithamar, "[poss.] *[is]land of palms; [father] of Tamar*":– Ithamar (19), Ithamar's (2)

H419 [1]אֵיתָן ***'êtān***[1], a. [12] [→ 420; cf. 3851]. ever-flowing, of a stream that is always filled with water; by extension: never-failing, steady, established, eternal:– rich (2), constant (1), enduring (1), ever-flowing (1), everlasting (1), flowing stream (1), long established (1), never-failing (1), place (1), secure (1), steady (1)

H420 [2]אֵיתָן ***'êtān***[2], n.pr.m. [8] [√ 419]. Ethan, "*long lived, ever-flowing [streams]*":– Ethan (8)

H421 אַךְ ***'ak***, adv. [161] [→ 434, 435]. but, surely, only, however:– but (29), surely (25), only (15), however (8), nevertheless (5), yet (5), but only (4), just (4), nothing but (4), truly (3), also (2), and (2), indeed (2), so (2), after (1), although (1), as long as (1), as surely as (1), be sure (1), both (1), but (1 [+3954]), but also (1), but too (1), complete (1), completely (1), except (1), furthermore (1), just after (1), once more (1 [+2021, 7193]), only (1 [+8370]), provided (1 [+561]), really (1), scarcely (1), surely (1 [+6964]), though (1), very (1), yes (1), NDT (28)

H422 אַכַּד ***'akkad***, n.pr.loc. [1] Akkad:– Akkad (1)

H423 אַכְזָב ***'akzāb***, a. [2] [√ 3941]. deceptive, deceitful, referring to a stream or a person:– deceptive (2)

H424 אַכְזִיב ***'akzîb***, n.pr.loc. [4] [√ 3941?]. Aczib, "*deceit*":– Akzib (4)

H425 אַכְזָר ***'akzār***, a. [4] [→ 426, 427]. deadly, ruthless, fierce, heartless:– deadly (1), fierce (1), heartless (1), ruthlessly (1 [+4200])

H426 אַכְזָרִי ***'akzārî***, a. [8] [√ 425]. cruel, merciless:– cruel (7), death (1)

H427 אַכְזְרִיּוּת ***'akzᵉriyyût***, n.f. [1] [√ 425]. cruelty:– cruel (1)

H428 אֲכִילָה ***'ᵃkîlâ***, n.f. [1] [√ 430]. food:– food (1)

H429 אָכִישׁ ***'ākîš***, n.pr.m. [21] Achish, "*the king gives*":– Achish (19), NDT (2)

H430 אָכַל ***'ākal***, v. [814] [→ 428, 431, 433, 4407, 4408, 4409, 4818; 10030]. [Q] to eat; [N] to be eaten; [Pu] be consumed, be destroyed; [H] to give to eat, feed; from the base meaning of eating food is the fig. extension of consuming and destroying something:– eat (358), ate (70), devour (43), consume (29), eating (25), be eaten (24), eaten (23), eats (22), devoured (20), consumed (19), devours (10), consuming (9), food (8), enjoy (7), consumes (6), eaten (6 [+430]), feed on (6), be consumed (5), ate up (4), burns (4), gave to eat (4), destroy (3), eater (3), feast (3), fed (3), be devoured (2), been destroyed (2), destroyed (2), devouring (2), eat up (2), eaten provisions (2 [+430]), feasting (2), feed (2), free to eat (2 [+430]), give[S] (2), had to eat (2), have plenty to eat (2 [+430]), is eaten (2 [+430]), make eat (2), make eat food (2), man-eater (2 [+132]), must eat (2 [+430]), needed (2), shared (2), used up (2 [+430]), burn up (1), burned (1), burned up (1), crushed completely (1 [+4730, 2256]), dine on (1), dined (1), dried up (1), earn (1), eat away (1), eat food (1), eaten away (1), eats away (1), enjoyed (1), feast on (1), feasting (1 [+2256, 9272]), feeding (1), feeds on (1), get food (1), give to eat (1), had food enough (1), have[S] (1), have food (1), is eaten (1), kept (1), lick up (1), like (1), live on (1), meal (1 [+4312]), need (1), pests (1), prepare food to eat (1), prepares (1), provided for (1 [+2118, 4200, 4312, 2256]), put an end (1), ruin (1), sap (1), scarce (1 [+928, 5017]), share in (1), sharing (1 [+4946]), stay for a meal (1 [+4312]), stripped (1), stripped clean (1), supposed to dine (1 [+3782, 3782]), swallowed up (1), taste (1), to eat (1), took space (1), use (1), would[S] (1), NDT (11)

H431 אֹכֶל ***'ōkel***, n.m. [39] [√ 430]. food; a general word for food as anything edible:– food (35), food (1 [+5762]), it[S] (1), mealtime (1 [+6961, 2021]), prey (1)

H432 אֻכָל ***'ukāl***, n.pr.m. Not used in NIVEBC [√ 3983]. Ucal, "[poss.] *I am consumed* or *I cease*"

H433 אָכְלָה ***'oklâ***, n.f. [18] [√ 430]. what is consumed, food, fuel:– food (11), fuel (3), devour (2), eat (2)

H434 [1]אָכֵן ***'ākēn***[1], adv. [18] [√ 421 + 2176]. Surely! Truly!, an exclamation to emphasize the unexpected:– surely (7), but (4), yet (2), actually (1), because surely (1), how (1), truly (1), NDT (1)

H435 [2]אָכֵן ***'ākēn***[2], adv. Not used in NIVEBC [√ 421 + 2176]. so that

H436 אָכַף ***'ākap***, v. [1] [→ 437]. [Q] to drive, press hard:– drives on (1)

H437 אֶכֶף ***'ekep***, n.m. [1] [√ 436]. hand, with a focus that this part of the body that can exert pressure or press hard:– hand (1)

H438 אִכָּר ***'ikkār***, n.m. [7] farmer, people who work in fields and vineyards:– farmers (4), farmer (1), people (1), work fields (1)

H439 אַכְשָׁף ***'akšāp***, n.pr.loc. [3] [√ 4175]. Acshaph, "*fascination*":– Akshaph (3)

H440 [1]אַל ***'al***[1], adv.neg. [731] [√ 10031]. no, not:– not (507), don't (63), no (55), nor (16), never (12), or (5), without (3), cannot (2), from (2), neither (2), never (2 [+4200, 6409]), nothing (2), or (2 [+2256]), stop (2), abstain from sexual relations (1 [+5602, 448, 851]), always (1 [+2893]), better than (1), beware (1 [+9068]), forget (1 [+2349]), immortality (1 [+4638]), instead of (1), neither (1 [+2256]), never (1 [+6524]), overlook (1 [+7155]), secure against (1 [+6640]), up not (1), NDT (44)

H441 [2]אַל *'al[2]*, l.art. the (Arabic art.)

H442 [1]אֵל *'ēl[1]*, n.m. Not used in NIVEBC [√ 380]. ram, man of power

H443 [2]אֵל *'ēl[2]*, n.m. Not used in NIVEBC [√ 381; cf. 380]. mighty tree

H444 [3]אֵל *'ēl[3]*, n.[m.] Not used in NIVEBC [√ 382; cf. 380]. doorpost

H445 [4]אֵל *'ēl[4]*, n.m. [6] [√ 446]. power:– power (3 [+3338]), God (1), powerless (1 [+401, 4200]), powerless (1 [+401, 4200, 3338])

H446 [5]אֵל *'ēl[5]*, n.m. [238] [→ 445, 466, 468; cf. 212?; *also used with compound proper names*]. God, the Mighty One, as a title of majesty and power, often used in combination with other titles; also any false god, gods; any person who is strong and capable: mighty one:– God (217), God's (7), gods (3), mighty (3), mighty one (3), great (1), heavenly (1 [+1201]), heavenly beings (1 [+1201]), highest (1), his[s] (1)

H447 [6]אֵל *'ēl[6]*, pr.pl.m. & f. [9] [→ 187, 465; 10032]. these:– these (7), those (2)

H448 אֶל *'el*, pp. [5511] [→ 492, 493]. to, toward; in, into; with regard to:– to (3047), into (157), on (133), against (127), in (105), at (91), for (76), toward (57), with (49), enter (36 [+995]), before (30), over (21), concerning (19), about (18), entered (17 [+995]), of (15), reached (14 [+995]), among (12), by (12), into (11 [+9348]), around (10), sleep with (8 [+995]), near (7), slept with (7 [+995]), made love to (6 [+995]), because of (5), enters (5 [+995]), along (4), arrived (4 [+995]), attack (4), attack (4 [+6590]), in front of (4 [+7156]), upon (4), after (3), as for (3), at (3 [+4578]), attack (3 [+995]), decorated (3), facedown (3 [+7156]), facing (3 [+7156]), from (3), in front of (3 [+4578]), straight ahead (3 [+6298, 7156]), together (3 [+285, 285]), up to (3), above (2), all the way to (2), along with (2), approaches (2 [+995]), be buried (2 [+665, 7700]), beside (2), down to (2), faced (2 [+7156]), facing each other (2 [+4691, 4691]), fall in (2 [+6015]), hands together (2 [+4090, 4090]), in addition to (2), in front of (2), include (2), inside (2 [+9348]), into presence (2), next to (2 [+3338]), next to (2 [+6298]), on (2 [+4578]), onto (2), reach (2 [+995]), received (2 [+995]), together (2 [+851, 295]), under (2), wherever (2 [+3972, 889]), above (1 [+1068]), abstain from sexual relations (1 [+440, 5602, 851]), abutted (1), according to (1), across (1), adjoining (1 [+7156]), among (1 [+9348]), among yourselves (1 [+408, 278]), and (1), approached (1 [+995]), arrive (1 [+995]), as (1), as far as (1), as far as (1 [+4578]), at the sight of (1), ate (1 [+995, 7931]), attack (1 [+7756]), attacked (1 [+7756]), attacking (1 [+6590]), attentive to (1), avoid (1 [+4202, 2143]), away (1 [+2021, 2575, 2025]), because (1), before (1 [+7156]), belonged to (1), belonged to (1 [+2118]), belongs to (1), beside (1 [+3338]), bordering (1), both and (1), buried (1 [+995, 7700]), call to mind (1 [+8740, 4213]), care (1 [+8492, 4213]), care about (1 [+8492, 4213]), checked on (1 [+8938]), committed adultery with (1 [+995]), concerned about (1 [+8492, 4213]), concerned for (1), consult (1), counting on (1 [+5951, 906, 5883]), covered (1), cupped (1 [+7023]), decorated with (1), definitely (1 [+3922]), did the same[s] (1 [+2489, 285, 285]), done so[s] (1 [+995, 7931]), during (1), entered (1 [+6073]), entering (1 [+995]), entrusted to (1 [+3338]), every kind (1 [+4946, 2385, 2385]), faced (1), faced forward (1 [+4578, 7156]), filled with gladness (1 [+8524, 1637]), find (1 [+995]), fit for (1), fixed on (1), follow (1 [+3338]), for the sake of (1), from (1 [+7156]), go sleep with (1 [+995]), guest (1 [+995, 1074]), had sexual relations with (1 [+995]), have (1), have on hand (1 [+9393, 3338]), have sexual relations with (1 [+7928]), here (1), high (1), impressed (1), in accordance with (1), in charge of (1), in front of (1 [+4578, 7156]), in vain (1 [+2855]), inherit (1 [+2118]), inquire of (1 [+2011]), inquire of (1 [+7928]), inquired of (1 [+606]), inside (1), inside (1 [+2021, 1074]), into (1 [+7163]), invade (1 [+995]), invaded (1 [+995]), invaded (1 [+6590]), invader (1 [+995]), join (1), join (1 [+3718]), keep away (1 [+7928, 3870]), listened attentively to (1 [+265]), look in the face (1 [+5951, 7156]), lusted after (1 [+6311]), lying on (1), made love to (1 [+7928]), make love to (1 [+995]), make turn (1 [+5989]), married (1 [+995]), meet (1), meet (1 [+7156]), occupied (1 [+6641]), occupy (1 [+995]), on account of (1), on the faces of (1), on the side of (1), onto (1 [+9348]), opposite (1), opposite (1 [+7156]), out in front (1 [+4578, 7156]), out of (1), over (1 [+1068]), overboard (1 [+2021, 3542]), overruled (1 [+2616]), overtake (1 [+628]), overtook (1 [+995]), reached (1 [+6590]), reaches (1 [+995]), reflected on (1 [+5989, 4213]), rejoined (1 [+2143]), replace (1 [+995, 9393]), required to give (1 [+2118]), returned (1 [+995]), right in (1), see (1 [+6524]), showed concern for (1 [+7155]), sleeping with (1 [+995]), sleeps with (1 [+995]), southern (1 [+6991, 5582]), southward (1 [+2021, 3545]), square (1 [+752, 8063]), square (1 [+8062, 752, 8063]), stops to think (1 [+8740, 4213]), surmounted by (1), that (1), their (1 [+2157]), thought (1 [+606, 3276]), to (1 [+4578]), to (1 [+9348]), took (1 [+995]), touched (1 [+995]), toward (1 [+2006]), toward (1 [+5790]), toward (1 [+7156]), use (1 [+2143]), went in to spend the night with (1 [+995]), NDT (1164)

H449 אֵל אֱלֹהֵי יִשְׂרָאֵל *'ēl 'ᵉlōhê yiśrā'ēl*, n.pr.loc. [1] [√ 446 + 466 + 3776]. El Elohe Israel, "*God, the God of Israel*":– El Elohe Israel (1)

H450 אֵל בֵּית־אֵל *'ēl bêt-'ēl*, n.pr.loc. [1] [√ 446 + 1074 + 446]. El Bethel, "*God [El] of Bethel*":– El Bethel (1)

H451 אֵל בְּרִית *'ēl bᵉrît*, n.pr.[loc.?] [1] [√ 446 + 1382]. El-Berith, "*god [El] of a covenant*":– El-Berith (1)

H452 אֵלָא *'ēlā'*, n.pr.m. [1] [cf. 462]. Ela:– Ela (1)

H453 אֶלְגָּבִישׁ *'elgābîš*, n.[m.] [3] [cf. 1486]. hail(stone) or clump of ice:– hailstones (3 [+74])

H454 אַלְגּוּמִּים *'algûmmîm*, n.[m.]pl. [3] [cf. 523]. algum (wood); a transliteration of the Hebrew, the exact identification of which is uncertain:– algumwood (2 [+6770]), algum (1)

H455 אֶלְדָּד *'eldād*, n.pr.m. [2] [√ 446 + 1856]. Eldad, "*beloved of God [El]*; [poss.] *Dadi is god*":– Eldad (2)

H456 אֶלְדָּעָה *'eldā'â*, n.pr.m. [2] [√ 446 + 1977?]. Eldaah, "*God [El] is [my] desire*":– Eldaah (2)

H457 [1]אָלָה *'ālâ[1]*, v. [10] [→ 460, 9297]. [Q] to utter a curse, swear an oath; [H] to bind under oath, take an oath:– swear the oath (2), take an oath (2), bound under an oath (1), cursing (1), swears (1), take oaths (1), utter a curse (1), NDT (1)

H458 [2]אָלָה *'ālâ[2]*, v. [1] [Q] to mourn, wail:– Mourn (1)

H459 [3]אָלָה *'ālâ[3]*, v. [Q] to be unfit to

H460 [4]אָלָה *'ālâ[4]*, n.f. [33] [√ 457]. curse, oath; sworn agreement; public charge:– oath (10), curse (9), curses (7), required (2 [+5957, 928]), curse (1 [+2256, 8652]), public charge (1), put curse (1 [+8678, 8652]), put under oath (1 [+9048]), sworn agreement (1)

H461 [1]אֵלָה *'ēlâ[1]*, n.f. [13] [→ 462; cf. 381, 380; 10027]. oak, terebinth, or any species of large tree:– oak (6), oak tree (3), terebinth (2), great tree (1), tree (1)

H462 [2]אֵלָה *'ēlâ[2]*, n.pr.m. [13] [√ 461; cf. 452]. Elah, "*species of a mighty tree*":– Elah (12), Elah's (1)

H463 [3]אֵלָה *'ēlâ[3]*, n.pr.loc. [3] [√ 380]. Elah, "*a mighty tree*":– Elah (3)

H464 אַלָּה *'allâ*, n.f. [1] [√ 380]. oak, or any species of large tree:– oak (1)

H465 אֵלֶּה *'ēlleh*, pr.pl.m. & f. [744] [√ 447; 10034]. these:– these (476), this (58), those (16), they (12), this[s] (12 [+2021, 1821, 2021]), them (11), such (10), others[s] (7), some time later (6 [+339, 2021, 1821, 2021]), some (5), the (5), following[s] (4), here (3), who (3), men[s] (2), one group[s] (2), that (2), us[s] (2), what[s] (2 [+2021, 1821, 2021]), after a while (1 [+339, 2021, 1821, 2021]), all[s] (1), all this (1), animals[s] (1), as follows (1), each other (1), everything (1 [+3972, 2021, 1821, 2021]), gave the message (1 [+1819, 3972, 2021, 2021, 1821]), here is a list of[s] (1), his[s] (1), impartially (1 [+6640, 465]), impartially (1 [+465, 6640]), later (1 [+339, 2021, 1821, 2021]), next[s] (1), now (1 [+928, 2021, 3427, 2021]), now (1 [+928, 2021, 3427, 2021]), share their duties (1 [+6640]), she (1), that[s] (1 [+2021, 1821, 2021]), that happened (1 [+1821, 2021, 2021]), the craftsmen[s] (1), the first[s] (1), the five men[s] (1), the gods[s] (1), the men[s] (1), the others[s] (1), the total[s] (1), their[s] (1 [+2021]), this is how (1 [+928, 3972]), this is how (1 [+3869, 2021, 1821, 2021]), this is why (1 [+6584]), two[s] (1), very (1), what (1), who[s] (1), whose[s] (1 [+1426, 2257]), your[s] (1), NDT (69)

H466 אֱלֹהִים *'ᵉlōhîm*, n.pl.m. & f. [2603] [√ 468; cf. 446]. God (plural of majesty: plural in form but singular in meaning, with a focus on great power); gods (true grammatical plural); any person characterized by greatness or power: mighty one, great one, judge:– God (2300), gods (205), God's (27), he[s] (7), he[s] (7 [+3378, 3870]), judges (4), him[s] (3 [+3378, 3870]), I[s] (2), angels (2 [+1201, 2021]), goddess (2), he[s] (2 [+2021]), his[s] (2 [+3378, 3870]), God's (1 [+4200]), God's (1 [+4946]), angels (1), angels (1 [+1201]), divine (1), ghostly figure (1), godly (1), great (1), he[s] (1 [+2021, 824]), he[s] (1 [+3378, 5646]), him[s] (1), him[s] (1 [+2021]), him[s] (1 [+3378, 4013]), his[s] (1 [+3276]), idols (1 [+5011]), it[s] (1 [+778, 2021]), lead to do the same[s] (1 [+2388, 339, 2177]), majestic (1), mighty (1), my[s] (1), sacred (1), shrine (1 [+1074]), them[s] (1 [+2157]), them[s] (1 [+3998, 1074, 2021]), there[s] (1 [+928, 1074]), very (1 [+4200]), NDT (14)

H467 אִלּוּ *'illû*, c. [2] [√ 561 + 4273]. if:– if (2)

H468 אֱלוֹהַּ *'ᵉlôah*, n.m. [57] [→ 466; cf. 446; 10033]. God; god; idol:– God (53), God's (4)

H469 [1]אֱלוּל *'ᵉlûl[1]*, n.pr. [1] Elul:– Elul (1)

H470 [2]אֱלוּל *'ᵉlûl[2]*, n.m.? Not used in NIVEBC [√ 496]. see 496

H471 [1]אֵלוֹן *'ēlôn[1]*, n.[f.] [10] [→ 472; cf. 380; 10027]. great tree, large tree of an unspecified species:– great tree (4), great trees (4), large tree (1), tree (1)

H472 [2]אֵלוֹן *'ēlôn[2]*, n.pr.m. [2] [→ 471, 533; cf. 381]. Elon, "*species of a mighty tree*":– Elon (2)

H473 [1]אַלּוֹן *'allôn[1]*, n.m. [8] [→ 474; cf. 380]. oak tree, large tree of an unspecified species:– oak (4), oaks (4)

H474 [2]אַלּוֹן *'allôn[2]*, n.pr.m. [1] [√ 473; cf. 380]. Allon, "*oak*":– Allon (1)

H475 אַלּוֹן בָּכוּת *'allôn bākût*, n.pr.loc. [1] [√ 380 + 1134]. Allon Bacuth, "*oak of weeping*":– Allon Bakuth (1)

H476 [1]אַלּוּף *'allûp[1]*, a. [9] [√ 544]. close friend, partner, ally, companion:– close friends (2), friend (2), allies (1), companion (1), gentle (1), oxen (1), partner (1)

H477 [2]אַלּוּף *'allûp[2]*, n.m. [60] [√ 545]. chief, leader:– chiefs (16), clans (2), clan (1), divisions (1), NDT (40)

H478 אָלוּשׁ *'ālûš*, n.pr.loc. [2] Alush:– Alush (2)

H479 אֶלְזָבָד *'elzābād*, n.pr.m. [2] [√ 446 + 2272]. Elzabad, "*God [El] has given*":– Elzabad (2)

H480 אָלַח *'ālaḥ*, v. [3] [N] to be, become (morally) corrupt, a fig. extension of milk turning sour, not found in the OT:– corrupt (3)

H481 אֶלְחָנָן *'elḥānān*, n.pr.m. [4] [√ 446 + 2860]. Elhanan, "*God [El] is gracious*":– Elhanan (4)

H482 אֱלִיאָב *'ᵉlî'āb*, n.pr.m. [21] [√ 446 + 3]. Eliab, "*God [El] is [my] father*":– Eliab (20), he[s] (1)

H483 אֱלִיאֵל *'ᵉlî'ēl*, n.pr.m. [10] [√ 446 + 3276 + 446]. Eliel, "*God [El] is [my] God*":– Eliel (10)

H484 אֱלִיאָתָה *'ᵉlî'ātâ*, n.pr.m. [1] [√ 446 + 910]. Eliathah, "*God [El] comes*":– Eliathah (1)

H485 אֱלִידָד *'ᵉlîdād*, n.pr.m. [1] [√ 446 + 1856]. Elidad, "*God [El] is [my] beloved*":– Elidad (1)

H486 אֶלְיָדָע *'elyādā'*, n.pr.m. [4] [√ 446 + 3359]. Eliada, "*God [El] knows*":– Eliada (4)

H487 אַלְיָה *'alyâ*, n.f. [5] fat tail (of a sheep):– fat tail (5)

H488 אֵלִיָּה *'ēliyyâ*, n.pr.m. [8] [√ 446 + 3378]. Elijah, "*Yahweh is [my] God*":– Elijah (8)

H489 אֵלִיָּהוּ *'ēliyyāhû*, n.pr.m. [63] [√ 446 + 3378]. Elijah, "*Yahweh is [my] God*":– Elijah (60), Elijah's (2), NDT (1)

H490 אֱלִיהוּ *'ᵉlîhû*, n.pr.m. [4] [√ 446 + 2085]. Elihu, "*Yahweh is [my] God*":– Elihu (4)

H491 אֱלִיהוּא *'ᵉlîhû'*, n.pr.m. [7] [√ 446 + 2085]. Elihu, "*Yahweh is [my] God*":– Elihu (6), he[s] (1)

H492 אֶלְיְהוֹעֵינַי *'elyᵉhô'ênay*, n.pr.m. [2] [√ 448 + 3378 + 6524]. Eliehoenai, "*my eyes [look] to Yahweh*":– Eliehoenai (2)

H493 אֶלְיוֹעֵינַי *'elyô'ênay*, n.pr.m. [7] [√ 448 + 3378 + 6524]. Elioenai, "*my eyes [look] to Yahweh*":– Elioenai (7)

H494 אֶלְיַחְבָּא *'elyaḥbā'*, n.pr.m. [2] [√ 446 + 2461]. Eliahba, "*God [El] hides*":– Eliahba (2)

H495 אֱלִיחֹרֶף *'ᵉlîḥōrep*, n.pr.m. [1] Elihoreph:– Elihoreph (1)

H496 אֱלִיל *'ᵉlîl*, n.m. [20] [→ 470]. idols, images, gods:– idols (15), worthless (2), idolatries (1), images (1), NDT (1)

H497 אֱלִימֶלֶךְ *'ᵉlîmelek*, n.pr.m. [6] [√ 446 + 4889]. Elimelech, "*God [El] is [my] king*":– Elimelek (6)

H498 אֶלְיָסָף *'elyāsāp*, n.pr.m. [6] [√ 446 + 3578]. Eliasaph, "*God [El] has added*":– Eliasaph (6)

H499 אֱלִיעֶזֶר *'ᵉlî'ezer*, n.pr.m. [14] [√ 446 + 6469]. Eliezer, "*God [El] is [my] help*":– Eliezer (14)

H500 אֱלִיעָם *'ᵉlî'ām*, n.pr.m. [2] [√ 446 + 6639]. Eliam, "*God [El] is [my] kinsman*":– Eliam (2)

H501 אֱלִיעֵינַי *'ᵉlî'ênay*, n.pr.m. [1] [√ 448 + 3378 + 6524]. Elienai, "*my eyes [look] to Yahweh*":– Elienai (1)

H502 אֱלִיפַז *'ᵉlîpaz*, n.pr.m. [15] [√ 446 + 7058]. Eliphaz, "*God [El] is fine gold* or *God crushes*":– Eliphaz (14), him[s] (1)

H503 אֱלִיפַל *'ᵉlîpal*, n.pr.m. [1] [√ 446 + 7136]. Eliphal, "*[my] God [El] sit in judgment*":– Eliphal (1)

H504 אֱלִיפְלֵהוּ *'ᵉlîpᵉlēhû*, n.pr.m. [2] [√ 446 + 7098?]. Eliphelehu, "*God [El] distinguish him!*":– Eliphelehu (2)

H505 אֱלִיפֶלֶט *'ᵉlîpeleṭ*, n.pr.m. [8] [√ 446 + 7118]. Eliphelet, "*God [El] is [my] deliverance*":– Eliphelet (8)

H506 אֱלִיצוּר *'ᵉlîṣûr*, n.pr.m. [5] [√ 446 + 7446]. Elizur, "*God [El] is [my] Rock*":– Elizur (5)

H507 אֱלִיצָפָן *'ᵉlîṣāpān*, n.pr.m. [4] [√ 446 + 7621]. Elizaphan, "*God [El] is [my] hiding place*":– Elizaphan (4)

H508 אֱלִיקָא *'ᵉlîqā'*, n.pr.m. [1] [√ 446 + 7756?]. Elika:– Elika (1)

H509 אֶלְיָקִים *'elyāqîm*, n.pr.m. [12] [√ 446 + 7756]. Eliakim, "*God [El] establishes*":– Eliakim (12)

H510 אֱלִישֶׁבַע *'ᵉlîšeba'*, n.pr.f. [1] [√ 446 + 8682]. Elisheba, "*God [El] is an oath; God [El] is my fill*":– Elisheba (1)

H511 אֱלִישָׁה *'ᵉlîšâ*, n.pr.loc. [3] Elishah, "*God [El] saves*":– Elishah (3)

H512 אֱלִישׁוּעַ ***'ᵉlîšûa'***, n.pr.m. [3] [√ 446 + 8775]. Elishua, "*God [El] is my salvation*":– Elishua (3)

H513 אֶלְיָשִׁיב ***'elyāšîb***, n.pr.m. [17] [√ 446 + 8740]. Eliashib, "*God [El] restores*":– Eliashib (15), Eliashib's (1), it[S] (1 [+1074])

H514 אֱלִישָׁמָע ***'ᵉlîšāmā'***, n.pr.m. [16] [√ 446 + 9048]. Elishama, "*God [El] has heard*":– Elishama (16)

H515 אֱלִישָׁע ***'ᵉlîšā'***, n.pr.m. [58] [√ 446 + 3828?]. Elisha, "*God [El] is [my] salvation*":– Elisha (54), Elisha's (3), he[S] (1)

H516 אֱלִישָׁפָט ***'ᵉlîšāpāṭ***, n.pr.m. [1] [√ 446 + 9149]. Elishaphat, "*God [El] is [my] judge*":– Elishaphat (1)

H517 אֱלִיָּתָה ***'ᵉliyyātâ***, n.pr.m. [1] [√ 446 + 910]. Eliathah, "*God [El] comes*":– Eliathah (1)

H518 אַלְלַי ***'allay***, interj. [2] Woe!, What misery!, Alas!:– what misery (1), woe (1)

H519 [1]אָלַם ***'ālam[1]***, v. [8] [→ 522, 532]. [N] to be silenced, be speechless:– silent (5), be silenced (1), speechless (1), utterly silent (1 [+1875])

H520 [2]אָלַם ***'ālam[2]***, v. [1] [→ 524]. [P] to bind:– binding (1)

H521 אֵלֶם ***'ēlem***, n.[m.] Not used in NIVEBC [cf. 519?, 520?]. silence [?]

H522 אִלֵּם ***'illēm***, a. [6] [√ 519]. mute, unable to speak:– mute (4), cannot speak (1), those who cannot speak (1)

H523 אַלְמֻגִּים ***'almuggîm***, n.[m.]pl. [3] [cf. 454]. almugwood; a transliteration of the Hebrew, the exact identification of which is uncertain:– almugwood (3 [+6770])

H524 אֲלֻמָּה ***'ᵃlummâ***, n.f. [5] [√ 520]. sheaf:– sheaves (2), it[S] (1), sheaf (1), sheaves of grain (1)

H525 אַלְמוֹדָד ***'almôdād***, n.pr. [2] Almodad, "*God [El] is loved*":– Almodad (2)

H526 אַלַּמֶּלֶךְ ***'allammelek***, n.pr.loc. [1] [√ 464? + 4889]. Allammelech, "*oak of the king* or *oak of Molech*":– Allammelek (1)

H527 [1]אַלְמָן ***'almān[1]***, a. [1] [√ 530]. widowed (one forsaken):– forsaken (1)

H528 [2]אַלְמָן ***'almān[2]***, n.[f.] [2] [cf. 810]. stronghold:– strongholds (2)

H529 אַלְמֹן ***'almōn***, n.[m.] [1] [√ 530]. widowhood:– widowhood (1)

H530 אַלְמָנָה ***'almānâ***, n.f. [54] [→ 527, 529, 531]. widow:– widow (31), widows (18), widow's (4), NDT (1)

H531 אַלְמָנוּת ***'almānût***, n.f. [4] [√ 530]. widowhood:– widow's (2), widowhood (1), widows (1)

H532 אַלְמֹנִי ***'almōnî***, a. [3] [√ 519; cf. 7140, 7141]. a certain so-and-so, whoever, wherever, with a focus that this is not named or spoken out loud:– certain (1 [+7141]), friend (1 [+7141]), such and such (1 [+7141])

H533 אֵלֹנִי ***'ēlōnî***, a.g. [1] [√ 472; cf. 391]. Elonite, "*of Elon*":– Elonite (1)

H534 אֶלְנָעַם ***'elnā'am***, n.pr.m. [1] [√ 446 + 5840]. Elnaam, "*God [El] is pleasantness*":– Elnaam (1)

H535 אֶלְנָתָן ***'elnātān***, n.pr.m. [7] [√ 446 + 5989]. Elnathan, "*God [El] is given*":– Elnathan (7)

H536 אֶלָּסָר ***'ellāsār***, n.pr.loc. [2] Ellasar:– Ellasar (2)

H537 אֶלְעָד ***'el'ād***, n.pr.m. [1] [√ 446 + 6386]. Elead, "*God [El] has testified*":– Elead (1)

H538 אֶלְעָדָה ***'el'ādâ***, n.pr.m. [1] [√ 446 + 6335]. Eleadah, "*God [El] has adorned*":– Eleadah (1)

H539 אֶלְעוּזַי ***'el'ûzay***, n.pr.m. [1] [√ 446 + 6437?]. Eluzai, "*God [El] is my strength*":– Eluzai (1)

H540 אֶלְעָזָר ***'el'āzār***, n.pr.m. [72] [√ 446 + 6468]. Eleazar, "*God [El] is a help*":– Eleazar (70), Eleazar's (2)

H541 אֶלְעָלֵא ***'el'ālē'***, n.pr.loc. [1] [√ 446 + 6590]. Elealeh, "*God [El] is high*":– Elealeh (1)

H542 אֶלְעָלֵה ***'el'ālēh***, n.pr.loc. [4] [√ 446? + 6590]. Elealeh, "*God [El] is high*":– Elealeh (4)

H543 אֶלְעָשָׂה ***'el'āśâ***, n.pr.m. [6] [√ 446 + 6913]. Eleasah, "*God [El] has fashioned*":– Eleasah (4), Elasah (2)

H544 [1]אָלַף ***'ālap[1]***, v. [4] [→ 476]. [Q] to learn, become familiar with; [P] to teach, instruct:– learn (1), prompts (1), teach (1), teaches (1)

H545 [2]אָלַף ***'ālap[2]***, v.den. [1] [→ 477, 547, 548; cf. 546]. [H] to increase by thousands, produce in abundance:– increase by thousands (1)

H546 [1]אֶלֶף ***'elep[1]***, n.m. [7] [→ 477, 548; cf. 544]. cattle herd; oxen:– herds (5), oxen (2)

H547 [2]אֶלֶף ***'elep[2]***, n.m. [495] [√ 545; 10038]. thousand:– thousand (222), thousands (33), 25,000 (14 [+2822, 2256, 6929]), 24,000 (13 [+6929, 2256, 752]), 10,000 (9 [+6930]), 4,500 (8 [+2822, 4395, 2256, 752]), 1,000 (5), million (4 [+547]), 1,254 (3 [+4395, 2822, 2256, 752]), 40,500 (3 [+752, 2256, 2822, 4395]), 5,000 (3 [+2822]), 53,400 (3 [+8993, 2256, 2822, 2256, 752, 4395]), eleven hundred (3 [+2256, 4395]), 1,052 (2 [+2822, 2256, 9109]), 1,247 (2 [+4395, 752, 2256, 8679]), 1,775 (2 [+2256, 8679, 4395, 2256, 2822, 2256, 8679]), 16,000 (2 [+9252, 6925]), 18,000 (2 [+9046, 6925]), 200,000 (2 [+4395]), 3,600 (2 [+8993, 2256, 9252, 4395]), 30,500 (2 [+8993, 2256, 2822, 4395]), 32,200 (2 [+9109, 2256, 8993, 2256, 4395]), 35,400 (2 [+2822, 2256, 8993, 2256, 752, 4395]), 36,000 (2 [+9252, 2256, 8993]), 4,600 (2 [+752, 2256, 9252, 4395]), 41,500 (2 [+285, 2256, 752, 2256, 2822, 4395]), 45,650 (2 [+2822, 2256, 752, 2256, 9252, 4395, 2256, 2822]), 46,500 (2 [+9252, 2256, 752, 2256, 2822, 4395]), 54,400 (2 [+752, 2256, 2822, 2256, 752, 4395]), 57,400 (2 [+8679, 2256, 2822, 2256, 752, 4395]), 59,300 (2 [+9596, 2256, 2822, 2256, 8993, 4395]), 6,720 (2 [+9252, 8679, 4395, 2256, 6929]), 62,700 (2 [+9109, 2256, 9252, 2256, 8679, 4395]), 7,337 (2 [+8679, 8993, 4395, 8993, 2256, 8679]), 70,000 (2 [+8679]), 74,600 (2 [+752, 2256, 8679, 2256, 9252, 4395]), 80,000 (2 [+9046]), fourteen hundred (2 [+2256, 752, 4395]), thousand generations (2), units of a thousand (2), 1,017 (1 [+8679, 6925]), 1,017 (1 [+2256, 8679, 6925]), 1,222 (1 [+4395, 6929, 2256, 9109]), 1,254 (1 [+4395, 2256, 752, 2822]), 1,290 (1 [+4395, 2256, 9596]), 1,335 (1 [+8993, 4395, 8993, 2256, 2822]), 1,365 (1 [+2822, 2256, 9252, 2256, 8993, 4395, 2256]), 1,760 (1 [+2256, 8679, 4395, 2256, 9252]), 108,100 (1 [+4395, 2256, 9046, 547, 2256, 4395]), 108,100 (1 [+4395, 547, 2256, 9046, 2256, 4395]), 120,000 (1 [+4395, 2256, 6929]), 14,700 (1 [+752, 6925, 2256, 8679, 4395]), 151,450 (1 [+4395, 2256, 285, 2822, 547, 752, 4395, 2822, 2256, 2256, 2256]), 151,450 (1 [+4395, 547, 2256, 285, 2822, 752, 4395, 2822, 2256, 2256, 2256]), 153,600 (1 [+4395, 2256, 2822, 2256, 8993, 547, 2256, 9252, 4395]), 153,600 (1 [+4395, 2256, 2822, 547, 2256, 8993, 2256, 9252, 4395]), 157,600 (1 [+4395, 2256, 8679, 2256, 2822, 547, 9252, 4395, 2256]), 157,600 (1 [+4395, 547, 2256, 8679, 2256, 2822, 9252, 4395, 2256]), 16,750 (1 [+9252, 6925, 8679, 4395, 2256, 2822]), 17,200 (1 [+8679, 6925, 2256, 4395]), 180,000 (1 [+4395, 2256, 9046]), 186,400 (1 [+4395, 2256, 9046, 547, 9252, 547, 752, 4395, 2256, 2256]), 186,400 (1 [+4395, 547, 2256, 9046, 9252, 547, 752, 4395, 2256, 2256]), 186,400 (1 [+4395, 547, 2256, 9046, 547, 9252, 752, 4395, 2256, 2256]), 2,000 (1), 2,056 (1 [+2822, 2256, 9252]), 2,067 (1 [+9252, 2256, 8679]), 2,172 (1 [+4395, 8679, 2256, 9109]), 2,172 (1 [+4395, 2256, 8679, 2256, 9109]), 2,200 (1 [+2256, 4395]), 2,300 (1 [+2256, 8993, 4395]), 2,322 (1 [+8993, 4395, 6929, 2256, 9109]), 2,400 (1 [+2256, 752, 4395]), 2,600 (1 [+2256, 9252, 4395]), 2,630 (1 [+2256, 9252, 4395, 2256, 8993]), 2,750 (1 [+8679, 4395, 2256, 2822]), 2,812 (1 [+9046, 4395, 2256, 9109, 6925]), 2,818 (1 [+2256, 9046, 4395, 9046, 6925]), 20,000 (1 [+6929]), 20,200 (1 [+6929, 2256, 4395]), 20,800 (1 [+6929, 2256, 9046, 4395]), 22,000 (1 [+9109, 2256, 6929]), 22,034 (1 [+6929, 2256, 9109, 2256, 8993, 2256, 752]), 22,200 (1 [+9109, 2256, 6929, 2256, 4395]), 22,273 (1 [+9109, 2256, 6929, 8993, 2256, 8679, 2256, 4395]), 22,600 (1 [+6929, 2256, 9109, 2256, 9252, 4395]), 23,000 (1 [+8993, 2256, 6929]), 24,000 (1 [+752, 2256, 6929]), 25,100 (1 [+6929, 2256, 2822, 2256, 4395]), 26,000 (1 [+6929, 2256, 9252]), 28,600 (1 [+6929, 2256, 9046, 2256, 9252, 4395]), 280,000 (1 [+4395, 2256, 9046]), 3,000 (1 [+8993]), 3,023 (1 [+8993, 2256, 6929, 2256, 8993]), 3,200 (1 [+8993, 2256, 4395]), 3,630 (1 [+8993, 2256, 9252, 4395, 2256, 8993]), 3,700 (1 [+8993, 2256, 8679, 4395]), 3,930 (1 [+8993, 9596, 4395, 2256, 8993]), 300,000 (1 [+8993, 4395]), 307,500 (1 [+8993, 4395, 2256, 8679, 547, 2256, 2822, 4395]), 307,500 (1 [+8993, 4395, 547, 2256, 8679, 2256, 2822, 4395]), 32,000 (1 [+9109, 2256, 8993]), 32,500 (1 [+9109, 2256, 8993, 2256, 2822, 4395]), 337,500 (1 [+8993, 4395, 2256, 8993, 547, 8679, 547, 2256, 2822, 4395]), 337,500 (1 [+8993, 4395, 547, 2256, 8993, 8679, 547, 2256, 2822, 4395]), 337,500 (1 [+8993, 4395, 547, 2256, 8993, 547, 8679, 2256, 2822, 4395]), 337,500 (1 [+8993, 4395, 2256, 8993, 547, 2256, 8679, 547, 2256, 2822, 4395]), 337,500 (1 [+8993, 4395, 547, 2256, 8993, 2256, 8679, 547, 2256, 2822, 4395]), 337,500 (1 [+8993, 4395, 547, 2256, 8993, 547, 2256, 8679, 2256, 2822, 4395]), 36,000 (1 [+8993, 2256, 9252]), 37,000 (1 [+8993, 2256, 8679]), 40,000 (1 [+752]), 42,360 (1 [+752, 8052, 8993, 4395, 9252]), 42,360 (1 [+752, 8052, 8993, 4395, 2256, 9252]), 43,730 (1 [+8993, 2256, 752, 2256, 8679, 4395, 2256, 8993]), 44,760 (1 [+752, 2256, 752, 2256, 8679, 4395, 2256, 9252]), 45,400 (1 [+2822, 2256, 752, 2256, 752, 4395]), 45,600 (1 [+2822, 2256, 752, 2256, 9252, 4395]), 5,400 (1 [+2822, 2256, 752, 4395]), 50,000 (1 [+2822]), 52,700 (1 [+9109, 2256, 2822, 2256, 8679, 4395]), 6,200 (1 [+9252, 2256, 4395]), 6,800 (1 [+9252, 2256, 9046, 4395]), 60,500 (1 [+9252, 2256, 2822, 4395]), 601,730 (1 [+9252, 4395, 2256, 547, 8679, 4395, 2256, 8993]), 601,730 (1 [+9252, 4395, 547, 2256, 8679, 4395, 2256, 8993]), 603,550 (1 [+9252, 4395, 2256, 8993, 547, 2822, 4395, 2822, 2256, 2256]), 603,550 (1 [+9252, 4395, 547, 2256, 8993, 2822, 4395, 2822, 2256, 2256]), 603,550 (1 [+9252, 4395, 8993, 547, 2822, 4395, 2822, 2256, 2256, 2256]), 603,550 (1 [+9252, 4395, 547, 8993, 2822, 4395, 2822, 2256, 2256, 2256]), 603,550 (1 [+9252, 4395, 2256, 8993, 547, 2256, 2822, 4395, 2256, 2822]), 603,550 (1 [+9252, 4395, 547, 2256, 8993, 2256, 2822, 4395, 2256, 2822]), 61,000 (1 [+9252, 8052, 2256]), 61,000 (1 [+285, 2256, 9252]), 64,300 (1 [+752, 2256, 9252, 2256, 8993, 4395]), 64,400 (1 [+752, 2256, 9252, 2256, 752, 4395]), 675,000 (1 [+9252, 4395, 2256, 8679, 547, 2256, 2822, 547]), 675,000 (1 [+9252, 4395, 547, 2256, 8679, 2256, 2822, 547]), 675,000 (1 [+9252, 4395, 547, 2256, 8679, 547, 2256, 2822]), 7,000 (1 [+8679]), 7,100 (1 [+8679, 2256, 4395]), 7,500 (1 [+8679, 2256, 2822, 4395]), 72,000 (1 [+9109, 2256, 8679]), 76,500 (1 [+9252, 2256, 8679, 2256, 2822, 4395]), 8,580 (1 [+9046, 2256, 2822, 4395, 2256, 9046]), 8,600 (1 [+9046, 2256, 9252, 4395]), 87,000 (1 [+9046, 2256, 8679]), eighteen thousand (1 [+8052, 2256, 9046]), seventeen hundred (1 [+8679, 4395, 2256]), seventeen hundred (1 [+2256, 8679, 4395]), thirty-three hundred (1 [+8993, 2256, 8993, 4395]), twelve hundred (1 [+2256, 4395]), twenty-seven hundred (1 [+2256, 8679, 4395]), twenty-six hundred (1 [+2256, 9252, 4395]), units of 1,000 (1), NDT (3)

H548 [3]אֶלֶף ***'elep[3]***, n.m. [12] [√ 545]. by extension from "thousand," this refers to any large unit or group: (family) clan, (military) unit:– clans (9), clan (1), unit (1), units (1)

H549 [4]אֶלֶף ***'elep[4]***, n.pr.loc. Eleph, see 2030

H550 אֱלִפֶּלֶט ***'elpelet***, n.pr.m. [1] [√ 446 + 7118]. Elpelet, "*God [El] is deliverance*":– Elpelet (1)

H551 אֶלְפַּעַל ***'elpa'al***, n.pr.m. [3] [√ 446 + 7188]. Elpaal, "*God [El] creates*":– Elpaal (3)

H552 אָלַץ ***'ālaṣ***, v. [1] [P] to prod, urge, a fig. extension of pressing one object hard against another, not found in the OT:– prodded (1)

H553 אֶלְצָפָן ***'elṣāpān***, n.pr.m. [2] [√ 446 + 7621]. Elzaphan, "*God [El] is [my] hiding place*":– Elzaphan (2)

H554 אַלְקוּם ***'alqûm***, n.[m.]? army

H555 אֶלְקָנָה ***'elqānâ***, n.pr.m. [21] [√ 446 + 7865]. Elkanah, "*God [El] has possessed*":– Elkanah (20), NDT (1)

H556 אֶלְקֹשִׁי ***'elqōšî***, a.g. [1] Elkoshite, "*of Elkosh*":– Elkoshite (1)

H557 אֶלְתּוֹלַד ***'eltôlad***, n.pr.loc. [2] [cf. 9351]. Eltolad, "*generation; kindred of God [El]; place where God [El] gives children*":– Eltolad (2)

H558 אֶלְתְּקֵא ***'eltᵉqē'***, n.pr.loc. [1] [→ 559]. Eltekeh, "*meeting place*":– Eltekeh (1)

H559 אֶלְתְּקֵה ***'eltᵉqēh***, n.pr.loc. [1] [√ 558]. Eltekeh, "*meeting place*":– Eltekeh (1)

H560 אֶלְתְּקֹן ***'eltᵉqōn***, n.pr.loc. [1] Eltekon, "*God [El] has arranged*":– Eltekon (1)

H561 אִם ***'im***, c. & pt.inter. [1072] [→ 467, 3955]. if, whether, or; whenever, as often as:– if (513), but (39 [+3954]), or (39), not (34), when (28), except (24 [+3954]), though (22), only (18), surely (14 [+4202]), whether (14), even if (9), if (9 [+3954]), that (8), no (7), but if (6), since (6), unless (6 [+3954]), although (5), or (5 [+2256]), never (4), unless (4 [+4202]), yet if (4), and (3), however (3 [+3954]), neither (3), only if (3), until (3 [+6330]), whenever (3), but only (2 [+3954]), don't (2), even (2), if only (2), instead (2 [+3954]), nor (2), other than (2 [+3954]), surely (2 [+3954]), than (2 [+3954]), that (2 [+4202]), though (2 [+3954]), whether (2 [+4202]), without (2 [+3954]), after (1 [+3983]), although (1 [+3954]), as (1), as if (1), as long as (1 [+6388]), because (1), because (1 [+4202, 3610]), but (1), but (1 [+4202]), but (1 [+4202]), cannot (1), certainly (1 [+4202]), even (1 [+3954]), even though (1), except (1 [+1194]), however (1), if (1 [+3907]), if (1 [+3907]), if indeed (1), indeed (1 [+3954]), never (1 [+2721]), never (1 [+4200, 5905]), never (1 [+6330, 6409]), nor (1 [+2256]), not (1 [+3954]), not even (1), not one (1), nothing (1 [+4946, 3972]), or (1 [+2256, 401]), other than (1), otherwise (1), please (1), provided (1 [+421]), rather (1), rather (1 [+3954]), so (1), so (1 [+4202, 3610]), suppose (1), surely (1 [+401]), till (1 [+4202]), till (1 [+6330]), unless (1 [+1194]), unless (1 [+4202, 3954]), unless (1 [+3954, 4200, 7156]), until (1 [+3954]), until (1 [+4202]), until (1 [+6330, 889]), until (1 [+6330, 889]), whether (1 [+2022, 4202]), while (1), why (1 [+4027, 4200, 4537]), won't until (1 [+3954]), yet (1 [+3954]), you (1 [+3870]), NDT (156)

H562 אֵם ***'ēm***, n.f. [220] [→ 566]. mother, grandmother, ancestress; by extension: a term of endearment; caregiver; fork (in a road):– mother (134), mother's (61), mothers (9), parents (3 [+3, 2256]), grandmother (2), she[S] (2 [+2257]), birth (1 [+1061]), brothers (1 [+278]), fork (1), grandmother's (1), uncle (1 [+278]), uncle's (1 [+278]), very own brother (1 [+278, 1201, 3870]), NDT (2)

H563 אָמָה ***'āmâ***, n.f. [56] slave woman; female servant, maidservant:– servant (15), female servants (9), female slave (6), female servant (5), female slaves (5), servant's (3), slave girls (2), slave woman (2), her[S] (1 [+3870]), just as mother did[S] (1), me[S] (1 [+3870]), serve just as mother (1), slave (1), slave born in household (1 [+1201]), slaves (1 [+6269, 2256]), woman (1), woman's (1)

H564 [1]אַמָּה ***'ammâ[1]***, n.f. [250] [√ 10039]. cubit (measurement of length, from the elbow to end of fingers, about 18 to 22 inches [about half a meter]); an unspecified unit of time:– cubits (185), cubit (38), long cubits (2), doorposts (1), time (1), NDT (23)

H565 [2]אַמָּה **'ammâ[2]**, n.pr.loc. [1] Ammah, "*cubit*":– Ammah (1)

H566 [3]אַמָּה **'ammâ[3]**, n.f. Not used in NIVEBC [√ 562]. mother-city, metropolis

H567 [4]אַמָּה **'ammâ[4]**, n.f. pivot (of a door)

H568 אֵמָה **'ēmâ**, n.f. Not used in NIVEBC [cf. 564]. see 4395

H569 אֻמָּה **'ummâ**, n.f. [3] [√ 10040]. tribe, clan:– tribal (2), peoples (1)

H570 [1]אָמוֹן **'āmôn[1]**, n.m. [1] [→ 588]. craftsman:– craftsmen (1)

H571 [2]אָמוֹן **'āmôn[2]**, n.pr.m. [17] [→ 577; cf. 572, 586]. Amon, "*trustworthy*":– Amon (15), Amon's (2)

H572 [3]אָמוֹן **'āmôn[3]**, n.pr.[m.] [1] [→ 5531; cf. 571, 586]. Amon (pagan god), "*trustworthy*":– Amon (1)

H573 [1]אֵמוּן **'ēmûn[1]**, n.[m.] [2] [√ 586]. faithful:– faithful (1), true (1)

H574 [2]אֵמוּן **'ēmûn[2]**, n.[m.] [6] [√ 586]. faithful, trustworthy:– faith (1), faithful (1), honest (1), loyal (1), trustworthy (1), unfaithful (1 [+4202])

H575 אֱמוּנָה **'ᵉmûnâ**, n.f. [49] [√ 586]. faithfulness, steadiness, trustworthiness:– faithfulness (23), faithful (5), faithfully (4 [+928]), truth (4), trustworthy (3), entrusted with (2 [+928]), honest (2), complete honesty (1), integrity (1), safe (1), steady (1), sure foundation (1), trust (1)

H576 אָמוֹץ **'āmôṣ**, n.pr.m. [13] [√ 599]. Amoz, "*strong*":– Amoz (13)

H577 אָמִי **'āmî**, n.pr.m. [1] [√ 571; cf. 586]. Ami, "*trustworthy, reliable, faithful*":– Ami (1)

H578 אֲמִינוֹן **'ᵃmînôn**, n.pr.m. [1] [√ 596; cf. 586]. Amnon, "*trustworthy*":– Amnon (1)

H579 אַמִּיץ **'ammîṣ**, a. [6] [√ 599]. strong, mighty, brave:– mighty (2), bravest (1 [+4213]), strength (1), strong (1), vast (1)

H580 אָמִיר **'āmîr**, n.m. [2] [√ 607]. branch:– branches (1), undergrowth (1)

H581 [1]אָמַל **'āmal[1]**, v. [15] [→ 583, 584; cf. 4908]. [Qp] to be weak-willed; [Pul] to wither, languish, fade away:– languish (2), wither (2), fade (1), fails (1), faint (1), languishes (1), pine away (1), pines away (1), waste away (1), wasted away (1), wastes away (1), withered (1), withers (1)

H582 [2]אָמַל **'āmal[2]**, v. [1] [cf. 4908]. [Qp] to be hot, feverish:– filled with fury against (1 [+4226])

H583 אֻמְלַל **'umlal**, a. [1] [√ 581]. faint, fading away:– faint (1)

H584 אֲמֵלָל **'ᵃmēlāl**, a. [1] [√ 581]. feeble, fading:– feeble (1)

H585 אֲמָם **'ᵃmām**, n.pr.loc. [1] [→ 5497]. Amam:– Amam (1)

H586 [1]אָמַן **'āman[1]**, v. [98] [→ 571, 572, 573, 574, 575, 577, 578, 587, 589, 590, 591, 593, 594, 595, 596, 597, 2124?; 10041, 10327]. [N] to be faithful, be trustworthy, be established; [H] to believe, trust, have confidence:– believe (20), faithful (14), trust (9), believed (6), trustworthy (5), be established (2), come true (2), firm (2), have faith (2), places trust (2), put trust (2), trusted (2), be confirmed (1), be trusted (1), be upheld (1), be verified (1), certain (1), confident (1), constantly (1), despairs (1 [+4202]), endure (1), enduring (1), fails (1 [+4202]), firmly (1), have assurance (1), lasting (1), lingering (1), loyal (1), never fail (1), not fail (1), prolonged (1), reliable (1), relies on (1), stand (1), stand firm (1 [+4394]), stand firm in faith (1), stand still (1), sure (1), trusted advisers (1), trusting (1), trustworthy (1 [+8120]), was attested (1)

H587 [2]אָמַן **'āman[2]**, v. [9] [√ 586]. [Q] to nurse, nurture, care for; be a trustee, be a guardian; [Qp, N] to be nurtured, cared for:– brought up (2), nurse (2), are carried (1), cared (1), foster fathers (1), guardians (1), guardians of children (1)

H588 אָמָּן **'ommān**, n.m. [1] [√ 570]. craftsman:– artist's (1)

H589 אָמֵן **'āmēn**, adv. [30] [√ 586]. amen, surely; truth:– amen (26), amen so be it (2 [+589]), true (2)

H590 אֹמֶן **'ōmen**, n.[m.] [1] [→ 597, 598; cf. 586]. faithfulness:– perfect (1)

H591 [1]אֲמָנָה **'ᵃmānâ[1]**, n.f. [2] [√ 586]. binding agreement, trustworthy agreement:– binding agreement (1), regulated (1)

H592 [2]אֲמָנָה **'ᵃmānâ[2]**, n.pr.loc. [1] [cf. 76]. Amana, "*constant*":– Amana (1)

H593 [1]אָמְנָה **'omnâ[1]**, adv. [2] [√ 586]. really, truly, indeed:– really (1), true (1)

H594 [2]אָמְנָה **'omnâ[2]**, n.f. [1] [√ 586]. bringing up, caring, tending, fostering:– bringing up (1)

H595 אֹמְנָה **'ōmᵉnâ**, subst. [1] [√ 586?]. doorpost:– doorposts (1)

H596 אַמְנוֹן **'amnôn**, n.pr.m. [27] [→ 578; cf. 586]. Amnon, "*trustworthy*":– Amnon (25), Amnon's (1), him[s] (1)

H597 אָמְנָם **'omnām**, adv. [9] [→ 598; cf. 590, 586]. indeed, truly, assuredly:– true (4), indeed (2), be assured (1), doubtless (1), unthinkable (1 [+4202])

H598 אֻמְנָם **'umnām**, adv. [5] [√ 597; cf. 590, 586]. really, indeed; used in interrogative sentences:– really (3), indeed (1), really (1 [+677])

H599 אָמֵץ **'āmēṣ**, v. [41] [→ 576, 579, 600, 601, 602, 4410; *also used with compound proper names*]. [Q] to be strong, courageous; [P] to strengthen, support, establish; harden; [Ht] to persist, determine:– courageous (11), strong (4), strengthen (3), managed (2), muster (2), raised up (2), determined (1), encourage (1), established (1), hardened (1), hardhearted (1 [+906, 4222]), let grow (1), marshal (1), obstinate (1), opposed (1 [+6584]), reinforced (1), steady (1), strengthened (1), stronger (1), supported (1), take heart (1 [+4213]), take heart (1 [+4222]), victorious (1)

H600 אָמֹץ **'āmōṣ**, a. [2] [√ 599]. powerful, strong:– powerful (2)

H601 אֹמֶץ **'ōmeṣ**, n.[m.] [1] [√ 599]. strength:– grow stronger (1 [+3578])

H602 אַמְצָה **'amṣâ**, n.f. [1] [√ 599]. strength:– strong (1)

H603 אַמְצִי **'amṣî**, n.pr.m. [2] [√ 599; cf. 604?]. Amzi, "[poss.] *[Yahweh is] my strength*":– Amzi (2)

H604 אֲמַצְיָה **'ᵃmaṣyâ**, n.pr.m. [9] [→ 603?, 605; cf. 599 + 3378]. Amaziah, "*Yahweh is powerful*":– Amaziah (9)

H605 אֲמַצְיָהוּ **'ᵃmaṣyāhû**, n.pr.m. [31] [√ 604; cf. 599 + 3378]. Amaziah, "*Yahweh is powerful*":– Amaziah (29), Amaziah's (2)

H606 [1]אָמַר **'āmar[1]**, v. [5273] [→ 223, 608, 609, 614, 615, 4411; 10042; *also used with compound proper names*]. [Q, H] to say, speak, think (say to oneself); [Qp, N] to be said; note the many contextual renderings in the NIV:– said (1958), says (608), say (508), asked (213), replied (188), answered (162), saying (137), tell (88), told (84), ask (45), thought (45), ordered (28), message (18), added (15), commanded (13), spoke (13), answer (12), speak (12), promised (11), declared (9), shouted (9), continued (8), word (8), spoke (7 [+5951, 2256]), called (6), cried (6), prayed (6), think (6), thinking (6), gave orders (5), tells (5), asking (4), be said (4), call (4), exclaimed (4), reply (4), reported (4), say (4 [+606]), spoken (4), asks (3), be called (3), called out (3), claim (3), cried out (3), declare (3), intend (3), suggested (3), announced (2), be (2), challenge (2), command (2), commands (2), complain (2), cry out (2), declares (2 [+606]), demanding (2), is said (2), keep saying (2 [+606]), name (2), order (2), promised (2 [+606]), read (2), replied (2 [+8938]), responded (2), set (2), shout (2), shouting (2), show (2), so sure (2 [+606]), talked (2), telling (2), thinks (2), want (2), add (1), advised (1), afraid[s] (1), agreed (1), assured (1), be named (1), be told (1), been given (1), boast (1), boasted (1), boasts (1), brought up (1), call out (1), calling out (1), calls (1), came (1), claimed (1), claims (1), commemorate (1), confessed (1), cries (1), cry (1), cry out (1 [+5951, 4200]), demand (1), demanded (1), demanded of (1), directed (1), exclaim (1), explain (1), gave (1), gave an order (1), gave the order (1), give (1), goes (1), greeted (1), heard (1 [+928, 265]), indicate (1), indicated (1), inquired of (1 [+448]), insisted (1), instructed (1), intended (1), issued orders (1), makes speech (1 [+609]), news (1), objected (1), offered (1), plan (1), plead (1), proclaiming (1), proposed (1), protest (1), provided (1), question (1), realize (1 [+4200, 4222]), recite (1), recite (1 [+6699, 2256]), repeated (1), replies (1), report (1), reporting (1), respond (1), say (1 [+6699, 2256]), saying (1 [+4200]), search (1 [+928]), sent word (1), snorts (1), solemnly swear (1), speaks (1), spoke up (1), spoken out (1 [+6218]), suggest (1), swear (1), talking (1), tell (1 [+1821]), tell story (1), think (1 [+928, 4213]), think (1 [+928, 4222]), thinking (1 [+928, 4222]), thought (1 [+448, 3276]), told (1 [+8938, 4200]), urged (1), use (1), used (1), uttered (1), wanted (1), warned (1), warning (1), was said (1), was told (1), words (1), NDT (835)

H607 [2]אָמַר **'āmar[2]**, v. [2] [→ 580, 610, 9473]. [Ht] to boast:– boast (1), full of boasting (1)

H608 אֹמֶר **'ōmer**, n.m. [5] [√ 606]. saying, word:– speech (2), promise (1), what[s] (1), word (1)

H609 [1]אֵמֶר **'ēmer[1]**, n.m. [48] [√ 606]. word, saying:– words (31), arguments (2), what say (2 [+7023]), words (2 [+7023]), appointed (1), commands (1), keeps saying (1 [+8740]), lies (1 [+9214]), makes speech (1 [+606]), pleading (1), reports (1), speak (1), what decreed (1 [+7023]), what said (1 [+7023]), what say (1)

H610 [2]אֵמֶר **'ēmer[2]**, n.m. Not used in NIVEBC [√ 607]. branched antlers or lamb

H611 [1]אִמֵּר **'immēr[1]**, n.m. [1] [→ 612, 613; 10043]. fawn, lamb:– fawns (1)

H612 [2]אִמֵּר **'immēr[2]**, n.pr.m. [8] [√ 611]. Immer, "*lamb*":– Immer (8)

H613 [3]אִמֵּר **'immēr[3]**, n.pr.loc. [2] [√ 611]. Immer, "*lamb*":– Immer (2)

H614 אִמְרָה **'imrâ**, n.f. [37] [√ 606]. word, saying, utterance:– word (12), promise (11), words (4), promises (2), speech (2), command (1), prayer (1), solemn decree (1), what have to say (1), what say (1), NDT (1)

H615 אֶמְרָה **'emrâ**, n.f. Not used in NIVEBC [√ 606]. see 614

H616 אֱמֹרִי **'ᵉmōrî**, a.g. [87] Amorite, "[poss.] *hill dwellers; westerners*":– Amorites (77), Amorite (9), it[s] (1 [+1473, 2021])

H617 אִמְרִי **'imrî**, n.pr.m. [2] [√ 606 + 3378]. Imri, "*Yahweh spoke*":– Imri (2)

H618 אֲמַרְיָה **'ᵃmaryâ**, n.pr.m. [13] [→ 619; cf. 606 + 3378]. Amariah, "*Yahweh has said*":– Amariah (12), Amariah's (1)

H619 אֲמַרְיָהוּ **'ᵃmaryāhû**, n.pr.m. [3] [√ 618; cf. 606 + 3378]. Amariah, "*Yahweh has said*":– Amariah (3)

H620 אַמְרָפֶל **'amrāpel**, n.pr.m. [2] Amraphel:– Amraphel (2)

H621 אֶמֶשׁ **'emeš**, adv. [5] [cf. 5406?]. last night; yesterday (evening):– last night (3), night (1), yesterday (1)

H622 אֱמֶת **'ᵉmet**, n.f. [127] [→ 624; cf. 586]. faithfulness, reliability, trustworthiness; truth, what conforms to reality in contrast to what is false; "the book of truth" is a reliable book, referring to heavenly scroll detailing future things:– faithfulness (39), truth (22), true (19), faithful (8), faithfully (4), faithfully (4 [+928]), sure (4), truthful (4), security (3), honorably (2 [+928]), right (2), truly (2 [+928]), trustworthy (2), assurance (1), assuredly (1 [+928]), fairly (1), fairness (1), faithful (1 [+2143, 928]), faithful care (1), faithfully (1 [+6913]), firm (1), integrity (1), lasting (1), really (1 [+928]), reliable (1)

H623 אַמְתַּחַת **'amtaḥat**, n.f. [15] [√ 5501]. sack:– sack (7), sacks (7), it[s] (1 [+2257])

H624 אֲמִתַּי **'ᵃmittay**, n.pr.m. [2] [√ 622; cf. 586]. Amittai, "*true*":– Amittai (2)

H625 אָן **'ān**, adv. [42] how long?; where?:– where (17 [+2025]), how long (12 [+6330, 2025]), anywhere else (2 [+2025, 2256, 625, 2025]), anywhere else (2 [+625, 2025, 2256, 2025]), where (2), anywhere (1 [+2025, 2256, 625, 2025]), anywhere (1 [+625, 2025, 2256, 2025]), how long (1 [+6330]), when (1 [+6330, 2025]), wherever (1 [+2025]), which way (1 [+2025]), which way (1 [+2025])

H626 אָנָּא **'onnā'**, interj. [6] [√ 629; cf. 5528]. I ask you!, O! (preceding a request):– I ask (1), oh (1), NDT (4)

H627 [1]אָנָה **'ānâ[1]**, v. [3] [→ 230, 640, 3433, 9302; cf. 634, 645]. [Q] to mourn, lament, groan:– groan (1), lament (1), mourning (1)

H628 [2]אָנָה **'ānâ[2]**, v. [4] [→ 9299, 9301]. [P] to make happen; [Pu] to befall, have happen to; [Ht] to pick a quarrel against:– lets happen (1 [+4200, 3338]), overtake (1 [+448]), overtakes (1 [+4200]), trying to pick a quarrel (1)

H629 אָנָּה **'onnâ**, interj. [6] [√ 626; cf. 5528]. I ask you!, O! (preceding a request):– NDT (6)

H630 אָנוּ **'ᵃnû**, p.com.pl. Not used in NIVEBC [√ 636]. we

H631 אָנוּשׁ **'ānûš**, a.vbl. [8] [√ 653; cf. 5683]. incurable, beyond cure; despairing:– incurable (3), beyond cure (1), despair (1), grievous (1), incurable wound (1), no cure (1)

H632 [1]אֱנוֹשׁ **'ᵉnôš[1]**, n.m. [42] [→ 633; cf. 653; 10046, 10050]. man, humankind, mortal, with an emphasis on frailty; "a man of peace" is a "friend":– mortal (9), mortals (9), people (4), human (3), one (3), mankind (2), enemies[s] (1), every (1 [+3972]), friends (1 [+8934]), man (1), mortals (1 [+1201]), mortals (1 [+4637]), ordinary (1), person (1), person's (1), their[s] (1), them[s] (1), very few (1 [+4663])

H633 [2]אֱנוֹשׁ **'ᵉnôš[2]**, n.pr.m. [7] [√ 632; cf. 653]. Enosh, "*[mortal] man*":– Enosh (7)

H634 אָנַח **'ānaḥ**, v. [13] [→ 635; cf. 627, 645, 5664]. [N] to groan, moan:– groan (7), groaning (2), grieve (1), groaned (1), groans (1), moan (1)

H635 אֲנָחָה **'ᵃnāḥâ**, n.f. [11] [√ 634]. groaning, sighing:– groaning (5), sighing (4), groan (1), groans (1)

H636 אֲנַחְנוּ **'ᵃnaḥnû**, p.com.pl. [120] [→ 630, 638, 644, 5721; 10047]. we:– we (103), us (6), we're (2), our (1), NDT (8)

H637 אֲנָחֲרַת **'ᵃnāḥarat**, n.pr.loc. [1] Anaharath:– Anaharath (1)

H638 אֲנִי **'ᵃnî**, p.com.sg. [874] [√ 636; 10044]. I:– I (784), me (30), myself (24), we (6), I'll (3), my (2), I'm (1), each of us (1 [+2256, 2085]), mine (1), my life (1), yes[s] (1), NDT (20)

H639 אֳנִי **'ᵒnî**, n.m. [7] [→ 641]. ships, fleet of ships:– ships (3), fleet (1), fleet of trading ships (1 [+9576]), galley (1), it[s] (1 [+9576])

H640 אֲנִיָּה **'ᵃniyyâ**, n.f. [2] [√ 627]. lamentation, mourning:– lament (1), lamentation (1)

H641 אֳנִיָּה **'ᵒniyyâ**, n.f. [31] [√ 639]. ship, trading ship; (pl.) fleet of ships:– ships (16), ship (3), boats (1), cargo (1 [+3998, 889, 928, 2021]), fleet of ships (1), fleet of trading ships (1 [+9576]), fleet of trading ships (1 [+2143, 9576]), fleet of trading ships (1 [+4200, 2143, 9576]), it[s] (1 [+9576]), sail (1 [+2143, 928, 2021]), sailors (1 [+408]), these[s] (1), they[s] (1), trading ship (1 [+9576])

H642 אֲנִיעָם **'anî'ām**, n.pr.m. [1] Aniam, "*I am kinsman*":– Aniam (1)

H643 אֲנָךְ **'ănāk**, n.[m.] [4] plummet, weight for a plumb line:– plumb line (3), true to plumb (1)

H644 אָנֹכִי **'ānōkî**, p.com.sg. [359] [√ 636]. I:– I (329), I'm (7), me (5), myself (5), I'll (3), it[S] (1), we (1), NDT (8)

H645 אָנַן **'ānan**, v. [2] [cf. 627 *or* 634]. [Htpol] to complain:– complain (1), complained (1)

H646 אָנַס **'ānas**, v. [1] [√ 10048]. [Q] to compel; "there is no compelling" means "to allow":– allowed (1 [+401])

H647 אָנַף **'ānap**, v. [14] [→ 678, 690, 691, 3018; 10049]. [Q] to be, become angry; [Ht] to feel angry:– angry (14)

H648 אָנָף **'ānāp**, n.m. Not used in NIVEBC [√ 678; cf. 647]. face

H649 אֲנָפָה **'ănāpâ**, n.f. [2] heron, an unclean bird:– heron (2)

H650 אָנַק **'ānaq**, v. [4] [→ 651; cf. 5543, 5544]. [Q, N] to groan, lament, sigh:– groan (3), lament (1)

H651 [1]אֲנָקָה **'ănāqâ[1]**, n.f. [4] [√ 650]. groaning, sighing:– groans (2), groan (1), wail (1)

H652 [2]אֲנָקָה **'ănāqâ[2]**, n.f. [1] gecko:– gecko (1)

H653 אָנַשׁ **'ānaš**, v. [1] [→ 631, 632, 633]. [N] be ill, sickly:– ill (1)

H654 אָסָא **'āsā'**, n.pr.m. [58] Asa, "[poss.] *healer; myrtle*":– Asa (50), Asa's (7), NDT (1)

H655 אָסוּךְ **'āsûk**, n.[m.] [1] [√ 6057]. small (oil) jar, flask:– small jar (1)

H656 אָסוֹן **'āsôn**, n.m. [5] serious injury, harm:– harm (3), serious injury (2)

H657 אֵסוּר **'ēsûr**, n.m. [3] [√ 673; 10054]. bindings, chains, fetters, shackles:– bindings (1), chains (1), imprisoned (1 [+5989, 1074, 2021])

H658 אָסִיף **'āsîp**, n.[m.] [3] [√ 665]. (Feast of) Ingathering; harvest (from a threshing floor and winepress before the rainy season):– ingathering (2), harvest (1)

H659 אָסִיר **'āsîr**, n.m. [12] [√ 673]. prisoner, captive:– prisoners (8), captives (2), captive (1), held (1)

H660 [1]אַסִּיר **'assîr[1]**, n.m.[col.] [4] [→ 661; cf. 673]. captive, prisoner:– captives (2), captive (1), prisoners (1)

H661 [2]אַסִּיר **'assîr[2]**, n.pr.m. [4] [√ 660; cf. 673]. Assir, "*prisoner*":– Assir (4)

H662 אָסָם **'āsām**, n.m. [2] barn, storehouse:– barns (2)

H663 אַסְנָה **'asnâ**, n.pr.m. [1] Asnah, "[poss.] *thornbush; he who belongs to Nah*":– Asnah (1)

H664 אָסְנַת **'āsᵉnat**, n.pr.f. [3] Asenath, "*[belonging to] Neith*":– Asenath (3)

H665 אָסַף **'āsap**, v. [200] [→ 658, 666, 667, 668, 669, 670, 671, 4417]. [Q] to store, gather, harvest; [Qp] to be a victim; [N] to be gathered, assembled; [P] to be a rear guard, to bring in, gather; [Pu] to be gathered, collected; [Ht] to assemble; [H] to bring together:– gathered (18), gather (16), assembled (12), be gathered (9), assemble (6), harvest (6), rear guard (5), was gathered (5), brought together (4), called together (4 [+8938, 2256]), gathered together (4), take away (4), are taken away (3), collected (3), cure (3), gather together (3), gathered up (3), mustered (3), accumulated (2), be buried (2 [+448, 7700]), be gathered (2 [+665]), bring (2), came together (2), gather in (2), gather up (2), gathers up (2), no longer shine (2 [+5586]), put (2), surely gather (2 [+665]), withdraw (2), admit (1), are gathered (1), assembled together (1), assembling (1), banded together (1 [+4200, 2021, 2653]), be[S] (1), be brought back (1), be collected (1), be gathered up (1), be herded together (1 [+669]), be recovered (1), been brought (1), been gathered (1), bring back (1), brought (1), brought back (1), called together (1), cured (1), destroy (1), do so more (1), drew up (1), gather around (1), gathering (1), gathers (1), gone (1), got together (1), had brought (1), harvested (1), is gathered in (1), is harvested (1), join (1), join forces (1), joined forces (1), joined forces (1 [+3481]), lose (1), massing together (1), muster (1), rallied (1), receive (1), regrouped (1 [+3480]), remove (1), return (1), returned (1), set aside (1), steal away (1), store away (1), summon (1), sweep away (1 [+6066]), swept away (1), take (1), taken (1), taken away (1), together (1), took (1), took into service (1), victims (1), wane (1), was[S] (1), were brought together (1), were caught (1), were gathered (1), were mustered (1), withdrawn (1), withdraws (1), withdrew (1)

H666 אָסָף **'āsāp**, n.pr.m. [46] [√ 665]. Asaph, "*gatherer*":– Asaph (45), Asaph's (1)

H667 אָסֹף **'āsōp**, n.[m.] [3] [√ 665]. storehouse, storeroom:– storehouse (1), storehouse (1 [+1074]), storerooms (1)

H668 אֹסֶף **'ōsep**, n.m. [3] [√ 665]. harvest (of fruit), gathering:– gathers (1), harvest of fruit (1), NDT (1)

H669 אֲסֵפָה **'ăsēpâ**, n.f.vbl. [1] [√ 665]. gathering (prisoners); imprisonment:– be herded together (1 [+665])

H670 אֲסֻפָּה **'ăsuppâ**, n.f. [1] [√ 665]. collection (of sayings):– collected sayings (1 [+1251])

H671 אֲסַפְסֻף **'ăsapsup**, n.[m.] [1] [√ 665]. rabble, collection (of grumblers):– rabble (1)

H672 אַסְפָּתָא **'aspātā'**, n.pr.m. [1] Aspatha, "[poss.] *given from a sacred horse*":– Aspatha (1)

H673 אָסַר **'āsar**, v. [73] [→ 657, 659, 660, 661, 674, 4591, 4593, 4594?, 5035?, 5037?]. [Q] to bind, tie up; to obligate; [Qp] to be confined, be bound; [N] to be tied, be kept in prison; [Pu] to be captured, be taken prisoner:– bound (9), obligated (4), obligates (4), be tied (2), hitch up (2), prison (2 [+1074]), prisoners (2), tie up (2), tie up (2 [+673]), tied (2), ties (2), ties securely (2 [+673]), are bound (1), be kept in prison (1), be tied up (1), been captured (1), bind (1), binding (1), captives (1), fetters (1), had made ready (1), harness (1), hitch (1), hitched (1), hitched up (1), instruct (1), is held captive (1), jammed (1), join in (1), made ready (1), obligate (1), obligation taken (1), prison (1 [+1074, 2021]), put (1), put in bonds (1), put in chains (1), start (1), stay (1), take prisoner (1), tether (1), tethered (1), was confined (1), went into (1), were bound (1), were confined (1), were held (1), were taken prisoner (1), wore (1), NDT (2)

H674 אִסָּר **'issār**, n.m. [11] [√ 673; 10057]. pledge, a binding obligation:– pledge (6), pledges (5)

H675 אֵסַר־חַדֹּן **'ēsar-ḥaddōn**, n.pr.m. [3] Esarhaddon, "*Ashur has given a brother [for a lost son]*":– Esarhaddon (3)

H676 אֶסְתֵּר **'estēr**, n.pr.f. [55] Esther, "[Persian] *star* [poss.] *Ishtar*":– Esther (41), Esther's (6), she[S] (4), her[S] (1), who[S] (1), NDT (2)

H677 [1]אַף **'ap[1]**, c. [134] [√ 10059]. how much (better, worse; more, less); really, truly; too, also, even more:– and (9), too (7), and (6 [+2256]), even (6), how much more (4), how much more (4 [+3954]), also (3), how much less (3 [+3954]), how much less (3 [+3954]), how much worse (3 [+3954]), indeed (3), no sooner (3 [+1153]), surely (3), all (2), and also (2), how much more so (2 [+3954]), now (2), then (2), too (2 [+2256]), yes (2), also (1 [+2256]), but also (1), but even (1), but now (1), even (1 [+2256]), even (1 [+2256, 3954]), even though (1), how (1), how much better (1 [+3954]), how much less (1 [+3954, 4202]), how much more (1 [+2256, 3954]), if (1), in all this (1), indeed (1 [+2256, 3954]), moreover (1), no (1), nor (1 [+401]), or (1), really (1), really (1 [+598]), really (1 [+3954]), rejoice greatly (1 [+1635, 1638]), till (1 [+2256]), together with (1 [+2256]), true (1), very (1), whether (1), yet (1 [+2256]), NDT (35)

H678 [2]אַף **'ap[2]**, n.m. [277] [→ 648, 690, 691; cf. 647; 10049]. nose (representing the face or some part of the face); "hot of nose" signifies anger; "long of nose" signifies patience; "high of nose" signifies arrogance:– anger (173), angry (15), wrath (15), face (14), nostrils (12), nose (10), faces (4), very angry (4 [+3013]), patient (3 [+800]), fury (2), noses (2), anger (1 [+3013]), angry (1 [+3019]), before (1 [+928]), before (1 [+4200]), breath (1), brow (1), double (1), fell facedown (1 [+2556, 4200]), furious (1 [+3013, 4394]), great rage (1 [+3034]), hot-tempered (1 [+3013]), life breath (1 [+8120]), long-suffering (1 [+800]), not angry (1 [+8740]), passion (1), patience (1 [+802]), pride (1 [+1470]), quick-tempered (1 [+7920]), resentment (1), snout (1), which[S] (1 [+2257]), yields patience (1 [+799]), NDT (1)

H679 אָפַד **'āpad**, v.den. [2] [→ 682]. [Q] to fasten:– fasten (1), tied (1)

H680 [1]אֵפֹד **'ēpōd[1]**, n.m. [49] [→ 681?; cf. 679]. ephod, a garment of a priest used for adornment and as an aid in priestly service:– ephod (46), it[S] (1 [+2021]), NDT (2)

H681 [2]אֵפֹד **'ēpōd[2]**, n.pr.m. [1] [√ 680?; cf. 679]. Ephod, "*ephod*":– Ephod (1)

H682 אֲפֻדָּה **'ăpuddâ**, n.f. [3] [√ 679]. skillfully woven covering:– skillfully woven (2), covered (1)

H683 אַפֶּדֶן **'appeden**, n.[m.] [1] palace tent, royal tent:– royal (1)

H684 אָפָה **'āpâ**, v. [13] [→ 685, 4418; cf. 9519?]. [Q] to bake; [N] to be baked:– bake (5), baked (5), bakes (1), baking (1), be baked (1)

H685 אֹפֶה **'ōpeh**, n.m. *or* v.ptcp. [11] [√ 684]. baker:– baker (8), bakers (2), baked goods (1 [+4407, 5126])

H686 אֵפוֹא **'ēpô'**, pt. [15] [√ 361? + 7024?]. then, so then:– then (6), now (3), so (3), how (1 [+928, 2021, 4537]), oh (1 [+4769, 5989]), where (1 [+180])

H687 אֲפוּנָה **'ăpûnâ**, n.f.? Not used in NIVEBC [√ 7041]. despair [?]

H688 אֲפִיחַ **'ăpîaḥ**, n.pr.m. [1] Aphiah:– Aphiah (1)

H689 אָפִיל **'āpîl**, a. [1] [√ 694]. late-ripening, late in the season:– ripen later (1)

H690 [1]אַפַּיִם **'appayim[1]**, n.m. Not used in NIVEBC [√ 691; cf. 678, 647]. face, anger

H691 [2]אַפַּיִם **'appayim[2]**, n.pr.m. [2] [√ 690; cf. 678, 647]. Appaim, "*[pair of] nostrils*":– Appaim (2)

H692 [1]אָפִיק **'āpîq[1]**, n.m. [18] [√ 706]. stream, water channel; valley, ravine, the deepest part of a valley flowing with water:– ravines (8), streams (4), valleys (2), channels (1), rows (1), streams (1 [+5707]), tubes (1)

H693 [2]אָפִיק **'āpîq[2]**, n.m. [1] [√ 706]. mighty, strong:– mighty (1)

H694 אֹפֶל **'ōpel**, n.m. [9] [→ 689, 695, 696, 4419?, 4420?]. darkness, the absence of light, often with the associative meaning of gloom, despair; shadows:– darkness (4), thick darkness (2), deepest night (1 [+6547, 4017]), gloom (1), shadows (1)

H695 אָפֵל **'āpēl**, a. [1] [√ 694]. dark, gloomy:– pitch-dark (1)

H696 אֲפֵלָה **'ăpēlâ**, n.f. [10] [√ 694]. the dark, darkness, with the associative meaning of mental gloom and despair:– gloom (2), dark (1), dark (1 [+413]), darkness (1), deep darkness (1), deep shadows (1), night (1), total darkness (1 [+3125]), utter darkness (1)

H697 אֶפְלָל **'eplāl**, n.pr.m. [2] [√ 7136]. Ephlal, "*judgment, arbitration*":– Ephlal (2)

H698 אֹפֶן **'ōpen**, n.[m.] [1] [cf. 236?]. (right) time; aptly:– rightly (1 [+6584])

H699 אָפֵס **'āpēs**, v. [5] [→ 700, 702]. [Q] to come to an end, cease:– all gone (1), come to an end (1), gone (1), vanish (1), vanished (1)

H700 אֶפֶס **'epes**, n.m. [43] [√ 699]. ends (of the earth); no, nothing; however, but, only, yet:– ends (14), no (5), none (5), but (3), without (3 [+928]), not (2), only (2), amount to nothing (1), however (1 [+3954]), lately (1 [+928]), nothing (1), nothing at all (1 [+401, 2256]), or (1 [+2256]), vanish away (1), whether (1 [+2256]), yet (1 [+3954])

H701 אֹפֶס **'ōpes**, n.[m.] [1] [cf. 7168]. an extremity of the body, which in context wades through shallow water: ankles, or possibly soles of the feet:– ankle-deep (1)

H702 אֶפֶס דַּמִּים **'epes dammîm**, n.pr.loc. [1] [√ 699 + 1956]. Ephes Dammim, "*border of Dammim [blood]*":– Ephes Dammim (1)

H703 אֶפַע **'epa'**, n. *or* a. [1] worthless:– worthless (1)

H704 אֶפְעֶה **'ep'eh**, n.[m.] [3] [√ 7184?]. snake, variously identified as an adder or viper:– adder (2), adders (1)

H705 אָפַף **'āpap**, v. [5] [Q] to surround, entangle, engulf:– entangled (2), engulfing (1), surround (1), swirled about (1)

H706 אָפַק **'āpaq**, v. [7] [→ 692, 693]. [Ht] to control oneself, restrain oneself; to feel compelled:– are withheld (1), control himself (1), controlling himself (1), felt compelled (1), held myself back (1), hold yourself back (1), restrained himself (1)

H707 אֲפֵק **'ăpēq**, n.pr.loc. [9] [→ 708]. Aphek, "*stronghold*":– Aphek (9)

H708 אֲפֵקָה **'ăpēqâ**, n.pr.loc. [1] [√ 707]. Aphekah, "*fortress*":– Aphekah (1)

H709 אֵפֶר **'ēper**, n.[m.] [22] [→ 234, 235]. ashes, dust:– ashes (20), dust (2)

H710 אֲפֵר **'ăpēr**, n.[m.] [2] headband:– headband (2)

H711 אֶפְרֹחַ **'eprōaḥ**, n.m. [4] [√ 7256]. young (of a bird), chick:– young (2), young ones (1), NDT (1)

H712 אַפִּרְיוֹן **'appiryôn**, n.[m.] [1] carriage; other sources: sedan chair, litter, or palanquin, a vehicle carried on poles by porters:– carriage (1)

H713 אֶפְרַיִם **'eprayim**, n.pr.m. [180] [√ 7238?]. Ephraim, "*doubly fruitful*":– Ephraim (146), Ephraim's (11), Ephraim (7 [+1201]), Ephraimites (4 [+1201]), Ephraim (2 [+824]), Ephraimite (2), Ephraimite (2 [+1201]), Ephraimites (2), Ephraim (1 [+1074]), Ephraimites (1 [+408]), Ephraimites (1 [+4946]), NDT (1)

H714 [1]אֶפְרָת **'eprāt[1]**, n.pr.loc. [4] [→ 715, 716, 717, 718]. Ephrath, "*fruitful land*":– Ephrath (4)

H715 [2]אֶפְרָת **'eprāt[2]**, n.pr.f. [1] [√ 714]. Ephrath, "*fruitful land*":– Ephrath (1)

H716 [1]אֶפְרָתָה **'eprātā[1]**, n.pr.loc. [3] [→ 3980; cf. 714]. Ephrathah, "*fruitful land*":– Ephrathah (3)

H717 [2]אֶפְרָתָה **'eprātā[2]**, n.pr.f. [2] [√ 714]. Ephrathah, "*fruitful land*":– Ephrathah (2)

H718 אֶפְרָתִי **'eprātî**, a.g. [5] [√ 714]. Ephraimite, "*of Ephraim*":– Ephraimite (3), Ephrathite (1), Ephrathites (1)

H719 אֶצְבֹּן **'eṣbōn**, n.pr.m. [2] Ezbon:– Ezbon (2)

H720 אֶצְבַּע **'eṣba'**, n.f. [31] [√ 10064]. digit appendage of hand or foot: finger, toe; "four fingers" is a measurement of width (Jer 52:21):– finger (17), fingers (11), forefinger (2), toes (1)

H721 [1]אָצִיל **'āṣîl[1]**, n.[m.] [1] [√ 724]. far corner, the remote areas of the earth:– farthest corners (1)

H722 [2]אָצִיל **'āṣîl[2]**, n.[m.] [1] [→ 727, 728]. leader, with an implication of being noble and distinguished:– leaders (1)

H723 אַצִּיל **'aṣṣîl**, n.[f.] [3] [√ 724]. joint (of shoulder or wrist); "a cubit of the joint" (Ezek 41:8) is an unknown length, translated as a "long cubit":– arms (1 [+3338]), long (1), wrists (1 [+3338])

H724 אָצַל **'āṣal**, v.den. [5] [→ 721, 723, 725, 729]. [Q] to turn aside; to take away; [N] to be smaller:– denied (1), reserved (1), smaller (1), take (1), took (1)

H725 [1]אֵצֶל **'ēṣel[1]**, subst.pp. [61] [√ 724]. beside, near, at the side:– beside (30), near (6), side (3), at (2), at side (2), away (2 [+4946]), by (2), next to (2), with (2), close to (1), close to (1 [+7940]), east (1 [+7711]), go to bed with (1 [+8886]), neared (1 [+2143]), next to (1 [+4946]), to (1), NDT (3)

H726 [2]אֵצֶל **'ēṣel[2]**, n.pr.loc. Not used in NIVEBC [→ 1089]. Ezel, see 1089

H727 [1]אָצֵל **'āṣēl[1]**, n.pr.m. [6] [√ 722]. Azel, *"noble"*:– Azel (6)

H728 [2]אָצֵל **'āṣēl[2]**, n.pr.loc. [1] [√ 722]. Azel, *"noble"*:– Azel (1)

H729 אֲצַלְיָהוּ **'ᵃṣalyāhû**, n.pr.m. [2] [√ 724 + 3378]. Azaliah, *"Yahweh is keeping in reserve"*:– Azaliah (2)

H730 אֹצֶם **'ōṣem**, n.pr.m. [2] Ozem:– Ozem (2)

H731 אֶצְעָדָה **'eṣ'ādâ**, n.f. [2] [√ 7575]. armlet, armband; an ornamental chain worn on the wrist or the ankle:– armlets (1), band (1)

H732 אָצַר **'āṣar**, v. [5] [→ 238, 733?]. [Q] to store up; [N] be stored; [H] to be in charge of a storeroom:– stored up (2), be stored up (1), put in charge of the storerooms (1 [+6584, 238]), store up (1)

H733 אֵצֶר **'ēṣer**, n.pr.m. [5] [√ 732?]. Ezer, *"help"*:– Ezer (5)

H734 אֶקְדָּח **'eqdāḥ**, n.[m.] [1] [√ 7706]. sparkling jewel; some sources: beryl stone:– sparkling jewels (1 [+74])

H735 אַקּוֹ **'aqqô**, n.m. [1] [√ 3567]. wild goat:– wild goat (1)

H736 אֲרָא **'ᵃrā'**, n.pr.m. [1] Ara:– Ara (1)

H737 אֶרְאֵל **'er'ēl**, n.[m.] [1] [√ 738?]. brave man, hero:– brave men (1)

H738 אֲרִאֵל **'ᵃri'ēl**, n.pr.m. [2] [√ 737?]. best man, warrior:– mightiest warriors (2)

H739 [1]אַרְאֵלִי **'ar'ēlî[1]**, n.pr.m. [2] [→ 740; cf. 9550?]. Areli:– Areli (2)

H740 [2]אַרְאֵלִי **'ar'ēlî[2]**, a.g. [1] [√ 739; cf. 9550?]. Arelite, *"of Areli"*:– Arelite (1)

H741 אָרַב **'ārab**, v. [41] [→ 743, 744, 747?, 4422]. [Q] to lay in wait against, hide in ambush; [P] to ambush, waylay; [H] to set an ambush:– ambush (10), lie in wait (6), lies in wait (5), set an ambush (3), hidden (2), in ambush (2), lay in wait (2), ambush set (1), ambushes (1), bandits (1), hide (1), lies in wait (1 [+928, 2021, 5041]), lurk (1), lurked (1), lurks (1), lying in wait (1), took up concealed positions (1), NDT (1)

H742 אֲרָב **'ᵃrāb**, n.pr.loc. [1] [cf. 750?]. Arab, *"desert or steppe"*:– Arab (1)

H743 אֶרֶב **'ereb**, n.[m.] [2] [√ 741]. cover, hiding place, lair; hiding place (for an ambush):– cover (1), wait (1)

H744 אֹרֶב **'ōreb**, n.[m.] [2] [√ 741]. trap, intrigue:– intrigue (1), traps (1)

H745 אַרְבֵּאל **'arbē'l**, n.loc. Not used in NIVEBC [→ 1079]. Arbel

H746 אַרְבֶּה **'arbeh**, n.m. [24] [√ 8049?]. locust, mature locust:– locusts (15), locust (5), great locusts (2), great locust (1), they[S] (1 [+2021])

H747 אָרְבָּה **'orbâ**, n.f. [1] [√ 741?]. cleverness; other sources: nimble movements (of the hands), perhaps some concrete survival skill, such as swimming:– cleverness (1)

H748 אֲרֻבָּה **'ᵃrubbâ**, n.f. [9] floodgate; window; nest (nesting hole):– floodgates (6), nests (1), window (1), windows (1)

H749 אֲרֻבּוֹת **'ᵃrubbôt**, n.pr.loc. [1] Arubboth:– Arubboth (1)

H750 אַרְבִּי **'arbî**, a.g. [1] [cf. 742?]. Arbite:– Arbite (1)

H751 ארנבן **'rnbn**, n.pr.loc. Aranabanim

H752 [1]אַרְבַּע **'arba'[1]**, n.m. & f. [455] [→ 753, 754, 2033, 7957, 7959, 8055, 8062, 8063?, 8065, 8067, 8068; 10065]. four, (pl.) forty; fourth, fortieth:– four (175), forty (79), fourteenth (19 [+6925]), 24,000 (13 [+6929, 2256, 547]), fourteen (12 [+6925]), 4,500 (8 [+2822, 4395, 2256, 547]), fourteen (7 [+6926]), twenty-fourth (7 [+6929, 2256]), fourth (5), twenty-four (5 [+6929, 2256]), all fours (4), forty-one (4 [+2256, 285]), forty-two (4 [+2256, 9109]), fourteenth (4 [+6926]), 1,254 (3 [+547, 4395, 2822, 2256]), 40,500 (3 [+547, 2256, 2822, 4395]), 430 (3 [+8993, 2256, 4395]), 53,400 (3 [+8993, 2256, 2822, 547, 2256, 4395]), fortieth (3), forty-five (3 [+2256, 2822]), 1,247 (2 [+547, 4395, 2256, 8679]), 245 (2 [+4395, 2256, 2822]), 345 (2 [+8993, 4395, 2256, 2822]), 35,400 (2 [+2822, 2256, 8993, 547, 2256, 4395]), 4,600 (2 [+547, 2256, 9252, 4395]), 403 (2 [+8993, 2256, 4395]), 41,500 (2 [+285, 2256, 547, 2256, 2822, 4395]), 42 (2 [+2256, 9109]), 435 (2 [+4395, 8993, 2256, 2822]), 45,650 (2 [+2822, 2256, 547, 2256, 9252, 4395, 2256, 2822]), 46,500 (2 [+9252, 2256, 547, 2256, 2822, 4395]), 54,400 (2 [+2256, 2822, 547, 2256, 752, 4395]), 54,400 (2 [+752, 2256, 2822, 547, 2256, 4395]), 57,400 (2 [+8679, 2256, 2822, 547, 2256, 4395]), 74 (2 [+8679, 2256]), 74,600 (2 [+2256, 8679, 547, 2256, 9252, 4395]), forty-eight (2 [+2256, 9046]), fourteen hundred (2 [+547, 2256, 4395]), twenty-fourth (2 [+2256, 6929]), 1,254 (1 [+547, 4395, 2256, 2822]), 14,700 (1 [+6925, 547, 2256, 8679, 4395]), 148 (1 [+4395, 2256, 9046]), 151,450 (1 [+4395, 547, 2256, 285, 2822, 547, 4395, 2822, 2256, 2256, 2256]), 186,400 (1 [+4395, 2256, 9046, 547, 9252, 547, 4395, 2256, 2256]), 2,400 (1 [+547, 2256, 4395]), 22,034 (1 [+6929, 2256, 9109, 547, 2256, 8993, 2256]), 24,000 (1 [+2256, 6929, 547]), 242 (1 [+4395, 2256, 9109]), 245 (1 [+4395, 2256, 2256, 2822]), 284 (1 [+4395, 9046, 2256]), 324 (1 [+8993, 4395, 6929, 2256]), 34 (1 [+2256, 8993]), 40 (1), 40,000 (1 [+547]), 410 (1 [+4395, 2256, 6927]), 42,360 (1 [+8052, 547, 8993, 4395, 9252]), 42,360 (1 [+8052, 547, 8993, 4395, 2256, 9252]), 420 (1 [+4395, 2256, 6929]), 43,730 (1 [+8993, 2256, 547, 2256, 8679, 4395, 2256, 8993]), 44,760 (1 [+2256, 752, 547, 2256, 8679, 4395, 2256, 9252]), 44,760 (1 [+752, 2256, 547, 2256, 8679, 4395, 2256, 9252]), 45,400 (1 [+2822, 2256, 547, 2256, 752, 4395]), 45,400 (1 [+2822, 2256, 752, 547, 2256, 4395]), 45,600 (1 [+2822, 2256, 547, 2256, 9252, 4395]), 454 (1 [+4395, 2822, 2256, 752]), 454 (1 [+752, 4395, 2822, 2256]), 468 (1 [+4395, 9252, 2256, 9046]), 5,400 (1 [+2822, 547, 2256, 4395]), 64,300 (1 [+2256, 9252, 547, 2256, 8993, 4395]), 64,400 (1 [+2256, 9252, 547, 2256, 752, 4395]), 64,400 (1 [+752, 2256, 9252, 547, 2256, 4395]), 642 (1 [+9252, 4395, 2256, 9109]), 642 (1 [+9252, 4395, 2256, 2256, 9109]), 648 (1 [+9252, 4395, 2256, 9046]), 743 (1 [+8679, 4395, 2256, 8993]), 743 (1 [+8679, 4395, 2256, 2256, 8993]), 745 (1 [+8679, 4395, 2256, 2822]), 840 (1 [+2256, 9046, 4395]), 845 (1 [+9046, 4395, 2256, 2822]), 945 (1 [+9596, 4395, 2256, 2256, 2822]), each[S] (1), forty-first (1 [+2256, 285]), forty-nine (1 [+2256, 9596]), forty-seven (1 [+2256, 8679]), four-fifths (1 [+3338]), square (1 [+448, 8063]), square (1 [+8062, 448, 8063]), two (0 [+2256, 9109]), NDT (5)

H753 [2]אַרְבַּע **'arba'[2]**, n.pr.m. Not used in NIVEBC [√ 752]. Arba

H754 אַרְבָּעִים **'arbā'îm**, n.pl.indecl. Not used in NIVEBC [√ 752]. forty (pl. of "four" [752])

H755 אָרַג **'ārag**, v. [15] [→ 756]. [Q] to weave, spin (a web):– weaver's (4), weaver (3), weavers (2), did weaving (1 [+1428]), spin (1), weave (1), wove (1), woven (1 [+5126]), NDT (1)

H756 אֶרֶג **'ereg**, n.[m.] [2] [√ 755]. weaver's loom, weaver's shuttle:– loom (1), weaver's shuttle (1)

H757 אַרְגָּב **'argāb**, n.m. Not used in NIVEBC [→ 758, 759; cf. 8073]. heap, mound

H758 [1]אַרְגֹּב **'argōb[1]**, n.pr.loc. [4] [√ 757; cf. 8073]. Argob, *"mound"*:– Argob (4)

H759 [2]אַרְגֹּב **'argōb[2]**, n.pr.m. [1] [√ 757; cf. 8073]. Argob, *"mound"*:– Argob (1)

H760 אַרְגְּוָן **'argᵉwān**, n.[m.] [1] [cf. 763]. purple (yarn):– purple (1)

H761 אַרְגַּז **'argaz**, n.m. [3] [√ 8074]. chest (containing objects); other sources: saddlebag:– chest (3)

H762 אֹרְגִים **'ōrᵉgîm**, n.pr.m. Not used in NIVEBC [cf. 3629]. Oregim

H763 אַרְגָּמָן **'argāmān**, n.[m.] [38] [cf. 760; 10066]. purple (yarn):– purple (36), purple material (1), tapestry (1)

H764 אַרְדְּ **'ard**, n.pr.m. [3] [→ 765?, 766, 769?]. Ard, *"hunchbacked"*:– Ard (3)

H765 אַרְדּוֹן **'ardôn**, n.pr.m. [1] [√ 764?]. Ardon, *"hunchbacked"*:– Ardon (1)

H766 אַרְדִּי **'ardî**, a.g. [1] [√ 764]. Ardite, *"of Ard"*:– Ardite (1)

H767 אֲרִידַי **'ᵃriday**, n.pr.m. [1] Aridai, "[perhaps] *delight of Hari*":– Aridai (1)

H768 אָרָה **'ārâ**, v. [2] [√ 251?]. [Q] to gather, pick (fruit):– gathered (1), pick (1)

H769 אֲרוֹד **'ᵃrôd**, n.pr.m. Not used in NIVEBC [√ 764?]. Arod, see 771

H770 אַרְוָד **'arwād**, n.pr.loc. [2] [→ 773]. Arvad:– Arvad (2)

H771 [1]אֲרוֹדִי **'ᵃrôdî[1]**, n.pr.m. [2] [→ 772]. Arodi, *"hunchbacked"*:– Arodi (2)

H772 [2]אֲרוֹדִי **'ᵃrôdî[2]**, a.g. [1] [√ 771]. Arodite, *"of Arodi"*:– Arodite (1)

H773 אַרְוָדִי **'arwādî**, a.g. [2] [√ 770]. Arvadite, *"of Arvad"*:– Arvadites (2)

H774 אֻרְוָה **'urwâ**, n.f. [4] [cf. 795]. (animal) stall, pen, stable:– stalls (3), pens (1)

H775 אָרוּז **'ārûz**, a. [1] [√ 780?]. tight, solid:– tightly knotted (1)

H776 אֲרוּכָה **'ᵃrûkâ**, n.f. [6] [√ 799]. healing, health; repair:– health (2), repairs (2), healing (1), healing for wound (1)

H777 אֲרוּמָה **'ᵃrûmâ**, n.pr.loc. [1] [cf. 8126]. Arumah, *"lofty"*:– Arumah (1)

H778 אֲרוֹן **'ᵃrôn**, n.m. & f. [202] ark, chest, box; coffin:– ark (185), chest (6), it[S] (3 [+2021]), it[S] (2), coffin (1), it (1 [+2021]), it[S] (1 [+2021, 466]), it[S] (1 [+2021, 1382]), NDT (2)

H779 אֲרַוְנָה **'ᵃrawnâ**, n.pr.m. [9] [cf. 819]. Araunah, *"strong"*:– Araunah (8), he[S] (1)

H780 אֶרֶז **'erez**, n.m. [73] [→ 775?, 781]. cedar; other sources: fir:– cedar (53), cedars (19), them[S] (1 [+6770])

H781 אַרְזָה **'arzâ**, n.f.col. [1] [√ 780]. beam of cedar; other sources: paneling (made of fir):– beams of cedar (1)

H782 [1]אָרַח **'āraḥ[1]**, v. [7] [→ 783?, 784, 785, 786?]. [Q] to go, travel; (ptcp.) traveler, wanderer; (ptcp.pl.) caravans:– traveler (4), going out (1), keeps company (1 [+4200, 2495]), travelers (1)

H783 [2]אָרַח **'āraḥ[2]**, n.pr.m. [4] [√ 782?]. Arah, *"he wanders"*:– Arah (4)

H784 אֹרַח **'ōraḥ**, n.m. [55] [√ 782; 10068]. road, way, path, thoroughfare; by extension: way of life, manner of conduct; "the way of a woman" means "childbirth":– path (18), paths (12), way (8), ways (5), course (4), age of childbearing (1 [+3869, 2021, 851]), conduct (1), destiny (1), highways (1), path (1 [+2006]), roads (1), siege ramps (1 [+369]), stay on path (1)

H785 אֹרְחָה **'ōrḥâ**, n.f. [4] [√ 782]. caravan:– caravans (3), caravan (1)

H786 אֲרֻחָה **'ᵃruḥâ**, n.f. [6] [√ 782?]. allowance, provision; portion:– allowance (2), provisions (1), small serving (1), NDT (2)

H787 אֲרִי **'ᵃrî**, n.m. [34] [→ 788]. (the African) lion, with the associative meanings of strength, fierceness, and sometimes nobility; sometimes fig. of people who are destructive:– lion (17), lions (14), fierce lion (1), lion's (1), young lion (1 [+4097])

H788 אוּרִי **'urî**, n.pr.m. [1] [√ 787]. Uri, *"Yahweh is [my] flame, light"*:– Uri (1)

H789 [1]אֲרִיאֵל **'ᵃrî'ēl[1]**, n.m. [3] [→ 738, 790, 791; cf. 2219]. altar hearth:– altar hearth (2), hearth (1)

H790 [2]אֲרִיאֵל **'ᵃrî'ēl[2]**, n.pr.f. [4] [√ 789]. Ariel, *"lioness of God [El]"*:– Ariel (4)

H791 [3]אֲרִיאֵל **'ᵃrî'ēl[3]**, n.pr.m. [1] [√ 789]. Ariel, *"lioness of God [El]"*:– Ariel (1)

H792 אֲרִידָתָא **'ᵃrîdātā'**, n.pr.m. [1] Aridatha, "[perhaps] *given by Hari*":– Aridatha (1)

H793 [1]אַרְיֵה **'aryēh[1]**, n.m. [44] [→ 794; 10069]. (the African) lion:– lion (34), lions (4), lion's (4), cubs (1 [+1594]), it[S] (1 [+1581, 2021])

H794 [2]אַרְיֵה **'aryēh[2]**, n.pr.m. [1] [√ 793]. Arieh, *"lion"*:– Arieh (1)

H795 אֻרְיָה **'uryâ**, n.f. Not used in NIVEBC [cf. 774]. manger, crib

H796 אַרְיוֹךְ **'aryôk**, n.pr.m. [2] [√ 10070]. Arioch:– Arioch (2)

H797 אוּרִים **'urîm**, n.[m.]pl. Not used in NIVEBC [√ 241]. (pl.) region of light, East

H798 אֲרִיסַי **'ᵃrîsay**, n.pr.m. [1] Arisai:– Arisai (1)

H799 אָרַךְ **'ārak**, v. [35] [→ 776, 800, 801, 802, 803; 10073]. [Q] to be, become long; [H] to lengthen, to have a long (life):– live long (8 [+3427]), long (4), lengthen (2), outlived (2 [+3427, 339]), prolong (2), been long (1), delay (1), endure (1), enjoy a long reign (1 [+3427]), enjoy long life (1 [+3427]), give long (1), go by (1), have long (1), live a long time (1), living long (1), made long (1), maintains (1), patient (1), remained (1), stayed (1 [+8905]), stick out (1), yields patience (1 [+678])

H800 אָרֵךְ **'ārēk**, a. [15] [√ 799]. slow (to anger), patient, long-suffering:– slow (9), patient (3 [+678]), long (1), long-suffering (1 [+678]), patience (1 [+8120])

H801 אָרֹךְ **'ārōk**, a. [3] [√ 799]. length (spatial and temporal):– long time (2), longer (1)

H802 אֹרֶךְ **'ōrek**, n.[m.] [94] [√ 799]. length (spatial and temporal):– long (65), length (12), wide (2), endless (1), extended (1), forever (1 [+4200, 3427]), lengthwise (1), longer (1), many years (1 [+3427]), patience (1 [+678]), prolong (1), so long (1 [+3427]), spreading (1), square (1 [+2256, 8145]), total wingspan (1 [+4053]), NDT (3)

H803 [1]אֶרֶךְ **'erek[1]**, a. Not used in NIVEBC [√ 799]. see 800

H804 [2]אֶרֶךְ **'erek[2]**, n.pr.loc. [1] [√ 10074]. Erech:– Uruk (1)

H805 אַרְכִּי **'arkî**, a.g. [6] Arkite:– Arkite (5), Arkites (1)

H806 אֲרָם **'ᵃrām**, n.pr.m. [129] [→ 811, 812, 7020; *also used with compound proper names*]. Aram:– Aram (69), Arameans (42), Aramean (7), Aramean kingdom (2), their[S] (2), them[S] (2), they[S] (2), it[S] (1), NDT (2)

H807 אֲרַם מַעֲכָה **'ᵃram ma'ᵃkâ**, n.pr.loc. [1] [√ 806 + 5081]. Aram Maacah:– Aram Maakah (1)

H808 אֲרַם נַהֲרַיִם **'ᵃram nahᵃrayim**, n.loc. [5] [√ 806 + 5645]. Aram Naharaim:– Aram Naharaim (5)

H809 אֲרַם צוֹבָה **'ᵃram ṣôbâ**, n.pr.loc. [1] [√ 806 + 7420]. Aram Zobah:– Aram Zobah (1)

H810 אַרְמוֹן **'armôn**, n.m. [32] [→ 813; cf. 528, 8227]. fortress, citadel, palace, stronghold, a military defensive building usually small of base but many floors high:–

fortresses (19), citadels (4), citadel (3), palaces (3), fortress (1), palace (1), stronghold (1)

H811 אֲרָמִי ***'arāmî***, adv. [5] [√ 806]. in Aramaic:– in Aramaic (4), NDT (1)

H812 אֲרַמִּי ***'arammî***, a.g. [12] [√ 806]. Aramean:– Aramean (8), Arameans (4)

H813 אַרְמֹנִי ***'armōnî***, n.pr.m. [1] [√ 810]. Armoni, *"one born in the dwelling tower, the palace"*:– Armoni (1)

H814 אֲרָן ***'arān***, n.pr.m. [2] Aran, *"wild goat"*:– Aran (2)

H815 1אֹרֶן ***'ōren1***, n.[m.] [1] [→ 816, 818?]. pine tree; other sources: laurel, sweet laurel, fir, cedar:– pine (1)

H816 2אֹרֶן ***'ōren2***, n.pr.m. [1] [√ 815]. Oren, *"fir or cedar; laurel"*:– Oren (1)

H817 אַרְנֶבֶת ***'arnebet***, n.f. [2] [cf. 4]. rabbit; other sources: hare:– rabbit (2)

H818 אַרְנוֹן ***'arnôn***, n.pr.loc. [25] [√ 815?]. Arnon:– Arnon (24), Arnon's (1)

H819 אֲרַנְיָה ***'aranyâ***, n.pr.m. Not used in NIVEBC [cf. 779]. Aranyah

H820 אַרְנָן ***'arnān***, n.pr.m. [1] Arnan:– Arnan (1)

H821 אָרְנָן ***'ornān***, n.pr.m. [12] Araunah, *"strong"*:– Araunah (9), heS (1), himS (1), NDT (1)

H822 אַרְפָּד ***'arpād***, n.pr.loc. [6] Arpad:– Arpad (6)

H823 אַרְפַּכְשַׁד ***'arpakšad***, n.pr.m. [9] Arphaxad:– Arphaxad (9)

H824 אֶרֶץ ***'ereṣ***, n.f. & m. [2493] [√ 10075, 10077]. world, earth, all inhabited lands; parts of the earth, land (in contrast to water), ground, soil; country, region, territory; "heaven and earth" means the totality of creation; "the ends of the earth" means "a very distant place":– land (1148), earth (511), Egypt (184 [+5213]), ground (158), country (90), countries (37), lands (37), Canaan (29 [+4046]), world (20), region (18), territory (17), wild (16), Edom (10 [+121]), Gilead (8 [+1680]), Israel (7 [+3776]), Judah (6 [+3373]), aroundS (6), itS (6 [+2021]), territories (6), Moab (5 [+4566]), area (5), earth's (5), fields (5), Goshen (4 [+1777]), countryside (4), district (4), land (4 [+299]), neighboring (4), soil (4), dust (3), floor (3), itsS (3 [+2021]), Assyria (2 [+855]), Ephraim (2 [+713]), JudahS (2 [+2021]), Midian (2 [+4518]), Negev (2 [+5582]), Shinar (2 [+9114]), cities (2 [+9133]), community (2), empire (2), lower Egypt (2 [+5213]), the otherS (2 [+7895, 2021]), thereS (2 [+2021]), theyS (2 [+6639, 2021]), upper Egypt (2 [+7356]), Babylon (1 [+951]), Babylon (1 [+4169]), Babylonia (1 [+9114]), Bashan (1 [+1421]), Benjamin (1 [+1228]), Galilee (1 [+1665]), Naphtali (1 [+5889]), Philistines (1 [+7149]), Tema (1 [+9401]), Uz (1 [+6420]), areas of land (1), army (1), battlefield (1), central hill (1 [+3179]), community (1 [+6639, 2021]), deep (1 [+6584, 7156, 2021]), desert (1 [+4497]), districts (1), down (1 [+2025]), earthly (1 [+4946, 2021]), everywhere (1 [+928, 3972, 2021]), fail (1 [+5877, 2025]), field (1), floor space (1), foreign (1), heS (1 [+466, 2021]), hereS (1 [+2021]), hereS (1 [+928, 2021]), homeland (1 [+4580]), homeland (1 [+5226]), in midair (1 [+1068, 2021, 9028, 2256, 1068, 2021]), itS (1 [+2021, 2021, 2296]), land's (1 [+928]), little distance (1 [+3896]), nations (1), nations (1 [+1580]), native land (1), native-born (1 [+275]), native-born (1 [+275, 2021]), native-born (1 [+3528, 928, 2021]), neighbors (1), on foot (1 [+6584, 2021]), other nationalities (1 [+6639, 2021]), peoples (1), place (1), plain (1 [+6677]), plateau (1 [+4793]), property (1 [+299]), shore (1), soil (1 [+6760]), some distance (1 [+3896]), some distance (1 [+3896, 2021]), suitable (1), surroundingS (1), theirS (1 [+6639, 2021]), themS (1 [+6551, 2021]), there (1 [+928]), thereS (1 [+928, 2257]), thereS (1 [+2025, 4046]), thereS (1 [+928, 2021]), tracts of land (1), vicinity (1), whereS (1), whole earth (1 [+9315]), whole world (1 [+9315]), whole world (1 [+2256, 9315]), whomS (1 [+6639, 2021]), wild animals (1 [+989]), NDT (30)

H825 אַרְצָא ***'arṣā'***, n.pr.m. [1] Arza, "[perhaps] *gracious*":– Arza (1)

H826 אָרַר ***'ārar***, v. [63] [→ 251?, 4423]. [Q] to curse, place a curse; [Qp] to be cursed, be under a curse; [N] to be cursed; [P] to bring a curse; [Ho] to bring a curse upon one:– cursed (30), curse (11), be cursed (7), brings a curse (6), curse bitterly (2 [+826]), put a curse on (2), under a curse (2), accursed (1), curse (1 [+4423]), cursed be (1)

H827 אֲרָרָט ***'ărāraṭ***, n.pr.loc. [4] Ararat:– Ararat (4)

H828 אֲרָרִי ***'arārî***, a.g. Not used in NIVEBC [cf. 2240]. Ararite, see 2240

H829 אָרַשׂ ***'āraś***, v. [11] [P] to betroth, pledge to marriage; [Pu] to be betrothed, be pledged to be married:– pledged to be married (4), betroth (3), betrothed (2), is pledged to be married (1), pledged (1)

H830 אֲרֶשֶׁת ***'arešet***, n.f. [1] [→ 4626]. request, desire:– request (1)

H831 אַרְתַּחְשַׁסְתְּא ***'artaḥšast'***, אַרְתַּחְשַׁשְׂתְּ ***'artaḥšaśt***, אַרְתַּחְשַׁשְׂתָּא ***'artaḥšaśtā'***, n.pr.m. [9] [√ 10078]. Artaxerxes:– Artaxerxes (9)

H832 אֲשַׂרְאֵל ***'aśar'ēl***, n.pr.m. [1] [→ 833, 834, 835]. Asarel:– Asarel (1)

H833 אֲשַׂרְאֵלָה ***'aśar'ēlâ***, n.pr.m. [1] [√ 832; cf. 3777]. Asarelah:– Asarelah (1)

H834 אַשְׂרִאֵלִי ***'aśri'ēlî***, a.g. [1] [√ 832]. Asrielite, *"of Asriel"*:– Asrielite (1)

H835 אַשְׂרִיאֵל ***'aśrî'ēl***, n.pr.m. [3] [√ 832]. Asriel, *"God has filled with joy* or *[the object of] joy is God"*:– Asriel (3)

H836 1אֵשׁ ***'ēš1***, n.f. & m. [376] [→ 852; 10080]. fire, flame; lightning:– fire (253), burned (10 [+8596, 928, 2021]), burn down (9 [+8596, 928, 2021]), set on fire (9 [+3675, 928, 2021]), fiery (8), lightning (7), burning (6), burn (5 [+8596, 928, 2021]), be burned up (4 [+8596, 928, 2021]), burning (4 [+6584, 2021]), set fire (4 [+3675]), set on fire (4 [+8596, 928, 2021]), burn up (3 [+8596, 928, 2021]), burned down (3 [+8596, 928, 2021]), burned up (3 [+8596, 928, 2021]), burning coals (3), flame (3), blazing (2), coals (2), fire (2 [+4258]), fires (2), flaming (2), itS (2 [+2021]), use for fuel (2 [+1277]), are burned up (1 [+8596, 928, 2021, 8596]), be burned (1 [+8596, 928, 2021]), be burned down (1 [+8596, 928, 2021]), burn (1 [+4805]), burn to death (1 [+8596, 928, 2021]), burned (1 [+8938, 928, 2021]), burned down (1 [+8596, 2021]), burned to death (1 [+8596, 928, 2021]), charred (1 [+1277, 928, 2021]), firepot (1 [+3963]), flashes (1 [+928]), fuel for fire (1 [+928, 1896]), fuel for flames (1 [+928, 1896]), kindled (1 [+7706]), lightning (1 [+4259]), lit (1 [+1277]), on fire (1 [+1277, 928, 2021]), set ablaze (1 [+3675, 928, 2021]), set fire to (1 [+8596, 928, 2021]), set fire to (1 [+8938, 928, 2021]), set on fire (1 [+3675]), used for fuel (1 [+8596, 1198]), NDT (2)

H837 2אֵשׁ ***'ēš2***, n.f. & m. trifle

H838 אִשׁ ***'iš***, subst. [1] [√ 3780]. there is:– one (1)

H839 אַשְׁבֵּל ***'ašbēl***, n.pr.m. [3] [→ 840; cf. 8670]. Ashbel, "[poss. a form of] *man of Baal; having a long upper lip*":– Ashbel (3)

H840 אַשְׁבֵּלִי ***'ašbēlî***, a.g. [1] [√ 839; cf. 8670]. Ashbelite, *"of Ashbel"*:– Ashbelite (1)

H841 אֶשְׁבָּן ***'ešbān***, n.pr.m. [2] Eshban, *"man of understanding"*:– Eshban (2)

H842 אַשְׁבֵּעַ ***'ašbēa'***, n.pr.loc. Not used in NIVEBC [→ 1080]. Ashbea, see 1080

H843 אֶשְׁבַּעַל ***'ešba'al***, n.pr.m. [2] [√ 408 + 1251]. Esh-Baal, *"man of Baal"*:– Esh-Baal (2)

H844 אֶשֶׁד ***'ešed***, n.f. [7] [→ 845, 850]. slopes, mountain slopes:– slopes (5), mountain slopes (2)

H845 אֶשֶׁד ***'ešed***, n.[m.] Not used in NIVEBC [√ 844]. foundation, bottom, lower part (slope)

H846 אַשְׁדּוֹד ***'ašdôd***, n.pr.loc. [17] [→ 847, 848]. Ashdod, "[perhaps] *fortress*":– Ashdod (15), NDT (2)

H847 אַשְׁדּוֹדִי ***'ašdôdî***, a.g. [5] [√ 846]. from Ashdod:– people of Ashdod (3), Ashdod (1), from Ashdod (1)

H848 אַשְׁדּוֹדִית ***'ašdôdît***, adv. [1] [√ 846]. language of Ashdod:– language of Ashdod (1)

H849 אַשְׁדּוֹת הַפִּסְגָּה ***'ašdôt happisgâ***, n.pr.loc. Not used in NIVEBC [√ 844 + 2021 + 7171]. Ashdoth Pisgah

H850 אֲשֵׁדָה ***'ēšdāt***, n.f. [1] [√ 844]. mountain slope:– mountain slopes (1)

H851 אִשָּׁה ***'iššâ***, n.f. [780] [√ 408; 10493]. woman, in contrast to man; wife, in contrast to husband; "to take a woman" means "to marry":– wife (254), woman (166), women (98), wives (91), married (10 [+4374]), wife's (9), each (7), give in marriage (6 [+5989, 4200]), herS (6 [+2021]), mother (6), one (6), sheS (6 [+2021]), widow (6), gave in marriage (5 [+5989, 4200]), harem (5 [+1074]), marry (5 [+2118, 4200]), married (4 [+4374, 4200]), marry (4 [+4374, 4200]), marry (4 [+4374]), woman's (4), married (3 [+2118, 4200]), weaklingsS (3), adulterous (2 [+2424]), harem (2), herS (2), mate (2), together (2 [+448, 295]), NaomiS (1 [+2021]), abstain from sexual relations (1 [+440, 5602, 448]), age of childbearing (1 [+784, 3869, 2021]), be given in marriage (1 [+5989, 4200]), become wife (1 [+4374, 4200]), commits adultery (1 [+5537]), female (1), gave in marriage (1 [+5989]), girl (1 [+3251]), give (1 [+5989, 4200]), give in marriage (1 [+5989, 2021]), herS (1 [+2257]), herS (1 [+123, 2257]), married (1 [+2118]), married (1 [+5951]), married (1 [+4374, 4200, 2257, 4200]), married to (1 [+2118, 4200]), mothers (1), othersS (1 [+2021]), period (1 [+2006]), queensS (1), sheS (1 [+2257]), stillborn child (1 [+5878]), themS (1), theyS (1 [+2021]), theyS (1 [+1201, 2021]), took in marriage (1 [+4374, 4200]), was given in marriage (1 [+5989, 4200]), weaklingsS (1 [+3869, 2021]), widow (1 [+4637]), wife (1 [+1249]), women's (1), NDT (30)

H852 אִשֶּׁה ***'iššeh***, n.m. [65] [√ 836; 10080]. offering made by fire:– food offering (39), food offerings (20), food (2), food offering (2 [+4312]), food offering (1 [+7933]), food offerings (1 [+7933])

H853 אֲשׁוּיָה ***'ašûyâ***, n.f. Not used in NIVEBC [cf. 859]. see 859

H854 אֱשׁוּן ***'ešûn***, n.[m.] [1] approach (of darkness):– pitch darkness (1 [+3125])

H855 אַשּׁוּר ***'aššûr***, n.pr.g. & loc. [151] [√ 894]. Asshur, Assyria:– Assyria (120), Ashur (7), Assyrian (7), Assyrians (7), Assyrians (5 [+1201]), Assyria (2 [+824]), Assyria's (1), ShalmaneserS (1 [+4889]), NDT (1)

H856 אַשּׁוּרִי ***'ašûrî***, a.g. [1] Ashuri:– Ashuri (1)

H857 אַשּׁוּרִם ***'aššûrim***, n.pr.g.pl. [1] Asshurite, *"of Asshur"*:– Ashurites (1)

H858 אַשְׁחוּר ***'ašḥûr***, n.pr.m. [2] Ashhur:– Ashhur (2)

H859 אָשְׁיָה ***'ošyâ***, n.f. [1] [cf. 853]. tower:– towers (1)

H860 אֲשִׁימָא ***'ašîmā'***, n.pr.[m.] [1] Ashima:– Ashima (1)

H861 אָשִׁישׁ ***'āšîš***, n.m. man

H862 אֲשִׁישָׁה ***'ašîšâ***, n.f. [5] [√ 899?]. cake of raisins, made of dried, compressed grapes; used as food and as an offering:– cake of raisins (2), raisin cakes (1), raisins (1), sacred cakes (1)

H863 אֶשֶׁךְ ***'ešek***, n.[m.] [1] testicle:– testicles (1)

H864 1אֶשְׁכּוֹל ***'eškôl1***, n.m. [9] [→ 865, 866; cf. 8897]. cluster of grapes:– cluster of grapes (3), cluster (2), clusters (2), clusters of fruit (1), clusters of grapes (1)

H865 2אֶשְׁכֹּל ***'eškôl2***, n.pr.loc. [4] [√ 864]. Eshcol, *"[grape] cluster"*:– Eshkol (4)

H866 אֶשְׁכֹּל ***'eškōl3***, n.pr.m. [2] [√ 864]. Eshcol, *"[grape] cluster"*:– Eshkol (2)

H867 אַשְׁכְּנַז ***'aškenaz***, n.pr.m. [3] Ashkenaz:– Ashkenaz (3)

H868 אֶשְׁכָּר ***'eškār***, n.[m.] [2] gifts; payment:– gifts (1), paid (1 [+8740])

H869 אֶשֶׁל ***'ēšel***, n.m. [3] tamarisk tree:– tamarisk tree (3)

H870 אָשַׁם ***'āšam***, v. [35] [→ 871, 872, 873]. [Q] to be guilty; to be in a state of liable for a wrongdoing, with an implication of that one will suffer or be punished for the guilt; [N] to be suffering; [H] to declare guilty:– guilty (7), realize guilt (6), bear guilt (3), condemned (2), guilty of wrongdoing (2 [+870]), sin (2), very guilty (2 [+870]), aware that guilty (1), borne guilt (1), declare guilty (1), devastated (1), held guilty (1), not be guilty (1), pay for it (1), realizes guilt (1), suffering (1), unpunished (1 [+4202]), wronged (1)

H871 אָשָׁם ***'āšām***, n.m. [47] [√ 870]. guilt offering, atoning sacrifice; guilt, penalty:– guilt offering (28), guilt offerings (5), penalty (4), guilt (2), wrong (2), itsS (1 [+2021]), making amends for sin (1), offering for sin (1), restitution (1 [+8740]), sins (1), NDT (1)

H872 אָשֵׁם ***'āšēm***, a. [2] [√ 870]. guilty, bearing guilt:– convict (1), punished (1)

H873 אַשְׁמָה ***'ašmâ***, n.f. [19] [√ 870]. guilt, guiltiness:– guilt (13), guilty (2), guilt offering (1), guilty of sins (1), requiring payment (1), sin (1)

H874 אַשְׁמוּרָה ***'ašmûrâ***, n.f. [7] [√ 9068]. watch of the night (middle or last):– watches of the night (3), watch (2), last watch of the night (1 [+1332]), last watch of the night (1 [+2021, 1332])

H875 אַשְׁמָן ***'ašmān***, n.[m.]pl. [1] [√ 9043?]. strong one:– strong (1)

H876 אֶשְׁנָב ***'ešnāb***, n.[m.] [2] [√ 5959]. lattice, a barred or grated window:– lattice (2)

H877 אַשְׁנָה ***'ašnâ***, n.pr.loc. [2] Ashnah:– Ashnah (2)

H878 אֶשְׁעָן ***'eš'ān***, n.pr.loc. [1] Eshan, *"support"*:– Eshan (1)

H879 אַשָּׁף ***'aššāp***, n.m. [2] [√ 10081]. enchanter, conjurer, one of the profession of the secret arts, in communication with the dead:– enchanters (2)

H880 אַשְׁפָּה ***'ašpâ***, n.f. [6] quiver (for arrows):– quiver (5), quivers (1)

H881 אַשְׁפְּנַז ***'ašpenaz***, n.pr.m. [1] Ashpenaz, *"guest"*:– Ashpenaz (1)

H882 אֶשְׁפָּר ***'ešpār***, n.m. [2] [√ 8795]. cake of dates:– cake of dates (2)

H883 אַשְׁפֹּת ***'ašpōt***, n.[m.] [7] [√ 9189]. ash heap; Dung (Gate):– dung (4), ash heap (2), ash heaps (1)

H884 אַשְׁקְלוֹן ***'ašqelôn***, n.pr.loc. [12] [→ 885]. Ashkelon:– Ashkelon (12)

H885 אֶשְׁקְלוֹנִי ***'ešqelônî***, a.g. [1] [√ 884]. Ashkelonite, *"of Ashkelon"*:– Ashkelon (1)

H886 1אָשַׁר ***'āšar1***, v. [7] [→ 892, 893]. [Q] to walk (straight); [P] to lead, guide; reprove; [Pu] to be guided:– walk (2), are guided (1), defend (1), guide (1), guides (1), set right (1)

H887 2אָשַׁר ***'āšar2***, v. [9] [→ 888, 890, 891, 896, 897]. [P] to call blessed, pronounce happy, speak well of; [Pu] to be blessed; in some contexts, to give a blessing is to act kindly and impart benefits to the one being blessed; to be blessed implies the happy state that results:– call blessed (4), be blessed (1), call happy (1), called blessed (1), counted among the blessed (1), spoke well of (1)

H888 אָשֵׁר ***'āšēr***, n.pr.m. [43] [√ 896; cf. 887]. Asher,

"*Happy One!*":– Asher (37), Asher (5 [+1201]), Asher's (1 [+4946])

H889 אֲשֶׁר **'ašer**, pt.rel. [5494] [→ 948, 3876, 4424]. (rel.) who, which, what; (c.) that, in order that, so that:– who (526), that (519), as (269 [+3869]), which (210), what (177), whom (120), where (78), just as (59 [+3869]), whose (42), those (41), when (41), when (38 [+3869]), whatever (31 [+3972]), until (30 [+6330]), for (28), how (28), because (27), just as (23 [+3869, 3972]), what (19 [+3869]), as (18), because (18 [+3610]), just as (17 [+3869, 4027]), whatever (17), after (14 [+3869]), because (14 [+6584]), like (12), wherever (12 [+928, 3972]), so that (11), administrator (10 [+6584]), if (10), the one[S] (10), as (8 [+3869, 4027]), though (7), anyone (6), because (6 [+9393]), since (6), so (6), them[S] (6), whatever (6 [+3869]), as (5 [+3869, 3972]), because (5 [+3869]), he[S] (5), things (5), whatever (5 [+3869, 3972]), whoever (5), as (4 [+4027, 3869]), it[S] (4), of (4), something (4), the covenant[S] (4), as soon as (3), at (3), because (3 [+6813]), before (3 [+6330, 4202]), for (3 [+3610]), if (3 [+3869]), just as (3), one (3), since (3 [+3610]), such as (3), territory[S] (3), the land[S] (3), these (3), wherever (3 [+928, 5226]), although (2), as much as (2 [+3869]), because (2 [+928]), even as (2 [+3869]), even though (2), exactly as (2 [+3869, 4027]), for (2 [+9393]), here (2), him[S] (2), how much (2), just the way (2 [+3869]), just what (2 [+3869, 4027]), one[S] (2), or (2 [+4202]), others[S] (2), someone (2), sometimes (2 [+3780]), such (2), the creatures[S] (2), the day[S] (2), the men[S] (2), the name[S] (2), the ones[S] (2), the property[S] (2), the steward[S] (2 [+6584]), the way[S] (2), the ways[S] (2), there (2), they[S] (2), this (2), what (2 [+3869, 4027]), where (2 [+928]), wherever (2), wherever (2 [+448, 3972]), wherever (2 [+928, 2021, 2006]), wherever (2 [+928, 3972, 2021, 5226]), whoever (2 [+408]), with (2), abundantly (1 [+6330, 6330, 3907]), according to (1 [+3869]), according to (1), although (1 [+928, 3972]), any (1), anything (1 [+3972]), as (1 [+928]), as (1 [+928, 3972]), as easily as (1 [+3869]), as long as (1 [+3869]), as though (1 [+3869]), because (1 [+4946]), because (1 [+3869, 7023]), because of (1 [+3869]), but (1), by (1), cargo (1 [+3998, 928, 2021, 641]), closest friend (1 [+8276, 3869, 5883, 3870]), covenant[S] (1), creature[S] (1), creatures[S] (1), crowd (1 [+3972, 6641]), disaster[S] (1), do not know where am going (1 [+2143, 6584, 2143]), edict[S] (1), else[S] (1), everyone else (1), everything (1), everything else (1), exactly as (1 [+3869, 3972]), exactly like (1 [+3869, 3972, 4027]), except (1 [+4202]), finally (1 [+6330]), followers (1 [+2021, 6639, 339]), followers (1 [+408, 2143, 6640]), for (1 [+928]), for (1 [+6584]), from (1 [+928]), gods[S] (1), governor[S] (1 [+6584]), have (1 [+4200]), heavy enough[S] (1), houses[S] (1), if only (1 [+3869]), in (1), in accordance with (1 [+3869]), in accordance with (1 [+3972]), in proportion to (1 [+5002, 3869]), in the end (1 [+6330]), in the manner (1 [+3869]), including (1), instead of (1 [+9393]), it (1), just as (1 [+3869, 3972]), just as (1 [+4200, 3972]), just as (1 [+3869, 3972, 4027]), keeper[S] (1 [+6584]), kind (1 [+3869]), life (1 [+3427, 2118]), like (1 [+3869, 4027]), like (1 [+3869, 3972]), living things[S] (1), make countless (1 [+8049, 4202, 6218]), man[S] (1), matters[S] (1), more (1 [+3869]), moving from place to place (1 [+2143, 928, 2143]), my people[S] (1), no sooner than (1 [+3869]), nothing (1 [+4202, 3972]), now that (1 [+3869]), or (1), other[S] (1 [+907]), otherwise (1 [+4200, 5100, 4202]), people[S] (1), people[S] (1 [+3972, 928]), peoples[S] (1), place[S] (1), possessions[S] (1), predecessor (1 [+2118, 4200, 7156]), proper place (1 [+5226, 2118, 9004]), property[S] (1), property[S] (1 [+2118, 4200]), replies[S] (1), responsible for (1 [+4200, 928]), robe[S] (1), same (1 [+3869]), same (1 [+3869, 4027]), same as (1), share (1 [+3869, 4200]), shared hardships (1 [+6700, 928, 6700]), she[S] (1), since (1 [+339]), since (1 [+928]), since (1 [+4946]), since (1 [+9393]), so (1 [+3869]), so that (1 [+3610]), so with (1 [+3869]), some[S] (1), some other place[S] (1), some territory[S] (1), steward[S] (1 [+6584, 1074]), steward[S] (1 [+2021, 408, 6584, 1074]), surviving (1 [+3856, 3855]), than (1 [+4946]), that (1 [+6330]), the areas[S] (1), the celebration[S] (1), the cup[S] (1), the gods[S] (1), the man[S] (1), the person[S] (1), the place[S] (1), the places[S] (1), the plans[S] (1), the quarters[S] (1), the ridge[S] (1), the storehouses[S] (1 [+928, 2157]), the temple[S] (1), the terms[S] (1), the totals[S] (1), the vineyards[S] (1), the words[S] (1), the young woman[S] (1), then (1), then (1 [+3869]), this is how (1 [+3869]), those[S] (1 [+2021, 6639, 339]), till (1 [+6330]), town[S] (1), under (1), unless (1 [+4200, 963, 4946]), until (1 [+6330, 561]), until (1 [+6330, 561]), very thing (1 [+3869, 4027]), vows[S] (1), what (1 [+4017]), whatever (1 [+3869, 4027]), whatever (1 [+3869, 3972, 4027]), when (1 [+6584]), whenever (1 [+3869]), whenever (1 [+928, 3972]), wherever (1 [+928]), wherever (1 [+4946]), wherever (1 [+9004, 2025]), wherever (1 [+3972, 9004]), wherever (1 [+2021, 928, 2006]), wherever (1 [+928, 2021, 5226]), wherever (1 [+6584, 3972, 2021, 5226]), wherever (1 [+928, 285, 2021, 5226]), which[S] (1 [+5226]), while (1), while (1 [+3869]), who (1 [+2021]), whoever (1 [+4769]), whoever (1 [+4769]), whoever (1 [+3972, 408]), whose (1 [+4200]), yet (1), yet (1 [+4946, 1172]), you[S] (1), NDT (2644)

H890 אֶשֶׁר **'ešer**, n.[m.] [1] [√ 887]. fortune, blessedness, happiness:– blessed (1)

H891 אֹשֶׁר **'ōšer**, n.[m.] [1] [→ 897; cf. 887]. fortune, blessedness, happiness:– happy (1)

H892 אֲשֻׁר **'ašur**, n.f. [9] [√ 886]. steps, tracks:– steps (4), feet (2), foothold (1), place to stand (1), tracked down (1)

H893 ¹אַשּׁוּר **'aššur[1]**, n.f. Not used in NIVEBC [√ 886]. step, track, see 892

H894 ²אַשּׁוּר **'aššur[2]**, n.pr.g. & loc. Not used in NIVEBC [→ 855]. Asshur, see 855

H895 אֲשֵׁרָה **'ašērâ**, n.pr.f. [40] [cf. 6958?]. Asherah (pagan god), Asherah pole:– Asherah poles (22), Asherah pole (12), Asherah (5), Asherahs (1)

H896 אָשֵׁרִי **'āšērî**, a.g. [1] [√ 888; cf. 887]. people of Asher:– Asherites (1)

H897 אַשְׁרֵי **'ašrê**, n.[m.] [44] [√ 891; cf. 887]. blessed!, happy!, a heightened state of happiness and joy, implying very favorable circumstances, often resulting from the kind acts of God:– blessed (37), how happy (4), happy (2), blessings (1)

H898 אַשֻּׁרִים **'ašurîm**, n.pr.m.? Not used in NIVEBC [√ 9309]. Ashurites [?]

H899 אשׁשׁ **'āšaš**, v. [1] [→ 862?; 10079]. [Htpol] to fix in one's mind:– keep in mind (1)

H900 אֶשְׁתָּאֹל **'eštā'ōl**, n.pr.loc. [7] [→ 901; cf. 8626]. Eshtaol, "*[place of oracles,] inquiry*":– Eshtaol (7)

H901 אֶשְׁתָּאֻלִי **'eštā'ulî**, a.g. [1] [√ 900]. Eshtaolite, "*of Eshtaol*":– Eshtaolites (1)

H902 אֶשְׁתּוֹן **'eštōn**, n.pr.m. [2] Eshton, "[poss.] *hen-pecked [husband]* or *effeminate*":– Eshton (2)

H903 אֶשְׁתְּמֹה **'ešt[e]mōh**, n.pr.loc. [1] [cf. 904]. Eshtemoh, "*[place where oracle is] heard*":– Eshtemoh (1)

H904 אֶשְׁתְּמוֹעַ **'ešt[e]mōa'**, n.pr.loc. & m. [5] [√ 9048; cf. 903]. Eshtemoa, "*[place where oracle is] heard*":– Eshtemoa (5)

H905 אַתְּ **'att**, p.f.sg. [60] [→ 911, 914, 917, 920]. you:– you (50), how did it go (1 [+4769]), NDT (9)

H906 ¹אֵת **'ēt[1]**, pt. [10901] [→ 254; 10337]. usually not translated: marks the direct object:– aloud (5 [+5951, 7754]), entreat (3 [+2704, 7156]), ordained (3 [+4848, 3338]), sought the favor of (3 [+2704, 7156]), take a census (3 [+5951, 8031]), to (3), enabled to conceive (2 [+7337, 8167]), installed (2 [+4848, 3338]), let know (2 [+1655, 265]), openhanded (2 [+7337, 3338, 7337]), ordination (2 [+4848, 3338]), tells (2 [+1655, 265]), accepted (1 [+5951, 7156]), began (1 [+5951, 7754]), come into presence (1 [+8011, 7156]), consecrated (1 [+4848, 3338]), count (1 [+5951, 8031]), counted (1 [+5951, 8031]), counting on (1 [+5951, 5883, 448]), did[S] (1 [+2520, 2995]), did[S] (1 [+3877, 4213, 4392]), did so[S] (1 [+6913, 2021, 7175]), disheartened (1 [+5022, 4222]), for (1), given word (1 [+7198, 7023]), hardhearted (1 [+599, 4222]), has sexual relations with (1 [+1655, 6872]), have sexual relations (1 [+8011, 6872]), helped (1 [+2616, 3338]), helped find strength (1 [+2616, 3338]), include in the census (1 [+5951, 8031]), inquire of (1 [+8626, 7023]), intercede with (1 [+2704, 7156]), interceded with (1 [+2704, 7156]), keep themselves alive (1 [+8740, 5883, 4392]), let go (1 [+5663, 3338]), letting know (1 [+1655, 265]), looked (1 [+6524]), on (1), ordain (1 [+4848, 3338]), out (1 [+5951]), relieve himself (1 [+6114, 8079, 2257]), relieving himself (1 [+6114, 8079, 2257]), revealed (1 [+1655, 265]), saw (1 [+5951, 6524]), seek favor (1 [+2704, 7156]), sent on way (1 [+8938]), sought favor (1 [+2704, 7156]), stared with a fixed gaze (1 [+6641, 7156, 2256, 8492]), sulking (1 [+6015, 7156]), sworn (1 [+5951, 3338]), tell (1 [+1655, 265]), tightfisted (1 [+7890, 3338]), undergo circumcision (1 [+4576, 1414, 6889]), uttered a word (1 [+3076, 4383]), want to kill (1 [+1335, 5883]), wanted (1 [+8626, 5883]), wanted to kill (1 [+1335, 5883]), wept so loudly (1 [+1140, 5989, 7754, 928]), worry (1 [+8492, 4213]), NDT (10821)

H907 ²אֵת **'ēt[2]**, pp. [935] [→ 909, 4425]. with, to, upon, beside, among, against:– with (405), from (93 [+4946]), against (34), to (30), along with (18), among (15), his (15 [+2257]), of (10), before (8 [+7156]), and (7), have (7), near (7), slept with (6 [+8886]), for (5), by (4), in (4), left (4 [+2143, 4946]), on (4), through (4 [+4946]), doing (3 [+4946]), had (3 [+5162]), pronounced on (3 [+1819]), the Lord's (3 [+4946, 3378]), allied with (2), away (2 [+4946]), away from (2 [+4946]), before (2), close to (2), has (2), have (2 [+3780]), in front of (2 [+7156]), leave (2 [+2143, 4946]), within (2), about (1), accompanied (1 [+2143]), accompanied (1 [+6590]), accompanied by (1), accompany (1 [+3655]), according to (1), account for (1 [+3108]), acquire (1 [+7864]), adding to (1 [+2256]), all around (1), alongside (1), among (1 [+4946]), among (1 [+8905]), and (1 [+2256]), and together (1), any of (1 [+4946]), as well as (1), ask (1 [+8626]), assist (1 [+6641]), because of (1), both and (1), bring (1 [+995]), by (1 [+4946]), by myself (1 [+4946, 3276]), company (1 [+2118]), concern (1), confide in (1 [+4213]), decreed (1), defend (1), determined (1 [+4946]), fighting with (1 [+2118]), following (1 [+6639]), for (1 [+4946]), forsaking (1 [+4946]), gain support (1 [+2118, 3338]), given to (1), gone from (1 [+401]), had (1), have with (1), help (1), help (1 [+2118]), help (1 [+6913]), helped (1), helping (1), in hand (1), in possession (1), in presence (1 [+7156]), in sight (1 [+7156]), in view (1 [+7156]), inquire of (1 [+2011, 4946]), into (1), know (1), leaves (1 [+2143, 4946]), left (1 [+4946]), like (1), lost (1 [+5877, 4946]), my (1 [+3276]), near (1 [+2143]), next to (1), on (1 [+4946]), on behalf of (1 [+4946]), on side (1), oppose (1), other[S] (1 [+889]), out of (1 [+4946]), over (1), past (1 [+4946]), representative (1 [+4946]), send (1 [+995, 4946]), sent by (1 [+4946]), served (1 [+6641, 7156]), shared with (1), show (1), sleeping with (1 [+8886]), sleeps with (1 [+8886, 8887, 2446]), some (1 [+4946]), supported (1 [+3338, 2118]), through (1), to (1 [+7156]), together (1), together (1 [+408, 8276, 2084]), together with (1), told (1 [+9048, 4946]), toward (1), under (1), under (1 [+7156]), under care (1), upon (1), with (1 [+7156]), with the help of (1), with the help of (1 [+4946]), within sight of (1 [+7156]), your (1 [+3870]), NDT (130)

H908 ³אֵת **'ēt[3]**, n.[m.] [5] plowshare, mattock:– plowshares (3), mattocks (2)

H909 אֶתְבַּעַל **'etba'al**, n.pr.m. [1] [√ 907 + 1251]. Ethbaal, "*with [him is] Baal*":– Ethbaal (1)

H910 אתה **'ātâ**, v. [21] [→ 415, 484, 517; 10085]. [Q] to come; [H] to bring:– come (7), bring (2), comes (2), advance (1), assembled (1), be restored (1), came (1), come forward (1), coming (1), holds (1), pass (1), sweeps over (1), things to come (1)

H911 אַתָּה **'attâ**, p.m.sg. [745] [√ 905; 10051, 10052]. you, your, yourself:– you (624), yourself (17), your (4), you alone (2 [+911]), your own (2), you're (2), it (1), you yourself (1), yours (1), you'll (1), NDT (90)

H912 אָתוֹן **'ātôn**, n.f. [34] female donkey:– donkey (13), donkeys (12), it[S] (3 [+2021]), female donkeys (3), colt (1 [+1201]), donkey's (1), them[S] (1 [+2021])

H913 אַתּוּק **'attûq**, n.m. Not used in NIVEBC [cf. 916]. see 916

H914 אַתִּי **'attî**, p.f.sg. Not used in NIVEBC [√ 905]. see 905

H915 אִתַּי **'ittay**, n.pr.m. [8] [cf. 416]. Ittai, "[poss.] *with me*":– Ittai (7), Ithai (1)

H916 אַתִּיק **'attîq**, n.m. [5] [cf. 913]. gallery, porch; other sources: street, passage:– galleries (3), gallery (2)

H917 אַתֶּם **'attem**, p.m.pl. [283] [√ 905; 10053]. you (all), yours, yourselves:– you (243), yourselves (10), your (3), yours (2), people[S] (1), you and your men (1), NDT (23)

H918 אֵתָם **'ētām**, n.pr.loc. [4] Etham, "[poss.] *fort*":– Etham (4)

H919 אֶתְמוֹל **'etmôl**, subst.adv. [8] [√ 9453]. yesterday; (adv.) before, formerly, lately, in the past:– before (2 [+8997]), day (1 [+3427]), formerly (1 [+4946, 8997]), in the past (1 [+1685, 1685, 8997]), lately (1), long (1 [+4946]), previously (1 [+3869, 8997])

H920 אַתֵּן **'attēn**, p.f.pl. [4] [√ 905]. you (all):– you (4)

H921 אֶתְנָה **'etnâ**, n.f. [1] [√ 924]. payment (of a prostitute):– pay (1)

H922 אֶתְנִי **'etnî**, n.pr.m. [1] Ethni, "*gift* or *hire*":– Ethni (1)

H923 אֵתָנִים **'ētānîm**, n.pr.[m.] [1] [√ 3851]. Ethanim, "*ever-flowing [streams]*":– Ethanim (1)

H924 אֶתְנַן **'etnan**, n.m. [11] [→ 921, 925, 9479; cf. 5989]. wages, payment (of a prostitute):– earnings (2), payment (2), wages (2), lucrative prostitution (1), pay (1 [+5989]), temple gifts (1), wages of a prostitute (1), NDT (1)

H925 אֶתְנָן **'etnān**, n.pr.m. [1] [√ 924]. Ethnan, "*hire [of a prostitute]*":– Ethnan (1)

H926 אֲתָרִים **'atārîm**, n.pr.loc. [1] Atharim, "[trad.] *way of the spies*":– Atharim (1)

H927 ב **b**, letter. Not used in NIVEBC [√ 10088]. letter of the Hebrew alphabet

H928 -בְּ **b[e]-**, pp.pref. [15533] [→ 948, 972, 1198, 1233, 1236, 1247, 1295, 1417; 10089]. in, on, among, over, through, against; when, whenever; a spatial, temporal, or logical marker to show relationship of objects, words, and phrases:– in (4595), with (1040), on (971), at (595), by (494), when (491), into (346), of (294), to (287), against (261), among (243), through (187), for (162), among (114 [+9348]), from (99), over (91), as (80), through (62 [+3338]), because of (59), during (58), according to (50), among (50 [+7931]), while (49), in (47 [+9348]), throughout (47 [+3972]), when (44 [+3427]), before (36 [+3270]), obey (35 [+9048, 7754]), under (34), followed (28 [+2143]), throughout (27), after (26), along (26), enter (26 [+995]), follow (26 [+2143]), in (24 [+7931]), there[S] (22 [+2023]), about (21), whenever (21), with (21 [+3338]), to (19 [+265]), within (19 [+7931]), by (18 [+3338]), near (18), obeyed (18 [+9048, 7754]), within (18), because (17), with (17 [+9348]), how (16 [+4537]), if (16), to (16 [+7754]), inquired of (15 [+8626]), inside (15 [+9348]), to (15 [+3338]), used (14), within (14 [+9348]), here (12 [+2296]), where (12), for the sake of (11 [+6288]), had (11), has (11), have (11), when (11 [+6961]), with (11 [+7931]), around (10), burned (10 [+8596, 2021, 836]), entered (10 [+995]), upon (10), wherever (10 [+3972]), because of (9 [+1673]), burn down (9 [+8596, 2021, 836]), east (9 [+6298]), inside (9), into (9 [+9348]), safely (9 [+8934]), seems (9 [+6524]), think (9 [+6524]), wherever (9 [+3972, 889]), without (9 [+4202]), and (8), in spite of (8), seemed (8 [+6524]), through (8 [+9348]), before (7), invade (7 [+995]), outside (7 [+2021, 2575]), pleased (7 [+3512, 6524]), that (7), along with (6 [+9348]), always (6 [+3972, 6961]), amid (6), because of (6 [+6288]), before (6 [+2021, 8037]), despite (6), hand over (6 [+5989, 3338]), like (6), secretly (6 [+2021, 6260]), set on fire (6 [+3675, 2021, 836]), there[s] (6 [+3731]), this is how (6 [+2296]), unintentionally (6 [+8705]), use (6), using (6), within (6 [+6388]), against (5 [+7156]), any (5), at the cost of (5), beyond (5 [+6298]), burn (5 [+8596, 2021, 836]), displeased (5 [+8317, 6524]), has (5 [+2118]), on account of (5), pleased with (5 [+5162, 2834, 6524]), ruthlessly (5 [+7266]), so that (5 [+6288]), stone (5 [+8083, 2021, 74]), very old (5 [+2416, 995, 2021, 3427]), accidentally (4 [+8705]), across (4), across (4 [+6298]), allotted (4 [+2021, 1598]), be burned up (4 [+8596, 2021, 836]), committing[s] (4), consult (4 [+2011]), every morning (4 [+2021, 1332, 928, 2021, 1332]), faithfully (4 [+575]), faithfully (4 [+622]), following (4 [+2143]), for sake (4 [+6288]), handed over (4 [+5989, 3338]), have (4 [+3338]), in exchange for (4), inner room (4 [+2540, 2540]), inquire of (4 [+2011]), invaded (4 [+995]), like (4 [+3202, 6524]), on (4 [+7931]), out of (4), proclaim (4 [+7924]), some (4), there[s] (4 [+2257]), there[s] (4 [+2021, 1195]), touch (4 [+2118]), unintentionally (4 [+1172, 1981]), wearing (4), whether (4), wish (4 [+3202, 6524]), with (4 [+6524]), as (3 [+2006]), at the risk of (3), at the time of (3), because (3 [+6288]), before (3 [+4202]), beside (3), between (3 [+9348]), burn up (3 [+8596, 2021, 836]), burned down (3 [+8596, 2021, 836]), burned up (3 [+8596, 2021, 836]), called out (3 [+7924, 7754, 1524]), cost (3), daily (3 [+3427, 3427]), each year (3 [+9102, 9102]), early (3 [+8040]), every last male (3 [+8874, 7815]), favorably disposed toward (3 [+2834, 6524]), fill (3), first (3 [+2021, 9378]), heard (3 [+265]), holding (3 [+3338]), including (3), king's (3 [+4889]), later (3), made (3), male (3 [+8874, 7815]), near (3 [+7931]), on high (3 [+2021, 5294]), on the basis of (3), peacefully (3 [+8934]), saw (3 [+6524]), secret (3 [+4537]), seem (3 [+6524]), set on fire (3 [+8596, 2021, 836]), set on fire (3 [+3675, 836, 2021]), share (3 [+5951]), stone (3 [+6232, 2021, 74]), there[s] (3 [+2023]), there[s] (3 [+2023]), though (3), through (3 [+7931]), throughout (3 [+3972, 1473]), to (3 [+6288]), toward (3), under (3 [+3338]), whenever (3 [+3972]), wherever (3 [+3972, 889]), wherever (3 [+5226, 889]), wild (3 [+2021, 8441]), without (3 [+700]), accompanied by (2), all (2), all day long (2 [+2021, 3427, 2021, 2085]), allotted (2 [+5989, 2021, 1598]), alone (2 [+1727, 2257]), along with (2), anywhere (2 [+3972, 5226]), as (2 [+6961]), as before (2 [+3869, 7193, 7193]), as long as (2), as long as live (2 [+6388]), as soon as (2), assassinate (2 [+8938, 3338]), associate with (2 [+995]), at (2 [+6961]), at (2 [+2021, 2942, 6330]), because (2 [+889]), before (2 [+265]), before (2 [+3270, 4202]), bloodshed (2 [+995, 1947]), bring (2), by (2 [+6524]), by what means (2 [+4537]), chosen (2 [+7924, 9005]), deceitfully (2 [+5327]), disobeyed (2 [+4202, 9048, 7754]), distressed (2 [+8317, 6524]), do (2), down (2), each (2), each day (2 [+3427, 3427]), earlier (2 [+2021, 9378]), entrusted with (2 [+575]), every morning (2 [+928, 2021, 1332, 2021, 1332]), every morning (2 [+928, 2021, 1332, 2021, 1332]), first (2 [+2021, 8037]), fleet-footed (2 [+7824, 8079]), following (2), following (2 [+8079]), follows (2 [+2143]), for (2 [+6288]), for each day (2 [+1821, 3427, 3427]), for nothing (2 [+1896, 8198]), from (2 [+9348]), fully obey (2 [+9048, 7754, 9048]), greatly (2 [+4394, 4394]), had (2 [+3338]), has (2 [+3780]), have respect for (2 [+3700, 6524]), honorably (2 [+622]), in charge of (2), in each corner (2 [+928, 5243, 5243]), in obedience to (2), in order to (2 [+6288]), in regard to (2), in return for (2), inside (2 [+2021, 1074]), intersecting (2 [+9348]), its (2 [+2023]), joyfully (2 [+8525]), just as (2), led by (2 [+8031]), listen closely (2 [+9048, 265]), look carefully (2 [+8011, 6524]), make a survey of (2 [+2143]), make want to (2 [+5989, 8120]), mark (2), my (2 [+8079, 3276]), near (2 [+6298]), obeying (2 [+9048, 7754]), on guard (2 [+9068, 8120]), over (2 [+8031]), overwhelmed (2 [+4202, 2118, 6388, 8120]), pierces (2 [+5918, 2256, 995]), play (2 [+5594, 3338]), playing the lyre (2 [+5594, 3338]), please (2 [+3202, 6524]), please (2 [+3837, 6524]), pleased (2 [+3202, 6524]), pleased (2 [+3837, 6524]), privately (2 [+2021, 6260]), quietly (2 [+2021, 4319]), reached (2 [+995]), required (2 [+5957, 460]), so (2 [+6288]), sold for (2 [+2118]), stoned (2 [+6232, 2021, 74]), struck (2 [+2118]), supervising (2), that (2 [+6288]), then (2 [+2021, 340]), there[s] (2 [+9076]), there[s] (2 [+2021, 1074]), there[s] (2 [+9348, 2023]), thought (2 [+6524]), throughout (2 [+6017]), throughout (2 [+9348]), to (2 [+6524]), truly (2 [+622]), under command (2 [+8079]), up to (2), very (2 [+4394, 4394]), what (2 [+4537]), what (2), where (2 [+889]), where[s] (2 [+2023]), wherever (2), wherever (2 [+2021, 2006, 889]), while (2 [+3427]), wholeheartedly (2 [+3972, 4222]), wholeheartedly (2 [+3972, 4213]), wholeheartedly (2 [+4222, 8969]), why (2 [+4537]), with help (2), without (2 [+401]), withstand (2 [+995]), withstand (2 [+6641, 7156]), yearly (2 [+9102, 285]), Israelite (1 [+3776]), Israelite (1 [+1201, 3776]), Israel's (1 [+3776]), ability (1 [+2683, 4213]), aboard (1), above (1 [+2021, 5294]), accuse (1 [+8492, 1821]), after (1 [+1821]), after (1 [+3427]), after (1 [+9005]), after (1 [+4946, 1896]), again (1 [+1685, 2021, 7193, 2021, 2085]), against (1 [+6330]), alive (1 [+5883]), all (1 [+285]), all night long (1 [+2021, 4326]), allotted (1 [+2118, 1598, 2021]), alone (1 [+285]), along (1 [+6298]), along (1 [+9348]), along with (1 [+3338]), along with (1 [+7931]), alongside (1), aloud (1 [+7754]), aloud (1 [+7754, 1524]), already (1 [+9378, 2021]), already (1 [+8611, 3893]), although (1 [+3972, 889]), among (1 [+2021, 9348]), angry (1 [+3013, 6524]), annual (1 [+7193, 2021, 9102]), annual (1 [+285, 2021, 9102]), annually (1 [+3972, 9102, 2256, 9102]), anywhere in (1 [+3972, 1473]), appealed to (1 [+3512, 6524]), appear (1 [+2118, 6524, 3869]), appointed (1 [+5989, 3338]), approve of (1 [+3202, 6524]), archers (1 [+4619, 2021, 8008]), archers (1 [+4619, 408, 2021, 8008]), are burned up (1 [+8596, 2021, 836, 8596]), arrayed in (1), arrest (1 [+8938, 3338]), as (1 [+889]), as (1 [+3972, 889]), as done before (1 [+3869, 7193, 7193]), as long as (1 [+3427]), as long as (1 [+3972, 6961]), as one (1 [+9348]), as sail[s] (1 [+4213]), as usually did (1 [+3869, 3427, 3427]), assault (1 [+8938]), assemble (1 [+6590, 2021, 7736]), assisted (1 [+2616, 3338]), assuredly (1 [+622]), at (1 [+6298]), at (1 [+7931]), at (1 [+9348]), at (1 [+2021, 2006]), at once (1 [+2021, 3427]), at once (1 [+2021, 6961, 2021, 2085]), at once (1 [+2021, 3427, 2021, 2085]), at other times (1 [+7193, 7193]), at stake (1), at the blast (1 [+1896]), at the time (1), attached to (1), attack (1 [+3718]), attack (1 [+5877]), attack (1 [+8938, 3338]), attacked (1 [+5877]), attacked (1 [+6590]), attacked (1 [+8938, 3338]), attacks (1 [+8938, 3338]), bare (1 [+4399, 401]), based on (1), be a virgin (1 [+1436]), be burned (1 [+8596, 2021, 836]), be burned down (1 [+8596, 2021, 836]), be defeated (1 [+5989, 3338]), be taken captive (1 [+9530, 2021, 4090]), bears (1), because (1 [+1673]), because (1 [+3610]), because (1 [+3610, 3610]), because (1 [+3610, 2256, 3610]), become allies (1 [+2118, 7931]), before (1 [+678]), before (1 [+2021, 9378]), beginning with (1), behind (1), belong to (1 [+2118]), belonged to (1 [+8079]), bent on (1), bent on (1 [+6783]), beset (1 [+995]), beside (1 [+2668]), beside (1 [+3338]), besiege (1 [+995, 2021, 5189]), besieged (1 [+2837]), between (1), bind themselves with (1 [+995]), blind (1 [+6427, 5782, 2021]), boasted (1 [+1540, 7023]), boldly (1 [+3338, 8123]), borrowed (1 [+5957]), bought (1 [+7864, 2021, 4084]), bring about (1 [+2118]), brought (1 [+3338]), brought with (1 [+2118, 3338]), brutally (1 [+7266]), burn (1 [+1277, 2021, 241]), burn to death (1 [+8596, 2021, 836]), burned (1 [+8938, 2021, 836]), burned to death (1 [+8596, 2021, 836]), buy (1 [+4084]), by (1 [+9348]), by day (1 [+3429]), by means (1), by means of (1), cargo (1 [+3998, 889, 2021, 641]), carried (1 [+4374, 3338]), carry off (1 [+995, 2021, 8660]), carrying (1), cause (1 [+3338]), charred (1 [+1277, 2021, 836]), claimed too soon (1 [+987, 2021, 8037]), close to (1), clung to (1), come into (1 [+5877]), commit (1 [+2143]), committed (1 [+2143]), compels (1), concealed in (1), conduct the affairs (1 [+2143, 7931]), consider (1 [+4222]), consider (1 [+6524]), considered (1 [+6524]), consult (1 [+2011, 1821]), containing (1), contrary to (1 [+4202, 3869]), counted off (1 [+6296, 5031]), counterattack (1 [+2200, 2021, 4878]), covered (1 [+2118]), covers (1 [+995]), cruelly (1 [+2622]), customary (1 [+7193, 7193, 3869]), daily (1 [+1821, 3427, 3427]), daily (1 [+3427, 3427, 2257]), day by day (1 [+1821, 3427, 3427]), day by day (1 [+1821, 3427, 3427, 2257]), dealing with (1), debtor (1 [+5957]), deceived (1 [+5792, 5793]), deceptively (1 [+6817]), defiantly (1 [+7418]), defiantly (1 [+3338, 8123]), delegation (1 [+3338, 6269]), deliberately (1 [+6893]), deliver (1 [+5989]), delivered (1 [+3338]), despise (1 [+1022, 6524]), despise (1 [+7837, 6524]), despises (1 [+1022, 6524]), despises (1 [+7837, 6524]), despite (1 [+8611, 4200]), diligently obey (1 [+9048, 7754, 9048]), disapprove (1 [+8317, 6524]), disobedience (1 [+4202, 9048, 7754]), disobey (1 [+1194, 9048, 7754]), displease (1 [+8273, 6524]), displease (1 [+4202, 5162, 2834, 6524]), displeased greatly (1 [+8317, 6524]), displeasing (1 [+8273, 6524]), displeasing (1 [+4202, 5162, 2834, 6524]), distributed among (1), do[s] (1), do that[s] (1 [+2118, 2257, 3338]), done (1 [+4848, 3338]), done by (1 [+3338]), doubly (1 [+2021, 9109]), drew (1 [+4848, 3338]), driving (1), due annually (1 [+4946, 1896, 9102, 9102]), during (1 [+3427]), each day's (1 [+3427, 3427]), each day's (1 [+3427, 3427, 2257]), each morning (1 [+2021, 1332, 928, 2021, 1332]), each morning (1 [+928, 2021, 1332, 2021, 1332]), eagerly (1 [+3972, 8356]), east (1 [+6298, 4667, 2025]), east (1 [+6298, 4667, 9087]), east (1 [+6298, 4667, 2025, 9087]), encounter (1 [+995]), end (1 [+2118, 2021, 340]), endures (1), enrich (1), entered (1 [+995, 9348]), entering (1 [+995]), entering (1 [+995, 7931]), entering (1 [+995, 9348]), enters (1 [+995]), entrusted to (1 [+3338]), even after (1), even if (1), even though (1), evening (1 [+2021, 6847, 928, 2021, 6847]), evening (1 [+928, 2021, 6847, 2021, 6847]), every (1), every day (1 [+3427, 3427]), every evening (1 [+2021, 6847, 928, 2021, 6847]), every evening (1 [+928, 2021, 6847, 2021, 6847]), every sabbath (1 [+8701, 8701]), everyone's (1 [+408]), everywhere (1 [+3972, 5226]), everywhere (1 [+3972, 2021, 824]), exceedingly (1 [+4394, 4394]), extort (1 [+2021, 6945]), fairly (1 [+7406]), faithful (1 [+2143, 622]), far back in (1 [+3752]), far off (1 [+8158]), far out (1 [+4213]), fault (1 [+8611, 4200]), favorable toward (1 [+5162, 2834, 6524]), few (1 [+5071, 5031]), fiercely (1 [+2021, 6677]), filled (1 [+2118, 3972]), filled with (1 [+7931]), flashed back and forth (1 [+4374, 9348]), flashes (1 [+836]), follow (1 [+2118]), follow (1 [+8079]), follow (1 [+2143, 8079]), followed (1), for (1 [+889]), for (1 [+6524]), for (1 [+9348]), for (1 [+8611, 1685]), for lack of (1), for this purpose (1 [+6288]), forcefully (1 [+3338]), formerly (1 [+2021, 8037]), fought in (1 [+3655]), free from (1 [+4202]), from (1 [+889]), from (1 [+3338]), from (1 [+6524]), from now (1 [+6388]), from the time (1), fuel for fire (1 [+1896, 836]), fuel for flames (1 [+1896, 836]), fully determined (1 [+4222, 8969]), gave in (1 [+9048, 7754]), gave victory (1 [+5989, 3338]), get (1), get the better of (1 [+5957]), give (1 [+5989, 3338]), given by (1), giving credit to (1 [+9005]), glad (1 [+3512, 6524]), gladly (1 [+3206, 4222]), go (1 [+2143, 2006]), gone (1 [+4202, 6641]), gone (1 [+4202, 2118]), grown old (1 [+2416, 995, 2021, 3427]), guilty (1 [+3338]), had (1 [+2118]), had (1 [+7023]), had (1 [+7931]), had chance (1 [+2118, 3338]), hand over (1 [+6037, 3338]), handed (1 [+5989, 3338]), handed over (1 [+5162, 3338]), handing over (1 [+5989, 3338]), harbor (1 [+4328, 7931]), harbor in (1), harshly (1 [+2622]), have (1 [+2118]), have (1 [+5055]), have (1 [+7023]), have (1 [+5162, 3338]), have a claim on (1), have in (1), have something to eat (1 [+5966, 9094]), having sexual relations with (1 [+5989, 8888]), heard (1 [+606, 265]), heard (1 [+7992, 7754]), here[s] (1 [+2023]), here[s] (1 [+5226]), here[s] (1 [+2021, 4497]), here[s] (1 [+2021, 824]), here[s] (1 [+2021, 5226, 2021, 2296]), his (1 [+2257]), his[s] (1 [+2021, 4889]), hold (1 [+2118, 3338]), holding (1), holds (1 [+2118, 3338]), how (1), how (1 [+2021, 4537, 686]), hurl insults (1 [+7080, 8557]), if (1 [+3427]), if (1 [+3427]), imagine (1 [+5381]), imprisoned (1 [+5989, 5464]), in (1 [+1068]), in (1 [+3427]), in (1 [+4213]), in (1 [+4595]), in accordance with (1), in charge of (1 [+3338]), in equal amounts (1 [+963, 963]), in keeping with (1), in payment for (1), in person (1 [+265]), in possession (1), in reliance on (1), in response to (1), in step with (1 [+6783]), in the name of (1), in the order (1), in view of (1), include (1 [+9348]), inquire of (1 [+8626]), inquires of (1 [+8626, 1821]), inquiring of (1 [+8626]), inserted into (1), inside (1 [+7931]), insist on paying for (1 [+7864, 4697, 7864]), inspire (1 [+5989, 4222]), intentionally (1 [+7402]), into (1 [+7931]), invade (1 [+6296]), invade (1 [+6590]), invaded (1 [+6590]), invading (1 [+995]), invoke (1 [+7924, 7023]), involved in (1), its[s] (1 [+2021, 6551]), join (1 [+2118]), joined in (1 [+9348]), just before (1 [+3270]), keep (1 [+2143]), keeping watch (1 [+8011, 6524]), kept (1 [+2143]), killing (1 [+8938, 3338]), know (1 [+3780, 1978]), lack (1 [+401]), lack (1 [+4202]), laden with (1), laid siege (1 [+995, 2021, 5189]), lamb (1 [+8445, 2021, 3897]), lamb (1 [+8445, 2021, 4166]), land's (1 [+824]), lately (1 [+700]), later (1 [+2021, 340]), later in time (1 [+344]), lead life (1 [+2143]), leads (1 [+2021, 8037]), leave (1), led life (1 [+2143]), left (1 [+3338]), let get away (1 [+8938, 2006]), let touch (1 [+995]), leveled completely (1 [+9164, 2021, 9168]), lie in state (1 [+8886, 3883]), lies in wait (1 [+741, 2021, 5041]), like (1 [+9348]), like (1 [+2021, 3202, 4200]), liked (1 [+3837, 6524]), listen carefully (1 [+9048, 7754]), listen carefully (1 [+265, 9048]), listened (1 [+265]), live (1 [+2143]), live (1 [+2021, 2644]), lived (1 [+2021, 1074]), long ago (1 [+2021, 8037]), look (1 [+6524]), looked (1 [+2118, 6524]), lose heart (1 [+1327, 8120, 7931]), lost self-confidence (1 [+5877, 4394, 6524]), loudly (1 [+7754, 1524]), made (1 [+4374]), made a fatal mistake (1 [+9494, 5883]), made pay for (1 [+8740, 8031]), made with (1), make enter (1 [+995]), make fine speeches (1 [+2488, 4863]), make full restitution (1 [+8740, 8031]), make sure hears (1 [+8492, 265]), makes (1), measured out (1 [+9419, 4500]), mention (1 [+9019, 7023]), monthly (1 [+2544, 2544]), mortal (1 [+5883]), mounted (1 [+2021, 6061]), moving from place to place (1 [+2143, 889, 2143]), must sell (1 [+4835, 2021, 4084, 4835]), my (1 [+3276]), nails down (1 [+2616, 5021]), named (1 [+7924, 9005]), native-born (1 [+3528, 2021, 824]), nomads (1 [+8905, 185]), not please (1 [+8317, 6524]), not want (1 [+8273, 6524]), now (1), now (1 [+2021, 3427, 2021, 465]), now (1 [+2021, 3427, 2021, 465]), obey (1 [+2143]), obey fully (1 [+9048, 7754, 9048]), obeys (1 [+9048, 7754]), of (1 [+9348]), off (1), offer (1), offered (1), on (1 [+9348]), on account of (1 [+6288]), on board (1), on board (1 [+9348]), on each side (1), on fire (1 [+1277, 2021, 836]), on high (1 [+7757]), on side (1), on the condition that (1 [+2296]), on the tip of tongue (1 [+4383, 2674]), once (1), one (1), one by one (1 [+5031]), one of[s] (1), one way (1 [+285]), only (1 [+1727, 2257]), only if (1), only to (1 [+6288]), oppose (1 [+995]), oppressed (1 [+6913, 2021, 6945]), out here (1 [+2021, 2575]), out in (1), outdoor (1 [+2021, 2575]), over

(1 [+9348]), over to (1), overrun (1), paid (1), parallel (1 [+7156]), part of (1), pay with (1), peaceably (1 [+8934]), penetrate (1 [+995]), penned up (1 [+3973, 1074, 2021]), people[S] (1 [+3972, 889]), pierce (1), pierce (1 [+995]), pierced (1 [+995]), pierced (1 [+5737]), placed seal (1 [+3159, 2597]), playing[S] (1), please (1 [+3838, 6524]), please (1 [+3202, 2256, 3838, 6524]), pleased (1 [+3838, 6524]), pleased (1 [+3201, 6524]), pleased with (1 [+3202, 6524]), pleased with (1 [+3512, 6524]), pleased with (1 [+3837, 6524]), pleased with (1 [+5951, 2834, 6524]), pleases (1 [+3512, 6524]), pleases (1 [+3202, 6524]), plot (1 [+3108, 4222]), plot against (1 [+3108, 4222]), prefer (1 [+3202, 6524]), present in (1), preserved (1 [+8492, 2021, 2645]), presumptuously (1 [+2295]), prevailed on (1 [+2616]), privately (1 [+2021, 4319]), privately (1 [+2021, 8952]), proclaimed (1 [+7924]), prone to (1), protect (1 [+8883, 3829]), pursues (1 [+8740]), put in jeopardy (1 [+5951, 1414, 9094]), put on (1 [+8492, 5516]), put on makeup (1 [+6167, 2021, 7037]), put up a bold front (1 [+6451, 7156]), quickly (1 [+4559]), raiding (1 [+995]), rationed (1 [+5374]), rationed (1 [+5486]), reached (1 [+2118]), reached (1 [+9048]), reaches to (1), ready for battle (1 [+7372, 2021, 4878]), really (1 [+622]), recently (1 [+7940]), regards (1 [+5162, 6524]), regular flow (1 [+2307, 1414]), regularly (1 [+4200, 3427, 3427]), rely on (1 [+2143]), repay (1 [+5989, 8031]), repay (1 [+8740, 8031]), residing in (1), responsible for (1 [+6015]), responsible for (1 [+4200, 889]), responsible for (1 [+8611, 4200]), result of (1), ride (1 [+2143]), risked (1), roars (1 [+5989, 7754]), sabbath after sabbath (1 [+3427, 2021, 8701, 928, 3427, 2021, 8701]), sabbath after sabbath (1 [+928, 3427, 2021, 8701, 3427, 2021, 8701]), sacrificed (1 [+5989, 6296]), said (1 [+1819, 7023]), said (1 [+2143, 2021, 641]), sandaled (1 [+2021, 5837]), satisfied (1 [+8934]), satisfied (1 [+3512, 6524]), scarce (1 [+430, 5017]), scorned the idea (1 [+1022, 6524]), screamed (1 [+7924, 7754, 1524]), search (1 [+606]), see (1 [+6524]), seem (1 [+4017, 6524]), seem (1 [+2118, 6524]), seemed (1 [+2118, 6524]), seen as (1 [+6524]), sees (1 [+6524]), seize (1 [+8492, 3338]), self-control (1 [+5440, 8120]), sell (1 [+5989, 4084]), sell (1 [+5989, 4084]), sell for (1 [+2118]), set ablaze (1 [+3675, 2021, 836]), set fire to (1 [+8596, 2021, 836]), set fire to (1 [+8938, 836, 2021]), set on (1), set on fire (1 [+8596, 836, 2021]), set with (1), shamefully (1 [+2365]), shared hardships (1 [+6700, 889, 6700]), shoot (1 [+2021, 8008]), shout (1 [+7924, 7754]), shout aloud (1 [+7924, 1744]), shouted (1 [+7924, 7754]), shouted (1 [+8123, 7754, 9558]), since (1), since (1 [+889]), sing (1 [+8492, 7023]), sins defiantly (1 [+6913, 3338, 8123]), sins unintentionally (1 [+6913, 8705]), sling stones (1 [+2021, 74]), smoothed (1 [+1760, 2021, 4490]), smoothly (1 [+4797]), so (1 [+4394, 4394]), so defiantly (1 [+6981, 7418]), so far as (1), so hard (1 [+5186]), so quickly (1 [+7328]), some of (1), someone else[S] (1 [+3338]), sound (1 [+9048, 7754]), speak (1 [+7023]), spreads feathers to run (1 [+5257, 2021, 5294]), stargazers (1 [+2600, 3919]), stationed at (1), stoned (1 [+8083, 2021, 74]), stoning (1 [+8083, 2021, 74]), store up (1 [+238, 5659]), strike (1 [+2118]), striking (1 [+2118]), suddenly (1 [+7353]), suddenly (1 [+7353, 7328]), suffer (1), suffered (1 [+2118]), surrender (1 [+6037, 3338]), surrounded by (1 [+9348]), sweep away (1 [+7674, 4053]), take great delight (1 [+8464, 8525]), take hold of (1 [+2118]), taken (1 [+3338]), taken great pains (1 [+6715]), taken into account (1), takes the stand (1 [+7756]), taking with (1 [+3338]), tell (1 [+1819, 265]), tell (1 [+6218, 265]), tent-dwelling (1 [+2021, 185]), terrorized (1 [+3154]), that (1 [+3907]), the storehouses[S] (1 [+889, 2157]), their (1 [+4090, 2157]), then (1 [+2296]), then (1 [+6288]), then[S] (1 [+2021, 3427, 2021, 2085]), there (1), there (1 [+824]), there (1 [+2021, 2215]), there (1 [+2021, 1195]), there[S] (1 [+951]), there[S] (1 [+2157]), there[S] (1 [+1078]), there[S] (1 [+8931]), there[S] (1 [+1618]), there[S] (1 [+1028]), there[S] (1 [+5213]), there[S] (1 [+2972]), there[S] (1 [+8148, 2023]), there[S] (1 [+824, 2257]), there[S] (1 [+1074, 466]), there[S] (1 [+9463, 2025]), there[S] (1 [+2023, 9348]), there[S] (1 [+9348, 4392]), there[S] (1 [+2021, 5207]), there[S] (1 [+5707, 7724]), there[S] (1 [+2021, 6551]), there[S] (1 [+2021, 2006]), there[S] (1 [+9348, 2257]), there[S] (1 [+2021, 4722]), there[S] (1 [+9348, 2023]), there[S] (1 [+2021, 824]), there[S] (1 [+2021, 1014]), there[S] (1 [+7931, 2257]), there[S] (1 [+2021, 2215]), there[S] (1 [+3752, 2021, 1074]), think (1 [+606, 4213]), think (1 [+606, 4222]), thinking (1 [+606, 4222]), this (1 [+3907]), this is how (1 [+3972, 465]), this is the way (1 [+4392]), thoughtlessly (1 [+4200, 1051, 8557]), thoughts (1 [+6783, 5883]), through contact with (1), through fault (1), throughout (1 [+7931]), thunders (1 [+5989, 7754]), till (1), timely (1 [+6961]), to (1 [+4213]), to (1 [+4200, 6288]), to avenge (1), to each man (1 [+9005]), to get (1), together with (1), told (1 [+1819, 265]), told (1 [+8492, 7023]), took (1), took with (1 [+3338]), towered (1 [+1467, 7757, 2256, 5989, 7550]), tried (1 [+9365, 4213]), troubled (1 [+8273, 6524]), troubled deeply (1 [+6662, 6524]), under cover (1 [+9564]), underfoot (1 [+8079]), unharmed (1 [+8934]), uninhabited (1 [+4202, 132, 2257]), unintentionally (1 [+4202, 7402]), unnoticed (1 [+2021, 4319]), upon (1 [+7931]), uprightly (1 [+3841]), upset (1 [+8317, 6524]), urgently (1 [+2622]), use name as a curse (1 [+8678]), used (1 [+3338]), used for (1), uses (1 [+3338]), value (1 [+1540, 6524]), valued (1 [+1540, 6524]), very old (1 [+2416, 995, 2021, 408]), very old (1 [+2418, 995, 2021, 3427]), vigorously (1 [+2622]), vigorously (1 [+6437]), vigorously (1 [+8044, 3946]), walk (1 [+2143, 2006]), walking along (1 [+2021, 2006]), wanted to do (1 [+3202, 6524]), watch (1 [+6524]), waylaid (1 [+8492, 2021, 2006]), wearing (1 [+265]), went aboard (1 [+3718]), wept so loudly (1 [+1140, 5989, 906, 7754]), were put in chains (1 [+8415, 2414]), west (1 [+6298]), when (1 [+8040]), when (1 [+2021, 3427]), when (1 [+2021, 3427]), when began (1 [+3427]), whenever (1 [+3427]), whenever (1 [+6961]), whenever (1 [+3972, 6961]), whenever (1 [+3972, 889]), where[S] (1 [+2177]), where[S] (1 [+2257]), where[S] (1 [+396]), where[S] (1 [+5226]), where[S] (1 [+6152, 8234]), where[S] (1 [+2021, 5226]), wherever (1 [+889]), wherever (1 [+3972, 2021, 5226]), wherever (1 [+2021, 889, 2006]), wherever (1 [+2021, 5226, 889]), wherever (1 [+3972, 2021, 5226, 889]), wherever (1 [+3972, 2021, 5226, 889]), wherever (1 [+285, 2021, 5226, 889]), wherever goes (1 [+995, 2256, 928, 3655]), wherever goes (1 [+3655, 2256, 928, 995]), wherever goes (1 [+928, 995, 2256, 3655]), wherever goes (1 [+928, 3655, 2256, 995]), while (1 [+6288]), while (1 [+6388]), wholeheartedly (1 [+4213, 8969]), willfully (1 [+4222]), wish (1 [+3512, 6524]), wished (1 [+3202, 6524]), wishes (1 [+3202, 6524]), with (1 [+2118]), with (1 [+6288]), with (1 [+8079]), with in hand (1), within (1 [+2668]), within (1 [+3752]), within (1 [+9348, 5055]), within very walls (1 [+7931]), without (1 [+1172]), without meaning (1 [+2021, 2039]), withstood (1 [+6641, 7156]), won (1 [+5951, 6524]), workers (1 [+6913, 2021, 4856]), worn (1 [+5432]), worth (1), your (1 [+2257]), your (1 [+3870]), NDT (2382)

H929 בִּאָה **bi'â**, n.f. [1] [√ 995]. entrance:– entrance (1)

H930 בָּאַר **bā'ar**, v. [3] [P] to make plain, make clear, expound:– clearly (1), expound (1), make plain (1)

H931 [1]בְּאֵר **be'ēr[1]**, n.f. [39] [→ 932, 933, 934, 935, 936, 937, 938, 939, 940, 941, 942, 1014, 1015, 1016, 1364, 1365; cf. 1071; *also used with compound proper names*]. well, a shaft in the ground for extraction of water; pit, a depression in the earth with no focus on water:– well (30), full of pits (2 [+931]), pit (2), wells (2), well (1 [+4784]), wells (1 [+4784]), well's (1)

H932 [2]בְּאֵר **be'ēr[2]**, n.pr.loc. [2] [√ 931]. Beer, "*cistern, well*":– Beer (2)

H933 [3]בְּאֵר **be'ēr[3]**, n.f. Not used in NIVEBC [√ 931]. Beer (used in compound names), "*cistern, well*"

H934 בֹּאר **bō'r**, n.m. Not used in NIVEBC [√ 1014; cf. 931]. see 1014

H935 בְּאֵר אֵילִים **be'ēr 'êlîm**, n.pr.loc. [1] [√ 931 + 381; cf. 380]. Beer Elim, "*cistern, well of Elim*":– Beer Elim (1)

H936 בְּאֵר לַחַי רֹאִי **be'ēr laḥay rō'î**, n.pr.loc. [3] [√ 931 + 4200 + 2649 + 8022]. Beer Lahai Roi, "*well that belongs to the Living One seeing me*":– Beer Lahai Roi (3)

H937 בְּאֵר שֶׁבַע **be'ēr šeba'**, n.pr.loc. [34] [√ 931 + 8679]. Beersheba, "*seventh well*":– Beersheba (34)

H938 בְּאֵרָא **be'ērā'**, n.pr.m. [1] [√ 931]. Beera, "*cistern, well*":– Beera (1)

H939 בְּאֵרָה **be'ērâ**, n.pr.m. [1] [√ 931]. Beerah, "*cistern, well*":– Beerah (1)

H940 בְּאֵרוֹת **be'ērôt**, n.pr.loc. [5] [√ 943; cf. 931]. Beeroth, "*cisterns, wells*":– Beeroth (5)

H941 בְּאֵרִי **be'ērî**, n.pr.m. [2] [√ 931]. Beeri, "*[my] cistern, well*":– Beeri (2)

H942 בְּאֵרֹת בְּנֵי־יַעֲקָן **be'ērōt bene-ya'aqān**, n.pr.loc. Not used in NIVEBC [√ 931 + 1201 + 3622]. Beeroth Bene-Jaakan, "*wells of the sons of Jaakan*"

H943 בְּאֵרֹתִי **be'ērōtî**, a.g. [5] [√ 940; cf. 1409]. Beerothite, "*of Beeroth*":– Beerothite (4), people of Beeroth (1)

H944 בָּאַשׁ **bā'aš**, v. [17] [→ 945, 946, 947; 10091]. [Q] to stink, smell; [N] to become a stench; [H] to make a stench, to cause a bad smell; [Ht] to make oneself a stench:– obnoxious (3), so obnoxious (2 [+944]), stink (2), give a bad smell (1 [+5580]), loathsome (1), made obnoxious (1 [+8194]), made yourself obnoxious (1), make a stench (1), making obnoxious (1), reeked (1), rot (1), smell (1), smelled bad (1)

H945 בְּאֹשׁ **be'ōš**, n.m. [3] [√ 944]. stench, stink:– stench (2), stink (1 [+6590])

H946 בְּאֻשִׁים **be'uš**, n.[m.]pl. [2] [√ 944]. bad (putrid) fruit, rotten grapes:– bad (1), bad fruit (1)

H947 בָּאְשָׁה **bo'šâ**, n.f. [1] [√ 944]. weeds, a plant of no value, variously identified:– stinkweed (1)

H948 בַּאֲשֶׁר **ba'ašer**, adv. & c. Not used in NIVEBC [√ 928 + 889]. because, for, since; where, wherever

H949 בָּבָה **bābâ**, n.f. [1] [√ 950?]. apple (of the eye), eyeball, formally, "little child of the eye," a term of endearment:– apple (1)

H950 בֵּבַי **bēbay**, n.pr.m. [6] [√ 949?]. Bebai, "*child*":– Bebai (6)

H951 בָּבֶל **bābel**, n.pr.loc. [262] [cf. 4169; 10093]. Babel, Babylon, "*gate of god[s]*; [Ge 11:9] *confused*":– Babylon (241), Babylon's (4), Babylonians (2 [+1201]), Babel (1), Babylon (1 [+824]), Babylonia (1), Babylonian (1 [+1201]), he[S] (1 [+4889]), him[S] (1 [+4889]), his[S] (1 [+4889]), there[S] (1 [+928]), NDT (7)

H952 בַּג **bag**, var. Not used in NIVEBC [cf. 1020, 7329?]. see 1020

H953 בָּגַד **bāgad**, v. [49] [→ 954, 955, 956, 957]. [Q] to be unfaithful, be faithless; to betray, act treacherously:– unfaithful (21), betrayed (5), treacherous (4), betray (2), betrays (2), broken faith (2), faithless (2), how treacherous (2 [+953]), utterly unfaithful (2 [+953]), acted treacherously (1), betrayer (1), betraying (1), faithless (1 [+954]), traitor (1), traitors (1), undependable (1)

H954 [1]בֶּגֶד **beged[1]**, n.[m.] [2] [√ 953]. treachery:– faithless (1 [+953]), treachery (1)

H955 [2]בֶּגֶד **beged[2]**, n.m. [215] [√ 953]. clothing, garment, cloak, robe:– clothes (79), garments (48), garment (16), robes (16), clothing (14), fabric (9), cloak (8), cloth (8), tunic (2), wardrobe (2), articles of clothing (1), blankets (1 [+2927]), cloaks (1), clothed (1), clothed (1 [+4252]), clothes (1 [+6886]), covers (1), rags (1), those[S] (1), NDT (4)

H956 בֹּגְדוֹת **bōgedôt**, n.pl.abst. [1] [√ 953]. treachery:– treacherous (1)

H957 בָּגוֹד **bāgôd**, a. [2] [√ 953]. unfaithful, pertaining to being adulterous, with the implication that the actions were deceptive and treacherous:– unfaithful (2)

H958 בִּגְוַי **bigway**, n.pr.m. [6] Bigvai, "*fortunate*":– Bigvai (6)

H959 בִּגְלַל **biglal**, n.m. Not used in NIVEBC [√ 1673]. because of

H960 בִּגְתָא **bigtā'**, n.pr.m. [1] [→ 961, 962]. Bigtha, "*gift of God*":– Bigtha (1)

H961 בִּגְתָן **bigtān**, n.pr.m. [1] [√ 960]. Bigthana, "*gift of God*":– Bigthana (1)

H962 בִּגְתָנָא **bigtānā'**, n.pr.m. [1] [√ 960]. Bigthana, "*gift of God*":– Bigthana (1)

H963 [1]בַּד **bad[1]**, n.m. [160] [√ 969; cf. 4224]. part, member, limb; alone, apart, only; in addition to:– alone (38 [+4200]), in addition to (18 [+4946, 4200]), only (17 [+4200]), only one (8 [+4200]), besides (7 [+4946, 4200]), by themselves (4 [+4200, 4392]), apart (3 [+4200]), as well as (2 [+4200, 4946]), besides (2 [+4200, 4946]), limbs (2), not including (2 [+4200, 4946]), set (2), all (1 [+4200]), all alone (1 [+4200]), all by myself (1 [+4200, 3276]), along with (1 [+4946, 4200]), also (1 [+4200]), anyone (1 [+4200]), besides (1 [+4200]), by himself (1 [+4200, 2257]), by itself (1 [+4200]), by itself (1 [+4200, 2257]), by myself (1 [+4200, 3276]), even though (1 [+4200]), in addition (1 [+4200]), in addition (1 [+4946, 4200]), in addition to (1 [+4200]), in addition to (1 [+4200]), in equal amounts (1 [+963, 928]), in equal amounts (1 [+928, 963]), into another set (1 [+4200]), into one set (1 [+4200]), more than (1 [+4946, 4200]), myself (1 [+3276]), not counting (1 [+4946, 4200]), not counting (1 [+4200, 4946]), only (1 [+2314, 4200]), only one (1 [+4200, 2257]), other than (1 [+4946, 4200]), other than (1 [+1194, 4200]), parts (1), separate (1 [+4200]), separate (1 [+3657, 4200]), this one (1 [+4200]), unless (1 [+4200, 4946, 889]), NDT (22)

H964 [2]בַּד **bad[2]**, n.m. [40] [√ 969]. pole, bar:– poles (31), carrying poles (2), their[S] (2 [+2021]), branches (1), gates (1), main branches (1 [+4751]), they[S] (1 [+2021]), NDT (1)

H965 [3]בַּד **bad[3]**, n.[m.] [23] [√ 969]. formally, a "(cut) piece (of a garment)," likely linen of the flax plant:– linen (22), undergarments (1 [+4829])

H966 [4]בַּד **bad[4]**, n.m. [3] [√ 968]. boasting, idle talk:– boasts (2), idle talk (1)

H967 [5]בַּד **bad[5]**, n.m. [3] [√ 968]. false prophet, with a focus on empty, idle talk:– false prophets (3)

H968 בָּדָא **bādā'**, v. [2] [→ 966, 967]. [Q] to choose; to make up, devise:– choosing (1), making up (1)

H969 בָּדַד **bādad**, v. [3] [→ 963, 964, 965, 970, 4224]. [Q] to be alone, isolated:– alone (1), straggler (1), wandering alone (1)

H970 בָּדָד **bādād**, n.[m.] [11] [√ 969]. alone, by oneself, apart:– alone (4), alone (1 [+4200]), apart (1 [+4200]), by itself (1 [+4200]), deserted (1), desolate (1), far from danger (1), secure (1)

H971 בְּדַד **bedad**, n.pr.m. [2] Bedad, "*solitary*":– Bedad (2)

H972 בְּדֵי **bedê**, subst. Not used in NIVEBC [√ 928 + 1896]. see 928 & 1896

H973 בֵּדְיָה **bēdeyâ**, n.pr.m. [1] Bedeiah, "*servant of Yahweh*":– Bedeiah (1)

H974 בְּדִיל **bedîl**, n.[m.] [4] [√ 976?]. tin, an inexpensive metal that could be used as a medium of exchange. Some read "a stone of tin" (Zech 4:10) as "a plumb line and weight":– tin (4)

H975 בָּדִיל **bādîl**, n.[m.] [2] [√ 976]. Negative: impurities, slag, the dross of the smelting process, used as a figure of moral and ceremonial impurities. Positive: something separated, therefore chosen:– chosen (1), impurities (1)

H976 בָּדַל ***bādal***, v. [42] [→ 974?, 975, 977, 4426]. [N] separate oneself, be expelled; [H] to separate, sever completely, distinguish between:– set apart (7), separate (5), separated (4), distinguish (3), separated themselves (3), set aside (3), dividing completely (2), separate yourselves (2), surely exclude (2 [+976]), be expelled (1), defected (1), dismissed (1), employed (1), excluded (1), kept themselves separate (1), make a distinction (1), selected (1), single out (1), singled out (1), was set apart (1)

H977 בָּדָל ***bādāl***, n.[m.] [1] [√ 976]. piece (of an ear):– piece (1)

H978 בְּדֹלַח ***b^e^dōlaḥ***, n.[m.] [2] aromatic resin; some sources: bdellium-gum (an aromatic, yellowish gum):– aromatic resin (1), resin (1)

H979 בְּדָן ***b^e^dān***, n.pr.m. [1] Bedan, *"son of judgment"*:– Bedan (1)

H980 בָּדַק ***bādaq***, v.den. [1] [→ 981; cf. 1438]. [Q] to repair, mend:– repaired (1)

H981 בֶּדֶק ***bedeq***, n.m. [9] [√ 980]. breach (of a temple or a ship):– damage (2), repair (1 [+2616]), repairing (1), seams (1), shipwrights (1 [+2616]), NDT (3)

H982 בִּדְקַר ***bidqar***, n.pr.m. [1] [√ 1201? + 1992?]. Bidkar, *"son of Deker [piercing]"*:– Bidkar (1)

H983 בֹּהוּ ***bōhû***, n.[m.] [3] emptiness, desolation, a void associated with chaos; "empty and void" is a state of total chaos:– empty (2), desolation (1)

H984 בְּהוֹן ***b^e^hôn***, n.[f.] [2] [√ 991]. thumb, big toe:– thumbs (2 [+3338])

H985 בַּהַט ***bahaṭ***, n.[m.] [1] porphyry (or some other precious stone):– porphyry (1)

H986 בָּהִיר ***bāhîr***, a. [1] [→ 994]. bright, brilliant:– bright (1)

H987 בָּהַל ***bāhal***, v. [39] [→ 988; cf. 1164; 10097, 10218]. [N] to be terrified, alarmed, dismayed, bewildered; [P] to make afraid, terrify; to make haste; [Pu] to be hastened, made to hurry; to cause terror; to cause to hurry:– terrified (10), dismayed (3), hurried (2), make afraid (2), terrifies (2), alarm (1), alarmed (1), am bewildered (1), anguish (1 [+4394]), claimed too soon (1 [+928, 2021, 8037]), eager (1), hurry (1), immediately (1), in a hurry (1), in agony (1), in anguish (1), quick (1), quickly (1), sudden (1), terrify (1), terror (1), terror seize (1), tremble (1), was shaken (1), went (1)

H988 בֶּהָלָה ***behālâ***, n.f. [4] [√ 987; 10096]. sudden terror; misfortune:– terror (2), misfortune (1), sudden terror (1)

H989 בְּהֵמָה ***b^e^hēmâ***, n.f. [189] [→ 990?]. beast, animal, livestock, herds, cattle:– animals (75), animal (39), livestock (32), cattle (15), beast (7), beasts (5), herds (3), another[S] (1), beasts of burden (1 [+2651, 2256]), brute beast (1), domestic (1), kinds of cattle (1 [+2256, 989]), kinds of cattle (1 [+989, 2256]), livestock (1 [+5238]), mount (1), mounts (1), one[S] (1), wild animals (1 [+824]), wild beasts (1), NDT (1)

H990 בְּהֵמוֹת ***b^e^hēmôt***, n.m. [1] [√ 989?]. behemoth; sources variously identify as hippopotamus, crocodile, elephant; the plural form may indicate this is the ultimate creature, a composite description of the strongest attributes of the animal kingdom:– Behemoth (1)

H991 בֹּהֶן ***bōhen***, n.[f.] [14] [→ 984, 992?]. thumb, big toe:– big toe (5), thumb (5), big toes (2), thumbs (2)

H992 בֹּהַן ***bōhan***, n.pr.m. [2] [√ 991?]. Bohan, *"thumb, big toe"*:– Bohan (2)

H993 בֹּהַק ***bōhaq***, n.m. [1] harmless rash:– harmless rash (1)

H994 בַּהֶרֶת ***baheret***, n.f. [12] [√ 986]. spot, bright spot (on the skin):– spot (6), shiny spot (3), spots (2), NDT (1)

H995 בּוֹא ***bô'***, v. [2558] [→ 929, 4427, 4569, 9311]. [Q] to come, go; [H] to bring, take; [Ho] to be brought:– come (378), came (285), bring (175), went (174), brought (167), go (106), coming (70), comes (62), arrived (46), enter (36 [+448]), enter (31), returned (29), enter (26 [+928]), bringing (20), took (20), entered (19), go in (19), entered (17 [+448]), went in (17), reached (14 [+448]), take (14), gone (13), come in (12), entering (12), bring in (11), brought in (11), came in (11), reached (11 [+6330]), bring back (10), entered (10 [+928]), brings (8), brought back (8), enters (8), put (8), sleep with (8 [+448]), went into (8), fulfilled (7), invade (7 [+928]), set (7), slept with (7 [+448]), followed (6 [+339]), get (6), go into (6), made love to (6 [+448]), reached (6), sunset (6 [+2021, 9087]), went back (6), attack (5 [+6584]), attack (5), bring into (5), enters (5 [+448]), flee (5), going (5), very old (5 [+2416, 928, 2021, 3427]), approached (4 [+6330]), arrived (4 [+448]), back (4), came back (4), carried off (4), certainly come (4 [+995]), entrance (4), flows (4), going on duty (4), happened (4), included (4), invaded (4 [+928]), overtake (4), reached (4 [+2025]), return (4), arriving (3), attack (3 [+4200]), bring about (3), brought into (3), comes true (3), entered (3 [+4200]), get in (3), goes (3), going in (3), is brought (3), marched (3), overtakes (3), present (3), presented (3), returning (3), sailed (3), setting (3), toward (3 [+3870, 2025]), was brought (3), actually come (2 [+995]), advance (2), approaches (2 [+448]), approaching (2), arrival (2), arrives (2), associate (2), associate with (2 [+928]), at hand (2), attacked (2 [+6584]), be brought (2), been brought into (2), bloodshed (2 [+928, 1947]), bow (2), bring down (2), bringing in (2), brought to pass (2), came home (2), came to pass (2), carried (2), come back (2), come into (2), comes (2 [+995]), comes true (2 [+995]), delivered (2), enter (2 [+6584]), entering (2 [+4200]), follows (2 [+339]), get there (2), give (2), go back (2), go now (2 [+2143]), goes down (2), goes in (2), happens (2), inserted (2), invade (2), kept (2), lead (2), led (2), led in campaigns (2 [+3655, 2256, 4200, 7156]), led on military campaigns (2 [+3655, 2256]), left (2 [+4946]), march (2), pierces (2 [+5918, 2256, 928]), placed (2), put in (2), reach (2 [+448]), reach (2 [+6330]), reached (2 [+928]), received (2 [+448]), return (2 [+995]), set out (2), sets (2), sunset (2 [+6961, 2021, 9087]), sweep on (2 [+995]), taken (2), went inside (2), were brought (2), withstand (2 [+928]), accompanied (1 [+8079]), admitted (1), advanced (1), advancing (1), all the way to (1), all the way to (1 [+6330]), all the way to (1 [+6330, 3870]), appear (1), appeared (1), apply (1), approach (1), approached (1), approached (1 [+448]), are (1), arrive (1), arrive (1 [+448]), arrive (1 [+6330]), arrived (1 [+6330]), arrives (1 [+7024]), assembled (1 [+7736]), at hand (1 [+7940]), at hand (1 [+7940, 4200]), ate (1 [+448, 7931]), attacking (1 [+6584]), attacks (1 [+6584]), awaits (1), away (1), be (1), be brought in (1), be heard[S] (1), be inserted (1), be right there (1), be taken (1), become (1), been brought (1), been taken into (1), begin (1), beset (1 [+928]), besiege (1 [+928, 2021, 5189]), bind themselves with (1 [+928]), blessed (1 [+1388]), border (1), bound (1), break into (1), bring (1 [+907]), bring home (1), bring out (1), bringing into (1), broke (1), brought about (1), brought in as wives (1), built up (1), buried (1), buried (1 [+448, 7700]), by all means go (1 [+2143]), calling together (1 [+8938, 2256]), came along (1), came back (1 [+2143, 2256]), came bringing (1), came into (1), came up (1), came with (1), carried away (1), carried back (1), carry (1), carry back (1), carry off (1), carry off (1 [+928, 2021, 8660]), carry out duties (1 [+3655, 2256]), caused to come (1), check (1 [+4200, 7156]), collapses (1 [+8691]), come home (1), come into view (1), come on (1), come to rest (1), come true (1), comes by (1), comes in (1), committed adultery with (1 [+448]), confront (1), covers (1 [+928]), crept (1), crowded into (1), deported (1 [+1583]), does[S] (1), done so[S] (1 [+448, 7931]), edge (1), encounter (1 [+928]), encroach (1), enter (1 [+4200]), entered (1 [+2025]), entered (1 [+6584]), entered (1 [+928, 9348]), entered and went (1), entering (1 [+448]), entering (1 [+928]), entering (1 [+2025]), entering (1 [+6330]), entering (1 [+928, 7931]), entering (1 [+928, 9348]), enters (1 [+928]), enters (1 [+2025]), enters (1 [+4200]), escort (1), every spring (1 [+9102]), extending (1), fallen (1), falls (1), find (1 [+448]), fled (1), float (1), flowing (1), follow (1 [+339]), followed in (1 [+339]), fulfill (1), future (1), gain (1), give (1 [+9202, 4200]), give children (1 [+6584]), give in (1), given (1), go (1 [+2143]), go about business (1 [+3655, 2256]), go at once (1 [+2143, 2256]), go down (1), go home (1), go in (1 [+2143, 2256]), go sleep with (1 [+448]), going down (1), gone into (1), granted (1), grown old (1 [+2416, 928, 2021, 3427]), guest (1 [+448, 1074]), had (1), had[S] (1), had brought (1), had brought in (1), had sexual relations with (1 [+448]), hand over (1), harvested (1), has (1), have (1), hid in (1), imported (1), in (1), insert (1), intermarry (1), into (1), invade (1 [+448]), invade (1 [+9004, 2025]), invaded (1 [+448]), invaded (1 [+6584]), invader (1 [+448]), invading (1 [+928]), invading (1 [+4200]), invited (1), is (1), join (1 [+6330]), journeyed (1), laid siege (1 [+928, 2021, 5189]), last (1), lead (1 [+3655, 2256]), lead (1 [+3655, 4200, 7156, 2256]), led into (1), ledges (1), let touch (1 [+928]), listed (1), made attack (1), make (1), make enter (1 [+928]), make go down (1), make love to (1 [+448]), make up mind (1 [+6783]), married (1 [+448]), migration (1), moved (1), moved into (1), moved out (1), moves (1), moving (1), occupy (1 [+448]), offer (1), on (1), on duty (1 [+2256, 3655]), oppose (1 [+928]), over (1), overtook (1 [+448]), overwhelm (1 [+6584]), pass (1), passed (1), penetrate (1 [+928]), pierce (1 [+928]), pierced (1 [+928]), place (1), placing (1), poured (1), produce (1), provide (1), pulled back (1), put (1 [+4200, 7156]), putting (1), raiding (1 [+928]), reach (1), reached (1 [+4200]), reaches (1 [+448]), received (1), received (1 [+4200]), reentered (1 [+2256, 8740]), replace (1 [+448, 9393]), report back (1), reported (1), resound (1), rest (1), return (1 [+2143]), return (1 [+6388]), returned (1 [+448]), rose (1), sank in (1), send (1), send (1 [+4946, 907]), sent (1), serve (1 [+3655, 2256]), set foot (1), share (1), shave head in mourning (1 [+7947]), shed (1), sleeping with (1 [+448]), sleeps with (1 [+448]), spread (1), stay (1 [+4202]), stayed away (1 [+4202]), stepped (1), stole into (1 [+1704, 4200]), successor (1 [+132, 8611, 339]), sunset (1 [+2021, 3064]), swarm (1), swept in (1), take (1 [+1198]), take (1 [+6584]), take along (1), take back (1), take home (1), take into (1), take out (1), take part (1), taken place (1), takes place (1), taking (1), time is ripe (1 [+7891]), to the vicinity of (1 [+6330, 3870]), took (1 [+448]), took back (1), took back (1 [+8938, 2256]), took into (1), touch (1), touched (1 [+448]), travel about (1 [+3655, 2256]), traveled (1), treads (1), turn (1), up (1), very old (1 [+2416, 928, 2021, 408]), very old (1 [+2418, 928, 2021, 3427]), visit (1), was brought into (1), was taken (1), went in to spend the night with (1 [+448]), went on (1), went out (1), went over (1), were (1), were taken (1), what[S] (1 [+2021]), wherever goes (1 [+928, 2256, 928, 3655]), wherever goes (1 [+928, 3655, 2256, 928]), wielding (1 [+4200, 5087, 2025]), will[S] (1), work (1), NDT (62)

H996 בּוּז ***bûz*^1^**, v. [14] [→ 997, 998?, 999, 1000, 1001]. [Q] to despise, scorn, deride:– despise (5), despises (2), scorns (2), utterly scorned (2 [+996]), dares despise (1), derides (1), scorn (1)

H997 בּוּז ***bûz*^2^**, n.m. [11] [√ 996]. contempt:– contempt (9), despised (1), laughingstock (1)

H998 בּוּז ***bûz*^3^**, n.pr.m. [3] [√ 996?]. Buz, *"contempt"*:– Buz (3)

H999 בּוּזָה ***bûzâ***, n.f. [1] [√ 996]. contempt:– despised (1)

H1000 בּוּזִי ***bûzî*^1^**, a.g. [2] [→ 1001; cf. 996]. Buzite, *"of Buz"*:– Buzite (2)

H1001 בּוּזִי ***bûzî*^2^**, n.pr.m. [1] [√ 1000; cf. 996]. Buzi, *"contempt"*:– Buzi (1)

H1002 בַּוַּי ***bawway***, n.pr.m. Not used in NIVEBC [cf. 1218]. Bavvai, see 1218

H1003 בּוּךְ ***bûk***, v. [3] [→ 4428]. [N] to wander around, mill about; to be bewildered:– bewildered (1), mill about (1), wandering around in confusion (1)

H1004 בּוּל ***bûl*^1^**, n.[m.] [1] Bul (month), the eighth month of the Canaanite calendar (modern October-November):– Bul (1)

H1005 בּוּל ***bûl*^2^**, n.[m.] [1] piece of wood, in context likely referring to a block of wood that has been crafted into an idol:– block (1)

H1006 בּוּל ***bûl*^3^**, n.[m.] [1] [→ 9315?]. produce; in context produce as a gift or tribute:– produce (1)

H1007 בּוּנָה ***bûnâ***, n.pr.m. [1] Bunah:– Bunah (1)

H1008 בּוּס ***bûs***, v. [12] [→ 4431, 9313]. [Q, P] to trample down; loathe; [Htpol] to kick about; [Ho] to be trodden down:– trample down (4), kicking about (2), loathes (1), trample (1), trampled (1), trampled down (1), trampled underfoot (1), trampling (1)

H1009 בּוּץ ***bûṣ***, n.[m.] [8] [→ 1010?, 1070]. fine linen; white linen:– fine linen (6), linen (1), white linen (1)

H1010 בּוֹצֵץ ***bôṣēṣ***, n.pr.loc. [1] [√ 1009? *or* 1288?]. Bozez, *"oozing place"*:– Bozez (1)

H1011 בּוּקָה ***bûqâ***, n.f. [1] [→ 4433, 6443?]. pillage, that which is made desolate and emptied:– pillaged (1)

H1012 בּוֹקֵר ***bôqēr***, n.m.den. [1] [√ 1330; cf. 1329]. herdsman, usually a shepherd:– shepherd (1)

H1013 בּוּר ***bûr***, v. [1] [Q] to conclude:– concluded (1)

H1014 בּוֹר ***bôr***, n.m. [71] [→ 934, 1015, 1016, 1071; cf. 931, 3930, 6941]. pit, well, cistern; dungeon; a cistern is usually a shaft in the ground, hewn out of soft stone and plastered to hold water:– pit (25), cistern (20), well (6), cisterns (5), dungeon (3), wells (3), dungeon (2 [+1074]), grave (1), hole (1), one[S] (1), quarry (1 [+5217]), realm of the dead (1), slimy pit (1 [+8622]), there[S] (1 [+928, 2021])

H1015 בּוֹר הַסִּרָה ***bôr hassirâ***, n.pr.loc. Not used in NIVEBC [√ 1014 + 2021 + 6241]. Bor Hasirah, see 1014 & 6241

H1016 בּוֹר־עָשָׁן ***bôr-'āšān***, n.pr.loc. [1] [√ 1014 + 6940; cf. 3930, 6941]. Bor Ashan, *"pit of smoke"*:– Bor Ashan (1)

H1017 בּוֹשׁ ***bôš*^1^**, v. [122] [→ 1019, 1423, 1425, 4434]. [Q] to be put to shame, be ashamed, be disgraced; [Htpolal] to feel ashamed; [H] to bring shame, to cause disgrace, act shamefully:– put to shame (44), ashamed (22), disgraced (8), shame (7), have shame at all (4 [+1017]), shamed (4), disgraceful (3), dismayed (3), be disgraced (2), despair (2), disappointed (2), disgrace (2), embarrassed (2), bear shame (1), bring shame (1), brings shame (1), disgraces (1), distressed (1), embarrassment (1), felt shame (1), frustrate (1), humiliated (1), let be dashed (1), let be put to shame (1), overwhelmed with shame (1), shame come on (1), shameful (1), shamelessly (1 [+4202]), utter shame (1 [+1425]), NDT (1)

H1018 בּוֹשׁ ***bôš*^2^**, v. [2] [Polal] to be delayed, be long:– long (1), so long (1)

H1019 בּוּשָׁה ***bûšâ***, n.f. [4] [√ 1017]. shame:– shame (4)

H1020 בַּז ***baz***, n.[m.] [25] [→ 4561; cf. 1024]. plunder, loot, despoiling:– plunder (15), plundered (4), loot (2 [+1024]), despoil (1 [+5989, 4200]), looted (1), plunder (1 [+1024]), taken captive (1)

H1021 בָּזָא ***bāzā'***, v. [2] [Q] to divide, likely referring to the washing out of rivers by force of the waters:– divided (2)

H1022 בָּזָה ***bāzâ***, v. [43] [→ 1025, 1026, 5802]. [Q] to despise, scorn, ridicule, show contempt for; [Qp] to be despised; [N] to be despised, be contemptible; [H] to cause to despise:– despised (18), despise (7), contemptible (3), was despised (3), be despised (2), despise (1 [+928, 6524]), despises (1), despises (1 [+928, 6524]), despising (1), is despised (1), ridiculed (1), scorned the idea (1 [+928, 6524]), show contempt (1), shown contempt (1), shows contempt (1)

H1023 בִּזָּה ***bizzâ***, n.f. [10] [√ 1024]. plunder, booty, spoils:– plunder (8), pillage (1), plundered (1)

H1024 בָּזַז ***bāzaz***, v. [43] [→ 1020, 1023]. [Q] to plunder, loot, carry off spoils; [Qp, N, Pu] to be plundered:– plunder (11), carried off (4), carry off (4), looted (3), loot (2), loot (2 [+1020]), plundered (2), took (2), totally plundered (2 [+1024]), be plundered (1), collect (1), make spoil (1), plunder (1 [+1020]), plunderers (1), robbing (1), snatch (1), take (1), taken plunder (1), taking as plunder (1), took as plunder (1)

H1025 בִּזָּיוֹן ***bizzāyôn***, n.[m.] [1] [→ 1026; cf. 1022]. disrespect, contempt:– disrespect (1)

H1026 בִּזְיוֹתְיָה ***bizyôtᵉyâ***, n.pr.loc. [1] [√ 1025 + 3378]. Biziothiah, "*contempt of Yahweh*":– Biziothiah (1)

H1027 בָּזָק ***bāzāq***, n.[m.] [1] flashes of lightning, lightning:– flashes of lightning (1)

H1028 בֶּזֶק ***bezeq***, n.pr.loc. [3] [→ 152]. Bezek, "*scattering, sowing*":– Bezek (2), there[S] (1 [+928])

H1029 בָּזַר ***bāzar***, v. [2] [cf. 7061; 10095]. [Q] to distribute; [P] to scatter:– distribute (1), scatter (1)

H1030 בִּזְּתָא ***bizzᵉtā'***, n.pr.m. [1] Biztha, "[perhaps] *eunuch* or *bound*":– Biztha (1)

H1031 בָּחוֹן ***bāḥôn***, n.[m.] [1] [√ 1043]. tester of metals, assayer:– tester of metals (1)

H1032 בַּחוּן ***baḥûn***, n.[m.] [1] [→ 1039, 1044]. siege tower, a moveable military engine used to attack a walled city:– siege towers (1)

H1033 [1]בָּחוּר ***bāḥûr[1]***, n.m. [50] [→ 1035, 1036, 1037]. young man, able (fighting) man; bridegroom:– young men (35), young man (4), able (3), able young men (2), men (1), sons (1), strong young men (1), young (1), younger men (1), youths (1)

H1034 [2]בָּחוּר ***bāḥûr[2]***, a. *or* v.ptcp. Not used in NIVEBC [cf. 1047]. see 1047

H1035 בְּחוּרוֹת ***bᵉḥûrôt***, n.f.pl.abst. [2] [√ 1033]. youth, as a state of being:– youth (2)

H1036 בְּחוּרִים ***bᵉḥûrîm***, n.m.pl.abst. [1] [√ 1033]. youth:– youth (1)

H1037 [1]בַּחוּרִים ***baḥûrîm[1]***, n.m. Not used in NIVEBC [√ 1033]. young men

H1038 [2]בַּחוּרִים ***baḥûrîm[2]***, n.pr.loc. [5] [cf. 1372]. Bahurim, "*young men*":– Bahurim (5)

H1039 בַּחִין ***baḥîn***, var. Not used in NIVEBC [√ 1032]. see 1032

H1040 בָּחִיר ***bāḥîr***, n.m. [13] [√ 1047]. chosen one, one preferred or selected by God with an implication of receiving special favor:– chosen (13)

H1041 [1]בָּחַל ***bāḥal[1]***, v. [1] [Q] to detest, disdain, feel an attitude of loathing:– detested (1)

H1042 [2]בָּחַל ***bāḥal[2]***, v. [Pu] to be gotten by greed

H1043 בָּחַן ***bāḥan***, v. [29] [→ 1031, 1045, 1046]. [Q] to test, try, probe, examine; [Qp, N, Pu] to be tested; to test and learn the genuineness of an object, fig. of assaying a metal to determine its purity or nature:– test (11), be tested (3), examine (3), tested (3), tests (2), examines (1), probe (1), probes (1), put to the test (1), testing (1), tried (1), NDT (1)

H1044 בַּחַן ***baḥan***, n.[m.] [1] [√ 1032]. watchtower:– watchtower (1)

H1045 [1]בֹּחַן ***bōḥan[1]***, n.[m.] Not used in NIVEBC [√ 1043]. testing, see 1043

H1046 [2]בֹּחַן ***bōḥan[2]***, n.[m.] [1] [√ 1043]. tested (stone):– tested (1)

H1047 [1]בָּחַר ***bāḥar[1]***, v. [164] [→ 1040, 3295, 4435, 4436, 4437; cf. 1034, 1048]. [Q] to choose, select, desire, prefer; [Qp, N] to be chosen, choice, the best, preferred:– chosen (57), choose (44), chose (27), chooses (6), able young (4), choice (4), best (3), prefer (3), select (2), selected (2), acceptable (1), adopt (1), decide (1), desirable (1), desire (1), discern (1), find (1), get (1 [+7864]), selects (1), sided with (1 [+4200]), tested (1), would rather be (1)

H1048 [2]בָּחַר ***bāḥar[2]***, v. Not used in NIVEBC [cf. 1034, 1047]. [Q] to enter into a covenant; [Pu] be joined

H1049 בַּחֲרוּמִי ***baḥᵃrûmî***, a.g. [1] [→ 1050]. Baharumite:– Baharumite (1)

H1050 בַּחֻרִמִי ***baḥurimî***, a.g. Not used in NIVEBC [cf. 1372]. Bahurimite, see 1372

H1051 בָּטָא ***bāṭā'***, v. [4] [→ 4439]. [Q, P] to speak thoughtlessly, to speak rashly, recklessly:– carelessly (1), rash words came (1), thoughtlessly (1 [+4200, 928, 8557]), words of reckless (1)

H1052 בָּטוּחַ ***bāṭûaḥ***, a. Not used in NIVEBC [√ 1053]. confident, see 1053

H1053 [1]בָּטַח ***bāṭaḥ[1]***, v. [119] [→ 19, 1052, 1055, 1057, 1058, 1059, 4440; cf. 1054]. [Q] to trust, rely on, put confidence in; [Qp] to be confident; [H] to lead to believe, make trust:– trust (47), trusted (10), trusts (10), depending (8), put trust (6), depend (4), feel secure (4), secure (4), rely (3), confident (2), let persuade to trust (2), on basing (2), persuaded to trust (2), put confidence (2), relied (2), trusting (2), basing confidence (1), bold (1), depended (1), feels secure (1), has full confidence (1 [+4213]), let depend (1), made trust (1), safe (1), unsuspecting (1)

H1054 [2]בָּטַח ***bāṭaḥ[2]***, v. [1] [cf. 1053]. [Q] to stumble, fall to the ground:– stumble (1)

H1055 [1]בֶּטַח ***beṭaḥ[1]***, n.[m.] [42] [√ 1053]. safety, security:– safety (24), secure (4), confidence (2), safely (2 [+4200]), unsuspecting (2), complacency (1), feeling of security (1), in safety (1), securely (1), security (1), trustfully (1 [+4200]), unsuspecting (1 [+4200]), without a care (1)

H1056 [2]בֶּטַח ***beṭaḥ[2]***, n.pr.loc. Not used in NIVEBC [cf. 3187]. Betah, see 3182

H1057 בִּטְחָה ***biṭḥâ***, n.f. [1] [√ 1053]. trust, confidence:– trust (1)

H1058 בַּטֻּחָה ***baṭṭuḥâ***, n.f.pl. [1] [√ 1053]. security, safety:– secure (1)

H1059 בִּטָּחוֹן ***biṭṭāḥôn***, n.m. [3] [√ 1053]. confidence, hope:– confidence (2), hope (1)

H1060 בָּטֵל ***bāṭal***, v. [1] [√ 10098]. [Q] to cease (activity):– cease (1)

H1061 [1]בֶּטֶן ***beṭen[1]***, n.f. [72] inmost part, viscera: abdomen, belly, stomach, womb; by extension: the inner person, the heart, the seat of emotion, thought, and desire:– womb (31), belly (4), abdomen (3), birth (3), stomach (3), body (2), heart (2), inmost parts (2 [+2540]), bellies (1), birth (1 [+562]), bodies (1), born (1), borne (1), bowl-shaped part (1), children (1 [+7262]), craving (1), deep (1), descendants (1 [+7262]), family (1 [+1201]), infants (1 [+7262]), inmost being (1 [+2540]), inmost being (1 [+3972, 2540]), inside (1), offspring (1), offspring (1 [+7262, 2021]), pregnancy (1), waist (1), within (1), NDT (2)

H1062 [2]בֶּטֶן ***beṭen[2]***, n.pr.loc. [1] [cf. 1063?]. Beten, "*womb, bowels*":– Beten (1)

H1063 בָּטְנָה ***boṭnâ***, n.[m.]pl. [1] [cf. 1062?, 1064?]. pistachio nut:– pistachio nuts (1)

H1064 בְּטֹנִים ***bᵉṭōnîm***, n.pr.loc. [1] [cf. 1063?]. Betonim, "*pistachio nuts*":– Betonim (1)

H1065 בִּי ***bî***, pt.entreaty [13] O!, please!:– pardon me (4), pardon (3), pardon your servant (2), please (2), beg pardon (1), pardon (1 [+2021, 6411])

H1066 בָּיַי ***bāyay***, v. Not used in NIVEBC [√ 14?]. to entreat

H1067 בִּין ***bîn***, v. [169] [→ 1068, 1069, 3296?, 9312]. [Q] to understand, discern, realize; be prudent; [N] to be discerning, be understanding; [Pol] to care for; to have skill, insight; to instruct, explain; [Htpolel/Htpolal] to look closely, consider with full attention, ponder:– understand (29), discerning (18), understanding (10), consider (7), understood (6), give understanding (4), have understanding (4), instructed (4), discern (3), give thought (3), perceive (3), ponder (3), understands (3), clever (2), discernment (2), gain (2), gain understanding (2), gives understanding (2), know (2), look (2), note well (2 [+1067]), realized (2), skilled (2), able (1), acted wisely (1), brilliant (1), cared for (1), cause to understand (1), checked (1), comprehended (1), consider carefully (1), considers (1), distinguish (1), dwell on (1), enlighten (1), explain (1), explaining (1), feel (1), find (1), gave full attention (1), give discernment (1), have concern (1 [+1981]), have regard (1), insight (1), insights have (1), instruct (1), instructing (1), intelligent (1), learned (1), learning (1), look lustfully (1), looked closely (1), master (1), noticed (1), observe (1), prudent (1), quick to understand (1 [+4529]), realize (1), regard (1), see (1), sensible (1), show (1), show favor (1), show regard (1), skillful (1), take note (1), take notice (1), takes notice (1), teacher (1), tell the meaning (1), think (1), thinking (1), understand clearly (1 [+1069]), well (1), NDT (1)

H1068 בַּיִן ***bayin***, subst. & pp. [406] [→ 1227; cf. 1067; 10099]. between; separate from; whether ... or:– between (163), among (31), at twilight (9 [+2021, 6847]), from (6), at (3), between (3 [+4946]), as (2), at twilight (2 [+6847, 2021]), on forehead (2 [+6524]), on foreheads (2 [+6524]), or (2), whether (2), with (2), above (1), above (1 [+448]), above (1 [+6584]), against (1), alternated with (1), among (1 [+4946]), attached to (1), difference between (1), distinction between (1), every (1), from (1 [+4200]), from (1 [+4946]), front of heads (1 [+6524]), have (1 [+2118]), in (1), in (1 [+928]), in midair (1 [+2021, 9028, 2256, 1068, 2021, 824]), in midair (1 [+1068, 2021, 9028, 2256, 2021, 824]), in the midst of (1), midst (1), of (1 [+4946]), on (1), out of (1 [+4946]), over (1 [+448]), relationships between (1), separate (1 [+5911]), separated (1 [+7233]), slung on back (1 [+4190]), the difference between (1), to (1), together (1), using (1), witness (1 [+9048]), womb (1 [+8079]), NDT (143)

H1069 בִּינָה ***bînâ***, n.f. [38] [√ 1067; 10100]. understanding, insight, discernment, good sense, wisdom, usually referring to the wisdom that responds to the Lord and his instruction:– understanding (19), insight (7), cleverness (1), discernment (1), good sense (1), great skill (1 [+2682, 3359]), incomprehensible (1 [+401]), intelligence (1), understand (1), understand (1 [+3359]), understand clearly (1 [+1067]), understood (1 [+3359]), wisdom (1), NDT (1)

H1070 בֵּיצָה ***bêṣâ***, n.f. [6] [√ 1009]. egg:– eggs (5), NDT (1)

H1071 בָּיִר ***bayir***, n.[f.] Not used in NIVEBC [√ 1014; cf. 931]. well

H1072 בִּירָה ***bîrâ***, n.f. [18] [cf. 1073; 10101]. citadel, fort, palatial structure:– citadel (14), forts (2), palatial structure (2)

H1073 בִּירָנִיָּה ***bîrāniyyâ***, n.f. Not used in NIVEBC [cf. 1072]. fortified place

H1074 [1]בַּיִת ***bayit[1]***, n.m. [2040] [→ 1131; 10103]. house, home; of royalty: palace; of deity: temple; a specific part of a house: room; place; by extension: household, family, clan, tribe:– house (553), temple (439), palace (118), people (91), household (86), houses (82), home (73), family (64), families (57 [+3]), Israel (39 [+3776]), family (32 [+3]), Israelites (30 [+3776]), descendants (16), palace (15 [+4889]), land (14), Judah (13 [+3373]), homes (12), tribe (9), tribes (9), hold (8), households (7), Jacob (6 [+3620]), buildings (6), prison (6 [+2021, 6045]), estate (5), families (5), harem (5 [+851]), inside (5 [+4946]), place (5), shrines (5), Israelite (4 [+408, 4946, 3776]), behind (4 [+4946]), building (4), hall (4), its[S] (4 [+2021]), prison (4 [+2021, 3975]), room (4), that[S] (4), dynasty (3), family line (3), nation (3), Esau (2 [+6916]), armory (2 [+3998]), center (2), court (2), division (2), dungeon (2 [+1014]), in (2 [+2025, 2021]), inside (2 [+2025]), inside (2 [+928, 2021]), its[S] (2 [+3378]), its[S] (2 [+2021]), kingdom (2), palace grounds (2 [+4889]), prison (2 [+673]), prison (2 [+3975]), prison (2 [+2021, 3989]), quarters (2), residence (2), sanctuary (2), shelter (2), storehouses (2 [+5800]), temple area (2), temples (2), there[S] (2 [+928, 2021]), those[S] (2), web (2), Ephraim (1 [+713]), Israel and Judah (1 [+3776]), Israelite (1 [+3776]), Israel's (1 [+3776]), Joseph (1 [+3441]), Rekabites (1 [+8209]), Rekabites (1 [+1201, 8211]), all[S] (1), apartment (1), at home (1 [+5661]), banquet hall (1 [+3516]), born in the same home (1 [+4580]), both Judah (1 [+3373]), bottles (1), city (1), clan (1 [+5476, 3]), clans (1 [+3]), descendants (1 [+5270]), dungeon (1 [+3975]), dwellings (1), family line (1 [+3]), full (1 [+6017]), group (1 [+2755, 3]), guest (1 [+995, 448]), guests (1 [+1591]), house (1 [+185]), house (1 [+4632]), imprisoned (1 [+5989, 2021, 657]), in (1 [+2021, 2025]), inner (1), inside (1), inside (1 [+448, 2021]), inside (1 [+4200, 4946]), interior (1), interior (1 [+4946, 2025]), inward (1 [+2025]), its[S] (1 [+513]), its[S] (1 [+1251]), its[S] (1 [+3378]), its[S] (1 [+3870]), kingdoms (1), kitchens (1 [+1418]), leaders (1), lived (1 [+928, 2021]), living with (1), lodge (1 [+4472]), main hall (1), mansions (1), mansions (1 [+8041]), members of family (1 [+3]), members of family (1 [+2256, 1074, 3]), members of family (1 [+1074, 2256, 3]), palace (1 [+4895]), palaces (1), pen up (1 [+2025]), penned up (1 [+3973, 928, 2021]), possessions (1), prison (1), prison (1 [+5464]), prison (1 [+2021, 673]), prison (1 [+2021, 4551]), prison (1 [+2021, 7213]), prisons (1 [+3975]), sanctuary (1 [+5219]), shrine (1), shrine (1 [+466]), site of palace (1), slave by birth (1 [+3535]), stall (1), steward[S] (1 [+889, 6584]), steward[S] (1 [+2021, 408, 889, 6584]), storehouse (1 [+238]), storehouse (1 [+667]), strong fortress (1 [+5181]), that[S] (1 [+2021, 2021, 2296]), them[S] (1 [+2023]), them[S] (1 [+3998, 2021, 466]), there[S] (1 [+7281]), there[S] (1 [+8235]), there[S] (1 [+928, 466]), there[S] (1 [+928, 3752, 2021]), they[S] (1 [+3441]), tomb (1), town (1), treasury (1 [+238]), tribes (1 [+3972]), under (1 [+4200]), under (1 [+4946]), wall (1), where[S] (1), whole family (1 [+3]), wine stewards (1 [+8042]), workers (1 [+6275]), NDT (39)

H1075 [2]בַּיִת ***bayit[2]***, pp. [3] between; among; at a crossroads:– among (1), between (1), meet (1)

H1076 [3]בַּיִת ***bayit[3]***, n.pr.loc. Bayit

H1077 בֵּית אָוֶן ***bêt 'āwen***, n.pr.loc. [7] [√ 1074 + 224]. Beth Aven, "*house of idolatry*":– Beth Aven (7)

H1078 בֵּית־אֵל ***bêt-'ēl***, n.pr.loc. [72] [√ 1074 + 446; cf. 2029]. Bethel, "*temple [house] of God [El]*":– Bethel (71), there[S] (1 [+928])

H1079 בֵּית אַרְבֵאל ***bêt 'arbē'l***, n.pr.loc. [1] [√ 1074 + 745]. Beth Arbel, "*house of Arbel*":– Beth Arbel (1)

H1080 בֵּית אַשְׁבֵּעַ ***bêt 'ašbēa'***, n.pr.loc. [1] [√ 1074 + 842]. Beth Ashbea, "*House of Ashbea*":– Beth Ashbea (1)

H1081 בֵּית בַּעַל מְעוֹן ***bêt ba'al mᵉ'ôn***, n.pr.loc. [1] [√ 1074 + 1260]. Beth Baal Meon, "*house of Baal Meon*":– Beth Baal Meon (1)

H1082 בֵּית בִּרְאִי ***bêt bir'î***, n.pr.loc. [1] [√ 1074 + 1348]. Beth Biri, "*house of Biri* or *den of a lioness*":– Beth Biri (1)

H1083 בֵּית בָּרָה ***bêt bārâ***, n.pr.loc. [2] [√ 1074 + [?]]. Beth Barah, "*house of Barah [the river ford]*":– Beth Barah (2)

H1084 בֵּית־גָּדֵר ***bêt-gādēr***, n.pr.loc. [1] [√ 1074 + 1554; cf. 1559]. Beth Gader, "*house of Gader* or *site of a stone hedge*":– Beth Gader (1)

H1085 בֵּית גָּמוּל ***bêt gāmûl***, n.pr.loc. [1] [√ 1074 + 1694]. Beth Gamul, *"house of recompense"*:– Beth Gamul (1)

H1086 בֵּית דִּבְלָתָיִם ***bêt diblātayim***, n.pr.loc. [1] [√ 1074 + 1814]. Beth Diblathaim, *"house of Diblathaim"*:– Beth Diblathaim (1)

H1087 בֵּית־דָּגוֹן ***bêt-dāgôn***, n.pr.loc. [2] [√ 1074 + 1837]. Beth Dagon, *"temple [house] of Dagon"*:– Beth Dagon (2)

H1088 בֵּית הָאֱלִי ***bêt hā'elî***, a.g. [1] [√ 1074 + 466; cf. 468]. the Bethelite, *"of Bethel"*:– of Bethel (1)

H1089 בֵּית הָאֵצֶל ***bêt hā'ēṣel***, n.pr.loc. [1] [√ 1074 + 2021 + 726]. Beth Ezel, *"house of Ezel* or *site nearby"*:– Beth Ezel (1)

H1090 בֵּית הַגִּלְגָּל ***bêt haggilgāl***, n.pr.loc. [1] [√ 1074 + 2021 + 1652]. Beth Gilgal:– Beth Gilgal (1)

H1091 בֵּית הַגָּן ***bêt haggān***, n.pr.loc.? [1] [√ 1074 + 2056]. Beth Haggan, *"house of Haggan* or *site of the garden"*:– Beth Haggan (1)

H1092 בֵּית הַמֶּרְחָק ***bêt hammerḥāq***, n.pr.loc. Not used in NIVEBC [√ 1074 + 2021 + 8178]. Beth Hamerhaq; see 1074 & 5305

H1093 בֵּית הַיְשִׁימוֹת ***bêt hayᵉšîmôt***, n.pr.loc. [4] [√ 1074 + 2127]. Beth Jeshimoth, *"house of Jeshimoth* or *site of desolation"*:– Beth Jeshimoth (4)

H1094 בֵּית־הַכֶּרֶם ***bêt-hakkerem***, n.pr.loc. [2] [√ 1074 + 2130]. Beth Hakkerem, *"house of Hakkerem* or *site of vineyard"*:– Beth Hakkerem (2)

H1095 בֵּית־הַלַּחְמִי ***bêt-hallaḥmî***, a.g. [4] [√ 1074 + 2140]. the Bethlehemite, *"of Bethlehem"*:– of Bethlehem (3), the Bethlehemite (1)

H1096 בֵּית־הַמַּרְכָּבוֹת ***bêt-hammarkābôt***, n.pr.loc. [1] [√ 1074 + 2175]. Beth Marcaboth, *"site [house] of Marcaboth [chariots]"*:– Beth Markaboth (1)

H1097 בֵּית הָעֵמֶק ***bêt hā'ēmeq***, n.pr.loc. [1] [√ 1074 + 2021 + 6677]. Beth Emek, *"house of Emek* or *site of the valley"*:– Beth Emek (1)

H1098 בֵּית הָעֲרָבָה ***bêt hāᵃrābâ***, n.pr.loc. [4] [√ 1074 + 2196]. Beth Arabah, *"house of Arabah [desert, plain]"*:– Beth Arabah (4)

H1099 בֵּית הָרָם ***bêt hārām***, n.pr.loc. [1] [√ 1074 + 2234]. Beth Haram:– Beth Haram (1)

H1100 בֵּית הָרָן ***bêt hārān***, n.pr.loc. [1] [√ 1074 + 2237]. Beth Haran, *"house of the mountaineer"*:– Beth Haran (1)

H1101 בֵּית הַשִּׁטָּה ***bêt haššiṭṭâ***, n.pr.loc. [1] [√ 1074 + 2242]. Beth Shittah, *"house of Shittah [acacias]"*:– Beth Shittah (1)

H1102 בֵּית־חָגְלָה ***bêt-ḥoglâ***, n.pr.loc. [3] [√ 1074 + 2519]. Beth Hoglah, *"house of Hoglah* or *site of the partridge"*:– Beth Hoglah (3)

H1103 בֵּית־חוֹרוֹן ***bêt-ḥôrôn***, n.pr.loc. [14] [√ 1074 + 2582]. Beth Horon, *"house of Horon* or *site of ravine"*:– Beth Horon (14)

H1104 בֵּית חָנָן ***bêt ḥānān***, n.pr.loc. Not used in NIVEBC [√ 1074 + 2860]. Bethhanan

H1105 בֵּית כָּר ***bêt kār***, n.pr.loc. [1] [√ 1074 + 4122]. Beth Car, *"site [house] of a lamb"*:– Beth Kar (1)

H1106 בֵּית לְבָאוֹת ***bêt lᵉbā'ôt***, n.pr.loc. [1] [√ 1074 + 4219]. Beth Lebaoth, *"house of Lebaoth* or *den of the lioness"*:– Beth Lebaoth (1)

H1107 בֵּית לֶחֶם ***bêt leḥem***, n.pr.loc. [41] [√ 1074 + 4312]. Bethlehem, *"house of bread;* [poss.] *temple [house] of Lakhmu"*:– Bethlehem (40), NDT (1)

H1108 בֵּית לְעַפְרָה ***bêt lᵉaprâ***, n.pr.loc. [1] [√ 1074 + 4364]. Beth Ophrah, *"house of Ophrah* or *house of dust"*:– Beth Ophrah (1)

H1109 בֵּית מִלּוֹא ***bêt millô'***, n.pr.loc. [4] [√ 1074 + 4848]. Beth Millo, *"house of Millo* or *site of earth fill"*:– Beth Millo (4)

H1110 בֵּית מְעוֹן ***bêt mᵉôn***, n.pr.loc. [1] [√ 1074 + 1260]. Beth Meon, *"house of habitation"*:– Beth Meon (1)

H1111 בֵּית מַעֲכָה ***bêt maᵃkâ***, n.pr.loc. Not used in NIVEBC [√ 1074 + 5081]. Beth Maacah

H1112 בֵּית מַרְכָּבוֹת ***bêt markābôt***, n.pr.loc. [1] [√ 1074 + 5325]. Beth Marcaboth:– Beth Markaboth (1)

H1113 בֵּית נִמְרָה ***bêt nimrâ***, n.pr.loc. [2] [√ 1074 + 5809]. Beth Nimrah, *"house of Nimrah [spotted leopard]; house of a basin of clear, limpid water"*:– Beth Nimrah (2)

H1114 בֵּית עֶדֶן ***bêt 'eden***, n.pr.loc. [1] [√ 1074 + 6361]. Beth Eden, *"house of Eden; garden place"*:– Beth Eden (1)

H1115 בֵּית־עַזְמָוֶת ***bêt-'azmāwet***, n.pr.loc. [1] [√ 1074 + 6462]. Beth Azmaveth, *"strong of death; house of Azmaveth [camel fodder]"*:– Beth Azmaveth (1)

H1116 בֵּית־עֲנוֹת ***bêt-ᵃnôt***, n.pr.loc. [1] [√ 1074 + 6742]. Beth Anoth, *"house of Anath [plural]"*:– Beth Anoth (1)

H1117 בֵּית־עֲנָת ***bêt-ᵃnāt***, n.pr.loc. [3] [√ 1074 + 6742]. Beth Anath, *"house of Anath"*:– Beth Anath (3)

H1118 בֵּית־עֵקֶד ***bêt-'ēqed***, n.pr.loc. [2] [√ 1074 + 6820]. Beth Eked:– Beth Eked (2)

H1119 בֵּית עַשְׁתָּרוֹת ***bêt 'aštārôt***, n.pr.loc.? Not used in NIVEBC [√ 1074 + 6958]. Beth Ashtaroth, *"temple of the Ashtoreths"*

H1120 בֵּית פֶּלֶט ***bêt peleṭ***, n.pr.loc. [2] [√ 1074 + 7118]. Beth Pelet, *"house of Pelet [escape]"*:– Beth Pelet (2)

H1121 בֵּית פְּעוֹר ***bêt pᵉ'ôr***, n.pr.loc. [4] [√ 1074 + 7186]. Beth Peor, *"house of Peor"*:– Beth Peor (4)

H1122 בֵּית פַּצֵּץ ***bêt paṣṣēṣ***, n.pr.loc. [1] [√ 1074 + 7208]. Beth Pazzez:– Beth Pazzez (1)

H1123 בֵּית־צוּר ***bêt-ṣûr***, n.pr.loc. [4] [√ 1074 + 7446]. Beth Zur, *"cliff house"*:– Beth Zur (4)

H1124 בֵּית־רְחוֹב ***bêt-rᵉḥôb***, n.pr.loc. [2] [√ 1074 + 8148]. Beth Rehob, *"house of Rehob [main street, market]"*:– Beth Rehob (2)

H1125 בֵּית רָפָא ***bêt rāpā'***, n.pr.[loc.?] [1] [√ 1074 + 8324]. Beth Rapha, *"house of Rapha [healing]"*:– Beth Rapha (1)

H1126 בֵּית־שְׁאָן ***bêt-šᵉ'ān***, n.pr.loc. [9] [√ 1074 + 8632]. Beth Shan, *"site [house] of Shan [repose]"*:– Beth Shan (9)

H1127 בֵּית שֶׁמֶשׁ ***bêt šemeš***, n.pr.loc. [20] [√ 1074 + 9087]. Beth Shemesh, *"temple [house] of Shemesh"*:– Beth Shemesh (20)

H1128 בֵּית־הַשִּׁמְשִׁי ***bêt-šimšî***, a.g. [2] [√ 1074 + 9090]. of Beth Shemesh:– of Beth Shemesh (2)

H1129 בֵּית תּוֹגַרְמָה ***bêt tôgarmâ***, n.pr.loc. [2] [√ 1074 + [?]]. Beth Togarmah, *"house of Togarmah"*:– Beth Togarmah (2)

H1130 בֵּית־תַּפּוּחַ ***bêt-tappûaḥ***, n.pr.loc. [1] [√ 1074 + 9515]. Beth Tappuah, *"house of Tappuah [apricot; apple]"*:– Beth Tappuah (1)

H1131 בִּיתָן ***bîtān***, n.[m.] [3] [√ 1074]. dwelling place, of royalty: palace, with a possible focus on the inner parts of the palace complex:– palace (3)

H1132 [1]בָּכָא ***bākā'***[1], n.[m.] [4] [√ 1134]. balsam tree; some sources: baka-shrub:– poplar trees (4)

H1133 [2]בָּכָא ***bākā'***[2], n.pr.loc. [1] [√ 1134]. Baca, *"balsam tree* or *weeping"*:– Baka (1)

H1134 בָּכָה ***bākâ***, v. [114] [→ 1132, 1133, 1135, 1139, 1140, 1143, 4441; cf. 1141]. [Q] to weep, wail, cry, sob, mourn; [P] to weep for, mourn for; this can refer to ritual mourning as well as personal sorrow:– wept (35), weep (26), weeping (16), wailing (5), mourned (3), wept (3 [+1140]), bitterly weeps (2 [+1134]), mourn (2), wailed (2), weep (2 [+1134]), weep at all (2 [+1134]), weep bitterly (2 [+1134]), weeping bitterly (2 [+1134]), wept aloud (2), cried (1), crying (1), grieved (1), mourning (1), sob (1), sobbing (1), tears (1), weeping (1 [+1140]), wept bitterly (1 [+2221, 1135]), wet with tears (1)

H1135 בֶּכֶה ***bekeh***, n.[m.] [1] [√ 1134]. weeping:– wept bitterly (1 [+1134, 2221])

H1136 בִּכּוּרָה ***bikkûrâ***, n.f. [4] [√ 1144]. early ripened fruit, usually ripening in June (late fruit ripens in August):– early figs (1), early fruit (1), figs ripe (1), ripen early (1)

H1137 בִּכּוּרִים ***bikkûrîm***, n.m. [16] [√ 1144]. firstfruits, first ripened produce:– firstfruits (12), first ripe (1), first ripe fruit (1), first ripe grain (1), NDT (1)

H1138 בְּכוֹרַת ***bᵉkôrat***, n.pr.m. [1] [√ 1144]. Becorath, *"firstborn"*:– Bekorath (1)

H1139 בָּכוּת ***bākût***, n.f. Not used in NIVEBC [√ 1134]. Bacuth

H1140 בְּכִי ***bᵉkî***, n.m. [29] [√ 1134]. weeping:– weeping (14), weep (4), wept (3 [+1134]), weeping bitterly (2 [+1140]), weeps (2), tears (1), weep (1 [+5951]), weeping (1 [+1134]), wept so loudly (1 [+5989, 906, 7754, 928])

H1141 בֹּכִים ***bōkîm***, n.pr.loc. [2] [cf. 1134]. Bokim, *"weepings"*:– Bokim (2)

H1142 בְּכִירָה ***bᵉkîrâ***, n.f. [6] [√ 1144]. first born (daughter):– older (6)

H1143 בְּכִית ***bᵉkît***, n.f. [1] [√ 1134]. mourning, weeping:– mourning (1)

H1144 בָּכַר ***bākar***, v. [4] [→ 1136, 1137, 1138, 1142, 1145, 1146, 1147, 1148, 1149, 1150, 1151, 1152]. [P] bear early fruit; give the rights of the firstborn; [Pu] be made a firstborn (dedication); [H] to bear one's first child:– bear fruit (1), bearing first child (1), firstborn belongs to (1 [+4200]), give the rights of the firstborn (1)

H1145 בֵּכֶר ***bēker***, n.f. [1] [→ 1146; cf. 1144]. young bull camel:– young camels (1)

H1146 בֶּכֶר ***beker***, n.pr.m. [5] [→ 1145, 1151, 1152; cf. 1144]. Beker, *"young male camel"*:– Beker (5)

H1147 בְּכֹר ***bᵉkōr***, n.m. [122] [√ 1144]. firstborn, first male offspring (human or animal), the oldest son, with associative meanings of honor, status, prominence, and privileges of inheritance to the firstborn; by extension: one in a special relationship with God:– firstborn (108), oldest (3), firstborn male (2), first (1), first male offspring (1), first male offspring (1 [+7081, 8167]), poorest of the poor (1 [+1924]), NDT (5)

H1148 בְּכֹרָה ***bᵉkōrâ***, n.f. [10] [√ 1144]. birthright, rights of the firstborn:– birthright (6), ages (1 [+7584]), firstborn (1), rights as firstborn (1), rights of the firstborn (1)

H1149 בִּכְרָה ***bikrâ***, n.f. [1] [√ 1144]. young cow-camel (having given birth to her first calf):– she-camel (1)

H1150 בֹּכְרוּ ***bōkᵉrû***, n.pr.m. [2] [√ 1144]. Bokeru, *"his first born"*:– Bokeru (2)

H1151 בַּכְרִי ***bakrî***, a.g. [1] [√ 1146; cf. 1144]. Bekerite, *"of Beker"*:– Bekerite (1)

H1152 בִּכְרִי ***bikrî***, n.pr.m. *or* a.g. [9] [√ 1146; cf. 1144]. Bicri, *"firstborn"*:– Bikri (8), Bikrites (1)

H1153 [1]בַּל ***bal***[1], adv. [69] [→ 66, 1187; cf. 1162]. no, not, cannot, never:– not (33), no (6), cannot (5), never (4), no sooner (3 [+677]), never (2 [+4200, 5905]), never (2 [+4200, 6409]), nor (2 [+2256]), blind (1 [+8011]), don't (1), ignorant (1 [+3359]), immovable (1 [+4572]), never (1 [+6388]), never (1 [+6409, 2256, 6329]), nothing (1), nothing (1 [+4537]), secure (1 [+4572]), untouched (1 [+7212]), worthless (1 [+3603]), NDT (1)

H1154 [2]בַּל ***bal***[2], adv. Not used in NIVEBC [√ 1162]. surely

H1155 בֵּל ***bēl***, n.pr.m. [3] [→ 1157, 1161, 1171, 1193]. Bel, *"Bel"*:– Bel (3)

H1156 בַּלְאֲדָן ***balᵃdān***, n.pr.m. [2] [→ 5282]. Baladan:– Baladan (2)

H1157 בֵּלְאשַׁצַּר ***bēl'šaṣṣar***, n.pr.m. [1] [√ 1155; 10105, 10109]. Belshazzar, *"Bel protect the king"*:– Belshazzar's (1)

H1158 בָּלַג ***bālag***, v. [4] [→ 1159, 1160]. [H] to flash (with a focus on suddenness); by extension: to smile, rejoice, gleam, have a cheerful attitude:– blinding flash (1), enjoy life (1), have joy (1), smile (1)

H1159 בִּלְגָּה ***bilgâ***, n.pr.m. [3] [√ 1158]. Bilgah, *"gleam, smile"*:– Bilgah (2), Bilgah's (1)

H1160 בִּלְגַּי ***bilgay***, n.pr.m. [1] [√ 1158]. Bilgai, *"gleam, smile"*:– Bilgai (1)

H1161 בִּלְדַּד ***bildad***, n.pr.m. [5] [√ 1155? + 1856]. Bildad, *"Bel has loved"*:– Bildad (5)

H1162 [1]בָּלָה ***bālâ***[1], v. [15] [→ 66, 1153, 1154, 1165, 1170, 1172, 1187, 1194, 4442, 9318; 10106]. [Q] to wear out, waste away; [P] to enjoy, use to the full; to decay; to grow old; to oppress:– wear out (6), worn out (2), decay (1), did[S] (1), long enjoy (1), made grow old (1), oppress (1), wasted away (1), wastes away (1)

H1163 [2]בָּלָה ***bālâ***[2], n.pr.loc. [1] [cf. 1168]. Balah, *"old, worn out"*:– Balah (1)

H1164 בָּלָה ***bālah***[3], v. Not used in NIVEBC [→ 1166, 1167?; cf. 987]. [P] to be troubled

H1165 בָּלֶה ***bāleh***, a. [5] [√ 1162]. old, worn-out:– old (2), worn (1), worn out (1), worn-out (1)

H1166 בַּלָּהָה ***ballāhâ***, n.f. [10] [√ 1164]. sudden terror, horrible end; in some contexts a horrible end refers to death:– terrors (6), horrible end (3), sudden terror (1)

H1167 [1]בִּלְהָה ***bilhâ***[1], n.pr.f. [10] [√ 1164?]. Bilhah, "[perhaps] *simplicity* or *modesty* or *to be without concern"*:– Bilhah (9), she[S] (1)

H1168 [2]בִּלְהָה ***bilhâ***[2], n.pr.loc. [1] [√ 1266; cf. 1163]. Bilhah:– Bilhah (1)

H1169 בִּלְהָן ***bilhān***, n.pr.m. [4] Bilhan, *"foolish"*:– Bilhan (4)

H1170 בְּלוֹי ***bᵉlôy***, n.[m.] [3] [√ 1162]. old, worn-out (things):– old (2), worn-out (1)

H1171 בֵּלְטְשַׁאצַּר ***bēlṭᵉša'ṣṣar***, n.pr.m. [2] [√ 1155; 10108]. Belteshazzar, *"protect his life"*:– Belteshazzar (2)

H1172 בְּלִי ***bᵉlî***, subst. [57] [→ 1174, 1175; cf. 1162]. lacking, without; nothing:– no (11), lack (6), not (6), without (5), unintentionally (4 [+928, 1981]), there is no (3 [+401]), deserted (1 [+4946, 408]), deserted (1 [+4946, 3782]), destruction (1), guiltless (1 [+7322]), lacking (1), lacking (1 [+4946]), nameless (1 [+9005]), no (1 [+4946]), no longer (1), no more (1), nothing (1 [+4537]), relentless (1 [+3104]), there were no (1 [+401]), unnoticed (1 [+4946, 8492]), untraveled (1 [+4946, 408, 6296]), wide (1 [+4200, 2976]), without (1 [+928]), without (1 [+3869]), without (1 [+4200]), without (1 [+4946]), yet (1 [+4946, 889]), NDT (1)

H1173 בְּלִיל ***bᵉlîl***, n.m. [3] [√ 1177]. fodder, mash, fermented matter:– fodder (3)

H1174 בְּלִימָה ***bᵉlîmâ***, n.[m.] Not used in NIVEBC [√ 1172 + 4537]. nothing

H1175 בְּלִיַּעַל ***bᵉliyya'al***, n.[m.] [27] [√ 1172 + 3603]. wicked one, vile one, evil one, worthless one, transliterated "Belial"; A "son of Belial" or "man of Belial" is a troublemaker and scoundrel:– wicked (6), scoundrels (5 [+1201]), destruction (2), vile (2), wicked (2 [+1201]), corrupt (1), evil men (1), scoundrel (1 [+408]), scoundrel (1 [+408, 2021]), troublemaker (1 [+132]), troublemaker (1 [+408]), troublemakers (1), troublemakers (1 [+408, 1201]), worthless (1), NDT (1)

H1176 [1]בָּלַל ***bālal***[1], v. [43] [→ 8671?, 9316, 9319; cf. 1182?]. [Q] to confuse; feed; pour upon; [Qp] to mix (with);

[Htpolal] to be thrown about, shaken back and forth:– mixed (33), mixed in (5), confuse (1), confused (1), fed (1), mixes (1), poured (1)

H1177 2בָּלַל **bālal2**, v.den. Not used in NIVEBC [→ 1173]. [Q] to give fodder, feed

H1178 בָּלַם **bālam**, v. [1] [Q] to be controlled, in check:– controlled (1)

H1179 בָּלַס **bālas**, v.den. [1] [Q] to nip (scratch open) unripe sycamore-fig fruit, so as to promote ripening and make more palatable:– took care of (1)

H1180 1בָּלַע **bāla'1**, v. [43] [→ 1183, 1185, 1186, 1188, 1189, 1190?, 3300?]. [Q] to swallow up; [N] to be swallowed; [P] to swallow up, gulp down, devour, consume; [Pu] be swallowed up, be devoured:– swallowed up (9), swallow up (7), swallowed (6), swallow (4), be swallowed up (2), destroy (2), swallows (2), consumed (1), destroying (1), devoured (1), for an instant (1 [+6330, 8371]), gulp (1), gulps down (1), is swallowed up (1), moment (1), ruin (1), torn (1), uneaten (1 [+4202])

H1181 2בָּלַע **bāla'2**, v. Not used in NIVEBC [→ 3300?]. [P] to communicate, spread abroad; [Pu] be communicated (to a person)

H1182 3בָּלַע **bāla'3**, v. [6] [→ 1184, 3300?; cf. 1176?]. [N] be befuddled, confused; [P] to confuse, turn away; [Pu] to be led astray; [Ht] to be confused thoroughly:– are led astray (1), at wits end (1 [+3972, 2683]), befuddled (1), bring to nothing (1), confuse (1), turn (1)

H1183 1בֶּלַע **bela'1**, n.[m.] [1] [√ 1180]. what is swallowed:– what swallowed (1)

H1184 2בֶּלַע **bela'2**, n.[m.] [1] [√ 1182]. harmful, with a likely focus on destruction, fig. of what is greedily swallowed up:– harmful (1)

H1185 3בֶּלַע **bela'3**, n.pr.m. [12] [√ 1180]. Bela, "*swallower, devourer*":– Bela (12)

H1186 4בֶּלַע **bela'4**, n.pr.loc. [2] [√ 1180]. Bela, "*swallower, devourer*":– Bela (2)

H1187 בַּלְעֲדֵי **bal'adê**, adv. [17] [√ 1153 + 6330]. apart from, except for, besides:– besides (4), apart from (3 [+4946]), cannot (2), other than (2 [+4946]), without (2 [+4946]), except (1 [+4946]), not (1 [+4946]), nothing (1), without (1)

H1188 בַּלְעִי **bal'î**, a.g. [1] [√ 1180]. Belaite, "*of Bela*":– Belaite (1)

H1189 1בִּלְעָם **bil'ām1**, n.pr.m. [60] [√ 1180]. Balaam, "[poss.] *Baal [lord] of the people;* [poss.] *the clan brings forth; devourer, glutton*":– Balaam (53), Balaam's (4), hes (1), hims (1), the two of thems (1 [+1192, 2256])

H1190 2בִּלְעָם **bil'ām2**, n.pr.loc. [1] [√ 1180?]. Bileam, "*[gift] brought to the people*":– Bileam (1)

H1191 בָּלַק **bālaq**, v. [2] [→ 1192, 4444]. [Q] to devastate; [Pu] to be stripped, devastated:– devastate (1), stripped (1)

H1192 בָּלָק **bālāq**, n.pr.m. [43] [√ 1191]. Balak, "*devastator*":– Balak (33), Balak's (3), the two of thems (1 [+2256, 1189]), thems (1 [+6269]), NDT (5)

H1193 בִּלְשָׁן **bilšān**, n.pr.m. [2] [√ 1155]. Bilshan, "*their Bel [lord]*":– Bilshan (2)

H1194 בִּלְתִּי **biltî**, subst. & adv. & pp. [112] [√ 1162]. no, not, without; except for; besides:– not (38), no (13), keep from (5), nothing (5), neither (4), without (3), except (2), fail (2), never (2), prevent (2 [+5989]), unless (2), avoid (1), be kept from (1 [+1757, 4200]), be nothing (1 [+401]), besides (1), but (1), ceremonially unclean (1 [+3196]), didn't (1), disobey (1 [+9048, 928, 7754]), except (1 [+561]), except for (1), failing (1), forbidden (1 [+7422]), free from (1), from (1), insatiable (1 [+8429]), instead of (1 [+4200]), no more (1), not (1 [+4946]), only (1 [+4202]), other than (1 [+4200, 963]), refusing (1), remain unmarried (1 [+6328, 4200, 2118, 4200, 408]), stop (1), unable (1), unceasing (1 [+6239]), unless (1 [+561]), worthless (1 [+3603]), NDT (7)

H1195 1בָּמָה **bāmâ1**, n.f. [101] [→ 192?, 1196, 1199, 1200]. high place, worship shrine (an elevated place, often artificial, for the worship of a god); heights:– high places (58), high place (20), heights (12), theres (4 [+928, 2021]), mound (2), gateway (1 [+9133]), there (1 [+928, 2021]), tops (1), waves (1), NDT (1)

H1196 2בָּמָה **bāmâ2**, n.pr.loc. [1] [√ 1195]. Bamah, "*high place*":– Bamah (1)

H1197 בִּמְהָל **bimhāl**, n.pr.m. [1] [√ 1201 + 4543]. Bimhal, "*son of circumcision*":– Bimhal (1)

H1198 בְּמוֹ **bemô**, pp. [10] [√ 928]. by, with, in:– in (2), with (2), from (1), take (1 [+995]), through (1), used for fuel (1 [+8596, 836]), NDT (2)

H1199 בָּמוֹת **bāmôt**, n.pr.loc. [2] [√ 1195]. Bamoth, "*high places [for cultic worship]*":– Bamoth (2)

H1200 בָּמוֹת בַּעַל **bāmôt ba'al**, n.pr.loc. [2] [√ 1195 + 1251]. Bamoth Baal, "*high places for Baal [worship]*":– Bamoth Baal (2)

H1201 1בֵּן **bēn1**, n.m. [4926] [→ 1202, 1217, 1232; cf. 1215, 1337; 10120; *also used with compound proper names*]. son, child (of either gender), descendant (in any generation), offspring (human or animal); by extension: a term of endearment; one of a class or kind or nation or family. A "son of man" is a "human being" (Nu 23:19), a term that often assumes messianic significance (Ps 8):– son (1833), sons (762), Israelites (486 [+3776]), descendants (236), children (213), old (154), people (93), Ammonites (80 [+6648]), young (54), Israelite (49 [+3776]), Israel (23 [+3776]), Benjamites (18 [+1228]), Reubenites (17 [+8017]), men (17), Gadites (16 [+1514]), Levites (15 [+4290]), people (14 [+6639]), Benjamin (13 [+1228]), Judah (13 [+3373]), mankind (13 [+132]), descendant (12), son's (12), thems (12 [+3776]), company (10), foreigners (10 [+5797]), Ammon (9 [+6648]), Danites (9 [+1968]), Hittites (9 [+3147]), Merarites (9 [+5356]), age (9), Ammonite (8 [+6648]), child (8), children's (8), grandchildren (8 [+1201]), Ephraim (7 [+713]), Gad (7 [+1514]), Kohathite (7 [+7740]), Merarite (7 [+5356]), people (7 [+132]), theys (7 [+3776]), Gershonites (6 [+1767]), Reuben (6 [+8017]), Simeon (6 [+9058]), exiles (6 [+1583]), grandson (6), grandson (6 [+1201]), grandsons (6 [+1201]), Asher (5 [+888]), Assyrians (5 [+855]), Manasseh (5 [+4985]), Naphtali (5 [+5889]), Zebulun (5 [+2282]), foreigner (5 [+5797]), line (5), peoples (5), scoundrels (5 [+1175]), year-old (5 [+9102]), Anakites (4 [+6737]), Dan (4 [+1968]), Ephraimites (4 [+713]), Issachar (4 [+3779]), Kohathites (4 [+7740]), Kohathites (4 [+7741]), Simeonites (4 [+9058]), able men (4 [+2657]), age (4 [+9102]), boy (4), brave (4 [+2657]), cousin (4 [+1856]), descended (4), grandsons (4), people (4 [+2021, 132]), Levites (3 [+4291]), human (3 [+132]), human beings (3 [+132]), human race (3 [+132]), princes (3), princes (3 [+4889]), theirs (3 [+3870]), theirs (3 [+2257]), whoses (3), Babylonians (2 [+951]), Ephraimite (2 [+713]), Gershonite (2 [+1767]), Israelite (2 [+4946, 3776]), Israelite (2 [+408, 4946, 3776]), Joseph (2 [+3441]), Manassites (2 [+4985]), ages (2 [+9102]), angels (2 [+2021, 466]), born (2), calf (2 [+1330]), calves (2), common people (2 [+6639]), condemned to (2), cubs (2), fathers (2), fruitful vine (2 [+7238]), grandchildren (2), hims (2 [+3870]), hostages (2 [+9510]), human (2 [+2021, 132]), human being (2 [+132]), lambs (2 [+7366]), lay people (2 [+6639]), levitical (2 [+4290]), man (2), man (2 [+132]), men (2 [+132]), mortals (2 [+132]), musts (2), nephew (2 [+278]), one (2 [+132]), ones (2), overnight (2 [+4326]), successors (2), theirs (2 [+2257]), theys (2 [+3776]), theys (2 [+5797]), valiant fighter (2 [+408, 2657]), wicked (2 [+1175]), wicked (2 [+6406]), young men (2), Aaronic (1 [+195]), Ahohite (1 [+292]), Babylonian (1 [+951]), Benjamin (1 [+408, 3549]), Edomites (1 [+121]), Egyptians (1 [+5213]), Gad (1 [+1532]), Gershonite (1 [+1769]), Gershonites (1 [+1768]), Gershonites (1 [+1769]), Gilead (1 [+1680]), Hakmonite (1 [+2685]), Is (1), Israelite (1 [+4200, 3776]), Israelite (1 [+928, 3776]), Israelites (1 [+4946, 3776]), Israelites (1 [+6639, 3776]), Judah's (1 [+3373]), Kedar (1 [+7723]), Korahites (1 [+7948]), Levi (1 [+4291]), Maakathite (1 [+5084]), Moabites (1 [+4566]), Rekabites (1 [+1074, 8211]), Reuben (1 [+8018]), Reubenite (1 [+8017]), Zadokites (1 [+7401]), Zerahites (1 [+2438]), able (1 [+2657]), able-bodied (1 [+2657]), all (1 [+132]), all mankind (1 [+132]), all people (1 [+2021, 132]), angels (1 [+466]), anointed (1 [+3658, 2021]), anyone (1), anyone (1 [+408]), anywhere in (1 [+4946]), army (1), arrows (1 [+8008]), arrowss (1), babies (1), birth (1), bravely (1 [+4200, 2657]), bravest soldier (1 [+2657]), brood (1), bull (1 [+1330]), calves (1 [+1330]), children (1 [+1887]), children's (1 [+4200]), choice (1), clans (1), colt (1 [+912]), courageous (1 [+2657]), cousins on their father's side (1 [+1856]), cushites (1 [+3934]), deserves (1), destitute (1 [+2710]), disciple (1), especially bred (1 [+2021, 8247]), everyone on earth (1 [+132]), evildoers (1 [+6594]), families (1), family (1), family (1 [+1061]), fertile (1 [+9043]), fighting (1 [+2657]), foal (1), foreigner (1 [+2021, 5797]), foreigners (1 [+2021, 5797]), goats (1 [+6436]), granddaughters (1 [+1426]), greeks (1 [+3436]), hes (1 [+281, 6687]), heavenly (1 [+446]), heavenly beings (1 [+446]), high (1 [+408]), highborn (1 [+408]), hims (1 [+2023]), hims (1 [+2021, 3778]), his peoples (1 [+3147]), human beings (1 [+2021, 132]), human hands (1 [+132]), humanity (1 [+132]), humans (1 [+2021, 132]), leading (1 [+2657]), low (1 [+132]), lowborn (1 [+132]), mankind (1 [+2021, 132]), man's (1 [+2021, 132]), members (1), mortals (1 [+632]), murderer (1 [+8357]), musicians (1 [+8876]), must die (1 [+4638]), my (1), mys (1 [+2257]), native (1 [+6639]), nephews (1 [+2157]), noisy boasters (1 [+8623]), of Gilead (1 [+1682]), of Judah (1 [+3373]), one (1), one who will inherit (1 [+5479]), oppressed (1 [+6715]), people (1 [+408]), people's (1 [+4946, 132]), people's (1 [+2021, 132]), person (1 [+132]), prince (1 [+4889]), prophets (1 [+5566]), proud (1 [+8832]), proud beasts (1 [+8832]), rebellious (1 [+5308]), servant (1), slave born in household (1 [+563]), soldiers (1 [+2657]), somes (1), son of (1), sparks (1 [+8404]), theirs (1), theirs (1 [+3871]), theirs (1 [+6648]), theirs (1 [+2021, 1769]), thems (1 [+4013]), thems (1 [+3620]), thems (1 [+6648]), theys (1 [+2257]), theys (1 [+2023]), theys (1 [+6648]), theys (1 [+1228]), theys (1 [+1968]), theys (1 [+2021, 851]), theys (1 [+1514, 2256, 1201, 8017]), theys (1 [+1201, 1514, 2256, 8017]), thoses (1), tribe (1), tribes (1), troops (1 [+1522]), troublemakers (1 [+408, 1175]), vassal (1), very own brother (1 [+278, 562, 3870]), vultures (1 [+5979]), whos (1 [+3776]), womb (1 [+5402]), worthy (1 [+2657]), NDT (223)

H1202 2בֵּן **bēn2**, n.pr.m. Not used in NIVEBC [√ 1201]. Ben

H1203 בֶּן־אֲבִינָדָב **ben-'abînādāb**, n.pr.m. [1] [√ 1201 + 3 + 5605]. Ben-Abinadab, "*son of Abinadab*":– Ben-Abinadab (1)

H1204 בֶּן־אוֹנִי **ben-'ônî**, n.pr.m. [1] [√ 1201 + 224]. Ben-Oni, "*son of my sorrow*":– Ben-Oni (1)

H1205 בֶּן־גֶּבֶר **ben-geber**, n.pr.m. [1] [√ 1201 + 1505]. Ben-Geber, "*son of strength*":– Ben-Geber (1)

H1206 בֶּן־דֶּקֶר **ben-deqer**, n.pr.[loc.?] [1] [√ 1201 + 1991]. Ben-Deker, "*son of Deker [pierces]*":– Ben-Deker (1)

H1207 בֶּן־הֲדַד **ben-hadad**, n.pr.m. [25] [√ 1201 + 2060]. Ben-Hadad, "*son of Hadad*":– Ben-Hadad (24), Ben-Hadad's (1)

H1208 בֶּן־הִנֹּם **ben-hinnōm**, n.pr.loc. [10] [√ 1201 + 2183]. Ben Hinnom, "*the son of Hinnom*":– Ben Hinnom (10)

H1209 בֶּן־זוֹחֵת **ben-zôḥēt**, n.pr.m. [1] [√ 1201 + 2311]. Ben-Zoheth, "*son of Zoheth*":– Ben-Zoheth (1)

H1210 בֶּן־חוּר **ben-ḥûr**, n.pr.m. [1] [√ 1201 + 2581]. Ben-Hur, "*son of Hur*":– Ben-Hur (1)

H1211 בֶּן־חַיִל **ben-ḥayil**, n.pr.m. [1] [√ 1201 + 2657]. Ben-Hail, "*son of strength*":– Ben-Hail (1)

H1212 בֶּן־חָנָן **ben-ḥānān**, n.pr.m. [1] [√ 1201 + 2860]. Ben-Hanan, "*son of grace*":– Ben-Hanan (1)

H1213 בֶּן־חֶסֶד **ben-ḥesed**, n.pr.m. [1] [√ 1201 + 2876]. Ben-Hesed, "*son of Hesed [loyal love]*":– Ben-Hesed (1)

H1214 בֶּן־עַמִּי **ben-'ammî**, n.pr.m. [1] [√ 1201 + 6639 + 3276]. Ben-Ammi, "*son of my people*":– Ben-Ammi (1)

H1215 בָּנָה **bānâ**, v. [377] [→ 1218, 1220, 1221, 1224, 1230, 4445, 4447, 9322; cf. 1201, 1426; 10111; *also used with compound proper names*]. [Q] to make, build, rebuild, establish; [Qp, N] to be built, established:– built (114), build (94), building (24), rebuilt (24), rebuild (16), be rebuilt (13), built up (12), builders (9), build up (7), builds (6), fortified (4), rebuilding (3), be built (2), been built (2), been rebuilt (2), build a family (2), erect (2), indeed built (2 [+1215]), is built (2), made (2), rebuilt (2 [+8740, 2256]), usings (2), be established (1), be restored (1), besieged (1 [+6584]), builder (1), builds up (1), constructed (1), construction (1), craftsmen (1), did work (1), done thiss (1 [+4640, 4200, 3378]), erected (1), establish (1), form (1), leave (1), lined (1), make firm (1), newly built (1), partitioned off (1), prosper (1), rebuild (1 [+8740, 2256]), repairing (1), restored (1), set up (1), stands firm (1), was built (1), were used (1), worked (1), NDT (4)

H1216 בְּנֹב **benōb**, n.pr.m. Not used in NIVEBC [→ 3785, 3787]. Benob

H1217 בְּנוֹ **benô**, n.pr.m. *or* n.m.+p.m.sg.suf. [2] [√ 1201]. Beno, "*his son*":– Beno (2)

H1218 בִּנּוּי **binnûy**, n.pr.m. [8] [√ 1215; cf. 1002]. Binnui, "*son*":– Binnui (8)

H1219 בְּנוֹת **benôt**, n.pr. Not used in NIVEBC [→ 6112]. Benoth, see 6112

H1220 בָּנִי **bānî**, n.pr.m. [14] [√ 1215]. Bani, "*descendant*":– Bani (14)

H1221 בֻּנִּי **bunnî**, n.pr.m. [3] [√ 1215]. Bunni:– Bunni (3)

H1222 בְּנֵי־בְרַק **benê-beraq**, n.pr.loc. [1] [√ 1201 + 1400]. Bene Berak, "*sons of Barak [lightning]*":– Bene Berak (1)

H1223 בְּנֵי יַעֲקָן **benê ya'aqān**, n.pr.loc. [3] Bene Jaakan, "[poss.] *son of Jaakan*":– Bene Jaakan (3)

H1224 בִּנְיָה **binyâ**, n.f. [1] [√ 1215]. building, physical structure:– building (1)

H1225 בְּנָיָה **benāyâ**, n.pr.m. [11] [√ 1215 + 3378]. Benaiah, "*Yahweh has built*":– Benaiah (11)

H1226 בְּנָיָהוּ **benāyāhû**, n.pr.m. [31] [√ 1215 + 3378]. Benaiah, "*Yahweh has built*":– Benaiah (31)

H1227 בֵּנַיִם **bēnayim**, subst.[du.] [2] [√ 1068]. champion, single fighter:– champion (2 [+408, 2021])

H1228 בִּנְיָמִין **binyāmîn**, בֶּן־יָמִין **ben-yāmîn**, n.pr.m. [166] [→ 1229, 3549; cf. 1201 + 3545]. Benjamin, "*son of [the] right hand; southerner*":– Benjamin (109), Benjamites (18 [+1201]), Benjamin (13 [+1201]), Benjamites (10), Benjamite (4), tribe of Benjamin (3), Benjamin's (2), Benjamin (1 [+824]), Benjamite (1 [+408]), Benjamite (1 [+4946]), Benjamites (1 [+408]), Benjamites (1 [+4946]), Benjamites (1 [+408, 4946]), theys (1 [+1201])

H1229 בֶּן־יְמִינִי **ben-yemînî**, בִּנְיָמִינִי **binyemînî**, a.g. [9] [√ 1128; cf. 1201 + 3545]. Benjamite, of Benjamin, "*of Benjamin*":– Benjamite (7), Benjamites (1), men of Benjamin (1)

H1230 בִּנְיָן **binyān**, n.m. [7] [√ 1215; 10112]. building, structure; outer wall:– building (4), outer wall (2), wall (1)

H1231 בְּנִינוּ **benînû**, n.pr.m. [1] [√ 1201]. Beninu, "*our son*":– Beninu (1)

HEBREW INDEX

H1232 בִּנְעָא ***bin'ā'***, n.pr.m. [2] [√ 1201 + *]. Binea:– Binea (2)

H1233 בְּסוֹדְיָה ***besôdeyâ***, n.pr.m. [1] [√ 928 + 6051 + 3378; cf. 1234?]. Besodeiah, "*in secret council of Yahweh*":– Besodeiah (1)

H1234 בְּסַי ***bēsay***, n.pr.m. [2] [cf. 1233?]. Besai, "*in secret council of Yahweh*":– Besai (2)

H1235 בֹּסֶר ***bōser***, n.m. [5] unripe grapes, sour grapes:– sour grapes (3), grape (1), unripe grapes (1)

H1236 בַּעֲבוּר ***ba'abûr***, pp.+c. Not used in NIVEBC [√ 928 + 6288]. for the sake of; on account of; for; in order that

H1237 בַּעַד1 ***ba'ad1***, subst.pp. [104] [→ 1238]. behind; through, over; around; from; on behalf of, for (benefit of):– for (47), through (8), behind (5), from (4), behind (3 [+4946]), in (3), around (2), on behalf of (2), around (1 [+6017, 4946]), barred in (1 [+1378]), by (1), for (1 [+3954]), kept the women from conceiving (1 [+6806, 8167, 6806]), of (1), on (1), on behalf (1), over (1), seals off (1 [+3159]), NDT (20)

H1238 בַּעַד2 ***ba'ad2***, subst. Not used in NIVEBC [√ 1237]. price, payment

H1239 בָּעָה1 ***bā'â1***, v. [3] [√ 10114]. [Q] to ask, inquire; [N] to be pillaged; other sources: searched out, with an implication that what is found would be taken and so ransacked:– ask (2), pillaged (1)

H1240 בָּעָה2 ***bā'â2***, v. [2] [Q] to boil; [N] to bulge, be swollen:– bulging (1), causes to boil (1)

H1241 בְּעוּלָה ***be'ûlâ***, n.pr.f. [1] [√ 1249]. Beulah:– Beulah (1)

H1242 בְּעוֹר ***be'ôr***, n.pr.m. [10] Beor, "[perhaps] *a burning*":– Beor (10)

H1243 בִּעוּת ***bi'ût***, n.m.pl. [2] [√ 1286]. terror:– terrors (2)

H1244 בֹּעַז1 ***bō'az1***, n.pr.m. [22] Boaz, "[prob.] *in him is strength*":– Boaz (22)

H1245 בֹּעַז2 ***bō'az2***, n.pr.m. [2] Boaz, "[prob.] *in him is strength*":– Boaz (2)

H1246 בָּעַט ***bā'aṭ***, v. [2] [Q] to kick (in scorn):– kicked (1), scorn (1)

H1247 בְּעִי ***be'î***, n[m.] Not used in NIVEBC [√ 928 + 6505]. ?

H1248 בְּעִיר ***be'îr***, n.m. [6] [→ 1279, 1280]. animals, livestock, cattle:– livestock (4), animals (1), cattle (1)

H1249 בָּעַל1 ***bā'al1***, v. [15] [→ 1241]. [Q] to rule over; to marry, be a husband; [Qp, N] to be married, have a husband:– husband (4), be married (1), has a husband (1), married (1), married (1 [+1251]), marries (1), marries (1 [+4374, 2256]), marry (1), marrying (1), ruled (1), ruled over (1), wife (1 [+851])

H1250 בָּעַל2 ***bā'al2***, v. [Q] to make

H1251 בַּעַל1 ***ba'al1***, n.m. [164] [→ 1252, 1266, 1272; cf. 1249; 10116; *also used with compound proper names*]. 1) Baal (pagan god); 2) husband, master, owner, citizen; used in many phrases to indicate mastery of an object: "lord of arrows" is a master archer; "lord of dreams" is an interpreter of dreams, etc., "*master, owner, lord*":– Baal (54), Baals (18), citizens (18), owner (11), husband (5), Baal worship (4), Baal's (3), husbands (2), owners (2), two-horned (2 [+2021, 7967]), accuser (1 [+5477]), allied (1 [+1382]), archers (1 [+2932]), betrothed (1 [+4053]), bird (1 [+4053]), bird on the wing (1 [+4053]), captain (1), charmer (1 [+4383]), collected sayings (1 [+670]), creditor (1 [+5408, 3338, 2257]), dreamer (1 [+2021, 2706]), drivers (1 [+7304]), filled with (1), given to gluttony (1 [+5883]), had (1), has (1), have (1), himS (1 [+2023]), hot-tempered (1 [+2779]), husband's (1), involved in (1), itS (1 [+1074]), man's (1), married (1 [+1249]), master (1), men (1), one who destroys (1 [+5422]), one who gives (1), openedS (1), owned (1), owner's (1), people (1), person (1), practice (1), prudentS (1 [+2257]), related by marriage (1), rulers (1), schemer (1 [+4659]), tenants (1), theyS (1 [+8901]), theyS (1 [+3972, 4463, 8901]), those to whom due (1), those who get (1), under oath (1 [+8652]), with (1)

H1252 בַּעַל2 ***ba'al2***, n.pr.m. [3] [√ 1251]. Baal, "*master, owner, lord*":– Baal (3)

H1253 בַּעַל בְּרִית ***ba'al berît***, n.pr. [2] [√ 1251 + 1382]. Baal-Berith, "*Baal [lord] of the covenant*":– Baal-Berith (2)

H1254 בַּעַל גָּד ***ba'al gād***, n.pr.loc. [3] [√ 1251 + 1514]. Baal Gad, "*lord [Baal] of good luck*":– Baal Gad (3)

H1255 בַּעַל הָמוֹן ***ba'al hāmôn***, n.pr.loc. [1] [√ 1251 + 2162]. Baal Hamon, "*lord [Baal] of Hamon* or *possessor of abundance*":– Baal Hamon (1)

H1256 בַּעַל זְבוּב ***ba'al zebûb***, n.pr. [4] [√ 1251 + 2279]. Baal-Zebub, "*Baal [lord] of the flies*":– Baal-Zebub (4)

H1257 בַּעַל חָנָן ***ba'al ḥānān***, n.pr.m. [5] [√ 1251 + 2860]. Baal-Hanan, "*lord [Baal] is gracious*":– Baal-Hanan (5)

H1258 בַּעַל חָצוֹר ***ba'al ḥāṣôr***, n.pr.loc. [1] [√ 1251 + 2959]. Baal Hazor, "*lord [Baal] of Hazor*":– Baal Hazor (1)

H1259 בַּעַל חֶרְמוֹן ***ba'al ḥermôn***, n.pr.loc. [2] [√ 1251 + 3056]. Baal Hermon, "*lord [Baal] of Hermon*":– Baal Hermon (2)

H1260 בַּעַל מְעוֹן ***ba'al me'ôn***, n.pr.loc. [3] [√ 1251 + 5061?]. Baal Meon:– Baal Meon (3)

H1261 בַּעַל פְּעוֹר ***ba'al pe'ôr***, n.pr.m. [2] [√ 1251 + 7186]. Baal Peor, "*lord [Baal] of Peor*":– Baal Peor (2)

H1262 בַּעַל־פְּרָצִים ***ba'al-perāṣîm***, n.pr.loc. [4] [√ 1251 + 7288]. Baal Perazim, "*lord [Baal] of making a breech, breaking through*":– Baal Perazim (4)

H1263 בַּעַל צְפֹן ***ba'al ṣepōn***, n.pr.loc. [3] [√ 1251 + 7600]. Baal Zephon, "*lord [Baal] of the north*":– Baal Zephon (3)

H1264 בַּעַל שָׁלִשָׁה ***ba'al šālišâ***, n.pr.loc. [1] [√ 1251 + 8995]. Baal Shalishah:– Baal Shalishah (1)

H1265 בַּעַל תָּמָר ***ba'al tāmār***, n.pr.loc. [1] [√ 1251 + 9469]. Baal Tamar, "*lord [Baal] of the palm tree*":– Baal Tamar (1)

H1266 בַּעֲלָה1 ***ba'alâ1***, n.f. [4] [→ 1168, 1267?, 1268; cf. 1251]. mistress (of sorceries); (female) owner:– medium (1 [+200]), mistress (1), oneS (1 [+200]), owned (1)

H1267 בַּעֲלָה2 ***ba'alâ2***, n.pr.loc. [6] [√ 1266?]. Baalah, "[fem. of Baal] *lady*":– Baalah (6)

H1268 בְּעָלוֹת ***be'ālôt***, n.pr.loc. [1] [√ 1266]. Bealoth, "[fem. pl. of Baal] *lady*":– Bealoth (1)

H1269 בְּעֶלְיָדָע ***be'elyādā'***, n.pr.m. [1] [√ 1251 + 3359]. Beeliada, "*the lord [Baal] knows*":– Beeliada (1)

H1270 בְּעַלְיָה ***be'alyâ***, n.pr.m. [1] [√ 1251 + 3359 + 3378]. Bealiah, "*Yahweh is Lord*":– Bealiah (1)

H1271 בַּעֲלִיס ***ba'alîs***, n.pr.m. [1] Baalis, "[poss.] *son of delight* or *Baals*":– Baalis (1)

H1272 בַּעֲלַת ***ba'alāt***, n.pr.loc. [4] [→ 1251]. Baalath, "*lady, goddess* [fem. of Baal]":– Baalath (4)

H1273 בַּעֲלַת בְּאֵר ***ba'alat be'ēr***, n.pr.loc. [1] [√ 1251 + 931]. Baalath Beer, "*lord [Baal] of the well*":– Baalath Beer (1)

H1274 בְּעֹן ***be'ōn***, n.pr.loc. [1] Beon:– Beon (1)

H1275 בַּעֲנָא ***ba'anā'***, n.pr.m. [3] [→ 1276]. Baana, "*son of affliction*":– Baana (3)

H1276 בַּעֲנָה ***ba'anâ***, n.pr.m. [9] [√ 1275]. Baanah, "*son of affliction*":– Baanah (9)

H1277 בָּעַר1 ***bā'ar1***, v. [63] [→ 1281, 1282, 9323; cf. 1278]. [Q] to burn; [P] to light a fire, set a blaze; [Pu] to be burning; [Ht] to start a fire, consume with fire:– burn (10), burned (5), burning (5), blazed (4), burn up (3), fire (3), light (3), use for fuel (3), ablaze (2), blazing (2), burned up (2), burns (2), set ablaze (2), wipe out (2), blazed forth (1), blazes (1), burn (1 [+928, 2021, 241]), charred (1 [+928, 2021, 836]), consumed (1), consumes (1), fires (1), flare up (1), kindled (1), lit (1 [+836]), on fire (1 [+928, 2021, 836]), raged (1), sacrificed (1), sets ablaze (1), started (1)

H1278 בָּעַר2 ***bā'ar2***, v. [24] [cf. 1277]. [N] to be purged; [P] to purge, remove, get rid of; [H] to graze:– purge (11), rid (3), destroyed (2), removed (2), got rid of (1), graze (1), grazes (1), laid waste (1), purged (1), ruined (1)

H1279 בָּעַר3 ***bā'ar3***, v.den. [7] [√ 1248]. [Q] to be senseless, to be brutal; [N] to behave senseless:– senseless (5), brutal (1), give senseless (1)

H1280 בַּעַר ***ba'ar***, n.m. [5] [√ 1248]. senselessness, stupidity, ignorance, comparable to an animal:– senseless (3), brute (1), stupid (1)

H1281 בַּעֲרָא ***ba'arā'***, n.pr.f. [1] [√ 1282; cf. 1277]. Baara, "*passionate [burning] one*":– Baara (1)

H1282 בְּעֵרָה ***be'ērâ***, n.f. [1] [→ 1281; cf. 1277]. fire:– fire (1)

H1283 בַּעֲשֵׂיָה ***ba'aśēyâ***, n.pr.m. [1] Baaseiah, "*Yahweh is bold*":– Baaseiah (1)

H1284 בַּעְשָׁא ***ba'šā'***, n.pr.m. [28] Baasha, "*boldness*":– Baasha (25), Baasha's (2), heS (1)

H1285 בְּעֶשְׁתְּרָה ***be'ešterâ***, n.pr.loc. [1] [cf. 6958?]. Be Eshtarah:– Be Eshterah (1)

H1286 בָּעַת ***bā'at***, v. [16] [→ 1287, 1243]. [N] to be afraid, be terrified; [P] to torment, terrify, overwhelm:– overwhelmed (2), terrified (2), terrify (2), afraid (1), alarm (1), fill with terror (1), frighten (1), frightening (1), makes tremble (1), overwhelm (1), startle (1), tormented (1), tormenting (1)

H1287 בְּעָתָה ***be'ātâ***, n.f. [2] [√ 1286]. terror:– terror (2)

H1288 בֹּץ ***bōṣ***, n.[m.] [1] [→ 1010?, 1289, 9324?]. mud, silt:– mud (1)

H1289 בִּצָּה ***biṣṣâ***, n.f. [3] [√ 1288]. marsh, swamp, waterlogged ground:– marsh (2), swamps (1)

H1290 בָּצוּר ***bāṣûr***, a. [25] [√ 1307]. fortified:– fortified (22), walls (2), unsearchable (1)

H1291 בֵּצַי ***bēṣay***, n.pr.m. [3] Bezai:– Bezai (3)

H1292 בָּצִיר1 ***bāṣîr1***, n.m. [7] [√ 1305]. grape harvest; grapes; vineyard:– grape harvest (4), full grape harvest (1), grapes (1), vineyard (1)

H1293 בָּצִיר2 ***bāṣîr2***, n.m. [1] [√ 1307]. dense, inaccessible (forest):– dense (1)

H1294 בָּצָל ***bāṣāl***, n.m. [1] [→ 1296?, 1297?]. onion:– onions (1)

H1295 בְּצַלְאֵל ***beṣal'ēl***, n.pr.m. [9] [√ 928 + 7498 + 446]. Bezalel, "*in the shadow of God [El]*":– Bezalel (9)

H1296 בַּצְלוּת ***baṣlût***, n.pr.m. [2] [√ 1294?]. Bazluth:– Bazluth (2)

H1297 בַּצְלִית ***baṣlît***, n.pr.m. Not used in NIVEBC [√ 1294?]. Bazlith

H1298 בָּצַע ***bāṣa'***, v. [16] [→ 1299]. [Q] to cut off; to be greedy, make unjust gain; [P] to cut off; to finish; to make unjust gain:– cut off (3), greedy (3), breaking ranks (1), bring down (1), builds (1), complete (1), finished (1), fulfilled (1), go after ill-gotten gain (1 [+1299]), greedy (1 [+1299]), make unjust gain (1 [+1299]), unjust gain (1)

H1299 בֶּצַע ***beṣa'***, n.m. [23] [√ 1298]. ill-gotten gain, dishonest gain; cutting off:– gain (8), dishonest gain (3), unjust gain (2), destroyed (1), gained (1), go after ill-gotten gain (1 [+1298]), greed (1), greedy (1 [+1298]), ill-gotten gain (1), ill-gotten gains (1), make unjust gain (1 [+1298]), plunder (1), selfish gain (1)

H1300 בְּצַעֲנַנִּים ***beṣa'annannîm***, n.pr.loc. Not used in NIVEBC [cf. 7588]. Bezaanannim

H1301 בָּצֵק1 ***bāṣēq1***, v. [2] [→ 1302, 1304]. [Q] to swell, become swollen:– swell (1), swollen (1)

H1302 בָּצֵק2 ***bāṣēq2***, n.[m.] [5] [√ 1301]. dough made of flour, not yet leavened:– dough (5)

H1303 בִּצְקָלוֹן ***biṣqālôn***, n.[m.] Not used in NIVEBC. head of grain

H1304 בָּצְקַת ***boṣqat***, n.pr.loc. [2] [√ 1301]. Bozkath, "*swollen or elevated spot*":– Bozkath (2)

H1305 בָּצַר1 ***bāṣar1***, v. [7] [→ 1292]. [Q] to harvest, gather grapes:– grape pickers (2), harvest (2), gathered (1), gathering grapes (1), harvest grapes (1)

H1306 בָּצַר2 ***bāṣar2***, v. [1] [→ 1314, 1316]. [Q] to humble, break (the spirit):– breaks (1)

H1307 בָּצַר3 ***bāṣar3***, v. [4] [→ 1290, 1293, 1310?, 1311, 1312, 1313, 1315, 4448, 4449, 4450?]. [N] to be impossible, be thwarted; [P] to strengthen, fortify:– be thwarted (1), fortifies (1), impossible (1), strengthen (1)

H1308 בָּצַר4 ***bāṣar4***, n.m. Not used in NIVEBC [→ 1309, 1310?, 4450]. [P] to test gold, assay

H1309 בֶּצֶר1 ***beṣer1***, n.[m.] [2] [√ 1308]. gold ore:– gold (1), nuggets (1)

H1310 בֶּצֶר2 ***beṣer2***, n.pr.m. [1] [√ 1308 *or* 1307]. Bezer, "*[metallic] ore* or *place of refuge*":– Bezer (1)

H1311 בֶּצֶר3 ***beṣer3***, n.pr.loc. [4] [√ 1307 *or possibly* 1308]. Bezer, "*[metallic] ore* or *place of refuge*":– Bezer (4)

H1312 בָּצְרָה1 ***boṣrâ1***, n.f. [1] [√ 1307]. pen, sheep-fold:– pen (1)

H1313 בָּצְרָה2 ***boṣrâ2***, n.pr.loc. [8] [√ 1307]. Bozrah, "*enclosure (for sheep), fortress*":– Bozrah (8)

H1314 בַּצָּרָה ***baṣṣārâ***, n.f. [3] [√ 1306]. drought; trouble:– trouble (2), drought (1)

H1315 בִּצָּרוֹן ***biṣṣārôn***, n.[m.] [1] [√ 1307]. fortress, stronghold:– fortress (1)

H1316 בַּצֹּרֶת ***baṣṣōret***, n.f. [1] [√ 1306]. drought:– drought (1)

H1317 בַּקְבּוּק ***baqbûq***, n.pr.m. [2] [√ 1318]. Bakbuk, "*gurgling (sound coming out of a bottle)*":– Bakbuk (2)

H1318 בַּקְבֻּק ***baqbuq***, n.[m.] [3] [→ 1317, 1319, 1321, 1322]. jar; in some contexts a flask:– jar (3)

H1319 בַּקְבֻּקְיָה ***baqbuqyâ***, n.pr.m. [3] [√ 1318 + 3378]. Bakbukiah, "*Yahweh pours out*":– Bakbukiah (3)

H1320 בַּקְבַּקַּר ***baqbaqqar***, n.pr.m. [1] Bakbakkar, "*investigator*":– Bakbakkar (1)

H1321 בֻּקִּי ***buqqî***, n.pr.m. [5] [√ 1318; cf. 1322]. Bukki, "*proved of Yahweh; mouth [gurgle sounds] of Yahweh*":– Bukki (5)

H1322 בֻּקִּיָּהוּ ***buqqiyyāhû***, n.pr.m. [2] [√ 1318 + 3378?; cf. 1321]. Bukkiah, "*proved of Yahweh*":– Bukkiah (2)

H1323 בְּקִיעַ ***bāqîa'***, n.[m.] [2] [√ 1324]. breach (in a defense); bits, debris:– bits (1), walls broken through (1)

H1324 בָּקַע ***bāqa'***, v. [51] [→ 1323, 1325, 1326]. [Q] to divide, split, tear open; [N] to be split, burst open; [P] to split open, burst forth; [Pu] to be cracked open, broken through, ripped open; [H] to break through, divide; [Ho] to be broken through; [Ht] to split apart:– divided (3), ripped open (3), split (3), was broken through (3), broke (2), burst forth (2), cracked (2), divide (2), hatch (2), opened up (2), split apart (2), were divided (2), be split (1), been broken through (1), break forth (1), break through (1), breaks up (1), burst (1), chopped up (1), conquer (1), cut (1), gush forth (1), invaded (1), is hatched (1), mauled (1), ready to burst (1), rip open (1), shook (1), splits (1), taken by storm (1), tear apart (1), tore open (1), tunnel (1 [+3284]), unleash (1), were dashed to pieces (1)

H1325 בֶּקַע ***beqa'***, n.[m.] [2] [√ 1324]. beka (half-shekel, one-fifth of an ounce [five or six grams]):– beka (2)

H1326 בִּקְעָה ***biq'â***, n.f. [20] [√ 1324; 10117]. valley, plain:– plain (9), valley (7), valleys (4)

H1327 [1]בָּקַק ***bāqaq***[1], v. [8] [cf. 3309?]. [Q] to lay waste, ruin, destroy; [N] to be laid waste; [P] to devastate:– be completely laid waste (2 [+1327]), destroyers (1), devastate (1), laid waste (1), lay waste (1), lose heart (1 [+8120, 928, 7931]), ruin (1)

H1328 [2]בָּקַק ***bāqaq***[2], v. [1] [Q] to grow abundantly, spread out:– spreading (1)

H1329 בָּקַר ***bāqar***, v. [7] [→ 1330, 1331, 1332, 1333, 1334; 10118]. [P] to inspect, seek; look after; consider:– look after (2), consider (1), look (1), pick out (1), seek (1), seeking guidance (1)

H1330 בָּקָר ***bāqār***, n.m. [184] [→ 1012; cf. 1329]. animal, cow, bull; cattle, oxen, herd:– cattle (40), herds (33), oxen (31), bull (27 [+7228]), bulls (14), herd (9), bulls (5 [+7228]), bull (4), ox (4), animals (2), calf (2 [+1201]), cows (2), heifer (2 [+6320]), bull (1 [+1201]), calves (1 [+1201]), cattle (1 [+5238]), cow (1), herds (1 [+5238]), herds (1 [+6373]), oxgoad (1 [+4913]), plowing (1), young cow (1 [+6320])

H1331 [1]בֹּקֶר ***bōqer***[1], n.m. Not used in NIVEBC [√ 1329]. sacrifice for omens

H1332 [2]בֹּקֶר ***bōqer***[2], n.m. [215] [√ 1329]. morning:– morning (179), every morning (4 [+928, 2021, 928, 2021, 1332]), dawn (3), dawn (2 [+240, 2021]), daybreak (2 [+240, 2021]), every morning (2 [+928, 2021, 1332, 928, 2021]), every morning (2 [+928, 2021, 1332, 928, 2021]), mornings (2), morning's (2), break of day (1 [+7155]), daybreak (1 [+7155]), daybreak (1 [+2021, 240]), daybreak (1 [+7155, 2021]), daylight (1 [+240, 2021]), each morning (1 [+928, 2021, 928, 2021, 1332]), each morning (1 [+928, 2021, 1332, 928, 2021]), each morning (1 [+4200, 2021, 4200, 2021, 1332]), each morning (1 [+4200, 2021, 1332, 4200, 2021]), hold back overnight (1 [+4328, 6330]), last watch of the night (1 [+874]), last watch of the night (1 [+874, 2021]), morning light (1), NDT (4)

H1333 בַּקָּרָה ***baqqārâ***, n.f.vbl. [1] [√ 1329]. looking after, caring for:– looks after (1)

H1334 בִּקֹּרֶת ***biqqōret***, n.f. [1] [√ 1329]. due punishment (after investigation):– due punishment (1)

H1335 בָּקַשׁ ***bāqaš***, v. [224] [→ 1336]. [P] to seek, search, look for, inquire about; [Pu] be sought, be investigated:– seek (44), look for (11), want to kill (11 [+5883]), looked for (10), search for (10), searched for (7), looking for (6), sought (5), tried (5), trying to kill (5 [+5883]), find (4), searched (4), seeking (4), hold accountable (3 [+4946, 3338]), search (3), search out (3), seeks (3), trying (3), want (3), call to account (2), conspired (2), demand (2), determined (2), foster (2), in search of (2), intended (2), intent on (2), searching for (2), seek out (2), sought out (2), take (2), about to (1), ask for (1), asked (1), asked for (1), asked for permission (1), asking for (1), be sought (1), beg (1), begging (1), bent on (1), call to account (1 [+4946, 3338]), carefully investigated (1 [+2011, 2256]), demanded (1), demanded payment (1), destroy (1 [+5883]), finds (1), go searching for (1), gone in search of (1), hold responsible (1 [+4946, 3338]), inquiring of (1), invites (1), looking for a chance (1), looks to (1), petitioned (1), plans (1), plead with (1), pleaded (1), pleaded with (1), promote (1), pursue (1), pursues (1), pursuing (1), questioned (1), search be made (1), search made for (1), searching (1), seek an audience with (1 [+7156]), seek help (1), seek to (1), set out (1), straining (1), threatening to kill (1 [+5883]), tried to kill (1 [+5883]), trying to (1), trying to get (1), want to (1), want to do (1), want to kill (1 [+906, 5883]), want to take (1), wanted to (1), wanted to kill (1 [+5883]), wanted to kill (1 [+906, 5883]), wanted to make (1 [+4200]), wants to kill (1 [+5883]), was investigated (1), went in search of (1)

H1336 בַּקָּשָׁה ***baqqāšâ***, n.m. [8] [√ 1335]. request:– request (7), asked (1)

H1337 [1]בַּר ***bar***[1], n.m. [4] [→ 1401; cf. 1201; 10120]. son (exclusively male in the OT); the phrase translated "Kiss the Son" (Ps 2:12) is an act of homage to a king:– son (4)

H1338 [2]בַּר ***bar***[2], a. [7] [√ 1405]. pure; empty; favorite; radiant, bright:– pure (3), bright (1), empty (1), favorite (1), radiant (1)

H1339 [3]בַּר ***bar***[3], n.m. [13] [√ 1405; cf. 1350?]. grain, wheat, that has been cleansed and threshed:– grain (11), wheat (2)

H1340 [4]בַּר ***bar***[4], n.m. [1] [√ 10119]. wilds, in the open field:– wilds (1)

H1341 [1]בֹּר ***bōr***[1], n.m. [5] [√ 1405]. cleanness:– cleanness (5)

H1342 [2]בֹּר ***bōr***[2], n.m. [2] [√ 1405]. soda, potash, lye, used in making soap:– cleansing powder (1), thoroughly purge away (1 [+7671, 3869, 2021])

H1343 [1]בָּרָא ***bārā'***[1], v. [48] [→ 1349, 1375]. [Q] to create, Creator; [N] to be created; can refers to creating from nothing as well as to reforming existing materials, as in "create in me a pure heart" (Ps 51:10):– created (20), create (10), were created (6), creator (4), are created (2), creating (2), brings about (1), creates (1), done (1), not yet created (1)

H1344 [2]בָּרָא ***bārā'***[2], v. [1] [→ 1374; cf. 5258]. [H] to fatten:– fattening (1)

H1345 [3]בָּרָא ***bārā'***[3], v. [5] [P] to cut, cut down, clear (a forest):– clear (1), clear land (1), cut down (1), make (1), NDT (1)

H1346 [4]בָּרָא ***bārā'***[4], v. Not used in NIVEBC [√ 1356]. see 1356

H1347 בְּרֹאדַךְ־בַּלְאֲדָן ***b^{e}rō'dak-bal'^{a}dān***, n.pr.m. Not used in NIVEBC [√ 5282]. Berodach-Baladan, see 5282

H1348 בִּרְאִי ***bir'î***, n.pr.loc. Not used in NIVEBC [→ 1082]. Biri

H1349 בְּרָאיָה ***b^{e}rā'yâ***, n.pr.m. [1] [√ 1343 + 3378]. Beraiah, "*Yahweh has created*":– Beraiah (1)

H1350 בַּרְבֻּר ***barbur***, n.m.pl. [1] [cf. 1339?]. fowl, bird (of various species):– fowl (1)

H1351 בָּרַד ***bārad***, v.den. [1] [→ 1352]. [Q] to shower hail:– hail (1)

H1352 בָּרָד ***bārād***, n.m. [28] [√ 1351]. hail, hailstones:– hail (21), hail (2 [+74]), hailstones (1), hailstorm (1), hailstorm (1 [+2443]), it^{s} (1 [+2021]), storm (1)

H1353 בָּרֹד ***bārōd***, a. [4] spotted, dappled:– dappled (2), spotted (2)

H1354 [1]בֶּרֶד ***bered***[1], n.pr.loc. [1] Bered, "[poss.] *freezing rain*":– Bered (1)

H1355 [2]בֶּרֶד ***bered***[2], n.pr.m. [1] Bered, "[poss.] *freezing rain*":– Bered (1)

H1356 [1]בָּרָה ***bārâ***[1], v. [6] [→ 1346, 1362, 1376]. [Q] to eat; [H] to give to eat, urge to eat:– eat (3), food (1), give to eat (1), urged to eat (1)

H1357 [2]בָּרָה ***bārâ***[2], v. [1] [√ 1382]. [Q] to enter into a covenant:– Choose (1)

H1358 בָּרוּךְ ***bārûk***, n.pr.m. [26] [√ 1385]. Baruch, "*be blessed*":– Baruch (26)

H1359 בָּרוּר ***bārûr***, a. *or* v.ptcp. [2] [√ 1405]. pure, sincere:– purify (1 [+2200]), sincerely (1)

H1360 בְּרוֹשׁ ***b^{e}rôš***, n.m. [20] [cf. 1361]. pine tree; some sources: cypress or fir:– juniper (11), junipers (6), castanets (1 [+6770]), juniper (1 [+6770]), spears of juniper (1)

H1361 בְּרוֹת ***b^{e}rôt***, n.m. [1] [cf. 1360]. fir tree; some sources: juniper or cypress:– firs (1)

H1362 בָּרוּת ***bārût***, n.f. [1] [√ 1356]. food:– food (1)

H1363 בֵּרוֹתָה ***bērôtâ***, n.pr.loc. [1] Berothah, "*well*":– Berothah (1)

H1364 בִּרְזָוִת ***birzāwit***, n.pr.f. Not used in NIVEBC [√ 1365]. Birzavith, see 1365

H1365 בִּרְזָיִת ***birzāyit***, n.pr.f. [1] [√ 931 + 2339]. Birzaith, "*well of olive oil*":– Birzaith (1)

H1366 בַּרְזֶל ***barzel***, n.m. [76] [→ 1367; 10591]. iron, iron (implements):– iron (62), iron-smelting (3), ax (2), iron tool (2), blacksmith (1 [+3093]), head (1), iron axhead (1), iron chains (1), irons (1), tool of iron (1), NDT (1)

H1367 בַּרְזִלַּי ***barzillay***, n.pr.m. [12] [√ 1366]. Barzillai, "*[made of] iron*":– Barzillai (12)

H1368 [1]בָּרַח ***bāraḥ***[1], v. [65] [→ 1371, 4451; cf. 1369, 1370]. [Q] to flee, run away, escape; [H] to drive out, make flee:– fled (32), flee (4), fleeing (4), running away (3), flees headlong (2 [+1368]), come away (1), drives out (1), drove away (1), drove out (1), escaping (1), extend (1), extended (1), flees (1), fleeting (1), fly away (1), go back (1), gone back (1), leave at once (1), make flee (1), put to flight (1), ran away (1), ran off (1), run away (1), run off (1), takes to flight (1)

H1369 [2]בָּרַח ***bāraḥ***[2], v. Not used in NIVEBC [cf. 1368, 1370]. [H] to injure

H1370 [3]בָּרַח ***bāraḥ***[3], v. Not used in NIVEBC [→ 1378; cf. 1368, 1369]. [H] to make impassable

H1371 בָּרִחַ ***bāriaḥ***, a. [4] [√ 1368]. gliding; fugitive:– fugitives (2), gliding (2)

H1372 בַּרְחֻמִי ***barḥumî***, a.g. [1] [cf. 1038, 1050]. Barhumite:– Barhumite (1)

H1373 בֵּרִי ***bērî***, n.pr.m. [1] Beri, "*wisdom*":– Beri (1)

H1374 בָּרִיא ***bārî'***, a. [14] [√ 1344; cf. 5258]. fat, choice, healthy:– fat (4), healthy (3), fat (2 [+1414]), choice (1), choice sheep (1), choicest (1), nourished (1 [+1414]), stall-fed (1)

H1375 בְּרִיאָה ***b^{e}rî'â***, n.f. [1] [√ 1343]. created thing, with a possible implication that it is something new:– something totally new (1)

H1376 בִּרְיָה ***biryâ***, n.f. [3] [√ 1356]. food; in context it refers to food for sick people:– food (3)

H1377 בָּרִיחַ ***bārîaḥ***, n.pr.m. [1] Bariah, "[poss.] *board, bar; fugitive; descendant*":– Bariah (1)

H1378 בְּרִיחַ ***b^{e}rîaḥ***, n.m. [40] [√ 1370]. bar, gate bar, crossbar:– bars (17), crossbars (11), crossbar (2), bar (1), barred gates (1), barred in (1 [+1237]), bars of gates (1), gate (1), gate bars (1), NDT (4)

H1379 בֵּרִים ***bērîm***, a.g. Berite

H1380 בְּרִיעָה ***b^{e}rî'â***, n.pr.m. [11] [→ 1381]. Beriah, "*prominent, excellent*":– Beriah (11)

H1381 בְּרִיעִי ***b^{e}rî'î***, a.g. [1] [√ 1380]. Beriite, "*of Beriah*":– Beriite (1)

H1382 בְּרִית ***b^{e}rît***, n.f. [284] [→ 451, 1253, 1357]. covenant, treaty, compact, agreement, an association between two parties with various responsibilities, benefits, and penalties; "to cut a covenant" is "make a covenant," a figure of the act of ceremonially cutting an animal into two parts, with an implication of serious consequences for not fulfilling the covenant:– covenant (249), treaty (26), agreement (3), agreements (1), alliance (1), allied (1 [+1251]), allies (1 [+408]), it^{s} (1 [+778, 2021]), marriage covenant (1)

H1383 בֹּרִית ***bōrît***, n.f. [2] [√ 1405]. soap, made from soap plants or potash:– cleansing powder (1), soap (1)

H1384 [1]בָּרַךְ ***bārak***[1], v. [3] [√ 1386; 10121]. [Q] to kneel down; [H] to make kneel:– had kneel down (1), kneel (1), knelt down (1 [+6584, 1386])

H1385 [2]בָּרַךְ ***bārak***[2], v. [326] [→ 1358, 1387, 1388, 3310; cf. 1386?; 10122]. [P] to bless, pronounce blessings, give praise, give thanks, extol; [Qp, N, Pu] to be blessed, be praised; [Ht] to bless oneself, be blessed; this can mean to speak words invoking divine favor (bless), or speak of the excellence of someone (praise):– blessed (83), bless (79), praise (65), be blessed (22), blesses (8), praised (8), give blessing (6), blessing (3), congratulate (3), cursed (3), extol (3), pronounce blessings (3), bless (2 [+1385]), bless abundant (2 [+1385]), bless at all (2 [+1385]), blessed (2 [+1385]), blessed again and again (2 [+1385]), curse (2), done nothing but bless (2 [+1385]), richly bless (2 [+1385]), surely bless (2 [+1385]), bid farewell (1), blessings given (1), commended (1), count blessed (1), curse^{s} (1), do so^{s} (1), gave blessing (1), give greetings (1), given (1), giving blessing (1 [+1388]), greet (1), greet (1 [+7925]), greeted (1), greets (1), invoke a blessing on themselves (1), invoke blessings (1), invokes a blessing (1), pronounce blessing (1), pronounced (1), thank (1), worships (1), NDT (1)

H1386 בֶּרֶךְ ***berek***, n.f. [25] [→ 1384, 1392, 1393; cf. 1385?; 10072, 10123]. knee, the "buckling of the knees" means to falter, implying great fear or despair; "to bow the knee" means to be reverent or submissive:– knees (15), lap (2), leg (2), for (1 [+6584]), knee (1), knee-deep (1), kneel (1), kneeling (1 [+4156, 6584]), knelt down (1 [+1384, 6584])

H1387 בַּרַכְאֵל ***barak'ēl***, n.pr.m. [2] [√ 1385 + 446]. Barakel, "*God [El] blesses*":– Barakel (2)

H1388 [1]בְּרָכָה ***b^{e}rākâ***[1], n.f. [68] [→ 1389, 1390; cf. 1385]. blessing; gift:– blessing (39), blessings (15), gift (3), blessed (2 [+5989]), peace (2), special favor (2), blessed (1), blessed (1 [+995]), generous (1), giving blessing (1 [+1385]), present (1)

H1389 [2]בְּרָכָה ***b^{e}rākâ***[2], n.pr.m. [1] [√ 1388; cf. 1385]. Beracah, "*blessing*":– Berakah (1)

H1390 [3]בְּרָכָה ***b^{e}rākâ***[3], n.pr.loc. [2] [√ 1388; cf. 1385]. Beracah, "*blessing*":– Berakah (2)

H1391 בְּרֵכָה ***b^{e}rēkâ***, n.f. [18] (man-made) pool, reservoir:– pool (13), pools (2), pool (1 [+4784]), reservoirs (1 [+4784]), NDT (1)

H1392 בֶּרֶכְיָה ***berekyâ***, n.pr.m. [7] [√ 1386 + 3378]. Berekiah, "*Yahweh blesses*":– Berekiah (7)

H1393 בֶּרֶכְיָהוּ ***berekyāhû***, n.pr.m. [4] [√ 1386 + 3378]. Berekiah, "*Yahweh blesses*":– Berekiah (4)

H1394 בְּרֹמִים ***b^{e}rōmîm***, n.[m.] [1] multicolored, a fabric of two-color webbing:– multicolored (1)

H1395 בַּרְנֵעַ ***barnēa'***, n.pr.loc. Not used in NIVEBC [→ 7732]. Barnea

H1396 בֶּרַע ***bera'***, n.pr.m. [1] Bera, "*gift*":– Bera (1)

H1397 בָּרַק ***bāraq***, v. [1] [→ 1398, 1399, 1402]. [Q] to flash lightning:– Send forth lightning (1 [+1398])

H1398 [1]בָּרָק ***bārāq***[1], n.m. [21] [→ 1399, 1402; cf. 1397]. lightning bolt, flash of lightning:– lightning (11), flash like lightning (2), bolts of lightning (1), flashing (1), gleaming point (1), glittering (1), great bolts of lightning (1), lightning bolts (1), send forth lightning (1 [+1397]), strike like lightning (1)

H1399 [2]בָּרָק ***bārāq***[2], n.pr.m. [14] [√ 1398; cf. 1397]. Barak, "*lightning*":– Barak (13), Barak's (1)

H1400 בְּרַק ***b^{e}raq***, n.pr.loc. Not used in NIVEBC [→ 1222]. Berak

H1401 בַּרְקוֹס ***barqôs***, n.pr.m. [2] [√ 1337 + *]. Barkos, "*son of Kos*":– Barkos (2)

H1402 בַּרְקֹן ***barqōn***, n.m.pl. [2] [√ 1398; cf. 1397]. brier, a thorny plant:– briers (2)

H1403 בָּרֶקֶת ***bāreqet***, n.f. [2] [→ 1404]. beryl (a green stone, exact identification uncertain):– beryl (2)

H1404 בָּרְקַת ***bār^{e}qat***, n.f. [1] [√ 1403]. beryl (a green stone, exact identification uncertain):– beryl (1)

H1405 [1]בָּרַר ***bārar***[1], v. [14] [→ 1338, 1339, 1341, 1342, 1359, 1383; cf. 1406]. [Q] to purge; [Qp] to be chosen, be choice; [N] to keep clean, be pure; [P] purify; [H] to cleanse; [Ht] to show oneself pure:– pure (3), choice (2), chosen (2), show yourself pure (2), be purified (1), cleanse (1), purge (1), purified (1), tests (1)

H1406 ²בָּרַר ***bārar2***, v. [2] [cf. 1405]. [Qp] to be sharpened, polished, [H] to sharpen:– polished (1), sharpen (1)

H1407 בִּרְשַׁע ***birša'***, n.pr.m. [1] Birsha, "*disagreeable in taste*":– Birsha (1)

H1408 בֵּרֹתַי ***bērōtay***, n.pr.loc. [1] Berothai:– Berothai (1)

H1409 בֵּרֹתִי ***bērōtî***, a.g. [1] [cf. 943]. Berothite, "*of Berothai [?]*":– Berothite (1)

H1410 בְּשׂוֹר ***beśôr***, n.pr.loc. [3] Besor:– Besor (2), NDT (1)

H1411 בֹּשֶׂם ***bōśem***, n.m. [30] [→ 1412, 3311]. spices, perfume, fragrance; this can refer to balsam oil or to perfume in general:– spices (21), spice (3), fragrance (2), fragrant (2), perfumes (1), spice-laden (1)

H1412 בָּשְׂמַת ***bāśemat***, n.pr.f. [7] [√ 1411]. Basemath, "*fragrant*":– Basemath (7)

H1413 בָּשַׂר ***bāśar***, v. [24] [→ 1415]. [P] to bring (good) news, proclaim (good) news; [Ht] to hear news:– proclaim (5), bring good news (3), bringing good news (2), brought the news (2), proclaim the news (2), take the news (2), bring tidings (1), bringing news (1), brings good news (1), do soS (1), hear good news (1), messenger of good news (1), proclaim good news (1), proclaiming (1)

H1414 בָּשָׂר ***bāśār***, n.m. [269] [√ 10125]. flesh, the soft tissue mass of any animal; the whole body; particular parts of the body: meat, skin, genitals, etc.; by extension: humankind, living things:– flesh (74), meat (64), body (20), people (9), skin (8 [+6425]), creature (7), himself (7 [+2257]), mankind (6), bodies (5), life (4), flesh and blood (3), themselves (3 [+2257]), creatures (2), fat (2 [+1374]), gaunt (2 [+1987]), genitals (2), itS (2), kind (2), living thing (2), living things (2), mortal (2), skin (2), be circumcised (1 [+4576, 6889]), blood relative (1 [+8638]), bodily (1 [+4946]), body (1 [+6872]), circumcised (1 [+4576, 6889]), close relative (1 [+8638]), completely (1 [+4946, 5883, 2256, 6330]), everyone (1 [+3972]), everyone (1 [+3972]), humanity (1), lean (1 [+8369]), mankind (1 [+408]), me (1 [+3276]), meal (1), mortals (1), myself (1 [+3276]), nothing but skin (1 [+6425, 2256]), nourished (1 [+1374]), oneS (1 [+3972]), put in jeopardy (1 [+5951, 928, 9094]), regular flow (1 [+2307, 928]), thatS (1), them (1 [+4392]), thoseS (1), undergo circumcision (1 [+4576, 906, 6889]), was circumcised (1 [+4576, 6889]), whole being (1), you (1 [+3870]), NDT (11)

H1415 בְּשׂרָה ***beśōrâ***, n.f. [6] [√ 1413]. news, good news:– news (3), good news (2), reward for news (1)

H1416 בַּשֶּׁבֶת ***baššebet***, n.pr.m. Not used in NIVEBC [→ 3783]. Basshebeth

H1417 בְּשַׁגַּם ***bešaggam***, pp. & rel. & adv. Not used in NIVEBC [√ 928 + 8611 + 1685]. see 928, 8611, 1685

H1418 בָּשַׁל ***bāšal***, v. [28] [→ 1419, 4453]. [Q] to ripen; boil; [P] to cook, boil, roast, bake; [Pu] to be cooked, be boiled; [H] ripen:– cook (10), cooked (5), boiled (3), boil (2), baked (1), boiled (1 [+1419]), burned to cook (1), kitchens (1 [+1074]), ripe (1), ripened (1), roast (1), roasted (1)

H1419 בָּשֵׁל ***bāšēl***, a. [2] [√ 1418]. cooked, boiled:– boiled (1), boiled (1 [+1418])

H1420 בִּשְׁלָם ***bišlām***, n.pr.m. [1] [cf. 8967]. Bishlam, "*son of Shalom [peace]*":– Bishlam (1)

H1421 ¹בָּשָׁן ***bāšān1***, n.pr.loc. [60] Bashan, "*fertile stoneless plain*":– Bashan (59), Bashan (1 [+824])

H1422 ²בָּשָׁן ***bāšān2***, n.m. serpent

H1423 בָּשְׁנָה ***bošnâ***, n.f. [1] [√ 1017]. disgrace, shame:– disgraced (1 [+4374])

H1424 בָּשַׁס ***bāšas***, v. [1] [Po] to trample:– levy a straw tax (1)

H1425 בֹּשֶׁת ***bōšet***, n.f. [30] [→ 410; cf. 1017]. shame, disgrace, humiliation:– shame (20), disgraced (2), disgrace (1 [+7156]), humiliation (1 [+7156]), shame (1 [+6872]), shameful god (1), shameful gods (1), shameful idol (1), shaming (1), utter shame (1 [+1017])

H1426 ¹בַּת ***bat1***, n.f. [586] [→ 1442, 1444, 1445; cf. 1215]. daughter, female child of any generation (granddaughter, etc.); by extension: any female, girl, woman; a term of endearment; fig., outlying village or settlement (of a "mother" city):– daughter (241), daughters (204), women (15), people (14 [+6639]), surrounding settlements (10), settlements (9), villages (7), surrounding villages (6), granddaughter (5), woman (5), young women (5), owls (4 [+3613]), daughter's (3), girl (3), city (2), horned owl (2 [+3613]), owl (2 [+3613]), queen city (2), year-old (2 [+9102]), Egypt (1 [+5213]), adopted (1 [+4374, 4200]), age (1 [+9102]), apple (1 [+413]), branches (1), cousin (1 [+1856]), daughters in marriage (1), descendant (1), eyes (1 [+6524]), granddaughters (1 [+1201]), inhabitants (1), old (1), outlying villages (1), people (1), princess (1 [+4889]), sheS (1 [+7281]), sister (1), songs (1 [+8877]), themS (1 [+8870]), whoseS (1 [+7524]), whoseS (1 [+465, 2257]), women who worship (1), young (1), NDT (22)

H1427 ²בַּת ***bat2***, n.m. & f. [14] [√ 10126]. bath (liquid measure, equal to an ephah, about six gallons [about 22 liters]; some sources: eight to nine gallons):– baths (8), bath (6)

H1428 ³בַּת ***bat3***, n.f. [1] woven garment:– did weaving (1 [+755])

H1429 בָּתָה ***bātâ***, n.f. [1] [→ 1431?]. wasteland:– wasteland (1)

H1430 בֹּתָה ***bōtâ***, var. see 2999

H1431 בַּתָּה ***battâ***, n.f. [1] [√ 1429?]. steep ravine, face of a cliff:– steep (1)

H1432 ¹בְּתוּאֵל ***betû'ēl1***, n.pr.m. [9] [√ 5493 + 446]. Bethuel, "*man of God [El]*":– Bethuel (9)

H1433 ²בְּתוּאֵל ***betû'ēl2***, n.pr.loc. [1] [cf. 1434?]. Bethuel, "*man of God [El]*":– Bethuel (1)

H1434 בְּתוּל ***betûl***, n.pr.loc. [1] [cf. 1433?]. Bethul:– Bethul (1)

H1435 בְּתוּלָה ***betûlâ***, n.f. [51] [→ 1436]. virgin, maiden; a marriageable woman who has never had sexual intercourse and still under the authority of her father; (unmarried) young woman:– virgin (25), young women (11), virgins (6), young woman (4), women (2), daughters (1), unmarried (1), young women (1 [+5855])

H1436 בְּתוּלִים ***betûlîm***, n.f. [9] [√ 1435]. virginity; proof of virginity, referring to a cloth with blood from a virgin's first sexual encounter:– proof of virginity (3), never marry (2), be a virgin (1 [+928]), proof that a virgin (1), to be a virgin (1), virgin (1)

H1437 בִּתְיָה ***bityâ***, n.pr.f. [1] Bithiah, "[*poss.*] *worshiper of Yahweh* or *queen*":– Bithiah (1)

H1438 בָּתַק ***bātaq***, v. [1] [cf. 980]. [P] to hack to pieces, slaughter:– hack to pieces (1)

H1439 בָּתַר ***bātar***, v. [2] [→ 1440, 1441, 1443]. [Q, P] to cut in pieces:– cut (1), cut in half (1)

H1440 ¹בֶּתֶר ***beter1***, n.m. [3] [√ 1439]. piece:– pieces (2), halves (1)

H1441 ²בֶּתֶר ***beter2***, n.m. [1] [√ 1439]. ruggedness, referring to mountains with rugged ravines:– rugged (1)

H1442 בַּת-רַבִּים ***bat-rabbîm***, n.pr.loc. [1] [√ 1426 + 8049]. Bath Rabbim, "*daughter of a multitude*":– Bath Rabbim (1)

H1443 בִּתְרוֹן ***bitrôn***, n.[pr.loc.?] [or m.?] [1] [√ 1439]. Traditionally Bithron, *"ravine"*, or a ravine. Others: morning time:– morning hours (1)

H1444 בַּת-שֶׁבַע ***bat-šeba'***, n.pr.f. [12] [√ 1426 + 8682]. Bathsheba, "*seventh daughter* or *daughter of an oath*":– Bathsheba (12)

H1445 בַּת-שׁוּעַ ***bat-šûa'***, n.pr.f. Not used in NIVEBC [√ 1426 + 8679?]. Bath-Shua

H1446 ג ***g***, letter. Not used in NIVEBC [√ 10127]. letter of the Hebrew alphabet

H1447 גֵּא ***gē'***, a. [1] [√ 1448]. proud, arrogant:– arrogance (1)

H1448 גָּאָה ***gā'â***, v. [7] [→ 1447, 1449, 1450, 1452, 1454, 1455, 1456, 1575]. [Q] to grow tall, be high, to rise up; by extension: to be exalted:– highly exalted (4 [+1448]), grow tall (1), hold head high (1), risen (1)

H1449 גֵּאָה ***gē'â***, n.f. [1] [√ 1448]. pride, arrogance:– pride (1)

H1450 גֵּאֶה ***gē'eh***, a. [8] [√ 1448]. proud, arrogant:– proud (6), arrogance (1), arrogant (1)

H1451 גְּאוּאֵל ***ge'û'ēl***, n.pr.m. [1] [√ 1447 + 446]. Geuel, "*splendor of God [El]*":– Geuel (1)

H1452 גַּאֲוָה ***ga'awâ***, n.f. [18] [√ 1448]. surging; majesty, glory, triumph; pride, arrogance, conceit:– pride (7), conceit (2), majesty (2), arrogance (1), arrogant (1), glorious (1), proud (1), proud (1 [+6913]), surging (1), triumph (1)

H1453 גְּאוּלִים ***ge'ûlîm***, n.m.pl.abst. [1] [√ 1457]. redemption, with an implication that the redemption involves recompense:– redeem (1)

H1454 גָּאוֹן ***gā'ôn***, n.m. [49] [√ 1448]. surging (waves), lush (high) thickets; majesty, splendor, glory; pride, arrogance:– pride (24), majesty (6), arrogance (5), proud (4), thickets (3), splendor (2), arrogant (1), glory (1), lush thicket (1), majestic (1), pomp (1)

H1455 גֵּאוּת ***gē'ût***, n.f. [8] [√ 1448]. surging (sea), rising (smoke); majesty, glory; pride, arrogance:– majesty (2), pride (2), arrogance (1), column (1), glorious things (1), surging (1)

H1456 גַּאֲיוֹן ***ga'ayôn***, a. [1] [√ 1448]. arrogant, proud:– proud (1)

H1457 ¹גָּאַל ***gā'al1***, v. [103] [→ 1453, 1460, 3319]. [Q] to redeem, deliver; (n.) avenger; kinsman-redeemer; [Qp] to be redeemed; [N] to be redeemed, redeem oneself; often this redemption is in the context of saving from danger or hostility, as a figure of purchasing a slave or indentured person. A "kinsman-redeemer" purchases a relative from slavery (actual or potential); a "kinsman-avenger" provides justice on behalf of a relative; both concepts are in the image of God as Redeemer:– redeemed (19), redeemer (17), redeem (16), avenger (13), redeem (6 [+1457]), guardian-redeemer (5), be redeemed (3), do itS (2), guardian-redeemer of family (2), relative (2), rescue (2), anotherS (1), claim (1), close relative (1), defender (1), delivered (1), do duty as guardian-redeemer (1), do soS (1), guardian-redeemers (1), has the right to do itS (1), is redeemed (1), redeem themselves (1), redeemable (1), redeems (1), NDT (3)

H1458 ²גָּאַל ***gā'al2***, v. [11] [→ 1459; cf. 1718]. [N] to be stained, defiled; [P] to defile; [Pu] to be unclean, defiled; [H/Aphel] to stain; [Ht] to defile oneself:– defiled (4), defile himself (2), unclean (2), are defiled (1), are stained (1), stained (1)

H1459 גֹּאַל ***gō'al***, n.[m.] [1] [√ 1458]. defilement:– defiled (1)

H1460 גְּאֻלָּה ***ge'ullâ***, n.f. [14] [√ 1457]. redemption (of a person or object); right of redemption; blood relatives; see also 1457:– redemption (4), redeem (3), right of redemption (2), as nearest relative duty (1), exiles (1 [+408]), itS (1 [+3276]), redeemed (1), right to redeem (1)

H1461 ¹גַּב ***gab1***, n.m. & f. [10] [→ 1462; 10128]. eyebrow; rim (of a wheel); mound, back:– rims (3), mounds (2), back (1), backs (1), eyebrows (1 [+6524]), mound (1), strong (1)

H1462 ²גַּב ***gab2***, n.m. [2] [√ 1461]. defense:– defenses (2)

H1463 ¹גֵּב ***gēb1***, n.[m.] [3] [→ 1481; 10129]. ditch; cistern:– pools of water (2 [+1463]), cisterns (1)

H1464 ²גֵּב ***gēb2***, n.[m.] [1] an architectural structure variously interpretated: beam, rafter, paneling:– beams (1)

H1465 גֶּבֶא ***gebe'***, n.m. [2] cistern; marsh:– cistern (1), marshes (1)

H1466 גֵּבָה ***gēbâ***, n.[m.] [1] [→ 1479]. swarm (of locust):– locusts (1)

H1467 גָּבַהּ ***gābah***, v. [33] [→ 1468, 1469, 1470, 1471, 1510, 3322]. [Q] to be tall, tower high; to exalt; to be proud, haughty, arrogant; [H] to make high, grow tall; exalt; the attitude of pride or arrogance is a fig. extension the base meaning of being tall or high; something that is "too high" cannot be understood:– haughty (4), proud (4), exalted (3), high (2), higher (2), soar (2), towered (2), arrogant (1), build high (1), builds high (1), devoted (1), exalts (1), highest (1), made higher (1), make grow tall (1), pride (1), pride (1 [+4213]), taller (1), tower proudly (1), towered (1 [+928, 7757, 2256, 5989, 7550]), upward (1)

H1468 גָּבֵהַּ ***gābēah***, a. [4] [√ 1467]. high, towered; proud, haughty; the attitude of pride or arrogance is a fig. extension the base meaning of being tall or high:– haughty (1), pride (1 [+8120]), proud (1), towered (1)

H1469 גָּבֹהַּ ***gābōah***, a. [38] [√ 1467]. high, tall; proud, haughty; the attitude of pride or arrogance is a fig. extension the base meaning of being tall or high:– high (17), height (2), lofty (2), so proudly (2 [+1469]), tall (2), arrogant (1), exalted (1), haughty (1), height (1 [+7757]), heights (1), long (1), longer (1), official (1), oneS (1), othersS (1), taller (1), towers (1), NDT (1)

H1470 גֹּבַהּ ***gōbah***, n.m. [18] [√ 1467]. tallness, height; splendor, majesty; pride, haughtiness, conceit; the attitude of pride or arrogance is a fig. extension the base meaning of being tall or high:– height (5), high (3), haughty (1), heights (1), higher (1), insolence (1), pride (1), pride (1 [+678]), raised (1), splendor (1), tall (1), NDT (1)

H1471 גַּבְהוּת ***gabhût***, n.f. [2] [√ 1467]. arrogance:– arrogance (1), arrogant (1 [+132])

H1472 גָּבֹל ***gābôl***, var. Not used in NIVEBC [cf. 1473]. boundary [?]

H1473 גְּבוּל ***gebûl***, n.m. [240] [→ 1474, 1487; cf. 1472]. territory, boundary, border:– territory (57), boundary (44), border (37), borders (10), itS (9 [+2021]), country (7), land (7), area (4), boundary stone (4), boundaries (3), rim (3), throughout (3 [+928, 3972]), boundary stones (2), coastline (2), region (2), vicinity (2), Egypt (1 [+5213]), allotted territory (1), anywhere (1 [+3972]), anywhere in (1 [+928, 3972]), areas (1), bank (1), borderland (1), coast (1), districts (1), domain (1), end (1 [+7895]), homeland (1), itS (1), itS (1 [+2021, 616]), limits (1), neighboring territory (1), part (1), parts (1), places (1), the borders (1), wall (1), walls (1), NDT (22)

H1474 גְּבוּלָה ***gebûlâ***, n.f. [10] [√ 1473]. boundary stone, border marker:– boundaries (6), allotted portions (1), boundary stones (1), field (1), territory (1)

H1475 גִּבּוֹר ***gibbôr***, a. [158] [√ 1504; 10132]. mighty one, mighty warrior, special guard:– warriors (31), mighty (22), fighting men (15), warrior (13), mighty warriors (12), brave warriors (5 [+2657]), mighty warrior (5), strong (5), heroes (3), mighty men (3), special guard (3), best fighting men (2 [+2657]), champion (2), hero (2), standing (2 [+2657]), valiant soldier (2 [+2657]), warrior's (2), able men (1 [+2657]), anotherS (1), blameless (1 [+9459]), brave fighting men (1 [+2657]), brave man (1 [+2657]), brave warrior (1 [+2657]), capable men (1 [+2657]), experienced fighting men (1 [+408, 4878, 2657]), fighter (1), fighters (1), good fighters (1), leaders (1), man (1), men (1), men of standing (1 [+2657]), mighty (1 [+3946]), mighty hero (1), mighty warrior (1 [+2657]), mighty warriors (1 [+2657]), military staff (1), noblest (1 [+4946]), officers (1), person (1), powerful (1), principal (1), soldiers (1), troops (1 [+2657]), very capable men (1 [+2657]), warriors (1 [+2657])

H1476 גְּבוּרָה ***gᵉbûrâ***, n.f. [61] [√ 1504; 10130]. power, strength, might, achievement:– power (15), might (13), strength (12), achievements (8), mighty acts (5), things[S] (2), acts of power (1), mighty power (1), mighty works (1), source of strength (1), victory (1), warriors (1)

H1477 גִּבֵּחַ ***gibbēaḥ***, a. [1] [→ 1478]. bald forehead:– bald forehead (1)

H1478 גַּבַּחַת ***gabbaḥat***, n.f. [4] [√ 1477]. bald spot on the forehead; bare spot on cloth:– forehead (3), NDT (1)

H1479 גֹּבַי ***gōbay***, n.m.col. [2] [√ 1466]. swarm of locust:– locusts (1), swarms of locusts (1)

H1480 גַּבַּי ***gabbay***, n.pr.m. [1] Gabbai, "*collector*":– Gabbai (1)

H1481 גֵּבִים ***gēbîm***, n.pr.loc. [1] [√ 1463]. Gebim, "*ditches*":– Gebim (1)

H1482 גְּבִינָה ***gᵉbînâ***, n.f. [1] [cf. 1492]. cheese:– cheese (1)

H1483 גָּבִיעַ ***gābîa'***, n.m. [14] [→ 1499, 4457?]. cup, (drinking) bowl:– cup (4), cups (4), flowerlike cups (2), bowls (1), one[S] (1), NDT (2)

H1484 גְּבִיר ***gᵉbîr***, n.m. [2] [→ 1484; cf. 1504]. lord, master:– lord (2)

H1485 גְּבִירָה ***gᵉbîrâ***, n.f. [13] [√ 1484; cf. 1504]. mistress (female lord); queen:– mistress (7), queen mother (3), position as queen mother (2), queen (1)

H1486 גָּבִישׁ ***gābîš***, n.m. [1] [cf. 453]. jasper:– jasper (1)

H1487 גָּבַל ***gābal***, v.den. [5] [√ 1473]. [Q] to set up a boundary; [H] to put limits around (a geographical area):– borders (1), formed the boundary (1), put limits (1), put limits around (1), set up (1)

H1488 גְּבַל ***gᵉbal***, n.pr.loc. [1] [→ 1490]. Gebal, "[poss.] *border; hill*":– Byblos (1)

H1489 גְּבָל ***gᵉbāl***, n.pr.loc. [1] Gebal, "[poss.] *border; hill*":– Byblos (1)

H1490 גִּבְלִי ***giblî***, a.g. [2] [√ 1488]. Gebalite, "*of Gebal*":– Byblos (1), workers from Byblos (1)

H1491 גַּבְלֻת ***gablut***, n.f. [2] [→ 4456]. braided (gold chain):– braided (2)

H1492 גִּבֵּן ***gibbēn***, a. [1] [→ 1493; cf. 1482]. hunchbacked:– hunchback (1)

H1493 גַּבְנֹן ***gabnōn***, n.[m.] [2] [√ 1492]. ruggedness; a many-peaked mountain range with an appearance that suggests wonder and majesty:– rugged (2)

H1494 גֶּבַע ***geba'***, n.pr.loc. [15] [√ 1496]. Geba, "*hill*":– Geba (15)

H1495 גִּבְעָא ***gib'ā'***, n.pr.m. [1] [√ 1496?]. Gibea, "*mound, hill*":– Gibea (1)

H1496 [1]גִּבְעָה ***gib'â[1]***, n.f. [67] [→ 1494, 1495?, 1497, 1500, 1501, 1502, 1648]. hill, hill top, height:– hills (36), hill (26), heights (2), hilltops (2), NDT (1)

H1497 [2]גִּבְעָה ***gib'â[2]***, n.pr.loc. [49] [→ 1503; cf. 1496]. Gibeah, "*mound, hill*":– Gibeah (48), NDT (1)

H1498 גִּבְעוֹנִי ***gib'ōnî***, a.g. [8] [√ 1500; cf. 1496]. Gibeonite, of Gibeon, "*of Gibeon*":– Gibeonites (6), Gibeonite (1), of Gibeon (1)

H1499 גִּבְעֹל ***gib'ōl***, n.[m.] [1] [√ 1483]. bloom:– in bloom (1)

H1500 גִּבְעוֹן ***gib'ōn***, n.pr.loc. [39] [→ 1498; cf. 1496]. Gibeon, "*mound, hill*":– Gibeon (38), Gibeonites (1 [+408])

H1501 גִּבְעַת ***gib'at***, n.pr.loc. Not used in NIVEBC [√ 1496]. Gibeath

H1502 גִּבְעַת הָעֲרָלוֹת ***gib'at hā'ᵃrālôt***, n.pr.loc. [1] [√ 1496 + 2197]. Gibeath Haaraloth, "*hill of foreskins*":– Gibeath Haaraloth (1)

H1503 גִּבְעָתִי ***gib'ātî***, a.g. [1] [√ 1497]. Gibeathite, "*of Gibeah*":– Gibeathite (1)

H1504 גָּבַר ***gābar***, v. [25] [→ 1475, 1476, 1484, 1485, 1505, 1506, 1507, 1508, 1509]. [Q] to rise, flood; to be greater, stronger; to prevail, overwhelm; [P] to strengthen; [H] to cause to triumph, confirm (a covenant); [Ht] to show oneself as a victor:– rose (3), great (2), strengthen (2), triumph (2), winning (2), arrogantly (1), confirm (1), flooded (1), greater (1), increasing (1), needed (1), overpowered (1), overwhelmed (1), prevail (1), prevailed (1), prevails (1), stronger (1), strongest (1), vaunts himself (1)

H1505 [1]גֶּבֶר ***geber[1]***, n.m. [66] [→ 1205, 1506, 1508; cf. 1504; 10131]. (strong, young) man:– man (21), one (9), men (6), strong man (4), people (2), person (2), anyone (1), blameless (1 [+9459]), boy (1), each[S] (1), families (1), he[S] (1), husband's (1), leaders (1 [+8031]), man's (1), men's (1), mighty man (1), person's (1), prevail (1), ruler (1 [+8031]), soldiers (1 [+408, 4878]), someone (1), them[S] (1), those[S] (1), who (1 [+4769]), NDT (3)

H1506 [2]גֶּבֶר ***geber[2]***, n.pr.m. [1] [√ 1505; cf. 1504]. Geber, "*[strong young] man*":– Geber (1)

H1507 גִּבָּר ***gibbār***, n.pr.m. [1] [√ 1504]. Gibbar, "*[young vigorous] man, hero*":– Gibbar (1)

H1508 גַּבְרִיאֵל ***gabrî'ēl***, n.pr.m. [2] [√ 1505 + 446]. Gabriel, "*[strong] man of God [El]*":– Gabriel (2)

H1509 גְּבֶרֶת ***gᵉberet***, n.f. [2] [√ 1504]. queen:– queen (2)

H1510 גִּבְּתוֹן ***gibbᵉtôn***, n.pr.loc. [6] [√ 1467]. Gibbethon, "*mound, hill*":– Gibbethon (5), it[S] (1)

H1511 גָּג ***gāg***, n.m. [30] roof, top:– roof (18), roofs (7), top (3), roof of house (1), top of the wall (1)

H1512 [1]גַּד ***gad[1]***, n.m. [2] coriander:– coriander (2)

H1513 [2]גַּד ***gad[2]***, n.[m.] [2] [→ 1514, 1534, 1535]. good fortune; (as a pagan god) Fortune:– fortune (1), good fortune (1)

H1514 גָּד ***gād***, n.pr.m. [70] [→ 1254, 1532, 1533; cf. 1513]. Gad, "*fortune*":– Gad (43), Gadites (16 [+1201]), Gad (7 [+1201]), Gad's (1), they[S] (1 [+1201, 2256, 1201, 8017]), NDT (2)

H1515 גִּדְגָּד ***gidgād***, n.pr.loc. Not used in NIVEBC [cf. 2044]. Gidgad, see 2988

H1516 גֻּדְגֹּדָה ***gudgōdâ***, n.pr.loc. [2] Gudgodah, "*cleft*":– Gudgodah (1), NDT (1)

H1517 [1]גָּדַד ***gādad[1]***, v. [6] [→ 1518, 1521, 1522, 1523, 1574?; 10134]. [Htpolal] to cut oneself, slash oneself:– cut themselves (2), cut yourselves (2), slash themselves appealing to their gods (1), slashed themselves (1)

H1518 [2]גָּדַד ***gādad[2]***, v. [3] [√ 1517]. [Q] to band together; [Htpolal] to band together against:– band together (1), marshal troops (1), thronged (1)

H1519 גָּדָה ***gādâ***, n.f. Not used in NIVEBC [→ 1536]. bank (of a river)

H1520 גַּדָּה ***gaddâ***, n.pr.loc. Not used in NIVEBC [→ 2961]. Gaddah

H1521 [1]גְּדוּד ***gᵉdûd[1]***, n.m. & f. [1] [√ 1517]. ridge (of a furrow):– ridges (1)

H1522 [2]גְּדוּד ***gᵉdûd[2]***, n.m. [33] [√ 1517]. band of raiders; band of rebels; bandits; troops, divisions:– troops (5), raiders (3), raiding bands (3), raiding party (3), band of raiders (2), troop (2), band (1), bandits (1), bands (1), bands of raiders (1), divisions (1), forces (1), invaders (1), marauders (1), men ready for battle (1 [+7372, 4878]), raid (1), them[S] (1 [+2021]), troops (1 [+1201]), NDT (3)

H1523 גְּדוּדָה ***gᵉdûdâ***, n.m. & f. [1] [√ 1517]. slash, cut (of the skin):– slashed (1)

H1524 גָּדוֹל ***gādôl***, a. [528] [→ 2045; cf. 1540]. great, large; much, more; this can refer to physical size, quantity, degree, and social status (great king, high priest):– great (229), large (42), high (23), greatest (17), loud (16), Mediterranean[S] (12), mighty (10), greater (9), older (9), heavy (8), old (7), vast (7), very (7), terrible (5), bitterly (4), greatly (4), much (4), oldest (4), powerful (4), strong (4), called out (3 [+7924, 928, 7754]), even more (3), huge (3), important (3), many (3), aloud (2 [+7754]), awful (2), became more and more powerful (2 [+2143, 2143, 2256]), deep (2), fierce (2), great (2 [+4394]), larger (2), louder (2), loudly (2), more (2), such (2), wealthy (2), wonders (2), all (1), aloud (1 [+928, 7754]), at all (1 [+7785, 2256]), at all (1 [+7785, 196]), awful (1 [+2098]), became more and more powerful (1 [+2143, 2256]), better (1), big (1), boastful (1 [+1819]), chief (1), deeds (1), defeated (1 [+5782, 4394, 4804]), defeated completely (1 [+5782, 4804]), devastated (1 [+5782, 4394, 4804]), difficult (1), far (1), feat (1 [+1821]), fine (1 [+2256, 3202]), great amount (1), grievous (1), hard (1), harsh (1), highly regarded (1 [+4394]), hot-tempered (1 [+2779]), huge (1 [+6330, 4200, 4394]), immense (1), imposing (1 [+4200, 5260]), intense (1 [+4394]), large (1 [+4394]), leaders (1), leading (1), loud (1 [+6330, 4394]), loudly (1 [+928, 7754]), main (1), most important (1), nobles (1), noisy din (1 [+7754]), older (1 [+4946]), power (1), preeminent (1), prominent (1), rich (1), screamed (1 [+7924, 928, 7754]), serious (1), shout (1 [+7924, 7754]), so much (1), solemn (1), strange (1), stronger (1), such (1 [+2296]), terrified (1 [+3707, 3711]), thick (1), top (1), total (1 [+4394]), trembled violently (1 [+3006, 6330, 4394, 3010]), upper (1), utterly (1), vast (1 [+4394]), vast (1 [+4394, 4394]), violent (1), well-to-do (1), NDT (1)

H1525 גְּדוּלָּה ***gᵉdûllâ***, n.f. [12] [√ 1540]. greatness, majesty, recognition, honor:– great (3), greatness (3), great thing (2), great deeds (1), honor (1), majesty (1), recognition (1)

H1526 גִּדּוּף ***giddûp***, n.m.pl. [2] [√ 1552]. taunt, scorn, reviling:– scorn (1), taunts (1)

H1527 גְּדוּפָה ***gᵉdûpâ***, n.f. [1] [√ 1552]. taunt, scorn, reviling:– taunt (1)

H1528 גִּדּוּפָה ***giddûpâ***, n.m.pl. [1] [√ 1552]. insult:– insults (1)

H1529 [1]גְּדוֹר ***gᵉdôr[1]***, n.pr.m. [4] [√ 1553]. Gedor, "*wall; pock-marked*":– Gedor (4)

H1530 [2]גְּדוֹר ***gᵉdôr[2]***, n.pr.loc. [3] Gedor, "*wall; pock-marked*":– Gedor (3)

H1531 גְּדִי ***gᵉdî***, n.m. [17] [→ 1537, 6527]. (male) young goat:– young goat (7 [+6436]), young goat (5), goat (1), goatskins (1 [+6425, 6436]), lambs (1), young goats (1), young goats (1 [+6436])

H1532 [1]גָּדִי ***gādî[1]***, a.g. [15] [√ 1514]. Gadite, of Gad, "*of Gad*":– Gadites (12), Gad (1), Gad (1 [+1201]), of Gad (1)

H1533 [2]גָּדִי ***gādî[2]***, n.pr.m. [2] [√ 1514]. Gadi, "*my fortune*":– Gadi (2)

H1534 גַּדִּי ***gaddî***, n.pr.m. [1] [√ 1513]. Gaddi, "*my fortune*":– Gaddi (1)

H1535 גַּדִּיאֵל ***gaddî'ēl***, n.pr.m. [1] [√ 1513 + 446]. Gaddiel, "*God [El] is my fortune; Gad is [my] God*":– Gaddiel (1)

H1536 גִּדְיָה ***gidyâ***, n.f. [4] [√ 1519]. bank (of a river):– banks (2), at flood stage (1 [+6584, 3972]), at flood stage (1 [+4848, 6584, 3972])

H1537 גְּדִיָּה ***gᵉdiyyâ***, n.f. [1] [√ 1531]. (female) young goat:– young goats (1)

H1538 [1]גָּדִישׁ ***gādîš[1]***, n.m. [3] [→ 1539]. shock of grain, sheaf of grain:– sheaves (1), shocks (1), shocks of grain (1)

H1539 [2]גָּדִישׁ ***gādîš[2]***, n.[m.] [1] [√ 1538]. tomb:– tombs (1)

H1540 גָּדַל ***gādal***, v. [116] [→ 1524, 1525, 1541, 1542, 1543, 1544?, 1547, 4460, 4463, 4464, 4465; *also used with compound proper names*]. [Q] to grow up; be great, exalted; [P] to grow long, make great; to exalt, honor, glorify; [Pu] to be well-nurtured; [H] to make great, cause greatness; [Ht] to magnify oneself, show greatness; see also 1524:– great (19), greater (8), grown up (7), grew up (6), exalt (5), grew (5), exalted (4), reared (4), defied (2 [+6584]), gives great (2), glorify (2), honored (2), make great (2), wealthy (2), boast (1), boast so much (1 [+7023, 3870]), boasted (1 [+928, 7023]), boosting (1), brought up (1), developed (1), displayed (1), exalt himself (1), great (1 [+4394]), great things done (1), greatness (1), grew older (1), grow long (1), grows up (1), increased (1), increased (1 [+2256, 3578]), made great (1), made grow (1), made threats (1), magnificent (1), magnify (1), make greater (1), make grow (1), make so much of (1), mocking (1), most (1), nourished (1), pile high (1), powerful (1), promoted (1), reached (1 [+6330]), rear (1), rearing (1), rich (1), rising (1), set up to be great (1), show greatness (1), superior (1), trained (1), triumphed (1), turned (1 [+6811]), undertook great (1), value (1 [+928, 6524]), valued (1 [+928, 6524]), well-nurtured (1), yielding (1)

H1541 גָּדֵל ***gādēl***, a.vbl. *or* v.ptcp. [4] [√ 1540]. great, powerful:– large (1), more and more powerful (1 [+2143, 2256, 6330, 4200, 5087, 2025]), stature (1), wealth (1)

H1542 גֹּדֶל ***gōdel***, n.m. [13] [√ 1540]. greatness, majesty, strength; pride, arrogance:– majesty (4), greatness (3), arrogance (1), beauty (1), great (1), great power (1), strong (1), willful pride (1 [+7262])

H1543 גִּדֵּל ***giddēl***, n.pr.m. [4] [√ 1540]. Giddel, "*big*":– Giddel (4)

H1544 גְּדִל ***gādil***, n.[m.]pl. [2] [√ 1540?]. tassel, festoon:– adorned (1), tassels (1)

H1545 גְּדַלְיָה ***gᵉdalyâ***, n.pr.m. [6] [√ 1540 + 3378]. Gedaliah, "*great is Yahweh*":– Gedaliah (6)

H1546 גְּדַלְיָהוּ ***gᵉdalyāhû***, n.pr.m. [26] [√ 1540 + 3378]. Gedaliah, "*great is Yahweh*":– Gedaliah (25), Gedaliah's (1)

H1547 גִּדַּלְתִּי ***giddaltî***, n.pr.m. [2] [√ 1540]. Giddalti, "*I pronounce [God as] Great; I reared up*":– Giddalti (2)

H1548 גָּדַע ***gāda'***, v. [22] [→ 1549, 1550, 1551]. [Q] to cut short, cut off, break; [P] to cut down, cut to pieces; [Qp, N, Pu] to be cut off, be cut down:– cut down (4), cut off (3), broke (2), cut to pieces (2), be cut off (1), be felled (1), be sheared off (1), been cast down (1), been felled (1), broken (1), broken down (1), cut short (1), cut through (1), cuts through (1), is cut off (1)

H1549 גִּדְעוֹן ***gid'ôn***, n.pr.m. [39] [→ 1551; cf. 1548]. Gideon, "*one who cuts, hacks*":– Gideon (35), he[S] (3), Gideon's (1)

H1550 גִּדְעֹם ***gid'ōm***, n.pr.loc. [1] [√ 1548]. Gidom, "*cutting off, stop pursuit*":– Gidom (1)

H1551 גִּדְעֹנִי ***gid'ōnî***, n.pr.m. [5] [√ 1549; cf. 1548]. Gideoni, "*one who cuts, hacks*":– Gideoni (5)

H1552 גָּדַף ***gādap***, v. [7] [→ 1526, 1527, 1528]. [P] to blaspheme, revile:– blasphemed (5), blasphemes (1), revile (1)

H1553 גָּדַר ***gādar***, v. [10] [→ 1529, 1554, 1555, 1556, 1557, 1558, 1560, 1561, 1562]. [Q] to built a stone wall, heap up stones for a wall:– masons (2), repair (2), barred (1), blocked (1), build up (1), repairer of Walls (1), wall in (1 [+1555]), walled (1)

H1554 גֶּדֶר ***geder***, n.pr.loc. [1] [→ 1084; cf. 1084, 1553]. Geder, "*wall [of stones]*":– Geder (1)

H1555 גָּדֵר ***gādēr***, n.m. [14] [√ 1553]. wall, fence, a wall made of loose stones from the field without mortar:– wall (7), walls (3), fence (1), wall in (1 [+1553]), wall of protection (1), NDT (1)

H1556 [1]גְּדֵרָה **gᵉdērâ[1]**, n.f. [9] [→ 1557, 1558, 1561, 1562; cf. 1553]. wall, pen (for sheep) made of stone walls:– pens (4), walls (3), pens (1 [+7366]), wall (1)

H1557 [2]גְּדֵרָה **gᵉdērâ[2]**, n.pr.loc. [2] [√ 1556; cf. 1553]. Gederah, "*stone pen, sheep corral*":– Gederah (2)

H1558 גְּדֵרוֹת **gᵉdērôt**, n.pr.loc. [2] [√ 1556; cf. 1553]. Gederoth, "*stone pens, sheep corrals*":– Gederoth (2)

H1559 גְּדֵרִי **gᵉdērî**, a.g. [1] [cf. 1084]. Gederite, "*of Geder*":– Gederite (1)

H1560 גְּדֶרֶת **gᵉderet**, n.f. Not used in NIVEBC [√ 1553]. wall of stones

H1561 גְּדֵרָתִי **gᵉdērātî**, a.g. [1] [√ 1556; cf. 1553]. Gederathite, "*of Geder[ath]*":– Gederathite (1)

H1562 גְּדֵרֹתַיִם **gᵉdērōtayim**, n.pr.loc. [1] [√ 1556; cf. 1553]. Gederothaim, "*two stone pens, two sheep corrals*":– Gederothaim (1)

H1563 גֵּה **gēh**, var. see 2296

H1564 גָּהָה **gāhâ**, v. [1] [→ 1565, 4443]. [Q] to heal:– heal (1)

H1565 גֵּהָה **gēhâ**, n.f. [1] [√ 1564]. healing, cure; that which promotes healing: medicine:– medicine (1)

H1566 גָּהַר **gāhar**, v. [3] [Q] to bow down; stretch out in prostration:– stretched out (2), bent down (1)

H1567 גַּו **gaw**, n.[m.] [3] [√ 1568]. back (of the body); "to thrust behind the back" means "to reject":– back (2), backs (1)

H1568 [1]גֵּו **gēw[1]**, n.[m.] [7] [→ 1567, 1576, 1581]. back (of the body); "to walk upon the back" is a sign of conquest and subjugation; "to send sin behind the back" is "to forgive":– back (5), backs (2)

H1569 [2]גֵּו **gēw[2]**, n.[m.] [1] [√ 1580?; 10135]. fellow people, community:– human society (1)

H1570 [1]גֹּב **gôb[1]**, n.pr.loc. [2] [√ 1572?]. Gob, "*cistern*":– Gob (2)

H1571 [2]גּוֹב **gôb[2]**, n.[m.] [1] locust:– swarms (1)

H1572 גּוּב **gûb**, v. Not used in NIVEBC [√ 1570?]. [Q] to dig

H1573 גּוֹג **gôg**, n.pr.m. [10] [→ 2163, 4470]. Gog, "*precious golden object*":– Gog (10)

H1574 גּוּד **gûd**, v. [3] [√ 1517?]. [Q] to attack, invade:– attack (1), attacked (1), invading (1)

H1575 [1]גֵּוָה **gēwâ[1]**, n.f. [3] [√ 1448; 10136]. pride, lifting up:– pride (2), lift up (1)

H1576 [2]גֵּוָה **gēwâ[2]**, n.f. [1] [√ 1568]. back (of the body):– back (1)

H1577 גּוּז **gûz**, v. [2] [Q] to pass along, pass away:– drove in (1), pass (1)

H1578 גּוֹזָל **gôzāl**, n.m. [2] young bird, hatchling:– young (1), young pigeon (1)

H1579 גּוֹזָן **gôzān**, n.pr.loc. [5] Gozan:– Gozan (5)

H1580 גּוֹי **gôy**, n.m. [555] [→ 1582]. people, nation; regularly in the OT, any people in contrast to Israel: the Gentiles, pagan, heathen, uncultured:– nations (412), nation (113), people (7), Gentiles (3), Gentile (2), each national group (2 [+1580]), peoples (2), another[S] (1), army (1), countries (1), foreign (1), it[S] (1 [+2021]), kind (1), nations (1 [+824]), pagan nations (1), people of nations (1), they[S] (1), NDT (4)

H1581 גְּוִיָּה **gᵉwiyyâ**, n.f. [13] [√ 1568]. dead body, corpse; carcass:– bodies (4), body (4), carcass (1), corpses (1), dead (1), it[S] (1 [+2021, 793]), NDT (1)

H1582 גּוֹיִם **gôyim**, n.pr.g. [3] [√ 1580]. Goiim, Goyim, "*nation, Gentiles*":– Goyim (3)

H1583 גּוֹלָה **gôlâ**, n.f. [41] [√ 1655; 10145]. exile, captive, people deported to another place:– exile (16), exiles (15), exiles (6 [+1201]), captive (1), deported (1 [+995]), those[S] (1 [+2021]), took (1 [+2143])

H1584 גּוֹלָן **gôlān**, n.pr.loc. [4] [→ 1660]. Golan:– Golan (4)

H1585 גּוּמָּץ **gûmmāṣ**, n.m. [1] pit:– pit (1)

H1586 [1]גּוּנִי **gûnî[1]**, n.pr.m. [4] [→ 1587]. Guni, "*spotted sand grouse*":– Guni (4)

H1587 [2]גּוּנִי **gûnî[2]**, a.g. [1] [√ 1586]. Gunite, "*of Guni*":– Gunite (1)

H1588 גָּוַע **gāwa'**, v. [24] [Q] to perish, die, breath one's last:– die (8), died (4), breathed his last (3), perish (3), perished (2), breathed last (1), breathes his last (1), close to death (1), fell dead (1)

H1589 גּוּף **gûp**, v. [1] [H] to shut (a door):– shut (1)

H1590 גּוּפָה **gûpâ**, n.f. [2] [√ 1727]. dead body, corpse:– bodies (1), NDT (1)

H1591 [1]גּוּר **gûr[1]**, v. [80] [→ 1595?, 1731, 1745, 4472]. [Q] to live as an alien, dwell as a stranger, implying less social rights than a native; [Htpol] to stay, gather together:– residing (19), dwell (8), live (7), living (7), settle (6), stay (4), live for a while (3), stayed (3), foreigners (2), lived (2), resides (2), stay for a while (2), staying (2), strangers (2), can[S] (1), dwellings (1), for a while stayed (1), foreigner (1), guests (1 [+1074]), linger (1), nomads (1), reside as a foreigner (1), resided as a foreigner (1), settled (1), welcome (1)

H1592 [2]גּוּר **gûr[2]**, v. [6] [cf. 1741, 1594?]. [Q] to attack, stir up:– attack (2 [+1592]), conspire (2), attacks (1), stir up (1)

H1593 [3]גּוּר **gûr[3]**, v. [10] [→ 4471, 4474, 4475; cf. 3336]. [Q] to be terrified, be afraid, fear; to revere:– afraid (2), fear (2), revere (2), terrified (2), alarmed (1), dreaded (1)

H1594 [4]גּוּר **gûr[4]**, n.m. [7] [→ 1596; cf. 1592?]. cub (young of lions, jackals):– cubs (3), cub (2), cubs (1 [+793]), young (1)

H1595 [5]גּוּר **gûr[5]**, n.pr.loc. [1] [√ 1591?]. Gur:– Gur (1)

H1596 גּוֹר **gôr**, n.[m.] [2] [√ 1594]. cub (of lion):– cubs (2)

H1597 גּוּר־בַּעַל **gûr-bā'al**, n.pr.loc. [1] [cf. 3327]. Gur Baal, "*sojourn of Baal*":– Gur Baal (1)

H1598 גּוֹרָל **gôrāl**, n.m. [78] lot, device by which a decision was made, often a pebble, stick, or pottery shard either thrown or blindly pulled from a container; by extension: what is decided by lot, allotment (of land):– lot (36), lots (18), allotment (5), allotted (4 [+928, 2021]), allotted (3), allotted (2 [+2118]), allotted (2 [+5989, 928, 2021]), allotted (1 [+2118, 928, 2021]), allotted inheritance (1), casting lots (1), in whatever order (1 [+4202, 5877, 6584]), portions (1), territory allotted (1), NDT (2)

H1599 גּוּשׁ **gûš**, n.[m.] [1] [→ 1641]. scab, something crusted:– scabs (1 [+6760])

H1600 גֵּז **gēz**, n.[m.] [4] [√ 1605]. fleece, sheared wool; grass mowed:– fleece (1), harvested (1), mown field (1), wool from shearing (1)

H1601 גִּזְבָּר **gizbār**, n.m. [1] [√ 10133, 10139]. treasurer:– treasurer (1)

H1602 גָּזָה **gāzâ**, v. [1] [→ 1607]. [Q] to bring forth, cut off (the umbilical cord):– brought forth (1)

H1603 גִּזָּה **gizzâ**, n.f. [7] [√ 1605]. wool fleece:– fleece (6), NDT (1)

H1604 גִּזוֹנִי **gizônî**, a.g. [1] Gizonite, "*of Gizon*":– Gizonite (1)

H1605 גָּזַז **gāzaz**, v. [15] [→ 1600, 1603, 1606]. [Q] to shear sheep; to shave one's head (in mourning):– shear (3), shearers (3), shearing (3), be destroyed (1), cut off (1), shave head (1 [+7942]), shaved (1), sheep-shearing time (1), sheepshearers (1)

H1606 גָּזֵז **gāzēz**, n.pr.m. [2] [√ 1605]. Gazez, "[poss.] *sheep shearer;* [poss.] *one born at the time of shearing*":– Gazez (2)

H1607 גָּזִית **gāzît**, n.f. [11] [√ 1602]. dressed stone, stone hewn or cut for masonry:– dressed (3), dressed stone (3), cut (2), blocks of stone (1), dressed stones (1), stone (1)

H1608 גָּזַל **gāzal**, v. [30] [→ 1609, 1610, 1611]. [Q] to rob, seize, snatch, take way; [Qp, N] to be robbed, be forcibly taken from:– rob (3), snatched (3), been robbed (2), commit robbery (2 [+1611]), seized (2), are robbed (1), be forcibly taken (1), caught (1), commit robbery (1 [+1610]), commits robbery (1 [+1611]), exploit (1), injured (1), robbed (1), robbed (1 [+1609]), robs (1), seize (1), snatch away (1), steal (1), stolen (1), stolen (1 [+1611]), take by force (1), tear (1), withhold (1)

H1609 גֶּזֶל **gēzel**, n.[m.] [2] [√ 1608]. denial of rights:– denied (1), robbed (1 [+1608])

H1610 גָּזֵל **gāzēl**, n.[m.] [4] [→ 1611; cf. 1608]. stealing, robbery, implying violence:– commit robbery (1 [+1608]), robbery (1), something stolen (1), stolen goods (1)

H1611 גְּזֵלָה **gᵉzēlâ**, n.f. [6] [√ 1610; cf. 1608]. plunder, spoil, stolen things:– commit robbery (2 [+1608]), commits robbery (1 [+1608]), plunder (1), stolen (1 [+1608]), what stolen (1)

H1612 גָּזָם **gāzām**, n.m. [3] [→ 1613; cf. 4080]. locust swarm; some sources: caterpillar or a specific state in the development of a locust:– locust swarm (2), locusts (1)

H1613 גַּזָּם **gazzām**, n.pr.m. [2] [√ 1612]. Gazzam, "*some kind of bird or insect*":– Gazzam (2)

H1614 גֶּזַע **geza'**, n.m. [3] stump, root stock:– stump (2), take root (1 [+9245])

H1615 [1]גָּזַר **gāzar[1]**, v. [12] [→ 1617, 1618?, 1619, 1620, 1621, 4477; cf. 1616, 1746; 10140, 10141]. [Q] to cut in two, divide, cut down; decide on; to disappear; [N] to be cut off, be excluded:– are cut off (2), banned (1), cut (1), cut down (1), cut in two (1), decide (1), decreed (1), divided (1), perish (1), there are no (1), was cut off (1)

H1616 [2]גָּזַר **gāzar[2]**, v. [1] [cf. 1615]. [Q] to devour, eat, with a possible focus on carving or chewing up food:– devour (1)

H1617 [1]גֶּזֶר **gezer[1]**, n.[m.] [2] [√ 1615]. pieces (something divided and cut up):– asunder (1), pieces (1)

H1618 [2]גֶּזֶר **gezer[2]**, n.pr.loc. [15] [→ 1621; cf. 1615?]. Gezer, "[poss.] *pieces*":– Gezer (14), there[S] (1 [+928])

H1619 גִּזְרָה **gizrâ**, n.f. [8] [√ 1615]. courtyard; appearance:– courtyard (7), appearance (1)

H1620 גְּזֵרָה **gᵉzērâ**, n.f. [1] [√ 1615; 10141]. solitary place, unfertile land:– remote (1)

H1621 גִּזְרִי **gizrî**, a.g. Not used in NIVEBC [√ 1618; cf. 1615, 1747]. Gizrite, see 1747

H1622 גָּחָה **gāḥâ**, v. Not used in NIVEBC [√ 1631]. [Q] to draw out (from womb)

H1623 גָּחוֹן **gāḥôn**, n.m. [2] belly (of reptile):– belly (2)

H1624 גַּחַל **gaḥal**, n.f. [15] [→ 1625]. burning coals, hot embers:– coals (6), burning coals (5), bolts (2), embers (1), hot coals (1)

H1625 גַּחֶלֶת **gaḥelet**, n.f. [2] [√ 1624]. burning coals:– burning coal (1), coals (1)

H1626 גַּחַם **gaḥam**, n.pr.m. [1] Gaham, "*burning brightly*":– Gaham (1)

H1627 גַּחַר **gaḥar**, n.pr.m. [2] Gahar, "*[born in the] year of little rain*":– Gahar (2)

H1628 גַּיְא **gay'**, n.m. & f. [57] [→ 1629]. valley:– valley (49), valleys (7), it[S] (1 [+2215])

H1629 גֵּיא חֲרָשִׁים **gê' ḥ^arāšîm**, n.pr.loc. [2] [√ 1628 + 3096]. Ge Harashim, "*valley of the craftsmen*":– Ge Harashim (2)

H1630 גִּיד **gîd**, n.m. [7] sinew, tendon:– sinews (2), tendon (2 [+5962]), tendons (2), muscles (1)

H1631 [1]גִּיחַ **gîaḥ[1]**, v. [6] [→ 1622, 1632, 1633; 10137]. [Q] to burst forth, surge, bring forth (a baby); [H] to charge; to thrash about:– brought (1), burst (1), charged out (1), in agony (1), surge (1), thrashing about (1)

H1632 [2]גִּיחַ **gîaḥ[2]**, n.pr.loc. [1] [√ 1631]. Giah, "*bubbling spring*":– Giah (1)

H1633 גִּיחוֹן **gîḥôn**, n.pr.loc. [6] [√ 1631]. Gihon, "*to gush forth*":– Gihon (6)

H1634 גֵּיחֲזִי **gêḥ^azî**, n.pr.m. [12] Gehazi, "[poss.] *valley of vision*":– Gehazi (12)

H1635 [1]גִּיל **gîl[1]**, v. [45] [→ 28?, 1636, 1637, 1638]. [Q] to rejoice, be glad, be joyful, the attitude and action of favorable circumstance, often expressed in shouts and song:– rejoice (23), glad (11), rejoices (3), great joy (2 [+1635]), joyful (2), celebrate (1), joy (1), rejoice greatly (1 [+677, 1638]), rejoiced (1)

H1636 [2]גִּיל **gîl[2]**, n.[m.] [1] [√ 1635]. age, stage in life:– age (1)

H1637 [3]גִּיל **gîl[3]**, n.[m.] [8] [√ 1635]. gladness, delight, jubilance; see also 1635:– gladness (5), delight (1), filled with gladness (1 [+8524, 448]), jubilant (1)

H1638 גִּילָה **gîlâ**, n.f. [2] [√ 1635]. rejoicing, delight:– delight (1), rejoice greatly (1 [+1635, 677])

H1639 גִּילֹנִי **gîlōnî**, a.g. [2] [√ 1656; cf. 1655]. Gilonite, "*of Gilon*":– Gilonite (2)

H1640 גִּינַת **gînat**, n.pr.m. [2] Ginath, "*protector*":– Ginath (2)

H1641 גִּישׁ **gîš**, var. Not used in NIVEBC [√ 1599]. see 1599

H1642 גֵּישָׁן **gêšān**, n.pr.m. [1] Geshan:– Geshan (1)

H1643 [1]גַּל **gal[1]**, n.m. [18] [→ 1668; cf. 1670]. heap, pile (of rocks, rubble):– heap (8), heap of ruins (2), pile (2), piles of stone (2 [+5898]), heap of rubble (1), pile of rocks (1), piles of stones (1), rubble (1)

H1644 [2]גַּל **gal[2]**, n.m. [16] [√ 1670]. waves, breaker waves, surging waves; fountain:– waves (13), breakers (1), fountain (1), surging (1)

H1645 גֵּל **gēl**, n.m. [3] [√ 1670]. dung, excrement, used for fuel in some contexts:– dung (1), excrement (1), excrement (1 [+7362])

H1646 גֹּל **gōl**, n.f.? Not used in NIVEBC [√ 1657]. see 1657

H1647 גַּלָּב **gallāb**, n.[m.] [1] barber:– barber's (1)

H1648 גִּלְבֹּעַ **gilbōa'**, n.pr.loc. [8] [√ 1496]. Gilboa, "*bubbling*":– Gilboa (8)

H1649 [1]גַּלְגַּל **galgal[1]**, n.m. [9] [→ 1650; cf. 1670; 10143]. wheel; whirlwind:– wheels (3), wagons (2), chariot wheels (1), wheel (1), whirling wheels (1), whirlwind (1)

H1650 [2]גַּלְגַּל **galgal[2]**, n.m. [2] [√ 1649; cf. 1670]. tumbleweed (a wheel-shaped plant):– tumbleweed (2)

H1651 [1]גִּלְגָּל **gilgāl[1]**, n.[m.] [1] [√ 1670; 10143]. wheel:– wheels (1)

H1652 [2]גִּלְגָּל **gilgāl[2]**, n.pr.loc. [40] [→ 1090; cf. 1670]. Gilgal, "*circle of stones*":– Gilgal (39), NDT (1)

H1653 גֻּלְגֹּלֶת **gulgōlet**, n.f. [12] [√ 1670]. skull; individual, person:– one by one (4 [+4200, 4392]), skull (2), each (1 [+5031]), each one (1), head (1), individually (1 [+4200]), person (1), total (1)

H1654 גֶּלֶד **gēled**, n.m. [1] skin:– skin (1)

H1655 גָּלָה **gālâ**, v. [189] [→ 1583, 1639, 1661, 1663, 1656; 10144]. [Q] to tell, uncover, reveal; depart, leave, be exiled, banished; [Qp] to be opened, unseal; be made known; [N] to be revealed, be exposed; [P] to reveal, expose (nakedness) = sexual relations; [Pu] to be opened, exiled; [H] to deport, exile:– carried into exile (11), have sexual relations with (11 [+6872]), deported (7), surely go into exile (6 [+1655]), be exposed (4), dishonored (4 [+6872]), expose (4), uncovered (4), exposed (3), go into exile (3), have sexual relations (3 [+6872]), open (3), opened (3), revealed (3), taken captive (3), taken into exile (3), be revealed (2), been carried into exile (2), been revealed (2), betray (2), betrays (2), carried into exile (2 [+1655]), clearly reveal myself (2 [+1655]), committed (2), departed (2), exile (2), exiled (2), go into exile (2 [+1655]), have relations with (2 [+6872]), laid bare (2), let know (2 [+906, 265]), made known (2), revealed (2 [+265]), revealed himself (2), sent into exile (2), tells (2 [+906, 265]), took captive (2), took into exile (2), uncover (2), unsealed (2), went into captivity (2), went into exile (2), airing (1), banished (1), bare (1), be carried into exile (1), be exiled (1), be laid bare (1), been shown (1), been torn off (1), being carried into exile (1), bring to attention (1 [+265]), brought (1), captive (1), captivity (1), carried away (1), carried on openly (1), carry away (1), carry into exile (1), carry off (1), disclose (1), dishonor bed (1 [+4053]), dishonor bed (1 [+6872]), dishonor by having sexual relations with (1 [+6872]), dishonor by to have sexual relations (1 [+6872]), dishonors bed (1 [+4053]), driven out (1), free (1), go (1), going around half-naked (1), gone into exile (1), has sexual relations with (1 [+906, 6872]), lay bare (1), led captive (1), let enjoy (1), let see (1), letting know (1 [+906, 265]), lift (1), makes listen (1 [+265]), remove (1), removed (1), revealed (1 [+906, 265]), revealing (1), reveals (1), send into exile (1), set out (1), showed themselves (1), speak (1), speaks (1 [+265]), strip (1 [+6872]), strip off (1), stripped (1), stripped away (1), take off (1), taken (1), tell (1 [+906, 265]), they were taken captive (1), was given (1), was uncovered (1), word come (1), would[S] (1 [+1655]), would[S] (1 [+1655]), NDT (2)

H1656 גִּלֹה ***gilōh***, n.pr.loc. [2] [→ 1639; cf. 1655]. Giloh:– Giloh (2)

H1657 גֻּלָּה ***gullâ***, n.f. [15] [→ 1646, 1684]. spring (of water); bowl-shaped capital (of a pillar):– bowl-shaped (6), springs (4), bowl (3), NDT (2)

H1658 גִּלּוּלִים ***gillûlîm***, n.m. [48] [√ 1670]. (pl.) idols:– idols (46), idolatry (2)

H1659 גְּלוֹם ***gᵉlôm***, n.[m.] [1] [√ 1676?]. fabric:– fabric (1)

H1660 גָּלוֹן ***gālôn***, n.pr.loc. Not used in NIVEBC [√ 1584]. Galon, see 1584

H1661 גָּלוּת ***gālût***, n.f. [15] [√ 1655; 10145]. exile, captive:– exiles (7), exile (5), captives (1), communities (1), communities of captives (1)

H1662 גָּלַח ***gālaḥ***, v. [22] [P] to shave off, cut off; [Pu] be shaved off; [Ht] to have oneself shaven, shave oneself:– shave (5), shave off (5), shaved off (3), cut hair (2), shaved (2), been shaved (1), shave themselves (1), were shaved (1), NDT (2)

H1663 גִּלָּיוֹן ***gillāyôn***, n.m. [2] [√ 1655]. scroll (some sources: wooden tablet with a wax cover); mirror:– mirrors (1), scroll (1)

H1664 1גָּלִיל ***gālîl[1]***, a. [3] [√ 1670]. turnable (door); rings; rods:– rings (1), rods (1), turned in sockets (1)

H1665 2גָּלִיל ***gālîl[2]***, n.pr.loc. [6] [→ 1666, 1667; cf. 1670]. Galilee, "*ring, circle,* hence *region*":– Galilee (5), Galilee (1 [+824])

H1666 גְּלִילָה ***gᵉlîlâ***, n.f. [3] [→ 1667; cf. 1665]. region, district:– regions (2), region (1)

H1667 גְּלִילוֹת ***gᵉlîlôt***, n.pr.loc. [3] [√ 1666]. Geliloth, "*region*":– Geliloth (3)

H1668 גַּלִּים ***gallîm***, n.pr.loc. [2] [√ 1643; cf. 1670]. Gallim, "*heaps*":– Gallim (2)

H1669 גָּלְיָת ***golyāt***, n.pr.m. [6] Goliath, "*exile*":– Goliath (6)

H1670 1גָּלַל ***gālal[1]***, v. [17] [→ 1643, 1644, 1645, 1649, 1650, 1651, 1652, 1653, 1658, 1664, 1665, 1666, 1667, 1668, 1672, 1674, 2055, 4479; cf. 1671, 4478?; 10146]. [Q] to roll down, roll away; to commit, turn over; [N] to be rolled; [P] to roll; [Polal] to be rolled; [Htpol] to roll about, wallow; "to commit, trust" is a figure of rolling care or responsibilty onto the Lord:– roll (4), rolled (3), commit (2), attack (1), come rolling in (1), lay wallowing (1), roll on (1), rolled away (1), rolled up (1), rolls (1), trusts (1)

H1671 2גָּלַל ***gālal[2]***, v. Not used in NIVEBC [cf. 1670]. [Polal, Htpol] to be befouled

H1672 1גָּלָל ***gālāl[1]***, n.[m.] [2] [√ 1670]. dung, filth:– dung (2)

H1673 2גָּלָל ***gālāl[2]***, n.[m.] [10] [√ 959]. because of, on account of, for the sake of:– because of (8 [+928]), because (1 [+928]), because of (1 [+928])

H1674 3גָּלָל ***gālāl[3]***, n.pr.m. [3] [→ 1675; cf. 1670]. Galal, "[poss.] *tortoise; roll away*":– Galal (3)

H1675 גִּלֲלַי ***gilᵃlay***, n.pr.m. [1] [√ 1674]. Gilalai:– Gilalai (1)

H1676 גָּלַם ***gālam***, v. [1] [→ 1659?, 1677]. [Q] to roll up (clothing in a tight ball):– rolled up (1)

H1677 גֹּלֶם ***gōlem***, n.[m.] [1] [√ 1676]. unformed body, embryo:– unformed body (1)

H1678 גַּלְמוּד ***galmûd***, a. [4] barren, haggard:– barren (3), haggard (1)

H1679 גָּלַע ***gālaʿ***, v. [3] [Ht] to burst out (in quarrel); to defy:– breaks out (1), quick to quarrel (1), starts quarrels (1)

H1680 גִּלְעָד ***gilʿād***, n.pr.loc. [& m.?] [102] [→ 1682, 3316, 8240]. Gilead, "[perhaps] *monument of stones*":– Gilead (85), Gilead (8 [+824]), Gileadites (3), Gilead (1 [+1201]), Gileadites (1 [+408]), Gilead's (1), them[S] (1 [+2418]), there[S] (1 [+5206]), NDT (1)

H1681 גַּלְעֵד ***galʿēd***, n.pr.loc. [2] [√ 10310]. Galeed; see also 3337, "*heap of [stones that are a] witness*":– Galeed (2)

H1682 גִּלְעָדִי ***gilʿādî***, a.g. [11] [√ 1680]. Gileadite, of Gilead, "*of Gilead*":– Gileadite (8), of Gilead (2), of Gilead (1 [+1201])

H1683 גָּלַשׁ ***gālaš***, v. [2] [Q] to descend; some sources: to leap, frisk:– descending (2)

H1684 גֻּלֹּת ***gullōt***, n.pr.loc. Not used in NIVEBC [√ 1657]. Gullot, "*springs*"

H1685 גַּם ***gam***, adv. [770] [→ 1417; cf. 4480]. also, surely, too; and, but, yet, even, moreover:– also (109), even (64), too (62), and (50 [+2256]), and (49), also (25 [+2256]), both (13), even (9 [+2256]), then (9), moreover (8 [+2256]), even (7 [+2256]), as well (6), but (6), moreover (6), or (6), yes (6), either (5), though (5), as well as (4), indeed (4), neither (4 [+4202]), now (4), or (4 [+2256]), so (4 [+2256]), too (4 [+2256]), again (3), just as (3), nor (3), nor (3 [+4202]), now (3 [+2256]), surely (3), then (3 [+2256]), and also (2), another (2), as for (2), besides (2 [+2256]), but also (2), in turn (2), indeed (2 [+2256]), more (2), neither (2), no (2), therefore (2 [+2256]), together with (2 [+2256]), yet (2), after (1 [+2256]), again (1 [+928, 2021, 7193, 2021, 2085]), along with (1 [+2256]), although (1 [+3954]), and even (1), and indeed (1), and now (1), both and (1), but (1 [+2256]), but (1), but even (1), but even (1 [+2256]), certainly (1), even (1 [+3954]), even (1 [+3954]), ever (1), finally (1 [+2256]), for (1 [+928, 8611]), for some time (1 [+9453, 1685, 8997]), for some time (1 [+1685, 9453, 8997]), furthermore (1), furthermore (1 [+2256]), in spite of (1), in the past (1 [+919, 1685, 8997]), in the past (1 [+1685, 919, 8997]), including (1 [+2256]), instead (1 [+2256]), joined (1 [+2256]), kept provoking (1 [+4087, 4088]), mere (1), moreover (1 [+3954]), near (1 [+2256]), next (1), no sooner than (1), nor (1 [+2256]), nor (1 [+2256, 401]), nor (1 [+2256, 4202]), or (1 [+3954]), since (1), so (1), so much as (1), still (1 [+2256]), than (1 [+2256]), that (1 [+2256]), therefore (1), very well (1), when (1), whether (1), with (1), with (1 [+2256]), yes (1 [+2256]), yes (1 [+2256]), yet (1 [+2256]), yet (1 [+2256]), NDT (196)

H1686 גָּמָא ***gāmāʾ***, v. [2] [→ 1687?]. [P] to eat up, swallow up; [H] to give water (to sip):– eats up (1), give (1)

H1687 גֹּמֶא ***gōmeʾ***, n.m. [4] [√ 1686?]. papyrus:– papyrus (4)

H1688 גֹּמֶד ***gōmed***, n.m. [1] [→ 1689?]. unit of measure: short cubit (the length from the elbow to the knuckles, about 12 to 18 inches):– about a cubit (1)

H1689 גַּמָּדִים ***gammādîm***, n.pr.g. [1] [√ 1688?]. men of Gammad, "[prob.] *valiant men*":– men of Gammad (1)

H1690 גָּמוּל ***gāmûl***, n.pr.m. [1] [√ 1694]. Gamul, "*weaned*":– Gamul (1)

H1691 גְּמוּל ***gᵉmûl***, n.m. [19] [√ 1694]. what is done; benefit; what is deserved, recompense:– what done (4), what deserve (3), retribution (2), according to what[S] (1), benefits (1), deeds (1), deserve (1), deserves (1 [+3338]), due (1), kindness (1), something done (1), what deserves (1), work (1)

H1692 גְּמוּלָה ***gᵉmûlâ***, n.f. [3] [√ 1694]. what is done; retribution, recompense:– retribution (1), way[S] (1), what done (1)

H1693 גִּמְזוֹ ***gimzô***, n.pr.loc. [1] Gimzo, "*place of sycamore trees*":– Gimzo (1)

H1694 גָּמַל ***gāmal***, v. [37] [→ 1085, 1690, 1691, 1692, 1695?, 1696, 1697, 9326]. [Q] to do, produce, deal fully; to wean; to repay (what is deserved); [Qp, N] to be weaned:– weaned (7), done (4), dealt with (2), good (2), repay (2), treated (2), was weaned (2), been good (1), benefit (1), brings (1), brought (1), brought up (1), committed (1), did (1), goodness (1), is weaned (1), paying back (1), produced (1), repaid (1), repaying (1), reward (1), ripening (1), young child (1)

H1695 גָּמָל ***gāmāl***, n.m. [54] [√ 1694?]. camel:– camels (48), camel (3), camel-loads (1 [+5362]), camel's (1), NDT (1)

H1696 גְּמַלִּי ***gᵉmallî***, n.pr.m. [1] [√ 1694]. Gemalli, "*my reward*":– Gemalli (1)

H1697 גַּמְלִיאֵל ***gamlîʾēl***, n.pr.m. [5] [√ 1694 + 446]. Gamaliel, "*recompense of God [El]*":– Gamaliel (5)

H1698 גָּמַר ***gāmar***, v. [5] [→ 1700, 1701, 1702; 10147]. [Q] to bring to an end, fail; fulfill:– bring to an end (1), failed (1), no anymore (1), vindicate (1), vindicates (1)

H1699 1גֹּמֶר ***gōmer[1]***, n.pr.m. [5] Gomer, "*complete*":– Gomer (5)

H1700 2גֹּמֶר ***gōmer[2]***, n.pr.f. [1] [√ 1698]. Gomer, "*complete*":– Gomer (1)

H1701 גְּמַרְיָה ***gᵉmaryâ***, n.pr.m. [1] [√ 1698 + 3378]. Gemariah, "*Yahweh has accomplished*":– Gemariah (1)

H1702 גְּמַרְיָהוּ ***gᵉmaryāhû***, n.pr.m. [4] [√ 1698 + 3378]. Gemariah, "*Yahweh has accomplished*":– Gemariah (4)

H1703 גַּן ***gan***, n.m. [41] [→ 1708; cf. 1713]. garden:– garden (39), gardens (2)

H1704 גָּנַב ***gānab***, v. [40] [→ 1705, 1706, 1707?]. [Q] to steal, be a thief, kidnap; to deceive; [Qp, N, Pu] to be stolen, forcibly carried off; [Ht] to steal oneself away, sneak in:– steal (9), stolen (4), steals (2), stole (2), stole away (2), was forcibly carried off (2 [+1704]), was stolen (2 [+1704]), are stolen (1), be considered stolen (1), deceive (1), deceived (1 [+4213]), deceived (1 [+4222]), kidnapping (1 [+5883]), kidnaps (1), snatches away (1), steal away (1), steal in (1), stealing (1), stole into (1 [+4200, 995]), swept away (1), thief (1), was secretly brought (1), was stolen (1), NDT (1)

H1705 גַּנָּב ***gannāb***, n.m. [17] [√ 1704]. thief; kidnapper:– thief (8), thieves (8), kidnapper (1)

H1706 גְּנֵבָה ***gᵉnēbâ***, n.f. [2] [√ 1704]. stolen possession:– stolen (1), theft (1)

H1707 גְּנֻבַת ***gᵉnubat***, n.pr.m. [2] [√ 1704?]. Genubath, "*thief*":– Genubath (2)

H1708 גַּנָּה ***gannâ***, n.f. [16] [√ 1703; cf. 1713]. garden, grove:– gardens (9), garden (6), grove (1)

H1709 1גֶּנֶז ***genez[1]***, n.[m.] [2] [→ 1711; 10148]. (royal) treasury:– treasury (2)

H1710 2גֶּנֶז ***genez[2]***, n.[m.] [1] rug:– rugs (1)

H1711 גַּנְזַךְ ***ganzak***, n.[m.] [1] [√ 1709]. (temple) storeroom, where treasures are kept:– storerooms (1)

H1712 גַּנִּים ***gannîm***, n.pr.loc. Not used in NIVEBC [→ 6528]. Gannim

H1713 גָּנַן ***gānan***, v. [8] [→ 1703, 1708, 4482]. [Q] to defend, shield, protect:– defend (4), shield (4)

H1714 גִּנְּתוֹי ***ginnᵉtôy***, n.pr.m. Not used in NIVEBC [cf. 1715]. Ginnethoi, see 1715

H1715 גִּנְּתוֹן ***ginnᵉtôn***, n.pr.m. [3] [cf. 1714]. Ginnethon:– Ginnethon (2), Ginnethon's (1)

H1716 גָּעָה ***gāʿâ***, v. [2] [cf. 7880]. [Q] to bellow, low (of cattle):– bellow (1), lowing (1)

H1717 גֹּעָה ***gōʿâ***, n.pr.loc. [1] Goah:– Goah (1)

H1718 גָּעַל ***gāʿal***, v. [10] [→ 1719, 1720; cf. 1458]. [Q] to abhor, despise, loathe; [N] to be defiled; [H] to cause defiling = fail to impregnate:– abhor (4), despised (2), abhorred (1), despise (1), fail (1), was despised (1)

H1719 גֹּעַל ***gōʿal***, n.m. [1] [√ 1718]. despising, loathing:– despised (1)

H1720 גַּעַל ***gaʿal***, n.pr.m. [9] [√ 1718]. Gaal, "*loathing*":– Gaal (9)

H1721 גָּעַר ***gāʿar***, v. [14] [→ 1722, 4486]. [Q] to rebuke, reprimand; prevent (insects):– rebuke (7), rebuked (3), rebukes (2), prevent (1), reprimanded (1)

H1722 גְּעָרָה ***gᵉʿārâ***, n.f. [15] [√ 1721]. rebuke; threat:– rebuke (11), threat (2), rebukes (1), threatening rebukes (1)

H1723 גָּעַשׁ ***gāʿaš***, v. [9] [Q] to shake, tremble; [Pu] to be shaken; [Ht] to shake back and forth, stagger, surge, tremble back and forth:– trembled (4), surging (2), are shaken (1), roll (1), stagger (1)

H1724 גַּעַשׁ ***gaʿaš***, n.pr.loc. [4] Gaash, "*rumble, quake*":– Gaash (4)

H1725 גַּעְתָּם ***gaʿtām***, n.pr.m. [3] Gatam:– Gatam (3)

H1726 1גַּף ***gap[1]***, n.m. [1] height, elevation:– highest point (1 [+5294])

H1727 2גַּף ***gap[2]***, n.m. [3] [→ 111, 1590]. body; by oneself [with 928]:– alone (2 [+928, 2257]), only (1 [+928, 2257])

H1728 גֶּפֶן ***gepen***, n.f. & m. [55] vine, grapevine:– vine (36), vines (16), grapevine (2 [+3516]), grapevines (1)

H1729 גֹּפֶר ***gōper***, n.[m] [1] cypress (wood); exact identity of the wood is uncertain; "gopher wood" is simply a transliteration of the Hebrew:– cypress (1)

H1730 גָּפְרִית ***goprît***, n.f. [7] sulfur; older versions: brimstone:– burning sulfur (4), sulfur (3)

H1731 גֵּר ***gēr***, n.m. [92] [→ 1745; cf. 1591]. alien, stranger (in a foreign land):– foreigner (51), foreigners (23), foreigner residing (5), foreigners residing (3), stranger (3), foreigner (1 [+408]), foreigner (1 [+9369]), foreigner living among (1), foreigners living among (1), foreigners reside (1), foreigner's (1), strangers (1)

H1732 גִּר ***gir***, n.[m.] [1] [√ 10142]. chalk:– limestone (1 [+74])

H1733 גֵּרָא ***gērā'***, n.pr.m. [9] Gera, "[perhaps] *sojourner*":– Gera (9)

H1734 גָּרָב ***gārāb***, n.[m.] [3] [→ 1735, 1736]. festering sore:– festering (2), festering sores (1)

H1735 [1]גָּרֵב ***gārēb[1]***, n.pr.m. [2] [√ 1734]. Gareb, "*scabby*":– Gareb (2)

H1736 [2]גָּרֵב ***gārēb[2]***, n.pr.loc. [1] [√ 1734]. Gareb, "*scabby*":– Gareb (1)

H1737 גַּרְגַּר ***gargar***, n.m. [1] ripe olives:– olives (1)

H1738 גַּרְגְּרוֹת ***garg^erôt***, n.f.pl. [4] neck, throat:– neck (4)

H1739 גִּרְגָּשִׁי ***girgāšî***, a.g. [7] Girgashite:– Girgashites (7)

H1740 גָּרַד ***gārad***, v. [1] [Ht] to scrape oneself (with a broken piece of pottery):– scraped himself (1)

H1741 גָּרָה ***gārâ***, v. [14] [→ 9327; cf. 1592]. [P] to stir up (a dispute); [Ht] to provoke (to war), engage (to battle):– ask (2), provoke to war (2), stirs up (2), carry the battle (1 [+8740, 2256]), engage (1), opposed (1), prepare for war (1), provoke (1), resist (1), stir up (1), wage war (1 [+4200, 2021, 4878])

H1742 [1]גֵּרָה ***gērâ[1]***, n.f. [11] [√ 1760]. cud:– cud (11)

H1743 [2]גֵּרָה ***gērâ[2]***, n.f. [5] gerah (measure, one-twentieth of a shekel, about half a gram):– gerahs (5)

H1744 גָּרוֹן ***gārôn***, n.m. [8] [√ 1760]. throat, neck; by extension: mouth; an "outstretched neck" is a sign of arrogance and possibly of sexual misconduct:– throat (3), mouths (1), neck (1), necks (1), shout aloud (1 [+7924, 928]), throats (1)

H1745 גֵּרוּת כִּמְהָם ***gērût kimhām***, n.f. [1] [√ 1731 + 4016]. Geruth Kimham:– Geruth Kimham (1)

H1746 גָּרַז ***gāraz***, v. [1] [→ 1749; cf. 1615]. [N] to be cut off, implying destruction:– am cut off (1)

H1747 גִּרְזִי ***girzî***, a.g. [1] [cf. 1621]. Girzite:– Girzites (1)

H1748 גְּרִזִים ***g^erizîm***, n.pr.loc. [4] Gerizim:– Gerizim (4)

H1749 גַּרְזֶן ***garzen***, n.m. [4] [√ 1746]. ax, chisel:– ax (3), chisel (1)

H1750 [1]גָּרַם ***gāram[1]***, v. [1] [Q] to leave, reserve:– leave (1)

H1751 [2]גָּרַם ***gāram[2]***, v.den. [2] [√ 1752]. [P] to break, to break bones:– break in pieces (1), chew (1)

H1752 גֶּרֶם ***gerem***, n.[m.] [5] [→ 1751, 1753?; 10150]. bone, rawboned, bony; bareness:– bare (1), bone (1), bones (1), limbs (1), rawboned (1)

H1753 גַּרְמִי ***garmî***, a.g. [1] [√ 1752?]. Garmite:– Garmite (1)

H1754 גָּרֹל ***gārōl***, a. see 1524

H1755 גֹּרֶן ***gōren***, n.m. [36] threshing floor:– threshing floor (32), threshing floors (3), threshing floor (1 [+1841])

H1756 גָּרַס ***gāras***, v. [2] [Q] to be crushed; [H] to break, crush:– broken (1), consumed (1)

H1757 [1]גָּרַע ***gāra'[1]***, v. [21] [→ 1758, 4492]. [Q] to take away, reduce, hinder; [Qp] to be cut off (of a beard); [N] to be reduced, be taken away, to disappear:– be reduced (2), be taken (2), cut off (2), be kept from (1 [+4200, 1194]), be taken away (1), deprive (1), disappear (1), have a monopoly on (1), hinder (1), omit (1), reduce (1), reduce the number (1), reduced (1), shave (1), subtract (1), take (1), take away (1), taken (1)

H1758 [2]גָּרַע ***gāra'[2]***, v. [1] [√ 1757]. [P] to draw up (drops of water):– draws up (1)

H1759 גָּרַף ***gārap***, v. [1] [→ 114, 4493]. [Q] to sweep away (of a river):– swept away (1)

H1760 גָּרַר ***gārar***, v. [5] [→ 1742, 1744, 4490; cf. 5599]. [Q] to chew; to drag away; [Polal] to be sawn; [Htpol] to drive, swirl:– catches (1), chew (1), drag away (1), driving (1), smoothed (1 [+928, 2021, 4490])

H1761 גְּרָר ***g^erār***, n.pr.loc. [10] Gerar, "*circle, region*":– Gerar (10)

H1762 גֶּרֶשׂ ***gereś***, n.[m.] [2] (coarse) crushed grain, grits, groats:– crushed (1), crushed grain (1)

H1763 [1]גָּרַשׁ ***gāraš[1]***, v. [46] [→ 1766, 4494, 4495; cf. 1764]. [Q] to drive out; [Qp] to be divorced; [N] to be banished; [P] to drive out, expel [Pu] to be banished:– drive out (8), drive (7), drove out (6), divorced (5), drove away (3), drive out (2 [+1763]), driven (2), driving out (2), be driven (1), been banished (1), been driven out (1), cast aside (1), drive away (1), driving (1), drove (1), emptied (1), get rid of (1), removed (1), were banished (1)

H1764 [2]גָּרַשׁ ***gāraš[2]***, v. [3] [√ 1765; cf. 1763]. [Q] to cast up, toss up; [N] to be tossed, be stirred up:– be stirred up (1), cast up (1), tossing (1)

H1765 גֶּרֶשׁ ***gereš***, n.[m.] [1] [√ 1764]. yield, produce:– yield (1)

H1766 גְּרֻשָׁה ***g^erušâ***, n.f. [1] [√ 1763]. dispossession:– dispossessing (1)

H1767 גֵּרְשׁוֹן ***gēršôn***, n.pr.m. [17] [→ 1768, 1769]. Gershon, "*temporary resident there*":– Gershon (9), Gershonites (6 [+1201]), Gershonite (2 [+1201])

H1768 גֵּרְשֹׁם ***gēršōm***, n.pr.m. [14] [√ 1767]. Gershom, Gershon, "*temporary resident there*":– Gershom (7), Gershon (6), Gershonites (1 [+1201])

H1769 גֵּרְשֻׁנִּי ***gēršunnî***, a.g. [13] [√ 1767]. Gershonite, "*of Gershon*":– Gershonite (7), Gershonites (3), Gershonite (1 [+1201]), Gershonites (1 [+1201]), their[S] (1 [+1201, 2021])

H1770 גְּשׁוּר ***g^ešûr***, n.pr.m. [9] [→ 1771]. Geshur, "*bridge*":– Geshur (8), they[S] (1 [+2256, 5083])

H1771 גְּשׁוּרִי ***g^ešûrî***, a.g. [6] [√ 1770]. Geshurite, people of Geshur, "*of Geshur*":– Geshurites (3), people of Geshur (3)

H1772 גָּשַׁם ***gāšam***, v.den. [3] [→ 1773, 1774, 1775, 1776]. [H] to bring rain:– bring rain (1), on (1), rained (1)

H1773 [1]גֶּשֶׁם ***gešem[1]***, n.m. [35] [→ 1774, 1775; cf. 1772]. rain, shower, downpour:– rain (24), showers (3), rains (2), rainy (2), abundant showers (1), downpour (1 [+4764]), shower (1), winter rains (1)

H1774 [2]גֶּשֶׁם ***gešem[2]***, n.pr.m. [3] [→ 1776; cf. 1772, 1773]. Geshem, "*rain shower*":– Geshem (3)

H1775 גֹּשֶׁם ***gōšem***, n.[m.] Not used in NIVEBC [√ 1773; cf. 1772]. shower, rain

H1776 גַּשְׁמוּ ***gašmû***, n.pr.m. [1] [√ 1774; cf. 1772]. Geshem, "*rain shower*":– Geshem (1)

H1777 גֹּשֶׁן ***gōšen***, n.pr.loc. [15] Goshen, "*mound of earth*":– Goshen (11), Goshen (4 [+824])

H1778 גִּשְׁפָּא ***gišpā'***, n.pr.m. [1] Gishpa, "*listener*":– Gishpa (1)

H1779 גָּשַׁשׁ ***gāšaš***, v. [2] [P] to grope along, feel one's way (as if blind):– feeling way (1), grope along (1)

H1780 [1]גַּת ***gat[1]***, n.f. [5] [→ 1781, 1782, 1783, 1784, 1785, 1786, 1787]. winepress; also used as a hiding place:– winepress (4), winepresses (1)

H1781 [2]גַּת ***gat[2]***, n.pr.loc. [34] [→ 1785, 1787; cf. 1780]. Gath, "*winepress*":– Gath (34)

H1782 [3]גַּת ***gat[3]***, n.pr.loc. Not used in NIVEBC [√ 1780]. Gath, see 1783, 1784

H1783 גַּת הַחֵפֶר ***gat haḥēper***, גַּת חֵפֶר ***gat ḥēper***, n.pr. loc. [2] [√ 1780 + 2021 + 2919]. Gath Hepher, "*winepress waterpit*":– Gath Hepher (2)

H1784 גַּת־רִמּוֹן ***gat-rimmôn***, n.pr.loc. [4] [√ 1780 + 8232]. Gath Rimmon, "*winepress of pomegranate*":– Gath Rimmon (4)

H1785 גִּתִּי ***gittî***, a.g. [10] [√ 1781; cf. 1780]. Gittite, "*of Gath*":– Gittite (8), Gath (1), Gittites (1)

H1786 גִּתַּיִם ***gittayim***, n.pr.loc. [2] [√ 1780]. Gittaim, "*two winepresses*":– Gittaim (2)

H1787 גִּתִּית ***gittît***, tt. [3] [√ 1781; cf. 1780]. gittith: unknown musical term, possibly the name of the tune, or the name of the instrument that played it, or even related in some way to ceremonies associated with the winepress:– gittith (3)

H1788 גֶּתֶר ***geter***, n.pr.m. [2] Gether:– Gether (2)

H1789 ד ***d***, letter. Not used in NIVEBC [√ 10152]. letter of the Hebrew alphabet

H1790 דָּאַב ***dā'ab***, v. [3] [→ 1791, 1792]. [Q] to be dim (of eyes); to sorrow:– dim (1), faint (1 [+5883]), sorrow (1)

H1791 דְּאָבָה ***d^e'ābâ***, n.f. [1] [√ 1790]. dismay, despair:– dismay (1)

H1792 דְּאָבוֹן ***d^e'ābôn***, n.[m.] [1] [√ 1790]. despair:– despairing (1)

H1793 דָּאַג ***dā'ag***, v. [7] [→ 1795, 1796, 1869]. [Q] to worry, dread, be troubled, be afraid:– afraid (1), dread (1), dreaded (1), has worries (1), troubled (1), worried (1), worrying (1)

H1794 דָּאג ***dā'g***, n.m. [1] [√ 1834]. fish:– fish (1)

H1795 דֹּאֵג ***dō'ēg***, n.pr.m. [6] [√ 1793]. Doeg, "*anxious*":– Doeg (6)

H1796 דְּאָגָה ***d^e'āgâ***, n.f. [6] [√ 1793]. fear, anxiety, restlessness:– anxiety (3), fear (2), restless (1)

H1797 [1]דָּאָה ***dā'â[1]***, v. [5] [→ 1798; cf. 1901]. [Q] to swoop down, pounce; to soar:– soared (2), swooping down (2), swoop down (1)

H1798 [2]דָּאָה ***dā'â[2]***, n.f. [1] [√ 1797]. red kite (bird):– red kite (1)

H1799 דֹּאר ***dō'r***, n.pr.loc. [1] [→ 1888, 2831, 5869, 6529; cf. 1883, 1884]. Dor:– Dor (1)

H1800 דֹּב ***dōb***, n.m. [12] [√ 1803; 10155]. bear (animal):– bear (10), bears (2)

H1801 דֹּבֶא ***dōbe'***, n.[m.] [1] strength:– strength (1)

H1802 דְּבָאָה ***d^ebā'â***, n.f. strength

H1803 דָּבַב ***dābab***, v. [1] [→ 1800, 1804?, 1807?]. [Q] to flow over gently:– flowing gently (1)

H1804 דִּבָּה ***dibbâ***, n.f. [9] [√ 1803?]. bad report, slander, bad reputation, whisper:– bad report (2), report (2), slander (2), whispering (2), charge (1)

H1805 [1]דְּבוֹרָה ***d^ebôrâ[1]***, n.f. [4] [→ 1806; cf. 1819]. wild honey bee; (pl.) swarm of bees:– bees (3), swarm of bees (1)

H1806 [2]דְּבוֹרָה ***d^ebôrâ[2]***, n.pr.f. [10] [√ 1805; cf. 1819]. Deborah, "*hornet, wasp, wild honey bee*":– Deborah (10)

H1807 דִּבְיוֹנִים ***dibyōnîm***, n.[m.] [1] [√ 1803? + 3433]. seed pods or doves' dung:– seed pods (1)

H1808 [1]דְּבִיר ***d^ebîr[1]***, n.m. [15] [→ 1809, 1810; cf. 1818?, 1819?]. inner sanctuary, referring to the Most Holy Place:– inner sanctuary (14), most holy place (1 [+7731])

H1809 [2]דְּבִיר ***d^ebîr[2]***, n.pr.m. [1] [√ 1808; cf. 1818]. Debir, "*back room [of a shrine temple for oracle pronouncement]*":– Debir (1)

H1810 [3]דְּבִיר ***d^ebîr[3]***, n.pr.loc. [13] [√ 1808; cf. 1818]. Debir, "*back room [of a shrine temple for oracle pronouncement]*":– Debir (11), NDT (2)

H1811 דְּבֵלָה ***d^ebēlâ***, n.f. [5] [→ 1813?]. pressed fig cakes; poultice of figs:– poultice (2), cake of pressed figs (1), cakes of pressed figs (1), fig cakes (1)

H1812 דִּבְלָה ***diblâ***, n.pr.loc. [1] Diblah:– Diblah (1)

H1813 דִּבְלַיִם ***diblayim***, n.pr.m. [1] [√ 1811?]. Diblaim, "*lump of [two dried fig] cakes*":– Diblaim (1)

H1814 דִּבְלָתַיִם ***diblātayim***, n.pr.loc. Not used in NIVEBC [→ 1086, 6627]. Diblathaim

H1815 דָּבַק ***dābaq***, v. [54] [→ 1816, 1817; 10158]. [Q] to be united, hold fast, keep, cling to; [H] to overtake, cause to cleave, press hard upon; [Pu] to be joined fast, be stuck together; [Ho] be made to cleave, stick to; from the base joining or fastening objects together comes the figure of close association of people:– hold fast (7), cling (5), in hot pursuit (3), bound (2), clung (2), held fast (2), keep (2), make stick (2), stay (2), sticks (2), ally (1), are joined fast (1), caught up (1), defiled (1 [+4583]), drawn (1), follow (1 [+339]), found (1), froze (1), have part (1), joined (1), laid low (1), not escape (1), overtake (1), overtook (1), plague (1), pressing (1), reduced to (1), stayed (1), stayed close (1), stick together (1), sticking (1), stuck (1), tightly joined (1), united (1), NDT (1)

H1816 דָּבֵק ***dābēq***, a. [3] [√ 1815]. holding fast, sticking to:– held fast (1), sticks closer (1), touched (1)

H1817 דֶּבֶק ***debeq***, n.m. [3] [√ 1815]. welding; sections (of armor):– breastplate (1), sections (1), welding (1)

H1818 [1]דָּבַר ***dābar[1]***, v. [5] [→ 1808?, 1809, 1810, 1822, 1823, 1824, 1827, 1829, 4497]. [P] to depart; to destroy; [H] to subdue:– departure (1), destroy (1), subdued (1), subdues (1), testify (1)

H1819 [2]דָּבַר ***dābar[2]***, v. [1137] [→ 1805, 1806, 1808?, 1821, 1825, 1826, 1830, 4498]. [Q. P, Ht] to say, speak, tell, command, promise; [Qp, Pu] to be spoken (of); [N] to speak together; a general term for verbal communication, note the specific contextual translations in the NIV:– said (199), speak (167), spoken (98), spoke (88), say (67), promised (50), tell (49), speaking (36), told (36), talked (16), says (15), speaks (14), talking (14), talk (11), saying (10), gave (6), pronounced (6), reported (6), declared (5), decreed (5), directed (5), given (5), made (5), proclaimed (5), repeated (5), replied (5), say (5 [+1821]), warned (5), asked (4), praying (4), promise (4), speak out (4), telling (4), words (4), ask (3), give (3), instructed (3), pronounce (3), pronounced on (3 [+907]), speak up (3), spoke up (3), threatened (3), announce (2), announced (2), answered (2), declare (2), foretold (2), full of (2), give answer (2 [+1821]), give word (2), inciting (2), liars (2 [+9214]), preached (2), proclaim (2), proclaiming (2), promises made (2), propose (2), sang (2), speak well (2 [+1819]), tells (2), threaten (2), used to say (2 [+1819]), utter (2), address (1), are said (1), argued (1), asking (1), asks (1), boastful (1 [+1524]), break out (1), commanded (1), contend (1), decree (1), dictate (1), discussed (1), encourage (1 [+6584, 4213]), encouraged (1 [+6584, 4222]), ever say (1 [+1821]), explained (1), fluent (1 [+4554, 4200]), gave the message (1 [+3972, 2021, 2021, 465, 1821]), give an answer (1), give opinion (1), gives (1), giving (1), harbor deception (1), imagine (1), instructed (1 [+7023]), invite (1), is spoken (1), lie (1 [+3942]), lie (1 [+9214]), lied (1 [+3942]), lies (1 [+8736]), lying (1 [+3942]), lying (1 [+9214]), made request (1), make (1), make many promises (1 [+1821]), make promise (1 [+1821]), make request (1), mention (1), mentioned (1), message (1), message came (1), named (1), ordered (1), persuade (1 [+6584, 4213]), plea (1), plead (1), pleaded (1), predicted (1), proclaims (1), promise (1 [+1821]), promises (1), promises (1 [+1821]), prophesied (1 [+5553]), rebukes (1), recited (1), reciting (1), recommended (1), request (1 [+1821]), requested (1), ridicule (1), said (1 [+928, 7023]), said (1 [+1821]), said (1 [+2021, 1821]), said a word (1), shouted (1), silent (1 [+4202]), slander (1), speak with words (1), speaking kindly (1 [+6584, 4213]), speech (1 [+4537]), spoken (1 [+7023]), spread (1), spreading (1), spreads (1), state (1), suggested (1), talking together (1), tell (1 [+928, 265]), testify (1), told (1 [+928, 265]), urging (1), uttered (1 [+1821]), verdict (1), wills[S] (1 [+1821]), NDT (24)

H1820 [3]דָּבַר ***dābar[3]***, v. [P] to have descendants

H1821 דָּבָר ***dābār***, n.m. [1442] [√ 1819]. what is said, word (or any unit of speech such as a clause, or the whole of communication); matter (any event); thing (any object):–

word (340), words (224), events (51), this[s] (38 [+2021, 2021, 2296]), annals (37 [+3427]), things (33), message (28), thing (26), what[s] (26 [+2021]), matter (23), what said (21), nothing (20 [+4202]), promise (16), anything (15), say (13), command (11), everything (11 [+3972, 2021]), this[s] (11 [+2021, 2021, 465]), what[s] (10), answer (9 [+8740]), said (9), answer (8), report (8), what say (8), anything (7 [+3972]), records (7), terms (7), because of (6 [+6584]), case (6), commandments (6), it[s] (6 [+2021]), reported (6 [+8740]), some time later (6 [+339, 2021, 2021, 465]), asked (5), cases (5), commanded (5), everything (5 [+3972]), instructions (5), promises (5), say (5 [+1819]), what[s] (5 [+2021]), account (4), advice (4), it[s] (4 [+2021, 2021, 2296]), plan (4), promised (4), request (4), sayings (4), something (4), told (4), affairs (3), annals (3), answered (3 [+8740]), because (3 [+6584]), commands (3), concerning (3 [+6584]), conversation (3), instruction (3), lies (3 [+9214]), mission (3), questions (3), speak (3), this[s] (3 [+2021]), this[s] (3 [+2021]), this[s] (3 [+2021, 2296, 2021]), this[s] (3 [+2021, 2021, 2296]), way (3), what[s] (3 [+2021, 2021, 2296]), about (2 [+6584]), achievements (2), bidding (2), charge (2), claims (2), conduct (2), counsel (2), deeds (2), dispute (2), doing (2), empty words (2 [+8557]), for each day (2 [+3427, 928, 3427]), give answer (2 [+1819]), incident (2), nothing (2 [+401]), occasion (2), order (2), predicting (2), regulations (2), relationship (2), required (2), requirement (2), requirements (2), saying (2), some (2), speaks (2), spoke (2), spoken (2), story (2), verdict (2 [+5477]), voice (2), what[s] (2 [+2021, 2021, 465]), what written (2), written (2), accusations (1), accuse (1 [+8492, 928]), activity (1), affair (1), after (1 [+928]), after a while (1 [+339, 2021, 2021, 465]), amount (1), animal[s] (1), answer (1 [+6699]), anything (1 [+3972, 2021]), anything (1 [+4946, 3972]), anything (1 [+4946, 3972, 2021, 1821]), anything (1 [+1821, 4946, 3972, 2021]), ask (1 [+2011]), at all (1), behavior (1), cases (1 [+8191]), cause (1), charges (1), compliments (1 [+5833]), concerned (1), conferred (1), conferred (1 [+2118]), consult (1 [+2011, 928]), covenant[s] (1), cries (1), curses (1), customary (1 [+4027]), daily (1 [+3427, 928, 3427]), danger (1), day by day (1 [+3427, 928, 3427]), day by day (1 [+3427, 928, 3427, 2257]), decided (1 [+6641]), decisions (1), decree (1), deed (1), defiance (1), demand (1), details (1), directed (1), disease (1), disputes (1), done (1), duties (1), duty (1), edict (1), eloquent (1 [+408]), else (1), enough (1), ever say (1 [+1819]), everything (1 [+3972, 2021, 2021, 465]), feat (1 [+1524]), flaw (1 [+8273]), for (1 [+6584]), for (1 [+6584]), fulfilled (1), gave the message (1 [+1819, 3972, 2021, 2021, 465]), harm (1 [+8273]), how (1), idea (1), in the cause of (1 [+6584]), incident[s] (1), inquires of (1 [+8626, 928]), instructed (1), it[s] (1), it[s] (1 [+3870]), later (1 [+339, 2021, 2021, 465]), lesson (1), lies (1 [+3942]), make many promises (1 [+1819]), make promise (1 [+1819]), matters (1), mere talk (1 [+8557]), need (1), nothing (1 [+4202, 3972]), nothing (1 [+4202, 3972]), nothing whatever (1 [+401, 3972]), offering (1), one[s] (1), ones[s] (1), ordered (1), plans (1), plot (1), prediction (1), promise (1 [+1819]), promises (1 [+1819]), prophecy (1), proposal (1), proposed (1), question (1), record (1), refrain (1), reports (1), request (1 [+1819]), requested (1), revelation (1), rule (1), ruling (1), said (1 [+1819]), said (1 [+1819, 2021]), says (1), secret (1), signs (1 [+253]), sins (1 [+6411]), situation (1), slandered (1 [+8492, 6613]), slanders (1 [+8492, 6613]), something to say (1), songs (1 [+8877]), speaking (1), speaking (1 [+7754]), speech (1), speeches (1), such[s] (1), suggested (1 [+2021, 2021, 2296]), suggestion (1), teachings (1), tell (1), tell (1 [+606]), text (1), that[s] (1 [+2021, 2021, 465]), that happened (1 [+2021, 465, 2021]), that said (1), the word (1), them[s] (1 [+3870]), them[s] (1 [+2021, 2021, 2296]), theme (1), they[s] (1 [+3870]), things promised (1), things threatened (1), this (1 [+2021, 2021, 2296]), this[s] (1), this[s] (1 [+2021, 465, 2021]), this is how (1 [+3869, 2021, 2021, 465]), thought (1), thoughts (1), threats (1), through (1 [+3869]), times (1), transfer of property (1 [+9455, 3972]), trouble (1), uttered (1 [+1819]), warning (1), what[s] (1 [+7754]), what asks (1), what foretold (1), what have to say (1), what said (1 [+7754]), what says (1), what spoke (1), whatever (1 [+4537]), whisper (1), why (1), will[s] (1 [+1819]), words (1 [+7023]), work (1), year (1 [+9102]), NDT (34)

H1822 [1]דֶּבֶר ***deber[1]***, n.m. [49] [√ 1818]. plague, pestilence, disease, a pandemic occurrence of sickness and death; some sources identify specific diseases in specific contexts:– plague (43), plagues (3), pestilence (2), diseases (1)

H1823 [2]דֶּבֶר ***deber[2]***, n.m. Not used in NIVEBC [√ 1818]. thorn

H1824 דֹּבֶר ***dōber***, n.[m.] [2] [√ 1818]. pasture, in a remote place:– pasture (2)

H1825 דִּבֵּר ***dibbēr***, n.[m.] [1] [√ 1819]. word (of God):– word (1)

H1826 דִּבְרָה ***dibrâ***, n.f. [5] [√ 1819; 10159]. cause; order; therefore, because:– as for (1 [+6584]), because (1 [+6584]), cause (1), order (1), therefore (1 [+6584, 8611])

H1827 דֹּבְרוֹת ***dōbᵉrôt***, n.f.pl. [1] [√ 1818]. raft, a collection of logs towed behind a ship:– rafts (1)

H1828 דִּבְרִי ***dibrî***, n.pr.m. [1] Dibri, "[poss.] *speak*":– Dibri (1)

H1829 דָּבְרַת ***dābᵉrat***, n.pr.loc. [3] [√ 1818]. Daberath, "*pasture*":– Daberath (3)

H1830 דַּבֶּרֶת ***dabberet***, n.f. [1] [√ 1819]. instruction, word:– instruction (1)

H1831 דְּבַשׁ ***dᵉbaš***, n.m. [54] [→ 3340]. honey:– honey (52), honeycomb (1 [+3626]), honeycomb (1 [+7430])

H1832 [1]דַּבֶּשֶׁת ***dabbešet[1]***, n.f. [1] [→ 1833?]. hump (of a camel):– humps (1)

H1833 [2]דַּבֶּשֶׁת ***dabbešet[2]***, n.pr.loc. [1] [√ 1832?]. Dabbesheth, "*hump*":– Dabbesheth (1)

H1834 דָּג ***dāg***, n.m. [18] [→ 1794, 1835?, 1836, 1854, 1855, 1900; cf. 1899]. fish:– fish (17), fishing (1)

H1835 [1]דָּגָה ***dāgâ[1]***, v. [1] [√ 1834?]. [Q] to increase, multiply:– increase (1)

H1836 [2]דָּגָה ***dāgâ[2]***, n.f. [15] [√ 1834]. fish:– fish (15)

H1837 דָּגוֹן ***dāgôn***, n.pr.m. [12] [→ 1087, 1841]. Dagon (pagan god), "*[god of] grain; fish*":– Dagon (8), Dagon's (2), his[s] (1), his body[s] (1)

H1838 [1]דָּגַל ***dāgal[1]***, v. [1] [√ 1840]. [Qp] to be outstanding, be conspicuous:– outstanding (1)

H1839 [2]דָּגַל ***dāgal[2]***, v.den. [3] [√ 1840]. [Q] to lift a banner; [N] be gathered around the banner(s), organized as troops:– in procession (1), lift up banners (1), troops with banners (1)

H1840 דֶּגֶל ***degel***, n.m. [14] [→ 1838, 1839, 5609]. standard, banner:– standard (11), standards (2), banner (1)

H1841 דָּגָן ***dāgān***, n.m. [40] [√ 1837]. grain:– grain (38), bread (1), threshing floor (1 [+1755])

H1842 דָּגַר ***dāgar***, v. [2] [Q] to care for; hatch eggs:– care for young (1), hatches eggs (1)

H1843 דַּד ***dad***, n.m. [4] bosom, breast:– bosom (2), bosoms (1), breasts (1)

H1844 דָּדָה ***dādâ***, v. [1] [Ht] to walk, lead:– walk humbly (1)

H1845 דֹּדָוָהוּ ***dōdāwāhû***, n.pr.m. [1] Dodavahu, "*beloved of Yahweh*":– Dodavahu (1)

H1846 דּוֹדִי ***dōdî***, n.pr.m. Not used in NIVEBC [√ 1856?]. Dodai, "*beloved*"

H1847 דְּדָן ***dᵉdān***, n.pr.loc. & g. [10] [→ 1848]. Dedan:– Dedan (10)

H1848 דְּדָנִי ***dᵉdānî***, a.g. [1] [√ 1847]. Dedanite, "*of Dedan*":– Dedanites (1)

H1849 דֹּדָנִים ***dōdānîm***, n.pr.g.pl. Not used in NIVEBC [cf. 8102]. Dodanim

H1850 דָּהַם ***dāham***, v. [1] [N] to be taken by surprise, be astounded:– taken by surprise (1)

H1851 דָּהַר ***dāhar***, v. [1] [→ 1852]. [Q] to gallop:– galloping (1)

H1852 דַּהֲרָה ***dahărâ***, n.f. [2] [√ 1851]. galloping:– galloping (2)

H1853 דּוּב ***dûb***, v. [2] [cf. 2307]. [H] to drain away, wear away; loss of life as a fig. extension of draining liquid out of a container:– sap (2)

H1854 דַּוָּג ***dawwāg***, n.m. [1] [√ 1834]. fisherman:– Fishermen (1)

H1855 דּוּגָה ***dûgâ***, n.f. [1] [√ 1834]. fishing (hooks):– fishhooks (1 [+6106])

H1856 דּוֹד ***dôd***, n.m. [61] [→ 455, 485, 1161, 1846?, 1858?, 1860, 1861?, 1862?]. uncle, cousin, relative; beloved one, lover; a term of endearment ranging from friendship and familial affection to romantic love:– beloved (30), uncle (11), love (9), cousin (4 [+1201]), others[s] (2), beloved's (1 [+4200]), cousin (1 [+1426]), cousins on their father's side (1 [+1201]), relative (1), NDT (1)

H1857 דּוּד ***dûd***, n.m. [8] basket; kettle, caldron, pot:– basket (3), baskets (2), caldrons (1), kettle (1), pot (1)

H1858 דָּוִד ***dāwid***, n.pr.m. [1075] [√ 1856?]. David, "*beloved one*":– David (909), David's (66), he[s] (47), him[s] (18), David's (8 [+4200]), his[s] (4), David's line (1), his own (1), you[s] (1), NDT (20)

H1859 דּוּדָאִים ***dûdā'îm***, n.m. [6] [√ 1863]. mandrake plant, thought to be a fertility aid or aphrodisiac:– mandrakes (5), mandrake plants (1)

H1860 דּוֹדָה ***dôdâ***, n.f. [3] [√ 1856]. aunt (father's sister):– aunt (2), father's sister (1)

H1861 דּוֹדוֹ ***dôdô***, n.pr.m. [3] [√ 1856?]. Dodo, "*beloved*":– Dodo (3)

H1862 דּוֹדַי ***dôday***, n.pr.m. [3] [√ 1856?]. Dodai, "*beloved*":– Dodai (3)

H1863 דּוּדַי ***dûday***, n.m. Not used in NIVEBC [→ 1859]. mandrakes

H1864 דָּוָה ***dāwâ***, v. [1] [→ 1865, 1867, 1868, 1902?, 4504]. [Q] to have a monthly period, menstruate:– monthly period (1 [+5614])

H1865 דָּוֶה ***dāweh***, a. [5] [√ 1864]. pertaining to the menstrual cycle; fainting:– faint (2), menstrual cloth (1), monthly period (1), monthly period (1 [+5614])

H1866 דּוּחַ ***dûaḥ***, v. [3] [cf. 5615]. [H] to rinse, wash, cleanse:– cleanse (1), rinsed (1), washed (1)

H1867 דְּוַי ***dᵉway***, n.[m.] [2] [√ 1864]. illness:– ill (1), sickbed (1 [+6911])

H1868 דַּוָּי ***dawwāy***, a. [3] [√ 1864]. faint; afflicted:– faint (2), afflicted (1)

H1869 דּוֹיֵג ***dôyēg***, n.pr.m. Not used in NIVEBC [√ 1793]. Doyeg, see 1795

H1870 דּוּךְ ***dûk***, v. [1] [→ 4521; cf. 1916, 1917, 1920, 1990]. [Q] to crush (in a mortar):– crushed (1)

H1871 דּוּכִיפַת ***dûkîpat***, n.f. [2] hoopoe:– hoopoe (2)

H1872 [1]דּוּמָה ***dûmâ[1]***, n.f. [3] [√ 1957]. silence:– place of silence (1), silence of death (1), silenced (1)

H1873 [2]דּוּמָה ***dûmâ[2]***, n.pr.loc. [1] Dumah, "*silence [name of the underworld]*":– Dumah (1)

H1874 [3]דּוּמָה ***dûmâ[3]***, n.pr.loc. [3] Dumah, "*silence*":– Dumah (3)

H1875 דּוּמִיָּה ***dûmiyyâ***, n.f. [4] [√ 1957; cf. 1949]. silence, stillness; rest:– rest (2), awaits (1), utterly silent (1 [+519])

H1876 דּוּמָם ***dûmām***, n.[m.] [3] [cf. 1957]. in silence, quietly; lifeless:– lifeless (1), quietly (1), silence (1)

H1877 דּוּמֶּשֶׂק ***dûmmeśeq***, n.pr.loc. [1] [√ 1966]. Damascus:– Damascus (1)

H1878 דּוֹן ***dôn***, v. [Q] to remain [?]

H1879 דּוּן ***dûn***, n.[m.] Not used in NIVEBC [√ 1906]. judgment

H1880 דּוֹנַג ***dônag***, n.m. [4] wax:– wax (4)

H1881 דּוּץ ***dûṣ***, v. [1] [Q] to leap:– goes (1)

H1882 דּוּק ***dûq***, v. Not used in NIVEBC [→ 1911]. [Q] to review

H1883 [1]דּוּר ***dûr[1]***, v. [1] [→ 4509; cf. 1799, 1884, 1888]. [Q] to pile logs (around):– Pile wood (1)

H1884 [2]דּוּר ***dûr[2]***, v. [1] [→ 126, 1885, 1886, 1887; cf. 1799, 1883, 1888; 10163]. [Q] to dwell:– dwell (1)

H1885 [3]דּוּר ***dûr[3]***, n.[m.] [2] [√ 1884; 10753]. all around, encircling; ball:– ball (1), on all sides (1 [+3869, 2021])

H1886 [1]דּוֹר ***dôr[1]***, n.m. [1] [√ 1884]. house, dwelling:– house (1)

H1887 [2]דּוֹר ***dôr[2]***, n.m. [166] [√ 1884; 10183]. generation, generation to come; descendant:– generation (45), generations to come (36), all generations (14 [+2256, 1887]), all generations (14 [+1887, 2256]), generations (12), descendants (5), all generations (4 [+1887]), those[s] (4), generations (3 [+2256, 1887]), generations (3 [+1887, 2256]), through all generations (2 [+1887]), age-old (1 [+2256, 1887]), age-old (1 [+1887, 2256]), all time (1 [+2256, 1887]), all time (1 [+1887, 2256]), another[s] (1), children (1 [+1201]), company (1), endless generations (1 [+2256, 1887]), endless generations (1 [+1887, 2256]), ever (1 [+4200, 2256, 1887]), ever (1 [+4200, 1887, 2256]), generations long past (1 [+9102, 2256, 1887]), generations long past (1 [+9102, 1887, 2256]), generations to come (1 [+2256, 1887]), generations to come (1 [+1887, 2256]), many generations (1 [+2256, 1887]), many generations (1 [+1887, 2256]), people of time (1), to come (1 [+2256, 1887]), to come (1 [+1887, 2256]), who have gone before (1 [+3]), wicked[s] (1 [+2306]), NDT (2)

H1888 [3]דּוֹר ***dôr[3]***, n.pr.loc. [3] [√ 1799; cf. 1883, 1884]. Dor:– Dor (3)

H1889 דּוּשׁ ***dûš***, v. [16] [→ 1912, 1913?, 4536; 10165]. [Q] to tread, trample, thresh; [Qp, N, Ho] be trampled, be threshed:– thresh (3), go on threshing (2 [+1889]), threshed (2), be trampled (1), is threshed (1), is trampled down (1), tear (1), threshing (1), threshing grain (1), threshing time (1), trample (1), treading out grain (1)

H1890 דָּחָה ***dāḥâ***, v. [8] [→ 1892, 4510; cf. 1891, 5615; 10166]. [Q] to push, push away; trip up; [Qp] to totter; [N] to be brought down; [Pu] to be thrown down:– was pushed back (2 [+1890]), are brought down (1), banished (1), driving away (1), thrown down (1), tottering (1), trip (1)

H1891 דָּחַח ***dāḥaḥ***, v. Not used in NIVEBC [cf. 1890, 5615]. [N] to be push, pushed out

H1892 דְּחִי ***dᵉḥî***, n.[m.] [2] [√ 1890]. stumbling:– stumbling (2)

H1893 דֹּחַן ***dōḥan***, n.m. [1] (sorghum) millet:– millet (1)

H1894 דָּחַף ***dāḥap***, v. [4] [→ 4511]. [Qp] to be spurred on, be in haste; [N] to be eager, be rushed, hurry:– spurred on (2), eager (1), rushed (1)

H1895 דָּחַק ***dāḥaq***, v. [2] [Q] to afflict, oppress:– afflicted (1), jostle (1)

H1896 דַּי ***day***, subst. [39] [→ 972, 1973, 3904, 4514]. enough, sufficient:– whenever (5 [+4946]), enough (4), from (3 [+4946]), as much as wanted (2), for nothing (2 [+928, 8198]), afford (1 [+5162, 3338]), afford (1 [+5595, 3338]), after (1 [+4946, 928]), as far as possible (1 [+3869]), as often as (1 [+4946]), as often as (1 [+4946]), at the blast (1 [+928]), deserves (1 [+3869]), due annually (1 [+4946, 9102, 928, 9102]), enough (1 [+4200, 4537]), fuel for fire (1 [+928, 836]), fuel for flames (1 [+928, 836]), just enough (1), means (1), no end (1 [+3869]), often (1 [+4946]), plenty (1), room enough to store (1), sufficient (1), sufficient means (1 [+3869]), swarms (1), whatever (1), whenever (1 [+3954, 4946])

H1897 דִּיבוֹן ***dîbôn***, n.pr.loc. [9] [→ 1898; cf. 1904, 1905]. Dibon:– Dibon (9)

H1898 דִּיבֹן גָּד ***dîbôn gād***, n.pr.loc. [2] [√ 1897 + 1514]. Dibon Gad:– Dibon Gad (2)

H1899 דִּיג ***dîg***, v.den. [1] [cf. 1834]. [Q] to catch fish:– catch (1)

H1900 דַּיָּג ***dayyāg***, n.m. [2] [√ 1834]. fisherman:– fishermen (2)

H1901 דַּיָּה ***dayyâ***, n.f. [2] [cf. 1797]. falcon:– falcon (1), falcons (1)

H1902 דְּיוֹ ***dᵉyô***, n.m. [1] [√ 1864?]. ink, a writing substance made of soot or metal shavings mixed with oil or resin:– ink (1)

H1903 דִּי זָהָב ***dî zāhāb***, n.pr.loc. [1] Dizahab, "*that which has gold*":– Dizahab (1)

H1904 דִּימוֹן ***dîmôn***, n.pr.loc. [2] [cf. 1897]. Dimon:– Dimon (2)

H1905 דִּימוֹנָה ***dîmônâ***, n.pr.loc. [1] [cf. 1897]. Dimonah:– Dimonah (1)

H1906 [1]דִּין ***dîn[1]***, v. [24] [→ 1879, 1907, 1908, 1909, 1968, 1969, 4506, 4507, 4519, 4528, 8723, 8726; 10169; *also used with compound proper names*]. [Q] to judge, punish; to plead, defend, vindicate, contend for; [N] to argue:– judge (7), vindicate (3), contend (2), administer (1), arguing among themselves (1), defend rights (1), defended (1), govern (1), governs (1), judges (1), plead (1), provide justice (1), punish (1), seek justice (1 [+1907]), vindicated (1)

H1907 [2]דִּין ***dîn[2]***, n.[m.] [20] [√ 1906; 10170]. cause, legal case; judgment, justice:– judgment (4), cause (3), justice (3), rights (3), case (2), judge (1), lawsuits (1 [+4200, 1907]), lawsuits (1 [+1907, 4200]), quarrels (1), seek justice (1 [+1906])

H1908 דַּיָּן ***dayyān***, n.m. [2] [√ 1906; 10171]. defender, judge:– defender (1), judge (1)

H1909 דִּינָה ***dînâ***, n.pr.f. [8] [√ 1906]. Dinah, "*female judge*":– Dinah (7), Dinah's (1)

H1910 דִּיפַת ***dîpat***, n.pr.m. Not used in NIVEBC [cf. 8196]. Diphath, see 8196

H1911 דָּיֵק ***dāyēq***, n.m. [6] [√ 1882]. siege works:– siege works (6)

H1912 דַּיִשׁ ***dayiš***, n.m. [1] [√ 1889]. threshing (season):– threshing (1)

H1913 [1]דִּישׁוֹן ***dîšôn[1]***, n.[m.] [1] [→ 1914?, 1915?; cf. 1889?]. ibex:– ibex (1)

H1914 [2]דִּישׁוֹן ***dîšôn[2]***, n.pr.m. [8] [√ 1913?]. Dishon, Dishan, "*ibex[?]*":– Dishon (7), Dishan (1)

H1915 דִּישָׁן ***dîšān***, n.pr.m. [4] [√ 1913?]. Dishan, "*ibex[?]*":– Dishan (4)

H1916 דַּךְ ***dak***, a. [4] [→ 1921; cf. 1870, 1917, 1920, 1990]. oppressed:– oppressed (3), hurts (1)

H1917 דָּכָא ***dākā'***, v. [18] [→ 1918, 1919; cf. 1870, 1916, 1920, 1990]. [N] to be contrite; [P] to crush; [Pu] to be crushed, be dejected, be humbled; [Ht] to lie crushed:– crush (7), crushed (4), broke (1), contrite (1), crushes (1), crushing (1), dejected (1), humbled themselves (1), was crushed (1)

H1918 [1]דַּכָּא ***dakkā'[1]***, a. [3] [√ 1917]. crushed, contrite:– contrite (1), crushed (1), crushing (1)

H1919 [2]דַּכָּא ***dakkā'[2]***, n.[m.] [1] [√ 1917]. dust:– dust (1)

H1920 דָּכָה ***dākâ***, v. [5] [→ 1922; cf. 1870, 1916, 1917, 1990]. [Q, P] to crush; [N] to be crushed, contrite:– crushed (4), contrite (1)

H1921 דַּכָּה ***dakkâ***, n.f. Not used in NIVEBC [√ 1916]. crushing (of testicle)

H1922 דֳּכִי ***dᵒkî***, n.[m.] [1] [√ 1920]. pounding (waves):– pounding waves (1)

H1923 [1]דַּל ***dal[1]***, n.[m.] [1] [→ 1928, 1946]. door:– door (1)

H1924 [2]דַּל ***dal[2]***, a. [48] [→ 1930; cf. 1937]. poor, needy, humble; weak, haggard, scrawny:– poor (36), weak (4), grew weaker and weaker (1 [+2143, 2256]), haggard (1), helpless (1), humble (1), needy (1), poorest of the poor (1 [+1147]), scrawny (1), weakest (1)

H1925 דָּלַג ***dālag***, v. [5] [Q, P] to scale, ascend, leap up over:– scale (2), avoid stepping (1), leap (1), leaping (1)

H1926 [1]דָּלָה ***dālâ[1]***, v. [5] [→ 1932, 1933, 1934; cf. 1927]. [Q, P] to draw up, draw water (from a well):– drew water (2 [+1926]), draw water (1), draws out (1), lifted out of the depths (1)

H1927 [2]דָּלָה ***dālâ[2]***, v. [1] [→ 1936; cf. 1926]. [Q] to hang limp, dangle:– useless (1)

H1928 [3]דָּלָה ***dālâ[3]***, n.f. Not used in NIVEBC [√ 1923]. door

H1929 [1]דַּלָּה ***dallâ[1]***, n.f. [2] [√ 1938]. threads remaining on the loom; flowing hair:– hair (1 [+8031]), loom (1)

H1930 [2]דַּלָּה ***dallâ[2]***, n.f. [5] [√ 1924; cf. 1937]. poor, a class of people with little status, influence, and social value:– poorest (5)

H1931 דָּלַח ***dālaḥ***, v. [3] [Q] to churn, stir up:– churning (1), muddied (1), stirred (1)

H1932 דְּלִי ***dᵉlî***, n.[m.] [2] [√ 1926]. (water) bucket, possibly made of leather:– bucket (1), buckets (1)

H1933 דְּלָיָה ***dᵉlāyâ***, n.pr.m. [4] [√ 1926 + 3378]. Delaiah, "*Yahweh draws up [like water in a bucket]*":– Delaiah (4)

H1934 דְּלָיָהוּ ***dᵉlāyāhû***, n.pr.m. [3] [√ 1926 + 3378]. Delaiah, "*Yahweh draws up [like water in a bucket]*":– Delaiah (3)

H1935 דְּלִילָה ***dᵉlîlâ***, n.pr.f. [6] [√ 1938]. Delilah, "*tease*":– Delilah (6)

H1936 דָּלִית ***dālît***, n.f. [8] [√ 1927]. branch, bough:– branches (6), boughs (2)

H1937 [1]דָּלַל ***dālal[1]***, v. [7] [→ 1924, 1930; cf. 1938]. [Q] to be in need, be weak, fade:– in need (2), brought low (1), dwindle (1), fade (1), impoverished (1), weak (1)

H1938 [2]דָּלַל ***dālal[2]***, v. [1] [→ 1929, 1935; cf. 1937]. [Q] to dangle:– dangle (1)

H1939 דִּלְעָן ***dil'ān***, n.pr.loc. [1] Dilean, "*cucumber; protrude*":– Dilean (1)

H1940 [1]דָּלַף ***dālap[1]***, v. [2] [→ 1942]. [Q] to leak; to pour out:– leaks (1), pour out tears (1)

H1941 [2]דָּלַף ***dālap[2]***, v. [1] [→ 1943, 3358]. [Q] to be weary, be sleepless:– weary (1)

H1942 דֶּלֶף ***delep***, n.m. [2] [√ 1940]. leaky roof:– leaky roof (2)

H1943 דַּלְפוֹן ***dalpôn***, n.pr.m. [1] [√ 1941]. Dalphon, "*crafty; sleepless*":– Dalphon (1)

H1944 דָּלַק ***dālaq***, v. [9] [→ 1945; 10178]. [Q] to set on fire; to hunt, chase, pursue; [H] to inflame, kindle:– chased (1), chasing (1 [+339]), fervent (1), flaming (1), hunt down (1), hunts down (1), inflamed (1), kindle (1), set on fire (1)

H1945 דַּלֶּקֶת ***dalleqet***, n.f. [1] [√ 1944]. inflammation:– inflammation (1)

H1946 דֶּלֶת ***delet***, n.f. [& m.?] [85] [√ 1923]. door, gate; column, lid, leaf (of a door):– doors (46), door (21), gates (10), leaves (2), columns (1), gate (1), it[S] (1 [+2021]), lid (1), outside (1 [+4946]), NDT (1)

H1947 דָּם ***dām***, n.m. [357] [cf. 1956?]. blood, lifeblood; by extension: bloodshed, death; blood-colored fluids: grape juice, wine; "to pour out blood" is "to kill" since life is in the blood:– blood (281), bloodshed (17), bloodthirsty (4), guilty of bloodshed (4), it[S] (4 [+2021]), guilt of blood (3), guilt of bloodshed (3), lifeblood (3 [+5883]), bleeding (2), bloodshed (2 [+995, 928]), bloodshed (2 [+4200, 1947]), bloodshed (2 [+1947, 4200]), guilt of shedding blood (2), blood shed (1), blood vengeance (1), blood-stained (1), bloodshed (1 [+5477]), bloodshed (1 [+9161]), bloodstains (1), bloodthirsty (1 [+408]), death (1), do anything that endangers life (1 [+6641, 6584]), flow (1), guilt of murder (1 [+5883]), guilty of blood (1), guilty of murder (1), innocent man (1 [+5929]), it[S] (1), it[S] (1 [+2257]), it[S] (1 [+4946, 2023]), killing (1), massacre (1), murder (1), murderer (1 [+408]), murderer (1 [+408, 2021]), murdering (1), other[S] (1), person[S] (1), shedding of blood (1), NDT (2)

H1948 [1]דָּמָה ***dāmâ[1]***, v. [29] [→ 1952, 1953, 1955; 10179]. [Q] to be like, liken, resemble; [N] to be like; [P] to think, plan, intend; to liken; [Ht] to consider oneself equal to:– compare (4), compared (3), is like (3), be like (2), am like (1), are like (1), been like (1), equal (1), intending (1), intends (1), like (1), liken (1), make myself like (1), match (1), meditate (1), plan (1), planned (1), plotted (1), think (1), thought (1), told parables (1)

H1949 [2]דָּמָה ***dāmâ[2]***, v. [4] [→ 1950, 1951?, 1954; cf. 1875, 1957, 1958]. [Q] to cease; to be silent; [N] to be silenced:– be silenced (1), ceasing (1), silence (1), unceasingly (1 [+4202])

H1950 [3]דָּמָה ***dāmâ[3]***, v. [13] [√ 1949]. [Q] to destroy; [N] to perish, be ruined, be destroyed, be wiped out:– ruined (3), be completely destroyed (2 [+1950]), destroy (2), perish (2), are destroyed (1), be destroyed (1), be wiped out (1), disaster awaits (1)

H1951 דּוּמָה ***dumâ***, n.f. [1] [√ 1949?]. one silenced:– silenced (1)

H1952 דְּמוּת ***dᵉmût***, n.f. [25] [√ 1948]. likeness, figure, image, form:– likeness (5), like (4), looked (3), looked like (3), figure (2), appearance (1), figures (1), form (1), image (1), like (1 [+3869]), looked something like (1), sketch (1), NDT (1)

H1953 דְּמִי ***dᵉmî***, n.[m.] [1] [√ 1948]. prime (of life), a fig. extension of being at a midway point in a journey:– prime (1)

H1954 דֳּמִי ***dᵒmî***, n.[m.] [3] [√ 1949]. silence, rest:– rest (2), silent (1)

H1955 דִּמְיוֹן ***dimyôn***, n.[m.] [1] [√ 1948]. likeness:– like (1)

H1956 דַּמִּים ***dammîm***, n.pr.loc. Not used in NIVEBC [→ 702, 7169; cf. 1947?]. Dammim, see 702

H1957 [1]דָּמַם ***dāmam[1]***, v. [25] [→ 1872, 1875, 1960; cf. 1876, 1949, 1959]. [Q] to be still, be silent, be quiet, rest; [N] to be silenced; [Po] to quiet:– silent (6), be silenced (3), be still (2), ceasing (1), find rest (1), keep quiet (1), quieted (1), quietly (1), rest (1), silence (1), silenced (1), stand still (1), still (1), stood still (1), stops (1), wait (1), waiting in silence (1)

H1958 [2]דָּמַם ***dāmam[2]***, v. Not used in NIVEBC [cf. 1949]. [Q] to wail

H1959 [3]דָּמַם ***dāmam[3]***, v. [4] [cf. 1957]. [Q] to perish; [N] to be laid waste, be destroyed; [H] to doom to perish:– be destroyed (1), doomed to perish (1), perish (1), will be laid waste (1)

H1960 דְּמָמָה ***dᵉmāmâ***, n.f. [3] [√ 1957]. hush, whisper:– hushed (1), whisper (1), whisper (1 [+7754])

H1961 דֹּמֶן ***dōmen***, n.m. [6] [→ 4523]. refuse, dung:– dung (6)

H1962 דִּמְנָה ***dimnâ***, n.pr.loc. [1] Dimnah, "*manure*":– Dimnah (1)

H1963 דָּמַע ***dāma'***, v. [2] [→ 1964, 1965]. [Q] to weep:– weep bitterly (2 [+1963])

H1964 דֶּמַע ***dema'***, n.[m.] [1] [√ 1963]. juice:– vats (1)

H1965 דִּמְעָה ***dim'â***, n.f. [23] [√ 1963]. tears, weeping:– tears (21), weeping (2)

H1966 דַּמֶּשֶׂק ***dammeśeq***, n.pr.loc. [36] [→ 1877, 1967?, 2008]. Damascus:– Damascus (36)

H1967 דְּמֶשֶׁק ***dᵉmešeq***, n.[m.?] [1] [√ 1966?]. a piece of fabric, damask [?]. Or perhaps a variant spelling of the place name Damascus:– piece of fabric (1)

H1968 [1]דָּן ***dān[1]***, n.pr.m. [48] [→ 1970, 1974; cf. 1906]. Dan, "*judge*":– Dan (33), Danites (9 [+1201]), Dan (4 [+1201]), Danite (1 [+4200, 4751]), they[S] (1 [+1201])

H1969 [2]דָּן ***dān[2]***, n.pr.loc. [20] [√ 1906]. Dan, "*judge*":– Dan (20)

H1969.5 דַּן ***dan***, n.m. [1] cask, container, barrel. Conjectured from Ugaritic, Akkadian and Arabic in Eze 27:19:– casks (1)

H1970 דָּן יַעַן ***dān ya'an***, n.pr.loc. [1] [√ 1968 + 3611]. Dan Jaan:– Dan Jaan (1)

H1971 דָּנִאֵל ***dāni'ēl***, n.pr.m. Not used in NIVEBC [√ 1906 + 446]. Danel, Daniel; this can refer to four different persons, the most prominent being the sage and prophet of the captivity, see 1975, "*God is [my] judge*"

H1972 דַּנָּה ***dannâ***, n.pr.loc. [1] [→ 4527]. Dannah, "*stronghold*":– Dannah (1)

H1973 דִּנְהָבָה ***dinhābâ***, n.pr.loc. [2] [√ 1896 + 5649]. Dinhabah:– Dinhabah (2)

H1974 דָּנִי ***dānî***, a.g. [5] [√ 1968]. Danite, men of Dan, "*of Dan*":– Dan (2), Danites (2), Danites (1 [+5476])

H1975 דָּנִיֵּאל ***dāniyyē'l***, n.pr.m. [29] [√ 1906 + 446; 10181]. Daniel, "*God [El] is my judge*":– Daniel (29)

H1976 דֵּעַ ***dēa'***, n.[m.] [5] [→ 1978; cf. 3359]. what is known, knowledge:– what know (3), knowledge (2)

H1977 דָּעָה ***dā'â***, v. Not used in NIVEBC [→ 456]. [Q] to seek, ask about

H1978 דֵּעָה ***dē'â***, n.f. [6] [√ 1976; cf. 3359]. knowledge:– knowledge (3), know (1 [+3780, 928]), knows (1), teach (1 [+3723])

H1979 דְּעוּאֵל ***dᵉ'û'ēl***, n.pr.m. [5] [√ 3359 + 446]. Deuel, "*known of God [El]*":– Deuel (5)

H1980 דָּעַךְ ***dā'ak***, v. [9] [cf. 2403]. [Q] to snuff out, extinguish; [N] to vanish; [Pu] to die out:– snuffed out (5), extinguished (1), goes out (1), vanish (1), were consumed (1)

H1981 [1]דַּעַת ***da'at[1]***, n.f. & m. [91] [√ 3359]. knowledge; understanding, learning:– knowledge (69), know (5), unintentionally (4 [+928, 1172]), acknowledgment (2), has knowledge (2 [+3359]), attained to knowledge (1 [+3359]), have concern (1 [+1067]), it[S] (1), learning (1), notions (1), understanding (1), well informed (1 [+3359]), what know (1), what teach (1)

H1982 [2]דַּעַת ***da'at[2]***, n.f. Not used in NIVEBC [√ 3359]. claim

H1983 [3]דַּעַת ***da'at[3]***, n.f. sweat

H1984 דֹּפִי ***dᵒpî***, n.[m.] [1] blemish, stain; slander:– slander (1 [+5989])

H1985 דָּפַק ***dāpaq***, v. [3] [→ 1986]. [Q] to drive hard; to knock hard (= worry); [Ht] to pound (on a door):– driven hard (1), knocking (1), pounding (1)

H1986 דָּפְקָה ***dopqâ***, n.pr.loc. [2] [√ 1985]. Dophkah, "*drive [sheep]*":– Dophkah (2)

H1987 דַּק ***daq***, a. [14] [√ 1990]. gaunt, thin, dwarfed;

finely ground (incense), fine (dust):– thin (6), fine (2), gaunt (2 [+1414]), dwarf (1), finely ground (1), gentle (1), NDT (1)

H1988 דֹּק ***dōq***, n.[m.] [1] [√ 1990]. canopy, thin veil:– canopy (1)

H1989 דִּקְלָה ***diqlâ***, n.pr.m.[loc.] [2] Diklah, "*[place of] date palms*":– Diklah (2)

H1990 דָּקַק ***dāqaq***, v. [13] [→ 1987, 1988; cf. 1870, 1916, 1917, 1920; 10182]. [Q] to finely crush or grind; [H] to grind to powder, break to pieces; [Ho] to be ground (to make bread):– powder (3), ground (2), be ground (1), break to pieces (1), broke to pieces (1), broke up (1), crush (1), fine (1), pounded (1), use to grind (1)

H1991 דָּקַר ***dāqar***, v. [11] [→ 1206, 1992, 4532]. [Q] to drive through, pierce, stab; [Qp, N, Pu] to be pierced:– run through (3), be thrust through (1), drove into (1), fatally wounded (1), pierced (1), racked with hunger (1), ran through (1), stab (1), wounded (1)

H1992 דֶּקֶר ***deqer***, n.pr.m. Not used in NIVEBC [√ 1991]. Deker, see 1206

H1993 דַּר ***dar***, n.[m.] [1] mother-of-pearl:– mother-of-pearl (1)

H1994 דֵּרָאוֹן ***dērā'ôn***, n.m. [2] loathing, contempt, aversion:– contempt (1), loathsome (1)

H1995 דָּרְבָן ***dorbān***, n.[m.] [1] [→ 1996]. (iron) goading stick:– goads (1)

H1996 דָּרְבֹנָה ***dorbōnâ***, n.[f.] [1] [√ 1995]. (iron) goading stick:– goads (1)

H1997 דַּרְדַּע ***darda'***, n.pr.m. [2] [cf. 2009]. Darda:– Darda (2)

H1998 דַּרְדַּר ***dardar***, n.[m.] [2] thistle:– thistles (2)

H1999 דָּרוֹם ***dārôm***, n.m. [19] south; south wind:– south (14), south (3 [+2006, 2021]), south wind (1), southward (1)

H2000 [1]דְּרוֹר ***d[e]rôr[1]***, n.f. [2] a kind of bird, perhaps swallow or dove:– swallow (2)

H2001 [2]דְּרוֹר ***d[e]rôr[2]***, n.[m.] [1] oil of myrrh, stacte:– liquid (1)

H2002 [3]דְּרוֹר ***d[e]rôr[3]***, n.[m.] [7] freedom, liberty; an event required every fifty years to restore Israelite slaves to freedom and Israelite land to tribal allotments:– freedom (5), freedom for slaves (1), liberty (1)

H2003 דָּרְיָוֶשׁ ***dār[e]yāweš***, n.pr.m. [10] [√ 10184]. Darius, "*he who upholds the good*":– Darius (10)

H2004 דָּרְיוֹשׁ ***daryôš***, v. see 2011

H2005 דָּרַךְ ***dārak***, v. [63] [→ 2006, 4534]. [Q] to go out, set out, march on, walk upon, trample; to bend (a bow); [Qp] to string (a bow), be bent (of a bow); [H] to shoot (a bow); to cause to tread, to enable to go; to lead, guide:– bend (4), trampled (4), tread (4), treads (4), draw (3), treading (3), guide (2), march (2), set (2), strung (2), trodden (2), aim (1), archer (1), bent (1), come (1), cross over (1), direct (1), directs (1), draw the bow (1), drew (1), enables to tread (1), go (1), guides (1), handle (1), lead (1), led (1), make ready to shoot (1), march on (1), overran (1), press (1), set feet (1), set foot on (1), step (1), string (1), treads out (1), trod (1), use (1), walked (1), walks (1), with bows (1 [+8008]), NDT (2)

H2006 דֶּרֶךְ ***derek***, n.m. [705] [√ 2005]. way, path, route, road, journey; by extension: conduct, way of life; a pagan god (Amos 8:14):– way (170), ways (166), road (60), journey (30), path (21), conduct (18), obedience (15), toward (15), direction (9), roads (8), through (8), route (7), paths (5), what done (5), east (4 [+2021, 7708]), obedience (4 [+3972]), pass by (4 [+6296]), side (4), to (4), as (3 [+928]), by (3), course (3), highway (3), mission (3), on (3), roadside (3), south (3 [+2021, 1999]), works (3), all do (2), do (2), go to (2), leads (2), life (2), main road (2 [+2006]), north (2 [+2021, 7600]), passageway (2), street (2), trackless (2 [+4202]), what[s] (2 [+2021]), wherever (2 [+928, 2021, 889]), action (1), along (1), at (1 [+928, 2021]), behavior (1), blameless (1 [+9447]), by way of (1), course of life (1), crossroads (1), custom (1), did (1), dispersed (1 [+2143, 4200]), distance (1), distances (1), distant (1 [+8049, 2021]), do so[s] (1 [+8740, 4946]), done (1), east (1 [+7156, 2021, 7708, 2025]), everything do (1), extending (1), facing (1), fate (1), favors (1), following (1), go (1 [+2143, 928]), god (1), going about (1), him (1 [+2257]), how behaved (1), how live (1), justice (1), leads to (1), let get away (1 [+8938, 928]), line (1), lives (1), long (1), march (1), military campaign (1), missions (1), north (1 [+7156, 2021, 7600]), northward (1 [+2021, 7600]), on way (1 [+6913]), path (1 [+784]), period (1 [+851]), person of integrity (1 [+9448]), place (1), room (1), routes (1), running here and there (1 [+8592]), siege ramp (1), skilled (1 [+3512]), streets (1), strength (1), that[s] (1), there[s] (1 [+928, 2021]), things did (1), toward (1 [+448]), toward (1 [+6584]), toward (1 [+6584, 7156]), travel (1 [+6296]), traveled (1), traveled (1 [+2143]), traveling (1), upright (1 [+3838]), vigor (1), walk (1), walk (1 [+2143, 928]), walked (1), walking along (1 [+928, 2021]), waylaid (1 [+8492, 928, 2021]), westward (1 [+339]), what did (1), where[s] (1 [+2021]), wherever (1 [+2021, 928, 889]), which way (1 [+361, 2296, 2021]), NDT (23)

H2007 דַּרְכְּמוֹנִים ***dark[e]mônîm***, n.[m.] [4] [→ 163]. (pl.) drachmas (Persian: a unit of weight used as a money, the value of which is uncertain):– darics (4)

H2008 דַּרְמֶשֶׂק ***darmeśeq***, n.pr.loc. [6] [√ 1966]. Damascus:– Damascus (6)

H2009 דָּרַע ***dāra'***, n.pr.m. Not used in NIVEBC [cf. 1997]. Daraa, see 1997

H2010 דַּרְקוֹן ***darqôn***, n.pr.m. [2] Darkon, "[perhaps] *rough* or *stern*":– Darkon (2)

H2011 דָּרַשׁ ***dāraš***, v. [162] [→ 4535]. [Q] to seek, inquire, consult; [Qp] to ponder, be sought after; [N] to let oneself be inquired of, to allow a search to be made:– seek (35), inquire of (19), sought (11), consult (5), seeking (5), consult (4 [+928]), inquire of (4 [+928]), call to account (3), demand an accounting (3), cares for (2), certainly demand (2 [+2011]), consults (2), inquired about (2 [+2011]), investigate (2), let inquire of (2 [+4200]), look (2), require (2), search for (2), searches (2), seek help (2), seek out (2), seeks (2), sought out (2), study (2), appeal (1), are pondered (1), ask (1), ask (1 [+1821]), asked (1), avenges (1), call to account (1 [+4946, 6640]), care about (1), care for (1), carefully investigated (1 [+2256, 1335]), cares (1), come looking for (1), consult (1 [+928, 1821]), consulted (1), find out (1), follow (1), give an accounting (1), guidance (1), hold accountable (1 [+4946, 3338]), inquire (1), inquire of (1 [+448]), inquire of (1 [+4200]), inquire of (1 [+4946, 907]), inquired of (1), inquiring (1), let inquire of (1), let inquire of at all (1 [+4200, 2011]), let inquire of at all (1 [+2011, 4200]), look to (1), make investigation (1), probe (1), rally (1), required (1 [+6584]), revealed myself (1), search was made (1), searched (1), searches for (1), seek will (1), selects (1), sought after (1), worked for (1), would (1), yield to plea (1)

H2012 דָּשָׁא ***dāšā'***, v. [2] [→ 2013]. [Q] to become green (of pastures); [H] to produce, cause to shoot forth:– green (1), produce (1)

H2013 דֶּשֶׁא ***deše'***, n.m. [14] [√ 2012; 10187]. (new) green vegetation, (new) green grass:– grass (4), green (4), vegetation (3), grass (1 [+4604]), new grass (1), new growth (1)

H2014 [1]דָּשֵׁן ***dāšēn[1]***, v. [11] [→ 2015, 2016]. [Q] to thrive, grow fat; [P] to anoint, give health; to remove the (fat) ashes; [Pu] to prosper, be satisfied, be soaked (with fat); [Hotpaal] to be covered with fat:– prosper (2), remove ashes (2), accept (1), anoint (1), are fully satisfied (1), be soaked (1), gives health (1), is covered (1), thrive (1)

H2015 [2]דָּשֵׁן ***dāšēn[2]***, a. [2] [√ 2014]. rich (pertaining to food which is fresh and possibly juicy), fresh:– fresh (1), rich (1)

H2016 דֶּשֶׁן ***dešen***, n.m. [16] [√ 2014]. fat; ashes (the burned wood of the altar fire soaked with fat); by extension: abundance, rich foods, choice food; in the ancient Near East fatness was a positive, enviable state, though extreme obesity could be denounced or ridiculed:– ashes (7), abundance (3), ash (1), choice food (1), oil (1), rich (1), richest of fare (1), richest of foods (1 [+2693, 2256])

H2017 דָּת ***dāt***, n.f. [21] [√ 10186]. command (either written or oral), prescription, custom, edict, law:– edict (8), law (6), laws (2), command (1), customs (1), order (1), orders (1), prescribed (1)

H2018 דָּתָן ***dātān***, n.pr.m. [10] Dathan, "*strong*":– Dathan (10)

H2019 דֹּתָן ***dōtān***, n.pr.loc. [3] Dothan, "*two wells*":– Dothan (3)

H2020 ה ***h***, letter. Not used in NIVEBC [√ 10189]. letter of the Hebrew alphabet

H2021 -הַ ***ha-***, art.pref. [30270] [√ 10002; *also used with compound proper names*]. the, a, who, this, that; often not translated:– the (16153), a (746), who (454), that (199), this (150), his[s] (146), those (146), today (139 [+3427]), their[s] (102), an (73), what (67), your[s] (60), these (55), each (38), today (38 [+3427, 2021, 2296]), today (38 [+2021, 3427, 2296]), he[s] (37), this[s] (34 [+1821, 2021, 2296]), my[s] (33), him[s] (29 [+4889]), this[s] (28 [+2021, 1821, 2296]), its[s] (26), anyone (24), her[s] (24), one (24), what[s] (23 [+1821]), you[s] (23), whoever (22), any (19), they[s] (19 [+6639]), always (18 [+3972, 3427]), which (18), now (17 [+2021, 3427, 2296]), them[s] (17 [+6639]), they[s] (17), birds (16 [+6416, 9028]), he[s] (16 [+3913]), he[s] (16 [+4889]), other[s] (16), now (15 [+3427, 2021, 2296]), our[s] (14), now (13 [+3427]), this[s] (12 [+2021, 1821, 2296]), at twilight (11 [+1068, 6847]), everything (11 [+3972, 1821]), this[s] (11 [+1821, 2021, 465]), this[s] (11 [+2021, 1821, 465]), whatever (11), burned (10 [+8596, 928, 836]), he[s] (10 [+4889]), burn down (9 [+8596, 928, 836]), some[s] (9), tonight (9 [+4326]), everyone (8 [+3972, 5883]), it[s] (8 [+1473]), what[s] (8 [+1821]), every (7), it[s] (7 [+6551]), outside (7 [+928, 2575]), they[s] (7 [+6639]), your Majesty (7 [+4889]), before (6 [+928, 8037]), her[s] (6 [+851]), him[s] (6), his[s] (6 [+4889]), prison (6 [+1074, 6045]), secretly (6 [+928, 6260]), set on fire (6 [+3675, 928, 836]), she[s] (6 [+851]), some time later (6 [+339, 1821, 2021, 465]), some time later (6 [+339, 2021, 1821, 465]), sunset (6 [+995, 9087]), they[s] (6 [+408]), this[s] (6 [+1821, 2021, 2296]), those[s] (6 [+6639]), as long as (5 [+3972, 3427]), burn (5 [+8596, 928, 836]), he[s] (5 [+408]), it[s] (5 [+1821]), stone (5 [+8083, 928, 74]), this[s] (5 [+1821]), very old (5 [+2416, 995, 928, 3427]), Trans-Euphrates (4 [+6298, 5643]), allotted (4 [+928, 1598]), anyone (4 [+4769, 408]), be burned up (4 [+8596, 928, 836]), burning (4 [+6584, 836]), day after day (4 [+3972, 3427]), east (4 [+2006, 7708]), every morning (4 [+928, 1332, 928, 2021, 1332]), falsely (4 [+4200, 9214]), first (4 [+3869, 3427]), in vain (4 [+4200, 8736]), it[s] (4), it[s] (4 [+1821, 2021, 2296]), it[s] (4 [+2021, 1821, 2296]), it[s] (4 [+6551]), its[s] (4 [+380]), people (4 [+1201, 132]), prison (4 [+1074, 3975]), set on fire (4 [+8596, 928, 836]), she[s] (4 [+5855]), them[s] (4), there[s] (4 [+928, 1195]), they[s] (4 [+2085, 2021, 5883]), they[s] (4 [+2021, 2085, 5883]), those[s] (4 [+408]), anyone (3 [+5883]), anyone (3 [+408]), burn up (3 [+8596, 928, 836]), burned down (3 [+8596, 928, 836]), burned up (3 [+8596, 928, 836]), east (3 [+4667, 9087]), ever since (3 [+6330, 3427, 2021, 2296]), ever since (3 [+6330, 2021, 3427, 2296]), everyone (3 [+3972, 132]), first (3 [+928, 9378]), forever (3 [+3972, 3427]), he[s] (3 [+7149]), her[s] (3 [+5855]), him[s] (3 [+408]), his own[s] (3), his own[s] (3 [+4889]), it[s] (3 [+5999]), it[s] (3 [+6219]), it[s] (3 [+4640]), it[s] (3 [+2215]), it[s] (3 [+912]), it[s] (3 [+5438]), it[s] (3 [+5596]), it[s] (3 [+1074]), its[s] (3 [+824]), its[s] (3 [+4640]), men[s] (3), misuse (3 [+5951, 4200, 8736]), on high (3 [+928, 5294]), set on fire (3 [+3675, 836, 928]), someone (3), south (3 [+2006, 1999]), stone (3 [+6232, 928, 74]), their own[s] (3), them (3 [+6639]), them[s] (3 [+3051]), them[s] (3 [+7931]), them[s] (3 [+7971]), them[s] (3 [+3913]), they[s] (3 [+6639]), they[s] (3 [+408]), this[s] (3 [+2021, 2296, 1821]), those[s] (3 [+408]), trees (3 [+6770, 8441]), what[s] (3), what[s] (3 [+5126]), what[s] (3 [+2021, 1821, 2296]), what[s] (3 [+1821, 2021, 2296]), who[s] (3 [+3913]), whose (3), wild (3 [+928, 8441]), you (3), Amaziah[s] (2 [+4889]), David's[s] (2), Judah[s] (2 [+824]), all[s] (2), all day long (2 [+928, 3427, 2021, 2085]), all day long (2 [+928, 2021, 3427, 2085]), allotted (2 [+5989, 928, 1598]), angels (2 [+1201, 466]), another[s] (2), anyone (2 [+3972, 132]), anyone (2 [+3972, 408]), anyone[s] (2), anything (2), anything (2 [+3972, 3998]), at (2 [+928, 2942, 6330]), certain (2), champion (2 [+408, 1227]), chief officer (2 [+8569, 7372]), completely (2 [+4200, 3972]), continual (2 [+3972, 3427]), continually (2 [+3972, 3427]), dawn (2 [+240, 1332]), daybreak (2 [+240, 1332]), daybreak (2 [+6590, 8840]), earlier (2 [+928, 9378]), east (2 [+4667, 2025, 9087]), ever (2 [+3972, 3427]), every morning (2 [+928, 2021, 1332, 928, 1332]), every morning (2 [+928, 2021, 1332, 928, 1332]), everyone (2 [+408]), everyone (2 [+3972, 6639]), first (2 [+928, 8037]), for life (2 [+3972, 3427]), forever (2 [+6330, 6409]), gave the message (2 [+1819, 3972, 2021, 465, 1821]), he[s] (2 [+466]), he[s] (2 [+408]), here[s] (2 [+5226, 2021, 2296]), here[s] (2 [+2021, 5226, 2296]), him[s] (2 [+5853]), him[s] (2 [+2085, 2021, 408]), him[s] (2 [+2021, 2085, 408]), his own[s] (2 [+3913]), human (2 [+1201, 132]), in (2 [+2025, 1074]), inside (2 [+928, 1074]), it (2), it[s] (2 [+7339]), it[s] (2 [+836]), it[s] (2 [+5577]), it[s] (2 [+3542]), it[s] (2 [+1947]), it[s] (2 [+380]), it[s] (2 [+824]), it[s] (2 [+9310]), it[s] (2 [+8120]), it[s] (2 [+824]), it[s] (2 [+185]), it[s] (2 [+778]), it[s] (2 [+3542]), it[s] (2 [+824]), it[s] (2 [+4966]), it[s] (2 [+1947]), it[s] (2 [+7228]), it[s] (2 [+4640]), its[s] (2 [+9133]), its[s] (2 [+1074]), its[s] (2 [+3284]), its[s] (2 [+2958]), its[s] (2 [+7228]), misuses (2 [+5951, 4200, 8736]), north (2 [+2006, 7600]), now (2 [+3869, 6961]), now (2 [+928, 3427, 2021, 465]), on high (2 [+4200, 5294]), one[s] (2 [+6639]), one[s] (2), one's (2), prison (2 [+1074, 3989]), privately (2 [+928, 6260]), quietly (2 [+928, 4319]), something[s] (2), still (2 [+6330, 3427, 2021, 2296]), still (2 [+6330, 2021, 3427, 2296]), stoned (2 [+6232, 928, 74]), such (2), sunrise (2 [+2436, 9087]), sunset (2 [+6961, 995, 9087]), the other[s] (2 [+7895, 824]), their[s] (2 [+964]), their[s] (2 [+6639]), them[s] (2 [+3338]), them[s] (2 [+8993]), them[s] (2 [+3972, 6639]), them[s] (2 [+2085, 2021, 408]), them[s] (2 [+2021, 2085, 408]), them[s] (2 [+408]), them[s] (2 [+4131]), them[s] (2 [+5853]), them[s] (2 [+408]), then (2 [+928, 340]), there[s] (2 [+824]), there[s] (2 [+928, 1074]), they[s] (2 [+7366]), they[s] (2 [+6639, 824]), they[s] (2 [+8357]), they[s] (2 [+3913]), this[s] (2 [+2296, 2021, 1821]), this[s] (2 [+2021, 1821, 2296]), this very (2), those[s] (2 [+408]), those[s] (2 [+5877]), two-horned (2 [+1251, 7967]), used to (2 [+4200, 8037]), what[s] (2 [+1821, 2021, 465]), what[s] (2 [+2021, 1821, 465]), what[s] (2 [+2006]), where[s] (2 [+5226]), wherever (2 [+928, 2006, 889]), wherever (2 [+928, 3972, 5226, 889]), whoever (2 [+4769, 408]), whose[s] (2), Boaz[s] (1 [+408]), Israelite (1 [+408, 3778]), Israel's[s] (1), Jacob's[s] (1), Jether[s] (1 [+5853]), Jonah's[s] (1), Naomi[s] (1 [+851]), O (1), Saul's[s] (1), Ziklag[s] (1 [+6551]), above (1 [+928, 5294]), accuses (1 [+7756, 4200, 5477]), after a while (1 [+339, 1821, 2021, 465]), after a while (1 [+339, 2021, 1821, 465]), afternoon (1 [+5742, 3427]), again (1 [+1685, 928, 7193, 2021, 2085]), again (1 [+1685, 928, 2021, 7193, 2085]), age of childbearing (1 [+784, 3869, 851]), ago (1 [+3427]), all (1 [+3972, 408]), all night long (1 [+928, 4326]), all people (1 [+1201, 132]), all-night (1 [+3972, 4326]), allotted (1 [+2118, 1598, 928]), already (1 [+9378, 928]), among (1 [+928, 9348]), annual (1 [+7193, 928, 9102]), annual (1 [+285, 928, 9102]), anointed

(1 [+3658, 1201]), another[s] (1 [+9019]), another[s] (1 [+132]), another[s] (1 [+2215, 4946, 2296]), anyone (1 [+3972, 5883]), anyone[s] (1 [+4637]), anything (1 [+3972, 1821]), anything (1 [+1821, 4946, 3972, 1821]), anything[s] (1), archers (1 [+4619, 928, 8008]), archers (1 [+4619, 408, 928, 8008]), are burned up (1 [+8596, 928, 836, 8596]), around (1 [+4200, 2575]), around (1 [+4946, 2575]), assemble (1 [+6590, 928, 7736]), at (1 [+928, 2006]), at last (1 [+7193]), at once (1 [+3427]), at once (1 [+928, 3427]), at once (1 [+928, 6961, 2021, 2085]), at once (1 [+928, 2021, 6961, 2085]), at once (1 [+928, 3427, 2021, 2085]), at once (1 [+928, 2021, 3427, 2085]), at this time (1 [+3427]), away (1 [+448, 2575, 2025]), banded together (1 [+665, 4200, 2653]), be burned (1 [+8596, 928, 836]), be burned down (1 [+8596, 928, 836]), be taken captive (1 [+9530, 928, 4090]), before (1 [+928, 9378]), beginning (1 [+3427]), below (1 [+6584, 141]), below deck (1 [+3752, 6208]), besiege (1 [+995, 928, 5189]), blind (1 [+6427, 5782, 928]), both[s] (1 [+170, 2256, 2021, 8533]), both[s] (1 [+2021, 170, 2256, 8533]), bought (1 [+7864, 928, 4084]), breeding (1 [+3501, 7366]), brings to ruin (1 [+6156, 4200, 8273]), burn (1 [+1277, 928, 241]), burn to death (1 [+8596, 928, 836]), burned (1 [+8938, 928, 836]), burned down (1 [+8596, 836]), burned to death (1 [+8596, 928, 836]), callous (1 [+3869, 2693]), captain (1 [+8042, 2480]), cargo (1 [+3998, 889, 928, 641]), carry off (1 [+995, 928, 8660]), charred (1 [+1277, 928, 836]), claimed too soon (1 [+987, 928, 8037]), commander in chief (1 [+6584, 7372]), community (1 [+6639, 824]), counterattack (1 [+2200, 928, 4878]), crops (1 [+7262, 141]), daily (1 [+4200, 3427]), daybreak (1 [+1332, 240]), daybreak (1 [+7155, 1332]), daylight (1 [+240, 1332]), deep (1 [+6584, 7156, 824]), did so[s] (1 [+6913, 906, 7175]), distant (1 [+8049, 2006]), doing this[s] (1 [+3569, 6894]), doubly (1 [+928, 9109]), down (1 [+4946, 9028]), dreamer (1 [+1251, 2706]), each[s] (1 [+4090]), each day (1 [+4200, 3427]), each day (1 [+4200, 3427, 4200, 2021, 3427]), each day (1 [+4200, 2021, 3427, 4200, 3427]), each morning (1 [+928, 1332, 928, 2021, 1332]), each morning (1 [+928, 2021, 1332, 928, 1332]), each morning (1 [+4200, 1332, 4200, 2021, 1332]), each morning (1 [+4200, 2021, 1332, 4200, 1332]), earthly (1 [+4946, 824]), east (1 [+7156, 2006, 7708, 2025]), end (1 [+2118, 928, 340]), enthrones (1 [+3782, 4200, 4058]), especially bred (1 [+1201, 8247]), evening (1 [+6961, 6847]), evening (1 [+928, 6847, 928, 2021, 6847]), evening (1 [+928, 2021, 6847, 928, 6847]), every day (1 [+4200, 3427]), every evening (1 [+928, 6847, 928, 2021, 6847]), every evening (1 [+928, 2021, 6847, 928, 6847]), everyone (1 [+3972, 408]), everyone[s] (1), everyone's (1 [+3972, 132]), everything (1 [+3972]), everything (1 [+3972, 4856]), everything (1 [+3972, 1821, 2021, 465]), everything (1 [+3972, 2021, 1821, 465]), everywhere (1 [+3972, 5226]), everywhere (1 [+928, 3972, 824]), extort (1 [+928, 6945]), fiercely (1 [+928, 6677]), fight (1 [+3655, 4200, 4878]), followers (1 [+6639, 889, 339]), for a while (1 [+3869, 3427]), foreigner (1 [+1201, 5797]), foreigners (1 [+1201, 5797]), forevermore (1 [+6330, 6409]), formerly (1 [+928, 8037]), furthermore (1 [+2256, 9108]), get out (1 [+8938, 2575, 2025]), give in marriage (1 [+5989, 851]), going up (1 [+6590, 9028, 2025]), grown old (1 [+2416, 995, 928, 3427]), hard (1 [+3668, 4200, 4607]), he[s] (1 [+4855]), he[s] (1 [+5853]), he[s] (1 [+3913]), he[s] (1 [+7595]), he[s] (1 [+3758, 5566]), he[s] (1 [+3381, 3913]), he[s] (1 [+466, 824]), he[s] (1 [+408, 5283]), he[s] (1 [+408, 2021, 340]), he[s] (1 [+2021, 5883, 2085]), he[s] (1 [+2021, 408, 340]), he[s] (1 [+5883, 2021, 2085]), he[s] (1 [+408, 2021, 8886, 6640]), he[s] (1 [+2021, 408, 8886, 6640]), he himself[s] (1 [+3913]), here[s] (1 [+824]), here[s] (1 [+5226]), here[s] (1 [+928, 4497]), here[s] (1 [+928, 824]), here[s] (1 [+928, 5226, 2021, 2296]), here[s] (1 [+928, 2021, 5226, 2296]), him[s] (1 [+7140]), him[s] (1 [+7127]), him[s] (1 [+3450]), him[s] (1 [+7149]), him[s] (1 [+8357]), him[s] (1 [+466]), him[s] (1 [+3759, 5566]), him[s] (1 [+1201, 3778]), himself[s] (1 [+408]), his[s] (1 [+408]), his[s] (1 [+5566]), his[s] (1 [+4637]), his[s] (1 [+928, 4889]), his own[s] (1 [+5566, 2021, 2418]), his own[s] (1 [+2021, 5566, 2418]), how (1 [+928, 4537, 686]), human beings (1 [+1201, 132]), humans (1 [+1201, 132]), immediately (1 [+3869, 3427]), imprisoned (1 [+5989, 1074, 657]), in (1 [+1074, 2025]), in broad daylight (1 [+5584, 9087]), in broad daylight (1 [+4200, 6524, 9087, 2021, 2296]), in broad daylight (1 [+4200, 6524, 2021, 9087, 2296]), in midair (1 [+1068, 9028, 2256, 1068, 2021, 824]), in midair (1 [+1068, 2021, 9028, 2256, 1068, 824]), in the west (1 [+4427, 9087]), infamous (1 [+3238, 9005]), inside (1 [+448, 1074]), it (1 [+778]), it (1 [+3136]), it (1 [+4058]), it (1 [+4114]), it (1 [+4640]), it[s] (1 [+8367]), it[s] (1 [+2162]), it[s] (1 [+5261]), it[s] (1 [+2706]), it[s] (1 [+258]), it[s] (1 [+1580]), it[s] (1 [+6770]), it[s] (1 [+2570]), it[s] (1 [+6322]), it[s] (1 [+7498]), it[s] (1 [+1946]), it[s] (1 [+8288]), it[s] (1 [+4223]), it[s] (1 [+680]), it[s] (1 [+2851]), it[s] (1 [+5120]), it[s] (1 [+1821]), it[s] (1 [+7663]), it[s] (1 [+4258]), it[s] (1 [+6320]), it[s] (1 [+6639]), it[s] (1 [+9024]), it[s] (1 [+1473]), it[s] (1 [+7815]), it[s] (1 [+185]), it[s] (1 [+6727]), it[s] (1 [+4784]), it[s] (1 [+8441]), it[s] (1 [+4722]), it[s] (1 [+8538]), it[s] (1 [+1074]), it[s] (1 [+6592]), it[s] (1 [+9043]), it[s] (1 [+2633]), it[s] (1 [+8701]), it[s] (1 [+3855]), it[s] (1 [+8407]), it[s] (1 [+8947]), it[s] (1 [+778]), it[s] (1 [+1352]), it[s] (1 [+6174]), it[s] (1 [+4084]), it[s] (1 [+8385]), it[s] (1 [+9133, 4889]), it[s] (1 [+778, 466]), it[s] (1 [+1581, 793]), it[s] (1 [+1473, 616]), it[s] (1 [+778, 1382]), it[s] (1 [+6551, 2021, 2296]), it[s] (1 [+5226, 2021, 2085]), it[s] (1 [+2021, 7606, 2645]), it[s] (1 [+2021, 6551, 2296]), it[s] (1 [+2021, 8878, 2296]), it[s] (1 [+2021, 5226, 2085]), it[s] (1 [+7606, 2021, 2645]), it[s] (1 [+824, 2021, 2296]), it[s] (1 [+2021, 824, 2296]), it[s] (1 [+8878, 2021, 2296]), its (1), its[s] (1 [+7407]), its[s] (1 [+3720]), its[s] (1 [+7175]), its[s] (1 [+871]), its[s] (1 [+6425]), its[s] (1 [+6592]), its[s] (1 [+2633]), its[s] (1 [+4963]), its[s] (1 [+4200, 4058]), its[s] (1 [+928, 6551]), it's[s] (1 [+3427]), just (1 [+3427]), just now (1 [+3427]), laid siege (1 [+995, 928, 5189]), lamb (1 [+8445, 928, 3897]), lamb (1 [+8445, 928, 4166]), last night (1 [+4326]), last watch of the night (1 [+874, 1332]), lasting (1 [+6330, 3427, 2021, 2296]), lasting (1 [+6330, 2021, 3427, 2296]), later (1 [+928, 340]), later (1 [+339, 1821, 2021, 465]), later (1 [+339, 2021, 1821, 465]), leads (1 [+928, 8037]), leveled completely (1 [+9164, 928, 9168]), lies in wait (1 [+741, 928, 5041]), like (1 [+928, 3202, 4200]), live (1 [+928, 2644]), lived (1 [+928, 1074]), long ago (1 [+928, 8037]), long life (1 [+4200, 2644]), mankind (1 [+1201, 132]), man's (1 [+1201, 132]), mealtime (1 [+6961, 431]), midnight (1 [+2942, 4326]), mounted (1 [+928, 6061]), murderer (1 [+408, 1947]), must sell (1 [+4835, 928, 4084, 4835]), native-born (1 [+275, 824]), native-born (1 [+3528, 928, 824]), natural (1 [+3869, 3972, 132]), never (1 [+4202, 3972, 3427]), nightfall (1 [+4326]), no (1 [+4202]), noon (1 [+4734, 3427]), north (1 [+7156, 2006, 7600]), northward (1 [+2006, 7600]), nothing (1 [+4202, 3972]), now (1 [+7193]), now (1 [+928, 2021, 3427, 465]), now (1 [+928, 2021, 3427, 465]), offspring (1 [+7262, 1061]), on all sides (1 [+3869, 1885]), on each side (1 [+4946, 6298, 4946, 2296, 4946, 2021, 6298, 4946, 2296]), on each side (1 [+4946, 2021, 6298, 4946, 2296, 4946, 6298, 4946, 2296]), on fire (1 [+1277, 928, 836]), on foot (1 [+6584, 824]), once a year (1 [+4946, 7891, 3427, 4200, 3427]), once again (1 [+3869, 8037]), once more (1 [+421, 7193]), one[s] (1 [+4131]), one[s] (1 [+5566]), one another (1 [+6639]), one's[s] (1), oppressed (1 [+6913, 928, 6945]), other nationalities (1 [+6639, 824]), others[s] (1), others[s] (1 [+6296]), others[s] (1 [+851]), out here (1 [+928, 2575]), outdoor (1 [+928, 2575]), outer (1 [+4200, 2575]), outside the family (1 [+2575, 2025, 2424]), overboard (1 [+448, 3542]), pardon (1 [+1065, 6411]), pardon (1 [+6411, 6584]), penned up (1 [+3973, 1074, 928]), people[s] (1), people[s] (1 [+8011]), people's (1 [+1201, 132]), perjurers (1 [+8678, 4200, 9214]), perjury (1 [+8678, 4200, 9214]), permanently (1 [+4200, 7552]), places[s] (1), plant (1 [+6912, 8441]), plotting (1 [+3086, 8288]), preserved (1 [+8492, 928, 2645]), priestly (1 [+4200, 3913]), prison (1 [+1074, 673]), prison (1 [+1074, 4551]), prison (1 [+1074, 7213]), privately (1 [+928, 4319]), privately (1 [+928, 8952]), put on makeup (1 [+6167, 928, 7037]), put out (1 [+3655, 2575]), ready for battle (1 [+7372, 928, 4878]), ready for battle (1 [+408, 7372, 4200, 4878]), recently (1 [+3427]), reflects (1 [+4200, 132]), reflects (1 [+4200, 7156]), regular (1 [+3972, 3427]), sabbath after sabbath (1 [+928, 3427, 8701, 928, 3427, 2021, 8701]), sabbath after sabbath (1 [+928, 3427, 2021, 8701, 928, 3427, 8701]), safely (1 [+4200, 8934]), said (1 [+1819, 1821]), sail (1 [+2143, 928, 641]), sandaled (1 [+928, 5837]), scoundrel (1 [+408, 1175]), see (1 [+8011, 4200, 6524]), set ablaze (1 [+3675, 928, 836]), set farther back (1 [+2958, 337]), set fire to (1 [+8596, 928, 836]), set fire to (1 [+8938, 928, 836]), seven-day periods (1 [+8679, 3427]), she[s] (1), she[s] (1 [+4893]), shoot (1 [+928, 8008]), shrub (1 [+3972, 8489, 8441]), similar (1 [+3869, 5260]), sling stones (1 [+928, 74]), smoothed (1 [+1760, 928, 4490]), sober (1 [+3655, 3516, 4946]), some distance (1 [+3896, 824]), someone (1 [+285, 6639]), someone (1 [+3972, 132]), someone[s] (1 [+5877]), southward (1 [+448, 3545]), spreads feathers to run (1 [+5257, 928, 5294]), spring (1 [+6524, 4784]), spring (1 [+9588, 9102]), steward[s] (1 [+408, 889, 6584, 1074]), still (1 [+3869, 3427, 2021, 2296]), still (1 [+3869, 2021, 3427, 2296]), stoned (1 [+8083, 928, 74]), stoning (1 [+8083, 928, 74]), such[s] (1 [+6913]), suggested (1 [+1821, 2021, 2296]), suggested (1 [+2021, 1821, 2296]), sunset (1 [+995, 3064]), tent-dwelling (1 [+928, 185]), that[s] (1 [+1821, 2021, 465]), that[s] (1 [+2021, 1074, 2296]), that[s] (1 [+2021, 1821, 465]), that[s] (1 [+1074, 2021, 2296]), that happened (1 [+1821, 465, 2021]), that happened (1 [+1821, 2021, 465]), the[s] (1), the place[s] (1), their (1), their[s] (1 [+3913]), their[s] (1 [+465]), their[s] (1 [+408]), their[s] (1 [+4131]), their[s] (1 [+1201, 1769]), their[s] (1 [+6639, 824]), their[s] (1 [+4200, 2498]), their own[s] (1 [+367]), them (1 [+3192]), them (1 [+4291]), them[s] (1 [+5566]), them[s] (1 [+132]), them[s] (1 [+5987]), them[s] (1 [+6109]), them[s] (1 [+7736]), them[s] (1 [+9149]), them[s] (1 [+7700]), them[s] (1 [+1522]), them[s] (1 [+912]), them[s] (1 [+2143]), them[s] (1 [+4291]), them[s] (1 [+5596]), them[s] (1 [+7194]), them[s] (1 [+3192]), them[s] (1 [+7983]), them[s] (1 [+4283]), them[s] (1 [+5999]), them[s] (1 [+6551, 824]), them[s] (1 [+36, 278]), them[s] (1 [+9109, 3192]), them[s] (1 [+9109, 74]), them[s] (1 [+6929, 7983]), them[s] (1 [+1821, 2021, 2296]), them[s] (1 [+3998, 1074, 466]), them[s] (1 [+2021, 1821, 2296]), them[s] (1 [+6639, 2021, 2296]), them[s] (1 [+2021, 6639, 2296]), then[s] (1 [+6961, 2021, 2085]), then[s] (1 [+2021, 6961, 2085]), then[s] (1 [+928, 3427, 2021, 2085]), then[s] (1 [+928, 2021, 3427, 2085]), there (1 [+928, 1195]), there (1 [+928, 2215]), there[s] (1 [+3720]), there[s] (1 [+9399]), there[s] (1 [+8441]), there[s] (1 [+928, 5207]), there[s] (1 [+928, 6551]), there[s] (1 [+928, 2006]), there[s] (1 [+928, 4722]), there[s] (1 [+928, 824]), there[s] (1 [+928, 1014]), there[s] (1 [+928, 2215]), there[s] (1 [+928, 3752, 1074]), these[s] (1 [+74]), these[s] (1 [+2693]), these men[s] (1 [+6913, 4856]), they (1), they (1 [+2085, 2021, 5883]), they (1 [+2021, 2085, 5883]), they[s] (1 [+8569]), they[s] (1 [+4855]), they[s] (1 [+5954]), they[s] (1 [+4784]), they[s] (1 [+6296]), they[s] (1 [+3374]), they[s] (1 [+4619]), they[s] (1 [+851]), they[s] (1 [+9133]), they[s] (1 [+7736]), they[s] (1 [+3452]), they[s] (1 [+8103]), they[s] (1 [+7665]), they[s] (1 [+964]), they[s] (1 [+746]), they[s] (1 [+4291]), they[s] (1 [+3972, 6639]), they[s] (1 [+1201, 851]), they[s] (1 [+2085, 2021, 408]), they[s] (1 [+2021, 2085, 408]), they[s] (1 [+5883, 2021, 2085]), they[s] (1 [+2021, 5883, 2085]), they[s] (1 [+3405, 2256, 8569, 2657]), this (1 [+1821, 2021, 2296]), this (1 [+2021, 1821, 2296]), this[s] (1 [+1821]), this[s] (1 [+9108]), this[s] (1 [+2296, 1821, 2021]), this[s] (1 [+5126, 2021, 2296]), this[s] (1 [+2021, 465, 1821]), this[s] (1 [+2021, 5126, 2296]), this[s] (1 [+465, 1821, 2021]), this is how (1 [+3869, 1821, 2021, 465]), this is how (1 [+3869, 2021, 1821, 465]), thoroughly purge away (1 [+7671, 3869, 1342]), those (1 [+3972, 5883]), those[s] (1), those[s] (1 [+8636]), those[s] (1 [+7156]), those[s] (1 [+1583]), those[s] (1 [+132]), those[s] (1 [+2651]), those[s] (1 [+8599]), those[s] (1 [+7239]), those[s] (1 [+6639, 889, 339]), those who[s] (1 [+408]), tomorrow[s] (1), unnoticed (1 [+928, 4319]), useless (1 [+4200, 9214]), very (1), very old (1 [+2416, 995, 928, 408]), very old (1 [+2418, 995, 928, 3427]), wage war (1 [+1741, 4200, 4878]), walking along (1 [+928, 2006]), waylaid (1 [+8492, 928, 2006]), we[s] (1 [+132]), weaklings[s] (1 [+3869, 851]), what[s] (1 [+4856]), what[s] (1 [+995]), what[s] (1 [+2021, 5184, 2296]), what[s] (1 [+5184, 2021, 2296]), whatever[s] (1 [+3655]), whatever[s] (1 [+9368]), when (1 [+928, 3427]), when (1 [+928, 3427]), where[s] (1 [+2006]), where[s] (1 [+928, 5226]), where[s] (1 [+2958, 2021, 2667]), where[s] (1 [+2021, 2958, 2667]), wherever (1 [+928, 3972, 5226]), wherever (1 [+4946, 3972, 5226]), wherever (1 [+928, 889, 2006]), wherever (1 [+928, 5226, 889]), wherever (1 [+6584, 3972, 5226, 889]), wherever (1 [+928, 285, 5226, 889]), whether a (1), which[s] (1 [+8965]), which[s] (1 [+7366]), which way (1 [+361, 2296, 2006]), who (1 [+889]), who (1 [+4769, 408]), who (1 [+408, 6504]), whoever (1 [+3972, 132]), whoever[s] (1), whom (1), whom[s] (1 [+6639, 824]), whose[s] (1 [+285, 2021, 9108]), whose[s] (1 [+2021, 285, 9108]), without meaning (1 [+928, 2039]), woman's monthly uncleanness (1 [+3240, 5614]), workers (1 [+6913, 928, 4856]), year (1 [+4200, 3427]), years (1 [+6961, 9102]), yet (1 [+3427]), yet (1 [+6330, 3427, 2021, 2085]), yet (1 [+6330, 2021, 3427, 2085]), yet (1 [+6330, 3427, 2021, 2156]), yet (1 [+6330, 2021, 3427, 2156]), you[s] (1 [+4889]), your[s] (1 [+4889]), NDT (9756)

H2022 -הֲ ***hᵃ-***, inter.pt.pref. [742] [√ 10190]. introduces a question; usually translated as a question mark:– whether (12), if (11), not (7), when (4), don't (3), as you know (2 [+4202]), or (2), rather (2), isn't (1), not only (1), only (1 [+4202]), so (1), surely (1), unless (1 [+4202]), what about (1 [+4202]), whether (1 [+561, 4202]), NDT (691)

H2023 הָ- ***-āh***, הָ- ***-hā***, הָ- ***-â***[1], הָא- ***-hā'***, p.f.sg.suf. [3088] [→ 2024, 2084, 2114, 2157, 2161, 2177, 2181, 2257, 4392, 4564, 5527, 5626, 5647]. she, her; it, its:– her (1121), it (541), its (256), the[s] (91), their (77), she (65), them (32), there[s] (26 [+928]), the city[s] (12), the land[s] (12), whose (12), your (9), herself (8), herself (7 [+5883]), this (7), which[s] (7), you (7), a[s] (5), her (5 [+4200]), her own (5), one (3), that city[s] (3), there[s] (3), there[s] (3 [+6584]), there[s] (3 [+6584]), there[s] (3 [+928, 9348]), this[s] (3), which (3), wisdom[s] (3), Hagar[s] (2), Jerusalem[s] (2), hers (2), its (2 [+928]), its[s] (2), its land[s] (2), land[s] (2), that[s] (2), the (2), the town[s] (2), there[s] (2 [+928]), where[s] (2 [+928]), Dinah's[s] (1), Edom[s] (1), Edom's[s] (1), Egypt[s] (1), Hannah[s] (1), Hannah's[s] (1), Israel's[s] (1), Judah[s] (1), Moab[s] (1), Nineveh[s] (1 [+5226]), Ruth's[s] (1), Samaria's[s] (1), Tyre[s] (1), Zion[s] (1), all this[s] (1), an[s] (1), another[s] (1), city[s] (1), he[s] (1 [+3]), here[s] (1 [+928]), hers (1 [+4200]), herself (1 [+4222]), herself (1 [+7931]), him (1), him[s] (1 [+1201]), him[s] (1 [+1251]), him[s] (1 [+3]), his (1), his daughter's[s] (1), his nurse[s] (1), in (1), it[s] (1 [+7023]), it[s] (1 [+4946, 1947]), its (1 [+4200]), its (1 [+4200]), its (1 [+6584]), its inhabitants[s] (1), its own (1), its people[s] (1), my law[s] (1), piece[s] (1), righteous[s] (1), she (1 [+5883]), she (1 [+5883]), that (1), that day[s] (1), that place[s] (1), that time[s] (1), that's (1), the altar[s] (1), the courtyard[s] (1), the donkey[s] (1), the dove[s] (1), the earth[s] (1), the fire[s] (1), the first woman[s] (1), the goat[s] (1), the kingdom[s] (1), the lampstand[s] (1), the pit[s] (1), the place[s] (1), the plot[s] (1), the spring[s] (1), the sword[s] (1), the temple[s] (1), the young woman[s] (1), their land[s] (1), their lands[s] (1), them[s] (1 [+1074]), themselves (1), there[s] (1 [+4200]), there[s] (1 [+5226]), there[s] (1 [+9348, 928]), there[s] (1 [+928, 8148]), these[s] (1), they[s] (1 [+1201]), this city[s] (1), this land[s] (1), those (1), tongue[s] (1), what happened[s] (1), whom (1), word[s] (1), your own (1), your wife[s] (1), yourself (1 [+4222]), NDT (646)

H2024 הֹ- ***-ōh***, p.m.sg.suf. [36] [√ 2023]. he, his, him:– his

HEBREW INDEX

(9), they (4), its (3), them (3), it (1), their (1), those (1), NDT (14)

H2025 הָ- ***-â[2]***, adv.suf. [1113] to, toward; a suffixed adverb or remnant of an archaic case ending:– to (292), on (90), at (58), there (56 [+9004]), into (49), in (39), more (36 [+5087]), west (28 [+3542]), north (25 [+7600]), toward (25), where (17 [+625]), where (16 [+9004]), how long (12 [+6330, 625]), east (11 [+7708]), for (9), northern (9 [+7600]), south (9 [+5582]), outside (8 [+2575]), east (7 [+7711]), east (7 [+4667]), upward (6 [+4200, 5087]), out (5 [+2575]), south (5 [+9402]), above (4 [+4946, 4200, 5087]), reached (4 [+995]), the Jordan[S] (4 [+9004]), above (3 [+4200, 5087]), against (3), eastern (3 [+7711]), from (3), in (3 [+2021, 1074]), in it[S] (3 [+9004]), on (3 [+5087]), south (3 [+5582, 9402]), southern (3 [+5582]), westward (3 [+3542]), after (2), anywhere else (2 [+625, 2256, 625, 2025]), anywhere else (2 [+625, 2025, 2256, 625]), east (2 [+4667, 2021, 9087]), eastern (2 [+4667]), eastern (2 [+7708]), head (2 [+4946, 8900, 2256, 5087]), higher (2 [+5087]), highly (2 [+4200, 5087]), in the presence of (2 [+5584]), inside (2), inside (2 [+1074]), it[S] (2 [+9004]), over (2 [+4946, 4200, 5087]), top (2 [+4946, 4200, 5087]), toward (2 [+995, 3870]), up (2 [+4200, 5087]), very (2 [+4200, 5087]), western (2 [+3542]), wherever (2 [+9004]), across (1), advance (1 [+7156]), along (1), among (1), annual (1 [+4946, 3427, 3427]), anywhere (1 [+625, 2256, 625, 2025]), anywhere (1 [+625, 2025, 2256, 625]), as far as (1), at each successive level (1 [+4200, 5087, 4200, 5087, 2025]), at each successive level (1 [+4200, 5087, 2025, 4200, 5087]), away (1 [+448, 2021, 2575]), back[S] (1 [+9004]), beyond (1 [+5087]), deep (1 [+5087]), depth (1 [+4200, 5087]), down (1 [+824]), downstream (1 [+5087, 4946, 4200]), each year (1 [+4946, 3427, 3427]), each year (1 [+4946, 3427, 3427]), east (1 [+6298, 4667]), east (1 [+928, 6298, 4667]), east (1 [+7156, 2006, 2021, 7708]), east (1 [+928, 6298, 4667, 9087]), eastward (1 [+4667]), eastward (1 [+7708]), eastward (1 [+7711]), eastward (1 [+7711, 4667, 2025]), eastward (1 [+7711, 2025, 4667]), entered (1 [+995]), entering (1 [+995]), enters (1 [+995]), exceedingly (1 [+4200, 5087]), extend (1 [+2575]), extend eastward (1 [+7708]), extend westward (1 [+3542]), facing (1), fail (1 [+5877, 824]), get out (1 [+8938, 2021, 2575]), going up (1 [+6590, 2021, 9028]), heights (1 [+4200, 5087]), here (1 [+2178]), here[S] (1 [+5213]), high above (1 [+4946, 4200, 5087]), higher than (1 [+8049, 4200, 5087]), in ascending stages (1 [+4200, 5087, 4200, 5087, 2025]), in ascending stages (1 [+4200, 5087, 2025, 4200, 5087]), in the vicinity of (1), inside[S] (1 [+9004]), interior (1 [+4946, 1074]), invade (1 [+995, 9004]), inward (1 [+1074]), join (1), magnificence (1 [+5087]), more (1 [+4200, 5087]), more and more powerful (1 [+2143, 2256, 1541, 6330, 4200, 5087]), north (1 [+4946, 7600]), northern (1 [+4946, 7600]), older (1 [+5087]), on to (1), onto (1), outer (1 [+4946, 4200, 5087]), outside (1 [+2667]), outside (1 [+7339]), outside (1 [+4946, 2575]), outside (1 [+4946, 2575]), outside the family (1 [+2021, 2575, 2424]), over (1), over (1 [+4946, 5087, 4200]), over and above (1 [+4200, 5087]), overturned (1 [+2200, 4200, 5087]), pen up (1 [+1074]), project upward (1 [+4200, 5087]), severe (1 [+4200, 5087]), south (1 [+5582, 9402, 2025]), south (1 [+2025, 5582, 9402]), southeast (1 [+7711, 5582]), southeast (1 [+7711, 5582, 2025]), southeast (1 [+7711, 2025, 5582]), southern (1 [+9402, 5582, 2025]), southern (1 [+9402, 2025, 5582]), the land[S] (1 [+9004]), there[S] (1 [+7730]), there[S] (1 [+824, 4046]), there[S] (1 [+928, 9463]), to (1 [+9004]), top (1 [+5087]), top of (1 [+4946, 4200, 5087]), toward (1 [+3870, 995]), upstream (1 [+4200, 5087]), upward (1 [+4946, 4200, 5087]), very (1 [+6330, 4200, 5087]), west (1 [+5115]), western[S] (1 [+4667]), when (1 [+6330, 625]), wherever (1 [+625]), wherever (1 [+889, 9004]), which way (1 [+625]), which way (1 [+625]), wielding (1 [+995, 4200, 5087]), young and old (1 [+2256, 5087]), NDT (112)

H2026 הֵא ***hē'***, interj. [2] [√ 10194, 10195]. surely! see!, a discourse marker of emphasis:– here (1), surely (1)

H2027 הֶאָח ***he'āḥ***, interj. [12] Ah!, Aha!:– aha (11), ah (1)

H2028 הָאֲחַשְׁתָּרִי ***hā'ᵃḥaštārî***, n.pr.m. *or* a.g. [1] [√ 349]. Haahashtari, "*the Ahashtarites*":– Haahashtari (1)

H2029 הָאֱלִי ***hā'ᵉlî***, a.g. Not used in NIVEBC [cf. 1088]. see 1088

H2030 הָאֶלֶף ***hā'elep***, n.pr.loc. [1] Haeleph:– Haeleph (1)

H2031 הָאַמָּה ***hā'ammâ***, n.pr.loc. Not used in NIVEBC [→ 1094]. Ha-Ammah, see 5497

H2032 הָאֵצֶל ***hā'ēṣel***, n.pr.loc. Not used in NIVEBC [→ 1089]. Ha-Ezel, see 1089

H2033 הָאַרְבַּע ***hā'arba'***, n.pr.loc. Not used in NIVEBC [√ 752]. Arba

H2034 הָאֲרָרִי ***hā'rārî***, var. Not used in NIVEBC [cf. 828]. see 2240

H2035 [1]הַב ***hab[1]***, v. [34] [cf. 3364]. come!, give!, put!, ascribe!:– give (10), ascribe (9), come (5), bring (2), respond with (2), appoint (1), choose (1), do (1), praise (1), put (1), speak up (1)

H2036 [2]הַב ***hab[2]***, n.m.? Not used in NIVEBC [→ 9105]. elephant [?]

H2037 הַבְהָב ***habhab***, n.m. [1] gift:– gifts (1)

H2038 הָבַל ***hābal***, v.den. [5] [√ 2039]. [Q] to be worthless, meaningless; be proud, vain; [H] to fill with false hopes, cause to become vain:– worthless (2), fill with false hopes (1), meaningless talk (1 [+2039]), put vain hope (1)

H2039 [1]הֶבֶל ***hebel[1]***, n.m. [73] [→ 2038; cf. 2040]. breath; by extension: something with no substance, meaninglessness, worthlessness, vanity, emptiness, futility; idol:– meaningless (34), worthless idols (9), breath (5), in vain (4), worthless (4), utterly meaningless (2 [+2039]), dishonest (1), empty talk (1), fleeting (1), futile (1), futility (1), less meaning (1 [+8049]), meaningless talk (1 [+2038]), mere breath (1), no meaning (1), nonsense (1), nothing at all (1 [+9332, 2256]), utterly useless (1 [+2256, 8198]), vapor (1), without meaning (1 [+928, 2021]), worthless idols (1 [+8736])

H2040 [2]הֶבֶל ***hebel[2]***, n.pr.m. [8] [cf. 2039?]. Abel, "*morning mist*":– Abel (8)

H2041 הָבְנִים ***hobnîm***, n.[m.] [1] ebony:– ebony (1)

H2042 הָבַר ***hābar***, v. [1] [Q] (ptcp.) astrologer, one who divides (classifies) the night sky for the purpose of telling the future:– astrologers (1 [+9028])

H2043 הֵגֵא ***hēgē'***, n.pr.m. [1] [cf. 2051]. Hegai:– Hegai (1)

H2044 הַגִּדְגָּד ***haggidgād***, n.pr.m. Not used in NIVEBC [→ 2988; cf. 1515]. Haggidgad, see 2988

H2045 הַגְּדוֹלִים ***haggᵉdôlîm***, n.pr.m. [1] [√ 1524]. Haggedolim, "*the great ones*":– Haggedolim (1)

H2046 הַגּוֹיִם ***haggôyim***, n.pr.loc. Not used in NIVEBC [→ 3099]. Haggoyim

H2047 [1]הָגָה ***hāgâ[1]***, v. [25] [→ 2049, 2050, 2053]. [Q] to utter a sound, moan, meditate; [H] to mutter; from the base meaning of uttering a sound of any kind comes figure of meditation, the act of thoughtful deliberation with the implication of speaking to oneself:– meditate (2), moan mournfully (2 [+2047]), plot (2), utter (2), consider (1), growls (1), lament (1), meditates (1), moan (1), moaned (1), mutter (1), mutters (1), ponder (1), proclaim (1), scheme (1), speaks (1), tell (1), think (1), utter a sound (1), uttering (1), weighs (1)

H2048 [2]הָגָה ***hāgâ[2]***, v. [3] [cf. 3325]. [Q] to expel, remove:– remove (2), drives out (1)

H2049 הֶגֶה ***hegeh***, n.m. [3] [√ 2047]. moaning, mourning, rumbling:– moan (1), mourning (1), rumbling (1)

H2050 הָגוּת ***hāgût***, n.f. [1] [√ 2047]. utterance, meditation, which can include thinking and planning:– meditation (1)

H2051 הֵגַי ***hēgay***, n.pr.m. [3] [cf. 2043]. Hegai:– Hegai (3)

H2052 הָגִיג ***hāgîg***, n.m. [2] sighing, meditation:– lament (1), meditated (1)

H2053 הִגָּיוֹן ***higgāyôn***, n.m. [3] [√ 2047]. muttering (sounds spoken to no one in particular), meditation see also 2047; Higgaion, melody:– meditation (1), melody (1), mutter (1)

H2054 הָגִין ***hāgîn***, a. [1] corresponding:– corresponding (1)

H2055 הַגִּלְגָּל ***haggilgāl***, n.pr.loc. Not used in NIVEBC [√ 1670]. Gilgal

H2056 הַגָּן ***haggān***, n.pr.loc.? Not used in NIVEBC [→ 1091]. Haggan, see 1091

H2057 הָגָר ***hāgār***, n.pr.f. [12] [→ 2058?]. Hagar, "*emigration, flight*":– Hagar (11), she[S] (1)

H2058 הַגְרִי ***hagrî***, a.g. [& n.pr.m.?] [7] [√ 2057?]. Hagrites, of Hagri, "*wanderer*":– Hagrites (4), Hagri (2), Hagrite (1)

H2059 הֵד ***hēd***, n.[m.] [1] [√ 2116]. joyous shout:– joy (1)

H2060 הֲדַד ***h[a]dad***, n.pr.m. [13] [→ 119, 1207, 2061, 2062, 2066, 2067, 2836]. Hadad, "*thunderer*":– Hadad (12), NDT (1)

H2061 הֲדַדְעֶזֶר ***h[a]dad'ezer***, n.pr.m. [21] [√ 2060 + 6469]. Hadadezer, "*Hadad is a help*":– Hadadezer (17), Hadadezer's (2), who[S] (2)

H2062 הֲדַד־רִמּוֹן ***h[a]dad-rimmôn***, n.pr.m.[loc.?] [1] [√ 2060 + 8235]. Hadad Rimmon:– Hadad Rimmon (1)

H2063 הָדָה ***hādâ***, v. [1] [Q] to put, stretch out:– put (1)

H2064 הֹדּוּ ***hōddû***, n.pr.loc. [2] India:– India (2)

H2065 הֲדוּרִים ***h[a]dûrîm***, n.[pl.m.] mountains

H2066 [1]הֲדוֹרָם ***h[a]dôrām[1]***, n.pr.m. [2] [√ 2060 + 8123]. Hadoram, "*Hadad is exalted*":– Hadoram (2)

H2067 [2]הֲדוֹרָם ***h[a]dôrām[2]***, n.pr.m. [2] [√ 2060 + 8123]. Hadoram; Adoniram:– Adoniram (1), Hadoram (1)

H2068 הִדַּי ***hidday***, n.pr.m. [1] [cf. 2583]. Hiddai:– Hiddai (1)

H2069 הֹדַיְוָהוּ ***hōdaywāhû***, n.pr.m. Not used in NIVEBC [√ 2089]. Hodayvahu, see 2089

H2070 הָדַךְ ***hādak***, v. [1] [Q] to crush by treading upon:– crush (1)

H2071 הֲדֹם ***h[a]dōm***, n.m. [6] footstool:– footstool (5 [+8079]), footstool (1)

H2072 הֲדַס ***h[a]das***, n.m. [6] [→ 2073]. myrtle tree:– myrtle trees (3), myrtle (2), myrtles (1)

H2073 הֲדַסָּה ***h[a]dassâ***, n.pr.f. [1] [√ 2072]. Hadassah, "*myrtle;* [poss.] *bride* or *myrtle*":– Hadassah (1)

H2074 הָדַף ***hādap***, v. [11] [Q] to shove, push, thrust, drive out:– depose (1), driven (1), driven out (1), push away (1), push down (1), push out (1), pushes (1), shove (1), shoves (1), thrusting out (1), thwarts (1)

H2075 הָדַר ***hādar***, v. [6] [→ 2077, 2078, 2079; 10198]. [Q] to show favoritism; show respect; [Qp] to be splendor; [N] to be shown respect; [Ht] to exalt oneself:– are shown respect (1 [+7156]), exalt yourself (1), favoritism (1 [+7156]), show favoritism (1), show respect (1), splendor (1)

H2076 הֲדַר ***h[a]dar***, n.pr.m. Not used in NIVEBC [→ 2080]. Hadar, see 2060

H2077 הָדָר ***hādār***, n.m. [30] [√ 2075; 10199]. majesty, splendor, glory, nobility; often related to the appearance of an object that is beautiful and instills awe:– splendor (13), majesty (9), majestic (2), blessing (1), dignity (1), glory (1), honor (1), luxuriant (1), nobles (1)

H2078 הֶדֶר ***heder***, n.[m.] [1] [√ 2075; 10199]. splendor; "the royal splendor" may refer to the land of Israel, with the focus that this land is an valued ornament of the king:– splendor (1)

H2079 הֲדָרָה ***h[a]dārâ***, n.f. [5] [√ 2075]. splendor, glory:– splendor (4), glory (1)

H2080 הֲדַרְעֶזֶר ***h[a]dar'ezer***, n.pr.m. Not used in NIVEBC [√ 2076 + 6469]. Hadarezer, see 2061

H2081 הָהּ ***hāh***, interj. [1] Alas!:– Alas (1)

H2082 הוֹ ***hô***, interj. [2] [→ 2098]. ah! (doubled for emphasis), with a strong implication of mourning or sorrow:– anguish (2 [+2082])

H2083 הוּ ***hû***, p.m.sg. [1] [√ 2085]. he, she, it; that, which:– it (1)

H2084 -הוּ ***-hû***, p.m.sg.suf. [1081] [√ 2023]. he, his, him; it, its:– him (443), it (155), his (82), them (60), their (51), a[S] (18), he (17), its (16), the[S] (10), their own (6), they (5), David[S] (4), her (4), your (4), someone (3), Moses[S] (2), Pekahiah[S] (2), a (2), each (2), one (2), that person[S] (2), which (2), whose (2), Abram[S] (1), Asahel's[S] (1), Ben-Hadad[S] (1), Cyrus[S] (1), God[S] (1), Joab[S] (1), Nadab[S] (1), another (1), both of you (1 [+3870, 2256]), his own (1), idol[S] (1), me (1), meal[S] (1), my (1), one's (1), she (1), that day[S] (1), the (1), the altar[S] (1), the child[S] (1), the clouds[S] (1), the honey[S] (1), the idol[S] (1), the inside[S] (1), the lamb[S] (1), the lion[S] (1), the manna[S] (1), the mountain[S] (1), the parties (1 [+408, 2256, 8276]), the stand[S] (1), the water[S] (1), theirs (1), this (1), together (1 [+408, 907, 8276]), which[S] (1), who (1), whom (1), you (1), NDT (149)

H2085 הוּא ***hû'***, p.m.sg. [1873] [→ 2083, 2115, 2156, 2160, 2179; 10200, 10205; *also used with compound proper names*]. he, it; this, that:– he (384), that (362), it (192), she (82), they (77), this (54), that is (35), who (30), himself (19), that same (19), one (11), which (11), same (9), him (8), those (6), his (5), that person[S] (4), these (4), they[S] (4 [+2021, 2021, 5883]), you (4), Jotham[S] (3), the man[S] (3), them (3), this city[S] (3), Abram[S] (2), all day long (2 [+928, 2021, 3427, 2021]), far and wide (2 [+4946, 2256, 2134]), her (2), him[S] (2 [+2021, 2021, 408]), that very (2), the Lord[S] (2), the animal[S] (2), them[S] (2 [+2021, 2021, 408]), what (2), whose (2), Baal[S] (1), Balaam[S] (1), Beerah[S] (1), David[S] (1), Edomites[S] (1), Elah[S] (1), Eleazar[S] (1), Elijah[S] (1), Elisha[S] (1), Gaal[S] (1), Gehazi[S] (1), Hannah[S] (1), Naaman[S] (1), Ruth[S] (1), Sarai[S] (1), Shem[S] (1), again (1 [+1685, 928, 2021, 7193, 2021]), any[S] (1), anyone (1), at once (1 [+928, 2021, 6961, 2021]), at once (1 [+928, 2021, 3427, 2021]), daughter[S] (1), death[S] (1), each of us (1 [+638, 2256]), else (1), fire[S] (1), he[S] (1 [+2021, 5883, 2021]), he alone (1), he himself (1), herself (1), his[S] (1), it[S] (1 [+2021, 5226, 2021]), its (1), joy[S] (1), let it be (1 [+4027]), man[S] (1), mine (1), my vow[S] (1), only (1), only[S] (1), other[S] (1), priests[S] (1), regular[S] (1), she's (1), something[S] (1), such (1), that man[S] (1), that other person[S] (1), that part[S] (1), that person's life[S] (1), that son[S] (1), that's (1), the Makirites[S] (1), the avenger[S] (1), the baby[S] (1), the city[S] (1), the father[S] (1), the key[S] (1), the prophet[S] (1), the slave[S] (1), the woman[S] (1), their (1), themselves (1), then[S] (1 [+2021, 6961, 2021]), then[S] (1 [+928, 2021, 3427, 2021]), they (1 [+2021, 2021, 5883]), they[S] (1), they[S] (1 [+2021, 2021, 408]), they[S] (1 [+2021, 5883, 2021]), things[S] (1), this man[S] (1), this same (1), very (1), which[S] (1), who[S] (1), whoever (1), yet (1 [+6330, 2021, 3427, 2021]), NDT (442)

H2086 [1]הוֹד ***hôd[1]***, n.m. [24] [→ 2087, 6654; cf. 3344; *also used with compound proper names*]. splendor, majesty, glory, strength:– splendor (10), honor (3), majesty (3), glory (2), proud (2), authority (1), face (1), glorious (1), majestic (1)

H2087 [2]הוֹד ***hôd[2]***, n.pr.m. [1] [√ 2086]. Hod, "*grandeur*":– Hod (1)

H2088 הוֹדְוָה ***hôdᵉwâ***, n.pr.m. [1] [→ 2089, 2090; cf. 3344 + 3378]. Hodaviah, "*give thanks to Yahweh*":– Hodaviah (1)

H2089 הוֹדַוְיָה ***hôdawyâ***, n.pr.m. [3] [→ 2069, 2088; cf.

HEBREW INDEX

3344 + 3378]. Hodaviah, "*give thanks to Yahweh*":– Hodaviah (3)

H2090 הוֹדַוְיָהוּ ***hôdawyāhû***, n.pr.m. [1] [√ 2088; cf. 3344 + 3378]. Hodaviah, "*give thanks to Yahweh*":– Hodaviah (1)

H2091 הוֹדִיָּה ***hôdiyyâ***, n.pr.m. [6] [√ 2086 + 3378]. Hodiah, "*grandeur is Yahweh*":– Hodiah (5), Hodiah's (1)

H2092 ¹הָוָה ***hāwâ¹***, v. [1] [→ 2095, 2096, 2119; cf. 2093]. [Q] to fall (on):– fall (1)

H2093 ²הָוָה ***hāwâ²***, v. [5] [cf. 2092, 2118; 10201]. [Q] to be, become; to get, have:– be (2), become (1), get (1), lie (1)

H2094 ¹הַוָּה ***hawwâ¹***, n.f. [3] [√ 205; cf. 203]. (evil) desire, craving:– craving (1), desire (1), evil desires (1)

H2095 ²הַוָּה ***hawwâ²***, n.f. [13] [→ 2119; cf. 2092]. destruction, ruin, corruption:– destroying (2), malice (2), ruin (2), corrupt (1), deadly (1), destruction (1), destructive (1), destructive forces (1), disaster (1), misery (1)

H2096 הֹוָה ***hōwâ***, n.f. [3] [√ 2092]. calamity, disaster:– calamity (3)

H2097 הוֹהָם ***hôhām***, n.pr.m. [1] Hoham:– Hoham (1)

H2098 הוֹי ***hôy***, interj. [51] [√ 2082]. woe!, ah!, oh!, alas!; (to invite) come!:– woe (38), alas (7), come (4), ah (1), awful (1 [+1524])

H2099 הוֹלֵלוֹת ***hôlēlôt***, n.f. [4] [√ 2147]. madness, delusion, folly:– madness (4)

H2100 הוֹלֵלוּת ***hôlēlût***, n.f. [1] [√ 2147]. madness, delusion, folly:– madness (1)

H2101 הוּם ***hûm***, v. [4] [→ 4539; cf. 2159, 2169, 5637]. [Q] to throw into confusion; [N] to be stirred up, be shook; [H] to be distraught; to throng:– distraught (1), shook (1), stirred (1), throng (1)

H2102 הוֹמָם ***hômām***, n.pr.m. [1] [→ 2123]. Homam:– Homam (1)

H2103 הוּן ***hûn***, v. [1] [→ 2104]. [H] to think it easy:– thinking it easy (1)

H2104 הוֹן ***hôn***, n.m. [26] [√ 2103]. wealth, riches, possessions:– wealth (15), enough (2), wealth of goods (2), money (1), pittance (1 [+4202]), rich (1), riches (1), riches (1 [+3701]), treasures (1), valuable things (1 [+3701])

H2105 הוֹר ***hôr***, n.m. Not used in NIVEBC [cf. 2215]. mountain

H2106 הוֹשָׁמָע ***hôšāmā'***, n.pr.m. [1] [√ 9048 + 3378]. Hoshama, "*Yahweh has heard*":– Hoshama (1)

H2107 הוֹשֵׁעַ ***hôšēa'***, n.pr.m. [16] [√ 3828 + 446 *or* 3378]. Hoshea; Joshua, "*salvation*":– Hoshea (12), Hosea (2), Joshua (1), him[s] (1)

H2108 הוֹשַׁעְיָה ***hôša'yâ***, n.pr.m. [3] [√ 3828 + 3378]. Hoshaiah, "*Yahweh has saved*":– Hoshaiah (3)

H2109 הוּת ***hût***, v. [1] [cf. 2254]. [Pol] to assault:– assault (1)

H2110 הוֹתִיר ***hôtîr***, n.pr.m. [2] [√ 3855]. Hothir, "*one who remains*":– Hothir (2)

H2111 הָזָה ***hāzâ***, v. [1] [Q] to dream:– dream (1)

H2112 הַחִירֹת ***haḥîrôt***, n.pr.loc. Not used in NIVEBC [√ 2672]. Hahiroth

H2113 הִי ***hî***, n.[m.] [1] woe!, an exclamation of sorrow:– woe (1)

H2114 הִי- ***-hî***, p.m.sg.suf. [1] [√ 2023]. his, him:– his (1)

H2115 הִיא ***hî'***, p.f.sg. [1] [√ 2085; 10205]. she, see 2085:– whose (1)

H2116 הֵידָד ***hêdād***, n.m. [7] [→ 2059]. shout (of joy):– shouts of joy (3), shout (1), shout in triumph (1 [+6702]), shouting (1), shouts (1)

H2117 הֻיְּדוֹת ***huyyedôt***, n.f.pl. [1] [√ 3344]. (pl.) songs of thanksgiving:– songs of thanksgiving (1)

H2118 הָיָה ***hāyâ***, v. [3555] [→ 181; cf. 2093; 10201]. [Q] to be, become, happen; [N] to be done, happen; the common verb of being, referring to state of being, change of state, existence, and the occurring of events, or even possession:– be (700), was (304), came (165), become (163), were (157), is (96), been (77), are (74), had (67), became (60), have (50 [+4200]), happened (26), come (24), am (19), will (19), happen (16), have (16), remain (14), belong to (12 [+4200]), lived (12 [+3427]), has (10), hold (10), becomes (9), fall (9), remained (9), become (8 [+4200]), comes (8), set (8), go (7), lived (7), done (6), fell (6), lie (6), serve (6), went (6), belonged to (5 [+4200]), consider (5 [+4200]), continue (5), ended (5 [+9362]), fallen (5), has (5 [+928]), has (5 [+4200]), left (5), made (5), marry (5 [+4200, 851]), stay (5), stayed (5), belongs to (4 [+4200]), bring (4), bring (4 [+4200]), endure (4), included (4), keep (4), last (4), leave (4), make (4), numbered (4), one day (4 [+2256]), took place (4), touch (4 [+928]), appears (3), coming (3), end (3 [+9362]), ending (3 [+9362]), extend (3), given (3), keep (3 [+4200]), kept (3), lay (3), married (3 [+4200, 851]), put (3), reach (3), rest (3), spread (3), stand (3), taken (3), use (3), used (3), wear (3 [+6584]), agree (2 [+3869, 285]), allotted (2 [+1598]), applies (2), are (2 [+2118]), arose (2), became (2 [+2725, 4200]), being (2), bind (2 [+4200, 3213]), brought (2), came (2 [+2118]), certainly come true (2 [+2118]), come into being (2 [+2118]), come what may (2 [+4537]), connecting (2), did (2), exists (2), extended (2), follow (2 [+339]), fulfilled (2), get (2), help (2 [+6640]), lies (2), lying (2), may (2), overwhelmed (2 [+4202, 6388, 8120, 928]), owned (2 [+5238]), reached (2), receive (2 [+4200]), regard as (2 [+4200]), resided (2), rule (2 [+6584]), serve as (2), served (2), settled (2), sold for (2 [+928]), spent (2), struck (2 [+928]), surely become (2 [+2118]), take in exchange (2), take place (2), turn to (2), turned into (2 [+4200]), was exactly (2 [+2118]), wear (2), abound (1 [+7172]), acquired (1 [+4200]), act (1), act (1 [+4200]), allotted (1 [+1598, 928, 2021]), amount to (1), amounted to (1), appear (1), appear (1 [+928, 6524, 3869]), appeared (1), apply (1), appointed (1), appointed[s] (1), aroused (1 [+6584]), arouses (1), arranged (1 [+4595]), attach (1), be treated as (1), bear (1 [+4200]), become allies (1 [+928, 7931]), becoming (1), began (1), beginning (1), belong (1), belong to (1 [+928]), belonged to (1 [+448]), belonging to (1 [+4200]), belongs (1), bring about (1 [+928]), brings (1), broke out (1), brought about (1 [+4946]), brought with (1 [+928, 3338]), came into being (1), came to (1), came to be (1), carried by (1 [+6584]), caught (1), cause (1 [+4946]), caused (1), comes of (1), committed (1), company (1 [+907]), compare with (1 [+3869]), complete (1 [+4946, 7891]), condemn (1 [+4200, 2631]), conferred (1 [+1821]), consist of (1), continued (1 [+2143]), controlled (1 [+4200]), could not (1 [+6584]), count (1 [+4200]), covered (1 [+928]), decide (1 [+6584, 7023]), decided (1 [+6640, 4213]), designate (1), do (1), do that[s] (1 [+928, 2257, 3338]), downcast (1 [+4200]), drove back (1 [+6584]), earlier (1), end (1 [+928, 2021, 340]), ends (1), endure (1 [+4200]), engaged in (1), escapes (1 [+7129]), extending (1), fared (1), feared (1 [+3007]), fighting with (1 [+907]), filled (1 [+928, 3972]), find (1), flee (1), follow (1), follow (1 [+928]), formed (1), fulfilled (1 [+4027]), future (1 [+4537, 8611]), gain support (1 [+3338, 907]), gained (1), give (1), give (1 [+4200]), give shelter (1 [+6261]), goes (1 [+8079]), gone (1), gone (1 [+4202, 928]), got (1 [+4200]), grew worse and worse (1 [+2716, 2617, 4394]), had (1 [+928]), had (1 [+6584]), had chance (1 [+928, 3338]), had part in (1 [+4946]), had to (1 [+6584]), happening (1), happens (1), harbor (1 [+6640, 4222]), harbored (1 [+4200]), has (1 [+6640]), have (1 [+928]), have (1 [+1068]), have (1 [+6584]), having (1 [+4200]), help (1 [+907]), help (1 [+4200]), hold (1 [+928, 3338]), holds (1 [+928, 3338]), in all (1), in office (1), inclined (1 [+2296]), include (1), increase (1), inherit (1 [+448]), interfere (1 [+8477]), into marry (1 [+4200]), join (1 [+928]), join (1 [+4222, 4200, 3480]), joined (1), lasted (1), led the way (1 [+3338, 8037]), left (1 [+4200]), let (1), life (1 [+3427, 889]), living (1), looked (1 [+928, 6524]), lusted[s] (1), made angry (1 [+7911]), made fall (1 [+4200, 4842]), make sport of (1 [+4200, 5442]), making (1), married (1 [+851]), married to (1 [+4200, 851]), marries (1 [+4200]), marries (1 [+4200, 408]), marries (1 [+4200, 408, 2118]), marries (1 [+2118, 4200, 408]), marry (1 [+4200, 408]), marry into (1 [+4200]), mattered (1), mount (1 [+4853]), moved (1), observe (1), occur (1), occurred (1), once (1), owes (1), own (1 [+4200]), passed (1), possessed (1 [+4200]), preceded (1 [+4200, 7156]), predecessor (1 [+889, 4200, 7156]), prepare (1 [+3922]), produced (1), proper place (1 [+5226, 889, 9004]), property[s] (1 [+889, 4200]), prove to be (1), proved to be (1), provided for (1 [+4200, 4312, 2256, 430]), raise (1), raised (1), reached (1 [+928]), reaching (1), ready (1), rebel (1 [+5308]), received (1), received (1 [+4200]), regard (1 [+4200, 7156]), reinforce (1 [+2432]), remain unmarried (1 [+6328, 4200, 1194, 4200, 408]), remains (1), required (1), required to give (1 [+448]), resting (1), restored (1), retain (1 [+4200]), retains (1), ruled (1 [+4889]), ruled (1 [+8037]), run (1), secure (1 [+4200]), seem (1), seem (1 [+928, 6524]), seemed (1), seemed (1 [+928, 6524]), sell for (1 [+928]), serve (1 [+4200]), serve (1 [+4200, 7156]), served (1 [+4200, 7156]), served as (1), serving (1), share (1 [+4200, 285]), shed (1), shine (1 [+240]), shows to be (1 [+4200]), sprang up (1), spreads (1), standing (1), start (1), started (1), started falling (1), staying (1), steals forth (1), stretched (1), strike (1), strike (1 [+928]), striking (1 [+928]), subject[s] (1), suffer (1), suffered (1 [+928]), suffered (1 [+4200]), supply (1 [+4200]), supported (1 [+339]), supported (1 [+3338, 907]), surely take place (1), surround (1 [+6017, 4946]), take (1), take (1 [+4200]), take care of (1 [+6125]), take care of (1 [+4200, 5466]), take command (1 [+4200, 5464]), take hold of (1 [+928]), take the place of (1 [+9393]), tasted (1), taught (1 [+3723]), tend livestock (1 [+408, 5238]), tended livestock (1 [+408, 5238]), testify (1 [+6332]), to come (1), took care of (1 [+6125]), touches (1 [+6584]), treat (1 [+4200]), treated (1), treated (1 [+6640]), treated as (1 [+4200]), treating (1), turn against (1 [+4200, 8477]), turned (1), turned out (1), unmarried (1 [+4202, 4200, 408]), use (1 [+4200]), use (1 [+4200]), used to (1), using (1), want[s] (1), was committed (1), wasn't (1 [+4202]), weighed (1), went over (1 [+6017]), weren't (1 [+4202]), when (1 [+4946]), will (1 [+401]), with (1 [+928]), work (1), worked[s] (1), worn out (1), you (1), NDT (857)

H2119 הַיָּה ***hayyâ***, n.f. Not used in NIVEBC [√ 2095; cf. 2092]. destruction

H2120 הֵיךְ ***hêk***, adv. [2] [cf. 375]. how?:– How (2)

H2121 הֵיכָל ***hêkāl***, n.m. [80] [√ 10206]. a building of some kind: temple, sanctuary, palace; main hall:– temple (52), main hall (13), palace (7), palaces (4), house (2), sanctuary (1), temples (1)

H2122 הֵילֵל ***hêlēl***, n.m.[pr.?] [1] [√ 2145]. from the base meaning "shining one," this refers to an object in the night sky, often translated "morning star," and possibly referring the planet Venus; fig. used as a title of the king of Babylon (Isa 14:12). The Latin "lucifer" also means "shining one," and has become a title of Satan due to a traditional equation of the king of Babylon with the devil:– morning star (1)

H2123 הֵימָם ***hêmām***, n.pr.m. [1] [√ 2102]. Homam:– Homam (1)

H2124 הֵימָן ***hêmān***, n.pr.m. [17] [√ 3545? *or* 586?]. Homam:– Heman (16), his[s] (1)

H2125 הִין ***hîn***, n.m. [22] hin (liquid measure of volume, one-sixth of a bath, about one gallon [four liters]):– hin (22)

H2126 הַיַּרְקוֹן ***hayyarqôn***, n.pr.loc. Not used in NIVEBC [→ 4770]. Jarkon

H2127 הַיְשִׁימוֹת ***hayeśîmôt***, n.pr.loc. Not used in NIVEBC [→ 1093; cf. 3811]. Jeshimoth

H2128 הָכַר ***hākar***, v. Not used in NIVEBC [cf. 2686]. see 2686

H2129 הַכָּרָה ***hakkārâ***, n.f. [1] [√ 5795]. look (on a face) as a non-verbal communication, which in context may refer to personal bias:– look (1)

H2130 הַכֶּרֶם ***hakkerem***, n.pr.loc. Not used in NIVEBC [→ 1094]. Hakkerem

H2131 הַל ***hal***, l.inter. Not used in NIVEBC [√ 2021 + 4200]. interrogative particle

H2132 הֲלֹא ***halō'***, pt.inter.+adv. Not used in NIVEBC [√ 2022 + 4202]. see 2022 & 4202

H2133 הָלָא ***hālā'***, v.den. [1] [N] to be driven away, be removed:– driven away (1)

H2134 הָלְאָה ***hāle'â***, adv. [16] beyond; far (and wide), some distance away; out of the way!:– on (4), beyond (2 [+4946, 2256]), far and wide (2 [+4946, 2085, 2256]), beyond (1 [+4946]), beyond (1 [+4946, 4200]), continuing (1), forward (1), on the other side of (1 [+4946, 6298, 2256]), outside (1 [+4946]), some distance away (1), way (1)

H2135 הַלּוֹחֵשׁ ***hallôḥēš***, n.pr.m. [2] [√ 2021 + 4317]. Hallohesh, "*the whisperer*":– Hallohesh (2)

H2136 הִלּוּלִים ***hillûlîm***, n.[m.] [2] [√ 2146]. offering of praise; festival (related to a god):– festival (1), offering of praise (1)

H2137 הַלָּז ***hallāz***, p.com.sg. [7] [√ 2138; cf. 4208]. this:– this (3), that (2), the (1), there's (1)

H2138 הַלָּזֶה ***hallāzeh***, p.m. [3] [→ 2137, 2139; cf. 2306]. this:– that (2), this (1)

H2139 הַלֵּזוּ ***hallēzû***, p.f. Not used in NIVEBC [√ 2138]. this

H2140 הַלַּחְמִי ***hallaḥmî***, a.g. Not used in NIVEBC [→ 1095]. see 1095

H2141 הָלִיךְ ***hālîk***, n.[m.] [1] [√ 2143]. path, steps:– path (1)

H2142 הֲלִיכָה ***halîkâ***, n.f. [6] [√ 2143]. procession, way, walk; traveling merchants; affairs:– procession (2), affairs (1), marches on (1), traveling merchants (1), way (1)

H2143 הָלַךְ ***hālak***, v. [1551] [→ 2141, 2142, 2144, 2168, 4544, 4907, 9336, 9354; 10207]. [Q] to walk, go, travel; [N] to fade away; [P] to walk about, go about, [H] to drive back, get rid of; enable to walk; to lead; bring; [Ht] to move to and fro, wander, walk about; by extension: to walk as a lifestyle, a pattern of conduct:– go (326), went (173), come (94), walk (79), followed (31), left (30), gone (29), followed (27 [+339]), follow (26 [+928]), follow (20 [+339]), going (15), moved (15), led (14), set out (14), walked (13), came (12), take (11), went away (11), went out (10), go about (7), go back (7), leave (7), continue (6), continued (6), following (6 [+339]), goes (6), live (6), marched (6), walking (6), walks (6), go out (5), left (5 [+4946]), returned (5), run (5), traveled (5), walked faithfully (5), went off (5), went on (5), became more and more powerful (4 [+2143, 2256, 1524]), brought (4), coming (4), fled (4), following (4 [+928]), go (4 [+2256, 8740]), go away (4), go off (4), lead (4), left (4 [+4946, 907]), taking (4), walk faithfully (4), be (3), did[s] (3), follow (3), go ahead (3), grow (3), leave (3 [+4946]), on way (3), ran (3), return (3), wandered (3), withdrew (3), advanced (2), away (2), be on way (2), been (2), began (2), carry (2), certainly go (2 [+2143]), depart (2), disappears (2), done[s] (2), flow (2), flowed (2), follows (2 [+928]), get (2), get out (2), go (2 [+2143]), go (2 [+2143]), go at once (2 [+2143]), go out (2 [+2143]), go way (2), goes about (2), going about (2), going back (2), going back and forth (2), gone (2 [+2143]), gone off (2 [+2143]), gossip (2 [+8215]), keeping all the way (2 [+2143]), kept coming (2 [+2143]), leader (2 [+4200, 7156]), leads away (2), leave (2 [+4946, 907]), lived (2), make a survey of (2 [+928]), march (2), marched out (2), marching (2), minister (2), move (2), moved about (2), remain (2), return (2 [+8740]), rode (2), sent (2), set sail (2), spread (2), stay (2), thief (2), took (2), travel (2), walk about (2), walked along (2 [+2143]), walking along (2 [+2143]), way (2), went (2 [+2143]), went along (2 [+2143]), went on way (2), went out (2 [+2143]), went over (2), went up (2), were on way (2), wet (2), about (1), accompanied (1 [+907]), accompanied by (1 [+6640]), accompany (1 [+4200, 5584]), advances (1), all the way (1), all this time (1), associates (1), attended by (1 [+4200, 8079]), avoid (1 [+4202, 448]), banish (1), be on way (1 [+5825, 2256]), became more and more powerful (1 [+2256, 1524]), blows (1), by all means go (1 [+995]), came back (1 [+2256, 995]), cause to live (1), climbed up (1), closer and closer (1 [+2256, 7929]), comes (1), commit (1 [+928]), committed (1 [+928]), concern (1), conduct (1), conduct the affairs (1 [+928, 7931]), continued (1 [+2118]), continued to grow (1), course (1), crawl (1), departed (1), departs (1), deported (1), devoted to (1), devoted to (1 [+339]), disappeared (1 [+4946, 6524]), dispersed (1 [+4200, 2006]), do not know where am going (1 [+2143, 6584, 889]), do not know where am going (1 [+6584, 889, 2143]), drive (1), driven (1), drove back (1), enabled to walk (1), entered (1 [+6330]), escape (1), escorted (1), exiled (1), fade away (1), faithful (1 [+928, 622]), flashed back and forth (1), flashed down (1), fleeing (1), fleet of trading ships (1 [+641, 9576]), fleet of trading ships (1 [+641, 4200, 9576]), floated (1), flowing (1), flows (1), flows away (1), flying (1), follow (1 [+928, 8079]), follow along (1), followers (1 [+339]), followers (1 [+408, 889, 6640]), freely strut (1), get away (1), get back (1), get rid of (1), go (1 [+995]), go (1 [+928, 2006]), go aside (1), go at once (1 [+2256, 995]), go forward (1), go in (1 [+2256, 995]), go now (1 [+995]), go now (1 [+995]), go on (1), go on way (1), go over (1), go to and fro (1), goes around (1), goes down (1), going around (1), going off (1), gone away (1), gone up (1), greedy (1 [+339]), grew even wilder (1 [+6192, 2256]), grew louder and louder (1 [+2256, 2618, 4394]), grew stronger and stronger (1 [+2256, 2618]), grew weaker and weaker (1 [+2256, 1924]), grope about (1), have go (1), hurry (1 [+4559]), increased more and more (1 [+2256, 8041, 2143]), increased more and more (1 [+2143, 2256, 8041]), invaded (1 [+4200]), join (1 [+6584]), join (1 [+6640]), journey (1), keep (1 [+928]), keep on (1), kept (1), kept (1 [+928]), kept on (1), kept on (1 [+8743]), lead (1 [+4200, 7156]), lead life (1 [+928]), lead lives (1), lead on (1 [+5627, 2256]), leading (1), leads (1), leave (1 [+4946, 6640]), leave (1 [+4946, 6643]), leaves (1 [+4946, 907]), leaving (1), led (1 [+339]), led life (1 [+928]), left (1 [+4946, 6640]), live (1 [+928]), live securely (1), made walk (1), made way (1), make flow (1), marches (1), melting away (1 [+4570, 2256]), more and more powerful (1 [+2256, 1541, 6330, 4200, 5087, 2025]), moved back and forth (1), moves (1), moves about (1), moves along (1), moving (1), moving about (1), moving from place to place (1), moving from place to place (1 [+2143, 928, 889]), moving from place to place (1 [+928, 889, 2143]), near (1 [+907]), neared (1 [+725]), obey (1 [+928]), off (1), passed away (1), passing (1), persisted (1), pressed harder and harder (1 [+2256, 7997]), proceed (1), proceeded (1), prowled (1), prowling (1), pursue (1 [+339]), pursued (1 [+339]), pursuing (1 [+339]), ran down (1), receded steadily (1 [+8740, 2256, 8740]), rejoined (1 [+448]), rely on (1 [+928]), resort to (1 [+4200, 7925]), return (1 [+995]), return (1 [+7155, 2256]), return (1 [+2256, 8740]), ride (1 [+928]), rides (1), roam (1 [+2256, 3718]), roamed (1), rode off (1), rougher and rougher (1 [+6192, 2256]), roving (1), runs along (1), sail (1 [+928, 2021, 641]), sending (1), sending on (1), set off (1), shining ever brighter (1 [+2256, 239]), slanderer (1 [+8215]), stalks (1), stream (1), strutting along with swaying hips (1 [+2256, 3262]), surely leave (1 [+4946, 6584, 2143]), surely leave (1 [+2143, 4946, 6584]), sweep (1), take back (1), take part (1 [+6640]), take possession (1), taken (1), themS (1 [+2021]), took (1 [+1583]), took to (1), travel along (1), traveled (1 [+2006]), travelers (1 [+5986]), traveling (1), trudge (1), turned (1), turning (1), use (1 [+448]), walk (1 [+928, 2006]), walk around (1), walked about (1), walked along (1), walked around (1), walked back and forth (1), walked on (1), walking along (1), walking around (1), wanders (1), ways (1), went about (1), went around (1), went back (1), went forth (1), went forward (1), went home (1), went in (1), willS (1), with (1), withdraw (1), withdrew (1 [+4946]), NDT (73)

H2144 הֵלֶךְ ***hēlek***, n.m. [2] [√2143]. oozing, flowing; visitor:– oozing out (1), traveler (1)

H2145 [1]הָלַל ***hālal***[1], v. [4] [→ 183, 2122]. [H] to flash, radiate, shine:– radiance (1), shone (1), show (1), throws out flashes (1)

H2146 [2]הָלַל ***hālal***[2], v. [146] [→ 2136, 2148, 2149, 4545, 9335; *also used with compound proper names*]. [P] to praise; give thanks; cheer, extol; [Pu] to be praised, be worthy of praise, be of renown; [Ht] to make one's boast in (the name of God); "Hallelujah" is a compound of the second person plural imperative and the personal name of God: hallelu-yah, praise Yah(weh); see 2149:– praise (87), boast (11), praised (8), worthy of praise (6), boasts (4), glory (4), give praise (3), praises (3), be praised (2), glory in (2), make boast (2), praising (2), bring praise (1), cheering (1), extol (1), gave thanks (1), giving praise (1), had wedding songs (1), is praised (1), renown (1), sang praises (1), sing praise (1), sing praises (1), that purposeS (1)

H2147 [3]הָלַל ***hālal***[3], v. [16] [→ 2099, 2100]. [Q] to be arrogant; [Po] to make a fool of, to mock, rail against; [Poal] to be foolish; [Htpo] to act like a madman; act furiously:– arrogant (3), go mad (2), makes fools of (2), acted like a madman (1), boast (1), drive furiously (1), gone mad (1), madness (1), mock (1), rail (1), storm (1), turns into a fool (1)

H2148 הִלֵּל ***hillēl***, n.pr.m. [2] [√2146]. Hillel, "*he has praises*":– Hillel (2)

H2149 הַלְלוּיָהּ ***halelûyāh***, v.+n.pr.m. *or* excl. Not used in NIVEBC [√2146 + 3378]. hallelujah (praise Yahweh)

H2150 הָלַם ***hālam***, v. [8] [→ 2153, 4547]. [Q] to strike, smash, beat, trample:– beat (1), laid low (1), smashed (1), strike (1), strikes (1), struck (1), thundered (1), trampled down (1)

H2151 הֲלֹם ***halōm***, adv. [12] to here:– here (4), this far (2 [+6330]), in all directions (1), now (1), over here (1), to (1), NDT (2)

H2152 הֶלֶם ***hēlem***, n.pr.m. [1] Helem, "*health*":– Helem (1)

H2153 הַלְמוּת ***halmût***, n.f. [1] [√2150]. hammer:– hammer (1)

H2154 [1]הָם ***hām***[1], n.pr.loc. [1] Ham:– Ham (1)

H2155 [2]הָם ***hām***[2], n.[m.] [1] [cf. 2166]. wealth:– wealth (1)

H2156 הֵם ***hēm***, p.m.pl. [558] [√2085; 10210]. they, them:– they (317), those (39), them (15), these (14), that (11), who (7), it (5), themselves (4), thingsS (3), indeed they (2 [+2156]), peopleS (2), suchS (2), the gatekeepersS (2), this (2), IsraelitesS (1), allS (1), his netS (1), our ownS (1), such (1), the (1), the BenjamitesS (1), the IsraelitesS (1), the othersS (1), the peopleS (1), the placesS (1), the priestsS (1), the spiesS (1), their idolsS (1), those same (1), yet (1 [+6330, 2021, 3427, 2021]), you (1), NDT (116)

H2157 הֶם- ***-hem***, הֵם- ***-hēm***, p.m.pl.suf. [3026] [→ 4548; cf. 2023]. they, them, their:– them (1100), their (907), they (122), theS (56), their (37 [+4200]), themselves (26), their own (20), those (18), the peopleS (11), it (8), these (6), who (6), whose (6), her (5), its (5), peopleS (5), his (4), menS (4), their own (4 [+4200]), theirs (4), whom (4), Moses and AaronS (3), him (3), my peopleS (3), the (3), the IsraelitesS (3), the idolsS (3), which (3), whichS (3), IsraelS (2), aS (2), each (2), its own (2), the GibeonitesS (2), the HagritesS (2), the envoysS (2), the postsS (2), theirs (2 [+4200]), themS (2 [+4053]), you (2), your (2), Elijah and ElishaS (1 [+9109]), IsraelitesS (1), bothS (1), doing soS (1), each otherS (1 [+9109]), enemiesS (1), godsS (1), his followersS (1), his preceptsS (1), itS (1), itself (1), loversS (1), man'sS (1), my accusersS (1), nephews (1 [+1201]), officialsS (1), oneS (1 [+4200]), one kind after another (1 [+4200, 5476]), othersS (1 [+4946]), people from Benjamin (1 [+278]), people from Judah (1 [+278]), peoplesS (1), priestsS (1 [+278]), relatedS (1), someone's (1), such godsS (1), such thingsS (1), that (1), the AmmonitesS (1), the EgyptiansS (1), the HebronitesS (1), the KohathiteS (1), the LevitesS (1), the PhilistinesS (1), the bodiesS (1), the brothersS (1), the cherubimS (1), the communityS (1), the deadS (1), the gatekeepersS (1), the heavensS (1), the man and the womanS (1), the potsS (1), the processionS (1), the shepherdsS (1), the spiesS (1), the standsS (1), the storehousesS (1 [+889, 928]), the storeroomsS (1), the waters (1), their (1 [+448]), their (1 [+4946]), their (1 [+6584]), their (1 [+928, 4090]), their descendantsS (1), their own (1 [+7156]), theirs (1 [+4946]), themS (1 [+8533]), themS (1 [+466]), themselves (1 [+7156]), thereS (1 [+928]), thereS (1 [+6584]), theseS (1), these daysS (1), these menS (1), these thingsS (1), this threatS (1), thornsS (1), those IsraelitesS (1), us (1 [+3276, 2256]), whereS (1 [+6584]), womenS (1), your troopsS (1), yours (1 [+4200]), NDT (546)

H2158 הַמְּדָתָא ***hammedātā'***, n.pr.m. [5] Hammedatha, "*given by the moon [god]*":– Hammedatha (5)

H2159 הָמָה ***hāmâ***, v. [33] [→ 2162, 2164?, 2166, 2167?; cf. 2101, 2169, 5637]. [Q] to make a noise, be tumultuous:– roar (5), disturbed (3), laments (3), growl (2), rage (2), roaring (2), snarling (2), unruly (2), brawler (1), cry out (1), groaned (1), in uproar (1), moan (1), noise (1 [+7754]), pound (1), pounds (1), raging (1), rush about (1), tumult (1), yearns (1)

H2160 הֵמָּה ***hēmmâ***, p.m.pl. Not used in NIVEBC [√2085; 10210]. they

H2161 הֵמָה- ***-hēmâ***, p.m.pl.suf. [1] [√2023]. they, them:– theS (1)

H2162 הָמוֹן ***hāmôn***, n.m. [82] [→ 1255, 2163, 2164; cf. 2159]. commotion, tumult, confusion; many, populace, hoards, army:– hordes (18), army (12), crowd (7), wealth (5), many (4), all (2 [+3972]), commotion (2), multitudes (2), noise (2), noisy (2), roar (2), vast army (2), abundance (1), army (1 [+2657]), clamor (1), common people (1), confusion (1), great amount (1), heavy (1), itS (1 [+2021]), large (1), masses (1), multitude (1), people (1), populace (1), rage (1), roaring (1), rumble (1), tenderness (1 [+5055]), throng (1), troops (1), tumult (1), turmoil (1), uproar (1 [+7754])

H2163 הֲמוֹן גּוֹג ***hemôn gôg***, n.pr.loc. [2] [√2162 + 1573]. Hamon Gog, "*multitude of Gog*":– Hamon Gog (2)

H2164 הֲמוֹנָה ***hemônâ***, n.pr.loc. [1] [√2162?; cf. 2159]. Hamonah, "*multitude*":– Hamonah (1)

H2165 הַמַּחְלְקוֹת ***hammaḥleqôt***, n.pl.f. Not used in NIVEBC [→ 6154; cf. 2745, 4712]. Hammahlekoth

H2166 הֶמְיָה ***hemyâ***, n.f. [1] [√2159; cf. 2155]. noise, sound, tone:– noise (1)

H2167 הֲמֻלָּה ***hemullâ***, n.f. [2] [√2159?]. tumult, sound, noise:– storm (1), tumult (1 [+7754])

H2168 הַמֹּלֶכֶת ***hammōleket***, n.pr.f. [1] [√2143; cf. 4907]. Hammoleketh, "*the queen*":– Hammoleketh (1)

H2169 [1]הָמַם ***hāmam***[1], v. [15] [cf. 2101, 2159, 5637]. [Q] to throw into confusion; to rout:– routed (3), threw into confusion (2), eliminated (1), resounds (1), rolled over (1), rout (1), ruin (1), threw into a panic (1), throw into confusion (1), throwing into confusion (1 [+4539]), thrown into confusion (1), troubling (1)

H2170 [2]הָמַם ***hāmam***[2], v. [Q] to drain

H2171 הָמַן ***hāman***, v.den.? [1] [Q] to rage, be turbulent:– unruly (1)

H2172 הָמָן ***hāmān***, n.pr.m. [54] Haman:– Haman (43), Haman's (5), heS (5), NDT (1)

H2173 הֲמָסִים ***hemāsîm***, n.[m.] [1] twigs, brushwood:– twigs (1)

H2174 הַמִּצְפֶּה ***hammiṣpeh***, n.pr.loc. Not used in NIVEBC [→ 8256; cf. 5205, 7595]. Ha-Mizpah, see 8256

H2175 הַמַּרְכָּבוֹת ***hammarkābôt***, n.pr.loc. Not used in NIVEBC [→ 1096]. Ha-Marcaboth

H2176 [1]הֵן ***hēn***[1], adv.demo. *or* interj. [99] [→ 434, 435, 2178, 2180, 6364; 10213]. see!, surely!; if, yet, but, then:– if (15), but (7), see (6), surely (6), look (4), now (4), yet (3), since (2), though (2), when (2), agreed (1), but if (1), even (1), for (1), full well (1), here (1), oh (1), only (1), true (1), what if (1), NDT (38)

H2177 הֵן- ***-hēn***[2], הֶן- ***-hen***, p.f.pl.suf. [183] [√2023]. they, them, their:– their (77), them (46), they (8), theS (3), it (2), its (2), their (2 [+4200]), their own (2), bothS (1), lead to do the sameS (1 [+2388, 339, 466]), the roomsS (1), the woman and her sisterS (1), the womenS (1), theirs (1), theseS (1), things (1), whereS (1 [+928]), which (1), whichS (1), NDT (30)

H2178 [1]הֵנָּה ***hēnnâ***[1], adv. [51] [→ 6364; cf. 2176]. here, to here; on this side, on the opposite side:– here (23), leftS (2), rightS (2), all this time (1 [+6330]), back and forth (1 [+285, 2256, 285, 2178]), back and forth (1 [+285, 2178, 2256, 285]), here (1 [+2025]), here (1 [+6330]), in any direction (1 [+2256, 2178]), in any direction (1 [+2178, 2256]), nearby (1), now (1), on this side (1), opposite (1), since (1 [+6330]), the present time (1), then (1), there (1), this (1), this dayS (1), thus far (1 [+6330]), to house (1), to houseS (1), toward it (1), yet (1 [+6330]), NDT (2)

H2179 [2]הֵנָּה ***hēnnâ***[2], p.f.pl. [45] [√2085]. they, these, those:– they (8), these (5), them (4), thingsS (2), those (2), both (1), cowsS (1), given even more (1 [+3578, 3869, 2256, 3869, 2179]), given even more (1 [+3578, 3869, 2179, 2256, 3869]), peopleS (1), plansS (1), such (1), their (1 [+4200]), themselves (1), what is the meaning (1 [+4537]), NDT (14)

H2180 הִנֵּה ***hinnēh***, pt.demo. [1060] [√2176]. look!, now!, here, there, a marker used to enliven a narrative, change a scene, emphasize an idea, or call attention to detail:– see (84), look (60), there (57), here (55), saw (44), now (33), if (27), surely (24), found (12), yes (9), how (6), indeed (6), listen (6), suddenly (6), but (5), this (5), beware (3), even (3), just then (3 [+2256]), that (3), already (2), appeared (2), as soon as (2), just (2), just as (2), remember (2), so (2), suppose (2), very well (2), very well then (2), what (2), when (2), I am (1), after all (1), all at once (1 [+2296]), be sure (1), certainly (1), come (1), come on then (1), consider (1), discovered (1), for (1), heard (1), here now (1), it is still there (1), look I know (1 [+6964]), meanwhile (1), nevertheless (1), not (1), now then (1), ready (1), ready to do (1), realized (1), right now (1), showed (1), since (1), soon (1), suddenly appeared (1), sure (1), surely (1 [+3954]), then (1), therefore (1), think (1), this is how (1), this is why (1), though (1), too (1), unless (1), very well (1 [+5528]), well (1), what can do (1), while (1), yes (1 [+3954]), NDT (544)

H2181 הֶנָה- ***-henâ***, הֵנָה- ***-henâ***, p.f.pl.suf. [3] [√2023]. they, them:– its (1), them (1), they (1)

H2182 הֲנָחָה ***hanāḥâ***, n.f. [1] [√5663]. holiday, an official day of rest and celebration:– holiday (1)

H2183 הִנֹּם ***hinnōm***, n.pr.m. & loc. [3] [→ 1208]. Hinnom:– Hinnom (3)

H2184 הֵנַע ***hēna'***, n.pr.loc. [3] Hena, "*Anath*":– Hena (3)

H2185 הֲנָפָה ***hanāpâ***, v. Not used in NIVEBC [√5677]. shaking, see 5677

H2186 הַנְּקֵב ***hanneqeb***, n.pr.loc. Not used in NIVEBC [→ 146; cf. 2021 + 5918]. Nekeb

H2187 הַס ***has***, interj. [7] [→ 2188]. Silence!, Quiet!, Hush!:– be silent (2), be still (2), hush (1), leave (1), silence (1)

H2188 הָסָה ***hāsâ***, v.den. [1] [√ 2187]. [H] to silence, cause to be still:– silenced (1)

H2189 הַסְּנָאָה ***hass^{e}nā'â***, n.pr.m. [1] [√ 2021 + 6171]. Hassenaah:– Hassenaah (1)

H2190 הַסְּנוּאָה ***hass^{e}nu'â***, n.pr.m. [2] [√ 2021 + 8533]. Hassenuah, "*the hated women*":– Hassenuah (2)

H2191 הַסֹּפֶרֶת ***hassōperet***, n.pr.m. [1] [√ 2021 + 6219]. Hassophereth, "*the scribes*":– Hassophereth (1)

H2192 הָעֲבָרִים ***hā'^{a}bārîm***, n.pr.loc. Not used in NIVEBC [→ 6516]. Abarim

H2193 הָעֵזֶר ***hā'ēzer***, n.pr.loc. Not used in NIVEBC [√ 6469]. Ha-Ezer, see 75, "*the rock*"

H2194 הָעַמֹּנִי ***hā'ammōnî***, a.g. Not used in NIVEBC [→ 4112; cf. 2021 + 6648, 6671]. Ha-Ammoni, see 4112, "*the Ammonite*"

H2195 הָעֵמֶק ***hā'ēmeq***, n.pr.loc. Not used in NIVEBC [√ 6676]. Ha-Emek, see 1097, "*the valley*"

H2196 הָעֲרָבָה ***hā'^{a}rābâ***, n.pr.loc. Not used in NIVEBC [→ 1098]. Ha-Arabah, see 1098, "*the desert*"

H2197 הָעֲרָלוֹת ***hā'^{a}rālôt***, n.f. Not used in NIVEBC [→ 1502; cf. 6889]. Haaraloth, see 1502, "*the foreskins*"

H2198 הֲפֻגָה ***h^{a}pugâ***, n.f. [1] [√ 7028]. relief, stopping:– relief (1)

H2199 הַפּוּךְ ***happûk***, n.pr.f. Not used in NIVEBC [→ 7968]. Happuch

H2200 הָפַךְ ***hāpak***, v. [94] [→ 2201, 2202, 2203, 4550, 4551, 9337; cf. 60]. [Q] to overthrow, overturn, turn around, change; [Qp] to be turned over; [N] to be changed, transformed, turned into; [Ho] to be overwhelmed; [Ht] to tumble around, flash back and forth, swirl; from the base meaning of turning an object over comes the fig. extension of "changing one's mind":– turned (20), turn (6), changed (4), overthrew (4), overthrow (4), be changed (2), be turned (2), turned back (2), turns (2), was changed (2), wheel around (2 [+3338]), are (1), be brought (1), be overthrown (1), been turned over (1), came tumbling (1), change (1), changed (1 [+337]), counterattack (1 [+928, 2021, 4878]), counterattacked (1), devastate (1), distort (1), disturbed (1), flashing back and forth (1), got down (1), is transformed (1), lay bare (1), left (1), overcome (1), overthrew destroying (1), overthrown (1), overthrows (1), overturn (1), overturned (1 [+4200, 5087, 2025]), overturns (1), overwhelm (1), perverse (1), purify (1 [+1359]), restores (1), routed (1 [+6902]), swirl (1), takes shape (1), the tables were turned (1), turn into (1), turned about (1 [+3338]), turned and became (1), turned around (1), turned into (1), turned over (1), turning (1), unreliable (1), was overcome (1), was overthrown (1), was sapped (1), was turned (1)

H2201 הֵפֶךְ ***hēpek***, n.m. [3] [√ 2200]. opposite, turning of things upside down, perversion:– opposite (1), turn upside down (1), very opposite (1)

H2202 הֲפֵכָה ***h^{a}pēkâ***, n.f. [1] [√ 2200]. catastrophe, demolition:– catastrophe (1)

H2203 הֲפַכְפַּךְ ***h^{a}pakpak***, a. [1] [√ 2200]. devious, crooked:– devious (1)

H2204 הַפִּצֵּץ ***happiṣṣēṣ***, n.pr.m. [1] [√ 2021 + 7207; cf. 7209]. Happizzez, "*the one who breaks*":– Happizzez (1)

H2205 הֻצַּב ***huṣṣab***, var. Not used in NIVEBC [√ 5893]. see 5893

H2206 הַצֹּבֵבָה ***haṣṣōbēbâ***, n.pr.m. [1] [√ 2021 + 7376]. Hazzobebah:– Hazzobebah (1)

H2207 הַצְּבָיִים ***haṣṣ^{e}bāyîm***, n.pr.m. Not used in NIVEBC [→ 7097]. Hazzebaim

H2208 הַצָּלָה ***haṣṣālâ***, n.f. [1] [√ 5911]. deliverance:– deliverance (1)

H2209 הַצְלֶלְפּוֹנִי ***haṣṣ^{e}lelpônî***, n.pr.f. [1] [√ 2021 + 7511 + 7156 + 3276]. Hazzelelponi:– Hazzelelponi (1)

H2210 הֹצֶן ***hōṣen***, n.[m.] [1] weapon (variously interpreted):– weapons (1)

H2211 הַצֻּרִים ***haṣṣurîm***, n.pr.loc. Not used in NIVEBC [→ 2763]. Hazzurim

H2212 הַקּוֹץ ***haqqôṣ***, n.pr.m. [5] [√ 2021 + 7764?]. Hakkoz, "*the thorn*":– Hakkoz (5)

H2213 הַקּוֹרֵא ***haqqōrē'***, n.pr.loc. Not used in NIVEBC [→ 6530]. Hakkore, see 6530

H2214 הַקָּטָן ***haqqāṭān***, n.pr.m. [1] [√ 2021 + 7783]. Hakkatan, "*the small one*":– Hakkatan (1)

H2215 הַר ***har***, n.m. [561] [→ 2216; cf. 2105]. hill, mountain, range (of hills, mountains); referring to low hills as well as high mountains:– mountains (139), mountain (121), mount (120), hill country (84), hills (39), hill (28), mountain shrines (4), mountaintops (4 [+8031]), it^{S} (3 [+2021]), another^{S} (1 [+2021, 4946, 2296]), hillside (1), hillside (1 [+7521]), hilltop (1), hilltop (1 [+8031]), hilltops (1 [+8031]), it^{S} (1 [+1628]), made mountain (1), mountain clefts (1), mountain haunts (1), mountain regions (1), mountaintop (1 [+8031]), range (1), there (1 [+928, 2021]), there^{S} (1 [+928, 2021]), NDT (4)

H2216 הֹר ***hōr***, n.pr.loc. [12] [√ 2215]. Hor, "[perhaps] *mountain*":– Hor (12)

H2217 הָרָא ***hārā'***, n.pr.loc. [1] Hara, "*hill, highland*":– Hara (1)

H2218 הָרֹאֶה ***hārō'eh***, n.pr.m. [1] [√ 8011]. Haroeh, "*the seer*":– Haroeh (1)

H2219 הַרְאֵל ***har'ēl***, n.[m.] [1] [cf. 789]. altar hearth:– altar hearth (1)

H2220 הַרְבָּה ***harbâ***, v. Not used in NIVEBC [√ 8049]. see 8049

H2221 הַרְבֵּה ***harbēh***, v.inf. (used as adv.) [50] [√ 8049]. great (number), many, much, abundance:– much (10), many (8), great (4), great quantity (4 [+4394]), more (3), quantities (2), abundance (1), abundance (1 [+4394]), abundant supply (1), all (1), extensive (1), full (1), great (1 [+4394]), great numbers (1 [+4394]), greatly (1), large (1), large amount (1 [+4394]), large number (1), overrighteous (1 [+7404]), overwicked (1 [+8399]), seldom (1 [+4202]), so much (1), terribly (1 [+4394]), very (1 [+4394]), wept bitterly (1 [+1134, 1135])

H2222 הָרַג ***hārag***, v. [167] [→ 2223, 2224]. [Q] to kill, put to death, murder, slaughter; [Qp, N, Pu] to be slain, be put to death, be slaughtered:– killed (55), kill (46), slain (8), put to death (7), killing (6), murdered (4), slay (4), kills (3), put (3), destroyed (2), kill (2 [+2222]), must certainly put to death (2 [+2222]), slayer (2), be killed (1), be ravaged (1), been killed (1), destroy (1), destroying (1), executed (1), face death (1), murder (1), murderer (1), murderers (1), murdering (1), murders (1), put to death (1 [+4638]), ravage (1), slaughter (1), slaughter (1 [+4200, 5422]), slaughter takes place (1 [+2223]), slaughtered (1), slaughtering (1), slew (1), NDT (3)

H2223 הֶרֶג ***hereg***, n.m. [5] [√ 2222]. slaughter, killing:– slaughter (2), killed (1), killing (1), slaughter takes place (1 [+2222])

H2224 הֲרֵגָה ***h^{a}rēgâ***, n.f. [5] [√ 2222]. slaughter:– slaughter (5)

H2225 הָרָה ***hārâ***, v. [45] [→ 2226, 2228, 2230, 2231]. [Q] to conceive, become pregnant, be with child; [Gp; Pu] to be conceived, born:– pregnant (21), conceived (14), conceive (4), conceives (1), gave birth (1), is conceived (1), with child (1), NDT (2)

H2226 הָרֶה ***hāreh***, a.f. [12] [√ 2225]. pregnant, expecting (child):– pregnant (8), conceive (1), enlarged (1), expectant mothers (1), pregnant women (1)

H2227 הָרוּם ***hārûm***, n.pr.m. [1] [cf. 2235]. Harum, "*consecrated*":– Harum (1)

H2228 הֵרוֹן ***hērôn***, n.[m.] [1] [√ 2225]. childbearing, pregnancy:– childbearing (1)

H2229 הֲרוֹרִי ***h^{a}rôrî***, a.g. [1] Harorite:– Harorite (1)

H2230 הָרִיָּה ***hāriyyâ***, a.f. [1] [√ 2225]. pregnant, expecting:– pregnant women (1)

H2231 הֵרָיוֹן ***hērāyôn***, n.[m.] [2] [√ 2225]. conception, pregnancy:– conceive (1), conception (1)

H2232 הֲרִיסָה ***h^{a}rîsâ***, n.f. [1] [√ 2238]. ruin:– ruins (1)

H2233 הֲרִיסוּת ***h^{a}rîsût***, n.f. [1] [√ 2238]. waste, ruin, destruction:– waste (1)

H2234 הָרָם ***hārām***, n.pr.loc. Not used in NIVEBC [→ 1099]. Haram

H2235 הֹרָם ***hōrām***, n.pr.m. [1] [cf. 2227]. Horam, "*height*":– Horam (1)

H2236 הַרְמוֹן ***harmôn***, n.pr.loc. [1] Harmon:– Harmon (1)

H2237 הָרָן ***hārān***, n.pr.m. [7] [→ 1100]. Haran, "*mountaineer* [perhaps *sanctuary*]":– Haran (7)

H2238 הָרַס ***hāras***, v. [43] [→ 2232, 2233]. [Q] to tear down, break down, destroy; [Qp] to be in ruins; [N] to be destroyed, in ruins; [P] to destroy:– tear down (8), torn down (4), overthrow (3), destroyed (2), force way through (2), must demolish (2 [+2238]), tears down (2), are torn down (1), be overturned (1), been broken down (1), been torn down (1), being destroyed (1), break (1), break down (1), demolish (1), demolished (1), destroy (1), in ruins (1), is destroyed (1), laid waste (1 [+2990, 2256]), left in ruins (1), ousted (1), overthrew (1), overthrown (1), pull down (1), threw down (1), was destroyed (1)

H2239 הֶרֶס ***heres***, n.[m.] Not used in NIVEBC [→ 6556]. destruction (= Heliopolis)

H2240 הֲרָרִי ***h^{a}rārî***, a.g. [5] Hararite:– Hararite (5)

H2241 הַשַּׁחַר ***haššaḥar***, n.pr.loc. Not used in NIVEBC [→ 7680]. Ha-Shahar, see 7680, "*the dawn*"

H2242 הַשִּׁטָּה ***haššiṭṭâ***, n.pr.loc. Not used in NIVEBC [→ 1101]. Ha-Shittah, see 1101, "*the acacia*"

H2243 הַשִּׁטִּים ***haššiṭṭîm***, n.pr.loc. Not used in NIVEBC [→ 69]. Ha-Shittim, see 69, "*the acacias*"

H2244 הָשֵׁם ***hāšēm***, n.pr.m. [1] Hashem:– Hashem (1)

H2245 הַשְׁמָעוּת ***hašmā'ût***, n.f. [1] [√ 9048]. news, communication, information:– news (1 [+265])

H2246 הַתַּאֲוָה ***hatta'^{a}wâ***, n.pr.loc. Not used in NIVEBC [→ 7701]. Hattaavah

H2247 הִתּוּךְ ***hittûk***, n.[m.] [1] [√ 5988]. melting:– melted (1)

H2248 הִתְחַבְּרוּת ***hitḥabb^{e}rût***, n. *or* v.ptcp. Not used in NIVEBC [√ 2489]. alliance, see 2489

H2249 הִתְיַחֵשׂ ***hityaḥēś***, v.den. Not used in NIVEBC [√ 3509]. registration

H2250 הַתִּיכוֹן ***hattîkôn***, n.pr.loc. Not used in NIVEBC [→ 2962; cf. 2021 + 9348]. Hatticon

H2251 הֲתָךְ ***h^{a}tāk***, n.pr.m. [4] Hathach, "*good*":– Hathak (3), him^{S} (1)

H2252 הָתַל ***hātal***, v. [1] [→ 2253; cf. 9438]. [P] to taunt, mock:– taunt (1)

H2253 הֲתֻלִּים ***h^{a}tulîm***, n.[m.]pl. [1] [√ 2252]. mockery:– mockers (1)

H2254 הָתַת ***hātat***, v. Not used in NIVEBC [cf. 2109]. [Po] to overwhelm with reproaches

H2255 ו ***w***, letter. Not used in NIVEBC [√ 10220]. letter of the Hebrew alphabet

H2256 -וְ ***w^{e}-***, c.pref. [50277] [√ 10221]. a marker showing the relationship between words, clauses, sentences, and sections; generally, coordinating: and, also; contrasting: but, yet, however; showing a logical relationship: because, so then; emphazing: even, indeed:– and (19120), but (1879), then (1831), so (1187), or (915), when (600), with (331), now (250), also (249), so that (243), that (177), yet (144), while (115), nor (107 [+4202]), and then (93), as (88), for (86), both and (79), after (77), together with (74), however (72), nor (68), as for (64), and when (63), and also (61), if (58), therefore (57), even (54), along with (51), and (50 [+1685]), and so (45), though (42), because (41), as well as (40), including (39), also (25 [+1685]), but when (25), twenty-five (23 [+6929, 2822]), even though (22), meanwhile (19), since (19), until (18), again (17), instead (17), even (16 [+1685]), in this way (16), twenty-two (15 [+6929, 9109]), 25,000 (14 [+2822, 6929, 547]), all generations (14 [+1887, 1887]), at this (14), 24,000 (13 [+6929, 752, 547]), nor (13 [+440]), or (13 [+4202]), both (12), thus (12), although (11), and now (11), and yet (11), next (11), whether or (11), 250 (10 [+2822, 4395]), but also (10), include (10), nevertheless (10), on each side (10 [+4946, 7024, 4946, 7024]), only (10), and that (9), but then (9), till (9), too (9), 4,500 (8 [+2822, 4395, 752, 547]), moreover (8), moreover (8 [+1685]), and too (7), but as for (7), either or (7), finally (7), spoke (7 [+5951, 606]), twenty-fourth (7 [+6929, 752]), and (6 [+677]), and though (6), besides (6), but now (6), on both sides^{S} (6 [+4946, 2296, 4946, 2296]), thirty-three (6 [+8993, 8993]), thirty-two (6 [+8993, 9109]), twenty-seventh (6 [+6929, 8679]), whenever (6), 120 (5 [+4395, 6929]), after that (5), but (5 [+219]), even if (5), indeed (5), just as (5), now that (5), or (5 [+561]), sent for (5 [+8938, 7924, 4200]), that is (5), to (5), twenty-four (5 [+6929, 752]), twenty-nine (5 [+6929, 9596]), 128 (4 [+4395, 6929, 9046]), 603,550 (4 [+9252, 4395, 547, 8993, 547, 2822, 4395, 2822, 2256, 2256]), afterward (4), and after (4), and as well (4), before (4), called together (4 [+8938, 665]), eighty-five (4 [+9046, 2822]), forty-one (4 [+752, 285]), forty-two (4 [+752, 9109]), go (4 [+2143, 8740]), nor (4 [+401]), on (4), on either side (4 [+4946, 7024, 4946, 7024]), one day (4), one day (4 [+2118]), or (4 [+1685]), so (4 [+1685]), so when (4), that is why (4), too (4 [+1685]), twenty-one (4 [+6929, 285]), twenty-third (4 [+8993, 6929]), twenty-three (4 [+6929, 8993]), yes (4), 1,254 (3 [+547, 4395, 2822, 752]), 127 (3 [+8679, 6929, 2256, 4395]), 127 (3 [+8679, 2256, 6929, 4395]), 151,450 (3 [+4395, 547, 2256, 285, 2822, 547, 752, 4395, 2822, 2256, 2256]), 29 (3 [+9596, 6929]), 40,500 (3 [+752, 547, 2822, 4395]), 430 (3 [+8993, 752, 4395]), 53,400 (3 [+8993, 2822, 547, 2256, 752, 4395]), 53,400 (3 [+8993, 2256, 2822, 547, 752, 4395]), and even (3), and since (3), and so that (3), as soon as (3), as well as (3 [+1685]), between (3 [+4946, 6330]), each people (3 [+6639, 6639]), each province (3 [+4519, 4519]), eleven hundred (3 [+547, 4395]), fifty-two (3 [+2822, 9109]), forty-five (3 [+752, 2822]), generations (3 [+1887, 1887]), idol (3 [+7181, 5011]), in (3), just then (3 [+2180]), neither (3 [+4202]), now (3 [+1685]), otherwise (3), parents (3 [+3, 562]), see (3 [+3359, 8011]), sent for (3 [+8938, 7924]), seventy-seven (3 [+8679, 8679]), so then (3), stark naked (3 [+6567, 6880]), then (3 [+1685]), thirty-five (3 [+8993, 2822]), thirty-ninth (3 [+8993, 9596]), thirty-one (3 [+8993, 285]), thirty-seventh (3 [+8993, 8679]), twenty-eight (3 [+6929, 9046]), twenty-fifth (3 [+6929, 2822]), twenty-third (3 [+6929, 8993]), 1,052 (2 [+547, 2822, 9109]), 1,247 (2 [+547, 4395, 752, 8679]), 1,775 (2 [+547, 8679, 4395, 2256, 2822, 2256, 8679]), 1,775 (2 [+547, 2256, 8679, 4395, 2822, 2256, 8679]), 1,775 (2 [+547, 2256, 8679, 4395, 2256, 2822, 8679]), 112 (2 [+4395, 9109, 6925]), 123 (2 [+4395, 6929, 8993]), 137 (2 [+8679, 8993, 2256, 4395]), 137 (2 [+8679, 2256, 8993, 4395]), 150 (2 [+4395, 2822]),

186,400 (2 [+4395, 547, 2256, 9046, 547, 9252, 547, 752, 4395, 2256]), 220 (2 [+4395, 6929]), 223 (2 [+4395, 6929, 8993]), 245 (2 [+4395, 752, 2822]), 3,600 (2 [+8993, 547, 9252, 4395]), 30,500 (2 [+8993, 547, 2822, 4395]), 32 (2 [+9109, 8993]), 32,200 (2 [+9109, 8993, 547, 2256, 4395]), 32,200 (2 [+9109, 2256, 8993, 547, 4395]), 320 (2 [+8993, 4395, 6929]), 345 (2 [+8993, 4395, 752, 2822]), 35,400 (2 [+2822, 8993, 547, 2256, 752, 4395]), 35,400 (2 [+2822, 2256, 8993, 547, 752, 4395]), 36,000 (2 [+9252, 8993, 547]), 372 (2 [+8993, 4395, 8679, 9109]), 390 (2 [+8993, 4395, 9596]), 392 (2 [+8993, 4395, 9596, 9109]), 4,600 (2 [+752, 547, 9252, 4395]), 403 (2 [+8993, 752, 4395]), 41,500 (2 [+285, 752, 547, 2256, 2822, 4395]), 41,500 (2 [+285, 2256, 752, 547, 2822, 4395]), 42 (2 [+752, 9109]), 435 (2 [+752, 4395, 8993, 2822]), 45,650 (2 [+2822, 752, 547, 2256, 9252, 4395, 2256, 2822]), 45,650 (2 [+2822, 2256, 752, 547, 9252, 4395, 2256, 2822]), 45,650 (2 [+2822, 2256, 752, 547, 2256, 9252, 4395, 2822]), 46,500 (2 [+9252, 752, 547, 2256, 2822, 4395]), 46,500 (2 [+9252, 2256, 752, 547, 2822, 4395]), 52 (2 [+2822, 9109]), 54,400 (2 [+752, 2822, 547, 2256, 752, 4395]), 54,400 (2 [+752, 2256, 2822, 547, 752, 4395]), 57,400 (2 [+8679, 2822, 547, 2256, 752, 4395]), 57,400 (2 [+8679, 2256, 2822, 547, 752, 4395]), 59,300 (2 [+9596, 2822, 547, 2256, 8993, 4395]), 59,300 (2 [+9596, 2256, 2822, 547, 8993, 4395]), 6,720 (2 [+9252, 547, 8679, 4395, 6929]), 603,550 (2 [+9252, 4395, 547, 2256, 8993, 547, 2822, 4395, 2822, 2256]), 62,700 (2 [+9109, 9252, 547, 2256, 8679, 4395]), 62,700 (2 [+9109, 2256, 9252, 547, 8679, 4395]), 621 (2 [+9252, 4395, 6929, 285]), 65 (2 [+2822, 9252]), 652 (2 [+9252, 4395, 2822, 9109]), 666 (2 [+9252, 4395, 9252, 9252]), 7,337 (2 [+8679, 547, 8993, 4395, 8993, 8679]), 736 (2 [+8679, 4395, 8993, 9252]), 74 (2 [+8679, 752]), 74,600 (2 [+752, 8679, 547, 2256, 9252, 4395]), 74,600 (2 [+752, 2256, 8679, 547, 9252, 4395]), 760 (2 [+8679, 4395, 9252]), 95 (2 [+9596, 2822]), 973 (2 [+9596, 4395, 8679, 8993]), 98 (2 [+9596, 9046]), and afterward (2), and because (2), and included (2), anywhere else (2 [+625, 2025, 625, 2025]), as well (2), at either ends (2 [+4946, 2296, 4946, 2296]), at that time (2), became more and more powerful (2 [+2143, 2143, 1524]), besides (2 [+1685]), beyond (2 [+4946, 2134]), but (2 [+1685]), but even (2), differing weights (2 [+74, 74]), each dish (2 [+4094, 4094]), each gate (2 [+9133, 9133]), each lampstand (2 [+4963, 4963]), even when (2), far and wide (2 [+4946, 2085, 2134]), fifty-five (2 [+2822, 2822]), followed by (2), forty-eight (2 [+752, 9046]), fourteen hundred (2 [+547, 752, 4395]), from (2), fully accomplishes (2 [+6913, 7756]), furthermore (2), head (2 [+4946, 8900, 5087, 2025]), here (2), how (2), idols (2 [+7178, 5011]), imported (2 [+6590, 3655]), in turn (2), included (2), indeed (2 [+1685]), led in campaigns (2 [+3655, 995, 4200, 7156]), led on military campaigns (2 [+3655, 995]), neither (2), ninety-nine (2 [+9596, 9596]), ninety-six (2 [+9596, 9252]), nor (2 [+1153]), now when (2), or (2 [+440]), or (2 [+3954]), otherwise (2 [+4202]), pierces (2 [+5918, 995, 928]), put to death (2 [+5782, 4637]), rather (2), rather than (2 [+4202]), rebuilt (2 [+8740, 1215]), seventy-five (2 [+8679, 2822]), sixty-six (2 [+9252, 9252]), sixty-two (2 [+9252, 9109]), slaves (2 [+6269, 9148]), still (2), summoned (2 [+8938, 7924]), thems (2 [+2286, 7518]), then when (2), therefore (2 [+1685]), thirty-eighth (2 [+8993, 9046]), thirty-second (2 [+8993, 9109]), thirty-seven (2 [+8993, 8679]), together with (2 [+1685]), too (2 [+677]), treaty of friendship (2 [+8934, 3208]), twenty-first (2 [+6929, 285]), twenty-first (2 [+285, 6929]), twenty-fourth (2 [+752, 6929]), twenty-second (2 [+9109, 6929]), twenty-seven (2 [+6929, 8679]), twenty-three (2 [+8993, 6929]), us (2 [+3276, 3870]), various kinds of service (2 [+6275, 6275]), with the help of (2), yet (2 [+1685]), 1,017 (1 [+547, 8679, 6925]), 1,222 (1 [+547, 4395, 6929, 9109]), 1,254 (1 [+547, 4395, 752, 2822]), 1,290 (1 [+547, 4395, 9596]), 1,335 (1 [+547, 8993, 4395, 8993, 2822]), 1,365 (1 [+2822, 9252, 2256, 8993, 4395, 2256, 547]), 1,365 (1 [+2822, 2256, 9252, 8993, 4395, 2256, 547]), 1,365 (1 [+2822, 2256, 9252, 2256, 8993, 4395, 547]), 1,760 (1 [+547, 8679, 4395, 2256, 9252]), 1,760 (1 [+547, 2256, 8679, 4395, 9252]), 105 (1 [+2822, 4395]), 108,100 (1 [+4395, 547, 9046, 547, 2256, 4395]), 108,100 (1 [+4395, 547, 2256, 9046, 547, 4395]), 110 (1 [+4395, 6927]), 119 (1 [+9596, 6926, 4395]), 120,000 (1 [+4395, 6929, 547]), 122 (1 [+4395, 6929, 9109]), 122 (1 [+4395, 6929, 2256, 9109]), 122 (1 [+4395, 2256, 6929, 9109]), 130 (1 [+8993, 4395]), 130 (1 [+4395, 8993]), 133 (1 [+8993, 8993, 2256, 4395]), 133 (1 [+8993, 2256, 8993, 4395]), 138 (1 [+4395, 8993, 9046]), 139 (1 [+4395, 8993, 9596]), 14,700 (1 [+752, 6925, 547, 8679, 4395]), 148 (1 [+4395, 752, 9046]), 151,450 (1 [+4395, 547, 285, 2822, 547, 752, 4395, 2822, 2256, 2256, 2256]), 153,600 (1 [+4395, 2822, 547, 2256, 8993, 547, 2256, 9252, 4395]), 153,600 (1 [+4395, 2256, 2822, 547, 8993, 547, 2256, 9252, 4395]), 153,600 (1 [+4395, 2256, 2822, 547, 2256, 8993, 547, 9252, 4395]), 156 (1 [+4395, 2822, 9252]), 157,600 (1 [+4395, 547, 8679, 2256, 2822, 547, 9252, 4395, 2256]), 157,600 (1 [+4395, 547, 2256, 8679, 2822, 547, 9252, 4395, 2256]), 157,600 (1 [+4395, 2256, 547, 2256, 8679, 2256, 2822, 547, 9252, 4395]), 16,750 (1 [+9252, 6925, 547, 8679, 4395, 2822]), 160 (1 [+4395, 9252]), 162 (1 [+9109, 9252, 2256, 4395]), 162 (1 [+9109, 2256, 9252, 4395]), 17,200 (1 [+8679, 6925, 547, 4395]), 172 (1 [+4395, 8679, 9109]), 180 (1 [+9046, 4395]), 180,000 (1 [+4395, 9046, 547]), 182 (1 [+9109, 9046, 2256, 4395]), 182 (1 [+9109, 2256, 9046, 4395]), 186,400 (1 [+4395, 547, 9046, 547, 9252, 547, 752, 4395, 2256, 2256]), 187 (1 [+8679, 9046, 2256, 4395]), 187 (1 [+8679, 2256, 9046, 4395]), 188 (1 [+4395, 9046, 9046]), 2,056 (1 [+547, 2822, 9252]), 2,067 (1 [+547, 9252, 8679]), 2,172 (1 [+547, 4395, 8679, 9109]), 2,172 (1 [+547, 4395, 8679, 2256, 9109]), 2,172 (1 [+547, 4395, 2256, 8679, 9109]), 2,200 (1 [+547, 4395]), 2,300 (1 [+547, 8993, 4395]), 2,322 (1 [+547, 8993, 4395, 6929, 9109]), 2,400 (1 [+547, 752, 4395]), 2,600 (1 [+547, 9252, 4395]), 2,630 (1 [+547, 9252, 4395, 2256, 8993]), 2,630 (1 [+547, 2256, 9252, 4395, 8993]), 2,750 (1 [+547, 8679, 4395, 2822]), 2,812 (1 [+547, 9046, 4395, 9109, 6925]), 2,818 (1 [+547, 9046, 4395, 9046, 6925]), 20,200 (1 [+6929, 547, 4395]), 20,800 (1 [+6929, 547, 9046, 4395]), 205 (1 [+2822, 4395]), 207 (1 [+8679, 4395]), 209 (1 [+9596, 4395]), 212 (1 [+4395, 9109, 6925]), 218 (1 [+4395, 9046, 6925]), 22 (1 [+6929, 9109]), 22,000 (1 [+9109, 6929, 547]), 22,034 (1 [+6929, 9109, 547, 2256, 8993, 2256, 752]), 22,034 (1 [+6929, 2256, 9109, 547, 8993, 2256, 752]), 22,034 (1 [+6929, 2256, 9109, 547, 2256, 8993, 752]), 22,200 (1 [+9109, 6929, 547, 2256, 4395]), 22,200 (1 [+9109, 2256, 6929, 547, 4395]), 22,273 (1 [+9109, 6929, 547, 8993, 2256, 8679, 2256, 4395]), 22,273 (1 [+9109, 2256, 6929, 547, 8993, 8679, 2256, 4395]), 22,273 (1 [+9109, 2256, 6929, 547, 8993, 2256, 8679, 4395]), 22,600 (1 [+6929, 9109, 547, 2256, 9252, 4395]), 22,600 (1 [+6929, 2256, 9109, 547, 9252, 4395]), 23,000 (1 [+8993, 6929, 547]), 232 (1 [+4395, 9109, 8993]), 24,000 (1 [+752, 6929, 547]), 242 (1 [+4395, 752, 9109]), 245 (1 [+4395, 752, 2256, 2822]), 245 (1 [+4395, 2256, 752, 2822]), 25,100 (1 [+6929, 2822, 547, 2256, 4395]), 25,100 (1 [+6929, 2256, 2822, 547, 4395]), 26,000 (1 [+6929, 9252, 547]), 273 (1 [+8993, 8679, 2256, 4395]), 273 (1 [+8993, 2256, 8679, 4395]), 28 (1 [+6929, 9046]), 28,600 (1 [+6929, 9046, 547, 2256, 9252, 4395]), 28,600 (1 [+6929, 2256, 9046, 547, 9252, 4395]), 280,000 (1 [+4395, 9046, 547]), 284 (1 [+4395, 9046, 752]), 288 (1 [+4395, 9046, 9046]), 3,023 (1 [+8993, 547, 6929, 2256, 8993]), 3,023 (1 [+8993, 547, 2256, 6929, 8993]), 3,200 (1 [+8993, 547, 4395]), 3,630 (1 [+8993, 547, 9252, 4395, 2256, 8993]), 3,630 (1 [+8993, 547, 2256, 9252, 4395, 8993]), 3,700 (1 [+8993, 547, 8679, 4395]), 3,930 (1 [+8993, 547, 9596, 4395, 8993]), 307,500 (1 [+8993, 4395, 547, 8679, 547, 2256, 2822, 4395]), 307,500 (1 [+8993, 4395, 547, 2256, 8679, 547, 2822, 4395]), 318 (1 [+9046, 6925, 8993, 4395]), 32 (1 [+8993, 9109]), 32,000 (1 [+9109, 8993, 547]), 32,500 (1 [+9109, 8993, 547, 2256, 2822, 4395]), 32,500 (1 [+9109, 2256, 8993, 547, 2822, 4395]), 323 (1 [+4395, 8993, 6929, 8993]), 324 (1 [+8993, 4395, 6929, 752]), 328 (1 [+8993, 4395, 6929, 9046]), 337,500 (1 [+8993, 4395, 547, 8993, 547, 8679, 547, 2256, 2822, 4395]), 337,500 (1 [+8993, 4395, 547, 2256, 8993, 547, 8679, 547, 2822, 4395]), 337,500 (1 [+8993, 4395, 547, 8993, 547, 2256, 8679, 547, 2256, 2822, 4395]), 337,500 (1 [+8993, 4395, 547, 2256, 8993, 547, 8679, 547, 2256, 2822, 4395]), 337,500 (1 [+8993, 4395, 547, 2256, 8993, 547, 2256, 8679, 547, 2822, 4395]), 34 (1 [+752, 8993]), 35 (1 [+2822, 8993]), 350 (1 [+8993, 4395, 2822]), 36,000 (1 [+8993, 9252, 547]), 365 (1 [+2822, 9252, 2256, 8993, 4395]), 365 (1 [+2822, 2256, 9252, 8993, 4395]), 37,000 (1 [+8993, 8679, 547]), 410 (1 [+752, 4395, 6927]), 42,360 (1 [+752, 8052, 547, 8993, 4395, 9252]), 420 (1 [+752, 4395, 6929]), 43,730 (1 [+8993, 752, 547, 2256, 8679, 4395, 2256, 8993]), 43,730 (1 [+8993, 2256, 752, 547, 8679, 4395, 2256, 8993]), 43,730 (1 [+8993, 2256, 752, 547, 2256, 8679, 4395, 8993]), 44,760 (1 [+752, 752, 547, 2256, 8679, 4395, 2256, 9252]), 44,760 (1 [+752, 2256, 752, 547, 8679, 4395, 2256, 9252]), 44,760 (1 [+752, 2256, 752, 547, 2256, 8679, 4395, 9252]), 45,400 (1 [+2822, 752, 547, 2256, 752, 4395]), 45,400 (1 [+2822, 2256, 752, 547, 752, 4395]), 45,600 (1 [+2822, 752, 547, 2256, 9252, 4395]), 45,600 (1 [+2822, 2256, 752, 547, 9252, 4395]), 454 (1 [+752, 4395, 2822, 752]), 468 (1 [+752, 4395, 9252, 9046]), 5,400 (1 [+2822, 547, 752, 4395]), 52,700 (1 [+9109, 2822, 547, 2256, 8679, 4395]), 52,700 (1 [+9109, 2256, 2822, 547, 8679, 4395]), 530 (1 [+2822, 4395, 8993]), 550 (1 [+2822, 2822, 4395]), 56 (1 [+2822, 9252]), 595 (1 [+2822, 9596, 2256, 2822, 4395]), 595 (1 [+2822, 2256, 9596, 2822, 4395]), 6,200 (1 [+9252, 547, 4395]), 6,800 (1 [+9252, 547, 9046, 4395]), 60,500 (1 [+9252, 547, 2822, 4395]), 601,730 (1 [+9252, 4395, 547, 547, 8679, 4395, 2256, 8993]), 601,730 (1 [+9252, 4395, 547, 2256, 547, 8679, 4395, 8993]), 603,550 (1 [+9252, 4395, 547, 8993, 547, 2256, 2822, 4395, 2256, 2822]), 603,550 (1 [+9252, 4395, 547, 2256, 8993, 547, 2822, 4395, 2256, 2822]), 603,550 (1 [+9252, 4395, 547, 2256, 8993, 547, 2256, 2822, 4395, 2822]), 61 (1 [+285, 9252]), 61,000 (1 [+9252, 8052, 547]), 61,000 (1 [+285, 9252, 547]), 62 (1 [+9252, 9109]), 623 (1 [+9252, 4395, 6929, 8993]), 628 (1 [+9252, 4395, 6929, 9046]), 64,300 (1 [+752, 9252, 547, 2256, 8993, 4395]), 64,300 (1 [+752, 2256, 9252, 547, 8993, 4395]), 64,400 (1 [+752, 9252, 547, 2256, 752, 4395]), 64,400 (1 [+752, 2256, 9252, 547, 752, 4395]), 642 (1 [+9252, 4395, 752, 9109]), 642 (1 [+9252, 4395, 752, 2256, 9109]), 642 (1 [+9252, 4395, 2256, 752, 9109]), 648 (1 [+9252, 4395, 752, 9046]), 650 (1 [+9252, 4395, 2822]), 655 (1 [+9252, 4395, 2822, 2822]), 666 (1 [+9252, 4395, 9252, 2256, 9252]), 666 (1 [+9252, 4395, 2256, 9252, 9252]), 667 (1 [+9252, 4395, 9252, 8679]), 67 (1 [+9252, 8679]), 675 (1 [+9252, 4395, 2822, 8679]), 675,000 (1 [+9252, 4395, 547, 8679, 547, 2256, 2822, 547]), 675,000 (1 [+9252, 4395, 547, 2256, 8679, 547, 2822, 547]), 690 (1 [+9252, 4395, 9596]), 7,100 (1 [+8679, 547, 4395]), 7,500 (1 [+8679, 547, 2822, 4395]), 72 (1 [+9109, 8679]), 72,000 (1 [+9109, 8679, 547]), 721 (1 [+8679, 4395, 6929, 2256, 285]), 721 (1 [+8679, 4395, 2256, 6929, 285]), 725 (1 [+8679, 4395, 6929, 2822]), 730 (1 [+8679, 4395, 8993]), 743 (1 [+8679, 4395, 752, 8993]), 743 (1 [+8679, 4395, 752, 2256, 8993]), 743 (1 [+8679, 4395, 2256, 752, 8993]), 745 (1 [+8679, 4395, 752, 2822]), 76,500 (1 [+9252, 8679, 547, 2256, 2822, 4395]), 76,500 (1 [+9252, 2256, 8679, 547, 2822, 4395]), 775 (1 [+8679, 4395, 2822, 8679]), 777 (1 [+8679, 8679, 2256, 8679, 4395]), 777 (1 [+8679, 2256, 8679, 8679, 4395]), 782 (1 [+9109, 9046, 2256, 8679, 4395]), 782 (1 [+9109, 2256, 9046, 8679, 4395]), 8,580 (1 [+9046, 547, 2822, 4395, 2256, 9046]), 8,580 (1 [+9046, 547, 2256, 2822, 4395, 9046]), 8,600 (1 [+9046, 547, 9252, 4395]), 807 (1 [+8679, 9046, 4395]), 815 (1 [+2822, 6926, 9046, 4395]), 822 (1 [+9046, 4395, 6929, 9109]), 830 (1 [+8993, 9046, 4395]), 832 (1 [+9046, 4395, 8993, 9109]), 840 (1 [+752, 9046, 4395]), 845 (1 [+9046, 4395, 2822, 752]), 87,000 (1 [+9046, 8679, 547]), 895 (1 [+2822, 9596, 2256, 9046, 4395]), 895 (1 [+2822, 2256, 9596, 9046, 4395]), 905 (1 [+2822, 9596, 4395]), 910 (1 [+6924, 9596, 4395]), 912 (1 [+9109, 6926, 9596, 4395]), 928 (1 [+9596, 4395, 6929, 9046]), 930 (1 [+9596, 4395, 8993]), 945 (1 [+9596, 4395, 752, 2256, 2822]), 945 (1 [+9596, 4395, 2256, 752, 2822]), 950 (1 [+9596, 4395, 2822]), 956 (1 [+9596, 4395, 2822, 2256, 9252]), 956 (1 [+9596, 4395, 2256, 2822, 9252]), 962 (1 [+9109, 9252, 2256, 9596, 4395]), 962 (1 [+9109, 2256, 9252, 9596, 4395]), 969 (1 [+9596, 9252, 2256, 9596, 4395]), 969 (1 [+9596, 2256, 9252, 9596, 4395]), accompanied by (1), acts of violence (1 [+8719, 8691]), adding to (1 [+907]), after (1 [+1685]), after this (1), again and again (1 [+8899, 8938]), age-old (1 [+1887, 1887]), all time (1 [+1887, 1887]), along with (1 [+1685]), also (1 [+677]), also included (1), alternates (1 [+7194, 2298, 8232]), alternateds (1 [+7194, 8232]), and (1 [+255]), and (1 [+907]), and again (1), and alike (1), and as (1), and as for (1), and even after (1), and even though (1), and likewise (1), and that is why (1), and what about (1), and whenever (1), and with (1), annually (1 [+928, 3972, 9102, 9102]), anyone among people (1 [+8276, 278]), anywhere (1 [+625, 2025, 625, 2025]), army (1 [+7736, 6639]), as far as (1), as surely as (1), as surely as live (1 [+2644, 2644, 5883]), as well as (1 [+3869]), assassinated (1 [+5782, 4637]), at all (1 [+7785, 1524]), at that (1), back and forth (1 [+285, 2178, 285, 2178]), be on way (1 [+5825, 2143]), bearing (1), beasts of burden (1 [+2651, 989]), became more and more powerful (1 [+2143, 1524]), because (1 [+4202]), because (1 [+3610, 928, 3610]), been brought to attention (1 [+5583, 9048]), bordering each sides (1 [+4946, 2296, 4946, 2296]), boths (1 [+2021, 170, 2021, 8533]), both of you (1 [+3870, 2084]), bring (1 [+4374, 3655]), but (1 [+8370]), but (1 [+3463]), but even (1 [+1685]), but if (1), but too (1), but while (1), by (1), by the time (1), by then (1), calling together (1 [+8938, 995]), came back (1 [+2143, 995]), carefully investigated (1 [+2011, 1335]), carry out duties (1 [+3655, 995]), carry the battle (1 [+8740, 1741]), cities (1 [+6551, 6551]), closer and closer (1 [+2143, 7929]), commander-in-chief (1 [+8031, 8569]), completely (1 [+4946, 5883, 6330, 1414]), cover up (1 [+8740, 4059]), crushed completely (1 [+4730, 430]), curse (1 [+460, 8652]), did sos (1 [+4374, 8008, 2932]), differing measures (1 [+406, 406]), each of us (1 [+638, 2085]), each table (1 [+8947, 8947]), each town (1 [+6551, 6551]), eighteen thousand (1 [+8052, 9046, 547]), eighty-six (1 [+9046, 9252]), eighty-three (1 [+9046, 8993]), endless generations (1 [+1887, 1887]), endowed with (1), enslaved (1 [+3899, 4200, 6269, 4200, 9148]), especially (1), even (1 [+677]), even (1 [+677, 3954]), even then (1), even while (1), ever (1 [+4200, 1887, 1887]), every city (1 [+6551, 6551]), every day (1 [+3972, 3427, 3427]), every family (1 [+5476, 5476]), every province (1 [+4519, 4519]), except for (1 [+4202]), executed (1 [+5782, 4637]), far too numerous (1 [+8041, 6786]), fatherless (1 [+3846, 401, 3]), feasting (1 [+430, 9272]), fifteen (1 [+2822, 6927]), fifty-second (1 [+2822, 9109]), finally (1 [+1685]), find out (1 [+8011, 3359]), find out (1 [+3359, 8011]), find out (1 [+3359, 8011]), fine (1 [+1524, 3202]), for instance (1), forty-first (1 [+752, 285]), forty-nine (1 [+752, 9596]), forty-seven (1 [+752, 8679]), fully obeyed (1 [+9048, 6913]), furthermore (1 [+6388]), furthermore (1 [+1685]), furthermore (1 [+6964]), furthermore (1 [+2021, 9108]), generations long past (1 [+9102, 1887, 1887]), generations to come (1 [+1887, 1887]), given even more (1 [+3578, 3869, 2179, 3869, 2179]), go about business (1 [+3655, 995]), go at once (1 [+2143, 995]), go in (1 [+2143, 995]), grapes or raisins (1 [+6694, 4300, 3313]), great wrath (1 [+2405, 7912]), grew even wilder (1 [+6192, 2143]), grew louder and louder (1 [+2143, 2618, 4394]), grew stronger and stronger (1 [+2143, 2618]), grew weaker and weaker (1 [+2143, 1924]), had brought

(1 [+8938, 4374]), had executed (1 [+5782, 4637]), had removed (1 [+8938, 4374]), harem (1 [+8721, 8721]), hearts (1 [+4213, 4213]), here is what (1 [+3869, 2296, 3869, 2296]), how much more (1), how much more (1 [+677, 3954]), however (1 [+219]), if then (1), in addition (1), in addition to (1), in any direction (1 [+2178, 2178]), in any direction (1 [+3907, 3907]), in midair (1 [+1068, 2021, 9028, 1068, 2021, 824]), in order for (1), in such a way that (1), including (1 [+1685]), including and (1), increased (1 [+1540, 3578]), increased more and more (1 [+2143, 8041, 2143]), indeed (1 [+677, 3954]), instead (1 [+1685]), invite (1 [+8938, 7924]), joined (1 [+1685]), kills (1 [+5782, 5883, 4637]), kinds of cattle (1 [+989, 989]), laid waste (1 [+2990, 2238]), later (1), lead (1 [+3655, 995]), lead (1 [+3655, 4200, 7156, 995]), lead on (1 [+5627, 2143]), likewise (1), loaded with (1), look around (1 [+5951, 6524, 8011]), made good escape (1 [+5674, 4880]), man (1 [+408, 408]), many generations (1 [+1887, 1887]), many years (1 [+3427, 9102]), marauding forces (1 [+6296, 8740]), marries (1 [+4374, 1249]), meanwhile (1 [+6330, 3907, 6330, 3907]), melting away (1 [+4570, 2143]), members of family (1 [+1074, 1074, 3]), more and more powerful (1 [+2143, 1541, 6330, 4200, 5087, 2025]), movements (1 [+4604, 4569]), near (1 [+1685]), neither (1 [+440]), never (1 [+1153, 6409, 6329]), nevertheless (1 [+219]), ninety-eight (1 [+9596, 9046]), no more than (1), nor (1 [+561]), nor (1 [+1685]), nor (1 [+4946, 401]), nor (1 [+1685, 401]), nor (1 [+1685, 4202]), not (1), nothing at all (1 [+401, 700]), nothing at all (1 [+9332, 2039]), nothing but skin (1 [+6425, 1414]), now (1 [+6964]), numbers increased greatly (1 [+8049, 7238]), obey (1 [+9068, 6913]), on both (1 [+4946, 2296, 4946, 2296]), on both sides (1 [+7156, 294]), on both sides[S] (1 [+4946, 2296, 2296]), on duty (1 [+995, 3655]), on each side[S] (1 [+4946, 2296, 4946, 2296]), on the other side of (1 [+4946, 6298, 2134]), once more (1), one of the other peoples (1 [+6639, 6639]), or (1 [+401]), or (1 [+700]), or (1 [+561, 401]), pay any attention (1 [+5564, 8011]), pay careful attention (1 [+8011, 5742, 265]), pay close attention (1 [+7992, 9048]), please (1 [+3202, 3838, 928, 6524]), pressed harder and harder (1 [+2143, 7997]), provided for (1 [+2118, 4200, 4312, 430]), raised (1 [+5951, 5989]), raped (1 [+8886, 6700]), raped (1 [+6700, 8886]), rapes (1 [+9530, 8886, 6640]), rapes (1 [+2616, 8886, 6640]), realize (1 [+3359, 8011]), realized (1 [+8011, 3359]), reappears (1 [+8740, 7255]), rebuild (1 [+1215, 8740]), recaptured (1 [+8740, 4374]), receded steadily (1 [+8740, 2143, 8740]), recite (1 [+6699, 606]), reentered (1 [+995, 8740]), reopened (1 [+8740, 2916]), return (1 [+7155, 2143]), return (1 [+2143, 8740]), richest of foods (1 [+2693, 2016]), roam (1 [+2143, 3718]), rougher and rougher (1 [+6192, 2143]), ruined (1 [+2472, 2476]), say (1 [+6699, 606]), scream for help (1 [+8123, 7754, 7924]), screamed for help (1 [+8123, 7754, 7924]), securely barred (1 [+6037, 6037]), send for (1 [+8938, 4374]), send for (1 [+8938, 4374]), sent for (1 [+8938, 4374]), sent word (1 [+8938, 5583]), sent word (1 [+8938, 7924]), serve (1 [+3655, 995]), seventeen (1 [+8679, 6927]), seventeen hundred (1 [+8679, 4395, 547]), seventeen hundred (1 [+547, 8679, 4395]), seventy-five (1 [+2822, 8679]), shining ever brighter (1 [+2143, 239]), shouted (1 [+5951, 7754, 7924]), similarly (1), sixty-eight (1 [+9252, 9046]), sixty-five (1 [+9252, 2822]), slaves (1 [+6269, 563]), so if (1), square (1 [+802, 8145]), square (1 [+4946, 7024, 4946, 7024]), staggering burden (1 [+7050, 4842]), stared with a fixed gaze (1 [+6641, 906, 7156, 8492]), stayed night (1 [+3782, 4328]), still (1 [+1685]), strip off fine clothes (1 [+7320, 6910]), strutting along with swaying hips (1 [+2143, 3262]), summon (1 [+8938, 4374]), suppose (1), surely (1), than (1 [+1685]), than (1 [+4202]), that (1 [+1685]), the (1), the parties (1 [+408, 8276, 2084]), the two of them[S] (1 [+1192, 1189]), them[S] (1 [+7401, 59]), then (1 [+339]), then (1 [+6964]), they[S] (1 [+1770, 5083]), they[S] (1 [+3405, 8569, 2021, 2657]), they[S] (1 [+1201, 1514, 1201, 8017]), thirty-eight (1 [+8993, 9046]), thirty-eight (1 [+8993, 9046]), thirty-fifth (1 [+8993, 2822]), thirty-first (1 [+8993, 285]), thirty-six (1 [+8993, 9252]), thirty-sixth (1 [+8993, 9252]), thirty-three hundred (1 [+8993, 547, 8993, 4395]), this is how (1), through (1), till (1 [+677]), time and again (1 [+4202, 285, 4202, 9109]), to come (1 [+1887, 1887]), together (1), together with (1 [+677]), together with (1 [+6330]), took (1 [+4374, 5011]), took back (1 [+8938, 995]), towered (1 [+1467, 928, 7757, 5989, 7550]), travel about (1 [+3655, 995]), traveled through (1 [+6296, 8740]), twelve hundred (1 [+547, 4395]), twenty-eight (1 [+9046, 6929]), twenty-seven hundred (1 [+547, 8679, 4395]), twenty-six (1 [+6929, 9252]), twenty-six hundred (1 [+547, 9252, 4395]), twenty-sixth (1 [+6929, 9252]), two differing measures (1 [+406, 406]), two differing weights (1 [+74, 74]), two men (1 [+408, 278, 3481]), undivided loyalty (1 [+4202, 4213, 4213]), upon (1), us (1 [+3276, 2157]), us (1 [+3276, 4013]), utterly useless (1 [+2039, 8198]), various gates (1 [+9133, 9133]), various peoples (1 [+6639, 6639]), various provinces (1 [+4519, 4519]), what (1 [+3869, 2296, 3869, 2296]), what (1 [+3869, 2297, 3869, 2296]), what about (1), when also (1), where (1), wherever goes (1 [+928, 995, 928, 3655]), wherever goes (1 [+928, 3655, 928, 995]), whether (1), whether (1 [+700]), whether the (1), who (1), who (1 [+4769, 4769]), whoever he may be (1 [+6424, 6699]), whole world (1 [+824, 9315]), with (1 [+1685]), with both (1), yes (1 [+1685]), yes (1 [+1685]), yet (1 [+677]), yet (1 [+6964]), yet also (1), young and old (1 [+5087, 2025]), two (0 [+752, 9109]), NDT (20103)

H2257 וֹ- ***-ô***, ו- ***-w***, וּ- ***-û***, p.m.sg.suf. [11854] [√ 2023]. he, him, his; it, its:– his (3899), him (1963), their (679), it (515), he (457), its (411), the[S] (345), them (326), they (91), his own (81), his (73 [+4200]), their own (60), whose (56), himself (50), a[S] (47), your (40), her (38), whom (27), one (16), his (15 [+907]), who (15), you (14), your own (11), David[S] (10), the altar[S] (10), God[S] (9), himself (9 [+4213]), himself (9 [+5883]), them[S] (9 [+3]), themselves (9 [+5883]), each (8), its own (8), Moses[S] (7), he (7 [+5883]), himself (7 [+1414]), the (7), the king's[S] (7), God's[S] (6), his own (6 [+4200]), that (6), the Lord[S] (6), the king[S] (6), the man[S] (6), their (6 [+4200]), those (6), anyone (5), that[S] (5), the value[S] (5), their[S] (5 [+1201]), this[S] (5), which (5), Aaron[S] (4), David's[S] (4), Elijah[S] (4), Elisha[S] (4), Israel's[S] (4), Jacob[S] (4), Jehoram[S] (4), Jehu[S] (4), Solomon[S] (4), a (4), an[S] (4), its (4 [+4200]), one's (4), the gateway[S] (4), the same[S] (4), themselves (4), there[S] (4 [+928]), those[S] (4), Abram[S] (3), Eliakim's[S] (3), Gideon[S] (3), Jehoiachin[S] (3), Joseph[S] (3), Saul's[S] (3), any[S] (3), my (3), our own (3), same[S] (3), she (3), that person[S] (3), the Lord's[S] (3), their own (3 [+4200]), theirs (3 [+4200]), them (3 [+5883]), themselves (3 [+1414]), there[S] (3), they (3 [+5883]), whose (3 [+4200]), Aaron's[S] (2), Abraham[S] (2), Ahab[S] (2), Ahaziah[S] (2), Amnon[S] (2), Gehazi[S] (2), Isaac[S] (2), Jehoiachin's[S] (2), Jehoram's[S] (2), Jeremiah[S] (2), Joab[S] (2), Joash[S] (2), Job's[S] (2), Joseph's[S] (2), Josiah[S] (2), Josiah's[S] (2), Nebuchadnezzar[S] (2), Noah[S] (2), Saul[S] (2), Solomon's[S] (2), Zedekiah's[S] (2), alone (2 [+928, 1727]), enemy[S] (2), here[S] (2), him[S] (2 [+3]), his (2 [+6640]), hosea[S] (2), man[S] (2), own (2), owner (2 [+4200]), person[S] (2), pillar[S] (2), she[S] (2 [+562]), someone else[S] (2), such[S] (2), the area[S] (2), the ark[S] (2), the defender[S] (2), the king (2), the king of the south[S] (2), the lamps[S] (2), the neighbor[S] (2), the offender[S] (2), the person[S] (2), the priest[S] (2), the table[S] (2), the wicked[S] (2), their[S] (2), them[S] (2 [+278]), them[S] (2 [+6269]), they[S] (2 [+6269]), this altar[S] (2), tribe[S] (2), Abijah's[S] (1), Abishai[S] (1), Abraham's[S] (1), Absalom's[S] (1), Achan[S] (1), Achish[S] (1), Adonijah[S] (1), Ahab's[S] (1), Ahaz[S] (1), Amasa[S] (1), Amon's[S] (1), Baal's[S] (1), Baruch[S] (1), Benaiah[S] (1), Egypt[S] (1), Ehud[S] (1), Eleazar[S] (1), Elisha's[S] (1), Gog[S] (1), Hadad[S] (1), Haman[S] (1), Hanun[S] (1), Heman's[S] (1), Israel (1), Jacob's[S] (1), Jehoahaz[S] (1), Jehoiakim's[S] (1), Jehu's[S] (1), Jeriah[S] (1), Jesse[S] (1), Jethro[S] (1), Joab's[S] (1), Job[S] (1), Joshua[S] (1), Judah's[S] (1), Kish[S] (1), Laban[S] (1), Leviathan's[S] (1), Lot's[S] (1), Manasseh[S] (1), Naaman's[S] (1), Naboth's[S] (1), Necho[S] (1), Obed-Edom[S] (1), Obed-Edom's[S] (1), Othniel[S] (1), Pharaoh's[S] (1), Potiphar[S] (1), Rehoboam[S] (1), Samuel's[S] (1), Sennacherib's[S] (1), Shalmaneser's[S] (1 [+4200]), Shaul's[S] (1), Sheba[S] (1), Sherebiah's[S] (1), Shimei[S] (1), Uzziah[S] (1), Zechariah[S] (1), Zechariah's[S] (1), an[S] (1 [+4200]), animal[S] (1), another[S] (1), any such thing[S] (1), anyone[S] (1), both[S] (1), by himself (1 [+4200, 963]), by itself (1 [+4200, 963]), consecrate themselves (1 [+4848, 3338]), creditor (1 [+1251, 5408, 3338]), daily (1 [+3427, 928, 3427]), day by day (1 [+1821, 3427, 928, 3427]), did[S] (1 [+5989, 3338]), did this[S] (1 [+5742, 3338]), do that[S] (1 [+2118, 928, 3338]), each (1 [+408, 278]), each day's (1 [+3427, 928, 3427]), equally (1 [+408, 3869, 278]), equally among them (1 [+408, 3869, 278]), every[S] (1), godless[S] (1), he (1 [+3338]), he (1 [+4213]), he himself (1), her[S] (1 [+851]), her[S] (1 [+851, 123]), her husband[S] (1), her son[S] (1), herself (1), him (1 [+2006]), him (1 [+3338]), him (1 [+5883]), him[S] (1), him[S] (1 [+3162]), himself (1 [+4222]), himself (1 [+9005]), his (1 [+928]), his[S] (1 [+3]), his father[S] (1), his father's[S] (1), his neighbor[S] (1), his own (1 [+4946, 4213]), home (1 [+185]), home (1 [+5226]), human[S] (1), inner sanctuary[S] (1), it[S] (1), it[S] (1 [+2942]), it[S] (1 [+9005]), it[S] (1 [+8031]), it[S] (1 [+1947]), it[S] (1 [+2308]), it[S] (1 [+623]), its[S] (1), its[S] (1 [+7933]), its own (1 [+5883]), itself (1), man's[S] (1), married (1 [+4374, 4200, 4200, 851]), my[S] (1 [+1201]), my companion[S] (1), not circumcised (1 [+6889, 4200]), of his own (1 [+3655, 3751]), one's[S] (1), only (1 [+928, 1727]), only one (1 [+4200, 963]), opposite[S] (1), others[S] (1), our (1), owners (1), owns[S] (1), people[S] (1 [+6524]), person's[S] (1), prudent[S] (1 [+1251]), relieve himself (1 [+6114, 906, 8079]), relieving himself (1 [+6114, 906, 8079]), riches[S] (1), royal[S] (1), same (1), servant[S] (1), she[S] (1 [+7108]), she[S] (1 [+3304]), she[S] (1 [+851]), soldier[S] (1), someone (1), something[S] (1), stolen goods (1 [+4202, 4200]), that man's line[S] (1), that month[S] (1), that nation[S] (1), the Benjamites[S] (1), the Nazirite[S] (1), the Nazirite's[S] (1), the Philistine's[S] (1), the accused[S] (1), the angel[S] (1), the animal[S] (1), the article[S] (1), the avenger[S] (1), the basket[S] (1), the bells[S] (1), the boy[S] (1), the boy's[S] (1), the bread[S] (1), the buyer's[S] (1), the calf[S] (1), the captain[S] (1), the cloud[S] (1), the coming storm[S] (1), the country[S] (1), the curtain[S] (1), the enemy's[S] (1), the ephod[S] (1), the fabric[S] (1), the false witness[S] (1), the fugitive[S] (1), the gold[S] (1), the grapes[S] (1), the great cedar[S] (1), the guilty party[S] (1), the injured person[S] (1), the kidnapper's[S] (1), the king's (1), the lambs[S] (1), the land[S] (1), the leader's[S] (1), the man himself (1), the man's[S] (1), the murderer[S] (1), the one (1), the other[S] (1), the other half of Manasseh[S] (1), the other man[S] (1), the owner[S] (1), the people[S] (1), the person being dedicated (1), the platform[S] (1), the pot[S] (1), the potter[S] (1), the rim[S] (1), the robe[S] (1), the scroll[S] (1), the servant[S] (1), the shore[S] (1), the slave[S] (1), the snake[S] (1), the spoiled part[S] (1), the successor[S] (1), the tribe[S] (1), the wood[S] (1), the wrongdoer[S] (1), their body[S] (1), their children[S] (1), their descendants[S] (1), their own (1 [+5883]), their very (1), their wealth[S] (1), theirs (1 [+6584]), them (1 [+8031]), them[S] (1 [+6639]), them[S] (1 [+7366]), themselves (1 [+4213]), themselves (1 [+8638]), there[S] (1 [+928, 824]), there[S] (1 [+928, 9348]), there[S] (1 [+928, 7931]), these (1), these[S] (1), they (1 [+3338]), they[S] (1), they[S] (1 [+1201]), this god's[S] (1), this matter[S] (1), today[S] (1), uninhabited (1 [+4202, 132, 928]), victim[S] (1), walled (1 [+4200, 2570]), where[S] (1 [+928]), which[S] (1 [+678]), which[S] (1 [+7366]), who[S] (1), whose[S] (1 [+465, 1426]), wicked (1), wicked[S] (1), your (1 [+928]), your (1 [+4200]), your ancestor[S] (1), your neighbor[S] (1), your side[S] (1), your tithe[S] (1), yourself (1), yourself (1 [+4213]), yourself (1 [+5883]), NDT (1941)

H2258 וְדָן ***wᵉdān***, n.pr.loc.? see 1968

H2259 וָהֵב ***wāhēb***, n.pr.loc.? Waheb

H2260 וָו ***wāw***, n.[m.] [13] hook, peg:– hooks (13)

H2261 וָזָר ***wāzār***, a. [1] guilty:– guilty (1)

H2262 וַיְזָתָא ***wayᵉzātā'***, n.pr.m. [1] Vaizatha, "[poss.] *given of the best one*":– Vaizatha (1)

H2263 וָלָד ***wālād***, n.m. [1] [√ 3528]. child:– able to conceive (1)

H2264 וַנְיָה ***wanyâ***, n.pr.m. [1] Vaniah, "[poss.] *worthy of love*":– Vaniah (1)

H2265 וָפְסִי ***wopsî***, n.pr.m. [1] Vophsi:– Vophsi (1)

H2266 וַשְׁנִי ***wašnî***, n.pr.m.? see 9108

H2267 וַשְׁתִּי ***waštî***, n.pr.f. [10] Vashti, "*one beautiful, desired*":– Vashti (10)

H2268 ז ***z***, letter. Not used in NIVEBC [√ 10222]. letter of the Hebrew alphabet

H2269 זְאֵב¹ ***zᵉ'ēb¹***, n.m. [7] [→ 2270]. wolf:– wolf (4), wolves (3)

H2270 זְאֵב² ***zᵉ'ēb²***, n.pr.m. [6] [√ 2269]. Zeeb, "*wolf*":– Zeeb (6)

H2271 זֹאת ***zō't***, p.demo. & adv. Not used in NIVEBC [√ 2296]. this, these

H2272 זָבַד ***zābad***, v. [1] [→ 2273, 2274, 2275, 2280, 2281, 2288; *also used with compound proper names*]. [Q] to give (a gift), bestow:– presented (1)

H2273 זֶבֶד ***zēbed***, n.m. [1] [√ 2272]. gift:– gift (1)

H2274 זָבָד ***zābād***, n.pr.m. [8] [√ 2272]. Zabad, "*he bestows*":– Zabad (8)

H2275 זַבְדִּי ***zabdî***, n.pr.m. [3] [√ 2272]. Zabdi, "*Yahweh bestows*":– Zabdi (3)

H2276 זַבְדִּיאֵל ***zabdî'ēl***, n.pr.m. [2] [√ 2272 + 446]. Zabdiel, "*God [El] bestows*":– Zabdiel (2)

H2277 זְבַדְיָה ***zᵉbadyâ***, n.pr.m. [6] [→ 2278; cf. 2272 + 3378]. Zebadiah, "*Yahweh bestows*":– Zebadiah (6)

H2278 זְבַדְיָהוּ ***zᵉbadyāhû***, n.pr.m. [3] [√ 2277; cf. 2272 + 3378]. Zebadiah, "*Yahweh bestows*":– Zebadiah (3)

H2279 זְבוּב ***zᵉbûb***, n.m. [2] [→ 1256]. fly (insect):– flies (2)

H2280 זָבוּד ***zābûd***, n.pr.m. [1] [√ 2272]. Zabud, "*[he has] bestowed upon*":– Zabud (1)

H2281 זְבוּדָּה ***zᵉbûddâ***, n.pr.f. Not used in NIVEBC [√ 2272; cf. 2288]. Zebuddah, see 2288

H2282 זְבוּלוּן ***zᵉbûlûn***, n.pr.m. [45] [→ 2283; cf. 2292]. Zebulun, "*honor* [Ge 30:20]":– Zebulun (40), Zebulun (5 [+1201])

H2283 זְבוּלֹנִי ***zᵉbûlōnî***, a.g. [3] [√ 2282; cf. 2292]. Zebulunite, "*of Zebulun*":– Zebulun (1), Zebulunite (1), NDT (1)

H2284 זָבַח ***zābaḥ***, v. [134] [→ 2285, 2286, 4640; 10156]. [Q, P] to offer a sacrifice; to slaughter, butcher:– sacrifice (40), offer sacrifices (18), sacrificed (18), offered (10), offer (9), offered sacrifices (8), sacrificing (6), sacrifices (3), slaughter (3), slaughtered (3), made sacrifices (2 [+2285]), preparing (2), sacrifice (2 [+2285]), butchered (1), do[S] (1), making (1), offered a sacrifice (1), offering (1), offering sacrifices (1), offers (1), sacrifices offer (1), NDT (2)

H2285 זֶבַח¹ ***zebaḥ¹***, n.m. [162] [→ 2286; cf. 2284; 10157]. sacrifice, offering:– sacrifices (56), sacrifice (48), offering (24), offerings (14), sacrificed (13), made sacrifices (2 [+2284]), sacrifice (2 [+2284]), feasting (1), food from offering (1), it[S] (1 [+8968])

H2286 זֶבַח² ***zebaḥ²***, n.pr.m. [12] [√ 2285; cf. 2284]. Zebah, "*sacrifice*":– Zebah (10), them[S] (2 [+2256, 7518])

H2287 זַבַּי ***zabbay***, n.pr.m. [2] Zabbai, "[perhaps] *God has given*":– Zabbai (2)

H2288 זְבִידָה ***zᵉbîdâ***, n.pr.f. [1] [√ 2272; cf. 2281]. Zebidah, "*given*":– Zebidah (1)

H2289 זְבִינָא ***zᵉbînā'***, n.pr.m. [1] Zebina, "*one bought, purchased*":– Zebina (1)

H2290 זָבַל ***zābal***, v. [1] [cf. 2292, 6022]. [Q] to honor, exalt; from the base meaning of lifting up or carrying an object, especially bringing presents, not found in the OT:– treat with honor (1)

H2291 [1]זְבֻל ***zᵉbul[1]***, n.pr.m. [6] [√ 2292]. Zebul, "*elevation, height, lofty [temple]*":– Zebul (6)

H2292 [2]זְבֻל ***zᵉbul[2]***, n.[m.] [5] [→ 374?, 2282, 2290, 2291]. magnificent dwelling, princely mansion, lofty dwelling:– magnificent (2), heavens (1), lofty throne (1), princely mansions (1)

H2293 זָג ***zāg***, n.[m.] [1] [cf. 2423]. skin, peel (of grape):– skins (1)

H2294 זֵד ***zēd***, a. [13] [→ 2295; cf. 2326]. arrogant, proud, haughty:– arrogant (9), arrogant foes (1), haughty (1), proud (1), willful sins (1)

H2295 זָדוֹן ***zādôn***, n.m. [11] [√ 2294]. pride, arrogance, contempt, presumption:– pride (4), arrogant (2), arrogance (1), conceited (1), contempt (1), insolent (1), presumptuously (1 [+928])

H2296 זֶה ***zeh***, p.demo. & adv. [1779] [→ 2271, 2297, 2305, 2306, 4208, 4643, 4644; cf. 2306]. this, these, such:– this (1082), these (108), that (48), this[s] (39 [+2021, 1821, 2021]), today (38 [+2021, 3427, 2021]), here (17), now (15 [+2021, 3427, 2021]), one (15), such (15), here (12 [+928]), it (12), he (11), this very (8), where (8 [+361]), another[s] (6), on both sides[s] (6 [+4946, 2256, 4946, 2296]), on both sides[s] (6 [+4946, 2296, 2256, 4946]), this is how (6 [+928]), other[s] (5), what (5), it[s] (4 [+2021, 1821, 2021]), side[s] (4), the (4), the other[s] (4), ever since (3 [+6330, 2021, 3427, 2021]), now (3), really (3), same (3), she (3), so (3 [+6584]), such (3 [+3869]), that same (3), them (3), this[s] (3 [+2021, 2021, 1821]), those (3), very (3), what (3 [+361]), what[s] (3 [+2021, 1821, 2021]), another messenger[s] (2), at either end[s] (2 [+4946, 2256, 4946, 2296]), at either end[s] (2 [+4946, 2296, 2256, 4946]), here[s] (2 [+2021, 5226, 2021]), how (2), others[s] (2), so (2 [+3869]), still (2 [+6330, 2021, 3427, 2021]), there (2), therefore (2 [+6584]), thing[s] (2), this[s] (2 [+2021, 1821, 2021]), this is how (2), which (2), which (2 [+361]), who (2), Leah[s] (1), all at once (1 [+2180]), an (1), another[s] (1 [+2021, 2215, 4946]), another messenger (1), back[s] (1), bordering each side[s] (1 [+4946, 2256, 4946, 2296]), bordering each side[s] (1 [+4946, 2296, 2256, 4946]), by what (1 [+361]), except for (1), from (1 [+4946]), front[s] (1), her (1), here[s] (1 [+928, 2021, 5226, 2021]), here is what (1 [+3869, 2256, 3869, 2296]), here is what (1 [+3869, 2296, 2256, 3869]), he's (1), how (1 [+4537]), in broad daylight (1 [+4200, 6524, 2021, 9087, 2021]), inclined (1 [+2118]), it[s] (1 [+2021, 6551, 2021]), it[s] (1 [+2021, 824, 2021]), it[s] (1 [+2021, 8878, 2021]), its[s] (1), just (1 [+6964]), lasting (1 [+6330, 2021, 3427, 2021]), later (1 [+339]), long for[s] (1), neither (1 [+4202]), now (1 [+3954]), now (1 [+6964]), now (1 [+2021, 2021, 3427]), on both (1 [+4946, 2256, 4946, 2296]), on both (1 [+4946, 2296, 2256, 4946]), on both sides[s] (1 [+4946, 2256, 2296]), on both sides[s] (1 [+4946, 2296, 2256]), on each side (1 [+4946, 2021, 6298, 4946, 4946, 2021, 6298, 4946, 2296]), on each side (1 [+4946, 2021, 6298, 4946, 2296, 4946, 2021, 6298, 4946]), on each side[s] (1 [+4946, 2256, 4946, 2296]), on each side[s] (1 [+4946, 2296, 2256, 4946]), on the condition that (1 [+928]), once (1), one[s] (1), one condition[s] (1), over a year (1 [+3427, 196, 2296, 9102]), over a year (1 [+2296, 3427, 196, 9102]), right where (1), same amount[s] (1), so (1), some (1), still (1 [+3869, 2021, 3427, 2021]), such (1 [+1524]), such offerings[s] (1), such questions[s] (1), suggested (1 [+2021, 1821, 2021]), that[s] (1 [+2021, 1074, 2021]), that's (1), the[s] (1), the condition[s] (1), the crown[s] (1), the first one[s] (1), the younger one[s] (1), them[s] (1 [+2021, 1821, 2021]), them[s] (1 [+2021, 6639, 2021]), then (1), then (1 [+928]), things[s] (1), this (1 [+2021, 1821, 2021]), this[s] (1 [+2021, 5126, 2021]), this fellow's[s] (1 [+4200]), this is what (1), today (1 [+3427]), what (1 [+4769]), what (1 [+3869, 2256, 3869, 2296]), what (1 [+3869, 2296, 2256, 3869]), what (1 [+3869, 2297, 2256, 3869]), what[s] (1 [+2021, 5184, 2021]), what do I care about (1 [+4200, 4537, 4200, 3276]), which way (1 [+361]), which way (1 [+361, 2021, 2006]), whom (1), why (1 [+6584]), why (1 [+361 + 4200]), why (1 [+4200, 4537]), you[s] (1), NDT (142)

H2297 זֹה ***zōh***, p.demo. & adv. [11] [→ 2305; cf. 2296; 10154]. this:– this (6), one (1), such (1 [+3869]), what (1 [+3869, 2256, 3869, 2296]), NDT (2)

H2298 [1]זָהָב ***zāhāb[1]***, n.m. [387] [→ 2298.5?, 4771; cf. 7410; 10160]. gold, nugget of gold, gold piece or coin:– gold (367), golden (9), pure gold (4 [+2298]), alternate[s] (1 [+7194, 2256, 8232]), nuggets of gold (1), NDT (5)

H2298.5 [2]זָהָב ***zāhāb[2]***, n.pr.loc. [1] [→ 2298]. Zahab, "*golden*" [?]. Conjectured in Nu 21:14:– Zahab (1)

H2299 זָהַם ***zāham***, v. [1] [→ 2300]. [P] to make repulsive, loathsome (to someone):– finds repulsive (1)

H2300 זַהַם ***zaham***, n.pr.m. [1] [√ 2299]. Zaham, "*putrid, loathsome*":– Zaham (1)

H2301 [1]זָהַר ***zāhar[1]***, v. [1] [→ 2303; cf. 7413, 7414]. [H] to shine:– shine (1)

H2302 [2]זָהַר ***zāhar[2]***, v. [21] [cf. 2319; 10224]. [N] to be warned, take warning; [H] to give warning, dissuade:– warn (8), dissuade (2), give warning (2), heed the warning (2), be warned (1), heed a warning (1), heeded the warning (1), is warned (1), teach (1), took warning (1), warned (1)

H2303 זֹהַר ***zōhar***, n.[m.] [2] [√ 2301]. brightness, shining:– bright (1), brightness (1)

H2304 זִו ***ziw***, n.pr. [2] [√ 10228]. Ziv, "*bright [as colorful flowers]*":– Ziv (2)

H2305 זוֹ ***zô***, p.demo. [2] [√ 2297; cf. 2296]. this:– for this (1), NDT (1)

H2306 זוּ ***zû***, p.demo. & rel. [15] [√ 2296; cf. 2138]. who, which, that:– the (4), as (1), it (1), that (1), things (1), where (1), who (1), whose (1), wicked[s] (1 [+1887]), NDT (3)

H2307 זוּב ***zûb***, v. [42] [→ 2308; cf. 1853]. [Q] to flow, gush out; discharge (of body fluids); "flowing with milk and honey" is a figure of sweet abundance:– flowing (19), discharge (8), gushed out (3), man[s] (3), bodily discharge (1), discharge (1 [+2308]), flow (1), fruitful (1), has a discharge (1 [+2308]), regular flow (1 [+928, 1414]), running sore (1), unusual discharge (1), waste away (1)

H2308 זוֹב ***zôb***, n.m. [13] [√ 2307]. discharge (of body fluids):– discharge (7), discharge (1 [+3240]), discharge (1 [+2307]), has a discharge (1 [+2307]), it[s] (1 [+2257]), NDT (2)

H2309 זוּזִים ***zûzîm***, n.pr.g. [1] Zuzite, "*strong nations; babblers*":– Zuzites (1)

H2310 זוּחַ ***zûaḥ***, v. Not used in NIVEBC [cf. 2322]. [N] to come loose, get out of place

H2311 זוֹחֵת ***zôḥēt***, n.pr.m. [1] [→ 1209]. Zoheth, "*proud*":– Zoheth (1)

H2312 זָוִית ***zāwît***, n.f. [2] [cf. 4646]. corner (of a palace, altar), pillar:– corners (1), pillars (1)

H2313 זוּל ***zûl***, v. [1] [→ 2314]. [Q] to pour out, weigh out:– pour out (1)

H2314 זוּלָה ***zûlâ***, n.[f.] pp.c. [16] [√ 2313]. but, only, except; apart from, besides:– but (6), except (4), besides (2), apart from (1), only (1), only (1 [+4202]), only (1 [+4200, 963])

H2315 זוּן ***zûn***, v. Not used in NIVEBC [→ 4648; 10226, 10410]. [Q] to feed

H2316 זוּעַ ***zûa'***, v. [3] [→ 2317; cf. 2398, 2400; 10227]. [Q] to show fear, tremble; [Pil] to make tremble:– make tremble (1), showed fear (1), tremble (1)

H2317 זְוָעָה ***zᵉwā'â***, n.f. [6] [√ 2316]. abhorrence, terror, object of dread:– abhorrent (4), object of dread (1), terror (1)

H2318 [1]זוּר ***zûr[1]***, v. [4] [Q] to squeeze, press upon, crush:– broken (1), cleansed (1), crush (1), squeezed (1)

H2319 [2]זוּר ***zûr[2]***, v. [6] [→ 2424; cf. 2302]. [Q, N, Ho] to go astray, turn aside, be estranged:– turned (2), deserted (1), estranged (1), foreigner (1), go astray (1)

H2320 [3]זוּר ***zûr[3]***, v. [1] [Q] to stink; by extension: to be offensive:– offensive (1)

H2321 זָזָא ***zāzā'***, n.pr.m. [1] Zaza, "*form of a shortened nick name; term of endearment*":– Zaza (1)

H2322 זָחַח ***zāḥaḥ***, v. [2] [cf. 2310]. [N] to swing out:– swing out (2)

H2323 [1]זָחַל ***zāḥal[1]***, v. [2] [→ 2325; cf. 2324]. [Q] to crawl, glide (of a snake):– crawl (1), glide (1)

H2324 [2]זָחַל ***zāḥal[2]***, v. [1] [cf. 2323; 10167]. [Q] to be afraid:– fearful (1)

H2325 זֹחֶלֶת ***zōḥelet***, n.pr.loc. [1] [√ 2323]. Zoheleth, "*crawling thing* or *fearsome thing*":– Zoheleth (1)

H2326 זִיד ***zîd***, v. [10] [→ 2327, 5686; cf. 2294; 10225]. [Q] to treat arrogantly, defy; [H] to cook; to act arrogantly, be contemptuous:– arrogant (2), arrogance (1), arrogantly treated (1), contemptuous (1), cooking (1), defied (1), presumes (1), schemes (1), treated arrogantly (1)

H2327 זֵידוֹן ***zêdôn***, a. [1] [√ 2326]. raging (water), implying it is out of control:– raging (1)

H2328 [1]זִיז ***zîz[1]***, n.m. [2] creatures:– insects (2)

H2329 [2]זִיז ***zîz[2]***, n.[m.] [1] nipple (of a lactating breast):– overflowing (1)

H2330 זִיזָא ***zîzā'***, n.pr.m. [3] [√ 2331?]. Ziza, "*(childish abbreviation, like 'mama,' as a name of endearment)*":– Ziza (3)

H2331 זִיזָה ***zîzâ***, n.pr.m. [1] [√ 2330?]. Ziza, "*(childish abbreviation, like 'mama,' as a term of endearment)*":– Ziza (1)

H2332 זִינָא ***zînā'***, n.pr.m. Not used in NIVEBC [cf. 2330]. Zina, see 2330

H2333 זִיעַ ***zîa'***, n.pr.m. [1] Zia, "[poss.] *trembler*":– Zia (1)

H2334 [1]זִיף ***zîp[1]***, n.pr.loc. [8] [→ 2337]. Ziph:– Ziph (7), there[s] (1 [+4497])

H2335 [2]זִיף ***zîp[2]***, n.pr.m. [2] Ziph:– Ziph (2)

H2336 זִיפָה ***zîpâ***, n.pr.m. [1] Ziphah:– Ziphah (1)

H2337 זִיפִי ***zîpî***, a.g. [3] [√ 2334]. Ziphite, "*of Ziph*":– Ziphites (3)

H2338 זִיקוֹת ***zîqôt***, n.[m.] [2] [→ 2415]. flaming torch:– flaming torches (1), torches (1)

H2339 זַיִת ***zayit***, n.m. [38] [→ 1364, 1365, 2340, 2457?]. olive (tree, grove, oil, leaf):– olive (9), olive tree (8), olive groves (7), olives (7), olive trees (4), olive grove (1), olive trees (1 [+3658]), olives from trees (1)

H2340 זֵיתָן ***zêtān***, n.pr.m. [1] [√ 2339]. Zethan, "*olive tree* or *one who deals in olives*":– Zethan (1)

H2341 זַךְ ***zak***, a. [11] [√ 2348]. pure, clear; flawless, innocent, upright:– pure (7), clear (2), flawless (1), upright (1)

H2342 זָכָה ***zākâ***, v. [8] [cf. 2348; 10229]. [Q] to be pure; be justified, be acquitted; [P] to keep pure; [Ht] to make oneself clean, pure; usually referring to moral purity as a superior quality:– kept pure (2), pure (2), acquit (1), justified (1), make yourselves clean (1), purity (1)

H2343 זְכוֹכִית ***zᵉkôkît***, n.[f.] [1] [√ 2348]. crystal, referring to a transparent ornament):– crystal (1)

H2344 זְכוּר ***zᵉkûr***, n.m. [4] [√ 2350]. male:– men (4)

H2345 זָכוּר ***zākûr***, n.m. Not used in NIVEBC [√ 2350]. male

H2346 זַכּוּר ***zakkûr***, n.pr.m. [10] [√ 2349]. Zaccur, "*remembering*":– Zakkur (10)

H2347 זַכַּי ***zakkay***, n.pr.m. [2] [√ 2349 + 3378?]. Zaccai, "*Yahweh has remembered,* [or perhaps] *Yahweh remember*":– Zakkai (2)

H2348 זָכַךְ ***zākak***, v. [4] [→ 2341, 2343; cf. 2342]. [Q] to be pure, bright, clean:– pure (2), brighter (1), NDT (1)

H2349 [1]זָכַר ***zākar[1]***, v. [222] [→ 260, 2345, 2346, 2352, 2353, 2354, 2355, 4654; *also used with compound proper names*]. [Q] to remember, commemorate, consider; [Qp] to remember; [N] to be remembered, be mentioned; [H] to bring to remembrance, remind, mention:– remember (116), remembered (23), be remembered (14), remembers (8), invoke (4), mention (4), consider (2), mentioned (2), petition (2), proclaim (2), recalled (2), reflect on (2), remember (2 [+2349]), remember well (2 [+2349]), remind (2), tell (2), well remember (2 [+2349]), are remembered (1), be invoked (1), brought to mind (1), burns memorial (1), call on (1), carry on the memory (1), cause to be honored (1), commemorate (1), disregarding (1 [+4202]), done this[s] (1), draw attention to (1), extol (1), forget (1 [+440]), hold (1), honor (1), is remembered (1), mindful (1), perpetuate memory (1 [+9005]), praise (1), recalling (1), record (1), reminded (1), reminder (1), review the past (1), spoken (1), summons (1), think about (1), thought (1), trust (1), worthy of mention (1), NDT (1)

H2350 [2]זָכַר ***zākar[2]***, n.m. & a. [1] [→ 2344, 2345, 2351]. [N] to be born male:– males (1)

H2351 זָכָר ***zākār***, n.m. & a. [82] [√ 2350; 10175]. male, man:– male (37), men (17), males (11), man (9), son (3), boy (1), boys (1 [+3251]), not a virgin (1 [+3359, 5435]), slept with (1 [+3359, 5435]), slept with (1 [+3359, 4200, 5435])

H2352 זֵכֶר ***zēker***, n.m. [23] [√ 2349]. memory, remembrance (with an implication of honor, worship, and celebration); fame, renown:– name (9), memory (4), renown (3), remembered (2), celebrate (1), fame (1), name call (1), name memory (1), proclaims name (1)

H2353 [1]זֶכֶר ***zeker[1]***, n.pr.m. [1] [√ 2349]. Zeker, "*memorial*":– Zeker (1)

H2354 [2]זֵכֶר ***zeker[2]***, n.m. Not used in NIVEBC [√ 2349]. memorial

H2355 זִכָּרוֹן ***zikkārôn***, n.m. [24] [√ 2349; 10176]. memorial, remembrance (with an implication of honor, worship, and celebration), commemoration, reminder:– memorial (9), remembered (2), reminder-offering (2 [+4966]), chronicles (1), commemorate (1), commemorated (1), historic right (1), maxims (1), pagan symbols (1), remembers (1), remembrance (1), remind (1), reminder (1), something remembered (1)

H2356 זִכְרִי ***zikrî***, n.pr.m. [12] [√ 2349? + 3378?]. Zicri, "*Yahweh remembers*":– Zikri (12)

H2357 זְכַרְיָה ***zᵉkaryâ***, n.pr.m. [25] [→ 2358; cf. 2349 + 3378; 10230]. Zechariah, "*Yahweh remembers*":– Zechariah (24), Zechariah's (1)

H2358 זְכַרְיָהוּ ***zᵉkaryāhû***, n.pr.m. [16] [√ 2357; cf. 2349 + 3378]. Zechariah, "*Yahweh remembers*":– Zechariah (16)

H2359 זֻלּוּת ***zullût***, n.f. [1] [√ 2361]. vileness:– vile (1)

H2360 זַלְזַל ***zalzal***, n.[m.] [1] [√ 2361; cf. 6149]. shoots, sprigs, tendrils:– shoots (1)

H2361 [1]זָלַל ***zālal[1]***, v. [7] [→ 2359, 2360; cf. 2362]. [Q] to be profligate, be a glutton, to gorge oneself; [H] to despise, treat contemptibly:– gluttons (2), despise (1), despised (1), glutton (1), gorge (1), worthless (1)

H2362 [2]זָלַל ***zālal[2]***, v. [3] [cf. 2361]. [N] to tremble (of mountains):– quaked (1), tremble (1), trembled (1)

H2363 זַלְעָפָה ***zal'āpâ***, n.f. [3] [√ 2406]. raging (wind);

indignation; fits of hunger:– feverish (1), indignation (1), scorching (1)

H2364 זִלְפָּה ***zilpâ***, n.pr.f. [7] Zilpah, *"short nosed person"*:– Zilpah (7)

H2365 [1]זִמָּה ***zimmâ***[1], n.f. [29] lewdness, shamelessness, evil:– lewdness (6), wicked (3), wicked schemes (3), wickedness (3), consequences of lewdness (2), lewd (2), evil intent (1), evil schemes (1), lewd act (1), lewd acts (1), penalty for lewdness (1), plans (1), schemes (1), shamefully (1 [+928]), shameless (1), NDT (1)

H2366 [2]זִמָּה ***zimmâ***[2], n.pr.m. [3] Zimmah, *"consider, plan"*:– Zimmah (3)

H2367 זְמוֹרָה ***z***[e]***môrâ***, n.[f.] [5] [√ 2377; cf. 2444]. vine branch:– branch (3), vines (2)

H2368 זַמְזֻמִּים ***zamzummîm***, n.pr.g. [1] [√ 2372?]. Zamzummite, *"babblers"*:– Zamzummites (1)

H2369 [1]זָמִיר ***zāmîr***[1], n.m. [7] [√ 2376]. song, music and song:– singing (2), songs (2), music and song (1), song (1), theme of song (1)

H2370 [2]זָמִיר ***zāmîr***[2], n.[m.] Not used in NIVEBC [√ 2377]. pruning (of vines); vintage

H2371 זְמִירָה ***z***[e]***mîrâ***, n.pr.m. [1] [√ 2379?; cf. 2376]. Zemirah, "[poss.] *song [with instrumental accompaniment];* [poss.] *Yahweh has helped*":– Zemirah (1)

H2372 זָמַם ***zāmam***, v. [13] [→ 2368?, 2373, 4659]. [Q] to determine, plan, plot, intend, resolve:– determined (3), plot (2), carry out purpose (1), considers (1), decided (1), intended (1), plan (1), plan evil (1), planned (1), planned evil (1)

H2373 זָמָם ***zāmām***, n.[m.] [1] [√ 2372]. plan, plot:– plans (1)

H2374 זָמַן ***zāman***, v. [3] [√ 2375; 10231]. [Pu] to be set, be designated, appointed:– set (2), designated (1)

H2375 זְמָן ***z***[e]***mān***, n.m. [4] [→ 2374; 10232]. time, appointed time:– time (2), designated times (1), time appointed (1)

H2376 [1]זָמַר ***zāmar***[1], v. [45] [→ 2369, 2371?, 2379, 2384, 4660; 10233, 10234]. [P] to sing, sing praises, to make music, to chant, sing, or play instruments to worship God and proclaim his excellence:– sing praise (13), make music (9), sing the praises (7), sing praises (6), sing (5), sing in praise (2), music (1), praise (1), praise in song (1)

H2377 [2]זָמַר ***zāmar***[2], v. [3] [→ 2367, 2370, 4661, 4662]. [Q] to prune (vines); [N] to be pruned:– prune (2), pruned (1)

H2378 זֶמֶר ***zemer***, n.[m.] [1] [cf. 2380?]. mountain sheep; some sources: gazelle:– mountain sheep (1)

H2379 [1]זִמְרָה ***zimrâ***[1], n.f. [4] [→ 2371?; cf. 2376]. singing, song, (instrumental) music:– music (2), singing (2)

H2380 [2]זִמְרָה ***zimrâ***[2], n.f. [4] [→ 2381; cf. 2378?]. best product, having a high value:– defense (3), best products (1)

H2381 [1]זִמְרִי ***zimrî***[1], n.pr.m. [17] [√ 2380]. Zimri, *"wild goats, sheep;* [poss.] *awe of Yahweh"*:– Zimri (16), Zimri's (1)

H2382 [2]זִמְרִי ***zimrî***[2], n.pr.loc. [1] Zimri, *"wild goats, sheep;* [poss.] *awe of Yahweh"*:– Zimri (1)

H2383 זִמְרָן ***zimrān***, n.pr.m. [2] Zimran, *"wild goats, sheep"*:– Zimran (2)

H2384 זִמְרָת ***zimrāt***, n.f. Not used in NIVEBC [√ 2376?]. song or strength

H2385 זַן ***zan***, n.[m.] [3] [√ 10235]. kind, sort:– every kind (1 [+4946, 448, 2385]), every kind (1 [+4946, 2385, 448]), various (1)

H2386 זָנַב ***zānab***, v.den. [2] [√ 2387]. [P] to cut off from the rear position, attack from the rear, as a fig. extension of the base meaning "to cut off a tail":– attack from the rear (1), attacked (1)

H2387 זָנָב ***zānāb***, n.m. [11] [→ 2386]. tail; stump:– tail (9), stubs (1), tails (1)

H2388 [1]זָנָה ***zānâ***[1], v. [61] [→ 2390, 2393, 2394, 9373]. [Q] to be, become a prostitute; to be sexually immoral, be promiscuous, commit adultery; [Pu] to be solicited for prostitution; [H] to make a prostitute, to turn to prostitution:– prostitute (12), prostituted (5), unfaithful (5), engaged in prostitution (4), turn to prostitution (3), adulterous (2), committed adultery (2), continue prostitution (2 [+2388]), prostitutes (2), carried on prostitution (1), caused to prostitute themselves (1), commit adultery (1), did[S] (1), engage in prostitution (1), engaging in prostitution (1), guilty of prostitution (1), guilty of unfaithfulness (1), indulge in sexual immorality (1), lead to do the same[S] (1 [+339, 466, 2177]), led to prostitute themselves (1), lust after (1 [+339]), lusted (1), lusted after (1 [+339]), making a prostitute (1), ply her trade[S] (1), promiscuous (1), prostituting (1), prostitution (1), runs after for favors (1 [+339]), that[S] (1 [+4392]), turned to prostitution (1), use as a prostitute (1 [+9373]), NDT (1)

H2389 [2]זָנָה ***zānâ***[2], v. [Q] to feel a dislike for

H2390 זֹנָה ***zōnâ***, n.f. *or* v.ptcp. [33] [√ 2388]. prostitute, harlot:– prostitute (20), prostitutes (8), prostitution (2), adulterous (1), harlots (1), prostitute's (1)

H2391 [1]זָנוֹחַ ***zānôaḥ***[1], n.pr.loc. [4] [→ 2392; cf. 2395 *or* 2396]. Zanoah, *"rejected"*:– Zanoah (4)

H2392 [2]זָנוֹחַ ***zānôaḥ***[2], n.pr.m. [1] [√ 2391; cf. 2395 *or* 2396]. Zanoah, *"rejected"*:– Zanoah (1)

H2393 זְנוּנִים ***z***[e]***nûnîm***, n.[m.] [12] [√ 2388]. wanton lust, prostitution, adultery; by extension: idolatry, as unfaithfulness to God:– prostitution (4), adulterous look (1), adultery (1), her[S] (1), idolatry (1), promiscuous (1), wanton lust (1), NDT (2)

H2394 זְנוּת ***z***[e]***nût***, n.f.abst. [9] [√ 2388]. prostitution, sexual immorality, unfaithfulness; by extension: idolatry, as unfaithfulness to God:– prostitution (7), immorality (1), unfaithfulness (1)

H2395 [1]זָנַח ***zānaḥ***[1], v. [1] [→ 2391?, 2392?]. [H] to stink:– stink (1)

H2396 [2]זָנַח ***zānaḥ***[2], v. [19] [→ 2391?, 2392?]. [Q] to reject, cast out; [H] to declare rejected; to remove:– rejected (11), reject (4), cast off (1), deprived (1), removed (1), throw out (1)

H2397 זָנַק ***zānaq***, v. [1] [P] to spring out:– springing out (1)

H2398 זָעָא ***zā'â***, v. Not used in NIVEBC [cf. 2316]. [Pil] to terrify

H2399 זֵעָה ***zē'â***, n.f. [1] [√ 3472]. sweat; the "sweat of the brow" refers to do heavy manual labor:– sweat (1)

H2400 זַעֲוָה ***za'***[a]***wâ***, n.f. [2] [→ 2401; cf. 2316]. thing of horror, terror:– terror (1), thing of horror (1)

H2401 זַעֲוָן ***za'***[a]***wān***, n.pr.m. [2] [√ 2400 + 5527?]. Zaavan, "[poss.] *trembling, terror*":– Zaavan (2)

H2402 זְעֵיר ***z***[e]***'êr***, n.[m.] [5] [→ 4663; cf. 7592; 10236]. little; a little longer:– little (4), little longer (1)

H2403 זָעַךְ ***zā'ak***, v. [1] [cf. 1980]. [N] to be extinguished:– are cut short (1)

H2404 זָעַם ***zā'am***, v. [12] [→ 2405]. [Q] to express wrath, show fury, denounce; [Qp] to be under wrath, be accursed; [N] to be scolded, be cursed:– denounce (2), denounced (2), accursed (1), angry (1), displays wrath (1), fury shown (1), horrified (1), under the wrath (1), under wrath (1), vent fury (1)

H2405 זַעַם ***za'am***, n.m. [22] [√ 2404]. wrath, anger, indignation, insolence:– wrath (15), indignation (3), anger (1), fierce (1), great wrath (1 [+2256, 7912]), insolent (1)

H2406 [1]זָעַף ***zā'ap***[1], v. [3] [→ 2363, 2408, 2409; cf. 2407]. [Q] to rage against, become angry:– angry (1), rages (1), raging (1)

H2407 [2]זָעַף ***zā'ap***[2], v. [2] [cf. 2406]. [Q] to look dejected, look pitiful:– dejected (1), looking worse (1)

H2408 זַעַף ***za'ap***, n.m. [6] [√ 2406]. rage, wrath:– rage (2), raging (2), enraged (1), wrath (1)

H2409 זָעֵף ***zā'ēp***, a. [2] [√ 2406]. angry, raging:– angry (2)

H2410 זָעַק ***zā'aq***, v. [73] [→ 2411; cf. 7590; 10237]. [Q] to cry out, call to, weep aloud, howl; [N] to be called, be summoned; be assembled; [H] to summon, cause to gather together, issue a proclamation:– cried out (19), cry out (18), cries out (4), cried (3), cry (3), called (2), crying out (2), summon (2), summoned (2), assembled (1), call out (1), called out to fight (1), calling to arms (1 [+339]), cried for help (1), cried out for help (1), cry for help (1 [+7754]), cry out for help (1), howl (1), make appeals (1), sent up a cry (1), summoning (1), the proclamation issued (1), wail (1), wailing (1 [+2411]), weeping aloud (1), were called (1), were called together (1)

H2411 זְעָקָה ***z***[e]***'āqâ***, n.f. [18] [√ 2410]. outcry, shout, lament, wail:– cry (7), outcry (3), cry out (1 [+7754]), cry out (1 [+9048]), crying (1), lament (1 [+6424]), lamentation (1), shouts (1), wailing (1), wailing (1 [+2410])

H2412 זִפְרֹון ***ziprôn***, n.pr.loc. [1] Ziphron:– Ziphron (1)

H2413 זֶפֶת ***zepet***, n.f. [3] pitch (resin):– pitch (3)

H2414 [1]זֵק ***zēq***[1], n.[m.] [4] [cf. 272]. chains, fetters:– chains (2), fetters (1), were put in chains (1 [+8415, 928])

H2415 [2]זֵק ***zēq***[2], n.[m.] [1] [√ 2338]. firebrands:– flaming (1)

H2416 [1]זָקֵן ***zāqēn***[1], v. [26] [√ 2417]. [Q] to be old; [H] to grow old; this can refer to maturity in contrast to youth or to advanced age:– old (16), very old (5 [+995, 928, 2021, 3427]), aged (1 [+4394]), grew old (1), grow old (1), grown old (1 [+995, 928, 2021, 3427]), very old (1 [+995, 928, 2021, 408])

H2417 זָקָן ***zāqān***, n.m. [19] [→ 2416, 2418, 2419, 2420, 2421]. beard, whiskers (a sign of maturity or age); chin:– beard (12), beards (4), chin (2), hair (1)

H2418 [2]זָקֵן ***zāqēn***[2], a. [179] [√ 2417; 10675]. elder, old, aged, veteran; (n.) elder, leader, dignitary; "elder" can refer to a formal position as a community leader and arbiter:– elders (121), old (29), aged (5), dignitaries (2), elderly (2), leaders (2), leading (2), of ripe old age (2), old age (2), elder (1), his own[S] (1 [+2021, 5566, 2021]), older (1), older (1 [+4200, 3427]), senior (1), them[S] (1 [+1680]), very old (1 [+995, 928, 2021, 3427]), veteran (1), NDT (4)

H2419 זֹקֶן ***zōqen***, n.[m.] [1] [√ 2417]. old age:– old age (1)

H2420 זִקְנָה ***ziqnâ***, n.f. [6] [√ 2417]. old age, growing old:– old age (3), old (2), grew old (1)

H2421 זְקֻנִים ***z***[e]***qunîm***, n.pl.[m.] [4] [√ 2417]. old age:– old age (4)

H2422 זָקַף ***zāqap***, v. [2] [√ 10238]. [Q] to lift up:– lifts up (2)

H2423 זָקַק ***zāqaq***, v. [7] [cf. 2293]. [Q] to refine, distill; [P] to refine; [Pu] to be refined, be purified:– refined (4), distill (1), finest (1), refine (1)

H2424 זָר ***zār***, a. *or* v.ptcp. [71] [√ 2319]. strange, foreign, alien, one of a different kind; unauthorized, illegitimate:– foreigners (16), foreign (10), strangers (8), anyone else (4), stranger (4), else (3), unauthorized (3), adulterous (2), adulterous (2 [+851]), another (2), anyone other than a priest (2), strange (2), arrogant foes (1), distant sources (1), enemies (1), foreigner (1), illegitimate (1), imported (1), one (1 [+408]), one[S] (1), other (1), outside a priest's family (1), outside the family (1 [+2021, 2575, 2025]), someone else (1), unauthorized person (1)

H2425 זֵר ***zēr***, n.m. [10] [√ 2452]. molding:– molding (10)

H2426 זָרָא ***zārā'***, n.[f.] [1] loathsome thing:– loathe (1)

H2427 זָרַב ***zārab***, v. [1] [Pu] to become dry:– dry (1)

H2428 זְרֻבָּבֶל ***z***[e]***rubbābel***, n.pr.m. [21] [√ 2445 + 951; 10239]. Zerubbabel, *"offspring [seed] of Babylon; scion* i.e., *one grafted into the [plant of] Babylon"*:– Zerubbabel (21)

H2429 זֶרֶד ***zered***, n.pr.loc. [4] Zered, *"[valley of some kind of] plant"*:– Zered (3), the[S] (1)

H2430 [1]זָרָה ***zārâ***[1], v. [38] [→ 4665, 4668; cf. 4664]. [Q, P] to scatter, spread out; winnow; [N, Pu] to be scattered, spread out:– scatter (18), scattered (5), winnow (4), spread (2), winnows out (2), are scattered (1), is scattered (1), smear (1), spread out (1), throw away (1), were scattered (1), winnowing (1)

H2431 [2]זָרָה ***zārâ***[2], v. [1] [√ 2455]. [P] to measure off, discern:– discern (1)

H2432 זְרוֹעַ ***z***[e]***rôa'***, n.f. [90] [cf. 274; 10013, 10185]. arm, forearm, shoulder; power, strength, force:– arm (52), arms (17), strength (5), power (4), shoulder (2), arm of power (1), armed (1), armed forces (1), army (1), forces (1), power (1 [+3946]), powerful (1), reinforce (1 [+2118]), shoulders (1), strong arms (1 [+3338])

H2433 זֵרוּעַ ***zērûa'***, n.[m.] [2] [√ 2445]. (plants from) seeds:– seeds (1), seeds (1 [+2446])

H2434 זַרְזִיף ***zarzîp***, n.[m.] Not used in NIVEBC [√ 2449]. dripping

H2435 זַרְזִיר ***zarzîr***, a. [1] [√ 2452?]. a strutting animal, variously interpreted: rooster, horse, greyhound:– strutting rooster (1 [+5516])

H2436 זָרַח ***zāraḥ***, v. [19] [→ 275, 276, 2437, 2438, 2439, 4667; *also used with compound proper names*]. [Q] to rise, dawn (of the sun); by extension: to appear bright red (as with a skin disorder):– rises (5), rise (2), rose (2), sunrise (2 [+2021, 9087]), appears (1), broke out (1), dawned (1), dawns (1), shine (1), shines (1), shining (1), sunrise (1 [+9087])

H2437 [1]זֶרַח ***zeraḥ***[1], n.[m.] [1] [→ 2438, 2439; cf. 2436]. dawning (of light):– dawn (1)

H2438 [2]זֶרַח ***zeraḥ***[2], n.pr.m. [21] [→ 276; cf. 2436, 2437]. Zerah, *"dawning, shining* or *flashing [red or scarlet] light"*:– Zerah (20), Zerahites (1 [+1201])

H2439 זַרְחִי ***zarḥî***, a.g. [6] [√ 2438; cf. 2436, 2437]. Zerahite, *"of Zerah"*:– Zerahite (4), Zerahites (2)

H2440 זְרַחְיָה ***z***[e]***raḥyâ***, n.pr.m. [5] [√ 2436 + 3378]. Zerahiah, *"Yahweh shines brightly [red or scarlet]; Yahweh has risen [like the sun]"*:– Zerahiah (5)

H2441 [1]זָרַם ***zāram***[1], v. [1] [cf. 2442]. [Q] to sweep away, put an end to:– sweep away (1)

H2442 [2]זָרַם ***zāram***[2], v. [1] [→ 2443; cf. 2441]. [Q] to sweep away (=2441?); [Po] to pour down:– poured down (1)

H2443 זֶרֶם ***zerem***, n.m. [9] [√ 2442]. rain, rainstorm, thunderstorm, torrent rains:– storm (4), driving rain (1 [+4784]), hailstorm (1 [+1352]), rains (1), thunderstorm (1), torrents (1)

H2444 זִרְמָה ***zirmâ***, n.f. [2] [cf. 2367]. male genitals or emission:– emission (1), that[S] (1)

H2445 זָרַע ***zāra'***, v. [55] [→ 2433, 2446, 2447, 2448, 4669; 10240; *also used with compound proper names*]. [Q] to sow seed, plant seed; [Qp] to be sown upon; [Pu] to be sown; [N] to be sown, be planted, to have children, have descendants; [H] to yield seed, to become pregnant; from the base meaning of scattering seed onto the ground comes the fig. extension "to have children":– sow (16), plant (9), planted (4), sown (4), planted crops (2), seed-bearing (2 [+2446]), sower (2), sows (2), be able to have children (1 [+2446]), be planted (1), bearing (1), have descendants (1), plant (1 [+2446]), plant seed (1), plant with seed (1), planting (1), pregnant (1), scatter (1), scattered (1), seed (1 [+2446]), sowed (1), sowing seed (1)

H2446 זֶרַע **zeraʿ**, n.m. [230] [√ 2445; 10240]. seed, semen, that which propagates a species; by extension: that which is propagated, child, offspring, descendant, line, race:– descendants (81), offspring (34), seed (24), children (19), family (5), grain (5), semen (5), line (4), people (4), descent (3), blood (2), child (2), descendant (2), descended (2), family line (2), posterity (2), seed-bearing (2 [+2445]), Israel (1 [+3776]), Jews[S] (1), armed men (1), be able to have children (1 [+2445]), brood (1), crops (1), descendant (1 [+408, 4946]), fertile (1), has sexual relations (1 [+8886, 8887]), have sexual relations (1 [+5989, 8888, 4200]), origin (1), plant (1), plant (1 [+2445]), planter (1 [+5432]), planting (1), produce (1 [+9311, 3655]), race (1), righteous (1 [+7404]), seed (1 [+2445]), seed to sow (1 [+5433]), seedlings (1), seeds (1 [+2433]), seedtime (1), sleeps with (1 [+8886, 8887, 907]), son (1 [+408]), sons (1), stock (1), their[S] (1 [+3870]), them[S] (1 [+3870]), various kinds (1), NDT (2)

H2447 זֵרֹעִים **zērōʿîm**, n.[m.] [1] [→ 2448; cf. 2445]. vegetables:– vegetables (1)

H2448 זֵרְעֹנִים **zērʿōnîm**, n.[m.] [1] [√ 2447; cf. 2445]. vegetables:– vegetables (1)

H2449 זָרַף **zārap**, n.[m.] [1] [→ 2434]. [Pil] to water, shower:– watering (1)

H2450 [1]זָרַק **zāraq[1]**, v. [35] [→ 4670]. [Q] to sprinkle, to scatter, to toss (in the air); [Pu] to be sprinkled:– splashed (12), splash (10), sprinkled (3), been sprinkled (2), scatter (2), scattered (1), splashes (1), splashing (1), sprinkle (1), toss (1), tossed (1)

H2451 [2]זָרַק **zāraq[2]**, v. [Q] to creep in

H2452 [1]זרר **zārar[1]**, v. Not used in NIVEBC [→ 2425, 2435?; cf. 2453]. [Qp] to be pressed out

H2453 [2]זרר **zārar[2]**, v. [1] [cf. 2452]. [Po] to sneeze:– sneezed (1)

H2454 זֶרֶשׁ **zereš**, n.pr.f. [4] Zeresh, "[poss.] *Kirsha; gold; mop-headed*":– Zeresh (4)

H2455 זֶרֶת **zeret**, n.f. [7] [→ 2431]. handbreadth, span (of an open hand, a measure of about nine inches [23 cm]):– span (6), breadth of hand (1)

H2456 זַתּוּא **zattûʾ**, n.pr.m. [5] Zattu:– Zattu (5)

H2457 זֵתָם **zētām**, n.pr.m. [2] [√ 2339?]. Zetham, "[poss.] *olive tree*":– Zetham (2)

H2458 זֵתַר **zētar**, n.pr.m. [1] Zethar, "[poss.] *conqueror; slayer*":– Zethar (1)

H2459 ח **ḥ**, letter. Not used in NIVEBC [√ 10241]. letter of the Hebrew alphabet

H2460 חֹב **ḥōb**, n.[m.] [1] [√ 2462; cf. 2461]. heart:– heart (1)

H2461 חָבָא **ḥābāʾ**, v. [34] [→ 494, 4675, 4676; cf. 2460, 2463?, 2464, 2465?]. [N] to be hidden, to hide oneself; [Pu] to keep oneself in hiding; [H] to hide (another); [Ho] to be hidden away; [Ht] to keep oneself hidden:– hid (7), hidden (7), hiding (5), hid themselves (2), be protected (1), become hard (1), force into hiding (1), hidden away (1), hidden himself (1), hide (1), hide themselves (1), hide yourselves (1), hushed (1), secretly (1), stay there (1), stepped aside (1), uses[S] (1)

H2462 חָבַב **ḥābab**, v. [1] [→ 2460, 2463?, 2465?]. [Q] to love:– love (1)

H2463 חֹבָב **ḥōbāb**, n.pr.m. [2] [√ 2462?; cf. 2461?]. Hobab, "*beloved;* [poss.] *deceit*":– Hobab (2)

H2464 חָבָה **ḥābâ**, v. [4] [→ 2469, 2470; cf. 2461]. [Q] to hide; [N] to conceal oneself:– hide (3), conceal himself (1)

H2465 חֻבָּה **ḥubbâ**, n.pr.m. [1] [√ 2462?; cf. 2461?, 3478]. Hubbah, "*God has hidden [someone from danger]*":– Hubbah (1)

H2466 חָבוֹר **ḥābôr**, n.pr.loc. [3] Habor:– Habor (3)

H2467 חַבּוּרָה **ḥabbûrâ**, n.f. [7] [√ 2488]. bruise, welt, wound, injury:– bruise (2), wounds (2), blows (1), injuring (1), welts (1)

H2468 חָבַט **ḥābaṭ**, v. [5] [Q] to thresh, beat out; [N] to be beaten:– beat (1), is beaten out (1), thresh (1), threshed (1), threshing (1)

H2469 חֳבַיָּה **ḥᵒbayyâ**, n.pr.m. [2] [√ 2464 + 3378]. Hobaiah, "*Yahweh has hidden*":– Hobaiah (2)

H2470 חֶבְיוֹן **ḥebyôn**, n.[m.] [1] [√ 2464]. hiding, covering:– hidden (1)

H2471 [1]חָבַל **ḥābal[1]**, v. [12] [→ 2478, 2481]. [Q] to require a pledge, demand a security:– hold in pledge (2), take as a pledge (2 [+2471]), demanded security (1), require a pledge for a loan (1 [+2478]), seized for a debt (1), take as a pledge (1), take as security for a debt (1), take in pledge (1), taken in pledge (1), taking as security (1)

H2472 [2]חָבַל **ḥābal[2]**, v. [12] [→ 2476; 10243]. [Q] to act wickedly, to offend; [P] to destroy, ruin, work havoc; [Pu] to be broken:– destroy (3), acted very wickedly (2 [+2472]), be broken (1), is broken (1), offend (1), pay for it (1), ruin (1), ruined (1 [+2256, 2476]), wreak havoc (1)

H2473 [3]חָבַל **ḥābal[3]**, v. [3] [→ 2477]. [P] to conceive, be pregnant, to be in labor:– conceived (1), in labor (1), pregnant (1)

H2474 [1]חֶבֶל **ḥebel[1]**, n.m. [2] [cf. 2475, 2480, 2482]. procession, group:– procession (2)

H2475 [2]חֶבֶל **ḥebel[2]**, n.m. [49] [cf. 2474, 2479, 2480, 2482]. rope, cord, line, rigging; share, portion, region, district:– cords (11), ropes (9), region (5), land (3), portion (3), rope (2), share (2), allotted (1), boundary lines (1), by (1), cord (1), fate (1), lands (1), length (1), length of cord (1), lengths (1), line (1), measured (1), noose (1), portions (1), rigging (1)

H2476 [3]חֶבֶל **ḥebel[3]**, n.m. [1] [√ 2472]. destruction, ruin:– ruined (1 [+2472, 2256])

H2477 חֵבֶל **ḥēbel**, n.m. [8] [√ 2473]. labor pains, anguish of birth pangs:– pain (3), pains (2), anguish (1), labor pains (1), pangs (1)

H2478 חֲבֹל **ḥᵃbōl**, n.[m.] [3] [√ 2471]. pledge for a loan:– require a pledge for a loan (1 [+2471]), what took in pledge (1), what took in pledge for a loan (1)

H2479 חִבֵּל **ḥibbēl**, n.[m.] [1] [√ 2475]. (ship's) rigging, mast:– rigging (1)

H2480 חֹבֵל **ḥōbēl**, n.m. [5] [cf. 2474, 2475, 2482]. seaman, sailor:– sailors (3), captain (1 [+8042, 2021]), sailors (1 [+3542])

H2481 חֲבֹלָה **ḥᵃbōlâ**, n.f. [1] [√ 2471]. pledge for a loan:– what took in pledge (1)

H2482 חֹבְלִים **ḥōbᵉlîm**, n.[m.]pl. [2] [cf. 2474, 2475, 2480]. union:– Union (2)

H2483 חֲבַצֶּלֶת **ḥᵃbaṣṣelet**, n.f. [2] rose; crocus:– crocus (1), rose (1)

H2484 חֲבַצִּנְיָה **ḥᵃbaṣṣinyâ**, n.pr.m. [1] Habazziniah, "[poss.] *exuberant in Yahweh*":– Habazziniah (1)

H2485 חָבַק **ḥābaq**, v. [13] [→ 2486]. [Q] to hold in one's arms, embrace; to fold one's hands; [P] to embrace, hug:– embrace (3), embraced (3), embraces (2), embracing (1), fold (1), hold in arms (1), hug (1), lie (1)

H2486 חִבֻּק **ḥibbuq**, n.[m.] [2] [√ 2485]. folding (of idle hands):– folding (2)

H2487 חֲבַקּוּק **ḥᵃbaqqûq**, n.pr.m. [2] Habakkuk, "*garden plant*":– Habakkuk (2)

H2488 [1]חָבַר **ḥābar[1]**, v. [1] [→ 2467, 2494]. [H] to make fine speeches:– make fine speeches (1 [+928, 4863])

H2489 [2]חָבַר **ḥābar[2]**, v. [28] [→ 2248, 2490, 2491, 2492, 2493, 2495, 2496, 2497, 2498, 2499, 2500, 2501, 4677, 4678]. [Q] to join, unite, be attached, to be touching; to cast spells, to enchant; [Qp] to be joined; [P] to fasten, join; [Pu] to be fastened, be closely compacted; [Ht] to make an alliance, become allies:– attached (2), be fastened (2), fasten (2), fasten together (2), joined (2), made an alliance (2), agreed (1), allied with (1), allies (1), among (1), casts spells (1 [+2490]), coming to an agreement (1), did the same[S] (1 [+285, 448, 285]), do the same[S] (1), enchanter (1 [+2490]), is closely compacted (1), join (1), join together (1), joined forces (1), joined to (1), touched (1), touching (1)

H2490 [1]חֶבֶר **ḥeber[1]**, n.[m.] [7] [√ 2489]. sharing; band, group; magic spell:– bands (1), casts spells (1 [+2489]), enchanter (1 [+2489]), magic spells (1), share (1), share with (1), spells (1)

H2491 [2]חֶבֶר **ḥeber[2]**, n.pr.m. [11] [→ 2499; cf. 2489]. Heber, "*associate*":– Heber (10), Heber's (1)

H2492 חָבֵר **ḥābēr**, a. & n.m. [12] [√ 2489; 10245, 10246]. companion, associate, partner, friend:– associated with (3), friends (2), companions (1), do that[S] (1), friend (1), one[S] (1), partner (1), partners (1), united (1)

H2493 חַבָּר **ḥabbār**, n.m. [1] [√ 2489]. (fellow) trader, one of a community of traders:– traders (1)

H2494 חֲבַרְבֻּרוֹת **ḥᵃbarburôt**, n.f. [1] [√ 2488]. spots (of a leopard):– spots (1)

H2495 חֶבְרָה **ḥebrâ**, n.f. [1] [√ 2489]. company, association:– keeps company (1 [+782, 4200])

H2496 [1]חֶבְרוֹן **ḥebrôn[1]**, n.pr.loc. [63] [√ 2489]. Hebron, "*association*":– Hebron (62), NDT (1)

H2497 [2]חֶבְרוֹן **ḥebrôn[2]**, n.pr.m. [10] [→ 2498; cf. 2489, 2496?]. Hebron, "*association*":– Hebron (10)

H2498 חֶבְרוֹנִי **ḥebrônî**, a.g. [6] [√ 2497; cf. 2489, 2496]. Hebronite, "*of Hebron*":– Hebronites (4), Hebronite (1), their[S] (1 [+4200, 2021])

H2499 חֶבְרִי **ḥebrî**, a.g. [1] [√ 2491; cf. 2489]. Heberite, "*of Heber*":– Heberite (1)

H2500 חֲבֶרֶת **ḥᵃberet**, n.f. [1] [√ 2489]. partner, (marriage) companion:– partner (1)

H2501 חֹבֶרֶת **ḥōberet**, n.f. [4] [√ 2489]. set (of curtains):– set (4)

H2502 חָבַשׁ **ḥābaš**, v. [32] [cf. 3109]. [Q] to tie, bind, saddle; [Qp] to be saddled; to be twisted, wrapped around; [P] to bind up; [Pu] to be bound, bandaged:– saddled (8), bind up (3), binds up (3), fastened (2), saddle (2), bandaged (1), been bound up (1), bound up (1), did so[S] (1), dressed (1), fasten (1), govern (1), have saddled (1), loaded (1), remedy (1), shroud (1), twisted (1), wrapped around (1), NDT (1)

H2503 חֲבִתִּים **ḥᵃbittîm**, n.[m.]pl. [1] [→ 4679]. offering bread (flat cakes, baked in a pan):– offering bread (1)

H2504 חַג **ḥag**, n.m. [62] [√ 2510]. religious feast, festival; festal procession:– festival (51), festivals (3), religious festivals (2), feast (1), feasts (1), festal procession (1), festival offerings (1), festival sacrifices (1), yearly festivals (1)

H2505 חָגָּא **ḥoggāʾ**, n.[f.] [1] terror; some sources: confusion:– terror (1)

H2506 [1]חָגָב **ḥāgāb[1]**, n.m. [5] [→ 2507, 2508, 2509]. grasshopper, locust (in some cultures distinguished from a grasshopper and used as a food source):– grasshopper (2), grasshoppers (2), locusts (1)

H2507 [2]חָגָב **ḥāgāb[2]**, n.pr.m. [1] [→ 2508, 2509; cf. 2506]. Hagab, "*locust*":– Hagab (1)

H2508 חֲגָבָא **ḥᵃgābāʾ**, n.pr.m. Not used in NIVEBC [√ 2507; cf. 2506]. Hagaba, "*locust*"

H2509 חֲגָבָה **ḥᵃgābâ**, n.pr.m. [2] [√ 2507; cf. 2506]. Hagabah, "*locust*":– Hagaba (1), Hagabah (1)

H2510 חָגַג **ḥāgag**, v. [15] [→ 2504, 2515, 2516, 2517, 2518; cf. 2552]. [Q] to hold a festival, celebrate a festival; this can refer to a religious celebration or a revel:– celebrate (9), celebrate a festival (1), celebrate the festival (1), festive (1), hold a festival (1), reeled (1), reveling (1)

H2511 חָגוּ **ḥāgû**, n.m.pl. [3] clefts (of a rock) that can be used as a hiding place or retreat from danger:– clefts (3)

H2512 חֲגוֹר **ḥᵃgôr**, n.[m.] [3] [√ 2520]. belt, sash:– belt (2), sashes (1)

H2513 חָגוֹר **ḥāgôr**, a. [1] [√ 2520]. belted (around the waist):– belts (1 [+258])

H2514 חֲגוֹרָה **ḥᵃgôrâ**, n.f. [5] [√ 2520]. covering; belt, sash:– bear arms (1 [+2520]), belt (1), coverings (1), sash (1), warrior's belt (1)

H2515 חַגִּי **ḥaggî**, n.pr.m. & a.g. [3] [√ 2510]. Haggi, "*festal; born on the feast day*":– Haggi (2), Haggite (1)

H2516 חַגַּי **ḥaggay**, n.pr.m. [9] [√ 2510; 10247]. Haggai, "*festal; born on the feast day*":– Haggai (9)

H2517 חַגִּיָּה **ḥaggiyyâ**, n.pr.m. [1] [√ 2510 + 3378]. Haggiah, "*feast of Yahweh*":– Haggiah (1)

H2518 חַגִּית **ḥaggît**, n.pr.f. [5] [√ 2510]. Haggith, "*festal; born on the feast day*":– Haggith (5)

H2519 חָגְלָה **ḥoglâ**, n.pr.f. [4] [→ 1102; cf. 3005]. Hoglah, "*partridge*":– Hoglah (4)

H2520 חָגַר **ḥāgar**, v. [43] [→ 2512, 2513, 2514, 4680]. [Q] to tie, strap, fasten; to tuck (lower robe) into one's belt, gird; [Qp] to be tucked in, girded:– put on (10), wearing (4), armed (3 [+3998]), tied around (3), tuck cloak into belt (2 [+5516]), wear (2), bear arms (1 [+2514]), belt (1), cloak tucked into belt (1 [+5516]), clothed (1), did[S] (1 [+906, 2995]), fastened (1), fastened on (1), gird (1), in (1), puts on armor (1), restrained (1), sets about work (1 [+5516]), strap on (1), strapped (1), strapped on (1), tie (1), tie around (1), was armed (1), wrap in rags (1 [+6584])

H2521 [1]חַד **ḥad[1]**, a. [4] [√ 2523]. sharp (sword):– sharp (3), sharpened (1)

H2522 [2]חַד **ḥad[2]**, a. [1] [cf. 285]. one, each:– each (1)

H2523 חָדַד **ḥādad**, v. [5] [→ 2521, 2529, 2531]. [Q] to be fierce, sharp; [Ho] to be sharpened; [Ht] to slash:– sharpened (2), fiercer (1), is sharpened (1), slash (1)

H2524 חֲדַד **ḥᵃdad**, n.pr.m. [2] Hadad, "*sharp, fierce*":– Hadad (2)

H2525 [1]חָדָה **ḥādâ[1]**, v. [2] [→ 2530, 3484, 3485; cf. 2526, 2527]. [Q] to be delighted; [P] to make glad:– delighted (1), made glad (1)

H2526 [2]חָדָה **ḥādâ[2]**, v. [1] [cf. 2525]. [N] to be seen:– be included (1)

H2527 [3]חָדָה **ḥādâ[3]**, v. [2] [cf. 2525]. [Q] to sharpen; [H] to sharpen:– sharpens (2)

H2528 חַדָּה **ḥaddâ**, n.pr.loc. Not used in NIVEBC [→ 6532]. Haddah

H2529 חַדּוּד **ḥaddûd**, a. [1] [√ 2523]. jagged, pointed:– jagged (1)

H2530 חֶדְוָה **ḥedwâ**, n.f. [2] [√ 2525; 10250]. joy:– joy (2)

H2531 חָדִיד **ḥādîd**, n.pr.loc. [3] [√ 2523]. Hadid, "*sharp*":– Hadid (3)

H2532 [1]חָדַל **ḥādal[1]**, v. [58] [→ 2534, 2536?; cf. 2533]. [Q] to stop, cease, refrain, fail:– stopped (10), stop (8), fail (5), not (5), give up (3), let alone (3), refrain (2), abandoned (1), always be (1 [+4202]), cease (1), do not (1), don't (1), ended (1), failing (1), fails (1), gone away (1), held back (1), keep (1), leave alone (1 [+4946]), no enough (1), no more (1), not trust (1), over (1), past (1), refrain from (1), refuse (1), silent (1), stop trusting in (1 [+4946]), would not (1)

H2533 [2]חָדַל ***ḥādal***[2], v. Not used in NIVEBC [cf. 2532, 2536?]. [Q] to become fat, have success

H2534 חָדֵל ***ḥādēl***, a. [3] [√ 2532]. refused, rejected, fleeting:– fleeting (1), refuse (1), rejected (1)

H2535 חֶדֶל ***ḥedel***, n.[m.] world (of the living); some sources: the Underworld, the realm of the dead

H2536 חַדְלָי ***ḥadlāy***, n.pr.m. [1] [√ 2432 *or* 2533]. Hadlai, "*resting; fat, stout*":– Hadlai (1)

H2537 חֵדֶק ***ḥēdeq***, n.[m.] [2] brier, thorn:– brier (1), thorns (1)

H2538 חִדֶּקֶל ***ḥiddeqel***, n.pr.loc. [2] Hiddekel = Tigris, "*arrow*":– Tigris (2)

H2539 חָדַר ***ḥādar***, v. [1] [→ 2540]. [Q] to close in on every side, surround:– closing in from every side (1)

H2540 חֶדֶר ***ḥeder***, n.m. [38] [√ 2539]. room, chamber, bedroom; shrine; "the chambers of the belly" means "the most inner parts"; "the chambers of death" means "Sheol":– room (6), bedroom (4 [+5435]), inner room (4 [+2540, 928]), inner room (4 [+928, 2540]), rooms (3), bedroom (2), bedroom (2 [+4753]), chambers (2), inmost parts (2 [+1061]), bedrooms (1), chamber (1), constellations (1), homes (1), inmost being (1 [+1061]), inmost being (1 [+3972, 1061]), inner room (1), private room (1), shrine (1)

H2541 חַדְרָךְ ***ḥadrāk***, n.pr.loc. [1] Hadrach:– Hadrak (1)

H2542 חָדַשׁ ***ḥādaš***, v. [10] [→ 2543, 2544, 2545, 2546, 2548]. [Q] to renew, restore, repair, reaffirm; [Ht] to renew oneself:– renew (5), restore (2), bring new (1), is renewed (1), repaired (1)

H2543 חָדָשׁ ***ḥādāš***, a. [53] [√ 2542; 10251]. new, recent, fresh:– new (50), fade (1), recently (1), recently (1 [+4946, 7940])

H2544 [1]חֹדֶשׁ ***ḥōdeš***[1], n.m. [& f.?] [281] [→ 2545; cf. 2542]. month; new moon, new moon festival:– month (192), months (30), new Moon (8), new Moons (7), new Moon feasts (4), new Moon feast (3), another[S] (1), feast[S] (1), mating time (1), month (1 [+4946, 4200, 2544]), month (1 [+4946, 2544, 4200]), monthly (1), monthly (1 [+2544, 928]), monthly (1 [+928, 2544]), new Moon feasts (1 [+8031]), whole month (1 [+3427]), NDT (27)

H2545 [2]חֹדֶשׁ ***ḥōdeš***[2], n.pr.f. [1] [√ 2544; cf. 2542]. Hodesh, "*new moon*":– Hodesh (1)

H2546 חֲדָשָׁה ***ḥ***^a^***dāšâ***, n.pr.loc. [1] [√ 2542]. Hadashah, "*new*":– Hadashah (1)

H2547 חָדְשִׁי ***ḥodšî***, n.pr.loc. Not used in NIVEBC [→ 9398]. Hodshi

H2548 חֲדַתָּה ***ḥ***^a^***dattâ***, n.pr.loc. Not used in NIVEBC [√ 2542]. Hadattah

H2549 חוּב ***ḥûb***, v. [1] [→ 2550]. [P] to forfeit (one's head):– because of (1)

H2550 חוֹב ***ḥôb***, n.[m.] [1] [√ 2549]. loan, debt:– loan (1)

H2551 חֹבָה ***ḥôbâ***, n.pr.loc. [1] Hobah:– Hobah (1)

H2552 [1]חוּג ***ḥûg***[1], v. [1] [→ 2553, 4684; cf. 2510]. [Q] to encircle:– marks out (1)

H2553 [2]חוּג ***ḥûg***[2], n.[m.] [3] [√ 2552]. circle, horizon:– circle (1), horizon (1), vaulted (1)

H2554 חוּד ***ḥûd***, v.den. [4] [√ 2648; cf. 284]. [Q] to tell a riddle, set forth an allegory:– tell (2), given (1), set forth (1)

H2555 [1]חָוָה ***ḥāwâ***[1], v. [6] [→ 289; 10018, 10252]. [P] to tell, explain, show, display:– tell (3), explain (1), reveal (1), show (1)

H2556 [2]חָוָה ***ḥāwâ***[2], v. [170] [cf. 8817]. [Hsh] to bow down low (in worship); prostrate oneself; pay one honor, homage:– worship (38), bow down (33), bowed down (29), worshiped (22), worshiping (7), bowed (6), bowing down (6), pay honor (6), bowed in worship (2), prostrated himself (2), prostrating herself (2), worships (2), bow (1), bow down in worship (1), bow down to worship (1), bowed down and worshiped (1), bowed low (1), bows down (1), fell facedown (1 [+4200, 678]), honor (1), humbly bow (1), paid homage (1), paid honor (1), prostrating (1), prostrating themselves (1), reverence (1), worshiped leaned (1)

H2557 [1]חַוָּה ***ḥawwâ***[1], n.f. [3] settlement, camp; an unwalled village, a tent camp of nomadic peoples, more or less permanent:– settlements (3)

H2558 [2]חַוָּה ***ḥawwâ***[2], n.pr.f. [2] [cf. 2649]. Eve, "*life*":– Eve (2)

H2559 חוֹזָי ***ḥôzāy***, n.m. Not used in NIVEBC [√ 2602; cf. 2600]. Hozai

H2560 [1]חוֹחַ ***ḥôaḥ***[1], n.m. [12] [cf. 2626]. thicket, thistle, thornbush, bramble, briers; hook:– thistle (4), hook (2), thorns (2), brambles (1), briers (1), thickets (1), thornbush (1)

H2561 [2]חוֹחַ ***ḥôaḥ***[2], n.m. hollows, cleft in rock

H2562 חוּט ***ḥûṭ***, n.m. [7] [√ 10253]. line, cord, ribbon, thread:– circumference (1 [+6015]), cord (1), cord (1 [+9535]), in circumference (1 [+6015]), ribbon (1), thread (1), threads (1)

H2563 חִוִּי ***ḥiwwî***, a.g. [25] Hivite:– Hivites (23), Hivite (2)

H2564 חֲוִילָה ***ḥ***^a^***wîlâ***, n.pr.loc. [7] [√ 2567]. Havilah, "*stretch of sand*":– Havilah (7)

H2565 [1]חוּל ***ḥûl***[1], v. [10] [→ 4688, 4689, 4703, 4714?; cf. 2658]. [Q] to swirl, turn, fall, dance; [Pol] to wait; to dance (the round dance); [Htpol] to wait patiently; to swirl down; in some contexts this refers to a whirlwind:– swirling down (2), dancing (1), fall (1), flash (1), join (1), turned (1), wait (1), wait patiently (1), NDT (1)

H2566 [2]חוּל ***ḥûl***[2], n.pr.m. [2] Hul:– Hul (2)

H2567 [1]חוֹל ***ḥôl***[1], n.m. [23] [→ 2564]. sand, grains of sand, with the associative meanings that the sands are vast and innumerable:– sand (21), grains of sand (2)

H2568 [2]חוֹל ***ḥôl***[2], n.m. palm tree or phoenix bird

H2569 חוּם ***ḥûm***, a. [4] [√ 2801]. dark-colored; some shade of gray:– dark-colored (4)

H2570 חוֹמָה ***ḥômâ***, n.f. [133] [→ 3503]. wall, with various associative meanings: protection, safety, or impenetrability:– wall (81), walls (44), city wall (2), walled (2), it[S] (1 [+2021]), walled (1 [+4200, 2257]), NDT (2)

H2571 חוּס ***ḥûs***, v. [24] [Q] to show pity, mercy, have compassion, spare:– look with pity (6 [+6524]), show pity (4 [+6524]), looked with pity (2 [+6524]), show mercy (2), concerned (1), have concern (1), have pity (1), look with compassion (1 [+6524]), mercy (1), mind (1), showing pity (1 [+6524]), spare (1), spared (1), take pity (1)

H2572 חוֹף ***ḥôp***, n.[m.] [7] [√ 2910]. coast, seashore, haven (for ships):– coast (4 [+3542]), coast (1), haven (1), seashore (1 [+3542])

H2573 חוּפָם ***ḥûpām***, n.pr.m. [1] [→ 2574]. Hupham:– Hupham (1)

H2574 חוּפָמִי ***ḥûpāmî***, a.g. [1] [√ 2573]. Huphamite, "*of Hupham*":– Huphamite (1)

H2575 חוּץ ***ḥûṣ***, n.[m.] [164] [→ 2667; cf. 2666]. out, outside; street, market area; countryside, fields, outdoors:– outside (49 [+4946]), streets (38), street (12), outside (8), outside (8 [+2025]), outside (7 [+928, 2021]), out (5 [+2025]), out (5), outer (3), fields (2), area (1 [+4946]), around (1 [+4200, 2021]), around (1 [+4946, 2021]), away (1 [+448, 2021, 2025]), countryside (1), elsewhere (1), extend (1 [+2025]), get out (1 [+8938, 2021, 2025]), land (1), market areas (1), open (1), out here (1 [+928, 2021]), outdoor (1 [+928, 2021]), outer (1 [+4200, 2021]), outside (1 [+4946, 2025]), outside (1 [+4946, 2025]), outside the family (1 [+2021, 2025, 2424]), put out (1 [+3655, 2021]), relieve yourself (1 [+3782]), without (1 [+4946]), NDT (7)

H2576 חוֹק ***ḥôq***, n.[m.] Not used in NIVEBC [√ 2980]. see 2668

H2577 חוּקֹק ***ḥûqōq***, n.pr.loc. [1] Hukok:– Hukok (1)

H2578 [1]חָוַר ***ḥāwar***[1], v. [1] [→ 2580, 2583, 3035; 10254]. [Q] to grow pale:– grow pale (1)

H2579 [2]חָוַר ***ḥāwar***[2], v. [Q] to become less

H2580 [1]חוּר ***ḥûr***[1], n.[m.] [2] [√ 2578]. white garments, white linen:– white (2)

H2581 [2]חוּר ***ḥûr***[2], n.pr.m. [15] [→ 1210, 6656?]. Hur, "[perhaps] *child*":– Hur (15)

H2582 חוֹרוֹן ***ḥôrôn***, n.pr.loc. Not used in NIVEBC [→ 1103]. Horon

H2583 חוֹרָי ***ḥôrāy***, n.m. [1] [√ 2578]. fine linen:– fine linen (1)

H2584 חוּרַי ***ḥûray***, n.pr.m. [1] Hurai:– Hurai (1)

H2585 חוּרִי ***ḥûrî***, n.pr.m. [1] Huri, "*linen weaver*":– Huri (1)

H2586 חוּרָם ***ḥûrām***, n.pr.m. [10] [√ 325?]. Huram, Hiram, "*[my] brother is elevated*":– Hiram (6), Huram (3), Hiram's (1)

H2587 חוּרָם אָבִי ***ḥûrām 'ābî***, n.pr.m. [2] [√ 325? + 3]. Huram-Abi, "*my father is Huram*":– Huram-Abi (2)

H2588 חַוְרָן ***ḥawrān***, n.pr.loc. [2] Hauran, "*black*":– Hauran (2)

H2589 חוֹרֹנַיִם ***ḥôrōnayim***, n.pr.loc. [5] Horonaim, "*twin hollows, twin caves*":– Horonaim (5)

H2590 [1]חוּשׁ ***ḥûš***[1], v. [16] [→ 2673, 4561; cf. 2591]. [Q] to go quickly, hasten, rush upon; [Qp] to be ready; [H] to make hurry, hasten:– come quickly (7), hasten (2), do swiftly (1), go quickly (1), hurried (1), hurry (1), rushes (1), sudden (1), swooping (1)

H2591 [2]חוּשׁ ***ḥûš***[2], v. [3] [cf. 2590]. [Q] to be greatly disturbed; to find enjoyment; [H] to be dismayed:– find enjoyment (1), greatly disturbed (1), stricken with panic (1)

H2592 חוּשָׁה ***ḥûšâ***, n.pr.m. [1] [→ 3144]. Hushah, "[perhaps] *haste*":– Hushah (1)

H2593 חוּשַׁי ***ḥûšay***, n.pr.m. [14] [cf. 8856?]. Hushai:– Hushai (12), NDT (2)

H2594 חוּשִׁים ***ḥûšîm***, n.pr.f. [2] [cf. 3123]. Hushim:– Hushim (2)

H2595 חוּשָׁם ***ḥûšām***, n.pr.m. [4] [cf. 3130]. Husham:– Husham (4)

H2596 חַוּוֹת יָאִיר ***ḥawwōt yā'îr***, n.pr.m. & n.f. [4] [cf. 3281]. Havvoth Jair, "*villages of Jair*":– Havvoth Jair (4)

H2597 [1]חוֹתָם ***ḥôtām***[1], n.m. [14] [→ 2598; cf. 3159]. seal, signet ring:– seal (10), signet ring (2), placed seal (1 [+3159, 928]), sealed together (1 [+6037])

H2598 [2]חוֹתָם ***ḥôtām***[2], n.pr.m. [2] [√ 2597; cf. 3159]. Hotham, "*signet ring, seal*":– Hotham (2)

H2599 חֲזָאֵל ***ḥ***^a^***zā'ēl***, n.pr.m. [23] [√ 2600 + 446]. Hazael, "*God [El] sees*":– Hazael (21), he[S] (1), his[S] (1)

H2600 חָזָה ***ḥāzâ***, v. [55] [→ 2559, 2602, 2606, 2607, 2608, 2612, 4690, 4691, 4692; 10255; *also used with compound proper names*]. [Q] to see, to look, observe, gaze; by extension: to choose (one thing over another); to have visions, to prophesy:– see (13), seen (5), visions (5), saw (4), sees (4), gaze (3), look (3), see visions (3), are[S] (1), gave (1), give visions (1), gloat (1), looked with lust (1), looks (1), observed (1), observes (1), prophesy (1), received (1), saw visions (1 [+2606]), select (1), stargazers (1 [+928, 3919]), the vision saw (1), vision saw (1)

H2601 חָזֶה ***ḥāzeh***, n.m. [13] [√ 10249]. breast (portion of sacrifice):– breast (11), breasts (2)

H2602 [1]חֹזֶה ***ḥōzeh***[1], n.m. [17] [→ 2559, 3997; cf. 2600]. seer, one who receives a communication from God, with a possible focus that the message has a visual component:– seer (11), seers (5), prophets (1)

H2603 [2]חֹזֶה ***ḥōzeh***[2], n.m. [1] agreement:– agreement (1)

H2604 חֲזָהאֵל ***ḥ***^a^***zāh'ēl***, n.pr.m. Not used in NIVEBC [√ 2600 + 446]. Haziel, see 2609

H2605 חֲזוֹ ***ḥ***^a^***zô***, n.pr.m. [1] Hazo:– Hazo (1)

H2606 חָזוֹן ***ḥāzôn***, n.m. [35] [√ 2600]. vision, revelation, a message from God, with a possible focus on the visual aspects of the message:– vision (22), visions (8), revelation (4), saw visions (1 [+2600])

H2607 חָזוּת ***ḥāzût***, n.f. [5] [√ 2600]. vision; prominent appearance:– prominent (2), vision (2), agreement (1)

H2608 חֲזוֹת ***ḥ***^a^***zôt***, n.[f.] [1] [√ 2600]. visions:– visions (1)

H2609 חֲזִיאֵל ***ḥ***^a^***zî'ēl***, n.pr.m. [1] [√ 2600 + 446]. Haziel, "*vision of God [El]*":– Haziel (1)

H2610 חֲזָיָה ***ḥ***^a^***zāyâ***, n.pr.m. [1] [√ 2600 + 3378]. Hazaiah, "*Yahweh sees*":– Hazaiah (1)

H2611 חֶזְיוֹן ***ḥezyôn***, n.pr.m. [1] Hezion, "*vision; one with floppy ears*":– Hezion (1)

H2612 חִזָּיוֹן ***ḥizzāyôn***, n.m. [9] [√ 2600]. vision, dream, revelation:– vision (5), visions (2), dreams (1), revelation (1)

H2613 חֲזִיז ***ḥ***^a^***zîz***, n.[m.] [3] storm cloud, dark and producing lightning and thunder:– thunderstorm (2 [+7754]), thunderstorms (1)

H2614 חֲזִיר ***ḥ***^a^***zîr***, n.m. [7] [→ 2615, 3492]. pig, boar:– pig (2), pigs (2), pig's (2), boars (1)

H2615 חֵזִיר ***ḥēzîr***, n.pr.m. [2] [√ 2614]. Hezir, "*boar*":– Hezir (2)

H2616 חָזַק ***ḥāzaq***, v. [290] [→ 2617, 2618, 2619, 2620, 2621, 2622; *also used with compound proper names*]. [Q] to be strong, hard, harsh, severe; [P] to harden (one's heart); to give strength, repair, encourage; [H] to grasp, seize, hold; to make repairs; [Ht] to establish oneself firmly; to encourage, to rally strength; from the base meaning of physical hardness come by extension: physical and internal strength of character; (negative) hardness of the heart, failure to respond to a person or message:– strong (41), repaired (18), made repairs (14), strengthen (12), repair (10), took hold (7), hardened (6), severe (5), strengthened (5), stronger (5), take hold (5), encourage (4), firmly (4), hard (4), repairs made (4), took (4), gripped (3), harden (3), hold fast (3), powerful (3), armed (2), cling (2), embraced (2), encouraged (2), encouraged (2 [+3338]), established himself firmly (2), fasten (2), fight bravely (2), grabbed (2), held (2), help (2), holds fast (2), seize (2), seizes (2), take (2), took courage (2), urged (2), arrogantly (1), assisted (1 [+3338]), assisted (1 [+928, 3338]), be sure (1), began (1 [+3338]), brace yourselves (1 [+5516]), captured (1), carried out repairs (1), caught (1), caught hold (1), caulk (1), come (1), conquered (1 [+6584]), courage (1), courageously (1), devote (1), devoted (1), do best (1), encourages (1), equipped (1), fortified (1), found strength (1), gave power (1), gave strength (1), gave strong support (1 [+6640]), give strength (1), given strength (1), gone[S] (1), grabs (1), grasped (1), grasping (1), grew in strength (1), grips (1), have strength (1), heavier (1), held secure (1), help (1 [+3338]), helped (1), helped (1 [+906, 3338]), helped find strength (1 [+906, 3338]), hold back (1), hold on (1), holding (1), join (1 [+6584]), kept (1), lay hold (1), leans (1), made harder (1), made strong (1), maintain (1), maintaining (1), maintains (1), marshaled strength (1), more resolute (1), nails down (1 [+928, 5021]), overpowered (1), overruled (1 [+448]), overruled (1 [+6584]), preserve (1), press (1), prevailed on (1 [+928]), proved stronger (1), rallied strength (1), rapes (1 [+2256, 8886, 6640]), recovery (1), reinforce (1), reinforced (1), repair (1 [+981]), repairing (1), resist (1), restored (1), restoring (1), seized (1), shipwrights (1 [+981]), showed strength (1), stay (1), strengthen position

(1), strengthened himself (1), strengthening his own position (1), strengthens (1), strong (1 [+3338]), support (1), supported (1), supports (1 [+6640]), take courage (1), take firm hold (1), take up (1), takes hold (1), triumphed (1), unswerving (1), victorious (1), was strengthened (1), worked hard (1), NDT (3)

H2617 חָזָק **ḥāzāq**, a. [57] [√ 2616]. mighty, powerful, strong, hard, severe; from the base meaning of physical hardness come by extension: physical and internal strength of character; (negative) hardness of the heart, failure to respond to a person or message:– mighty (23), strong (12), powerful (6), hardened (2 [+5195]), power (2), stronger (2), bitter (1), fiercest (1), good (1), grew worse and worse (1 [+2118, 2716, 4394]), hard (1), harder (1), loud (1), severe (1), stubborn (1 [+4213]), unyielding (1 [+7156])

H2618 חָזֵק **ḥāzēq**, a.vbl. [2] [√ 2616]. strong, loud:– grew louder and louder (1 [+2143, 2256, 4394]), grew stronger and stronger (1 [+2143, 2256])

H2619 חֵזֶק **ḥēzeq**, n.[m.] [1] [√ 2616]. strength:– strength (1)

H2620 חֹזֶק **ḥōzeq**, n.m. [5] [√ 2616]. might, strength, power:– mighty (3), power (1), strength (1)

H2621 חֶזְקָה **ḥezqâ**, n.f. [4] [√ 2616]. strength, power:– became powerful (1), become strong (1), gained power (1), strong (1)

H2622 חָזְקָה **ḥozqâ**, n.f. [5] [√ 2616]. force, harshness, urgency:– cruelly (1 [+928]), force (1), harshly (1 [+928]), urgently (1 [+928]), vigorously (1 [+928])

H2623 חִזְקִי **ḥizqî**, n.pr.m. [1] [√ 2616 + 3378]. Hizki, "*Yahweh is [my] strength* or *my strength*":– Hizki (1)

H2624 חִזְקִיָּה **ḥizqiyyâ**, n.pr.m. [13] [√ 2616 + 3378]. Hezekiah, "*Yahweh is [my] strength*":– Hezekiah (9), Hezekiah's (1), Hezekiah's (1 [+4200]), Hizkiah (1), he^{S} (1)

H2625 חִזְקִיָּהוּ **ḥizqiyyāhû**, n.pr.m. [74] [√ 2616 + 3378]. Hezekiah, "*Yahweh is [my] strength*":– Hezekiah (66), Hezekiah's (5), he^{S} (2), Hezekiah's (1 [+4200])

H2626 חָח **ḥāḥ**, n.m. [7] [cf. 2560]. hook; brooch:– hooks (4), hook (2), brooches (1)

H2627 חָטָא **ḥāṭā'**, v. [237] [→ 2628, 2629, 2630, 2631, 2632, 2633]. [Q] to sin, do wrong, miss the way; [P] to purify, cleanse, to offer a sin offering; [H] to bring a sin upon, cause to commit a sin; [Ht] to purify oneself; "to sin," to willfully act contrary to the will and law of God, is a figure of missing or moving from a standard or mark:– sinned (68), sin (26), committed (23), caused to commit (20), sins (16), purify (9), sinning (7), caused to sin (4), sinner (4), wronged (4), purify themselves (3), sinful (3), bear the blame (2), do wrong (2), done wrong (2), led into sin (2), purified (2), wrongs (2), a sin committed (1 [+2631]), be purified (1), bore the loss (1), bring sin (1), cause to sin (1), cleanse (1), commit (1), commit a sin (1), committed (1 [+2628]), committed a sin (1 [+2631]), crime committed (1), fail to find (1), failed to do (1), fails to reach (1), fault (1), find missing (1), forfeit (1), forfeiting (1), lead into sin (1), make out to be guilty (1), make sin (1), miss (1), miss the way (1), offended (1), offered for a sin offering (1), offers (1), presented for a sin offering (1), purified themselves (1), purify yourselves (1), purifying (1), retreat (1), sin offerings (1), sinned greatly (1 [+2628]), sinner's (1), wicked (1), NDT (3)

H2628 חֵטְא **ḥēṭ'**, n.m. [33] [√ 2627; 10259]. sin, action contrary to the will and law of God, with a strong implication that guilt follows, error; see also 2627:– sin (7), sins (6), guilty of sin (3), consequences of sin (2), guilty (2), held responsible (2 [+5951]), sinful (2), become guilty (1 [+5951, 6584]), committed (1 [+2627]), consequences of sins (1), guilt (1), guilty (1 [+5951]), offenses (1), punished for sins (1), shortcomings (1), sinned greatly (1 [+2627])

H2629 חַטָּא **ḥaṭṭā'**, a. & n.m. [19] [√ 2627]. sinful, guilty; (n.) sinner, wicked one; see also 2627:– sinners (12), sinful (2), criminals (1), sinned (1), sinner (1), sinning (1), wicked people (1)

H2630 חֶטְאָה **ḥeṭ'â**, n.[f.] [1] [√ 2627]. sin; see also 2627:– sinning (1)

H2631 חֲטָאָה **ḥ^{a}ṭā'â**, n.f. [8] [√ 2627]. sin, guilt, condemnation; sin offering; see also 2627:– sin (2), a sin committed (1 [+2627]), committed a sin (1 [+2627]), condemn (1 [+2118, 4200]), guilt (1), sin offerings (1), sins (1)

H2632 חַטָּאָה **ḥaṭṭā'â**, n.f. [2] [√ 2627]. sin, wickedness, fault; see also 2627:– sin (1), wickedness (1)

H2633 חַטָּאת **ḥaṭṭā't**, n.f. [292] [√ 2627; 10258, 10260]. sin, wrong, iniquity; sin offering, purification offering; see also 2627:– sin offering (105), sin (83), sins (75), sin offerings (8), punishment (2), wronged (2), cleansing (1), iniquities (1), it^{S} (1 [+2021]), its^{S} (1 [+2021]), offense (1), purification from sin (1), purification offering (1), sin and death (1), sinful thing (1), sinner (1), sinning (1), that^{S} (1), wickedness (1), wrongs (1), wrongs (1 [+6913]), NDT (2)

H2634 חָטַב **ḥāṭab**, v. [9] [Q] to cut, chop (wood); (n.) woodcutter, woodsman; [Pu] to carve:– woodcutters (3 [+6770]), cut (2), carved (1), chop (1), cut down (1), woodsmen (1)

H2635 חֲטֻבוֹת **ḥ^{a}ṭubôt**, n.f.pl. [1] colored, embroidered (fabric):– colored (1)

H2636 חִטָּה **ḥiṭṭâ**, n.f. [30] [√ 2845; 10272]. wheat:– wheat (30)

H2637 חַטּוּשׁ **ḥaṭṭûš**, n.pr.m. [5] Hattush:– Hattush (5)

H2638 חֲטִיטָא **ḥ^{a}ṭîṭā'**, n.pr.m. [2] Hatita:– Hatita (2)

H2639 חַטִּיל **ḥaṭṭîl**, n.pr.m. [2] Hattil, "*talkative*":– Hattil (2)

H2640 חֲטִיפָא **ḥ^{a}ṭîpā'**, n.pr.m. [2] [√ 2642]. Hatipha, "*taken captive*":– Hatipha (2)

H2641 חָטַם **ḥāṭam**, v. [1] [→ 3033]. [Q] to hold back, restrain:– hold back (1)

H2642 חָטַף **ḥāṭap**, v. [3] [→ 2640]. [Q] to seize, carry off (by force):– catch (1), catches (1), seize (1)

H2643 חֹטֶר **ḥōṭer**, n.m. [2] rod, switch; shoot, twig:– lashes out (1), shoot (1)

H2644 ^{1}חַי **ḥay^{1}**, n.m. [235] [→ 2652; cf. 2649]. life, state of living (in contrast to death), lifetime; "as I live" is a formula for an oath, implying death should follow if what is sworn is not true:– life (107), as surely lives (46), as surely as live (23), live (13), lived (8), as live (6), lives (6), as lives (3), living (3), as surely as live (2 [+5883]), lifetime (2), as surely as live (1 [+2256, 2644, 5883]), as surely as live (1 [+2644, 2256, 5883]), creature (1), everything you do (1), life will not be worth living (1 [+4200, 4537]), life-giving (1), lifetime (1 [+3427]), live (1 [+928, 2021]), long life (1 [+4200, 2021]), nourish (1), old (1 [+3427, 9102]), NDT (5)

H2645 ^{2}חַי **ḥay^{2}**, a. [145] [√ 2649; 10261]. living, alive, with an implication that life has movement and vigor; "living meat" is "raw meat"; "living water" is "fresh, running water":– living (61), alive (34), live (15), fresh (8), raw (5), lives (3), life (2), lifetime (2), next year (2), next year (2 [+6961]), as surely as live (1), flowing (1), green (1), it^{S} (1 [+2021, 7606, 2021]), lived (1), living (1 [+132]), living creatures (1), living thing (1), others^{S} (1), preserved (1 [+8492, 928, 2021]), raw (1 [+4695])

H2646 ^{3}חַי **ḥay^{3}**, n.[m.] [1] [√ 2649; 10261]. family, kin:– family (1)

H2647 חִיאֵל **ḥî'ēl**, n.pr.m. [1] [√ 278 + 446]. Hiel, "*God [El] lives here*":– Hiel (1)

H2648 חִידָה **ḥîdâ**, n.f. [17] [→ 2554; 10019]. riddle, hard question, allegory; hidden things, intrigue; scorn (the asking of a riddle as a game could imply scorn and ridicule toward the person asked):– riddle (8), hard questions (2), riddles (2), allegory (1), answer (1), hidden things (1), intrigue (1), scorn (1)

H2649 חָיָה **ḥāyâ**, v. [279] [→ 2644, 2645, 2646, 2650, 2651, 2652, 2653, 2654, 4695; cf. 2558; 10262; *also used with compound proper names*]. [Q] to live; recover, revive; [P] to keep alive, preserve life; [H] to keep alive, save a life, spare a life, restore a life:– live (90), lived (43), surely live (18 [+2649]), preserve life (11), spared (10), long live (9), keep alive (8), let live (7), recover (6), revive (5), certainly recover (4 [+2649]), save life (4), kept alive (3), leave alive (3), preserve (3), restored to life (3), allowed to live (2), bring back to life (2), came to life (2), come to life (2), preserves (2), revived (2), save (2), save lives (2), spare (2), survive (2), survived (2), allow to live (1), bring to life (1), brought back to life (1), choose life (1), die (1 [+4202]), flourish (1), give life (1), gives life (1), healed (1), live again (1), live on (1), lives (1), makes alive (1), preserved life (1), preserves life (1), raised (1), recovered (1), recovery (1 [+4946, 2716]), repeat (1), restore life (1), restored (1), safety (1), saved lives (1), saving (1), spare lives (1), spared lives (1), spares lives (1), sparing (1), stay alive (1), will^{S} (1)

H2650 חָיֶה **ḥāyeh**, a. [1] [√ 2649]. vigorous:– vigorous (1)

H2651 ^{1}חַיָּה **ḥayyâ^{1}**, n.f. [104] [√ 2649; 10263]. animal, beast, livestock, living creature:– animals (35), beasts (17), living creatures (13), living (8), animal (7), wild animals (5), beast (4), creatures (3), living creature (2), wild beasts (2), animal (1 [+7473]), animal wild (1), beasts of burden (1 [+2256, 989]), creature (1), living things (1), ones^{S} (1), those^{S} (1 [+2021]), wild animal (1)

H2652 ^{2}חַיָּה **ḥayyâ^{2}**, n.f. [12] [√ 2644; cf. 2649]. life, one's very being; hunger (of lions):– life (2), lives (2), body (1), hunger (1), live (1), me (1 [+3276]), renewal (1), them (1 [+4392]), NDT (2)

H2653 ^{3}חַיָּה **ḥayyâ^{3}**, n.f. [3] [√ 2649]. band, army; people, home:– band (1), banded together (1 [+665, 4200, 2021]), people (1)

H2654 חַיּוּת **ḥayyût**, n.f.abst. [1] [√ 2649]. lifetime:– living (1)

H2655 ^{1}חִיל **ḥîl^{1}**, v. [46] [→ 2659, 2660, 2714]. [Q] to writhe, tremble, be in labor, give birth; [Pol] to give birth, bring forth; be in deep anguish, to twist; [Polal] to be brought forth, be given birth; [H] to shake; [Ho] to be born; [Htpalpal] be in distress; [Htpol] to be in torment:– in anguish (4), in labor (4), tremble (4), gave birth (2), shakes (2), was given birth (2), wounded (2), writhe (2), writhe in agony (2 [+2655]), writhe in pain (2), writhed (2), writhes (2), at birth (1), be born (1), bears (1), brings (1), brought forth (1), brought to birth (1), felt pain (1), goes into labor (1), in deep anguish (1), in distress (1), suffers torment (1), trembles (1), twists (1), were brought forth (1), writhe in agony (1 [+4394]), writhed in labor (1)

H2656 ^{2}חִיל **ḥîl^{2}**, v. [2] [→ 2657]. [Q] to endure, prosper:– endure (1), prosperous (1)

H2657 חַיִל **ḥayil**, n.m. [244] [→ 35, 38, 1211; cf. 2656; 10264]. strength, capability, skill, valor, wealth; army, troop, warrior:– army (78), wealth (25), fighting men (12 [+1475]), strength (11), brave warriors (5 [+1475]), riches (5), able men (4 [+1201]), brave (4 [+1201]), troops (4), valiant (4), capable (3), force (3), forces (3), noble character (3), soldiers (3), standing (3), strong (3), able-bodied (2), best fighting men (2 [+1475]), brave (2), caravan (2), might (2), mighty things (2), power (2), standing (2 [+1475]), valiant fighter (2 [+1201, 408]), valiant fighters (2 [+408]), valiant soldier (2 [+1475]), victory (2), warriors (2 [+408]), able (1 [+1201]), able men (1 [+1475]), able-bodied (1 [+1201]), armed (1), armed forces (1 [+7372]), armies (1), army (1 [+2162]), army (1 [+7372]), battle (1), brave fighting men (1 [+1475]), brave man (1 [+1475]), brave warrior (1 [+1475]), bravely (1 [+4200, 1201]), bravest soldier (1 [+1201]), capable men (1 [+1475]), champions (1 [+408]), company (1), courageous (1 [+1201]), experienced fighting men (1 [+408, 4878, 1475]), fighting (1), fighting (1 [+1201]), goods (1), leading (1 [+1201]), men of standing (1 [+1475]), mighty (1), mighty warrior (1 [+1475]), mighty warriors (1 [+1475]), military (1), military leaders (1), noble (1), one^{S} (1), profit (1), skills (1), soldiers (1 [+1201]), special ability (1), strongest defenders (1 [+408]), they^{S} (1 [+3405, 2256, 8569, 2021]), troops (1 [+1475]), valiantly (1), very capable men (1 [+1475]), warriors (1 [+1475]), wealthy (1), worthy (1), worthy (1 [+1201]), NDT (1)

H2658 חֵיל **ḥêl**, n.m. [7] [cf. 2565]. ramparts, outer fortification, defense walls:– ramparts (3), defense (1), outer fortifications (1), wall (1), walls (1)

H2659 ^{3}חִיל **ḥîl^{3}**, n.m. [6] [√ 2655]. pain, anguish:– pain (5), anguish (1)

H2660 חִילָה **ḥîlâ**, n.f. [1] [√ 2655]. pain, any kind of physical trauma, as a fig. extension of the labor pains of birth:– pain (1)

H2661 חִילֵז **ḥîlēz**, n.pr.loc. Not used in NIVEBC [cf. 2664]. Hilez, see 2664

H2662 חֵילֵךְ **ḥêlēk**, n.pr.loc. [1] Helech:– Helek (1)

H2663 חֵילָם **ḥêlām**, n.pr.loc. [2] [cf. 2691]. Helam, "*health*":– Helam (2)

H2664 חִילֵן **ḥîlēn**, n.pr.loc. [1] [cf. 2661]. Hilen:– Hilen (1)

H2665 חִין **ḥîn**, n.[m.] [1] [√ 2858]. gracefulness:– graceful (1)

H2666 חַיִץ **ḥayiṣ**, n.[m.] [1] [cf. 2575]. flimsy wall, inner wall:– flimsy wall (1)

H2667 חִיצוֹן **ḥîṣôn**, a. [25] [√ 2575]. outer, outside, exterior:– outer (20), away from (1), both outer (1), outside (1), outside (1 [+2025]), where^{S} (1 [+2021, 2958, 2021])

H2668 חֵיק **ḥêq**, n.[m.] [38] lap, bosom, the area to which one holds and cradles a loved one; by extension: the inner person, heart, seat of affection; fold of a cloak, gutter:– arms (7), cloak (5), laps (4), gutter (3), lap (3), breast (2), heart (2), loves (2), beside (1 [+928]), bosom (1), embrace (1), floor (1), garment (1), love (1), returned unanswered (1 [+8740]), secret (1), within (1 [+928]), NDT (1)

H2669 חִירָה **ḥîrâ**, n.pr.m. [2] Hirah:– Hirah (2)

H2670 חִירוֹם **ḥîrôm**, n.pr.m. [3] [√ 325?]. Hiram, "*[my] brother is elevated*":– Hiram (2), he^{S} (1)

H2671 חִירָם **ḥîrām**, n.pr.m. [20] [√ 325?]. Hiram, "*[my] brother is elevated*":– Hiram (15), Huram (3), Hiram's (1), he^{S} (1)

H2672 חִירֹת **ḥîrōt**, n.pr.loc. Not used in NIVEBC [→ 2112, 7084]. Hiroth

H2673 חִישׁ **ḥîš**, adv. [1] [√ 2590]. quickly, in haste:– quickly (1)

H2674 חֵךְ **ḥēk**, n.m. [19] (area of the) mouth: lips, tongue (taste), roof of the mouth:– mouth (7), roof of mouth (3), taste (3), tongue (2), lips (1), on the tip of tongue (1 [+4383, 928]), roof of mouths (1), speech (1)

H2675 חָכָה **ḥākâ**, v. [14] [Q] to wait; [P] to lie in wait (ambush); hope for, long for:– wait (7), delay (1), lie in ambush (1), long for (1), longs (1), wait in hope (1), waited (1), waits for (1)

H2676 חַכָּה **ḥakkâ**, n.f. [3] fishhook:– hooks (2), fishhook (1)

H2677 חֲכִילָה **ḥ^{a}kîlâ**, n.pr.loc. [3] [√ 2679]. Hakilah:– Hakilah (3)

H2678 חֲכַלְיָה **ḥ^{a}kalyâ**, n.pr.m. [2] [√ 2679 + 3378]. Hacaliah, "*dark*":– Hakaliah (2)

H2679 חַכְלִילִי **ḥaklîlî**, a. [1] [→ 2677, 2678, 2680]. darker; some sources: sparkling:– darker (1)

H2680 חַכְלִלוּת ***ḥaklilût***, n.f. [1] [√ 2679]. bloodshot (eyes); some sources: sparkling:– bloodshot (1)

H2681 חָכַם ***ḥākam***, v. [27] [→ 2682, 2683, 2684, 2685?; 10265]. [Q] to be wise, be skillful, gain wisdom; [P] to make wiser, to teach wisdom; [Pu] to be skillful; [H] to make wise; [Ht] to deal shrewdly; to show oneself wise; to be wise implies understanding and acting in a manner that is effective and usually moral:– wise (12), skillful (2), wisdom (2), wiser (2), counted among the wise (1), deal shrewdly (1), extremely wise (1 [+2682]), make wiser (1), makes wiser (1), making wise (1), overwise (1 [+3463]), skill (1), teach wisdom (1)

H2682 חָכָם ***ḥākām***, a. [138] [√ 2681; 10265]. wise, skilled, shrewd, craftsman; (n.) wise person, sage, one who interprets divination or prophecy, one who has fear of the Lord and understanding that leads to effective (moral) action; see also 2681:– wise (104), skilled (7), skilled (5 [+4213]), wisdom (4), skilled workers (3), skilled workers (2 [+4213]), wiser (2), advisers (1), craftsmen (1), extremely wise (1 [+2681]), great skill (1 [+3359, 1069]), shrewd (1), skillful (1), thoseS (1), unwise (1 [+4202]), wise (1 [+408]), wise (1 [+4213]), wisest (1)

H2683 חָכְמָה ***ḥokmâ***, n.f. [149] [√ 2681; 10266]. wisdom, skill, learning; this can refer to skill in life, trade, war, or spiritual things; see also 2681:– wisdom (133), skill (4), learning (2), ability (1), ability (1 [+928, 4213]), at wits end (1 [+3972, 1182]), skill (1 [+4213]), skilled (1), thatS (1), wisdom (1 [+8120]), wisdom's (1), wise (1), wise advice (1)

H2684 חָכְמוֹת ***ḥokmôt***, n.f.pl.abst. [4] [√ 2681]. wisdom; the plural form may imply in its essential or supreme condition; see also 2681:– wisdom (4)

H2685 חַכְמֹנִי ***ḥakmōnî***, n.pr.m.[g.?] [2] [√ 2681?]. Hacmoni; Hacmonite, *"wise"*:– Hakmoni (1), Hakmonite (1 [+1201])

H2686 חָכַר ***ḥākar***, v. [1] [cf. 2128]. [Q] to attack (vigorously):– attack (1)

H2687 חֹל ***ḥōl***, n.[m.] [7] [√ 2725]. common use, not holy, ordinary:– common (4), common use (1), not holy (1), ordinary (1)

H2688 חָלָא ***ḥālā'***, v. [1] [→ 2689, 2690, 9377; cf. 2703]. [Q] to be ill:– afflicted with a disease (1)

H2689 1חֶלְאָה ***ḥel'â1***, n.f. [5] [→ 2690; cf. 2688]. deposit, encrustation, rust:– deposit (3), encrusted (1), NDT (1)

H2690 2חֶלְאָה ***ḥel'â2***, n.pr.f. [2] [√ 2689; cf. 2688]. Helah, *"necklace; rust"*:– Helah (2)

H2691 חֵלָאם ***ḥēlā'm***, n.pr.loc. Not used in NIVEBC [cf. 2663]. Helam, see 2663

H2692 חָלָב ***ḥālāb***, n.m. [45] [→ 2697]. milk:– milk (40), cheeses (1 [+3043]), cream (1), curds (1), suckling (1), well nourished (1 [+4848])

H2693 1חֵלֶב ***ḥēleb1***, n.m. [91] fat, fat portions; by extension: finest, best part; callous (heart that is dull and unresponsive):– fat (64), fat portions (7), finest (5), best (3), callous hearts (2), callous (1 [+3869, 2021]), fattened (1), flesh (1), richest of foods (1 [+2256, 2016]), theseS (1 [+2021]), NDT (5)

H2694 2חֵלֶב ***ḥēleb2***, n.pr.m. Not used in NIVEBC [cf. 2699]. Heleb, see 2699

H2695 חֶלְבָּה ***ḥelbâ***, n.pr.loc. [1] Helbah, *"fertile region"*:– Helbah (1)

H2696 חֶלְבּוֹן ***ḥelbôn***, n.pr.loc. [1] Helbon, *"fertile"*:– Helbon (1)

H2697 חֶלְבְּנָה ***ḥelbenâ***, n.f. [1] [√ 2692]. galbanum (aromatic gum resin used to make incense):– galbanum (1)

H2698 חֶלֶד ***ḥeled***, n.[m.] [6] [→ 2699, 2702]. life, duration of life; this world:– world (2), fleeting life (1), life (1), span of years (1), this world (1)

H2699 חֵלֶד ***ḥēled***, n.pr.m. [2] [√ 2698]. Heled, *"mole"*:– Heled (2)

H2700 חֹלֶד ***ḥōled***, n.[m.] [1] [→ 2701]. weasel; some sources: rat or mole:– weasel (1)

H2701 חֻלְדָּה ***ḥuldâ***, n.pr.m. [2] [√ 2700]. Huldah, *"weasel"*:– Huldah (2)

H2702 חֶלְדַּי ***ḥelday***, n.pr.m. [3] [√ 2698]. Heldai, *"mole"*:– Heldai (3)

H2703 1חָלָה ***ḥālâ1***, v. [56] [→ 2716, 4700, 4701, 4705?, 4706?, 4707?, 4708, 5710; cf. 2688, 2704]. [Q] to be ill, be weak, be faint, become diseased, be wounded; [N] to be made sick, be incurable; [P] to afflict; [Pu] to become weak; [H] to make ill, to cause to suffer; [Ho] to be wounded; [Ht] to pretend to be ill, to feel sick:– ill (13), weak (8), diseased (3), faint (3), illness (3), wounded (3), been wounded (2), grievous (2), afflicted (1), beyond healing (1), cause to suffer (1), concerned (1), crushing (1 [+4394]), fatal (1), grieve (1), hurt (1), incurable (1), inflamed (1 [+2779]), injured (1), lay exhausted (1), made himself ill (1), makes sick (1), pretend to be ill (1), pretended to be ill (1), sick (1), suffering (1), wear themselves out (1)

H2704 2חָלָה ***ḥālâ2***, v. [17] [→ 4714?; cf. 2703]. [P] to entreat, implore, seek favor, intercede:– entreat (3 [+906, 7156]), sought the favor of (2 [+906, 7156]), appeal (1), court favor (1 [+7156]), curry favor with (1 [+7156]), intercede with (1 [+906, 7156]), interceded with (1 [+906, 7156]), plead with (1 [+7156]), seek favor (1 [+7156]), seek favor (1 [+906, 7156]), sought (1), sought favor (1 [+7156]), sought favor (1 [+906, 7156]), sought the favor of (1 [+7156, 906])

H2705 חַלָּה ***ḥallâ***, n.f. [14] [√ 2726]. (ring-shaped) bread cakes:– thick loaves (6), loaf (3), thick loaf (3), loaves of bread (1), thick loaf (1 [+4312])

H2706 חֲלוֹם ***ḥalôm***, n.m. [65] [√ 2731; 10267]. dream, dreamer; this can refer to a supernatural revelation by God by words and images:– dream (29), dreams (13), had a dream (6 [+2731]), dream had (2 [+2731]), dreamer (2 [+2731]), had dream (2 [+2731]), had dreams (2 [+2731]), dreamed (1), dreamer (1 [+1251, 2021]), dreaming (1), dreams (1 [+2731]), dreams encourage to have (1 [+2731]), foretells by dreams (1 [+2731]), interpreters of dreams (1), itS (1 [+2021]), NDT (1)

H2707 חַלּוֹן ***ḥallôn***, n.m. & f. [31] [√ 2726]. window, narrow openings, parapet openings:– window (13), windows (10), openings (7), parapet openings (1)

H2708 חֹלוֹן ***ḥōlôn***, n.pr.loc. [3] Holon, "[perhaps] *sandy*":– Holon (3)

H2709 חַלּוֹנַי ***ḥallônāy***, n.m. & f. window

H2710 חֲלוֹף ***ḥalôp***, n.m. [1] [√ 2736]. destitute, vanishing:– destitute (1 [+1201])

H2711 חֲלוּשָׁה ***ḥalûšâ***, n.f. [1] [√ 2765]. defeat:– defeat (1)

H2712 חֲלַח ***ḥalaḥ***, n.pr.loc. [3] Halah:– Halah (3)

H2713 חַלְחוּל ***ḥalḥûl***, n.pr.loc. [1] Halhul:– Halhul (1)

H2714 חַלְחָלָה ***ḥalḥālâ***, n.f. [4] [√ 2655]. anguish, pain, trembling:– anguish (2), pain (1), tremble (1)

H2715 חָלַט ***ḥālaṭ***, v. [1] [Q] to accept a statement:– pick up (1)

H2716 חֳלִי ***ḥolî***, n.m. [24] [√ 2703]. illness, sickness, affliction; wound, injury:– disease (5), illness (5), sickness (4), pain (2), affliction (1), evil (1), grew worse and worse (1 [+2118, 2617, 4394]), ill (1), illnesses (1), injured (1), injury (1), recovery (1 [+2649, 4946])

H2717 1חֲלִי ***ḥalî1***, n.m. [2] [→ 2719]. ornament, jewel:– jewels (1), ornament (1)

H2718 2חֲלִי ***ḥalî2***, n.pr.loc. [1] Hali, *"adornment"*:– Hali (1)

H2719 חֶלְיָה ***ḥelyâ***, n.f. [1] [√ 2717]. jewelry, ornament:– jewelry (1)

H2720 1חָלִיל ***ḥālîl1***, n.m. [6] [→ 2727, 5704?; cf. 2726]. flute:– pipes (4), pipe (2)

H2721 2חָלִילָה ***ḥālîl2***, subst. [21] [√ 2725]. far be it!, never!:– far be it (12), forbid (4), never (3), never (1 [+561]), of course not (1)

H2722 חֲלִיפָה ***ḥalîpâ***, n.f. [12] [√ 2736]. set, sequence, shift; renewal, relief:– sets (6), change (1), clothes (1), new (1), renewal (1), shifts (1), wave upon wave (1)

H2723 חֲלִיצָה ***ḥalîṣâ***, n.f. [2] [√ 2741]. belongings, equipment:– everythingS (1), weapons (1)

H2724 חֵלְכָה ***ḥēlkâ***, a. [3] victim:– victims (3)

H2725 1חָלַל ***ḥālal1***, v. [134] [→ 2687, 2721, 9378]. [N] to defile oneself, be profaned, be desecrated; [P] to defile, profane, desecrate; to enjoy; [Pu] to be defiled; [H] to begin, to proceed, launch; [Ho] to be begun:– began (26), desecrated (11), profane (11), begin (7), profaned (7), begun (6), defile (6), desecrate (6), defiled (5), desecrating (5), enjoy (4), beginning (3), being profaned (3), started (3), became (2 [+4200, 2118]), first time (2), take the lead (2), violate (2), am profaned (1), be defamed (1), be desecrated (1), becoming (1), been defiled (1), been profaned (1), break (1), bring down (1), defiles herself (1), degrade (1), desecrates (1), disgraced (1), disgraces (1), dishonor (1), drove in disgrace (1), let be profaned (1), proceeded (1), treating with contempt (1), undertook (1), violates (1), was desecrated (1), NDT (2)

H2726 2חָלַל ***ḥālal2***, v. [8] [→ 2705, 2707, 2720, 2727, 2728, 2729, 4704, 5704?]. [Q] to be wounded; [P] to pierce, wound; [Pu] to be killed; [Pol] to pierce, wound; [Polal] to be wounded:– killed (1), pierce (1), pierced (1), pierced through (1), slay (1), was pierced (1), wounded (1), wounds (1)

H2727 3חָלַל ***ḥālal3***, v.den. [2] [√ 2720; cf. 2726]. [Q, P] to play the flute:– make music (1), playing (1)

H2728 1חָלָל ***ḥālāl1***, n.m. [91] [√ 2726]. dead, slain, casualty:– slain (36), killed (21), dead (8), casualties (4), wounded (4), body (3), victims (3), slaughter (2), bodies (1), dead bodies (1), die (1), fall in battle (1 [+5877]), hurt (1), killed (1 [+5877]), mortally wounded man (1), people (1), slain in battle (1), violent (1)

H2729 2חָלָל ***ḥālāl2***, a. [3] [√ 2726]. defiled, profane (moral or ceremonial failure):– defiled (2), profane (1)

H2730 1חָלַם ***ḥālam1***, v. [2] [cf. 2731]. [Q] to grow strong; [H] to restore to health:– grow strong (1), restored to health (1)

H2731 2חָלַם ***ḥālam2***, v. [27] [→ 2706; cf. 2730]. [Q] to dream; [H] to encourage one to have dreams:– had a dream (6 [+2706]), had a dream (5), dream had (2 [+2706]), dreamer (2 [+2706]), dreams (2), had dream (2 [+2706]), had dreams (2 [+2706]), dream (1), dreamed (1), dreams (1 [+2706]), dreams encourage to have (1 [+2706]), foretells by dreams (1 [+2706]), NDT (1)

H2732 חֵלֶם ***ḥēlem***, n.pr.m. Not used in NIVEBC [cf. 2702]. Helem, see 2702

H2733 חַלָּמוּת ***ḥallāmût***, n.f. [1] egg or mallow:– mallow (1)

H2734 חַלָּמִישׁ ***ḥallāmîš***, n.m. [5] flinty rock, hard rock:– flint (1), flinty (1), flinty rock (1), hard (1), hard rock (1)

H2735 חֵלֹן ***ḥēlōn***, n.pr.m. [5] Helon, *"strength, power"*:– Helon (5)

H2736 1חָלַף ***ḥālap1***, v. [26] [→ 2710, 2722, 2739, 4709?, 4710; 10268]. [Q] to go by, pass on, sweep by; to be new; [P] to change; [H] to change, exchange, replace, renew:– changed (3), new (3), change (2), changing (1), comes along (1), disappear (1), discarded (1), exchange (1), glided past (1), go (1), goes by (1), let renew (1), over (1), renew (1), replace (1), skim past (1), sprout (1), sweep on (1), sweep past (1), sweeping (1), violated (1)

H2737 2חָלַף ***ḥālap2***, v. [2] [→ 2738?]. [Q] to pierce, cut through:– pierced (1), pierces (1)

H2738 1חֵלֶף ***ḥēlep1***, n.pr.loc. [1] [√ 2737?]. Heleph, "[poss.] *sharp, cutting*":– Heleph (1)

H2739 2חֵלֶף ***ḥēlep2***, n.[m.] [2] [√ 2736]. in return for:– for (1), in return for (1)

H2740 1חָלַץ ***ḥālaṣ1***, v. [23] [→ 4711; cf. 2741, 2742]. [Q] to take off; [Qp] to be taken off; [N] to be delivered, be rescued; [P] to rescue, deliver; to tear out, rob:– deliver (4), rescued (3), be delivered (2), delivers (2), torn out (2), delivered (1), escape (1), is rescued (1), offer (1), rescue (1), robbed (1), take off (1), unsandaled (1 [+5837]), withdrawn (1), NDT (1)

H2741 2חָלַץ ***ḥālaṣ2***, v. [21] [→ 2723, 2742; cf. 2740]. [Qp] to be armed (for battle); [N] to arm oneself; [H] to strengthen:– armed (12), armed guard (2), arm (1), arm ourselves (1), arm yourselves (1), armed for battle (1), army (1), soldiers (1), strengthen (1)

H2742 חֶלֶץ ***ḥeleṣ***, n.pr.m. [5] [√ 2740 *or* 2741]. Helez, *"vigor; he has saved"*:– Helez (5)

H2743 חֲלָצַיִם ***ḥalāṣayim***, n.[f.] [10] [√ 10284]. waist, stomach, the area between the lowest ribs and the hip-bones; by extension: body, flesh; the inner person, heart:– brace (2 [+273]), flesh and blood (2 [+3655, 4946]), waist (2), descendantsS (1 [+4946]), hearts (1), stomach (1), yourselvesS (1)

H2744 1חָלַק ***ḥālaq1***, v. [9] [→ 2747, 2748, 2749, 2752, 2753, 2756, 2761, 4712]. [Q] to be smooth, slippery; deceitful; [H] to speak deceit, flatter, be seductive:– flatter (2), seductive (2), deceitful (1), flattering (1), smooth (1), smooths (1), tell lies (1)

H2745 2חָלַק ***ḥālaq2***, v. [56] [→ 2165, 2750, 2754, 2755, 2758, 2759, 2760, 2762, 4713]. [Q] to divide, apportion, assign; [N] to be divided, be dispersed, be distributed; [P] to divide, allot, apportion; [Pu] to be divided; [H] to get one's share; [Ht] to divide among themselves:– divide (9), divided (5), dividing (3), share (3), be divided up (2), distribute (2), gave (2), parcel out (2), accomplices (1 [+6640]), allots (1), allotting (1), apportioned (1), assigns (1), be allotted (1), be distributed (1), be divided (1), distributed (1), distributes (1), distributing supplies (1), divide up (1), divided up (1), divides (1), get share of property (1), give a portion (1), give a share (1), given (1), is dispersed (1), is distributed (1), made assignments (1), received (1), scatter (1), scattered (1), separated (1), separated into divisions (1), took some of the things (1), were split (1)

H2746 3חָלַק ***ḥālaq3***, v. [P] to destroy

H2747 1חָלָק ***ḥālāq1***, a. [10] [√ 2744]. smooth, slippery, pleasant, flattering:– flattering (3), smooth (2), flatter (1), flattery (1), pleasant (1), slippery (1), smoother (1)

H2748 2חָלָק ***ḥālāq2***, n.pr.loc. [2] [√ 2744]. Halak:– Halak (2)

H2749 1חֵלֶק ***ḥēleq1***, n.[m.] [1] [√ 2744]. smoothness:– smooth (1)

H2750 2חֵלֶק ***ḥēleq2***, n.m. [66] [→ 2754, 2762; cf. 2745; 10269; *also used with compound proper names*]. share, portion, allotment, plot of ground:– share (16), portion (13), lot (6), allotment (4), parts (3), portions (3), reward (3), fate (2), plot of ground (2), benefits (1), fields (1), have say (1 [+6699]), inheritance (1), invest (1 [+5989]), land (1), lives (1), own (1), part (1), plot (1), portion (1 [+4987]), possession (1), thatS (1), NDT (1)

H2751 3חֵלֶק ***ḥēleq3***, n.pr.m. [2] [→ 2757; cf. 2759?, 2760?]. Helek, *"portion, lot"*:– Helek (2)

H2752 חַלֻּק ***ḥalluq***, a. [1] [√ 2744]. smooth (stones):– smooth (1)

H2753 1חֶלְקָה ***ḥelqâ1***, n.f. [2] [√ 2744]. smoothness:– smooth (2)

H2754 2חֶלְקָה ***ḥelqâ2***, n.f. [23] [√ 2750; cf. 2745]. plot, field, tract:– field (10), field (4 [+8441]), plot (2), plot of ground (2), portion (2), anotherS (1), piece (1), tract (1)

H2755 חֲלֻקָּה ***ḥªluqqâ***, n.f. [1] [√ 2745]. part, portion, division:– group (1 [+1074, 3])

H2756 חֲלַקָּה ***ḥªlaqqâ***, n.f. Not used in NIVEBC [√ 2744]. smoothness, flattery

H2757 חֶלְקִי ***ḥelqî***, a.g. [1] [√ 2751]. Helekite, "*of Helek*":– Helekite (1)

H2758 חֶלְקַי ***ḥelqāy***, n.pr.m. [1] [√ 2750 + 3378?]. Helkai, "*Yahweh is [my] portion*":– Helkai (1)

H2759 חִלְקִיָּה ***ḥilqiyyâ***, n.pr.m. [15] [→ 2760; cf. 2750 + 3378, 2751?]. Hilkiah, "*Yahweh is [my] portion*":– Hilkiah (13), Hilkiah's (1), he[S] (1)

H2760 חִלְקִיָּהוּ ***ḥilqiyyāhû***, n.pr.m. [19] [√ 2759; cf. 2750 + 3378, 2751?]. Hilkiah, "*Yahweh is [my] portion*":– Hilkiah (18), he[S] (1)

H2761 חֲלַקְלַק ***ḥªlaqlaq***, n.f.abst. [4] [√ 2744]. slippery, slick and hard to walk on; by extension: slippery words, intrigue, insincere:– slippery (2), intrigue (1), not sincere (1)

H2762 חֶלְקַת ***ḥelqat***, n.pr.loc. [2] [→ 2763; cf. 2745, 2750]. Helkath, "*portion*":– Helkath (2)

H2763 חֶלְקַת הַצֻּרִים ***ḥelqat haṣṣurîm***, n.pr.loc. [1] [√ 2762 + 2211]. Helkath Hazzurim, "[poss.] *portion [field] of rock* or *swords; portion [field] of snare*":– Helkath Hazzurim (1)

H2764 [1]חָלַשׁ ***ḥālaš[1]***, v. [1] [→ 2766; cf. 2765]. [Q] to be laid low:– laid low (1)

H2765 [2]חָלַשׁ ***ḥālaš[2]***, v. [2] [→ 2711; cf. 2764]. [Q] to overcome, defeat:– laid low (1), overcame (1)

H2766 חַלָּשׁ ***ḥallāš***, a. [1] [√ 2764]. weak, weakling:– weakling (1)

H2767 [1]חָם ***ḥām[1]***, n.m. [4] [→ 2782, 2792]. father-in-law:– father-in-law (4)

H2768 [2]חָם ***ḥām[2]***, a. [2] [√ 2801]. hot, sweltering:– swelter (1), warm (1)

H2769 [3]חָם ***ḥām[3]***, n.pr.m. & loc. [16] [→ 2781, 2795]. Ham:– Ham (15), Hamites (1)

H2770 חֹם ***ḥōm***, n.m. [9] [√ 2801]. heat:– heat (8), hot (1)

H2771 חֵמָא ***ḥēmā'***, n.f. Not used in NIVEBC [√ 3501; cf. 2779]. see 2779

H2772 חֶמְאָה ***ḥem'â***, n.f. [10] [cf. 4717]. curds, curdled milk; butter, cream:– curds (6), cream (2), butter (1), curdled milk (1)

H2773 חָמַד ***ḥāmad***, v. [21] [→ 2774, 2775, 2776, 2777, 4718, 4719]. [Q] to covet, lust, desire; delight in; [Qp] (n.) what is coveted: treasure, wealth; [N] to be pleasing, be desirable; [P] to delight; this can refer to proper delight and fondness, as well as to improper lust and desire:– covet (6), desire (2), treasure (2), choice (1), chooses (1), coveted (1), delight (1), delight in (1), delighted (1), desirable (1), lust after (1), pleasing (1), precious (1), wealth (1)

H2774 חֶמֶד ***ḥemed***, n.[m.] [6] [√ 2773]. fruitfulness, lushness; pleasantness; handsomeness:– handsome (3), fruitful (1), lush (1), pleasant (1)

H2775 חֶמְדָּה ***ḥemdâ***, n.f. [16] [√ 2773]. desirable, pleasant, fine, valuable (things):– pleasant (4), desired (2), treasures (2 [+3998]), best (1), desire (1), fine (1), regret (1), stately (1), valuable (1), valuables (1), value (1)

H2776 חֲמֻדוֹת ***ḥªmudôt***, n.f. [9] [√ 2773]. esteemed, precious, costly (things):– highly esteemed (3), best (1), choice (1), costly gifts (1), precious (1), riches (1), value (1)

H2777 חֶמְדָּן ***ḥemdān***, n.pr.m. [2] [√ 2773; cf. 2820]. Hemdan, "*desirable*":– Hemdan (2)

H2778 חָמָה ***ḥāmâ***, n.f. [1] [Q] to watch, be careful:– careful (1)

H2779 חֵמָה ***ḥēmâ***, n.f. [123] [√ 3501; cf. 2771; 10270]. anger, wrath, fury, rage, from the base meaning of heat (as in "hot-headed"); by extension: venom (poison that causes a burning sensation):– wrath (75), anger (11), fury (8), rage (5), venom (4), furious (3), angry (2), burning (2), fierce (2), poison (2), easily angered (1), enraged (1 [+4848]), hot (1), hot-tempered (1), hot-tempered (1 [+1251]), hot-tempered (1 [+1524]), indignation (1), inflamed (1 [+2703]), stinging (1)

H2780 חַמָּה ***ḥammâ***, n.f. [6] [√ 2801]. heat (of the sun):– sun (4), sunlight (1 [+240]), warmth (1)

H2781 חַמּוּאֵל ***ḥammû'ēl***, n.pr.m. [1] [√ 2769 + 446; cf. 2795]. Hammuel, "*God [El] of Ham*":– Hammuel (1)

H2782 חֲמוּטַל ***ḥªmûṭal***, n.pr.f. [3] [√ 2767 + 3228]. Hamutal, "*my husband's father is like dew*":– Hamutal (3)

H2783 חָמוּל ***ḥāmûl***, n.pr.m. [3] [→ 2784; cf. 2798]. Hamul, "*pitied*":– Hamul (3)

H2784 חָמוּלִי ***ḥāmûlî***, a.g. [1] [√ 2783; cf. 2798]. Hamulite, "*of Hamul*":– Hamulite (1)

H2785 חַמּוֹן ***ḥammôn***, n.pr.loc. [2] [√ 2801]. Hammon, "*hot springs*":– Hammon (2)

H2786 חָמוּץ ***ḥāmûṣ***, a. Not used in NIVEBC [√ 2808]. crimson, see 2808

H2787 חָמוֹץ ***ḥāmôṣ***, n.[m.] [1] [√ 2807]. oppressor; oppressed:– oppressed (1)

H2788 חַמּוּק ***ḥammûq***, n.m. [1] [√ 2811]. gracefulness, curve:– graceful (1)

H2789 [1]חֲמוֹר ***ḥªmôr[1]***, n.m. [98] [→ 2791; cf. 2790, 2813]. donkey:– donkey (47), donkeys (45), donkey's (3), donkeys (2 [+2789]), male donkeys (1)

H2790 [2]חֲמוֹר ***ḥªmôr[2]***, n.[m.] Not used in NIVEBC [√ 2813; cf. 2789]. heap

H2791 [3]חֲמוֹר ***ḥªmôr[3]***, n.pr.m. [13] [√ 2789; cf. 2813]. Hamor, "*male donkey*":– Hamor (12), his[S] (1)

H2792 חָמוֹת ***ḥāmôt***, n.f. [11] [√ 2767]. mother-in-law:– mother-in-law (11)

H2793 חֹמֶט ***ḥōmeṭ***, n.[m.] [1] skink (lizard):– skink (1)

H2794 חֻמְטָה ***ḥumṭâ***, n.pr.loc. [1] Humtah, "*[unclean] reptile*":– Humtah (1)

H2795 חֲמִיטַל ***ḥªmîṭal***, n.pr.f. Not used in NIVEBC [√ 2769; cf. 2782]. Hamital, see 2782

H2796 חָמִיץ ***ḥāmîṣ***, a. [1] [√ 2806]. sour mash, sorrel-fodder:– mash (1)

H2797 חֲמִישִׁי ***ḥªmîšî***, a.num.ord. [45] [√ 2822]. fifth:– fifth (44), one fifth (1)

H2798 חָמַל ***ḥāmal***, v. [41] [→ 2783, 2784, 2799, 2800, 2857, 4720?]. [Q] to spare, take pity on, have mercy on:– spare (13), pity (6), spared (3), had pity (2), have pity (2), mercy (2), allow pity (1), bear (1), compassion (1), concern (1), felt sorry (1), had compassion (1), had concern (1), has compassion and spares (1), mercilessly (1 [+4202]), refrained (1), show mercy (1), took pity (1), unrelenting (1 [+4202])

H2799 חֶמְלָה ***ḥemlâ***, n.f. [2] [√ 2798]. mercy:– merciful (1), mercy (1)

H2800 חֻמְלָה ***ḥumlâ***, n.[f.] *or* v.inf. Not used in NIVEBC [√ 2798]. compassion

H2801 חָמַם ***ḥāmam***, v. [22] [→ 2569, 2768, 2770, 2780, 2785, 2802, 2829, 2832, 2833; cf. 3501]. [Q] to be hot, be warm; by extension: to be aroused; be in a rage; [N] to burn with lust; [P] to let warm; [Ht] to warm oneself:– warm (7), hot (6), warms (2), aroused (1), burn with lust (1), heat (1), in a rage (1 [+4222]), lets warm (1), warming (1), warmth (1)

H2802 חַמָּן ***ḥammān***, n.m. [8] [√ 2801]. incense altar:– incense altars (8)

H2803 [1]חָמַס ***ḥāmas[1]***, v. [8] [→ 2805, 9379?; cf. 2804]. [Q] to do violence, harm, to lay waste; to be stripped off; [N] to be mistreated:– do violence (2), harm (1), laid waste (1), mistreated (1), stripped (1), violence (1), wrong (1)

H2804 [2]חָמַס ***ḥāmas[2]***, v. Not used in NIVEBC [cf. 2803]. [Q] to think up, devise

H2805 חָמָס ***ḥāmās***, n.m. [60] [√ 2803]. violence, destruction, malice, ruthlessness, fierceness:– violence (39), violent (4), violent (4 [+408]), malicious (3), destroyed (2), crime (1), fiercely (1), plundered (1), poison (1), ruthless (1), terror (1), violent (1 [+4848]), wrong (1)

H2806 [1]חָמֵץ ***ḥāmēṣ[1]***, v. [4] [→ 2786, 2796, 2809, 2810, 4721]. [Q] to have yeast added, be leavened; by extension: [Ht] to be grieved, embittered:– rises (1), was grieved (1), yeast (1), yeast added (1)

H2807 [2]חָמֵץ ***ḥāmēṣ[2]***, v. [1] [→ 2787]. [Q] to be cruel, oppress:– cruel (1)

H2808 [3]חָמֵץ ***ḥāmēṣ[3]***, v. [1] [→ 2786]. [Qp] to be stained crimson:– stained crimson (1)

H2809 [4]חָמֵץ ***ḥāmēṣ[4]***, n.m. [11] [√ 2806]. something leavened, made with yeast:– yeast (3), anything containing yeast (2), anything with yeast in it (1), bread made with yeast (1), containing yeast (1), leavened bread (1), made with yeast (1), with yeast in it (1)

H2810 חֹמֶץ ***ḥōmeṣ***, n.m. [6] [√ 2806]. vinegar, wine vinegar:– vinegar (4), wine vinegar (1), NDT (1)

H2811 חָמַק ***ḥāmaq***, v. [2] [→ 2788]. [Q] to leave, turn away; [Ht] to wander, turn here and there:– left (1), wander (1)

H2812 [1]חָמַר ***ḥāmar[1]***, v. [2] [→ 2815, 2816, 2819; cf. 2814]. [Q] to foam:– foam (1), foaming (1)

H2813 [2]חָמַר ***ḥāmar[2]***, v. [3] [→ 2789, 2790, 2791, 2817, 3502]. [Poalal] to be reddened, glow:– in torment (2), red (1)

H2814 [3]חָמַר ***ḥāmar[3]***, v.den. [1] [cf. 2812]. [Q] to coat, cover, to apply pitch as a sealant:– coated (1)

H2815 חֶמֶר ***ḥemer***, n.[m.] [1] [√ 2812; 10271]. (foaming, fermenting) wine:– foaming (1)

H2816 [1]חֹמֶר ***ḥōmer[1]***, n.[m.] [1] [√ 2812]. churning, storming (sea waters):– churning (1)

H2817 [2]חֹמֶר ***ḥōmer[2]***, n.m. [17] [√ 2813]. clay, mortar, mud; "defenses of clay" are weak arguments:– clay (11), mortar (4), mud (2)

H2818 [3]חֹמֶר ***ḥōmer[3]***, n.m. [13] homer (dry measure of volume, roughly the amount a donkey could carry, variously reckoned from six to eleven bushels [220 to 394 liters]):– homer (10), heaps (2 [+2818]), homers (1)

H2819 חֵמָר ***ḥēmār***, n.[m.] [3] [√ 2812]. tar (used in waterproofing or mortar):– tar (3)

H2820 חַמְרָן ***ḥamrān***, n.pr.m. Not used in NIVEBC [cf. 2777]. Hamran, see 2777

H2821 חָמַשׁ ***ḥāmaš***, v.den. [6] [→ 2826; cf. 2822]. [Qp] to be organized for war; [P] to take a fifth:– ready for battle (3), battle (1), outposts (1 [+7895]), take a fifth (1)

H2822 חָמֵשׁ ***ḥāmēš***, n.m. & f. [507] [→ 2797, 2821, 2823, 2825, 2826]. five, (pl.) fifty:– five (165), fifty (80), twenty-five (23 [+6929, 2256]), fifteenth (15 [+6925]), 25,000 (14 [+2256, 6929, 547]), 250 (10 [+2256, 4395]), fifteen (9 [+6926]), 4,500 (8 [+4395, 2256, 752, 547]), fifteen (6 [+6925]), 500 (5 [+4395]), captain (5 [+8569]), fifth (5), 1,254 (4 [+547, 4395, 2256, 752]), eighty-five (4 [+9046, 2256]), fifties (4), 40,500 (3 [+752, 547, 2256, 4395]), 5,000 (3 [+547]), 50 (3), 53,400 (3 [+8993, 2256, 547, 2256, 752, 4395]), fiftieth (3), fifty-two (3 [+2256, 9109]), forty-five (3 [+752, 2256]), thirty-five (3 [+8993, 2256]), twenty-fifth (3 [+6929, 2256]), 1,052 (2 [+547, 2256, 9109]), 1,775 (2 [+547, 2256, 8679, 4395, 2256, 2256, 8679]), 150 (2 [+4395, 2256]), 245 (2 [+4395, 752, 2256]), 30,500 (2 [+8993, 547, 2256, 4395]), 345 (2 [+8993, 4395, 752, 2256]), 35,400 (2 [+2256, 8993, 547, 2256, 752, 4395]), 41,500 (2 [+285, 2256, 752, 547, 2256, 4395]), 435 (2 [+752, 4395, 8993, 2256]), 45,650 (2 [+2822, 2256, 752, 547, 2256, 9252, 4395, 2256]), 45,650 (2 [+2256, 752, 547, 2256, 9252, 4395, 2256, 2822]), 46,500 (2 [+9252, 2256, 752, 547, 2256, 4395]), 52 (2 [+2256, 9109]), 54,400 (2 [+752, 2256, 547, 2256, 752, 4395]), 57,400 (2 [+8679, 2256, 547, 2256, 752, 4395]), 59,300 (2 [+9596, 2256, 547, 2256, 8993, 4395]), 65 (2 [+2256, 9252]), 652 (2 [+9252, 4395, 2256, 9109]), 95 (2 [+9596, 2256]), fifteenth (2 [+6926]), fifty-five (2 [+2822, 2256]), fifty-five (2 [+2256, 2822]), men[S] (2), seventy-five (2 [+8679, 2256]), 1,335 (1 [+547, 8993, 4395, 8993, 2256]), 1,365 (1 [+2256, 9252, 2256, 8993, 4395, 2256, 547]), 105 (1 [+2256, 4395]), 151,450 (1 [+4395, 547, 2256, 285, 547, 752, 4395, 2822, 2256, 2256, 2256]), 151,450 (1 [+4395, 547, 2256, 285, 2822, 547, 752, 4395, 2256, 2256, 2256]), 153,600 (1 [+4395, 2256, 547, 2256, 8993, 547, 2256, 9252, 4395]), 156 (1 [+4395, 2256, 9252]), 157,600 (1 [+4395, 547, 2256, 8679, 2256, 547, 9252, 4395, 2256]), 16,750 (1 [+9252, 6925, 547, 8679, 4395, 2256]), 2,056 (1 [+547, 2256, 9252]), 2,750 (1 [+547, 8679, 4395, 2256]), 205 (1 [+2256, 4395]), 245 (1 [+4395, 2256, 752, 2256]), 25,100 (1 [+6929, 2256, 547, 2256, 4395]), 307,500 (1 [+8993, 4395, 547, 2256, 8679, 547, 2256, 4395]), 32,500 (1 [+9109, 2256, 8993, 547, 2256, 4395]), 337,500 (1 [+8993, 4395, 547, 2256, 8993, 547, 8679, 547, 2256, 4395]), 337,500 (1 [+8993, 4395, 547, 2256, 8993, 547, 2256, 8679, 547, 2256, 4395]), 35 (1 [+2256, 8993]), 350 (1 [+8993, 4395, 2256]), 365 (1 [+2256, 9252, 2256, 8993, 4395]), 45,400 (1 [+2256, 752, 547, 2256, 752, 4395]), 45,600 (1 [+2256, 752, 547, 2256, 9252, 4395]), 454 (1 [+752, 4395, 2256, 752]), 5,400 (1 [+547, 2256, 752, 4395]), 50,000 (1 [+547]), 52,700 (1 [+9109, 2256, 547, 2256, 8679, 4395]), 530 (1 [+4395, 2256, 8993]), 550 (1 [+2256, 2822, 4395]), 550 (1 [+2822, 2256, 4395]), 56 (1 [+2256, 9252]), 595 (1 [+2256, 9596, 2256, 2822, 4395]), 595 (1 [+2822, 2256, 9596, 2256, 4395]), 60,500 (1 [+9252, 547, 2256, 4395]), 603,550 (1 [+9252, 4395, 547, 2256, 8993, 547, 4395, 2822, 2256, 2256]), 603,550 (1 [+9252, 4395, 547, 2256, 8993, 547, 2822, 4395, 2256, 2256]), 603,550 (1 [+9252, 4395, 547, 8993, 547, 4395, 2822, 2256, 2256, 2256]), 603,550 (1 [+9252, 4395, 547, 8993, 547, 2822, 4395, 2256, 2256, 2256]), 603,550 (1 [+9252, 4395, 547, 2256, 8993, 547, 2256, 4395, 2256, 2822]), 603,550 (1 [+9252, 4395, 547, 2256, 8993, 547, 2256, 2822, 4395, 2256]), 650 (1 [+9252, 4395, 2256]), 655 (1 [+9252, 4395, 2256, 2822]), 655 (1 [+9252, 4395, 2822, 2256]), 675 (1 [+9252, 4395, 2256, 8679]), 675,000 (1 [+9252, 4395, 547, 2256, 8679, 547, 2256, 547]), 7,500 (1 [+8679, 547, 2256, 4395]), 725 (1 [+8679, 4395, 6929, 2256]), 745 (1 [+8679, 4395, 752, 2256]), 76,500 (1 [+9252, 2256, 8679, 547, 2256, 4395]), 775 (1 [+8679, 4395, 2256, 8679]), 8,580 (1 [+9046, 547, 2256, 4395, 2256, 9046]), 815 (1 [+6926, 2256, 9046, 4395]), 845 (1 [+9046, 4395, 2256, 752]), 895 (1 [+2256, 9596, 2256, 9046, 4395]), 905 (1 [+2256, 9596, 4395]), 945 (1 [+9596, 4395, 2256, 752, 2256]), 950 (1 [+9596, 4395, 2256]), 956 (1 [+9596, 4395, 2256, 2256, 9252]), captains (1 [+8569]), fifteen (1 [+2256, 6927]), fifty-second (1 [+2256, 9109]), seventy-five (1 [+2256, 8679]), sixty-five (1 [+9252, 2256]), thirty-fifth (1 [+8993, 2256]), NDT (11)

H2823 [1]חֹמֶשׁ ***ḥōmeš[1]***, n.[m.] [1] [√ 2822]. fifth:– fifth (1)

H2824 [2]חֹמֶשׁ ***ḥōmeš[2]***, n.m. [4] stomach, belly:– stomach (3), belly (1)

H2825 חֲמִשִּׁים ***ḥªmiššîm***, n.pl. Not used in NIVEBC [√ 2822]. fifty (pl. of "five" [2822])

H2826 חֲמֻשִׁים ***ḥªmušîm***, a.pl. Not used in NIVEBC [√ 2821; cf. 2822]. in battle array

H2827 חֵמֶת ***ḥēmet***, n.[m.] [4] skin (for water or wine):– skin (3), wineskin (1)

H2828 חֲמָת ***ḥªmāt***, n.pr.loc. [24] [→ 2832, 2833, 4217]. Hamath, "*fortress*":– Hamath (24)

H2829 [1]חַמַּת ***ḥammat[1]***, n.pr.loc. [1] [→ 2831; cf. 2801]. Hammath, "*hot springs*":– Hammath (1)

H2830 [2]חַמַּת **ḥammat[2]**, n.pr.m. [1] Hammath, "*hot springs*":– Hammath (1)

H2831 חַמֹּת דֹּאר **ḥammōt dō'r**, n.pr.loc. [1] [√ 2829 + 1799]. Hammoth Dor, "*hot spring of Dor*":– Hammoth Dor (1)

H2832 חֲמָת צוֹבָה **ḥ[a]māt ṣôbâ**, n.pr.loc. [1] [√ 2828 + 7420]. Hamath Zobah:– Hamath Zobah (1)

H2833 חֲמָתִי **ḥ[a]mātî**, a.g. [2] [√ 2828; cf. 2801]. Hamathite, "*of Hamath*":– Hamathites (2)

H2834 [1]חֵן **ḥēn[1]**, n.m. [69] [→ 2836, 2839, 2855; cf. 2858; *also used with compound proper names*]. favor, grace; charm; grace is the moral quality of kindness, displaying a favorable disposition; "to find grace in someone's eyes" means to be in a state of favor:– favor (42), grace (5), pleased with (5 [+5162, 928, 6524]), favorably disposed toward (3 [+928, 6524]), bless (2), alluring (1 [+3202]), charm (1), charm (1 [+74]), displease (1 [+4202, 5162, 928, 6524]), displeasing (1 [+4202, 5162, 928, 6524]), esteemed (1), favorable toward (1 [+5162, 928, 6524]), graceful (1), gracious (1), kindhearted (1), ornament to grace (1), pleased with (1 [+5951, 928, 6524])

H2835 [2]חֵן **ḥēn[2]**, n.pr.m. [1] [√ 2858]. Hen, "*gracious*":– Hen (1)

H2836 חֵנָדָד **ḥēnādād**, n.pr.m. [4] [√ 2834 + 2060]. Henadad, "*favor of Hadad*":– Henadad (4)

H2837 [1]חָנָה **ḥānâ[1]**, v. [143] [→ 2844, 4722, 4724, 9381, 9386?]. [Q] to set up camp, pitch camp, encamp:– camped (76), encamped (13), camp (11), encamp (10), set up camp (4), took up positions (3), besiege (2 [+6584]), made camp (2), pitched camp (2), set up tents (2), attacked (1), besieged (1 [+928]), besieged (1 [+6584]), camping (1), encamps (1), laid siege to (1 [+6584]), living (1), nearly over (1), remain in camp (1), remained in camp (1), set up (1), settle (1), settled (1), stay (1), NDT (4)

H2838 [2]חָנָה **ḥānâ[2]**, v. see 2858

H2839 חַנָּה **ḥannâ**, n.pr.f. [13] [√ 2834; cf. 2858]. Hannah, "*favor*":– Hannah (12), her[S] (1)

H2840 [1]חֲנוֹךְ **ḥ[a]nôk[1]**, n.pr.m. [16] [→ 2841, 2854; cf. 2849, 2852]. Enoch; Hanoch, "*initiated; follower*":– Enoch (10), Hanok (6)

H2841 [2]חֲנוֹךְ **ḥ[a]nôk[2]**, n.pr.loc. Not used in NIVEBC [√ 2840; cf. 2852]. Enoch

H2842 חָנוּן **ḥānûn**, n.pr.m. [11] [√ 2858]. Hanun, "*favored*":– Hanun (11)

H2843 חַנּוּן **ḥannûn**, a. [13] [√ 2858]. gracious, compassionate:– gracious (12), compassionate (1)

H2844 חָנוּת **ḥānût**, n.f. [1] [√ 2837]. vaulted cell:– vaulted cell (1)

H2845 [1]חָנַט **ḥānaṭ[1]**, v. [1] [→ 2636]. [Q] to ripen:– forms (1)

H2846 [2]חָנַט **ḥānaṭ[2]**, v. [3] [→ 2847]. [Q] to embalm:– embalmed (2), embalm (1)

H2847 חֲנֻטִים **ḥ[a]nuṭîm**, n.[m.]pl.abst. [1] [√ 2846]. embalming:– embalming (1)

H2848 חַנִּיאֵל **ḥannî'ēl**, n.pr.m. [2] [√ 2858 + 446]. Hanniel, "*favored of God [El]*":– Hanniel (2)

H2849 חָנִיךְ **ḥānîk**, a. [1] [√ 2852; cf. 2840]. trained (and trusted person):– trained men (1)

H2850 חֲנִינָה **ḥ[a]nînâ**, n.f. [1] [√ 2858]. favor, kindness:– favor (1)

H2851 חֲנִית **ḥ[a]nît**, n.f. [48] spear:– spear (38), spears (8), it[S] (1 [+2021]), its[S] (1)

H2852 חָנַךְ **ḥānak**, v. [5] [→ 2840, 2841, 2849, 2853, 2854]. [Q] to dedicate, to devote an object to deity; to train (morally and religiously):– dedicated (2), live in (2), start off (1)

H2853 חֲנֻכָּה **ḥ[a]nukkâ**, n.f. [8] [√ 2852; 10273]. dedication, offering for dedication:– dedication (6), offerings for dedication (2)

H2854 חֲנֹכִי **ḥ[a]nōkî**, a.g. [1] [√ 2840; cf. 2852]. Hanochite, "*of Hanoch*":– Hanokite (1)

H2855 חִנָּם **ḥinnām**, subst.adv. [33] [√ 2834; cf. 2858]. without cause, for no reason; for nothing:– without cause (8), for nothing (5), for no reason (4), needless (2), useless (2), without reason (2), at no cost (1), cost nothing (1), costs nothing (1), harmless soul (1 [+5929]), in vain (1 [+448]), innocent (1), undeserved (1), without any payment (1 [+401]), without any reason (1), without paying anything (1)

H2856 חֲנַמְאֵל **ḥ[a]nam'ēl**, n.pr.m. [4] [√ 2834 + 446]. Hanamel, "*God [El] is gracious*":– Hanamel (4)

H2857 חֲנָמַל **ḥ[a]nāmal**, n.[m.] [1] [√ 2798]. sleet:– sleet (1)

H2858 [1]חָנַן **ḥānan[1]**, v. [77] [→ 2665, 2834, 2835, 2839, 2842, 2843, 2850, 2855, 2860, 9380?, 9382, 9383, 9384, 9385?; 10274; *also used with compound proper names*]. [Q] to be gracious, to have mercy, to take pity, be kind; [Pol] to move to pity, be kind, be charming; [Ho] to be shown compassion, mercy; [Ht] to plead for grace, beg for mercy; this word implies acts of kindness, not simply feelings of pity:– have mercy (16), gracious (13), merciful (6), kind (4), plead (3), begged (2), generous (2), gracious (2 [+2858]), have pity (2), making supplication (2), pleaded (2), show mercy (2), beg (1), beg for mercy (1), begged for favor (1), charming (1), cried for mercy (1), do the favor (1), favor (1), generously (1), get mercy (1), grace is shown (1), graciously given (1), lift up for mercy (1), made[S] (1), moves to pity (1), pity (1), plead for mercy (1), prayed (1), show favor (1), shows favor (1), shows mercy (1), take pity (1)

H2859 [2]חָנַן **ḥānan[2]**, v. [1] [Q] to be loathsome:– loathsome (1)

H2860 חָנָן **ḥānān**, n.pr.m. [12] [√ 2858; *also used with compound proper names*]. Hanan, "*gracious*":– Hanan (12)

H2861 חֲנַנְאֵל **ḥ[a]nan'ēl**, n.pr.m. [4] [√ 2858 + 446]. Hananel, "*God [El] is gracious*":– Hananel (4)

H2862 חֲנָנִי **ḥ[a]nānî**, n.pr.m. [11] [√ 2858 + 3378]. Hanani, "*gracious*":– Hanani (11)

H2863 חֲנַנְיָה **ḥ[a]nanyâ**, n.pr.m. [25] [√ 2858 + 3378; 10275]. Hananiah, "*Yahweh is gracious*":– Hananiah (24), he[S] (1)

H2864 חֲנַנְיָהוּ **ḥ[a]nanyāhû**, n.pr.m. [3] [√ 2858 + 3378]. Hananiah, "*Yahweh is gracious*":– Hananiah (3)

H2865 חָנֵס **ḥānēs**, n.pr.loc. [1] Hanes:– Hanes (1)

H2866 [1]חָנֵף **ḥānēp[1]**, v. [11] [→ 2868, 2869, 2870]. [Q] to be desecrated, be defiled; [H] to corrupt, defile, pollute:– defiled (4), completely defiled (2 [+2866]), corrupt (1), desecrated (1), godless (1), pollute (1), pollutes (1)

H2867 [2]חָנֵף **ḥānēp[2]**, a. [Q] to limp, see 2868

H2868 [3]חָנֵף **ḥānēp[3]**, a. [13] [√ 2866]. godless, ungodly:– godless (9), ungodly (3), godless (1 [+132])

H2869 חֹנֶף **ḥōnep**, n.[m.] [1] [√ 2866]. ungodliness, godlessness:– ungodliness (1)

H2870 חֲנֻפָּה **ḥ[a]nuppâ**, n.f. [1] [√ 2866]. ungodliness, godlessness:– ungodliness (1)

H2871 חָנַק **ḥānaq**, v. [2] [→ 4725]. [N] to hang oneself; [P] to strangle:– hanged himself (1), strangled (1)

H2872 חַנָּתֹן **ḥannātôn**, n.pr.loc. [1] Hannathon:– Hannathon (1)

H2873 [1]חָסַד **ḥāsad[1]**, v. [1] [→ 2875]. [P] to put to shame, reproach, with the strong implication of an insult:– shame (1)

H2874 [2]חָסַד **ḥāsad[2]**, v. [2] [→ 1213, 2876, 2877, 2883, 2884]. [Ht] to conduct oneself as faithful:– show yourself faithful (2)

H2875 [1]חֶסֶד **ḥesed[1]**, n.m. [3] [√ 2873]. disgrace:– disgrace (2), condemns (1)

H2876 [2]חֶסֶד **ḥesed[2]**, n.m. [244] [→ 1213, 2877, 2878?, 2883; cf. 2874]. unfailing love, loyal love, devotion, kindness, often based on a prior relationship, especially a covenant relationship:– love (126), kindness (41), unfailing love (39), great love (5), mercy (4), kindnesses (3), unfailing kindness (3), acts of devotion (2), favor (2), loving (2), rely (2), God's love (1), approval (1), devotion (1), devout (1 [+408]), faithful (1), faithfully (1), faithfulness (1), good favor (1), kind (1), kindly (1), loving deeds (1), loyal (1), loyalty (1), merciful (1), well (1)

H2877 [3]חֶסֶד **ḥesed[3]**, n.pr.m. Not used in NIVEBC [√ 2876; cf. 2874]. Hesed

H2878 חֲסַדְיָה **ḥ[a]sadyâ**, n.pr.m. [1] [√ 2876 + 3378]. Hasadiah, "*Yahweh is faithful*":– Hasadiah (1)

H2879 חָסָה **ḥāsâ**, v. [37] [→ 335, 2882, 4726; *also used with compound proper names*]. [Q] to take refuge in, to trust in:– take refuge (25), takes refuge (3), find refuge (2), taken refuge (2), trust (2), refuge (1), seek refuge (1), took refuge (1)

H2880 [1]חֹסָה **ḥōsâ[1]**, n.pr.m. [4] Hosah, "*refuge*":– Hosah (4)

H2881 [2]חֹסָה **ḥōsâ[2]**, n.pr.loc. [1] Hosah, "*refuge*":– Hosah (1)

H2882 חָסוּת **ḥāsût**, n.f. [1] [√ 2879]. refuge:– NDT (1)

H2883 חָסִיד **ḥāsîd**, a.m. [33] [→ 2884; cf. 2874, 2876]. godly, saints, the people of God with a focus on their faithfulness; this can refer to a prominent individual, with messianic significance (Ps 16:10):– faithful (15), faithful people (10), faithful servants (4), consecrated people (1), faithful servant (1), own people (1), unfaithful (1 [+4202])

H2884 חֲסִידָה **ḥ[a]sîdâ**, n.f. [6] [√ 2883; cf. 2874]. stork; some sources: heron:– stork (6)

H2885 חָסִיל **ḥāsîl**, n.m. [6] [√ 2887]. grasshoppers, locusts at a particular stage of development:– grasshoppers (2), locusts (2), grasshopper (1), young locusts (1)

H2886 חֲסִין **ḥ[a]sîn**, a. [1] [→ 2891]. mighty, strong:– mighty (1)

H2887 חָסַל **ḥāsal**, v. [1] [→ 2885]. [Q, H] to devour, consume:– devour (1)

H2888 חָסַם **ḥāsam**, v. [2] [→ 4727]. [Q] to muzzle (an animal); to block (the way):– block the way (1), muzzle (1)

H2889 חָסַן **ḥāsan**, v.den. [1] [→ 2890; 10277]. [N] to be stored up:– hoarded (1)

H2890 חֹסֶן **ḥōsen**, n.m. [5] [√ 2889; 10278]. stored treasure, riches, wealth:– rich store (1), riches (1), treasure (1), treasures (1), wealth (1)

H2891 חָסֹן **ḥāsōn**, a. [2] [√ 2886]. mighty, strong:– mighty (1), strong (1)

H2892 חִסְפַּס **ḥaspas**, v. [1] [Pualal] to flake; some sources: to be scale-like, pertaining to the shape of an object; to crisp, crackle, pertaining to the brittleness of an object:– flakes (1)

H2893 [1]חָסֵר **ḥāsēr[1]**, v. [23] [→ 2894, 2895, 2896, 2898, 4728]. [Q] to lack; to have nothing; to go down, recede; [P] to make lower; to deprive; [H] to cause to lack, withhold:– lack (5), lacked (2), lacks (2), run dry (2), always (1 [+440]), depriving (1), goes hungry (1), gone down (1), had nothing (1 [+3972]), have too little (1), made lower (1), need (1 [+4728]), number is less than (1), recede (1), scarce (1), withhold (1)

H2894 [2]חָסֵר **ḥāsēr[2]**, a. [17] [√ 2893]. lacking; wanting:– has no (6), have no (3), lack (2), had no (1), lacked (1), lacks (1), no (1), short (1), tyrannical (1 [+9312])

H2895 חֶסֶר **ḥeser**, n.m. [2] [√ 2893]. poverty, lack:– poverty (1), want (1)

H2896 חֹסֶר **ḥōser**, n.[m.] [3] [√ 2893]. poverty, lack:– lack (1), need (1), poverty (1)

H2897 חַסְרָה **ḥasrâ**, n.pr.m. [1] [cf. 3030]. Hasrah:– Hasrah (1)

H2898 חֶסְרוֹן **ḥesrôn**, n.m. [1] [√ 2893]. what is lacking:– lacking (1)

H2899 [1]חַף **ḥap[1]**, a. [1] [√ 2910]. clean, pure:– clean (1)

H2900 [2]חַף **ḥap[2]**, n.pr.m. Apis

H2901 חָפָא **ḥāpā'**, v. [1] [P] to do secretly:– secretly did (1)

H2902 חָפָה **ḥāpâ**, v. [12] [→ 2903, 2904; cf. 2910]. [Q] to cover; [Qp] to be covered; [N] to be sheathed, be covered; [P] to panel, overlay, cover:– covered (4), overlaid (3), cover (2), are sheathed (1), paneled (1), was covered (1)

H2903 [1]חֻפָּה **ḥuppâ[1]**, n.f. [3] [→ 2904; cf. 2902]. canopy, shelter; chamber, pavilion (of marriage ceremony):– chamber (2), canopy (1)

H2904 [2]חֻפָּה **ḥuppâ[2]**, n.pr.m. [1] [√ 2903; cf. 2902]. Huppah, "*canopy,* hence *protection*":– Huppah (1)

H2905 חָפַז **ḥāpaz**, v. [9] [→ 2906]. [Q] to hurry away (in alarm or terror):– alarm (3), fled (1), headlong flight (1), hurried (1), hurrying (1), panic (1), took to flight (1)

H2906 חִפָּזוֹן **ḥippāzôn**, n.[m.] [3] [√ 2905]. haste:– haste (3)

H2907 חֻפִּים **ḥuppîm**, n.pr.m. & a.g. [3] Huppim; Huppite, "*coast people*":– Huppites (2), Huppim (1)

H2908 חֹפֶן **ḥōpen**, n.[m.] [6] hollow of the hand, handful (sometimes as a measure of volume):– hands (3), handfuls (2 [+4850]), two handfuls (1 [+4850])

H2909 חָפְנִי **ḥopnî**, n.pr.m. [5] Hophni, "*tadpole*":– Hophni (5)

H2910 חָפַף **ḥāpap**, v. [1] [→ 2572, 2899; cf. 2902]. [Q] to shield, shelter:– shields (1)

H2911 [1]חָפֵץ **ḥāpēṣ[1]**, v. [74] [→ 2913, 2914, 2915]. [Q] to desire, delight in, be pleased with, have pleasure:– pleased (8), delights (6), desire (6), delighted (5), want (5), delight (4), pleases (4), desires (3), delight in (2), displeases (2 [+4202]), eager (2), find delight (2), find pleasure (2), take any pleasure in (2 [+2911]), take pleasure (2), will (2), delights in (1), desired (1), desired (1 [+3139]), favors (1), found pleasure (1), have delight (1), have desire (1), have pleasure (1), likes (1), meant (1), please (1), pleasure (1), rather (1), take delight (1), taken a liking (1), willing (1), wished (1)

H2912 [2]חָפֵץ **ḥāpaṣ[2]**, v. [1] [Q] to sway; some sources: to hang:– sways (1)

H2913 [3]חָפֵץ **ḥāpēṣ[3]**, a.vbl. [12] [√ 2911]. desire, delight, pleasure:– desire (3), delight (2), delight in (1), delights in (1), loves (1), pleased with (1), prefer (1), wanted (1), willing (1)

H2914 חֵפֶץ **ḥēpeṣ**, n.m. [38] [√ 2911]. desire, delight, pleasure:– please (5), wants (4), delight (3), desire (3), desired (3), pleasure (3), activity (2), wanted (2), care (1), delightful (1), desires (1), eager (1), just right (1), matter (1), pleased (1), precious (1), purpose (1), such things[S] (1), want (1), will (1), wish (1)

H2915 חֶפְצִי־בָהּ **ḥepṣî-bāh**, n.pr.f. [2] [√ 2911 + 928 + 2023]. Hephzibah, "*my pleasure is in her*":– Hephzibah (2)

H2916 [1]חָפַר **ḥāpar[1]**, v. [22] [→ 1783, 2919, 2921, 2923, 7249]. [Q] to dig, scoop, to paw, to make a hole of any depth in soil; by extension: to spy out, search for, look about, seek out:– dug (10), spy out (3), dig a hole (1), digs (1), dug up (1), look about (1), looks for (1), paws (1), reopened (1 [+8740, 2256]), scoops out (1), search for (1)

H2917 [2]חָפֵר **ḥāpar[2]**, v. [17] [Q] to feel dismay, be disgraced, be humiliated, be in confusion; [H] to bring disgrace, be ashamed, be humiliated:– confusion (4), disgraced (3), disgrace (2), humiliated (2), ashamed (1), bring shame (1), covered with shame (1), disappointed (1), dismay (1), dismayed (1)

H2918 [1]חֵפֶר **ḥēper[1]**, n.pr.m. [7] [→ 2920]. Hepher, "[perhaps] *help*":– Hepher (7)

H2919 2חֵפֶר **ḥēper2**, n.pr.loc. [2] [→ 1783; cf. 2916]. Hepher, "[perhaps] *help*":– Hepher (2)

H2920 חֶפְרִי **ḥeprî**, a.g. [1] [√ 2918]. Hepherite, "*of Hepher*":– Hepherite (1)

H2921 חֲפָרַיִם **ḥapārayim**, n.pr.loc. [1] [√ 2916]. Hapharaim, "*place of two trenches*":– Hapharaim (1)

H2922 חָפְרַע **ḥopra'**, n.pr.m. [1] Hophra:– Hophra (1)

H2923 חֲפַרְפָּרָה **ḥaparpārâ**, n.f. [1] [√ 2916]. rodent (an object of worship):– moles (1)

H2924 חָפַשׂ **ḥāpaś**, v. [24] [→ 2925]. [Q] to search for, examine, plot; [N] to be ransacked; [P] to search, look around, track down, hunt down; [Pu] to go into hiding, to devise; [Ht] to disguise oneself, become like:– disguised himself (5), search (4), in disguise (2), asked (1), be ransacked (1), becomes like (1), devised (1), examine (1), go into hiding (1), hunt down (1), look around (1), plot (1), search for (1), searched (1), sheds light on (1), track down (1)

H2925 חֵפֶשׂ **ḥēpeś**, n.[m.] [1] [√ 2924]. plan, plot:– plan (1)

H2926 חָפַשׁ **ḥāpaš**, v. [1] [√ 2930]. [Pu] to be freed:– been freed (1)

H2927 חֹפֶשׁ **ḥōpeš**, n.[m.] [1] material (for saddle blanket):– blankets (1 [+955])

H2928 חֻפְשָׁה **ḥupšâ**, n.f. [1] [√ 2930]. freedom:– freedom (1)

H2929 חָפְשׁוּת **ḥopšût**, n.f. Not used in NIVEBC [√ 2930]. see 2931

H2930 חָפְשִׁי **ḥopšî**, a. [17] [→ 2926, 2928, 2929, 2931]. free; set apart, exempt:– free (9), free (2 [+8938]), exempt from taxes (1 [+6913]), freed (1), freed (1 [+8938]), set apart (1), set free (1 [+8938]), NDT (1)

H2931 חָפְשִׁית **ḥopšît**, n.f. [2] [√ 2930]. separation, exemption (from duties):– separate (2)

H2932 חֵץ **ḥēṣ**, n.m. [52] [→ 2943]. arrow; archer:– arrows (38), arrow (12), archers (1 [+1251]), did so[S] (1 [+4374, 8008, 2256])

H2933 1חָצַב **ḥāṣēb1**, v. [15] [→ 2935, 4732; cf. 2934]. [Q] to dig; hew out, cut out; [Qp, N, Pu] to be dug, be engraved, be cut out; [H] to cut in pieces:– dug (3), cut out (2), dig (2), cut in pieces (1), cut to pieces (1), engraved (1), hewing (1), prepare (1), swings (1), were cut (1), NDT (1)

H2934 2חָצַב **ḥāṣab2**, v. [1] [cf. 2933]. [Q] to strike (with lightning):– strikes (1)

H2935 חֹצֵב **ḥōṣēb**, n.[m.] *or* v.ptcp. [8] [√ 2933]. stonecutter, mason:– stonecutters (5), masons (2), stonecutters (1 [+74])

H2936 חָצָה **ḥāṣâ**, v. [15] [→ 2940, 2942, 2944, 3505, 3507, 4733, 4734; cf. 2951, 2952, 2953]. [Q] to divide; set apart; to rise up to; [N] to be divided, be parceled out:– divided (5), divide equally (2), be divided (1), divide up (1), dividing (1), live out half (1), parceled out (1), rising up (1), set apart (1), NDT (1)

H2937 1חָצוֹר **ḥāṣôr1**, n.pr.loc. [15] [→ 6533; cf. 2958]. Hazor, "*enclosure*":– Hazor (15)

H2938 2חָצוֹר **ḥāṣôr2**, n.pr.loc. [3] [√ 2958]. sedentary Arabs:– Hazor (3)

H2939 חָצוֹר חֲדַתָּה **ḥāṣôr ḥadattâ**, n.pr.loc. [1] [√ 2958]. Hazor Hadattah, "*new Hazor*":– Hazor Hadattah (1)

H2940 חֲצוֹת **ḥaṣôt**, n.f. [3] [√ 2936]. middle (of the night), mid(night):– midnight (2 [+4326]), middle (1)

H2941 חֻצוֹת **ḥuṣôt**, n.pr.loc. Not used in NIVEBC [→ 7960]. Huzoth

H2942 חֲצִי **ḥaṣî**, n.m. [125] [√ 2936]. half, halfway, middle, midst:– half (80), half-tribe (19 [+8657]), half-tribe (5 [+4751]), half-district (4 [+7135]), middle (4), at (2 [+928, 2021, 6330]), halfway (2), two (2), half-tribe (1), its[S] (1 [+2257]), midnight (1 [+2021, 4326]), midst (1), NDT (3)

H2943 1חֵצִי **ḥēṣî1**, n.m. [5] [√ 2932]. arrow:– arrow (5)

H2944 2חֵצִי **ḥēṣî2**, n.m. Not used in NIVEBC [√ 2936]. see 2942

H2945 1חָצִיר **ḥāṣîr1**, n.m. [20] (green) grass; hay:– grass (19), hay (1)

H2946 2חָצִיר **ḥāṣîr2**, n.m. [1] [→ 2947, 2955, 2956, 2968, 2969, 2974]. leeks:– leeks (1)

H2947 3חָצִיר **ḥāṣîr3**, n.[m.] & n.m. Not used in NIVEBC [√ 2946]. reed

H2948 4חָצִיר **ḥāṣîr4**, n.[m.] [1] home, abode, haunt:– home (1)

H2949 חֵצֶן **ḥēṣen**, n.m. Not used in NIVEBC [→ 2950, 3079?]. bosom (of a garment)

H2950 חֹצֶן **ḥōṣen**, n.m. [3] [√ 2949]. arms, folds of a robe:– arms (2), folds of robe (1)

H2951 1חָצַץ **ḥāṣaṣ1**, v. [2] [cf. 2936]. [Q] to be in order, in ranks; [P] to divide, share; [Pu] to come to an end:– come to an end (1), in ranks (1)

H2952 2חָצַץ **ḥāṣaṣ2**, v.den. [1] [cf. 2936]. [P] to sing; some sources: to distribute water:– singers (1)

H2953 חָצָץ **ḥāṣāṣ**, n.[m.] [2] [cf. 2936]. gravel:– gravel (2)

H2954 חַצְצוֹן תָּמָר **ḥaṣeṣôn tāmār**, n.pr.loc. [2] [cf. 9469]. Hazazon Tamar, "*Hazazon of the palm trees*":– Hazezon Tamar (2)

H2955 חָצַר **ḥaṣṣar**, v.den. [6] [√ 2956; cf. 2946]. [P] to sound a trumpet, play a trumpet:– blew (1), blew trumpets (1), blow (1), sounded (1), sounding (1), trumpeters (1)

H2956 חֲצֹצְרָה **ḥaṣōṣerâ**, n.f. [29] [→ 2955, 2957; cf. 2946]. trumpet, a metal instrument used for signaling and music:– trumpets (26), trumpeters (2), horn (1)

H2957 חָצַר **ḥāṣar**, v. Not used in NIVEBC [√ 2956]. see 2955

H2958 1חָצֵר **ḥāṣēr1**, n.m. [190] [→ 2937, 2938, 2939, 2959, 2962, 2973]. courtyard, court of a house, enclosed areas; village, a permanent settlement but without walls:– courtyard (60), court (48), villages (45), courts (21), courtyards (4), its[S] (2 [+2021]), settlements (2), enclosed (1), set farther back (1 [+2021, 337]), surrounding villages (1), where[S] (1 [+2021, 2021, 2667]), NDT (4)

H2959 2חָצֵר **ḥāṣēr2**, n.m. Not used in NIVEBC [→ 1258, 2960, 2961, 2963, 2964, 2965, 2966, 2967, 2975; cf. 2958]. Hazar

H2960 חֲצַר־אַדָּר **ḥaṣar-'addār**, n.pr.loc. [1] [√ 162 + 2959]. Hazar Addar, "*settlement of Addar*":– Hazar Addar (1)

H2961 חֲצַר גַּדָּה **ḥaṣar gaddâ**, n.pr.loc. [1] [√ 2959 + 1520]. Hazar Gaddah, "*settlement of Gad*":– Hazar Gaddah (1)

H2962 חָצֵר הַתִּיכוֹן **ḥāṣēr hattîkôn**, n.pr.loc. [1] [√ 2958 + 2250]. Hazer Hatticon, "*place of Hatticon*":– Hazer Hattikon (1)

H2963 חֲצַר סוּסָה **ḥaṣar sûsâ**, n.pr.loc. [1] [√ 2959 + 6063]. Hazar Susah, "*settlement of Susah [horse]*":– Hazar Susah (1)

H2964 חֲצַר סוּסִים **ḥaṣar sûsîm**, n.pr.loc. [1] [√ 2959 + 6065]. Hazar Susim, "*settlement of Susah [horse]*":– Hazar Susim (1)

H2965 חֲצַר עֵינוֹן **ḥaṣar 'ênôn**, n.pr.loc. [1] [√ 2959 + 6541]. Hazar Enan, "*settlement of Enan*":– Hazar Enan (1)

H2966 חֲצַר עֵינָן **ḥaṣar 'ênān**, n.pr.loc. [3] [√ 2959 + 6544]. Hazar Enan, "*settlement of Enan*":– Hazar Enan (3)

H2967 חֲצַר שׁוּעָל **ḥaṣar šû'āl**, n.pr.loc. [4] [√ 2959 + 8785]. Hazar Shual, "*settlement of Shual [jackal]*":– Hazar Shual (4)

H2968 חֶצְרוֹ **ḥeṣrô**, n.pr.m. [2] [√ 2946; cf. 2974]. Hezro:– Hezro (2)

H2969 1חֶצְרוֹן **ḥeṣrôn1**, n.pr.m. [16] [→ 2971; cf. 2946, 2970]. Hezron, "*enclosure*":– Hezron (16)

H2970 2חֶצְרוֹן **ḥeṣrôn2**, n.pr.loc. [1] [√ 7955; cf. 2969]. Hezron, "*enclosure*":– Hezron (1)

H2971 חֶצְרוֹנִי **ḥeṣrônî**, a.g. [2] [√ 2969; cf. 2946]. Hezronite, "*of Hezron*":– Hezronite (2)

H2972 חֲצֵרוֹת **ḥaṣērôt**, n.pr.loc. [6] Hazeroth, "*settlements*":– Hazeroth (5), there[S] (1 [+928])

H2973 חֲצֵרִים **ḥaṣērîm**, n.pr.loc. Not used in NIVEBC [√ 2958]. Hazerim

H2974 חֶצְרַי **ḥeṣray**, n.pr.m. Not used in NIVEBC [√ 2946; cf. 2968]. Hezrai, see 2968

H2975 חֲצַרְמָוֶת **ḥaṣarmāwet**, n.pr.m. [2] [√ 2959 + 4638]. Hazarmaveth, "*village of Maveth [death]*":– Hazarmaveth (2)

H2976 חֹק **ḥōq**, n.m. [128] [→ 2978, 2981; cf. 2980]. decree, statute, prescription, a clear communication of what someone should do; allotment, share, portion, prescribed amount of something:– decrees (76), share (11), decree (8), statutes (3), limits (2), ordinance (2), tradition (2), allotment (1), barrier (1), boundaries (1), boundary (1), conditions (1), daily bread (1), daily bread (1 [+4312]), horizon (1), law (1), laws (1), make laws (1 [+2980]), perpetual share (1), portions (1), precepts (1), prescribed portion (1), quota (1), regular allotment (1), regulations (1), ruling (1), statute (1), territory (1), time (1), wide (1 [+4200, 1172]), NDT (1)

H2977 חָקָה **ḥāqâ**, v. [4] [cf. 2980]. [Pu] to be carved, be portrayed; [Ht] mark for oneself; from the base meaning of carving or engraving is by extension of the act of writing; the communication itself, regulation:– portrayed (2), carvings (1), putting marks (1)

H2978 חֻקָּה **ḥuqqâ**, n.f. [104] [√ 2976; cf. 2980]. decree, ordinance, regulation, statute:– decrees (55), ordinance (23), regulations (7), practices (4), rules (3), customs (2), force of law (2 [+5477]), laws (2), instructions (1), regular (1), requirement (1), share (1), statutes (1), what is required (1)

H2979 חֲקוּפָא **ḥaqûpā'**, n.pr.m. [2] Hakupha, "*crooked*":– Hakupha (2)

H2980 חָקַק **ḥāqaq**, v. [19] [→ 2576, 2976, 2978; cf. 2977]. [Q] to mark out, inscribe, chisel, engrave; [Qp] to be portrayed; [Po] to command, be a leader, ruler; staff (of a commander); [Pu] to be decreed; [Ho] to be written:– marked out (2), scepter (2), been decreed (1), captains (1), chiseling (1), draw (1), engraved (1), inscribe (1), issue decrees (1), lawgiver (1), leader's (1), make laws (1 [+2976]), portrayed (1), princes (1), ruler's staff (1), scepters (1), were written (1)

H2981 חֵקֶק **ḥēqeq**, var. Not used in NIVEBC [√ 2976]. see 2976

H2982 חֻקֹּק **ḥuqqōq**, n.pr.loc. [1] Hukkok:– Hukkok (1)

H2983 חָקַר **ḥāqar**, v. [27] [→ 2984, 4736]. [Q] to explore, search out, probe; [N] to be determined, be searched; [P] to search out:– explore (4), examined (2), search (2), be calculated (1), be searched out (1), carry out a more detailed search (1), cross-examines (1), dense (1 [+4202]), discovered (1), probe (1), sample (1), search out (1), search out for (1), searched (1), searched out (1), searching for (1), sees (1), surely sound out (1), test (1), tested (1), took up (1), was determined (1)

H2984 חֵקֶר **ḥēqer**, n.m. [13] [√ 2983]. searching, finding out, often negatively stated: what cannot be search thoroughly or found out:– fathom (2), fathomed (2), searching (2), finding out (1), inquiry (1), mysteries (1), recesses (1), search out (1), unsearchable (1 [+401]), what learned (1)

H2985 1חֹר **ḥōr1**, n.m. [13] noble, free person:– nobles (12), noble (1)

H2986 2חֹר **ḥōr2**, n.[m.] [7] [→ 2987, 2988]. hole (in various forms):– hole (2), holes (2), lairs (1), latch-opening (1), sockets (1)

H2987 חֻר **ḥur**, n.[m.] [2] [√ 2986]. hole, pit:– den (1), pits (1)

H2988 חֹר הַגִּדְגָּד **ḥōr haggidgād**, n.pr.loc. [2] [√ 2986 + 2044]. Hor Haggidgad, "*cavern of the Gidgad*":– Hor Haggidgad (2)

H2989 חֲרָאִים **ḥarā'îm**, n.[m.] [2] [→ 4738; cf. 3039]. filth, excrement:– excrement (2)

H2990 1חָרֵב **ḥārēb1**, v. [37] [→ 2992, 2993, 2994, 2996, 2997, 2998?, 2999, 3000, 3001; 10281]. [Q] to be dried up, be parched; be desolate, lay in ruins; [N] to be ruined, be desolate; [Pu] to be dried up; [H] to lay waste, devastate, cause to dry up; [Ho] to lie in ruins:– laid waste (6), dried up (5), dry up (5), desolate (3), ruined (3), been dried (2), dry (2), parched (2), utterly ruined (2 [+2990]), devastated (1), horror (1), laid waste (1 [+2256, 2238]), lay waste (1), left deserted (1), lies in ruins (1), makes run dry (1)

H2991 2חָרֵב **ḥārēb2**, v. [4] [√ 2995]. [Q] to kill; [N] to be slaughtered:– kill (2), must have fought (2 [+2991])

H2992 3חָרֵב **ḥārēb3**, a. [10] [√ 2990]. dry, desolate, wasted, in ruins:– in ruins (3), dry (2), ruin (2), desolate (1), desolate waste (1), ruined (1)

H2993 4חָרֵב **ḥārēb4**, v. Not used in NIVEBC [√ 2990]. to be desolate

H2994 5חָרֵב **ḥārēb5**, a. Not used in NIVEBC [√ 2990]. waste, desolate

H2995 חֶרֶב **ḥereb**, n.f. [409] [→ 2991]. sword; dagger; knife; cutting tool; by extension: battle, war; used fig. of God's judgment:– sword (363), swords (29), swordsmen (5 [+408, 8990]), dagger (3), knives (2), war (2), did[S] (1 [+2520, 906]), killed (1 [+5782, 4200, 7023]), tool (1), weapons (1), NDT (1)

H2996 1חֹרֶב **ḥōreb1**, n.m. [13] [√ 2990]. heat, dryness, drought, fever:– heat (6), drought (3), dry (3), fever (1)

H2997 2חֹרֶב **ḥōreb2**, n.[m.] [4] [√ 2990]. waste, rubble, object of horror, desolation:– object of horror (1), rubble (1), ruined (1), waste (1)

H2998 חֹרֵב **ḥōrēb**, n.pr.loc. [17] [√ 2990?]. Horeb, "*dry, desolate*":– Horeb (17)

H2999 חָרְבָּה **ḥorbâ**, n.f. [43] [√ 2990]. ruins, desolate place:– ruins (21), ruin (7), desolate (5), in ruins (3), deserts (1), desolation (1), places lying in ruins (1), ruined (1), ruined homes (1), waste (1), wasteland (1)

H3000 חָרָבָה **ḥārābâ**, n.f. [8] [√ 2990]. dry land, dry ground:– dry ground (4), dry land (3), dry up (1 [+5989])

H3001 חֲרָבוֹן **ḥarābôn**, n.m. [1] [√ 2990]. dry heat, implying a drought:– heat (1)

H3002 חַרְבוֹנָא **ḥarbônā'**, n.pr.m. [1] [cf. 3003]. Harbona, "*donkey driver*":– Harbona (1)

H3003 חַרְבוֹנָה **ḥarbônâ**, n.pr.m. [1] [cf. 3002]. Harbona, "*donkey driver*":– Harbona (1)

H3004 חָרַג **ḥārag**, v. [2] [Q] to come out trembling:– come trembling (2)

H3005 חַרְגֹּל **ḥargōl**, n.[m.] [1] [cf. 2519]. cricket; some sources: locust, grasshopper:– cricket (1)

H3006 חָרַד **ḥārad**, v. [39] [→ 3007, 3008?, 3009, 3010, 3011?, 3012?]. [Q] to tremble, quake, shudder, be startled; [H] to make afraid, frighten, make tremble:– make afraid (9), tremble (5), trembled (4), trembling (3), frighten away (2), alarm (1), come trembling (1), fear (1), frighten (1), gone to trouble (1 [+3010]), pounds (1), quaking with fear (1), routing (1), shudder (1), startled (1), strike with terror (1), terrify (1), terror filled (1 [+4394]), trembled violently (1 [+1524, 6330, 4394, 3010]), trembles (1), NDT (1)

H3007 חָרֵד **ḥārēd**, a.vbl. [6] [√ 3006]. trembling, fearful:– tremble (2), fear (1), feared (1 [+2118]), trembled (1), trembles (1)

H3008 1חֲרֹד ***ḥᵃrōd1***, n.pr.loc. [1] [→ 3009?, 3012, 6534; cf. 3006?]. Harod, "*trembling*":– Harod (1)

H3009 2חֲרֹד ***ḥᵃrōd2***, a.g. *or* n.pr. Not used in NIVEBC [√ 3006?; cf. 3008?]. see 3012

H3010 1חֲרָדָה ***ḥᵃrādâ1***, n.f. [9] [√ 3006]. panic, fear, terror, horror:– fear (2), panic (2), terror (2), gone to trouble (1 [+3006]), horror (1), trembled violently (1 [+3006, 1524, 6330, 4394])

H3011 2חֲרָדָה ***ḥᵃrādâ2***, n.pr.loc. [2] [√ 3006?]. Haradah, "*place of fear*":– Haradah (2)

H3012 חֲרֹדִי ***ḥᵃrōdî***, a.loc. [2] [√ 3008; cf. 3006?]. Harodite:– Harodite (2)

H3013 1חָרָה ***ḥārâ1***, v. [92] [→ 3019, 3034; cf. 3081]. [Q] to be angry, be aroused; to burn with anger; [N] to rage; [H] to be jealous; [Tiphel] to compete, contend with; [Ht] to fret:– angry (23), burned (18), angry (11 [+678]), burn (6), aroused (4), burns (4), fret (4), very angry (4 [+678]), burned (2 [+4394]), furious (2 [+4394]), loses temper (2 [+3013]), anger (1 [+678]), angry (1 [+928, 6524]), burning (1), compete (1), flared (1), flared up (1), furious (1 [+678, 4394]), have more and more (1), rage (1), raged (1), zealously (1), NDT (1)

H3014 2חָרָה ***ḥārâ2***, v. [Q] to become few in number

H3015 חַרְהֲיָה ***ḥarhᵃyâ***, n.pr.m. [1] [cf. 3029]. Harhaiah:– Harhaiah (1)

H3016 חֲרוּזִים ***ḥᵃrûzîm***, n.[m.]pl. [1] string of jewels; some sources: string of beads or shells:– strings of jewels (1)

H3017 חָרוּל ***ḥārûl***, n.[m.] [3] weeds, undergrowth, variously identified:– weeds (2), undergrowth (1)

H3018 חֲרוּמַף ***ḥᵃrûmap***, n.pr.m. [1] [√ 3050 + 678]. Harumaph, "*disfigured nose*":– Harumaph (1)

H3019 חָרוֹן ***ḥārôn***, n.m. [40] [√ 3013]. fierce (anger), burning (anger), wrath:– fierce (28), wrath (5), burning (2), angry (1 [+678]), burning anger (1), dry (1), heat (1), hot (1)

H3020 חֲרוּפִי ***ḥᵃrûpî***, a.g. [1] [cf. 3042]. Haruphite:– Haruphite (1)

H3021 1חָרוּץ ***ḥārûṣ1***, n.m. [7] gold:– gold (6), NDT (1)

H3022 2חָרוּץ ***ḥārûṣ2***, n.[m.] [1] [√ 3076]. trench, ditch, moat, a military defense:– trench (1)

H3023 3חָרוּץ ***ḥārûṣ3***, a. [4] [√ 3076]. threshing sledge, sharp instrument for harvest:– sharp (1), sledge (1), sledges (1), threshing sledge (1)

H3024 4חָרוּץ ***ḥārûṣ4***, a.vbl. [1] [√ 3076]. maimed, mutilated, pertaining to what has been cut:– maimed (1)

H3025 5חָרוּץ ***ḥārûṣ5***, n.[m.] [2] [√ 3076]. decision:– decision (2)

H3026 6חָרוּץ ***ḥārûṣ6***, a. [5] [√ 3077]. diligent, industrious:– diligent (5)

H3027 7חָרוּץ ***ḥārûṣ7***, n.pr.m. [1] [√ 3077?]. Haruz, "[perhaps] *gold* or *eager*":– Haruz (1)

H3028 חַרְחוּר ***ḥarḥûr***, n.pr.m. [2] [√ 3031; cf. 3081]. Harhur, "[poss.] *fever;* [poss.] *raven; one born during mother's fever*":– Harhur (2)

H3029 חַרְחֲיָה ***ḥarḥᵃyâ***, n.pr.m. Not used in NIVEBC [cf. 3015]. see 3015

H3030 חַרְחַס ***ḥarḥas***, n.pr.m. [1] [cf. 2897]. Harhas:– Harhas (1)

H3031 חַרְחֻר ***ḥarḥur***, n.m. [1] [→ 3028; cf. 3081]. scorching heat; some souces: fever:– scorching heat (1)

H3032 חֶרֶט ***ḥereṭ***, n.[m.] [2] pen; fashioning tool, stylus:– pen (1), tool (1)

H3033 חַרְטֹם ***ḥarṭōm***, n.m. [11] [√ 2641; 10282]. magician:– magicians (10), themS (1)

H3034 חֳרִי ***ḥᵒrî***, n.m. [6] [√ 3013]. hot, burning, fierce (anger):– fierce (3), burning (1), great rage (1 [+678]), hot (1)

H3035 1חֹרִי ***ḥōrî1***, n.[m.] [1] [√ 2578]. (white) bread or cake:– bread (1)

H3036 2חֹרִי ***ḥōrî2***, n.pr.m. [3] Hori, "*cave-dweller*":– Hori (3)

H3037 3חֹרִי ***ḥōrî3***, a.g. [7] Horite, "*of Hor[i]*":– Horite (4), Horites (3)

H3038 חָרִיט ***ḥārîṭ***, n.m. [2] bag, purse:– bags (1), purses (1)

H3039 חִרְיוֹנִים ***ḥiryyônîm***, n.[m.] Not used in NIVEBC [cf. 2989 + 3433]. dove's dung [?], see 2989

H3040 חָרִיף ***ḥārîp***, n.pr.m. [2] [→ 3042; cf. 3069]. Hariph, "*one born at harvest time*":– Hariph (2)

H3041 חֲרִיפוֹת ***ḥᵃrîpôt***, n.[f.] Not used in NIVEBC [√ 3070]. grains of sand

H3042 חֲרִיפִי ***ḥᵃrîpî***, a.g. Not used in NIVEBC [√ 3040; cf. 3020, 3069, 3070?]. Hariphite, see 3020

H3043 1חָרִיץ ***ḥārîṣ1***, n.m. [1] [√ 3076]. portion, slice:– cheeses (1 [+2692])

H3044 2חָרִיץ ***ḥārîṣ2***, n.m. [2] [√ 3076]. pick, hoe, an iron tool:– picks (2)

H3045 חָרִישׁ ***ḥārîš***, n.m. [3] [√ 3086]. plowing, time of plowing:– ground (1), plowing (1), plowing season (1)

H3046 חֲרִישִׁי ***ḥᵃrîšî***, a. [1] [√ 3086?]. scorching:– scorching (1)

H3047 חָרַךְ ***ḥārak***, v. [1] [Q] to roast; some sources: to capture:– roast (1)

H3048 חֲרַכִּים ***ḥᵃrakkîm***, n.[m.]pl. [1] lattice, a window covered by crossed strips of wood:– lattice (1)

H3049 1חָרַם ***ḥāram1***, v. [50] [→ 1259, 3051, 3055, 3056, 3057]. [H] to completely destroy, devote to destruction, exterminate, annihilate [Ho] to be destroyed, be devoted to destruction; this can refer to anything which is under the ban from common use, some things are set apart for use by priests, other things are destroyed utterly as devoted to the LORD:– totally destroyed (13), completely destroyed (6), completely destroy (5), totally destroy (3), completely destroy (2 [+3049]), destroy completely (2), destroyed (2), destroying completely (2), must destroy totally (2 [+3049]), annihilate (1), be destroyed (1), bring about destruction (1), destroy (1), destroy totally (1), destroying (1), devote (1), devoted and destroyed (1), devoted to destruction (1 [+3051]), devotes (1), exterminate (1), forfeit (1), kill (1)

H3050 2חָרַם ***ḥāram2***, v. [1] [→ 3018, 3052, 3053?]. [Qp] to be disfigured, mutilated, any split portion of the face, possibly a cleft palate:– disfigured (1)

H3051 1חֵרֶם ***ḥērem1***, n.m. [29] [√ 3049]. devoted, set apart for destruction; this can refer to anything which is under the ban from common use, some things are set apart for use by priests, other things are destroyed utterly as devoted to the LORD:– devoted things (7), devoted (4), destruction (3), themS (3 [+2021]), set apart for destruction (2), condemned things (1), destroyed (1), determined should die (1), devoted to God (1), devoted to destruction (1), devoted to destruction (1 [+3049]), devoted to the Lord (1), total destruction (1), totally destroyed (1), NDT (1)

H3052 2חֵרֶם ***ḥērem2***, n.m. [9] [√ 3050]. net, fishnet, trap:– net (4), fishnets (2), nets (2), trap (1)

H3053 חָרִם ***ḥārim***, n.pr.m. [11] [√ 3050?]. Harim, "*consecrated [to Yahweh]*":– Harim (10), Harim's (1)

H3054 חֹרֵם ***ḥōrēm***, n.pr.loc. [1] Horem, "*consecrated*":– Horem (1)

H3055 חָרְמָה ***ḥormâ***, n.pr.loc. [9] [√ 3049]. Hormah, "*consecration*":– Hormah (9)

H3056 חֶרְמוֹן ***ḥermôn***, n.pr.loc. [14] [→ 1259, 3057; cf. 3049]. Hermon, "*consecrated place*":– Hermon (13), heights of Hermon (1)

H3057 חֶרְמֹנִים ***ḥermōnîm***, n.pr.loc. Not used in NIVEBC [√ 3056; cf. 3049]. heights of Hermon, see 3056

H3058 חֶרְמֵשׁ ***ḥermēš***, n.[m.] [3] sickle (for harvest of grain):– sickle (2), sickles (1)

H3059 1חָרָן ***ḥārān1***, n.pr.loc. [10] Haran, "*mountaineer* perhaps *sanctuary*":– Harran (10)

H3060 2חָרָן ***ḥārān2***, n.pr.m. [2] Haran, "*mountaineer* perhaps *sanctuary*":– Haran (2)

H3061 חֹרֹנִי ***ḥōrōnî***, a.g. [3] Horonite:– Horonite (3)

H3062 חַרְנֶפֶר ***ḥarneper***, n.pr.m. *or* loc. [1] Harnepher, "*Horus is merciful*":– Harnepher (1)

H3063 1חֶרֶס ***ḥeres1***, n.[m.] [1] itch, any eruptive skin rash:– itch (1)

H3064 2חֶרֶס ***ḥeres2***, n.m. [3] [→ 3065, 3066, 6557, 9467]. sun:– sun (2), sunset (1 [+995, 2021])

H3065 3חֶרֶס ***ḥeres3***, n.pr.loc. [2] [√ 3064, 9466]. Heres, "*sun*":– Heres (2)

H3066 חַרְסָה ***ḥarᵉsâ***, n.m. Not used in NIVEBC [√ 3064]. sun, see 3064

H3067 חַרְסוּת ***ḥarsût***, n.f.col. Not used in NIVEBC [√ 3084]. potsherd, see 3068

H3068 חַרְסִית ***ḥarsît***, n.f.col. [1] [√ 3084]. potsherd:– Potsherd (1)

H3069 1חָרַף ***ḥārap1***, v.den. [1] [→ 3040, 3042, 3073, 3074; cf. 3072]. [Q] (to spend the time of) winter:– all winter (1)

H3070 2חָרַף ***ḥārap2***, v. [39] [→ 3041, 3075; cf. 3042?]. [Q] to treat with contempt, insult, reproach, taunt; [P] to defy, ridicule, taunt, mock, insult:– ridicule (4), ridiculed (4), taunted (4), defied (3), defy (3), mocked (3), insulting (2), reproach (2), shows contempt (2), taunt (2), discredit (1), hurled (1), insult (1), insulted (1), mock (1), rebuking (1), ridiculing (1), risked (1 [+4200, 4637]), taunts (1), treats with contempt (1)

H3071 3חָרַף ***ḥārap3***, v. [P] to disillusion, confuse

H3072 4חָרַף ***ḥārap4***, v. [1] [cf. 3069]. [N] to be promised to a man, engaged:– promised (1)

H3073 חָרֵף ***ḥārēp***, n.pr.m. [1] [√ 3069]. Hareph, "*autumn* or *sharp; scornful*":– Hareph (1)

H3074 חֹרֶף ***ḥōrep***, n.m. [7] [√ 3069]. winter (the early time of the harvest cycle); prime (the early time of one's youth):– winter (5), prime (1), season (1)

H3075 חֶרְפָּה ***ḥerpâ***, n.f. [73] [√ 3070]. disgrace, contempt, scorn, insult:– disgrace (16), reproach (13), scorn (10), insults (5), object of scorn (5), contempt (4), shame (4), object of reproach (3), scorned (3), insolence (2), humiliation (1), insult (1), insulted (1), mock (1), mocked (1), objects of contempt (1), offensive (1), slur (1)

H3076 1חָרַץ ***ḥāraṣ1***, v. [10] [→ 3022, 3023, 3024, 3025, 3043, 3044]. [Q] to pronounce, determine; [Qp, N] to be determined, be decreed:– been decreed (2), decreed (2), bark (1 [+4383]), been determined (1), determined (1), is decreed (1), pronounced (1), uttered a word (1 [+906, 4383])

H3077 2חָרַץ ***ḥāraṣ2***, v. [1] [√ 3026 *or* 3027?]. [Q] to pay attention, act quickly:– move quickly (1)

H3078 חַרְצֹב ***ḥarṣōb***, n.[f.] [2] struggle; chains:– chains (1), struggles (1)

H3079 חַרְצָן ***ḥarṣān***, n.m.pl. [1] [√ 2949?]. seeds (of grapes); some sources: unripe fruit:– seeds (1)

H3080 חָרַק ***ḥāraq***, v. [5] [Q] to gnash, grind (teeth):– gnash (3), gnashed (1), gnashes (1)

H3081 1חָרַר ***ḥārar1***, v. [9] [→ 3028, 3031, 3083; cf. 3013]. [Q] to burn; (heated metal) glow; [N] be parched, burned, charred; [Pil] to kindle, cause to burn, glow; by extension: to have a fever:– be charred (1), burn (1), burned up (1), burns (1), chars (1), glows (1), is charred (1), kindling (1), parched (1)

H3082 2חָרַר ***ḥārar2***, v. [N] to be hoarse

H3083 חֲרֵרִים ***ḥᵃrērîm***, n.[m.] [1] [√ 3081]. parched place, a hot, lifeless desert place:– parched places (1)

H3084 חֶרֶשׂ ***ḥereś***, n.[m.] [17] [→ 3067, 3068, 3085, 7818, 7819]. clay pot, earthenware; potsherd, fragment of pottery:– clay (9), potsherds (3), earthenware (1), fragment (1), piece of broken pottery (1), pieces (1), potsherd (1)

H3085 חֲרֶשֶׂת ***ḥᵃreśet***, n.pr.loc. Not used in NIVEBC [√ 3084]. Hareseth, see 7819

H3086 1חָרַשׁ ***ḥāraš1***, v. [27] [→ 3045, 3046?, 3088, 3093, 3096, 3098, 4739]. [Q] to plow; engrave; plan, plot; [Qp] to be inscribed; [N] to be plowed; [H] to plot against:– plow (6), plot (3), be plowed (2), plowed (2), plowing (2), devises (1), farmer (1), inscribed (1), plan (1), planted (1), plots (1), plotting (1 [+2021, 8288]), plowman (1), plowmen (1), plows (1), skilled craftsman (1), tools (1)

H3087 2חָרֵשׁ ***ḥārēš2***, v. [47] [→ 3089, 3090?, 3094, 3095?]. [Q] to be silent, be quiet; to become deaf; [H] to be quiet, say nothing, be silent; [Ht] to make no moves, keep silent:– silent (15), quiet (6), says nothing (3), altogether silent (2 [+3087]), deaf (2), remain silent (2 [+3087]), says nothing (2 [+3087]), turn a deaf ear (2), did nothing (1), fail to speak (1), holds tongue (1), keep silent (1), made no move (1), no longer rebuke (1), reduce to silence (1), said no more (1), say nothing (1), saying nothing (1), still (1), stop (1), without saying a word (1)

H3088 1חֶרֶשׁ ***ḥereš1***, n.[m.] Not used in NIVEBC [√ 3086]. magic, sorcery

H3089 2חֶרֶשׁ ***ḥereš2***, n.[m.] (used as adv.) [1] [√ 3087]. secretly, silently:– secretly (1)

H3090 3חֶרֶשׁ ***ḥereš3***, n.pr.m. [1] [√ 3087?]. Heresh, "*deaf, silent*":– Heresh (1)

H3091 1חֹרֶשׁ ***ḥōreš1***, n.m. [3] [→ 3092?; cf. 3099]. wooded place, forest, thicket:– forest (1), thickets (1), wooded areas (1)

H3092 2חֹרֶשׁ ***ḥōreš2***, n.pr.loc. [4] [√ 3091? *or* 3093?]. Horesh, "*woodsman* or *craftsman*":– Horesh (4)

H3093 חָרָשׁ ***ḥārāš***, n.m. [37] [√ 3086, 3092?]. skilled craftsman: blacksmith, carpenter, stonemason, gemcutter, idol-maker, etc.; the ironic phrase "craftsman of destruction" means people who are very good at destroying things (Ezek 21:31):– skilled workers (5), carpenters (4), craftsmen (4), carpenters (3 [+6770]), craftsman (3), metalworker (3), blacksmith (2), skilled (2), blacksmith (1 [+1366]), carpenter (1 [+6770]), cutter (1), engraver (1), engravers (1), makers (1), masons (1 [+74]), stonemasons (1 [+7815]), stonemasons (1 [+74, 7815]), worker (1), workers (1)

H3094 חֵרֵשׁ ***ḥērēš***, a. [9] [√ 3087]. deaf (one):– deaf (8), NDT (1)

H3095 חַרְשָׁא ***ḥaršā'***, n.pr.m. [2] [→ 9426; cf. 3087?]. Harsha, "*deaf*":– Harsha (2)

H3096 חֲרָשִׁים ***ḥᵃrāšîm***, n.pr.loc. Not used in NIVEBC [→ 1629; cf. 3086]. Harashim, see 1629

H3097 חֲרֶשֶׁת ***ḥᵃrešet***, n.pr.loc. Not used in NIVEBC [√ 7819]. Haresheth, see 7819

H3098 חֲרֹשֶׁת ***ḥᵃrōšet1***, n.f. [4] [√ 3086]. cutting (stone), working (wood):– cut (2), work (2)

H3099 חֲרֹשֶׁת הַגּוֹיִם ***ḥᵃrōšet haggôyim***, n.pr.loc. [3] [√ 2046; cf. 2046, 3091]. Harosheth Haggoyim, "*Harosheth of the nations*":– Harosheth Haggoyim (3)

H3100 חָרַת ***ḥārat***, v. [1] [Qp] to be engraved:– engraved (1)

H3101 חֶרֶת ***ḥeret***, n.pr.loc. [1] Hereth:– Hereth (1)

H3102 חֲשׂוּפָא ***ḥᵃśûpā'***, n.pr.m. [2] Hasupha:– Hasupha (2)

H3103 חֲשׂוּפַי ***ḥᵃśûpay***, v. Not used in NIVEBC [√ 3106]. see 3106

H3104 חָשַׂךְ ***ḥāśak***, v. [27] [Q] to keep back, to withhold, halt, spare; [N] to be spared, be relieved:– hold back (3), withheld (3), kept (2), are spared (1), bring relief (1), halted (1), hesitate (1), hold (1), is relieved (1), keep (1), keep silent (1 [+7023]), preserve (1), punished less (1 [+4200, 4752]), relentless (1 [+1172]), reserve (1), restrain (1), spare (1), spares (1), sparing (1), too easy on (1), uses with restraint (1), withholds (1)

H3105 חָשִׂף ***ḥāśip***, n.m. [1] [√ 3107]. small flock:– small flocks (1)

H3106 [1]חָשַׂף ***ḥāśap[1]***, v. [11] [→ 3103, 4741]. [Q] to strip bare, lay bare; to scoop out, draw out; [Qp] to be bared:– bared (2), stripped off bark (2 [+3106]), draw (1), lay bare (1), lift up (1), pull up (1), scooping (1), strip bare (1), strips bare (1)

H3107 [2]חָשַׂף ***ḥāśap[2]***, v. Not used in NIVEBC [→ 3105]. [P] to bring to premature birth

H3108 חָשַׁב ***ḥāšab***, v. [112] [→ 3110, 3112, 3113, 3114, 3115, 3116, 3117, 3121, 4742; 10285]. [Q] to plan, plot, purpose, consider; to credit, account, impute; [N] to be thought, considered, regarded; be reckoned, accounted; [P] to determine, plan, plot; to compute, account; [Ht] to consider oneself:– plot (6), devised (5), think (5), plan (4), are regarded (3), count (3), devise (3), plots (3), plotting (3), thought (3), was considered (3), are considered (2), be reckoned (2), considered (2), determine (2), devises (2), intended (2), make (2), planning (2), purposed (2 [+4742]), seem (2), seems (2), were considered (2), account for (1 [+907]), am counted (1), are thought (1), be considered (1), be considered as (1), be reckoned credit (1), be taken (1), care for (1), compute (1), consider (1), consider themselves (1), considers (1), counted (1), counts (1), credited (1), determine the value (1), determined (1), devise plans (1), devise ways (1), devising (1), execute (1), has in mind (1 [+4222]), held in esteem (1), hold (1), hold in esteem (1), honored (1), imagine (1), improvise (1), is considered (1), make plans (1 [+4742]), mean (1), planned (1), plans have (1 [+4742]), plot (1 [+928, 4222]), plot against (1 [+928, 4222]), plotted (1), plotted (1 [+4742]), regard (1), regarded (1), require an accounting (1), respected (1), scheming (1), threatened (1), treats (1), tried (1), was credited (1), were thought (1)

H3109 חֵשֶׁב ***ḥēšeb***, n.m. [8] [cf. 2502]. waistband:– waistband (7), decorative waistband (1)

H3110 חֹשֵׁב ***ḥōšēb***, n.[m.] *or* v.ptcp. [12] [√ 3108]. skilled craftsman, designer:– skilled hands (3), skilled worker (3), designer (1), designers (1), designers (1 [+4742]), expert hands (1), invented (1 [+4742]), skilled craftsman (1)

H3111 חַשְׁבַּדָּנָה ***ḥašbaddānâ***, n.pr.m. [1] [cf. 3116]. Hashbaddanah, "[prob.] *Yahweh has considered me*":– Hashbaddanah (1)

H3112 חֲשֻׁבָה ***ḥᵃšubâ***, n.pr.m. [1] [√ 3108]. Hashubah, "*consideration*":– Hashubah (1)

H3113 [1]חֶשְׁבּוֹן ***ḥešbôn[1]***, n.m. [3] [√ 3108]. scheme, plan:– scheme of things (2), planning (1)

H3114 [2]חֶשְׁבּוֹן ***ḥešbôn[2]***, n.pr.loc. [38] [√ 3108]. Heshbon, "*reckoning*":– Heshbon (37), Heshbon's dominion (1)

H3115 חִשָּׁבוֹן ***ḥiššābôn***, n.m. [2] [√ 3108]. catapult machine (for hurling against ramparts); scheme:– devices (1), schemes (1)

H3116 חֲשַׁבְיָה ***ḥᵃšabyâ***, n.pr.m. [12] [√ 3108 + 3378; cf. 3111]. Hashabiah, "*Yahweh has reckoned*":– Hashabiah (12)

H3117 חֲשַׁבְיָהוּ ***ḥᵃšabyāhû***, n.pr.m. [3] [√ 3108 + 3378]. Hashabiah, "*Yaweh has reckoned*":– Hashabiah (3)

H3118 חֲשַׁבְנָה ***ḥᵃšabnâ***, n.pr.m. [1] Hashabnah, "[prob.] *Yahweh has considered me*":– Hashabnah (1)

H3119 חֲשַׁבְנְיָה ***ḥᵃšabnᵉyâ***, n.pr.m. [2] Hashabneiah, "[prob.] *Yahweh has considered me*":– Hashabneiah (2)

H3120 חָשָׁה ***ḥāšâ***, v. [16] [Q] to be silent, be hushed; [H] to keep silent; to do nothing, hesitate:– silent (8), quiet (2), aren't do something (1), calmed (1), doing nothing (1), hushed (1), keeping it to ourselves (1), not saying (1)

H3121 חַשּׁוּב ***ḥaššûb***, n.pr.m. [5] [√ 3108]. Hasshub, "*considerate*":– Hasshub (5)

H3122 חָשׁוּק ***ḥāšûq***, n.[m.] [8] [√ 3138]. band, binding:– bands (8)

H3123 חֻשִׁים ***ḥušîm***, n.pr.m. [1] [cf. 2594]. Hushim:– Hushim (1)

H3124 חָשַׁךְ ***ḥāšak***, v. [17] [→ 3125, 3126, 3127, 3128, 4743]. [Q] to grow dark, be dim, be black; [H] to darken, make dark; often darkness has the associative meanings of gloom, despair, terror, ignorance, or hard to understand:– dark (5), darkened (3), dim (2), black (1), blacker (1), brings darkness (1), darken (1), darkens (1), made dark (1), obscures (1)

H3125 חֹשֶׁךְ ***ḥōšek***, n.m. [80] [√ 3124; 10286]. darkness, dark; blackness, gloom; often darkness has the associative meanings of gloom, despair, terror, ignorance, or hard to understand:– darkness (63), dark (4), realm of darkness (4), gloom (2), black (1), deep shadow (1), dusk (1), hidden (1), pitch darkness (1 [+854]), place of darkness (1), total darkness (1 [+696])

H3126 חָשֹׁךְ ***ḥāšōk***, a. [1] [√ 3124]. obscure, dark, unknown:– officials of low rank (1)

H3127 חָשְׁכָה ***ḥoškâ***, n.f. [1] [√ 3124]. darkness:– darkness (1)

H3128 חֲשֵׁכָה ***ḥᵃšēkâ***, n.f. [7] [√ 3124]. darkness:– darkness (4), dark (3)

H3129 חָשַׁל ***ḥāšal***, v. [1] [N] to lag (behind), be worn out:– lagging (1)

H3130 חָשֻׁם ***ḥāšum***, n.pr.m. [5] [→ 3131, 3132, 3135; cf. 2595]. Hashum, "*broad-nosed*":– Hashum (5)

H3131 חֻשִׁם ***ḥušim***, n.pr.m.[g.] [1] [√ 3130]. Hushite:– Hushites (1)

H3132 חֶשְׁמוֹן ***ḥešmôn***, n.pr.loc. [1] [√ 3130]. Heshmon:– Heshmon (1)

H3133 חַשְׁמַל ***ḥašmal***, n.[m.] [3] glowing metal; some sources: electrum:– glowing metal (3)

H3134 חַשְׁמַן ***ḥašman***, n.m. [1] envoy:– Envoys (1)

H3135 חַשְׁמֹנָה ***ḥašmōnâ***, n.pr.loc. [2] [√ 3130]. Hashmonah:– Hashmonah (2)

H3136 חֹשֶׁן ***ḥōšen***, n.m. [24] breastpiece:– breastpiece (23), it (1 [+2021])

H3137 [1]חָשַׁק ***ḥāšaq[1]***, v. [8] [→ 3139; cf. 3138]. [Q] to set one's affection, desire, love, be attached to:– desired (2 [+3139]), set affection (2), attracted (1), in love kept (1), loves (1), set (1)

H3138 [2]חָשַׁק ***ḥāšaq[2]***, v.den. [3] [→ 3122, 3140; cf. 3137]. [P] to make bands, make joints for binding; [Pu] to have bands:– bands (2), make bands (1)

H3139 חֵשֶׁק ***ḥēšeq***, n.m. [4] [√ 3137]. thing desired, thing longed for:– desired (1 [+2911]), desired (1 [+3137]), desired (1 [+3137]), longed for (1)

H3140 חִשֻּׁק ***ḥiššuq***, n.[m.] [1] [√ 3138]. spokes (of a wheel):– spokes (1)

H3141 חִשֻּׁר ***ḥiššur***, n.[m.] [1] [→ 3142]. hub (of a wheel):– hubs (1)

H3142 חַשְׁרָה ***ḥašrâ***, n.f. Not used in NIVEBC [√ 3141]. collection, mass

H3143 חֲשַׁשׁ ***ḥᵃšaš***, n.m. [2] chaff, dry grass:– chaff (1), dry grass (1)

H3144 חֻשָׁתִי ***ḥušātî***, a.g. [5] [√ 2592]. Hushathite:– Hushathite (5)

H3145 [1]חַת ***ḥat[1]***, n.m. [2] [√ 3169]. fear, dread, terror:– dread (1), fear (1)

H3146 [2]חַת ***ḥat[2]***, a. [2] [√ 3169]. terrified, broken:– broken (1), terrified (1)

H3147 חֵת ***ḥēt***, n.pr.m. [14] [→ 3153]. Hittite, "*descendants of Heth*":– Hittites (9 [+1201]), Hittite (2), Hittites (2), his people[s] (1 [+1201])

H3148 חָתָא ***ḥātā'***, v. [N] to be destroyed, see 9393

H3149 חָתָה ***ḥātâ***, v. [4] [→ 4746]. [Q] to get, snatch, take away:– heap (1), scoop (1), snatch up (1), taking (1)

H3150 חִתָּה ***ḥittâ***, n.f. [1] [√ 3169]. terror:– terror (1)

H3151 חִתּוּל ***ḥittûl***, n.[m.] [1] [√ 3156]. splint, bandage:– splint (1)

H3152 חַתְחַת ***ḥatḥat***, n.[m.] [1] [√ 3169]. horror, terror, danger:– dangers (1)

H3153 חִתִּי ***ḥittî***, a.g. [48] [√ 3147]. Hittite, "*descendants of Heth*":– Hittites (25), Hittite (23)

H3154 חִתִּית ***ḥittît***, n.f. [8] [√ 3169]. terror:– terror (7), terrorized (1 [+928])

H3155 חָתַךְ ***ḥātak***, v. [1] [N] to be decreed:– are decreed (1)

H3156 חָתַל ***ḥātal***, v. [2] [→ 3151, 3157]. [Pu, Ho] to be wrapped in strips of cloth:– wrapped in cloths (2 [+3156])

H3157 חֲתֻלָּה ***ḥᵃtullâ***, n.f. [1] [√ 3156]. band (of cloth) for wrapping:– wrapped (1)

H3158 חֶתְלוֹן ***ḥetlôn***, n.pr.loc. [2] Hethlon:– Hethlon (2)

H3159 חָתַם ***ḥātam***, v. [25] [→ 2597, 2598, 3160; 10291]. [Q] to seal (with a signet ring); to seal up; by extension: to be a model; [Qp] to be sealed, be enclosed; [N] to be sealed; [P] to seal in; [H] to block, obstruct:– sealed (12), seal (3), seal up (2), affixing seals (1), be sealed up (1), blocked (1), enclosed (1), placed seal (1 [+928, 2597]), seals off (1 [+1237]), shut in (1), stops (1)

H3160 חֹתֶמֶת ***ḥōtemet***, n.f. [1] [√ 3159]. signet ring seal:– seal (1)

H3161 חָתַן ***ḥātan***, v.den. [11] [√ 3163]. [Q, Ht] to intermarry; to become a son-in-law:– son-in-law (5), intermarry (4), allied himself by marriage (1), made an alliance (1)

H3162 חֹתֵן ***ḥōtēn***, n.vbl. [21] [√ 3163]. father-in-law:– father-in-law (19), brother-in-law (1), him[s] (1 [+2257])

H3163 חָתָן ***ḥātān***, n.m. [20] [→ 3161, 3162, 3164, 3165]. son-in-law; bridegroom:– bridegroom (10), son-in-law (6), sons-in-law (3), related by marriage (1)

H3164 חֲתֻנָּה ***ḥᵃtunnâ***, n.f. [1] [√ 3163]. wedding, marriage:– wedding (1)

H3165 חֹתֶנֶת ***ḥōtenet***, n.f.vbl. [1] [√ 3163]. mother-in-law (she who has a son-in-law):– mother-in-law (1)

H3166 חָתַף ***ḥātap***, v. [1] [→ 3167]. [Q] to snatch away:– snatches away (1)

H3167 חֶתֶף ***ḥetep***, n.[m.] [1] [√ 3166]. bandit, robber:– bandit (1)

H3168 חָתַר ***ḥātar***, v. [8] [→ 4747]. [Q] to dig, break into; row (in rough seas):– dug (3), dig (2), break into (1), dig down (1), row (1)

H3169 חָתַת ***ḥātat***, v. [54] [→ 3145, 3146, 3150, 3152, 3154, 3170, 3171?, 4744?, 4745]. [Q] to be shattered, dismayed, terrified; [N] to be discouraged, terrified; [P] to frighten; break; [H] to shatter, terrify:– discouraged (10), terrified (9), dismayed (8), shattered (7), filled with terror (3), terrify (3), shatter (2), afraid (1), be broken (1), be shattered (1), broken (1), cracked (1), dreaded (1), fail (1), frighten (1), frightened (1), panic (1), stood in awe (1), terror (1)

H3170 [1]חֲתַת ***ḥᵃtat[1]***, n.[m.] [1] [→ 3170; cf. 3169]. something dreadful, horrible:– something dreadful (1)

H3171 [2]חֲתַת ***ḥᵃtat[2]***, n.pr.m. [1] [√ 3170?; cf. 3169?]. Hathath, "[poss.] *terror;* [poss.] *weakness*":– Hathath (1)

H3172 ט ***ṭ***, letter. Not used in NIVEBC [√ 10292]. letter of the Hebrew alphabet

H3173 טֵאטֵא ***ṭē'ṭē'***, v. [1] [→ 4748; cf. 3226]. [Pil] to sweep away:– sweep (1)

H3174 טָבְאַל ***ṭābᵉ'al***, n.pr.m. [1] [√ 3202 + 446]. Tabeel, "*God [El] is good*":– Tabeel (1)

H3175 טָבְאֵל ***ṭābᵉ'ēl***, n.pr.m. [1] [√ 3202 + 446]. Tabeel, "*God [El] is good*":– Tabeel (1)

H3176 טָבַב ***ṭābab***, v. Not used in NIVEBC [√ 3201]. [Q] to speak

H3177 טִבָּה ***ṭibbâ***, n.f. rumor

H3178 טְבוּלִים ***ṭᵉbûlîm***, n.m. [1] turban:– turbans (1)

H3179 טַבּוּר ***ṭabbûr***, n.[m.] [2] center (of the land), as a fig. extension of the navel of the body, not found in the OT:– center (1), central hill (1 [+824])

H3180 טָבַח ***ṭābaḥ***, v. [11] [→ 3181, 3184, 3185, 3186, 4749]. [Q] to slaughter, butcher; [Qp] to be slaughtered:– slaughter (3), slaughtered (3), be slaughtered (1), prepared (1), slaughter (1 [+3181]), slaughters (1), slay (1)

H3181 [1]טֶבַח ***ṭebaḥ[1]***, n.m. [13] [→ 3182; cf. 18, 3180]. slaughtering:– slaughter (10), animal (1), meat (1), slaughter (1 [+3180])

H3182 [2]טֶבַח ***ṭebaḥ[2]***, n.pr.m. [1] [√ 3181]. Tebah, "[poss.] *one born at the time or place of the slaughtering*":– Tebah (1)

H3183 [3]טֶבַח ***ṭebaḥ[3]***, n.pr.loc. [1] [cf. 3187]. Tebah, "[poss.] *one born at the time or place of slaughtering*":– Tebah (1)

H3184 טַבָּח ***ṭabbāḥ***, n.m. [32] [→ 3185; cf. 3180; 10295]. cook, butcher; by extension: executioner; guard, imperial guard:– guard (13), imperial guard (12), cook (2), NDT (5)

H3185 טַבָּחָה ***ṭabbāḥâ***, n.f. [1] [√ 3184; cf. 3180]. (female) cook (of meat):– cooks (1)

H3186 טִבְחָה ***ṭibḥâ***, n.f. [3] [√ 3180]. slaughtered meat, butchered meat:– butchered (1), meat (1), slaughtered (1)

H3187 טִבְחַת ***ṭibḥat***, n.pr.loc. [1] [cf. 1056, 3183]. Tebah, "[poss.] *one born at the time or place of slaughtering*":– Tebah (1)

H3188 טָבַל ***ṭābal***, v. [16] [Q] to dip, plunge; bathe, soak; [N] to be dipped:– dip (8), dipped (4), bathe (1), plunge (1), soaked (1), touched (1)

H3189 טְבַלְיָהוּ ***ṭᵉbalyāhû***, n.pr.m. [1] [√ 3228 + 4200? + 3378?]. Tabaliah, "*Yahweh has dipped*":– Tabaliah (1)

H3190 טָבַע ***ṭāba'***, v. [10] [→ 3191, 3192]. [Q] to sink down, to fall into; [Pu] to be drowned; [Ho] to be sunk, be settled into:– sink (2), sunk (2), are drowned (1), fallen (1), sank (1), sank down (1), were set (1), were settled in place (1)

H3191 טַבָּעוֹת ***ṭabbā'ôt***, n.pr.m. [2] [√ 3192; cf. 3190]. Tabbaoth, "*[ornamental or signet] ring*":– Tabbaoth (2)

H3192 טַבַּעַת ***ṭabba'at***, n.f. [49] [→ 3191; cf. 3190]. ring; signet ring:– rings (34), ring (5), signet ring (5), signet rings (2), them (1 [+2021]), them[s] (1 [+2021]), them[s] (1 [+9109, 2021])

H3193 טַבְרִמֹּן ***ṭabrimmōn***, n.pr.m. [1] [√ 3202 + 8235]. Tabrimmon, "*Rimmon is good*":– Tabrimmon (1)

H3194 טֵבֵת ***ṭēbēt***, n.pr. [1] Tebeth:– Tebeth (1)

H3195 טַבָּת ***ṭabbāt***, n.pr.loc. [1] Tabbath, "[poss.] *good*":– Tabbath (1)

H3196 טָהוֹר ***ṭāhôr***, a. [95] [√ 3197]. clean, pure, flawless, free from impurity; moral or ceremonial purity as a fig. extension of an object being free from defect or filth:– pure (42), clean (34), ceremonially clean (13), unclean (3 [+4202]), ceremonially unclean (1 [+1194]), flawless (1), unclean (1 [+401])

H3197 טָהֵר **ṭāhēr**, v. [94] [→ 3196, 3198, 3199, 3200, 4756]. [Q] to be (ceremonially) clean, purified; [P] to pronounce clean, cleanse, make ceremonially clean, to purify; [Ht] to cleanse oneself, purify oneself; this can mean moral or ceremonial purity; see also 3196:– clean (23), be cleansed (12), cleanse (11), pronounce clean (9), cleansed (8), purify (7), purified (4), ceremonially clean (3), purify themselves (3), purified themselves (2), been cleansed (1), cleansing (1), make ceremonially clean (1), pronounces clean (1), pronouncing clean (1), pure (1), purge (1), purged (1), purified themselves ceremonially (1), purifier (1), purify yourselves (1), unclean (1 [+4202])

H3198 טֹהַר **ṭōhar**, n.[m.] [3] [√ 3197]. purity; cleanness; clearness, brightness:– purification (2), bright blue[S] (1)

H3199 טְהָר **ṭ[e]hār**, n.[m.] [1] [√ 3197]. splendor, purity:– splendor (1)

H3200 טָהֳרָה **ṭoh[o]râ**, n.f. [13] [√ 3197]. cleansing, purification; pronouncement of (ceremonial) cleansing:– cleansing (3), ceremonial cleansing (2), pronounced clean (2), purification (2), purified (2), clean (1), cleansed (1)

H3201 [1]טוֹב **ṭôb[1]**, v. [28] [→ 3176, 3202, 3203, 3204, 3205, 3206, 3208; cf. 3512; 10293, 10320]. [Q] to be good, well, pleasing; [H] to do well, do good, prosper; this can refer to quality as well as to moral goodness:– pleases (7), in high spirits (5 [+4213]), any better (2 [+3201]), did well (2), feel better (2), beautiful (1), doing good (1), done well (1), favorably disposed (1), go well (1), make prosper (1), pleased (1 [+928, 6524]), pleasing (1), prosper (1), well off (1)

H3202 [2]טוֹב **ṭôb[2]**, a. & n.m. [489] [→ 3204, 3208; cf. 3201; 10294; *also used with compound proper names*]. good, pleasing, desirable; goodness; this can refer to quality as well as to moral goodness:– good (240), better (64), best (17), well (11), fine (9), prosperity (9), right (7), beautiful (6 [+5260]), better off (6), pleases (6), favorable (4), goodness (4), gracious (4), like (4 [+928, 6524]), precious (4), wish (4 [+928, 6524]), choice (3), kind (3), beautiful (2), favorably (2), glad (2), handsome (2), happy (2), please (2), please (2 [+928, 6524]), pleased (2 [+928, 6524]), pleasing (2), prosper (2 [+5162]), rich (2), satisfaction (2), success (2), very well (2), alluring (1 [+2834]), approve of (1 [+928, 6524]), as[S] (1), attractive (1), benefited (1), better (1 [+4946]), bounty (1), celebrating (1 [+3427]), celebration (1), cheerful (1), delightful (1), enjoyable (1), favor (1), festive (1), fine (1 [+1524, 2256]), finest (1), flourishing (1), generous (1 [+6524]), good (1 [+408]), graciously (1), handsome (1 [+5260]), handsome (1 [+9307]), happiness (1), healthier (1), help (1), intelligent (1 [+8507]), joyful (1), like (1 [+928, 2021, 4200]), lovely (1), mean more (1), noble (1), pleasant (1), please (1 [+2256, 3838, 928, 6524]), pleased with (1 [+928, 6524]), pleases (1 [+928, 6524]), prefer (1 [+928, 6524]), profitable (1), profitable (1 [+6087]), prosper (1), prospered (1), prosperous (1), prospers (1 [+5162]), relief (1), sinful (1 [+4202]), sound (1), the other[S] (1), valid (1), wanted to do (1 [+928, 6524]), wealth (1), well off (1), well-being (1), wicked (1 [+4202]), wished (1 [+928, 6524]), wishes (1 [+928, 6524]), wrong (1 [+4202]), NDT (1)

H3203 [3]טוֹב **ṭôb[3]**, a. [1] [√ 3201]. sweet(-smelling), perfume:– sweet (1)

H3204 [4]טוֹב **ṭôb[4]**, n.pr.loc. [4] [√ 3202; cf. 3201]. Tob, "*good*":– Tob (4)

H3205 [5]טוֹב **ṭôb[5]**, n.m. Not used in NIVEBC [√ 3201]. see 3202

H3206 טוּב **ṭûb**, n.m. [32] [√ 3201]. good, best; goodness, prosperity; this can refer to quality as well as to moral goodness:– good things (7), goodness (5), good (4), prosperity (3), best (2), bounty (2), attractive (1), best things (1), blessings (1), fair (1), finest wares (1), gladly (1 [+928, 4222]), joy (1), prosper (1), rich produce (1)

H3207 טוֹב אֲדוֹנִיָּה **ṭôb '[a]dôniyyâ**, n.pr.m. [1] [√ 3204 + 125]. Tob-Adonijah, "*good is [my] Lord Yahweh*":– Tob-Adonijah (1)

H3208 טוֹבָה **ṭôbâ**, n.f. [67] [√ 3202; cf. 3201]. good, well-being; this can refer to quality as well as to moral goodness:– good (21), prosperity (9), good things (7), favor (3), well (3), bounty (2), good thing (2), kindly (2), treaty of friendship (2 [+8934, 2256]), covenant blessing (1), enjoyment (1), fair (1), good deeds (1), good do (1 [+3512]), good work (1), goodness (1), goods (1), gracious (1), in behalf (1 [+6584]), joy (1), prosperous (1), satisfaction (1), unharmed (1), welfare (1), well-being (1)

H3209 טוֹבִיָּה **ṭôbiyyâ**, n.pr.m. [17] [√ 3202 + 3378]. Tobiah; Tobijah, "*Yahweh is good*":– Tobiah (14), Tobijah (2), Tobiah's (1)

H3210 טוֹבִיָּהוּ **ṭôbiyyāhû**, n.pr.m. [1] [√ 3202 + 3378]. Tobijah, "*Yahweh is good*":– Tobijah (1)

H3211 טָוָה **ṭāwâ**, v. [2] [→ 4757]. [Q] to spin (yarn):– spun (2)

H3212 טוּחַ **ṭûaḥ**, v. [11] [→ 3225; cf. 3220]. [Q] to cover with whitewash; overlay with plaster; [N] to be plastered, be coated:– covered (3), cover (2), been plastered (1), overlaying (1), plaster (1), plastered (1), whitewash (1 [+9521]), whitewashed (1)

H3213 טוֹטָפֹת **ṭôṭāpōt**, n.f.pl. [3] [√ 5752]. symbol, sign (later, phylactery, a small box of Scripture verses worn as a sign of obedience to the covenant):– bind (2 [+2118, 4200]), symbol (1)

H3214 טוּל **ṭûl**, v. [14] [→ 3232]. [P] to hurl; [H] to thrown, hurl; [Ho] to be overpowered, be fallen, be hurled:– hurl (2), hurled (2), threw (2), throw (2), be hurled out (1), fall (1), hurl away (1 [+3232]), is cast (1), overpowering (1), sent (1)

H3215 טוּר **ṭûr**, n.m. [26] [→ 3227]. row, course:– row (9), rows (9), course (2), courses (2), ledge of stone (1), sets (1), NDT (2)

H3216 טוּשׂ **ṭûś**, v. [1] [Q] to swoop down; some sources: to flutter:– swooping down (1)

H3217 טָחָה **ṭāḥâ**, v. [1] [Pil] to shoot (an arrow the distance of a bowshot; the distance of a bowshot is still in sight, though it is out of hearing range):– bowshot (1 [+8008])

H3218 טְחוֹן **ṭ[e]ḥôn**, n.[m.] [1] [√ 3221]. hand-mill, grinding-mill:– millstones (1)

H3219 טֻחוֹת **ṭuḥôt**, n.f.pl. [2] inner parts; heart, with a possible focus that this is a mysterious and unknowable part of a person:– ibis (1), womb (1)

H3220 טָחַח **ṭāḥaḥ**, v. [1] [cf. 3212]. [Q] to be smeared over:– plastered over (1)

H3221 טָחַן **ṭāḥan**, v. [7] [→ 3218, 3222, 3223]. [Q] to grind to flour, crush to powder:– ground (2), grind (1), grind grain (1), grinding (1), grinding grain (1), ground to powder (1 [+3512])

H3222 טַחֲנָה **ṭaḥ[a]nâ**, n.f. [1] [√ 3221]. grinding-mill:– grinding (1)

H3223 טֹחֲנָה **ṭōḥ[a]nâ**, n.f. [1] [√ 3221]. grinder (= molar tooth):– grinders (1)

H3224 טְחֹרִים **ṭ[e]ḥōrîm**, n.m. [2] tumor, hemorrhoids:– tumors (2)

H3225 טִיחַ **ṭîaḥ**, n.[m.] [1] [√ 3212]. coating (of whitewash); some sources: coating of clay:– whitewash (1)

H3226 טִיט **ṭîṭ**, n.m. [13] [→ 3173, 4748; 10298]. mud, dirt, mire, clay:– mud (8), clay (2), mire (2), dirt (1)

H3227 טִירָה **ṭîrâ**, n.f. [7] [√ 3215; cf. 3515?, 7652]. camp (protected by stone walls); tower, battlement:– camps (3), ledge (1), locations (1), place (1), towers (1)

H3228 טַל **ṭal**, n.m. [31] [→ 40, 2782, 3189; 10299]. dew, night mist:– dew (31)

H3229 טָלָא **ṭālā'**, v. [8] [Qp] to be spotted; be variegated; [Pu] to be patched:– spotted (6), gaudy (1), patched (1)

H3230 טְלָאִים **ṭ[e]lā'îm**, n.pr.loc. [1] [√ 3231]. Telaim, "*lambs*":– Telaim (1)

H3231 טָלֶה **ṭāleh**, n.m. [3] [√ 3230]. lamb:– lamb (2), lambs (1)

H3232 טַלְטֵלָה **ṭalṭēlâ**, n.f. [1] [√ 3214]. hurling, throwing:– hurl away (1 [+3214])

H3233 טָלַל **ṭālal**, v. [1] [cf. 7511]. [P] to cover with a roof:– roofing over (1)

H3234 [1]טֶלֶם **ṭelem[1]**, n.pr.loc. [1] [√ 3235; cf. 3236]. Telem, "*brightness*":– Telem (1)

H3235 [2]טֶלֶם **ṭelem[2]**, n.pr.m. [1] [→ 3234; cf. 3236]. Telem, "*brightness*":– Telem (1)

H3236 טַלְמוֹן **ṭalmôn**, n.pr.m. [5] [cf. 3234, 3235]. Talmon, "[perhaps] *brightness*":– Talmon (5)

H3237 [1]טָמֵא **ṭāmē'[1]**, v. [163] [→ 3238, 3239, 3240, 3241?]. [Q] to be unclean, defiled; [N] to be made unclean, become defiled, impure; [P] to make unclean, defile, desecrate; [Pu] to become defiled; [Ht] to make oneself unclean, defiled; [Hotpaal] to be defiled; this can mean to be ceremonially impure or to be immoral in action:– unclean (62), defiled (29), defile (12), pronounce unclean (8), defile yourselves (6), defiles (4), ceremonially unclean (3), defiling (3), desecrated (3), make himself unclean (3), defile themselves (2), defiled herself (2), desecrate (2), impure (2), made herself impure (2), make yourselves unclean (2), pronounce unclean (2 [+3237]), be made unclean (1), became defiled (1), been defiled (1), corrupt (1), defile himself (1), defiled yourself (1), defiled yourselves (1), impurity (1), made yourself impure (1), make himself ceremonially unclean (1), make themselves ceremonially unclean (1), make unclean (1), makes herself impure (1), pronounce ceremonially unclean (1), pronounced unclean (1), remain unclean (1 [+3238])

H3238 [2]טָמֵא **ṭāmē'[2]**, a. [87] [√ 3237]. unclean, defiled, impure; this can mean to be ceremonial impurity or active immorality:– unclean (63), ceremonially unclean (12), defiled (7), impure (1), infamous (1 [+2021, 9005]), pagan (1), remain unclean (1 [+3237]), NDT (1)

H3239 טָמְאָה **ṭom'â**, n.f. Not used in NIVEBC [√ 3237]. uncleanness, see 3237

H3240 טֻמְאָה **ṭum'â**, n.f. [36] [√ 3237]. uncleanness, impurity, filthiness; this can mean ceremonial impurity or a physical impurity on the body or in an object:– uncleanness (16), unclean (6), impurity (4), impurities (2), ceremonially unclean (1), discharge (1 [+2308]), filthiness (1), impure (1), things that make unclean (1), unclean practices (1), woman's monthly uncleanness (1 [+2021, 5614]), NDT (1)

H3241 טָמָה **ṭāmâ**, v. [1] [√ 3237?]. [N] to be considered stupid; some sources: to be regarded as unclean:– considered stupid (1)

H3242 טָמַם **ṭāmam**, v. [N] to be stopped up

H3243 טָמַן **ṭāman**, v. [31] [→ 4759]. [Q] to hide; bury; [Qp] to be hidden; [N] to hide oneself; [H] to keep hidden:– hidden (9), hid (6), hide (3), buried (2), buries (2), bury (2), hiding (2), grave (1), hidden away (1), lies in wait (1), set (1), treasures hidden (1 [+8561])

H3244 טֶנֶא **ṭene'**, n.m. [4] basket:– basket (4)

H3245 טָנַף **ṭānap**, v. [1] [P] to soil, make dirty:– soil (1)

H3246 טָעָה **ṭā'â**, v. [1] [cf. 9494]. [H] to lead astray:– lead astray (1)

H3247 טָעַם **ṭā'am**, v. [11] [→ 3248, 4761; 10301]. [Q] to taste; to see, discover by experience:– taste (4), tasted (2), tasted (2 [+3247]), tastes (2), sees (1)

H3248 טַעַם **ṭa'am**, n.m. [13] [√ 3247; 10302]. taste; discretion; discernment; decree, judgment; "to turn from discernment" means "to pretend to be insane" (1Sa 21:13):– pretended to be insane (2 [+9101]), tasted (2), decree (1), discernment (1), discreetly (1), discretion (1), flavor (1), good judgment (1), judgment (1), tastes (1), NDT (1)

H3249 [1]טָעַן **ṭā'an[1]**, v. [1] [Pu] to be pierced:– pierced (1)

H3250 [2]טָעַן **ṭā'an[2]**, v. [1] [Q] to load:– Load (1)

H3251 [1]טַף **ṭap[1]**, n.m. [42] [→ 3262; cf. 3252]. (little) children, women and children, those (as a class) not able or barely able to march:– children (28), women and children (6), little ones (4), boys (1 [+2351]), families (1), girl (1 [+851]), little children (1)

H3252 [2]טַף **ṭap[2]**, n.m. Not used in NIVEBC [cf. 3251]. drops

H3253 [1]טָפַח **ṭāpaḥ[1]**, v. [1] [→ 3255, 3256, 3257, 3258; cf. 3254?]. [P] to spread out:– spread out (1)

H3254 [2]טָפַח **ṭāpaḥ[2]**, v.den. [1] [→ 3259, 4762; cf. 3253?]. [P] to care for; some sources: to bear healthy children:– cared for (1)

H3255 טֶפַח **ṭepaḥ**, n.[m.] [2] [→ 3256; cf. 3253]. span, handbreadth (the width of the hand at the base of the four fingers, about three inches (8 cm):– handbreadth (2)

H3256 טֹפַח **ṭōpaḥ**, n.m. [5] [√ 3255; cf. 3253]. handbreadth, span of the hand; see also 3255:– handbreadth (5)

H3257 [1]טְפָחָה **ṭ[e]pāḥâ[1]**, n.[m.] [1] [√ 3253]. handbreadth, a figure of a short unit of time, a few years; see also 3255:– handbreadth (1)

H3258 [2]טְפָחָה **ṭ[e]pāḥâ[2]**, n.[m.] [1] [√ 3253]. eaves:– eaves (1)

H3259 טִפֻּחִים **ṭippuḥîm**, n.[m.]pl.abst. [1] [√ 3254]. caring for (children):– cared for (1)

H3260 טָפַל **ṭāpal**, v. [3] [cf. 9521]. [Q] to smear, cover:– cover (1), smear (1), smeared (1)

H3261 טִפְסַר **ṭipsār**, n.[m.] [2] official, clerk:– commander (1), officials (1)

H3262 טָפַף **ṭāpap**, v. [1] [√ 3251]. [Q] to take little steps, trip along:– strutting along with swaying hips (1 [+2143, 2256])

H3263 טָפַשׁ **ṭāpaš**, v. [1] [Q] to be unfeeling, insensible:– unfeeling (1)

H3264 טָפַת **ṭāpat**, n.pr.f. [1] Taphath, "[poss.] *little child*":– Taphath (1)

H3265 טָרַד **ṭārad**, v. [2] [→ 4765; 10304]. [Q] to constantly drip:– constant dripping (1), dripping (1)

H3266 טְרוֹם **ṭ[e]rôm**, adv.temp. Not used in NIVEBC [→ 3269, 3270]. before

H3267 טָרַח **ṭāraḥ**, v. [1] [→ 3268]. [H] to load down, burden with:– loads (1)

H3268 טֹרַח **ṭōraḥ**, n.m. [2] [√ 3267]. burden, problem, load:– burden (1), problems (1)

H3269 טָרִי **ṭārî**, a. [2] [√ 3266]. fresh (bone); open, moist (sore):– fresh (1), open (1)

H3270 טֶרֶם **ṭerem**, adv.temp. & c. [56] [√ 3266]. a marker of time: before; negative: not, not yet:– before (29 [+928]), before (9), before (7 [+928]), not yet (4), before (2 [+928, 4202]), before (1 [+4946]), just before (1 [+928]), no yet (1), no yet (1 [+3972]), still not (1)

H3271 טָרַף **ṭārap**, v. [25] [→ 3272, 3273, 3274]. [Q] to tear, mangle; [Qp, N, Pu] to be torn (to pieces); [H] to provide (to enjoy):– tear to pieces (4), tearing (3), been torn to pieces (2 [+3271]), surely been torn to pieces (2 [+3271]), tear (2), was torn to pieces by a wild animal (2 [+3271]), give (1), killed (1), mangles (1), prey (1), raged (1), ravenous (1), tear apart (1), tear prey (1), tears (1), torn to pieces (1)

H3272 טֶרֶף **ṭerep**, n.m. [22] [√ 3271]. prey (food for wild animals):– prey (13), food (4), victims (2), game (1), kill (1), torn (1)

H3273 טָרָף **ṭārāp**, a. [2] [√ 3271]. fresh-picked (leaf or vegetation):– freshly plucked (1), new (1)

H3274 טְרֵפָה **ṭᵉrēpâ**, n.f. [9] [√ 3271]. animal torn by wild beasts:– torn by wild animals (5), animal torn by beasts (1), animals torn by wild beasts (1), prey (1), remains (1)

H3275 י **y**, letter. Not used in NIVEBC [√ 10306]. letter of the Hebrew alphabet

H3276 ־ִי **-î**, p.sg.com.suf. [6486] [→ 483, 5646, 5761]. I, me, my:– my (3455), me (1798), I (389), my (79 [+4200]), the[s] (52), my own (45), me (44 [+5883]), I (39 [+5883]), mine (31 [+4200]), myself (27), our (26), us (17), mine (15), a[s] (11), myself (10 [+5883]), myself (7 [+4213]), I'm (5), my (4 [+5883]), my own (4 [+4200]), you[s] (4 [+123]), me (3 [+7156]), this[s] (3), I've (2), her (2), here[s] (2), his (2), me (2 [+3883]), my (2 [+928, 8079]), them[s] (2 [+6639]), us (2 [+2256, 3870]), we (2), you (2), I (1 [+4213]), I (1 [+5055]), I (1 [+7023]), I (1 [+8120]), all by myself (1 [+4200, 963]), an[s] (1), by myself (1 [+4946, 907]), by myself (1 [+4200, 963]), he[s] (1 [+3]), her (1 [+4200]), here[s] (1 [+6584]), here[s] (1 [+6640]), him (1), him[s] (1 [+3]), him[s] (1 [+123]), his[s] (1 [+466]), it[s] (1 [+1460]), it[s] (1 [+4213]), it[s] (1 [+274]), it[s] (1 [+7754]), its (1), me (1 [+1414]), me (1 [+2652]), me (1 [+4213]), me (1 [+8120]), me (1 [+9005]), mine (1 [+6643]), mine (1 [+9393]), mine (1 [+8611, 4200]), my (1 [+907]), my (1 [+928]), my (1 [+6640]), my (1 [+7156]), my (1 [+4200, 7156]), my life (1), my life's (1), my own (1 [+8611, 4200]), myself (1 [+963]), myself (1 [+1414]), myself (1 [+3338]), our own (1), ours (1 [+4200]), their[s] (1 [+6639, 3776]), they[s] (1 [+7366]), thought (1 [+606, 448]), us (1 [+2256, 2157]), us (1 [+2256, 4013]), what do I care about (1 [+4200, 4537, 2296, 4200]), your (1), your[s] (1 [+123]), NDT (348)

H3277 יָאַב **yā'ab**, v. [1] [→ 95?, 3365?; cf. 14?, 9289?]. [Q] to long for:– longing for (1)

H3278 יָאָה **yā'â**, v. [1] [Q] to be fitting, be proper:– due (1)

H3279 יַאֲזַנְיָה **ya'ᵃzanyâ**, n.pr.m. [2] [→ 3280; cf. 263 + 3378]. Jaazaniah, *"Yahweh listens"*:– Jaazaniah (2)

H3280 יַאֲזַנְיָהוּ **ya'ᵃzanyāhû**, n.pr.m. [2] [√ 3279; cf. 263 + 3378]. Jaazaniah, *"Yahweh listens"*:– Jaazaniah (2)

H3281 יָאִיר **yā'îr**, n.pr.m. [8] [→ 2596, 3285]. Jair, *"he gives light"*:– Jair (8)

H3282 ¹יָאַל **yā'al¹**, v. [4] [cf. 211]. [N] to become foolish, act foolish:– become fools (2), foolish (1), foolishly (1)

H3283 ²יָאַל **yā'al²**, v. [19] [cf. 215, 4578]. [H] to begin; to determine; be intent upon; to agree to; to be content, be pleased; to be bold:– determined (3), pleased (3), agreed (2), bold (2), be so kind as (1), began (1), by all means (1), content (1), intent on (1), please (1 [+5528]), tried (1), willing (1), NDT (1)

H3284 יְאֹר **yᵉ'ōr**, n.m. [64] river, stream, the Nile river; likely the Tigris river in Daniel:– nile (32), river (13), streams (9), canals (2), its[s] (2 [+2021]), riverbank (1 [+3338]), riverbank (1 [+8557]), tunnel (1 [+1324]), waters of the nile (1), NDT (2)

H3285 יָאִרִי **yā'irî**, a.g. [1] [√ 3281]. Jairite, *"of Jair"*:– Jairite (1)

H3286 יָאַשׁ **yā'aš**, v. [6] [N] to be despairing of, be without hope, give up; [P] to let despair:– despair (1), desperate (1), give up (1), hopeless (1), no use (1), use (1)

H3287 יֹאשִׁיָּה **yō'šiyyâ**, n.pr.m. [1] [→ 3288 [+ 3378]. Josiah, *"let or may Yahweh give"*:– Josiah (1)

H3288 יֹאשִׁיָּהוּ **yō'šiyyāhû**, n.pr.m. [52] [√ 3287 [+ 3378]. Josiah, *"let or may Yahweh give"*:– Josiah (47), Josiah's (3), him[s] (1), NDT (1)

H3289 יַאתוֹן **yi'tôn**, n.m. Not used in NIVEBC [cf. 415]. see 415

H3290 יְאָתְרַי **yᵉ'āṯᵉray**, n.pr.m. [1] Jeatherai:– Jeatherai (1)

H3291 יָבַב **yābab**, v. [1] [√ 3412]. [P] to cry out, lament:– cried out (1)

H3292 יְבוּל **yᵉbûl**, n.m. [12] [√ 3297]. crops, produce, harvest:– crops (7), harvest (2), grapes (1), harvests (1), produce (1)

H3293 יְבוּס **yᵉbûs**, n.pr.loc. [4] [→ 3294]. Jebus:– Jebus (3), NDT (1)

H3294 יְבוּסִי **yᵉbûsî**, a.g. [41] [√ 3293]. Jebusite, *"of Jebus"*:– Jebusites (32), Jebusite (9)

H3295 יִבְחָר **yibḥār**, n.pr.m. [3] [√ 1047]. Ibhar, *"he chooses"*:– Ibhar (3)

H3296 יָבִין **yābîn**, n.pr.m. [8] [√ 1067]. Jabin, *"perceptive"*:– Jabin (6), Jabin's (1), him[s] (1 [+4889, 4046])

H3297 יָבַל **yābal**, v. [18] [→ 64, 201, 3292, 3298, 3299, 3414; 10308]. [H] to bring, take (a gift); [Ho] to be brought, be led, be carried off:– bring (5), are carried (1), are delivered (1), be brought (1), be carried (1), be led forth (1), been carried (1), bring back (1), is led (1), led (1), led in (1), sends (1), taken (1), was led (1)

H3298 ¹יָבָל **yābāl¹**, n.[m.] [3] [√ 3297]. stream, watercourse:– flood (1), flow (1), flowing streams (1 [+4784])

H3299 ²יָבָל **yābāl²**, n.pr.m. [1] [√ 3297]. Jabal:– Jabal (1)

H3300 יִבְלְעָם **yiblᵉ'ām**, n.pr.loc. [3] [√ 1180? or 1182?]. Ibleam:– Ibleam (3)

H3301 יַבֶּלֶת **yabbelet**, a. [1] [→ 3413]. wart; some sources: running sore:– anything with warts (1)

H3302 יָבַם **yābam**, v.den. [3] [√ 3303]. [P] to fulfill the procreational duty of the brother-in-law:– fulfill the duty of a brother-in-law (2), fulfill duty as a brother-in-law (1)

H3303 יָבָם **yābām**, n.m. [2] [→ 3302, 3304]. husband's brother:– husband's brother (2)

H3304 יְבָמָה **yᵉbāmâ**, n.f. [5] [√ 3303]. brother's widow; sister-in-law, husband's brother's widow:– brother's widow (1), brother's wife (1), her[s] (1 [+3871]), she[s] (1 [+2257]), sister-in-law (1)

H3305 יַבְנְאֵל **yabnᵉ'ēl**, n.pr.loc. [2] [√ 1215 + 446; cf. 3306]. Jabneel, *"God [El] will build"*:– Jabneel (2)

H3306 יַבְנֶה **yabnēh**, n.pr.loc. [1] [cf. 3305]. Jabneh:– Jabneh (1)

H3307 יִבְנְיָה **yibnᵉyâ**, n.pr.m. [1] [√ 1215 + 3378]. Ibneiah, *"Yahweh built"*:– Ibneiah (1)

H3308 יִבְנִיָּה **yibniyyâ**, n.pr.m. [1] [√ 1215 + 3378]. Ibnijah, *"Yahweh built"*:– Ibnijah (1)

H3309 יַבֹּק **yabbōq**, n.pr.loc. [7] [√ 1327? or 84?]. Jabbok, *"flowing or wrestling"*:– Jabbok (7)

H3310 יְבֶרֶכְיָהוּ **yᵉberekyāhû**, n.pr.m. [1] [√ 1385 + 3378]. Jeberekiah, *"Yahweh blesses"*:– Jeberekiah (1)

H3311 יִבְשָׂם **yibśām**, n.pr.m. [1] [√ 1411]. Ibsam, *"fragrance"*:– Ibsam (1)

H3312 ¹יָבֵשׁ **yābēš¹**, v. [62] [→ 3313, 3314?, 3315?, 3316, 3317, 3318]. [Q] to dry up, be dry, be withered, be shriveled up; [P] to make wither, dry up; [H] to make wither, dry up:– dried up (15), withered (8), dry up (7), wither (6), dry (5), withers (5), completely withered (2 [+3312]), dries up (2), wither away (2), wither completely (2 [+3312]), completely dry (1), drought (1), fail (1), made shrivel (1), make dry (1), parched (1), shriveled up (1), withered away (1)

H3313 ²יָבֵשׁ **yābēš²**, a.vbl. or v.ptcp. [10] [√ 3312]. dry, withered, by extension: a paralyzed person (whose limbs have a shriveled appearance):– dry (8), grapes or raisins (1 [+6694, 4300, 2256]), lost (1)

H3314 ³יָבֵשׁ **yābēš³**, n.pr.m. [3] [√ 3312?]. Jabesh, *"dry"*:– Jabesh (3)

H3315 ⁴יָבֵשׁ **yābēš⁴**, n.pr.loc. [9] [√ 3312?]. Jabesh, *"dry"*:– Jabesh (8), they[s] (1 [+408])

H3316 יָבֵשׁ גִּלְעָד **yābēš gil'ād**, n.pr.loc. [12] [√ 3312 + 1680]. Jabesh Gilead, *"dry Gilead"*:– Jabesh Gilead (11), them[s] (1 [+408])

H3317 יַבָּשָׁה **yabbāšâ**, n.f. [14] [√ 3312; 10309]. dry ground, dry land (in contrast to bodies of water):– dry ground (10), dry land (3), land (1)

H3318 יַבֶּשֶׁת **yabbešet**, n.f. [2] [√ 3312]. dry ground, dry land:– dry land (1), ground (1)

H3319 יִגְאָל **yig'āl**, n.pr.m. [3] [√ 1457]. Igal, *"he redeems"*:– Igal (3)

H3320 יָגַב **yāgab**, v. [2] [→ 3321]. [Q] to work a field, do farm work:– fields (2)

H3321 יָגֵב **yāgēb**, n.m. [1] [√ 3320]. field:– fields (1)

H3322 יָגְבְּהָה **yogbᵉhâ**, n.pr.loc. [2] [√ 1467]. Jogbehah, *"height"*:– Jogbehah (2)

H3323 יִגְדַּלְיָהוּ **yigdalyāhû**, n.pr.m. [1] [√ 1540 + 3378]. Igdaliah, *"Yahweh is great"*:– Igdaliah (1)

H3324 ¹יָגָה **yāgâ¹**, v. [7] [→ 3326, 9342; cf. 3325]. [N] to be grieved; [P] to bring grief; [H] to torment, bring grief:– brings grief (1), brought (1), brought grief (1), grief (1), grieve (1), torment (1), tormentors (1)

H3325 ²יָגָה **yāgâ²**, v. [1] [cf. 2048, 3324]. [H] to remove:– been removed (1)

H3326 יָגוֹן **yāgôn**, n.[m.] [14] [√ 3324]. sorrow, anguish, grief:– sorrow (13), anguish (1)

H3327 יָגוּר **yāgûr**, n.pr.loc. [1] [cf. 1597]. Jagur:– Jagur (1)

H3328 יָגוֹר **yāgôr**, a.vbl. [2] [√ 3336]. fearing, filled with fear:– fear (2)

H3329 יָגִיעַ **yāgîa'**, a. [1] [√ 3333]. weary, exhausted:– weary (1 [+3946])

H3330 יְגִיעַ **yᵉgîa'**, n.m. [16] [√ 3333]. labor, heavy work; the result of labor: produce, gain:– labor (4), fruits of labor (2), products (2), fruit of labor (1 [+4090]), heavy work (1), possessions (1), produce (1), toil (1), wealth (1), work (1), worked (1)

H3331 יְגִיעָה **yᵉgî'â**, n.f. [1] [√ 3333]. weariness:– wearies (1)

H3332 יָגְלִי **yoglî**, n.pr.m. [1] Jogli, "[perhaps] *may God reveal*":– Jogli (1)

H3333 יָגַע **yāga'**, v. [26] [→ 3329, 3330, 3331, 3334, 3335]. [Q] to labor, toil, be weary; [P] to make weary; [H] to make weary:– wearied (6), weary (5), worn out (3), labor (2), labored (2), dealt with (1), exhaust (1), struggle (1), tired (1), toil (1), toiled (1), wear out (1), wearies (1)

H3334 יָגָע **yāgā'**, n.[m.] [1] [√ 3333]. what is toiled for, the produce of labor:– What toiled for (1)

H3335 יָגֵעַ **yāgēa'**, a. [3] [√ 3333]. worn out, weary, wearisome:– wearisome (1), weary (1), worn out (1)

H3336 יָגֹר **yāgōr**, v. [5] [→ 3328; cf. 1593]. [Q] to fear, dread:– dread (2), dreaded (2), feared (1)

H3337 יְגַר שָׂהֲדוּתָא **yᵉgar śāhᵃdûtā'**, n.[m.] & n.m. [1] [√ 10310 + 10679]. Jegar Sahadutha, the Aramaic name of a stone monument, "witness heap"; see also 1681:– Jegar Sahadutha (1)

H3338 יָד **yād**, n.f. & m. [1614] [√ 10311]. hand, by extension: arm, finger; fig. of control, power, strength, direction, care:– hand (535), hands (419), through (62 [+928]), from (32 [+4946]), power (32), with (21 [+928]), by (18 [+928]), to (15 [+928]), care (14), to (13 [+6584]), afford (7 [+5952]), arm (7), next to (7 [+6584]), command (6), arms (6), direction (5), hand over (5 [+5989, 928]), next section (5 [+6584]), possession (5), side (5), supervision (5), against (4 [+4946, 9393]), finger (4), handed over (4 [+5989, 928]), have (4 [+928]), monument (4), spacious (4 [+8146]), along (3), clutches (3), control (3), fist (3), hands (3 [+4090]), hold accountable (3 [+1335, 4946]), holding (3 [+928]), next (3 [+6584]), ordained (3 [+4848, 906]), power (3 [+445]), special gifts (3 [+9556]), strength (3), under (3 [+928]), armrests (2), as much as pleases (2 [+5522]), assassinate (2 [+8938, 928]), authority (2), axles (2), be sure of this (2 [+4200, 3338]), be sure of this (2 [+3338, 4200]), by (2 [+6584]), encouraged (2 [+2616]), grasp (2), had (2 [+928]), handed (2), installed (2 [+4848, 906]), left-handed (2 [+360, 3545]), liberality (2), next to (2 [+448]), of (2 [+4946]), openhanded (2 [+7337, 906, 7337]), ordain (2 [+4848]), ordination (2 [+4848, 906]), paw (2), place (2), play (2 [+5594, 928]), playing the lyre (2 [+5594, 928]), projection (2), projections (2), prosper (2 [+5952]), rebelled (2 [+8123]), seized (2 [+8492]), supports (2), them[s] (2 [+2021]), thumbs (2 [+984]), times (2), wheel around (2 [+2200]), wrist (2), wrists (2), you (2 [+3870]), abandon (1 [+8332, 4946]), accompanied by (1 [+6584]), adjoining (1 [+6584]), adjoining section (1 [+6584]), afford (1 [+5162, 1896]), afford (1 [+5595, 1896]), against (1 [+4946]), agent (1 [+4200]), along (1 [+4200]), along with (1 [+928]), appointed (1 [+5989, 928]), arms (1 [+723]), arrest (1 [+8938, 928]), as a direct result (1 [+9393]), as prescribed by (1 [+6584]), assistant (1 [+6584]), assisted (1 [+2616]), assisted (1 [+6584]), assisted (1 [+2616, 928]), attack (1 [+8938, 928]), attack (1 [+6590, 6584]), attacked (1 [+8938, 928]), attacks (1 [+8938, 928]), bank (1), be defeated (1 [+5989, 928]), beckon (1 [+5677]), beckon (1 [+5951]), began (1 [+2616]), beside (1 [+6584]), beside (1 [+448]), beside (1 [+928]), beside (1 [+4200]), body (1), boldly (1 [+928, 8123]), border (1), borders (1), bounty (1), bracelets (1 [+7543, 6584]), bring (1 [+8883, 6584]), broad (1 [+8146]), brought (1 [+928]), brought with (1 [+2118, 928]), call to account (1 [+1335, 4946]), carried (1 [+4374, 928]), cause (1 [+928]), commanded (1), companies (1), consecrate himself (1 [+4848]), consecrate themselves (1 [+4848, 906]), consecrated (1 [+4848, 906]), creditor (1 [+1251, 5408, 2257]), custody (1), customers (1 [+6086]), customers (1 [+6088]), debts (1 [+5391]), dedicate (1 [+4848]), dedicated (1 [+4848]), defiantly (1 [+928, 8123]), delegation (1 [+928, 6269]), delivered (1 [+928]), deserves (1 [+1691]), did[s] (1 [+5989, 2257]), did this[s] (1 [+5742, 2257]), discourage (1 [+8332]), discouraging (1 [+8332]), do (1 [+5126]), do that[s] (1 [+2118, 928, 2257]), done (1 [+4848, 928]), done by (1 [+928]), don't say a word (1 [+8492, 6584, 7023]), drew (1 [+4848, 928]), entrusted to (1 [+448]), entrusted to (1 [+928]), escape (1 [+4880, 4946]), fists (1), follow (1 [+448]), force (1), forcefully (1 [+928]), four-fifths (1 [+752]), from (1 [+928]), gain support (1 [+2118, 907]), gave victory (1 [+5989, 928]), give (1 [+5989, 928]), give up (1 [+8332]), given over (1 [+5599, 6584]), guilty (1 [+928]), had chance (1 [+2118, 928]), hand over (1 [+6037, 928]), hand over (1 [+928, 5989]), handed (1 [+4946]), handed (1 [+5989, 928]), handed over (1 [+5162, 928]), handing over (1 [+5989, 928]), handiwork (1 [+5126]), have (1 [+5162, 928]), have (1 [+3780, 9393]), have on hand (1 [+448, 9393]), have on hand (1 [+3780, 9393]), he (1 [+2257]), help (1 [+2616]), help (1 [+4200]), help (1 [+6640]), help (1 [+8883, 6640]), helped (1 [+2616, 906]), helped find strength (1 [+2616, 906]), him (1 [+2257]), hold (1), hold (1 [+2118, 928]), hold accountable (1 [+2011, 4946]), hold responsible (1 [+1335, 4946]), holds (1 [+2118, 928]), in charge of (1 [+928]), it[s] (1 [+3870]), killing (1 [+8938, 928]), labor (1), large (1 [+8146]), leadership (1), led the way (1 [+2118, 8037]), left (1 [+928]), let go (1 [+5663, 906]), lets happen (1 [+628, 4200]), little by little (1 [+6584]), lost courage (1 [+8332]), made subject to (1 [+4044, 9393]), man-made (1 [+5126, 132]), marched past (1 [+6296, 6584]), memorial (1), myself (1 [+3276]), naked bodies (1), near (1 [+6584]), nearby (1 [+6584]),

HEBREW INDEX

ordain (1 [+4848, 906]), ordained (1 [+4848]), ordered (1), overpowered (1 [+6451, 6584]), pledged (1 [+5989]), plenty of room (1 [+8146]), portion (1), powerless (1 [+401, 4200, 445]), put in charge (1 [+6641, 6584]), put up security (1 [+9546, 4200]), reach out (1 [+5742]), reached out (1 [+8938]), reaches out (1 [+8938]), reaching (1 [+8938]), remaining (1), rich (1 [+5952]), riverbank (1 [+3284]), ruled (1 [+4939]), seize (1 [+8492, 928]), seize the opportunity (1 [+5162]), set apart (1 [+4848]), set free (1 [+8938, 4946]), shapes (1 [+5126]), shares (1), shed by (1 [+4946]), shores (1), sided with (1 [+6640]), signpost (1), sins defiantly (1 [+6913, 928, 8123]), skin^S (1), snare (1), someone else^S (1 [+928]), stroke (1), strong (1 [+2616]), strong arms (1 [+2432]), subdue (1 [+5447]), submit (1 [+5989]), submit (1 [+8132]), submitted (1 [+5989]), supported (1 [+2118, 907]), surrender (1 [+6037, 928]), surrenders (1 [+5989]), swore (1 [+5951]), sworn (1 [+5951, 906]), take charge of (1 [+9393]), taken (1 [+928]), taking with (1 [+928]), they (1 [+2257]), things did (1 [+5126]), those^S (1), tightfisted (1 [+7890, 906]), to (1 [+9393]), took with (1 [+928]), turned about (1 [+2200]), unable to support (1 [+4572]), under care (1), used (1 [+928]), uses (1 [+928]), vicinity (1), wants to give (1 [+5952]), war clubs (1 [+5234]), waves (1), weak (1 [+8333]), with (1 [+4200]), with (1 [+6584]), wrists (1 [+723]), NDT (57)

H3339 יִדְאֲלָה ***yid'^{a}lâ***, n.pr.loc. [1] Idalah:– Idalah (1)

H3340 יִדְבָּשׁ ***yidbāš***, n.pr.m. [1] [√ 1831]. Idbash, "*honey*":– Idbash (1)

H3341 יָדַד ***yādad***, v. [3] [cf. 3343]. [Q] to cast (lots for decision making):– cast (3)

H3342 יְדִדוּת ***y^{e}didût***, n.f. [1] [√ 3351]. loved one, beloved:– love (1)

H3343 ¹יָדָה ***yādā^1***, v. [3] [cf. 3341]. [Q] to shoot (a bow); [P] to throw (down):– shoot (1), threw (1), throw down (1)

H3344 ²יָדָה ***yādā^2***, v. [111] [→ 2086, 2088, 2089, 2090, 2117, 9343; 10312]. [H] to express praise, give thanks, extol, make a public confession, make an admission; to praise is to speak of the excellence of someone or something; to give thanks has a focus on the gratitude of the speaker:– praise (48), give thanks (27), confess (6), give praise (6), thanksgiving (3), confessed (2), confessing (2), extol (2), give praise to (2), thank (2), admit (1), brings praise (1), confesses (1), confession (1), gave thanks (1), led in thanksgiving (1 [+9378]), praised (1), praises (1), praising (1), thanking (1), thanks (1)

H3345 יַדּוֹ ***yaddaw***, n.pr.m. Not used in NIVEBC [√ 3351?]. Jaddaw, see 3350

H3346 יִדּוֹ ***yiddô***, n.pr.m. [1] [√ 3351; cf. 3350]. Iddo, "[prob.] *Yahweh has adorned*":– Iddo (1)

H3347 יָדוֹן ***yādôn***, n.pr.m. [1] Jadon, "*frail one* or *Yahweh rules*":– Jadon (1)

H3348 יַדּוּעַ ***yaddûa'***, n.pr.m. [3] [√ 3359]. Jaddua, "*one known*":– Jaddua (3)

H3349 יְדוּתוּן ***y^{e}dûtûn***, n.pr.m. [16] [→ 3357]. Jeduthun:– Jeduthun (15), his^S (1)

H3350 יַדַּי ***yadday***, n.pr.m. [1] [cf. 3346]. Jaddai:– Jaddai (1)

H3351 יָדִיד ***yādîd***, a. [8] [→ 3342, 3345?, 3346, 3352, 3353, 3354]. lovely, beloved:– love (3), beloved (2), loved one (1), lovely (1), loves (1)

H3352 יְדִידָה ***y^{e}dîdâ***, n.pr.f. [1] [√ 3351]. Jedidah, "*beloved; lovely, beloved*":– Jedidah (1)

H3353 יְדִידֹת ***y^{e}dîdôt***, a. [1] [√ 3351]. love (song, referring to a wedding song):– wedding (1)

H3354 יְדִידְיָהּ ***y^{e}dîd^{e}yāh***, n.pr.m. [1] [√ 3351 + 3378]. Jedidiah, "*beloved of Yahweh*":– Jedidiah (1)

H3355 יְדָיָה ***y^{e}dāyâ***, n.pr.m. [2] Jedaiah, "*Yahweh has favored* or *Yahweh knows*":– Jedaiah (2)

H3356 יְדִיעֲאֵל ***y^{e}dî'^{a}'ēl***, n.pr.m. [6] [√ 3359 + 446]. Jediael, "*known of God [El]*":– Jediael (6)

H3357 יְדִיתוּן ***y^{e}dîtûn***, n.pr.m. [1] [√ 3349]. Jeduthun:– Jeduthun (1)

H3358 יִדְלָף ***yidlāp***, n.pr.m. [1] [√ 1941]. Jidlaph, "*he weeps*":– Jidlaph (1)

H3359 יָדַע ***yāda'***, v. [946] [→ 1976, 1978, 1981, 1982, 3348, 3362, 4529, 4530, 4531; cf. 1983; 10313; *also used with compound proper names*]. [Q] to know, recognize, understand; to have sexual relations; [Qp] to be respected; [N] to be known, make oneself known; [P] to cause to know; [Pu] to be well known; [H] to show, teach, make known; [Ho] to be made aware; [Ht] to make oneself known; this can range in meaning from the mere acquisition and understanding of information to intimacy in relationship, including sexual relations:– know (425), knew (39), knows (39), known (25), acknowledge (20), make known (13), understand (13), realize (12), teach (12), be sure (11), tell (11), learned (9), aware (8), find out (8), know how (8), made known (8), show (8), knew about (6), know (6 [+3359]), knowing (6), learn (6), know about (5), realized (5), experienced (4), knowledge (4), knows how (4), made love to (4), see (4), understanding (4), unknown (4 [+4202]), acknowledged (3), answer (3), be known (3), closest friends (3), confront (3), consider (3), observe (3), see (3 [+2256, 8011]), skilled (3), assured (2 [+3359]), be sure (2 [+3359]), be sure know (2 [+3359]), care for (2), chosen (2), concern (2), concerned about (2), found out (2), gain (2), had the least inkling (2 [+3359]), has knowledge (2 [+1981]), have (2), have sex with (2), ignorant (2 [+4202]), is known (2), know for certain (2 [+3359]), knows very well (2 [+3359]), let know (2), make myself known (2), must understand (2 [+3359]), recognized (2), respected (2), revealed myself (2), slept with (2), take notice (2), understood (2), able (1), acknowledges (1), acquaintances (1), agreed (1), apply (1), approval (1), are known (1), assured (1), attained to knowledge (1 [+1981]), be found out (1), be made known (1), be recognized (1), be remembered (1), become known (1), been discovered (1), been known (1), behaved (1), by surprise (1 [+4202]), can (1), can read (1 [+6219]), cannot read (1 [+4202, 6219]), care about (1), cared for (1), cares for (1), close friend (1), close friends (1), closest friend (1), come to (1), comprehends (1), decide (1), display (1), displayed (1), embrace (1), endowed with (1), enjoy (1), experience (1), experts (1), familiar with (1), feel (1), find (1), find out (1 [+8011, 2256]), find out (1 [+2256, 8011]), find out (1 [+2256, 8011]), foresee (1), gaining (1), great skill (1 [+2682, 1069]), had experience (1), had regard for (1), had sexual relations with (1), have concern for (1), have to do with (1), ignorant (1 [+1153]), indicate (1), inform (1), instruct (1), is renowned (1), is respected (1), know (1 [+7188]), know all about (1), know how to read (1 [+6219]), know what it is like (1), know what means (1), knowing about (1), knowing how (1), leading (1), learn the difference between (1), learned about (1), learning (1), lets be known (1), letting know (1), made himself known (1), make himself known (1), make myself fully known (1), make predictions (1), makes known (1), meant (1), mourners (1 [+5631]), not a virgin (1 [+5435, 2351]), note (1), notice (1), noticed (1), perceive (1), perceiving (1), proclaim (1), raped (1), realize (1 [+2256, 8011]), realized (1 [+8011, 2256]), realizing (1), recognizes (1), remember (1), reveal myself (1), revealed (1), sees (1), show how to distinguish (1), showed (1), shown (1), shown himself (1), skillful (1), sleep with (1), slept with (1 [+5435]), slept with (1 [+5435, 2351]), slept with (1 [+4200, 5435, 408]), slept with (1 [+4200, 5435, 2351]), stranger (1 [+4202]), strangers (1 [+4202]), submit (1), suffer (1), taught (1), taught a lesson (1), teaching (1), tell the difference (1), think (1), think it over (1), think over (1), told (1), trained (1), unaware (1 [+4202]), under care (1), understand (1 [+1069]), understands (1), understood (1 [+1069]), unfamiliar (1 [+4202]), virgin (1 [+4202, 408]), want to do with (1), was discovered (1), was known (1), watch over (1), watched over (1), watches over (1), well informed (1 [+1981]), were seen (1), NDT (5)

H3360 יָדָע ***yādā'***, n.pr.m. [2] Jada, "*shrewd one; [God] has cared*":– Jada (2)

H3361 יְדַעְיָה ***y^{e}da'yâ***, n.pr.m. [11] [√ 3359 + 3378]. Jedaiah, "*Yahweh has favored* or *Yahweh knows*":– Jedaiah (9), Jedaiah's (2)

H3362 יִדְּעֹנִי ***yidd^e'ōnî***, n.m. [11] [√ 3359]. spiritist, soothsayer:– spiritists (9), spiritist (2)

H3363 יָהּ ***yāh***, n.pr.m. [49] [√ 3378]. LORD (Yahweh):– the Lord (42), Lord (4), the Lord himself (2 [+3363]), he^S (1)

H3364 יָהַב ***yāhab***, v. Not used in NIVEBC [cf. 2035; 10314]. [Q] to give; see 2035

H3365 יְהָב ***y^{e}hāb***, n.[m.] [1] [√ 3277?]. care, burden:– cares (1)

H3366 יָהַד ***yāhad***, v.den. [1] [√ 3374; cf. 3373]. [Ht] to become a Jew, this can mean to join the Jewish faith or simply to act like a Jew:– became Jews (1)

H3367 יָהְדַּי ***yāhdāy***, n.pr.m. [1] Jahdai, "*Yahweh lead*":– Jahdai (1)

H3368 יְהֻדִיָּה ***y^{e}hudiyyâ***, a.g. Not used in NIVEBC [√ 3373]. Jewish, Judean

H3369 יֵהוּא ***yēhû'***, n.pr.m. [58] [√ 3378 + 2085]. Jehu, "*Yahweh is he*":– Jehu (52), he^S (4), Jehu's (2)

H3370 יְהוֹאָחָז ***y^{e}hô'āḥāz***, n.pr.m. [20] [√ 3378 + 296]. Jehoahaz, "*Yahweh holds*":– Jehoahaz (18), Ahaziah (2)

H3371 יְהוֹאָשׁ ***y^{e}hô'āš***, n.pr.m. [17] [√ 3378 + 408]. Joash; Jehoash, "*Yahweh bestows; man of Yahweh*":– Jehoash (9), Joash (8)

H3372 יְהוּד ***y^{e}hûd***, n.pr.loc. [1] Jehud, "*declare*":– Jehud (1)

H3373 יְהוּדָה ***y^{e}hûdâ***, n.pr.m. & loc. [820] [→ 3366, 3368, 3374, 3375, 3376, 3377; 10315]. Judah, of Judah, Judean, "*praised*":– Judah (763), Judah (13 [+1074]), Judah (13 [+1201]), Judah's (11), Judah (6 [+824]), Jews (3), Hodaviah (1), Judah's (1 [+1201]), both Judah (1 [+1074]), of Judah (1 [+1201]), quarrel Judah (1), their^S (1 [+408]), they^S (1), NDT (4)

H3374 ¹יְהוּדִי ***y^{e}hûdî^1***, a.g. [76] [→ 3366, 3375, 3377; cf. 3373; 10316]. (person) of Judah, Judean, Jew, Jewish, "*of Judah*":– Jews (58), Jew (9), men of Judah (3), Jewish (2), Hebrew (1), people of Judah (1), they^S (1 [+2021]), tribe of Judah (1)

H3375 ²יְהוּדִי ***y^{e}hûdî^2***, n.pr.m. [4] [√ 3374; cf. 3373]. Jehudi, Yaudi, "*of Judah*":– Jehudi (4)

H3376 ¹יְהוּדִית ***y^{e}hûdît^1***, a.g.f. (used as adv.) [6] [√ 3373]. in Hebrew (language), in the language of Judah:– in Hebrew (5), language of Judah (1)

H3377 ²יְהוּדִית ***y^{e}hûdît^2***, n.pr.f. [1] [√ 3374; cf. 3373]. Judith, "*Jewess or Judahite*":– Judith (1)

H3378 יהוה ***yhwh***, יְהוִה ***yehwih***, n.pr.m. [6827] [→ 3363 *also used with compound proper names*]. LORD (Yahweh), the proper name of the one true God; knowledge and use of the name implies personal or covenant relationship; the name pictures God as the one who exists and/or causes existence:– the LORD (6016), LORD (400), the LORD's (258), he^S (36), the LORD's (23 [+4200]), him^S (17), his^S (13), he^S (6 [+466, 3870]), him^S (3 [+466, 3870]), the LORD's (3 [+4200]), the LORD's (3 [+4946, 907]), his^S (2 [+466, 3870]), its^S (2 [+1074]), me^S (2), LORD's (1), done this^S (1 [+1215, 4640, 4200]), he^S (1 [+4855]), he^S (1 [+466, 3870]), he^S (1 [+466, 5646]), him^S (1 [+466, 4013]), it^S (1 [+1074]), the LORD (1 [+9005]), the LORD himself (1 [+7156]), the LORD's (1 [+4946, 6640]), the angel (1 [+4855]), NDT (32)

H3379 יְהוֹזָבָד ***y^{e}hôzābād***, n.pr.m. [4] [√ 3378 + 2272]. Jehozabad, "*Yahweh endows*":– Jehozabad (4)

H3380 יְהוֹחָנָן ***y^{e}hôḥānān***, n.pr.m. [9] [√ 3378 + 2858]. Jehohanan, "*Yahweh has been gracious*":– Jehohanan (9)

H3381 יְהוֹיָדָע ***y^{e}hôyādā'***, n.pr.m. [51] [√ 3378 + 3359]. Jehoiada, "*Yahweh has known*":– Jehoiada (50), he^S (1 [+2021, 3913])

H3382 יְהוֹיָכִין ***y^{e}hôyākîn***, n.pr.m. [10] [→ 3518, 3526, 3527, 4037; cf. 3378 + 3922]. Jehoiachin, "*Yahweh supports*":– Jehoiachin (10)

H3383 יְהוֹיָקִים ***y^{e}hôyāqîm***, n.pr.m. [36] [√ 3378 + 7756]. Jehoiakim, "*Yahweh lifts up, establishes*":– Jehoiakim (34), Jehoiakim's (2)

H3384 יְהוֹיָרִיב ***y^{e}hôyārîb***, n.pr.m. [2] [√ 3378 + 8189]. Jehoiarib, "*Yahweh argues [for me]*":– Jehoiarib (2)

H3385 יְהוּכַל ***y^{e}hûkal***, n.pr.m. [1] [√ 3378 + 3523; cf. 3426]. Jehucal, "*Yahweh is capable*":– Jehukal (1)

H3386 יְהוֹנָדָב ***y^{e}hônādāb***, n.pr.m. [8] [√ 3378 + 5605]. Jonadab; Jehonadab, "*Yahweh is generous, noble*":– Jehonadab (7), Jonadab (1)

H3387 יְהוֹנָתָן ***y^{e}hônātān***, n.pr.m. [82] [√ 3378 + 5989]. Jonathan; Jehonathan, "*gift of Yahweh*":– Jonathan (69), Jonathan's (3), he^S (3), Jehonathan (2), NDT (5)

H3388 יְהוֹסֵף ***y^{e}hôsēp***, n.pr.m. [1] [cf. 3578]. Joseph, "*he will add*":– Joseph (1)

H3389 יְהוֹעַדָּה ***y^{e}hô'addâ***, n.pr.m. [2] Jehoaddah:– Jehoaddah (2)

H3390 יְהוֹעַדִּין ***y^{e}hô'addîn***, n.pr.f. Jehoaddin

H3391 יְהוֹעַדָּן ***y^{e}hô'addān***, n.pr.f. [2] Jehoaddin, "[prob.] *Yahweh is delight*":– Jehoaddan (2)

H3392 יְהוֹצָדָק ***y^{e}hôṣādāq***, n.pr.m. [8] [√ 3378 + 7405; 10318]. Jehozadak, "*Yahweh is just*":– Jozadak (8)

H3393 יְהוֹרָם ***y^{e}hôrām***, n.pr.m. [29] [√ 3378 + 8123]. Joram; Jehoram, "*Yahweh exalts*":– Jehoram (16), Joram (13)

H3394 יְהוֹשֶׁבַע ***y^{e}hôšeba'***, n.pr.f. [1] [√ 3378 + 8682]. Jehosheba, "*Yahweh is an oath; Yahweh gives plenty, satisfies*":– Jehosheba (1)

H3395 יְהוֹשַׁבְעַת ***y^{e}hôšab'at***, n.pr.f. [2] [√ 3378 + 8682]. Jehosheba, "*Yahweh is an oath; Yahweh gives plenty, satisfies*":– Jehosheba (2)

H3396 יְהוֹשָׁמָע ***y^{e}hôšāmā'***, n.pr.m. Not used in NIVEBC [√ 3378 + 9052]. Jehoshama

H3397 יְהוֹשֻׁעַ ***y^{e}hôšua'***, n.pr.m. [218] [√ 3378 + 8775]. Joshua, "*Yahweh saves*":– Joshua (203), he^S (8), him^S (2), NDT (5)

H3398 ¹יְהוֹשָׁפָט ***y^{e}hôšāpāṭ^1***, n.pr.m. [83] [√ 3378 + 9149]. Jehoshaphat, "*Yahweh has judged*":– Jehoshaphat (79), Jehoshaphat's (2), NDT (2)

H3399 ²יְהוֹשָׁפָט ***y^{e}hôšāpāṭ^2***, n.pr.loc. [2] [√ 3378 + 9149]. Jehoshaphat, "*[valley] of Yahweh's judgment*":– Jehoshaphat (2)

H3400 יָהִיר ***yāhîr***, a. [2] arrogant, haughty:– arrogant (2)

H3401 יְהַלֶּלְאֵל ***y^{e}hallel'ēl***, n.pr.[m.] [2] [√ 3401 + 446]. Jehallelel, "*he shall praise God [El]; God [El] shines forth*":– Jehallelel (2)

H3402 יַהֲלֹם ***yāh^{a}lōm***, n.[m.] [3] emerald (precious stone, exact identification uncertain):– emerald (3)

H3403 יַהַץ ***yahaṣ***, n.pr.loc. [7] Jahaz, "[perhaps] *a trodden* or *open place*":– Jahaz (7)

H3404 יַהְצָה ***yahṣâ***, n.pr.loc. [2] Jahzah:– Jahzah (2)

H3405 יוֹאָב ***yô'āb***, n.pr.m. [145] [→ 6502; cf. 3378 + 3]. Joab, "*Yahweh is father*":– Joab (132), Joab's (8), he^S (2), they^S (1 [+2256, 8569, 2021, 2657]), who^S (1), NDT (1)

H3406 יוֹאָח ***yô'āḥ***, n.pr.m. [11] [√ 3378 + 278]. Joah, "*Yahweh is brother*":– Joah (11)

H3407 יוֹאָחָז ***yô'āḥāz***, n.pr.m. [4] [√ 3378 + 296]. Jehoahaz; Joahaz, "*Yahweh grips, holds*":– Jehoahaz (3), Joahaz (1)

H3408 יוֹאֵל ***yô'ēl***, n.pr.m. [20] [√ 3378 + 446]. Joel, "*Yahweh is God [El]*":– Joel (20)

H3409 יוֹאָשׁ ***yô'āš***, n.pr.m. [47] [√ 3378 + 408]. Joash; Jehoash:– Joash (30), Jehoash (16), him[S] (1)

H3410 יוֹב ***yôb***, n.pr.m. Job

H3411 [1]יוֹבָב ***yôbāb***[1], n.pr.m. [2] Jobab, "*howl*":– Jobab (2)

H3412 [2]יוֹבָב ***yôbāb***[2], n.pr.m. [7] [√ 3291]. Jobab, "*howl*":– Jobab (7)

H3413 יוֹבֵל ***yôbēl***, n.m. [27] [√ 3301]. ram's horn; (blowing of ram's horn) jubilee, (Year of) Jubilee:– jubilee (20), trumpets (3 [+8795]), rams horns (1), ram's horn (1), trumpets (1 [+7967]), year of jubilee (1)

H3414 [1]יוּבַל ***yûbal***[1], n.[m.] [1] [√ 3297]. stream, watercourse:– stream (1)

H3415 [2]יוּבָל ***yûbal***[2], n.pr.m. [1] Jubal:– Jubal (1)

H3416 יוֹזָבָד ***yôzābād***, n.pr.m. [11] [√ 3378 + 2272]. Jozabad, "*Yahweh bestowed*":– Jozabad (11)

H3417 יוֹזָכָר ***yôzākār***, n.pr.m. Jozakar

H3418 יוֹחָא ***yôḥā'***, n.pr.m. [2] Joha:– Joha (2)

H3419 יוֹחָנָן ***yôḥānān***, n.pr.m. [24] [√ 3378 + 2858]. Johanan, "*Yahweh is gracious*":– Johanan (24)

H3420 יוּטָּה ***yûṭṭâ***, n.pr.loc. [3] Juttah, "*extended, inclined*":– Juttah (3)

H3421 יוֹיָדָע ***yôyādā'***, n.pr.m. [5] [√ 3378 + 3359]. Joiada, "*Yahweh knows*":– Joiada (5)

H3422 יוֹיָכִין ***yôyākîn***, n.pr.m. [1] [√ 3378 + 3922]. Jehoiachin, "*Yahweh supports*":– Jehoiachin (1)

H3423 יוֹיָקִים ***yôyāqîm***, n.pr.m. [4] [√ 3378 + 7756]. Joiakim, "*Yahweh lifts up*":– Joiakim (4)

H3424 יוֹיָרִיב ***yôyārîb***, n.pr.m. [5] [√ 3378 + 8189]. Joiarib, "*Yahweh contends, pleads [your case]*":– Joiarib (4), Joiarib's (1)

H3425 יוֹכֶבֶד ***yôkebed***, n.pr.f. [2] [√ 3378 + 3877]. Jochebed, "*Yahweh is glorious*":– Jochebed (2)

H3426 יוּכַל ***yûkal***, n.pr.m. [1] [cf. 3385]. Jehucal, "*Yahweh is capable*":– Jehukal (1)

H3427 [1]יוֹם ***yôm***[1], n.m. [2299] [→ 3429; 10317]. day (24 hours), daytime (in contrast to night); by extension: an indefinite period of time, an era with a certain characteristic, such as "the day of the LORD" and the prophetic "on that day":– day (946), days (475), today (139 [+2021]), time (122), when (44 [+928]), today (38 [+2021, 2021, 2296]), annals (37 [+1821]), always (18 [+3972, 2021]), life (17), reign (17), now (16 [+2021, 2021, 2296]), years (15), now (13 [+2021]), lived (12 [+2118]), as long as (9 [+3972]), lifetime (9), period (9), live long (8 [+799]), times (8), years (8 [+9102]), year (7), reigns (6), as long as (5 [+3972, 2021]), very old (5 [+2416, 995, 928, 2021]), daily (4 [+3427]), day after day (4 [+3972, 2021]), day's (4), first (4 [+3869, 2021]), three-day (4 [+8993]), annual (3), as long as lived (3 [+3972]), daily (3 [+3427, 928]), daily (3 [+928, 3427]), ever since (3 [+6330, 2021, 2021, 2296]), forever (3 [+3972, 2021]), some time (3), those[S] (3), all day long (2 [+928, 2021, 2021, 2085]), always (2 [+3972]), annual (2 [+4946, 3427, 2025]), as long as lives (2 [+3972]), continual (2 [+3972, 2021]), continually (2 [+3972, 2021]), date (2), during (2), each day (2 [+3427, 928]), each day (2 [+928, 3427]), each day's (2 [+3427]), each year (2 [+4946, 3427, 2025]), each year (2 [+4946, 3427, 2025]), ever (2 [+3972, 2021]), for each day (2 [+1821, 928, 3427]), for each day (2 [+1821, 3427, 928]), for life (2 [+3972, 2021]), live (2), other days (2 [+3427]), outlived (2 [+799, 339]), rest (2 [+3972]), some time later (2 [+4946]), still (2 [+6330, 2021, 2021, 2296]), that day (2 [+3427]), weeks (2 [+8651]), whole (2), after (1 [+928]), afternoon (1 [+5742, 2021]), age (1), age (1 [+8044]), ago (1 [+2021]), allotted time (1), altogether a total (1 [+3972]), as long as (1 [+928]), as long as endure (1 [+3869]), as long as live (1 [+3972]), as long as live (1 [+4946]), as long as live (1 [+3972, 4200, 6409]), as usually did (1 [+3869, 928, 3427]), as usually did (1 [+3869, 3427, 928]), at once (1 [+2021]), at once (1 [+928, 2021]), at once (1 [+928, 2021, 2021, 2085]), at this time (1 [+2021]), based on the rate paid (1 [+3869]), beginning (1 [+2021]), birthday (1 [+3528]), birthdays (1), blackness (1 [+4025]), broad daylight (1 [+240]), celebrating (1 [+3202]), daily (1 [+4200, 2021]), daily (1 [+4200, 285]), daily (1 [+1821, 928, 3427]), daily (1 [+1821, 3427, 928]), daily (1 [+3427, 928, 2257]), daily (1 [+928, 3427, 2257]), day (1 [+919]), day after day (1), day by day (1 [+1821, 928, 3427]), day by day (1 [+1821, 3427, 928]), day by day (1 [+1821, 928, 3427, 2257]), day by day (1 [+1821, 3427, 928, 2257]), daylight (1), days (1 [+9102]), days as (1), days of life (1), daytime (1), distant future (1 [+8041]), during (1 [+928]), during that time (1), each[S] (1), each day (1 [+4200, 2021]), each day (1 [+4200, 2021, 4200, 2021, 3427]), each day (1 [+4200, 2021, 3427, 4200, 2021]), each day's (1 [+3427, 928]), each day's (1 [+928, 3427]), each day's (1 [+928, 3427, 2257]), each day's (1 [+3427, 928, 2257]), endures (1), enjoy a long reign (1 [+799]), enjoy long life (1 [+799]), enjoyed long life (1 [+8428]), ever (1 [+3972]), ever (1 [+4946]), ever since (1 [+4946]), every day (1), every day (1 [+4200, 2021]), every day (1 [+3427, 928]), every day (1 [+928, 3427]), every day (1 [+3972, 2256, 3427]), every day (1 [+3972, 3427, 2256]), fate (1), first (1 [+3869]), for a while (1 [+285]), for a while (1 [+3869, 2021]), forever (1 [+4200, 802]), full (1), full moon (1 [+4057]), full years (1 [+9102]), future (1 [+344]), future (1 [+4737]), grown old (1 [+2416, 995, 928, 2021]), how long must wait (1 [+3869, 4537]), if (1 [+928]), if (1 [+928]), immediately (1 [+3869, 2021]), in (1 [+928]), in lifetime (1 [+3972]), in little more than (1 [+6584]), in the course of time (1 [+4200, 4946, 3427]), in the course of time (1 [+4200, 3427, 4946]), in trouble (1 [+7997]), it[S] (1), it's[S] (1 [+2021]), just (1 [+2021]), just now (1 [+2021]), lasting (1 [+6330, 2021, 2021, 2296]), later on (1 [+4946]), life (1 [+889, 2118]), life span (1 [+5031]), lifetime (1 [+2644]), lingering (1 [+6584, 3427]), lingering (1 [+3427, 6584]), lived (1), lives (1), lives (1 [+9102]), long ago (1 [+4946, 7710]), many years (1 [+802]), many years (1 [+2256, 9102]), never (1 [+4202, 4946]), never (1 [+4202, 3972, 2021]), night (1), noon (1 [+4734, 2021]), now (1 [+928, 2021, 2021, 465]), now (1 [+928, 2021, 2021, 465]), old (1 [+9102, 2644]), old (1 [+4946, 7710]), older (1 [+3888]), older (1 [+2418, 4200]), once a year (1 [+4946, 7891, 4200, 2021, 3427]), once a year (1 [+4946, 7891, 3427, 4200, 2021]), one month (1 [+3732]), over a year (1 [+2296, 196, 2296, 9102]), past (1 [+8037]), recently (1 [+2021]), regular (1 [+3972, 2021]), regularly (1 [+4200, 928, 3427]), regularly (1 [+4200, 3427, 928]), sabbath after sabbath (1 [+928, 2021, 8701, 928, 3427, 2021, 8701]), sabbath after sabbath (1 [+928, 3427, 2021, 8701, 928, 2021, 8701]), season (1), select a day (1 [+4946, 4200, 3427]), select a day (1 [+4946, 3427, 4200]), set time (1 [+4595]), seven-day (1 [+8679]), seven-day periods (1 [+8679, 2021]), since (1 [+4200, 4946]), so long (1 [+802]), span of life (1), still (1 [+3869, 2021, 2021, 2296]), sun (1), then[S] (1 [+928, 2021, 2021, 2085]), this[S] (1), today (1), today (1 [+2296]), tomorrow (1 [+4737]), two[S] (1), used to be (1 [+6409]), very old (1 [+2418, 995, 928, 2021]), when (1), when (1 [+4946]), when (1 [+928, 2021]), when (1 [+928, 2021]), when began (1 [+928]), whenever (1 [+928]), while (1 [+928]), while (1 [+928]), while (1 [+3972]), while continues (1 [+3972]), whole month (1 [+2544]), year (1 [+4200, 2021]), yet (1 [+2021]), yet (1 [+6330, 2021, 2021, 2085]), yet (1 [+6330, 2021, 2021, 2156]), younger (1 [+7582, 4200]), NDT (60)

H3428 [2]יוֹם ***yôm***[2], n.m. storm, wind; breath

H3429 יוֹמָם ***yômām***, subst. & adv. [51] [√ 3427]. day; in the daytime, by day:– day (23), by day (19), in the daytime (2), by day (1 [+928]), constant (1), day after day (1), day after day (1 [+9458]), during the day (1), during the daytime (1), in daytime (1)

H3430 יָוָן ***yāwān***, n.pr.g. [10] [→ 3436]. Javan; Greeks; Greece:– Greece (6), Javan (4)

H3431 יָוֵן ***yāwēn***, n.[m.] [2] mire, mud, sediment:– mire (1), miry (1)

H3432 יוֹנָדָב ***yônādāb***, n.pr.m. [7] [√ 3378 + 5605]. Jonadab, "*Yahweh is generous, noble*":– Jonadab (4), Jehonadab (3)

H3433 [1]יוֹנָה ***yônâ***[1], n.f. [32] [→ 1807, 3434; cf. 627, 3039]. dove; pigeon:– dove (14), doves (8), pigeons (8), pigeon (2)

H3434 [2]יוֹנָה ***yônâ***[2], n.pr.m. [19] [√ 3433]. Jonah, "*dove*":– Jonah (18), Jonah's (1)

H3435 [3]יוֹנָה ***yônâ***[3], n.[m.] *or* v.ptcp. Not used in NIVEBC [cf. 3561]. see 3561

H3436 יְוָנִי ***yewānî***, a.g. [1] [√ 3430]. Javanite = Greek:– Greeks (1 [+1201])

H3437 יוֹנֵק ***yônēq***, n.m. [12] [√ 3567]. infant, one nursing; tender shoot:– infants (6), infant (2), infant's (1), nursed (1), nursing (1), tender shoot (1)

H3438 יוֹנֶקֶת ***yôneqet***, n.f. [6] [√ 3567]. new shoot, young shoot (of a plant):– shoots (4), new shoots (1), young shoots (1)

H3439 יוֹנַת אֵלֶם רְחֹקִים ***yônat 'ēlem reḥōqîm***, tt. Not used in NIVEBC [√ 3433 + 381 + 8178]. Dove of the Distant Oaks

H3440 יוֹנָתָן ***yônātān***, n.pr.m. [43] [√ 3378 + 5989]. Jonathan, "*gift of Yahweh*":– Jonathan (43)

H3441 יוֹסֵף ***yôsēp***, n.pr.m. [213] [√ 3578]. Joseph, "*he will add*":– Joseph (178), Joseph's (20), he[S] (5), him[S] (4), Joseph (2 [+1201]), Joseph (1 [+1074]), his[S] (1), they[S] (1 [+1074]), NDT (1)

H3442 יוֹסִפְיָה ***yôsipyâ***, n.pr.m. [1] [√ 3578 + 3378]. Josiphiah, "*Yahweh will add*":– Josiphiah (1)

H3443 יוֹעֵאלָה ***yô'ē'lâ***, n.pr.m. [1] Joelah, "*let him help*":– Joelah (1)

H3444 יוֹעֵד ***yô'ēd***, n.pr.m. [1] [√ 3378 + 6332]. Joed, "*Yahweh is witness*":– Joed (1)

H3445 יוֹעֶזֶר ***yô'ezer***, n.pr.m. [1] [√ 3378 + 6469]. Joezer, "*Yahweh is help*":– Joezer (1)

H3446 יוֹעֵץ ***yô'ēṣ***, n.m. *or* v.ptcp. [21] [√ 3619]. counselor, adviser, one who gives advice and direction, with the implication that the advice given is wise and valuable:– advisers (6), counselor (6), rulers (3), adviser (1), counselors (1), encouraged (1), give counsel (1), officials (1), ruler (1)

H3447 יוֹעָשׁ ***yô'āš***, n.pr.m. [2] [√ 3378 + 6429]. Joash, "*Yahweh has bestowed*":– Joash (2)

H3448 יוֹצֵאת ***yôṣē't***, n.f. *or* v.ptcp. [1] [√ 3655]. going into captivity, departure; some sources: miscarriage (of cattle):– going into captivity (1)

H3449 יוֹצָדָק ***yôṣādāq***, n.pr.m. [4] [√ 3378 + 7405]. Jozadak, "*Yahweh is righteous*":– Jozadak (4)

H3450 יוֹצֵר ***yôṣēr***, n.[m.] *or* v.ptcp. [20] [√ 3670]. potter:– potter (11), potter's (4), him[S] (1 [+2021]), potters (1), pottery (1), pottery (1 [+3998]), pottery (1 [+5574])

H3451 יוֹקִים ***yôqîm***, n.pr.m. [1] [√ 3378? + 7756]. Jokim, "*Yahweh lifts up*":– Jokim (1)

H3452 [1]יוֹרֶה ***yôreh***[1], n.[m.] *or* v.ptcp. [2] [√ 3721]. archer:– archers (1), they[S] (1 [+2021])

H3453 [2]יוֹרֶה ***yôreh***[2], n.[m.] [2] [√ 8115]. autumn (i.e., the time of the early rains, from the end of October to the beginning of December):– autumn rains (2)

H3454 יוֹרָה ***yôrâ***, n.pr.m. [1] Jorah, "*one born during harvest*":– Jorah (1)

H3455 יוֹרַי ***yôray***, n.pr.m. [1] Jorai, "[poss.] *Yahweh sees; whom Yahweh teaches*":– Jorai (1)

H3456 יוֹרָם ***yôrām***, n.pr.m. [20] [√ 3378 + 8123]. Joram; Jehoram, "*Yahweh is exalted*":– Joram (14), Jehoram (4), Jehoram's (1), him[S] (1)

H3457 יוּשַׁב חֶסֶד ***yûšab ḥesed***, n.pr.m. [1] Jushab-Hesed, "*loyal love will be returned*":– Jushab-Hesed (1)

H3458 יוֹשִׁבְיָה ***yôšibyâ***, n.pr.m. [1] [√ 3782 + 3378]. Joshibiah, "*Yahweh places*":– Joshibiah (1)

H3459 יוֹשָׁה ***yôšâ***, n.pr.m. [1] Joshah, "*gift of Yahweh*":– Joshah (1)

H3460 יוֹשַׁוְיָה ***yôšawyâ***, n.pr.m. [1] [√ 3782 + 3378]. Joshaviah, "*Yahweh places*":– Joshaviah (1)

H3461 יוֹשָׁפָט ***yôšāpāṭ***, n.pr.m. [2] [√ 3378 + 9149]. Joshaphat, "*Yahweh judges*":– Joshaphat (2)

H3462 יוֹתָם ***yôtām***, n.pr.m. [24] [√ 3378 + 9447]. Jotham, "*Yahweh will complete*":– Jotham (22), Jotham's (2)

H3463 יוֹתֵר ***yôtēr***, n.m. *or* v.ptcp. [10] [√ 3855]. the rest; gain, advantage, profit; more than:– advantage (1), anything in addition (1), benefits (1), but (1 [+2256]), gain (1), not only (1), overwise (1 [+2681]), profit (1), rest (1), than (1 [+4946])

H3464 יְזוּאֵל ***yezû'ēl***, n.pr.m. Not used in NIVEBC [cf. 3465]. Jezuel, see 3465

H3465 יְזִיאֵל ***yezî'ēl***, n.pr.m. [1] [cf. 3464, 3466?, 3467?]. Jeziel:– Jeziel (1)

H3466 יִזִּיָּה ***yizziyyâ***, n.pr.m. [1] [cf. 3465?]. Izziah, "*may Yahweh sprinkle [in atonement]; Yahweh unites*":– Izziah (1)

H3467 יָזִיז ***yāzîz***, n.pr.m. [1] [cf. 3465?]. Jaziz:– Jaziz (1)

H3468 יִזְלִיאָה ***yizlî'â***, n.pr.m. [1] Izliah, "*long living, eternal; Yahweh delivers*":– Izliah (1)

H3469 יָזַן ***yāzan***, v. [1] [Pu] to be lusty, be in the rut:– lusty (1)

H3470 יְזַנְיָה ***yezanyâ***, n.pr.m. [1] Jezaniah, "*Yahweh gives ear*":– Jezaniah (1)

H3471 יְזַנְיָהוּ ***yezanyāhû***, n.pr.m. [1] Jaazaniah, "*Yahweh listens*":– Jaazaniah (1)

H3472 יֶזַע ***yeza'***, n.[m.] [1] [→ 2399]. perspiration, sweat:– perspire (1)

H3473 יִזְרָח ***yizrāḥ***, a.g. [1] Izrahite:– Izrahite (1)

H3474 יִזְרַחְיָה ***yizraḥyâ***, n.pr.m. [3] [√ 2436 + 3378]. Izrahiah; Jezrahiah, "*Yahweh shines* or *will arise*":– Izrahiah (2), Jezrahiah (1)

H3475 [1]יִזְרְעֶאל ***yizre'e'l***[1], n.pr.m. [2] [→ 3476, 3477; cf. 2445 + 446]. Jezreel, "*God [El] will sow*":– Jezreel (2)

H3476 [2]יִזְרְעֶאל ***yizre'e'l***[2], n.pr.loc. [34] [√ 3475]. Jezreel, "*God [El] will sow*":– Jezreel (34)

H3477 יִזְרְעֵאלִי ***yizre'ē'lî***, a.g. [13] [√ 3475]. Jezreelite, of Jezreel, "*of Jezreel*":– Jezreelite (7), of Jezreel (5), NDT (1)

H3478 יְחֻבָּה ***yeḥubbâ***, n.pr.m. Not used in NIVEBC [√ 2465]. Jehubbah, see 2465

H3479 יָחַד ***yāḥad***, v. [3] [→ 3480, 3481, 3495]. [Q] to join, be united; [P] to unite:– join (2), give undivided (1)

H3480 יַחַד ***yaḥad***, n.[m.] (used as adv.) [44] [√ 3479]. together, along with, in close proximity or concord either in space or time; by extension: close association in relationships, unity:– together (14), all (8), alike (2), also (2), completely (2), each other (2), alone (1), along with (1), both (1), by no means (1 [+4202]), in force (1), join (1 [+2118, 4222, 4200]), regrouped (1 [+665]), side by side (1), they (1), together in unity (1), with (1), NDT (3)

H3481 יַחְדָּו **yaḥdāw**, adv. [96] [√3479]. together; altogether; at the same time:– together (55), all (9), both (4), alike (3), as well (2), fitted (2 [+9447]), together with (2), all of them (1), alone (1), assemble (1 [+5602]), assemble (1 [+7695]), came together (1 [+7695]), come together (1 [+7695]), each other (1), even (1), joined forces (1 [+665]), people[S] (1), two men (1 [+408, 2256, 278]), with (1), with one accord (1), NDT (6)

H3482 יַחְדּוֹ **yaḥdô**, n.pr.m. [1] [cf. 3483]. Jahdo, "*[God] gives joy*":– Jahdo (1)

H3483 יַחְדֹּי **yaḥdōy**, n.pr.m. Not used in NIVEBC [cf. 3482]. see 3482

H3484 יַחְדִּיאֵל **yaḥdî'ēl**, n.pr.m. [1] [√2525 + 446]. Jahdiel, "*God [El] gives joy*":– Jahdiel (1)

H3485 יֶחְדְּיָהוּ **yeḥd^{e}yāhû**, n.pr.m. [2] [√2525 + 3378]. Jehdeiah, "*Yahweh rejoices [in his works]*":– Jehdeiah (2)

H3486 יְחוּאֵל **y^{e}ḥû'ēl**, n.pr.m. Not used in NIVEBC [cf. 3493]. Jehuel, see

H3487 יַחֲזִיאֵל **yaḥ^{a}zî'ēl**, n.pr.m. [6] [√2600 + 446]. Jahaziel, "*God [El] will see*":– Jahaziel (6)

H3488 יַחְזְיָה **yaḥz^{e}yâ**, n.pr.m. [1] [√2600 + 3378]. Jahzeiah, "*Yahweh sees*":– Jahzeiah (1)

H3489 יְחֶזְקֵאל **y^{e}ḥezqē'l**, n.pr.m. [3] [√2616 + 446]. Ezekiel; Jehezkel, "*God [El] gives strength*":– Ezekiel (2), Jehezkel (1)

H3490 יְחִזְקִיָּה **y^{e}ḥizqiyyâ**, n.pr.m. [3] [√2616 + 3378]. Hezekiah, "*Yahweh is [my] strength*":– Hezekiah (3)

H3491 יְחִזְקִיָּהוּ **y^{e}ḥizqiyyāhû**, n.pr.m. [41] [√2616 + 3378]. Hezekiah; Jehizkiah, "*Yahweh gives strength*":– Hezekiah (37), Hezekiah's (2), Jehizkiah (1), he[S] (1)

H3492 יַחְזֵרָה **yaḥzērâ**, n.pr.m. [1] [√2614]. Jahzerah, "[poss.] *prudent*":– Jahzerah (1)

H3493 יְחִיאֵל **y^{e}ḥî'ēl**, n.pr.m. [14] [→ 3494; cf. 2649 + 446, 3486]. Jehiel, "*God [El] lives*":– Jehiel (14)

H3494 יְחִיאֵלִי **y^{e}ḥî'ēlî**, n.pr.m. [2] [√3493]. Jehieli, "*of Jehiel*":– Jehieli (2)

H3495 יָחִיד **yāḥîd**, a. & subst. [12] [√3479]. only son, only child (special and unique to the parents); precious life; alone, solitary:– only son (5), lonely (2), only child (2), precious life (2), cherished (1)

H3496 יְחִיָּה **y^{e}ḥiyyâ**, n.pr.m. [1] [√2649 + 3378]. Jehiah, "*Yahweh lives*":– Jehiah (1)

H3497 יָחִיל **yāḥîl**, a.vbl. [1] [√3498]. waiting:– wait (1)

H3498 יָחַל **yāḥal**, v. [43] [→ 3497, 3499, 3500, 9347]. [N] to wait; [P] to wait for, put hope in, expect; [H] to wait, put hope in:– put hope (14), hope (7), wait (7), waited (6), depend (1), expect (1), expectantly (1), given hope (1), hope unfulfilled (1), looked (1), looking (1), wait for (1), wait in hope (1)

H3499 יַחְלְאֵל **yaḥl^{e}'ēl**, n.pr.m. [2] [→ 3500; cf. 3498 + 446]. Jahleel, "*wait for God [El];* [poss.] *may God [El] show himself friendly*":– Jahleel (2)

H3500 יַחְלְאֵלִי **yaḥl^{e}'ēlî**, a.g. [1] [√3499; cf. 3498 + 446]. Jahleelite, "*of Jahleel*":– Jahleelite (1)

H3501 יָחַם **yāḥam**, v. [6] [→ 2771, 2779; cf. 2801]. [Q] to be in (breeding) heat, be in the rut; [P] to be in (breeding) heat, to mate, to conceive:– in heat (2), breeding (1 [+2021, 7366]), conceived (1), mate (1), mated (1)

H3502 יַחְמוּר **yaḥmûr**, n.[m.] [2] [√2813]. roebuck, the roe deer:– roe deer (1), roebucks (1)

H3503 יַחְמַי **yaḥmay**, n.pr.m. [1] [√2570]. Jahmai, "*protect*":– Jahmai (1)

H3504 יָחֵף **yāḥēp**, a. [5] barefoot:– barefoot (4), bare (1)

H3505 יַחְצְאֵל **yaḥṣ^{e}'ēl**, n.pr.m. [2] [→ 3506; cf. 2936 + 446]. Jahziel, Jahzeel, "*God [El] apportions*":– Jahzeel (1), Jahziel (1)

H3506 יַחְצְאֵלִי **yaḥṣ^{e}'ēlî**, a.g. [1] [√3505; cf. 2936 + 446]. Jahzeelite, "*of Jahzeel*":– Jahzeelite (1)

H3507 יַחְצִיאֵל **yaḥ^{a}ṣî'ēl**, n.pr.m. [1] [√2936 + 446]. Jahziel:– Jahziel (1)

H3508 יָחַר **yāḥar**, v.? Not used in NIVEBC [cf. 336]. see 336

H3509 יָחַשׂ **yāḥaś**, v. [20] [→ 2249, 3510]. [Ht] to enroll oneself in a genealogical record, be in a family register:– family (2), listed (2), listed in genealogy (2), be listed in the genealogical record (1), deal with genealogies (1), enrolled in the genealogical records (1), genealogical record listed (1), kept a genealogical record (1), listed in genealogical records (1), names in the genealogical records (1), registered (1), registration by families (1), was listed in the genealogies (1), were entered in the genealogical records (1), were recorded in the genealogies (1), were registered (1), were registered by genealogy (1)

H3510 יַחַשׂ **yaḥaś**, n.[m.] [1] [√3509]. (book of) genealogy:– genealogical (1)

H3511 יַחַת **yaḥat**, n.pr.m. [8] Jahath, "*snatch up*":– Jahath (8)

H3512 יָטַב **yāṭab**, v. [115] [→ 3513, 3514, 4541, 4774; cf. 3201; 10293, 10320]. [Q] to be good, go well; to be glad, pleased; [H] to do good, right; to make successful, cause to prosper; "to be good in the eyes" indicates pleasure in and acceptance of a person or situation:– go well (14), do good (10), good (10), pleased (7 [+928, 6524]), reform (4), well (3), do what is right (2), enjoy (2), make prosper (2), prosper (2), really change (2 [+3512]), right (2), surely make prosper (2 [+3512]), thoroughly (2), treated well (2), adorned (1), adorns (1), appealed to (1 [+928, 6524]), arranged (1), best (1), better (1), brought success (1), cheer up (1 [+4213]), correctly (1), delighted (1), do right (1), doing good (1), enjoying (1), found favor (1), give joy (1), gives (1), glad (1 [+928, 6524]), goes well (1), good do (1 [+3208]), good done (1), greater (1), ground to powder (1 [+3221]), in good spirits (1 [+4213]), intends (1), is[S] (1), kind (1), make famous (1), make more prosperous (1), makes cheerful (1), please (1), pleased (1), pleased with (1 [+928, 6524]), pleases (1 [+928, 6524]), satisfied (1 [+928, 6524]), share (1), show kindness (1), skilled (1), skilled (1 [+2006]), skillfully (1), stately (1), stately bearing (1), tends (1), thorough (1), to pieces (1), treat well (1), very (1), very pleased (1 [+4213]), well provided for (1), wish (1 [+928, 6524])

H3513 יָטְבָה **yoṭbâ**, n.pr.loc. [1] [√3512]. Jotbah, "*good, pleasant*":– Jotbah (1)

H3514 יָטְבָתָה **yoṭbātâ**, n.pr.loc. [3] [√3512]. Jotbathah, "*good, pleasant*":– Jotbathah (3)

H3515 יְטוּר **y^{e}ṭûr**, n.pr.m. & g. [3] [cf. 3227?]. Jetur:– Jetur (3)

H3516 יַיִן **yayin**, n.m. [142] wine, an alcoholic beverage made of naturally fermented fruit juice (usually grapes), usually diluted with water for general consumption:– wine (133), grapevine (2 [+1728]), wineskins (2 [+5532]), banquet (1 [+5492]), banquet hall (1 [+1074]), old wine (1), sober (1 [+3655, 2021, 4946]), wine offerings (1)

H3517 יַךְ **yak**, var. see 3338

H3518 יְכוֹנְיָה **y^{e}kôn^{e}yâ**, n.pr.m. Not used in NIVEBC [√3382; cf. 3378 + 3922]. Jeconiah

H3519 יָכַח **yākaḥ**, v. [59] [→ 9349, 9350]. [N] to reason together (in a legal case); to be vindicated; [H] to rebuke, discipline, punish; decide, argue, defend, judge; [Ho] to be chastened; [Ht] to lodge a charge against:– rebuke (12), punish (3), rebuked (3), rebukes (3), chosen (2), judge (2), rebuke frankly (2 [+3519]), settle disputes (2), surely call to account (2 [+3519]), accuse (1), accuses (1), are vindicated (1), argue (1), argue case (1), arguments (1), arraign (1), be chastened (1), bring charges (1), complained (1), convict (1), correct (1), correction (1), corrects (1), decide (1), defend (1), defender (1), disciplines (1), establish innocence (1), give decisions (1), lodging a charge (1), mediate (1), pleads (1), prove (1), proved wrong (1), settle the matter (1), upholds justice (1), use[S] (1)

H3520 ¹יָכִין **yākîn[1]**, n.pr.m. [6] [√3922]. Jakin, "*he establishes*":– Jakin (6)

H3521 ²יָכִין **yākîn[2]**, n.pr.m. [2] [→ 3522; cf. 3922]. Jakin, "*he establishes*":– Jakin (2)

H3522 יָכִינִי **yākînî**, a.g. [1] [√3521; cf. 3922]. Jakinite, "*of Jakin*":– Jakinite (1)

H3523 יָכֹל **yākōl**, v. [194] [→ 3524, 3525; 10321; *also used with compound proper names*]. [Q] to be able, capable; overcome, prevail, have victory:– cannot (44 [+4202]), could (38), able (23), can (22), can't (7 [+4202]), overcome (5), must (4), prevail (4), allowed (3), overpower (3), succeed (3), bear (2), can certainly do (2 [+3523]), can do (2), can't (2 [+3523]), ever able (2 [+3523]), overcame (2), surely triumph (2 [+3523]), allowed to (1), attain (1), avail (1), cannot bear (1 [+4202]), cannot stand (1 [+4202]), could do (1), could risk (1), dare (1), dares (1), failed (1 [+4202]), gained the victory (1), have time (1 [+4538]), incapable (1 [+4202]), powerless (1 [+4202]), prevailed (1), tolerate (1), too heavy a burden to carry (1 [+4202, 5951]), troubled (1 [+4202, 9200]), unable (1 [+4202]), will (1), won (1), NDT (3)

H3524 יְכָלְיָה **y^{e}kolyâ**, n.pr.f. [1] [√3523 + 3378]. Jecoliah, "*Yahweh is able*":– Jekoliah (1)

H3525 יְכָלְיָהוּ **y^{e}kolyāhû**, n.pr.f. [1] [√3523 + 3378]. Jecoliah, "*Yahweh is able*":– Jekoliah (1)

H3526 יְכָנְיָה **y^{e}konyâ**, n.pr.m. [6] [√3382; cf. 3378 + 3922]. Jehoiachin, "*Yahweh supports*":– Jehoiachin (6)

H3527 יְכָנְיָהוּ **y^{e}konyāhû**, n.pr.m. [1] [√3382; cf. 3378 + 3922]. Jehoiachin, "*Yahweh supports*":– Jehoiachin (1)

H3528 יָלַד **yālad**, v. [490] [→ 2263, 3529, 3530, 3531, 3533, 3535, 4256, 4580, 4582, 9351?, 9352]. [Q] to give birth to, have a child, become the father of; [Qp, N, Pu, Ho] to be born, be a descendant; [P] to assist in childbirth, be a midwife; [H] to become the father of, cause to come to birth:– father (147), bore (48), gave birth (46), had (31), born (24), were born (20), give birth (17), borne (13), in labor (12), have (8), gives birth (7), midwives (7), was born (7), is born (5), be born (4), bear children (4), mother (4), bear (3), bears (3), given birth (3), has (3), having children (3), baby (2), been born (2), birth (2), borne children (2), childless (2 [+4202]), descendants (2), had a baby (2), had a son (2), had children (2), have a child (2), have children (2), in childbirth (2), midwife (2), was descended (2), be brought forth (1), bear a child (1), bearing children (1), bears a son (1), begotten (1), birthday (1 [+3427]), bore a child (1), bore young (1), bring (1), bring to delivery (1), child was born (1), childbirth (1), children (1), children born (1), daughter (1), descendant (1), fathered (1), fathers (1), forefather (1), gave life (1), give delivery (1), giving birth (1), had sons (1), helping during childbirth (1), lay (1), making bud (1), man fathers son (1), men[S] (1), mother bore (1), native-born (1 [+928, 2021, 824]), near the time of delivery (1), newborn (1), placed at birth (1), registered ancestry (1), son be born (1), takes effect (1), women[S] (1), yet unborn (1), NDT (5)

H3529 יֶלֶד **yeled**, n.m. [89] [√3528]. male child, young boy; this can refer to a wide range of ages, from infant to young adult:– child (21), children (20), young men (11), boy (8), boys (6), baby (4), boy's (3), young (3), sons (2), youth (2), babies (1), baby's (1), brood (1), gives birth prematurely (1 [+3655]), little ones (1), pagan (1 [+5799]), son (1), young man (1), NDT (1)

H3530 יַלְדָּה **yaldâ**, n.f. [3] [√3528]. female child, young girl; this can refer to a wide range of ages, from infant to young adult:– girls (2), girl (1)

H3531 יַלְדוּת **yaldût**, n.f. [3] [√3528]. youth, childhood:– young (2), youth (1)

H3532 יָלָה **yālah**, v. [1] [cf. 4263]. [Q] to waste away, languish, implying anxiety and consternation:– wasted away (1)

H3533 יִלּוֹד **yillôd**, a. [5] [√3528]. born (children):– born (4), children born (1)

H3534 יָלוֹן **yālôn**, n.pr.m. [1] Jalon:– Jalon (1)

H3535 יָלִיד **yālîd**, a. [13] [√3528]. born (child, slave child); (pl.) descendants, children:– descendants (5), born (3), those born (3), slave by birth (1 [+1074]), sons (1)

H3536 יָלַל **yālal**, v. [29] [→ 3537, 3538]. [H] to wail, howl:– wail (26), turn to wailing (1), wails (1), weep (1)

H3537 יְלֵל **y^{e}lēl**, n.[m.] [1] [√3536]. howling, wailing-cry:– howling (1)

H3538 יְלָלָה **y^{e}lālâ**, n.f. [5] [√3536]. wailing, lamentation, howling:– wailing (3), lamentation (1), wail (1)

H3539 יַלֶּפֶת **yallepet**, n.f. [2] running sore; some sources: scab, ringworm:– running sores (2)

H3540 יֶלֶק **yeleq**, n.m. [9] locust, grasshopper; young locust, possibly some stage in the development of the locust:– grasshoppers (2), locusts (2), swarm of locusts (2), young locusts (2), young locust (1)

H3541 יַלְקוּט **yalqûṭ**, n.[m.] [1] [√4377]. pouch:– pouch (1)

H3542 יָם **yām**, n.m. [396] [cf. 42; 10322]. sea; seashore; the west (the direction of the Mediterranean Sea relative to the Near East); by extension: a large container for holding water; the recurring image of the sea as a terrifying danger and opponent of the LORD has its source in the Sea (Yamm) as a hostile Canaanite god:– sea (249), west (36), west (28 [+2025]), seas (21), Mediterranean sea (9), western (6), seashore (5), seashore (5 [+8557]), coast (4 [+2572]), it[S] (4 [+2021]), high seas (3 [+4213]), westward (3 [+2025]), coast (2), dead sea (2 [+6858]), lake (2), river (2), western (2 [+2025]), Mediterranean[S] (1), Mediterranean sea (1 [+7149]), coast (1 [+8557]), distant shores (1 [+362]), extend westward (1 [+2025]), overboard (1 [+448, 2021]), sailors (1 [+2480]), seafarers (1 [+6296]), seashore (1 [+2572]), shore (1 [+8557]), waters (1), NDT (2)

H3543 יְמוּאֵל **y^{e}mû'ēl**, n.pr.m. [2] [cf. 5803]. Jemuel:– Jemuel (2)

H3544 יְמִימָה **y^{e}mîmâ**, n.pr.f. [1] [√3553?]. Jemimah, "*dove*":– Jemimah (1)

H3545 ¹יָמִין **yāmîn[1]**, n.f. [140] [→ 1228, 1229, 2124?, 3546, 3547, 3548, 3554, 3556, 9402, 9405]. (direction) right; south, southward (south is right when facing east, the direction of orientation in the ancient Near East); the right is considered culturally to be stronger and of greater prestige than the left; to be seated on the right side of a ruler is a greater position than on the left side:– right (118), south (13), left-handed (2 [+360, 3338]), south (2 [+4946]), hand (1), southward (1 [+448, 2021]), which way (1 [+6584, 196, 6584, 8520]), NDT (2)

H3546 ²יָמִין **yāmîn[2]**, n.pr.m. [6] [→ 3547; cf. 3545]. Jamin, "[poss.] *right hand; south, an indication of [good] fortune*":– Jamin (6)

H3547 יָמִינִי **yāmînî**, a.g. [1] [√3546; cf. 3545]. Jaminite, "*of Jamin*":– Jaminite (1)

H3548 יְמָינִי **y^{e}māynî**, a. Not used in NIVEBC [√3545]. see 3556

H3549 יְמִינִי **y^{e}mînî**, a.g. [4] [√1228]. Benjamite, "*of Benjamin*":– Benjamin (1), Benjamin (1 [+1201, 408]), Benjamite (1 [+408]), tribe of Benjamin (1 [+408])

H3550 יִמְלָא ***yimlā'***, n.pr.m. [2] [√ 4848]. Imlah, *"fullness"*:– Imlah (2)

H3551 יִמְלָה ***yimlâ***, n.pr.m. [2] [√ 4848]. Imlah, *"fullness"*:– Imlah (2)

H3552 יַמְלֵךְ ***yamlēk***, n.pr.m. [1] [√ 4887?]. Jamlech, *"he will reign"*:– Jamlech (1)

H3553 יֵמִם ***yēmim***, n.[m.] [1] [√ 3544?]. hot springs; traditionally: mules; others: adders:– hot springs (1)

H3554 יָמַן ***yāman***, v.den. [5] [√ 3545]. [H] to go the right; (ptcp.) right-handed:– turn to the right (2), go to the right (1), right-handed (1), to the right (1)

H3555 יִמְנָה ***yimnâ***, n.pr.m. [5] [√ 4948]. Imnah; Imnite, *"good fortune"*:– Imnah (4), Imnite (1)

H3556 יְמָנִי ***yᵉmānî***, a. [33] [→ 3548; cf. 3545]. (direction) right:– right (24), south (9)

H3557 יִמְנָע ***yimnā'***, n.pr.m. [1] [√ 4979]. Imna, "[poss.] *he is withheld; luck, fortune*":– Imna (1)

H3558 יָמַר ***yāmar***, v. [1] [H] to change, exchange:– changed (1)

H3559 יִמְרָה ***yimrâ***, n.pr.m. [1] [√ 5286]. Imrah, *"he rebels"*:– Imrah (1)

H3560 יָמַשׁ ***yāmaš***, v. Not used in NIVEBC [cf. 4630, 5491]. [H] to touch

H3561 יָנָה ***yānâ***, v. [19] [Q] to oppress, to crush; [H] to mistreat, take advantage of, oppress:– oppress (5), oppressor (3), mistreat (2), oppressors (2), take advantage of (2), crush (1), do wrong (1), driving (1), mistreated (1), oppresses (1)

H3562 יָנוֹחַ ***yānôaḥ***, n.pr.loc. [3] [√ 5663]. Janoah, *"resting place"*:– Janoah (3)

H3563 יָנוֹחָה ***yānôḥâ***, n.pr.loc. Not used in NIVEBC [√ 5663]. Janohah

H3564 יָנוּם ***yānûm***, n.pr.loc. Not used in NIVEBC [√ 5670?]. Janum

H3565 יָנִים ***yānîm***, n.pr.loc. [1] [√ 5670?]. Janim:– Janim (1)

H3566 יְנִיקָה ***yᵉniqâ***, n.f. [1] [√ 3567]. shoot (of a plant):– shoot (1)

H3567 יָנַק ***yānaq***, v. [16] [→ 735, 3437, 3438, 3566, 4787; cf. 5682]. [Q] to suck, be nursing; [H] to give nourishment, nurse:– nurse (7), nursed (4), drink (1), feast on (1), female (1), nourished (1), suck (1)

H3568 יַנְשׁוּף ***yanšûp***, n.[m.] [3] [√ 5973]. great owl (an unclean bird, variously identified):– great owl (3)

H3569 [1]יָסַד ***yāsad***[1], v. [41] [→ 3571, 3572, 3573, 4586, 4587, 4588, 4589, 4996]. [Q] to lay a foundation, establish, ordain; [N] to be founded; [P] to lay a foundation, establish; [Pu, Ho] to be founded, have a foundation laid:– established (4), laid the foundations (4), the foundation was laid (4), laid the foundation (3), founded (2), set (2), the foundation laid (2), assigned (1), assigned to positions (1), begun (1), doing this[s] (1 [+2021, 6894]), foundations (1), foundations be laid (1), instructed (1), laid foundations (1), lay (1), lay foundations (1), lays the foundation (1), lays the foundations (1), made a place (1), ordained (1), provide a foundation (1), sets (1), sure (1), the foundation been laid (1), the foundations were laid (1), was founded (1)

H3570 [2]יָסַד ***yāsad***[2], v. [2] [cf. 6051]. [N] to associate, conspire (together):– band (1), conspire (1)

H3571 יְסֻד ***yᵉsud***, n.[m.] Not used in NIVEBC [√ 3569]. foundation, beginning

H3572 יְסוֹד ***yᵉsôd***, n.f. & m. [20] [√ 3569]. foundation; base (of an altar); foot (base of the body); by extension: what is firm or enduring:– base (9), foundations (6), foundation (2), foot (1), restoration (1), stand firm (1)

H3573 יְסוּדָה ***yᵉsûdâ***, n.f. [1] [√ 3569]. foundation:– founded (1)

H3574 יִסּוֹר ***yissôr***, n.m. [1] [√ 3579]. corrector, fault-finder, reprover:– correct (1)

H3575 יָסַךְ ***yāsak***, v. Not used in NIVEBC [cf. 5818, 6057]. see 6057

H3576 יִסְכָּה ***yiskâ***, n.pr.f. [1] Iscah:– Iskah (1)

H3577 יִסְמַכְיָהוּ ***yismakyāhû***, n.pr.m. [1] [√ 6164 + 3378]. Ismakiah, *"Yahweh sustains"*:– Ismakiah (1)

H3578 יָסַף ***yāsap***, v. [215] [→ 25, 47, 498, 3441, 3442, 6231; cf. 3388, 10323]. [Q] to add to, to do once more, to do again; [N] to be added to, to gain more, to be joined; [H] to increase, to cause to add to, to continue on, to add to, to happen again:– again (29), again (21 [+6388]), add (19), severely (12), more (9), longer (8), added (7), more (6 [+6388]), longer (5 [+6388]), once more (5), anymore (4 [+6388]), continued (4), make even heavier (4), anymore (3), do again (3), multiply (3), adding (2), all the more (2 [+6388]), enlarged (2), far exceeded (2), never (2 [+4202]), once again (2 [+6388]), once more (2 [+6388]), promote (2), stopped (2 [+4202, 6388]), adds (1), adds length (1), another (1), another (1 [+6388]), any longer (1), any longer (1 [+6388]), attracts (1), back (1 [+6388]), be added (1), bring (1), bring more and more (1), by far (1), carried still further (1), cause to flourish (1), continued (1 [+6388]), do again (1 [+6388]), else (1), ever (1), farther (1), gains (1), gave (1), given even more (1 [+3869, 2179, 2256, 3869, 2179]), grow stronger (1 [+601]), had reaffirm (1), heap (1), heaping (1), increase (1), increase (1 [+6584]), increased (1), increased (1 [+1540, 2256]), join (1), later (1), make again (1 [+6388]), making more (1), more (1 [+8041]), more and more (1), more and more (1 [+6584, 3972]), more besides (1), multiplies (1), over (1), pay an additional (1), persist (1), prolong (1), reach out[s] (1), still another (1 [+6388]), still more (1), stirring up more (1), stop (1 [+4202]), were added (1 [+6388]), without (1 [+4202]), NDT (5)

H3579 [1]יָסַר ***yāsar***[1], v. [42] [→ 3574, 3581, 4592, 5036; cf. 3580]. [Q] to correct, discipline; [N] to accept correction, be warned, be disciplined; [P] to punish, correct, discipline; to instruct, train, discipline; [H] to catch; [Nitpael] to let oneself take warning:– discipline (11), punish (5), scourged (4), disciplines (3), chastened severely (2 [+3579]), instructs (2), scourge (2), take warning (2), accept correction (1), be corrected (1), be warned (1), been disciplined (1), catch (1), corrects (1), disciplined (1), instructed (1), taught (1), trained (1), warning (1)

H3580 [2]יָסַר ***yāsar***[2], v. Not used in NIVEBC [cf. 3579]. [P] to strengthen

H3581 יָסֹר ***yāsōr***, n.[m.] Not used in NIVEBC [√ 3579]. inspector, instructor

H3582 יָע ***yā'***, n.[m.] [9] [√ 3589]. shovel (for altar fires):– shovels (9)

H3583 [1]יַעְבֵּץ ***ya'bēṣ***[1], n.pr.loc. [1] [√ 3584]. Jabez, *"to grieve"*:– Jabez (1)

H3584 [2]יַעְבֵּץ ***ya'bēṣ***[2], n.pr.m. [3] [→ 3583]. Jabez, *"to grieve"*:– Jabez (3)

H3585 יָעַד ***yā'ad***, v. [28] [→ 4595, 4596, 4597, 5676; cf. 6337]. [Q] to select, appoint, set out; [N] to meet with, assemble, band together, join forces; [H] to summon, challenge; [Ho] to be set, be ordered:– meet (8), banded together (3), challenge (3), assemble (2), gathered (2), joined forces (2), appointed (1), met by agreement (1), ordered (1), placed (1), selected (1), selects (1), set (1), turned (1)

H3586 יַעְדָּה ***ya'dâ***, n.pr.m. [2] [√ 6334? *or* 6335?]. Jadah, *"honeycomb"*:– Jadah (2)

H3587 יֶעְדּוֹ ***ye'dô***, n.pr.m. [1] [√ 6335 *or* 6344]. Iddo, "[prob.] *Yahweh has adorned*":– Iddo (1)

H3588 יֶעְדִּי ***ye'dî***, n.pr.m. Not used in NIVEBC [√ 6334? *or* 6335?]. Iddi

H3589 יָעָה ***yā'â***, v. [1] [→ 3582, 3590?, 3599?]. [Q] to sweep away:– sweep away (1)

H3590 יְעוּאֵל ***yᵉ'û'ēl***, n.pr.m. [2] [→ 3599; cf. 3589? + 446]. Jeuel, *"God [El] has preserved"*:– Jeuel (2)

H3591 יְעוּץ ***yᵉ'ûṣ***, n.pr.m. [1] Jeuz, *"he comes to help;* [poss.] *encouraged"*:– Jeuz (1)

H3592 יָעוּר ***yā'ûr***, n.pr.m. Not used in NIVEBC [cf. 3600]. Jaur

H3593 יְעוּשׁ ***yᵉ'ûš***, n.pr.m. [9] [√ 6429; cf. 3601]. Jeush, "[perhaps] *may God aid*":– Jeush (9)

H3594 יָעַז ***yā'az***, v. [1] [cf. 6451]. [N] to be arrogant, be insolent:– arrogant (1)

H3595 יַעֲזִיאֵל ***ya'ᵃzî'ēl***, n.pr.m. [1] Jaaziel, *"God [El] strengthens"*:– Jaaziel (1)

H3596 יַעֲזִיָּהוּ ***ya'ᵃziyyāhû***, n.pr.m. [2] Jaaziah, *"may Yahweh nourish"*:– Jaaziah (2)

H3597 יַעְזֵיר ***ya'zêr***, n.pr.loc. [13] [√ 6468]. Jazer, *"he helps"*:– Jazer (13)

H3598 יָעַט ***yā'aṭ***, v. [1] [cf. 6486]. [Q] to array, cover:– arrayed (1)

H3599 יְעִיאֵל ***yᵉ'î'ēl***, n.pr.m. [13] [→ 3590; cf. 3589? + 446]. Jeiel, *"God [El] has preserved;* [poss.] *God [El] sweeps up"*:– Jeiel (12), Jaaziel (1)

H3600 יָעִיר ***yā'îr***, n.pr.m. [2] [√ 6424; cf. 3592]. Jair, *"he gives light"*:– Jair (2)

H3601 יְעִישׁ ***yᵉ'îš***, n.pr.m. Not used in NIVEBC [√ 6429; cf. 3593]. Jeish

H3602 יַעְכָּן ***ya'kān***, n.pr.m. [1] Jacan:– Jakan (1)

H3603 יָעַל ***yā'al***, v. [23] [→ 1175]. [H] to have value, have use, have value, have benefit:– gain (3), benefit in the least (2 [+3603]), succeed (2), worthless idols (2 [+4202]), advantage (1), benefit (1), best (1), did good (1), do good (1), have lasting value (1), have value (1), of value (1), profit (1), unprofitable (1 [+4202]), useless (1 [+4202]), worthless (1 [+1153]), worthless (1 [+1194]), worthless (1 [+4202])

H3604 [1]יָעֵל ***yā'ēl***[1], n.[m.] [3] [→ 3605, 3606, 3607, 3608]. mountain goat, wild goat:– wild Goats (2), goats (1)

H3605 [2]יָעֵל ***yā'ēl***[2], n.pr.f. [6] [√ 3604]. Jael, *"mountain goat"*:– Jael (6)

H3606 יַעְלָא ***ya'lā'***, n.pr.m. [1] [√ 3607; cf. 3604]. Jaala:– Jaala (1)

H3607 [1]יַעֲלָה ***ya'ᵃlâ***[1], n.f. [1] [→ 3606, 3608; cf. 3604]. (female) mountain goat, ibex; deer:– deer (1)

H3608 [2]יַעֲלָה ***ya'ᵃlâ***[2], n.pr.m. [1] [√ 3607; cf. 3604]. Jaala:– Jaala (1)

H3609 יַעְלָם ***ya'lām***, n.pr.m. [4] [√ 6596]. Jalam:– Jalam (4)

H3610 [1]יַעַן ***ya'an***[1], subst.pp.c. [99] [√ 6701]. for, because, since:– because (34), because (11 [+889]), because (7 [+889]), because (3 [+3954]), because of (3), for (3 [+889]), since (3 [+889]), for (2), since (2), because (1 [+928]), because (1 [+3610, 928]), because (1 [+928, 3610]), because (1 [+561, 4202]), because (1 [+3610, 2256, 928]), because (1 [+2256, 928, 3610]), in (1), since (1 [+3954]), so (1 [+561, 4202]), so that (1 [+889]), therefore (1 [+4200, 4027]), while (1), why (1 [+4537]), NDT (18)

H3611 [2]יַעַן ***ya'an***[2], n.pr.loc. Not used in NIVEBC [→ 1970]. Jaan, see 1970

H3612 יָעֵן ***yā'ēn***, n.[m.] [1] [cf. 3613]. (male) ostrich:– ostriches (1)

H3613 יַעֲנָה ***ya'ᵃnâ***, n.f. [8] [cf. 3612, 6720]. owl; horned owl:– owls (4 [+1426]), horned owl (2 [+1426]), owl (2 [+1426])

H3614 יַעְנַי ***ya'nay***, n.pr.m. [1] [√ 6699?]. Janai, *"he will answer"*:– Janai (1)

H3615 [1]יָעֵף ***yā'ēp***[1], v. [8] [→ 3617, 3618; cf. 6545, 6546]. [Q] to grow tired, be faint, exhaust oneself:– faint (2), tired (2), exhaust (1), fall (1), labor (1), tire (1)

H3616 [2]יָעֵף ***yā'ēp***[2], v. [1] [→ 3618]. [Ho] to be in swift flight:– swift flight (1 [+3618])

H3617 [3]יָעֵף ***yā'ēp***[3], a. [4] [√ 3615]. weary, exhausted, fatigued:– exhausted (2), weary (2)

H3618 יְעָף ***yᵉ'āp***, n.[m.] [1] [√ 3616]. flight; some source: tiredness, weariness:– swift flight (1 [+3616])

H3619 יָעַץ ***yā'aṣ***, v. [59] [→ 3446, 4600, 6783; cf. 6418; 10324, 10325]. [Q] to give advise, give counsel; to purpose, plan, plot, determine; [Qp] to be determined; [N] to seek advise, consult; to confer, to plot (together); [Ht] to consult together, conspire against:– consulted (5), advice gave (3 [+6783]), advise (3), advised (3), planned (3), plotted (3), advice (2), advice given (2 [+6783]), determined (2), planned (2 [+6783]), plot (2), purposed (2), advice offered (1), advise (1 [+6783]), agreed (1), conferred (1), conferring (1), conspire (1), consult (1), consulted advisers (1), consulting (1), counsel (1), counsels (1), decided (1), devises plans (1), give advice (1), give counsel (1), giving advice (1 [+6783]), intend (1), make plans (1), make up (1), meet (1), planning (1 [+6783]), plotted (1 [+6783]), promote (1), seeking advice (1), take advice (1), take counsel (1), warn (1)

H3620 יַעֲקֹב ***ya'ᵃqōb***, n.pr.m. & g. [349] [cf. 6811?, 6812?]. Jacob, *"follower, replacer, one who follows at the heel"*:– Jacob (310), Jacob's (17), he[s] (7), Jacob (6 [+1074]), him[s] (5), his[s] (2), Jacob's (1 [+4200]), them[s] (1 [+1201])

H3621 יַעֲקֹבָה ***ya'ᵃqōbâ***, n.pr.m. [1] Jaakobah, *"may [deity] protect"*:– Jaakobah (1)

H3622 יַעֲקָן ***ya'ᵃqān***, n.pr.loc. Not used in NIVEBC [→ 942; cf. 6826?]. Jaakan

H3623 [1]יַעַר ***ya'ar***[1], n.m. [57] [→ 3625, 3627]. forest, woods, thicket; (cultivated) tree groves:– forest (38), forests (7), thickets (3), woods (3), finest of forests (2 [+4149]), thicket (2), forested (1), groves (1)

H3624 [2]יַעַר ***ya'ar***[2], n.[m.] [1] [→ 3626]. honeycomb:– honeycomb (1)

H3625 [3]יַעַר ***ya'ar***[3], n.pr.m. *or* loc. [1] [√ 3623]. Jaar:– Jaar (1)

H3626 [1]יַעְרָה ***ya'ᵃrâ***[1], n.f. [1] [√ 3624]. honeycomb:– honeycomb (1 [+1831])

H3627 [2]יַעְרָה ***ya'ᵃrâ***[2], n.m. Not used in NIVEBC [√ 3623]. forest

H3628 יַעְרָה ***ya'râ***, n.pr.m. [1] Jarah, see 3586

H3629 יַעְרֵי אֹרְגִים ***ya'ᵃrê 'ōrᵉgîm***, n.pr.m. Not used in NIVEBC [cf. 762]. Jaare-Oregim

H3630 יְעָרִים ***yᵉ'ārîm***, n.pr.loc. [1] [→ 7961]. Jearim, *"timberlands"*:– Jearim (1)

H3631 יַעֲרֶשְׁיָה ***ya'ᵃrešyâ***, n.pr.m. [1] [√ 3378]. Jaareshiah, *"Yahweh plants"*:– Jaareshiah (1)

H3632 יַעֲשׂוּ ***ya'ᵃśû***, n.pr.m. [1] [√ 6913]. Jaasu:– Jaasu (1)

H3633 יַעֲשַׂי ***ya'ᵃśāy***, n.pr.m. Not used in NIVEBC [√ 6913]. Jaasai

H3634 יַעֲשִׂיאֵל ***ya'ᵃśî'ēl***, n.pr.m. [2] [√ 6913 + 446]. Jaasiel, *"God [El] does"*:– Jaasiel (2)

H3635 יִפְדְיָה ***yipdᵉyâ***, n.pr.m. [1] Iphdeiah, *"Yahweh redeems"*:– Iphdeiah (1)

H3636 יָפָה ***yāpâ***, v. [8] [→ 3637, 3638, 3639?, 3642, 3645; cf. 6993]. [Q] to be beautiful, delightful; [P] to adorn, make beautiful; [Ht] to adorn oneself:– beautiful (3), adorn (1), adorn yourself (1), delightful (1), majestic (1), most excellent (1)

H3637 יָפֶה ***yāpeh***, a. [42] [√ 3636]. beautiful, fair, lovely, handsome:– beautiful (23), beautiful (3 [+5260]), lovely (3), beautiful (2 [+9307]), handsome (2 [+5260]), sleek (2 [+5260]), appropriate (1), fair (1), fine (1), handsome (1), handsome appearance (1), sleek (1 [+9307]), well-built (1 [+9307])

H3638 יְפֵה־פִיָּה ***yᵉpēh-piyyâ***, a.f. Not used in NIVEBC [√ 3636; cf. 3645]. beautiful, pretty

H3639 יָפוֹ ***yāpô***, n.pr.loc. [4] [√ 3636?]. Joppa, "*beautiful*":– Joppa (4)

H3640 יָפַח ***yāpaḥ***, v. [1] [→ 3641; cf. 7032]. [Ht] to gasp for breath:– gasping for breath (1)

H3641 יָפֵחַ ***yāpēaḥ***, a. [1] [√ 3640]. breathing out, with a strong implication that this breath results in an action or communication:– spouting accusations (1)

H3642 יְפִי ***yᵉpî***, n.m. [19] [√ 3636]. beauty:– beauty (18), beautiful (1)

H3643 ¹יָפִיעַ ***yāpîa'¹***, n.pr.loc. [1] [√ 3649]. Japhia, "[perhaps] *may the deity shine*":– Japhia (1)

H3644 ²יָפִיעַ ***yāpîa'²***, n.pr.m. [4] [√ 3649]. Japhia, "[perhaps] *may the deity shine*":– Japhia (4)

H3645 יְפֵיפִיָּה ***yᵉpêpiyyâ***, a.[f.] [1] [√ 3636; cf. 3638]. beautiful:– beautiful (1)

H3646 יַפְלֵט ***yaplēṭ***, n.pr.m. [3] [→ 3647; cf. 7117]. Japhlet, "*he delivers;* [poss.] *he escapes*":– Japhlet (2), Japhlet's (1)

H3647 יַפְלֵטִי ***yaplēṭî***, a.g. [1] [√ 3646; cf. 7117]. Japhletite, "*of Japhlet*":– Japhletites (1)

H3648 יְפֻנֶּה ***yᵉpunneh***, n.pr.m. [16] [√ 7155]. Jephunneh, "[perhaps] *may he [God] turn* or *turned*":– Jephunneh (16)

H3649 יָפַע ***yāpa'***, v. [8] [→ 3643, 3644, 3650]. [H] to shine forth, flash; smile:– shine forth (2), light (1), makes flash (1), shine (1), shines forth (1), shone forth (1), smile (1)

H3650 יִפְעָה ***yip'â***, n.f. [2] [√ 3649]. shining splendor:– shining splendor (1), splendor (1)

H3651 יֶפֶת ***yepet***, n.pr.m. [11] [√ 7332]. Japheth, "*enlarge*":– Japheth (10), Japheth's (1 [+4200])

H3652 ¹יִפְתָּח ***yiptāḥ¹***, n.pr.loc. [1] [√ 7337]. Iphtah, "*he opens*":– Iphtah (1)

H3653 ²יִפְתָּח ***yiptāḥ²***, n.pr.m. [29] [√ 7337]. Jephthah, "*Yahweh opens, frees*":– Jephthah (22), him[S] (2), Jephthah's (1), he[S] (1), his[S] (1), NDT (2)

H3654 יִפְתַּח־אֵל ***yiptaḥ-'ēl***, n.pr.loc. [2] [√ 7337 + 446]. Iphtah El, "*God [El] opens*":– Iphtah El (2)

H3655 יָצָא ***yāṣā'***, v. [1067] [→ 3448, 3665, 4604, 4605, 4606, 7368, 7556, 9362]. [Q] to go out, come out; [H] to bring out, lead forth; produce; [Ho] to be brought out; emptied; by extension: to grow (of plants), to have offspring:– brought out (101), went out (83), came out (82), go out (58), go (41), come out (38), left (37), bring out (35), leave (24), went (20), come (19), serve (14), marched out (13), out (11), gone out (10), set out (10), bring (9), coming out (9), brought (8), came (7), comes (7), get out (7), going out (7), spread (7), take (6), comes out (5), escape (5), extending (5), goes out (5), leaving (5), took (5), bring forth (4), brings out (4), go free (4), gone (4), march out (4), produces (4), released (4), removed (4), returned (4), spreading (4), surrender (4), took out (4), bringing out (3), came forward (3), coming (3), fell (3), going (3), had brought (3), lead out (3), led out (3), marching out (3), produce (3), projecting (3), send out (3), sent (3), take out (3), went on (3), withdrew (3), be brought out (2), began (2), bringing (2), burst out (2), came out (2 [+3655]), come forth (2), come up (2), continued (2), depart (2), departed (2), departure (2), drive out (2), ever goes outside (2 [+3655]), experienced soldiers (2 [+7372]), exported (2), flesh and blood (2 [+4946, 2743]), flesh and blood (2 [+4946, 5055]), flow out (2), flows (2), forth (2), free (2), going off duty (2), gone from (2), has (2), imported (2 [+6590, 2256]), is (2), led (2), led in campaigns (2 [+2256, 995, 4200, 7156]), led on military campaigns (2 [+2256, 995]), left (2 [+3655]), marches out (2), move out (2), promised (2 [+4946, 7023]), ready to go out (2 [+7372]), remove (2), said (2 [+4946, 7023]), sank (2), spring up (2), stepped forward (2), surely come out (2 [+3655]), surely march out (2 [+3655]), surrender (2 [+3655]), taken (2), taken out (2), took from (2), utter (2), your own flesh and blood (2 [+4946, 3870]), accompany (1 [+907]), advance (1), advanced (1), advancing (1), among[S] (1), announced (1), appearing (1), arise (1), arisen (1), arises (1), avoid (1), away (1), become known (1), been brought out (1), born (1 [+4946, 8167]), break out (1), breaks out (1), breathed her last (1 [+5883]), bring (1 [+4374, 2256]), bringing forth (1), brings (1), budded (1 [+7258]), burst forth (1), call out (1), came out together (1), came together (1), carried away (1), carried out (1), carry (1), carry out (1), carry out duties (1 [+2256, 995]), charges (1), cleared (1), collapse (1), continue (1), crawling out (1), crossed (1), dart (1), departs (1), descendants (1 [+5883, 3751]), descended (1), did[S] (1), direct descendants (1 [+3751]), discharged (1), do[S] (1), draw (1), drawn (1), drew out (1), empties (1), encamped (1 [+4722]), end (1), escaped (1), exacted (1), extend (1), extended (1), falls (1), fight (1 [+4200, 2021, 4878]), fit for military service (1 [+7372]), flare up (1), flash (1), flashed out (1), flowed (1), flying (1), follow (1), follow (1 [+339]), followed (1), followed (1 [+339]), followed (1 [+6640]), forges (1), fought in (1 [+928]), fought in (1 [+4200]), found (1), freed (1), from gone out (1), give vent to (1), given (1), gives (1), gives birth prematurely (1 [+3529]), go about (1), go about business (1 [+2256, 995]), go forth (1), go into (1), go off (1), go off duty (1), go off to war (1), go up (1), goes (1), goes over (1), grows out (1), gushed out (1 [+8041]), gushing out (1), have leave (1), headed (1), imported (1), is[S] (1 [+4946]), issue (1), joined (1), keep free (1), lay (1), lead (1 [+2256, 995]), lead (1 [+4200, 7156, 2256, 995]), leads out (1), leaves (1), led out (1 [+4200, 7156]), lost (1), made come out (1), make shine (1), make spew out (1 [+4946, 7023]), makes come up (1), march on (1), met expenses (1), of his own (1 [+3751, 2257]), on duty (1 [+995, 2256]), on the way (1), on way (1), out came (1), out goes (1), paid (1), passing (1), pierced (1), pour out (1), pours (1), prevails (1), produce (1 [+9311, 2446]), produced (1), promote (1), pursue (1 [+339]), put away (1), put out (1 [+2021, 2575]), reached (1), ready for military service (1 [+7372]), release (1), risen (1), rises (1), rising (1), rode out (1), rush (1), rushed out (1), say (1 [+4946, 7023]), send away (1), sent out (1), serve (1 [+2256, 995]), serve in (1), set free (1), sets free (1), shines out (1), slip out (1), sober (1 [+2021, 3516, 4946]), sow (1), speak (1), spoke (1), spreads (1), spring (1), starting (1), stepped out (1), stretch (1), surrendered (1), take back (1), telling (1), took part in (1 [+4200]), travel about (1 [+2256, 995]), turned (1), undertook (1), unsheathed (1 [+4946, 9509]), uttered (1 [+4946]), venture out (1), vindicated (1 [+7407]), was[S] (1), was brought out (1), went away (1), went outside (1), were (1), whatever[S] (1 [+2021]), wherever goes (1 [+928, 995, 2256, 928]), wherever goes (1 [+928, 2256, 928, 995]), NDT (9)

H3656 יָצַב ***yāṣab***, v. [49] [cf. 5893, 5895; 10326]. [Ht] to stand one's ground, confront; to stand before, present oneself, commit oneself:– stand (6), stood (6), took stand (3), confront (2), present themselves (2), present yourselves (2), presented themselves (2), serve (2), stand up (2), stay (2), take positions (2), argue case (1), commit themselves (1), kept distance (1 [+4946, 5584]), place (1), present himself (1), rise up (1), sided (1), stand firm (1), stand out (1), stand still (1), standing (1), station myself (1), take a stand (1), take place (1), take up positions (1), took places (1), wait (1), withstand (1 [+6640])

H3657 יָצַג ***yāṣag***, v. [16] [cf. 3668]. [H] to set, place, present; touch; [Ho] to be left behind:– set (4), made (2), placed (2), leave (1), leave behind (1), maintain (1), make bare (1), place (1), presented (1), separate (1 [+4200, 963]), touch (1)

H3658 ¹יִצְהָר ***yiṣhār¹***, n.[m.] [23] [→ 3659, 3660; cf. 7414]. olive oil:– olive oil (19), oil (2), anointed (1 [+1201, 2021]), olive trees (1 [+2339])

H3659 ²יִצְהָר ***yiṣhār²***, n.pr.m. [9] [√ 3658; cf. 7414]. Izhar, "*the shining one*":– Izhar (9)

H3660 יִצְהָרִי ***yiṣhārî***, a.g. [4] [√ 3658; cf. 7414]. Izharite, "*of Izhar*":– Izharites (4)

H3661 ¹יָצוּעַ ***yāṣûa'¹***, n.[m.] [5] [√ 3667]. bed, couch:– bed (2), bed (1 [+6911]), couch (1), marriage bed (1)

H3662 ²יָצוּעַ ***yāṣûa'²***, n.[m.] Not used in NIVEBC. see 3666

H3663 יִצְחָק ***yiṣḥāq***, n.pr.m. [108] [√ 7464; cf. 3773]. Isaac, "*he laugh, he will laugh* or *mock; [God] laughs*":– Isaac (101), Isaac's (2), he[S] (2), his[S] (1), who[S] (1), NDT (1)

H3664 יִצְחָר ***yiṣḥār***, n.pr.m. Not used in NIVEBC [cf. 7468]. Jizhar

H3665 יָצִיא ***yāṣî'***, a. [1] [√ 3655]. coming forth:– sons (1)

H3666 יָצִיעַ ***yāṣîa'***, n.m. [3] [√ 3667]. structure, room, often referring to an annex, wing, or level of a building:– floor (1), side rooms (1), structure (1)

H3667 יָצַע ***yāṣa'***, v. [4] [→ 3661, 3666, 5201]. [H] to spread out bedding; [Ho] to be spread out:– are spread out (1), lay (1), lying (1), make bed (1)

H3668 יָצַק ***yāṣaq***, v. [51] [→ 3669, 4607, 4609, 5187?, 7440?; cf. 3657]. [Q] to pour out, cast out; [Qp] be cast out, be poured out, be smelted; [H] to pour out, spread out; [Ho] to be poured out, be washed away; be anointed:– pour (11), cast (10), poured (6), poured out (4), firm (2), hard (2), pouring (2), were cast (2), afflicted (1), been anointed (1), frozen (1), hard (1 [+4200, 2021, 4607]), is smelted (1), pour out (1), ran (1), serve (1), served (1), set down (1), spread out (1), washed away (1)

H3669 יְצֻקָה ***yᵉṣuqâ***, n.f. [1] [√ 3668]. casting (of metal), with a focus that this is one piece:– one piece with (1)

H3670 יָצַר ***yāṣar***, v. [42] [→ 3450, 3671, 3672, 3673, 3674]. [Q] to form, fashion, shape, create; (of God) the Maker, the Creator; [N] to be formed; [Pu] to be formed; [Ho] to be forged, be formed; usually from existing material; God as Creator or Maker, has its focus his planning and forming the creation as a skilled craftsman:– formed (15), maker (4), planned (4), forms (3), made (2), preparing (2), shapes (2), brings on (1), craftsman (1), creator (1), fashioned (1), forged (1), form (1), make (1), makes (1), ordained (1), was formed (1)

H3671 ¹יֵצֶר ***yēṣer¹***, n.m. [9] [→ 3672; cf. 3670]. something formed, creation; inclination, disposition, motivation:– inclination (2), creation (1), desire (1), desires (1), disposed (1), formed (1), minds (1), pot (1)

H3672 ²יֵצֶר ***yēṣer²***, n.pr.m. [3] [→ 3673; cf. 3670, 3671]. Jezer, "*formed, fashioned*":– Jezer (3)

H3673 יִצְרִי ***yiṣrî***, a.g. & n.pr.m. [2] [√ 3672; cf. 3670]. Izri; Jezerite, "*Yahweh designs*":– Izri (1), Jezerite (1)

H3674 יְצֻרִים ***yᵉṣurîm***, n.m.pl. [1] [√ 3670]. frame, body, limbs, that which gives visible form to a person:– frame (1)

H3675 יָצַת ***yāṣat***, v. [26] [cf. 7455]. [Q] to set ablaze; [N] to burn, be burned; [H] to kindle, set on fire:– set on fire (6 [+928, 2021, 836]), set fire (4 [+836]), kindle (3), set on fire (3 [+836, 928, 2021]), been burned (2), are burned (1), burn (1), burns (1), kindled (1), set ablaze (1 [+928, 2021, 836]), set on fire (1), set on fire (1 [+836]), sets ablaze (1)

H3676 יֶקֶב ***yeqeb***, n.m. [16] [cf. 5918]. winepress; (wine or oil) vat:– winepress (7), vats (3), winepresses (3), presses (2), wine vat (1)

H3677 יְקַבְצְאֵל ***yᵉqabṣᵉ'ēl***, n.pr.loc. [1] [√ 7695 + 446]. Jekabzeel, "*God [El] gathers*":– Jekabzeel (1)

H3678 יָקַד ***yāqad***, v. [8] [→ 3679, 3683, 4611, 4612; 10328, 10329]. [Q] to burn; to kindle a fire; [Ho] to be burning, be kindled:– be kept burning (3), burn (2), burning (1), burns (1), kindled (1)

H3679 יְקֹד ***yᵉqōd***, n.[m.] [2] [√ 3678]. blazing, burning:– blazing (1), fire (1)

H3680 יָקְדְעָם ***yoqdᵉ'ām***, n.pr.loc. [1] Jokdeam:– Jokdeam (1)

H3681 יָקֶה ***yāqeh***, n.pr.m. [1] Jakeh, "*prudent*":– Jakeh (1)

H3682 יְקָהָה ***yᵉqāhâ***, n.f. [1] obedience:– obedience (1)

H3683 יָקוּד ***yāqûd***, n.[m.] [1] [√ 3678]. hearth (of a fireplace):– hearth (1)

H3684 יָקוֹט ***yāqôṭ***, a. [1] [cf. 7753]. fragile (thing); possibly referring to a spider's web:– fragile (1)

H3685 יְקוּם ***yᵉqûm***, n.[m.] [3] [√ 7756]. living thing, living creature:– living thing (2), living creature (1)

H3686 יָקוֹשׁ ***yāqôš***, n.[m.] Not used in NIVEBC [√ 3704]. fowler, bait-layer

H3687 יָקוּשׁ ***yāqûš***, n.[m.] [4] [√ 3704]. fowler, one who snares birds:– fowler (1), fowler's (1), men who snare birds (1), snares (1 [+7062])

H3688 יְקוּתִיאֵל ***yᵉqûtî'ēl***, n.pr.m. [1] Jekuthiel, "*God [El] will nourish*":– Jekuthiel (1)

H3689 יָקַח ***yāqaḥ***, v. [1] [H] to become insolent, have audacity:– insolent (1)

H3690 יָקְטָן ***yoqṭān***, n.pr.m. [6] [√ 3699]. Joktan, "*smaller*":– Joktan (6)

H3691 יָקִים ***yāqîm***, n.pr.m. [2] [√ 7756]. Jakim, "*he will establish*":– Jakim (2)

H3692 יַקִּיר ***yaqqîr***, a. [1] [√ 3700; 10330]. dear, precious:– dear (1)

H3693 יְקַמְיָה ***yᵉqamyâ***, n.pr.m. [3] [√ 7756 + 3378]. Jekamiah, "*Yahweh will establish*":– Jekamiah (3)

H3694 יְקַמְעָם ***yᵉqam'ām***, n.pr.m. [2] [√ 7756 + 6639]. Jekameam, "*[my] kinsman establishes*":– Jekameam (2)

H3695 יָקְמְעָם ***yoqmᵉ'ām***, n.pr.loc. [2] [√ 3696?]. Jokmeam, "*let the people arise*":– Jokmeam (2)

H3696 יָקְנְעָם ***yoqnᵉ'ām***, n.pr.loc. [4] [√ 3695?]. Jokneam:– Jokneam (4)

H3697 יָקַע ***yāqa'***, v. [8] [cf. 5936]. [Q] to turn (away), wrench; [H] to kill and expose; [Ho] to be killed and exposed:– killed and exposed (2), turned away in disgust (2), been killed and exposed (1), kill and expose (1), turn away (1), wrenched (1)

H3698 יְקִפָּאוֹן ***yᵉqippā'ôn***, v. Not used in NIVEBC [√ 7884]. see 7885

H3699 יָקַץ ***yāqaṣ***, v. [11] [→ 3690; cf. 7810]. [Q] to wake up, awake:– awoke (6), woke up (3), awakened (1), wake up (1)

H3700 יָקַר ***yāqar***, v. [11] [→ 3692, 3701, 3702]. [Q] to be precious, be costly; become well known; [H] to make scarce:– precious (4), have respect for (2 [+928, 6524]), costly (1), make scarcer (1), seldom (1), valued (1), well known (1 [+4394])

H3701 יָקָר ***yāqār***, a. [34] [√ 3700]. precious, valuable, quality, pertaining to items that are rare, beloved, or splendid:– precious (18), high-grade (3), rare (2), fine (1), flowers (1), good quality (1), honored (1), outweighs (1 [+4946]), priceless (1), riches (1 [+2104]), splendor (1), valuable things (1 [+2104]), very (1), worthy (1)

H3702 יְקָר ***yᵉqār***, n.m. [17] [√ 3700; 10331]. honor, splendor, riches, valuable things:– honor (7), wealth (2), honor (1 [+6913]), precious things (1), price (1), rare (1), respect (1 [+5989]), splendor (1), treasures (1), valuables (1)

H3703 יִקְרָה ***yiqrâ***, a. Not used in NIVEBC [√ 7936]. meeting

H3704 יָקֹשׁ ***yāqaš***, v. [9] [→ 3686, 3687, 3705, 4613; cf. 5943, 7772]. [Q] to lay a bird snare, set a trap; [N, Pu] to be ensnared, be trapped:– are ensnared (1), are trapped (1), be ensnared (1), be snared (1), been trapped (1), fowler's (1), laid (1), set a trap (1), snared (1)

H3705 יָקְשָׁן ***yoqšān***, n.pr.m. [4] [√ 3704]. Jokshan:– Jokshan (4)

H3706 יָקְתְאֵל ***yoqtᵉ'ēl***, n.pr.loc. [2] [√ 446]. Joktheel:– Joktheel (2)

H3707 יָרֵא¹ ***yārē'¹***, v. [332] [→ 3710, 3711, 4616; cf. 4624]. [Q] to be afraid, be frightened; to revere, respect; [N] to be awesome, be dreadful, be feared; [P] to frighten, terrify, intimidate; in some contexts fear relates to terror and fright, in other contexts fear relates to honor, respect and awe, as in "the fear of the LORD":– afraid (120), fear (92), awesome (24), feared (12), worship (10), revere (9), be feared (4), dreadful (4), terrified (4 [+4394]), awesome wonders (3), intimidate (3), alarmed (2), despair (2), frightened (2), have fear (2), revered (2), revering (2), stand in awe (2), stood in awe (2), worshiped (2), awesome works (1), believer (1), dreaded (1), dreadful (1 [+4394]), feared (1 [+3711]), fearfully (1), fearing (1), fears (1), filled with awe (1), filled with fear (1 [+4394]), frighten (1), have reverence (1), have reverence for (1), held in awe (1), is feared (1), made afraid (1), more awesome (1), not daring (1), overawed (1), respect (1), respects (1), reverent (1), shown reverence (1), stood in awe (1 [+4394]), terrified (1 [+4394, 4394]), terrified (1 [+1524, 3711]), terrify (1), terror (1), with reverence serve (1)

H3708 ²יָרֵא ***yārē'²***, v. Not used in NIVEBC [cf. 3721]. see 3721

H3709 ³יָרֵא ***yārē'³***, v. Not used in NIVEBC [cf. 3722]. see 3722

H3710 ⁴יָרֵא ***yārē'⁴***, a.vbl. [52] [√ 3707]. fear; worship; see also 3707:– fear (34), fears (6), afraid (4), feared (3), worshiped (2), revere (1), worship (1), worshiping (1)

H3711 יִרְאָה ***yir'â***, n.f. [45] [√ 3707]. fear, reverence, piety; see also 3707:– fear (34), piety (3), reverence (2), awesome (1), feared (1), feared (1 [+3707]), fears (1), revere (1), terrified (1 [+3707, 1524])

H3712 יִרְאוֹן ***yir'ôn***, n.pr.loc. [1] Iron:– Iron (1)

H3713 יִרְאִיָּיה ***yir'iyyāyh***, n.pr.m. [2] [√ 8011 + 3378]. Irijah, "*Yahweh sees*":– Irijah (2)

H3714 יָרֵב ***yārēb***, n.m. [2] [√ 8045]. great (king):– great (2)

H3715 יְרֻבַּעַל ***yᵉrubba'al***, n.pr.m. [14] [√ 8045 + 1251]. Jerub-Baal, "*Baal contends*":– Jerub-Baal (11), Jerub-Baal's (3)

H3716 יָרָבְעָם ***yārob'ām***, n.pr.m. [104] [√ 8045 + 6639]. Jeroboam, "*the people increase*":– Jeroboam (94), Jeroboam's (6), he^S (4)

H3717 יְרֻבֶּשֶׁת ***yᵉrubbešet***, n.pr.m. [1] [√ 8045 + 1017]. Jerub-Besheth, "*Shame [Baal] contends*":– Jerub-Besheth (1)

H3718 יָרַד ***yārad***, v. [381] [→ 3720, 4618]. [Q] to come down, go down, descend; [H] to bring down, lower; [Ho] to be brought down, be taken down:– went down (63), go down (62), come down (28), came down (25), bring down (19), down (13), brought down (8), go (7), gone down (7), take down (7), coming down (6), fall (6), going down (4), took down (4), come (3), comes down (3), descend (3), descended (3), gone (3), leave (3 [+4946]), let down (3), lowered (3), overflow (3), pull down (3), be brought down (2), came down (2 [+3718]), continued down (2), descending (2), falling (2), fell (2), flowing (2), goes down (2), lead down (2), went (2), abandon (1 [+4946]), are brought down (1), attack (1), attack (1 [+928]), been brought down (1), been taken down (1), bowed (1), brings down (1), brought (1), came out (1), carried down (1), climbed down (1), consign (1), continued (1), cut down (1), descends (1), do so^S (1), fail (1), fall down (1), fallen (1), falls (1), flattens (1), flow (1), flow from (1), flowed down (1), flowing down (1), goes down (1 [+4200, 4752]), gone down (1 [+345]), got down (1), got off (1 [+4946, 6584]), haul down (1), join (1 [+448]), leading down (1), leave (1 [+4946, 9348]), led down (1), let flow (1), let go down (1), letting run down (1), made flow down (1), march down (1), moved down (1), overflowing (1), poured (1), prostrate (1), puts (1), ran down (1), removed (1), road down (1), roam (1 [+2143, 2256]), running down (1), sank (1), sank down (1), send down (1), sends (1), sent down (1), settled (1), sink (1), so^S (1), step down (1), stepped down (1), subdued (1), take (1), take off (1 [+4946, 6584]), taken (1), toward evening (1 [+4394]), was taken down (1), went aboard (1 [+928]), went out (1), will^S (1), NDT (3)

H3719 יֶרֶד ***yered***, n.pr.m. [7] Jared; Jered, "*rose; servant*":– Jared (6), Jered (1)

H3720 יַרְדֵּן ***yardēn***, n.pr.loc. [181] [√ 3718]. Jordan, "*descending*":– Jordan (172), Jordan's (3), river (2), its^S (1 [+2021]), there^S (1 [+2021]), NDT (2)

H3721 ¹יָרָה ***yārâ¹***, v. [25] [→ 3452, 3725, 3748, 3754, 3755, 3756, 4619; cf. 3708]. [Q] to throw, cast; shoot; [N] to be shot through; [H] to shoot (an arrow), to hurl:– shoot (10), shot (3), shot with arrows (2 [+3721]), cast (1), fallen (1), hurled (1), laid (1), overthrown (1), set up (1), shoot arrows (1), shooting (1), shot arrows (1), throws (1)

H3722 ²יָרָה ***yārâ²***, v. [3] [→ 4620; cf. 3709]. [H] to water upon, rain, shower; [Ho] to be refreshed:– be refreshed (1), showers (1), water (1)

H3723 ³יָרָה ***yārâ³***, v. [46] [→ 4621, 4622, 9368]. [H] to teach, instruct, give guidance, in a formal or informal setting, with an implied authority for the teacher and the content of what is taught:– teach (25), instruct (5), teaches (3), taught (2), achieve (1), determine (1), get directions (1), give guidance (1), instructed (1), instruction (1), instructs (1), motions (1), showed (1), taught (1 [+2118]), teach (1 [+1978])

H3724 יָרַה ***yārah***, v. [1] [cf. 8109]. [Q] to be frozen in fear:– afraid (1)

H3725 יְרוּאֵל ***yᵉrû'ēl***, n.pr.loc. [1] [√ 3721 + 446]. Jeruel, "*God [El] is a foundation*":– Jeruel (1)

H3726 יָרוֹחַ ***yārôaḥ***, n.pr.m. [1] [√ 3732]. Jaroah, "*soft, delicate*":– Jaroah (1)

H3727 יָרוּם ***yārûm***, a.vbl. *or* v.ptcp. Not used in NIVEBC [→ 3753; cf. 8123]. high, exalted

H3728 יָרוֹק ***yārôq***, n.[m.] [1] [√ 3764]. green plant:– green thing (1)

H3729 יְרוּשָׁא ***yᵉrûšā'***, n.pr.f. [1] [√ 3769]. Jerusha, "*possession*":– Jerusha (1)

H3730 יְרוּשָׁה ***yᵉrûšâ***, n.pr.f. [1] [√ 3769]. Jerusha, "*possession*":– Jerusha (1)

H3731 יְרוּשָׁלַםִ ***yᵉrûšālaim***, n.pr.loc. [643] [√ 10332]. Jerusalem, "*foundation of Shalem [peace]*":– Jerusalem (631), there^S (6 [+928]), Jerusalem's (3), the city^S (1), NDT (2)

H3732 ¹יֶרַח ***yeraḥ¹***, n.m. [12] [→ 3726, 3733, 3734, 3735, 3747; cf. 782; 10333]. moon; (lunar) month:– month (5), months (5), moon (1), one month (1 [+3427])

H3733 ²יֶרַח ***yeraḥ²***, n.pr.m. [2] [√ 3732]. Jerah, "*moon [god?]*":– Jerah (2)

H3734 יָרֵחַ ***yārēaḥ***, n.m. [27] [√ 3732]. moon:– moon (27)

H3735 יְרִחוֹ ***yᵉriḥô***, n.pr.loc. [57] [√ 3732]. Jericho, "*moon city*":– Jericho (55), there^S (1), NDT (1)

H3736 יְרֹחָם ***yᵉrōḥām***, n.pr.m. [10] [√ 8163]. Jeroham, "*he will be compassionate*":– Jeroham (10)

H3737 יְרַחְמְאֵל ***yᵉraḥmᵉ'ēl***, n.pr.m. [8] [√ 8163 + 446]. Jerahmeel, "*God [El] will have compassion*":– Jerahmeel (8)

H3738 יְרַחְמְאֵלִי ***yᵉraḥmᵉ'ēlî***, a.g. [2] [√ 8163 + 446]. Jerahmeelite, "*of Jerahmeel*":– Jerahmeel (1), Jerahmeelites (1)

H3739 יַרְחָע ***yarḥā'***, n.pr.m. [2] Jarha:– Jarha (2)

H3740 יָרַט ***yāraṭ***, v. [2] [Q] to throw (into someone's custody); to be reckless, a fig. extension of going down a steep ravine:– reckless (1), thrown (1)

H3741 יְרִיאֵל ***yᵉrî'ēl***, n.pr.m. [1] [cf. 3746]. Jeriel, "*founded of God [El]; God [El] will see*":– Jeriel (1)

H3742 ¹יָרִיב ***yārîb¹***, n.[m.] [3] [√ 8189]. contender, accuser, adversary, opponent:– contend (2), accusers (1)

H3743 ²יָרִיב ***yārîb²***, n.pr.m. [3] Jarib, "*Yahweh contends*":– Jarib (3)

H3744 יְרִיבַי ***yᵉrîbay***, n.pr.m. [1] [→ 8192?]. Jeribai, "*Yahweh pleads*":– Jeribai (1)

H3745 יְרִיָּה ***yᵉriyyâ***, n.pr.m. [1] [√ 3746]. Jeriah, "*Yahweh founds*":– Jeriah (1)

H3746 יְרִיָּהוּ ***yᵉriyyāhû***, n.pr.m. [2] [→ 3745; cf. 3741]. Jeriah, "*Yahweh founds*":– Jeriah (2)

H3747 יְרִיחוֹ ***yᵉriḥōh***, n.pr.loc. Not used in NIVEBC [√ 3732]. Jericho

H3748 יְרִימוֹת ***yᵉrîmôt***, n.pr.m. [7] [√ 3721? + 4637?]. Jerimoth, "*swollen* or *obese*":– Jerimoth (7)

H3749 יְרִיעָה ***yᵉrî'â***, n.f. [51] [√ 3760]. tent curtain; tent, shelter, dwelling:– curtains (18), curtain (14), other^S (4), tent (3), shelter (2), dwellings (1), shelters (1), tent curtains (1), NDT (7)

H3750 יְרִיעוֹת ***yᵉrî'ôt***, n.pr.m. [1] [√ 3760]. Jerioth, "*tents*":– Jerioth (1)

H3751 יָרֵךְ ***yārēk***, n.f. [34] [→ 3752; 10334]. the area and components of the torso: thigh, hip, breast, leg, side; by extension: side, base, of any object:– side (9), thigh (6), hip (5), base (3), womb (3), breast (2), attacked viciously (1 [+5782, 8797, 6584]), descendants (1 [+5883, 3655]), direct descendants (1 [+3655]), leg (1), legs (1), of his own (1 [+3655, 2257])

H3752 יְרֵכָה ***yᵉrēkâ***, n.[f.] [28] [√ 3751]. far end, ends (of the earth); remote area: heights, depths:– far end (6), ends (4), far (3), utmost heights (3), depths (2), remote area (2), below deck (1 [+2021, 6208]), border (1), end (1), far back in (1 [+928]), heights (1), rear (1), there^S (1 [+928, 2021, 1074]), within (1 [+928])

H3753 יָרַם ***yāram***, v. Not used in NIVEBC [√ 3727; cf. 8123]. [Qp] to be high, exalted

H3754 יַרְמוּת ***yarmût***, n.pr.loc. [7] [√ 3721 + 4637?]. Jarmuth, "*height*":– Jarmuth (7)

H3755 יְרָמוֹת ***yᵉrāmôt***, n.pr.m. Not used in NIVEBC [√ 3721]. Jeramoth

H3756 יְרֵמוֹת ***yᵉrēmôt***, n.pr.m. [7] [√ 3721]. Jeremoth; Jerimoth, "*swollen* or *obese*":– Jeremoth (5), Jerimoth (2)

H3757 יְרֵמַי ***yᵉrēmay***, n.pr.m. [1] [cf. 3758?]. Jeremai, "[poss.] *fat*":– Jeremai (1)

H3758 יִרְמְיָה ***yirmᵉyâ***, n.pr.m. [18] [→ 3759; cf. 3757?, 8227 + 3378]. Jeremiah, "*Yahweh loosens [the womb]; Yahweh lifts up*; [poss.] *Yahweh shoots, establishes*":– Jeremiah (16), Jeremiah's (1), he^S (1 [+2021, 5566])

H3759 יִרְמְיָהוּ ***yirmᵉyāhû***, n.pr.m. [129] [√ 3758; cf. 8227 + 3378]. Jeremiah, "*Yahweh loosens [the womb]; Yahweh lifts up*; [poss.] *Yahweh shoots, establishes*":– Jeremiah (123), he^S (2), him^S (2), Jeremiah's (1), him^S (1 [+2021, 5566])

H3760 יָרַע ***yāra'***, v. [1] [→ 3749, 3750]. [Q] to tremble, be faint-hearted:– faint (1)

H3761 יִרְפְּאֵל ***yirpᵉ'ēl***, n.pr.loc. [1] [√ 8324 + 446]. Irpeel, "*God [El] heals*":– Irpeel (1)

H3762 יָרַק ***yāraq***, v. [3] [→ 3765?; cf. 8394]. [Q] to spit (in the face as an act of contempt):– spit (2 [+3762]), spit (1)

H3763 יָרָק ***yārāq***, n.[m.] [3] [√ 3764]. vegetables, vegetable greens:– vegetable (2), vegetables (1)

H3764 יֶרֶק ***yereq***, n.m. [8] [→ 3728, 3763, 3765?, 3766, 3768]. green (of plants, foliage, shoots, grass):– green (4), tender shoots (2), grass (1), plants (1)

H3765 יַרְקוֹן ***yarqôn***, n.pr.loc. Not used in NIVEBC [√ 3762? 3764?]. Jarkon

H3766 יֵרָקוֹן ***yērāqôn***, n.m. [6] [√ 3764]. paleness (of face); mildew (of grain):– mildew (5), deathly pale (1)

H3767 יָרְקְעָם ***yorqᵉ'ām***, n.pr.m. [1] [√ 8392]. Jorkeam:– Jorkeam (1)

H3768 יְרַקְרַק ***yᵉraqraq***, a. [3] [√ 3764]. yellowish-green, pale-green (mildew); shining-yellowish (gold):– greenish (2), shining (1)

H3769 ¹יָרַשׁ ***yāraš¹***, v. [231] [→ 3729, 3730, 3771, 3772, 4625, 4627, 8397, 8407, 9408; cf. 3770, 8133]. [Q] to be an heir, gain an inheritance, have as a possession; [N] to become destitute, to be poor; [P] to take possession of; [H] to drive away, push out, destroy; to cause to inherit; many of these meanings have a common element of gaining (by right or violence) or losing possession (by force or circumstance):– possess (48), take possession (31), drive out (26), driven out (11), inherit (11), drove out (9), took possession (9), take over (6), took over (6), dispossess (5), heir (5), taken over (5), occupy (4), taken possession (4), certainly drive out (2 [+3769]), destroy (2), dislodge (2), drive out completely (2 [+3769]), drove out completely (2 [+3769]), possessed (2), take (2), become poor (1), belonged (1), capturing (1), conquer (1), conqueror (1), destitute (1), displaces (1), dispossessing (1), drive (1), drive from (1), drove (1), fell heir (1), gain possession (1), gave as an inheritance (1), give (1), given (1), gives (1), grow poor (1), inheritance (1), inherited (1), inherits (1), leave as an inheritance (1), make reap (1), make vomit up (1), new owners (1), occupied (1), own (1), poor (1), prosperous (1 [+6807]), seize (1), seized property (1), sends poverty (1), share in the inheritance (1), steal property (1), take away possessions (1), won (1), NDT (1)

H3770 ²יָרַשׁ ***yāraš²***, n.m. Not used in NIVEBC [cf. 3769]. [Q] to press (grapes)

H3771 יְרֵשָׁה ***yᵉrēšâ***, n.f. [2] [√ 3769]. possession conquered:– conquered (2)

H3772 יְרֻשָּׁה ***yᵉruššâ***, n.f. [14] [√ 3769]. possession, inheritance:– possession (7), own (2), heirs (1), heritage (1), inheritance (1), part (1), possess (1)

H3773 יִשְׂחָק ***yiśḥāq***, n.pr.m. [4] [√ 8471; cf. 3663]. Isaac, "*he laughs, he will laugh* or *mock; [God] laughs*":– Isaac (4)

H3774 יְשִׂימִאֵל ***yᵉśîmi'ēl***, n.pr.m. [1] [√ 8492 + 446]. Jesimiel, "*God [El] will establish*":– Jesimiel (1)

H3775 יָשַׂם ***yāśam***, v. Not used in NIVEBC [cf. 8492]. see 8492

H3776 יִשְׂרָאֵל ***yiśrā'ēl***, n.pr.m. & g. [2506] [→ 449, 3778; cf. 8575; 10335]. Israel, "*he struggles with God* [El]":– Israel (1631), Israelites (486 [+1201]), Israelites (68), Israelite (49 [+1201]), Israel's (40), Israel (39 [+1074]), Israelites (30 [+408]), Israelites (30 [+1074]), Israel (23 [+1201]), Israelite (17), them^S (8 [+1201]), Israel (7 [+824]), them^S (7), they^S (5 [+1201]), Israelite (4 [+408]), Israelite (4 [+408, 4946, 1074]), Israel's (4 [+4200]), them^S (4 [+1201]), they^S (4 [+1201]), Israelite (2 [+4946, 1201]), Israelite (2 [+408, 4946, 1201]), their^S (2), Israel (1 [+408]), Israel (1 [+2446]), Israel (1 [+6639]), Israel and Judah (1 [+1074]), Israelite (1 [+928]), Israelite (1 [+1074]), Israelite (1 [+4946]), Israelite (1 [+4200, 1201]), Israelite (1 [+928, 1201]), Israelites (1 [+4946]), Israelites (1 [+4946, 1201]), Israelites (1 [+6639, 1201]), Israel's (1 [+928]), Israel's (1 [+1074]), her^S (1 [+141]), the whole land^S (1), their^S (1 [+6584]), their^S (1 [+6639, 3276]), them^S (1 [+3972]), them^S (1 [+3972,

7736]), them[S] (1 [+3972, 7736]), they[S] (1 [+3972]), who[S] (1 [+1201]), NDT (17)

H3777 יְשַׂרְאֵלָה **yeśar'ēlâ**, n.pr.m. [1] [cf. 833]. Jesarelah:– Jesarelah (1)

H3778 יִשְׂרְאֵלִי **yiśre'ēlî**, a.g. [4] [√ 3776]. Israelite, "*of Israel*":– Israelite (2), Israelite (1 [+408, 2021]), him[S] (1 [+1201, 2021])

H3779 יִשָּׂשכָר **yiśśāśkār**, n.pr.m. [43] [√ 408 + 8510]. Issachar, "*there is reward* [Ge. 30:18]; *may [God] show mercy; hired hand*":– Issachar (38), Issachar (4 [+1201]), NDT (1)

H3780 יֵשׁ **yēš**, subst. [140] [→ 409, 838, 3807?, 3808?; cf. 9370; 10029]. there is, it exists:– there is (27), is (13), have (12 [+4200]), is there (8), be (5), are (4), have (4), there are (4), will (4), am (3), there was (3), has (2), has (2 [+928]), have (2 [+907]), owned (2 [+4200]), sometimes (2 [+889]), are there (1), continue (1), had (1), had (1 [+4200]), have (1 [+9393, 3338]), have on hand (1 [+9393, 3338]), it is (1), know (1 [+928, 1978]), lies (1), may (1), owns (1 [+4200]), rich (1), so[S] (1), there were (1), there will be (1), were (1), yes (1), NDT (26)

H3781 יִשְׁאָל **yiš'āl**, n.pr.m. Not used in NIVEBC [√ 8626]. Ishal

H3782 יָשַׁב **yāšab**, v. [1086] [→ 4632, 8699, 8859?, 9369; 10338; *also used with compound proper names*]. [Q] to live, inhabit, dwell, stay; [N] to be settled, be inhabited; [P] to set up; to cause to settle, make dwell, to cause to sit; by extension: to marry, with a focus that the spouses live together:– live (140), lived (91), live in (68), people (65), sit (59), settled (43), living (41), sitting (40), stay (37), inhabitants (35), living in (32), stayed (32), sat (29), sat down (23), remained (17), dwell (14), inhabited (13), enthroned (12), lived in (12), settle (12), sits (11), dwelling (10), lives (10), remain (9), seated (9), dwell in (8), occupied (8), reigned (8), staying (7), sit enthroned (6), wait (6), married (5), settle down (5), men (4), sits enthroned (4), be (3), inhabitant (3), sit down (3), are (2), at rest (2), be inhabited (2), dwells (2), dwelt (2), everyone (2 [+3972]), king (2), left (2), lies (2), lived at (2), make dwell (2), marrying (2), meet (2), occupy (2), reign (2), resettle (2), resettled (2), residents (2), ruling (2), seat (2), seats (2), situated (2), stand (2), stay (2 [+3782]), stays (2), supposed to dine (2 [+3782, 430]), took seat (2), took up residence (2), were (2), avoid (1 [+4946]), based (1), brought to live (1), citizens (1), crouching (1), deserted (1 [+401]), deserted (1 [+4202]), deserted (1 [+4946, 401]), deserted (1 [+4946, 1172]), did so[S] (1), dwellers (1), dwellings (1), empty (1 [+4946, 401]), endures (1), enthrones (1 [+4200, 2021, 4058]), give (1), go (1), had live (1), have a home (1), held court (1), hide in (1), hold out (1), intact (1), kings (1), lay in wait (1), left behind (1), let live (1), lie (1), live on (1), live securely (1), living at (1), lounging (1), made dwell (1), make live (1), makes dwell (1), meeting (1), mounted like jewels (1 [+6584, 4859]), occupants (1), peopled (1), peoples (1), reigns (1), relieve yourself (1 [+2575]), remains (1), resided (1), rest (1), rested (1), restore (1), sat up (1), sat waiting (1), securely (1), set up (1), sets (1), settle in (1), settle on (1), settles (1), sit as judge (1), spend (1), spent (1), stay at home (1), stay in (1), stay up (1), stayed at home (1), stayed night (1 [+2256, 4328]), stopping (1), succeeded (1), successor (1), taken seat (1), takes (1 [+6584]), takes seat (1), thrones (1), took place (1), took places (1), took seats (1), was (1), whole earth (1 [+7921]), withdrew (1), NDT (18)

H3783 יֹשֵׁב בַּשֶּׁבֶת **yōšēb baššebet**, n.pr.m. [1] [cf. 1416]. Josheb-Basshebeth, "*one sitting in the seat*":– Josheb-Basshebeth (1)

H3784 יֶשֶׁבְאָב **yešeb'āb**, n.pr.m. [1] [√ 8740 + 3]. Jeshebeab, "*father lives*":– Jeshebeab (1)

H3785 יִשְׁבּוֹ בְנֹב **yišbô benōb**, n.pr.m. Not used in NIVEBC [cf. 1216]. Ishbo-Benob

H3786 יִשְׁבָּח **yišbāḥ**, n.pr.m. [1] [√ 8655]. Ishbah, "*he boasts, congratulates*":– Ishbah (1)

H3787 יִשְׁבִּי בְנֹב **yišbî benōb**, n.pr.m. [1] [cf. 1216]. Ishbi-Benob:– Ishbi-Benob (1)

H3788 יָשֻׁבִי לֶחֶם **yāšubî leḥem**, n.pr.m. [1] [√ 3794 + 4312]. Jashubi Lehem, "*[they] returned to Lehem*":– Jashubi Lehem (1)

H3789 יִשְׁבַּעַל **yišba'al**, n.pr.m. Not used in NIVEBC [√ 408 + 1251]. Ish-Baal

H3790 יָשָׁבְעָם **yāšob'ām**, n.pr.m. [3] Jashobeam, "*the people return*":– Jashobeam (3)

H3791 יִשְׁבָּק **yišbāq**, n.pr.m. [2] [→ 8749]. Ishbak:– Ishbak (2)

H3792 יָשְׁבְּקָשָׁה **yošbeqāšâ**, n.pr.m. [2] Joshbekashah, "*one sitting in request [prayer?]*":– Joshbekashah (2)

H3793 [1]יָשׁוּב **yāšûb[1]**, n.pr.m. [4] [→ 3795; cf. 3806, 8740]. Jashub, "*he returns*":– Jashub (4)

H3794 [2]יָשׁוּב **yāšûb[2]**, n.loc. Not used in NIVEBC [→ 3788]. Jashub

H3795 יָשׁוּבִי **yāšûbî**, a.g. [1] [√ 3793; cf. 8740]. Jashubite, "*of Jashub*":– Jashubite (1)

H3796 יִשְׁוָה **yišwâ**, n.pr.m. [2] [√ 8750]. Ishvah, "*he will level*":– Ishvah (2)

H3797 יְשׁוֹחָיָה **yešôḥāyâ**, n.pr.m. [1] [√ 3378 + 8820?]. Jeshohaiah, "[poss.] *Yahweh humbles*":– Jeshohaiah (1)

H3798 [1]יִשְׁוִי **yišwî[1]**, n.pr.m. [4] [√ 8750]. Ishvi:– Ishvi (4)

H3799 [2]יִשְׁוִי **yišwî[2]**, a.g. [1] [√ 8750]. Ishvite, "*of Ishvi*":– Ishvite (1)

H3800 [1]יֵשׁוּעַ **yēšûa'[1]**, n.pr.m. [28] [√ 3801; cf. 3828; 10336]. Jeshua, "*Yahweh saves*":– Jeshua (16), Joshua (12)

H3801 [2]יֵשׁוּעַ **yēšûa'[2]**, n.pr.loc. [1] [√ 3800; cf. 3828]. Jeshua, "*Yahweh saves*":– Jeshua (1)

H3802 יְשׁוּעָה **yešû'â**, n.f. [78] [√ 3828]. salvation, deliverance, help, rescue from a dangerous circumstance or harmful state by a savior; divine salvation usually has its focus on rescue from earthly enemies, occasionally referring to salvation from guilt, sin, and punishment:– salvation (45), deliverance (9), savior (6), victories (5), victory (4), save (2), deliver (1), deliverer (1), rescue (1), safety (1), saves (1), saving (1), saving help (1)

H3803 יֶשַׁח **yešaḥ**, n.[m.] [1] emptiness; some sources: filth, dung:– empty (1)

H3804 יָשַׁט **yāšaṭ**, v. [3] [H] to extend; hold out:– extended (1), extends (1), held out (1)

H3805 יִשַׁי **yišay**, n.pr.m. [41] [→ 414]. Jesse:– Jesse (34), Jesse's (5), him[S] (1), NDT (1)

H3806 יָשִׁיב **yāšib**, n.pr.m. Not used in NIVEBC [cf. 3793]. Jashib

H3807 יִשִּׁיָּה **yiššiyyâ**, n.pr.m. [6] [√ 3780? + 3378]. Isshiah; Ishijah, "*Yahweh forgets*":– Ishiah (5), Ishijah (1)

H3808 יִשִּׁיָּהוּ **yiššiyyāhû**, n.pr.m. [1] [√ 3780? + 3378]. Isshiah, "*Yahweh forgets*":– Ishiah (1)

H3809 יְשִׁימָה **yešîmâ**, n.f. Not used in NIVEBC [√ 3815]. desolation

H3810 יְשִׁימוֹן **yešîmôn**, n.m. [13] [√ 3815]. Jeshimon; wasteland:– wasteland (5), Jeshimon (4), wilderness (2), waste (1), wastelands (1)

H3811 יְשִׁימוֹת **yešîmôt**, n.pr.loc. Not used in NIVEBC [→ 1093, 2127]. Jeshimoth

H3812 יַשִּׁימָוֶת **yaššîmāwet**, n.f. Not used in NIVEBC [√ 3815]. devastation

H3813 יָשִׁישׁ **yāšîš**, a. [4] [→ 3814?; cf. 3844]. old, aged:– aged (2), old (1), old men (1)

H3814 יְשִׁישַׁי **yešîšay**, n.pr.m. [1] [√ 3813?]. Jeshishai, "*aged*":– Jeshishai (1)

H3815 יָשַׁם **yāšam**, v. Not used in NIVEBC [→ 3809, 3810, 3812; cf. 9037]. [Q] to be desolate

H3816 יִשְׁמָא **yišmā'**, n.pr.m. [1] [√ 3817]. Ishma, "*desolate; God [El] he heard*":– Ishma (1)

H3817 יִשְׁמָעֵאל **yišmā'ē'l**, n.pr.m. [48] [→ 3816, 3818; cf. 9048 + 446]. Ishmael, "*God [El] he heard*":– Ishmael (47), he[S] (1)

H3818 יִשְׁמְעֵאלִי **yišme'ē'lî**, a.g. [9] [√ 3817]. Ishmaelite, "*of Ishmael*":– Ishmaelites (6), Ishmaelite (3)

H3819 יִשְׁמַעְיָה **yišma'yâ**, n.pr.m. [1] [→ 3820, 3821?; cf. 9048 + 3378]. Ishmaiah, "*Yahweh heard*":– Ishmaiah (1)

H3820 יִשְׁמַעְיָהוּ **yišma'yāhû**, n.pr.m. [1] [√ 3819; cf. 9048 + 3378]. Ishmaiah, "*Yahweh heard*":– Ishmaiah (1)

H3821 יִשְׁמְרַי **yišmeray**, n.pr.m. [1] [√ 3819?; cf. 9048 + 3378]. Ishmerai, "*Yahweh guards*":– Ishmerai (1)

H3822 [1]יָשֵׁן **yāšēn[1]**, v. [18] [→ 3823?, 3825, 3826?, 9104, 9097]. [Q] to sleep, fall asleep; [P] to put to sleep:– sleep (7), fell asleep (2), sleep (2 [+9104]), sleeping (2), asleep (1), putting to sleep (1), rest (1), sleeps (1), smolders (1)

H3823 [2]יָשֵׁן **yāšēn[2]**, v. [3] [→ 3824; cf. 3822?]. [N] to live a long time, be old, chronic:– chronic (1), last year's harvest (1 [+3824]), lived a long time (1)

H3824 יָשָׁן **yāšān**, a. [6] [→ 3827?; cf. 3823]. old; pertaining to last year:– old (3), it[S] (2), last year's harvest (1 [+3823])

H3825 [3]יָשֵׁן **yāšēn[3]**, a. [7] [√ 3822]. sleeping, pertaining to sleep:– asleep (2), sleep (2), sleeping (2), slept (1)

H3826 [4]יָשֵׁן **yāšēn[4]**, n.pr.m. [1] [√ 3822?]. Jashen, "[poss.] *asleep*":– Jashen (1)

H3827 יְשָׁנָה **yešānâ**, n.pr.loc. [3] [√ 3824?]. Jeshanah, "*old*":– Jeshanah (3)

H3828 יָשַׁע **yāša'**, v. [184] [→ 3802, 3829, 3830, 4635, 4636, 4795, 4796, 9591; *also used with compound proper names*]. [N] to be rescued, be delivered, be saved; [H] to save, rescue, deliver; divine salvation has its focus on rescue from earthly enemies, occasionally referring to salvation from guilt, sin, and punishment:– save (85), saved (23), be saved (11), saves (10), rescue (8), help (7), deliver (4), gave victory (4), give victory (3), achieved salvation (2), avenging (2), been saved (2), bring victory (2), help at all (2 [+3828]), rescued (2), are saved (1), avenge (1), avenged (1), be delivered (1), brought about victory (1 [+9591]), came to rescue (1), delivering (1), get help for (1), gives victory (1), is saved (1), kept safe (1), preserve (1), salvation (1), saving (1), spare (1), victorious (1), worked salvation (1)

H3829 יֶשַׁע **yēša'**, n.m. [36] [→ 3801; cf. 3828; *also used with compound proper names*]. salvation, deliverance, protection, often implying a victory is at hand; (of God) Savior, a title of God that focuses on rescue from earthly enemies, occasionally referring to salvation from guilt, sin, and punishment:– salvation (15), savior (13), safety (2), saving help (2), deliver (1), protect (1 [+8883, 928]), save (1), victorious (1)

H3830 יֹשַׁע **yōša'**, n.[m.] Not used in NIVEBC [√ 3828]. help

H3831 יִשְׁעִי **yiš'î**, n.pr.m. [5] [√ 3828? + 3378?]. Ishi, "*God has saved*":– Ishi (4), who[S] (1)

H3832 יְשַׁעְיָה **yeša'yâ**, n.pr.m. [4] [√ 3828 + 3378]. Jeshaiah, "*Yahweh will save*":– Jeshaiah (4)

H3833 יְשַׁעְיָהוּ **yeša'yāhû**, n.pr.m. [35] [√ 3828 + 3378]. Isaiah; Jeshaiah, "*Yahweh saves*":– Isaiah (30), Jeshaiah (3), NDT (2)

H3834 יִשְׁפָּה **yišpâ**, n.pr.m. [1] [√ 9142]. Ishpah, "[poss.] *barren way, empty path*":– Ishpah (1)

H3835 יָשְׁפֵה **yāšepēh**, n.[m.] [3] jasper (exact identification uncertain):– jasper (3)

H3836 יִשְׁפָּן **yišpān**, n.pr.m. [1] [√ 9142?]. Ishpan, "[poss.] *may God judge*":– Ishpan (1)

H3837 יָשַׁר **yāšar**, v. [25] [→ 3838, 3839, 3840, 3841, 3842, 3843, 4793, 4797, 9227, 9228]. [Q] to do good, do right, be straight; [P] to make straight, make smooth; [Pu] to be evenly hammered; [H] to make straight, gaze straight; from the base meaning of straightening out a crooked object comes the fig. extension of doing an act that is not perverse, but right or just:– make straight (4), right (3), please (2 [+928, 6524]), pleased (2 [+928, 6524]), best (1), channeled (1), consider right (1), fix directly (1), go straight (1), good (1), hammered evenly (1), keeps straight (1), level (1), liked (1 [+928, 6524]), makes straight (1), pleased with (1 [+928, 6524]), upright (1), went straight (1)

H3838 [1]יָשָׁר **yāšār[1]**, a. [117] [√ 3837]. straight (not crooked or twisted); by extension, something morally straight: right, upright, innocent; (n.) upright person:– upright (50), right (43), fit (3), just (2), straight (2), alliance (1), conscientious (1 [+4222]), in accord with (1 [+4222]), innocent (1), level (1), please (1 [+928, 6524]), please (1 [+3202, 2256, 928, 6524]), pleased (1 [+928, 6524]), reliable (1), right and true (1), righteous (1), safe (1), stretched out (1), upright (1 [+2006]), uprightness (1), what right (1), worthy (1)

H3839 [2]יָשָׁר **yāšār[2]**, n.pr.m. [2] [√ 3837]. Jashar:– Jashar (2)

H3840 יֵשֶׁר **yēšer**, n.pr.m. [1] [√ 3837]. Jesher, "[perhaps] *the deity shows himself just*":– Jesher (1)

H3841 יֹשֶׁר **yōšer**, n.m. [14] [√ 3837]. uprightness, straightness, honesty, integrity:– upright (4), honest (2), straight (2), uprightness (2), integrity (1 [+4222]), right (1), unduly (1 [+4946]), uprightly (1 [+928])

H3842 יִשְׁרָה **yišrâ**, n.f. [1] [√ 3837]. uprightness:– upright (1)

H3843 יְשֻׁרוּן **yešurûn**, n.pr.m. [4] [√ 3837]. Jeshurun, "*upright*":– Jeshurun (4)

H3844 יָשֵׁשׁ **yāšēš**, a. [1] [→ 3813]. aged, decrepit:– infirm (1)

H3845 יָתֵד **yātēd**, n.f. [25] tent peg, stake, pin (of a loom); tool for digging:– tent pegs (7), peg (4), pin (3), tent peg (3), stakes (2), those[S] (2), firm place (1), pegs (1), something to dig with (1), NDT (1)

H3846 יָתוֹם **yātôm**, n.[m.] [42] fatherless, orphan:– fatherless (37), fatherless children (2), fatherless (1 [+2256, 401, 3]), fatherless child (1), orphan's (1)

H3847 יְתוּר **yetûr**, var. Not used in NIVEBC [cf. 9365]. see 9365

H3848 יַתִּיר **yattîr**, n.pr.loc. [4] [√ 3855]. Jattir, "[poss.] *preeminence*":– Jattir (4)

H3849 יִתְלָה **yitlâ**, n.pr.loc. [1] [√ 9434; cf. 9002]. Ithlah, "*hanging, lofty place*":– Ithlah (1)

H3850 יִתְמָה **yitmâ**, n.pr.m. [1] Ithmah, "*fatherless; purity*":– Ithmah (1)

H3851 [1]יָתַן **yātan[1]**, v. Not used in NIVEBC [→ 419, 923, 3853, 3854]. [Q] to be constant, be durable

H3852 [2]יָתַן **yātan[2]**, v. Not used in NIVEBC [cf. 5989]. [Q] to give

H3853 יַתְנִיאֵל **yatnî'ēl**, n.pr.m. [1] [√ 3851 + 446]. Jathniel, "*God [El] hires; God [El] is forever*":– Jathniel (1)

H3854 יִתְנָן **yitnān**, n.pr.loc. [1] [√ 3851]. Ithnan:– Ithnan (1)

H3855 יָתַר **yātar**, v. [105] [→ 2110, 3463, 3848?, 3856, 3858, 3859, 3860, 3861, 3862, 3863, 3864, 3866, 4639, 4798; 10339; *also used with compound proper names*]. [N] to remain, be left over, the rest; [H] to have left over, spare, preserve:– left (22), rest (20), remaining (7), left over (6), remain (4), be left (3), leave (3), spare (3), had left over (2), remains (2), some (2), still left (2), allow to remain (1), are left (1), be left alive (1), been left alive (1), escaped (1), excel (1), grant abundant (1), had some left over (1), have left over (1), holding out (1), it^{S} (1 [+2021]), keep (1), kept (1), leaving (1), lying (1), more (1), most (1), preserve (1), remained (1), sparing (1), still (1), stopped (1 [+4202]), survived (1), surviving (1 [+3856, 889]), survivors (1), was detained (1), was left (1), NDT (2)

H3856 ^{1}יֶתֶר ***yeter^{1}***, n.m. [95] [→ 3658; cf. 3855]. remainder, remnant, the rest, what is left over:– other (45), rest (21), left (6), survivors (3), excelling (2), last (2 [+8636, 4946]), remaining (2), eloquent (1), even far (1 [+4394]), full (1), last (1), leftovers (1), little left (1 [+7129, 8636]), others (1), power (1), surviving (1), surviving (1 [+889, 3855]), wealth (1), NDT (3)

H3857 ^{2}יֶתֶר ***yeter^{2}***, n.m. [6] [→ 4798]. thong, cord, bowstring:– bowstrings (3), bow (1), cords of tent (1), strings (1)

H3858 ^{3}יֶתֶר ***yeter^{3}***, n.pr.m. [9] [→ 3863; cf. 3855, 3856]. Jether; Jethro:– Jether (8), Jethro (1)

H3859 יִתְרָא ***yitrā'***, n.pr.m. [1] [√ 3855]. Jether, "*abundance*":– Jether (1)

H3860 יִתְרָה ***yitrâ***, n.f. [2] [√ 3855]. wealth, abundance:– wealth (2)

H3861 יִתְרוֹ ***yitrô***, n.pr.m. [9] [√ 3855]. Jethro, "*remainder*":– Jethro (8), he^{S} (1)

H3862 יִתְרוֹן ***yitrôn***, n.[m.] [10] [√ 3855]. profit, gain, increase:– gain (3), better (2), advantage (1), fee (1), gained (1), increase (1), success (1)

H3863 יִתְרִי ***yitrî***, a.g. [5] [√ 3858; cf. 3855]. Ithrite:– Ithrite (4), Ithrites (1)

H3864 יִתְרָן ***yitrān***, n.pr.m. [3] [√ 3855]. Ithran, "*what is over, profit; excellent*":– Ithran (3)

H3865 יִתְרְעָם ***yitreʿām***, n.pr.m. [2] [√ 3856 + 6639]. Ithream, "*remainder of the people*":– Ithream (2)

H3866 יֹתֶרֶת ***yōteret***, n.f. [11] [√ 3855]. covering, lobe (of certain animal livers):– long lobe (11)

H3867 יְתֵת ***yetēt***, n.pr.m. [2] Jetheth:– Jetheth (2)

H3868 כ ***k***, letter. Not used in NIVEBC [√ 10340]. letter of the Hebrew alphabet

H3869 כְּ- ***ke-***, subst.pref. [2908] [→ 3876, 3904, 4015, 4017; 10341]. marker of comparison: as, like; marker of similarity or correspondence: according to; marker of time: when, as soon as, about:– like (896), as (426), as (269 [+889]), when (112), according to (84), just as (59 [+889]), about (40), when (38 [+889]), in accordance with (32), in (30), as soon as (24), just as (24 [+3972, 889]), what (21), for (20), what (19 [+889]), just as (17 [+889, 4027]), just as (16), same (16), after (14 [+889]), such (14), after (12), at (12), as if (11), like (11 [+889]), same as (11), to (11), while (9), with (9), as (8 [+889, 4027]), such as (8), as though (7), by (7), because (6), like (6 [+5126]), similar (6), whatever (6 [+889]), as (5 [+3972, 889]), because (5 [+889]), whatever (5 [+3972, 889]), as (4 [+4027, 889]), first (4 [+2021, 3427]), in keeping with (4), soon (4 [+5071]), whenever (4), alike (3), as common as (3), following (3), how (3 [+4537]), if (3 [+889]), into (3), like (3 [+5260]), so (3), such (3 [+2296]), whatever (3), according to (2 [+6584]), agree (2 [+2118, 285]), almost (2 [+5071]), and (2), as before (2 [+7193, 928, 7193]), as much as (2 [+889]), as soon as (2 [+889]), at once (2 [+8092]), because of (2), but (2), compared to (2), conformed to (2 [+6913]), engaging in (2), equal (2), even as (2 [+889]), exactly as (2 [+889, 4027]), follow (2 [+6913]), followed (2), had (2), how many (2 [+6330, 4537]), imitate (2 [+6913]), in the order of (2), in way (2), indeed (2), just the way (2 [+889]), just what (2 [+889, 4027]), leaving none alive (2 [+408, 285]), now (2 [+2021, 6961]), numbered (2 [+285]), out of (2), so (2 [+2296]), unlike (2 [+4202]), unlike (2 [+4202]), way (2), what (2 [+889, 4027]), what deserve (2 [+5126]), whatever (2 [+3972]), according to (1 [+889]), according to (1 [+7023]), according to the rules (1), accordingly (1 [+7023]), adhere to (1 [+6913]), after (1 [+9005]), against (1 [+4202]), age of childbearing (1 [+784, 2021, 851]), all (1), among (1), appear (1 [+2118, 928, 6524]), appropriate (1), as (1 [+6961]), as (1 [+4027]), as (1 [+6795]), as (1 [+8611]), as deserve (1), as done before (1 [+7193, 928, 7193]), as easily as (1 [+889]), as far as (1), as far as possible (1 [+1896]), as for (1), as good as (1), as in the case of (1), as in times past (1 [+3972]), as is the case (1), as long as (1 [+889]), as long as endure (1 [+3427]), as many (1), as many as (1), as measureless as (1), as much as (1), as much as (1 [+7023]), as soon as (1 [+4027]), as surely as (1), as though (1 [+889]), as usual (1 [+9453, 8997]), as usually (1), as usually did (1 [+3427, 928, 3427]), as well as (1), as well as (1 [+2256]), as with (1), at (1 [+6590]), based on the rate paid (1 [+3427]), because (1 [+7023, 889]), because of (1 [+889]), both (1), both alike (1), both and (1), by the time (1), callous (1 [+2021, 2693]), closest friend (1 [+8276, 889, 5883, 3870]), compare with (1), compare with (1 [+2118]), contrary to (1 [+4202]), contrary to (1 [+928, 4202]), customary (1 [+7193, 7193, 928]), deserves (1 [+1896]), desire (1), equal to (1), equally (1), equally (1 [+285]), equally (1 [+408, 278, 2257]), equally among them (1 [+408, 278, 2257]), even (1), even for (1), exactly as (1 [+3972, 889]), exactly like (1 [+4027]), exactly like (1 [+3972, 889, 4027]), fared like (1), few (1 [+5071]), first (1 [+3427]), follow (1), followed the example (1 [+6913, 6913]), for a while (1 [+2021, 3427]), from (1), fulfill (1 [+6913, 7023, 4027]), ghostlike (1 [+200]), given even more (1 [+3578, 2179, 2256, 3869, 2179]), given even more (1 [+3578, 3869, 2179, 2256, 2179]), heart and soul (1 [+4222]), here is what (1 [+2296, 2256, 3869, 2296]), here is what (1 [+3869, 2296, 2256, 2296]), how (1), how long (1 [+4537]), how long must wait (1 [+4537, 3427]), how many (1 [+4537]), how many more (1 [+4537]), how often (1 [+4537]), how often (1 [+4537]), how quickly (1 [+5071]), if (1), if only (1 [+889]), immediately (1 [+2021, 3427]), in a moment (1 [+5071]), in accordance with (1 [+889]), in accordance with (1 [+4027]), in proportion to (1), in proportion to (1 [+7023]), in proportion to (1 [+5002, 889]), in spite of (1), in the manner (1 [+889]), in the way (1), in unison (1 [+285]), interwoven (1 [+8054]), joined together (1 [+6641, 285]), just as (1 [+3972]), just as (1 [+4027]), just as (1 [+3972, 889, 4027]), just like (1 [+4027]), kind (1), kind (1 [+889]), large enough (1), like (1 [+1952]), like (1 [+5477]), like (1 [+6524]), like (1 [+6886]), like (1 [+3972, 889]), like (1 [+889, 4027]), might well have (1 [+5071]), mistake for (1 [+8011]), more (1 [+889]), more (1 [+8045]), natural (1 [+3972, 2021, 132]), nearly (1 [+401]), no end (1 [+1896]), no sooner than (1), no sooner than (1 [+889]), not^{S} (1), nothing but (1), nothing more than (1), now that (1 [+889]), obeyed (1 [+7756]), of (1), of little value (1 [+5071]), of one mind (1 [+285, 408]), on all sides (1 [+2021, 1885]), once again (1 [+2021, 8037]), one for each (1 [+5031]), only (1), or (1), outcome different (1 [+4202]), persisted in (1 [+6913]), prescribed (1 [+5477]), previously (1 [+919, 8997]), quotas (1 [+5477]), remains (1), same (1 [+889]), same (1 [+889, 4027]), scarcely (1 [+5071]), share (1 [+889, 4200]), similar (1 [+2021, 5260]), so (1 [+6584]), so (1 [+889]), so many (1 [+4537]), so that (1 [+7023]), so with (1), so with (1 [+889]), some (1), some (1 [+5071]), soon (1 [+5071, 7775]), sort (1), spokesman (1 [+7023]), standing (1), still (1 [+2021, 3427, 2021, 2296]), such (1 [+2297]), suddenly (1 [+8092]), sufficient means (1 [+1896]), suitable (1 [+5584]), suitable for (1 [+5584]), than (1), the same as (1), the same as (1 [+7023]), then (1 [+889]), this is how (1 [+889]), this is how (1 [+2021, 1821, 2021, 465]), thoroughly purge away (1 [+7671, 2021, 1342]), though (1), through (1 [+1821]), together (1 [+285]), too (1), treated as (1), up to (1), using (1), usual (1), very thing (1 [+889, 4027]), weaklings^{S} (1 [+2021, 851]), what (1 [+2296, 2256, 3869, 2296]), what (1 [+3869, 2296, 2256, 2296]), what (1 [+2297, 2256, 3869, 2296]), what (1 [+3869, 2297, 2256, 2296]), what deserve (1), what deserve for (1), what deserves (1), whatever (1 [+889, 4027]), whatever (1 [+3972, 889, 4027]), whenever (1 [+889]), whether (1), while (1 [+889]), without (1 [+1172]), yet (1), NDT (256)

H3870 ךָ- ***-kā***, ךְ- ***-āk***, כָה- ***-kēh***, p.m.sg.suf. [7062] [→ 3871, 4013, 4032]. you, your:– your (3437), you (2608), the^{S} (84), your own (67), yourself (41), your (36 [+4200]), yours (23 [+4200]), you (22 [+5883]), yours (20), a^{S} (10), him (10), he^{S} (7 [+3378, 466]), yourselves (7), his (6), its (4), my (4), your own (4 [+4200]), yourself (4 [+4222]), yourself (4 [+5883]), any^{S} (3), him^{S} (3 [+3378, 466]), their^{S} (3 [+1201]), they^{S} (3 [+278]), toward (3 [+995, 2025]), what are you doing (3 [+4537, 4200]), an^{S} (2), he^{S} (2 [+3]), him^{S} (2 [+1201]), his^{S} (2 [+3378, 466]), the (2), this^{S} (2), us (2 [+3276, 2256]), you (2 [+3338]), your own flesh and blood (2 [+3655, 4946]), your very own (2 [+4200]), yourself (2 [+4213]), yourselves (2 [+4222]), yourselves (2 [+5883]), I^{S} (1 [+6269]), all the way to (1 [+6330, 995]), boast so much (1 [+1540, 7023]), both of you (1 [+2256, 2084]), closest friend (1 [+8276, 889, 3869, 5883]), he^{S} (1 [+6269]), her (1), her^{S} (1 [+563]), here^{S} (1 [+6584]), him^{S} (1 [+6269]), it^{S} (1 [+1821]), it^{S} (1 [+1074]), it^{S} (1 [+3338]), its^{S} (1), keep away (1 [+7928, 448]), lead on (1 [+339]), me (1), me^{S} (1 [+6269]), me^{S} (1 [+563]), one^{S} (1), their^{S} (1 [+367]), their^{S} (1 [+2446]), their^{S} (1 [+8276]), them^{S} (1 [+1821]), them^{S} (1 [+4621]), them^{S} (1 [+3]), them^{S} (1 [+2446]), they^{S} (1 [+1821]), to the vicinity of (1 [+6330, 995]), toward (1 [+995]), very own brother (1 [+278, 1201, 562]), what right have you (1 [+4537, 4200]), whose (1), you (1 [+561]), you (1 [+1414]), you (1 [+4213]), you (1 [+8120]), you^{S} (1), you with food (1), you yourself (1 [+7156]), your (1 [+907]), your (1 [+928]), your (1 [+5580]), your (1 [+5742]), your body (1), your own self (1), NDT (574)

H3871 ךְ- ***-k***, כִי- ***-kî***, p.f.sg.suf. [1269] [√ 3870]. you, your:– your (614), you (487), the^{S} (14), your (10 [+4200]), you (4 [+5883]), yourself (3), her (2), whose (2), you (2 [+7156]), your own (2), yours (2), her^{S} (1 [+3304]), their^{S} (1 [+1201]), these^{S} (1), what is the matter (1 [+4537, 4200]), whom (1), your (1 [+6584]), yours (1 [+4200]), yourself (1 [+4213]), yourself (1 [+4222]), yourselves (1), NDT (117)

H3872 כָּאַב ***kā'ab***, v. [8] [→ 3873, 4799]. [Q] to feel pain, ache; [H] to bring pain:– in pain (2), ache (1), brought grief (1), feel pain (1), ruin (1), sharp (1), wounds (1)

H3873 כְּאֵב ***ke'ēb***, n.m. [6] [√ 3872]. pain, anguish, suffering:– pain (3), anguish (2), suffering (1)

H3874 כָּאָה ***kā'â***, v. [3] [→ 3875; cf. 3909]. [N] to be brokenhearted, lose heart; [H] to dishearten, cause to lose heart:– brokenhearted (1 [+4222]), disheartened (1 [+4213]), lose heart (1)

H3875 כָּאֶה ***kā'eh***, a. Not used in NIVEBC [√ 3874]. disheartened

H3876 כַּאֲשֶׁר ***ka'ašer***, c. Not used in NIVEBC [√ 3869 + 889]. as, just as, because

H3877 ^{1}כָּבֵד ***kābēd^{1}***, v. [114] [→ 3878, 3879, 3880, 3881, 3883, 3884, 3885]. [Q] to be heavy; to be wealthy, honored, glorified; to be failing, dull; [N] to be glorified, honored, renowned; [P] to honor, glorify, reward; [Pu] to be honored; [H] to make heavy, make hard; [Ht] to make numerous; honor oneself. If the base meaning is "to be weighty or heavy," then by extension, negatively: hard, dull, stubborn, difficult in circumstance; positively: substantial, honored, glorious, wealthy:– honor (20), heavy (8), honored (7), hardened (4), be honored (3), honors (3), display glory (2), gain glory (2), glorify (2), glorious (2), highly respected (2), honorable (2), honoring (2), made heavy (2), multiply (2), nobles (2), put heavy (2), renowned (2), reward handsomely (2 [+3877]), was held in honor (2), am honored (1), be held in honor (1), bring glory (1), bring honor (1), burden (1), covered (1 [+4946, 9048]), did^{S} (1 [+906, 4213, 4392]), distinguished (1), distinguished himself (1), dull (1), failing (1), fierce (1), gain glory for myself (1), gained glory for yourself (1), give glory (1), glorified (1), glory (1), grew fierce (1), grievous (1), harden (1), harder (1), heavy (1 [+4394]), heavy (1 [+3878]), held in honor (1), increased (1), is honored (1), laid heavy (1), make dull (1), makes wealthy (1), outweigh (1 [+4946]), overflowing (1), placed a heavy burden (1), pretend to be somebody (1), proud (1), reward (1), reward handsomely (1 [+4394, 3877]), reward handsomely (1 [+3877, 4394]), unyielding (1), was honored (1), wealthy (1), weighed down (1)

H3878 ^{2}כָּבֵד ***kābēd^{2}***, a. [40] [√ 3877]. heavy, severe, difficult, an extended degree or amount, positive or negative; see also 3877:– heavy (8), great (5), large (4), severe (4), strange (2), worst (2 [+4394]), bitterly (1 [+4394]), dense (1), great numbers (1 [+4394]), heavier (1), heavy (1 [+3877]), large (1 [+4394]), severe (1 [+4394]), slow (1), solemn (1), strong (1), terrible (1 [+4394]), thick (1), tired (1), unyielding (1), NDT (1)

H3879 ^{3}כָּבֵד ***kābēd^{3}***, n.m. [14] [√ 3877]. liver; heart:– liver (13), heart (1)

H3880 כֹּבֶד ***kōbed***, n.[m.] [4] [√ 3877]. heaviness; heavy mass (density, piles):– dense (1), heat (1), heavy (1), piles (1)

H3881 כְּבֵדֻת ***kebēdut***, n.f. [1] [√ 3877]. difficulty, awkwardness:– difficulty (1)

H3882 כָּבָה ***kābâ***, v. [24] [Q] to be quenched, snuffed out; [P] to quench, put out, snuff out:– quenched (7), quench (4), go out (3), put out (2), snuff out (2), extinguished (1), goes out (1), gone out (1), quench fire (1), snuffed out (1), unquenchable (1 [+4202])

H3883 ^{1}כָּבוֹד ***kābôd^{1}***, n.m. [200] [→ 376; cf. 3877]. glory, honor, splendor, wealth; while related words can be positive or negative in context, this word is almost exclusively positive in the OT; "the Glory" a title for God focuses on his splendor and high status; "my glory" means "myself" (Ge 49:8); see also 3879:– glory (118), honor (32), glorious (10), splendor (7), glorious God (3), wealth (3), dignity (2), me (2 [+3276]), pomp (2), riches (2), soul (2), vast (2), abundance (1), deep (1), glorious one (1), heart (1), honor (1 [+5989]), honorable (1), honored (1), honored (1 [+6913]), honoring (1), lie in state (1 [+8886, 928]), nobles (1), of high rank (1), proud (1), rewarded (1), tongue (1)

H3884 ^{2}כָּבוֹד ***kābôd^{2}***, a. [2] [√ 3877]. glorious, elegant:– elegant (1), glorious (1)

H3885 כְּבוּדָּה ***kebûddâ***, n.f. [1] [√ 3877]. possession, valuable property:– possessions (1)

H3886 כָּבוּל ***kābûl***, n.pr.loc. [2] [√ 3890]. Cabul, "*good for nothing*":– Kabul (2)

H3887 כַּבּוֹן ***kabbôn***, n.pr.loc. [1] Cabbon:– Kabbon (1)

H3888 כַּבִּיר ***kabbîr***, a. [10] [√ 3892]. great, mighty (of God and humans), with a focus on potency or ability:– mighty (4), blustering (1), feeble (1 [+4202]), flooding downpour (1 [+8851]), fortune (1), great (1), older (1 [+3427])

H3889 כָּבִיר ***kābîr***, n.[m.] [2] [√ 3892]. something braided; in context referring to goat's hair:– goats hair (2 [+6436])

H3890 כֶּבֶל ***kebel***, n.[m.] [2] [→ 3886]. shackles, fetters:– shackles (2)

H3891 כָּבַס ***kābas***, v. [51] [cf. 3899]. [Q] (ptcp.) washer, fuller; [P] to wash, launder; [Pu] to be washed; [Hotpael] to be washed off:– wash (36), washed (5), launderer's (3), be washed (2), been washed (2), wash away (1), washerman's (1), NDT (1)

H3892 כָּבַר ***kābar***, v. [2] [→ 3888, 3889, 3893, 3894, 3895, 3896, 4802]. [H] to multiply; provide in abundance:– abundance (1), multiplies (1)

H3893 כְּבָר[1] ***kᵉbār¹***, adv. [9] [√ 3892]. already, before:– already (6), already (1 [+928, 8611]), before (1), long since (1)

H3894 [2]כְּבָר ***kᵉbār²***, n.pr.loc. [8] [√ 3892]. Kebar:– Kebar (8)

H3895 כְּבָרָה[1] ***kᵉbārâ¹***, n.f. [1] [√ 3892]. sieve:– sieve (1)

H3896 [2]כִּבְרָה ***kᵉbārâ²***, n.f. [3] [√ 3892]. (a certain) distance; some sources: as far as a horse can run; as far as one can see; about seven miles:– little distance (1 [+824]), some distance (1 [+824]), some distance (1 [+2021, 824])

H3897 כֶּבֶשׂ ***kebeś***, n.m. [105] [→ 3898; cf. 4166]. ram-lamb, young ram sheep:– male lambs (35), lambs (25), lamb (19), male lamb (15), sheep (3), lamb (1 [+8445, 928, 2021]), lambs (1 [+7366]), NDT (6)

H3898 כִּבְשָׂה ***kibśâ***, n.f. [8] [√ 3897]. ewe-lamb, young female sheep:– ewe lamb (4), ewe lambs (2), lamb (1), lambs (1)

H3899 כָּבַשׁ ***kābaš***, v. [14] [→ 3900, 3901; cf. 3891, 4115]. [Q] to subdue, overcome, enslave; [N] be subdued, be subject, be brought under control; [P] to subdue; [H] subdue, subjugate:– is subdued (2), been enslaved (1), enslaved (1 [+4200, 6269, 2256, 4200, 9148]), forced (1), is subject (1), make men slaves (1 [+6269]), molest (1), overcome (1), subdue (1), subdued (1), subject (1), tread underfoot (1), was brought under control (1)

H3900 כֶּבֶשׁ ***kebeš***, n.[m.] [1] [√ 3899]. footstool:– footstool (1)

H3901 כִּבְשָׁן ***kibšān***, n.m. [4] [√ 3899]. furnace, likely in context referring to a kiln or forge for making glass, pottery, smelting, etc:– furnace (4)

H3902 כַּד ***kad***, n.f. [18] jar, pitcher (of the size that could by carried on the shoulder):– jar (12), jars (3), large jars (1), pitcher (1), NDT (1)

H3903 כִּדּוּר ***kaddûr***, n.[m.] Not used in NIVEBC [√ 3960]. ball

H3904 כְּדֵי ***kᵉdê***, subst. Not used in NIVEBC [√ 3869 + 1896]. see 1896 & 3869

H3905 כַּדְכֹּד ***kadkōd***, n.[m.] [2] ruby (exact identification unknown):– rubies (2)

H3906 כְּדָרְלָעֹמֶר ***kᵉdorlā'ōmer***, כְּדָר-לָעֹמֶר ***kᵉdor-lā'ōmer***, n.pr.m. [5] Kedorlaomer, *"servant of [the deity] Lagamar"*:– Kedorlaomer (5)

H3907 כֹּה ***kōh***, adv.demo. [576] [→ 3970; 10345]. this is what, thus:– this is what (473), this (15), ever so (12), here (4), now (3), so (3), this is how (2), abundantly (1 [+6330, 889, 6330]), if (1 [+561]), if (1 [+561]), in any direction (1 [+3907, 2256]), in any direction (1 [+2256, 3907]), like this (1), meanwhile (1 [+6330, 2256, 6330, 3907]), meanwhile (1 [+6330, 3907, 2256, 6330]), over there (1), same (1), such (1), that (1), that (1 [+928]), that is what (1), there (1), this (1 [+928]), this way (1), what (1), what happened (1), NDT (45)

H3908 כָּהָה[1] ***kāhâ¹***, v. [9] [→ 3910, 3911; cf. 3909]. [Q] to grow dim, be weak; [P] to fade, become faint:– faded (2), totally blinded (2 [+3908]), weak (2), faint (1), falter (1), grown dim (1)

H3909 [2]כָּהָה ***kāhâ²***, v. [1] [cf. 3908, 3874]. [P] to rebuke, set (someone) right, with an implication that future bad behavior is curtailed:– restrain (1)

H3910 כֵּהֶה ***kēheh***, a. [7] [√ 3908]. dull; weak; smoldering; despairing:– faded (3), despair (1), dull (1), smoldering (1), weak (1)

H3911 כֵּהָה ***kēhâ***, n.f. [1] [√ 3908]. healing, relief:– heal (1 [+4200, 8691])

H3912 כָּהַן ***kāhan***, v.den. [23] [√ 3913]. [P] to serve as a priest; see also 3913:– serve as priests (12), priest (2), priests (2), serve as priest (2), served as priests (2), high priest (1), served as priest (1), serving as priests (1)

H3913 כֹּהֵן ***kōhēn***, n.m. [747] [→ 3912, 3914; 10347]. priest, who not only had religious duties, but also examined persons and things for medical diagnosis, policed the unruly, and taught the word of God:– priest (387), priests (301), he[S] (17 [+2021]), priest's (7), them[S] (3 [+2021]), who[S] (3 [+2021]), his own[S] (2 [+2021]), priestly (2), they[S] (2 [+2021]), he[S] (1 [+3381, 2021]), he himself[S] (1 [+2021]), idolatrous priests (1 [+4024, 6640]), priesthood (1), priestly (1 [+4946]), priestly (1 [+4200, 2021]), their[S] (1 [+2021]), NDT (16)

H3914 כְּהֻנָּה ***kᵉhunnâ***, n.f. [14] [√ 3913]. priesthood, priestly office; see also 3913:– priesthood (9), priestly office (2), priests (2), priestly service (1)

H3915 כּוּב ***kûb***, n.pr.g. [1] Kub:– Kub (1)

H3916 כּוֹבַע ***kôba'***, n.m. [6] [cf. 7746]. helmet:– helmets (4), helmet (2)

H3917 כָּוָה ***kāwâ***, v. [2] [→ 3918, 3953, 4805]. [N] to be burned, be scorched:– be burned (1), being scorched (1)

H3918 כְּוִיָּה ***kᵉwiyyâ***, n.f. [2] [√ 3817]. burn spot, scar (of a burn):– burn (2)

H3919 כּוֹכָב ***kôkāb***, n.m. [37] star, planet, a luminary in the night sky; by extension: human power (such as a king), heavenly power (that serve God); stargazer, one who studies the movements of the stars to predict the future:– stars (33), star (2), stargazers (1 [+2600, 928]), starry (1)

H3920 כּוּל ***kûl***, v. [38] [cf. 4005?]. [Q] to hold, seize; [Pil] to hold; to provide, supply, sustain; [H] to hold; to bear, endure:– endure (4), contain (3), held (3), hold (3), provide (3), provided (3), supplied (2), supplied provisions (2), sustain (2), bear (1), conduct (1), consume (1), feed (1), given provisions (1), hold in (1), holding (1), holding in (1), holds (1), provide supplies (1), supply (1), supply with food (1), sustained (1)

H3921 כּוּמָז ***kûmāz***, n.[m.] [2] ornament, necklace:– necklaces (1), ornaments (1)

H3922 כּוּן[1] ***kûn¹***, v. [217] [→ 3382, 3422, 3520, 3521, 3925, 4026, 4042, 4806, 4807, 4828, 5788, 5789, 9414; cf. 4029]. [N] to be established, be steadfast, be firm, be prepared; [Pol] to establish, set in place, make secure; [Polal] to be made firm, be prepared; [H] to establish, make preparations, provide; [Ho] to be made ready, be established, be attached:– established (23), prepared (13), establish (11), be established (10), prepare (10), provided (9), steadfast (7), ready (5), formed (4), founded (4), made preparations (4), set (4), establishes (3), get ready (3), provide (3), set in place (3), set up (3), was established (3), been proved (2), direct (2), is established (2), is firmly established (2), loyal (2), made ready (2), truth (2), turn (2), was carried out (2), about to (1), aim (1), appear (1 [+4604]), appointed (1), are established (1), are prepared (1), be restored (1), be set (1), be trusted (1), been firmly decided (1), been made ready (1), bent on (1), brought about (1), built (1), commit (1), confirmed (1), could (1), definite information (1), definitely (1 [+448]), determine (1), devote (1), devoted (1), done[S] (1), encourage (1 [+4213]), endure (1), establishing (1), fashions (1), find out (1), form (1), full (1), gave a firm (1), get information (1), have ready (1), is (1), is established firm (1), is made ready (1), keep loyal (1), lays up (1), made plans (1), make preparations (1), make secure (1), makes firm (1), makes secure (1), on the alert (1), ordained (1), piles (1), prepare (1 [+2118]), preparing (1), provides (1), put in order (1), put in place (1), refreshed (1), right (1), secure (1), set in order (1), set on (1), sets (1), spread (1), stand (1), standing (1 [+5163, 8079]), steadfastly (1), stood (1), stopped (1), store up (1), stores (1), string (1), supplied provisions (1), supplies (1), supply (1), support (1), sustain (1), took (1), was arranged (1), was reestablished (1), were attached (1), were prepared (1), NDT (1)

H3923 [2]כּוּן ***kûn²***, n.pr.loc. [1] Cun, *"chosen"*:– Kun (1)

H3924 כַּוָּן ***kawwān***, n.[m.] [2] cake of bread (presented as an offering):– cakes (2)

H3925 כּוֹנַנְיָהוּ ***kônanyāhû***, n.pr.m. Not used in NIVEBC [√ 3922 + 3378]. Conaniah

H3926 כּוֹס[1] ***kôs¹***, n.f. [31] cup:– cup (26), goblet (2 [+7694]), cups (1), give a drink (1 [+9197]), lot (1 [+4987])

H3927 [2]כּוֹס ***kôs²***, n.[m.] [3] little owl:– little owl (2), owl (1)

H3928 כּוּר[1] ***kûr¹***, v. Not used in NIVEBC [cf. 4839]. [Q] to bore, dig, hew

H3929 [2]כּוּר ***kûr²***, n.[m.] [9] [cf. 3968]. (little) furnace (for smelting metals); by extension: the testing and purification process:– furnace (9)

H3930 כּוֹר עָשָׁן ***kôr 'āšān***, n.pr.loc. Not used in NIVEBC [cf. 1014, 1016]. Kor Ashan

H3931 כּוֹרֶשׁ ***kôreš***, n.pr.m. [15] [√ 10350]. Cyrus:– Cyrus (15)

H3932 כּוּשׁ[1] ***kûš¹***, n.pr.loc. [29] [→ 3934, 3935]. Cush:– Cush (28), Cushite (1)

H3933 [2]כּוּשׁ ***kûš²***, n.pr.m. [1] Cush:– Cush (1)

H3934 כּוּשִׁי[1] ***kûšî¹***, a.g. [25] [√ 3932]. Cushite, *"of Cush"*:– cushite (14), cushites (8), Ethiopian (1), cushites (1 [+1201]), NDT (1)

H3935 [2]כּוּשִׁי ***kûšî²***, n.pr.m. [2] [√ 3932]. Cushi:– Cushi (2)

H3936 כּוּשָׁן ***kûšān***, n.pr.loc. [1] Cushan:– Cushan (1)

H3937 כּוּשַׁן רִשְׁעָתַיִם ***kûšan riš'ātayim***, n.pr.m. [4] [cf. 8403]. Cushan-Rishathaim, *"man of Cush, doubly guilty"*:– Cushan-Rishathaim (2), him[S] (1), whom[S] (1)

H3938 כּוֹשָׁרָה ***kôšārâ***, n.f. [1] [cf. 8876]. singing or prosperity, fortune:– singing (1)

H3939 כּוּת ***kût***, n.pr.loc. [1] [→ 3940]. Cuthah:– Kuthah (1)

H3940 כּוּתָה ***kûtâ***, n.pr.loc. [1] [√ 3939]. Cuthah:– Kuthah (1)

H3941 כָּזַב ***kāzab***, v. [16] [→ 423, 424?, 3942, 3943, 3945]. [Q] to lie; [N] to be proven a liar, be false; [P] to lie, deceive, prove false; to fail; [H] to prove someone a liar:– lie (3), lying (2), prove false (2), considered a liar (1), deceive (1), fail (1), false (1), liar (1), liar (1 [+8120]), mislead (1), not true (1), prove a liar (1)

H3942 כָּזָב ***kāzāb***, n.m. [31] [√ 3941; 10343, 10344]. lie, falsehood; by extension: delusion; false god (worshiped by a deluded person):– lies (10), lying (5), lie (4), false gods (3), false (2), deceptive (1), falsely (1), liar (1 [+408]), lie (1 [+1819]), lied (1 [+1819]), lies (1 [+1821]), lying (1 [+1819])

H3943 כֹּזֵבָא ***kōzēbā'***, n.pr.loc. [1] [√ 3941]. Cozeba, *"liar"*:– Kozeba (1)

H3944 כָּזְבִּי ***kozbî***, n.pr.f. [2] Cozbi, *"deceitful; luxuriant"*:– Kozbi (2)

H3945 כְּזִיב ***kᵉzîb***, n.pr.loc. [1] [√ 3941]. Kezib, *"deceit"*:– Kezib (1)

H3946 כֹּחַ[1] ***kōaḥ¹***, n.m. [124] strength, power, might, ability; often physical strength and the vigor of good health, sometimes simply ability to accomplish an action:– strength (55), power (30), might (4), powerful (4), ability (2), able (2 [+6806]), powerless (2 [+4202]), wealth (2), cannot (1 [+401]), crops (1), feel very weak (1 [+4202, 6806]), firm (1), great (1), helpless (1 [+4946]), helpless (1 [+4202, 6806]), mighty (1), mighty (1 [+1475]), power (1 [+2432]), powerless (1 [+401]), qualified (1), resources (1), shout (1), strengthened (1), very strong (1 [+6793]), vigorous (1), vigorously (1 [+928, 8044]), weakness (1 [+4202]), weary (1 [+3329]), yield (1), NDT (2)

H3947 [2]כֹּחַ ***kōaḥ²***, n.[m.] [1] monitor lizard; some sources: any kind of lizard:– monitor lizard (1)

H3948 כָּחַד ***kāḥad***, v. [32] [N] to be hidden; be destroyed, perish; [P] to hide, conceal, keep from; [H] to hide; to destroy, annihilate, get rid of:– hide (8), hidden (3), conceal (2), hiding (2), annihilated (1), are destroyed (1), denied (1), destroy (1), got rid of (1), hides (1), keep (1), keep back (1), led to downfall (1), lost (1), perish (1), perishing (1), ruined (1), was hidden (1), were destroyed (1), wipe out (1), wiped (1)

H3949 כָּחַל ***kāḥal***, v. [1] [Q] to paint (eyes):– applied makeup (1)

H3950 כָּחַשׁ ***kāḥaš***, v. [22] [→ 3951, 3952]. [Q] to be thin; [N] to cringe, feign obedience; [P] to lie, deceive; fail; to cringe, feign obedience; [Ht] to cringe, feign obedience:– cower (3), lied (3), cringe (2), lie (2), lying (2), deceive (1), deceiving (1), disown (1), disowns (1), fail (1), fails (1), thin (1), treachery (1), unfaithful (1), untrue (1)

H3951 כַּחַשׁ ***kaḥaš***, n.m. [6] [√ 3950]. lie, deception; gauntness, thinness, leanness:– lies (4), deception (1), gauntness (1)

H3952 כֶּחָשׁ ***keḥāš***, a. [1] [√ 3950]. deceitful, untruthful:– deceitful (1)

H3953 כִּי[1] ***kî¹***, n.[m.] [1] [√ 3917]. branding:– branding (1)

H3954 [2]כִּי ***kî²***, c. [4481] [→ 3955, 3956]. a marker that shows the relationship between clauses, sentences, or sections; logical: for, that, because; contrast: but, except; introducing a statement, often untranslated:– for (1053), that (563), because (529), when (218), if (137), but (104), though (53), surely (49), since (43), but (39 [+561]), how (38), except (24 [+561]), and (22), yet (17), even (14), so (14), although (12), only (11 [+561]), only (11), if (9 [+561]), why (9), now (8), as (7), by (7), indeed (7), even though (6), unless (6 [+561]), because (5 [+6584]), because of (5), whenever (5), yes (5), after (4), how much more (4 [+677]), however (4), if not (4 [+4295]), then (4), as for (3), because (3 [+3610]), even if (3), how much less (3 [+677]), how much less (3 [+677]), how much worse (3 [+677]), however (3 [+561]), if not (3), instead (3), just (3), now that (3), or (3), other than (3), still (3), until (3 [+6330]), while (3), after all (2), because (2 [+6813]), but (2 [+700]), but only (2), but only (2 [+561]), certainly (2), even (2 [+1685]), how much more so (2 [+677]), in fact (2), instead (2 [+561]), nevertheless (2), no (2), or (2 [+2256]), out of (2), perhaps (2), so that (2), suppose (2), surely (2 [+561]), than (2 [+561]), therefore (2), this (2), though (2 [+561]), too (2), what (2), whether (2), without (2 [+561]), all (1), although (1 [+561]), although (1 [+1685]), as well (1), at (1), at all (1), at least (1), because (1 [+9393]), because (1 [+6584, 4027]), because (1 [+6584, 4027]), because (1 [+4200, 4537]), because of (1 [+4946, 7156]), because that will mean (1), before (1 [+401]), but (1 [+421]), clearly (1 [+8011]), despite (1), even (1 [+561]), even (1 [+2256, 677]), even when (1), ever (1), for (1 [+1237]), for (1 [+6584, 4027]), for (1 [+6584, 4027]), for otherwise (1), greater (1), how much better (1 [+677]), how much less (1 [+677, 4202]), how much more (1 [+2256, 677]), how well (1), however (1 [+700]), if even (1), if so (1 [+6964]), in doing this (1), in order to (1), indeed (1 [+561]), indeed (1 [+2256, 677]), is that why (1), it was the custom of (1), just because (1), moreover (1), moreover (1 [+1685]), not (1 [+561]), not only (1), now (1 [+2296]), on the contrary (1), once (1), or (1 [+1685]), rather (1), rather (1 [+561]), rather (1 [+4202]), really (1), really (1 [+677]), rightly (1), since (1 [+3610]), since (1 [+9393]), since (1 [+6584, 4027]), so (1 [+4394]), surely (1 [+2180]), surely (1 [+6964]), that if (1), that really (1), till (1 [+6330]), truly (1), unless (1 [+561,

4202]), unless (1 [+561, 4200, 7156]), until (1 [+561]), very well then (1), well (1), what more (1 [+4537]), when (1 [+4200, 7023]), whenever (1 [+4946, 1896]), where (1), with (1), won't until (1 [+561]), yes (1 [+2180]), yes (1 [+4202]), yet (1 [+700]), yet (1 [+561]), NDT (1252)

H3955 כִּי־אִם ***kî-'im***, c. *or* pt. Not used in NIVEBC [√ 3954 + 561]. but, except

H3956 כִּי עַל כֵּן ***kî 'al kēn***, c.+pp.+adv. Not used in NIVEBC [√ 3954 + 6586]. forasmuch as

H3957 כִּיד ***kîd***, n.[m.] [1] destruction:– destruction (1)

H3958 כִּידוֹד ***kîdôd***, n.m. [1] spark:– sparks (1)

H3959 כִּידוֹן ***kîdôn***, n.[m.] [9] [→ 3961?]. javelin, lance, spear:– javelin (5), lance (2), spear (1), spears (1)

H3960 כִּידוֹר ***kîdôr***, n.[m.] [1] [→ 3903]. attack, battle:– attack (1)

H3961 כִּידֹן ***kîdōn***, n.pr.m. [1] [√ 3959?]. Kidon:– Kidon (1)

H3962 כִּיּוּן ***kiyyûn***, n.m. [1] pedestal:– pedestal (1)

H3963 כִּיּוֹר ***kiyyôr***, n.m. [22] basin, pan, firepot:– basin (12), basins (5), firepot (1 [+836]), pan (1), platform (1), NDT (2)

H3964 כִּילַי ***kîlay***, n.m. [2] [√ 5792?]. scoundrel:– scoundrel (1), scoundrels (1)

H3965 כֵּילַפּוֹת ***kêlappôt***, n.[f.] [1] [√ 3990?]. an iron-tipped tool: ax, crowbar, pickax, etc:– hatchets (1)

H3966 כִּימָה ***kîmâ***, n.f. [3] Pleiades (a constellation):– Pleiades (3)

H3967 כִּיס ***kîs***, n.m. [5] bag, purse:– bag (3), bags (1), loot (1)

H3968 כִּיר ***kîr***, n.[m.] [1] [cf. 3929]. cooking pot, stove, a small portable cooking hearth, the form of the word suggesting it is large enough for a pair of pots:– cooking pot (1)

H3969 כִּישׁוֹר ***kîšôr***, n.[m.] [1] distaff, spindle, whorl, the small disk at the bottom of a distaff to promote turning:– distaff (1)

H3970 כָּכָה ***kākâ***, adv. [37] [√ 3907]. this is what, this is how, thus:– so (6), this (4), this is how (4), this is what (4), in this way (3), in the same way (2), such a thing (2), as (1), because of (1 [+6584]), in this manner (1), like this (1), such (1), such and such (1), that (1), true (1), NDT (4)

H3971 כִּכָּר ***kikkār***, n.f. [68] [√ 4159; 10352]. plain (geographical area); loaf of bread; cover (of lead); talent (unit of weight or value, about 75 pounds [34 kg]):– talents (38), plain (10), talent (9), loaf (4), bread (1 [+4312]), cover (1), loaves (1), region (1), round (1), surrounding region (1), whole region (1)

H3972 כֹּל ***kōl***, n.m. [5413] [→ 3997; cf. 4005; 10353, 10354]. all, everyone, everything, totality of a mass or collective; every, any, a particular of a totality:– all (3246), every (302), whole (258), everything (187), any (150), entire (77), everyone (48), throughout (47 [+928]), anyone (44), anything (36), whatever (31 [+889]), no (30 [+4202]), each (24), just as (24 [+3869, 889]), always (18 [+2021, 3427]), whatever (17), a (16), total (16), whoever (16), none (13 [+4202]), one (13), rest (13), throughout (13), those[s] (12), wherever (12 [+928, 889]), everything (11 [+2021, 1821]), nothing (11 [+4202]), wherever (10 [+928]), as long as (9 [+3427]), everyone (9 [+408]), other[s] (9), altogether a total (8), completely (8), everyone (8 [+2021, 5883]), anything (7 [+1821]), anywhere (7), full (7), always (6 [+928, 6961]), altogether (5), as (5 [+3869, 889]), as long as (5 [+2021, 3427]), everything (5 [+1821]), whatever (5 [+3869, 889]), day after day (4 [+2021, 3427]), everything (4 [+5126]), much (4), obedience (4 [+2006]), some (4 [+4946]), any (3 [+285]), as long as lived (3 [+3427]), at all (3), both (3), everyone (3 [+2021, 132]), everything (3 [+4213]), everywhere (3), forever (3 [+2021, 3427]), fully (3), in all (3), nothing (3 [+401]), throughout (3 [+4200]), throughout (3 [+928, 1473]), what[s] (3), whenever (3 [+928]), all (2 [+2162]), always (2 [+3427]), an (2), any (2 [+4769]), any (2 [+408]), anyone (2 [+5883]), anyone (2 [+2021, 132]), anyone (2 [+2021, 408]), anything (2 [+4399]), anything (2 [+2021, 3998]), anywhere (2 [+928, 5226]), as long as (2 [+6388]), as long as lives (2 [+3427]), completely (2 [+4200, 2021]), continual (2 [+2021, 3427]), continually (2 [+2021, 3427]), dire (2), during (2), even (2), ever (2), ever (2 [+2021, 3427]), everyone (2 [+132]), everyone (2 [+132]), everyone (2 [+3782]), everyone (2 [+1414]), everyone (2 [+2021, 6639]), everything (2 [+3998]), everywhere (2 [+5226]), for life (2 [+2021, 3427]), great (2), great (2 [+8044]), in full force (2), it[s] (2), no (2 [+4202, 4946]), nothing (2 [+4202, 1821]), rest (2 [+3427]), something (2), them[s] (2 [+2021, 6639]), this[s] (2), through (2), together (2), totaled (2), various (2), whatever (2 [+3869]), wherever (2 [+448, 889]), wherever (2 [+928, 2021, 5226, 889]), wholeheartedly (2 [+928, 4222]), wholeheartedly (2 [+928, 4213]), abundant (1), all (1 [+2021, 408]), all kinds (1 [+4946]), all over (1), all-night (1 [+2021, 4326]), although (1 [+928, 889]), altogether a total (1 [+3427]), among (1 [+4200]), an[s] (1), annually (1 [+928, 9102, 2256, 9102]), anyone (1 [+408]), anyone (1 [+2021, 5883]), anything (1 [+889]), anything (1 [+3998]), anything (1 [+2021, 1821]), anything (1 [+1821, 4946]), anything (1 [+1821, 4946, 2021, 1821]), anywhere (1 [+1473]), anywhere in (1 [+928, 1473]), as (1), as (1 [+6645, 8611]), as (1 [+928, 889]), as in times past (1 [+3869]), as long as (1), as long as (1 [+928, 6961]), as long as live (1 [+3427]), as long as live (1 [+3427, 4200, 6409]), at flood stage (1 [+6584, 1536]), at flood stage (1 [+4848, 6584, 1536]), at random (1), at wits end (1 [+2683, 1182]), body (1), covered with (1), crowd (1 [+889, 6641]), depth (1), detailed (1), details (1), distant (1 [+362]), eagerly (1 [+928, 8356]), ever (1 [+3427]), everlasting (1 [+6409]), every (1 [+632]), every day (1 [+3427, 2256, 3427]), every way (1), everyone (1 [+4392]), everyone (1 [+5883]), everyone (1 [+5883]), everyone (1 [+2021, 408]), everyone else (1 [+7736]), everyone's (1), everyone's (1 [+2021, 132]), everything (1 [+5626]), everything (1 [+2021]), everything (1 [+8214]), everything (1 [+2021, 4856]), everything (1 [+2021, 1821, 2021, 465]), everywhere (1 [+928, 5226]), everywhere (1 [+2021, 5226]), everywhere (1 [+928, 2021, 824]), exactly as (1 [+3869, 889]), exactly like (1 [+3869, 889, 4027]), farthest recesses (1 [+9417]), filled (1 [+2118, 928]), four[s] (1), full force (1), gave the message (1 [+1819, 2021, 2021, 465, 1821]), had nothing (1 [+2893]), in (1), in accordance with (1 [+889]), in lifetime (1 [+3427]), inmost being (1 [+2540, 1061]), just as (1 [+3869]), just as (1 [+4200, 889]), just as (1 [+3869, 889, 4027]), like (1 [+3869, 889]), long (1), main (1), many (1), more (1), more and more (1 [+3578, 6584]), natural (1 [+3869, 2021, 132]), never (1 [+4202, 2021, 3427]), no yet (1 [+3270]), none (1 [+4202, 4946]), none (1 [+4202, 5883]), nothing (1 [+4202, 889]), nothing (1 [+4202, 2021]), nothing (1 [+561, 4946]), nothing but (1), nothing whatever (1 [+401, 1821]), numbered (1), one[s] (1 [+1414]), open (1), people[s] (1), people[s] (1 [+889, 928]), person (1), prosperity (1 [+8044]), regular (1 [+2021, 3427]), rest[s] (1), serious (1), shrub (1 [+8489, 2021, 8441]), so far as (1 [+4200]), solid (1), someone (1 [+2021, 132]), something (1 [+3998]), sound (1), stark naked (1 [+6872]), still (1 [+6388]), such (1 [+4946]), surpasses (1 [+6584]), that[s] (1), the (1), the[s] (1), the things[s] (1), them (1 [+7736, 3776]), them[s] (1 [+3776]), them[s] (1 [+6551]), them[s] (1 [+7736, 3776]), there is no (1 [+401]), there is nothing (1 [+401]), these[s] (1), they[s] (1), they[s] (1 [+3776]), they[s] (1 [+2021, 6639]), they[s] (1 [+1251, 4463, 8901]), things (1 [+3998]), this is how (1 [+928, 465]), those (1), those (1 [+2021, 5883]), throng (1), throughout (1 [+4946]), throughout (1 [+6584, 7156]), total (1 [+7212]), total (1 [+4200, 5031]), transfer of property (1 [+9455, 1821]), tribes (1 [+1074]), vast (1), whatever (1 [+3869, 889, 4027]), whenever (1), whenever (1 [+4200]), whenever (1 [+928, 6961]), whenever (1 [+928, 889]), wherever (1 [+889, 9004]), wherever (1 [+928, 2021, 5226]), wherever (1 [+4946, 2021, 5226]), wherever (1 [+6584, 2021, 5226, 889]), while (1 [+3427]), while continues (1 [+3427]), who[s] (1), whoever (1 [+408, 889]), whoever (1 [+2021, 132]), your[s] (1), NDT (302)

H3973 [1]כָּלָא ***kālā'[1]***, v. [17] [→ 3975, 3989, 4813; cf. 3974, 3983, 3984; cf. 3998]. [Q] to stop, withhold, contain; [Qp] to be confined; [N] to be restrained:– were restrained (2), am confined (1), confined (1), contain (1), hold back (1), imprisoned (1), keeping (1), kept (1), penned up (1 [+1074, 928, 2021]), refuse (1), seal (1), stop (1), stopped falling (1), withheld (1), withhold (1), NDT (1)

H3974 [2]כָּלָא ***kālā'[2]***, v. [1] [cf. 3973, 3998]. [P] to finish:– finish (1)

H3975 כֶּלֶא ***kele'***, n.[m.] [10] [√ 3973; cf. 3999]. prison, (house of) imprisonment:– prison (4 [+1074, 2021]), prison (2), prison (2 [+1074]), dungeon (1 [+1074]), prisons (1 [+1074])

H3976 כִּלְאָב ***kil'āb***, n.pr.m. [1] Kileab:– Kileab (1)

H3977 כִּלְאַיִם ***kil'ayim***, n.[m.] [4] (things of) two kinds:– two kinds (3), different kinds (1)

H3978 כֶּלֶב ***keleb***, n.m. [32] [→ 3979; cf. 3990]. dog; by extension of a person of low status: a dead dog; an immoral person: male prostitute:– dogs (19), dog (10), dog's (2), male prostitute (1)

H3979 כָּלֵב ***kālēb***, n.pr.m. [35] [→ 3980, 3981, 3982, 3990, 3992; cf. 3978]. Caleb, "*dog; snappish, warding off*":– Caleb (29), Caleb's (6)

H3980 כָּלֵב אֶפְרָתָה ***kālēb 'eprātâ***, n.pr.loc. [1] [√ 3979 + 716]. Caleb Ephrathah:– Caleb Ephrathah (1)

H3981 כָּלִבּוֹ ***kālibbiw***, a.g. Not used in NIVEBC [√ 3979]. see 3982

H3982 כָּלִבִּי ***kālibbî***, a.g. [1] [√ 3979]. Calebite, "*of Caleb*":– Calebite (1)

H3983 [1]כָּלָה ***kālâ[1]***, v. [205] [→ 432, 3985, 3986, 4001, 4002, 4816, 9416, 9417; cf. 3973, 3974, 3998, 4005, 5801]. [Q] to finish, fulfill, complete; to fail, cease, perish; [P] to finish, complete, fulfill; to destroy, end, wipe out; [Pu] to be completed, be concluded:– finished (54), destroyed (12), destroy (10), fail (10), completed (6), spend (6), finish (5), perish (5), end (4), put an end (4), consume (3), consumed (3), ended (3), gone (3), spent (3), cease (2), come to an end (2), complete (2), destroy completely (2), determined (2), finishing (2), fulfill (2), made an end (2), pour out (2), used up (2), very (2), after (1), after (1 [+561]), all (1), bent on (1), broken (1), came to an end (1), completely (1), completely (1 [+6330]), completely (1 [+6330, 9462]), completely destroyed (1 [+6330]), completion (1), concludes (1), crushed (1), decided (1), destroys (1), devour (1), disappear (1), done (1), eliminate (1), ending (1), failed (1), fails (1), faints (1), faints with longing (1), finally (1), full (1), given full vent (1), go up (1), grow weary (1), had enough (1), hanging (1), intended (1), leaving (1), longed (1), make an end (1), met (1), no more (1), overcome (1), ravage (1), settled (1), stopped (1), strip bare (1), vanish (1), vanishes (1), wastes away (1), were completed (1), wipe (1), wiped (1), wiped out (1), yearns (1), NDT (2)

H3984 [2]כָּלָה ***kālâ[2]***, v. Not used in NIVEBC [cf. 3973]. see 3973

H3985 כָּלֶה ***kāleh***, a. [1] [√ 3983]. failing with desire, longing:– wear out (1)

H3986 כָּלָה ***kālâ[3]***, n.f. [21] [√ 3983]. destruction, complete destruction:– end (6), completely destroy (5 [+6913]), destroy completely (3 [+6913]), destruction (2), bad (1), completely (1), destructive (1), power to destroy (1), totally (1)

H3987 כַּלָּה ***kallâ***, n.f. [34] [→ 3994]. (before marriage) bride; daughter-in-law:– bride (15), daughter-in-law (14), daughters-in-law (5)

H3988 כְּלֻהַי ***k[e]luhî***, n.pr.m. [1] [cf. 3993]. Keluhi:– Keluhi (1)

H3989 כְּלוּא ***k[e]lû'***, n.[m.] [2] [√ 3973]. imprisonment:– prison (2 [+1074, 2021])

H3990 [1]כְּלוּב ***k[e]lûb[1]***, n.m. [3] [→ 3965?, 3978, 3979, 3990, 3991?]. (fruit) basket; (bird) cage:– basket (2), cages (1)

H3991 [2]כְּלוּב ***k[e]lûb[2]***, n.pr.m. [2] [√ 3990?]. Kelub, "*basket*":– Kelub (2)

H3992 כְּלוּבָי ***k[e]lûbāy***, n.pr.m. [1] [√ 3979]. Caleb, "*dog; snappish warding off*":– Caleb (1)

H3993 כְּלוּהוּ ***k[e]lûhû***, n.pr.m. Not used in NIVEBC [cf. 3988]. Keluhu

H3994 כְּלוּלֹת ***k[e]lûlōt***, n.f. [1] [√ 3987]. time of betrothal, state of betrothal:– bride (1)

H3995 [1]כֶּלַח ***kelaḥ[1]***, n.m. [2] full vigor:– full vigor (1), vigor (1)

H3996 [2]כֶּלַח ***kelaḥ[2]***, n.pr.loc. [2] Calah, "*strength, vigor*":– Calah (2)

H3997 כָּל־חֹזֶה ***kol-ḥōzeh***, n.pr.m. [2] [√ 3972 + 2602]. Col-Hozeh, "*every seer*":– Kol-Hozeh (2)

H3998 כְּלִי ***k[e]lî***, n.m. [323] [cf. 3973?, 3974?, 3983?]. article, utensil, thing; a general term that can be used of any object:– articles (70), armor-bearer (19 [+5951]), furnishings (19), utensils (13), weapons (12), instruments (10), equipment (9), jar (9), pot (9), article (8), weapon (8), accessories (7), jars (6), jewelry (5), supplies (5), things (5), armor (4), belongings (4), goods (4), objects (4), armed (3 [+2520]), object (3), anything (2), anything (2 [+3972, 2021]), armor-bearers (2 [+5951]), armory (2 [+1074]), bag (2), bags (2), everything (2 [+3972]), goblets (2 [+5482]), household articles (2), instruments (2 [+8877]), jewels (2), one[s] (2), packed (2), treasures (2 [+2775]), vessels (2), another[s] (1), anything (1 [+3972]), basket (1), boats (1), bodies (1), cargo (1 [+889, 928, 2021, 641]), clothing (1), container (1), dishes (1), goblets (1), it[s] (1), jewel (1), kinds (1), methods (1), other[s] (1), pitchers (1), possessions (1), pots (1), pottery (1), pottery (1 [+3450]), sacks (1), something (1), something (1 [+3972]), specific things (1 [+5466]), storage jar (1), storage jars (1), them[s] (1 [+1074, 2021, 466]), things (1 [+3972]), tool (1), vessel (1), weapon (1 [+4878]), weapon (1 [+5424]), weapon (1 [+7372, 4878]), weapons (1 [+4878]), yokes (1), NDT (22)

H3999 כְּלִיא ***k[e]lî'***, n.[m.] Not used in NIVEBC [cf. 3975]. imprisonment

H4000 כִּלְיָה ***kilyâ***, n.f. [31] kidney; by extension: inmost being: heart, mind, spirit, the seat of thought and emotion of the inner person; kernel (of wheat):– kidneys (18), heart (4), mind (3), inmost being (2), hearts (1), kernels (1), minds (1), spirit (1)

H4001 כִּלָּיוֹן ***killāyôn***, n.m. [2] [√ 3983]. destruction, annihilation; weariness, failure (of the eyes):– destruction (1), weary with longing (1)

H4002 כִּלְיוֹן ***kilyôn***, n.pr.m. [3] [√ 3983]. Kilion, "*annihilation*":– Kilion (3)

H4003 כָּלִיל ***kālîl***, a. & subst. [15] [√ 4005]. entire, whole, perfect; whole burnt offering:– perfect (3), completely (2), entirely (2), whole (2), offered whole (1), perfection (1), solid (1), totally (1), whole burnt offering (1), whole burnt offerings (1)

H4004 כַּלְכֹּל ***kalkōl***, n.pr.m. [2] [√ 4005?]. Calcol:– Kalkol (2)

H4005 כָּלַל ***kālal***, v. [2] [→ 3972, 3997, 4003, 4004?, 4006,

4814, 4815, 4817; cf. 3920?, 3983; 10353, 10354]. [Q] to bring to perfection, make complete:– brought to perfection (2)

H4006 כְּלָל **kelāl**, n.pr.m. [1] [√ 4005]. Kelal, *"perfection, completeness"*:– Kelal (1)

H4007 כָּלַם **kālam**, v. [38] [→ 4009, 4010]. [N] to be disgraced, be humiliated, be put to shame; [H] to disgrace, humble, bring to shame; [Ho] to be mistreated, be despairing:– ashamed (6), disgraced (6), humiliated (3), blush (2), disgrace (2), mistreat (2), be disgraced (1), be put to shame (1), been in disgrace (1), blush with shame (1), despairing (1), disgraces (1), fear disgrace (1), humbled (1), in disgrace (1), lacked (1), put to shame (1), puts to shame (1), rebuke (1), reprimand (1), reproached (1), shameful treatment (1), were shocked (1)

H4008 כִּלְמַד **kilmad**, n.pr.loc. [1] Kilmad:– Kilmad (1)

H4009 כְּלִמָּה **kelimmâ**, n.f. [30] [√ 4007]. disgrace, shame, scorn:– disgrace (12), shame (9), scorn (3), dishonor (1), dishonors (1), humiliation (1), mocking (1), shamed (1), taunts (1)

H4010 כְּלִמּוּת **kelimmût**, n.f. [1] [√ 4007]. shame, disgrace, insult:– shame (1)

H4011 כַּלְנֵה **kalnēh**, n.pr.loc. [2] [cf. 4012]. Calneh, *"all of them"*:– Kalneh (2)

H4012 כַּלְנוֹ **kalnô**, n.pr.loc. [1] [cf. 4011]. Calno, *"all of them"*:– Kalno (1)

H4013 כֶם- **-kem**, p.m.pl.suf. [2648] [√ 3870]. you, your:– you (1269), your (931), theS (52), your (47 [+4200]), yourselves (35), your own (20), yourselves (12 [+5883]), their (4), you (4 [+5883]), yours (4 [+4200]), your own (3 [+4200]), yours (3), themS (2 [+7700]), yourselves (2 [+7156]), aS (1), anS (1), everyS (1), himS (1 [+3378, 466]), see for yourselves (1 [+8011, 6524]), the (1), the peopleS (1), them (1), themS (1 [+278]), themS (1 [+1201]), themS (1 [+3]), theyS (1 [+3]), us (1 [+3276, 2256]), what do you mean (1 [+4537, 4200]), you (1 [+6795]), you (1 [+7156]), your (1 [+4946]), your (1 [+6584]), yourselves (1 [+4222]), yourselves (1 [+7418]), you're (1), NDT (239)

H4014 כָּמַהּ **kāmah**, v. [1] [→ 4016]. [Q] to long for, yearn for:– longs for (1)

H4015 כַּמָּה **kammâ**, pp.+p.inter. Not used in NIVEBC [√ 3869 + 4537; 10356]. why?, see 3869 & 4537

H4016 כִּמְהָם **kimhām**, n.pr.m. [3] [→ 1745; cf. 4014, 4018]. Kimham:– Kimham (3)

H4017 כְּמוֹ **kemô**, adv. & c. [140] [√ 3869 + 4537]. like, as; for, with, when:– like (79), as (26), according to (2), with (2), all (1), as though (1), as well as (1), but (1), deepest night (1 [+6547, 694]), equal (1), equal to (1), even so (1), for (1), in a moment (1 [+8092]), kind (1), like that (1), or (1), same (1), seem (1 [+928, 6524]), such (1 [+4027]), such as (1), what (1 [+889]), whether (1), worse (1 [+4202]), worth (1), NDT (10)

H4018 כִּמְוהָם **kimwhām**, n.pr.m. Not used in NIVEBC [cf. 4016]. Kimuham

H4019 כְּמוֹשׁ **kemôš**, n.pr. [8] [cf. 4020]. Chemosh (pagan god):– Chemosh (8)

H4020 כְּמִישׁ **kemîš**, var. Not used in NIVEBC [cf. 4019]. see 4019

H4021 כַּמֹּן **kammōn**, n.m. [3] cummin (a small, flavorful seed of the carrot family):– cumin (3)

H4022 כָּמַס **kāmas**, v. [1] [→ 4820, 4825]. [Qp] to be kept in reserve:– kept in reserve (1)

H4023 כָּמַר **kāmar**, v. [4] [→ 4024]. [N] to become hot; become aroused, be excited (with compassion):– aroused (1), deeply moved (1), deeply moved (1 [+8171]), hot (1)

H4024 כֹּמֶר **kōmer**, n.m. [3] [√ 4023]. priest, in the OT always one who serves a foreign god, with a possible focus on manic rituals and altered states of awareness:– idolatrous priests (2), idolatrous priests (1 [+6640, 3913])

H4025 כַּמְרִיר **kamrîr**, n.m. [1] blackness, deep gloom:– blackness (1 [+3427])

H4026 ¹כֵּן **kēn1**, a. [20] [→ 4027; cf. 3922]. honest; right, correct, orderly:– right (7), honest (5), agreed (1), correctly (1), order (1), truly (1), unjustly (1 [+4202]), upright (1), yes (1), NDT (1)

H4027 ²כֵּן **kēn2**, adv. [748] [→ 4026, 4338, 6586; 10357]. marker to show sequence of logic: so, thus, therefore; marker to show sequence of events: so, then:– therefore (147 [+4200]), so (86), therefore (51 [+6584]), that is why (34 [+6584]), this (32), so (25 [+6584]), same (24), that (18), just as (17 [+3869, 889]), afterward (15 [+339]), as (12 [+3869, 889]), so (10 [+4200]), in the course of time (8 [+339]), such (7), as (6), because (5 [+6584]), but (5 [+4200]), this is why (5 [+6584]), true (4), what (4), after (3 [+339]), for (3), in this way (3), itS (3), later (3 [+339]), like (3), more (3), some time later (3 [+339]), that is what (3), then (3 [+4200]), this is what (3), and (2), and so (2 [+6584]), exactly (2), exactly as (2 [+3869, 889]), in way (2), just what (2 [+3869, 889]), like that (2), like this (2), no (2 [+4202]), so that (2 [+6584]), such a thing (2), surely (2 [+4200]), that is how (2), that is the way (2), then (2 [+339]), this is how (2), very well (2 [+4200]), what (2 [+3869, 889]), accordingly (1), alike (1), also (1), and (1 [+4200]), and (1 [+6584]), as (1 [+3869]), as soon as (1 [+3869]), as well (1), because (1 [+4200]), because (1 [+3954, 6584]), because (1 [+3954, 6584]), because of (1 [+6584]), because of this (1 [+4200]), because of this (1 [+6584]), custom (1 [+6913]), customary (1 [+1821]), empty (1 [+4202]), enough (1), exactly like (1 [+3869]), exactly like (1 [+3869, 3972, 889]), follow (1 [+6913]), follow lead (1 [+6913]), followed (1 [+6913]), follows (1 [+339]), for (1 [+3954, 6584]), for (1 [+3954, 6584]), from then on (1 [+4946, 339]), fulfill (1 [+6913, 7023, 3869]), fulfilled (1 [+2118]), futile (1 [+4202]), greatly (1), happeningS (1), how (1 [+6584]), however (1 [+4200]), in accordance with (1 [+3869]), in the course of time (1 [+4946, 339]), in the same order (1), in the same way (1), it must be (1), just as (1), just as (1 [+3869]), just as (1 [+3869, 3972, 889]), just for that (1 [+4200]), just like (1 [+3869]), later (1 [+4946, 339]), let it be (1 [+2085]), like (1 [+3869, 889]), nevertheless (1 [+4200]), no wonder (1 [+6584]), no wonder (1 [+6584]), not (1), nothing (1 [+4202]), only then (1 [+339]), particularly (1 [+4200]), same (1 [+3869, 889]), similar (1), since (1 [+6584]), since (1 [+3954, 6584]), so much (1), so then (1 [+4200]), still (1 [+4200]), such (1 [+4017]), that (1 [+6584]), that is what (1 [+6584]), that was how (1), that's why (1 [+6584]), then (1), then (1 [+6584]), therefore (1 [+4200, 3610]), this was the kind (1), this was what (1), this way (1), too (1), tried (1 [+6913]), very thing (1 [+3869, 889]), very well (1), whatever (1 [+3869, 889]), whatever (1 [+3869, 3972, 889]), why (1 [+561, 4200, 4537]), yes (1), yet (1), yet (1 [+4200]), NDT (82)

H4028 ³כֵּן **kēn3**, pt.rel. which

H4029 ⁴כֵּן **kēn4**, n.m. [10] [→ 4030, 4039, 4040, 4041; cf. 3922]. stand (of a basin):– stand (8), basework (1 [+5126]), mast (1 [+9568])

H4030 ⁵כֵּן **kēn5**, n.m. [6] [√ 4029]. position; place:– position (2), instead of (1 [+6584]), place (1), succeeded (1 [+6641, 6584]), successor (1 [+6641, 6584])

H4031 ⁶כֵּן **kēn6**, n.[m.] [5] [→ 4038]. gnats, flies:– gnats (4), flies (1)

H4032 כֶן- **-ken**, כֶנָה- **-kenâ**, p.f.pl.suf. [19] [√ 3870]. you, your:– your (13), you (5), your own (1)

H4033 כָּנָה **kānâ**, v. [4] [P] to bestow a title or name of honor; to flatter by giving a name of honor:– bestow a title of honor (1), flatter (1), flattery (1), take (1)

H4034 כַּנֵּה **kannēh**, n.pr.loc. [1] Canneh:– Kanneh (1)

H4035 כַּנָּה **kannâ**, n.f. [1] root:– root (1)

H4036 כִּנּוֹר **kinnôr**, n.m. [42] a stringed instrument: harp, lyre, lute, zither:– harps (19), harp (15), lyre (6), lyres (1), stringed instruments (1)

H4037 כָּנְיָהוּ **konyāhû**, n.pr.m. [3] [√ 3382; cf. 3378 + 3922]. Jehoiachin:– Jehoiachin (3)

H4038 כִּנָּם **kinnām**, n.[m.] [2] [√ 4031]. gnats:– gnats (2)

H4039 כְּנָנִי **kenānî**, n.pr.m. [1] [→ 4040; cf. 4029 + 3378]. Kenani, *"Yahweh strengthens"*:– Kenani (1)

H4040 כְּנַנְיָה **kenanyâ**, n.pr.m. [1] [√ 4039; cf. 4029 + 3378]. Kenaniah, *"Yahweh strengthens"*:– Kenaniah (1)

H4041 כְּנַנְיָהוּ **kenanyāhû**, n.pr.m. [2] [√ 4039; cf. 4029 + 3378]. Kenaniah, *"Yahweh strengthens"*:– Kenaniah (2)

H4042 כָּנַנְיָהוּ **kānanyāhû**, n.pr.m. [3] [√ 3378 + 3922]. Conaniah, *"Yahweh sustains"*:– Konaniah (3)

H4043 כָּנַס **kānas**, v. [11] [→ 4829; 10359]. [Q, P] to assemble, gather, store up; [Ht] to wrap around:– gather (3), gathers (2), amassed (1), assemble (1), bring (1), gather together (1), storing up wealth (1), wrap around (1)

H4044 כָּנַע **kāna'**, v. [36] [→ 4045]. [N] to be humbled, be subdued, be subjected; [H] to subdue, humble, subject:– humbled himself (5), subdued (5), humbled themselves (4), humbled yourself (3), subdue (3), humble himself (2), subjected (2), were subdued (2), are humbled (1), humble (1), humble themselves (1), humbled (1), made subject to (1 [+9393, 3338]), repented (1), silence (1), was subdued (1), were subjugated (1), NDT (1)

H4045 כִּנְעָה **kin'â**, n.f. [1] [√ 4044]. bundle of belongings:– belongings (1)

H4046 ¹כְּנַעַן **kena'an1**, n.pr.m. & loc. [88] [→ 4049?, 4050]. Canaan; Canaanite, *"land of purple,* hence *merchant, trader"*:– Canaan (53), Canaan (29 [+824]), Canaanite (3), Phoenicia (1), himS (1 [+3296, 4889]), thereS (1 [+824, 2025])

H4047 ²כְּנַעַן **kena'an2**, n.[m.] [4] [→ 4048, 4051]. merchant, trader:– merchants (2), merchant (1), merchants (1 [+6639])

H4048 כִּנְעָן **kin'ān**, n.m. [1] [√ 4047]. trader, merchant:– traders (1)

H4049 כְּנַעֲנָה **kena'ănâ**, n.pr.m. [5] [√ 4046?]. Kenaanah, *"toward Canaan"*:– Kenaanah (5)

H4050 ¹כְּנַעֲנִי **kena'ănî1**, a.g. [71] [√ 4046]. Canaanite, of Canaan, in Canaan, *"of Canaan"*:– Canaanites (56), Canaanite (13), Canaan (1), in Canaan (1)

H4051 ²כְּנַעֲנִי **kena'ănî2**, n.m. [2] [√ 4047]. merchant, trader:– merchants (2)

H4052 כָּנַף **kānap**, v.den. [1] [√ 4053]. [N] to hide oneself, be hidden:– hidden (1)

H4053 כָּנָף **kānāp**, n.f. [108] [→ 4052]. extreme part: wing (of creatures that fly); corner, hem (of garment); ends (of the earth):– wings (55), wing (13), corner (3), corners (3), corner of garment (2), ends (2), fold (2), themS (2 [+2157]), bird (1 [+1251]), bird (1 [+7606]), bird on the wing (1 [+1251]), birds (1 [+7606]), birds (1 [+6416]), clothes (1), dishonor bed (1 [+1655]), dishonors bed (1 [+1655]), eachS (1), edges (1), flying (1), folds of garment (1), hem (1), hem of robe (1), kindS (1), kindsS (1), otherS (1), piece (1), quarters (1), rays (1), sweep away (1 [+7674, 928]), thoseS (1), total wingspan (1 [+802]), winged (1), NDT (2)

H4054 כִּנְרוֹת **kinrôt**, כִּנֲרוֹת **kinarôt**, n.pr.loc. [3] [→ 4055]. Kinnereth, *"zithers, lyres"*:– Kinnereth (2), Galilee (1)

H4055 כִּנֶּרֶת **kinneret**, n.pr.loc. [4] [√ 4054]. Kinnereth, *"zithers, lyres"*:– Galilee (2), Kinnereth (2)

H4056 כְּנָת **kenāt**, n.f. [1] [√ 10360]. associate, companion:– associates (1)

H4057 כֶּסֶא **kese'**, n.[m.] [3] [→ 4060, 4061]. full moon:– full moon (1), full moon (1 [+3427]), moon full (1)

H4058 כִּסֵּא **kissē'**, n.m. [135] [→ 4066; 10372]. seat, chair; in a public or civic setting: place of authority, seat of honor; of royalty or deity: throne:– throne (109), thrones (8), chair (4), seat (3), seat of honor (3), thoseS (2), authority (1), enthroned (1 [+4200]), enthrones (1 [+3782, 4200, 2021]), it (1 [+2021]), itsS (1 [+4200, 2021]), NDT (1)

H4059 כָּסָה **kāsâ**, v. [151] [→ 4062, 4064, 4832, 4833]. [Qp] to be covered; [N] to be covered; [P] to cover, conceal; to decorate; to overwhelm; [Pu] to be covered, be shrouded; [Ht] to cover oneself, put on clothing:– covered (37), cover (25), covers (11), covering (6), decorating (4), be covered (3), conceals (3), cover (3 [+4832]), cover up (3), hide (3), put on (3), wearing (3), were covered (3), clothed (2), conceal (2), concealed (2), keep (2), on (2), provides (2), put over (2), are covered (1), bathing (1), blindfolds (1 [+7156]), buried (1), closed (1), clothe (1), cover themselves (1), cover up (1 [+2256, 8740]), covered herself (1), covered up (1), covers over (1), decorate (1), does (1), engulf (1), engulfed (1), fills (1), flood (1), is shrouded (1), keeps (1), overlook (1), overwhelm (1), overwhelmed (1), overwhelms (1), shield (1), was covered (1), wear (1), NDT (4)

H4060 כֶּסֶה **kēseh**, n.[m.] Not used in NIVEBC [√ 4057]. full moon

H4061 כִּסֵּה **kissēh**, n.m. Not used in NIVEBC [√ 4058]. see 4057

H4062 כָּסוּי **kāsûy**, n.[m.] [2] [√ 4059]. covering:– cover (1 [+5989]), covering (1)

H4063 כְּסֻלּוֹת **kesûlôt**, n.pr.loc. [1] [√ 4071]. Kesulloth, *"loins or flanks [of Mt. Tabor]"*:– Kesulloth (1)

H4064 כְּסוּת **kesût**, n.f. [8] [√ 4059]. covering, cloak, clothing:– covering (2), cloak (1), clothing (1), cover (1), cover the offense (1 [+6524]), garments (1), uncovered (1 [+401])

H4065 כָּסַח **kāsaḥ**, v. [2] [Qp] to be cut down (of brush):– cut (1), is cut down (1)

H4066 כֵּסְיָה **kēsyāh**, n.m. Not used in NIVEBC [√ 4058]. see 3363 & 4058

H4067 ¹כְּסִיל **kesîl1**, n.m. [70] [→ 4068; cf. 4071]. foolish, stupid, insolent; (n.) fool, insolent person:– fools (33), fool (26), foolish (7), fool's (2), fool (1 [+408]), fools (1 [+132])

H4068 ²כְּסִיל **kesîl2**, n.m. [4] [√ 4067; cf. 4071]. Orion (and its adjoining constellations):– Orion (2), Orion's (1), constellations (1)

H4069 ³כְּסִיל **kesîl3**, n.pr.loc. [1] Kesil:– Kesil (1)

H4070 כְּסִילוּת **kesîlût**, n.f. [1] [√ 4071]. folly, stupidity, insolence, with a possible implication of rebellion:– Folly (1)

H4071 כָּסַל **kāsal**, v. [1] [→ 4063, 4067, 4068, 4070, 4072?, 4073, 4074, 4076, 4077]. [Q] to be foolish, be stupid:– foolish (1)

H4072 ¹כֶּסֶל **kesel1**, n.m. [7] [→ 4079?; cf. 4071]. waist, back; (pl.) loins:– loins (5), back (1), waist (1)

H4073 ²כֶּסֶל **kesel2**, n.m. [6] [√ 4071]. trust, confidence; stupidity:– trust (3), side (1), stupidity (1), trust in (1)

H4074 כִּסְלָה **kislâ**, n.f. [2] [√ 4071]. confidence; folly:– confidence (1), folly (1)

H4075 כִּסְלֵו **kislēw**, n.pr.[m.] [2] Kislev:– Kislev (2)

H4076 כְּסָלוֹן **kesālôn**, n.pr.loc. [1] [√ 4071]. Kesalon:– Kesalon (1)

H4077 כִּסְלוֹן **kislôn**, n.pr.m. [1] [√ 4071]. Kislon, *"slow; strength"*:– Kislon (1)

H4078 כַּסְלֻחִים **kasluḥîm**, n.pr.g. [2] Casluhite:– Kasluhites (2)

H4079 כִּסְלֹת תָּבוֹר **kislōt tābôr**, n.pr.loc. [1] [√ 4072? + 9314]. Kisloth Tabor:– Kisloth Tabor (1)

H4080 כָּסַם ***kāsam***, v. [2] [→ 4081; cf. 1612, 4155]. [Q] to trip, clip (hair):– keep hair trimmed (2 [+4080])

H4081 כֻּסֶּמֶת ***kussemet***, n.f. [3] [√ 4080]. spelt, emmer wheat:– spelt (3)

H4082 כָּסַס ***kāsas***, v. [1] [→ 4830, 4831]. [Q] to determine, reckon, compute:– determine amount needed (1)

H4083 כָּסַף ***kāsap***, v. [6] [→ 4084]. [Q] to long for; be hungry; [N] to long for, yearn for; to be ashamed:– longed (2 [+4083]), hungry (1), long for (1), shameful (1 [+4202]), yearns (1)

H4084 כֶּסֶף ***kesep***, n.m. [403] [√ 4083; 10362]. silver, silver piece = money:– silver (304), money (60), price (7), silver (4 [+4084]), bought (2 [+5239]), shekels (2), value (2 [+6886]), bought (1 [+7864, 928, 2021]), buy (1 [+928]), it[S] (1 [+2021]), must sell (1 [+4835, 928, 2021, 4835]), pay (1 [+5989]), pay (1 [+9202]), pay for the loss (1 [+8966]), payment (1), property (1), sell (1 [+5989, 928]), sell (1 [+5989, 928]), value (1), what paid (1), NDT (9)

H4085 כָּסִפְיָא ***kāsipyā'***, n.pr.loc. [2] Casiphia:– Kasiphia (2)

H4086 כֶּסֶת ***keset***, n.f. [2] magic charm band:– magic charms (2)

H4087 כָּעַס ***kā'as***, v. [54] [→ 4088; cf. 4089]. [Q] to be angry, be vexed, be incensed; [P] to anger, provoke; [H] to provoke to anger:– aroused anger (17), arouse anger (7), arousing anger (6), angered (3), aroused the anger (3), provoked (3), angry (2), arouse anger (1 [+4088]), arouse the anger (1), aroused anger (1 [+4088]), aroused the anger (1 [+4088]), frustration (1), incensed (1), kept provoking (1 [+1685, 4088]), make angry (1), provoke (1), provoking (1), thrown insults (1), trouble (1), vexed (1)

H4088 כַּעַס ***ka'as***, n.m. [21] [√ 4087]. sorrow, grief, anxiety; anger, displeasure, annoyance:– grief (4), sorrow (3), anger (1), angered (1), annoyance (1), anxiety (1), arouse anger (1 [+4087]), aroused anger (1), aroused anger (1 [+4087]), aroused the anger (1 [+4087]), displeasure (1), frustration (1), kept provoking (1 [+4087, 1685]), nagging (1), provocation (1), taunt (1)

H4089 כַּעַשׂ ***ka'aś***, n.m. [4] [√ 4088; cf. 4087]. general uneasiness and anxiety, inwardly focused: anguish, grief; focused toward an object: anger, resentment:– anger (1), anguish (1), grief (1), resentment (1)

H4090 כַּף ***kap***, n.f. [192] [√ 4104]. hand (of a person), palm of the hand, sole of the foot, paw (of an animal); by extension: power, strength; something hollowed: socket, (shallow) dish; a measure of quantity: handful:– hands (76), hand (31), dish (12), dishes (12), palm (6), soles (6), feet (4 [+8079]), foot (4 [+8079]), sole (4), hands (3 [+3338]), socket (3), grasp (2), handful (2 [+4850]), hands together (2 [+4090, 448]), hands together (2 [+448, 4090]), palm of hand (2), arms (1), be taken captive (1 [+9530, 928, 2021]), clutches (1), each[S] (1 [+2021]), earnings (1 [+7262]), fingers (1), from (1 [+4946]), fruit of labor (1 [+3330]), handles (1), palms of hands (1), paws (1), perch (1 [+4200, 8079]), pocket (1), reach out (1 [+5951]), their (1 [+928, 2157]), those[S] (1 [+8079]), took a handful (1 [+4848]), NDT (4)

H4091 כֵּף ***kēp***, n.[m.] [2] rock:– rocks (2)

H4092 כָּפָה ***kāpâ***, v. [1] [Q] to soothe, avert (anger):– soothes (1)

H4093 כִּפָּה ***kippâ***, n.f. [4] [√ 4104]. palm branch, palm frond:– palm branch (2), branches (1), NDT (1)

H4094 [1]כְּפוֹר ***kᵉpôr[1]***, n.m. [9] bowl, dish (made of gold or silver):– bowls (3), each dish (2 [+4094, 2256]), each dish (2 [+2256, 4094]), NDT (2)

H4095 [2]כְּפוֹר ***kᵉpôr[2]***, n.m. [3] [√ 4105]. frost:– frost (3)

H4096 כָּפִיס ***kāpîs***, n.m. [1] beam (of woodwork); some sources: rafter:– beams (1)

H4097 כְּפִיר ***kᵉpîr***, n.m. [30] [√ 4105]. young lion:– lion (7), lions (7), great lion (3), strong lion (3), young lions (3), fierce lion (1), great lions (1), it[S] (1), them[S] (1), young (1), young lion (1), young lion (1 [+787])

H4098 כְּפִירָה ***kᵉpîrâ***, n.pr.loc. [4] [√ 4107]. Kephirah, "*village*":– Kephirah (4)

H4099 כְּפִירִים ***kᵉpîrîm***, n.m.[loc.?] [2] [√ 4107]. villages:– villages (2)

H4100 כָּפַל ***kāpal***, v. [4] [→ 4101, 4834]. [Q] to fold double; [Qp] to be folded double; [N] to be doubled:– folded double (2), fold double (1), strike twice (1)

H4101 כֶּפֶל ***kepel***, n.[m.] [3] [√ 4100]. double; two sides:– double (2), two sides (1)

H4102 כָּפַן ***kāpan***, v. [1] [→ 4103]. [Q] to hunger, send out roots in hunger:– sent out (1)

H4103 כָּפָן ***kāpān***, n.[m.] [2] [√ 4102]. hunger, famine:– famine (1), hunger (1)

H4104 כָּפַף ***kāpap***, v. [5] [→ 4090, 4093]. [Q] to bow down in distress; [Qp] be bowed down; [N] bow down (before):– are bowed down (2), bow down (1), bowed down in distress (1), bowing (1)

H4105 [1]כָּפַר ***kāpar[1]***, v. [100] [→ 4095, 4097, 4106, 4109, 4111, 4113, 4114; cf. 4106, 4109]. [Nitpael] to be atoned (for); [P] to make atonement; make amends, pardon, release, appease, forgive; [Pu] to be atoned for, be annulled; [Ht] to allow for atonement; atonement may be a figure of covering over and therefore forgetting (forgiving) sin:– make atonement (59), making atonement (6), atonement made (5), made atonement (4), atone (3), be atoned for (3), forgave (2), forgive (2), makes atonement (2), accept atonement (1), appease (1), atoned for (1), atonement (1), atonement be made (1), atonement made (1 [+4113]), atonement was made (1), be annulled (1), be atoned (1), is atoned for (1), pacify (1 [+7156]), pardon (1), ward off with a ransom (1), NDT (1)

H4106 [2]כָּפַר ***kāpar[2]***, v.den. [1] [√ 4109; cf. 4105]. [Q] to coat, cover (with pitch):– coat (1)

H4107 כָּפָר ***kāpār***, n.m. [2] [→ 4098, 4099, 4108, 4112]. (unwalled) village:– villages (2)

H4108 [1]כֹּפֶר ***kōper[1]***, n.[m.] [1] [√ 4107]. (unwalled) village:– villages (1)

H4109 [2]כֹּפֶר ***kōper[2]***, n.m. [1] [→ 4106; cf. 4105]. pitch (used to cover and seal the ark of Noah):– pitch (1)

H4110 [3]כֹּפֶר ***kōper[3]***, n.m. [2] henna, henna blossom:– henna (1), henna blossoms (1)

H4111 [4]כֹּפֶר ***kōper[4]***, n.m. [13] [√ 4105]. ransom, compensation, payment; bribe:– ransom (8), bribe (2), bribes (1), compensation (1), payment (1)

H4112 כְּפַר הָעַמֹּנִי ***kᵉpar hā'ammōnî***, n.pr.loc. [1] [√ 4107 + 2194; cf. 6671]. Kephar Ammoni, "*village of Ammonites*":– Kephar Ammoni (1)

H4113 כִּפֻּרִים ***kippurîm***, n.pl.abst. [8] [√ 4105]. atonement; atonement may be a figure of covering over and therefore forgetting (forgiving) sin; "day of Atonement" is an annual day of rest and with ceremonies accomplishing full atonement for the nation of Israel:– atonement (6), atonement made (1 [+4105]), atoning (1)

H4114 כַּפֹּרֶת ***kappōret***, n. [27] [√ 4105]. atonement cover (traditionally: mercy seat); the golden cover on the ark of the covenant, the place where atonement is made; see also 4113:– atonement cover (15), cover (10), atonement (1), it (1 [+2021])

H4115 כָּפַשׁ ***kāpaš***, v. [1] [cf. 3899]. [H] to trample down:– trampled (1)

H4116 [1]כַּפְתּוֹר ***kaptôr[1]***, n.pr.loc. [3] [→ 4118]. Caphtor:– Caphtor (3)

H4117 [2]כַּפְתּוֹר ***kaptôr[2]***, n.m. [18] bud; top of a pillar or column:– buds (8), bud (6), columns (1), tops of the pillars (1), NDT (2)

H4118 כַּפְתֹּרִי ***kaptōrî***, a.g. [3] [√ 4116]. Caphtorite, "*of Caphtor*":– Caphtorites (3)

H4119 [1]כַּר ***kar[1]***, n.[m.] [12] [√ 4159]. ram-lamb, (young) ram; battering ram:– lambs (8), battering rams (3), choice lambs (1 [+4946, 7366])

H4120 [2]כַּר ***kar[2]***, n.m. [3] meadow, pastureland:– meadows (2), field (1)

H4121 [3]כַּר ***kar[3]***, n.[m.] [1] saddle, saddle-bag:– saddle (1)

H4122 כָּר ***kār***, n.pr.loc. Not used in NIVEBC [→ 1105]. Car

H4123 כֹּר ***kōr***, n.[m.] [7] [√ 10367]. cor (measure of dry or liquid volume, about 60 gallons [220 liters]):– cors (6), cor (1)

H4124 כִּרְבֵּל ***kirbēl***, v.den. [1] [√ 10368]. [Pu] to be clothed, be wrapped:– was clothed (1)

H4125 [1]כָּרָה ***kārâ[1]***, v. [15] [→ 4129, 4808, 4838]. [Q] to dig; to hew (stone); to hollow out:– dug (5), digs (3), cut out (1), dig (1), is dug (1), opened (1), pierce (1), plots (1), sank (1)

H4126 [2]כָּרָה ***kārâ[2]***, v. [4] [Q] to barter; purchase:– barter (1), barter away (1), bought (1), NDT (1)

H4127 [3]כָּרָה ***kārâ[3]***, v. [1] [√ 4130]. [Q] to prepare a feast:– prepared a feast (1 [+4130])

H4128 [4]כָּרָה ***kārâ[4]***, v. [Q] to tie together

H4129 [5]כָּרָה ***kārâ[5]***, n.f. Not used in NIVEBC [√ 4125]. cistern, well

H4130 כֵּרָה ***kērâ***, n.f. [1] [→ 4127]. feast, banquet:– prepared a feast (1 [+4127])

H4131 [1]כְּרוּב ***kᵉrûb[1]***, n.m. [91] cherub, (pl.) cherubim, a class of supernatural beings that serve in the presence of God; used as ornamental figures on the atonement cover of the ark of the covenant and in the temple as well as on the walls and doors of the temple:– cherubim (66), cherub (15), them[S] (2 [+2021]), one[S] (1 [+2021]), their[S] (1 [+2021]), NDT (6)

H4132 [2]כְּרוּב ***kᵉrûb[2]***, n.pr.loc. [2] Kerub:– Kerub (2)

H4133 כָּרִי ***kārî***, a.g. [2] Carite:– Carites (2)

H4134 כְּרִית ***kᵉrît***, n.pr.loc. [2] [√ 4162]. Kerith, "*cut off, perish*":– Kerith (2)

H4135 כְּרִיתוּת ***kᵉrîtût***, n.f. [4] [√ 4162]. divorce:– divorce (4)

H4136 כַּרְכֹּב ***karkōb***, n.[m.] [2] ledge, rim, edge:– ledge (2)

H4137 כַּרְכֹּם ***karkōm***, n.[m.] [1] saffron (plant):– saffron (1)

H4138 כַּרְכְּמִישׁ ***karkᵉmîš***, n.pr.loc. [3] Carchemish:– Carchemish (3)

H4139 כַּרְכַּס ***karkas***, n.pr.m. [1] Carcas, "[perhaps] *vulture*":– Karkas (1)

H4140 כִּרְכָּרָה ***kirkārâ***, n.f. [1] [√ 4159]. (fast running) female camel:– camels (1)

H4141 כָּרַם ***kāram***, v. Not used in NIVEBC [√ 4142]. [Q] to tend a vineyard

H4142 [1]כֶּרֶם ***kerem[1]***, n.m. [93] [→ 4141, 4143, 4144, 4145?, 4146?, 4149]. vineyard:– vineyards (49), vineyard (41), grapes (1), vintage (1), NDT (1)

H4143 [2]כֶּרֶם ***kerem[2]***, n.pr.loc. Not used in NIVEBC [√ 4142]. Kerem

H4144 כֹּרֵם ***kōrēm***, n.m. *or* v.ptcp. [5] [√ 4142]. worker in the vineyard, vine growers, vinedressers:– work vineyards (2), vine growers (1), vineyards (1), working fields and vineyards (1)

H4145 [1]כַּרְמִי ***karmî[1]***, n.pr.m. [8] [→ 4146; cf. 4142?]. Carmi, "[poss.] *[fruitful] vine, vineyard owner*":– Karmi (8)

H4146 [2]כַּרְמִי ***karmî[2]***, a.g. [1] [√ 4145; cf. 4142?]. Carmite, "*of Carmi*":– Karmite (1)

H4147 כַּרְמִיל ***karmîl***, n.[m.] [3] crimson (yarn):– crimson (3)

H4148 כְּרָמִים ***kᵉrāmîm***, n.pr.loc. Not used in NIVEBC [→ 70]. Keramim

H4149 [1]כַּרְמֶל ***karmel[1]***, n.m. [14] [→ 4150, 4151, 4153; cf. 4142]. fertile land, fruitful land; this can refer to an orchard or plantation:– fertile field (5), finest of forests (2 [+3623]), orchards (2), fertile (1), fertile fields (1), fertile lands (1), fertile pasturelands (1), fruitful land (1)

H4150 [2]כַּרְמֶל ***karmel[2]***, n.pr.loc. [7] [→ 4153; cf. 4149]. Carmel (city), "*orchard planted with vine and fruit trees*":– Carmel (7)

H4151 [3]כַּרְמֶל ***karmel[3]***, n.pr.loc. [15] [√ 4149]. Carmel (hill), "*orchard planted with vine and fruit trees*":– Carmel (15)

H4152 [4]כַּרְמֶל ***karmel[4]***, n.m. [3] new grain, newly ripe grain:– new grain (2), heads of new grain (1)

H4153 כַּרְמְלִי ***karmᵉlî***, a.g. [7] [√ 4150; cf. 4149]. Carmelite, of Carmel, "*of Carmel*":– of Carmel (5), Carmelite (2)

H4154 כְּרָן ***kᵉrān***, n.pr.m. [2] Keran:– Keran (2)

H4155 כִּרְסֵם ***kirsēm***, v. [1] [cf. 4080]. [P] to ravage, eat away:– ravage (1)

H4156 כָּרַע ***kāra'***, v. [36] [√ 4157]. [Q] to kneel down, crouch, often with the associative meaning of respect and honor or of readiness for action; [H] to make bow down, make kneel (an act of oppression), make miserable:– sank (3), bow (2), bow down (2), brought down (2 [+4156]), fell (2), humbled (2), kneel down (2), knelt down (2), bowed down (1), bows down (1), bring down (1), brought to knees (1), cringe (1), crouch (1), crouch down (1), crouches (1), cutting down (1), down (1), fall (1), faltering (1), got down (1), kneel (1), kneeling (1 [+6584, 1386]), knelt (1), sleep with (1 [+6584]), slumped down (1), went into labor (1)

H4157 כֶּרַע ***kera'***, n.[f.] [9] [→ 4156]. leg bone (the shank bone, between the knee and ankle):– legs (8), leg bones (1)

H4158 כַּרְפַּס ***karpas***, n.m. [1] (fine) linen:– hangings of linen (1)

H4159 כָּרַר ***kārar***, v. [2] [→ 3929?, 3971, 4119, 4140]. [Pil] to dance:– dancing (2)

H4160 כָּרֵשׂ ***kārēś***, n.[m.] [1] stomach, belly:– stomach (1)

H4161 כַּרְשְׁנָא ***karšᵉnā'***, n.pr.m. [1] Carshena, "[poss.] *black*":– Karshena (1)

H4162 כָּרַת ***kārat***, v. [288] [→ 4134?, 4135, 4164]. [Q] to cut off, cut down; to make (a covenant, agreement); [Qp] to be cut off, broken off; [N] to be cut off, be destroyed; [Pu] to be cut down; [H] to cut off, get rid of, destroy, kill; [Ho] to be cut off; "to cut a covenant" is "make a covenant," a figure of the act of ceremonially cutting an animal into two parts, with an implication of serious consequences for not fulfilling the covenant:– made (45), cut off (38), make (27), be cut off (26), cut down (20), destroy (16), be destroyed (9), cut (8), fail to have (8 [+4200]), destroyed (6), kill (6), wipe out (5), making (4), be cut down (3), made a covenant (3), remove (3), covenanted (2), endure forever (2 [+4202]), must surely be cut off (2 [+4162]), put an end (2), renewed (2), was cut off (2), are destroyed (1), banish (1), be blotted out (1), be broken (1), be consumed (1), be put to death (1), be released from (1), be removed from (1), be rid of (1), be ruined (1), be silenced (1), be struck down (1), be taken (1), be without (1 [+4946]), been broken off (1), been cut off (1), been snatched (1), blot out (1), chop down (1), conquered (1), cut up (1), cutting (1), cutting (1 [+9163]), cutting off (1), destroy completely (1), destruction (1), disappear (1), entered (1), fell (1), felling (1), form (1), is cut down (1), kill off (1), killing (1), killing off (1), leave no (1), made a pact (1), make a treaty (1), makes (1), makes a covenant (1), no (1), out (1), perish (1), put an end to (1), removed (1), silence (1), take away (1), vanished (1), were cut off (1)

H4163 כְּרֹת ***kerōt***, var. Not used in NIVEBC [cf. 4165]. see 4165

H4164 כְּרֻתוֹת ***kerutôt***, n.[f.pl.] [3] [√ 4162]. beams (trimmed and cut):– trimmed beams (3)

H4165 כְּרֵתִי ***kerētî***, a.g. [10] [cf. 7152?]. Kerethite:– Kerethites (9), Kerethite (1)

H4166 כֶּשֶׂב ***keśeb***, n.[m.] [13] [→ 4167; cf. 3897]. ram-lamb, young sheep:– lamb (5), sheep (4), lamb (1 [+8445, 928, 2021]), lambs (1), sheep (1 [+8445]), young of the flock (1)

H4167 כִּשְׂבָּה ***kiśbâ***, n.f. [1] [√ 4166]. ewe-lamb, young sheep:– lamb (1)

H4168 כֶּשֶׂד ***keśed***, n.pr.m. [1] [√ 4169]. Kesed, *"Chaldean, Babylonian"*:– Kesed (1)

H4169 כַּשְׂדִּים ***kaśdîm***, n.pr.g. [80] [→ 4168; cf. 951; 10361, 10373]. Chaldean, Babylonian, astrologers:– Babylonians (50), Babylonian (12), Chaldeans (8), Babylonia (5), Chaldea (2), astrologers (2), Babylon (1 [+824])

H4170 כָּשָׂה ***kāśâ***, v. [1] [Q] to become sleek, heavy; stubborn, headstrong:– sleek (1)

H4171 כָּשַׁח ***kāšaḥ***, v. [Q] to become lame, crippled

H4172 כַּשִּׁיל ***kaššîl***, n.[m.] [1] [√ 4173]. axe:– axes (1)

H4173 כָּשַׁל ***kāšal***, v. [62] [→ 4172, 4174, 4842, 4843]. [Q] to stumble, falter, fail; [N] be caused to stumble, be brought down; [H] to cause to stumble, overthrow, bring to ruin; [Ho] to be overthrown:– stumble (25), fall (4), stumbled (4), be brought down (2), downfall (2), give way (2), overthrow (2), stumble and fall (2 [+4173]), stumbles (2), bring condemnation (1), bring to ruin (1), cause to fall (1), caused to stumble (1), fails (1), faltered (1), feeblest (1), giving out (1), made stumble (1), make stumble (1), overthrown (1), sapped (1), stagger (1), staggers (1), stumbling (1), weak (1), without success (1)

H4174 כִּשָּׁלוֹן ***kiššālôn***, n.[m.] [1] [√ 4173]. falling down, stumbling:– fall (1)

H4175 כָּשַׁף ***kāšap***, v.den. [6] [→ 439, 4176, 4177]. [P] to engage in witchcraft, be a sorcerer:– sorcerers (3), engages in witchcraft (1), sorceress (1), sought omens (1)

H4176 כֶּשֶׁף ***kešep***, n.m. [6] [√ 4175]. witchcraft, sorcery, often with the associative meanings of rebellion and seduction into false religion:– sorceries (3), witchcraft (3)

H4177 כַּשָּׁף ***kaššāp***, n.m. [1] [√ 4175]. sorcerer:– sorcerers (1)

H4178 כָּשֵׁר ***kāšēr***, v. [3] [→ 4179]. [Q] to be right, successful; [H] to bring success:– bring (1), succeed (1), thinks right (1)

H4179 כִּשְׁרוֹן ***kišrôn***, n.[m.] [3] [√ 4178]. skill, achievement; benefit:– achievement (1 [+5126]), benefit (1), skill (1)

H4180 כָּתַב ***kātab***, v. [221] [→ 4181, 4182, 4844; 10374]. [Q] to write, engrave (on stone tablets); [Qp] to be written, be inscribed; [N] to be written down, be listed, be recorded; [P] to issue a written statement; writing can refer to ink on leather or papyrus, stylus on wax or clay, or carving in stone:– written (105), write (25), wrote (25), recorded (9), write down (6), wrote down (5), be written (3), inscribed (3), signed (3), were recorded (3), be listed (2), engraved (2), issue decrees (2 [+4180]), was recorded (2), were written (2), write a description (2), writes (2), wrote out (2), been recorded (1), decree be issued (1), listed (1), lodged (1), map out (1), order be written (1), put in writing (1), putting in writing (1), record (1), record (1 [+9005]), register (1), was written (1), was written down (1), were listed (1), words (1), writing (1), written descriptions (1), wrote description (1)

H4181 כְּתָב ***ketāb***, n.m. [17] [√ 4180; 10375]. written communication in various forms: script, text, record, book (as a scroll or tablet):– script (5), records (3), text (3), book (1), document (1), instructions written (1), letter (1), prescribed (1), writing (1)

H4182 כְּתֹבֶת ***ketōbet***, n.f. [1] [√ 4180]. tattoo mark:– marks (1)

H4183 כִּתִּיִּים ***kittiyyîm***, a. & n.g. [8] Kittim, Cyprus; western coastlands:– Cyprus (5), Kittites (2), western coastlands (1)

H4184 כָּתִית ***kātît***, a. [5] [√ 4198]. beaten or pressed olives; in some contexts this refers to virgin olive oil:– pressed (2), pressed olives (2), pressed olive (1)

H4185 כֹּתֶל ***kōtel***, n.[m.] [1] [√ 10376]. wall (of a house):– wall (1)

H4186 כִּתְלִישׁ ***kitlîš***, n.pr.loc. [1] Kitlish:– Kitlish (1)

H4187 כָּתַם ***kātam***, v. [1] [N] be stained, be defiled:– stain (1)

H4188 כֶּתֶם ***ketem***, n.m. [9] [cf. 4846?]. gold, pure gold:– gold (5), fine gold (2), pure gold (1), purest gold (1 [+7058])

H4189 כֻּתֹּנֶת ***kuttōnet***, n.f. [29] garment, robe, tunic:– robe (13), tunics (6), tunic (5), garments (4), garment (1)

H4190 כָּתֵף ***kātēp***, n.f. [68] shoulder, the part an animal or human that carries a load; by extension: shoulder piece; slope (of a hill), side, wall (of a building):– side (18), shoulders (9), shoulder pieces (8), slope (8), shoulder (5), backs (3), projecting walls (2), slopes (2), arm (1), flank (1), handles (1), hips (1), one[S] (1), sides (1), sidewalls (1), slung on back (1 [+1068]), supports (1 [+7193]), wall (1), NDT (3)

H4191 כְּתֹף ***ketōp***, var. Not used in NIVEBC [√ 9512]. see 3869 & 9512

H4192 כָּתַר¹ ***kātar***[1], v. [1] [→ 4194; cf. 4193, 4194]. [P] to bear with, have patience with:– Bear (1)

H4193 כָּתַר² ***kātar***[2], v. [4] [√ 4195?, 4196?; cf. 4192, 4194]. [P] to surround, encircle; [H] to gather about; hem in:– encircle (1), gather about (1), hem in (1), surrounded (1)

H4194 כָּתַר³ ***kātar***[3], v. [1] [√ 4195?, 4196?; cf. 4192, 4193]. [H] to crown, wear as a headdress:– crowned (1)

H4195 כֶּתֶר ***keter***, n.m. [3] [√ 4194 *or* 4193]. crown (probably not jeweled), royal headdress, crest, high turban:– crown (2), crest (1)

H4196 כֹּתֶרֶת ***kōteret***, n.f. [21] [√ 4194 *or* 4193]. capital (of a pillar or column):– capitals (11), capital (5), circular frame (1), NDT (4)

H4197 כָּתַשׁ ***kātaš***, v. [1] [→ 4847]. [Q] to grind, pound (in a mortar):– grind (1)

H4198 כָּתַת ***kātat***, v. [17] [→ 4184, 4185]. [Q] to crush, beat; [Qp] to be crushed, be shattered; [P] to beat, crush, break to pieces; [Pu] to be crushed; [H] to beat down; [Ho] to be battered to pieces:– beat (3), crushed (3), beat down (2), are broken to pieces (1), are defeated (1), battered to pieces (1 [+8625]), be broken to pieces (1), broke into pieces (1), crush (1), devastate (1), shattered (1), were crushed (1)

H4199 ל ***l***, letter. Not used in NIVEBC [√ 10377]. letter of the Hebrew alphabet

H4200 לְ-1 ***le-1***, pp.pref. [20654] [→ 2131, 3189?, 4210, 4240, 4307, 4338, 4342, 4344, 4345, 4346, 4348, 4359, 4367, 4368; cf. 4201?; 10378]. to, toward; in, through; before, at, with; temporally: before, until, when; logically: so that, in order to; agency: by means of:– to (4684), for (1677), of (747), before (542 [+7156]), in (370), with (219), as (208), by (189), why (166 [+4537]), from (158), on (149), therefore (147 [+4027]), forever (134 [+6409]), into (110), at (106), have (95), against (91), according to (88), had (88), my (79 [+3276]), so that (77 [+5100]), through (77), his (73 [+2257]), that (73), so that (70), before (69), in front of (65 [+7156]), had (50 [+2118]), have (50 [+2118]), to (50 [+7156]), has (49), your (47 [+4013]), ahead (44 [+7156]), about (42), over (42), alone (38 [+963]), their (37 [+2157]), your (36 [+3870]), to (35 [+5100]), belong to (31), mine (31 [+3276]), belongs to (30), so (26), the Lord's (26 [+3378]), belonging to (25), to (25 [+7023]), that (24 [+5100]), when (24), before (23 [+4946, 7156]), yours (23 [+3870]), for sake (22 [+5100]), for the sake of (22 [+5100]), in order to (22), by (21 [+7156]), among (20), our (20 [+5646]), presence (19 [+7156]), every (18), in addition to (18 [+4946, 963]), like (18), so (18 [+5100]), concerning (17), forever (17 [+5905]), only (17 [+963]), because of (16 [+5100]), belonged to (16), presented to (16), toward (16), and (14), against (13 [+7156]), forever (13 [+6329]), as for (12), belong to (12 [+2118]), have (12 [+3780]), after (11), before (11 [+5584]), from (11 [+4946, 7156]), then (11 [+5100]), for (10 [+7156]), so (10 [+4027]), to (10 [+7754]), under (10), your (10 [+3871]), David's (8 [+1858]), become (8 [+2118]), fail to have (8 [+4162]), from (8 [+7156]), never (8 [+4202, 6409]), only one (8 [+963]), upon (8), with (8 [+7156]), Solomon's (7 [+8976]), and (7 [+5100]), besides (7 [+4946, 963]), formerly (7 [+7156]), have to do with (7), meet (7 [+7156]), near (7), on behalf (7), serve (7 [+6641, 7156]), because of (6), before (6 [+6524]), give in marriage (6 [+5989, 851]), his own (6 [+2257]), in order to (6 [+5100]), near (6 [+7156]), their (6 [+2257]), upward (6 [+5087, 2025]), always (5 [+6409]), belonged to (5 [+2118]), but (5 [+4027]), close to (5 [+6645]), consider (5 [+2118]), destined for (5), for (5 [+5100]), for sake (5), gave in marriage (5 [+5989, 851]), has (5 [+2118]), her (5 [+2023]), marry (5 [+2118, 851]), on side (5), sent for (5 [+8938, 2256, 7924]), their (5 [+4564]), throughout (5), used to (5 [+7156]), what (5 [+4537]), while (5), with (5 [+7023]), Israel's (4 [+3776]), Saul's (4 [+8620]), above (4 [+4946, 5087, 2025]), awaits (4), belongs to (4 [+2118]), between (4), bring (4 [+2118]), by themselves (4 [+963, 4392]), concerns (4), escape with (4 [+8965]), ever (4 [+6409]), falsely (4 [+2021, 9214]), father's (4 [+3]), given to (4), great (4 [+8044]), greet (4 [+8626, 8934]), in behalf of (4), in honor (4), in vain (4 [+8198]), in vain (4 [+2021, 8736]), its (4 [+2257]), lord's (4 [+123]), married (4 [+4374, 851]), marry (4 [+4374, 851]), my own (4 [+3276]), never (4 [+4202, 5905]), one by one (4 [+1653, 4392]), owned (4), owns (4), plentiful (4 [+8044]), received (4), their own (4 [+2157]), till (4), within (4), your own (4 [+3870]), yours (4 [+4013]), above (3 [+5087, 2025]), along (3), always (3 [+5905]), apart (3 [+963]), as if (3), as soon as (3), attack (3 [+995]), become (3), below (3 [+4752]), by (3 [+7023]), down (3 [+4752]), entered (3 [+995]), eternal (3 [+6409]), face (3 [+7156]), faced (3), get (3), great amount (3 [+8044]), greatly (3 [+8044]), in abundance (3 [+8044]), keep (3 [+2118]), king's (3 [+4889]), large numbers (3 [+8044]), leading (3 [+7156]), leads to (3), married (3 [+2118, 851]), misuse (3 [+5951, 2021, 8736]), opposite (3 [+7156]), over (3 [+4946, 5087, 2025]), regard as (3), related to (3), sight (3 [+7156]), their own (3 [+2257]), theirs (3 [+2257]), then (3 [+4027]), therefore (3 [+5100]), throughout (3 [+3972]), to belonged (3), until (3), watch (3 [+6524]), watched (3 [+6524]), what are you doing (3 [+4537, 3870]), when (3 [+6961]), whose (3 [+2257]), without (3 [+4202]), your own (3 [+4013]), Pharaoh's (2 [+7281]), a matter of (2), accompanies (2 [+7156]), according to (2 [+7023]), across (2), along with (2 [+6645]), any (2), appears (2 [+7156]), applies to (2), around (2), as (2 [+6645]), as long as (2 [+7156]), as well as (2 [+963, 4946]), assigned to (2), at (2 [+7156]), at random (2 [+9448]), at table[S] (2 [+7156]), at the point of (2), attack (2 [+6913]), be sure of this (2 [+3338, 3338]), became (2 [+2725, 2118]), because (2), beside (2 [+6645]), beside (2 [+7156]), besides (2 [+963, 4946]), bind (2 [+2118, 3213]), bloodshed (2 [+1947, 1947]), bottom (2 [+4946, 4752]), causes (2), clan by clan (2 [+5476]), completely (2 [+2021, 3972]), covered with (2 [+7156]), do for (2), during (2), each (2), entered service (2 [+6641, 7156]), entering (2 [+995]), extensive (2 [+8044]), find (2), finds (2), for (2 [+4027]), forever (2 [+6330, 6409]), from (2 [+4974]), gently (2 [+351]), give (2), given (2), greeted (2 [+8626, 8934]), highly (2 [+5087, 2025]), his[S] (2 [+8976]), holding (2), how were (2 [+8934]), in (2 [+5584]), in (2 [+6961]), in accordance with (2), in addition to (2 [+963]), in behalf (2), in connection with (2), in front of (2 [+5584]), in order that (2), in presence (2 [+5584, 6524]), in such a way that (2), in way (2 [+7156]), inside (2 [+7156]), just as (2 [+6645]), large quantities (2 [+8044]), leader (2 [+2143, 7156]), led in campaigns (2 [+3655, 2256, 995, 7156]), let inquire of (2 [+2011]), liable to (2), long ago (2 [+4946, 8158]), many (2 [+8044]), mean by (2), mean to (2), misuses (2 [+5951, 2021, 8736]), much (2 [+8044]), never (2 [+440, 6409]), never again (2 [+4202, 6409]), not including (2 [+963, 4946]), of (2 [+4946, 7156]), on account of (2), on behalf of (2), on high (2 [+2021, 5294]), opposite (2 [+5584]), ours (2 [+5646]), own (2), owned (2 [+3780]), owner (2 [+2257]), parallel to (2 [+6645]), plenty (2 [+8044]), preceded (2 [+7156]), receive (2 [+2118]), regard as (2 [+2118]), regarded as by (2), representing (2), resist (2 [+6641, 7156]), safely (2 [+1055]), see (2 [+7156]), served (2 [+6641, 7156]), serving (2 [+6641, 7156]), some (2), surely (2 [+4027]), their (2 [+2177]), theirs (2 [+2157]), to (2 [+6524]), to belong (2), to belongs (2), top (2 [+4946, 5087, 2025]), turned into (2 [+2118]), under (2 [+7156]), up (2 [+5087, 2025]), used as (2), used in (2), used to (2 [+2021, 8037]), very (2 [+5087, 2025]), very well (2 [+4027]), watching (2 [+6524]), when (2 [+7023]), whose (2 [+4769]), withstand (2 [+6641, 7156]), won (2 [+5951, 7156]), worship (2 [+7156]), your very own (2 [+3870]), Aaron's (1 [+195]), Absalom's (1 [+94]), Adonijah's (1 [+154]), Danite (1 [+4751, 1968]), God's (1 [+466]), Hezekiah's (1 [+2624]), Hezekiah's (1 [+2625]), Israelite (1 [+1201, 3776]), Jacob's (1 [+3620]), Japheth's (1 [+3651]), Nebuchadnezzar's (1 [+5557]), Shalmaneser's[S] (1 [+2257]), Shimei's (1 [+9059]), Solomon's (1 [+8611, 8976]), Zedekiah's (1 [+7409]), above (1), above (1 [+4946, 5087, 4946, 6645]), abundant (1 [+8044]), accompanied (1), accompany (1 [+2143, 5584]), accused of (1), accuses (1 [+7756, 2021, 5477]), acquired (1 [+2118]), act (1 [+2118]), adjoining (1 [+6645]), adopted (1 [+4374, 1426]), adorned (1 [+7596, 9514]), affects (1), after (1 [+7891]), after (1 [+7891]), again (1 [+6409]), against (1 [+5100]), agent (1 [+3338]), agreed with (1 [+9048, 7754]), ahead (1), ahead (1 [+4946, 7156]), alike (1 [+6645]), all (1 [+963]), all alone (1 [+963]), all around (1 [+4946, 5087]), all by myself (1 [+963, 3276]), allotted (1), allowed (1), alone (1 [+970]), along (1 [+3338]), along with (1), along with (1 [+4946, 963]), alongside (1 [+6645]), alongside of (1 [+6645]), also (1 [+963]), among (1 [+3972]), an[S] (1 [+2257]), and (1 [+4027]), and so (1), anyone (1 [+963]), apart (1 [+970]), around (1 [+2021, 2575]), as (1 [+6961]), as a result (1), as in (1), as long as live (1 [+3972, 3427, 6409]), as much as (1 [+7023]), as well as (1 [+6645]), asked how they were (1 [+8934, 8626]), asked how were (1 [+8626, 8934]), assaults (1 [+5596, 5596]), assigned (1), assistant (1 [+6641, 7156]), associated with (1), at (1 [+6645]), at (1 [+7023]), at advance (1 [+7156]), at each successive level (1 [+5087, 2025, 4200, 5087, 2025]), at each successive level (1 [+4200, 5087, 2025, 5087, 2025]), at hand (1 [+7940, 995]), at sanctuary[S] (1 [+7156]), at the head of (1 [+7156]), attain (1), attend (1 [+7156]), attended by (1 [+2143, 8079]), attending (1 [+7156]), attention (1 [+7156]), avoid (1 [+4202, 6843]), awaits (1 [+7156]), backward (1 [+294]), bake thoroughly (1 [+8596, 8599]), banded together (1 [+665, 2021, 2653]), be given in marriage (1 [+5989, 851]), be kept from (1 [+1757, 1194]), bear (1 [+2118]), became (1), because (1 [+4027]), because (1 [+3954, 4537]), because of (1 [+4946, 7156]), because of this (1 [+4027]), become wife (1 [+4374, 851]), before (1 [+678]), before eyes (1 [+7156]), before time (1 [+4946, 7156]), beforehand (1 [+4946, 7156]), belonging to (1 [+2118]), beloved's (1 [+1856]), bent on (1), bent on (1 [+5100]), beside (1 [+3338]), besides (1), besides (1 [+963]), beyond (1 [+4946, 2134]), bodyguard (1 [+9068,

8031]), bordering (1 [+6645]), borne by (1), bravely (1 [+1201, 2657]), bringing (1), brings (1), brings to ruin (1 [+6156, 2021, 8273]), brought (1), but (1), but why (1 [+4537]), by (1 [+4946]), by (1 [+6524]), by himself (1 [+963, 2257]), by itself (1 [+963]), by itself (1 [+970]), by itself (1 [+963, 2257]), by myself (1 [+963, 3276]), call in honor of (1 [+7727]), check (1 [+995, 7156]), children's (1 [+1201]), choose (1), come across (1 [+7925, 7156]), committed (1), completely (1 [+6409]), condemn (1 [+2118, 2631]), confront (1 [+5893, 7925]), consult (1), consult (1 [+7156]), contains (1), continually (1 [+6329]), continually (1 [+8092]), controlled (1), controlled (1 [+2118]), corresponding to (1), count (1 [+2118]), covered (1 [+8492]), crown (1), cry out (1 [+5951, 606]), daily (1 [+7156]), daily (1 [+3427, 285]), daily (1 [+2021, 3427]), dedicated to (1), depth (1 [+2025, 5087]), despite (1 [+928, 8611]), despoil (1 [+5989, 1020]), directed to (1), directly in front of (1 [+5790]), directly opposite (1 [+5790, 7156]), dispersed (1 [+2143, 2006]), done this[s] (1 [+1215, 4640, 3378]), doomed to (1), downcast (1 [+2118]), downstream (1 [+5087, 4946, 2025]), droves (1 [+8044]), each[s] (1 [+5031]), each day (1 [+2021, 3427]), each day (1 [+2021, 3427, 4200, 2021, 3427]), each day (1 [+4200, 2021, 3427, 2021, 3427]), each morning (1 [+2021, 1332, 4200, 2021, 1332]), each morning (1 [+4200, 2021, 1332, 2021, 1332]), endless (1 [+5905]), endure (1 [+2118]), enough (1 [+4537, 1896]), enslaved (1 [+3899, 6269, 2256, 4200, 9148]), enslaved (1 [+3899, 4200, 6269, 2256, 9148]), enter (1 [+995]), enter service (1 [+6641, 7156]), entered the service (1 [+6641, 7156]), enters (1 [+995]), enthroned (1 [+4058]), enthrones (1 [+3782, 2021, 4058]), eternal (1 [+6329]), even though (1 [+963]), ever (1 [+6329]), ever (1 [+7156]), ever (1 [+1887, 2256, 1887]), ever again (1 [+5905, 5905]), ever since (1 [+4946]), everlasting (1 [+5905]), everlasting (1 [+6409]), every day (1 [+2021, 3427]), exceedingly (1 [+5087, 2025]), extends to (1 [+4946]), eyes[s] (1 [+5584]), faced (1 [+7156]), far and wide (1 [+6330, 4946, 8158]), far away (1 [+6330, 4946, 8158]), fault (1 [+928, 8611]), fell facedown (1 [+2556, 678]), fight (1 [+3655, 2021, 4878]), firstborn belongs to (1 [+1144]), fit for (1), fleet of trading ships (1 [+641, 2143, 9576]), fluent (1 [+4554, 1819]), for front of (1 [+7156]), for life (1 [+6409]), for relief from (1 [+4946, 7156]), for the sake of (1), for then (1 [+5100]), forced to (1), forever (1 [+802, 3427]), forward (1 [+7156]), fought in (1 [+3655]), found (1 [+8011, 7156]), from (1 [+1068]), from (1 [+4946]), from among (1), from place to place (1 [+5023]), gain (1), gave permission (1), give (1 [+2118]), give (1 [+7156]), give (1 [+5989, 851]), give (1 [+9202, 995]), give in marriage (1 [+5989, 408]), given over to (1), goes down (1 [+3718, 4752]), going (1), got (1 [+2118]), great number (1 [+8044]), great numbers (1 [+8044]), great quantities (1 [+8044, 4394]), had (1 [+3780]), had (1 [+5162]), had been (1 [+7156]), harbored (1 [+2118]), hard (1 [+3668, 2021, 4607]), has (1 [+5162]), has to do with (1), have (1 [+889]), have (1 [+5989]), have part (1), have regard (1 [+8492, 5584]), have regard for (1 [+5564]), have right (1), have sexual relations (1 [+5989, 8888, 2446]), have the right (1), having (1), having (1 [+2118]), heal (1 [+3911, 8691]), hear (1 [+5877, 7156]), heights (1 [+5087, 2025]), help (1), help (1 [+2118]), help (1 [+3338]), help (1 [+6913]), her (1 [+3276]), here (1 [+7156]), hers (1 [+2023]), high above (1 [+4946, 5087, 2025]), higher than (1 [+8049, 5087, 2025]), his (1 [+4564]), his[s] (1 [+5557]), his[s] (1 [+5407]), his[s] (1 [+90]), his[s] (1 [+8620]), his[s] (1 [+4889, 5213]), hold (1), how was (1 [+8934]), how was going (1 [+8934]), however (1 [+4027]), huge (1 [+1524, 6330, 4394]), hunt down (1 [+7421, 4511]), imposing (1 [+1524, 5260]), in (1 [+7156]), in accordance with (1 [+7023]), in addition (1 [+963]), in addition (1 [+4946, 963]), in ascending stages (1 [+5087, 2025, 4200, 5087, 2025]), in ascending stages (1 [+4200, 5087, 2025, 5087, 2025]), in behalf of (1 [+5100]), in broad daylight (1 [+6524, 2021, 9087, 2021, 2296]), in charge of (1), in debt (1 [+5957]), in earlier times (1 [+7156]), in eyes (1 [+7156]), in front of (1 [+6524]), in fulfillment of (1), in full view of (1 [+6524]), in large numbers (1 [+8044]), in opposition to (1), in path (1 [+7156]), in possession (1), in preparation for (1), in service (1 [+7156]), in sight (1), in the course of time (1 [+3427, 4946, 3427]), in the eyes of (1 [+7156]), in the face of (1 [+5584]), in the region of (1), in the service of (1), in the sight of (1), in this way (1), in this way (1 [+5100]), inclines to (1), individually (1 [+1653]), inner (1 [+7156]), inner (1 [+7163]), inquire of (1 [+2011]), inside (1 [+7163]), inside (1 [+4946, 1074]), instead of (1), instead of (1 [+1194]), intent on (1), intimate with (1), into (1 [+7163]), into another set (1 [+963]), into marry (1 [+2118]), into one set (1 [+963]), invaded (1 [+2143]), invading (1 [+995]), involve (1), involved in (1), it means (1), its (1 [+2023]), its (1 [+2023]), its[s] (1 [+2021, 4058]), join (1 [+2118, 4222, 3480]), jointed (1 [+4946, 5087, 8079]), just as (1 [+3972, 889]), just as much as (1 [+7023]), just for that (1 [+4027]), just imagine (1 [+8492]), keep (1), keeps company (1 [+782, 2495]), kept (1), killed (1 [+5782, 7023, 2995]), lack (1 [+401]), large amount (1 [+8044]), larger (1 [+8044]), lasting (1 [+6409]), later (1), later (1 [+7891]), lawsuits (1 [+1907, 1907]), lead (1 [+7156]), lead (1 [+2143, 7156]), lead (1 [+3655, 7156, 2256, 995]), lead across (1 [+6296, 7156]), lead to (1), leading into (1), leading into (1 [+7023]), leading to (1), learned (1 [+5583]), leave (1), leaves (1), led (1 [+7156]), led out (1 [+3655, 7156]), led to (1), left (1 [+2118]), length (1 [+6645]), let inquire of at all (1 [+2011, 2011]), lets happen (1 [+628, 3338]), life will not be worth living (1 [+2644, 4537]), like (1 [+6645]), like (1 [+928, 2021, 3202]), long (1 [+6409]), long ago (1 [+6409]), long life (1 [+2021, 2644]), look with approval (1 [+8883, 5584, 6524]), made fall (1 [+2118, 4842]), make (1), make serve (1 [+8492]), make sport of (1 [+2118, 5442]), married (1 [+4374, 2257, 4200, 851]), married (1 [+4374, 4200, 2257, 851]), married to (1 [+2118, 851]), marries (1 [+2118]), marries (1 [+2118, 408]), marries (1 [+2118, 408, 2118]), marry (1 [+4374]), marry (1 [+2118, 408]), marry into (1 [+2118]), match for (1), mighty (1 [+8044]), mindful (1 [+5584, 6524]), mine (1 [+8611, 3276]), month (1 [+4946, 2544, 2544]), more (1 [+401]), more (1 [+8044]), more (1 [+5087, 2025]), more and more powerful (1 [+2143, 2256, 1541, 6330, 5087, 2025]), more for (1), more quickly than (1 [+7156]), more readily than (1 [+7156]), more than (1 [+401]), more than (1 [+4946, 963]), my (1 [+7156, 3276]), my own (1 [+8611, 3276]), namely (1), never (1 [+6329]), never (1 [+6409, 1153]), never (1 [+5905, 1153]), never (1 [+561, 5905]), never (1 [+1153, 6409]), never (1 [+1153, 5905]), never (1 [+401, 6409]), never (1 [+4202, 7156]), nevertheless (1 [+4027]), next to (1), next to (1 [+5584]), next to (1 [+6298]), not circumcised (1 [+6889, 2257]), not counting (1 [+4946, 963]), not counting (1 [+963, 4946]), numerous (1 [+8044]), obey (1), obey (1 [+9048, 7754]), of (1 [+7156]), of (1 [+4946, 8611]), of what use (1 [+4537]), offered a kiss of homage (1 [+5975, 7023]), older (1 [+2418, 3427]), on (1 [+8031]), on behalf of (1 [+5466]), on behalf of (1 [+5790]), once a year (1 [+4946, 7891, 3427, 2021, 3427]), once for all (1 [+5905]), one[s] (1 [+2157]), one kind after another (1 [+5476, 2157]), only (1 [+2314, 963]), only one (1 [+963, 2257]), open (1 [+7156]), opposite (1 [+6645]), other than (1 [+4946, 963]), other than (1 [+1194, 963]), otherwise (1 [+5100, 889, 4202]), ours (1 [+3276]), ours (1 [+7156, 5646]), out (1), out of way (1 [+4946, 7156]), outer (1 [+2021, 2575]), outer (1 [+4946, 5087, 2025]), over (1 [+7156]), over (1 [+4946, 6584]), over and above (1 [+5087, 2025]), over here (1 [+6298, 285]), over there (1 [+6298, 285]), overlooking (1 [+7156]), overtake (1), overtakes (1), overtakes (1 [+628]), overturned (1 [+2200, 5087, 2025]), own (1 [+2118]), owning (1), owns (1 [+3780]), paid any attention (1 [+5742, 265, 9048]), particularly (1 [+4027]), pay (1), people's (1 [+132]), people's (1 [+6639]), per (1), perch (1 [+4090, 8079]), perjurers (1 [+8678, 2021, 9214]), perjury (1 [+8678, 2021, 9214]), permanently (1 [+7552]), permanently (1 [+2021, 7552]), piece by piece (1 [+5984]), plentifully (1 [+7859]), possessed (1 [+2118]), powerless (1 [+401, 445]), powerless (1 [+401, 445, 3338]), preceded (1 [+2118, 7156]), preceding (1 [+7156]), predecessor (1 [+889, 2118, 7156]), present (1 [+7156]), present (1 [+5877, 7156]), previous (1 [+7156]), priestly (1 [+2021, 3913]), project upward (1 [+5087, 2025]), property[s] (1 [+889, 2118]), provide with (1), provided for (1 [+2118, 4312, 2256, 430]), provides for (1), publicly (1 [+6524]), punished less (1 [+3104, 4752]), put (1 [+7156, 995]), put up security (1 [+9546, 3338]), quantities (1 [+8044]), quite innocently (1 [+9448]), reached (1 [+995]), ready for (1), ready for battle (1 [+408, 7372, 2021, 4878]), ready to (1), realize (1 [+606, 4222]), receive (1 [+5989]), received (1 [+995]), received (1 [+2118]), receives (1), reduced to servitude (1 [+6268, 6269]), referring to (1), reflects (1 [+2021, 132]), reflects (1 [+2021, 7156]), regard (1 [+8492, 5584]), regard (1 [+2118, 7156]), regarded (1), regarded as (1), regardless (1 [+401, 9068]), regards (1 [+5162, 7156]), regularly (1 [+3427, 928, 3427]), relating to (1), relationship to (1), remain unmarried (1 [+6328, 1194, 2118, 4200, 408]), remain unmarried (1 [+6328, 4200, 1194, 2118, 408]), renowned (1 [+9005]), represent (1), represented (1), resisted (1 [+6641, 5584]), resort to (1 [+2143, 7925]), responding to (1 [+6645]), responsible for (1), responsible for (1 [+5584]), responsible for (1 [+928, 889]), responsible for (1 [+928, 8611]), rests with (1), retain (1 [+2118]), reward (1), right before (1), right before (1 [+5584]), right for (1), risked (1 [+3070, 4637]), royal (1 [+4889]), ruined (1 [+7914]), ruthlessly (1 [+425]), safely (1 [+2021, 8934]), same as (1), saying (1 [+606]), secure (1 [+2118]), see (1 [+6524]), see (1 [+8011, 2021, 6524]), see to it (1 [+6524]), seek (1), select a day (1 [+4946, 3427, 3427]), self-control (1 [+5110, 8120]), sent for (1 [+8938, 7924]), separate (1 [+963]), separate (1 [+3657, 963]), servants (1 [+6269]), serve (1 [+2118]), serve (1 [+7156]), serve (1 [+2118, 7156]), served (1 [+2118, 7156]), service of (1), setting the time (1 [+5503]), severe (1 [+5087, 2025]), share (1 [+2118, 285]), share (1 [+3869, 889]), show (1 [+7156]), shows to be (1 [+2118]), sided with (1 [+1047]), since (1 [+4946, 3427]), slaughter (1 [+2222, 5422]), slept with (1 [+3359, 5435, 408]), slept with (1 [+3359, 5435, 2351]), slow down (1 [+6806, 8206]), slowly (1 [+351]), so as to (1), so far as (1 [+3972]), so many (1 [+8044]), so then (1 [+4027]), some years later (1 [+7891, 9102]), started (1 [+6991]), stationed at (1), still (1 [+4027]), stole into (1 [+1704, 995]), stolen goods (1 [+4202, 2257]), stood before (1 [+7156]), storerooms (1 [+5969, 238]), straight ahead (1 [+5790]), straight to (1), struck (1), subject to (1), succeed against (1 [+5584]), successfully (1 [+5905]), such as (1), suffered (1 [+2118]), summoned (1 [+8938, 7924]), supply (1 [+2118]), take (1 [+2118]), take care of (1 [+2118, 5466]), take command (1 [+2118, 5464]), take for (1 [+5989, 7156]), taken (1), taken from (1 [+4946, 7156]), testify (1 [+6699, 6332]), than (1), that is why (1 [+5100]), their (1 [+2179]), their[s] (1 [+2021, 2498]), there[s] (1 [+2023]), therefore (1 [+4027, 3610]), this fellow's[s] (1 [+2296]), this one (1 [+963]), though (1), thoughtlessly (1 [+1051, 928, 8557]), thus (1), thus (1 [+5100]), till (1 [+5100]), to (1 [+4946]), to (1 [+928, 6288]), to (1 [+6584, 7156]), to fulfill (1), to honor (1), to mark (1), to provide for the needs of (1), to serve as (1), to the very end (1 [+6409, 6813]), to turned (1), to use (1), told (1 [+8938, 606]), took in marriage (1 [+4374, 851]), took part in (1 [+3655]), top of (1 [+4946, 5087, 2025]), total (1), total (1 [+3972, 5031]), treat (1 [+2118]), treated as (1 [+2118]), treated the same as (1 [+6645]), troubles (1), trustfully (1 [+1055]), tuned to (1), turn against (1 [+2118, 8477]), turn into (1), two parties (1 [+408, 408]), under (1 [+1074]), under blessing (1 [+7156]), under direction (1 [+7156]), under supervision (1 [+7156]), unending (1 [+6329]), unintentionally (1 [+8705]), unless (1 [+963, 4946, 889]), unless (1 [+3954, 561, 7156]), unmarried (1 [+4202, 2118, 408]), unsuspecting (1 [+1055]), unto (1), upstream (1 [+5087, 2025]), upward (1 [+4946, 5087, 2025]), use (1 [+2118]), use (1 [+2118]), used by (1), used for (1), useless (1 [+2021, 9214]), uses (1), valued at (1), very (1 [+466]), very (1 [+6330, 5087, 2025]), wage war (1 [+1741, 2021, 4878]), walled (1 [+2257, 2570]), want (1), want to (1), wanted to make (1 [+1335]), was given in marriage (1 [+5989, 851]), watched (1 [+7156]), wear (1), were fettered (1 [+5602, 5733]), what do I care about (1 [+4537, 2296, 4200, 3276]), what do I care about (1 [+4200, 4537, 2296, 3276]), what do you mean (1 [+4537, 4013]), what is doing (1 [+4537]), what is the matter (1 [+4537, 3871]), what right have you (1 [+4537, 3870]), what's the meaning of (1 [+4769]), when (1 [+3954, 7023]), whenever (1 [+3972]), whenever (1 [+7023]), where[s] (1 [+4564]), where[s] (1 [+7156]), wherever (1), wherever (1 [+8079]), whether (1), while (1 [+6961]), whose (1 [+889]), why (1 [+361, 2296]), why (1 [+4537, 2296]), why (1 [+8611, 4537]), why (1 [+561, 4027, 4537]), wide (1 [+1172, 2976]), wielding (1 [+995, 5087, 2025]), wish well (1 [+8934]), with (1 [+3338]), with (1 [+6645]), without (1 [+401]), without (1 [+1172]), year (1 [+2021, 3427]), yet (1 [+4027]), young woman's (1 [+5855]), younger (1 [+7582, 3427]), your (1 [+2257]), yours (1 [+2157]), yours (1 [+3871]), NDT (7297)

H4201 ־לְ *lᵉ-2*, pt.pref. Not used in NIVEBC [cf. 4200?]. emphatic, vocative prefix

H4202 לֹא *lōʾ*, adv. [5166] [→ 218?, 4203, 4204, 4205, 4257, 4274; 10379, 10384; *also used with compound proper names*]. no, not:– not (2937), no (625), never (156), nor (107 [+2256]), cannot (97), nothing (69), without (62), cannot (44 [+3523]), neither (44), don't (35), no (30 [+3972]), didn't (29), none (29), nothing (20 [+1821]), haven't (14), isn't (14), or (14), surely (14 [+561]), none (13 [+3972]), or (13 [+2256]), won't (13), before (12), nor (11), nothing (11 [+3972]), refused (11 [+14]), without (9 [+928]), never (8 [+4200, 6409]), unwilling (8 [+14]), can't (7 [+3523]), failed (7), nothing (7 [+4399]), refused (7), aren't (5), forbidden (5 [+6913]), hasn't (5), never (5 [+6388]), none (5 [+408]), refuse (5), wouldn't (5), fail (4), little (4), neither (4 [+1685]), never (4 [+4200, 5905]), unjust (4 [+9419]), unknown (4 [+3359]), unless (4 [+561]), before (3 [+6330, 889]), before (3 [+928]), beyond (3), doesn't (3), injustice (3 [+5477]), instead of (3), lack (3), more than (3), neither (3 [+2256]), nor (3 [+1685]), unable (3), unclean (3 [+3196]), unlike (3), without (3 [+4200]), as you know (2 [+2022]), before (2 [+928, 3270]), can't (2), childless (2 [+3528]), disobeyed (2 [+9048]), disobeyed (2 [+9048, 928, 7754]), displeases (2 [+2911]), endure forever (2 [+4162]), fails (2), forbidden (2 [+7422]), free from (2), from (2), hardly (2), never (2 [+3578]), never (2 [+6330, 6409]), never again (2 [+4200, 6409]), no (2 [+4027]), no (2 [+4946, 3972]), nothing (2 [+3972, 1821]), nowhere (2), or (2 [+889]), otherwise (2 [+2256]), overwhelmed (2 [+2118, 6388, 8120, 928]), powerless (2 [+3946]), rather than (2), rather than (2 [+2256]), refuse (2 [+14]), shouldn't (2), stopped (2 [+3578, 6388]), that (2 [+561]), trackless (2 [+2006]), unlike (2 [+3869]), useless (2 [+7503]), whether (2 [+561]), worthless idols (2 [+3603]), against (1 [+3869]), agreed (1), always be (1 [+2532]), always be (1 [+4631]), anything[s] (1), as[s] (1), avoid (1 [+2143, 448]), avoid (1 [+6843, 4200]), barely (1), because (1 [+2256]), because (1 [+561, 3610]), before (1 [+6330]), before (1 [+6388]), before elapsed (1 [+4848]), better than (1), bottled-up (1 [+7337]), but (1), but (1 [+561]), but (1 [+561]), by no means (1 [+3480]), by surprise (1 [+3359]), can hardly breathe (1 [+5972, 8636]), cannot bear (1 [+3523]), cannot read (1 [+3359, 6219]), cannot stand (1 [+3523]), certainly (1 [+561]), cloudless (1 [+6265]), contrary (1), contrary to (1), contrary to (1 [+3869]), contrary to (1 [+928, 3869]), couldn't (1), delayed (1 [+237]), dense (1 [+2983]), denying (1), deserted (1 [+3782]), despairs (1 [+586]), die (1 [+2649]), disobedience (1 [+9048, 928, 7754]), disobey (1 [+9048]), disorder (1 [+6043]), displease (1 [+5162, 2834, 928, 6524]), displeasing (1 [+5162, 2834, 928, 6524]), disregarding (1 [+2349]), either (1), else (1), empty (1 [+4027]), ever (1), except (1 [+889]), except for (1 [+2256]), fail (1 [+8505]), failed (1 [+3523]), failed (1 [+7756, 6388]), fails (1 [+586]), feeble (1 [+3888]), feeble (1 [+6437]), feel very weak (1 [+6806, 3946]), free from (1 [+928]), free of (1), futile (1 [+4027]), gives way (1 [+6641]), go unanswered (1 [+6699]), gone (1 [+6641, 928]), gone (1 [+2118, 928]), helpless (1 [+6806, 3946]), hidden (1 [+8011]), how much less (1 [+677, 3954]), if (1), ignorant (1 [+3359]), ignorant (1 [+3359]), ignored (1 [+8492, 4213]), in vain (1), in whatever order (1 [+5877, 1598, 6584]), incapable (1 [+3523]), keep (1 [+4631]), lack (1 [+928]), little value (1 [+4399]), low (1), make countless (1 [+8049, 889, 6218]), many (1 [+5071]), measureless (1 [+4499]), mercilessly (1 [+2798]), must[s] (1), neglect (1 [+5757]), neither (1 [+2296]), never (1 [+6362]), never (1 [+6409]), never (1 [+8041]), never (1 [+9458]), never (1 [+4946, 3427]), never (1 [+4200, 7156]), never (1 [+3972, 2021, 3427]), never again (1 [+6330, 5905]), no (1 [+2021]), nobody (1 [+132]), none (1 [+4399]), none (1 [+285]), none (1 [+4946, 3972]), none (1 [+3972, 5883]), nor (1 [+2256, 1685]), nothing (1 [+4027]), nothing (1 [+4312]), nothing (1 [+5126]), nothing (1 [+3972, 889]), nothing (1 [+2021, 3972]), nowhere (1 [+4955]), of no account (1), only (1 [+2314]), only (1 [+8370]), only (1 [+1194]), only (1 [+2022]), only[s] (1), other than (1), otherwise (1 [+4200, 5100, 889]), outcome different (1 [+3869]), past (1), pittance (1 [+2104]), powerless (1), powerless (1 [+3523]), precious (1 [+5877]), rather (1 [+3954]), refused (1 [+9048]), refuses (1), resent (1 [+170]), scarcely (1), seldom (1 [+2221]), shameful (1 [+4083]), shamelessly (1 [+1017]), silent (1 [+1819]), since (1), sinful (1 [+3202]), so (1 [+561, 3610]), stand (1 [+8740]), stay (1 [+995]), stayed away (1 [+995]), stench (1 [+8193]), still to come (1 [+6913]), stolen goods (1 [+4200, 2257]), stop (1), stop (1 [+3578]), stopped (1 [+3855]), stops (1), stranger (1 [+3359]), strangers (1 [+3359]), surely (1), than (1 [+2256]), till (1), till (1 [+561]), time and again (1 [+285, 2256, 4202, 9109]), time and again (1 [+4202, 285, 2256, 9109]), too (1), too heavy a burden to carry (1 [+3523, 5951]), troubled (1 [+3523, 9200]), true (1 [+9213]), turned a deaf ear (1 [+263]), unable (1 [+3523]), unafraid (1 [+7064]), unaware (1 [+3359]), unceasingly (1 [+1949]), unchanged (1 [+4614]), unclean (1 [+3197]), uncut (1 [+7786]), undivided loyalty (1 [+4213, 2256, 4213]), uneaten (1 [+1180]), unfaithful (1 [+574]), unfaithful (1 [+2883]), unfamiliar (1 [+3359]), unfanned (1 [+5870]), uninhabited (1 [+132, 928, 2257]), unintentionally (1 [+928, 7402]), unjust (1 [+5477]), unjustly (1 [+4026]), unless (1), unless (1 [+2022]), unless (1 [+561, 3954]), unmarried (1 [+2118, 4200, 408]), unprofitable (1 [+3603]), unpunished (1 [+870]), unquenchable (1 [+3882]), unrelenting (1 [+2798]), unrighteousness (1 [+7406]), unruly (1 [+4340]), unsharpened (1 [+7837]), unsuccessful (1 [+7503]), unsuited (1 [+5534]), unthinkable (1 [+597]), until (1 [+561]), untiring (1 [+7028]), unwise (1 [+2682]), useless (1), useless (1 [+3603]), useless (1 [+6122]), virgin (1 [+3359, 408]), wasn't (1 [+2118]), weakness (1 [+3946]), weren't (1), weren't (1 [+2118]), what about (1 [+2022]), whether (1 [+2022, 561]), who[s] (1), wicked (1 [+3202]), withheld[s] (1 [+4763]), withhold (1), without (1 [+3578]), worse (1 [+4017]), worthless (1 [+3603]), wrong (1 [+3202]), yes (1 [+3954]), NDT (306)

H4203 לֹא דָבָר ***lō' dābār,*** לֹא דְבָר ***lō' dᵉbār***, n.pr.loc. [2] [√ 4202 + 1818]. Lo Debar, "*no pasture*":– Lo Debar (2)

H4204 לֹא עַמִּי ***lō' 'ammî***, n.pr.m. [1] [√ 4202 + 6652]. Lo-Ammi, "*not my people*":– Lo-Ammi (1)

H4205 לֹא רֻחָמָה ***lō' ruḥāmâ***, n.pr.f. [2] [√ 4202 + 8170]. Lo-Ruhamah, "*no compassion*":– Lo-Ruhamah (2)

H4206 לָאָה ***lā'â***, v. [20] [→ 9430; cf. 4264]. [Q] to be weary; [N] to wear oneself out, be weary; [H] to wear someone out, try one's patience, frustrate:– weary (4), worn out (3), try patience (2), am tired (1), burdened (1), cannot (1), could not (1), discouraged (1), frustrated (1), impatient (1), lazy (1), not be able (1), wears herself out (1), weary themselves (1)

H4207 לֵאָה ***lē'â***, n.pr.f. [34] Leah, "[poss.] *wild-cow; wild cow, gazelle; cow*":– Leah (28), Leah's (5), NDT (1)

H4208 לָאז ***lā'z***, adv.? Not used in NIVEBC [√ 2296; cf. 2137]. see 262

H4209 לָאַט ***lā'aṭ***, v. Not used in NIVEBC [cf. 4286]. [Q] to cover

H4210 לָאֵל ***lā'ēl***, n.pr.m. [1] [√ 4200 + 446]. Lael, "*[belonging] to God [El]*":– Lael (1)

H4211 לְאֹם ***lᵉ'ōm***, n.m. [35] people, nation:– peoples (18), nations (10), people (3), nation (1), other[s] (1), others[s] (1), subjects (1)

H4212 לְאֻמִּים ***lᵉ'ummîm***, n.pr.g. [1] Leummite:– Leummites (1)

H4213 לֵב ***lēb***, n.m. [600] [→ 4214, 4221, 4222, 4223; 10380]. heart; by extension: the inner person, self, the seat of thought and emotion: conscience, courage, mind, understanding:– heart (289), hearts (84), mind (22), sense (11), himself (9 [+2257]), attention (7), minds (7), myself (7 [+3276]), in high spirits (5 [+3201]), skilled (5 [+2682]), understanding (5), brokenhearted (3 [+8689]), everything (3 [+3972]), high seas (3 [+3542]), tenderly (3 [+6584]), arrogant (2 [+5951]), conscience-stricken (2 [+5782]), considered (2 [+8492]), courage (2), imagination (2), resolved (2 [+8492, 6584]), senseless (2 [+401]), skilled workers (2 [+2682]), thoughts (2), wholehearted devotion (2 [+8969]), wholeheartedly (2 [+928, 3972]), will (2), willing (2 [+5618]), willing (2 [+5951]), wise (2), yourself (2 [+3870]), I (1 [+3276]), ability (1), ability (1 [+2683, 928]), able to understand (1), accord (1), again give allegiance (1 [+8740]), anxious striving (1 [+8301]), as sail[s] (1 [+928]), attitude (1), bravest (1 [+579]), call to mind (1 [+8740, 448]), care (1 [+8492, 448]), care about (1 [+8492, 448]), careful attention (1), cares (1 [+8492, 6584]), cheer up (1 [+3512]), chest (1), concerned about (1 [+8492, 448]), confide in (1 [+907]), conscience (1), consider (1 [+8492]), consider (1 [+8492, 6584]), consider well (1 [+8883]), dared (1 [+4848]), dead (1 [+4637, 4946]), deceived (1 [+1704]), decided (1 [+2118, 6640]), did[s] (1 [+3877, 906, 4392]), discourage (1 [+5648]), discouraged (1 [+5648]), disheartened (1 [+3874]), encourage (1 [+3922]), encourage (1 [+1819, 6584]), encouragingly (1 [+6584]), enraged (1 [+6192]), faithless (1 [+6047]), far out (1 [+928]), has full confidence (1 [+1053]), have sense (1), he (1 [+2257]), head (1), heartache (1 [+6780]), hearts (1 [+4213, 2256]), hearts (1 [+2256, 4213]), heart's (1), his own (1 [+4946, 2257]), idea (1 [+4946]), ignored (1 [+4202, 8492]), in (1 [+928]), in good spirits (1 [+3512]), inclined (1 [+5742]), intent (1), intention (1 [+8492]), it[s] (1 [+3276]), kindly (1), led astray (1 [+5742]), me (1 [+3276]), merrymakers (1 [+8524]), obstinate (1 [+7997]), opinions (1), persist in own way (1 [+9244]), persuade (1 [+1819, 6584]), pride (1 [+1467]), proud (1 [+8123]), purpose (1), reason (1), reflected on (1 [+5989, 448]), refreshed (1 [+6184]), resolve (1 [+8492, 6584]), rip open (1 [+7973, 6033]), skill (1 [+2683]), speaking kindly (1 [+1819, 6584]), spirit (1), stops to think (1 [+8740, 448]), stubborn (1 [+2617]), stubborn-hearted (1 [+52]), stunned (1 [+7028]), take heart (1 [+599]), take note (1 [+8883]), them (1 [+4392]), themselves (1 [+2257]), themselves (1 [+4392]), think (1 [+5989]), think (1 [+606, 928]), to (1 [+928]), tried (1 [+9365, 928]), undivided loyalty (1 [+4202, 2256, 4213]), undivided loyalty (1 [+4202, 4213, 2256]), valiant (1 [+52]), very (1), very pleased (1 [+3512]), voluntarily (1 [+6590, 6584, 408]), wholeheartedly (1 [+9459]), wholeheartedly (1 [+928, 8969]), willful (1), willing (1 [+5605]), willingly (1 [+4946]), wisdom (1), wise (1 [+2682]), worry (1 [+8492, 906]), you (1 [+3870]), yourself (1 [+2257]), yourself (1 [+3871]), NDT (2)

H4214 לֵב קָמָי ***lēb qāmāy***, n.pr.loc. [1] [√ 4213 + 7856]. Leb Kamai:– Leb Kamai (1)

H4215 לְבֹא ***lābō'***, n.pr.loc. Not used in NIVEBC [→ 4217]. entrance, see 4217

H4216 לֶבֶא ***lebe'***, n.m. [1] [→ 1106, 4218, 4219, 4232, 4233, 4234]. lion:– lions (1)

H4217 לְבוֹא חֲמָת ***lᵉbō' ḥᵃmāt***, n.pr.loc. [12] [√ 4215 + 2828]. Lebo Hamath, "*entrance to Hamath*":– Lebo Hamath (12)

H4218 לִבְאָה ***lib'â***, n.f. [1] [√ 4216]. lioness:– mate (1)

H4219 לְבָאוֹת ***lᵉbā'ôt***, n.pr.loc. [1] [→ 1106; cf. 4216]. Lebaoth, "*lionesses*":– Lebaoth (1)

H4220 ¹לָבַב ***lābab[1]***, v.den. [3] [→ 4226]. [N] to be made wise, be made intelligent; [P] to steal one's heart (from a lover's glance):– stolen heart (2), become wise (1)

H4221 ²לָבַב ***lābab[2]***, v.den. [2] [√ 4223; cf. 4213]. [P] to make special bread or pastry (heart-shaped?):– made bread (1), make special bread (1 [+4223])

H4222 לֵבָב ***lēbāb***, n.m. & f. [251] [√ 4213; 10381]. heart; by extension: the inner person, self, the seat of thought and emotion: conscience, courage, mind, understanding:– heart (115), hearts (48), mind (10), give careful thought (5 [+8492]), yourself (4 [+3870]), conscience (3), heart's (2), understanding (2), wholehearted devotion (2 [+8969]), wholeheartedly (2 [+928, 8969]), wholeheartedly (2 [+928, 3972]), yourselves (2 [+3870]), breasts (1), brokenhearted (1 [+3874]), conscientious (1 [+3838]), consider (1 [+928]), consider better (1 [+8123]), convictions (1 [+6640]), courage (1), deceived (1 [+1704]), disheartened (1 [+5022, 906]), downhearted (1 [+8317]), encouraged (1 [+1819, 6584]), enticed (1 [+7331]), evil imaginations (1 [+5381]), fainthearted (1 [+8205]), fainthearted (1 [+8216]), filled with pride (1 [+8123]), fully determined (1 [+928, 8969]), gladly (1 [+928, 3206]), harbor (1 [+2118, 6640]), hardhearted (1 [+599, 906]), has in mind (1 [+3108]), heart and soul (1 [+3869]), herself (1 [+2023]), himself (1 [+2257]), in a rage (1 [+2801]), in accord with (1 [+3838]), indecisive (1 [+8205]), inspire (1 [+5989, 928]), integrity (1 [+3841]), intend (1 [+6640]), intent (1), join (1 [+2118, 4200, 3480]), made hearts (1), minds (1), plot (1 [+3108, 928]), plot against (1 [+3108, 928]), profound (1), proud (1 [+8123]), purpose (1), realize (1 [+606, 4200]), take heart (1 [+599]), themselves (1 [+4392]), think (1 [+5989]), think (1 [+606, 928]), thinking (1 [+606, 928]), willfully (1 [+928]), yourself (1 [+2023]), yourself (1 [+3871]), yourselves (1 [+4013]), NDT (5)

H4223 לְבִבָה ***lᵉbibâ***, n.f. [3] [→ 4221; cf. 4213]. special bread (heart-shaped?):– bread (1), it[s] (1 [+2021]), make special bread (1 [+4221])

H4224 לְבַד ***lᵉbad***, n.m. Not used in NIVEBC [√ 969]. alone, see 963 & 4200

H4225 לַבָּה ***labbâ***, n.f. [1] [cf. 4259]. flame:– flames (1)

H4226 לִבָּה ***libbâ***, n.[f.] [1] [√ 4220]. rage:– filled with fury against (1 [+582])

H4227 ¹לְבוֹנָה ***lᵉbônâ[1]***, n.f. Not used in NIVEBC [→ 4228; cf. 4237]. frankincense

H4228 ²לְבוֹנָה ***lᵉbônâ[2]***, n.pr.loc. [1] [√ 4227]. Lebonah, "*frankincense*":– Lebonah (1)

H4229 לָבוּשׁ ***lābûš***, n.m. [15] [√ 4252]. clothing, garments:– clothed (7), in (3), armed (1), covered (1), dress (1), dressed (1), wore (1)

H4230 לְבוּשׁ ***lᵉbûš***, n.m. [31] [√ 4252; 10382]. clothing, garment, robe:– garments (5), clothing (4), garment (4), robe (4), clothed (3), clothes (2), coat (1), dressed (1), gown (1), military tunic (1 [+4496]), protect (1), put on (1), put on (1 [+5989]), robed (1), robes (1)

H4231 לָבַט ***lābaṭ***, v. [3] [N] to come to ruin, be trampled:– comes to ruin (2), come to ruin (1)

H4232 לְבִי ***lᵉbî***, n.[m. & f.] Not used in NIVEBC [√ 4216]. lion

H4233 לָבִיא ***lābî'***, n.m. & f. [11] [√ 4216]. lion, lioness:– lioness (7), lion (3), lionesses (1)

H4234 לְבִיָּא ***lᵉbiyyā'***, n.f. [1] [√ 4216]. lioness:– lioness (1)

H4235 ¹לָבַן ***lāban[1]***, v. [5] [→ 4227, 4228, 4237, 4238, 4239, 4242, 4243?, 4244, 4245, 4247, 4248]. [H] to make white, be whitened; [Ht] to show oneself spotless, purified:– made spotless (2), leaving white (1), white (1), whiter (1)

H4236 ²לָבַן ***lāban[2]***, v.den. [3] [√ 4246]. [Q] to make bricks:– bricks (1), make bricks (1 [+4246]), making bricks (1 [+4246])

H4237 ¹לָבָן ***lābān[1]***, a. [29] [→ 4227, 4238, 4239?, 4244, 4247; cf. 4235]. white:– white (24), reddish-white (4 [+140]), whiter (1)

H4238 ²לָבָן ***lābān[2]***, n.pr.m. [54] [√ 4237]. Laban, "*white*":– Laban (45), Laban's (5), he[s] (2), him[s] (1), NDT (1)

H4239 ³לָבָן ***lābān[3]***, n.pr.loc. [1] [√ 4237?]. Laban, "*white*":– Laban (1)

H4240 לַבֵּן ***labbēn***, tt. Not used in NIVEBC [√ 4200 + 2021 + 1201]. of the son [?]

H4241 לְבָנָהּ ***lᵉbānāh'***, var. Not used in NIVEBC [√ 4244]. Lebana, see 4245

H4242 לִבְנֶה ***libneh***, n.[m.] [2] [√ 4235]. poplar tree; some sources: storax tree:– poplar (2)

H4243 לִבְנָה ***libnâ***, n.pr.loc. [18] [√ 4235?]. Libnah, "*white*":– Libnah (17), it[s] (1)

H4244 ¹לְבָנָה ***lᵉbānâ[1]***, n.f. [3] [→ 4241, 4245; cf. 4237]. bright (full) moon:– moon (3)

H4245 ²לְבָנָה ***lᵉbānâ[2]***, n.pr.loc. [2] [√ 4244; cf. 4241]. Lebanah; Lebana, "*white*":– Lebana (1), Lebanah (1)

H4246 לְבֵנָה ***lᵉbēnâ***, n.f. [12] [→ 4236, 4861]. brick; tablet:– bricks (5), brick (2), altars of brick (1), block of clay (1), make bricks (1 [+4236]), making bricks (1 [+4236]), pavement (1)

H4247 לְבֹנָה ***lᵉbōnâ***, n.f. [21] [√ 4237]. frankincense (a fragrant, resinous gum):– incense (20), frankincense (1)

H4248 לְבָנוֹן ***lᵉbānôn***, n.pr.loc. [71] [√ 4235]. Lebanon, "*white, snow*":– Lebanon (68), cedar of Lebanon (2), there[s] (1)

H4249 ¹לִבְנִי ***libnî[1]***, n.pr.m. [5] [→ 4250]. Libni, "*[descendant of] Libni* or *white*":– Libni (5)

H4250 ²לִבְנִי ***libnî[2]***, a.g. [2] [√ 4249]. Libnite, "*of Libni*":– Libnite (1), Libnites (1)

H4251 לִבְנַת ***libnāt***, n.pr.loc. Not used in NIVEBC [→ 8866]. Libnath, see 8866

H4252 לָבַשׁ ***lābaš***, v. [97] [→ 4229, 4230, 4860, 9432; 10383]. [Q] to put on clothing, dress, clothe; [Qp] to be dressed; [Pu] to be dressed; [H] to dress another, clothe someone:– put on (23), clothed (15), clothe (10), wear (9), dress (5), came on (3), dressed (3), dressed in (3), robed (3), covered (2), wore (2), clad (1), clothed (1 [+955]), clothes (1), dress in (1), provide (1), provided with clothes (1), put clothes on (1), put on (1 [+9432]), put on as clothing (1), put on clothes (1), put on robes (1), puts on (1), putting on (1), robe (1), vestments (1), wear clothes (1), worn (1), NDT (2)

H4253 לֹג ***lōg***, n.m. [5] log (liquid measure, about a third of a quart or liter):– log (5)

H4254 לֹד ***lōd***, n.pr.loc. [4] Lod:– Lod (4)

H4255 לִדְבִר ***lidbir***, n.pr.loc. Lidbir, see 1810 & 4200

H4256 לֵדָה ***lēdâ***, n.[f.] *or* v.inf. [4] [√ 3528]. delivery (of birth):– deliver (2), birth (1), in labor (1)

H4257 לֹה ***lōh***, adv. [1] [√ 4202]. not:– NDT (1)

H4258 לַהַב ***lahab***, n.m. [12] [→ 4259, 8927]. flame of fire; by extension: flash (of a blade), blade of a sword:– flames (3), fire (2 [+836]), flame (2), flashing (2), aflame (1), blade (1), it[S] (1 [+2021])

H4259 לֶהָבָה ***lehābâ***, n.f. [19] [√ 4258; cf. 4225]. flame, blaze, flash; (iron) point (of a blade):– flame (6), flames (3), flaming (3), blaze (2), blazing (1), burned (1), flashes (1), lightning (1 [+836]), point (1)

H4260 לְהָבִים ***lehābîm***, n.pr.g. [2] Lehabite:– Lehabites (2)

H4261 לַהַג ***lahag***, n.m. [1] study, devotion to books:– study (1)

H4262 לַהַד ***lāhad***, n.pr.m. [1] Lahad, "[perhaps] *slow, indolent*":– Lahad (1)

H4263 לָהַהּ ***lāhah***, v. [1] [cf. 3532, 4271]. [Ht] to behave like a madman:– maniac (1)

H4264 לָהָה ***lāhâ***, v. Not used in NIVEBC [cf. 4206]. [Q] to languish, faint

H4265 ¹לָהַט ***lāhaṭ***[1], v. [10] [→ 4266, 4267; cf. 4358]. [Q] to burn, flame; [P] to set afire, set ablaze, consume:– sets ablaze (2), blazes (1), burned up (1), consumed (1), consumes (1), flames (1), in flames (1), set afire (1), set on fire (1)

H4266 ²לָהַט ***lāhaṭ***[2], v. [1] [√ 4265]. [Q] to devour; (n.) ravenous beast:– ravenous beasts (1)

H4267 לַהַט ***lahaṭ***, n.[m.] [1] [√ 4265]. flame; referring to the supernatural blade of a sword:– flaming (1)

H4268 לְהָטִים ***lehāṭîm***, n.m.pl. [1] [cf. 4286]. secret arts, sorceries:– secret arts (1)

H4269 לָהַם ***lāham***, v. [2] [Ht] to let oneself swallow greedily; (ptcp.) choice morsels:– choice morsels (2)

H4270 לָהֵן ***lāhēn***, c. Not used in NIVEBC [√ 10385]. therefore

H4271 לִהְלֵהַּ ***lihlēah***, v. Not used in NIVEBC [cf. 4263]. [Htpal] to amaze, startle; (n.) madman

H4272 לַהֲקָה ***lahᵃqâ***, n.f. [2] group, community:– aged (1), group (1)

H4273 לוּ ***lû***, c. [24] [→ 467, 4295]. if! if only!; O that!:– if (11), if only (9), let (1), oh (1), what if (1), will (1)

H4274 לֹו דְבָר ***lô debār***, n.pr.loc. [2] [√ 4202 + 1818]. Lo Debar, "*no pasture*":– Lo Debar (2)

H4275 לוּב ***lûb***, n.g.pl. [4] Libya, Libyan:– Libyans (3), Libya (1)

H4276 לוּד ***lûd***, n.pr.m. & g. [8] Lud, Ludite; Lydia, Lydians:– Lud (2), Ludites (2), Lydia (2), Lydians (1), men of Lydia (1)

H4277 ¹לָוָה ***lāwâ***[1], v. [12] [→ 4290, 4291, 4292, 4293; cf. 4339]. [Q] to accompany; [N] to be joined, be attached, be bound to:– join (5), bind themselves (2), accompany (1), attached (1), be joined (1), bound (1), joined (1)

H4278 ²לָוָה ***lāwâ***[2], v. [14] [Q] to borrow; [H] to lend:– lend (4), borrow (3), borrower (2), lend freely (2), lender (2), lends (1)

H4279 ¹לוּז ***lûz***[1], v. [6] [→ 4299]. [Q] to depart (from one's sight); [N] to be devious, be perverse, be deceitful; [H] to depart (from one's sight):– devious (2), let out (2), deceit (1), perverse (1)

H4280 ²לוּז ***lûz***[2], n.[m.] [1] [→ 4281]. almond tree (branch):– almond (1)

H4281 ³לוּז ***lûz***[3], n.pr.loc. [8] [→ 4282; cf. 4280]. Luz, "*almond tree*":– Luz (7), NDT (1)

H4282 לוּזָה ***lûzâ***, n.pr.loc. Not used in NIVEBC [√ 4281 + 2025]. Luzah, see 4281

H4283 לוּחַ ***lûaḥ***, n.m. [43] [→ 4284; cf. 4300]. tablets (of stone); board, panel (of wood); plate (metal):– tablets (33), tablet (3), boards (2), panels (1), surfaces (1), them[S] (1 [+2021]), they[S] (1), timbers (1)

H4284 לוּחִית ***lûḥît***, n.pr.loc. [2] [√ 4283; cf. 4300, 4304]. Luhith:– Luhith (2)

H4285 לוֹחֵשׁ ***lôḥēš***, n.pr.m. Not used in NIVEBC [√ 4317]. Lohesh, see 2135

H4286 לוּט ***lûṭ***, v. [4] [→ 4287, 4319, 4320; cf. 4209, 4268]. [Q] to cover, enfold; [Qp] to be wrapped up; [H] to cover, wrap up:– covered (1), enfolds (1), pulled over (1), wrapped (1)

H4287 ¹לוֹט ***lôṭ***[1], n.m. [1] [√ 4286]. shroud, covering:– shroud (1)

H4288 ²לוֹט ***lôṭ***[2], n.pr.m. [33] [→ 4289]. Lot:– Lot (28), Lot's (3), he[S] (1), NDT (1)

H4289 לוֹטָן ***lôṭān***, n.pr.m. [7] [√ 4288]. Lotan, "*of Lot*":– Lotan (5), Lotan's (2)

H4290 ¹לֵוִי ***lēwî***[1], n.pr.m. [62] [√ 4277; 10387]. Levi; Levite, "*of Levi*":– Levi (40), Levites (15 [+1201]), Levite (2), Levites (2), Levitical (2 [+1201]), Levites (1 [+4751])

H4291 ²לֵוִי ***lēwî***[2], a.g. [287] [√ 4277; 10387]. Levite, of Levi, "*of Levi*":– Levites (234), Levite (26), levitical (14), Levi (3), Levites (3 [+1201]), Levi (1 [+1201]), Levites (1 [+5476]), them (1 [+2021]), them[S] (1 [+2021]), they[S] (1 [+2021]), NDT (2)

H4292 לִוְיָה ***liwyâ***, n.f. [2] [√ 4277]. garland, wreath:– garland (2)

H4293 לִוְיָתָן ***liwyātān***, n.m. [6] [√ 4277]. Leviathan, sea-monster; this refers both to a serpent-like sea creature and to a mythological monster of chaos opposed to the true God:– Leviathan (6)

H4294 לוּל ***lûl***, n.[m.] [1] stairway; some sources: trap door:– stairway (1)

H4295 לוּלֵא ***lûlē'***, c. [14] [√ 4273]. if not, unless:– if not (5), if not (4 [+3954]), unless (2), but (1), not (1), remain (1)

H4296 לוּן ***lûn***, v. [15] [→ 9442]. [N] to grumble against, blame; [H] to grumble against, blame:– grumbled (7), grumble (3), constant grumbling (1 [+9442]), grumbling (1), grumbling (1 [+9442]), howl (1), made grumble (1)

H4297 לוּשׁ ***lûš***, v. [5] [Q] to knead (bread dough):– knead (2), kneaded (2), kneading (1)

H4298 לָוִשׁ ***lāwiš***, n.pr.m. Not used in NIVEBC [√ 4330]. Lawish, see 4331

H4299 לָזוּת ***lāzût***, n.f. [1] [√ 4279]. crookedness, perversity, referring to a kind of speech:– corrupt talk (1)

H4300 לַח ***laḥ***, a. [6] [→ 4283, 4284, 4301]. fresh, fresh-cut, still moist:– fresh (2), green (2), fresh-cut (1), grapes or raisins (1 [+6694, 2256, 3313])

H4301 לֵחַ ***lēaḥ***, n.m. [1] [√ 4300]. strength:– strength (1)

H4302 ¹לְחוּם ***leḥûm***[1], n.[m.] [1] entrails:– entrails (1)

H4303 ²לְחוּם ***leḥûm***[2], n.[m.] [1] [√ 4309]. blow, wound:– blows (1)

H4304 לֻחוֹת ***luḥôt***, n.pr.loc. Not used in NIVEBC [cf. 4284]. Luhoth, see 4284

H4305 ¹לְחִי ***leḥî***[1], n.m. [20] [→ 4306?, 8257?]. jaw, jawbone; by extension: cheek, jowl:– cheek (4), cheeks (4), jawbone (4), jaws (3), face (2), jaw (2), meat from the head (1)

H4306 ²לְחִי ***leḥî***[2], n.pr.loc. [4] [√ 4305?]. Lehi, "*jawbone*":– Lehi (4)

H4307 לַחַי רֹאִי ***laḥay rō'î***, n.pr.loc. Not used in NIVEBC [√ 4200 + 2649 + 8022]. Lahai Roi

H4308 לָחַךְ ***lāḥak***, v. [6] [Q] to lick up; [P] to lick up, subdue:– lick (3), lick up (1), licked up (1), licks up (1)

H4309 ¹לָחַם ***lāḥam***[1], v. [171] [→ 4303, 4311, 4878]. [Q] to fight against, attack; [N] to fight against, attack:– fight (71), fought (30), attacked (16), fighting (12), attack (6), attacking (6), battle (5), fights (3), go to war (3), war (3), fight (2 [+4309]), wage war (2), at war (1), engage in battle (1), fight battle (1), military (1), military exploits (1), overpower (1), overpower (1 [+6584]), pressed attack (1), waged war (1), waging war (1), wars (1), NDT (1)

H4310 ²לָחַם ***lāḥam***[2], v. [6] [√ 4312]. [Q] to eat, dine; [Qp] to be consumed:– eat (4), consuming (1), dine (1)

H4311 לָחֶם ***lāḥem***, n.[m.] [1] [√ 4309]. war; other sources vary:– war (1)

H4312 לֶחֶם ***leḥem***, n.m. & f. [298] [→ 1107, 3788, 4310; 10389]. bread, bread loaf; any kind of food; time or act of eating, meal; "bread of the Presence" is a regular offering to the LORD presented on a designated table in the tabernacle and temple:– food (118), bread (115), loaves of bread (6), meal (3), something[S] (3), eat (2), food offering (2 [+852]), provisions (2), something to eat (2 [+7326]), baked (1), bread (1 [+3971]), crops (1), daily bread (1 [+2976]), devour (1), feast (1), feed (1), food (1 [+7326]), fruit (1), grain (1), loaf (1), loaves (1), meal (1 [+430]), nothing (1 [+4202]), overfed (1 [+8430]), provided for (1 [+2118, 4200, 2256, 430]), round loaves (1), stay for a meal (1 [+430]), thick loaf (1 [+2705]), NDT (26)

H4313 לַחְמִי ***laḥmî***, n.pr.m. [1] Lahmi:– Lahmi (1)

H4314 לַחְמָס ***laḥmās***, n.pr.loc. [1] Lahmas:– Lahmas (1)

H4315 לָחַץ ***lāḥaṣ***, v. [19] [→ 4316; cf. 5722]. [Q] to oppress, crush, confine; [N] to be pressed close:– oppressed (6), oppress (4), oppressors (2), confined (1), crushing (1), hold shut (1), oppressing (1), press (1), pressed close (1), severely oppressing (1 [+4316])

H4316 לַחַץ ***laḥaṣ***, n.m. [12] [√ 4315]. oppression, affliction; short ration (of bread or water):– affliction (2), nothing but (2), oppressed (2), oppression (2), severely oppressing (1 [+4315]), way[S] (1), NDT (2)

H4317 לָחַשׁ ***lāḥaš***, v. [3] [→ 2135, 4285, 4318; cf. 5727]. [P] to charm, enchant (i.e., whisper); [Ht] to whisper together:– charmer (1), whisper (1), whispering among themselves (1)

H4318 לַחַשׁ ***laḥaš***, n.[m.] [5] [√ 4317]. charming, whispering; charm, enchanter:– charmed (2), barely whisper a prayer (1 [+7440]), charms (1), enchanter (1)

H4319 לָט ***lāṭ***, n.[m.] [7] [√ 4286]. quietly, privately, secretly, a fig. extension of the base meaning "no physical sound"; (pl.) secret arts, with a focus on mysterious and hidden elements of this magic:– secret arts (3), quietly (2 [+928, 2021]), privately (1 [+928, 2021]), unnoticed (1 [+928, 2021])

H4320 לֹט ***lōṭ***, n.[m.] [2] [√ 4286]. myrrh (a resinous, fragrant and slightly bitter to the taste); some sources: mastic bark (a resinous gum of the rockrose plant):– myrrh (2)

H4321 לְטָאָה ***leṭā'â***, n.f. [1] wall lizard; some sources: gecko:– wall lizard (1)

H4322 לְטוּשִׁים ***leṭûšim***, n.pr.g. [1] [√ 4323]. Letushite, "*sharpened*":– Letushites (1)

H4323 לָטַשׁ ***lāṭaš***, v. [5] [→ 4322]. [Q] to sharpen; to forge, hammer; to pierce (with the eyes); [Pu] to be sharpened:– sharpened (2), fastens piercing (1), forged (1), sharpen (1)

H4324 לֹיָה ***lōyâ***, n.f. [3] [cf. 4339]. wreath, garland; some translate as a technical architectural term: border, rim:– wreaths (3)

H4325 לַיִל ***layil***, n.m. [6] [→ 4326, 4327; cf. 4328; 10391]. night:– night (6)

H4326 לַיְלָה ***laylâ***, n.m. [227] [√ 4325; cf. 4328; 10391]. night; sometimes with the implication that it is the time of illicit, illegal, or immoral activity:– night (192), nights (14), tonight (9 [+2021]), midnight (2 [+2940]), overnight (2 [+1201]), all night long (1 [+928, 2021]), all-night (1 [+3972, 2021]), last night (1 [+2021]), midnight (1 [+2942, 2021]), nightfall (1), nightfall (1 [+2021]), nocturnal (1), NDT (1)

H4327 לִילִית ***lîlît***, n.f. [1] [√ 4325; cf. 4328]. night creature; Lilith, a female demon of the night:– night creatures (1)

H4328 לִין ***lîn***, v. [69] [→ 4349, 4869, 4870; cf. 4325, 4326, 4327]. [Q] to spend the night, stay the night; [H] to hold back overnight, leave overnight; [Htpolal] to stay for the night; by extension: to stay, dwell an indeterminate amount of time:– spend the night (17), stay (7), spent the night (6), remain (3), spent (3), dwell (2), spend (2), stay at night (2), at home (1), camp (1), camped (1), endure (1), for the night (1), harbor (1 [+928, 7931]), hold back overnight (1 [+6330, 1332]), kept (1), left (1), lie all night (1), overnight (1), remains (1), resides (1), rest (1), resting (1), rests (1), roost (1), sleeping (1), spend days (1), spend nights (1), spent the nights (1), stay night (1), stay tonight (1), stayed night (1 [+3782, 2256]), stays at night (1), stays only a night (1 [+5742]), stopped for the night (1)

H4329 לִיץ ***lîṣ***, v. [6] [→ 4370, 4371, 4372, 4885, 4886]. [Q] to mock, scorn, talk big; [H] to mock; [Htpolal] to show oneself a mocker:– mock (2), mocks (2), mocker (1), mocking (1)

H4330 ¹לַיִשׁ ***layiš***[1], n.m. [3] [→ 4298, 4331, 4332, 4333]. lion:– lion (2), lions (1)

H4331 ²לַיִשׁ ***layiš***[2], n.pr.m. [2] [√ 4330]. Laish, "*lion*":– Laish (2)

H4332 ³לַיִשׁ ***layiš***[3], n.pr.loc. [4] [√ 4330; cf. 4386]. Laish, "*lion*":– Laish (4)

H4333 לַיְשָׁה ***layešâ***, n.pr.loc. [1] [√ 4330]. Laishah, "*lion*":– Laishah (1)

H4334 לָכַד ***lākad***, v. [121] [→ 4335, 4892]. [Q] to capture, seize, take as a possession; [N] to be taken captive, be seized, be taken:– captured (33), took (15), capture (9), be captured (6), was taken (5), be caught (4), take (4), caught (3), chooses (3), taken (3), was chosen (3), captures (2), caught (2 [+4334]), ensnare (2), was captured (2), are caught (1), are trapped (1), assumed (1), be taken captive (1), catch (1), catches (1), chosen (1), cling together (1), conquered (1), ensnared (1), entangle (1), frozen (1), held fast (1), is captured (1), is caught (1), seize (1), seized (1), takes (1), took possession (1), took prisoner (1), trapped (1), was caught (1), was taken by lot (1), were caught (1), were taken (1)

H4335 לֶכֶד ***leked***, n.[m.] [1] [√ 4334]. snaring, capturing:– snared (1)

H4336 לֵכָה ***lēkâ***, n.pr.loc. [1] Lecah, "*to you*":– Lekah (1)

H4337 לָכִישׁ ***lākîš***, n.pr.loc. [24] Lachish:– Lachish (24)

H4338 לָכֵן ***lākēn***, adv. & pp. Not used in NIVEBC [√ 4200 + 4027]. therefore, see 4200 & 4027

H4339 לֻלָאוֹת ***lulā'ōt***, n.f. [13] [cf. 4277, 4324]. (pl.) loops:– loops (11), NDT (2)

H4340 לָמַד ***lāmad***, v. [86] [→ 4341, 4913, 9441]. [Q] to learn, train for; [Qp] to be trained; [P] to teach, instruct, cause to learn; [Pu] to be trained; with implication that the learning will be put to use:– teach (30), learn (15), taught (13), learned (3), teaches (3), trains (3), learn well (2 [+4340]), teaching (2), train (2), trained (2), accept (1), adopted (1), been taught (1), cultivated (1), experienced (1), imparted (1), instructors

(1), teachers (1), unruly (1 [+4202]), were trained (1), NDT (1)

H4341 לִמֻּד ***limmud***, a. [6] [√ 4340]. accustomed to; (n.) a disciple, one who is taught, a follower:– accustomed to (2), disciples (1), one instructed (1), taught (1), well-instructed (1)

H4342 לָמָּה ***lāmmâ***, p.inter. & indef. Not used in NIVEBC [√ 4200 + 4537]. why?, see 4200 & 4537

H4343 לָמוֹ ***lāmô***, pp.+p.suf. Not used in NIVEBC [√ 4200 + 4564]. to him, his, see 4200 & 4564

H4344 לְמוֹ ***lᵉmô***, pp. [4] [√ 4200]. for, in, over:– for (1), in (1), over (1), NDT (1)

H4345 לְמוּאֵל ***lᵉmû'ēl***, n.pr.m. [2] [√ 4200 + 446]. Lemuel, "*[belonging] to God [El]*":– Lemuel (2)

H4346 לְמוֹאֵל ***lᵉmô'ēl***, n.pr.m. Not used in NIVEBC [√ 4200 + 4578]. see 4200 & 4578

H4347 לֶמֶךְ ***lemek***, n.pr.m. [11] Lamech:– Lamech (11)

H4348 לְמַעַן ***lᵉma'an***, pr.+subst. Not used in NIVEBC [√ 4200 + 6701]. so that, that; to; for the sake of

H4349 לֵן ***lēn***, n.[m.] *or* v.ptcp. Not used in NIVEBC [√ 4328]. spending the night, see 4328

H4350 לֹעַ ***lōa'***, n.[m.] [1] [√ 4363]. throat:– throat (1)

H4351 לָעַב ***lā'ab***, v. [1] [H] to mock, make sport of (someone), make a game of (someone):– mocked (1)

H4352 לָעַג ***lā'ag***, v. [20] [→ 4353, 4354; cf. 6589]. [Q] to mock, scoff, ridicule; [N] to stammer, speak as a foreigner; [H] to mock, ridicule:– mock (6), mocks (6), maliciously mocked (2 [+4352]), ridiculed (2), mocked (1), scoff (1), scoffs (1), strange (1)

H4353 לַעַג ***la'ag***, n.[m.] [8] [√ 4352]. scorn, ridicule, derision:– scorn (3), ridiculed (2), derision (1), foreign (1), ridicule (1)

H4354 לָעֵג ***lā'ēg***, a. Not used in NIVEBC [√ 4352]. people of stammering lips or foreign language

H4355 לַעְדָּה ***la'dâ***, n.pr.m. [1] [→ 4356]. Laadah, "[perhaps] *having a fat throat or neck*":– Laadah (1)

H4356 לַעְדָּן ***la'dān***, n.pr.m. [7] [√ 4355]. Ladan:– Ladan (7)

H4357 לָעַז ***lā'az***, v. [1] [Q] to speak a foreign tongue, speak an unintelligible language:– foreign tongue (1)

H4358 לָעַט ***lā'aṭ***, v. [1] [cf. 4265]. [H] to let (someone) gulp down:– let have (1)

H4359 לָעִיר ***lā'îr***, n.[pr.loc.?] [2] [√ 4200 + 6551]. Lair, Laair, "*of* or *to the city*"; see 4200 & 6551:– Lair (2)

H4360 לַעֲנָה ***la'ᵃnâ***, n.f. [8] gall (bitter to the taste, possibly poisonous); by extension: bitterness as a concept:– bitter (3), gall (3), bitterness (2)

H4361 לְעַנּוֹת ***lᵉ'annôt***, n.[pl.] *or* v.ptcp. [1] [√ 6700?]. leannoth [t.t. in Psalms]:– leannoth (1)

H4362 לָעַע ***lā'a'[1]***, v. [2] [Q] to talk impetuously, to dedicate (something) rashly; a fig. extension of drinking in a hurried, careless manner:– impetuous (1), rashly (1)

H4363 ²לָעַע ***lā'a'[2]***, v. [1] [→ 4350; cf. 6633]. [Q] to sip, lap, slurp:– drink (1)

H4364 לְעָפְרָה ***lᵉ'aprâ***, n.pr.loc. Not used in NIVEBC [→ 1108; cf. 6765]. Ophrah

H4365 לַפִּיד ***lappîd***, n.m. [13] [→ 4366?]. torch, firebrand; by extension: lightning:– torches (5), torch (4), flames (1), flaming torches (1), lightning (1), NDT (1)

H4366 לַפִּידוֹת ***lappîdôt***, n.pr.m. [1] [√ 4365?]. Lappidoth, "*flames*":– Lappidoth (1)

H4367 לִפְנֵי ***lipnê***, pp.+n.m. Not used in NIVEBC [√ 4200 + 7155]. to, for, before, see 4200 & 7155

H4368 לִפְנָי ***lipnāy***, pp.+n. Not used in NIVEBC [√ 4200 + 7155]. see 4200 & 7156

H4369 לָפַת ***lāpat***, v. [3] [Q] to reach toward; [N] be turned aside; in some contexts there is an implication of touching or grasping the object reached toward:– reached toward (1), turn aside (1), turned (1)

H4370 לֵץ ***lēṣ***, n.[m.] *or* v.ptcp. [16] [√ 4329]. mocker, babbler, scoffer:– mocker (9), mockers (6), proud mockers (1)

H4371 לָצוֹן ***lāṣôn***, n.[m.] [3] [√ 4329]. mockery, scoffing, hostile speech of fools:– mockers (1 [+408]), mockery (1), scoffers (1 [+408])

H4372 לָצַץ ***lāṣaṣ***, n.[m.] *or* v.ptcp. [1] [√ 4329]. mocker, scoffer, with an implication that this class of person is foolish and rebellious:– mockers (1)

H4373 לַקּוּם ***laqqûm***, n.pr.loc. [1] Lakkum:– Lakkum (1)

H4374 לָקַח ***lāqaḥ***, v. [963] [→ 4375, 4376, 4917, 4918?, 4920, 5228, 5229]. [Q] to take, receive; [Qp] to be led away; [N] to be captured, taken away; [Pu] to be taken away, brought; [Ht] to flash back and forth; by extension: to gain possession, exercise authority; "to take a woman" means "to marry a wife":– take (235), took (235), get (47), taken (33), accept (24), bring (20), brought (20), married (16), taking (16), take away (12), receive (11), received (11), married (10 [+851]), took away (10), marry (8), accepted (7), choose (7), got (6), selected (6), takes (6), accepts (5), capture (5), captured (5), marries (5), be taken (4), married (4 [+4200, 851]), marry (4 [+851]), put (4), seize (4), seized (4), taken away (4), was taken (4), been captured (3), bring back (3), carried (3), carried away (3), carried off (3), collected (3), marry (3 [+4200, 851]), respond to (3), select (3), took hold (3), use (3), am taken (2), carry away (2), chose (2), collect (2), found (2), is taken (2), keep (2), kill (2 [+5883]), led away (2), made off with (2), picked up (2), purchased (2), take up (2), takes away (2), took as prisoners (2), was taken away (2), were taken (2), accepting (1), adopted (1 [+4200, 1426]), appoint (1), are gathered (1), are taken (1), arrest (1), be brought (1), become wife (1 [+4200, 851]), been taken (1), been taken away (1), being led away (1), blow away (1), bring (1 [+2256, 3655]), brought back (1), buy (1), buys (1), captivate (1), carried (1 [+928, 3338]), catch (1), caught (1), choose as wives (1), come back (1), did (1), did so[S] (1), did so[S] (1 [+8008, 2256, 2932]), disgraced (1 [+1423]), drew (1), find (1), flashed back and forth (1 [+928, 9348]), flashing (1), get back (1), grabbed (1), had brought (1), had brought (1 [+8938, 2256]), had removed (1 [+8938, 2256]), have (1), have come (1), impose (1), invites (1), kept (1), learn (1), learned (1), loaded (1), made (1 [+928]), make (1), married (1 [+4200, 2257, 4200, 851]), marries (1 [+2256, 1249]), marry (1 [+4200]), marry (1 [+851, 4200]), need (1), no longer (1 [+4946]), open to (1), pledged to marry (1), prefer (1), prepare (1), recaptured (1 [+8740, 2256]), receives (1), receiving (1), removed (1), responded to (1), retake (1), sampled (1), saves (1), send for (1 [+8938, 2256]), send for (1 [+8938, 2256]), sent for (1), sent for (1 [+8938, 2256]), share (1), snatched (1), strip of (1), stripped (1), suffer (1), summon (1 [+8938, 2256]), takes life (1), taking hold (1), took (1 [+2256, 5011]), took down (1), took in marriage (1 [+4200, 851]), took out (1), took over (1), took prisoner (1), use as (1), wag (1), want (1), was captured (1), NDT (19)

H4375 לֶקַח ***leqaḥ***, n.m. [9] [√ 4374]. teaching, instruction, learning:– instruction (3), learning (3), beliefs (1), persuasive words (1), teaching (1)

H4376 לִקְחִי ***liqḥî***, n.pr.m. [1] [√ 4374]. Likhi, "*take, marry*":– Likhi (1)

H4377 לָקַט ***lāqaṭ***, v. [37] [→ 3541, 4378]. [Q] to gather; [P] to gather, pick up, glean; [Pu] to be gathered up; [Ht] to gather oneself about; this act of gathering is general, and can refer to the second or final gleanings of the field or orchard:– gather (12), gathered (7), glean (6), pick up (3), be gathered up (1), collected (1), gather up (1), gathering (1), gleaned (1), gleans (1), picked (1), picked up (1), picked up scraps (1)

H4378 לֶקֶט ***leqeṭ***, n.[m.] [2] [√ 4377]. gleanings (of a harvest):– gleanings (2)

H4379 לָקַק ***lāqaq***, v. [7] [Q, P] to lap up, lick up:– licked up (2), drank lapping (1), lap (1), lapped (1), laps (1), lick up (1)

H4380 לָקַשׁ ***lāqaš***, v.den. [1] [→ 4381, 4919]. [P] to glean:– glean (1)

H4381 לֶקֶשׁ ***leqeš***, n.[m.] [2] [√ 4380]. second crop, late grass at spring time:– late crops (1), NDT (1)

H4382 לָשָׁד ***lāšād***, n.m. [2] moist (food), strength:– something made (1), strength (1)

H4383 לָשׁוֹן ***lāšôn***, n.m. [117] [→ 4387; 10392]. tongue; by extension: language, speech, noise (of an animal); something tongue-shaped: wedge (of precious metal), bay, gulf, flame of fire:– tongue (58), tongues (25), language (12), languages (4), bay (3), words (3), bar (2), bark (1 [+3076]), charmer (1 [+1251]), fangs (1), gulf (1), lips (1), object of malicious talk (1 [+6590, 6584, 8557]), on the tip of tongue (1 [+928, 2674]), slanderers (1 [+408]), talk (1), uttered a word (1 [+3076, 906])

H4384 לִשְׁכָּה ***liškâ***, n.f. [46] [cf. 5969]. room, chamber; hall; storeroom:– rooms (21), room (13), storerooms (5), side rooms (2), chambers (1), hall (1), priests rooms (1 [+7731]), that[S] (1), NDT (1)

H4385 לֶשֶׁם ***lešem[1]***, n.[m.] [2] jacinth (exact identification is uncertain):– jacinth (2)

H4386 ²לֶשֶׁם ***lešem[2]***, n.pr.loc. [2] [cf. 4332]. Leshem, "*lion*":– Leshem (2)

H4387 לָשַׁן ***lāšan***, v.den. [2] [√ 4383]. [Po] to slander; [H] to slander:– slander (1), slanders (1)

H4388 לֶשַׁע ***leša'***, n.pr.loc. [1] Lasha:– Lasha (1)

H4389 לַשָּׁרוֹן ***laššārôn***, n.pr.loc. [1] [cf. 9227]. Lasharon, "*[belonging to] Sharon*":– Lasharon (1)

H4390 לֶתֶךְ ***letek***, n.[m.] [1] lethek (a dry measure, half a cor, about 6 bushels [220 liters]):– lethek (1)

H4391 מ ***m***, letter. Not used in NIVEBC [√ 10393]. letter of the Hebrew alphabet

H4392 ־ָם ***-ām***, ־ם ***-m***, p.m.pl.suf. [3926] [→ 307?, 2023]. they, them, their:– them (1547), their (1010), they (255), the[S] (125), their own (44), it (32), its (28), a[S] (15), whose (15), themselves (14), you (12), the people[S] (10), those (10), these (8), Israel[S] (6), which[S] (6), his (5), the Israelites[S] (5), them (5 [+5883]), they (5 [+5883]), who (5), your (5), by themselves (4 [+4200, 963]), he (4), one by one (4 [+4200, 1653]), the creatures[S] (4), each (3), her (3), him (3), my people[S] (3), our (3), people[S] (3), she (3), that[S] (3), the Levites[S] (3), the cherubim[S] (3), the rest[S] (3), their bodies[S] (3), us (3), which (3), Judah[S] (2), all[S] (2), courts[S] (2), gods[S] (2), our ancestors[S] (2), that (2), the enemy[S] (2), the men[S] (2), the shields[S] (2), the wicked[S] (2), these[S] (2), these articles[S] (2), things[S] (2), this (2), this[S] (2), whom (2), Babylon[S] (1), Egypt[S] (1), Moses and Aaron[S] (1), anyone (1), army[S] (1), battle[S] (1), buyer and seller[S] (1), creatures[S] (1), did[S] (1 [+3877, 906, 4213]), each[S] (1), else's (1), everyone (1 [+3972]), extremes[S] (1), his enemies[S] (1), his sons[S] (1), human[S] (1), its people[S] (1), keep themselves alive (1 [+8740, 906, 5883]), man[S] (1), man's[S] (1), matters[S] (1), people (1), priests[S] (1), prophets[S] (1), that[S] (1 [+2388]), that person[S] (1), the Arameans[S] (1), the Canaanites[S] (1), the Gibeonites[S] (1), the Horites[S] (1), the Midianites[S] (1), the Midianites (1), the army[S] (1), the case[S] (1), the censers[S] (1), the days[S] (1), the enemy (1), the flock[S] (1 [+5883]), the goats[S] (1), the gods[S] (1), the hair[S] (1), the kings[S] (1), the nations[S] (1), the needy[S] (1), the nobles and officials[S] (1), the others[S] (1), the people (1), the priests[S] (1), the ropes[S] (1), the servants[S] (1), the stones[S] (1), the things[S] (1), the water[S] (1), their[S] (1), their enemies[S] (1), their gods[S] (1), their leaders[S] (1), their offerings[S] (1), their temples[S] (1), them (1 [+1414]), them (1 [+2652]), them (1 [+4213]), themselves (1 [+4213]), themselves (1 [+4222]), there[S] (1 [+928, 9348]), these days[S] (1), these offerings[S] (1), they (1 [+9307]), this is the way (1 [+928]), this people[S] (1), those nations[S] (1), whom[S] (1), young men[S] (1), your children[S] (1), your lovers[S] (1), yourselves (1), NDT (593)

H4393 מַאֲבוּס ***ma'ᵃbûs***, n.[m.] [1] [√ 80]. granary:– granaries (1)

H4394 מְאֹד ***mᵉ'ōd***, n.m. (used as adv.) [300] a marker of great degree or quanity: very, greatly, exceedingly, much:– very (70), greatly (22), great (20), so (7), large (6), most (6), very (6 [+6330]), exceedingly (4 [+4394]), great quantity (4 [+2221]), terrified (4 [+3707]), very much (4), beyond measure (3 [+6330]), deep (3), greatly (3 [+928, 4394]), how (3), very (3 [+928, 4394]), all (2), burned (2 [+3013]), closely (2), desperate (2), exceedingly (2 [+928, 4394]), fully (2), furious (2 [+3013]), great (2 [+1524]), greatly (2 [+4394]), large (2 [+8041]), much (2), so (2 [+4394]), so (2 [+928, 4394]), strength (2), terrified (2 [+3707, 4394]), thoroughly (2), utterly (2), utterly (2 [+6330]), vast (2 [+1524, 4394]), worst (2 [+3878]), abundance (1 [+2221]), abundantly (1), accumulate large amounts (1 [+8049]), aged (1 [+2416]), almost (1), anguish (1 [+987]), at a distance (1 [+8158]), badly (1), behaved in the vilest manner (1 [+9493]), beyond number (1 [+8041]), bitterly (1), bitterly (1 [+3878]), boundless (1 [+8146]), come quickly (1 [+4554]), coming quickly (1 [+4554]), completely (1), critically (1), crushing (1 [+2703]), defeated (1 [+5782, 1524, 4804]), devastated (1 [+5782, 1524, 4804]), devout (1), dreadful (1 [+3707]), enough (1), even far (1 [+3856]), even more (1), ever-present (1 [+5162]), exceedingly (1), exhausted (1 [+6545]), far (1), filled with fear (1 [+3707]), firmly (1), full well (1), furious (1 [+7911]), furious (1 [+3013, 678]), gorged (1 [+8425]), great (1 [+1540]), great (1 [+2221]), great numbers (1 [+2221]), great numbers (1 [+3878]), great quantities (1 [+4200, 8044]), greatly (1 [+4394, 928]), grew louder and louder (1 [+2143, 2256, 2618]), grew worse and worse (1 [+2118, 2716, 2617]), heavy (1 [+3877]), highly (1), highly regarded (1 [+1524]), how great (1), huge (1), huge (1 [+1524, 6330, 4200]), intense (1 [+1524]), kept bringing pressure (1 [+7210]), large (1 [+1524]), large (1 [+3878]), large amount (1 [+2221]), least (1), long way (1 [+8158]), lost self-confidence (1 [+5877, 928, 6524]), loud (1 [+1524, 6330]), make as great as you like (1 [+8049]), many (1 [+8041]), more (1), much (1 [+6330]), quickly (1), reward handsomely (1 [+3877, 3877]), severe (1 [+3878]), severe (1 [+8041]), so (1 [+3954]), so highly (1), so much (1), stand firm (1 [+586]), stood in awe (1 [+3707]), strongly (1), tempest rages (1 [+8548]), terrible (1 [+3878]), terribly (1 [+2221]), terror filled (1 [+3006]), too (1), total (1 [+1524]), toward evening (1 [+3718]), trembled violently (1 [+3006, 1524, 6330, 3010]), unmercifully (1 [+6330]), utter (1), vast (1 [+1524]), very (1 [+2221]), very (1 [+6786]), very (1 [+4394, 928]), violently (1), well known (1 [+3700]), writhe in agony (1 [+2655]), NDT (3)

H4395 ¹מֵאָה ***mē'â[1]***, n.f. [580] [→ 4396?, 4405; 10395]. hundred:– hundred (236), hundreds (18), 250 (10 [+2822, 2256]), 100 (8), 4,500 (8 [+2822, 2256, 752, 547]), units of a hundred (6), 120 (5 [+2256, 6929]), 200 (5), 500 (5 [+2822]), 128 (4 [+6929, 2256, 9046]), 1,254 (3 [+547, 2822, 2256, 752]), 127 (3 [+8679, 2256, 6929, 2256]), 40,500 (3 [+752, 547, 2256, 2822]), 430 (3 [+8993, 2256, 752]), 53,400 (3 [+8993, 2256, 2822, 547, 2256, 752]), eleven hundred (3 [+547, 2256]), 1,247 (2 [+547, 752, 2256, 8679]), 1,775 (2 [+547, 2256, 8679, 2256, 2822, 2256, 8679]), 112 (2 [+2256, 9109, 6925]), 123 (2 [+6929, 2256, 8993]), 137 (2 [+8679, 2256, 8993, 2256]), 150 (2 [+2256, 2822]), 200,000 (2 [+547]), 220 (2 [+2256, 6929]), 223 (2 [+6929, 2256, 8993]), 245 (2 [+752, 2256, 2822]), 3,600 (2 [+8993, 547, 2256, 9252]), 30,500 (2 [+8993, 547, 2256, 2822]), 300 (2 [+8993]), 32,200 (2 [+9109, 2256, 8993, 547, 2256]), 320 (2 [+8993, 2256, 6929]), 345 (2 [+8993, 752, 2256, 2822]),

35,400 (2 [+2822, 2256, 8993, 547, 2256, 752]), 372 (2 [+8993, 8679, 2256, 9109]), 390 (2 [+8993, 2256, 9596]), 392 (2 [+8993, 9596, 2256, 9109]), 4,600 (2 [+752, 547, 2256, 9252]), 403 (2 [+8993, 2256, 752]), 41,500 (2 [+285, 2256, 752, 547, 2256, 2822]), 435 (2 [+752, 8993, 2256, 2822]), 45,650 (2 [+2822, 2256, 752, 547, 2256, 9252, 2256, 2822]), 46,500 (2 [+9252, 2256, 752, 547, 2256, 2822]), 54,400 (2 [+752, 2256, 2822, 547, 2256, 752]), 57,400 (2 [+8679, 2256, 2822, 547, 2256, 752]), 59,300 (2 [+9596, 2256, 2822, 547, 2256, 8993]), 6,720 (2 [+9252, 547, 8679, 2256, 6929]), 62,700 (2 [+9109, 2256, 9252, 547, 2256, 8679]), 621 (2 [+9252, 6929, 2256, 285]), 652 (2 [+9252, 2822, 2256, 9109]), 666 (2 [+9252, 9252, 2256, 9252]), 7,337 (2 [+8679, 547, 8993, 8993, 2256, 8679]), 736 (2 [+8679, 8993, 2256, 9252]), 74,600 (2 [+752, 2256, 8679, 547, 2256, 9252]), 760 (2 [+8679, 2256, 9252]), 800 (2 [+9046]), 973 (2 [+9596, 8679, 2256, 8993]), fourteen hundred (2 [+547, 2256, 752]), units of hundreds (2), 1,222 (1 [+547, 6929, 2256, 9109]), 1,254 (1 [+547, 2256, 752, 2822]), 1,290 (1 [+547, 2256, 9596]), 1,335 (1 [+547, 8993, 8993, 2256, 2822]), 1,365 (1 [+2822, 2256, 9252, 2256, 8993, 2256, 547]), 1,760 (1 [+547, 2256, 8679, 2256, 9252]), 105 (1 [+2822, 2256]), 108,100 (1 [+4395, 547, 2256, 9046, 547, 2256]), 108,100 (1 [+547, 2256, 9046, 547, 2256, 4395]), 110 (1 [+2256, 6927]), 112 (1 [+9109, 6925]), 119 (1 [+9596, 6926, 2256]), 120,000 (1 [+2256, 6929, 547]), 122 (1 [+6929, 2256, 9109]), 122 (1 [+2256, 6929, 2256, 9109]), 130 (1 [+8993, 2256]), 130 (1 [+2256, 8993]), 133 (1 [+8993, 2256, 8993, 2256]), 138 (1 [+8993, 2256, 9046]), 139 (1 [+8993, 2256, 9596]), 14,700 (1 [+752, 6925, 547, 2256, 8679]), 148 (1 [+752, 2256, 9046]), 151,450 (1 [+547, 2256, 285, 2822, 547, 752, 4395, 2822, 2256, 2256, 2256]), 151,450 (1 [+4395, 547, 2256, 285, 2822, 547, 752, 2822, 2256, 2256, 2256]), 153,600 (1 [+2256, 2822, 547, 2256, 8993, 547, 2256, 9252, 4395]), 153,600 (1 [+4395, 2256, 2822, 547, 2256, 8993, 547, 2256, 9252]), 156 (1 [+2822, 2256, 9252]), 157,600 (1 [+547, 2256, 8679, 2256, 2822, 547, 9252, 4395, 2256]), 157,600 (1 [+4395, 547, 2256, 8679, 2256, 2822, 547, 9252, 2256]), 16,750 (1 [+9252, 6925, 547, 8679, 2256, 2822]), 160 (1 [+2256, 9252]), 162 (1 [+9109, 2256, 9252, 2256]), 17,200 (1 [+8679, 6925, 547, 2256]), 172 (1 [+8679, 2256, 9109]), 180 (1 [+9046, 2256]), 180,000 (1 [+2256, 9046, 547]), 182 (1 [+9109, 2256, 9046, 2256]), 186,400 (1 [+547, 2256, 9046, 547, 9252, 547, 752, 4395, 2256, 2256]), 186,400 (1 [+4395, 547, 2256, 9046, 547, 9252, 547, 752, 2256, 2256]), 187 (1 [+8679, 2256, 9046, 2256]), 188 (1 [+9046, 2256, 9046]), 2,172 (1 [+547, 8679, 2256, 9109]), 2,172 (1 [+547, 2256, 8679, 2256, 9109]), 2,200 (1 [+547, 2256]), 2,300 (1 [+547, 2256, 8993]), 2,322 (1 [+547, 8993, 6929, 2256, 9109]), 2,400 (1 [+547, 2256, 752]), 2,600 (1 [+547, 2256, 9252]), 2,630 (1 [+547, 2256, 9252, 2256, 8993]), 2,750 (1 [+547, 8679, 2256, 2822]), 2,812 (1 [+547, 9046, 2256, 9109, 6925]), 2,818 (1 [+547, 2256, 9046, 9046, 6925]), 20,200 (1 [+6929, 547, 2256]), 20,800 (1 [+6929, 547, 2256, 9046]), 205 (1 [+2822, 2256]), 207 (1 [+8679, 2256]), 209 (1 [+9596, 2256]), 212 (1 [+2256, 9109, 6925]), 218 (1 [+2256, 9046, 6925]), 22,200 (1 [+9109, 2256, 6929, 547, 2256]), 22,273 (1 [+9109, 2256, 6929, 547, 8993, 2256, 8679, 2256]), 22,600 (1 [+6929, 2256, 9109, 547, 2256, 9252]), 232 (1 [+9109, 2256, 8993]), 242 (1 [+752, 2256, 9109]), 245 (1 [+2256, 752, 2256, 2822]), 25,100 (1 [+6929, 2256, 2822, 547, 2256]), 273 (1 [+8993, 2256, 8679, 2256]), 28,600 (1 [+6929, 2256, 9046, 547, 2256, 9252]), 280,000 (1 [+2256, 9046, 547]), 284 (1 [+9046, 2256, 752]), 288 (1 [+9046, 2256, 9046]), 3,200 (1 [+8993, 547, 2256]), 3,630 (1 [+8993, 547, 2256, 9252, 2256, 8993]), 3,700 (1 [+8993, 547, 2256, 8679]), 3,930 (1 [+8993, 547, 9596, 2256, 8993]), 300,000 (1 [+8993, 547]), 307,500 (1 [+8993, 547, 2256, 8679, 547, 2256, 2822, 4395]), 307,500 (1 [+8993, 4395, 547, 2256, 8679, 547, 2256, 2822]), 318 (1 [+9046, 6925, 2256, 8993]), 32,500 (1 [+9109, 2256, 8993, 547, 2256, 2822]), 323 (1 [+8993, 6929, 2256, 8993]), 324 (1 [+8993, 6929, 2256, 752]), 328 (1 [+8993, 6929, 2256, 9046]), 337,500 (1 [+8993, 547, 2256, 8993, 547, 8679, 547, 2256, 2822, 4395]), 337,500 (1 [+8993, 4395, 547, 2256, 8993, 547, 8679, 547, 2256, 2822]), 337,500 (1 [+8993, 547, 2256, 8993, 547, 2256, 8679, 547, 2256, 2822, 4395]), 337,500 (1 [+8993, 4395, 547, 2256, 8993, 547, 2256, 8679, 547, 2256, 2822]), 350 (1 [+8993, 2256, 2822]), 365 (1 [+2822, 2256, 9252, 2256, 8993]), 410 (1 [+752, 2256, 6927]), 42,360 (1 [+752, 8052, 547, 8993, 9252]), 42,360 (1 [+752, 8052, 547, 8993, 2256, 9252]), 420 (1 [+752, 2256, 6929]), 43,730 (1 [+8993, 2256, 752, 547, 2256, 8679, 2256, 8993]), 44,760 (1 [+752, 2256, 752, 547, 2256, 8679, 2256, 9252]), 45,400 (1 [+2822, 2256, 752, 547, 2256, 752]), 45,600 (1 [+2822, 2256, 752, 547, 2256, 9252]), 454 (1 [+752, 2822, 2256, 752]), 468 (1 [+752, 9252, 2256, 9046]), 5,400 (1 [+2822, 547, 2256, 752]), 52,700 (1 [+9109, 2256, 2822, 547, 2256, 8679]), 530 (1 [+2822, 2256, 8993]), 550 (1 [+2822, 2256, 2822]), 595 (1 [+2822, 2256, 9596, 2256, 2822]), 6,200 (1 [+9252, 547, 2256]), 6,800 (1 [+9252, 547, 2256, 9046]), 60,500 (1 [+9252, 547, 2256, 2822]), 601,730 (1 [+9252, 547, 2256, 547, 8679, 4395, 2256, 8993]), 601,730 (1 [+9252, 4395, 547, 2256, 547, 8679, 2256, 8993]), 603,550 (1 [+9252, 547, 2256, 8993, 547, 2822, 4395, 2822, 2256, 2256]), 603,550 (1 [+9252, 4395, 547, 2256, 8993, 547, 2822, 2822, 2256, 2256]), 603,550 (1 [+9252, 547, 8993, 547, 2822, 4395, 2822, 2256, 2256, 2256]), 603,550 (1 [+9252, 4395, 547, 8993, 547, 2822, 2822, 2256, 2256, 2256]), 603,550 (1 [+9252, 547, 2256, 8993, 547, 2256, 2822, 4395, 2256, 2822]), 603,550 (1 [+9252, 4395, 547, 2256, 8993, 547, 2256, 2822, 2256, 2822]), 623 (1 [+9252, 6929, 2256, 8993]), 628 (1 [+9252, 6929, 2256, 9046]), 64,300 (1 [+752, 2256, 9252, 547, 2256, 8993]), 64,400 (1 [+752, 2256, 9252, 547, 2256, 752]), 642 (1 [+9252, 752, 2256, 9109]), 642 (1 [+9252, 2256, 752, 2256, 9109]), 648 (1 [+9252, 752, 2256, 9046]), 650 (1 [+9252, 2256, 2822]), 655 (1 [+9252, 2822, 2256, 2822]), 666 (1 [+9252, 2256, 9252, 2256, 9252]), 667 (1 [+9252, 9252, 2256, 8679]), 675 (1 [+9252, 2822, 2256, 8679]), 675,000 (1 [+9252, 547, 2256, 8679, 547, 2256, 2822, 547]), 690 (1 [+9252, 2256, 9596]), 7,100 (1 [+8679, 547, 2256]), 7,500 (1 [+8679, 547, 2256, 2822]), 721 (1 [+8679, 2256, 6929, 2256, 285]), 725 (1 [+8679, 6929, 2256, 2822]), 730 (1 [+8679, 2256, 8993]), 743 (1 [+8679, 752, 2256, 8993]), 743 (1 [+8679, 2256, 752, 2256, 8993]), 745 (1 [+8679, 752, 2256, 2822]), 76,500 (1 [+9252, 2256, 8679, 547, 2256, 2822]), 775 (1 [+8679, 2822, 2256, 8679]), 777 (1 [+8679, 2256, 8679, 2256, 8679]), 782 (1 [+9109, 2256, 9046, 2256, 8679]), 8,580 (1 [+9046, 547, 2256, 2822, 2256, 9046]), 8,600 (1 [+9046, 547, 2256, 9252]), 807 (1 [+8679, 2256, 9046]), 815 (1 [+2822, 6926, 2256, 9046]), 822 (1 [+9046, 6929, 2256, 9109]), 830 (1 [+8993, 2256, 9046]), 832 (1 [+9046, 8993, 2256, 9109]), 840 (1 [+752, 2256, 9046]), 845 (1 [+9046, 2256, 2822, 752]), 895 (1 [+2822, 2256, 9596, 2256, 9046]), 905 (1 [+2822, 2256, 9596]), 910 (1 [+6924, 2256, 9596]), 912 (1 [+9109, 6926, 2256, 9596]), 928 (1 [+9596, 6929, 2256, 9046]), 930 (1 [+9596, 2256, 8993]), 945 (1 [+9596, 2256, 752, 2256, 2822]), 950 (1 [+9596, 2256, 2822]), 956 (1 [+9596, 2256, 2822, 2256, 9252]), 962 (1 [+9109, 2256, 9252, 2256, 9596]), 969 (1 [+9596, 2256, 9252, 2256, 9596]), hundredfold (1 [+9134]), hundredth (1), one percent (1), seventeen hundred (1 [+8679, 2256, 547]), seventeen hundred (1 [+547, 2256, 8679]), thirty-three hundred (1 [+8993, 547, 2256, 8993]), twelve hundred (1 [+547, 2256]), twenty-seven hundred (1 [+547, 2256, 8679]), twenty-six hundred (1 [+547, 2256, 9252]), two hundred (1), NDT (2)

H4396 ²מֵאָה ***mēʾâ²***, n.pr.loc. [2] [√ 4395?; 10395]. (the Tower of) the Hundred:– Hundred (2)

H4397 מַאֲוַיִּים ***maʾᵃwiyyîm***, n.[m.pl.] [1] [√ 203]. desires:– desires (1)

H4398 מְאוּם ***mᵉʾûm***, n.m. Not used in NIVEBC [→ 4399; cf. 4583]. defect, blemish, see 4583

H4399 מְאוּמָה ***mᵉʾûmâ***, p.indef. [32] [√ 4398]. something, anything; (with negation) nothing:– anything (9), nothing (7 [+4202]), anything (2 [+3972]), nothing (2 [+401]), all (1), any kind (1), bare (1 [+401, 928]), fault (1), little value (1), little value (1 [+4202]), none (1 [+4202]), something (1), there is nothing (1 [+401]), there is nothing (1 [+401]), whatever (1), NDT (1)

H4400 מָאוֹס ***māʾôs***, n.[m.] [1] [√ 4415]. refuse, trash:– refuse (1)

H4401 מָאוֹר ***māʾôr***, n.m. [19] [√ 239]. light source, luminary, light-bearer:– light (14), lights (4), moon (1)

H4402 מְאוּרָה ***mᵉʾûrâ***, n.f. [1] [√ 239?]. nest hole (of a viper):– nest (1)

H4403 מֵאָז ***mēʾāz***, pp. & adv. Not used in NIVEBC [√ 4946 + 255]. from that time, ever since; of long ago, see 4946 & 255

H4404 מֹאזְנַיִם ***mōʾznayim***, n.[m.]du. [15] [√ 10396]. set of scales, (two) balance pans for weight measurement, with an emphasis on honesty and standardized measurements; by extension: righteous evaluation of motives and actions:– scales (12), balance (2), set of scales (1 [+5486])

H4405 מְאָיוֹת ***mᵉʾāyôt***, var. Not used in NIVEBC [√ 4395]. see 4395

H4406 מֵאַיִן ***mēʾayin***, adv. Not used in NIVEBC [√ 4946 + 402]. from where?, see 402 & 4946

H4407 מַאֲכָל ***maʾᵃkāl***, n.m. & f. [30] [√ 430]. food, supplies, something to eat:– food (21), fruit (4), baked goods (1 [+5126, 685]), devoured (1), meal (1), something to eat (1), supplies (1)

H4408 מַאֲכֶלֶת ***maʾᵃkelet***, n.f. [4] [√ 430]. (butcher) knife, sometimes with a ceremonial or sacrificial focus:– knife (3), knives (1)

H4409 מַאֲכֹלֶת ***maʾᵃkōlet***, n.f. [2] [√ 430]. fuel (for a fire); a fig. extension of food that is consumed:– fuel (2)

H4410 מַאֲמָץ ***maʾᵃmāṣ***, n.[m.] [1] [√ 599]. effort, exertion:– efforts (1)

H4411 מַאֲמָר ***maʾᵃmār***, n.m. [3] [√ 606; 10397]. command, decree, instruction:– command (1), decree (1), instructions (1)

H4412 מָאֵן ***māʾan***, v. [46] [→ 4413, 4414]. [P] to refuse, reject:– refused (21), refuse (16), absolutely refuses (2 [+4412]), refuses (2), refusing (2), incurable (1 [+8324]), resist (1), would not (1)

H4413 מָאֵן ***māʾēn***, a.vbl. Not used in NIVEBC [√ 4412]. refusing

H4414 מֵאֵן ***mēʾēn***, a. Not used in NIVEBC [√ 4412]. refusing

H4415 ¹מָאַס ***māʾas¹***, v. [75] [→ 4400]. [Q] to reject, despise, spurn, disdain; [N] to be rejected, become vile:– rejected (34), reject (13), despise (8), despised (3), despises (3), rejected completely (2 [+4415]), utterly rejected (2 [+4415]), be rejected (1), denied (1), disdained (1), refuse (1), ridiculed (1), scorn (1), spurn (1), spurned (1), vile (1), withholds (1)

H4416 ²מָאַס ***māʾas²***, v. [2] [cf. 4998, 5022]. [N] to be festering, be dissolving; be vanishing:– festering (1), vanish (1)

H4417 מְאַסֵּף ***mᵉʾassēp***, n.m. *or* v.ptcp. Not used in NIVEBC [√ 665]. rear guard, see 665

H4418 מַאֲפֶה ***maʾᵃpeh***, n.[m.] [1] [√ 684]. something baked:– baked (1)

H4419 מַאֲפֵל ***maʾᵃpēl***, n.[m.] [1] [√ 694?]. darkness:– darkness (1)

H4420 מַאְפֵּלְיָה ***maʾpēlyâ***, n.f. [1] [√ 694?]. great darkness:– great darkness (1)

H4421 מָאַר ***māʾar***, v. [4] [H] to be destructive; to be painful:– persistent (3), painful (1)

H4422 מַאֲרָב ***maʾᵃrāb***, n.m. [5] [√ 741]. ambush; troops in an ambush:– ambush (1), hiding place (1), place of ambush (1), troops (1), wait (1)

H4423 מְאֵרָה ***mᵉʾērâ***, n.f. [5] [√ 826]. curse:– curse (2), curses (2), curse (1 [+826])

H4424 מֵאֲשֶׁר ***mēʾᵃšer***, adv. & c. Not used in NIVEBC [√ 4946 + 889]. from which, from whom, see 889 & 4946

H4425 מֵאֵת ***mēʾēt***, pp.+pp. Not used in NIVEBC [√ 4946 + 907]. from (with), see 4946 & 907

H4426 מִבְדָּלוֹת ***mibdālôt***, n.f. [1] [√ 976]. set aside, selected, singled out:– set aside (1)

H4427 מָבוֹא ***mābôʾ***, n.m. [25] [→ 4569; cf. 995]. entrance, entryway, gateway; "the place where the sun goes (sets)" is the direction west:– entrance (7), enter (2), west (2 [+9087]), where sets (2), do^S (1), entrance (1 [+7339]), entryway (1), gateway (1), go down (1), harbor (1), how to get into (1), in the west (1 [+2021, 9087]), outskirts (1), place where sets (1), setting (1), NDT (1)

H4428 מְבוּכָה ***mᵉbûkâ***, n.f. [2] [√ 1003]. confusion, confused terror:– confusion (1), terror (1)

H4429 מַבּוּל ***mabbûl***, n.m. [13] [√ 5574]. flood (waters):– flood (10), floodwaters (3 [+4784])

H4430 מְבוֹנִים ***mᵉbônîm***, var. see 1067

H4431 מְבוּסָה ***mᵉbûsâ***, n.f. [3] [√ 1008]. trampling down, implying subjugation:– aggressive (2), trampling (1)

H4432 מַבּוּעַ ***mabbûaʿ***, n.[m.] [3] [√ 5580]. (a bubbling) spring (of water):– bubbling springs (1 [+4784]), spring (1), springs (1)

H4433 מְבוּקָה ***mᵉbûqâ***, n.f. [1] [√ 1011]. plundering, devastation, desertion:– plundered (1)

H4434 מְבוּשִׁים ***mᵉbûšîm***, n.[m.] [1] [√ 1017]. private parts, (male) genitals, with a possible focus on shame if exposed:– private parts (1)

H4435 מִבְחוֹר ***mibḥôr***, n.[m.] [2] [√ 1047]. choicest (trees); major (towns):– choicest (1), major (1)

H4436 ¹מִבְחָר ***mibḥār¹***, n.[m.] & f. [13] [→ 4437; cf. 1047]. choicest, best, elite, finest (persons or things):– choicest (4), best (3), choice (1), choice possessions (1), elite (1), fine (1), finest (1), pick (1)

H4437 ²מִבְחָר ***mibḥār²***, n.pr.m. [1] [√ 4436; cf. 1047]. Mibhar, *"choice"*:– Mibhar (1)

H4438 מַבָּט ***mabbāṭ***, n.m. [3] [√ 5564]. hope, trust in, relying on:– hope (1), relied on (1), trusted in (1)

H4439 מִבְטָא ***mibṭāʾ***, n.[m.] [2] [√ 1051]. rash promise, rashness:– rash promise (2)

H4440 מִבְטָח ***mibṭāḥ***, n.[m.] [15] [√ 1053]. security, trust, confidence:– trust (3), confidence (2), secure (2), security (2), hope (1), reliance (1), source of confidence (1), trusted (1), trusts (1 [+8492]), what rely on (1)

H4441 מַבָּךְ ***mabbāk***, n.m. [1] [√ 1134]. source:– sources (1)

H4442 מַבֵּל ***mabbēl***, n.[m.] [1] [√ 1162]. fire:– Fire (1)

H4443 מַבְלִיגִית ***mablîgît***, n.f. [1] [√ 1564]. comfort, smile, cheerfulness:– Comforter (1)

H4444 מְבֻלָּקָה ***mᵉbulāqâ***, n.[f.] *or* v.ptcp. Not used in NIVEBC [√ 1191]. destruction, see 1191

H4445 מִבְנֶה ***mibneh***, n.m. [1] [√ 1215]. building, structure:– buildings (1)

H4446 מְבֻנַּי ***mᵉbunnay***, n.pr.m. Mebunnai, *"well built"*

H4447 מַבְנִית ***mabnît***, n.f. Not used in NIVEBC [√ 1067]. structure, frame, body

H4448 ¹מִבְצָר ***mibṣār¹***, n.m. [36] [→ 4449; cf. 1307]. fortress, fortification, stronghold:– fortified (21), strongholds

(5), fortresses (3), fortified cities (2), defenses (1), fortified city (1), fortified places (1), fortress (1), mightiest fortresses (1 [+5057])

H4449 ²מִבְצָר ***mibṣār²***, n.pr.m. [2] [√ 4448; cf. 1307]. Mibzar, "*bastion*":– Mibzar (2)

H4450 ³מִבְצָר ***mibṣār³***, n.m. [1] [√ 1308]. ore:– ore (1)

H4451 מִבְרָח ***mibrāḥ***, n.m. Not used in NIVEBC [√ 1368]. fleeing, refugee

H4452 מִבְשָׂם ***mibśām***, n.pr.m. [3] Mibsam, "*sweet odor*":– Mibsam (3)

H4453 מְבַשְּׁלוֹת ***mᵉbaššᵉlôt***, n.f.pl. [1] [√ 1418]. places for fire, cooking-places:– places for fire (1)

H4454 מָג ***māg***, n.m. [2] [→ 8059]. official (used with 8042):– official (2)

H4455 מַגְבִּישׁ ***magbîš***, n.pr.m. [1] Magbish, "[perhaps] *thick*":– Magbish (1)

H4456 מִגְבָּלוֹת ***migbālôt***, n.f.pl. [1] [√ 1491]. (braided) chains, (twisted) cords:– braided (1)

H4457 מִגְבָּעָה ***migbā'â***, n.f.pl. [4] [√ 1483?]. headband:– caps (3), caps (1 [+6996])

H4458 מֶגֶד ***meged***, n.m. [12] [→ 4459, 4461, 4462, 4469]. choice things, best gifts:– best (2), choice (2), valuable gifts (2), articles of value (1), costly gifts (1), delicacy (1), finest (1), fruitfulness (1), precious (1)

H4459 מְגִדּוֹ ***mᵉgiddô***, n.pr.loc. [11] [→ 4461; cf. 4458]. Megiddo, "*place of troops*":– Megiddo (11)

H4460 מִגְדּוֹל ***migdôl***, n.m. Not used in NIVEBC [√ 1540]. great, see 1540

H4461 מְגִדּוֹן ***mᵉgiddôn***, n.pr.loc. [1] [√ 4459; cf. 4458]. Megiddo, "*place of troops*":– Megiddo (1)

H4462 מַגְדִּיאֵל ***magdî'ēl***, n.pr.m. [2] [√ 4458 + 446]. Magdiel, "*choice gift of God [El]*":– Magdiel (2)

H4463 ¹מִגְדָּל ***migdāl¹***, n.m. [48] [→ 4464, 4465, 4466, 4467, 4468; cf. 1540]. tower, watchtower, usually a tall, narrow building used for defense; high platform (made of wood and used for public speaking to crowds); an elevated area such as a garden with mounds, terraces:– tower (28), towers (13), watchtower (2), watchtower (2 [+5915]), high platform (1), theyˢ (1 [+3972, 1251, 8901]), watchtowers (1)

H4464 ²מִגְדָּל ***migdāl²***, n.pr.loc. Not used in NIVEBC [√ 4463; cf. 1540]. Migdal

H4465 מִגְדֹּל ***migdōl***, n.pr.loc. [6] [√ 4463; cf. 1540]. Migdol, "*tower*":– Migdol (6)

H4466 מִגְדַּל־אֵל ***migdal-'ēl***, n.pr.loc. [1] [√ 4463 + 446; cf. 1540]. Migdal El, "*tower of God [El]*":– Migdal El (1)

H4467 מִגְדַּל־גָּד ***migdal-gad***, n.pr.loc. [1] [√ 4463 + 1514; cf. 1540]. Migdal Gad, "*tower of Gad*":– Migdal Gad (1)

H4468 מִגְדַּל־עֵדֶר ***migdal-'ēder***, n.pr.loc. [1] [√ 4463 + 6374]. Migdal Eder, "*tower of Eder [flock]*":– Migdal Eder (1)

H4469 מִגְדָּנוֹת ***migdānôt***, n.f.[pl.] Not used in NIVEBC [√ 4458]. costly gifts, articles of value

H4470 מָגוֹג ***māgôg***, n.pr.loc. [4] [√ 1573]. Magog, "[perhaps] *land of Gog*":– Magog (4)

H4471 ¹מָגוֹר ***māgôr¹***, n.m. [8] [→ 4475; cf. 1593]. terror, horror:– terror (7), terrors (1)

H4472 ²מָגוֹר ***māgôr²***, n.[m.] [11] [√ 1591]. to live as an alien, stay as a stranger; place to live, place to lodge:– pilgrimage (2), reside as a foreigner (2), lived (1), living (1), lodge (1 [+1074]), lodging (1), stayed (1), staying (1), where resided (1)

H4473 ³מָגוֹר ***māgôr³***, n.[m.] Not used in NIVEBC [→ 4476, 4923]. grain pit, storage chamber = heart, mind

H4474 מָגוֹר מִסָּבִיב ***māgôr missābîb***, n.pr.m. [1] [√ 1593 + 4992]. Magor-Missabib, "*terror on every side*":– Terror (1)

H4475 מְגוֹרָה ***mᵉgôrâ***, n.f. [3] [√ 4471; cf. 1593]. dread, fear:– dread (2), fears (1)

H4476 מְגוּרָה ***mᵉgûrâ***, n.f. [1] [√ 4473]. barn, grain-pit, storage chamber:– barn (1)

H4477 מַגְזֵרָה ***magzērâ***, n.f. [1] [√ 1615]. ax:– axes (1)

H4478 מַגָּל ***maggāl***, n.[m.] [2] [cf. 1670?]. sickle:– sickle (2)

H4479 מְגִלָּה ***mᵉgillâ***, n.f. [21] [√ 1670; 10399]. scroll (a rolled up document made of leather or papyrus):– scroll (17), scroll (4 [+6219])

H4480 מְגַמָּה ***mᵉgammâ***, n.f. [1] [cf. 1685]. horde:– hordes (1)

H4481 מָגַן ***māgan***, v. [4] [→ 4484]. [P] to hand over, deliver to, present with:– delivered (1), given over (1), hand over (1), present (1)

H4482 ¹מָגֵן ***māgēn¹***, n.m. [63] [√ 1713]. (small) shield used for defense, usually of oiled leather; by extension: ruler, a leader who protects; fig. of the impregnable scales of leviathan:– shield (32), shields (19), small shields (6), armed (2), kings (1), large shields (1), rulers (1), shields small (1)

H4483 ²מָגֵן ***māgēn²***, n.m. *or* a. Not used in NIVEBC [→ 4485]. insolent

H4484 מֶגֶן ***megen***, n.m. & f. Not used in NIVEBC [√ 4481]. gift, present (gifts made in return)

H4485 מְגִנָּה ***mᵉginnâ***, n.f. [1] [√ 4483]. veil, covering:– veil (1)

H4486 מִגְעֶרֶת ***mig'eret***, n.f. [1] [√ 1721]. rebuke, reproach:– rebuke (1)

H4487 מַגֵּפָה ***maggēpâ***, n.f. [25] [√ 5597]. plague; blow, strike, slaughter:– plague (19), blow (2), casualties (1), losses (1), plagues (1), slaughter (1)

H4488 מַגְפִּיעָשׁ ***magpî'āš***, n.pr.m. [1] Magpiash, "*moth killer*":– Magpiash (1)

H4489 מָגַר ***māgar***, v. [2] [√ 10400]. [Qp] to be thrown; [P] to cast, throw down:– cast (1), thrown (1)

H4490 מְגֵרָה ***mᵉgērâ***, n.f. [4] [√ 1760]. saw (stone-cutting tool):– saws (2), axes (1), smoothed (1 [+1760, 928, 2021])

H4491 מִגְרוֹן ***migrôn***, n.pr.loc. [2] Migron, "*precipice*":– Migron (2)

H4492 מִגְרָעוֹת ***migrā'ôt***, n.f. [1] [√ 1757]. offset ledge, recess, rebatement (of a wall):– offset ledges (1)

H4493 מֶגְרָפָה ***megrāpâ***, n.f. [1] [√ 1759]. clods (of earth) or a digging instrument: hoe, spade, shovel:– clods (1)

H4494 מִגְרָשׁ ***migrāš***, n.m. [101] [√ 1763]. pastureland, untilled open land (belonging to a town):– pasturelands (41), pastureland (5), farmlands (1 [+8441]), open land (1), pastureland (1 [+8441]), shorelands (1), NDT (51)

H4495 מִגְרְשׁוֹת ***migrᵉšōt***, var. Not used in NIVEBC [√ 1763]. see 4494

H4496 מַד ***mad***, n.m. [11] [√ 4499; cf. 4503]. clothing, garment; measure, decree:– tunic (3), clothes (2), clothing (1), decreed (1), garment (1), military tunic (1 [+4230]), robe (1), saddle blankets (1)

H4497 ¹מִדְבָּר ***midbār¹***, n.m. [270] [√ 1818]. desert, wasteland, barren wilderness, desolate land that supports little life; open country, suitable for grazing:– wilderness (129), desert (128), wasteland (5), barren wilderness (1), country (1), desert (1 [+824]), deserts (1), hereˢ (1 [+928, 2021]), open country (1), thereˢ (1), thereˢ (1 [+2334])

H4498 ²מִדְבָּר ***midbār²***, n.m. [1] [√ 1819]. mouth, instrument of speech:– mouth (1)

H4499 מָדַד ***mādad***, v. [51] [→ 4496, 4500, 4924]. [Q] to measure a distance; consider a plan; [N] to be measured; [P] to measure off; [Htpol] to stretch oneself out:– measured (30), measured off (5), measure off (3), be measured (2), measure (2), consider (1), drags on (1), measure distance (1), measure the full payment (1), measureless (1 [+4202]), poured into measures (1), stretched himself out (1), NDT (2)

H4500 ¹מִדָּה ***middâ¹***, n.f. [54] [√ 4499; cf. 4515]. measurement, size, length; section (of a wall), length of life:– measurements (12), size (10), measuring (9), section (7), huge (2), at regular intervals (1), district (1), great (1), great size (1), length (1), long (1), measure (1), measured out (1 [+9419, 928]), measures (1), number (1), standard (1), tall (1), tall (1 [+408]), NDT (1)

H4501 ²מִדָּה ***middâ²***, n.f. [1] [cf. 5989; 10402, 10429]. tax:– tax (1)

H4502 מַדְהֵבָה ***madhēbâ***, n.f. Not used in NIVEBC [cf. 5290, 8104]. fury

H4503 מַדּוּ ***mādû***, מַדְוֶה ***madweh¹***, n.m. [2] [cf. 4496]. garment:– garments (2)

H4504 מַדְוֶה ***madweh²***, n.m. [2] [√ 1864]. disease, sickness:– diseases (2)

H4505 מַדּוּחִים ***maddûḥîm***, n.[m.] [1] [√ 5615]. misleading, able to deceive:– misleading (1)

H4506 ¹מָדוֹן ***mādôn¹***, n.m. [21] [→ 4517; cf. 1906, 4515]. dissension, quarrel, strife, contention:– conflict (8), quarrelsome (6), disputes (2), quarrel (2), strife (2), contends (1)

H4507 ²מָדוֹן ***mādôn²***, n.pr.loc. [2] [√ 1906]. Madon, "*contention*":– Madon (2)

H4508 מַדּוּעַ ***maddûa'***, adv. [72] Why?, What is the meaning?:– why (70), what (1), what's the meaning of (1)

H4509 מְדוּרָה ***mᵉdûrâ***, n.f. [2] [√ 1883]. (circular) pile of wood, fire pit:– fire pit (1), wood (1)

H4510 מִדְחֶה ***midḥeh***, n.m. [1] [√ 1890]. ruin, downfall:– ruin (1)

H4511 מַדְחֵפָה ***madḥēpâ***, n.f. [1] [√ 1894]. blow, thrust; (pl.) blow after blow:– hunt down (1 [+7421, 4200])

H4512 מָדַי ***māday***, n.pr.g. & loc. [16] [→ 4513; 10404, 10405]. Madai; Media, Medes:– Media (7), Medes (5), Madai (2), Mede (1), Median (1)

H4513 מָדִי ***mādî***, a.g. [1] [√ 4512]. Mede:– Mede (1)

H4514 מַדַּי ***madday***, pp.+subst. Not used in NIVEBC [√ 1896 + 4537 *or* 4946]. see 4537 or 4946 & 1896

H4515 מָדִין ***mādîn***, n.m. Not used in NIVEBC [√ 4506 *or* 4500]. see 4506 or 4500

H4516 מִדִּין ***middîn***, n.pr.loc. [1] Middin:– Middin (1)

H4517 ¹מִדְיָן ***midyān¹***, n.m. Not used in NIVEBC [→ 4506, 4518, 4520; cf. 1906]. quarrel, strife, contention

H4518 ²מִדְיָן ***midyān²***, n.pr.m. & loc. [59] [→ 4520; cf. 1906, 4506, 4517]. Midian, Midianite:– Midian (32), Midianites (12), Midianite (8), Midian (2 [+824]), Midian's (2), themˢ (1), NDT (2)

H4519 מְדִינָה ***mᵉdînâ***, n.f. [53] [√ 1906; 10406]. province, district, region:– provinces (20), province (10), provincial (5), each province (3 [+4519, 2256]), each province (3 [+2256, 4519]), district (1), every province (1 [+4519, 2256]), every province (1 [+2256, 4519]), parts (1), regions (1), various provinces (1 [+4519, 2256]), various provinces (1 [+2256, 4519]), NDT (5)

H4520 מִדְיָנִי ***midyānî***, a.g. [8] [√ 4518; cf. 1906, 4517]. Midianite, "*of Midian*":– Midianite (5), Midianites (3)

H4521 מְדֹכָה ***mᵉdōkâ***, n.f. [1] [√ 1870]. mortar:– mortar (1)

H4522 מַדְמֵן ***madmēn***, n.pr.loc. [1] [→ 4524, 4526]. Madmen, "*[sounds like] be silenced*":– Madmen (1)

H4523 ¹מַדְמֵנָה ***madmēnâ¹***, n.f. [1] [√ 1961]. manure-pile, dung-heap:– manure (1)

H4524 ²מַדְמֵנָה ***madmēnâ²***, n.pr.loc. [1] [√ 4522]. Madmenah, "*dunghill*":– Madmenah (1)

H4525 ¹מַדְמַנָּה ***madmannâ¹***, n.pr.m. [1] Madmannah, "*dung place*":– Madmannah (1)

H4526 ²מַדְמַנָּה ***madmannâ²***, n.pr.loc. [1] [√ 4522]. Madmannah, "*dung place*":– Madmannah (1)

H4527 ¹מְדָן ***mᵉdān¹***, n.pr.m. [2] [√ 1972]. Medan, "*dissension*":– Medan (2)

H4528 ²מְדָן ***mᵉdān²***, n.m. Not used in NIVEBC [√ 1906]. dissension, see 4506

H4529 מַדָּע ***maddā'***, n.m. [6] [√ 3359; 10430]. knowledge:– knowledge (4), quick to understand (1 [+1067]), thoughts (1)

H4530 מֹדָע ***mōdā'***, n.m. [2] [→ 4531; cf. 3359]. (distant) relative, kinsman:– relative (2)

H4531 מֹדַעַת ***mōda'at***, n.f. [1] [√ 4530; cf. 3359]. (distant) kinsman:– relative (1)

H4532 מַדְקֵרָה ***madqērâ***, n.f. [1] [√ 1991]. piercing (of a sword):– pierce (1)

H4533 מַדְרֵגָה ***madrēgâ***, n.f. [2] cliff, (steep) mountainside (with footholds and hiding places):– cliffs (1), mountainside (1)

H4534 מִדְרָךְ ***midrāk***, n.[m.] [1] [√ 2005]. foot-width, footprint:– put on (1)

H4535 מִדְרָשׁ ***midrāš***, n.[m.] [2] [√ 2011]. annotation, study, writing, exposition:– annotations (2)

H4536 מְדֻשָׁה ***mᵉdušâ***, n.f. [1] [√ 1889]. that which is crushed (by trampling on a threshing floor):– crushed (1)

H4537 מָה ***mâ***, p.inter. & indef. [752] [→ 1174, 4015, 4017, 4342, 4548, 4643, 4943, 5505, 8975; cf. 4768, 4942; 10394, 10408]. why?, what?, how?; O!, who, whoever, whatever:– what (342), why (166 [+4200]), how (68), why (33), why (13 [+6584]), how (9 [+928]), how (7 [+928]), whatever (6), what (5 [+4200]), how long (4 [+6330]), what mean (4), who (4), how (3 [+3869]), listen (3), secret (3 [+928]), what are you doing (3 [+4200, 3870]), what's the matter (3), by what means (2 [+928]), come what may (2 [+2118]), how many (2 [+6330, 3869]), not (2), what (2 [+928]), why (2 [+928]), anything (1), because (1 [+3954, 4200]), but why (1 [+4200]), enough (1 [+4200, 1896]), ever so (1), future (1 [+8611, 2118]), how (1 [+2296]), how (1 [+928, 2021, 686]), how find things (1), how long (1 [+3869]), how long must wait (1 [+3869, 3427]), how many (1 [+3869]), how many more (1 [+3869]), how much (1), how often (1 [+3869]), how often (1 [+3869]), if (1 [+196]), life will not be worth living (1 [+2644, 4200]), notˢ (1), nothing (1 [+1153]), nothing (1 [+1172]), of what use (1 [+4200]), so many (1 [+3869]), speech (1 [+1819]), that (1), this is how (1), what (1 [+6584]), what about (1), what do I care about (1 [+4200, 2296, 4200, 3276]), what do you mean (1 [+4200, 4013]), what is doing (1 [+4200]), what is the matter (1 [+4200, 3871]), what is the meaning (1), what is the meaning (1 [+2179]), what is the meaning of (1), what is troubling (1), what is wrong (1), what kind (1), what like (1), what more (1 [+3954]), what right have you (1 [+4200, 3870]), whatever (1 [+1821]), whatever (1 [+8611]), what's (1), when (1 [+6330]), where (1), whether (1), which (1), why (1 [+3610]), why (1 [+9393]), why (1 [+4200, 2296]), why (1 [+8611, 4200]), why (1 [+561, 4027, 4200]), NDT (11)

H4538 מָהַהּ ***māhah***, v. [8] [Htpal] to wait, delay, linger, hesitate:– wait (2), delay (1), delayed (1), have time (1 [+3523]), hesitated (1), linger (1), waited (1)

H4539 מְהוּמָה ***mᵉhûmâ***, n.f. [12] [√ 2101]. turmoil, confusion, panic, discomfiture:– panic (4), turmoil (3), confusion (2), throwing into confusion (1 [+2169]), tumult (1), unrest (1)

H4540 מְהוּמָן ***mᵉhûmān***, n.pr.m. [1] Mehuman:– Mehuman (1)

H4541 מְהֵיטַבְאֵל ***mehêṭab'ēl***, n.pr.m. & f. [3] [√ 3512 + 446]. Mehetabel, "*God [El] does good*":– Mehetabel (3)

H4542 מָהִיר ***māhîr***, a. [4] [√ 4554]. skilled, well versed, experienced; speedy, prompt:– skilled (1), skillful (1), speeds (1), well versed (1)

H4543 מָהַל ***māhal***, v. [1] [→ 1197; cf. 4576]. [Qp] to be diluted, changed to an adulterated state; referring to dilution by water:– diluted (1)

H4544 מַהֲלָךְ ***mahălāk***, n.m. [5] [√ 2143]. passageway; journey:– journey (2), go through (1), passageway (1), place (1)

H4545 מַהֲלָל ***mahălāl***, n.[m.] [1] [→ 4546; cf. 2146]. praise, good reputation:– praise (1)

H4546 מַהֲלַלְאֵל ***mahălal'ēl***, n.pr.m. [7] [√ 4545 + 446]. Mahalalel, "*praise of God [El]*":– Mahalalel (7)

H4547 מַהֲלֻמוֹת ***mahălumôt***, n.f.pl. [2] [√ 2150]. (pl.) beating, thrashing, repeated blows to the body:– beating (1), beatings (1)

H4548 מָהֵם ***māhēm***, var. Not used in NIVEBC [√ 4537 + 2157]. see 4537 & 2156

H4549 מַהֲמֹרוֹת ***mahămōrôt***, n.f.[pl.] [1] miry pits, pits filled with rain water:– miry pits (1)

H4550 מַהְפֵּכָה ***mahpēkâ***, n.f. [6] [√ 2200]. overthrow, destruction, demolishing:– overthrown (3), overthrew (2), destruction (1)

H4551 מַהְפֶּכֶת ***mahpeket***, n.f. [4] [√ 2200]. stocks (confining a prisoner, suggesting in a crooked posture or distortion):– stocks (3), prison (1 [+1074, 2021])

H4552 מְהוֹלָה ***mehôlâ***, n.pr.loc. Not used in NIVEBC [→ 71]. Meholah

H4553 מְהֻקְצָעוֹת ***mehuqṣā'ôt***, n.[pl.] *or* v.ptcp. Not used in NIVEBC [√ 7910]. made with corners

H4554 [1]מָהַר ***māhar[1]***, v. [82] [→ 4542, 4556, 4557, 4559, 4561]. [N] to be swept away; to be impetuous, rash, disturbed; [P] to be quick, hasten, hurry, do at once:– quickly (27), hurried (8), quick (6), at once (4), hurry (4), bring at once (3), soon (3), swift (3), fearful (2), immediately (2), act at once (1), acted quickly (1), all at once (1), are swept away (1), come quickly (1), come quickly (1 [+4394]), coming quickly (1 [+4394]), darting (1), dash (1), do now (1), early (1), fluent (1 [+4200, 1819]), go at once (1), hasten (1), hastily (1), hasty (1), impetuous (1), move quickly (1), run (1), sudden (1)

H4555 [2]מָהַר ***māhar[2]***, v.den. [2] [√ 4558]. [Q] to pay the purchase price for a bride:– must pay bride-price (2 [+4555])

H4556 [1]מַהֵר ***mahēr[1]***, a. Not used in NIVEBC [√ 4554]. swift

H4557 [2]מַהֵר ***mahēr[2]***, adv. Not used in NIVEBC [√ 4554]. swiftly

H4558 מֹהַר ***mōhar***, n.m. [3] [→ 4555, 4560]. bride-price, compensation to the father of the bride:– bride-price (1), price for bride (1), price for the bride (1)

H4559 מְהֵרָה ***mehērâ***, n.f. [20] [√ 4554]. haste, quickness, speed; (adv.) quickly, swiftly, soon, at once:– quickly (6), at once (4), soon (2), hurriedly (1), hurry (1), hurry (1 [+2143]), quickly (1 [+928]), speedily (1), swiftly (1), swiftly (1 [+6330]), very soon (1)

H4560 מַהֲרַי ***mahăray***, n.pr.m. [3] [√ 4558]. Maharai, "*impetuous*":– Maharai (3)

H4561 מַהֵר שָׁלָל חָשׁ בַּז ***mahēr šālāl ḥāš baz***, n.pr.m. [2] [√ 4554 + 8965 + 2590 + 1020]. Maher-Shalal-Hash-Baz, "*quick to the plunder, swift to the spoil*":– Maher-Shalal-Hash-Baz (2)

H4562 מַהֲתַלָּה ***mahătallâ***, n.f. [1] [√ 9438]. illusion, deception:– illusions (1)

H4563 מוֹ ***mô***, n.? see 4784

H4564 מוֹ- ,מוּ- ,-מוֹ ***-mô, -mû, -mô***, p.suf. [118] [√ 2023]. he, him; they, them:– them (44), their (23), their (5 [+4200]), themselves (5), him (4), it (3), they (3), us (3), the[S] (2), Japheth[S] (1), Shem[S] (1), each other[S] (1), he (1), his (1), his (1 [+4200]), his people[S] (1), its (1), my enemies[S] (1), them up (1), those (1), water[S] (1), where[S] (1 [+4200]), who (1), your enemies[S] (1), NDT (11)

H4565 [1]מוֹאָב ***mô'āb[1]***, n.pr.m. [2] [→ 4566, 4567, 7075]. Moab:– Moab (2)

H4566 [2]מוֹאָב ***mô'āb[2]***, n.pr.m. & loc. [179] [√ 4565]. Moab, Moabite:– Moab (132), Moabites (13), Moabite (10), Moab (7 [+8441]), Moab's (7), Moab (5 [+824]), Moabites (1 [+408]), Moabites (1 [+1201]), its[S] (1), there[S] (1 [+8441]), they[S] (1)

H4567 מוֹאָבִי ***mô'ābî***, a.g. [16] [√ 4565]. Moabite, from Moab, "*of Moab*":– Moabite (11), Moabites (4), Moab (1)

H4568 מוֹאל ***mô'l***, subst. & pp. Not used in NIVEBC [cf. 4578]. see 4578

H4569 מוֹבָא ***môbā'***, n.[m.] [2] [√ 4427; cf. 995]. coming in; entrance (way):– entrances (1), movements (1 [+4604, 2256])

H4570 מוּג ***mûg***, v. [16] [Q] to melt, waste away; [N] to melt away (in fear), be disheartened; to collapse; [Pol] to soften; to toss about; [Htpol] to melt away, flow from; from the base meaning the melting of a substance is the fig. extension of the inner person melting is fear:– melt away (3), melting in fear (2), melts (2), collapses (1), disheartened (1), flow (1), melt with fear (1), melted away (1), melting away (1 [+2256, 2143]), quake (1), soften (1), toss about (1)

H4571 מוּד ***môd***, v. [1] [Pol] to shake, convulse, set into motion:– shook (1)

H4572 [1]מוֹט ***môṭ[1]***, v. [40] [→ 4573, 4574]. [Q] to slip, fall, totter, stagger; [N] to be shaken, be caused to move, be toppled; [H] to bring down, to cause to fall; [Htpol] to be thoroughly shaken, be continually shaken:– be shaken (8), fall (5), be moved (3), slip (3), is violently shaken (2 [+4572]), removed (2), slipping (2), topple (2), are shaken (1), be uprooted (1), be uprooted (1 [+9247]), bring down (1), give way (1), immovable (1 [+1153]), quaking (1), secure (1 [+1153]), shake (1), shaken (1), staggering (1), stumbled (1), unable to support (1 [+3338])

H4573 [2]מוֹט ***môṭ[2]***, n.[m.] [4] [√ 4572]. carrying frame; pole; yoke bar:– carrying frame (2), pole (1), yoke (1)

H4574 מוֹטָה ***môṭâ***, n.f. [12] [√ 4572]. yoke bar, pole, bar; by extension: oppression of subjected people:– yoke (8), bars (2), crossbars (1), poles (1)

H4575 מוּךְ ***mûk***, v. [5] [cf. 4812]. [Q] to become poor:– poor (4), poor to pay (1)

H4576 [1]מוּל ***mûl[1]***, v. [30] [→ 4581; cf. 4543, 4909]. [Q] to circumcise; [Qp] to be circumcised; [N] to be circumcised, undergo circumcision, circumcise oneself; "to circumcise the heart" means to commit to covenant obedience from within, not only formally:– circumcised (7), be circumcised (4), been circumcised (2), must be circumcised (2 [+4576]), was circumcised (2), are[S] (1), be circumcised (1 [+1414, 6889]), been circumcised (1 [+6889]), circumcise (1), circumcise (1 [+6889]), circumcise yourselves (1), circumcised (1 [+1414, 6889]), circumcising (1), did so[S] (1), had[S] (1), undergo circumcision (1 [+906, 1414, 6889]), was circumcised (1 [+1414, 6889]), were circumcised (1)

H4577 [2]מוּל ***mûl[2]***, v. [3] [H] to cut off, ward off:– cut down (3)

H4578 [3]מוּל ***mûl[3]***, subst. & pp. [35] [cf. 3283, 4568]. before, opposite, in front of:– at (3 [+448]), in front of (3 [+448]), corner (2), in front of (2 [+4946]), near (2), on (2 [+448]), on (2 [+4946]), opposite (2), toward (2), as far as (1 [+448]), before (1), border (1), faced forward (1 [+448, 7156]), facing (1), from (1 [+4946]), in front of (1 [+448, 7156]), in the front part (1), in the vicinity of (1), next to (1 [+4946]), off (1 [+4946]), opposite direction (1), out in front (1 [+448, 7156]), to (1), to (1 [+448])

H4579 מוֹלָדָה ***môlādâ***, n.pr.loc. [4] Moladah, "*generation*":– Moladah (4)

H4580 מוֹלֶדֶת ***môledet***, n.f. [22] [√ 3528]. family, relatives, children; (land of) birth, native (land):– native (4), relatives (3), birth (2), family (2), family background (2), people (2), born (1), born in the same home (1 [+1074]), children (1), homeland (1 [+824]), natives (1), NDT (2)

H4581 מוּלָה ***mûlâ***, n.f. [1] [√ 4576]. circumcision:– circumcision (1)

H4582 מוֹלִיד ***môlîd***, n.pr.m. [1] [√ 3528]. Molid, "*descendant*":– Molid (1)

H4583 מוּם ***mûm***, n.m. [21] [cf. 4398]. defect, blemish, flaw, injury; by extension: shame, defilement:– defect (8), blemish (3), flaw (2), abuse (1), defects (1), defiled (1 [+1815]), fault (1), injures (1 [+5989]), injury (1), physical defect (1), shame (1)

H4584 מוּמְכָן ***mewmukān***, n.pr.m. Not used in NIVEBC [√ 4925]. Mumecan, see 4925

H4585 מוּסָב ***mûsāb***, n.m. Not used in NIVEBC [√ 6015]. encompassing, surrounding

H4586 מוּסָד ***mûsād***, n.m. [2] [→ 4588; cf. 3569]. foundation, laying the foundation stone:– foundation (1), foundation laid (1)

H4587 מוֹסָד ***môsād***, n.m. [8] [→ 4589; cf. 3569]. foundation:– foundations (8)

H4588 מוּסָדָה ***mûsādâ***, n.f. [1] [√ 4586; cf. 3569]. foundation:– foundation (1)

H4589 מוֹסָדָה ***môsādâ***, n.m. [5] [√ 4587; cf. 3569]. foundation:– foundations (3), foundation (1), founded (1)

H4590 מוּסָךְ ***mûsāk***, n.m. [1] [√ 6114; cf. 4788]. canopy:– canopy (1)

H4591 מוֹסֵר ***môsēr***, n.m. [5] [→ 4593, 5035; cf. 673]. chains, shackles, fetters:– chains (3), noose (1), shackles (1)

H4592 מוּסָר ***mûsār***, n.m. [50] [→ 5036; cf. 3579]. discipline, instruction, correction; wisdom and teaching that imply correcting errant behavior:– discipline (18), instruction (15), correction (6), lesson (2), punishment (2), disciplined (1), punished (1), punishing (1), rebuke (1), taught (1), warning (1), warnings (1)

H4593 [1]מוֹסֵרָה ***môsērâ[1]***, n.m. [8] [√ 4591; cf. 673]. bonds, shackles, straps, chains, fetters:– bonds (3), chains (2), ropes (1), shackles (1), yoke of straps (1)

H4594 [2]מוֹסֵרָה ***môsērâ[2]***, n.pr.loc. [1] [√ 673?; cf. 5035]. Moserah, "*bond, prison [?]*":– Moserah (1)

H4595 מוֹעֵד ***mô'ēd***, n.m. [223] [√ 3585]. (Tent of) Meeting; appointed time, designated time, season:– meeting (146), appointed festivals (24), appointed time (15), time (7), festivals (3), appointed (2), anniversary (1), appointed festival (1), appointed seasons (1), appointed times (1), army (1), arranged (1 [+2118]), assembly (1), assigned portion (1), certain place (1), council (1), designated (1), feast (1), festival offerings (1), in (1 [+928]), occasion (1), opportunity (1), place of meeting (1), place where met (1), place where worshiped (1), ready (1), sacred times (1), seasons (1), set time (1 [+3427]), time set (1), times (1), NDT (1)

H4596 מוֹעָד ***mô'ād***, n.[m.] [1] [√ 3585]. ranks, appointed place of a soldier:– ranks (1)

H4597 מוּעָדָה ***mû'ādâ***, n.f. [1] [√ 3585]. designation, appointment:– designated (1)

H4598 מוֹעַדְיָה ***mô'adyâ***, n.pr.m. [1] [√ 5048 + 3378; cf. 5049]. Moadiah, "[perhaps] *Yahweh assembles* or *Yahweh promises*":– Moadiah's (1)

H4599 מוּעָף ***mû'āp***, n.[m.] [1] [√ 6415]. gloom, darkness; fig. of the emotional state of sadness and despondency:– gloom (1)

H4600 מוֹעֵצָה ***mô'ēṣâ***, n.f. [7] [√ 3619]. plan, scheme, device, intrigue:– counsel (1), devices (1), inclinations (1), intrigues (1), plans (1), schemes (1), traditions (1)

H4601 מוּעָקָה ***mû'āqâ***, n.f. [1] [√ 6421?]. burden, misery, hardship:– burdens (1)

H4602 מוֹפַעַת ***môpa'at***, n.pr.loc. Not used in NIVEBC [cf. 4789]. Mophaath, see 4789

H4603 מוֹפֵת ***môpēt***, n.m. [36] wonder, sign, miracle, portent; symbol:– wonders (17), sign (8), wonder (3), miracles (2), miraculous sign (2), miracle (1), portent (1), symbolic of things to come (1), symbols (1)

H4604 [1]מוֹצָא ***môṣā'[1]***, n.m. [27] [√ 3655]. act of going out, springing out, exiting, moving on; by extension, (n.) what goes out: spring (of water), mine shaft, sunrise, east:– exits (3), flowing springs (2 [+4784]), imported (2), spring (2 [+4784]), stages (2), appear (1 [+3922]), came from (1), east (1), go (1), goes out (1), grass (1 [+2013]), mine (1), movements (1 [+2256, 4569]), outlet (1), rises (1), springs (1 [+4784]), utter (1), what passes (1), what uttered (1), where dawns (1), word that comes from (1)

H4605 [2]מוֹצָא ***môṣā'[2]***, n.pr.m. [5] [√ 3655]. Moza, "*sunrise*":– Moza (5)

H4606 מוֹצָאָה ***môṣā'â***, n.f. [1] [√ 3655]. origin, coming out; latrine:– origins (1)

H4607 [1]מוּצָק ***mûṣāq[1]***, n.m. [7] [→ 4609; cf. 3668]. casting (of metal):– cast metal (3), cast (1), cast bronze (1), cast in molds (1), hard (1 [+3668, 4200, 2021])

H4608 [2]מוּצָק ***mûṣāq[2]***, n.[m.] [2] [√ 7439]. restriction, constraint; distress, hardship:– distress (1), restriction (1)

H4609 מוּצָקָה ***mûṣāqâ***, n.f. [2] [√ 4607; cf. 3668]. casting (into one piece); channel, spout or lip (of a lamp):– channels (1), one piece with (1)

H4610 מוּק ***mûq***, v. [1] [H] to scoff:– scoff (1)

H4611 מוֹקֵד ***môqēd***, n.[m.] [2] [→ 4612; cf. 3678]. hearth, (place of) glowing embers, burning embers:– burning (1), glowing embers (1)

H4612 מוֹקְדָה ***môqedâ***, n.f. [1] [√ 4611; cf. 3678]. hearth, place of burning:– hearth (1)

H4613 מוֹקֵשׁ ***môqēš***, n.m. [28] [√ 3704]. snare, trap, that which captures prey; by extension: ensnarement, entrapment (of a person):– snare (11), snares (7), trap (3), traps (3), bait (1), ensnared (1), snared (1), trapped (1)

H4614 [1]מוּר ***mûr[1]***, v. [14] [→ 9455; cf. 4615]. [N] to be changed; [H] to exchange, substitute, change:– exchanged (3), make a substitution (2 [+4614]), substitute (2 [+4614]), change mind (1), divided up (1), exchange (1), give way (1), make substitution (1), substitute (1), unchanged (1 [+4202])

H4615 [2]מוּר ***mûr[2]***, v. Not used in NIVEBC [cf. 4614]. [N] to shake, quake

H4616 מוֹרָא ***môrā'***, n.m. [12] [√ 3707; cf. 4624]. fear, terror, respect, reverence; awesome deed:– fear (4), terror (3), awesome (1), awesome deeds (1), feared (1), respect (1), reverence (1)

H4617 מוֹרַג ***môrag***, n.m. [3] threshing sledge:– threshing sledges (2), threshing sledge (1)

H4618 מוֹרָד ***môrād***, n.[m.] [5] [√ 3718]. slope, road going down; something hammered down:– road down (2), hammered (1), slope (1), slopes (1)

H4619 [1]מוֹרֶה ***môreh[1]***, n.[m.] *or* v.ptcp. [4] [√ 3721]. archer:– archers (1), archers (1 [+928, 2021, 8008]), archers (1 [+408, 928, 2021, 8008]), they[S] (1 [+2021])

H4620 [2]מוֹרֶה ***môreh[2]***, n.m. [3] [√ 3722]. autumn rains:– autumn rains (2), autumn (1)

H4621 [3]מוֹרֶה ***môreh[3]***, n.m. [4] [√ 3723]. teacher:– teachers (2), teacher (1), them[S] (1 [+3870])

H4622 [4]מוֹרֶה ***môreh[4]***, n.pr.[loc.?] [3] [√ 3723]. Moreh:– Moreh (3)

H4623 [1]מוֹרָה ***môrâ[1]***, n.m. [3] [√ 6867]. razor:– razor (3)

H4624 [2]מוֹרָא ***môrâ[2]***, n.[m.] Not used in NIVEBC [cf. 3707]. terror, see 4616

H4625 [1]מוֹרָשׁ ***môrāš[1]***, n.[m.] [2] [→ 4627; cf. 3769]. possession, inheritance:– inheritance (1), place (1)

H4626 [2]מוֹרָשׁ ***môrāš[2]***, n.[m.] [1] [√ 830]. desire:– desires (1)

H4627 מוֹרָשָׁה ***môrāšâ***, n.f. [9] [√ 4625; cf. 3769]. possession:– possession (9)

H4628 מוֹרֶשֶׁת גַּת ***môrešet gat***, n.pr.loc. [1] [→ 4629]. Moresheth Gath, *"possession of Gath"*:– Moresheth Gath (1)

H4629 מוֹרַשְׁתִּי ***môraštî***, a.g. [2] [√ 4628]. of Moresheth:– of Moresheth (2)

H4630 [1]מוּשׁ ***mûš[1]***, v. [3] [cf. 3560, 5491]. [Q] to touch, feel; [H] be able to feel, touch:– feel (2), touch (1)

H4631 [2]מוּשׁ ***mûš[2]***, v. [20] [Q] to depart, leave, move away, vanish; [H] to remove:– leave (3), shaken (2), always be (1 [+4202]), departed (1), fails (1), give way (1), go away (1), keep (1 [+4202]), left place (1), move (1), moved (1), moving (1), remove (1), save (1), takes (1), vanish (1), without (1)

H4632 מוֹשָׁב ***môšāb***, n.m. [43] [√ 3782]. dwelling, settlement, place to live, place:– live (12), settlements (5), dwelling (2), seat (2), seating (2), where settle (2), company (1), council (1), dwelling place (1), dwellings (1), home (1), house (1 [+1074]), houses (1), length of time (1), members (1), place (1), places where lived (1), region where lived (1), settle (1), settled (1), situated (1), stood (1), throne (1), NDT (1)

H4633 [1]מוּשִׁי ***mûšî[1]***, n.pr.m. [8] [→ 4634]. Mushi:– Mushi (8)

H4634 [2]מוּשִׁי ***mûšî[2]***, a.g. [2] [√ 4633]. Mushite, *"of Mushi"*:– Mushite (1), Mushites (1)

H4635 מוֹשִׁיעַ ***môšîaʻ***, n.[m.] *or* v.ptcp. [21] [√ 3828]. savior, deliverer, rescuer; the OT concept of God as Savior has its focus on rescue from earthly enemies, occasionally referring to salvation from guilt, sin, and punishment:– savior (11), deliverer (3), rescue (3), deliverers (2), rescues (1), save (1)

H4636 מוֹשָׁעָה ***môšāʻâ***, n.f. [1] [√ 3828]. act of salvation, act of helping; see also 4635:– saves (1)

H4637 מוּת ***mût***, v. [846] [→ 4638, 4926, 9456; *also used with compound proper names*]. [Q] to die, be killed, be dead; [Pol] to kill, slay, put to death; [H] to kill, make die, put to death, assassinate; [Ho] to be put to death, be murdered:– die (202), died (163), dead (100), put to death (46), kill (34), death (30), killed (29), be put to death (28 [+4637]), be put to death (24), dies (19), put to death (18 [+4637]), certainly die (10 [+4637]), die (10 [+4637]), surely die (10 [+4637]), is to be put to death (8 [+4637]), kill (8 [+4637]), must die (8 [+4637]), assassinated (5), dying (5), slay (4), fatal (3), putting to death (3), be murdered (2), brings death (2), causing to die (2), corpse (2), destroy (2), died a natural death (2), doomed to die (2 [+4637]), in fact die (2 [+4637]), killing (2), must be put to death (2 [+4637]), perish (2), put[S] (2), put to death (2 [+5782, 2256]), slain (2), surely be put to death (2 [+4637]), anyone[S] (1 [+2021]), as good as dead (1), assassinated (1 [+5782, 2256]), assassination (1), be killed (1), body (1), bring about death (1), dead (1 [+4946, 4213]), die out (1), end (1), executed (1 [+5782, 2256]), failed (1), fatal blow (1), go down (1), had executed (1 [+5782, 2256]), his[S] (1 [+2021]), is put to death (1), killed (1 [+5782]), killing off (1), kills (1), kills (1 [+5782, 5883, 2256]), lifeless (1), lose life (1), make die (1), messengers of death (1), mortals (1 [+632]), murder (1), person[S] (1), put death (1), ready to die (1), risked (1 [+3070, 4200]), slays (1), someone[S] (1), stillborn infant (1), struck down and died (1), to be put to death (1), was killed (1), was put to death (1), were put to death (1), widow (1 [+851]), with a fatal blow (1), NDT (8)

H4638 מָוֶת ***māwet***, n.m. [151] [→ 2975; cf. 4637; 10409]. death, dying:– death (111), die (12), died (11), dead (3), dies (3), deadly (2), capital offense (1 [+5477]), deadly plague (1), death's (1), dying (1), immortality (1 [+440]), kill (1), must die (1 [+1201]), plague (1), put to death (1 [+2222])

H4639 מוֹתָר ***môtār***, n.m. [3] [√ 3855]. profit, advantage:– profit (2), advantage (1)

H4640 מִזְבֵּחַ ***mizbēaḥ***, n.m. [401] [√ 2284; 10401]. altar:– altar (337), altars (50), it[S] (5 [+2021]), its[S] (3 [+2021]), done this[S] (1 [+1215, 4200, 3378]), it (1 [+2021]), NDT (4)

H4641 מֶזֶג ***mezeg***, n.m. [1] blended wine, mixed wine (likely spiced):– blended wine (1)

H4642 מָזֶה ***māzeh***, a. [1] empty (from hunger), implying an unhealthy loss of weight and breakdown in health:– wasting (1)

H4643 מַזֶּה ***mazzeh***, var. Not used in NIVEBC [√ 4537 + 2296]. see 4537 & 2296

H4644 מִזֶּה ***mizzeh***, var. Not used in NIVEBC [√ 4946 + 2296]. from this, from here, see 4946 & 2296

H4645 מִזָּה ***mizzâ***, n.pr.m. [3] Mizzah, *"terror"*:– Mizzah (3)

H4646 מָזוּ ***māzû***, n.m. [1] [cf. 2312]. barn, granary:– barns (1)

H4647 מְזוּזָה ***mezûzâ***, n.f. [19] doorframe, doorpost, doorjamb:– doorframes (4), doorposts (4), doorframe (3), doorpost (2), doorway (1 [+7339]), doorways (1 [+7339]), gatepost (1 [+9133]), gateposts (1 [+9133]), posts (1), width[S] (1 [+382])

H4648 מָזוֹן ***māzôn***, n.m. [2] [√ 2315]. provisions, food:– provisions (2)

H4649 [1]מָזוֹר ***māzôr[1]***, n.[m.] [3] sore, boil, ulcer:– sores (2), sore (1)

H4650 [2]מָזוֹר ***māzôr[2]***, n.m. [1] trap, ambush:– trap (1)

H4651 [1]מֵזַח ***mēzaḥ[1]***, n.m. [1] [→ 4685]. harbor; an area in which wind and wave are restricted as a fig. extension of a girdle or belt that restrains:– harbor (1)

H4652 [2]מֵזַח ***mēzaḥ[2]***, n.m. [1] [→ 4653]. belt, leather girdle worn next to the skin:– belt (1)

H4653 מָזִיחַ ***māzîaḥ***, n.m. [1] [√ 4652]. belt, girdle:– disarms (1 [+8332])

H4654 מַזְכִּיר ***mazkîr***, n.m. *or* v.ptcp. [9] [√ 2349]. recorder, clerk, secretary:– recorder (9)

H4655 מַזָּל ***mazzāl***, n.[f.]pl. [1] [cf. 4666]. constellation (possibly of the zodiac signs):– constellations (1)

H4656 מִזְלָג ***mizlāg***, n.m. & f. Not used in NIVEBC [→ 4657, 4658]. (three-tined) meat fork

H4657 מַזְלֵג ***mazlēg***, n.m. [7] [√ 4656]. (three-tined) meat fork:– meat forks (4), fork (2), forks (1)

H4658 מִזְלָגָה ***mizlāgâ***, n.[f.] Not used in NIVEBC [√ 4656]. (three-tined) meat fork, see 4656

H4659 מְזִמָּה ***mezimmâ***, n.f. [19] [√ 2372]. discretion; scheme, plan, purpose, intent:– discretion (5), wicked schemes (3), evil schemes (2), purpose (2), purposes (2), schemes (2), evil intent (1), schemer (1 [+1251]), thoughts (1)

H4660 מִזְמוֹר ***mizmôr***, n.m. [57] [√ 2376]. psalm, melody:– psalm (57)

H4661 מַזְמֵרָה ***mazmērâ***, n.f. [4] [√ 2377]. pruning hook, pruning knife, vine-knife:– pruning hooks (3), pruning knives (1)

H4662 מְזַמֶּרֶת ***mezammeret***, n.f. [5] [√ 2377]. wick trimmer (scissors, possibly also used as a snuffer):– wick trimmers (5)

H4663 מִזְעָר ***mizʻār***, n.[m.] [4] [√ 2402]. small matter, few:– in a very short time (1 [+6388, 5071]), very few (1 [+632]), very few (1 [+5071]), very soon (1 [+6388, 5071])

H4664 מָזַר ***māzar***, v. Not used in NIVEBC [cf. 2430]. [Qp] to be spread out (a net)

H4665 מִזְרֶה ***mizreh***, n.[m.] [2] [√ 2430]. winnowing fork, shovel:– shovel (1), winnowing fork (1)

H4666 מַזָּרוֹת ***mazzārôt***, n.[f.]pl. [1] [cf. 4655]. constellations, variously specified:– constellations (1)

H4667 מִזְרָח ***mizrāḥ***, n.[m.] [74] [√ 2436]. direction of the sunrise, east, eastern; the east was the direction of orientation in the ancient Near East:– east (34), east (7 [+2025]), rising (5), sunrise (5), east (3 [+2021, 9087]), sunrise (3 [+9087]), east (2 [+9087]), east (2 [+2025, 2021, 9087]), eastern (2 [+2025]), east (1 [+6298, 2025]), east (1 [+928, 6298, 2025]), east (1 [+928, 6298, 9087]), east (1 [+928, 6298, 2025, 9087]), eastern (1), eastern (1 [+9087]), eastward (1 [+2025]), eastward (1 [+7711, 2025, 2025]), western[S] (1 [+2025]), where rises (1), NDT (1)

H4668 מְזָרִים ***mezārîm***, n.m. *or* v.ptcp. [1] [√ 2430]. driving (north) winds:– driving winds (1)

H4669 מִזְרָע ***mizrāʻ***, n.[m.] [1] [√ 2445]. seeded field, land sown:– sown field (1)

H4670 מִזְרָק ***mizrāq***, n.m. [32] [√ 2450]. sacred bowl used for sprinkling (the altar):– sprinkling bowls (15), sprinkling bowl (13), bowl used for sprinkling (1), bowlful (1), bowls (1), sacred bowls (1)

H4671 מֵחַ ***mēaḥ***, n.[m.] [2] [→ 4672; cf. 4683]. fat sheep; (representing) the rich:– fat animals (1), rich (1)

H4672 מֹחַ ***mōaḥ***, n.m. [1] [√ 4671; cf. 4683]. marrow (of the bones):– marrow (1)

H4673 [1]מָחָא ***māḥāʼ[1]***, v. [3] [→ 4686; cf. 4682; 10411]. [Q] to clap (hands in joy):– clap (2), clapped (1)

H4674 [2]מָחָא ***māḥāʼ[2]***, v.den. Not used in NIVEBC [cf. 4683]. see 4683

H4675 מַחֲבֵא ***maḥabēʼ***, n.[m.] [1] [√ 2461]. shelter, hiding place (from wind):– shelter (1)

H4676 מַחֲבֹא ***maḥabōʼ***, n.[m.] [1] [√ 2461]. hiding place:– hiding places (1)

H4677 מְחַבְּרוֹת ***meḥabberôt***, n.f. [2] [√ 2489]. fittings, braces (of iron), joists, truss (of timber):– fittings (1), joists (1)

H4678 מַחְבֶּרֶת ***maḥberet***, n.f. [8] [√ 2489]. place of joining, seam, set (of curtains):– set (6), seam (2)

H4679 מַחֲבַת ***maḥabat***, n.f. [5] [√ 2503]. (metal) griddle or baking pan:– griddle (3), baking (1), pan (1)

H4680 מַחֲגֹרֶת ***maḥagōret***, n.f. [1] [√ 2520]. girding (of sackcloth wrapped around the body):– sackcloth (1 [+8566])

H4681 [1]מָחָה ***māḥâ[1]***, v. [34] [→ 9457?]. [Q] to wash off, wipe out, blot out, destroy; [N] be blotted out, be wiped out, be exterminated; [H] to cause to blot out:– blot out (11), be blotted out (3), blotted out (2), completely blot out (2 [+4681]), wipe (2), wiped out (2), wipes (2), be wiped away (1), be wiped out (1), blots out (1), ruin (1), swept away (1), wash off (1), wipe away (1), wipe out (1), wiped (1), wiping (1)

H4682 [2]מָחָה ***māḥâ[2]***, v. [1] [√ 4693; cf. 4673; 10411]. [Q] to continue along, stretch along:– continue (1)

H4683 [3]מָחָה ***māḥâ[3]***, v.den. [1] [cf. 4674, 4671, 4672]. [Pu] (choice food-dishes) to be filled with marrow:– meats (1)

H4684 מְחוּגָה ***meḥûgâ***, n.f. [1] [√ 2552]. compass (for making circles):– compasses (1)

H4685 מָחוֹז ***māḥôz***, n.[m.] [1] [√ 4651]. haven, harbor, which might include a population center like a repair yard and city:– haven (1)

H4686 מְחוּיָאֵל ***meḥûyāʼēl***, n.pr.m. [2] [√ 4673 + 446; cf. 4696]. Mehujael:– Mehujael (2)

H4687 מַחֲוִים ***maḥawîm***, a.g. [1] Mahavite:– Mahavite (1)

H4688 [1]מָחוֹל ***māḥôl[1]***, n.m. [6] [→ 4689, 4703; cf. 2565]. circle-dancing, round-dancing:– dancing (4), dance (2)

H4689 [2]מָחוֹל ***māḥôl[2]***, n.pr.m. [1] [√ 4688; cf. 2565]. Mahol, *"place of round dancing"*:– Mahol (1)

H4690 מַחֲזֶה ***maḥazeh***, n.[m.] [4] [√ 2600]. vision:– vision (3), visions (1)

H4691 מֶחֱזָה ***meḥezâ***, n.f. [4] [√ 2600]. light, place of seeing, in some contexts referring to a window:– facing each other (2 [+4691, 448]), facing each other (2 [+448, 4691])

H4692 מַחֲזִיאוֹת ***maḥazîʼôt***, n.pr.m. [2] [√ 2600]. Mahazioth, *"visions"*:– Mahazioth (2)

H4693 מְחִי ***meḥî***, n.[m.] [1] [√ 4682]. blow (of a battering ram):– blows (1)

H4694 מְחִידָא ***meḥîdāʼ***, n.pr.m. [2] Mehida, "[poss.] *bought as slave*":– Mehida (2)

H4695 מִחְיָה ***miḥyâ***, n.f. [8] [√ 2649]. saving of a life; raw flesh; food, sustenance; relief, recovering:– food (1), living thing (1), new life (1), raw (1 [+2645]), raw flesh (1), recover (1), relief (1), save lives (1)

H4696 מְחִיָּיאֵל ***meḥiyyāyʼēl***, n.pr.m. Not used in NIVEBC [cf. 4686]. Mehijael

H4697 [1]מְחִיר ***meḥîr[1]***, n.m. [15] [→ 4698]. price, cost, money:– price (6), current price (2), charge (1), cost (1), insist on paying for (1 [+7864, 928, 7864]), money (1), sale (1), worth (1), NDT (1)

H4698 [2]מְחִיר ***meḥîr[2]***, n.pr.m. [1] [√ 4697]. Mehir, *"hired hand"*:– Mehir (1)

H4699 מַחְלֵב ***maḥalēb***, n.pr.loc. Mahaleb, see 2475

H4700 מַחֲלֶה ***maḥaleh***, n.[m.] [2] [→ 4701; cf. 2703]. sickness, disease:– disease (1), sickness (1)

H4701 מַחֲלָה ***maḥalâ***, n.f. [4] [√ 4700; cf. 2703]. disease, sickness:– disease (2), diseases (1), sickness (1)

H4702 מַחְלָה ***maḥlâ***, n.pr.f. [& m.?] [5] Mahlah, "[perhaps] *weak one*":– Mahlah (5)

H4703 מְחֹלָה ***meḥōlâ***, n.f. [8] [√ 4688; cf. 71, 2565]. circle-dance, round-dance:– dancing (5), dances (2), dance (1)

H4704 מְחִלָּה ***meḥillâ***, n.f. [1] [√ 2726]. hole:– holes (1)

H4705 מַחְלוֹן ***maḥlôn***, n.pr.m. [4] [√ 2703?]. Mahlon:– Mahlon (3), Mahlon's (1)

H4706 [1]מַחְלִי ***maḥlî[1]***, n.pr.m. [12] [√ 2703?]. Mahli, "[perhaps] *shrewd, cunning*":– Mahli (12)

H4707 [2]מַחְלִי ***maḥlî[2]***, a.g. [2] [√ 2703?]. Mahlite, *"of Mahli"*:– Mahlite (1), Mahlites (1)

H4708 מַחֲלֻיִים ***maḥaluyîm***, n.m. [1] [√ 2703]. sickness (caused by wounding):– wounded (1)

H4709 מַחֲלָף ***maḥalāp***, n.m. [1] [√ 2736?]. utensil, perhaps a pan:– pans (1)

H4710 מַחְלָפָה ***maḥalāpâ***, n.f. [3] [√ 2736]. braids (of hair):– braids (3)

H4711 מַחֲלָצוֹת ***maḥalāṣôt***, n.f.[pl.] [2] [√ 2740]. fine robes, fine, white, festival garments:– fine garments (1), fine robes (1)

H4712 מַחְלְקוֹת ***maḥleqôt***, n.f.pl. Not used in NIVEBC [√ 2744; cf. 2165, 6154]. smoothness, slipperiness, see 6154

H4713 מַחֲלֹקֶת ***maḥalōqet***, n.f. [42] [√ 2745; 10412]. portion, share (of land); division, group (of people):– divisions (20), division (17), tribal divisions (2), army divisions (1), portions (1), NDT (1)

H4714 ¹מָחֲלַת ***māḥ***ª***lat¹***, n.f. [2] [√ 2565? *or* 2704?]. mahalath (t.t. in the Psalms):– mahalath (2)

H4715 ²מָחֲלַת ***māḥ***ª***lat²***, n.pr.f. [2] Mahalath, "*suffering of affliction* [NIV]; *sickness or suffering poem* [JB]":– Mahalath (2)

H4716 מְחֹלָתִי ***m***ᵉ***ḥōlātî***, a.g. [2] [cf. 71?]. Meholathite, of Meholah, "*of Meholah*":– Meholathite (1), of Meholah (1)

H4717 מַחְמָאֹת ***maḥmā'ōt***, n.f.pl. [1] [cf. 2772]. butter; some sources: curds, yogurt:– butter (1)

H4718 מַחְמָד ***maḥmād***, n.m. [13] [√ 2773]. thing of value, something of delight, treasure; "the delight of the eyes" is someone or something especially cherished:– treasures (4), delight (3), cherished (1), lovely (1), pleasing (1), treasured (1), value (1), value (1 [+6524])

H4719 מַחְמֹד ***maḥmōd***, n.[m.] [1] [√ 2773]. treasure, something precious:– treasures (1)

H4720 מַחְמָל ***maḥmāl***, n.[m.] [1] [√ 2798?]. yearning:– object (1)

H4721 מַחְמֶצֶת ***maḥmeṣet***, n.f. [2] [√ 2806]. something made with yeast, with a sour taste:– anything with yeast in it (1), made with yeast (1)

H4722 מַחֲנֶה ***maḥ***ª***neh***, n.m. & f. [213] [→ 4724; cf. 2837]. camp, group (military or civilian):– camp (144), army (23), camps (9), forces (5), troops (3), armies (2), dwelling (2), fighting (2), group (2), lines (2), Midianites^S (1), attendants (1), band (1), company (1), encamped (1 [+3655]), flocks and herds (1), force (1), groups (1), it^S (1 [+5213]), it^S (1 [+2021]), there^S (1 [+928, 2021]), tribes (1), units (1), unwalled (1), NDT (5)

H4723 מַחֲנֵה־דָן ***maḥ***ª***nēh-dān***, n.pr.loc. [2] Mahaneh Dan, "*camp of Dan*":– Mahaneh Dan (2)

H4724 מַחֲנַיִם ***maḥ***ª***nayim***, n.pr.loc. [14] [√ 4722; cf. 2837]. Mahanaim, "*double camp*":– Mahanaim (14)

H4725 מַחֲנָק ***maḥ***ª***nāq***, n.[m.] [1] [√ 2871]. strangling, suffocation:– strangling (1)

H4726 מַחְסֶה ***maḥseh***, n.m. [20] [→ 4729; cf. 2879]. refuge, shelter:– refuge (18), shelter (2)

H4727 מַחְסוֹם ***maḥsôm***, n.m. [1] [√ 2888]. muzzle, a covering for the mouth to keep silence:– muzzle (1)

H4728 מַחְסוֹר ***maḥsôr***, n.[m.] [13] [√ 2893]. need, lack of, scarcity, hence poverty:– poverty (4), lack (2), need (2), scarcity (2), lacks (1), need (1 [+2893]), poor (1)

H4729 מַחְסֵיָה ***maḥsēyâ***, n.pr.m. [2] [√ 4726 + 3378]. Mahseiah:– Mahseiah (2)

H4730 מָחַץ ***māḥaṣ***, v. [13] [→ 4731; 10411]. [Q] to beat to pieces, crush, shatter:– crush (3), crushed (2), crushed completely (1 [+2256, 430]), crushing (1), cut to pieces (1), injures (1), pierce (1), shattered (1), strike down (1 [+5516]), wounded (1)

H4731 מַחַץ ***maḥaṣ***, n.[m.] [1] [√ 4730]. wound (from a blow):– wounds (1)

H4732 מַחְצֵב ***maḥṣēb***, n.[m.] [3] [√ 2933]. dressed (stone), hewn (stone):– dressed (3)

H4733 מֶחֱצָה ***meḥ***ᵉ***ṣâ***, n.f. [2] [√ 2936]. half:– half (2)

H4734 מַחֲצִית ***maḥ***ª***ṣît***, n.f. [16] [√ 2936]. half; noon, middle of the day:– half (13), half as much (1), half share (1), noon (1 [+2021, 3427])

H4735 מָחַק ***māḥaq***, v. [1] [Q] to crush, smash, pierce:– crushed (1)

H4736 מֶחְקָר ***meḥqār***, n.m. [1] [√ 2983]. (unexplored) depths (of the earth):– depths (1)

H4737 מָחָר ***māḥār***, n.m. (used as adv.) [52] [→ 4740; cf. 336]. tomorrow, the next day, in the future:– tomorrow (43), in the future (4), days to come (1), ever (1), future (1 [+3427]), some day (1), tomorrow (1 [+3427])

H4738 מַחֲרָאָה ***maḥ***ª***rā'â***, n.f. [1] [√ 2989]. latrine:– latrine (1)

H4739 מַחֲרֵשָׁה ***maḥ***ª***rēšâ***, n.f. [2] [√ 3086]. plowshare:– plow points (2)

H4740 מָחֳרָת ***moḥ***º***rāt***, n.f. [32] [√ 4737; cf. 336]. the next day, the day after:– next day (22), day after (6), next (3), following (1)

H4741 מַחְשֹׂף ***maḥśōp***, n.m. [1] [√ 3106]. exposing, laying bare (of wood):– exposing (1)

H4742 מַחֲשָׁבָה ***maḥ***ª***šābâ***, n.f. [56] [√ 3108]. thought, plan, scheme, plot, design:– thoughts (11), plans (10), schemes (4), plan (3), plots (3), purposes (3), artistic designs (2), purposed (2 [+3108]), scheme (2), artistic crafts (1), design (1), designers (1 [+3110]), devised (1), imaginations (1), invented (1 [+3110]), make plans (1 [+3108]), overthrow (1), plans have (1 [+3108]), plotted (1 [+3108]), things planned (1), thought (1), ways (1), what planned (1), what thinking (1), NDT (1)

H4743 מַחְשָׁךְ ***maḥšāk***, n.m. [7] [√ 3124]. place of darkness, hiding place:– darkness (5), dark places (1), darkest (1)

H4744 מַחַת ***maḥat***, n.pr.m. [3] [√ 3169?]. Mahath, "[perhaps] *tough*":– Mahath (3)

H4745 מְחִתָּה ***m***ᵉ***ḥittâ***, n.f. [11] [√ 3169]. ruin, undoing; terror, horror:– ruin (4), terror (3), object of horror (1), ruined (1), ruins (1), undoing (1)

H4746 מַחְתָּה ***maḥtâ***, n.f. [22] [√ 3149]. censer, firepan, tray:– censers (11), censer (4), firepans (3), trays (3), it^S (1)

H4747 מַחְתֶּרֶת ***maḥteret***, n.m. [2] [√ 3168]. (the act of) breaking into (a house) and so trespassing:– breaking in (2)

H4748 מַטְאֲטֵא ***maṭ'ªṭē'***, n.[m.] [1] [√ 3173; cf. 3226]. broom:– broom (1)

H4749 מַטְבֵּחַ ***maṭbēaḥ***, n.[m.] [1] [√ 3180]. place of slaughter, slaughter yard:– place to slaughter (1)

H4750 מָטֶה ***māṭeh***, n.m. Not used in NIVEBC [√ 5742; 10413]. one approaching death

H4751 מַטֶּה ***maṭṭeh***, n.m. [& f.?] [252] [√ 5742]. staff, rod, club, a stick used to assist in walking, discipline, and guidance, often highly individualized and used for identification; of royalty: scepter; by extension: tribe, as a major unit of national group or clan (fig. identified with or under authority of a leader's staff):– tribe (122), staff (37), tribes (21), tribal (8), half-tribe (5 [+2942]), rod (5), staffs (5), club (4), supply (4), another^S (2), branches (2), scepter (2), Danite (1 [+4200, 1968]), Levites (1 [+4290]), arrows (1), bar (1), branch (1), family (1), main branches (1 [+964]), one^S (1), spear (1), supplies (1), them^S (1), NDT (24)

H4752 מַטָּה ***maṭṭâ***, adv. [19] [√ 5742]. below, beneath, lower, bottom:– below (3 [+4200]), bottom (3), down (3 [+4200]), bottom (2 [+4946, 4200]), lower (2), goes down (1 [+3718, 4200]), going down to (1), less (1), punished less (1 [+3104, 4200]), NDT (2)

H4753 מִטָּה ***miṭṭâ***, n.f. [28] [√ 5742]. bed, couch, a piece of furniture on which one reclines for rest or sleep; by extension: bier, to carry the dead; carriage or palanquin (a vehicle carried on poles by porters):– bed (18), couch (4), bedroom (2 [+2540]), beds (1), bier (1), carriage (1), couches (1)

H4754 מֻטֶּה ***muṭṭeh***, n.[m.] [1] [√ 5742]. injustice, warping (of justice), crookedness (of law):– injustice (1)

H4755 מֻטָּה ***muṭṭâ***, n.f. Not used in NIVEBC [√ 5742]. outspreading (of wings)

H4756 מִטְהָר ***miṭhār***, n.[m.] Not used in NIVEBC [√ 3197]. purity, splendor

H4757 מַטְוֶה ***maṭweh***, n.[m.] [1] [√ 3211]. that which is spun, yarn:– what spun (1)

H4758 מָטִיל ***māṭîl***, n.m. [1] (iron) rod:– rods (1)

H4759 מַטְמוֹן ***maṭmôn***, n.m. [5] [√ 3243]. (hidden) treasure, (hidden) riches:– hidden treasure (2), hidden (1), riches (1), treasure (1)

H4760 מַטָּע ***maṭṭā'***, n.m. [6] [√ 5749]. (the act or place of) planting:– planted (2), planting (2), base (1), land for crops (1)

H4761 מַטְעָם ***maṭ'ām***, n.m. [8] [√ 3247]. tasty food, delicacy:– tasty food (6), delicacies (2)

H4762 מִטְפַּחַת ***miṭpaḥat***, n.f. [2] [√ 3254]. cloak, shawl:– cloaks (1), shawl (1)

H4763 מָטַר ***māṭar***, v.den. [17] [√ 4764]. [N] to be rained upon; [H] to send rain down on; [Ho] to be rained upon; rain has a generally positive associations of growth and refreshment, though excessive or ill-timed rain is potentially destructive to crops and even life-threatening:– rained down (3), rain down (2), sent rain (2), had^S (1), had rain (1), pour down (1), rain (1), rain (1 [+4764]), rained (1), send (1), send rain (1), water (1), withheld^S (1 [+4202])

H4764 מָטָר ***māṭār***, n.m. [38] [→ 4763, 4767]. rain, rain shower; see also 4763:– rain (34), showers (2), downpour (1 [+1773]), rain (1 [+4763])

H4765 מַטְרֵד ***maṭrēd***, n.pr.f. [2] [√ 3265]. Matred, "[perhaps] *spear*":– Matred (2)

H4766 מַטָּרָה ***maṭṭārâ***, n.f. [16] [√ 5757]. (the court of the) guard, i.e., place of confinement; (the Gate of the) Guard (a place); target:– guard (13), target (3)

H4767 מַטְרִי ***maṭrî***, a.g. [1] [√ 4764]. Matri:– Matri's (1)

H4768 מַי ***may***, var. Not used in NIVEBC [cf. 4537]. see 4537

H4769 מִי ***mî***, p.inter. [422] [→ 4775?, 4776, 4777, 4778, 4779, 4780, 4781, 4792]. who?, what?, which?; anyone, whoever:– who (287), whom (30), what (13), whose (13), which (11), if only (10 [+5989]), oh (8 [+5989]), anyone (5), whoever (5), anyone (4 [+2021, 408]), if only (4), someone (3), any (2 [+3972]), how (2), whoever (2 [+2021, 408]), I wish (1 [+5989]), how I long for (1 [+5989, 5761]), how did it go (1 [+905]), is there (1), oh (1 [+5989, 686]), oh how I wish (1 [+5989]), one (1), others^S (1), what (1 [+2296]), what's the meaning of (1 [+4200]), who (1 [+1505]), who (1 [+2021, 408]), who (1 [+4769, 2256]), who (1 [+2256, 4769]), whoever (1 [+889]), whoever (1 [+889]), whose (1 [+4200]), whose (1 [+4200]), why (1), NDT (4)

H4770 מֵי הַיַּרְקוֹן ***mê hayyarqôn***, n.pr.loc. [1] [√ 4784 + 2126]. Me Jarkon, "*waters of Jarkon [greenish?]*":– Me Jarkon (1)

H4771 מֵי זָהָב ***mê zāhāb***, n.pr.m. [2] [√ 4784 + 2298]. Me-Zahab, "*waters of gold*":– Me-Zahab (2)

H4772 מֵידְבָא ***mêd***ᵉ***bā'***, n.pr.loc. [5] Medeba:– Medeba (5)

H4773 מֵידָד ***mêdād***, n.pr.m. [2] Medad, "*beloved*":– Medad (2)

H4774 מֵיטָב ***mêṭāb***, n.[m.] [6] [√ 3512]. best (part of something):– best (5), NDT (1)

H4775 מִיכָא ***mîkā'***, n.pr.m. [4] [→ 4776?, 4777; cf. 4769?]. Mica, "*Who is like Yahweh?*":– Mika (4)

H4776 מִיכָאֵל ***mîkā'ēl***, n.pr.m. [13] [√ 4775?; cf. 4769 + 3869 + 446]. Michael, "*Who is like God [El]?*":– Michael (13)

H4777 מִיכָה ***mîkâ***, n.pr.m. [33] [√ 4775; cf. 4769 + 3869 + 3378]. Micah; Mica; Micaiah, "*Who is like Yahweh?*":– Micah (24), Micah's (6), Micaiah (1), Mika (1), his^S (1)

H4778 מִיכָהוּ ***mîkāhû***, n.pr.m. Not used in NIVEBC [√ 4769 + 3869 + 2084]. Micahu, see 4780

H4779 מִיכָיָה ***mîkāyâ***, n.pr.m. [3] [→ 4780, 4781; cf. 4769 + 3869 + 3378]. Micaiah, "*Who is like Yahweh?*":– Micaiah (3)

H4780 מִיכָיָהוּ ***mîkāyāhû***, n.pr.m. & f. [1] [√ 4779; cf. 4769 + 3869 + 3378]. Micaiah, "*Who is like Yahweh?*":– Micaiah (1)

H4781 מִיכָיְהוּ ***mîkāy***ᵉ***hû***, n.pr.m. [21] [√ 4779; cf. 4769 + 3869 + 3378]. Micaiah; Micah, "*Who is like Yahweh?*":– Micaiah (19), Micah (1), Micah's (1)

H4782 מִיכַל ***mîkāl***, n.[m.] [1] [→ 4783]. brook, stream; some sources: pool, reservoir:– brook (1 [+4784])

H4783 מִיכַל ***mîkal***, n.pr.f. [17] [√ 4782]. Michal, "*Who is like God [El]?*":– Michal (17)

H4784 מַיִם ***mayim***, n.m. [578] [→ 72, 4770, 4771, 5387]. water; in nature: ocean, lake, flood, river; from the body: tears, urine:– water (355), waters (138), river (4), flood (3), floodwaters (3 [+4429]), rain (3), sea (3), springs (3 [+5078]), tears (3), flowing springs (2 [+4604]), spring (2), spring (2 [+4604]), spring (2 [+6524]), springs (2 [+6524]), that^S (2), urine (2), waterless (2 [+401]), well-watered (2 [+9272]), brook (1 [+4782]), brooks (1 [+5707]), bubbling springs (1 [+4432]), dam (1), driving rain (1 [+2443]), floodwaters (1 [+8041]), floodwaters (1 [+8673]), flow (1), flowing streams (1 [+3298]), it^S (1 [+2021]), melted (1), pool (1), pool (1 [+106]), pool (1 [+1391]), reservoirs (1 [+1391]), reservoirs (1 [+5224]), seas (1), spring (1 [+6524, 2021]), spring of water (1), springs (1), springs (1 [+4604]), stream (1), swampland (1 [+106]), they^S (1 [+2021]), water supply (1), watering (1), water's (1), waves (1), well (1 [+931]), wells (1 [+931]), NDT (15)

H4785 מִיָּמִן ***miyyāmîn***, n.pr.m. [4] [√ 4975]. Mijamin, "*from the right hand*":– Mijamin (4)

H4786 מִין ***mîn***, n.[m.] [31] [→ 9454]. kind: genus or species:– kind (18), kinds (9), various kinds (1), NDT (3)

H4787 מֵינֶקֶת ***mêneqet***, n.[f.] *or* v.ptcp. [6] [√ 3567]. nursing woman, wet-nurse:– nurse (4), nursing mothers (1), NDT (1)

H4788 מֵיסָךְ ***mêsāk***, n.m. Not used in NIVEBC [√ 4590]. see 4590

H4789 מֵיפַעַת ***mêpa'at***, n.pr.loc. [4] [cf. 4602]. Mephaath, "*splendor*":– Mephaath (4)

H4790 מִיץ ***mîṣ***, n.m. [3] [→ 5160]. pressing, squeezing:– churning (1), stirring up (1), twisting (1)

H4791 מֵישָׁא ***mêšā'***, n.pr.m. [1] Mesha:– Mesha (1)

H4792 מִישָׁאֵל ***mîšā'ēl***, n.pr.m. [7] [√ 4769 + 8611 + 446; 10414]. Mishael, "*Who belongs to God [El]?*":– Mishael (7)

H4793 מִישׁוֹר ***mîšôr***, n.m. [23] [√ 3837]. (geographical) plateau, plain, level ground; (of ruling and right living) uprightness, justice, straightness:– plateau (9), justice (2), level (2), level ground (2), plains (2), plain (1), plateau (1 [+824]), smooth (1), straight (1), uprightness (1), with equity (1)

H4794 מֵישַׁךְ ***mêšak***, n.pr.m. [1] [√ 10415]. Meshach, "[perhaps] *I have become weak*":– Meshach (1)

H4795 מֵישַׁע ***mêša'***, n.pr.m. [1] [√ 3828]. Mesha:– Mesha (1)

H4796 מֵישָׁע ***mêšā'***, n.pr.m. [1] [√ 3828]. Mesha:– Mesha (1)

H4797 מֵישָׁרִים ***mêšārîm***, n.m. [19] [√ 3837]. uprightness, fairness, equity, justice; moral uprightness and justice are fig. extensions of an object that is straight rather than crooked:– right (6), equity (5), fair (2), alliance (1), integrity (1), level (1), smoothly (1 [+928]), straight (1), with equity (1)

H4798 מֵיתָר ***mêtār***, n.m. [9] [√ 3857]. rope, cord; bow-string:– ropes (7), cords (1), drawn bow (1)

H4799 מַכְאֹב ***mak'ōb***, n.m. [16] [√ 3872]. pain, grief, sorrow, suffering:– pain (7), suffering (6), grief (1), pains (1), woes (1)

H4800 מַכְבֵּנָה ***makbēnâ***, n.pr.loc. [1] [cf. 4801]. Macbenah, "*bond*":– Makbenah (1)

H4801 מַכְבַּנַּי ***makbannay***, n.pr.m. [1] [cf. 4800]. Macbannai, "*clad with a cloak*":– Makbannai (1)

H4802 מַכְבֵּר ***makbēr***, n.[m.] [1] [→ 4803]. thick cloth, with a focus that it is twisted, braided, or woven:– thick cloth (1)

H4803 מִכְבָּר ***mikbār***, n.m. [6] [√ 4802]. grating, latticework:– grating (6)

H4804 מַכָּה ***makkâ***, n.f. [48] [√ 5782]. wound, injury, physical damage to the body; by extension: plague, affliction, calamity, disaster:– wounds (9), wound (4), losses (3), struck down (3), blow (2), plague (2), plagues (2), slaughter (2), afflictions (1), attack (1), beatings (1), blows (1), calamities (1), casualties (1), defeated (1 [+5782, 1524, 4394]), defeated completely (1 [+5782, 1524]), devastated (1 [+5782, 1524, 4394]), disaster (1), disasters (1), flogged (1 [+5782]), force (1), ground (1), inflicted (1), injury (1), slaughtered (1), sores (1), struck down (1 [+5782]), NDT (2)

H4805 מִכְוָה ***mikwâ***, n.f. [5] [√ 3917]. burn (on the skin), scar; in context this is not an intentional mark or tattoo:– burn (4), burn (1 [+836])

H4806 מָכוֹן ***mākôn***, n.m. [17] [√ 3922]. (established) place, site; foundation (of earth or throne):– place (10), foundation (2), dwelling place (1), foundations (1), site (1), NDT (2)

H4807 מְכוֹנָה ***mᵉkônâ***, n.f. [23] [√ 3922]. movable stand; (established) place, foundation:– movable stands (7), stand (6), stands (6), foundation (1), place (1), NDT (2)

H4808 מְכוּרָה ***mᵉkûrâ***, n.f. [3] [√ 4125]. ancestry, origin, parentage:– ancestry (3)

H4809 מָכִי ***mākî***, n.pr.m. [1] Maki, "[perhaps] *reduced* or *bought*":– Maki (1)

H4810 מָכִיר ***mākîr***, n.pr.m. [22] [→ 4811]. Makir, Makirite, "*bought*":– Makir (20), Makirites (1), Makir's (1)

H4811 מָכִירִי ***mākîrî***, a.g. [1] [√ 4810]. Makirite, "*of Makir*":– Makirite (1)

H4812 מָכַךְ ***mākak***, v. [3] [cf. 4575]. [Q] to sink, go down, waste away; [N] to sag, be sunk down; [Ho] to be brought low:– are brought low (1), sag (1), wasted away (1)

H4813 מִכְלָא ***miklāʼ***, n.[m.] [3] [√ 3973]. pen, fold (for sheep or goats):– pens (2), pen (1)

H4814 מִכְלוֹל ***miklôl***, n.m. [2] [√ 4005]. fullness, completeness, perfection:– full (1), fully (1)

H4815 מַכְלוּל ***maklûl***, n.m. [1] [√ 4005]. beautiful garment, finery, with a focus the excellence of the item:– beautiful garments (1)

H4816 מִכְלוֹת ***miklôt***, n.[f.] [1] [√ 3983]. solid (gold), purest (gold):– solid (1)

H4817 מִכְלָל ***miklāl***, n.m. [1] [√ 4005]. perfection:– perfect (1)

H4818 מַכֹּלֶת ***makkōlet***, n.f. [1] [√ 430]. food:– food (1)

H4819 מִכְמָן ***mikmān***, n.[m.] [1] (hidden) treasure:– treasures (1)

H4820 מִכְמָס ***mikmās***, n.pr.loc. [2] [→ 4825; cf. 4022]. Micmash, "[perhaps] *hidden place*":– Mikmash (2)

H4821 מִכְמָר ***mikmār***, n.[m.] [2] [→ 4822, 4823, 4824]. net, snare (for capture of game):– net (1), nets (1)

H4822 מַכְמֹר ***makmōr***, n.[m.] Not used in NIVEBC [√ 4821]. net, snare

H4823 מִכְמֶרֶת ***mikmeret***, n.f. [3] [→ 4824; cf. 4821]. fishing net, dragnet (for fish):– dragnet (2), nets (1)

H4824 מִכְמֹרֶת ***mikmōret***, n.f. Not used in NIVEBC [√ 4823; cf. 4821]. fishing net, dragnet (for fish)

H4825 מִכְמָשׂ ***mikmāś***, n.pr.loc. [9] [√ 4820; cf. 4022]. Micmash, "[perhaps] *hidden place*":– Mikmash (9)

H4826 מִכְמְתָת ***mikmᵉtāt***, n.pr.loc. [2] Micmethath:– Mikmethath (2)

H4827 מַכְנַדְבַי ***maknadbay***, n.pr.m. [1] Macnadebai, "[poss.] *possession of Nebo*":– Maknadebai (1)

H4828 מְכֹנָה ***mᵉkōnâ***, n.pr.loc. [1] [√ 3922]. Meconah, "*foundation*":– Mekonah (1)

H4829 מִכְנָס ***miknās***, n.m. [5] [√ 4043]. undergarment, some kind of shorts or trousers:– undergarments (4), undergarments (1 [+965])

H4830 מֶכֶס ***mekes***, n.m. [6] [√ 4082]. tribute, cultic dues or taxes:– tribute (6)

H4831 מִכְסָה ***miksâ***, n.f. [2] [√ 4082]. number (of persons); amount, valuation (of a thing):– number (1), value (1 [+6886])

H4832 מִכְסֶה ***mikseh***, n.[m.] [16] [√ 4059]. covering:– covering (12), cover (3 [+4059]), coverings (1)

H4833 מְכַסֶּה ***mᵉkasseh***, n.m. [4] [√ 4059]. covering (of a body or building); layer of fat (on the kidneys):– awnings (1), clothes (1), cover (1), layer of fat (1)

H4834 מַכְפֵּלָה ***makpēlâ***, n.pr.loc. [6] [√ 4100]. Machpelah, "*double [cave]*":– Machpelah (6)

H4835 מָכַר ***mākar***, v. [80] [→ 4836, 4837?, 4928, 4929]. [Q] to sell; [N] to be sold; [Ht] to sell oneself:– sold (21), sell (17), selling (7), be sold (5), sells (5), sold themselves (4), sell themselves (3), seller (3), been sold (2), were sold (2), be sold back (1), deliver (1), enslaved (1), must be sold (1 [+4929]), must sell (1 [+928, 2021, 4084, 4835]), must sell (1 [+4835, 928, 2021, 4084]), offer yourselves for sale (1), sell land (1 [+4928]), sellers (1), sold himself (1), sold yourself (1)

H4836 מֶכֶר ***meker***, n.m. [3] [√ 4835]. worth, value; merchandise:– merchandise (1), pay (1 [+5989]), worth (1)

H4837 מַכָּר ***makkār***, n.m. [2] [√ 4835?]. treasurer:– treasurers (2)

H4838 מִכְרֶה ***mikreh***, n.m. [1] [√ 4125]. (salt) pit:– pits (1)

H4839 מְכֵרָה ***mᵉkērâ***, n.[f.] [1] [cf. 3928]. sword, weapon:– swords (1)

H4840 מִכְרִי ***mikrî***, n.pr.m. [1] Micri:– Mikri (1)

H4841 מְכֵרָתִי ***mᵉkērātî***, a.g. [1] Mekerathite:– Mekerathite (1)

H4842 מִכְשׁוֹל ***mikšôl***, n.m. [14] [√ 4173]. stumbling block, obstacle; (occasion of) stumbling, downfall:– stumbling block (4), obstacles (2), downfall (1), fallen (1), made fall (1 [+2118, 4200]), make stumble (1), makes fall (1), staggering burden (1 [+7050, 2256]), stumble (1), stumbling blocks (1)

H4843 מַכְשֵׁלָה ***makšēlâ***, n.f. [2] [√ 4173]. heap of ruins, heap of rubble:– heap of ruins (1), idols that cause to stumble (1)

H4844 מִכְתָּב ***miktāb***, n.m. [9] [√ 4180]. writing, inscription, letter:– writing (5), inscription (1 [+7334]), letter (1), written (1), NDT (1)

H4845 מְכִתָּה ***mᵉkittâ***, n.f. [1] [√ 4198]. pieces, crushed fragments:– pieces (1)

H4846 מִכְתָּם ***miktām***, n.[m.] [6] [√ 4188?]. miktam (t.t. in the Psalms, of uncertain meaning):– miktam (6)

H4847 מַכְתֵּשׁ ***maktēš***, n.m. [3] [√ 4197]. hollow place; mortar; market district (at a hollow place in the city?):– hollow place (1), market district (1), mortar (1)

H4848 [1]מָלֵא ***mālēʼ[1]***, v. [249] [→ 3550, 3551, 4849, 4850, 4851, 4852, 4853, 4854, 4859, 4864; cf. 4862; 10416; *also used with compound proper names*]. [Q] to fill up, be full; [Qp] to be ordained, fulfilled; [N] to be filled, become filled up; [P] to fill up, satisfy; ordain, consecrate; [Pu] to be set; [Ht] to unite together; "to fill the hand" means to ordain or consecrate for service to God:– filled (46), fill (39), full (32), be filled (10), over (8), wholeheartedly (7), completed (5), covered (5), fulfilled (5), was filled (4), filling (3), fills (3), ordained (3 [+906, 3338]), satisfy (3), set (3), installed (2 [+906, 3338]), laden with (2), ordain (2 [+3338]), ordination (2 [+906, 3338]), passed (2), add word to (1), aloud (1), are filled (1), at flood stage (1 [+6584, 3972, 1536]), bathed in (1), bear (1), before elapsed (1 [+4202]), came (1), come (1), come to an end (1), consecrate himself (1 [+3338]), consecrate themselves (1 [+3338, 2257]), consecrated (1 [+906, 3338]), counted out the full number (1), cover (1), cover (1 [+7156]), crowded (1), dared (1 [+4213]), dedicate (1 [+3338]), dedicated (1 [+3338]), did completely (1), done (1 [+928, 3338]), drenched (1), drew (1 [+3338, 928]), enraged (1 [+2779]), enriched (1), filled with (1), finish (1), finished (1), fulfilling (1), fulfillment (1), give full (1), given (1), gorge (1), grant (1), have fill (1), heaping up (1), is satisfied (1), last (1), live out (1), make succeed (1), making full (1), midst (1), mount (1 [+4853]), mounted (1), numbered (1), ordain (1 [+906, 3338]), ordained (1 [+3338]), overflowing (1), prosper (1), provide (1), racked with (1), set apart (1 [+3338]), take up (1), taking full (1), took a handful (1 [+4090]), unite (1), uses (1), violent (1 [+2805]), well nourished (1 [+2692]), were filled (1), NDT (2)

H4849 [2]מָלֵא ***mālēʼ[2]***, a. [62] [√ 4848]. filled, full; "full of days" means "very old":– filled (32), full (23), abundance (1), loaded (1), loud (1), mother's[S] (1), strewn with (1), strong (1), weighed down (1)

H4850 מְלֹא ***mᵉlōʼ***, n.m. [38] [√ 4848]. what fills, what makes something full; fullness, everything:– everything in (8), all that is in (5), full (3), all (2), handful (2 [+4090]), handfuls (2 [+2908]), take a handful (2 [+7858, 7859]), all that in (1), all who live in (1), all who were in (1), as many as could hold (1), bowlful (1 [+6210]), cover (1), fullness (1), group (1), length (1), take (1), third[S] (1), two handfuls (1 [+2908]), whole band (1), NDT (1)

H4851 מִלֹּא ***millōʼ***, n.pr.loc. Not used in NIVEBC [√ 4864; cf. 4848]. Millo

H4852 מְלֵאָה ***mᵉlēʼâ***, n.f. [3] [√ 4848]. full yield (of crops):– crops (1), granaries (1), juice (1)

H4853 מִלֻּאָה ***milluʼâ***, n.f. [3] [√ 4848]. mounting (of jewels), setting (of jewels):– mount (1 [+2118]), mount (1 [+4848]), settings (1)

H4854 מִלֻּאִים ***milluʼîm***, n.m. [15] [√ 4848]. ordination, consecration (of a priest); mounting, setting (of gem stones):– ordination (7), mounted (3), ordination offering (2), ordination offerings (1), ordination ram (1), settings (1)

H4855 מַלְאָךְ ***malʼāk***, n.m. [213] [→ 4856, 4857, 4858?; 10417]. messenger, a human representative; angel, a supernatural representative of God, sometimes delivering messages, sometimes protecting God's people; the "angel of the LORD" sometimes shares divine characteristics and is sometimes thought to be an manifestation of God himself, or of the preincarnate Christ:– angel (98), messengers (59), messenger (24), angels (9), men (8), envoys (7), delegation (1), he[S] (1 [+3378]), he[S] (1 [+2021]), men[S] (1), spies (1), the angel (1 [+3378]), they[S] (1 [+2021]), NDT (1)

H4856 מְלָאכָה ***mᵉlāʼkâ***, n.f. [167] [√ 4855]. work, deed, duty, craft, service; thing, something:– work (86), regular work (12 [+6275]), workers (10), anything (3), duties (3), task (3), administrators (2 [+6913]), project (2), property (2), service (2), skills (2), use (2 [+6913]), anything useful (1), assist (1), been used (1 [+6913]), building (1), business (1), crafts (1), deeds (1), details (1), done (1), everything (1 [+3972, 2021]), flocks and herds (1), kinds (1), labored (1), made (1), matter (1), merchants (1 [+6913]), part (1), performed (1), projects (1), purpose (1), responsible (1), responsible (1 [+6275]), settings (1 [+9513]), skilled workers (1 [+6913]), something useful (1), supplies (1), these men[S] (1 [+6913, 2021]), what[S] (1), what[S] (1 [+2021]), work (1 [+6913]), worked (1), workers (1 [+6913, 8441]), workers (1 [+6913, 928, 2021]), working (1 [+6913]), NDT (4)

H4857 מַלְאֲכוּת ***malʼăkût***, n.f. [1] [√ 4855]. message (from a commissioned messenger):– message (1)

H4858 מַלְאָכִי ***malʼākî***, n.pr.m. [1] [√ 4855?]. Malachi, "*my messenger* or *messenger of Yahweh*":– Malachi (1)

H4859 מִלֵּאת ***millēʼt***, n.f. [1] [√ 4848]. setting, mounting, the solid base in which a gem is set:– mounted like jewels (1 [+3782, 6584])

H4860 מַלְבּוּשׁ ***malbûš***, n.m. [8] [√ 4252]. clothing, robe, attire, garment:– robes (4), clothes (3), clothing (1)

H4861 מַלְבֵּן ***malbēn***, n.[m.] [3] [√ 4246; cf. 4905]. brickwork, brick pavement; (the act of) brickmaking:– brick pavement (1), brickmaking (1), brickwork (1)

H4862 מָלָה ***mālâ***, v. Not used in NIVEBC [cf. 4848]. [P] to fill; [N] be filled

H4863 מִלָּה ***millâ***, n.f. [38] [√ 4910; 10418]. word, what is said; the act of speaking, speech:– words (23), speaking (2), speeches (2), what say (2), word (2), anything to say (1), byword (1), make fine speeches (1 [+2488, 928]), reply (1 [+8740]), said (1), say (1), what[S] (1)

H4864 מִלּוֹא ***millôʼ***, n.pr.loc. [6] [→ 4851; cf. 4848]. supporting terrace (cf. Beth Millo):– terraces (6)

H4865 מַלּוּחַ ***mallûaḥ***, n.[m.] [1] [√ 4875]. salt herb (collected by the destitute and banished):– salt herbs (1)

H4866 מַלּוּךְ ***mallûk***, n.pr.m. [6] [√ 4889; cf. 4887]. Malluch, "*counselor; king*":– Malluk (6)

H4867 מְלוּכָה ***mᵉlûkâ***, n.f. [24] [√ 4887]. kingship, rulership, royalty:– kingdom (10), royal (7), kingship (3), dominion (1), king (1), queen (1), rule (1)

H4868 מַלּוּכִי ***mallûkî***, n.pr.m. [1] [cf. 4883]. Malluch, "*counselor; king*":– Malluk's (1)

H4869 מָלוֹן ***mālôn***, n.m. [8] [√ 4328]. place of overnight lodging, place where one spends the night:– lodging place (2), camp (1), camp overnight (1), parts (1), place (1), place where they stopped for the night (1), place where we stopped for the night (1)

H4870 מְלוּנָה ***mᵉlûnâ***, n.f. [2] [√ 4328]. hut, structure (of a watchman in the field):– hut (2)

H4871 מַלּוֹתִי ***mallôtî***, n.pr.m. [2] [√ 4910]. Mallothi, "*my expression*":– Mallothi (2)

H4872 [1]מָלַח ***mālaḥ[1]***, v. [1] [→ 4874]. [N] to vanish, be dispersed:– vanish (1)

H4873 [2]מָלַח ***mālaḥ[2]***, v.den. [4] [√ 4875]. [Q] to season with salt; [Pu] to be salted; [Ho] to be rubbed with salt:– were rubbed with salt (2 [+4873]), be salted (1), season (1)

H4874 [1]מֶלַח ***melaḥ[1]***, n.[m.] [2] [√ 4872]. worn-out clothes, rags:– clothes (2)

H4875 [2]מֶלַח ***melaḥ[2]***, n.m. [29] [→ 4865, 4873, 4876, 4877, 6558, 9427; 10419, 10420]. salt, a staple of the ancient world; positively: for flavoring, as a nutrient, as a food preservative; as a medicine; for curing animal skins; negatively: used on fields to prevent or inhibit productive plant growth:– salt (20), dead[S] (9)

H4876 מַלָּח ***mallāḥ***, n.m. [4] [√ 4875]. sailor, mariner:– mariners (2), sailors (2)

H4877 מְלֵחָה ***mᵉlēḥâ***, n.f. [3] [√ 4875]. salt flat, salt wastelands, barren country:– salt (1), salt flats (1), salt waste (1)

H4878 מִלְחָמָה ***milḥāmâ***, n.f. [319] [√ 4309]. fighting, battle (a particular engagement), war (as an ongoing event):– battle (132), war (76), fight (16), fighting (14), soldiers (12 [+408]), warrior (6 [+408]), wars (6), army (4 [+408]), army (4 [+6639]), battles (4), warfare (3), at war with (2 [+408]), battle formation (2), battle lines (2), military age (2), armed (1), at war (1), at war (1 [+6913]), attack (1), attacked (1), battle (1 [+7372]), counterattack (1 [+2200, 928, 2021]), experienced fighter (1 [+408]), experienced fighting men (1 [+408, 1475, 2657]), fight (1 [+3655, 4200, 2021]), fit for battle (1 [+408]), force (1 [+6639]), great soldiers (1 [+408]), men ready for battle (1 [+1522, 7372]), military (1), ready for battle (1 [+7372, 928, 2021]), ready for battle (1 [+408, 7372, 4200, 2021]), soldiers (1 [+9530]), soldiers (1 [+1505, 408]), struggle (1), that[s] (1), time of war (1), wage war (1 [+1741, 4200, 2021]), war cry (1), weapon (1 [+3998]), weapon (1 [+3998, 7372]), weapons (1 [+3998]), well-trained (1 [+6913]), went to war (1 [+6913]), NDT (5)

H4879 מֶלֶט **melet**, n.[m.] [1] [√ 4881?]. clay flooring:– clay (1)

H4880 [1]מלט **mālaṭ[1]**, v. [95] [→ 4882; cf. 7117]. [N] to deliver oneself, escape, flee; [P] to save, deliver, rescue; [H] to rescue; to deliver (a child); [Ht] to shoot out (of sparks); to escape:– escaped (20), escape (15), save (6), flee (5), run (4), be delivered (3), rescue (3), rescued (3), saved (3), deliver (2), delivers (2), escape (2 [+4880]), go free (2), got away (2), let get away (2), save (2 [+4880]), are kept safe (1), be rescued (1), be saved (1), escape (1 [+5883]), escape (1 [+7127]), escape (1 [+4946, 3338]), escaping (1), get away (1), get away with (1), lay eggs (1), made escape (1), made good escape (1 [+5674, 2256]), release (1), retrieved (1), shoot out (1), slip out (1), slipped away (1), spared (1), were saved (1)

H4881 [2]מלט **mālaṭ[2]**, v. Not used in NIVEBC [→ 4879?]. [Ht] to be bald

H4882 מְלַטְיָה **m[e]laṭyâ**, n.pr.m. [1] [√ 4880 + 3378]. Melatiah, "*Yahweh sets free*":– Melatiah (1)

H4883 מְלִיכוּ **m[e]lîkû**, n.pr.m. Not used in NIVEBC [cf. 4868]. Melichu, see 4868

H4884 מְלִילָה **m[e]lîlâ**, n.f. [1] [√ 4908]. (rubbed) kernels (of grain):– kernels (1)

H4885 מֵלִיץ **mēlîṣ**, n.[m.] *or* v.ptcp. [5] [√ 4329]. intercessor, mediator (in various capacities); this can refer both to human and heavenly beings:– envoys (1), intercessor (1), interpreter (1), messenger (1), sent to teach (1)

H4886 מְלִיצָה **m[e]lîṣâ**, n.[f.] [2] [√ 4329]. allusive saying, parable; ridicule:– parables (1), ridicule (1)

H4887 [1]מלך **mālak[1]**, v.den. [346] [→ 3552?, 4867 4888, 4889, 4930, 4931]. [Q] to reign as king; [H] to make one a king, have a coronation; [Ho] be made a king:– king (152), reigned (70), reign (37), made king (24), reigns (10), ruled (9), make king (7), rule (4), proclaimed king (3), intend to reign (2 [+4887]), set up king (2 [+4889]), surely be king (2 [+4887]), acknowledged as king (1), appoint as king (1), came to power (1), crown (1), extend (1), give king (1 [+4889]), king (1 [+4889]), kingship (1), made king (1 [+4889]), made queen (1), make king (1 [+4889]), making king (1), put on throne (1), queen (1), reigned (1 [+4889]), ruled over (1), ruling (1), set a king (1 [+4889]), set up kings (1), took control (1), was made ruler (1), NDT (3)

H4888 [2]מלך **mālak[2]**, v. [1] [√ 4887; 10422]. [N] to ponder, consider carefully within oneself:– pondered (1)

H4889 [1]מֶלֶךְ **melek[1]**, n.m. [2522] [→ 4866, 4890, 4891, 4893, 4894, 4895, 4904, 4906; cf. 4887; 10421; *also used with compound proper names*]. king, royal ruler, human and divine; "the great king" is the more prominent of the leaders in a convenant agreement and is used of God (Ps 48:2); the "king of kings" is the supreme sovereign and is not used of God in the OT:– king (1829), kings (275), king's (173), royal (65), him[s] (29 [+2021]), he[s] (26 [+2021]), palace (15 [+1074]), your Majesty (7 [+2021]), his[s] (6 [+2021]), his own[s] (3 [+2021]), king's (3 [+928]), king's (3 [+4200]), princes (3 [+1201]), reign (3), Amaziah[s] (2 [+2021]), palace grounds (2 [+1074]), ruled (2), set up king (2 [+4887]), Shalmaneser[s] (1 [+855]), give king (1 [+4887]), he[s] (1 [+951]), him[s] (1 [+951]), him[s] (1 [+3296, 4046]), his[s] (1 [+951]), his[s] (1 [+4200, 5213]), his[s] (1 [+928, 2021]), it[s] (1 [+9133, 2021]), king (1 [+4887]), kingdom (1), kingdoms (1), made king (1 [+4887]), make king (1 [+4887]), prince (1 [+1201]), princess (1 [+1426]), reigned (1 [+4887]), royal (1 [+4200]), rule over (1), ruled (1 [+2118]), rulers (1), set a king (1 [+4887]), you[s] (1 [+2021]), your[s] (1 [+2021]), NDT (50)

H4890 [2]מֶלֶךְ **melek[2]**, n.pr.m. [2] [√ 4889; cf. 4887]. Melech, "*king*":– Melek (2)

H4891 מֹלֶךְ **mōlek**, n.pr.[m.] [9] [√ 4889]. Molech (pagan god), "*(shameful) king*":– Molek (9)

H4892 מַלְכֹּדֶת **malkōdet**, n.f. [1] [√ 4334]. trap, snare:– trap (1)

H4893 מַלְכָּה **malkâ**, n.f. [35] [√ 4889; cf. 4887; 10423]. queen (outside Israel), a female ruler of a kingdom; wife of a king, royalty but without much actual governmental power:– queen (30), queens (2), queen's (2), she[s] (1 [+2021])

H4894 מִלְכָּה **milkâ**, n.pr.f. [11] [√ 4889; cf. 4887]. Milcah, "*queen*":– Milkah (11)

H4895 מַלְכוּת **malkût**, n.f. [91] [√ 4889; cf. 4887; 10424]. kingdom, empire, realm; reign, royal power, position as a king:– kingdom (36), reign (19), royal (16), realm (5), empire (2), kingdoms (2), royal position (2), became king (1), king (1), kingship (1), palace (1 [+1074]), position as king (1), royalty (1), rule (1), NDT (2)

H4896 מַלְכִּיאֵל **malkî'ēl**, n.pr.m. [3] [→ 4897; cf. 4889 + 446]. Malkiel, "*God [El] is [my] king*":– Malkiel (3)

H4897 מַלְכִּיאֵלִי **malkî'ēlî**, a.g. [1] [√ 4896; cf. 4889 + 446]. Malkielite, "*of Malkiel*":– Malkielite (1)

H4898 מַלְכִּיָּה **malkiyyâ**, n.pr.m. [15] [√ 4889 + 3378]. Malkijah, "*Yahweh is [my] king*":– Malkijah (15)

H4899 מַלְכִּיָּהוּ **malkiyyāhû**, n.pr.m. [1] [√ 4889 + 3378]. Malkijah, "*Yahweh is [my] king*":– Malkijah (1)

H4900 מַלְכִּי־צֶדֶק **malkî-ṣedeq**, n.pr.m. [2] [√ 4889 + 7406]. Melchizedek, "*[my] king is Zedek [just]*":– Melchizedek (2)

H4901 מַלְכִּירָם **malkîrām**, n.pr.m. [1] [√ 4889 + 8123]. Malkiram, "*[my] king is exalted*":– Malkiram (1)

H4902 מַלְכִּי־שׁוּעַ **malkî-šûa'**, n.pr.m. [5] [√ 4889 + 8775]. Malki-Shua, "*[my] king saves*":– Malki-Shua (5)

H4903 מַלְכָּם **malkām**, n.pr.m. [4] [√ 4889 + 4392]. Malcam, Molech, "*their king* or *[servant of] Malk*":– Molek (3), Malkam (1)

H4904 מִלְכֹּם **milkōm**, n.pr.[m.] [3] [√ 4889]. Milcom, Molech, "*their king* or *[servant of] Malk*":– Molek (3)

H4905 מַלְכֵּן **malkēn**, n.[m.] Not used in NIVEBC [cf. 4861]. see 4861

H4906 מְלֶכֶת **m[e]leket**, n.f. [5] [√ 4889]. Queen (of Heaven):– Queen (5)

H4907 מֹלֶכֶת **mōleket**, n.pr.f. Not used in NIVEBC [√ 2143]. Moleketh, see 2168

H4908 [1]מלל **mālal[1]**, v. [6] [→ 4884; cf. 581, 582]. [Q] to wither away; [Pol] to wither; [Htpol] be blunted (of arrows):– wither (3), dry (1), fall short (1), wither away (1)

H4909 [2]מלל **mālal[2]**, v. [2] [cf. 4576]. [Q] to circumcise; [N] to be cut off:– are cut off (1), circumcise (1)

H4910 [3]מלל **mālal[3]**, v. [4] [→ 4863, 4871; cf. 4911; 10425]. [P] to say, speak, proclaim:– proclaim (1), said (1), say (1), speak (1)

H4911 [4]מלל **mālal[4]**, v. [1] [cf. 4910]. [Q] to signal by rubbing or scraping:– signals (1)

H4912 מִלֲלַי **mil[a]lay**, n.pr.m. [1] Milalai:– Milalai (1)

H4913 מַלְמָד **malmād**, n.[m.] [1] [√ 4340]. oxgoad, cattle prod, a (metal-tipped) poker used to guide animals, which could also be used as a weapon:– oxgoad (1 [+1330])

H4914 מלץ **mālaṣ**, v. [1] [→ 6666]. [N] to be smooth, pleasant, palatable, sweet:– sweet (1)

H4915 מֶלְצַר **melṣar**, n.m. [2] [√ 5915]. guard, guardian, official:– guard (2)

H4916 מלק **mālaq**, v. [2] [Q] to wring off, pinch off (the head of a bird):– wring (1), wring off (1)

H4917 מַלְקוֹחַ **malqôaḥ**, n.m. [7] [√ 4374]. spoils of war, plunder, war-booty:– spoils (4), plunder (2), all[s] (1)

H4918 מַלְקוֹחַיִם **malqôḥayim**, n.[m.] [1] [√ 4374?]. roof of the mouth, palate:– roof of mouth (1)

H4919 מַלְקוֹשׁ **malqôš**, n.m. [8] [√ 4380]. spring rains, latter rains of March-April:– spring rains (4), rain in spring (1), spring (1), spring rain (1), springtime (1 [+6961])

H4920 מֶלְקָחַיִם **melqāḥayim**, n.[m.]du. [6] [√ 4374]. (pair of) wick trimmers; (pair of) tongs:– tongs (3), wick trimmers (3)

H4921 מֶלְתָּחָה **meltāḥâ**, n.f. [1] wardrobe:– wardrobe (1)

H4922 מַלְתָּעוֹת **maltā'ôt**, n.f.pl. [1] [→ 5506]. fangs, teeth; some sources: jawbone:– fangs (1)

H4923 מַמְּגֻרָה **mamm[e]gûrâ**, n.f.pl. [1] [√ 4473]. granary, grain-pit:– granaries (1)

H4924 מֵמַד **mēmād**, n.[m.] [1] [√ 4499]. dimensions, measurement:– dimensions (1)

H4925 מְמוּכָן **m[e]mûkān**, n.pr.m. [3] [→ 4584]. Memucan:– Memukan (3)

H4926 מָמוֹת **māmôt**, n.[m.] [2] [√ 4637]. death:– deadly (1), death (1)

H4927 מַמְזֵר **mamzēr**, n.m. [2] one born of a forbidden marriage; foreigner; this can have the associative meaning of being an unprivileged or despised class:– mongrel people (1), one born of a forbidden marriage (1)

H4928 מִמְכָּר **mimkār**, n.m. [10] [√ 4835]. what is sold, goods, merchandise:– sold (2), what sold (2), goods (1), money from sale (1), property sold (1), release (1), sale (1), sell land (1 [+4835])

H4929 מִמְכֶּרֶת **mimkeret**, n.f. [1] [√ 4835]. selling, sale:– must be sold (1 [+4835])

H4930 מַמְלָכָה **mamlākâ**, n.f. [117] [√ 4887]. kingdom, royal dominion, reign:– kingdom (58), kingdoms (45), royal (7), kings (2), kingship (2), reign (2), royal power (1)

H4931 מַמְלָכוּת **mamlākût**, n.f. [9] [√ 4887]. kingdom, realm, royal dominion:– kingdom (4), realm (3), reign (1), royal (1)

H4932 מִמְסָךְ **mimsāk**, n.m. [2] [√ 5007]. bowl of mixed wine, with a focus on the wine:– bowls of mixed wine (2)

H4933 מֶמֶר **memer**, n.[m.] [1] [√ 5352]. bitterness, annoyance:– bitterness (1)

H4934 [1]מַמְרֵא **mamrē'[1]**, n.pr.loc. [8] [√ 5258?]. Mamre, "*strength*":– Mamre (8)

H4935 [2]מַמְרֵא **mamrē'[2]**, n.pr.m. [2] [√ 5258?]. Mamre, "*strength*":– Mamre (2)

H4936 מַמְּרֹרִים **mamm[e]rōrîm**, n.m.[pl.] [1] [√ 5352]. misery, bitterness:– misery (1)

H4937 מִמְשַׁח **mimšaḥ**, n.[m.] [1] [√ 5417]. anointing:– anointed (1)

H4938 מִמְשָׁל **mimšāl**, n.[m.] [3] [√ 5440]. leader, ruler; power, dominion, sovereign authority:– power (2), leaders (1)

H4939 מֶמְשָׁלָה **memšālâ**, n.f. [17] [√ 5440]. dominion, power to govern, authority to rule:– dominion (4), govern (4), kingdom (3), ruled (2), authority (1), forces (1), rule (1), ruled (1 [+3338])

H4940 מִמְשָׁק **mimšāq**, n.[m.] [1] [→ 5479]. place, ground (overgrown with weeds):– place (1)

H4941 מַמְתַקִּים **mamtaqqîm**, n.m.[pl.] [2] [√ 5517]. sweetness, sweet things:– sweet (1), sweetness (1)

H4942 [1]מָן **mān[1]**, n.m. [13] [cf. 4537]. manna, a food given by God to the generation of the Exodus: "the grain of heaven":– manna (13)

H4943 [2]מָן **mān[2]**, inter. [1] [√ 4537; 10426]. what?:– What (1)

H4944 [1]מֵן **mēn[1]**, n.[m.] [2] (music of) stringed instruments:– music of strings (1), strings (1)

H4945 [2]מֵן **mēn[2]**, n.[m.] [1] [√ 4948]. share, portion:– share (1)

H4946 מִן **min**, pp. [7516] [→ 4403, 4406, 4424, 4425, 4514, 4644, 4974, 5088, 5136, 5456; 10427]. marker of a source or extension from a source: from, out of, of; temporary: since, after; logically: because of; of degree: more than:– from (2538), of (570), than (179), out of (176), from (155 [+6584]), some (122), in (116), on (102), at (93), from (93 [+907]), more than (92), before (82 [+7156]), because of (55 [+7156]), too (53), outside (49 [+2575]), with (48), by (46), from (45 [+7156]), because of (43), any (40), for (40), to (37), from (32 [+3338]), one (30), from (26 [+6640]), among (25), before (23 [+4200, 7156]), above (19 [+5087]), since (19), because (17), in addition to (17 [+4200, 963]), of (17 [+7156]), below (16 [+9393]), from (16 [+7931]), not (16), on every side (16 [+6017]), from (15 [+9348]), through (14), above (13 [+6584]), as (13), no (13), out of (13 [+9348]), from (12 [+339]), without (12), above (11), after (11), away from (11), from (11 [+4200, 7156]), from among (11), part (11), rather than (11), against (10), away from (10 [+6584]), on (10 [+6584]), on each side (10 [+4946, 7024, 2256, 7024]), when (10), behind (9 [+339]), of one piece with (9), on each side (9 [+7024, 2256, 4946, 7024]), so (9), without (9 [+401]), because (8 [+7156]), besides (8 [+4200, 963]), by (8 [+7156]), off (8 [+6584]), whether (8), around (7 [+6017]), under (7 [+9393]), better than (6), from (6 [+5584]), north (6 [+7600]), of (6 [+907]), on both sides[s] (6 [+2296, 2256, 4946, 2296]), on both sides[s] (6 [+4946, 2296, 2256, 2296]), over (6), before (5), far away (5 [+8158]), greater than (5), inside (5 [+1074]), left (5 [+2143]), long ago (5 [+255]), off (5), south (5 [+5582]), toward (5), whenever (5 [+1896]), where (5 [+402]), Israelite (4 [+408, 1074, 3776]), above (4 [+4200, 5087, 2025]), against (4 [+9393, 3338]), among (4 [+7931]), away (4), behind (4 [+1074]), beneath (4 [+9393]), beyond (4), both (4), later (4 [+7891]), leave (4), left (4 [+2143, 907]), malice aforethought (4 [+8533, 9453, 8997]), most (4), of (4 [+6640]), of (4 [+9348]), on either side (4 [+7024, 2256, 4946, 7024]), on either side (4 [+4946, 7024, 2256, 7024]), out (4 [+2575]), out of (4 [+6584]), some (4 [+3972]), some of (4), that (4), through (4 [+907]), until (4), within (4), across (3 [+6298]), after (3 [+7891]), against (3 [+6584]), against (3 [+7156]), ancient (3 [+6409]), apart from (3 [+1187]), at (3 [+7156]), back (3 [+9004]), behind (3 [+1237]), belong to (3), besides (3 [+1187]), between (3 [+1068]), between (3 [+2256, 6330]), cannot (3), dictated (3 [+7023]), doing (3 [+907]), east (3 [+7710]), either (3), escape (3 [+7156]), ever since (3), far from (3), from (3 [+1896]), higher than (3 [+6584]), hold accountable (3 [+1335, 3338]), into (3), leave (3 [+2143]), left (3 [+7756]), no (3 [+401]), northern (3 [+7600]), on[s] (3), out (3 [+9004]), so that (3), the Lord's (3 [+907, 3378]), under (3), Israelite (2 [+1201, 3776]), Israelite (2 [+408, 1201, 3776]), about (2), after (2 [+7895]), all around (2 [+6017]), along (2), as often as (2 [+1896]), as well as (2 [+4200, 963]), at either end[s] (2 [+2296, 2256, 4946, 2296]), at either end[s] (2 [+4946, 2296, 2256, 2296]), at set times (2 [+6961, 6330, 6961]), away (2 [+725]), away (2 [+907]), away from (2 [+339]), away from (2 [+907]), away from (2 [+6640]), away from (2 [+7156]), back (2 [+339]), before (2 [+6584]), beside (2 [+7396]), between (2), beyond (2 [+6298]), beyond (2 [+2256, 2134]), bottom (2 [+4200, 4752]), by (2 [+6640]), caused by (2), distant (2 [+5305]), distant (2 [+8158]), east (2 [+6298]), even more than (2), ever (2 [+6409]), ever since (2 [+255]), excluded from (2), extend from (2), extended from (2), extending from

(2), far and wide (2 [+2085, 2256, 2134]), flesh and blood (2 [+3655, 2743]), flesh and blood (2 [+3655, 5055]), from (2 [+9393]), from (2 [+6584, 7156]), from every side (2 [+6017]), from out of (2 [+9348]), future (2 [+8158]), got off (2 [+7563, 6584]), had the habit (2 [+9453, 8997]), head (2 [+8900, 2256, 5087, 2025]), in front of (2 [+4578]), in regard to (2), instead of (2), just above (2 [+5087]), last (2 [+8636, 3856]), leave (2 [+2143, 907]), leave alone (2 [+6073]), left (2 [+995]), left of (2), less than (2), like (2), long ago (2 [+6409]), long ago (2 [+7710]), long ago (2 [+8158]), long ago (2 [+4200, 8158]), made of (2), mine (2 [+5761]), never (2), no (2 [+4202, 3972]), north (2 [+8520]), not counting (2 [+4200, 963]), not including (2 [+4200, 963]), of (2 [+3338]), of (2 [+6584]), of (2 [+4200, 7156]), of one piece (2), on (2 [+4578]), only (2), other than (2 [+1187]), out (2), out from (2), over (2 [+5087]), over (2 [+6584]), over (2 [+4200, 5087, 2025]), promised (2 [+3655, 7023]), pursuing (2 [+339]), said (2 [+3655, 7023]), separated from (2 [+6584]), since (2 [+255]), so many (2 [+8044]), so not (2), so that not (2), some (2 [+7921]), some time later (2 [+3427]), south (2 [+3545]), speak (2 [+7023]), to (2 [+6640]), top (2 [+4200, 5087, 2025]), turning from (2), unaware of (2 [+6623]), where (2 [+9004]), without (2 [+1187]), your own flesh and blood (2 [+3655, 3870]), Asher's (1 [+888]), Benjamite (1 [+1228]), Benjamites (1 [+1228]), Benjamites (1 [+408, 1228]), Ephraimites (1 [+713]), God's (1 [+466]), Israelite (1 [+3776]), Israelites (1 [+3776]), Israelites (1 [+1201, 3776]), abandon (1 [+3718]), abandon (1 [+8332, 3338]), about to (1 [+6964, 7940]), above (1 [+5087, 6584]), above (1 [+5087, 4946, 4200, 6645]), above (1 [+4946, 5087, 4200, 6645]), according to (1), across from (1 [+6298]), across the way (1 [+5584]), after (1 [+339]), after (1 [+7921]), after (1 [+1896, 928]), against (1 [+3338]), ahead (1 [+4200, 7156]), all around (1 [+4200, 5087]), all kinds (1 [+3972]), all life (1 [+6388]), all sorts (1 [+7896]), all the way from (1), allots (1), along (1 [+6298]), along with (1 [+4200, 963]), alongside (1 [+6298]), aloof (1 [+5584]), already (1 [+255]), always (1 [+6388]), among (1 [+907]), among (1 [+1068]), annual (1 [+3427, 3427, 2025]), another[S] (1 [+2021, 2215, 2296]), any (1 [+6388]), any of (1 [+907]), anything (1 [+1821, 3972]), anything (1 [+1821, 3972, 2021, 1821]), anywhere in (1 [+1201]), area (1 [+2575]), around (1 [+6017, 1237]), around (1 [+2021, 2575]), as a result of (1), as long as (1), as long as live (1 [+3427]), as much as (1 [+8049]), avert (1 [+6296, 6584]), avoid (1), avoid (1 [+3782]), away (1 [+6584]), away (1 [+6640]), away (1 [+9004]), away from (1 [+5584]), be without (1 [+4162]), because (1 [+889]), because of (1 [+5584]), because of (1 [+9004]), because of (1 [+4200, 7156]), because of (1 [+3954, 7156]), before (1 [+3270]), before (1 [+6640]), before (1 [+9453, 8997]), before time (1 [+4200, 7156]), beforehand (1 [+4200, 7156]), behind (1 [+294]), belonging to (1), belongs to (1), beside (1 [+6584]), besides (1 [+963, 4200]), better (1 [+3202]), beyond (1 [+2134]), beyond (1 [+2134, 4200]), bodily (1 [+1414]), bordering each side[S] (1 [+2296, 2256, 4946, 2296]), bordering each side[S] (1 [+4946, 2296, 2256, 2296]), born (1 [+3655, 8167]), branch of (1 [+9348]), brief (1 [+7940]), broke camp (1 [+5825, 185]), broke off (1 [+8740]), brought about (1 [+2118]), by (1 [+907]), by (1 [+4200]), by (1 [+5584]), by (1 [+6298]), by (1 [+6584]), by (1 [+7023]), by (1 [+9348]), by myself (1 [+907, 3276]), by not (1), call to account (1 [+1335, 3338]), call to account (1 [+2011, 6640]), cause (1 [+2118]), causes (1), certain (1), choice lambs (1 [+7366, 4119]), citizens of[S] (1), come from (1), complete (1 [+2118, 7891]), completely (1 [+5883, 2256, 6330, 1414]), concerning (1), confront (1), confronting (1 [+7156]), consent (1), constant (1 [+5584]), covered (1 [+3877, 9048]), dead (1 [+4637, 4213]), deaf (1 [+9048]), defense against (1 [+7156]), deprived of (1), descendant (1 [+408, 2446]), descendants[S] (1 [+2743]), deserted (1 [+401, 3782]), deserted (1 [+401, 132]), deserted (1 [+6590, 339]), deserted (1 [+1172, 408]), deserted (1 [+1172, 3782]), determined (1 [+907]), dictate (1 [+7023]), dictated (1 [+7924, 7023]), dictation (1 [+7023]), different from (1), directed by (1), directly from (1), disappeared (1 [+2143, 6524]), do away with (1 [+6073, 9348]), do so[S] (1 [+8740, 2006]), down (1), down (1 [+8031]), down (1 [+2021, 9028]), downstream (1 [+5087, 4200, 2025]), driven from (1), due annually (1 [+1896, 9102, 928, 9102]), during (1), each year (1 [+3427, 3427, 2025]), each year (1 [+3427, 3427, 2025]), earthly (1 [+2021, 824]), eastward (1 [+7710]), eluded (1 [+6015, 7156]), empty (1 [+401, 3782]), entire (1 [+7895]), enveloped (1 [+6017]), escape (1 [+4880, 3338]), escape from (1 [+6584]), escaped from (1), even beyond (1 [+6584]), ever (1 [+3427]), ever since (1 [+4200]), ever since (1 [+3427]), every (1 [+7891]), every kind (1 [+2385, 448, 2385]), excelled (1), except (1 [+1187]), except for (1), extends to (1 [+4200]), face (1 [+7156]), faced (1), facing (1), facing (1 [+5584]), fail (1 [+6073]), failed (1 [+6980]), failed to keep (1 [+6073]), far and wide (1 [+6330, 4200, 8158]), far away (1 [+5305]), far away (1 [+6330, 4200, 8158]), far from (1 [+6640]), far from (1 [+5584]), few (1), follow (1 [+7756, 339]), for (1 [+907]), for (1 [+6584]), for (1 [+7156]), for fear of (1), for fear of (1 [+7156]), for lack of (1), for relief from (1 [+4200, 7156]), for sake (1 [+7156]), former (1 [+7710]), formerly (1 [+919, 8997]), forsaking (1 [+907]), found[S] (1 [+401]), free from (1), free of (1), from (1 [+255]), from (1 [+1068]), from (1 [+2296]), from (1 [+4090]), from (1 [+4200]), from (1 [+4578]), from (1 [+6017]), from (1 [+6298]), from (1 [+6524]), from (1 [+6640, 7156]), from among (1 [+9348]), from inside (1), from then on (1 [+339, 4027]), frontal (1 [+5584]), gaunt (1 [+9043]), give up (1 [+8740]), gone from (1 [+9348]), got off (1 [+3718, 6584]), had part in (1 [+2118]), handed (1 [+3338]), have no (1 [+6]), have no (1 [+6259, 6524]), have nowhere (1 [+6]), helpless (1 [+3946]), high above (1 [+4200, 5087, 2025]), higher (1 [+5087]), higher (1 [+6584]), his (1 [+5647]), his own (1 [+4213, 2257]), hold accountable (1 [+2011, 3338]), hold responsible (1 [+1335, 3338]), idea (1 [+4213]), in (1 [+6584]), in (1 [+7931]), in (1 [+9348]), in addition (1 [+4200, 963]), in addition to (1 [+963, 4200]), in deference to (1 [+7156]), in front of (1 [+7156]), in presence (1), in the course of time (1 [+339, 4027]), in the course of time (1 [+4200, 3427, 3427]), including (1), inquire of (1 [+2011, 907]), inside (1 [+7163]), inside (1 [+4200, 1074]), interior (1 [+1074, 2025]), is[S] (1 [+3655]), it[S] (1 [+1947, 2023]), its[S] (1 [+5288]), jointed (1 [+5087, 4200, 8079]), just (1 [+6964]), keep from (1), kept distance (1 [+3656, 5584]), kept from (1), lacking (1 [+1172]), larger share of (1), later (1), later (1 [+339, 4027]), later on (1 [+3427]), leave (1 [+6015]), leave (1 [+6590]), leave (1 [+9004]), leave (1 [+2143, 6640]), leave (1 [+2143, 6643]), leave (1 [+3718, 9348]), leave alone (1 [+2532]), leave alone (1 [+6641]), leaves (1 [+2143, 907]), leaving (1 [+5825]), leaving (1 [+6296]), left (1), left (1 [+339]), left (1 [+907]), left (1 [+5825]), left (1 [+6590]), left (1 [+2143, 6640]), left (1 [+7756, 9348]), lived (1), long (1 [+919]), long (1 [+6409]), long (1 [+8158]), long ages ago (1 [+6409]), long ago (1 [+3427, 7710]), loss (1), lost (1), lost (1 [+5877]), lost (1 [+5877, 907]), lower (1 [+9393]), made from (1), made up of (1), make room for (1 [+7156]), make spew out (1 [+3655, 7023]), meet (1 [+7156]), member (1), month (1 [+2544, 4200, 2544]), more (1), more numerous than (1), more than (1), more than (1 [+4200, 963]), move about (1 [+7756, 9393]), much more than (1), near (1), near (1 [+7396]), nearby (1 [+7940]), neither (1 [+401]), never (1 [+4202, 3427]), next to (1 [+725]), next to (1 [+4578]), next to (1 [+7396]), no (1 [+1172]), no longer (1 [+4374]), no longer be (1 [+6073]), no more (1), no other will be (1 [+401]), noblest (1 [+1475]), none (1 [+401]), none (1 [+4202, 3972]), nor (1 [+2256, 401]), north (1 [+7600, 2025]), northern (1 [+7600, 2025]), not (1 [+1187]), not (1 [+1194]), not harm (1 [+5927]), nothing (1 [+561, 3972]), nothing but (1), now (1 [+255]), obscure (1 [+6680, 9048]), of (1 [+1068]), of (1 [+7895]), of (1 [+8611, 4200]), of old (1 [+6409]), off (1 [+4578]), often (1 [+1896]), old (1 [+3427, 7710]), older (1 [+1524]), on (1 [+907]), on behalf of (1 [+907]), on both (1 [+2296, 2256, 4946, 2296]), on both (1 [+4946, 2296, 2256, 2296]), on both sides[S] (1 [+2296, 2256, 2296]), on each side (1 [+7024, 4946, 2256, 7024]), on each side (1 [+2021, 6298, 4946, 2296, 4946, 2021, 6298, 4946, 2296]), on each side (1 [+4946, 2021, 6298, 2296, 4946, 2021, 6298, 4946, 2296]), on each side (1 [+4946, 2021, 6298, 4946, 2296, 2021, 6298, 4946, 2296]), on each side (1 [+4946, 2021, 6298, 4946, 2296, 4946, 2021, 6298, 2296]), on each side[S] (1 [+2296, 2256, 4946, 2296]), on each side[S] (1 [+4946, 2296, 2256, 2296]), on high (1 [+5087]), on high (1 [+5294]), on reaching (1), on terms (1 [+6640]), on the basis of (1), on the other side of (1 [+6298, 2256, 2134]), on this side of (1 [+6298]), once (1), once a year (1 [+7891, 3427, 4200, 2021, 3427]), one of (1), opposing (1), opposite (1 [+5584]), or (1), other than (1 [+4200, 963]), others[S] (1 [+2157]), out (1 [+7156]), out of (1 [+907]), out of (1 [+1068]), out of (1 [+5584]), out of (1 [+7156]), out of (1 [+7931]), out of way (1 [+4200, 7156]), outer (1 [+4200, 5087, 2025]), outnumber (1 [+8045]), outnumber (1 [+8049]), outside (1 [+1946]), outside (1 [+2134]), outside (1 [+9393]), outside (1 [+2575, 2025]), outside (1 [+2575, 2025]), outweigh (1 [+3877]), outweighs (1 [+3701]), over (1 [+6584, 4200]), over (1 [+5087, 4200, 2025]), pad (1 [+9393]), past (1 [+907]), past (1 [+6584]), peels (1 [+6584]), people's (1 [+1201, 132]), permission (1), poured out (1 [+9161]), presence (1 [+6584]), prevent from (1), priestly (1 [+3913]), projecting from (1), protection from (1 [+7156]), received from (1), recently (1 [+2543, 7940]), recovery (1 [+2649, 2716]), reject (1 [+8959, 6584, 7156]), reject (1 [+8938, 6584, 7156]), representative (1 [+907]), represented (1), rest of (1), resting on (1 [+9393]), revoke (1 [+8740]), rid (1 [+8959, 6584]), risked (1 [+8959, 5584]), say (1 [+3655, 7023]), select a day (1 [+3427, 4200, 3427]), send (1 [+995, 907]), sent by (1 [+907]), set free (1 [+8938, 3338]), sharing (1 [+430]), shed by (1 [+3338]), side (1 [+6298]), sides (1 [+6298, 6017]), since (1 [+889]), since (1 [+4200, 3427]), so cannot (1), so that no (1), sober (1 [+3655, 2021, 3516]), some (1 [+907]), some distance away (1 [+8158]), some distance away (1 [+8178]), some distance from (1 [+7156]), southern (1 [+5582]), southernmost (1 [+7895]), southward (1 [+9402]), spared from (1 [+7156]), spoke the word (1 [+7023]), square (1 [+7024, 2256, 4946, 7024]), square (1 [+4946, 7024, 2256, 7024]), started (1), starting out from (1), stop trusting in (1 [+2532]), stopped (1), stopped (1 [+6590]), stopped (1 [+8740]), such (1 [+3972]), surely leave (1 [+2143, 6584, 2143]), surpasses (1), surround (1 [+2118, 6017]), take off (1 [+3718, 6584]), taken (1), taken from (1 [+4200, 7156]), than (1 [+889]), than (1 [+3463]), than deserved (1), the (1), the Lord's (1 [+6640, 3378]), their (1 [+2157]), theirs (1 [+2157]), there (1 [+9004]), there (1 [+5584]), there is no (1 [+401]), those[S] (1), though (1), throughout (1 [+3972]), till no more (1), to (1 [+339]), to (1 [+4200]), to (1 [+6584]), to (1 [+7156]), to (1 [+9393]), to nothing (1 [+8024]), told (1 [+9048, 907]), top of (1 [+4200, 5087, 2025]), unaware (1 [+6623]), unaware (1 [+6623, 6524]), under (1 [+1074]), under (1 [+7156]), underneath (1 [+9393]), unduly (1 [+3841]), unless (1 [+4200, 963, 889]), unnoticed (1 [+1172, 8492]), unsheathed (1 [+3655, 9509]), untraveled (1 [+1172, 408, 6296]), upward (1 [+4200, 5087, 2025]), used (1), uttered (1 [+3655]), utterly (1), was spent for making (1 [+6913]), west (1 [+6298]), what said (1 [+7023]), when (1 [+2118]), when (1 [+255]), when (1 [+3427]), when (1 [+6961]), when came to be (1 [+7710]), whenever (1 [+3954, 1896]), wherever (1 [+889]), wherever (1 [+3972, 2021, 5226]), while (1), will (1), willingly (1 [+4213]), with (1 [+7396]), with the help of (1 [+907]), withdrew (1 [+2143]), without (1 [+1172]), without (1 [+2575]), without being aware (1 [+6524]), worked (1), worse than (1), yet (1 [+1172, 889]), your (1 [+4013]), NDT (1128)

H4947 מַנְגִּינָה ***mangînâ***, n.f. [1] [√ 5594]. mocking song:– mock in songs (1)

H4948 מָנָה ***mānâ[1]***, v. [28] [→ 3555, 4945, 4949, 4950, 4951, 4972, 4987, 9463?, 9464, 9466?, 9467?; 10431]. [Q] to count, number, take a census; [N] to be counted, be numbered; [P] to assign, appoint, provide; [Pu] to be assigned, be appointed:– counted (4), provided (4), assigned (3), count (3), be counted (2), number (2), take a census (2), appoint (1), appointed (1), counts (1), destine (1), determines (1), raise (1), was numbered (1), were assigned (1)

H4949 מָנֶה ***māneh***, n.m. [5] [√ 4948; 10428]. mina (unit of weight, about 1.25 pounds [0.6 kg]):– minas (4), mina (1)

H4950 מָנָה ***mānâ[2]***, n.f. [12] [√ 4948]. share, portion, piece:– share (3), piece of meat (1), portion (1), portions (1), portions of food (1), portions of meat (1), presents (1), presents of food (1), some[S] (1), special food (1)

H4951 מֹנֶה ***mōneh***, n.[m.] [2] [√ 4948]. time, occurrence:– times (2)

H4952 מִנְהָג ***minhāg***, n.m. [2] [√ 5627]. driving (of a chariot):– driving (1), that[S] (1)

H4953 מִנְהָרָה ***minhārâ***, n.f. [1] shelter, hole, cave (in mountain clefts):– shelters (1)

H4954 מָנוֹד ***mānôd***, n.[m.] [2] [√ 5653]. shaking of the head (in scorn or derision):– object of derision (1), shake (1)

H4955 מָנוֹחַ ***mānôaḥ[1]***, n.m. [7] [→ 4956, 4957, 4967; cf. 5663]. resting place; the home of a person or the lair of an animal, with the focus that this is a place of rest, satisfaction, and contentment:– resting place (2), came to rest (1), home (1), nowhere (1 [+4202]), places of rest (1), rest (1)

H4956 [2]מָנוֹחַ ***mānôaḥ[2]***, n.pr.m. [18] [√ 4955; cf. 5663]. Manoah, "*rest*":– Manoah (15), he[S] (1), NDT (2)

H4957 מְנוּחָה ***m[e]nûḥâ***, n.f. [21] [√ 4955; cf. 5663]. resting place; see also 4955:– resting place (7), rest (5), easily (1), inheritance (1), peace and rest (1), place of rest (1), place to rest (1), places of rest (1), quiet (1), resting (1), staff (1)

H4958 מָנוֹל ***mānôl***, n.[m.] Not used in NIVEBC [cf. 4978]. property, possessions

H4959 מָנוֹן ***mānôn***, n.m. [1] grief:– insolent (1)

H4960 מָנוֹס ***mānôs***, n.m. [8] [→ 4961; cf. 5674]. place to flee, place of escape, refuge:– refuge (4), escape (1), flee (1), flee in haste (1 [+5674]), not escape (1 [+6])

H4961 מְנוּסָה ***m[e]nûsâ***, n.f. [2] [√ 4960; cf. 5674]. flight, fleeing:– fleeing (1), flight (1)

H4962 מָנוֹר ***mānôr***, n.m. [4] (weaver's) rod, beam (of weavers):– rod (4)

H4963 מְנוֹרָה ***m[e]nôrâ***, n.f. [42] [√ 5944]. lampstand (holding an oil lamp; not a candlestick, holding a wax candle):– lampstand (26), lampstands (5), each lampstand (2 [+4963]), each lampstand (2 [+4963, 2256]), each lampstand (2 [+2256, 4963]), its[S] (1 [+2021]), lamp (1), NDT (3)

H4964 מִנְּזָר ***minn[e]zār***, n.[m.]pl. [1] [cf. 5692]. guard, watchman, with a possible implication of status and rank:– guards (1)

H4965 מֻנָּח ***munnāḥ***, n.m. *or* v.ptcp. [3] [√ 5663]. open area:– open area (3)

H4966 מִנְחָה ***minḥâ***, n.f. [210] [√ 10432]. grain offering; animal offering or sacrifice; gift, tribute, present:– grain offering (92), grain offerings (42), offering (17), tribute (13), gift (11), gifts (8), offerings (8), sacrifice (5), grain (2), it[S] (2 [+2021]), offering of grain (2), reminder-offering (2 [+2355]), sacrifices (2), evening sacrifice (1 [+6590]), sacrifice (1 [+6590]), NDT (2)

H4967 מְנֻחוֹת ***mᵉnuḥôt***, var. Not used in NIVEBC [√ 4955]. Manuhoth, see 4971

H4968 מְנַחֵם ***mᵉnaḥēm***, n.pr.m. [8] [√ 5714]. Menahem, *"comforter"*:– Menahem (7), Menahem's (1)

H4969 [1]מָנַחַת ***mānaḥat[1]***, n.pr.m. [2] [√ 5663]. Manahath, *"resting place"*:– Manahath (2)

H4970 [2]מָנַחַת ***mānaḥat[2]***, n.pr.loc. [1] [→ 4971; cf. 5663]. Manahath, *"resting place"*:– Manahath (1)

H4971 מָנַחְתִּי ***mānaḥtî***, a.g. [2] [√ 4970; cf. 5663]. Manahathite, *"of Manahath"*:– Manahathites (2)

H4972 מְנִי ***mᵉnî***, n.pr. [1] [√ 4948]. Destiny (pagan god):– Destiny (1)

H4973 [1]מִנִּי ***minnî[1]***, n.pr.loc. [1] Minni:– Minni (1)

H4974 [2]מִנִּי ***minnî[2]***, pp. [34] [√ 4946]. from, out of; more than:– from (11), than (3), with (3), by (2), from (2 [+4200]), of (2), out of (2), since (2), before (1), ever since (1), NDT (5)

H4975 מִנְיָמִין ***minyāmîn***, n.pr.m. [3] [→ 4785]. Miniamin, *"from the right, good, fortune"*:– Miniamin (2), Miniamin's (1)

H4976 [1]מִנִּית ***minnît[1]***, n.pr.loc. [2] Minnith:– Minnith (2)

H4977 [2]מִנִּית ***minnît[2]***, n.pr.loc. rice [?]

H4978 מִנְלֶה ***minleh***, n.[m.] [1] [cf. 4958]. possession, acquisition:– possessions (1)

H4979 מָנַע ***māna'***, v. [29] [→ 3557]. [Q] to keep from, withhold, deny, refuse; [N] to be kept from, be withheld, be denied:– kept (4), withheld (4), withhold (4), keep (2), refuse (2), are denied (1), been withheld (1), denied (1), deprived (1), do not run (1), held back (1), hoards (1), keep back (1), keeps (1), linger (1), not set (1), refused (1), restrain (1)

H4980 מַנְעוּל ***man'ûl***, n.[m.] [6] [√ 5835]. bolt, lock (of a door):– bolts (5), bolt (1)

H4981 מִנְעָל ***min'āl***, n.m. [1] [√ 5835]. bolt (on a gate):– bolts of gates (1)

H4982 מַנְעַמִּים ***man'ammîm***, n.[m.]pl. [1] [√ 5838]. (edible) delicacies:– delicacies (1)

H4983 מְנַעַנְעִים ***mᵉna'an'îm***, n.[m.pl.] [1] [√ 5675]. sistrum, rattle, percussion instrument not precisely identified:– sistrums (1)

H4984 מְנַקִּית ***mᵉnaqqît***, n.f. [4] [√ 5927]. bowl (used for drink offering):– bowls (3), bowls used for drink offerings (1)

H4985 מְנַשֶּׁה ***mᵉnaššeh***, n.pr.m. [145] [→ 4986; cf. 5960]. Manasseh, *"one that makes to forget"*:– Manasseh (129), Manasseh's (6), Manasseh (5 [+1201]), Manassites (2 [+1201]), tribe of Manasseh (2), NDT (1)

H4986 מְנַשִּׁי ***mᵉnaššî***, a.g. [4] [√ 4985; cf. 5960]. Manassite, of Manasseh, *"of Manasseh"*:– Manasseh (3), Manassites (1)

H4987 מְנָת ***mᵉnāt***, n.f. [9] [√ 4948]. portion, lot, assigned share:– portions (3), portion (2), contributed (1), food (1), lot (1 [+3926]), portion (1 [+2750])

H4988 מָס ***mās***, a. Not used in NIVEBC [√ 5022]. despairing (man)

H4989 מַס ***mas***, n.m. [23] forced labor, slave labor:– forced labor (15), slave (2), forced laborers (1), labor (1), laborers (1), slave labor (1), tribute (1), NDT (1)

H4990 מֵסַב ***mēsab***, n.[m.] [4] [→ 4991; cf. 6015]. surrounding; round table, circle of feasters; (adv.) around, round about:– around (2), surround (1), table (1)

H4991 מְסִבָּה ***mᵉsibbâ***, n.[f.] (used as adv.) [1] [√ 4990; cf. 6015]. (adv.) around, round about:– around (1)

H4992 מִסָּבִיב ***missābîb***, n.pr.m. Not used in NIVEBC [→ 4474]. Missabib, see 4474

H4993 [1]מַסְגֵּר ***masgēr[1]***, n.[m.] [3] [→ 4994; cf. 6037]. prison, dungeon:– prison (3)

H4994 [2]מַסְגֵּר ***masgēr[2]***, n.[m.] [4] [√ 4993; cf. 6037]. artisan, craftsman; some sources: metalworker, locksmith:– artisans (4)

H4995 מִסְגֶּרֶת ***misgeret***, n.f. [17] [√ 6037]. side panels (of a building); rim (of a table and base); stronghold; den:– rim (6), panels (5), side panels (2), strongholds (2), dens (1), NDT (1)

H4996 מַסָּד ***massad***, n.[m.] [1] [√ 3569]. foundation:– foundation (1)

H4997 מִסְדְּרוֹן ***misdᵉrôn***, n.[m.] [1] [√ 6043?]. porch, vestibule:– porch (1)

H4998 מָסָה ***māsâ***, v. [4] [cf. 4416, 5022]. [H] to melt, dissolve; to consume; to drench (with tears):– consume (1), drench (1), made melt in fear (1), melts (1)

H4999 [1]מַסָּה ***massâ[1]***, n.f. [3] [→ 5001; cf. 5814]. trial, test, temptation:– trials (2), testings (1)

H5000 [2]מַסָּה ***massâ[2]***, n.f. [1] [√ 5022]. despair:– despair (1)

H5001 [3]מַסָּה ***massâ[3]***, n.pr.loc. [5] [√ 4999?; cf. 5814?]. Massah, *"test, try"*:– Massah (5)

H5002 מִסָּה ***missâ***, n.f. [1] proportion, measure:– in proportion to (1 [+3869, 889])

H5003 מַסְוֶה ***masweh***, n.[m.] [3] [√ 6078]. veil, covering:– veil (3)

H5004 מְסוּכָה ***mᵉsûkâ***, n.f. [1] [→ 5379; cf. 6056]. thorn hedge:– thorn hedge (1)

H5005 מַסָּח ***massāḥ***, n.m. *or* adv. [1] [cf. 5815?]. in turn, taking turns:– take turns (1)

H5006 מִסְחָר ***misḥār***, n.m. [1] [cf. 6086]. revenue:– revenues (1)

H5007 מָסַךְ ***māsak***, v. [5] [→ 4932, 5008]. [Q] to mingle, mix (substances into drinks):– mixed (2), mingle (1), mixing (1), poured (1)

H5008 מֶסֶךְ ***mesek***, n.[m.] [1] [√ 5007]. mixture (of spices):– mixed with spices (1)

H5009 מָסָךְ ***māsāk***, n.[m.] [25] [√ 6114]. curtain, covering; by extension: shield, defense:– curtain (17), shielding (3), covering (2), curtains (1), defenses (1), shields (1)

H5010 מְסֻכָה ***mᵉsukâ***, n.f. [1] [√ 6114]. (woven) covering:– adorned (1)

H5011 [1]מַסֵּכָה ***massēkâ[1]***, n.f. [26] [√ 5818]. image, idol (of cast metal):– idol (3 [+7181, 2256]), idol cast (3), idols (3), idols (2 [+7178, 2256]), image (2), images (2), cast (1), forming an alliance (1 [+5818]), idol (1), idol cast from metal (1), idols (1 [+466]), idols cast (1), idols made of metal (1), metal (1), overlaid (1), overlaid with silver (1), took (1 [+4374, 2256])

H5012 [2]מַסֵּכָה ***massēkâ[2]***, n.f. [2] [√ 5819]. (woven) blanket, (interwoven) covering:– blanket (1), sheet (1)

H5013 [3]מַסֵּכָה ***massēkâ[3]***, n.f. Not used in NIVEBC [√ 5819]. alliance

H5014 מִסְכֵּן ***miskēn***, a. [4] [→ 5017; cf. 6123]. poor, needy (one):– poor (4)

H5015 מְסֻכָּן ***mᵉsukkān***, n.[m.] *or* v.ptcp. Not used in NIVEBC [cf. 6123]. a kind of tree [?], see 6123

H5016 מִסְכְּנוֹת ***miskᵉnôt***, n.f.pl. [7] [√ 6122]. storage places, warehouses:– store (6), buildings to store (1)

H5017 מִסְכֵּנֻת ***miskēnut***, n.f. [1] [√ 5014; cf. 6123]. scarcity, poverty:– scarce (1 [+430, 928])

H5018 מַסֶּכֶת ***masseket***, n.f. [3] [√ 5819]. warp-threads (the lengthwise threads of a loom):– fabric (3)

H5019 מְסִלָּה ***mᵉsillâ***, n.f. [27] [√ 6148]. main road; (raised) highway, ramp, stairs; by extension: lifestyle, conduct in life:– road (10), highway (6), roads (3), highways (2), courses (1), main road (1), pilgrimage (1), steps (1), straight ahead (1), ways (1)

H5020 מַסְלוּל ***maslûl***, n.m. [1] [√ 6148]. highway:– highway (1)

H5021 מַסְמֵר ***masmēr***, n.m. [4] [√ 6169]. nail:– nails (3), nails down (1 [+2616, 928])

H5022 מָסַס ***māsas***, v. [21] [→ 4988, 5000, 9468; cf. 4416, 4998, 5376, 5806]. [Q] to waste away, dissolve; [N] to be melted, dissolved; [H] to cause to melt:– melt (3), melt with fear (3), melted in fear (3), melt with fear (2 [+5022]), be soaked (1), disheartened (1 [+906, 4222]), dropped (1), melt in fear (1), melted (1), melted away (1), melts (1), waste away (1), wastes away (1), weak (1)

H5023 מַסַּע ***massa'***, n.[m.] [12] [√ 5825]. journey, travels from place to place:– journey (2), travels (2), from place to place (1 [+4200]), having set out (1), order of march (1), setting out (1), stages in journey (1), traveled from place to place (1), traveling from place to place (1), way (1)

H5024 [1]מַסָּע ***massā'[1]***, n.[m.] [1] [√ 5825]. quarry:– quarry (1)

H5025 [2]מַסָּע ***massā'[2]***, n.m. [1] a weapon probably thrown like a spear or javelin; dart:– dart (1)

H5026 מִסְעָד ***mis'ād***, n.[m.] [1] [√ 6184]. supports (for a building):– supports (1)

H5027 מִסְפֵּד ***mispēd***, n.m. [16] [√ 6199]. wailing, howling, weeping, mourning:– wailing (5), mourning (4), wail (2), weeping (2), howl (1 [+6913]), lamented (1 [+6199]), mourns (1)

H5028 מִסְפּוֹא ***mispô'***, n.m. [5] fodder, animal feed:– fodder (4), feed (1)

H5029 מִסְפָּחָה ***mispāḥâ***, n.f. [2] [√ 6202]. veil, (head) covering:– veils (2)

H5030 מִסְפַּחַת ***mispaḥat***, n.f. [3] [√ 6204]. (uninfectious) breaking out of skin, rash or scab; referring to something relatively harmless:– rash (3)

H5031 [1]מִסְפָּר ***mispār[1]***, n.m. [132] [→ 5032?, 5033?; cf. 6219]. number, quantity; listing, inventory, census:– number (47), listed (15), counted (8), few (7), list (6), as many as (3), how many (2), number (2 [+5152]), numbered (2), numbers (2), account (1), all (1), allotted (1), any (1), archers (1 [+8008]), census (1), count (1), counted off (1 [+6296, 928]), countless (1 [+401]), during (1), each (1 [+1653]), each[S] (1 [+4200]), few (1 [+5071, 928]), in all (1), innumerable (1 [+401]), inventory (1), length (1), life span (1 [+3427]), limit (1), listing (1), many (1), measure (1), one by one (1 [+928]), one for each (1 [+3869]), only a few (1), only a few (1 [+5493]), so many (1 [+8041]), total (1 [+3972, 4200]), very few (1 [+5493]), NDT (9)

H5032 [2]מִסְפָּר ***mispār[2]***, n.pr.m. [1] [→ 5033; cf. 5031?, 6219]. Mispar, *"number"*:– Mispar (1)

H5033 מִסְפֶּרֶת ***misperet***, n.pr.m. [1] [√ 5032; cf. 5031?]. Mispereth:– Mispereth (1)

H5034 מָסַר ***māsar***, v. [2] [→ 5037?]. [Q] to supply, deliver; [N] to be supplied:– enticed (1), supplied (1)

H5035 מֹסֵרוֹת ***mōsērôt***, n.pr.loc. [2] [√ 673?; cf. 4594]. Moseroth, *"bonds, prison [?]"*:– Moseroth (2)

H5036 מֹסָרָם ***mōsārām***, n.m. Not used in NIVEBC [√ 4592; cf. 3579]. see 4592

H5037 מָסֹרֶת ***māsōret***, n.f. [1] [√ 673? *or* 5034?]. bond, obligation, duty:– bond (1)

H5038 מִסַּת ***missat***, n. see 5002

H5039 מִסְתּוֹר ***mistôr***, n.[m.] [1] [√ 6259]. hiding place, shelter (from the elements):– hiding place (1)

H5040 מַסְתֵּר ***mastēr***, n.[m.] [1] [√ 6259]. (the act of) hiding:– hide (1)

H5041 מִסְתָּר ***mistār***, n.[m.] [10] [√ 6259]. hiding place, covered place (from which to ambush):– ambush (2), hiding (2), secret places (2), cover (1), hiding places (1), lies in wait (1 [+741, 928, 2021]), secret (1)

H5042 מַעֲבָד ***ma'ᵃbād***, n.[m.] [1] [√ 6268; 10434]. deed, action:– deeds (1)

H5043 מַעֲבֶה ***ma'ᵃbeh***, n.[m.] [1] [√ 6286]. mold, foundry:– molds (1)

H5044 מַעֲבָר ***ma'ᵃbār***, n.[m.] [3] [√ 6296]. stroke (of a rod); (geographical) pass; ford (of a river):– ford (1), pass (1), stroke (1)

H5045 מַעְבָּרָה ***ma'bārâ***, n.f. [8] [√ 6296]. ford, river crossing; (geographical) pass:– fords (5), pass (2), river crossings (1)

H5046 [1]מַעְגָּל ***ma'gāl[1]***, n.m. [3] [√ 6318]. (circled) camp, encampment:– camp (3)

H5047 [2]מַעְגָּל ***ma'gāl[2]***, n.m. [13] [√ 6318]. (rutted) path (of a cart or wagon):– paths (8), path (2), carts (1), way (1), ways (1)

H5048 מָעַד ***mā'ad***, v. [8] [→ 4598, 5049, 5050]. [Q] to slip, waver, wobble; [Pu] to become lame; [H] cause to wobble, to bend, wrench (one's back):– give way (2), bent (1), faltered (1), lame (1), slip (1), slipping (1), wrenched (1)

H5049 מַעַדַי ***ma'ᵃday***, n.pr.m. [1] [→ 5050; cf. 4598, 5048 + 3378]. Maadai, *"ornaments"*:– Maadai (1)

H5050 מַעַדְיָה ***ma'adyâ***, n.pr.m. [1] [√ 5049; cf. 5048 + 3378]. Moadiah, "[perhaps] *Yahweh assembles* or *Yahweh promises*":– Moadiah (1)

H5051 מַעֲדַנּוֹת ***ma'ᵃdannōt***, n.[f.pl.] [2] [√ 6357; cf. 6698]. chains, bands, cords used for binding; others: beautiful; (adv.) confidently:– chains (2)

H5052 מַעֲדַנִּים ***ma'ᵃdannîm***, n.[m.pl.] [3] [√ 6357]. delicacy; delight:– delicacies (2), delights (1)

H5053 מַעְדֵּר ***ma'dēr***, n.[m.] [1] [√ 6371]. hoe (to cultivate ground):– hoe (1)

H5054 מָעָה ***mā'â***, n.f. [1] grain (of sand):– numberless grains (1)

H5055 מֵעֶה ***mē'eh***, n.m. [33] [√ 10435]. viscera: stomach, heart, bowels, womb; (body as a whole); by extension: of the inner person, the seat of emotions: anguish, tenderness:– bowels (4), heart (4), anguish (2), body (2), flesh and blood (2), flesh and blood (2 [+3655, 4946]), inside (2), stomach (2), within (2), womb (2), I (1 [+3276]), belly (1), children (1 [+7368]), have (1 [+928]), intestines (1), line (1), stomachs (1), tenderness (1 [+2162]), within (1 [+928, 9348])

H5056 מָעוֹג ***mā'ôg***, n.[m.] [1] [√ 6383]. provision, supply; some sources: flat bread:– bread (1)

H5057 מָעוֹז ***mā'ôz***, n.m. [34] [→ 5058; cf. 6451]. refuge, stronghold, fortress, place of protection; (used with "head") helmet:– fortress (8), refuge (8), stronghold (7), fortresses (2), helmet (2 [+8031]), protection (2), height (1), mightiest fortresses (1 [+4448]), protect (1), strength (1), strong (1)

H5058 מָעוֹזֶן ***mā'ôzen***, n.m. [1] [√ 5057; cf. 6451]. fortress, refuge:– fortresses (1)

H5059 מָעוֹךְ ***mā'ôk***, n.pr.m. [1] [cf. 5082]. Maoch, *"poor one"*:– Maok (1)

H5060 [1]מָעוֹן ***mā'ôn[1]***, n.[m.] Not used in NIVEBC. help

H5061 [2]מָעוֹן ***mā'ôn[2]***, n.[m.] [18] [→ 1110, 1260, 5062, 5063, 5104; cf. 6410]. dwelling place:– dwelling (6), dwelling place (4), haunt (4), den (1), place of refuge (1), refuge (1), where live (1)

H5062 [3]מָעוֹן ***mā'ôn[3]***, n.pr.m. & g. [3] [√ 5061]. Maon; Maonite, *"dwelling"*:– Maon (2), Maonites (1)

H5063 [4]מָעוֹן ***mā'ôn[4]***, n.pr.loc. [5] [√ 5061]. Maon, *"dwelling"*:– Maon (5)

H5064 מְעוּנִים ***mᵉ'ûnîm***, n.pr.g. [5] [cf. 5079]. Meunim, Meunite, *"people of Maon"*:– Meunites (3), Meunim (2)

H5065 מְעוֹנֹתַי ***mᵉ'ônōtay***, n.pr.m. [2] Meonothai, *"my dwellings"*:– Meonothai (2)

H5066 מָעוּף **mā'ûp**, n.[m.] [1] [√ 6415]. gloom, darkness:– gloom (1)

H5067 מָעוֹר **mā'ôr**, n.[m.] [1] [√ 6423]. exposed genitals, nakedness:– naked bodies (1)

H5068 מַעֲזְיָה **ma'azyâ**, n.pr.m. [1] [→ 5069]. Maaziah, "*Yahweh is a refuge*":– Maaziah (1)

H5069 מַעַזְיָהוּ **ma'azyāhû**, n.pr.m. [1] [√ 5068]. Maaziah, "*Yahweh is a refuge*":– Maaziah (1)

H5070 מָעַט **mā'aṭ**, v. [22] [→ 5071]. [Q] to dwindle, decrease, become few; [P] to become few; [H] to let reduce, make diminish, make collect little:– few (4), decrease (2), smaller (2), decreased (1), dwindles away (1), gathered little (1), give less (1), just a few (1), let diminish (1), little (1), make few in number (1), make weak (1), no less than (1), numbers decreased (1), reduce to nothing (1), small (1), trifling (1)

H5071 מְעַט **me'aṭ**, subst. [101] [√ 5070]. little (of size), few (of quantity), short (of time):– little (33), few (12), not enough (5), only a few (5), soon (4 [+3869]), little while (3), smaller (3), almost (2 [+3869]), isn't enough (2), short distance (2), soon (2 [+6388]), almost (1 [+6388]), brief (1), few (1 [+3869]), few (1 [+928, 5031]), few in number (1 [+5493]), fewest (1), how quickly (1 [+3869]), in a moment (1 [+3869]), in a very short time (1 [+6388, 4663]), little more (1), little while (1 [+6388]), little while (1 [+8092]), many (1 [+4202]), might well have (1 [+3869]), moment's (1), of little value (1 [+3869]), only a little (1), scarcely (1 [+3869]), short (1), some (1), some (1 [+3869]), soon (1 [+3869, 7775]), too few (1), too little (1), very few (1 [+4663]), very soon (1 [+6388, 4663]), wasn't enough (1), waste away (1)

H5072 מְעֻטָּה **me'uṭṭâ**, var. see 6487

H5073 מַעֲטֶה **ma'aṭeh**, n.[m.] [1] [√ 6486]. garment, mantle, wrap:– garment (1)

H5074 מַעֲטָפָה **ma'aṭepet**, n.f. [1] [√ 6493]. cape, outer garment:– capes (1)

H5075 מְעִי **me'î**, n.[m.] [1] [√ 6505]. heap (of ruins):– heap (1)

H5076 מָעַי **mā'ay**, n.pr.m. [1] Maai, "*to be compassionate*":– Maai (1)

H5077 מְעִיל **me'îl**, n.m. [28] robe, cloak:– robe (20), cloak (4), robes (2), garment (1), NDT (1)

H5078 מַעְיָן **ma'yān**, n.m. [23] [√ 6524]. spring, fountain, well; by extension: source of life (satisfaction, blessing):– springs (10), spring (5), springs (3 [+4784]), fountain (2), fountains (1), well (1), wells (1)

H5079 מְעִינִים **me'înîm**, n.pr.g. Not used in NIVEBC [cf. 5064]. Meinites, see 5064

H5080 מָעַךְ **mā'ak**, v. [4] [Qp] be pressed (into the ground), be crushed, be bruised; [Pu] be fondled:– bruised (1), fondled (1), stuck (1), were fondled (1)

H5081 מַעֲכָה[1] **ma'akâ[1]**, n.pr.g. [3] [→ 5082, 5083, 5084; *also used with compound proper names*]. Maacah, "[perhaps] *dull, stupid*":– Maakah (3)

H5082 מַעֲכָה[2] **ma'akâ[2]**, n.pr.m. & f. [19] [√ 5081; cf. 5059]. Maacah, "[perhaps] *dull, stupid*":– Maakah (19)

H5083 מַעֲכַת **ma'akāt**, n.pr.g. [1] [√ 5081]. Maacah:– they[S] (1 [+1770, 2256])

H5084 מַעֲכָתִי **ma'akātî**, a.g. [8] [√ 5081]. Maacathite, of Maacah, "*of Maacah*":– Maakah (3), Maakathite (3), Maakathite (1 [+1201]), Maakathites (1)

H5085 מָעַל **mā'al**, v. [35] [→ 5086]. [Q] to act unfaithfully, break faith, commit a violation:– unfaithful (14), unfaithful (10 [+5086]), betray (1), break faith (1 [+5086]), broke faith (1), is unfaithful (1 [+5086]), more and more unfaithful (1 [+8049, 5086]), most unfaithful (1 [+5086]), unfaithfulness (1 [+5086]), unfaithfulness (1 [+5086]), unfaithfulness guilty of (1 [+5086]), unfaithfulness showed (1 [+5086]), violating the ban (1)

H5086 מַעַל[1] **ma'al[1]**, n.m. [29] [√ 5085]. unfaithfulness:– unfaithful (11), unfaithfulness (6), unfaithfulness (2 [+5085]), break faith (1 [+5085]), disobedience (1), falsehood (1), is unfaithful (1 [+5085]), matter (1), more and more unfaithful (1 [+8049, 5085]), most unfaithful (1 [+5085]), unfaithfulness guilty of (1 [+5085]), unfaithfulness showed (1 [+5085]), NDT (1)

H5087 מַעַל[2] **ma'al[2]**, subst.adv. & pp. [140] [√ 6590]. above, beyond; this refer to spatial position, to degree, and to time (afterward):– more (36 [+2025]), above (19 [+4946]), upward (6 [+4200, 2025]), above (4 [+4946, 4200, 2025]), above (3 [+4200, 2025]), on (3 [+2025]), over (3 [+4946, 4200, 2025]), head (2 [+4946, 8900, 2256, 2025]), higher (2 [+2025]), highly (2 [+4200, 2025]), just above (2 [+4946]), over (2 [+4946]), top (2 [+4946, 4200, 2025]), up (2 [+4200, 2025]), very (2 [+4200, 2025]), above (1 [+4946, 6584]), above (1 [+4946, 4946, 4200, 6645]), all around (1 [+4946, 4200]), at each successive level (1 [+4200, 2025, 4200, 5087, 2025]), at each successive level (1 [+4200, 5087, 2025, 4200, 2025]), beyond (1 [+2025]), deep (1 [+2025]), depth (1 [+2025, 4200]), downstream (1 [+4946, 4200, 2025]), exceedingly (1 [+4200, 2025]), heights (1 [+4200, 2025]), high above (1 [+4946, 4200, 2025]), higher (1 [+4946]), higher than (1 [+8049, 4200, 2025]), in ascending stages (1 [+4200, 2025, 4200, 5087, 2025]), in ascending stages (1 [+4200, 5087, 2025, 4200, 2025]), jointed (1 [+4946, 4200, 8079]), magnificence (1 [+2025]), more (1 [+4200, 2025]), more and more powerful (1 [+2143, 2256, 1541, 6330, 4200, 2025]), older (1 [+2025]), on high (1 [+4946]), outer (1 [+4946, 4200, 2025]), over and above (1 [+4200, 2025]), overturned (1 [+2200, 4200, 2025]), project upward (1 [+4200, 2025]), severe (1 [+4200, 2025]), top (1), top (1 [+2025]), top of (1 [+4946, 4200, 2025]), upstream (1 [+4200, 2025]), upward (1 [+4946, 4200, 2025]), very (1 [+6330, 4200, 2025]), wielding (1 [+995, 4200, 2025]), young and old (1 [+2256, 2025]), NDT (15)

H5088 מֵעַל **mē'al**, pp.+pp. Not used in NIVEBC [√ 4946 + 6584]. see 4946 & 6584

H5089 מֹעַל **mō'al**, n.[m.] [1] [√ 6590]. lifting (of hands):– lifted (1)

H5090 מַעֲלֶה **ma'aleh**, n.m. [16] [√ 6590]. and ascent: hill, mount, (geographical) pass; stairs:– pass (7), hill (4), ascent (1), going up (1), mount (1), stairs (1), way up (1)

H5091 מַעֲלָה[1] **ma'alâ[1]**, n.f. [1] [√ 6590]. what goes through (or rises into) one's mind:– what is going through (1)

H5092 מַעֲלָה[2] **ma'alâ[2]**, n.f. [46] [√ 6590]. ascent: steps, stairway, paces:– steps (22), ascents (15), stairway (2), flight of stairs (1), journey (1), lofty palace (1), most exalted (1 [+9366]), NDT (3)

H5093 מַעְלָה **ma'elâ**, adv. & pp. Not used in NIVEBC [√ 6590]. above

H5094 מַעֲלִיל **ma'alîl**, n.m. Not used in NIVEBC [√ 6618]. see 5095

H5095 מַעֲלָל **ma'alāl**, n.m. [41] [√ 6618]. deeds, actions, practices, what is done:– deeds (16), actions (8), done (6), practices (3), dealings (1), do (1), evil practices (1), sins (1), ways (1), what doing (1), wicked deeds (1), work (1)

H5096 מַעֲמָד **ma'amād**, n.[m.] [5] [√ 6641]. attendance, serving; position of attendant:– attending (2), duty (1), places (1), position (1)

H5097 מָעֳמָד **mo'omād**, n.[m.] [1] [√ 6641]. foothold, firm ground:– foothold (1)

H5098 מַעֲמָסָה **ma'amāsâ**, n.f. [1] [√ 6673]. heavy stone, hard-to-lift rock:– immovable (1)

H5099 מַעֲמַקִּים **ma'amaqqîm**, n.m.pl. [5] [√ 6676]. depths (of waters or seas):– depths (3), deep (2)

H5100 מַעַן **ma'an**, subst.pp.c. [271] [√ 6701]. for the sake of, on account of, because; therefore, so that:– so that (77 [+4200]), to (35 [+4200]), that (24 [+4200]), for sake (22 [+4200]), for the sake of (22 [+4200]), so (18 [+4200]), because of (16 [+4200]), then (11 [+4200]), and (7 [+4200]), in order to (6 [+4200]), for (5 [+4200]), therefore (3 [+4200]), against (1 [+4200]), bent on (1 [+4200]), for then (1 [+4200]), in behalf of (1 [+4200]), in this way (1 [+4200]), otherwise (1 [+4200, 889, 4202]), that is why (1 [+4200]), thus (1 [+4200]), till (1 [+4200]), NDT (16)

H5101 מַעֲנֶה[1] **ma'aneh[1]**, n.m. [7] [√ 6699]. reply, answer, response:– answer (3), giving an apt reply (1 [+7023]), respond (1), say (1), way to refute (1)

H5102 מַעֲנֶה[2] **ma'aneh[2]**, n.m. [1] [√ 6701]. purpose:– proper end (1)

H5103 מַעֲנָה **ma'anâ**, n.f. [2] [→ 5105; cf. 6701]. furrow, plow path:– acre (1 [+7538]), furrows (1)

H5104 מְעוֹנָה **me'ōnâ**, n.f. [9] [√ 5061]. hiding place, refuge; dwelling place, (animal) den:– dens (5), refuge (2), den (1), dwelling place (1)

H5105 מַעֲנִית **ma'anît**, var. Not used in NIVEBC [√ 5103; cf. 6701]. see 5103

H5106 מַעַץ **ma'aṣ**, n.pr.m. [1] [→ 318]. Maaz, "[perhaps] *angry* or *wrath*":– Maaz (1)

H5107 מַעֲצֵבָה **ma'aṣēbâ**, n.f. [1] [√ 6772]. place of torment, place of pain:– torment (1)

H5108 מַעֲצָד **ma'aṣād**, n.[m.] [2] chiseling tool (for wood carving); some sources: ax, adze:– chisel (1), tool (1)

H5109 מַעְצוֹר **ma'ṣôr**, n.[m] [1] [√ 6806]. hindrance:– hinder (1)

H5110 מַעְצָר **ma'ṣār**, n.[m.] [1] [√ 6806]. self-control:– self-control (1 [+4200, 8120])

H5111 מַעֲקֶה **ma'aqeh**, n.[m.] [1] parapet, a short wall around the upper level of a house:– parapet (1)

H5112 מַעֲקַשִּׁים **ma'aqaššîm**, n.[m.] [1] [√ 6835]. rough places, uneven terrain, rugged country:– rough places (1)

H5113 מַעַר **ma'ar**, n.[m.] [2] [√ 5116]. nakedness; available space:– available space (1), nakedness (1)

H5114 מַעֲרָב[1] **ma'arāb[1]**, n.m. [8] [√ 6842]. wares, goods (for trade, exchange, or barter):– wares (7), merchants (1 [+6842])

H5115 מַעֲרָב[2] **ma'arāb[2]**, n.[m.] [15] [√ 6845]. west (the place of the sunset):– west (12), place of setting (1), west (1 [+2025]), NDT (1)

H5116 מַעֲרֶה **ma'areh**, n.[m.] Not used in NIVEBC [→ 5113]. approaches, vicinity

H5117 מְעָרָה[1] **me'ārâ[1]**, n.f. [38] [√ 6869?]. cave:– cave (30), caves (6), den (1), NDT (1)

H5118 מְעָרָה[2] **me'ārâ[2]**, n.f. [1] [→ 5125; cf. 6867]. wasteland, bare field:– wasteland (1)

H5119 מַעֲרָךְ **ma'arāk**, n.[m.] [1] [√ 6885]. plan, consideration, arrangement:– plans (1)

H5120 מַעֲרָכָה **ma'arākâ**, n.f. [19] [√ 6885]. things arranged in a row: battle line, row of army ranks; row, layer (of things); by extension: proper arrangement of something fitting and suitable:– armies (4), battle line (3), lines (2), ranks (2), battle lines (1), battle positions (1), battlefield (1 [+8441]), facing each other (1 [+7925]), forces (1), it[S] (1 [+2021]), proper kind (1), row (1)

H5121 מַעֲרֶכֶת **ma'areket**, n.f. [10] [√ 6885]. (consecrated) bread set in rows; see also 5120:– set out on the table (3), consecrated bread (2), stack (2), set out (1), setting out the consecrated bread (1), stacks (1)

H5122 מַעֲרֹם **ma'arōm**, n.m. [1] [√ 6867]. nakedness, naked person:– naked (1)

H5123 מַעֲרָץ **ma'arāṣ**, n.[m.] Not used in NIVEBC [√ 6907]. terror, see 6907

H5124 מַעֲרָצָה **ma'arāṣâ**, n.f. [1] [√ 6907]. terrifying power:– great power (1)

H5125 מַעֲרָת **ma'arāt**, n.pr.loc. [1] [√ 5118?; cf. 6867]. Maarath, "*barren*":– Maarath (1)

H5126 מַעֲשֶׂה **ma'aśeh**, n.m. [236] [→ 5127, 5128, 5129; cf. 6913]. work, labor, deed; something made, something done:– work (61), works (16), what done (12), made (10), what made (10), deeds (8), things (7), like (6 [+3869]), everything (4 [+3972]), woven (4), do (3), does (3), done (3), like (3), practices (3), what[S] (3 [+2021]), crops (2), deed (2), done (2 [+6913]), fashioned (2), labor (2), network (2 [+8407]), objects (2), occupation (2), products (2), shape (2), what deserve (2 [+3869]), what did (2), working (2), accomplished (1), achievement (1 [+4179]), acting (1), acts (1), baked goods (1 [+4407, 685]), baking (1), basework (1 [+4029]), construction (1), crafted (1), creature made (1), crime (1 [+8288]), crop (1), customs (1), design (1), do (1 [+3338]), formed (1), fruit (1), handiwork (1 [+3338]), how[S] (1), how made (1), idols made (1), interwoven chains (1 [+9249]), is done (1 [+6913]), made of (1), making (1), man-made (1 [+3338, 132]), network (1 [+8422, 8422]), nothing (1 [+4202]), performance (1), perfumes (1 [+5351]), projects (1), property (1), sculptured (1 [+7589]), shapes (1 [+3338]), structure (1), that does (1), that done (1), that made (1), things did (1), things did (1 [+3338]), this[S] (1 [+2021, 2021, 2296]), trouble (1), undertook (1), verses (1), way (1), well-dressed hair (1 [+5250]), what do (1), what make (1), whatever do (1), work (1 [+6913]), woven (1 [+755]), wrongdoing (1), NDT (2)

H5127 מַעֲשַׂי **ma'śay**, n.pr.m. [1] [√ 5126 + 3378]. Maasai, "*work of Yahweh*":– Maasai (1)

H5128 מַעֲשֵׂיָה **ma'aśēyâ**, n.pr.m. [16] [√ 5126 + 3378]. Maaseiah, "*Yahweh is a refuge*":– Maaseiah (16)

H5129 מַעֲשֵׂיָהוּ **ma'aśēyāhû**, n.pr.m. [7] [√ 5126 + 3378; cf. 6913]. Maaseiah, "*Yahweh is a refuge*":– Maaseiah (7)

H5130 מַעֲשֵׂר **ma'aśēr**, n.m. [32] [√ 6923]. tithe, setting aside a tenth:– tithe (13), tithes (13), tenth (5), setting aside a tenth (1 [+6923])

H5131 מַעֲשַׁקּוֹת **ma'aśaqqôt**, n.f. [2] [√ 6921]. (col.pl) extortion:– extortion (2)

H5132 מֹף **mōp**, n.pr.loc. [1] [cf. 5862]. Moph = Memphis:– Memphis (1)

H5133 מִפְגָּע **mipgā'**, n.[m.] [1] [√ 7003]. target:– target (1)

H5134 מַפָּח **mappāḥ**, n.[m.] [1] [√ 5870]. (a dying) gasp, exhaling (of soul), with an implication of despair and affliction:– gasp (1)

H5135 מַפֻּחַ **mappuaḥ**, n.m. [1] [√ 5870]. bellows:– bellows (1)

H5136 מְפִיבֹשֶׁת **mepîbōšet**, מְפִי-בֹשֶׁת **mepî-bōšet**, n.pr.m. [15] [√ 4946 + 7023 + 1425]. Mephibosheth, "*from the mouth of Shame [a derogatory name for Baal]*":– Mephibosheth (15)

H5137 מֻפִּים **muppîm**, n.pr.m. [1] Muppim:– Muppim (1)

H5138 מֵפִיץ **mēpîṣ**, n.m. [1] [√ 7046]. war club:– club (1)

H5139 מַפָּל **mappāl**, n.m. [2] [→ 5142, 5143; cf. 5877]. sweepings, waste, refuse (of wheat); (fleshy) folds (of the leviathan):– folds (1), sweepings (1)

H5140 מִפְלָאוֹת **miplā'ôt**, n.f.[pl.] [1] [√ 7098]. wonders, marvelous works:– wonders (1)

H5141 מִפְלַגָּה **miplaggâ**, n.f. [1] [√ 7103]. division (of family groups), subgroup of a clan:– subdivisions (1)

H5142 מַפָּלָה **mappālâ**, n.f. [1] [√ 5139; cf. 5877]. ruin, heap of rubble:– ruins (1)

H5143 מַפֵּלָה **mappēlâ**, n.f. [2] [√ 5139; cf. 5877]. ruin, heap of rubble:– ruin (2)

H5144 מִפְלָט **miplāṭ**, n.[m.] [1] [√ 7117]. place of shelter, refuge, escape:– place of shelter (1)

H5145 מִפְלֶצֶת **mipleṣet**, n.f. [4] [√ 7145]. repulsive image, disgraceful (idol):– it[S] (2), repulsive image (2)

H5146 מִפְלָשׂ **miplāś**, n.[m.] [1] floating, hovering (clouds):– hang poised (1)

H5147 מַפֶּלֶת **mappelet**, n.f. [8] [√ 5877]. downfall, collapse; (something downfallen) a shipwreck; carcass:– fall (3), downfall (2), carcass (1), fallen (1), shipwreck (1)

H5148 מִפְעָל **mip'āl**, n.[m.] [1] [√ 7188]. deed, work:– deeds (1)

H5149 מִפְעָלָה **mip'ālâ**, n.[f.] [2] [√ 7188]. deed, work:– what done (2)

H5150 מַפָּץ **mappāṣ**, n.[m.] [1] [√ 5879]. shattering, wrecking (weapon), implying death will follow its effective use:– deadly (1)

H5151 מַפֵּץ **mappēṣ**, n.m. [1] [√ 5879]. war club:– war club (1)

H5152 מִפְקָד **mipqād**, n.[m.] [5] [√ 7212]. appointment (by a king); number, counting (of the people); Inspection (Gate):– number (2 [+5031]), appointment (1), designated part (1), inspection (1)

H5153 מִפְרָץ **miprāṣ**, n.[m.] [1] [√ 7287]. cove, inlet, landing-place:– coves (1)

H5154 מַפְרֶקֶת **mapreqet**, n.f. [1] [√ 7293]. neck:– neck (1)

H5155 מִפְרָשׂ **miprāś**, n.[m.] [2] [√ 7298]. spreading (used of clouds and canvas sail):– sail (1), spreads out (1)

H5156 מִפְשָׂעָה **mipśā'â**, n.f. [1] [cf. 7314]. buttocks, posterior area:– buttocks (1)

H5157 מִפְתָּח **miptāḥ**, n.[m.] [1] [√ 7337]. opening (of lips):– open (1)

H5158 מַפְתֵּחַ **maptēaḥ**, n.m. [3] [√ 7337]. key:– key (2), key for opening (1)

H5159 מִפְתָּן **miptān**, n.[m.] [8] [cf. 7327]. threshold:– threshold (8)

H5160 מֵץ **mēṣ**, n.m. [1] [√ 4790]. oppressor:– oppressor (1)

H5161 מֹץ **mōṣ**, n.m. [8] chaff:– chaff (7), windblown chaff (1)

H5162 מָצָא **māṣā'**, v. [454] [Q] to find, find out, discover, uncover; [N] to be found out; be caught; [H] to hand over, present; to bring upon, cause to encounter; "to find favor in the eyes" means to "be please":– found (110), find (87), be found (23), was found (12), finds (11), is found (11), were (9), been found (8), were found (8), meet (7), come on (6), discovered (6), finding (6), met (6), pleased with (5 [+2834, 928, 6524]), present (5), is caught (4), are (3), discover (3), had (3 [+907]), handed (3), acquire (2), came (2), came upon (2), comprehend (2), fathom (2), happened (2), have enough (2), is (2), is found (2 [+5162]), lived (2), overtook (2), prosper (2 [+3202]), reach (2), still (2), survives (2), was (2), acquired (1), afford (1 [+3338, 1896]), are found (1), be room enough (1), be seen (1), become (1), been brought (1), before (1), bring a reward (1), brings (1), brings on (1), came across (1), came over (1), captured (1), catch (1), caught (1), caught up (1), come upon (1), comes (1), detect (1), discover meaning (1), displease (1 [+4202, 2834, 928, 6524]), displeasing (1 [+4202, 2834, 928, 6524]), do (1), doing (1), enough (1), ever-present (1 [+4394]), fall on (1), favorable toward (1 [+2834, 928, 6524]), find out (1), following (1), found courage (1), found out (1), found to be true (1), gain (1), gained (1), get (1), give (1), had (1), had (1 [+4200]), handed over (1 [+928, 3338]), happened to (1), has (1 [+4200]), have (1 [+928, 3338]), here (1), hit (1), is[S] (1), is attained (1), is captured (1), lay hold (1), lay on (1), left (1), lies (1), lift (1), looking for (1), lot (1), overcome (1), overtake (1), possess (1), probe (1), prospers (1 [+3202]), reaches (1), reaped (1), receive (1), regards (1 [+928, 6524]), regards (1 [+4200, 7156]), search (1), seize (1), seize the opportunity (1 [+3338]), seized (1), solved (1), spreads (1), still out (1), took (1), uncovered (1), was caught (1), were caught (1), will be found (1), win (1), NDT (7)

H5163 מַצָּב **maṣṣāb**, n.m. [10] [→ 5165; cf. 5893]. standing place; office; outpost, garrison:– outpost (4), detachment (1), garrison (1), office (1), outposts (1), standing (1 [+8079, 3922]), stood (1 [+8079])

H5164 מֻצָּב **muṣṣāb**, n.[m.] [2] [√ 5893]. pillar, tower:– pillar (1), towers (1)

H5165 מַצָּבָה **maṣṣābâ**, n.f. [1] [√ 5163]. outpost, garrison of soldiers on the perimeter of a guarded area:– outpost (1)

H5166 מִצָּבָה **miṣṣābâ**, n.f. [1] [√ 5893]. guard, watch:– guard (1)

H5167 מַצֵּבָה **maṣṣēbâ**, n.f. [34] [→ 5170; cf. 5893]. sacred (upright) stone, stone pillar:– sacred stones (14), pillar (10), sacred stone (5), monument (1), pillars (1), sacred pillars (1), stone pillars (1), NDT (1)

H5168 מְצֹבָיָה **m[e]ṣōbāyâ**, a.g. [1] Mezobaite:– Mezobaite (1)

H5169 מַצֶּבֶת[1] **maṣṣebet[1]**, n.f. [2] [√ 5893]. (tree) stump:– stump (1), stumps (1)

H5170 מַצֶּבֶת[2] **maṣṣebet[2]**, n.f. [2] [√ 5167; cf. 5893]. sacred (upright) stone, stone pillar:– pillar (2)

H5171 מְצָד **m[e]ṣād**, n.f. [11] [√ 7421; cf. 5181]. stronghold, fortress (with difficult access):– strongholds (7), fortress (2), stronghold (2)

H5172 מָצָה **māṣâ**, v. [7] [cf. 5209]. [Q] to squeeze out; to drain dry; [N] to be drained out:– be drained out (2), drain dry (1), drained to dregs (1 [+9272]), drink down (1), drink up (1), wrung out (1)

H5173 מֹצָה **mōṣâ**, n.pr.loc. [1] Mozah:– Mozah (1)

H5174 מַצָּה[1] **maṣṣâ[1]**, n.f. [53] [cf. 5209?]. unleavened bread, bread made without yeast; bread quickly made, without waiting for the dough to rise:– unleavened bread (20), bread made without yeast (12), without yeast (7), bread without yeast (4), made without yeast (4), bread (1), festival of unleavened Bread (1), prepared without yeast (1), NDT (3)

H5175 מַצָּה[2] **maṣṣâ[2]**, n.f. [3] [√ 5897]. quarrel, strife:– strife (2), quarrel (1)

H5176 מֻצְהָב **muṣhāb**, n.[m.] or v.ptcp. Not used in NIVEBC [√ 7410]. brass, see 7410

H5177 מִצְהָלוֹת **miṣhālôt**, n.f.[pl.] [2] [√ 7412]. neighing:– lustful neighings (1), neighing (1 [+7754])

H5178 מָצוֹד[1] **māṣôd[1]**, n.[m.] [3] [√ 7421]. (hunting) snare, net:– net (1), snare (1), stronghold (1)

H5179 מָצוֹד[2] **māṣôd[2]**, n.m. Not used in NIVEBC [√ 7421]. plunder; stronghold

H5180 מְצוּדָה[1] **m[e]ṣûdâ[1]**, n.f. [4] [√ 7421]. (hunting) snare, net; prey:– snare (2), prey (1), prison (1)

H5181 מְצוּדָה[2] **m[e]ṣûdâ[2]**, n.f. [18] [√ 7421?; cf. 5171]. stronghold, fortress, prison (a place difficult to access):– fortress (9), stronghold (7), prison (1), strong fortress (1 [+1074])

H5182 מְצוֹדָה[1] **m[e]ṣôdâ[1]**, n.f. [1] [√ 7421]. net:– net (1)

H5183 מְצוֹדָה[2] **m[e]ṣôdâ[2]**, n.f. [1] [√ 7421]. fortress, prison (a place difficult to access):– fortress (1)

H5184 מִצְוָה **miṣwâ**, n.f. [181] [√ 7422]. command, order, prescription, instruction:– commands (132), command (13), commandments (8), commanded (4), ordered (4), prescribed (3), law (2), warning (2), commanded (1 [+7422]), commanded (1 [+7422]), commandment (1), gave (1), instructions (1), laws (1), order (1), orders (1), rules (1), terms (1), way prescribed (1), what[S] (1 [+2021, 2021, 2296]), what ordered (1)

H5185 מְצוֹלָה **m[e]ṣôlâ**, n.f. [12] [√ 7425]. depths, the deep:– depths (10), deep (1), ravine (1)

H5186 מָצוֹק **māṣôq**, n.[m.] [6] [→ 5188; cf. 7439]. distress, suffering, stress, hardship:– suffering (3), distress (2), so hard (1 [+928])

H5187 מָצוּק **māṣûq**, n.m. [2] [√ 3668?]. foundation, pillar, support:– foundations (1), stood (1)

H5188 מְצוּקָה **m[e]ṣûqâ**, n.f. [7] [√ 5186; cf. 7439]. distress, anguish, stress, affliction:– distress (4), anguish (3)

H5189 מָצוֹר[1] **māṣôr[1]**, n.[m.] [22] [√ 5190; cf. 7443]. siege; siege works, ramparts:– siege (15), siege works (2), besiege (1 [+995, 928, 2021]), besieged (1), laid siege (1 [+995, 928, 2021]), ramparts (1), under siege (1)

H5190 מָצוֹר[2] **māṣôr[2]**, n.[m.] [4] [→ 5189, 5193; cf. 7443]. stronghold, fortification, defense:– fortified (2), defense (1), stronghold (1)

H5191 מָצוֹר[3] **māṣôr[3]**, n.pr.loc. [5] [√ 5213]. Egypt:– Egypt (5)

H5192 מָצוֹר[4] **māṣôr[4]**, n.[m.] Not used in NIVEBC [√ 7443]. lock up, custody

H5193 מְצוּרָה **m[e]ṣûrâ**, n.f. [8] [√ 5190; cf. 7443]. fortification, defense, fortress:– fortified (5), defenses (1), fortress (1), siege works (1)

H5194 מַצּוּת **maṣṣût**, n.f. [1] [√ 5897]. enemy, person of strife:– enemies (1 [+408])

H5195 מֵצַח **mēṣaḥ**, n.m. [12] [→ 5196; cf. 7458?]. forehead:– forehead (8), hardened (2 [+2617]), brazen look (1), foreheads (1)

H5196 מִצְחָה **miṣḥâ**, n.f. [1] [√ 5195; cf. 7458?]. greaves (armor for the front or back of leg from ankle to knee):– greaves (1)

H5197 מְצִלָּה **m[e]ṣillâ**, n.f. [1] [√ 7509]. (small) bell (on a horse):– bells (1)

H5198 מְצֻלָה **m[e]ṣulâ**, n.f. Not used in NIVEBC [√ 7425]. depth, the deep

H5199 מְצִלְתַּיִם **m[e]ṣiltayim**, n.f.du. [13] [√ 7509]. (pair of) cymbals:– cymbals (13)

H5200 מִצְנֶפֶת **miṣnepet**, n.f. [12] [√ 7571]. turban, headband:– turban (11), NDT (1)

H5201 מַצָּע **maṣṣā'**, n.m. [1] [√ 3667]. bed, couch:– bed (1)

H5202 מִצְעָד **miṣ'ād**, n.[m.] [3] [√ 7575]. step; (position of submission in a) train:– steps (2), submission (1)

H5203 מִצְעָר[1] **miṣ'ār[1]**, n.m. [5] [√ 7592]. small quantity, few:– small (2), humble (1), little while (1), only a few (1)

H5204 מִצְעָר[2] **miṣ'ār[2]**, n.pr.loc. [1] [√ 7592]. Mizar, "*small*":– Mizar (1)

H5205 מִצְפֶּה[1] **miṣpeh[1]**, n.m. [2] [→ 2174, 5206, 5207; cf. 7595]. watchtower (used for military defense and surveillance), any place that overlooks:– place that overlooks (1), watchtower (1)

H5206 מִצְפֶּה[2] **miṣpeh[2]**, n.pr.loc. [5] [√ 5205; cf. 7595]. Mizpah, "*lookout point*":– Mizpah (4), there[S] (1 [+1680])

H5207 מִצְפָּה **miṣpâ**, n.pr.loc. [40] [√ 5205; cf. 7595]. Mizpah, "*lookout point*":– Mizpah (39), there[S] (1 [+928, 2021])

H5208 מַצְפּוֹן **maṣpôn**, n.[m.] [1] [√ 7621]. hidden treasure, hiding place:– hidden treasures (1)

H5209 מָצַץ **māṣaṣ**, v. [1] [cf. 5172?]. [Q] to drink deeply, quaff:– drink deeply (1)

H5210 מֵצַר **mēṣar**, n.[m.] [3] [√ 7674]. anguish, distress, hardship:– anguish (1), distress (1), hard pressed (1)

H5211 מַצָּרָה **maṣṣārâ**, n.f. Not used in NIVEBC [√ 5915]. guard, watch

H5212 מִצְרִי **miṣrî**, a.g. [24] [√ 5213]. Egyptian:– Egyptian (19), Egyptian (2 [+408]), Egyptian's (2), Egyptians (1)

H5213 מִצְרַיִם **miṣrayim**, n.pr.loc. & g. [686] [→ 73, 5191, 5212]. Mizraim; Egypt, Egyptian:– Egypt (377), Egypt (184 [+824]), Egyptians (83), Egyptian (10), Egypt's (5), lower Egypt (2 [+824]), them[S] (2), Egypt (1 [+1426]), Egypt (1 [+1473]), Egyptians (1 [+1201]), country (1), here[S] (1 [+2025]), his[S] (1 [+4200, 4889]), it[S] (1 [+4722]), lower Egypt (1), the Egyptians (1), there[S] (1), there[S] (1 [+928]), they[S] (1), who[S] (1), NDT (10)

H5214 מַצְרֵף **maṣrēp**, n.[m.] [2] [√ 7671]. crucible, melting pot for metal:– crucible (2)

H5215 מַק **maq**, n.m. [2] [√ 5245]. stench, smell of decay:– decay (1), stench (1)

H5216 מַקֶּבֶת[1] **maqqebet[1]**, n.f. [4] [√ 5918]. hammer:– hammer (3), hammers (1)

H5217 מַקֶּבֶת[2] **maqqebet[2]**, n.f. [1] [√ 5918]. quarry:– quarry (1 [+1014])

H5218 מַקֵּדָה **maqqēdâ**, n.pr.loc. [9] [√ 5923]. Makkedah, "*locality of shepherds*":– Makkedah (9)

H5219 מִקְדָּשׁ **miqdāš**, n.m. [75] [√ 7727]. holy place, sanctuary, shrine:– sanctuary (59), sanctuaries (4), holy place (3), holiest (1), holy places (1), holy things (1), it[S] (1), most holy place (1 [+7731]), sanctuary (1 [+1074]), sanctuary (1 [+5226]), shrine (1), temple (1)

H5220 מַקְהֵל **maqhēl**, n.[m.] [2] [√ 7736]. assembly, congregation:– great congregation (2)

H5221 מַקְהֵלֹת **maqhēlôt**, n.pr.loc. [2] [√ 7736]. Makheloth, "*assemblies*":– Makheloth (2)

H5222 מִקְוֵא **miqwē'**, n.pr.loc.? Not used in NIVEBC [cf. 7745]. see 2256 & 7745

H5223 מִקְוֶה[1] **miqweh[1]**, n.[m.] [5] [√ 7747]. hope:– hope (5)

H5224 מִקְוֶה[2] **miqweh[2]**, n.[m.] [3] [√ 7748]. collection (of water), reservoir:– collecting (1), gathered (1), reservoirs (1 [+4784])

H5225 מִקְוָה **miqwâ**, n.f. [1] [√ 7748]. reservoir:– reservoir (1)

H5226 מָקוֹם **māqôm**, n.m. [400] [√ 7756]. place, site:– place (255), home (14), places (12), area (9), land (5), room (5), site (4), spot (4), where[S] (4), wherever (3 [+928, 889]), anywhere (2 [+928, 3972]), dwell (2), dwelling place (2), everywhere (2 [+3972]), here[S] (2 [+2021, 2021, 2296]), seat (2 [+8699]), sites (2), space (2), there[S] (2), where[S] (2 [+2021]), wherever (2 [+928, 3972, 2021, 889]), Nineveh[S] (1 [+2023]), base (1), channels (1), commands (1), countries (1), direction (1), dwelling (1), everywhere (1 [+928, 3972]), everywhere (1 [+3972, 2021]), haunt (1), here[S] (1 [+928]), here[S] (1 [+2021]), here[S] (1 [+928, 2021, 2021, 2296]), home (1 [+2257]), homeland (1), homeland (1 [+824]), homes (1), hometown (1 [+9133]), it[S] (1), it[S] (1 [+2021, 2021, 2085]), lair (1), lands (1), locality (1), place where standing (1), points (1), position (1), positions (1), post (1), proper place (1 [+889, 2118, 9004]), regions (1), reside (1), rest (1), sanctuary (1 [+5219]), sanctuary (1 [+7731]), seated (1 [+5989]), somewhere (1), suitable (1), there[S] (1 [+2023]), town (1), way (1), where (1 [+361]), where[S] (1 [+928]), where[S] (1 [+928, 2021]), where dwells (1), where lived (1), wherever (1 [+928, 3972, 2021]), wherever (1 [+4946, 3972, 2021]), wherever (1 [+928, 2021, 889]), wherever (1 [+6584, 3972, 2021, 889]), wherever (1 [+928, 285, 2021, 889]), which[S] (1 [+889]), NDT (12)

H5227 מָקוֹר **māqôr**, n.m. [18] [√ 7769]. fountain, spring, source (of a flow), often with an implication of abundance or freshness:– fountain (9), spring (3), assembly (1), flow (1), it[S] (1), source of (1), springs (1), well (1)

H5228 מִקָּח ***miqqāḥ***, n.[m.] [1] [√ 4374]. taking, accepting (a bribe):– bribery (1 [+8816])

H5229 מַקָּחוֹת ***maqqāḥôt***, n.f. [1] [√ 4374]. (pl.) merchandise, wares:– merchandise (1)

H5230 מִקְטָר ***miqṭār***, n.m. [1] [√ 7787]. burning:– burning (1)

H5231 מֻקְטָר ***muqṭār***, n.m. [1] [√ 7787]. incense:– incense (1)

H5232 מְקַטֶּרֶת ***meqaṭṭeret***, n.f. [1] [√ 7787]. incense altar:– incense altars (1)

H5233 מִקְטֶרֶת ***miqṭeret***, n.f. [2] [√ 7787]. censer, incense burner:– censer (2)

H5234 מַקֵּל ***maqqēl***, n.m. & f. [18] branch, stick; staff, a stick used to assist in walking, discipline, and guidance; war club:– staff (7), branches (6), branch (1), diviner's rod (1), staffs (1), sticks (1), war clubs (1 [+3338])

H5235 מִקְלוֹת ***miqlôt***, n.pr.m. [4] Mikloth, "*rods*":– Mikloth (4)

H5236 מִקְלָט ***miqlāṭ***, n.[m.] [20] [√ 7832]. refuge, place of protection:– refuge (17), place of refuge (1), protection (1), NDT (1)

H5237 מִקְלַעַת ***miqla'at***, n.f. [4] [√ 7844]. carving, engraving (on wood):– carved (2 [+7844]), carved (1), engraving (1)

H5238 מִקְנֶה ***miqneh***, n.m. [76] [→ 5240; cf. 7864]. livestock, (animals from) herds and flocks:– livestock (45), cattle (4), flocks (4), owned (2 [+2118]), acquired (1), animal (1), animals (1), bought (1), cattle (1 [+1330]), droves of livestock (1), flocks (1 [+7366]), flocks and herds (1), herders (1), herders (1 [+8286]), herds (1), herds (1 [+1330]), herds and flocks (1), herds of livestock (1), livestock (1 [+989]), sheep and goats (1 [+7366]), tend livestock (1 [+408, 2118]), tended livestock (1 [+408, 2118]), that[S] (1), NDT (2)

H5239 מִקְנָה ***miqnâ***, n.f. [15] [√ 7864]. something bought, purchased, acquisition:– bought (4), purchase (3), bought (2 [+4084]), price (2), paid (1), property (1), NDT (2)

H5240 מִקְנֵיָהוּ ***miqnēyāhû***, n.pr.m. [2] [√ 5238 + 3378; cf. 7864]. Mikneiah, "*Yahweh acquires*":– Mikneiah (2)

H5241 מִקְסָם ***miqsām***, n.[m.] [2] [√ 7876]. divination:– divinations (2)

H5242 מָקַץ ***māqaṣ***, n.pr.loc. [1] Makaz:– Makaz (1)

H5243 מִקְצוֹעַ ***miqṣôa'***, n.m. [12] [√ 7910]. corner (of a base); angle of a wall:– corners (5), angle (4), in each corner (2 [+928, 928, 5243]), angle of the wall (1)

H5244 מַקְצֻעָה ***maqṣu'â***, n.[f.] [1] [√ 7909]. (wood) chisel:– chisels (1)

H5245 מָקַק ***māqaq***, v. [10] [→ 5215]. [N] to rot, waste away, fester; dissolve; [H] to cause to rot:– waste away (4), rot (3), be dissolved (1), fester (1), wasting away (1)

H5246 מִקְרָא ***miqrā'***, n.m. [23] [√ 7924]. assembly, calling the community together, usually for a religious ceremony:– assembly (15), assemblies (3), another[S] (1 [+7731]), assemble (1), calling together (1), convocations (1 [+7924]), read (1)

H5247 מִקְרֶה ***miqreh***, n.m. [10] [√ 7936]. happening by chance; fate, destiny:– fate (4), destiny (2), as it turned out (1 [+7936]), by chance (1), something happened (1), that[S] (1)

H5248 מְקָרֶה ***meqāreh***, n.[m.] [1] [√ 7939]. rafters, roof beams:– rafters (1)

H5249 מְקֵרָה ***meqērâ***, n.f. [2] [√ 7981]. coolness; cool room, summer home:– palace (2)

H5250 מִקְשֶׁה ***miqšeh***, n.[m.] [1] [→ 5251]. well-dressed hair:– well-dressed hair (1 [+5126])

H5251 [1]מִקְשָׁה ***miqšâ[1]***, n.f. [9] [√ 5250]. hammered work; some sources: embossed metal work:– hammered (5), hammered out (2), hammer out (1 [+6913]), NDT (1)

H5252 [2]מִקְשָׁה ***miqšâ[2]***, n.f. [2] [→ 7991]. melon field, cucumber field:– cucumber field (2)

H5253 [1]מַר ***mar[1]***, a. & subst. [38] [→ 5287; cf. 5352]. bitter; bitterness, ranging from being merely disagreeable to the taste to being poisonous; by extension: anxiety, despair:– bitter (16), bitterness (6), bitterly (4), anguish (3), bitter suffering (2), angry (1 [+5883]), cruel (1), deep anguish (1 [+5883]), discontented (1 [+5883]), fierce (1 [+5883]), in anguish (1 [+5883]), ruthless (1)

H5254 [2]מַר ***mar[2]***, n.[m.] [1] drop (in a bucket):– drop (1)

H5255 מֹר ***mōr***, n.m. [12] [√ 5352]. myrrh:– myrrh (12)

H5256 [1]מָרָא ***mārā'[1]***, v. Not used in NIVEBC [cf. 5286]. [Ho] to be obstinate

H5257 [2]מָרָא ***mārā'[2]***, v. [1] [Q] to flap, spread the feathers as it runs; this can also refer to the feet kicking up dirt:– spreads feathers to run (1 [+928, 2021, 5294])

H5258 [3]מָרָא ***mārā'[3]***, n.[m.] Not used in NIVEBC [→ 1344, 1374, 4934?, 4935?, 5309, 5319?]. [Q] to fatten, graze

H5259 [4]מָרָא ***mārā'[4]***, n.pr.f. [1] [√ 5352]. Mara, "*bitter*":– Mara (1)

H5260 מַרְאֶה ***mar'eh***, n.m. [103] [√ 8011]. what is seen with the eye, appearance; by extension: vision, supernatural revelation with a focus on visual communication, but can include verbal content:– appearance (14), looked (10), vision (10), beautiful (6 [+3202]), appears (5), appear (3), appeared (3), beautiful (3 [+3637]), like (3 [+3869]), that[S] (3), face (2), handsome (2 [+3637]), sight (2), sleek (2 [+3637]), ugly (2 [+8273]), what sees (2), clearly (1), eye (1), handsome (1 [+3202]), huge (1), imposing (1 [+1524, 4200]), look (1), look at (1), looked (1 [+8011]), pattern (1), saw (1 [+6524]), see (1), see (1 [+6524]), seem (1), sights (1), sights (1 [+6524]), similar (1 [+3869, 2021]), what[S] (1), NDT (14)

H5261 [1]מַרְאָה ***mar'â[1]***, n.f. [11] [√ 8011]. vision:– vision (5), visions (5), it[S] (1 [+2021])

H5262 [2]מַרְאָה ***mar'â[2]***, n.f. [1] [√ 8011]. mirror:– mirrors (1)

H5263 מֻרְאָה ***mur'â***, n.f. [1] [cf. 5286]. crop (of a bird):– crop (1)

H5264 מֵרֹאן ***mer'ôn***, n.pr.loc. Not used in NIVEBC [cf. 9077]. Meron

H5265 מְרַאֲשׁוֹת ***mera'ašôt***, n.[f.]pl.den. [10] [→ 5358; cf. 8039]. head rest, place near the head:– near head (4), head (2), under head (2), by head (1), heads (1)

H5266 מֵרַב ***mērab***, n.pr.f. [4] [√ 8045]. Merab, "*abundant*":– Merab (4)

H5267 מַרְבַד ***marbad***, n.[m.] [2] [√ 8048]. covering:– covered (1 [+8048]), coverings bed (1)

H5268 מִרְבָּה ***mirbâ***, n.f. [1] [√ 8049]. so much:– so much (1)

H5269 מַרְבֶּה ***marbeh***, n.[m.] [2] [√ 8049]. abundance, increase:– abundance (1), greatness (1)

H5270 מַרְבִּית ***marbît***, n.f. [5] [√ 8049]. great number; most, majority; profit:– most (2), descendants (1 [+1074]), greatness (1), profit (1)

H5271 מַרְבֵּץ ***marbēṣ***, n.[m.] [2] [√ 8069]. lair, resting place, place to lie down:– lair (1), resting place (1)

H5272 מַרְבֵּק ***marbēq***, n.[m.] [4] fattening (of a calf):– fattened (3), well-fed (1)

H5273 מַרְגּוֹעַ ***margôa'***, n.[m.] [1] [√ 8089]. resting place:– rest (1)

H5274 מַרְגְּלוֹת ***margelôt***, n.[f.]pl.den. [5] [√ 8079]. (place of) the feet:– feet (4), legs (1)

H5275 מַרְגֵּמָה ***margēmâ***, n.f. [1] [√ 8083]. sling:– sling (1)

H5276 מַרְגֵּעָה ***margē'â***, n.f. [1] [√ 8089]. place of repose, resting-place:– place of repose (1)

H5277 מָרַד ***mārad***, v. [25] [→ 5278, 5279?, 5280]. [Q] to rebel, revolt:– rebelled (12), rebel (7), revolt (2), rebelling (1), rebellion (1), rebellious (1), NDT (1)

H5278 [1]מֶרֶד ***mered[1]***, n.[m.] [1] [→ 5279; cf. 5277; 10438]. rebellion:– rebellion (1)

H5279 [2]מֶרֶד ***mered[2]***, n.pr.m. [2] [√ 5278?; cf. 5277]. Mered, "*rebel*":– Mered (2)

H5280 מַרְדּוּת ***mardût***, n.f. [1] [√ 5277]. rebellion, revolt:– rebellious (1)

H5281 מְרֹדָךְ ***merōdāk***, n.pr. [1] [→ 5282, 5283]. Marduk, Merodak (pagan god):– Marduk (1)

H5282 מְרֹדַךְ-בַּלְאֲדָן ***merōdak-bal'adān***, n.pr.m. [2] [√ 5281 + 1156; cf. 1347]. Merodach-Baladan, "*Marduk has given a son*":– Marduk-Baladan (2)

H5283 מָרְדֳּכַי ***mordokay***, n.pr.m. [60] [√ 5281]. Mordecai, "*Marduk*":– Mordecai (49), Mordecai's (5), he[S] (3), him[S] (2), he[S] (1 [+2021, 408])

H5284 מֻרְדָּף ***murdāp***, n.f. & m. [1] [√ 8103]. aggression:– aggression (1)

H5285 מָרָּה ***morrâ***, n.f. Not used in NIVEBC [√ 5352]. bitterness

H5286 [1]מָרָה ***mārâ[1]***, v. [44] [→ 3559, 5308, 5318?, 5361; cf. 5256, 5263]. [Q] to rebel, defy, become disobedient; [H] to act as a rebel, defy by one's action:– rebelled (20), rebellious (9), rebel (3), defied (2), most rebellious (2 [+5286]), rebels (2), defying (1), disobedient (1), disobeyed (1), hostility (1), rebelling (1), rebellion (1)

H5287 [2]מָרָה ***mārâ[2]***, a. Not used in NIVEBC [√ 5253; cf. 5352]. bitter[ness]

H5288 [3]מָרָה ***mārâ[3]***, n.pr.f. [5] [→ 5300; cf. 5352]. Marah, "*bitter*":– Marah (4), its[S] (1 [+4946])

H5289 מֹרָה ***mōrâ***, n.f. [2] [√ 5352]. bitterness, grief:– bitterness (1), source of grief (1 [+8120])

H5290 מַרְהֵבָה ***marhēbâ***, n.f. [1] [√ 8104; cf. 4502]. attack, assault:– fury (1)

H5291 מָרוּד ***mārûd***, n.[m.] [3] [√ 8113]. wandering; wanderer; homeless, with a focus on poverty:– wandering (2), wanderer (1)

H5292 מֵרוֹז ***mērôz***, n.pr.loc. [1] Meroz:– Meroz (1)

H5293 מָרוֹחַ ***mārôaḥ***, n.[m.] [1] [√ 5302]. damaged (by pounding or grinding):– damaged (1)

H5294 מָרוֹם ***mārôm***, n.m. [53] [√ 8123]. heights, (place) on high, being in an elevated position; by extension: pride, haughtiness, arrogance, an improperly high opinion of oneself; exaltation, high in honor and status:– on high (10), heights (8), heavens (6), exalted (3), high (3), on high (3 [+928, 2021]), pride (3), on high (2 [+4200, 2021]), above (1 [+928, 2021]), arrogance (1), heaven (1), height (1), heights above (1), heights of heaven (1), high positions (1), highest point (1), highest point (1 [+1726]), highest point (1 [+8031]), lofty (1), on heights (1), on high (1 [+4946]), spreads feathers to run (1 [+5257, 928, 2021]), terraced (1)

H5295 מֵרוֹם ***mērôm***, n.pr.loc. [2] [√ 8123]. Merom, "*high place*":– Merom (2)

H5296 מֵרוֹץ ***mērôṣ***, n.[m.] [1] [√ 8132]. foot race, running:– race (1)

H5297 [1]מְרוּצָה ***merûṣâ[1]***, n.f. [4] [√ 8132]. manner or mode of running; course of a race:– course (2), runs (1), NDT (1)

H5298 [2]מְרוּצָה ***merûṣâ[2]***, n.f. [1] [√ 8368]. extortion:– extortion (1)

H5299 מְרוּקִים ***merûqîm***, n.[m.] [1] [√ 5347]. beauty treatments (including massage and ointments):– beauty treatments (1)

H5300 מָרוֹת ***mārôt***, n.pr.loc. [1] [√ 5288; cf. 5352]. Maroth, "*bitterness*":– Maroth (1)

H5301 מַרְזֵחַ ***marzēaḥ***, n.m. [2] funeral meal; cultic feast:– feasting (1), funeral meal (1)

H5302 מָרַח ***māraḥ***, v. [1] [→ 5293]. [Q] to apply by spreading on or rubbing in:– apply (1)

H5303 מֶרְחָב ***merḥāb***, n.[m.] [6] [→ 5304; cf. 8143]. spaciousness, wideness, with the associative meaning that such a wide area is comfortable, and possibly safe and free:– spacious place (4), meadow (1), whole (1)

H5304 מֶרְחֳבְיָה ***merḥobyâ***, var. Not used in NIVEBC [√ 5303 + 3378]. see 3378 & 5303

H5305 מֶרְחָק ***merḥāq***, n.m. [18] [√ 8178]. distance, far away:– afar (4), distant (4), distant (2 [+4946]), far away (2), distant lands (1), edge (1), far away (1 [+4946]), far-off (1), faraway (1), stretches afar (1)

H5306 מַרְחֶשֶׁת ***marḥešet***, n.f. [2] [√ 8180]. cooking pan (with a lid):– pan (2)

H5307 מָרַט ***māraṭ***, v. [14] [√ 10440, 10441]. [Q] to pull out (hair); [Qp] to be polished, rubbed; [N] to lose one's hair, become bald; [Pu] to be polished, burnished, smooth (skinned):– polished (5), lost hair (2 [+8031]), smooth-skinned (2), burnished (1), made raw (1), pulled (1), pulled out beard (1), pulled out hair (1)

H5308 מְרִי ***merî***, n.m. [23] [√ 5286]. rebellion:– rebellious (17), rebellion (3), bitter (1), rebel (1 [+2118]), rebellious (1 [+1201])

H5309 מְרִיא ***merî'***, n.[m.] [8] [√ 5258; cf. 5263]. fattened animal (choice for consumption):– fattened calves (3), fattened animals (2), choice (1), fattened calf (1), yearling (1)

H5310 מֵרִיב ***mērîb***, n.pr.m. Not used in NIVEBC [→ 5311; cf. 8189]. antagonist (of Baal)

H5311 מְרִיב בַּעַל ***merîb ba'al***, n.pr.m. [3] [√ 5310 + 1251; cf. 5314]. Merib-Baal, "*Baal contends*":– Merib-Baal (2), who[S] (1)

H5312 [1]מְרִיבָה ***merîbâ[1]***, n.f. [2] [→ 5313, 5315; cf. 8189]. quarreling, strife; rebellion, with a focus on the feelings of enmity:– quarreling (1), rebelled (1)

H5313 [2]מְרִיבָה ***merîbâ[2]***, n.pr.loc. [7] [√ 5312; cf. 8189]. Meribah:– Meribah (7)

H5314 מְרִי-בַעַל ***merî-ba'al***, n.pr.m. [1] [√ 5310 + 1251; cf. 5311]. Merib-Baal, "*Baal contends*":– who[S] (1)

H5315 מְרִיבַת קָדֵשׁ ***merîbat qādēš***, n.pr.loc. [4] [√ 5312 + 7729]. Meribah Kadesh, "*quarrelling of Kadesh*":– Meribah Kadesh (4)

H5316 מְרָיָה ***merāyâ***, n.pr.m. [1] Meraiah, "*loved by Yahweh*":– Meraiah (1)

H5317 מֹרִיָּה ***mōriyyâ***, n.pr.loc. [2] Moriah:– Moriah (2)

H5318 מְרָיוֹת ***merāyôt***, n.pr.m. [6] [√ 5286?]. Meraioth, "*rebellious*":– Meraioth (6)

H5319 מִרְיָם ***miryām***, n.pr.f. & m. [15] [√ 5258?]. Miriam, "[variously] *bitterness; plump one; wished-for child; one who loves or is loved*":– Miriam (12), Miriam's (1), her[S] (1), she[S] (1)

H5320 מְרִירוּת ***merîrût***, n.f. [1] [√ 5352]. bitterness:– bitter grief (1)

H5321 מְרִירִי ***merîrî***, a. [1] [√ 5352]. bitter, in context referring to something deadly:– deadly (1)

H5322 מֹרֶךְ ***mōrek***, n.[m.] [1] [√ 8216]. fearfulness, despondency:– fearful (1)

H5323 מֶרְכָּב ***merkāb***, n.m. [3] [√ 8206]. seat, saddle, chariot:– chariot (1), seat (1), sits (1)

H5324 מֶרְכָּבָה ***merkābâ***, n.f. [44] [√ 8206]. chariot:– chariots (21), chariot (20), NDT (3)

H5325 מַרְכָּבוֹת ***markābôt***, n.pr.loc. Not used in NIVEBC [→ 1112]. Marcaboth

H5326 מַרְכֹּלֶת ***markōlet***, n.f. [1] [√ 8217]. marketplace, place of merchandising:– marketplace (1)

H5327 [1]מִרְמָה ***mirmâ[1]***, n.f. [39] [→ 5328; cf. 8228]. deceit, deception, dishonesty, treachery:– deceit (11), deceitful (7), dishonest (4), lies (4), false (3), deceitful (2 [+408]), deceitfully (2), deceitfully (2 [+928]), deception (2), lie (1), treachery (1)

H5328 [2]מִרְמָה ***mirmâ[2]***, n.pr.m. [1] [√ 5327?; cf. 8228?]. Mirmah, "*deceit*":– Mirmah (1)

H5329 מְרֵמוֹת ***m[e]rēmôt***, n.pr.m. [7] Meremoth, "*elevations*":– Meremoth (6), Meremoth's (1)

H5330 מִרְמָס ***mirmās***, n.[m.] [7] [√ 8252]. trampling down, running over:– beaten down (1), trample down (1 [+8492]), trampled (1), trampled underfoot (1), trampling underfoot (1), what trampled (1 [+8079]), where run (1)

H5331 מֵרֹנֹתִי ***mērōnōtî***, a.g. [2] Meronothite, of Meronoth, "*of Meronoth*":– Meronothite (1), of Meronoth (1)

H5332 מֶרֶס ***meres***, n.pr.m. [1] Meres, "*worthy*":– Meres (1)

H5333 מַרְסְנָא ***mars[e]nā'***, n.pr.m. [1] Marsena:– Marsena (1)

H5334 מֵרַע ***mēra'***, n.m. *or* v.ptcp. [1] [√ 8317]. evil, atrocity:– evil (1)

H5335 [1]מֵרֵעַ ***mērēa'[1]***, n.[m.] *or* v.ptcp. [8] [√ 8287]. close friend, companion, personal adviser:– companion (2), companions (2), friends (2), friend (1), personal adviser (1)

H5336 [2]מֵרֵעַ ***mērēa'[2]***, n.[m.] *or* v.ptcp. Not used in NIVEBC [√ 8317]. see 8317

H5337 מִרְעֶה ***mir'eh***, n.m. [13] [√ 8286]. pasture, grazing place:– pasture (12), place where fed (1)

H5338 מַרְעִית ***mar'ît***, n.f. [10] [√ 8286]. pasture, place of grazing:– pasture (8), fed (1), flock (1)

H5339 מַרְעֲלָה ***mar'[a]lâ***, n.pr.loc. [1] [√ 8302]. Maralah:– Maralah (1)

H5340 [1]מַרְפֵּא ***marpē'[1]***, n.m. [14] [→ 5342; cf. 8324]. healing, remedy:– healing (7), remedy (3), healed (1), health (1), incurable (1 [+401]), soothing (1)

H5341 [2]מַרְפֵּא ***marpē'[2]***, n.m. [2] [√ 8332]. calmness, composure:– at peace (1), calmness (1)

H5342 מַרְפֵּה ***marpēh***, n.m. Not used in NIVEBC [√ 5340; cf. 8324]. healing, see 5340

H5343 מִרְפָּשׂ ***mirpāś***, n.[m.] [1] [√ 8346]. what is muddy, fouled (by trampling):– what muddied (1)

H5344 מָרַץ ***māraṣ***, v. [4] [N] to be painful, hurtful; [H] to provoke, irritate:– ails (1), beyond all remedy (1), bitter (1), painful (1)

H5345 מַרְצֵעַ ***marṣēa'***, n.[m.] [2] [√ 8361]. awl (piercing tool):– awl (2)

H5346 מַרְצֶפֶת ***marṣepet***, n.f. [1] [√ 8362]. (stone) base, stone-layer:– base (1)

H5347 מָרַק ***māraq***, v. [3] [→ 5299, 5348, 9475]. [Q] to polish; [Qp] to be polished; [Pu] to be thoroughly scoured; [H] to cleanse:– be scoured (1), polish (1), polished (1)

H5348 מָרָק ***mārāq***, n.m. [3] [√ 5347]. broth (juice stewed out of meat):– broth (3)

H5349 מֶרְקָח ***merqāḥ***, n.[m.] [1] [√ 8379]. aromatic herb, scented spice, perfume:– perfume (1)

H5350 מֶרְקָחָה ***merqāḥâ***, n.f. [2] [√ 8379]. ointment jar, spice-pot:– pot of ointment (1), spices (1)

H5351 מִרְקַחַת ***mirqaḥat***, n.f. [3] [√ 8379]. mixture of fragrant spices, blend of perfumes:– fragrant (1), perfumes (1 [+5126]), took care of mixing (1 [+8379])

H5352 מָרַר ***mārar***, v. [17] [→ 4933, 4936, 5253, 5255, 5259, 5285, 5287, 5288, 5289, 5300, 5320, 5321, 5353, 5354, 5355, 9476]. [Q] to be bitter; suffer anguish; [P] to make bitter, weep bitterly; [H] to make bitter; to grieve bitterly; [Htpal] to enrage oneself, be furious; from the base meaning "to taste bitter" come extensions of bitter feelings: anger, fury, anguish, rebellion:– bitter (4), made bitter (3), bitterly (1), bitterness attacked (1), furiously (1), grieve bitterly (1), grieves (1), in bitter anguish (1), in bitter distress (1), rage (1), rebel (1), suffered (1)

H5353 מָרֹר ***mārōr***, n.m. [5] [√ 5352]. bitter things:– bitter herbs (3), bitter things (1), bitterness (1)

H5354 מְרֵרָה ***m[e]rērâ***, n.f. [1] [√ 5352]. gall (bitter fluid from the gall bladder):– gall (1)

H5355 מְרֹרָה ***m[e]rōrâ***, n.f. [2] [√ 5352]. gall bladder; venom, poison (of snakes):– liver (1), venom (1)

H5356 [1]מְרָרִי ***m[e]rārî[1]***, n.pr.m. [39] [→ 5357]. Merari; Merarite, "*bitter*":– Merari (21), Merarites (9 [+1201]), Merarite (7 [+1201]), Merarite (2)

H5357 [2]מְרָרִי ***m[e]rārî[2]***, a.g. [1] [√ 5356]. Merarite, "*of Merari*":– Merarite (1)

H5358 [1]מָרֵשָׁה ***mārēšâ[1]***, n.pr.loc. [6] [→ 5265, 5359?]. Mareshah, "[perhaps] *head place*":– Mareshah (6)

H5359 [2]מָרֵשָׁה ***mārēšâ[2]***, n.pr.m. [2] [√ 5358?]. Mareshah, "[perhaps] *head place*":– Mareshah (2)

H5360 מִרְשַׁעַת ***mirša'at***, n.f. [1] [√ 8399]. wickedness, of a person (that) wicked woman:– wicked (1)

H5361 מְרָתַיִם ***m[e]rātayim***, n.pr.f. [1] [√ 5286]. Merathaim, "*double rebellion*":– Merathaim (1)

H5362 [1]מַשָּׂא ***maśśā'[1]***, n.m. [36] [√ 5951]. burden, load, what is lifted and carried; by extension: oppression; singing (lifting the voice):– burden (8), load (7), carry (5), carrying (3), singing (2), what to carry (2), burdens (1), camel-loads (1 [+1695]), carried about (1), desire (1), loads (1), oppression (1), take away (1 [+5911]), that[S] (1), tribute (1)

H5363 [2]מַשָּׂא ***maśśā'[2]***, n.m. [30] [√ 5951]. oracle, prophetic utterance, pronouncement, with the focus on the content of the message:– prophecy (18), message (8), inspired utterance (2), prophecies (2)

H5364 [3]מַשָּׂא ***maśśā'[3]***, n.pr.g. & loc. [2] [→ 5392?]. Massa, "*burden, oracle*":– Massa (2)

H5365 מַשֹּׂא ***maśśō'***, n.m. [1] [√ 5951]. partiality:– partiality (1 [+7156])

H5366 מַשָּׂאָה ***maśśā'â***, n.f. [1] [√ 5951]. uplifted (clouds of smoke):– clouds of smoke (1)

H5367 מַשְׂאוֹת ***maś'ôt***, n.f.? Not used in NIVEBC [√ 5951]. see 5363 & 5368

H5368 מַשְׂאֵת ***maś'ēt***, n.f. [15] [√ 5951]. what is lifted up: portion (of food), tax, tribute, gift, burden:– tax (3), gifts (2), burden (1), cloud (1), gift (1), lifting up (1), portion (1), portions (1), present (1), signal (1), smoke (1), NDT (1)

H5369 [1]מִשְׂגָּב ***miśgāb[1]***, n.[m.] [17] [√ 8435]. fortress, refuge, stronghold:– fortress (9), stronghold (5), refuge (2), high (1)

H5370 [2]מִשְׂגָּב ***miśgāb[2]***, n.pr.loc. Not used in NIVEBC [√ 8435]. Misgab, see 5369

H5371 מַשֶּׂגֶת ***maśśeget***, n.[f.] *or* v.ptcp. Not used in NIVEBC [√ 5952]. overtaking, see 5952

H5372 מְשׂוּכָּה ***m[e]śûkkâ***, n.f. [1] [√ 8504]. thorn-hedge:– hedge (1)

H5373 מַשּׂוֹר ***maśśôr***, n.m. [1] saw (cutting tool):– saw (1)

H5374 מְשׂוּרָה ***m[e]śûrâ***, n.f. [4] (liquid) measure of quantity, measure of capacity:– measure out (1), measurements of quantity (1), quantity (1), rationed (1 [+928])

H5375 [1]מָשׂוֹשׂ ***māśôś[1]***, n.m. [16] [√ 8464]. joy, delight, celebration:– joy (6), delight (2), joyful (2), rejoices (2), celebrations (1), joyful sounds (1), merriment (1), rejoice greatly (1 [+8464])

H5376 [2]מָשׂוֹשׂ ***māśôś[2]***, n.m. [1] [cf. 5022]. wasting away, rotting away:– withers away (1)

H5377 מִשְׂחָק ***miśḥāq***, n.[m.] [1] [√ 8471]. (scoffing) laughter:– scoff (1)

H5378 מַשְׂטֵמָה ***maśṭēmâ***, n.f. [2] [√ 8475]. hostility, animosity, enmity:– hostility (2)

H5379 מְשֻׂכָה ***m[e]śukâ***, n.f. [1] [√ 5004; cf. 6056]. (thorn) hedge (which impedes movement):– blocked (1)

H5380 מַשְׂכִּיל ***maśkîl***, n.m. [14] [√ 8505]. maskil (t.t. in the Psalms, perhaps "wisdom song"):– maskil (13), psalm of praise (1)

H5381 מַשְׂכִּית ***maśkît***, n.f. [6] [√ 8495]. carved image, sculpture, figurine; what is imagined, imagination:– carved (1), carved images (1), evil imaginations (1 [+4222]), idol (1), imagine (1 [+928]), settings (1)

H5382 מַשְׂכֹּרֶת ***maśkōret***, n.f. [4] [√ 8509]. wage:– wages (3), rewarded (1)

H5383 מַשְׂמְרָה ***maśmērâ***, n.m. [1] [cf. 6169]. nail (on the end of a goad):– nails (1)

H5384 מִשְׂפָּח ***miśpāḥ***, n.[m.] [1] [cf. 6203]. bloodshed, with a focus on violence:– bloodshed (1)

H5385 מִשְׂרָה ***miśrâ***, n.f. [2] [√ 8606]. dominion, rule:– government (2)

H5386 מִשְׂרָפוֹת ***miśrāpôt***, n.[f.pl.] [2] [√ 8596]. (complete) burning, funeral fire:– burned (1), funeral fire (1)

H5387 מִשְׂרְפוֹת מַיִם ***miśr[e]pôt mayim***, n.pr.loc. [2] [√ 8596 + 4784]. Misrephoth Maim, "*waters of Misrephoth [lime burning]*":– Misrephoth Maim (2)

H5388 מַשְׂרֵקָה ***maśrēqâ***, n.pr.loc. [2] [√ 8601]. Masrekah, "[perhaps] *vineyard*":– Masrekah (2)

H5389 מַשְׂרֵת ***maśrēt***, n.m. [1] [√ 8419]. cooking pan:– pan (1)

H5390 מַשׁ ***maš***, var. see 5434

H5391 מַשָּׁא ***maššā'***, n.m. [3] [√ 5957]. debt; exacting of usury:– charging interest (1), debts (1 [+3338]), interest (1)

H5392 מֵשָׁא ***mēšā'***, n.pr.loc. [1] [√ 5364?]. Mesha:– Mesha (1)

H5393 מַשְׁאָב ***maš'āb***, n.[m.] [1] [√ 8612]. watering channel, place to draw water:– watering places (1)

H5394 מַשָּׁאָה ***maššā'â***, n.f. [2] [√ 5957]. (secured) loan:– debts (1), make a loan (1 [+5957])

H5395 מַשֻּׁאָה ***maššu'â***, n.[f.] Not used in NIVEBC [√ 5958]. deceiving, see 8420

H5396 מַשָּׁאוֹן ***maššā'ôn***, n.[m.] [1] [√ 5958]. deception:– deception (1)

H5397 מַשֻּׁאוֹת ***maššu'ôt***, n.f.pl. [2] ruin, rubble, desolation:– ruin (1), ruins (1)

H5398 מִשְׁאָל ***miš'āl***, n.pr.loc. [2] [cf. 5443]. Mishal:– Mishal (2)

H5399 מִשְׁאָלָה ***miš'ālâ***, n.f. [2] [√ 8626]. desire:– desires (1), requests (1)

H5400 מִשְׁאֶרֶת ***miš'eret***, n.f. [4] [√ 8419]. kneading trough:– kneading trough (2), kneading troughs (2)

H5401 מִשְׁבְּצוֹת ***mišb[e]ṣôt***, n.f.pl. [9] [√ 8687]. filigree settings (ornamental work with fine gold wire usually for setting jewels):– filigree (3), settings (3), filigree settings (2), interwoven (1)

H5402 מַשְׁבֵּר ***mašbēr***, n.[m.] [3] [√ 8689]. opening of the womb, the point where birth first occurs:– moment of birth (2), womb (1 [+1201])

H5403 מִשְׁבָּר ***mišbār***, n.[m.] [5] [√ 8689]. breakers, waves:– waves (3), breakers (2)

H5404 מִשְׁבָּת ***mišbāt***, n.[m.] [1] [√ 8697]. destruction, cessation, finish:– destruction (1)

H5405 מִשְׁגֶּה ***mišgeh***, n.m. [1] [√ 8706]. inadvertent mistake, oversight:– mistake (1)

H5406 מָשָׁה ***māšâ***, v. [3] [→ 5407; cf. 621?]. [Q] to draw out; [H] to cause to draw out:– drew out (2), drew (1)

H5407 מֹשֶׁה ***mōšeh***, n.pr.m. [767] [√ 5406]. Moses, "*drawn out* [Ex 2:10]; Egyptian for *child*":– Moses (723), he[S] (18), him[S] (17), his[S] (3), his[S] (1 [+4200]), NDT (5)

H5408 מַשֶּׁה ***maššeh***, n.m. [1] [√ 5957]. credit, loan; "the lord of the loan" is a "creditor":– creditor (1 [+1251, 3338, 2257])

H5409 מְשׁוֹאָה ***m[e]šō'â***, n.f. [3] [√ 8735]. wasteland, desolate land:– ruin (1), wasteland (1), wastelands (1)

H5410 מַשּׁוּאָה ***maššû'â***, n.[m.] Not used in NIVEBC [√ 5958]. deception

H5411 מְשׁוֹבָב ***m[e]šôbāb***, n.pr.m. [1] [√ 8740]. Meshobab:– Meshobab (1)

H5412 מְשׁוּבָה ***m[e]šûbâ***, n.f. [13] [√ 8740]. waywardness, backsliding, faithlessness, apostasy:– faithless (4), backsliding (3), waywardness (2), backslidings (1), rebelled (1), turn away (1), turn from (1)

H5413 מְשׁוּגָה ***m[e]šûgâ***, n.f. [1] [cf. 8704, 8706]. error:– error (1)

H5414 מָשׁוֹט ***māšôṭ***, n.[m.] [1] [√ 8763]. oar:– oars (1)

H5415 מִשּׁוֹט ***miššôṭ***, n.[m.] [1] [√ 8763]. oar:– oars (1)

H5416 מְשׁוּסָּה ***m[e]šiwssâ***, var. Not used in NIVEBC [cf. 5468]. see 5468

H5417 מָשַׁח ***māšaḥ***, v. [71] [→ 4937, 5418, 5420, 5431; 10442]. [Q] to anoint; [Qp] to be spread, be anointed; [N] to be anointed; usually referring to pouring or smearing sacred oil on a person in a ceremony of dedication, possibly symbolizing divine empowering to accomplish the task or office:– anointed (33), anoint (24), brushed (4), anointing (3), was anointed (2), been anointed (1), decorates (1), oil (1), rubbed (1), use (1)

H5418 [1]מִשְׁחָה ***mišḥâ[1]***, n.f. [21] [√ 5417]. anointing (oil), anointment; usually referring to pouring or smearing sacred oil on a person in a ceremony of dedication, possibly symbolizing divine empowering to accomplish the task or office:– anointing (21)

H5419 [2]מִשְׁחָה ***mišḥâ[2]***, n.f. [2] [→ 5421]. portion:– portion (1), NDT (1)

H5420 [1]מָשְׁחָה ***mošḥâ[1]***, n.f. [1] [√ 5417]. anointing, see 5417:– anointing (1)

H5421 [2]מָשְׁחָה ***mošḥâ[2]***, n.f. [1] [√ 5419]. portion:– portion (1)

H5422 מַשְׁחִית ***mašḥît***, n.[m.] [16] [√ 8845]. destroyer, one who destroys; destruction, corruption; bird trap:– destroyer (4), destructive (2), corruption (1), deathly pale (1), destroy (1), destroyers (1), destroys (1), destruction (1), one who destroys (1 [+1251]), slaughter (1 [+2222, 4200]), traps (1), undoing (1)

H5423 מִשְׁחָר ***mišḥār***, n.[m.] [1] [√ 8837]. dawn, early morning light:– morning's (1)

H5424 מַשְׁחֵת ***mašḥēt***, n.[m.] [1] [√ 8845]. destruction, annihilation:– weapon (1 [+3998])

H5425 מִשְׁחַת ***mišḥat***, n.[m.] [1] [√ 8845]. disfigurement, implying ugliness and repulsion:– disfigured (1)

H5426 מָשְׁחָת ***mošḥāt***, n.[m.] [1] [√ 8845]. deformity, defect, corruption:– deformed (1)

H5427 מִשְׁטוֹחַ ***mišṭôaḥ***, n.[m.] [3] [√ 8848]. place for spreading out nets, drying yard for nets:– place to spread (2), places for spreading (1)

H5428 מִשְׁטָר ***mišṭār***, n.m. [1] [√ 8853]. dominion, rule; some sources: heavenly writing (the starry sky as God's communication):– dominion (1)

H5429 מֶשִׁי ***mešî***, n.[m.] [2] costly fabric for garments; possibly referring to silk:– costly fabric (1), costly garments (1)

H5430 מְשֵׁיזַבְאֵל ***m^{e}šêzab'ēl***, n.pr.m. [3] [√ 10706]. Meshezabel, "*God [El] delivers*":– Meshezabel (3)

H5431 מָשִׁיחַ ***māšîaḥ***, n.m. [38] [√ 5417]. anointed (one), usually refers to pouring or smearing sacred oil on a person in a ceremony of dedication, possibly symbolizing divine empowering to accomplish the task or office; the Anointed One, the Messiah, God's ultimate chosen one, identified in the NT as Jesus:– anointed (38)

H5432 מָשַׁךְ ***māšak***, v. [36] [→ 5433, 5436]. [Q] to draw up, drag; to extend, spread out; [N] to be prolonged, delayed; [Pu] to be deferred; to be tall:– drew (2), tall (2), archers (1 [+8008]), be delayed (1), be prolonged (1), bear (1), cheering (1), continue (1), deferred (1), delay (1), drag away (1), dragged off (1), drags away (1), drags off (1), draw along (1), drawn (1), extend (1), follows (1), go at once (1), joins (1), lead (1), lead up (1), led (1), patient (1), planter (1 [+2446]), prolong (1), pull in (1), pulled (1), pulled up (1), sound long (1), sounds a long blast (1), spread out (1), take away (1), worn (1 [+928])

H5433 מֶשֶׁךְ¹ ***mešek[1]***, n.[m.] [2] [√ 5432]. (leather) bag, pouch (= price):– price (1), seed to sow (1 [+2446])

H5434 מֶשֶׁךְ² ***mešek[2]***, n.pr.g. [10] Meshech:– Meshek (10)

H5435 מִשְׁכָּב ***miškāb***, n.m. [46] [√ 8886; 10444]. bed, couch, used as a place for sleep, meditation, convalescence, marital relations, and worship:– bed (22), beds (7), bedroom (4 [+2540]), does[S] (2), bedding (1), bier (1), couch (1), lie in death (1), mat (1), not a virgin (1 [+3359, 2351]), slept with (1 [+3359]), slept with (1 [+3359, 2351]), slept with (1 [+3359, 4200, 408]), slept with (1 [+3359, 4200, 2351]), taking rest (1 [+8886])

H5436 מֹשְׁכוֹת ***mōš^{e}kôt***, n.f. [1] [√ 5432]. cords, chains, fetters:– belt (1)

H5437 מְשַׁכֶּלֶת ***m^{e}šakkelet***, n.f.abst. Not used in NIVEBC [√ 8897]. miscarriage

H5438 מִשְׁכָּן ***miškān***, n.m. [139] [√ 8905; 10445]. dwelling place, habitat, tent, tabernacle, the tent used as the central place of worship before the temple:– tabernacle (102), dwelling place (8), dwellings (5), tents (5), dwelling (3), it[S] (3 [+2021]), where dwells (2), dwelling places (1), habitat (1), homes (1), houses (1), lived (1), place where dwell (1), resting place (1), tent (1), NDT (3)

H5439 מָשָׁל¹ ***māšal[1]***, v. [17] [→ 5441, 5442, 5444, 5446]. [Q] to quote (a proverb or saying), to make up a proverb; [N] to liken, be like; [P] to tell a proverb; [H] to liken, compare to; [Ht] to show oneself like:– are like (2), be like (2), quote (2), tell (2), become like (1), byword (1), liken (1), poets (1), quote proverb (1), quotes proverbs (1), quoting (1), reduced to (1), telling (1)

H5440 מָשַׁל² ***māšal[2]***, v. [80] [→ 4938, 4939, 5445]. [Q] to rule, govern, control; [H] make one a ruler, (n.) dominion:– rule (30), ruler (17), rules (7), ruled (6), rulers (4), ruler's (3), actually rule (2 [+5440]), dominion (1), exercised (1), gain control (1), govern (1), has right (1), in charge (1), made rulers (1), make rulers (1), ruling (1), self-control (1 [+928, 8120]), NDT (1)

H5441 מָשַׁל³ ***māšal[3]***, v.den. Not used in NIVEBC [√ 5439]. [Q, P] to speak a proverb

H5442 מָשָׁל¹ ***māšāl[1]***, n.m. [40] [√ 5439]. wisdom sayings of various types: proverb, a short, pithy saying, easy to remember; parable, a brief story with a symbolic meaning; oracle, a discourse type of prophecy; taunt, ridicule, a stylized form for mocking an enemy:– byword (7), message (7), proverb (7), proverbs (7), parable (3), discourse (2), saying (2), make sport of (1 [+2118, 4200]), parables (1), ridicule (1 [+5951]), taunt (1), taunt (1 [+5951])

H5443 מָשָׁל² ***māšāl[2]***, n.pr.loc. [1] [cf. 5398]. Mashal:– Mashal (1)

H5444 מֹשֶׁל¹ ***mōšel[1]***, n.[m.] [1] [√ 5439]. likeness, similarity:– equal (1)

H5445 מֹשֶׁל² ***mōšel[2]***, n.[m.] [2] [√ 5440]. power, dominion:– power (1), rule (1)

H5446 מְשֹׁל ***m^{e}šōl***, n.[m.] Not used in NIVEBC [√ 5439]. byword, see 5439

H5447 מִשְׁלוֹחַ ***mišlôaḥ***, n.[m.] [3] [√ 8938]. giving, sending (presents); laying on (hands):– giving (2), subdue (1 [+3338])

H5448 מִשְׁלָח ***mišlāḥ***, n.[m.] [7] [√ 8938]. stretching out (of the hand):– put to (6), places where turned loose (1)

H5449 מִשְׁלַחַת ***mišlaḥat***, n.f. [2] [√ 8938]. discharge (from military); band, company (of angels):– band (1), discharged (1)

H5450 מְשֻׁלָּם ***m^{e}šullām***, n.pr.m. [25] [→ 5452, 5453; cf. 8966]. Meshullam, "*restitution*":– Meshullam (25)

H5451 מְשִׁלֵּמוֹת ***m^{e}šillēmôt***, n.pr.m. [2] [→ 5454; cf. 8966]. Meshillemoth, "*restitution*":– Meshillemoth (2)

H5452 מְשֶׁלֶמְיָה ***m^{e}šelemyâ***, n.pr.m. [1] [√ 5450 + 3378]. Meshelemiah, "*Yahweh repays*":– Meshelemiah (1)

H5453 מְשֶׁלֶמְיָהוּ ***m^{e}šelemyāhû***, n.pr.m. [3] [√ 5450 + 3378]. Meshelemiah, "*Yahweh repays*":– Meshelemiah (3)

H5454 מְשִׁלֵּמִית ***m^{e}šillēmît***, n.pr.m. [1] [√ 5451; cf. 8966]. Meshillemith, "*restitution*":– Meshillemith (1)

H5455 מְשֻׁלֶּמֶת ***m^{e}šullemet***, n.pr.f. [1] [√ 8966]. Meshullemeth, "*restitution*":– Meshullemeth (1)

H5456 מִשְׁלֹשׁ ***mišlōš***, n.[m.] Not used in NIVEBC [√ 4946 + 8993]. period of three (months), see 8993

H5457 מְשַׁמָּה ***m^{e}šammâ***, n.f. [7] [√ 9037]. object of horror, desolate waste, dried up place:– waste (4), dried up (2), object of horror (1)

H5458 מִשְׁמָן ***mišmān***, n.m. [5] [√ 9043]. fatness; by extension: sturdiness, stoutness; richness, fertility, abundance, prosperity:– fat (2), richest (1), sturdiest (1), sturdy (1)

H5459 מִשְׁמַנָּה ***mišmannâ***, n.pr.m. [1] [√ 9043]. Mishmannah, "*fatness*":– Mishmannah (1)

H5460 מַשְׁמַנִּים ***mašmannîm***, n.[m.] [1] [√ 9043]. choice food, festive food, rich with oil or fat (rare and valued in the ancient Near East):– choice food (1)

H5461 מִשְׁמָע¹ ***mišmā'[1]***, n.[m.] [1] [→ 5462; cf. 9048]. what one hears, rumor, hearsay:– what hears (1)

H5462 מִשְׁמָע² ***mišmā'[2]***, n.pr.m. [4] [√ 5461; cf. 9048]. Mishma, "*rumor*":– Mishma (4)

H5463 מִשְׁמַעַת ***mišma'at***, n.f. [4] [√ 9048]. bodyguard; subject, one obligated to allegiance:– bodyguard (3), subject to (1)

H5464 מִשְׁמָר¹ ***mišmār[1]***, n.[m.] [22] [√ 9068]. guard or guarding, custody, imprisonment:– custody (6), guard (4), else[S] (1), guarded (1 [+9068]), guards (1), guards (1 [+408]), imprisoned (1 [+5989, 928]), other[S] (1), posts (1), prison (1 [+1074]), section (1), services (1), take command (1 [+2118, 4200]), under guard (1 [+6584])

H5465 מִשְׁמָר² ***mišmār[2]***, n.[m.] Not used in NIVEBC [√ 9068]. muzzle

H5466 מִשְׁמֶרֶת ***mišmeret***, n.f. [78] [√ 9068]. responsibility, duty, service; requirement, obligation; guard, watch, what is cared for:– duties (8), care (5), requirements (5), responsibilities (4), guard (3 [+9068]), responsible (3), service (3), guarding (2 [+9068]), guards (2), keep (2), kept (2), order (2), responsible for care (2), what requires (2), command (1), duty (1), everything required (1), guard (1), guarded (1 [+9068]), guarding (1), in charge (1), lead (1), loyal (1 [+9068]), mission (1), obligations (1), on behalf of (1 [+4200]), part[S] (1), positions (1), post (1), preserved (1), responsibility (1), responsible (1 [+9068]), safe (1), services (1), serving (1), specific things (1 [+3998]), take care of (1), take care of (1 [+2118, 4200]), to guard (1 [+9068]), under guard (1), use (1), watch (1), NDT (5)

H5467 מִשְׁנֶה ***mišneh***, n.[m.] [34] [√ 9101]. second, next (in a series); twice, double:– second (7), next in rank (6), double (4), new Quarter (4), twice as much (4), copy (2), double portion (2), matching (1), other (1), second in rank (1), second-in-command (1), twice (1)

H5468 מְשִׁסָּה ***m^{e}šissâ***, n.f. [6] [√ 9116; cf. 5416]. plunder, loot, booty:– plundered (3), loot (2), prey (1)

H5469 מִשְׁעוֹל ***miš'ôl***, n.m. [1] [√ 9123]. narrow path:– narrow path (1)

H5470 מִשְׁעִי ***miš'î***, n.f. [1] cleansing, implying cleansing by washing and rubbing:– make clean (1)

H5471 מִשְׁעָם ***miš'ām***, n.pr.m. [1] Misham:– Misham (1)

H5472 מִשְׁעָן ***miš'ān***, n.[m.] [4] [√ 9128]. support, supplies:– supplies (2), support (2)

H5473 מַשְׁעֵן ***maš'ēn***, n.f. [1] [√ 9128]. support, supply:– supply (1)

H5474 מַשְׁעֵנָה ***maš'ēnâ***, n.f. [1] [√ 9128]. support, supply:– support (1)

H5475 מִשְׁעֶנֶת ***miš'enet***, n.f. [11] [√ 9128]. staff, stick:– staff (9), cane (1), staffs (1)

H5476 מִשְׁפָּחָה ***mišpāḥâ***, n.f. [303] [√ 9148]. clan, family, people:– clans (149), clan (102), families (8), peoples (8), family (7), clan by clan (2 [+4200]), each clan (2 [+5476]), people (2), Danites (1 [+1974]), Danites[S] (1), Levites (1 [+4291]), clan (1 [+3]), clan (1 [+1074, 3]), every family (1 [+5476, 2256]), every family (1 [+2256, 5476]), kinds (1), kingdoms (1), nation (1), one kind after another (1 [+4200, 2157]), NDT (12)

H5477 מִשְׁפָּט ***mišpāṭ***, n.m. [422] [→ 6535; cf. 9149]. justice, judgment; law, regulation, prescription, specification:– justice (89), laws (85), just (28), judgment (23), cause (12), regulations (12), right (12), judgments (11), specified (8), punishment (6), sentence (5), case (4), law (4), prescribed (4), standards (4), decision (3), due measure (3), injustice (3 [+4202]), justly (3), ordinance (3), prescribed way (3), requirements (3), rights (3), what requires (3), claim as rights[S] (2), commands (2), court (2), custom (2), decisions (2), force of law (2 [+2978]), judge (2), judging (2), ordinances (2), practice (2), practices (2), proper procedure (2), sentenced (2), specifications (2), trial (2), verdict (2 [+1821]), vindication (2), accuser (1 [+1251]), accuses (1 [+7756, 4200, 2021]), acts of justice (1), always do (1), bloodshed (1 [+1947]), capital offense (1 [+4638]), charges (1), customs (1), decided (1), decrees (1), defense (1), deserve (1), deserving (1), dimensions (1), disputes decided (1), do (1), due (1), honest (1), honestly (1), inquiring (1), instruction (1), judge (1 [+9149]), judges (1 [+6913]), just cause (1), kind (1), lawsuits (1), like (1 [+3869]), making decisions (1), manner (1), means of making decisions (1), place of judgment (1), plan (1), precepts (1), prescribed (1 [+3869]), proper place (1), punish (1 [+6913]), put on trial (1), quotas (1 [+3869]), regulation (1), regulations prescribed (1), render judgment (1 [+9149]), right way (1), rightfully (1), rights and duties (1), rule that governs (1), share (1), standards measuring (1), statutes (1), unjust (1 [+4202]), verdict (1), way prescribed (1), what right (1), NDT (2)

H5478 מִשְׁפְּתַיִם ***mišp^{e}tayim***, n.[m.]du. [2] [√ 9189]. (dual) campfires or two saddlebags:– sheep pens (2)

H5479 מֶשֶׁק ***mešeq***, n.[m.] [1] [√ 4940]. inheritance, possession:– one who will inherit (1 [+1201])

H5480 מַשָּׁק ***maššāq***, n.[m.] [1] [√ 9212]. onslaught, assault; formally "rushing," this is the sudden, aggressive movement of a swarm:– swarm (1)

H5481 מְשֻׁקָּד ***m^{e}šuqqād***, n.m. [6] [√ 9195; cf. 9193]. shape of almond flowers:– shaped like almond flowers (4), NDT (2)

H5482 מַשְׁקֶה¹ ***mašqeh[1]***, n.m. [19] [√ 9197]. cupbearer; drink (liquid); drinking vessel:– cupbearer (10), cupbearers (2), goblets (2 [+3998]), liquid (1), position (1), water (1), well watered (1), well-watered (1)

H5483 מַשְׁקֶה² ***mašqeh[2]***, n.m. Not used in NIVEBC [√ 9197]. irrigation, drink

H5484 מִשְׁקוֹל ***mišqôl***, n.[m.] [1] [√ 9202]. weight:– Weigh out (1)

H5485 מַשְׁקוֹף ***mašqôp***, n.[m.] [3] [√ 9207]. top (upper crosspiece of a door), lintel:– top (2), tops (1)

H5486 מִשְׁקָל ***mišqāl***, n.m. [49] [√ 9202]. weight:– weight (19), weighing (16), weighed (7), exact weight (1), force (1), paid (1 [+5989]), rationed (1 [+928]), set of scales (1 [+4404]), weighed out (1), NDT (1)

H5487 מִשְׁקֶלֶת ***mišqelet***, n.f. [2] [√ 9202?]. plumb line, leveling instrument:– plumb line (2)

H5488 מִשְׁקָע ***mišqā'***, n.[m.] [1] [√ 9205]. clear (settled) water:– clear (1)

H5489 מִשְׁרָה ***mišrâ***, n.f. [1] [√ 9223]. (grape) juice:– juice (1)

H5490 מִשְׁרָעִי ***mišrā'î***, a.g. [1] Mishraite:– Mishraites (1)

H5491 מָשַׁשׁ ***māšaš***, v. [9] [cf. 3560, 4630]. [Q] to touch, feel; [P] to grope, search thoroughly; [H] to let one feel:– grope (2), searched through (2), felt (1), grope about (1), touched (1), touches (1), NDT (1)

H5492 מִשְׁתֶּה ***mišteh***, n.m. [46] [√ 9272; 10447]. feast, banquet, dinner, with an focus on drinking:– banquet (13), feast (12), feasting (8), drink (3), drinking (2), banquet (1 [+3516]), banquets (1), feasts (1), meal (1), table (1), that[S] (1), NDT (2)

H5493 מֹת¹ ***mōt[1]***, n.m. [20] [→ 1432, 5500]. men; few (people):– few (3), men (3), people (3), those[S] (2), deceitful (1 [+8736]), deceivers (1 [+8736]), few in number (1 [+5071]), friends (1), little (1), only a few (1 [+5031]), others (1), very few (1 [+5031]), wicked (1 [+224])

H5494 מֹת² ***mōt[2]***, n.m. louse (insect)

H5495 מַתְבֵּן ***matbēn***, n.[m.] [1] [√ 9320]. heap of straw:– straw (1)

H5496 מֶתֶג ***meteg***, n.m. [4] [→ 5497]. bridle or bit:– bit (3), bridle (1)

H5497 מֶתֶג הָאַמָּה ***meteg hā'ammâ***, n.pr.loc. [1] [√ 5496 + 2021 + 585]. Metheg Ammah:– Metheg Ammah (1)

H5498 מָתוֹק ***mātôq***, a. [12] [√ 5517]. sweet, sweetness; by extension: pleasant, delightful:– sweet (10), sweeter (2)

H5499 מְתוּשָׁאֵל ***m^{e}tûšā'ēl***, n.pr.m. [2] [√ 4637 + 8611 + 446]. Methushael, "[perhaps] *man of God*":– Methushael (2)

H5500 מְתוּשֶׁלַח ***m^{e}tûšelaḥ***, n.pr.m. [6] [√ 5493 + 8938?]. Methuselah, "*man of the javelin*":– Methuselah (6)

H5501 מָתַח ***mātaḥ***, v. [1] [→ 623, 5502]. [Q] to spread out:– spreads out (1)

H5502 מִתְחָה ***mitḥâ***, n.[f.] Not used in NIVEBC [√ 5501]. spreading out

H5503 מָתַי ***mātay***, adv.inter. [43] How long?; When?:– how long (27 [+6330]), when (11), how long (2), for how long (1 [+6330]), how long (1 [+339, 6388]), setting the time (1 [+4200])

H5504 מַתְכֹּנֶת ***matkōnet***, n.f. [5] [√ 9419]. measure, formula:– formula (2), number (1), original design (1), standard measure (1)

H5505 מַתְּלָאָה ***matt^{e}lā'â***, p.indef.+n.f. Not used in NIVEBC [√ 4537 + 9430]. see 4537 & 9430

H5506 מְתַלְּעוֹת ***m^{e}tall^e'ôt***, n.f.pl. [3] [√ 4922]. jaw; teeth:– fangs (2), jaws (1)

H5507 מְתֹם **mᵉtōm**, n.m. [4] [√ 9462]. health, soundness:– health (2), all (1), soundness (1)

H5508 [1]מַתָּן **mattān[1]**, n.m.col. [5] [→ 5509, 5513, 5514, 5515; cf. 5989; 10448]. gift, present:– gift (3), gifts (2)

H5509 [2]מַתָּן **mattān[2]**, n.pr.m. [3] [√ 5508; cf. 5989]. Mattan, "*gift*":– Mattan (3)

H5510 [1]מַתָּנָה **mattānâ[1]**, n.f. [17] [→ 5511; cf. 5989]. gift, something given, such as an offering to deity or a bribe:– gifts (9), gift (5), bribe (1), bribes (1), given (1)

H5511 [2]מַתָּנָה **mattānâ[2]**, n.pr.loc. [2] [√ 5510; cf. 5989]. Mattanah, "*gift*":– Mattanah (2)

H5512 מִתְנִי **mitnî**, a.g. [1] [√ 5516?]. Mithnite:– Mithnite (1)

H5513 מַתְּנַי **mattᵉnay**, n.pr.m. [3] [√ 5508 + 3378]. Mattenai, "*gift*":– Mattenai (3)

H5514 מַתַּנְיָה **mattanyâ**, n.pr.m. [13] [√ 5508 + 3378]. Mattaniah, "*gift of Yahweh*":– Mattaniah (13)

H5515 מַתַּנְיָהוּ **mattanyāhû**, n.pr.m. [3] [√ 5508 + 3378]. Mattaniah, "*gift of Yahweh*":– Mattaniah (3)

H5516 מָתְנַיִם **motnayim**, n.m.du. [47] [→ 5512?]. (dual) waist, lower back (lumbar region), loins; "girding the loins" involves tucking the skirt of a tunic or robe into the belt, thus preparing for action: running, working, fighting, etc:– waist (16), side (4), waists (4), backs (3), body (2), there[S] (2), tuck cloak into belt (2 [+2520]), armor (1), belt (1 [+258]), bodies (1), brace yourselves (1 [+2616]), cloak tucked into belt (1 [+2520]), get ready (1 [+273]), heart (1), loins (1), make wear (1 [+6590, 6584]), put on (1 [+8492, 928]), sets about work (1 [+2520]), strike down (1 [+4730]), strutting rooster (1 [+2435]), tucking cloak into belt (1 [+9113])

H5517 מָתַק **mātaq**, v. [6] [→ 4941, 5498, 5518, 5519, 5520?]. [Q] to be, become sweet; [H] to taste sweet, enjoy sweetness:– sweet (3), enjoyed sweet (1), feasts on (1), fit to drink (1)

H5518 מֶתֶק **mātēq**, n.m. [2] [√ 5517]. sweetness; by extension: pleasantness:– gracious (1), pleasantness (1)

H5519 מֹתֶק **mōteq**, n.[m.] [1] [√ 5517]. sweetness:– sweet (1)

H5520 מִתְקָה **mitqâ**, n.pr.loc. [2] [√ 5517?]. Mithcah, "*sweetness*":– Mithkah (2)

H5521 מִתְרְדָת **mitrᵉdāt**, n.pr.m. [2] Mithredath, "*gift to Mithra*":– Mithredath (2)

H5522 מַתָּת **mattat**, n.f. [6] [→ 5524, 5525; cf. 5989]. gift, something given:– gift (3), as much as pleases (2 [+3338]), gifts never given (1 [+9214])

H5523 מַתַּתָּה **mattattâ**, n.pr.m. [1] [√ 5989]. Mattattah, "*gift*":– Mattattah (1)

H5524 מַתִּתְיָה **mattityâ**, n.pr.m. [4] [√ 5522 + 3378]. Mattithiah, "*gift of Yahweh*":– Mattithiah (4)

H5525 מַתִּתְיָהוּ **mattityāhû**, n.pr.m. [4] [√ 5522 + 3378]. Mattithiah, "*gift of Yahweh*":– Mattithiah (4)

H5526 נ **n**, letter. Not used in NIVEBC [√ 10449]. letter of the Hebrew alphabet

H5527 ן- **-ān**, ן- **-n**, p.f.pl.suf. [35] [√ 2023, 2401]. they, them, their:– their (9), they (5), them (4), each (2), the[S] (1), the creatures[S] (1), the rooms[S] (1), you (1), NDT (11)

H5528 [1]נָא **nā'[1]**, pt. [405] [→ 626, 629]. often not translated, marks entreaty or exhortation: please!, I beg you!, now!:– please (60), now (22), I beg you (5), then (4), come now (3 [+6964]), I would like (2), I ask (1), I pray (1), all right (1), but (1), if you will (1), please (1 [+3283]), quick (1), so (1), therefore (1), very well (1 [+2180]), we pray (1), NDT (298)

H5529 [2]נָא **nā'[2]**, a. [1] raw (meat):– raw (1)

H5530 נֹא **nō'**, n.pr.loc. [4] [→ 5531]. No = Thebes:– Thebes (4)

H5531 נֹא אָמוֹן **nō' 'āmôn**, n.pr.loc. [1] [√ 5530 + 572]. No Amon = Thebes, "*city of Amon*":– Thebes (1)

H5532 נֹאד **nō'd**, n.m. [7] skin vessel (skinned in one piece, the appendages tied or sewn, the neck the funnel, used to hold liquid):– skin (2), wineskins (2 [+3516]), jars (1), scroll (1), wineskin (1)

H5533 נָאָה **nā'â**, v. [3] [→ 5534; cf. 5658]. [Pilel] to be beautiful, adorn:– beautiful (2), adorns (1)

H5534 נָאוֶה **nā'weh**, a. [10] [√ 5533]. lovely, fitting, suited:– fitting (4), lovely (4), beautiful (1), unsuited (1 [+4202])

H5535 נָאַם **nā'am**, v.den. [1] [→ 5536]. [Q] to declare as a prophet:– declare (1)

H5536 נְאֻם **nᵉ'um**, n.m. [376] [√ 5535]. declaration, oracle, utterance; often a marker introducing or punctuating prophetic discourse:– declares (364), prophecy (6), says (2), utterance (2), inspired utterance (1), message from God (1)

H5537 נָאַף **nā'ap**, v. [31] [→ 5538, 5539; cf. 5677]. [Q, P] to commit adultery; [ptcp.] adulterer, adulteress; by extension: to be unfaithful to God (by having illicit relations with other gods):– commit adultery (7), adulterers (6), committed adultery (5), adulterous (3), adulterer (2), adulteress (2), adultery (2), adulteries (1), commits adultery (1), commits adultery (1 [+851]), NDT (1)

H5538 נַאֲפוּפִים **na'ᵃpûpîm**, n.[m.pl.] [1] [√ 5537]. (marks of) unfaithfulness, adultery; such marks might refer to jewelry or adornments which signal that a woman is available for illicit sex:– unfaithfulness (1)

H5539 נִאֻפִים **ni'upîm**, n.[m.] [2] [√ 5537]. adultery:– adulteries (1), adultery (1)

H5540 נָאַץ **nā'aṣ**, v. [24] [→ 5541, 5542]. [Q] to spurn, despise, reject; [P] to treat with contempt, revile, despise; [Htpo] be blasphemed, be reviled:– spurned (5), despise (4), revile (2), shown utter contempt (2 [+5540]), treated with contempt (2), despised (1), is blasphemed (1), rejected (1), rejecting (1), reviled (1), reviles (1), spurns (1), treat with contempt (1), treating with contempt (1)

H5541 נְאָצָה **nᵉ'āṣâ**, n.f. [2] [√ 5540]. disgrace, shame:– disgrace (2)

H5542 נֶאָצָה **ne'āṣâ**, n.f. [3] [√ 5540]. contemptible things, blasphemies:– blasphemies (2), contemptible things (1)

H5543 נָאַק **nā'aq**, v. [2] [→ 5544; cf. 650]. [Q] to groan:– groan (1 [+5544]), groans (1)

H5544 נְאָקָה **nᵉ'āqâ**, n.f. [4] [√ 5543; cf. 650]. groaning:– groaning (3), groan (1 [+5543])

H5545 נָאַר **nā'ar**, v. [2] [P] to renounce, abandon:– abandoned (1), renounced (1)

H5546 נֹב **nōb**, n.pr.loc. [6] Nob:– Nob (6)

H5547 נָבָא **nābā'**, v.den. [115] [√ 5566; 10451]. [N, Ht] to prophesy, speak as a prophet; prophecy has its focus on encouraging or restoring covenant faithfulness, the telling of future events encourages obedience or warns against disobedience:– prophesy (47), prophesying (28), prophesied (26), prophesies (8), acts like a prophet (1), frantic prophesying (1), poses as a prophet (1), prophetic (1), NDT (2)

H5548 נָבַב **nābab**, v. Not used in NIVEBC [→ 5554]. [Q] to hollow out

H5549 [1]נְבוֹ **nᵉbô[1]**, n.pr.loc. [11] Nebo, "*height* or *Mount of Nabu [Nebo]*":– Nebo (11)

H5550 [2]נְבוֹ **nᵉbô[2]**, n.pr.[m.] [1] [→ 5551, 5589; *also used with compound proper names*]. Nebo (pagan god), "*height* or *Mount of Nabu [Nebo]*":– Nebo (1)

H5551 [3]נְבוֹ **nᵉbô[3]**, n.pr.m. [1] [√ 5550]. Nebo, "*height* or *Mount of Nabu [Nebo]*":– Nebo (1)

H5552 נְבוּ שַׂר־סְכִים **nᵉbû śar-sᵉkîm**, n.pr.m. [1] [√ 5550 + 8569; cf. 8593]. Nebo-Sarsekim:– Nebo-Sarsekim (1)

H5553 נְבוּאָה **nᵉbû'â**, n.f. [3] [√ 5566; 10452]. prophecy, the word of the prophet; prophecy has its focus on encouraging or restoring covenant faithfulness, the telling of future events encourages obedience or warns against disobedience:– prophecy (2), prophesied (1 [+1819])

H5554 נָבוּב **nābûb**, n.m. *or* v.ptcp. [4] [√ 5548]. hollow thing; witless person:– hollow (3), witless (1 [+408])

H5555 נְבוּזַרְאֲדָן **nᵉbûzar'ᵃdān**, נְבוּזַר־אֲדָן, **nᵉbûzar-'ᵃdān**, n.pr.m. [15] [√ 5550 + 2445]. Nebuzaradan, "*Nebo [Nabu] has given seed [offspring]*":– Nebuzaradan (15)

H5556 נְבוּכַדְנֶאצַּר **nᵉbûkadne'ṣṣar**, נְבוּכַדְנֶצַּר **nᵉbûkadneṣṣar**, נְבוּכַדְנֶצּוֹר **nᵉbûkadneṣṣôr**, n.pr.m. [27] [√ 5550; 10453]. Nebuchadnezzar, "*Nebo protect my boundary stone; Nebo protect my son!*":– Nebuchadnezzar (26), his[S] (1)

H5557 נְבוּכַדְרֶאצַּר **nᵉbûkadre'ṣṣar**, נְבוּכַדְרֶאצּוֹר **nebûkadre'ṣṣôr**, n.pr.m. [33] [√ 5550; 10453]. Nebuchadnezzar, "*Nebo protect my boundary stone; Nebo protect my son!*":– Nebuchadnezzar (31), Nebuchadnezzar's (1 [+4200]), his[S] (1 [+4200])

H5558 נְבוּשַׁזְבָּן **nᵉbûšazbān**, נְבוּשַׁז־בָּן **nᵉbûšaz-bān**, n.pr.m. [1] [√ 5550]. Nebushazban, "*Nebo [Nabu] save me!*":– Nebushazban (1)

H5559 נָבוֹת **nābôt**, n.pr.m. [22] Naboth, "*sprout*":– Naboth (17), Naboth's (4), he[S] (1)

H5560 נָבַח **nābaḥ**, v. [1] [→ 5561?]. [Q] to bark:– bark (1)

H5561 [1]נֹבַח **nōbaḥ[1]**, n.pr.m. [1] [√ 5560?]. Nobah, "*barking*":– Nobah (1)

H5562 [2]נֹבַח **nōbaḥ[2]**, n.pr.loc. [2] Nobah, "*barking*":– Nobah (2)

H5563 נִבְחַז **nibḥaz**, n.pr.[m.] [1] Nibhaz (pagan god):– Nibhaz (1)

H5564 נָבַט **nābaṭ**, v. [69] [→ 4438, 5565]. [P] to look at; [H] to look at, gaze at, consider:– look (19), looked (7), consider (6), see (3), tolerate (3), gaze (2), have regard for (2), look down (2), look up (2), looks (2), seen (2), detect (1), have regard for (1 [+4200]), let look (1), look around (1), look on (1), look on with favor (1), look with favor (1 [+7156]), looked around (1), looked over (1), looks down (1), observe (1), pay any attention (1 [+2256, 8011]), sees (1), stare (1), viewed (1), views (1), watch (1), watches over (1), watching (1)

H5565 נְבָט **nᵉbāṭ**, n.pr.m. [25] [√ 5564]. Nebat, "*look to, regard [approvingly]*":– Nebat (25)

H5566 נָבִיא **nābî'**, n.m. [314] [→ 5547, 5553, 5567; 10455]. prophet (true or false), see also 5547:– prophet (154), prophets (150), he[S] (1 [+3758, 2021]), him[S] (1 [+3759, 2021]), his[S] (1 [+2021]), his own[S] (1 [+2021, 2021, 2418]), one[S] (1 [+2021]), prophecy (1), prophesy (1), prophets (1 [+1201]), them[S] (1 [+2021]), those who prophesy (1)

H5567 נְבִיאָה **nᵉbî'â**, n.f. [6] [√ 5566]. prophetess (true or false), see also 5547:– prophet (5), prophetess (1)

H5568 נְבָיוֹת **nᵉbāyôt**, n.pr.g. [5] Nebaioth:– Nebaioth (5)

H5569 נֵבֶךְ **nēbek**, n.[m.] [1] source springs (of the sea):– springs (1)

H5570 [1]נָבֵל **nābēl[1]**, v. [20] [→ 5577, 5578?]. [Q] to wither, shrivel, fade, decay:– fading (3), fall (3), wither (3), lose heart (2), only wear out (2 [+5570]), withers (2), crumbles (1), die away (1), shrivel up (1), shriveled (1), withered (1)

H5571 [2]נָבַל **nābal[2]**, v. [5] [→ 5572, 5573, 5576]. [Q] to play the fool, act disdainfully; [P] to treat with contempt, dishonor, reject:– dishonor (1), dishonors (1), play the fool (1), rejected (1), treat with contempt (1)

H5572 [1]נָבָל **nābāl[1]**, a. [19] [→ 5573; cf. 5571]. foolish, lacking understanding, (n.) fool; often pertaining to insolence, pride, and disobedience to God:– fool (4), foolish (4), fools (4), godless fool (3), base (1), lawless (1), no understanding (1), wicked fools (1)

H5573 [2]נָבָל **nābāl[2]**, n.pr.m. [21] [√ 5572; cf. 5571]. Nabal, "*fool*":– Nabal (18), Nabal's (2), he[S] (1)

H5574 [1]נֵבֶל **nēbel[1]**, n.m. [11] [→ 4429, 5575?]. (wine) skin; water jar, jug, pot (of clay):– skin (3), jars (2), wineskin (2), pots (1), pottery (1 [+3450]), skins (1), water jars (1)

H5575 [2]נֵבֶל **nēbel[2]**, n.m. [27] [√ 5574?]. lyre, harp (stringed instrument):– lyres (15), lyre (7), harps (4), harp (1)

H5576 נְבָלָה **nᵉbālâ**, n.f. [13] [√ 5571]. (very) wicked thing, disgraceful thing; vileness, something a fool would do:– folly (4), outrageous thing (4), outrageous (2), outrageous act (1), outrageous things (1), wicked thing (1)

H5577 נְבֵלָה **nᵉbēlâ**, n.f. [48] [√ 5570]. dead body, carcass:– body (13), carcasses (12), carcass (6), dead bodies (4), anything found dead (3), it[S] (2 [+2021]), already dead (1), animal found dead (1), bodies (1), dead bodies (1 [+132]), found dead (1), lifeless forms (1), NDT (2)

H5578 נַבְלוּת **nablût**, n.f. [1] [√ 5570?]. (female) genitals:– lewdness (1)

H5579 נְבַלָּט **nᵉballāṭ**, n.pr.loc. [1] Neballat:– Neballat (1)

H5580 נָבַע **nāba'**, v. [11] [→ 81, 4432]. [H] to gush forth, bubble out, spew forth:– gushes (2), pour out (2), give a bad smell (1 [+944]), overflow (1), pour forth (1), rushing (1), spew (1), utter (1), your (1 [+3870])

H5581 נִבְשָׁן **nibšān**, n.pr.loc. [1] Nibshan:– Nibshan (1)

H5582 נֶגֶב **negeb**, n.[pr.m.] [111] [→ 8241]. south, the Negev:– south (37), Negev (36), south (9 [+2025]), southern (6), south (5 [+4946]), south (3 [+9402, 2025]), southern (3 [+2025]), Negev (2 [+824]), south (2 [+9402]), south (1 [+2025, 9402, 2025]), southeast (1 [+7711, 2025]), southeast (1 [+7711, 2025, 2025]), southern (1 [+4946]), southern (1 [+448, 6991]), southern (1 [+9402, 2025, 2025]), southland (1), southland (1 [+8441])

H5583 נָגַד **nāgad**, v. [371] [→ 5584, 5592; 10457]. [H] to tell, report, inform; [Ho] to be told, have reported to:– tell (93), told (87), was told (23), reported (15), declare (14), proclaim (10), announce (8), explain (6), give (4), inform (4), revealed (4), said (4), answered (3), declared (3), explained (3), foretold (3), report (3), show (3), tells (3), assured (2 [+5583]), be sure to tell (2 [+5583]), been told about (2 [+5583]), brought report (2), denounce (2), denounces (2), foretell (2), give answer (2 [+5583]), heard (2), informed (2), messenger (2), must report (2 [+5583]), proclaiming (2), shown (2), speak (2), telling (2), warned (2), were clearly told (2 [+5583]), admit (1), announces (1), announcing (1), been brought to attention (1 [+2256, 9048]), been shown (1), been told (1), confess (1), confront (1), declares (1), declaring (1), describe (1), disclose (1), do so[S] (1), explaining (1), expose (1), exposed (1), give an answer (1), kept secret (1 [+401]), learn (1), learned (1 [+4200]), let know (1), made clear (1), make known (1), message (1), messenger[S] (1), parade (1), report came back (1), reveals (1), sent word (1 [+8938, 2256]), speak up (1), speaks (1), spoke (1), tell answer (1), tell the news (1), testify (1), told answer (1), utter (1), was reported (1), word came (1), NDT (3)

H5584 נֶגֶד **neged**, subst. & adv. & pp. [151] [√ 5583; 10458]. before, in front of, opposite of, beyond:– before (27), opposite (15), before (11 [+4200]), in the presence of (7), from (6 [+4946]), in front of (6), facing (3), in (3), near (3), before (2 [+7156]), by (2), distance (2), in (2 [+4200]), in front of (2 [+4200]), in presence (2 [+4200, 6524]), in the presence of (2 [+2025]), in the sight of (2), opposite (2 [+4200]), presence (2), straight in (2), to (2), accompany (1 [+2143, 4200]), across the way (1 [+4946]), against (1), aloof (1 [+4946]), away from (1 [+4946]), because of

HEBREW INDEX

(1 [+4946]), bent on (1 [+7156]), beyond (1), by (1 [+4946]), constant (1 [+4946]), defend (1 [+6641]), directly (1), eyes[S] (1 [+4200]), facing (1 [+4946]), far from (1 [+4946]), frontal (1 [+4946]), have regard (1 [+8492, 4200]), in broad daylight (1 [+2021, 9087]), in sight (1), in the face of (1 [+4200]), kept distance (1 [+3656, 4946]), known to (1), live in (1), look with approval (1 [+8883, 4200, 6524]), mindful (1 [+4200, 6524]), next to (1 [+4200]), opposite (1 [+4946]), out of (1 [+4946]), presence of (1), regard (1 [+8492, 4200]), resisted (1 [+6641, 4200]), responsible for (1 [+4200]), right before (1 [+4200]), risked (1 [+8959, 4946]), some distance (1), straight (1), straight through (1), succeed against (1 [+4200]), suitable (1 [+3869]), suitable for (1 [+3869]), there (1 [+4946]), with (1), NDT (4)

H5585 נָגַהּ ***nāgah***, v. [6] [→ 5586, 5587, 5588]. [Q] to shine; [H] to cause to shine, give light:– turns into light (2), burning (1), dawned (1), give (1), shine (1)

H5586 [1]נֹגַהּ ***nōgah[1]***, n.f. [19] [→ 5587; cf. 5585; 10459]. brightness, radiance, splendor, brilliance:– brightness (5), brilliant light (2), no longer shine (2 [+665]), radiance (2), bright (1), dawn (1), flashing (1), glow (1), light (1), morning (1), ray of brightness (1), splendor (1)

H5587 [2]נֹגַהּ ***nōgah[2]***, n.pr.m. [2] [√ 5586; cf. 5585]. Nogah, *"joy, splendor"*:– Nogah (2)

H5588 נְגֹהָה ***nᵉgōhâ***, n.f. [1] [√ 5585]. brightness, luster:– brightness (1)

H5589 נְגוֹ ***nᵉgô***, n.pr.m. Not used in NIVEBC [√ 6269 + 5550]. Nego, see 6284

H5590 נָגַח ***nāgaḥ***, v. [11] [→ 5591]. [Q] to gore (a bull into a person); [P] to gore, push back, butt; to engage in pushing back, butting, thrusting:– gore (3), gores (3), butting (1), charged (1), engage in battle (1), push back (1), NDT (1)

H5591 נַגָּח ***naggāḥ***, a. [2] [√ 5590]. (the act of) goring (a bull into a person):– goring (2)

H5592 נָגִיד ***nāgîd***, n.m. [44] [√ 5583]. leader, ruler, official, officer:– ruler (22), leader (4), official in charge (4), commanders (2), prince (2), in charge (1), leaders (1), nobles (1), officer in charge (1), officers (1), official (1), officials in charge (1), overseer (1), rulers (1), trustworthy things (1)

H5593 נְגִינָה ***nᵉgînâ***, n.f. [14] [√ 5594]. stringed instrument; song that mocks, taunts:– stringed instruments (9), mock in song (2), music (1), song (1), songs (1)

H5594 נָגַן ***nāgan***, v. [15] [→ 4947, 5593]. [Q] to play a stringed instrument, (n.) musician; [P] to play a stringed instrument:– harpist (2), play (2), play (2 [+928, 3338]), playing the lyre (2 [+928, 3338]), musicians (1), play the harp (1), play the lyre (1), playing (1), plays (1), plays an instrument (1), sing (1)

H5595 נָגַע ***nāga'***, v. [150] [→ 5596]. [Q] to touch; to strike; [Qp] to be plagued, be stricken; [N] to let oneself be driven back (in a battle); [P] to inflict, afflict; [Pu] to be plagued; [H] to extend, reach out, cause to touch; ranging in meaning from simple contact to violence:– touches (40), touched (24), touch (19), came (7), come (4), reached (4), afflicted (3), arrived (3), reaches (3), struck (3), get (2), reach (2), reaching (2), strike (2), strikes (2), touching (2), add (1), afford (1 [+3338, 1896]), approach (1), are plagued (1), attack (1), bother (1), bring down (1), brought down (1), casts down (1), draws near (1), drew near (1), extend (1), follows (1), happened (1), harm (1), harms (1), inflicted (1), is (1), laid (1), lay a hand on (1), let themselves be driven back (1), level (1), near (1), pierces (1), punished (1), put (1), seize (1), NDT (1)

H5596 נֶגַע ***nega'***, n.m. [78] [√ 5595]. plague, blow (of various kinds): mildew, infection, sores, scourge, disaster:– defiling (11), mold (11), sore (11), affected person (3), article[S] (3), defiling mold (3), disaster (3), it[S] (3 [+2021]), affected area (2), afflictions (2), spoiled (2), affected person (1 [+5999]), assault (1), assaults (1 [+5596, 4200]), assaults (1 [+4200, 5596]), blows (1), contaminated (1), defiling disease (1), disease (1), diseases (1), flogging (1), floggings (1), plague (1), punished (1), scourge (1), skin diseases (1), sore (1 [+5999]), sores (1), spoiled article (1), spreading mold (1 [+7669]), them[S] (1 [+2021]), wounds (1), NDT (3)

H5597 נָגַף ***nāgap***, v. [49] [→ 4487, 5598]. [Q] to strike, afflict (with a plague); [N] to be defeated:– be defeated (5), strike (5), been routed (4), strike down (3), struck down (3), were defeated (3), afflicted (2), been defeated (2), defeating (2 [+5597]), struck (2), stumble (2), was routed (2), were routed (2), bring defeat on (1), defeated (1), defeating (1), hit (1), inflicts (1), injures (1), routed (1), send a plague (1), strike with a plague (1), struck with a plague (1), was defeated (1), were beaten (1)

H5598 נֶגֶף ***negep***, n.m. [7] [√ 5597]. plague; stumbling (caused by a stone):– plague (6), causes to stumble (1)

H5599 נָגַר ***nāgar***, v. [10] [→ 5600; cf. 1760]. [N] to be spilled, flow; [H] to pour out, hand over, deliver over; [Ho] to be poured down (a slope):– rushing (2), delivered over (1), flow (1), given over (1 [+6584, 3338]), hand over (1), pour (1), pours out (1), spilled (1), stretched out (1)

H5600 נִגֶּרֶת ***niggeret***, n.[f.] *or* v.ptcp. Not used in NIVEBC [√ 5599]. torrent, see 5599

H5601 נָגַשׂ ***nāgaś***, v. [23] [cf. 5602]. [Q] to oppress, exploit, (n.) a slave driver; [N] to be oppressed, be hard pressed:– slave drivers (5), oppressor (3), require payment (2), ruler (2), driver's (1), exacted (1), exploit (1), hard pressed (1), in distress (1), oppress (1), oppress each other (1), oppressors (1), slave driver's (1), tax collector (1), was oppressed (1)

H5602 נָגַשׁ ***nāgaš***, v. [125] [cf. 5601]. [Q] to come near, approach; [N] to come near, approach; [H] to bring forth, present; [Ho] to be brought, be presented; [Ht] to draw near, assemble:– approached (12), come near (11), bring (10), brought (7), came (7), approach (6), went up (5), come (4), take (4), went (3), advanced (2), brought close (2), came up (2), close (2), come close (2), come forward (2), come here (2), get so close (2), go (2), go up (2), presented (2), abstain from sexual relations (1 [+440, 448, 851]), assemble (1 [+3481]), be brought (1), be overtaken (1), bring near (1), brings (1), came forward (1), came near (1), came over (1), confront (1), done so[S] (1), draw near (1), drew near (1), get out (1), give more space (1), go near (1), march out (1), moved forward (1), offer (1), offered (1), offering (1), overtake (1), present (1), sacrifice (1), set (1), set forth (1), step forward (1), stepped forward (1), took (1), touch (1), went close (1), went over (1), were fettered (1 [+4200, 5733]), NDT (1)

H5603 נֵד ***nēd***, n.m. [4] heap, wall, barrier, dam:– heap (2), wall (2)

H5604 נָדָא ***nādā'***, v. Not used in NIVEBC [cf. 5610, 5612, 5653]. [H] detach, remove from

H5605 נָדַב ***nādab***, v. [17] [→ 5606, 5607, 5618, 5619; 10219, 10461; *also used with compound proper names*]. [Q] to be willing; to prompt, incite; [Ht] to willingly offer oneself, volunteer, give a freewill offering:– brought as freewill offerings (1 [+5607]), freewill offerings (1), gave freewill offerings (1), gave willingly (1), give generously (1), given freely (1), given willingly (1), prompts to give (1), volunteered (1), volunteered himself for service (1), willing (1), willing (1 [+4213]), willing (1 [+8120]), willing response (1), willing volunteers (1), willingly given (1), willingly offer themselves (1)

H5606 נָדָב ***nādāb***, n.pr.m. [20] [→ 5608; cf. 5605]. Nadab, *"volunteer, free will offering"*:– Nadab (19), Nadab's (1)

H5607 נְדָבָה ***nᵉdābâ***, n.f. [26] [√ 5605]. free, voluntary; freewill offering:– freewill offerings (10), freewill offering (7), freely (2), willing (2), abundant (1), brought as freewill offerings (1 [+5605]), freewill (1), voluntarily (1), NDT (1)

H5608 נְדַבְיָה ***nᵉdabyâ***, n.pr.m. [1] [√ 5606; cf. 5605 + 3378]. Nedabiah, *"Yahweh volunteers"*:– Nedabiah (1)

H5609 נִדְגָּלוֹת ***nidgālôt***, n.? Not used in NIVEBC [√ 1840]. see 1839

H5610 נָדַד ***nādad***, v. [28] [→ 5611; cf. 5604, 5612, 5653; 10463]. [Q] to flee, be a fugitive; to wander, stray; [Pol] to flee away; [H] to banish, put to flight; [Ho] to be banished, be cast aside:– flee (5), fled (3), banished (2), flee in haste (2 [+5610]), flees (2), fugitives (2), be cast aside (1), could not (1), flapped (1), flown away (1), fluttering (1), fly away (1), in flight (1), nothing (1), refugees (1), strayed (1), wanderers (1), wanders about (1)

H5611 נְדֻדִים ***nᵉdudîm***, n.[m.pl.] [1] [√ 5610]. tossing and turning, restlessness (in bed in the night):– toss and turn (1 [+8425])

H5612 נָדָה ***nādâ***, v. [2] [→ 5614, 5765; cf. 5604, 5610, 5653]. [P] to exclude; to put off thoughts, suppose to be far off:– exclude (1), put off (1)

H5613 נֵדֶה ***nēdeh***, n.m. [1] gift, reward; likely referring to a fee for service:– gifts (1)

H5614 נִדָּה ***niddâ***, n.[m.] [29] [→ 5765; cf. 5612]. period of menstruation; (water used in) cleansing, "unclean" water; (act of) impurity, corruption, defilement:– period (7), cleansing (6), monthly period (3), thing unclean (2), act of impurity (1), corruption (1), defilement (1), impurity (1), impurity of monthly period (1), monthly flow (1), monthly period (1 [+1865]), monthly period (1 [+1864]), polluted (1), unclean thing (1), woman's monthly uncleanness (1 [+3240, 2021])

H5615 [1]נָדַח ***nādaḥ[1]***, v. [53] [→ 4505; cf. 1866, 1890, 1891, 5616]. [N] to be scattered, be exiled, be outcast; [Pu] be thrust into; [H] to cause to scatter, banish, drive out; [Ho] to be driven, be hunted:– banish (6), banished (6), exiles (6), been scattered (2), drive (2), fugitives (2), led astray (2), strays (2), are drawn away (1), be driven away (1), be enticed (1), be thrust (1), been banished (1), been driven (1), chased away (1), disperses (1), drive out (1), driven (1), driven away (1), enticed (1), exiled (1), hunted (1), outcast (1), pushing (1), scatter (1), scattered (1), seduced (1), spewed out (1), straying (1), topple (1), turn (1), turn away (1), were exiled (1)

H5616 [2]נָדַח ***nādaḥ[2]***, v. [3] [cf. 5615]. [Q] to wield (an ax); (to have hand) be put (to the ax); [H] to bring:– bring (1), putting (1), swings (1)

H5617 נֹדִי ***nōdî***, n.[m.] Not used in NIVEBC. see 5654

H5618 נָדִיב ***nādîb***, a. (used as noun) [27] [→ 5619; cf. 5605]. willing, generous; prince, noble, ruler, official:– nobles (9), princes (5), willing (3), noble (2), ruler (2), willing (2 [+4213]), great (1), honest officials (1), prince's (1), royal (1)

H5619 נְדִיבָה ***nᵉdîbâ***, n.f. [3] [√ 5618; cf. 5605]. something noble; dignity, nobility:– noble (2), dignity (1)

H5620 [1]נָדָן ***nādān[1]***, n.[m.] [1] [√ 10464]. sheath (of a sword):– sheath (1)

H5621 [2]נָדָן ***nādān[2]***, n.[m.] [1] [cf. 5989]. gift, wages of illicit sexual favors:– gifts (1)

H5622 נָדַף ***nādap***, v. [9] [Q] to blow away, scatter; [N] to be windblown, be fleeting:– windblown (3), blow away (2), blows away (1), fleeting (1), refute (1), NDT (1)

H5623 נָדַר ***nādar***, v. [31] [→ 5624; cf. 5692, 5693, 5694]. [Q] to make a vow:– made a vow (4 [+5624]), vowed (3 [+5624]), made vow (2 [+5624]), make a vow (2 [+5624]), makes a vow (2 [+5624]), vows made (2 [+5624]), made a vow (1), made vow (1), made vows (1 [+5624]), make a special vow (1 [+7098]), make a vow (1), make one[S] (1), make vows (1), make vows (1 [+5624]), makes a vow (1), making a vow (1), making vow (1), vow (1), vow made (1 [+5624]), vowed (1), vows (1), vows to give (1)

H5624 נֶדֶר ***neder***, n.m. [60] [√ 5623]. vow:– vows (20), vow (12), made a vow (4 [+5623]), vowed (3), vowed (3 [+5623]), made vow (2 [+5623]), make a vow (2 [+5623]), makes a vow (2 [+5623]), vows made (2 [+5623]), Nazirite vow (1 [+5694]), answer to prayers (1), fulfill a special vow (1 [+7098]), made vows (1 [+5623]), make vows (1 [+5623]), makes a special vow to dedicate (1 [+7098]), special vow (1 [+7098]), special vows (1 [+7098]), vow made (1 [+5623]), what promised (1)

H5625 נֹהַּ ***nōah***, n.[m.] [1] value, distinction:– value (1)

H5626 -נָה ***-nâ***, p.f.sg.suf. [212] [√ 2023]. her; it, its:– it (81), her (22), them (11), its (5), which[S] (5), they (4), she (3), the lampstand[S] (3), that (2), the[S] (2), this (2), everything (1 [+3972]), him (1), incense[S] (1), oath[S] (1), one (1), so[S] (1), the animal[S] (1), the city[S] (1), the flock[S] (1), the food[S] (1), the land[S] (1), the roof[S] (1), their (1), themselves (1), which (1), widow[S] (1), NDT (56)

H5627 [1]נָהַג ***nāhag[1]***, v. [30] [→ 4952]. [Q] to drive, lead, guide; [Qp] to be led; [P] to drive, lead forth, guide:– carried off (3), guiding (3), lead (3), led (3), drive (2), guide (2), made blow (2), drive away (1), driven away (1), drives (1), driving (1), drove (1), drove ahead (1), guided (1), lead away (1), lead on (1 [+2256, 2143]), led in triumphal procession (1), led out (1), take (1)

H5628 [2]נָהַג ***nāhag[2]***, v. [1] [cf. 5640]. [P] to moan, sob, lament:– moan (1)

H5629 [1]נָהָה ***nāhâ[1]***, v. [2] [→ 5631, 5632, 5760]. [Q] to mourn, wail; [N] to be taunted (with a mournful song):– taunt (1), wail (1)

H5630 [2]נָהָה ***nāhâ[2]***, v. [1] [N] to keep close, stay loyal:– turned (1)

H5631 נְהִי ***nᵉhî***, n.[m.] [7] [→ 5760; cf. 5629]. wailing, mourning, often related to mournful songs: lamentation:– wail (2), mourners (1 [+3359]), mournful song (1), mourning (1), wail (1 [+5951]), wailing (1)

H5632 נִהְיָה ***nihyâ***, n.f. Not used in NIVEBC [√ 5629]. wailing, lamentation, mourning

H5633 נָהַל ***nāhal***, v. [10] [→ 5634, 5635, 5636]. [P] guide, bring along, lead; [Ht] to move along:– guide (3), brought (1), gently leads (1), lead (1), leads (1), move along (1), put (1), took care of (1)

H5634 נַהֲלָל ***nahᵃlāl***, n.pr.loc. [2] [√ 5633]. Nahalal, *"watering place"*:– Nahalal (2)

H5635 [1]נַהֲלֹל ***nahᵃlōl[1]***, n.m. [1] [→ 5636; cf. 5633]. watering hole:– water holes (1)

H5636 [2]נַהֲלֹל ***nahᵃlōl[2]***, n.pr.loc. [1] [√ 5635; cf. 5633]. Nahalol, *"watering place"*:– Nahalol (1)

H5637 נָהַם ***nāham***, v. [5] [→ 5638, 5639; cf. 2101, 2159, 2169]. [Q] to growl, roar; to groan:– groan (2), growl (1), roar (1), roaring (1)

H5638 נַהַם ***naham***, n.[m.] [2] [√ 5637]. roaring, growling:– roar (2)

H5639 נְהָמָה ***nᵉhāmâ***, n.f. [2] [√ 5637]. roaring, growling; anguish, groaning:– anguish (1), roaring (1)

H5640 נָהַק ***nāhaq***, v. [2] [cf. 5628]. [Q] to bray (of a donkey):– bray (1), brayed (1)

H5641 [1]נָהַר ***nāhar[1]***, v. [3] [√ 5643]. [Q] to stream to (like a river flow):– stream (3)

H5642 [2]נָהַר ***nāhar[2]***, v. [3] [→ 5644; cf. 5944]. [Q] to be radiant (with joy), beam (with joy):– radiant (2), rejoice (1)

H5643 נָהָר ***nāhār***, n.m. [118] [→ 808, 5641, 5645; 10468]. river, stream, canal; the River, which can refer to the Euphrates, Tigris, or Nile:– river (40), rivers (23), Euphrates river (13), streams (12), Euphrates (4), Trans-Euphrates (4 [+6298, 2021]), canal (3), seas (3), Euphrates[S] (2), flood (2), riverbed (2), waters (2), canals (1), currents (1), rivers (1 [+5707]), wadi (1), NDT (4)

H5644 נְהָרָה ***nehārâ***, n.f. [1] [√ 5642; 10465, 10466, 10467]. (beaming) light:– light (1)

H5645 נַהֲרַיִם ***naharayim***, n.pr.loc. Not used in NIVEBC [→ 808; cf. 5643]. Naharaim, see 808, "*two rivers*"

H5646 נוּ- ***-nû[1]***, p.com.pl.suf. [1642] [√ 3276]. us, our:– us (703), our (670), we (94), our (20 [+4200]), our own (13), ourselves (10), ours (7), the[s] (6), it (5), we (5 [+5883]), ourselves (3 [+5883]), us (3 [+5883]), me (2), ours (2 [+4200]), a[s] (1), each other (1 [+9109]), he[s] (1 [+3378, 466]), here[s] (1), one (1), ours (1 [+4200, 7156]), that (1), us (1 [+6524]), us deserve (1), we're (1), what[s] (1), you (1), NDT (87)

H5647 נוּ- ***-nû[2]***, נוֹ- ***-nô***, p.m.sg.suf. [512] [√ 2023]. him, his; it, its:– him (116), it (90), them (81), he (18), they (13), his (9), one (4), their (3), animal[s] (2), its (2), the Lord[s] (2), the altar[s] (2), the ephod[s] (2), the slave[s] (2), their own (2), themselves (2), whom (2), Abimelek[s] (1), Absalom[s] (1), Edom[s] (1), Jeremiah[s] (1), Judah[s] (1), all[s] (1), another[s] (1), any[s] (1), at fault[s] (1), drink[s] (1), grain[s] (1), hers (1), his (1 [+4946]), his words[s] (1), manna[s] (1), person (1), return (1), that (1), that person[s] (1), the blood[s] (1), the guilt[s] (1), the meat[s] (1), the murderer[s] (1), the oil[s] (1), the one[s] (1), the roof[s] (1), the sacred portion[s] (1), the wicked[s] (1), theirs down (1), there[s] (1), these tithes[s] (1), this bread[s] (1), those[s] (1), what (1), who (1), NDT (125)

H5648 נוא ***nû'***, v. [8] [→ 9481]. [Q] to hinder; [H] to forbid, thwart, discourage:– forbids (2), discourage (1 [+4213]), discouraged (1 [+4213]), forbid (1), forbidden (1), refuse (1), thwarts (1)

H5649 נוב ***nûb***, v. [4] [→ 1973, 5650, 5762, 9482]. [Q] to bring forth, bear fruit, increase; [Pol] to make thrive:– bear fruit (1), comes the fruit (1), increase (1), make thrive (1)

H5650 נוֹב ***nôb***, n.[m.] Not used in NIVEBC [√ 5649]. see 5762

H5651 נוֹבַי ***nôbay***, n.pr.m. Not used in NIVEBC [cf. 5763]. Nobai, see 5763

H5652 נוּג ***nûg***, n.[m.] [1] sorrow:– mourn (1)

H5653 נוּד ***nûd***, v. [25] [→ 4954, 5654, 5655, 5764; cf. 5604, 5610, 5612; 10469]. [Q] to sway, wander, be aimless, become homeless; to mourn, express sympathy (by shaking the head:– flee (3), mourn (3), wanderer (2), away (1), comfort (1), comforted (1), drive away (1), fluttering (1), go astray (1), make wander (1), moaning (1), mourn loss (1), shake (1), shake head in scorn (1), shake heads in scorn (1), show sympathy (1), swaying (1), sways (1), sympathize (1), sympathy (1)

H5654 נוֹד ***nôd[1]***, n.[m.] [1] [√ 5653]. lament; some sources: wandering, homelessness:– misery (1)

H5655 נוֹד ***nôd[2]***, n.pr.loc. [1] [√ 5653]. Nod, "*wandering*":– Nod (1)

H5656 נוֹדָב ***nôdāb***, n.pr.g. [1] Nodab:– Nodab (1)

H5657 נָוָה ***nāwâ[1]***, v.den. [1] [√ 5659]. [Q] to be at rest, reach one's aim:– at rest (1)

H5658 נָוָה ***nāwâ[2]***, v. [1] [cf. 5533]. [H] to praise:– praise (1)

H5659 נָוֶה ***nāweh[1]***, n.m. [32] [→ 5657, 5661]. pasture, pastureland, with a possible focus that this is a place of rest and peace; (generally) abode, dwelling, house:– pasture (9), dwelling (2), grazing land (2), homeland (2), house (2), pastureland (2), abode (1), city (1), dwelling place (1), dwelling places (1), haunt (1), haunts (1), home (1), land (1), pastures (1), pleasant place (1), property (1), settlement (1), store up (1 [+238, 928])

H5660 נָוֶה ***nāweh[2]***, a. Not used in NIVEBC [√ 5659; cf. 5533]. dwelling, abiding

H5661 נָוָה ***nāwâ[3]***, n.f. [15] [√ 5959]. pasture, pastureland; (generally) abode, dwelling, camp, place:– pastures (7), grasslands (2), at home (1 [+1074]), dwellings (1), haunts (1), meadows (1), pasturelands (1), state (1)

H5662 נָוֹת ***nāwôt***, n.pr.loc. Not used in NIVEBC [cf. 5766]. Navoth, see 5766

H5663 נוּחַ ***nûaḥ[1]***, v. [139] [→ 2182, 3562, 3563, 4955, 4956, 4957, 4965, 4969, 4970, 4971, 5665, 5666?, 5739, 5740, 5767]. [Q] to settle, rest, wait; [H] to put, keep, settle, rest; to leave, allow; [Ho] to be placed, find rest:– leave (11), given rest (8), put (8), rest (7), give rest (5), left (5), rested (5), set (5), at rest (4), kept (4), leave alone (4), place (4), placed (4), find rest (3), gave rest (3), gives rest (3), settle (3), subside (3), allowed (2), came to rest (2), granted rest (2), laid (2), put down (2), set up (2), allied (1), allowed to remain (1), be (1), be set (1), cast (1), comes to rest (1), deposited (1), forsake (1), get relief (1), give peace (1), gives relief (1), got relief (1), have rest (1), lay (1), lay to rest (1), lays (1), left unweighed (1), let be idle (1), let go (1 [+906, 3338]), let remain (1), lowered (1), permits (1), remain (1), reposes (1), resides (1), resting (1), safely (1), save (1), saved (1), set down (1), settled down (1), store (1), subsided (1), throw (1), tolerate (1), touch (1), wait patiently (1), waited (1)

H5664 נוּחַ ***nûaḥ[2]***, v. Not used in NIVEBC [cf. 634]. [Q] to lament, wail

H5665 נוֹחַ ***nôaḥ***, n.f. [1] [→ 5666; cf. 5663]. resting place:– resting place (1)

H5666 נוֹחָה ***nôḥâ***, n.pr.m. [1] [√ 5665?; cf. 5663?]. Nohah, "*rest*":– Nohah (1)

H5667 נוּט ***nûṭ***, v. [1] [Q] to shake, quake:– shake (1)

H5668 נָוִית ***nāwît***, n.pr.loc. Not used in NIVEBC [cf. 5766]. Navith, see 5766

H5669 נָוֶל ***nāwel***, n. thread

H5670 נוּם ***nûm***, v. [6] [→ 3564?, 3565?, 5671, 9484]. [Q] to sleep, slumber, implying detachment from activities and others; by extension: to be dead:– slumber (3), sleep (2), slumbers (1)

H5671 נוּמָה ***nûmâ***, n.f. [1] [√ 5670]. drowsiness:– drowsiness (1)

H5672 נוּן ***nûn[1]***, v. [1] [cf. 5673?, 5768]. [N] to propagate, increase:– continue (1)

H5673 נוּן ***nûn[2]***, n.pr.m. [30] [cf. 5672?]. Nun, "*fish hence fertile, productive*":– Nun (30)

H5674 נוּס ***nûs***, v. [159] [→ 4960, 4961, 5771]. [Q] to flee away, escape; [Pol] to drive along; [H] to put to flight, get to safety:– fled (65), flee (39), fleeing (6), ran (6), flees (5), run (5), escape (3), flee away (3), escaped (2), forced to flee (2 [+5674]), fugitives (2), get away (2 [+5674]), draining away (1), drives along (1), fled back (1), fled up (1), flee for refuge (1), flee in haste (1 [+4960]), get away (1), gone (1), hurried to bring (1), keep (1), leave (1), made good escape (1 [+2256, 4880]), on the run (1), put to flight (1), retreat (1), routed (1), running away (1), seek refuge (1), turned and ran (1)

H5675 נוּעַ ***nûa'***, v. [39] [→ 4983]. [Q] to shake, sway, swagger, wander; [N] to be shaken; [H] to make wander, to set trembling, shake, toss:– shake (5), hold sway (3), shaken (3), reels (2 [+5675]), restless (2), stagger (2), staggered (2), tosses (2), wander about (2), disturb (1), grope (1), is shaken (1), made wander (1), make wander about (1), moving (1), set trembling (1), shaking (1), shook (1), sway (1), tremble (1), trembled (1), uproot (1), wander (1), wander aimlessly (1), wandering (1)

H5676 נוֹעַדְיָה ***nô'adyâ***, n.pr.m. & f. [2] [√ 3585 + 3378]. Noadiah, "*meet with Yahweh*":– Noadiah (2)

H5677 נוּף ***nûp[1]***, v. [35] [→ 2185, 5864, 9485; cf. 5537]. [Pol] to wave (the fist) threateningly; [H] to wave, present (an offering) by waving; to shake, wield, sweep; [Ho] to be waved:– wave (12), waved (4), presented (3), present (2), use (2), beckon (1 [+3338]), put (1), raise (1), raised (1), raises (1), shake (1), shakes (1), sweep (1), used (1), uses (1), was waved (1 [+9485]), wield (1)

H5678 נוּף ***nûp[2]***, v. [2] [→ 5885]. [Q] to sprinkle with myrrh (a bed); [H] to cause (rain) to fall:– gave (1), perfumed (1)

H5679 נוֹף ***nôp***, n.[m.] [1] [→ 5865, 5868, 5869, 5884]. loftiness, elevation, height:– loftiness (1)

H5680 נוּץ ***nûṣ***, v. [1] [Q] to leave, go away:– flee (1)

H5681 נוֹצָה ***nôṣâ***, n.f. [3] [cf. 5901, 5902]. plumage, feathers:– plumage (2), feathers (1)

H5682 נוּק ***nûq***, v. Not used in NIVEBC [cf. 3567]. [H] to suckle, nurse

H5683 נוּשׁ ***nûš***, v. [1] [cf. 631]. [Q] to be sick:– helpless (1)

H5684 נָזָה ***nāzâ[1]***, v. [24] [Q] to spatter; [H] to sprinkle:– sprinkle (16), spattered (2), sprinkled (2), is spattered (1), splash (1), sprinkles (1), NDT (1)

H5685 נָזָה ***nāzâ[2]***, v. [H] to leap, spring

H5686 נָזִיד ***nāzîd***, n.[m.] [6] [√ 2326]. stew, thick boiled food:– stew (6)

H5687 נָזִיר ***nāzîr***, n.m. [16] [√ 5693]. Nazirite, with the designated meaning of separation; a class of people dedicated to God; untended vine, dedicated to God in the sabbatical year of rest:– Nazirite (8), Nazirites (2), prince (2), untended vines (2), dedication (1), princes (1)

H5688 נָזַל ***nāzal***, v. [10] [→ 5689]. [Q] to flow down, pour down, stream down; [H] to make flow:– flow (2), descend (1), flowing (1), made flow (1), pour down moisture (1), shower down (1), spread everywhere (1), streaming down (1), streams (1)

H5689 נֹזֵל ***nōzēl***, n.[m.] *or* v.ptcp. [5] [√ 5688]. streams; surging waters:– streams (3), running water (1), surging (1)

H5690 נֶזֶם ***nezem***, n.m. [17] ring (in the nose or ear of male or female):– ring (5), earrings (4), rings (4), earring (2), nose ring (2)

H5691 נֵזֶק ***nēzeq***, n.[m.] [1] [√ 10472]. burden, trouble:– disturbing (1)

H5692 נָזַר ***nāzar[1]***, v. [5] [→ 5693; cf. 4964, 5623]. [N] to separate oneself, consecrate oneself; [H] to keep separate:– consecrated themselves (1), fast (1), keep separate (1), separate themselves (1), treat with respect (1)

H5693 נָזַר ***nāzar[2]***, v.den. [5] [→ 5687, 5692, 5694; cf. 5623]. [H] to abstain, separate as a Nazirite; see also 5687:– dedication (2), Nazirite (1), abstain (1), rededicate (1)

H5694 נֵזֶר ***nēzer***, n.m. [25] [√ 5693; cf. 5623]. separation, dedication (to God); diadem, crown (as a sign of consecration); Nazirite, a class of people dedicated to God:– crown (7), dedication (7), emblem (3), Nazirite (1), Nazirite vow (1 [+5624]), dedicated (1), hair (1), period of dedication (1), symbol of dedication (1), under Nazirite vow (1), NDT (1)

H5695 נֹחַ ***nōaḥ***, n.pr.m. [47] [√ 5714]. Noah, "*rest, comfort*":– Noah (40), Noah's (3), he[s] (2), his[s] (2)

H5696 נַחְבִּי ***naḥbî***, n.pr.m. [1] Nahbi, "[perhaps] *hidden* or *timid*":– Nahbi (1)

H5697 נָחָה ***nāḥâ[1]***, v. [39] [Q, H] to lead, guide:– lead (12), guide (8), led (6), guided (4), guides (2), brought (1), disperses (1), kept (1), lead out (1), left (1), settled (1), ushers (1)

H5698 נָחָה ***nāḥâ[2]***, v. [Q] lean upon

H5699 נַחוּם ***naḥûm***, n.pr.m. [1] [√ 5714]. Nahum, "*comfort*":– Nahum (1)

H5700 נְחוּם ***neḥûm***, n.pr.m. [1] [cf. 8156]. Nehum, "*comfort*":– Nehum (1)

H5701 נָחוֹר ***nāḥôr***, n.pr.m. [18] Nahor, "*the mound of Nahuru*":– Nahor (16), Nahor's (2)

H5702 נָחוּשׁ ***nāḥûš***, a. [1] [√ 5733]. (made) of bronze:– bronze (1)

H5703 נְחוּשָׁה ***neḥûšâ***, n.f. [10] [√ 5733; 10473]. copper, bronze:– bronze (8), bronze-tipped (1), copper (1)

H5704 נְחִילוֹת ***neḥîlôt***, n.f. [1] [√ 2720?; cf. 2726?]. flutes (a t.t. in Ps 5):– pipes (1)

H5705 נָחִיר ***nāḥîr***, n.[m.] [1] [√ 5723]. (dual) nostrils:– nostrils (1)

H5706 נָחַל ***nāḥal***, v.den. [59] [→ 5709]. [Q] to take as an appearance, take possession; [P] to assign an inheritance, allot; [H] to cause to inherit, give an inheritance; [Ho] to be allotted; [Ht] to obtain an inheritance for oneself; to distribute an inheritance:– inherit (6), assign as an inheritance (2), distribute (2), divide as inheritance (2), gave inheritance (2), giving as an inheritance (2), inheritance (2), lead to inherit (2), receive inheritance (2), received (2), received inheritance (2), take possession (2), allotted (1), assign inheritance (1), assigned (1), been allotted (1), bequeath (1), bestowing a inheritance (1), cause to inherit (1), divide (1), dividing (1), gave (1), get inheritance (1), give as an inheritance (1), give inheritance (1), has inherit (1), have inheritance (1), have inheritance (1 [+5709]), help assign (1), heritage (1), inherit land (1), inheritance given (1), inherits (1), leaves an inheritance (1), pass on as an inheritance (1), possessed (1), reassign (1), receive (1), receive inheritance (1 [+5709]), received as an inheritance (1), take as inheritance (1), wills (1), NDT (1)

H5707 נַחַל ***naḥal[1]***, n.m. [139] [→ 5708?, 5711, 5712]. river, stream, brook, wadi torrent; ravine, gorge, valley:– valley (37), gorge (19), river (17), streams (11), ravines (9), stream (9), ravine (8), wadi (7), brook (4), torrent (3), torrents (2), valleys (2), brooks (1 [+4784]), course (1), intermittent streams (1), rivers (1), rivers (1 [+5643]), shaft (1), stream beds (1), streams (1 [+692]), there[s] (1 [+928, 7724]), willows (1 [+6857]), NDT (1)

H5708 נַחַל ***naḥal[2]***, n.[m.] Not used in NIVEBC [√ 5707?]. date palm

H5709 נַחֲלָה ***naḥalâ[1]***, n.f. [222] [√ 5706]. inheritance, property:– inheritance (186), heritage (5), inherit (3), part (3), property (3), inheritances (2), one[s] (2), territory (2), that[s] (2), ancestral property (1), estate (1), have inheritance (1 [+5706]), inherited (1), it[s] (1), land (1), land inherits (1), lands (1), place (1), receive inheritance (1 [+5706]), territories (1), territory inherit (1), NDT (2)

H5710 נַחֲלָה ***naḥalâ[2]***, n.[m.] *or* v.ptcp. [1] [√ 2703]. disease:– disease (1)

H5711 נַחֲלָה ***naḥalâ[3]***, n.[pr.loc.?] [2] [→ 5712; cf. 5707]. wadi (of Egypt):– Wadi (2)

H5712 נַחֲלִיאֵל ***naḥalî'ēl***, n.pr.loc. [2] [√ 5711 + 446]. Nahaliel, "*wadi of God [El]*":– Nahaliel (2)

H5713 נֶחֱלָמִי ***neḥelāmî***, a.g. [3] Nehelamite:– Nehelamite (3)

H5714 נָחַם ***nāḥam***, v. [108] [→ 4968, 5695, 5699, 5700, 5715, 5716, 5717, 5718, 5719, 5720, 9487, 9488, 9489]. [N] to relent, repent, change one's mind; be grieved; [P] to comfort, console, express sympathy; [Pu] to be comforted, be consoled; [Ht] to console oneself; to change one's mind; avenge oneself:– comfort (23), relented (8), relent (7), comforted (5), express sympathy (5), be comforted (4), change mind (4), comforts (4), console (3), be consoled (2), comforter (2), comforters (2), consoled (2), give comfort (2), grieved (2), have compassion (2), regret (2), regretted (2), relents (2), repent (2), be avenged (1), change minds (1), compassion (1), find comfort (1), giving comfort (1), holding back (1), look with compassion (1), pity (1), planning to avenge himself (1), put at ease (1), reassured (1), reconsider (1), recovered from grief (1), relent and do not bring (1), relent and not bring (1), relent so that not bring (1), relented

HEBREW INDEX

and did not (1), repented (1), showed pity (1), vent wrath (1), was comforted (1), was consoled (1), were consoled (1)

H5715 נחם **naḥam**, n.pr.m. [1] [√ 5714]. Naham, *"repent, console"*:– Naham (1)

H5716 נֹחַם **nōḥam**, n.m. [1] [√ 5714]. compassion, pity:– compassion (1)

H5717 נֶחָמָה **neḥāmâ**, n.f. [2] [√ 5714]. comfort, consolation:– comfort (1), consolation (1)

H5718 נְחֶמְיָה **nᵉḥemyâ**, n.pr.m. [8] [√ 5714 + 3378]. Nehemiah, *"Yahweh has comforted"*:– Nehemiah (8)

H5719 נִחוּמִים **niḥumîm**, n.m.[pl.] [3] [√ 5714]. comfort, compassion:– comfort (1), comforting (1), compassion (1)

H5720 נַחֲמָנִי **naḥᵃmānî**, n.pr.m. [1] [√ 5714]. Nahamani, *"Yahweh has consoled"*:– Nahamani (1)

H5721 נַחְנוּ **naḥnû**, p.com.pl. [6] [√ 636]. we:– we (5), NDT (1)

H5722 נָחַץ **nāḥaṣ**, v. [1] [cf. 4315]. [Qp] to be urgent:– urgent (1)

H5723 נָחַר **nāḥar**, v. [2] [→ 5705, 5724, 5725]. [Q] to blow; [P] to snort:– angry (1), blow fiercely (1)

H5724 נַחַר **naḥar**, n.[m.] [1] [√ 5723]. snorting (of a horse):– snorting (1)

H5725 נַחֲרָה **naḥᵃrâ**, n.f. [1] [√ 5723]. snorting (of a horse):– snorting (1)

H5726 נַחְרַי **naḥray**, n.pr.m. [2] Naharai:– Naharai (2)

H5727 נָחַשׁ **nāḥaš**, v.den. [11] [→ 5728; cf. 4317]. [P] to practice divination, interpret omens and signs:– find things out by divination (2 [+5727]), sought omens (2), uses for divination (2 [+5727]), interprets omens (1), learned by divination (1), practice divination (1), took as a good sign (1), witchcraft (1)

H5728 נַחַשׁ **naḥaš**, n.[m.] [2] [√ 5727]. sorcery, magic curse, spell:– divination (2)

H5729 [1]נָחָשׁ **nāḥāš[1]**, n.m. [31] [→ 5731, 5732]. snake, serpent; by extension: a mythological creature of chaos opposed to God:– snake (15), serpent (10), snakes (3), serpent's (2), venomous snakes (1)

H5730 [2]נָחָשׁ **nāḥāš[2]**, n.pr.loc. Not used in NIVEBC [√ 5733; cf. 5736]. Nahash, see 6560

H5731 [3]נָחָשׁ **nāḥāš[3]**, n.pr.m. [9] [√ 5729]. Nahash, *"viper or copper"*:– Nahash (8), him[S] (1)

H5732 נַחְשׁוֹן **naḥšôn**, n.pr.m. [10] [√ 5729]. Nahshon, *"small viper"*:– Nahshon (10)

H5733 [1]נְחֹשֶׁת **nᵉḥōšet[1]**, n.m. [140] [→ 5702, 5703, 5730; cf. 5736; 10473]. copper, bronze; this can refer to bronze as a medium of exchange:– bronze (128), bronze shackles (5), copper (4), chains (1), lust (1), were fettered (1 [+5602, 4200])

H5734 [2]נְחֹשֶׁת **nᵉḥōšet[2]**, n.[f.] Not used in NIVEBC. menstruation

H5735 נְחֻשְׁתָּא **nᵉḥuštāʾ**, n.pr.f. [1] Nehushta, *"[strong as or color of] bronze"*:– Nehushta (1)

H5736 נְחֻשְׁתָּן **nᵉḥuštān**, n.pr. [1] [cf. 5730, 5733]. Nehushtan, *"bronze viper"*:– Nehushtan (1)

H5737 נָחַת **nāḥat**, v. [10] [→ 5738, 5741; cf. 9393; 10474]. [Q] to descend, go down; [N] to be pierced, penetrate; [P] to bend (a bow); to level off; [H] to bring down:– bend (2), bring down (1), come (1), come down (1), descend (1), go down (1), impresses (1), level (1), pierced (1 [+928])

H5738 [1]נַחַת **naḥat[1]**, n.[m.] [1] [√ 5737]. coming down, descending:– coming down (1)

H5739 [2]נַחַת **naḥat[2]**, n.f. & m. [6] [→ 5740; cf. 5663]. rest, peace, tranquillity:– rest (2), comfort (1), peace (1), quiet (1), tranquillity (1)

H5740 [3]נַחַת **naḥat[3]**, n.pr.m. [5] [√ 5739; cf. 5663]. Nahath, *"descent; [poss.] rest"*:– Nahath (5)

H5741 נָחֵת **nāḥēt**, a. [1] [√ 5737]. going down, descending:– going down (1)

H5742 נָטָה **nāṭâ**, v. [215] [→ 4750, 4751, 4752, 4753, 4754, 4755; cf. 352]. [Q] to spread out, stretch out; [Qp] to be outstretched, be spread out, be extended; [N] to be spread out, be stretched out; [H] to turn aside, pervert, lead astray; [Ho] to be outspread:– stretch out (24), outstretched (18), turn (18), stretched out (15), pitched (10), stretches out (8), turned (7), pay attention (6 [+265]), upraised (5), deprive (4), give ear (4 [+265]), deny (3), pervert (3), spread out (3), turn aside (3), turned away (3), deprive of justice (2), evening (2), extended (2), held out (2), parted (2), pitch (2), spread (2), took (2), afternoon (1 [+2021, 3427]), applying (1), be stretched out (1), bend (1), bent down (1), brandishes (1), channels (1), conspired (1), did this[S] (1 [+3338, 2257]), do let be drawn (1), extend (1), get back on (1), get off (1), giving (1), go ahead (1), go forward (1), grow long (1), hear (1 [+265]), hold out (1), inclined (1 [+4213]), kept away (1), lead (1), leaning (1), led astray (1), led astray (1 [+4213]), let down (1), lie down (1), listen (1 [+265]), measures (1), misleads (1), outspread (1), paid any attention (1 [+265, 4200, 9048]), paid attention (1 [+265]), part (1), pay careful attention (1 [+8011, 2256, 265]), perverted (1), plot (1), pushed (1), raised (1), reach out (1 [+3338]), set (1), shakes (1), showed (1), shown (1), siding (1), slipped (1), spreads out (1), stay (1), stays only a night (1 [+4328]), strayed (1), stretch wide (1), stretched (1), throw (1), thrust (1), took aside (1), turn away (1), turned aside (1), turning (1), turning aside (1), went over (1), withholds (1), won over (1), yield (1), your (1 [+3870]), NDT (1)

H5743 נְטוֹפָתִי **nᵉṭôpātî**, a.g. [11] [√ 5756; cf. 5752]. Netophathite, *"of Netophah"*:– Netophathite (8), Netophathites (3)

H5744 נָטִיל **nāṭîl**, a. [1] [√ 5747]. weighing (of precious metals); by extension, trading: buying, selling, and bartering:– who trade with (1)

H5745 נָטִיעַ **nāṭîaʿ**, n.[m.] [1] [√ 5749]. shoot (of a young plant):– plants (1)

H5746 נְטִישׁוֹת **nᵉṭîšôt**, n.f. [3] [√ 5759]. spreading branches, tendrils:– branches (2), spreading branches (1)

H5747 נָטַל **nāṭal**, v. [4] [→ 5744, 5748; 10475]. [Q] to lay upon; to weigh; [P] to lift:– giving (1), laid (1), lifted up (1), weighs (1)

H5748 נֵטֶל **nēṭel**, n.[m.] [1] [√ 5747]. burden, load:– burden (1)

H5749 נָטַע **nāṭaʿ**, v. [57] [→ 4760, 5745, 5750, 5751]. [Q] to plant (seed or stock); by extension: to place, set, set up (any object on any surface):– plant (28), planted (19), are planted (1), farmers (1), fashioned (1), firmly embedded (1), pitch (1), plants (1), replanted (1), set in place (1), set out (1), set up (1)

H5750 נֶטַע **neṭaʿ**, n.[m.] [4] [√ 5749]. garden, plants; young plant:– plant (1), plants (1), set out (1), vines (1)

H5751 נְטָעִים **nᵉṭāʿîm**, n.pr.loc. [1] [√ 5749]. Netaim:– Netaim (1)

H5752 נָטַף **nāṭap**, v. [18] [→ 3213, 5743, 5753, 5754, 5755, 5756]. [Q] to pour down; gently fall, drip; [H] to (drip words) preach, prophesy:– drip (3), prophesy (3), preach (2), dripped (1), dripping (1), drop (1), fell gently (1), poured (1), poured down (1), poured down rain (1), preaching (1), prophet (1), prophets say (1)

H5753 נָטָף **nāṭāp**, n.[m.] [1] [√ 5752]. gum resin, drops of stacte (the resin of a shrub):– gum resin (1)

H5754 נֶטֶף **neṭep**, n.m. [1] [√ 5752]. drop (of water):– drops (1)

H5755 נְטִפָה **nᵉṭipâ**, n.[f.] [2] [√ 5752]. pendant, a drop-shaped ornament:– earrings (1), pendants (1)

H5756 נְטֹפָה **nᵉṭōpâ**, n.pr.loc. [2] [√ 5743; cf. 5752]. Netophah, *"trickle, drip"*:– Netophah (2)

H5757 [1]נָטַר **nāṭar[1]**, v. [9] [→ 4766; cf. 5758, 5915]. [Q] to care for, tend; to be angry, harbor a grudge:– angry (2), bear a grudge against (1), harbor anger (1), neglect (1 [+4202]), take care of (1), tenants (1), tend (1), vents wrath (1)

H5758 [2]נָטַר **nāṭar[2]**, v. Not used in NIVEBC [cf. 5757]. [Q] to be angry, harbor a grudge

H5759 נָטַשׁ **nāṭaš**, v. [40] [→ 5746]. [Q] to abandon, forsake, reject; [Qp] to be scattered; [N] to spread out; to be deserted; [Pu] to be abandoned:– abandoned (5), forsake (5), left (4), leave (3), reject (3), spread out (3), scattered (2), abandon (1), be abandoned (1), cast out (1), deserted (1), drawn (1), drop (1), forgo (1), hangs loose (1), let (1), rejected (1), spread (1), spreading out (1), stopped thinking (1), throw (1), unused (1)

H5760 נִי **nî**, n.[m.] [1] [√ 5631; cf. 5629]. wailing:– wail (1)

H5761 -נִי **-nî**, p.com.sg.suf. [1307] [√ 3276]. I, me, my:– me (995), I (204), my (43), us (12), myself (3), mine (2 [+4946]), we (2), I'll (1), I'm (1), how I long for (1 [+4769, 5989]), my life (1), NDT (42)

H5762 נִיב **nîb**, n.[m.] [2] [√ 5649]. fruit; "fruit of the lips" is praise:– food (1 [+431]), praise (1)

H5763 נֵיבַי **nêbāy**, n.pr.m. [1] [√ 5651?]. Nebai, *"thrive"*:– Nebai (1)

H5764 ניד **nîd**, n.m. [1] [√ 5653]. comfort:– comfort (1)

H5765 נִידָה **nîdâ**, n.f. [1] [√ 5614; cf. 5612]. uncleanness, impurity:– unclean (1)

H5766 נָיוֹת **nāyôt**, n.pr.loc. [6] [cf. 5662, 5668]. Naioth, *"dwellings"*:– Naioth (6)

H5767 נִיחֹחַ **nîḥōaḥ**, n.[m.] [43] [√ 5663; 10478]. pleasing, soothing, appeasing:– pleasing (38), fragrant incense (4 [+8194]), offering pleasing (1)

H5768 [1]נִין **nîn[1]**, v. Not used in NIVEBC [→ 5769; cf. 5672]. [Q] to sprout forth

H5769 [2]נִין **nîn[2]**, n.[m.] [3] [√ 5768]. offspring, children, posterity:– offspring (2), children (1)

H5770 נִינְוֵה **nînᵉwēh**, n.pr.loc. [17] Nineveh:– Nineveh (16), Ninevites (1 [+408])

H5771 נִיס **nîs**, n.m. *or* v.inf. Not used in NIVEBC [√ 5674]. flight, fleeing

H5772 נִיסָן **nîsān**, n.pr. [2] Nisan:– Nisan (2)

H5773 נִיצוֹץ **nîṣôṣ**, n.[m.] [1] [√ 5913]. spark:– spark (1)

H5774 [1]נִיר **nîr[1]**, v. [2] [→ 5776]. [Q] to break up, bring into cultivation:– break up (2)

H5775 [2]נִיר **nîr[2]**, n.[m.] [4] [√ 5944]. lamp; by extension: descendant (continuing of a line as the burning of a lamp):– lamp (4)

H5776 [3]נִיר **nîr[3]**, n.[m.] [4] [√ 5774]. unplowed ground, likely referring to ground not plowed for the current season:– unplowed field (2), unplowed ground (2)

H5777 [1]נָכָא **nākāʾ[1]**, v. [1] [→ 5778, 5779, 5780?; cf. 5782]. [N] to be driven out (by whipping or scourging):– were driven out (1)

H5778 [2]נָכָא **nākāʾ[2]**, a. [1] [√ 5777]. grieving (as one unmercifully beaten):– grieve (1)

H5779 נָכֵא **nākēʾ**, a. [3] [√ 5777]. crushed, beaten, broken:– crushed (2), crushes (1)

H5780 נְכֹאת **nᵉkōʾt**, n.f. [2] [√ 5777?]. spices, resin:– spices (2)

H5781 נֶכֶד **neked**, n.[m.] [3] descendant, progeny:– descendants (3)

H5782 נָכָה **nākâ**, v. [499] [→ 4804, 5783, 5784, 5787; cf. 5777]. [N] to be struck; [Pu] to be destroyed; [H] to kill, slaughter, destroy, defeat; [Ho] to be beat, be struck, be wounded, be killed:– struck down (56), killed (40), defeated (33), struck (33), strike (28), put (24), attacked (22), kill (15), attack (13), beat (10), kills (10), strike down (9), inflicted (7), conquered (5), destroy (5), afflict (4), afflicted (4), attacks (4), murdered (4), slain (4), subdued (4), take (4), assassinated (3), cut down (3), defeat (3), hit (3), hits (3), killing (3), pin (3), punished (3), put to death (3), slaughtered (3), stabbed (3), strikes a blow (3), striking down (3), beat down (2), beaten (2), broke through (2), conscience-stricken (2 [+4213]), destroyed (2), flog (2), fought (2), had beaten (2), indeed defeated (2 [+5782]), inflict (2), kill (2 [+5883]), must certainly put (2 [+5782]), overpowered (2), punish (2), put to death (2 [+2256, 4637]), slapped (2), slaughtering (2), strike together (2), strikes (2), striking (2), struck (2 [+5782]), takes life (2 [+5883]), victory (2), were destroyed (2), wounded (2), accused[S] (1), annihilate (1), assailant (1), assailants (1), assassinated (1 [+2256, 4637]), assassins (1), attacked viciously (1 [+8797, 6584, 3751]), be beaten (1), be struck down (1), beating (1), beats (1), being beaten (1), blazed (1), blighted (1), blind (1 [+6427, 928, 2021]), break up (1), chewed (1), clapped (1), conquers (1), dealt (1), defeated (1 [+1524, 4394, 4804]), defeated completely (1 [+1524, 4804]), defeating (1), devastated (1 [+1524, 4394, 4804]), drove (1), executed (1), executed (1 [+2256, 4637]), fall (1), fallen (1), flogged (1 [+4804]), had executed (1 [+2256, 4637]), had struck down (1), harm (1), have flogged (1), hitting (1), impose lashes (1), inflicted casualties (1), injured (1), is blighted (1), is struck (1), killed (1 [+4637]), killed (1 [+8357]), killed (1 [+4200, 7023, 2995]), killed off (1), killer (1), kills (1 [+5883, 2256, 4637]), lashes (1), overthrow (1), person[S] (1), plunge (1), plunged (1), putting to death (1), putting to rout (1), routed (1), sacked (1), send down (1), shot (1), slay (1), smash (1), stricken (1), strikes down (1), struck down (1 [+4804]), struck the blow (1), tear down (1), thrust (1), was killed (1), was put to death (1), were afflicted (1), wound (1), wounds was given (1), NDT (2)

H5783 נָכֶה **nākeh**, a. [3] [√ 5782]. lame, crippled; contrite:– lame (2), contrite (1)

H5784 נֵכֶה **nēkeh**, a. Not used in NIVEBC [√ 5782]. attacker

H5785 נְכֹה **nᵉkōh**, n.pr.m. [3] [→ 5786]. Neco:– Necho (3)

H5786 נְכוֹ **nᵉkô**, n.pr.m. [4] [√ 5785]. Neco:– Necho (4)

H5787 [1]נָכוֹן **nākôn[1]**, n.[m.] [1] [√ 5782]. strike, blow:– fate (1)

H5788 [2]נָכוֹן **nākôn[2]**, a. *or* v.ptcp. Not used in NIVEBC [√ 3922]. something prepared, fate

H5789 [3]נָכוֹן **nākôn[3]**, n.pr.m. [1] [√ 3922]. Nacon, *"established"*:– Nakon (1)

H5790 נֹכַח **nōkaḥ**, subst. (used as pp. & adv.) [25] [→ 5791]. opposite, before, in front of:– opposite (5), before (3), facing (3), faces (2), approval (1), directly in front of (1 [+4200]), directly opposite (1 [+4200, 7156]), in front of (1), in full view (1 [+6524]), in the presence of (1 [+7156]), on behalf of (1 [+4200]), open before (1 [+7156]), straight ahead (1 [+4200]), toward (1 [+448]), toward (1 [+6330]), vicinity (1)

H5791 נָכֹחַ **nākōaḥ**, a. & subst. [8] [√ 5790]. proper, right, honest, what is straight:– right (3), honest (1), honesty (1), proper (1), uprightly (1), uprightness (1)

H5792 נָכַל **nākal**, v. [4] [→ 3964?, 5793]. [Q, P] to cheat, treat cunningly; [Ht] to conspire, plot:– cheat (1), conspire (1), deceived (1 [+928, 5793]), plotted (1)

H5793 נֵכֶל **nēkel**, n.[m.] [1] [√ 5792]. deception, cunning:– deceived (1 [+5792, 928])

H5794 נְכָסִים **nᵉkāsîm**, n.m.[pl.] [5] [√ 10479]. riches, wealth, possessions:– possessions (4), wealth (1)

H5795 [1]נָכַר **nākar[1]**, v. [44] [→ 2129, 5798; cf. 5796]. [N] to disguise oneself, be not recognized; [P] to regard, consider; to favor; to misunderstand; [H] to recognize, acknowledge; [Ht] to make known:– recognized (9), recognize (5), acknowledge (4), show partiality (4 [+7156]), know (2), are known (1), are recognized (1), concerned (1), disguise themselves (1), distinguish (1), examine to see (1), favor (1), know how (1), make friends with (1), misunderstand (1), notice (1), paid regard (1), realized (1), regard (1), remembers (1), see (1), takes note of (1), tell (1), took note (1), took notice (1)

H5796 ^{2}נָכַר ***nākar^{2}***, v.den. [5] [→ 5797, 5799; cf. 5795]. [P] to treat as foreign; [Ht] to pretend to be a stranger:– delivered (1), made foreign (1), pretend to be someone else (1), pretended to be a stranger (1), pretense (1)

H5797 נֵכָר ***nēkār***, n.[m.] [36] [√ 5796]. (one from a foreign land) foreigner, alien, stranger:– foreign (16), foreigners (10 [+1201]), foreigner (5 [+1201]), they^{S} (2 [+1201]), foreigner (1 [+1201, 2021]), foreigners (1 [+1201, 2021]), other than^{S} (1)

H5798 נֶכֶר ***neker***, n.[m.] [2] [√ 5795]. misfortune, disaster:– disaster (1), misfortune (1)

H5799 נָכְרִי ***nokrî***, a. [45] [√ 5796]. foreign, alien; (n.) foreigner:– foreign (14), foreigner (10), wayward (5), foreigners (4), outsider (3), stranger (2), alien (1), another (1), any^{S} (1), foreigners (1 [+6639]), pagan (1 [+3529]), strangers (1 [+408]), wild (1)

H5800 נְכֹת ***n^{e}kōt***, n.[f.] [2] treasure, storage:– storehouses (2 [+1074])

H5801 נָלָה ***nālâ***, v. [1] [cf. 3983]. [H] to stop:– stop (1)

H5802 נְמִבְזָה ***n^{e}mibzâ***, var. Not used in NIVEBC [√ 1022]. see 1022

H5803 נְמוּאֵל ***n^{e}mû'ēl***, n.pr.m. [3] [→ 5804; cf. 3543, 5832?]. Nemuel:– Nemuel (3)

H5804 נְמוּאֵלִי ***n^{e}mû'ēlî***, a.g. [1] [√ 5803]. Nemuelite, "*of Nemuel*":– Nemuelite (1)

H5805 נְמָלָה ***n^{e}mālâ***, n.f. [2] ant:– ant (1), ants (1)

H5806 נָמַס ***nāmēs***, v. Not used in NIVEBC [√ 5022]. see 5022

H5807 נָמֵר ***nāmēr***, n.m. [6] [√ 10480]. leopard:– leopard (4), leopards (2)

H5808 נִמְרֹד ***nimrōd***, n.pr.m. [4] Nimrod, "[perhaps] *to rebel* or *the Arrow, the mighty hero*":– Nimrod (4)

H5809 נִמְרָה ***nimrâ***, n.pr.loc. [1] [→ 1113, 5810]. Nimrah, "*spotted leopard; basin of limpid [clear] water*":– Nimrah (1)

H5810 נִמְרִים ***nimrîm***, n.pr.loc. [2] [√ 5809]. Nimrim, "*limpid [clear] waters; wholesome waters*; [poss.] *waters of leopards*":– Nimrim (2)

H5811 נִמְשִׁי ***nimšî***, n.pr.m. [5] Nimshi:– Nimshi (5)

H5812 נֵס ***nēs***, n.[m.] [21] [√ 5824; cf. 5823, 5824]. banner, standard, signal pole:– banner (14), battle standard (2), pole (2), sail (1), signal (1), warning sign (1)

H5813 נְסִבָּה ***n^{e}sibbâ***, n.f. [1] [√ 6015]. turn of events:– turn of events (1)

H5814 נָסָה ***nāsâ***, v. [36] [→ 4999, 5001?]. [P] to test (usually to prove character or faithfulness), to attempt; to test God implies a lack of confidence in his revealed character, thus is wicked:– test (13), put to the test (8), tested (7), used to (2), did^{S} (1), testing (1), tried (1), try (1), venture (1), ventures (1)

H5815 נָסַח ***nāsaḥ***, v. [4] [cf. 5005?; 10481]. [Q] to tear down; [N] to be uprooted, be torn down:– be uprooted (1), pluck (1), tears down (1), torn (1)

H5816 ^{1}נָסִיךְ ***nāsîk^{1}***, n.m. [2] [→ 5817; cf. 5818]. drink offering; metal image, idol:– drink offerings (1), metal images (1)

H5817 ^{2}נָסִיךְ ***nāsîk^{2}***, n.m. [4] [√ 5816; cf. 5818, 5820]. prince, leader:– princes (3), commanders (1 [+132])

H5818 ^{1}נָסַךְ ***nāsak^{1}***, v. [23] [→ 5011, 5816, 5817, 5821, 5822; cf. 3575, 6057; 10482]. [Q] to pour out; [N] to be poured out; [P] to pour out; [H] to pour out; [Ho] to be poured out; usually of pouring out a drink offering to deity:– poured out (7), pour out (6), pouring out (3), casts (2), brought (1), forming an alliance (1 [+5011]), pour (1), pouring out of drink offerings (1), pouring out of offerings (1)

H5819 ^{2}נָסַךְ ***nāsak^{2}***, v. [1] [→ 5012, 5013, 5018; cf. 6115, 8455, 8504]. [Qp] to be woven:– covers (1)

H5820 ^{3}נָסַךְ ***nāsak^{3}***, v. [2] [cf. 5817, 6057]. [Q] to install, set; [N] to be appointed:– installed (1), was formed (1)

H5821 ^{1}נֶסֶךְ ***nesek^{1}***, n.m. [60] [√ 5818; 10483]. drink offering:– drink offerings (32), drink offering (27), libations (1)

H5822 ^{2}נֶסֶךְ ***nesek^{2}***, n.m. [4] [√ 5818]. metal image, idol:– images (3), metal god (1)

H5823 ^{1}נָסַס ***nāsas^{1}***, v. [1] [cf. 5812, 5824]. [Q] to falter:– sick (1)

H5824 ^{2}נָסַס ***nāsas^{2}***, v. [2] [→ 5812; cf. 5812, 5823]. [Htpol] to unfurl; to sparkle:– be unfurled (1), sparkle (1)

H5825 נָסַע ***nāsa'***, v. [146] [→ 5023, 5024]. [Q] to set out, move on, leave, travel on; [N] to be pulled up; [H] to lead, bring out; to pull out:– set out (49), left (43), moved on (6), traveled (5), went (5), move (3), broke camp (2), move on (2), moved (2), pulled up (2), withdrew (2), advance (1), are pulled up (1), be on way (1 [+2256, 2143]), been pulled down (1), broke camp (1 [+4946, 185]), brought out (1), journeyed (1), leaving (1 [+4946]), led (1), left (1 [+4946]), let loose (1), marching (1), move about (1), move out (1), out (1), put to one side (1), quarries (1), removed from quarry (1), setting out (1), tore loose (1), transplanted (1), uproots (1), wander (1), went out (1), NDT (1)

H5826 נָסַק ***nāsaq***, v. see 6158

H5827 נִסְרֹךְ ***nisrōk***, n.pr.[m.] [2] Nisroch (pagan god):– Nisrok (2)

H5828 נֵעָה ***nē'â***, n.pr.loc. [1] Neah:– Neah (1)

H5829 נֹעָה ***nō'â***, n.pr.f. [4] Noah, "*rest, comfort*":– Noah (4)

H5830 נְעוּרִים ***n^{e}'ûrîm***, n.[m.]pl. [46] [√ 5849]. youth, childhood, boyhood:– youth (37), young (5), childhood (3), boyhood (1)

H5831 נְעוּרוֹת ***n^{e}'ûrôt***, n.[f.]pl. [1] [√ 5853]. youth:– youth (1)

H5832 נְעִיאֵל ***n^{e}'î'ēl***, n.pr.loc. [1] [cf. 5803?]. Neiel:– Neiel (1)

H5833 ^{1}נָעִים ***nā'îm^{1}***, a. [11] [√ 5838]. pleasant, charming:– pleasant (4), admired (1), beautiful (1), charming (1), compliments (1 [+1821]), contentment (1), pleasing (1), pleasures (1)

H5834 ^{2}נָעִים ***nā'îm^{2}***, a. [2] [√ 5838]. singing, sweetly sounding, musical:– hero (1), melodious (1)

H5835 ^{1}נָעַל ***nā'al^{1}***, v. [6] [→ 4980, 4981; cf. 5837]. [Q] to lock up, bolt; [Qp] to be locked up, be sealed:– locked (2), bolt (1), bolted (1), locked up (1), sealed (1)

H5836 ^{2}נָעַל ***nā'al^{2}***, v.den. [2] [√ 5837]. [Q] to put on a sandal; [H] to provide with sandals:– put sandals on (1), sandals (1)

H5837 נַעַל ***na'al***, n.f. [22] [→ 5836; cf. 5835]. sandal (normal footware); not to wear sandals could have the associative meaning of being in poverty, misery, or disgrace:– sandals (14), sandal (6), sandaled (1 [+928, 2021]), unsandaled (1 [+2740])

H5838 נָעֵם ***nā'ēm***, v. [8] [→ 45, 321, 534, 4982, 5833, 5834, 5839, 5840, 5841, 5842, 5843, 5844, 5845, 5846]. [Q] to be pleasant, be dear, be favored:– pleasant (2), dear (1), delicious (1), go well (1), more favored (1), pleasing (1), well (1)

H5839 נַעַם ***na'am***, n.pr.m. [1] [√ 5838]. Naam, "*pleasant*":– Naam (1)

H5840 נֹעַם ***nō'am***, n.m. [7] [→ 45, 321, 534; cf. 5838]. pleasantness, favor:– favor (3), gracious (2), beauty (1), pleasant (1)

H5841 ^{1}נַעֲמָה ***na'^{a}mâ^{1}***, n.pr.f. [4] [√ 5838]. Naamah, "*pleasant*":– Naamah (4)

H5842 ^{2}נַעֲמָה ***na'^{a}mâ^{2}***, n.pr.loc. [1] [√ 5838]. Naamah, "*pleasant*":– Naamah (1)

H5843 נָעֳמִי ***no'^{o}mî***, n.pr.f. [21] [√ 5838]. Naomi, "*my joy*":– Naomi (19), Naomi's (1), she^{S} (1)

H5844 נַעֲמִי ***na'^{a}mî***, a.g. [1] [√ 5843; cf. 5838]. Naamite, "*of Naaman*":– Naamite (1)

H5845 נַעֲמָן ***na'^{a}mān***, n.pr.m. [16] [→ 5844; cf. 5838]. Naaman, "*pleasantness*":– Naaman (14), Naaman's (2)

H5846 נַעֲמָנִים ***na'^{a}mānîm***, n.[m.] [1] [√ 5838]. finest (of Adonis [?]):– finest (1)

H5847 נַעֲמָתִי ***na'^{a}mātî***, a.g. [4] Naamathite:– Naamathite (4)

H5848 נַעֲצוּץ ***na'^{a}ṣûṣ***, n.[m.] [2] thornbush:– thornbush (1), thornbushes (1)

H5849 ^{1}נָעַר ***nā'ar^{1}***, v. [1] [→ 5830, 5852?, 5853?]. [Q] to growl:– growl (1)

H5850 ^{2}נָעַר ***nā'ar^{2}***, v. [11] [→ 5861]. [Q] to shake off; to refuse; [Qp] be shaken out; [N] to shake oneself free, be shaken off; [P] to shake off, sweep away; [Ht] to shake oneself free:– swept (2), am shaken off (1), drop leaves (1), keep (1), shake (1), shake myself free (1), shake off (1), shake out (1), shaken out (1), shook out (1)

H5851 ^{3}נָעַר ***nā'ar^{3}***, v. [Q] to dry out

H5852 ^{1}נַעַר ***na'ar^{1}***, n.[m.] Not used in NIVEBC [√ 5849?]. scattering, shaking; (n.) scattered ones

H5853 ^{2}נַעַר ***na'ar^{2}***, n.m. [239] [→ 5831, 5854, 5855, 5856, 5859?; cf. 5849?]. young man, boy, child, ranging in age from infancy to young adulthood; by extension: servant, attendant, steward, with a possible focus on lower social status:– boy (47), servant (28), young (27), men (22), young man (21), servants (14), child (10), young men (10), boy's (4), children (4), junior officers (4), boys (3), steward (3), him^{S} (2 [+2021]), overseer (2 [+5893]), them^{S} (2 [+2021]), too young (2), underlings (2), youth (2), youths (2), Jether^{S} (1 [+2021]), aide (1), assistants (1), attendants (1), attendants (1 [+9250]), boy (1 [+7783]), boys (1 [+7783]), child's (1), he^{S} (1), he^{S} (1 [+2021]), helper (1), man (1), men's (1), personal attendants (1 [+9250]), personal servant (1 [+9250]), servant's (1), small children (1), sons (1), workers (1), young person (1), NDT (8)

H5854 נֹעַר ***nō'ar***, n.m. [4] [√ 5853]. youth:– youth (3), child's (1)

H5855 ^{1}נַעֲרָה ***na'^{a}râ^{1}***, n.f. [63] [→ 5856; cf. 5853]. young woman, girl, ranging in age from infancy to young adulthood; by extension: servant, maid, with a possible focus on lower social status:– young woman (13), woman's (5), attendants (4), she^{S} (4 [+2021]), woman (4), female servants (3), girl (3), her^{S} (3 [+2021]), young (3), young woman's (3), young women (3), female attendants (2), women (2), women who work (2), her^{S} (1), servants (1), she^{S} (1), young woman's (1 [+4200]), young women (1 [+1435]), NDT (4)

H5856 ^{2}נַעֲרָה ***na'^{a}râ^{2}***, n.pr.f. [3] [→ 5855, 5858?; cf. 5853, 5857?]. Naarah, "*[young] woman*":– Naarah (3)

H5857 ^{3}נַעֲרָה ***na'^{a}râ^{3}***, n.pr.loc. [1] [cf. 5856?, 5858?, 5860]. Naarah:– Naarah (1)

H5858 נַעֲרַי ***na'^{a}ray***, n.pr.m. [1] [cf. 5856?, 5857?]. Naarai, "*young man of Yahweh*":– Naarai (1)

H5859 נְעַרְיָה ***n^{e}'aryâ***, n.pr.m. [3] [√ 5853? + 3378]. Neariah, "*[young] man of Yahweh*":– Neariah (3)

H5860 נַעֲרָן ***na'^{a}rān***, n.pr.loc. [1] [cf. 5857]. Naaran:– Naaran (1)

H5861 נְעֹרֶת ***n^{e}'ōret***, n.f. [2] [√ 5850]. tinder (broken fibers shaken off flax):– piece of string (1 [+7348]), tinder (1)

H5862 נֹף ***nōp***, n.pr.loc. [7] [cf. 5132]. Noph = Memphis:– Memphis (7)

H5863 נֶפֶג ***nepeg***, n.pr.m. [4] Nepheg, "*sprout, shoot*":– Nepheg (4)

H5864 ^{1}נָפָה ***nāpâ^{1}***, n.f. [1] [√ 5677]. sieve (winnowing device):– sieve (1)

H5865 ^{2}נָפָה ***nāpâ^{2}***, n.f. Not used in NIVEBC [√ 5679; cf. 5868]. height, yoke

H5866 נְפוּסִים ***n^{e}pûsîm***, n.pr.[g.?] [1] [→ 5867, 5873, 5875]. Nephussim:– Nephusim (1)

H5867 נְפוּשְׁסִים ***n^{e}pûš^{e}sîm***, n.pr.[g.?] [1] [√ 5866]. Nephushsim:– Nephusim (1)

H5868 נָפוֹת ***nāpôt***, n.pr.loc. [1] [√ 5679; cf. 5865]. Naphoth, "*heights*":– Naphoth (1)

H5869 נָפוֹת דֹּאר ***nāpôt dō'r***, נָפוֹת דּוֹר ***nāpôt dôr***, n.pr. loc. [3] [√ 5679 + 1799]. Naphoth Dor, "*heights of Dor*":– Naphoth Dor (3)

H5870 נָפַח ***nāpaḥ***, v. [12] [→ 5134, 5135, 9515; cf. 7031]. [Q] to blow upon, breathe upon; [Qp, Pu] to be blown upon; [H] to sniff out; to cause to breathe out:– boiling (2), blast (1), blew away (1), blow (1), breathe (1), breathe last (1 [+5883]), breathed (1), broken (1), fans (1), sniff contemptuously (1), unfanned (1 [+4202])

H5871 נֹפַח ***nōpaḥ***, n.pr.loc. [1] Nophah:– Nophah (1)

H5872 נְפִילִים ***n^{e}pîlîm***, n.m.pl. [3] [√ 5877]. Nephilim:– Nephilim (3)

H5873 נְפִיסִים ***n^{e}pîsîm***, n.pr.g.? Not used in NIVEBC [√ 5866]. Nephissim

H5874 נָפִישׁ ***nāpîš***, n.pr.m. [3] [√ 5882]. Naphish, "*refreshed*":– Naphish (3)

H5875 נְפִישְׁסִים ***n^{e}pîš^{e}sîm***, n.pr.g.? Not used in NIVEBC [√ 5866]. Nephishsim [?]

H5876 נֹפֶךְ ***nōpek***, n.[m.] [4] turquoise (green semi-precious stone):– turquoise (4)

H5877 נָפַל ***nāpal***, v. [435] [→ 5139, 5142, 5143, 5147, 5872, 5878; 10484]. [Q] to fall, fail; [Pilal?] to fall; [H] to cause to fall, to cast down, drop; (used of casting lots) to allocate; [Ht] to fall prostrate (to worship); to fall upon (to attack); by extension: to happen (of circumstance falling on a person):– fall (101), fell (67), fallen (41), falls (23), cast (14), allotted (4), collapsed (4), down (4), downfall (4), failed (4), make fall (4), allot (3), bring down (3), came (3), cut down (3), fall down (3), falling (3), fell down (3), put (3), bring (2), brought down (2), defected (2), deserted (2), deserting (2), downcast (2), falls prostrate (2), fell prostrate (2), going to death (2), gone over (2), got down (2), have cut down (2), inferior (2), lay (2), lie fallen (2), lying (2), miscarry (2), seized (2 [+6584]), surely come to ruin (2 [+5877]), surrender (2), those^{S} (2 [+2021]), threw (2), threw arms around (2 [+6584, 7418]), threw down (2), afraid (1 [+7065, 6584]), allocate (1), allots (1), attack (1 [+928]), attacked (1), attacked (1 [+928]), become (1), bowed down (1 [+6584, 7156]), bowed down to the ground (1 [+6584, 7156]), brings on (1), cast down (1), cause to fall (1), caused to fall (1), collapse (1), collapses (1), come into (1 [+928]), come over (1), come to life (1), confined (1), consisted of (1), cracked (1 [+7288]), crumble (1), cutting down (1), defeated (1), deserts (1), died (1), do not count (1), down came (1), dropped out (1), drops (1), erodes (1), fail (1 [+824, 2025]), fall in battle (1 [+2728]), fall limp (1), fallen down (1), falls down (1), fell dead (1), frown (1 [+7156]), give birth (1), give up (1), gone down (1), happens (1), have fall (1), hear (1 [+4200, 7156]), hurtling down (1), in whatever order (1 [+4202, 1598, 6584]), killed

(1), killed (1 [+2728]), knocks out (1), lay prostrate (1), left (1), let fall (1), lie (1), lived in hostility toward (1 [+6584, 7156]), lose (1), lost (1 [+4946, 907]), lost self-confidence (1 [+4394, 928, 6524]), made come down (1), make (1), make drop (1), make lie down (1), making (1), miscarries (1), neglect (1), overpower (1), overwhelmed (1 [+6584]), perish (1), pleading (1 [+9382]), plunge (1), precious (1 [+4202]), present (1 [+4200, 7156]), reach (1), settled (1), settles (1), sink (1), slaughter (1), slay (1), someone[S] (1 [+2021]), stilled (1), strewn (1), stumble (1), such force[S] (1), surrenders (1), swoop down (1), those[S] (1), threw arms around (1 [+6584]), throw (1), throwing himself down (1), thrown (1), tumbles (1), were[S] (1), NDT (1)

H5878 נֵפֶל ***nēpel***, n.m. [3] [√ 5877]. stillborn child, miscarriage:– stillborn child (2), stillborn child (1 [+851])

H5879 [1]נָפַץ ***nāpaṣ***[1], v. [18] [→ 5150, 5151, 5881; cf. 5880, 7046, 7207]. [Q] to shatter; [P] to shatter; (of log raft) to separate; [Pu] to be crushed:– shatter (9), broken (2), smash (2), broke (1), crushed to pieces (1), dash to pieces (1), dashes (1), separate (1)

H5880 [2]נָפַץ ***nāpaṣ***[2], v. [3] [cf. 5879]. [Q] to scatter:– scatter (1), scattered (1), scattering (1)

H5881 נֶפֶץ ***nepeṣ***, n.[m.] [1] [√ 5879]. bursting, pelting (of rain):– cloudburst (1)

H5882 נָפַשׁ ***nāpaš***, v.den. [3] [→ 5874, 5883]. [N] to be refreshed, refresh oneself:– be refreshed (1), refreshed himself (1), was refreshed (1)

H5883 נֶפֶשׁ ***nepeš***, n.f. [754] [√ 5882]. breath; by extension: life, life force, soul, an immaterial part of a person, the seat of emotion and desire; a creature or person as a whole: self, body, even corpse:– life (110), soul (66), me (44 [+3276]), I (39 [+3276]), lives (36), you (22 [+3870]), heart (14), yourselves (12 [+4013]), people (11), want to kill (11 [+1335]), anyone (10), myself (10 [+3276]), himself (9 [+2257]), themselves (9 [+2257]), themselves (9 [+4392]), everyone (8 [+3972, 2021]), person (8), he (7 [+2257]), herself (7 [+2023]), one (7), appetite (6), creatures (6), desire (6), hearts (5), spirit (5), them (5 [+4392]), they (5 [+4392]), trying to kill (5 [+1335]), we (5 [+5646]), creature (4), dead body (4), death (4), my (4 [+3276]), they[S] (4 [+2021, 2085, 2021]), those[S] (4), you (4 [+3871]), you (4 [+4013]), yourself (4 [+3870]), anyone (3 [+2021]), breath (3), dead (3), lifeblood (3 [+1947]), needs (3), ourselves (3 [+5646]), someone (3), them (3 [+2257]), they (3 [+2257]), us (3 [+5646]), anyone (2 [+3972]), as surely as live (2 [+2644]), body (2), desires (2), human (2 [+132]), hunger (2), hungry (2 [+8281]), kill (2 [+4374]), kill (2 [+5782]), long (2 [+5951]), members (2), mind (2), neck (2), persons (2), put trust (2 [+5951]), souls (2), strength (2), takes life (2 [+5782]), thing (2), thirsty (2 [+8799]), yourselves (2 [+3870]), affection (1), alive (1 [+928]), all (1), all being (1), angry (1 [+5253]), another[S] (1), anyone (1 [+3972, 2021]), appetite (1 [+203]), appetites (1), as surely as live (1 [+2644, 2256, 2644]), be a willing party (1 [+5951]), being (1), breathe last (1 [+5870]), breathed her last (1 [+3655]), closest friend (1 [+8276, 889, 3869, 3870]), completely (1 [+4946, 2256, 6330, 1414]), corpse (1), cost (1), counting on (1 [+5951, 906, 448]), courage (1), craved (1), craving (1 [+205]), deep anguish (1 [+5253]), descendants (1 [+3655, 3751]), desires (1 [+5951]), destroy (1 [+1335]), die (1), discontented (1 [+5253]), dying (1), earnestness (1 [+205]), enemies (1 [+8533]), escape (1 [+4880]), everyone (1 [+3972]), everyone (1 [+3972]), faint (1 [+1790]), fierce (1 [+5253]), given to gluttony (1 [+1251]), greed (1), greedy (1 [+8146]), guilt of murder (1 [+1947]), he[S] (1 [+2021, 2021, 2085]), heartfelt (1), heart's (1), herself (1), him (1 [+2257]), him[S] (1), how it feels (1), human beings (1 [+132]), hungry (1 [+8199]), impatient (1 [+7918]), in all[S] (1), in anguish (1 [+5253]), its own (1 [+2257]), jaws (1), just what wanted (1), keep themselves alive (1 [+8740]), keep themselves alive (1 [+8740, 906, 4392]), kidnapping (1 [+1704]), kill (1), kills (1 [+5782, 2256, 4637]), livelihood (1), made a fatal mistake (1 [+9494, 928]), man (1), member (1), minds (1), mortal (1 [+928]), murders (1 [+8357]), none (1 [+3972, 4202]), people (1 [+132]), perfume (1), personal vows (1 [+6886]), pleased (1), relish (1 [+5951]), she (1 [+2023]), she (1 [+2023]), shiftless (1 [+8244]), slave (1), that[S] (1), the flock[S] (1 [+4392]), their own (1 [+2257]), these[S] (1), they (1 [+2021, 2085, 2021]), they[S] (1 [+2021, 2021, 2085]), those (1 [+3972, 2021]), thoughts (1 [+6783, 928]), threatened (1 [+6330]), threatening to kill (1 [+1335]), throats (1), tried to kill (1 [+1335]), trust (1 [+5951]), wait to kill (1 [+9068]), want to kill (1 [+1335, 906]), wanted (1 [+8626, 906]), wanted to kill (1 [+1335]), wanted to kill (1 [+1335, 906]), wants to kill (1 [+1335]), weary (1 [+6546]), whole being (1), wicked (1 [+8401]), willing (1), wished (1), wishes (1), with a passion (1), yourself (1 [+2257]), NDT (45)

H5884 נֶפֶת ***nepet***, n.f. Not used in NIVEBC [√ 5679]. Nephet or hill, see 5868

H5885 נֹפֶת ***nōpet***, n.m. [5] [√ 5678]. honey of the honeycomb:– honey (2), honey from the comb (2), sweetness as the honeycomb (1)

H5886 נֶפְתּוֹחַ ***neptôaḥ***, n.pr.loc. [2] Nephtoah, "*opening*":– Nephtoah (2)

H5887 נַפְתּוּלִים ***naptûlîm***, n.[m.pl.] [1] [√ 7349]. struggles, wrestlings:– had a struggle (1 [+7349])

H5888 נַפְתֻּחִים ***naptuḥîm***, n.pr.loc. & a.g. [2] Naphtuhite:– Naphtuhites (2)

H5889 נַפְתָּלִי ***naptālî***, n.pr.m. [50] [√ 7349?]. Naphtali, "*wrestling*":– Naphtali (44), Naphtali (5 [+1201]), Naphtali (1 [+824])

H5890 [1]נֵץ ***nēṣ***[1], n.m. [2] [√ 5914]. blossom:– blossomed (1 [+6590]), flowers (1)

H5891 [2]נֵץ ***nēṣ***[2], n.m. [3] [√ 5892]. hawk or falcon (bird of prey):– hawk (3)

H5892 נָצָא ***nāṣā'***, v. Not used in NIVEBC [→ 5891; cf. 5899]. [Q] to fly

H5893 [1]נָצַב ***nāṣab***[1], v. [75] [→ 2205, 5163, 5164, 5165, 5166, 5167, 5169, 5170, 5895, 5896, 5907, 5908; cf. 3656, 5894]. [N] to stand oneself before; (n.) officer, official; [H] to station, set up, establish; [Ho] to be set up, be decreed:– standing (14), set up (11), set (5), stood (5), district governors (3), stand (3), officials (2), overseer (2 [+5853]), attendants (1), attending (1), confront (1 [+4200, 7925]), decreed (1), erected as a monument (1), foremen (1 [+8569]), healthy (1), is (1), leader (1), made (1), made stand up (1), piled up (1), present yourself (1), presides (1), provincial governor (1), ready (1), repointing (1), resting (1), secure (1), sets in place (1), stands firm (1), stay (1), stood by (1), stood up (1), stood upright (1), takes place (1), takes stand (1), waiting (1), NDT (2)

H5894 [2]נָצַב ***nāṣab***[2], v. Not used in NIVEBC [cf. 5893]. [N] to be wretched, exhausted

H5895 [1]נִצָּב ***niṣṣāb***[1], n.[m.] *or* v.ptcp. Not used in NIVEBC [√ 5893; cf. 3656]. see 5893

H5896 [2]נִצָּב ***niṣṣāb***[2], n.m. [1] [√ 5893]. handle, hilt (of sword, dagger or knife):– handle (1)

H5897 [1]נָצָה ***nāṣâ***[1], v. [8] [→ 5175, 5194]. [N] to fight (quarreling that can come to blows and struggles); [H] to rebel, engage in a struggle:– fighting (3), rebelled (2), fight broke out (1), fought (1), got into a fight (1)

H5898 [2]נָצָה ***nāṣâ***[2], v. [8] [Q] to lie in ruins; [N] to be laid waste, be desolate:– laid waste (2 [+5898]), lie in ruins (2), piles of stone (2 [+1643]), desolate (1), laid waste (1)

H5899 [3]נָצָה ***nāṣâ***[3], v. Not used in NIVEBC [→ 5902; cf. 5892]. [Q] to fly

H5900 נִצָּה ***niṣṣâ***, n.f. [2] [√ 5914]. blossom:– blossoms (1), flower (1)

H5901 [1]נֹצָה ***nōṣâ***[1], n.f. [1] [cf. 5681, 5902]. contents (of a bird's crop):– feathers (1)

H5902 [2]נֹצָה ***nōṣâ***[2], n.f. Not used in NIVEBC [√ 5899; cf. 5681, 5901]. falcon

H5903 נְצֻרִים ***neṣûrîm***, n.[m.] Not used in NIVEBC [√ 5915]. secret places, see 5915

H5904 נָצַח ***nāṣaḥ***, v. [65] [→ 5905, 5909; 10488]. [N] to be enduring, lasting; [P] to direct, supervise; (n.) director (of music, 55 times in the Psalms), supervisor:– director of music (55), foremen (2), direct (1), directing (1), director music (1), does always (1), in charge (1), supervise (1), supervised (1), supervising (1)

H5905 [1]נֵצַח ***nēṣaḥ***[1], n.m. [43] [√ 5904]. glory, majesty, splendor; forever, unending, everlasting, always; "the Glory of Israel" as a title of God probably emphasizes both glory and eternity:– forever (18), never (4 [+4202, 4200]), always (3 [+4200]), ever again (2 [+4200, 5905]), endless (1 [+4200]), eternal (1), everlasting (1), everlasting (1 [+4200]), flamed unchecked (1 [+9068]), glory (1), majesty (1), never (1 [+4200, 1153]), never (1 [+561, 4200]), never (1 [+1153, 4200]), never again (1 [+6330, 4202]), once for all (1 [+4200]), splendor (1), successfully (1 [+4200]), unending (1), utmost (1)

H5906 [2]נֵצַח ***nēṣaḥ***[2], n.m. [2] juice (= blood):– blood (2)

H5907 [1]נְצִיב ***neṣîb***[1], n.m. [11] [→ 5908; cf. 5893]. garrison, outpost; pillar:– garrisons (4), outpost (3), garrison (1), governor (1), pillar (1), NDT (1)

H5908 [2]נְצִיב ***neṣîb***[2], n.pr.loc. [1] [√ 5907; cf. 5893]. Nezib, "*pillar, garrison*":– Nezib (1)

H5909 נְצִיחַ ***neṣîaḥ***, n.pr.m. [2] [√ 5904]. Neziah, "*director [of worship]*":– Neziah (2)

H5910 נָצִיר ***nāṣîr***, a. Not used in NIVEBC [√ 5915]. preserved, see 5915

H5911 נָצַל ***nāṣal***, v. [213] [→ 2208; 10489]. [N] to be saved, be delivered, be spared; [P] to plunder, take away, tear away; [H] to deliver, save, rescue; [Ho] to be snatched; [Ht] to strip off oneself:– rescue (43), deliver (41), save (29), delivered (16), rescued (14), delivers (6), saved (6), surely deliver (4 [+5911]), rescues (3), be delivered (2), be rescued (2), be saved (2), defended (2), escape (2), ever delivered (2 [+5911]), free yourself (2), protect (2), recovered (2), rescued at all (2 [+5911]), snatched (2), succeed in the rescue (2 [+5911]), take (2), come to rescue (1), count for (1), defender (1), deliverance (1), delivering (1), ease (1), escapes (1), free (1), plunder (1), plundered (1), protected (1), rescuing (1), retake (1), safe (1), saves (1), separate (1 [+1068]), spared (1), stripped off (1), take away (1 [+5362]), take back (1), taken away (1), taken refuge (1), took away (1), was spared (1), NDT (1)

H5912 נִצָּנִים ***niṣṣānîm***, n.[m.] Not used in NIVEBC [√ 5914]. blossom

H5913 [1]נָצַץ ***nāṣaṣ***[1], v. [1] [→ 5773; cf. 5914]. [Q] to gleam, sparkle:– gleamed (1)

H5914 [2]נָצַץ ***nāṣaṣ***[2], v.den. [3] [→ 5890, 5900, 5912; cf. 5913]. [H] to bloom, blossom:– in bloom (2), blossoms (1)

H5915 נָצַר ***nāṣar***, v. [59] [→ 4915, 5211, 5903, 5910, 5917; cf. 5757; 10476]. [Q] to guard, watch, protect, keep, preserve; [Qp] to be kept secret, be hidden:– keep (13), protect (8), guard (6), guards (4), obey (4), guarded (2), preserve (2), watch over (2), watchtower (2 [+4463]), crafty (1), follow (1), guard well (1), heeds (1), hidden (1), is spared (1), keep safe (1), keep watch over (1), keeping secret vigil (1), kept (1), maintaining (1), observe (1), preserves (1), see (1), watchman (1), watchmen (1)

H5916 נֵצֶר ***nēṣer***, n.m. [4] branch, shoot (of a plant):– branch (2), family line (1 [+9247]), shoot (1)

H5917 נִצְּרָה ***niṣṣerâ***, n.f. *or* v.ptcp. [1] [√ 5915 not in KB]. watching, guarding:– watch (1)

H5918 [1]נָקַב ***nāqab***[1], v. [16] [→ 2186, 5216, 5217, 5920, 5921, 5922; cf. 3676, 5919, 7686]. [Q] to bore (a hole), pierce; to designate, bestow; [Qp] to have a hole; to be notable; [N] to be designated, be registered:– designated (3), pierce (2), pierces (2 [+2256, 995, 928]), been specified (1), bestow (1), bored (1), holes (1), name (1), notable (1), pierced (1), were designated (1), were registered (1)

H5919 [2]נָקַב ***nāqab***[2], v. [3] [cf. 5918, 7686]. [Q] to blaspheme, with a focus on marring someone's reputation:– blaspheme (1), blasphemed (1), blasphemes (1)

H5920 [1]נֶקֶב ***neqeb***[1], n.[m.] [1] [√ 5918]. mounting (used in gold jewelry):– mountings (1)

H5921 [2]נֶקֶב ***neqeb***[2], n.pr.loc. Not used in NIVEBC [√ 5918]. Nekeb

H5922 נְקֵבָה ***neqēbâ***, n.f. [22] [√ 5918]. female, woman:– female (16), woman (3), daughter (1), girl (1), women (1)

H5923 נָקֹד ***nāqōd***, a. [9] [→ 5218, 5925, 5926]. speckled, spotted:– speckled (9)

H5924 נֹקֵד ***nōqēd***, n.m. [2] shepherd, one who raises sheep:– raised sheep (1), shepherds (1)

H5925 נְקֻדָּה ***nequddâ***, n.f. [1] [√ 5923]. point, drops (of silver on a gold earring):– studded (1)

H5926 נִקֻּדִים ***niqqudîm***, n.[m.] [3] [√ 5923]. (small) cakes; crumbling (food supplies):– moldy (2), cakes (1)

H5927 נָקָה ***nāqâ***, v. [44] [→ 4984, 5929, 5930, 5931]. [Q] to go unpunished; [N] be innocent, be released, go unpunished; [P] to leave unpunished, consider innocent, pardon:– go unpunished (9), leave the guilty unpunished (6 [+5927]), let go entirely unpunished (4 [+5927]), innocent (3), be banished (2), be released (2), go unpunished (2 [+5927]), hold guiltless (2), indeed go unpunished (2 [+5927]), be cleared of guilt (1), consider innocent (1), destitute (1), forgive (1), guiltless (1), have a right to get even (1), hold innocent (1), leave unavenged (1), let go unpunished (1), not[S] (1), not be held liable (1), not harm (1 [+4946])

H5928 נְקוֹדָא ***neqôdā'***, n.pr.m. [4] Nekoda:– Nekoda (4)

H5929 נָקִי ***nāqî***, a. [43] [√ 5927]. innocent, free of blame, not guilty:– innocent (30), released (2), clean (1), exempt (1), free (1), free from blame (1), free from obligation (1), harmless soul (1 [+2855]), innocent man (1 [+1947]), not binding (1), not held responsible (1), not responsible (1), without guilt (1)

H5930 נָקִיא ***nāqî'***, a. Not used in NIVEBC [√ 5927; 10490]. innocent

H5931 נִקָּיוֹן ***niqqāyôn***, n.[m.] [5] [√ 5927]. cleanness, purity; by extension: moral or ceremonial innocence, purity, cleanness; "cleanness of teeth" is a sign of lack of food in famine:– innocence (2), clean (1), empty stomachs (1 [+9094]), purity (1)

H5932 נָקִיק ***nāqîq***, n.m. [3] crevice, cleft, crack:– crevices (2), crevice (1)

H5933 נָקַם ***nāqam***, v. [35] [→ 5934, 5935]. [Q] to seek vengeance, avenge; [N] to be avenged, avenge oneself; [P] to avenge; [Ho or Qp] to be avenged; [Ht] to take one's own vengeance:– avenge (6), must be punished (2 [+5933]), takes vengeance (2), took revenge (2 [+5934]), avenge (1 [+5935]), avenge (1 [+5934]), avenge myself (1), avenge themselves (1), avenge wrongs (1), avenged (1), avenged myself (1), avenger (1), avenging (1), be punished (1), bent on revenge (1), doing so (1), get revenge (1), get revenge (1 [+5934]), is avenged (1), punished (1), seek revenge (1), suffer vengeance (1), take revenge (1), take revenge (1 [+5934]), take vengeance (1), take vengeance (1 [+5935]), vengeance (1)

H5934 נָקָם ***nāqām***, n.m. [17] [→ 5935; cf. 5933]. vengeance, revenge:– vengeance (7), take vengeance (2 [+8740]), took revenge (2 [+5933]), avenge (1), avenge (1 [+5933]), avenged (1), get revenge (1 [+5933]), revenge (1), take revenge (1 [+5933])

H5935 נְקָמָה ***n^{e}qāmâ***, n.f. [27] [√ 5934; cf. 5933]. vengeance, revenge:– vengeance (17), avenges (2), avenges (2 [+5989]), avenge (1), avenge (1 [+5933]), avenged (1 [+5989]), avenged (1 [+6913]), revenge (1), take vengeance (1 [+5933])

H5936 נָקַע ***nāqa'***, v. [3] [cf. 3697]. [Q] to turn away in disgust:– turned away in disgust (2), turned away (1)

H5937 ^{1}נָקַף ***nāqap^1***, v. [2] [→ 5939]. [P] to cut down; to be destroyed:– cut down (1), destroyed (1)

H5938 ^{2}נָקַף ***nāqap^2***, v. [17] [→ 5940; cf. 9543]. [Q] to go through a yearly cycle; [H] to surround, encircle, engulf:– surrounded (2), circling (1), cut hair (1), cycle go on (1), drawn (1), echoes along (1), encircles (1), engulfed (1), go around (1), march around (1 [+6015]), run course (1), station themselves (1), station yourselves (1), surround (1), NDT (2)

H5939 נֹקֶף ***nōqep***, n.[m.] [2] [√ 5937]. beating (fruit off olive tree in harvest):– beaten (2)

H5940 נִקְפָּה ***niqpâ***, n.f. [1] [√ 5938]. rope (around waist):– rope (1)

H5941 נָקַר ***nāqar***, v. [6] [→ 5942]. [Q] to gouge out, peck out (an eye); [P] to gouge out; to pierce; [Pu] to be hewn out (of quarry rock):– gouge out (1), gouged out (1), pecked out (1), pierces (1), treat like slaves (1 [+6524]), were hewn (1)

H5942 נְקָרָה ***n^{e}qārâ***, n.f. [2] [√ 5941]. cleft; cavern:– caverns (1), cleft (1)

H5943 נָקַשׁ ***nāqaš***, v. [4] [cf. 3704, 7772; 10491]. [N] to be ensnared; [P] to lay out snares; [Ht] to lay out traps, set a trap:– be ensnared (1), seize (1), set a trap (1), set traps (1)

H5944 ^{1}נֵר ***nēr^1***, n.m. [43] [→ 46, 79, 4963, 5775, 5945, 5949, 5950; cf. 5642; 10471]. lamp (fueled by olive oil); by extension: life (as a burning lamp); light (showing the way of truth):– lamps (25), lamp (16), them^S (1), NDT (1)

H5945 ^{2}נֵר ***nēr^2***, n.pr.m. [17] [√ 5944]. Ner, "*lamp*":– Ner (17)

H5946 נֵרְגַל ***nēr^{e}gal***, n.pr. [1] [→ 5947]. Nergal (pagan god):– Nergal (1)

H5947 נֵרְגַל שַׂר־אֶצֶר ***nērgal śar-'eṣer***, n.pr.m. [3] [√ 5946 + 8570]. Nergal-Sharezer, "*Nergal protect the prince!*":– Nergal-Sharezer (3)

H5948 נֵרְדְּ ***nērd***, n.m. [3] nard (aromatic ointment):– nard (2), perfume (1)

H5949 נֵרִיָּה ***nēriyyâ***, n.pr.m. [7] [→ 4950; cf. 5944 + 3378]. Neriah, "*lamp of Yahweh*":– Neriah (7)

H5950 נֵרִיָּהוּ ***nēriyyāhû***, n.pr.m. [3] [√ 5949; cf. 5944 + 3378]. Neriah, "*lamp of Yahweh*":– Neriah (3)

H5951 נָשָׂא ***nāśā'***, v. [653] [→ 5362, 5363, 5365, 5366, 5367, 5368, 5953, 5954, 5955, 8420, 8421, 8480?, 8481?; 10492]. [Q] to bear, carry, lift up; forgive; [Qp] to be forgiven, honored, carried; [N] to be carried off, lifted up; [P] to elevate, carry along; [H] to cause to carry, to bring; [Ht] to exalt oneself, lift up oneself; from the base meaning of rise in elevation come fig. extensions "to exalt, honor," as the lifting up of a person in status, and "to forgive," as the removal of guilt and its penalties; "to lift up the eyes" means "to look up":– bear (35), carry (35), carrying (26), lift up (26), carried (25), up (25), armor-bearer (19 [+3998]), lifted up (16), take up (14), took (13), forgive (10), raise (10), brought (8), take (8), held responsible (7 [+6411]), lifted (7), spoke (7 [+2256, 606]), bring (6), carried off (6), took up (6), aloud (5 [+906, 7754]), carries (5), exalted (5), look (5 [+6524]), swore with uplifted (5), accept (4 [+7156]), aloud (4 [+7754]), bearing (4), carry off (4), endure (4), get (4), lift (4), loaded (4), pick up (4), picks up (4), rose (4), show partiality (4 [+7156]), spread (4), suffer (4), take away (4), be carried off (3), be exalted (3), bore (3), forgiving (3), lofty (3), looked (3 [+6524]), married (3), misuse (3 [+4200, 2021, 8736]), offer (3), picked up (3), put (3), share (3 [+928]), sworn with uplifted (3), take a census (3 [+906, 8031]), armor-bearers (2 [+3998]), arrogant (2 [+4213]), at all forgive (2 [+5951]), be lifted up (2), bearer (2), brought back (2), carried away (2), forgave (2), held responsible (2 [+2628]), long (2 [+5883]), misuses (2 [+4200, 2021, 8736]), must be carried (2 [+5951]), pay (2), pray (2 [+9525]), put trust (2 [+5883]), receive (2), released (2 [+8031]), rise (2), rise up (2), share (2), shows partiality (2 [+7156]), spare (2), support (2), take a census (2 [+8031]), taken (2), taken anything (2 [+5951]), wear (2), willing (2 [+4213]), with uplifted swore (2), won (2 [+4200, 7156]), abounds (1), accept (1), accepted (1 [+906, 7156]), are forgiven (1), armed (1), around (1), be a willing party (1 [+5883]), be carried (1), be forgiven (1), be raised up (1), be taken away (1), bear the consequences (1), bear up (1), bear with (1), beckon (1 [+3338]), become guilty (1 [+2628, 6584]), been exalted (1), began (1 [+906, 7754]), begin (1), borne (1), borne fruit (1), bring upon (1), carried (1 [+6673]), carriers (1 [+6025]), carries off (1), carry about (1), carry away (1), carry back (1), casts (1), caught up (1), chose (1), clothed with (1), containing (1), continued on journey (1 [+8079]), count (1 [+906, 8031]), counted (1 [+906, 8031]), counting on (1 [+906, 5883, 448]), cry out (1 [+4200, 606]), desires (1 [+5883]), dignitaries (1 [+7156]), disdainful (1), ease (1), elevated (1), elevating (1), entrust (1), equipped (1), exalt itself (1), exalt yourself (1), gather (1), gave assistance (1), grant (1 [+7156]), granted request (1 [+7156]), guilty (1), guilty (1 [+2628]), had (1), handle (1), have respect for (1), helped (1), high (1), highly regarded (1 [+7156]), honored (1 [+7156]), include in the census (1 [+906, 8031]), incur (1), is carried off (1), is exalted (1), let shine (1), lifts up (1), loaded up (1), look around (1 [+6524, 2256, 8011]), look in the face (1 [+7156, 448]), look up (1 [+6524]), look with longing (1 [+6524]), looked about (1 [+6524]), looks (1 [+6524]), loudly (1 [+7754]), make (1), man of rank (1 [+7156]), married (1 [+851]), mount up (1), mourn (1 [+7806]), moved (1), out (1), out (1 [+906]), pardon (1), pardoned (1), pardons (1), partial (1 [+7156]), placed (1), pleased with (1 [+2834, 928, 6524]), prepare (1), produce (1), provide (1), pull up (1), put himself forward (1), put in jeopardy (1 [+1414, 928, 9094]), raised (1), raised (1 [+2256, 5989]), raising (1), reach out (1 [+4090]), rear (1), rebel (1), receive (1 [+7156]), relish (1 [+5883]), respect (1 [+7156]), ridicule (1 [+5442]), rise again (1), rises high (1), rouse themselves (1), saw (1 [+906, 6524]), served (1), set yourselves (1), share in (1 [+6584]), shouted (1 [+7754, 2256, 7924]), showed partiality (1 [+7156]), shown honor (1 [+7156]), shown partiality (1 [+7156]), sing (1), snatch up (1), spoke (1), suffer for (1), suffered (1), suffering for (1), supplied (1), swear with uplifted (1), sweep away (1), sweeps away (1), swore (1 [+3338]), sworn (1 [+906, 3338]), take in marriage (1), taken as wives (1), taken up (1), takes up (1), taunt (1 [+5442]), toil (1), too heavy a burden to carry (1 [+4202, 3523]), took away (1), took notice (1 [+6524]), transport (1), trembles (1), trust (1 [+5883]), turn (1), uplifted (1), wail (1 [+5631]), was highly regarded (1), was raised (1), wearing (1), weep (1 [+1140]), won (1 [+928, 6524]), wore (1), NDT (8)

H5952 נָשַׂג ***nāśag***, v. [50] [→ 5371]. [H] to overtake, catch up, attain; to reach, to be able to afford:– overtake (14), afford (7 [+3338]), overtook (6), catch up (2), certainly overtake (2 [+5952]), continue until (2), overtaken (2), prosper (2 [+3338]), accompany (1), attain (1), catch (1), caught up (1), equal (1), move (1), overtaking (1), put (1), reach (1), reaches (1), rich (1 [+3338]), wants to give (1 [+3338]), NDT (1)

H5953 נְשׂוּאָה ***n^{e}śû'â***, n.f. [1] [√ 5951]. burden, load (of images that are carried about):– images that are carried about (1)

H5954 ^{1}נָשִׂיא ***nāśî'^{1}***, n.m. [131] [√ 5951]. leader, ruler, chief, prince:– leader (43), leaders (30), prince (29), princes (10), chiefs (3), ruler (3), chief leader (2 [+5954]), rulers (2), chief (1), himself^S (1), they^S (1 [+2021]), NDT (6)

H5955 ^{2}נָשִׂיא ***nāśî'^{2}***, n.[m.] [4] [√ 5951]. cloud, rising mist, damp fog:– clouds (4)

H5956 נָשַׂק ***nāśaq***, v. [3] [cf. 8519]. [N] to be kindled; [H] to kindle a fire, burn:– broke out (1), burn up (1), kindles a fire (1)

H5957 ^{1}נָשָׁא ***nāšā'^{1}***, v. [18] [→ 5391, 5394, 5408, 5963; cf. 5961, 5968, 8735]. [Q] to give a loan, be a creditor; [H] to make a loan; to subject one to tribute:– creditor (3), required (2 [+460, 928]), borrowed (1 [+928]), business deal (1), charging (1), creditors (1), debtor (1 [+928]), get the better of (1 [+928]), in debt (1 [+4200]), interest charging (1), lending (1), lent (1), loan made (1), make a loan (1 [+5394]), making loan (1)

H5958 ^{2}נָשָׁא ***nāšā'^{2}***, v. [15] [→ 5395, 5396, 5410; cf. 8735]. [N] to be deceived; [H] to deceive:– deceive (5), deceived (3), let deceive (3), completely deceived (2 [+5958]), are deceived (1), take by surprise (1)

H5959 נָשַׁב ***nāšab***, v. [3] [√ 876; cf. 5971, 5973]. [Q] to blow; [H] to cause to blow; to drive away:– blows (1), drove away (1), stirs up (1)

H5960 ^{1}נָשָׁה ***nāšâ^1***, v. [9] [→ 4985, 4986, 5964; cf. 8861]. [Q] to forget; [N] to be forgotten; [P] to make forget; [H] to make one forget; to allow one to forget:– forget (3), forgotten (2), surely forget (2 [+5960]), made forget (1), not endow (1)

H5961 ^{2}נָשָׁה ***nāšâ^2***, v. Not used in NIVEBC [cf. 5957]. see 5957

H5962 נָשֶׁה ***nāšeh***, n.[m.] [2] tendon (attached to the hip), perhaps the sciatic nerve:– tendon (2 [+1630])

H5963 נְשִׁי ***n^{e}šî***, n.[m.] [1] [√ 5957]. debt:– debts (1)

H5964 נְשִׁיָּה ***n^{e}šiyyâ***, n.f. [1] [√ 5960]. oblivion, place forgotten (by the LORD):– oblivion (1)

H5965 נְשִׁיקָה ***n^{e}šîqâ***, n.f. [2] [√ 5975]. kiss:– kisses (2)

H5966 ^{1}נָשַׁךְ ***nāšak^1***, v. [11] [cf. 5968]. [Q] to bite; [Qp] to be bitten; [P] to bite:– bite (3), bites (3), bitten (2), bit (1), have something to eat (1 [+928, 9094]), is bitten (1)

H5967 ^{2}נָשַׁךְ ***nāšak^2***, v.den. [5] [√ 5968]. [Q] to earn interest; to claim interest against one; [H] to charge interest:– charge interest (1), charge interest (1 [+5968]), creditors (1), earn interest (1), NDT (1)

H5968 נֶשֶׁךְ ***nešek***, n.[m.] [12] [→ 5967; cf. 5957, 5966]. interest, usury:– interest (8), charge interest (1 [+5967]), taking interest (1), NDT (2)

H5969 נִשְׁכָּה ***niškâ***, n.f. [3] [cf. 4384]. room (for various uses: living, storage, etc.):– living quarters (1), room (1), storerooms (1 [+4200, 238])

H5970 נָשַׁל ***nāšal***, v. [7] [Q] to take off, come off; to drive out:– take off (2), drive out (1), drives out (1), driving out (1), drop off (1), fly off (1)

H5971 נָשַׁם ***nāšam***, v. [1] [→ 5972, 9491, 9492; cf. 5959, 5973]. [Q] to gasp, pant:– gasp (1)

H5972 נְשָׁמָה ***n^{e}šāmâ***, n.f. [24] [√ 5971; 10494]. breath, blast of breath; by extension: life, life force, spirit:– breath (10), breathed (4), blast (2), spirit (2), breath (1 [+8120]), breathes (1), breathing (1), can hardly breathe (1 [+4202, 8636]), life (1), very people^S (1)

H5973 נָשַׁף ***nāšap***, v. [2] [→ 3568, 5974; cf. 5959, 5971]. [Q] to blow:– blew (1), blows (1)

H5974 נֶשֶׁף ***nešep***, n.m. [12] [√ 5973]. dusk, dawn (of morning); twilight (of evening):– dusk (4), twilight (3), dawn (2), darkening (1), morning (1), night (1)

H5975 ^{1}נָשַׁק ***nāšaq^1***, v. [30] [→ 5965]. [Q] to kiss; [P] to kiss (repeatedly or intensely); a kiss can show familial or romantic affection, as well as homage and submission:– kissed (16), kiss (9), kiss goodbye (2), kissed goodbye (2), offered a kiss of homage (1 [+4200, 7023])

H5976 ^{2}נָשַׁק ***nāšaq^2***, v. [5] [√ 5977]. [Q] to be equipped, arm oneself; [H] to brush against, touch up against:– armed (2), armed (1 [+8227]), brushing (1), submit (1)

H5977 ^{1}נֶשֶׁק ***nešeq^1***, n.m. [10] [→ 5976]. weapon; armory:– weapons (6), armory (1), battle (1), fray (1), weapon (1)

H5978 ^{2}נֶשֶׁק ***nešeq^2***, n.[m.] Not used in NIVEBC. kind of fragrance substance

H5979 נֶשֶׁר ***nešer***, n.m. [26] [√ 10495]. eagle; vulture:– eagle (16), eagles (6), eagle's (2), vulture (1), vultures (1 [+1201])

H5980 נָשַׁת ***nāšat***, v. [4] [Q] to be dry, be parched; [N] to be dried up:– dry up (1), exhausted (1), parched (1), stop (1)

H5981 נִשְׁתְּוָן ***ništ^{e}wān***, n.[m.] [2] [√ 10496]. letter, writing, see 10496:– letter (2)

H5982 נְתוּנִים ***n^{e}tûnîm***, v.ptcp. *or* n.m.[pl.] Not used in NIVEBC [√ 5987; cf. 5989]. see 5989 & 5987

H5983 נָתַח ***nātaḥ***, v. [9] [→ 5984]. [P] to cut into pieces:– cut (4), cut into pieces (4), cut up (1)

H5984 נֵתַח ***nētaḥ***, n.m. [13] [√ 5983]. piece (of butchered things or persons):– pieces (8), piece (2), parts (1), piece by piece (1 [+4200]), pieces of meat (1)

H5985 נָתִיב ***nātîb***, n.m. [5] [→ 5986]. path:– path (3), hidden path (1), wake (1)

H5986 נְתִיבָה ***n^{e}tîbâ***, n.f. [21] [√ 5985]. path, way, road; by extension: behavior, lifestyle:– paths (11), path (3), way (2), byways (1), road (1), roads (1), streets (1), travelers (1 [+2143])

H5987 נָתִין ***nātîn***, n.m. [17] [→ 5982; cf. 5989; 10497]. servant:– temple servants (15), them^S (1 [+2021]), NDT (1)

H5988 נָתַךְ ***nātak***, v. [21] [→ 2247]. [Q] to pour out; [N] to be poured out, be melted; [H] to pour out (liquid or money); to melt; [Ho] to be melted:– poured out (7), be melted (3), paid out (2), pour out (2), poured down (2), be poured out (1), been poured out (1), is poured out (1), melt (1), melted (1)

H5989 נָתַן ***nātan***, v. [2011] [→ 921, 924, 925, 5508, 5509, 5510, 5511, 5522, 5523, 5987, 5990; cf. 3852, 4501, 5621; 10498; *also used with compound proper names*]. [Q] to give, put; [Qp] to be given, dedicated; [N] to be given; [Ho or Qp] to be given; note the many contextual translations in the NIV:– give (351), gave (239), put (165), given (152), make (59), giving (58), gives (40), made (35), set (35), be given (25), deliver (24), placed (23), delivered (19), let (19), place (14), grant (13), pay (13), yield (13), appointed (12), bring (11), granted (10), if only (10 [+4769]), send (9), spread (9), assigned (8), entrusted (8), hand over (8), oh (8 [+4769]), give over (7), sent (7), give in marriage (6 [+4200, 851]), lay (6), offered (6), repay (6), sell (6), show (6), allow (5), attach (5), been given (5), exchanged (5), gave in marriage (5 [+4200, 851]), get (5), give in marriage (5), give up (5), hand over (5 [+928, 3338]), paid (5), provide (5), provides (5), set up (5), take (5), allowed (4), applied (4), be given wholly (4 [+5989]), certainly be given (4 [+5989]), fasten (4), fastened (4), handed over (4 [+928, 3338]), laid (4), offer (4), provided (4), setting (4), thunders (4 [+7754]), turn over (4), was given (4), appoint (3), attached (3), bring down (3), bringing down (3), brought (3), caused (3), deal (3), gave over (3), give back (3), given over (3), left (3), makes (3), produce (3), providing (3), resounded (3), stationed (3), treat (3), turned (3), was issued (3), yields (3), allotted (2 [+928, 2021, 1598]), announces (2), are (2), are given (2), attaching

(2), avenges (2 [+5935]), be issued (2), been put (2), blessed (2 [+1388]), cause (2), contributed (2), dedicated (2), deliver (2 [+5989]), deliver over (2), delivered over (2), delivers (2), direct (2), distributing (2), do (2), do so[S] (2), entrust (2), established (2), gifts (2), give (2 [+5989]), give generously (2 [+5989]), glad to give (2 [+5989]), hang (2), honor (2 [+9343]), is given (2), issued (2), keeps (2), kept (2), lend (2), lends (2), made turn (2), maintain (2), making (2), must certainly give (2 [+5989]), paying (2), permit (2), presented (2), prevent (2 [+1194]), proclaim (2), puts (2), raised (2), received (2), reported (2), reward (2), sacrifices (2), share (2), thrown (2), thunder (2 [+7754]), traded (2), treating (2), turn (2), turn into (2), wrap (2), I wish (1 [+4769]), abandoned (1), allotted (1), allow to possess (1), allowing (1), allows (1), appointed (1 [+928, 3338]), appoints (1), are laid (1), are put (1), arranged (1), ascribe (1), avenged (1 [+5935]), barter (1), be (1), be[S] (1), be betrayed (1), be bought (1), be defeated (1 [+928, 3338]), be delivered (1), be given in marriage (1 [+4200, 851]), be left (1), be supplied (1), bears (1), became (1), been allotted (1), been committed (1), been published (1), been subjected (1), bestow (1), bestowed (1), bestows (1), bow (1), bowed (1), bringing (1), brings (1), bury (1), buy (1), called together (1), came (1), carry out (1), cast (1), cause to become (1), causes (1), charge (1), charging (1), choose (1), consigned (1), costs (1), cover (1 [+4062]), credited (1), cry aloud (1 [+7754]), cut (1 [+8582]), deliver (1 [+928]), demand (1), designate (1), designated (1), despoil (1 [+4200, 1020]), destined (1), devote (1), did[S] (1 [+3338, 2257]), dispenses (1), display (1), distribute (1), distributed (1), do[S] (1), drop (1), dry up (1 [+3000]), enabled (1), endow (1), endures (1), establish (1), exchange (1), falls (1), feed (1 [+6584, 7023]), fill (1), from (1), gave in marriage (1), gave in marriage (1 [+851]), gave in pledge (1), gave up (1), gave victory (1 [+928, 3338]), give (1 [+928, 3338]), give (1 [+4200, 851]), give away (1), give in marriage (1 [+4200, 408]), give in marriage (1 [+2021, 851]), give permission (1), given in pledge (1), given up (1), gives gifts (1), gives over (1), granted requests (1), granting (1), grants (1), growl (1 [+7754]), growled (1 [+7754]), hand over (1 [+3338, 928]), handed (1 [+928, 3338]), handed over (1), handing over (1 [+928, 3338]), hands over (1), has sexual relations (1 [+8888]), have (1), have (1 [+4200]), have sexual relations (1 [+8888]), have sexual relations (1 [+8888, 4200, 2446]), having sexual relations with (1 [+928, 8888]), hold (1), hold accountable (1 [+6584]), honor (1), honor (1 [+3883]), how I long for (1 [+4769, 5761]), impart (1), imposed (1), imprisoned (1 [+928, 5464]), imprisoned (1 [+1074, 2021, 657]), in exchange (1), inflict (1), inflicted (1), injures (1 [+4583]), inserted (1), inspire (1 [+928, 4222]), instruct (1), invest (1 [+2750]), is (1), is drawn (1), is thrown (1), join (1), keep (1), leave (1), let be (1), let be heard (1), let have (1), let out (1), lifting (1), lifts (1), lose (1), made face (1 [+7156]), made ready (1), make restitution (1), make turn (1 [+448]), make want to (1 [+8120, 928]), make want to (1 [+928, 8120]), marry (1), oh (1 [+4769, 686]), oh how I wish (1 [+4769]), open (1 [+7341]), ordained (1), paid (1 [+5486]), pay (1 [+924]), pay (1 [+4084]), pay (1 [+4836]), pay (1 [+8510]), payment (1), perform (1), permitted to do (1), pile (1), piled (1), pitch (1), plant (1), pledged (1 [+3338]), pour (1), pour out (1), produces (1), prove to be (1), pulled (1), push (1), put in place (1), put on (1 [+4230]), put out (1), put up (1), putting (1), raise (1), raised (1 [+5951, 2256]), raises (1), raising (1), receive (1), receive (1 [+4200]), reduced (1), reflected on (1 [+448, 4213]), repay (1 [+928, 8031]), replaced (1 [+9393]), resolved (1 [+7156]), resound (1), respect (1 [+3702]), reward (1 [+7190]), rewarded (1 [+8510]), rises (1), roared (1 [+7754]), roars (1 [+928, 7754]), sacrificed (1 [+928, 6296]), sacrificing (1), seated (1 [+5226]), sell (1 [+928, 4084]), sell (1 [+928, 4084]), send down (1), send out (1), sends (1), shows (1), sing (1 [+7754]), slander (1 [+1984]), sparkles (1 [+6524]), spend (1), spreads (1), stained (1), store (1), stored (1), strike (1), subjected (1), subjecting (1), submit (1 [+3338]), submitted (1 [+3338]), suffer (1), suffer (1 [+6584]), supplied (1), supplies (1), supply (1), surely deliver (1 [+5989]), surely deliver (1 [+5989]), surrender (1), surrenders (1 [+3338]), take for (1 [+4200, 7156]), think (1 [+4213]), think (1 [+4222]), thunders (1 [+928, 7754]), tie (1 [+6584]), tie up (1), towered (1 [+1467, 928, 7757, 2256, 7550]), treated (1), turned (1 [+7156]), turned into (1), turned over (1), turns (1), use (1), was entrusted (1), was given in marriage (1 [+4200, 851]), was left hanging (1), wept so loudly (1 [+1140, 906, 7754, 928]), were assigned (1), were given (1), were given over (1), wins (1), NDT (28)

H5990 נָתָן ***nātān***, n.pr.m. [42] [√ 5989]. Nathan, "*gift*":– Nathan (42)

H5991 נְתַנְאֵל ***nᵉtan'ēl***, n.pr.m. [14] [√ 5889 + 446]. Nethanel, "*God [El] has given*":– Nethanel (14)

H5992 נְתַנְיָה ***nᵉtanyâ***, n.pr.m. [15] [√ 5989 + 3378]. Nethaniah, "*Yahweh has given*":– Nethaniah (15)

H5993 נְתַנְיָהוּ ***nᵉtanyāhû***, n.pr.m. [5] [√ 5989 + 3378]. Nethaniah, "*Yahweh has given*":– Nethaniah (5)

H5994 נְתַן־מֶלֶךְ ***nᵉtan-melek***, n.pr.m. [1] [√ 5989 + 4889]. Nathan-Melech, "*gift of king* or *gift of Melek, Molech, Malk*":– Nathan-Melek (1)

H5995 נָתַס ***nātas***, v. [1] [cf. 5996, 5997, 6004]. [Q] to break up, tear up:– break up (1)

H5996 נָתַע ***nāta'***, v. [1] [cf. 5995, 5997, 6004]. [N] to be broken down, be knocked out (of teeth):– are broken (1)

H5997 נָתַץ ***nātaṣ***, v. [42] [cf. 5995, 5996, 6004]. [Q] to break down, tear down, demolish; [Qp] to be broken down; [N] to be shattered, lay in ruins; [P] to tear down, break down, shatter, destroy; [Pu] to be demolished; [Ho] to be broken up:– broke down (6), tore down (6), break down (4), demolished (4), tear down (3), torn down (3), demolish (2), destroyed (2), pulled down (2), be broken up (1), been torn down (1), breaks down (1), bring down to ruin (1), broken down (1), destroy (1), lay in ruins (1), shattered (1), tear out (1), tears down (1)

H5998 נָתַק ***nātaq***, v. [27] [→ 5999]. [Q] to draw away, pull off; [Qp] to be torn; [N] to be lured away, be shattered, be torn, be broken; [P] to break, tear; [H] to lure away, drag off; [Ho] to be drawn away:– break (2), broken (2), snapped (2), are purged out (1), are shattered (1), are snapped (1), broke away (1), drag off (1), draw away (1), is broken (1), is torn (1), lured away (1), pull off (1), set (1), snaps (1), tear (1), tear away (1), tear off (1), tore off (1), torn (1), torn off (1), uprooted (1 [+9247]), were drawn away (1), were lured away (1)

H5999 נֶתֶק ***neteq***, n.m. [14] [√ 5998]. diseased area of skin: itch; some sources: ringworm, eczema:– sore (5), it[S] (3 [+2021]), affected area (1), affected person (1), affected person (1 [+5596]), defiling skin disease (1 [+7669]), sore (1 [+5596]), them[S] (1 [+2021])

H6000 ¹נָתַר ***nātar¹***, v. [1] [cf. 6002]. [H] to let loose, withdraw:– let loose (1)

H6001 ²נָתַר ***nātar²***, v. [3] [Q] to leap up; [P] to hop up; [H] to make leap up, jump up:– hopping (1), leaps (1), made tremble (1)

H6002 ³נָתַר ***nātar³***, v. [3] [cf. 6000]. [H] to set free, release, untie:– released (1), sets free (1), untie (1)

H6003 נֶתֶר ***neter***, n.[m.] [2] natron (a sodium carbonate for washing):– soap (1), wound (1)

H6004 נָתַשׁ ***nātaš***, v. [20] [cf. 5995, 5996, 5997]. [Q] to uproot; [N] to be uprooted; [Ho] to be uprooted:– uproot (11), be uprooted (3), uprooted (3), completely uproot (2 [+6004]), was uprooted (1)

H6005 ס ***s***, letter. Not used in NIVEBC [→ 6163; 10500]. letter of the Hebrew alphabet

H6006 סְאָה ***sᵉ'â***, n.f. [9] seah (dry measure, one-third of an ephah, about seven quarts or liters):– seahs (6), seah (3)

H6007 סְאוֹן ***sᵉ'ôn***, n.[m.] [1] [→ 6008]. boot:– boot (1)

H6008 סָאַן ***sā'an***, v.den. [1] [√ 6007]. [Q] to tramp along in boots:– warrior's (1)

H6009 סַאסְּאָה ***sa'ssᵉ'â***, n.f. [1] warfare, chasing away:– warfare (1)

H6010 ¹סָבָא ***sābā'¹***, v. [6] [√ 6011]. [Q] to be a drunkard, drink too much; [Qp] to be drunk:– drunkards (2), drink fill (1), drink too much (1), drunk (1), drunkard (1)

H6011 סֹבֶא ***sōbe'***, n.m. [3] [→ 6010]. wine, drink, implying drunkenness:– choice wine (1), drinks (1), wine (1)

H6012 ²סָבָא ***sābā'²***, n.m. Not used in NIVEBC [√ 6015?]. bind-weed, shrub

H6013 סְבָא ***sᵉbā'***, n.pr.m. [4] [→ 6014]. Seba:– Seba (4)

H6014 סְבָאִי ***sᵉbā'î***, n.pl.g. [1] [√ 6013]. Sabean:– Sabeans (1)

H6015 סָבַב ***sābab***, v. [163] [→ 4585, 4990, 4991, 5813, 6012?, 6016, 6017]. [Q] to go around, surround, encircle, engulf; [N] to change direction; to be surrounded; [P] to change; [Pol] to surround, shield, go about; [H] to turn about, circle around; [Ho] to be set, mounted, surrounded; to be changed:– surrounded (14), turned (11), surround (10), turn (10), changed (4), go about (3), moved (3), prowl about (3), turning (3), circle around (2), coiled around (2), curved (2), fall in (2 [+448]), led around (2), made rounds (2), made way around (2), march around (2), marched around (2), measure around (2 [+6017]), pass (2), round (2), settings (2), turned around (2), turned away (2), turns (2), went around (2), winds through (2), all around (1), be turned over (1), become (1), began (1), bring back (1), bring over (1), brought around (1), carried around (1), change (1), change direction (1), changing (1), circled (1), circuit (1), circumference (1 [+2562]), coming around (1), cross (1), curved around (1), dragged (1), eluded (1 [+4946, 7156]), encircled (1 [+6017]), encircled (1 [+6017, 6017]), encircling (1), engulf (1), gather around (1), gathered around (1), go (1), go around (1), hinged (1), in circumference (1 [+2562]), is rolled (1), leave (1 [+4946]), march around (1 [+5938]), on every side (1), once more (1), put around (1), responsible for (1 [+928]), return (1), returned home (1), roundabout (1), sent around (1), shielded (1), sit down (1), skirted (1), stand aside (1), stepped aside (1), sulking (1 [+906, 7156]), surrounding (1), surrounds (1), swarmed around (1), swirled about (1), swung open (1), took away (1), turn about (1), turn against (1), turn away (1 [+7156]), turn over (1), turned (1 [+7156]), turned over (1), waged against from all sides (1), walk about (1), walk through (1), went (1), went throughout (1), were changed (1), were mounted (1), NDT (1)

H6016 סִבָּה ***sibbâ***, n.f. [1] [√ 6015]. turning, arrangement (of events):– turn of events (1)

H6017 סָבִיב ***sābîb***, subst. (used as pp. & adv.) [334] [√ 6015]. all around, on all sides, surrounding, encircling:– around (108), all around (34 [+6017]), surrounding (27), on every side (25), all around (23), sides (12), around (7 [+4946]), around (6 [+6017]), all (5), neighbors (5), surround (5), every side (4), surrounded (4), about (2), all around (2 [+4946]), all over (2 [+6017, 6584]), back and forth (2 [+6017]), circular in shape (2 [+6318]), completely surrounding (2 [+6017]), covered with (2 [+8470, 6017]), from every side (2 [+4946]), measure around (2 [+6015]), neighboring (2), surrounding (2 [+6017]), surrounds (2), throughout (2 [+928]), along (1), area around (1), around (1 [+4946, 1237]), circular band (1 [+6318]), completely (1), course (1), encircled (1 [+6015]), encircled (1 [+6017, 6015]), encircled (1 [+6017, 6015]), encircling (1), enveloped (1 [+4946]), escorted by (1), everything around (1), everywhere (1), from (1 [+4946]), full (1 [+1074]), in (1), on (1), on all sides (1), outside walls (1), overrun (1), ringed about (1), round about (1), sides (1 [+6298, 4946]), stationed around (1), surround (1 [+2118, 4946]), went over (1 [+2118]), NDT (16)

H6018 סָבַךְ ***sābak***, v. [2] [→ 6019, 6020; cf. 8449]. [Qp, Pu] to be entangled, entwined:– entangled (1), entwines (1)

H6019 סְבַךְ ***sᵉbak***, n.[m.] [3] [√ 6018]. thicket, underbrush:– thickets (2), thicket (1)

H6020 סְבֹךְ ***sᵉbōk***, n.[m.] [2] [√ 6018]. thicket, underbrush (where animals can live or hide):– lair (1), thicket (1)

H6021 סִבְּכַי ***sibbᵉkay***, n.pr.m. [5] Sibbecai:– Sibbekai (5)

H6022 סָבַל ***sābal***, v. [9] [→ 6023, 6024, 6025, 6026; cf. 2290; 10502]. [Q] to bear, carry, sustain; [Pu] to be (heavy) laden; [Ht] to drag oneself along:– bear (2), sustain (2), bore (1), burden (1), carry (1), drags itself along (1), draw heavy loads (1)

H6023 סֵבֶל ***sēbel***, n.[m.] [3] [√ 6022]. burden; forced labor:– burden (1), labor force (1), materials (1)

H6024 סֹבֶל ***sōbel***, n.m. [3] [√ 6022]. burden:– burden (2), burdens (1)

H6025 סַבָּל ***sabbāl***, n.[m.] [5] [√ 6022]. carrier, burden-bearer:– carriers (2), laborers (2), carriers (1 [+5951])

H6026 סִבְלוֹת ***siblôt***, n.f. [6] [√ 6022]. forced labor, burden-bearer:– yoke (2), forced labor (1), hard labor (1), work (1), working (1)

H6027 סִבֹּלֶת ***sibbōlet***, n.f. [1] [cf. 8672, 8673]. Sibboleth, "*ear of grain* or *torrent of water*":– Sibboleth (1)

H6028 סִבְרַיִם ***sibrayim***, n.pr.loc. [1] Sibraim:– Sibraim (1)

H6029 סַבְתָּא ***sabtā'***, n.pr.g. [1] [→ 6030]. Sabta:– Sabta (1)

H6030 סַבְתָּה ***sabtâ***, n.pr.g. [1] [√ 6029]. Sabtah:– Sabtah (1)

H6031 סַבְתְּכָא ***sabtᵉkā'***, n.pr.g. [2] Sabteca:– Sabteka (2)

H6032 סָגַד ***sāgad***, v. [4] [√ 10504]. [Q] to bow down (in worship):– bow down (2), bows down (2)

H6033 סְגוֹר ***sᵉgôr***, n.[m.] [1] [√ 6037]. enclosure, closing (of the heart):– rip open (1 [+7973, 4213])

H6034 סָגוּר ***sāgûr***, n.m. [9] [cf. 6037?]. purity (of gold):– pure (8), finest gold (1)

H6035 סְגֻלָּה ***sᵉgullâ***, n.f. [8] treasured possession, personal property:– treasured possession (6), personal treasures (1), treasure (1)

H6036 סֶגֶן ***segen***, n.m. [17] [cf. 6122, 6125; 10505]. official, officer, commander:– officials (12), commanders (3), officers (1), rulers (1)

H6037 סָגַר ***sāgar***, v. [82] [→ 4993, 4994, 4995, 6033, 6050; cf. 6034?, 6126; 10506]. [Q] to shut, close; [Qp] to be shut; [N] to be confined, to be shut up, be imprisoned; [P] to deliver; [Pu] to be shut up, be barred, be closed; [H] to surrender, give over, deliver up; to put in isolation:– shut (21), isolate (8), be shut (4), gave over (3), be shut up (2), close (2), close up (2), closed (2), closed up (2), delivered (2), given (2), hand over (2), sold (2), surrender (2), are closed (1), closed in (1), confine (1), confined (1), confines in prison (1), deliver (1), deliver up (1), delivered up (1), filled in (1), given up (1), giving (1), hand over (1 [+928, 3338]), hemmed in (1), imprisoned himself (1), imprisons (1), is barred (1), keep isolated (1), locked (1), sealed together (1 [+2597]), securely barred (1 [+2256, 6037]), securely barred (1 [+6037, 2256]), shut yourself (1), shuts (1), surrender (1 [+928, 3338]), turned over (1), will[S] (1)

H6038 סָגָר ***sāgār***, n.m. [1] javelin, (battle) ax:– javelin (1)

H6039 סַגְרִיר ***sagrîr***, n.[m.] [1] heavy rain, downpour of rain:– rainstorm (1)

H6040 סַד ***sad***, n.[m.] [2] [cf. 8440]. shackles:– shackles (2)

HEBREW INDEX

H6041 סָדִין ***sādîn***, n.[m.] [4] linen garment:– linen garments (4)

H6042 סְדֹם ***sᵉdōm***, n.pr.loc. [39] Sodom:– Sodom (38), the city[S] (1)

H6043 סֵדֶר ***sēder***, n.[m.] [1] [→ 4997?; cf. 8444]. order, arrangement; "the land of disorder" refers to the Underworld, the region of darkness and chaos:– disorder (1 [+4202])

H6044 סַהַר ***sahar***, n.[m.] [1] [→ 6045]. roundness; referring to the shape of a bowl:– rounded (1)

H6045 סֹהַר ***sōhar***, n.[m.] [8] [√ 6044]. prison:– prison (6 [+1074, 2021]), NDT (2)

H6046 סוֹא ***sôʾ***, n.pr.m. [1] So:– So (1)

H6047 [1]סוּג ***sûg[1]***, v. [24] [cf. 6048, 6092, 8450, 8485]. [Q] to turn away, be faithless, be disloyal; [N] to be turned back, be disloyal, be faithless; [H] to move, displace; [Ho] to be driven back:– be turned (5), move (4), turned (2), deserted (1 [+294]), disloyal (1), faithless (1 [+4213]), is driven back (1 [+294]), moves (1), overtake (1), retreating (1 [+294]), store up (1), turn (1), turn away (1), turn back (1), turned away (1), turning (1)

H6048 [2]סוּג ***sûg[2]***, v. [1] [cf. 6047, 8451?]. [Qp] to be encircled, be bordered (by lilies):– encircled (1)

H6049 [3]סוּג ***sûg[3]***, n.[m.] Not used in NIVEBC [cf. 6092]. dross, see 6092

H6050 סוּגַר ***sûgar***, n.[m.] [1] [√ 6037]. cage; some sources: neck-stock (of iron or wood):– cage (1)

H6051 סוֹד ***sôd***, n.[m.] [21] [→ 1233; cf. 3570]. confidential talk, conspiracy; council, confidant:– council (7), confidence (4), company (1), confides (1), conspiracy (1), conspire (1), counsel (1), fellowship (1), gathered (1), intimate (1), intimate friendship (1), plan (1)

H6052 סוֹדִי ***sôdî***, n.pr.m. [1] Sodi, "*Yahweh confides*":– Sodi (1)

H6053 סוּחַ ***sûaḥ***, n.pr.m. [1] Suah, "[poss.] *offal, dung, viscera*":– Suah (1)

H6054 סוּחָה ***sûḥâ***, n.f. [1] [→ 6082; cf. 8472]. refuse, garbage, offal:– refuse (1)

H6055 סוֹטַי ***sôṭay***, n.pr.m. [2] Sotai:– Sotai (2)

H6056 [1]סוּךְ ***sûk[1]***, v. [2] [→ 5004, 5379; cf. 8504]. [Pil] to spur on, stir up:– spurred on (1), stir up (1)

H6057 [2]סוּךְ ***sûk[2]***, v. [10] [→ 655; cf. 3575, 5818, 5820]. [Q] to anoint, to use oils or perfumes or lotions; [H] to put on lotions; [Ho] to be poured on; this can refer to the application of oils, perfumes, lotions, or resins to the body:– use (3), used lotions at all (2 [+6057]), healing balm (1), pour (1), put on (1), put on lotions (1), put on perfume (1)

H6058 [3]סוּךְ ***sûk[3]***, v. Not used in NIVEBC [cf. 8455]. [Q, H] to hedge about, fence in

H6059 סְוֵנֵה ***sᵉwēnēh***, n.pr.loc. [3] [→ 6060]. Syene = Aswan:– Aswan (3)

H6060 סְוֵנִים ***sᵉwēnîm***, n.pr.pl. Not used in NIVEBC [√ 6059; cf. 6100]. of Syene (Aswan), "*of Syene (Aswan)*"

H6061 [1]סוּס ***sûs[1]***, n.m. [137] [→ 6063, 6064]. (male) horse, stallion:– horses (90), horse (30), horseman (3 [+8206]), horseback (2), mounted (2 [+8206]), warhorses (2), chariot horses (1), horsemen (1 [+8206]), horse's (1), mounted (1 [+928, 2021]), stallions (1), them[S] (1), NDT (2)

H6062 [2]סוּס ***sûs[2]***, n.[m.] Not used in NIVEBC [cf. 6101]. swallow, swift

H6063 סוּסָה ***sûsâ***, n.f. [1] [→ 2963; cf. 6061]. (female) horse, mare:– mare (1)

H6064 סוּסִי ***sûsî***, n.f. [1] [√ 6061]. Susi, "*[my] horse*":– Susi (1)

H6065 סוּסִים ***sûsîm***, n.pr.loc. Not used in NIVEBC [→ 2964]. Susim

H6066 [1]סוּף ***sûp[1]***, v. [6] [→ 6067, 6070; 10508]. [Q] to come to an end; demolish; die; [H] to sweep away:– sweep away (2), demolished (1), die out (1), meet end (1), sweep away (1 [+665])

H6067 סוֹף ***sôp***, n.m. [5] [√ 6066; 10509]. end, conclusion, destiny; rear guard:– end (2), conclusion (1), destiny (1), western ranks (1)

H6068 [1]סוּף ***sûp[2]***, n.m. [28] [→ 6069, 6071]. reed; Reed Sea (traditionally, Red Sea):– red (24), reeds (2), rushes (1), seaweed (1)

H6069 [2]סוּף ***sûp[3]***, n.pr.loc. [1] [√ 6068]. Suph, "*reeds, bushes*":– Suph (1)

H6070 [1]סוּפָה ***sûpâ[1]***, n.f. [15] [√ 6066]. storm wind, whirlwind, tempest, gale:– whirlwind (6), gale (2), storm (2), tempest (2), stormy (1), whirlwinds (1), windstorm (1)

H6071 [2]סוּפָה ***sûpâ[2]***, n.pr.loc. [1] [√ 6068]. Suphah, "*reeds, bushes*":– Suphah (1)

H6072 סוֹפֶרֶת ***sôperet***, n.pr.m. [1] [√ 6219]. Sophereth, "*scribe*":– Sophereth (1)

H6073 [1]סוּר ***sûr[1]***, v. [300] [→ 6239; cf. 6074, 6075]. [Q] to turn away, depart, leave; [Qp] to be rejected; [Pol] to drag from, turn aside; [H] to remove, get rid of, take off; [Ho] to be removed, be abolished; by extension: to forsake, reject:– removed (31), remove (28), turn away (22), turn (10), turned away (9), away (7), take away (7), cut off (6), leave (6), turn aside (6), departed (5), stop (5), take (5), turned (5), come (4), depart (4), got rid of (4), took off (4), keep (3), left (3), lifted (3), rejected (3), shun (3), shuns (3), taken away (3), turned aside (3), turning (3), turning aside (3), deny (2), deposed (2), get rid of (2), go (2), gone (2), is removed (2), keep free (2), leave alone (2 [+4946]), put away (2), rid (2), stopped (2), stray (2), take off (2), throw away (2), took (2), took away (2), turned in (2), abolish (1), avoided (1), avoids (1), banish (1), been removed (1), broke away (1), carry away (1), circumcise (1 [+6889]), clear (1), cleared away (1), come over (1), denied (1), denies (1), deprives (1), dethroned (1), deviate (1), did away with (1), do away with (1 [+4946, 9348]), dragged (1), end (1), entered (1 [+448]), escape (1), expelled (1), fade (1), fail (1), fail (1 [+4946]), failed to keep (1 [+4946]), far (1), give up (1), give up pursuit (1), go away (1), go over (1), gone over (1), hardened rebels (1 [+6253]), instead of (1), is abolished (1), lay aside (1), led astray (1), left undone (1), make leave (1), move (1), move back (1), moved away (1), no longer be (1 [+4946]), pass away (1), past (1), put aside (1), put out (1), removal (1), removes (1), return (1), sent away (1), set aside (1), shows no (1), shunned (1), silences (1), snatch away (1), stay (1), strip off (1), take back (1), taken (1), turns (1), turns away (1), vanish (1), ward off (1), went over (1), went up (1), NDT (1)

H6074 [2]סוּר ***sûr[2]***, a.vbl. [1] [cf. 6073]. corrupt:– corrupt (1)

H6075 [3]סוּר ***sûr[3]***, n.pr.loc. [1] [cf. 6073]. Sur:– Sur (1)

H6076 סוֹרִי ***sôrî***, a. stinking, foul-smelling

H6077 [1]סוּת ***sût[1]***, v. [18] [H] to incite, entice, urge, mislead:– incited (4), urged (3), entices (2), misleading (2), drew away (1), inciting (1), let mislead (1), mislead (1), misled (1), urged on (1), wooing (1)

H6078 [2]סוּת ***sût[2]***, n.[m.] [1] [→ 5003]. robe, garment:– robes (1)

H6079 סָחַב ***sāḥab***, v. [5] [→ 6080]. [Q] to drag down:– dragged away (3), drag away (1), drag down (1)

H6080 סְחָבָה ***sᵉḥābâ***, n.f. [2] [√ 6079]. rag:– rags (2)

H6081 סָחָה ***sāḥâ***, v. [1] [cf. 6082]. [P] to scrape away:– scrape away (1)

H6082 סְחִי ***sᵉḥî***, n.[m.] [1] [√ 6054; cf. 6081]. scum, refuse:– scum (1)

H6083 סְחִיפָה ***sᵉḥîpâ***, n.[m.] Not used in NIVEBC [√ 6085]. downpour (of rain)

H6084 סָחִישׁ ***sāḥîš***, n.[m.] [1] [cf. 8826]. grain that shoots up on its own (in the second year):– what springs from (1)

H6085 סָחַף ***sāḥap***, v. [2] [→ 6083]. [Q] to wash away (of rain); [N] to be washed away, be laid low:– be laid low (1), driving (1)

H6086 סָחַר ***sāḥar***, v. [21] [→ 6087, 6088; cf. 5006]. [Q] to be a trader, a merchant; [Pealal] to pound, throb (of the heart):– merchants (8), did business with (4), trade (3), customers (1 [+3338]), gone (1), labored (1), merchant (1), pounds (1), traders (1)

H6087 סַחַר ***saḥar***, n.m. [7] [√ 6086]. profit (from merchandising in the marketplace):– marketplace (1), merchandise (1), profit (1), profitable (1 [+3202]), profits (1), trading (1), NDT (1)

H6088 סְחֹרָה ***sᵉḥōrâ***, n.f. [1] [√ 6086]. customer:– customers (1 [+3338])

H6089 סֹחֵרָה ***sōḥērâ***, n.f. [1] rampart, wall:– rampart (1)

H6090 סֹחֶרֶת ***sōḥeret***, n.f. [1] costly stone (not specifically defined):– costly stones (1)

H6091 סֵט ***sēṭ***, n.[m.] [1] [cf. 8454]. faithlessness, transgression:– faithless (1)

H6092 סִיג ***sîg***, n.[m.] [8] [cf. 6047, 6049, 6213, 8485]. dross (usually of silver):– dross (8)

H6093 סִיד ***sîd***, n.[m.] Not used in NIVEBC [cf. 6167, 8487]. lime

H6094 סִיוָן ***siwān***, n.pr. [1] Sivan:– Sivan (1)

H6095 סִיחוֹן ***sîḥôn***, n.pr.m. [37] Sihon:– Sihon (34), he[S] (2), Sihon's (1)

H6096 [1]סִין ***sîn[1]***, n.pr.loc. [2] Sin = Pelusium:– Pelusium (2)

H6097 [2]סִין ***sîn[2]***, n.pr.loc. [4] Sin (a desert area between Sinai and Elim, having nothing to do with sinfulness), "*[desert] of clay* [or poss.] *[desert] of Sin*":– Sin (4)

H6098 סִינִי ***sînî***, a.g. [2] Sinite:– Sinites (2)

H6099 סִינַי ***sînay***, n.pr.loc. [35] Sinai, "*Sin; glare [from white chalk]*":– Sinai (35)

H6100 סִינִים ***sînîm***, a.g.pl. Not used in NIVEBC [cf. 6060]. Sinim, Chinese [?]

H6101 סִיס ***sîs***, n.[m.] [2] [cf. 6062]. swift, swallow:– swift (2)

H6102 סִיסְרָא ***sîsᵉrāʾ***, n.pr.m. [21] Sisera:– Sisera (19), Sisera's (2)

H6103 סִיעָא ***sîʿāʾ***, n.pr.m. [1] [→ 6104]. Sia, "*assembly*":– Sia (1)

H6104 סִיעֲהָא ***sîʿᵃhāʾ***, n.pr.m. [1] [√ 6103]. Siaha, "*assembly*":– Siaha (1)

H6105 סִיר ***sîr***, n.m. & f. [30] [√ 6106?]. pot, pan, caldron, washbasin:– pot (12), pots (12), washbasin (2 [+8176]), caldron (1), cooking pot (1), cooking pots (1), pan (1)

H6106 סִירָה ***sîrâ***, n.[m.] [5] [√ 6105?; cf. 6241]. thorn, thornbush; fishhook, barb:– thorns (3), fishhooks (1 [+1855]), thornbushes (1)

H6107 סָךְ ***sāk***, n.[m.] Not used in NIVEBC [√ 6115]. multitude, throng

H6108 סֹךְ ***sōk***, n.[m.] [5] [→ 6109, 6111; cf. 8494]. covering, dwelling (of human or lion):– cover (1), dwelling (1), lair (1), protection (1), tent (1)

H6109 סֻכָּה ***sukkâ***, n.f. [32] [→ 6111; cf. 6108]. tabernacle, shrine; booth, shelter, dwelling, tent:– tabernacles (9), temporary shelters (6), shelter (4), tents (3), canopy (2), shelters (2), dwelling (1), hut (1), pavilion (1), shrine (1), them[S] (1 [+2021]), thicket (1)

H6110 סִכּוּת ***sikkût***, n.pr.? Sikkut (pagan god?), see 6109

H6111 סֻכּוֹת ***sukkôt***, n.pr.loc. [18] [√ 6109; cf. 6108]. Succoth, "*booths*":– Sukkoth (18)

H6112 סֻכּוֹת בְּנוֹת ***sukkôt bᵉnôt***, n.pr. [1] [cf. 1219]. Succoth Benoth (pagan god):– Sukkoth Benoth (1)

H6113 סֻכִּיִּים ***sukkiyyîm***, n.pr.m.pl. [1] Sukkite:– Sukkites (1)

H6114 [1]סָכַךְ ***sākak[1]***, v. [18] [→ 4590, 5009, 5010, 6116, 6117; cf. 8503]. [Q] to cover, conceal, overshadow, shield; [H] to cover, shield; to relieve oneself:– covered (2), guardian (2), overshadowing (2), shield (2), conceal (1), cover (1), hedged in (1), overshadow (1), overshadowed (1), relieve himself (1 [+906, 8079, 2257]), relieving himself (1 [+906, 8079, 2257]), shielded (1), shut up (1), spread protection (1)

H6115 [2]סָכַךְ ***sākak[2]***, v. [2] [→ 6107; cf. 5819, 8455, 8504]. [Q] to knit together; [Pol] to knit together:– knit together (2)

H6116 סֹכֵךְ ***sōkēk***, n.[m.] [1] [√ 6114]. protective shield (a portable roof):– protective shield (1)

H6117 סְכָכָה ***sᵉkākâ***, n.pr.loc. [1] [√ 6114]. Secacah, "*thicket, cover*":– Sekakah (1)

H6118 סָכַל ***sākal***, v. [8] [→ 6119, 6120, 6121]. [N] to do a foolish thing; [P] to turn into foolishness; [H] to act like a fool:– done a foolish thing (4), acted like a fool (1), foolish (1), turn into foolishness (1), turns into nonsense (1)

H6119 סָכָל ***sākāl***, n.m. [7] [√ 6118]. foolish (one), senseless, stupid:– foolish (2), fools (2), fool (1), senseless (1), stupid (1)

H6120 סֶכֶל ***sekel***, n.m. [1] [√ 6118]. foolishness, fool:– Fools (1)

H6121 סִכְלוּת ***siklût***, n.f. [6] [√ 6118; cf. 8508]. folly:– folly (6)

H6122 [1]סָכַן ***sākan[1]***, v. [9] [→ 5016, 6125; cf. 6036]. [Q] to be of use, benefit, profit; [H] to be in the habit; be familiar with; to get along well with:– been in the habit of (2 [+6122]), profit (2), be of benefit (1), benefit (1), familiar with (1), submit (1), useless (1 [+4202])

H6123 [2]סָכַן ***sākan[2]***, v. [1] [cf. 5014, 5017]. [Pu] to be poor:– too poor (1)

H6124 [3]סָכַן ***sākan[3]***, v. [1] [N] to be endangered:– be endangered (1)

H6125 סֹכֵן ***sōkēn***, n.[m.] *or* v.ptcp. [3] [√ 6122; cf. 6036]. steward, nurse, attendant:– steward (1), take care of (1 [+2118]), took care of (1 [+2118])

H6126 [1]סָכַר ***sākar[1]***, v. [2] [cf. 6037, 6127]. [N] to be closed; be silent:– be silenced (1), been closed (1)

H6127 [2]סָכַר ***sākar[2]***, v. [1] [cf. 6126]. [P] to hand over, deliver:– hand over (1)

H6128 [3]סָכַר ***sākar[3]***, v. [1] [cf. 8509]. [Q] to hire:– bribed (1)

H6129 סָכַת ***sākat***, v. [1] [H] to be silent, be still:– silent (1)

H6130 סַל ***sal***, n.m. [15] basket:– basket (12), baskets (2), NDT (1)

H6131 סָלָא ***sālāʾ***, v. [1] [→ 6139, 6140?, 6141?; cf. 6137]. [Pu] to be weighed (in correlation to gold):– worth their weight (1)

H6132 סַלֻּא ***salluʾ***, n.pr.m. [2] [√ 6140?]. Sallu, "[poss.] *he restores*":– Sallu (2)

H6133 סִלָּא ***sillāʾ***, n.pr.loc. [1] Silla, "*embankment*":– Silla (1)

H6134 סָלַד ***sālad***, v. [1] [→ 6135?]. [P] to skip (for joy):– joy (1)

H6135 סֶלֶד ***seled***, n.pr.m. [2] [√ 6134?]. Seled, "*jump for joy*":– Seled (2)

H6136 [1]סָלָה ***sālâ[1]***, v. [2] [Q] to reject, toss aside; [P] to reject:– reject (1), rejected (1)

H6137 ²סָלָה ***sālâ²***, v. [2] [cf. 6131]. [Pu] to be bought, be paid for:– be bought (2)

H6138 סֶלָה ***selâ***, n.[f.] [35] [cf. 6148?]. selah (t.t. in the Psalms):– NDT (35)

H6139 סַלּוּ ***sallû***, n.pr.m. [2] [√ 6131; cf. 6144]. Sallu, "[poss.] *he restores*":– Sallu (1), Sallu's (1)

H6140 סָלוּא ***sālû'***, n.pr.m. [1] [√ 6131? *or* 6132?]. Salu, "*restored*":– Salu (1)

H6141 סִלּוֹן ***sillôn***, n.m. [2] [√ 6131?]. thorn, brier:– briers (1), thorns (1)

H6142 סָלַח ***sālaḥ***, v. [46] [→ 6143, 6145]. [Q] to forgive, release, pardon; [N] to be forgiven:– forgive (26), be forgiven (13), release (3), forgiven (2), forgives (1), pardon (1)

H6143 סַלָּח ***sallāḥ***, a. [1] [√ 6142]. forgiving:– forgiving (1)

H6144 סַלַּי ***sallay***, n.pr.m. [1] [cf. 6139]. Sallai, "[poss.] *God had restored*":– Sallai (1)

H6145 סְלִיחָה ***s^e^līḥâ***, n.f. [3] [√ 6142]. forgiveness, pardon:– forgiving (2), forgiveness (1)

H6146 סַלְכָה ***salkâ***, n.pr.loc. [4] Salecah:– Salekah (4)

H6147 ¹סָלַל ***sālal¹***, v. [3] [cf. 6148]. [Pil] to esteem, cherish; [Htpol] to behave haughtily, insolently:– cherish (1), proudly (1), set yourself (1)

H6148 ²סָלַל ***sālal²***, v. [10] [→ 5019, 5020, 6149, 6150, 6151; cf. 6138?, 6147]. [Q] to build up, heap up (a highway), extol; to pile up:– build up (4), build (2), built up (1), extol (1), is a highway (1), pile up (1)

H6149 סֹלְלָה ***sōl^e^lâ***, n.f. [11] [√ 6148; cf. 2360]. siege ramp, siege mound:– siege ramps (4), ramp (3), siege ramp (3), ramps (1)

H6150 סֻלָּם ***sullām***, n.m. [1] [√ 6148]. stairway; some sources: ladder:– stairway (1)

H6151 סַלְסִלָּה ***salsillâ***, n.[f.] [1] [√ 6148]. branch, shoot; some sources: basket:– branches (1)

H6152 ¹סֶלַע ***sela'¹***, n.m. [58] [→ 6153, 6154, 6255?]. rock, stone; rock formation: cliff, crag; by extension: stronghold, fortress; God as a "Rock" focuses on stability, faithfulness, and protection:– rock (30), rocks (9), crags (4), cliff (2), cliffs (2), mountain (2), cliff (1 [+9094]), rocky (1), rocky crag (1), rocky crags (1), stone (1), stronghold (1), where^S^ (1 [+928, 8234]), NDT (2)

H6153 ²סֶלַע ***sela'²***, n.pr.loc. [4] [√ 6152]. Sela, "*rock crags, cliffs*":– Sela (4)

H6154 סֶלַע הַמַּחְלְקוֹת ***sela' hammaḥl^e^qôt***, n.pr.loc. [1] [√ 6152 + 2165; cf. 4712]. Sela Hammahlekoth:– Sela Hammahlekoth (1)

H6155 סָלְעָם ***sol'ām***, n.m. [1] [√ 6152?]. edible locust or katydid:– katydid (1)

H6156 סָלַף ***sālap***, v. [7] [→ 6157]. [P] to twist; to overthrow; to frustrate:– overthrows (2), twists (2), brings to ruin (1 [+4200, 2021, 8273]), frustrates (1), ruin (1)

H6157 סֶלֶף ***selep***, n.m. [2] [√ 6156]. duplicity, perversity, deceit:– duplicity (1), perverse (1)

H6158 סָלַק ***sālaq***, v. [1] [√ 10513]. [Q] to go up, ascend, climb up:– go up (1)

H6159 סֹלֶת ***sōlet***, n.f. [53] fine flour (likely wheat flour):– finest flour (47), flour (3), special flour (2), finest (1)

H6160 סַם ***sam***, n.m. [16] [√ 6167]. fragrant perfume:– fragrant (14), fragrant spices (1), NDT (1)

H6161 סַמְגַּר ***samgar***, n.pr.m. [1] [→ 6162]. Samgar:– Samgar (1)

H6162 סַמְגַּר־נְבוֹ ***samgar-n^e^bô***, n.pr.m. Not used in NIVEBC [√ 6161 + 5550]. Samgar-Nebo, see 5552 & 6161

H6163 סְמָדַר ***s^e^mādar***, n.m. [3] [√ 6005 + *]. blossom (of a vine):– blossoming (1), blossoms (1), in bloom (1)

H6164 סָמַךְ ***sāmak***, v. [48] [→ 322, 3577, 6165; cf. 8527]. [Q] to sustain, uphold; to lay (one's hand upon); [Qp] to be braced, be steadfast; [N] to lean upon, rely upon, gain confidence; [P] to strengthen, refresh:– lay (17), laid (6), sustained (3), upholds (3), leans (2), sustain (2), sustains (2), allies (1), bracing (1), established (1), gained confidence (1), gave support (1), laid siege (1), lies heavily (1), relied (1), rely (1), rested (1), secure (1), steadfast (1), strengthen (1)

H6165 סְמַכְיָהוּ ***s^e^makyāhû***, n.pr.m. [1] [√ 6164]. Semakiah, "*Yahweh sustains, consecrates*":– Semakiah (1)

H6166 סֶמֶל ***semel***, n.m. [5] image, idol:– idol (2), image (1), image (1 [+7181]), shape (1)

H6167 סָמַם ***sāmam***, v. [1] [→ 6160; cf. 6093, 8487, 8531]. [H] to dye (i.e., to smear with paste or perfume):– put on makeup (1 [+928, 2021, 7037])

H6168 סָמַן ***sāman***, v. [1] [N] to be appointed, apportioned:– plot (1)

H6169 סָמַר ***sāmar***, v. [2] [→ 5021, 6170; cf. 5383]. [Q] to tremble, shudder (i.e., to have goose bumps, gooseflesh); [P] to bristle, stand on end (of hair):– stood on end (1), trembles (1)

H6170 סָמָר ***sāmār***, a. [1] [√ 6169]. bristling (locust):– swarm (1)

H6171 סְנָאָה ***s^e^nā'â***, n.pr.m. [2] [√ 8533, 6176]. Senaah, "*hated one*":– Senaah (2)

H6172 סַנְבַלַּט ***sanballaṭ***, n.pr.m. [10] Sanballat, "*Sin has given life*":– Sanballat (10)

H6173 סַנָּה ***sannâ***, n.pr.loc. Not used in NIVEBC [→ 7962]. Sannah

H6174 סְנֶה ***s^e^neh***, n.m. [6] bush, thorny shrub:– bush (5), it^S^ (1 [+2021])

H6175 סֶנֶּה ***senneh***, n.pr.loc. [1] Seneh, "*thorny;* [poss.] *[cliff shaped like] a tooth*":– Seneh (1)

H6176 סְנוּאָה ***s^e^nû'â***, n.pr.m. Not used in NIVEBC [√ 8533; cf. 2190, 6171]. Senuah, see 2190, "*hated one*"

H6177 סַנְוֵרִים ***sanwērîm***, n.[m.pl.] [3] blindness:– blindness (3)

H6178 סַנְחֵרִיב ***sanḥērîb***, n.pr.m. [13] Sennacherib, "*Sin has increased the brothers*; *Sin replace the [lost] brothers!*":– Sennacherib (13)

H6179 סַנְסַנָּה ***sansannâ***, n.pr.loc. [1] Sansannah, "*palm branch*":– Sansannah (1)

H6180 סַנְסִנָּה ***sansinnâ***, n.[m.]pl. [1] fruit cluster (of date tree):– fruit (1)

H6181 סְנַפִּיר ***s^e^nappîr***, n.[m.] [5] fin:– fins (5)

H6182 סָס ***sās***, n.m. [1] (garment) moth; some sources: worm:– worm (1)

H6183 סִסְמַי ***sismay***, n.pr.m. [2] Sismai, "[poss.] *belonging to Sisam*":– Sismai (2)

H6184 סָעַד ***sā'ad***, v. [12] [→ 5026; 10514]. [Q] to sustain, support, refresh:– sustains (3), refresh (2), for a meal (1), grant support (1), made secure (1), refreshed (1 [+4213]), supported (1), uphold (1), upholding (1)

H6185 סָעָה ***sā'â***, v. [1] [Q] to slander, defame, speak with malice:– tempest (1 [+8120])

H6186 ¹סָעִיף ***sā'îp¹***, n.[m.] [4] [→ 6187, 6188, 6189, 6190, 6191; cf. 6187]. cleft, crag:– cave (2), overhanging (2)

H6187 ²סָעִיף ***sā'îp²***, n.[m.] [2] [→ 6188, 6190, 6250; cf. 6186]. bough, branch:– boughs (1), branches (1)

H6188 סָעַף ***sā'ap***, v.den. [1] [√ 6187; cf. 6186]. [P] to lop off, trim down:– lop off (1)

H6189 סֵעֵף ***sē'ēp***, a. [1] [→ 6191; cf. 6186]. double-minded, divided in heart:– double-minded (1)

H6190 סְעַפָּה ***s^e^'appâ***, n.f. [2] [√ 6187; cf. 6186]. bough:– boughs (2)

H6191 סְעִפִּים ***s^e^'ippîm***, n.f. [1] [√ 6189; cf. 6186]. division, divided opinion, a fig. extension of hobbling on crutches made of boughs:– opinions (1)

H6192 סָעַר ***sā'ar***, v. [7] [→ 6193, 6194; cf. 8548]. [Q] to grow stormier, rougher; [N] to be enraged; [P] to scatter in a wind; [Po] to scatter, swirl; [Pu] to be lashed by storms:– enraged (1 [+4213]), grew even wilder (1 [+2143, 2256]), lashed by storms (1), rougher and rougher (1 [+2143, 2256]), scattered with a whirlwind (1), stormed out (1), swirling (1)

H6193 סַעַר ***sa'ar***, n.m. [8] [→ 6194; cf. 6192]. windstorm, tempest, gale:– storm (4), tempest (1), violent winds (1), whirlwind (1), wind (1)

H6194 סְעָרָה ***s^e^'ārâ***, n.f. [16] [√ 6193; cf. 6192]. windstorm, tempest, gale:– storm (5), whirlwind (3), gale (1), storms (1), stormy (1), tempest (1), tempest (1 [+8120]), violent wind (1 [+8120]), violent winds (1 [+8120]), windstorm (1 [+8120])

H6195 ¹סַף ***sap¹***, n.m. [7] [cf. 6196]. basin, bowl:– basins (3), basin (1), bowls (1), cup (1), NDT (1)

H6196 ²סַף ***sap²***, n.m. Not used in NIVEBC [cf. 6195]. wool, hide, skin

H6197 ³סַף ***sap³***, n.m. [25] [→ 6214]. threshold, door frame, entrance, doorway; doorkeeper:– threshold (7), thresholds (5), doorkeepers (4 [+9068]), doorway (2), doorframes (1), doorkeeper (1 [+9068]), doors (1), doorways (1), entrance (1), gatekeepers (1 [+9068]), NDT (1)

H6198 ⁴סַף ***sap⁴***, n.pr.m. [1] [cf. 6205]. Saph, "*basin, threshold*":– Saph (1)

H6199 סָפַד ***sāpad***, v. [30] [→ 5027, 6252?]. [Q] to beat the breast, mourn, lament, weep; [N] to be mourned:– mourn (12), mourned (8), lament (3), be mourned (2), beat (1), lamented (1 [+5027]), mourners (1), walk in mourning (1), weep (1)

H6200 סָפָה ***sāpâ***, v. [16] [Q] to sweep away; take away; bring disaster; [N] to be swept away; be destroyed:– be swept away (3), perish (2), sweep away (2), are caught (1), be destroyed (1), being swept away (1), bring disaster (1), cut off (1), perished (1), sweeps away (1), swept away (1), take (1)

H6201 סָפוֹן ***sāpôn***, n.[m.] Not used in NIVEBC [√ 6211]. paneling

H6202 ¹סָפַח ***sāpaḥ¹***, v. [4] [→ 5029, 6206, 6207; cf. 8558?, 9148]. [Q] to associate, attach to; [N] to be attached, be united; [Pu] be joined together; [Ht] to feel oneself attached to:– appoint (1), huddled (1), share (1), unite (1)

H6203 ²סָפַח ***sāpaḥ²***, v. [1] [cf. 5384, 8558?, 9148]. [P] to pour out:– pouring (1)

H6204 סַפַּחַת ***sappaḥat***, n.f. [2] [→ 5030]. rash, skin eruption:– rash (2)

H6205 סִפַּי ***sippay***, n.pr.m. [1] [cf. 6198]. Sippai:– Sippai (1)

H6206 ¹סָפִיחַ ***sāpîaḥ¹***, n.[m.] [4] [√ 6202]. what grows on its own, after-growth in a fallow year:– what grows by itself (2), what grows of itself (2)

H6207 ²סָפִיחַ ***sāpîaḥ²***, n.[m.] [1] [√ 6202]. torrent, downpour:– torrents (1)

H6208 סְפִינָה ***s^e^pînâ***, n.f. [1] [√ 6211]. ship (with a covering or deck):– below deck (1 [+3752, 2021])

H6209 סַפִּיר ***sappîr***, n.[m.] [11] sapphire; some sources: lapis lazuli:– lapis lazuli (9), lapis lazuli (2 [+74])

H6210 סֵפֶל ***sēpel***, n.[m.] [2] bowl (for water or curdled milk):– bowl (1), bowlful (1 [+4850])

H6211 סָפַן ***sāpan***, v. [6] [→ 6201, 6208, 6212; cf. 8561]. [Q] to cover; [Qp] to be roofed, be paneled, be roofed:– covered (1), paneled (1), panels (1), roofing (1), was kept (1), was roofed (1)

H6212 סִפֻּן ***sippun***, n.[m.] [1] [√ 6211]. ceiling:– ceiling (1)

H6213 סַפְסִיג ***sapsîg***, n.[m.] Not used in NIVEBC [cf. 6092]. glaze

H6214 סָפַף ***sāpap***, v.den. [1] [√ 6197]. [Htpol] to stand at the threshold:– doorkeeper (1)

H6215 ¹סָפַק ***sāpaq¹***, v. [6] [cf. 6216, 8562]. [Q] to clap hands; beat one's breast; to punish, slap:– beat (2), clap (1), punishes (1), scornfully claps hands (1), struck together (1)

H6216 ²סָפַק ***sāpaq²***, v. [1] [cf. 6215]. [Q] to wallow, splash:– wallow (1)

H6217 סֶפֶק ***sepeq***, n.[m.] [1] [cf. 8563]. riches, abundance:– riches (1)

H6218 סָפַר ***sāpar***, v. [104] [√ 6219]. [Q] to count, number, take a census; [N] to be counted, be recorded; by extension: [P] to tell, proclaim, recount (an event or principle); [Pu] to be told:– told (17), tell (16), count (11), count off (6), declare (6), proclaim (5), counted (3), telling (3), be recorded (2), be told (2), recount (2), talk (2), were told (2), acknowledge (1), appraised (1), be counted (1), boasted (1), census taken (1 [+6222]), conscripted (1), counted out (1), declared (1), gave account (1), gave an account (1), inform (1), is declared (1), keeping records (1), make countless (1 [+8049, 889, 4202]), on display (1), proclaimed (1), recite (1), record (1), repeated (1), spoken out (1 [+606]), state (1), tell (1 [+928, 265]), took a census (1), utter (1), wait (1), were counted (1), write (1)

H6219 ¹סֵפֶר ***sēper¹***, n.m. [186] [→ 2191, 5031, 5032?, 5033, 6072, 6218, 6221, 6222, 6225, 6228, 6229, 6230, 7963; cf. 6220; 10515]. book (as a scroll or tablet), scroll, letter, certificate, deed, dispatch:– book (104), scroll (23), letter (12), letters (10), deed (6), certificate (4), dispatches (4), scroll (4 [+4479]), it^S^ (3 [+2021]), literature (2), written (2), books (1), can read (1 [+3359]), cannot read (1 [+4202, 3359]), deeds (1), documents (1), indictment (1), know how to read (1 [+3359]), record (1), records (1), scriptures (1), them^S^ (1), NDT (1)

H6220 ²סֵפֶר ***sēper²***, n.m. Not used in NIVEBC [cf. 6219]. plate, panel

H6221 סֹפֵר ***sōpēr***, n.m. [56] [√ 6219; 10516]. learned writer, scribe, secretary:– secretary (28), teacher of the law (6), scribe (5), secretaries (4), scribes (2), teacher (2), writing (2), chief officer (1), commander's (1), man learned (1), officer in charge (1), scribe's (1), secretary's (1), writer (1)

H6222 ¹סְפָר ***s^e^pār¹***, n.[m.] [1] [√ 6219]. census:– census taken (1 [+6218])

H6223 ²סְפָר ***s^e^pār²***, n.pr.loc. [1] [cf. 9184]. Sephar:– Sephar (1)

H6224 סְפָרַד ***s^e^pārad***, n.pr.loc. [1] Sepharad:– Sepharad (1)

H6225 סִפְרָה ***siprâ***, n.f. [1] [√ 6219]. record, writing, scroll:– record (1)

H6226 סְפַרְוַיִם ***s^e^parwayim***, n.pr.loc. [6] [→ 6227]. Sepharvaim:– Sepharvaim (6)

H6227 סְפַרְוִים ***s^e^parwîm***, a.g. [1] [√ 6226]. Sepharvite, "*of Sepharvaim*":– Sepharvites (1)

H6228 סְפֹרוֹת ***s^e^pōrôt***, n.f. [1] [√ 6219]. measure, number; some sources: art of writing:– relate (1)

H6229 סֹפְרִים ***sōp^e^rîm***, n.[m.pl.] *or* v.ptcp. Not used in NIVEBC [√ 6219]. see 6221

H6230 סֹפֶרֶת ***sōperet***, n.pr.m. Not used in NIVEBC [√ 6219]. (office of) scribes

H6231 סֶפֶת ***sepet***, v. Not used in NIVEBC [√ 3578]. see 3578

H6232 סָקַל ***sāqal***, v. [22] [Q] to stone (as an execution); [N] to be stoned; [P] to throw stones (out or away), pelt with stones; [Pu] to be stoned:– stone (4), stone (3 [+928, 2021, 74]), be stoned (2 [+6232]), be stoned to death (2 [+6232]), been stoned (2), stoned (2 [+928, 2021, 74]), be stoned (1), be stoned to death (1), cleared of stones (1), pelted (1), remove (1), stoning (1), throwing (1)

H6233 סַר ***sār***, n.m. [1] [√ 6254; cf. 8606]. captain:– captain (1)

H6234 סַר ***sar***, a. [3] [√ 6253]. sullen, dejected, discouraged:– sullen (3)

H6235 סָרָב ***sārāb***, n.m. [1] briers:– briers (1)

H6236 סַרְגוֹן ***sargôn***, n.pr.m. [1] Sargon, "*firm, faithful king; the king is legitimate*":– Sargon (1)

H6237 סֶרֶד ***sered***, n.pr.m. [2] [→ 6238]. Sered:– Sered (2)

H6238 סַרְדִּי ***sardî***, a.g. [1] [√ 6237]. Seredite, "*of Sered*":– Seredite (1)

H6239 [1]סָרָה ***sārâ[1]***, n.f. [1] [√ 6073]. ceasing, stopping:– unceasing (1 [+1194])

H6240 [2]סָרָה ***sārâ[2]***, n.f. [7] [√ 6253]. rebellion, revolt:– rebellion (4), crime (1), revolt (1), revolted against (1)

H6241 סִרָה ***sirâ***, n.pr.[loc.] [1] [→ 1015; cf. 6106]. Sirah:– Sirah (1)

H6242 סָרוּחַ ***sārûaḥ***, a. *or* v.ptcp. [3] [√ 6243]. flowing, lounging:– flowing (1), lounge (1), lounging (1)

H6243 [1]סָרַח ***sāraḥ[1]***, v. [3] [→ 6242, 6245; cf. 8580]. [Q] to hang down, overhang, spread over; [Qp] to be overhanged:– hang (1), hang down (1), spreading (1)

H6244 [2]סָרַח ***sāraḥ[2]***, v. [1] [N] to be decayed, be spoiled, become stinking:– decayed (1)

H6245 סֶרַח ***seraḥ***, n.m. [1] [√ 6243]. overhang, what projects over:– length (1)

H6246 סִרְיוֹן ***siryôn***, n.[m.] [3] [cf. 8590, 9234]. (scale) armor, coat of mail:– armor (2), coat of armor (1)

H6247 סָרִיס ***sārîs***, n.m. [45] [→ 8060]. court official, palace officer, eunuch:– eunuchs (10), official (9), officials (9), officer (5), court officials (4), eunuch (4), officers (2), attendants (1), palace officials (1)

H6248 [1]סֶרֶן ***seren[1]***, n.[m.] [1] axle:– axles (1)

H6249 [2]סֶרֶן ***seren[2]***, n.m. [21] ruler, prince:– rulers (21)

H6250 סַרְעַפָּה ***sarʿappâ***, n.f. [1] [√ 6187]. bough:– boughs (1)

H6251 סָרַף ***sārap***, v. [1] [cf. 8596]. [P] to burn:– burn (1)

H6252 סִרְפָּד ***sirpād***, n.[m.] [1] [√ 6199?]. briers, stinging nettles:– briers (1)

H6253 [1]סָרַר ***sārar[1]***, v. [17] [→ 6234, 6240; cf. 6254]. [Q] to be stubborn, be obstinate, be rebellious:– stubborn (6), rebellious (4), obstinate (2), stubbornly (2), defiant (1), hardened rebels (1 [+6073]), rebels (1)

H6254 [2]סָרַר ***sārar[2]***, v.den. [1] [→ 6233; cf. 6253, 8569, 8606]. [Q] to be in charge, superintend:– in charge (1)

H6255 סְתָו ***s^e^tāw***, n.m. [1] [cf. 6257]. winter, rainy season:– winter (1)

H6256 סְתוּר ***s^e^tûr***, n.pr.m. [1] [√ 6259]. Sethur, "*concealed [by deity]*":– Sethur (1)

H6257 סְתָיו ***s^e^tāyw***, n.m. Not used in NIVEBC [cf. 6255]. winter, see 6255

H6258 סָתַם ***sātam***, v. [12] [cf. 8608]. [Q] to stop up, block off, seal; [Qp] to be closed up, (by extension) to be in a secret place; [N] to be closed; [P] to stop up:– stopped up (3), blocked (2), being closed (1), blocking off (1), roll up (1), rolled up (1), seal up (1), secret place (1), stop up (1)

H6259 סָתַר ***sātar***, v. [82] [→ 5039, 5040, 5041, 6256, 6260, 6261; 10519]. [Q] to be hidden, be concealed, have a refuge; [P] to hide; [Pu] to be hidden; [H] to hide, conceal; [Ht] to hide oneself, keep oneself hidden:– hide (35), hidden (10), hid (9), hiding (4), certainly hide (2 [+6259]), conceal (2), concealed (2), secret (2), take refuge (2), are hidden (1), away (1), be sheltered (1), covers (1), go into hiding (1), have no (1 [+4946, 6524]), hide yourself (1), hides (1), hiding himself (1), hiding place (1), is deprived (1), is hidden (1), undetected (1), vanish (1)

H6260 סֵתֶר ***sēter***, n.[m.] [35] [→ 6261; cf. 6259]. hiding place, secret place, shelter; covering, veil; (adv.) secretly, in secret:– secret (8), secretly (6 [+928, 2021]), shelter (5), hiding place (2), privately (2 [+928, 2021]), refuge (2), concealed (1), covering (1), hidden (1), hiding (1), hiding places (1), ravine (1), secret place (1), sly (1), thundercloud (1 [+8308]), veil (1)

H6261 סִתְרָה ***sitrâ***, n.f. [1] [√ 6260; cf. 6259]. shelter, hiding-place, refuge:– give shelter (1 [+2118])

H6262 סִתְרִי ***sitrî***, n.pr.m. [1] Sithri, "[poss.] *Yahweh is my hiding place*":– Sithri (1)

H6263 ע ***ʿ***, letter. Not used in NIVEBC [√ 10521]. letter of the Hebrew alphabet

H6264 [1]עָב ***ʿāb[1]***, n.m. [3] overhang, overhanging roof:– overhang (1), overhanging roof (1), overhangs (1)

H6265 [2]עָב ***ʿāb[2]***, n.m. [30] [√ 6380]. clouds:– clouds (19), cloud (7), clouds of the sky (2 [+8836]), cloudless (1 [+4202]), thick clouds (1)

H6266 [3]עָב ***ʿāb[3]***, n.m. [1] [√ 6380?]. thicket:– thickets (1)

H6267 עַב ***ʿab***, n.[m.] Not used in NIVEBC [√ 6286]. denseness, see 6295

H6268 עָבַד ***ʿābad***, v. [291] [→ 5042, 6269, 6271, 6272, 6275, 6276, 6285, 6381; *also used with compound proper names*; 10522]. [Q] to work, serve, labor, do; to worship, minister, work in ministry; [N] to be plowed, be cultivated; [Pu] to be worked; [H] to reduce to servitude, enslave, cause to serve; [Ho] to be caused to serve, worship (a god):– serve (91), worship (37), served (28), work (13), worshiped (12), do (11), serving (8), servants (6), subject to (6), worked (4), worshiping (4), enslave (3), enslaved (3), labor (3), subject (3), work for (3), worked for (3), burdened (2), farm (2), hold in bondage (2), till (2), work (2 [+6275]), workers (2), be cultivated (1), be plowed (1), been[S] (1), been plowed (1), been worked (1), cultivate (1), do[S] (1), do work (1), doing (1), done (1), drove (1), efforts (1), enslaving (1), farmer (1 [+408, 141]), forced (1), fulfilling by doing (1), keep working (1), laborer (1), led (1), made work (1), make slaves (1), make work (1), observe (1), perform (1), profits (1), put to work (1), reduced to servitude (1 [+4200, 6269]), servant (1), serve as slave (1), serve as slaves (1), serves (1), services (1), subjects (1), subjugate (1), submit (1), to subject (1), used (1), worship (1 [+6275]), NDT (3)

H6269 [1]עֶבֶד ***ʿebed[1]***, n.m. [803] [→ 5589, 6268, 6270, 6277, 6278, 6279, 6280; 10523; *also used with compound proper names*]. servant, slave, attendant; indentured servants and owned slaves had varying levels of status and responsibilities; according to the OT Law, a Hebrew slave could be sold to a Hebrew master for only six years, but there was no time limit for Gentile slaves:– servant (318), servants (159), officials (75), men (36), slaves (31), attendants (22), slave (16), officers (15), slavery (14), male servants (13), male slaves (10), servant's (7), subject (7), envoys (6), male servant (4), male slave (4), official (4), subjects (3), at service (2), attendant (2), in bondage (2), lowest of slaves (2 [+6269]), officer (2), retinue (2), service (2), slaves (2 [+2256, 9148]), them[S] (2 [+2257]), they[S] (2 [+2257]), vassal (2), vassals (2), I[S] (1 [+3870]), as slaves (1 [+6275]), court (1), delegation (1 [+928, 3338]), enslaved (1 [+3899, 4200, 2256, 4200, 9148]), fellow officers (1 [+123]), government officials (1), he[S] (1 [+3870]), him[S] (1 [+3870]), in service (1), make men slaves (1 [+3899]), me[S] (1 [+3870]), messengers (1), officials (1 [+408]), reduced to servitude (1 [+6268, 4200]), sailors[S] (1), servants (1 [+4200]), servants male (1), servants men (1), servants the (1), served (1), serves (1), slaves (1 [+2256, 563]), slaves male (1), subordinates (1), them[S] (1 [+1192]), they[S] (1 [+8620]), NDT (6)

H6270 [2]עֶבֶד ***ʿebed[2]***, n.pr.m. [6] [√ 6269]. Ebed, "*servant*":– Ebed (6)

H6271 עֲבָד ***ʿ^a^bād***, n.m. [1] [√ 6268]. what is done, deed, act:– what do (1)

H6272 עַבְדָּא ***ʿabdāʾ***, n.pr.m. [2] [√ 6268]. Abda, "*servant of Yahweh*":– Abda (2)

H6273 עֹבֵד־אֱדוֹם ***ʿōbēd-ʾ^e^dôm***, n.pr.m. [20] [√ 6268 + 139]. Obed-Edom, "*servant [worshiper] of Edom*":– Obed-Edom (18), him[S] (1), his[S] (1)

H6274 עַבְדְּאֵל ***ʿabd^e^ʾēl***, n.pr.m. [1] [√ 6269 + 446; cf. 6280]. Abdeel, "*servant of God [El]*":– Abdeel (1)

H6275 עֲבֹדָה ***ʿ^a^bōdâ***, n.f. [145] [√ 6268; 10525]. work, service, labor, task, duty, job; special work and service to God: service, ministry; forced labor: slavery:– work (39), service (24), regular work (12 [+4856]), labor (9), duties (5), serving (5), use (5), ceremony (3), ministering (3), campaign (2), constructing (2), job (2), ministry (2), slavery (2), task (2), various kinds of service (2 [+6275, 2256]), various kinds of service (2 [+2256, 6275]), work (2 [+6268]), as slaves (1 [+6269]), assist (1), by (1), craft (1), cultivate (1), demands (1), doing (1), doing work (1), effect (1), farmed (1), posts (1), regular service (1 [+7372]), required (1), responsible (1), responsible (1 [+4856]), served (1), slaves (1), tasks (1), workers (1 [+1074]), worship (1 [+6268]), NDT (2)

H6276 עֲבֻדָּה ***ʿ^a^buddâ***, n.f. [2] [√ 6268]. servant, slave:– servants (2)

H6277 [1]עַבְדּוֹן ***ʿabdôn[1]***, n.pr.m. [6] [√ 6278; cf. 6269]. Abdon, "*servant*":– Abdon (6)

H6278 [2]עַבְדּוֹן ***ʿabdôn[2]***, n.pr.loc. [3] [√ 6277; cf. 6269]. Abdon, "*servant*":– Abdon (3)

H6279 עַבְדִּי ***ʿabdî***, n.pr.m. [3] [√ 6280?]. Abdi, "*servant of Yahweh* or *my servant*":– Abdi (3)

H6280 עַבְדִּיאֵל ***ʿabdîʾēl***, n.pr.m. [1] [→ 6274, 6279?; cf. 6269 + 446, 6274]. Abdiel, "*servant of God [El]*":– Abdiel (1)

H6281 עֹבַדְיָה ***ʿōbadyâ***, n.pr.m. [11] [√ 6268 + 3378]. Obadiah, "*servant [worshiper] of Yahweh*":– Obadiah (11)

H6282 עֹבַדְיָהוּ ***ʿōbadyāhû***, n.pr.m. [9] [√ 6268 + 3378]. Obadiah, "*servant [worshiper] of Yahweh*":– Obadiah (9)

H6283 עֶבֶד־מֶלֶךְ ***ʿebed-melek***, n.pr.m. [6] [√ 6269 + 4889]. Ebed-Melech, "*servant of Melek [king]* or *Malk*":– Ebed-Melek (6)

H6284 עֲבֵד נְגוֹ ***ʿ^a^bēd n^e^gô***, n.pr.m. [1] [√ 6269 + 5550; 10460, 10524]. Abednego, "*servant of Nego* or *Nebo*":– Abednego (1)

H6285 עַבְדוּת ***ʿabdut***, n.f. [3] [√ 6268]. slavery, servitude:– bondage (2), slavery (1)

H6286 עָבָה ***ʿābâ***, v. [3] [→ 5043, 6267, 6295]. [Q] to be thick:– thicker (2), heavy (1)

H6287 עֲבוֹט ***ʿ^a^bôṭ***, n.[m.] [4] [→ 6292, 6294]. pledge, (garment) security (for a loan):– pledge (2), offered as a pledge (1), NDT (1)

H6288 [1]עֲבוּר ***ʿ^a^bûr[1]***, pp. & c. [49] [→ 1236]. marker of cause or reason: for, because; marker of purpose or intent: on account of; in order to; a marker of result: then; benefit: for:– for the sake of (11 [+928]), because of (6 [+928]), so that (5 [+928]), for sake (4 [+928]), because (3 [+928]), to (3 [+928]), for (2 [+928]), in order to (2 [+928]), so (2 [+928]), that (2 [+928]), for this purpose (1 [+928]), on account of (1 [+928]), only to (1 [+928]), then (1 [+928]), to (1 [+4200, 928]), while (1 [+928]), with (1 [+928]), NDT (2)

H6289 [2]עֲבוּר ***ʿ^a^bûr[2]***, n.[m.] [2] [√ 6296]. produce, yield:– food (1), produce (1)

H6290 [1]עָבוֹת ***ʿābôt[1]***, a. [4] [√ 6309]. leafy, dense, interwoven foliage:– leafy (3), shade (1)

H6291 [2]עָבוֹת ***ʿābôt[2]***, n.m. & f. [5] [√ 6309]. thick foliage:– thick foliage (4), boughs (1)

H6292 [1]עָבַט ***ʿābaṭ[1]***, v.den. [5] [√ 6287]. [Q] to borrow, i.e., take or receive a pledge; [H] to lend on a pledge:– freely lend (2 [+6292]), borrow (1), get (1), lend (1)

H6293 [2]עָבַט ***ʿābaṭ[2]***, v.den. [1] [P] to swerve, change (a course), implying a lack of purpose:– swerving (1)

H6294 עַבְטִיט ***ʿabṭîṭ***, n.[m.]intens. [1] [√ 6287]. heavy pledges, excessive mortgage for a debt; there may be an implication of undue force being used to keep the pledge:– extortion (1)

H6295 עֳבִי ***ʿ^o^bî***, n.[m.] [6] [√ 6286]. thickness, density, mold:– thick (2), thickness (2), dense (1), molds (1)

H6296 [1]עָבַר ***ʿābar[1]***, v. [543] [→ 5044, 5045, 6289, 6298, 6299, 6300, 6302, 6305]. [Q] to pass over, cross over, travel through; [N] to be crossed; [P] to extend; to breed; [H] to make pass through, let pass over, send over; by extensions: to forgive, as the passing over of guilt:– crossed (32), pass (30), cross (28), cross over (24), passed (20), crossed over (17), go (15), crossing (11), went (10), pass by (9), passed by (9), pass through (8), went on (8), go over (6), sacrificed (6), violated (6), come (5), go on (5), moved on (5), swept (5), pass by (4 [+2006]), sacrifice (4), take away (4), advanced (3), came along (3), come over (3), continued (3), going (3), led (3), over (3), pass away (3), passed through (3), passes (3), spread (3), traveled (3), bring across (2), bring across (2 [+6296]), broken (2), came by (2), comes (2), cross over without fail (2 [+6296]), crossing over (2), disobey (2), fail (2), get through (2), give (2), go beyond (2), go on way (2), go past (2), going down (2), gone (2), gone by (2), had pass (2), journey (2), led through (2), make (2), marched (2), passed along (2), passing by (2), passing through (2), past (2), put (2), send (2), spare (2), sweep through (2), sweeps by (2), swept by (2), taken away (2), transgressed (2), travel (2), travelers (2), travels (2), walked (2), according to the weight current (1), advance (1), avert (1 [+4946, 6584]), be over (1), been (1), beyond (1), blown (1), blows (1), breed (1), brought (1), brought over (1), came to the other side (1), carried over (1), carry over (1), cast off (1), cause to pass (1), census (1 [+408]), coming (1), coming over (1), continue on (1), continued along (1), continued on (1), counted off (1 [+928, 5031]), cover (1), cover (1 [+6584]), crosses over (1), did so[S] (1), disobeyed (1), disobeying (1), disregarded (1), driven (1), enter (1), exceed (1), expelled (1), explored (1 [+9365]), extended (1), fall (1), felt (1), fleeting (1), flowing (1), follow (1 [+339]), forded (1), forgive (1), forgives (1), forth (1), give over (1), go away (1), go out (1), goes (1), goes across (1), goes through (1), gone on (1), had pass by (1), have no limit (1), have no limits (1), have shave (1 [+9509]), have sounded (1), invade (1), invade (1 [+928]), irresistible (1), issued (1), jealous (1 [+8120, 7863, 6584]), kept on going (1), laid (1), lead across (1 [+4200, 7156]), leaving (1 [+4946]), led around (1), let pass (1), make cross (1), marauding forces (1 [+2256, 8740]), march on (1), marched on (1), marched past (1 [+6584, 3338]), marching (1), missed (1), moved (1), moved on ahead (1), moved on beyond (1), moves on (1), on the way (1), on way (1), others[S] (1 [+2021]), outran (1), over going (1), overcome (1), overflow (1), overlook (1), overrun (1), overstep (1), overwhelmed (1 [+8031]), overwhelming (1), pass into other hands (1), pass on (1), passed away (1), passer-by (1), passes by (1), passing (1), perish (1), perishing (1), provide safe-conduct (1), put a yoke (1), put an end (1), ran (1), ran past (1), reclaimed (1), remove (1), removed (1), repealed (1), roam (1), sacrificed (1 [+5989, 928]), sacrifices (1), sail (1), seafarers (1 [+3542]), send out (1), sent (1), sent across (1), sent over (1), sent throughout (1), set free (1), shave (1), someone[S] (1), sound (1), spread out (1), spreading

HEBREW INDEX

among (1), surrounded (1), sweep (1), swept away (1), swim (1), take note as pass (1), take over (1), taken from (1), taken over (1), they[S] (1 [+2021]), through (1), took (1), took off (1), transfer (1), travel (1 [+2006]), traveled along (1), traveled through (1 [+2256, 8740]), traveling through (1), turn away (1), turned aside (1), untraveled (1 [+4946, 1172, 408]), used (1), vanishes (1), violate (1), violation (1), wade through (1), walk on (1), walked on (1), went as far as (1), went away (1), went forward (1), went over (1), went up (1), NDT (4)

H6297 [2]עָבַר **'ābar[2]**, v.den. [8] [→ 6301]. [Ht] to be very angry, show oneself angry:– furious (3), anger (1), angry (1), hotheaded (1), rushes (1), very angry (1)

H6298 [1]עֵבֶר **'ēber[1]**, n.m. [90] [√ 6296; 10526]. what is on the other side, what is beyond, across; i.e., east or west; Trans-Euphrates:– east (9 [+928]), side (8), other side (6), beyond (5), beyond (5 [+928]), Trans-Euphrates (4 [+2021, 5643]), across (4 [+928]), across (4), straight ahead (3 [+448, 7156]), beyond (2 [+4946]), east (2 [+4946]), near (2 [+928]), next to (2 [+448]), across from (1 [+4946]), along (1 [+928]), along (1 [+4946]), alongside (1 [+4946]), at (1 [+928]), by (1 [+4946]), east (1), east (1 [+4667, 2025]), east (1 [+928, 4667, 2025]), east (1 [+928, 4667, 9087]), east (1 [+928, 4667, 2025, 9087]), east side (1), from (1 [+4946]), go on (1), land beyond (1), next to (1 [+4200]), on each side (1 [+4946, 2021, 4946, 2296, 4946, 2021, 6298, 4946, 2296]), on each side (1 [+4946, 2021, 6298, 4946, 2296, 4946, 2021, 4946, 2296]), on the other side (1 [+4946, 2256, 2134]), on this side of (1 [+4946]), over here (1 [+4200, 285]), over there (1 [+4200, 285]), side (1 [+4946]), sides (1), sides (1 [+4946, 6017]), space (1), this side (1), west (1), west (1 [+928]), west (1 [+4946]), NDT (4)

H6299 [2]עֵבֶר **'ēber[2]**, n.pr.m. [15] [√ 6296]. Eber, "*[regions] beyond [the river]*":– Eber (15)

H6300 עֲבָר **'ăbār**, n.pr.loc. Not used in NIVEBC [√ 6296]. crossing, see 6305

H6301 עֶבְרָה **'ebrâ**, n.f. [34] [√ 6297]. wrath, anger, fury, rage; insolence:– wrath (20), fury (6), anger (4), insolence (2), rage (2)

H6302 עֲבָרָה **'ᵃbārâ**, n.f. [3] [→ 6305; cf. 6296]. ford, crossing:– fords (2), ford (1)

H6303 [1]עִבְרִי **'ibrî[1]**, a. & n.g. [34] [→ 6304]. Hebrew:– Hebrews (16), Hebrew (15), Hebrew (1 [+408]), Hebrews (1 [+408]), NDT (1)

H6304 [2]עִבְרִי **'ibrî[2]**, n.pr.m. [1] [√ 6303]. Ibri, "*Hebrew*":– Ibri (1)

H6305 עֲבָרִים **'ᵃbārîm**, n.pr.loc. [5] [√ 6302; cf. 6296]. Abarim, "*geographical regions beyond*":– Abarim (5)

H6306 עֶבְרֹן **'ebrōn**, n.pr.loc. Not used in NIVEBC [cf. 6278]. Ebron, see 6278

H6307 עַבְרֹנָה **'abrōnâ**, n.pr.loc. [2] Abronah:– Abronah (2)

H6308 עָבַשׁ **'ābaš**, v. [1] [Q] to shrivel, wither, dry up:– shriveled (1)

H6309 עָבַת **'ābat**, v. [1] [→ 6290, 6291, 6310]. [P] to conspire, twist:– conspire (1)

H6310 עֲבֹת **'ᵃbōt**, n.m. [19] [√ 6309]. rope, cord, chains, ties; fetters, harness:– ropes (7), chains (4), rope (3), chains (1 [+9249]), cords (1), harness (1), shackles (1), ties (1)

H6311 עָגַב **'āgab**, v. [7] [→ 6312, 6311; cf. 6385]. [Q] to lust, have sensual desire for:– lusted after (3 [+6584]), lovers (1), lusted (1), lusted after (1), lusted after (1 [+448])

H6312 עֲגָבָה **'ᵃgābâ**, n.f. [2] [√ 6311]. lust, sensual desire:– love (1), lust (1)

H6313 עֲגָבִים **'ᵃgābîm**, n.[m.] [1] [√ 6311]. devotion, love:– love (1)

H6314 עֻגָה **'ugâ**, n.f. [7] [√ 6383]. (round, flat) bread cakes:– bread (2), loaf of bread (2), loaves (2), flat loaf (1)

H6315 עָגוּר **'āgûr**, n.[m.] [2] (short footed) thrush (a bird):– thrush (2)

H6316 עָגִיל **'āgîl**, n.[m.] [2] [√ 6318]. earring:– earrings (2)

H6317 עֲגִילָה **'ᵃgîlâ**, n.f. [1] [√ 6318]. circular shield:– shields (1)

H6318 עָגֹל **'āgōl**, a. [6] [→ 5046, 5047, 6316, 6317, 6318, 6319, 6320, 6321, 6322, 6323]. circular, round:– circular in shape (2 [+6017]), round (2), circular band (1 [+6017]), rounded (1)

H6319 עֵגֶל **'ēgel**, n.m. [36] [√ 6318]. bull-calf; calf-shaped idol:– calf (19), calves (10), shape of a calf (3), calf-idol (2), calf-idols (1), shape of calves (1)

H6320 [1]עֶגְלָה **'eglâ[1]**, n.f. [11] [→ 6321; cf. 6318]. heifer-calf, young cow:– heifer (6), heifer (2 [+1330]), heifer's (1), it[S] (1 [+2021]), young cow (1 [+1330])

H6321 [2]עֶגְלָה **'eglâ[2]**, n.pr.f. [2] [√ 6320]. Eglah, "*heifer*":– Eglah (2)

H6322 עֲגָלָה **'ᵃgālâ**, n.f. [24] [√ 6318]. cart:– cart (14), carts (8), it[S] (1 [+2021]), threshing cart (1)

H6323 [1]עֶגְלוֹן **'eglôn[1]**, n.pr.m. [5] [√ 6318]. Eglon, "*circle; young bull*":– Eglon (4), who[S] (1)

H6324 [2]עֶגְלוֹן **'eglôn[2]**, n.pr.loc. [8] Eglon, "*circle; young bull*":– Eglon (8)

H6325 עֶגְלַיִם **'eglayim**, n.pr.loc. Not used in NIVEBC [→ 6536]. Eglaim

H6326 עֶגְלַת שְׁלִשִׁיָּה **'eglat šᵉlišiyyâ**, n.pr.loc. [2] [cf. 8999]. Eglath Shelishiyah, "[poss.] *the third Eglath*":– Eglath Shelishiyah (2)

H6327 עָגַם **'āgam**, v. [1] [cf. 108]. [Q] to grieve for, have pity on:– grieved (1)

H6328 עָגַן **'āgan**, v. [1] [N] to keep withdrawn (from marital relations):– remain unmarried (1 [+4200, 1194, 2118, 4200, 408])

H6329 [1]עַד **'ad[1]**, n.m. [48] a unit of time, referring to the past: old, ancient; without limit: forever, eternal, for ever and ever; continual, always:– ever (16), forever (14), forever (3 [+6330]), ancient (2), ever and ever (2), everlasting (2), continually (1 [+4200]), eternal (1), eternal (1 [+4200]), ever (1 [+4200]), ever (1 [+6330]), never (1 [+4200]), never (1 [+1153, 6409, 2256]), of old (1), unending (1 [+4200])

H6330 [2]עַד **'ad[2]**, pp. [1259] [→ 1187, 6364; cf. 6334?; 10527]. until, up to, as far as (1 [+2178]), yet (1 [+6964]), NDT (91):– to (322), until (224), till (92), as far as (71), forever (44 [+6409]), until (30 [+889]), how long (27 [+5503]), up to (20), and (14), all the way to (12), how long (12 [+625, 2025]), reached (11 [+995]), before (9), or (8), as (7), by (7), at (6), for (6), until (6 [+8611]), very (6 [+4394]), ever (5 [+6409]), forevermore (5 [+6409]), while (5), after (4), approached (4 [+995]), even (4), from (4), how long (4 [+4537]), still (4), always (3 [+6409]), among (3), and alike (3), before (3 [+889, 4202]), between (3 [+4946, 2256]), beyond measure (3 [+4394]), but (3), ever since (3 [+2021, 3427, 2021, 2296]), forever (3 [+6329]), in (3), out to (3), reaches to (3), through (3), until (3 [+561]), until (3 [+3954]), when (3), as far away as (2), at (2 [+928, 2021, 2942]), at set times (2 [+4946, 6961, 6961]), down to (2), everlasting (2 [+6409]), forever (2 [+2021, 6409]), forever (2 [+4200, 6409]), from beginning to (2), how many (2 [+3869, 4537]), in the end (2), lasts (2), more (2 [+6409]), never (2 [+4202, 6409]), of (2), reach (2 [+995]), still (2 [+2021, 3427, 2021, 2296]), this far (2 [+2151]), till (2 [+8611]), up (2), utterly (2 [+4394]), with (2), abundantly (1 [+889, 6330, 3907]), abundantly (1 [+6330, 889, 3907]), against (1 [+928]), all the way to (1 [+995]), all the way to (1 [+995, 3870]), all the way up (1), all this time (1 [+2178]), arrive (1 [+995]), arrived (1 [+995]), as far as[S] (1), as long as (1), at the point of (1), before (1 [+4202]), by then (1), come to (1), completely (1 [+3983]), completely (1 [+3983, 9462]), completely (1 [+4946, 5883, 2256, 1414]), completely destroyed (1 [+3983]), down to (1 [+9462]), end (1), endless (1 [+6409]), ends (1), enough (1), entered (1 [+2143]), entering (1 [+995]), even enough (1), ever (1 [+6329]), extends to (1), far and wide (1 [+8158]), far and wide (1 [+4200, 4946, 8158]), far away (1 [+4200, 4946, 8158]), finally (1 [+889]), for an instant (1 [+1180, 8371]), for how long (1 [+5503]), forevermore (1 [+2021, 6409]), founded on (1), had for (1), here (1 [+2178]), hold back overnight (1 [+4328, 1332]), how long (1 [+625]), huge (1 [+1524, 4200, 4394]), in the end (1 [+889]), including (1), into (1), join (1 [+995]), lasted so long (1), lasting (1 [+6409]), lasting (1 [+2021, 3427, 2021, 2296]), led to (1), loud (1 [+1524, 4394]), meanwhile (1 [+3907, 2256, 6330, 3907]), meanwhile (1 [+6330, 3907, 2256, 3907]), more and more powerful (1 [+2143, 2256, 1541, 4200, 5087, 2025]), much (1 [+4394]), near (1), never (1 [+561, 6409]), never again (1 [+5905, 4202]), on (1 [+6964]), only (1), over (1), prior (1), reach to (1), reached (1 [+1540]), reached height (1 [+8003]), reaching to (1), since (1), since (1 [+2178]), so (1), so much (1), so much that (1), still in force (1), swiftly (1 [+4559]), that (1 [+889]), this far (1 [+7024]), though (1), threatened (1 [+5883]), thus far (1 [+2178]), till (1 [+561]), till (1 [+889]), till (1 [+3954]), till (1 [+6961]), to the point of (1), to the vicinity of (1 [+995, 3870]), together with (1 [+2256]), toward (1), toward (1 [+5790]), trembled violently (1 [+3006, 1524, 4394, 3010]), unmercifully (1 [+4394]), until (1 [+889, 561]), until (1 [+889, 561]), until the end of (1), until the time for (1), utter destruction (1 [+7]), very (1 [+4200, 5087, 2025]), waited (1), when (1 [+4537]), when (1 [+8611]), when (1 [+625, 2025]), while (1 [+8611]), while still (1), without (1 [+401]), yet (1), yet (1 [+2178]), yet (1 [+6964]), yet (1 [+2021, 3427, 2021, 2085]), yet (1 [+2021, 3427, 2021, 2156]), NDT (89)

H6331 [3]עַד **'ad[3]**, n.[m.] [1] [√ 6334]. prey, plunder:– prey (1)

H6332 עֵד **'ēd**, n.m. [73] [→ 3444; cf. 6386]. witness, testimony; an object that serves as a memorial or a person giving of legal evidence:– witness (38), witnesses (18), testify (3), testimony (3), called in as witnesses (1 [+6386]), evidence (1), had witnessed (1 [+6386]), have the transaction witnessed (1 [+6386]), testify (1 [+2118]), testify (1 [+6699, 4200]), those who speak up for (1), witnessed (1 [+6386]), NDT (3)

H6333 עִדֹּא **'iddō'**, n.pr.m. [1] [√ 6341]. Iddo, "[prob.] *Yahweh has adorned*":– Iddo (1)

H6334 [1]עָדָה **'ādâ[1]**, v. [2] [→ 3586?, 3588?, 6330?, 6331; 10528]. [Q] to prowl; [H] to take away, remove:– prowls (1), takes away (1)

H6335 [2]עָדָה **'ādâ[2]**, v. [8] [→ 538, 3586?, 3587, 3588?, 6336, 6344]. [Q] to adorn oneself, put on jewelry:– adorned (2), adorn (1), adorns (1), decked (1), put on (1), put on jewelry (1 [+6344]), take up (1)

H6336 [3]עָדָה **'ādâ[3]**, n.pr.f. [8] [√ 6344; cf. 6335]. Adah, "*adornment*":– Adah (8)

H6337 [1]עֵדָה **'ēdâ[1]**, n.f. [148] [cf. 3585]. community, assembly, with a possible focus on the unity of the congregation; this can refer to good or evil groups; human or animal groups:– community (67), assembly (52), followers (10), people (4), company (2), God's people (1), assembled (1), community's (1), flocking together (1), herd (1), household (1), nation (1), pack (1), swarm (1), NDT (4)

H6338 [2]עֵדָה **'ēdâ[2]**, n.f. [5] [√ 6386]. witness:– witness (4), witnesses (1)

H6339 [3]עֵדָה **'ēdâ[3]**, n.f. Not used in NIVEBC [√ 6386]. testimony

H6340 עִדָּה **'iddâ**, n.f. [1] menstruation:– filthy (1)

H6341 עִדּוֹ **'iddô**, n.pr.m. [4] [→ 6333, 6342; 10529]. Iddo, "[prob.] *Yahweh has adorned*":– Iddo (4)

H6342 עִדּוֹא **'iddô'**, n.pr.m. [3] [√ 6341; 10529]. Iddo, "[prob.] *Yahweh has adorned*":– Iddo (2), Iddo's (1)

H6343 עֵדוּת **'ēdût**, n.f. [83] [√ 6386]. testimony, statute, stipulation, regulation; this can also mean "the Testimony" as a formal written copy of the precepts and stipulations of a covenant:– statutes (34), covenant law (29), tablets of the covenant law (6), stipulations (4), copy of covenant (2), covenant (2), statute (2), demands (1), law (1), regulations (1), NDT (1)

H6344 עֲדִי **'ᵃdî**, n.[m.] [14] [√ 3587, 6336, 6346, 6348; cf. 6335; *also used with compound proper names*]. ornament, beautiful jewelry:– ornaments (5), jewelry (2), beautiful jewelry (1 [+7382]), bridle (1 [+8270]), desires (1), jewels (1), puberty[S] (1 [+6344]), puberty[S] (1 [+6344]), put on jewelry (1 [+6335])

H6345 עֲדָיָא **'ᵃdāyā'**, n.pr.m. Not used in NIVEBC [cf. 6347]. Adaia, see 6342

H6346 עֲדִיאֵל **'ᵃdî'ēl**, n.pr.m. [3] [√ 6344 + 446]. Adiel, "*adornment of God [El]*":– Adiel (3)

H6347 עֲדָיָה **'ᵃdāyâ**, n.pr.m. [8] [√ 6344 + 3378; cf. 6345]. Adaiah, "*adornment of Yahweh*":– Adaiah (8)

H6348 עֲדָיָהוּ **'ᵃdāyāhû**, n.pr.m. [1] [√ 6344 + 3378]. Adaiah, "*adornment of Yahweh*":– Adaiah (1)

H6349 [1]עָדִין **'ādîn[1]**, a. [1] [√ 6357]. voluptuous, wantonness:– lover of pleasure (1)

H6350 [2]עָדִין **'ādîn[2]**, n.pr.m. [4] [√ 6357]. Adin, "*voluptuous, luxurious*":– Adin (4)

H6351 עֲדִינָא **'ᵃdînā'**, n.pr.m. [1] [√ 6357]. Adina, "*adorned*":– Adina (1)

H6352 עֲדִינוֹ **'ᵃdînô**, n.pr.m. Adino

H6353 עֲדִיתַיִם **'ᵃdîtayim**, n.pr.loc. [1] Adithaim, "*double [row] of adornments*":– Adithaim (1)

H6354 עַדְלַי **'adlay**, n.pr.m. [1] Adlai, "*be just*":– Adlai (1)

H6355 עֲדֻלָּם **'ᵃdullām**, n.pr.loc. [8] [→ 6356]. Adullam, "*retreat or refuge;* [poss.] *[they are] just*":– Adullam (8)

H6356 עֲדֻלָּמִי **'ᵃdullāmî**, a.g. [3] [√ 6355]. Adullamite, of Adullam, "*of Adullam*":– Adullamite (2), of Adullam (1)

H6357 עָדַן **'ādan**, v.den. [1] [→ 5051, 5052, 6349, 6350, 6351, 6366; cf. 6367?]. [Ht] to revel in the good life, luxuriate:– reveled (1)

H6358 [1]עֵדֶן **'ēden[1]**, n.[m.] [3] [→ 6360, 6365; cf. 6363]. delight, delicacy; finery:– delicacies (1), delights (1), finery (1)

H6359 [2]עֵדֶן **'ēden[2]**, n.pr.loc. [14] Eden, "*paradise, delight,* [poss.] *flat land*":– Eden (14)

H6360 [3]עֵדֶן **'ēden[3]**, n.pr.m. [2] [√ 6358]. Eden, "*paradise, delight,* [poss.] *flat land*":– Eden (2)

H6361 עֶדֶן **'eden**, n.pr.loc. [3] [→ 1114]. Eden, "*paradise, delight,* [poss.] *flat land*":– Eden (3)

H6362 עֲדֶן **'ᵃden**, adv. [1] yet:– never (1 [+4202])

H6363 עַדְנָא **'adnā'**, n.pr.m. [2] [cf. 6358, 6365]. Adna, "*delight*":– Adna (2)

H6364 עֲדֶנָה **'ᵃdenâ**, adv. [1] [√ 6330 + 2178]. still:– still (1)

H6365 עַדְנָה **'adnâ**, n.pr.m. [1] [√ 6358; cf. 6363]. Adnah, "*delight*":– Adnah (1)

H6366 עֶדְנָה **'ednâ**, n.f. [1] [√ 6357]. (sexual) pleasure, delight:– pleasure (1)

H6367 עַדְנַח **'adnaḥ**, n.pr.m. [1] [cf. 6357?]. Adnah, "*delight*":– Adnah (1)

H6368 עַדְעָדָה **'ad'ādâ**, n.pr.loc. [1] Adadah:– Adadah (1)

H6369 עָדַף **'ādap**, v. [9] [Q] (ptcp.) what is left over, what is additional; [H] to have a surplus:– additional (2), left (2), balance (1), exceed number (1), exceeded number (1), have too much (1), left over (1)

H6370 עָדַר ***'ādar*[1]**, v. [2] [cf. 6468]. [Q] to help, serve; referring to a fighting unit that acts as a group:– help (1), volunteered to serve (1)

H6371 עָדַר ***'ādar*[2]**, v. [2] [→ 5053]. [N] to be cultivated, be weeded:– cultivated (2)

H6372 עָדַר ***'ādar*[3]**, v. [7] [→ 6373]. [N] to be missing; be lacking; [P] to let be lacking:– missing (3), fail (1), left (1), nowhere to be found (1), saw to it that was lacking (1)

H6373 עֵדֶר ***'ēder*[1]**, n.m. [38] [→ 6372]. flock, herd:– flock (15), flocks (15), herds (3), each herd (2 [+6373]), flocks and herds (1), herds (1 [+1330]), sheep (1)

H6374 עֵדֶר ***'ēder*[2]**, n.pr.m. [2] [→ 4468, 6375?, 6376, 6377]. Eder, *"flock"*:– Eder (2)

H6375 עֵדֶר ***'ēder*[3]**, n.pr.loc. [1] [√ 6374?]. Eder, *"flock"*:– Eder (1)

H6376 עֵדֶר ***'eder***, n.pr.m. [1] [√ 6374]. Eder, *"flock"*:– Eder (1)

H6377 עַדְרִיאֵל ***'adrî'ēl***, n.pr.m. [2] [√ 6374 + 446]. Adriel, *"[my] help is God [El]"*:– Adriel (2)

H6378 עֲדָשִׁים ***'ᵃdāšîm***, n.f. [4] lentils:– lentils (3), lentil (1)

H6379 עַוָּא ***'awwā'***, n.pr.loc. [1] [cf. 6393]. Avva:– Avva (1)

H6380 עוּב ***'ûb***, v.den. [1] [→ 6265, 6266?]. [H] to cover with a cloud:– covered with the cloud (1)

H6381 עוֹבֵד ***'ôbēd***, n.pr.m. [10] [√ 6268]. Obed, *"servant [worshiper]"*:– Obed (10)

H6382 עוֹבָל ***'ôbāl***, n.pr.g. [2] [cf. 6508]. Obal:– Obal (2)

H6383 עוּג ***'ûg***, v.den. [1] [→ 5056, 6314]. [Q] to bake a (round, flat) cake of bread:– bake (1)

H6384 עוֹג ***'ôg***, n.pr.m. [22] Og:– Og (20), Og's (2)

H6385 עוּגָב ***'ûgāb***, n.m. [4] [cf. 6311]. flute:– pipe (3), pipes (1)

H6386 עוּד ***'ûd*[1]**, v.den. [44] [→ 537, 6332, 6338, 6339, 6343, 6388, 6389, 9496; cf. 6387]. [P] to surround (with ropes); [Pil] to sustain, relieve; [H] to admonish, warn, charge, declare; to testify, to call on a witness; [Ho] to be warned; [Htpol] to hold each other up; from the base meaning of binding (with ropes) come the fig. extensions of "to warn, charge, testify" (bind with words) and "to help, sustain" (bind oneself to another in aid and comfort):– warned (7), warn (4), testify (3), call as witnesses (2), sustains (2), warn solemnly (2 [+6386]), warned (2 [+6386]), warned solemnly (2 [+6386]), warned to keep (2), been warned (1), bind (1), brought charges against (1), call to testify (1), called in as witnesses (1 [+6332]), commended (1), gave charge (1), give warning (1), had witnessed (1 [+6332]), have bring charges (1), have the transaction witnessed (1 [+6332]), say (1), solemnly declared (1), stand firm (1), testified (1), witness (1), witnessed (1 [+6332]), NDT (1)

H6387 עוּד ***'ûd*[2]**, v. Not used in NIVEBC [cf. 6386]. [Q, H] to bear witness

H6388 עוֹד ***'ôd***, subst. (used as adv.) [489] [√ 6386; 10531]. longer, again, still, more:– longer (74), again (72), still (54), more (36), again (21 [+3578]), while still (16), other (11), another (9), anymore (9), continued (8), yet (7), more (6 [+3578]), within (6 [+928]), further (5), longer (5 [+3578]), never (5 [+4202]), also (4), anymore (4 [+3578]), besides (4), else (4), once again (4), another (3 [+337]), any longer (3), all the more (2 [+3578]), any more (2), as long as (2 [+3972]), as long as live (2 [+928]), even (2), left (2), more (2 [+337]), once again (2 [+3578]), once more (2 [+3578]), overwhelmed (2 [+4202, 2118, 8120, 928]), remain (2), remained (2), remains (2), soon (2 [+5071]), still another (2), stopped (2 [+4202, 3578]), while (2), added (1), all life (1 [+4946]), almost (1 [+5071]), always (1 [+4946]), another (1 [+3578]), any (1 [+4946]), any longer (1 [+3578]), as long as (1), as long as (1 [+561]), awaits (1), back (1), back (1 [+3578]), before (1 [+4202]), but also (1), continue (1), continued (1 [+3578]), do again (1 [+3578]), even as (1), even more (1), ever (1), ever again (1), failed (1 [+4202, 7756]), for (1), from now (1 [+928]), from now on (1), furthermore (1 [+2256]), how long (1 [+339, 5503]), in (1), in a very short time (1 [+5071, 4663]), kept on (1), left now (1), little while (1 [+5071]), long time (1), make again (1 [+3578]), moreover (1), never (1 [+1153]), next (1), not enough (1 [+7781]), now (1), on (1), once more (1), only (1), others (1), reappears (1 [+8011]), reconsider (1 [+8740]), regain (1 [+6806]), return (1 [+995]), since then (1), something else (1), stands (1), still (1 [+3972]), still (1 [+8636]), still another (1 [+3578]), time (1), very soon (1 [+5071, 4663]), were added (1 [+3578]), while (1 [+928]), yet to come (1), NDT (27)

H6389 עוֹדֵד ***'ōdēd***, n.pr.m. [3] [√ 6386]. Oded, *"restorer"*:– Oded (3)

H6390 עָוָה ***'āwâ*[1]**, v. [17] [→ 6392, 6411, 6412, 6413, 6505; cf. 6391]. [Q] to do wrong; [N] to be perverse, be warped; [P] to ruin, make crooked; [H] to do wrong, pervert; from the base meaning of twisting an object comes the fig. extension of twisting morality: to be perverse, to do wrong:– done wrong (6), perverted (2), am staggered (1), bowed down (1), did wrong (1), does wrong (1), made crooked (1), perverse (1), ruin (1), sinning (1), warped (1)

H6391 עָוָה ***'āwâ*[2]**, v.den. Not used in NIVEBC [cf. 6390]. [Q] to do wrong; [H] to commit iniquity

H6392 עַוָּה ***'awwâ*[1]**, n.f. [3] [→ 6504, 6509; cf. 6390]. ruin, wreckage, rubble:– ruin (3)

H6393 עַוָּה ***'awwâ*[2]**, n.pr.loc. Not used in NIVEBC [→ 6398, 6399; cf. 6379]. Avvah, see 6394

H6394 עִוָּה ***'iwwâ***, n.pr.loc. [3] [√ 6399]. Ivvah:– Ivvah (3)

H6395 עוּז ***'ûz***, v. [5] [→ 6437; cf. 6451]. [Q] to take refuge; [H] to bring to refuge, give shelter:– flee for safety (2), bring to a place of shelter (1), look for help (1), take cover (1)

H6396 עֲוִיל ***'ᵃwîl*[1]**, n.m. [2] [√ 6402]. little boys:– children (1), little boys (1)

H6397 עֲוִיל ***'ᵃwîl*[2]**, n.m. [1] [√ 6401]. evil one, unjust one:– ungodly (1)

H6398 עַוִּים ***'awwîm*[1]**, a.g. [3] [√ 6393]. Avvite:– Avvites (3)

H6399 עַוִּים ***'awwîm*[2]**, n.pr.loc. [1] [√ 6393; cf. 6394]. Avvim:– Avvim (1)

H6400 עֲוִית ***'ᵃwît***, n.pr.loc. [2] [cf. 6511]. Avith:– Avith (2)

H6401 עָוַל ***'āwal*[1]**, v.den. [2] [→ 6397, 6404, 6405, 6406, 6637]. [P] to do evil, act wrong:– doing evil (1), evil (1)

H6402 עוּל ***'ûl*[2]**, v. [5] [→ 6396, 6403, 6407, 6408]. [Q] to nurse, suckle:– calved (1), have young (1), nursing young (1), sheep (1), such[S] (1)

H6403 עוּל ***'ûl*[3]**, n.m. [4] [√ 6402]. nursing infant, baby:– infant (2), baby at breast (1), little child (1)

H6404 עָוֶל ***'āwel***, n.m. [21] [√ 6401]. wrong, evil, sin, injustice, what is morally perverted, warped, and twisted, an extension of the base meaning of a physically twisted, crooked object (not found in the OT):– evil (5), dishonest (3), sin (3), wrong (3), dishonestly (1), doing wrong (1), fault (1), guilt (1), pervert (1 [+6913]), unjust (1), ways (1)

H6405 עַוָּל ***'awwāl***, n.m. [6] [√ 6401]. wicked one, evil one, unjust one:– wicked (2), evil man (1), unjust (1), unrighteous (1), wrongdoers (1)

H6406 עַוְלָה ***'awlâ***, n.f. & m. [32] [√ 6401; cf. 6593, 6637]. wickedness, evil, injustice:– wicked (6), injustice (5), wickedness (5), wrong (5), evil (4), wicked (2 [+1201]), anything wicked (1), false (1), unjust (1), wickedly (1), wrongdoing (1)

H6407 עוֹלֵל ***'ôlēl***, n.m. [11] [√ 6402]. child, little one:– children (6), little ones (2), infant (1), infants (1), little children (1)

H6408 עוֹלָל ***'ôlāl***, n.m. [9] [√ 6402]. child, little one:– children (7), infants (2)

H6409 עוֹלָם ***'ôlām***, n.m. [440] [cf. 6518; 10550]. everlasting, forever, eternity; from of old, ancient, lasting, for a duration:– forever (134 [+4200]), everlasting (56), forever (44 [+6330]), lasting (26), forever (21), ancient (13), ever (9), perpetual (9), never (8 [+4202, 4200]), of old (7), always (5 [+4200]), ever (5 [+6330]), for ever (5), forevermore (5 [+6330]), eternal (4), ever (4 [+4200]), long ago (4), always (3), always (3 [+6330]), ancient (3 [+4946]), ancient times (3), eternal (3 [+4200]), for life (3), age-old (2), ever (2 [+4946]), everlasting (2 [+6330]), forever (2 [+6330, 2021]), forever (2 [+6330, 4200]), long (2), long ago (2 [+4946]), more (2 [+6330]), never (2 [+440, 4200]), never (2 [+4202, 6330]), never again (2 [+4202, 4200]), old (2), permanent (2), again (1 [+4200]), ages (1), all eternity (1), all time (1), any time (1), as long as live (1 [+3972, 3427, 4200]), completely (1 [+4200]), continue (1), continued (1), early times (1), endless (1 [+6330]), eternity (1), everlasting (1 [+3972]), everlasting (1 [+4200]), for life (1 [+4200]), forevermore (1 [+6330, 2021]), gone by (1), lasting (1 [+4200]), lasting (1 [+6330]), lasting (1 [+9458]), life (1), long (1 [+4200]), long (1 [+4946]), long ages ago (1 [+4946]), long ago (1 [+4200]), long time (1), never (1 [+4202]), never (1 [+4200, 1153]), never (1 [+401, 4200]), never (1 [+1153, 4200]), never (1 [+561, 6330]), never (1 [+1153, 2256, 6329]), of old (1 [+4946]), to come (1), to the very end (1 [+4200, 6813]), used to be (1 [+3427]), NDT (1)

H6410 עוּן ***'ûn***, v. [2] [→ 5061]. [Q] to dwell:– dwell (1), inhabit (1)

H6411 עָוֹן ***'āwōn***, n.m. [233] [√ 6390; 10532]. sin, wickedness, iniquity, often with a focus on the guilt or liability incurred, and the punishment to follow:– sin (60), sins (50), guilt (32), iniquity (12), wickedness (12), iniquities (10), punishment (9), held responsible (7 [+5951]), crime (4), guilty (4), wicked (4), consequences of sin (3), responsibility for offenses (3), wrongdoing (3), offense (2), sinful (2), wrong (2), affliction (1), crimes (1), evil deeds (1), fault (1), faults (1), offenses (1), pardon (1 [+1065, 2021]), pardon (1 [+2021, 6584]), punished (1), punished (1 [+7936]), sins (1 [+1821]), wrongdoings (1), wrongs (1), NDT (1)

H6412 עוֹנָה ***'ônâ***, n.f. Not used in NIVEBC [√ 6390]. sin, see 6411

H6413 עִוְעִים ***'iw'îm***, n.pl.abst. [1] [√ 6390]. (col. pl.) dizziness, staggering, frenzy:– dizziness (1)

H6414 עוּף ***'ûp*[1]**, v. [24] [→ 6416]. [Q] to fly; [Pol] to dart about (of a flying bird or a snake); [H] to let (eyes) glance; [Ht] to fly away:– fly away (4), darting (3), flew (3), fly (3), flying (3), flies (2), cast (1), flies away (1), fly along (1), fly off (1), hovering overhead (1), swoop down (1)

H6415 עוּף ***'ûp*[2]**, v. Not used in NIVEBC [→ 4599, 5066, 6757, 9507; cf. 6547]. [Q] to be dark

H6416 עוֹף ***'ôp***, n.m. [71] [√ 6414; 10533]. bird, winged creatures, flying creatures:– birds (37), birds (16 [+2021, 9028]), bird (12), flying (4), birds (1 [+4053]), winged creature (1)

H6417 עוֹפַי ***'ôpay***, n.pr.m. Not used in NIVEBC [cf. 6550]. Ophai, see 6550

H6418 עוּץ ***'ûṣ*[1]**, v. [2] [cf. 3619]. [Q] to consider, devise, plan:– devise (1), must do something (1)

H6419 עוּץ ***'ûṣ*[2]**, n.pr.m. [5] Uz:– Uz (5)

H6420 עוּץ ***'ûṣ*[3]**, n.pr.loc. [3] Uz:– Uz (2), Uz (1 [+824])

H6421 עוּק ***'ûq***, v. [2] [→ 4601?, 6821]. [Q] to crush, totter; [H] to crush, cause to totter:– crush (1), crushes (1)

H6422 עָוַר ***'āwar*[1]**, v. [5] [→ 6426, 6427, 6428]. [P] to make blind:– put out (3), blinds (2)

H6423 עוּר ***'ûr*[2]**, v. [1] [→ 5067, 6425?; cf. 6867]. [N] to be uncovered, be laid bare:– uncovered (1 [+6880])

H6424 עוּר ***'ûr*[3]**, v. [81] [→ 3600, 6552, 6555, 6749, 6841, 6878, 6879]. [Q] to awake; [N] to be aroused, stirred up, wakened; [Pol] to awaken, arouse, raise up; [Pil] to raise, keep up; [H] to stir up, rouse, waken; [Htpol] to rouse oneself:– awake (16), stir up (8), awaken (6), rouse (6), stirred up (6), wake up (5), raised (4), arouse (3), moved (3), arise (2), aroused (2), be roused (2), stirs up (2), wakens (2), awakened (1), being stirred up (1), gloated (1), lament (1 [+2411]), lash (1), raise up (1), rising (1), roused (1), roused himself (1), rouses (1), stir (1), strives (1), whoever he may be (1 [+2256, 6699]), woke up (1)

H6425 עוֹר ***'ôr***, n.m. [99] [√ 6423?]. skin, hide, leather:– skin (39), leather (20), hide (8), skin (8 [+1414]), durable leather (6), skins (6), face (3 [+7156]), flesh (1), goatskins (1 [+1531, 6436]), hides (1), its[S] (1 [+2021]), nothing but skin (1 [+2256, 1414]), NDT (4)

H6426 עִוֵּר ***'iwwēr***, a. [26] [√ 6422]. blind:– blind (26)

H6427 עִוָּרוֹן ***'iwwārôn***, n.[m.] [2] [√ 6422]. blindness, blinding:– blind (1 [+5782, 928, 2021]), blindness (1)

H6428 עַוֶּרֶת ***'awweret***, n.f. [1] [√ 6422]. blindness:– blind (1)

H6429 עוּשׁ ***'ûš***, v. [1] [→ 3447, 3593, 3601; cf. 6431]. [Q] to be quick or to help:– quickly (1)

H6430 עָוַת ***'āwat***, v. [11] [→ 6432]. [P] to make crooked, pervert; [Pu] to be twisted, be made crooked; [Ht] to stoop down, bend over; from the base meaning of twisting an object comes the fig. extension of twisting morality: to pervert:– pervert (3), cheating (1), deprive (1), frustrates (1), is crooked (1), made crooked (1), stoop (1), wronged (1), wronging (1)

H6431 עוּת ***'ût***, v. [1] [√ 6433; cf. 6429]. [Q] to sustain, help:– sustains (1)

H6432 עַוָּתָה ***'awwātâ***, n.f. [1] [√ 6430]. wrong:– wrong done (1)

H6433 עוּתַי ***'ûtay***, n.pr.m. [2] [√ 6431]. Uthai, "[poss.] *superiority of Yahweh;* [poss.] *[my] restoration"*:– Uthai (2)

H6434 עַז ***'az***, a. [23] [→ 6456?; cf. 6451]. strong, mighty, powerful, fierce:– strong (5), mighty (4), fierce (3), powerful (3), fierce-looking (2 [+7156]), fortified (1), great (1), harshly (1), strength (1), stronger (1), stronghold (1)

H6435 עַז ***'āz***, n.m. [1] [√ 6451]. power, strength:– power (1)

H6436 עֵז ***'ēz***, n.m. [74] [√ 6451?; 10535]. goat; goat hair:– male goat (24 [+8538]), goats (12), goat (8), goat hair (7), young goat (7 [+1531]), goat (2 [+7618]), goat (2 [+8538]), goat (2 [+8544]), goats hair (2 [+3889]), male goats (2 [+8538]), goat (1 [+8445]), goats (1 [+1201]), goatskins (1 [+6425, 1531]), male goats (1 [+7618]), young goat (1), young goats (1 [+1531])

H6437 עֹז ***'ōz***, n.m. [92] [→ 6454, 6459, 6460; cf. 6395, 6451]. strength, power, might; stronghold, fortification; strong-willed, stubborn;:– strength (38), power (12), strong (10), mighty (8), might (5), fortified (4), stronghold (4), feeble (1 [+4202]), firm (1), fortress (1), great (1), great power (1), greatly emboldened (1 [+8104]), hard (1), resounding (1), strongholds (1), stubborn (1), vigorously (1 [+928])

H6438 עֻזָּא ***'uzzā'***, n.pr.m. [11] [→ 6446]. Uzza, Uzzah, *"strong, fierce one"*:– Uzzah (6), Uzza (5)

H6439 עֲזָאזֵל ***'ᵃzā'zēl***, n.[m. *or* pr.] [4] scapegoat, a goat sent into the wilderness of the Day of Atonement, symbolically carrying away the sin of the community; some see this word as the name of the desert spirit (Azazel) to whom the goat is sent:– scapegoat (4)

H6440 עָזַב ***'āzab*[1]**, v. [212] [→ 6442, 6447, 6448]. [Q] to leave, abandon, reject, desert; [Qp] be left, be abandoned, be freed; [N] be abandoned, be forsaken, be neglected; [Pu] be deserted, be abandoned:– forsake (37), forsaken (36), leave (25), left (20), abandoned (18), deserted (10), forsook (8), abandon (6), forsaking (5), free (5), rejected (4), leaves (3), neglect (3), desert (2), deserts (2), fails (2), rejecting (2), be abandoned (1), be laid waste (1), be left (1), been abandoned (1), change (1), commit (1), forsakes (1), gave up (1), give free rein (1), give up (1), go (1), ignores (1), is forsaken (1), is neglected (1), lays (1), leaving (1), left behind (1), left destitute (1), renounces (1), stop (1), stopped showing (1), turn away from (1), turn from (1), vanish (1)

H6441 [2]עָזַב **'āzab[2]**, v. [4] [Q] to restore, help:– be sure help (2 [+6441]), restore wall (1), restored (1)

H6442 עִזְבוֹנִים **'izbônîm**, n.[m.] [7] [√ 6440]. merchandise, goods:– merchandise (6), wares (1)

H6443 עַזְבּוּק **'azbûq**, n.pr.m. [1] [√ 1011?]. Azbuk:– Azbuk (1)

H6444 עַזְגָּד **'azgād**, n.pr.m. [4] Azgad, "*strong is Gad*":– Azgad (4)

H6445 עַזָּה **'azzâ**, n.pr.loc. [20] [→ 6484]. Gaza, "*strong*":– Gaza (20)

H6446 עֻזָּא **'uzzā**, n.pr.m. [3] [→ 7290; cf. 6438]. Uzzah, "*strong, fierce*":– Uzzah (3)

H6447 [1]עֲזוּבָה **'azûbâ[1]**, n.f. Not used in NIVEBC [√ 6440]. forsaking, desolation

H6448 [2]עֲזוּבָה **'azûbâ[2]**, n.pr.f. [4] [√ 6440]. Azubah, "*adornment*":– Azubah (4)

H6449 עֱזוּז **'ezûz**, n.[m.] [3] [√ 6451]. power, strength:– power (2), violence (1)

H6450 עִזּוּז **'izzûz**, a. [2] [√ 6451]. strong, powerful:– reinforcements (1), strong (1)

H6451 עָזַז **'āzaz**, v. [11] [→ 5057, 5058, 6434, 6435, 6436?, 6449, 6450, 6452, 6453, 6456, 6461, 6464; cf. 3594, 6395, 6437]. [Q] to be strong, overpower; [H] to put on a bold face, be brazen:– strong (2), brazen (1), fixed securely (1), makes powerful (1), oppressive (1), overpowered (1 [+3338, 6584]), put up a bold front (1 [+928, 7156]), show strength (1), triumph (1), triumphant (1)

H6452 עָזָז **'āzāz**, n.pr.m. [1] [√ 6451]. Azaz, "*strong*":– Azaz (1)

H6453 עֲזַזְיָהוּ **'azazyāhû**, n.pr.m. [3] [√ 6451 + 3378]. Azaziah, "*Yahweh is strong*":– Azaziah (3)

H6454 עֻזִּי **'uzzî**, n.pr.m. [11] [√ 6437]. Uzzi, "*Yahweh is [my] strength*":– Uzzi (11)

H6455 עֻזִּיָּא **'uzziyyā'**, n.pr.m. [1] [cf. 6459]. Uzzia, "*[my] strength* or *Yahweh is [my] strength*":– Uzzia (1)

H6456 עֲזִיאֵל **'azî'ēl**, n.pr.m. [1] [√ 6434? + 446?]. Aziel, "*God is my strength*":– Jaaziel (1)

H6457 עֻזִּיאֵל **'uzzî'ēl**, n.pr.m. [16] [→ 6458; cf. 6437 + 446]. Uzziel, "*God [El] is [my] strength*":– Uzziel (16)

H6458 עָזִּיאֵלִי **'ozzî'ēlî**, a.g. [2] [√ 6457; cf. 6437 + 446]. Uzzielite, "*of Uzziel*":– Uzzielites (2)

H6459 עֻזִּיָּה **'uzziyyâ**, n.pr.m. [8] [√ 6437 + 3378; cf. 6455]. Uzziah, "*Yahweh is [my] strength*":– Uzziah (8)

H6460 עֻזִּיָּהוּ **'uzziyyāhû**, n.pr.m. [19] [√ 6437 + 3378]. Uzziah, "*Yahweh is [my] strength*":– Uzziah (18), Uzziah's (1)

H6461 עֲזִיזָא **'azîzā'**, n.pr.m. [1] [√ 6451]. Aziza, "*powerful*":– Aziza (1)

H6462 [1]עַזְמָוֶת **'azmāwet[1]**, n.pr.m. [6] [→ 1115, 6463]. Azmaveth, "*strong one of death; camel fodder, plant of the plumose family*":– Azmaveth (6)

H6463 [2]עַזְמָוֶת **'azmāwet[2]**, n.pr.loc. [2] [√ 6462]. Azmaveth, "*strong one of death; camel fodder, plant of the plumose family*":– Azmaveth (2)

H6464 עַזָּן **'azzān**, n.pr.m. [1] [√ 6451]. Azzan, "*strong*":– Azzan (1)

H6465 עָזְנִיָּה **'ozniyyâ**, n.f. [2] black vulture:– black vulture (2)

H6466 עָזַק **'āzaq**, v. [1] [P] to dig:– dug up (1)

H6467 עֲזֵקָה **'azēqâ**, n.pr.loc. [7] Azekah, "[poss.] *hoe [the ground]*":– Azekah (7)

H6468 עָזַר **'āzar**, v. [81] [→ 540, 3597, 6469, 6470, 6474, 6475, 6478, 6479, 6481; cf. 6370]. [Q] to help, support; [Qp] to be helped; [N] to be helped:– help (45), helped (12), helps (5), helper (2), allied with (1), allies (1), are helped (1), assist (1), came to rescue (1), cohorts (1), gave support (1 [+339]), give support (1), helpers (1), protect (1), receive help (1 [+6469]), support (1), supported (1), sustain (1), was helped (1), went too far (1), were helped (1)

H6469 [1]עֵזֶר **'ēzer[1]**, n.m. [21] [→ 2193, 6470, 6471, 6472, 6476, 6477; cf. 6468; *also used with compound proper names*]. help, helper:– help (13), helper (5), receive help (1 [+6468]), staff (1), strength (1)

H6470 [2]עֵזֶר **'ēzer[2]**, n.pr.m. [4] [√ 6469; cf. 6468]. Ezer, "*help*":– Ezer (4)

H6471 [1]עֶזֶר **'ezer[1]**, n.pr.loc. Not used in NIVEBC [√ 6469]. Ezer, see 75, "*help*"

H6472 [2]עֶזֶר **'ezer[2]**, n.pr.m. [1] [√ 6469]. Ezer, "*help*":– Ezer (1)

H6473 עַזּוּר **'azzur**, n.pr.m. [3] Azzur, "*help*":– Azzur (3)

H6474 עֶזְרָא **'ezrā'**, n.pr.m. [22] [√ 6468; 10537]. Ezra, "*help*":– Ezra (21), Ezra's (1)

H6475 עֲזַרְאֵל **'azar'ēl**, n.pr.m. [6] [√ 6468 + 446]. Azarel, "*God [El] has helped*":– Azarel (6)

H6476 [1]עֶזְרָה **'ezrâ[1]**, n.f. [28] [→ 6477; cf. 6469]. help, aid, support; helper, ally:– help (21), aid (3), allies (1), helper (1), influence (1), support (1)

H6477 [2]עֶזְרָה **'ezrâ[2]**, n.pr.m. [1] [√ 6476]. Ezrah:– Ezrah (1)

H6478 עֲזָרָה **'azārâ**, n.f. [9] [√ 6468]. court, enclosure; ledge, barrier:– ledge (4), court (2), ledge that goes around (2), outer court (1)

H6479 עֶזְרִי **'ezrî**, n.pr.m. [1] [√ 6468 + 3378? *or* 3276?]. Ezri, "*my help*":– Ezri (1)

H6480 עַזְרִיאֵל **'azrî'ēl**, n.pr.m. [3] [√ 6469 + 446]. Azriel, "*God [El] is [my] help*":– Azriel (3)

H6481 עֲזַרְיָה **'azaryâ**, n.pr.m. [32] [√ 6468 + 3378; 10538]. Azariah, "*Yahweh has helped*":– Azariah (31), Azariah's (1)

H6482 עֲזַרְיָהוּ **'azaryāhû**, n.pr.m. [16] [√ 6469 + 3378]. Azariah; Azariahu, "*Yahweh has helped*":– Azariah (14), Azariahu (1), Azariah's (1)

H6483 עַזְרִיקָם **'azrîqām**, n.pr.m. [6] [√ 6469 + 7756]. Azrikam, "*[my] help arises*":– Azrikam (6)

H6484 עַזָּתִי **'azzātî**, a.g. [2] [√ 6445]. Gazite, "*of Gaza*":– Gaza (1), people of Gaza (1)

H6485 עֵט **'ēṭ**, n.m. [4] (iron) engraving tool, stylus; (reed) pen:– pen (2), tool (2)

H6486 [1]עָטָה **'āṭâ[1]**, v. [13] [→ 5073; cf. 3598]. [Q] to cover, wrap oneself; [H] cover, wrap another (thing):– cover (5), wrapped (2), covered (1), covered with a mantle (1), veiled (1), wearing (1), wrapped himself (1), wraps himself (1)

H6487 [2]עָטָה **'āṭâ[2]**, v. [5] [Q] to grasp; to pick clean of lice; [Pu] to be grasped:– take firm hold (2 [+6487]), is grasped (1), pick clean (1), picks clean of lice (1)

H6488 עָטוּף **'āṭûp**, a. *or* v.ptcp. [2] [√ 6494]. weak, faint:– faint (1), weak (1)

H6489 עֲטִין **'aṭîn**, n.[m.] [1] body, part of body; or pail, bucket:– body (1)

H6490 עֲטִישָׁה **'aṭîšâ**, n.f. [1] snorting, sneezing:– snorting (1)

H6491 עֲטַלֵּף **'aṭallēp**, n.[m.] [3] [√ 6493 + 4200]. bat (animal):– bat (2), bats (1)

H6492 עֲטָם **'āṭām**, n.f. Not used in NIVEBC [√ 6793]. thigh

H6493 [1]עָטַף **'āṭap[1]**, v. [3] [→ 5074, 6491; cf. 6495]. [Q] to clothe, mantle; to turn aside:– clothe (1 [+8884]), mantled (1), turns (1)

H6494 [2]עָטַף **'āṭap[2]**, v. [11] [→ 6488]. [Q] to grow faint; [N] to be faint; [H] to be feeble; [Ht] to ebb away, grow faint:– faint (6), weak (2), ebbed away (1), ebbing away (1), faint away (1)

H6495 [3]עָטַף **'āṭap[3]**, v. Not used in NIVEBC [cf. 6493]. [Q, N, H, Ht] to be feeble

H6496 [1]עָטַר **'āṭar[1]**, v. [2] [→ 6497, 6498, 6499, 6500, 6501, 6502, 6503]. [Q] to surround, close in upon:– closing in (1), surround (1)

H6497 [2]עָטַר **'āṭar[2]**, v.den. [5] [√ 6496]. [P] to crown, place a wreath (on the head); [H] to bestow a crown:– crowned (2), bestower of crowns (1), crown (1), crowns (1)

H6498 [1]עֲטָרָה **'aṭārâ[1]**, n.f. [23] [√ 6496]. crown, wreath, placed on the head as a symbol of celebration or status; can be made of plants or precious metals:– crown (18), wreath (3), crowns (2)

H6499 [2]עֲטָרָה **'aṭārâ[2]**, n.pr.f. [1] [√ 6496]. Atarah, "*circlet, wreath*":– Atarah (1)

H6500 עֲטָרוֹת **'aṭārôt**, n.pr.loc. [4] [→ 6501, 6502; cf. 6496]. Ataroth, "*circlets, wreaths*":– Ataroth (4)

H6501 עַטְרוֹת אַדָּר **'aṭrôt 'addār**, n.pr.loc. [2] [√ 6500 + 162]. Ataroth Addar, "*wreaths of majesty*":– Ataroth Addar (2)

H6502 עַטְרוֹת בֵּית יוֹאָב **'aṭrôt bêt yô'āb**, n.pr.loc. [1] [√ 6500 + 1074 + 3405]. Atroth Beth Joab, "*circlets, folds of the house of Joab*":– Atroth Beth Joab (1)

H6503 עַטְרוֹת שׁוֹפָן **'aṭrôt šôpān**, n.pr.loc. [1] [√ 6496 + 8794]. Atroth Shophan, "*circlets, folds of Shophan*":– Atroth Shophan (1)

H6504 עַי **'ay**, n.pr.loc. [38] [→ 6509; cf. 6392]. Ai, "*ruin, the heap*":– Ai (36), city[s] (1), who[s] (1 [+408, 2021])

H6505 עִי **'î**, n.[m.] [7] [→ 1247, 5075, 6510, 6516, 6517; cf. 6390]. heap of rubble; (of a person) a broken man:– heap of rubble (5), broken man (1), rubble (1)

H6506 [1]עֵיבָל **'êbāl[1]**, n.pr.loc. [4] [→ 6507]. Ebal:– Ebal (4)

H6507 [2]עֵיבָל **'êbāl[2]**, n.pr.m. & g. [3] [√ 6506]. Ebal:– Ebal (3)

H6508 [3]עֵיבָל **'êbāl[3]**, n.pr.m. Not used in NIVEBC [cf. 6382]. Ebal, see 6382

H6509 עַיָּה **'ayyâ**, n.pr.loc. [2] [√ 6504; cf. 6569]. Ayyah; Aija, "*ruin, heap*":– Aija (1), Ayyah (1)

H6510 עִיּוֹן **'iyyôn**, n.pr.loc. [3] [√ 6505]. Ijon, "*place of heaps [of stone]*":– Ijon (3)

H6511 עַיּוֹת **'ayôt**, n.pr.loc. Not used in NIVEBC [cf. 6400]. Aioth, see 6400

H6512 [1]עִיט **'îṭ[1]**, v. [1] [cf. 6513]. [Q] to hurl insults:– hurled insults (1)

H6513 [2]עִיט **'îṭ[2]**, v.den. [2] [→ 6514, 6515?; cf. 6512]. [Q] to pounce upon (with shrieks and screams):– pounce (1), pounced (1)

H6514 עַיִט **'ayiṭ**, n.m. [8] [→ 6515?; cf. 6513]. (coll) birds of prey, carrion birds:– bird of prey (3), birds of prey (3), birds (1), carrion birds (1 [+7606])

H6515 עֵיטָם **'êṭām**, n.pr.loc. [5] [√ 6514? + 4392?]. Etam, "[poss.] *place of birds of prey*":– Etam (5)

H6516 עִיֵּי הָעֲבָרִים **'iyyê hā'abārîm**, n.pr.loc. [2] [√ 6505 + 2192]. Iye Abarim, "*heaps of Abarim [regions beyond]*":– Iye Abarim (2)

H6517 עִיִּים **'iyyîm**, n.pr.loc. [2] [√ 6505]. Iyim; Iim, "*heaps, ruins*", a shortened form of Iye Abarim [6516]:– Iye Abarim (1), Iyim (1)

H6518 עֵילוֹם **'êlôm**, n.m. Not used in NIVEBC [cf. 6409]. forever, see 6409

H6519 עִילַי **'îlay**, n.pr.m. [1] Ilai:– Ilai (1)

H6520 [1]עֵילָם **'êlām[1]**, n.pr.g. & loc. [15] [→ 6521; 10551]. Elam, "*highland*":– Elam (14), Elam's (1)

H6521 [2]עֵילָם **'êlām[2]**, n.pr.m. [13] [√ 6520; 10551]. Elam, "*highland*":– Elam (13)

H6522 עַיָם **'ayām**, n.[m.] [1] scorching (of wind):– scorching (1)

H6523 עָיַן **'āyan**, v.den. [1] [√ 6524]. [Q] to keep an eye on, look at (with suspicion or jealousy):– kept a close eye on (1)

H6524 [1]עַיִן **'ayin[1]**, n.f. & m. [884] [→ 5078, 6523, 6526, 6543, 6544; cf. 6525; 10540; *also used with compound proper names*]. eye; by extension: sight; spring, fountain; to be "evil of eye" is to be displeased; to be "good of eye" is to be pleased; to be "good in one's eyes" is to be pleasing "right in one's eyes" means acceptable by one's personal standards:– eyes (430), sight (63), eye (40), looked (25), presence (14), seems (9 [+928]), spring (9), think (9 [+928]), seemed (8 [+928]), before (6 [+4200]), look with pity (6 [+2571]), displeased (5 [+8317, 928]), face (5), look (5 [+5951]), look (5), pleased (5 [+3512, 928]), pleased with (5 [+5162, 2834, 928]), like (4 [+3202, 928]), show pity (4 [+2571]), wish (4 [+3202, 928]), with (4 [+928]), favorably disposed toward (3 [+2834, 928]), fountain (3), looked (3 [+5951]), saw (3 [+928]), seem (3 [+928]), watch (3 [+4200]), watched (3 [+4200]), appearance (2), by (2 [+928]), distressed (2 [+8317, 928]), have respect for (2 [+3700, 928]), in presence (2 [+4200, 5584]), look after (2 [+8492, 6584]), look carefully (2 [+8011, 928]), looked with pity (2 [+2571]), on forehead (2 [+1068]), on foreheads (2 [+1068]), please (2 [+3837, 928]), please (2 [+3202, 928]), pleased (2 [+3202, 928]), pleased (2 [+3837, 928]), pleased (2 [+3512, 928]), see (2), sparkled (2), spring (2 [+4784]), springs (2 [+4784]), thought (2 [+928]), to (2 [+928]), watching (2), watching (2 [+4200]), angry (1 [+3013, 928]), appealed to (1 [+3512, 928]), appear (1 [+2118, 928, 3869]), approve of (1 [+3202, 928]), begrudge (1 [+8317]), begrudging host (1 [+8273]), by (1 [+4200]), consider (1 [+928]), considered (1 [+928]), cover the offense (1 [+4064]), despise (1 [+1022, 928]), despise (1 [+7837, 928]), despises (1 [+1022, 928]), despises (1 [+7837, 928]), disappeared (1 [+2143, 4946]), disapprove (1 [+8317, 928]), displease (1 [+8273, 928]), displease (1 [+4202, 5162, 2834, 928]), displeased greatly (1 [+8317, 928]), displeasing (1 [+8273, 928]), displeasing (1 [+4202, 5162, 2834, 928]), downcast (1 [+8814]), eyebrows (1 [+1461]), eyes (1 [+1426]), favorable toward (1 [+5162, 2834, 928]), for (1 [+928]), fountains (1), from (1 [+928]), from (1 [+4946]), front of heads (1 [+1068]), full view (1), generous (1 [+3202]), glad (1 [+3512, 928]), glance (1), gleam (1), have no (1 [+6259, 4946]), have no compassion (1 [+8317]), in broad daylight (1 [+4200, 2021, 9087, 2021, 2296]), in front of (1 [+4200]), in full view (1 [+5790]), in full view of (1 [+4200]), keeping watch (1 [+8011, 928]), like (1 [+3869]), liked (1 [+3837, 928]), look (1 [+928]), look around (1 [+5951, 2256, 8011]), look up (1 [+5951]), look with approval (1 [+8883, 4200, 5584]), look with compassion (1 [+2571]), look with longing (1 [+5951]), looked (1 [+906]), looked (1 [+2118, 928]), looked about (1 [+5951]), looks (1 [+5951]), lost self-confidence (1 [+5877, 4394, 928]), mindful (1 [+4200, 5584]), never (1 [+440]), not please (1 [+8317, 928]), not want (1 [+8273, 928]), outward appearance (1), people[s] (1 [+2257]), please (1 [+3838, 928]), please (1 [+3202, 2256, 3838, 928]), pleased (1 [+3838, 928]), pleased (1 [+3201, 928]), pleased with (1 [+3202, 928]), pleased with (1 [+3512, 928]), pleased with (1 [+3837, 928]), pleased with (1 [+5951, 2834, 928]), pleases (1 [+3512, 928]), pleases (1 [+3202, 928]), prefer (1 [+3202, 928]), publicly (1 [+4200]), regards (1 [+5162, 928]), satisfied (1 [+3512, 928]), saw (1 [+5260]), saw (1 [+5951, 906]), scorned the idea (1 [+1022, 928]), see (1 [+448]), see (1 [+928]), see (1 [+4200]), see (1 [+5260]), see (1 [+8011]), see (1 [+8492]), see (1 [+8011, 4200, 2021]), see for yourselves (1 [+8011, 4013]), see to it (1 [+4200]), seem (1 [+4017, 928]), seem (1 [+2118, 928]), seemed (1 [+2118, 928]), seen as (1 [+928]), sees (1 [+928]), show (1), show ill will (1 [+8317]), showing pity (1 [+2571]), sights (1 [+5260]), sparkles (1 [+5989]), sparkling (1), spring (1 [+2021, 4784]), springs (1), stay awake (1 [+7219]), stingy (1 [+8273, 408]), streams (1), those[s] (1), to (1 [+4200]), to (1 [+4200]), took notice (1 [+5951]), treat like slaves (1 [+5941]), troubled (1 [+8273, 928]), troubled deeply (1 [+6662, 928]), unaware (1 [+6623, 4946]), upset (1 [+8317, 928]), us (1 [+5646]), value (1 [+4718]), value (1 [+1540, 928]), valued (1 [+1540, 928]), wanted to do (1 [+3202, 928]), watch (1 [+928]), watches (1), well (1), what see (1), winks maliciously (1 [+7975]), wish (1 [+3512, 928]), wished (1 [+3202, 928]), wishes (1 [+3202, 928]), without being aware (1 [+4946]), won (1 [+5951, 928]), NDT (25)

H6525 ²עַיִן **'ayin²**, n.f. Not used in NIVEBC [cf. 6524]. spring, fountain

H6526 ³עַיִן **'ayin³**, n.pr.loc. [5] [√ 6524]. Ain, "*eye[ball]* or *spring [of water]*":– Ain (5)

H6527 עֵין גֶּדִי **'ên gedî**, n.pr.loc. [6] [√ 6524 + 1531]. En Gedi, "*spring of young goat*":– En Gedi (6)

H6528 עֵין גַּנִּים **'ên gannîm**, n.pr.loc. [3] [√ 6524 + 1712]. En Gannim, "*spring of gardens*":– En Gannim (3)

H6529 עֵין־דֹּאר **'ên-dō'r**, עֵין־דּוֹר **'ên-dôr**, n.pr.loc. [3] [√ 6524 + 1799]. Endor, "*spring of Dor*":– Endor (3)

H6530 עֵין הַקּוֹרֵא **'ên haqqôrē'**, n.pr.loc. [1] [√ 6524 + 2213]. En Hakkore, "*spring of the partridge* or *caller*":– En Hakkore (1)

H6531 עֵין הַתַּנִּין **'ên hattannîn**, n.pr.loc. Not used in NIVEBC [√ 6524 + 2021 + 9490]. En Hattannin, see 6524 & 9490, "*well of the jackals*"

H6532 עֵין חַדָּה **'ên ḥaddâ**, n.pr.loc. [1] [√ 6524 + 2528]. En Haddah, "*spring of gladness*":– En Haddah (1)

H6533 עֵין חָצוֹר **'ên ḥāṣôr**, n.pr.loc. [1] [√ 6524 + 2937]. En Hazor, "*spring of Hazor*":– En Hazor (1)

H6534 עֵין חֲרֹד **'ên ḥᵃrōd**, n.pr.loc. Not used in NIVEBC [√ 6524 + 3008]. En Harod, see 6524 & 3008, "*spring of Harod*"

H6535 עֵין מִשְׁפָּט **'ên mišpāṭ**, n.pr.loc. [1] [√ 6524 + 5477]. En Mishpat, "*spring of judgment*":– En Mishpat (1)

H6536 עֵין עֶגְלַיִם **'ên 'eglayim**, n.pr.loc. [1] [√ 6524 + 6325]. En Eglaim, "*spring of two calves*":– En Eglaim (1)

H6537 עֵין רֹגֵל **'ên rōgēl**, n.pr.loc. [4] [√ 6524 + 8080]. En Rogel, "*spring of the fuller* or *wanderer* or *spy*":– En Rogel (4)

H6538 עֵין רִמּוֹן **'ên rimmôn**, n.pr.loc. [1] [√ 6524 + 8235]. En Rimmon, "*spring of Rimmon*":– En Rimmon (1)

H6539 עֵין שֶׁמֶשׁ **'ên šemeš**, n.pr.loc. [2] [√ 6524 + 9087]. En Shemesh, "*spring of Shemesh*":– En Shemesh (2)

H6540 עֵין תַּפּוּחַ **'ên tappûaḥ**, n.pr.loc. [1] [√ 6524 + 9517]. En Tappuah, "*spring of apple*":– En Tappuah (1)

H6541 עֵינוֹן **'ênôn**, n.pr.loc. Not used in NIVEBC [→ 2965]. Enan

H6542 עֵינַיִם **'ênayim**, n.pr.loc. [2] [cf. 6543?]. Enaim, "*two springs*":– Enaim (2)

H6543 עֵינָם **'ênām**, n.pr.loc. [1] [√ 6524 + 4392; cf. 6542?]. Enam:– Enam (1)

H6544 עֵינָן **'ênān**, n.pr.m. [5] [→ 2966; cf. 6524 + 5527]. Enan, "*spring*":– Enan (5)

H6545 עִיף **'îp**, v. [5] [→ 6546; cf. 3615]. [Q] to be faint, be exhausted:– exhausted (2), exhausted (1 [+4394]), faint (1), fainting (1)

H6546 עָיֵף **'āyēp**, a. [17] [√ 6545; cf. 3615]. weary, faint; famished, parched:– weary (5), exhausted (3), famished (2), parched (2), faint (1), thirsty (1), tired (1), weary (1 [+5883]), worn out (1)

H6547 ¹עֵיפָה **'êpâ¹**, n.f. [2] [→ 6548, 6549; cf. 6415]. darkness:– darkness (1), deepest night (1 [+4017, 694])

H6548 ²עֵיפָה **'êpâ²**, n.pr.g. [1] [√ 6549; cf. 6547]. Ephah, "*darkness*":– Ephah (1)

H6549 ³עֵיפָה **'êpâ³**, n.pr.m. & f. [4] [→ 6548; cf. 6547]. Ephah, "*darkness*":– Ephah (4)

H6550 עֵיפַי **'êpay**, n.pr.m. [1] [cf. 6417]. Ephai, "*my bird*":– Ephai (1)

H6551 ¹עִיר **'îr¹**, n.f. [1085] [→ 6840? [also found with compound proper names]]. city, town, village, a general term for a population center:– city (511), towns (264), cities (125), town (99), its[s] (11 [+2021]), villages (8), hometown (3), each towns (2 [+6551]), townspeople (2 [+408]), Ziklag[s] (1 [+2021]), another[s] (1), citadel (1), cities (1 [+6551, 2256]), cities (1 [+2256, 6551]), each town (1 [+6551, 2256]), each town (1 [+2256, 6551]), every city (1 [+6551, 2256]), every city (1 [+2256, 6551]), inner shrine (1), it[s] (1 [+2021, 2021, 2296]), its[s] (1), its[s] (1 [+928, 2021]), places (1), them[s] (1), them[s] (1 [+3972]), them[s] (1 [+2021, 824]), there[s] (1 [+928, 2021]), villages (1 [+7252]), which[s] (1), NDT (40)

H6552 ²עִיר **'îr²**, n.[m.] [1] [√ 6424]. anguish, terror, wrath:– anguish (1)

H6553 ³עִיר **'îr³**, n.pr.m. [1] [√ 6554]. Ir, "[poss.] *stallion donkey*":– Ir (1)

H6554 ⁴עִיר **'îr⁴**, n.m. [1] [→ 6553, 6562, 6565, 6566]. (male) donkey (young and robust):– donkey (1)

H6555 עַיִר **'ayir**, n.m. [7] [√ 6424]. (male) donkey:– donkeys (4), colt (2), male donkeys (1)

H6556 עִיר הַהֶרֶס **'îr haheres**, n.pr.loc. Not used in NIVEBC [√ 6551 + 2021 + 2239]. Ir Haheres, see 6551 & 2021 & 2239, "*the city of destruction*"

H6557 עִיר הַחֶרֶס **'îr haḥeres**, n.pr.loc. Not used in NIVEBC [√ 6551 + 2021 + 3064]. Ir Haheres, see 6551 & 2021 & 3064, "*the city of the sun*"

H6558 עִיר הַמֶּלַח **'îr hammelaḥ**, n.pr.loc. Not used in NIVEBC [√ 6551 + 2021 + 4875]. Ir Hammelak, see 6551 & 2021 & 4875, "*the city of salt*"

H6559 עִיר הַתְּמָרִים **'îr hattᵉmārîm**, n.pr.loc. Not used in NIVEBC [√ 6551 + 2021 + 9469]. Ir Hattemarim, see 6551 & 2021 & 9468, "*the city of palms*"

H6560 עִיר נָחָשׁ **'îr nāḥāš**, n.pr.loc. [1] [√ 6551 + 5730]. Ir Nahash, "*city of Nahash*":– Ir Nahash (1)

H6561 עִיר שֶׁמֶשׁ **'îr šemeš**, n.pr.loc. [1] [√ 6551 + 9087]. Ir Shemesh, "*city of Shemesh*":– Ir Shemesh (1)

H6562 עִירָא **'îrā'**, n.pr.m. [6] [√ 6554]. Ira, "[poss.] *stallion donkey*":– Ira (6)

H6563 עִירָד **'îrād**, n.pr.m. [2] [√ 6871]. Irad:– Irad (2)

H6564 עִירוּ **'îrû**, n.pr.m. [1] Iru:– Iru (1)

H6565 עִירִי **'îrî**, n.pr.m. [1] [√ 6554]. Iri, "[perhaps] *donkey's colt*":– Iri (1)

H6566 עִירָם **'îrām**, n.pr.m. [2] [√ 6554 + 4392]. Iram:– Iram (2)

H6567 עֵירֹם **'êrōm**, a. (used as noun) [10] [√ 6867]. naked; nakedness:– naked (6), stark naked (3 [+2256, 6880]), nakedness (1)

H6568 עַיִשׁ **'ayiš**, n.f. [1] [→ 6933]. constellation: the Bear or the Lion, or some other constellation:– Bear (1)

H6569 עַיַּת **'ayyat**, n.pr.loc. [1] [cf. 6509]. Aiath, "[poss.] *ruin, heap*":– Aiath (1)

H6570 עַכְבּוֹר **'akbôr**, n.pr.m. [7] [√ 6572]. Acbor, "*mouse* or *jerboa*":– Akbor (7)

H6571 עַכָּבִישׁ **'akkābîš**, n.m. [2] spider:– spider's (2)

H6572 עַכְבָּר **'akbār**, n.m. [6] [→ 6570]. (jumping) rat, jerboa:– rats (5), rat (1)

H6573 עַכּוֹ **'akkô**, n.pr.loc. [1] Acco:– Akko (1)

H6574 עָכוֹר **'ākôr**, n.pr.loc. [5] [√ 6579]. Achor, "*trouble*":– Achor (5)

H6575 עָכָן **'ākān**, n.pr.m. [6] Achan, "*troubler*":– Achan (6)

H6576 עָכַס **'ākas**, v.den. [2] [→ 6577, 6578]. [P] to jingle, rattle (of ankle ornaments):– ornaments jingling (1), stepping (1)

H6577 עֶכֶס **'ekes**, n.[m.] [1] [√ 6576]. bangle, ankle ornament:– bangles (1)

H6578 עַכְסָה **'aksâ**, n.pr.f. [5] [√ 6576]. Acsah, "*decorative anklet*":– Aksah (5)

H6579 עָכַר **'ākar**, v. [14] [→ 6574, 6580, 6581]. [Q] to bring trouble, make trouble; [N] to be troubled, be anguished:– brought trouble (3), bring ruin (2), bring trouble (2), brings ruin (2), made trouble (2), devastated (1), increased (1), troubler (1)

H6580 עָכָר **'ākār**, n.pr.m. [1] [√ 6579]. Achar, "*trouble*":– Achar (1)

H6581 עָכְרָן **'okrān**, n.pr.m. [5] [√ 6579]. Ocran, "*trouble*":– Okran (5)

H6582 עַכְשׁוּב **'akšûb**, n.m. [1] (horned) viper; other sources: asp:– vipers (1)

H6583 ¹עַל **'al¹**, subst. [5] [√ 6590; cf. 6584; 10546]. (the) Most High:– Most High (5)

H6584 ²עַל **'al²**, pp. & c. [5761] [→ 5088, 6586, 6629; cf. 6583; 10542]. marker of relationship: spatial: on, upon, over, against, toward; logical: because of, according to; temporal: on, when, during:– on (1242), against (405), over (371), to (319), for (248), in (247), from (155 [+4946]), at (129), by (93), with (78), of (59), because of (55), about (54), therefore (51 [+4027]), upon (46), above (43), in charge of (40), concerning (35), along (34), that is why (34 [+4027]), because (29), near (27), around (26), beside (26), so (25 [+4027]), into (24), according to (18), from (18), facedown (15 [+7156]), under (15), because (14 [+889]), on (14 [+7156]), above (13 [+4946]), to (13 [+3338]), why (13 [+4537]), toward (11), administrator (10 [+889]), attack (10), away from (10 [+4946]), bears (10 [+7924]), border (10), on (10 [+4946]), over (10 [+7156]), within (9), after (8), along with (8), near (8 [+7156]), off (8 [+4946]), on top of (8), together with (8), as (7), before (7), next to (7 [+3338]), wearing (7), attacked (6 [+6590]), because of (6 [+1821]), in (6 [+7156]), in front of (6 [+7156]), next to (6), there[s] (6 [+2023]), among (5), attack (5 [+995]), attack (5 [+6590]), because (5 [+3954]), because (5 [+4027]), before (5 [+7156]), east (5 [+7156]), for sake (5), had charge of (5), next section (5 [+3338]), than (5), this is why (5 [+4027]), across (4), bear (4 [+7924]), because of (4 [+128]), burning (4 [+2021, 836]), connected to (4), covered with (4), enter (4 [+6590]), have (4), in accordance with (4), in addition to (4), in command (4 [+7372]), out of (4 [+4946]), about (3 [+128]), according to (3 [+7023]), across (3 [+7156]), against (3 [+4946]), at side (3), attacking (3 [+7756]), because (3 [+1821]), concerning (3 [+1821]), faces (3 [+7156]), facing (3 [+7156]), had to (3), higher than (3 [+4946]), in opposition to (3), in spite of (3), invaded (3 [+6590]), lusted after (3 [+6311]), next (3 [+3338]), on account of (3), oppose (3), past (3), responsible for (3), rested on (3), so (3 [+2296]), tenderly (3 [+4213]), throughout (3), top (3), toward (3 [+7156]), up to (3), wear (3 [+2118]), when (3), about (2 [+1821]), across from (2 [+7156]), along (2 [+3338]), and (2), and so (2 [+4027]), as for (2), as though (2), as well as (2), at fate (2), attached to (2), attacked (2 [+995]), await (2), before (2 [+4946]), besides (2), besiege (2 [+2837]), by (2 [+3338]), cover (2), crown (2), decorated with (2), defied (2 [+1540]), enter (2 [+995]), fighting (2), for (2 [+1821]), from (2 [+7156]), from (2 [+4946, 7156]), got off (2 [+7563, 4946]), inner (2), look after (2 [+8492, 6524]), lying on (2 [+7156]), mating with (2 [+6590]), more than (2), of (2 [+4946]), on (2 [+7023]), on behalf (2), onto (2), outside (2), over (2 [+4946]), prostrate (2 [+7156]), protect (2 [+6641]), resolved (2 [+8492, 4213]), responsibility for (2), rests on (2), rule (2 [+2118]), rule over (2), seized (2 [+5877]), separated from (2 [+4946]), set on (2), shields (2), so that (2 [+4027]), the stewards[s] (2 [+889]), therefore (2 [+2296]), though (2), threw arms around (2 [+5877, 7418]), to (2 [+7931]), too (2), wore (2), above (1 [+1068]), above (1 [+4946, 5087]), accompanied by (1 [+3338]), according to (1 [+3869]), according to (1 [+3869]), accuse (1 [+7212]), add (1), adjoining (1 [+3338]), adjoining section (1 [+3338]), administrator (1), adorned (1 [+6590]), adorned with (1), afraid (1 [+5877, 7065]), against (1 [+7156]), against side (1), ahead (1 [+7156]), all over (1 [+6017, 6017]), all the way to (1), aloft (1 [+89]), although (1), and (1 [+4027]), and alike (1), anoint (1), apart from (1), aroused (1 [+2118]), as a result of (1), as far as (1), as for (1 [+1826]), as part of (1), as prescribed by (1 [+3338]), assail (1 [+8883]), assaults (1 [+7756]), assistant (1 [+3338]), assisted (1 [+3338]), assume the responsibility for carrying out (1 [+6641]), at (1 [+6813]), at (1 [+7156]), at flood stage (1 [+3972, 1536]), at flood stage (1 [+4848, 3972, 1536]), at heels (1 [+7418]), attack (1 [+6590, 3338]), attacked (1 [+7320]), attacked (1 [+7756]), attacked viciously (1 [+5782, 8797, 3751]), attacking (1), attacking (1 [+995]), attacks (1 [+995]), attacks (1 [+7756]), attendants (1 [+6641]), avert (1 [+6296, 4946]), away (1 [+4946]), because (1 [+1826]), because (1 [+3954, 4027]), because (1 [+3954, 4027]), because of (1 [+4027]), because of (1 [+3970]), because of (1 [+6813]), because of this (1 [+4027]), become guilty (1 [+2628, 5951]), been under (1 [+6590]), belonging to (1), below (1 [+2021, 141]), beside (1 [+3338]), beside (1 [+4946]), beside (1 [+7156]), besieged (1 [+1215]), besieged (1 [+2837]), better than (1), between (1), beyond (1), binding on (1), blessed (1), bordering (1), bowed down (1 [+5877, 7156]), bowed down to the ground (1 [+5877, 7156]), bracelets (1 [+7543, 3338]), bring (1 [+8883, 3338]), by (1 [+4946]), by (1 [+7023]), care for (1), cares (1 [+8492, 4213]), carried by (1 [+2118]), carry on (1 [+7756]), charged against (1), commander in chief (1 [+2021, 7372]), confronted (1 [+6641]), confronted (1 [+7756]), conquered (1 [+2616]), consider (1 [+8492, 4213]), contact with (1), contribute (1), corresponding to (1 [+7156]), could not (1 [+2118]), cover (1 [+6296]), credited to (1), crossing (1 [+7156]), crowns (1), deal with (1), decide (1 [+2118, 7023]), deep (1 [+7156, 2021, 824]), demanded (1 [+7023]), depend on (1), directed to (1), do anything that endangers life (1 [+6641, 1947]), do not know where am going (1 [+2143, 889, 2143]), don't say a word (1 [+8492, 3338, 7023]), drove back (1 [+2118]), during (1), east (1 [+7156, 7710]), embraced (1 [+7418]), encircle (1 [+7443]), encourage (1 [+1819, 4213]), encouraged (1 [+1819, 4222]), encouragingly (1 [+4213]), entered (1 [+995]), escape from (1 [+4946]), even beyond (1 [+4946]), express (1 [+7023]), extend toward (1), extended (1 [+7156]), falsely (1 [+9214]), feed (1 [+5989, 7023]), feed on (1), fight (1), follows (1 [+7925]), for (1 [+889]), for (1 [+1386]), for (1 [+4946]), for (1 [+7156]), for (1 [+3954, 4027]), for (1 [+3954, 4027]), for sake (1 [+128]), gave a high rank in (1 [+8492]), give children (1 [+995]), given over (1 [+5599, 3338]), got off (1 [+3718, 4946]), governor[s]

(1 [+889]), guarded (1), had (1), had (1 [+2118]), had mount (1 [+8206]), had to (1 [+2118]), hanging on (1), has (1), have (1 [+2118]), have mount (1 [+8206]), help (1), here[S] (1 [+3870]), here[S] (1 [+3276]), here by (1), high (1 [+8031]), higher (1 [+4946]), highest (1 [+8031]), hold accountable (1 [+5989]), how (1), how (1 [+4027]), in (1 [+4946]), in accordance with (1 [+7023]), in behalf (1), in behalf (1 [+3208]), in behalf of (1), in charge (1 [+6641]), in control (1), in front of (1), in hands (1), in hostility toward (1 [+7156]), in little more than (1 [+3427]), in preference to (1 [+7156]), in presence (1), in presence of (1), in store for (1), in the care of (1), in the cause of (1 [+1821]), in the presence of (1), in view of (1), in whatever order (1 [+4202, 5877, 1598]), including (1), increase (1 [+3578]), instead of (1 [+4030]), invade (1 [+6590]), invaded (1 [+995]), involving (1), its (1 [+2023]), jealous (1 [+8120, 7863, 6296]), join (1 [+2143]), join (1 [+2616]), keeper[S] (1 [+889]), kneeling (1 [+4156, 1386]), knelt down (1 [+1384, 1386]), laid siege to (1 [+2837]), leader (1), leads to (1), lingering (1 [+3427, 3427]), little by little (1 [+3338]), lived in hostility toward (1 [+5877, 7156]), load (1), loaded with (1), longed for (1), lying on (1), make wear (1 [+6590, 5516]), marched past (1 [+6296, 3338]), more and more (1 [+3578, 3972]), mounted like jewels (1 [+3782, 4859]), near (1 [+3338]), nearby (1), nearby (1 [+3338]), nearest (1 [+7156]), no wonder (1 [+4027]), no wonder (1 [+4027]), not (1), object of malicious talk (1 [+6590, 8557, 4383]), obligates (1), on behalf of (1), on foot (1 [+2021, 824]), opposed (1 [+599]), opposed (1 [+6641]), over (1 [+4946, 4200]), over higher (1), overflow (1 [+6590]), overpower (1 [+4309]), overpowered (1 [+6451, 3338]), overruled (1 [+2616]), overwhelm (1 [+995]), overwhelmed (1 [+5877]), pardon (1 [+2021, 6411]), part (1), part of (1), past (1 [+4946]), peels (1 [+4946]), persuade (1 [+1819, 4213]), placed on (1), presence (1 [+4946]), protects (1 [+6641]), put in charge (1 [+6641, 3338]), put in charge of the storerooms (1 [+732, 238]), reaches to (1), reason (1), received gladly (1 [+8523]), reclining (1), regarding (1), reign over (1), reject (1 [+8959, 4946, 7156]), reject (1 [+8938, 4946, 7156]), repay (1 [+8740, 8031]), required (1 [+2011]), required of (1), resolve (1 [+8492, 4213]), responsible (1), rid (1 [+8959, 4946]), rightly (1 [+698]), ring (1), ruled over (1), serve (1 [+6641]), set against (1), share in (1 [+5951]), shave (1 [+7947]), simply (1 [+7023]), since (1), since (1 [+4027]), since (1 [+3954, 4027]), sleep with (1 [+4156]), so (1 [+3869]), speaking kindly (1 [+1819, 4213]), stand up (1 [+6641, 6642]), steward[S] (1 [+889, 1074]), steward[S] (1 [+2021, 408, 889, 1074]), strike (1), succeeded (1 [+6641, 4030]), successor (1 [+6641, 4030]), suffer (1 [+5989]), supervised (1), supporting (1), surely leave (1 [+2143, 4946, 2143]), surpasses (1 [+3972]), take (1 [+995]), take care of (1), take off (1 [+3718, 4946]), takes (1 [+3782]), that (1 [+4027]), that is what (1 [+4027]), that's why (1 [+4027]), the duty of (1), their (1 [+2157]), their[S] (1 [+3776]), theirs (1 [+2257]), then (1 [+4027]), there[S] (1 [+2157]), therefore (1 [+1826, 8611]), this is why (1 [+465]), threw arms around (1 [+5877]), throughout (1 [+7156, 3972]), tie (1 [+5989]), to (1 [+4946]), to (1 [+4200, 7156]), to reach (1), took up (1 [+6641]), touched (1 [+6590]), touches (1 [+2118]), toward (1 [+2006]), toward (1 [+7156, 2006]), under guard (1 [+5464]), upon (1 [+7156]), upside down (1 [+7156]), used (1), used for (1), using (1), voluntarily (1 [+6590, 4213, 408]), watch over (1 [+8492]), wear (1 [+6590]), wearing around (1), weigh down (1), what (1 [+4537]), when (1 [+889]), where[S] (1 [+2157]), where[S] (1 [+6642]), wherever (1 [+3972, 2021, 5226, 889]), which way (1 [+3545, 196, 6584, 8520]), which way (1 [+6584, 3545, 196, 8520]), while still alive (1 [+7156]), why (1 [+2296]), will (1 [+7023]), windblown (1 [+7156, 8120]), with (1 [+3338]), with (1 [+7156]), with still inside (1), worn (1), wrap in rags (1 [+2520]), yet (1), your (1 [+3871]), your (1 [+4013]), NDT (891)

H6585 עֹל **ʿōl**, n.m. [39] [√ 6619]. yoke, placed on draft animals; by extension: a figure of oppression or of proper training:– yoke (35), it[S] (3), yoked (1 [+6590])

H6586 עַל־כֵּן **ʿal-kēn**, pp.+adv. Not used in NIVEBC [→ 3956; cf. 6584 + 4027]. see 6584 & 4027

H6587 עֻלָּא **ʿullāʾ**, n.pr.m. [1] [√ 6590]. Ulla:– Ulla (1)

H6588 עַלְבוֹן **ʿalbôn**, n.pr.m. Not used in NIVEBC [→ 50]. Albon, see 50

H6589 עִלֵּג **ʿillēg**, a. [1] [cf. 4352]. speaking inarticulately; (pl.n.) stammerers:– stammering (1)

H6590 עָלָה **ʿālâ**, v. [893] [→ 541, 5087, 5089, 5090, 5091, 5092, 5093, 6583, 6587, 6591, 6592, 6595, 6597, 6603, 6604, 6605, 6606, 6607, 6608, 6609, 6610, 9498?, 9499]. [Q] to go up, ascend, rise; [N] to be lifted up, withdraw, be exalted; [H] to take up, set up, offer a sacrifice; [Ho] to be offered up, be carried away, be recorded; [Ht] to raise oneself up; from the base meaning of rise in elevation comes the fig. extension "to exalt, honor," as the lifting up of a person in status:– went up (112), go up (74), brought up (44), came up (31), bring up (24), come up (24), go (23), offered (14), sacrificed (14), come (12), offer (12), up (12), attack (11), sacrifice (11), gone up (10), bring (9), coming up (9), lifted (9), rise (8), rises (8), set up (8), climbed (7), went (7), attacked (6 [+6584]), led up (6), marched up (6), ascended (5), attack (5 [+6584]), attacked (5), chews (5), invaded (5), marched (5), presented (5), sacrificing (5), take up (5), ascend (4), attack (4 [+448]), brought (4), came (4), chew (4), climb up (4), conscripted (4), enter (4 [+6584]), goes up (4), grow (4), return (4), returned (4), rising (4), rose (4), took (4), approach (3), going up (3), grew up (3), growing (3), lying on (3), makes rise (3), march (3), offered sacrifices (3), offerings (3), present (3), send up (3), withdraw (3), withdrew (3), advance (2), advances (2), aroused (2), assemble (2), attacking (2), bringing up (2), call (2), carried (2), carried up (2), carry up (2), climb (2), climbed up (2), climbing up (2), climbs (2), daybreak (2 [+2021, 8840]), get (2), get out of here (2), go back (2), gone (2), got on (2), imported (2 [+2256, 3655]), is (2), lift (2), mating with (2 [+6584]), offering (2), raged (2), reached (2), should go up (2 [+6590]), soar (2), spring up (2), sprinkled (2), surely bring back (2 [+6590]), take (2), taken (2), used (2), withdrawn (2), accompanied (1 [+907]), adorned (1 [+6584]), advanced (1), appeared (1), are exalted (1), are recorded (1), ascending (1), ascends (1), ascent (1), assemble (1 [+928, 2021, 7736]), at (1 [+3869]), attack (1 [+6584, 3338]), attacked (1 [+928]), attacking (1 [+448]), back (1), been under (1 [+6584]), billowed up (1), blazed up (1), blossomed (1 [+5890]), blow away (1), blowing in (1), bring back (1), brought along (1), brought back (1), building (1), burning (1), burnt offerings (1), carried away (1), casting up (1), charge (1), charged (1), charging (1), chosen (1), climbed in (1), come back (1), comes (1), comes out (1), coming (1), coming out (1), consider (1), continued (1), continued up (1), decorated (1), deserted (1 [+4946, 339]), drag away (1), entered (1), evening sacrifice (1 [+4966]), exalted (1), falls (1), filled (1), first light of dawn (1 [+8840]), flare up (1), flared (1), flourishing (1), flowed over (1), gathered (1), go directly (1), go off (1), go straight up (1), goes (1), going (1), going up (1 [+2021, 9028, 2025]), gone ahead (1), grow up (1), had come up (1), had go up (1), haul up (1), have (1), headed (1), helped up (1), hung (1), invade (1 [+928]), invade (1 [+6584]), invaded (1 [+448]), invaded (1 [+928]), is on way (1), kept burning (1), lead (1), leading to (1), leave (1 [+4946]), left (1 [+4946]), lights (1), made (1), made[S] (1), made come up (1), made grow up (1), make come (1), make come up (1), make offerings (1), make wear (1 [+6584, 5516]), makes offering (1), making (1), mount (1), mounted up (1), move away (1), moved away (1), moved up (1), object of malicious talk (1 [+6584, 8557, 4383]), offer up (1), offered up (1), offers (1), on (1), on way (1), on way up (1), overflow (1 [+6584]), overgrown (1), overrun (1), paid (1), passed (1), presented offerings (1), progressed (1), pull out (1), pulls up (1), put on (1), raises up (1), ran (1), ran up (1), reached (1 [+448]), reaches (1), restore (1), retreated (1), rising up (1), sacrifice (1 [+4966]), sacrifice (1 [+6592]), scale (1), send (1), serve (1), set out (1), sprinkle (1), stepped out (1), steps (1), stink (1 [+945]), stir up (1), stirs up (1), stopped (1 [+4946]), surpass (1), swarm (1), take away (1), taken up (1), took up (1), touched (1 [+6584]), upper (1), voluntarily (1 [+6584, 4213, 408]), walking (1), wear (1), wear (1 [+6584]), weighed (1), went back (1), went off (1), went over (1), worked (1), yoked (1 [+6585]), NDT (14)

H6591 עָלֶה **ʿāleh**, n.m. [18] [√ 6590]. leaves, foliage:– leaves (7), leaf (5), branches (1), green leaf (1), NDT (4)

H6592 [1]עֹלָה **ʿōlâ[1]**, n.f. [286] [√ 6590; 10545]. burnt offering, wholly dedicated to God:– burnt offering (159), burnt offerings (108), offering (7), sacrifice (2), burnt (1), it[S] (1 [+2021]), its[S] (1 [+2021]), offerings (1), sacrifice (1 [+6590]), sacrifices (1), them[S] (1), NDT (3)

H6593 [2]עֹלָה **ʿōlâ[2]**, n.f. Not used in NIVEBC [cf. 6406]. see 6406

H6594 [1]עַלְוָה **ʿalwâ[1]**, n.f. [1] evil, wickedness:– evildoers (1 [+1201])

H6595 [2]עַלְוָה **ʿalwâ[2]**, n.pr.m. [2] [√ 6590]. Alvah:– Alvah (2)

H6596 עֲלוּמִים **ʿalûmîm**, n.pl.abst. [4] [→ 3609, 6624, 6625, 6628]. (abst.pl.) youthfulness, (the vigor of) youth:– youth (3), youthful vigor (1)

H6597 עַלְוָן **ʿalwān**, n.pr.m. [2] [√ 6590; cf. 6615]. Alvan, "[poss.] *ascending one* or *tall*":– Alvan (2)

H6598 עֲלוּקָה **ʿalûqâ**, n.f. [1] leech:– leech (1)

H6599 עָלוֹת **ʿālôt**, n.pr.loc. [1] Aloth:– Aloth (1)

H6600 עָלַז **ʿālaz**, v. [16] [→ 6601, 6611; cf. 6632]. [Q] to rejoice, be jubilant:– rejoice (7), jubilant (2), triumph (2), glad (1), leaps for joy (1), made merry (1), reveling (1), shout with laughter (1)

H6601 עָלֵז **ʿālēz**, a. (used as n.) [1] [√ 6600]. reveling, exultant; (n.) reveler:– revelers (1)

H6602 עֲלָטָה **ʿalāṭâ**, n.f. [4] darkness, dusk:– dusk (3), darkness (1)

H6603 [1]עֵלִי **ʿēlî[1]**, n.pr.m. [33] [√ 3378 *or* 446 + 6590]. Eli, "*Yahweh is exalted; God [El] is exalted*":– Eli (27), Eli's (4), who[S] (1), NDT (1)

H6604 [2]עֵלִי **ʿēlî[2]**, n.[m.] [1] [√ 6590; 10546]. Most High:– Most High (1)

H6605 עֱלִי **ʿelî**, n.[m.] [1] [√ 6590]. pestle (of a mortar):– pestle (1)

H6606 עִלִּי **ʿillî**, a. [2] [√ 6590; 10547]. upper:– upper (2)

H6607 עַלְיָה **ʿalyâ**, n.pr.m. Not used in NIVEBC [√ 6590]. Aliah, see 6595

H6608 עֲלִיָּה **ʿaliyyâ**, n.f. [19] [√ 6590; 10547]. upper room, upper parts:– upper room (6), room (4), room above (2), upper chambers (2), upper parts (2), upper rooms (2), room over (1)

H6609 [1]עֶלְיוֹן **ʿelyôn[1]**, a. [20] [√ 6590; 10548]. upper, also used in place names:– upper (15), high (2), top (2), most exalted (1)

H6610 [2]עֶלְיוֹן **ʿelyôn[2]**, n.m. [31] [√ 6590; 10546, 10548]. (the) Most High, a title of God with a focus on supremacy in status and power:– Most High (31)

H6611 עַלִּיז **ʿallîz**, a. [7] [√ 6600; cf. 6616]. rejoicing, exulting; reveling, wild:– revelry (4), boasters (1), rejoice (1), revelers (1)

H6612 עֲלִיל **ʿalîl**, n.[m.] [1] [√ 6619]. furnace:– crucible (1)

H6613 עֲלִילָה **ʿalîlâ**, n.f. [24] [√ 6618]. what is done, deed, action:– actions (6), deeds (5), what done (5), did (1), do (1), done (1), mighty deeds (1), misdeeds (1), practices (1), slandered (1 [+8492, 1821]), slanders (1 [+8492, 1821])

H6614 עֲלִילִיָּה **ʿalîliyyâ**, n.f. [1] deed:– deeds (1)

H6615 עַלְיָן **ʿalyān**, n.pr.m. Not used in NIVEBC [cf. 6597]. Alian, see 6597

H6616 עָלִיץ **ʿālîṣ**, a. Not used in NIVEBC [cf. 6611]. haughty, insolent

H6617 עֲלִיצֻת **ʿalîṣut**, n.f. [1] [√ 6636; cf. 6632]. rejoicing, exaltation, including verbal expressions of joy and praise; from a negative perspective: haughtiness, presumption, gloating:– gloating (1)

H6618 [1]עָלַל **ʿālal[1]**, v. [18] [→ 5094, 5095, 6613, 6622, 9500; cf. 6621]. [Po] to deal with; to glean, go over a second time; [Poal] to be dealt with (in a way that causes suffering); [Ht] to deal harshly, abuse, mistreat; [Htpo] to take part in (wickedness):– abuse (2), dealt harshly (2), glean thoroughly (2 [+6618]), abused (1), brings grief (1), cut down (1), deal (1), dealt (1), go over a second time (1), go over the vines again (1), made a fool (1), mistreat (1), take part in (1), treated (1), was inflicted (1)

H6619 [2]עָלַל **ʿālal[2]**, v. [1] [→ 6585, 6612; 10549]. [Po] to thrust (in):– buried (1)

H6620 [3]עָלַל **ʿālal[3]**, v.den. [1] [Po] to act or play the child; (n.) youths:– Youths (1)

H6621 [4]עָלַל **ʿālal[4]**, v.den. Not used in NIVEBC [cf. 6618]. [Po] to glean

H6622 עֹלֵלוֹת **ʿōlēlôt**, n.f.pl.intens. [6] [√ 6618]. gleanings:– few grapes (2), gleanings (2), gleaning (1), gleanings of grapes (1)

H6623 עָלַם **ʿālam**, v. [29] [→ 9501, 9502]. [Qp] to be in secret; [N] to be concealed, be hidden, be unaware; [H] to hide, shut off, conceal; [Ht] to hide oneself from, ignore:– hidden (4), ignore (4), close (2), close (2 [+6623]), hard (2), hide (2), unaware of (2 [+4946]), bring (1), hiding (1), hypocrites (1), make shut (1), obscures (1), secret (1), shut (1), swollen (1), turn away (1), unaware (1 [+4946]), unaware (1 [+4946, 6524])

H6624 עֶלֶם **ʿelem**, n.m. [2] [√ 6596]. boy, young man:– boy (1), young man (1)

H6625 עַלְמָה **ʿalmâ**, n.f. [7] [√ 6596; cf. 6628]. girl, young woman, (in certain contexts) virgin:– young woman (2), young women (2), girl (1), virgin (1), virgins (1)

H6626 עַלְמוֹן **ʿalmôn**, n.pr.loc. [1] [→ 6627]. Almon:– Almon (1)

H6627 עַלְמֹן דִּבְלָתָיִם **ʿalmôn diblātayim**, n.pr.loc. [2] [√ 6626 + 1814]. Almon Diblathaim, "*way of the double fig cakes*":– Almon Diblathaim (2)

H6628 עֲלָמוֹת **ʿalāmôt**, n.f. [2] [√ 6596; cf. 6625]. alamoth (t.t. in the Psalms):– alamoth (2)

H6629 עַל־מוּת **ʿal-mût**, tt. Not used in NIVEBC [√ 6584 + 4637]. Al-Muth, see 6584 & 4637

H6630 [1]עָלֶמֶת **ʿālemet[1]**, n.pr.loc. [1] [√ 6631?]. Alemeth, "*concealment*":– Alemeth (1)

H6631 [2]עָלֶמֶת **ʿālemet[2]**, n.pr.m. [3] [√ 6630?]. Alemeth, "*concealment*":– Alemeth (3)

H6632 עָלַס **ʿālas**, v. [3] [cf. 6600, 6617, 6636]. [Q] to enjoy; [N] to appear glad; [Ht] to enjoy one another:– enjoy (1), enjoy ourselves (1), flap joyfully (1)

H6633 עָלַע **ʿālaʿ**, v. [1] [cf. 4363]. [Palpal] to drink, feast on:– feast on (1)

H6634 עָלַף **ʿālap**, v. [6] [Pu] to faint; to be withered; be decorated, covered; [Ht] to disguise oneself; to grow faint:– faint (2), decorated (1), disguise herself (1), fainted (1), withered away (1)

H6635 עֻלְפֶּה **ʿulpeh**, var. see 6634

H6636 עָלַץ **'ālaṣ**, v. [8] [→ 6617; cf. 6632]. [Q] to rejoice, be jubilant:– rejoice (3), rejoices (2), triumph (2), jubilant (1)

H6637 עֹלָתָה **'ōlātâ**, n.f. [1] [√ 6401; cf. 6406]. injustice:– injustice (1)

H6638 1עַם **'am1**, n.[m.] Not used in NIVEBC [√ 6639; 10553]. father's relatives, one's people

H6639 2עַם **'am2**, n.m. [1867] [→ 6638; 10553; *also used with compound proper names*]. people, nation, countrymen; army, troop:– people (1270), peoples (102), nations (89), men (62), army (60), troops (37), theyS (29 [+2021]), themS (17 [+2021]), people (14 [+1426]), people (14 [+1201]), nation (9), soldiers (9), people's (7), fighting men (6), thoseS (6 [+2021]), IsraelitesS (4), army (4 [+4878]), members (4), nationality (4), othersS (4), each people (3 [+6639, 2256]), each people (3 [+2256, 6639]), everyone (3), them (3 [+2021]), common people (2 [+1201]), creatures (2), humble (2 [+6714]), lay people (2 [+1201]), oneS (2 [+2021]), others (2), theirS (2 [+2021]), themS (2 [+3972, 2021]), theyS (2 [+2021, 824]), thoseS (2), Israel (1 [+3776]), Israelite (1), Israelites (1 [+1201, 3776]), anyone elseS (1), army (1 [+7736, 2256]), common people (1), community (1 [+2021, 824]), elseS (1), everyone (1 [+3972, 2021]), everyone (1 [+3972, 2021]), followers (1 [+2021, 889, 339]), following (1 [+907]), force (1 [+4878]), forces (1), foreigners (1 [+5799]), group of people (1), guests (1), inhabitants (1), itS (1 [+2021]), leaders (1 [+8031]), lives (1), merchants (1 [+4047]), multitude (1), nationalities (1), native (1), native (1 [+1201]), one another (1 [+2021]), one of the other peoples (1 [+6639, 2256]), one of the other peoples (1 [+2256, 6639]), other nationalities (1 [+2021, 824]), people's (1 [+4200]), person (1), population (1), soldier (1), soldiers (1 [+7372]), someone (1 [+285, 2021]), theirS (1 [+3276, 3776]), theirS (1 [+2021, 824]), themS (1 [+2257]), themS (1 [+3276]), themS (1 [+3276]), themS (1 [+2021, 2021, 2296]), theyS (1), theyS (1 [+3972, 2021]), thoseS (1 [+2021, 889, 339]), throngs (1 [+6786]), various peoples (1 [+6639, 2256]), various peoples (1 [+2256, 6639]), whomS (1 [+2021, 824]), NDT (35)

H6640 עִם **'im**, pp. [1050] [→ 6672; cf. 6669; 10554]. marker of association or proximity: to, toward; with, among:– with (524), to (63), against (45), from (26 [+4946]), and (24), among (23), for (14), along with (12), near (12), in (11), toward (10), at (8), together with (8), before (7), like (7), sleep with (5 [+8886]), sleeps with (5 [+8886]), join (4), of (4 [+4946]), slept with (4 [+8886]), beside (3), by (3), have (3), help (3), on (3), accompanied by (2), accompany (2), also (2), as well as (2), away from (2 [+4946]), by (2 [+4946]), come to bed with (2 [+8886]), has sexual relations with (2 [+8886]), help (2 [+2118]), his (2 [+2257]), in company with (2), into (2), to (2 [+4946]), to belong (2), accompanied by (1 [+2143]), accomplices (1 [+2745]), alliesS (1 [+8611]), allots to (1), and alike (1), and all (1), around (1), as long as (1), aside (1), attitude (1), away (1 [+4946]), because of (1), bed with (1 [+8886]), before (1 [+4946]), belong to (1), besides (1), both and (1), call to account (1 [+2011, 4946]), concerning (1), convictions (1 [+4222]), decided (1 [+2118, 4213]), demand (1), desire (1), despite (1), done thisS (1 [+8886]), dwell with (1), endowed with (1), even as (1), far from (1 [+4946]), followed (1), followed (1 [+3655]), followers (1 [+408, 889, 2143]), from (1), from (1 [+4946, 7156]), gave strong support (1 [+2616]), give (1), had (1), harbor (1 [+2118, 4222]), has (1), has (1 [+2118]), heS (1 [+2021, 408, 2021, 8886]), help (1 [+3338]), help (1 [+8883, 3338]), here (1), hereS (1 [+3276]), idolatrous priests (1 [+4024, 3913]), impartially (1 [+465, 465]), in mind (1), in spite of (1), in store (1), in the care of (1), in the presence of (1), intend (1 [+4222]), join (1 [+2143]), leave (1 [+2143, 4946]), left (1 [+2143, 4946]), made love to (1 [+8886]), make love to (1 [+8886]), manned by (1), my (1 [+3276]), of (1), on terms (1 [+4946]), present (1), rapes (1 [+9530, 2256, 8886]), rapes (1 [+2616, 2256, 8886]), secure against (1 [+440]), share their duties (1 [+465]), sided with (1 [+3338]), sleeping with (1 [+8886]), support (1), supports (1 [+2616]), take part (1 [+2143]), the Lord's (1 [+4946, 3378]), took care of (1), treated (1 [+2118]), treated (1 [+6913]), with help (1), with the help of (1), withstand (1 [+3656]), NDT (112)

H6641 עָמַד **'āmad**, v. [522] [→ 5096, 5097, 6642, 6643, 6644, 6647]. [Q] to stand, stand up, stand still; [H] to cause to stand, present; to appoint, assign; [Ho] to be presented, be caused to stand:– stood (82), stand (66), standing (53), stopped (19), appointed (11), stationed (8), serve (7 [+4200, 7156]), stay (7), stop (7), arise (6), assigned (6), stands (6), stood still (6), endure (5), present (5), stand up (5), stood up (5), endures (4), have stand (4), ministering (4), presented (4), put in place (4), set (4), stayed (4), had stand (3), raised (3), remain (3), remained (3), remains (3), serve (3), stand firm (3), appoint (2), came to a halt (2), causes to stand (2), confirmed (2), delay (2), entered service (2 [+4200, 7156]), last (2), minister (2), perform (2), propped up (2), protect (2 [+6584]), resist (2 [+4200, 7156]), rise (2), rose up (2), served (2), served (2 [+4200, 7156]), serving (2 [+4200, 7156]), set in place (2), set up (2), stand ground (2), stayed behind (2), take stand (2), took places (2), took stand (2), unchanged (2), unchanged (2 [+9393]), upright (2), wait (2), withstand (2 [+4200, 7156]), withstand (2 [+928, 7156]), act (1), arisen (1), as didS (1), assist (1 [+907]), assistant (1 [+4200, 7156]), assume the responsibility for carrying out (1 [+6584]), attendants (1 [+6584]), avoid (1), be (1), be presented (1), broke out (1), built (1), calm (1), canS (1), claim (1), come (1), come forward (1), confronted (1 [+6584]), crowd (1 [+3972, 889]), decided (1 [+1821]), defend (1 [+5584]), do anything that endangers life (1 [+6584, 1947]), emerge (1), enduring (1), enter service (1 [+4200, 7156]), entered the service (1 [+4200, 7156]), establish (1), established (1), face (1), fulfillment (1), gives stability (1), gives way (1 [+4202]), gone (1 [+4202, 928]), had pledge (1), had serve (1), halt (1), halted (1), held (1), in charge (1 [+6584]), installed (1), joined together (1 [+3869, 285]), keep on (1), leave alone (1 [+4946]), linger (1), live (1), making strong (1), muster (1), occupied (1 [+448]), on duty (1), opposed (1 [+6584]), performed (1), persists (1), pledged (1), position (1), post (1), posted (1), posting (1), protects (1 [+6584]), put in charge (1 [+6584, 3338]), putting in place (1), raise (1), raised up (1), reach (1), rebuilding (1), rebuilt (1), recovers (1), rely (1), repair (1), replaced (1 [+9393]), represent (1), resist (1), resisted (1 [+4200, 5584]), rise up (1), rises (1), serve (1 [+6584]), served (1 [+907, 7156]), sets up (1), stand the strain (1), stand up (1 [+6584, 6642]), standing trial (1), stands firm (1), stared with a fixed gaze (1 [+906, 7156, 2256, 8492]), staying (1), stays (1), stirred up (1), stood by (1), stood firm (1), stood in places (1), stood waiting (1), succeed (1), succeeded (1 [+6584, 4030]), successor (1 [+9393]), successor (1 [+6584, 4030]), surviving (1), to feet (1), tolerated (1), took (1), took up (1 [+6584]), uphold (1), was (1), were (1), withstood (1 [+928, 7156]), NDT (7)

H6642 עֹמֶד **'ōmed**, n.[m.] [9] [√ 6641]. standing-place (a position, station, or post):– feet (1), pillar (1), place where standing (1), places (1), positions (1), posts (1), stand up (1 [+6641, 6584]), standing (1), whereS (1 [+6584])

H6643 עִמָּד **'immād**, pp. [45] [√ 6641]. with:– with (16), to (6), against (2), in (2), besides (1), for (1), leave (1 [+2143, 4946]), mine (1 [+3276]), oppose (1), oppose (1 [+8189]), surround (1), toward (1), NDT (11)

H6644 עֶמְדָּה **'emdâ**, n.f. [1] [√ 6641]. place to stand, protection:– protects (1)

H6645 1עֻמָּה **'ummâ1**, n.f. (used as pp.) [32] [√ 6669]. close by; alongside; adjoining:– close to (5 [+4200]), along with (2 [+4200]), as (2 [+4200]), beside (2 [+4200]), just as (2 [+4200]), parallel to (2 [+4200]), above (1 [+4946, 5087, 4946, 4200]), adjoining (1 [+4200]), alike (1 [+4200]), alongside (1 [+4200]), alongside of (1 [+4200]), as (1 [+3972, 8611]), as well as (1 [+4200]), at (1 [+4200]), bordering (1 [+4200]), length (1 [+4200]), like (1 [+4200]), opposite (1 [+4200]), responding to (1 [+4200]), treated the same as (1 [+4200]), with (1 [+4200]), NDT (2)

H6646 2עֻמָּה **'ummâ2**, n.pr.loc. [1] Ummah:– Ummah (1)

H6647 עַמּוּד **'ammûd**, n.m. [110] [√ 6641]. pillar, post, column; used fig. of the pillar-shaped cloud of God's presence:– pillars (37), posts (36), pillar (26), columns (2), colonnade (1 [+395]), column (1), oneS (1), NDT (6)

H6648 עַמּוֹן **'ammôn**, n.pr.[loc.] [106] [→ 2194, 6649; cf. 6639]. Ammonite; Ammon, "*my people* [Ge 19:38]":– Ammonites (80 [+1201]), Ammon (9 [+1201]), Ammonite (8 [+1201]), Ammon (4), Ammonites (1), theirS (1 [+1201]), themS (1 [+1201]), theyS (1 [+1201]), NDT (1)

H6649 עַמּוֹנִי **'ammônî**, a.g. [20] [√ 6648]. Ammonite, from Ammon, "*of Ammon*":– Ammonite (13), Ammonites (6), Ammon (1)

H6650 עָמוֹס **'āmôs**, n.pr.m. [7] [√ 6673?]. Amos, "*burden bearer*":– Amos (7)

H6651 עָמוֹק **'āmôq**, n.pr.m. [2] [√ 6676]. Amok, "*capable*":– Amok (1), Amok's (1)

H6652 עַמִּי **'ammî**, n.pr.m. Not used in NIVEBC [→ 4204]. Ammi

H6653 עַמִּיאֵל **'ammî'ēl**, n.pr.m. [6] [√ 6639 + 446]. Ammiel, "*God [El] is my kinsman*":– Ammiel (6)

H6654 עַמִּיהוּד **'ammîhûd**, n.pr.m. [10] [√ 6639 + 2086]. Ammihud, "*[my] people have majesty*":– Ammihud (10)

H6655 עַמִּיזָבָד **'ammîzābād**, n.pr.m. [1] [√ 6639 + 2272]. Ammizabad, "*[my] people have given a gift*":– Ammizabad (1)

H6656 עַמִּיחוּר **'ammîḥûr**, n.pr.m. Not used in NIVEBC [√ 6639 + 2581?]. Ammihur, see 6654

H6657 עַמִּינָדָב **'ammînādāb**, n.pr.m. [13] [√ 6639 + 5605]. Amminadab, "*[my] people are generous*":– Amminadab (13)

H6658 עָמִיר **'āmîr**, n.[m.] [5] [√ 6682]. (newly) cut grain:– sheaves (2), cut grain (1), grain (1), thrive (1)

H6659 עַמִּישַׁדָּי **'ammîšadday**, n.pr.m. [5] [√ 6639 + 8724]. Ammishaddai, "*Shaddai is [my] kinsman*":– Ammishaddai (5)

H6660 עָמִית **'āmît**, n.m. [12] [√ 6669]. neighbor, countryman, associate (one in close, united relation):– neighbor (5), people (2), anotherS (1), close (1), neighbor's (1), otherS (1), themS (1)

H6661 עָמַל **'āmal**, v. [11] [→ 6662, 6663, 6664, 6665]. [Q] to labor, toil, pour forth effort:– labor (3), toil (2), toiled (2), efforts (1), poured effort (1), tend (1), works (1)

H6662 1עָמָל **'āmāl1**, n.m. & f. [55] [√ 6661]. trouble, work, labor, toil:– trouble (14), toil (13), misery (5), labor (4), toilsome (2), wrongdoing (2), abuse (1), bitter labor (1), burdens (1), distress (1), fruit of toil (1), labors (1), making trouble (1), mischief (1), miserable (1), oppressive (1), suffered (1), thingsS (1), troubled deeply (1 [+928, 6524]), whatS (1), what toiled for (1)

H6663 2עָמָל **'āmāl2**, n.pr.m. [1] [√ 6662; cf. 6661]. Amal, "*laborer, troubler*":– Amal (1)

H6664 1עָמֵל **'āmēl1**, n.m. [4] [√ 6661]. misery; workman, laborer:– misery (2), laborers (1), workman's (1)

H6665 2עָמֵל **'āmēl2**, a.vbl. [5] [√ 6661]. toiling, laboring:– labor (1), toil (1), toiled for (1), toiling (1), toilsome (1)

H6666 עַמְלָץ **'amlāṣ**, n.[m.] Not used in NIVEBC [√ 4914]. shark

H6667 עֲמָלֵק **'ᵃmālēq**, n.pr.m. [39] [→ 6668]. Amalek; Amalekite:– Amalekites (25), Amalek (12), Amalekite (1), theirS (1)

H6668 עֲמָלֵקִי **'ᵃmālēqî**, a.g. [12] [√ 6667]. Amalekite, "*of Amalek*":– Amalekites (9), Amalekite (3)

H6669 1עָמַם **'āmam1**, v. [1] [→ 6640, 6645, 6660]. [Q] to be rival to, be equal to:– rival (1)

H6670 2עָמַם **'āmam2**, v. [2] [Q] to grow dark; [Ho] to lose luster, grow dark:– hidden (1), lost luster (1)

H6671 עַמֹּנָה **'ammōnâ**, var. Not used in NIVEBC [cf. 2194, 4112]. see 4112

H6672 עִמָּנוּ אֵל **'immānû 'ēl**, n.pr.m. [2] [√ 6640 + 5646 + 446]. Immanuel, "*God with us*":– Immanuel (2)

H6673 עָמַס **'āmas**, v. [9] [→ 5098, 6650?, 6674]. [Q] to load a burden, carry a burden; [Qp] to be burdensome, be upheld; [H] to lay a burden upon:– laid (2), bears burdens (1), burdensome (1), carried (1 [+5951]), loaded (1), loading (1), move (1), upheld (1)

H6674 עֲמַסְיָה **'ᵃmasyâ**, n.pr.m. [1] [√ 6673 + 3378]. Amasiah, "*Yahweh carries a load*":– Amasiah (1)

H6675 עַמְעָד **'am'ād**, n.pr.loc. [1] Amad:– Amad (1)

H6676 עָמַק **'āmaq**, v. [9] [→ 1097, 2195, 5099, 6651, 6677, 6678, 6679, 6680, 6681]. [Q] to be profound; [H] to make deep (in various senses):– deep (2), deepest (1), go to great depths (1), greatly (1), knee-deep (1), made deep (1), profound (1), sunk deep (1)

H6677 עֵמֶק **'ēmeq**, n.m. [68] [→ 1097; cf. 6676]. valley; (low-lying) plain:– valley (52), valleys (11), plain (2), fiercely (1 [+928, 2021]), plain (1 [+824]), plains (1)

H6678 עָמֹק **'āmōq**, a. [17] [√ 6676; 10555]. deep; profound:– deep (13), most profound (2 [+6678]), cunning (1), deeper (1)

H6679 עֹמֶק **'ōmeq**, n.[m.] [2] [√ 6676]. depth:– deep (2)

H6680 עָמֵק **'āmēq**, a. [3] [√ 6676]. obscure, unintelligible, by extension of what is physically deep (not found in the OT):– obscure (2), obscure (1 [+4946, 9048])

H6681 עֵמֶק קְצִיץ **'ēmeq qᵉṣîṣ**, n.pr.loc. [1] [√ 6676 + 7906]. Emek Keziz, "*valley of Keziz*":– Emek Keziz (1)

H6682 1עָמַר **'āmar1**, v.den. [1] [→ 6658, 6684, 6685, 6890, 6891; cf. 6890]. [P] to bind sheaves (of newly cut grain):– gathers (1)

H6683 2עָמַר **'āmar2**, v. [2] [→ 6686, 6688, 6689]. [Ht] to treat brutally, deal tyrannically with:– treat as a slave (1), treating as a slave (1)

H6684 1עֹמֶר **'ōmer1**, n.m. [8] [√ 6682]. sheaf of grain:– sheaf (4), sheaves (3), sheaf of grain (1)

H6685 2עֹמֶר **'ōmer2**, n.m. [6] [√ 6682]. omer (dry measure, one-tenth of an ephah, about two quarts or liters):– omer (5), omers (1)

H6686 עֲמֹרָה **'ᵃmōrâ**, n.pr.loc. [19] [√ 6683]. Gomorrah, "*to overwhelm with water*":– Gomorrah (19)

H6687 עָמְרִי **'omrî**, n.pr.m. [18] Omri, "*thrive, live long*":– Omri (15), Omri's (2), heS (1 [+281, 1201])

H6688 עַמְרָם **'amrām**, n.pr.m. [14] [→ 6689; cf. 6683? *or* 6639? + 8123?]. Amram, "*exalted people*":– Amram (13), Amram's (1)

H6689 עַמְרָמִי **'amrāmî**, a.g. [2] [√ 6688]. Amramite, "*of Amram*":– Amramites (2)

H6690 עֲמָשָׂא **'ᵃmāśā'**, n.pr.m. [16] [→ 6691]. Amasa, "*[my] people are from Jesse*":– Amasa (15), whoseS (1)

H6691 עֲמָשַׂי **'ᵃmāśay**, n.pr.m. [5] [√ 6690]. Amasai, "*[my] people are from Jesse*":– Amasai (5)

H6692 עֲמַשְׁסַי **'ᵃmašsay**, n.pr.m. [1] Amashai:– Amashsai (1)

H6693 עֲנָב **'ᵃnāb**, n.pr.loc. [2] [√ 6694]. Anab, "*grape*":– Anab (2)

H6694 עֵנָב **'ēnāb**, n.m. [19] [→ 6693]. cluster of grapes:–

grapes (12), good grapes (2), grape (2), grapes or raisins (1 [+4300, 2256, 3313]), raisin (1), NDT (1)

H6695 עָנַג ***ʿānag***, v. [10] [→ 6696, 6697, 9503]. [Pu] to be delicate; [Ht] to delight oneself, enjoy, to mock:– delight (2), find delight (2), delicate (1), enjoy (1), find joy (1), mocking (1), sensitive (1), take delight (1)

H6696 עֹנֶג ***ʿōneg***, n.[m.] [2] [√ 6695]. delight, luxury, enjoyment:– delight (1), luxurious (1)

H6697 עָנֹג ***ʿānōg***, a. [3] [√ 6695]. sensitive, delicate:– sensitive (2), delicate (1)

H6698 עָנַד ***ʿānad***, v. [2] [cf. 5051]. [Q] to bind around, bind upon:– fasten (1), put on (1)

H6699 [1]עָנָה ***ʿānâ[1]***, v. [314] [→ 3614?, 5101, 6717; 10558]. [Q] to answer, reply, respond; [N] to be answered; usually verbal, the response can involve action:– answer (74), answered (73), replied (42), said (29), answers (7), asked (7), respond (7), responded (6), testify (5), spoke (4), testifies (4), reply (3), answering (2), declare (2), give (2), help (2), said in reply (2), spoke up (2), accept (1), accuse (1), answer (1 [+1821]), answer given (1), arguing (1), be answered (1), brought (1), come to relief (1), dispute (1), echo (1), explained (1), gave ruling (1), get response (1), give answer (1), give testimony (1), gives (1), gives back answer (1), giving testimony (1), go unanswered (1 [+4202]), had[S] (1), have answer (1), have say (1 [+2750]), recite (1 [+2256, 606]), reported (1), responds (1), said a word (1), save (1), say (1), say (1 [+2256, 606]), says (1), shout (1), shouted (1), tell (1), testified (1), testify (1 [+4200, 6332]), testimony (1), told (1), whoever he may be (1 [+6424, 2256]), NDT (3)

H6700 [2]עָנָה ***ʿānâ[2]***, v. [81] [→ 4361?, 5103, 6703? 6705, 6708, 6709, 6713, 6714, 6715, 9504]. [Q] to be afflicted; to stoop down; [N] to be afflicted, humbled, oppressed; [P] to afflict, oppress, subdue, humble, mistreat; [Pu] to be afflicted, deny oneself; [H] to afflict another, oppress; [Ht] to humble oneself; humbling by force implies dishonor:– afflicted (12), deny (6), humble (5), oppress (5), oppressed (4), humbled (3), subdue (3), violated (3), humble yourself (2), mistreated (2), raped (2), afflict (1), be afflicted (1), bring affliction (1), broke (1), bruised (1), deny themselves (1), disgraced (1), dishonored (1), disturbed (1), do[S] (1 [+6700]), do[S] (1 [+6700]), force (1), humble ourselves (1), made suffer (1), mistreat (1), oppressors (1), overwhelmed (1), punish (1), raped (1 [+8886, 2256]), raped (1 [+2256, 8886]), respond (1), self-denial (1), shared hardships (1 [+928, 889, 6700]), shared hardships (1 [+6700, 928, 889]), stilled (1), subdued (1), submit (1), suffered (1), suffered affliction (1), take advantage of (1), use (1), violate women (1), violates (1), NDT (1)

H6701 [3]עָנָה ***ʿānâ[3]***, v. [3] [→ 3610, 4348, 5100, 5102, 6703?, 6721, 6961, 6964, 6967, 6968]. [Q] to be concerned about, be worried about; [H] to keep occupied, keep oneself busy:– burden (2 [+6721]), keeps occupied (1)

H6702 [4]עָנָה ***ʿānâ[4]***, v. [13] [Q] to sing; [P] to sing to or sing about:– sing (5), sang (4), sound (2 [+7754]), shout in triumph (1 [+2116]), singing (1)

H6703 עֹנָה ***ʿōnâ***, n.f. [1] [√ 6700? *or* 6701?]. marital rights (of intercourse):– marital rights (1)

H6704 עֲנָה ***ʿ^{a}nâ***, n.pr.m. [12] [√ 6742]. Anah:– Anah (12)

H6705 עָנָו ***ʿānāw***, n.m. [22] [→ 6718; cf. 6700; 10559]. humble, afflicted, poor, oppressed:– humble (6), afflicted (4), poor (4), oppressed (2), afflicted (1 [+6714]), helpless (1), humble and oppressed (1), meek (1), needy (1), them[S] (1)

H6706 עֻנּוֹ ***ʿunnô***, n.pr.m. Not used in NIVEBC [cf. 6716]. Unno, see 6716

H6707 עָנוּב ***ʿānûb***, n.pr.m. [1] Anub, "*fruitful*":– Anub (1)

H6708 עֲנָוָה ***ʿ^{a}nāwâ***, n.f. [5] [√ 6700]. humility:– humility (5)

H6709 עַנְוָה ***ʿanwâ***, n.f. Not used in NIVEBC [√ 6700]. humility

H6710 עֲנוֹק ***ʿ^{a}nôq***, n.pr.[m. *or* loc.] [1] [→ 6737]. Anak, "*neck*":– Anak (1)

H6711 עֲנוּשִׁים ***ʿ^{a}nûšîm***, n.[m.pl.] *or* v.ptcp. [1] [√ 6740]. (punishing) fines:– fines (1)

H6712 עֲנוֹת ***ʿ^{a}nôt***, n.pr.m. & loc. Not used in NIVEBC [√ 6742]. Anoth, see 1116

H6713 עֱנוּת ***ʿ^{e}nût***, n.f. [1] [√ 6700]. suffering, affliction:– suffering (1)

H6714 עָנִי ***ʿānî***, a. [75] [√ 6700; 10559]. needy, poor, afflicted, oppressed, often referring to a class of persons of low status and lacking resources:– poor (42), afflicted (13), oppressed (5), needy (3), helpless (2), humble (2 [+6639]), afflicted (1 [+6705]), humble (1), lowly (1), meek (1), suffer (1), suffered (1), weak (1), wretched (1)

H6715 עֳנִי ***ʿ^{o}nî***, n.m. [37] [√ 6701]. affliction, suffering, misery:– affliction (14), misery (9), suffering (9), grief (1), hardship (1), oppressed (1 [+1201]), persecute (1), taken great pains (1 [+928])

H6716 עֻנִּי ***ʿunnî***, n.pr.m. [3] [cf. 6706]. Unni, "*Yahweh has answered*":– Unni (3)

H6717 עֲנָיָה ***ʿ^{a}nāyâ***, n.pr.m. [2] [√ 6699 + 3378]. Anaiah, "*Yahweh responds*":– Anaiah (2)

H6718 עָנָיו ***ʿānāyw***, n.m. Not used in NIVEBC [√ 6705; cf. 6701]. see 6705

H6719 עָנִים ***ʿānîm***, n.pr.loc. [1] Anim, "*springs*":– Anim (1)

H6720 עֵנִים ***ʿēnîm***, n.[m.] Not used in NIVEBC [cf. 3613]. see 3612

H6721 עִנְיָן ***ʿinyān***, n.m. [8] [√ 6701]. task, work, labor; misfortune, cares, troubles:– burden (2 [+6701]), business (1), cares (1), labor (1), misfortune (1 [+8273]), task (1), work (1)

H6722 עָנֵם ***ʿānēm***, n.pr.loc. [1] Anem, "*springs*":– Anem (1)

H6723 עֲנָמִים ***ʿ^{a}nāmîm***, n.pr.g. [2] Anamite:– Anamites (2)

H6724 עֲנַמֶּלֶךְ ***ʿ^{a}nammelek***, n.pr.[m.] [1] [√ 6742 + 4889]. Anammelech (pagan god), "*Anath is king*":– Anammelek (1)

H6725 [1]עָנַן ***ʿānan[1]***, v.den. [1] [→ 6727, 6728, 6729, 6730, 6731]. [P] to bring clouds:– bring clouds (1 [+6727])

H6726 [2]עָנַן ***ʿānan[2]***, v. [10] [√ 6701]. [Po] to practice sorcery, practice divination, cast spells:– practiced divination (2), cast spells (1), diviners (1), mediums (1), practice divination (1), practice sorcery (1), seek omens (1), sorceress (1), sorcery (1)

H6727 [1]עָנָן ***ʿānān[1]***, n.m. [87] [√ 6729; cf. 6725; 10560]. cloud, of moisture or smoke, natural or supernatural:– cloud (63), clouds (17), mist (2), bring clouds (1 [+6725]), it[S] (1 [+2021]), morning mist (1), smoke (1), them[S] (1)

H6728 [2]עָנָן ***ʿānān[2]***, n.pr.m. [1] [√ 6727; cf. 6725]. Anan, "*cloud*":– Anan (1)

H6729 עֲנָנָה ***ʿ^{a}nānâ***, n.f. [1] [√ 6727; cf. 6725]. cloud, likely referring to a dense rain cloud:– cloud (1)

H6730 עֲנָנִי ***ʿ^{a}nānî***, n.pr.m. [1] [√ 6725 + 3378]. Anani, "*Yahweh is a covering*":– Anani (1)

H6731 [1]עֲנַנְיָה ***ʿ^{a}nān^{e}yâ[1]***, n.pr.m. [1] [√ 6725 + 3378]. Ananiah, "*Yahweh is a covering*":– Ananiah (1)

H6732 [2]עֲנַנְיָה ***ʿ^{a}nān^{e}yâ[2]***, n.pr.loc. [1] Ananiah, "*Yahweh is a covering*":– Ananiah (1)

H6733 עָנָף ***ʿānāp***, n.[m.] [7] [→ 6734; 10561]. branches:– branches (5), branch (1), NDT (1)

H6734 עָנֵף ***ʿānēp***, a. [1] [√ 6733]. full of branches:– full of branches (1)

H6735 עָנַק ***ʿānaq***, v.den. [3] [√ 6736]. [Q] to put on (as a necklace); [H] to supply, a fig. extension of putting an adornment around the neck:– supply liberally (2 [+6735]), necklace (1)

H6736 [1]עֲנָק ***ʿ^{a}nāq[1]***, n.m. [3] [→ 6735]. necklace chain:– chain (1), chains (1), jewel (1)

H6737 [2]עֲנָק ***ʿ^{a}nāq[2]***, n.[m.] & g. [17] [√ 6710]. Anak, Anakites (with 1201):– Anakites (7), Anak (6), Anakites (4 [+1201])

H6738 [1]עָנֵר ***ʿānēr[1]***, n.pr.[m.] [2] Aner:– Aner (2)

H6739 [2]עָנֵר ***ʿānēr[2]***, n.pr.loc. [1] Aner:– Aner (1)

H6740 עָנַשׁ ***ʿānaš***, v.den. [8] [→ 6711, 6741; 10562]. [Q] to levy a fine (as a punishment or recompense); [N] to be fined, be punished:– must be fined (2 [+6740]), pay the penalty (2), fine (1), imposed a levy (1), imposing a fine (1), punished (1)

H6741 עֹנֶשׁ ***ʿōneš***, n.[m.] [2] [√ 6740]. levy, penalty, fine:– levy (1), penalty (1)

H6742 עֲנָת ***ʿ^{a}nāt***, n.pr.m. [2] [→ 1116, 1117, 6704, 6712, 6724, 6743, 6744, 6745]. Anath, "*Semitic goddess*":– Anath (2)

H6743 [1]עֲנָתוֹת ***ʿ^{a}nātôt[1]***, n.pr.loc. [13] [√ 6742]. Anathoth, "*plural of Anath*":– Anathoth (13)

H6744 [2]עֲנָתוֹת ***ʿ^{a}nātôt[2]***, n.pr.m. [2] [√ 6742]. Anathoth, "*plural of Anath*":– Anathoth (2)

H6745 עַנְּתֹתִי ***ʿann^{e}tōtî***, a.g. [5] [√ 6742]. Anathothite, from Anathoth, "*of Anathoth*":– from Anathoth (3), Anathothite (2)

H6746 עַנְתֹתִיָּה ***ʿantōtiyyâ***, n.pr.m. [1] Anthothijah:– Anthothijah (1)

H6747 עָסִיס ***ʿāsîs***, n.m. [5] [√ 6748]. new wine (relatively sweet); nectar:– new wine (3), nectar (1), wine (1)

H6748 עָסַס ***ʿāsas***, v. [1] [→ 6747]. [Q] to trample down:– trample on (1)

H6749 עָעַר ***ʿāʿar***, v. Not used in NIVEBC [√ 6424]. see 6424

H6750 עֳפָאִים ***ʿ^{o}pāʾyim***, n.m.pl. Not used in NIVEBC [→ 6751]. foliage

H6751 עֳפִי ***ʿ^{o}pî***, n.[m.] [1] [√ 6750; 10564]. branch:– branches (1)

H6752 [1]עָפַל ***ʿāpal[1]***, v. [1] [→ 6754, 6755; cf. 6753]. [Pu] to be puffed up, be swelled:– puffed up (1)

H6753 [2]עָפַל ***ʿāpal[2]***, v. [1] [cf. 6752]. [H] to have presumption, to have the audacity to:– presumption (1)

H6754 [1]עֹפֶל ***ʿōpel[1]***, n.m. [6] [√ 6752]. tumor, hemorrhoid, abscess:– tumors (6)

H6755 [2]עֹפֶל ***ʿōpel[2]***, n.[m.] [8] [√ 6754]. hill; (as a proper name) the hill of Ophel:– hill of Ophel (4), Ophel (1), citadel (1), hill (1), stronghold (1)

H6756 עָפְנִי ***ʿopnî***, n.pr.loc. [1] Ophni:– Ophni (1)

H6757 עַפְעַפַּיִם ***ʿapʿappayim***, n.m. [10] [√ 6415]. flashing rays (of dawn); glances or flitting of eyes or eyelids:– eyelids (3), eyes (3), first rays (1), gaze (1), glances (1), rays (1)

H6758 עָפַף ***ʿāpap***, v. [1] [Po] to brandish, cause to fly to and fro:– brandish (1)

H6759 עָפַר ***ʿāpar***, v.den. [1] [√ 6760]. [P] to shower (with dust or dirt):– showering (1)

H6760 עָפָר ***ʿāpār***, n.m. [110] [→ 6759; cf. 6762]. dust, earth, soil in any form; used as a figure of something that cannot be counted:– dust (81), earth (5), rubble (5), soil (4), ground (3), ashes (2), powder (2), clay (1), dirt (1), earthen ramps (1), material (1), plaster (1), sand (1), scabs (1 [+1599]), soil (1 [+824])

H6761 עֵפֶר ***ʿēper***, n.pr.m. [4] [→ 6766, 6767, 6768]. Epher, "*[small] gazelle*":– Epher (4)

H6762 עֹפֶר ***ʿōper***, n.m. [5] [→ 6763, 6764, 6765; cf. 6760]. fawn (of a deer or gazelle):– young stag (3 [+385]), fawns (2)

H6763 [1]עָפְרָה ***ʿoprâ[1]***, n.pr.m. [1] [→ 6764; cf. 6762]. Ophrah, "*young gazelle*":– Ophrah (1)

H6764 [2]עָפְרָה ***ʿoprâ[2]***, n.pr.loc. [7] [√ 6763; cf. 6762]. Ophrah, "*[young] gazelle*":– Ophrah (7)

H6765 עַפְרָה ***ʿaprâ***, n.pr.loc. Not used in NIVEBC [√ 4364; cf. 6762?]. Ophrah

H6766 [1]עֶפְרוֹן ***ʿeprôn[1]***, n.pr.m. [12] [→ 6767?, 6768; cf. 6761]. Ephron, "*gazelle*":– Ephron (8), Ephron's (2), he[S] (1), him[S] (1)

H6767 [2]עֶפְרוֹן ***ʿeprôn[2]***, n.pr.loc. [2] [√ 6766?; cf. 6761]. Ephron, "*gazelle*":– Ephron (2)

H6768 עֶפְרַיִן ***ʿeprayin***, n.pr.loc. Not used in NIVEBC [√ 6766; cf. 6761]. Ephrayin, see 6761

H6769 עֹפֶרֶת ***ʿōperet***, n.m. [9] lead (a mineral):– lead (9)

H6770 עֵץ ***ʿēṣ***, n.m. [330] [→ 6785; 10058]. tree; by extension, the product of the tree: wood, any wooden object:– wood (100), trees (64), tree (56), timber (12), pole (10), logs (9), wooden (9), poles (6), stick (6), shaft (4), almugwood (3 [+523]), carpenters (3 [+3093]), stick of wood (3), sticks (3), trees (3 [+2021, 8441]), woodcutters (3 [+2634]), algumwood (2 [+454]), timbers (2), beams (1), branches (1 [+8457]), carpenter (1 [+3093]), carpenters (1), castanets (1 [+1360]), firewood (1), it[S] (1 [+2021]), juniper (1 [+1360]), leave pole (1), loads of wood (1), lumber (1), olive (1 [+9043]), olive-wood (1 [+9043]), paneling (1 [+7596]), piece of wood (1), plant life (1), stalks (1), that[S] (1), them[S] (1 [+780]), vessels of wood (1), wooden idol (1), woodpile (1), woodwork (1), NDT (9)

H6771 [1]עָצַב ***ʿāṣab[1]***, v. [2] [→ 6773, 6775, 6777]. [P] to shape; [H] to make an image (of the Queen of Heaven):– impressed with image (1), shaped (1)

H6772 [2]עָצַב ***ʿāṣab[2]***, v. [15] [→ 5107, 6774, 6776, 6778, 6779, 6780; 10565]. [Q] to interfere with; [Qp] to be distressed; [N] to be grieved, be distressed; [P] to grieve; [H] to grieve; [Ht] to be filled with grief, be filled with pain:– distressed (2), grieve (2), grieved (2), be grieved (1), be injured (1), grieving (1), pain (1), rebuked (1), shocked (1), twist (1), was deeply troubled (1), was grieved (1)

H6773 עָצָב ***ʿāṣāb***, n.[m.] [17] [√ 6771]. idol, image, a crafted object believed to represent or even possess a spirit or god:– idols (13), images (4)

H6774 עַצָּב ***ʿaṣṣāb***, n.[m.] [1] [√ 6772]. (hard) worker, toiler:– workers (1)

H6775 [1]עֶצֶב ***ʿeṣeb[1]***, n.m. [1] [√ 6771]. pot, vessel:– pot (1)

H6776 [2]עֶצֶב ***ʿeṣeb[2]***, n.[m.] [6] [√ 6772]. pain, toil, hard work:– hard work (1), harsh (1), painful labor (1), painful toil (1), toil (1), toiling (1)

H6777 [1]עֹצֶב ***ʿōṣeb[1]***, n.m. [1] [√ 6771]. idol:– images (1)

H6778 [2]עֹצֶב ***ʿōṣeb[2]***, n.[m.] [3] [√ 6772]. pain, toil:– offensive (1), pain (1), suffering (1)

H6779 עִצָּבוֹן ***ʿiṣṣābôn***, n.[m.] [3] [√ 6772]. pain, hardship, distress:– painful toil (2), pains (1)

H6780 עַצֶּבֶת ***ʿaṣṣebet***, n.f. [5] [√ 6772]. pain, sorrow, grief:– grief (1), heartache (1 [+4213]), suffer (1), sufferings (1), wounds (1)

H6781 עָצָה ***ʿāṣâ***, v. [1] [Q] to wink (the eye), as a non-verbal communication of what is evil, malicious, or lurid:– winks (1)

H6782 עָצֶה ***ʿāṣeh***, n.[m.] [1] backbone, tailbone:– backbone (1)

H6783 [1]עֵצָה ***ʿēṣâ[1]***, n.f. [88] [√ 3619; 10539]. advice, counsel, plan, purpose, scheme:– advice (16), counsel (15), plans (15), plan (6), advice gave (3 [+3619]), purpose (3), advice given (2 [+3619]), planned (2 [+3619]), purposes (2), schemes (2), advise (1 [+3619]), alliances (1), bent on (1 [+928]), consultation (1), counselor (1 [+408]), counselors (1 [+408]), decision (1), giving advice (1 [+3619]), harmony (1 [+8934]), in step with (1 [+928]), make up mind (1 [+995]), planned (1), planning (1 [+3619]), plot (1), plots (1), plotted (1 [+3619]), predictions (1), sense (1), strategy

(1), that[S] (1), thoughts (1 [+928, 5883]), what decided to do (1)

H6784 [2]עֵצָה **'ēṣâ[2]**, n.f. revolt, resistance, disobedience

H6785 [3]עֵצָה **'ēṣâ[3]**, n.f.col. [1] [√ 6770]. (coll.) wood; this can refer to wooden idols:– trees (1)

H6786 עָצוּם **'āṣûm**, a. [31] [→ 6802; cf. 6793]. strong, mighty, powerful:– mighty (9), powerful (6), stronger (6), strong (4), far too numerous (1 [+8041, 2256]), great (1), power (1), strength (1), throngs (1 [+6639]), very (1 [+4394])

H6787 עֶצְיוֹן גֶּבֶר **'eṣyôn geber**, n.pr.loc. [7] Ezion Geber, "*giant, the giant backbone*":– Ezion Geber (7)

H6788 עָצַל **'āṣal**, v. [1] [→ 6789, 6790, 6791, 6792]. [N] to hesitate, be sluggish, be slow:– hesitate (1)

H6789 עָצֵל **'āṣēl**, a. [14] [√ 6788]. sluggish, slow, lazy; (n.) sluggard, one with no discipline or motivation, a moral failure:– sluggard (11), sluggards (2), sluggard's (1)

H6790 עַצְלָה **'aṣlâ**, n.f. [1] [√ 6788]. laziness, slowness, sluggishness:– Laziness (1)

H6791 עַצְלוּת **'aṣlût**, n.f. [1] [√ 6788]. idleness, sluggishness, laziness:– idleness (1)

H6792 עֲצַלְתַּיִם **'ᵃṣaltayim**, n.f.du. [1] [√ 6788]. extreme laziness, indolence:– laziness (1)

H6793 [1]עָצַם **'āṣam[1]**, v. [18] [→ 6492, 6786, 6795, 6796, 6797, 6798, 6799, 6800, 6801, 9508]. [Q] to be vast, powerful, numerous; [P] to crush his bone; [H] to make numerous, make powerful, make vast:– many (6), numerous (3), crush bones (1), height of power (1), made numerous (1), more (1), power (1), powerful (1), strength (1), vast (1), very strong (1 [+3946])

H6794 [2]עָצַם **'āṣam[2]**, v. [2] [Q] to close (the eyes); [P] to tightly shut (the eyes):– sealed (1), shut (1)

H6795 [1]עֶצֶם **'eṣem[1]**, n.f. [126] [→ 6796; cf. 6793]. bone; by extension: the whole body, any part of the body, limb; strength of the body, vigor; (adv.) that very (day); "one's bone and flesh" is a close relative:– bones (80), very (12), blood (6), bone (6), body (3), bodies (2), same (2), as (1 [+3869]), being (1), frame (1), limb (1), those[S] (1), vigor (1), you (1 [+4013]), NDT (8)

H6796 [2]עֶצֶם **'eṣem[2]**, n.pr.loc. [3] [√ 6795; cf. 6793]. Ezem, "*bone [strength]*":– Ezem (3)

H6797 [1]עֹצֶם **'ōṣem[1]**, n.[m.] [3] [√ 6793]. might, strength:– strength (2), might (1)

H6798 [2]עֹצֶם **'ōṣem[2]**, n.[m.] [1] [√ 6793]. framework (of bones of the human body):– frame (1)

H6799 עַצְמָה **'aṣmâ**, n.f. Not used in NIVEBC [√ 6793]. evil deeds; severe suffering

H6800 עָצְמָה **'oṣmâ**, n.f. [2] [√ 6793]. power, potency, might:– potent (1), power (1)

H6801 עַצְמוֹן **'aṣmôn**, n.pr.loc. [3] [√ 6795; cf. 6793]. Azmon, "*strongly [built body]*":– Azmon (2), where[S] (1)

H6802 עֲצֻמוֹת **'ᵃṣumôt**, n.f.[pl.] [1] [√ 6786]. defensive arguments, strong words:– arguments (1)

H6803 עֵצֶן **'ēṣen**, var. Ezen, see 2851

H6804 עֶצְנִי **'eṣnî**, n.pr. *or* a.g.? Eznite, see 2851

H6805 עָצַץ **'āṣaṣ**, v. [Q] to fix one's eyes on

H6806 עָצַר **'āṣar**, v. [46] [→ 5109, 5110, 6807, 6808, 6809]. [Q] to refrain, hold back, restrain; [Qp] to be enslaved, be constrained; [N] to be stopped, be detained:– shut up (5), slave (5), able (2 [+3946]), be stopped (2), retain (2), stopped (2), was stopped (2), able (1), been kept (1), close up (1), confined (1), detain (1), detained (1), feel very weak (1 [+4202, 3946]), govern (1), helpless (1 [+4202, 3946]), holds back (1), keep (1), kept (1), kept the women from conceiving (1 [+1237, 8167, 6806]), kept the women from conceiving (1 [+6806, 1237, 8167]), prevail (1), refrained (1), regain (1 [+6388]), restricted (1), seized (1), slow down (1 [+4200, 8206]), stay (1), stops (1), was banished (1), was checked (1), was confined (1), was shut in (1)

H6807 עֶצֶר **'eṣer**, n.[m.] [1] [√ 6806]. restraint, oppression:– prosperous (1 [+3769])

H6808 עֹצֶר **'ōṣer**, n.[m.] [3] [√ 6806]. oppression; barrenness:– oppression (2), barren (1)

H6809 עֲצָרָה **'ᵃṣārâ**, n.f. [11] [√ 6806]. assembly, usually on a festive day:– assembly (4), assemblies (2), closing special assembly (2), sacred assembly (2), crowd (1)

H6810 עָקַב **'āqab**, v. [5] [√ 6812; cf. 6811, 6812, 7693]. [Q] to deceive; to grasp at the heel; [P] to hold the heel, to hold back:– deceiver (2 [+6810]), grasped heel (1), holds back (1), taken advantage of (1)

H6811 [1]עָקֵב **'āqēb[1]**, n.m. [13] [→ 6813, 6814; cf. 3620, 6810, 6812]. heel, hoof; footstep, footprint; by extension: rear guard of a military formation; a euphemism for private parts:– heel (3), heels (2), ambush (1), body (1), footprints (1), hooves (1), step (1), steps (1), tracks (1), turned (1 [+1540])

H6812 [2]עָקֵב **'āqēb[2]**, a.vbl. [1] [→ 6810, 6815, 6816, 6817; cf. 3620, 6810, 6811, 7693]. deceiver:– deceivers (1)

H6813 עֵקֶב **'ēqeb**, n.[m.] (used as adv. & c.) [15] [√ 6811]. (c.) because; (n.) a reward; unto the end:– because (3 [+889]), because (2 [+3954]), for (2), at (1 [+6584]), because (1), because of (1 [+6584]), if (1), reward (1), to the end (1), to the very end (1 [+4200, 6409]), wages (1)

H6814 [1]עָקֹב **'āqōb[1]**, a. [1] [√ 6811]. footprint:– footprints (1)

H6815 [2]עָקֹב **'āqōb[2]**, a. [2] [√ 6812]. deceitful; rough, bumpy:– deceitful (1), rough ground (1)

H6816 עֹקֶב **'ōqeb**, n.[m.] Not used in NIVEBC [√ 6812]. insidiousness

H6817 עָקְבָּה **'oqbâ**, n.f. [1] [√ 6812]. deceptiveness, cunning, craftiness:– deceptively (1 [+928])

H6818 עָקַד **'āqad**, v. [1] [→ 6819, 6820]. [Q] to bind (feet):– bound (1)

H6819 עָקֹד **'āqōd**, a. [7] [√ 6818]. streaked, striped:– streaked (7)

H6820 עֵקֶד **'ēqed**, n.pr.loc. Not used in NIVEBC [→ 1118; cf. 6818]. Eked, see 1118

H6821 עָקָה **'āqâ**, n.f. [1] [√ 6421]. pressure; oppressive look, stare, or actions:– threats (1)

H6822 עַקּוּב **'aqqûb**, n.pr.m. [8] Akkub, "*guard*":– Akkub (8)

H6823 עָקַל **'āqal**, v. [1] [→ 6824, 6825]. [Pu] to be perverted, be distorted, be crooked:– perverted (1)

H6824 עֲקַלְקַל **'ᵃqalqāl**, a.intens. [2] [√ 6823]. crooked, winding:– crooked ways (1), winding (1)

H6825 עֲקַלָּתוֹן **'ᵃqallātôn**, a. [1] [√ 6823]. coiling (serpent):– coiling (1)

H6826 עַקָּן **'aqān**, n.pr.m. [2] [→ 3622?]. Akan:– Akan (2)

H6827 [1]עָקַר **'āqar[1]**, v.den. [2] [→ 6829, 6830, 6831; cf. 6828; 10566, 10567]. [Q] to root up; [N] to be uprooted:– uproot (1), uprooted (1)

H6828 [2]עָקַר **'āqar[2]**, v.den. [5] [cf. 6827]. [P] to hamstring (to cut the tendon and render helpless or useless):– hamstring (4), hamstring (1)

H6829 עָקָר **'āqār**, a. [12] [√ 6827]. barren, sterile, without children:– childless (6), barren (5), without young (1)

H6830 [1]עֵקֶר **'ēqer[1]**, n.m. [1] [√ 6827]. offspring, as the fig. extension of a plant that grows up from a root:– member (1)

H6831 [2]עֵקֶר **'ēqer[2]**, n.pr.m. [1] [√ 6827?]. Eker, "[poss.] *offspring*":– Eker (1)

H6832 עַקְרָב **'aqrāb**, n.m. [9] [√ 7930]. scorpion:– scorpions (6), scorpion (3)

H6833 עֶקְרוֹן **'eqrôn**, n.pr.loc. [22] [→ 6834]. Ekron, "[perhaps] *barren place* or *fertile place*":– Ekron (22)

H6834 עֶקְרוֹנִי **'eqrônî**, a.g. [2] [√ 6833]. Ekronite, of Ekron, "*of Ekron*":– Ekron (1), people of Ekron (1)

H6835 עָקַשׁ **'āqaš**, v. [5] [→ 5112, 6836, 6837, 6838]. [N] to be perverse, be crooked; [P] to take crooked paths; to distort; [H] to pronounce guilty:– distort (1), perverse (1), pronounce guilty (1), takes crooked (1), turned crooked (1)

H6836 [1]עִקֵּשׁ **'iqqēš[1]**, a. [11] [→ 6837; cf. 6835]. perverse, crooked, warped:– perverse (5), devious (2), corrupt (1), crooked (1), warped (1), wicked (1)

H6837 [2]עִקֵּשׁ **'iqqēš[2]**, n.pr.m. [3] [√ 6836; cf. 6835]. Ikkesh, "*crooked, perverted*":– Ikkesh (3)

H6838 עִקְּשׁוּת **'iqqᵉšût**, n.f. [2] [√ 6835]. perversion, corruption, crookedness:– corrupt (1), perversity (1)

H6839 [1]עָר **'ār[1]**, n.m. [2] [√ 6910?]. enemy, adversary:– adversaries (1), enemy (1)

H6840 [2]עָר **'ār[2]**, n.pr.loc. [6] [√ 6551?]. Ar, "[poss.] *city*":– Ar (6)

H6841 עֵר **'ēr**, n.pr.m. [10] [√ 6424; 10541]. Er, "*watchful, watcher*":– Er (9), NDT (1)

H6842 [1]עָרַב **'ārab[1]**, v. [17] [→ 5114, 6859, 6860, 9510; cf. 6843?, 6845]. [Q] to put up a security, make a guarantee, give a pledge; [Ht] to make a bargain, make a wager:– puts up security (4), make a bargain (2), come to aid (1), devote (1), ensure (1), guarantee safety (1), guaranteed safety (1), merchants (1 [+5114]), mortgaging (1), pledge (1), put up security (1), puts up security (1 [+6859]), trade (1)

H6843 [2]עָרַב **'ārab[2]**, v. [5] [→ 6849, 6850, 6856; cf. 6842?; 10569]. [Ht] to mingle, join in with, share with:– mingled (2), avoid (1 [+4202, 4200]), join (1), share (1)

H6844 [3]עָרַב **'ārab[3]**, v. [8] [→ 6853]. [Q] to be pleasing, be pleasant, be acceptable:– please (2), sweet (2), acceptable (1), found pleasure (1), pleasant (1), pleasing (1)

H6845 [4]עָרַב **'ārab[4]**, v.den. [3] [→ 5115, 6847; cf. 6842]. [Q] to become evening; (opposite of joy) turn to gloom; [H] to do something in the evening:– evening (2), turns to gloom (1)

H6846 [1]עֶרֶב **'ereb[1]**, n.m. Not used in NIVEBC [cf. 6850]. see 6850

H6847 [2]עֶרֶב **'ereb[2]**, n.[m.] [134] [√ 6845]. evening, twilight, dusk, the fading of the day; twilight can extend into the dark of the night:– evening (110), at twilight (11 [+1068, 2021]), dusk (2), evenings (2), night (2), evening (1 [+6961, 2021]), evening (1 [+928, 2021, 928, 2021, 6847]), evening (1 [+928, 2021, 6847, 928, 2021]), every evening (1 [+928, 2021, 928, 2021, 6847]), every evening (1 [+928, 2021, 6847, 928, 2021]), fading (1), NDT (1)

H6848 [3]עֶרֶב **'ereb[3]**, n.m. Not used in NIVEBC [cf. 6851, 6858]. see 6851

H6849 [1]עֵרֶב **'ēreb[1]**, n.[m.] [9] [√ 6843]. knitted or woven material:– knitted material (9)

H6850 [2]עֵרֶב **'ēreb[2]**, n.m. [5] [cf. 6843, 6846]. foreign people:– foreign people (2), foreigners (1), of foreign descent (1), other people (1)

H6851 [1]עֲרָב **'ᵃrab[1]**, n.pr.loc. & g. [7] [√ 6858; cf. 6848]. Arabia, Arab:– Arabia (6), Arabian (1)

H6852 [2]עֲרָב **'ᵃrab[2]**, n.[pr.loc.?] Not used in NIVEBC [√ 6858]. see 6851 & 6858

H6853 עָרֵב **'ārēb**, a. [2] [√ 6844]. pleasant, sweet (voice):– sweet (1), tastes sweet (1)

H6854 [1]עֹרֵב **'ōrēb[1]**, n.m. [10] [→ 6855]. raven:– raven (6), ravens (4)

H6855 [2]עֹרֵב **'ōrēb[2]**, n.pr.m. [7] [√ 6854]. Oreb, "*raven*":– Oreb (7)

H6856 עָרֹב **'ārōb**, n.m. [9] [√ 6843]. swarms of flies:– swarms of flies (5), flies (4)

H6857 [1]עֲרָבָה **'ᵃrābâ[1]**, n.[f.] [5] [→ 6863]. poplar tree:– poplars (3), poplar trees (1), willows (1 [+5707])

H6858 [2]עֲרָבָה **'ᵃrābâ[2]**, n.f. [57] [→ 6851, 6852, 6861, 6862; cf. 6848]. plains (a geographical region of desert, wilderness or wasteland); (pr.n.) Arabah:– Arabah (26), plains (17), desert (5), wasteland (3), Dead Sea (2 [+3542]), wastelands (2), deserts (1), wilderness (1)

H6859 עֲרֻבָּה **'ᵃrubbâ**, n.f. [2] [√ 6842]. security, pledge; assurance:– assurance (1), puts up security (1 [+6842])

H6860 עֵרָבוֹן **'ērābôn**, n.[m.] [3] [√ 6842]. pledge, security:– pledge (3)

H6861 עַרְבִי **'arbî**, a.g. [7] [√ 6858]. Arab, of Arabia; may also refer to bedouin in general:– Arabs (5), Arab (2)

H6862 עֲרָבִי **'ᵃrābî**, n.g. [2] [√ 6858]. Arab, nomad:– nomad (1), nomads (1)

H6863 עַרְבָתִי **'arbātî**, a.g. [2] [√ 6857]. Arbathite, "*of Arabah*":– Arbathite (2)

H6864 עָרַג **'ārag**, v. [3] [√ 6870?]. [Q] to pant for, long for (as a thirsty animal):– pants (2), pant (1)

H6865 [1]עֲרָד **'ᵃrād[1]**, n.pr.m. [1] [√ 6871]. Arad:– Arad (1)

H6866 [2]עֲרָד **'ᵃrād[2]**, n.pr.loc. [4] [√ 6871]. Arad, "*wild donkey*":– Arad (4)

H6867 [1]עָרָה **'ārâ[1]**, v. [14] [→ 4623, 5118, 5122, 6567, 6872, 6873, 6880, 6895, 9509; cf. 6910, 6423]. [N] to be poured; [P] to lay bare, empty, expose, strip; [H] to make exposed; to cause to pour out; to dishonor; [Ht] to show oneself naked:– exposed (2), tear down (2), dishonor (1), emptied (1), empty (1), give over to death (1), is poured (1), make bald (1), poured out (1), stripped (1), stripped naked (1), uncovers (1)

H6868 [2]עָרָה **'ārâ[2]**, n.f. [1] plants, bulrushes:– plants (1)

H6869 [3]עָרָה **'ārâ[3]**, n.pr.loc. [1] [→ 5117?]. Arah:– Arah (1)

H6870 עֲרוּגָה **'ᵃrûgâ**, n.f. [4] [√ 6864?]. garden bed, garden plot:– beds (2), plot (2)

H6871 עָרוֹד **'ārôd**, n.[m.] [1] [→ 6563, 6865, 6866; 10570]. wild donkey:– its[S] (1)

H6872 עֶרְוָה **'erwâ**, n.f. [53] [√ 6867; 10571]. nakedness (indecent or shameful in certain situations); "to expose the nakedness" is to have sexual relations:– have sexual relations with (11 [+1655]), naked body (5), dishonored (4 [+1655]), naked (4), dishonor (3), have sexual relations (3 [+1655]), have relations with (2 [+1655]), indecent (2), shame (2), unprotected (2), body (1 [+1414]), dishonor bed (1 [+1655]), dishonor by having sexual relations with (1 [+1655]), dishonor by to have sexual relations (1 [+1655]), has sexual relations with (1 [+1655, 906]), have sexual relations (1 [+8011, 906]), nakedness (1), private parts (1), shame (1 [+1425]), stark naked (1 [+3972]), strip (1 [+1655]), NDT (4)

H6873 עָרוֹם **'ārôm**, a. [16] [√ 6873]. naked, stripped:– naked (13), stripped (3)

H6874 עָרוּם **'ārûm**, a. [11] [√ 6891]. wise and understanding; with a positive connotation: prudent, clever; with a negative connotation: crafty:– prudent (7), crafty (3), prudent (1 [+132])

H6875 [1]עֲרוֹעֵר **'ᵃrô'ēr[1]**, n.[m.] Not used in NIVEBC [→ 6876; cf. 6910]. bush

H6876 [2]עֲרוֹעֵר **'ᵃrô'ēr[2]**, n.pr.loc. [16] [→ 6901; cf. 6875, 6910]. Aroer, "*juniper*":– Aroer (16)

H6877 עָרוּץ **'ārûṣ**, a. [1] [√ 6907]. dry or dreadful:– dry (1)

H6878 [1]עֵרִי **'ērî[1]**, n.pr.m. [2] [→ 6879; cf. 6424]. Eri, "*watcher*":– Eri (2)

H6879 [2]עֵרִי **'ērî[2]**, a.g. [1] [√ 6878; cf. 6424]. Erite, "*of Eri*":– Erite (1)

H6880 עֶרְיָה *'eryâ*, n.f. [6] [√ 6867]. bareness, nakedness, the state of being uncovered:– stark naked (3 [+6567, 2256]), bare (1), naked (1), uncovered (1 [+6423])

H6881 עֲרִיסָה *'arîsâ*, n.f. [4] ground meal (dough in the first phase of bread making):– ground meal (4)

H6882 עֲרִיפִים *'arîpîm*, n.[m.pl.] [1] [√ 6903]. cloud:– clouds (1)

H6883 עָרִיץ *'ārîṣ*, a. [21] [√ 6907]. ruthless, cruel, fierce:– ruthless (17), fierce (2), cruel (1), mighty (1)

H6884 עֲרִירִי *'arîrî*, a. [4] [√ 6910]. childless, very undesireable and even shameful in the ancient Near East:– childless (4)

H6885 עָרַךְ *'ārak*, v.[den.] [74] [→ 6886, 5119, 5120, 5121]. [Q] to arrange in rows; put in order, take up (battle) positions; [Qp] to be arranged, be put in order, be put in formation; [H] to set a value:– took up positions (5), arrange (4), deployed (4), prepared (4), arranged (3), compare (3), spread (3), drew up (2), drew up line (2), formed battle lines (2), judge quality (2), marshaled (2), prepare (2), set (2), set out (2), take up positions (2), been prepared (1), compare with (1), deployed forces (1), draw up case (1), drawing up (1), drawn up (1), drew up lines (1), formation (1), formed lines (1), handle (1), in formation (1), keep (1), laid out (1), lay (1), lay out (1), liken (1), line up (1), ready (1), set accusations (1), set out (1 [+6886]), set up (1), set value (1), stand up (1), state (1), stationed (1), sustain (1), taxed (1), tend (1), tended (1), value sets (1)

H6886 עֵרֶךְ *'ērek*, n.m. [33] [√ 6885]. proper estimated value:– value (11), proper value (3), set value (3), value (2 [+4084]), assessments (1), clothes (1 [+955]), equivalent value (1), form (1), like (1 [+3869]), personal vows (1 [+5883]), price set (1), set out (1 [+6885]), specified amount (1), that[S] (1), value (1 [+4831]), what belongs (1), worth (1), NDT (1)

H6887 עָרֵל *'āral*, v.den. [2] [√ 6889]. [Q] to regard as forbidden, leave unharvested:– nakedness be exposed (1), regard as forbidden (1 [+6889])

H6888 עָרֵל *'ārēl*, a. [34] [√ 6889]. uncircumcised (i.e., having a foreskin of the penis):– uncircumcised (28), faltering (2), closed (1), forbidden (1), NDT (2)

H6889 עָרְלָה *'orlâ*, n.f. [14] [→ 1502, 6887, 6888]. foreskin (of the penis):– foreskins (3), be circumcised (1 [+4576, 1414]), been circumcised (1 [+4576]), circumcise (1 [+6073]), circumcise (1 [+4576]), circumcised (1 [+4576, 1414]), flesh (1), foreskin (1), not circumcised (1 [+4200, 2257]), regard as forbidden (1 [+6887]), undergo circumcision (1 [+4576, 906, 1414]), was circumcised (1 [+4576, 1414])

H6890 1עָרַם *'āram[1]*, v. [1] [→ 6894; cf. 6682]. [N] to be piled up, be dammed up:– piled up (1)

H6891 2עָרַם *'āram[2]*, v. [6] [→ 6874, 6892, 6893]. [Q] to be crafty, show prudence; [H] to initiate cunning plans:– very crafty (2 [+6891]), craftiness (1), cunning (1), learn prudence (1), shows prudence (1)

H6892 עֹרֶם *'ōrem*, n.[m.] Not used in NIVEBC [√ 6891]. craftiness

H6893 עָרְמָה *'ormâ*, n.f. [5] [√ 6891]. prudence, cunning:– prudence (3), deliberately (1 [+928]), ruse (1)

H6894 עֲרֵמָה *'arēmâ*, n.f. [11] [√ 6890]. heap, mound (of grain):– heaps (3), in heaps (2 [+6894]), doing this[S] (1 [+3569, 2021]), grain (1), grain pile (1), heap (1), heaps of grain (1), mound (1)

H6895 עַרְמוֹן *'ermôn*, n.[m.] [2] [√ 6867]. plane tree:– plane trees (2)

H6896 עֵרָן *'ērān*, n.pr.m. [1] [→ 6897]. Eran, "*watcher, watchful*":– Eran (1)

H6897 עֵרָנִי *'ērānî*, a.g. [1] [√ 6896]. Eranite, "*of Eran*":– Eranite (1)

H6898 עַרְעוֹר *'ar'ôr*, n.pr.loc. Not used in NIVEBC [cf. 6876]. see 6876

H6899 עַרְעָר *'ar'ār*, a. [3] [→ 6900; cf. 6910]. destitute, naked, stripped; (juniper) bush:– bush (2), destitute (1)

H6900 עַרְעָרָה *'ar'ārâ*, n.pr.loc. Not used in NIVEBC [cf. 6368, 6899]. Ararah, see 6899 & 6368

H6901 עֲרֹעֵרִי *'arō'ērî*, a.g. [1] [√ 6876; cf. 6910]. Aroerite, "*of Aroer*":– Aroerite (1)

H6902 עֹרֶף *'ōrep*, n.m. [33] [→ 6905]. neck; to be "stiff of neck" is to be obstinate, stubborn, implying rebellion:– stiff-necked (11 [+7996]), backs (7), stiff-necked (7 [+7997]), neck (4), back (2), routed (1 [+2200]), NDT (1)

H6903 1עָרַף *'ārap[1]*, v. [2] [→ 6882, 6906?; cf. 8319]. [Q] to trickle, drip:– drop (1), fall (1)

H6904 2עָרַף *'ārap[2]*, v.den. [6] [Q] to break; [Qp] be broken:– break neck (3), breaks neck (1), demolish (1), neck was broken (1)

H6905 עָרְפָּה *'orpâ*, n.pr.f. [2] [√ 6902]. Orpah, "*neck, the girl with the full mane[?]*":– Orpah (2)

H6906 עֲרָפֶל *'arāpel*, n.m. [15] [√ 6903?]. dark or thick clouds; deep gloom:– thick darkness (4), blackness (2), dark cloud (2), dark clouds (2), darkness (2), deep darkness (2), deep gloom (1)

H6907 עָרַץ *'āraṣ*, v. [15] [→ 5123, 5124, 6877, 6883]. [Q] to shake, to shake in terror; [N] to be feared; [H] to dread, stand in awe:– terrified (4), dread (2), shake (2), afraid (1), cause terror (1), feared (1), is feared (1), stand in awe (1), strike terror (1), torment (1)

H6908 עָרַק *'āraq*, v. [2] [Q] to gnaw:– gnawing pains (1), roamed (1)

H6909 עַרְקִי *'arqî*, a.g. [2] Arkite:– Arkites (2)

H6910 עָרַר *'ārar*, v. [4] [→ 6839?, 6875, 6876, 6884, 6899, 6901; cf. 6867]. [Q] to strip off; [Po] to strip; [Pil] to level, demolish; [Htpal] to be laid utterly bare:– be leveled (2 [+6910]), strip off fine clothes (1 [+7320, 2256]), stripped bare (1)

H6911 עֶרֶשׂ *'ereś*, n.f. [10] bed, couch:– bed (4), couch (2), bed (1 [+3661]), couches (1), sickbed (1 [+1867]), NDT (1)

H6912 עֵשֶׂב *'ēśeb*, n.m. [33] [√ 10572]. green plant, vegetation, grass:– grass (11), plants (8), growing (4), plant (3), vegetation (2), food (1), green thing (1), plant (1 [+2021, 8441]), tender plants (1), NDT (1)

H6913 1עָשָׂה *'āśâ[1]*, v. [2617] [→ 543, 3632, 3633, 3634, 5126, 5127, 5128, 5129, 6914, 6915, 6918, 6919]. [Q] to do, make; [Qp] to be done; [N] to be done, be made; [Pu] to be made; a generic of action, seen in the many contextual translations of the NIV:– do (408), did (285), made (266), done (260), make (161), doing (62), does (50), follow (39), celebrate (24), deal (23), maker (22), show (22), obey (21), act (20), built (20), prepare (20), carry out (18), be done (17), offer (16), sacrifice (16), inflict (15), provide (14), celebrated (13), committed (13), prepared (13), keep (11), workers (11), acted (10), observe (10), been done (9), bring (9), gave (9), performed (9), shown (9), accomplish (8), makes (8), present (8), treated (8), work (8), brought (7), treat (7), bear (6), build (6), is done (6), making (6), obeys (6), worked (6), commits (5), completely destroy (5 [+3986]), deal with (5), forbidden (5 [+4202]), grant (5), perform (5), produce (5), set up (5), showed (5), uphold (5), yield (5), acquired (4), appointed (4), be made (4), brought about (4), carried out (4), deal (4 [+6913]), exploits (4), gain (4), give (4), held (4), observed (4), practice (4), provided (4), put (4), sends (4), used (4), used to make (4), working (4), achieve (3), acting (3), be granted (3), carrying out (3), caused (3), destroy completely (3 [+3986]), do work (3), engage (3), gained (3), instituted (3), offered (3), performs (3), produced (3), showing (3), shows (3), supervise (3), use (3), waged (3), were carved (3), works (3), achieved (2), administrators (2 [+4856]), are done (2), attack (2 [+4200]), bake (2), be fulfilled (2), be prepared (2), been made (2), been observed (2), behave (2), behaved (2), careful to carry out (2 [+6913]), carved (2), certainly carry out (2 [+6913]), certainly do (2 [+6913]), certainly make (2 [+6913]), commit (2), conduct (2), conformed to (2 [+3869]), consulted (2), created (2), deals (2), dealt (2), do (2 [+6913]), do great things (2 [+6913]), done (2 [+5126]), dug (2), fight (2), follow (2 [+3869]), formed (2), fought (2), fulfill (2), fulfilled (2), fully accomplishes (2 [+2256, 7756]), get (2), happen (2), happens (2), harm (2 [+8273]), harm (2 [+8288]), imitate (2 [+3869]), inflicted (2), introduced (2), kept (2), maintain (2), obeyed (2), open (2), ordained (2), pack (2), put into practice (2), responsible (2), serve (2), shaping (2), surely show (2 [+6913]), surely sprout (2 [+6913]), undertaken (2), upholds (2), use (2 [+4856]), wage (2), was celebrated (2), worship (2), yielded (2), accomplished (1), accomplishing (1), acts (1), add (1), adhere to (1 [+3869]), administer (1), am (1), amassed (1), answer (1), applies (1), apply (1), are (1), artificial (1), assign (1), assigned (1), at war (1 [+4878]), at work (1), attend to (1), avenged (1 [+5935]), be (1), be carried out (1), be completed (1), be injured (1), be offered (1), be paid back (1), be presented (1), be used (1), bearing (1), became famous (1 [+9005]), been (1), been committed (1), been constructed (1), been followed (1), been used (1 [+4856]), began (1), behaves (1), bent on (1), bring up (1), bulges with flesh (1 [+7089]), busy (1), cancel debts (1 [+9024]), carried on (1), carried through (1), carrying on (1), cast (1), celebrating (1), celebration (1), comes (1), construct (1), constructed (1), continue (1), continued (1), cooked (1), copied (1), creature (1), crop (1), custom (1), custom (1 [+4027]), customary (1), dealings (1), defends (1), deserve (1), did so[S] (1 [+906, 2021, 7175]), diligent (1), displayed (1), do something (1), dressed (1), earners (1), earns (1), enacted (1), engaged in (1), erected (1), establish (1), established (1), establishes (1), evildoer (1 [+8288]), evildoer (1 [+8402]), evildoers (1 [+8402]), executed (1), exempt from taxes (1 [+2930]), exercises (1), faithfully (1 [+622]), fashion (1), fashioned (1), fill (1), finished (1), fit for (1), follow (1 [+4027]), follow lead (1 [+4027]), followed (1 [+4027]), followed the example (1 [+6913, 3869]), followed the example (1 [+3869, 6913]), founded (1), fulfill (1 [+7023, 3869, 4027]), fulfills (1), fully obeyed (1 [+9048, 2256]), get ready (1), give over (1), given (1), goes on (1), going (1), got ready (1), granted (1), grow (1), hammer (1 [+8393]), hammer out (1 [+5251]), handle (1), handled (1), have (1), have[S] (1), help (1), help (1 [+907]), help (1 [+4200]), hold (1), honor (1 [+3702]), honored (1 [+3883]), howl (1 [+5027]), in charge (1), is built (1), is carried out (1), is done (1 [+5126]), is forged (1), judge[S] (1), judges (1 [+5477]), keeping (1), keeps (1), make provision (1), manage (1), may do (1), measured (1), meet (1), merchants (1 [+4856]), molded (1), mount (1), mounted (1), mourn (1 [+65]), move (1), obey (1 [+9068, 2256]), observance (1), occurs (1), officiate (1), on way (1 [+2006]), oppressed (1 [+928, 2021, 6945]), pass through (1), persist (1), persisted in (1 [+3869]), pervert (1 [+6404]), piled (1), practices (1), presents (1), proclaimed (1), proud (1 [+1452]), provides (1), providing (1), punish (1 [+5477]), put forth (1), put in jeopardy (1 [+9214]), ready (1), received (1), reduces (1), render (1), rescued (1 [+9591]), resist (1), resorted (1), rich (1), roughs out (1), sacrificed (1), schemes (1), secures (1), serve (1 [+7372]), set (1), shapes (1), sins defiantly (1 [+928, 3338, 8123]), sins unintentionally (1 [+928, 8705]), skilled workers (1 [+4856]), speak (1), still to come (1 [+4202]), stir up (1), such[S] (1 [+2021]), take (1), take action (1), take part (1 [+7928]), take place (1), taken care of (1), taking place (1), these men[S] (1 [+2021, 4856]), trained (1), treated (1 [+6640]), tried (1 [+4027]), trim (1), trimmed (1), turns to (1), upheld (1), use to make (1), useful (1), using (1), was happening (1), was made (1), was spent for making (1 [+4946]), ways (1), well-trained (1 [+4878]), went about (1), went on (1), went to war (1 [+4878]), were[S] (1), were made (1), were practiced (1), were prepared (1), won (1), work (1 [+4856]), work (1 [+5126]), workers (1 [+408]), workers (1 [+4856, 8441]), workers (1 [+928, 2021, 4856]), working (1 [+4856]), works out (1), wrongdoing (1 [+8400]), wrongs (1 [+2633]), NDT (75)

H6914 2עָשָׂה *'āśâ[2]*, v. [3] [√ 6913]. [P] to caress, squeeze:– caressed (3)

H6915 עֲשָׂהאֵל *'aśāh'ēl,* עֲשָׂה־אֵל *'aśāh-'ēl*, n.pr.m. [18] [√ 6913 + 446]. Asahel, "*God [El] has made*":– Asahel (17), he[S] (1)

H6916 עֵשָׂו *'ēśāw*, n.pr.m. [97] Esau, "*hairy*":– Esau (77), Esau's (14), he[S] (3), Esau (2 [+1074]), NDT (1)

H6917 עָשׂוֹר *'āśôr*, n.[m.] [16] [√ 6923]. (group of) ten:– tenth (12), ten-stringed (3), ten (1)

H6918 עֲשִׂיאֵל *'aśî'ēl*, n.pr.m. [1] [√ 6913 + 446]. Asiel, "*God [El] has made*":– Asiel (1)

H6919 עֲשָׂיָה *'aśāyâ*, n.pr.m. [7] [√ 6913 + 3378]. Asaiah, "*Yahweh has made*":– Asaiah (7)

H6920 עֲשִׂירִי *'aśîrî*, a.num.ord. [29] [√ 6923]. tenth:– tenth (28), one-tenth (1)

H6921 עָשַׂק *'āśaq*, v. [1] [→ 5131]. [Ht] to dispute, quarrel:– disputed (1)

H6922 עֵשֶׂק *'ēśeq*, n.pr.loc. [1] Esek, "*dispute*":– Esek (1)

H6923 עָשַׂר *'āśar*, v.den. [9] [→ 5130, 6917, 6920, 6924, 6925, 6926, 6927, 6928, 6929, 6930]. [Q] to take a tenth; [P] to give a tenth, set aside a tenth; [H] to give or receive a tenth:– be sure to set aside a tenth (2 [+6923]), give a tenth (2 [+6923]), take a tenth (2), collect tithes (1), receive tithes (1), setting aside a tenth (1 [+5130])

H6924 עֶשֶׂר *'eśer*, n.m. & f. [59] [√ 6923; 10573]. ten:– ten (58), 910 (1 [+2256, 9596, 4395])

H6925 עָשָׂר *'āśār*, n. *or* a.num. [205] [√ 6923]. ten (always used in combined numbers):– twelve (51 [+9109]), 12 (24 [+9109]), fourteenth (19 [+752]), fifteenth (15 [+2822]), twelfth (15 [+9109]), fourteen (12 [+752]), eleventh (9 [+6954]), thirteenth (8 [+8993]), fifteen (6 [+2822]), eighteen (4 [+9046]), seventeenth (4 [+8679]), sixteen (4 [+9252]), eleven (3 [+285]), sixteenth (3 [+9252]), 112 (2 [+4395, 2256, 9109]), 16,000 (2 [+9252, 547]), 18 (2 [+9046]), 18,000 (2 [+9046, 547]), eighteenth (2 [+9046]), nineteenth (2 [+9596]), thirteen (2 [+8993]), 1,017 (1 [+547, 8679]), 1,017 (1 [+547, 2256, 8679]), 112 (1 [+4395, 9109]), 13 (1 [+8993]), 14,700 (1 [+752, 547, 2256, 8679, 4395]), 16,750 (1 [+9252, 547, 8679, 4395, 2256, 2822]), 17,200 (1 [+8679, 547, 2256, 4395]), 2,812 (1 [+547, 9046, 4395, 2256, 9109]), 2,818 (1 [+547, 2256, 9046, 4395, 9046]), 212 (1 [+4395, 2256, 9109]), 218 (1 [+4395, 2256, 9046]), 318 (1 [+9046, 2256, 8993, 4395]), eleven (1 [+6954]), nineteen (1 [+9596])

H6926 עֶשְׂרֵה *'eśrēh*, n.f. [136] [√ 6923]. ten (used in compound numbers):– twelve (30 [+9109]), sixteen (14 [+9252]), thirteen (10 [+8993]), eighteenth (9 [+9046]), fifteen (9 [+2822]), eighteen (8 [+9046]), twelfth (8 [+9109]), fourteen (7 [+752]), eleven (6 [+285]), seventeen (5 [+8679]), eleven (4 [+6954]), eleventh (4 [+285]), eleventh (4 [+6954]), fourteenth (4 [+752]), thirteenth (3 [+8993]), fifteenth (2 [+2822]), nineteenth (2 [+9596]), seventeenth (2 [+8679]), 119 (1 [+9596, 2256, 4395]), 815 (1 [+2822, 2256, 9046, 4395]), 912 (1 [+9109, 2256, 9596, 4395]), hundred and twenty thousand (1 [+8052, 9109]), nineteen (1 [+9596])

H6927 עֲשָׂרָה *'aśārâ*, n.m. [64] [√ 6923; 10573]. ten:– ten (59), 110 (1 [+4395, 2256]), 410 (1 [+752, 4395, 2256]), fifteen (1 [+2822, 2256]), seventeen (1 [+8679, 2256]), NDT (1)

H6928 עִשָּׂרוֹן *'iśśārôn*, n.m. [29] [√ 6923]. tenth part:– two-tenths (11 [+9109]), three-tenths (8 [+8993]), one-tenth (4), tenth (4), one-tenth (1 [+285])

H6929 עֶשְׂרִים ***'eśrîm***, n.pl.indecl. [315] [√ 6923; 10574]. twenty (pl. of "ten" [6924]):– twenty (120), twenty-five (23 [+2256, 2822]), twenty-two (15 [+2256, 9109]), 25,000 (14 [+2822, 2256, 547]), 24,000 (13 [+2256, 752, 547]), twentieth (9), twenty-fourth (7 [+2256, 752]), twenty-seventh (6 [+2256, 8679]), 120 (5 [+4395, 2256]), twenty-four (5 [+2256, 752]), twenty-nine (5 [+2256, 9596]), 128 (4 [+4395, 2256, 9046]), twenty-one (4 [+2256, 285]), twenty-third (4 [+8993, 2256]), twenty-three (4 [+2256, 8993]), 127 (3 [+8679, 2256, 2256, 4395]), 29 (3 [+9596, 2256]), twenty-eight (3 [+2256, 9046]), twenty-fifth (3 [+2256, 2822]), twenty-third (3 [+2256, 8993]), 123 (2 [+4395, 2256, 8993]), 20 (2), 220 (2 [+4395, 2256]), 223 (2 [+4395, 2256, 8993]), 320 (2 [+8993, 4395, 2256]), 6,720 (2 [+9252, 547, 8679, 4395, 2256]), 621 (2 [+9252, 4395, 2256, 285]), twenty-first (2 [+2256, 285]), twenty-first (2 [+285, 2256]), twenty-fourth (2 [+752, 2256]), twenty-second (2 [+9109, 2256]), twenty-seven (2 [+2256, 8679]), twenty-three (2 [+8993, 2256]), 1,222 (1 [+547, 4395, 2256, 9109]), 120,000 (1 [+4395, 2256, 547]), 122 (1 [+4395, 2256, 9109]), 122 (1 [+4395, 2256, 2256, 9109]), 2,322 (1 [+547, 8993, 4395, 2256, 9109]), 20,000 (1 [+547]), 20,200 (1 [+547, 2256, 4395]), 20,800 (1 [+547, 2256, 9046, 4395]), 22 (1 [+2256, 9109]), 22,000 (1 [+9109, 2256, 547]), 22,034 (1 [+2256, 9109, 547, 2256, 8993, 2256, 752]), 22,200 (1 [+9109, 2256, 547, 2256, 4395]), 22,273 (1 [+9109, 2256, 547, 8993, 2256, 8679, 2256, 4395]), 22,600 (1 [+2256, 9109, 547, 2256, 9252, 4395]), 23,000 (1 [+8993, 2256, 547]), 24,000 (1 [+752, 2256, 547]), 25,100 (1 [+2256, 2822, 547, 2256, 4395]), 26,000 (1 [+2256, 9252, 547]), 28 (1 [+2256, 9046]), 28,600 (1 [+2256, 9046, 547, 2256, 9252, 4395]), 3,023 (1 [+8993, 547, 2256, 2256, 8993]), 323 (1 [+4395, 8993, 2256, 8993]), 324 (1 [+8993, 4395, 2256, 752]), 328 (1 [+8993, 4395, 2256, 9046]), 420 (1 [+752, 4395, 2256]), 623 (1 [+9252, 4395, 2256, 8993]), 628 (1 [+9252, 4395, 2256, 9046]), 721 (1 [+8679, 4395, 2256, 2256, 285]), 725 (1 [+8679, 4395, 2256, 2822]), 822 (1 [+9046, 4395, 2256, 9109]), 928 (1 [+9596, 4395, 2256, 9046]), thems (1 [+2021, 7983]), twenty-eight (1 [+9046, 2256]), twenty-six (1 [+2256, 9252]), twenty-sixth (1 [+2256, 9252]), NDT (1)

H6930 עֲשֶׂרֶת ***'ᵃśeret***, n.f. [52] [√ 6923]. (group of) ten:– ten (39), 10,000 (9 [+547]), tens (3), ten-acre (1 [+7538])

H6931 1עָשׁ ***'āš1***, n.m. [7] [√ 6949]. moth, which consumes some natural fabrics:– moth (4), moths (2), moth's cocoon (1)

H6932 2עָשׁ ***'āš2***, n.m. Not used in NIVEBC [√ 6949]. pus

H6933 3עָשׁ ***'āš3***, n.[f.] [1] [√ 6568]. Bear or Lion (a constellation):– Bear (1)

H6934 עָשׁוֹק ***'āšôq***, n.[m.] [1] [√ 6943]. oppressor:– oppressor (1)

H6935 עֲשׁוּקִים ***'ᵃšûqîm***, n.pl.abst. [3] [√ 6943]. oppression:– oppression (3)

H6936 עָשׁוֹת ***'āšôt***, a. [1] [√ 6950]. wrought, fashioned (iron):– wrought (1)

H6937 עַשְׁוָת ***'ašwāt***, n.pr.m. [1] Ashvath, "[poss.] *wrought iron*":– Ashvath (1)

H6938 עָשִׁיר ***'āšîr***, a. (used as n.) [23] [√ 6947]. rich, wealthy; (n.) the rich, rich person:– rich (20), rich (1 [+408]), wealth (1), wealthy (1)

H6939 עָשַׁן ***'āšan***, v.den. [6] [→ 6940, 6942]. [Q] to envelope in smoke, smolder:– smoke (2), anger smolder (1), burn (1), covered with smoke (1), smolder (1)

H6940 1עָשָׁן ***'āšān1***, n.m. [25] [→ 1016; cf. 6939]. smoke (billowing, ascending, blowing):– smoke (23), cloud of smoke (1), smoking (1)

H6941 2עָשָׁן ***'āšān2***, n.pr.loc. [4] [cf. 1014, 1016]. Ashan, "*smoke*":– Ashan (4)

H6942 עָשֵׁן ***'āšēn***, a. [2] [√ 6939]. smoking, smoldering:– in smoke (1), smoldering (1)

H6943 עָשַׁק ***'āšaq***, v. [37] [→ 6934, 6935, 6944, 6945, 6946]. [Q] to oppress, mistreat; to defraud, extort; [Qp] to be oppressed, be tormented; [Pu] to be crushed:– oppress (7), oppressed (7), defraud (4), oppresses (3), cheated (2), oppressor (2), oppressors (2), cheat (1), crushed (1), mistreat (1), oppression (1), practice extortion (1 [+6945]), practiced extortion (1 [+6945]), raging (1), take advantage (1), taken by extortion (1 [+6945]), tormented (1)

H6944 עֵשֶׁק ***'ēšeq***, n.pr.m. [1] [√ 6943]. Eshek, "*oppressor*":– Eshek (1)

H6945 עֹשֶׁק ***'ōšeq***, n.m. [15] [√ 6943]. oppression, tyranny; extortion:– oppression (6), extortion (2), extort (1 [+928, 2021]), oppressed (1), oppressed (1 [+6913, 928, 2021]), practice extortion (1 [+6943]), practiced extortion (1 [+6943]), taken by extortion (1 [+6943]), tyranny (1)

H6946 עָשְׁקָה ***'ošqâ***, n.f. [1] [√ 6945; cf. 6943]. trouble, oppression:– threatened (1)

H6947 עָשַׁר ***'āšar***, v. [17] [→ 6938, 6948]. [Q] to be, become rich; [H] to make rich, bring wealth:– rich (7), bring wealth (1), brings wealth (1), enrich (1), enriched (1), get rich (1), give wealth (1 [+6948]), made rich (1), pretends to be rich (1), richer (1 [+6948]), wealth (1)

H6948 עֹשֶׁר ***'ōšer***, n.m. [37] [√ 6947]. wealth, riches:– wealth (22), riches (13), give wealth (1 [+6947]), richer (1 [+6947])

H6949 עָשֵׁשׁ ***'āšaš***, v. [3] [→ 6931, 6932]. [Q] to grow weak:– weak (3)

H6950 1עָשַׁת ***'āšat1***, v. [1] [→ 6936, 6952]. [Q] to grow sleek (i.e., smooth or shiny):– sleek (1)

H6951 2עָשַׁת ***'āšat2***, v. [1] [→ 6953, 6955; 10575]. [Ht] to take notice:– take notice (1)

H6952 עֶשֶׁת ***'ešet***, n.[m.] [1] [√ 6950]. polished piece, slab, plate:– polished (1)

H6953 עַשְׁתּוּת ***'aštût***, n.f. [1] [√ 6951]. thought:– have (1)

H6954 עַשְׁתֵּי ***'aštê***, n. *or* a.num. [18] eleven, eleventh:– eleventh (9 [+6925]), eleven (4 [+6926]), eleventh (4 [+6926]), eleven (1 [+6925])

H6955 עֶשְׁתֹּנָת ***'eštōnet***, n.f. [1] [√ 6951]. plan, thought:– plans (1)

H6956 עַשְׁתֹּרֶת ***'aštōret***, n.pr.f. [9] [√ 6958]. Ashtoreth (pagan god):– Ashtoreths (6), Ashtoreth (3)

H6957 עַשְׁתְּרֹת ***'ašteret***, n.f. [4] lamb or ewe:– lambs (4)

H6958 עַשְׁתָּרֹת ***'aštārōt***, n.pr.loc. [6] [→ 1119, 6956, 6959, 6960; cf. 895, 1285?]. Ashtaroth:– Ashtaroth (6)

H6959 עַשְׁתְּרֹת קַרְנַיִם ***'ašᵉrōt qarnayim***, n.pr.loc. [1] [√ 6958 + 7969]. Ashteroth Karnaim, "*Ashteroth of the pair of horns [twin peaks?]*":– Ashteroth Karnaim (1)

H6960 עַשְׁתְּרָתִי ***'ašᵉrātî***, a.g. [1] [√ 6958]. Ashterathite:– Ashterathite (1)

H6961 עֵת ***'ēt***, n.f. [298] [√ 6701]. time (in general); a unit of time (of various lengths), season:– time (178), times (26), when (13), season (12), always (6 [+928, 3972]), when (3 [+4200]), as (2 [+928]), at (2 [+928]), at set times (2 [+4946, 6330, 6961]), at set times (2 [+4946, 6961, 6330]), days (2), in (2 [+4200]), next year (2 [+2645]), now (2 [+3869, 2021]), now (2), proper time (2), sunset (2 [+995, 2021, 9087]), appointed time (1), as (1 [+3869]), as (1 [+4200]), as long as (1 [+928, 3972]), at once (1 [+928, 2021, 2021, 2085]), circumstances (1), doom (1), due time (1), end (1), evening (1 [+2021, 6847]), future (1), hour (1), mealtime (1 [+2021, 431]), occasion (1), old (1), past (1 [+8037]), punishment (1), ripens (1), seasons (1), spring (1 [+9588, 9102]), springtime (1 [+4919]), thens (1 [+2021, 2021, 2085]), till (1 [+6330]), time after time (1 [+8041]), timely (1 [+928]), when (1 [+4946]), whenever (1 [+928]), whenever (1 [+928, 3972]), while (1 [+4200]), years (1 [+2021, 9102]), NDT (8)

H6962 עֵת קָצִין ***'ēt qāṣîn***, n.pr.loc. [1] [cf. 7903]. Eth Kazin:– Eth Kazin (1)

H6963 עָתַד ***'ātad***, v. [2] [→ 6965, 6966?, 6969]. [P] to make ready; [Ht] to be destined:– crumbling (1), get ready (1)

H6964 עַתָּה ***'attâ***, adv. [432] [√ 6701]. now:– now (317), then (10), come now (3 [+5528]), therefore (3), when (3), already (2), but (2), longer (2), soon (2), about to (1 [+4946, 7940]), although (1), always (1), further (1), furthermore (1), furthermore (1 [+2256]), going to (1), if so (1 [+3954]), just (1 [+2296]), just (1 [+4946]), look I know (1 [+2180]), now (1 [+2256]), now (1 [+2296]), now then (1), on (1 [+6330]), right now (1), so (1), surely (1 [+421]), surely (1 [+3954]), that day (1), that time on (1), then (1 [+2256]), this (1), this day (1), this time on (1), yet (1 [+2256]), yet (1 [+6330]), NDT (61)

H6965 עָתוּד ***'ātûd***, a. [1] [√ 6963]. supply, treasure:– treasures (1)

H6966 עַתּוּד ***'attûd***, n.m. [29] [√ 6963?]. male goat; (of humans) a leader:– male goats (15), goats (12), leaders (2)

H6967 עִתִּי ***'ittî***, a. [1] [√ 6701]. available:– appointed for the task (1)

H6968 עַתַּי ***'attay***, n.pr.m. [4] [√ 6701]. Attai, "*timely,* [or perhaps] *an abbreviation of Athaiah*":– Attai (4)

H6969 עָתִיד ***'ātîd***, a. [5] [√ 6963; 10577]. ready, prepared:– ready (3), doom (1), poised (1)

H6970 עֲתָיָה ***'ᵃtāyâ***, n.pr.m. [1] Athaiah, "[poss.] *[the] superiority of Yahweh*":– Athaiah (1)

H6971 עָתִיק ***'ātîq***, a. [1] [√ 6980]. fine, choice, select:– fine (1)

H6972 עַתִּיק ***'attîq***, a. [2] [√ 6980]. taken, removed (from place or time):– from ancient times (1), taken (1)

H6973 עֲתָךְ ***'ᵃtāk***, n.pr.loc. [1] Athach:– Athak (1)

H6974 עַתְלַי ***'atlay***, n.pr.m. & f. [1] [→ 6975, 6976]. Athlai, "[poss.] *Yahweh is exalted; oldest of Yahweh*":– Athlai (1)

H6975 עֲתַלְיָה ***'ᵃtalyâ***, n.pr.m. & f. [7] [√ 6474]. Athaliah, "[poss.] *Yahweh is exalted; oldest of Yahweh*":– Athaliah (7)

H6976 עֲתַלְיָהוּ ***'ᵃtalyāhû***, n.pr.m. & f. [10] [√ 6974]. Athaliah, "[poss.] *Yahweh is exalted; oldest of Yahweh*":– Athaliah (10)

H6977 עָתַם ***'ātam***, v. [1] [N] to be destroyed; in context, to be scorched:– be scorched (1)

H6978 עָתְנִי ***'otnî***, n.pr.m. [1] [→ 6979]. Othni:– Othni (1)

H6979 עָתְנִיאֵל ***'otnî'ēl***, n.pr.m. [7] [√ 6978 + 446]. Othniel:– Othniel (7)

H6980 עָתַק ***'ātaq***, v. [9] [→ 6971, 6972, 6981, 6982; 10578]. [Q] to move; to grow old, grow weak; [H] to move on; to fail; to copy:– moved (2), compiled (1), fail (1), failed (1 [+4946]), growing old (1), moved on (1), moves (1), went on (1)

H6981 עָתָק ***'ātāq***, a. [4] [√ 6980]. arrogant, insolent, outstretched:– arrogance (1), arrogant (1), arrogantly (1), so defiantly (1 [+928, 7418])

H6982 עָתֵק ***'ātēq***, a. [1] [√ 6980]. enduring (wealth):– enduring (1)

H6983 1עָתַר ***'ātar1***, v. [20] [→ 6985, 6986, 6987?; cf. 6984?]. [Q] to pray; [N] to respond to prayer, be moved by an entreaty; [H] to pray, make entreaty:– pray (8), answered prayer (4), prayed (4), was moved by entreaty (2), answered prayers (1), respond to pleas (1)

H6984 2עָתַר ***'ātar2***, v. [2] [→ 6988; cf. 6983?]. [N] to be multiplied; [H] to multiply:– multiplies (1), without restraint (1)

H6985 1עָתָר ***'ātār1***, n.[m.] [1] [√ 6983]. worshiper:– worshipers (1)

H6986 2עָתָר ***'ātār2***, n.[m.] [1] [√ 6983]. fragrance, perfume:– fragrant (1)

H6987 עֶתֶר ***'eter***, n.pr.loc. [2] [√ 6983?]. Ether, "[perhaps] *perfume*":– Ether (2)

H6988 עֲתֶרֶת ***'ᵃteret***, n.f. [1] [√ 6984]. abundance:– abundant (1)

H6989 פ ***p***, letter. Not used in NIVEBC [√ 10579]. letter of the Hebrew alphabet

H6990 פָּאָה ***pā'â***, v. [1] [→ 6991?, 6992]. [H] to split into pieces, scatter:– scatter (1)

H6991 1פֵּאָה ***pē'â1***, n.f. [85] [√ 6990?]. side, edge, boundary; forehead or crown of the head:– side (33), boundary (4), edges (4), end (4), distant places (3 [+7916]), corners (2), foreheads (2), border (1), front (1), head (1), sides (1), southern (1 [+448, 5582]), started (1 [+4200]), NDT (27)

H6992 2פֵּאָה ***pē'â2***, n.f. [1] [√ 6990]. piece, part; possibly the same as 6991:– remotest frontiers (1)

H6993 3פֵּאָה ***pē'â3***, n.f. Not used in NIVEBC [cf. 3636]. splendor, luxury

H6994 1פָּאַר ***pā'ar1***, v.den. [1] [√ 6998]. [P] to knock down olives a second time:– go over the branches a second time (1 [+339])

H6995 2פָּאַר ***pā'ar2***, v. [13] [→ 6996?, 9514]. [P] to honor, adorn, endow with splendor; [Ht] to glorify oneself, display one's splendor; (negatively) to boast:– display splendor (3), adorn (2), endowed with splendor (2), boast (1), bring honor (1), crowns (1), displays glory (1), leave the honor (1), raise itself (1)

H6996 פְּאֵר ***pᵉ'ēr***, n.m. [7] [√ 6995?]. turban, headdress:– turbans (2), adorns head (1), caps (1 [+4457]), crown of beauty (1), headdresses (1), turban (1)

H6997 פֹּארָה ***pō'râ***, n.f. [6] branch, leafy bough:– branches (5), leafy boughs (1)

H6998 פֻּארָה ***pu'râ***, n.f.col. [1] [→ 6994]. bough:– boughs (1)

H6999 פָּארוּר ***pā'rûr***, n.[m.] [2] [√ 7248]. growing pale, turning pale; some sources: to burn, glow:– grows pale (1 [+7695]), turns pale (1 [+7695])

H7000 פָּארָן ***pā'rān***, n.pr.loc. [11] [→ 386; cf. 7230?]. Paran, "*plain*":– Paran (11)

H7001 פַּג ***pag***, n.f. [1] early fruit, in context, unripe fig buds:– early fruit (1)

H7002 פִּגּוּל ***piggûl***, n.m. [4] (ceremonially) unclean meat, kept too long after a sacrifice:– impure (3), impure meat (1)

H7003 פָּגַע ***pāga'***, n.m. [46] [→ 5133, 7004, 7005]. to strike, touch; intercede for, plead with; [H] to make intercession, intervene; strike; cause to encounter:– touched (6), strike down (4), struck down (4), meet (3), plead (2), strike (2), attack (1), attacked (1), bordered (1), come across (1), come to the help of (1), comes upon (1), dos (1), extended (1), find (1), found (1), harmed (1), intercede (1), intervene (1), kill (1), laid (1), made intercession (1), make plead (1), met (1), praying (1), reached (1), spare (1), strike mark (1), urge (1), urged (1), NDT (1)

H7004 פֶּגַע ***pega'***, n.m. [2] [√ 7003]. chance, occurrence:– chance (1), disaster (1 [+8273])

H7005 פַּגְעִיאֵל ***pag'î'ēl***, n.pr.m. [5] [√ 7003 + 446]. Pagiel:– Pagiel (5)

H7006 פָּגַר ***pāgar***, v. [2] [→ 7007]. [P] to be exhausted:– exhausted (2)

H7007 פֶּגֶר ***peger***, n.m. [21] [√ 7006]. dead body, corpse; carcass; by extension: lifeless idol, with a focus that it is unclean and impotent:– bodies (7), dead bodies (7), carcasses (2), funeral offerings (2), corpse (1), dead (1), lifeless forms (1)

H7008 פָּגַשׁ ***pāgaš***, v. [14] [Q] to meet; to attack; [N] to have in common, to meet together; [P] to come upon, encounter:– met (6), have in common (2), meet (2), attack (1), comes (1), meet together (1), meets (1)

H7009 פָּדָה ***pādâ***, v. [59] [→ 7012, 7013, 7014, 7017, 7018; *also used with compound proper names*]. [Q] to redeem, ransom, deliver, rescue, buy; [Qp] to be redeemed, be ransomed; [N] to be ransomed, be redeemed; [H] to let be ransomed; [Ho] to be brought to ransomed; this can mean to purchase a devoted animal from sacrifice or to purchase a person from slavery to freedom or new ownership; by extension: divine salvation from oppression, death, or sin:– redeem (16), redeemed (13), deliver (8), delivered (4), rescue (3), rescued (3), been ransomed (2 [+7009]), must redeem (2 [+7009]), redeem (2 [+7009]), be delivered (1), be ransomed (1), bought back (1), let be redeemed (1), redemption (1), rescues (1)

H7010 פְּדַהְאֵל ***pedah'ēl***, n.pr.m. [1] [√ 7009 + 446]. Pedahel, "*God [El] ransoms*":– Pedahel (1)

H7011 פְּדָהצוּר ***pedāhṣûr***, פְּדָה־צוּר ***pedāh-ṣûr***, n.pr.m. [5] [√ 7009 + 7446]. Pedahzur, "*the Rock ransoms*":– Pedahzur (5)

H7012 פְּדוּיִם ***pedûyim***, n.[m.]pl.abst. [3] [√ 7009]. redemption, ransom, paid to purchase firstborn Israelites from dedication to God:– redemption (2), redeem (1)

H7013 פָּדוֹן ***pādôn***, n.pr.m. [2] [√ 7009]. Padon, "*ransom*":– Padon (2)

H7014 פְּדוּת ***pedût***, n.f. [3] [√ 7009]. redemption, ransom, always of divine action:– redemption (2), deliver (1)

H7015 פְּדָיָה ***pedāyâ***, n.pr.m. [7] [√ 7009 + 3378]. Pedaiah, "*Yahweh ransoms*":– Pedaiah (7)

H7016 פְּדָיָהוּ ***pedāyāhû***, n.pr.m. [1] [√ 7009 + 3378]. Pedaiah, "*Yahweh ransoms*":– Pedaiah (1)

H7017 פִּדְיוֹם ***pidyôm***, n.m. [1] [√ 7009]. redemption, ransom:– redemption (1)

H7018 פִּדְיוֹן ***pidyôn***, n.m. [2] [√ 7009]. redemption money, ransom payment:– ransom (1), redeem (1)

H7019 פַּדָּן ***paddān***, n.pr.loc. [1] [→ 7020]. Paddan, "*plain*":– Paddan (1)

H7020 פַּדַּן אֲרָם ***paddan 'arām***, n.pr.loc. [10] [√ 7019 + 806]. Paddan Aram, "*plain of Aram*":– Paddan Aram (10)

H7021 פָּדַע ***pāda'***, v. [1] [Q] to spare, deliver:– Spare (1)

H7022 פֶּדֶר ***peder***, n.[m.] [3] suet (the hard fat about kidney's and loins of animals):– fat (3)

H7023 פֶּה ***peh***, n.m. [497] [→ 7092; 10588]. mouth (human or animal); by extension: speech, command, testimony; any opening; edge (of a sword):– mouth (186), mouths (47), command (39), to (25 [+4200]), lips (17), opening (8), face (7), with (5 [+4200]), word (5), commanded (4), end (4), testimony (4), according to (3 [+6584]), by (3 [+4200]), dictated (3 [+4946]), number (3), speech (3), spoken (3), according to (2 [+4200]), commands (2), on (2 [+6584]), other[S] (2), promised (2 [+3655, 4946]), pronounced (2), required (2), said (2), said (2 [+3655, 4946]), sneer (2 [+8143]), speak (2), speak (2 [+4946]), speak up (2 [+7337]), what say (2 [+609]), words (2 [+609]), I (1 [+3276]), according to (1 [+3869]), accordingly (1 [+3869]), amount (1), as much as (1 [+3869]), as much as (1 [+4200]), at (1 [+4200]), beak (1), because (1 [+3869, 889]), big talk (1), boast so much (1 [+1540, 3870]), boasted (1 [+1540, 928]), by (1 [+4946]), by (1 [+6584]), collar (1), collar (1 [+9389]), consulting (1 [+8626]), cupped (1 [+448]), decide (1 [+2118, 6584]), demanded (1 [+6584]), dictate (1 [+4946]), dictated (1), dictated (1 [+7924, 4946]), dictation (1 [+4946]), direction (1), don't say a word (1 [+8492, 3338, 6584]), double-edged (1), double-edged (1 [+9109]), drank in (1 [+7196]), express (1 [+6584]), feed (1 [+5989, 6584]), fruit (1), fulfill (1 [+6913, 3869, 4027]), give command (1 [+7337]), given word (1 [+7198, 906]), giving an apt reply (1 [+5101]), had (1 [+928]), have (1 [+928]), hunger (1), in accordance with (1 [+4200]), in accordance with (1 [+6584]), in proportion to (1 [+3869]), inquire of (1 [+8626, 906]), instructed (1 [+1819]), invoke (1 [+7924, 928]), it[S] (1 [+2023]), jaws (1), just as much as (1 [+4200]), keep silent (1 [+3104]), killed (1 [+5782, 4200, 2995]), leading into (1 [+4200]), made a vow (1 [+7198]), make spew out (1 [+3655, 4946]), mention (1 [+9019, 928]), neck (1), offered a kiss of homage (1 [+5975, 4200]), orders (1), portion (1), praise (1), requires (1), said (1 [+1819, 928]), say (1), say (1 [+3655, 4946]), sayings (1), share (1), simply (1 [+6584]), sing (1 [+8492, 928]), so that (1 [+3869]), speak (1 [+928]), speak (1 [+7337]), speaks (1 [+7337]), spoke the word (1 [+4946]), spoken (1 [+1819]), spokesman (1 [+3869]), talk (1), taste (1), the same as (1 [+3869]), told (1 [+8492, 928]), two-thirds (1 [+9109]), what decreed (1 [+609]), what said (1 [+609]), what said (1 [+4946]), when (1 [+4200]), when (1 [+4200]), when (1 [+3954, 4200]), whenever (1 [+4200]), will (1 [+6584]), without exception (1 [+285]), without exception[S] (1 [+285]), words (1 [+1821]), NDT (8)

H7024 פֹּה ***pōh***, adv.loc. [82] [→ 407, 686?]. here:– here (42), on each side (9 [+4946, 2256, 4946, 7024]), on each side (9 [+4946, 7024, 2256, 4946]), on either side (4 [+4946, 2256, 4946, 7024]), on either side (4 [+4946, 7024, 2256, 4946]), other[S] (2), side (2), arrives (1 [+995]), on each side (1 [+4946, 2256, 4946, 7024]), on each side (1 [+4946, 7024, 4946, 2256]), square (1 [+4946, 2256, 4946, 7024]), square (1 [+4946, 7024, 2256, 4946]), there (1), this far (1 [+6330]), NDT (3)

H7025 פּוּאָה ***pû'â***, n.pr.m. [4] [→ 7026, 7027, 7030; cf. 7043]. Puah, "[perhaps] *girl*":– Puah (4)

H7026 פּוּאָה ***puû'â***, n.pr.m. Not used in NIVEBC [√ 7025]. Puah, "[perhaps] *girl*"

H7027 פּוּאִי ***pû'î***, a.g. [1] [√ 7025]. Puite, "*of Puah*":– Puite (1)

H7028 פּוּג ***pûg***, v. [4] [→ 2198, 7029]. [Q] to grow numb, be feeble; [N] to be benumbed, be feeble:– feeble (1), paralyzed (1), stunned (1 [+4213]), untiring (1 [+4202])

H7029 פּוּגָה ***pûgâ***, n.f. [1] [√ 7028]. relief, relaxation:– relief (1)

H7030 פֻּוָּה ***puwwâ***, n.pr.m. Not used in NIVEBC [√ 7025]. Puvah, see 7026

H7031 פּוּחַ1 ***pûaḥ[1]***, v. [3] [→ 7086; cf. 5870, 7032]. [Q] to blow, become dawn (of the day); [H] to blow (of wind):– breaks (2), blow (1)

H7032 פּוּחַ2 ***pûaḥ[2]***, v. [11] [cf. 3640, 7031?]. [Q] to breathe out; [H] to breathe out, sneer, malign:– pours out (4), witness (2), breathe out (1), malign (1), sneers (1), speaks (1), stir up (1)

H7033 פּוּט ***pûṭ***, n.pr.g. [8] Put; Libya, Libyans:– Put (6), Libya (1), Libyans (1)

H7034 פּוּטִיאֵל ***pûṭî'ēl***, n.pr.m. [1] [√ 446]. Putiel, "*he whom God [El] gives*":– Putiel (1)

H7035 פּוֹטִיפַר ***pôṭîpar***, n.pr.m. [2] [cf. 7036]. Potiphar, "*he whom Ra gives*":– Potiphar (2)

H7036 פּוֹטִי פֶרַע ***pôṭî pera'***, n.pr.m. [3] [cf. 7280]. Potiphera, "*he whom Ra gives*":– Potiphera (3)

H7037 פּוּךְ ***pûk***, n.[m.] [4] turquoise (stone); (eye) paint, possibly derived from turquoise:– turquoise (2), makeup (1), put on makeup (1 [+6167, 928, 2021])

H7038 פּוֹל ***pôl***, n.[m.]col. [2] beans:– beans (2)

H7039 פּוּל1 ***pûl[1]***, n.pr.loc.? see 4275

H7040 פּוּל2 ***pûl[2]***, n.pr.m. [3] [√ 7189; cf. 7188]. Pul:– Pul (2), him[S] (1)

H7041 פּוּן ***pûn***, v. [1] [→ 687]. [Q] to be in despair:– in despair (1)

H7042 פּוֹנֶה ***pôneh***, n.f. Not used in NIVEBC [cf. 7157]. see 7157

H7043 פּוּנִי ***pûnî***, a.g. Not used in NIVEBC [cf. 7025]. Punite, see 7027

H7044 פּוּנֹן ***pûnōn***, n.pr.loc. [2] [cf. 7091]. Punon:– Punon (2)

H7045 פּוּעָה ***pû'â***, n.pr.f. [1] Puah, "[perhaps] *girl*":– Puah (1)

H7046 פּוּץ1 ***pûṣ[1]***, v. [65] [→ 5138, 9518; cf. 5879, 7207, 7047]. [Q] to be scattered; [Qp] to be scattered; [N] to be scattered; [H] to cause to scatter:– scattered (21), scatter (11), disperse (7), were scattered (5), been scattered (4), dispersed (2), overflow (2), attacker (1), be scattered (1), blow away (1), dog (1), driven (1), go out (1), is scattered (1), scattering (1), scatters (1), separated (1), sow (1), spread out (1), unleash (1)

H7047 פּוּץ2 ***pûṣ[2]***, v. Not used in NIVEBC [cf. 7046]. [Q] flow, overflow

H7048 פּוּק1 ***pûq[1]***, v. [2] [→ 7050; cf. 7049, 7211]. [Q] to stumble, totter; [H] to totter:– stumble (1), totter (1)

H7049 פּוּק2 ***pûq[2]***, v. [7] [cf. 7048]. [H] to bring out, furnish, promote:– gain (1), let succeed (1), obtain (1), provision (1), receive (1), receives (1), spend (1)

H7050 פּוּקָה ***pûqâ***, n.f. [1] [√ 7048]. staggering, stumbling:– staggering burden (1 [+2256, 4842])

H7051 פּוּר1 ***pûr[1]***, v. Not used in NIVEBC [cf. 7296]. [H] to destroy

H7052 פּוּר2 ***pûr[2]***, n.m. [8] pur (the lot), pebbles, sticks, or pottery shards that were thrown to make decisions; (pl.) Purim, a Jewish festival celebrating God's control over the casting of lots:– Purim (5), pur (3)

H7053 פּוּרָה ***pûrâ***, n.f. [2] trough of the winepress; measure (equal to the filling of the winepress):– measures (1), winepress (1)

H7054 פּוֹרָתָא ***pôrātā'***, n.pr.m. [1] Poratha:– Poratha (1)

H7055 פּוּשׁ1 ***pûš[1]***, v. [3] [Q] to leap, frolic, gallop; this may refer to the playful pawing action of a young animal:– frolic (2), gallops headlong (1)

H7056 פּוּשׁ2 ***pûš[2]***, v. [1] [N] to be scattered:– scattered (1)

H7057 פּוּתִי ***pûtî***, a.g. [1] Puthite:– Puthites (1)

H7058 פָּז ***paz***, n.m. [9] [→ 502, 7059]. pure gold:– pure gold (5), gold (2), fine gold (1), purest gold (1 [+4188])

H7059 פָּזַז1 ***pāzaz[1]***, v. [1] [√ 7058]. [Ho] to be set with pure gold:– fine (1)

H7060 פָּזַז2 ***pāzaz[2]***, v. [2] [Q] to be limber; [P] to leap:– leaping (1), limber (1)

H7061 פָּזַר ***pāzar***, v. [10] [cf. 1029]. [Qp] to be scattered; [P] to scatter; [N] to be scattered; [Pu] to be dispersed:– scattered (5), been scattered (1), dispersed (1), freely scattered (1), gives freely (1), scatters (1)

H7062 פַּח1 ***paḥ[1]***, n.m. [24] [→ 7072]. snare, bird-trap:– snare (14), snares (4), trap (4), pitfalls (1), snares (1 [+3687])

H7063 פַּח2 ***paḥ[2]***, n.[m.] [2] thin sheets (of hammered metal):– sheets (1), thin sheets (1)

H7064 פָּחַד ***pāḥad***, v. [25] [→ 7065, 7067]. [Q] to tremble, be afraid; [P] to live in terror, fear; [H] to make shake, make tremble:– afraid (3), fear (2), overwhelmed with dread (2 [+7065]), terrified (2), trembles (2), brought down to terror (1), come trembling (1), feared (1), fill (1), filled with dread (1), in awe (1), live in terror (1), looked in fear (1), made shake (1), showed fear (1), throb (1), tremble (1), turn in fear (1), unafraid (1 [+4202])

H7065 פַּחַד1 ***paḥad[1]***, n.m. [49] [√ 7064; cf. 7524]. fear, terror, dread:– fear (14), terror (13), dread (4), fearful presence (3), calamity (2), overwhelmed with dread (2 [+7064]), afraid (1 [+5877, 6584]), awe (1), cares (1), disaster (1), dreaded (1), object of dread (1), peril (1), terrifying (1), terrors (1), threat (1), what[S] (1)

H7066 פַּחַד2 ***paḥad[2]***, n.[m.] [1] thigh:– thighs (1)

H7067 פַּחְדָּה ***paḥdâ***, n.f. [1] [√ 7064]. awe, dread:– awe (1)

H7068 פֶּחָה ***peḥâ***, n.m. [28] [→ 7075?; 10580]. governor, officer:– governors (15), governor (10), officer (2), officers (1)

H7069 פָּחַז ***pāḥaz***, v. [2] [→ 7070, 7071]. [Q] to be arrogant, be insolent:– scoundrels (1), unprincipled (1)

H7070 פַּחַז ***paḥaz***, n.[m.] [1] [√ 7069]. turbulence, recklessness:– Turbulent (1)

H7071 פַּחֲזוּת ***paḥazût***, n.f. [1] [√ 7069]. insolence, arrogance, with an implication of recklessness:– reckless (1)

H7072 פָּחַח ***pāḥaḥ***, v.den. [1] [√ 7062]. [H] to trap; [Ho] to be entrapped:– trapped (1)

H7073 פֶּחָם ***peḥām***, n.[m.] [4] coal, charcoal:– coals (3), charcoal (1)

H7074 פַּחַת ***paḥat***, n.m. [10] [→ 7076]. pit, cave:– pit (7), cave (2), pitfalls (1)

H7075 פַּחַת מוֹאָב ***paḥat mô'āb***, n.pr.m. [6] [√ 7068? + 4565]. Pahath-Moab, "*supervisor of Moab*":– Pahath-Moab (6)

H7076 פְּחֶתֶת ***peḥetet***, n.m. [1] [√ 7074]. mildew (that eats away at a garment):– spoiled (1)

H7077 פִּטְדָה ***piṭdâ***, n.f. [*or* m.?] [4] topaz; some sources: chrysolite:– chrysolite (3), topaz (1)

H7078 פְּטִירִים ***peṭîrîm***, var. Not used in NIVEBC [√ 7080]. see 7080

H7079 פַּטִּישׁ ***paṭṭîš***, n.m. [3] (sledge-)hammer:– hammer (3)

H7080 פָּטַר ***pāṭar***, v. [9] [→ 7078, 7081, 7082]. [Q] to elude, escape, release; [Qp] to be opened; [H] to open wide the mouth (as an insult):– open (4), breaching (1), eluded (1), hurl insults (1 [+928, 8557]), released (1), were exempt from duties (1)

H7081 פֶּטֶר ***peṭer***, n.[m.] [11] [→ 7082; cf. 7080]. first offspring, firstborn:– first offspring (5), firstborn (3), first male offspring (1 [+1147, 8167]), firstborn (1 [+8167]), firstborn (1 [+8715])

H7082 פִּטְרָה ***piṭrâ***, n.f. [1] [√ 7081; cf. 7080]. firstborn:– firstborn (1)

H7083 פִּי־בֶסֶת ***pî-beset***, n.pr.loc. [1] Bubastis (Piy-Beset), "*house of the cat goddess Basht*":– Bubastis (1)

H7084 פִּי הַחִירֹת ***pî haḥîrôt***, n.pr.loc. [4] [√ 2672]. Pi Hahiroth, "*temple [house] of Hathor*":– Pi Hahiroth (4)

H7085 פִּיד ***pîd***, n.[m.] [4] misfortune, distress, calamity:– misfortune (2), calamities (1), distress (1)

H7086 פִּיחַ ***pîaḥ***, n.[m.] [2] [√ 7031]. soot (from a furnace):– soot (2)

H7087 פִּיכֹל ***pîkōl***, n.pr.m. [3] Phicol:– Phicol (3)

H7088 פִּים ***pîm***, n.[m.] [1] pim (two-thirds of a shekel, about one-third of an ounce [7.6 grams]):– two-thirds of a shekel (1)

H7089 פִּימָה ***pîmâ***, n.f. [1] fat, referring to an abundant life:– bulges with flesh (1 [+6913])

H7090 פִּינְחָס ***pînehās***, n.pr.m. [25] [cf. 9387]. Phinehas, "*the black man*":– Phinehas (25)

H7091 פִּינֹן ***pînōn***, n.pr.m. [2] [cf. 7044]. Pinon, "*darkness* [name related to famous copper mines]":– Pinon (2)

H7092 פִּיפִיּוֹת ***pîpiyyôt***, n.[f.pl.?] [2] [√ 7023]. double-edged, with many teeth:– double-edged (1), many teeth (1)

H7093 פִּישׁוֹן ***pîšôn***, n.pr.loc. [1] Pishon:– Pishon (1)

H7094 פִּיתוֹן ***pîtôn***, n.pr.m. [2] Pithon:– Pithon (2)

H7095 פַּךְ ***pak***, n.m. [3] [→ 7096]. flask, (small) jug:– flask (3)

H7096 פָּכָה ***pākâ***, v. [1] [√ 7095]. [P] to trickle:– trickling (1)

H7097 פֹּכֶרֶת הַצְּבָיִים ***pōkeret haṣṣᵉbāyîm***, n.pr.m. [2] [cf. 2207]. Pokereth-Hazzebaim, "*pitfall of gazelles, i.e., gazelle hunter*":– Pokereth-Hazzebaim (2)

H7098 פָּלָא ***pālā'***, v.den. [73] [→ 504?, 5140, 7098, 7099, 7100, 7101, 7102, 7112; cf. 7111]. [N] to be wonderful, be marvelous, be amazing; to be hard, be amazing; [P] to fulfill; [H] to show a wonder, to cause to astound; [Ht] to show oneself marvelous:– wonderful (16), wonders (15), marvelous (10), miracles (5), amazing (3), hard (3), difficult (2), am wonderfully made (1), are wonderful (1), astound (1), astounding (1), display awesome power (1), fulfill a special vow (1 [+5624]), greatly (1), impossible (1), magnificent (1), make a special vow (1 [+5623]), makes a special vow to dedicate (1 [+5624]), send fearful (1), show wonders (1), showed wonders (1), special vow (1 [+5624]), special vows (1 [+5624]), unheard-of (1), wonder (1), wonderful deeds (1)

H7099 פֶּלֶא ***pele'***, n.m. [13] [√ 7098]. wonder, miracle, astounding thing:– wonders (4), miracles (3), wonderful (2), astonishing things (1), astounding (1), wonder (1), wonderful things (1)

H7100 פִּלְאִי ***pil'î***, a. [2] [√ 7098]. wonderful, beyond understanding:– beyond understanding (1), wonderful (1)

H7101 פַּלֻּאִי ***pallu'î***, a.g. [1] [√ 7112; cf. 7098]. Palluite, "*wonderful*":– Palluite (1)

H7102 פְּלָאיָה ***pᵉlā'yâ***, n.pr.m. [2] [√ 7098 + 3378]. Pelaiah, "*Yahweh is spectacular*":– Pelaiah (2)

H7103 פָּלַג ***pālag***, v. [4] [→ 5141, 7104, 7106, 7107; cf. 7135; 10583, 10584]. [N] to be divided; [P] to cut open, divide:– was divided (2), confound (1), cuts (1)

H7104 פֶּלֶג1 ***peleg[1]***, n.m. [10] [√ 7103]. stream, artificial irrigation canal:– streams (9), stream (1)

H7105 פֶּלֶג2 ***peleg[2]***, n.pr.m. [7] Peleg, "*water canal*":– Peleg (7)

H7106 פְּלַגָּה ***pᵉlaggâ***, n.f. [3] [√ 7103]. district, division; stream:– districts (2), streams (1)

H7107 פְּלֻגָּה ***pᵉluggâ***, n.f. [1] [√ 7103; 10585]. division (of a clan or family):– subdivision (1)

H7108 פִּילֶגֶשׁ ***pîlegeš***, n.f. [37] concubine, a female consort generally with lower status and fewer rights than a wife, with the function of giving social status or pleasure to the husband; once this refers to a woman's male consorts (Ezek 23:20):– concubine (21), concubines (14), lovers (1), she[S] (1 [+2257])

H7109 פִּלְדָּשׁ ***pildāš***, n.pr.m. [1] Pildash, "*steely; spider*":– Pildash (1)

H7110 פְּלָדֹת ***pᵉlādōt***, n.f. [1] (polished) metal:– metal (1)

H7111 פָּלָה ***pālâ***, v. [5] [→ 7113, 7126, 7141, 7151; cf. 7098]. [N] to be distinguished; [H] to deal differently, make a distinction:– deal differently (1), distinguish (1), make a distinction (1), makes a distinction (1), set apart (1)

H7112 פַּלּוּא ***pallû'***, n.pr.m. [5] [→ 7101; cf. 7098]. Pallu, "*wonderful*":– Pallu (5)

H7113 פְּלוֹנִי ***pᵉlônî***, a.g. [3] [√ 7111]. Pelonite:– Pelonite (3)

H7114 פָּלַח ***pālaḥ***, v. [5] [→ 7115, 7116; 10586]. [Q] to plow; [P] to cut up, pierce; to bring forth (from the womb):– pierces (2), bring forth (1), cut up (1), plows (1)

H7115 פֶּלַח ***pelaḥ***, n.f. [6] [√ 7114]. millstone; half (of a pomegranate); slice (of a cake):– millstone (3), halves (2), part (1)

H7116 פִּלְחָא ***pilḥā'***, n.pr.m. [1] [√ 7114]. Pilha, "*millstone; plowman; harelip*":– Pilha (1)

H7117 פָּלַט ***pālaṭ***, v. [26] [→ 3646, 3647, 5144, 7118, 7119, 7122, 7123, 7124, 7125, 7127, 7128, 7129; cf. 4880]. [Q] to escape; [P] to rescue, deliver; [H] to bring to safety:– deliverer (5), rescue (5), delivered (4), deliver (3), delivers (2), save (2), calve (1), carry off (1), escape (1), let escape (1), saves (1)

H7118 פֶּלֶט ***peleṭ***, n.pr.m. [2] [→ 7121; cf. 7117; *also used with compound proper names*]. Pelet, "*rescue*":– Pelet (2)

H7119 פַּלֵּט ***pallēṭ***, n[.m.] [1] [√ 7117]. deliverance:– deliverance (1)

H7120 פַּלְטִי1 ***palṭî[1]***, n.pr.m. [2] [√ 7123]. Palti; Paltiel, "*God [El] is [my] deliverance*":– Palti (1), Paltiel (1)

H7121 פַּלְטִי2 ***palṭî[2]***, a.g. [1] [√ 7118]. Paltite:– Paltite (1)

H7122 פִּלְטַי ***pilṭay***, n.pr.m. [1] [√ 7117]. Piltai, "*Yahweh rescues*":– Piltai (1)

H7123 פַּלְטִיאֵל ***palṭî'ēl***, n.pr.m. [2] [→ 7120; cf. 7117 + 446]. Paltiel, "*God [El] is [my] deliverance*":– Paltiel (2)

H7124 פְּלַטְיָה ***pᵉlaṭyâ***, n.pr.m. [3] [√ 7117 + 3378]. Pelatiah, "*Yahweh rescues*":– Pelatiah (3)

H7125 פְּלַטְיָהוּ ***pᵉlaṭyāhû***, n.pr.m. [2] [√ 7117 + 3378]. Pelatiah, "*Yahweh rescues*":– Pelatiah (2)

H7126 פְּלָיָה ***pᵉlāyâ***, n.pr.m. [1] [√ 7111 + 3378]. Pelaiah, "*Yahweh is spectacular*":– Pelaiah (1)

H7127 פָּלִיט ***pālîṭ***, n.m. [19] [√ 7117]. fugitive, one who escapes:– escape (5), fugitives (4), escaped (2), anyone[S] (1), escape (1 [+4880]), fugitive (1), him[S] (1 [+2021]), man[S] (1), man who escaped (1), renegades (1), survivor (1)

H7128 פָּלֵיט ***pālêṭ***, n.m. [5] [√ 7117]. fugitive, one who escapes:– fugitives (2), escaped (1), refugees (1), survive (1)

H7129 פְּלֵיטָה ***pᵉlêṭâ***, n.f. [28] [√ 7117]. fugitive, one who escapes, survivors, remnant:– remnant (6), deliverance (4), escape (4), survivors (4), escaped (3), band of survivors (2), escapes (1 [+2118]), fugitives (1), little left (1 [+3856, 8636]), place to escape (1), survivor (1)

H7130 פָּלִיל ***pālîl***, n.m. [2] [√ 7136]. judge:– concede (1), court (1)

H7131 פְּלִילָה ***pᵉlîlâ***, n.f. [1] [√ 7136]. decision:– decision (1)

H7132 פְּלִילִי ***pᵉlîlî***, a. [2] [√ 7136]. for a judge, calling for judgment:– to be judged (2)

H7133 פְּלִילִיָּה ***pᵉlîliyyâ***, n.f. [1] [√ 7136]. rendering of a decision, the calling for a judgment:– rendering decisions (1)

H7134 פֶּלֶךְ1 ***pelek[1]***, n.[m.] [2] spindle-whorl, which could be used as a crutch:– crutch (1), spindle (1)

H7135 פֶּלֶךְ2 ***pelek[2]***, n.[m.] [8] [cf. 7103]. district:– district (4), half-district (4 [+2942])

H7136 פָּלַל1 ***pālal[1]***, v. [4] [→ 697, 7130, 7131, 7132, 7133, 7138, 7139; *also used with compound proper names*]. [P] to mediate, intervene; to expect; to furnish justification:– expected (1), furnished justification (1), intervened (1), mediate (1)

H7137 פָּלַל2 ***pālal[2]***, v. [80] [→ 9525]. [Ht] to pray:– pray (33), prayed (28), praying (10), prays (3), intercede (2), prayer (2), plead (1), NDT (1)

H7138 פָּלָל ***pālāl***, n.pr.m. [1] [√ 7136]. Palal, "*he has judged*":– Palal (1)

H7139 פְּלַלְיָה ***pᵉlalyâ***, n.pr.m. [1] [√ 7136 + 3378]. Pelaliah, "*Yahweh intercedes in arbitration*":– Pelaliah (1)

H7140 פַּלְמֹנִי ***palmōnî***, p. [1] [cf. 532, 7141]. certain one:– him[S] (1 [+2021])

H7141 פְּלֹנִי ***pᵉlōnî***, p. [3] [√ 7111; cf. 532, 7140]. certain one:– certain (1 [+532]), friend (1 [+532]), such and such (1 [+532])

H7142 פָּלַס1 ***pālas[1]***, v.den. [3] [P] to make level, make smooth, prepare:– make smooth (1), mete out (1), prepared (1)

H7143 פָּלַס2 ***pālas[2]***, v.den. [3] [→ 7144]. [P] to examine, observe:– examines (1), give careful thought (1), gives thought (1)

H7144 פֶּלֶס ***peles***, n.[m.] [2] [√ 7143]. balance, scale:– balances (1), scales (1)

H7145 פָּלַץ ***pālaṣ***, v. [1] [→ 5145, 7146, 9526]. [Ht] to tremble, shake:– makes tremble (1)

H7146 פַּלָּצוּת ***pallāṣût***, n.f. [4] [√ 7145]. trembling, shuddering, shaking:– fear (1), horror (1), terror (1), trembling (1)

H7147 פָּלַשׁ ***pālaš***, v. [4] [Ht] to roll oneself (in the dust or ash):– roll (4)

H7148 פְּלֶשֶׁת ***pᵉlešet***, n.pr.loc. [9] [→ 7149]. Philistia; Philistine:– Philistia (7), Philistines (2)

H7149 פְּלִשְׁתִּי ***pᵉlištî***, a.g. [287] [√ 7148]. Philistine:– Philistines (199), Philistine (62), they[S] (8), Philistine's (4), he[S] (3 [+2021]), them[S] (3), Mediterranean sea (1 [+3542]), Philistia (1), Philistines (1 [+824]), him[S] (1 [+2021]), his[S] (1), their[S] (1), NDT (2)

H7150 פֶּלֶת ***pelet***, n.pr.m. [2] Peleth, "*[perhaps] swift or swiftness*":– Peleth (2)

H7151 פְּלוּת ***pᵉlut***, n.f. [1] [√ 7111]. distinction:– distinction (1)

H7152 פְּלֵתִי ***pᵉlētî***, a.g. [7] [cf. 4165?]. Pelethite:– Pelethites (7)

H7153 פֶּן ***pen***, c. [133] [√ 7155?]. lest, not:– or (52), not (15), otherwise (10), lest (6), so that not (6), if (4), might (4), and (3), no (3), because (2), for (2), so not (2), that no (2), that not (2), for if (1), may (1), not be allowed (1), or else (1), perhaps (1), so cannot (1), so that can't (1), so that no (1), that (1), that won't (1), too (1), would (1), NDT (8)

H7154 פַּנַּג ***pannag***, n.[m.] [1] food, confection:– confections (1)

H7155 פָּנָה ***pānâ***, v. [134] [→ 3648, 4367, 4368, 7153?, 7156, 7157, 7158, 7159, 7160, 7161, 7163, 7164]. [Q] to turn (in various senses); [P] to prepare; to turn away; [H] to turn; [Ho] to be caused to turn:– turned (27), turn (19), facing (14), looked (4), prepare (4), look (3), return (3), turning (3), faces (2), give attention (2), left (2), look with favor (2), looking (2), turned back (2), turns (2), turns away (2), accept (1), approaches (1), back (1), back (1 [+339]), break camp (1), break of day (1 [+1332]), cleared ground (1), daybreak (1 [+1332]), daybreak (1 [+2021, 1332]), emptied (1), expected (1), face (1), faced (1), fading (1), fled (1), go (1), goes (1), looked around (1), looking back (1), looks with favor (1), notice (1), overlook (1 [+440]), pass away (1), prepared (1), respond (1), return (1 [+2256, 2143]), showed concern for (1 [+448]), surveyed (1), tied (1), turn around (1), turn back (1), turn to help (1), turned (1 [+8900]), turned around (1), turned away (1), turns back (1), NDT (5)

H7156 פָּנֶה ***pāneh***, n.m. & f. [2124] [→ 2209, 7163; cf. 7155]. face; by extension: appearance, presence; (pp.) before, in front of, in the presence of; to "show one's face" is a sign of favor; to "turn" or "hide one's face" is a sign of rejection:– before (542 [+4200]), face (210), presence (108), before (100), in front of (65 [+4200]), because of (55 [+4946]), to (50 [+4200]), from (45 [+4946]), ahead (44 [+4200]), faces (36), front (25), before (23 [+4946, 4200]), by (21 [+4200]), presence (19 [+4200]), sight (19), of (17 [+4946]), facedown (15 [+6584]), on (14 [+6584]), against (13 [+4200]), from (11 [+4946, 4200]), for (10 [+4200]), over (10 [+6584]), surface (10), because (8 [+4946]), before (8 [+907]), by (8 [+4946]), from (8 [+4200]), near (8 [+6584]), open (8), with (8 [+4200]), facing (7), formerly (7 [+4200]), meet (7 [+4200]), serve (7 [+6641, 4200]), in (6 [+6584]), in front of (6 [+6584]), near (6 [+4200]), against (5 [+928]), before (5 [+6584]), east (5 [+6584]), used to (5 [+4200]), accept (4 [+5951]), determined (4 [+8492]), in front of (4 [+448]), show partiality (4 [+5795]), show partiality (4 [+5951]), across (3 [+6584]), against (3 [+4946]), at (3 [+4946]), entreat (3 [+2704, 906]), escape (3 [+4946]), face (3 [+4200]), face (3 [+6425]), facedown (3 [+448]), faces (3 [+6584]), facing (3 [+448]), facing (3 [+6584]), leading (3 [+4200]), me (3 [+3276]), opposite (3 [+4200]), sight (3 [+4200]), sought the favor of (3 [+2704, 906]), straight ahead (3 [+448, 6298]), toward (3 [+6584]), accompanies (2 [+4200]), across from (2 [+6584]), advisers (2 [+8011]), appears (2 [+4200]), as long as (2 [+4200]), at (2 [+4200]), at table[S] (2 [+4200]), attitude (2), audience (2), away from (2 [+4946]), before (2 [+5584]), beside (2 [+4200]), covered with (2 [+4200]), east (2), entered service (2 [+6641, 4200]), face each other in battle (2 [+8011]), faced (2), faced (2 [+448]), faced each other (2 [+8011]), fierce-looking (2 [+6434]), floor (2), from (2 [+6584]), from (2 [+4946, 6584]), in front of (2), in front of (2 [+907]), in way (2 [+4200]), inside (2 [+4200]), leader (2 [+2143, 4200]), led in campaigns (2 [+3655, 2256, 995, 4200]), look (2), looking (2), lying on (2 [+6584]), of (2 [+4946, 4200]), preceded (2 [+4200]), prostrate (2 [+6584]), reject (2 [+8740]), repulse (2 [+8740]), resist (2 [+6641, 4200]), see (2 [+4200]), served (2 [+6641, 4200]), serving (2 [+6641, 4200]), shows partiality (2 [+5951]), top (2), under (2 [+4200]), withstand (2 [+6641, 4200]), withstand (2 [+6641, 928]), won (2 [+5951, 4200]), worship (2 [+4200]), you (2 [+3871]), yourselves (2 [+4013]), accepted (1 [+5951, 906]), adjoining (1 [+448]), advance (1 [+2025]), against (1 [+6584]), ahead (1 [+6584]), ahead (1 [+4946, 4200]), all (1), appear (1), appear before (1 [+8011]), appearance (1), approach (1), are shown respect (1 [+2075]), assistant (1 [+6641, 4200]), at (1 [+6584]), at advance (1 [+4200]), at sanctuary[S] (1 [+4200]), at the head of (1 [+4200]), attend (1 [+4200]), attending (1 [+4200]), attention (1), attention (1 [+4200]), awaits (1 [+4200]), because of (1 [+4946, 4200]), because of (1 [+3954, 4946]), before (1 [+448]), before eyes (1 [+4200]), before time (1 [+4946, 4200]), beforehand (1 [+4946, 4200]), beginning (1), bent on (1 [+5584]), beside (1 [+6584]), blade (1), blindfolds (1 [+4059]), border (1), bowed down (1 [+5877, 6584]), bowed down to the ground (1 [+5877, 6584]), check (1 [+995, 4200]), come across (1 [+7925, 4200]), come into presence (1 [+8011, 906]), condition (1), confronting (1 [+4946]), consult (1 [+4200]), corresponding to (1 [+6584]), countenance (1), court favor (1 [+2704]), cover (1 [+4848]), crossing (1 [+6584]), curry favor with (1 [+2704]), daily (1 [+4200]), deep (1 [+6584, 2021, 824]), defense against (1 [+4946]), determine (1 [+8492]), determined (1 [+8492, 8492]), dignitaries (1 [+5951]), directly opposite (1 [+5790, 4200]), disgrace (1 [+1425]), earlier times (1), east (1 [+6584, 7710]), east (1 [+2006, 2021, 7708, 2025]), eastern border (1), eastern ranks (1), edge (1), eluded (1 [+6015, 4946]), end (1), enter service (1 [+6641, 4200]), entered the service (1 [+6641, 4200]), ever (1 [+4200]), expression (1), extended (1 [+6584]), face (1 [+4946]), faced (1 [+4200]), faced forward (1 [+448, 4578]), favoritism (1 [+2075]), field (1), for (1), for (1 [+4946]), for (1 [+6584]), for fear of (1 [+4946]), for front of (1 [+4200]), for relief from (1 [+4946, 4200]), for sake (1 [+4946]), forward (1 [+4200]), found (1 [+8011, 4200]), from (1 [+448]), from (1 [+4946, 6640]), frown (1 [+5877]), give (1 [+4200]), grant (1 [+5951]), granted request (1 [+5951]), ground (1), had been (1 [+4200]), had special access to (1 [+8011]), head (1), hear (1 [+5877, 4200]), here (1 [+4200]), highly regarded (1 [+5951]), honored (1 [+5951]), humiliation (1 [+1425]), in (1), in (1 [+4200]), in deference to (1 [+4946]), in earlier times (1 [+4200]), in eyes (1 [+4200]), in front (1), in front of (1 [+4946]), in front of (1 [+448, 4578]), in hostility toward (1 [+6584]), in path (1 [+4200]), in preference to (1 [+6584]), in presence

(1 [+907]), in service (1 [+4200]), in sight (1 [+907]), in the eyes of (1 [+4200]), in the presence of (1 [+5790]), in view (1 [+907]), inner (1 [+4200]), intended (1), intercede with (1 [+2704, 906]), interceded with (1 [+2704, 906]), lead (1), lead (1 [+4200]), lead (1 [+2143, 4200]), lead (1 [+3655, 4200, 2256, 995]), lead across (1 [+6296, 4200]), led (1 [+4200]), led out (1 [+3655, 4200]), lifetime (1), lived in hostility toward (1 [+5877, 6584]), look in the face (1 [+5951, 448]), look with favor (1 [+239]), look with favor (1 [+5564]), looked (1), looked (1 [+8492]), made face (1 [+5989]), make room for (1 [+4946]), man of rank (1 [+5951]), meet (1 [+448]), meet (1 [+4946]), meet with (1 [+8011]), more quickly than (1 [+4200]), more readily than (1 [+4200]), mouth (1), my (1 [+3276]), my (1 [+4200, 3276]), nearest (1 [+6584]), never (1 [+4202, 4200]), north (1 [+2006, 2021, 7600]), obstinate (1 [+7997]), of (1 [+4200]), on both sides (1 [+2256, 294]), open (1 [+4200]), open before (1 [+5790]), opening (1), opposite (1 [+448]), ours (1 [+4200, 5646]), out (1 [+4946]), out in front (1 [+448, 4578]), out of (1 [+4946]), out of way (1 [+4946, 4200]), outer (1), over (1 [+4200]), overlooking (1 [+4200]), pacify (1 [+4105]), parallel (1 [+928]), partial (1 [+5951]), partiality (1 [+5365]), plead with (1 [+2704]), preceded (1 [+2118, 4200]), preceding (1 [+4200]), predecessor (1 [+889, 2118, 4200]), present (1), present (1 [+4200]), present (1 [+5877, 4200]), previous (1 [+4200]), protection from (1 [+4946]), put (1 [+4200, 995]), put up a bold front (1 [+6451, 928]), receive (1 [+5951]), reflects (1 [+4200, 2021]), regard (1 [+2118, 4200]), regards (1 [+5162, 4200]), region (1), reject (1 [+8959, 4946, 6584]), reject (1 [+8938, 4946, 6584]), renounce (1 [+8740]), resist (1), resolved (1 [+5989]), respect (1 [+5951]), sake (1), scalp (1), see (1 [+8011]), seek an audience with (1 [+1335]), seek favor (1 [+2704]), seek favor (1 [+2704, 906]), seen for myself (1 [+8011]), serve (1 [+4200]), serve (1 [+2118, 4200]), served (1 [+6641, 907]), served (1 [+2118, 4200]), show (1 [+4200]), showed partiality (1 [+5951]), shown honor (1 [+5951]), shown partiality (1 [+5951]), some distance from (1 [+4946]), sought favor (1 [+2704]), sought favor (1 [+2704, 906]), spared from (1 [+4946]), stared with a fixed gaze (1 [+6641, 906, 2256, 8492]), stood before (1 [+4200]), sulking (1 [+6015, 906]), table[S] (1), take for (1 [+5989, 4200]), taken from (1 [+4946, 4200]), that[S] (1), the Lord himself (1 [+3378]), their own (1 [+2157]), themselves (1 [+2157]), those[S] (1 [+2021]), throughout (1 [+6584, 3972]), tilting toward (1), to (1 [+907]), to (1 [+4946]), to (1 [+6584, 4200]), toward (1), toward (1 [+448]), toward (1 [+6584, 2006]), turn away (1 [+6015]), turned (1 [+5989]), turned (1 [+6015]), turned (1 [+8492]), under (1 [+907]), under (1 [+4946]), under blessing (1 [+4200]), under direction (1 [+4200]), under supervision (1 [+4200]), unless (1 [+3954, 561, 4200]), unyielding (1 [+2617]), upon (1 [+6584]), upside down (1 [+6584]), watched (1 [+4200]), where[S] (1 [+4200]), while still alive (1 [+6584]), windblown (1 [+6584, 8120]), with (1 [+907]), with (1 [+6584]), within sight of (1 [+907]), withstood (1 [+6641, 928]), you (1 [+4013]), you yourself (1 [+3870]), NDT (117)

H7157 פִּנָּה ***pinnâ***, n.f. [31] [√ 7155]. corner (of a structure), cornerstone (as a crucial element); stronghold; by extension: leader:– corner (15), corners (5), cornerstone (3), leaders (2), corner defenses (1), cornerstone (1 [+74]), cornerstone (1 [+8031]), cornerstones (1), street corner (1), strongholds (1)

H7158 [1]פְּנוּאֵל ***pᵉnû'ēl[1]***, n.pr.m. [2] [√ 7159; cf. 7155 + 446]. Penuel, *"face of God [El]"*:– Penuel (2)

H7159 [2]פְּנוּאֵל ***pᵉnû'ēl[2]***, n.pr.loc. [6] [√ 7158; cf. 7155 + 446]. Peniel, *"face of God [El]"*:– Peniel (5), they[S] (1 [+408])

H7160 [1]פְּנִיאֵל ***pᵉnî'ēl[1]***, n.pr.m. Not used in NIVEBC [√ 7161; cf. 7155 + 446]. Peniel, see 7158, *"face of God [El]"*

H7161 [2]פְּנִיאֵל ***pᵉnî'ēl[2]***, n.pr.loc. [1] [√ 7160; cf. 7155 + 446]. Peniel, *"face of God [El]"*:– Peniel (1)

H7162 פְּנִיִּים ***pᵉnîyyim***, var. Not used in NIVEBC [√ 7165]. see 7165

H7163 פְּנִימָה ***pᵉnîmâ***, adv. *or* pp. [13] [→ 7164; cf. 7156, 7155]. inner, inside, within:– inside (2), in (1), inner (1 [+4200]), inner sanctuary (1), inside (1 [+4200]), inside (1 [+4946]), into (1 [+448]), into (1 [+4200]), inward (1), within (1), within chamber (1), NDT (1)

H7164 פְּנִימִי ***pᵉnîmî***, a. [31] [√ 7163]. inner:– inner (25), inner sanctuary (2), innermost (2), far end (1), inside (1)

H7165 פְּנִינִים ***pᵉnînîm***, n.[f.]pl. [6] [→ 7162, 7166]. rubies or corals:– rubies (6)

H7166 פְּנִנָּה ***pᵉninnâ***, n.pr.f. [3] [√ 7165]. Peninnah, "[poss.] *pearls, coral branches; woman with rich hair*":– Peninnah (3)

H7167 פָּנַק ***pānaq***, v. [1] [P] to pamper:– pampered (1)

H7168 פַּס ***pas***, n.[m.] [5] [→ 7169; cf. 701; 10589]. ornamentation, many-colored or long-sleeved garment:– ornate (5)

H7169 פַּס דַּמִּים ***pas dammîm***, n.pr.loc. [1] [√ 7168 + 1956]. Pas Dammim, *"place of blood"*:– Pas Dammim (1)

H7170 פָּסַג ***pāsag***, v. [1] [P] to look over or to walk among:– view (1)

H7171 פִּסְגָּה ***pisgâ***, n.pr.loc. [8] [→ 849]. Pisgah:– Pisgah (8)

H7172 פִּסָּה ***pissâ***, n.f. [1] abundance, plenty:– abound (1 [+2118])

H7173 [1]פָּסַח ***pāsaḥ[1]***, v. [4] [→ 7175, 9527; cf. 7174]. [Q] to pass over:– pass over (3), passed over (1)

H7174 [2]פָּסַח ***pāsaḥ[2]***, v. [3] [→ 7176, 7177; cf. 7173]. [Q] to be limp; [N] to become crippled; to worship in a limping dance:– became disabled (1), danced (1), waver (1)

H7175 פֶּסַח ***pesaḥ***, n.m. [49] [√ 7173]. Passover; this can refer to the festival, the meal, or the lamb sacrificed at the festival:– Passover (35), Passover lamb (4), Passover lambs (3), Passover offerings (3), Passover animals (1), Passover meal (1), did so[S] (1 [+6913, 906, 2021]), its[S] (1 [+2021])

H7176 פָּסֵחַ ***pāsēaḥ***, n.pr.m. [4] [√ 7174]. Paseah, *"hobbling one"*:– Paseah (4)

H7177 פִּסֵּחַ ***pissēaḥ***, a. [14] [√ 7174]. lame, crippled:– lame (14)

H7178 פָּסִיל ***pāsîl***, n.m. [23] [√ 7180]. idol, carved image:– idols (14), images (5), idols (2 [+2256, 5011]), stone images (2)

H7179 פָּסַךְ ***pāsak***, n.pr.m. [1] Pasach, *"to divide"*:– Pasak (1)

H7180 פָּסַל ***pāsal***, v. [6] [→ 7178, 7181]. [Q] to chisel out, carve (stone or wood):– chisel out (2), chiseled out (2), carved (1), cut (1)

H7181 פֶּסֶל ***pesel***, n.m. [31] [√ 7180]. idol, usually an image carved of wood or stone:– idol (13), image (6), idols (5), idol (3 [+2256, 5011]), images (2), carved (1), image (1 [+6166])

H7182 פָּסַס ***pāsas***, v. [1] [Q] to vanish:– vanished (1)

H7183 פִּסְפָּה ***pispâ***, n.pr.m. [1] Pispah:– Pispah (1)

H7184 פָּעָה ***pā'â***, v. [1] [√ 704?]. [Q] to cry out, groan (in childbirth):– cry out (1)

H7185 פָּעוּ ***pā'û***, n.pr.loc. [2] [cf. 7187]. Pau, *"groaning, bleating"*:– Pau (2)

H7186 פְּעוֹר ***pᵉ'ôr***, n.pr.loc. [9] [→ 1121, 1261; cf. 7196?]. Peor, *"opening"*:– Peor (8), that[S] (1)

H7187 פָּעִי ***pā'î***, n.pr.loc. Not used in NIVEBC [cf. 7185]. Pai, see 7185

H7188 פָּעַל ***pā'al***, v. [57] [→ 551, 5148, 5149, 7040, 7189, 7190, 7191]. [Q] to do, make:– evildoers (16 [+224]), do (12), done (9), does (2), made (2), act (1), affect (1), bestow (1), brings (1), devise (1), did (1), evildoer (1 [+224]), fashions (1), forges (1), know (1 [+3359]), maker (1), makes ready (1), plot (1), practice (1), works (1), works out (1)

H7189 פֹּעַל ***pō'al***, n.m. [37] [→ 7040; cf. 7188]. work, deed, labor:– deeds (8), work (7), works (5), what done (4), conduct (2), labor (2), acts (1), did (1), exploits (1), made (1), paid (1), performed exploits (1), something (1), what[S] (1), what did (1)

H7190 פְּעֻלָּה ***pᵉ'ullâ***, n.f. [14] [→ 7191; cf. 7188]. work, deed, recompense:– wages (3), deeds (2), recompense (2), reward (2), work (2), bribe (1), payment (1), reward (1 [+5989])

H7191 פְּעֻלְּתַי ***pᵉ'ullᵉtay***, n.pr.m. [1] [√ 7190; cf. 7188]. Peullethai, *"worker, wage earner"*:– Peullethai (1)

H7192 פָּעַם ***pā'am***, v. [5] [→ 7193, 7194]. [Q] to push, impel; [N] to be troubled; [Ht] to be troubled:– troubled (3), stir (1), troubles (1)

H7193 פַּעַם ***pa'am***, n.f. [118] [→ 7194; cf. 7192]. step, foot; time, occurrence:– times (43), time (15), feet (10), twice (5), now (3), once (3 [+285]), once more (3), as before (2 [+3869, 928, 7193]), as before (2 [+3869, 7193, 928]), customary (2 [+7193, 3869, 928]), encounter (2), footsteps (2), one more (2), steps (2), again (1 [+1685, 928, 2021, 2021, 2085]), annual (1 [+928, 2021, 9102]), anvil (1), as done before (1 [+3869, 928, 7193]), as done before (1 [+3869, 7193, 928]), at last (1 [+2021]), at other times (1 [+7193, 928]), at other times (1 [+928, 7193]), campaign (1), clatter (1), forms (1), level (1), moment (1), now (1 [+2021]), once (1), once more (1 [+421, 2021]), other[S] (1), sets (1), supports (1 [+4190]), thrust (1), twice over (1), NDT (1)

H7194 פַּעֲמוֹן ***pa'ᵃmôn***, n.[m.] [7] [√ 7193; cf. 7192]. bell (on a robe):– bells (4), alternate[S] (1 [+2298, 2256, 8232]), alternated[S] (1 [+2256, 8232]), them[S] (1 [+2021])

H7195 פַּעְנֵחַ ***pa'nēaḥ***, n.pr.m. Not used in NIVEBC [√ 7624]. Paneah

H7196 פָּעַר ***pā'ar***, v. [4] [cf. 7186?, 7197?]. [Q] to open wide (mouth):– open (2), drank in (1 [+7023]), opening (1)

H7197 פַּעֲרַי ***pa'ᵃray***, n.pr.m. [1] [cf. 7196?]. Paarai, *"devotee of Peor"*:– Paarai (1)

H7198 פָּצָה ***pāṣâ***, v. [15] [Q] to open (mouth); to deliver, set free:– opened (3), deliver (2), open wide (2), opens (2), delivers (1), given word (1 [+906, 7023]), made a vow (1 [+7023]), open (1), opened wide (1), promised (1)

H7199 [1]פָּצַח ***pāṣaḥ[1]***, v. [Q] to be serene

H7200 [2]פָּצַח ***pāṣaḥ[2]***, v. [8] [Q] to break forth, burst forth; [P] to break (in pieces):– burst (6), break (1), break in pieces (1)

H7201 פְּצִירָה ***pᵉṣîrâ***, n.f. [1] sharpening (of plowshare):– sharpening (1)

H7202 פָּצַל ***pāṣal***, v. [2] [→ 7203]. [P] to peel (bark off boughs):– peeled (1), peeling (1)

H7203 פְּצָלוֹת ***pᵉṣālôt***, n.f.pl. [1] [√ 7202]. stripes (made by peeling bark):– stripes (1)

H7204 פָּצַם ***pāṣam***, v. [1] [Q] to tear open:– torn open (1)

H7205 פָּצַע ***pāṣa'***, v. [3] [→ 7206]. [Q] to bruise, wound; [Qp] to be emasculated (by crushing):– been emasculated (1), bruised (1), wounded (1)

H7206 פֶּצַע ***peṣa'***, n.m. [8] [√ 7205]. wound, bruise:– wounds (4), wound (2), bruises (1), wounding (1)

H7207 פָּצַץ ***pāṣaṣ***, v. [3] [→ 1122, 2204, 7209; cf. 5879, 7046]. [Pol] to break to pieces, shatter; [Pil] to crush, smash; [Htpol] to be crumbled, be shattered:– breaks in pieces (1), crumbled (1), crushed (1)

H7208 פַּצֵּץ ***paṣṣēṣ***, n.pr.loc. Not used in NIVEBC [√ 7207]. Pazzez, see 1122, *"one who breaks"*

H7209 פִּצֵּץ ***piṣṣēṣ***, n.pr.m. Not used in NIVEBC [√ 7207]. Pizzez, see 2204, *"one who breaks"*

H7210 פָּצַר ***pāṣar***, v. [7] [cf. 7287]. [Q] to insist on, bring pressure, persuade; [H] to be arrogant:– insisted (2), arrogance (1), kept bringing pressure (1 [+4394]), persisted (1), persuaded (1), urged (1)

H7211 פִּק ***piq***, n.[m.] [1] [cf. 7048]. giving way, shaking (of knees):– give way (1)

H7212 פָּקַד ***pāqad***, v. [301] [→ 5152, 7213, 7214, 7215, 7216, 7217, 7218, 7224]. [Q] to pay attention, care for; to count, number; to punish; [Qp] to be counted, listed; [N] to be missing, empty; [P] to muster; [Pu] to be robbed; to be recorded; [H] to appoint, give a charge; [Ho] to be appointed; [Ht] be mustered, counted; [Hotpaal] to be counted:– punish (45), counted (23), number (18), numbered (13), numbers (12), appoint (11), were counted (10), appointed (9), assigned (9), count (9), mustered (8), care for (6), missing (6), put in charge (6), surely come to aid (6 [+7212]), appointed as governor (5), punished (5), come (3), empty (3), punishes (3), assign (2), be punished (2), counted (2 [+7212]), deal (2), enroll (2), examine (2), gracious (2), misses at all (2 [+7212]), missing (2 [+7212]), mobilized (2), officers (2), punishing (2), supervisors (2), total (2), was counted (2), watched over and seen (2 [+7212]), were appointed (2), accuse (1 [+6584]), assembled (1), be called to arms (1), be missed (1), be missing (1), be robbed (1), bestow punishment (1), bestowed care on (1), bring (1), bring punishment (1), called to account (1), came (1), come to aid (1), come to the aid of (1), commit (1), concerned about (1), destroy (1), did[S] (1), fails to come (1), harm (1), in charge (1), in charge of (1), lack (1), listed (1), longed for (1), missed (1), muster forces (1), mustering (1), numbering (1), placed (1), post (1), posted (1), prescribed (1), punishments come (1), put (1), put away (1), see (1), send (1), sets (1), store (1), suffer (1), summoned (1), take care of (1), take stock of (1), total (1 [+3972]), untouched (1 [+1153]), visit (1), was entrusted (1 [+7214]), watch over (1), were counted in the census (1), were found missing (1), were recorded (1), were registered (1), NDT (4)

H7213 פְּקֻדָּה ***pᵉquddâ***, n.f. [32] [√ 7212]. positive: appointment, charge, visitation; negative: punishment:– punished (4), punishment (3), appointed (2), appointed order (2), judgment (2), appointed to execute judgment (1), assignment (1), charge (1), enrollment (1), fate (1), governor (1), guards (1), having charge (1), in charge (1), mustered (1), officials (1), oversight (1), place of leadership (1), prison (1 [+1074, 2021]), providence (1), reckoning (1), responsible (1), stored up (1), visits (1)

H7214 פִּקָּדוֹן ***piqqādôn***, n.m. [3] [√ 7212]. something entrusted, something in reserve:– held in reserve (1), something entrusted (1), was entrusted (1 [+7212])

H7215 פְּקִדֻת ***pᵉqidut***, n.f. [1] [√ 7212]. (captain of the) guard:– guard (1)

H7216 פְּקוֹד ***pᵉqôd***, n.pr.loc. [2] [√ 7212]. Pekod, *"visitation"*:– Pekod (2)

H7217 פְּקוּדִים ***pᵉqûdîm***, n.pl.[m.] [1] [√ 7212]. accounting (of materials):– amounts (1)

H7218 פִּקּוּדִים ***piqqûdîm***, n.m.pl. [24] [√ 7212]. precepts, directions, orders:– precepts (24)

H7219 פָּקַח ***pāqaḥ***, v. [19] [→ 7220?, 7221, 7222, 7223]. [Q] to open; [Qp] to be opened; [N] to be opened:– open (7), opened (4), be opened (2), fix (1), gives sight (1), keep watchful (1), opens (1), stay awake (1 [+6524]), were opened (1)

H7220 פֶּקַח ***peqaḥ***, n.pr.m. [11] [√ 7219?]. Pekah, *"he has opened"*:– Pekah (10), Pekah's (1)

H7221 פִּקֵּחַ ***piqqēaḥ***, a. [2] [√ 7219]. (normal) sighted:– see (1), sight (1)

H7222 פְּקַחְיָה **pᵉqaḥyâ**, n.pr.m. [3] [√ 7219 + 3378]. Pekahiah, *"Yahweh opens"*:– Pekahiah (2), Pekahiah's (1)

H7223 פְּקַח־קוֹחַ **pᵉqaḥ-qôaḥ**, n.[m.] [1] [√ 7219; cf. 7751]. opening (of eyesight); some sources: opening a prison house to release prisoners:– release from darkness (1)

H7224 פָּקִיד **pāqîd**, n.m. [13] [√ 7212]. chief officer, supervisor, commissioner:– chief officer (3), in charge (3), commissioners (2), assistants (1), deputy (1), direction (1), officer (1), official (1)

H7225 פְּקָעִים **pᵉqā'îm**, n.m.pl. [3] [→ 7226]. gourds:– gourds (3)

H7226 פַּקֻּעֹת **paqqu'ōt**, n.[f.]pl. [1] [√ 7225]. gourds:– gourds (1 [+8441])

H7227 פֶּקֶר **peqer**, n.[m.] licentiousness

H7228 פַּר **par**, n.m. [132] [→ 7239]. bull:– bull (47), bulls (30), bull (27 [+1330]), bull's (9), bulls (5 [+1330]), young bulls (3), its[S] (2 [+2021]), its[S] (2 [+2021]), bull calves (1), its[S] (1), one[S] (1), oxen (1), NDT (3)

H7229 פָּרָא **pārā'**, v. [1] [cf. 7238]. [H] to thrive in fruitfulness:– thrives (1)

H7230 פֶּרֶא **pere'**, n.m. *or* f. [9] [→ 7000?, 7231; cf. 7241]. wild donkey; some sources: zebra, onager:– wild donkey (4), wild donkeys (3), donkeys (1), wild donkey's (1)

H7231 פִּרְאָם **pir'ām**, n.pr.m. [1] [√ 7230]. Piram, "[poss.] *wild donkey; indomitable*; [poss.] *zebra*":– Piram (1)

H7232 פַּרְבָּר **parbār**, n.[m.] [2] [cf. 7247]. court (of the temple):– court (2)

H7233 פָּרַד **pārad**, v. [26] [→ 7234, 7235, 7237]. [Qp] to be spread out; [N] to be separated, be parted; [P] to consort with; [Pu] to be scattered; [H] to set apart, divide, separate; [Ht] to be scattered, be parted:– separates (3), spread out (2), are scattered (1), be parted (1), be scattered (1), be separated (1), consort (1), deserts (1), divided (1), keep separate (1), keeps apart (1), left (1), out of joint (1), part company (1), parted (1), parted company (1), separated (1), separated (1 [+1068]), set apart by themselves (1), spreading out (1), unfriendly (1), was separated (1), were parted (1)

H7234 פֶּרֶד **pered**, n.m. [15] [→ 7235; cf. 7233]. mule:– mules (11), mule (4)

H7235 פִּרְדָּה **pirdâ**, n.f. [5] [√ 7234]. (female) mule:– mule (3)

H7236 פַּרְדֵּס **pardēs**, n.[m.] [3] park, forest, orchard:– orchard (1), park (1), parks (1)

H7237 פְּרֻדֹת **pᵉrudōt**, n.f. [1] [√ 7233]. grain (of seed); some sources: dried fig:– seeds (1)

H7238 [1]פָּרָה **pārâ[1]**, v. [29] [→ 713?, 7242, 7262, 7311; cf. 7229]. [Q] to be fruitful, flourish; [H] to make fruitful:– fruitful (13), make fruitful (5), fruitful vine (2 [+1201]), made fruitful (2), bear fruit (1), exceedingly fruitful (1), flourish (1), increased (1), numbers increased greatly (1 [+8049, 2256]), produces (1), spring up (1)

H7239 [2]פָּרָה **pārâ[2]**, n.f. [26] [√ 7228]. cow, heifer:– cows (18), heifer (6), cow (1), those[S] (1 [+2021])

H7240 [3]פָּרָה **pārâ[3]**, n.pr.loc. [1] Parah, *"cow"*:– Parah (1)

H7241 פֶּרֶה **pereh**, n.m. [1] [cf. 7230]. wild donkey:– wild donkey (1)

H7242 פּוּרָה **purâ**, n.pr.m. [2] [√ 7238]. Purah, *"branch; imposing"*:– Purah (2)

H7243 פְּרוּדָא **pᵉrûdā'**, n.pr.m. [1] [cf. 7263]. Peruda, *"single, unique"*:– Peruda (1)

H7244 פְּרוֹזִים **pᵉrôzîm**, n.[m.] Not used in NIVEBC [√ 7253; cf. 7252]. see 7253

H7245 פָּרוּחַ **pārûaḥ**, n.pr.m. [1] [√ 7255]. Paruah, *"blooming; cheerful"*:– Paruah (1)

H7246 פַּרְוַיִם **parwayim**, n.pr.loc. [1] Parvaim:– Parvaim (1)

H7247 פַּרְוָר **parwār**, n.[m.] [1] [cf. 7232]. court:– court (1)

H7248 פָּרוּר **pārûr**, n.[m.] [3] [→ 6999]. cooking pot:– pot (3)

H7249 פֵּרוֹת **pērôt**, n.f. Not used in NIVEBC [√ 2916]. see 2923

H7250 פָּרָז **pārāz**, n.[m.] [1] warrior:– warriors (1)

H7251 פְּרָזוֹן **pᵉrāzôn**, n.[m.] [2] [√ 7252]. dwellers in the open country; warriors:– villagers (2)

H7252 פְּרָזוֹת **pᵉrāzôt**, n.f.[pl.] [3] [→ 7244, 7251, 7253, 7254]. rural, open country:– city without walls (1), unwalled villages (1), villages (1 [+6551])

H7253 פְּרָזִי **pᵉrāzî**, n.[m.] [3] [√ 7244; cf. 7252]. rural, open country:– country (1), rural (1), unwalled (1)

H7254 פְּרִזִּי **pᵉrizzî**, a.g. [23] [√ 7252]. Perizzite:– Perizzites (23)

H7255 [1]פָּרַח **pāraḥ[1]**, v. [34] [→ 7245, 7258, 7259?; cf. 7257]. [Q] to sprout, blossom; break out, flourish; [H] to make flourish, bring to bud:– flourish (5), blossom (4), broken out (3), budded (3), breaks out all over (2 [+7255]), bud (2), burst into bloom (2 [+7255]), spring up (2), blossomed (1), break out (1), breaking out (1), bring to bud (1), broke out (1), make flourish (1), reappears (1 [+8740, 2256]), spreading (1), sprout (1), sprouted (1), thrive (1)

H7256 [2]פָּרַח **pāraḥ[2]**, v. [2] [→ 711]. [Q] to fly; (n.) a bird:– birds (2)

H7257 [3]פָּרַח **pāraḥ[3]**, v. Not used in NIVEBC [cf. 7255]. [Q] to break out

H7258 פֶּרַח **peraḥ**, n.m. [17] [√ 7255]. blossom, bud; floral work:– blossoms (8), blossom (3), floral work (2), budded (1 [+3655]), flowers (1), NDT (2)

H7259 פִּרְחָח **pirḥaḥ**, n.m.col. [1] [√ 7255?]. offspring, brood, tribe, with a focus on energetic behavior:– tribe (1)

H7260 פָּרַט **pāraṭ**, v. [1] [→ 7261?]. [Q] to strum, improvise (on a musical instrument):– strum away (1)

H7261 פֶּרֶט **pereṭ**, n.[m.]col. [1] [√ 7260?]. fallen grapes:– grapes that have fallen (1)

H7262 פְּרִי **pᵉrî**, n.m. [120] [√ 7238]. fruit, produce, crops; by extension: offspring of any creature; result of any action; "fruit of the lips" is speech, praise; "fruit of the hand" is something earned:– fruit (78), crops (8), produce (4), young (4), fruits (3), deserve (2), firstfruits (2 [+8040]), fruitful (2), all done (1), branches (1), children (1 [+1061]), crops (1 [+2021, 141]), crops[S] (1), descendants (1), descendants (1 [+1061]), earnings (1 [+4090]), fruitfulness (1), infants (1 [+1061]), offspring (1), offspring (1 [+2021, 1061]), result (1), rewarded (1), what deserve (1), willful pride (1 [+1542]), NDT (1)

H7263 פְּרִידָא **pᵉrîdā'**, n.pr.m. [1] [cf. 7243]. Perida, *"single, unique"*:– Perida (1)

H7264 [1]פָּרִיץ **pārîṣ[1]**, n.m. [1] [√ 7287]. ferocious (animal):– ravenous (1)

H7265 [2]פָּרִיץ **pārîṣ[2]**, n.m. [5] [√ 7287]. robber; violent one:– violent (3), robbers (2)

H7266 פֶּרֶךְ **perek**, n.[m.] [6] ruthlessness, brutality, violence:– ruthlessly (5 [+928]), brutally (1 [+928])

H7267 פָּרֹכֶת **pārōket**, n.f. [25] curtain:– curtain (25)

H7268 פָּרַם **pāram**, v. [3] [Q] to tear; [Qp] to be torn:– tear (2), torn (1)

H7269 פַּרְמַשְׁתָּא **parmašᵉtā'**, n.pr.m. [1] Parmashta, *"very first"*:– Parmashta (1)

H7270 פַּרְנָךְ **parnāk**, n.pr.m. [1] Parnach:– Parnak (1)

H7271 [1]פָּרַס **pāras[1]**, v. [14] [→ 7272?, 7274; 10592]. [Q] to offer food, share food; [H] to have a divided hoof:– divided (11), hooves (1), offer food (1), share (1)

H7272 פֶּרֶס **peres**, n.[m.] [2] [√ 7271?]. vulture:– vulture (2)

H7273 [2]פָּרַס **pāras[2]**, n.pr.loc. [28] [→ 7275; 10594, 10595]. Persia; Persian:– Persia (26), Persian (2)

H7274 פַּרְסָה **parsâ**, n.f. [21] [√ 7271]. hoof:– hoof (12), hooves (6), NDT (3)

H7275 פָּרְסִי **pārᵉsî**, a.g. [1] [√ 7273; 10595]. Persian:– Persian (1)

H7276 [1]פָּרַע **pāra'[1]**, v.den. [1] [→ 7278; cf. 7277]. [Q] to take the lead:– take the lead (1)

H7277 [2]פָּרַע **pāra'[2]**, v. [15] [cf. 7276]. [Q] to be out of control, be unkempt; to ignore, avoid; [Qp] to be unkempt, be running wild; [N] to be unrestrained; [H] to let neglect; to promote wickedness:– disregard (3), unkempt (3), avoid (1), cast off restraint (1), disregards (1), get out of control (1), hold back (1), loosen (1), promoted wickedness (1), running wild (1), taking away (1)

H7278 [1]פֶּרַע **pera'[1]**, n.[m.] [2] [√ 7276; cf. 7279?]. leader, prince:– leaders (1), princes (1)

H7279 [2]פֶּרַע **pera'[2]**, n.[m.] [2] [cf. 7278?]. long hair of head:– hair (1 [+8552, 8031]), hair long (1)

H7280 [3]פֶּרַע **pera'[3]**, n.pr.m. Not used in NIVEBC [cf. 7036]. Pera, see 7036

H7281 פַּרְעֹה **par'ōh**, n.m. [273] Pharaoh:– Pharaoh (205), Pharaoh's (52), his[S] (5), he[S] (4), Pharaoh's (2 [+4200]), him[S] (2), royal (1), she[S] (1 [+1426]), there[S] (1 [+1074])

H7282 [1]פַּרְעֹשׁ **par'ōš[1]**, n.m. [2] [→ 7283]. flea:– flea (2)

H7283 [2]פַּרְעֹשׁ **par'ōš[2]**, n.pr.m. [6] [√ 7282]. Parosh, *"flea"*:– Parosh (6)

H7284 פִּרְעָתוֹן **pir'ātôn**, n.pr.loc. [1] [→ 7285]. Pirathon:– Pirathon (1)

H7285 פִּרְעָתוֹנִי **pir'ātônî**, a.g. [5] [√ 7284]. Pirathonite, from Pirathon, *"of Pirathon"*:– Pirathonite (3), from Pirathon (1), NDT (1)

H7286 פַּרְפַּר **parpar**, n.pr.loc. [1] Pharpar:– Pharpar (1)

H7287 פָּרַץ **pāraṣ**, v. [49] [→ 1262, 5153, 7264, 7265, 7288, 7289, 7290, 7291, 7292; cf. 7210]. [Q] to break out, burst forth; [Qp] to be broken through; [N] to be spread abroad; [Pu] to be broken down; [Ht] to break oneself away:– broken out (4), broke down (3), broken down (3), urged (3), break down (2), break out (2), increased (2), spread (2), spread out (2), again and again bursts (1 [+7288, 7288]), are broken through (1), break (1), break all bounds (1), breaking away (1), breaks open (1), breaks through (1), brim over (1), broke out (1), broke out in anger (1), broken (1), broken into (1), broken out (1 [+7288]), broken through (1), burst upon (1), cut (1), destroy (1), dispersing (1), far and wide (1), flourish (1), gaps (1), many (1), prosperous (1), tear down (1), urging (1), went out (1)

H7288 [1]פֶּרֶץ **pereṣ[1]**, n.m. [19] [→ 1262, 8236; cf. 7287]. breech, break, gap caused by something breaking through; by extension: outburst of anger:– gap (3), breach (2), break out (2), wrath (2), again and again bursts (1 [+7287, 7288]), again and again bursts (1 [+7287, 7288]), breaches (1), breaches in the wall (1), breaching of walls (1), broken (1), broken out (1 [+7287]), broken walls (1), cracked (1 [+5877]), gap in the wall (1)

H7289 [2]פֶּרֶץ **pereṣ[2]**, n.pr.m. [15] [→ 7291; cf. 7287]. Perez, *"breaking out"*:– Perez (15)

H7290 פֶּרֶץ עֻזָּא **pereṣ 'uzzā'**, פֶּרֶץ עֻזָּה **pereṣ 'uzzâ**, n.pr.loc. [2] [√ 7288 + 6446]. Perez Uzzah, *"breaking out of Uzzah"*:– Perez Uzzah (2)

H7291 פַּרְצִי **parṣî**, a.g. [1] [√ 7289; cf. 7287]. Perezite:– Perezite (1)

H7292 פְּרָצִים **pᵉrāṣîm**, n.pr.loc. [1] [√ 7288; cf. 7287]. Perazim, *"breaking out"*:– Perazim (1)

H7293 פָּרַק **pāraq**, v. [10] [→ 5154, 7294, 7295; 10596]. [Q] to rip to pieces; to free (by tearing away); [P] to take off, tear off; [Ht] to take off from oneself, tear off from oneself:– take off (2), free (1), freed (1), rip to pieces (1), tearing off (1), throw off (1), took off (1), tore apart (1), was stripped (1)

H7294 פֶּרֶק **pereq**, n.[m.] [2] [√ 7293]. crossroad; plunder:– crossroads (1), plunder (1)

H7295 פָּרָק **pārāq**, n.[m.] Not used in NIVEBC [√ 7293]. fragment

H7296 [1]פָּרַר **pārar[1]**, v. [49] [cf. 7051]. [H] to break, violate, nullify; [Ho] to be broken, revoked, thwarted:– break (8), breaking (6), broken (6), nullifies (4 [+7296]), broke (3), foils (2), frustrate (2), be broken (1), be thwarted (1), discredit (1), fail (1), frustrated (1), frustrating (1), no longer stirred (1), nullified (1), nullifies (1), nullify (1), put away (1), revoking (1), take (1), thwart (1), thwarts (1), undermine (1), violate (1), was revoked (1)

H7297 [2]פָּרַר **pārar[2]**, v. [4] [Q] to split asunder; [Pil] to shatter; [Pol] to split open; [Htpol] to split asunder:– is split asunder (2 [+7297]), shattered (1), split open (1)

H7298 פָּרַשׂ **pāraś**, v. [69] [→ 5155; cf. 7299]. [Q] to spread out, scatter; [Qp] to be spread out; [N] to be scattered; [P] to scatter, spread out:– spread (21), spread out (18), spreading (5), scattered (3), stretch out (3), spreading out (2), throw (2), be scattered (1), cast (1), chop up (1), display (1), expose (1), extended (1), gives (1), held out (1), laid (1), opens (1), scatters (1), spreads (1), stretches out (1), stretching out (1), unrolled (1)

H7299 פַּרְשֵׂז **paršēz**, a.vbl. *or* v. Not used in NIVEBC [cf. 7298]. spreading

H7300 [1]פָּרַשׁ **pāraš[1]**, v. [3] [→ 7304, 7305, 7308; cf. 7301; 10597]. [Q] to make clear; [N] to be given; [Pu] to be made clear:– clear (1), made clear (1), making clear (1)

H7301 [2]פָּרַשׁ **pāraš[2]**, v. [1] [cf. 7300, 7302]. [H] to secrete poison:– poisons (1)

H7302 [1]פֶּרֶשׁ **pereš[1]**, n.[m.] [7] [→ 7303; cf. 7301]. offal, dung or intestinal contents of a butchered animal:– intestines (5), dung (1), NDT (1)

H7303 [2]פֶּרֶשׁ **pereš[2]**, n.pr.m. [1] [√ 7302]. Peresh, *"offal eviscerated; dung; contents of stomach [not intestine]"*:– Peresh (1)

H7304 [1]פָּרָשׁ **pārāš[1]**, n.[m.] [18] [√ 7300]. horse:– horses (14), cavalry horses (1), drivers (1 [+1251]), steeds (1), warhorses (1)

H7305 [2]פָּרָשׁ **pārāš[2]**, n.m. [38] [√ 7300]. horseman:– horsemen (27), charioteers (6), cavalry (5)

H7306 פַּרְשֶׁגֶן **paršegen**, n.m. [1] [cf. 7358; 10598]. copy:– copy (1)

H7307 פַּרְשְׁדֹן **paršᵉdōn**, n.[m] [1] back (of a person), back door [?]:– bowels (1)

H7308 פָּרָשָׁה **pārāšâ**, n.f. [2] [√ 7300]. exact amount, exact statement:– exact amount (1), full account (1)

H7309 פַּרְשַׁנְדָּתָא **paršandātā'**, n.pr.m. [1] Parshandatha:– Parshandatha (1)

H7310 פְּרָת **pᵉrāt**, n.pr.loc. [19] Euphrates (mighty river of Mesopotamia); Perath (small river or valley in the book of Jeremiah):– Euphrates (15), Perath (4)

H7311 פֹּרָת **pōrāt**, var. Not used in NIVEBC [√ 7238]. see 7238

H7312 פַּרְתְּמִים **partᵉmîm**, n.m.pl. [3] nobles, princes:– most noble (1), nobility (1), princes (1)

H7313 פָּשָׂה **pāśâ**, v. [22] [Q] to spread:– spread (14), spread (4 [+7313]), spreading (4 [+7313])

H7314 פָּשַׂע **pāśa'**, v. [1] [→ 7315; cf. 5156]. [Q] to march, step forth:– march (1)

H7315 פֶּשַׂע **peśa'**, n.[m.] [1] [√ 7314]. step:– step (1)

HEBREW INDEX

H7316 פָּשַׂק ***pāśaq***, v. [2] [Q] to open wide (the lips in talking or smirking); [P] to spread the feet or legs (in immorality):– speak rashly (1 [+8557]), spreading (1)

H7317 פַּשׁ ***paš***, n.[m.] [1] wickedness or weakness, foolishness:– wickedness (1)

H7318 פָּשַׁח ***pāšaḥ***, v. [1] [P] to mangle:– mangled (1)

H7319 פַּשְׁחוּר ***pašḥûr***, n.pr.m. [14] Pashhur, "[perhaps] *be quiet* and *round about*":– Pashhur (13), he[S] (1)

H7320 פָּשַׁט ***pāšaṭ***, v. [43] [Q] to take off, strip; to make a sudden dash, raid; [P] to strip; [H] to take off, strip off; [Ht] to strip oneself:– raided (7), strip (7), stripped (4), take off (4), skin (2), stripped off (2), took off (2), advance (1), attacked (1 [+6584]), go raiding (1), made a dash (1), raiding (1), remove (1), removed (1), rob (1), rushed forward (1), skinned (1), strip off (1), strip off fine clothes (1 [+2256, 6910]), strip the dead (1), swept down (1), taken off (1)

H7321 פָּשַׁע ***pāša'***, v. [41] [→ 7322]. [Q] to rebel, revolt (against human or divine authority):– rebelled (13), in rebellion (4), rebels (3), transgressors (3), committed (2), rebel (2), rebellion (2), revolted (2), sin (2), sinned (2), do wrong (1), in revolt (1), rebellious (1), sinners (1), wronged (1), wrongs (1)

H7322 פֶּשַׁע ***peša'***, n.m. [93] [√ 7321]. rebellion, revolt, sin, transgression (against human or divine authority):– sins (20), offenses (14), rebellion (13), transgressions (11), transgression (8), sin (6), offense (4), rebellious (3), wrong (2), crime (1), disobeys (1), guilt of rebellion (1), guiltless (1 [+1172]), illegal possession (1), penalty of sin (1), presumption (1), rebels (1), sinful (1), sinfulness (1), sinned (1), wrongs (1)

H7323 פֵּשֶׁר ***pēšer***, n.[m.] [1] [√ 10599, 10600]. explanation, interpretation:– explanation (1)

H7324 פֵּשֶׁת ***pēšet***, n.[m.] [16] [→ 7325]. flax, linen (made of flax):– linen (12), flax (4)

H7325 פִּשְׁתָּה ***pištâ***, n.f. [4] [√ 7324]. flax, wick (made of flax):– flax (2), wick (2)

H7326 פַּת ***pat***, n.f. [14] [→ 7329; cf. 7359]. little piece, morsel (of food):– piece (2), something to eat (2 [+4312]), bread (1), crumble (1 [+7359]), crust (1), food (1), food (1 [+4312]), it[S] (1), little (1), pebbles (1), pieces (1), some (1)

H7327 פֹּת ***pōt***, n.[f.] [2] [cf. 5159]. scalp, forehead; socket (for doors):– scalps (1), sockets (1)

H7328 פִּתְאֹם ***pit'ōm***, subst. (used as adv.) [25] [√ 7353]. suddenly, unexpectedly, all at once, in an instant:– suddenly (13), sudden (4), in an instant (2), all at once (1), at once (1), by surprise (1), so quickly (1 [+928]), suddenly (1 [+928, 7353]), unexpectedly (1)

H7329 פַּת־בַּג ***pat-bag***, n.[m.] [6] [√ 7326 + 952 [?]]. (fine) food, choice provisions:– food (4), choice food (1), provisions (1)

H7330 פִּתְגָם ***pitgām***, n.m. [2] [√ 10601]. edict, decree; sentence (for a crime):– edict (1), sentence (1)

H7331 פָּתָה[1] ***pātâ[1]***, v.den. [27] [→ 7343, 7344, 7346]. [Q] to be simple, easily deceived, enticed; [P] to seduce, entice, deceive, allure; [N] to be enticed, deceived; [Pu] to be deceived, enticed, persuaded:– entice (5), enticed (2), enticing (2), allure (1), be deceived (1), be persuaded (1), been enticed (1), coax (1), deceive (1), deceived (1), easily deceived (1), enticed (1 [+4222]), entices (1), flatter (1), is enticed (1), lure (1), mislead (1), seduces (1), simple (1), talks too much (1 [+8557]), was deceived (1)

H7332 פָּתָה[2] ***pātâ[2]***, v. [1] [→ 3651; 10603]. [H] to provide ample space, make spacious:– extend territory (1)

H7333 פְּתוּאֵל ***p^{e}tû'ēl***, n.pr.m. [1] [√ 7343 + 446]. Pethuel, "*God's opening*":– Pethuel (1)

H7334 פִּתּוּחַ ***pittûaḥ***, n.m. [11] [√ 7338]. engraving, inscription:– engraved (2), art of engraving (1 [+7338]), carved paneling (1), engrave (1 [+7338]), engraved (1 [+7338]), engraves (1), experienced in engraving (1 [+7338]), inscription (1), inscription (1 [+4844]), NDT (1)

H7335 פְּתוֹר ***p^{e}tôr***, n.pr.loc. [2] Pethor:– Pethor (2)

H7336 פְּתוֹת ***p^{e}tôt***, n.[m.] [1] [√ 7359]. scrap, morsel (of food):– scraps (1)

H7337 פָּתַח[1] ***pātaḥ[1]***, v. [136] [→ 3652, 3653, 3654, 5157, 5158, 7339, 7340, 7341, 7342, 7347; 10602]. [Q] to open; [Qp] to be opened; [N] to be opened; [P] to loosen, release, take off; [Ht] to free oneself:– open (44), opened (31), be opened (4), enabled to conceive (2 [+906, 8167]), speak up (2 [+7023]), takes off (2), were opened (2), wide open (2 [+7337]), are opened (1), be poured out (1), be released (1), be set free (1), bottled-up (1 [+4202]), break open (1), breaking up (1), draw (1), drawn (1), expose (1), expound (1), free yourself (1), freed (1), freeing (1), give command (1 [+7023]), go (1), loose (1), loosen (1), loosened (1), make flow (1), market (1), open wide (1), opened up (1), openhanded (1 [+3338, 906, 7337]), openhanded (1 [+7337, 3338, 906]), openhanded (1 [+906, 3338, 7337]), openhanded (1 [+7337, 906, 3338]), opens (1), reach (1), release (1), removed (1), set free (1), speak (1 [+7023]), speaks (1 [+7023]), strip (1), take off (1), throw open (1), thrown open (1), uncovers (1), unloaded (1), unlocked (1), unsealed (1), unstopped (1), unstrung (1), untied (1), was opened (1), NDT (1)

H7338 פָּתַח[2] ***pātaḥ[2]***, v. [9] [→ 7334]. [P] to engrave, carve; [Pu] to be engraved:– engrave (3), art of engraving (1 [+7334]), carved (1), engrave (1 [+7334]), engraved (1), engraved (1 [+7334]), experienced in engraving (1 [+7334])

H7339 פֶּתַח ***petaḥ***, n.m. [163] [√ 7337]. entrance, opening; of a building or city: door, gate:– entrance (110), door (15), doorway (9), doors (5), entrances (3), doorways (2), gate (2), gates (2), it[S] (2 [+2021]), doorway (1 [+4647]), doorways (1 [+4647]), entrance (1 [+4427]), entrance (1 [+9133]), gate (1 [+9133]), mouth (1), one[S] (1), outside (1), outside (1 [+2025]), parapet opening (1), words (1), NDT (2)

H7340 פֵּתַח ***pētaḥ***, n.m. [1] [√ 7337]. revelation, disclosure, an extension opening a door or gate:– unfolding (1)

H7341 פִּתָּחוֹן ***pittāḥôn***, n.[m.] [2] [√ 7337]. opening (of mouth for communication):– open (1), open (1 [+5989])

H7342 פְּתַחְיָה ***p^{e}taḥyâ***, n.pr.m. [4] [√ 7337 + 3378]. Pethahiah, "*Yahweh opens*":– Pethahiah (4)

H7343 פֶּתִי[1] ***petî[1]***, a. [16] [√ 7331, 7333]. simple, naÔve, someone easily deceived or persuaded:– simple (15), unwary (1)

H7344 פֶּתִי[2] ***petî[2]***, n.f. [3] [√ 7331]. simple ways, simplemindedness:– simple ways (2), ignorance (1)

H7345 פְּתִיגִיל ***p^{e}tîgîl***, n.[m.] [1] fine clothing:– fine clothing (1)

H7346 פְּתַיּוּת ***p^{e}tayyût***, n.f. [1] [√ 7331]. undisciplined, deceptive:– simple (1)

H7347 פְּתִיחָה ***p^{e}tîḥâ***, n.[f.] [2] [√ 7337]. drawn sword:– drawn sword (1), drawn swords (1)

H7348 פָּתִיל ***pātîl***, n.m. [11] [√ 7349]. cord, strands, string:– cord (8), fastened (1), piece of string (1 [+5861]), strands (1)

H7349 פָּתַל ***pātal***, v. [5] [→ 5887, 5889?, 7348, 7350]. [N] to have a struggle; to be wily, be crooked; [Ht] to show oneself shrewd:– show yourself shrewd (2), crooked (1), had a struggle (1 [+5887]), wily (1)

H7350 פְּתַלְתֹּל ***p^{e}taltōl***, a. [1] [√ 7349]. crooked, perverse:– crooked (1)

H7351 פִּתֹם ***pitōm***, n.pr.loc. [1] Pithom, "*temple [house] of Atum*":– Pithom (1)

H7352 פֶּתֶן ***peten***, n.m. [6] cobra, serpent; some sources: viper:– cobra (2), serpents (2), cobras (1), cobra's (1)

H7353 פֶּתַע ***peta'***, subst. (used as adv.) [7] [→ 7328]. instant; (adv.) suddenly, in an instant:– suddenly (3), instant (2), suddenly (1 [+928]), suddenly (1 [+928, 7328])

H7354 פָּתַר ***pātar***, v. [9] [→ 7355; 10599, 10600]. [Q] to interpret, give the meaning (of a dream):– interpret (4), interpreted (2), given interpretation (1), giving interpretation (1), said in interpretation (1)

H7355 פִּתְרוֹן ***pittārôn***, n.m. [5] [√ 7354]. interpretation, meaning:– meaning (2), means (2), interpretations (1)

H7356 פַּתְרוֹס ***patrôs***, n.pr.loc. [5] [→ 7357]. Upper Egypt (Patros):– upper Egypt (2), upper Egypt (2 [+824]), upper (1)

H7357 פַּתְרֻסִים ***patrusîm***, a.g.pl. [2] [√ 7356]. Pathrusite:– Pathrusites (2)

H7358 פַּתְשֶׁגֶן ***patšegen***, n.m. [3] [cf. 7306; 10598]. copy (of a text):– copy (3)

H7359 פָּתַת ***pātat***, v. [1] [→ 7326, 7336]. [Q] to crumble:– Crumble (1 [+7326])

H7360 צ ***ṣ***, letter. Not used in NIVEBC [√ 10604]. letter of the Hebrew alphabet

H7361 צֵא ***ṣē'***, n.[m.] Not used in NIVEBC [→ 7362, 7363, 7364]. dirt

H7362 צֵאָה ***ṣē'â***, n.f. [2] [√ 7361]. excrement, dung:– excrement (1), excrement (1 [+1645])

H7363 צֹאָה ***ṣō'â***, n.f. [3] [√ 7361]. filth, excrement, dung; by extension: moral filth:– filth (3)

H7364 צֹאִי ***ṣō'î***, a. [2] [√ 7361]. filthy, befouled (with excrement):– filthy (2)

H7365 צֶאֱלִים ***ṣe'^{e}lîm***, n.m.pl. [2] lotus plant:– lotus plants (1), lotuses (1)

H7366 צֹאן ***ṣō'n***, n.col.f. *or* m. [275] [→ 7555, 7556; cf. 3655]. flock, sheep, goats (in contrast to larger mammals: cattle, donkeys, camels, etc.):– sheep (98), flocks (71), flock (65), sheep and goats (11), animals (6), shepherds (3 [+8286]), lambs (2 [+1201]), they[S] (2 [+2021]), animal from flock (1), breeding (1 [+3501, 2021]), choice lambs (1 [+4946, 4119]), ewes (1), flocks (1 [+5238]), goats (1), lambs (1 [+3897]), pens (1 [+1556]), rest[S] (1), sheep and goats (1 [+5238]), them[S] (1 [+2257]), they[S] (1 [+3276]), which[S] (1 [+2257]), which[S] (1 [+2021]), NDT (3)

H7367 צַאֲנָן ***ṣa'^{a}nān***, n.pr.loc. [1] [cf. 7569?]. Zaanan:– Zaanan (1)

H7368 צֶאֱצָאִים ***ṣe'^{e}ṣā'îm***, n.m.[pl.] [11] [√ 3655]. offspring, descendant:– offspring (4), descendants (3), all that springs from (1), children (1 [+5055]), crops (1), that comes out (1)

H7369 צָב[1] ***ṣāb[1]***, n.[m.] [2] [→ 7376]. (covered) wagon; some sources: litter without wheels:– covered (1), wagons (1)

H7370 צָב[2] ***ṣāb[2]***, n.[m.] [1] [√ 7377?]. lizard (of unspecified species):– great lizard (1)

H7371 צָבָא[1] ***ṣābā'[1]***, v. [14] [→ 7372]. [Q] to fight, do battle; to serve in (temple) corps:– conscripting (2), fight (2), fought (2), served (2 [+7371]), attack (1), do battle (1), fighting (1), serve (1 [+7372]), served (1), take part (1 [+7372])

H7372 צָבָא[2] ***ṣābā'[2]***, n.m. & f. [485] [√ 7371]. army, host, divisions (of an army); as a title of God: of Hosts (the heavenly armies), the Almighty, with a focus on great power to conquer or rule, a fig. extension of the leader of an great army:– almighty (285), army (60), divisions (21), division (20), battle (12), hosts (8), armies (6), war (6), forces (4), in command (4 [+6584]), serve (4), starry host (4), stars (4), hard service (3), host (3), multitudes (3), chief officer (2 [+8569, 2021]), experienced soldiers (2 [+3655]), heavenly hosts (2), ready to go out (2 [+3655]), the Lord's people (2), troops (2), armed forces (1 [+2657]), army (1 [+2657]), array (1), battle (1 [+4878]), commander in chief (1 [+6584, 2021]), commanders (1 [+8569]), fit for military service (1 [+3655]), men ready for battle (1 [+1522, 4878]), powers (1), ready for battle (1 [+928, 2021, 4878]), ready for battle (1 [+408, 4200, 2021, 4878]), ready for military service (1 [+3655]), regular service (1 [+6275]), serve (1 [+6913]), serve (1 [+7371]), soldier (1 [+408]), soldiers (1), soldiers (1 [+408]), soldiers (1 [+6639]), starry hosts (1), take part (1 [+7371]), throng (1), vast array (1), weapon (1 [+3998, 4878]), NDT (2)

H7373 צְבָא[3] ***ṣābā'[3]***, n.m. [1] [→ 7374; cf. 7475, 7383]. gazelle:– gazelles (1)

H7374 צְבָאָה ***ṣ^{e}bā'â***, n.f. [2] [√ 7373]. (female) gazelle:– gazelles (2)

H7375 צְבֹאִים ***ṣ^{e}bō'îm***, n.pr.loc. [5] [cf. 7373, 7387]. Zeboiim, "*gazelles*":– Zeboyim (5)

H7376 צֹבֵבָה ***ṣōbēbâ***, n.pr.m. Not used in NIVEBC [→ 2206, 7369]. Zobebah, see 2206

H7377 צָבָה ***ṣābâ***, v. [2] [→ 7370?, 7379]. [Q] to swell; [H] to cause to swell:– swell (1), swells (1)

H7378 צֹבֶה ***ṣōbeh***, var. see 7371

H7379 צָבֶה ***ṣābeh***, a. [1] [√ 7377]. swollen:– swell (1)

H7380 צָבוּעַ ***ṣābûa'***, a. [1] [√ 7388]. speckled, variegated, pertaining to the pattern on a winged creature:– speckled (1)

H7381 צָבַט ***ṣābaṭ***, v. [1] [cf. 7395]. [Q] to offer (food to another person):– offered (1)

H7382 צְבִי[1] ***ṣ^{e}bî[1]***, n.m. [17] [√ 10605]. ornament, beautiful (thing), glory:– beautiful (6), beauty (2), glory (2), most beautiful (2), most beautiful (2 [+7382]), beautiful jewelry (1 [+6344]), jewel (1), splendor (1)

H7383 צְבִי[2] ***ṣ^{e}bî[2]***, n.m. [12] [→ 7384, 7385, 7386; cf. 7373, 7387]. gazelle:– gazelle (11), gazelles (1)

H7384 צִבְיָא ***ṣibyā'***, n.pr.m. [1] [√ 7383]. Zibia, "*gazelle*":– Zibia (1)

H7385 צִבְיָה ***ṣibyâ***, n.pr.f. [2] [√ 7383]. Zibiah, "*gazelle*":– Zibiah (2)

H7386 צְבִיָּה ***ṣ^{e}biyyâ***, n.f. [2] [√ 7383]. (female) gazelle:– gazelle (2)

H7387 צְבֹיִים ***ṣ^{e}bōyîm***, n.pr.loc. Not used in NIVEBC [cf. 7375, 7383]. Zeboiim, see 7375, "*gazelles*"

H7388 צָבַע ***ṣāba'***, v. Not used in NIVEBC [→ 7380, 7389; 7390, 7391; 10607]. [Ht] to be dyed

H7389 צֶבַע ***ṣeba'***, n.[m.] [3] [√ 7388; 10607]. colorful (dyed) garment:– colorful garments (2), garments (1)

H7390 צִבְעוֹן ***ṣib'ôn***, n.pr.m. [8] [cf. 7388, 7391]. Zibeon, "*hyena*":– Zibeon (8)

H7391 צְבֹעִים ***ṣ^{e}bō'îm***, n.pr.loc. [2] [cf. 7388, 7390]. Zeboim, "*hyenas*":– Zeboim (1), Zeboyim (1)

H7392 צָבַר ***ṣābar***, v. [7] [→ 7393, 7394]. [Q] to store up, heap up, pile up:– building (1), heaped up (1), heaping up wealth (1), heaps up (1), piled (1), store up (1), stored up (1)

H7393 צִבֻּר ***ṣibbur***, n.m. [1] [√ 7392]. pile, heap:– piles (1)

H7394 צִבָּרוֹן ***ṣibbārôn***, n.m. Not used in NIVEBC [√ 7392]. heap

H7395 צֶבֶת ***ṣebet***, n.[m.]pl. [1] [cf. 7381]. bundle (of grain with the stalk):– bundles (1)

H7396 צַד[1] ***ṣad[1]***, n.m. [33] [→ 7398; 10608]. side (of something):– side (14), sides (4), beside (2 [+4946]), opposite sides (2 [+7521]), arm (1), backs (1), flank (1), hip (1), near (1 [+4946]), next to (1 [+4946]), other[S] (1), vicinity (1), with (1 [+4946]), NDT (2)

H7397 צַד[2] ***ṣad[2]***, n.m. [1] [cf. 7403]. snare:– traps (1)

H7398 צְדָד ***ṣ^{e}dād***, n.pr.loc. [2] [√ 7396]. Zedad, "*side*":– Zedad (2)

H7399 צָדָה[1] ***ṣādâ[1]***, v. [2] [→ 7402]. [Q] to lie in wait, hunt down a person:– done intentionally (1), hunting down (1)

H7400 2צָדָה **ṣādâ2**, v. [1] [N] to be destroyed, be laid waste:– are laid waste (1)

H7401 צָדוֹק **ṣādôq**, n.pr.m. [53] [√ 7405]. Zadok, *"righteous one"*:– Zadok (51), Zadokites (1 [+1201]), thems (1 [+2256, 59])

H7402 צְדִיָּה **ṣediyyâ**, n.f. [2] [√ 7399; 10216, 10609]. ambush, lying-in-wait (with malicious intent):– intentionally (1 [+928]), unintentionally (1 [+928, 4202])

H7403 צִדִּים **ṣiddîm**, n.pr.loc. [1] [cf. 7397]. Ziddim, *"place on the sides or flanks [of the hill]"*:– Ziddim (1)

H7404 צַדִּיק **ṣaddîq**, a. [205] [√ 7405]. righteous, upright, just, innocent; in accordance with a proper (God's) standard, and so implying innocence:– righteous (174), innocent (17), just (2), right (2), righteous one (2), upright (2), honest (1), in the right (1), overrighteous (1 [+2221]), righteous (1 [+2446]), righteousness (1), NDT (1)

H7405 צָדַק **ṣādaq**, v.den. [41] [→ 3392, 3449, 7401, 7404, 7406, 7407, 7408, 7409]. [Q] to be righteous, be innocent, be vindicated; in accordance with a proper (God's) standard, and so implying innocence:– righteous (9), innocent (4), acquit (2), acquitting (2), justify (2), prove innocence (2), right (2), vindicated (2), vindicating (2), admit in the right (1), appear righteous (1), be reconsecrated (1), find deliverance (1), innocence (1), justifying (1), lead to righteousness (1), made appear righteous (1), made seem righteous (1), prove right (1), see that receive justice (1), uphold the cause (1), vindicate (1), vindicates (1)

H7406 צֶדֶק **ṣedeq**, n.m. [118] [→ 155, 4900, 7408, 7409; cf. 7405]. righteousness, justice, rightness, acting according to a proper (God's) standard, doing what is right, being in the right:– righteousness (46), righteous (19), honest (7), justice (6), right (6), just (4), accurate (3), fairly (3), truth (3), vindication (3), prosperous (2), righteous savior (2), fairly (1 [+928]), in the right (1), integrity (1), justly (1), righteous deeds (1), righteous reward (1), righteously (1), rights (1), saving acts (1), unrighteousness (1 [+4202]), verdant (1), vindicated (1), NDT (2)

H7407 צְדָקָה **ṣedāqâ**, n.f. [157] [√ 7405; 10610]. righteousness, acting according to a proper (God's) standard, doing what is right, being in the right:– righteousness (89), right (20), righteous (8), righteous acts (6), righteous things (4), innocence (3), righteous deeds (3), justice (2), prosperity (2), victories (2), vindication (2), well-being (2), claim (1), deliverance (1), faithful (1), full well-being (1), honesty (1), integrity (1), itss (1 [+2021]), just (1), righteous act (1), righteous will (1), righteously (1), salvation (1), victory (1), vindicated (1 [+3655])

H7408 צִדְקִיָּה **ṣidqiyyâ**, n.pr.m. [7] [√ 7406 + 3378]. Zedekiah, *"Yahweh is [my] righteousness"*:– Zedekiah (7)

H7409 צִדְקִיָּהוּ **ṣidqiyyāhû**, n.pr.m. [57] [√ 7406 + 3378]. Zedekiah, *"Yahweh is [my] righteousness"*:– Zedekiah (53), Zedekiah's (2), Zedekiah's (1 [+4200]), hiss (1)

H7410 צָהַב **ṣāhab**, v. [1] [→ 5176, 7411, 7419, 7420; cf. 2298]. [Ho] to be polished, gleaming copper color:– polished (1)

H7411 צָהֹב **ṣāhōb**, a. [3] [√ 7410]. yellow, blond; some sources: gleaming red:– yellow (3)

H7412 1צָהַל **ṣāhal1**, v. [8] [→ 5177]. [Q] to shout out, celebrate; to neigh (of a horse):– acclaim (1), cry out (1 [+7754]), held a celebration (1), neigh (1), neighing (1), shout (1), shout aloud (1), shout for joy (1)

H7413 2צָהַל **ṣāhal2**, v. [1] [cf. 2301, 7414]. [H] to make shine:– make shine (1)

H7414 צָהַר **ṣāhar**, v.den. [1] [→ 3658, 3659, 3660, 7415, 7416; cf. 2301, 7413]. [H] to press olives; some sources relate to 7416 and translate "to spend the noontime":– crush olives (1)

H7415 צֹהַר **ṣōhar**, n.f. [1] [√ 7414]. roof, covering (for the ark of Noah):– roof (1)

H7416 צָהֳרַיִם **ṣohorayim**, n.[m.] [23] [√ 7414]. noon, noonday, midday:– noon (11), midday (7), noonday (3), high noon (1), noonday sun (1)

H7417 צַו **ṣaw**, n.[m.] [1] [√ 8736? *or* 7422?]. worthless thing, an idol or utterance (perhaps a nonsense syllable, a mocking sound):– idols (1)

H7418 צַוָּאר **ṣawwā'r**, n.m. [41] [→ 7454; 10611]. (back of) neck:– neck (24), necks (7), threw arms around (2 [+5877, 6584]), at heels (1 [+6584]), defiantly (1 [+928]), embraced (1 [+6584]), head (1), shoulders (1), so defiantly (1 [+928, 6981]), yourselves (1 [+4013]), NDT (1)

H7419 צוֹבָא **ṣôbā'**, n.pr.loc. [2] [cf. 7420]. Zobah:– Zobah (2)

H7420 צוֹבָה **ṣôbâ**, n.pr.loc. [10] [→ 809, 2832; cf. 7410, 7419]. Zobah:– Zobah (10)

H7421 צוּד **ṣûd**, v. [17] [→ 5171, 5178, 5179, 5180, 5181?, 5182, 5183, 7473, 7475]. [Q] to hunt, stalk; [Pil] to ensnare; by extension to stalk people for capture or oppression:– ensnare (4), hunt (4), hunted (2 [+7421]), hunt down (1), hunt down (1 [+4200, 4511]), hunted (1), hunts (1), preys on (1), stalk (1), stalked (1)

H7422 צָוָה **ṣāwâ**, v. [502] [→ 5184, 7417?]. [P] to command, order, instruct, give direction; [Pu] to be commanded, be directed, be ordered:– commanded (206), command (46), gave (25), ordered (22), commands (13), giving (13), gave orders (10), give (10), instructed (9), appointed (8), directed (8), told (8), gave order (7), gave command (5), order (5), been commanded (4), do (4), give command (4), given (4), orders (4), tell (4), commission (3), decreed (3), gave instructions (3), give orders (3), ordained (3), put in order (3), was commanded (3), charged (2), commanded (2 [+5184]), forbidden (2 [+4202]), given order (2), given orders (2), giving orders (2), instructions (2), laid down (2), mades (2), send (2), thats (2), thiss (2), appoint (1), are directed (1), authorize (1), bestows (1), commander (1), commanding (1), commissioned (1), decree (1), decrees (1), determined (1), direct (1), directs (1), dispatch (1), forbidden (1), forbidden (1 [+1194]), gave a charge (1), gave an order (1), gave commands (1), gave the order (1), give a message (1), give commands (1), give the order (1), given a command (1), given an order (1), given the command (1), giving instructions (1), instruct (1), issue an order (1), left instructions (1), marshaled (1), prescribed (1), put in charge (1), puts in command (1), say (1), sent (1), sent word (1), summon (1), NDT (1)

H7423 צָוַח **ṣāwaḥ**, v. [1] [→ 7424]. [Q] to shout, cry aloud:– shout (1)

H7424 צְוָחָה **ṣewāḥâ**, n.f. [4] [√ 7423]. cry of distress, wail:– cries (1), cry (1), cry of distress (1), cry out (1)

H7425 צוּלָה **ṣûlâ**, n.f. [1] [→ 5185, 5198; cf. 7510]. the watery deep, the ocean abyss:– watery deep (1)

H7426 צוּם **ṣûm**, v. [21] [→ 7427]. [Q] to fast, to voluntarily abstain from food as dedication to deity, as a sign of mourning, or possibly as a medical treatment:– fasted (12), fast (4), fasted (2 [+7426]), fasting (2), fasted (1 [+7427])

H7427 צוֹם **ṣôm**, n.m. [26] [√ 7426]. fast, time of fasting, act of fasting; see also 7426:– fasting (10), fast (9), day of fasting (1), fasted (1 [+7426]), fasts (1), time of fasting (1), NDT (3)

H7428 צוּעָר **ṣû'ār**, n.pr.m. [5] [√ 7592]. Zuar, *"little one"*:– Zuar (5)

H7429 1צוּף **ṣûp1**, v. [3] [→ 7430, 7431?, 7433, 7487, 7597?]. [Q] to flow; [H] to make float; to overwhelm (with water):– closed (1), made float (1), overwhelmed (1)

H7430 2צוּף **ṣûp2**, n.m. [2] [√ 7429]. honeycomb (dripping with honey):– honeycomb (1), honeycomb (1 [+1831])

H7431 3צוּף **ṣûp3**, n.pr.m.[loc.?] [3] [√ 7429?]. Zuph:– Zuph (3)

H7432 צוֹפַח **ṣôpaḥ**, n.pr.m. [2] [√ 7613]. Zophah, *"bellied jug"*:– Zophah (2)

H7433 צוֹפַי **ṣôpay**, n.pr.m. [1] [√ 7429; cf. 7434]. Zophai, *"[dripping, full] honeycomb"*:– Zophai (1)

H7434 צוּפִי **ṣûpî**, a.g. [1] [cf. 7433]. Zuphite:– Zuphite (1)

H7435 צוֹפִים **ṣôpîm**, a.g. Not used in NIVEBC [cf. 7434, 7614]. Zophim

H7436 צוֹפַר **ṣôpar**, n.pr.m. [4] [√ 7606?]. Zophar, "[poss.] *peep, twitter [as a bird]*":– Zophar (4)

H7437 1צוּץ **ṣûṣ1**, v. [8] [→ 7488, 7490, 7491, 7492]. [Q] to bud, blossom; [H] to put forth blossoms; to cause to flourish:– flourish (3), blossomed (1 [+7488]), bud (1), budded (1), radiant (1), springs up (1)

H7438 2צוּץ **ṣûṣ2**, v. [1] [H] to peer at, look at:– peering (1)

H7439 1צוּק **ṣûq1**, v. [11] [→ 4608, 5186, 5188, 7441, 7442; cf. 7636]. [H] to oppress, compel, nag, inflict:– inflict (3), besiege (2), oppressor (2), press (2), compels (1), nagging (1)

H7440 2צוּק **ṣûq2**, v. [1] [√ 3668?]. [Q] to pour out:– barely whisper a prayer (1 [+4318])

H7441 צוֹק **ṣôq**, n.[m.] [1] [√ 7439]. trouble, oppression:– trouble (1)

H7442 צוּקָה **ṣûqâ**, n.f. [3] [√ 7439]. trouble, distress, oppression:– distress (1), fearful (1), trouble (1)

H7443 1צוּר **ṣûr1**, v. [35] [→ 5189, 5190, 5192, 5193; cf. 7493, 7674]. [Q] to siege, besiege, enclose:– besieging (7), besieged (6), laid siege (5), besiege (3), lay siege (3), besieges (1), encircle (1 [+6584]), enclose (1), hem in (1), put into bags (1), siege (1), stirring up (1), take (1), tied up (1), tuck away (1), under siege (1)

H7444 2צוּר **ṣûr2**, v. [4] [√ 7496?]. [Q] to oppose, harass:– harass (2), attack (1), oppose (1)

H7445 3צוּר **ṣûr3**, v. [2] [→ 7451, 7497?]. [Q] to fashion, shape:– cast (1), fashioning (1)

H7446 4צוּר **ṣûr4**, n.m. [74] [→ 506, 1123, 7011, 7448, 7449?, 7452, 7453; 10296]. rock; stone mass, rocky crag; a title of God, with a focus of stability, and possibly as a place of security and safety:– rock (60), rocks (8), rocky (3), crag (1), crags (1), strength (1)

H7447 5צוּר **ṣûr5**, n.m. Not used in NIVEBC [√ 7644]. pebble, flint

H7448 6צוּר **ṣûr6**, n.pr.m. [5] [√ 7446]. Zur, *"rock"*:– Zur (5)

H7449 7צוּר **ṣûr7**, n.pr.loc. Not used in NIVEBC [√ 7446?]. Zur, see 1123, *"Zur [the Rock]"*

H7450 צֹר **ṣôr**, n.pr.loc. [42] [√ 7645; cf. 7644]. Tyre, *"rocky place"*:– Tyre (42)

H7451 צוּרָה **ṣûrâ**, n.f. [5] [√ 7445]. design, form:– design (3), forms (1), NDT (1)

H7452 צוּרִיאֵל **ṣûrî'ēl**, n.pr.m. [1] [√ 7446 + 446]. Zuriel, *"God [El] is [my] rock"*:– Zuriel (1)

H7453 צוּרִישַׁדָּי **ṣûrîšadday**, צוּרִי־שַׁדָּי **ṣûrî-šadday**, n.pr.m. [5] [√ 7446 + 8724]. Zurishaddai, *"Shaddai is [my] rock"*:– Zurishaddai (5)

H7454 צַוְּרֹנִים **ṣawwerōnîm**, n.[m.]pl. [1] [√ 7418]. necklace:– necklace (1)

H7455 צוּת **ṣût**, v. [1] [cf. 3675]. [H] to set on fire:– set on fire (1)

H7456 צַח **ṣaḥ**, a. [4] [√ 7458]. radiant, shimmering, scorching, clear:– clear (1), radiant (1), scorching (1), shimmering (1)

H7457 צִחֶה **ṣiḥeh**, a. [1] [cf. 7458]. parched:– parched (1)

H7458 צָחַח **ṣāḥaḥ**, v. [1] [→ 5195?, 5196?, 7456, 7460, 7461, 7463; cf. 7457, 7459]. [Q] to be white:– whiter (1)

H7459 צְחִחִי **ṣeḥiḥî**, n.[m.] Not used in NIVEBC [cf. 7458, 7460]. see 7460

H7460 צָחִיחַ **ṣāḥîaḥ**, n.[m.] [5] [√ 7458; cf. 7459]. bare (rock or place in a wall):– bare (4), exposed places (1)

H7461 צְחִיחָה **ṣeḥîḥâ**, n.f. [1] [√ 7458]. bare, (sun-)scorched land:– sun-scorched land (1)

H7462 צַחֲנָה **ṣaḥanâ**, n.f. [1] putrid smell, stench:– smell (1)

H7463 צַחְצָחוֹת **ṣaḥṣāḥôt**, n.[f.pl.] [1] [√ 7458]. bare, (sun-)scorched land:– sun-scorched land (1)

H7464 צָחַק **ṣāḥaq**, v. [13] [→ 3663, 7465; cf. 8471]. [Q] to laugh; [P] to mock, make sport, caress; this can mean to laugh with delight or in scorn:– laugh (4), laughed (2), make sport (2), caressing (1), indulge in revelry (1), joking (1), mocking (1), performed (1)

H7465 צְחֹק **ṣeḥōq**, n.[m.] [2] [√ 7464]. laughter, scorn:– laughter (1), scorn (1)

H7466 צַחַר **ṣāḥar**, n.[m.] [1] [√ 7467]. Zahar, *"yellowish red, tawny"*:– Zahar (1)

H7467 צָחֹר **ṣāḥōr**, a. [1] [→ 7466, 7468]. white, yellowish red, tawny:– white (1)

H7468 צֹחַר **ṣōḥar**, n.pr.m. [5] [√ 7467; cf. 3664]. Zohar, *"yellowish red, tawny"*:– Zohar (5)

H7469 1צִי **ṣî1**, n.m. [4] ship:– ships (3), ship (1)

H7470 2צִי **ṣî2**, n.m. [6] [√ 7480]. desert creature, referring to known animals or presumed spirits or demons; tribe of the desert:– desert creatures (4), creatures of the desert (1), desert tribes (1)

H7471 צִיבָא **ṣîbā'**, n.pr.m. [16] Ziba, *"gazelle"*:– Ziba (15), Ziba's (1)

H7472 צִיד **ṣîd**, v.den. [1] [→ 7474, 7476]. [Ht] to pack provisions for oneself:– packed (1)

H7473 1צַיִד **ṣayid1**, n.m. [14] [√ 7421]. (hunting) game; hunter:– game (7), hunter (2), wild game (2), animal (1 [+2651]), hunter (1 [+408]), hunting (1)

H7474 2צַיִד **ṣayid2**, n.[m.] [5] [√ 7472]. food supply, provision:– food (2), provisions (2), food supply (1)

H7475 צַיָּד **ṣayyād**, n.m. [1] [√ 7421]. hunter:– hunters (1)

H7476 צֵידָה **ṣêdâ**, n.f. [9] [√ 7472]. food, provisions, supplies:– provisions (7), food (2)

H7477 צִידוֹן **ṣîdôn**, n.pr.loc. [20] [→ 7478, 7479]. Sidon, *"fishery"*:– Sidon (20)

H7478 צִידוֹן רַבָּה **ṣîdôn rabbâ**, n.pr.loc. [2] [√ 7477 + 8045]. Greater Sidon:– Greater Sidon (2)

H7479 צִידֹנִי **ṣîdōnî**, a.g. [16] [√ 7477]. Sidonian, people of Sidon:– Sidonians (15), people of Sidon (1)

H7480 צִיָּה **ṣiyyâ**, n.f. [16] [→ 7470, 7481]. desert, parched land, dry land, waterless region:– dry (5), parched (4), drought (2), parched land (2), desert (1), dry land (1), wilderness (1)

H7481 צָיוֹן **ṣāyôn**, n.[m.] [2] [√ 7480]. desert, waterless country:– desert (2)

H7482 צִיּוֹן **ṣiyyôn**, n.pr.loc. [154] Zion, *"citadel"*:– Zion (152), Zion's (2)

H7483 צִיּוּן **ṣiyyûn**, n.m. [3] sign, stone marker:– marker (1), road signs (1), tombstone (1)

H7484 צִיחָא **ṣîḥā'**, n.pr.m. [3] Ziha:– Ziha (3)

H7485 צִינֹק **ṣînōq**, n.[m.] [1] neck-iron, iron collar:– neck-irons (1)

H7486 צִיעֹר **ṣî'ōr**, n.pr.loc. [1] [√ 7592]. Zior, *"small, insignificant"*:– Zior (1)

H7487 צִיף **ṣîp**, n.pr.m. Not used in NIVEBC [√ 7430; cf. 7431]. Ziph, see 7431

H7488 [1]צִיץ **ṣîṣ[1]**, n.m. [14] [→ 7491, 7492; cf. 7437]. flower, blossom; (ornamental) plate:– flowers (8), plate (3), flower (2), blossomed (1 [+7437])

H7489 [2]צִיץ **ṣîṣ[2]**, n.pr.loc. [1] Ziz, "[poss.] *ascent where the flowers grow*":– Ziz (1)

H7490 [3]צִיץ **ṣîṣ[3]**, n.[m.] [1] [√ 7437]. salt:– salt (1)

H7491 צִיצָה **ṣîṣâ**, n.f. [1] [√ 7488; cf. 7437]. flower:– flower (1)

H7492 צִיצִת **ṣîṣit**, n.f. [4] [√ 7488; cf. 7437]. tassel of threads; tuft of hair:– tassels (2), hair (1), tassel (1)

H7493 [1]צִיר **ṣîr[1]**, v.den. [1] [cf. 7443]. [Ht] to act as a delegation:– delegation (1)

H7494 [2]צִיר **ṣîr[2]**, n.[m.] [1] hinge, (door-)pivot:– hinges (1)

H7495 [3]צִיר **ṣîr[3]**, n.m. [6] envoy, messenger:– envoy (3), ambassadors (1), envoys (1), messenger (1)

H7496 [4]צִיר **ṣîr[4]**, n.[m.] [5] [√ 7444?]. pains, pangs, anguish:– anguish (1), labor pains (1), pain (1), pangs (1), those[S] (1)

H7497 [5]צִיר **ṣîr[5]**, n.m. [1] [√ 7445?]. idol:– idols (1)

H7498 צֵל **ṣēl**, n.m. [53] [→ 1295, 7500, 7516, 7524; cf. 7511]. shadow, shade, protection:– shadow (26), shade (16), shadows (5), protection (2), shelter (2), evening shadows (1), it[S] (1 [+2021])

H7499 צָלָה **ṣālâ**, v. [3] [→ 7507]. [Q] to roast (meat):– roast (1), roasted (1), roasts (1)

H7500 צִלָּה **ṣillâ**, n.pr.f. [3] [√ 7498; cf. 5511]. Zillah, "*[God is my] shadow*, i.e., *protection*":– Zillah (3)

H7501 צְלוּל **ṣᵉlûl**, n.m. [1] [cf. 7508]. round loaf:– round loaf (1)

H7502 [1]צָלַח **ṣālaḥ[1]**, v. [10] [Q] to be powerful, come forcefully; to rush:– came powerfully (6), came forcefully (1), come powerfully (1), rushed (1), sweep through (1)

H7503 [2]צָלַח **ṣālaḥ[2]**, v. [55] [√ 10613]. [Q] to prosper, prevail, succeed, avail; [H] to make a success, grant prosperity, make victorious:– prosper (7), succeed (7), prospered (5), victorious (4), gave success (3), successful (3), give success (2), grant success (2), have success (2), thrive (2), useless (2 [+4202]), achieve purpose (1), avail (1), granted success (1), helped (1), made successful (1), make success (1), prevail (1), promote (1), prosperous (1), prospers (1), rose (1), succeeded (1), succeeded in carrying out (1), unsuccessful (1 [+4202]), useful (1), victoriously (1)

H7504 צְלֹחִית **ṣᵉlōḥit**, n.f. [1] [√ 7505]. (shallow) bowl; some sources: pan, cruse, dish:– bowl (1)

H7505 צַלַּחַת **ṣallaḥat**, n.[f.] [4] [→ 7504, 7506]. dish, pan:– dish (3), pans (1)

H7506 צֵלָחַת **ṣēlaḥat**, n.[f.] Not used in NIVEBC [√ 7505]. pot for cooking

H7507 צָלִי **ṣālî**, a. [3] [√ 7499]. roasted (meat):– meat (1), roast (1), roasted (1)

H7508 צְלִיל **ṣᵉlîl**, n.m. Not used in NIVEBC [cf. 7501]. cake, round loaf

H7509 [1]צָלַל **ṣālal[1]**, v. [4] [→ 5197, 5199, 7526, 7527, 7528?, 7529]. [Q] to tingle; to quiver:– tingle (2), make tingle (1), quivered (1)

H7510 [2]צָלַל **ṣālal[2]**, v. [1] [cf. 7425]. [Q] to sink down:– sank (1)

H7511 [3]צָלַל **ṣālal[3]**, v. [2] [→ 1295, 2209, 7498, 7500, 7516, 7524; cf. 3233; 10300]. [Q] to grow dark; [H] to give shade:– evening shadows fell (1), overshadowing (1)

H7512 [1]צֶלֶם **ṣelem[1]**, n.m. [15] [→ 7513, 7514?; 10614]. image (usually referring to an object of worship), idol:– idols (6), image (5), models (2), figures (1), NDT (1)

H7513 [2]צֶלֶם **ṣelem[2]**, n.m. [2] [√ 7512]. phantom, fantasy, shadowy thing:– fantasies (1), phantom (1)

H7514 [1]צַלְמוֹן **ṣalmôn[1]**, n.pr.m. [1] [√ 7512?]. Zalmon, "*in his image, copy*":– Zalmon (1)

H7515 [2]צַלְמוֹן **ṣalmôn[2]**, n.pr.loc. [2] Zalmon, "*black hill*":– Zalmon (2)

H7516 צַלְמָוֶת **ṣalmāwet**, n.[m.] [18] [√ 7498 + 4637]. shadow, darkness, gloom, blackness:– utter darkness (9), deep darkness (2), midnight (2), blackest (1), dark shadows (1), darkest (1), darkness (1), deepest darkness (1)

H7517 צַלְמֹנָה **ṣalmōnâ**, n.pr.loc. [2] Zalmonah, "*dark, gloomy, shaded place*":– Zalmonah (2)

H7518 צַלְמֻנָּע **ṣalmunnā'**, n.pr.m. [12] Zalmunna, "*protection refused*":– Zalmunna (10), them[S] (2 [+2286, 2256])

H7519 צָלַע **ṣāla'**, v. [4] [→ 7520]. [Q] to be lame, limp:– lame (3), limping (1)

H7520 צֶלַע **ṣela'**, n.[m.] [4] [√ 7519]. stumbling, falling, slipping:– fall (1), falls (1), slip (1), stumbled (1)

H7521 [1]צֵלָע **ṣēlā'[1]**, n.f. & m. [40] [→ 7522; 10552]. side:– side (10), side rooms (9), sides (4), boards (2), opposite sides (2 [+7396]), another[S] (1), beams (1), floor (1), hillside (1 [+2215]), leaves (1), one[S] (1), planks (1), rib (1), ribs (1), side room (1), NDT (3)

H7522 [2]צֵלָע **ṣēlā'[2]**, n.pr.loc. [2] [√ 7521]. Zela, Zelah, "*side, slope*":– Zela (1), Zelah (1)

H7523 צָלָף **ṣālāp**, n.pr.m. [1] Zalaph, "*low, prickly shrub [caper plant]*":– Zalaph (1)

H7524 צְלָפְחָד **ṣᵉlopḥād**, n.pr.m. [11] [√ 7498 + 7065]. Zelophehad, "*shadow of dread, terror* i.e., *protection from terror or dread*":– Zelophehad (5), Zelophehad's (4), who[S] (1), whose[S] (1 [+1426])

H7525 צֶלְצַח **ṣelṣaḥ**, n.pr.loc. [1] Zelzah:– Zelzah (1)

H7526 צְלָצַל **ṣᵉlāṣal**, n.m. [1] [√ 7509]. (swarm of) locust; some sources: cricket:– Swarms of locusts (1)

H7527 [1]צִלְצָל **ṣilṣāl[1]**, n.[m.] [1] [√ 7509]. whirring, buzzing:– whirring (1)

H7528 [2]צִלְצָל **ṣilṣāl[2]**, n.[m.] [1] [√ 7509?]. (fishing) spear:– spears (1)

H7529 צֶלְצְלִים **ṣelṣelîm**, n.m.pl. [3] [√ 7509]. cymbals:– cymbals (3)

H7530 צֶלֶק **ṣeleq**, n.pr.m. [2] Zelek, "*cry aloud*":– Zelek (2)

H7531 צִלְּתַי **ṣillᵉtay**, n.pr.m. [2] Zillethai, "*shadow of Yahweh*":– Zillethai (2)

H7532 [1]צָמֵא **ṣāmē'[1]**, v. [10] [→ 7533, 7534, 7535, 7536]. [Q] to thirst, be thirsty:– thirsty (5), thirst (3), suffer thirst (1), thirsts (1)

H7533 צָמָא **ṣāmā'**, n.[m.] [17] [√ 7532]. thirst (of humans and animals); used fig. of parched ground:– thirst (15), parched ground (1), thirsty (1)

H7534 [2]צָמֵא **ṣāmē'[2]**, a. [10] [√ 7532]. thirsty, used of humans and animals; used fig. of parched ground:– thirsty (9), dry (1)

H7535 צִמְאָה **ṣim'â**, n.f. [1] [√ 7532]. thirst:– dry (1)

H7536 צִמָּאוֹן **ṣimmā'ôn**, n.[m.] [3] [√ 7532]. thirsty ground:– thirsty ground (2), thirsty (1)

H7537 צָמַד **ṣāmad**, v. [5] [→ 7538, 7543, 7544]. [N] to be joined together; [Pu] to be strapped on; [H] to harness, attach to:– yoked themselves (3), harness (1), strapped (1)

H7538 צֶמֶד **ṣemed**, n.m. [15] [√ 7537]. yoke, team of two, pair; this can refer to a measurement of land, as the acreage a team of animals can plow:– yoke (3), pair (2), two (2), acre (1 [+5103]), oxen (1), string (1), team (1), teams (1), ten-acre (1 [+6930]), together (1), yoke of oxen (1)

H7539 צַמָּה **ṣammâ**, n.f. [4] veil:– veil (4)

H7540 צִמּוּקִים **ṣimmûqîm**, n.m.[pl.] [4] [√ 7546]. raisin cakes:– cakes of raisins (3), raisin cakes (1)

H7541 צָמַח **ṣāmaḥ**, v. [33] [→ 7542]. [Q] to sprout up, spring up; [P] to grow; [H] to cause to grow, bring to fruition:– grown (4), sprouted (3), flourish (2), grow (2), make grow (2), make sprout (2), makes grow (2), appear (1), branch out (1), bring to fruition (1), causes to grow (1), flourishing (1), growing (1), made grow (1), make spring up (1), produce (1), spring into being (1), spring up (1), springs forth (1), springs up (1), sprout (1), sprouting (1), sprung up (1)

H7542 צֶמַח **ṣemaḥ**, n.m. [12] [√ 7541]. growth (which sprouts); (as a messianic title) the Branch:– branch (5), crops (1), grew (1), growth (1), head (1), plant (1), sprout (1), vegetation (1)

H7543 [1]צָמִיד **ṣāmîd[1]**, n.m. [6] [√ 7537]. bracelet:– bracelets (5), bracelets (1 [+6584, 3338])

H7544 [2]צָמִיד **ṣāmîd[2]**, n.[m.] [1] [√ 7537]. lid, cover:– lid (1)

H7545 צַמִּים **ṣammîm**, n.m. [1] snare:– snare (1)

H7546 צָמַק **ṣāmaq**, v. [1] [→ 7540]. [Q] to be dry, shriveled (of breasts):– dry (1)

H7547 צֶמֶר **ṣemer**, n.m. [16] [→ 7549, 7550; 10556]. wool:– wool (13), woolen (2), woolen garment (1)

H7548 צְמָרִי **ṣᵉmārî**, a.g. [2] Zemarite:– Zemarites (2)

H7549 צְמָרַיִם **ṣᵉmārayim**, n.pr.loc. [2] [√ 7547]. Zemaraim, "[poss.] *double peak*":– Zemaraim (2)

H7550 צַמֶּרֶת **ṣammeret**, n.f. [5] [√ 7547]. top (of a tree):– top (2), shoot (1), tops (1), towered (1 [+1467, 928, 7757, 2256, 5989])

H7551 צָמַת **ṣāmat**, v. [15] [→ 7552]. [Q] to silence; [N] to be silenced; [Pil] to destroy; [P] to wear out; [H] to put to silence, destroy:– destroy (4), destroyed (3), put to silence (2), end (1), seek to destroy (1), silence (1), silenced (1), stop flowing (1), wears out (1)

H7552 צְמִתֻת **ṣᵉmitut**, n.f. [2] [√ 7551]. permanence, finality:– permanently (1 [+4200]), permanently (1 [+4200, 2021])

H7553 צֵן **ṣēn**, n.[m.] [3] [→ 7559, 7564]. thorn; hook:– hooks (1), snares (1), thorns (1)

H7554 צִן **ṣin**, n.pr.loc. [10] Zin:– Zin (10)

H7555 צֹנֶא **ṣōnē'**, [n.m.] Not used in NIVEBC [√ 7366]. flocks

H7556 צֹנֶה **ṣōneh**, [n.m.] [1] [√ 7366; cf. 3655]. flocks (of sheep and goats):– flocks (1)

H7557 [1]צִנָּה **ṣinnâ[1]**, n.f. [1] coolness:– snow-cooled drink (1 [+8920])

H7558 [2]צִנָּה **ṣinnâ[2]**, n.f. [21] (large) shield:– shield (9), large shields (7), shields (4), armor (1)

H7559 [3]צִנָּה **ṣinnâ[3]**, n.f. Not used in NIVEBC [√ 7553]. hook, see 7553

H7560 צָנוּעַ **ṣānûa'**, a. [1] [√ 7570]. humble, modest:– humility (1)

H7561 צָנוּף **ṣānûp**, n.m. Not used in NIVEBC [√ 7571; cf. 7565]. turban, see 7565

H7562 צִנּוֹר **ṣinnôr**, n.m. [2] [→ 7574]. water shaft; waterfall:– water shaft (1), waterfalls (1)

H7563 צָנַח **ṣānaḥ**, v. [3] [Q] to get down; to go down:– got off (2 [+4946, 6584]), NDT (1)

H7564 צְנִינִים **ṣᵉnînîm**, n.[m.pl.] [2] [√ 7553]. thorns:– thorns (2)

H7565 צָנִיף **ṣānîp**, n.m. [4] [→ 7566; cf. 7561, 7571]. turban:– turban (3), diadem (1)

H7566 צְנִיפָה **ṣᵉnîpâ**, n.m. [1] [√ 7565; cf. 7571]. turban (of woman), an ornamental head wrap:– tiaras (1)

H7567 צָנַם **ṣānam**, v. Not used in NIVEBC [→ 7568]. [Q] to dry up, harden, see 7568

H7568 צָנֻם **ṣānum**, a. *or* v.ptcp. [1] [√ 7567]. withered:– withered (1)

H7569 צְנָן **ṣᵉnān**, n.pr.loc. [1] [cf. 7367?]. Zenan, "*place of flocks*":– Zenan (1)

H7570 צָנַע **ṣāna'**, v. [1] [→ 5760]. [H] to show a humble (walk with God), as an extension of acting in a cautious manner:– humbly (1)

H7571 צָנַף **ṣānap**, v. [3] [→ 5200, 7561, 7565, 7566, 7572]. [Q] to wrap around, wind around:– roll up tightly (2 [+7571, 7572]), put on (1)

H7572 צְנֵפָה **ṣᵉnēpâ**, n.f. [1] [√ 7571]. winding, wrapping:– roll up tightly (1 [+7571, 7571])

H7573 צִנְצֶנֶת **ṣinṣenet**, n.f. [1] vessel, receptacle, likely referring to a jar:– jar (1)

H7574 צַנְתָּרוֹת **ṣantārôt**, n.m.pl. [1] [√ 7562]. pipes:– pipes (1)

H7575 צָעַד **ṣā'ad**, v. [8] [→ 731, 5202, 7576, 7577, 7578]. [Q] to step, march; [H] to make march:– marched (2), climb (1), marched off (1), strode through (1), taken steps (1 [+7576]), walk (1), walking along (1)

H7576 צַעַד **ṣa'ad**, n.m. [14] [√ 7575]. step, stride:– step (5), steps (5), path (2), stride (1), taken steps (1 [+7575])

H7577 [1]צְעָדָה **ṣᵉ'ādâ[1]**, n.f. [2] [√ 7575]. marching:– marching (2)

H7578 [2]צְעָדָה **ṣᵉ'ādâ[2]**, n.f. [1] [√ 7575]. ankle chains:– anklets (1)

H7579 צָעָה **ṣā'â**, v. [5] [Q] to lay down, stoop, incline; [P] to tip, pour out:– cowering prisoners (1), lay down (1), pour (1), pour out (1), striding forward (1)

H7580 צָעוֹר **ṣā'ôr**, a. Not used in NIVEBC [√ 7592]. see 7582

H7581 צָעִיף **ṣā'îp**, n.[m.] [3] veil:– veil (3)

H7582 [1]צָעִיר **ṣā'îr[1]**, a. [23] [√ 7592; cf. 7580, 7584]. younger, small, little, lowly:– younger (7), young (3), youngest (3), least (2), little (2), small (2), lowly (1), servants (1), smallest (1), younger (1 [+4200, 3427])

H7583 [2]צָעִיר **ṣā'îr[2]**, n.pr.loc. [1] Zair, "*small, insignificant*, hence *narrow pass*":– Zair (1)

H7584 צְעִירָה **ṣᵉ'îrâ**, n.f. [1] [cf. 7582]. youth, youngest (offspring):– ages (1 [+1148])

H7585 צָעַן **ṣā'an**, v. [1] [Q] to pack up, move (a tent):– moved (1)

H7586 צֹעַן **ṣō'an**, n.pr.loc. [7] Zoan:– Zoan (7)

H7587 צְעַנִּים **ṣᵉ'annîm**, n.pr.loc. Not used in NIVEBC [cf. 7588]. Zeannim, see 7588

H7588 צַעֲנַנִּים **ṣa'ănannîm**, n.pr.loc. [2] [cf. 1300, 7587]. Zaanannim:– Zaanannim (2)

H7589 צַעֲצֻעִים **ṣa'ăṣu'îm**, n.[m.]pl. [1] sculptured work (by metal casting):– sculptured (1 [+5126])

H7590 צָעַק **ṣā'aq**, v. [55] [→ 7591; cf. 2410; 10237]. [Q] to cry; [N] to be called out, be summoned; [P] to keep crying; [H] to call together, summon:– cried out (16), cry out (10), cried for help (3), were called out (3), appeal (2), cried (2), cries out (2), cry out (2 [+7590]), crying out (2), appealed (1), burst out (1), called out (1), cried out for help (1 [+7754]), cry (1), cry aloud (1), scream for help (1), screamed (1), shout (1), summoned (1), summoned (1), was called up (1), were called to arms (1), were summoned (1)

H7591 צְעָקָה **ṣᵉ'āqâ**, n.f. [21] [√ 7590]. cry of distress, outcry, wailing:– cry (8), outcry (3), cries (2), cry (2 [+7754]), wailing (2), cries of anguish (1 [+7754]), cries of distress (1), crying out (1), outcry (1 [+7754])

H7592 צָעַר **ṣā'ar**, v. [3] [→ 5203, 5204, 7428, 7486, 7580,

7582, 7593; cf. 2402]. [Q] to be trivial, insignificant, little:– brought low (1), disdained (1), little ones (1)

H7593 צֹעַר ***ṣō'ar***, n.pr.loc. [10] [√ 7592]. Zoar, "*small, insignificant*":– Zoar (10)

H7594 צָפַד ***ṣāpad***, v. [1] [Q] to shrivel:– shriveled (1)

H7595 [1]צָפָה ***ṣāpâ[1]***, v. [36] [→ 2174, 5205, 5206, 5207, 7600, 7601, 7603, 7610, 7611?]. [Q] to keep watch, be a lookout; [Qp] to be spied out; [P] to watch, lookout:– watchman (11), lookout (4), watchmen (4), watch (3), he[S] (1 [+2021]), keep watch (1), keeping watch (1), lie in wait (1), look (1), looking (1), lookouts (1), marked (1), standing watch (1), wait expectantly (1), watch in hope (1), watched (1), watches over (1), watching (1)

H7596 [2]צָפָה ***ṣāpâ[2]***, v. [47] [→ 7599, 7620, 7633, 7634?]. [Q] to arrange; [P] to overlay, cover, adorn; [Pu] to be overlaid, be coated:– overlaid (27), overlay (11), covered (4), adorned (1 [+4200, 9514]), coating (1), paneling (1 [+6770]), spread (1), NDT (1)

H7597 [3]צָפָה ***ṣāpâ[3]***, n.f. [1] [√ 7429?]. out-flow, discharge:– flowing (1)

H7598 צְפוֹ ***ṣᵉpô***, n.pr.m. [3] [cf. 7609]. Zepho, "[poss.] *gaze*":– Zepho (3)

H7599 צִפּוּי ***ṣippûy***, n.[m.] [5] [√ 7596]. overlaying, (metal) plating:– overlaid (3), overlay (2)

H7600 [1]צָפוֹן ***ṣāpôn[1]***, n.f. [150] [→ 1263, 7601, 7603; cf. 7595]. north, northern:– north (94), north (25 [+2025]), northern (9 [+2025]), north (6 [+4946]), northern (5), northern (3 [+4946]), north (2 [+2006, 2021]), north (1 [+4946, 2025]), north (1 [+7156, 2006, 2021]), north wind (1), northern (1 [+4946, 2025]), northward (1 [+2006, 2021]), NDT (1)

H7601 [2]צָפוֹן ***ṣāpôn[2]***, n.pr.loc. [4] [√ 7600; cf. 7595]. Zaphon, "[poss.] *North* or *[proper name of a god], Zephon*":– Zaphon (4)

H7602 צְפוֹן ***ṣᵉpôn***, n.pr.m. [2] [→ 7604; cf. 7611]. Zephon, "[poss.] *gaze*; [poss.] *look out [tower], watch*":– Zephon (2)

H7603 [1]צְפוֹנִי ***ṣᵉpônî[1]***, a. [1] [√ 7600; cf. 7595]. northern; (n.) northerner:– northern (1)

H7604 [2]צְפוֹנִי ***ṣᵉpônî[2]***, a.g. [1] [√ 7602]. Zephonite, "*of Zephon*":– Zephonite (1)

H7605 צָפוּעַ ***ṣāpûa'***, n.[m.] Not used in NIVEBC [cf. 7616]. see 7616

H7606 [1]צִפּוֹר ***ṣippôr[1]***, n.f. & m. [40] [→ 7436?, 7607, 7631]. bird (individual and collective):– bird (18), birds (11), bird's (2), sparrow (2), bird (1 [+4053]), birds (1 [+4053]), carrion birds (1 [+6514]), it[S] (1 [+2021, 2021, 2645]), poultry (1), sparrows (1), NDT (1)

H7607 [2]צִפּוֹר ***ṣippôr[2]***, n.pr.m. [7] [√ 7606; 10616]. Zippor, "*bird, swallow*":– Zippor (7)

H7608 צַפַּחַת ***ṣappaḥat***, n.f. [7] [√ 7613]. jug, jar (for liquid), a portable convex or spherical shape, with a lid or plug for transport:– jug (6), jar (1)

H7609 צְפִי ***ṣᵉpî***, n.pr.m. Not used in NIVEBC [cf. 7598]. Zephi, see 7598

H7610 צִפִּיָּה ***ṣippiyyâ***, n.f. [1] [√ 7595]. watchtower, lookout:– towers (1)

H7611 צִפְיוֹן ***ṣipyôn***, n.pr.m. Not used in NIVEBC [→ 7612; cf. 7595?, 7602]. Ziphion, see 7602

H7612 צִפְיוֹנִי ***ṣipyônî***, a.g. Not used in NIVEBC [√ 7611]. Ziphionite

H7613 צַפִּיחִת ***ṣappîḥit***, n.f. [1] [→ 7432, 7608]. wafer, flat-cake:– wafers (1)

H7614 צֹפִים ***ṣōpîm***, n.pr.[loc.?] [1] [cf. 7435]. Zophim:– Zophim (1)

H7615 צָפִין ***ṣāpîn***, n.[m.] Not used in NIVEBC [√ 7621]. see 7621

H7616 צָפִיעַ ***ṣāpîa'***, n.[m.] [1] [cf. 7605]. manure, dung:– dung (1)

H7617 צְפִיעָה ***ṣᵉpî'â***, n.f. [1] offshoots, leaf:– offshoots (1)

H7618 צָפִיר ***ṣāpîr***, n.m. [6] [√ 10615]. (male) goat:– goat (2 [+6436]), goat (1), male goats (1), male goats (1 [+6436]), NDT (1)

H7619 צְפִירָה ***ṣᵉpîrâ***, n.f. [3] crown, wreath; doom:– doom (2), crown (1)

H7620 צָפִית ***ṣāpît***, n.f. [1] [√ 7596]. rug, carpet:– rugs (1)

H7621 צָפַן ***ṣāpan***, v. [32] [→ 5208, 7615; *also used with compound proper names*]. [Q] to hide, conceal, store up; [Qp] to be treasured, be cherished; [N] to be stored up, be concealed; [H] to hide:– stored up (4), store up (3), ambush (2), hidden (2), hide (2), keep safe (2), restraining (2), cherish (1), closed (1), concealed (1), hid (1), holds in store (1), is concealed (1), is stored up (1), kept on record (1), lurk (1), secret (1), set (1), stores up (1), treasure (1), treasured (1), treasures (1)

H7622 צְפַנְיָה ***ṣᵉpanyâ***, n.pr.m. [8] [√ 7621 + 3378]. Zephaniah, "*Yahweh has hidden [to shelter]* or *Yahweh has hidden [as a treasure]*":– Zephaniah (8)

H7623 צְפַנְיָהוּ ***ṣᵉpanyāhû***, n.pr.m. [2] [√ 7621 + 3378]. Zephaniah, "*Yahweh has hidden [to shelter]* or *Yahweh has hidden [as a treasure]*":– Zephaniah (2)

H7624 צָפְנַת פַּעְנֵחַ ***ṣāpᵉnat pa'nēaḥ***, n.pr.m. [1] [√ 7195]. Zaphenath-Paneah, "*the [pagan] god speaks and he [the newborn] lives*":– Zaphenath-Paneah (1)

H7625 צֶפַע ***ṣepa'***, n.m. [1] [→ 7626]. viper, serpent:– viper (1)

H7626 צִפְעֹנִי ***ṣip'ōnî***, n.m. [4] [√ 7625]. viper:– vipers (2), viper (1), viper's (1)

H7627 צָפַף ***ṣāpap***, v. [4] [→ 7628]. [Pil] to chirp; to whisper:– whisper (2), chirp (1), cried (1)

H7628 צַפְצָפָה ***ṣapṣāpâ***, n.f. [1] [√ 7627]. willow:– willow (1)

H7629 צָפַר ***ṣāpar***, v. [1] [Q] to leave, depart:– leave (1)

H7630 צְפַרְדֵּעַ ***ṣᵉpardēa'***, n.f. [13] frogs:– frogs (13)

H7631 צִפֹּרָה ***ṣippōrâ***, n.pr.f. [3] [√ 7606]. Zipporah, "*bird, swallow*":– Zipporah (3)

H7632 צִפֹּרֶן ***ṣippōren***, n.[m.] [2] [√ 10303]. nail (of finger or toe); (flint or hard stone) point (of a stylus):– nails (1), point (1)

H7633 צֶפֶת ***ṣepet***, n.f. [1] [√ 7596]. capital (of a pillar):– capital (1)

H7634 צְפַת ***ṣᵉpat***, n.pr.loc. [1] [√ 7596?]. Zephath, "*watcher*":– Zephath (1)

H7635 צְפָתָה ***ṣᵉpātâ***, n.pr.loc. [1] Zephathah, "*watchtower*":– Zephathah (1)

H7636 צָקוּן ***ṣāqûn***, var. Not used in NIVEBC [cf. 7439]. see 7440

H7637 צִקְלַג ***ṣiqlag***, n.pr.loc. [15] Ziklag:– Ziklag (14), it[S] (1)

H7638 צִקְלוֹן ***ṣiqqālôn***, n.[m] [1] Not used in NIVEBC. garment, bag:– NDT (1)

H7639 [1]צַר ***ṣar[1]***, a. & n.m. [47] [√ 7674]. (n.) trouble, distress, anguish; (a.) narrow:– distress (20), trouble (11), narrow (3), small (3), distressed (2), adversity (1), anguish (1), anguished (1), critical (1), grieve (1), misery (1), pent-up (1), tightly (1)

H7640 [2]צַר ***ṣar[2]***, n.f. [68] [√ 7675; 10568]. enemy, foe, adversary, opponent:– enemies (29), foes (19), enemy (10), foe (3), adversaries (2), adversary (2), hostile (1), opponent (1), oppressor (1)

H7641 [3]צַר ***ṣar[3]***, a. *or* n.[m.] [1] [√ 7644]. flint, known for is hardness:– flint (1)

H7642 [4]צַר ***ṣar[4]***, n.m. *or* a. see 7639

H7643 צֵר ***ṣēr***, n.pr.loc. [1] Zer:– Zer (1)

H7644 [1]צֹר ***ṣōr[1]***, n.[m.] [5] [→ 7447, 7450, 7641, 7645, 7656, 7660]. flint knife:– flint (3), edge (1), flint knife (1)

H7645 [2]צֹר ***ṣōr[2]***, n.pr.loc. Not used in NIVEBC [→ 7450, 7660; cf. 7644]. Tyre

H7646 צָרַב ***ṣārab***, v. [1] [→ 7647, 7648]. [N] to be scorched:– be scorched (1)

H7647 צָרָב ***ṣārāb***, a. [1] [√ 7646]. scorching:– scorching (1)

H7648 צָרֶבֶת ***ṣārebet***, n.f. [2] [√ 7646]. scar:– scar (2)

H7649 צְרֵדָה ***ṣᵉrēdâ***, n.pr.loc. [2] Zeredah:– Zarethan (1), Zeredah (1)

H7650 [1]צָרָה ***ṣārâ[1]***, n.f. [70] [√ 7639; cf. 7674]. trouble, distress, calamity, anguish:– distress (24), trouble (22), troubles (8), anguish (4), calamities (4), calamity (2), adversity (1), distressed (1), groan (1), hardship (1), hostility (1), oppressed (1)

H7651 [2]צָרָה ***ṣārâ[2]***, n.f. [1] [√ 7675]. rival-wife:– rival (1)

H7652 צִרָה ***ṣirâ***, n.f. Not used in NIVEBC [cf. 3227]. (stone) sheep pen, fold

H7653 צְרוּיָה ***ṣᵉrûyâ***, n.pr.f. [26] Zeruiah, "*perfumed resin*":– Zeruiah (25), Zeruiah's (1)

H7654 צְרוּעָה ***ṣᵉrû'â***, n.pr.loc. [1] [√ 7665]. Zeruah, "*one with skin disease*":– Zeruah (1)

H7655 [1]צְרוֹר ***ṣᵉrôr[1]***, n.m. [7] [→ 7657?; cf. 7674]. pouch, purse, sachet, bag:– purse (2), bag (1), bundle (1), pouch (1), pouches (1), sachet (1)

H7656 [2]צְרוֹר ***ṣᵉrôr[2]***, n.m. [2] [→ 7657?; cf. 7644]. pebble:– pebble (2)

H7657 [3]צְרוֹר ***ṣᵉrôr[3]***, n.pr.m. [1] [√ 7656? *or* 7655?]. Zeror, "*money bag, pouch,* [or poss.] *pebbles*":– Zeror (1)

H7658 צָרַח ***ṣāraḥ***, v. [2] [→ 7659]. [Q] to shout, cry out; [H] to raise the battle cry:– raise the battle cry (1), shouts battle cry (1)

H7659 צְרַח ***ṣeraḥ***, n.[m.] Not used in NIVEBC [√ 7658]. war-cry, shriek

H7660 צֹרִי ***ṣōrî***, a.g. [5] [√ 7645]. Tyrian, of Tyre:– Tyre (2), Tyrians (1), from Tyre (1), people from Tyre (1)

H7661 צְרִי ***ṣᵉrî***, n.[m.] [6] [→ 7662]. balm, mastic (resin), usually obtained from processing from the bark of a tree:– balm (6)

H7662 צְרִי ***ṣᵉrî***, n.pr.m. [1] [√ 7661]. Zeri, "*balsam*":– Zeri (1)

H7663 צְרִיחַ ***ṣᵉrîaḥ***, n.[m.] [4] pit, (underground) stronghold, likely referring to a man-made pit:– stronghold (2), it[S] (1 [+2021]), pits (1)

H7664 צֹרֶךְ ***ṣōrek***, n.[m.] [1] need:– need (1)

H7665 צָרַע ***ṣāra'***, v.den. [20] [→ 7654, 7665?, 7669]. [Qp, Pu] to be leprous, afflicted with an infectious skin disease:– had leprosy (5), leprosy (4), leprous (3), diseased (2), defiling skin disease (1), disease (1), had a defiling skin disease (1), has a defiling skin disease (1), skin was leprous (1), they[S] (1 [+2021])

H7666 צָרְעָה ***ṣor'â***, n.pr.loc. [10] [→ 7668, 7670]. Zorah:– Zorah (10)

H7667 צִרְעָה ***ṣir'â***, n.f.col. [3] [√ 7665?]. hornets or discouragement:– hornet (3)

H7668 צָרְעִי ***ṣor'î***, a.g. [1] [√ 7666]. Zorite:– Zorites (1)

H7669 צָרַעַת ***ṣāra'at***, n.f. [35] [√ 7665]. infectious skin disease; (of clothing) mildew:– skin disease (10), defiling disease (5), defiling mold (5), leprosy (5), disease (2), defiling (1), defiling molds (1), defiling skin disease (1), defiling skin disease (1 [+5999]), defiling skin diseases and defiling molds (1), it[S] (1), molds (1), spreading mold (1 [+5596])

H7670 צָרְעָתִי ***ṣārᵉ'ātî***, a.g. [2] [√ 7666]. Zorathite, "*of Zorah*":– Zorathites (2)

H7671 צָרַף ***ṣārap***, v. [33] [→ 5214, 7672]. [Q] to smelt, refine (metals); (n.) (gold- or silver-)smith:– goldsmith (6), refined (4), flawless (3), goldsmiths (2), refine (2), refining goes on (2 [+7671]), silversmith (2), been tested (1), examine (1), fashions (1), proved true (1), purified (1), refiner (1), refiner's (1), test (1), thin out (1), thoroughly purge away (1 [+3869, 2021, 1342]), NDT (2)

H7672 צֹרְפִי ***ṣōrᵉpî***, n.[m.]col. [1] [√ 7671]. (member of the) goldsmiths:– goldsmiths (1)

H7673 צָרְפַת ***ṣārᵉpat***, n.pr.loc. [3] Zarephath, "[poss.] *smelting place; place of pigmenting, staining*":– Zarephath (3)

H7674 [1]צָרַר ***ṣārar[1]***, v. [30] [→ 5210, 7639, 7650, 7655, 7676; cf. 7443, 7675]. [Q] to bind up, wrap up, tie up; to hamper, oppress, be in distress; [Qp] be bound, be confined; [Pu] to be mended; [H] to bring trouble, distress, oppress:– distress (3), bring distress (2), in distress (2), in labor (2), besiege (1), bind up (1), bound securely (1), distressed (1), gave trouble (1), hampered (1), kept in confinement (1), lay siege (1), mended (1), obsessed (1), oppress (1), oppressed (1), small (1), stored up (1), sweep away (1 [+928, 4053]), trouble (1), tying (1), weakened (1), wrapped (1), wrapped up (1), wraps up (1)

H7675 [2]צָרַר ***ṣārar[2]***, v. [26] [→ 7640, 7651, 7677; cf. 7674]. [Q] to be a rival-wife; to be an enemy, adversary:– enemies (7), enemy (4), foes (4), oppressed (2), adversaries (1), foe (1), give trouble (1), hostile (1), oppose (1), oppressing (1), rival wife (1), treat as enemies (1), treated as enemies (1)

H7676 [3]צָרַר ***ṣārar[3]***, v.den. Not used in NIVEBC [√ 7674]. [H] to suffer distress

H7677 [4]צָרַר ***ṣārar[4]***, v.den. Not used in NIVEBC [√ 7675]. [Q] to be a rival wife

H7678 צְרֵרָה ***ṣᵉrērâ***, n.p.loc. [1] Zererah:– Zererah (1)

H7679 צֶרֶת ***ṣeret***, n.pr.m. [1] [→ 7680]. Zereth, "*splendor*":– Zereth (1)

H7680 צֶרֶת הַשַּׁחַר ***ṣeret haššaḥar***, n.pr.loc. [1] [√ 7679 + 2241]. Zereth Shahar, "*glory of dawn*":– Zereth Shahar (1)

H7681 צָרְתָן ***ṣārᵉtān***, n.pr.loc. [3] Zarethan:– Zarethan (3)

H7682 ק ***q***, letter. Not used in NIVEBC [√ 10617]. letter of the Hebrew alphabet

H7683 קֵא ***qē'***, n.[m.] [1] [√ 7794]. vomit:– vomit (1)

H7684 קָאַת ***qā'at***, n.[f.] [5] desert owl:– desert owl (4), owl (1)

H7685 קַב ***qab***, n.[m.] [1] [→ 7688]. cab (dry measure, one-eighteenth of an ephah, about one quart or liter):– cab (1)

H7686 קָבַב ***qābab***, v. [14] [cf. 5918, 5919]. [Q] to curse:– curse (7), cursed (3), curse at all (2 [+7686]), put a curse on (2)

H7687 קֵבָה ***qēbâ***, n.f. [2] maw (4th stomach of cud-chewing animals); (of humans) belly, stomach area:– internal organs (1), stomach (1)

H7688 קֻבָּה ***qubbâ***, n.f. [1] [√ 7685]. woman's section (of a tent):– tent (1)

H7689 קִבּוּץ ***qibbûṣ***, n.m. [1] [√ 7695]. collection (of idols):– collection (1)

H7690 קְבוּרָה ***qᵉbûrâ***, n.f. [14] [√ 7699]. tomb, grave, burial:– tomb (6), grave (3), burial (1), buried (1), cemetery (1 [+8441]), have burial (1 [+7699]), proper burial (1)

H7691 קָבַל ***qābal***, v. [13] [→ 7692; 10618]. [P] to receive, take; [H] to match, correspond:– accept (3), took (3), opposite (2), received (2), agreed (1), take choice (1), NDT (1)

H7692 קְבֹל **qebōl**, n.[m.] [2] [√ 7691]. (something) in front of, battering ram:– battering rams (1), in front of (1)

H7693 קָבַע **qāba'**, v. [6] [cf. 6810, 6812]. [Q] to rob, plunder:– rob (2), robbing (2), exact (1), NDT (1)

H7694 קֻבַּעַת **qubba'at**, n.f. [2] cup, goblet:– goblet (2 [+3926])

H7695 קָבַץ **qābaṣ**, v. [127] [→ 7689, 7697, 7698; *also used with compound proper names*]. [Q] to collect, gather, assemble; [Qp] to be assembled; [N] to be gathered, be assembled, be joined; [P] to gather, assemble; [Pu] to be gathered; [Ht] to gather (themselves) together:– gather (38), gathered (17), assembled (11), assemble (10), called together (4), gathers (4), brought together (3), gather together (3), bring (2), came together (2), collect (2), come together (2), surely bring together (2 [+7695]), were assembled (2), amasses (1), assemble (1 [+3481]), assemble yourselves (1), be gathered (1), bring back (1), bring together (1), came together (1 [+3481]), collected (1), come and join (1), come together (1 [+3481]), gather in (1), gathered together (1), grows pale (1 [+6999]), join (1), joined forces (1), mobilized (1), mustered (1), picked up (1), rallied (1), shepherd (1), stored up (1), takes captive (1), turns pale (1 [+6999]), were brought (1), were gathered (1)

H7696 קַבְצְאֵל **qabṣe'ēl**, n.pr.loc. [3] [√ 7695 + 446]. Kabzeel, "*God [El] collects*":– Kabzeel (3)

H7697 קְבֻצָה **qebuṣâ**, n.f. [1] [√ 7695]. gathering:– gathered (1)

H7698 קִבְצַיִם **qibṣayim**, n.pr.loc. [1] [√ 7695]. Kibzaim:– Kibzaim (1)

H7699 קָבַר **qābar**, v. [132] [→ 7690, 7700, 7701]. [Q] to store up, pile up, heap up:– buried (53), bury (31), was buried (31), burying (7), be buried (4), be sure to bury (2 [+7699]), gravediggers (1), have burial (1 [+7690]), is buried (1), NDT (1)

H7700 קֶבֶר **qeber**, n.m. [68] [→ 7701]. burial site, tomb, grave:– grave (18), tomb (16), graves (10), tombs (9), burial (5), be buried (2 [+665, 448]), buried (2), themS (2 [+4013]), burial place (1), burial site (1), buried (1 [+995, 448]), themS (1 [+2021])

H7701 קִבְרוֹת הַתַּאֲוָה **qibrôt hatta'awâ**, n.pr.loc. [5] [√ 7700 + 2246]. Kibroth Hattaavah, "*graves of lust, greed*":– Kibroth Hattaavah (5)

H7702 קָדַד **qādad**, v. [15] [√ 7721?]. [Q] to bow low, bow down:– bowed down (13), bowed (1), bowed low (1)

H7703 קִדָּה **qiddâ**, n.f. [2] cassia (a spice):– cassia (2)

H7704 קְדוּמִים **qedûmîm**, n.[m.pl.] [1] [√ 7709]. age-old, ancient:– age-old (1)

H7705 קָדוֹשׁ **qādôš**, a. [115] [√ 7727; 10620]. holy, sacred, consecrated, set apart as dedicated to God; by extension: pure, innocent, free from impurity; (n.) holy people of God, saints; as a title of God, "the Holy One" focuses on God as unique, wholly other:– holy (58), holy one (43), sanctuary (7), consecrated (4), holy people (2), sacred (1)

H7706 קָדַח **qādaḥ**, v. [5] [→ 734, 7707]. [Q] to kindle, light (a fire):– kindle (1), kindled (1), kindled (1 [+836]), light (1), sets ablaze (1)

H7707 קַדַּחַת **qaddaḥat**, n.f. [2] [√ 7706]. fever, inflammation:– fever (2)

H7708 קָדִים **qādîm**, n.m. [67] [√ 7709]. east, eastern, the direction of orientation in the ancient Near East (facing the sunrise); east is also the direction of the great desert, thus an east or desert wind is particularly hot:– east (34), east (11 [+2025]), east wind (7), east (4 [+2006, 2021]), eastern (2 [+2025]), eastward (2), desert wind (1), east (1 [+7156, 2006, 2021, 2025]), east winds (1), eastward (1 [+2025]), extend eastward (1 [+2025]), hot east wind (1), NDT (1)

H7709 קָדַם **qādam**, v.den. [27] [→ 7704, 7708, 7710, 7711, 7712, 7713, 7714, 7715, 7716, 7717, 7718, 7719, 7720; 10621, 10623]. [P] to be in front of, meet, confront:– come before (4), confronted (4), come to meet (2), confront (2), bring (1), came to greet (1), come (1), comes before (1), forestall (1), go (1), go before (1), has a claim against (1), in front (1), meet (1), met (1), opposite (1), receive (1), rise (1), stay open (1)

H7710 קֶדֶם **qedem**, n.[m.] [61] [√ 7709]. (as a direction) east, eastern; the direction of orientation in the ancient Near East (facing the sunrise); (used of time) ancient, eternal, long ago, possibly relating to east as the direction of origin (as the sunrise):– east (17), eastern (7), long ago (7), of old (6), ancient (3), east (3 [+4946]), before (2), gone by (2), long ago (2 [+4946]), ancient times (1), days of old (1), east (1 [+6584, 7156]), eastward (1 [+4946]), eternal (1), everlasting (1), former (1 [+4946]), from of old (1), long ago (1 [+4946, 3427]), old (1 [+4946, 3427]), past (1), when came to be (1 [+4946])

H7711 קֵדְמָה **qēdem**, adv. [26] [→ 7714; cf. 7709]. eastern, (toward the) east; see also 7710:– east (9), east (7 [+2025]), eastern (3 [+2025]), east (1 [+725]), eastward (1 [+2025]), eastward (1 [+2025, 4667, 2025]), southeast (1 [+2025, 5582]), southeast (1 [+2025, 5582, 2025]), NDT (2)

H7712 קַדְמָה **qadmâ**, n.f. [6] [√ 7709; 10622]. past, antiquity; ancient (city); see also 7710:– before (3), old (1), past (1), NDT (1)

H7713 קִדְמָה **qidmâ**, n.f. [4] [√ 7709]. east; see also 7710:– east (4)

H7714 1קֵדְמָה **qēdemâ1**, adv. Not used in NIVEBC [√ 7711; cf. 7709]. eastward, see 7711 & 2025

H7715 2קְדֵמָה **qēdemâ2**, n.pr.m. [2] [√ 7709]. Kedemah, "*east*":– Kedemah (2)

H7716 קַדְמוֹן **qadmôn**, a. [1] [→ 7719, 7720; cf. 7709]. eastern; see also 7710:– eastern (1)

H7717 קְדֵמוֹת **qedēmôt**, n.pr.loc. [4] [√ 7709]. Kedemoth, "*east*":– Kedemoth (4)

H7718 קַדְמִיאֵל **qadmî'ēl**, n.pr.m. [8] [√ 7709 + 446]. Kadmiel, "*[stand] before God [El]*":– Kadmiel (8)

H7719 1קַדְמֹנִי **qadmōnî1**, a. [10] [√ 7716; cf. 7709]. (of a direction) eastern; (of time) old, former, past; see also 7710:– east (3), deadS (2), former (2), old (1), past (1), NDT (1)

H7720 2קַדְמֹנִי **qadmōnî2**, a.g. [1] [√ 7716; cf. 7709]. Kadmonite:– Kadmonites (1)

H7721 קָדְקֹד **qodqōd**, n.[m.] [12] [√ 7702?]. top or crown of the head:– brow (2), heads (2), skulls (2), top of head (2), crown of head (1), crowns (1), head (1), skull (1)

H7722 קָדַר **qādar**, v. [17] [→ 7723, 7724, 7725, 7726]. [Q] to grow dark, be black; to mourn, wail, grieve; [H] to make dark, bring gloom; [Ht] to grow dark:– darkened (3), mourning (3), darken (2), mourn (2), black (1), blackened (1), clothed with gloom (1), dark (1), go dark (1), grief (1), wail (1)

H7723 קֵדָר **qēdār**, n.pr.g. [12] [√ 7722]. Kedar, "*mighty*":– Kedar (10), Kedar (1 [+1201]), Kedar's (1)

H7724 קִדְרוֹן **qidrôn**, n.pr.loc. [11] [√ 7722]. Kidron:– Kidron (10), thereS (1 [+928, 5707])

H7725 קַדְרוּת **qadrût**, n.f. [1] [√ 7722]. darkness, blackness:– darkness (1)

H7726 קְדֹרַנִּית **qedōrannît**, adv. [1] [√ 7722]. in mourner's attire, in an unkempt manner:– mourners (1)

H7727 קָדַשׁ **qādaš**, v.den. [171] [→ 5219, 7705, 7728, 7729, 7730, 7731, 7732]. [Q] to be holy, sacred, consecrated; [N] to show oneself holy, be consecrated; [P] to consecrate, make holy; [Pu] to be dedicated, consecrated; [Ht] to consecrate oneself; [H] to set apart, consecrate, dedicate, regard as holy; to set apart as dedicated to God; by extension: pure, innocent, free from impurity:– consecrate (29), consecrated (23), dedicated (10), consecrate yourselves (9), consecrated themselves (7), keep holy (7), holy (6), makes holy (6), set apart (6), be proved holy (5), dedicates (5), prepare (5), dedicate (4), made holy (4), consecration (3), proved holy (3), been consecrated (2), declare holy (2), honor as holy (2), keeping holy (2), make holy (2), regard as holy (2), sacred (2), set aside (2), solemnly consecrate (2 [+7727]), acknowledge holiness (1), be acknowledged as holy (1), be consecrated (1), call in honor of (1 [+4200]), celebrate holy (1), consecrate themselves (1), consecrating (1), consecrating themselves (1), consecrating themselves (1 [+7731]), defiled (1), doneS (1), holiness (1), prepared (1), proved to be holy (1), purified (1), purifying herself (1), send (1), set apart as holy (1), show holiness (1), uphold holiness (1), NDT (1)

H7728 1קָדֵשׁ **qādēš1**, n.m. [10] [√ 7727]. (male or female) shrine prostitute:– shrine prostitutes (5), shrine prostitute (4), prostitutes of the shrines (1)

H7729 2קָדֵשׁ **qādēš2**, n.pr.loc. [14] [→ 5315; cf. 7727]. Kadesh, "*sacred place*":– Kadesh (14)

H7730 קֶדֶשׁ **qedeš**, n.pr.loc. [12] [√ 7727]. Kedesh, "*sacred place*":– Kedesh (11), thereS (1 [+2025])

H7731 קֹדֶשׁ **qōdeš**, n.m. [469] [√ 7727]. holy or sacred thing, holy or sacred place, sanctuary; holiness, set apart as dedicated to God; the "holy of holies" is the most holy place, set apart exclusively for the Presence of God, with very limited high priestly access; see also 7727:– holy (134), sanctuary (74), sacred (65), most holy (42 [+7731]), most holy place (20), holy place (14), holy things (10), most holy offerings (10 [+7731]), holiness (9), sacred offerings (8), consecrated (7), most holy place (7 [+7731]), most holy place (6 [+7731]), most holy things (6 [+7731]), holy offerings (5), sacred offering (3), dedicated (2), dedicated things (2), holy furnishings (2), sacred objects (2), sacred things (2), something holy (2), things dedicated (2), anotherS (1 [+5246]), consecrated gifts (1 [+7731]), consecrated gifts (1 [+7731]), consecrated things (1), consecrating themselves (1 [+7727]), dedicate (1), dedicated gifts (1), gifts dedicated (1), holy one (1), holy ones (1), holy precincts (1), itS (1), most holy (1 [+7731]), most holy (1 [+7731]), most holy place (1 [+1808]), most holy place (1 [+5219]), most sacred (1 [+7731]), most sacred (1 [+7731]), most sacred food (1 [+7731]), most sacred food (1 [+7731]), offering (1), offerings (1), priests rooms (1 [+4384]), sacred gifts (1), sacred portion (1), sanctuary (1 [+5226]), set apart (1), temple (1), thingsS (1), what holy (1), NDT (5)

H7732 קָדֵשׁ בַּרְנֵעַ **qādēš barnēa'**, n.pr.loc. [10] [√ 7727 + 1395]. Kadesh Barnea, "*sacred place of Barnea*":– Kadesh Barnea (10)

H7733 קָהָה **qāhâ**, v. [4] [→ 7734]. [Q] to be dull, blunt (of teeth); [P] to be dull:– set on edge (3), dull (1)

H7734 קֵהָיוֹן **qēhāyôn**, n.[m.] Not used in NIVEBC [√ 7733]. bluntness

H7735 קָהַל **qāhal**, v.den. [39] [√ 7736]. [N] to be gathered, be assembled; [H] to summon, call together, cause to assemble:– gathered (9), assembled (8), assemble (5), came together (3), gather (2), gathered together (2), mustered (2), summoned (2), called together (1), came as a group (1), convenes a court (1), crowded (1), gather together (1), summoned to assemble (1)

H7736 קָהָל **qāhāl**, n.m. [123] [→ 5220, 5221, 7735, 7736, 7737, 7738, 7739, 7827; cf. 7754]. assembly, community, often of Israel assembled for religious ceremony:– assembly (74), community (13), company (5), horde (4), crowd (3), mob (3), throng (3), army (2), gathered (2), hordes (2), alliance (1), army (1 [+2256, 6639]), assemble (1 [+6590, 928, 2021]), assembled (1 [+995]), everyone else (1 [+3972]), members (1), them (1 [+3972, 3776]), themS (1 [+2021]), themS (1 [+3972, 3776]), theyS (1 [+2021]), NDT (2)

H7737 קְהִלָּה **qehillâ**, n.f. [2] [√ 7736]. assembly, meeting:– assembly (1), meeting (1)

H7738 קֹהֶלֶת **qōhelet**, n.m. [7] [√ 7736]. (as a title or name) the Teacher, one who calls together and instructs the assembly:– Teacher (7)

H7739 קְהֵלָתָה **qehēlātâ**, n.pr.loc. [2] [√ 7736]. Kehelathah, "*assembly*":– Kehelathah (2)

H7740 קְהָת **qehāt**, n.pr.m. [32] [→ 7741]. Kohath, Kohathite:– Kohath (18), Kohathite (7 [+1201]), Kohathites (4 [+1201]), Kohath's (2), NDT (1)

H7741 קְהָתִי **qehātî**, a.g. [15] [√ 7740]. Kohathite, "*of Kohath*":– Kohathite (7), Kohathites (4 [+1201]), Kohathites (3), Kohath (1)

H7742 1קַו **qāw1**, n.m. [20] [√ 7747?; cf. 7749]. measuring line, ruler:– measuring line (7), line (4), rule (4), measure (1), that (1), thatS (1), this (1), thisS (1)

H7743 2קַו **qāw2**, n.m. [4] [√ 7744?; cf. 7768]. strange speech:– strange speech (4 [+7743])

H7744 3קַו **qāw3**, n.m. Not used in NIVEBC [√ 7743?]. qav (a mocking sound, like blah-blah)

H7745 קְוֵא **qewē'**, n.pr.loc. [2] [cf. 7750]. Kue:– Kue (2)

H7746 קוֹבַע **qôba'**, n.[m.] [2] [cf. 3916]. helmet:– helmet (1), helmets (1)

H7747 1קָוָה **qāwâ1**, v. [47] [→ 5223, 7742?, 9535, 9536, 9537]. [Q] to hope in; [P] to hope for, wait for, look for:– hope in (7), wait (6), look (5), hope (4), looked for (4), hoped (2), trusted (2), wait for (2), waited patiently for (2 [+7747]), waiting (2), expect (1), hope for (1), hoped for (1), hopes in (1), hoping (1), long for (1), look for (1), look in hope (1), put trust (1), waited for (1), waits (1)

H7748 2קָוָה **qāwâ2**, v. [2] [→ 5224, 5225]. [N] to be gathered:– be gathered (1), gather (1)

H7749 קָוֶה **qāweh**, n.m. Not used in NIVEBC [cf. 7742]. see 7742

H7750 קְוֵה **qewēh**, n.pr.loc. [2] [cf. 7745]. Kue:– Kue (2)

H7751 קוֹחַ **qôaḥ**, n.[m.] Not used in NIVEBC [cf. 7223]. see 7223

H7752 קוּט **qûṭ**, v. [7] [cf. 7762, 9210]. [Q] to feel anger, loathing; [N] to feel loathing; [Htpolal] to loathe, abhor:– loathe (4), abhor (1), angry (1), loathing (1)

H7753 קוֹט **qôṭ**, v. *or* n.m. Not used in NIVEBC [cf. 3684]. [Q] to be fragile, see 3684

H7754 קוֹל **qôl**, n.m. [506] [→ 7755?, 7826; cf. 7736; 10631]. sound, voice, noise:– voice (93), sound (63), obey (35 [+9048, 928]), obeyed (18 [+9048, 928]), voices (17), to (16 [+928]), thunder (12), listen (11), noise (11), to (10 [+4200]), cry (8), cry for mercy (6 [+9384]), sounds (6), aloud (5 [+5951, 906]), proclamation (5), roar (5), aloud (4 [+5951]), thunders (4 [+5989]), blast (3), called out (3 [+7924, 928, 1524]), cries (3), plea (3), word (3), aloud (2), aloud (2 [+1524]), crackling (2), cry (2 [+7591]), crying (2), disobeyed (2 [+4202, 9048, 928]), fully obey (2 [+9048, 928, 9048]), hear (2), heard (2), heard (2 [+9048]), lowing (2), obeying (2 [+9048, 928]), response (2), shout (2), shouts (2), shouts of joy (2 [+8262]), sound (2 [+6702]), sounding (2), speech (2), thunder (2 [+5989]), thunderstorm (2 [+2613]), what say (2), what saying (2), what says (2), words (2), acclamation (1), agreed with (1 [+9048, 4200]), aloud (1 [+928]), aloud (1 [+928, 1524]), argue (1 [+9048]), began (1 [+5951, 906]), blast (1 [+8795]), bleating (1), call out (1 [+7924]), calling (1 [+7924]), clamor (1), clatter (1 [+8323]), command (1), cooing (1), crack (1), cried out (1), cried out for help (1 [+7590]), cries of anguish (1 [+7591]), cry aloud (1 [+5989]), cry for help (1 [+2410]), cry for help (1 [+8776]), cry out (1 [+7412]), cry out (1 [+2411]), diligently obey (1 [+9048, 928, 9048]), disobedience (1 [+4202, 9048, 928]), disobey (1 [+1194, 9048, 928]), gave in (1 [+9048, 928]), give a hearing (1 [+263]), growl (1), growl (1 [+5989]), growled (1 [+5989]), hear (1 [+263]), hear (1 [+9048]), heard (1 [+7992, 928]), hears (1 [+9048, 9048]), hiss (1), hooting (1), it[s] (1 [+3276]), listen (1 [+9048]), listen carefully (1 [+9048, 928]), loudly (1 [+5951]), loudly (1 [+928, 1524]), music (1), neighing (1 [+5177]), news (1), noise (1 [+2159]), noisy din (1 [+1524]), obey (1 [+9048, 4200]), obey fully (1 [+9048, 928, 9048]), obeys (1 [+9048, 928]), outcry (1 [+7591]), rebuke (1), resound (1), roared (1 [+5989]), roaring (1 [+8614]), roars (1 [+5989, 928]), say (1), scream for help (1 [+8123, 2256, 7924]), screamed (1 [+7924, 928, 1524]), screamed for help (1 [+8123, 2256, 7924]), shout (1 [+8123]), shout (1 [+7924, 928]), shout (1 [+7924, 1524]), shouted (1 [+7924, 928]), shouted (1 [+5951, 2256, 7924]), shouted (1 [+8123, 928, 9558]), shouting (1 [+9558]), sing (1 [+5989]), sound (1 [+8123]), sound (1 [+9048, 928]), speaking (1 [+1821]), taunts (1), thunders (1 [+5989, 928]), tumult (1 [+2167]), tune (1), uproar (1), uproar (1 [+2162]), uproar (1 [+9558]), very (1), war cry (1), weeping (1), wept so loudly (1 [+1140, 5989, 906, 928]), what[s] (1), what[s] (1 [+1821]), what have to say (1), what said (1), what said (1 [+1821]), whisper (1 [+1960]), NDT (24)

H7755 קוֹלָיָה ***qôlāyâ***, n.pr.m. [2] [√ 7754?]. Kolaiah, "*Yahweh's voice*":– Kolaiah (2)

H7756 קוּם ***qûm***, v. [627] [→ 3685, 3691, 5226, 7757, 7758, 7799, 7800, 7850, 9538, 9539; 10624; *also used with compound proper names*]. [Q] to get up, arise, stand, establish; [P] to establish, confirm, restore; [Pol] to raise up; [H] to set up, establish, restore; [Ho] to be set up, be raised up; [Htpol] to raise up against:– got up (50), rise (29), get up (25), rise up (24), arise (22), set up (17), stand (16), rose (15), establish (13), raise up (12), fulfill (11), set out (11), come (9), go (9), raised up (9), stand up (9), at once (8), established (8), rose up (8), stood up (8), restore (7), foes (5), stood (5), arose (4), attacking (4), confirm (4), erected (4), keep (4), prepared (4), carried out (3), confirms (3), endure (3), enemies (3), help up (3), kept (3), left (3 [+4946]), now (3), proceeded (3), rises up (3), standing (3), up (3), adversaries (2), begin (2), build (2), came (2), changed (2 [+7756]), confirmed (2), decreed (2), deeded (2), fulfilled (2), fully accomplishes (2 [+6913, 2256]), get it to its feet (2 [+7756]), get ready (2), got ready (2), hurry (2), keep (2 [+7756]), maintain (2), place (2), raise (2), raises (2), raising up (2), rise to power (2), risen up (2), rises (2), rouse (2), set (2), start (2), stepped forward (2), succeeded (2 [+9393]), supported (2), surely stand (2 [+7756]), survive (2), accomplish (1), accuses (1 [+4200, 2021, 5477]), adversary (1), all right do it[s] (1), appear (1), appears (1), appointed (1), arise and come (1), arisen (1), assaults (1 [+6584]), attack (1), attack (1 [+448]), attacked (1 [+448]), attacked (1 [+6584]), attacks (1), attacks (1 [+6584]), be (1), become (1), been kept (1), began (1), belong (1), binding (1), break out (1), brighter (1), bring (1), came out (1), came to power (1), carries out (1), carry on (1), carry on (1 [+6584]), carry out (1), come forward (1), come on (1), come out (1), confirming (1), confronted (1 [+6584]), confronts (1), convict (1), crept up (1), do[s] (1), done (1), endures (1), erect (1), establish the custom (1), exalted (1), failed (1), failed (1 [+4202, 6388]), final (1), follow (1 [+339]), follow (1 [+4946, 339]), followed (1 [+339]), gave (1), get away (1), gets up (1), go up (1), gone (1), grew up (1), happen (1), has effect (1), have (1), heaped up (1), hold (1), hurried (1), in rebellion (1), in turn (1), incited (1), left (1), left (1 [+4946, 9348]), lift up (1), made (1), make good (1), makes rise (1), move about (1 [+4946, 9393]), moved (1), moved out (1), obeyed (1 [+3869]), opposed (1), piled up (1), prevails (1), provide (1), raised (1), rebelled (1), remain (1), remains (1), revolt (1), revolted (1), risen (1), send (1), set to work (1), setting up (1), sit up (1), soon (1), started (1), station (1), stilled (1), stir up (1), stood ground (1), strengthen (1), succeed (1), surged forward (1), take place (1), takes the stand (1 [+928]), turned (1), undertakes (1), uphold (1), was set up (1), went (1), went in (1), went out (1), went to work (1), withdrew (1), withstand (1), NDT (63)

H7757 קוֹמָה ***qômâ***, n.f. [44] [√ 7756]. height:– high (28), height (2), tallest (2), deep (1), diameter (1), height (1 [+1469]), higher (1), length (1), lengths (1), lofty trees (1 [+8123]), low (1 [+9166]), on high (1), on high (1 [+928]), stature (1), towered (1 [+1467, 928, 2256, 5989, 7550])

H7758 קוֹמְמִיּוּת ***qômᵉmiyyût***, n.f. [1] [√ 7756]. (adv.) with head held high:– with heads held high (1)

H7759 קוֹנֵן ***qônēn***, var. Not used in NIVEBC [cf. 7801]. see 7801

H7760 קוֹעַ ***qôaʿ***, n.pr.g. [1] [cf. 8778]. Koa:– Koa (1)

H7761 קוֹף ***qôp***, n.[m.] [2] ape:– apes (2)

H7762 [1]קוּץ ***qûṣ[1]***, v. [8] [→ 7764?; cf. 7752, 9210]. [Q] to detest, be disgusted, loathe:– dread (2), abhorred (1), detest (1), disgusted (1), filled with dread (1), hostile (1), resent (1)

H7763 [2]קוּץ ***qûṣ[2]***, v. [1] [H] to tear apart:– tear apart (1)

H7764 [1]קוֹץ ***qôṣ[1]***, n.m. [12] [→ 2212?, 7766?; cf. 7762?]. thorns, thornbush:– thorns (10), thornbushes (2)

H7765 [2]קוֹץ ***qôṣ[2]***, n.pr.m. Not used in NIVEBC [√ 7916; cf. 7891]. shreds of a wick

H7766 [3]קוֹץ ***qôṣ[3]***, n.pr.m. [1] [√ 7764?]. Koz, "*thorn*":– Koz (1)

H7767 קְוֻצּוֹת ***qᵉwuṣṣôt***, n.f.pl. [2] (locks) of hair:– hair (2)

H7768 קַוְקָו ***qawqāw***, n.[m.] Not used in NIVEBC [cf. 7743]. power, suppleness, strange speech

H7769 [1]קוּר ***qûr[1]***, v. [2] [→ 5227, 7981?]. [Q] to dig (a well or water hole):– dug wells (2)

H7770 [2]קוּר ***qûr[2]***, n.m. [2] thread (of a spider cobweb):– cobwebs (1), web (1)

H7771 קוֹרָה ***qôrâ***, n.f. [6] [√ 7939]. beam, pole, roof beams, tree:– beams (1), ceiling (1), ceiling beams (1), pole (1), roof (1), tree (1)

H7772 קוּשׁ ***qûš***, v. [1] [cf. 3704, 5943]. [Q] to set a snare:– ensnare (1)

H7773 קוּשָׁיָהוּ ***qûšāyāhû***, n.pr.m. [1] [cf. 7823]. Kushaiah:– Kushaiah (1)

H7774 קָה ***qāh***, n.[m.] willow

H7775 קָט ***qāṭ***, pt. [1] little; soon (with 3869 & 5071):– soon (1 [+3869, 5071])

H7776 קֶטֶב ***qeṭeb***, n.m. [4] plague, destruction:– plague (2), destruction (1), destructive (1)

H7777 קְטוֹרָה ***qᵉṭôrâ***, n.m. [1] [√ 7787]. smoke (of sacrifice):– incense (1)

H7778 קְטוּרָה ***qᵉṭûrâ***, n.pr.f. [4] [√ 7787]. Keturah, "*incense, scented one*":– Keturah (4)

H7779 קָטַל ***qāṭal***, v. [3] [→ 7780; 10625]. [Q] to slay, kill:– slay (2), kills (1)

H7780 קֶטֶל ***qeṭel***, n.[m.] [1] [√ 7779]. slaughter:– slaughter (1)

H7781 [1]קָטֹן ***qāṭōn[1]***, v. [4] [→ 7782, 7783, 7784, 7785]. [Q] to be unworthy, not enough, trifling; [H] to make a (measure) small:– not enough (1), not enough (1 [+6388]), skimping (1), unworthy (1)

H7782 קֹטֶן ***qōṭen***, n.m. [2] [√ 7781]. little finger; possibly a euphemism for penis:– little finger (2)

H7783 [1]קָטָן ***qāṭān[1]***, a. [47] [→ 2214, 7784; cf. 7781]. small (in size); few (in quantity); by extension, of status: lesser, insignificant; of age: young(est):– small (12), least (9), younger (8), young (4), youngest (4), little (3), boy (1 [+5853]), boys (1 [+5853]), lesser (1), light (1), low (1), lower (1), smallest (1)

H7784 [2]קָטָן ***qāṭān[2]***, n.pr.m. Not used in NIVEBC [√ 7783; cf. 7781]. Katan, see 2214, "*small one*"

H7785 [2]קָטֹן ***qāṭōn[2]***, a. [54] [√ 7781]. small (in size); by extension, of status: least, insignificant; of age: young(est):– small (14), youngest (14), least (7), young (7), little (3), younger (3), simple (2), at all (1 [+2256, 1524]), at all (1 [+196, 1524]), brief (1), lesser (1)

H7786 קָטַף ***qāṭap***, v. [5] [Q] to pick off (grain), break off (twigs); [N] to be picked off:– break off (1), broke off (1), gathered (1), pick (1), uncut (1 [+4202])

H7787 [1]קָטַר ***qāṭar[1]***, v.den. [114] [→ 5230, 5231, 5232, 5233, 7777, 7778, 7789, 7790, 7792, 7798]. [P] to burn an offering (of incense smoke); [Pu] to be perfumed; [H] to make a burned smoking offering; [Ho] to be burned as an offering:– burn (35), burn incense (18), burned incense (15), burned (12), burning incense (11), burn sacrifices (3), burned sacrifices (3), burned (2 [+7787]), make offerings (2), be burned (1), burn offerings (1), burning (1), burns incense (1), make offering (1), offer (1), offer sacrifices (1), offered up (1), perfumed (1), present (1), presented offerings (1), presenting (1), NDT (1)

H7788 [2]קָטַר ***qāṭar[2]***, v. [1] [√ 7791]. [Qp] to be enclosed:– enclosed (1)

H7789 קִטֵּר ***qiṭṭēr***, n.f. [1] [√ 7787]. incense, often as or accompanying an offering to God:– incense (1)

H7790 קִטְרוֹן ***qiṭrôn***, n.pr.loc. [1] [√ 7787]. Kitron, "*incense, [sacrificial] smoke*":– Kitron (1)

H7791 קְטֻרוֹת ***qᵉṭurôt***, n.[f.pl.] Not used in NIVEBC [√ 7788]. enclosures, see 7788

H7792 קְטֹרֶת ***qᵉṭōret***, n.f. [60] [√ 7787]. incense, smoke offering, its pleasant fragrance symbolic of God's acceptance:– incense (59), offering (1)

H7793 קַטָּת ***qaṭṭāt***, n.pr.loc. [1] Kattath:– Kattath (1)

H7794 [1]קִיא ***qîʾ[1]***, v. [9] [→ 7683, 7795; cf. 7796]. [Q] to vomit; [H] to vomit out, spit out:– vomit (2), vomit out (2), vomited out (2), spit out (1), vomit up (1), vomited (1)

H7795 [2]קִיא ***qîʾ[2]***, n.m. [3] [√ 7794]. vomit:– vomit (3)

H7796 קָיָה ***qāyâ***, v. Not used in NIVEBC [cf. 7794]. [Q] to vomit

H7797 קַיִט ***qayiṭ***, n.m. Not used in NIVEBC [cf. 7811; 10627]. summer

H7798 קִיטוֹר ***qîṭôr***, n.m. [4] [√ 7787]. smoke:– smoke (2), clouds (1), dense smoke (1)

H7799 קִים ***qîm***, n.m. [1] [√ 7756]. foe, adversary:– foes (1)

H7800 קִימָה ***qîmâ***, n.f. [1] [√ 7756]. standing up:– standing (1)

H7801 קִין ***qîn***, v.den. [8] [→ 7806; cf. 7759]. [Pol] to chant a lament, sing a dirge:– chant (3), composed laments (1), sang lament (1), take up a lament (1), took up lament (1 [+7806]), wailing (1)

H7802 [1]קַיִן ***qayin[1]***, n.[m.] [1] spearhead, spear:– spearhead (1)

H7803 [2]קַיִן ***qayin[2]***, n.pr.m. [16] [→ 7804?, 7808, 7809, 9340; cf. 7864, 7865]. Cain, "*metal worker; brought forth, acquired* [Ge 4:1]":– Cain (16)

H7804 [3]קַיִן ***qayin[3]***, n.pr.g. [2] [→ 7808, 7803?]. Kenite, "*metal workers*":– Kenites (2)

H7805 [4]קַיִן ***qayin[4]***, n.pr.loc. [1] [√ 7803]. Kain, "*place of metal workers [?]*":– Kain (1)

H7806 [1]קִינָה ***qînâ[1]***, n.f. [18] [√ 7801]. lament, mourning song, dirge:– lament (13), laments (2), mourn (1 [+5951]), took up lament (1 [+7801]), weeping (1)

H7807 [2]קִינָה ***qînâ[2]***, n.pr.loc. [1] Kinah, "*lament, dirge*":– Kinah (1)

H7808 קֵינִי ***qênî***, a.g. [12] [√ 7804; cf. 7803]. Kenite:– Kenites (7), Kenite (5)

H7809 קֵינָן ***qênān***, n.pr.m. [6] [√ 7803]. Kenan:– Kenan (6)

H7810 קִיץ ***qîṣ***, v. [23] [→ 7811; cf. 3699]. [Q] to pass the summer; [H] to rouse, awaken:– awake (7), wake up (4), awakens (2), rouse (2), all summer (1), awakened (1), awakes (1), awoke (1), come to life (1), rise (1), roused (1), wake (1)

H7811 קַיִץ ***qayiṣ***, n.m. [20] [√ 7810; cf. 7797; 10627]. summer; by extension, summer fruit, ripe fruit:– summer (10), summer fruit (3), ripe fruit (2), ripened fruit (2), cakes of figs (1), fruit (1), harvest (1)

H7812 קִיצוֹן ***qîṣôn***, a. [4] [√ 7891]. end, outermost:– end (4)

H7813 קִיקָיוֹן ***qîqāyôn***, n.m. [5] caster-oil vine; some sources: cucumber plant:– plant (4), leafy plant (1)

H7814 קִיקָלוֹן ***qîqālôn***, n.[m.] [1] [√ 7837]. disgrace:– disgrace (1)

H7815 [1]קִיר ***qîr[1]***, n.m. [74] [→ 7816, 7817; cf. 7984; *also used with compound proper names*]. wall (of a building or city); by extension, any surface of a construction: side, ceiling, surface; one who "urinates on a wall" is male:– wall (38), walls (16), every last male (3 [+8874, 928]), male (3 [+8874, 928]), sides (3), side (2), agony (1), ceiling (1), city (1), it[s] (1 [+2021]), roof (1), stonemasons (1 [+3093]), stonemasons (1 [+3093, 74]), NDT (2)

H7816 [2]קִיר ***qîr[2]***, n.pr.loc. [1] [√ 7815]. Kir, "*walled enclosure*":– Kir (1)

H7817 [3]קִיר ***qîr[3]***, n.pr.loc. [4] [√ 7815]. Kir, "*walled enclosure*":– Kir (4)

H7818 קִיר-חֶרֶשׂ ***qîr-ḥereś***, n.pr.loc. [3] [√ 7815 + 3084]. Kir Hareseth, "*walled [city] of pottery fragments*":– Kir Hareseth (3)

H7819 קִיר חֲרֶשֶׂת ***qîr ḥᵃreśet***, n.pr.loc. [2] [√ 7815 + 3084]. Kir Hareseth, "*walled [city] of pottery fragments*":– Kir Hareseth (2)

H7820 קֵירֹס ***qêrōs***, n.pr.m. [2] Keros:– Keros (2)

H7821 קִישׁ ***qîš***, n.pr.m. [21] Kish, "*bow, power*":– Kish (21)

H7822 קִישׁוֹן ***qîšôn***, n.pr.loc. [6] Kishon, "*cunning*":– Kishon (6)

H7823 קִישִׁי ***qîšî***, n.pr.m. [1] [cf. 7773]. Kishi, "[poss.] *gift; snarer*":– Kishi (1)

H7824 קַל ***qal***, a. [13] [√ 7837]. fleet-footed, swift, speedy:– swift (7), fleet-footed (2 [+928, 8079]), foam (1), speedily (1), swifter (1), swiftly (1)

H7825 [1]קֹלִי ***qōl[1]***, n.[m.] [1] [√ 7837]. lightness, (i.e., frivolity or light-heartedness):– little (1)

H7826 [2]קֹל ***qōl[2]***, n.m. Not used in NIVEBC [√ 7754]. voice, see 7754

H7827 קָלַה ***qālah***, v.den. Not used in NIVEBC [√ 7736]. see 7735

H7828 [1]קָלָה ***qālâ[1]***, v. [4] [→ 7833]. [Q] to burn; [Qp] to be roasted; [N] to have a burning sensation:– burned (1), roasted (1), roasted grain (1), searing pain (1)

H7829 [2]קָלָה ***qālâ[2]***, v. [7] [→ 7830; cf. 7837]. [N] to lightly esteemed, to be a nobody, be degraded; [H] to dishonor, treat with contempt:– be a nobody (1), be degraded (1), be despised (1), dishonors (1), little known (1), nobody (1), small (1)

H7830 קָלוֹן ***qālôn***, n.m. [17] [√ 7829]. shame, disgrace, dishonor:– shame (9), disgrace (3), insults (2), disgraceful (1), insult (1), shameful ways (1)

H7831 קַלַּחַת ***qallaḥat***, n.f. [2] caldron, (cooking) pot:– caldron (1), pot (1)

H7832 קָלַט ***qālaṭ***, v. [1] [→ 5236, 7836]. [Qp] to be stunted:– stunted (1)

H7833 קָלִי ***qālî***, n.m. [5] [√ 7828]. roasted grain, parched grain:– roasted grain (4), roasted (1)

H7834 קַלָּי **qallāy**, n.pr.m. [1] Kallai, *"swift"*:– Kallai (1)

H7835 קֵלָיָה **qēlāyâ**, n.pr.m. [1] Kelaiah, "[perhaps] *Yahweh has dishonored*":– Kelaiah (1)

H7836 קְלִיטָא **qᵉlîṭā'**, n.pr.m. [3] [√ 7832]. Kelita:– Kelita (3)

H7837 קָלַל **qālal**, v. [81] [→ 7814, 7824, 7825, 7838, 7839, 7848; cf. 7829]. [Q] to recede, grow smaller; to be vile, to disdain, despise; to be swift; [N] to be trivial, insignificant; to be swift; [P] to curse, blaspheme, revile; [Pu] to be accursed; [H] to lighten; to humble; to treat with contempt; [Htpal] to be shaken:– curse (12), cursed (8), curses (7), lighten (5), swifter (5), cursing (3), make lighter (3), blasphemer (2), not serious (2), receded (2), be considered accursed (1), become undignified (1), blaspheme (1), blasphemed (1), call a curse down (1), called curses down (1), called down a curse (1), called down curses (1 [+7839]), cast lots (1), comes easily (1), considered trivial (1), despise (1 [+928, 6524]), despises (1 [+928, 6524]), disdained (1), easy (1), humble (1), humbled (1), is cursed (1), lift (1), pronounce a curse on (1), put a curse on (1), revile (1), simple (1), small (1), swaying (1), swift (1), treat with contempt (1), treated with contempt (1), trivial (1), unsharpened (1 [+4202]), unworthy (1), vile (1)

H7838 קָלָל **qālāl**, a. [2] [√ 7837]. burnished, polished:– burnished (2)

H7839 קְלָלָה **qᵉlālâ**, n.f. [33] [√ 7837]. curse, condemnation:– curse (23), curses (7), called down curses (1 [+7837]), cursing (1), pronounce curses (1)

H7840 קָלַס **qālas**, v. [4] [→ 7841, 7842]. [P] to scorn; [Ht] to make fun of:– mock (2), jeered (1), scorned (1)

H7841 קֶלֶס **qeles**, n.[m.] [3] [√ 7840]. derision, reproach:– derision (2), reproach (1)

H7842 קַלָּסָה **qallāsâ**, n.f. [1] [√ 7840]. laughingstock, object of derision:– laughingstock (1)

H7843 קָלַע **qāla'**[1], v. [4] [√ 7845]. [Q, P] to hurl a stone (from a sling):– hurl away (1), hurl out (1), sling (1), slung (1)

H7844 [2]קָלַע **qāla'**[2], v. [3] [→ 5237, 7846]. [Q] to carve:– carved (2 [+5237]), carved (1)

H7845 קֶלַע **qela'**[1], n.[m.] [6] [→ 7843, 7847]. sling (a weapon):– sling (3), slingstones (3 [+74])

H7846 [2]קֶלַע **qela'**[2], n.[m.] [15] [√ 7844]. curtains:– curtains (15)

H7847 קַלָּע **qallā'**, n.m. [1] [√ 7845]. slinger (one who uses a sling):– men armed with slings (1)

H7848 קְלֹקֵל **qᵉlōqēl**, a. [1] [√ 7837]. miserable (food), starvation (rations):– miserable (1)

H7849 קִלְּשׁוֹן **qillᵉšôn**, n.[m.] [1] (sharp pointed, three-pronged) fork:– forks (1)

H7850 קָמָה **qāmâ**, n.f. [10] [√ 7756]. standing grain:– standing grain (6), grows up (2), grainfield (1), stalk (1)

H7851 קְמוּאֵל **qᵉmû'ēl**, n.pr.m. [3] [√ 7756 + 446]. Kemuel, *"God's [El's] mound"*:– Kemuel (3)

H7852 קָמוֹן **qāmôn**, n.pr.loc. [1] Kamon:– Kamon (1)

H7853 קִמּוֹשׂ **qimmôś**, n.m. [3] thorns, nettles, briers (weeds of all kinds):– briers (1), nettles (1), thorns (1)

H7854 קֶמַח **qemaḥ**, n.[m.] [14] flour:– flour (13), meal (1)

H7855 קָמַט **qāmaṭ**, v. [2] [Q] to seize; [Pu] to be seized:– shriveled up (1), were carried off (1)

H7856 קָמַי **qāmāy**, n.pr.loc. Not used in NIVEBC [→ 4214]. Kamai, see 4214

H7857 קָמַל **qāmal**, v. [2] [Q] to wither:– wither (1), withers (1)

H7858 קָמַץ **qāmaṣ**, v. [3] [→ 7859]. [Q] to take a handful:– take a handful (2 [+4850, 7859]), take a handful (1)

H7859 קֹמֶץ **qōmeṣ**, n.[m.] [4] [√ 7858]. handful; (pl.) abundance:– take a handful (2 [+7858, 4850]), handful (1), plentifully (1 [+4200])

H7860 קֵן **qēn**, n.m. [13] [√ 7873]. nest:– nest (11), house (1), rooms (1)

H7861 קָנָא **qānā'**, v.den. [34] [→ 7862, 7863, 7868]. [P] (of negative attitude) to be jealous, be envious; (of positive attitude) to be zealous:– jealous (5), envy (4), very zealous (4 [+7861]), envious (3), suspects (3), zealous (3), envied (2), jealous (2 [+7863]), made jealous (2), aroused jealousy (1), jealousy (1), make envious (1), provokes to jealousy (1), stirred up jealous anger (1), zeal (1)

H7862 קַנָּא **qannā'**, a. [6] [→ 7868; cf. 7861]. jealous; an adjective or title used exclusively of God, focusing on his desire for exclusive relationships:– jealous (6)

H7863 קִנְאָה **qin'â**, n.f. [43] [√ 7861]. jealousy, envy, zeal:– jealousy (15), zeal (15), jealous anger (4), envy (3), jealous (2 [+7861]), am[S] (1), jealous (1), jealous (1 [+8120, 6296, 6584]), NDT (1)

H7864 [1]קָנָה **qānâ**[1], v. [77] [→ 5238, 5239, 5240, 7871; cf. 7803, 7865; 10632]. [Q] to buy, acquire, get; [N] to be bought:– buy (21), bought (19), buyer (6), get (6), be bought (2), insist on paying (2 [+7864]), purchase (2), purchased (2), acquire (1), acquire (1 [+907]), acquired (1), acquires (1), bought (1 [+928, 2021, 4084]), bought back (1), buyers (1), buying (1), buys (1 [+7871]), gains (1), get (1 [+1047]), gets (1), insist on paying for (1 [+928, 4697, 7864]), insist on paying for (1 [+7864, 928, 4697]), master (1), reclaim (1), taken (1)

H7865 [2]קָנָה **qānâ**[2], v. [6] [→ 555; cf. 7803, 7864]. [Q] to create, bring forth; (as a title of God) Creator:– creator (3), brought forth (2), created (1)

H7866 קָנֶה **qāneh**, n.m. [57] [→ 7867]. branch, rod; (calamus) reed, stalk, shaft, cane; by extension: a measure of length, variously reckoned:– rod (12), branches (10), reed (5), branch (4), calamus (4), reeds (4), shaft (2), stalk (2), fragrant calamus (1), joint (1), measuring rod (1), scales (1), NDT (10)

H7867 קָנָה **qānâ**[3], n.pr.loc. [3] [√ 7866]. Kanah, *"reed"*:– Kanah (3)

H7868 קַנּוֹא **qannô'**, a. [2] [√ 7862; cf. 7861]. jealous:– jealous (2)

H7869 קְנַז **qᵉnaz**, n.pr.m. [11] [→ 7870]. Kenaz, *"hunting"*:– Kenaz (11)

H7870 קְנִזִּי **qᵉnizzî**, a.g. [4] [√ 7869]. Kenizzite:– Kenizzite (3), Kenizzites (1)

H7871 קִנְיָן **qinyān**, n.[m.] [11] [√ 7864]. goods, property, possessions:– goods (3), buys (1 [+7864]), creatures (1), have (1), herds (1), livelihood (1), possessed (1), property (1), NDT (1)

H7872 קִנָּמוֹן **qinnāmôn**, n.m. [3] cinnamon (a spice from the far east):– cinnamon (3)

H7873 קָנַן **qānan**, v.den. [5] [→ 7860]. [P] to make a nest; [Pu] to be nestled, nested:– make nests (1), makes nest (1), nest (1), nested (1), nestled (1)

H7874 קֶנֶץ **qeneṣ**, n.[m.] [1] [cf. 7891]. end, an extension of a snare or net that captures or restrains (not found in the OT):– end (1 [+8492])

H7875 קְנָת **qᵉnāt**, n.pr.loc. [2] Kenath, *"possession"*:– Kenath (2)

H7876 קָסַם **qāsam**, v.den. [20] [→ 5241, 7877]. [Q] to practice divination, be a soothsayer, seek an omen:– diviners (6), divination (2), divinations (2), consult (1), diviner (1), omen (1), practice divination (1 [+7877]), practiced divination (1), practiced divination (1 [+7877]), practices divination (1 [+7877]), seek an omen (1 [+7877]), tell fortunes (1), utter divinations (1)

H7877 קֶסֶם **qesem**, n.[m.] [11] [√ 7876]. divination: pagan practice of determining the future by examining the position of stars, communication with the dead or with spirits, examining animal organs, or casting lots:– divinations (2), divination (1), evil omens (1), fee for divination (1), lot (1), oracle (1), practice divination (1 [+7876]), practiced divination (1 [+7876]), practices divination (1 [+7876]), seek an omen (1 [+7876])

H7878 קָסַס **qāsas**, v. [1] [cf. 7989]. [Pol] to strip off:– stripped (1)

H7879 קֶסֶת **qeset**, n.[f.] [3] writing kit, writing-case:– kit (2), writing kit (1)

H7880 קָעָה **qā'â**, v. Not used in NIVEBC [cf. 1716]. [Q] to cry out

H7881 קְעִילָה **qᵉ'îlâ**, n.pr.loc. [18] Keilah:– Keilah (18)

H7882 קַעֲקַע **qa'ᵃqa'**, n.[m.] [1] tattoo:– tattoo (1)

H7883 קְעָרָה **qᵉ'ārâ**, n.f. [17] [√ 9206]. plate, dish:– plate (13), plates (4)

H7884 קָפָא **qāpā'**, v. [3] [→ 3698, 7885]. [Q, N] to congeal, thicken; [H] to curdle:– complacent (1), congealed (1), curdle (1)

H7885 קִפָּאוֹן **qippā'ôn**, n.[m.] [1] [√ 7884]. frost:– frosty darkness (1)

H7886 קָפַד **qāpad**, v. [1] [→ 7887, 7888; cf. 7889]. [P] to roll up:– rolled up (1)

H7887 קִפֹּד **qippōd**, n.[m.] [3] [√ 7886]. screech owl; some sources: hedgehog:– screech owl (2), owls (1)

H7888 קְפָדָה **qᵉpādâ**, n.[f.] [1] [√ 7886]. terror, anguish:– terror (1)

H7889 קִפּוֹז **qippôz**, n.f. [1] [cf. 7886, 7890]. owl; some sources: tree snake:– owl (1)

H7890 קָפַץ **qāpaṣ**, v. [7] [cf. 7889]. [Q] to draw together, shut; [N] to be gathered up; [P] to bound, leap:– shut (2), bounding (1), gathered up (1), shuts (1), tightfisted (1 [+906, 3338]), withheld (1)

H7891 קֵץ **qēṣ**, n.m. [67] [→ 7812, 7916; cf. 7874, 7915]. end, limit, boundary:– end (40), later (4 [+4946]), after (3 [+4946]), climax (3), remotest (2), afar (1), after (1 [+4200]), after (1 [+4200]), complete (1 [+2118, 4946]), course (1), endless (1 [+401]), every (1 [+4946]), fulfilled (1), later (1 [+4200]), limit (1), once a year (1 [+4946, 3427, 4200, 2021, 3427]), passed (1), prospects (1), some years later (1 [+4200, 9102]), time is ripe (1 [+995])

H7892 קָצַב **qāṣab**, v. [2] [→ 7893]. [Q] to cut off; [Qp] to be shorn, be cut off:– cut (1), sheep just shorn (1)

H7893 קֶצֶב **qeṣeb**, n.m. [3] [√ 7892]. shape, foundation:– shape (2), roots (1)

H7894 קָצָה **qāṣâ**[1], v. [4] [→ 7895, 7896, 7897, 7898, 7899?, 7901, 7921; cf. 7915]. [P] to cut off, reduce; [H] to scrape off:– cutting off (1), reduce size (1), scraped (1), scraped off (1)

H7895 קָצֶה **qāṣeh**, n.[m.] [93] [√ 7894]. end, limit, outskirts, edge:– end (27), ends (16), edge (11), outskirts (5), border (3), mouth (3), other[S] (3), after (2 [+4946]), foot (2), frontier (2), the other[S] (2 [+2021, 824]), delta (1), end (1 [+1473]), entire (1 [+4946]), every part (1), extreme (1), far end (1), farthest (1), most distant land (1), of (1 [+4946]), other (1), other[S] (1 [+9028]), outposts (1 [+2821]), southernmost (1 [+4946]), tip (1), NDT (3)

H7896 קָצָה **qāṣâ**[2], n.f. & m.[pl.] [35] [√ 7894]. end, fringe, edge:– ends (11), corners (9), end (4), all sorts (2), tip (2), all (1), all sorts (1 [+4946]), other[S] (1), outer fringe (1), quarters (1), ruin (1), NDT (1)

H7897 קֵצֶה **qēṣeh**, n.[m.] [5] [√ 7894]. end, boundary, limit:– end (2), boundless (1 [+401]), endless (1 [+401]), number (1)

H7898 קָצוּ **qāṣû**, n.[m.] [3] [√ 7894]. ends, borders (of the earth):– ends (2), borders (1)

H7899 קָצוּץ **qāṣûṣ**, n. *or* v.ptcp. Not used in NIVEBC [√ 7916 *or* 7894]. distant or cut off

H7900 קָצוּר **qāṣûr**, a. *or* v.ptcp. [1] [√ 7918]. narrow, short:– narrower (1)

H7901 קְצוֹת **qᵉṣôt**, n.[m.] Not used in NIVEBC [√ 7894]. end

H7902 קֶצַח **qeṣaḥ**, n.m. [3] caraway, cummin:– caraway (3)

H7903 קָצִין **qāṣîn**, n.m. [12] [→ 6962]. commander, ruler, leader:– commander (4), rulers (3), leader (2), commanders (1), leaders (1), ruler (1)

H7904 [1]קְצִיעָה **qᵉṣî'â**[1], n.f. [1] [√ 7905; cf. 7909]. cassia:– cassia (1)

H7905 [2]קְצִיעָה **qᵉṣî'â**[2], n.pr.f. [1] [√ 7904; cf. 7909]. Keziah, *"cassia [cinnamon]"*:– Keziah (1)

H7906 קְצִיץ **qᵉṣîṣ**, n.pr.loc. Not used in NIVEBC [√ 6681; cf. 7916, 7891]. Keziz

H7907 [1]קָצִיר **qāṣîr**[1], n.m. [49] [√ 7917]. harvest, time of reaping:– harvest (37), harvests (3), harvest time (2), harvesting (2 [+7917]), harvesting grain (1), reap (1 [+7917]), reapers (1), reaping (1), NDT (1)

H7908 [2]קָצִיר **qāṣîr**[2], n.m. [5] [√ 7918?]. branch, bough, twig, shoot:– branches (3), shoots (1), twigs (1)

H7909 קָצַע **qāṣa'**[1], v. [1] [→ 5244, 7904, 7905]. [H] to scrape off:– have scraped (1)

H7910 [2]קָצַע **qāṣa'**[2], v.den. [3] [→ 4553, 5243]. [Pu, Ho] to be made with corners:– corners (3)

H7911 קָצַף **qāṣap**, v. [34] [→ 7912; 10633]. [Q] to be angry; [H] to provoke to anger; [Ht] to be enraged:– angry (23), angered (2), enraged (2), anger (1), angry (1 [+7912]), aroused anger (1), aroused wrath (1), furious (1 [+4394]), made angry (1 [+2118]), very angry (1 [+7912])

H7912 [1]קֶצֶף **qeṣep**[1], n.m. [28] [√ 7911; 10634]. wrath, anger, fury:– wrath (13), anger (7), angry (3), angry (1 [+7911]), discord (1), fury (1), great wrath (1 [+2405, 2256]), very angry (1 [+7911])

H7913 [2]קֶצֶף **qeṣep**[2], n.[m.] [1] [→ 7914]. twig (snapped off):– twig (1)

H7914 קְצָפָה **qᵉṣāpâ**, n.f. [1] [√ 7913]. stump, splintering:– ruined (1 [+4200])

H7915 [1]קָצַץ **qāṣaṣ**[1], v. [11] [cf. 7891, 7894]. [Q] to cut off; [P] to cut off, take away; [Pu] to be cut off, maimed:– cut off (5), cut (1), cut free (1), cut in pieces (1), cut up (1), shatters (1), stripped off (1)

H7916 [2]קָצַץ **qāṣaṣ**[2], v. [3] [→ 7765, 7899?, 7906; cf. 7891]. [H] to come to an end:– distant places (3 [+6991])

H7917 [1]קָצַר **qāṣar**[1], v. [34] [→ 7907]. [Q] to reap, harvest, gather:– reap (15), harvesters (5), harvesting (3), reaper (3), gather (1), gathering (1), harvest (1), reap (1 [+7907]), reaped (1), reapers (1), reaps (1), NDT (1)

H7918 [2]קָצַר **qāṣar**[2], v. [14] [→ 7900, 7908?, 7919, 7920]. [Q] to be short; (by extension) to be impatient, angry; [P] to cut short; [H] to shorten, cut short:– cut short (3), short (2), short (2 [+7918]), bear no longer (1), grew weary (1), impatient (1), impatient (1 [+5883]), impatient (1 [+8120]), sick (1), too short (1)

H7919 קֹצֶר **qōṣer**, n.[m.] [1] [√ 7918]. discouragement, despondency, an extension of shortness or lack (of spirit):– discouragement (1 [+8120])

H7920 קָצֵר **qāṣēr**, a. [5] [√ 7918]. shortened: quick-tempered, impatient:– drained (2), few (1), quick-tempered (1 [+678]), quick-tempered (1 [+8120])

H7921 קְצָת **qᵉṣāt**, n.f. [7] [√ 7894; 10636]. end, extremity:– end (2), after (1 [+4946]), corners (1), some (1 [+4946]), some (1 [+4946]), whole earth (1 [+3782])

H7922 קַר ***qar***, a. [3] [√ 7981]. cool, cold (water); cool-headed, even-tempered (of one's spirit):– cold (1), cool (1), even-tempered (1 [+8120])

H7923 קֹר ***qōr***, n.[m.] [1] [√ 7981]. cold:– cold (1)

H7924 ¹קָרָא ***qārā'¹***, v. [733] [→ 5246, 7926, 7927, 7951, 7952; 10637]. [Q] to call, summon, announce, proclaim; [Qp] to be invited as a guest, be appointed; [N] to be called, be summoned; [Pu] to be called; "to call on the name of the LORD" means to proclaim or praise the excellence of Yahweh, to worship Yahweh, or to summon Yahweh by name for help:– called (138), call (76), named (60), summoned (46), read (33), called (26 [+9005]), proclaim (23), summon (18), be called (14), calls (14), invited (12), proclaimed (12), called out (11), calling (11), cried out (11), bears (10 [+6584]), invite (8), call on (7), call out (7), cry out (7), gave (7), call (6 [+9005]), shouted (6), cry (5), is called (5), proclaiming (5), sent for (5 [+8938, 2256, 4200]), bear (4 [+6584]), called together (4), name (4), proclaim (4 [+928]), summons (4), are called (3), called out (3 [+928, 7754, 1524]), guests (3), sent for (3 [+8938, 2256]), was called (3), announced (2), asks (2), be called (2 [+9005]), be known as (2), be reckoned (2), call in (2), chosen (2 [+928, 9005]), famous (2 [+9005]), gave name (2), read aloud (2), say (2), summoned (2 [+8938, 2256]), were summoned (2), announce (1), appeal (1), be mentioned (1), be named (1 [+9005]), been called (1), been invited as guests (1), been named (1 [+9005]), being called (1), being summoned (1), bleat (1), blurts out (1), brag (1), bring out (1), call back (1), call for help (1), call out (1 [+7754]), call yourselves (1), called down (1), called in (1), calling (1 [+7754]), calling (1 [+9005]), calling down (1), calling for help (1), calling forth (1), calling out (1), calls forth (1), calls in (1), claim (1), convocations (1 [+5246]), cried (1), cries out (1), declared (1), decreed (1), dictated (1 [+4946, 7023]), did[s] (1), exclaim (1), foretold (1), gave the name (1), get (1), give (1), given (1), got (1), grasping (1), herald (1), invitation (1), invite (1 [+8938, 2256]), invoke (1 [+928, 7023]), is called (1 [+9005]), is called together (1), known as (1), make an offer (1), make proclamation (1), men of high rank (1), name (1 [+9005]), named (1 [+928, 9005]), offer (1), pray (1), prayed (1), preach (1), proclaimed (1 [+928]), pronounced (1), raised a cry (1), reading (1), scream for help (1 [+8123, 7754, 2256]), screamed (1 [+928, 7754, 1524]), screamed for help (1 [+8123, 7754, 2256]), sent for (1 [+8938, 4200]), sent word (1 [+8938, 2256]), shout (1), shout (1 [+928, 7754]), shout (1 [+7754, 1524]), shout aloud (1 [+928, 1744]), shouted (1 [+928, 7754]), shouted (1 [+5951, 7754, 2256]), shouted the news (1), summoned (1 [+8938, 4200]), voices (1), was called (1 [+9005]), was read aloud (1), were appointed (1), were called (1), were counted (1), were invited (1), word (1), NDT (5)

H7925 ²קָרָא ***qārā'²***, v. [138] [cf. 7936]. [Q] to meet, encounter, happen; [N] to have met, have happened, [H] to cause to happen:– meet (77), against (13), met (5), happened (4), toward (3), attack (2), came toward (2), come upon (2), follows (2), meet in battle (2), oppose (2), breaks out (1), brought on (1), come (1), come across (1 [+4200, 7156]), comes (1), confront (1 [+5893, 4200]), facing each other (1 [+5120]), fall on (1), fight (1), follows (1 [+6584]), greet (1 [+1385]), happen (1), happened to be (1 [+7936]), help (1), into (1), opposite (1), out came to meet (1), resort to (1 [+2143, 4200]), seized (1), wage (1), welcomed (1), went to meet (1), NDT (2)

H7926 ¹קֹרֵא ***qōrē'¹***, n.m. [2] [→ 7927; cf. 7924]. partridge:– partridge (2)

H7927 ²קֹרֵא ***qōrē'²***, n.pr.m. [3] [√ 7926; cf. 7924]. Kore, "*proclaimer*":– Kore (3)

H7928 קָרַב ***qārab***, v. [280] [→ 6832, 7929, 7930, 7932, 7933, 7934, 7940; 10638]. [Q] to come near, approach; [N] to present oneself, be brought near; [P] to bring near, approach; [H] to bring near, offer, present:– present (38), bring (36), offer (26), brought (15), come (10), come near (10), presented (10), approached (8), go near (7), brings (6), came (6), near (6), approach (5), offered (5), brought forward (4), had come forward (4), went (4), bring near (3), came forward (3), came near (3), come forward (3), drew near (3), offers (3), about (2), acceptable (2), advance (2), brought near (2), come here (2), draw near (2), join (2), made an offering (2), offering (2), presenting (2), sacrificed (2), add (1), appear (1), approaches (1), approaching (1), bring forward (1), bringing (1), bringing near (1), brought offering (1), brought to a close (1), came together (1), cause to come near (1), closer (1), come closer (1), comes (1), comes near (1), encroach (1), go (1), gone near (1), have brought (1), have come near (1), have sexual relations with (1 [+448]), inquire of (1 [+448]), joined (1), keep away (1 [+448, 3870]), made love to (1 [+448]), made offerings (1), march up (1), meet (1), offer sacrifices (1), offer up (1), present yourselves (1), presents (1), reach (1), reached (1), soon (1), stood (1), take part (1 [+6913]), went near (1), NDT (2)

H7929 קָרֵב ***qārēb***, a.vbl. [12] [√ 7928]. approaching, coming near:– approaches (2), draw near (2), even comes near (2 [+7929]), approached (1), came (1), closer (1), closer and closer (1 [+2143, 2256]), comes near (1), going (1)

H7930 קְרָב ***qerāb***, n.[m.] [9] [→ 6832; cf. 7928; 10639]. war, battle:– war (5), battle (4)

H7931 קֶרֶב ***qereb***, n.[m.] [224] inner parts; by extension: heart or mind as the seat of thought and emotion; interior, midst; (pp.) among, in the midst of:– among (68), in (24 [+928]), within (19 [+928]), from (16 [+4946]), internal organs (16), with (11 [+928]), midst (6), among (4 [+4946]), on (4 [+928]), heart (3), hearts (3), near (3 [+928]), them[s] (3 [+2021]), through (3 [+928]), inmost being (2), to (2 [+6584]), along with (1 [+928]), at (1 [+928]), ate (1 [+995, 448]), become allies (1 [+2118, 928]), body (1), conduct the affairs (1 [+2143, 928]), done so[s] (1 [+995, 448]), entering (1 [+995, 928]), filled with (1 [+928]), folds (1), had (1 [+928]), harbor (1 [+4328, 928]), herself (1 [+2023]), in (1 [+4946]), inside (1 [+928]), into (1 [+928]), lose heart (1 [+1327, 8120, 928]), middle (1), mind (1), minds (1), out of (1 [+4946]), presence (1), ranks (1), stomach (1), there[s] (1 [+928, 2257]), thick (1), throughout (1 [+928]), upon (1 [+928]), within very walls (1 [+928]), NDT (8)

H7932 קִרְבָה ***qirbâ***, n.f. [2] [√ 7928]. nearness, approach:– come near (1), near (1)

H7933 קָרְבָּן ***qorbān***, n.m. [79] [√ 7928]. gift, offering, sacrifice:– offering (56), offerings (7), gifts (2), offer (2), food offering (1 [+852]), food offerings (1 [+852]), gift (1), its[s] (1 [+2257]), offered (1), sacrifice (1), NDT (6)

H7934 קֻרְבָּן ***qurbān***, n.[m.] [2] [√ 7928]. contribution, supply (of wood):– contribution (1), contributions (1)

H7935 קַרְדֹּם ***qardōm***, n.[m.] [5] ax; some sources: adze:– axes (4), ax (1)

H7936 קָרָה ***qārâ¹***, v. [27] [→ 3703, 5247, 7937, 7950; cf. 7925]. [Q] to happen, meet, encounter; [N] to meet with, have happen; [P] to make beams, build beams; [H] to give success, to select oneself:– met (4), happen (3), happened (3), laid beams (2), as it turned out (1 [+5247]), beams (1), come (1), come true (1), comes (1), gave success (1), happened to be (1 [+7925]), lays beams (1), make beams (1), make successful (1), meet (1), overtake (1), overtakes (1), punished (1 [+6411]), select (1)

H7937 קָרֶה ***qāreh***, n.[m.] [1] [√ 7936]. emission (at night):– emission (1)

H7938 ¹קָרָה ***qārâ²***, n.f. [6] [√ 7981]. cold:– cold (5), icy blast (1)

H7939 ²קָרָה ***qārâ³***, v.den. Not used in NIVEBC [→ 5248, 7771]. [P] to lay the beams of

H7940 קָרוֹב ***qārôb***, a. [77] [√ 7928]. near, close:– near (38), nearest (5), neighbors (3), approach (2), close (2), closely related (2), warriors (2), about to (1 [+6964, 4946]), always (1), at hand (1 [+995]), at hand (1 [+4200, 995]), brief (1 [+4946]), close at hand (1), close relative (1), close relative (1 [+8638]), close to (1 [+725]), close to heart (1), closely associated (1), closest (1), come near (1), dependent (1), invites (1), nearby (1), nearby (1 [+4946]), neighbor (1), others (1), recently (1 [+928]), recently (1 [+2543, 4946]), relatives (1), shorter (1)

H7941 קָרוּת ***qārût***, n.f. Not used in NIVEBC [√ 7981]. cold, see 7938

H7942 קָרַח ***qāraḥ***, v. [5] [→ 7944, 7945, 7946, 7947, 7948, 7949]. [Q] to shave, make bald; [N] to shave oneself, make oneself bald; [H] to shave another, make bald; [Ho] to be rubbed bare, be make bald:– must shave (1 [+7947]), shave head (1), shave head (1 [+1605]), shave heads (1 [+7947]), was rubbed bare (1)

H7943 קֶרַח ***qeraḥ***, n.m. [7] ice, frost, hail:– ice (3), cold (1), crystal (1), frost (1), hail (1)

H7944 קֵרֵחַ ***qērēaḥ***, a. [3] [√ 7942]. bald, bald-headed:– baldy (2), bald (1)

H7945 קָרֵחַ ***qārēaḥ***, n.pr.m. [14] [√ 7942]. Kareah, "*bald head*":– Kareah (14)

H7946 קֹרַח ***qōraḥ***, n.pr.m. [37] [→ 7948; cf. 7942]. Korah, "*shaven, bald*":– Korah (35), Korah's (2)

H7947 קָרְחָה ***qorḥâ***, n.f. [11] [√ 7942]. baldness, shaving the head:– shaved (3), baldness (1), make bald (1 [+8143]), must shave (1 [+7942]), shave (1 [+6584]), shave (1 [+8492]), shave head in mourning (1 [+995]), shave heads (1 [+7942]), tear out hair (1)

H7948 קָרְחִי ***qorḥî***, a.g. [8] [√ 7946; cf. 7942]. Korahite, "*of Korah*":– Korahite (3), Korahites (3), Korah (1), Korahites (1 [+1201])

H7949 קָרַחַת ***qāraḥat***, n.f. [4] [√ 7942]. bald spot (not the forehead area); bare spot (of articles):– head (2), bald head (1), side (1)

H7950 קְרִי ***qerî***, n.[m.] [7] [√ 7936]. hostile encounter, hostility:– hostile (6), hostility (1)

H7951 קָרִיא ***qārî'***, a. [2] [√ 7924]. summoned, called:– appointed (1), officials (1)

H7952 קְרִיאָה ***qerî'â***, n.f. [1] [√ 7924]. message, appeal:– message (1)

H7953 קִרְיָה ***qiryâ***, n.f. [29] [√ 7984; 10640]. city, town:– city (20), town (5), cities (3), one[s] (1)

H7954 קְרִיּוֹת ***qeriyyôt***, n.pr.loc. [3] [√ 7984]. Kerioth, "*town*":– Kerioth (3)

H7955 קְרִיּוֹת חֶצְרוֹן ***qeriyyôt ḥeṣrôn***, n.pr.loc. [1] [√ 7984 + 2970]. Kerioth Hezron, "*town of Hezron*":– Kerioth Hezron (1)

H7956 קִרְיַת ***qiryat***, n.f. [1] [√ 7984]. Kiriath:– Kiriath (1)

H7957 קִרְיַת אַרְבַּע ***qiryat 'arba'***, n.pr.loc. [7] [√ 7984 + 752]. Kiriath Arba, "*city of four*":– Kiriath Arba (7)

H7958 קִרְיַת־בַּעַל ***qiryat-ba'al***, n.pr.loc. [2] [√ 7984 + 1251]. Kiriath Baal:– Kiriath Baal (2)

H7959 קִרְיַת הָאַרְבַּע ***qiryat hā'arba'***, n.pr.loc. [2] [√ 7984 + 752]. Kiriath Arba, "*city of four*":– Kiriath Arba (2)

H7960 קִרְיַת חֻצוֹת ***qiryat ḥuṣôt***, n.pr.loc. [1] [√ 7984 + 2941]. Kiriath Huzoth, "*city of Huzoth [outside spaces]*":– Kiriath Huzoth (1)

H7961 קִרְיַת יְעָרִים ***qiryat ye'ārîm***, n.pr.loc. [19] [√ 7984 + 3630]. Kiriath Jearim, "*city of timberlands*":– Kiriath Jearim (19)

H7962 קִרְיַת־סַנָּה ***qiryat-sannâ***, n.pr.loc. [1] [√ 7984 + 6173]. Kiriath Sannah, "*city of Sannah*":– Kiriath Sannah (1)

H7963 קִרְיַת־סֵפֶר ***qiryat-sēper***, n.pr.loc. [4] [√ 7984 + 6219]. Kiriath Sepher, "*city of scribe*":– Kiriath Sepher (4)

H7964 קִרְיָתַיִם ***qiryātayim***, n.pr.loc. [6] [√ 7984]. Kiriathaim, "*two cities*":– Kiriathaim (6)

H7965 קָרַם ***qāram***, v. [2] [Q] to cover with, spread; [N] to be spread over:– cover (1), covered (1)

H7966 קָרַן ***qāran***, v.den. [4] [√ 7967]. [Q] to be radiant; [H] to be with horns:– radiant (3), horns (1)

H7967 קֶרֶן ***qeren***, n.f. [75] [→ 7966, 7968, 7969; 10641]. horn, (pair) of horns; something made of horns: wind instrument, container; horn often symbolizes strength and status, as in "horn of salvation":– horns (44), horn (23), two-horned (2 [+1251, 2021]), brow (1), hillside (1), him[s] (1), rays (1), trumpets (1 [+3413]), tusks (1)

H7968 קֶרֶן הַפּוּךְ ***qeren happûk***, n.pr.f. [1] [√ 7967 + 2199]. Keren-Happuch, "*horn of [cosmetic] eye shadow*; i.e., *cosmetic case*":– Keren-Happuch (1)

H7969 קַרְנַיִם ***qarnayim***, n.pr.loc. [1] [→ 6959; cf. 7967]. Karnaim, "*horns*":– Karnaim (1)

H7970 קָרַס ***qāras***, v. [2] [→ 7971, 7972]. [Q] to stoop low, bend down:– stoop (1), stoops low (1)

H7971 קֶרֶס ***qeres***, n.[m.] [10] [√ 7970]. clasp, hook (of curtains):– clasps (7), them[s] (3 [+2021])

H7972 קַרְסֹל ***qarsōl***, n.[f.] [2] [√ 7970]. (dual) ankles:– ankles (2)

H7973 קָרַע ***qāra'***, v. [63] [→ 7974]. [Q] to tear, rend, rip; [Qp] to be torn; [N] to be torn to pieces, be split apart:– tore (26), torn (12), tear (10), most certainly tear away (2 [+7973]), rend (2), tore away (2), be split apart (1), cut off (1), highlight (1), makes large (1), rip open (1 [+6033, 4213]), slandered (1), tear off (1), tore (1 [+7974]), was split apart (1)

H7974 קְרָעִים ***qerā'îm***, n.m.[pl.] [4] [√ 7973]. torn pieces (of a garment), rags:– pieces (2), rags (1), tore (1 [+7973])

H7975 קָרַץ ***qāraṣ***, v. [5] [→ 7976; 10642]. [Q] to maliciously wink, purse (the lips); [Pu] to be shaped:– maliciously wink (1), piece (1), purses (1), winks maliciously (1), winks maliciously (1 [+6524])

H7976 קֶרֶץ ***qereṣ***, n.m. [1] [√ 7975]. gadfly; some sources: mosquito:– gadfly (1)

H7977 ¹קַרְקַע ***qarqa'¹***, n.[m.] [7] [→ 7978, 7980]. floor:– floor (5), bottom (1), floors (1)

H7978 ²קַרְקַע ***qarqa'²***, n.pr.loc. [1] [√ 7977]. Karka, "*floor, ground*":– Karka (1)

H7979 קַרְקַר ***qarqar***, var. see 7721

H7980 קַרְקֹר ***qarqōr***, n.pr.loc. [1] [√ 7977]. Karkor:– Karkor (1)

H7981 ¹קָרַר ***qārar¹***, v. [2] [√ 7769 *or* root of: 5249, 7922, 7923, 7938, 7941; cf. 7982]. [H] to pour out or to keep cool:– pours out (2)

H7982 ²קָרַר ***qārar²***, v. [1] [cf. 7981]. [Pil] to tear down:– battering down (1)

H7983 קֶרֶשׁ ***qereš***, n.m. [46] frame:– frames (27), frame (8), those[s] (2), deck (1), them[s] (1 [+2021]), them[s] (1 [+2021, 6929]), NDT (6)

H7984 קֶרֶת ***qeret***, n.f. [5] [→ 7953, 7954, 7956, 7964, 7985, 7986; cf. 7815; *also used with compound proper names*]. city, town:– city (5)

H7985 קַרְתָּה ***qartâ***, n.pr.loc. [2] [√ 7984]. Kartah, "*city*":– Kartah (2)

H7986 קַרְתָּן ***qartān***, n.pr.loc. [1] [√ 7984]. Kartan:– Kartan (1)

H7987 קַשְׂוָה ***qaśwâ***, n.f. [4] pitcher, jar:– pitchers (3), jars (1)

H7988 קְשִׂיטָה ***qeśîṭâ***, n.f. [3] piece of silver (unknown unit of weight or value):– pieces of silver (2), piece of silver (1)

H7989 קַשְׂקֶשֶׂת ***qaśqeśet***, n.f. [8] [cf. 7878]. scales (as on skin of marine creatures); scale armor:– scales (7), coat of scale armor (1 [+9234])

H7990 קַשׁ ***qaš***, n.m. [16] [√ 8006]. stubble, chaff, straw:– stubble (7), chaff (6), straw (2), piece of straw (1)

H7991 קִשֻּׁאָה ***qiššu'â***, n.f. [1] [√ 5252]. cucumber:– cucumbers (1)

H7992 קָשַׁב ***qāšab***, v. [46] [→ 7993, 7994, 7995]. [Q] to listen; [H] to pay attention, give heed, listen:– listen (13), pay attention (12), hear (5), listened (3), listens (2), paid attention (2), alert (1 [+7993]), attendance (1), attentively (1), heard (1 [+928, 7754]), heed (1), listen (1 [+265]), pay close attention (1 [+2256, 9048]), pays attention (1), turning (1)

H7993 קֶשֶׁב ***qešeb***, n.m. [4] [√ 7992]. paying attention, responding:– alert (1), alert (1 [+7992]), paid attention (1), response (1)

H7994 קַשָּׁב ***qaššāb***, a. [2] [√ 7992]. attentive:– attentive (2)

H7995 קַשֻּׁב ***qaššub***, a. [3] [√ 7992]. attentive:– attentive (3)

H7996 קָשָׁה ***qāšâ***, v. [28] [→ 7997, 8001]. [Q] to be hard, harsh, cruel; [N] to be distressed; [P] to have great difficulty (in labor); [H] to make stiff, harden, be difficult:– stiff-necked (11 [+6902]), harden (2), put heavy (2), cruel (1), difficult (1), distressed (1), great difficulty (1), hard (1), hardens (1), hardship (1), having great difficulty (1), heavy (1), made stubborn (1), pressed forcefully (1), resisted (1), stubbornly refused (1)

H7997 קָשֶׁה ***qāšeh***, a. [36] [√ 7996]. hard, harsh, difficult, fierce; stubborn, stiff(-necked), obstinate:– stiff-necked (7 [+6902]), harsh (6), harshly (5), fierce (3), stubborn (2), bad news (1), cruel (1), deeply troubled (1 [+8120]), desperate times (1), difficult (1), dire (1), in trouble (1 [+3427]), obstinate (1 [+4213]), obstinate (1 [+7156]), pressed harder and harder (1 [+2143, 2256]), strong (1), surly (1), unyielding (1)

H7998 קָשַׁח ***qāšaḥ***, v. [2] [H] to harden:– harden (1), treats harshly (1)

H7999 קֹשְׁטְ ***qōšṭ***, n.m. [1] [√ 10643]. true:– honest (1)

H8000 קֹשֶׁט ***qōšeṭ***, n.[m.?] [1] [cf. 8008]. bow (weapon):– bow (1)

H8001 קְשִׁי ***q^{e}šî***, n.[m.] [1] [√ 7996]. stubbornness:– stubbornness (1)

H8002 קִשְׁיוֹן ***qišyôn***, n.pr.loc. [2] Kishion:– Kishion (2)

H8003 קָשַׁר ***qāšar***, v. [44] [→ 8004, 8005]. [Q] to tie, bind; to plot, conspire; [Qp] to be bound up; be strong; [N] to be joined with; [P] to bind; [Pu] to be strong; [Ht] to conspire together:– conspired (10), plotted (7), bind (4), conspired (4 [+8004]), tie (3), tied (3), became one with (1), carried out (1), closely bound up (1), conspiracy led (1 [+8004]), conspirators (1), hold (1), is bound up (1), put on (1), put on a leash (1), raising a conspiracy (1), reached height (1 [+6330]), strong (1), stronger (1)

H8004 קֶשֶׁר ***qešer***, n.m. [16] [√ 8003]. conspiracy, treason:– conspiracy (5), conspired (4 [+8003]), treason (4), conspiracy led (1 [+8003]), rebellion (1), traitor (1)

H8005 קִשֻּׁרִים ***qiššurîm***, n.[m.]pl. [2] [√ 8003]. sashes, wedding ornaments:– sashes (1), wedding ornaments (1)

H8006 [1]קָשַׁשׁ ***qāšaš[1]***, v.den. [8] [→ 7990; cf. 8007]. [Q] to gather together; [Pol] to gather; [Htpol] to gather together:– gathering (4), gather (2), gather together (2)

H8007 [2]קָשַׁשׁ ***qāšaš[2]***, v. Not used in NIVEBC [cf. 8006]. [Q, Htpol] to gather together, assemble

H8008 קֶשֶׁת ***qešet***, n.f. [& m.?] [76] [→ 8009; cf. 8000]. bow (weapon); by extension, something bow shaped: rainbow:– bow (45), bows (14), rainbow (4), archer (1 [+9530]), archers (1 [+5031]), archers (1 [+5432]), archers (1 [+8227]), archers (1 [+4619, 928, 2021]), archers (1 [+4619, 408, 928, 2021]), arrow (1), arrows (1), arrows (1 [+1201]), bowshot (1 [+3217]), did so[S] (1 [+4374, 2256, 2932]), shoot (1 [+928, 2021]), with bows (1 [+2005])

H8009 קַשָּׁת ***qaššāt***, n.m. [1] [√ 8008]. archer:– archer (1 [+8050])

H8010 ר ***r***, letter. Not used in NIVEBC [√ 10645]. letter of the Hebrew alphabet

H8011 [1]רָאָה ***rā'â[1]***, v. [1295] [→ 2218, 4307, 5260, 5261, 5262, 8012?, 8013, 8014, 8015, 8016, 8019, 8021, 8022, 8023, 8024, 8026; *also used with compound proper names*]. [Q] to see, look, view; to realize, know, consider; [Qp] to be selected; [N] to become visible, appear, show oneself; [Pu] to be seen; [H] to cause to see, show; [Ho] to be shown; [Ht] to look at each other, meet with; a general word for visual perception; note the many contextual translations in the NIV:– see (348), saw (304), seen (102), look (53), looked (37), appeared (32), examine (25), sees (23), show (22), appear (20), showed (17), shown (12), consider (10), realized (10), be seen (9), find out (8), appears (7), seeing (7), watching (7), examines (6), enjoy (5), watch (5), find (4), have regard for (4), learned (4), noticed (4), watched (4), been seen (3), observed (3), remember (3), see (3 [+3359, 2256]), advisers (2 [+7156]), be shown (2), decide (2), ever seeing (2 [+8011]), face (2), face each other in battle (2 [+7156]), faced each other (2 [+7156]), find out (2 [+3359, 2256]), gloat over (2), had[S] (2), here (2), indeed seen (2 [+8011]), inspect (2), knows (2), let see (2), look after (2), look around (2), look carefully (2 [+928, 6524]), look for (2), look over (2), looking (2), looks (2), observe (2), only look (2 [+8011]), provide (2), revealed (2), saw clearly (2 [+8011]), understand (2), view (2), were exposed (2), ah (1), allowed to see (1), appear before (1 [+7156]), appearing (1), are given (1), attract (1), be found (1), be provided (1), bear in mind (1), beheld (1), being seen (1), blind (1 [+1153]), bring (1), catch glimpse (1), caught sight of (1), cherished (1), choose (1), chose (1), chosen (1), clearly (1 [+3954]), come into presence (1 [+906, 7156]), come into view (1), compare (1), consider carefully (1), conspicuous (1), contemplating (1), display (1), displayed (1), experienced (1), faced (1), find out (1 [+2256, 3359]), found (1), found (1 [+4200, 7156]), gaze (1), gazing (1), getting[S] (1), glimpse (1), gloat (1), had a vision (1), had special access to (1 [+7156]), have sexual relations (1 [+906, 6872]), hidden (1 [+4202]), inspected (1), keeping watch (1 [+928, 6524]), knew (1), knowing (1), let gloat (1), listen (1), listen carefully (1), look around (1 [+5951, 6524, 2256]), looked (1 [+5260]), looked things over (1), looking at each other (1), lookout (1), looks down on (1), looks kindly (1), made see (1), make look (1), make see (1), meet with (1 [+7156]), met (1), mistake for (1 [+3869]), notice (1), paid attention (1), pay any attention (1 [+5564, 2256]), pay careful attention (1 [+2256, 5742, 265]), people[S] (1 [+2021]), please (1), present (1), present himself (1), present myself (1), present themselves (1), present yourself (1), probe (1), realize (1), realize (1 [+3359, 2256]), realized (1 [+2256, 3359]), realizing (1), reappears (1 [+6388]), reason (1), regard (1), regarded (1), respect (1), revealing (1), reveals (1), see (1 [+6524]), see (1 [+7156]), see (1 [+4200, 2021, 6524]), see for yourselves (1 [+6524, 4013]), see visions (1), seems (1), seen for myself (1 [+7156]), selected (1), show himself (1), showing (1), sight (1), stare (1), suffered (1), took note (1), turn (1), uncovered (1), very well (1), viewed (1), visible (1), visit (1), was seen (1), were shown (1), NDT (27)

H8012 [2]רָאָה ***rā'â[2]***, n.f. [1] [√ 8011?]. red kite:– red kite (1)

H8013 רָאֶה ***rā'eh***, a. Not used in NIVEBC [√ 8011]. seeing

H8014 [1]רֹאֶה ***rō'eh[1]***, n.[m.] [11] [√ 8011]. seer:– seer (9), seers (1), seer's (1)

H8015 [2]רֹאֶה ***rō'eh[2]***, n.[m.] [1] [√ 8011]. vision:– seeing visions (1)

H8016 [3]רֹאֶה ***rō'eh[3]***, n.pr.m. Not used in NIVEBC [√ 8011; cf. 2218]. Roeh, see 2218

H8017 רְאוּבֵן ***r^{e}'ûbēn***, n.pr.m. [72] [→ 8018; cf. 8011 + 1201]. Reuben, *"see, a son!* [Ge 29:32]; *substitute a son"*:– Reuben (45), Reubenites (17 [+1201]), Reuben (6 [+1201]), Reubenite (1 [+1201]), they[S] (1 [+1201, 1514, 2256, 1201]), NDT (2)

H8018 רְאוּבֵנִי ***r^{e}'ûbēnî***, a.g. [18] [√ 8017]. Reubenite, of Reuben, *"of Reuben"*:– Reubenites (13), Reuben (3), Reuben (1 [+1201]), Reubenite (1)

H8019 רַאֲוָה ***ra'^{a}wâ***, n.f. [1] [√ 8011]. spectacle, sight:– spectacle (1)

H8020 רְאוּמָה ***r^{e}'ûmâ***, n.pr.f. [1] [√ 8163? *or* 8028?]. Reumah:– Reumah (1)

H8021 רְאוּת ***r^{e}'ût***, n.f. [1] [√ 8011]. look:– feast on (1)

H8022 רֹאִי ***rō'î***, n.pr.loc. Not used in NIVEBC [√ 8011; cf. 936]. Roi, see 936

H8023 רְאִי ***r^{e}'î***, n.m. [1] [√ 8011]. mirror:– mirror (1)

H8024 רֳאִי ***r^{o}'î***, n.[m.] [4] [√ 8011; 10657]. appearance, spectacle:– features (1), sees (1), spectacle (1), to nothing (1 [+4946])

H8025 רְאָיָה ***r^{e}'āyâ***, n.pr.m. [4] [√ 8011 + 3378]. Reaiah, *"Yahweh has seen"*:– Reaiah (4)

H8026 רְאִית ***r^{e}'ît***, n.f. Not used in NIVEBC [√ 8011]. look, sight

H8027 רָאַם ***rā'am***, v. [1] [→ 8030; cf. 8123]. [Q] to rise up high:– raised up high (1)

H8028 רְאֵם ***r^{e}'ēm***, n.m. [9] [√ 8020?]. wild oxen:– wild ox (6), wild oxen (2), it[S] (1)

H8029 [1]רָאמוֹת ***rā'môt[1]***, n.[f.pl.] [2] coral:– coral (2)

H8030 [2]רָאמוֹת ***rā'môt[2]***, n.pr.loc. [5] [√ 8027; cf. 8123]. Ramoth, *"height"*:– Ramoth (5)

H8031 [1]רֹאשׁ ***rō'š[1]***, n.m. [601] [→ 8033, 8035, 8034?, 8036, 8037, 8038, 8040, 8396; 10646]. head (of the body); by extension: top (of an object); high in status or authority: leader, chief; source or origin: first, beginning; "to lift up the head" can mean to take a census, to behead, or to restore to a position:– head (204), heads (127), top (45), chief (29), leaders (21), first (16), tops (10), hair (9), beginning (7), chiefs (6), companies (6), corner (6), leader (6), mountaintops (4 [+2215]), highest (3), summit (3), take a census (3 [+5951, 906]), topmost (3), ends (2), finest (2), helmet (2 [+5057]), highest point (2), led by (2 [+928]), lost hair (2 [+5307]), over (2 [+928]), prominent place (2), released (2 [+5951]), take a census (2 [+5951]), all (1), any (1), authority (1), begin (1), bodyguard (1 [+9068, 4200]), branches off (1), choicest gifts (1), command (1), commander-in-chief (1 [+2256, 8569]), commanders (1), company (1), cornerstone (1 [+7157]), count (1 [+5951, 906]), counted (1 [+5951, 906]), crest (1), crown (1), detachments (1), director (1), directors (1), divisions (1), down (1 [+4946]), each (1), fine (1), foremost (1), full (1), hair (1 [+1929]), hair (1 [+7279, 8552]), headwaters (1), high (1 [+6584]), highest (1 [+6584]), highest point (1 [+5294]), hilltop (1 [+2215]), hilltops (1 [+2215]), include in the census (1 [+5951, 906]), it[S] (1 [+2257]), it[S] (1 [+8552]), junction (1), leaders (1 [+408]), leaders (1 [+1505]), leaders (1 [+6639]), leading (1), made pay for (1 [+8740, 928]), make full restitution (1 [+8740, 928]), masters (1), men (1), mountaintop (1 [+2215]), new Moon feasts (1 [+2544]), oldest (1), on (1 [+4200]), outstanding (1), overwhelmed (1 [+6296]), peaks (1), raiding parties (1), reaches (1), repay (1 [+5989, 928]), repay (1 [+8740, 928]), repay (1 [+8740, 6584]), ruler (1 [+1505]), rulers (1), special (1), sum (1), them (1 [+2257]), tip (1), very beginning (1), NDT (9)

H8032 [2]רֹאשׁ ***rō'š[2]***, n.m. [12] poison; gall; bitterness:– poison (5), poisoned (3), bitterness (2), gall (1), poisonous weeds (1)

H8033 [3]רֹאשׁ ***rō'š[3]***, n.pr.m. [1] [√ 8031]. Rosh, *"head, leader"*:– Rosh (1)

H8034 [4]רֹאשׁ ***rō'š[4]***, n.pr.g. Not used in NIVEBC [√ 8031?]. Rosh

H8035 רִאשָׁה ***ri'šâ***, n.f. [1] [√ 8031]. beginning, before:– before (1)

H8036 רֹאשָׁה ***rō'šâ***, n.f. [1] [√ 8031]. uppermost, cap[stone]:– capstone (1 [+74])

H8037 רִאשׁוֹן ***ri'šôn***, a. [182] [→ 8038; cf. 8031]. (of position) first, foremost; (of time) former, beginning, earlier:– first (100), former (19), beginning (12), before (6 [+928, 2021]), before (5), earlier (5), first (2 [+928, 2021]), old (2), previous (2), used to (2 [+4200, 2021]), ancestors (1), ancestors (1 [+3]), chief (1), chief officials (1), claimed too soon (1 [+987, 928, 2021]), days of old (1), formerly (1 [+928, 2021]), front (1), highest (1), lead (1), leads (1 [+928, 2021]), led the way (1 [+3338, 2118]), long (1), long ago (1 [+928, 2021]), older (1), once again (1 [+3869, 2021]), one in the lead (1), past (1), past (1 [+3427]), past (1 [+6961]), past generations (1), predecessors (1), ruled (1 [+2118]), used to (1), NDT (3)

H8038 רִאשֹׁנִי ***ri'šōnî***, a. [1] [√ 8037; cf. 8031]. first:– first (1)

H8039 רַאֲשׁוֹת ***ra'^{a}šôt***, n.[f.]pl.den. Not used in NIVEBC [√ 8031; cf. 5265]. head, place of the head, see 5265

H8040 רֵאשִׁית ***rē'šît***, n.f. [51] [√ 8031]. what is first; beginning:– first (12), firstfruits (8), beginning (7), best (6), early (3), firstfruits (2 [+7262]), began (1), beginnings (1), choice (1), choice parts (1), early (1 [+928]), finest (1), firstfruits of harvest (1), foremost (1), former part (1), leaders (1), mainstay (1), starting (1), when (1 [+928])

H8041 [1]רַב ***rab[1]***, a. [423] [→ 8051; cf. 8045; 10647]. many, much; great, abundant, numerous:– many (162), great (71), long (18), abundant (13), numerous (13), mighty (11), abounding (8), large (8), much (8), enough (6), larger (6), vast (6), full (4), more (4), greatly (3), number (3), plenty (3), crowd (2), deep (2), fully (2), gone too far (2), great deal (2), heavy (2), large (2 [+4394]), large amount (2), long enough (2), no end (2), rushing (2), so great (2), so many (2), abundantly (1), all abound (1), beyond number (1 [+4394]), chief (1), convinced (1), distant (1), distant future (1 [+3427]), far too numerous (1 [+2256, 6786]), floodwaters (1 [+4784]), gone far enough (1), great quantities (1), greater (1), greater power (1), gushed out (1 [+3655]), high (1), huge (1), increased more and more (1 [+2143, 2256, 2143]), increasing (1), larger number (1), mansions (1 [+1074]), many (1 [+4394]), more (1 [+3578]), most (1), multitude (1), multitudes (1), never (1 [+4202]), numbers (1), old (1), older (1), powerful (1), practices (1), quantities (1), quantity (1), rich (1), richly (1), severe (1 [+4394]), severely (1), so (1), so many (1 [+5031]), so much (1), stronger (1), surging (1), time after time (1 [+6961]), too long (1), very (1), weighed down (1), weighs heavily (1), what (1), whole (1), wide (1)

H8042 [2]רַב ***rab[2]***, n.m. [33] [→ 8059, 8060, 8072; 10652]. commander, chief officer, high official:– commander (23), chief (3), high (2), officers (2), captain (1 [+2021, 2480]), wine stewards (1 [+1074]), NDT (1)

H8043 [3]רַב ***rab[3]***, n.m. [3] [√ 8046]. archer:– archers (2), archer (1)

H8044 רֹב ***rōb***, n.m. [150] [√ 8045]. greatness, abundance; multitude:– many (29), great (22), numerous (7), all (4), great (4 [+4200]), in abundance (4), much (4), plentiful (4 [+4200]), abundant (3), great amount (3 [+4200]), greatly (3 [+4200]), large numbers (3 [+4200]), abundance (2), extensive (2 [+4200]), great (2 [+3972]), great numbers (2), greatness (2), large (2), large quantities (2 [+4200]), many (2 [+4200]), much (2 [+4200]), plenty (2 [+4200]), so many (2 [+4946]), abound (1), advanced (1), age (1 [+3427]), droves (1 [+4200]), great number (1), great number (1 [+4200]), great numbers (1 [+4200]), great quantities (1 [+4200, 4394]), harsh (1), in large numbers (1 [+4200]), increased (1), large amount (1 [+4200]), larger (1 [+4200]), load (1), long (1), mighty (1 [+4200]), more (1 [+4200]), multiplying (1), multitude (1), numerous (1 [+4200]), produces (1), prosperity (1), prosperity (1 [+3972]), quantities (1 [+4200]), rabble (1 [+132]), size (1), so many (1), so many (1 [+4200]), such[S] (1), surpassing (1), thick (1), vigorously (1 [+928, 3946]), widespread (1), NDT (5)

H8045 [1]רָבַב ***rābab***[1], v. [22] [→ 3714, 3715, 3716, 3717, 5266, 7478, 8041, 8044, 8047, 8051, 8052, 8053, 8056; cf. 8049]. [Q] to abound, increase, be great; [Pu] to increase by tens of thousands:– many (7), numerous (5), great (2), abound (1), do[S] (1), increase in number (1), more (1 [+3869]), often (1), outnumber (1 [+4946]), tens of thousands (1), utterly (1)

H8046 [2]רָבַב ***rābab***[2], v. [1] [→ 8043; cf. 8050]. [Q] to shoot (an arrow):– shot (1)

H8047 רְבָבָה ***r***[e]***bābâ***, n.f. [16] [√ 8045]. ten thousand, myriad; (virtually) countless number:– ten thousand (6), tens of thousands (5), countless (1), grow (1), myriads (1), ten thousands (1), thousands (1)

H8048 רָבַד ***rābad***, v. [1] [→ 5267, 8054]. [Q] to cover:– covered (1 [+5267])

H8049 [1]רָבָה ***rābâ***[1], v. [174] [→ 746?, 1442, 2220, 2221, 5268, 5269, 5270, 9551, 9552; 8045; 10648]. [Q] to increase in number, multiply, grow large; [P] to rear (offspring); to gain; make numerous; [H] to cause to increase, make numerous, enlarge:– increase (13), many (10), increase in number (9), increased (9), increase numbers (8), numerous (8), multiplied (5), make numerous (4), multiply (4), thrive (4), great (3), greater (3), increases (3), much (3), gave many (2), give larger (2), greatly (2), had many (2), increase so much (2 [+8049]), increase the number (2), increasing (2), keep (2), long (2), made great (2), make numerous (2 [+8049]), make very severe (2 [+8049]), more (2), more and more (2), multiplies (2), reared (2), take many (2), abundant (1), accumulate large amounts (1 [+4394]), acquire great numbers (1), add to numbers (1), adding (1), as much as (1 [+4946]), before[S] (1), built many (1), built more (1), cause many (1), distant (1 [+2021, 2006]), done more (1), enlarge (1), enlarged (1), freely (1), gaining (1), gathered much (1), generously gave (1), get more (1), give more (1), grew (1), grow large (1), have many (1), heap (1), higher than (1 [+4200, 5087, 2025]), increased in number (1), increased in numbers (1), increased number (1), increased numbers (1), kept on (1), lavished (1), less meaning (1 [+2039]), made many (1), made numerous (1), make as great as you like (1 [+4394]), make countless (1 [+889, 4202, 6218]), make many (1), make plentiful (1), makes grow (1), many times (1), more and more unfaithful (1 [+5085, 5086]), numbers increased (1), numbers increased greatly (1 [+2256, 7238]), offer many (1), outnumber (1 [+4946]), piles up (1), repeatedly (1), so does[S] (1), time after time (1), too much (1), try many (1), use an abundance (1), whole (1), yet more (1)

H8050 [2]רָבָה ***rābâ***[2], v. [1] [cf. 8046]. [Q] to shoot; (ptcp.) archer:– archer (1 [+8009])

H8051 רַבָּה ***rabbâ***, n.pr.loc. [15] [√ 8041; cf. 8045]. Rabbah, "*chief, capital [city]*":– Rabbah (15)

H8052 רִבּוֹא ***ribbô'***, n.f. [10] [√ 8045; 10649]. ten thousand; myriad, (virtually) countless number:– 20,000 (2 [+9109]), 42,360 (1 [+752, 547, 8993, 4395, 9252]), 42,360 (1 [+752, 547, 8993, 4395, 2256, 9252]), 61,000 (1 [+9252, 2256, 547]), eighteen thousand (1 [+2256, 9046, 547]), hundred and twenty thousand (1 [+9109, 6926]), many thousands (1), ten thousand (1), tens of thousands (1)

H8053 רְבִיבִים ***r***[e]***bîbîm***, n.m. [6] [√ 8045]. rain shower, abundant rain, gentle rain:– showers (5), abundant rain (1)

H8054 רָבִיד ***rābîd***, n.[m.] [3] [√ 8048]. necklace, ornamental chain:– chain (1), interwoven (1 [+3869]), necklace (1)

H8055 רְבִיעִי ***r***[e]***bî'î***, a.num.ord. [58] [√ 752; 10651]. fourth:– fourth (45), quarter (9), fourth generation (2), one fourth (1), square (1)

H8056 רַבִּית ***rabbît***, n.pr.loc. [1] [√ 8045]. Rabbith, "*great*":– Rabbith (1)

H8057 רָבַךְ ***rābak***, v. [3] [Ho] to be kneaded, mixed (of dough):– mixing (1), well-kneaded (1), well-mixed (1)

H8058 רִבְלָה ***riblâ***, n.pr.loc. [11] Riblah:– Riblah (11)

H8059 רַב מָג ***rab māg***, n.m. Not used in NIVEBC [√ 8042 + 4454]. high official

H8060 רַב־סָרִיס ***rab-sārîs***, n.m. Not used in NIVEBC [√ 8042 + 6247]. chief officer

H8061 [1]רָבַע ***rāba'***[1], v.den. [4] [cf. 8069]. [Q] to lie down with, have sexual relations with; [H] to mate, cross-breed:– have sexual relations (1), have sexual relations with (1), lying down (1), mate (1)

H8062 [2]רָבַע ***rāba'***[2], v.den. [12] [√ 752]. [Qp, P] to be squared, have four corners:– square (9), rectangular (2), square (1 [+448, 752, 8063])

H8063 [1]רֶבַע ***reba'***[1], n.m. [7] [→ 8064?; cf. 752?]. fourth-part, quarter; side (of a square thing):– directions (2), quarter (2), sides (1), square (1 [+448, 752]), square (1 [+8062, 448, 752])

H8064 [2]רֶבַע ***reba'***[2], n.m. [2] [√ 8063?; cf. 752?]. Reba:– Reba (2)

H8065 [1]רֹבַע ***rōba'***[1], n.[m.] [2] [√ 752]. fourth-part, quarter:– fourth (1), quarter (1)

H8066 [2]רֹבַע ***rōba'***[2], n.[m.] Not used in NIVEBC. dust, rubbish

H8067 רִבֵּעַ ***ribbēa'***, a. [4] [√ 752]. fourth; (n.) the fourth generation:– fourth generation (4)

H8068 רְבֻעַת ***r***[e]***bu'at***, var. Not used in NIVEBC [√ 752]. square

H8069 רָבַץ ***rābaṣ***, v. [30] [→ 5271, 8070; cf. 8061]. [Q] to lie down; [H] to make lie down; to cause to rest:– lie down (11), lay down (2), lie (2), lying (2), rest (2), crouching (1), fall (1), fallen down (1), have lie down (1), lies down (1), lying down (1), makes lie down (1), rebuild (1), rest flocks (1), sitting (1), NDT (1)

H8070 רֵבֶץ ***rēbeṣ***, n.[m.] [4] [√ 8069]. resting place:– resting place (2), dwelling place (1), where lay (1)

H8071 רִבְקָה ***ribqâ***, n.pr.f. [30] Rebekah, "[poss.] *choice calf*":– Rebekah (29), Rebekah's (1)

H8072 רַב־שָׁקֵה ***rab-šāqēh***, n.m. [16] [√ 8042 + 9197]. Assyrian officer: (field) commander, cupbearer:– field commander (12), commander (4)

H8073 רֶגֶב ***regeb***, n.m. [2] [→ 757, 758, 759]. clod of dirt:– clods of earth (1), soil (1)

H8074 רָגַז ***rāgaz***, v. [41] [→ 761, 8075, 8076, 8077; 10653]. [Q] to quake, shake, tremble; to be angry, be in anguish; [H] to cause to shake, make tremble, cause a disturbance; [Ht] to enrage oneself (against):– tremble (8), rage (4), shook (4), disturbed (3), shakes (2), trembled (2), all astir (1), come trembling (1), convulsed (1), enraged (1), in anguish (1), made tremble (1), make tremble (1), pounded (1), provoke (1), quake (1), quarrel (1), rages (1), rouse (1), shake (1), shaken (1), shudder (1), trembles (1), unrest (1)

H8075 רֹגֶז ***rōgez***, n.m. [7] [√ 8074; 10654]. turmoil, excitement, tumult:– turmoil (3), excitement (1), roar (1), trouble (1), wrath (1)

H8076 רַגָּז ***raggāz***, a. [1] [√ 8074]. anxious, trembling:– anxious (1)

H8077 רָגְזָה ***rogzâ***, n.f. [1] [√ 8074]. shuddering, agitation:– shudder (1)

H8078 רָגַל ***rāgal***, v.den. [26] [√ 8079]. [Q] to slander; [P] to spy, explore:– spies (8), spied out (4), spy out (4), spying (2), explore (1), explored (1), scouts (1), secret messengers (1), slandered (1), spies (1 [+408]), taught to walk (1), utters slander (1)

H8079 רֶגֶל ***regel***, n.f. [245] [→ 5274, 8078, 8081; 10655]. foot; by extension, body parts associated with the foot: sole, legs, big toe, ankle; a euphemism for the genitals; footing or base of an object; footstep, as a measure of length:– feet (134), foot (40), legs (6), footstool (5 [+2071]), feet (4 [+4090]), foot (4 [+4090]), times (4), steps (3), big toes (2), fleet-footed (2 [+7824, 928]), following (2 [+928]), footsteps (2), my (2 [+928, 3276]), pace (2), under command (2 [+928]), accompanied (1 [+995]), ankles (1), attended by (1 [+2143, 4200]), belonged to (1 [+928]), continued on journey (1 [+5951]), follow (1 [+928]), follow (1 [+2143, 928]), goes (1 [+2118]), jointed (1 [+4946, 5087, 4200]), letting range free (1 [+8938]), perch (1 [+4200, 4090]), private parts (1 [+8552]), relieve himself (1 [+6114, 906, 2257]), relieving himself (1 [+6114, 906, 2257]), service (1), standing (1 [+5163, 3922]), step (1), stood (1 [+5163]), those[S] (1 [+4090]), underfoot (1 [+928]), underfoot (1 [+9393]), what trampled (1 [+5330]), wherever (1 [+4200]), with (1 [+928]), womb (1 [+1068]), NDT (6)

H8080 רֹגֵל ***rōgēl***, n.pr.loc. Not used in NIVEBC [√ 6537]. Rogel, see 6537

H8081 רַגְלִי ***raglî***, a. [13] [√ 8079]. (persons) on foot (i.e., not riding):– foot soldiers (6), foot soldiers (3 [+408]), on foot (2), foot (1), men (1 [+408])

H8082 רֹגְלִים ***rōg***[e]***lîm***, n.pr.loc. [2] Rogelim, "*[place of] treaders, fullers [one who cleans clothes by kneading with no soap)*":– Rogelim (2)

H8083 רָגַם ***rāgam***, v. [16] [→ 5275, 8086]. [Q] to execute by hurling stones:– stone (5 [+928, 2021, 74]), stoned (4 [+74]), must stone (2 [+8083]), stone (1), stone (1 [+74]), stoned (1 [+928, 2021, 74]), stoned to death (1 [+74]), stoning (1 [+928, 2021, 74])

H8084 רֶגֶם ***regem***, n.pr.m. [1] [→ 8085; cf. 9553]. Regem, "*friend*":– Regem (1)

H8085 רֶגֶם מֶלֶךְ ***regem melek***, n.pr.m. [1] [√ 8084 + 4889]. Regem-Melech, "*friend of the king;* [poss.] *chief of troops of the king*":– Regem-Melek (1)

H8086 רִגְמָה ***rigmâ***, n.f. [1] [√ 8083]. great throng, crowd, a bustling, noisy group:– great throng (1)

H8087 רָגַן ***rāgan***, v. [7] [Q] to complain; [N] to be grumbling, be gossiping:– gossip (4), grumbled (2), complain (1)

H8088 [1]רָגַע ***rāga'***[1], v. [8] [cf. 8089]. [Q] to stir up, churn up; [H] to do something in an instant:– stirs up (2), churned up (1), in an instant (1), instant (1), moment (1), speedily (1), NDT (1)

H8089 [2]רָגַע ***rāga'***[2], v. [5] [→ 5273, 5276, 8091, 8092; cf. 8088, 8090]. [N] to cease; [H] to find repose, bring rest:– bring rest (1), cease (1), find repose (1), give rest (1), lie down (1)

H8090 [3]רָגַע ***rāga'***[3], v. [1] [cf. 8089]. [Q] to harden, crust over:– broken (1)

H8091 רָגֵעַ ***rāgēa'***, a. [1] [√ 8089]. quiet, resting:– live quietly (1)

H8092 רֶגַע ***rega'***, n.m. [22] [√ 8089]. moment, instant; peace, tranquillity:– moment (9), at once (2 [+3869]), in a moment (2), at another time (1), at any time (1), continually (1 [+4200]), in a moment (1 [+4017]), in an instant (1), little while (1 [+5071]), peace (1), suddenly (1), suddenly (1 [+3869])

H8093 רָגַשׁ ***rāgaš***, v. [1] [→ 8094, 8095; 10656]. [Q] to be restless, be in tumult, likely referring to a rebellious conspiracy:– conspire (1)

H8094 רֶגֶשׁ ***regeš***, n.[m.] [1] [√ 8093]. throng:– worshipers (1)

H8095 רִגְשָׁה ***rigšâ***, n.f. [1] [√ 8093]. crowd, throng:– plots (1)

H8096 רָדַד ***rādad***, v. [3] [→ 8100]. [Q] to subdue, beat down; [H] to hammer out flat:– hammered (1), subdue (1), subdues (1)

H8097 [1]רָדָה ***rādâ***[1], v. [23] [→ 8099]. [Q] to rule over; [H] to cause to dominate:– rule (10), ruled (3), officials (2), directed (1), leading (1), prevail (1), rule over (1), ruler (1), subdued (1), subdues (1), trample the grapes (1)

H8098 [2]רָדָה ***rādâ***[2], v. [2] [Q] to scoop out, scrape out:– scooped out (1), taken (1)

H8099 רַדַּי ***radday***, n.pr.m. [1] [√ 8097]. Raddai, "[poss.] *beating down; Yahweh rules*":– Raddai (1)

H8100 רְדִיד ***r***[e]***dîd***, n.[m.] [2] [√ 8096]. cloak, shawl, something wrapped around:– cloak (1), shawls (1)

H8101 רָדַם ***rādam***, v. [7] [→ 9554]. [N] to be in a heavy sleep:– fell into a deep sleep (2), in a deep sleep (1), lay fast asleep (1), lie still (1), sleep (1), sleeps (1)

H8102 רֹדָן ***rōdān***, n.pr.loc. *or* g. [3] [→ 8114; cf. 1849]. Rodanim; Rhodes, "*people of Rhodes*":– Rodanites (2), Rhodes (1)

H8103 רָדַף ***rādap***, v. [143] [→ 5284]. [Q] to pursue, chase, persecute; [N] to be pursued, be hounded; [P] to pursue, chase; [Pu] to be chased; [H] to chase:– pursue (33), pursued (27), pursuing (11), chased (8), pursuers (7), pursues (7), chase (6), persecute (4), persecutors (4), follow (3), pursuit (3), went in pursuit (3), chase after (2), go (2), in pursuit (2), came by in pursuit (1), comes in pursuit (1), devise (1), driven (1), driven away (1), hound (1), hounded (1), hunts (1), hurried (1), past (1), persecuted (1), plague (1), press on (1), pursuer (1), put to flight (1), routs (1), run after (1), seek to do (1), set out in pursuit (1), they[S] (1 [+2021]), NDT (1)

H8104 רָהַב ***rāhab***, v. [4] [→ 5290, 8105, 8106, 8107; cf. 4502]. [Q] to rise up against; press one's plea; [H] to overwhelm; make bold:– give no rest (1), greatly emboldened (1 [+6437]), overwhelm (1), rise up (1)

H8105 רַהַב ***rahab***, n.pr. [6] [√ 8104]. Rahab, a sea monster of chaos that opposes God; used of the land of Egypt, with a focus on affliction or arrogance:– Rahab (6)

H8106 רֹהַב ***rōhab***, n.[m.] [1] [√ 8104]. pride or hurry, see 8145:– best (1)

H8107 רָהָב ***rāhāb***, a. [1] [√ 8104]. proud, defiant:– proud (1)

H8108 רָהְגָּה ***rohgâ***, n.pr.m. [1] [→ 8117]. Rohgah:– Rohgah (1)

H8109 רָהָה ***rāhâ***, v. Not used in NIVEBC [cf. 3724]. [Q] to fear

H8110 [1]רַהַט ***rahaṭ***[1], n.[m.] [3] [cf. 8111]. watering trough:– troughs (2), troughs (1 [+9216])

H8111 [2]רַהַט ***rahaṭ***[2], n.[m.] [1] [→ 8112; cf. 8110]. tress, rafter:– tresses (1)

H8112 רָהִיט ***rāhîṭ***, n.m.col. [1] [√ 8111]. rafters:– rafters (1)

H8113 רוּד ***rûd***, v. [4] [→ 5291]. [Q] to roam; [H] to grow restless, cause restlessness:– restless (1), roam (1), trouble (1), unruly (1)

H8114 רוֹדָנִים ***rôdānîm***, n.pr.g.pl. Not used in NIVEBC [√ 8102]. Rhodians

H8115 רָוָה ***rāwâ***, v. [14] [→ 3453, 8116, 8122, 8188]. [Q] to drink to satisfaction, quench the thirst; [P] to drench, refresh, satisfy; [H] to lavish upon, cause to refresh; from the base meaning of quenching thirst come the fig. extensions of refreshment, satisfaction, and fulfillment:– drench (2), satisfy (2), drenched (1), drink deeply (1), drunk its fill (1), feast (1), given to drink (1), lavished on (1), quenched its thirst (1), refresh (1), refreshes (1), watering (1)

H8116 רָוֶה ***rāweh***, a. [4] [√ 8115]. well-watered, drenched:– well-watered (2), drowned (1), watered land (1)

H8117 רוֹהֲגָה ***rôhᵃgâ***, n.pr.m. Not used in NIVEBC [√ 8108]. Rohagah, see 8108

H8118 רָוַח ***rāwaḥ***, v. [3] [→ 8119, 8120, 8121, 8193, 8194]. [Q] to feel relief; [Pu] to be spacious:– find relief (1), relief come (1), spacious (1)

H8119 רֶוַח ***rewaḥ***, n.m. [2] [√ 8118]. relief; space:– relief (1), space (1)

H8120 רוּחַ ***rûaḥ***, n.f. [378] [√ 8118; 10658]. breath, wind; by extension: spirit, mind, heart, as the immaterial part of a person that can respond to God, the seat of life; spirit being, especially the Spirit of God:– spirit (166), wind (78), breath (33), winds (13), mind (4), side (4), blast (3), heart (3), sides (3), courage (2), feelings (2), itS (2 [+2021]), make want to (2 [+5989, 928]), on guard (2 [+9068, 928]), overwhelmed (2 [+4202, 2118, 6388, 928]), power of the spirit (2), rage (2), spirits (2), I (1 [+3276]), air (1), anger (1), animosity (1 [+8273]), breath (1 [+5972]), breeze (1), breezes (1), cool (1), deep sleep (1 [+9554]), deeply troubled (1 [+7997]), discouragement (1 [+7919]), empty (1), even-tempered (1 [+7922]), hostility (1), impatient (1 [+7918]), inspired (1), inspires (1), jealous (1 [+7863, 6296, 6584]), liar (1 [+3941]), life (1), life breath (1 [+678]), long-winded (1), lose heart (1 [+1327, 928, 7931]), me (1 [+3276]), motives (1), pant (1 [+8634]), patience (1 [+800]), pride (1 [+1468]), quick-tempered (1 [+7920]), resentment (1), revived (1 [+8740]), self-control (1 [+5440, 928]), self-control (1 [+5110, 4200]), source of grief (1 [+5289]), spirit of leadership (1), strength (1), tempest (1 [+6185]), tempest (1 [+6194]), theyS (1), thoughts (1), trustworthy (1 [+586]), violent wind (1 [+6194]), violent winds (1 [+6194]), whirlwind (1), willing (1 [+5605]), windblown (1 [+6584, 7156]), windstorm (1 [+6194]), wisdom (1 [+2683]), you (1 [+3870]), NDT (4)

H8121 רְוָחָה ***rᵉwāḥâ***, n.f. [2] [√ 8118]. relief, respite:– relief (2)

H8122 רְוָיָה ***rᵉwāyâ***, n.f. [2] [√ 8115]. place of abundance, overflowing:– overflows (1), place of abundance (1)

H8123 1רוּם ***rûm[1]***, v. [192] [→ 5294, 5295, 8027, 8124, 8125, 8126, 8127, 8128, 8129, 8225, 8226, 9556, 9557; cf. 3727, 3753, 8229, 8250; 10659; *also used with compound proper names*]. [Q] to be high, raise up; to be proud, haughty; [Pol] to exalt, lift high; [Polal] to be exalted, be lifted up; [H] to cause to lift up, present (an offering); to raise up against, rebel; [Ho] to be presented, be taken away; to exalt oneself; from the base meaning of being high in spatial position come the fig. extensions of being high in status: exalted, and high in attitude: proud, arrogant:– exalted (20), exalt (16), present (10), high (8), raised (6), remove (6), haughty (5), lift up (5), lifted high (5), raise (5), provided (4), raised up (4), tall (4), exalts (3), lift (3), lifts (3), rose (3), be exalted (2), brought up (2), lifted up (2), lofty (2), offer (2), presenting (2), rebelled (2 [+3338]), rise up (2), as a special gift set aside (1), be lifted up (1), boldly (1 [+928, 3338]), brandish (1), build on high (1), celebrate (1), consider better (1 [+4222]), contributed (1), defiantly (1 [+928, 3338]), displays (1), donated (1), exalt himself (1), filled with pride (1 [+4222]), get (1), greater (1), heights (1), held up (1), higher (1), highest (1), honored (1), is removed (1), let triumph (1), lift high (1), lift out (1), lifted (1), lifts high (1), lifts up (1), lofty trees (1 [+7757]), loud (1), made grow tall (1), make (1), picked up (1), present (1 [+9556]), present a portion (1), presented (1), proud (1), proud (1 [+4213]), proud (1 [+4222]), raised sworn an oath (1), rear (1), rebuild (1), rise (1), scream for help (1 [+7754, 2256, 7924]), screamed for help (1 [+7754, 2256, 7924]), set apart (1), set high (1), set up (1), shout (1 [+7754]), shouted (1 [+7754, 928, 9558]), sins defiantly (1 [+6913, 928, 3338]), sound (1 [+7754]), stop (1), take (1), take out (1), take up (1), taller (1), took away (1), took up (1), towering (1), triumph (1), triumphed (1), turn (1), upraised (1), very top (1), was presented (1 [+9556]), NDT (1)

H8124 2רוּם ***rûm[2]***, n.[m.] [6] [√ 8123; 10660]. height; haughtiness, pride:– haughty (2), pride (2), haughtiness (1), high (1)

H8125 רוֹם ***rôm***, adv. [1] [√ 8123]. on high:– high (1)

H8126 רוּמָה ***rûmâ***, n.pr.loc. [1] [√ 8123; cf. 777]. Rumah, "*height*":– Rumah (1)

H8127 רוֹמָה ***rômâ***, adv. [1] [√ 8123]. proudly, haughtily:– proudly (1)

H8128 רוֹמָם ***rômām***, n.[m.] [2] [√ 8123]. praise, exaltation:– praise (2)

H8129 רוֹמֵמֻת ***rômēmut***, n.f. [1] [√ 8123]. rising up, lifting up:– rise up (1)

H8130 רוּן ***rûn***, v. [1] [Htpol] to awake from a stupor, become sober:– wakes from stupor (1)

H8131 רוּעַ ***rûaʿ***, v. [45] [→ 8275, 9558]. [H] to raise a battle cry; sound a trumpet blast; shout in triumph or exaltation:– shout (8), shout for joy (5), shout aloud (4), shouted (3), gave a shout (2 [+9558]), shout in triumph (2), shouting (2), cry aloud (1 [+8275]), cry out (1), crying out (1), extol (1), give a shout (1 [+9558]), give a war cry (1), made noise (1 [+9558]), raise the battle cry (1), raise the war cry (1), raised a shout (1 [+9558]), raised the battle cry (1), shouted for joy (1), shouts (1), signal (1), sound (1), sound a blast (1), sound alarm (1), sound of battle cry (1), triumph (1)

H8132 רוּץ ***rûṣ***, v. [103] [→ 5296, 5297, 8350; cf. 8351?]. [Q] to run, hurry, be a messenger; [Pol] to dart about, run to and fro; [H] to chase; to bring quickly:– run (20), ran (19), guards (10), couriers (6), hurried (4), running (4), guard (3), hurry (3), rush (3), advance (2), chase (2), guardroom (2 [+9288]), runner (2), anotherS (1), attack (1), busy (1), charge (1), charged (1), charging (1), come running (1), courier (1), dart about (1), gallop along (1), go (1), go quickly (1), quickly brought (1), raced (1), ran off (1), runs (1), rushed forward (1), rushes (1), served quickly (1), submit (1 [+3338]), throw down (1), NDT (2)

H8133 רוּשׁ ***rûš***, v. [23] [→ 8203; cf. 3769]. [Q] to be poor, be in poverty, be oppressed; [Htpol] to pretend to be poor:– poor (18), poverty (2), oppressed (1), pretends to be poor (1), weak (1)

H8134 רוּת ***rût***, n.pr.f. [12] [√ 8287?]. Ruth, "*friendship; refreshed [as with water]*; [poss.] *comrade, companion*":– Ruth (12)

H8135 רָזָה ***rāzâ***, v. [2] [→ 8136, 8137, 8140]. [Q] to destroy; [N] to waste away:– destroys (1), waste away (1)

H8136 רָזֶה ***rāzeh***, a. [2] [√ 8135]. lean; barren:– lean (1), poor (1)

H8137 1רָזוֹן ***rāzôn[1]***, n.[m.] [3] [√ 8135]. wasting disease; short, scrimped (ephah):– wasting disease (2), short (1)

H8138 2רָזוֹן ***rāzôn[2]***, n.m. [1] [√ 8142]. prince, dignitary:– prince (1)

H8139 רְזוֹן ***rᵉzôn***, n.pr.m. [1] [√ 8142]. Rezon, "*prince; high official*":– Rezon (1)

H8140 רָזִי ***rāzî***, n.[m.] [2] [√ 8135]. wasting away, leanness:– waste away (2)

H8141 רָזַם ***rāzam***, v. [1] [Q] to wink, flash the eyes:– flash (1)

H8142 רָזַן ***rāzan***, v. [6] [→ 8138, 8139]. [Q] to be a ruler; (ptcp.) a prince, ruler:– rulers (5), princes (1)

H8143 רָחַב ***rāḥab***, v. [25] [→ 5303, 5304, 8144, 8145, 8146, 8147, 8148, 8152, 8153, 8154]. [Q] to be wide; to swell (with joy); to boast; [N] to be roomy, be broad; [H] to enlarge, broaden, make wide:– enlarge (2), enlarges (2), sneer (2 [+7023]), boasts (1), broad (1), broadened (1), enlarged (1), expands (1), extend (1), give relief (1), given room (1), greedy (1), make bald (1 [+7947]), open wide (1), opened wide (1), opens the way (1), provide a broad (1), provide broad (1), relieve (1), swell with joy (1), wide (1), wider (1)

H8144 רַחַב ***raḥab***, n.[m.] [2] [√ 8143]. spacious place, vast expanse:– spacious place (1), vast expanses (1)

H8145 רֹחַב ***rōḥab***, n.[m.] [100] [√ 8143]. breadth, width:– wide (69), width (11), breadth (3), thick (3), deep (2), distance (2), broad (1), from front to back (1), length (1), projected (1), square (1 [+802, 2256]), widened (1), NDT (4)

H8146 1רָחָב ***rāḥāb[1]***, a. [21] [→ 8147?; cf. 8143]. spacious, broad, roomy:– spacious (4 [+3338]), broad (2), proud (2), spacious (2), boundless (1 [+4394]), broad (1 [+3338]), freedom (1), gaping (1), greedy (1 [+5883]), large (1), large (1 [+3338]), plenty of room (1 [+3338]), spread out (1), thick (1), wider (1)

H8147 2רָחָב ***rāḥāb[2]***, n.pr.f. [5] [√ 8146?; cf. 8143]. Rahab, "*spacious, broad*":– Rahab (5)

H8148 1רְחֹב ***rᵉḥōb[1]***, n.f. [43] [→ 1124, 8149, 8150?, 8151, 8155; cf. 8143]. public square, open street:– streets (14), square (10), public square (8), public squares (4), squares (4), oneS (1), open square (1), thereS (1 [+928, 2023])

H8149 2רְחֹב ***rᵉḥōb[2]***, n.pr.loc. [7] [√ 8148]. Rehob, "*broad, wide [place, market]*":– Rehob (7)

H8150 3רְחֹב ***rᵉḥōb[3]***, n.pr.m. [3] [√ 8148?]. Rehob, "*broad, wide [place, market]*":– Rehob (3)

H8151 רְחֹבוֹת ***rᵉḥōbôt***, n.pr.loc. [3] [√ 8148]. Rehoboth, "*broad, wide [places, markets]*":– Rehoboth (3)

H8152 רְחַבְיָה ***rᵉḥabyâ***, n.pr.m. [2] [√ 8143 + 3378]. Rehabiah, "*Yahweh has enlarged*":– Rehabiah (2)

H8153 רְחַבְיָהוּ ***rᵉḥabyāhû***, n.pr.m. [3] [√ 8143 + 3378]. Rehabiah, "*Yahweh has enlarged*":– Rehabiah (2), hisS (1)

H8154 רְחַבְעָם ***rᵉḥabʿām***, n.pr.m. [49] [√ 8143 + 6639]. Rehoboam, "*[my] people will enlarge, expand*":– Rehoboam (42), Rehoboam's (3), heS (3), NDT (1)

H8155 רְחֹבֹת עִיר ***rᵉḥōbōt ʿîr***, n.pr.loc. [1] [√ 8148 + 6551]. Rehoboth Ir, "*streets of [the] city* or *spacious city*":– Rehoboth Ir (1)

H8156 רְחוּם ***rᵉḥûm***, n.pr.m. [4] [√ 8163; cf. 5700; 10662]. Rehum, "*[he] is compassionate*":– Rehum (4)

H8157 רַחוּם ***raḥûm***, a. [13] [√ 8163]. compassionate, merciful:– compassionate (10), merciful (3)

H8158 רָחוֹק ***rāḥôq***, a. (used as noun) [85] [√ 8178; 10663]. far, distant; (n.) distance, afar:– far (12), distant (11), afar (10), distance (10), far away (9), far away (5 [+4946]), distant (2 [+4946]), distant place (2), future (2 [+4946]), long ago (2 [+4946]), long ago (2 [+4200, 4946]), long way (2), at a distance (1 [+4394]), away (1), beyond (1), beyond reach (1), far and wide (1 [+6330]), far and wide (1 [+6330, 4200, 4946]), far away (1 [+6330, 4200, 4946]), far off (1), far off (1 [+928]), far-off (1), farthest (1), long (1 [+4946]), long way (1 [+4394]), past (1), some distance away (1 [+4946]), widely (1)

H8159 רָחִיט ***rāḥîṭ***, n.m. Not used in NIVEBC [cf. 8112]. see 8112

H8160 רֵחַיִם ***rēḥayim***, n.[m.] [5] handmill; pair of mill stones:– hand mill (2), millstones (2), pair of millstones (1)

H8161 1רָחֵל ***rāḥēl[1]***, n.f. [4] [→ 8162]. ewe-sheep:– sheep (3), ewes (1)

H8162 2רָחֵל ***rāḥēl[2]***, n.pr.f. [47] [√ 8161]. Rachel, "*ewe*":– Rachel (40), Rachel's (5), herS (1), sheS (1)

H8163 רָחַם ***rāḥam***, v.den. [47] [→ 3736, 3737, 3738, 8020?, 8156, 8157, 8172; cf. 8167]. [Q] to love; [P] to have compassion on, show mercy, take pity on; [Pu] to find compassion, be loved; feelings of compassion are usually accompanied by acts of compassion:– have compassion (15), compassion (4), has compassion (4), show love (4), mercy (3), show compassion (3), have great compassion (2 [+8163]), have mercy (2), loved (2), show mercy (2), find compassion (1), finds mercy (1), full of compassion (1), had compassion (1), love (1), pity (1)

H8164 רָחָם ***rāḥām***, n.[m.] [1] [→ 8165, 8168]. carrion-vulture; some sources: osprey:– osprey (1)

H8165 1רַחַם ***raḥam[1]***, n.pr.m. [1] [√ 8164]. Raham, "*compassion*":– Raham (1)

H8166 2רַחַם ***raḥam[2]***, n.m. Not used in NIVEBC [√ 8167]. see 8167

H8167 רֶחֶם ***reḥem***, n.m. [31] [→ 8166, 8169, 8171; cf. 8163]. womb; by extension: mother, any female, birth; an "open womb" is able to conceive; a "closed womb" cannot conceive:– womb (17), birth (3), enabled to conceive (2 [+7337, 906]), woman (2), born (1), born (1 [+3655, 4946]), first male offspring (1 [+1147, 7081]), firstborn (1 [+7081]), kept the women from conceiving (1 [+6806, 1237, 6806]), mothers (1), wombs (1)

H8168 רָחָמָה ***rāḥāmâ***, n.[m.] [1] [√ 8164]. carrion-vulture; some sources: osprey:– osprey (1)

H8169 רַחֲמָה ***raḥᵃmâ***, n.f. [1] [√ 8167]. womb; slang for woman:– twoS (1)

H8170 רֻחָמָה ***ruḥāmâ***, n.pr.f. Not used in NIVEBC [→ 4205]. Ruhamah

H8171 רַחֲמִים ***raḥᵃmîm***, n.m.pl.abst. [39] [√ 8167; 10664]. compassion, mercy, pity:– compassion (17), mercy (12), compassions (1), deeply moved (1 [+4023]), favor (1), great mercy (1), kindest acts (1), love (1), merciful (1), pity (1), women (1), NDT (1)

H8172 רַחֲמָנִי ***raḥᵃmānî***, a. [1] [√ 8163]. compassionate:– compassionate (1)

H8173 1רָחַף ***rāḥap[1]***, v. [3] [Q] to tremble, shake; [P] to hover:– hovering (1), hovers (1), tremble (1)

H8174 2רָחַף ***rāḥap[2]***, v. [Q] to grow soft, relax

H8175 רָחַץ ***rāḥaṣ***, v. [73] [→ 8176, 8177]. [Q] to wash, bathe; [Pu] to be cleansed; [Ht] to wash oneself:– bathe (24), wash (23), washed (10), bathed (4), washing (4), are cleansed (1), bathing (1), dip (1), drenched (1), wade (1), wash away (1), washed myself (1), were washed (1)

H8176 רַחַץ ***raḥaṣ***, n.[m.] [2] [√ 8175]. washing:– washbasin (2 [+6105])

H8177 רַחְצָה ***raḥṣâ***, n.f. [2] [√ 8175]. washing:– washing (2)

H8178 רָחַק ***rāḥaq***, v. [58] [→ 1092, 3439, 5305, 8158, 8179]. [Q] to be far off; to avoid, stand aloof; [P] to send far away, extend; [H] to remove far away, drive far off, go very far:– far (12), far away (7), drive far (3), keep far (3), must very far (2 [+8178]), put away (2), remove far (2), sent far away (2), stand aloof (2), taken (2), alienated (1), avoid (1), away (1), distance away (1), extended (1), extending (1), far from (1), far removed (1), go far (1), gone some distance (1), have nothing to do (1), is severed (1), keep distance (1), no near (1), refrain (1), send far (1), some distance away (1 [+4946]), stay far (1), strayed far (1), went far (1), withdraw far (1)

H8179 רָחֵק ***rāḥēq***, a.vbl. [1] [√ 8178]. one who is far away:– far (1)

H8180 רָחַשׁ ***rāḥaš***, v. [1] [→ 5306]. [Q] to be stirred up (one's heart):– stirred (1)

H8181 רַחַת ***raḥat***, n.f. [1] winnowing fork, shovel:– fork (1)

H8182 רָטַב ***rāṭab***, v. [1] [→ 8183]. [Q] to be drenched, be wet:– drenched (1)

H8183 רָטֹב ***rāṭōb***, a. [1] [√ 8182]. well-watered (plant):– well-watered plant (1)

H8184 רָטָה ***rāṭâ***, v. [Q] to wring out

H8185 רֶטֶט ***reṭeṭ***, n.[m.] [1] [cf. 8417]. panic:– panic (1)

H8186 רֻטֲפַשׁ ***ruṭᵉpaš***, v. [1] [Qp] to be renewed:– be renewed (1)

H8187 רָטַשׁ ***rāṭaš***, v. [6] [P] to dash to pieces; [Pu] to be dashed to pieces:– be dashed to pieces (1), be dashed to the ground (1), dash to the ground (1), strike down (1), were dashed to pieces (1), were dashed to the ground (1)

H8188 רִי ***rî***, n.[m.] [1] [√ 8115]. moisture:– moisture (1)

H8189 1רִיב ***rîb1***, v. [68] [→ 3384, 3424, 3742, 5310, 5311, 5312, 5313, 5315, 8190, 8191]. [Q] to quarrel, contend, plead for:– quarreled (7), bring charges (6), contend (4), defend (4), accuse (3), quarrel (3), rebuked (3), complain (2), quarrel (2 [+8189]), rebuke (2), take up (2), vigorously defend (2 [+8189]), accused (1), argue the case (1), bring a case (1), bring a charge (1), challenged (1), charges (1), contended (1), contends (1), defender (1), defends (1), defends cause (1), dispute (1), fights (1), in court (1), judgment (1), oppose (1), oppose (1 [+6643]), plead (1), plead case (1), plead cause (1), plead the case (1), pleads (1), take to court (1 [+8190]), took to task (1), took up (1), upheld (1), uphold (1), uphold cause (1)

H8190 2רִיב ***rîb2***, n.m. [60] [√ 8189]. contention, grievance, strife, legal dispute:– case (9), cause (9), strife (7), dispute (4), lawsuit (3), attacks (2), charge (2), complaint (2), disputes (2), quarrel (2), quarreling (2), accusation (1), accuser (1 [+408]), accusing (1), cases of dispute (1), charges (1), contend (1), court (1), distress (1), grievance (1), justice (1), lawsuits (1), oppose (1), strives (1), struggle (1), take to court (1 [+8189]), taunts (1)

H8191 רִיבָה ***rîbâ***, n.m. [2] [√ 8189]. legal plea:– cases (1 [+1821]), pleas (1)

H8192 רִיבַי ***rîbay***, n.pr.m. [2] [√ 3744?]. Ribai, "*opponent*":– Ribai (2)

H8193 רִיחַ ***rîaḥ***, v. [11] [→ 8194; cf. 8118]. [H] to smell (an aroma or odor):– smell (2), accept (1), catches the scent (1), caught the smell (1 [+8194]), comes close (1), delight (1), enjoy fragrance (1), smelled (1), stench (1 [+4202]), take delight (1)

H8194 רֵיחַ ***rêaḥ***, n.m. [58] [√ 8193; cf. 8118; 10666]. aroma; pleasing and acceptable: fragrance; unpleasing and unacceptable: stench; both connotations are used of sacrifices as accepted or rejected by God:– aroma (40), fragrance (8), fragrant incense (4 [+5767]), smell (2), caught the smell (1 [+8193]), fragranceS (1), made obnoxious (1 [+944]), scent (1)

H8195 רִיפוֹת ***rîpôt***, n.[f.] [2] grain:– grain (2)

H8196 רִיפַת ***rîpat***, n.pr.g. [2] [cf. 1910]. Riphath:– Riphath (2)

H8197 1רִיק ***rîq1***, v. [18] [→ 8198, 8199, 8200]. [H] to pour forth, empty out; to draw (a sword):– draw (3), drawn (3), emptying (2), pour out (2), brandish (1), called out (1), draw out (1), empty (1), leave empty (1), pour (1), poured (1), poured out (1)

H8198 2רִיק ***rîq2***, n.[m.] [12] [√ 8197]. emptiness, nothingness, vanity:– in vain (4 [+4200]), for nothing (2 [+928, 1896]), in vain (2), delusions (1), empty (1), utterly useless (1 [+2039, 2256]), vain (1)

H8199 רֵיק ***rêq***, a. [14] [√ 8197]. empty; idle, worthless:– empty (4), fantasies (2), worthless (2), emptied (1), hungry (1 [+5883]), idle (1), reckless (1), scoundrels (1), vulgar (1)

H8200 רֵיקָם ***rêqām***, adv. [16] [√ 8197]. empty-handed, without cause or satisfaction:– empty-handed (9), empty (2), without cause (2), unfilled (1), unsatisfied (1), without a gift (1)

H8201 1רִיר ***rîr1***, v. [1] [→ 8202]. [Q] to flow:– flowing (1)

H8202 2רִיר ***rîr2***, n.m. [2] [√ 8201]. saliva; white (of an egg); some sources: a kind of plant juice:– saliva (1), sap (1)

H8203 רֵישׁ ***rêš***, n.m. [7] [√ 8133]. poverty:– poverty (7)

H8204 רֹךְ ***rōk***, n.[m.] [1] [√ 8216]. gentleness, tenderness, softness:– gentle (1)

H8205 רַךְ ***rak***, a. [16] [√ 8216]. gentle, tender, weak, soft:– gentle (5), tender (5), inexperienced (2), weak (2), fainthearted (1 [+4222]), indecisive (1 [+4222])

H8206 רָכַב ***rākab***, v. [78] [→ 5323, 5324, 8207, 8208, 8209, 8210, 8211, 8213]. [Q] to ride or mount an riding animal:– riding (9), mounted (7), rider (4), rode (4), driver (3), horseman (3 [+6061]), put (3), ride (3), riders (3), rides (3), drive (2), mounted (2 [+6061]), ridden (2), ride on (2), rode off (2), came riding (1), cause to ride in triumph (1), drivers (1), got into chariot (1), got on (1), had mount (1 [+6584]), had ride (1), had ride along (1), have mount (1 [+6584]), horsemen (1 [+6061]), in a chariot (1), lead (1), led on horseback (1), let ride (1), made ride (1), mount (1), moved (1), ride forth (1), ride off (1), rides across (1), riding in chariots (1), set (1), slow down (1 [+6806, 4200]), take (1), taken (1), took by chariot (1)

H8207 רֶכֶב ***rekeb***, n.m. [120] [√ 8206]. chariot; large upper mill stone:– chariots (77), chariot (26), chariot horses (3), charioteers (3), riders (3), upper (2), charioteers (1 [+132]), chariots and charioteers (1), upper one (1), NDT (3)

H8208 רַכָּב ***rakkāb***, n.m. [3] [√ 8206]. chariot driver, horseman:– chariot driver (2), horseman (1)

H8209 רֵכָב ***rēkāb***, n.pr.m. [13] [→ 8211; cf. 8206]. Recab, "[prob.] *rider* or *horseman [from to ride, mount]*":– Rekab (12), Rekabites (1 [+1074])

H8210 רִכְבָּה ***rikbâ***, n.f. [1] [√ 8206]. act of riding:– saddle (1)

H8211 רֵכָבִי ***rēkābî***, a.g. [4] [√ 8209; cf. 8206]. Recabite, "*of Recab*":– Rekabites (2), Rekabite (1), Rekabites (1 [+1201, 1074])

H8212 רֵכָה ***rēkâ***, n.pr.loc. [1] Recah:– Rekah (1)

H8213 רְכוּב ***rᵉkûb***, n.[m.] [1] [√ 8206]. chariot:– chariot (1)

H8214 רְכוּשׁ ***rᵉkûš***, n.m. [28] [√ 8223]. possessions, property, goods, equipment:– possessions (11), goods (7), property (3), wealth (2), equipment (1), equipped (1), everything (1 [+3972]), own (1), riches (1)

H8215 רָכִיל ***rākîl***, n.[m.] [6] [√ 8217?]. slanderer, gossip:– gossip (2 [+2143]), slander (1), slanderer (1 [+2143]), slanderers (1 [+408]), spreading slander (1)

H8216 רָכַךְ ***rākak***, v. [8] [→ 5322, 8204, 8205]. [Q] to be soft, faint-hearted; [Pu] to be soothed; [H] to make faint:– lose (2), responsive (2), fainthearted (1 [+4222]), made faint (1), soothed (1), soothing (1)

H8217 רָכַל ***rākal***, v. [17] [→ 5326, 8215?, 8218?, 8219]. [Q] to do trade, act as a merchant; (n.) trader, merchant:– merchants (6), traded (5), merchant (2), traders (2), did business with (1), traded with (1)

H8218 רָכָל ***rākāl***, n.pr.loc. [1] [√ 8217?]. Racal, "*trade*":– Rakal (1)

H8219 רְכֻלָּה ***rᵉkullâ***, n.f. [4] [√ 8217]. trading of merchandise:– trade (2), merchandise (1), trading (1)

H8220 רָכַס ***rākas***, v. [2] [→ 8221, 8222?; cf. 8224]. [Q] to tie, bind:– tied (2)

H8221 רֶכֶס ***rekes***, n.[m.] [1] [√ 8220]. rugged place:– rugged places (1)

H8222 רֹכֶס ***rōkes***, n.[m.] [1] [√ 8220?]. intrigue, plot, conspiracy:– intrigues (1)

H8223 רָכַשׁ ***rākaš***, v. [5] [→ 8214]. [Q] to tie, bind:– accumulated (2), acquired (2), NDT (1)

H8224 רֶכֶשׁ ***rekeš***, n.m.col. [4] [cf. 8220]. team of horses; fast horses (for couriers):– fast horses (2), chariot horses (1), horses (1)

H8225 1רָם ***rām1***, a.vbl. *or* v.ptcp. Not used in NIVEBC [√ 8123]. high, exalted

H8226 2רָם ***rām2***, n.pr.m. [7] [√ 8123]. Ram, "*high, exalted*":– Ram (7)

H8227 1רָמָה ***rāmâ1***, v. [4] [→ 810, 8239, 3758, 3759; 10667]. [Q] to hurl (horse and rider); to shoot (arrows):– hurled (2), archers (1 [+8008]), armed (1 [+5976])

H8228 2רָמָה ***rāmâ2***, v. [8] [→ 5327, 5328, 8244, 8245, 9564, 9566, 9567; cf. 8332?]. [P] to deceive, betray:– betrayed (2), deceive (2), deceived (2), betray (1), deceives (1)

H8229 3רָמָה ***rāmâ3***, n.f. [5] [→ 8230, 8238, 8240, 8241, 8255, 8256, 8257, 8258, 8259; cf. 8123]. lofty shrine; height:– lofty shrines (3), hill (1), lofty shrine (1)

H8230 4רָמָה ***rāmâ4***, n.pr.loc. [35] [√ 8229]. Ramah; Ramoth, "*elevated spot, height*":– Ramah (33), Ramoth (2)

H8231 רִמָּה ***rimmâ***, n.f. [7] [√ 8249]. worm, maggot:– maggots (2), worm (2), worms (2), maggot (1)

H8232 1רִמּוֹן ***rimmôn1***, n.m. [31] [→ 1784, 8233, 8234, 8236, 8237]. pomegranate: the tree, its fruit, or decorative objects shaped like the fruit:– pomegranates (24), pomegranate (4), alternateS (1 [+7194, 2298, 2256]), alternatedS (1 [+7194, 2256]), pomegranate tree (1)

H8233 2רִמּוֹן ***rimmôn2***, n.pr.m. [3] [√ 8232 *or* 8235]. Rimmon, "*pomegranate* or *Rimmon*":– Rimmon (3)

H8234 3רִמּוֹן ***rimmôn3***, n.pr.loc. [9] [√ 8232 *or* 8235]. Rimmon, "*pomegranate* or *Rimmon*":– Rimmon (8), whereS (1 [+928, 6152])

H8235 4רִמּוֹן ***rimmôn4***, n.pr.m. [3] [→ 2062, 3193, 6538; cf. 8233, 8234]. Rimmon (pagan god), "*Rimmon*":– Rimmon (2), thereS (1 [+1074])

H8236 רִמּוֹן פֶּרֶץ ***rimmôn pereṣ***, n.pr.loc. [2] [√ 8232 + 7288]. Rimmon Perez, "*pomegranate pass [breach]*":– Rimmon Perez (2)

H8237 רִמּוֹנוֹ ***rimmônô***, n.pr.loc. [1] [√ 8234]. Rimmono, "*pomegranate* or *Rimmon*":– Rimmono (1)

H8238 רָמוֹת ***rāmôt***, n.pr.loc. Not used in NIVEBC [√ 8229]. Ramoth

H8239 רָמוּת ***rāmût***, n.f. [1] [√ 8227]. remains, refuse, rubbish:– remains (1)

H8240 רָמוֹת גִּלְעָד ***rāmôt gilʿād***, n.pr.loc. [20] [√ 8229 + 1680]. Ramoth Gilead, "*heights in Gilead*":– Ramoth Gilead (20)

H8241 רָמוֹת־נֶגֶב ***rāmôt-negeb***, n.pr.loc. [1] [√ 8241 + 5582]. Ramoth Negev, "*heights of Negev [the south]*":– Ramoth Negev (1)

H8242 רֹמַח ***rōmaḥ***, n.[m.] [15] spear:– spears (10), spear (5)

H8243 רַמְיָה ***ramyâ***, n.pr.m. [1] [√ 8123? + 3378?]. Ramiah, "*Yahweh is exalted*":– Ramiah (1)

H8244 1רְמִיָּה ***rᵉmiyyâ1***, n.f. [7] [√ 8228]. laziness, laxness, slackness:– faulty (2), lazy (2), lax (1), laziness (1), shiftless (1 [+5883])

H8245 2רְמִיָּה ***rᵉmiyyâ2***, n.f. [8] [√ 8228]. deceit:– deceit (3), deceitful (2), deceitfully (2), lies (1)

H8246 רַמִּים ***rammîm***, n.pr. Ramites

H8247 רַמָּכָה ***rammākâ***, n.[f.] [1] fast mare:– especially bred (1 [+1201, 2021])

H8248 רְמַלְיָהוּ ***rᵉmalyāhû***, n.pr.m. [13] [√ 3378]. Remaliah, "*Yahweh has adorned*":– Remaliah (11), Remaliah's (2)

H8249 1רָמַם ***rāmam1***, v.den. [1] [→ 8231]. [Q] to be full of maggots, be wormy:– full (1)

H8250 2רָמַם ***rāmam2***, v. [5] [cf. 8123]. [Q] to be exalted; [N] to rise upward; to get away:– rose (2), exalted (1), get away (1), rose upward (1)

H8251 רֹמַמְתִּי עֶזֶר ***rōmamtî ʿezer***, n.pr.m. [2] [√ 8123 + 6469]. Romamti-Ezer, "*[he is my] highest help*":– Romamti-Ezer (2)

H8252 רָמַס ***rāmas***, v. [19] [→ 5330]. [Q] to trample, tread upon; [N] to be trampled:– trample (4), trampled (4), trampled underfoot (3), aggressor (1), be trampled (1), mauls (1), trample down (1), trampling (1), tread (1), treading (1), trod down (1)

H8253 רָמַשׂ ***rāmaś***, v. [17] [→ 8254]. [Q] to move along (ground or in the water):– moves (5), move (4), moves about (2), moves along (2), creature that moves (1), creatures that move (1), moved (1), prowl (1)

H8254 רֶמֶשׂ ***remeś***, n.m. [17] [√ 8253]. creatures that move along (ground or sea):– creatures that move (5), creature (2), creatures (2), crawling things (1), creature that moves (1), creatures that move along the ground (1), moves about (1), reptiles (1), sea creatures (1), small creatures (1), teeming creatures (1)

H8255 רֶמֶת ***remet***, n.pr.loc. [1] [√ 8229]. Remeth, "*heights*":– Remeth (1)

H8256 רָמַת הַמִּצְפֶּה ***rāmat hammiṣpeh***, n.pr.loc. [1] [√ 8229 + 2174]. Ramath Mizpah, "*height [hill] of Mizpah [watch tower]*":– Ramath Mizpah (1)

H8257 רָמַת לְחִי ***rāmat lᵉḥî***, n.pr.loc. [1] [√ 8229 + 4305?]. Ramath Lehi, "*height [hill] of Lehi*":– Ramath Lehi (1)

H8258 רָמָתִי ***rāmātî***, a.g. [1] [√ 8229]. Ramathite, "*of Ramah*":– Ramathite (1)

H8259 רָמָתַיִם ***rāmātayim***, n.pr.loc. [1] [√ 8229]. Ramathaim, "*two heights*":– Ramathaim (1)

H8260 רֹן ***rōn***, n.[m.] [1] [√ 8264]. (joyful) song:– songs (1)

H8261 רָנָה ***rānâ***, v. [1] [→ 8262, 8263; cf. 8264]. [Q] to rattle:– rattles (1)

H8262 1רִנָּה ***rinnâ1***, n.f. [33] [→ 8263; cf. 8261, 8264]. shout of joy, song of joy; cry of pleading:– cry (10), singing (4), song (4), songs of joy (4), shouts of joy (3), plea (2), shouts of joy (2 [+7754]), joy (1), pride (1), rejoicing (1), sing (1)

H8263 2רִנָּה ***rinnâ2***, n.pr.m. [1] [√ 8262; cf. 8261]. Rinnah, "*ringing cry [of joy] to Yahweh*":– Rinnah (1)

H8264 רָנַן ***rānan***, v. [53] [→ 8260, 8265, 8266; cf. 8261, 8262]. [Q] to shout for joy, sing for joy; to cry, plead; [P] to sing for joy; [Polal] to sing for joy; [H] to make sing, call for songs of joy:– sing for joy (15), shout for joy (12), sing (8), cry out (2), ever sing for joy (2 [+8264]), rejoice (2), call forth songs of joy (1), calls aloud (1), cries aloud (1), joyfully sing (1), jubilant song (1), made sing (1), sang (1), shout (1), shouted for joy (1), sing joyfully (1), sings (1), songs of joy (1)

H8265 רְנָנָה ***rᵉnānâ***, n.f. [4] [√ 8264]. shout of joy, joyful song:– joyful songs (1), mirth (1), shout of joy (1), singing (1)

H8266 רְנָנִים ***rᵉnānîm***, n.[m.]pl. [1] [√ 8264]. female ostrich:– ostrich (1)

H8267 רִסָּה ***rissâ***, n.pr.loc. [2] [√ 8272?]. Rissah, "*dew*":– Rissah (2)

H8268 1רְסִיס ***rāsîs1***, n.[m.] [1] [√ 8272]. drop (of moisture):– dampness (1)

H8269 2רָסִיס ***rāsîs2***, n.[m.] [1] broken piece (of rubble):– pieces (1)

H8270 1רֶסֶן ***resen1***, n.m. [3] bridle:– bit (1), bridle (1 [+6344]), restraint (1)

H8271 2רֶסֶן ***resen2***, n.pr.loc. [1] Resen:– Resen (1)

H8272 רָסַס ***rāsas***, v. [1] [→ 8267?, 8268]. [Q] to moisten, sprinkle:– moisten (1)

H8273 1רַע ***raʿ1***, a. [350] [→ 8274, 8288; cf. 8317]. bad, disagreeable, inferior in quality; by extension: evil, wicked in ethical quality; what is disagreeable to God is ethically evil; God's actions of judgment are disagreeable to the

HEBREW INDEX

wicked (Ezek 14:21), but are not ethically evil:– evil (179), bad (26), wicked (24), wrong (10), harm (8), trouble (8), disaster (6), evildoers (5), wild (4), ugly (3), deadly (2), evildoer (2), evildoers (2 [+408]), ferocious (2), grievous (2), harm (2 [+6913]), heavy (2), malice (2), no good (2), painful (2), ruin (2), sad (2), terrible (2), ugly (2 [+5260]), animosity (1 [+8120]), begrudging host (1 [+6524]), bitter (1), brings to ruin (1 [+6156, 4200, 2021]), crimes (1), cruel (1), destroying (1), destruction (1), difficult (1), disaster (1 [+7004]), displease (1 [+928, 6524]), displeasing (1 [+928, 6524]), distressing (1), dreadful (1), evildoers (1 [+132]), flaw (1 [+1821]), great (1), hardships (1), harm (1 [+1821]), harmful (1), horrible (1), hurt (1), impure (1), look sad (1), mean (1), miserable (1), misery (1), misfortune (1 [+6721]), not[s] (1), not want (1 [+928, 6524]), one way[s] (1), savage (1), serious (1), severe (1), sin (1), stern (1), stingy (1 [+6524, 408]), surely suffer (1 [+8317]), troubled (1 [+928, 6524]), ugly (1 [+9307]), undesirable (1), unfavorable (1), unjust (1), vile (1), violence (1), worse (1), worst (1), wretched (1), NDT (1)

H8274 [2]רֵעַ ***ra'***[2], n.m. Not used in NIVEBC [√ 8273; cf. 8317]. evil, distress, misery, injury, calamity

H8275 [1]רֵעַ ***rēa'***[1], n.m.vbl. [3] [√ 8131]. shouting, roar:– cry aloud (1 [+8131]), shouting (1), thunder (1)

H8276 [2]רֵעַ ***rēa'***[2], n.m. [187] [√ 8287]. neighbor; friend, companion, associate:– neighbor (45), other[s] (27), friend (23), neighbor's (19), friends (18), neighbors (13), another[s] (11), another (2), companion (2), other person's (2), someone (2), adviser (1), another's[s] (1), anyone among people (1 [+2256, 278]), associates (1), closest friend (1 [+889, 3869, 5883, 3870]), companions (1), confidant (1), each other[s] (1), fellow (1), fellow Israelite (1), husband (1), lovers (1), making own people (1), opponent (1), opponent's (1), other (1), own people (1), own people (1 [+278]), someone else's (1), the parties (1 [+408, 2256, 2084]), their[s] (1 [+3870]), together (1 [+408, 907, 2084]), NDT (1)

H8277 [3]רֵעַ ***rēa'***[3], n.[m.] [2] [√ 8290]. thought, intention:– thoughts (2)

H8278 רֹעַ ***rōa'***, n.[m.] [19] [√ 8317]. bad, disagreeable, inferior in quality; by extension: evil, wicked in ethical quality:– evil (9), bad (4), wicked (2), sad (1), sadness (1), sinful (1), ugly (1)

H8279 [1]רָעֵב ***rā'ēb***[1], v. [13] [→ 8280, 8281, 8282]. [Q] to be hungry, be famished, be starving:– hungry (6), causing to hunger (1), famished (1), feel the famine (1), go hungry (1), hunger (1), let go hungry (1), starving (1)

H8280 רָעָב ***rā'āb***, n.m. [101] [√ 8279]. hunger, famine, starvation:– famine (91), hunger (6), starvation (2), starve (2)

H8281 [2]רָעֵב ***rā'ēb***[2], a. [20] [√ 8279]. hungry:– hungry (17), hungry (2 [+5883]), starving (1)

H8282 רְעָבוֹן ***r***[e]***'ābôn***, n.[m.] [3] [√ 8279]. hunger, famine, starvation:– starving (2), famine (1)

H8283 רָעַד ***rā'ad***, v. [3] [→ 8284, 8285]. [Q, H] to tremble:– greatly distressed (1), trembles (1), trembling (1)

H8284 רַעַד ***ra'ad***, n.m. [2] [√ 8283]. trembling:– trembling (2)

H8285 רְעָדָה ***r***[e]***'ādâ***, n.f. [4] [√ 8283]. trembling:– trembling (4)

H8286 [1]רָעָה ***rā'â***[1], v. [172] [→ 5337, 5338, 8297]. [Q] to be a shepherd, to care for flocks, graze; by extension: to rule, with a focus on care and concern:– shepherd (46), shepherds (38), tend (8), feed (7), graze (7), tending (6), pasture (4), feed on (3), feeds on (3), grazing (3), shepherded (3), shepherds (3 [+7366]), take care of (3), browse (2), browses (2), eat (2), find pasture (2), grazed (2), herders (2), shepherd's (2), cared for (1), devour (1), drive away (1), enjoy pasture (1), graze flock (1), grazing flocks (1), grazing the flocks (1), herders (1 [+5238]), herding (1), keeping (1), kept (1), lead (1), leaders (1), nourish (1), prey on (1), rule (1), shepherd flock (1), tends (1), those[s] (1), NDT (5)

H8287 [2]רָעָה ***rā'â***[2], v. [5] [→ 5335, 8134?, 8276, 8291, 8292, 8293, 8294, 8295, 8296, 8298, 8299, 8300; cf. 8289]. [Q] to be a companion, be a friend; [P] to be an attendant of the groom (of a wedding):– companion (3), attended at feast (1), make friends (1)

H8288 [3]רָעָה ***rā'â***[3], n.f. [316] [√ 8273; cf. 8317]. bad, disaster, harm, trouble; by extension: ethical evil, wickedness; what is "bad" to God is ethically evil; God's actions of judgment are "bad" to the wicked (Jer 18:8), but are not ethically evil:– disaster (81), evil (47), wickedness (32), harm (26), trouble (17), calamity (15), ruin (8), wrong (8), disasters (5), troubles (5), wicked (5), bad (3), calamities (3), distress (3), wrongdoing (3), badly (2), crimes (2), danger (2), evil deeds (2), evil thing (2), harm (2 [+6913]), harming (2), misery (2), misfortune (2), punishment (2), wickedness is great (2 [+8288]), another[s] (1), awful crime (1), awful thing (1), crime (1 [+5126]), cruelty (1), deeds of evildoers (1), defeat (1), destroy (1), destruction (1), discomfort (1), downfall (1), evil intent (1), evildoer (1 [+6913]), fate (1), fault (1), guilty of wrongdoing (1), it[s] (1 [+2021]), malice (1), offense (1), peril (1), plotting (1 [+3086, 2021]), seemed wrong (1 [+8317]), sin (1), sins (1), something desperate (1), very disturbed (1 [+8317]), wicked (1 [+408]), wicked thing (1), worst (1), wrongs (1), NDT (3)

H8289 [4]רָעָה ***rā'â***[4], v.den. Not used in NIVEBC [cf. 8287]. [P] to be an attendant of a groom, see 8287

H8290 [5]רָעָה ***rā'â***[5], v. [Q] to desire, long for

H8291 רֵעֶה ***rē'eh***, n.m. [4] [√ 8287]. friend, personal advisor:– confidant (2), adviser (1), one who is close (1)

H8292 רֵעָה ***rē'â***, n.f. [3] [√ 8287]. companion, friend:– friends (2), companions (1)

H8293 רְעוּ ***r***[e]***'û***, n.pr.m. [5] [√ 8287; cf. 8298]. Reu, *"friend [of God]"*:– Reu (5)

H8294 רְעוּאֵל ***r***[e]***'û'ēl***, n.pr.m. [10] [√ 8287 + 446]. Reuel, *"friend of God [El]"*:– Reuel (10)

H8295 [1]רְעוּת ***r***[e]***'ût***[1], n.f. [6] [√ 8287]. (female) neighbor; fellow (female):– mate (2), another[s] (1), another's[s] (1), someone else (1), NDT (1)

H8296 [2]רְעוּת ***r***[e]***'ût***[2], n.f. [7] [√ 8290; 10668]. chasing after:– chasing after (7)

H8297 רְעִי ***r***[e]***'î***, n.[m.] [1] [√ 8286]. pastured (cattle):– pasture-fed (1)

H8298 רֵעִי ***rē'î***, n.pr.m. [1] [√ 8287; cf. 8293]. Rei, *"friendly or [my] friend"*:– Rei (1)

H8299 רַעְיָה ***ra'yâ***, n.f. [9] [√ 8287]. darling, beloved, formally, companion, a woman who is the object of a man's love and affection:– darling (9)

H8300 רֵעְיָה ***rē'yâ***, n.f. Not used in NIVEBC [√ 8287]. companion

H8301 רַעְיוֹן ***ra'yôn***, n.[m.] [3] [√ 8290]. chasing after, striving for:– chasing after (2), anxious striving (1 [+4213])

H8302 רָעַל ***rā'al***, v. [1] [→ 5339, 8303, 8304, 9570]. [Ho] to be made to quiver:– brandished (1)

H8303 רַעַל ***ra'al***, n.[m.] [1] [√ 8302]. reeling:– reeling (1)

H8304 רְעָלָה ***r***[e]***'ālâ***, n.[f.] [1] [√ 8302]. veil:– veils (1)

H8305 רְעֵלָיָה ***r***[e]***'ēlāyâ***, n.pr.m. [1] [cf. 8313]. Reelaiah:– Reelaiah (1)

H8306 [1]רָעַם ***rā'am***[1], v.den. [11] [→ 8308, 8312, 8313]. [Q] to storm, thunder; [H] to make thunder, make storm:– resound (3), thundered (3), thunders (3), thunder (2)

H8307 [2]רָעַם ***rā'am***[2], v.den. [2] [Q] to be confused, distorted; [H] to irritate, agitate:– distorted with fear (1), irritate (1)

H8308 רַעַם ***ra'am***, n.[m.] [6] [√ 8306]. thunder; thunderous shout:– thunder (4), shout (1), thundercloud (1 [+6260])

H8309 רַעְמָא ***ra'mā'***, n.pr.m. [2] [cf. 8311]. Raamah:– Raamah (2)

H8310 [1]רַעְמָה ***ra'mâ***[1], n.f. [1] mane (of a horse):– flowing mane (1)

H8311 [2]רַעְמָה ***ra'mâ***[2], n.pr.m. [3] [cf. 8309]. Raamah:– Raamah (3)

H8312 [3]רַעְמָה ***ra'mâ***[3], n.f. Not used in NIVEBC [√ 8306]. thunder

H8313 רַעַמְיָה ***ra'amyâ***, n.pr.m. [1] [√ 8306 + 3378; cf. 8305]. Raamiah, *"Yahweh has thundered"*:– Raamiah (1)

H8314 רַעְמְסֵס ***ra'm***[e]***sēs***, n.pr.loc. [5] Rameses, a town in Egypt and a region in the Nile Delta, *"Ra created him"*:– Rameses (5)

H8315 רָעַן ***rā'an***, v. [1] [→ 8316]. [Palel] to flourish:– flourish (1)

H8316 רַעֲנָן ***ra'***[a]***nān***, a. [19] [√ 8315; 10670]. spreading (tree), verdant, luxuriant:– spreading (11), flourishing (2), green (2), fine (1), luxuriant tree (1), thriving (1), verdant (1)

H8317 [1]רָעַע ***rā'a'***[1], v.den. [94] [→ 5334, 5336, 8273, 8274, 8278, 8288]. [Q] to be distressed, be displeased; (by extension) to be bad, be evil; [N] to suffer harm; [H] to do wickedness; bring trouble, mistreat; this refers to what is displeasing from a personal perspective; what is displeasing to God is ethically evil:– wicked (11), evil (7), evildoers (6), harm (6), displeased (5 [+928, 6524]), bring disaster (4), brought trouble (3), do harm (3), bad (2), distressed (2 [+928, 6524]), doing evil (2), mistreated (2), persist in doing evil (2 [+8317]), acted wickedly (1), begrudge (1 [+6524]), bring trouble (1), broken (1), brought misfortune (1), brought to grief (1), brought tragedy (1), crushed (1), destruction brought (1), did evil (1), disapprove (1 [+928, 6524]), displeased (1), displeased greatly (1 [+928, 6524]), do evil (1), do wicked thing (1), doing wrong (1), done evil (1), done wrong (1), downhearted (1 [+4222]), grudging (1), harming (1), have no compassion (1 [+6524]), hurts (1), leads to evil (1), look sad (1), not please (1 [+928, 6524]), seemed wrong (1 [+8288]), show ill will (1 [+6524]), sinned (1), suffers harm (1), surely suffer (1 [+8273]), treat worse (1), trouble came (1), upset (1 [+928, 6524]), very disturbed (1 [+8288]), vile (1), villains (1), wickedly (1), wronged (1)

H8318 [2]רָעַע ***rā'a'***[2], v. [9] [cf. 8320, 8368]. [Q] to break, shatter; [H] to break down; [Htpol] to come to ruin:– break (2), is broken up (2 [+8318]), broke down (1), broken (1), comes to ruin (1), cracked (1), shatters (1)

H8319 רָעַף ***rā'ap***, v. [5] [cf. 6903]. [Q] to drop, fall, overflow; [H] to cause to rain:– overflow (2), let drop (1), rain down (1), showers fall (1)

H8320 רָעַץ ***rā'aṣ***, v. [2] [cf. 8318, 8368]. [Q] to shatter:– shattered (2)

H8321 [1]רָעַשׁ ***rā'aš***[1], v. [30] [→ 8323]. [Q] to shake, quake, tremble; [N] to be made to quake; [H] to cause to shake, make to tremble:– tremble (7), shake (6), quake (3), quaked (3), trembles (3), made tremble (2), shook (2), make leap (1), quaking (1), shaken (1), sway (1)

H8322 [2]רָעַשׁ ***rā'aš***[2], v. [Q] to be abundant

H8323 רַעַשׁ ***ra'aš***, n.m. [17] [√ 8321]. commotion, rattling, earthquake; this can mean a quaking motion and the sounds from a quaking motion; by extension: any clamor, discord, or frenzy:– earthquake (7), rumbling (2), battle (1), clatter (1 [+7754]), commotion (1), frenzied (1), noise (1), rattling (1), rattling sound (1), tremble (1)

H8324 [1]רָפָא ***rāpā'***[1], v. [67] [→ 5340, 5342, 8325, 8326, 8334?, 8335?, 8336, 8337, 9559; *also used with compound proper names*]. [Q] to heal; [N] to be healed, be cured; [P] to heal, repair; [Ht] to recover:– heal (21), healed (10), heals (5), be healed (4), physicians (4), recover (3), be cured (2), cure (2), dress (2), fresh (2), see that is completely healed (2 [+8324]), are healed (1), be repaired (1), been healed (1), gone (1), incurable (1 [+4412]), makes fresh (1), mend (1), physician (1), pure (1), repaired (1)

H8325 [2]רָפָא ***rāpā'***[2], n.pr.m. [3] [√ 8324; cf. 8330]. Rapha, "[poss.] *one healed*":– Rapha (3)

H8326 רִפְאוּת ***rip'ût***, n.f. [1] [√ 8324]. health, healing:– health (1)

H8327 [1]רְפָאִים ***r***[e]***pā'îm***[1], n.m. [8] [cf. 8332?]. dead, the spirits of the departed:– dead (4), spirits (2), spirits of the dead (1), spirits of the departed (1)

H8328 [2]רְפָאִים ***r***[e]***pā'îm***[2], n.pr.g. [11] [cf. 8332?]. Rephaite, *"mighty"*:– Rephaites (10), who[s] (1)

H8329 [3]רְפָאִים ***r***[e]***pā'îm***[3], n.pr.g. [8] [cf. 8332?]. Rephaim, *"sunken, powerless ones [giants];* [poss.] *shades, ghosts of the dead ones [giants]"*:– Rephaim (8)

H8330 רְפָאֵל ***r***[e]***pā'ēl***, n.pr.m. [1] [√ 8324 + 446; cf. 8325]. Rephael, *"God [El] heals"*:– Rephael (1)

H8331 רָפַד ***rāpad***, v. [3] [→ 8339, 8340]. [Q] to spread (mud, so as to leave a trail); [P] to spread out; to refresh:– leaving a trail (1), refresh (1), spread out (1)

H8332 [1]רָפָה ***rāpâ***[1], v. [47] [→ 5341, 8333, 8342; cf. 8228?, 8327?, 8328?, 8329?]. [Q] to hang limp, sink down, be feeble; [N] to be lazy; [P] to lower; discourage; [H] to leave alone, abandon, withdraw; [Ht] to show oneself slack:– leave (4), go limp (3), hang limp (3), lazy (3), let alone (3), let go (3), abandon (2), give (2), lowered (2), withdraw (2), abandon (1 [+3338, 4946]), almost (1), disarms (1 [+4653]), discourage (1 [+3338]), discouraging (1 [+3338]), enough (1), fail (1), falter (1), feeble (1), give up (1 [+3338]), leave alone (1), lost courage (1 [+3338]), refrain (1), sinks down (1), slack (1), still (1), subsided (1), to the point of exhaustion (1), wait (1), weak (1)

H8333 רָפֶה ***rāpeh***, a. [4] [√ 8332]. weak, feeble:– feeble (2), weak (1), weak (1 [+3338])

H8334 [2]רָפָה ***rāpâ***[2], n.pr.m. [1] [√ 8324?]. Raphah, "[poss.] *one healed*":– Raphah (1)

H8335 [3]רָפָה ***rāpâ***[3], n.pr.m. [4] [√ 8324?]. Rapha, "[poss.] *one healed*":– Rapha (4)

H8336 רָפוּא ***rāpû'***, n.pr.m. [1] [√ 8324]. Raphu, *"healed"*:– Raphu (1)

H8337 רְפוּאָה ***r***[e]***pû'â***, n.f. [3] [√ 8324]. healing:– healed (1), medicines (1), remedy (1)

H8338 רֶפַח ***repaḥ***, n.pr.m. [1] Rephah, "[poss.] *rich; easy [life]*":– Rephah (1)

H8339 רְפִידָה ***r***[e]***pîdâ***, n.f. [1] [√ 8331]. base (of a royal carriage); some sources: seat cover:– base (1)

H8340 רְפִידִים ***r***[e]***pîdîm***, n.pr.loc. [5] [√ 8331]. Rephidim, "[poss.] *supports, rests; resting place*":– Rephidim (5)

H8341 רְפָיָה ***r***[e]***pāyâ***, n.pr.m. [5] [cf. 8334?]. Rephaiah, *"Yahweh heals"*:– Rephaiah (5)

H8342 רִפָּיוֹן ***rippāyôn***, n.[m.] [1] [√ 8332]. hanging limp, possibly referring to despair:– hang limp (1)

H8343 רַפְסֹדוֹת ***rapsōdôt***, n.[f.pl.] [1] (log) rafts:– rafts (1)

H8344 רָפַף ***rāpap***, v. [1] [Poal] to quake, shake:– quake (1)

H8345 רָפַק ***rāpaq***, v. [1] [Ht] to lean oneself (upon):– leaning (1)

H8346 רָפַשׂ ***rāpaś***, v. [4] [→ 5343; 10672]. [Q] to muddy (a stream by trampling through); [N] to be muddied; [Ht] to be humbled, humble oneself:– humbled (1), muddied (1), muddy (1), muddying (1)

H8347 רֶפֶשׁ ***repeš***, n.[m.] [1] mire (of the sea):– mire (1)

H8348 רֶפֶת ***repet***, n.[m.] [1] stall, enclosure for cattle:– stalls (1)

H8349 רַץ ***raṣ***, n.[m.] [1] bar (of silver):– bars (1)

H8350 רָץ **rāṣ**, n.m. *or* v.ptcp. Not used in NIVEBC [√ 8132]. runner, guard, see 8132

H8351 1רָצָא **rāṣā'1**, v. [1] [cf. 8132?]. [Q] to run forth:– sped forth (1)

H8352 2רָצָא **rāṣā'2**, v. Not used in NIVEBC [√ 8354]. [Q] to take pleasure in, accept, see 8354

H8353 רָצַד **rāṣad**, v. [1] [P] to gaze in hostility:– gaze in envy (1)

H8354 1רָצָה **rāṣâ1**, v. [53] [→ 8352, 8356, 8359?, 8360?, 9573, 9574]. [Q] to be pleased, delight in, accept; [Qp] to be favored, be esteemed; [N] to be accepted; [H] to enjoy; [Ht] to regain favor:– accept (10), be accepted (5), pleased with (4), enjoy (3), pleased (3), delight (2), delights in (2), please (2), approve (1), approved (1), be acceptable (1), dear to (1), devotion (1), enjoyed (1), favored (1), find favor with (1), held in high esteem (1), in delight (1), join (1), loved (1), put in (1), received favorably (1), regain favor (1), show favor (1), showed favor (1), take delight in (1), take pleasure (1), take pleasure in (1), takes delight (1), takes pleasure (1)

H8355 2רָצָה **rāṣâ2**, v. [4] [Q] to pay for (sin); [N] to be paid for; [P] to make amends:– pay for (2), been paid for (1), make amends (1)

H8356 רָצוֹן **rāṣôn**, n.[m.] [56] [√ 8354]. pleasure, acceptance, favor, will:– favor (16), accepted (7), acceptable (5), pleased (4), pleases (4), will (4), delights (3), desires (2), please (2), pleasure (2), eagerly (1 [+928, 3972]), favored (1), find favor (1), finds favor (1), goodwill (1), pleasing (1), wished (1)

H8357 רָצַח **rāṣaḥ**, v. [46] [→ 8358]. [Q] to murder, kill; [N] to be murdered, killed; [P] to murder, kill:– murderer (12), accused of murder (7), murder (6), accused (2), killed (2), murdered (2), theyS (2 [+2021]), anyoneS (1), be killed (1), fugitiveS (1), himS (1 [+2021]), kill (1), killed (1 [+5782]), killed a person (1), kills a person (1), kills someone (1), murderer (1 [+1201]), murderers (1), murders (1 [+5883]), put to death (1)

H8358 רֶצַח **reṣaḥ**, n.[m.] [2] [√ 8357]. slaughter, murder, agony of death:– mortal agony (1), slaughter (1)

H8359 רִצְיָא **riṣyā'**, n.pr.m. [1] [√ 8354?]. Rizia, "[poss.] *pleasant one*":– Rizia (1)

H8360 רְצִין **rᵉṣîn**, n.pr.m. [11] [√ 8354?]. Rezin:– Rezin (10), Rezin's (1)

H8361 רָצַע **rāṣa'**, v. [1] [→ 5345]. [Q] to pierce (ear):– pierce (1)

H8362 רָצַף **rāṣap**, v. [1] [→ 5346, 8367]. [Qp] to be inlaid, be fitted:– inlaid (1)

H8363 1רֶצֶף **reṣep1**, n.f. [1] [→ 8364, 8365, 8366]. hot coals, live coals:– baked over hot coals (1)

H8364 2רֶצֶף **reṣep2**, n.pr.loc. [2] [√ 8363]. Rezeph, "*heated stones, live coals*":– Rezeph (2)

H8365 1רִצְפָּה **riṣpâ1**, n.f. [1] [√ 8363]. live coal, hot coal:– live coal (1)

H8366 2רִצְפָּה **riṣpâ2**, n.pr.f. [4] [√ 8363]. Rizpah, "*heated stones, live coals*":– Rizpah (4)

H8367 רִצְפָה **riṣᵉpâ**, n.f. [7] [√ 8362]. (stone) pavement:– pavement (5), itS (1 [+2021]), mosaic pavement (1)

H8368 רָצַץ **rāṣaṣ**, v. [20] [→ 5298; cf. 8318, 8320; 10671]. [Q] break, smash, oppress; [Qp] to be smashed, broken, splintered, oppressed; [N] to be broken, splintered; [P] to oppress, crush; [H] to crush to pieces; [Htpol] to jostle each other:– oppressed (4), splintered (3), broken (2), crushed (2), bruised (1), brutally oppressed (1), cracked (1), cruel (1), crush (1), discouraged (1), jostled each other (1), smashed to pieces (1), trampled (1)

H8369 1רַק **raq1**, a. [3] [→ 8370, 8377, 8378, 8386, 8395]. lean, thin, lank:– lean (2), lean (1 [+1414])

H8370 2רַק **raq2**, adv. [109] [√ 8369]. only, but, however, except:– only (28), but (22), however (13), except (5), nevertheless (4), surely (3), yet (3), always (2), except that (2), although (1), and (1), as for (1), be sure (1), but (1 [+2256]), but also (1), but only (1), moreover (1), nothing but (1), only (1 [+4202]), only (1 [+421]), really (1), sheer (1), NDT (14)

H8371 רֹק **rōq**, n.[m.] [3] [√ 8394]. spit, saliva; "to swallow one's spit" means a very brief time:– for an instant (1 [+6330, 1180]), spit (1), spitting (1)

H8372 רָקַב **rāqab**, v. [2] [→ 8373, 8374, 8375]. [Q] to rot, become worm-eaten:– rot (2)

H8373 רָקָב **rāqāb**, n.[m.] [5] [√ 8372]. rottenness, decay:– decay (2), rot (1), rots (1), something rotten (1)

H8374 רֹקֶב **rōqeb**, n.[m.] Not used in NIVEBC [√ 8372]. wine-skin

H8375 רִקָּבוֹן **riqqābôn**, n.[m.] [1] [√ 8372]. rottenness:– rotten (1)

H8376 רָקַד **rāqad**, v. [9] [Q] to skip, dance; [P] to leap about, dance; [H] to make skip:– leap (2), dance (1), dance about (1), dancing (1), jolting (1), leap about (1), leaped (1), makes leap (1)

H8377 רַקָּה **raqqâ**, n.f. [5] [√ 8369]. temple (of the head):– temple (3), temples (2)

H8378 רַקּוֹן **raqqôn**, n.pr.loc. [1] [√ 8369]. Rakkon, "*narrow place*":– Rakkon (1)

H8379 רָקַח **rāqaḥ**, v. [8] [→ 5349, 5350, 5351, 8380, 8381, 8382, 8383, 8384]. [Q] to make perfume, mix spices; [Pu] to be blended (of perfume); [H] to mix spices:– perfumer (3), blended (1), makes perfume (1), mixing in (1), perfume (1 [+9043]), took care of mixing (1 [+5351])

H8380 רֶקַח **reqaḥ**, n.[m.] [1] [→ 8381; cf. 8379]. (powdered) spice:– spiced (1)

H8381 רֹקַח **rōqaḥ**, n.[m.] [2] [√ 8380; cf. 8379]. fragrant blend, spice-blend:– blend (1), fragrant blend (1)

H8382 רַקָּח **raqqāḥ**, n.m. [1] [√ 8379]. perfume-maker, ointment-mixer:– perfume-makers (1)

H8383 רִקֻּחַ **riqquaḥ**, n.[m.] [1] [√ 8379]. perfume, ointment:– perfumes (1)

H8384 רַקָּחָה **raqqāḥâ**, n.f. [1] [√ 8379]. perfume-maker, ointment-mixer:– perfumers (1)

H8385 רָקִיעַ **rāqia'**, n.m. [17] [√ 8392]. expanse (of the sky or heaven); the space above the earth that holds visible objects: clouds, planets, stars:– vault (13), heavens (2), itS (1 [+2021]), skies (1)

H8386 רָקִיק **rāqîq**, n.m. [8] [√ 8369]. wafer, (thin, flat) cake:– thin loaves (5), thin loaf (3)

H8387 רָקַם **rāqam**, v. [9] [→ 8388?, 8389?, 8390?, 8391]. [Q] to embroider, weave colored thread; [Pu] to be woven together:– embroiderer (7), embroiderers (1), was woven together (1)

H8388 רָקֶם **rāqem**, n.pr.m. [1] [√ 8387?]. Rakem, "*weaver, embroider*":– Rakem (1)

H8389 1רֶקֶם **reqem1**, n.pr.loc. [1] [√ 8387?]. Rekem, "*friendship*":– Rekem (1)

H8390 2רֶקֶם **reqem2**, n.pr.m. [4] [√ 8387?]. Rekem, "*friendship*":– Rekem (4)

H8391 רִקְמָה **riqmâ**, n.f. [12] [√ 8387]. embroidered work; varied colored things:– embroidered (4), embroidered work (2), embroidered cloth (1), embroidered dress (1), embroidered garments (1), highly embroidered (1), varied colors (1), various colors (1)

H8392 רָקַע **rāqa'**, v. [12] [→ 3767, 8385, 8393]. [Q] to spread out; stamp upon, trample; [P] to hammer out thin, overlay (with precious metal); [Pu] to be hammered, be beaten thin; [H] to cause to spread out, make into plated metal:– hammered out (2), spreads out (2), trampled (2), hammered (1), overlays (1), spread out (1), spreading out (1), stamp (1), stamped (1)

H8393 רִקֻּעַ **riqqua'**, n.[m.] [1] [√ 8392]. sheet, something beaten thin:– Hammer (1 [+6913])

H8394 רָקַק **rāqaq**, v. [1] [→ 8371; cf. 3762]. [Q] to spit saliva:– spits (1)

H8395 רַקַּת **raqqat**, n.pr.loc. [1] [√ 8369]. Rakkath, "*narrow place*":– Rakkath (1)

H8396 רֹשׁ **rōš**, n.pr.loc. & g. Not used in NIVEBC [√ 8031; cf. 8034]. Rosh

H8397 רִשְׁיוֹן **rišyôn**, n.[m.] [1] [√ 3769]. authorization, permission:– authorized (1)

H8398 רָשַׁם **rāšam**, v. [1] [√ 10673]. [Qp] to be written, be inscribed:– written (1)

H8399 רָשַׁע **rāša'**, v.den. [34] [→ 5360, 8400, 8401, 8402]. [Q] to do evil, act wickedly; to be guilty; [H] to declare guilty, condemn, inflict punishment; to do wrong:– condemn (6), guilty (5), acted wickedly (4), condemning (3), wicked (3), condemns (2), declare guilty (2), act wickedly (1), condemned (1), do wrong (1), done wrong (1), inflicted punishment (1), let be condemned (1), overwicked (1 [+2221]), refute (1), violated (1)

H8400 רֶשַׁע **reša'**, n.m. [30] [√ 8399]. evil, wickedness, wrongdoing:– wickedness (16), wicked (5), ill-gotten (2), dishonest (1), evil (1), evil deeds (1), injustice (1), wicked (1 [+408]), wrongdoing (1 [+6913]), NDT (1)

H8401 רָשָׁע **rāšā'**, a. [263] [√ 8399]. wicked, evil, guilty:– wicked (232), guilty (10), evil (3), wickedness (3), themS (2), theyS (2), deserves (1), evildoers (1), heS (1), in the wrong (1), one in the wrong (1), thief (1), ungodly (1), whoS (1), wicked (1 [+408]), wicked (1 [+5883]), NDT (1)

H8402 רִשְׁעָה **riš'â**, n.f. [15] [√ 8399]. wickedness:– wickedness (11), crime (1), evildoer (1 [+6913]), evildoers (1 [+6913]), wicked (1)

H8403 רִשְׁעָתַיִם **riš'ātayim**, n.pr.m. Not used in NIVEBC [→ 3937]. Rishathaim

H8404 1רֶשֶׁף **rešep1**, n.m. [7] [→ 8405]. flame:– pestilence (2), blazing (1), bolts of lightning (1), burns (1), flashing (1), sparks (1 [+1201])

H8405 2רֶשֶׁף **rešep2**, n.pr.m. [1] [√ 8404]. Resheph, "*flame, flash of fire*":– Resheph (1)

H8406 רָשַׁשׁ **rāšaš**, v. [2] [→ 9576?, 9577?, 9578?]. [Pol] to destroy, shatter; [Pu] to be crushed, shattered:– been crushed (1), destroy (1)

H8407 רֶשֶׁת **rešet**, n.f. [22] [√ 3769]. net, snare, trap (for catching game); network (net-like metal grating):– net (15), network (2 [+5126]), itS (1 [+2021]), nets (1), network (1), snare (1), trap (1)

H8408 רַתּוֹק **rattôq**, n.[m.] [1] [√ 8415]. chain:– chains (1)

H8409 רָתַח **rātaḥ**, v. [3] [→ 8410]. [P] to bring to a boil; [Pu] to be caused to churn; [H] to make to churn:– bring to a boil (1 [+8410]), churning (1), makes churn (1)

H8410 רֶתַח **retaḥ**, n.[m.] [1] [√ 8409]. boiling:– bring to a boil (1 [+8409])

H8411 רַתִּיקָה **rattîqâ**, n.f. [1] [√ 8415]. chain:– chains (1)

H8412 רָתַם **rātam**, v. [1] [→ 8413, 8414?]. [Q] to tie up, harness (horse team):– harness (1)

H8413 רֹתֶם **rōtem**, n.m. [4] [→ 8414; cf. 8412?]. broom tree:– broom bush (3), bush (1)

H8414 רִתְמָה **ritmâ**, n.pr.loc. [2] [√ 8413; cf. 8412?]. Rithmah, "*[place of] broom plants*":– Rithmah (2)

H8415 רָתַק **rātaq**, v. [1] [→ 8408, 8411, 8416]. [Pu] to be bound with chains:– were put in chains (1 [+2414, 928])

H8416 רְתֻקוֹת **rᵉtuqôt**, n.[f.pl.] [1] [√ 8415]. chains:– chains (1)

H8417 רְתֵת **rᵉtēt**, n.m. [1] [cf. 8185]. trembling, fright:– trembled (1)

H8418 שׂ **ś**, letter. Not used in NIVEBC [√ 10674]. letter of the Hebrew alphabet

H8419 שְׂאֹר **śᵉ'ōr**, n.m. [5] [→ 5389, 5400]. yeast, leaven:– yeast (5)

H8420 1שְׂאֵת **śᵉ'ēt1**, n.f. [7] [→ 8480?, 8481?; cf. 5951]. splendor, honor, loftiness, acceptance:– honor (2), splendor (2), accepted (1), lofty place (1), rises up (1)

H8421 2שְׂאֵת **śᵉ'ēt2**, n.f. [7] [√ 5951]. swelling:– swelling (6), swollen (1)

H8422 שְׂבָכָה **śᵉbākâ**, n.f. [16] [√ 8449; 10676]. network, lattice, interwoven mesh:– network (12), lattice (1), mesh (1), network (1 [+8422, 5126]), network (1 [+5126, 8422])

H8423 שְׂבָם **śᵉbām**, n.pr.loc. [1] [→ 8424]. Sebam, "*sweet smell*":– Sebam (1)

H8424 שִׂבְמָה **śibmâ**, n.pr.loc. [5] [√ 8423]. Sibmah:– Sibmah (5)

H8425 שָׂבַע **śāba'**, v. [98] [→ 8426, 8427, 8428, 8429, 8430]. [Q] to be satisfied, have enough, be satiated; the filling and even overfilling of appetites and desires:– satisfied (29), filled (9), satisfy (9), full (4), get enough (3), have enough (3), satisfies (3), endured (2), fill (2), gorge (2), has enough (2), have abundant (2), too much (2), all want (1), all wanted (1), areS (1), been filled (1), content (1), eat fill (1), eats fill (1), enjoy (1), enjoy plenty (1), feast on (1), fed well (1), fully repaid (1), gets plenty (1), gorged (1 [+4394]), had enough (1), had plenty (1), have fill (1), have more than enough (1), have to spare (1), have too much (1), overwhelm (1), overwhelmed (1), satisfy fully (1), supplied all needs (1), toss and turn (1 [+5611]), well watered (1)

H8426 שָׂבָע **śābā'**, n.m. [8] [√ 8425]. abundance, overflowing:– abundance (7), overflowing (1)

H8427 שֹׂבַע **śōba'**, n.[m.] [8] [√ 8425]. one's fill to contentment, all one wants:– all want (2), fill (2), all could eat (1), all wanted (1), content (1), eaten enough (1)

H8428 שָׂבֵעַ **śābēa'**, a. [10] [√ 8425]. full, abounding:– full (7), abounding (1), content (1), enjoyed long life (1 [+3427])

H8429 שָׂבְעָה **śob'â**, n.f. [5] [√ 8425]. abundance, satisfaction, enough:– abundant (1), enough (1), glutted (1), insatiable (1 [+1194]), satisfy (1)

H8430 שִׂבְעָה **śib'â**, n.f. [1] [√ 8425]. abundance, plenty:– overfed (1 [+4312])

H8431 1שָׂבַר **śābar1**, v. [2] [√ 10503]. [Q] to examine:– examining (2)

H8432 2שָׂבַר **śābar2**, v. [6] [→ 8433]. [P] to wait for, hope for:– look (2), wait (2), hope (1), hoped (1)

H8433 שֵׂבֶר **śēber**, n.m. [2] [√ 8432]. hope:– hope (1), hopes (1)

H8434 שָׂגָא **śāgā'**, v. [2] [√ 8438; cf. 8436; 10677]. [H] to make great, extol:– extol (1), makes great (1)

H8435 שָׂגַב **śāgab**, v. [20] [→ 5369, 5370, 8437]. [Q] to be too strong for; [N] to be lofty, be exalted; [P] to lift high; to protect; [Pu] to be kept safe; [H] to act exalted:– protect (3), be exalted (2), exalted (2), is exalted (2), lifted (2), lofty (2), fortress (1), high (1), is kept safe (1), safe (1), strengthened (1), strong (1), too high to scale (1)

H8436 שָׂגָה **śāgâ**, v. [4] [cf. 8434]. [Q] to be prosperous, thrive, grow; [H] to increase (in wealth):– go on amassing (1), grow (1), prosperous (1), thrive (1)

H8437 שְׂגוּב **śᵉgûb**, n.pr.m. [3] [√ 8435; cf. 8439]. Segub, "*exalted*":– Segub (3)

H8438 שַׂגִּיא **śaggî'**, a. [2] [√ 8434; 10678]. exalted:– exalted (1), great (1)

H8439 שְׂגִיב **śᵉgîb**, n.pr.m. Not used in NIVEBC [cf. 8437]. Sebig, see 8437

H8440 שָׂדַד **śādad**, v. [3] [→ 8443; cf. 6040, 8444]. [P] to till, harrow, break up the ground:– break up the ground (1), till (1), working (1)

H8441 שָׂדֶה **śādeh**, n.m. [320] [→ 8442]. area of land, usually cultivated: field, open country, countryside:– field (114), fields (74), wild (29), country (18), land (12), open country (9), Moab (7 [+4566]), field (4 [+2754]), ground (4), open (4), territory (4), family land (3 [+299]), region (3), trees (3 [+6770, 2021]), wild (3 [+928, 2021]), area (2), countryside (2), mainland (2), open field (2), soil (2), battlefield (1 [+5120]), cemetery (1 [+7690]), city (1), farmlands (1 [+4494]), forest (1), gourds (1 [+7226]), it[S] (1 [+2021]), outlying districts (1), pastureland (1 [+4494]), place (1), plant (1 [+6912, 2021]), shrub (1 [+3972, 8489, 2021]), southland (1 [+5582]), there[S] (1 [+4566]), there[S] (1 [+2021]), workers (1 [+6913, 4856]), NDT (3)

H8442 שָׂדַי **śāday**, n.m. [13] [√ 8441]. field; see also 8441:– field (6), fields (4), wild (2), slopes (1)

H8443 שִׂדִּים **śiddîm**, n.pr.loc. [3] [√ 8440]. Siddim:– Siddim (3)

H8444 שְׂדֵרָה **śᵉdērâ**, n.f. [4] [cf. 6043, 8440]. ranks, rows; planks (architectural term):– ranks (3), planks (1)

H8445 שֶׂה **śeh**, n.m. & f. [47] sheep, lamb:– sheep (26), lamb (11), another[S] (2), flock (2), animals (1), goat (1 [+6436]), lamb (1 [+928, 2021, 3897]), lamb (1 [+928, 2021, 4166]), one[S] (1), sheep (1 [+4166])

H8446 שָׂהֵד **śāhēd**, n.[m.] [1] [√ 10679]. witness:– advocate (1)

H8447 שָׂהֲדוּתָא **śāhᵃdûtâ'**, n.f. Not used in NIVEBC [√ 10679]. Sahadutha

H8448 שַׂהֲרֹנִים **śahᵃrōnîm**, n.m. [3] ornamental crescent (or moon shaped) necklace:– ornaments (2), crescent necklaces (1)

H8449 שׂוֹבֶךְ **śôbek**, n.[m.] [1] [√ 8422; cf. 6018]. tangle of branches:– thick branches (1)

H8450 שׂוּג[1] **śûg[1]**, v. Not used in NIVEBC [cf. 6047]. see 6047

H8451 שׂוּג[2] **śûg[2]**, v. [1] [cf. 6048?]. [Pil] to cause growth, raise:– make grow (1)

H8452 שׂוּחַ **śûaḥ**, v. [1] [Q] to meditate:– meditate (1)

H8453 שַׂוְחָט **śawḥāṭ**, n.[?] Not used in NIVEBC [√ 8759]. see 8821

H8454 שׂוּט **śûṭ**, v. [1] [→ 8473?; cf. 6091, 8474]. [Q] to turn aside (to false gods):– turn aside (1)

H8455 שׂוּךְ **śûk**, v. [2] [→ 8456, 8457, 8458?, 8459; cf. 5819, 6115, 6058, 8504]. [Q] to block with thorn hedges:– block (1), put a hedge (1)

H8456 שׂוֹךְ **śôk**, n.[m.] [1] [√ 8455]. branch or brushwood:– branches (1)

H8457 שׂוֹכָה **śôkâ**, n.f. [1] [√ 8455]. branch or brushwood:– branches (1 [+6770])

H8458 שׂוֹכֹה **śôkōh**, n.pr.loc. [5] [√ 8455?]. Socoh, "[poss.] *thorny place*":– Sokoh (5)

H8459 שׂוֹכוֹ **śôkô**, n.pr.loc. [3] [√ 8455]. Soco, "[perhaps] *thorny place*":– Soko (3)

H8460 שׂוּכָתִי **śûkātî**, a.g. [1] Sucathite:– Sucathites (1)

H8461 שׂוּמָה **śûmâ**, n.f. [1] [√ 8492]. intention:– intention (1)

H8462 שׂוּר **śûr**, v. Not used in NIVEBC [√ 8463?]. [Q] to saw

H8463 שׂוֹרָה **śôrâ**, n.[f.] [1] [√ 8462?; cf. 8555?]. place, row or a type of grain:– place (1)

H8464 שׂוּשׂ **śûś**, v. [27] [→ 5375, 5376, 8607]. [Q] to rejoice, be pleased, be delighted:– rejoice (11), delight (2), delight greatly (2 [+8464]), glad (2), rejoicing (2), delighted (1), gladly (1), happy (1), please (1), pleased (1), rejoice greatly (1 [+5375]), take delight (1), take great delight (1 [+928, 8525])

H8465 שֵׂחַ **śēaḥ**, n.[m.] [1] [√ 8488]. thoughts:– thoughts (1)

H8466 שָׂחָה **śāḥâ**, v. [3] [→ 8467]. [Q] to swim; [H] to make swim, flood:– flood (1), swim (1), swimmers (1)

H8467 שָׂחוּ **śāḥû**, n.[m.] [1] [√ 8466]. water deep enough to swim in:– deep enough to swim in (1)

H8468 שְׂחוֹק **śᵉḥôq**, n.[m.] [15] [√ 8471]. laughter, which can communicate joy or ridicule; object of ridicule: laughingstock:– laughter (7), laughingstock (3), object of ridicule (3), pleasure (1), ridiculed (1)

H8469 שָׂחַט **śāḥaṭ**, v. [1] [Q] to squeeze out (juice from grapes):– squeezed (1)

H8470 שָׂחִיף **śāḥîp**, a. [1] covered, paneled:– covered with (1 [+6017, 6017])

H8471 שָׂחַק **śāḥaq**, v. [36] [→ 3773, 5377, 8468; cf. 7464]. [Q] to laugh, be amused; to laugh at, mock, scoff; [P] to celebrate, rejoice, frolic; [H] to scorn; this can communicate joy or ridicule:– laugh (7), laughs (6), entertaining (3), rejoicing (3), celebrate (1), danced (1), entertain (1), fight hand to hand (1), frolic (1), joking (1), joyful (1), laughed (1), make a pet (1), mock (1), perform (1), play (1), playing (1), revelers (1), scoffs (1), scorned (1), smiled (1)

H8472 שֻׂחֹת **śuḥōt**, n.f. Not used in NIVEBC [cf. 6054]. filth

H8473 שֵׂט **śēṭ**, n.[m.] [1] [√ 8454?]. rebel:– rebels (1)

H8474 שָׂטָה **śāṭâ**, v. [6] [cf. 8454]. [Q] to go astray:– goes astray (2), gone astray (2), turn (2)

H8475 שָׂטַם **śāṭam**, v. [6] [√ 5378; cf. 8476]. [Q] to hold a grudge, hold hostility toward:– assail (1), assails (1), attack (1), held a grudge against (1), holds a grudge against (1), hostility (1)

H8476 שָׂטַן **śāṭan**, v.den. [6] [→ 8477, 8478, 8479; cf. 8475]. [Q] to accuse, slander:– accusers (3), accuse (2), lodge accusations against (1)

H8477 שָׂטָן **śāṭān**, n.m.[pr.] [27] [√ 8476]. (human) adversary, accuser, one who opposes, slanderer; (as a proper name) Satan, the spirit being who is an opponent of God and slanderer of his creation:– Satan (18), adversary (4), oppose (2), accuser (1), interfere (1 [+2118]), turn against (1 [+2118, 4200])

H8478 שִׂטְנָה[1] **śiṭnâ[1]**, n.f. [1] [→ 8479; cf. 8476]. accusation:– accusation (1)

H8479 שִׂטְנָה[2] **śiṭnâ[2]**, n.pr.loc. [1] [√ 8478]. Sitnah, "*hostility*":– Sitnah (1)

H8480 שִׂיא **śî'**, n.m. [1] [→ 8481; cf. 5951?, 8420?]. height:– pride (1)

H8481 שִׂיאֹן **śî'ôn**, n.pr.loc. Not used in NIVEBC [√ 8480; cf. 5951?, 8420]. Siyon

H8482 שִׂיב **śîb**, v. [2] [→ 8483, 8484; 10681]. [Q] to be gray(-haired); hence, old:– gray (1), gray-haired (1)

H8483 שֵׂיב **śêb**, n.[m.] [1] [√ 8482]. gray-headedness, old age:– age (1)

H8484 שֵׂיבָה **śêbâ**, n.f. [19] [√ 8482]. gray-haired (person), old age:– old age (6), gray head (5), gray hair (3), aged (1), gray (1), gray hairs (1), hair gray (1), white hair (1)

H8485 שִׂיג **śîg**, n.[m.] [1] [cf. 6047, 6092]. busyness; perhaps: bowel movement:– busy (1)

H8486 שִׂיד[1] **śîd[1]**, v.den. [2] [√ 8487]. [Q] to coat with (a whitewash) plaster:– coat (2)

H8487 שִׂיד[2] **śîd[2]**, n.[m.] [4] [→ 8486; cf. 6093, 6167]. lime, plaster (used as a whitewash):– ashes (2), plaster (2)

H8488 שִׂיחַ[1] **śîaḥ[1]**, v.den. [20] [→ 8465, 8490, 8491]. [Q] to meditate, muse on, consider, think on:– meditate (8), consider (2), meditated (2), speak (2), tell (2), complain (1), in distress (1), mock (1), protested (1)

H8489 שִׂיחַ[2] **śîaḥ[2]**, n.[m.] [4] bush, shrub:– bushes (2), brush (1), shrub (1 [+3972, 2021, 8441])

H8490 שִׂיחַ[3] **śîaḥ[3]**, n.m. [14] [√ 8488]. complaint, lament:– complaint (7), anguish (1), complaints (1), deep in thought (1), lament (1), meditation (1), sort of things he says (1), thoughts (1)

H8491 שִׂיחָה **śîḥâ**, n.f. [3] [√ 8488]. meditation:– meditate (2), devotion (1)

H8492 שִׂים **śîm**, v. [582] [→ 3774, 8461, 9582; cf. 3775; 10682]. [Q] to place, put, establish, appoint; [Qp] to be placed, set upon; [H] to cause to place, put; [Ho] to be set:– put (109), make (48), set (46), made (35), placed (16), set up (13), give (11), laid (10), appointed (8), lay (7), place (7), turn (7), makes (6), gave (5), give careful thought (5 [+4222]), took (5), appoint (4), bring (4), determined (4 [+7156]), established (4), put in place (4), put up (4), putting (4), turned (4), brought (3), fasten (3), named (3 [+9005]), performed (3), provide (3), take (3), assign (2), attached (2), be sure to appoint (2 [+8492]), charges (2), considered (2 [+4213]), consigning to labor (2), fastened (2), given (2), giving (2), keep (2), leaving (2), look after (2 [+6524, 6584]), mark out (2), pay (2), planted (2), posted (2), prepare (2), puts (2), reduce (2), reduced (2), resolved (2 [+6584, 4213]), seized (2 [+3338]), served (2), setting (2), turn into (2), accuse (1 [+1821, 928]), added (1), applied (1), arrange (1), attach (1), avenged (1), be (1), become (1), care (1 [+4213, 448]), care about (1 [+4213, 448]), cares (1 [+6584, 4213]), caused to turn (1), charge (1), clap (1), concerned about (1 [+448, 4213]), consider (1), consider (1 [+4213]), consider (1 [+6584, 4213]), controls (1), covered (1 [+4200]), designate (1), destroy (1 [+9039]), determine (1 [+7156]), determined (1 [+7156, 8492]), determined (1 [+8492, 7156]), did[S] (1), displayed (1), does (1), don't say a word (1 [+3338, 6584, 7023]), draws from (1), end (1 [+7874]), erected (1), establish (1), establishes (1), exacted (1), examine (1), fastens (1), fix (1), float (1), formed (1), gave a high rank in (1 [+6584]), get dressed (1), grants (1), had (1), had brought (1), harbor (1), have regard (1 [+4200, 5584]), headed for (1), hung (1), ignored (1 [+4202, 4213]), imposed (1), increased (1), inflict (1), intention (1 [+4213]), issued (1), just imagine (1 [+4200]), keeps (1), lay up (1), left (1), lifted (1), light (1), list (1), loaded (1), looked (1 [+7156]), make serve (1 [+4200]), make sure hears (1 [+928, 265]), making (1), marked off (1), offers (1), piled (1), pitched (1), plant (1), poured (1), prepared (1), prepares (1), presented (1), preserve (1), preserved (1 [+928, 2021, 2645]), press charges (1), pressed (1), provided (1), put in charge (1), put on (1 [+928, 5516]), reaffirmed (1), regard (1 [+4200, 5584]), repay (1), replace (1 [+9393]), replaced (1), require (1), resolve (1 [+6584, 4213]), see (1 [+6524]), seize (1 [+928, 3338]), separated (1), serve (1), set in place (1), sets (1), sets up (1), shave (1 [+7947]), shedding (1), showed (1), shrouded (1), sing (1 [+928, 7023]), slandered (1 [+6613, 1821]), slanders (1 [+6613, 1821]), spread (1), stared with a fixed gaze (1 [+6641, 906, 7156, 2256]), stationed (1), stirs up (1), strap (1), take up positions (1), taken (1), takes (1), throw (1), thrown (1), told (1 [+928, 7023]), took up positions (1), trample down (1 [+5330]), treat (1), trusts (1 [+4440]), turned (1 [+7156]), turned into (1), unnoticed (1 [+4946, 1172]), use (1), used (1), was placed (1), was set (1), watch over (1 [+6584]), waylaid (1 [+928, 2021, 2006]), worry (1 [+906, 4213]), NDT (15)

H8493 שֵׂךְ **śēk**, n.[m.] [1] [√ 8504]. barb, splinter, thorn:– barbs (1)

H8494 שֹׂךְ **śōk**, n.[m.] [1] [cf. 6108]. dwelling place:– dwelling (1)

H8495 שָׂכָה **śākâ**, n.[m.] Not used in NIVEBC [→ 5381, 8499; cf. 8498?]. [Q] to look out for

H8496 שֻׂכָּה **śukkâ**, n.f. [1] [√ 8504]. harpoon:– harpoons (1)

H8497 שֵׂכוּ **śekû**, n.pr.loc. [1] Secu, "*lookout point*":– Seku (1)

H8498 שֶׂכְוִי **śekwî**, n.[m.] [1] [cf. 8495?]. mind; some sources: mist:– rooster (1)

H8499 שָׂכְיָה **śākᵉyâ**, n.pr.m. [1] [√ 8495 + 3378]. Sakia, "[poss.] *one who looks to Yahweh*":– Sakia (1)

H8500 שְׂכִיָּה **śᵉkiyyâ**, n.f. [1] marine vessel, ship:– vessel (1)

H8501 שַׂכִּין **śakkîn**, n.[m.] [1] [√ 8504]. knife:– knife (1)

H8502 שָׂכִיר **śākîr**, a. [18] [√ 8509]. hired worker, servant under contract:– hired worker (6), hired (2), hired laborer (2), servant bound by contract (2), hired hand (1), hired laborers (1), hired workers (1), laborers (1), mercenaries (1), workers hired (1)

H8503 שָׂכַךְ[1] **śākak[1]**, v. [1] [cf. 6058, 6114]. [Q] to cover (with the purpose to hide or screen):– cover (1)

H8504 שָׂכַךְ[2] **śākak[2]**, v. Not used in NIVEBC [→ 5372, 8493, 8496, 8501; cf. 5819, 6056, 6115, 8455]. [Pol] to knit or weave together, to be pointed

H8505 שָׂכַל[1] **śākal[1]**, v. [61] [→ 5380, 8507; cf. 8506; 10683]. [Q] to have success; [H] to have insight, wisdom, understanding; to prosper, successful; the potent capacity to understand and so exercise skill in life, a state caused by proper training and teaching, enhanced by careful observation:– wise (8), prudent (6), understand (6), successful (5), prosper (3), act wisely (2), instruct (2), understanding (2), careful (1), enabled to understand (1), fail (1 [+4202]), gaining wisdom (1), gave thought (1), give attention (1), give insight (1), gives heed (1), giving attention (1), had great success (1), had regard for (1), have insight (1), have regard for (1), have understanding (1), insight (1), make prudent (1), met with success (1), paying attention (1), ponder (1), prudence (1), prudent behavior (1), showed understanding (1 [+8507]), showing aptitude (1), skilled (1), success come (1), takes note (1), wisely (1)

H8506 שָׂכַל[2] **śākal[2]**, v. [1] [cf. 8505]. [P] to cross (the hands and arms in an extended motion):– crossing (1)

H8507 שֶׂכֶל **śekel**, n.m. [16] [√ 8505; 10684]. understanding, wisdom, discretion; see alse 8505:– prudence (2), understanding (2), capable (1), discretion (1), intelligence (1), intelligent (1 [+3202]), judgment (1), meaning (1), name (1), prudent (1), showed understanding (1 [+8505]), wisdom (1), wise (1), NDT (1)

H8508 שִׂכְלוּת **śiklût**, n.f. [1] [cf. 6121]. folly:– folly (1)

H8509 שָׂכַר **śākar**, v. [20] [→ 3779, 5382, 8502, 8510, 8511, 8512; cf. 6128]. [Q] to hire; [Qp] to be hired; [N] to hire oneself; [Ht] to earn wages for oneself:– hired (9), hire (3), earn wages (2 [+8509]), hired (2 [+8509]), been hired (1), hire themselves out (1), hires (1), NDT (1)

H8510 שָׂכָר[1] **śākār[1]**, n.m. [28] [→ 8511; cf. 8509; *also used with compound proper names*]. wage, reward:– wages (10), reward (6), pay (2), rewarded (2), fare (1), hire (1), money paid for hire (1), paid (1 [+9202]), pay (1 [+5989]), return (1), rewarded (1 [+5989]), worth (1)

H8511 שָׂכָר[2] **śākār[2]**, n.pr.m. [2] [√ 8510; cf. 8509]. Sacar, "*reward [given by God],* [poss.] *hired hand*":– Sakar (2)

H8512 שֶׂכֶר **śeker**, n.[m.] [2] [√ 8509]. wage, reward:– reward (1), wage (1)

H8513 שְׂלָו **śᵉlāw**, n.f. [4] quail:– quail (4)

H8514 שַׂלְמָא **śalmā'**, n.pr.m. [2] [→ 8516, 8517]. Salma, "*little spark*":– Salma (2)

H8515 שַׂלְמָה[1] **śalmâ[1]**, n.f. [16] [cf. 8529]. clothing, garment, cloak, robe:– clothes (5), cloak (4), garment (2), robes (2), clothing (1), garments (1), robe (1)

H8516 [2]שַׂלְמָה **śalmâ[2]**, n.pr.m. Not used in NIVEBC [√ 8514]. Salmah, see 8517

H8517 שַׂלְמוֹן **śalmôn**, n.pr.m. [4] [√ 8514]. Salmon, "*little spark*":– Salmon (4)

H8518 שַׂלְמַי **śalmay**, n.pr.m. Not used in NIVEBC [cf. 8978]. Salmai, see 8978

H8519 שָׂלַק **śālaq**, v. Not used in NIVEBC [cf. 5956]. [N] to be kindled; [H] to make a fire burn

H8520 שְׂמֹאל **śemō'l**, n.[m.] [54] [→ 8521, 8522; cf. 8619]. left (opposite of right); north:– left (45), north (6), north (2 [+4946]), which way (1 [+6584, 3545, 196, 6584])

H8521 שִׂמְאֵל **śim'ēl**, v.den. [5] [√ 8520]. [H] to go to the left; be left-handed:– to the left (3), go to the left (1), left-handed (1)

H8522 שְׂמָאלִי **śemā'lî**, a. [9] [√ 8520]. on the left; northern:– north (4), left (3), NDT (2)

H8523 שָׂמַח **śāmaḥ**, v. [154] [→ 8524, 8525]. [Q] to rejoice, be glad, delight in:– rejoice (43), glad (29), rejoiced (11), gloat (6), rejoices (6), brings joy (4), bring joy (3), delight (3), happy (3), joy (3), make glad (3), rejoicing (3), enjoy (2), gladly (2), joyful (2), let gloat (2), made very glad (2 [+8523]), pleased (2), be[S] (1), bring happiness (1), cheers (1), cheers up (1), elated (1), filled with joy (1), give joy (1), given cause to rejoice (1), given joy (1 [+8525]), giving joy (1), gladdens (1), gladness (1), glee (1), happy (1 [+8525]), held a celebration (1), joyous (1), made rejoice (1), make merry (1), makes glad (1), makes merry (1), received gladly (1 [+6584]), rejoiced (1 [+8525]), share joy (1 [+8525]), shines brightly (1), take pleasure (1)

H8524 שָׂמֵחַ **śāmēaḥ**, a.vbl. [21] [√ 8523]. rejoicing, gladness, delight:– happy (4), joyful (2), rejoicing (2), cheerful (1), cheering (1), delight (1), delight in (1), enjoy (1), filled with gladness (1 [+448, 1637]), filled with joy (1), gloat (1), gloats (1), joy (1), merrymakers (1 [+4213]), rejoice (1), rejoicing (1 [+8525])

H8525 שִׂמְחָה **śimḥâ**, n.f. [94] [√ 8523]. joy, gladness, pleasure, delight:– joy (46), gladness (10), rejoicing (7), pleasure (5), rejoice (3), joyful (2), joyfully (2), joyfully (2 [+928]), rejoiced (2), celebrate (1), delight (1), enjoyment (1), given joy (1 [+8523]), glad occasions (1), glee (1), happiness (1), happy (1 [+8523]), joyful songs (1), pleased (1), rejoiced (1 [+8523]), rejoicing (1 [+8524]), revelry (1), share joy (1 [+8523]), take great delight (1 [+8464, 928])

H8526 שְׂמִיכָה **śemîkâ**, n.f. [1] [√ 8527]. covering:– blanket (1)

H8527 שָׂמַךְ **śāmak**, v. Not used in NIVEBC [→ 8526; cf. 6164]. [Q] to cover

H8528 שַׂמְלָה **śamlâ**, n.pr.m. [4] [→ 8529, 8530]. Samlah:– Samlah (4)

H8529 שִׂמְלָה **śimlâ**, n.f. [29] [√ 8528; cf. 8515]. clothing, garment, cloak:– clothes (12), clothing (7), cloak (4), garment (3), cloth (2), best clothes (1)

H8530 שַׂמְלַי **śamlay**, n.pr.m. Not used in NIVEBC [√ 8528]. Samlai, see 8978

H8531 שָׂמַם **śāmam**, v. Not used in NIVEBC [cf. 6167]. [H] to paint or perfume

H8532 שְׂמָמִית **śemāmît**, n.f. [1] lizard; some sources: gecko:– lizard (1)

H8533 שָׂנֵא **śānē'**, v. [146] [→ 2190, 6171, 6176, 8534, 8535; 10686]. [Q] to hate, be an enemy; [Qp] to be unloved; [N] to be hated, be shunned; [P] to be an adversary, be a foe; "hate" can be active, as an enemy or adversary; or passive, as someone unloved or shunned:– hate (60), hated (16), hates (13), enemies (11), foes (11), malice aforethought (4 [+4946, 9453, 8997]), adversaries (3), dislikes (3), enemy (2), foe (2), hated (2 [+8533]), abhor (1), am not loved (1), are shunned (1), both[S] (1 [+2021, 170, 2256, 2021]), contemptible (1), detest (1), enemies (1 [+5883]), enemy's (1), hate (1 [+8534]), have hatred (1 [+8534]), hostile (1), is hated (1), not[S] (1), not love (1), not loved (1), refuses (1), shunned (1), them[S] (1 [+2157]), unloved (1)

H8534 שִׂנְאָה **śin'â**, n.f. [17] [√ 8533]. hatred, malice:– hatred (8), hate (2), hate (1 [+8533]), hated (1), hates (1), have hatred (1 [+8533]), malice (1), malice aforethought (1), NDT (1)

H8535 שָׂנִיא **śānî'**, a. [1] [√ 8533]. not loved, disdained:– not love (1)

H8536 שְׂנִיר **śenîr**, n.pr.loc. [4] Senir:– Senir (4)

H8537 [1]שָׂעִיר **śā'îr[1]**, a. [3] [→ 8538, 8539, 8544; cf. 8547]. hairy, shaggy:– hairy (2), shaggy (1)

H8538 [2]שָׂעִיר **śā'îr[2]**, n.m. [54] [√ 8537; cf. 8547]. male goat:– male goat (31), goat (10), goats (3), goat's (3), goat (2 [+6436]), male goats (2 [+6436]), wild goats (2), it[S] (1 [+2021])

H8539 [3]שָׂעִיר **śā'îr[3]**, n.m. [2] [√ 8537; cf. 8547]. goat idol:– goat idols (2)

H8540 [4]שָׂעִיר **śā'îr[4]**, n.[m.] [1] rain shower:– showers (1)

H8541 [1]שֵׂעִיר **śē'îr[1]**, n.pr.loc. [35] [→ 8542, 8543, 8545; cf. 8547]. Seir, "*hairy, shaggy, covered with trees*; [poss.] *the place of the goats* or *the place of Esau* [Ge 25:25 BDB]; *small forest, rich forest*":– Seir (35)

H8542 [2]שֵׂעִיר **śē'îr[2]**, n.pr.loc. [1] [√ 8541; cf. 8547]. Seir, "*hairy, shaggy*":– Seir (1)

H8543 [3]שֵׂעִיר **śē'îr[3]**, n.pr.m. [3] [√ 8541; cf. 8547]. Seir, "*hairy, shaggy*":– Seir (3)

H8544 [1]שְׂעִירָה **śe'îrâ[1]**, n.f. [2] [√ 8537]. female goat:– goat (2 [+6436])

H8545 [2]שְׂעִירָה **śe'îrâ[2]**, n.pr.loc. [1] [√ 8541]. Seirah, "*place of the goats;* [poss.] *woody hills; shaggy forest*":– Seirah (1)

H8546 שְׂעִפִּים **śe'ippîm**, n.[m.]pl. [2] [√ 8595]. disquieted thoughts, troubled thoughts:– disquieting (1), troubled thoughts (1)

H8547 [1]שָׂעַר **śā'ar[1]**, v.den. [3] [→ 8537, 8538, 8539, 8541, 8542, 8543, 8544, 8545, 8550, 8552, 8553, 8555]. [Q] to shudder, bristle with horror:– shudder (3)

H8548 [2]שָׂעַר **śā'ar[2]**, v. [4] [→ 8551, 8554; cf. 6192]. [Q] to sweep away (by the wind); [N] to be in a storm; [P] to sweep away (by a wind); [Ht] to storm against:– storm out (1), sweeps out (1), swept away (1), tempest rages (1 [+4394])

H8549 [3]שָׂעַר **śā'ar[3]**, v. [1] [Q] to know about, be acquainted with:– fear (1)

H8550 [1]שַׂעַר **śa'ar[1]**, n.[m.] [3] [√ 8547]. horror, shudder, an extension of the bristling of hair (in excitement or fear):– horror (3)

H8551 [2]שַׂעַר **śa'ar[2]**, n.[m.] [1] [√ 8548]. wind storm, gale:– wind (1)

H8552 שֵׂעָר **śē'ār**, n.m. [28] [√ 8547; 10687]. hair:– hair (22), hairy (2), garment of hair (1), hair (1 [+7279, 8031]), it[S] (1 [+8031]), private parts (1 [+8079])

H8553 שַׂעֲרָה **śa'arâ**, n.f. [7] [√ 8547]. hair:– hair (3), hair of head (2), hairs (2)

H8554 שְׂעָרָה **śe'ārâ**, n.f. [2] [√ 8548]. storm, gale:– storm (2)

H8555 שְׂעֹרָה **śe'ōrâ**, n.f. [34] [√ 8547; cf. 8463?]. barley:– barley (33), NDT (1)

H8556 שְׂעֹרִים **śe'ōrîm**, n.pr.m. [1] Seorim, "*one born at the time of the barley [harvest]*":– Seorim (1)

H8557 שָׂפָה **śāpâ**, n.f. & m. [176] [→ 8559]. lips (of the mouth); by extension: speech, language; edge of an object, rim, border; the "lip of the sea" is the seashore:– lips (98), rim (14), edge (10), bank (7), language (5), seashore (5 [+3542]), speech (3), chattering (2), empty words (2 [+1821]), mouth (2), talk (2), tongues (2), band (1), banks (1), border (1), coast (1 [+3542]), hurl insults (1 [+7080, 928]), mere talk (1 [+1821]), object of malicious talk (1 [+6590, 6584, 4383]), riverbank (1 [+3284]), shore (1), shore (1 [+3542]), speak rashly (1 [+7316]), speaks (1), talker (1 [+408]), talks too much (1 [+7331]), thoughtlessly (1 [+4200, 1051, 928]), voice (1), what said (1), whisper (1), words (1), NDT (5)

H8558 שָׂפַח **śāpaḥ**, v.den. [1] [cf. 6202?, 6203?]. [P] to bring sores, make scabby:– bring sores on (1)

H8559 שָׂפָם **śāpām**, n.[m.] [5] [√ 8557]. (the area of the) mustache; lower part of the face:– mustache and beard (2), faces (1), lower part of face (1), mustache (1)

H8560 שִׂפְמוֹת **śipmôt**, n.pr.loc. [1] [cf. 9174]. Siphmoth:– Siphmoth (1)

H8561 שָׂפַן **śāpan**, v. [1] [cf. 6211]. [Qp] to be hidden:– treasures hidden (1 [+3243])

H8562 [1]שָׂפַק **śāpaq[1]**, v. [2] [→ 8564; cf. 6215]. [Q] to clap one's hands (in derision); [H] to clasp hands:– claps in derision (1), embrace customs (1)

H8563 [2]שָׂפַק **śāpaq[2]**, v. [1] [→ 8565; cf. 6217]. [Q] to be enough:– enough (1)

H8564 שֶׂפֶק **śepeq**, n.[m.] Not used in NIVEBC [√ 8562]. hand-clapping, i.e., mockery

H8565 שֵׂפֶק **śēpeq**, n.[m.] [1] [√ 8563]. plenty, sufficiency:– plenty (1)

H8566 שַׂק **śaq**, n.m. [49] sackcloth; sack:– sackcloth (43), sack (3), sacks (2), sackcloth (1 [+4680])

H8567 שָׂקַד **śāqad**, v. [1] [N] to be bound:– been bound (1)

H8568 שָׂקַר **śāqar**, v. [1] [P] to flirt, ogle (with the eyes):– flirting (1)

H8569 שַׂר **śar**, n.m. [421] [→ 5552, 5947, 8576, 8593; cf. 6254, 8606]. ruler of various spheres (military, religious, governmental): commander, official, prince, chief, leader; "Prince of Peace" is a title of the child who would rule on David's throne, referring to the Messiah:– officials (91), commanders (76), commander (39), leaders (30), officers (30), princes (29), chief (17), nobles (16), ruler (14), prince (8), captain (7), leader (7), rulers (6), captain (5 [+2822]), leading (3), officials in charge (3), warden (3), chief officer (2 [+2021, 7372]), command (2), governor (2), in charge (2), captains (1 [+2822]), chief men (1), chief officials (1), commander-in-chief (1 [+8031, 2256]), commanders (1 [+7372]), dignitaries (1), foremen (1 [+5893]), head (1), heads (1), masters (1), mighty (1), officer (1), they[S] (1 [+2021]), they[S] (1 [+3405, 2256, 2021, 2657]), NDT (15)

H8570 שַׂר־אֶצֶר **śar'eṣer,** שַׂר־אֶצֶר **śar-'eṣer**, n.pr.m. [3] [→ 5947]. Sharezer, "*[god] protect the king!*":– Sharezer (3)

H8571 שָׂרַג **śārag**, v. [2] [→ 8585]. [Pu] to be close-knit, be intertwined; [Ht] to be woven together:– close-knit (1), woven together (1)

H8572 שָׂרַד **śārad**, v. [1] [→ 8586]. [Q] to run away, escape:– survivors (1)

H8573 שְׂרָד **śerād**, n.[m.] [4] [√ 8574?]. woven material (with some kind of braiding woven in it):– woven (4)

H8574 שֶׂרֶד **śered**, n.[m.] [1] [√ 8573?]. marker (for wood chiseling):– marker (1)

H8575 [1]שָׂרָה **śārâ[1]**, v. [3] [→ 449, 3776, 3778, 8588, 8589]. [Q] to struggle, contend:– struggled (3)

H8576 [2]שָׂרָה **śārâ[2]**, n.f. [5] [→ 8569, 8577; cf. 8606]. woman of nobility, lady of royal birth, queen:– ladies (1), of royal birth (1), queen (1), queens (1), women of nobility (1)

H8577 [3]שָׂרָה **śārâ[3]**, n.pr.f. [38] [√ 8576; cf. 8584]. Sarah, "*princess*":– Sarah (35), Sarah's (1), she[S] (1), NDT (1)

H8578 שְׂרוּג **śerûg**, n.pr.m. [5] Serug, "*descendant* i.e., *younger branch*":– Serug (5)

H8579 שְׂרוֹךְ **śerôk**, n.[m.] [2] [√ 8592]. thong (of a sandal):– strap (2)

H8580 שֶׂרַח **śeraḥ**, n.pr.f. [3] [cf. 6243]. Serah, "*one who explains, opens, extends; abundance*":– Serah (3)

H8581 שָׂרַט **śāraṭ**, v. [3] [→ 8582, 8583]. [Q] to make a cut, incise the skin; [N] to make oneself incised, cut oneself:– injure themselves (2 [+8581]), cut (1 [+8583])

H8582 שֶׂרֶט **śereṭ**, n.[m.] [1] [√ 8581]. cut, incision:– cut (1 [+5989])

H8583 שָׂרֶטֶת **śāreṭet**, n.f. [1] [√ 8581]. cut, incision; this may refer to a tattoo:– cut (1 [+8581])

H8584 שָׂרַי **śāray**, n.pr.f. [17] [cf. 8577]. Sarai, "*princess*":– Sarai (15), she[S] (1), NDT (1)

H8585 שָׂרִיג **śārîg**, n.m. [3] [√ 8571]. branch, tendril (of grape vines and fig trees):– branches (3)

H8586 [1]שָׂרִיד **śārîd[1]**, n.m. [28] [√ 8572]. survivor; those left:– survivors (17), survive (4), left (2), survivor (2), few (1), remnant (1), survived (1)

H8587 [2]שָׂרִיד **śārîd[2]**, n.pr.loc. [2] Sarid, "*survivor*":– Sarid (2)

H8588 שְׂרָיָה **śerāyâ**, n.pr.m. [18] [√ 8575 + 3378]. Seraiah, "*Yahweh persists; Yahweh is prince; Yahweh contends*":– Seraiah (17), Seraiah's (1)

H8589 שְׂרָיָהוּ **śerāyāhû**, n.pr.m. [1] [√ 8575 + 3378]. Seraiah, "*Yahweh persists; Yahweh is prince; Yahweh contends*":– Seraiah (1)

H8590 שִׂרְיוֹן **śiryôn**, n.pr.loc. [3] [cf. 6246]. Sirion, "*coat of mail*":– Sirion (3)

H8591 שָׂרִיק **śārîq**, a. [1] [√ 8600]. combed (flax, as a first step for making linen):– combed (1)

H8592 שָׂרַךְ **śārak**, v. [1] [→ 8579]. [P] to run here and there (aimlessly):– running here and there (1 [+2006])

H8593 שַׂר־סְכִים **śar-sekîm**, n.pr.m. Not used in NIVEBC [√ 8569; cf. 5552]. Sarsekim

H8594 שָׂרַע **śāra'**, v. [3] [Qp] to be deformed; [Ht] to stretch oneself:– deformed (2), stretch out (1)

H8595 שַׂרְעַפִּים **śar'appîm**, n.[m.]pl. [2] [→ 8546]. anxiety, anxious thoughts:– anxiety (1), anxious thoughts (1)

H8596 שָׂרַף **śārap**, v. [115] [→ 5386, 5387, 8597, 8598, 8599; cf. 6251]. [Q] to burn, set a fire; [Qp, N, Pu] to be burned up:– burned (26), burn (13), burned (10 [+928, 2021, 836]), burn down (9 [+928, 2021, 836]), burn (5 [+928, 2021, 836]), be burned up (4 [+928, 2021, 836]), burns (4), burn up (3 [+928, 2021, 836]), burned down (3 [+928, 2021, 836]), burned up (3 [+928, 2021, 836]), set fire to (3), set on fire (3 [+928, 2021, 836]), be burned (2), are burned up (1 [+928, 2021, 836, 8596]), are burned up (1 [+8596, 928, 2021, 836]), bake thoroughly (1 [+4200, 8599]), be burned (1 [+928, 2021, 836]), be burned down (1 [+928, 2021, 836]), be destroyed (1), been burned to death (1), been burned up (1), being burned (1), burn as sacrifices (1), burn down (1), burn to death (1 [+928, 2021, 836]), burn up (1), burned as sacrifices (1), burned down (1 [+2021, 836]), burned to death (1), burned to death (1 [+928, 2021, 836]), burned up (1), destroy (1), destroyed (1), destroyed by fire (1), is burned (1), made (1), make a fire (1), set fire to (1 [+928, 2021, 836]), set on fire (1 [+928, 836, 2021]), used for fuel (1 [+1198, 836])

H8597 [1]שָׂרָף **śārāp[1]**, n.m. [7] [→ 8598; cf. 8596]. venomous snake; seraph (six-winged being):– seraphim (2), venomous (2), snake (1), snakes (1), venomous serpent (1)

H8598 [2]שָׂרָף **śārāp[2]**, n.pr.m. [1] [√ 8597; cf. 8596]. Saraph, "*burning one, serpent*":– Saraph (1)

H8599 שְׂרֵפָה **śerēpâ**, n.f. [13] [√ 8596]. burning:– fire (3), burned (2), burning (2), bake thoroughly (1 [+8596, 4200]), burned-out (1), burning waste (1), charred remains (1), those[S] (1 [+2021]), NDT (1)

H8600 שָׂרַק ***śāraq***, a. Not used in NIVEBC [→ 8591]. to comb or card flax

H8601 ¹שָׂרֹק ***śārōq¹***, a. [1] [→ 5388, 8602, 8603, 8604, 8605]. brown, dark red (color of grapes):– brown (1)

H8602 ²שָׂרֹק ***śārōq²***, n.[m.] [1] [√ 8601]. choice vines:– choicest vines (1)

H8603 ¹שֹׂרֵק ***śōrēq¹***, n.[m.] [2] [√ 8601]. choice vines:– choice vine (1), choicest vines (1)

H8604 ²שֹׂרֵק ***śōrēq²***, n.pr.loc. [1] [√ 8601]. Sorek, "*blood red grapes*":– Sorek (1)

H8605 שְׂרֵקָה ***śᵉrēqâ***, n.f. [1] [√ 8601]. choice vine:– choicest branch (1)

H8606 שָׂרַר ***śārar***, v.den. [7] [→ 5385, 8569; cf. 6233, 6254]. [Q] to rule, govern; [H] to choose a prince; [Ht] to act out as a ruler:– lord it (2 [+8606]), choose princes (1), govern (1), governed (1), rule (1), ruler (1)

H8607 שָׂשׂוֹן ***śāśôn***, n.m. [22] [√ 8464]. joy, gladness:– joy (15), gladness (5), joyful (1), rejoicing (1)

H8608 שָׂתַם ***śātam***, v. [1] [cf. 6258]. [Q] to shut out, obstruct:– shuts out (1)

H8609 שָׂתַר ***śātar***, v. [1] [√ 10520]. [N] to be broken out (with tumors):– outbreak (1)

H8610 שׁ ***š***, letter. Not used in NIVEBC [√ 10688]. letter of the Hebrew alphabet

H8611 -שֶׁ ***ša-***, pt.rel.pref. [140] [→ 1417, 4792, 5499, 8724, 8975]. who, that, because:– that (16), who (13), which (7), until (6 [+6330]), the one[S] (4), whose (4), because (3), whom (3), he[S] (2), till (2 [+6330]), Solomon's (1 [+4200, 8976]), allies[S] (1 [+6640]), already (1 [+928, 3893]), as (1 [+3869]), as (1 [+3972, 6645]), body[S] (1), despite (1 [+928, 4200]), fault (1 [+928, 4200]), for (1 [+928, 1685]), future (1 [+4537, 2118]), he (1), how (1), it[S] (1), mine (1 [+4200, 3276]), my own (1 [+4200, 3276]), of (1 [+4946, 4200]), responsible for (1 [+928, 4200]), since (1), so that (1), successor (1 [+132, 995, 339]), than (1), the produce[S] (1), therefore (1 [+6584, 1826]), until (1), whatever (1 [+4537]), when (1 [+6330]), where (1), while (1 [+6330]), why (1 [+4200, 4537]), NDT (51)

H8612 שָׁאַב ***šā'ab***, v. [19] [→ 5393]. [Q] to draw and carry water:– draw water (5), draw (4), drew (4), carriers (3), carry (1), drew water (1), filled (1)

H8613 שָׁאַג ***šā'ag***, v. [20] [→ 8614]. [Q] to roar:– roar (7), roaring (4), roared (3), roar mightily (2 [+8613]), roars (2), comes roar (1), groan (1)

H8614 שְׁאָגָה ***šᵉ'āgâ***, n.f. [7] [√ 8613]. roar, groan:– roar (3), anguish (1), groaning (1), groans (1), roaring (1 [+7754])

H8615 ¹שָׁאָה ***šā'â¹***, v. [4] [→ 8619, 8622, 8625, 8643, 8858?, 8885?]. [Q] to lie wasted; [N] to be ruined; [H] to turn into desolation:– turned into (2), lie ruined (1), ruined (1)

H8616 ²שָׁאָה ***šā'â²***, v. [2] [→ 8623, 9583, 9589, 9594]. [N] to roar:– roar (2)

H8617 ³שָׁאָה ***šā'â³***, v. [1] [cf. 9120]. [Ht] to watch closely, gaze at:– watched closely (1)

H8618 שַׁאֲוָה ***ša'ᵃwâ***, n.f. devastating storm

H8619 שְׁאוֹל ***šᵉ'ôl***, n.f. & m. [66] [√ 8615; cf. 8520, 8628]. grave; by extension, realm of death, deepest depths, transliterated "Sheol":– grave (29), realm of the dead (25), death (7), depths (2), depths below (2), die (1)

H8620 שָׁאוּל ***šā'ûl***, n.pr.m. [405] [→ 8621; cf. 8626]. Saul, Shaul, "*asked,* [poss.] *dedicated to God*":– Saul (326), Saul's (34), he[S] (13), Shaul (9), him[S] (6), Saul's (4 [+4200]), his[S] (3), his[S] (1 [+4200]), they[S] (1 [+6269]), NDT (8)

H8621 שָׁאוּלִי ***šā'ûlî***, a.g. [1] [√ 8620]. Shaulite, "*of Shaul*":– Shaulite (1)

H8622 ¹שָׁאוֹן ***šā'ôn¹***, n.m. [1] [√ 8615]. waste, desolation; a slime pit that may refer to Sheol (8619):– slimy pit (1 [+1014])

H8623 ²שָׁאוֹן ***šā'ôn²***, n.m. [17] [√ 8616]. roar, uproar, tumult, loud noise:– uproar (4), roar (3), roaring (3), brawlers (1), great tumult (1), loud noise (1), noise (1), noisy boasters (1 [+1201]), roar of battle (1), tumult (1)

H8624 שְׁאָט ***šᵉ'āṭ***, n.[m.] [3] malice:– malice (3)

H8625 שְׁאִיָּה ***šᵉ'iyyâ***, n.f. [1] [√ 8615]. desolation, ruin:– battered to pieces (1 [+4198])

H8626 שָׁאַל ***šā'al***, v. [171] [→ 900, 901, 3781, 5399, 8620, 8621, 8924, 8927, 8929; 10689; *also used with compound proper names*]. [Q] to ask, inquire, request; [Qp] to be given over; [N] to ask permission; [P] to ask intently, beg; [H] to give what is asked for:– ask (39), asked (37), inquired of (15 [+928]), question (6), asks (4), greet (4 [+4200, 8934]), request (4), consult (3), questioned (3), asking (2), earnestly asked for permission (2 [+8626]), earnestly asked permission (2 [+8626]), get answer (2 [+8626]), greeted (2 [+4200, 8934]), have request to make (2 [+8629]), questioned closely (2 [+8626]), ask (1 [+907]), asked how they were (1 [+4200, 8934]), asked how were (1 [+4200, 8934]), be given over (1), beg (1), beggars (1), borrows (1), consulted (1), consulting (1 [+7023]), demand (1), demanding (1), demands (1), desired (1), find out (1), gave (1), gave what asked for (1), give (1), have request (1 [+8629]), inquire (1), inquire of (1 [+928]), inquire of (1 [+906, 7023]), inquires of (1 [+928, 1821]), inquiring of (1 [+928]), investigate (1), invoking (1), look (1), make[S] (1), medium (1 [+200]), obtain decisions (1), pray (1), prayed (1), require (1), said (1), tell (1), took (1), wanted (1 [+906, 5883]), was borrowed (1), wish (1), NDT (4)

H8627 שְׁאָל ***šᵉ'āl***, n.pr.m. [1] [√ 8626]. Sheal, "*May God grant!, asking*":– Sheal (1)

H8628 שְׁאָלָה ***šᵉ'ālâ***, var. Not used in NIVEBC [√ 8619 + 2025]. in [the] depths, see 8619

H8629 שְׁאֵלָה ***šᵉ'ēlâ***, n.f. [13] [→ 8924; cf. 8626; 10690]. petition, request:– petition (6), have request to make (2 [+8626]), have request (1 [+8626]), prayed for (1), request (1), what[S] (1), what asked for (1)

H8630 שְׁאַלְתִּיאֵל ***šᵉ'altî'ēl***, n.pr.m. [6] [√ 8626 + 446; cf. 9003]. Shealtiel, "*I have asked [him] of God [El]*; [poss.] *God [El] is a shield, God [El] is a victor*":– Shealtiel (6)

H8631 שָׁאַן ***šā'an***, v. [5] [→ 8633, 8916]. [Palpal] to be at ease, be at rest, be secure:– security (2), at ease (1), at rest (1), enjoy ease (1)

H8632 שְׁאָן ***šᵉ'ān***, n.pr.loc. Not used in NIVEBC [→ 1126, 9093]. Shan, see 1126

H8633 שַׁאֲנָן ***ša'ᵃnān***, a. [10] [√ 8631]. at ease, complacent, secure; insolent, proud:– complacent (3), insolence (2), arrogant (1), at ease (1), feel secure (1), peaceful (1), undisturbed (1)

H8634 ¹שָׁאַף ***šā'ap¹***, v. [11] [cf. 8635]. [Q] to pant after, long for, pursue:– pant (3), hotly pursue (1), hurries back (1), in hot pursuit (1), long for (1), longing for (1), pant (1 [+8120]), pursue (1), sniffing (1)

H8635 ²שָׁאַף ***šā'ap²***, v. [3] [cf. 8634, 8789, 8790]. [Q] to trample, crush:– trample (2), crushed (1)

H8636 שָׁאַר ***šā'ar***, v. [132] [→ 8637, 8639, 8641, 8642; 10692]. [Q] to remain; [N] to be left, remain; [H] to leave, spare:– left (50), remained (10), remain (9), leave (7), left behind (6), leaving (5), rest (5), survived (4), survive (3), survivors (3), have left (2), last (2 [+4946, 3856]), leave alive (2), spare (2), been kept (1), can hardly breathe (1 [+5972, 4202]), left alone (1), left survivor (1), little left (1 [+3856, 7129]), remains (1), remnant (1), remnant spare (1), reserve (1), sparing (1), still (1), still (1 [+6388]), survives (1), surviving (1), those[S] (1 [+2021]), NDT (7)

H8637 שְׁאָר ***šᵉ'ār***, n.m. [25] [√ 8636; 10692]. remainder, remnant, the rest:– rest (10), remnant (9), survivors (3), other (1), remainder (1), remaining (1)

H8638 שְׁאֵר ***šᵉ'ēr***, n.m. [18] [√ 8640]. flesh, meat; by extension: the body as a whole; blood relative, as one's "flesh and blood":– flesh (4), close relative (3), body (2), meat (2), blood relative (1 [+1414]), close relative (1 [+1414]), close relative (1 [+7940]), close relatives (1), food (1), relative (1), themselves (1 [+2257])

H8639 שְׁאָר יָשׁוּב ***šᵉ'ār yāšûb***, n.pr.m. [1] [√ 8636 + 3782]. Shear-Jashub, "*remnant will return*":– Shear-Jashub (1)

H8640 שַׁאֲרָה ***ša'ᵃrâ***, var. Not used in NIVEBC [√ 8638 + 2023]. see 8638

H8641 שֶׁאֱרָה ***šᵉ'ᵉrâ***, n.pr.f. [1] [√ 8636; cf. 267]. Sheerah, "*blood relationship* or *female relative; remainder*":– Sheerah (1)

H8642 שְׁאֵרִית ***šᵉ'ērît***, n.f. [67] [√ 8636]. remnant, remainder, the rest:– remnant (45), rest (7), survivors (6), remaining (2), descendant (1), last (1), left (1), other (1), remain (1), survived (1), NDT (1)

H8643 שֵׁאת ***šē't***, n.f. [1] [√ 8615]. ruin, desolation:– ruin (1)

H8644 שְׁבָא ***šᵉbā'***, n.pr.loc. & m. [23] [→ 8645]. Sheba, "*seven* or *oath*":– Sheba (22), Sabeans (1)

H8645 שְׁבָאִים ***šᵉbā'îm***, a.g. [1] [√ 8644]. Sabeans:– Sabeans (1)

H8646 שְׁבָבִים ***šᵉbābîm***, n.[m.]pl. [1] [√ 8663]. broken pieces, splinters:– broken in pieces (1)

H8647 שָׁבָה ***šābâ***, v. [47] [→ 8649, 8654, 8659, 8660, 8664, 8665, 8669, 8860]. [Q] to take captive; [Qp, N] to be taken captive:– captors (6), carried off (4), taken captive (4), captured (3), took captive (3), are held captive (2), captives (2), take captive (2 [+8647]), take captive (2), takes captive (2 [+8647]), be taken captive (1), been captured (1), been carried captive (1), been taken captive (1), captured (1 [+8660]), carried away (1), held captive (1), is taken away (1), made captives of (1), make captives (1), seized (1), take captives (1 [+8660]), taken (1), taken as prisoners (1 [+8664]), takes captive (1), took as prisoners (1 [+8664]), took many captives (1 [+8660])

H8648 שְׁבוֹ ***šᵉbô***, n.[f.] [2] agate (exact identification is uncertain):– agate (2)

H8649 שְׁבוּאֵל ***šᵉbû'ēl***, n.pr.m. Not used in NIVEBC [√ 8647? + 446; cf. 8742]. Shubael, "[poss.] *captive of God [El]* or *God [El] restores*"

H8650 שְׁבִיל ***šᵉbûl***, n.[m.] Not used in NIVEBC [cf. 8666]. path, see 8666

H8651 שָׁבוּעַ ***šābûa'***, n.m. [19] [√ 8678]. week (a time period of seven); Feast of Weeks, a festival celebrating the first produce of the harvest; a unit of time used in the book of Daniel, possibly a "week" of seven years:– weeks (7), sevens (4), seven (3), weeks (2 [+3427]), bridal week (1), festival of weeks (1), week (1)

H8652 שְׁבוּעָה ***šᵉbû'â***, n.f. [29] [√ 8678]. sworn oath:– oath (17), swear (2), curse (1 [+460, 2256]), curses (1), oath swore (1), put curse (1 [+460, 8678]), sworn (1), sworn allegiance (1 [+8678]), sworn judgments (1), takes an oath (1 [+8678]), them[S] (1), under oath (1 [+1251])

H8653 שָׁבוּר ***šābûr***, a. *or* v.ptcp. [1] [√ 8689]. injury (by fracture):– injured (1)

H8654 שְׁבוּת ***šᵉbût***, n.f. [24] [√ 8647]. captivity, exile; fortunes:– fortunes (14), captivity (6), restores (2 [+8740]), exile (1), NDT (1)

H8655 ¹שָׁבַח ***šābaḥ¹***, v. [9] [→ 3786; 10693]. [P] to glorify, commend, extol; [Ht] to glory in:– extol (2), glory (2), commend (1), commends (1), declared (1), glorify (1), receive praise (1)

H8656 ²שָׁבַח ***šābaḥ²***, v. [3] [P] to keep still; [H] to cause stillness:– bring calm (1), still (1), stilled (1)

H8657 שֵׁבֶט ***šēbeṭ***, n.m. [190] [→ 9222; 10694]. rod, staff, a stick used to assist in walking, discipline, and guidance, often highly individualized and used for identification; of royalty: scepter; by extension: tribe, as a major unit of national group or clan (fig. identified with or under authority of a leader's staff), people, clan, family:– tribes (74), tribe (40), rod (25), half-tribe (19 [+2942]), scepter (13), people (3), tribal (3), club (2), staff (2), chief men (1), javelins (1), peoples (1), punish (1), rulers (1), shepherd's rod (1), stick (1), NDT (2)

H8658 שְׁבָט ***šᵉbāṭ***, n.pr.m. [1] Shebat, "*[month of] destroying [rain]*":– Shebat (1)

H8659 שָׁבִי ***šābî***, a. *or* n.m. Not used in NIVEBC [√ 8647]. captive

H8660 שְׁבִי ***šᵉbî***, n.m. [48] [√ 8647]. captivity, exile; captive, prisoner:– captivity (17), exile (13), captives (7), captured (4), prisoners (2), captured (1 [+8647]), carry off (1 [+995, 928, 2021]), prisoner (1), take captives (1 [+8647]), took many captives (1 [+8647])

H8661 שֹׁבִי ***šōbî***, n.pr.m. [1] Shobi, "[poss.] *captive* or *Yahweh returns*":– Shobi (1)

H8662 שֹׁבַי ***šōbay***, n.pr.m. [2] Shobai, "[poss.] *captive* or *Yahweh returns*":– Shobai (2)

H8663 שָׁבִיב ***šābîb***, n.m. [1] [→ 8646; 10695]. flame; some sources: spark:– flame (1)

H8664 שִׁבְיָה ***šibyâ***, n.f. [9] [√ 8647]. captive, prisoner; captivity:– prisoners (3), captives (2), captivity (2), taken as prisoners (1 [+8647]), took as prisoners (1 [+8647])

H8665 שְׁבִיָּה ***šᵉbiyyâ***, n.f. [1] [√ 8647]. captive:– captive (1)

H8666 שְׁבִיל ***šᵉbîl***, n.[m.] [2] [√ 8670; cf. 8650]. way, path:– paths (1), way (1)

H8667 שָׁבִיס ***šābîs***, n.[m.] [1] headband:– headbands (1)

H8668 שְׁבִיעִי ***šᵉbî'î***, a.num.ord. [97] [√ 8679]. seventh:– seventh (97)

H8669 שְׁבִית ***šᵉbît***, n.f. [9] [√ 8647]. captivity, fortune:– fortunes (5), captives (1), NDT (3)

H8670 שֹׁבֶל ***šōbel***, n.[m.] [1] [→ 839, 840, 8666, 8672, 8673]. skirt, hem of skirt:– skirts (1)

H8671 שַׁבְּלוּל ***šabbᵉlûl***, n.m. [1] [√ 1176?]. slug, snail; some sources: miscarriage:– slug (1)

H8672 ¹שִׁבֹּלֶת ***šibbōlet¹***, n.f. [16] [√ 8670; cf. 6027]. head of grain:– heads of grain (8), heads (3), grain (2), branches (1), leftover grain (1), shibboleth (1)

H8673 ²שִׁבֹּלֶת ***šibbōlet²***, n.f. [3] [√ 8670; cf. 6027]. flood, torrent, flow:– floods (1), floodwaters (1 [+4784]), flowing (1)

H8674 שֶׁבְנָא ***šebnā'***, n.pr.m. [7] [√ 8676?; cf. 8675]. Shebna, "*[Yahweh] return now*":– Shebna (7)

H8675 שֶׁבְנָה ***šebnâ***, n.pr.m. [2] [cf. 8674]. Shebna, "*[Yahweh] return now*":– Shebna (2)

H8676 שְׁבַנְיָה ***šᵉbanyâ***, n.pr.m. [5] [→ 8674?, 8677]. Shebaniah:– Shebaniah (5)

H8677 שְׁבַנְיָהוּ ***šᵉbanyāhû***, n.pr.m. [1] [√ 8676]. Shebaniah:– Shebaniah (1)

H8678 שָׁבַע ***šāba'***, v. [186] [→ 937, 8651, 8652, 8668, 8679, 8684, 8685, 8686]. [N] to swear an oath, make a sworn promise; [H] to make one swear an oath, give a charge:– swore (35), swear (30), promised on oath (21), sworn (21), took an oath (7), swore an oath (6), charge (5), made swear (4), take oaths (4), made swear an oath (3), made take an oath (3), make swear (3), put under oath (3), taken an oath (3), bound under a strict oath (2 [+8678]), made swear an oath (2 [+8678]), oath (2), solemnly swore (2), swore oath (2), takes an oath (2), bound with the oath (1), confirmed by oath (1), declared on oath (1), gave oath (1), gave solemn oath

(1), given oath (1), keeps an oath (1), perjurers (1 [+4200, 2021, 9214]), perjury (1 [+4200, 2021, 9214]), pledged on oath (1), pronounced solemn oath (1), put curse (1 [+460, 8652]), ratified by oath (1), solemnly promised (1), swear allegiance (1), swearing (1), swears (1), swears falsely (1), sworn allegiance (1 [+8652]), sworn an oath (1), taken oath (1), takes an oath (1 [+8652]), took oath (1), took the oath (1), use name as a curse (1 [+928]), want to swear (1)

H8679 [1]שֶׁבַע ***šeba'***[1], n.m. & f. [490] [→ 937, 1445?, 8668, 8685; cf. 8678; 10696]. seven; (pl.) seventy:– seven (286), seventy (56), seventh (9), twenty-seventh (6 [+6929, 2256]), 70 (5), seventeen (5 [+6926]), seven pairs (4 [+8679]), seventeenth (4 [+6925]), 127 (3 [+2256, 6929, 2256, 4395]), seventy-seven (3 [+8679, 2256]), seventy-seven (3 [+2256, 8679]), thirty-seventh (3 [+8993, 2256]), 1,247 (2 [+547, 4395, 752, 2256]), 1,775 (2 [+547, 2256, 4395, 2256, 2822, 2256, 8679]), 1,775 (2 [+547, 2256, 8679, 4395, 2256, 2822, 2256]), 137 (2 [+2256, 8993, 2256, 4395]), 372 (2 [+8993, 4395, 2256, 9109]), 57,400 (2 [+2256, 2822, 547, 2256, 752, 4395]), 6,720 (2 [+9252, 547, 4395, 2256, 6929]), 62,700 (2 [+9109, 2256, 9252, 547, 2256, 4395]), 7,337 (2 [+8679, 547, 8993, 4395, 8993, 2256]), 7,337 (2 [+547, 8993, 4395, 8993, 2256, 8679]), 70,000 (2 [+547]), 736 (2 [+4395, 8993, 2256, 9252]), 74 (2 [+2256, 752]), 74,600 (2 [+752, 2256, 547, 2256, 9252, 4395]), 760 (2 [+4395, 2256, 9252]), 973 (2 [+9596, 4395, 2256, 8993]), seventeenth (2 [+6926]), seventy-five (2 [+2256, 2822]), thirty-seven (2 [+8993, 2256]), twenty-seven (2 [+6929, 2256]), 1,017 (1 [+547, 6925]), 1,017 (1 [+547, 2256, 6925]), 1,760 (1 [+547, 2256, 4395, 2256, 9252]), 14,700 (1 [+752, 6925, 547, 2256, 4395]), 157,600 (1 [+4395, 547, 2256, 2256, 2822, 547, 9252, 4395, 2256]), 16,750 (1 [+9252, 6925, 547, 4395, 2256, 2822]), 17,200 (1 [+6925, 547, 2256, 4395]), 172 (1 [+4395, 2256, 9109]), 187 (1 [+2256, 9046, 2256, 4395]), 2,067 (1 [+547, 9252, 2256]), 2,172 (1 [+547, 4395, 2256, 9109]), 2,172 (1 [+547, 4395, 2256, 2256, 9109]), 2,750 (1 [+547, 4395, 2256, 2822]), 207 (1 [+2256, 4395]), 22,273 (1 [+9109, 2256, 6929, 547, 8993, 2256, 2256, 4395]), 273 (1 [+8993, 2256, 2256, 4395]), 3,700 (1 [+8993, 547, 2256, 4395]), 307,500 (1 [+8993, 4395, 547, 2256, 547, 2256, 2822, 4395]), 337,500 (1 [+8993, 4395, 2256, 8993, 547, 547, 2256, 2822, 4395]), 337,500 (1 [+8993, 547, 4395, 2256, 8993, 547, 2256, 547, 2256, 2256, 2822, 4395]), 37,000 (1 [+8993, 2256, 547]), 43,730 (1 [+8993, 2256, 752, 547, 2256, 4395, 2256, 8993]), 44,760 (1 [+752, 2256, 752, 547, 2256, 4395, 2256, 9252]), 52,700 (1 [+9109, 2256, 2822, 547, 2256, 4395]), 601,730 (1 [+9252, 4395, 547, 2256, 547, 4395, 2256, 8993]), 667 (1 [+9252, 4395, 9252, 2256]), 67 (1 [+9252, 2256]), 675 (1 [+9252, 4395, 2822, 2256]), 675,000 (1 [+9252, 4395, 547, 2256, 547, 2256, 2822, 547]), 7,000 (1 [+547]), 7,100 (1 [+547, 2256, 4395]), 7,500 (1 [+547, 2256, 2822, 4395]), 72 (1 [+9109, 2256]), 72,000 (1 [+9109, 2256, 547]), 721 (1 [+4395, 2256, 6929, 2256, 2256, 285]), 725 (1 [+4395, 6929, 2256, 2822]), 730 (1 [+4395, 2256, 8993]), 743 (1 [+4395, 752, 2256, 8993]), 743 (1 [+4395, 2256, 752, 2256, 8993]), 745 (1 [+4395, 752, 2256, 2822]), 76,500 (1 [+9252, 2256, 547, 2256, 2822, 4395]), 775 (1 [+8679, 4395, 2822, 2256]), 775 (1 [+4395, 2822, 2256, 8679]), 777 (1 [+2256, 8679, 2256, 8679, 4395]), 777 (1 [+8679, 2256, 2256, 8679, 4395]), 777 (1 [+8679, 2256, 8679, 2256, 4395]), 782 (1 [+9109, 2256, 9046, 2256, 4395]), 807 (1 [+2256, 9046, 4395]), 87,000 (1 [+9046, 2256, 547]), forty-seven (1 [+752, 2256]), many (1), seven-day (1 [+3427]), seven-day periods (1 [+2021, 3427]), sevenfold (1), seventeen (1 [+2256, 6927]), seventeen hundred (1 [+4395, 2256, 547]), seventeen hundred (1 [+547, 2256, 4395]), seventy-five (1 [+2822, 2256]), twenty-seven hundred (1 [+547, 2256, 4395]), NDT (4)

H8680 [2]שֶׁבַע ***šeba'***[2], n.pr.m. [9] [√ 8682]. Sheba, "*seven* or *oath*":– Sheba (9)

H8681 [3]שֶׁבַע ***šeba'***[3], n.pr.loc. [1] [√ 8682]. Sheba, "*seven* or *oath*":– Sheba (1)

H8682 [4]שֶׁבַע ***šeba'***[4], n.m. Not used in NIVEBC [→ 510, 1444, 3394, 3395, 8680, 8681, 8683]. abundance

H8683 שִׁבְעָה ***šib'â***, n.pr.loc. [1] [√ 8682]. Shibah:– Shibah (1)

H8684 שִׁבְעִים ***šib'îm***, n.pl. Not used in NIVEBC [√ 8678]. seventy (pl. of "seven" [8679])

H8685 שִׁבְעָנָה ***šib'ānâ***, n.m. [1] [√ 8679; cf. 8678]. seven:– seven (1)

H8686 שִׁבְעָתַיִם ***šib'ātayim***, n.f.du. Not used in NIVEBC [√ 8678]. seven-fold, seven times

H8687 שָׁבַץ ***šābaṣ***, v. [2] [→ 5401, 8688, 9587]. [P] to weave; [Pu] to be woven (of fine metal), (n.) a filigree setting:– filigree settings (1), weave (1)

H8688 שָׁבָץ ***šābāṣ***, n.m. [1] [√ 8687]. seizure, cramp, referring to death throes:– throes of death (1)

H8689 [1]שָׁבַר ***šābar***[1], v. [146] [→ 5402, 5403, 8653, 8691, 8693, 8695, 8696; 10752]. [Q] to break, destroy, crush; [Qp] to be broken; [N] to be destroyed, be smashed, be broken; [P] to break, smash, shatter; [H] to bring to break through (of birth); [Ho] to be crushed:– break (19), broken (16), smashed (10), be broken (9), broke (9), be destroyed (5), break down (4), cut off (4), shattered (4), smash (4), brokenhearted (3 [+4213]), injured (3), is broken (3), are broken (2), are crushed (2), break to pieces (2 [+8689]), breaking to pieces (2), breaks (2), broke up (2), crush (2), destroy (2), destroyed (2), is injured (2), mauled (2), was broken off (2), were wrecked (2), abolish (1), are broken off (1), are shattered (1), be broken off (1), be broken up (1), be injured (1), be smashed (1), been broken (1), been grieved (1), break to pieces (1), break up (1), breaks down (1), breaks in pieces (1), bring to the moment of birth (1), broke off (1), broken off (1), crushed (1), demolish (1), desolate (1), fixed (1), is shattered (1), quench (1), shattering (1), stripped (1), suffered (1), was broken (1), were crushed (1)

H8690 [2]שָׁבַר ***šābar***[2], v.den. [21] [√ 8692]. [Q] to buy grain or food; [H] to sell, allow to buy grain:– buy (11), sell (3), buy grain (2), sold grain (2), buying (1), pay for (1), selling (1)

H8691 [1]שֶׁבֶר ***šeber***[1], n.m. [44] [→ 8696; cf. 8689]. destruction, brokenness, injury; "destruction of spirit" is discouragement, and so lacking motivation and being faint-hearted:– destruction (13), wound (6), destroyed (3), disaster (2), fracture (2), acts of violence (1 [+8719, 2256]), break in pieces (1), broken (1), brokenness (1), bruises (1), collapses (1 [+995]), crash (1), crippled (1), crushed (1), crushes (1), downfall (1), fractures (1), heal (1 [+3911, 4200]), injury (1), ruin (1), thrashing (1), NDT (2)

H8692 [2]שֶׁבֶר ***šeber***[2], n.[m.] [9] [→ 8690]. grain:– grain (9)

H8693 [3]שֶׁבֶר ***šeber***[3], n.pr.m. [1] [√ 8691 *or* 8692]. Sheber, "[poss.] *lion;* [poss.] *breaking* or *crushing* or *roughly broken grain*":– Sheber (1)

H8694 שֵׁבֶר ***šēber***, n.m. [1] interpretation (of a dream):– interpretation (1)

H8695 שִׁבָּרוֹן ***šibbārôn***, n.[m.] [2] [√ 8689]. destruction, brokenness:– broken (1), destruction (1)

H8696 שְׁבָרִים ***šᵉbārîm***, n.m.[pl.] [1] [√ 8691]. stone quarry:– stone quarries (1)

H8697 [1]שָׁבַת ***šābat***[1], v. [72] [→ 5404, 8698, 8700, 8701, 8702, 8703; cf. 8697]. [Q] to rest, observe the Sabbath; [N] to come to an end, disappear; [H] to put to an end, stop:– put an end (14), rested (5), stopped (4), come to an end (3), remove (3), rest (3), stop (3), bring an end (2), cease (2), ended (2), gone (2), put a stop (2), abandoned (1), bring to an end (1), cause to stop (1), did away with (1), disappear (1), discard (1), do away with (1), do not work (1), erase (1), have[S] (1), have rest (1), leave (1), left without (1), makes cease (1), must observe a sabbath (1 [+8701]), need not (1), no (1), observe sabbath (1 [+8701]), removed (1), revert (1), rid (1), ruined (1), settles (1), silence (1), stilled (1), stopping (1), wipe (1)

H8698 [2]שָׁבַת ***šābat***[2], v.den. Not used in NIVEBC [√ 8697]. [Q] to keep, observe (the Sabbath)

H8699 [1]שֶׁבֶת ***šebet***[1], n.f. [6] [√ 3782]. place of sitting or settling, site, seat:– seat (2 [+5226]), home (1), lie (1), reign (1), settlement (1)

H8700 [2]שֶׁבֶת ***šebet***[2], n.f. [2] [√ 8697]. cessation, doing-nothing:– do-nothing (1), loss of time (1)

H8701 שַׁבָּת ***šabbāt***, n.f. & m. [111] [→ 8702, 8703; cf. 8697]. Sabbath, the seventh day of the week in the Hebrew calendar (modern Saturday) with a focus of this day as a day of rest and worship; by extension: sabbath, any day or year or period of rest:– sabbath (62), sabbaths (28), day of sabbath rest (5 [+8702]), every sabbath (2 [+8701]), another[S] (1), every sabbath (1 [+8701, 928]), every sabbath (1 [+928, 8701]), it[S] (1 [+2021]), must observe a sabbath (1 [+8697]), observe sabbath (1 [+8697]), sabbath after sabbath (1 [+928, 3427, 2021, 928, 3427, 2021, 8701]), sabbath after sabbath (1 [+928, 3427, 2021, 8701, 928, 3427, 2021]), sabbath days (1), sabbath rest (1 [+8702]), sabbath rests (1), weeks (1), NDT (2)

H8702 שַׁבָּתוֹן ***šabbātôn***, n.m. [11] [√ 8701]. (day of) rest:– day of sabbath rest (5 [+8701]), day of sabbath rest (4), rest (1), sabbath rest (1 [+8701])

H8703 שַׁבְּתַי ***šabbᵉtay***, n.pr.m. [3] [√ 8701]. Shabbethai, "*one born at Sabbath*":– Shabbethai (3)

H8704 שָׁגַג ***šāgag***, v. [4] [→ 54; cf. 5413, 8706]. [Q] to err unintentionally, go astray:– deceived (1), erred (1), went astray (1), wrong committed unintentionally (1 [+8705])

H8705 שְׁגָגָה ***šᵉgāgâ***, n.f. [19] [cf. 8706]. unintentional wrong, accidental error:– unintentionally (6 [+928]), accidentally (4 [+928]), mistake (2), error (1), not intentional (1), sins unintentionally (1 [+6913, 928]), unintentional wrong (1), unintentionally (1 [+4200]), wrong (1), wrong committed unintentionally (1 [+8704])

H8706 שָׁגָה ***šāgâ***, v. [21] [→ 5405; cf. 5413, 8704, 8705, 8707?, 8709]. [Q] to sin unintentionally, go astray, wander:– stagger (3), stray (3), intoxicated (2), led astray (2), sins unintentionally (2), wrong (2), deceiver (1), gone astray (1), leads (1), leads astray (1), let stray (1), unintentionally (1), wandered (1)

H8707 שָׁגֵה ***šāgēh***, n.pr.m. [1] [√ 8706?]. Shagee, "*wanderer, meanderer [like grazing sheep]*":– Shagee (1)

H8708 שָׁגַח ***šāgaḥ***, v. [3] [H] to gaze, stare:– gazing (1), stare (1), watches (1)

H8709 שְׁגִיאָה ***šᵉgî'â***, n.f. [1] [cf. 8706]. error, mistake:– errors (1)

H8710 שִׁגָּיוֹן ***šiggāyôn***, tt. *or* n.m. [2] shiggaion, shigionoth:– shiggaion (1), shigionoth (1)

H8711 שָׁגַל ***šāgal***, v. [4] [√ 8712]. [Q] to ravish, sexually violate; [Qp, N, Pu] to be ravished, be raped:– been ravished (1), rape (1), raped (1), violated (1)

H8712 שֵׁגָל ***šēgal***, n.f. [2] [→ 8711; 10699]. queen, royal bride:– queen (1), royal bride (1)

H8713 שָׁגַע ***šāga'***, v. [7] [→ 8714]. [Pu] to be mad, act like a maniac; [Ht] to carry on like a madman:– maniac (2), carry on (1), drive mad (1), insane (1), madmen (1), maniac (1 [+408])

H8714 שִׁגָּעוֹן ***šiggā'ôn***, n.m. [3] [√ 8713]. madness:– madness (2), maniac (1)

H8715 שֶׁגֶר ***šeger***, n.f. [5] calf, offspring (of cattle):– calves (4), firstborn (1 [+7081])

H8716 שַׁד ***šad***, n.m. [21] [→ 8718, 8721]. (female) breast:– breasts (17), breast (4)

H8717 שֵׁד ***šēd***, n.[m.] [2] demon, evil spirit:– false gods (2)

H8718 [1]שֹׁד ***šōd***[1], n.m. [3] [√ 8716]. (female) breast:– breasts (2), breast (1)

H8719 [2]שֹׁד ***šōd***[2], n.m. [24] [√ 8720]. destruction, ruin, violence:– destruction (12), ruin (3), violence (3), acts of violence (1 [+2256, 8691]), destroys (1), havoc (1), looted (1), oppression (1), plundered (1)

H8720 שָׁדַד ***šādad***, v. [59] [→ 8719, 8722]. [Q] to devastate, devastate; [Qp] to be destroyed; [H] to be ruined; [P, Pol] to ravage, destroy; [Pu] to be destroyed, be ruined; [Ho] to be ruined:– destroyed (7), destroyer (7), destroy (5), ruined (4), destroyers (3), is destroyed (3), are destroyed (2), be destroyed (2), destroying (2), destroys (2), devastated (2), marauders (2), utterly ruined (2 [+8720]), are ruined (1), be devastated (1), be ruined (1), been destroyed (1), dead (1), doomed to destruction (1), in ruins (1), lies in ruins (1), looter (1), out to destroy (1), plunder (1), ravage (1), robbers (1), robs (1), shatter (1), takes loot (1)

H8721 שִׁדָּה ***šiddâ***, n.f. [2] [√ 8716]. lady, concubine; (pl.) harem:– harem (1 [+8721, 2256]), harem (1 [+2256, 8721])

H8722 שָׁדוּד ***šādûd***, n.pr.loc. Not used in NIVEBC [√ 8720; cf. 8587]. Shadud, see 8587

H8723 שַׁדּוּן ***šaddûn***, n.[m.] Not used in NIVEBC [√ 1906; cf. 8726]. judgment

H8724 שַׁדַּי ***šadday***, n.[pr.m.] [48] [→ 7453, 8725?; cf. 8716 *or* 8717 *or* 8720 *or* 8611 + 1896; *also used with compound proper names*]. Almighty:– Almighty (48)

H8725 שְׁדֵיאוּר ***šᵉdê'ûr***, n.pr.m. [5] [√ 8724? + 329]. Shedeur, "*Shaddai is light* or *Shaddai is fire*":– Shedeur (5)

H8726 שַׁדִּין ***šaddîn***, n.m. Not used in NIVEBC [√ 1906; cf. 8723]. judgment

H8727 שְׁדֵמָה ***šᵉdēmâ***, n.f. [5] (cultivated) field; terrace:– fields (4), terraces (1)

H8728 שָׁדַף ***šādap***, v. [3] [→ 8729, 8730; cf. 8812]. [Qp] to be scorched:– scorched (3)

H8729 שְׁדֵפָה ***šᵉdēpâ***, n.f. [2] [√ 8728]. scorching:– scorched (2)

H8730 שִׁדָּפוֹן ***šiddāpôn***, n.m. [5] [√ 8728]. blight:– blight (5)

H8731 שַׁדְרַךְ ***šadrak***, n.pr.m. [1] [√ 10701]. Shadrach, "*servant of Aku*":– Shadrach (1)

H8732 [1]שֹׁהַם ***šōham***[1], n.m. [11] [→ 8733]. onyx (exact identification is uncertain):– onyx (9), onyx (2 [+74])

H8733 [2]שֹׁהַם ***šōham***[2], n.pr.m. [1] [√ 8732]. Shoham, "*carnelian [precious stone]*":– Shoham (1)

H8734 שָׁו ***šāw***, n.[m.] Not used in NIVEBC [√ 8736]. worthless, see 8736

H8735 שׁוּא ***šû'***, v. Not used in NIVEBC [→ 5409, 8738, 8739; cf. 5957, 5958; cf. 8615]. [H] to treat badly

H8736 שָׁוְא ***šāw'***, n.[m.] [53] [→ 7417?, 8734]. worthlessness, vanity, falseness:– false (15), in vain (4 [+4200, 2021]), worthless (4), in vain (3), lies (3), misuse (3 [+5951, 4200, 2021]), falsehood (2), futility (2), misuses (2 [+5951, 4200, 2021]), deceit (1), deceitful (1 [+5493]), deceivers (1 [+5493]), destruction (1), empty plea (1), falsely (1), futile (1), idol (1), idols (1), lies (1 [+1819]), meaningless (1), nothing (1), worthless idols (1), worthless idols (1 [+2039]), worthless things (1)

H8737 שְׁוָא ***šᵉwā'***, n.pr.m. [2] [√ 8750; cf. 8857]. Sheva, "*vanity, emptiness; one who will emulate*":– Sheva (2)

H8738 שׁוֹא ***šô'***, n.[m.] [1] [√ 8735]. ravage:– ravages (1)

H8739 שׁוֹאָה ***šô'â***, n.f. [12] [√ 8735]. trouble, ruin, disaster, desolation:– ruin (3), desolate (2), storm (2), catastrophe (1), destroyed (1), disaster (1), ruins (1), trouble (1)

H8740 [1]שׁוּב ***šûb*[1]**, v. [1052] [→ 3793, 3795, 5411, 5412, 8743, 8744, 8745, 8746, 9588; 10754; *also used with compound proper names*]. [Q] to turn back, turn to, return; [Qp] to return; [Pol] to restore, bring back; [Polal] to be recovered; [H] to restore, recover, bring back; [Ho] to be returned, be brought back; from the base meaning of turning back comes the fig. extension of restoration of relationship, as when one returns in repentance to God:– return (157), returned (98), turn (50), bring back (38), restore (38), go back (37), again (35), turn back (27), come back (22), went back (22), brought back (20), back (18), turn away (17), turned (17), restored (15), turned away (13), relent (12), repent (11), put back (10), answer (9 [+1821]), give back (9), send back (9), came back (8), turned back (8), recovered (7), take back (7), repay (6), reported (6 [+1821]), returns (6), turns (6), answer (5), bring (5), go (5), took back (5), turns away (5), change (4), ever return (4 [+8740]), go (4 [+2143, 2256]), pay back (4), refuse (4), rewarded (4), take (4), turn away (4 [+8740]), withdrew (4), answered (3 [+1821]), bringing back (3), make return (3), returning (3), started back (3), stop (3), stopped (3), turned around (3), again and again (2), be sure to return (2 [+8740]), be sure to take back (2 [+8740]), bring down (2), by all means send (2 [+8740]), coming back (2), depart (2), keep (2), left (2), oppose (2), pay (2), pays back (2 [+8740]), rebuilt (2 [+2256, 1215]), refreshes (2), regain (2), reject (2 [+7156]), repaid (2), repented (2), repents (2), reply (2), repulse (2 [+7156]), restores (2 [+8654]), restrain (2), retreat (2), return (2 [+2143]), return (2 [+8740]), revert (2), revoked (2), sent (2), sent back (2), surely return (2 [+8740]), take back (2 [+8740]), take vengeance (2 [+5934]), takes back (2 [+8740]), turn around (2), turning (2), withdraw (2), withholds (2), again (1 [+9108]), again be used (1), again give allegiance (1 [+4213]), another (1), answer give (1), answered (1), arrived (1), back again (1), be brought back (1), been returned (1), break (1), brings reward (1), broke off (1 [+4946]), brought (1), brought down (1), call to mind (1 [+448, 4213]), came again (1), carry the battle (1 [+2256, 1741]), catch (1), caused to roam (1), changed (1), changed minds (1), changes (1), come (1), condemning (1), continually (1), cover up (1 [+2256, 4059]), did[S] (1), do so[S] (1 [+4946, 2006]), dole out (1), draw back (1), drew back (1), drives (1), escaping (1), flow back (1), flowed back (1), forced to restore (1), gave (1), get back (1), give (1), give up (1 [+4946]), go back (1 [+345]), go down (1), go on (1), going back (1), haul in (1), hold back (1), keep themselves alive (1 [+5883]), keep themselves alive (1 [+906, 5883, 4392]), keeps saying (1 [+609]), made go back (1), made pay for (1 [+928, 8031]), made retreat (1 [+294]), make full restitution (1 [+928, 8031]), make go (1), make right (1), marauding forces (1 [+6296, 2256]), mislead (1), no longer (1), not angry (1 [+678]), once more (1), overruling (1), overthrows (1 [+294]), paid (1), paid (1 [+868]), paid back (1), pass again (1), passed (1), pay a tribute (1), pays back (1), penitent (1), prompt to answer (1), pull back (1), pursues (1 [+928]), raised (1), ran (1), reappears (1 [+2256, 7255]), rebuild (1 [+1215, 2256]), recaptured (1 [+2256, 4374]), receded steadily (1 [+8740, 2143, 2256]), receded steadily (1 [+2143, 2256, 8740]), recoil (1), recoils (1), reconsider (1 [+6388]), recover (1), reentered (1 [+995, 2256]), refreshing (1), refund (1), renew (1), renounce (1 [+7156]), reopened (1 [+2256, 2916]), repay (1 [+928, 8031]), repay (1 [+6584, 8031]), reply (1 [+4863]), report back (1), rescue (1), respond (1), rest (1), restitution (1 [+871]), restitution made (1), restore again (1), restorer (1), restrained (1), retire (1), retreats (1), return (1 [+2143, 2256]), returned unanswered (1 [+2668]), reverse (1), reversed (1), revived (1 [+8120]), revoke (1 [+4946]), rewards (1), roll back (1), say (1), send (1), sending back (1), shy away (1), something else (1), stand (1 [+4202]), stopped (1 [+4946]), stops to think (1 [+448, 4213]), strayed (1), subsides (1), take away (1), taken back (1), traveled through (1 [+6296, 2256]), try again (1), turn again (1), turned again (1), turned to go (1), turning away (1), vent (1), ward off (1), were brought back (1), withdrawn (1 [+294]), withheld (1), withhold (1), NDT (16)

H8741 [2]שׁוּב ***šûb*[2]**, n.f. see 8740

H8742 שׁוּבָאֵל ***šûbā'ēl***, n.pr.m. [6] [cf. 8649]. Shubael, "[poss.] *captive of God [El]* or *God [El] restores*":– Shubael (6)

H8743 [1]שׁוֹבָב ***šôbāb*[1]**, a. [3] [√ 8740]. faithless, rebellious, apostate:– faithless (2), kept on (1 [+2143])

H8744 [2]שׁוֹבָב ***šôbāb*[2]**, n.pr.m. [4] [√ 8740]. Shobab, "*one who turns back, repents*":– Shobab (4)

H8745 שׁוֹבֵב ***šôbēb***, a. [3] [√ 8740]. unfaithful, traitorous, apostate:– unfaithful (2), traitors (1)

H8746 שׁוּבָה ***šûbâ***, n.f. [1] [√ 8740]. returning, i.e., repentance:– repentance (1)

H8747 שׁוֹבַךְ ***šôbak***, n.pr.m. [2] [cf. 8791]. Shobach:– Shobak (2)

H8748 שׁוֹבָל ***šôbāl***, n.pr.m. [9] Shobal, "*basket*":– Shobal (9)

H8749 שׁוֹבֵק ***šôbēq***, n.pr.m. [1] [√ 3791]. Shobek, "*victor*":– Shobek (1)

H8750 [1]שָׁוָה ***šāwâ*[1]**, v. [14] [→ 3796, 3798, 3799, 8737, 8752, 8753, 8754, 8856, 9590; 10702]. [Q] to be like, be equal; to be appropriate, be deserved; [N] to be like; [P] to make smooth; [H] to liken; to count as equal:– compare (2), be just like (1), calmed (1), count equal (1), equal (1), get what deserved (1), gives satisfaction (1), in best interest (1), is like (1), justify (1), leveled (1), liken (1), waited patiently (1)

H8751 [2]שָׁוָה ***šāwâ*[2]**, v. [7] [P] to set, place, bestow:– bestowed (2), makes (2), brought forth (1), keep (1), set heart (1)

H8752 שָׁוֶה ***šāweh***, n.m.[loc.?] Not used in NIVEBC [→ 8753; cf. 8750]. see 8753 & 8754

H8753 שָׁוֵה ***šāwēh***, n.pr.loc. [1] [√ 8752; cf. 8750]. Shaveh, "*level [valley]*":– Shaveh (1)

H8754 שָׁוֵה קִרְיָתַיִם ***šāwēh qiryātayim***, n.pr.loc. [1] [√ 8750 + 7984]. Shaveh Kiriathaim:– Shaveh Kiriathaim (1)

H8755 [1]שׁוּחַ ***šûaḥ*[1]**, v. [1] [→ 8757, 8758?, 8846; cf. 8817, 8820]. [Q] sink down:– leads down (1)

H8756 [2]שׁוּחַ ***šûaḥ*[2]**, n.pr.m. [2] [→ 8760]. Shuah, "*depression, lowland [an Aramean land on the Euphrates River]*":– Shuah (2)

H8757 [1]שׁוּחָה ***šûḥâ*[1]**, n.f. [5] [→ 8758?; cf. 8755, 8864]. pit, rift:– pit (4), ravines (1)

H8758 [2]שׁוּחָה ***šûḥâ*[2]**, n.pr.[m.?] [1] [√ 8757?; cf. 8755?]. Shuhah, "*pit, depression*":– Shuhah's (1)

H8759 שָׁוְחַט ***šawḥaṭ***, v. Not used in NIVEBC [→ 8453]. see 8821

H8760 שׁוּחִי ***šûḥî***, a.g. [5] [√ 8756]. Shuhite:– Shuhite (5)

H8761 שׁוּחָם ***šûḥām***, n.pr.m. [1] [→ 8762]. Shuham:– Shuham (1)

H8762 שׁוּחָמִי ***šûḥāmî***, a.g. [2] [√ 8761]. Shuhamite, "*of Shuham*":– Shuhamite (2)

H8763 [1]שׁוּט ***šûṭ*[1]**, v.den. [13] [→ 5414, 5415, 8765, 8849, 8868]. [Q] to roam, go about; to oar (a boat); [Pol] to wander, go here and there; [Htpol] to rush here and there:– oarsmen (2), range (2), roaming (2), go (1), go here and there (1), go up and down (1), gone (1), rush here and there (1), wander (1), went around (1)

H8764 [2]שׁוּט ***šûṭ*[2]**, v. [3] [Q] to malign, act malicious:– despise (1), malicious (1), maligned (1)

H8765 [1]שׁוֹט ***šôṭ*[1]**, n.m. [11] [→ 8849; cf. 8763, 8867]. whip, lash:– whips (5), scourge (3), whip (2), lash (1)

H8766 [2]שׁוֹט ***šôṭ*[2]**, n.m. (sudden) flood

H8767 שׁוּל ***šûl***, n.m. [11] [cf. 8870]. hem (of a robe); skirt:– hem (5), skirts (4), train of robe (1), NDT (1)

H8768 שׁוֹלָל ***šôlāl***, a. [3] [√ 8964; cf. 8871]. barefoot, stripped:– stripped (2), barefoot (1)

H8769 שׁוּלַמִּית ***šûlammît***, a.g.[f.] [2] Shulammite:– Shulammite (2)

H8770 שׁוּמִים ***šûmîm***, n.[m.] [1] garlic:– garlic (1)

H8771 [1]שׁוּנִי ***šûnî*[1]**, n.pr.m. [2] [→ 8772]. Shuni:– Shuni (2)

H8772 [2]שׁוּנִי ***šûnî*[2]**, a.g. [1] [√ 8771]. Shunite, "*of Shuni*":– Shunite (1)

H8773 שׁוּנֵם ***šûnēm***, n.pr.loc. [3] [→ 8774]. Shunem:– Shunem (3)

H8774 שׁוּנַמִּי ***šûnammî***, a.g. [8] [√ 8773]. Shunammite, "*of Shunem*":– Shunammite (8)

H8775 שָׁוַע ***šāwa'***, v. [22] [→ 8776, 8779, 8780, 8784; cf. 8782; *also used with compound proper names*]. [P] to cry for help, plead:– cry for help (7), cried for help (4), call for help (3), called for help (3), cry out (3), cry out for help (1), plead for relief (1)

H8776 שֶׁוַע ***šewa'***, n.[m.] [1] [√ 8775]. cry for help:– cry for help (1 [+7754])

H8777 [1]שׁוֹעַ ***šôa'*[1]**, a. [2] [→ 55, 8781, 8782]. highly respected, noble; (n.) the rich:– highly respected (1), rich (1)

H8778 [2]שׁוֹעַ ***šôa'*[2]**, n.pr.g. [1] [cf. 7760]. Shoa, "*rich*":– Shoa (1)

H8779 [3]שׁוֹעַ ***šôa'*[3]**, n.[m.] [1] [√ 8775]. crying out:– crying out (1)

H8780 [1]שׁוּעַ ***šûa'*[1]**, n.[m.] [1] [√ 8775]. cry for help:– cries for help (1)

H8781 [2]שׁוּעַ ***šûa'*[2]**, n.pr.m. [3] [√ 8782; cf. 8777]. Shua, "*prosperity*":– Shua (3)

H8782 [3]שׁוּעַ ***šûa'*[3]**, n.m. [1] [→ 8781; cf. 8775, 8777]. wealth:– wealth (1)

H8783 שׁוּעָא ***šû'ā'***, n.pr.f. [1] Shua, "*prosperity*":– Shua (1)

H8784 שַׁוְעָה ***šaw'â***, n.f. [11] [√ 8775]. cry for help:– cry (7), cry for help (3), outcry (1)

H8785 [1]שׁוּעָל ***šû'āl*[1]**, n.m. [7] [→ 2967, 8786, 8787]. fox; jackal:– foxes (3), jackals (3), fox (1)

H8786 [2]שׁוּעָל ***šû'āl*[2]**, n.pr.m. [1] [√ 8785]. Shual, "*fox or jackal*":– Shual (1)

H8787 [3]שׁוּעָל ***šû'āl*[3]**, n.pr.loc. [1] [√ 8785]. Shual, "*fox or jackal*":– Shual (1)

H8788 שׁוֹעֵר ***šō'ēr***, n.m. [37] [√ 9133; 10777]. gatekeeper, doorkeeper:– gatekeepers (31), doorkeepers (2), gatekeeper (2), keep watch (1), keeper of gate (1)

H8789 [1]שׁוּף ***šûp*[1]**, v. [3] [cf. 8790, 8635]. [Q] to crush; some sources: bruise, a wound that is not fatal:– crush (2), hide (1)

H8790 [2]שׁוּף ***šûp*[2]**, v. [1] [cf. 8789, 8635]. [Q] to strike:– strike (1)

H8791 שׁוֹפָךְ ***šôpak***, n.pr.m. [2] [cf. 8747]. Shophach:– Shophak (2)

H8792 שׁוּפָם ***šûpām***, n.pr.m. [1] [→ 8793; cf. 9145]. Shupham:– Shupham (1)

H8793 שׁוּפָמִי ***šûpāmî***, a.g. [1] [√ 8792]. Shuphamite, "*of Shupham*":– Shuphamite (1)

H8794 שׁוֹפָן ***šôpān***, n.pr.loc. Not used in NIVEBC [→ 6503]. Shophan

H8795 שׁוֹפָר ***šôpār***, n.m. [72] [→ 882; cf. 9182]. trumpet, ram's horn:– trumpet (44), trumpets (18), trumpets (3 [+3413]), ram's horn (2), blast (1 [+7754]), horns (1), rams horns (1), trumpet (1 [+9558]), NDT (1)

H8796 [1]שׁוּק ***šûq*[1]**, v. [3] [→ 8797, 8798, 8799; cf. 9212?]. [H] to prove narrow, overflow; [Polel] to water abundantly:– overflow (2), water (1)

H8797 שׁוֹק ***šôq***, n.[f.] [19] [√ 8796; 10741]. (lower) thigh; leg:– thigh (13), legs (5), attacked viciously (1 [+5782, 6584, 3751])

H8798 [2]שׁוּק ***šûq*[2]**, n.m. [4] [√ 8796]. street:– street (2), streets (2)

H8799 שׁוֹקֵק ***šôqēq***, a. *or* v.ptcp. [2] [√ 8796]. thirsty, unquenched:– thirsty (2 [+5883])

H8800 [1]שׁוּר ***šûr*[1]**, v. [14] [→ 8803, 8804?, 8805, 9224]. [Q] to see, look, view:– see (5), behold (1), care for (1), gaze (1), lie in wait (1), look (1), lurk (1), pays attention (1), perceives (1), view (1)

H8801 [2]שׁוּר ***šûr*[2]**, v. [4] [Q] to travel, descend:– carriers (1), descend (1), go (1), went (1)

H8802 שׁוֹר ***šôr***, n.m. [79] [→ 56, 9593; 10756]. bull, ox:– ox (37), bull (16), cattle (13), animal (2), bulls (2), calf (2), cow (2), herd (2), cows (1), one[S] (1), oxen (1)

H8803 [3]שׁוּר ***šûr*[3]**, n.[m.] [3] [→ 8804; cf. 8800; 10703]. wall:– wall (3)

H8804 [4]שׁוּר ***šûr*[4]**, n.pr.loc. [6] [√ 8803?; cf. 8800?]. Shur, "*wall*":– Shur (6)

H8805 שׁוּרָה ***šûrâ***, n.f. [1] [→ 9224; cf. 8800]. supporting wall (of a terrace):– terraces (1)

H8806 שׁוֹרֵר ***šôrēr***, n.m. [6] enemy, adversary:– adversaries (2), slander (2), enemies (1), oppressors (1)

H8807 שַׁוְשָׁא ***šawšā'***, n.pr.m. [1] Shavsha:– Shavsha (1)

H8808 [1]שׁוּשַׁן ***šûšan*[1]**, n.m. [17] lily plant; some sources: lotus plant:– lilies (11), lily (6)

H8809 [2]שׁוּשַׁן ***šûšan*[2]**, n.pr.loc. [21] [√ 10704]. Susa:– Susa (21)

H8810 שׁוּשַׁק ***šûšaq***, n.pr.m. Not used in NIVEBC [cf. 8882]. Shushak, see 8882

H8811 שׁוּתֶלַח ***šûtelaḥ***, n.pr.m. [4] [→ 9279]. Shuthelah:– Shuthelah (4)

H8812 שָׁזַף ***šāzap***, v. [3] [cf. 8728]. [Q] to see; to be darkened:– darkened (1), saw (1), seen (1)

H8813 שָׁזַר ***šāzar***, v. [21] [Ho] to be finely twisted:– finely twisted (21)

H8814 שַׁח ***šaḥ***, a. [1] [√ 8820]. downward, bent, low:– downcast (1 [+6524])

H8815 שָׁחַד ***šāḥad***, v. [2] [→ 8816; cf. 8610]. [Q] to give a gift; pay a bribe; pay a ransom:– bribing (1), pay a ransom (1)

H8816 שֹׁחַד ***šōḥad***, n.m. [23] [√ 8815]. bribe, gift:– bribe (11), bribes (7), gift (2), bribery (1 [+5228]), reward (1), those who love bribes (1)

H8817 שָׁחָה ***šāḥâ***, v. [2] [cf. 2556, 8755, 8820]. [Q] to bow down; [H] to weigh down, cause to bow:– fall prostrate (1), weighs down (1)

H8818 שְׁחוֹר ***šᵉḥôr***, n.[m.] [1] [√ 8837]. soot:– soot (1)

H8819 שְׁחוּת ***šᵉḥût***, n.f. [1] [→ 8827]. trap, pit:– trap (1)

H8820 שָׁחַח ***šāḥaḥ***, v. [18] [→ 8814; cf. 8755, 8817]. [Q] to bow down, bend low; [N] to be brought low; [H] to humble, bring low:– brought low (3), be brought low (2), bow down (1), bowed head (1), bowing (1), bring down (1), collapse (1), collapsed (1), cowered (1), crouch (1), downcast (1), faint (1), humbled (1), humbles (1), mumble (1)

H8821 [1]שָׁחַט ***šāḥaṭ*[1]**, v. [80] [→ 8823, 8824]. [Q] to slaughter, kill; [Qp, N] to be killed, be slaughtered:– slaughtered (33), slaughter (23), killed (6), sacrificed (2), sacrifices (2), be slaughtered (1), butchered (1), dead (1), deadly (1), kill (1), killing (1), offer (1), sacrifice (1), sacrifices slaughtered (1), slaughtering (1), slay (1), was killed (1), were slaughtered (1), NDT (1)

H8822 [2]שָׁחַט ***šāḥaṭ*[2]**, v. [5] [Qp] to be hammered, beaten;

some sources: to be alloyed, blended, referring to the mixing of metals:– hammered (5)

H8823 שְׁחָטָה **šaḥ^{a}ṭâ**, n.f. [1] [√ 8821]. slaughter:– slaughter (1)

H8824 שְׁחִיטָה **š^{e}ḥîṭâ**, n.f. [1] [√ 8821]. killing, slaughter:– kill (1)

H8825 שְׁחִין **š^{e}ḥîn**, n.m. [13] boils, skin sores:– boil (6), boils (5), sores (1), NDT (1)

H8826 שָׁחִיס **šāḥîs**, n.[m.] [1] [cf. 6084]. growth, what springs up:– what springs from (1)

H8827 שְׁחִית **š^{e}ḥît**, n.f. [2] [√ 8819]. pit, trap, grave:– grave (1), traps (1)

H8828 שַׁחַל **šaḥal**, n.m. [7] [√ 8829]. lion:– lion (6), NDT (1)

H8829 שְׁחֵלֶת **š^{e}ḥēlet**, n.f. [1] [→ 8828]. onycha (a fragrant spice):– onycha (1)

H8830 שַׁחַף **šaḥap**, n.[m.] [2] gull or possibly bat:– gull (2)

H8831 שַׁחֶפֶת **šaḥepet**, n.f. [2] wasting disease, consumption:– wasting disease (1), wasting diseases (1)

H8832 שַׁחַץ **šaḥaṣ**, n.[m.] [2] [→ 8833, 8834]. pride, dignity:– proud (1 [+1201]), proud beasts (1 [+1201])

H8833 שַׁחֲצוּמָה **šaḥ^{a}ṣûmâ**, n.pr.loc. [1] [√ 8832]. Shahazumah, "*elevated place*":– Shahazumah (1)

H8834 שַׁחֲצִימָה **šaḥ^{a}ṣîmâ**, n.pr.loc. Not used in NIVEBC [√ 8832]. Shahazimah, see 8833

H8835 שָׁחַק **šāḥaq**, v. [4] [→ 8836]. [Q] to grind, wear away:– beat fine (2), grind (1), wears away (1)

H8836 שַׁחַק **šaḥaq**, n.m. [21] [√ 8835]. clouds, skies:– clouds (7), skies (6), heavens (3), clouds of the sky (2 [+6265]), dust (1), skies above (1), sky (1)

H8837 [1]שָׁחַר **šāḥar[1]**, v. [1] [→ 328, 5423, 8818, 8839, 8040, 8841, 8842, 8844]. [Q] to become black:– grows black (1)

H8838 [2]שָׁחַר **šāḥar[2]**, v.den. [13] [→ 8843; cf. 8840?]. [Q] to seek, look; [P] to earnestly seek, search for:– earnestly seek (2), careful (1), conjure away (1), eagerly (1), foraging (1), longs for (1), look for (1), looked for (1), search for (1), seek (1), seek earnestly (1), seeks (1)

H8839 שָׁחֹר **šāḥōr**, a. [6] [√ 8837]. black, dark:– black (5), dark (1)

H8840 שַׁחַר **šaḥar**, n.m. [23] [√ 8037, 8844; cf. 8838?]. dawn, daybreak:– dawn (14), daybreak (2), daybreak (2 [+6590, 2021]), day dawns (1), first light of dawn (1 [+6590]), light of dawn (1), morning (1), sun rises (1)

H8841 שַׁחֲרוּת **šaḥ^{a}rût**, n.f. [1] [√ 8837]. vigor, prime of youth, an extension of dark hair color (or perhaps of the dawn):– vigor (1)

H8842 שְׁחַרְחֹר **š^{e}ḥarḥōr**, a. [1] [√ 8837]. dark, swarthy (complexion):– dark (1)

H8843 שְׁחַרְיָה **š^{e}ḥaryâ**, n.pr.m. [1] [√ 8838]. Shehariah, "*he seeks Yahweh*":– Shehariah (1)

H8844 שַׁחֲרַיִם **šaḥ^{a}rayim**, n.pr.m. [1] [√ 8840; cf. 8837]. Shaharaim, "*one born at early [reddish] dawn*":– Shaharaim (1)

H8845 שָׁחַת **šāḥat**, v. [146] [→ 5422, 5424, 5425, 5426; 10705]. [N] to be corrupt, be ruined, be marred; [P] to corrupt, destroy, ruin; [H] to destroy, corrupt, bring to ruin:– destroy (61), corrupt (11), destroyed (11), destroying (5), cut down (3), ruin (3), ruined (3), act corruptly (2), corrupted (2), depraved (2), destroys (2), destruction (2), devastate (2), raiding parties (2), ravage (2), sure to become utterly corrupt (2 [+8845]), afflicting (1), allowed to fall into ruin (1), battering (1), blemished (1), cause devastation (1), cause of destruction (1), clip off (1), corrupt practices (1), corruption (1), devastated (1), devouring (1), doing so^{S} (1), downfall (1), endanger (1), given to corruption (1), killed (1), laid waste (1), overthrow (1), polluted (1), ravaging (1), ravenous (1), slaughtered (1), spilled (1), steal (1), struck down (1), tear down (1), violated (1), was marred (1), was ruined (1), wasted (1), NDT (1)

H8846 שַׁחַת **šaḥat**, n.f. [24] [√ 8755]. pit, dungeon; corruption, decay:– pit (18), decay (3), corruption (1), dungeon (1), slime pit (1)

H8847 שִׁטָּה **šiṭṭâ**, n.f. [29] [→ 8850]. acacia wood:– acacia (25), acacia wood (3), acacias (1)

H8848 שָׁטַח **šāṭaḥ**, v. [6] [→ 5427]. [Q] to spread out, enlarge, scatter; [P] to spread out:– spread out (2 [+8848]), enlarges (1), exposed (1), scattered (1), spread out (1)

H8849 שֹׁטֵט **šōṭēṭ**, n.[m.] [1] [√ 8765; cf. 8763]. whip, scourge:– whips (1)

H8850 שִׁטִּים **šiṭṭîm**, n.pr.loc. [4] [√ 8847]. Shittim, "*acacia trees*":– Shittim (4)

H8851 שָׁטַף **šāṭap**, v. [31] [→ 8852; cf. 9192]. [Q] to overflow, flood, wash away; [N] to be rinsed, be swept away; [Pu] to be rinsed:– overwhelming (3), torrents (3), engulf (2), flood (2), overflow (2), washed (2), be rinsed (1), be swept away (1), charging (1), engulfed (1), flooding (1), flooding downpour (1 [+3888]), flowed (1), flowed abundantly (1), overflowing (1), rinsed (1), rinsing (1), rushing (1), sweep away (1), sweep over (1), swept away (1), swirling over (1), wash away (1)

H8852 שֶׁטֶף **šeṭep**, n.m. [6] [√ 8851; cf. 9192]. flood, torrents (of rain):– flood (2), overwhelming (2), rising (1), torrents of rain (1)

H8853 שָׁטַר **šāṭar**, n.m. [25] [→ 5428, 8854, 8855]. [Q] to keep a record; (n.) official, officer, foreman:– officials (10), officers (6), overseers (5), officer (1), overseer (1), scribes (1), serve as officials (1)

H8854 שֹׁטֵר **šōṭēr**, n.m. Not used in NIVEBC [√ 8853]. oversee, officer

H8855 שִׁטְרַי **šiṭray**, n.pr.m. [1] [√ 8853; cf. 9231]. Shitrai, "*scribe, officer*":– Shitrai (1)

H8856 שַׁי **šay**, n.m. [3] [√ 8750; cf. 2593?]. gift:– gifts (3)

H8857 שְׁיָא **š^{e}yā'**, n.pr.m. Not used in NIVEBC [cf. 8737]. Sheya, see 8737

H8858 שִׁיאֹן **šî'ōn**, n.pr.loc. [1] [√ 8615?]. Shion:– Shion (1)

H8859 [1]שִׁיבָה **šîbâ[1]**, n.f. [1] [√ 3782?]. stay:– stay (1)

H8860 [2]שִׁיבָה **šîbâ[2]**, n.f. Not used in NIVEBC [√ 8647; cf. 8669]. captives

H8861 שָׁיָה **šāyâ**, v. [1] [cf. 5960]. [Q] to desert, forget:– deserted (1)

H8862 שִׁיזָא **šîzā'**, n.pr.m. [1] Shiza:– Shiza (1)

H8863 שִׁיחַ **šîaḥ**, v. [5] [Q] to disintegrate away (to dust):– downcast (4), down (1)

H8864 שִׁיחָה **šîḥâ**, n.f. [2] [cf. 8757]. pit, pitfall:– pit (1), pits (1)

H8865 שִׁיחוֹר **šîḥôr**, n.pr.loc. [4] [→ 8866]. Shihor, "[poss.] *black water*; [Egyptian] *Canal of Horus*":– Shihor (3), Nile (1)

H8866 שִׁיחוֹר לִבְנָת **šîḥôr libnāt**, n.pr.loc. [1] [√ 4251 + 8865]. Shihor Libnath:– Shihor Libnath (1)

H8867 שִׁיט **šîṭ**, n.[m.] Not used in NIVEBC [cf. 8765]. scourge, see 8765

H8868 שַׁיִט **šayiṭ**, n.[m.] [1] [√ 8763]. oar:– oars (1)

H8869 שִׁילֹה **šîlōh**, n.pr.loc.? Not used in NIVEBC [√ 8870]. Shiloh

H8870 שִׁילוֹ **šîlô**, n.pr.loc. [3] [→ 8869, 8872; cf. 8767]. Shiloh:– Shiloh (2), them^{S} (1 [+1426])

H8871 שֵׁילָל **šêlāl**, a. Not used in NIVEBC [cf. 8768]. see 8768

H8872 שִׁילֹנִי **šîlōnî**, a.g. [6] [√ 8870; cf. 8926]. Shilonite, of Shiloh, "*of Shiloh*":– Shilonite (4), Shelanites (1), of Shiloh (1)

H8873 שִׁימוֹן **šîmôn**, n.pr.m. [1] Shimon:– Shimon (1)

H8874 שִׁין **šîn**, v. [6] [→ 8875; cf. 9282]. [Hiphil] to urinate (on a wall), i.e., a male:– every last male (3 [+928, 7815]), male (3 [+928, 7815])

H8875 שַׁיִן **šayin**, n.[m.] [2] [√ 8874]. urine:– urine (2)

H8876 [1]שִׁיר **šîr[1]**, v. [86] [→ 8877, 8878; cf. 3938]. [Q] to sing; [P ptcp.] singer, musician:– sing (32), musicians (27), singers (11), sang (4), choirs (2), be sung (1), echo (1), musician (1), musicians (1 [+1201]), played (1), praised in song (1), sang song (1), sing praise (1), singing (1), sings (1)

H8877 [2]שִׁיר **šîr[2]**, n.m. [77] [√ 8876]. song, music:– song (47), songs (10), music (5), musical (5), singing (4), instruments (2 [+3998]), musicians (1), sing (1), songs (1 [+1426]), songs (1 [+1821])

H8878 שִׁירָה **šîrâ**, n.f. [13] [√ 8876]. song:– song (11), it^{S} (1 [+2021, 2021, 2296]), songs (1)

H8879 שְׁיָרָה **š^{e}yārâ**, n.[f.] Not used in NIVEBC. caravan, see 8801

H8880 שַׁיִשׁ **šayiš**, n.[m.] [1] [√ 9253]. alabaster:– marble (1 [+74])

H8881 שִׁישָׁא **šîšā'**, n.pr.m. [1] Shisha:– Shisha (1)

H8882 שִׁישַׁק **šîšaq**, n.pr.m. [7] [cf. 8810]. Shishak:– Shishak (7)

H8883 [1]שִׁית **šît[1]**, v. [83] [→ 8884, 9269; cf. 9286]. [Q] to place, put, set; [Ho] to be demanded:– make (8), put (8), made (6), set (6), bring (2), give (2), granted (2), is demanded (2), lay (2), place (2), placed (2), posted (2 [+8883]), take (2), turn (2), alert (1), applied (1), apply (1), appointed (1), assail (1 [+6584]), assign (1), bring (1 [+3338, 6584]), burn^{S} (1), change (1), close (1), consider well (1 [+4213]), demands (1), establish (1), gave a place (1), gives (1), halt (1), harbor (1), have (1), help (1 [+3338, 6640]), hold (1), laid (1), look with approval (1 [+4200, 5584, 6524]), make turn (1), makes (1), pay (1), perform (1), placing (1), protect (1 [+928, 3829]), set out (1), strike (1), take note (1 [+4213]), treat (1), turned (1), wrestle (1), NDT (1)

H8884 [2]שִׁית **šît[2]**, n.m. [2] [√ 8883]. garment:– clothe (1 [+6493]), dressed (1)

H8885 שַׁיִת **šayit**, n.[m.] [7] [√ 8615?]. thorns, thorn-bushes:– thorns (7)

H8886 שָׁכַב **šākab**, v. [207] [→ 5435, 8887, 8888]. [Q] to lie down, rest; sleep with; (as a euphemism of sexual intercourse) to lie with, sleep with; [H] to make lie down; [Ho] to be laid down:– rested (36), lie down (20), lie (17), lay down (13), lying (10), lay (8), rest (8), lies (7), has sexual relations (6), slept with (6 [+907]), sleep (5), sleep with (5 [+6640]), sleeps with (5 [+6640]), lying down (4), slept with (4 [+6640]), laid (3), lies down (3), be laid (2), come to bed with (2 [+6640]), has sexual relations (2 [+8886]), has sexual relations with (2 [+6640]), put (2), slept (2), bed with (1 [+6640]), done this^{S} (1 [+6640]), dwell (1), go (1), go to bed with (1 [+725]), go to sleep (1), gone to bed (1), had sexual relations (1), has sexual relations (1 [+8887, 2446]), have sexual relations (1), he^{S} (1 [+2021, 408, 2021, 6640]), laid low (1), laid to rest (1), lain down (1), lay down to sleep (1), lie around (1), lie in state (1 [+928, 3883]), made lie down (1), made love to (1 [+6640]), make love to (1 [+6640]), raped (1 [+6700, 2256]), raped (1 [+2256, 6700]), rapes (1 [+9530, 2256, 6640]), rapes (1 [+2616, 2256, 6640]), resting (1), sleeping (1), sleeping with (1 [+907]), sleeping with (1 [+6640]), sleeps (1), sleeps with (1 [+8887, 2446, 907]), stayed (1), take rest (1), taking rest (1 [+5435]), tip over (1), NDT (1)

H8887 שִׁכְבָה **šikbâ**, n.f. [9] [√ 8886]. emission, discharge:– emission (4), has sexual relations (1 [+8886, 2446]), layer (1), sleeps with (1 [+8886, 2446, 907]), NDT (2)

H8888 שְׁכֹבֶת **š^{e}kōbet**, n.f. [4] [√ 8886]. sexual relations, sexual intercourse:– has sexual relations (1 [+5989]), have sexual relations (1 [+5989]), have sexual relations (1 [+5989, 4200, 2446]), having sexual relations with (1 [+5989, 928])

H8889 שָׁכָה **šākâ**, v. [1] [H] to be well-fed; lusting:– well-fed (1)

H8890 שְׁכוֹל **š^{e}kôl**, n.[m.] [3] [√ 8897]. forlornness, loss of children:– loss of children (2), bereaved (1)

H8891 שַׁכּוּל **šakkûl**, a. [6] [√ 8897]. pertaining to the loss of offspring:– robbed of cubs (2), alone (1), childless (1), missing (1), robbed (1)

H8892 שְׁכוּלָה **š^{e}kûlâ**, a. [1] [√ 8897]. bereaved (of children):– bereaved (1)

H8893 שִׁכּוֹר **šikkôr**, a. [13] [√ 8910]. drunk, drunkenness; (n.) a drunkard:– drunkards (5), drunk (2), drunkard (2), getting drunk (2 [+9272]), drunkard's (1), drunken (1)

H8894 שָׁכַח **šākaḥ**, v. [101] [→ 8895; 10708]. [Q] to forget; [N] to be forgotten; [P] to make forget; [H] to make forget; [Ht] to be forgotten:– forget (43), forgotten (20), forgot (11), be forgotten (7), ignore (4), ever forget (2 [+8894]), forgets (2), ignored (2), am forgotten (1), been forgotten (1), is forgotten (1), made forget (1), make forget (1), neglect (1), never notice (1), overlook (1), unmindful (1), untouched (1)

H8895 שָׁכֵחַ **šākēaḥ**, a. [2] [√ 8894]. forgetting:– forget (2)

H8896 שָׁכַךְ **šākak**, v. [5] [Q] to recede, reside; [H] to get rid of:– subsided (2), receded (1), rid (1), NDT (1)

H8897 שָׁכֹל **šākal**, v. [23] [→ 864, 5437, 8890, 8891, 8892, 8898]. [Q] to be bereaved (of children); [P] to make childless, bring bereavement, suffer miscarriage; [H] to miscarry:– miscarry (3), bereaved (2), deprive of children (2), leave childless (2), make childless (2), bereave (1), bereaves (1), bring bereavement (1), childless (1), deprived of children (1), drop fruit before it is ripe (1), lose (1), made childless (1), make unproductive (1), miscarried (1), rob of children (1), unproductive (1)

H8898 שִׁכֻּלִים **šikkulîm**, n.[m.]pl.abst. [1] [√ 8897]. (state of) bereavement (of children):– bereavement (1)

H8899 שָׁכַם **šākam**, v.den. [65] [√ 8900]. [H] to do early in the morning; to do again and again:– early (18), again and again (11), got up early (5), get up early (4), got up (4), early got up (3), early in the morning (3), rose (3), rose early (3), early the next morning (2), again and again (1 [+2256, 8938]), eager (1), early arose (1), early morning get up (1), go early (1), morning (1), rise early (1), NDT (2)

H8900 [1]שְׁכֶם **š^{e}kem[1]**, n.m. [22] [→ 8899, 8901, 8902, 8903, 8904]. shoulder (upper part of the back); by extension: ridge of land:– shoulders (9), shoulder (7), head (2 [+4946, 2256, 5087, 2025]), backs (1), ridge of land (1), shoulder to shoulder (1 [+285]), turned (1 [+7155])

H8901 [2]שְׁכֶם **š^{e}kem[2]**, n.pr.loc. [48] [√ 8900]. Shechem, "*shoulders [and upper part of the back]*; [poss.] *shoulder [saddle of a hill]*":– Shechem (43), there^{S} (2), its^{S} (1), they^{S} (1 [+1251]), they^{S} (1 [+3972, 1251, 4463])

H8902 [3]שְׁכֶם **š^{e}kem[3]**, n.pr.m. [15] [√ 8900]. Shechem, "*shoulders [and upper part of the back]*; [poss.] *shoulder [saddle of a hill]*":– Shechem (11), Shechem's (3), Shechemites (1)

H8903 שֶׁכֶם **šekem**, n.pr.m. [3] [→ 8904; cf. 8900]. Shechem, "*shoulders [and upper part of the back]*":– Shechem (3)

H8904 שִׁכְמִי **šikmî**, a.g. [1] [√ 8903]. Shechemite, "*of Shechem*":– Shechemite (1)

H8905 שָׁכַן **šākan**, v. [130] [→ 5438, 8906, 8907, 8908, 8909; 10709]. [Q] to dwell, abide, live among, stay; [P] to make to dwell, make a home; [H] to cause to dwell, settle in, set up a dwelling:– live (26), dwell (21), dwelling (8), live in (6), settled (5), dwell in (4), dwells (4), nest (3), stayed (3), dwelt (2), dwelt in (2), have a home (2 [+9393]), let live (2), lived in (2), lives (2), living (2), remain (2), rest (2), set up (2), settle (2), abode (1), allow to dwell (1), among (1 [+907]), at rest (1), came to rest (1), camp (1), come to dwell (1), dwells in (1), encamped (1), find shelter (1), inhabit (1), inhabited (1), let settle (1), lie (1), lie down to rest (1), lived (1), lives in (1), made a dwelling (1), make home (1), make sleep (1), nomads (1 [+928, 185]), placed (1), resides (1), rests (1), settled in (1), stands (1), stay (1), stayed (1 [+799])

H8906 שָׁכֵן **šēken**, n.m. Not used in NIVEBC [√ 8905]. dwelling

H8907 שָׁכֵן **šākēn**, a. [20] [√ 8905]. neighbor; inhabitant:– neighbors (11), neighbor (3), neighboring (2), living (1), neighboring peoples (1), one living in (1), people who live in (1)

H8908 שְׁכַנְיָה **šᵉkanyâ**, n.pr.m. [9] [√ 8905 + 3378]. Shecaniah, "*Yahweh has taken up his abode*":– Shekaniah (8), Shekaniah's (1)

H8909 שְׁכַנְיָהוּ **šᵉkanyāhû**, n.pr.m. [2] [√ 8905 + 3378]. Shecaniah, "*Yahweh has taken up his abode*":– Shekaniah (2)

H8910 שָׁכַר **šākar**, v. [18] [→ 8893, 8911, 8912, 8913]. [Q] to become drunk, drink to one's fill; [P] to make drunk; [H] to make drunk; [Ht] to behave drunken:– drunk (6), make drunk (4), made drunk (3), drank freely (1), drink fill (1), get drunk (1), have fill (1), stay drunk (1)

H8911 שֵׁכָר **šēkār**, n.[m.] [23] [√ 8910]. fermented drink, beer:– beer (11), fermented drink (9), drinks (2), drunkards (1 [+9272])

H8912 שָׁכֻר **šākur**, a. *or* v.ptcp. [1] [√ 8910]. drunken:– made drunk (1)

H8913 [1]שִׁכָּרוֹן **šikkārôn[1]**, n.[m.] [3] [√ 8910]. drunkenness:– drunkenness (2), drunk (1)

H8914 [2]שִׁכָּרוֹן **šikkārôn[2]**, n.pr.loc. [1] Shikkeron, "[poss.] *drunkenness; hog bean plant*":– Shikkeron (1)

H8915 שַׁל **šal**, n.[m.] [1] irreverent act:– irreverent act (1)

H8916 שַׁלְאֲנָן **šal'ᵃnan**, a. [1] [√ 8631]. secure:– secure (1)

H8917 שָׁלַב **šālab**, v. [2] [√ 8918]. [Pu] to be joined, set parallel, dovetailed:– set parallel (2)

H8918 שָׁלָב **šālāb**, n.[m.]pl. [3] [→ 8917]. upright, crossbar:– uprights (3)

H8919 שָׁלַג **šālag**, v.den. [1] [√ 8920]. [H] to snow:– snow fallen (1)

H8920 [1]שֶׁלֶג **šeleg[1]**, n.m. [19] [→ 8919, 8921; 10758]. snow:– snow (13), snowy (2), white as snow (2), snow-cooled drink (1 [+7557]), snows (1)

H8921 [2]שֶׁלֶג **šeleg[2]**, n.m. [1] [√ 8920]. soap (processed from the soapwort plant):– soap (1)

H8922 [1]שָׁלָה **šālā[1]**, v. [7] [→ 8929, 8930, 8932, 8937, 8952, 8953; cf. 8923]. [Q] to be at ease, have peace; [N] to give oneself to rest; [H] to raise hopes:– at ease (1), have peace (1), live at ease (1), negligent (1), raise hopes (1), secure (1), undisturbed (1)

H8923 [2]שָׁלָה **šālâ[2]**, v. [1] [cf. 8922]. [Q] to take away, extract:– takes away (1)

H8924 [1]שֵׁלָה **šēlâ[1]**, n.f. [1] [√ 8629; cf. 8626]. petition:– what[S] (1)

H8925 [2]שֵׁלָה **šēlâ[2]**, n.pr.m. [8] [→ 8924, 8989]. Shelah, "*missile [a weapon], sprout*":– Shelah (8)

H8926 שִׁלֹה **šilōh**, n.pr.loc. [22] [cf. 8872, 8931, 9304]. Shiloh:– Shiloh (22)

H8927 שַׁלְהֶבֶת **šalhebet**, n.f. [2] [√ 4258]. flame:– flame (2)

H8928 שַׁלְהֶבֶתְיָה **šalhebetyâ**, n.f. [+n.pr.?] [1] mighty flame (or 8927 + 3363):– mighty flame (1)

H8929 שָׁלֵו **šālēw**, a. [8] [√ 8922; 10710]. quiet, at ease, carefree:– at ease (2), carefree (1), free of care (1), prosperous (1), quiet (1), respite (1), well (1)

H8930 שָׁלוּ **šālû**, n.[m.] [1] [√ 8922; 10711, 10712]. secure feeling, ease:– felt secure (1)

H8931 שִׁלוֹ **šilô**, n.pr.loc. [7] [cf. 8926]. Shiloh:– Shiloh (6), there[S] (1 [+928])

H8932 שַׁלְוָה **šalwâ**, n.f. [8] [√ 8922; 10713]. security, ease:– feel secure (3), complacency (1), felt secure (1), peace and quiet (1), security (1), unconcerned (1 [+9200])

H8933 שִׁלּוּחִים **šillûḥîm**, n.[m.]pl. [3] [√ 8938]. parting gifts; sending away:– parting gifts (1), sent away (1), wedding gift (1)

H8934 שָׁלוֹם **šālôm**, n.m. [235] [→ 58, 94, 8976, 8979, 8984, 8985; cf. 8966; 10720]. peace, safety, prosperity, well-being; intactness, wholeness; peace can have a focus of security, safety which can bring feelings of satisfaction, well-being, and contentment:– peace (111), all right (9), safe (9), safely (9 [+928]), come in peace (5), greet (4 [+8626, 4200]), prosperity (4), well (4), how are (3), peacefully (3 [+928]), success (3), blessing (2), cordially (2), good health (2), greeted (2 [+8626, 4200]), how were (2 [+4200]), in peace (2), peace and prosperity (2), peaceful (2), peacefully (2), perfect peace (2 [+8934]), prosper (2), treaty of friendship (2 [+2256, 3208]), triumph (2), all is well (1), alliance (1), asked how they were (1 [+4200, 8626]), asked how were (1 [+8626, 4200]), benefit (1), close friend (1 [+408]), completely (1), contentment (1), desires (1), friends (1), friends (1 [+408]), friends (1 [+632]), good (1), goodwill (1), greet (1), grow well (1), harmony (1 [+6783]), how is (1), how was (1), how was (1 [+4200]), how was going (1 [+4200]), kind (1), order (1), peaceably (1), peaceably (1 [+928]), peaceful relations (1), peacetime (1), prospers (1), safely (1 [+4200, 2021]), satisfied (1 [+928]), secure (1), sound (1), soundness (1), trusted friends (1 [+408]), unharmed (1), unharmed (1 [+928]), unscathed (1), welcome (1), welfare (1), well-being (1), wish well (1 [+4200]), yes[S] (1), NDT (3)

H8935 שַׁלּוּם **šallûm**, n.pr.m. [26] [√ 8966]. Shallum, "*peace, well-being, prosperity*":– Shallum (25), Shallum's (1)

H8936 שִׁלּוּם **šillûm**, n.[m.] [4] [√ 8966]. retribution, reckoning; bribe, gift:– retribution (2), bribes (1), reckoning (1)

H8937 שַׁלּוּן **šallûn**, n.pr.m. [1] [√ 8922]. Shallun, "*recompense*":– Shallun (1)

H8938 שָׁלַח **šālaḥ**, v. [848] [→ 5447, 5448, 5449, 8933, 8939, 8940, 8941, 8942, 8943, 8944; 10714]. [Q] to send out; [Qp] to be sent away; [N] to be sent; [P] to send away, let go, release; [Pu] to be sent away, thrust out; [H] to send out; "to let go" from a marriage relationship is to divorce:– sent (309), send (112), let go (54), sending (21), sent away (21), sent out (17), lay (13), sent word (11), reached out (10), sends (10), send away (8), stretched out (7), send on way (6), sent for (5 [+2256, 7924, 4200]), sent on way (5), set free (5), called together (4 [+2256, 665]), release (4), send word (4), sent off (4), set (4), stretch out (4), dismissed (3), reach out (3), reached (3), send back (3), sent back (3), sent for (3), sent for (3 [+2256, 7924]), shoot (3), stirs up (3), assassinate (2 [+3338, 928]), be sure to let go (2 [+8938]), been sent (2), divorce (2), divorced (2), divorces (2), do let go (2 [+8938]), drive out (2), extend (2), free (2), free (2 [+2930]), gave orders (2), gave over (2), pursue (2 [+339]), raise (2), reached down (2), replied (2 [+606]), send out (2), send urgent (2 [+8938]), sent message (2), shot (2), summoned (2 [+2256, 7924]), thrust (2), unleashed (2), was sent (2), abandoned (1), again and again (1 [+8899, 2256]), appealed (1), arrest (1 [+3338, 928]), assault (1 [+928]), assigned (1), attack (1 [+3338, 928]), attacked (1 [+3338, 928]), attacks (1 [+3338, 928]), banished (1), be sent (1), being sent (1), brought (1), burned (1 [+928, 2021, 836]), calling together (1 [+2256, 995]), checked on (1 [+448]), come back (1), delivered (1), demanded (1), directed (1), dispatched (1), does[S] (1), ended (1), exile (1), extends (1), force (1), freed (1 [+2930]), gave (1), gave away in marriage (1), get out (1 [+2021, 2575, 2025]), give an order (1), had brought (1 [+2256, 4374]), had removed (1 [+2256, 4374]), holds (1), investigated (1), invite (1 [+2256, 7924]), killing (1 [+3338, 928]), laid (1), lay snares (1), lays (1), leave (1), left undisciplined (1), let down (1), let get away (1), let get away (1 [+928, 2006]), let grow (1), let loose (1), lets loose (1), lets stray (1), letting go (1), letting range free (1 [+8079]), lift (1), lowered (1), made flourish (1), make arrangements (1), makes pour (1), ordered (1), pointing (1), provided (1), pushed (1), put (1), put out (1), putting (1), reach down (1), reached out (1 [+3338]), reaches out (1 [+3338]), reaching (1 [+3338]), reject (1 [+4946, 6584, 7156]), released (1), releases (1), remove (1), return (1), see on way (1), seize (1), send a message (1), send for (1 [+2256, 4374]), send for (1 [+2256, 4374]), send forth (1), sending away (1), sends forth (1), sends out (1), sent a message (1), sent for (1 [+2256, 4374]), sent for (1 [+4200, 7924]), sent for help (1), sent messengers (1), sent on way (1 [+906]), sent word (1 [+2256, 5583]), sent word (1 [+2256, 7924]), serve (1), set fire to (1 [+928, 836, 2021]), set free (1 [+2930]), set free (1 [+4946, 3338]), ship (1), shooting (1), spared (1), specify (1), spreading (1), stirred up (1), summon (1), summon (1 [+2256, 4374]), summoned (1), summoned (1 [+4200, 7924]), swing (1), throw off (1), told (1 [+4200, 606]), took back (1 [+2256, 995]), turned (1), unleash (1), use (1), use to do (1), vent (1), was sent away (1), were sent (1), were sent on way (1), NDT (18)

H8939 [1]שֶׁלַח **šelaḥ[1]**, n.[m.] [7] [√ 8938]. weapon, sword, javelin:– weapon (3), sword (2), defenses (1), weapons (1)

H8940 [2]שֶׁלַח **šelaḥ[2]**, n.pr.loc. [1] [√ 8938]. Siloam, "*sent*":– Siloam (1)

H8941 [3]שֶׁלַח **šelaḥ[3]**, n.pr.m. [9] [→ 8939?; cf. 8938]. Shelah, "*missile [a weapon], sprout*":– Shelah (9)

H8942 שִׁלֹחַ **šilōaḥ**, n.pr.loc. [1] [√ 8938]. Shiloah:– Shiloah (1)

H8943 שְׁלֻחוֹת **šᵉluḥôt**, n.f. [1] [√ 8938]. shoot (of a vine):– shoots (1)

H8944 שִׁלְחִי **šilḥî**, n.pr.m. [2] [√ 8938]. Shilhi, "[poss.] *[my] javelin [thrower?]*":– Shilhi (2)

H8945 שְׁלָחִים **šᵉlāḥîm**, n.[m.] [1] [√ 8938]. shoots, sprouts of a plant (in a closed, private garden):– plants (1)

H8946 שִׁלְחִים **šilḥîm**, n.pr.loc. [1] Shilhim:– Shilhim (1)

H8947 שֻׁלְחָן **šulḥān**, n.m. [70] table:– table (52), tables (12), each table (1 [+8947, 2256]), each table (1 [+2256, 8947]), it[S] (1 [+2021]), NDT (3)

H8948 שָׁלַט **šālaṭ**, v. [8] [→ 8950, 8951, 8954; 10715]. [Q] to control, lord over; [H] to let rule, enable:– ability (1), got the upper hand (1), grant the ability (1), have control (1), let rule (1), lorded it over (1), lords it over (1), overpower (1)

H8949 שֶׁלֶט **šeleṭ**, n.m. [7] small (round) shield:– shields (6), small shields (1)

H8950 שִׁלְטוֹן **šilṭôn**, n.[m.] [2] [√ 8948; 10717]. supremacy:– power (1), supreme (1)

H8951 שַׁלֶּטֶת **šalleṭet**, a. [1] [√ 8948]. brazen, domineering:– brazen (1)

H8952 שְׁלִי **šᵉlî**, n.[m.] [1] [√ 8922]. privateness, uninterruptedness:– privately (1 [+928, 2021])

H8953 שִׁלְיָה **šilyâ**, n.f. [1] [√ 8922]. afterbirth:– afterbirth (1)

H8954 שַׁלִּיט **šallîṭ**, a. [4] [√ 8948; 10718]. ruler, governor:– governor (1), power (1), ruler (1), rulers (1)

H8955 [1]שָׁלִישׁ **šālîš[1]**, n.[m.] [2] [√ 8993]. bowlful, basketful (a unit of measure, probably of one-third of something):– basket (1), bowlful (1)

H8956 [2]שָׁלִישׁ **šālîš[2]**, n.[m.] [1] [√ 8993]. lute:– lyres (1)

H8957 [3]שָׁלִישׁ **šālîš[3]**, n.m. [14] [√ 8993; 10761]. officer:– officers (5), officer (3), captains (2), chariot officers (2), chariot officer (1), chief officers (1)

H8958 שְׁלִישִׁי **šᵉlîšî**, a.num.ord. [105] [√ 8993; 10759, 10761]. third:– third (93), three (7), day after (1), day after tomorrow (1), one-third (1), that[S] (1), upper (1)

H8959 שָׁלַךְ **šālak**, v. [125] [→ 8960?, 8961]. [H] to throw, hurl, scatter; [Ho] to be thrown, be cast:– threw (26), throw (12), cast (8), thrown (6), thrust (5), put (4), throw down (4), hurled (3), throw away (3), get rid of (2), lying (2), threw down (2), thrown away (2), thrown out (2), throws (2), toss (2), turned (2), are cast (1), banish (1), be thrown (1), be thrown out (1), cast away (1), cast out (1), did[S] (1), divide (1), drop (1), dropped (1), dropping (1), flung (1), hurl (1), hurled down (1), hurls (1), hurls down (1), in ruins (1), knocked (1), left lying (1), pelt (1), pushed back (1), pushed down (1), reject (1 [+4946, 6584, 7156]), rid (1 [+4946, 6584]), risked (1 [+4946, 5584]), scatter (1), scattered (1), set down (1), shedding (1), snatched (1), sprinkle (1), threw away (1), threw out (1), throw off (1), thrown aside (1), turned (1 [+339]), was thrown down (1), were thrown out (1)

H8960 שָׁלָךְ **šālāk**, n.[m.] [2] [√ 8959?]. cormorant:– cormorant (2)

H8961 [1]שַׁלֶּכֶת **šalleket[1]**, n.f. [1] [√ 8959]. cutting down:– cut down (1)

H8962 [2]שַׁלֶּכֶת **šalleket[2]**, n.pr.loc. [1] Shalleketh, "[poss.] *[gate of] sending forth*":– Shalleketh (1)

H8963 [1]שָׁלַל **šālal[1]**, v. [2] [Q] to pull out:– pull out (2 [+8963])

H8964 [2]שָׁלַל **šālal[2]**, v. [14] [→ 8768, 8965]. [Q] to plunder, loot; [Htpol] to be plundered:– plunder (4), plundered (4), plunder (2 [+8965]), seize (2), becomes prey (1), loot (1 [+8965])

H8965 שָׁלָל **šālāl**, n.m. [73] [→ 4561; cf. 8964]. plunder, spoil, loot:– plunder (48), escape with (4 [+4200]), spoils (4), loot (3), plunder (2 [+8964]), goods (1), loot (1 [+8964]), plundered (1), possessions plundered (1), prey (1), property (1), share of plunder (1), spoil (1), spoils of war (1), value (1), which[S] (1 [+2021]), NDT (1)

H8966 שָׁלֵם **šālēm[1]**, v. [118] [→ 5450, 5451, 5454, 5455, 8934, 8935, 8936, 8967, 8968, 8969, 8970, 8971, 8972, 8973, 8974, 8976, 8977, 8979, 8980, 8984, 8985, 8986, 8988; *also used with compound proper names*]. [Q] to be finished, be completed; be at peace; [Qp] to be at peace; [P] to repay, make restitution, fulfill (a vow); [Pu] to be repaid, be fulfilled; [H] to make peace; cause to fulfill; [Ho] to be brought into peace:– repay (19), fulfill (13), pay (8), pay back (6), make restitution (5), reward (5), must make restitution (4 [+8966]), at peace (3), finished (3), made peace (3), repays (3), made a treaty of peace (2), made an end (2), must certainly make restitution (2 [+8966]), must pay (2 [+8966]), repay in full (2 [+8966]), repaying (2), restore (2), accomplish (1), ally (1), be fulfilled (1), be repaid (1), bring punishment (1), carries out (1), causes to make peace (1), completed (1), end (1), fulfilled (1), fulfilled obligations (1), fulfills (1), in covenant with (1), is rewarded (1), keep (1), make good (1), make pay (1), make peace (1), offer (1), paid back (1), pay back in full (1), pay for the loss (1 [+4084]), pays back (1), peaceful (1), present (1), receive due (1), repaid (1), restitution (1), restitution made (1), return (1), rewarded (1), unscathed (1)

H8967 שְׁלָם **šᵉlām**, n.m. Not used in NIVEBC [→ 1420; cf. 8966; 10720]. agreement

H8968 שֶׁלֶם **šelem**, n.[m.] [87] [√ 8966]. fellowship (offering):– fellowship (34), fellowship offerings (31), fellowship offering (21), it[S] (1 [+2285])

H8969 [1]שָׁלֵם **šālēm**[2], a. [27] [√ 8966; 10719]. safe, complete, whole:– fully committed (4), accurate (2), fully devoted (2), whole (2), wholehearted devotion (2 [+4213]), wholehearted devotion (2 [+4222]), wholeheartedly (2 [+928, 4222]), allies (1), dressed (1), fieldstones (1 [+74]), friendly (1), full measure (1), fully determined (1 [+928, 4222]), richly (1), safely (1), uncut (1), wholeheartedly (1 [+928, 4213]), NDT (1)

H8970 [2]שָׁלֵם **šālēm**[3], n.pr.loc. [2] [√ 8966]. Salem, *"peace"*:– Salem (2)

H8971 [3]שָׁלֵם **šālēm**[4], v.den. Not used in NIVEBC [√ 8966]. [P] to make a covenant of peace, be at peace

H8972 [1]שִׁלֵּם **šillēm**[1], n.pr.loc. Not used in NIVEBC [√ 8966]. recompense

H8973 [2]שִׁלֵּם **šillēm**[2], n.pr.m. [3] [→ 8980; cf. 8966]. Shillem, *"recompense;* [poss.] *whole, healthy, complete"*:– Shillem (3)

H8974 שִׁלֻּמָה **šillumâ**, n.f. [1] [√ 8966]. punishment, retribution:– punishment (1)

H8975 שַׁלָּמָה **šallāmâ**, rel.+pp.+p.indef. Not used in NIVEBC [√ 8611 + 4200 + 4537]. see 8611 & 4200 & 4537

H8976 שְׁלֹמֹה **šᵉlōmōh**, n.pr.m. [293] [√ 8934; cf. 8966]. Solomon, *"peace, well-being"*:– Solomon (235), Solomon's (26), he[s] (12), Solomon's (7 [+4200]), him[s] (6), his[s] (2), his[s] (2 [+4200]), Solomon's (1 [+8611, 4200]), NDT (2)

H8977 שְׁלֹמוֹת **šᵉlōmôt**, n.pr.m. [3] [√ 8966]. Shelomoth, *"at peace"*:– Shelomoth (3)

H8978 שַׁלְמַי **šalmay**, n.pr.m. [2] [cf. 8518, 9036]. Shalmai, "[perhaps] *Yahweh is well-being"*:– Shalmai (2)

H8979 שְׁלֹמִי **šᵉlōmî**, n.pr.m. [1] [→ 8984, 8985; cf. 8934]. Shelomi, *"at peace"*:– Shelomi (1)

H8980 שִׁלֵּמִי **šillēmî**, a.g. [1] [√ 8973]. Shillemite, *"of Shillem"*:– Shillemite (1)

H8981 שְׁלֻמִיאֵל **šᵉlumî'ēl**, n.pr.m. [5] [√ 8966 + 446]. Shelumiel, *"God [El] is [my] peace"*:– Shelumiel (5)

H8982 שֶׁלֶמְיָה **šelemyâ**, n.pr.m. [5] [√ 8966 + 3378]. Shelemiah, *"Yahweh pays back* [poss.] *he restores peace offering of Yahweh"*:– Shelemiah (5)

H8983 שֶׁלֶמְיָהוּ **šelemyāhû**, n.pr.m. [5] [√ 8966 + 3378]. Shelemiah, *"Yahweh pays back,* [poss.] *he restores peace offering of Yahweh"*:– Shelemiah (5)

H8984 [1]שְׁלֹמִית **šᵉlōmît**[1], n.pr.m. [6] [√ 8979; cf. 8966]. Shelomith, *"at peace"*:– Shelomith (6)

H8985 [2]שְׁלֹמִית **šᵉlōmît**[2], n.pr.f. [2] [√ 8979; cf. 8966]. Shelomith, *"at peace"*:– Shelomith (2)

H8986 שַׁלְמַן **šalman**, n.pr.m. [1] [√ 8966]. Shalman, "[abbreviation of] *Shalmaneser"*:– Shalman (1)

H8987 שַׁלְמַנְאֶסֶר **šalman'eser**, n.pr.m. [2] Shalmaneser, *"Shulman is chief* or *Sulmanu is leader"*:– Shalmaneser (2)

H8988 שַׁלְמֹנִים **šalmōnîm**, n.[m.pl.] [1] [√ 8966]. gifts:– gifts (1)

H8989 שֵׁלָנִי **šēlānî**, a.g. [3] [√ 8925]. Shelanite, of Shelah, *"of Shelah"*:– Asaiah (1), Shelanite (1), of Shelah (1)

H8990 שָׁלַף **šālap**, v. [25] [Q] to draw out (a sword); remove (a sandal); [Qp] to be drawn (sword):– swordsmen (5 [+408, 2995]), draw (4), drawn (4), armed (3), handle (2), drew (1), grow (1), pull out (1), pulls (1), removed (1), took off (1), NDT (1)

H8991 שֶׁלֶף **šelep**, n.pr.m. [2] Sheleph, *"one plucked out, drawn out"*:– Sheleph (2)

H8992 שָׁלַשׁ **šālaš**, v.den. [10] [√ 8993]. [P] to do a third time, on the third day; [Pu] to be three years old, in three parts:– did the third time (1), divide into three (1), do a third time (1), the day after tomorrow (1), three (1), three years old (1), three-year-old (1), top[s] (1), NDT (2)

H8993 שָׁלֹשׁ **šālōš**, n.m. & f. [604] [→ 5456, 8955, 8956, 8957, 8958, 8992, 8994, 8996, 8997, 8998, 8999, 9000, 9001; 10760]. three; (pl.) thirty:– three (284), thirty (84), third (12), thirteen (10 [+6926]), thirteenth (8 [+6925]), three-tenths (8 [+6928]), thirty-three (6 [+8993, 2256]), thirty-three (6 [+2256, 8993]), thirty-two (6 [+2256, 9109]), 30 (5), three-day (4 [+3427]), twenty-third (4 [+2256, 6929]), twenty-three (4 [+6929, 2256]), 430 (3 [+2256, 752, 4395]), 53,400 (3 [+2256, 2822, 547, 2256, 752, 4395]), thirteenth (3 [+6926]), thirty-five (3 [+2256, 2822]), thirty-ninth (3 [+2256, 9596]), thirty-one (3 [+2256, 285]), thirty-seventh (3 [+2256, 8679]), twenty-third (3 [+6929, 2256]), 123 (2 [+4395, 6929, 2256]), 137 (2 [+8679, 2256, 2256, 4395]), 223 (2 [+4395, 6929, 2256]), 3,600 (2 [+547, 2256, 9252, 4395]), 30,500 (2 [+547, 2256, 2822, 4395]), 300 (2 [+4395]), 32 (2 [+9109, 2256]), 32,200 (2 [+9109, 2256, 547, 2256, 4395]), 320 (2 [+4395, 2256, 6929]), 345 (2 [+4395, 752, 2256, 2822]), 35,400 (2 [+2822, 2256, 547, 2256, 752, 4395]), 36,000 (2 [+9252, 2256, 547]), 372 (2 [+4395, 8679, 2256, 9109]), 390 (2 [+4395, 2256, 9596]), 392 (2 [+4395, 9596, 2256, 9109]), 403 (2 [+2256, 752, 4395]), 435 (2 [+752, 4395, 2256, 2822]), 59,300 (2 [+9596, 2256, 2822, 547, 2256, 4395]), 7,337 (2 [+8679, 547, 4395, 8993, 2256, 8679]), 7,337 (2 [+8679, 547, 8993, 4395, 2256, 8679]), 736 (2 [+8679, 4395, 2256, 9252]), 973 (2 [+9596, 4395, 8679, 2256]), them[s] (2 [+2021]), thirteen (2 [+6925]), thirty-eighth (2 [+2256, 9046]), thirty-second (2 [+2256, 9109]), thirty-seven (2 [+2256, 8679]), twenty-three (2 [+2256, 6929]), 1,335 (1 [+547, 4395, 8993, 2256, 2822]), 1,335 (1 [+547, 8993, 4395, 2256, 2822]), 1,365 (1 [+2822, 2256, 9252, 2256, 4395, 2256, 547]), 13 (1 [+6925]), 130 (1 [+4395, 2256]), 130 (1 [+2256, 4395]), 133 (1 [+2256, 8993, 2256, 4395]), 133 (1 [+8993, 2256, 2256, 4395]), 138 (1 [+4395, 2256, 9046]), 139 (1 [+4395, 2256, 9596]), 153,600 (1 [+4395, 2256, 2822, 547, 2256, 547, 2256, 9252, 4395]), 2,300 (1 [+547, 2256, 4395]), 2,322 (1 [+547, 4395, 6929, 2256, 9109]), 2,630 (1 [+547, 2256, 9252, 4395, 2256]), 22,034 (1 [+6929, 2256, 9109, 547, 2256, 2256, 752]), 22,273 (1 [+9109, 2256, 6929, 547, 2256, 8679, 2256, 4395]), 23,000 (1 [+2256, 6929, 547]), 232 (1 [+4395, 9109, 2256]), 273 (1 [+2256, 8679, 2256, 4395]), 3,000 (1 [+547]), 3,023 (1 [+8993, 547, 2256, 6929, 2256]), 3,023 (1 [+547, 2256, 6929, 2256, 8993]), 3,200 (1 [+547, 2256, 4395]), 3,630 (1 [+8993, 547, 2256, 9252, 4395, 2256]), 3,630 (1 [+547, 2256, 9252, 4395, 2256, 8993]), 3,700 (1 [+547, 2256, 8679, 4395]), 3,930 (1 [+8993, 547, 9596, 4395, 2256]), 3,930 (1 [+547, 9596, 4395, 2256, 8993]), 300,000 (1 [+4395, 547]), 307,500 (1 [+4395, 547, 2256, 8679, 547, 2256, 2822, 4395]), 318 (1 [+9046, 6925, 2256, 4395]), 32 (1 [+2256, 9109]), 32,000 (1 [+9109, 2256, 547]), 32,500 (1 [+9109, 2256, 547, 2256, 2822, 4395]), 323 (1 [+4395, 6929, 2256, 8993]), 323 (1 [+4395, 8993, 6929, 2256]), 324 (1 [+4395, 6929, 2256, 752]), 328 (1 [+4395, 6929, 2256, 9046]), 337,500 (1 [+4395, 547, 2256, 8993, 547, 8679, 547, 2256, 2822, 4395]), 337,500 (1 [+8993, 4395, 547, 2256, 547, 8679, 547, 2256, 2822, 4395]), 337,500 (1 [+4395, 547, 2256, 8993, 547, 2256, 8679, 547, 2256, 2822, 4395]), 337,500 (1 [+8993, 4395, 547, 2256, 547, 2256, 8679, 547, 2256, 2822, 4395]), 34 (1 [+752, 2256]), 35 (1 [+2822, 2256]), 350 (1 [+4395, 2256, 2822]), 36,000 (1 [+2256, 9252, 547]), 365 (1 [+2822, 2256, 9252, 2256, 4395]), 37,000 (1 [+2256, 8679, 547]), 42,360 (1 [+752, 8052, 547, 4395, 9252]), 42,360 (1 [+752, 8052, 547, 4395, 2256, 9252]), 43,730 (1 [+8993, 2256, 752, 547, 2256, 8679, 4395, 2256]), 43,730 (1 [+2256, 752, 547, 2256, 8679, 4395, 2256, 8993]), 530 (1 [+2822, 4395, 2256]), 601,730 (1 [+9252, 4395, 2256, 547, 2256, 547, 8679, 4395, 2256]), 603,550 (1 [+9252, 4395, 547, 2256, 547, 2822, 4395, 2822, 2256, 2256]), 603,550 (1 [+9252, 4395, 547, 547, 2822, 4395, 2822, 2256, 2256, 2256]), 603,550 (1 [+9252, 4395, 547, 2256, 547, 2256, 2822, 4395, 2256, 2822]), 623 (1 [+9252, 4395, 6929, 2256]), 64,300 (1 [+752, 2256, 9252, 547, 2256, 4395]), 730 (1 [+8679, 4395, 2256]), 743 (1 [+8679, 4395, 752, 2256]), 743 (1 [+8679, 4395, 2256, 752, 2256]), 830 (1 [+2256, 9046, 4395]), 832 (1 [+9046, 4395, 2256, 9109]), 930 (1 [+9596, 4395, 2256]), eighty-three (1 [+9046, 2256]), people[s] (1 [+9109]), thirtieth (1), thirty-eight (1 [+2256, 9046]), thirty-eight (1 [+2256, 9046]), thirty-fifth (1 [+2256, 2822]), thirty-first (1 [+2256, 285]), thirty-six (1 [+2256, 9252]), thirty-sixth (1 [+2256, 9252]), thirty-three hundred (1 [+547, 2256, 8993, 4395]), thirty-three hundred (1 [+8993, 547, 2256, 4395]), this time[s] (1 [+9102]), three-pronged (1 [+9094]), NDT (5)

H8994 שֶׁלֶשׁ **šeleš**, n.pr.m. [1] [√ 8993]. Shelesh, *"triplet;* [poss.] *obedient* or *gentle"*:– Shelesh (1)

H8995 שָׁלִשָׁה **šālišâ**, n.pr.loc. [1] [→ 1264]. Shalisha, *"third part"*:– Shalisha (1)

H8996 שִׁלְשָׁה **šilšâ**, n.pr.m. [1] [√ 8993]. Shilshah, "[poss.] *obedient* or *gentle; third [part, child?], triplet"*:– Shilshah (1)

H8997 שִׁלְשׁוֹם **šilšôm**, adv. [23] [√ 8993]. formally, three days ago; used with 9453, "yesterday and three days ago," as an adverb of time: formerly, previously:– before (6 [+9453]), malice aforethought (4 [+8533, 4946, 9453]), before (2 [+919]), had the habit (2 [+4946, 9453]), as usual (1 [+3869, 9453]), before (1 [+4946, 9453]), for some time (1 [+1685, 9453, 1685]), formerly (1 [+4946, 919]), had been (1 [+9453]), in the past (1 [+9453]), in the past (1 [+1685, 919, 1685]), past (1 [+9453]), previously (1 [+3869, 919])

H8998 שְׁלִשִׁי **šālišî**, a.num.ord. (used as noun) [2] [√ 8993]. [the] Three:– Three (2)

H8999 שְׁלִשִׁיָּה **šᵉlišiyyâ**, n.pr.loc. Not used in NIVEBC [→ 6326; cf. 8993]. Shelishiyah, see 6326

H9000 שִׁלֵּשִׁים **šillēšîm**, a. [5] [√ 8993]. third (generation):– third (4), third generation (1)

H9001 שְׁלֹשִׁים **šᵉlōšîm**, n.indecl. Not used in NIVEBC [√ 8993]. thirty (pl. of "three" [7969])

H9002 שִׁלְתָּה **šiltâ**, n.pr.loc. Not used in NIVEBC [√ 9434; cf. 3849]. Shiltah

H9003 שַׁלְתִּיאֵל **šaltî'ēl**, n.pr.m. [3] [cf. 8630]. Shealtiel, *"I have asked [him] of God [El];* [poss.] *God [El] is a shield, God [El] is a victor"*:– Shealtiel (3)

H9004 שָׁם **šām**, adv. [826] [√ 10764]. there, where:– there (397), where (100), there (56 [+2025]), which[s] (18), it[s] (17), where (16 [+2025]), here (9), in which[s] (5), back (4), in it[s] (4), the Jordan[s] (4 [+2025]), in it[s] (3 [+2025]), out (3 [+4946]), behind (2), in (2), in Zion[s] (2), that place[s] (2), them[s] (2), where (2 [+4946]), whom[s] (2), Gath[s] (1), Hebron[s] (1), Samaria[s] (1), among which[s] (1), at Pas Dammim[s] (1), away (1 [+4946]), back[s] (1 [+2025]), because of (1 [+4946]), beside (1), in such places[s] (1), in them[s] (1), inside[s] (1 [+2025]), into it[s] (1), invade (1 [+995, 2025]), it[s] (1 [+2025]), it[s] (1 [+2025]), leave (1 [+4946]), nearby (1), one of these cities[s] (1), place (1), proper place (1 [+5226, 889, 2118]), right there (1), see (1), that land[s] (1), the chest[s] (1), the city[s] (1), the land[s] (1 [+2025]), the north[s] (1), them (1), there (1 [+4946]), there[s] (1), to (1 [+2025]), what[s] (1), when (1), wherever (1), wherever (1 [+2025]), wherever (1 [+2025]), wherever (1 [+3972, 889]), wherever (1 [+889, 2025]), with (1), NDT (136)

H9005 [1]שֵׁם **šēm**[1], n.m. [863] [→ 9006?, 9017, 9026, 9027; 10721]. name, a proper designation of a person, place, or thing; by extension: renown, fame; "to call on the name of the LORD" means to proclaim or praise the excellence of Yahweh, to worship Yahweh, or to summon Yahweh by name for help:– name (558), names (63), named (57 [+7924]), named (44), called (36), fame (11), name's (7), call (6 [+7924]), renown (6), famous (5), name (4 [+7924]), honor (3), named (3 [+8492]), be called (2 [+7924]), chosen (2 [+7924, 928]), famous (2 [+7924]), after (1 [+928]), after (1 [+3869]), be known as (1 [+7924]), be named (1 [+7924]), became famous (1 [+6913]), been named (1 [+7924]), byword (1), calling (1 [+7924]), famous (1 [+408]), giving credit to (1 [+928]), himself (1 [+2257]), infamous (1 [+3238, 2021]), is called (1 [+7924]), it[s] (1 [+2257]), me (1 [+3276]), memorable (1), named (1 [+7924, 928]), nameless (1 [+1172]), perpetuate memory (1 [+2349]), record (1 [+4180]), renowned (1 [+4200]), that[s] (1), the Lord (1 [+3378]), to each man (1 [+928]), was called (1 [+7924]), well-known (1 [+408]), word (1), NDT (27)

H9006 [2]שֵׁם **šēm**[2], n.pr.m. [17] [√ 9005?]. Shem, *"name, fame"*:– Shem (16), Shem's (1)

H9007 שַׁמָּא **šammā'**, n.pr.m. [2] [cf. 9015]. Shamma; Shammah, *"astonishment"*:– Shamma (1), Shammah (1)

H9008 שֶׁמְאֵבֶר **šem'ēber**, n.pr.m. [1] Shemeber:– Shemeber (1)

H9009 שִׁמְאָה **šim'â**, n.pr.m. [1] [cf. 9010]. Shimeah, *"he has heard* or *he is obedient"*:– Shimeah (1)

H9010 שִׁמְאָם **šim'ām**, n.pr.m. [1] [cf. 9009]. Shimeam:– Shimeam (1)

H9011 שַׁמְגַּר **šamgar**, n.pr.m. [2] Shamgar, *"Shimke gave [a son]"*:– Shamgar (2)

H9012 שָׁמַד **šāmad**, v. [91] [√ 10722]. [N] to be destroyed; [H] to destroy, demolish, annihilate:– destroy (31), destroyed (25), be destroyed (7), are destroyed (5), certainly be destroyed (2 [+9012]), demolish (2), destruction (2), totally destroy (2 [+9012]), wipe out (2), annihilate (1), annihilation (1), be overthrown (1), been decimated (1), been destroyed (1), brought to ruin (1), completely destroyed (1), crushed (1), cut off (1), exterminating (1), get rid of (1), perished (1), shatter (1)

H9013 שֶׁמֶד **šemed**, n.pr.m. [1] Shemed, *"destruction"*:– Shemed (1)

H9014 [1]שַׁמָּה **šammâ**[1], n.f. [40] [√ 9037]. thing of horror; desolation, devastation, what is laid waste:– object of horror (10), desolate (8), waste (6), ruin (4), laid waste (3), horror (2), desolation (2), desolations (1), destroyed (1), horrible (1), in ruins (1), thing of horror (1), wasteland (1)

H9015 [2]שַׁמָּה **šammâ**[2], n.pr.m. [7] [→ 9016, 9021, 9025?; cf. 9007, 9048? *or* 9087?]. Shammah, *"waste"*:– Shammah (7)

H9016 שַׁמְהוּת **šamhût**, n.pr.m. [1] [√ 9021; cf. 9015]. Shamhuth, "[poss.] *one born at a time of a horrible event"*:– Shamhuth (1)

H9017 שְׁמוּאֵל **šᵉmû'ēl**, n.pr.m. [141] [√ 9005 + 446]. Samuel; Shemuel, *"his name is God [El]; heard of God; the unnamed god is El"*:– Samuel (127), he[s] (5), Samuel's (4), him[s] (2), Shemuel (1), NDT (2)

H9018 שַׁמּוּעַ **šammûa'**, n.pr.m. [5] [√ 9048 + 3378?]. Shammua, "[poss.] *[Yahweh] hears; rumor"*:– Shammua (5)

H9019 שְׁמוּעָה **šᵉmû'â**, n.f. [27] [√ 9048]. message, rumor, report:– news (8), report (7), message (5), rumor (3), another[s] (1 [+2021]), mention (1 [+928, 7023]), reports (1), rumors (1)

H9020 שָׁמוּר **šāmûr**, n.pr.m. Not used in NIVEBC [cf. 9033]. Shamur, see 9033

H9021 שַׁמּוֹת **šammôt**, n.pr.m. [1] [→ 9016; cf. 9015]. Shammoth, *"desolation"*:– Shammoth (1)

H9022 שָׁמַח **šāmaḥ**, v. [Q] to be magnanimous, see 8523

H9023 שָׁמַט **šāmaṭ**, v. [9] [→ 9024]. [Q] to drop down, stumble; to lie unplowed; [N] to be thrown down; [H] to cancel a debt:– stumbled (2), be thrown down (1), cancel (1), cancel debt (1), lie unplowed (1), lose (1), threw down (1), throw down (1)

H9024 שְׁמִטָּה **šᵉmiṭṭâ**, n.f. [5] [√ 9023]. canceling of debt:– canceling debts (2), cancel debts (1 [+6913]), it[s] (1 [+2021]), time for canceling debts (1)

H9025 שַׁמַּי **šammay**, n.pr.m. [6] [√ 9048? *or* 9015?].

Shammai, "*Yahweh has heard*":– Shammai (5), Shammai's (1)

H9026 שְׁמִידָע **šᵉmîdāʿ**, n.pr.m. [3] [→ 9027; cf. 9005 + 3359]. Shemida, "[poss.] *the name knows*; [poss.] *Eshmun has known*":– Shemida (3)

H9027 שְׁמִידָעִי **šᵉmîdāʿî**, a.g. [1] [√ 9026; cf. 9005]. Shemidaite, "*of Shemida*":– Shemidaite (1)

H9028 שָׁמַיִם **šāmayim**, n.m. [421] [√ 10723]. region above the earth: the heavens: place of the stars, sky, air; heaven: the invisible realm of God:– heavens (150), heaven (147), sky (60), birds (16 [+6416, 2021]), highest heavens (10 [+9028]), starry (9), skies (7), highest heavens (4 [+9028]), air (3), heavenly (3), astrologers (1 [+2042]), down (1 [+4946, 2021]), going up (1 [+6590, 2021, 2025]), heavens above (1), heaven's (1), highest heaven (1 [+9028]), highest heaven (1 [+9028]), horizon (1), in midair (1 [+1068, 2021, 2256, 1068, 2021, 824]), others (1 [+7895]), NDT (2)

H9029 שְׁמִינִי **šᵉmînî**, a.num.ord. [28] [√ 9046]. eighth:– eighth (27), followings (1)

H9030 שְׁמִינִית **šᵉmînît**, tt. [3] [√ 9046]. sheminith:– sheminith (3)

H9031 1שָׁמִיר **šāmîr1**, n.m. [8] [√ 9068; cf. 9033?]. briers:– briers (8)

H9032 2שָׁמִיר **šāmîr2**, n.m. [3] [cf. 9033?]. hardest stone; (other contexts) flint or emery:– as hard as flint (1), flint (1), hardest stone (1)

H9033 3שָׁמִיר **šāmîr3**, n.pr.m. [1] [cf. 9020, 9031?, 9032?]. Shamir, "[poss.] *thorny* or *emery [flint]*":– Shamir (1)

H9034 4שָׁמִיר **šāmîr4**, n.pr.loc. [3] Shamir, "[poss.] *thorny* or *emery [flint]*":– Shamir (3)

H9035 שְׁמִירָמוֹת **šᵉmîrāmôt**, n.pr.m. [4] [cf. 9082]. Shemiramoth, "*heights, heavens;* [poss. pr.n. of pagan goddess]":– Shemiramoth (4)

H9036 שַׁמְלַי **šamlay**, n.pr.m. Not used in NIVEBC [cf. 8978]. Shamlai, see 8978

H9037 1שָׁמֵם **šāmēm1**, v. [93] [→ 5457, 9014, 9038, 9039, 9040, 9041; cf. 3815; 10724]. [Q] to be desolate, be appalled; [N] to become desolate, be appalled; [Pol] to cause desolation, be appalled; [H] to bring to devastation, cause to be appalled; [Ho] to lie desolate; [Htpol] to destroy oneself, be appalled:– appalled (23), desolate (16), devastated (5), causes desolation (4), deserted (4), lay waste (4), lies desolate (4), demolished (2), destitute (2), ruin (2), was laid waste (2), are appalled (1), are demolished (1), be demolished (1), be destroyed (1), be laid waste (1), brought devastation (1), cause to be appalled (1), deeply distressed (1), desolation (1), desolations (1), destroy yourself (1), destroyed (1), dismayed (1), fill with horror (1), hims (1), horrified (1), in ruins (1), laid waste (1), made desolate (1), ravaged (1), ruined (1), strip (1), stripped (1), were terrified (1), without help (1)

H9038 2שָׁמֵם **šāmēm2**, a. [2] [√ 9037]. desolate, deserted:– desolate (2)

H9039 שְׁמָמָה **šᵉmāmâ**, n.f. [56] [√ 9037]. desolation, ruin, wasteland:– desolate (30), waste (5), desolation (3), ruins (3), wasteland (3), desolate place (2), laid waste (2), barren (1), demolished (1), desolate waste (1), despair (1), destroy (1 [+8492]), ravaged (1), ruined (1), utterly desolate (1)

H9040 שִׁמְמָה **šimᵉmâ**, n.f. [1] [√ 9037]. desolation:– desolate (1)

H9041 שִׁמָּמוֹן **šimmāmôn**, n.[m.] [2] [√ 9037]. despair, which may border on feelings of horror and shuddering:– despair (2)

H9042 שָׁמֵן **šāmēn1**, v. [5] [√ 9043]. [Q] to grow fat; [H] to show as well-fed; by extension: to be calloused, unresponsive of heart:– fat (1), filled with food (1), grew fat (1), make calloused (1), well-nourished (1)

H9043 שֶׁמֶן **šemen**, n.m. [193] [→ 875?, 5458, 5459, 5460, 9042, 9044, 9045]. olive, the tree and its products: olive berry, olive oil, olive wood; olive oil was a staple of diet in biblical times, and was also used as a medicine, lamp fuel, and in religious offerings and ritual:– oil (94), olive oil (74), olive (3), perfume (3), fertile (2), best (1), cosmetic lotions (1), fat (1), fertile (1 [+1201]), fine perfume (1), gaunt (1 [+4946]), its (1 [+2021]), lotions (1), oils (1), ointments (1), olive (1 [+6770]), olive-wood (1 [+6770]), perfume (1 [+8379]), perfumes (1), rich food (1), wild olive (1), NDT (1)

H9044 שָׁמָן **šāmān**, n.[m.] [2] [√ 9043]. richness, fatness:– richness (2)

H9045 שָׁמֵן **šāmēn2**, a. [10] [√ 9043]. rich, fertile:– fertile (3), rich (3), luxury (1), plentiful (1), sleek (1), vigorous (1)

H9046 שְׁמֹנֶה **šᵉmōneh**, n.m. & f. [147] [→ 9029, 9030, 9047]. eight; (pl.) eighty:– eight (29), eighty (15), eighteenth (9 [+6926]), eighteen (8 [+6926]), 128 (4 [+4395, 6929, 2256]), eighteen (4 [+6925]), eighty-five (4 [+2256, 2822]), eighth (3), twenty-eight (3 [+6929, 2256]), 18 (2 [+6925]), 18,000 (2 [+6925, 547]), 80 (2), 80,000 (2 [+547]), 800 (2 [+4395]), 98 (2 [+9596, 2256]), eighteenth (2 [+6925]), forty-eight (2 [+752, 2256]), thirty-eighth (2 [+8993, 2256]), 108,100 (1 [+4395, 547, 2256, 547, 2256, 4395]), 138 (1 [+4395, 8993, 2256]), 148 (1 [+4395, 752, 2256]), 180 (1 [+2256, 4395]), 180,000 (1 [+4395, 2256, 547]), 182 (1 [+9109, 2256, 2256, 4395]), 186,400 (1 [+4395, 547, 2256, 547, 9252, 547, 752, 4395, 2256, 2256]), 187 (1 [+8679, 2256, 2256, 4395]), 188 (1 [+4395, 2256, 9046]), 188 (1 [+4395, 9046, 2256]), 2,812 (1 [+547, 4395, 2256, 9109, 6925]), 2,818 (1 [+547, 2256, 4395, 9046, 6925]), 2,818 (1 [+547, 2256, 9046, 4395, 6925]), 20,800 (1 [+6929, 547, 2256, 4395]), 218 (1 [+4395, 2256, 6925]), 28 (1 [+6929, 2256]), 28,600 (1 [+6929, 2256, 547, 2256, 9252, 4395]), 280,000 (1 [+4395, 2256, 547]), 284 (1 [+4395, 2256, 752]), 288 (1 [+4395, 2256, 9046]), 288 (1 [+4395, 9046, 2256]), 318 (1 [+6925, 2256, 8993, 4395]), 328 (1 [+8993, 4395, 6929, 2256]), 468 (1 [+752, 4395, 9252, 2256]), 6,800 (1 [+9252, 547, 2256, 4395]), 628 (1 [+9252, 4395, 6929, 2256]), 648 (1 [+9252, 4395, 752, 2256]), 782 (1 [+9109, 2256, 2256, 8679, 4395]), 8,580 (1 [+9046, 547, 2256, 2822, 4395, 2256]), 8,580 (1 [+547, 2256, 2822, 4395, 2256, 9046]), 8,600 (1 [+547, 2256, 9252, 4395]), 807 (1 [+8679, 2256, 4395]), 815 (1 [+2822, 6926, 2256, 4395]), 822 (1 [+4395, 6929, 2256, 9109]), 830 (1 [+8993, 2256, 4395]), 832 (1 [+4395, 8993, 2256, 9109]), 840 (1 [+752, 2256, 4395]), 845 (1 [+4395, 2256, 2822, 752]), 87,000 (1 [+2256, 8679, 547]), 895 (1 [+2822, 2256, 9596, 2256, 4395]), 928 (1 [+9596, 4395, 6929, 2256]), eighteen thousand (1 [+8052, 2256, 547]), eightieth (1), eighty-six (1 [+9252, 2256]), eighty-three (1 [+2256, 8993]), ninety-eight (1 [+9596, 2256]), sixty-eight (1 [+9252, 2256]), thirty-eight (1 [+8993, 2256]), thirty-eight (1 [+8993, 2256]), twenty-eight (1 [+2256, 6929])

H9047 שְׁמֹנִים **šᵉmōnîm**, n.pl.indecl. Not used in NIVEBC [√ 9046]. eighty (pl. of "eight" [9046])

H9048 שָׁמַע **šāmaʿ**, v. [1159] [→ 904, 2245, 3816-3821, 5461, 5462, 5463, 9015, 9016, 9021, 9019, 9025, 9049, 9050, 9051, 9053, 9054, 9056, 9057, 9058, 9059, 9060, 9063, 9064, 9065; cf. 1072]. [Q] to hear, listen, obey; [N] to be heard; [P] to summon, call together; [H] to proclaim, summon, make hear; from the base meaning of hearing come the extensions of understanding and obedience:– heard (293), hear (234), listen (226), obey (49), listened (40), obeyed (31), hears (27), proclaim (15), agreed (9), be heard (9), listening (9), hearing (8), understand (8), is heard (6), obey (5 [+928, 7754]), listen carefully (4 [+9048]), listen carefully (4 [+9048]), paid attention (4), pay attention (4), was heard (4), do (3), heed (3), let hear (3), obedient (3), proclaimed (3), resound (3), sound (3), agree (2), are heard (2), careful to obey (2 [+9048]), certainly hear (2 [+9048]), declare (2), discerning (2), disobeyed (2 [+4202]), disobeyed (2 [+4202, 928, 7754]), ever hearing (2 [+9048]), faithfully obey (2 [+9048]), foretold (2), fully obey (2 [+928, 7754, 9048]), fully obey (2 [+9048, 928, 7754]), give (2), heard (2 [+7754]), heard definitely (2 [+9048]), hears (2 [+9048]), listen closely (2 [+928, 265]), mark my words (2), obeying (2 [+928, 7754]), proclaiming (2), raise (2), received a report (2), sang (2), summon (2), surely heard (2 [+9048]), administering (1), agreed with (1 [+4200, 7754]), announce (1), announced (1), answer (1), are heeded (1), argue (1 [+7754]), be heeded (1), beens (1), been brought to attention (1 [+5583, 2256]), been heard (1), been heard of (1), been proclaimed (1), boast (1), bring word (1), called up (1), careful listener (1 [+408]), cause to hear (1), caused to hear (1), complied (1), comply (1), covered (1 [+3877, 4946]), cry out (1), cry out (1 [+2411]), deaf (1 [+4946]), did (1), diligently obey (1 [+928, 7754, 9048]), diligently obey (1 [+9048, 928, 7754]), disobedience (1 [+4202, 928, 7754]), disobey (1 [+4202]), disobey (1 [+1194, 928, 7754]), expect to be heard (1), find out (1), fully obeyed (1 [+2256, 6913]), gave in (1 [+928, 7754]), get back to (1), haves (1), hear (1 [+7754]), heard (1 [+9051]), hears (1 [+7754, 9048]), hears (1 [+9048, 7754]), heeds (1), heeds (1 [+265]), is proclaimed (1), is reported (1), issued an order (1), learn (1), let be heard (1), listen (1 [+7754]), listen carefully (1 [+928, 265]), listen carefully (1 [+928, 7754]), listen in (1), listened to (1), listens (1), made hear (1), made known (1), made proclamation (1), make hear (1), make heard (1), obey (1 [+4200, 7754]), obey fully (1 [+928, 7754, 9048]), obey fully (1 [+9048, 928, 7754]), obeying (1), obeys (1), obeys (1 [+928, 7754]), obscure (1 [+6680, 4946]), overheard (1), paid any attention (1 [+5742, 265, 4200]), pay close attention (1 [+7992, 2256]), playing (1), plots (1), proclaims (1), pronounced (1), put under oath (1 [+460]), reached (1), reached (1 [+928]), received (1), received message (1), refused (1 [+4202]), resounds (1), respond (1), respond to (1), sound (1 [+928, 7754]), sound be heard (1), sounding (1), summoned (1), tell (1), told (1), told (1 [+4946, 907]), was overheard (1), were heard (1), witness (1 [+1068]), word came (1), NDT (4)

H9049 1שֶׁמַע **šemaʿ1**, n.[m.] [1] [→ 9050; cf. 9048]. clash, sound:– clash (1)

H9050 2שֶׁמַע **šemaʿ2**, n.pr.m. [5] [√ 9049]. Shema, "*he hears*":– Shema (5)

H9051 שֵׁמַע **šēmaʿ**, n.[m.] [17] [√ 9048]. what is heard, report, news, rumor:– fame (4), report (3), reports (3), hear (2), news (2), heard (1 [+9048]), rumor (1), word (1)

H9052 שָׁמָע **šāmāʿ**, n.pr.m. [1] [√ 9048 + 3378?]. Shama, "*one obedient [to Yahweh]*":– Shama (1)

H9053 שֹׁמַע **šōmaʿ**, n.m. [4] [√ 9048]. report; reputation:– reports (2), fame (1), reputation (1)

H9054 שְׁמַע **šᵉmaʿ**, n.pr.loc. [1] [√ 9048]. Shema, "*he hears*":– Shema (1)

H9055 שִׁמְעָא **šimʿāʾ**, n.pr.m. [5] [√ 9048 + 3378?]. Shimea; Shammua, "*he has heard* or *obedient one*":– Shimea (4), Shammua (1)

H9056 שִׁמְעָה **šimʿâ**, n.pr.m. [3] [→ 9065; cf. 9048 + 3378?]. Shimeah, "*he has heard* or *he is obedient*":– Shimeah (3)

H9057 שְׁמָעָה **šᵉmāʿâ**, n.pr.m. [1] [√ 9048]. Shemaah, "[poss.] *Yahweh hears*":– Shemaah (1)

H9058 שִׁמְעוֹן **šimʿôn**, n.pr.m. [44] [→ 9063; cf. 9048]. Simeon, Simeonite, "*he has heard* or *obedient one*":– Simeon (29), Simeon (6 [+1201]), Simeonites (4 [+1201]), Simeonites (3), Shimeon (1), NDT (1)

H9059 1שִׁמְעִי **šimʿî1**, n.pr.m. [44] [→ 9060; cf. 9048 + 3378?]. Shimei, "*Yahweh has heard* or *famous*":– Shimei (42), Shimei's (1 [+4200]), hes (1)

H9060 2שִׁמְעִי **šimʿî2**, a.g. [2] [√ 9059]. Shimeites, of Shimei, "*of Shimei*":– Shimei (1), Shimeites (1)

H9061 שְׁמַעְיָה **šᵉmaʿyâ**, n.pr.m. [34] [√ 9048 + 3378]. Shemaiah, "*Yahweh hears*":– Shemaiah (32), Shemaiah's (1), hiss (1)

H9062 שְׁמַעְיָהוּ **šᵉmaʿyāhû**, n.pr.m. [7] [√ 9048 + 3378]. Shemaiah, "*Yahweh hears*":– Shemaiah (7)

H9063 שִׁמְעֹנִי **šimʿōnî**, a.g. [4] [√ 9058]. Simeonite, of Simeon, "*of Simeon*":– Simeon (2), Simeonite (1), Simeonites (1)

H9064 שִׁמְעָת **šimʿāt**, n.pr.f. [2] [√ 9048]. Shimeath, "*guardian, watcher*":– Shimeath (2)

H9065 שִׁמְעָתִי **šimʿātî**, a.g. [1] [√ 9056]. Shimeathite, "*of Shimeath*":– Shimeathites (1)

H9066 שֵׁמֶץ **šēmeṣ**, n.[m.] [2] [→ 9067?]. whisper:– faint (1), whisper (1)

H9067 שִׁמְצָה **šimṣâ**, n.f. [1] [√ 9066?]. laughingstock, derision:– laughingstock (1)

H9068 שָׁמַר **šāmar**, v. [467] [→ 874, 5464, 5465, 5466, 9031, 9069, 9070?, 9072, 9073, 9074, 9076, 9078, 9081, 9085, 9086; *also used with compound proper names*]. [Q] to keep, watch, observe, guard; [Qp] to be set aside, be secured; [N] to be careful, beware; [P] to cling to; [Ht] to keep oneself; to observe for oneself:– keep (84), careful (45), observe (21), kept (18), guard (17), obey (17), carefully (16), keeps (10), watch (9), watchmen (7), keeping (6), obeyed (6), watches over (6), keeper (5), protects (5), take care of (5), watch over (5), celebrate (4), doorkeepers (4 [+6197]), heeds (4), in charge (4), keep safe (4), maintain (4), preserve (4), protect (4), responsible (4), be sure (3), care (3), do (3), guard (3 [+5466]), guarded (3), guarding (3), make sure (3), on guard (3), serve (3), watched over (3), watchman (3), be careful (2), be sure to keep (2 [+9068]), beware (2), careful (2 [+9068]), carefully observe (2 [+9068]), carried out (2), carrying out (2), cling (2), faithful (2), follow (2), followed (2), guarding (2 [+5466]), guards (2), heed (2), kept myself (2), obeying (2), observed (2), on guard (2 [+928, 8120]), pay attention (2), perform (2), protected (2), safekeeping (2), waiting (2), watches (2), watching (2), watching over (2), act (1), assures (1), beware (1 [+440]), bodyguard (1 [+4200, 8031]), cared for (1), careful to do (1), cherishes (1), consider (1), continue (1), continued (1), defending (1), did (1), dids (1), done (1), doorkeeper (1 [+6197]), eyed (1), flamed unchecked (1 [+5905]), gatekeepers (1 [+6197]), give (1), guarded (1 [+5466]), guarded (1 [+5464]), had charge of (1), have charge of (1), hoarded (1), keep away (1), keep close watch on (1), keep penned up (1), keep track of (1), keepers (1), keeps close watch (1), kept a record (1), kept in mind (1), kept penned up (1), kept themselves (1), kept watch (1), living (1), loyal (1 [+5466]), must (1), obey (1 [+2256, 6913]), obeys (1), observing (1), on duty (1), on duty at (1), performed (1), performing (1), preserved (1), put (1), regardless (1 [+401, 4200]), remains (1), responsible (1 [+5466]), responsible for (1), secured (1), see (1), see to it (1), shepherd (1), spare (1), spies (1), take care (1), tended sheep (1), to guard (1 [+5466]), under siege (1), wait to kill (1 [+5883]), was set aside (1), watch carefully (1)

H9069 1שֶׁמֶר **šemer1**, n.m. [5] [→ 9070?; cf. 9068]. dregs (of wine); aged wine:– dregs (3), aged wine (1), wines (1)

H9070 2שֶׁמֶר **šemer2**, n.pr.m. [3] [√ 9069?]. Shemer, "[poss.] *watch;* [poss.] *sediment of wine from which clear wine is made*":– Shemer (3)

H9071 שֹׁמֵר **šōmēr**, n.pr.m. [3] [√ 9083]. Shomer, "*guardian, watchman*":– Shomer (3)

H9072 שָׁמְרָה **šomrâ**, n.f. [1] [√ 9068]. guard, watch:– guard (1)

H9073 שְׁמֻרָה **šᵉmurâ**, n.f. [1] [√ 9068]. eyelid (that covers and protects the eye):– kept from closing (1 [+296])

H9074 1שִׁמְרוֹן **šimrôn1**, n.pr.loc. [2] [√ 9068]. Shimron, "*guardian, watchman*":– Shimron (2)

H9075 ²שִׁמְרוֹן **šimrôn²**, n.pr.m. [3] [→ 9084]. Shimron:– Shimron (3)

H9076 שֹׁמְרוֹן **šōmᵉrôn**, n.pr.m. [109] [→ 9085; cf. 9068; 10726]. Samaria, the capital city of northern kingdom of Israel; by extension, the northern kingdom itself, *"belonging to the clan of Shemer* [1Ki 16:24]":– Samaria (104), the cityˢ (2), thereˢ (2 [+928]), Samaria's (1)

H9077 שִׁמְרוֹן מְרֹאון **šimrôn mᵉr'ôn**, n.pr.loc. [1] [cf. 5264]. Shimron Meron:– Shimron Meron (1)

H9078 שִׁמְרִי **šimrî**, n.pr.m. [4] [√ 9068]. Shimri, *"Yahweh guards, preserves"*:– Shimri (4)

H9079 שְׁמַרְיָה **šᵉmaryâ**, n.pr.m. [3] [√ 9068 + 3378]. Shemariah, *"Yahweh guards, preserves"*:– Shemariah (3)

H9080 שְׁמַרְיָהוּ **šᵉmaryāhû**, n.pr.m. [1] [√ 9068 + 3378]. Shemariah, *"Yahweh guards, preserves"*:– Shemariah (1)

H9081 שִׁמֻּרִים **šimmurîm**, n.[m.pl.] [2] [√ 9068]. vigil, night-watch:– vigil (2)

H9082 שְׁמִירִימוֹת **šᵉmîrîmôt**, n.pr.m. Not used in NIVEBC [cf. 9035]. Shemirimoth, see 9035

H9083 שִׁמְרִית **šimrît**, n.pr.f. [1] [→ 9071]. Shimrith, *"guardianess, watch woman"*:– Shimrith (1)

H9084 שִׁמְרֹנִי **šimrōnî**, a.g. [1] [√ 9075]. Shimronite, *"of Shimron"*:– Shimronite (1)

H9085 שֹׁמְרֹנִי **šōmᵉrōnî**, a.g. [1] [√ 9076]. of Samaria, *"of Samaria"*:– people of Samaria (1)

H9086 שִׁמְרָת **šimrāt**, n.pr.m. [1] [√ 9068]. Shimrath, *"guardian, watchman"*:– Shimrath (1)

H9087 שֶׁמֶשׁ **šemeš**, n.f. & m. [135] [→ 1127, 1128, 6539, 6561, 9015, 9088, 9089, 9090; 10728]. sun:– sun (102), sunset (6 [+995, 2021]), east (3 [+4667, 2021]), sunrise (3 [+4667]), east (2 [+4667]), east (2 [+4667, 2025, 2021]), sunrise (2 [+2436, 2021]), sunset (2 [+6961, 995, 2021]), west (2 [+4427]), battlements (1), broad daylight (1), east (1 [+928, 6298, 4667]), east (1 [+928, 6298, 4667, 2025]), eastern (1 [+4667]), in broad daylight (1 [+5584, 2021]), in broad daylight (1 [+4200, 6524, 2021, 2021, 2296]), in the west (1 [+4427, 2021]), sunlight (1), sunrise (1 [+2436]), sunshine (1)

H9088 שִׁמְשׁוֹן **šimšôn**, n.pr.m. [38] [√ 9087]. Samson, *"little one of Shemesh* or *strong"*:– Samson (33), Samson's (3), heˢ (2)

H9089 שִׁמְשַׁי **šimšay**, n.pr.m. Not used in NIVEBC [√ 9087; 10729]. Shimshai, see 10729, *"one given to Shemesh"*

H9090 שִׁמְשִׁי **šimšî**, n.pr. *or* a.g. Not used in NIVEBC [→ 1128; cf. 9087]. see 1128

H9091 שַׁמְשְׁרַי **šamšᵉray**, n.pr.m. [1] Shamsherai, *"may Shemesh guard"*:– Shamsherai (1)

H9092 שֻׁמָתִי **šumātî**, a.g. [1] Shumathite:– Shumathites (1)

H9093 שַׁן **šan**, n.pr.loc. Not used in NIVEBC [√ 8632]. Shan

H9094 ¹שֵׁן **šēn¹**, n.f. & m. [56] [→ 9105; cf. 9111; 10730]. tooth (human or animal); by extension, anything tooth shaped: rocky crag; "cleanness of teeth" is a sign of lack of food in famine:– teeth (26), ivory (10), tooth (9), cliff (1), cliff (1 [+6152]), crag (1), empty stomachs (1 [+5931]), fangs (1), have something to eat (1 [+5966, 928]), put in jeopardy (1 [+5951, 1414, 928]), three-pronged (1 [+8993]), NDT (3)

H9095 ²שֵׁן **šēn²**, n.pr.loc. [1] [√ 9111]. Shen, *"tooth, crag [of rock]"*:– Shen (1)

H9096 שָׁנֵא **šānēʾ**, v. [1] [√ 9091?]. [Q] to become dull:– dull (1)

H9097 שְׁנָא **šēnāʾ**, n.f. [1] [√ 9104; cf. 3822]. sleep:– sleep (1)

H9098 שִׁנְאָב **šinʾāb**, n.pr.m. [1] Shinab, *"Sin is his father"*:– Shinab (1)

H9099 שִׁנְאָן **šinʾān**, n.[m.] [1] [√ 9091?]. high in rank or number:– thousands (1)

H9100 שֶׁנְאַצַּר **šenʾaṣṣar**, n.pr.m. [1] Shenazzar, *"may Sin protect"*:– Shenazzar (1)

H9101 ¹שָׁנָה **šānâ¹**, v. [24] [→ 5467, 9096?, 9099?, 9102, 9103, 9106?, 9108, 9109; cf. 9112; 10731]. [Q] to repeat, do again; [N] to be repeated; [P] to change, alter; to pretend; [Pu] to be changed; [Ht] to disguise oneself:– change (2), different (2), do again (2), pretended to be insane (2 [+3248]), put aside (2), again (1), alter (1), changes (1), changing (1), deprive (1), did again (1), disguise yourself (1), more (1), moved (1), rebellious (1), repeat (1), repeats (1), strike twice (1), was given (1)

H9102 ²שָׁנָה **šānâ²**, n.f. [868] [√ 9101; 10732]. year:– years (408), year (303), years (8 [+3427]), year-old (5 [+1201]), age (4 [+1201]), each year (3 [+9102, 928]), each year (3 [+9102, 9102]), spring (3 [+9588]), ages (2 [+1201]), each year (2 [+9102]), themˢ (2), year-old (2 [+1426]), yearly (2 [+928, 285]), age (1 [+1426]), ages (1), annual (1 [+7193, 928, 2021]), annual (1 [+285, 928, 2021]), annually (1 [+928, 3972, 2256, 9102]), annually (1 [+928, 3972, 9102, 2256]), day (1), days (1 [+3427]), due annually (1 [+4946, 1896, 928, 9102]), due annually (1 [+4946, 1896, 9102, 928]), every spring (1 [+995]), full years (1 [+3427]), generations long past (1 [+1887, 2256, 1887]), itˢ (1), itsˢ (1), lives (1 [+3427]), many years (1 [+3427, 2256]), old (1 [+3427, 2644]), over a year (1 [+2296, 3427, 196, 2296]), some years later (1 [+4200, 7891]), spring (1 [+9588, 2021]), spring (1 [+6961, 9588]), successive years (1 [+9102, 339]), successive years (1 [+339, 9102]), this timeˢ (1 [+8993]), time (1), year (1 [+1821]), years (1 [+2021, 6961]), year's (1), NDT (92)

H9102.5 ³שָׁנָה **šānâ³**, n.f. [1] dignity, honor. Conjectured in Pr 5:9:– dignity (1)

H9103 ⁴שָׁנָה **šānâ⁴**, v. Not used in NIVEBC [√ 9101]. [Q] to repeat, do again; [N] to be repeated

H9104 שֵׁנָה **šēnâ**, n.f. [23] [√ 3822; cf. 9097; 10733]. sleep, with a focus of rest and inactivity, sometimes laziness; by extension: death:– sleep (20), sleep (2 [+3822]), sleep of death (1)

H9105 שֶׁנְהַבִּים **šenhabbîm**, n.m.[pl.] [2] [√ 9094 + 2036]. ivory:– ivory (2)

H9106 ¹שָׁנִי **šānî¹**, n.[m.] [42] [√ 9101?]. scarlet, crimson (thread):– scarlet yarn (31 [+9357]), scarlet (7), scarlet thread (2), scarlet (1 [+9357]), scarlet wool (1 [+9357])

H9107 ²שָׁנִי **šānî²**, a. full grown

H9108 שֵׁנִי **šēnî**, a.num.ord. [152] [√ 9109; cf. 9101; 10765, 10766]. second:– second (75), other (33), another (12), second time (10), again (5), after (1), again (1 [+8740]), all alone (1 [+401]), another part (1), each (1), following (1), furthermore (1 [+2256, 2021]), middle (1), next (1), one (1), second in command (1), thisˢ (1 [+2021]), this time (1), whoseˢ (1 [+2021, 285, 2021]), NDT (3)

H9109 שְׁנַיִם **šᵉnayim**, n.m. & f. [765] [→ 9108; cf. 9101; 10775]. two:– two (375), twelve (51 [+6925]), both (49), twelve (30 [+6926]), 12 (24 [+6925]), each (16), twelfth (15 [+6925]), twenty-two (15 [+6929, 2256]), second (12), two-tenths (11 [+6928]), pair (9), double (8), twelfth (8 [+6926]), thirty-two (6 [+8993, 2256]), forty-two (4 [+752, 2256]), pairs (4 [+9109]), together (4), fifty-two (3 [+2822, 2256]), 1,052 (2 [+547, 2822, 2256]), 112 (2 [+4395, 2256, 6925]), 20,000 (2 [+8052]), 32 (2 [+2256, 8993]), 32,200 (2 [+2256, 8993, 547, 2256, 4395]), 372 (2 [+8993, 4395, 8679, 2256]), 392 (2 [+8993, 4395, 9596, 2256]), 42 (2 [+752, 2256]), 52 (2 [+2822, 2256]), 62,700 (2 [+2256, 9252, 547, 2256, 8679, 4395]), 652 (2 [+9252, 4395, 2822, 2256]), sides (2), sixty-two (2 [+9252, 2256]), thirty-second (2 [+8993, 2256]), twenty-second (2 [+2256, 6929]), twice (2), two at a time (2 [+9109]), 1,222 (1 [+547, 4395, 6929, 2256]), 112 (1 [+4395, 6925]), 122 (1 [+4395, 6929, 2256]), 122 (1 [+4395, 2256, 6929, 2256]), 162 (1 [+2256, 9252, 2256, 4395]), 172 (1 [+4395, 8679, 2256]), 182 (1 [+2256, 9046, 2256, 4395]), 2,172 (1 [+547, 4395, 8679, 2256]), 2,172 (1 [+547, 4395, 2256, 8679, 2256]), 2,322 (1 [+547, 8993, 4395, 6929, 2256]), 2,812 (1 [+547, 9046, 4395, 2256, 6925]), 212 (1 [+4395, 2256, 6925]), 22 (1 [+6929, 2256]), 22,000 (1 [+2256, 6929, 547]), 22,034 (1 [+6929, 2256, 547, 2256, 8993, 2256, 752]), 22,200 (1 [+6929, 547, 2256, 4395]), 22,273 (1 [+2256, 6929, 547, 8993, 2256, 8679, 2256, 4395]), 22,600 (1 [+6929, 2256, 547, 2256, 9252, 4395]), 232 (1 [+4395, 2256, 8993]), 242 (1 [+4395, 752, 2256]), 32 (1 [+8993, 2256]), 32,000 (1 [+2256, 8993, 547]), 32,500 (1 [+2256, 8993, 547, 2256, 2822, 4395]), 52,700 (1 [+2256, 2822, 547, 2256, 8679, 4395]), 62 (1 [+9252, 2256]), 642 (1 [+9252, 4395, 752, 2256]), 642 (1 [+9252, 4395, 2256, 752, 2256]), 72 (1 [+2256, 8679]), 72,000 (1 [+2256, 8679, 547]), 782 (1 [+2256, 9046, 2256, 8679, 4395]), 822 (1 [+9046, 4395, 6929, 2256]), 832 (1 [+9046, 4395, 8993, 2256]), 912 (1 [+6926, 2256, 9596, 4395]), 962 (1 [+2256, 9252, 2256, 9596, 4395]), Elijah and Elishaˢ (1 [+2157]), another (1), both sides (1), double-edged (1 [+7023]), doubly (1 [+928, 2021]), eachˢ (1), each other (1 [+5646]), each otherˢ (1 [+2157]), few (1), fifty-second (1 [+2822, 2256]), hundred and twenty thousand (1 [+8052, 6926]), inner and outerˢ (1), one pair (1), other (1), otherˢ (1), peopleˢ (1 [+8993]), someˢ (1), themˢ (1 [+2021, 3192]), themˢ (1 [+2021, 74]), time and again (1 [+4202, 285, 2256, 4202]), two-thirds (1 [+7023]), two (0 [+752, 2256]), NDT (32)

H9110 שְׁנִינָה **šᵉnînâ**, n.f. [4] [√ 9111]. object of ridicule:– object of ridicule (4)

H9111 ¹שָׁנַן **šānan¹**, v. [8] [→ 9094, 9095, 9105, 9110]. [Q] to sharpen; [Qp] be sharpened; [Htpol] to be embittered:– sharp (4), sharpen (2), embittered (1), make sharp (1)

H9112 ²שָׁנַן **šānan²**, v. [1] [cf. 9101]. [P] to impress, repeat:– Impress (1)

H9113 שָׁנַס **šānas**, v. [1] [P] to tuck up the cloak (into the belt):– tucking cloak into belt (1 [+5516])

H9114 שִׁנְעָר **šinʿār**, n.pr.loc. [8] Shinar; Babylonia:– Babylonia (3), Shinar (2), Shinar (2 [+824]), Babylonia (1 [+824])

H9115 שָׁסָה **šāsâ**, v. [11] [cf. 9116]. [Q] to raid, loot, plunder; [Qp] to be looted:– plundered (4), raiders (2), loot (1), looted (1), looting (1), pillage (1), plunderers (1)

H9116 שָׁסַס **šāsas**, v. [6] [→ 5468; cf. 9115]. [Q] to plunder, ransack; [N] to be looted, be ransacked:– plundered (3), be looted (1), plunder (1), ransacked (1)

H9117 שָׁסַע **šāsaʿ**, v. [9] [→ 9118]. [Q] to divide; [Qp] be divided; [P] to tear apart:– sharply rebuked (1), tear open (1), tore apart (1), torn (1), NDT (5)

H9118 שֶׁסַע **šesaʿ**, n.[m.] [4] [√ 9117]. cleft (split hoof):– NDT (4)

H9119 שָׁסַף **šāsap**, v. [1] [P] to hack to pieces (for execution):– put to death (1)

H9120 שָׁעָה **šāʿâ**, v. [11] [cf. 8617, 9283]. [Q] to look with favor, have regard for, pay attention to:– look (6), have regard (1), look with favor (1), looked with favor (1), pay attention (1), turn away (1)

H9121 שַׁעֲטָה **šaʿăṭâ**, n.f. [1] galloping, pounding (hooves):– galloping (1)

H9122 שַׁעַטְנֵז **šaʿaṭnēz**, n.m. [2] woven cloth; likely referring to a wide mesh:– woven (1), woven material (1)

H9123 שֹׁעַל **šōʿal**, n.[m.] [3] [→ 5469, 9127?]. hollow of the hand; handful, a measure of volume:– handful (1), handfuls (1), hollow of hand (1)

H9124 שַׁעַלְבִים **šaʿalbîm**, n.pr.loc. [2] [→ 9125]. Shaalbim, *"site of foxes"*:– Shaalbim (2)

H9125 שַׁעַלַבִּין **šaʿᵃlabbîn**, n.pr.loc. [1] [√ 9124]. Shaalabbin, *"site of foxes"*:– Shaalabbin (1)

H9126 שַׁעַלְבֹנִי **šaʿalbōnî**, a.g. [2] Shaalbonite:– Shaalbonite (2)

H9127 שַׁעֲלִים **šaʿᵃlîm**, n.pr.loc. [1] [√ 9123?]. Shaalim, "[poss.] *[land of] hollow depth*":– Shaalim (1)

H9128 שָׁעַן **šāʿan**, v. [22] [→ 5472, 5473, 5474, 5475]. [N] to lean oneself upon, rely on:– rely (5), lean (3), leaning (3), relied (3), leaned (2), rest (2), depended (1), lie (1), look for support (1), NDT (1)

H9129 ¹שָׁעַע **šāʿaʿ¹**, v. [4] [Q] be blinded; [H] to make close the eyes; [Htpal] to blind oneself; a fig. extension of smearing over or pasting objects together:– blind yourselves (1), close (1), closed (1), sightless (1)

H9130 ²שָׁעַע **šāʿaʿ²**, v. [6] [→ 9141]. [Pil] to take joy in, delight in; [Pulpal] to be dandled; [Htpal] to delight oneself in:– delight (3), brought joy (1), dandled (1), play (1)

H9131 שַׁעַף **šaʿap**, n.pr.m. [2] Shaaph:– Shaaph (2)

H9132 שָׁעַר **šāʿar**, v. [1] [→ 9134]. [Q] to think, estimate, calculate:– thinking (1)

H9133 ¹שַׁעַר **šaʿar¹**, n.m. [374] [→ 8788, 9135, 9139; 10776]. gate, gateway; often referring to the entrance to a city, a key point of the city's defense and a place for public hearings and decisions:– gate (177), gates (70), gateway (28), towns (20), city gate (11), entrance (10), cities (7), court (6), city gates (4), courts (4), gateways (4), town (4), cities (2 [+824]), each gate (2 [+9133, 2256]), each gate (2 [+2256, 9133]), itsˢ (2 [+2021]), town gate (2), assembly at the gate (1), endˢ (1), entrance (1 [+7339]), gate (1 [+7339]), gatepost (1 [+4647]), gateposts (1 [+4647]), gateway (1 [+1195]), hometown (1 [+5226]), inner chamber (1), itˢ (1 [+2021, 4889]), oppositeˢ (1), otherˢ (1), theyˢ (1 [+2021]), various gates (1 [+9133, 2256]), various gates (1 [+2256, 9133]), NDT (4)

H9134 ²שַׁעַר **šaʿar²**, n.[m.] [1] [√ 9132]. measure (of grain):– hundredfold (1 [+4395])

H9135 שֹׁעָר **šōʿār**, a. [1] [√ 9133]. burst open, i.e., poor quality (figs):– NDT (1)

H9136 שַׁעֲרוּר **šaʿᵃrûr**, n.f. [2] [→ 9137]. something horrible, shocking thing:– shocking thing (1), something horrible (1)

H9137 שַׁעֲרוּרִי **šaʿᵃrûrî**, n.f. [2] [√ 9136]. horrible thing:– horrible thing (2)

H9138 שְׁעַרְיָה **šᵉʿaryâ**, n.pr.m. [2] [√ 3378]. Sheariah, "[poss.] *Yahweh breaks*":– Sheariah (2)

H9139 שַׁעֲרַיִם **šaʿᵃrayim**, n.pr.loc. [3] [√ 9133]. Shaaraim, *"double gates"*:– Shaaraim (3)

H9140 שַׁעַשְׁגַּז **šaʿašgaz**, n.pr.m. [1] Shaashgaz:– Shaashgaz (1)

H9141 שַׁעֲשׁוּעִים **šaʿᵃšûʿîm**, n.[m.]pl.intens. [9] [√ 9130]. delight:– delight (6), delighted (1), delighting (1), filled with delight (1)

H9142 שָׁפָה **šāpâ**, v. [2] [→ 3834, 3836?, 9143?, 9147?, 9155, 9156]. [N, Pu] to be swept bare:– bare (1), stick out (1)

H9143 שְׁפוֹ **šᵉpô**, n.pr.m. [2] [√ 9142?; cf. 9156]. Shepho, "[poss.] *barren way, empty path*":– Shepho (2)

H9144 שְׁפוֹט **šᵉpôṭ**, n.m. [2] [√ 9149]. judgment, punishment:– judgment (1), punishment (1)

H9145 שְׁפוּפָם **šᵉpûpām**, n.pr.m. Not used in NIVEBC [cf. 8792]. Shephupham, "[perhaps] *serpent*"

H9146 שְׁפוּפָן **šᵉpûpān**, n.pr.m. [1] [√ 9159?]. Shephuphan, "[perhaps] *serpent*":– Shephuphan (1)

H9147 שְׁפוֹת **šᵉpôt**, n.f. [1] [√ 9142?]. milk product: cream, curds, cheese, etc:– cheese (1)

H9148 שִׁפְחָה **šipḥâ**, n.f. [63] [→ 5476; cf. 6202, 6203].

maidservant, female slave:– servant (25), female servants (10), female slaves (9), slave (8), attendant (2), female slave (2), slaves (2 [+6269, 2256]), women (2), enslaved (1 [+3899, 4200, 6269, 2256, 4200]), female servant (1), serve (1)

H9149 שָׁפַט ***šāpaṭ***, v. [202] [→ 5477, 9143, 9144, 9150, 9151, 9154; 10735; *also used with compound proper names*]. [Q] to judge, decide; lead, defend, vindicate; [N] to execute judgment, be brought to trial; to argue a matter; [Po] (ptcp.) judge:– judge (66), judges (24), led (12), rulers (8), execute judgment (6), govern (5), leaders (5), vindicate (5), decide (4), defend (4), judged (3), judging (3), lead (3), governed (2), play the judge (2 [+9149]), rule (2), ruler (2), sentence (2), vindicated (2), administer (1), argue (1), be judged (1), bring into judgment (1), bring judgment (1), bring justice (1), brought to trial (1), condemn (1), confront with evidence (1), decide dispute (1), decided (1), defend the cause (1), defending (1), executing judgment (1), given[S] (1), goes to court (1), held court (1), is tried (1), judge (1 [+5477]), judge in office (1), judges decide (1), judges in office (1), leader (1), leading (1), pass judgment (1), pleads a case (1), punish (1), put on trial (1), render judgment (1 [+5477]), renders judgment (1), ruled (1), rules (1), serve as judge (1), serve as judges (1), served (1), served as judges (1), serving as leader (1), take up the cause (1), them[S] (1 [+2021]), uphold (1), NDT (2)

H9150 שֶׁפֶט ***šepeṭ***, n.m. [16] [√ 9149]. judgment, punishment:– punishment (9), judgment (3), acts of judgment (2), judgments (1), penalties (1)

H9151 שָׁפָט ***šāpāṭ***, n.pr.m. [8] [√ 9149]. Shaphat, "*he judges*":– Shaphat (8)

H9152 שְׁפַטְיָה ***šᵉpaṭyâ***, n.pr.m. [10] [√ 9149 + 3378]. Shephatiah, "*Yahweh has judged*":– Shephatiah (10)

H9153 שְׁפַטְיָהוּ ***šᵉpaṭyāhû***, n.pr.m. [3] [√ 9149 + 3378]. Shephatiah, "*Yahweh has judged*":– Shephatiah (3)

H9154 שִׁפְטָן ***šipṭān***, n.pr.m. [1] [√ 9149]. Shiphtan, "*he has judged*":– Shiphtan (1)

H9155 1שְׁפִי ***šᵉpî[1]***, n.m. [9] [→ 9156; cf. 9142]. barren height:– barren heights (7), barren height (1), barren hill (1)

H9156 2שְׁפִי ***šᵉpî[2]***, n.pr.m. Not used in NIVEBC [√ 9155? compare 9143]. Shephi, see 9143

H9157 1שֻׁפִּים ***šuppîm[1]***, n.pr.m. [1] Shuppim:– Shuppim (1)

H9158 2שֻׁפִּים ***šuppîm[2]***, a.g.[pl.] [2] [√ 9172]. Shuppites:– Shuppites (2)

H9159 שְׁפִיפֹן ***šᵉpîpōn***, n.[m.] [1] [→ 9146?]. viper:– viper (1)

H9160 שָׁפִיר ***šāpîr***, n.pr.loc. [1] [√ 9182]. Shaphir, "*lovely*":– Shaphir (1)

H9161 שָׁפַךְ ***šāpak***, v. [115] [→ 9162, 9163]. [Q] to pour out, shed, spill; [Qp, N, Pu] to be outpoured, be shed; [Ht] be scattered, ebb away; "to shed blood" means to kill:– pour out (33), shed (25), poured out (11), build (6), shedding (4), outpoured (3), pours out (3), be poured out (2), be shed (2), built (2), pour (2), pours (2), sheds (2), am poured out (1), be poured (1), been shed (1), bloodshed (1 [+1947]), build up (1), drain out (1), dumped (1), ebb away (1), ebbs away (1), flowed (1), lavished (1), lost (1), outpouring (1), poured out (1 [+4946]), pouring out (1), scattered (1), spilled out (1), spills (1)

H9162 שֶׁפֶךְ ***šepek***, n.[m.] [2] [√ 9161]. dump (for throwing out ash refuse):– heap (1), where thrown (1)

H9163 שָׁפְכָה ***šopkâ***, n.f. [1] [√ 9161]. male organ (fluid duct):– cutting (1 [+4162])

H9164 שָׁפֵל ***šāpēl[1]***, v. [30] [→ 9165, 9166, 9167, 9168, 9169, 9170; 10737, 10738]. [Q] to be humbled, be brought low; [H] to humble, bring low:– humbled (6), brought low (4), bring low (3), bring down (2), brings down (1), brings low (1), casts (1), come down (1), descended (1), fades (1), humble (1), humbles (1), humiliate (1), lay low (1), lays low (1), leveled completely (1 [+928, 2021, 9168]), levels (1), low (1), stoops down (1)

H9165 שֵׁפֶל ***šēpel***, n.[m.] [2] [√ 9164]. low estate, humble condition:– low (1), low estate (1)

H9166 שָׁפָל ***šāpāl***, a. [18] [√ 9164]. low, deep:– lowly (8), deep (3), humiliated (2), low (2), deeper (1), low (1 [+7757]), lowliest (1)

H9167 שָׁפֵל ***šāpēl[2]***, a. Not used in NIVEBC [√ 9164]. low

H9168 שִׁפְלָה ***šiplâ***, n.f. [1] [√ 9164]. state of lowliness, condition of humiliation:– leveled completely (1 [+9164, 928, 2021])

H9169 שְׁפֵלָה ***šᵉpēlâ***, n.f. [20] [√ 9164]. (western) foothills, Shephelah, a major buffer area between the (Philistine) coastal plain and the highlands of Judah:– western foothills (13), foothills (7)

H9170 שִׁפְלוּת ***šiplût***, n.f. [1] [√ 9164]. idleness, inactivity, an extension of lowering the hands to a position of rest:– idle (1)

H9171 שָׁפָם ***šāpām***, n.pr.m. [1] Shapham:– Shapham (1)

H9172 שְׁפָם ***šᵉpām***, n.pr.loc. [2] [→ 9175?]. Shepham, "*nakedness*":– Shepham (2)

H9173 שֻׁפָּם ***šuppim***, n.pr.m. Not used in NIVEBC [√ 9158]. Shuppites, see 9158

H9174 שִׁפְמוֹת ***šipᵉmôt***, n.pr.loc. Not used in NIVEBC [cf. 8560]. Shiphamot, see 8560

H9175 שִׁפְמִי ***šipmî***, a.g. [1] [√ 9172?]. Shiphmite:– Shiphmite (1)

H9176 1שָׁפָן ***šāpān[1]***, n.m. [4] [→ 9177]. coney:– hyrax (3), hyraxes (1)

H9177 2שָׁפָן ***šāpān[2]***, n.pr.m. [30] [√ 9176]. Shaphan, "*rock badger*":– Shaphan (30)

H9178 שָׁפַע ***šāpa'***, v. Not used in NIVEBC [→ 9179, 9180, 9181]. [Q] to flow abundantly

H9179 שֶׁפַע ***šepa'***, n.[m.] [1] [√ 9178]. abundance:– abundance (1)

H9180 שִׁפְעָה ***šip'â***, n.f. [6] [√ 9178]. (of water) flood; mass (of humans or animals):– flood (2), troops (2), herds (1), many (1)

H9181 שִׁפְעִי ***šip'î***, n.pr.m. [1] [√ 9178]. Shiphi, "*flowing abundance*":– Shiphi (1)

H9182 שָׁפַר ***šāpar***, v. [1] [→ 9160, 9183, 9185, 9186, 9188; cf. 8795; 10739]. [Q] to be delightful, pleasing:– delightful (1)

H9183 1שֶׁפֶר ***šeper[1]***, n.m. [1] [√ 9182]. beauty, loveliness:– beautiful (1)

H9184 2שֶׁפֶר ***šeper[2]***, n.pr.loc. [2] [cf. 6223]. Shepher:– Shepher (2)

H9185 1שִׁפְרָה ***šiprâ[1]***, n.f. [1] [√ 9182]. fairness, clearness (of skies):– fair (1)

H9186 2שִׁפְרָה ***šiprâ[2]***, n.pr.f. [1] [√ 9182]. Shiphrah, "*beautiful, fair*":– Shiphrah (1)

H9187 שַׁפְרוּר ***šaprûr***, n.[m.] Not used in NIVEBC [cf. 9188]. see 9188

H9188 שַׁפְרִיר ***šaprîr***, n.[m.] [1] [√ 9182; cf. 9187]. royal canopy, pavilion:– royal canopy (1)

H9189 שָׁפַת ***šāpat***, v.den. [5] [→ 883, 5478, 9190, 9191]. [Q] to place, put:– put on (3), establish (1), lay (1)

H9190 1שְׁפַתַּיִם ***šᵉpattayim[1]***, n.[m.]du. [1] [√ 9189]. an area of inactivity: (place of the) fireplaces; some sources: saddlebags or sheepfolds:– sheep pens (1)

H9191 2שְׁפַתַּיִם ***šᵉpattayim[2]***, n.[m.]du. [1] [√ 9189]. double-pronged hooks:– double-pronged hooks (1)

H9192 שֶׁצֶף ***šeṣep***, n.m. [1] [cf. 8851, 8852]. surging, flooding (of anger):– surge (1)

H9193 1שָׁקַד ***šāqad[1]***, v. [12] [→ 5481, 9195, 9196]. [Q] to be awake, watch, stand guard:– watching (3), did not hesitate (1), guard (1), have an eye for (1), lie awake (1), lie in wait (1), stand watch (1), watch (1), watch kept (1), watched (1)

H9194 2שָׁקַד ***šāqad[2]***, v. [Q] to be emaciated

H9195 3שָׁקַד ***šāqad[3]***, v.den. Not used in NIVEBC [→ 5481, 9196; cf. 9193]. [P] to be shaped like an almond blossom

H9196 שָׁקֵד ***šāqēd***, n.[m.] [4] [√ 9195; cf. 9193]. almond tree, almond nuts:– almond tree (2), almonds (2)

H9197 שָׁקָה ***šāqâ***, v. [61] [→ 5482, 5483, 9198, 9216; cf. 9272]. [N] to be given a drink; [Pu] to be moistened; [H] to give a drink to:– water (10), watered (6), drink (5), made drink (4), gave a drink (3), give to drink (3), gave (2), get a drink (2), get to drink (2), give drink (2), got to drink (2), make drink (2), drench (1), gave water (1), give (1), give a drink (1), give a drink (1 [+3926]), give water (1), given (1), given a drink (1), given to drink (1), gives drink (1), have drink (1), irrigated (1), let drink (1), made to drink (1), rich (1), watering (1), waters (1), wine served (1)

H9198 שִׁקּוּי ***šiqqûy***, n.[m.] [3] [√ 9197]. drink; nourishing drink:– drink (2), nourishment (1)

H9199 שִׁקּוּץ ***šiqqûṣ***, n.m. [28] [√ 9210]. detestable thing, vileness, abomination:– vile images (10), abomination (3), detestable god (3), detestable idols (3), abominations (1), detestable acts (1), detestable images (1), detestable things (1), filth (1), forbidden food (1), vile (1), vile god (1), vile goddess (1)

H9200 שָׁקַט ***šāqaṭ***, v. [41] [→ 9201; cf. 9284]. [Q] to be at rest, be at peace; [H] to keep silent, remain quiet, remain calm:– at peace (7), calm (4), had peace (4), rest (4), quiet (3), quietness (3), had rest (2), have peace (2), in peace (2), peaceful (2), calms (1), grant relief (1), left (1), lies hushed (1), silent (1), stand aloof (1), troubled (1 [+4202, 3523]), unconcerned (1 [+8932])

H9201 שֶׁקֶט ***šeqeṭ***, n.[m.] [1] [√ 9200]. quietness:– quiet (1)

H9202 שָׁקַל ***šāqal***, v. [22] [→ 5484, 5486, 5487?, 9203; 10769]. [Q] to weigh out, make payment; [N] to be weighed:– weighed out (7), be weighed (2 [+9202]), pay (2), weigh (2), weigh out (2), be weighed out (1), give (1 [+4200, 995]), paid (1 [+8510]), pay (1 [+4084]), spend (1), took revenue (1), weighed (1)

H9203 שֶׁקֶל ***šeqel***, n.m. [88] [√ 9202; 10770]. shekel (a unit of weight and value, about two-fifths of an ounce [11.5 grams]):– shekels (45), shekel (39), price (1), weighs (1), which[S] (1), NDT (1)

H9204 שִׁקְמָה ***šiqmâ***, n.f. [7] sycamore-fig tree:– sycamore-fig trees (5), fig trees (1), sycamore-figs (1)

H9205 שָׁקַע ***šāqa'***, v. [6] [→ 5488]. [Q] to sink down; [N] to sink; [H] to make sink down, make settle:– sink (2), died down (1), let settle (1), sinks (1), tie down (1)

H9206 שְׁקַעֲרוּרָה ***šᵉqa'ᵃrûrâ***, n.f. [1] [→ 7883]. depression, hollow:– depressions (1)

H9207 שָׁקַף ***šāqap***, v. [22] [→ 5485, 9208?, 9209]. [N] to look down on, overlook; [H] to look down on:– looked down (7), looks down (4), overlooking (2), watched (2), appears (1), look down (1), looked (1), looked out (1), looms (1), overlooks (1), peered (1)

H9208 שֶׁקֶף ***šāqep***, n.[m.] [1] [√ 9207?]. frame work (of a door):– frames (1)

H9209 שְׁקֻפִים ***šᵉqupîm***, n.m. [2] [√ 9207]. clerestory window (a high place window):– high up (1), windows placed high (1)

H9210 שָׁקַץ ***šāqaṣ***, v. [7] [→ 9199, 9211; cf. 7752, 7762]. [P] to detest, abhor, defile:– defile (2), regard as unclean (2), regard as vile (2 [+9210]), scorned (1)

H9211 שֶׁקֶץ ***šeqeṣ***, n.m. [10] [√ 9210]. detestable thing:– unclean (8), regarded as unclean (1), unclean things (1)

H9212 שָׁקַק ***šāqaq***, v. [4] [→ 5480; cf. 8796?]. [Q] to rush forth, charge forth; [Htpal] to rush back and forth:– charging (1), pounce (1), rush (1), rushing back and forth (1)

H9213 שָׁקַר ***šāqar***, v.den. [6] [→ 9214, 9215]. [Q] to deal falsely with; [P] to deceive, lie, betray:– betray (1), deal falsely (1), deceive (1), false (1), lie (1), true (1 [+4202])

H9214 שֶׁקֶר ***šeqer***, n.m. [113] [√ 9213]. lie, falseness, deception; vanity:– lies (21), false (14), lying (12), deceiving (4), deceptive (4), falsely (4), falsely (4 [+4200, 2021]), without cause (4), deceit (3), deceitful (3), falsehood (3), fraud (3), lie (3), lies (3 [+1821]), not true (3), false gods (2), liar (2), liars (2 [+1819]), wrong (2), come to nothing (1), deceiver (1), deception (1), disillusionment (1), falsely (1 [+6584]), gifts never given (1 [+5522]), liars (1), lie (1 [+1819]), lies (1 [+609]), lying (1 [+1819]), perjurers (1 [+8678, 4200, 2021]), perjury (1 [+8678, 4200, 2021]), pretense (1), put in jeopardy (1 [+6913]), useless (1 [+4200, 2021]), vain hope (1), without reason (1)

H9215 שַׁקָּר ***šaqqār***, n.m. Not used in NIVEBC [√ 9213]. liar, slanderer

H9216 שֹׁקֶת ***šōqet***, n.f. [2] [√ 9197]. watering-trough:– trough (1), troughs (1 [+8110])

H9217 1שֵׁר ***šēr[1]***, n.[f.] [1] [→ 9225]. bracelet:– bracelets (1)

H9218 2שֵׁר ***šēr[2]***, n.[m.] Not used in NIVEBC [cf. 9219]. see 9219

H9219 שֹׁר ***šōr***, n.[m.] [3] [√ 9242; cf. 9218]. navel; umbilical cord:– body (1), cord (1), navel (1)

H9220 שָׁרָב ***šārāb***, n.m. [2] [→ 9221?]. parching heat; burning hot sand:– burning sand (1), desert heat (1)

H9221 שֵׁרֵבְיָה ***šērēbyâ***, n.pr.m. [8] [√ 9220? + 3378]. Sherebiah, "[poss.] *Yahweh has sent burning heat*":– Sherebiah (8)

H9222 שַׁרְבִיט ***šarbîṭ***, n.m. [4] [√ 8657]. scepter, staff:– scepter (4)

H9223 1שָׁרָה ***šārâ[1]***, v. [2] [→ 5489, 9233; 10742]. [Q] to unleash; to deliver, set free:– deliver (1), unleashes (1)

H9224 2שָׁרָה ***šārâ[2]***, n.[m.] [1] [√ 8805; cf. 8800]. vineyard:– vineyards (1)

H9225 שֵׁרָה ***šērâ***, n.[f.] Not used in NIVEBC [√ 9217]. bracelet

H9226 שָׁרוּחֶן ***šārûḥen***, n.pr.loc. [1] Sharuhen:– Sharuhen (1)

H9227 שָׁרוֹן ***šārôn***, n.pr.loc. [6] [→ 9228; cf. 3837, 4389]. Sharon, "*plain, level country*":– Sharon (6)

H9228 שָׁרוֹנִי ***šārônî***, a.g. [1] [√ 9227; cf. 3837]. Sharonite, "*of Sharon*":– Sharonite (1)

H9229 שְׁרוּקָה ***šᵉrûqâ***, n.[f.] Not used in NIVEBC [cf. 9239?, 9240]. scorn, see 9241

H9230 שֵׁרוּת ***šērût***, var. Not used in NIVEBC [cf. 9223]. see 9223

H9231 שִׁרְטַי ***širṭay***, n.pr.m. Not used in NIVEBC [cf. 8855]. Shirtai, see 8855

H9232 שָׁרַי ***šāray***, n.pr.m. [1] Sharai:– Sharai (1)

H9233 שִׁרְיָה ***širyâ***, n.f. [1] [√ 9223]. a weapon that is thrown: javelin, lance, light spear; some sources: arrowhead:– javelin (1)

H9234 שִׁרְיוֹן ***širyôn***, n.[m.] [8] [cf. 6246]. coat of scale armor:– armor (2), breastplate (1), coat of armor (1), coat of scale armor (1 [+7989]), coats of armor (1), scale armor (1), NDT (1)

H9235 שָׁרִיר ***šārîr***, n.[m.] [1] [√ 9242]. muscle:– muscles (1)

H9236 שְׁרֵמוֹת ***šᵉrēmôt***, n.f. see 8727

H9237 שָׁרַץ **šāraṣ**, v. [14] [→ 9238]. [Q] to teem, swarm, move about; move greatly:– moves (3), multiply (2), move (1), multiplied greatly (1), swarm (1), swarms (1), teem (1), teem (1 [+9238]), teemed (1), teems (1), NDT (1)

H9238 שֶׁרֶץ **šereṣ**, n.m. [16] [√ 9237]. creatures that teem, swarm, move about:– insects (4), creature (3), creature that moves along the ground (2), creatures (2), animals (1), crawling thing (1), move along (1), swarming things (1), teem (1 [+9237])

H9239 שָׁרַק **šāraq**, v. [12] [→ 9240, 9241; cf. 9229?]. [Q] to whistle, hiss, scoff:– scoff (8), hisses (1), signal (1), whistle (1), whistles (1)

H9240 שְׁרֵקָה **š^{e}rēqâ**, n.f. [7] [√ 9239; cf. 9229]. object of scorn, thing of derision, something held in contempt; an extension of the act of whistling or shrieking in derision:– scorn (6), derision (1)

H9241 שְׁרִיקָה **š^{e}riqâ**, n.[f.] [2] [√ 9239]. whistling; scorn; some sources: flute playing:– scorn (1), whistling (1)

H9242 שָׁרַר **šārar**, v. Not used in NIVEBC [→ 9219, 9235, 9243, 9244]. [Q] to be firm, hard

H9243 שָׁרָר **šārār**, n.pr.m. [1] [√ 9242]. Sharar, "*firm*":– Sharar (1)

H9244 שְׁרִירוּת **š^{e}rirût**, n.f. [10] [√ 9242]. stubbornness:– stubbornness (7), stubborn (2), persist in own way (1 [+4213])

H9245 שָׁרַשׁ **šāraš**, v.den. [8] [√ 9247]. [P] to uproot; [Poel/Poal] to take root; [Pu] to be uprooted; [H] to take root:– be uprooted (1), take root (1), take root (1 [+1614]), taken root (1), taking root (1), took root (1 [+9247]), uproot (1), uprooted (1)

H9246 שֶׁרֶשׁ **šereš**, n.pr.m. [1] [√ 9247]. Sheresh, "*root, rootstock, sucker [of a plant]*":– Sheresh (1)

H9247 שֹׁרֶשׁ **šōreš**, n.m. [33] [→ 9245, 9246; 10743]. root of a plant; by extension: base or bottom of any object; source of a family line; "the Root of Jesse" is a messianic title, emphasizing Davidic origin:– roots (15), root (12), be uprooted (1 [+4572]), depths (1), family line (1 [+5916]), soles (1), took root (1 [+9245]), uprooted (1 [+5998])

H9248 שַׁרְשָׁה **šaršâ**, n.f. Not used in NIVEBC [√ 9249]. chain, see 9249

H9249 שַׁרְשְׁרָה **šarš^{e}râ**, n.f. [8] [→ 9248]. chain:– chains (5), chain (1), chains (1 [+6310]), interwoven chains (1 [+5126])

H9250 שָׁרַת **šārat**, v. [97] [→ 9251]. [P] to minister, serve, attend:– minister (30), ministering (14), serve (7), service (5), aide (4), assist (4), servant (4), servants (4), served (4), ministered (3), attending (2), ministers (2), attendant (1), attendants (1), attendants (1 [+5853]), attended (1), ministering (1 [+9251]), officials (1), on duty (1), personal attendants (1 [+5853]), personal servant (1 [+5853]), serving (1), supply (1), take care of (1), waited on (1), NDT (1)

H9251 שָׁרֵת **šārēt**, n.m. [2] [√ 9250]. cultic service:– ministering (1 [+9250]), service (1)

H9252 שֵׁשׁ[1] **šēš[1]**, n.m. [274] [→ 9261, 9262; 10747]. six; (pl.) sixty:– six (117), sixty (23), sixteen (14 [+6926]), sixteen (4 [+6925]), sixteenth (3 [+6925]), 16,000 (2 [+6925, 547]), 3,600 (2 [+8993, 547, 2256, 4395]), 36,000 (2 [+2256, 8993, 547]), 4,600 (2 [+752, 547, 2256, 4395]), 45,650 (2 [+2822, 2256, 752, 547, 2256, 4395, 2256, 2822]), 46,500 (2 [+2256, 752, 547, 2256, 2822, 4395]), 6,720 (2 [+547, 8679, 4395, 2256, 6929]), 62,700 (2 [+9109, 2256, 547, 2256, 8679, 4395]), 621 (2 [+4395, 6929, 2256, 285]), 65 (2 [+2822, 2256]), 652 (2 [+4395, 2822, 2256, 9109]), 666 (2 [+9252, 4395, 2256, 9252]), 666 (2 [+9252, 4395, 9252, 2256]), 666 (2 [+4395, 9252, 2256, 9252]), 736 (2 [+8679, 4395, 8993, 2256]), 74,600 (2 [+752, 2256, 8679, 547, 2256, 4395]), 760 (2 [+8679, 4395, 2256]), ninety-six (2 [+9596, 2256]), sixty-six (2 [+9252, 2256]), sixty-six (2 [+2256, 9252]), sixty-two (2 [+2256, 9109]), 1,365 (1 [+2822, 2256, 2256, 8993, 4395, 2256, 547]), 1,760 (1 [+547, 2256, 8679, 4395, 2256]), 153,600 (1 [+4395, 2256, 2822, 547, 2256, 8993, 547, 2256, 4395]), 156 (1 [+4395, 2822, 2256]), 157,600 (1 [+4395, 547, 2256, 8679, 2256, 2822, 547, 4395, 2256]), 16,750 (1 [+6925, 547, 8679, 4395, 2256, 2822]), 160 (1 [+4395, 2256]), 162 (1 [+9109, 2256, 2256, 4395]), 186,400 (1 [+4395, 547, 2256, 9046, 547, 547, 752, 4395, 2256, 2256]), 2,056 (1 [+547, 2822, 2256]), 2,067 (1 [+547, 2256, 8679]), 2,600 (1 [+547, 2256, 4395]), 2,630 (1 [+547, 2256, 4395, 2256, 8993]), 22,600 (1 [+6929, 2256, 9109, 547, 2256, 4395]), 26,000 (1 [+6929, 2256, 547]), 28,600 (1 [+6929, 2256, 9046, 547, 2256, 4395]), 3,630 (1 [+8993, 547, 2256, 4395, 2256, 8993]), 36,000 (1 [+8993, 2256, 547]), 365 (1 [+2822, 2256, 2256, 8993, 4395]), 42,360 (1 [+752, 8052, 547, 8993, 4395]), 42,360 (1 [+752, 8052, 547, 8993, 4395, 2256]), 44,760 (1 [+752, 2256, 752, 547, 2256, 8679, 4395, 2256]), 45,600 (1 [+2822, 2256, 752, 547, 2256, 4395]), 468 (1 [+752, 4395, 2256, 9046]), 56 (1 [+2822, 2256]), 6,200 (1 [+547, 2256, 4395]), 6,800 (1 [+547, 2256, 9046, 4395]), 60 (1), 60,500 (1 [+547, 2256, 2822, 4395]), 601,730 (1 [+4395, 547, 2256, 547, 8679, 4395, 2256, 8993]), 603,550 (1 [+4395, 547, 2256, 8993, 547, 2822, 4395, 2822, 2256, 2256]), 603,550 (1 [+4395, 547, 8993, 547, 2822, 4395, 2822, 2256, 2256, 2256]), 603,550 (1 [+4395, 547, 2256, 8993, 547, 2256, 2822, 4395, 2256, 2822]), 61 (1 [+285, 2256]), 61,000 (1 [+8052, 2256, 547]), 61,000 (1 [+285, 2256, 547]), 62 (1 [+2256, 9109]), 623 (1 [+4395, 6929, 2256, 8993]), 628 (1 [+4395, 6929, 2256, 9046]), 64,300 (1 [+752, 2256, 547, 2256, 8993, 4395]), 64,400 (1 [+752, 2256, 547, 2256, 752, 4395]), 642 (1 [+4395, 752, 2256, 9109]), 642 (1 [+4395, 2256, 752, 2256, 9109]), 648 (1 [+4395, 752, 2256, 9046]), 650 (1 [+4395, 2256, 2822]), 655 (1 [+4395, 2822, 2256, 2822]), 666 (1 [+4395, 2256, 9252, 2256, 9252]), 666 (1 [+9252, 4395, 2256, 2256, 9252]), 666 (1 [+9252, 4395, 2256, 9252, 2256]), 667 (1 [+4395, 9252, 2256, 8679]), 667 (1 [+9252, 4395, 2256, 8679]), 67 (1 [+2256, 8679]), 675 (1 [+4395, 2822, 2256, 8679]), 675,000 (1 [+4395, 547, 2256, 8679, 547, 2256, 2822, 547]), 690 (1 [+4395, 2256, 9596]), 76,500 (1 [+2256, 8679, 547, 2256, 2822, 4395]), 8,600 (1 [+9046, 547, 2256, 4395]), 956 (1 [+9596, 4395, 2256, 2822, 2256]), 962 (1 [+9109, 2256, 2256, 9596, 4395]), 969 (1 [+9596, 2256, 2256, 9596, 4395]), eighty-six (1 [+9046, 2256]), sixth (1), sixty-eight (1 [+2256, 9046]), sixty-five (1 [+2256, 2822]), thirty-six (1 [+8993, 2256]), thirty-sixth (1 [+8993, 2256]), twenty-six (1 [+6929, 2256]), twenty-six hundred (1 [+547, 2256, 4395]), twenty-sixth (1 [+6929, 2256]), NDT (2)

H9253 שֵׁשׁ[2] **šēš[2]**, n.m. [3] [→ 8880, 9254, 9260]. alabaster:– marble (3)

H9254 שֵׁשׁ[3] **šēš[3]**, n.m. [38] [→ 9260; cf. 9253]. fine linen, byssus (processed from the flax plant):– linen (21), fine linen (17)

H9255 שָׁשָׁא **šāšā'**, v.intens. [1] [P] to lead along:– drag along (1)

H9256 שֵׁשְׁבַּצַּר **šēšbaṣṣar**, n.pr.m. [2] [cf. 9256]. Sheshbazzar, "*may Sin protect [the father]*":– Sheshbazzar (2)

H9257 שָׁשָׁה **šāšâ**, v.den. [1] [P] to give a sixth part:– sixth (1)

H9258 שָׁשַׁי **šāšay**, n.pr.m. [1] Shashai, "*noble*":– Shashai (1)

H9259 שֵׁשַׁי **šēšay**, n.pr.m. [3] Sheshai, "[poss.] *sixth [child]*":– Sheshai (3)

H9260 שֵׁשִׁי **šēšî**, n.m. Not used in NIVEBC [√ 9254; cf. 9253]. linen, see 9254

H9261 שִׁשִּׁי **šiššî**, a.num.ord. [28] [√ 9252]. sixth:– sixth (28)

H9262 שִׁשִּׁים **šiššîm**, n.indecl. Not used in NIVEBC [√ 9252; 10749]. sixty (pl. of "six" [9252])

H9263 שֵׁשַׁךְ **šēšak**, n.pr.loc. [2] Sheshach, "[cryptogram for] *Babel*":– Sheshak (2)

H9264 שֵׁשָׁן **šēšān**, n.pr.m. [5] Sheshan:– Sheshan (4), he^{S} (1)

H9265 שָׁשָׁק **šāšāq**, n.pr.m. [2] Shashak:– Shashak (2)

H9266 שָׁשַׁר **šāšar**, n.[m.] [2] red color (from lead, iron rust, or insects):– red (2)

H9267 שָׁת **šāt**, n.m. Not used in NIVEBC [√ 9268]. foundation, see 9268

H9268 שֵׁת[1] **šēt[1]**, n.[m.] [3] [→ 9267, 9273]. foundation; buttocks:– buttocks (2), foundations (1)

H9269 שֵׁת[2] **šēt[2]**, n.pr.m. [9] [√ 8883]. Seth, "*determined, granted* [Ge 4:25]; *restitution*":– Seth (8), Sheth (1)

H9270 שֵׁת[3] **šēt[3]**, n.pr.m. defiance

H9271 שָׁתָה[1] **šātâ[1]**, n.m. [1] [→ 9272?, 9274]. worker in weaving:– workers in cloth (1)

H9272 שָׁתָה[2] **šātâ[2]**, v. [217] [→ 5492, 9275, 9276; cf. 9197; 10748]. [Q] to drink; by extension: to be drunk; [N] to be drunken:– drink (128), drank (28), drinking (22), drinks (8), drunk (7), must drink (6 [+9272]), drinkers (2), getting drunk (2 [+8893]), well-watered (2 [+4784]), banquet (1), drained to dregs (1 [+5172]), drink up (1), drinks in (1), drunkards (1 [+8911]), feasted (1), feasting (1 [+430, 2256]), get a drink (1), have a drink (1), refresh (1), NDT (2)

H9273 שָׁתוֹת **šātôt**, n.m. Not used in NIVEBC [√ 9268 & 9272]. see 9268 & 9272

H9274 שְׁתִי[1] **š^{e}tî[1]**, n.m. [9] [√ 9271]. woven material, made on a loom; some sources: warp, the vertical threads on a loom:– woven (9)

H9275 שְׁתִי[2] **š^{e}tî[2]**, n.[m.] [1] [√ 9272]. drunkenness, drinking:– drunkenness (1)

H9276 שְׁתִיָּה **š^{e}tiyyâ**, n.f. [1] [√ 9272]. (manner of) drinking:– drink with no restrictions (1)

H9277 שָׁתִיל **šātîl**, n.[m.] [1] [√ 9278]. slip, cutting (of a plant):– shoots (1)

H9278 שָׁתַל **šātal**, v. [10] [→ 9277]. [Q] to plant; [Qp] to be planted:– planted (5), been planted (2), plant (2), is planted (1)

H9279 שֻׁתַלְחִי **šutalḥî**, a.g. [1] [√ 8811]. Shuthelahite, "*of Shuthelah*":– Shuthelahite (1)

H9280 שָׁתַם **šātam**, v. [2] [→ 9281]. [Qp] to be opened:– sees clearly (2)

H9281 שְׁתֻם **š^{e}tum**, a. *or* v.ptcp. Not used in NIVEBC [√ 9280]. see 9280

H9282 שָׁתַן **šātan**, v. Not used in NIVEBC [cf. 8874]. [H] to urinate

H9283 שָׁתַע **šāta'**, v. [2] [cf. 9120]. [Q] to be dismayed:– dismayed (2)

H9284 שָׁתַק **šātaq**, v. [4] [cf. 9200]. [Q] to become calm, die down:– calm (2), calm down (1), dies down (1)

H9285 שֵׁתָר **šētār**, n.pr.m. [1] Shethar:– Shethar (1)

H9286 שָׁתַת **šātat**, v. [2] [cf. 8883]. [Q] to be destined, appoint, lay claim:– destined (1), lay claim (1)

H9287 ת **t**, letter. Not used in NIVEBC [√ 10751]. letter of the Hebrew alphabet

H9288 תָּא **tā'**, n.m. [13] alcove for guards, guardroom:– alcoves (8), alcove (2), guardroom (2 [+8132]), alcoves for the guards (1)

H9289 תָּאַב[1] **tā'ab[1]**, v. [2] [→ 9291; cf. 14? *or* 3277?]. [Q] to long for, desire:– long for (2)

H9290 תָּאַב[2] **tā'ab[2]**, v. [1] [cf. 9493]. [P] to abhor, loathe:– abhor (1)

H9291 תַּאֲבָה **ta'^{a}bâ**, n.f. [1] [√ 9289]. longing, desiring:– longing (1)

H9292 תָּאָה **tā'â**, v. [2] [cf. 204, 9344]. [P] to draw a line, mark out (territory):– run a line (1), NDT (1)

H9293 תְּאוֹ **t^{e}'ô**, n.m. [2] antelope; some sources: wild ox or sheep:– antelope (2)

H9294 תַּאֲוָה[1] **ta'^{a}wâ[1]**, n.f. [21] [√ 203]. longing, desire, craving:– desire (5), longing (2), longings (2), bounty (1), choicest (1), crave other food (1 [+203]), craved (1), craves for more (1 [+203]), craving (1), cravings (1), desires (1), gave in to craving (1 [+203]), pleasing (1), selfish ends (1), what craved (1)

H9295 תַּאֲוָה[2] **ta'^{a}wâ[2]**, n.f. Not used in NIVEBC [√ 9344]. boundary

H9296 תְּאוֹמִים **t^{e}'ômîm**, n.m. Not used in NIVEBC [√ 9339]. twins, see 9339

H9297 תַּאֲלָה **ta'^{a}lâ**, n.f. [1] [√ 457]. curse:– curse (1)

H9298 תָּאַם **tā'am**, v.den. [2] [√ 9339]. [H] to have twins:– has twin (2)

H9299 תַּאֲנָה **ta'^{a}nâ**, n.f. [1] [√ 628]. (time of) heat, rut:– in heat (1)

H9300 תְּאֵנָה **t^{e}'ēnâ**, n.f. [39] fig; fig tree:– fig tree (15), figs (13), fig trees (6), fig (2), ones^{S} (1), those^{S} (1), tree (1)

H9301 תֹּאֲנָה **tō'^{a}nâ**, n.f. [1] [√ 628]. occasion, opportunity:– occasion (1)

H9302 תַּאֲנִיָּה **ta'^{a}niyyâ**, n.f. [2] [√ 627]. mourning:– mourn (1), mourning (1)

H9303 תְּאֻנִים **t^{e}'unîm**, n.[m.] [1] [√ 224?]. efforts, toil:– efforts (1)

H9304 תַּאֲנַת שִׁלֹה **ta'^{a}nat šilōh**, n.pr.loc. [1] [cf. 8926]. Taanath Shiloh, "[poss.] *approach to Shiloh*":– Taanath Shiloh (1)

H9305 תָּאַר[1] **tā'ar[1]**, v. [6] [cf. 9306, 9365?]. [Q] to turn toward; [Pu] to be turned toward:– turned (3), curved (1), headed (1), went down (1)

H9306 תָּאַר[2] **tā'ar[2]**, v.den. [2] [→ 9307; cf. 9305]. [P] to mark out a form, make an outline:– makes an outline (1), marks (1)

H9307 תֹּאַר **tō'ar**, n.m. [15] [√ 9306]. form, shape; beauty, fine-looking person:– beautiful (2 [+3637]), figure (2), form (2), bearing (1), beauty (1), fine-looking (1), handsome (1 [+3202]), look like (1), sleek (1 [+3637]), they (1 [+4392]), ugly (1 [+8273]), well-built (1 [+3637])

H9308 תַּאְרֵעַ **ta'rēa'**, n.pr.m. [1] [cf. 9390]. Tarea:– Tarea (1)

H9309 תְּאַשּׁוּר **t^{e}'aššûr**, n.f. [3] [→ 898]. cypress tree, cypress wood:– cypress (2), cypress wood (1)

H9310 תֵּבָה **tēbâ**, n.f. [28] box-shaped thing: chest, ark, basket:– ark (24), basket (2), it^{S} (2 [+2021])

H9311 תְּבוּאָה **t^{e}bû'â**, n.f. [42] [√ 995]. harvest, crops, produce:– harvest (10), crops (6), produce (4), income (3), brings forth (1), comes (1), crop (1), crop comes in (1), earnings (1), enough (1), fruit (1), gain (1), harvesting crops (1), harvests (1), produce (1 [+2446, 3655]), produced (1), produces (1), product (1), revenue (1), what is taken (1), yield (1), yields returns (1), NDT (1)

H9312 תְּבוּנָה **t^{e}bûnâ**, n.f. [42] [→ 9341; cf. 1067]. understanding, insight; ability, skill, wisdom:– understanding (30), insight (3), ability (1), cleverly fashioned (1), detect (1), discernment (1), reasoning (1), skillful (1), tyrannical (1 [+2894]), wisdom (1), words of insight (1)

H9313 תְּבוּסָה **t^{e}bûsâ**, n.f. [1] [√ 1008]. downfall, ruin:– downfall (1)

H9314 תָּבוֹר **tābôr**, n.pr.loc. [10] [→ 4079; cf. 268]. Tabor:– Tabor (10)

H9315 תֵּבֵל **tēbēl**, n.f. & m. [36] [√ 1006?]. world, earth:–

world (29), earth (4), whole earth (1 [+824]), whole world (1 [+824]), whole world (1 [+824, 2256])

H9316 תֶּבֶל ***tebel***, n.[m.] [2] [√ 1176]. perversion, abominable confusion:– perversion (2)

H9317 תֻּבַל ***tubal***, n.pr.loc. [8] Tubal:– Tubal (8)

H9318 תַּבְלִית ***tablît***, n.f. [1] [√ 1162]. destruction:– destruction (1)

H9319 תְּבַלֻּל ***teballul***, n.[m.] [1] [√ 1176]. defect (obscuring vision); likely referring to a cataract:– defect (1)

H9320 תֶּבֶן ***teben***, n.m. [17] [→ 5495]. straw:– straw (17)

H9321 תִּבְנִי ***tibnî***, n.pr.m. [3] Tibni:– Tibni (3)

H9322 תַּבְנִית ***tabnît***, n.f. [20] [√ 1215]. image, form, shape:– plans (3), looked like (2), pattern (2), plan (2), adorn (1), form (1), formed (1), image (1), kinds (1), replica (1), NDT (5)

H9323 תַּבְעֵרָה ***tab'ērâ***, n.pr.loc. [2] [√ 1277]. Taberah, "*burning*":– Taberah (2)

H9324 תֵּבֵץ ***tēbēṣ***, n.pr.loc. [3] [√ 1288?]. Thebez:– Thebez (2), it^S (1)

H9325 תִּגְלַת פִּלְאֶסֶר ***tiglat pil'eser***, n.pr.m. [3] [cf. 9433]. Tiglath-Pileser, "*my trust is in the son of [the temple] Esharra*":– Tiglath-Pileser (3)

H9326 תַּגְמוּל ***tagmûl***, n.m. [1] [√ 1694]. benefit, gracious act:– goodness (1)

H9327 תִּגְרָה ***tigrâ***, n.f. [1] [√ 1741]. agitation, blow:– blow (1)

H9328 תֹּגַרְמָה ***tōgarmâ***, n.pr.loc. [2] Togarmah:– Togarmah (2)

H9329 תִּדְהָר ***tidhār***, n.[m.] [2] fir tree; some sources: elm or ash tree:– fir (2)

H9330 תַּדְמֹר ***tadmōr***, n.pr.loc. [2] Tadmor, "*palm tree*":– Tadmor (2)

H9331 תִּדְעָל ***tid'āl***, n.pr.m. [2] Tidal:– Tidal (2)

H9332 תֹּהוּ ***tōhû***, n.m. [20] formless, waste, empty; (of speech) useless, confused, vain:– empty (2), formless (2), nothing (2), waste (2), barren (1), chaos (1), confusion (1), empty space (1), false (1), in vain (1), nothing at all (1 [+2256, 2039]), ruined (1), useless (1), useless idols (1), wasteland (1), worthless (1)

H9333 תְּהוֹם ***tehôm***, n.f. & m. [36] the deep, depths, with the associative meanings of darkness and secrecy, controlled or inhabited by mysterious powers; "the depths of the earth" is the abode of the dead:– deep (17), depths (6), deep springs (4), deep waters (3), watery depths (3), ocean depths (2), seas (1)

H9334 תָּהֳלָה ***tohºlâ***, n.f. [1] error:– error (1)

H9335 תְּהִלָּה ***tehillâ***, n.f. [57] [√ 2146]. praise, renown, glory; praise is proclaiming the excellence of a person or object:– praise (45), praises (3), praised (2), boast (1), glory (1), hymn of praise (1), praiseworthy deeds (1), psalm of praise (1), renown (1), theme of praise (1)

H9336 תַּהֲלוּכָה ***tahalûkâ***, n.f. Not used in NIVEBC [√ 2143]. procession

H9337 תַּהְפֻּכוֹת ***tahpukôt***, n.f. [10] [√ 2200]. perversity, confusing things:– perverse (6), confusing things (1), deceit (1), perverseness (1), perversity (1)

H9338 תָּו ***tāw***, n.m. [3] [√ 9344]. mark (on the forehead); signing (a document):– mark (1), put a mark (1 [+9344]), sign (1)

H9339 תּוֹאֲמִים ***tô'ªmîm***, n.m. [6] [→ 9296, 9298]. twins, (something) double:– twin (4), double (2)

H9340 תּוּבַל קַיִן ***tûbal qayin***, n.pr.m. [2] [√ 7803]. Tubal-Cain:– Tubal-Cain (1), Tubal-Cain's (1)

H9341 תּוּבְנָה ***tûbnâ***, n.f. Not used in NIVEBC [√ 9312; cf. 1067]. see 9312

H9342 תּוּגָה ***tûgâ***, n.f. [4] [√ 3324]. grief, sorrow:– grief (3), sorrow (1)

H9343 תּוֹדָה ***tôdâ***, n.f. [32] [√ 3344]. thank offering; thanksgiving, confession of thankfulness; song of thanksgiving; thanks is the speaking of the excellence of a person or object, with a focus on the personal gratitude of the speaker:– thank offerings (8), thanksgiving (6), thank (4), grateful praise (2), honor (2 [+5989]), praise (2), songs of thanksgiving (2), choir (1), choirs that gave thanks (1), choirs to give thanks (1), expression of thankfulness (1), giving grateful praise (1), thank offering (1)

H9344 [1]תָּוָה ***tāwâ[1]***, v.den. [2] [→ 9295, 9338; cf. 204, 9292]. [P] to put a mark, place a sign:– making marks (1), put a mark (1 [+9338])

H9345 [2]תָּוָה ***tāwâ[2]***, v. [1] [H] to vex, bring pain:– vexed (1)

H9346 תּוֹחַ ***tôaḥ***, n.pr.m. [1] [cf. 9375]. Toah:– Toah (1)

H9347 תּוֹחֶלֶת ***tôḥelet***, n.f. [5] [√ 3498]. hope, expectation:– hope (2), hoped (1), promise (1), prospect (1)

H9348 תָּוֶךְ ***tāwek***, subst. [418] [→ 2250, 9399]. middle, midst, center, among, within:– among (114 [+928]), in (47 [+928]), middle (27), with (17 [+928]), from (15 [+4946]), inside (15 [+928]), within (14 [+928]), among (13), out of (13 [+4946]), center (11), into (11 [+448]), midst (11), into (9 [+928]), through (8 [+928]), along with (6 [+928]), within (5), of (4 [+4946]), between (3 [+928]), from (2 [+928]), from out of (2 [+4946]), heart (2), inside (2 [+448]), intersecting (2 [+928]), presence (2), there^S (2 [+928, 2023]), throughout (2 [+928]), along (1 [+928]), among (1 [+448]), among (1 [+928, 2021]), as one (1 [+928]), at (1 [+928]), branch of (1 [+4946]), by (1 [+928]), by (1 [+4946]), central (1), do away with (1 [+6073, 4946]), entered (1 [+995, 928]), entering (1 [+995, 928]), flashed back and forth (1 [+4374, 928]), for (1 [+928]), from among (1 [+4946]), gone from (1 [+4946]), in (1 [+4946]), include (1 [+928]), inner part (1), interior (1), joined in (1 [+928]), leave (1 [+3718, 4946]), left (1 [+7756, 4946]), like (1 [+928]), of (1 [+928]), on (1 [+928]), on board (1 [+928]), onto (1 [+448]), over (1 [+928]), ranks (1), surrounded by (1 [+928]), there^S (1 [+2023, 928]), there^S (1 [+928, 4392]), there^S (1 [+928, 2257]), there^S (1 [+928, 2023]), to (1 [+448]), two (1), within (1 [+928, 5055]), NDT (21)

H9349 תּוֹכֵחָה ***tôkēḥâ***, n.f. [4] [√ 3519]. rebuke, punishment, correction:– rebuke (2), punishment (1), reckoning (1)

H9350 תּוֹכַחַת ***tôkaḥat***, n.f. [24] [√ 3519]. correction, rebuke, punishment:– correction (9), rebuke (7), argument (1), arguments (1), complaint (1), punish (1), punishments (1), rebukes (1), reply (1), reprimand (1)

H9351 תּוֹלָד ***tôlād***, n.pr.loc. [1] [√ 3528?; cf. 557]. Tolad, "*birth, generation [?]*":– Tolad (1)

H9352 תּוֹלֵדוֹת ***tôlēdôt***, n.f.pl. [39] [√ 3528]. account, record, genealogy, family line:– records (14), account of family line (4), account of the family line (4), listed genealogy (3), account (2), genealogical records (2), genealogy (2), account of family (1), account of the family (1), birth (1), descendants (1), family line (1), genealogical record (1), lines of descent (1), order of birth (1)

H9353 תּוֹלוֹן ***tôlôn***, n.pr.m. Not used in NIVEBC [cf. 9400]. Tolon, see 9400

H9354 תּוֹלָל ***tôlāl***, n.m. [1] [√ 2143]. tormentor, oppressor:– tormentors (1)

H9355 [1]תּוֹלָע ***tôlā'[1]***, n.[m.] [2] [→ 9356, 9357, 9358, 9443]. (deep) red, purple:– crimson (1), royal purple (1)

H9356 [2]תּוֹלָע ***tôlā'[2]***, n.pr.m. [6] [→ 9358; cf. 9355]. Tola:– Tola (6)

H9357 תּוֹלֵעָה ***tôlē'â***, n.f. [41] [√ 9355]. scarlet yarn, scarlet yarn; worm, maggot:– scarlet yarn (31 [+9106]), worm (4), worms (3), maggots (1), scarlet (1 [+9106]), scarlet wool (1 [+9106])

H9358 תּוֹלָעִי ***tôlā'î***, a.g. [1] [√ 9356; cf. 9355]. Tolaite, "*of Tola*":– Tolaite (1)

H9359 תּוֹעֵבָה ***tô'ēbâ***, n.f. [117] [√ 9493?]. detestable thing, loathsome thing, abomination:– detestable practices (32), detestable (21), detestable things (18), detests (14), detestable thing (7), detest (6), detestable idols (6), things detestable (3), things^S (2), abominations (1), detestable god (1), detestable offense (1), detestable sins (1), detestable ways (1), repulsive (1), thing detestable (1), what detestable (1)

H9360 תּוֹעָה ***tô'â***, n.f. [2] [√ 9494]. trouble, error:– error (1), trouble (1)

H9361 תּוֹעָפוֹת ***tô'āpôt***, n.f. [4] best, choice; strength; some sources: horns:– strength (2), choicest (1), peaks (1)

H9362 תּוֹצָאוֹת ***tôṣā'ôt***, n.f. [23] [√ 3655]. end, limit, starting point:– ended (5 [+2118]), out (5), end (3 [+2118]), ending (3 [+2118]), escape (1), exits (1), extended (1), farthest limits (1), flows from (1), NDT (2)

H9363 תּוֹקְהַת ***towqºhat***, n.pr.m. Not used in NIVEBC [cf. 9534]. Tokehath, see 9534

H9364 תּוֹקְעִים ***tôqº'îm***, n.m.[pl.] *or* v.ptcp. [1] [√ 9546]. striking of hands in pledge:– shake hands in pledge (1)

H9365 תּוּר ***tûr***, v. [24] [cf. 3847, 9305?]. [Q] to explore, investigate, search out; [H] to send out to spy:– explore (6), explored (5), merchants (2 [+408]), chasing (1), choose carefully (1), explored (1 [+6296]), exploring (1), find (1), investigate (1), ranges (1), search out (1), searched out (1), sent to spy out (1), tried (1 [+928, 4213])

H9366 [1]תּוֹר ***tôr[1]***, n.m. [5] turning; earring:– earrings (2), turn (2), most exalted (1 [+5092])

H9367 [2]תּוֹר ***tôr[2]***, n.f. & m. [14] dove:– doves (9), dove (5)

H9368 תּוֹרָה ***tôrâ***, n.f. [220] [√ 3723]. law, regulation, teaching, instruction; often referring to the five books of Moses in whole and in part:– law (156), regulations (15), laws (13), instruction (12), teaching (9), instructions (6), God's instruction (2), decree (1), instruction in the law (1), it^S (1), matters of law (1), teaching of law (1), teachings (1), whatever^S (1 [+2021])

H9369 תּוֹשָׁב ***tôšāb***, n.m. [13] [√ 3782]. temporary resident, stranger, alien:– stranger (3), residing (2), temporary resident (2), temporary residents (2), foreigner (1 [+1731]), guest (1), reside as strangers (1), strangers (1)

H9370 תּוּשִׁיָּה ***tûšiyyâ***, n.f. [11] [cf. 3780]. success, victory; sound judgment, wisdom:– sound judgment (3), success (3), insight (2), wisdom (2), true wisdom (1)

H9371 תּוֹתָח ***tôtāḥ***, n.m. [1] (stout) club:– club (1)

H9372 תָּזַז ***tāzaz***, v. [1] [H] to cut down:– cut down (1)

H9373 תַּזְנוּת ***taznût***, n.f.abst. [20] [√ 2388]. promiscuity, prostitution, act of lust:– prostitution (8), promiscuity (5), lust (2), favors (1), illicit favors (1), promiscuous (1), prostitute (1), use as a prostitute (1 [+2388])

H9374 תַּחְבֻּלוֹת ***taḥbulôt***, n.f. [6] guidance, advice, giving direction:– guidance (4), advice (1), direction (1)

H9375 תֹּחוּ ***tōḥû***, n.pr.m. [1] [cf. 9346]. Tohu:– Tohu (1)

H9376 תַּחְכְּמֹנִי ***taḥkºmōnî***, a.g. [1] Tahkemonite:– Tahkemonite (1)

H9377 תַּחֲלֻאִים ***taḥªlu'îm***, n.pl.m. [5] [√ 2688]. diseases:– diseases (3), pain (1), ravages (1)

H9378 תְּחִלָּה ***teḥillâ***, n.f. [22] [√ 2725]. beginning, at first:– beginning (7), first (5), began (2), earlier (2 [+928, 2021]), first time (2), already (1 [+928, 2021]), before (1 [+928, 2021]), led in thanksgiving (1 [+3344]), NDT (1)

H9379 תַּחְמָס ***taḥmās***, n.[m.] [2] [√ 2803?]. screech owl:– screech owl (2)

H9380 תַּחַן ***taḥan***, n.pr.m. [2] [→ 9385; cf. 2858?]. Tahan, "[poss.] *grace, favor*":– Tahan (2)

H9381 תַּחֲנָה ***taḥªnâ***, n.f. [1] [√ 2837; cf. 9386]. encampment:– set up camp (1)

H9382 [1]תְּחִנָּה ***teḥinnâ[1]***, n.f. [25] [→ 9383; cf. 2858]. plea, petition, request, supplication:– plea (10), petition (4), plea for mercy (2), supplication (2), cry for mercy (1), gracious (1), mercy (1), pleading (1 [+5877]), pleas (1), request (1), supplications (1)

H9383 [2]תְּחִנָּה ***teḥinnâ[2]***, n.pr.m. [1] [√ 9382; cf. 2858]. Tehinnah, "*supplication for favor*":– Tehinnah (1)

H9384 תַּחֲנוּן ***taḥªnûn***, n.[m.]pl.abst. [18] [√ 2858]. plea for mercy, petition, supplication:– cry for mercy (6 [+7754]), cry for mercy (2), pray (2), begging for mercy (1), mercy (1), petition (1), petitions (1), pleading (1), requests (1), supplication (1), supplications (1)

H9385 תַּחֲנִי ***taḥªnî***, a.g. [1] [√ 9380; cf. 2858?]. Tahanite, "*of Tahan*":– Tahanite (1)

H9386 תַּחֲנֹתִי ***taḥªnōtî***, n.f. Not used in NIVEBC [√ 2837?]. see 9381

H9387 תַּחְפַּנְחֵס ***taḥpanḥēs***, n.pr.loc. [7] [cf. 7090]. Tahpanhes, "*fortress of Penhase [the black man]*":– Tahpanhes (7)

H9388 תַּחְפְּנֵיס ***taḥpºnês***, n.pr.f. [3] Tahpenes, "*wife of the king*":– Tahpenes (3)

H9389 תַּחְרָא ***taḥrā'***, n.[m.] [2] collar, edge around an opening in a garment:– collar (1), collar (1 [+7023])

H9390 תַּחְרֵעַ ***taḥrēa'***, n.pr.m. [1] [cf. 9308]. Tahrea, "[poss.] *clever one*":– Tahrea (1)

H9391 [1]תַּחַשׁ ***taḥaš[1]***, n.m. [14] [→ 9392]. (leather of) a sea cow:– durable^S (6), other^S (3), another type^S (2), another^S (1), durable leather^S (1), fine leather (1)

H9392 [2]תַּחַשׁ ***taḥaš[2]***, n.pr.m. [1] [√ 9391]. Tahash, "*species of dolphin*":– Tahash (1)

H9393 [1]תַּחַת ***taḥat[1]***, n.[m.] & adv. & pp. [500] [→ 9394, 9395, 9396, 9397; cf. 5737; 10757]. under, in place of, succeeding (on a sequence):– under (150), succeeded (65), for (33), in place of (24), in place (23), instead of (19), below (16 [+4946]), beneath (13), below (10), under (7 [+4946]), because (6 [+889]), succeed (5), against (4 [+4946, 3338]), beneath (4 [+4946]), instead (4), where (4), with (4), in (3), in return for (3), replace (3), while married to (3), among (2), at the foot of (2), before (2), for feet (2), from (2 [+4946]), have a home (2 [+8905]), in exchange for (2), on (2), place (2), succeeded (2 [+7756]), to (2), to compensate for (2), unchanged (2 [+6641]), underneath (2), although (1), amid (1), as a direct result (1 [+3338]), at feet (1), at foot of (1), at the spot (1), because (1 [+3954]), by (1), for (1 [+889]), for (1 [+889]), from (1 [+889]), have (1 [+3780, 3338]), have on hand (1 [+448, 3338]), have on hand (1 [+3780, 3338]), homes (1), in exchange (1), in land (1), in position (1), in stead (1), in the place of (1), instead of (1 [+889]), land^S (1), legs (1), lower (1 [+4946]), made subject to (1 [+4044, 3338]), mine (1 [+3276]), move about (1 [+7756, 4946]), on behalf (1), on the spot (1), outside (1 [+4946]), pad (1 [+4946]), position (1), replace (1 [+8492]), replace (1 [+995, 448]), replaced (1 [+5989]), replaced (1 [+6641]), resting on (1 [+4946]), riding (1), since (1 [+889]), since (1 [+3954]), submission (1), succeeds (1), successor (1 [+6641]), supported (1), take charge of (1 [+3338]), take the place of (1), take the place of (1 [+2118]), though (1), to (1 [+3338]), to (1 [+4946]), underfoot (1 [+8079]), underneath (1 [+4946]), undersides (1), where stand (1), why (1 [+4537]), NDT (14)

H9394 [2]תַּחַת ***taḥat[2]***, n.pr.m. [4] [√ 9393]. Tahath, "*compensation*":– Tahath (4)

H9395 [3]תַּחַת ***taḥat[3]***, n.pr.loc. [2] [√ 9393]. Tahath, "*compensation*":– Tahath (2)

H9396 תַּחְתּוֹן ***taḥtôn***, a. [14] [√ 9393]. lower:– lower (11), lowest (3)

H9397 תַּחְתִּי ***taḥtî***, a. & subst. [19] [√ 9393]. lower; (n.) depths, below, sometimes referring to the underworld, the realm of the dead:– below (7), depths (4), lower (4), lowest (2), beneath (1), foot (1)

H9398 תַּחְתִּים חָדְשִׁי ***taḥtîm ḥodšî***, n.pr.loc. [1] [cf. 2547]. Tahtim Hodshi:– Tahtim Hodshi (1)

H9399 תִּיכוֹן ***tîkôn***, a. [10] [√ 9348]. middle, center:– middle (7), center (2), there[S] (1 [+2021])

H9400 תִּילוֹן ***tîlôn***, n.pr.m. [1] [cf. 9353]. Tilon:– Tilon (1)

H9401 תֵּימָא ***têmā'***, n.pr.loc. [& m.?] [5] Tema, *"on the right [not left] side, hence south country"*:– Tema (4), Tema (1 [+824])

H9402 [1]תֵּימָן ***têmān[1]***, n.f. [23] [→ 9403; cf. 3545]. south, southward, south wind:– south (8), south (5 [+2025]), south (3 [+5582, 2025]), south (2 [+5582]), south wind (2), south (1 [+2025, 5582, 2025]), southern (1 [+2025, 5582, 2025]), southward (1 [+4946])

H9403 [2]תֵּימָן ***têmān[2]***, n.pr.loc. [11] [→ 9404; cf. 3545, 9402]. Teman, *"on the right [not left] side, hence south country"*:– Teman (11)

H9404 תֵּימָנִי ***têmānî***, a.g. [8] [√ 9403]. Temanite, *"of Teman"*:– Temanite (6), Temanites (2)

H9405 תֵּימְנִי ***têmᵉnî***, n.pr.m. [1] [√ 3545]. Temeni, *"one from the right* [not left], *hence southerner"*:– Temeni (1)

H9406 תִּימָרָה ***tîmārâ***, n.f. [2] [→ 9473?, 9477; cf. 9469]. column (of smoke):– billows (1), column (1)

H9407 תִּיצִי ***tîṣî***, a.g. [1] Tizite:– Tizite (1)

H9408 תִּירוֹשׁ ***tîrôš***, n.m. [38] [√ 3769]. new wine:– new wine (35), grapes (1), juice (1), wine (1)

H9409 תִּירְיָא ***tîrᵉyā'***, n.pr.m. [1] Tiria:– Tiria (1)

H9410 תִּירָס ***tîrās***, n.pr.loc. [& m.?] [2] Tiras:– Tiras (2)

H9411 תַּיִשׁ ***tayiš***, n.m. [4] male goat:– male goats (2), goats (1), he-goat (1)

H9412 תֹּךְ ***tōk***, n.m. [4] oppression, threat:– threats (2), oppression (1), oppressor (1 [+408])

H9413 תָּכָה ***tākâ***, v. [1] [Pu] to bow down:– bow down (1)

H9414 תְּכוּנָה ***tᵉkûnâ***, n.f. [3] [√ 3922]. dwelling; arrangement, supply:– arrangement (1), dwelling (1), supply (1)

H9415 תֻּכִּיִּים ***tukkiyyîm***, n.m.[pl.] [2] baboons; some sources: monkeys, peacocks, poultry:– baboons (2)

H9416 תִּכְלָה ***tiklâ***, n.f. [1] [√ 3983]. perfection:– perfection (1)

H9417 תַּכְלִית ***taklît***, n.f. [5] [√ 3983]. end, limit, boundary:– boundary (1), end (1), farthest recesses (1 [+3972]), limits (1), nothing but (1)

H9418 תְּכֵלֶת ***tᵉkēlet***, n.f. [49] blue material:– blue (42), blue yarn (3), blue cloth (2), blue material (2)

H9419 תָּכַן ***tākan***, v. [18] [→ 5504, 9420, 9422; cf. 9545; 10771]. [Q] to weigh, estimate; [N] to be just, be weighted; [P] to hold firm, mark off, understand; [Pu] to be determined:– just (5), unjust (4 [+4202]), weighs (2), amount been determined (1), are weighed (1), fathom (1), hold firm (1), marked off (1), measured out (1 [+928, 4500]), weighed (1)

H9420 [1]תֹּכֶן ***tōken[1]***, n.m. [2] [√ 9419]. full quota, fixed measure; size, measurement:– full quota (1), size (1)

H9421 [2]תֹּכֶן ***tōken[2]***, n.pr.loc. [1] Token, *"measure"*:– Token (1)

H9422 תָּכְנִית ***toknît***, n.f. [2] [√ 9419]. (perfect) example, design:– perfection (2)

H9423 תַּכְרִיךְ ***takrîk***, n.m. [1] robe, mantle:– robe (1)

H9424 תֵּל ***tēl***, n.[m.] [5] [→ 9425, 9426, 9427, 9435, 9446?]. mound, heap, ruin:– heap of ruins (1), mound (1), mounds (1), ruin (1), ruins (1)

H9425 תֵּל אָבִיב ***tēl 'ābîb***, n.pr.loc. [1] [√ 9424 + 26]. Tel Abib, *"mound of barley; mound of storm tide; mound of flood"*:– Tel Aviv (1)

H9426 תֵּל חַרְשָׁא ***tēl haršā'***, n.pr.loc. [2] [√ 9424 + 3091 *or* 3093]. Tel Harsha, *"mound of the forest* or *craftsman"*:– Tel Harsha (2)

H9427 תֵּל מֶלַח ***tēl melaḥ***, n.pr.loc. [2] [√ 9424 + 4875]. Tel Melah, *"mound of salt"*:– Tel Melah (2)

H9428 תָּלָא ***tālā'***, v. [3] [cf. 9434]. [Q] to hang; [Qp] to be suspended, be determined:– determined (1), hung (1), suspense (1)

H9429 תַּלְאֻבוֹת ***tal'ubôt***, n.f. [1] burning heat:– burning heat (1)

H9430 תְּלָאָה ***tᵉlā'â***, n.f. [5] [→ 5505; cf. 4206]. hardship, burden:– hardship (2), hardships (2), burden (1)

H9431 תְּלַאשָּׂר ***tᵉla'śśār***, n.pr.loc. [2] [√ 9445]. Tel Assar, *"ruined city, mound of Assar"*:– Tel Assar (2)

H9432 תִּלְבֹּשֶׁת ***tilbōšet***, n.f. [1] [√ 4252]. clothing, what is worn:– put on (1 [+4252])

H9433 תִּגְלַת פִּלְאֶסֶר, תִּלְּגַת פִּלְנְאֶסֶר ***tillᵉgat pilnᵉ'eser***, ***tillᵉgat pilneser***, n.pr.m. [3] [cf. 9325]. Tiglath-Pileser (Tilgat-Pilneser), *"my trust is in the son of [the temple] Esharra"*:– Tiglath-Pileser (3)

H9434 תָּלָה ***tālâ***, v. [27] [→ 3849, 9002, 9437; cf. 9428]. [Q, P] to hang, suspend; [Qp, N] to be hung:– impaled (9), hung (4), hang (3), exposed (2), hanging (2), impale (2), been hung up (1), impaling (1), is hung (1), suspends (1), were impaled (1)

H9435 תָּלוּל ***tālûl***, a. [1] [√ 9424]. lofty, towering:– lofty (1)

H9436 תֶּלַח ***telaḥ***, n.pr.m. [1] Telah, *"fissure, split, fracture"*:– Telah (1)

H9437 תְּלִי ***tᵉlî***, n.[m.] [1] [√ 9434]. quiver (case to hold arrows that hangs or dangles):– quiver (1)

H9438 תָּלַל ***tālal***, v. [9] [→ 4562; cf. 2252]. [H] to make a fool of, deceive, cheat; [Ho] to be deluded:– deceive (2), made a fool of (2), act deceitfully (1), cheated (1), deceives (1), deluded (1), making a fool of (1)

H9439 תֶּלֶם ***telem***, n.m. [5] [→ 9440]. furrow, plowed line:– furrows (2), plowed (2), furrow (1)

H9440 תַּלְמַי ***talmay***, n.pr.m. [6] [√ 9439]. Talmai, "[poss.] *[my] furrow maker"*:– Talmai (6)

H9441 תַּלְמִיד ***talmîd***, n.[m.] [1] [√ 4340]. student, pupil:– student (1)

H9442 תְּלֻנּוֹת ***tᵉlunnôt***, n.f. [8] [√ 4296]. grumbling, complaint:– grumbling (5), complaints (1), constant grumbling (1 [+4296]), grumbling (1 [+4296])

H9443 תָּלַע ***tāla'***, v.den. [1] [√ 9355]. [Pu] to be clad in scarlet material:– clad in scarlet (1)

H9444 תַּלְפִּיּוֹת ***talpiyyôt***, n.f.pl. [1] elegance or courses of stones:– courses of stone (1)

H9445 תְּלַשָּׂר ***tᵉlaśśār***, n.pr.loc. Not used in NIVEBC [√ 9431]. Telassar, see 9431

H9446 תַּלְתַּל ***taltāl***, n.f.? [1] [√ 9424?]. wavy:– wavy (1)

H9447 תָּם ***tām***, a. [17] [→ 3462; cf. 9462]. blameless, flawless, perfect:– blameless (8), fitted (2 [+3481]), blameless (1 [+2006]), content (1), flawless (1), innocent (1), integrity (1), perfect (1), strong (1)

H9448 תֹּם ,תֹּם ***tōm***, n.[m.] [23] [→ 9460; cf. 9462]. blamelessness, integrity, innocence:– blameless (9), integrity (6), at random (2 [+4200]), clear (2), full (1), full measure (1), person of integrity (1 [+2006]), quite innocently (1 [+4200])

H9449 תָּמַהּ ***tāmah***, v. [10] [→ 9451; 10755, 10763]. [Q] to be astonished, be astounded, be stunned; [Htpal] to be stunned in oneself:– utterly amazed (2 [+9449]), aghast (1), amazed (1), appalled (1), astounded (1), look aghast (1), looked in astonishment (1), stunned (1), surprised (1)

H9450 תֻּמָּה ***tummâ***, n.f. [5] [√ 9462]. integrity, blamelessness:– integrity (4), blameless (1)

H9451 תִּמָּהוֹן ***timmāhôn***, n.[m.] [2] [√ 9449]. confusion, panic:– confusion (1), panic (1)

H9452 תַּמּוּז ***tammûz***, n.pr.[m.] [1] Tammuz (pagan god):– god Tammuz (1)

H9453 תְּמוֹל ***tᵉmôl***, subst.adv. [22] [→ 919]. yesterday; (generally) before, in the past:– before (6 [+8997]), malice aforethought (4 [+8533, 4946, 8997]), yesterday (4), had the habit (2 [+4946, 8997]), as usual (1 [+3869, 8997]), before (1 [+4946, 8997]), for some time (1 [+1685, 1685, 8997]), had been (1 [+8997]), in the past (1 [+8997]), past (1 [+8997])

H9454 תְּמוּנָה ***tᵉmûnâ***, n.f. [10] [√ 4786]. form, image, likeness:– form (7), image (1), kind (1), likeness (1)

H9455 תְּמוּרָה ***tᵉmûrâ***, n.f. [6] [√ 4614]. substitution, transfer, exchange:– substitute (2), had for (1), return (1), trading (1), transfer of property (1 [+3972, 1821])

H9456 תְּמוּתָה ***tᵉmûtâ***, n.f. [2] [√ 4637]. death:– death (1), die (1)

H9457 תֶּמַח ***temaḥ***, n.pr.m. [2] [√ 4681?]. Temah:– Temah (2)

H9458 תָּמִיד ***tāmîd***, n.m. (used as adv.) [104] (adv.) continually, constantly, regularly, daily:– always (24), regular (23), continually (13), regularly (11), ever (8), daily sacrifice (5), constantly (2), forever (2), at all times (1), constant (1), continual (1), continued (1), continuing (1), continuously (1), daily (1), day after day (1 [+3429]), endless (1), keep on (1), kept (1), lasting (1 [+6409]), long (1), never (1 [+4202]), often (1), NDT (1)

H9459 תָּמִים ***tāmîm***, a. [90] [√ 9462]. without defect, blameless, perfect:– without defect (47), blameless (18), perfect (6), full (3), good faith (2), secure (2), whole (2), all (1), blameless (1 [+1475]), blameless (1 [+1505]), entire (1), thummim (1), truth (1), wholeheartedly (1 [+4213]), NDT (3)

H9460 תֻּמִּים ***tummîm***, n.m.[pl.] [5] [√ 9448; cf. 9462]. Thummim, formally "Perfections," devices used by the high priest to make God's will known, possibly related to the casting of lots:– Thummim (5)

H9461 תָּמַךְ ***tāmak***, v. [21] [Q] to take hold of, grasp, hold secure; [N] to be seized:– uphold (3), gain (2), hold fast (2), holds (2), accepting (1), gains (1), grasps (1), held (1), held up (1), hold back (1), lead straight (1), make secure (1), take hold (1), taken hold (1), took hold (1), upholds (1)

H9462 תָּמַם ***tāmam***, v. [64] [→ 3462, 5507, 9447, 9448, 9450, 9459, 9460]. [Q] to complete, finish, perfect; [H] to end, stop, complete; [Ht] to show oneself blameless:– gone (5), completely (4), end (4), perish (3), all (2), blameless (2), completed (2), finished (2), last (2), over (2), put an end (2), show yourself blameless (2), vanish (2), all gone (1), burn away (1), burned (1), burned away (1), completely (1 [+3983, 6330]), consumed (1), cook well (1), destroy (1), destroyed (1), die (1), died (1), done (1), doomed (1), down to (1 [+6330]), ended (1), fail (1), full (1), have get ready (1), meet end (1), overtaken (1), perfect (1), perished (1), perishing (1), settled (1), spent (1), stop (1), NDT (4)

H9463 תִּמְנָה ***timnâ***, n.pr.loc. [12] [→ 9464; cf. 4948?]. Timnah, *"lot, portion"*:– Timnah (11), there[S] (1 [+928, 2025])

H9464 תִּמְנִי ***timnî***, a.g. [1] [√ 9463; cf. 4948?]. Timnite, *"of Timnah"*:– Timnite's (1)

H9465 תִּמְנָע ***timna'***, n.pr.m. & f. [6] Timna, *"lot, portion"*:– Timna (6)

H9466 תִּמְנַת־חֶרֶס ***timnat-ḥeres***, n.pr.loc. [1] [√ 4948? + 3065]. Timnath Heres, *"place of the sun [worship]"*:– Timnath Heres (1)

H9467 תִּמְנַת־סֶרַח ***timnat-seraḥ***, n.pr.loc. [2] [√ 4948? + 3064]. Timnath Serah, *"place of the sun [worship]"*:– Timnath Serah (2)

H9468 תֶּמֶס ***temes***, n.m. [1] [√ 5022]. melting away:– melts away (1)

H9469 [1]תָּמָר ***tāmār[1]***, n.m. [12] [→ 1265, 2954, 6559, 9470, 9471, 9472, 9474; cf. 9406]. palm tree:– palms (6), palm (2), palm tree (2), palm trees (2)

H9470 [2]תָּמָר ***tāmār[2]***, n.pr.f. [22] [√ 9469]. Tamar, *"date palm"*:– Tamar (22)

H9471 [3]תָּמָר ***tāmār[3]***, n.pr.loc. [3] [√ 9469]. Tamar, *"date palm"*:– Tamar (3)

H9472 [1]תֹּמֶר ***tōmer[1]***, n.m.loc. [1] [√ 9469]. the Palm (of Deborah: a location), *"date palm"*:– Palm (1)

H9473 [2]תֹּמֶר ***tōmer[2]***, n.m. [1] [√ 607, 9406?]. scarecrow:– scarecrow (1)

H9474 תִּמֹרָה ***timōrâ***, n.f. [19] [√ 9469]. palm tree:– palm trees (14), palm tree (2), palm tree decorations (2), palm tree designs (1)

H9475 תַּמְרוּק ***tamrûq***, n.[m.] [4] [√ 5347]. beauty treatment (including massages and cleansing rituals), cosmetics:– beauty treatments (2), cosmetics (1), scrub away (1)

H9476 [1]תַּמְרוּרִים ***tamrûrîm[1]***, n.m. [3] [√ 5352]. bitterness:– bitter (2), great (1)

H9477 [2]תַּמְרוּרִים ***tamrûrîm[2]***, n.m. [1] [√ 9406]. guidepost:– guideposts (1)

H9478 תַּן ***tan***, n.[m. & f.] [14] [√ 9490]. jackal:– jackals (13), jackal (1)

H9479 [1]תָּנָה ***tānâ[1]***, v. [2] [√ 924]. [Q, H] to sell oneself as a prostitute:– sold (2)

H9480 [2]תָּנָה ***tānâ[2]***, v. [2] [P] to commemorate, recount:– commemorate (1), recite (1)

H9481 תְּנוּאָה ***tᵉnû'â***, n.f. [2] [√ 5648]. fault, opposition, what one has against another:– against (1), fault (1)

H9482 תְּנוּבָה ***tᵉnûbâ***, n.f. [5] [√ 5649]. crop, produce:– fruit (3), crops (1), food (1)

H9483 תְּנוּךְ ***tᵉnûk***, n.[m.] [8] lobe (of the ear):– lobe (5), lobes (2), NDT (1)

H9484 תְּנוּמָה ***tᵉnûmâ***, n.f. [5] [√ 5670]. slumber, sleep:– slumber (5)

H9485 תְּנוּפָה ***tᵉnûpâ***, n.f. [30] [√ 5677]. wave offering, what it waved:– wave offering (21), waved (5), blows (1), uplifted (1), was waved (1 [+5677]), wave offerings (1)

H9486 תַּנּוּר ***tannûr***, n.m. [15] oven, furnace, firepot (a portable oven for cooking bread):– oven (8), furnace (3), ovens (3), firepot (1)

H9487 תַּנְחוּמוֹת ***tanḥûmôt***, n.[m.pl.] [2] [√ 5714]. consolation:– consolation (1), consolations (1)

H9488 תַּנְחוּמִים ***tanḥûmîm***, n.m.[pl.] [3] [√ 5714]. consolation, comfort:– comforting (1), consolation (1), console (1)

H9489 תַּנְחֻמֶת ***tanḥumet***, n.pr.m. [2] [√ 5714]. Tanhumeth, *"comfort"*:– Tanhumeth (2)

H9490 תַּנִּין ***tannîn***, n.m. [15] [→ 6531, 9478]. serpent, snake; monster of the deep; (pr.n.) Jackal (Well); can refer to large sea creatures as well as to mythological monsters of chaos opposed to God:– monster (5), snake (3), serpent (2), Jackal (1), creatures of the sea (1), great sea creatures (1), monster of the deep (1), serpents (1)

H9491 [1]תִּנְשֶׁמֶת ***tinšemet[1]***, n.f. [1] [√ 5971]. chameleon:– chameleon (1)

H9492 [2]תִּנְשֶׁמֶת ***tinšemet***[2], n.f. [2] [√ 5971]. white owl:– white owl (2)

H9493 תָּעַב ***tā'ab***, v.den. [22] [→ 9359?; cf. 9290]. [N] to be repulsive, be vile, be rejected; [P] to detest, abhor, loathe, despise; [H] to behave in a vile manner:– detest (6), vile (4), despise (3), abhorred (2), utterly detest (2 [+9493]), behaved in the vilest manner (1 [+4394]), degraded (1), loathed (1), rejected (1), repulsive (1)

H9494 תָּעָה ***tā'â***, v. [50] [→ 9360; cf. 3246]. [Q] to wander, go astray; [N] to deceive oneself; to stagger around (as a drunk); [H] to lead astray, make wander, mislead:– led astray (6), leads astray (4), go astray (3), lead astray (3), wandered (3), went astray (3), reel (2), stray (2), strayed (2), wayward (2), deceive himself (1), did[s] (1), error (1), falters (1), go about (1), gone astray (1), had wander (1), made a fatal mistake (1 [+928, 5883]), made wander (1), make stagger (1), make wander (1), makes stagger (1), makes wander (1), mislead (1), spread (1), staggers around (1), strays (1), wander about (1), wandering around (1), wandering off (1)

H9495 תֹּעוּ ***tō'û***, n.pr.m. [2] [cf. 9497]. Tou:– Tou (2)

H9496 תְּעוּדָה ***tᵉ'ûdâ***, n.f. [3] [√ 6386]. testimony; method of legalizing transactions (sandal transaction):– testimony of warning (2), method of legalizing transactions (1)

H9497 תֹּעִי ***tō'î***, n.pr.m. [3] [cf. 9495]. Tou (Toi):– Tou (2), he[s] (1)

H9498 [1]תְּעָלָה ***tᵉ'ālâ***[1], n.f. [9] [√ 6590?]. trench, channel, aqueduct:– aqueduct (3), trench (3), channel (1), channels (1), tunnel (1)

H9499 [2]תְּעָלָה ***tᵉ'ālâ***[2], n.f. [2] [√ 6590]. healing:– healing (2)

H9500 תַּעֲלוּלִים ***ta'ᵃlûlîm***, n.m.pl.abst. [2] [√ 6618]. wantonness; harsh treatment, referring to impulsive people:– children (1), harsh treatment (1)

H9501 תַּעֲלֻם ***ta'ᵃlum***, n.f. Not used in NIVEBC [√ 6623]. hidden thing

H9502 תַּעֲלֻמָה ***ta'ᵃlumâ***, n.f. [3] [√ 6623]. secret; hidden thing:– secrets (2), hidden things (1)

H9503 תַּעֲנוּג ***ta'ᵃnûg***, n.[m.] [5] [√ 6695]. delight, pleasure; living in luxury:– delight (1), delights (1), delights of a heart (1), live in luxury (1), pleasant (1)

H9504 תַּעֲנִית ***ta'ᵃnît***, n.f. [1] [√ 6700]. self-abasement, mortification:– self-abasement (1)

H9505 תַּעְנָךְ ***ta'ᵃnak***, n.pr.loc. [7] Taanach:– Taanach (7)

H9506 תָּעַע ***tā'a'***, v. [2] [→ 9511]. [Pil] to mock; [Htpal] to scoff at:– scoffed (1), tricking (1)

H9507 תְּעֻפָה ***tᵉ'upâ***, n.f. [1] [√ 6415]. darkness:– darkness (1)

H9508 תַּעֲצֻמוֹת ***ta'ᵃṣumôt***, n.f.[pl.] [1] [√ 6793]. strength, might:– strength (1)

H9509 תַּעַר ***ta'ar***, n.m. [13] [√ 6867]. razor, knife, scabbard:– sheath (6), razor (4), have shave (1 [+6296]), knife (1), unsheathed (1 [+3655, 4946])

H9510 תַּעֲרוּבוֹת ***ta'ᵃrûbôt***, n.f.[pl.] [2] [√ 6842]. hostage, formally "son of a pledge":– hostages (2 [+1201])

H9511 תַּעְתֻּעִים ***ta'tu'îm***, n.[m.]pl.abst. [2] [√ 9506]. mockery:– mockery (2)

H9512 [1]תֹּף ***tōp***[1], n.m. [16] [→ 4191, 9528; cf. 9513]. tambourine, timbrel:– timbrels (9), timbrel (4), music of timbrels (2), music of timbrel (1)

H9513 [2]תֹּף ***tōp***[2], n.m. [1] [cf. 9512]. setting, jewelry; some sources uncertain in meaning:– settings (1 [+4856])

H9514 תִּפְאֶרֶת ***tip'eret***, n.f. [51] [√ 6995]. glory, splendor, honor:– glorious (12), glory (11), splendor (8), honor (7), fine (3), beautiful (2), boasted (2), adorned (1 [+7596, 4200]), elation (1), finery (1), look (1), pride (1), NDT (1)

H9515 [1]תַּפּוּחַ ***tappûaḥ***[1], n.[m.] [6] [→ 1130, 9516, 9517; cf. 5870]. apple, apple tree:– apple tree (3), apples (3)

H9516 [2]תַּפּוּחַ ***tappûaḥ***[2], n.pr.m. [1] [√ 9515; cf. 5870]. Tappuah, "*apple*":– Tappuah (1)

H9517 [3]תַּפּוּחַ ***tappûaḥ***[3], n.pr.loc. [5] [→ 6540; cf. 5870, 9515]. Tappuah, "*apple*":– Tappuah (5)

H9518 תְּפוּצָה ***tᵉpûṣâ***, n.f.pl. [1] [√ 7046]. shattering, dispersing:– NDT (1)

H9519 תֻּפִינִים ***tupînîm***, n.[m.]pl. [1] [cf. 684?]. broken into pieces:– broken (1)

H9520 תָּפַל ***tāpal***, v. Not used in NIVEBC [→ 9522, 9524]. see 7349

H9521 [1]תָּפֵל ***tāpēl***[1], n.[m.] [5] [cf. 3260]. whitewash:– whitewash (4), whitewash (1 [+3212])

H9522 [2]תָּפֵל ***tāpēl***[2], a. [2] [→ 9524; cf. 9520]. tasteless (food); worthless (prophetic visions):– tasteless (1), worthless (1)

H9523 תֹּפֶל ***tōpel***, n.pr.loc. [1] [→ 330?]. Tophel, "*cement*":– Tophel (1)

H9524 תִּפְלָה ***tiplâ***, n.f. [3] [√ 9522; cf. 9520]. repulsiveness, wrongdoing:– wrongdoing (2), repulsive thing (1)

H9525 תְּפִלָּה ***tᵉpillâ***, n.f. [77] [√ 7137]. prayer, plea, petition:– prayer (61), prayers (10), petition (2), pray (2 [+5951]), plea (1), pray (1)

H9526 תִּפְלֶצֶת ***tipleṣet***, n.f. [1] [√ 7145]. terror, horror, a state of great fear even to the point of shuddering:– terror (1)

H9527 תִּפְסַח ***tipsaḥ***, n.pr.loc. [2] [√ 7173]. Tiphsah:– Tiphsah (2)

H9528 תָּפַף ***tāpap***, v.den. [2] [√ 9512]. [Q] to tap (play) a tambourine; [Pol] to beat (the breast):– beat (1), playing timbrels (1)

H9529 תָּפַר ***tāpar***, v. [4] [Q] to sew, mend; [P] to sew (together):– mend (1), sew (1), sewed (1), sewed together (1)

H9530 תָּפַשׂ ***tāpaś***, v. [65] [Q] to take hold of, seize, capture; [Qp] to be covered; [N] to be seized, be caught, be captured; [P] to catch (a lizard):– captured (8), seize (4), seized (4), take (4), took (4), capture (3), arrested (2), be caught (2), caught (2), grasped (2), surely be captured (2 [+9530]), taken (2), was trapped (2), archer (1 [+8008]), are caught (1), be captured (1), be taken captive (1 [+928, 2021, 4090]), been caught in the act (1), brandishing (1), capturing (1), carry (1), covered (1), deal with (1), dishonor (1), handle (1), hold (1), occupy (1), play (1), rapes (1 [+2256, 8886, 6640]), reaper (1), recapture (1), soldiers (1 [+4878]), take captive (1), take hold (1), taken over (1), took hold (1), NDT (1)

H9531 [1]תֹּפֶת ***tōpet***[1], n.f. [1] spitting:– spit (1)

H9532 [2]תֹּפֶת ***tōpet***[2], n.pr.loc. [9] Topheth:– Topheth (9)

H9533 תָּפְתֶּה ***topteh***, n.pr.loc. [1] Topheth:– Topheth (1)

H9534 תָּקְהַת ***toqhat***, n.pr.m. [1] [cf. 9363]. Tokhath:– Tokhath (1)

H9535 [1]תִּקְוָה ***tiqwâ***[1], n.f. [2] [√ 7747]. cord:– cord (1), cord (1 [+2562])

H9536 [2]תִּקְוָה ***tiqwâ***[2], n.f. [32] [→ 9537; cf. 7747]. hope, expectation:– hope (29), hopes (2), expectation (1)

H9537 [3]תִּקְוָה ***tiqwâ***[3], n.pr.m. [2] [√ 9536; cf. 7747]. Tikvah, "*hope*":– Tikvah (2)

H9538 תְּקוּמָה ***tᵉqûmâ***, n.f. [1] [√ 7756]. ability to stand:– able to stand (1)

H9539 תְּקוֹמֵם ***tᵉqômēm***, v. Not used in NIVEBC [√ 7756]. see 7756

H9540 תָּקוֹעַ ***tāqôa'***, n.[m.] [1] [√ 9546]. trumpet, for battle signals:– trumpet (1)

H9541 תְּקוֹעַ ***tᵉqôa'***, n.pr.loc. [7] [→ 9542; cf. 9546]. Tekoa:– Tekoa (7)

H9542 תְּקוֹעִי ***tᵉqô'î***, a.g. [7] [√ 9541]. Tekoite, of Tekoa, "*of Tekoa*":– from Tekoa (4), men of Tekoa (2), Tekoite (1)

H9543 תְּקוּפָה ***tᵉqûpâ***, n.f. [4] [cf. 5938]. turning, course:– turn (2), circuit (1), course (1)

H9544 תַּקִּיף ***taqqîp***, a. [1] [√ 9548; 10768]. strong, mighty:– stronger (1)

H9545 תָּקַן ***tāqan***, v. [3] [cf. 9419; 10771]. [Q] to be straight; [P] to straighten, set in order:– set in order (1), straighten (1), straightened (1)

H9546 תָּקַע ***tāqa'***, v. [68] [→ 9364, 9540, 9541, 9542, 9547]. [Q] to sound (a trumpet); to pitch, camp; to strike, clap; [Qp] to be driven; [N] to be sounded (a trumpet); to put up a security:– sounded (10), blow (9), blew (7), sound (7), blowing (5), sounding (3), clap (2), plunged (2), shakes in pledge (2), sounds (2), blow trumpets (1), blown (1), blows (1), camped (1), carried (1), drive (1), driven (1), drove (1), fastened (1), had blown (1), hung up (1), pitch (1), pitched (1), put up security (1 [+4200, 3338]), shaken in pledge (1), signal (1), sounded blast (1), tighten (1), tightened (1)

H9547 תֵּקַע ***tēqa'***, n.[m.] [1] [√ 9546]. sounding, blast (of a trumpet):– sounding (1)

H9548 תָּקַף ***tāqap***, v. [3] [→ 9544, 9549; 10772]. [Q] to overpower, overwhelm:– overpower (1), overpowered (1), overwhelm (1)

H9549 תֹּקֶף ***tōqep***, n.m. [3] [→ 9548; 10773]. power, might, authority:– authority (1), might (1), power (1)

H9550 תַּרְאֲלָה ***tar'ᵃlâ***, n.pr.loc. [1] [→ 739?, 740?]. Taralah:– Taralah (1)

H9551 תַּרְבּוּת ***tarbût***, n.f. [1] [√ 8049]. a group of the same kind, brood:– brood (1)

H9552 תַּרְבִּית ***tarbît***, n.f. [6] [√ 8049]. excessive interest, exorbitant interest:– profit (6)

H9553 תִּרְגֵּם ***tirgēm***, v. [1] [→ 8084]. [Pu] to be interpreted, be translated:– language (1)

H9554 תַּרְדֵּמָה ***tardēmâ***, n.f. [7] [√ 8101]. deep (supernatural) sleep, often a state of divine revelation and activity:– deep sleep (6), deep sleep (1 [+8120])

H9555 תִּרְהָקָה ***tirhāqâ***, n.pr.m. [2] Tirhakah:– Tirhakah (2)

H9556 תְּרוּמָה ***tᵉrûmâ***, n.f. [75] [√ 8123]. offering, special gift, contribution:– offering (19), portion (12), contributions (8), offerings (6), presented (4), contribution (3), special gifts (3 [+3338]), part (2), set aside (2), bribes (1), district (1), gift (1), portion as a special gift (1), present (1 [+8123]), present an offering (1), special gift (1), special gifts (1), special offering (1), special portion (1), terraced (1), was presented (1 [+8123]), NDT (4)

H9557 תְּרוּמִיָּה ***tᵉrûmiyyâ***, n.f.den. [1] [√ 8123]. special gift, tribute:– special gift (1)

H9558 תְּרוּעָה ***tᵉrû'â***, n.f. [36] [√ 8131]. trumpet blast, battle cry:– battle cry (5), shouts (3), shouts of joy (3), blast (2), cry (2), gave a shout (2 [+8131]), shout for joy (2), war cries (2), acclaim (1), give a shout (1 [+8131]), made noise (1 [+8131]), raised a shout (1 [+8131]), resounding (1), shout (1), shouted (1 [+8123, 7754, 928]), shouting (1), shouting (1 [+7754]), signaling (1), sound the trumpets (1), trumpet (1 [+8795]), trumpet blast (1), trumpet blasts (1), uproar (1 [+7754])

H9559 תְּרוּפָה ***tᵉrûpâ***, n.f. [1] [√ 8324]. healing:– healing (1)

H9560 תִּרְזָה ***tirzâ***, n.f. [1] cypress tree:– cypress (1)

H9561 תֶּרַח ***teraḥ***, n.pr.m. [11] [√ 9562]. Terah:– Terah (9), Terah's (1), he[s] (1)

H9562 תָּרַח ***tāraḥ***, n.pr.loc. [2] [√ 9561]. Terah:– Terah (2)

H9563 תִּרְהֲנָה ***tirhᵃnâ***, n.pr.[f.?] [1] Tirhanah:– Tirhanah (1)

H9564 תָּרְמָה ***tormâ***, n.[f.] [1] [√ 8228]. (under) cover:– Under cover (1 [+928])

H9565 תַּרְמוּק ***tarmûq***, n.m. pavement

H9566 תַּרְמוּת ***tarmût***, n.f. Not used in NIVEBC [√ 9567; cf. 8228]. see 9567

H9567 תַּרְמִית ***tarmît***, n.f. [5] [→ 9566; cf. 8228]. deceitfulness, delusion:– delusions (3), deceit (1), deceitful (1)

H9568 תֹּרֶן ***tōren***, n.m. [3] (sailing) mast; flagstaff (on top of hill):– flagstaff (1), mast (1), mast (1 [+4029])

H9569 תַּרְעִית ***tar'ît***, n.f. Not used in NIVEBC [√ 8290]. speculation

H9570 תַּרְעֵלָה ***tar'ēlâ***, n.f. [3] [√ 8302]. staggering, reeling:– makes stagger (2), made stagger (1)

H9571 תִּרְעָתִים ***tir'ātîm***, n.pr.m.pl. [1] Tirathite:– Tirathites (1)

H9572 תְּרָפִים ***tᵉrāpîm***, n.m.pl. [15] household god, idol:– household gods (10), idol (2), idols (2), idolatry (1)

H9573 [1]תִּרְצָה ***tirṣâ***[1], n.pr.f. [4] [√ 8354]. Tirzah, "*pleasant one* or *compensation*":– Tirzah (4)

H9574 [2]תִּרְצָה ***tirṣâ***[2], n.pr.loc. [14] [√ 8354]. Tirzah, "*pleasant one* or *compensation*":– Tirzah (14)

H9575 תֶּרֶשׁ ***tereš***, n.pr.m. [2] Teresh, "[perhaps] *desire*":– Teresh (2)

H9576 [1]תַּרְשִׁישׁ ***taršîš***[1], n.pr.loc. [24] [√ 8406?]. Tarshish, ships of Tarshish = trading ships, "[poss.] *yellow jasper*; [poss.] *greedy one; foundry, refinery*":– Tarshish (15), fleet of trading ships (1 [+639]), fleet of trading ships (1 [+641]), fleet of trading ships (1 [+641, 2143]), fleet of trading ships (1 [+641, 4200, 2143]), it[s] (1 [+641]), it[s] (1 [+639]), that port[s] (1), trade (1), trading ship (1 [+641])

H9577 [2]תַּרְשִׁישׁ ***taršîš***[2], n.m. [7] [√ 8406?]. chrysolite:– topaz (6), topaz (1 [+74])

H9578 [3]תַּרְשִׁישׁ ***taršîš***[3], n.pr.m. [4] [√ 8406?]. Tarshish, "[poss.] *yellow jasper;* [poss.] *greedy one; foundry, refinery*":– Tarshish (4)

H9579 תִּרְשָׁתָא ***tiršātā'***, n.m. [5] governor:– governor (5)

H9580 תַּרְתָּן ***tartān***, n.m. [2] [√ 10775, 10778]. supreme commander, second in command:– supreme commander (2)

H9581 תַּרְתָּק ***tartāq***, n.pr.[m.] [1] Tartak (pagan god):– Tartak (1)

H9582 תְּשׂוּמֶה ***tᵉśûmâ***, n.f. [1] [√ 8492]. pledge, security:– left (1)

H9583 תְּשֻׁאָה ***tᵉšu'â***, n.f. [5] [√ 8616; cf. 9589, 9594]. shouting, commotion, thundering:– commotion (1), shout (1), shouts (1), storm (1), thunders (1)

H9584 תִּשְׁבֶּה ***tišbeh***, n.pr.loc. Not used in NIVEBC [√ 9586]. Tishbeh

H9585 תִּשְׁבִּי ***tišbî***, a.g. [6] [√ 9586]. Tishbite, "*of Tishbe*":– Tishbite (6)

H9586 תִּשְׁבֵּי ***tišbê***, n.pr.loc. [1] [→ 9584, 9585]. Tishbe:– Tishbe (1)

H9587 תַּשְׁבֵּץ ***tašbēṣ***, n.[m.] [1] [√ 8687]. woven or checkered fabric:– woven (1)

H9588 תְּשׁוּבָה ***tᵉšûbâ***, n.f. [8] [√ 8740]. spring [time of year]; answer:– spring (3 [+9102]), answering (1), answers (1), spring (1 [+2021, 9102]), spring (1 [+6961, 9102]), went back (1)

H9589 תְּשֻׁוָּה ***tᵉšuwwâ***, n.f. Not used in NIVEBC [√ 8616; cf. 9594]. storm, noise, see 9583

H9590 תַּשְׁוִית ***tašwît***, n.f. Not used in NIVEBC [√ 8750]. cushioned couch, ottoman

H9591 תְּשׁוּעָה ***tᵉšû'â***, n.f. [34] [√ 3828]. deliverance, salvation, victory; divine salvation has its focus on rescue from earthly enemies, occasionally referring to salvation from guilt, sin, and punishment:– victory (12), salvation (9), help (2), saving help (2), savior (2), brought about victory

(1 [+3828]), deliverance (1), rescue (1), rescued (1), rescued (1 [+6913]), save (1), saving acts (1)

H9592 תְּשׁוּקָה ***tešûqâ***, n.f. [3] desire, longing:– desire (2), desires (1)

H9593 תְּשׁוּרָה ***tešûrâ***, n.f. [1] [√ 8802]. gift, present:– gift (1)

H9594 תֻּשִׁיָּה ***tušiyyâ***, n.f. Not used in NIVEBC [√ 8616; cf. 9589]. storm, noise, see 9583

H9595 תְּשִׁיעִי ***tešî'î***, a.num.ord. [18] [√ 9596]. ninth:– ninth (18)

H9596 תֵּשַׁע ***tēša'***, n.m. & f. [78] [→ 9595, 9597]. nine, (pl.) ninety:– nine (14), ninth (5), twenty-nine (5 [+6929, 2256]), 29 (3 [+2256, 6929]), thirty-ninth (3 [+8993, 2256]), 390 (2 [+8993, 4395, 2256]), 392 (2 [+8993, 4395, 2256, 9109]), 59,300 (2 [+2256, 2822, 547, 2256, 8993, 4395]), 95 (2 [+2256, 2822]), 973 (2 [+4395, 8679, 2256, 8993]), 98 (2 [+2256, 9046]), nineteenth (2 [+6925]), nineteenth (2 [+6926]), ninety (2), ninety-nine (2 [+9596, 2256]), ninety-nine (2 [+2256, 9596]), ninety-six (2 [+2256, 9252]), 1,290 (1 [+547, 4395, 2256]), 119 (1 [+6926, 2256, 4395]), 139 (1 [+4395, 8993, 2256]), 209 (1 [+2256, 4395]), 3,930 (1 [+8993, 547, 4395, 2256, 8993]), 595 (1 [+2822, 2256, 2256, 2822, 4395]), 690 (1 [+9252, 4395, 2256]), 895 (1 [+2822, 2256, 2256, 9046, 4395]), 90 (1), 905 (1 [+2822, 2256, 4395]), 910 (1 [+6924, 2256, 4395]), 912 (1 [+9109, 6926, 2256, 4395]), 928 (1 [+4395, 6929, 2256, 9046]), 930 (1 [+4395, 2256, 8993]), 945 (1 [+4395, 2256, 752, 2256, 2822]), 950 (1 [+4395, 2256, 2822]), 956 (1 [+4395, 2256, 2822, 2256, 9252]), 962 (1 [+9109, 2256, 9252, 2256, 4395]), 969 (1 [+2256, 9252, 2256, 9596, 4395]), 969 (1 [+9596, 2256, 9252, 2256, 4395]), forty-nine (1 [+752, 2256]), nineteen (1 [+6925]), nineteen (1 [+6926]), ninety-eight (1 [+2256, 9046])

H9597 תִּשְׁעִים ***tiš'îm***, n.indecl. Not used in NIVEBC [√ 9596]. ninety (pl. of "nine" [9596])

FEATURES OF THE ARAMAIC TO ENGLISH DICTIONARY-INDEX

G/K NUMBER
Matches the number at the end of context lines; Aramaic G/K numbers start with "A" (see pages xii, xv, xvi).

LEXICAL FORM and TRANSLITERATION
See the table of transliteration and pronunciation below.

PART OF SPEECH
The part of speech is abbreviated (see the table of abbreviations below).

FREQUENCY COUNT
Indicates the total in the NIV Hebrew text; if a Hebrew word is not in the NIV Hebrew text, it is noted by "Not used in the NIVEBC" (see page xvii).

A10009 אֲדָר ***ʼ^{a}dār***, n.pr.month [1] [√ 160].

RELATED WORDS LIST
Aramaic words related by common elements are listed by five-digit G/K number; Hebrew by one- to four-digits (see page xvii).

Adar, "[poss.] *dark, clouded*":–

DEFINITION and ETYMOLOGY
Words are defined, often with expanded explanations. If a proper name, the possible definition (etymology) is given in italics (see page xvi).

Adar (1)

NIV WORD and FREQUENCY COUNT
Following the symbol :– NIV words are listed according to their exact textual spelling and are organized according to frequency (see page xvi).

he^{S} (2), him^{S} (1), his^{S} (1)

RAISED LETTER "S"
Indicates "substitution" translation (see pages xiv, xvi).

members of family (1 [+1074])

MULTIPLE WORDS / MULTIPLE NUMBERS
More than one NIV word and/or more than one G/K number indicate multiple-word translations (see pages xi, xiii, xvi).

NDT (2)

NDT (NOT DIRECTLY TRANSLATED)
Always the final entry, this indicates the number of times the Aramaic word was not translated in the NIV for stylistic reasons (see pages xiv, xvi).

TABLE OF SIMPLIFIED TRANSLITERATION AND PRONUNCIATION

Consonants

א	ʼ	[no sound]
ב, בּ	*b*	*b*oy
ג, גּ	*g*	*g*irl
ד, דּ	*d*	*d*og
ה	*h*	*h*ot
ו	*w*	*v*ote
ז	*z*	*z*ip
ח	*ḥ*	Ba*ch*
ט	*ṭ*	*t*ip
י	*y*	*y*es
ךּ, כ, כּ	*k*	*k*it
ל	*l*	*l*et
ם, מ	*m*	*m*other
ן, נ	*n*	*n*ot
ס	*s*	*s*ip
ע	ʻ	[no sound]
ף, פ, פּ	*p*	*p*et
ץ, צ	*ṣ*	si*ts*
ק	*q*	tor*q*ue
ר	*r*	*r*ot
שׂ	*ś*	*s*ip
שׁ	*š*	*sh*ip
ת, תּ	*t*	*t*ip

Vowels

הָ	*â*	f*a*ther
◌ָ	*ā*	f*a*ther
◌ַ	*a*	f*a*ther
◌ֲ	^{a}	b*a*ton
וּ	*û*	t*u*ne
◌ֻ	*u*	s*u*re
◌ֵי	*ê*	th*ey*
◌ֵ	*ē*	th*ey*
◌ֶ	*e*	g*e*t
◌ְ if (vocal)	^{e}	s*e*lect
◌ֱ	^{e}	s*e*lect
◌ִי	*î*	mach*i*ne
◌ִ	*i*	p*i*n
וֹ	*ô*	ph*o*ne
◌ֹ	*ō*	ph*o*ne
◌ָ	*o*	ph*o*ne
◌ֳ	^{o}	m*o*tel

TABLE OF ARAMAIC DICTIONARY ABBREVIATIONS

&	and	excl.	exclamation	pp.	preposition	[Ho]	Hophal
+	plus: in combination with	f.	feminine	pr.	proper [noun]	[Hp]	Haphel passive
?	uncertain	fig.	figurative(ly)	pref.	prefix	[Hsh]	Hishtaphel
[]	uncertain part of speech	g.	gentilic	prob.	probably	[Hth]	Hithaphal
→	see these related words	indecl.	indeclinable	pt.	particle	[Htpa]	Hitpaal
√	see this organizing word	indef.	indefinite	ptcp.	participle	[Htpe]	Hitpeel
1.	first person	inf.	infinitive	rel.	relative	[Htpol]	Hitpolel
2.	second person	intens.	intensive	s.	singular	[Htt]	Ettaphal
3.	third person	inter.	interrogative	subst.	substantive	[Itpa]	Itpaal
a.	adjective	interj.	interjection	suf.	suffix	[Itpe]	Itpeel
abst.	abstract	l.	loanword	temp.	temporal	[Itpo]	Itpoal
adv.	adverb	loc.	location	v.	verb	[P]	Peal
art.	article	m.	masculine	var.	variant	[Pa]	Pael
c.	conjunction	n.	noun	vbl.	verbal	[Pap]	Pael passive
col.	collective	neg.	negative			[Peil]	Peil
com.	common gender	num.	numeral			[Po]	Poel
demo.	demonstrative	ord.	ordinal			[Pol]	Polel
den.	denominative	p.	pronoun	Aramaic Verbal Stems		[Pp]	Peal passive (participle)
du.	dual number	pl.	plural	[A]	Aphel	[Pu]	Pual
emph.	emphatic	poss.	possibly	[H]	Haphel	[Sh]	Shaphel

ARAMAIC TO ENGLISH DICTIONARY-INDEX

A10001 א **'**, letter. Not used in NIVEBC [√ 1]. letter of the Aramaic alphabet

A10002 אָ- **-ā'**, art.suf. [813] [√ 10191]. the, a; indicates vocative: O; indicates emphatic state:– the (402), your Majesty (19 [+10421]), a (16), this (7), these (5), his[S] (4), him[S] (3 [+10421]), that (3), an (2), birds (2 [+10616, 10723]), continually (2 [+10089, 10753]), cordial greetings (2 [+10720, 10353, 10002]), ever (2 [+10550]), he[S] (2 [+10421]), my[S] (2), Trans-Euphrates (1 [+10526, 10468]), as soon as (1 [+10089, 10530, 10168]), as soon as (1 [+10232, 10341, 10168]), certainly (1 [+10327]), ever (1 [+10527, 10550]), forever (1 [+10550]), forever (1 [+10527, 10509]), forever (1 [+10527, 10550]), forever (1 [+10378, 10550]), he (1 [+10421]), he[S] (1 [+10453, 10421]), he[S] (1 [+10453, 10421]), his[S] (1 [+10421]), his[S] (1 [+10421]), immediately (1 [+10734]), immediately (1 [+10734]), it[S] (1), it[S] (1 [+10424]), it[S] (1 [+10418]), it[S] (1 [+10614]), its[S] (1), never end (1 [+10527, 10509]), order (1 [+10682, 10302]), she[S] (1 [+10423]), sundown (1 [+10436, 10728]), them[S] (1 [+10038]), they[S] (1 [+10353, 10553]), this[S] (1 [+10418]), what[S] (1 [+10418]), when (1 [+10089, 10530]), who[S] (1 [+10131]), your Majesty's (1 [+10421]), NDT (308)

A10003 אַב **'ab**, n.m. [9] [√ 3]. father, predecessor, ancestor (not necessarily male):– father (5), ancestors (2), predecessors (1), NDT (1)

A10004 אֵב **'ēb**, n.m. [3] [√ 4]. fruit:– fruit (3)

A10005 אבד **'abad**, v. [7] [√ 6]. [P] to perish; [H] to execute; [Ho] to be destroyed:– execute (2), completely destroyed (1 [+10722, 10221]), destroyed (1), executed (1), execution (1), perish (1)

A10006 אֶבֶן **'eben**, n.f. [8] [√ 74]. rock, stone, including hewn or unhewn stones, stone slabs and bricks:– rock (3), stone (3), large stones (2 [+10146])

A10007 אִגְּרָה **'iggᵉrâ**, n.f. [3] [√ 115]. letter:– letter (3)

A10008 אֱדַיִן **'ᵉdayin**, adv. [57] [√ 255]. then, thus, so then:– then (13 [+10089]), then (11), so (8 [+10089]), so (3), when (2 [+10089]), also (1 [+10358]), and (1 [+10221]), as soon as (1 [+10427, 10168]), at this (1), finally (1), now (1), that day[S] (1), therefore (1 [+10089]), thus (1 [+10089]), NDT (11)

A10009 אֲדָר **'ᵃdār**, n.pr.month [1] [√ 160]. Adar, "[poss.] *dark, clouded*":– Adar (1)

A10010 אִדַּר **'iddar**, n.m. [1] threshing floor:– threshing floor (1)

A10011 אֲדַרְגָּזַר **'ᵃdargāzar**, n.m. [2] adviser, counselor, likely the king's "minister of information":– advisers (2)

A10012 אַדְרַזְדָּא **'adrazdā'**, adv. [1] with diligence, zealously:– with diligence (1)

A10013 אֶדְרָע **'edrā'**, n.[f.] [1] [√ 10185; 274, 2432]. arm; fig., power, force:– force (1)

A10014 אַזְדָּא **'azdā'**, a. [2] firm, assured:– firmly (2)

A10015 אזה **'azâ**, v. [3] [P] to heat; [Pp] to be heated:– heated (1), hot (1), hotter (1)

A10016 אזל **'azal**, v. [7] [√ 261]. [P] to go, return:– returned (2), went (2), go (1), NDT (2)

A10017 אַח **'aḥ**, n.m. [1] [√ 278]. brother:– fellow Israelites (1)

A10018 אַחֲוָיָה **'aḥᵃwāyâ**, n.f. Not used in NIVEBC [√ 10252]. declaring

A10019 אֲחִידָה **'ᵃḥîdâ**, n.f. [1] [√ 2648]. riddle:– riddles (1)

A10020 אַחְמְתָא **'aḥmᵉtā'**, n.pr.loc. [1] Ecbatana, "[perhaps] *place of gathering*":– Ecbatana (1)

A10021 אחר **'aḥar**, pp. [3] [→ 10022, 10024; 339]. after, in the future:– after (1), in the future (1 [+10180]), to come (1 [+10201, 10180])

A10022 אָחֳרִי **'āḥᵒrî**, n.f.constr. [1] [√ 10021; 344]. end (of days), (days) to come:– to come (1)

A10023 אָחֳרִי **'oḥᵒrî**, a.f. [6] [√ 10025]. other, another:– another (3), a[S] (1), one (1), other (1)

A10024 אָחֳרֵין **'oḥᵒrên**, adv. [1] [√ 10021]. finally, at last:– Finally (1 [+10221, 10527])

A10025 אָחֳרָן **'oḥᵒrān**, a.m. [5] [→ 10023]. other, another, someone else:– another (2), one (1), other (1), someone else (1)

A10026 אֲחַשְׁדַּרְפַּן **'ᵃḥašdarpan**, n.m. [9] [√ 346]. satrap, a viceroy or governor having considerable power:– satraps (9)

A10027 אִילָן **'îlān**, n.m. [6] [√ 471]. tree:– tree (6)

A10028 אֵימְתָן **'êmᵉtān**, a. [1] frightening, terrible:– frightening (1)

A10029 אִיתַי **'îtay**, pt. [17] [√ 3780]. there is, there are; a marker of existence often called a "quasi-verb":– there is (3), are (2), do (1), have (1 [+10089]), in fact (1), there are (1), unharmed (1 [+10244, 10379]), will be left with (1 [+10378]), NDT (6)

A10030 אכל **'ᵃkal**, v. [7] [√ 430]. [P] to eat (food); to destroy, devastate, devour (an object):– devoured (2), ate (1), denounced (1 [+10642]), devour (1), eat (1), falsely accused (1 [+10642])

A10031 אַל **'al**, neg.adv. [4] [√ 440]. not:– don't (2), not (2)

A10032 אֵל **'ēl**, p.demo.pl. [1] [√ 10180; 447]. these:– these (1)

A10033 אֱלָהּ **'ᵉlāh**, n.m. [95] [√ 468]. God, in the singular usually the true God, but see Da 4:8; 6:7 for a pagan god; gods, in the plural:– God (79), gods (15), NDT (1)

A10034 אֵלֶּה **'ēlleh**, p.demo.pl. Not used in NIVEBC [√ 10180; 465]. these

A10035 אֲלוּ **'ᵃlû**, interj. [5] [√ 10067]. there!, behold!; a discourse marker of transition, emphasis, or attention:– there (4), NDT (1)

A10036 אִלֵּין **'illên**, p.demo.pl. [5] [√ 10180]. these:– the others[S] (1), those (1), NDT (3)

A10037 אִלֵּךְ **'illēk**, p.demo.pl [14] [√ 10180]. these:– these (7), their[S] (1 [+10378, 10131]), NDT (6)

A10038 אֲלַף **'ᵃlap**, n.m. [4] [√ 547]. thousand; the phrase "thousands upon thousands" is an indefinitely large number:– thousands (2), them[S] (1 [+10002]), thousand (1)

A10039 אַמָּה **'ammâ**, n.f. [4] [√ 564]. cubit (measurement of distance from the elbow to the end of the fingers, about 18 to 22 inches):– cubits (4)

A10040 אֻמָּה **'ummâ**, n.f. [8] [√ 569]. nation, people:– peoples (6), nation (1), people (1)

A10041 אמן **'ᵃman**, v. [3] [√ 586]. [H] to trust in; [Hp] be trustworthy:– trustworthy (2), trusted (1)

A10042 אמר **'ᵃmar**, v. [71] [→ 10397; 606]. [P] to say, tell; to command:– said (6), tell (6), told (5), asked (3), command (3), commanded (2), gave orders (2), interpret (2 [+10600]), ordered (2), say (2), decreed (1), gave explanation (1), gave the order (1), saying (1), spoke (1), summoned (1 [+10378, 10085]), NDT (32)

A10043 אִמַּר **'immar**, n.m. [3] male lamb:– male lambs (3)

A10044 אֲנָה **'ᵃnâ**, p.1.com.sg. [16] [√ 638]. I:– I (15), me (1)

A10045 אִנּוּן **'innûn**, p.3.m.pl. [4] [√ 10200]. they; those:– those (1), NDT (3)

A10046 אֱנוֹשׁ **'ᵉnôš**, n.m. Not used in NIVEBC [√ 10050; 632]. man, person, see 10050

A10047 אֲנַחְנָא **'ᵃnaḥnā'**, p.1.com.pl. [4] [√ 636]. we:– we (4)

A10048 אנס **'ᵃnas**, v. [1] [√ 646]. [P] to oppress, make difficult:– difficult (1)

A10049 אֲנַף **'ᵃnap**, n.m. [2] [√ 647]. face; "to fall on the face" is to assume a position of honor or reverence:– attitude (1 [+10614]), prostrate (1 [+10542])

A10050 אֱנָשׁ **'ᵉnāš**, n.m. [25] [→ 10046; 632]. man, human being; humankind, people, often in contrast to animals; "son of man" often means a human being, but in Da 7:13 assumes messianic significance:– human being (4), on earth[S] (4), people (4), anyone (2 [+10353]), human (2), man (2), all mankind (1 [+10120]), everyone (1 [+10353]), one (1), people (1 [+10120]), people (1 [+10240]), whoever (1 [+10353, 10168]), NDT (1)

A10051 אַנְתְּ **'ant**, p.2.sg.m. Not used in NIVEBC [cf. 10052; 911]. you, your, see 10052

A10052 אַנְתָּה **'antā**, p.2.m.sg. [15] [cf. 10051; 911]. you:– you (10), NDT (5)

A10053 אַנְתּוּן **'antûn**, p.2.m.pl. [1] [√ 917]. you (all):– you (1)

A10054 אֱסוּר **'ᵉsûr**, n.[m.] [3] [→ 10057; 657]. bond, fetter; (pl.) imprisonment:– bound (2), imprisonment (1)

A10055 אָסְנַפַּר **'āsᵉnappar**, n.pr.m. [1] Ashurbanipal, "*Ashur creates a son*":– Ashurbanipal (1)

A10056 אָסְפַּרְנָא **'osparnā'**, adv. [7] with diligence, surely, fully:– with diligence (3), be sure (1), diligence (1), fully (1), surely (1)

A10057 אֱסָר **'ᵉsār**, n.m. [7] [√ 10054; 674]. (enforced) decree, i.e., a legally binding edict, a fig. extension of a bond or fetter that inhibits or controls:– decree (7)

A10058 אָע **'ā'**, n.m. [5] [√ 6770]. wood, timber:– timbers (2), wood (2), beam (1)

A10059 אַף **'ap**, c. [4] [√ 677]. even, also:– also (1 [+10221]), also (1 [+10221]), even (1 [+10221]), nor (1 [+10221, 10379])

A10060 אֲפָרְסָי **'ᵃpārᵉsāy**, n.pr.pl.g. [1] [√ 7273?]. Persian, from Persia:– people from Persia (1)

A10061 אֲפַרְסְכָי **'ᵃparsᵉkāy**, n.m.pl.[pr.g.?] [2] officials; transliterated in the KJV and ASV as the proper name "Apharsachites":– officials (2)

A10062 אֲפַרְסַתְכָי **'ᵃparsatkāy**, n.pr.m.pl.[pr.g.?] [1] officials:– officials (1)

A10063 אַפְּתֹם **'appᵉtōm**, n.m. [1] revenue, treasury:– revenues (1)

A10064 אֶצְבַּע **'eṣba'**, n.f. [3] [√ 720]. toe, finger:– fingers (1), toes (1), toes (1 [+10655])

A10065 אַרְבַּע **'arba'**, n.m. & f. [8] [√ 10651; 752]. four:– four (8)

A10066 אַרְגְּוָן **'argᵉwān**, n.m. [3] [√ 763]. purple (clothing), a sign of rulership:– purple (3)

A10067 אֲרוּ **'ᵃrû**, interj. [5] [√ 10035]. there!, behold!, i.e., a discourse marker of introduction, transition, or emphasis:– there (5)

A10068 אֲרַח **'ᵃraḥ**, n.[m.?] [2] [√ 784]. road, way; fig., conduct or way of life (only used fig. in the Aramaic portion of the Bible):– ways (2)

A10069 אַרְיֵה **'aryēh**, n.m. [10] [√ 793]. lion, an animal with the associative meanings of being fierce and powerful, and so causing fear:– lions (9), lion (1)

A10070 אַרְיוֹךְ **'aryôk**, n.pr.m. [5] [√ 796]. Arioch:– Arioch (4), NDT (1)

A10071 אַרִיךְ **'arîk**, a.vbl. [1] proper, fitting:– proper (1)

A10072 אַרְכֻבָּה **'arkubbâ**, n.f. [1] [√ 1384]. knee; "knocking of the knees" indicates fear:– knees (1)

A10073 אַרְכָה **'arkâ**, n.f. [2] [√ 801]. continuing, prolongation, lengthening of time:– continue (1), live (1 [+10089, 10261])

A10074 אַרְכְּוָי **'arkᵉwāy**, n.pr.g. [1] [√ 804]. Erech:– Uruk (1)

A10075 אֲרַע **'ᵃra'**, n.[f.] [21] [→ 10076, 10077; 824]. earth, world, the dwelling place of all peoples; land, ground, the dwelling place of a specific people:– earth (16), ground (3), inferior (1), land (1)

A10076 אַרְעִי ***'ar'î***, n.f.den. [1] [√ 10075]. floor, bottom:– floor (1)

A10077 אֲרַק ***'ᵃraq***, n.[f.] [1] [√ 10075; 824]. earth:– earth (1)

A10078 אַרְתַּחְשַׁשְׂתְּא ***'artaḥšaśt'***, אַרְתַּחְשַׁשְׂתְּא ***'artaḥšast'***, אַרְתַּחְשַׁשְׂתְּ ***'artaḥšaśt***, n.pr.m. [6] [√ 831]. Artaxerxes, "*kingdom of righteousness*":– Artaxerxes (6)

A10079 אֹשׁ ***'ōš***, n.m. [3] [√ 9268]. foundation:– foundations (3)

A10080 אֶשָּׁא ***'eššā'***, n.[f.] [1] [√ 836, 852]. fire:– fire (1)

A10081 אָשַׁף ***'āšap***, n.m. [6] [√ 879]. enchanter, conjurer:– enchanters (4), enchanter (2)

A10082 אֻשַּׁרְנָא ***'uššarnā'***, n.m. [2] structure, a building or part of a building (various sources translate more specifically: "beams, roofing, paneling, scaffolding," etc.):– it[S] (2 [+10180])

A10083 אֶשְׁתַּדּוּר ***'eštaddûr***, n.m. [2] [√ 10700]. rebellion, sedition, revolt:– sedition (1), sedition (1 [+10522])

A10084 אָת ***'āt***, n.m. [3] [√ 253]. miraculous sign:– signs (2), miraculous signs (1)

A10085 אֲתָה ***'ᵃtâ***, v. [16] [√ 910]. [P] to come, go; [H] to bring; [Hp] to be brought:– brought (3), brought in (2), came (2), come (2), bring in (1), coming (1), gone (1), summoned (1 [+10042, 10378]), was brought (1), went (1), were brought (1)

A10086 אַתּוּן ***'attûn***, n.m. [& f.?] [10] furnace:– furnace (10)

A10087 אֲתַר ***'ᵃtar***, n.m. [5] [→ 10092; 889]. site, place; "not any place" (Da 2:35) is translated idiomatically as "not a trace.":– site (2), place (1), places (1), trace (1)

A10088 ב ***b***, letter. Not used in NIVEBC [√ 927]. letter of the Aramaic alphabet

A10089 בְּ- ***bᵉ-***, pp.pref. [226] [→ 10092; 928]. in, with, by:– in (80), then (13 [+10008]), with (11), on (9), at (8), so (8 [+10008]), over (7), by (6), of (6), from (4), have (3), continually (2 [+10753, 10002]), into (2), to (2), under (2), underfoot (2 [+10655]), when (2 [+10008]), Daniel's (1 [+10181]), about (1), among (1), as soon as (1 [+10530, 10002, 10168]), because (1), daily (1 [+10317, 10317]), during (1), had (1), have (1 [+10029]), his (1 [+10192]), immediately (1 [+10096]), in (1 [+10135]), in (1 [+10135, 10464]), live (1 [+10073, 10261]), loudly (1 [+10264]), on (1 [+10135]), place[S] (1 [+10193]), place[S] (1 [+10135, 10193]), possess (1 [+10311]), something to do with (1), summoned (1 [+10637, 10264, 10378, 10549]), therefore (1 [+10008]), throughout (1 [+10353]), thus (1 [+10008]), wearing (1), when (1 [+10530, 10002]), wherever (1 [+10353, 10168]), while (1), with regard to (1), NDT (30)

A10090 בְּאִישׁ ***bi'yš***, a. [1] [√ 10091]. wicked, evil, bad:– wicked (1)

A10091 בְּאֵשׁ ***bᵉ'ēš***, v. [1] [→ 10090; 944]. [P] to be distressed:– distressed (1)

A10092 בָּאתַר ***bā'tar***, pp. + n.m. [3] [√ 10089 & 10087]. after:– After (3)

A10093 בָּבֶל ***bābel***, n.pr.loc. [25] [→ 10094; 951]. Babylon, "*gate of god(s)*":– Babylon (24), its[S] (1)

A10094 בָּבְלָי ***bābᵉlî***, a.g. [1] [√ 10093]. Babylonian, from Babylon:– Babylon (1)

A10095 בְּדַר ***bᵉdar***, v. [1] [√ 1029, 7061]. [Pa] to scatter:– scatter (1)

A10096 בְּהִילוּ ***bᵉhîlû***, n.f. [1] [√ 10097; 987]. hurry, haste; (as adv.) immediately:– immediately (1 [+10089])

A10097 בְּהַל ***bᵉhal***, v. [11] [→ 10096, 10218; 987]. [Pa] to frighten, terrify; [Htpe] to hurry, be at once; [Htpa] to be frightened:– terrified (3), alarm (1), alarmed (1), amazement (1 [+10755]), at once (1), disturbed (1), frightened (1), hurried (1), troubled (1)

A10098 בְּטֵל ***bᵉṭal***, v. [6] [√ 1060]. [P] to come to a standstill; [Pa] to stop (another):– stop (2), came to a standstill (1), stop work (1), stopped (1), NDT (1)

A10099 בֵּין ***bên***, pp. [2] [√ 1068]. between, among:– among (1), between (1)

A10100 בִּינָה ***bînâ***, n.f. [1] [√ 1069]. discernment, insight:– discerning (1 [+10313])

A10101 בִּירָה ***bîrâ***, n.f. [1] [√ 1072]. citadel, fortress:– citadel (1)

A10102 בִּית ***bît***, v.den. [1] [√ 10103]. [P] to spend the night:– spent the night (1)

A10103 בַּיִת ***bayit***, n.m. [44] [→ 10102; 1074]. a place of residence: house, home; residence of royalty: palace; residence of God or a god: temple:– house (17), temple (16), home (2), houses (2), archives (1 [+10148]), archives (1 [+10515]), hall (1), residence (1), treasury (1), treasury (1 [+10148]), NDT (1)

A10104 בָּל ***bāl***, n.[m.] [1] heart, mind:– determined (1 [+10682])

A10105 בֵּלְשַׁאצַּר ***bēl'šaṣṣar***, n.pr.m. [2] [√ 10109; 1157]. Belshazzar, "*Bel protect the king*":– Belshazzar (2)

A10106 בְּלָה ***bᵉlâ***, v. [1] [√ 1162]. [Pa] to oppress, wear down:– oppress (1)

A10107 בְּלוֹ ***bᵉlô***, n.[m.] [3] tribute, tax:– tribute (3)

A10108 בֵּלְטְשַׁאצַּר ***bēlṭᵉša'ṣṣar***, n.pr.m. [8] [cf. 10109; 1171]. Belteshazzar, "*protect his life*":– Belteshazzar (8)

A10109 בֵּלְשַׁאצַּר ***bēlša'ṣṣar***, n.pr.m. [5] [√ 10105; 1157]. Belshazzar, "*Bel protect the king*":– Belshazzar (4), Belshazzar's (1)

A10110 בֵּן ***bēn***, n.m. see 10120

A10111 בְּנָה ***bᵉnâ***, v. [22] [→ 10112; 1215]. [P] to build, construct, rebuild; [Pp] to be built; [Htpe] to be built, be constructed, be rebuilt:– rebuild (7), built (3), be rebuilt (2), building (2), is built (2), rebuilding (2), build (1), constructing (1), construction (1), under construction (1)

A10112 בִּנְיָן ***binyān***, n.[m.] [1] [√ 10111; 1230]. building:– building (1)

A10113 בְּנַס ***bᵉnas***, v. [1] [P] to become angry:– angry (1)

A10114 בְּעָה ***bᵉ'â***, v. [12] [→ 10115; 1239]. [P] to ask for, request; when petitioning deity: pray for, plead for:– asked (2), prays (2 [+10115]), asked for (1), look for (1), plead (1), praying (1), prays (1), request (1), sought out (1), tried (1)

A10115 בָּעוּ ***bā'û***, n.f. [2] [√ 10114]. prayer, petition, request:– prays (2 [+10114])

A10116 בְּעֵל ***bᵉ'ēl***, n.m. [3] [√ 1251]. with 10302, "lord of the decree" is translated "commanding officer":– commanding officer (3 [+10302])

A10117 בִּקְעָה ***biq'â***, n.f. [1] [√ 1326]. plain, (broad) valley:– plain (1)

A10118 בְּקַר ***bᵉqar***, v. [5] [√ 1329]. [Pa] to make a search, inquire; [Htpa] to let a search be made:– a search made (2), a search be made (1), inquire (1), searched (1)

A10119 [1]בַּר ***bar[1]***, n.[m.] [8] [√ 1340]. open field, the wild, an area not populated by people, the place of undomesticated animals:– wild (5), field (3)

A10120 [2]בַּר ***bar[2]***, n.m. [19] [√ 1337, 1201]. a direct descendant, human or animal, male or of either gender: son, child; a distant descendant: grandson, grandchild, descendant; fig., one of a class or kind:– son (5), exiles (4 [+10145]), descendant (2), sons (2), age (1 [+10732]), all mankind (1 [+10050]), children (1), people (1), people (1 [+10050]), young (1)

A10121 [1]בְּרַךְ ***bᵉrak[1]***, v. [1] [→ 10123; 1384]. [P] to kneel, an act of reverence to authority, often referring to God:– got down (1)

A10122 [2]בְּרַךְ ***bᵉrak[2]***, v. [4] [√ 1385]. [Pp] to be praised; [Pa] to praise; [Pap] to be praised, to give or receive words of excellence:– praise (2), praised (2)

A10123 בְּרֵךְ ***bᵉrēk***, n.[f.] [1] [√ 10121; 1386]. knee; "to kneel down on the knees" is to assume a position of reverence or worship:– knees (1)

A10124 בְּרַם ***bᵉram***, adv.advers. [5] but, however, nevertheless:– but (3), however (1), nevertheless (1)

A10125 בְּשַׂר ***bᵉśar***, n.m. [3] [√ 1414]. flesh (human or creatures):– creature (1), flesh (1), humans (1)

A10126 בַּת ***bat***, n.[m.] [2] [√ 1427]. bath (liquid measure):– baths (2)

A10127 ג ***g***, letter. Not used in NIVEBC [√ 1446]. letter of the Aramaic alphabet

A10128 גַּב ***gab***, n.[m.] [1] [√ 10129?]. the back (body part):– back (1)

A10129 גֹּב ***gōb***, n.m. [10] [√ 10128?; 1463]. den, pit (of lions), often an excavated hole:– den (10)

A10130 גְּבוּרָה ***gᵉbûrâ***, n.f. [2] [√ 10131; 1476]. power, might, strength:– power (2)

A10131 גְּבַר ***gᵉbar***, n.m. [21] [→ 10130, 10132; 1505]. (mighty) man; in some contexts an indefinite pronoun: certain ones:– men (10), some[S] (3), man (2), soldiers (1), their[S] (1 [+10378, 10037]), those[S] (1), who[S] (1 [+10002]), NDT (2)

A10132 גִּבָּר ***gibbar***, n.m. [1] [√ 10131; 1475]. strong man, mighty one:– strongest soldiers (1 [+10264])

A10133 גְּדָבַר ***gᵉdābar***, n.m. [2] [cf. 10139; 1601]. treasurer:– treasurers (2)

A10134 גְּדַד ***gᵉdad***, v. [2] [√ 1517]. [P] to cut down:– Cut down (2)

A10135 גַּו ***gaw***, n.m. [13] [√ 1569]. middle, interior:– into (6 [+10378]), in (1 [+10089]), in (1 [+10089, 10464]), middle (1), of (1 [+10427]), on (1 [+10089]), place[S] (1 [+10089, 10193]), NDT (1)

A10136 גֵּוָה ***gēwâ***, n.f. [1] [√ 1575]. pride:– pride (1)

A10137 גּוּחַ ***gûaḥ***, v. [1] [√ 1631]. [H] to churn up, stir up (the sea):– churning up (1)

A10138 גּוֹן ***gôn***, var. see 10135 & 10464

A10139 גִּזְבַּר ***gizbar***, n.m. [1] [cf. 10133; 1601]. treasurer:– treasurers (1)

A10140 גְּזַר ***gᵉzar***, v. [6] [→ 10141; 1615]. [P] to determine; (as noun) diviner, astrologer; note that a diviner determines the future through interpretations of omens, such as the movement of the stars (astrologer), or through interpreting the fissures in bodily organs of animals, such as livers; [Htpe] to cut out; [Itpe] to cut out:– diviners (3), cut out (1), diviner (1), was cut out (1)

A10141 גְּזֵרָה ***gᵉzērâ***, n.f. [2] [√ 10140; 1620]. decree, decision:– announced (1), decree (1)

A10142 גִּיר ***gîr***, n.[m.] [1] [√ 1732]. plaster:– plaster (1)

A10143 גַּלְגַּל ***galgal***, n.m. [1] [√ 10146; 1649, 1651]. wheel:– wheels (1)

A10144 גְּלָה ***gᵉlâ***, v. [9] [√ 1655]. [P] to reveal (mysteries); [Peil] to be revealed (i.e., mysteries); [H] to deport:– deported (2), revealer (2), reveals (2), been revealed (1), reveal (1), was revealed (1)

A10145 גָּלוּ ***gālû***, n.f. [4] [√ 1661]. exile:– exiles (4 [+10120])

A10146 גְּלָל ***gᵉlāl***, n.[m.] [2] [→ 10143, 10399; 1670]. (col.) stone blocks, formally, "stones of rolling" i.e., stones too large to carry:– large stones (2 [+10006])

A10147 גְּמַר ***gᵉmar***, v. [1] [√ 1698]. [Pp] to be finished; (as an introduction in a letter) Greetings:– Greetings (1)

A10148 גְּנַז ***gᵉnaz***, n.m. [3] [√ 1709]. place of treasure and archived documents:– archives (1 [+10103]), treasury (1), treasury (1 [+10103])

A10149 גַּף ***gap***, n.f. [3] wing:– wings (3)

A10150 גְּרַם ***gᵉram***, n.[m.] [1] [√ 1752]. bone:– bones (1)

A10151 גְּשֵׁם ***gᵉšēm***, n.m. [5] body; the phrase "give up the body" is translated "to die":– body (3), bodies (1), lives (1)

A10152 ד ***d***, letter. Not used in NIVEBC [√ 1789]. letter of the Aramaic alphabet

A10153 דְּ- ***dᵉ-***, pt.rel. Not used in NIVEBC [√ 10168]. who, that, of

A10154 דָּא ***dā'***, p.demo.f. [6] [√ 2297, 2305, 2296]. this, this one:– this (2), each (1), knocking (1 [+10491, 10378, 10154]), knocking (1 [+10491, 10154, 10378]), others[S] (1)

A10155 דֹּב ***dōb***, n.m. [1] [√ 1800]. bear:– bear (1)

A10156 [1]דְּבַח ***dᵉbaḥ[1]***, v. [1] [→ 10157, 10401; 2284]. [P] to present a sacrifice as an act of worship:– present (1)

A10157 [2]דְּבַח ***dᵉbaḥ[2]***, n.[m.] [1] [√ 10156; 2285]. sacrifice (i.e., animal):– sacrifices (1)

A10158 דְּבַק ***dᵉbaq***, v. [1] [√ 1815]. [P] to be united, having a very close association:– united (1 [+10180, 10554, 10180])

A10159 דִּבְרָה ***dibrâ***, n.f. [2] [√ 1826]. affair, matter:– so that (1 [+10527, 10168]), so that (1 [+10542, 10168])

A10160 דְּהַב ***dᵉhab***, n.m. [23] [√ 2298]. gold:– gold (23)

A10161 דֶּהוּא ***dᵉhû'***, pt. + pr. Not used in NIVEBC [√ 10168 + 10200]. that is (10168 + 10200)

A10162 דֶּהָיֵא ***dehāyē'***, pt. + pr. Not used in NIVEBC [√ 10168 + 10200]. that is (10168 + 10200 son of man")

A10163 דּוּר ***dûr***, v. [7] [→ 10183, 10403, 10407, 10753; 1884]. [P] to live, dwell:– live (2), peoples (2), lived (1), shelter (1), NDT (1)

A10164 דּוּרָא ***dûrā'***, n.pr.loc. [1] Dura:– Dura (1)

A10165 דּוּשׁ ***dûš***, v. [1] [√ 1889]. [P] to trample, tread down:– trampling down (1)

A10166 דַּחֲוָה ***daḥᵃwâ***, n.f. [1] entertainment, variously interpreted as musical, dancing, sexual, culinary, etc:– entertainment (1)

A10167 דְּחַל ***dᵉḥal***, v. [6] [√ 2324]. [P] to fear, reverence; [Pp] to be terrified, be awesome; [Pa] to make afraid:– terrifying (2), awesome (1), feared (1), made afraid (1), reverence (1)

A10168 דִּי ***dî***, pt.rel. & c. [345] [→ 10153; 2296, 2306]. who, that, of:– that (47), of (46), who (19), which (9), until (8 [+10527]), whom (8), so that (6), those (5), anyone (4 [+10426]), because (4 [+10353, 10619]), from (4), because (3), for (3 [+10353, 10619]), in (3), when (3 [+10341]), with (3), but (2), for (2), just as (2), what (2), any more than (1 [+10195, 10341]), as (1), as (1 [+10527]), as soon as (1 [+10008, 10427]), as soon as (1 [+10089, 10530, 10002]), as soon as (1 [+10232, 10002, 10341]), because (1 [+10427]), because of (1 [+10378, 10619]), by (1 [+10353, 10619]), during (1), even as (1 [+10353, 10619]), hoping (1 [+10527]), if (1), just as (1 [+10353, 10619]), one (1), over (1), since (1 [+10353, 10619]), so that (1 [+10527, 10159]), so that (1 [+10542, 10159]), surely (1 [+10427, 10643]), this is the meaning (1 [+10353, 10619]), though (1 [+10353, 10619]), whatever (1 [+10353]), whatever (1 [+10353]), whatever (1 [+10408]), when (1 [+10427]), wherever (1 [+10089, 10353]), while (1 [+10527]), whoever (1 [+10353]), whoever (1 [+10426]), whoever (1 [+10426]), whoever (1 [+10353, 10050]), whose (1), NDT (129)

A10169 [1]דִּין ***dîn[1]***, v. [1] [→ 10170, 10171, 10172, 10406; 1906]. [P] to administer justice, judge:– administer justice (1)

A10170 [2]דִּין ***dîn[2]***, n.m. [5] [√ 10169; 1907]. judgment, court (place of judgment):– court (2), judgment (1), just (1), punished (1 [+10522, 10191])

A10171 דַּיָּן ***dayyān***, n.m. [2] [√ 10169; 1908]. judge:– judges (2)

A10172 דִּינָיֵא ***dînāyē'***, n.pr.g. Not used in NIVEBC [√ 10169]. judge

A10173 דֵּךְ ***dēk***, p.demo.com. [13] [→ 10174]. this:– this (12), NDT (1)

A10174 דִּכֵּן ***dikkēn***, p.demo.com. [3] [√ 10173]. that:– that (1), this (1), NDT (1)

A10175 דְּכַר ***dekar***, n.m. [3] [√ 2351]. ram (male animal):– rams (3)

A10176 דִּכְרוֹן ***dikrôn***, n.[m.] [1] [→ 10177; 2355]. memorandum, record:– Memorandum (1)

A10177 דָּכְרָן ***dokrān***, n.[m.] [2] [√ 10176; 2355]. memorandum, archived record:– archives (1 [+10515]), records (1 [+10515])

A10178 דְּלַק ***delaq***, v. [1] [√ 1944]. [P] to be ablaze, burn:– all ablaze (1 [+10471])

A10179 דְּמָה ***demâ***, v. [2] [√ 1948]. [P] to look like, resemble:– like (1), looked like (1)

A10180 דְּנָה ***denâ***, p.demo.com. [58] [→ 10032, 10034, 10036, 10037]. this, that:– this (27), itS (2 [+10082]), that (2), ago (1 [+10427, 10622]), as follows (1 [+10341]), before (1 [+10427, 10622]), here (1), in the future (1 [+10021]), so (1 [+10353, 10619]), such (1 [+10341]), that is why (1 [+10542]), the (1), then (1 [+10353, 10619]), therefore (1 [+10353, 10619]), these (1), this (1 [+10341]), this made (1 [+10353, 10619]), to come (1 [+10201, 10021]), united (1 [+10158, 10554, 10180]), united (1 [+10158, 10180, 10554]), NDT (10)

A10181 דָּנִיֵּאל ***dāniyyē'l***, n.pr.m. [52] [√ 1975]. Daniel, "*God (El) is my judge*":– Daniel (46), Daniel's (1), Daniel's (1 [+10089]), heS (1), himS (1), NDT (2)

A10182 דְּקַק ***deqaq***, v. [10] [√ 1990]. [P] to break to pieces; [H] to crush, smash, pulverize:– crushed (3), crush (2), breaks (1), broke to pieces (1), broken to pieces (1), crushing (1), smashed (1)

A10183 דָּר ***dār***, n.[m.] [4] [√ 10163; 1887]. generation; the phrase "from generation to generation" indicates an unlimited span of time: "eternal, forever":– generation (4)

A10184 דָּרְיָוֶשׁ ***dāreyāweš***, n.pr.m. [15] [√ 2003]. Darius, "*he who upholds the good*":– Darius (15)

A10185 דְּרָע ***derā'***, n.[f.] [1] [→ 10013; 2432]. arm:– arms (1)

A10186 דָּת ***dāt***, n.f. [14] [√ 2017]. law, decree, usually a written, codified prescription by either human or deity; the "Law of God" can refer to the Torah, the first five books of the Hebrew Bible:– law (9), decree (2), laws (2), penalty (1)

A10187 דֶּתֶא ***dete'***, n.[m.] [2] [√ 2013]. grass (of the open country):– grass (2)

A10188 דְּתָבַר ***detābar***, n.m. [2] [√ 2017]. judge:– judges (2)

A10189 ה ***h***, letter. Not used in NIVEBC [√ 2020]. letter of the Aramaic alphabet

A10190 הֲ־ ***ha-***, inter.pt. [6] [→ cf. 10216; 2022]. introduces a question, translated as a question mark rather than as a word:– is it true (1 [+10609]), NDT (5)

A10191 ־ָה ***-â***, art.suf. [50] [√ 10002]. the, a:– the (15), Trans-Euphrates (12 [+10526, 10468]), itsS (2), immediately (1 [+10734]), itS (1 [+10424]), punished (1 [+10522, 10170]), suddenly (1 [+10734]), that (1), that provinceS (1 [+10526, 10468]), this (1), yourS (1), NDT (13)

A10192 ־ֵהּ ***-ēh***, p.suf.3.m.sg. [159] [√ 10204; 2024]. he, him, his; it, its:– his (45), him (23), it (16), its (11), he (7), their (5), theS (4), aS (1), his (1 [+10089]), his (1 [+10378]), his own (1), manS (1), same (1), NDT (42)

A10193 ־ַהּ ***-ah***, p.suf.3.f.sg. [44] [√ 2023]. she, her; it, its:– it (15), its (7), them (5), placeS (1 [+10089]), placesS (1 [+10089, 10135]), theS (1), which (1), NDT (13)

A10194 הָא ***hā'***, demo.pt. [1] [√ 2026]. look!, there!:– Look (1)

A10195 הֵא ***hē'***, demo.pt. [1] [√ 2026]. just as:– any more than (1 [+10341, 10168])

A10196 הַדָּבַר ***haddābar***, n.m. [4] royal adviser, official of the king:– advisers (4)

A10197 הַדָּם ***haddām***, n.[m.] [2] pieces, members (of an execution by dismemberment):– pieces (2)

A10198 הֲדַר[1] ***hadar1***, v. [3] [→ 10199; 2075]. [Pa] to glorify, honor, to speak words that elevate the status of another:– glorified (1), glorify (1), honor (1)

A10199 הֲדַר[2] ***hadar2***, n.[m.] [3] [√ 10198; 2077, 2078]. splendor, honor, majesty:– honor (1), majesty (1), splendor (1)

A10200 הוּא ***hû'***, p.3.m.sg. [15] [→ 10045, 10205; 2085]. he, it:– he (5), it (1), that (1), that treeS (1), NDT (7)

A10201 הֲוָה ***hawâ***, v. [71] [√ 2118, 2093]. [P] to be, become, happen:– be (10), was (7), became (2), happen (2), were (2), appear (1), continued (1), fall (1), had (1 [+10542]), have (1), keep (1), kept (1), must (1), remain (1), stay (1), take place (1), to come (1 [+10021, 10180]), NDT (36)

A10202 הוך ***hûk***, v. Not used in NIVEBC [√ 10207]. see 10207

A10203 ־הוֹן ***-hôn***, p.suf.3.m.pl. [51] [√ 2157]. they, them, their:– them (17), their (16), theS (3), their own (1), they (1), NDT (13)

A10204 ־הִי ***-hî***, p.suf.3.m.sg. [76] [√ 10192; 2114]. he, his, him; it, its:– his (26), its (14), him (11), he (5), it (4), one (1), theS (1), NDT (14)

A10205 הִיא ***hî'***, p.3.f.sg. [7] [√ 10200; 2085]. she, it:– it (1), itself (1), there (1), this (1), NDT (3)

A10206 הֵיכַל ***hêkal***, n.m. [13] [√ 2121]. residence of a deity: temple; residence of royalty: palace:– temple (8), palace (5)

A10207 הֲלַךְ ***halak***, v. [7] [→ 10208; cf. 10202; 2143]. [P] to go; [Pa] to walk about; [H] to walk around:– go (3), walk (1), walking (1), walking around (1), NDT (1)

A10208 הֲלָךְ ***halāk***, n.[m.] [3] [√ 10207]. duty, toll, tax:– duty (3)

A10209 ־הֹם ***-hōm***, p.suf.3.m.pl. [12] [√ 10214; 2157]. they, them, their:– their (5), them (4), NDT (3)

A10210 הִמּוֹ ***himmô***, p.3.pl. [12] [√ 2156, 2160]. they, them:– them (6), they (1), NDT (5)

A10211 המונך ***hmwnk***, n.[m.] Not used in NIVEBC. necklace

A10212 הַמְיָנַךְ ***hamyānak***, n.[m.] [3] chain, necklace:– chain (3)

A10213 הֵן ***hēn***, c. [16] [√ 2176, 561?]. if, then, whether:– if (11), even if (1), then (1), NDT (3)

A10214 ־הֵן ***-hēn***, p.suf.3.f.pl. [8] [√ 10209, 10386; 2157]. they, them, their:– the othersS (1), them (1), NDT (6)

A10215 הַנְזָקָה ***hanzāqâ***, n.[f.] *or* v.inf. Not used in NIVEBC [√ 10472]. injury, disadvantage

A10216 הַצְדָּא ***haṣdā'***, inter. [+ n.?] Not used in NIVEBC [√ 10190 + 10609]. truly? really?, see 10190 & 10609

A10217 הַרְהֹר ***harhōr***, n.[m.] [1] mental image (in a dream-like state):– images (1)

A10218 הִתְבְּהָלָה ***hitbehālâ***, n. *or* v. Not used in NIVEBC [√ 10097]. hurry, see 10097

A10219 הִתְנַדָּבוּ ***hitnaddābû***, n.m. *or* v. Not used in NIVEBC [√ 10461]. gift, see 10461

A10220 ו ***w***, letter. Not used in NIVEBC [√ 2255]. letter of the Aramaic alphabet

A10221 וְ־ ***we-***, c.pref. [731] [√ 2256]. (connecting) and; (contrasting) or, but, however; (furthering) then, now:– and (400), or (20), but (19), then (9), now (5), so (5), so that (5), moreover (3), nor (3 [+10379]), that (3), together with (3), with (3), also (2), 120 (1 [+10395, 10574]), also (1 [+10059]), also (1 [+10059]), and (1 [+10008]), and now (1), and that (1), and when (1), as (1), as for (1), at this (1), completely destroyed (1 [+10722, 10005]), even (1 [+10059]), finally (1), finally (1 [+10527, 10024]), furthermore (1), including (1), instead (1), next (1), nor (1), nor (1 [+10059, 10379]), period of time (1 [+10232, 10530]), set to work (1 [+10624, 10742]), sixty-two (1 [+10749, 10775]), therefore (1), till (1), until (1), when (1), while (1), yes (1), yet (1), NDT (221)

A10222 ז ***z***, letter. Not used in NIVEBC [√ 2268]. letter of the Aramaic alphabet

A10223 זְבַן ***zeban***, v. [1] [P] to try to gain (time), buy (time):– gain (1)

A10224 זְהִיר ***zehîr***, v. [1] [√ 2302]. careful, cautious:– careful (1)

A10225 זוּד ***zûd***, v. [1] [√ 2326]. [H] to act proudly, act haughtily:– pride (1)

A10226 זוּן ***zûn***, v. [1] [→ 10410; 2315]. [Htpe] to be fed, live on:– was fed (1)

A10227 זוּעַ ***zûa'***, v. [2] [√ 2316]. [P] to dread, fear, to have an attitude of terror or worship, a fig. extension of "to shake, tremble.":– dreaded (1), fear (1)

A10228 זִיו ***zîw***, n.m. [6] radiant appearance: dazzling, splendor; terrified appearance: flushed, pale:– face pale (3), dazzling (1), look so pale (1 [+10731]), splendor (1)

A10229 זָכוּ ***zākû***, n.f. [1] [√ 2342]. innocence:– innocent (1)

A10230 זְכַרְיָה ***zekaryâ***, n.pr.m. [2] [√ 2357]. Zechariah, "*Yahweh remembers*":– Zechariah (2)

A10231 זְמַן[1] ***zeman1***, v.den. [1] [√ 10232; 2374]. [Htpe] to conspire, agree to; [H] to decide:– conspired (1)

A10232 זְמַן[2] ***zeman2***, n.m. [11] [→ 10232; 2375]. time, event, occurrence; a unit of time: indefinite period of time, set time, season:– time (5), times (2), as soon as (1 [+10002, 10341, 10168]), period of time (1 [+10221, 10530]), seasons (1), set times (1)

A10233 זְמָר ***zemār***, n.[m.] [4] [→ 10234; 2376]. music in general, or string music in particular:– music (4)

A10234 זַמָּר ***zammār***, n.m. [1] [√ 10233; 2376]. singer:– musicians (1)

A10235 זַן ***zan***, n.[m.] [4] [√ 2385]. kind, sort:– kinds (4)

A10236 זְעֵיר ***ze'êr***, a. [1] [√ 2402]. little, small; fig., insignificant, light in status:– little (1)

A10237 זְעִק ***ze'iq***, v. [1] [√ 4210, 7590]. [P] to call out, shout:– called (1)

A10238 זְקַף ***zeqap***, v. [1] [√ 2422]. [Pp] to be lifted up:– NDT (1)

A10239 זְרֻבָּבֶל ***zerubbābel***, n.pr.m. [1] [√ 2428]. Zerubbabel, "*seed of Babylon* or *one grafted into Babylon*":– Zerubbabel (1)

A10240 זְרַע ***zera'***, n.[m.] [1] [√ 2446]. seed, "seed" of a person is translated "descendant":– people (1 [+10050])

A10241 ח ***ḥ***, letter. Not used in NIVEBC [√ 2459]. letter of the Aramaic alphabet

A10242 חֲבוּלָה ***ḥabûlâ***, n.f. [1] [√ 10243]. wrong, crime:– wrong (1)

A10243 חֲבַל ***ḥabal***, v. [6] [→ 10242, 10244; 2472]. [Pa] to destroy, hurt; [Htpa] to be destroyed:– be destroyed (3), destroy (2), hurt (1)

A10244 חֲבָל ***ḥabāl***, n.m. [3] [√ 10243]. physical harm, wound, hurt; fig., damage resulting from the lowering of status:– threat (1), unharmed (1 [+10379, 10029]), wound (1)

A10245 חֲבַר ***ḥabar***, n.m. [3] [→ 10246; 2492]. friend, companion:– friends (3)

A10246 חַבְרָה ***ḥabrâ***, n.f. [1] [√ 10245; 2492]. companion (horn):– others (1)

A10247 חַגַּי ***ḥaggay***, n.pr.m. [2] [√ 2516]. Haggai, "*festal; born on the feast day*":– Haggai (2)

A10248 חַד ***ḥad***, a. & subst. [15] [√ 285]. one, first, a; time, occurrence:– a (5), one (5), first (3), all (1 [+10341]), times (1)

A10249 חֲדֵה ***ḥadēh***, n.m. [1] [√ 2601]. chest, breast:– chest (1)

A10250 חֶדְוָה ***ḥedwâ***, n.f. [1] [√ 2530]. joy:– joy (1)

A10251 חֲדַת ***ḥadat***, a. Not used in NIVEBC [√ 2543]. new

A10252 חֲוָה ***ḥawâ***, v. [15] [→ 10018; 2555]. [Pa] to reveal, tell, show; [H, A] tell, explain, make known, interpret:– interpret (5 [+10600]), tell (4), explain (2), do (1), explain (1 [+10600]), reveal (1), tells (1)

A10253 חוּט ***ḥûṭ***, v. [1] [H] to repair:– repairing (1)

A10254 חִוָּר ***ḥiwwār***, a. [1] white, a color of purity and lack of defilement:– white (1)

A10255 חֲזָה ***ḥazâ***, v. [31] [→ 10256, 10257; 2600]. [P] to see, look, watch, realize; [Pp] to be usual, be customary:– looked (8), saw (7), hadS (3), see (3), watched (3), looking (1), realize (1), usual (1), vision (1), watch (1), watching (1), NDT (1)

A10256 חֱזוּ ***ḥezû***, n.m. [12] [√ 10255]. vision, appearance:– visions (6), vision (4), dream (1 [+10267]), looked (1)

A10257 חֲזוֹת ***ḥazôt***, n.f. [2] [√ 10255]. visible sight:– visible (2)

A10258 חַטָּאָה ***ḥaṭṭā'â***, n.f. Not used in NIVEBC [√ 10259; 2633]. sin offering, see 10260

A10259 חֲטָי ***ḥaṭāy***, n.[m.] [1] [→ 10258, 10260; 2628]. sin:– sins (1)

A10260 חַטָּיָא ***ḥaṭṭāyā'***, n.f. [1] [√ 10259; 2633]. sin offering:– sin offering (1)

A10261 חַי ***ḥay***, a. [7] [√ 10262; 2644, 2645]. living, alive:– living (3), alive (1), live (1 [+10073, 10089]), lives (1), well-being (1)

A10262 חֲיָה ***ḥayâ***, v. [6] [→ 10261, 10263; 2649]. [P] to live; [H] to spare, let live:– live (5), spared (1)

A10263 חֵיוָא ***ḥêwâ***, n.f. [20] [√ 10262; 2651]. beast, animal; this can refer to physical creatures of earth as well as to fig. creatures of visions and parables:– animals (7), beast (6), beasts (5), animal (2)

A10264 חַיִל ***ḥayil***, n.m. [7] [√ 2657]. strength, power; an army:– army (1), compelled (1), loud (1), loudly (1 [+10089]), powers (1), strongest soldiers (1 [+10132]), summoned (1 [+10637, 10089, 10378, 10549])

A10265 חַכִּים ***ḥakkîm***, n.m. [14] [√ 10266; 2682]. wise man (usually pertaining to a social class):– wise (14)

A10266 חָכְמָה ***ḥokmâ***, n.f. [8] [→ 10265; 2683]. wisdom:– wisdom (7), thatS (1)

A10267 חֵלֶם ***ḥēlem***, n.m. [22] [√ 2706]. dream:– dream (20), dream (1 [+10256]), dreams (1)

A10268 חֲלַף ***ḥalap***, v. [4] [√ 2736]. [P] to pass by, pass over:– pass by (4)

A10269 חֲלָק ***ḥalāq***, n.[m.] [3] [→ 10412; 2750]. portion, lot in life:– live (2), nothing (1 [+10379])

A10270 חֱמָא ***ḥamâ***, n.f. [2] [√ 2779]. fury, rage; "to be in fury and rage" refers to anger of highest degree:– furious (1), furious (1 [+10416])

A10271 חֲמַר ***ḥamar***, n.m. [6] [√ 2815]. wine:– wine (6)

A10272 חִנְטָה ***ḥinṭâ***, n.f. [2] [√ 2636]. wheat:– wheat (2)

A10273 חֲנֻכָּה ***ḥanukkâ***, n.f. [4] [√ 2853]. (ceremonial religious) dedication:– dedication (4)

A10274 חֲנַן ***ḥanan***, v. [2] [√ 2858]. [P] to be kind, show mercy; [Htpa] to ask, implore:– asking for help (1), kind (1)

A10275 חֲנַנְיָה ***ḥananyâ***, n.pr.m. [1] [√ 2863]. Hananiah, "*Yahweh is gracious*":– Hananiah (1)

A10276 חַסִּיר ***ḥassîr***, a. [1] [√ 2894]. wanting, lacking in quality or quantity, deficient:– wanting (1)

A10277 חֲסַן ***ḥasan***, v. [2] [→ 10278; 2889]. [H] to take possession of, occupy:– possess (1), possessed (1)

A10278 חֱסֵן ***ḥesēn***, n.m. [2] [√ 10277; 2890]. power, might, force:– mighty (1), power (1)

A10279 חֲסַף ***ḥasap***, n.[m.] [9] (formed, molded) clay, baked clay:– clay (5), baked clay (2), baked clay (1 [+10298]), clay (1 [+10298])

A10280 חֲצַף ***ḥasap***, v. [2] [H] to show harshness:– harsh (1), urgent (1)

A10281 חֲרַב ***ḥarab***, v. [1] [√ 2990]. [Ho] to be destroyed, be devastated:– was destroyed (1)

A10282 חַרְטֹם ***ḥarṭōm***, n.m. [5] [√ 3033]. magician:– magicians (3), magician (2)

A10283 חֲרַךְ ***ḥarak***, v. [1] [Htpa] to be singed (i.e., hair burnt):– was singed (1)

A10284 חֲרַץ ***ḥaraṣ***, n.[m.] [1] [√ 2743]. hips, hip joints:– legs (1 [+10626])

A10285 חֲשַׁב ***ḥašab***, v. [1] [√ 3108]. [Pp] to be regarded, be respected:– are regarded (1)

A10286 חֲשׁוֹךְ ***ḥašôk***, n.[m.] [1] [√ 3125]. darkness:– darkness (1)

A10287 חֲשַׁח ***ḥašaḥ***, v. [1] [→ 10288, 10289]. [P] to be in need:– need (1)

A10288 חַשְׁחָה ***hašḥâ***, n.f. [1] [√ 10287]. need:– needed (1)

A10289 חַשְׁחוּ ***ḥašḥû***, n.f.col. [1] [√ 10287]. what is needed:– needed (1)

A10290 חֲשַׁל ***ḥašal***, v. [1] [P] to smash, pulverize:– smashes (1)

A10291 חֲתַם ***ḥatam***, v. [1] [√ 3159]. [P] to seal (with a signet ring):– sealed (1)

A10292 ט ***ṭ***, letter. Not used in NIVEBC [√ 3172]. letter of the Aramaic alphabet

A10293 טְאֵב ***ṭe'ēb***, v. [1] [→ 10294; cf. 10320; 3201, 3512]. [P] to be good = to have joy:– overjoyed (1 [+10678])

A10294 טָב ***ṭāb***, a. [2] [√ 10293; 3202]. good, pleasing, pure:– pleases (1), pure (1)

A10295 טַבָּח ***ṭabbāḥ***, n.m. [1] [√ 3184]. (royal) body-guard, executioner; an elite unit guarding a king, execution only one of its functions:– guard (1)

A10296 טוּר ***ṭûr***, n.m. [2] [√ 7446]. mountain:– mountain (2)

A10297 טְוָת ***ṭewāt***, adv. [1] without eating, in hunger, in fasting:– without eating (1)

A10298 טִין ***ṭîn***, n.[m.] [2] [√ 3226]. (wet) clay:– baked clay (1 [+10279]), clay (1 [+10279])

A10299 טַל ***ṭal***, n.[m.] [5] [√ 3228]. dew:– dew (5)

A10300 טְלַל ***ṭelal***, v. [1] [√ 7511]. [H] to find shelter:– found shelter (1)

A10301 טְעֵם[1] ***ṭe'ēm***[1], v. [3] [→ 10302; 3247]. [Pa] to eat:– eat (2), ate (1)

A10302 טְעֵם[2] ***ṭe'ēm***[2], n.m. [30] [√ 10301; 3248]. order, decree, command; tact, good sense; report, advice; with 10271 "under the command of wine" means "to be intoxicated"; with 10116, "lord of the decree" is translated "commanding officer":– decree (5), decree (5 [+10682]), commanding officer (3 [+10116]), order (3), attention (2), authorized (2 [+10682]), accountable (1), command (1), commanded (1 [+10682]), decreed (1 [+10682]), decrees (1), drinking (1), order (1 [+10682, 10002]), prescribed (1 [+10427]), report (1), tact (1)

A10303 טְפַר ***ṭepar***, n.m. [2] [√ 7632]. finger and toe nails (of a human); claws (of an animal):– claws (1), nails (1)

A10304 טְרַד ***ṭerad***, v. [4] [√ 3265]. [P] to drive away (as noun) one driven away; [Peil] to be driven away:– driven away (2), was driven away (2)

A10305 טַרְפְּלָי ***ṭarpelāy***, n.pr.g. [1] from Tripolis:– administrators (1)

A10306 י ***y***, letter. Not used in NIVEBC [√ 3275]. letter of the Aramaic alphabet

A10307 ־ִי ***-î***, p.suf.1.com.sg. [70] [√ 10477; 3276]. I, me, my:– my (30), I (14), me (12), my (1 [+10621]), myself (1 [+10380]), NDT (12)

A10308 יְבַל ***yebal***, v. [3] [√ 3297]. [H] to bring, take:– brought (2), take (1)

A10309 יַבֶּשְׁתָּא ***yabbešâ***, n.f. [1] [√ 3317]. earth; dry land (in contrast to the sea):– earth (1)

A10310 יְגַר ***yegar***, n.[m.] Not used in NIVEBC [√ 1681, 3337]. Jegar, see 3337

A10311 יַד ***yad***, n.f. [17] [√ 3338]. hand (of a human), paw (of an animal); fig., power, control, action:– hand (7), hands (5), hand (2 [+10589]), direction (1), possess (1 [+10089]), power (1)

A10312 יְדָה ***yedâ***, v. [2] [√ 3344]. [H] to give thanks, confess praise:– giving thanks (1), thank (1)

A10313 יְדַע ***yeda'***, v. [47] [→ 10430; 3359]. [P] to know, understand, acknowledge; [Pp] to be known; [H] to make known, tell, inform:– know (11), tell (8), acknowledge (3), interpret (3 [+10600]), explained (2), inform (2), made known (2), shown (2), understand (2), acknowledged (1), certain (1 [+10427, 10327]), discerning (1 [+10100]), gave (1), information (1), knew (1), knows (1), learned (1), remember (1), showed (1), teach (1), NDT (1)

A10314 יְהַב ***yehab***, v. [28] [→ cf. 10498; 3364]. [P] to give; [Pp] to be given; [Htpe] to be given as payment; be entrusted:– gave (4), given (4), was given (3), be delivered (1), be given (1), be handed over (1), be paid (1), entrusted (1), give (1), give up (1), gives (1), laid (1), lavished (1), made (1), paid (1), placed (1), pronounced (1), thrown (1), were allowed (1), were paid (1)

A10315 יְהוּד ***yehûd***, n.pr.loc. [7] [→ 10316; 3373]. Judah, "*praised*":– Judah (6), NDT (1)

A10316 יְהוּדָי ***yehûdāy***, n.g. [10] [√ 10315; 3374]. Jew:– Jews (8), Jewish (1), people[S] (1)

A10317 יוֹם ***yôm***, n.m. [16] [√ 3427]. a period of time which is indefinite in scope: it can range widely in meaning from "daytime" (in contrast to night); "day," a period of time approximately 24 hours; to longer periods (seasons or years). The title "Ancient of Days" is a title of God as old (eternal), emphasizing wisdom and power:– days (6), day (3), time (3), daily (1 [+10317, 10089]), daily (1 [+10089, 10317]), history (1), long history (1 [+10427, 10550])

A10318 יוֹצָדָק ***yôṣādāq***, n.pr.m. [1] [√ 3392]. Jozadak, "*Yahweh is righteous*":– Jozadak (1)

A10319 יְחַט ***yeḥaṭ***, v. [Pa] to lay a foundation, see 10253

A10320 יְטַב ***yeṭab***, v. [1] [cf. 10293; 3512]. [P] to seem best, be pleasing:– seems best (1)

A10321 יְכִל ***yekil***, v. [12] [cf. 10346; 3523]. [P] to be able:– able (5), can (5), defeating (1), unable (1 [+10379])

A10322 יַם ***yam***, n.m. [2] [√ 3542]. a body of water usually referring to ocean, sea, or lake; fig., the nether regions of mystery, chaos, and monsters:– sea (2)

A10323 יְסַף ***yesap***, v. [1] [√ 3578]. [Ho] to be added:– became even greater (1 [+10650, 10339])

A10324 יְעַט ***ye'aṭ***, v. [1] [→ 10325, 10539; 3619]. [Itpa] to take counsel together, implying mutual agreement and choices:– agreed (1)

A10325 יָעֵט ***yā'ēṭ***, n.m. *or* v.ptcp. [2] [√ 10324; 3619]. adviser, counselor:– advisers (2)

A10326 יְצַב ***yeṣab***, v. [1] [→ 10327; 3656]. [Pa] to make certain, to know the truth:– know the meaning (1)

A10327 יַצִּיב ***yaṣṣîb***, a. [5] [√ 10326]. certain, true, reliable:– certain (1 [+10427, 10313]), certainly (1 [+10002]), meaning (1), stands (1), true (1)

A10328 יְקַד ***yeqad***, v. [8] [→ 10329; 3678]. [P] to burn:– blazing (8 [+10471])

A10329 יְקֵדָה ***yeqēdâ***, n.f. [1] [√ 10328]. blazing, burning:– blazing (1)

A10330 יַקִּיר ***yaqqîr***, a. [2] [√ 10331; 3692]. honorable; difficult, with an implication that such difficulty makes something unlikely or improbable:– honorable (1), too difficult (1)

A10331 יְקָר ***yeqār***, n.m. [7] [→ 10330; 3702]. glory, honor, majesty:– glory (6), honor (1)

A10332 יְרוּשְׁלֶם ***yerûšelem***, n.pr.loc. [26] [√ 3731]. Jerusalem, "*foundation of Shalem (peace)*":– Jerusalem (26)

A10333 יְרַח ***yeraḥ***, n.m. [2] [√ 3732]. month:– month (1), months (1)

A10334 יַרְכָה ***yarkâ***, n.f. [1] [√ 3751]. (upper) thigh; some sources translate as "loin" (the lower back, as the soft area between the lower ribs and the hip joints):– thighs (1)

A10335 יִשְׂרָאֵל ***yiśrā'ēl***, n.pr.g. [8] [√ 3776]. Israel, "*he struggles with God (El)*":– Israel (7), Israelites (1 [+10553])

A10336 יֵשׁוּעַ ***yēšûa'***, n.pr.m. [1] [√ 3800]. Jeshua, "*Yahweh saves*":– Joshua (1)

A10337 יָת ***yāt***, pt. [1] [√ 906]. not translated, indicates the direct object:– NDT (1)

A10338 יְתִב ***yetib***, v. [5] [√ 3782]. [P] to live in, dwell; to sit, be seated; [H] to cause to settle, cause to dwell in:– living (1), seated (1), settled (1), sit (1), took seat (1)

A10339 יַתִּיר ***yattîr***, a. [8] [√ 3835]. exceptional, outstanding; (as adv.) so, very, exceedingly:– became even greater (1 [+10650, 10323]), exceptional (1), keen (1), most (1), outstanding (1), so (1), very (1), NDT (1)

A10340 כ ***k***, letter. Not used in NIVEBC [√ 3868]. letter of the Aramaic alphabet

A10341 כְּ־ ***ke-***, pp.pref. [41] [√ 3869]. as, like, according to:– like (14), as (6), in accordance with (4), when (3 [+10168]), according to (1), after (1), all (1 [+10248]), any more than (1 [+10195, 10168]), as follows (1 [+10180]), as soon as (1 [+10232, 10002, 10168]), at (1), for (1), how (1 [+10408]), how (1 [+10408]), in way (1), such (1 [+10180]), this (1 [+10180]), when (1)

A10342 ־ךְ ***-k***, p.suf.2.m.sg. [99] [√ 3870]. you, your:– your (43), you (40), there[S] (1 [+10444]), yours (1), yourself (1), yourself (1 [+10381]), NDT (12)

A10343 כְּדַב ***kedab***, a. [1] [→ 10344; 3942]. misleading, false:– misleading (1)

A10344 כִּדְבָה ***kidbâ***, a. Not used in NIVEBC [√ 10323; 3942]. lie

A10345 כָּה ***kâ***, adv. [1] [√ 3907]. here, up to this point:– This (1 [+10527])

A10346 כְּהַל ***kehal***, v. [4] [cf. 10321]. [P] to be able:– could (2), able (1), can (1)

A10347 כָּהֵן ***kāhēn***, n.m. [8] [√ 3913]. priest:– priests (6), priest (2)

A10348 כַּוָּה ***kawwâ***, n.f. [1] window:– windows (1)

A10349 ־כוֹן ***-kôn***, p.suf.2.m.pl. [10] [√ 10355; 4013]. you, your:– you (8), your (2)

A10350 כּוֹרֶשׁ ***kôreš***, n.pr.m. [8] [√ 3931]. Cyrus:– Cyrus (7), NDT (1)

A10351 כִּיל ***kîl***, v. Not used in NIVEBC [√ 3920?]. [Itpe] to be fixed

A10352 כַּכַּר ***kakkar***, n.[f.] [1] [√ 3971]. talent (unit of weight or value, probably about 75 lbs [34 k]):– talents (1)

A10353 כֹּל ***kōl***, n.m. [104] [√ 10354; 3972]. all, totality, completion of an event; a part of a totality: any, every:– all (38), any (9), whole (6), because (4 [+10619, 10168]), no (4 [+10379]), for (3 [+10619, 10168]), anyone (2 [+10050]), every (2), everything (2), a[S] (1), anyone (1), anyone[S] (1), by (1 [+10619, 10168]), cordial greetings (1 [+10720, 10002, 10002]), do so[S] (1 [+10708, 10544]), entire (1), even as (1 [+10619, 10168]), everyone (1 [+10050]), just as (1 [+10619, 10168]), none (1 [+10379]), since (1 [+10619, 10168]), so (1 [+10619, 10180]), then (1 [+10619, 10180]), therefore (1 [+10619, 10180]), they[S] (1 [+10553, 10002]), this is the meaning (1 [+10619, 10168]), this made (1 [+10619, 10180]), though (1 [+10619, 10168]), throughout (1 [+10089]), whatever (1 [+10168]), whatever (1 [+10168]), wherever (1 [+10089, 10168]), whoever (1 [+10168]), whoever (1 [+10050, 10168]), NDT (9)

A10354 כְּלַל ***kelal***, v. [7] [→ 10353; 4005]. [Sh] to finish, restore; [Hsh] to be finished:– are restored (2), finish (2), finished (2), restoring (1)

A10355 ־כֹם ***-kōm***, p.suf.2.m.pl. [5] [√ 10349; 4013]. you, your:– you (3), your (2)

A10356 כְּמָה ***kemâ***, pp. & p.inter. Not used in NIVEBC [√ 10341 + 10408]. how?. see 10341 & 10408

A10357 כֵּן ***kēn***, adv. [8] [√ 4027]. this is what, thus:– this (2), NDT (6)

A10358 כְּנֵמָא ***kenēmā'***, adv. [5] as follows, thus:– also (1 [+10008]), as follows (1), this (1), NDT (2)

A10359 כְּנַשׁ ***kenaš***, v. [3] [√ 4043]. [P] to assemble (persons); [Htpa] to be assembled:– assembled (1), crowded around (1), summoned (1 [+10714, 10378])

A10360 כְּנָת ***kenāt***, n.m. [7] [√ 4056]. associate, colleague:– associates (6), other (1)

A10361 כַּשְׂדָּי ***kasdāy***, n.pr.g. Not used in NIVEBC [cf. 10373]. Chaldean

A10362 כְּסַף ***kesap***, n.m. [13] [√ 4084]. silver:– silver (12), money (1)

A10363 כְּעַן ***ke'an***, adv. [13] [→ 10364, 10365]. now, furthermore, to the present:– now (6), furthermore (1), now then (1), the present (1), NDT (4)

A10364 כְּעֶנֶת ***ke'enet***, adv. [3] [√ 10363]. (and) now, a marker to connect what follows:– now (1), NDT (2)

A10365 כְּעֶת ***ke'et***, adv. [1] [√ 10363]. (and) now; the phrase "Peace and now" is a formal greeting in a letter:– NDT (1)

A10366 כְּפַת ***kepat***, v. [4] [Peil] to be bound; [Pa] to tie up; [Pap] to be tied:– firmly tied (1), tie up (1), tied up (1), were bound (1)

A10367 כֹּר ***kōr***, n.[m.] [1] [√ 4123]. cor (dry measure):– cors (1)

A10368 כַּרְבְּלָה ***karbelâ***, n.f. [1] headdress of some kind: turban, cap; the etymology suggests something wrapped around the head:– turbans (1)

A10369 כְּרָה ***kerâ***, v. [1] [Itpe] to be troubled, distressed:– troubled (1)

A10370 כָּרוֹז ***kārôz***, n.m. [1] [→ 10371]. herald, proclaimer:– herald (1)

A10371 כְּרַז ***keraz***, v.den. [1] [→ 10370]. [H] to proclaim:– proclaimed (1)

A10372 כָּרְסֵא ***korsē'***, n.m. [3] [√ 4058]. seat, chair; of power and position: throne; "to come down from the throne" means to be deposed and so lose power:– throne (2), thrones (1)

A10373 כַּשְׂדָּי ***kaśdāy***, n.pr.g. [9] [cf. 10361; 4169]. Chaldean; Babylonian; (as a common noun) astrologer:– astrologers (6), Babylonians (1), Chaldean (1), astrologer (1)

A10374 כְּתַב ***ketab***, v. [8] [→ 10375; 4180]. [P] to write; [Pp, Peil] to be written:– wrote (4), read (1), was written (1), write down (1), wrote down (1)

A10375 כְּתָב ***ketāb***, n.m. [12] [√ 10374; 4181]. writing, inscription, decree:– writing (5), inscription (2), put in writing (2 [+10673]), decree (1), limit (1), what written (1)

A10376 כְּתַל ***ketal***, n.[m.] [2] wall:– wall (1), walls (1)

A10377 ל ***l***, letter. Not used in NIVEBC [√ 4199]. letter of the Aramaic alphabet

A10378 לְ- ***le-***, pp.pref. [356] [√ 4200]. to, for, toward, into; belonging to, with regard to:– to (103), for (21), of (10), into (7), forever (6 [+10550]), had (6), into (6 [+10135]), in (3), against (2), as (2), before (2 [+10619]), on (2), why (2 [+10408]), against (1 [+10608]), applied to (1), at (1), because of (1 [+10619, 10168]), by (1), extends to (1), forever (1 [+10550, 10002]), his (1 [+10192]), in favor of (1), knocking (1 [+10491, 10154, 10154]), later (1 [+10636]), near (1 [+10619]), never (1 [+10379, 10550]), responsible (1 [+10484]), so that (1), summoned (1 [+10042, 10085]), summoned (1 [+10714, 10359]), summoned (1 [+10637, 10089, 10264, 10549]), their[S] (1 [+10037, 10131]), toward (1), what (1 [+10408]), will be left with (1 [+10029]), with (1), with (1 [+10619]), NDT (160)

A10379 לָא ***lā'***, adv.neg. [82] [cf. 10384; 4202]. no, not, never:– not (37), no (11), cannot (4), no (4 [+10353]), without (4), nor (3 [+10221]), never (2), before (1), neither (1), never (1 [+10378, 10550]), none (1 [+10353]), nor (1 [+10221, 10059]), nothing (1), nothing (1 [+10269]), rather than (1), unable (1 [+10321]), unharmed (1 [+10244, 10029]), weren't (1), NDT (6)

A10380 לֵב ***lēb***, n.[m.] [1] [√ 10381; 4213]. heart, mind:– myself (1 [+10307])

A10381 לְבַב ***lebab***, n.m. [7] [→ 10380; 4222]. heart (a physical organ); fig., the inner person that thinks, feels, and chooses: mind, heart, will; "one's heart" can mean "oneself":– mind (4), heart (1), mind (1 [+10669]), yourself (1 [+10342])

A10382 לְבוּשׁ ***lebûš***, n.m. [2] [√ 10383; 4230]. clothing, garment:– clothes (1), clothing (1)

A10383 לְבַשׁ ***lebaš***, v. [3] [→ 10382; 4252]. [P] to be clothed; [H] to clothe (another):– clothed (3)

A10384 לָה ***lâ***, adv.neg. Not used in NIVEBC [cf. 10379; 4202]. see 10379

A10385 לָהֵן ***lāhēn[1]***, c. [3] [√ 4270]. so then, therefore:– so (1), so then (1), therefore (1)

A10386 לָהֵן² ***lāhēn[2]***, c. [7] [√ 10379 & 10214]. except, but, unless:– except (4), but (2), unless (1)

A10387 לֵוָי ***lēwāy***, n.g. [4] [√ 4290, 4291]. Levite:– Levites (4)

A10388 לְוָת ***lewāt***, pp. [1] [cf. 10378 + 10337]. near, beside:– from (1 [+10427])

A10389 לְחֶם ***leḥem***, n.m. [1] [√ 4312]. bread; banquet meal:– banquet (1)

A10390 לְחֵנָה ***leḥēnâ***, n.f. [3] concubine, a class of spouse generally of lower status than a wife (the exact marriage relationship of a concubine varied in different cultures), usually for status and pleasure of the husband, also translated "mistress, consort":– concubines (3)

A10391 לֵילֵי ***lêlê***, n.[m.] [5] [√ 4325]. night:– night (5)

A10392 לִשָּׁן ***liššān***, n.m. [7] [√ 4383]. language, tongue:– language (7)

A10393 מ ***m***, letter. Not used in NIVEBC [√ 4391]. letter of the Aramaic alphabet

A10394 מָא ***mā'***, p.inter. & indef. Not used in NIVEBC [√ 10408; 4537]. what?, see 10408

A10395 מְאָה ***me'â***, n.f. [8] [√ 4395, 4396]. hundred; (dual) two hundred:– hundred (7), 120 (1 [+10221, 10574])

A10396 מֹאזְנֵא ***mō'znē'***, n.m.emph. [1] [√ 4404]. scale, balance, with a focus that the device is an objective implement for judging truth:– scales (1)

A10397 מֵאמַר ***mē'mar***, n.[m.] [2] [√ 10042; 4411]. declaration, request:– declare (1), requested (1)

A10398 מָאן ***mā'n***, n.m. [7] article, container, goblet:– articles (4), goblets (3)

A10399 מְגִלָּה ***megillâ***, n.f. [1] [√ 10146; 4479]. scroll:– scroll (1)

A10400 מְגַר ***megar***, v. [1] [√ 4489]. [Pa] to overthrow:– overthrow (1)

A10401 מַדְבַּח ***madbaḥ***, n.[m.] [1] [√ 10156; 4640]. altar:– altar (1)

A10402 מִדָּה ***middâ***, n.f. [4] [cf. 10429; 4501]. tax, revenue, tribute:– taxes (3), revenues (1)

A10403 מְדוֹר ***medôr***, n.[m.] [3] [√ 10163]. living, dwelling:– live (2), lived (1)

A10404 מָדַי ***māday***, n.pr.g. [6] [→ 10405; 4512]. Mede; Media:– Medes (4), Mede (1), Media (1)

A10405 מָדָיָא ***mādāyā'***, n.g. Not used in NIVEBC [√ 10404; 4512]. the Mede, see 10404

A10406 מְדִינָה ***medînâ***, n.f. [11] [√ 10169; 4519]. province, district:– province (7), provincial (2), district (1), provinces (1)

A10407 מְדָר ***medār***, n.m. [1] [√ 10163]. living, dwelling (place):– live (1)

A10408 מָה ***mâ***, p.inter. & indef. [14] [→ 10308; cf. 10426; 4537]. why?, what?; that which, what:– what (5), why (2 [+10378]), how (1 [+10341]), how (1 [+10341]), things (1), what (1 [+10378]), whatever (1), whatever (1 [+10168]), why (1 [+10542])

A10409 מוֹת ***môt***, n.[m.] [1] [√ 4638]. death:– death (1)

A10410 מָזוֹן ***māzôn***, n.[m.] [2] [√ 10226; 2315]. food:– food (2)

A10411 מְחָא ***meḥā'***, v. [4] [√ 4730]. [P] to strike; [Pa] to hold back, prevent; [Htpe] to be impaled:– struck (2), be impaled (1), hold back (1)

A10412 מַחְלְקָה ***maḥleqâ***, n.f. [1] [√ 10269; 4713]. group, division (of priests):– groups (1)

A10413 מְטָא ***meṭā'***, v. [8] [root of:]. [P] to reach out, extend towards:– approached (1), came (1), happened (1), issued (1), reached (1), reaches (1), touched (1), touching (1)

A10414 מִישָׁאֵל ***mîšā'ēl***, n.pr.m. [1] [√ 4792]. Mishael, "*who belongs to God (El)?*":– Mishael (1)

A10415 מֵישַׁךְ ***mêšak***, n.pr.m. [14] [√ 4794]. Meshach, "[perhaps] *I have become weak*":– Meshach (13), NDT (1)

A10416 מְלָא ***melā'***, v. [2] [√ 4848]. [P] to fill; [Htpe] to be filled:– filled (1), furious (1 [+10270])

A10417 מַלְאַךְ ***mal'ak***, n.m. [2] [√ 4855]. messenger; angel, a class of being that serves God, often to communicate with or rescue his faithful on earth:– angel (2)

A10418 מִלָּה ***millâ***, n.f. [24] [√ 10425; 4863]. word, command; matter, thing, affair; a general term like the English "thing":– matter (4), words (3), command (2), decided (2), things (2), decree (1), dream[S] (1), it[S] (1 [+10002]), speak (1 [+10425]), substance (1 [+10646]), thing (1), this[S] (1 [+10002]), voices (1), what[S] (1 [+10002]), what asks (1), what said (1)

A10419 מְלַח¹ ***melaḥ[1]***, v.den. [1] [→ 10420; 4873]. [P] to eat salt (i.e., be under obligation to); "to eat the salt of the palace" is to be under the solemn obligation to the king's interests:– under obligation (1 [+10420])

A10420 מְלַח² ***melaḥ[2]***, n.m. [3] [√ 10419; 4875]. salt, a condiment for food; also used in ceremonies (see 10419):– salt (2), under obligation (1 [+10419])

A10421 מֶלֶךְ ***melek***, n.m. [180] [→ 10423, 10424; 4889]. king, royal ruler:– king (116), your Majesty (19 [+10002]), kings (12), royal (9), king's (6), him[S] (3 [+10002]), he[S] (2 [+10002]), he (1 [+10002]), he[S] (1 [+10453, 10002]), he[S] (1 [+10453, 10002]), his[S] (1 [+10002]), his[S] (1 [+10002]), others[S] (1), royal interests (1), your Majesty's (1 [+10002]), NDT (5)

A10422 מְלַךְ ***melak***, n.m. [1] [√ 4888]. advice, counsel:– advice (1)

A10423 מַלְכָּה ***malkâ***, n.f. [2] [√ 10421; 4893]. queen, the wife of a king, with very high status but not likely equal status to the king; queen mother, mother or grandmother of a king:– queen (1), she[S] (1 [+10002])

A10424 מַלְכוּ ***malkû***, n.f. [57] [√ 10421; 4895]. kingdom, dominion, reign:– kingdom (30), kingdoms (7), reign (5), royal (4), sovereignty (2), dominion (1), government affairs (1), it[S] (1 [+10002]), it[S] (1 [+10191]), realm (1), royal authority (1), sovereign power (1), throne (1), NDT (1)

A10425 מְלַל ***melal***, v. [5] [→ 10418; 4910]. [Pa] to speak:– spoke (2), answered (1), speak (1 [+10418]), speaking (1)

A10426 מַן ***man***, p.inter. & indef. [10] [cf. 10408; 4943]. who? what?; anyone, whoever:– anyone (4 [+10168]), what (2), who (2), whoever (1 [+10168]), whoever (1 [+10168])

A10427 מִן ***min***, pp. [119] [√ 4946]. from, to, out of, more than:– from (40), of (8), partly (7), to (5), with (4), because of (2), before (2 [+10621]), from (2 [+10621]), one (2), out of (2), according to (1), ago (1 [+10622, 10180]), among (1), as soon as (1 [+10008, 10168]), because (1 [+10168]), before (1 [+10622, 10180]), by (1), by (1 [+10621]), certain (1 [+10327, 10313]), for (1), from (1 [+10388]), greater than (1), in (1 [+10608]), issue (1 [+10621]), long history (1 [+10317, 10550]), more than (1), of (1 [+10135]), on (1), over (1 [+10543]), partly (1 [+10636]), prescribed (1 [+10302]), some (1), surely (1 [+10643, 10168]), when (1 [+10168]), NDT (21)

A10428 מְנֵא ***menē'***, n.[m.] [3] [√ 10431; 4948]. mene (unit of weight, about 1.25 lbs. [0.6 kg]):– mene (3)

A10429 מִנְדָּה ***mindâ***, n.f. Not used in NIVEBC [cf. 10402]. tribute, see 10402

A10430 מַנְדַּע ***manda'***, n.[m.] [4] [√ 10313; 4529]. knowledge, understanding; in some contexts, sanity:– knowledge (2), sanity (2)

A10431 מְנָה ***menâ***, v. [5] [→ 10428, 10433; 4948]. [P] to number; [Pa] to appoint, set (over):– appointed (2), appoint (1), numbered (1), set (1)

A10432 מִנְחָה ***minḥâ***, n.f. [2] [√ 4966]. offering, gift; grain offering:– grain offerings (1), offering (1)

A10433 מִנְיָן ***minyān***, n.[m.] [1] [√ 10431]. number:– each (1)

A10434 מַעֲבָד ***ma'ăbād***, n.[m.] [1] [√ 10522; 5042]. what one does, work:– does (1)

A10435 מְעֵה ***me'ēh***, n.[m.]pl. [1] [√ 5055]. belly:– belly (1)

A10436 מֶעָל ***me'āl***, n.[m.] [1] [√ 10549]. going in, (+ 10728) sunset:– sundown (1 [+10728, 10002])

A10437 מָרֵא ***mārē'***, n.m. [4] lord; (of God) the Lord; "Lord of kings" is one who is an authority over any and all other authorities:– lord (4)

A10438 מְרַד ***merad***, n.[m.] [1] [→ 10439; 5278]. rebellion:– rebellion (1)

A10439 מָרָד ***mārād***, a. [2] [√ 10438]. rebellious:– rebellious (2)

A10440 מְרַט ***meraṭ***, v. [1] [√ 5307]. [Peil] to be torn off, plucked out:– were torn off (1)

A10441 מֹשֶׁה ***mōšeh***, n.pr.m. [1] [√ 5407]. Moses, "*drawn out* [Ex 2:10]; [Egyptian for] *child*":– Moses (1)

A10442 מְשַׁח¹ ***mešaḥ[1]***, n.[m.] [2] [√ 5418]. olive oil, used for food, lamp oil, and ceremonies:– olive oil (2)

A10443 מְשַׁח² ***mešaḥ[2]***, n.[m.] Not used in NIVEBC [√ 5419]. measure

A10444 מִשְׁכַּב ***miškab***, n.[m.] [6] [√ 5435]. bed, formally "a place for lying," which can refer to simple mats and even outer cloaks, as well as to pieces of furniture:– bed (5), there[S] (1 [+10342])

A10445 מִשְׁכַּן ***miškan***, n.[m.] [1] [√ 10709; 5438]. dwelling, abode:– dwelling (1)

A10446 מַשְׁרוֹקִי ***mašrôqî***, n.f. [4] flute, musical pipe, a cylinder-shaped instrument producing a high shrill sound, made of wood, reed, or bone:– flute (4)

A10447 מִשְׁתֵּא ***mištē'***, n.m. [1] [√ 10748; 5492]. banquet (hall); feast (hall), a place of merriment and celebration, often associated with drinking bouts:– banquet (1)

A10448 מַתְּנָה ***mattenâ***, n.f. [3] [√ 10498; 5508]. gift:– gifts (3)

A10449 נ ***n***, letter. Not used in NIVEBC [√ 5526]. letter of the Aramaic alphabet

A10450 -נָא ***-nā'***, p.suf.1.com.pl. [10] [√ 5646]. we, our:– us (7), our (1), the[S] (1), we (1)

A10451 נְבָא ***nebā'***, v. [1] [→ 10452, 10455; 5547]. [Htpa] to prophesy, act as a prophet:– prophesied (1)

A10452 נְבוּאָה ***nebû'â***, n.f. [1] [√ 10451; 5553]. prophesying, preaching:– preaching (1)

A10453 נְבוּכַדְנֶצַּר ***nebûkadneṣṣar***, n.pr.m. [31] [√ 5556, 5557]. Nebuchadnezzar, "*Nebo protect my boundary stone* or *Nebo protect my son!*":– Nebuchadnezzar (28), he[S] (1 [+10421, 10002]), he[S] (1 [+10421, 10002]), NDT (1)

A10454 נְבִזְבָּה ***nebizbâ***, n.f. [2] present, gift; this can be a gift given as a recompense for a proper service, a reward:– rewards (2)

A10455 נְבִיא ***nebî'***, n.m. [4] [√ 10451; 5566]. prophet, one who speaks for God in inspired utterance, often including the application of the message:– prophet (3), prophets (1)

A10456 נֶבְרְשָׁה ***nebrešâ***, n.f.emph. [1] lampstand:– lampstand (1)

A10457 נְגַד ***negad***, v. [1] [→ 10458; 5583]. [P] to flow:– flowing (1)

A10458 נֶגֶד ***neged***, pp. [1] [√ 10457; 5584]. toward, before, facing:– toward (1)

A10459 נְגַהּ ***negah***, n.[f.] [1] [√ 5586]. brightness (i.e., first light of dawn):– first light (1)

A10460 נְגוֹ ***negô***, n.pr.m. Not used in NIVEBC [cf. 10524]. Nego, see 10524

A10461 נְדַב ***nedab***, v. [4] [→ 10219; 5605]. [Htpa] to be willing, to give freely; (as noun) a freewill offering:– freely given (1), freewill offerings (1), volunteer (1), NDT (1)

A10462 נִדְבָּךְ ***nidbāk***, n.m. [2] course (of timber or stone in building):– courses (1), NDT (1)

A10463 נְדַד ***nedad***, v. [1] [cf. 10469; 5610]. [P] to flee (i.e., sleep flees = insomnia):– could not (1)

A10464 נִדְנֶה ***nidneh***, n.[m.] [1] sheath (of the spirit = the body):– in (1 [+10089, 10135])

A10465 נְהוֹר ***nehôr***, n.m. Not used in NIVEBC [→ 10466, 10467; 5644]. light

A10466 נְהִיר ***nehîr***, n.m. [1] [√ 10465; 5644]. light:– light (1)

A10467 נַהִירוּ ***nahîrû***, n.f. [2] [√ 10465; 5644]. insight, illumination (of the mind):– insight (2)

A10468 נְהַר ***nehar***, n.m. [15] [√ 5643]. river, stream:– Trans-Euphrates (12 [+10526, 10191]), Trans-Euphrates (1 [+10526, 10002]), river (1), that province^S (1 [+10526, 10191])

A10469 נוּד ***nûd***, v. [1] [cf. 10463; 5653]. [P] to flee:– flee (1)

A10470 נְוָלוּ ***newālû***, n.f. [3] pile of rubble, garbage-heap:– piles of rubble (2), pile of rubble (1)

A10471 נוּר ***nûr***, n.f. & m. [17] [√ 5775]. fire; used for heat, purification, and as a form of execution:– blazing (8 [+10328]), fire (8), all ablaze (1 [+10178])

A10472 נְזַק ***nezaq***, v. [4] [→ 10215; 5691]. [P] to suffer loss; [H] to cause to suffer, be a detriment, be troublesome:– detriment (1), suffer (1), suffer loss (1), troublesome (1)

A10473 נְחָשׁ ***nehāš***, n.m. [9] [√ 5703, 5733]. bronze material; "brass" is a copper alloy dating from Roman times:– bronze (9)

A10474 נְחַת ***nehat***, v. [6] [√ 5737]. [P] to come down; [H, A] to deposit, store; [Ho] to be deposed:– coming down (2), deposit (1), deposited (1), stored (1), was deposed (1)

A10475 נְטַל ***neṭal***, v. [2] [√ 5747]. [P] to raise up, lift up; [Peil] to be lifted up:– raised (1), was lifted (1)

A10476 נְטַר ***neṭar***, v. [1] [√ 5915]. [P] to keep (in one's mind or heart):– kept (1)

A10477 -נִי ***-nî***, p.suf.1.com.sg. [18] [√ 10307; 5761]. I, me, my:– me (17), NDT (1)

A10478 נִיחוֹחַ ***niḥôah***, n.[m.] [2] [√ 5767]. incense, pleasing scent:– incense (1), pleasing (1)

A10479 נְכַס ***nekas***, n.[m.] [2] [√ 5794]. treasury; fine:– property (1), treasury (1)

A10480 נְמַר ***nemar***, n.[m.] [1] [√ 5807]. leopard, panther:– leopard (1)

A10481 נְסַח ***nesah***, v. [1] [√ 5815]. [Htpe] to be pulled out:– be pulled (1)

A10482 ¹נְסַךְ ***nesak¹***, v. [1] [→ 10483; 5818]. [Pa] to present (an offering):– presented (1)

A10483 ²נְסַךְ ***nesak²***, n.[m.] [1] [√ 10482; 5821]. drink offering, libation:– drink offerings (1)

A10484 נְפַל ***nepal***, v. [11] [√ 5877]. [P] to fall:– fall down (5), fell (3), came (1), fell down (1), responsible (1 [+10378])

A10485 נְפַק ***nepaq***, v. [11] [→ 10486]. [P] to go out, come out; [H] to take out, remove:– taken (3), appeared (1), came out (1), come out (1), coming out (1), gone out (1), issued (1), removed (1), took (1)

A10486 נִפְקָה ***nipqâ***, n.f. [2] [√ 10485]. expense, cost:– costs (1), expenses (1)

A10487 נִצְבָּה ***nişbâ***, n.f. [1] hardness, firmness, a quality of strength of a metal:– strength (1)

A10488 נְצַח ***neṣah***, v. [1] [√ 5904]. [Htpa] to distinguish oneself:– distinguished himself (1)

A10489 נְצַל ***neṣal***, v. [3] [√ 5911]. [H] to save, rescue, deliver:– save (2), saves (1)

A10490 נְקֵא ***neqē'***, a. [1] [√ 5929]. pure, clean; this purity can be symbolized by the color white, as of lamb's wool:– white (1)

A10491 נְקַשׁ ***neqaš***, v. [1] [√ 5943]. [P] to knock (together):– knocking (1 [+10154, 10378, 10154])

A10492 נְשָׂא ***neśā'***, v. [3] [√ 5951]. [P] to take away, carry away; [Htpa] to revolt, rise up:– revolt (1), swept away (1), take (1)

A10493 נְשִׁין ***nešîn***, n.f.pl. [1] [√ 851]. wives, women:– wives (1)

A10494 נִשְׁמָה ***nišmâ***, n.f. [1] [√ 5972]. breath, air that enters and exhales the lungs; fig., that which is animate and conscious: life:– life (1)

A10495 נְשַׁר ***nešar***, n.m. [2] [√ 5979]. eagle, vulture:– eagle (2)

A10496 נִשְׁתְּוָן ***ništewān***, n.m. [3] [√ 5981]. official letter, decree:– letter (2), written reply (1)

A10497 נְתִין ***netîn***, n.m.pl. [1] [√ 10498; 5987]. temple servant:– temple servants (1)

A10498 נְתַן ***netan***, v. [7] [→ 10448, 10497; cf. 10314; 5989]. [P] to give, provide, supply:– gives (3), paid (1), provide (1), supply (1), NDT (1)

A10499 נְתַר ***netar***, v. [1] [H/A] to strip off, shake off:– strip off (1)

A10500 ס ***s***, letter. Not used in NIVEBC [√ 6005]. letter of the Aramaic alphabet

A10501 סַבְּכָא ***sabbekā'***, n.[f.] Not used in NIVEBC [cf. 10676]. lyre

A10502 סְבַל ***sebal***, v. [1] [√ 6022]. [Po] to be laid:– be laid (1)

A10503 סְבַר ***sebar***, v. [1] [√ 8431, 8432]. [P] to try, strive, seek:– try (1)

A10504 סְגִד ***segid***, v. [12] [√ 6032]. [P] to worship, pay honor:– worship (10), paid honor (1), worshiped (1)

A10505 סְגַן ***segan***, n.m. [5] [√ 6036]. prefect, governor:– prefects (4), in charge (1 [+10647])

A10506 סְגַר ***segar***, v. [1] [√ 6037]. [P] to shut, close up:– shut (1)

A10507 סוּמְפֹּנְיָה ***sûmpōneyâ***, n.f. [3] [cf. 10510, 10512]. musical instrument; sources vary widely: a wind instrument: pipe, bagpipe, double flute; a stringed instrument: dulcimer; a percussion instrument: drum, cymbal:– pipe (3)

A10508 סוּף ***sûp***, v. [2] [→ 10509; 6066]. [P] to be fulfilled; [H] to bring to an end:– bring to an end (1), fulfilled (1)

A10509 סוֹף ***sôp***, n.[m.] [5] [√ 10508; 6067]. end (of space, time, or circumstance):– distant parts (1), end (1), ends (1), forever (1 [+10527, 10002]), never end (1 [+10527, 10002])

A10510 סוּפֹּנְיָא ***sûppōneyā'***, n.f. Not used in NIVEBC [cf. 10507]. pipes, see 10507

A10511 סְטַר ***seṭar***, n.m. Not used in NIVEBC [cf. 10680]. see 10680

A10512 סִיפֹּנְיָא ***sîppōneyā'***, n.f. Not used in NIVEBC [cf. 10507]. pipes, see 10507

A10513 סְלִק ***selaq***, v. [8] [√ 6158]. [P] to come up, go up; [H] to lift up; [Ho] to be lifted up:– came up (4), lift out (1), took up (1), turned (1), was lifted (1)

A10514 סְעַד ***se'ad***, v. [1] [√ 6184]. [Pa] to help, support:– supporting (1)

A10515 סְפַר ***separ***, n.m. [5] [→ 10516; 6219]. record, archive, book (though not a book in the sense of a codex with bound pages); the phrase "book of Moses" means the first five books of the Bible:– archives (1 [+10103]), archives (1 [+10177]), book (1), books (1), records (1 [+10177])

A10516 סָפַר ***sāpar***, n.m. [6] [√ 10515; 6221]. teacher of the Law; secretary (an official), scribe:– secretary (4), teacher (2)

A10517 סַרְבָּל ***sarbāl***, n.[m.] [2] robe, garment; variously translated as "hose, trousers, tunic, mantle, coat, cloak":– robes (2)

A10518 סָרַךְ ***sārak***, n.m. [5] administrator:– administrators (5)

A10519 ¹סְתַר ***setar¹***, v. [1] [√ 6259]. [Pap] to be hidden; (as noun) hidden things:– hidden (1)

A10520 ²סְתַר ***setar²***, v. [1] [√ 8609]. [P] to destroy, demolish:– destroyed (1)

A10521 ע ***'***, letter. Not used in NIVEBC [√ 6263]. letter of the Aramaic alphabet

A10522 עֲבַד ***'abad***, v. [28] [→ 10434, 10523, 10525; 6268]. [P] to do, make; [Htpe] to be done, be made, be turned into; a general word of activity and occurrence; the context determines the best translation, "do, make, obey, happen," etc:– done (3), do (2), made (2), be carried out (1), be cut into (1), be done (1), be made (1), being carried on (1), carried out (1), celebrated (1), cut into (1), does (1), gave (1), make (1), neglect (1 [+10712]), obey (1), performed (1), performs (1), provide (1), punished (1 [+10170, 10191]), sedition (1 [+10083]), waging (1), NDT (2)

A10523 עֲבֵד ***'abēd***, n.m. [7] [√ 10522; 6269]. servant:– servants (6), servant (1)

A10524 עֲבֵד נְגוֹ ***'abēd negô***, n.pr.m. [14] [√ 10523 & ?; 6284]. Abednego, "*servant of Nego* or *Nebo*":– Abednego (13), NDT (1)

A10525 עֲבִידָה ***'abîdâ***, n.f. [6] [√ 10522; 6275]. work, service, administration:– work (3), administrators (1), affairs (1), service (1)

A10526 עֲבַר ***'abar***, n.m. [14] [√ 6298]. the opposite bank (of a river); Trans(-Euphrates) or "beyond (the River)" is to the east of Israel:– Trans-Euphrates (12 [+10468, 10191]), Trans-Euphrates (1 [+10468, 10002]), that province^S (1 [+10468, 10191])

A10527 עַד ***'ad***, pp. & c. [35] [√ 10528?; 6330]. up to, until:– until (8 [+10168]), until (4), for (3), during (2), as (1 [+10168]), ever (1 [+10550, 10002]), finally (1 [+10221, 10024]), forever (1 [+10509, 10002]), forever (1 [+10550, 10002]), hoping (1 [+10168]), never end (1 [+10509, 10002]), on (1), so that (1 [+10159, 10168]), this (1 [+10345]), to (1), up to (1), while (1 [+10168]), NDT (5)

A10528 עֲדָה ***'adâ***, v. [9] [→ 10527?; 6334]. [P] to be taken, be repealed; [H] to take away:– repealed (2), stripped (2), deposes (1), pass away (1), taken (1), taken away (1), was (1)

A10529 עִדּוֹא ***'iddô***, n.pr.m. [2] [√ 6341, 6342]. Iddo:– Iddo (2)

A10530 עִדָּן ***'iddān***, n.m. [13] time (general or specific period); "time, times, and half a time" likely means three-and-one-half periods of time:– times (6), time (3), as soon as (1 [+10089, 10002, 10168]), period of time (1 [+10232, 10221]), situation (1), when (1 [+10089, 10002])

A10531 עוֹד ***'ôd***, adv. [1] [√ 6388]. still, yet:– Even as (1)

A10532 עֲוָיָה ***'awāyâ***, n.f. [1] wickedness, iniquity:– wickedness (1)

A10533 עוֹף ***'ôp***, n.[m.] [2] [√ 6416]. bird; a "bird of heaven" is any wild bird:– bird (1), birds (1)

A10534 עוּר ***'ûr***, n.[m.] [1] chaff, the husk particles of threshed grain, used fig. to indicate something worthless:– chaff (1)

A10535 עֵז ***'ēz***, n.[f.] [1] goat (male and female):– male goats (1 [+10615])

A10536 עִזְקָה ***'izqâ***, n.f. [2] signet-ring, used to validate official business:– rings (1), signet ring (1)

A10537 עֶזְרָא ***'ezrā'***, n.pr.m. [3] [√ 6474]. Ezra, "*help*":– Ezra (3)

A10538 עֲזַרְיָה ***'azaryâ***, n.pr.m. [1] [√ 6481]. Azariah, "*Yahweh has helped*":– Azariah (1)

A10539 עֵטָה ***'ēṭâ***, n.f. [1] [√ 10324; 6783]. counsel, wisdom:– wisdom (1)

A10540 עַיִן ***'ayin***, n.f. [5] [√ 6524]. eye:– eyes (4), eye (1)

A10541 עִיר ***'îr***, n.m. [3] [√ 6424]. messenger (of God), watcher, one who is a sentinel to guard and protect:– messenger (2), messengers (1)

A10542 עַל ***'al***, pp. [104] [→ 10543, 10545, 10546, 10547, 10548; 6584]. upon, over, against, toward, concerning:– to (16), on (13), over (8), for (7), against (5), in (5), about (4), lying in (4), around (3), of (3), among (1), concerning (1), had (1 [+10201]), lying (1), prostrate (1 [+10049]), rule (1), so that (1 [+10159, 10168]), than (1), that is why (1 [+10180]), toward (1), why (1 [+10408]), NDT (25)

A10543 עֵלָּא ***'ēllā'***, adv. [1] [√ 10542; 6584]. over, above:– over (1 [+10427])

A10544 עִלָּה ***'illâ***, n.f. [3] [√ 6618]. grounds, basis, pretext (for charges):– basis for charges (1), do so^S (1 [+10708, 10353]), grounds for charges (1)

A10545 עֲלָוָה ***'alāwâ***, n.f. [1] [√ 10542; 6592]. burnt offering:– burnt offerings (1)

A10546 עִלָּי ***'illāy***, a. [10] [√ 10542; 6604]. highest, superior; the Most High, a title of God indicating his supreme status and power:– Most High (10)

A10547 עִלִּי ***'illî***, n.f. [1] [√ 10542; 6606]. upstairs room, a storage or guest room on the flat roof of a house:– upstairs room (1)

A10548 עֶלְיוֹן ***'elyôn***, a. [4] [√ 10542; 6610]. highest, superior; (as a title) the Most High:– most high (3), his^S (1)

A10549 עֲלַל ***'alal***, v. [14] [→ 10436; 6619]. [P] to go in; [H] to take in, bring before; [Ho] to be brought in, introduced before:– brought (2), came (2), went (2), came in (1), came into (1), summoned (1 [+10637, 10089, 10264, 10378]), take (1), took (1), was brought (1), went in (1), were brought (1)

A10550 עָלַם ***'ālam***, n.[m.] [20] [√ 6409]. forever, eternal, everlasting; ancient, a long time ago:– forever (6 [+10378]), eternal (2), ever (2 [+10002]), everlasting (2), ever (1), ever (1 [+10527, 10002]), forever (1 [+10002]), forever (1 [+10527, 10002]), forever (1 [+10378, 10002]), long (1), long history (1 [+10427, 10317]), never (1 [+10379, 10378])

A10551 עֵלְמָי ***'ēlmāy***, n.g.pl. [1] [√ 6520]. Elamite:– Elamites (1)

A10552 עֲלַע ***'ala'***, n.f. [1] [√ 7521]. rib:– ribs (1)

A10553 עַם ***'am***, n.m. [15] [√ 6639]. people, nation:– people (7), nations (6), Israelites (1 [+10335]), they^S (1 [+10353, 10002])

A10554 עִם ***'im***, pp. [22] [√ 6640]. with, along with, to, for; a marker showing association in various meanings:– with (11), for (2), to (2), against (1), among (1), as well as (1), at (1), of (1), united (1 [+10158, 10180, 10180]), NDT (1)

A10555 עַמִּיק ***'ammîq***, a. [1] [√ 6678]. deep; (as noun) the deep things, which are normally impenetrable and so secret and hidden, with the implication that such things are mysterious, profound, and valuable:– deep (1)

A10556 עֲמַר ***'amar***, n.m. [1] [√ 7547]. wool:– wool (1)

A10557 עַן ***'an***, adv. Not used in NIVEBC [cf. 10363]. see 10363

A10558 עֲנָה ***'anâ***, v. [30] [√ 6699]. [P] to answer, reply; usually a reaction to a direct question, but can be a more general response:– said (13), answered (5), replied (5), asked (3), ordered (1), shouted (1), NDT (2)

A10559 עֲנֵה ***'anēh***, a. [1] [√ 6714, 6705]. oppressed, needy, poor, implying that such persons are miserable in their life situation:– oppressed (1)

A10560 עֲנָן ***'anān***, n.[m.] [1] [√ 6727]. cloud:– clouds (1)

A10561 עֲנַף ***'anap***, n.[m.] [4] [√ 6733]. branch, bough:– branches (4)

A10562 עֲנָשׁ ***'anāš***, n.[m.] [1] [√ 6741]. confiscation; some sources translate as "fine," a monetary penalty without the necessary confiscation of property:– confiscation (1)

A10563 עֶנֶת ***'enet***, adv. Not used in NIVEBC [cf. 10364]. see 10364

A10564 עֳפִי **ʿopî**, n.m. [3] [√ 6751]. leaves, foliage:– leaves (3)

A10565 עֲצִיב **ʿᵃṣîb**, a.vbl. [1] anguished, sorrowful:– anguished (1)

A10566 עֲקַר **ʿᵃqar**, v.den. [1] [→ 10567; 6827]. [Itpe] to be uprooted, plucked out:– were uprooted (1)

A10567 עִקַּר **ʿiqqar**, n.[m.] [3] [√ 10566]. stump, root:– stump (3)

A10568 עָר **ʿār**, n.m. [1] [√ 7640]. adversary, foe:– adversaries (1)

A10569 עֲרַב **ʿᵃrab**, v. [4] [√ 6843]. [Pap] to be mixed; [Htpa] (ptcp.) mixture:– mixed (2), mixes (1), mixture (1)

A10570 עֲרָד **ʿᵃrād**, n.m. [1] [√ 6871]. wild donkey:– wild donkeys (1)

A10571 עַרְוָה **ʿarwâ**, n.f. [1] [√ 6872]. nakedness; fig., dishonor, lowering of one's status in a community resulting in disgrace or shame:– dishonored (1)

A10572 עֲשַׂב **ʿᵃśab**, n.[m.] [5] [√ 6912]. grass, (green) plants:– grass (4), plants (1)

A10573 עֲשַׂר **ʿᵃśar**, n.m. & f. [6] [→ 10574; 6924, 6927]. ten:– ten (4), twelve (1 [+10775]), twelve (1 [+10775])

A10574 עֶשְׂרִין **ʿeśrîn**, n.pl.indecl. [1] [√ 10573; 6929]. twenty; note that this is the grammatical plural of "ten":– 120 (1 [+10395, 10221])

A10575 עֲשִׁת **ʿᵃšat**, v. [1] [√ 6951]. [P] to plan, intend:– planned (1)

A10576 עֵת **ʿet**, adv. Not used in NIVEBC [cf. 10365]. see 10365

A10577 עֲתִיד **ʿᵃtîd**, a. [1] [√ 6969]. ready:– ready (1)

A10578 עַתִּיק **ʿattîq**, a. [3] old, ancient; (as a title) the Ancient (of Days), a title of veneration and honor emphasizing wisdom and power:– Ancient (3)

A10579 פ **p**, letter. Not used in NIVEBC [√ 6989]. letter of the Aramaic alphabet

A10580 פֶּחָה **peḥâ**, n.m. [10] [√ 7068]. governor:– governor (6), governors (4)

A10581 פֶּחָר **peḥār**, n.m. [1] potter; sources translate "clay":– NDT (1)

A10582 פַּטִּישׁ **paṭṭîš**, n.[m.] [1] trousers, leggings; some sources identify as other parts of clothing: coat, tunic, shirt, trousers, hose, hat, etc:– trousers (1)

A10583 1פְּלַג **pᵉlag[1]**, v. [1] [→ 10584, 10585; 7103]. [Pp] to be divided:– divided (1)

A10584 2פְּלַג **pᵉlag[2]**, n.[m.] [1] [√ 10583; 7104]. half:– half (1)

A10585 פְּלֻגָּה **pᵉluggâ**, n.f. [1] [√ 10583; 7107]. division (of priests):– divisions (1)

A10586 פְּלַח **pᵉlaḥ**, v. [10] [→ 10587; 7114?]. [P] to serve, worship, work for (deity or deities):– serve (7), workers (1), worship (1), worshiped (1)

A10587 פָּלְחָן **polḥān**, n.[m.] [1] [√ 10586]. worship, service, work (for deity):– worship (1)

A10588 פֻּם **pum**, n.m. [6] mouth:– mouth (4), lips (1), mouths (1)

A10589 פַּס **pas**, n.m. [2] [√ 7168]. (palm of) hand; this may also refer to the entire hand:– hand (2 [+10311])

A10590 פְּסַנְתֵּרִין **pᵉsantērîn**, n.[m.] [4] harp (triangular stringed instrument):– harp (4)

A10591 פַּרְזֶל **parzel**, n.m. [20] [√ 1366]. iron:– iron (20)

A10592 פְּרַס **pᵉras**, v. [1] [→ 10593; 7271]. [Peil] to be divided:– is divided (1)

A10593 פְּרֵס **pᵉrēs**, n.[m.] [2] [√ 10592]. parsin, peres (unit of measure & weight):– parsin (1), peres (1)

A10594 פָּרַס **pāras**, n.pr.loc. & g. [6] [→ 10595; 7273]. Persia, Persian:– Persians (4), Persia (2)

A10595 פַּרְסָי **parsāy**, a.g. [1] [√ 10594; 7275]. Persian:– Persian (1)

A10596 פְּרַק **pᵉraq**, v. [1] [√ 7293]. [P] to break off, tear away; to loosen, abolish; to renounce:– Renounce (1)

A10597 פְּרַשׁ **pᵉraš**, v. [1] [√ 7298]. [Pap] to be translated, be made clear, with an implication that each and every element of the letter be read and made clear:– translated (1)

A10598 פַּרְשֶׁגֶן **paršegen**, n.m. [3] [√ 7358]. copy (of a document):– copy (3)

A10599 1פְּשַׁר **pᵉšar[1]**, v. [2] [→ 10600; 7323, 7354]. [P] to give an interpretation; [Pa] to interpret; (as noun) an interpreter:– give interpretations (1 [+10600]), interpret (1)

A10600 2פְּשַׁר **pᵉšar[2]**, n.m. [31] [√ 10599; 7323]. interpretation, explanation, what something means:– means (7), interpret (5 [+10252]), interpretation (4), interpret (3), interpret (3 [+10313]), interpret (2 [+10042]), meaning (2), explain (1), explain (1 [+10252]), give interpretations (1 [+10599]), mean (1), meant (1)

A10601 פִּתְגָם **pitgām**, n.m. [6] [√ 7330]. word: report, reply, edict, decision, decree:– answer (1), decision (1), defend (1 [+10754]), edict (1), reply (1), report (1)

A10602 פְּתַח **pᵉtaḥ**, v. [2] [√ 7337]. [Pp, Peil] to be opened:– opened (1), were opened (1)

A10603 פְּתָי **pᵉtāy**, n.[m.] [2] width, breadth:– wide (2)

A10604 צ **ṣ**, letter. Not used in NIVEBC [√ 7360]. letter of the Aramaic alphabet

A10605 צְבָה **ṣᵉbâ**, v. [10] [→ 10606]. [P] to wish, desire, want, long for:– wanted to (4), wishes (4), pleases (1), wanted (1)

A10606 צְבוּ **ṣᵉbû**, n.f. [1] [√ 10605]. situation, matter, affair, thing:– situation (1)

A10607 צְבַע **ṣᵉbaʿ**, v. [5] [√ 7388]. [Pa] to drench, make wet; [Htpa] to be drenched, made wet:– be drenched (2), was drenched (2), drenched (1)

A10608 צַד **ṣad**, n.[m.] [2] [√ 7396]. side:– against (1 [+10378]), in (1 [+10427])

A10609 צְדָא **ṣᵉdāʾ**, n.[m.] [1] [cf. 10216]. purpose, (with 10190) is it true?:– Is it true (1 [+10190])

A10610 צִדְקָה **ṣidqâ**, n.f. [1] [√ 7407]. what is right:– right (1)

A10611 צַוַּאר **ṣawwaʾr**, n.m. [3] [√ 7418]. neck:– neck (3)

A10612 צְלָה **ṣᵉlâ**, v. [2] [Pa] to pray:– pray (1), prayed (1)

A10613 צְלַח **ṣᵉlaḥ**, v. [4] [√ 7503]. [H] to cause to prosper; to promote; to make progress:– making rapid progress (1), promoted (1), prosper (1), prospered (1)

A10614 צְלֵם **ṣᵉlēm**, n.m. [17] [√ 7512]. sculptured image, statue; this can refer to a statue, not necessarily worshiped, or to an idol, which is:– image (10), statue (5), attitude (1 [+10049]), it[S] (1 [+10002])

A10615 צְפִיר **ṣᵉpîr**, n.m. [1] [√ 7618]. male goat:– male goats (1 [+10535])

A10616 צִפַּר **ṣippar**, n.f. [4] [√ 7607]. bird:– birds (2 [+10002, 10723]), bird (1), birds (1)

A10617 ק **q**, letter. Not used in NIVEBC [√ 7682]. letter of the Aramaic alphabet

A10618 קְבַל **qᵉbal**, v.den. [3] [→ 10619; 7691]. [Pa] to receive; to take over:– receive (2), took over (1)

A10619 קֳבֵל **qᵒbēl**, subst. & pp. & c. [29] [√ 10618]. before, in front of; since, because of:– because (4 [+10353, 10168]), for (3 [+10353, 10168]), before (2 [+10378]), because of (1 [+10378, 10168]), by (1 [+10353, 10168]), even as (1 [+10353, 10168]), just as (1 [+10353, 10168]), near (1 [+10378]), since (1 [+10353, 10168]), so (1 [+10353, 10180]), then (1 [+10353, 10180]), therefore (1 [+10353, 10180]), this is the meaning (1 [+10353, 10168]), this made (1 [+10353, 10180]), though (1 [+10353, 10168]), with (1 [+10378]), NDT (7)

A10620 קַדִּישׁ **qaddîš**, a. [13] [√ 7705]. holy, ceremonial or moral purity; (as noun) holy one, saint, which can refer to human beings or angels:– holy (8), holy people (4), they[S] (1)

A10621 קֳדָם **qᵒdām**, pp. [42] [→ 10622, 10623; 7710]. before, in the presence of:– to (11), before (7), before (2 [+10427]), from (2 [+10427]), by (1 [+10427]), former (1), in presence (1), in sight (1), into presence (1), issue (1 [+10427]), my (1 [+10307]), presence (1), NDT (12)

A10622 קַדְמָה **qadmâ**, n.f. [2] [√ 10621; 7712]. before times; (as adv.) formerly:– ago (1 [+10427, 10180]), before (1 [+10427, 10180])

A10623 קַדְמָי **qadmāy**, a. [3] [√ 10621; 7710]. first; earlier, former:– first (2), earlier (1)

A10624 קוּם **qûm**, v. [35] [→ 10628?, 10629; 7756]. [P] to stand, rise up; [Pa] to issue (a decree); [H, A] to set up, establish; [Ho] to be set up, be established; from the base meaning of "standing up" (in contrast to sitting or lying) comes fig. extension of causing something to be or come into existence, implying a lively, active state:– set up (9), stood (4), arise (2), issue (2), sets (2), appoint (1), appointed (1), come (1), endure (1), get up (1), got up (1), installed (1), issues (1), leaped to feet (1), raises up (1), rise (1), set (1), set to work (1 [+10221, 10742]), standing (1), was raised up (1), NDT (1)

A10625 קְטַל **qᵉṭal**, v. [7] [√ 7779]. [P] to put to death, kill; [Peil] to be slain; [Htpe] to be put to death; [Pa] to kill; [Htpa] to be put to death:– put to death (4), was slain (2), killed (1)

A10626 קְטַר **qᵉṭar**, n.m. [3] joint (of the hip); difficult problem, "to solve a difficult problem" means to explain an enigma, as a fig. extension of untying a tight, hard-to-undo, knot:– difficult problems (2), legs (1 [+10284])

A10627 קַיִט **qayiṭ**, n.[m.] [1] [√ 7811]. summer:– summer (1)

A10628 קְיָם **qᵉyām**, n.[m.] [2] [√ 10624?]. edict, statute, decree:– edict (2)

A10629 קַיָּם **qayyām**, a. [2] [√ 10624]. enduring:– endures (1), restored (1)

A10630 קִיתְרֹס **qîtᵉrōs**, n.[m.] [4] a stringed instrument, translated variously as "zither, lute, lyre," etc:– zither (4)

A10631 קָל **qāl**, n.m. [7] [√ 7754]. sound, voice:– sound (4), voice (2), NDT (1)

A10632 קְנָה **qᵉnâ**, v. [1] [√ 7864]. [P] to buy:– buy (1)

A10633 1קְצַף **qᵉṣap[1]**, v. [1] [→ 10634; 7911]. [P] to become furious:– furious (1)

A10634 2קְצַף **qᵉṣap[2]**, n.[m.] [1] [√ 10633; 7912]. wrath, fury:– wrath (1)

A10635 קְצַץ **qᵉṣaṣ**, v. [1] [√ 7915]. [Pa] to trim off, cut off:– trim off (1)

A10636 קְצָת **qᵉṣāt**, n.f. [3] [√ 7921]. part; the end:– end (1), later (1 [+10378]), partly (1 [+10427])

A10637 קְרָא **qᵉrāʾ**, v. [11] [√ 7924]. [P] to call, proclaim, read out loud; [Pp, Peil] to be read out loud; [Htpe] to be called, be summoned:– read (4), been read (1), call (1), called (1), proclaimed (1), reads (1), summoned (1 [+10089, 10264, 10378, 10549]), was read (1)

A10638 קְרֵב **qᵉrēb**, v. [9] [→ 10639; 7928]. [P] to come near, approach; [Pa] to offer (a sacrifice); [H] to bring near, offer (a sacrifice):– approached (2), came forward (1), came near (1), led (1), offer sacrifices (1), offered (1), sacrifice (1), went (1)

A10639 קְרָב **qᵉrāb**, n.[m.] [1] [√ 10638; 7930]. war:– war (1)

A10640 קִרְיָה **qiryâ**, n.f. [9] [√ 7953]. city, town:– city (9)

A10641 קֶרֶן **qeren**, n.f. [14] [√ 7967]. horn (of an animal), also referring to a musical instrument:– horn (9), horns (5)

A10642 קְרַץ **qᵉraṣ**, n.[m.] [2] piece, "to eat pieces" is slander, denouncement:– denounced (1 [+10030]), falsely accused (1 [+10030])

A10643 קְשֹׁט **qᵉšōṭ**, n.[m.] [2] [√ 7999]. truth; (as adv.) surely, truly, rightly:– right (1), surely (1 [+10427, 10168])

A10644 קַתְרוֹס **qatrôs**, n.[m.] Not used in NIVEBC [cf. 10630]. zither, lyre, see 10630

A10645 ר **r**, letter. Not used in NIVEBC [√ 8010]. letter of the Aramaic alphabet

A10646 רֵאשׁ **rēʾš**, n.m. [14] [√ 8031]. head (for functions of sight and thought as a crucial part of the body); fig., leader; or the very first part of an event, the beginning:– head (4), mind (4), heads (2), saw (2), leaders (1), substance (1 [+10418])

A10647 רַב **rab**, a. [23] [√ 10648; 8041]. great, large, many, chief; this can refer to a large object (great, large), a large amount of objects (many, much), or high status (chief):– great (11), boastfully (2), chief (2), boastful (1), commander (1), enormous (1), huge (1), imposing (1), in charge (1 [+10505]), large (1), many (1 [+10678])

A10648 רְבָה **rᵉbâ**, v. [6] [→ 10647, 10649?, 10650, 10652; 8049]. [P] to become large, be great; [Pa] to place in a high position, make great:– grew large (2), great (1), grew (1), grown (1), placed in a high position (1)

A10649 רִבּוֹ **ribbô**, n.f. [2] [√ 10648?; 8052]. ten thousand, myriad, (virtually) countless number:– ten thousand (2)

A10650 רְבוּ **rᵉbû**, n.f. [5] [√ 10648]. greatness, high position:– greatness (3), became even greater (1 [+10339, 10323]), high position (1)

A10651 רְבִיעָי **rᵉbîʿāy**, a.num.ord. [6] [√ 10065; 8055]. fourth:– fourth (6)

A10652 רַבְרְבָנִין **rabrᵉbānîn**, n.m.pl. [8] [√ 10648]. nobles, lords:– nobles (8)

A10653 1רְגַז **rᵉgaz[1]**, v. [1] [→ 10654; 8074]. [H] to anger, enrage:– angered (1)

A10654 2רְגַז **rᵉgaz[2]**, n.m. [1] [√ 10653; 8075]. rage:– rage (1)

A10655 רְגַל **rᵉgal**, n.[f.] [7] [√ 8079]. foot:– feet (4), underfoot (2 [+10089]), toes (1 [+10064])

A10656 רְגַשׁ **rᵉgaš**, v. [3] [√ 8093]. [H] to go in as a group (causing an uproar), implying that those in the group are bumping into one another:– went as a group (3)

A10657 רֵו **rēw**, n.m. [2] appearance:– appearance (1), looks (1)

A10658 רוּחַ **rûaḥ**, n.f. [11] [cf. 10666; 8120]. wind, breath, spirit; from the base meaning of "wind" (or "breath") come the meaning of "spirit" as an immaterial supernatural being, and as the immaterial part of the inner person, with a possible focus on the reasoning and thinking faculty: "mind" or "heart":– spirit (6), mind (1), qualities (1), wind (1), winds (1), NDT (1)

A10659 1רוּם **rûm[1]**, v. [4] [→ 10660; 8123]. [P] to become arrogant; [Pol] to exalt, praise; [H] to promote, cause to rise (in rank); [Htpol] to rise up (against); all of these meanings are from the base meaning of "high" (see also 10660):– arrogant (1), exalt (1), promoted (1), set up (1)

A10660 2רוּם **rûm[2]**, n.m. [5] [√ 10659; 8124?]. height; the top:– high (2), top (2), height (1)

A10661 רָז **rāz**, n.m. [9] mystery, secret:– mystery (6), mysteries (3)

A10662 רְחוּם **rᵉḥûm**, n.pr.m. [4] [cf. 10664; 8156]. Rehum, *"(he) is compassionate"*:– Rehum (4)

A10663 רַחִיק **raḥîq**, a. [1] [√ 8158]. far away:– away (1)

A10664 רַחֲמִין **raḥ^{a}mîn**, n.[m.]pl.intens. [1] [cf. 10662; 8171]. mercy, compassion:– mercy (1)

A10665 רְחַץ **r^{e}haṣ**, v. [1] [Htpe] to put one's trust in, rely on:– trusted (1)

A10666 רֵיחַ **rêaḥ**, n.f. [1] [cf. 10658; 8194]. (singed, scorched) smell:– smell (1)

A10667 רְמָה **r^{e}mâ**, v. [12] [√ 8227]. [P] to throw; to impose; [Peil] to be thrown, be set in place; [Htpe] to be thrown:– be thrown (5), threw (2), thrown (2), impose (1), throw (1), were set in place (1)

A10668 רְעוּ **r^{e}'û**, n.f. [2] [→ 10669; 8296]. will, decision:– decision (1), will (1)

A10669 רַעְיוֹן **ra'yôn**, n.m. [6] [√ 10668; 8301]. thought (in one's mind):– thoughts (2), mind (1), mind (1 [+10381]), NDT (2)

A10670 רַעֲנַן **ra'^{a}nan**, a. [1] [√ 8316?]. prosperous, flourishing:– prosperous (1)

A10671 רְעַע **r^{e}'a'**, v. [2] [√ 8368]. [P] to break, crush; [Pa] to break to pieces, shatter:– break (1), breaks to pieces (1)

A10672 רְפַס **r^{e}pas**, v. [2] [√ 8346]. [P] to trample down:– trampled (2)

A10673 רְשַׁם **r^{e}šam**, v. [7] [√ 8398]. [P] to put in writing, publish; [Peil] to be written, be published:– put in writing (2 [+10375]), been published (1), publish (1), put in writing (1), was written (1), wrote (1)

A10674 שׂ **ś**, letter. Not used in NIVEBC [√ 8418]. letter of the Aramaic alphabet

A10675 שָׂב **śāb**, n.m. *or* v.ptcp. [5] [√ 10681]. elder, a community leader with considerable political, social, and judicial authority, as a fig. extension of being white-haired, implying wisdom and honor:– elders (5)

A10676 שַׂבְּכָא **śabb^{e}kā'**, n.[f.] [4] [cf. 10501; 8422]. lyre (triangular instrument with four strings):– lyre (4)

A10677 שְׂגָא **ś^{e}gā'**, v. [3] [→ 10678; 8434, 8436]. [P] to grow great:– greatly (2), grow (1)

A10678 שַׂגִּיא **śaggî'**, a. [13] [√ 10677; 8438]. great, large, abundant:– abundant (2), deeply (1), enormous (1), even more (1), fill (1), great (1), greatly (1), large (1), many (1), many (1 [+10647]), overjoyed (1 [+10293]), so (1)

A10679 שָׂהֲדוּ **śāh^{a}dû**, n.f. Not used in NIVEBC [√ 3337, 8447]. witness, see 3337

A10680 שְׂטַר **ś^{e}ṭar**, n.m. [1] [cf. 10511]. side:– sides (1)

A10681 שִׂיב **śîb**, v. Not used in NIVEBC [→ 10675; 8482]. [P] to be gray-haired

A10682 שִׂים **śîm**, v. [26] [√ 8492]. [P] to place (an order), issue (a decree); [Peil] to be placed, be issued; [Htpe] to be put, be laid (to rubble):– decree (5 [+10302]), issued (5), issue (3), authorized (2 [+10302]), appointed (1), called (1 [+10721]), commanded (1 [+10302]), decreed (1 [+10302]), determined (1 [+10104]), order (1 [+10302, 10002]), pay (1), pays (1), placed (1), placing (1), turned into (1)

A10683 שְׂכַל **ś^{e}kal**, v. [1] [→ 10684; 8505]. [Htpa] to think about, consider:– thinking (1)

A10684 שָׂכְלְתָנוּ **śokl^{e}tānû**, n.f. [3] [√ 10683]. intelligence, understanding, insight:– intelligence (2), understanding (1)

A10685 שִׂלָּה **śillâ**, n.f. Not used in NIVEBC [√ 6136]. insolence, rebellion

A10686 שְׂנָא **ś^{e}nā'**, v. [1] [√ 8533]. [P] to hate; (as noun) an enemy:– enemies (1)

A10687 שְׂעַר **ś^{e}'ar**, n.m. [3] [√ 8552]. hair (of the head or body):– hair (3)

A10688 שׁ **š**, letter. Not used in NIVEBC [√ 8610]. letter of the Aramaic alphabet

A10689 שְׁאֵל **š^{e}'ēl**, v. [6] [→ 10690; 8626]. [P] to ask, question:– asked (3), ask (1), asks (1), questioned (1)

A10690 שְׁאֵלָה **š^{e}'ēlâ**, n.f. [1] [√ 10689; 8629]. verdict, decision:– verdict (1)

A10691 שְׁאַלְתִּיאֵל **š^{e}'altî'ēl**, n.pr.m. [1] [√ 8630]. Shealtiel:– Shealtiel (1)

A10692 שְׁאָר **š^{e}'ār**, n.m. [12] [√ 8637]. the rest, remainder:– rest (5), elsewhere (2), left (2), other (2), anything else (1)

A10693 שְׁבַח **š^{e}baḥ**, v. [5] [√ 8655]. [Pa] to praise, honor:– praise (2), praised (2), honored (1)

A10694 שְׁבַט **š^{e}baṭ**, n.m. [1] [√ 8657]. tribe, a subgroup of a nation:– tribes (1)

A10695 שְׁבִיב **š^{e}bîb**, n.[m.] [2] [√ 8663]. flame:– flames (1), flaming (1)

A10696 שְׁבַע **š^{e}ba'**, n.m. & f. [6] [√ 8679]. seven; the phrase "seven times" (Da 3:19) likely means to be as hot as possible:– seven (6)

A10697 שְׁבַק **š^{e}baq**, v. [5] [P] to leave, have remain; [Htpe] to be left:– leave (2), be left (1), not interfere (1), remain (1)

A10698 שְׁבַשׁ **š^{e}baš**, v. [1] [Htpa] to be baffled, be perplexed:– baffled (1)

A10699 שֵׁגַל **šēgal**, n.f. [3] [√ 8712?]. wife, concubine:– wives (3)

A10700 שְׁדַר **š^{e}dar**, v. [1] [→ 10083]. [Htpa] to make every effort, strive:– made every effort (1)

A10701 שַׁדְרַךְ **šadrak**, n.pr.m. [14] [√ 8731]. Shadrach, "*servant of the (pagan moon god) Aku*":– Shadrach (13), NDT (1)

A10702 שְׁוָה **š^{e}wâ**, v. [2] [√ 8750]. [Peil] to be made like; [Pa] to make like; [Htpa] to be made into:– be turned into (1), given (1)

A10703 שׁוּר **šûr**, n.m. [3] [√ 8803]. wall:– walls (3)

A10704 שׁוּשַׁנְכָי **šûšankāy**, n.pr.g. & loc. [1] [√ 8809]. of Susa:– of Susa (1)

A10705 שְׁחַת **š^{e}ḥat**, v. [3] [√ 8845]. [Pp] to be corrupt, wicked; (as noun) corruption:– corrupt (1), corruption (1), wicked (1)

A10706 שֵׁיזִב **šêzib**, v. [9] [Sh] to rescue, save:– rescue (4), deliver (2), rescued (2), rescues (1)

A10707 שֵׁיצִיא **šêṣî'**, v. [1] [Sh] to complete, finish:– completed (1)

A10708 שְׁכַח **š^{e}kaḥ**, v. [17] [√ 8894]. [H] to find; [Htpe] to be found:– was found (5), find (4), found (4), do so[S] (1 [+10353, 10544]), leaving (1), obtain (1), NDT (1)

A10709 שְׁכַן **š^{e}kan**, v. [2] [→ 10445; 8905]. [P] to dwell; [Pa] to cause to dwell:– caused to dwell (1), nesting places (1)

A10710 שְׁלֵה **š^{e}lēh**, a. [1] [→ 10711, 10712, 10713; 8929]. contented, at ease:– contented (1)

A10711 שָׁלוּ **šāluh**, n.f. Not used in NIVEBC [√ 10710]. see 10712

A10712 שָׁלוּ **šālû**, n.f. [4] [√ 10710; 8930]. negligence:– anything (1), fail (1), neglect (1 [+10522]), negligent (1)

A10713 שְׁלֵוָה **š^{e}lēwâ**, n.f. [1] [√ 10710; 8932]. prosperity:– prosperity (1)

A10714 שְׁלַח **š^{e}laḥ**, v. [14] [√ 8938]. [P] to send out; [Pp, Peil] to be sent:– sent (9), are sent (1), lifts (1), send (1), sending message (1), summoned (1 [+10378, 10359])

A10715 שְׁלֵט **š^{e}lēṭ**, v. [7] [→ 10716, 10717, 10718; 8948]. [P] to rule over, overpower; [H] to make rule over:– made ruler (2), ruler (2), harmed (1), overpowered (1), rule (1)

A10716 שִׁלְטוֹן **šilṭōn**, n.m. [2] [√ 10715; 8950]. high official:– officials (2)

A10717 שָׁלְטָן **šolṭān**, n.m. [14] [√ 10715; 8950?]. dominion, power, authority:– dominion (7), authority (2), power (2), authority to rule (1), part (1), rulers (1)

A10718 שַׁלִּיט **šallîṭ**, a. [10] [√ 10715; 8954]. mighty, powerful, sovereign, ruling:– sovereign (4), authority (1), mighty (1), officer (1), ruler (1), rules (1), ruling (1)

A10719 שְׁלִם **š^{e}lim**, v. [3] [→ 10720; 8966]. [P] to be finished; [H] to (deliver) completely, bring to an end:– brought to an end (1), deliver (1), finished (1)

A10720 שְׁלָם **š^{e}lām**, n.m. [4] [√ 10719; 8934]. (as salutation) cordial greetings!; prosperity, well-being, good health:– prosper (2), cordial greetings (1 [+10353, 10002, 10002]), greetings (1)

A10721 שֻׁם **šum**, n.m. [12] [√ 9005]. name, what someone is called:– name (4), called (3), names (3), called (1 [+10682]), named (1)

A10722 שְׁמַד **š^{e}mad**, v. [1] [√ 9012]. [H] to completely destroy, exterminate:– completely destroyed (1 [+10221, 10005])

A10723 שְׁמַיִן **š^{e}mayin**, n.m.pl. [38] [√ 9028]. the heavens (of this world), sky, air; heaven (the realm of God); "heaven" is also a euphemism for "God"; the phrase "heaven and earth" combine into one meaning "the universe," the totality of all that exists:– heaven (29), sky (4), heavens (3), birds (2 [+10616, 10002])

A10724 שְׁמַם **š^{e}mam**, v. [1] [√ 9037]. [Itpo] to be greatly perplexed, implying one is in a state of severe distress, a fig. extension of destroying an object:– greatly perplexed (1)

A10725 שְׁמַע **š^{e}ma'**, v. [9] [√ 9048]. [P] to hear; [Htpa] to obey:– heard (4), hear (3), hears (1), obey (1)

A10726 שָׁמְרַיִן **šām^{e}rayin**, n.pr.loc. [2] [√ 9076]. Samaria, "*belonging to the clan of Shemer*":– Samaria (2)

A10727 ¹שְׁמַשׁ **š^{e}maš^{1}**, v. [1] [→ 10728?]. [Pa] to attend to, serve:– attended (1)

A10728 ²שְׁמַשׁ **š^{e}maš^{2}**, n.[m.] [1] [√ 10727?, 10728; 9087]. sun:– sundown (1 [+10436, 10002])

A10729 שִׁמְשַׁי **šimšay**, n.pr.m. [4] [√ 10728]. Shimshai, "*one given to (pagan sun god) Shemesh*":– Shimshai (4)

A10730 שֵׁן **šēn**, n.[f.] [3] [√ 9094]. tooth; in the dual number it is a set of teeth, the upper and lower rows of teeth in a mouth:– teeth (3)

A10731 ¹שְׁנָא **š^{e}nâ^{1}**, v. [21] [→ 10732; 9101]. [P] to be changed, be different; [Pa] to change; defy; [Pap] to be different; [H] to change, alter; [Itpa] to be changed, be turned into:– different (5), changed (4), change (3), turned (2), altered (1), changes (1), defied (1), defies (1), grew (1), look so pale (1 [+10228]), scorched (1)

A10732 ²שְׁנָה **š^{e}nâ^{2}**, n.f. [7] [√ 10731; 9102]. year:– year (5), age (1 [+10120]), years (1)

A10733 ³שְׁנָה **š^{e}nâ^{3}**, n.f. [1] [√ 9104]. sleep:– sleep (1)

A10734 שָׁעָה **šā'â**, n.f. [5] moment, short time; (as adv.) immediately, suddenly, for a time:– immediately (2 [+10002]), immediately (1 [+10191]), suddenly (1 [+10191]), time (1)

A10735 שְׁפַט **š^{e}paṭ**, v. [1] [√ 9149]. [P] to judge; (as noun) judge:– magistrates (1)

A10736 שַׁפִּיר **šappîr**, a. [2] [√ 10739]. beautiful, fair, lovely:– beautiful (2)

A10737 ¹שְׁפַל **š^{e}pal^{1}**, v. [4] [→ 10738; 9164]. [H] to humble, subdue, bring low:– humbled (2), humble (1), subdue (1)

A10738 ²שְׁפַל **š^{e}pal^{2}**, a. [1] [√ 10737; 9166]. low; (as superlative) lowliest:– lowliest (1)

A10739 שְׁפַר **š^{e}par**, v. [3] [→ 10736, 10740?; 9182]. [P] to be pleased, have pleasure:– pleased (2), pleasure (1)

A10740 שְׁפַרְפָּר **š^{e}parpār**, n.[m.] [1] [√ 10739?]. dawn:– dawn (1)

A10741 שָׁק **šāq**, n.[m.] [1] [√ 8797]. lower leg, shank:– legs (1)

A10742 שְׁרָה **š^{e}râ**, v. [6] [√ 9223]. [P] to loosen, solve (a problem); [Pp] to be loosened; to dwell; [Pa] to begin; [Htpa] to be loose and shaking (of legs giving way):– solve (2), dwells (1), set to work (1 [+10624, 10221]), unbound (1), weak (1)

A10743 שְׁרֹשׁ **š^{e}rōš**, n.m. [3] [→ 10744, 10745; 9247]. root:– roots (3)

A10744 שְׁרֹשׁוּ **š^{e}rōšû**, n.f. [1] [√ 10743]. banishment, uprooting (from community):– banishment (1)

A10745 שְׁרֹשִׁי **š^{e}rōšî**, n.f. Not used in NIVEBC [√ 10743]. banishment, uprooting (from community), see 10744

A10746 שֵׁשְׁבַּצַּר **šēšbaṣṣar**, n.pr.m. [2] [√ 9256]. Sheshbazzar, "*may (the pagan moon god) Sin protect (the father)*":– Sheshbazzar (2)

A10747 שֵׁת **šēt**, n.m. & f. [2] [→ 10749; 9252]. six:– six (1), sixth (1)

A10748 שְׁתָה **š^{e}tâ**, v. [5] [→ 10447; 9272]. [P] to drink; this can refer to common consumption of liquid, or it can refer to drinking in worship to pagan gods and in insult to the true God (by drinking with his vessels):– drank (4), drink (1)

A10749 שִׁתִּין **šittîn**, n.indecl. [4] [√ 10747; 9262]. sixty:– sixty (3), sixty-two (1 [+10221, 10775])

A10750 שְׁתַר בּוֹזְנַי **š^{e}tar bôz^{e}nay**, n.pr.m. [4] Shethar-Bozenai:– Shethar-Bozenai (4)

A10751 ת **t**, letter. Not used in NIVEBC [√ 9287]. letter of the Aramaic alphabet

A10752 תְּבַר **t^{e}bar**, v. [1] [√ 8689]. [Pp] to be brittle, not to have flexibility, implying such an object is fragile and easy to break:– brittle (1)

A10753 תְּדִיר **t^{e}dîr**, n.f. [2] [√ 10163]. duration, encircling; (as adv.) continually:– continually (2 [+10089, 10002])

A10754 תּוּב **tûb**, v. [8] [√ 8740]. [P] to return, restore; [H] to give back, return, answer:– restored (2), returned (2), defend (1 [+10601]), gave (1), received (1), spoke (1)

A10755 תְּוַהּ **t^{e}wah**, v. [1] [√ 9449]. [P] to be amazed, be alarmed, an attitude or emotion that shows either fear or awe:– amazement (1 [+10097])

A10756 תּוֹר **tôr**, n.m. [7] [√ 8802]. young bull or castrated bull, steer, ox, easier to handle for plowing, pulling, and threshing:– ox (4), bulls (3)

A10757 תְּחוֹת **t^{e}ḥôt**, pp. [5] [√ 9393]. under:– under (4), NDT (1)

A10758 תְּלַג **t^{e}lag**, n.[m.] [1] [√ 8920]. snow:– snow (1)

A10759 תְּלִיתָי **t^{e}lîtāy**, a. [1] [√ 10760; 8958]. third:– third (1)

A10760 תְּלָת **t^{e}lāt**, n.m. [11] [→ 10759, 10761, 10762; 8993]. three:– three (10), third (1)

A10761 תַּלְתָּא **taltā'**, a.den. [3] [√ 10760; 8958]. third highest; this can refer to ruling over a third of the kingdom, or ruling as third in command, or ruling in a triumvirate; some sources translate less specifically as a high official of indeterminate rank:– third highest (3)

A10762 תְּלָתִין **t^{e}lātîn**, n.indecl. [2] [√ 10760; 9001]. thirty:– thirty (2)

A10763 תְּמַהּ **t^{e}mah**, n.m. [3] wonder, miracle:– wonders (3)

A10764 תַּמָּה **tammâ**, adv. [4] [√ 9004]. there:– there (2), NDT (2)

A10765 תִּנְיָן **tinyān**, a. [1] [√ 10775]. second:– second (1)

A10766 תִּנְיָנוּת **tinyānût**, adv. [1] [√ 10775]. once more, in the second time:– Once more (1)

A10767 תִּפְתָּי **tiptāy**, n.m.pl. [2] magistrate, a general or legal authority such as a chief of police:– magistrates (2)

A10768 תַּקִּיף ***taqqîp***, a. [5] [√ 10772; 9544]. strong, powerful, mighty:– powerful (2), strong (2), mighty (1)

A10769 תְּקַל ***t^{e}qal***, v. [1] [→ 10770; 9202]. [Peil] to be weighed:– been weighed (1)

A10770 תְּקֵל ***t^{e}qēl***, n.[m.] [2] [√ 10769; 9203]. tekel, (i.e., shekel of weight):– tekel (2)

A10771 תְּקַן ***t^{e}qan***, v. [1] [√ 9545, 9419]. [Ho] to be restored, be reestablished:– was restored (1)

A10772 תְּקֵף ***t^{e}qip***, v. [5] [→ 10768, 10773, 10774; 9548]. [P] to become strong, become hard; [Pa] to enforce, make hard:– strong (3), enforce (1), hardened (1)

A10773 תְּקֹף ***t^{e}qōp***, n.[m.] [1] [√ 10772; 9549]. might, strength:– might (1)

A10774 תְּקָף ***t^{e}qāp***, n.[m.] [1] [√ 10772]. power, strength:– power (1)

A10775 תְּרֵין ***t^{e}rên***, n.m. & f. [4] [→ 10765, 10766, 10778; 9109]. two:– second (1), sixty-two (1 [+10749, 10221]), twelve (1 [+10573]), twelve (1 [+10573])

A10776 תְּרַע ***t^{e}ra'***, n.[m.] [2] [→ 10777; 9133]. gate, door; opening (of a furnace); (royal) court, the entourage of a king:– court (1), opening (1)

A10777 תָּרָע ***tārā'***, n.m. [1] [√ 10776; 8788]. gatekeeper, doorkeeper:– gatekeepers (1)

A10778 תַּרְתֵּין ***tartên***, n.m. & f. Not used in NIVEBC [√ 10775]. two, see 10775

A10779 תַּתְּנַי ***tatt^{e}nay***, n.pr.m. [4] Tattenai:– Tattenai (4)

FEATURES OF THE GREEK TO ENGLISH DICTIONARY-INDEX

G/K NUMBER
Matches the number at the end of context lines; Greek G/K numbers start with "*G*" and are in *italics* (see pages xii, xv, xvi).

LEXICAL FORM AND TRANSLITERATION
See the table of transliteration and pronunciation below.

PART OF SPEECH
The part of speech is abbreviated (see the table of abbreviations below).

FREQUENCY COUNT
Indicates the total in the NIV Greek text; if a Greek word is not in the NIV Greek text, it is noted by "Not used in the NIVEBC" (see page xvii).

G235 **Ἀλέξανδρος** ***Alexandros***, n. pr. [6] [→ *233, 234*].

RELATED WORDS LIST
Greek words related by common elements are listed by *italic* G/K number (see page xvii).

Alexander, "*defender of men*":–

DEFINITION and ETYMOLOGY
Words are defined, often with expanded explanations. If a proper name, the possible definition (etymology) is given in italics (see page xvi).

Alexander (5),

NIV WORD and FREQUENCY COUNT
Following the symbol :– NIV words are listed according to their exact textual spelling and are organized according to frequency (see page xvi).

he[S] (1)

RAISED LETTER "S"
Indicates "substitution" translation (see pages xiv, xvi).

one another (1 [+*257, 4639*]),

MULTIPLE WORDS / MULTIPLE NUMBERS
More than one NIV word and/or more than one G/K number indicate multiple-word translations (see pages xi, xiii, xvi).

NDT (3)

NDT (NOT DIRECTLY TRANSLATED)
Always the final entry, this indicates the number of times the Greek word was not translated in the NIV for stylistic reasons (see pages xiv, xvi).

TABLE OF TRANSLITERATION AND PRONUNCIATION

A, α	*A, a*	f*a*ther	Λ, λ	*L, l*	*l*et	Φ, φ	*Ph, ph*	*ph*one	γξ	*nx*	thi*nks*
B, β	*B, b*	*b*oy	M, μ	*M, m*	*m*other	X, χ	*Ch, ch*	Ba*ch*	γχ	*nch*	thi*nk*
Γ, γ	*G, g*	*g*irl	N, ν	*N, n*	*n*ot	Ψ, ψ	*Ps, ps*	li*ps*			
Δ, δ	*D, d*	*d*og	Ξ, ξ	*X, x*	fo*x*	Ω, ω	*Ō, ō*	ph*o*ne	αι	*ai*	*ai*sle
E, ε	*E, e*	g*e*t	O, ο	*O, o*	h*o*t				αυ	*au*	kr*au*t
Z, ζ	*Z, z*	a*dz*e	Π, π	*P, p*	*p*ot				ει	*ei*	*ei*ght
H, η	*Ē, ē*	th*ey*	P, ρ	*R, r*	*r*ot	Ῥ, ῥ	*Rh, rh*	myr*rh*	ευ, ηυ	*eu, ēu*	*you*
Θ, θ	*Th, th*	*th*ey	Σ, σ, ς	*S, s, s*	*s*ip	ʽ	*H, h*	*h*ot	οι	*oi*	*oi*l
I, ι	*I, i*	p*i*n, mach*i*ne	T, τ	*T, t*	*t*ip	γγ	*ng*	thi*ng*	ου	*ou*	thr*ough*
K, κ	*K, k*	*k*it	Y, υ	*Y, y*	p*u*t	γκ	*nk*	thi*nk*	υι	*ui*	*we*

TABLE OF GREEK DICTIONARY ABBREVIATIONS

&	and	comp.	comparative	inter.	interrogative	pl.	plural
?	uncertain	cond.	conditional	interj.	interjection	poss.	possessive
+	plus: in combination with	contr.	contraction	intr.	intransitive	pp.	preposition
[]	uncertain part of speech	demo.	demonstrative	l.	loanword	pp.*	improper preposition
→	see these related words	disj.	disjunctive	letter	letter of the alphabet	pr.	proper [noun]
√	see this organizing word	emph.	emphatic	mid.	middle	pt.	particle
a.	adjective	excl.	exclamation	n.	noun	recip.	reciprocal
act.	active	fig.	figurative(ly)	neg.	negative	reflex.	reflexive
adv.	adverb	g.	gentilic	neu.	neuter	rel.	relative
adver.	adversative	imper.	impersonal	num.	numeral	super.	superlative
aff.	affirmative	indef.	indefinite	p.	pronoun	temp.	temporal
art.	article	infer.	inferential	pass.	passive	trans.	transitional
c.	conjunction	inten.	intensive	pers.	personal	v.	verb

GREEK TO ENGLISH DICTIONARY-INDEX

G1* α *a, letter. Not used in NIVEBC. [→*270; 1.1: 4, 23, 37, 38, 47, 51, 52, 53, 57, 58, 63, 78, 83, 84, 85, 88, 89, 90, 91, 92, 93, 94, 95, 96, 97, 99, 100, 104, 105, 109, 112, 114, 115, 117, 118, 119, 120, 126, 127, 174, 175, 176, 177, 178, 179, 182, 183, 184, 185, 186, 187, 188, 189, 190, 191, 193, 195, 202, 203, 204, 218, 219, 220, 227, 228, 237, 238, 239, 240, 242, 263, 267, 269, 276, 277, 278, 282, 285, 288, 289, 290, 291, 292, 293, 294, 295, 296, 298, 299, 305, 318, 320, 357, 360, 383, 387, 394, 395, 396, 397, 406, 410, 440, 441, 442, 443, 444, 446, 447, 450, 451, 453, 454, 455, 460, 466, 480, 481, 485, 486, 490, 491, 492, 493, 495, 536, 537, 538, 543, 548, 553, 563, 564, 574, 577, 578, 579, 585, 586, 596, 597, 598, 601, 602, 603, 679, 680, 717, 718, 719, 720, 731, 733, 734, 777, 778, 779, 810, 812, 813, 814, 815, 816, 817, 819, 820, 821, 822, 826, 827, 831, 834, 836, 841, 844, 845, 846, 850, 851, 852, 853, 854, 855, 856, 857, 858, 859, 860, 861, 862, 863, 864, 865, 866, 869, 870, 871, 872, 873, 875, 876, 905, 906, 907, 908, 910, 911, 914, 915, 916, 917, 920, 921, 925, 932, 933, 936, 940, 942, 945, 946, 947, 950, 953, 1389, 1989, 2934; 1.2: 12, 867; 1.3: 80, 287?, 1979, 2051, 2887, 4158, 5258, 5788, 5789, 5790, 6012*]. 1) letter of the Greek alphabet; 2) inseparable prefix: 1.1 alpha privative (as non- or un- in English), 1.2 prefix of intensity, 1.3 prefix of similarity, collectivity or association; also used as the numeral "1" in the superscriptions of some Greek manuscripts

G2* Ἀαρών *Aarōn, n. pr. [5] Aaron (referring to both the person and his priesthood):– Aaron (4), Aaron's (1)

G3* Ἀβαδδών *Abaddōn, n. pr. [1] Abaddon, "*destruction*":– Abaddon (1)

G4* ἀβαρής *abarēs, a. [1] [√*1.1 + 983*]. not burdensome:– burden (1)

G5* ἀββά *abba, l.[n.] [3] Aramaic for "father":– Abba (3)

G6* Ἅβελ *Habel, n. pr. [4] Abel, "*morning mist*":– Abel (4)

G7* Ἀβιά *Abia, n. pr. [3] Abijah, "*[my] father is Yahweh*":– Abijah (3)

G8* Ἀβιαθάρ *Abiathar, n. pr. [1] Abiathar, "*[my] father gives abundance* or *the father is preeminent*":– Abiathar (1)

G9* Ἀβιληνή *Abilēnē, n. pr. [1] Abilene, a territory on the south end of the Ante-Lebanon mountain range, "[prob.] *meadow*":– Abilene (1)

G10* Ἀβιούδ *Abioud, n. pr. [2] Abiud, "*[my] father has majesty*":– Abihud (2)

G11* Ἀβραάμ *Abraam, n. pr. [73] Abraham, "*father of many*":– Abraham (64), Abraham's (9)

G12* ἄβυσσος *abyssos, n. [9] [√*1.2 + 1113*]. Abyss, the deep place, the underworld, the abode of the dead and demons, "*unfathomable depth*":– abyss (8), deep (1)

G13* Ἅγαβος *Hagabos, n. pr. [2] Agabus:– Agabus (2)

G14* ἀγαθοεργέω *agathoergeō, v. [2] [√*19 + 2240*]. to do good:– do good (1), shown kindness (1)

G15* ἀγαθοεργός *agathoergos, a. Not used in NIVEBC. [√*19 + 2240*]. one who does good

G16* ἀγαθοποιέω *agathopoieō, v. [9] [√*19 + 4472*]. to do good, to do right:– do good (3), doing good (3), do right (1), does good (1), good (1)

G17* ἀγαθοποιΐα *agathopoiia, n. [1] [√*19 + 4472*]. doing good:– do good (1)

G18* ἀγαθοποιός *agathopoios, a. [1] [√*19 + 4472*]. one who does good, right:– those who do right (1)

G19* ἀγαθός *agathos, a. [102] [→*14, 15, 16, 17, 18, 20, 920, 2817, 5787*]. good; good as a positive quality (vs. bad), good as a moral quality (vs. evil):– good (88), clear (2), right (2), better (1), favor (1), fully (1 [*+4246*]), generous (1), grain[S] (1), helpful (1), kind (1), pleasant (1), surplus (1 [*+4246, 2779*]), useful (1)

G20* ἀγαθωσύνη *agathōsynē, n. [4] [√*19*]. goodness:– goodness (4)

G21* ἀγαλλίασις *agalliasis, n. [5] [√*22*]. delight, great joy:– joy (2), delight (1), glad (1), great joy (1)

G22* ἀγαλλιάω *agalliaō, v. [11] [→*21*]. to be filled with delight, with great joy:– glad (2), rejoices (2), enjoy (1), filled with joy (1), filled with joy (1 [*+5915*]), full of joy (1), greatly rejoice (1), overjoyed (1 [*+5897*]), rejoiced (1)

G23* ἄγαμος *agamos, n. [4] [√*1.1 + 1141*]. unmarried (man or woman):– unmarried (4)

G24* ἀγανακτέω *aganakteō, v. [7] [→*25*]. to be indignant:– indignant (6), saying indignantly (1)

G25* ἀγανάκτησις *aganaktēsis, n. [1] [√*24*]. indignation:– indignation (1)

G26* ἀγαπάω *agapaō, v. [143] [→*27, 28*]. to love; in the NT usually the active love of God for his Son and his people, and the active love his people are to have for God, each other, and even enemies:– love (76), loved (39), loves (22), dearly loved (1), have[S] (1), longed for (1), love shown (1), loving (1), NDT (1)

G27* ἀγάπη *agapē, n. [115] [√*26*]. love, in the NT usually the active love of God for his Son and his people, and the active love his people are to have for God, each other, and even enemies; love feast, the common meal shared by Christians in connection with church meetings:– love (111), love (2 [*+2400*]), love feasts (1), loves (1)

G28* ἀγαπητός *agapētos, a. [61] [√*26*]. dearly loved one; the object of special affection and of special relationship, as with Jesus the beloved of the Father:– dear friends (22), dear (13), dear friend (10), love (10), loved (3), dearly loved (1), friends (1), loved so much (1 [*+1181*])

G29* Ἁγάρ *Hagar, n. pr. [2] Hagar:– Hagar (2)

G30* ἀγγαρεύω *angareuō, v. [3] to force, compel, press into service in military or civil matters:– forced (2), forces to go (1)

G31* ἀγγεῖον *angeion, n. [1] [√*35*]. jar, flask, a container for liquid:– jars (1)

G32* ἀγγελία *angelia, n. [2] [√*34*]. message:– message (2)

G33* ἀγγέλλω *angellō, v. [1] [√*34*]. to bring news, be a messenger:– with the news (1)

G34* ἄγγελος *angelos, n. [175] [→*32, 33, 334, 550, 791, 1334, 1972, 2039, 2040, 2041, 2294, 2295, 2296, 2694, 2858, 2859, 4132, 4133, 4600, 4603, 4615; cf. 72*]. angel, messenger; this can refer to a human messenger, such as John the Baptist, or messengers sent by John the Baptist or Jesus, or to the supernatural class of being that serves God: the angel:– angel (85), angels (81), messenger (4), angel's (2), messengers (2), spies (1)

G35* ἄγγος *angos, n. [1] [→*31*]. basket:– baskets (1)

G36* ἀγέλη *agelē, n. [7] [√*72*]. herd (of pigs):– herd (7)

G37* ἀγενεαλόγητος *agenealogētos, a. [1] [√*1.1 + 1181 + 3306*]. without genealogy:– without genealogy (1)

G38* ἀγενής *agenēs, a. [1] [√*1.1 + 1181*]. lowly, insignificant, implying low social standing:– lowly (1)

G39* ἁγιάζω *hagiazō, v. [28] [√*41*]. to sanctify, set apart, make holy; this can mean active dedication and service to God or the act of regarding or honoring as holy:– sanctified (9), made holy (4), sanctify (4), hallowed (2), make holy (2), makes sacred (2), consecrated (1), holy (1), makes holy (1), revere (1), set apart as very own (1)

G40* ἁγιασμός *hagiasmos, n. [10] [√*41*]. holiness:– holiness (4), holy (3), sanctifying work (2), sanctified (1)

G41* ἅγιος *hagios, a. [239] [→*39, 40, 42, 43; cf. 54*]. holy (moral quality), consecrated ([ceremonially] acceptable to God); holy person/people = saint(s), holy place = sanctuary:– holy (158), the Lord's people (19), God's people (13), most holy place (12 [*+41*]), God's holy people (9), sacred (4), his holy people (3), his people (3), holy people (3), sanctuary (3), Lord's people (2), people of God (2), Spirit (1), believers (1), consecrated (1 [*+2813*]), devoted to the Lord (1), holy place (1), the Lord's holy people (1), your holy people (1), your people (1)

G42* ἁγιότης *hagiotēs, n. [1] [√*41*]. holiness, a characteristic of God, shared by his people, requiring a lifestyle acceptable to God:– holiness (1)

G43* ἁγιωσύνη *hagiōsynē, n. [3] [√*41*]. holiness, a characteristic of God, shared by his people, requiring a lifestyle acceptable to God:– holiness (2), holy (1)

G44* ἀγκάλη *ankalē, n. [1] [→*1878*]. arm:– arms (1)

G45* ἄγκιστρον *ankistron, n. [1] [√*46*]. fish-hook, fish line with a hook on it:– line (1)

G46* ἄγκυρα *ankyra, n. [4] [→*45*]. anchor; used fig. of security:– anchors (3), anchor (1)

G47* ἄγναφος *agnaphos, a. [2] [√*1.1 + 1187*]. unshrunk, new cloth that has not been laundered:– unshrunk (2)

G48* ἁγνεία *hagneia, n. [2] [√*54*]. purity, in the sense of moral purity and proper sexual conduct:– purity (2)

G49* ἁγνίζω *hagnizō, v. [7] [√*54*]. to purify, ceremonially cleanse:– purified (2), purify (2), ceremonial cleansing (1), ceremonially clean (1), purification rites (1)

G50* ἁγνισμός *hagnismos, n. [1] [√*54*]. purification:– purification (1)

G51* ἀγνοέω *agnoeō, v. [22] [√*1.1 + 1182*]. to be ignorant, not know, not understand:– ignorant (3), not understand (3), uninformed (3), not know (2), unaware (2), unknown (2), don't know (1), ignorance (1), ignorant of the fact (1), ignored (1), ignores (1), not realizing (1), not recognize (1)

G52* ἀγνόημα *agnoēma, n. [1] [√*1.1 + 1182*]. sin committed in ignorance:– sins committed in ignorance (1)

G53* ἄγνοια *agnoia, n. [4] [√*1.1 + 1182*]. ignorance:– ignorance (4)

G54* ἁγνός *hagnos, a. [8] [→*48, 49, 50, 55, 56; cf. 41*]. pure (in some contexts morally pure), innocent:– pure (6), innocent (1), purity (1)

G55* ἁγνότης *hagnotēs, n. [2] [√*54*]. purity:– pure (1), purity (1)

G56* ἁγνῶς *hagnōs, adv. [1] [√*54*]. sincerely, purely:– sincerely (1)

G57* ἀγνωσία *agnōsia, n. [2] [√*1.1 + 1182*]. ignorance, with a focus on talk or action that opposes God:– ignorant (2)

G58* ἄγνωστος *agnōstos, a. [1] [√*1.1 + 1182*]. unknown:– unknown (1)

G59* ἀγορά *agora, n. [11] [√*60*]. marketplace (as a center of social and commercial life):– marketplaces (6), marketplace (5)

G60* ἀγοράζω *agorazō, v. [30] [→*59, 61, 251, 1319, 1973; cf. 72*]. to buy, purchase; this refers to buying and acquiring possessions, as in a market place, and to setting a slave free through purchase, often to God's purchase (redemption) of sinners:– buy (13), bought (9), purchased (2), selling (2), buying (1), buys (1), redeemed (1), spend (1)

G61* ἀγοραῖος *agoraios, a. [2] [√*60*]. marketplace, place where the courts meet:– courts (1), marketplace (1)

G62* ἄγρα *agra, n. [2] [→*65, 70, 71, 2436*]. catch (of fish), a net full:– catch (2)

G63* ἀγράμματος *agrammatos, a. [1] [√*1.1 + 1211*]. unschooled, probably in the sense of not having a formal rabbinic education:– unschooled (1)

G64 **ἀγραυλέω agrauleō**, v. [1] [√*69 + 885*]. to live outdoors, spend a night in the elements:– living out (1)

G65 **ἀγρεύω agreuō**, v. [1] [√*62*]. to catch:– catch (1)

G66 **ἀγριέλαιος agrielaios**, n. [2] [√*69 + 1777*]. wild olive tree:– olive tree that is wild (1), wild olive shoot (1)

G67 **ἄγριος agrios**, a. [3] [√*69*]. wild; undomesticated as well as uncontrolled:– wild (3)

G68 **Ἀγρίππας Agrippas**, n. pr. [11] [√*69 + 2691*]. Agrippa, "*wild horse*":– Agrippa (11)

G69 **ἀγρός agros**, n. [36] [→*64, 66, 67, 68*]. field, countryside, both tilled and untilled ground:– field (22), countryside (5), fields (5), country (3), it^{S} (1 [+*3836, 1697*])

G70 **ἀγρυπνέω agrypneō**, v. [4] [√*62 + 5678*]. to keep awake, keep alert:– alert (2), keep watch (1), on the watch (1)

G71 **ἀγρυπνία agrypnia**, n. [2] [√*62 + 5678*]. sleeplessness, wakefulness:– gone without sleep (1), sleepless nights (1)

G72 **ἄγω agō**, v. [69] [→*36, 73, 343, 442, 552, 795, 1341, 1455, 1456, 1524, 1652, 1687, 1974, 2007, 2042, 2056, 2081, 2190, 2220, 2221, 2448, 2449, 2450, 2451, 2762, 2864, 2989, 3555, 3842, 3843, 4080, 4108, 4135, 4206, 4207, 4219, 4310, 4575, 4605, 4641, 4642, 4643, 5130, 5194, 5251, 5252, 5270, 5632, 5902, 5932, 5933, 5961; cf. 34, 60, 545, 2989*]. to bring, lead; as a command: look, pay attention, listen:– brought (22), bring (9), go (6), led (5), brought in (4), took (3), bringing (2), listen (2), take (2), bring in (1), brought to trial (1), for (1), influenced (1), is (1), lead (1), leave (1 [+*1949*]), led away (1), led off (1), led out (1), open (1), swayed (1), taken (1), took home (1)

G73 **ἀγωγή agōgē**, n. [1] [√*72*]. way of life, personal conduct:– way of life (1)

G74 **ἀγών agōn**, n. [6] [→*75, 76, 497, 2043, 2865, 5253*]. struggle, fight, often an athletic contest:– fight (2), contending (1), opposition (1), race (1), struggle (1)

G75 **ἀγωνία agōnia**, n. [1] [√*74*]. anguish, anxiety:– anguish (1)

G76 **ἀγωνίζομαι agōnizomai**, v. [8] [√*74*]. to fight, struggle, often an athletic contest:– fight (2), competes in the games (1), contend (1), fought (1), make every effort (1), strive (1), wrestling (1)

G77 **Ἀδάμ Adam**, n. pr. [9] Adam, "*[red] earth* or *[ruddy] skin color*":– Adam (9)

G78 **ἀδάπανος adapanos**, a. [1] [√*1.1 + 1252*]. free of charge, without payment:– free of charge (1)

G79 **Ἀδδί Addi**, n. pr. [1] Addi, "[poss.] *my witness* or *adorned*":– Addi (1)

G80 **ἀδελφή adelphē**, n. [25] [√*81 [1.3]*]. sister, fellow countrywoman; by extension a female believer, a sister in the family of faith:– sister (16), sisters (8), believing (1)

G81 **ἀδελφός adelphos**, n. [342] [→*1.3, 80, 82, 5788, 5789, 5790, 6012*]. brother, fellow countryman, neighbor (often inclusive in gender); by extension a fellow believer in the family of faith; in the plural "brothers" regularly refers to men and women:– brothers and sisters (106), brother (73), brothers (48), brother or sister (22), believers (21), brothers and sisters (16 [+*467*]), brother's (7), brothers (6 [+*467*]), people (6), brother and sister (4), brothers (3 [+*467*]), them^{S} (3 [+*3836*]), brothers or sisters (2), fellow (2 [+*467*]), fellow (2), fellow believers (2), man (2), them^{S} (2), God's family (1 [+*3836*]), God's people (1), another^{S} (1), associates (1), believer (1), each other (1), fellow Israelites (1), fellow believer (1), friends (1 [+*467*]), fully human (1), him^{S} (1), husband (1), one another (1), our people (1), them^{S} (1 [+*5148*])

G82 **ἀδελφότης adelphotēs**, n. [2] [√*81*]. brotherhood, fellowship of believers (men and women):– family of believers (2)

G83 **ἄδηλος adēlos**, a. [2] [√*1.1 + 1316*]. not clear:– not clear (1), unmarked (1)

G84 **ἀδηλότης adēlotēs**, n. [1] [√*1.1 + 1316*]. uncertainty:– uncertain (1)

G85 **ἀδήλως adēlōs**, adv. [1] [√*1.1 + 1316*]. aimlessly, uncertainly:– aimlessly (1)

G86 **ἀδημονέω adēmoneō**, v. [3] to be troubled, distressed:– troubled (2), distressed (1)

G87 **ᾅδης hadēs**, n. [10] Hades, the grave, the place of the dead, "*the underworld*":– Hades (8), realm of the dead (2)

G88 **ἀδιάκριτος adiakritos**, a. [1] [√*1.1 + 1328 + 3212*]. impartial, free from prejudice:– impartial (1)

G89 **ἀδιάλειπτος adialeiptos**, a. [2] [√*1.1 + 1328 + 3309*]. constant, unceasing:– constantly (1), unceasing (1)

G90 **ἀδιαλείπτως adialeiptōs**, adv. [4] [√*1.1 + 1328 + 3309*]. constantly, unceasingly:– continually (3), constantly (1)

G91 **ἀδιαφθορία adiaphthoria**, n. Not used in NIVEBC. [√*1.1 + 1328 + 5780*]. sincerity, integrity

G92 **ἀδικέω adikeō**, v. [28] [√*1.1 + 1472*]. to do wrong, mistreat:– harm (6), did wrong (2), does wrong (2), done wrong (2), hurt (2), wronged (2), cheat (1), damage (1), do wrong (1), guilty (1), harm done (1), inflict injury (1), injured (1), mistreated (1), mistreating (1), torment (1), unfair (1), wrongs (1)

G93 **ἀδίκημα adikēma**, n. [3] [√*1.1 + 1472*]. crime, unrighteous or unjust act:– crime (1), crimes (1), misdemeanor (1)

G94 **ἀδικία adikia**, n. [25] [√*1.1 + 1472*]. wickedness, evil, wrongdoing:– wickedness (10), evil (3), unjust (2), unrighteousness (2), dishonest (2), evildoers (1 [+*2239*]), false (1), harm (1), sin (1), worldly (1), wrong (1), wrongdoing (1)

G95 **ἀδικοκρίτης adikokritēs**, n. Not used in NIVEBC. [√*1.1 + 1472 + 3212*]. unjust judge

G96 **ἄδικος adikos**, a. [12] [√*1.1 + 1472*]. unjust, unrighteous, used of things and persons; as a noun: unbeliever, wicked person:– unrighteous (3), dishonest (2), unjust (2), evildoers (1), ungodly (1), wicked (1), worldly (1), wrongdoers (1)

G97 **ἀδίκως adikōs**, adv. [1] [√*1.1 + 1472*]. unjustly:– unjust (1)

G98 **Ἀδμίν Admin**, n. pr. Not used in NIVEBC. [√*cf. 730*]. Admin

G99 **ἀδόκιμος adokimos**, a. [8] [√*1.1 + 1312*]. failing the test, rejected:– depraved (1), disqualified (1), fail the test (1 [+*1639*]), failed (1), failed the test (1 [+*1639*]), rejected (1), unfit (1), worthless (1)

G100 **ἄδολος adolos**, a. [1] [√*1.1 + 1515*]. pure, uncontaminated or tainted:– pure (1)

G101 **Ἀδραμυττηνός Adramyttēnos**, a. pr. g. [1] of Adramyttium:– from Adramyttium (1)

G102 **Ἀδρίας Adrias**, n. pr. [1] Adriatic Sea:– Adriatic sea (1)

G103 **ἁδρότης hadrotēs**, n. [1] liberal gift, liberality:– liberal gift (1)

G104 **ἀδυνατέω adynateō**, v. [2] [√*1.1 + 1538*]. to be impossible:– fail (1), impossible (1)

G105 **ἀδύνατος adynatos**, a. [10] [√*1.1 + 1538*]. impossible, powerless:– impossible (7), lame (1 [+*3836, 4546*]), powerless (1), weak (1)

G106 **ᾄδω adō**, v. [5] [√*6046*]. to sing:– sang (3), sing (1), singing (1)

G107 **ἀεί aei**, adv. [7] [→*132*]. always:– always (7)

G108 **ἀετός aetos**, n. [5] eagle (a noble, powerful bird), vulture (a carrion bird):– eagle (3), vultures (2)

G109 **ἄζυμος azymos**, a. [9] [√*1.1 + 2434*]. unleavened, (the Feast of) Unleavened Bread, made without yeast; fig. of purity:– festival of unleavened Bread (5), unleavened Bread (3), unleavened (1)

G110 **Ἀζώρ Azōr**, n. pr. [2] Azor:– Azor (2)

G111 **Ἄζωτος Azōtos**, n. pr. [1] Azotus, another name for Ashdod:– Azotus (1)

G112 **ἀηδία aēdia**, n. Not used in NIVEBC. [√*1.1 + 2454*]. enmity

G113 **ἀήρ aēr**, n. [7] [→*874; cf. 150, 885*]. air, sky:– air (6), sky (1)

G114 **ἀθανασία athanasia**, n. [3] [√*1.1 + 2569*]. immortality:– immortality (2), immortal (1)

G115 **ἀθάνατος athanatos**, a. Not used in NIVEBC. [√*1.1 + 2569*]. immortal

G116 **ἀθέμιτος athemitos**, a. Not used in NIVEBC. unlawful, detestable€ [2]:– against law (1), detestable (1)

G117 **ἄθεος atheos**, a. [1] [√*1.1 + 2536*]. without God, excluded from the heritage of Israel:– without God (1)

G118 **ἄθεσμος athesmos**, a. [2] [√*1.1 + 5502*]. lawless, unprincipled:– lawless (2)

G119 **ἀθετέω atheteō**, v. [16] [√*1.1 + 5502*]. to reject, set aside:– rejects (6), reject (2), rejected (2), set aside (2), broken (1), frustrate (1), refuse (1), setting aside (1)

G120 **ἀθέτησις athetēsis**, n. [2] [√*1.1 + 5502*]. setting aside, doing away with:– do away with (1), set aside (1)

G121 **Ἀθῆναι Athēnai**, n. pr. [4] [→*122*]. Athens:– Athens (4)

G122 **Ἀθηναῖος Athēnaios**, a. pr. g. [2] [√*121*]. Athenian, resident of Athens:– Athenians (1), of Athens (1)

G123 **ἀθλέω athleō**, v. [2] [→*124, 5254*]. to compete in a contest:– competes as an athlete (1), competing (1)

G124 **ἄθλησις athlēsis**, n. [1] [√*123*]. contest, struggle:– conflict (1)

G125 **ἀθροίζω athroizō**, v. [1] [→*2044, 5255; cf. 275, 2577*]. to assemble together, implying compactness or solidarity:– assembled together (1)

G126 **ἀθυμέω athymeō**, v. [1] [√*1.1 + 2596*]. to be discouraged, lose heart:– discouraged (1)

G127 **ἀθῷος athōos**, a. [2] [√*1.1 + 5502*]. innocent:– innocent (2)

G128 **αἴγειος aigeios**, a. [1] [√*144*]. of a goat:– goatskins (1 [+*1293*])

G129 **αἰγιαλός aigialos**, n. [6] [√*229*]. shore, beach:– shore (3), beach (2), sandy beach (1)

G130 **Αἰγύπτιος Aigyptios**, a. pr. g. [5] [√*131*]. Egyptian, person of Egypt:– Egyptian (3), Egyptians (2)

G131 **Αἴγυπτος Aigyptos**, n. pr. [25] [→*130*]. Egypt:– Egypt (20), Egypt (5 [+*1178*])

G132 **ἀΐδιος aidios**, a. [2] [√*107*]. eternal (referring to God's power, chains of punishment):– eternal (1), everlasting (1)

G133 **αἰδώς aidōs**, n. [1] [→*357*]. decency, modesty:– decency (1)

G134 **Αἰθίοψ Aithiops**, n. pr. g. [2] Ethiopian, person of Ethiopia:– Ethiopian (1 [+*467*]), Ethiopians (1)

G135 **αἷμα haima**, n. [97] [→*136, 137*]. blood; extended meanings: killing, death, sacrifice:– blood (88), bleeding (2 [+*4868*]), shedding blood (2), bleeding (1 [+*4380*]), blood red (1 [+*6055*]), human being (1 [+*4922, 2779*]), natural descent (1), subject to bleeding (1 [+*1877, 4868*])

G136 **αἱματεκχυσία haimatekchysia**, n. [1] [√*135 + 1772*]. shedding, pouring out of blood:– shedding of blood (1)

G137 **αἱμορροέω haimorroeō**, v. [1] [√*135 + 4835*]. to be subject to bleeding, to experience loss of blood:– subject to bleeding (1)

G138 **Αἰνέας Aineas**, n. pr. [2] [√*142*]. Aeneas, "[poss.] *praise*":– Aeneas (2)

G139 **αἴνεσις ainesis**, n. [1] [√*142*]. praise, speaking of the excellence of someone or something:– praise (1)

G140 **αἰνέω aineō**, v. [8] [√*142*]. to praise; in the NT, speaking of the excellence of God:– praising (5), praise (3)

G141 **αἴνιγμα ainigma**, n. [1] poor reflection, indistinct image:– reflection (1)

G142 **αἶνος ainos**, n. [2] [→*138, 139, 140, 2045, 2046, 2047, 4147*]. praise:– praise (1), praised (1 [+*1443*])

G143 **Αἰνών Ainōn**, n. pr. [1] Aenon, "*spring*":– Aenon (1)

G144 **αἴξ aix**, n. Not used in NIVEBC. [→*128*]. goat

G145 **αἱρέομαι haireomai**, v. [3] [→*146, 147, 148, 358, 359, 882, 904, 1348, 1349, 1975, 2746, 2747, 4311, 4576*]. to choose:– chose (2), choose (1)

G146 **αἵρεσις hairesis**, n. [9] [√*145*]. sect (religious party), faction, heresy:– sect (4), party (2), differences (1), factions (1), heresies (1)

G147 **αἱρετίζω hairetizō**, v. [1] [√*145*]. to choose (for the purpose of showing special favor):– chosen (1)

G148 **αἱρετικός hairetikos**, a. [1] [√*145*]. divisive:– divisive (1)

G149 **αἴρω airō**, v. [101] [→*554, 1976, 2048, 3558, 5256, 5512, 5513, 5643*]. to take up, take away:– take (15), picked up (9), take away (7), taken (7), get (6), pick up (6), took (5), taken away (4), takes away (4), carry (3), take up (3), takes (3), took away (3), go (2), lift up (2), pull away (2), raised (2), away with (1), carried (1), cuts off (1), deprived of (1), get rid of (1), get rid of (1 [+*608*]), hoisted aboard (1), in a loud voice (1 [+*5889*]), keep in suspense (1 [+*3836, 6034*]), looked (1 [+*3836, 4057*]), put (1), removed (1), rid (1), take out (1), taken down (1), taking out (1), weighed anchor (1), NDT (1)

G150 **αἰσθάνομαι aisthanomai**, v. [1] [→*151, 152; cf. 113*]. to grasp, understand, to have the capacity to perceive something clearly:– grasp (1)

G151 **αἴσθησις aisthēsis**, n. [1] [√*150*]. insight:– insight (1)

G152 **αἰσθητήριον aisthētērion**, n. [1] [√*150*]. sense, faculty:– themselves^{S} (1)

G153 **αἰσχροκερδής aischrokerdēs**, a. [2] [√*156 + 3046*]. pursuing dishonest gain:– pursuing dishonest gain (2)

G154 **αἰσχροκερδῶς aischrokerdōs**, adv. [1] [√*156 + 3046*]. in greediness for money:– pursuing dishonest gain (1)

G155 **αἰσχρολογία aischrologia**, n. [1] [√*156 + 3306*]. filthy language, vulgar speech:– filthy language (1)

G156 **αἰσχρός aischros**, a. [4] [→*153, 154, 155, 157, 158, 159, 454, 2049, 2875*]. disgraceful, shameful:– disgrace (1), disgraceful (1), dishonest (1), shameful (1)

G157 **αἰσχρότης *aischrotēs***, n. [1] [√*156*]. obscenity:– obscenity (1)

G158 **αἰσχύνη *aischynē***, n. [6] [√*156*]. shamefulness:– shame (3), shameful (2), humiliated (1 [+*3552*])

G159 **αἰσχύνομαι *aischynomai***, v. [5] [√*156*]. to be ashamed:– ashamed (4), unashamed (1 [+*3590*])

G160 **αἰτέω *aiteō***, v. [70] [→ *161, 555, 1977, 2050, 4148, 4644, 4645*]. to ask, ask for (of other humans or God), demand:– ask (27), asked (15), asks (7), ask for (6), asked for (4), asking (2), asks for (2), beg (1 [+*1797*]), called for (1), demand (1), demanded (1), favor (1 [+*5921*]), pray (1), request (1)

G161 **αἴτημα *aitēma***, n. [3] [√*160*]. request:– demand (1), requests (1), what[s] (1 [+*3836*])

G162 **αἰτία *aitia***, n. [20] [→ *163, 164, 165, 166, 360, 4577*]. (legal) charge; reason, cause:– basis for a charge (3), reason (3), charge (2), why (2 [+*1328, 4005*]), charge (1 [+*5770*]), charges (1), crime deserving (1), proper ground (1), situation (1), so (1 [+*1328, 4005*]), that is why (1 [+*1328, 4005*]), therefore (1 [+*1328, 4005*]), why (1 [+*5515, 3836*]), why (1 [+*3836, 1328, 4005*])

G163 **αἰτίαμα *aitiama***, n. Not used in NIVEBC. [√*162*]. charge, complaint

G164 **αἰτιάομαι *aitiaomai***, v. Not used in NIVEBC. [√*162*]. to charge

G165 **αἴτιος *aitios***, a. [5] [√*162*]. basis, reason or cause (for legal charges), source:– basis (1), basis for a charge (1), grounds for the death penalty (1 [+*2505*]), reason (1), source (1)

G166 **αἰτίωμα *aitiōma***, n. [1] [√*162*]. (legal) charge:– charges (1)

G167 **αἰφνίδιος *aiphnidios***, a. [2] [→ *924?, 1978, 1988, 2005*]. sudden, unexpected:– suddenly (2)

G168 **αἰχμαλωσία *aichmalōsia***, n. [3] [√*171*]. captivity:– captivity (2), took many captives (1 [+*169*])

G169 **αἰχμαλωτεύω *aichmalōteuō***, v. [1] [√*171*]. to take captive:– took many captives (1 [+*168*])

G170 **αἰχμαλωτίζω *aichmalōtizō***, v. [4] [√*171*]. to take captive, take prisoner:– gain control over (1), making a prisoner (1), take captive (1), taken as prisoners (1)

G171 **αἰχμάλωτος *aichmalōtos***, n. [1] [→ *168, 169, 170, 5257; cf. 274*]. prisoner:– prisoners (1)

G172 **αἰών *aiōn***, n. [123] [→ *173*]. eternity, age (time period); "this age" can mean the universe or even the current world system, the "god of this age" refers to the devil:– ever (44), age (20), forever (17 [+*1650, 3836*]), ages (5), forever (5 [+*1650, 3836*]), never (5 [+*4024, 3590, 1650, 3836*]), world (4), long ago (3), eternal (2), life (2), universe (2), again (1 [+*1650, 3836*]), ages past (1), ever (1 [+*1650, 3836*]), ever (1 [+*1666, 3836*]), forever (1 [+*1650*]), forever (1 [+*1650, 3836*]), forever (1 [+*1650, 2465*]), forevermore (1 [+*1650, 4246, 3836*]), never (1 [+*4024, 1650, 3836*]), never again (1 [+*4024, 3590, 1650, 3836*]), no never (1 [+*4024, 3590, 1650, 3836*]), permanent (1 [+*1650, 3836*]), time (1), ways (1)

G173 **αἰώνιος *aiōnios***, a. [70] [√*172*]. eternal, long ago:– eternal (64), beginning of time (2 [+*5989*]), forever (2), ages past (1), everlasting (1)

G174 **ἀκαθαρσία *akatharsia***, n. [10] [√*1.1 + 2754*]. impurity, a state of moral filthiness, especially in relation to sexual sin:– impurity (6), impure (2), sexual impurity (1), unclean (1)

G175 **ἀκαθάρτης *akathartēs***, n. Not used in NIVEBC. [√*1.1 + 2754*]. uncleanness

G176 **ἀκάθαρτος *akathartos***, a. [32] [√*1.1 + 2754*]. unclean, evil:– impure (24), unclean (7), filth (1)

G177 **ἀκαιρέομαι *akaireomai***, v. [1] [√*1.1 + 2789*]. to have no opportunity, have no time:– had no opportunity (1)

G178 **ἀκαίρως *akairōs***, adv. [1] [√*1.1 + 2789*]. out of season, lack of a favorable opportunity:– out of season (1)

G179 **ἄκακος *akakos***, a. [2] [√*1.1 + 2805*]. blameless, innocent, unsuspecting:– blameless (1), naive (1)

G180 **ἄκανθα *akantha***, n. [14] [√*216*]. thorn, thornbush:– thorns (9), thornbushes (2), which[s] (2 [+*3836*]), which[s] (1)

G181 **ἀκάνθινος *akanthinos***, a. [2] [√*216*]. of thorns, thorny:– of thorns (2)

G182 **ἄκαρπος *akarpos***, a. [7] [√*1.1 + 2843*]. unfruitful, unproductive, something generally useless:– unfruitful (3), unproductive (2), fruitless (1), without fruit (1)

G183 **ἀκατάγνωστος *akatagnōstos***, a. [1] [√*1.1 + 2848 + 1182*]. not condemned, what cannot be criticized:– cannot be condemned (1)

G184 **ἀκατακάλυπτος *akatakalyptos***, a. [2] [√*1.1 + 2848 + 2821*]. uncovered:– uncovered (2)

G185 **ἀκατάκριτος *akatakritos***, a. [2] [√*1.1 + 2848 + 3212*]. uncondemned, not condemned without a proper trial:– hasn't been found guilty (1), without a trial (1)

G186 **ἀκατάλυτος *akatalytos***, a. [1] [√*1.1 + 2848 + 3395*]. indestructible, unstoppable:– indestructible (1)

G187 **ἀκατάπαστος *akatapastos***, a. Not used in NIVEBC. [√*1.1 + 2848 + 4264*]. unceasing, restless

G188 **ἀκατάπαυστος *akatapaustos***, a. [1] [√*1.1 + 2848 + 4264*]. never stopping:– never stop (1)

G189 **ἀκαταστασία *akatastasia***, n. [5] [√*1.1 + 2848 + 2705*]. disorder, rebellion, riot:– disorder (3), riots (1), uprisings (1)

G190 **ἀκατάστατος *akatastatos***, a. [2] [√*1.1 + 2848 + 2705*]. unstable, restless:– restless (1), unstable (1)

G191 **ἀκατάσχετος *akataschetos***, a. Not used in NIVEBC. [√*1.1 + 2848 + 2400*]. uncontrollable

G192 **Ἀκελδαμάχ *Hakeldamach***, n. pr. [1] Akeldama (traditionally located south of the valley of Hinnom), "*field of blood*":– Akeldama (1)

G193 **ἀκέραιος *akeraios***, a. [3] [√*1.1 + 3042*]. innocent, pure, not mixed with evil:– innocent (2), pure (1)

G194 **ἀκηδεμονέω *akēdemoneō***, v. Not used in NIVEBC. be in distress, troubled

G195 **ἀκλινής *aklinēs***, a. [1] [√*1.1 + 3111*]. unswerving, without wavering:– unswervingly (1)

G196 **ἀκμάζω *akmazō***, v. [1] [√*216*]. to be or become ripe:– ripe (1)

G197 **ἀκμήν *akmēn***, adv. [1] [√*216*]. still, even yet:– still (1)

G198 **ἀκοή *akoē***, n. [25] [√*201*]. (act of) hearing, what is heard:– ears (3), ever hearing (3 [+*201*]), heard (3), message (2), news (2), rumors (2), what heard (2), ear (1), hearing message (1), listening (1), message heard (1), reports (1), say what itching ears want to hear (1 [+*3117*]), sense of hearing (1), understand (1)

G199 **ἀκολουθέω *akoloutheō***, v. [90] [→ *1.3, 1979, 2051, 2887, 4158, 5258*]. to follow; accompany; fig., to follow or be a disciple of a leader's teaching:– followed (42), follow (33), following (7), accompanied (2), be disciple (1 [+*3958*]), behind (1), follows (1), is one of (1 [+*3552*]), was one of (1), went (1)

G200 **ἀκουστός *akoustos***, a. Not used in NIVEBC. [√*201*]. audible

G201 **ἀκούω *akouō***, v. [427] [→ *198, 200, 1358, 1653, 2052, 4157, 4159, 4578, 5633, 5634, 5675*]. to hear, pay attention, understand, obey:– heard (205), hear (100), listen (37), hears (18), hearing (14), listening (8), listens (7), heard about (6), listened (6), listen to (4), ever hearing (3 [+*198*]), understand (2), accept (1), aware of what says (1), heard (1 [+*1639*]), heard of (1), hearers (1), it[s] (1 [+*4005, 608, 794*]), learned (1), listening to (1), obeyed (1), reached (1 [+*1650*]), report (1), reported (1), say (1 [+*1666*]), told (1), understands (1), whispered[s] (1), words (1)

G202 **ἀκρασία *akrasia***, n. [2] [√*1.1 + 3197*]. lack of self-control:– lack of self-control (1), self-indulgence (1)

G203 **ἀκρατής *akratēs***, a. [1] [√*1.1 + 3197*]. without self-control:– without self-control (1)

G204 **ἄκρατος *akratos***, a. [1] [√*1.1 + 3042*]. undiluted (of wine not watered down):– full strength (1)

G205 **ἀκρίβεια *akribeia***, n. [1] [√*207*]. thoroughness, strictness:– thoroughly (1 [+*2848*])

G206 **ἀκριβέστατος *akribestatos***, a. Not used in NIVEBC. [√*207*]. strictest

G207 **ἀκριβής *akribēs***, a. [1] [→ *205, 206, 208, 209*]. strict:– strictest (1)

G208 **ἀκριβόω *akriboō***, v. [2] [√*207*]. to find out exactly:– found out exact (1), learned (1)

G209 **ἀκριβῶς *akribōs***, adv. [9] [√*207*]. accurately, carefully, well:– carefully (2), more accurate (2), accurately (1), be very careful (1 [+*1063*]), more adequately (1), very well (1), well (1)

G210 **ἀκρίς *akris***, n. [4] locust (in some cultures distinguished from a grasshopper and used as a food source):– locusts (4)

G211 **ἀκροατήριον *akroatērion***, n. [1] [√*212*]. audience room (of the procurator), in which hearings were held and justice was privately dispensed:– audience room (1)

G212 **ἀκροατής *akroatēs***, n. [4] [→ *211, 2053*]. hearer:– hear (1), heard (1 [+*1181*]), listen (1), listens (1)

G213 **ἀκροβυστία *akrobystia***, n. [20] [√*216*]. uncircumcision, foreskin; fig., not of the Mosaic covenant, a Gentile:– uncircumcised (5), not circumcised (4), uncircumcision (4), before[s] (2 [+*1877*]), uncircumcised (2 [+*1877*]), before circumcised (1 [+*1877*]), they[s] (1 [+*3836, 899*]), uncircumcised (1 [+*2400*])

G214 **ἀκρογωνιαῖος *akrogōniaios***, a. [2] [√*216 + 1224*]. cornerstone, an essential stone in the construction of a building:– chief cornerstone (1), cornerstone (1)

G215 **ἀκροθίνιον *akrothinion***, n. [1] [√*216*]. plunder, booty, fine spoils:– plunder (1)

G216 **ἄκρον *akron***, n. [6] [→ *180, 181, 196, 197, 213, 214, 215, 948, 5644*]. end, top:– ends (2), end (1), other[s] (1), tip (1), top (1)

G217 **Ἀκύλας *Akylas***, n. pr. [6] Aquila, "*eagle*":– Aquila (6)

G218 **ἀκυρόω *akyroō***, v. [3] [√*1.1 + 3263*]. to nullify, make void:– nullify (2), set aside (1)

G219 **ἀκωλύτως *akōlytōs***, adv. [1] [√*1.1 + 3266*]. without hinderance:– without hindrance (1)

G220 **ἄκων *akōn***, a. [1] [√*1.1 + 1776*]. not voluntary, unwilling:– not voluntarily (1)

G221 **ἅλα *hala***, n. Not used in NIVEBC. [√*229*]. salt

G222 **ἀλάβαστρον *alabastron***, n. Not used in NIVEBC. [→ *223*]. alabaster jar

G223 **ἀλάβαστρος *alabastros***, n. [4] [√*222*]. alabaster jar; a long-necked flask, the top of which was broken off to empty its contents:– alabaster jar (3), jar (1)

G224 **ἀλαζονεία *alazoneia***, n. [2] [→ *225, 226*]. boasting, pretension, arrogance:– arrogant schemes (1), pride (1)

G225 **ἀλαζών *alazōn***, n. [2] [√*224*]. boaster, braggart:– boastful (2)

G226 **ἀλαλάζω *alalazō***, v. [2] [√*224*]. to clang, wail:– clanging (1), wailing (1)

G227 **ἀλάλητος *alalētos***, a. [1] [√*1.1 + 3281*]. inexpressible, unspeakable:– wordless (1)

G228 **ἄλαλος *alalos***, a. [3] [√*1.1 + 3281*]. mute, unable to speak:– mute (2), robbed of speech (1)

G229 **ἅλας *halas***, n. [8] [→ *129, 221, 243, 244, 245, 265, 266, 383, 1879, 4163; cf. 2498*]. salt; the impure salt of the ancient could become tasteless in adverse conditions, and its residue useless:– salt (6), it[s] (2 [+*3836*])

G230 **ἀλείφω *aleiphō***, v. [9] [→ *1981*]. to pour on, anoint (usually with olive oil):– poured on (4), anoint (2), anointed (1), put oil on (1), put on (1)

G231 **ἀλεκτοροφωνία *alektorophōnia***, n. [1] [√*232 + 5889*]. crowing of a rooster; the third Roman watch of the night (about midnight to 3:00 a.m.):– when the rooster crows (1)

G232 **ἀλέκτωρ *alektōr***, n. [11] [→ *231*]. rooster:– rooster (11)

G233 **Ἀλεξανδρεύς *Alexandreus***, n. pr. g. [2] [√*235*]. Alexandrian, person of Alexandria:– Alexandria (1), of Alexandria (1)

G234 **Ἀλεξανδρῖνος *Alexandrinos***, a. pr. g. [2] [√*235*]. Alexandrian, of Alexandria:– Alexandrian (2)

G235 **Ἀλέξανδρος *Alexandros***, n. pr. [6] [→ *233, 234*]. Alexander, "*defender of men*":– Alexander (5), he[s] (1)

G236 **ἄλευρον *aleuron***, n. [2] [√*241*]. flour:– flour (2)

G237 **ἀλήθεια *alētheia***, n. [109] [√*1.1 + 3291*]. truth, truthfulness; corresponding to reality:– truth (90), true (6), truly (2 [+*1877*]), assure (1 [+*2093, 3306*]), certainly (1 [+*2093*]), faithful (1), how true (1 [+*2093*]), indeed (1 [+*1142, 2093*]), it[s] (1), right (1 [+*2093*]), truthful (1), truthfully (1), truthfulness (1), very truly (1)

G238 **ἀληθεύω *alētheuō***, v. [2] [√*1.1 + 3291*]. to be truthful, tell the truth:– speaking the truth (1), telling the truth (1)

G239 **ἀληθής *alēthēs***, a. [26] [√*1.1 + 3291*]. true, genuine, reliable, trustworthy, valid:– true (12), real (3), truth (3), integrity (2), valid (2), genuine (1), really (1), trustworthy (1), truthful (1)

G240 **ἀληθινός *alēthinos***, a. [28] [√*1.1 + 3291*]. true, genuine:– true (27), sincere (1)

G241 **ἀλήθω *alēthō***, v. [2] [→ *236*]. to grind grain (with a handmill operated by two women):– grinding (1), grinding grain (1)

G242 **ἀληθῶς *alēthōs***, adv. [18] [√*1.1 + 3291*]. truly, surely:– surely (6), truly (6), really (2), actually (1), really (1 [+*3607*]), with certainty (1), without a doubt (1)

G243 **ἁλιεύς *halieus***, n. [5] [√*229*]. fisherman (by occupation):– fishermen (3), fish (1), fish (1 [+*1181*])

G244 **ἁλιεύω *halieuō***, v. [1] [√*229*]. to catch fish, either by net or by line:– fish (1)

G245 **ἁλίζω *halizō***, v. [2] [√*229*]. to salt, make salty:– made salty (1), salted (1)

G246 **ἀλίσγημα *alisgēma***, n. [1] pollution, ritually defiled:– polluted (1)

G247 ἀλλά *alla*, pt. adver. [639] [√*257*]. but, instead, yet, except:– but (409), instead (20), rather (17), yet (15), no (13), on the contrary (10), only (8), nevertheless (6), what (6), and (5), in fact (5), but rather (4), indeed (4), but instead (3), however (3), more than (3 [+*4024*]), now (3), but only (2), if not (2), on the contrary (2 [+*5539*]), so (2), what is more (2 [+*4024, 3667, 1254, 2779*]), again (1), although (1), and (1 [+*1145, 2779*]), because (1), but (1 [+*2445*]), cannot (1 [+*2445*]), certainly (1), even (1), even though (1), except (1 [+*3668*]), for (1), if (1), in addition (1 [+*2779*]), indeed (1 [+*2779*]), instead (1 [+*4047, 3437*]), instead of (1), just (1), no but (1), on the contrary (1 [+*4498, 3437*]), so much as (1), surely (1 [+*1145*]), the only thing that counts (1), then (1), though (1 [+*1623*]), though (1), what counts (1), what counts[S] (1), yes (1), yes (1 [+*2779*]), yet (1 [+*3437*]), NDT (65)

G248 ἀλλάσσω *allassō*, v. [6] [→*498, 557, 639, 1367, 2903, 2904, 3563, 4164, 5261; cf. 257*]. to change, exchange:– changed (3), change (2), exchanged (1)

G249 ἀλλαχόθεν *allachothen*, adv. pl. [1] [√*257*]. from another way:– by some other way (1)

G250 ἀλλαχοῦ *allachou*, adv. pl. [1] [√*257*]. elsewhere, somewhere else:– somewhere else (1)

G251 ἀλληγορέω *allēgoreō*, v. [1] [√*257 + 60*]. to take figuratively, speak allegorically, to employ an analogy or likeness in communication:– taken figuratively (1)

G252 ἀλληλουϊά *hallēlouia*, l.[v.+n. pr.] [4] hallelujah; from Hebrew hallelu-yah, praise Yah(weh):– hallelujah (4)

G253 ἀλλήλων *allēlōn*, p. recip. [100] [√*257*]. one another, each other:– one another (49), each other (29), themselves (3), each other's (2 [+*1877*]), others (2), together (2 [+*4639*]), all (1), mutual (1 [+*1650*]), one another's (1), one body (1), talked the matter over (1 [+*1368, 4639*]), them (1), yourselves (1), NDT (6)

G254 ἀλλογενής *allogenēs*, a. [1] [√*257 + 1181*]. foreigner:– foreigner (1)

G255 ἀλλοιόω *alloioō*, v. Not used in NIVEBC. [√*257*]. to change

G256 ἅλλομαι *hallomai*, v. [3] [→*380, 1880, 1982, 2383; cf. 4888*]. to jump up, well up, quick movement of both humans and water:– jumped up (1), jumping (1), welling up (1)

G257 ἄλλος *allos*, a. & n. [155] [→*247, 249, 250, 251, 253, 254, 255, 258, 259, 260, 261, 558; cf. 248*]. another, other:– another (43), others (36), other (33), someone else (6), else (5), more (4), some (4), a (2), one kind (2), that (2), another (1 [+*5516*]), another's (1), any other (1), anyone else (1), gospel[S] (1), one (1), one another (1 [+*4639, 257*]), one another (1 [+*257, 4639*]), some (1 [+*1254*]), other (1 [+*1254*]), other than (1), second (1), some more (1), someone (1), then (1), NDT (3)

G258 ἀλλοτριεπίσκοπος *allotriepiskopos*, n. [1] [√*257 + 2093 + 5023*]. meddler, busybody; formally rendered "one who oversees what belongs to another" (in an unwarranted manner):– meddler (1)

G259 ἀλλότριος *allotrios*, a. [14] [√*257*]. belonging to another:– someone else's (4), others (3), foreign (1), not his own (1), not their own (1), of others (1), stranger (1), stranger in a foreign country (1), stranger's (1)

G260 ἀλλόφυλος *allophylos*, a. [1] [√*257 + 5876*]. Gentile, foreigner:– gentile (1)

G261 ἄλλως *allōs*, adv. [1] [√*257*]. differently:– not obvious[S] (1)

G262 ἀλοάω *aloaō*, v. [3] [→*272, 3617, 3618, 4254, 4260*]. to tread, thresh, to separate grain kernels from the husks by beating or treading on:– treading out the grain (2), threshes (1)

G263 ἄλογος *alogos*, a. [3] [√*1.1 + 3306*]. unreasonable, without reason, brutish and living by instinct:– irrational (1), unreasonable (1), unreasoning (1)

G264 ἀλόη *aloē*, n. [1] aloes:– aloes (1)

G265 ἅλς *hals*, n. Not used in NIVEBC. [√*229*]. salt

G266 ἁλυκός *halykos*, a. [1] [√*229*]. salt spring, salty:– salt spring (1)

G267 ἄλυπος *alypos*, a. [1] [√*1.1 + 3383*]. free from anxiety; in the comparative, less anxiety:– less anxiety (1)

G268 ἅλυσις *halysis*, n. [11] chain (the state of imprisonment):– chains (6), chain (3), chained hand (1 [+*1297*]), chained hand (1 [+*1313*])

G269 ἀλυσιτελής *alysitelēs*, a. [1] [√*1.1 + 3395 + 5465*]. unadvantageous, without special benefit:– of no benefit (1)

G270 ἄλφα *alpha*, n. pr. [3] [√*1*]. Alpha, "*First* or *Beginning*":– Alpha (3)

G271 Ἀλφαῖος *Halphaios*, n. pr. [5] Alphaeus:– Alphaeus (5)

G272 ἅλων *halōn*, n. [2] [√*262*]. threshing floor:– threshing floor (2)

G273 ἀλώπηξ *alōpēx*, n. [3] fox; this can refer to a wicked person with the probable implication of being cunning or treacherous:– foxes (2), fox (1)

G274 ἅλωσις *halōsis*, n. [1] [→*379, 384, 2914, 4648, 4649, 5260; cf. 171*]. capture, catch:– caught (1)

G275 ἅμα *hama*, adv. & pp.* [11] [→*570, 761; cf. 125, 604*]. together, at the same time:– together (3), at the same time (2), early in the morning (2 [+*4745*]), and (1), besides (1), one thing more (1), with (1)

G276 ἀμαθής *amathēs*, a. [1] [√*1.1 + 3443*]. ignorant, without a formal education:– ignorant (1)

G277 ἀμαράντινος *amarantinos*, a. [1] [√*1.1 + 3447*]. unfading, without loss of pristine character:– never fade away (1)

G278 ἀμάραντος *amarantos*, a. [1] [√*1.1 + 3447*]. never fading:– never fade (1)

G279 ἁμαρτάνω *hamartanō*, v. [43] [→*280, 281, 283, 387, 4579*]. to sin, do wrong; usually to do any act contrary to the will and law of God:– sin (14), sinned (12), sinning (8), sins (4), commit a sin (1 [+*281*]), doing wrong (1), done wrong (1), leave life of sin (1 [+*3600*]), sinful (1)

G280 ἁμάρτημα *hamartēma*, n. [4] [√*279*]. sin, wrongdoing; usually any act contrary to the will and law of God:– sins (3), sin (1)

G281 ἁμαρτία *hamartia*, n. [173] [√*279*]. sin, wrongdoing; usually any act contrary to the will and law of God:– sin (77), sins (74), sinful (4), guilty of sin (3 [+*2400*]), sin offering (2), sin offerings (2 [+*4309*]), sinning (2), sins (2 [+*4472, 3836*]), commit a sin (1 [+*279*]), guilt (1), guilty of sin (1), sin (1 [+*2237*]), sin (1 [+*4472*]), sinned (1 [+*1639, 4472*]), sin's (1)

G282 ἀμάρτυρος *amartyros*, a. [1] [√*1.1 + 3459*]. without testimony, without witness:– without testimony (1)

G283 ἁμαρτωλός *hamartōlos*, a. [47] [√*279*]. (a.) sinful, as an absolute moral failure; (n.) sinner, one who violates God's will or law; in some contexts, one who does not keep orthodox traditions and behaviors:– sinners (29), sinner (9), sinful (5), sinful life (1), sinner (1 [+*467*]), sinner (1 [+*476*]), sinners (1 [+*476*])

G284 Ἀμασίας *Amasias*, n. pr. Not used in NIVEBC. Amaziah, "*Yahweh is powerful*"

G285 ἄμαχος *amachos*, a. [2] [√*1.1 + 3480*]. peaceable, not quarrelsome, without conflict:– not quarrelsome (1), peaceable (1)

G286 ἀμάω *amaō*, v. [1] to mow, cut down:– mowed (1)

G287 ἀμέθυστος *amethystos*, n. [1] [√*1.3 [?]* + 3501]. amethyst, usually purple or violet in color:– amethyst (1)

G288 ἀμελέω *ameleō*, v. [4] [√*1.1 + 3508*]. to neglect, ignore:– ignore (1), neglect (1), paid no attention (1), turned away from (1)

G289 ἄμεμπτος *amemptos*, a. [5] [√*1.1 + 3522*]. blameless, faultless:– blameless (2), blamelessly (1), faultless (1), nothing wrong (1)

G290 ἀμέμπτως *amemptōs*, adv. [2] [√*1.1 + 3522*]. blamelessly:– blameless (2)

G291 ἀμέριμνος *amerimnos*, a. [2] [√*1.1 + 3533*]. free from concern, free from care:– free from concern (1), out of trouble (1)

G292 ἀμετάθετος *ametathetos*, a. [2] [√*1.1 + 3552 + 5502*]. unchangeable, unchanging:– unchangeable (1), unchanging (1)

G293 ἀμετακίνητος *ametakinētos*, a. [1] [√*1.1 + 3552 + 3075*]. not moveable, immovable:– nothing move (1)

G294 ἀμεταμέλητος *ametamelētos*, a. [2] [√*1.1 + 3552 + 3508*]. without regret, so, not revocable:– irrevocable (1), no regret (1)

G295 ἀμετανόητος *ametanoētos*, a. [1] [√*1.1 + 3552 + 3808*]. unrepentant:– unrepentant (1)

G296 ἄμετρος *ametros*, a. [2] [√*1.1 + 3586*]. beyond limits, immeasurable:– limits (2)

G297 ἀμήν *amēn*, l.[adv.] [130] amen, the truth; a formula of solemn expression of certainty. In the Gospel of John it is doubled in the sayings of Jesus for emphasis:– truly (50), very truly (50 [+*297*]), amen (30)

G298 ἀμήτωρ *amētōr*, a. [1] [√*1.1 + 3613*]. without a mother:– without mother (1)

G299 ἀμίαντος *amiantos*, a. [4] [√*1.1 + 3620*]. pure:– pure (2), faultless (1), never spoil (1)

G300 Ἀμιναδάβ *Aminadab*, n. pr. [3] Amminadab, "*my people are generous*":– Amminadab (3)

G301 ἄμμον *ammon*, n. Not used in NIVEBC. [√*302*]. sand

G302 ἄμμος *ammos*, n. [5] [→*301*]. sand, often used as a figure of things that cannot be counted:– sand (4), shore (1)

G303 ἀμνός *amnos*, n. [4] lamb:– lamb (4)

G304 ἀμοιβή *amoibē*, n. [1] repayment, recompense:– repaying (1 [+*625*])

G305 ἄμορφος *amorphos*, a. Not used in NIVEBC. [√*1.1 + 3671*]. misshapen, ugly

G306 ἄμπελος *ampelos*, n. [9] [→*307, 308*]. vine, grapevine:– vine (7), grapes (1), grapevine (1)

G307 ἀμπελουργός *ampelourgos*, n. [1] [√*306 + 2240*]. one who takes care of a vineyard:– man who took care of the vineyard (1)

G308 ἀμπελών *ampelōn*, n. [23] [√*306*]. vineyard:– vineyard (23)

G309 Ἀμπλιᾶτος *Ampliatos*, n. pr. [1] Ampliatus:– Ampliatus (1)

G310 ἀμύνομαι *amynomai*, v. [1] to defend, help, come to the aid of:– went to defense (1)

G311 ἀμφιβάλλω *amphiballō*, v. [1] [→*312; cf. 965*]. to cast a fishnet (a round net with small weights along its edge):– casting a net (1)

G312 ἀμφίβληστρον *amphiblēstron*, n. [1] [√*311*]. casting net, fishing net (not a dragnet):– net (1)

G313 ἀμφιέζω *amphiezō*, v. [1] [→*314; cf. 2667*]. to clothe, dress:– clothes (1)

G314 ἀμφιέννυμι *amphiennymi*, v. [3] [√*313*]. to dress, clothe:– dressed (2), clothes (1)

G315 Ἀμφίπολις *Amphipolis*, n. pr. [1] [√*4484*]. Amphipolis, "*a city surrounded* or *a city conspicuous*":– Amphipolis (1)

G316 ἄμφοδον *amphodon*, n. [1] [√*3847*]. street, usually within a city:– street (1)

G317 ἀμφότεροι *amphoteroi*, a. Not used in NIVEBC. both, all€ [14]:– both (11), all (1), all things (1), two (1)

G318 ἀμώμητος *amōmētos*, a. [1] [√*1.1 + 3522*]. blameless, unblemished:– blameless (1)

G319 ἄμωμον *amōmon*, n. [1] spice, a general term for any kind of spice:– spice (1)

G320 ἄμωμος *amōmos*, a. [8] [√*1.1 + 3522*]. unblemished, blameless:– blameless (3), without blemish (2), without fault (2), unblemished (1)

G321 Ἀμών *Amōn*, n. pr. Not used in NIVEBC. Amon, "*trustworthy*"

G322 Ἀμώς *Amōs*, n. pr. [3] Amos, "*burden bearer*":– Amon (2), Amos (1)

G323 ἄν *an*, pt. [166] [→*1569, 1570, 2054, 2829, 4020, 6056*]. not easily translated: indicates potential or condition:– would have (22), would (17), whoever (15 [+*4005*]), until (13 [+*2401*]), if (12), anyone (8 [+*4005*]), before (4 [+*2401*]), whoever (4 [+*4005*]), anyone (3), anyone (2 [+*4005*]), a (2 [+*4005*]), might (2), the one (2 [+*4005*]), until (2 [+*2401*]), whatever (2 [+*4005, 5516*]), when (2 [+*6055*]), wherever (2 [+*3963*]), who (2 [+*4005*]), who (2 [+*5516*]), whoever (2 [+*4015*]), whom (2 [+*4005*]), a (1 [+*4005, 1254*]), all (1 [+*4012*]), all whom (1 [+*4012*]), whom (1 [+*4005*]), anyone (2 [+*4005*]), any (1 [+*4005*]), any (1 [+*4005, 5516*]), anyone (1 [+*5516*]), as soon as (1 [+*6055, 1994*]), before (1 [+*4570, 2445*]), can (1), could have (1), everything (1 [+*4246, 4012*]), how (1 [+*4802*]), if any (1 [+*4005*]), may (1), meaning (1 [+*5515, 1639*]), once (1 [+*608, 4005*]), perhaps (1), so that (1 [+*3968*]), so that (1 [+*3968*]), somehow or other (1 [+*6055*]), that (1 [+*3968*]), till (1 [+*2401*]), trying to (1 [+*6055*]), until (1 [+*948, 4005*]), what (1 [+*5515, 5516*]), what (1 [+*5515, 4047*]), whatever (1 [+*4005*]), whatever (1 [+*4005*]), whatever (1 [+*4005, 1254*]), whatever (1 [+*1877, 4005, 1254*]), whatever (1 [+*4012*]), whatever (1 [+*5516*]), whatever (1 [+*4246, 4012*]), whatever (1 [+*4005, 3836, 5516*]), when (1 [+*2471*]), which (1 [+*5515*]), which one (1 [+*5515*]), whoever (1 [+*4246, 4005*]), NDT (3)

G324 ἀνά *ana*, pp. [11] [→*327, 329, 330, 331, 332, 333, 334, 335, 336, 341, 342, 343, 344, 345, 346, 347, 348, 349, 350, 351, 352, 353, 355, 358, 359, 361, 362, 363, 364, 365, 366, 367, 368, 369, 370, 371, 372, 373, 374, 375, 376, 377, 378, 379, 380, 381, 382, 384, 385, 386, 388, 389, 390, 391, 392, 398, 399, 400, 401, 402, 404, 405, 407, 408, 409, 411, 412, 413, 414, 415, 416, 417, 418, 419, 420, 421, 423, 426, 427, 428, 429, 430, 431, 432, 433, 434, 445, 452, 456, 457, 461, 462, 465, 479, 482, 488, 494, 496, 499, 1983, 1985, 2056, 2057, 2058, 2059, 2060, 2061, 2914, 4646, 4647, 4648, 4649, 4650, 4651, 4652, 5262, 5263, 5264, 5265, 5266; cf. 403, 424, 458, 487, 539*]. each, in turn, among:– each (4), among (1 [+*3545*]), between (1 [+*3545*]), by (1), each (1 [+*1651, 1667*]), into (1 [+*3545*]), one at a time (1 [+*3538*]), NDT (1)

G325 ἀναβαθμός *anabathmos*, n. [2] [√*326*]. step; (pl.) a flight of steps:– steps (2)

GREEK INDEX

G326 **ἀναβαίνω** ***anabainō***, v. [82] [→*325, 328, 563, 609, 957, 1000, 1010, 1011, 1012, 1013, 1014, 1037, 1117, 1329, 1331, 1674, 1676, 1832, 1836, 1837, 2094, 2097, 2849, 2853, 2854, 3028, 3553, 4124, 4126, 4127, 4581, 4583, 4584, 4585, 4586, 4646, 5160, 5201, 5204, 5262, 5648*]. to go up, rise:– went up (22), going up (7), come up (5), ascended (4), go up (4), ascend (3), came up (3), climbed (3), went (3), ascending (2), coming (2), coming up (2), grew up (2), rise (2), catch (1), climbed back into (1), climbs in (1), comes up (1), conceived (1 [+*2093*]), decided (1 [+*2093, 3836, 2840*]), go (1), goes up (1), gone (1), grows (1), left (1), marched (1), on way up (1), reached (1), rose (1), up (1), went aboard (1), went upstairs (1)

G327 **ἀναβάλλω** ***anaballō***, v. [1] [√*324 + 965*]. to adjourn a proceeding (a legal term):– adjourned (1)

G328 **ἀναβιβάζω** ***anabibazō***, v. [1] [√*326*]. to pull up, bring up:– pulled up (1)

G329 **ἀναβλέπω** ***anablepō***, v. [25] [√*324 + 1063*]. to look up, receive sight:– looked up (5), received sight (5), receive sight (4), looking up (3), see (3), see again (2), able to see (1), man's (1), restore sight (1)

G330 **ἀνάβλεψις** ***anablepsis***, n. [1] [√*324 + 1063*]. recovery of sight:– recovery of sight (1)

G331 **ἀναβοάω** ***anaboaō***, v. [1] [√*324 + 1068*]. to cry out:– cried out (1)

G332 **ἀναβολή** ***anabolē***, n. [1] [√*324 + 965*]. delay, postponement:– delay (1 [+*4472*])

G333 **ἀνάγαιον** ***anagaion***, n. [2] [√*324 + 1178*]. upper room:– room upstairs (2)

G334 **ἀναγγέλλω** ***anangellō***, v. [14] [√*324 + 34*]. to tell, report, announce:– told (3), make known (2), reported (2), declare (1), explain (1), openly confessed (1 [+*2018, 2779*]), preach (1), proclaim (1), tell (1), told about (1)

G335 **ἀναγεννάω** ***anagennaō***, v. [2] [√*324 + 1181*]. to give new birth, cause to be born again; used in the sense of spiritual rebirth, similar to being born again/from above (see *540 + 1164*):– born again (1), given new birth (1)

G336 **ἀναγινώσκω** ***anaginōskō***, v. [32] [√*324 + 1182*]. to read, read aloud:– read (23), reading (5), reader (2), have read (1), reads aloud (1)

G337 **ἀναγκάζω** ***anankazō***, v. [9] [√*340*]. to compel, force:– compel (2), compelled (2), force (2), made (2), drove to it (1)

G338 **ἀναγκαῖος** ***anankaios***, a. [8] [√*340*]. necessary, indispensable:– necessary (3), friends (1), had to (1 [+*1639*]), indispensable (1), more necessary (1), urgent (1)

G339 **ἀναγκαστῶς** ***anankastōs***, adv. [1] [√*340*]. a must, by compulsion:– must (1)

G340 **ἀνάγκη** ***anankē***, n. [17] [→*337, 338, 339, 2055*]. necessity; distress, hardship:– necessary (3), compulsion (2), distress (2), hardships (2), I must (1 [+*2400*]), compelled (1), compelled (1 [+*2130*]), crisis (1), forced (1 [+*2848*]), must (1), must (1 [+*1666*]), need (1 [+*2400*])

G341 **ἀναγνωρίζω** ***anagnōrizō***, v. [1] [√*324 + 1182*]. to tell, make known again:– told who was (1)

G342 **ἀνάγνωσις** ***anagnōsis***, n. [3] [√*324 + 1182*]. reading, public reading:– public reading (1), read (1), reading (1)

G343 **ἀνάγω** ***anagō***, v. [23] [√*324 + 72*]. to lead up, bring up; (mid.) to put out to sea:– put out to sea (5), sail (4), brought (2), sailed (2), set sail (2), bring out (1), bring up (1), brought back (1), led (1), led up (1), set out (1), taken (1), took (1)

G344 **ἀναδείκνυμι** ***anadeiknymi***, v. [2] [√*324 + 1259*]. to show, appoint:– appointed (1), show (1)

G345 **ἀνάδειξις** ***anadeixis***, n. [1] [√*324 + 1259*]. public appearance:– appeared publicly (1)

G346 **ἀναδέχομαι** ***anadechomai***, v. [2] [√*324 + 1312*]. to receive, welcome:– embraced (1), welcomed to home (1)

G347 **ἀναδίδωμι** ***anadidōmi***, v. [1] [√*324 + 1443*]. to deliver, hand over:– delivered (1)

G348 **ἀναζάω** ***anazaō***, v. [2] [√*324 + 2409*]. to become alive again:– alive again (1), sprang to life (1)

G349 **ἀναζητέω** ***anazēteō***, v. [3] [√*324 + 2426*]. to look for, search for:– look for (2), looking for (1)

G350 **ἀναζώννυμι** ***anazōnnymi***, v. [1] [√*324 + 2439*]. to gird (the loins), bind (to prepare for action); used fig. of "girding the loins of the mind" (1Pe 1:13) to prepare mentally for action:– alert (1 [+*3836, 4019*])

G351 **ἀναζωπυρέω** ***anazōpyreō***, v. [1] [√*324 + 2409 + 4786*]. to fan a flame, rekindle:– fan into flame (1)

G352 **ἀναθάλλω** ***anathallō***, v. [1] [√*324 + 2558*]. to renew, cause to grow or bloom again:– renewed (1)

G353 **ἀνάθεμα** ***anathema***, n. [6] [→*354, 356, 2912, 2913; cf. 324 + 5502*]. curse, oath; one cursed:– cursed (3), under God's curse (2), taken a solemn oath (1 [+*354*])

G354 **ἀναθεματίζω** ***anathematizō***, v. [4] [√*353*]. to bind with an oath:– bound with an oath (1), call down curses (1), taken a solemn oath (1 [+*353*]), taken an oath (1)

G355 **ἀναθεωρέω** ***anatheōreō***, v. [2] [√*324 + 2555*]. to look carefully at:– consider (1), looked carefully at (1)

G356 **ἀνάθημα** ***anathēma***, n. [1] [√*353*]. gifts dedicated to God, devoted exclusively to the service of deity:– gifts dedicated to God (1)

G357 **ἀναίδεια** ***anaideia***, n. [1] [√*1.1 + 133*]. boldness:– shameless audacity (1)

G358 **ἀναίρεσις** ***anairesis***, n. [1] [√*324 + 145*]. death:– killing (1)

G359 **ἀναιρέω** ***anaireō***, v. [24] [√*324 + 145*]. to kill, put to death; (mid.) take for oneself:– kill (8), killed (4), put to death (4), executed (2), killing (2), get rid of (1), overthrow (1), sets aside (1), took (1)

G360 **ἀναίτιος** ***anaitios***, a. [2] [√*1.1 + 162*]. innocent:– innocent (2)

G361 **ἀνακαθίζω** ***anakathizō***, v. [2] [√*324 + 2767*]. to sit up (from a reclining or lying position):– sat up (2)

G362 **ἀνακαινίζω** ***anakainizō***, v. [1] [√*324 + 2785*]. to bring back, restore:– brought back (1 [+*4099*])

G363 **ἀνακαινόω** ***anakainoō***, v. [2] [√*324 + 2785*]. to renew:– renewed (2)

G364 **ἀνακαίνωσις** ***anakainōsis***, n. [2] [√*324 + 2785*]. renewal:– renewal (1), renewing (1)

G365 **ἀνακαλύπτω** ***anakalyptō***, v. [2] [√*324 + 2821*]. to unveil, uncover:– removed (1), unveiled (1)

G366 **ἀνακάμπτω** ***anakamptō***, v. [4] [√*324 + 2828*]. to return, come back:– return (2), come back (1), go back (1)

G367 **ἀνάκειμαι** ***anakeimai***, v. [14] [√*324 + 3023*]. to recline for a meal, dine (reclining was the normal posture at meals):– reclining at the table (3), at the table (2), guests (2), at the meal (1), dinner guests (1), eating (1), having dinner (1), reclining (1), reclining at table (1), seated (1)

G368 **ἀνακεφαλαιόω** ***anakephalaioō***, v. [2] [√*324 + 3051*]. to bring together under one head, summarize:– bring unity (1), summed up (1)

G369 **ἀνακλίνω** ***anaklinō***, v. [6] [√*324 + 3111*]. to cause to lie down, recline (to eat):– take places at the feast (2), have recline at the table (1), have sit down (1), placed (1), sit down (1)

G370 **ἀνακόπτω** ***anakoptō***, v. Not used in NIVEBC. [√*324 + 3164*]. to hinder, restrain

G371 **ἀνακράζω** ***anakrazō***, v. [5] [√*324 + 3189*]. to cry out:– cried out (4), shouted (1)

G372 **ἀνακραυγάζω** ***anakraugazō***, v. Not used in NIVEBC. [√*324 + 3189*]. to cry out

G373 **ἀνακρίνω** ***anakrinō***, v. [16] [√*324 + 3212*]. to examine, judge (in both a general and a legal sense):– examined (3), raising questions (2), brought under judgment (1), called to account (1), cross-examined (1), discerned (1), examining (1), judge (1), judged (1), judges (1), makes judgments about (1), sit in judgment (1), subject to judgments (1)

G374 **ἀνάκρισις** ***anakrisis***, n. [1] [√*324 + 3212*]. investigation:– investigation (1)

G375 **ἀνακυλίω** ***anakyliō***, v. Not used in NIVEBC. [√*324 + 3244*]. to roll away

G376 **ἀνακύπτω** ***anakyptō***, v. [4] [√*324 + 3252*]. to straighten up, stand erect:– straightened up (2), stand up (1), straighten up (1)

G377 **ἀναλαμβάνω** ***analambanō***, v. [13] [√*324 + 3284*]. to take up, lift up, bring up:– taken up (5), get (1), put on (1), take aboard (1), take up (1), taken (1), taken back (1), took (1), took aboard (1)

G378 **ἀνάλημψις** ***analēmpsis***, n. [1] [√*324 + 3284*]. taking up, ascension:– taken up to heaven (1)

G379 **ἀναλίσκω** ***analiskō***, v. Not used in NIVEBC. [√*324 + 274*]. to consume, destroy

G380 **ἀνάλλομαι** ***anallomai***, v. Not used in NIVEBC. [√*324 + 256*]. to jump up

G381 **ἀναλογία** ***analogia***, n. [1] [√*324 + 3306*]. proportion, right relationship:– in accordance with (1 [+*2848, 3836*])

G382 **ἀναλογίζομαι** ***analogizomai***, v. [1] [√*324 + 3306*]. to consider, think carefully:– consider (1)

G383 **ἄναλος** ***analos***, a. [1] [√*1.1 + 229*]. not salty:– loses saltiness (1 [+*1181*])

G384 **ἀναλόω** ***analoō***, v. [2] [√*324 + 274*]. to destroy, consume (with a possible implication of being used up):– destroy (1), destroyed (1)

G385 **ἀνάλυσις** ***analysis***, n. [1] [√*324 + 3395*]. departure (death):– departure (1)

G386 **ἀναλύω** ***analyō***, v. [2] [√*324 + 3395*]. to depart (die), return:– depart (1), return (1)

G387 **ἀναμάρτητος** ***anamartētos***, a. [1] [√*1.1 + 279*]. without sin:– without sin (1)

G388 **ἀναμένω** ***anamenō***, v. [1] [√*324 + 3531*]. to wait for, expect:– wait for (1)

G389 **ἀναμιμνήσκω** ***anamimnēskō***, v. [6] [√*324 + 3648*]. to remember, remind:– remembered (2), remind (2), remember (1), remembers (1)

G390 **ἀνάμνησις** ***anamnēsis***, n. [4] [√*324 + 3648*]. reminder, remembrance:– remembrance (3), reminder (1)

G391 **ἀνανεόομαι** ***ananeoomai***, v. [1] [√*324 + 3742*]. to be made new, renewed:– made new (1)

G392 **ἀνανήφω** ***ananēphō***, v. [1] [√*324 + 3768*]. to come to one's senses:– come to senses (1)

G393 **Ἀνανίας** ***Hananias***, n. pr. [11] Ananias, "*Yahweh is gracious*":– Ananias (11)

G394 **ἀναντίρρητος** ***anantirrētos***, a. [1] [√*1.1 + 505 + 4839*]. undeniable, indisputable:– undeniable (1)

G395 **ἀναντιρρήτως** ***anantirrētōs***, adv. [1] [√*1.1 + 505 + 4839*]. without raising any objection, indisputable:– without raising any objection (1)

G396 **ἀνάξιος** ***anaxios***, a. [1] [√*1.1 + 545*]. not competent, unworthy:– not competent (1)

G397 **ἀναξίως** ***anaxiōs***, adv. [1] [√*1.1 + 545*]. in an unworthy manner, possibly in a careless manner:– in an unworthy manner (1)

G398 **ἀνάπαυσις** ***anapausis***, n. [5] [√*324 + 4264*]. rest, resting place:– rest (4), stop (1 [+*2400*])

G399 **ἀναπαύω** ***anapauō***, v. [12] [√*324 + 4264*]. to rest, be refreshed; (act.) to give rest:– refreshed (3), resting (2), get rest (1), give rest (1), refresh (1), rest (1), rests (1), take life easy (1), wait (1)

G400 **ἀναπείθω** ***anapeithō***, v. [1] [√*324 + 4275*]. to persuade, with an implication of inciting resistance:– persuading (1)

G401 **ἀνάπειρος** ***anapeiros***, a. [2] [√*324 + 4386*]. crippled:– crippled (2)

G402 **ἀναπέμπω** ***anapempō***, v. [5] [√*324 + 4287*]. to send:– sent back (2), send (1), sending back (1), sent (1)

G403 **ἀναπηδάω** ***anapēdaō***, v. [1] [→*1659, 1737, 324*]. jump up, stand up:– jumped to feet (1)

G404 **ἀναπίπτω** ***anapiptō***, v. [12] [√*324 + 4406*]. recline, sit down, lie down (usually referring to the normal posture at meals):– sit down (3), reclined at the table (2), sat down (2), leaned back (1), leaning back (1), returned to place (1 [+*4099*]), sit down to eat (1), take (1 [+*1650*])

G405 **ἀναπληρόω** ***anaplēroō***, v. [6] [√*324 + 4444*]. to fulfill, make complete:– fulfill (1), fulfilled (1), heap up to the limit (1), make up for (1), put in (1), supplied (1)

G406 **ἀναπολόγητος** ***anapologētos***, a. [2] [√*1.1 + 608 + 3306*]. without excuse:– no excuse (1), without excuse (1)

G407 **ἀναπράσσω** ***anaprassō***, v. Not used in NIVEBC. [√*324 + 4556*]. to demand

G408 **ἀναπτύσσω** ***anaptyssō***, v. [1] [√*324 + 4771*]. to unroll (a scroll):– unrolling (1)

G409 **ἀνάπτω** ***anaptō***, v. [2] [√*324 + 721*]. to set on fire:– kindled (1), set on fire (1)

G410 **ἀναρίθμητος** ***anarithmētos***, a. [1] [√*1.1 + 750*]. countless:– countless (1)

G411 **ἀνασείω** ***anaseiō***, v. [2] [√*324 + 4940*]. to stir up, incite:– stirred up (1), stirs up (1)

G412 **ἀνασκευάζω** ***anaskeuazō***, v. [1] [√*324 + 5007*]. to trouble, upset:– troubling (1)

G413 **ἀνασπάω** ***anaspaō***, v. [2] [√*324 + 5060*]. to pull up, draw out:– pull out (1), pulled up (1)

G414 **ἀνάστασις** ***anastasis***, n. [42] [√*324 + 2705*]. resurrection, rising to life; from the base meaning of the act of rising from a prone or sitting position to a standing position. In the NT it means returning to life after death, usually referring to the raising to life of Jesus Christ:– resurrection (37), rise (3), raised to life again (1), rising (1)

G415 **ἀναστατόω** ***anastatoō***, v. [3] [√*324 + 2705*]. to cause trouble, start a revolt:– agitators (1), caused trouble (1), started a revolt (1)

G416 **ἀνασταυρόω** ***anastauroō***, v. [1] [√*324 + 5089*]. to crucify again:– crucifying all over again (1)

G417 **ἀναστενάζω** ***anastenazō***, v. [1] [√*324 + 5101*]. to sigh deeply:– sighed deeply (1 [+*3836, 4460*])

G418 **ἀναστρέφω** ***anastrephō***, v. [9] [√*324 + 5138*]. to conduct oneself, live (in a certain way); to return:– live (2), conduct (1), conducted (1), live out (1), lived (1), return (1), treated (1), went back (1)

G419 **ἀναστροφή** ***anastrophē***, n. [13] [*√324 + 5138*]. way of life, behavior:– way of life (4), behavior (2), conduct (2), lives (2), do (1), life (1), live (1)

G420 **ἀνασῴζω** ***anasōzō***, v. Not used in NIVEBC. [*√324 + 5392*]. to save

G421 **ἀνατάσσομαι** ***anatassomai***, v. [1] [*√324 + 5435*]. to draw up (an account), compile:– draw up (1)

G422 **ἀνατέλλω** ***anatellō***, v. [9] [*√424*]. to rise, dawn:– came up (2), rises (2), causes to rise (1), dawned (1), descended (1), just after sunrise (1 [*+3836, 2463*]), rising (1)

G423 **ἀνατίθημι** ***anatithēmi***, v. [2] [*√324 + 5502*]. to set before, declare before:– discussed (1), presented to (1)

G424 **ἀνατολή** ***anatolē***, n. [10] [*→422, 425, 1984, 324*]. east, rising of the sun; note that the east is the compass direction of orientation in the ancient Near East, just as the north is in the modern western world:– east (5), rose (2), east (1 [*+2463*]), east (1 [*+2463*]), rising sun (1)

G425 **ἀνατολικός** ***anatolikos***, a. Not used in NIVEBC. [*√424*]. eastern

G426 **ἀνατρέπω** ***anatrepō***, v. [3] [*√324 + 5572*]. to overturn, destroy:– destroy (1), disrupting (1), overturned (1)

G427 **ἀνατρέφω** ***anatrephō***, v. [3] [*√324 + 5555*]. to bring up, care for:– brought up (2), cared for (1)

G428 **ἀναφαίνω** ***anaphainō***, v. [2] [*√324 + 5743*]. to appear:– appear (1), sighting (1)

G429 **ἀναφέρω** ***anapherō***, v. [10] [*√324 + 5770*]. to lead up, offer (a sacrifice), bear (sin):– led up (2), offer (2), offered (2), bore (1), offering (1), take away (1), taken up (1)

G430 **ἀναφωνέω** ***anaphōneō***, v. [1] [*√324 + 5889*]. to exclaim, cry out loudly:– exclaimed (1)

G431 **ἀνάχυσις** ***anachysis***, n. [1] [*√1772; cf. 324*]. flood, wide stream:– reckless (1)

G432 **ἀναχωρέω** ***anachōreō***, v. [14] [*√324 + 6003*]. to withdraw, leave:– withdrew (7), left (3), drew (1), go away (1), gone (1), returned (1)

G433 **ἀνάψυξις** ***anapsyxis***, n. [1] [*√324 + 6038*]. refreshment, relaxation, relief:– refreshing (1)

G434 **ἀναψύχω** ***anapsychō***, v. [1] [*√324 + 6038*]. to refresh, revive:– refreshed (1)

G435 **ἀνδραποδιστής** ***andrapodistēs***, n. [1] [*√467 + 4546*]. slave trader, kidnapper:– slave traders (1)

G436 **Ἀνδρέας** ***Andreas***, n. pr. [13] [*√467*]. Andrew, "*manly*":– Andrew (13)

G437 **ἀνδρίζομαι** ***andrizomai***, v. [1] [*√467*]. to act courageously:– courageous (1)

G438 **Ἀνδρόνικος** ***Andronikos***, n. pr. [1] [*√467 + 3772*]. Andronicus, "*victor over men*":– Andronicus (1)

G439 **ἀνδροφόνος** ***androphonos***, n. [1] [*√467 + 5840*]. murderer:– murderers (1)

G440 **ἀνεγκλησία** ***anenklēsia***, n. Not used in NIVEBC. [*√1.1 + 1877 + 2813*]. blamelessness

G441 **ἀνέγκλητος** ***anenklētos***, a. [5] [*√1.1 + 1877 + 2813*]. blameless, free from accusation:– blameless (3), free from accusation (1), nothing against (1)

G442 **ἀνεκδιήγητος** ***anekdiēgētos***, a. [1] [*√1.1 + 1666 + 1328 + 72*]. indescribable, with the associative meanings of marvelous and wonderful:– indescribable (1)

G443 **ἀνεκλάλητος** ***aneklalētos***, a. [1] [*√1.1 + 1666 + 3281*]. inexpressible:– inexpressible (1)

G444 **ἀνέκλειπτος** ***anekleiptos***, a. [1] [*√1.1 + 1666 + 3309*]. not exhaustible, unfailing:– never fail (1)

G445 **ἀνεκτός** ***anektos***, a. [5] [*√324 + 2400*]. bearable, tolerable; used only in the comparative: more bearable:– more bearable (5)

G446 **ἀνελεήμων** ***aneleēmōn***, a. [1] [*√1.1 + 1799*]. ruthless, merciless:– no mercy (1)

G447 **ἀνέλεος** ***aneleos***, a. [1] [*√1.1 + 1799*]. merciless:– without mercy (1)

G448 **ἀνεμίζω** ***anemizō***, v. [1] [*√449*]. to be moved by the wind:– blown by the wind (1)

G449 **ἄνεμος** ***anemos***, n. [31] [*→448*]. wind, gale:– wind (19), winds (10), squall (2 [*+3278*])

G450 **ἀνένδεκτος** ***anendektos***, a. [1] [*√1.1 + 1877 + 1312*]. impossible:– bound to (1 [*+3590*])

G451 **ἀνεξεραύνητος** ***anexeraunētos***, a. [1] [*√1.1 + 1666 + 2236*]. unsearchable, inscrutable:– unsearchable (1)

G452 **ἀνεξίκακος** ***anexikakos***, a. [1] [*√324 + 2400 + 2805*]. not resentful, patient:– not resentful (1)

G453 **ἀνεξιχνίαστος** ***anexichniastos***, a. [2] [*√1.1 + 1666 + 2717*]. unsearchable, incomprehensible:– beyond tracing out (1), boundless (1)

G454 **ἀνεπαίσχυντος** ***anepaischyntos***, a. [1] [*√1.1 + 2093 + 156*]. unashamed:– not ashamed (1)

G455 **ἀνεπίλημπτος** ***anepilēmptos***, a. [3] [*√1.1 + 2093 + 3284*]. above reproach, not open to blame:– above reproach (1), blame (1), no open to blame (1)

G456 **ἀνέρχομαι** ***anerchomai***, v. [3] [*√324 + 2262*]. to go up:– went up (2), go up (1)

G457 **ἄνεσις** ***anesis***, n. [5] [*√918; cf. 324*]. rest, relaxation, relief:– freedom (1), peace (1), relief (1), relieved (1), rest (1)

G458 **ἀνετάζω** ***anetazō***, v. [2] [*→2004; cf. 324*]. to question, examine, interrogate:– interrogate (1), interrogated (1)

G459 **ἄνευ** ***aneu***, pp.* [3] without, apart from:– without (2), outside (1)

G460 **ἀνεύθετος** ***aneuthetos***, a. [1] [*√1.1 + 2292 + 5502*]. unsuitable, poor:– unsuitable (1)

G461 **ἀνευρίσκω** ***aneuriskō***, v. [2] [*√324 + 2351*]. to find:– found (1), sought out (1)

G462 **ἀνέχομαι** ***anechomai***, v. [15] [*√324 + 2400*]. to put up with, endure:– put up with (9), bear with (2), bearing with (1), endure (1), enduring (1), listen (1)

G463 **ἀνεψιός** ***anepsios***, n. [1] cousin:– cousin (1)

G464 **ἄνηθον** ***anēthon***, n. [1] dill, a plant used for seasoning:– dill (1)

G465 **ἀνήκω** ***anēkō***, v. [3] [*√324 + 2457*]. to be fitting, proper; to do one's duty:– fitting (1), ought to do (1), out of place (1 [*+4024*])

G466 **ἀνήμερος** ***anēmeros***, a. [1] [*√1.1*]. brutal, savage:– brutal (1)

G467 **ἀνήρ** ***anēr***, n. [231] [*→435, 436, 437, 438, 439, 3770, 5635, 5791*]. man, male, husband; usually an adult male, but in some contexts the emphasis is on maturity rather than gender (1Co 13:11; Eph 4:13; Jas 3:2):– man (60), men (54), husband (34), brothers and sisters (16 [*+81*]), husbands (12), brothers (6 [*+81*]), fellow (5), brothers (3 [*+81*]), faithful to his wife (3 [*+1651, 1222*]), people (3), Jews (2 [*+2681*]), fellow (2 [*+81*]), one (2), a (1 [*+5516*]), am a virgin (1 [*+4024, 1182*]), characters (1), divorced woman (1 [*+668, 608*]), Ethiopian (1 [*+134*]), faithful to her husband (1 [*+1651, 1222*]), friends (2), friends (1 [*+81*]), him^S (1), him^S (1 [*+3836*]), human (1), husband's (1), Jew (2 [*+2681*]), man's (1), mature (1 [*+5455*]), murderer (1 [*+5838*]), owner of (1 [*+4005*]), person (1), prophet (1 [*+4737*]), sinner (1 [*+283*]), someone (1), terrorists (1 [*+3836, 4974*]), NDT (5)

G468 **ἀνθίστημι** ***anthistēmi***, v. [18] [*√505 + 2705*]. to resist, oppose, rebel, withstand:– do so^S (5), resist (5), opposed (4), oppose (1), rebelling against (1), stand ground (1), stand up against (1)

G469 **ἀνθομολογέομαι** ***anthomologeomai***, v. [1] [*√505 + 3933*]. to give thanks, praise:– gave thanks (1)

G470 **ἄνθος** ***anthos***, n. [4] flower, blossom:– flowers (2), blossom (1), wild flower (1 [*+5965*])

G471 **ἀνθρακιά** ***anthrakia***, n. [2] [*√472*]. charcoal fire:– fire (1), fire of burning coals (1)

G472 **ἄνθραξ** ***anthrax***, n. [1] [*→471*]. coal, charcoal:– coals (1)

G473 **ἀνθρωπάρεσκος** ***anthrōpareskos***, a. [2] [*√476 + 743*]. one who wins favor, who pleases people:– curry favor (1), win favor (1)

G474 **ἀνθρώπινος** ***anthrōpinos***, a. [7] [*√476*]. human, common to mankind:– human (4), from everyday life (1), mankind (1 [*+5882, 3836*]), what is common to mankind (1)

G475 **ἀνθρωποκτόνος** ***anthrōpoktonos***, n. [3] [*√476 + 650*]. murderer:– murderer (3)

G476 **ἄνθρωπος** ***anthrōpos***, n. [555] [*→473, 474, 475, 1881, 5792, 5793*]. human being, person; humankind, people; man, husband; used of human beings in contrast to animals or deity; in some contexts it is used of male/husband in contrast to female/wife. "The Son of Man" is an OT phrase usually meaning "human being," that in the NT is used almost exclusively as a messianic title (see Da 7:13), emphasizing Jesus' humanity. "The outer person" is the corporeal body in contrast to "the inner (or hidden) person" of the spirit:– man (229), people (64), human (40), person (25), men (18), others (17), mankind (11), human being (9), human beings (9), everyone (8 [*+4246*]), one (8), someone (6), roman citizen (5 [*+4871*]), anyone (4), man's (4), self (4), them^S (4), them^S (4 [*+3836*]), everyone (3), people's (3), you^S (3), being (2), boy (2), everyone (2 [*+4246*]), fellow (2), glutton (2 [*+5741*]), he^S (2 [*+3836, 1697*]), humans (2), king (2 [*+995*]), landowner (2 [*+3867*]), people (2 [*+3836, 5626, 3836*]), person's (2), roman citizens (2 [*+4871*]), those^S (2), Jew (1 [*+2681*]), all (1 [*+4246*]), any (1 [*+5515, 5516*]), anyone (1 [*+3594*]), anyone (1 [*+5516*]), child (1), enemy (1 [*+2398*]), everyone (1 [*+4246, 3836*]), everyone^S (1), everyone's (1 [*+4246*]), evildoers (1 [*+4505*]), friend (1), from everyday life (1 [*+2848*]), him^S (1 [*+3836, 4047*]), human argument (1 [*+2848*]), human standards (1), humanity (1), husband (1), individuals (1), merchant (1 [*+1867*]), mortals (1), nations (1 [*+1620*]), one (1 [*+5516*]), one (1 [*+5515, 5516*]), other people (1), outwardly (1 [*+3836, 2032*]), owner of a house (1 [*+3867*]), pay attention to who they are (1 [*+1063, 1650, 4725*]), people (1 [*+3950*]), self (1 [*+2840*]), servant (1), servants^S (1), show favoritism (1 [*+4725, 3284*]), sinner (1 [*+283*]), sinners (1 [*+283*]), some (1 [*+5516*]), their own^S (1 [*+3836*]), they^S (1 [*+3836*]), they^S (1 [*+3836*]), underfoot^S (1 [*+5679, 3836*]), ungodly (1 [*+815*]), which (1 [*+5515*]), who (1 [*+5515*]), who^S (1 [*+3836, 4047*]), who they are (1 [*+4725*]), witnesses (1), world (1), NDT (4)

G477 **ἀνθυπατεύω** ***anthypateuō***, v. Not used in NIVEBC. [*√478*]. to be proconsul

G478 **ἀνθύπατος** ***anthypatos***, n. [5] [*→477; cf. 505*]. proconsul:– proconsul (4), proconsuls (1)

G479 **ἀνίημι** ***aniēmi***, v. [4] [*√918; cf. 324*]. loosen, untie; leave, abandon:– came loose (1), leave (1), not (1), untied (1)

G480 **ἀνίλεως** ***anileōs***, a. Not used in NIVEBC. [*√1.1 + 2661*]. merciless

G481 **ἄνιπτος** ***aniptos***, a. [2] [*√1.1 + 3782*]. unwashed:– unwashed (2)

G482 **ἀνίστημι** ***anistēmi***, v. [107] [*√324 + 2705*]. to get up, stand up, come back to life:– got up (16), get up (13), stood up (13), rise (9), raise up (7), rose (5), rise again (4), stand up (4), appeared (2), arise (2), come back to life (2), left (2), appears (1), came forward (1), came to power (1), come (1), got ready (1), helped to feet (1), left (1 [*+608*]), opposes (1 [*+2093*]), opposition arose (1), raised (1), raised again (1), raised from the dead (1), raised to life (1), raised up (1), raising (1), raising up (1), risen (1), rises (1), rising (1), rose again (1), set out (1), standing up (1), NDT (6)

G483 **Ἄννα** ***Hanna***, n. pr. [1] Anna, "*grace*":– Anna (1)

G484 **Ἄννας** ***Hannas***, n. pr. [4] Annas, "*grace*":– Annas (4)

G485 **ἀνόητος** ***anoētos***, a. [6] [*√1.1 + 3808*]. foolish, senseless:– foolish (5), how foolish (1 [*+6043, 1639, 6042*])

G486 **ἄνοια** ***anoia***, n. [2] [*√1.1 + 3808*]. folly, senselessness; fury:– folly (1), furious (1 [*+4398*])

G487 **ἀνοίγω** ***anoigō***, v. [77] [*→489, 1380, 1986; cf. 324*]. to open:– opened (38), open (22), opening (3), opens (3), standing open (2), began^S (1 [*+3836, 5125*]), began to speak (1 [*+3836, 5125, 3306*]), broke open (1), flew open (1), restored (1), sight (1 [*+3836, 4057*]), speak (1 [*+3836, 5125*]), spoken freely (1 [*+3836, 5125*]), NDT (1)

G488 **ἀνοικοδομέω** ***anoikodomeō***, v. [2] [*√324 + 3875 + 1560*]. to rebuild:– rebuild (2)

G489 **ἄνοιξις** ***anoixis***, n. [1] [*√487*]. (the act of) opening:– speak (1 [*+3836, 5125*])

G490 **ἀνομία** ***anomia***, n. [15] [*√1.1 + 3795*]. wickedness, lawlessness, lawless deed:– wickedness (5), lawlessness (3), breaks law (1 [*+4472*]), ever-increasing wickedness (1 [*+1650, 490*]), ever-increasing wickedness (1 [*+490, 1650*]), evil (1), evildoers (1 [*+2237, 3836*]), lawless acts (1), transgressions (1)

G491 **ἄνομος** ***anomos***, a. [9] [*√1.1 + 3795*]. without law, transgressing law (by not regarding it); as a noun this can mean a Gentile (without God's covenant law); Paul uses the definite article to speak of "the lawless one" (1Th. 2:8), often considered a title of the antichrist:– not having the law (3), lawless (2), free from law (1), lawbreakers (1), transgressors (1), wicked (1)

G492 **ἀνόμως** ***anomōs***, adv. [2] [*√1.1 + 3795*]. apart from law, without law:– apart from the law (2)

G493 **ἀνόνητος** ***anonētos***, a. Not used in NIVEBC. [*√1.1 + 3949*]. useless

G494 **ἀνορθόω** ***anorthoō***, v. [3] [*√324 + 3981*]. to restore, rebuild, strengthen:– restore (1), straightened up (1), strengthen (1)

G495 **ἀνόσιος** ***anosios***, a. [2] [*√1.1 + 4008*]. unholy, wicked:– unholy (2)

G496 **ἀνοχή** ***anochē***, n. [2] [*√324 + 2400*]. tolerance, forbearance, clemency:– forbearance (2)

G497 **ἀνταγωνίζομαι** ***antagōnizomai***, v. [1] [*√505 + 74*]. to struggle against:– struggle against (1)

G498 **ἀντάλλαγμα** ***antallagma***, n. [2] [*√505 + 248*]. something given in exchange:– in exchange for (2)

G499 **ἀνταναπληρόω** ***antanaplēroō***, v. [1] [*√505 + 324 + 4444*]. to fill up, complete:– fill up (1)

G500 **ἀνταποδίδωμι** ***antapodidōmi***, v. [7] [*√505 + 608 +*

1443]. to repay, return:– repay (4), in return (1), pay back (1), repaid (1)

G501 ἀνταπόδομα *antapodoma*, n. [2] [√*505* + *608* + *1443*]. repayment, retribution:– repaid (1), retribution (1)

G502 ἀνταπόδοσις *antapodosis*, n. [1] [√*505* + *608* + *1443*]. reward, repayment:– reward (1)

G503 ἀνταποκρίνομαι *antapokrinomai*, v. [2] [√*505* + *608* + *3212*]. to talk back, answer (with implication of contradicting someone):– say (1), talk back (1)

G504 ἀντέχω *antechō*, v. [4] [√*505* + *2400*]. to be devoted, hold firmly to; pay attention to:– devoted to (2), help (1), hold firmly (1)

G505 ἀντί *anti*, pp. [21] [→*394, 395, 468, 469, 497, 498, 499, 500, 501, 502, 503, 504, 506, 507, 508, 509, 510, 511, 512, 513, 514, 515, 516, 517, 518, 519, 520, 521, 524, 525, 526, 527, 528, 529, 530, 531, 532, 535, 560, 561, 1882, 2918, 5267, 5268, 5269, 5636, 5637; cf. 478, 1882*]. in exchange for (often as a sign of benefaction), in place of (often as a sign of contrast), instead of (often as a sign of an exchange of a relationship), one after another (often as a sign of purpose or result). Note that this preposition used in absolute does not mean to be "against" or "in opposition to" something:– for (9), because (4 [+*4005*]), instead (2), with (2), as (1), in place of (1), in place of already given (1), NDT (1)

G506 ἀντιβάλλω *antiballō*, v. [1] [√*505* + *965*]. to discuss, exchange (words):– discussing (1)

G507 ἀντιδιατίθημι *antidiatithēmi*, v. [1] [√*505* + *1328* + *5502*]. to oppose:– opponents (1)

G508 ἀντίδικος *antidikos*, n. [5] [√*505* + *1472*]. enemy, opponent (in battle or in court):– adversary (3), adversary who is taking to court (1), enemy (1)

G509 ἀντίθεσις *antithesis*, n. [1] [√*505* + *5502*]. opposition, objection:– opposing (1)

G510 ἀντικαθίστημι *antikathistēmi*, v. [1] [√*505* + *2848* + *2705*]. to resist, oppose, contest against:– resisted (1)

G511 ἀντικαλέω *antikaleō*, v. [1] [√*505* + *2813*]. to invite in reciprocation:– invite back (1)

G512 ἀντίκειμαι *antikeimai*, v. [8] [√*505* + *3023*]. to be an opponent, in conflict:– oppose (3), adversaries (1), contrary to (1), enemy (1), in conflict (1), opponents (1)

G513 ἄντικρυς *antikrys*, adv. [1] [√*505*]. opposite of, in proximity to:– off (1)

G514 ἀντιλαμβάνω *antilambanō*, v. [3] [√*505* + *3284*]. to help, come to the aid of, benefit:– devoted to (1), help (1), helped (1)

G515 ἀντιλέγω *antilegō*, v. [10] [√*505* + *3306*]. to speak against, talk back, contradict:– contradict (2), objected (1), obstinate (1), oppose (1), opposes (1), say (1), spoken against (1), talk back (1), talking against (1)

G516 ἀντίλημψις *antilēmpsis*, n. [1] [√*505* + *3284*]. help, ability to aid:– helping (1)

G517 ἀντιλογία *antilogia*, n. [4] [√*505* + *3306*]. argument, opposition, rebellion:– argument (1), doubt (1), opposition (1), rebellion (1)

G518 ἀντιλοιδορέω *antiloidoreō*, v. [1] [√*505* + *3368*]. to retaliate:– retaliate (1)

G519 ἀντίλυτρον *antilytron*, n. [1] [√*505* + *3395*]. ransom; the purchase price to bring liberation from oppression; it is the means to redemption. This refers to Jesus (in person and work) as the price of salvation:– ransom (1)

G520 ἀντιμετρέω *antimetreō*, v. [1] [√*505* + *3586*]. to measure in return:– measured (1)

G521 ἀντιμισθία *antimisthia*, n. [2] [√*505* + *3635*]. an exchange; penalty:– exchange (1), penalty (1)

G522 Ἀντιόχεια *Antiocheia*, n. pr. [18] [→*523*]. Antioch:– Antioch (18)

G523 Ἀντιοχεύς *Antiocheus*, n. pr. g. [1] [√*522*]. from Antioch:– from Antioch (1)

G524 ἀντιπαρέρχομαι *antiparerchomai*, v. [2] [√*505* + *4123* + *2262*]. to pass by on the opposite side:– passed by on the other side (2)

G525 Ἀντιπᾶς *Antipas*, n. pr. [1] [√*505* + *4252*]. Antipas:– Antipas (1)

G526 Ἀντιπατρίς *Antipatris*, n. pr. [1] [√*505* + *4252*]. Antipatris:– Antipatris (1)

G527 ἀντιπέρα *antipera*, adv. [1] [√*505* + *4305*]. across from, opposite of:– across from (1)

G528 ἀντιπίπτω *antipiptō*, v. [1] [√*505* + *4406*]. to resist, oppose:– resist (1)

G529 ἀντιστρατεύομαι *antistrateuomai*, v. [1] [√*505* + *5131*]. to wage war against:– waging war against (1)

G530 ἀντιτάσσω *antitassō*, v. [5] [√*505* + *5435*]. to oppose, rebel, resist:– opposes (2), opposed (1), opposing (1), rebels against (1)

G531 ἀντίτυπος *antitypos*, a. [2] [√*505* + *5597*]. copy, representation:– copy (1), symbolizes (1)

G532 ἀντίχριστος *antichristos*, n. [5] [√*505* + *5986*]. antichrist:– antichrist (4), antichrists (1)

G533 ἀντλέω *antleō*, v. [4] [√*534*]. to draw (water):– draw (1), draw out (1), draw water (1), drawn (1)

G534 ἄντλημα *antlēma*, n. [1] [→*533*]. container to draw water with:– to draw with (1)

G535 ἀντοφθαλμέω *antophthalmeō*, v. [1] [√*505* + *4057*]. to head into, face (the wind):– head into (1)

G536 ἄνυδρος *anydros*, a. [4] [√*1.1* + *5623*]. arid, without water:– arid (2), without rain (1), without water (1)

G537 ἀνυπόκριτος *anypokritos*, a. [6] [√*1.1* + *5679* + *3212*]. sincere, genuine, without hypocrisy; of good character, lacking pretense and prideful show:– sincere (6)

G538 ἀνυπότακτος *anypotaktos*, a. [4] [√*1.1* + *5679* + *5435*]. rebellious, disobedient; not made subject to, independent:– disobedient (1), not subject (1), rebellious (1), rebels (1)

G539 ἄνω *anō*, adv. pl. [9] [→*540, 541, 542, 1382, 2062, 5645; cf. 324*]. above, upward, heavenward, top:– above (5), up (2), brim (1), heavenward (1)

G540 ἄνωθεν *anōthen*, adv. pl. [13] [√*539*]. from above; from the beginning; again, anew:– from above (3), top (3), again (2), from heaven (2), all over again (1 [+*4099*]), for a long time (1), from the beginning (1)

G541 ἀνωτερικός *anōterikos*, a. [1] [√*539*]. interior, upper (regions):– interior (1 [+*3538*])

G542 ἀνώτερος *anōteros*, a. [2] [√*539*]. higher, better in social standing; earlier, previously, first:– better (1), first (1)

G543 ἀνωφελής *anōphelēs*, a. [2] [√*1.1* + *6067*]. unprofitable, useless:– unprofitable (1), useless (1)

G544 ἀξίνη *axinē*, n. [2] [√*2862*]. ax:– ax (2)

G545 ἄξιος *axios*, a. [41] [→*396, 397, 546, 547, 2921; cf. 72*]. worthy, deserving, in keeping with, corresponding to:– worthy (17), deserves (5), deserving (4), deserve (3), in keeping with (2), worth (2), advisable (1), as deserve (1 [+*1639*]), demonstrate (1 [+*4556*]), deserve (1 [+*1639*]), deserved (1), deserves (1 [+*1639*]), rightly (1), NDT (1)

G546 ἀξιόω *axioō*, v. [7] [√*545*]. to consider worthy, consider wise or fitting:– consider worthy (1), deserves (1), found worthy (1), make worthy (1), think it wise (1), want (1), worthy (1)

G547 ἀξίως *axiōs*, adv. [6] [√*545*]. in a worthy manner, suitably:– worthy (2), in a manner that honors (1), in a manner worthy (1), in a way worthy (1), worthy of (1)

G548 ἀόρατος *aoratos*, a. [5] [√*1.1* + *3972*]. invisible, not seen:– invisible (5)

G549 Ἀουλία *Aoulia*, n. pr. Not used in NIVEBC. [√*2685*]. Julia, "*of Julian [the family of Julius Caesar]*"

G550 ἀπαγγέλλω *apangellō*, v. [45] [√*608* + *34*]. to tell, report, proclaim, announce:– reported (12), told (11), tell (8), report (4), proclaim (3), confirm (1), declare (1), exclaimed (1), exclaiming (1), preached (1), said (1), told (1 [+*3836, 3364, 4047*])

G551 ἀπάγχω *apanchō*, v. [1] to hang (oneself):– hanged (1)

G552 ἀπάγω *apagō*, v. [15] [√*608* + *72*]. to lead away, bring before (an official):– led away (3), leads (2), took (2), brought (1), executed (1), lead away (1), lead out (1), led (1), led astray (1), take (1), they led away (1)

G553 ἀπαίδευτος *apaideutos*, a. [1] [√*1.1* + *4090*]. stupid, uneducated:– stupid (1)

G554 ἀπαίρω *apairō*, v. [3] [√*608* + *149*]. to take away:– taken (2), taken from (1)

G555 ἀπαιτέω *apaiteō*, v. [2] [√*608* + *160*]. to demand back:– demand back (1), demanded (1)

G556 ἀπαλγέω *apalgeō*, v. [1] to lose all sensitivity, become callous:– lost all sensitivity (1)

G557 ἀπαλλάσσω *apallassō*, v. [3] [√*608* + *248*]. (act.) to set free, release; (pass.) to be reconciled, come to a settlement (in court); to be cured:– cured (1), free (1), reconciled (1)

G558 ἀπαλλοτριόω *apallotrioō*, v. [3] [√*608* + *257*]. to be excluded, separated, alienated:– alienated from (1), excluded (1), separated (1)

G559 ἁπαλός *hapalos*, a. Not used in NIVEBC. tender (referring to sprouts)€ [2]:– tender (2)

G560 ἀπαντάω *apantaō*, v. [2] [√*608* + *505*]. to meet, encounter:– meet (1), met (1)

G561 ἀπάντησις *apantēsis*, n. [3] [√*608* + *505*]. (the act of) meeting, encountering:– meet (3)

G562 ἅπαξ *hapax*, adv. [14] [→*2384*]. once, once more, once for all; the Greek idiom "once and yet twice" means to do something repeatedly, "again and again" (Php 4:16):– once (8), once for all (3), again (1), at one time (1), more than once (1 [+*2779, 1489*])

G563 ἀπαράβατος *aparabatos*, a. [1] [√*1.1* + *4123* + *326*]. permanent, unchangeable:– permanent (1)

G564 ἀπαρασκεύαστος *aparaskeuastos*, a. [1] [√*1.1* + *4123* + *5007*]. unprepared, unready:– unprepared (1)

G565 ἀπαρνέομαι *aparneomai*, v. [11] [√*608* + *766*]. to disown, deny, repudiate:– disown (7), deny (3), disowned (1)

G566 ἀπαρτί *aparti*, adv. Not used in NIVEBC. [√*608* + *785*]. exactly, certainly

G567 ἀπάρτι *aparti*, adv. [pp.+adv.] Not used in NIVEBC. [√*608* + *785*]. from now on, again

G568 ἀπαρτισμός *apartismos*, n. [1] [√*608* + *785*]. completion, finishing:– complete (1)

G569 ἀπαρχή *aparchē*, n. [9] [√*608* + *806*]. firstfruits, the first of any crop or livestock offered to God before the rest could be used:– firstfruits (6), first convert (1), first converts (1), part offered as firstfruits (1)

G570 ἅπας *hapas*, a. [34] [√*275* + *4246*]. all, every, whole:– all (18), everything (7), everyone (3), whole (3), immense (1), none (1 [+*4024*]), NDT (1)

G571 ἀπασπάζομαι *apaspazomai*, v. [1] [√*608* + *832*]. to say farewell:– saying goodbye (1)

G572 ἀπατάω *apataō*, v. [3] [√*573*]. to deceive, cheat, trick:– deceive (2), deceived (1)

G573 ἀπάτη *apatē*, n. [7] [→*572, 1987, 5854, 5855*]. deception, deceitfulness:– deceitfulness (3), deceitful (1), deceives (1), deceptive (1), pleasures (1)

G574 ἀπάτωρ *apatōr*, a. [1] [√*1.1* + *4252*]. fatherless:– without father (1)

G575 ἀπαύγασμα *apaugasma*, n. [1] [√*608* + *879*]. radiance, brilliance:– radiance (1)

G576 ἀπαφρίζω *apaphrizō*, v. Not used in NIVEBC. [√*608* + *931*]. to cast off like foam

G577 ἀπείθεια *apeitheia*, n. [6] [√*1.1* + *4275*]. disobedience:– disobedience (4), disobedient (2)

G578 ἀπειθέω *apeitheō*, v. [14] [√*1.1* + *4275*]. to disobey, be disobedient:– disobedient (5), refused to believe (2), disobey (1), disobeyed (1), not believe (1), not obey (1), reject (1), rejects (1), unbelievers (1)

G579 ἀπειθής *apeithēs*, a. [6] [√*1.1* + *4275*]. disobedient:– disobedient (5), disobey (1)

G580 ἀπειλέω *apeileō*, v. [2] [√*581*]. to threaten, warn:– made threats (1), warn (1)

G581 ἀπειλή *apeilē*, n. [3] [→*580, 4653*]. threat:– threats (2), threaten (1)

G582 ἄπειμι[1] *apeimi[1]*, v. [7] [√*608* + *1639*]. to be absent:– absent (4), away (1), in absence (1), not (1)

G583 ἄπειμι[2] *apeimi[2]*, v. [1] [√*608* + *1640*]. to go away:– went (1)

G584 ἀπεῖπον *apeipon*, v. [1] [√*608* + *3306*]. to renounce, disown:– renounced (1)

G585 ἀπείραστος *apeirastos*, a. [1] [√*1.1* + *4278*]. incapable of being tempted, without temptation:– cannot tempted (1)

G586 ἄπειρος *apeiros*, a. [1] [√*1.1* + *4278*]. not acquainted with:– not acquainted with (1)

G587 ἀπεκδέχομαι *apekdechomai*, v. [8] [√*608* + *1666* + *1312*]. wait eagerly for:– eagerly await (2), eagerly wait for (1), wait eagerly (1), wait for (1), waited (1), waiting for (1), waits (1)

G588 ἀπεκδύομαι *apekdyomai*, v. [2] [√*608* + *1666* + *1544*]. to take off, disarm:– disarmed (1), taken off (1)

G589 ἀπέκδυσις *apekdysis*, n. [1] [√*608* + *1666* + *1544*]. removal, putting off:– put off (1)

G590 ἀπελαύνω *apelaunō*, v. [1] [√*608* + *1785*]. to eject from (court), drive away:– drove off (1)

G591 ἀπελεγμός *apelegmos*, n. [1] [√*608* + *1794*]. disrepute, discredit:– lose good name (1 [+*1650, 2262*])

G592 ἀπελεύθερος *apeleutheros*, n. [1] [√*608* + *1801*]. freedman, one no longer a slave:– freed person (1)

G593 Ἀπελλῆς *Apellēs*, n. pr. [1] Apelles:– Apelles (1)

G594 ἀπελπίζω *apelpizō*, v. [1] [√*608* + *1828*]. to expect nothing in return:– expecting to get back (1)

G595 ἀπέναντι *apenanti*, pp.* [5] [√*608* + *1882*]. opposite, in front of, against (opposition to):– before (1), defying (1 [+*4556*]), in front of (1), opposite (1), see (1)

G596 ἀπέραντος *aperantos*, a. [1] [√*1.1* + *4305*]. endless, unlimited:– endless (1)

G597 **ἀπερισπάστως** ***aperispastōs***, adv. [1] [√*1.1 + 4309 + 5060*]. undivided, without distraction:– undivided (1)

G598 **ἀπερίτμητος** ***aperitmētos***, a. [1] [√*1.1 + 4309 + 5533*]. uncircumcised (with a possible implication of being stubborn and obstinate):– uncircumcised (1)

G599 **ἀπέρχομαι** ***aperchomai***, v. [118] [√*608 + 2262*]. to go away, withdraw:– went (24), go (22), went away (18), left (7), went back (5), went off (5), gone (4), go away (3), leave (3), crossed (2), passed away (2), returned (2), went out (2), away (1), came (1), cross (1), drew back (1 [+*1650, 3836, 3958*]), followed (1 [+*3958*]), go on (1), go over (1), goes away (1), going away (1), gone away (1), on way (1), passed (1), past (1), perversion (1 [+*3958, 4922, 2283*]), spread (1), turned (1), went up (1), withdraw (1), withdrew (1)

G600 **ἀπέχω** ***apechō***, v. [19] [√*608 + 2400*]. to receive (in full); to be distant; (mid.) to abstain, avoid:– received in full (3), abstain (2), was from (2), a way off (1), about seven miles (1 [+*5084, 2008*]), abstain from (1), are (1), avoid (1), enough (1), far (1 [+*4522*]), have back (1), order to abstain (1), received (1), received payment (1), reject (1)

G601 **ἀπιστέω** ***apisteō***, v. [8] [√*1.1 + 4412*]. to disbelieve, be faithless, unfaithful. In some contexts unbelief has no implication of faithlessness or hardheartedness (Lk 24:11); in other contexts unbelief is a moral failure, not acting like a true follower (2Ti 2:13):– not believe (6), faithless (1), unfaithful (1)

G602 **ἀπιστία** ***apistia***, n. [11] [√*1.1 + 4412*]. unbelief, lack of faith (often with the implication of stubbornly refusing to believe or act in accord with God's will or law):– unbelief (6), lack of faith (3), unbelieving (1), unfaithfulness (1)

G603 **ἄπιστος** ***apistos***, a. [23] [√*1.1 + 4412*]. unbelieving, lacking in trust, doubting; as a noun: an unbeliever or outsider, one who does not believe the Gospel:– unbelievers (7), unbelieving (6), unbeliever (5), not a believer (2), doubting (1), incredible (1), not believe (1)

G604 **ἁπλόος** ***haploos***, a. Not used in NIVEBC. [→*605, 606, 607; cf. 275*]. good; same as *606*

G605 **ἁπλότης** ***haplotēs***, n. [8] [√*604*]. Formally "the quality of singleness," translated "generosity," the state of giving things in a manner that shows liberality; "sincerity," the moral quality of honesty expressing singleness of purpose or motivation:– generosity (2), sincerity (2), generous (1), generously (1 [+*1877*]), integrity (1), sincere devotion (1)

G606 **ἁπλοῦς** ***haplous***, a. [2] [√*604*]. good in the sense of healthy, formally, "singleness." Some think "a good eye" means to be generous and liberal in giving. Same as *604*.:– healthy (2)

G607 **ἁπλῶς** ***haplōs***, adv. [1] [√*604*]. generously, without reserve:– generously (1)

G608 **ἀπό** ***apo***, pp. [643] [→*406, 500, 501, 502, 503, 550, 552, 554, 555, 557, 558, 560, 561, 565, 566, 567, 568, 569, 571, 575, 576, 582, 583, 584, 587, 588, 589, 590, 591, 592, 594, 595, 599, 600, 609, 610, 611, 612, 613, 614, 615, 616, 617, 618, 619, 620, 621, 622, 623, 624, 625, 626, 627, 628, 629, 630, 631, 632, 633, 634, 635, 636, 637, 638, 639, 640, 641, 642, 643, 644, 645, 646, 647, 648, 649, 652, 653, 654, 655, 656, 657, 658, 659, 660, 661, 664, 665, 666, 667, 668, 669, 670, 671, 672, 673, 674, 675, 676, 677, 678, 681, 682, 683, 684, 685, 686, 687, 688, 689, 690, 691, 694, 695, 696, 697, 698, 699, 700, 701, 702, 703, 704, 705, 706, 707, 708, 709, 710, 711, 712, 713, 714, 715, 724, 904, 909, 919, 922, 923, 926, 927, 928, 929, 934, 935, 3632, 3633, 4467, 4534, 4535, 5270, 5271, 5272; cf. 723, 918*]. from, away from; by means of; out of; against:– from (345), of (33), by (24), in (14), since (12), for (11), on (11), at (10), against (8), with (7), away (4), because of (4), out of (4), far off (3 [+*3427*]), some of (3), as for (2), belonged to (2), since (2 [+*4005*]), some (2), to (2), after (1), again (1 [+*785*]), again (1 [+*3836, 3814*]), ago (1 [+*4005*]), alike (1 [+*1651*]), as (1), at the hands of (1), before (1), before (1 [+*4725*]), beginning with (1 [+*2779, 3836, 2759*]), beyond (1), both and (1 [+*2401*]), cut off from (1), depended on (1), divorced woman (1 [+*668, 467*]), ever since (1 [+*4005*]), far away (1 [+*3427*]), for a distance of (1), from (1 [+*4725*]), from among (1), from the time (1 [+*4005*]), from the time of (1), get rid of (1 [+*149*]), given (1 [+*2400*]), it[s] (1 [+*4005, 794, 201*]), leaving (1 [+*4513*]), left (1), left (1 [+*482*]), left (1 [+*4513, 4725*]), now (1 [+*785*]), now (1 [+*4005*]), now (1 [+*3836, 3814*]), of accord (1), on authority (1), on my own authority (1 [+*1831*]), once (1 [+*4005, 323*]), over (1), part of (1), sent from (1), separated from (1), so overjoyed (1 [+*3836, 5915*]), some time ago (1 [+*2465, 792*]), sound asleep (1 [+*2965, 3836, 5678*]), three ago (1 [+*5480*]), touched (1 [+*3836, 5999*]), with ever-increasing glory (1 [+*1518, 1650, 1518*]), woke up (1 [+*1586, 3836, 5678*]), your own idea (1 [+*4932, 3306*]), NDT (92)

G609 **ἀποβαίνω** ***apobainō***, v. [4] [√*608 + 326*]. to leave, get out; to result in, turn to, lead to:– bear testimony (1 [+*1650, 3457*]), landed (1 [+*1650, 3836, 1178*]), left (1), turn out (1)

G610 **ἀποβάλλω** ***apoballō***, v. [2] [√*608 + 965*]. to throw away:– throw away (1), throwing aside (1)

G611 **ἀποβλέπω** ***apoblepō***, v. [1] [√*608 + 1063*]. to look ahead, pay attention:– looking ahead (1)

G612 **ἀπόβλητος** ***apoblētos***, a. [1] [√*608 + 965*]. rejected (as unclean):– rejected (1)

G613 **ἀποβολή** ***apobolē***, n. [2] [√*608 + 965*]. rejection; loss:– lost (1), rejection (1)

G614 **ἀπογίνομαι** ***apoginomai***, v. [1] [√*608 + 1181*]. to die:– die (1)

G615 **ἀπογραφή** ***apographē***, n. [2] [√*608 + 1211*]. census, registration:– census (2)

G616 **ἀπογράφω** ***apographō***, v. [4] [√*608 + 1211*]. to take a census, register, record:– register (2), census be taken (1), written (1)

G617 **ἀποδείκνυμι** ***apodeiknymi***, v. [4] [√*608 + 1259*]. to display, exhibit, proclaim; prove, accredit, attest:– accredited (1), proclaiming (1), prove (1), put on display (1)

G618 **ἀπόδειξις** ***apodeixis***, n. [1] [√*608 + 1259*]. demonstration, proof:– demonstration (1)

G619 **ἀποδεκατεύω** ***apodekateuō***, v. Not used in NIVEBC. [√*608 + 1274*]. to tithe, give one-tenth of

G620 **ἀποδεκατόω** ***apodekatoō***, v. [4] [√*608 + 1274*]. to give a tenth, tithe; collect a tithe:– give a tenth (3), collect a tenth (1)

G621 **ἀπόδεκτος** ***apodektos***, a. [2] [√*608 + 1312*]. pleasing, pleasant:– pleases (1), pleasing (1)

G622 **ἀποδέχομαι** ***apodechomai***, v. [7] [√*608 + 1312*]. to welcome, accept, receive; acknowledge, acclaim:– welcomed (3), accepted (1), acknowledge (1), received (1), welcome (1)

G623 **ἀποδημέω** ***apodēmeō***, v. [6] [√*608 + 1322*]. to go away on a journey:– moved to another place (2), going on a journey (1), set off (1), went away (1), went on journey (1)

G624 **ἀπόδημος** ***apodēmos***, a. [1] [√*608 + 1322*]. going away on a journey:– going away (1)

G625 **ἀποδίδωμι** ***apodidōmi***, v. [48] [√*608 + 1443*]. give, give away; pay, pay back:– give (6), pay back (6), give back (4), repay (4), reward (4), pay (3), fulfill (2), given (2), paid (2), account (1 [+*3364*]), award (1), back (1), gave back (1), give share (1), got (1), pays back (1), produces (1), reimburse (1), repay debt (1), repaying (1 [+*304*]), sold (1), sold as a slave (1), testify (1 [+*3836, 3457*]), yielding (1)

G626 **ἀποδιορίζω** ***apodiorizō***, v. [1] [√*608 + 1328 + 4000*]. to divide, separate, cause a division:– divide (1)

G627 **ἀποδοκιμάζω** ***apodokimazō***, v. [9] [√*608 + 1312*]. to reject:– rejected (9)

G628 **ἀποδοχή** ***apodochē***, n. [2] [√*608 + 1312*]. acceptance, approval:– acceptance (2)

G629 **ἀπόθεσις** ***apothesis***, n. [2] [√*608 + 5502*]. removal, putting aside, getting rid of; this can be a euphemism for death (2Pe 1:14):– put aside (1 [+*1639*]), removal (1)

G630 **ἀποθήκη** ***apothēkē***, n. [6] [√*608 + 2565*]. barn, storehouse:– barn (4), barns (2)

G631 **ἀποθησαυρίζω** ***apothēsaurizō***, v. [1] [√*608 + 2565*]. to store up treasure:– lay up treasure (1)

G632 **ἀποθλίβω** ***apothlibō***, v. [1] [√*608 + 2567*]. to press against, crowd up to:– pressing against (1)

G633 **ἀποθνῄσκω** ***apothnēskō***, v. [111] [√*608 + 2569*]. to die (in a literal or fig. sense); to be about to die, be mortal:– died (48), die (34), dies (10), dead (9), dying (5), death (2), did[s] (1), face death (1), killed (1 [+*1877, 5840*])

G634 **ἀποκαθιστάνω** ***apokathistanō***, v. Not used in NIVEBC. [√*608 + 2848 + 2705*]. to restore, re-establish, cure

G635 **ἀποκαθίστημι** ***apokathistēmi***, v. [8] [√*608 + 2848 + 2705*]. to (completely) restore:– completely restored (3), restore (2), restored (2), restores (1)

G636 **ἀποκαλύπτω** ***apokalyptō***, v. [26] [√*608 + 2821*]. to reveal, disclose:– revealed (19), reveal (3), disclosed (2), make clear (1), revelation comes (1)

G637 **ἀποκάλυψις** ***apokalypsis***, n. [18] [√*608 + 2821*]. revelation, what is revealed, disclosure, to make information known with an implication that the information can be understood. This refers in the NT to God making information known, especially to his close associates:– revelation (9), revealed (7), revelations (2)

G638 **ἀποκαραδοκία** ***apokaradokia***, n. [2] [√*608 + 3191 + 1506*]. eager expectation:– eager expectation (1), eagerly expect (1)

G639 **ἀποκαταλλάσσω** ***apokatallassō***, v. [3] [√*608 + 2848 + 248*]. to reconcile, reunite:– reconcile (2), reconciled (1)

G640 **ἀποκατάστασις** ***apokatastasis***, n. [1] [√*608 + 2848 + 2705*]. restoration:– restore (1)

G641 **ἀπόκειμαι** ***apokeimai***, v. [4] [√*608 + 3023*]. to be stored up, destined:– destined (1), in store (1), laid away (1), stored up (1)

G642 **ἀποκεφαλίζω** ***apokephalizō***, v. [4] [√*608 + 3051*]. to behead:– beheaded (4)

G643 **ἀποκλείω** ***apokleiō***, v. [1] [√*608 + 3091*]. to close:– closes (1)

G644 **ἀποκόπτω** ***apokoptō***, v. [6] [√*608 + 3164*]. to cut off; emasculate:– cut off (3), cut (1), cutting off (1), emasculate (1)

G645 **ἀπόκριμα** ***apokrima***, n. [1] [√*608 + 3212*]. sentence, verdict:– sentence (1)

G646 **ἀποκρίνομαι** ***apokrinomai***, v. [230] [√*608 + 3212*]. to answer, reply; sometimes used in the NT in the Hebraic sense of continuing a discourse:– answered (78), replied (65), said (30), asked (19), answer (11), gave answer (4), spoke up (3), declared (2), made reply (2), reply (2), responded (2), say (2), spoke (2), answers (1), given a answer (1), in defense said (1), insisted (1), retorted (1), say in reply (1), tell (1), told (1)

G647 **ἀπόκρισις** ***apokrisis***, n. [4] [√*608 + 3212*]. answer:– answer (3), answers (1)

G648 **ἀποκρύπτω** ***apokryptō***, v. [4] [√*608 + 3221*]. to hide, conceal:– hidden (4)

G649 **ἀπόκρυφος** ***apokryphos***, a. [3] [√*608 + 3221*]. concealed, hidden, secret:– concealed (2), hidden (1)

G650 **ἀποκτείνω** ***apokteinō***, v. [74] [→*475, 651*]. to kill (either natural life or spiritual life):– kill (35), killed (27), put to death (4), kills (2), die (1), died (1), execute (1), strike dead (1 [+*1877, 2505*]), take life (1), NDT (1)

G651 **ἀποκτέννω** ***apoktennō***, v. Not used in NIVEBC. [√*650*]. to kill

G652 **ἀποκυέω** ***apokyeō***, v. [2] [√*608 + 3246*]. to give birth to, bring into being:– give birth (1), gives birth to (1)

G653 **ἀποκυλίω** ***apokyliō***, v. [4] [√*608 + 3244*]. to roll away, roll back:– rolled away (2), rolled back (1), will roll away (1)

G654 **ἀπολαλέω** ***apolaleō***, v. Not used in NIVEBC. [√*608 + 3281*]. to speak about freely

G655 **ἀπολαμβάνω** ***apolambanō***, v. [10] [√*608 + 3284*]. to receive, be repaid:– receive (3), received (2), getting (1), has back (1), repaid (1), rewarded (1 [+*3635*]), took away (1)

G656 **ἀπόλαυσις** ***apolausis***, n. [2] [√*608*]. enjoyment, pleasure:– enjoyment (1), pleasures (1)

G657 **ἀπολείπω** ***apoleipō***, v. [7] [√*608 + 3309*]. to leave behind:– left (4), remains (2), abandoned (1)

G658 **ἀπολείχω** ***apoleichō***, v. Not used in NIVEBC. [√*608 + 3314*]. lick, lick off

G659 **ἀπολιμπάνω** ***apolimpanō***, v. Not used in NIVEBC. [√*608 + 3309*]. leave behind

G660 **ἀπόλλυμι** ***apollymi***, v. [90] [√*608 + 3897*]. to destroy (an inanimate object), to kill (by taking a life), cause to lose (especially a life); to die or perish. Violence and strife is often the associative meaning related to this word:– lose (14), lost (11), perish (10), destroyed (9), destroy (8), kill (8), loses (7), killed (4), perishing (4), drown (3), ruined (3), die (2), bring to a end (1), death (1), have executed (1), perishes (1), spoils (1), vanished (1), wasted (1)

G661 **Ἀπολλύων** ***Apollyōn***, n. pr. [1] [√*608 + 3897*]. Apollyon, "*destroyer*":– Apollyon (1)

G662 **Ἀπολλωνία** ***Apollōnia***, n. pr. [1] [√*663*]. Apollonia:– Apollonia (1)

G663 **Ἀπολλῶς** ***Apollōs***, n. pr. [10] [→*662*]. Apollos:– Apollos (10)

G664 **ἀπολογέομαι** ***apologeomai***, v. [10] [√*608 + 3306*]. to defend oneself, speak in one's own behalf:– defend (2), defending (2), defense (2), make defense (2), made defense (1), make a defense (1)

G665 **ἀπολογία** ***apologia***, n. [8] [√*608 + 3306*]. defense; answer or reply (of reason or accounting):– defense (4), answer (1), defend (1), defending (1), eagerness to clear (1)

G666 **ἀπολούω** ***apolouō***, v. [2] [√*608 + 3374*]. to wash away:– wash away (1), washed (1)

G667 **ἀπολύτρωσις** ***apolytrōsis***, n. [10] [√*608 + 3395*]. redemption, ransom, release:– redemption (8), ransom to set free (1), released (1)

G668 **ἀπολύω** ***apolyō***, v. [66] [√*608 + 3395*]. to release (forgive, grant clemency); divorce, send away:– release (15), send away (7), divorces (6), dismissed (5), let go (5), released (5), divorce (4), sent away (3), sent off (3), set free (3), canceled (1), dismiss (1), divorced (1), divorced woman (1 [+*608, 467*]), forgive (1), forgiven (1), free (1), leave (1), send (1), sent on way (1)

G669 **ἀπομάσσω** ***apomassō***, v. [1] [√*608 + 3463*]. to wipe off (this refers to an action of protest):– wipe from as a warning (1)

GREEK INDEX

G670 ἀπομένω *apomenō*, v. Not used in NIVEBC. [√*608 + 3531*]. to remain behind

G671 ἀπονέμω *aponemō*, v. [1] [√*608 + 3795*]. to treat with, show, pay (respect):– treat with (1)

G672 ἀπονίπτω *aponiptō*, v. [1] [√*608 + 3782*]. to wash off:– washed (1)

G673 ἀποπέμπω *apopempō*, v. Not used in NIVEBC. [√*608 + 4287*]. to send out

G674 ἀποπίπτω *apopiptō*, v. [1] [√*608 + 4406*]. to fall away, drop off:– fell from (1)

G675 ἀποπλανάω *apoplanaō*, v. [2] [√*608 + 4415*]. to deceive, mislead; (pass.) to wander:– deceive (1), wandered (1)

G676 ἀποπλέω *apopleō*, v. [4] [√*608 + 4434*]. to sail away from:– sail (1), sailed (1), sailed back (1), set sail (1)

G677 ἀποπλύνω *apoplynō*, v. Not used in NIVEBC. [√*608 + 4459*]. to wash off, wash out

G678 ἀποπνίγω *apopnigō*, v. [2] [√*608 + 4464*]. to choke, smother; (pass.) to be drowned, choked (with water):– choked (1), drowned (1)

G679 ἀπορέω *aporeō*, v. [6] [√*1.1 + 4513*]. to be puzzled, at a loss, in wonder:– perplexed (2), at a loss (1), at a loss to know (1), puzzled (1), wondering (1)

G680 ἀπορία *aporia*, n. [1] [√*1.1 + 4513*]. perplexity, consternation:– perplexity (1)

G681 ἀπορίπτω *aporiptō*, v. [1] [√*608 + 4849*]. to jump into, throw oneself into:– jump overboard (1)

G682 ἀπορφανίζω *aporphanizō*, v. [1] [√*608 + 4003*]. to make an orphan of:– orphaned (1)

G683 ἀποσκευάζω *aposkeuazō*, v. Not used in NIVEBC. [√*608 + 5007*]. to pack up

G684 ἀποσκίασμα *aposkiasma*, n. [1] [√*608 + 5014*]. shadow:– shadows (1)

G685 ἀποσπάω *apospaō*, v. [4] [√*608 + 5060*]. to draw out, draw away, attract; (pass.) to withdraw:– draw away (1), drew out (1), torn away (1), withdrew (1)

G686 ἀποστασία *apostasia*, n. [2] [√*608 + 2705*]. turning away, rebellion, abandonment, apostasy:– rebellion (1), turn away (1)

G687 ἀποστάσιον *apostasion*, n. [3] [√*608 + 2705*]. divorce:– divorce (2), certificate of divorce (1)

G688 ἀποστάτης *apostatēs*, n. Not used in NIVEBC. [√*608 + 2705*]. deserter, apostate

G689 ἀποστεγάζω *apostegazō*, v. [1] [√*608 + 5095*]. to make an opening in a roof, remove a roof:– made an opening (1)

G690 ἀποστέλλω *apostellō*, v. [132] [→*692, 693, 1990, 5273, 6013; cf. 608 + 5097*]. to send, send out, send away (especially used of the official sending out of the disciples):– sent (94), send (17), sending (5), send out (3), sent out (3), sending out (2), gave orders (1), given orders (1), ordered (1), puts to (1), sent away (1), sent for (1 [+*3559*]), sent word (1), set free (1 [+*1877, 912*])

G691 ἀποστερέω *apostereō*, v. [6] [√*608*]. to defraud, cheat, steal; deprive, deny, withhold:– cheated (1), defraud (1), deprive (1), do wrong (1), failed to pay (1), robbed (1)

G692 ἀποστολή *apostolē*, n. [4] [√*690*]. apostleship, ministry / office of an apostle:– apostleship (2), apostle (1), apostolic (1)

G693 ἀπόστολος *apostolos*, n. [79] [√*690*]. apostle, representative, messenger, envoy; often used in a technical sense for the divinely appointed founders of the church:– apostles (55), apostle (19), messenger (2), super-apostles (2 [+*5663*]), representatives (1)

G694 ἀποστοματίζω *apostomatizō*, v. [1] [√*608 + 5125*]. to besiege with questions, interrogate closely:– besiege with questions (1 [+*4309, 4498*])

G695 ἀποστρέφω *apostrephō*, v. [9] [√*608 + 5138*]. to turn away from, rebel, mislead; to desert, reject; to return, put back:– turn away (3), deserted (1), inciting to rebellion (1), put back (1), reject (1), turn away from (1), turning from (1)

G696 ἀποστυγέω *apostygeō*, v. [1] [√*608 + 5144*]. to hate, abhor, loathe:– hate (1)

G697 ἀποσυνάγωγος *aposynagōgos*, a. [3] [√*608 + 5252*]. put out of the synagogue, excommunicated:– put out of the synagogue (2), out of the synagogue (1)

G698 ἀποτάσσω *apotassō*, v. [6] [√*608 + 5435*]. to say good-by, leave; give up, renounce, forsake:– left (2), give up (1), leaving (1), said goodbye (1), say goodbye (1)

G699 ἀποτελέω *apoteleō*, v. [2] [√*608 + 5465*]. to bring to completion; (pass.) to be full-grown, mature, completed:– full-grown (1), healing (1 [+*2617*])

G700 ἀποτίθημι *apotithēmi*, v. [9] [√*608 + 5502*]. to put aside, get rid of:– put off (2), rid of (2), get rid of (1), laid (1), put (1), put aside (1), throw off (1)

G701 ἀποτινάσσω *apotinassō*, v. [2] [√*1753; cf. 608*]. to shake off, stomp off:– shake off (1), shook off (1)

G702 ἀποτίνω *apotinō*, v. [1] [√*608 + 5514*]. to pay back, make restitution:– pay back (1)

G703 ἀποτολμάω *apotolmaō*, v. [1] [√*608 + 5528*]. to bring forth boldly:– boldly (1)

G704 ἀποτομία *apotomia*, n. [2] [√*608 + 5533*]. sternness, severity:– sternness (2)

G705 ἀποτόμως *apotomōs*, adv. [2] [√*608 + 5533*]. harshly, sharply, severely, rigorously:– harsh (1), sharply (1)

G706 ἀποτρέπω *apotrepō*, v. [1] [√*608 + 5572*]. to have nothing to do with, turn away from completely, avoid:– have nothing to do with (1)

G707 ἀπουσία *apousia*, n. [1] [√*608 + 1639*]. absence:– absence (1)

G708 ἀποφέρω *apopherō*, v. [6] [√*608 + 5770*]. to carry away, lead away:– carried away (2), carried (1), led away (1), taken (1), with (1)

G709 ἀποφεύγω *apopheugō*, v. [3] [√*608 + 5771*]. to escape (from):– escaped (2), escaping from (1)

G710 ἀποφθέγγομαι *apophthengomai*, v. [3] [√*608 + 5779*]. to say, speak out, address, declare, in some contexts with the inference of urgency or boldness:– addressed (1), enabled (1 [+*1443*]), saying (1)

G711 ἀποφορτίζομαι *apophortizomai*, v. [1] [√*608 + 5770*]. to unload:– unload (1)

G712 ἀπόχρησις *apochrēsis*, n. [1] [√*608 + 5968*]. using up, consumption:– use (1)

G713 ἀποχωρέω *apochōreō*, v. [3] [√*608 + 6003*]. to go away from, leave:– away (1), leaves (1), left (1)

G714 ἀποχωρίζω *apochōrizō*, v. [2] [√*608 + 6006*]. to part company, be separated; to recede, be split:– parted company (1), receded (1)

G715 ἀποψύχω *apopsychō*, v. [1] [√*608 + 6038*]. to faint (some translate "to die"):– faint (1)

G716 Ἄππιος *Appios*, n. pr. [1] Appius:– Appius (1)

G717 ἀπρόσιτος *aprositos*, a. [1] [√*1.1 + 4639 + 1640*]. unapproachable:– unapproachable (1)

G718 ἀπρόσκοπος *aproskopos*, a. [3] [√*1.1 + 4639 + 3164*]. blameless, clear; not causing one to stumble, not giving offense:– blameless (1), clear (1), not cause to stumble (1)

G719 ἀπροσωπολήμπτως *aprosōpolēmptōs*, adv. [1] [√*1.1 + 4725 + 3284*]. impartially, without prejudice:– impartially (1)

G720 ἄπταιστος *aptaistos*, a. [1] [√*1.1 + 4760*]. without falling, without stumbling:– from stumbling (1)

G721 ἅπτω *haptō*, v. [39] [→*409, 913, 2750, 4312*]. to touch, hold, handle; (act.) to start a fire; "to touch a woman" means "to get married":– touched (20), touch (8), lights (2), place hands on (2), built (1), handle (1), harm (1), have sexual relations (1), hold on (1), light (1), touching (1)

G722 Ἀπφία *Apphia*, n. pr. [1] Apphia:– Apphia (1)

G723 ἀπωθέω *apōtheō*, v. [6] [→*2034; cf. 608*]. to reject, repudiate, push aside:– reject (3), rejected (2), pushed aside (1)

G724 ἀπώλεια *apōleia*, n. [18] [√*608 + 3897*]. destruction, ruin, waste:– destruction (12), waste (2), destroyed (1), destroyed (1 [+*1650*]), destructive (1), perish (1 [+*1639, 1650*])

G725 ἀρά *ara*, n. [1] [→*2063, 2129, 2932, 2933*]. curse:– cursing (1)

G726 ἄρα *ara*, pt. infer. [49] then, so, therefore, consequently:– then (16), so (5), therefore (3 [+*4036*]), consequently (2 [+*4036*]), in that case (2 [+*2075*]), therefore (2 [+*4036*]), therefore (2), as to (1), consequently (1), if (1 [+*1623*]), in fact (1), in the hope that (1 [+*1623*]), otherwise (1 [+*2075*]), perhaps (1 [+*1623, 1145*]), so then (1), then (1 [+*1145*]), thus (1 [+*1145*]), NDT (7)

G727 ἆρα *ara*, pt. inter. [3] difficult to translate directly: introduces direct questions, showing anxiety or impatience:– doesn't that mean that (1), NDT (2)

G728 Ἀραβία *Arabia*, n. pr. [2] [√*732*]. Arabia, "*desert or steppe*":– Arabia (2)

G729 Ἄραβοι *Araboi*, n. pr. g. Not used in NIVEBC. [√*732*]. Arabs, "*desert dwellers*"

G730 Ἀράμ *Aram*, n. pr. [3] [√*cf. 98, 747, 763, 767*]. Ram, Aram, "*high, exalted*":– Ram (3)

G731 ἄραφος *araphos*, a. [1] [√*1.1 + 4827*]. seamless:– seamless (1)

G732 Ἄραψ *Araps*, n. pr. g. [1] [→*728, 729*]. Arab, "*desert dweller*":– Arabs (1)

G733 ἀργέω *argeō*, v. [1] [√*1.1 + 2240*]. to be idle, grow weary:– hanging over (1 [+*4024*])

G734 ἀργός *argos*, a. [8] [√*1.1 + 2240*]. idle, lazy; useless, ineffective; careless:– doing nothing (2), empty (1), idle (1), idlers (1), ineffective (1), lazy (1), useless (1)

G735 ἀργύρεος *argyreos*, a. Not used in NIVEBC. [√*738*]. (made of) silver; same as *739*

G736 ἀργύριον *argyrion*, n. [20] [√*738*]. silver (always referring to money):– money (12), pieces of silver (3), silver (3), coins (1), drachmas (1)

G737 ἀργυροκόπος *argyrokopos*, n. [1] [√*738 + 3164*]. silversmith:– silversmith (1)

G738 ἄργυρος *argyros*, n. [5] [→*735, 736, 737, 739, 921, 5794, 5795*]. silver:– silver (5)

G739 ἀργυροῦς *argyrous*, a. [3] [√*738*]. (made of) silver; same as *735*:– silver (3)

G740 Ἄρειος πάγος *Areios pagos*, n. pr. [2] [√*4076*]. meeting of the Areopagus; Mars' Hill, "*hill of the Greek god Ares*":– meeting of the Areopagus (2)

G741 Ἀρεοπαγίτης *Areopagitēs*, n. pr. g. [1] [√*4076*]. member of the Areopagus:– member of the Areopagus (1)

G742 ἀρεσκεία *areskeia*, n. [1] [√*743*]. pleasing, striving to please:– please (1)

G743 ἀρέσκω *areskō*, v. [17] [→*473, 742, 744, 2297, 2298, 2299*]. to please, accommodate:– please (13), pleased (3), displease (1 [+*3590*])

G744 ἀρεστός *arestos*, a. [4] [√*743*]. pleasing, desirable, right:– pleases (2), approval (1), right (1)

G745 Ἀρέτας *Haretas*, n. pr. [1] Aretas, "*virtuous*":– Aretas (1)

G746 ἀρετή *aretē*, n. [5] (moral) goodness, excellence, virtue:– goodness (3), excellent (1), praises (1)

G747 Ἀρηί *Arēi*, n. pr. Not used in NIVEBC. [√*cf. 730*]. Arei

G748 ἀρήν *arēn*, n. [1] [→*768*]. lamb:– lambs (1)

G749 ἀριθμέω *arithmeō*, v. [3] [√*750*]. to count:– numbered (2), count (1)

G750 ἀριθμός *arithmos*, n. [18] [→*410, 749, 2935*]. number:– number (13), numbering (1 [+*1639, 3836*]), numbers (1), one of (1 [+*1666, 3836*]), NDT (2)

G751 Ἀριμαθαία *Harimathaia*, n. pr. [4] Arimathea:– Arimathea (4)

G752 Ἀρίσταρχος *Aristarchos*, n. pr. [5] [√*806*]. Aristarchus, "*best ruler*":– Aristarchus (5)

G753 ἀριστάω *aristaō*, v. [3] [√*756*]. to eat (breakfast):– eat (1), eating (1), have breakfast (1)

G754 ἀριστερός *aristeros*, a. Not used in NIVEBC. left side, left hand; the left is considered culturally to be weaker than the right; a weapon in the left hand is a defensive weapon; to be seated on the left side of a ruler is a lesser position than on the right side€ [4]:– left (3), left hand (1)

G755 Ἀριστόβουλος *Aristoboulos*, n. pr. [1] [√*1089*]. Aristobulus, "*best advisor*":– Aristobulus (1)

G756 ἄριστον *ariston*, n. [4] [→*753*]. meal, feast:– dinner (1), feast (1), luncheon (1), meal (1)

G757 ἀρκετός *arketos*, a. [3] [√*758*]. enough, sufficient:– enough (3)

G758 ἀρκέω *arkeō*, v. [8] [→*757, 894, 895, 2064*]. (mid./pass.) to be content, satisfied; (act.) to be sufficient:– content (3), enough (3), satisfied (1), sufficient (1)

G759 ἄρκος *arkos*, n. [1] [→*760*]. bear:– bear (1)

G760 ἄρκτος *arktos*, n. Not used in NIVEBC. [√*759*]. bear

G761 ἅρμα *harma*, n. [4] [√*275*]. chariot, carriage (for traveling or military uses):– chariot (3), chariots (1)

G762 Ἁρμαγεδών *Harmagedōn*, n. pr. [1] [√*cf. 3403*]. Armageddon, "*Mount Megiddo*":– Armageddon (1)

G763 Ἀρμίν *Armin*, n. pr. Not used in NIVEBC. [√*cf. 730*]. Armin

G764 ἁρμόζω *harmozō*, v. [1] [→*765, 5274*]. to promise for marriage, betroth:– promised (1)

G765 ἁρμός *harmos*, n. [1] [√*764*]. joint (where bones connect):– joints (1)

G766 ἀρνέομαι *arneomai*, v. [33] [→*565*]. to deny, disown, renounce, repudiate:– denied (10), disown (5), deny (4), denying (3), denies (2), disowned (2), disowns (2), fail (1), refused (1), rejected (1), renounce (1), say no to (1)

G767 Ἀρνί *Arni*, n. pr. Not used in NIVEBC. [√*cf. 730*]. Arni

G768* ἀρνίον *arnion, n. [30] [√ *748*]. lamb, sheep; the Lamb (a title of Christ):– lamb (27), lamb's (2), lambs (1)

G769* ἀροτριάω *arotriaō, v. [2] [→ *770*]. to plow, furrow:– plowing (1), plows (1)

G770* ἄροτρον *arotron, n. [1] [√ *769*]. plow, furrow-maker:– plow (1)

G771* ἁρπαγή *harpagē, n. [3] [√ *773*]. greediness, confiscation, robbery, plunder:– greed (2), confiscation (1)

G772* ἁρπαγμός *harpagmos, n. [1] [√ *773*]. something to hold onto:– something used to own advantage (1)

G773* ἁρπάζω *harpazō, v. [14] [→ *771, 772, 774, 1395, 5275*]. to catch, steal, carry off:– caught up (3), snatch (2), attacks (1), carry off (1), force (1), raiding (1), snatched up (1), snatches away (1), snatching (1), suddenly took away (1), take by force (1)

G774* ἅρπαξ *harpax, a. [5] [√ *773*]. swindling, robbing, implying violence in the process; (destructively) ferocious, ravenous; as a noun, a (violent) robber or swindler:– swindlers (2), ferocious (1), robbers (1), swindler (1)

G775* ἀρραβών *arrabōn, n. [3] deposit which guarantees, downpayment, pledge:– deposit guaranteeing what is to come (2), deposit guaranteeing (1)

G776* ἄρρην *arrēn, n. Not used in NIVEBC. [√ *781*]. male

G777* ἄρρητος *arrētos, a. [1] [√ *1.1 + 4839*]. inexpressible, not to be spoken (in context, things or words too sacred to tell):– inexpressible (1)

G778* ἀρρωστέω *arrōsteō, v. Not used in NIVEBC. [√ *1.1 + 4874*]. to be ill

G779* ἄρρωστος *arrōstos, a. [5] [√ *1.1 + 4874*], sick, ill:– sick (5)

G780* ἀρσενοκοίτης *arsenokoitēs, n. [2] [√ *781 + 3023*]. one engaging in homosexual acts (likely referring to the active male partner), sexual deviant:– men who have sex with men (1 [*+3434*]), practicing homosexuality (1)

G781* ἄρσην *arsēn, a. [9] [→ *776, 780*]. male:– male (6), men (3)

G782* Ἀρτεμᾶς *Artemas, n. pr. [1] [√ *783 + 1443*]. Artemas, "*[given by] Artemis*":– Artemas (1)

G783* Ἄρτεμις *Artemis, n. pr. [5] [→ *782*]. Artemis:– Artemis (5)

G784* ἀρτέμων *artemōn, n. [1] foresail, sail:– foresail (1)

G785* ἄρτι *arti, adv. [36] [→ *566, 567, 568, 786, 787, 1992, 2936, 2937, 2938, 4616*]. now, at once, immediately:– now (21), now on (4), still (3 [*+2401*]), again (1 [*+608*]), at once (1), just (1), just now (1), now (1 [*+608*]), this moment (1), this very (1), this very day (1)

G786* ἀρτιγέννητος *artigennētos, a. [1] [√ *785 + 1181*]. newborn:– newborn (1)

G787* ἄρτιος *artios, a. [1] [√ *785*]. thorough, complete, capable, proficient, able to meet all demands:– equipped (1)

G788* ἄρτος *artos, n. [95] (loaf of) bread, food:– bread (63), loaves (17), food (5), loaf (3), loaves of bread (3), eat (2 [*+2266*]), small loaves (1), NDT (1)

G789* ἀρτύω *artyō, v. [3] to make salty, season:– made salty (1), make salty (1), seasoned (1)

G790* Ἀρφαξάδ *Arphaxad, n. pr. [1] Arphaxad:– Arphaxad (1)

G791* ἀρχάγγελος *archangelos, n. [2] [√ *806 + 34*]. archangel:– archangel (2)

G792* ἀρχαῖος *archaios, a. [11] [√ *806*]. ancient, of old:– ancient (3), long ago (2), people long ago (2), earliest (1), early (1), old (1), some time ago (1 [*+608, 2465*])

G793* Ἀρχέλαος *Archelaos, n. pr. [1] [√ *806 + 3295*]. Archelaus, "*ruler of people*":– Archelaus (1)

G794* ἀρχή *archē, n. [55] [√ *806*]. beginning, origin, first; ruler, power, authority; position of authority, domain:– beginning (32), rulers (5), first (3), corners (2), power (2), demons (1), dominion (1), early days (1), elementary (1), elementary truths (1 [*+5122, 3836*]), it[S] (1 [*+4005, 608, 201*]), original (1), positions of authority (1), powers (1), rule (1), ruler (1)

G795* ἀρχηγός *archēgos, n. [4] [√ *806 + 72*]. author, originator, founder; leader, ruler:– pioneer (2), author (1), prince (1)

G796* ἀρχιερατικός *archieratikos, a. [1] [√ *806 + 2641*]. of the high priest:– high priest's (1)

G797* ἀρχιερεύς *archiereus, n. [122] [√ *806 + 2641*]. chief priest, high priest:– chief priests (64), high priest (51), high priest's (3), high priests (2), chief priest (1), high-priesthood (1)

G798* ἀρχιλῃστής *archilēstēs, n. Not used in NIVEBC. [√ *806 + 3334*]. head of a rebellion

G799* ἀρχιποίμην *archipoimēn, n. [1] [√ *806 + 4478*]. chief shepherd:– chief shepherd (1)

G800* Ἄρχιππος *Archippos, n. pr. [2] [√ *806 + 2691*]. Archippus, "*master of the horse*":– Archippus (2)

G801* ἀρχισυνάγωγος *archisynagōgos, n. [9] [√ *806 + 5252*]. leader of the synagogue, an official whose duty it was to care for the physical needs for the worship service:– synagogue leader (6), him[S] (1 [*+3836*]), leaders of the synagogue (1), synagogue leaders (1)

G802* ἀρχιτέκτων *architektōn, n. [1] [√ *806 + 5492*]. expert builder:– builder (1)

G803* ἀρχιτελώνης *architelōnēs, n. [1] [√ *806 + 5467*]. chief tax collector:– chief tax collector (1)

G804* ἀρχιτρίκλινος *architriklinos, n. [3] [√ *806 + 5552 + 3111*]. master of the banquet, head waiter:– master of the banquet (2), he[S] (1)

G805* ἀρχοστασία *archostasia, n. Not used in NIVEBC. election of magistrates

G806* ἄρχω *archō, v. [86] [→ *569, 752, 791, 792, 793, 794, 795, 796, 797, 798, 799, 800, 801, 802, 803, 804, 807, 825, 1617, 1672, 1673, 1887, 2065, 2066, 2067, 4256, 4272, 4485, 4599, 4732, 5134, 5135, 5489, 5490, 5638, 5639, 5941*]. (act.) to rule; (mid.) to begin:– began (51), beginning (7), will (5), begin (3), begins (2), became (1), began ministry (1), first (1), late in the afternoon (1 [*+3836, 2465, 3111*]), presented case (1 [*+2989*]), rule (1), rulers (1), started (1), starting from the beginning (1), went on (1), NDT (8)

G807* ἄρχων *archōn, n. [37] [√ *806*]. ruler, leader, official:– rulers (12), prince (7), ruler (7), leaders (3), authorities (2), leader (1), magistrate (1), prominent (1), ruling council (1), synagogue leader (1), synagogue leader's (1)

G808* ἄρωμα *arōma, n. [4] spices, salves, scented oils, perfumes:– spices (4)

G809* Ἀσά *Asa, n. pr. Not used in NIVEBC. [√ *cf. 811*]. Asa, "[poss.] *healer; myrtle*"

G810* ἀσάλευτος *asaleutos, a. [2] [√ *1.1 + 4888*]. unshakable, immovable, fixed:– cannot be shaken (1), not move (1 [*+3531*])

G811* Ἀσάφ *Asaph, n. pr. [2] [√ *cf. 809*]. Asaph, "*gatherer*":– Asa (2)

G812* ἄσβεστος *asbestos, a. [3] [√ *1.1 + 4931*]. unquenchable, inextinguishable:– unquenchable (2), never goes out (1)

G813* ἀσέβεια *asebeia, n. [6] [√ *1.1 + 4936*]. ungodliness, godlessness, impiety (in thought and act):– ungodly (3), godlessness (2), ungodliness (1)

G814* ἀσεβέω *asebeō, v. [1] [√ *1.1 + 4936*]. to do ungodly acts, act impiously:– committed in ungodliness (1)

G815* ἀσεβής *asebēs, a. [9] [√ *1.1 + 4936*]. ungodly, wicked, impious:– ungodly (8), ungodly (1 [*+476*])

G816* ἀσέλγεια *aselgeia, n. [10] [√ *1.1*]. debauchery, sensuality, lewdness:– debauchery (4), depraved (1), depraved conduct (1), lewdness (1), license for immorality (1), lustful (1), sensuality (1)

G817* ἄσημος *asēmos, a. [1] [√ *1.1 + 4956*]. ordinary, obscure, insignificant:– ordinary (1)

G818* Ἀσήρ *Asēr, n. pr. [2] Asher, "*happy one*":– Asher (2)

G819* ἀσθένεια *astheneia, n. [24] [√ *1.1 + 4964*]. weakness, illness, infirmity:– weakness (9), weaknesses (4), crippled (1 [*+2400*]), diseases (1), illness (1 [*+3836, 4922*]), illnesses (1), infirmities (1), infirmity (1), invalid (1 [*+2400, 1877, 3836*]), limitations (1), sick (1 [*+2400*]), sickness (1), sicknesses (1)

G820* ἀσθενέω *astheneō, v. [33] [√ *1.1 + 4964*]. to be weak, ill:– sick (14), weak (12), ill (2), disabled people (1), invalid (1), sickness (1 [*+3798*]), weakened (1), weakening (1)

G821* ἀσθένημα *asthenēma, n. [1] [√ *1.1 + 4964*]. failing, weakness:– failings (1)

G822* ἀσθενής *asthenēs, a. [26] [√ *1.1 + 4964*]. weak, ill (of physical weakness or illness, also of moral or spiritual weakness):– weak (14), sick (6), weaker (2), lame (1), powerless (1), unimpressive (1), weakness (1)

G823* Ἀσία *Asia, n. pr. [18] [→ *824, 825*]. Asia:– province of Asia (15), Asia (2), provinces of Asia (1)

G824* Ἀσιανός *Asianos, n. pr. g. [1] [√ *823*]. one from the Roman province of Asia:– from the province of Asia (1)

G825* Ἀσιάρχης *Asiarchēs, n. pr. [1] [√ *823 + 806*]. official of the province of Asia, Asiarch, a wealthy and influential man, probably connected with the Imperial cult:– officials of the province (1)

G826* ἀσιτία *asitia, n. [1] [√ *1.1 + 4992*]. going without food:– without food (1)

G827* ἄσιτος *asitos, a. [1] [√ *1.1 + 4992*]. going without food:– without food (1)

G828* ἀσκέω *askeō, v. [1] to strive, do one's best:– strive (1)

G829* ἀσκός *askos, n. [12] wineskin, leather bag holding wine:– wineskins (9), skins (3)

G830* ἀσμένως *asmenōs, adv. [1] [√ *2454*]. warmly, gladly:– warmly (1)

G831* ἄσοφος *asophos, a. [1] [√ *1.1 + 5055*]. unwise, foolish:– unwise (1)

G832* ἀσπάζομαι *aspazomai, v. [59] [→ *571, 833*]. to give greetings (hello or good-bye):– greet (30), send greetings (11), sends greetings (7), greeted (4), call out (1), give greeting (1), give greetings (1), greets (1), pay respects (1), said goodbye (1), welcomed (1)

G833* ἀσπασμός *aspasmos, n. [10] [√ *832*]. greeting:– greeting (6), greeted with respect (3), respectful greetings (1)

G834* ἄσπιλος *aspilos, a. [4] [√ *1.1 + 5070*]. without spot, defect or blemish:– defect (1), from being polluted (1), spotless (1), without spot (1)

G835* ἀσπίς *aspis, n. [1] [→ *5646*]. viper, asp, cobra:– vipers (1)

G836* ἄσπονδος *aspondos, a. [1] [√ *1.1 + 5064*]. unforgiving, not reconcilable:– unforgiving (1)

G837* ἀσσάριον *assarion, n. [2] assarion (coin worth one-sixteenth of a day's wage):– pennies (1), penny (1)

G838* Ἀσσάρων *Assarōn, n. pr. Not used in NIVEBC. [√ *cf. 4926*]. Assaron

G839* ἆσσον *asson, adv. [1] nearer:– along the shore (1)

G840* Ἆσσος *Assos, n. pr. [2] Assos:– Assos (2)

G841* ἀστατέω *astateō, v. [1] [√ *1.1 + 2705*]. to be homeless, a vagabond:– homeless (1)

G842* ἀστεῖος *asteios, a. Not used in NIVEBC. not ordinary, beautiful, pleasing€ [2]:– no ordinary (1), no ordinary (1 [*+3836, 2536*])

G843* ἀστήρ *astēr, n. [24] [→ *849*]. star:– stars (13), star (11)

G844* ἀστήρικτος *astēriktos, a. [2] [√ *1.1 + 5114*]. unstable, weak:– unstable (1), unstable (1 [*+6034*])

G845* ἄστοργος *astorgos, a. [2] [√ *1.1*]. without love, heartless:– no love (1), without love (1)

G846* ἀστοχέω *astocheō, v. [3] [√ *1.1*]. to wander away, miss the mark; to turn to, deviate from:– departed (3)

G847* ἀστραπή *astrapē, n. [9] [→ *848, 1993, 4313*]. lightning; light, ray of light:– flashes of lightning (4), lightning (4), light (1)

G848* ἀστράπτω *astraptō, v. [2] [√ *847*]. to flash, gleam like lightning:– flashes (1), gleamed like lightning (1)

G849* ἄστρον *astron, n. [4] [√ *843*]. star, constellation:– stars (3), star (1)

G850* Ἀσύγκριτος *Asynkritos, n. pr. [1] [√ *1.1 + 5250 + 3212*]. Asyncritus, "*incomparable*":– Asyncritus (1)

G851* ἀσύμφωνος *asymphōnos, a. [1] [√ *1.1 + 5250 + 5889*]. disagreeable, not harmonious:– disagreed (1 [*+1639*])

G852* ἀσύνετος *asynetos, a. [5] [√ *918; cf. 1.1 + 5250*]. senseless, dull, without understanding, foolish:– dull (2), no understanding (2), foolish (1)

G853* ἀσύνθετος *asynthetos, a. [1] [√ *1.1 + 5250 + 5502*]. faithless, untrustworthy:– no fidelity (1)

G854* ἀσφάλεια *asphaleia, n. [3] [√ *1.1 + 5378*]. security, safety; certainty, truth:– certainty (1), safety (1), securely (1 [*+1877, 4246*])

G855* ἀσφαλής *asphalēs, a. [5] [√ *1.1 + 5378*]. safe, firm, certain; definite; the truth:– definite (1), exactly (1), firm (1), get at truth (1 [*+1182*]), safeguard (1)

G856* ἀσφαλίζω *asphalizō, v. [4] [√ *1.1 + 5378*]. to make secure; fasten:– made secure (2), fastened (1), make secure (1)

G857* ἀσφαλῶς *asphalōs, adv. [3] [√ *1.1 + 5378*]. carefully, securely; under guard; assuredly, beyond a doubt:– assured (1), carefully (1), under guard (1)

G858* ἀσχημονέω *aschēmoneō, v. [2] [√ *1.1 + 5386*]. to act improperly, dishonorably, indecently, rudely:– dishonor (1), not acting honorably (1)

G859* ἀσχημοσύνη *aschēmosynē, n. [2] [√ *1.1 + 5386*]. indecent act, shame:– shameful acts (1), shamefully (1)

G860* ἀσχήμων *aschēmōn, a. [1] [√ *1.1 + 5386*]. unpresentable, shameful, indecent:– unpresentable (1)

G861* ἀσωτία *asōtia, n. [3] [√ *1.1 + 5392*]. debauchery, dissipation, wildness:– debauchery (1), wild (1), wild living (1)

G862 **ἀσώτως** ***asōtōs***, adv. [1] [√1.1 + 5392]. wildly, in debauchery, in dissipation:– wild (1)

G863 **ἀτακτέω** ***atakteō***, v. [1] [√1.1 + 5435]. to be idle, lazy:– idle (1)

G864 **ἄτακτος** ***ataktos***, a. [1] [√1.1 + 5435]. idle, lazy:– idle and disruptive (1)

G865 **ἀτάκτως** ***ataktōs***, adv. [2] [√1.1 + 5435]. idly, irresponsibly:– idle and disruptive (2)

G866 **ἄτεκνος** ***ateknos***, a. [2] [√1.1 + 5503]. childless, without children:– childless (1), no children (1)

G867 **ἀτενίζω** ***atenizō***, v. [14] [√1753 [1.2]]. to look intently, gaze, stare:– looked straight at (2), fastened on (1), look steadily (1), looked (1), looked (1 [+2917]), looked closely at (1), looked directly at (1), looked intently (1), looked straight (1), looking intently up (1), seeing (1), stare (1), stared (1)

G868 **ἄτερ** ***ater***, pp.* [2] without, apart from:– when no was present (1), without (1)

G869 **ἀτιμάζω** ***atimazō***, v. [7] [√1.1 + 5507]. to dishonor, disgrace, treat shamefully, insult:– dishonor (2), treated shamefully (2), degrading (1), dishonored (1), suffering disgrace (1)

G870 **ἀτιμάω** ***atimaō***, v. Not used in NIVEBC. [√1.1 + 5507]. to treat shamefully, dishonor, disgrace

G871 **ἀτιμία** ***atimia***, n. [7] [√1.1 + 5507]. dishonor, disgrace, shame; common use:– common use (2), dishonor (2), disgrace (1), shame (1), shameful (1)

G872 **ἄτιμος** ***atimos***, a. [4] [√1.1 + 5507]. without honor, dishonored, despised:– without honor (2), dishonored (1), less honorable (1)

G873 **ἀτιμόω** ***atimoō***, v. Not used in NIVEBC. [√1.1 + 5507]. to disgrace

G874 **ἀτμίς** ***atmis***, n. [2] [√113]. mist, vapor; billows (of smoke):– billows (1), mist (1)

G875 **ἄτομος** ***atomos***, a. [1] [√1.1 + 5533]. in a flash, in a moment, an indivisible unit of time:– flash (1)

G876 **ἄτοπος** ***atopos***, a. [4] [√1.1 + 5536]. wrong, wicked; unusual, surprising:– wrong (2), unusual (1), wicked (1)

G877 **Ἀττάλεια** ***Attaleia***, n. pr. [1] Attalia:– Attalia (1)

G878 **αὐγάζω** ***augazō***, v. [1] [√879]. to see:– see (1)

G879 **αὐγή** ***augē***, n. [1] [→575, 878, 1315, 1419, 1420, 2964, 5495]. daylight, dawn:– daylight (1)

G880 **Αὔγουστος** ***Augoustos***, n. pr. [1] Augustus, *"reverant, holy"*:– Augustus (1)

G881 **αὐθάδης** ***authadēs***, a. [2] [√899 + 2454]. overbearing, arrogant, stubborn, self-willed:– arrogant (1), overbearing (1)

G882 **αὐθαίρετος** ***authairetos***, a. [2] [√899 + 145]. on one's own initiative, of one's own accord:– entirely on their own (1), on own initiative (1)

G883 **αὐθεντέω** ***authenteō***, v. [1] [√899]. to have authority over:– assume authority over (1)

G884 **αὐλέω** ***auleō***, v. [3] [√888]. to play the flute:– played the pipe (2), tune played (1 [+2445, 3068])

G885 **αὐλή** ***aulē***, n. [12] [→64, 2068, 4580; cf. 113, 887]. palace, house; courtyard, sheepfold:– courtyard (6), palace (2), court (1), house (1), pen (1), sheep pen (1)

G886 **αὐλητής** ***aulētēs***, n. [2] [√888]. flute player:– people playing pipes (1), pipers (1)

G887 **αὐλίζομαι** ***aulizomai***, v. [2] [→5276; cf. 885]. to spend the night, find lodging:– spend the night (1), spent the night (1)

G888 **αὐλός** ***aulos***, n. [1] [→884, 886]. flute:– pipe (1)

G889 **αὐξάνω** ***auxanō***, v. [23] [→890, 891, 5277, 5647]. to cause to grow; (intr.) grow, increase:– grew (4), grow (4), growing (2), grows (2), spread (2), enlarge (1), greater (1), grow to become mature (1), grow up (1), makes grow (1), making grow (1), number greatly increased (1 [+2779, 4437]), rises (1), spread widely (1)

G890 **αὔξησις** ***auxēsis***, n. [2] [√889]. growth, increase:– causes to grow (1), grows (1 [+4472])

G891 **αὔξω** ***auxō***, v. Not used in NIVEBC. [√889]. to cause to grow; (intr.) to grow, increase

G892 **αὔριον** ***aurion***, adv. [14] [→2069]. tomorrow, the next day:– tomorrow (11), next day (3)

G893 **αὐστηρός** ***austēros***, a. [2] [→903]. hard, severe, strict, exacting:– hard (2)

G894 **αὐτάρκεια** ***autarkeia***, n. [2] [√899 + 758]. contentment, having all of one's needs, sufficiency:– contentment (1), need (1)

G895 **αὐτάρκης** ***autarkēs***, a. [1] [√899 + 758]. content; (possibly) self-sufficient:– content (1)

G896 **αὐτοκατάκριτος** ***autokatakritos***, a. [1] [√899 + 2848 + 3212]. self-condemned:– self-condemned (1)

G897 **αὐτόματος** ***automatos***, a. [2] [√899]. by itself, automatic:– all by itself (1), by itself (1)

G898 **αὐτόπτης** ***autoptēs***, n. [1] [√899 + 3972]. eyewitness:– eyewitnesses (1)

G899 **αὐτός** ***autos***, p. inten. [5558] [→881, 882, 883, 894, 895, 896, 897, 898, 900, 901, 1571, 1831, 1929, 1994, 2070, 4194, 4932, 5437, 5796, 6058]. he, she, it; also used as inten.p., himself, herself, itself, themselves; the same one; also an adv. of place: here, there, where:– him (1288), them (885), his (781), their (338), her (204), he (196), it (180), they (151), Jesus[S] (149), its (67), same (42), himself (41), the man[S] (21), Paul[S] (19), Jesus[S] (17), she (17), his own (14), you (13), God's[S] (12), themselves (10), yourselves (10), home (9 [+3875]), myself (9), the man's[S] (9), your (9), that person (8), these (8), those (8), John[S] (7), that (7), whose (7), God[S] (6), very (6), his disciples[S] (5), others (5), the child[S] (5), the crowd[S] (5), their own (5), this (5), which (5), who (5), whom (5), Christ[S] (4), beast[S] (4), itself (4), ourselves (4), the boy[S] (4), the disciples[S] (4), there (4 [+1877]), together (4 [+2093, 3836]), I (3), John's[S] (3), Stephen[S] (3), Moses[S] (3), Christ[S] (6), Abraham[S] (3), Jesus and his disciples[S] (3), own (3), Peter and John[S] (3), the apostles[S] (5), the Jews[S] (3), the men[S] (3), the women[S] (3), theirs (3), them[S] (3 [+3836, 3412]), yourself (3), here (2), he's (2), himself (2 [+3836, 2840]), Joseph[S] (2), one's (2), Paul and Barnabas[S] (2), Paul and Silas[S] (2), Peter's[S] (2), Lazarus[S] (2), people[S] (4), Peter[S] (2), that (2 [+3836]), that is how (2 [+2848, 3836]), that very (2), the body[S] (2), the Lord[S] (2), the pigs[S] (2), the plants[S] (2), the servant[S] (2), the vineyard[S] (2), we (3), young man[S] (2), agree in what say (1 [+3836, 3306]), alive (1 [+3836, 6034, 1877, 1639]), as did (1 [+4047]), as usual (1 [+2848, 3836]), at once (1 [+3836, 6052]), Barnabas and Saul[S] (1), believers[S] (1 [+1666]), both of you (1 [+5148, 2779]), by himself (1 [+3668]), come together (1 [+5302, 2093, 3836]), comes together (1 [+5302, 2093, 3836]), done this[S] (1 [+5718, 3836, 4246]), each (1), figure (1), for this very reason (1 [+4047]), for the express purpose (1 [+1650, 4047]), Galilee[S] (1), Festus[S] (1), Elizabeth[S] (1), Elymas[S] (1), Israel[S] (1), fair (1), girl[S] (1), governing[S] (1 [+4047]), harvest[S] (1), Crete's[S] (1), disciples[S] (1), one (1 [+3836]), nearby (1 [+3836]), equal (1 [+3836]), got together (1 [+5251, 2093, 3836]), he (1 [+3836, 4725]), he (1 [+1328, 3836, 5931]), he[S] (1 [+3836, 4460, 1877, 899]), he[S] (1 [+3836, 4460, 899, 1877]), he and his disciples[S] (1), he himself (1), here (1 [+1877]), herself (1), him (1 [+3836, 3950]), his master[S] (1), his money[S] (1), immediately (1 [+1877, 3836, 6052]), in the same way (1 [+3836]), Isaac (1), it[S] (1 [+3836, 3456]), its (1 [+1877]), its[S] (1 [+3836, 4725]), its own (1), Jesus body[S] (1), Jesus himself[S] (1), lies[S] (1), Levi's[S] (1), Levi[S] (1), like-minded (1 [+3836, 5858]), live in harmony (1 [+3836, 5858]), love[S] (2), on board (1 [+1650]), one (1), one another (1), one place (1 [+3836]), Paul (2), Samaria[S] (1), Saul[S] (1), Paul's[S] (1), such (1), such beings (1), such branches[S] (1), that country[S] (1), that one (1), that one sheep[S] (1), that same (1), the child's[S] (1), the gentiles[S] (1), the star[S] (1), the altar[S] (1), the ark[S] (1), the blessing[S] (1), the boy's[S] (1), the builder[S] (1), the children[S] (1), the coast[S] (1), the commander[S] (1), the commander's[S] (1), the commandment[S] (1), the council[S] (1), the cross[S] (1), the disobedient[S] (1), the entrance[S] (1), the firstborn of Israel[S] (1), the flock[S] (1), the following (1), the island[S] (1), the Israelites[S] (1), the kings[S] (1), the land[S] (1), the master[S] (1), the messengers[S] (1), the money[S] (1), the net[S] (1), the new believers[S] (1), the officers[S] (1), the Pharisees and the teachers of the law[S] (1), the proceedings[S] (1), the prophets[S] (1), the same as (1 [+1651, 2779, 3836]), the sanhedrin[S] (1), the scrolls[S] (1), the servants[S] (1), the son[S] (1), the spirit[S] (1), the sun[S] (1), the synagogue[S] (1), the tongue[S] (1), the tree[S] (1), the two[S] (1), the two of you (1 [+5148, 2779]), the very one (1), the widow[S] (1), the wine[S] (1), their body[S] (1), their very (1), them (1 [+6034]), them[S] (1 [+3836, 5284]), them[S] (1 [+3836, 4546]), themselves (1 [+2840]), themselves (1 [+3836, 6034]), themselves (1 [+3836, 2840]), they[S] (1 [+3836, 5125]), they[S] (1 [+3836, 213]), they[S] (1 [+3836, 6001]), they[S] (1 [+3836, 4057]), things (1), this man[S] (1), this perfume[S] (1), this is why (1 [+1328]), those churches[S] (1), to their number (1 [+2093, 3836]), too (1 [+3836, 2779]), turned against (1 [+2048, 3836, 4761]), two Israelites[S] (1), united (1 [+1877, 3836]), where they were staying[S] (1), which[S] (1 [+3836, 3364]), whole (1), with this in mind (1 [+1650]), writing[S] (1), your slaves[S] (1), Zechariah's[S] (1), Apollos[S] (1), animals[S] (1), faith[S] (1), Christ's[S] (1), Saul[S] (2), Saul's[S] (1), Simeon[S] (1), Pilate[S] (1), people's[S] (1), plants[S] (1), James[S] (1), Jairus[S] (1), death[S] (1), Jesus (1), Lydda[S] (1), Ananias[S] (1), second beast[S] (1), strong man's[S] (1), that (1 [+3836]), these men[S] (1), NDT (661)

G900 **αὐτόφωρος** ***autophōros***, a. [1] [√899]. in the act:– act (1)

G901 **αὐτόχειρ** ***autocheir***, a. *or* n. [1] [√899 + 5931]. with one's own hand:– with their own hands (1)

G902 **αὐχέω** ***aucheō***, v. [1] [→3482]. to boast:– makes boasts (1)

G903 **αὐχμηρός** ***auchmēros***, a. [1] [√893]. dark:– dark (1)

G904 **ἀφαιρέω** ***aphaireō***, v. [10] [√608 + 145]. to take away from, remove; to cut (off):– cutting off (3), take away (3), taken away (2), takes away (1), taking away (1)

G905 **ἀφανής** ***aphanēs***, a. [1] [√1.1 + 5743]. hidden, invisible:– hidden from (1)

G906 **ἀφανίζω** ***aphanizō***, v. [5] [√1.1 + 5743]. to destroy, disfigure; to perish, vanish, disappear:– destroy (2), disfigure (1), perish (1), vanishes (1)

G907 **ἀφανισμός** ***aphanismos***, n. [1] [√1.1 + 5743]. disappearance, destruction:– disappear (1)

G908 **ἄφαντος** ***aphantos***, a. [1] [√1.1 + 5743]. disappearing, invisible:– disappeared from sight (1 [+1181])

G909 **ἀφεδρών** ***aphedrōn***, n. [2] [√608 + 1612]. latrine:– out of the body (1 [+1650, 1675]), out of the body[S] (1 [+1650, 3836, 1744])

G910 **ἀφειδία** ***apheidia***, n. [1] [√1.1 + 5767]. harsh treatment, unsparing:– harsh treatment (1)

G911 **ἀφελότης** ***aphelotēs***, n. [1] [√1.1]. sincerity, simplicity:– sincere (1)

G912 **ἄφεσις** ***aphesis***, n. [17] [√918]. forgiveness, pardon, release, cancellation of a debt:– forgiveness (12), forgive (1), forgiven (1), forgiven (1 [+2400]), freedom (1), set free (1 [+690, 1877])

G913 **ἁφή** ***haphē***, n. [2] [√721]. ligament, joint:– ligament (1), ligaments (1)

G914 **ἀφθαρσία** ***aphtharsia***, n. [7] [√1.1 + 5780]. imperishableness, immortality:– imperishable (3), immortality (2), imperishable (1 [+1877]), undying (1)

G915 **ἄφθαρτος** ***aphthartos***, a. [7] [√1.1 + 5780]. imperishable, immortal, lasting forever:– immortal (2), imperishable (2), never perish (1), that will last forever (1), unfading (1)

G916 **ἀφθονία** ***aphthonia***, n. Not used in NIVEBC. [√1.1 + 5784]. willingness

G917 **ἀφθορία** ***aphthoria***, n. [1] [√1.1 + 5780]. integrity, soundness, purity:– integrity (1)

G918 **ἀφίημι** ***aphiēmi***, v. [143] [→457, 479, 852, 912, 1588, 1889, 4217, 4223, 5304, 5305, 5317, 5320; cf. 608]. to forgive, pardon, remit, cancel; to leave, abandon; to allow, permit, tolerate:– left (36), forgive (22), forgiven (22), let (19), leave (7), leave alone (5), leaving (4), divorce (3), let go (3), deserted (2), abandoned (1), abandons (1), allow (1), canceled (1), consented (1), forgives (1), forsaken (1), gave up (1), hand over (1), leaves (1), leaving behind (1), let go of (1), let go on (1), move beyond (1), neglected (1), neglecting (1), refuse (1 [+4024]), tolerate (1), with (1), NDT (1)

G919 **ἀφικνέομαι** ***aphikneomai***, v. [1] [√608 + 2653]. to reach:– heard about (1 [+1650])

G920 **ἀφιλάγαθος** ***aphilagathos***, a. [1] [√1.1 + 5813 + 19]. not loving good:– not lovers of the good (1)

G921 **ἀφιλάργυρος** ***aphilargyros***, a. [2] [√1.1 + 5813 + 738]. not loving money, not greedy:– free from the love of money (1), not a lover of money (1)

G922 **ἄφιξις** ***aphixis***, n. [1] [√608 + 2653]. leaving, departure:– leave (1)

G923 **ἀφίστημι** ***aphistēmi***, v. [14] [√608 + 2705]. to leave, withdraw, abandon; to revolt, mislead:– left (4), abandon (1), away (1), deserted (1), fall away (1), leave alone (1), led in revolt (1 [+3958]), take away (1), turn away (1), turns away (1), withdrew (1)

G924 **ἄφνω** ***aphnō***, adv. [3] [√167?]. suddenly:– suddenly (3)

G925 **ἀφόβως** ***aphobōs***, adv. [4] [√1.1 + 5832]. fearlessly, without the slightest qualm, boldly:– without fear (2), nothing to fear (1), without the slightest qualm (1)

G926 **ἀφομοιόω** ***aphomoioō***, v. [1] [√608 + 3927]. (pass.) to be like, similar:– resembling (1 [+2400])

G927 **ἀφοράω** ***aphoraō***, v. [2] [√608 + 3972]. to fix one's eyes; look away:– fixing eyes on (1), see (1)

G928 **ἀφορίζω** ***aphorizō***, v. [10] [√608 + 4000]. to separate, set apart, exclude:– separate (4), set apart (3), exclude (1), separates (1), took (1)

G929 **ἀφορμή** ***aphormē***, n. [7] [√608 + 3995]. opportunity, opening, pretext:– opportunity (5), ground (1), indulge (1)

G930 **ἀφρίζω** ***aphrizō***, v. [2] [√931]. to foam at the mouth:– foaming at the mouth (1), foams at the mouth (1)

G931 **ἀφρός** ***aphros***, n. [1] [→576, 930, 2072]. foam, froth:– foams at the mouth (1 [+3552])

G932 **ἀφροσύνη** ***aphrosynē***, n. [4] [√1.1 + 5856]. foolishness, lack of sense:– fool (2), folly (1), foolishness (1)

G933 **ἄφρων** ***aphrōn***, a. [11] [√1.1 + 5856]. foolish, ignorant:– fool (5), foolish (5), fools (1)

G934 ἀφυπνόω *aphypnoō*, v. [1] [√*608 + 5678*]. to fall asleep:– fell asleep (1)

G935 ἀφυστερέω *aphystereō*, v. Not used in NIVEBC. [√*608 + 5731*]. withhold, keep back

G936 ἄφωνος *aphōnos*, a. [4] [√*1.1 + 5889*]. silent, mute, without speech; without meaning:– mute (1), silent (1), without meaning (1), without speech (1)

G937 Ἀχάζ *Achaz*, n. pr. [2] [→*941*]. Ahaz, *"he has grasped"*:– Ahaz (2)

G938 Ἀχαΐα *Achaia*, n. pr. [10] [→*939*]. Achaia:– Achaia (10)

G939 Ἀχαϊκός *Achaikos*, n. pr. [1] [√*938*]. Achaicus, *"belonging to Achaia"*:– Achaicus (1)

G940 ἀχάριστος *acharistos*, a. [2] [√*1.1 + 5897*]. ungrateful:– ungrateful (2)

G941 Ἀχάς *Achas*, n. pr. Not used in NIVEBC. [√*937*]. Ahaz, *"he has grasped"*

G942 ἀχειροποίητος *acheiropoiētos*, a. [3] [√*1.1 + 5931 + 4472*]. not made by human hands, implying not of human origin:– not built by human hands (1), not made with hands (1), not performed by human hands (1)

G943 Ἀχίμ *Achim*, n. pr. [2] Akim, *"Yahweh is my brother"*:– Akim (2)

G944 ἀχλύς *achlys*, n. [1] mistiness, dimness of sight:– mist (1)

G945 ἀχρεῖος *achreios*, a. [2] [√*1.1 + 5968*]. worthless, useless, unworthy:– unworthy (1), worthless (1)

G946 ἀχρειόω *achreioō*, v. [1] [√*1.1 + 5968*]. (pass.) to become worthless, depraved:– worthless (1)

G947 ἄχρηστος *achrēstos*, a. [1] [√*1.1 + 5968*]. useless, worthless:– useless (1)

G948 ἄχρι *achri*, pp.* & c. [48] [√*216*]. until, up to, as far as, as long as:– until (16), to (9), until (5 [+*4005*]), as far as (2), up to (2), as high as (1), as long as (1 [+*4005*]), before (1), even to (1), even to the point of (1), for (1), includes (1 [+*2391*]), just before (1 [+*4005*]), later (1), right up to (1), so much as to shrink from (1), then (1 [+*4005*]), to where (1), until (1 [+*4005, 323*])

G949 ἄχυρον *achyron*, n. [2] chaff:– chaff (2)

G950 ἀψευδής *apseudēs*, a. [1] [√*1.1 + 6017*]. not a liar, free from deceit, trustworthy:– not lie (1)

G951 ἀψίνθιον *apsinthion*, n. Not used in NIVEBC. [√*952*]. wormwood

G952 ἄψινθος *apsinthos*, n. [2] [→*951*]. (m.) Wormwood, referring to a bitter herb (absinthe); (f.) bitterness:– bitter (1), wormwood (1)

G953 ἄψυχος *apsychos*, a. [1] [√*1.1 + 6038*]. lifeless, inanimate:– lifeless (1)

G954 β *b*, letter. Not used in NIVEBC. letter of the Greek alphabet; also used as the numeral "2" in the superscriptions of some Greek manuscripts

G955 Βάαλ *Baal*, n. pr. [1] Baal, *"master, owner, lord"*:– Baal (1)

G956 Βαβυλών *Babylōn*, n. pr. [12] Babylon, *"gate of god[s]"*:– Babylon (11), NDT (1)

G957 βαθμός *bathmos*, n. [1] [√*326*]. standing, rank:– standing (1)

G958 βάθος *bathos*, n. [8] [√*960*]. depth, deep thing; extreme:– deep (3), depth (2), extreme (1 [+*2848*]), shallow (1 [+*3590*]), shallow (1 [+*3590, 2400*])

G959 βαθύνω *bathynō*, v. [1] [√*960*]. to go down deep, dig deep:– down deep (1)

G960 βαθύς *bathys*, a. [4] [→*958, 959*]. deep; (as a time of day) early:– deep (3), very (1)

G961 βάϊον *baion*, n. [1] (palm) branch:– branches (1)

G962 Βαλαάμ *Balaam*, n. pr. [3] Balaam, "[poss.] *Baal [lord] of the people* or *the clan brings forth*":– Balaam (2), Balaam's (1)

G963 Βαλάκ *Balak*, n. pr. [1] Balak, *"devastator"*:– Balak (1)

G964 βαλλάντιον *ballantion*, n. [4] purse, money-bag:– purse (3), purses (1)

G965 βάλλω *ballō*, v. [122] [→*327, 332, 506, 610, 612, 613, 1017, 1018, 1064, 1074, 1075, 1076, 1286, 1330, 1333, 1675, 1678, 1833, 2095, 2099, 2850, 2856, 3344, 3554, 4125, 4129, 4130, 4212, 4213, 4314, 4316, 4582, 5202, 5560, 5649, 5650, 5651, 5680; cf. 311*]. to throw, pour; to put, set:– thrown (26), throw (15), put (13), threw (5), put in (4), bring (3), cast (3), casting (3), hurled (3), hurled down (3), lying (3), gave (2), pour (2), poured (2), pours (2), putting (2), spewed (2), swung (2), toss (2), did[S] (1), drives (1), drop (1), entice to sin (1 [+*4998, 1967*]), fertilize (1 [+*3162*]), flinging (1), flung (1), help (1), impose (1), jumped (1 [+*1571*]), laid (1), lay (1), let down (1), lies (1), others[S] (1), planted (1), prompted (1 [+*1650, 3836, 2840*]), put on deposit (1), scatters (1), stone (1 [+*2093*]), swept down (1), threw in (1), throw out (1), thrown down (1), NDT (1)

G966 βαπτίζω *baptizō*, v. [77] [√*970*]. to baptize, wash; the baptizer:– baptized (49), baptize (12), baptizing (7), baptist (3), baptism (2), wash (2), baptized (1 [+*3836, 967*]), undergo[S] (1)

G967 βάπτισμα *baptisma*, n. [19] [√*970*]. baptism:– baptism (17), baptized (1 [+*966, 3836*]), baptizing (1)

G968 βαπτισμός *baptismos*, n. [4] [√*970*]. baptism, ceremonial washing:– baptism (1), ceremonial washings (1), cleansing rites (1), washing (1)

G969 βαπτιστής *baptistēs*, n. [12] [√*970*]. Baptist, a surname of John:– baptist (12)

G970 βάπτω *baptō*, v. [4] [→*966, 967, 968, 969, 1834, 1835*]. to dip (in):– dipped (2), dip (1), dipping (1)

G971 βαρ *bar*, l.[n.] Not used in NIVEBC. Not used in NIVEBC. son

G972 Βαραββᾶς *Barabbas*, n. pr. [11] Barabbas, *"son of a father* poss. *son of a rabbi"*:– Barabbas (11)

G973 Βαράκ *Barak*, n. pr. [1] Barak, *"lightning"*:– Barak (1)

G974 Βαραχίας *Barachias*, n. pr. [1] Berekiah, *"Yahweh blesses"*:– Berekiah (1)

G975 βάρβαρος *barbaros*, a. Not used in NIVEBC. non-Greek, foreign, "barbarian"; someone who speaks an unintelligible language€ [6]:– foreigner (2), islanders (2), barbarian (1), non-greeks (1)

G976 βαρέω *bareō*, v. [6] [√*983*]. (pass.) to be burdened, under pressure:– burdened (2), heavy (1), under pressure (1), very sleepy (1 [+*5678*]), weighed down (1)

G977 βαρέως *bareōs*, adv. [2] [√*983*]. with difficulty:– hardly (2)

G978 Βαρθολομαῖος *Bartholomaios*, n. pr. [4] Bartholomew, *"son of Talmai"*:– Bartholomew (4)

G979 Βαριησοῦς *Bariēsous*, n. pr. [1] Bar-Jesus, *"son of Jesus [Joshua]"*:– Bar-Jesus (1)

G980 Βαριωνᾶ *Bariōna*, n. pr. [1] [→*981*]. son of Jonah, Bar-Jona, *"son of Jonah* or *John"*:– son of Jonah (1)

G981 Βαριωνᾶς *Bariōnas*, n. pr. Not used in NIVEBC. [√*980*]. son of Jonah, Bar-Jona, *"son of Jonah* or *John"*

G982 Βαρναβᾶς *Barnabas*, n. pr. [28] Barnabas, *"son of comfort"*:– Barnabas (28)

G983 βάρος *baros*, n. [6] [→*4, 976, 977, 986, 987, 988, 2096, 2851, 2852*]. burden, weight; this can refer either to difficulty or importance:– burden (2), asserted authority (1 [+*1877, 1639*]), burden (1 [+*2202*]), burdens (1), far outweighs them all (1 [+*2848, 5651, 1650, 5651*])

G984 Βαρσαββᾶς *Barsabbas*, n. pr. [2] Barsabbas, *"son of the Sabbath* or *son of Saba"*:– Barsabbas (2)

G985 Βαρτιμαῖος *Bartimaios*, n. pr. [1] Bartimaeus, *"son of Timai* or *son of uncleanness"*:– Bartimaeus (1)

G986 βαρύνω *barynō*, v. Not used in NIVEBC. [√*983*]. to burden, grieve

G987 βαρύς *barys*, a. [6] [√*983*]. burdensome, heavy, important; savage, fierce:– burdensome (1), heavy (1), more important matters (1), savage (1), serious (1), weighty (1)

G988 βαρύτιμος *barytimos*, a. [1] [√*983 + 5507*]. very expensive:– very expensive (1)

G989 βασανίζω *basanizō*, v. [12] [√*992*]. to torture, torment; (pass.) to be tortured, tormented, in pain:– tormented (4), torture (4), buffeted (1), pain (1 [+*6048, 2779*]), straining (1), suffering (1)

G990 βασανισμός *basanismos*, n. [6] [√*992*]. torment, torture, agony:– torment (4), agony (1), sting (1)

G991 βασανιστής *basanistēs*, n. [1] [√*992*]. torturer:– jailers to be tortured (1)

G992 βάσανος *basanos*, n. [3] [→*989, 990, 991*]. torment, severe pain, torture:– torment (2), severe pain (1)

G993 βασιλεία *basileia*, n. [162] [√*995*]. kingdom, kingship, royal rule:– kingdom (154), kingdoms (3), appointed king (1 [+*3284*]), it[S] (1 [+*3836*]), made king (1 [+*3284, 3836*]), royal authority (1), rules (1 [+*2400*])

G994 βασίλειος *basileios*, a. [2] [√*995*]. royal, kingly; as a noun, a residence of royalty: palace:– palaces (1), royal (1)

G995 βασιλεύς *basileus*, n. [115] [→*993, 994, 996, 997, 998, 999, 5203*]. king:– king (80), kings (28), emperor (2), king (2 [+*476*]), king's (2), he[S] (1 [+*3836*])

G996 βασιλεύω *basileuō*, v. [21] [√*995*]. to reign as a king, become king:– reign (12), reigned (4), king (2), kings (1), reigning (1), reigns (1)

G997 βασιλικός *basilikos*, a. [5] [√*995*]. royal, noble, kingly; as a noun, royal official (possibly of the Herodian family):– royal (2), royal official (2), king's (1)

G998 βασιλίσκος *basiliskos*, n. Not used in NIVEBC. [√*995*]. petty king

G999 βασίλισσα *basilissa*, n. [4] [√*995*]. queen:– queen (4)

G1000 βάσις *basis*, n. [1] [√*326*]. foot:– feet (1)

G1001 βασκαίνω *baskainō*, v. [1] to bewitch:– bewitched (1)

G1002 βαστάζω *bastazō*, v. [27] [→*1546*]. to carry, bear up, carry off; to tolerate, help, support:– carry (4), bear (3), carrying (3), carried (2), bear with (1), bearers (1), bore (1), borne (1), carried away (1), endured hardships (1), gave birth (1), help himself to (1), pay (1), picked up (1), proclaim (1), rides (1), support (1), take (1), tolerate (1)

G1003 βάτος[1] *batos[1]*, n. [5] bush, brier, thornbush:– bush (4), briers (1)

G1004 βάτος[2] *batos[2]*, n. [1] bath (a unit of liquid measure, between eight and nine gallons):– nine hundred gallons (1 [+*1669*])

G1005 βάτραχος *batrachos*, n. [1] frog:– frogs (1)

G1006 βατταλογέω *battalogeō*, v. [1] [√*3306*]. to babble, prattle:– babbling (1)

G1007 βδέλυγμα *bdelygma*, n. [6] [→*1008, 1009*]. abomination, something detestable:– abomination (2), abominable (1), abominations (1), detestable (1), shameful (1)

G1008 βδελυκτός *bdelyktos*, a. [1] [√*1007*]. detestable, abominable:– detestable (1)

G1009 βδελύσσομαι *bdelyssomai*, v. [2] [√*1007*]. (mid.) to abhor, detest; (pass.) to be vile, abhorrent:– abhor (1), vile (1)

G1010 βέβαιος *bebaios*, a. [8] [√*326*]. firm, sure, certain, binding:– binding (1), completely reliable (1), confirm (1 [+*4472*]), firm (1), firmly (1), guaranteed (1), in force (1), secure (1)

G1011 βεβαιόω *bebaioō*, v. [8] [√*326*]. to confirm; keep strong:– confirmed (3), strengthened (2), confirming (1), keep firm (1), makes stand firm (1)

G1012 βεβαίωσις *bebaiōsis*, n. [2] [√*326*]. confirmation:– confirming (1), confirms (1 [+*1650*])

G1013 βέβηλος *bebēlos*, a. [5] [√*326*]. godless, irreligious, profane, worldly:– godless (4), irreligious (1)

G1014 βεβηλόω *bebēloō*, v. [2] [√*326*]. to desecrate, profane:– desecrate (2)

G1015 Βεελζεβούλ *Beelzeboul*, n. pr. [7] Beelzebub, *"lord [baal] of the flies"*:– Beelzebul (7)

G1016 Βελιάρ *Beliar*, n. pr. [1] Belial, *"wicked, without use"*:– Belial (1)

G1017 βελόνη *belonē*, n. [1] [√*965*]. needle:– needle (1)

G1018 βέλος *belos*, n. [1] [√*965*]. arrow:– arrows (1)

G1019 βελτίων *beltiōn*, a. Not used in NIVEBC. having a detailed knowledge, translated "better, very well"€ [1]:– very well (1)

G1020 Βενιαμείν *Beniamein*, n. pr. Not used in NIVEBC. [√*1021*]. Benjamin, *"son of the right hand* or *Southerner"*

G1021 Βενιαμίν *Beniamin*, n. pr. [4] [→*1020*]. Benjamin, *"son of the right hand* or *Southerner"*:– Benjamin (4)

G1022 Βερνίκη *Bernikē*, n. pr. [3] [√*5770 + 3772*]. Bernice, *"victorious"*:– Bernice (3)

G1023 Βέροια *Beroia*, n. pr. [2] [→*1024*]. Berea:– Berea (2)

G1024 Βεροιαῖος *Beroiaios*, a. pr. g. [1] [√*1023*]. Berean, person of Berea:– from Berea (1)

G1025 Βέρος *Beros*, n. pr. Not used in NIVEBC. Beros

G1026 Βεωορσόρ *Beōorsor*, n. pr. Not used in NIVEBC. [√*1027*]. Bosor

G1027 Βεώρ *Beōr*, n. pr. Not used in NIVEBC. [→*1026, 1082*]. Beor, "[perhaps] *a burning*"

G1028 Βηθαβαρά *Bēthabara*, n. pr. Not used in NIVEBC. Bethabara

G1029 Βηθανία *Bēthania*, n. pr. [12] Bethany, *"House of Ananiah* [or *the poor* or *unripe figs*]*"*:– Bethany (12)

G1030 Βηθαραβά *Bētharaba*, n. pr. Not used in NIVEBC. Betharaba

G1031 Βηθεσδά *Bēthesda*, n. pr. [1] Bethesda, *"site [house] of mercy"*:– Bethesda (1)

G1032 Βηθζαθά *Bēthzatha*, n. pr. Not used in NIVEBC. Bethzatha

G1033 Βηθλέεμ *Bēthleem*, n. pr. [8] Bethlehem, *"house of bread* poss. *temple of Lakhmu"*:– Bethlehem (8)

G1034 **Βηθσαϊδά** ***Bēthsaida***, n. pr. [7] Bethsaida, "*site [house] of fishing*":– Bethsaida (7)

G1035 **Βηθσαϊδάν** ***Bēthsaidan***, n. pr. Not used in NIVEBC. Bethsaida

G1036 **Βηθφαγή** ***Bēthphagē***, n. pr. [3] Bethphage, "*house of unripe figs*":– Bethphage (3)

G1037 **βῆμα** ***bēma***, n. [12] [√*326*]. judicial court, judge's seat; this can refer to human or divine judgment:– convened the court (2 [+*2767, 2093, 3836*]), judge's seat (2), judgment seat (2), court (1), place of judgment (1), proconsul (1), set on (1), throne (1), NDT (1)

G1038 **Βηρεύς** ***Bēreus***, n. pr. Not used in NIVEBC. Bereus

G1039 **βήρυλλος** ***bēryllos***, n. [1] beryl, a semi-precious stone of sea-green color:– beryl (1)

G1040 **βία** ***bia***, n. [3] [→*1041, 1042, 1043, 4128*]. force, violence, pounding (of surf):– force (1), pounding (1), violence (1)

G1041 **βιάζω** ***biazō***, v. [2] [√*1040*]. (mid.) to force one's way:– forcing way (1), subjected to violence (1)

G1042 **βίαιος** ***biaios***, a. [1] [√*1040*]. violent, strong:– violent (1)

G1043 **βιαστής** ***biastēs***, n. [1] [√*1040*]. forceful one:– violent (1)

G1044 **βιβλαρίδιον** ***biblaridion***, n. [3] [√*1047*]. little scroll:– little scroll (3)

G1045 **βιβλιδάριον** ***biblidarion***, n. Not used in NIVEBC. [√*1047*]. little scroll

G1046 **βιβλίον** ***biblion***, n. [34] [√*1047*]. scroll, book, certificate:– scroll (19), book (6), books (3), certificate (2), it[S] (2 [+*3836*]), scroll (1 [+*3053*]), scrolls (1)

G1047 **βίβλος** ***biblos***, n. [10] [→*1044, 1045, 1046*]. book, scroll:– book (8), genealogy (1 [+*1161*]), scrolls (1)

G1048 **βιβρώσκω** ***bibrōskō***, v. [1] [→*1109, 1110, 1111, 4963, 5037*]. to eat:– eaten (1)

G1049 **Βιθυνία** ***Bithynia***, n. pr. [2] Bithynia:– Bithynia (2)

G1050 **βίος** ***bios***, n. [9] [→*1051, 1052, 1053, 4259*]. (everyday) life; what one lives on, property, possessions:– property (2), civilian affairs (1 [+*4548*]), life (1), life's (1), live on (1), lives (1), possessions (1), to live on (1)

G1051 **βιόω** ***bioō***, v. [1] [√*1050*]. to live:– live (1)

G1052 **βίωσις** ***biōsis***, n. [1] [√*1050*]. the way one lives:– way lived (1)

G1053 **βιωτικός** ***biōtikos***, a. [3] [√*1050*]. (lesser things) of this life:– of life (1), such matters[S] (1), things of this life (1)

G1054 **βλαβερός** ***blaberos***, a. [1] [√*1055*]. harmful:– harmful (1)

G1055 **βλάπτω** ***blaptō***, v. [2] [→*1054*]. to hurt, injure:– hurt (1), injuring (1)

G1056 **βλαστάνω** ***blastanō***, v. [4] [→*1057, 1058, 1677*]. to sprout, bud:– budded (1), produced (1), sprouted (1), sprouts (1)

G1057 **βλαστάω** ***blastaō***, v. Not used in NIVEBC. [√*1056*]. to sprout, bud

G1058 **Βλάστος** ***Blastos***, n. pr. [1] [√*1056*]. Blastus, "*sprout [of a vine or branch]*":– Blastus (1)

G1059 **βλασφημέω** ***blasphēmeō***, v. [34] [→*1060, 1061; cf. 5774*]. to blaspheme, insult, slander, curse:– blaspheme (3), blaspheming (3), cursed (3), slander (3), blasphemed (2), blasphemes (2), heap abuse (2), hurled insults (2), abusive (1), blasphemy (1), bring into disrepute (1), denounced (1), heap abuse on (1), heaped abuse (1), hurled insults at (1), insulting (1), malign (1), slandered (1), slanderously (1), spoken blasphemy (1), spoken of as evil (1), utter (1)

G1060 **βλασφημία** ***blasphēmia***, n. [18] [√*1059*]. blasphemy, slander, malicious talk:– slander (8), blasphemy (5), blasphemous (2), blaspheme (1), blasphemies (1), malicious talk (1)

G1061 **βλάσφημος** ***blasphēmos***, a. [4] [√*1059*]. blasphemous, slanderous, abusive, evil, hurtful (speech); as a noun, a reviler, blasphemer:– abuse (1), abusive (1), blasphemer (1), blasphemous (1)

G1062 **βλέμμα** ***blemma***, n. [1] [√*1063*]. act of seeing:– saw (1)

G1063 **βλέπω** ***blepō***, v. [132] [→*329, 330, 611, 1062, 1332, 1838, 2098, 4315, 4587*]. to see, look at; to watch out, beware, pay attention:– see (51), saw (9), watch out (7), ever seeing (6 [+*1063*]), seen (6), see to it (5), seeing (5), sees (4), look (3), on guard (3), blind (2 [+*3590*]), careful (2), consider carefully (2), look at (2), unseen (2 [+*3590*]), already have (1), be very careful (1 [+*209*]), before eyes (1), consider (1), do (1), do yet have (1), exposed (1), facing (1), gaze (1), judging (1), looked in (1), looks (1), looks at (1), pay attention (1), pay attention to who they are (1 [+*1650, 4725, 476*]), sight (1), stared (1), take care (1), think (1), watch out for (1), with care (1 [+*4802*]), NDT (2)

G1064 **βλητέος** ***blēteos***, a. [1] [√*965*]. must be put:– must be poured (1)

G1065 **Βοανηργές** ***Boanērges***, l.[pr. n.] [1] Boanerges, "*sons of thunder*":– Boanerges (1)

G1066 **βοάω** ***boaō***, v. [12] [√*1068*]. to call, cry out, shout:– calling (4), called out (2), shouting (2), cried out (1), cry aloud (1), cry out (1), shrieks (1 [+*5889, 3489*])

G1067 **Βόες** ***Boes***, n. pr. [2] [→*1077, 1078*]. Boaz, "[perhaps] *in him is strength*":– Boaz (2)

G1068 **βοή** ***boē***, n. [1] [→*331, 1066, 1069, 1070, 1071, 2100, 2855*]. cry, shout:– cries (1)

G1069 **βοήθεια** ***boētheia***, n. [2] [√*1068*]. help; support (to hold something together with ropes or cables):– help (1), ropes (1)

G1070 **βοηθέω** ***boētheō***, v. [8] [√*1068*]. to help, come to the aid of:– help (6), helped (2)

G1071 **βοηθός** ***boēthos***, a. [1] [√*1068*]. helpful (one):– helper (1)

G1072 **βόθρος** ***bothros***, n. Not used in NIVEBC. [→*1073*]. pit, cistern

G1073 **βόθυνος** ***bothynos***, n. [3] [√*1072*]. pit, cistern:– pit (3)

G1074 **βολή** ***bolē***, n. [1] [√*965*]. throwing:– throw (1)

G1075 **βολίζω** ***bolizō***, v. [2] [√*965*]. to take a sounding (a nautical technical term):– took soundings (2)

G1076 **βολίς** ***bolis***, n. Not used in NIVEBC. [√*965*]. missile, arrow, javelin

G1077 **Βοόζ** ***Booz***, n. pr. Not used in NIVEBC. [√*1067*]. Boaz, "[perhaps] *in him is strength*"

G1078 **Βόος** ***Boos***, n. pr. [1] [√*1067*]. Boaz, "[perhaps] *in him is strength*":– Boaz (1)

G1079 **βόρβορος** ***borboros***, n. [1] mud, filth, slime:– mud (1)

G1080 **βορρᾶς** ***borras***, n. [2] the north:– north (2)

G1081 **βόσκω** ***boskō***, v. [9] [→*1083*]. to feed, tend; (pass.) to eat, graze:– feed (3), feeding (3), tending (3)

G1082 **Βοσόρ** ***Bosor***, n. pr. [1] [√*1027*]. Bosor:– Bezer (1)

G1083 **βοτάνη** ***botanē***, n. [1] [√*1081*]. crop (from any kind of plant or vegetation):– crop (1)

G1084 **βότρυς** ***botrys***, n. [1] grape cluster, bunch of grapes:– clusters of grapes (1)

G1085 **βουλευτής** ***bouleutēs***, n. [2] [√*1089*]. member of a council (an advisory or legislative body):– member of the council (2)

G1086 **βουλεύω** ***bouleuō***, v. [6] [√*1089*]. to make plans, consider, decide, plot:– consider (1), decided (1), made plans (1), make plans (1), plotted (1), NDT (1)

G1087 **βουλή** ***boulē***, n. [12] [√*1089*]. plan, purpose, will, decision:– purpose (5), will (2), decided (1 [+*5502*]), decision (1), motives (1), plan (1), planned (1 [+*1181*])

G1088 **βούλημα** ***boulēma***, n. [3] [√*1089*]. plan, will, choice:– choose (1), plan (1), will (1)

G1089 **βούλομαι** ***boulomai***, v. [37] [→*755, 1085, 1086, 1087, 1088, 2101, 2300, 4131, 5205, 5206, 5207*]. to wish, will, desire; to choose, determine, plan:– wanted (10), want (6), chooses (3), intended (2), like (2), want to (2), wanting (2), willing (2), chose (1), counsel (1), determined (1), determines (1), had in mind (1), liked (1), wants (1), will (1)

G1090 **βουνός** ***bounos***, n. [2] hill:– hill (1), hills (1)

G1091 **βοῦς** ***bous***, n. [8] ox, cattle:– ox (4), cattle (2), oxen (2)

G1092 **βραβεῖον** ***brabeion***, n. [2] [√*1093*]. prize (from a contest or foot race):– prize (2)

G1093 **βραβεύω** ***brabeuō***, v. [1] [→*1092, 2857*]. to rule:– rule (1)

G1094 **βραδύνω** ***bradynō***, v. [2] [√*1096*]. to delay, hesitate:– delayed (1), slow (1)

G1095 **βραδυπλοέω** ***bradyploeō***, v. [1] [√*1096 + 4434*]. to sail slowly:– made slow headway (1)

G1096 **βραδύς** ***bradys***, a. [3] [→*1094, 1095, 1097*]. slow:– slow (2), how slow (1 [+*3836, 2840*])

G1097 **βραδύτης** ***bradytēs***, n. [1] [√*1096*]. slowness:– slowness (1)

G1098 **βραχίων** ***brachiōn***, n. [3] [√*1099*]. arm; a figure of power and authority:– arm (2), power (1)

G1099 **βραχύς** ***brachys***, a. [7] [→*1098*]. little, short:– little (3), bite (1), for a little while (1), quite briefly (1 [+*1328*]), short (1)

G1100 **βρέφος** ***brephos***, n. [8] baby, infant:– baby (4), babies (2), infancy (1), newborn babies (1)

G1101 **βρέχω** ***brechō***, v. [7] [→*1104*]. to rain down (water or sulfur); to make wet:– rain (2), wet (2), rain (1 [+*5624*]), rained down (1), sends rain (1)

G1102 **βριμάομαι** ***brimaomai***, v. Not used in NIVEBC. [→*1839*]. to be indignant

G1103 **βροντή** ***brontē***, n. [12] thunder:– peals of thunder (4), thunder (4), thunders (3), thundered (1 [+*1181*])

G1104 **βροχή** ***brochē***, n. [2] [√*1101*]. rain:– rain (1), the (1)

G1105 **βρόχος** ***brochos***, n. [1] restriction, restraint (from the base meaning of a snare or noose, not found in the NT):– restrict (1 [+*2095*])

G1106 **βρυγμός** ***brygmos***, n. [7] [√*1107*]. gnashing, grinding:– gnashing (7)

G1107 **βρύχω** ***brychō***, v. [1] [→*1106*]. to gnash, grind:– gnashed (1)

G1108 **βρύω** ***bryō***, v. [1] to flow, pour forth:– flow (1)

G1109 **βρῶμα** ***brōma***, n. [17] [√*1048*]. food, what is eaten:– food (10), foods (2), what eat (2), eating (1), eating foods (1), solid food (1)

G1110 **βρώσιμος** ***brōsimos***, a. [1] [√*1048*]. eatable:– eat (1)

G1111 **βρῶσις** ***brōsis***, n. [11] [√*1048*]. consumable, food, rust, corrosion:– food (5), eating (2), vermin (2), eat (1), meal (1)

G1112 **βυθίζω** ***bythizō***, v. [2] [√*1113*]. (act.) to plunge; (pass.) to sink:– plunge (1), sink (1)

G1113 **βυθός** ***bythos***, n. [1] [→*12, 1112*]. open sea, the deep:– open sea (1)

G1114 **βυρσεύς** ***byrseus***, n. [3] tanner:– tanner (3)

G1115 **βύσσινος** ***byssinos***, a. [5] [√*1116*]. made of fine linen, a product of the flax plant:– fine linen (5)

G1116 **βύσσος** ***byssos***, n. [1] [→*1115, 3327*]. fine linen:– fine linen (1)

G1117 **βωμός** ***bōmos***, n. [1] [√*326*]. altar:– altar (1)

G1118 **γ** ***g***, letter. Not used in NIVEBC. letter of the Greek alphabet; also used as the numeral "3" in the superscriptions of some Greek manuscripts

G1119 **Γαββαθα** ***Gabbatha***, n. pr. [1] Gabbatha, "[poss.] *height, ridge*":– Gabbatha (1)

G1120 **Γαβριήλ** ***Gabriēl***, n. pr. [2] Gabriel, "*[strong] man of God [El]*":– Gabriel (2)

G1121 **γάγγραινα** ***gangraina***, n. [1] gangrene:– gangrene (1)

G1122 **Γάδ** ***Gad***, n. pr. [1] Gad, "*fortune*":– Gad (1)

G1123 **Γαδαρηνός** ***Gadarēnos***, a. pr. g. [1] Gadarene, "*from Gadara*":– Gadarenes (1)

G1124 **Γάζα**[1] ***Gaza***[1], n. pr. [1] Gaza, "*strong*":– Gaza (1)

G1125 **γάζα**[2] ***gaza***[2], n. [1] [→*1126*]. treasury:– treasury (1)

G1126 **γαζοφυλάκιον** ***gazophylakion***, n. [5] [√*1125 + 5875*]. treasury, place where offerings are put:– place where the offerings were put (2), temple treasury (2), treasury (1)

G1127 **Γάϊος** ***Gaios***, n. pr. [5] [√*1178*]. Gaius:– Gaius (5)

G1128 **γάλα** ***gala***, n. [5] milk:– milk (5)

G1129 **Γαλάτης** ***Galatēs***, n. pr. g. [1] [√*1130*]. Galatian, "*from Galatia*":– Galatians (1)

G1130 **Γαλατία** ***Galatia***, n. pr. [4] [→*1129, 1131*]. Galatia:– Galatia (3), Galatian (1)

G1131 **Γαλατικός** ***Galatikos***, a. pr. g. [2] [√*1130*]. Galatian:– Galatia (1), of Galatia (1)

G1132 **γαλήνη** ***galēnē***, n. [3] calm:– calm (3)

G1133 **Γαλιλαία** ***Galilaia***, n. pr. [61] [→*1134*]. Galilee, "*ring, circle, hence region*":– Galilee (61)

G1134 **Γαλιλαῖος** ***Galilaios***, a. pr. g. [11] [√*1133*]. Galilean, "*from Galilee*":– Galileans (5), Galilean (4), of Galilee (2)

G1135 **Γαλλία** ***Gallia***, n. pr. Not used in NIVEBC. Gaul

G1136 **Γαλλίων** ***Galliōn***, n. pr. [3] Gallio:– Gallio (3)

G1137 **Γαμαλιήλ** ***Gamaliēl***, n. pr. [2] Gamaliel, "*recompense of God [El]*":– Gamaliel (2)

G1138 **γαμέω** ***gameō***, v. [28] [√*1141*]. to marry:– marry (12), marries (7), married (6), marrying (2), got married (1 [+*1222*])

G1139 **γαμίζω** ***gamizō***, v. [7] [√*1141*]. to give in marriage, marry:– given in marriage (4), giving in marriage (1), marries (1), marry (1)

G1140 **γαμίσκω** ***gamiskō***, v. [1] [√*1141*]. (pass.) to be given in marriage:– given in marriage (1)

G1141 **γάμος** ***gamos***, n. [16] [→*23, 1138, 1139, 1140,*

1432, 1433, 1679, 1680, 2102]. wedding banquet (a festive time in the community):– wedding (6), wedding banquet (5), banquet (2), marriage (1), wedding feast (1), wedding hall (1)

G1142 **γάρ** ***gar***, c. [1035] [→ *5521*]. shows inference or continuation: for, because, indeed, but:– for (515), because (85), and (8), but (8), now (7), since (7), in fact (6), indeed (4), so (4), after all (3), as for (3), why (3), as (2), yes (2), again (1), and (1 [+*4048*]), and indeed (1), as it is (1), because of (1), even (1), even so (1 [+*2779*]), even though (1 [+*3525*]), for example (1), for this reason (1), for this very reason (1 [+*1650, 4047*]), how (1 [+*3590*]), indeed (1 [+*2093, 237*]), moreover (1), no doubt (1), or (1), rather (1), suppose (1), surely (1), that (1), the fact is (1), this is why (1 [+*1328, 4047*]), though (1), to be sure (1), yet (1), you see (1), NDT (352)

G1143 **γαστήρ** ***gastēr***, n. [9] belly, womb, gluttony:– pregnant (6 [+*1877, 2400*]), conceive (1 [+*1877, 2400*]), conceive (1 [+*5197, 1877*]), gluttons (1)

G1144 **Γαύδη** ***Gaudē***, n. pr. Not used in NIVEBC. [√*cf. 3007*]. Gauda

G1145 **γέ** ***ge***, pt. emph. [25] [→ *2301, 2781, 2793, 3529, 3591, 3615, 4007, 5522*]. emphatic particle: indeed, surely:– do[S] (2 [+*3590*]), otherwise (2 [+*1623, 1254, 3590*]), really (2), yet (2), and (1 [+*247, 2779*]), because (1 [+*1623, 2779*]), even (1 [+*2779*]), perhaps (1 [+*1623, 726*]), surely (1 [+*1623*]), surely (1 [+*247*]), then (1), then (1 [+*726*]), though (1 [+*2779*]), thus (1 [+*726*]), when (1 [+*1623*]), NDT (6)

G1146 **Γεδεών** ***Gedeōn***, n. pr. [1] Gideon, "*one who cuts, hacks*":– Gideon (1)

G1147 **γέεννα** ***geenna***, n. [12] Gehenna, hell, "*Valley of Hinnom*":– hell (12)

G1148 **Γεθσημανῆ** ***Gethsēmanē***, n. pr. Not used in NIVEBC. [√*cf. 1149*]. Gethsemane, "*olive oil press*"

G1149 **Γεθσημανί** ***Gethsēmani***, n. pr. [2] [√*cf. 1148*]. Gethsemane, "*olive oil press*":– Gethsemane (2)

G1150 **γείτων** ***geitōn***, n. [4] neighbor:– neighbors (4)

G1151 **γελάω** ***gelaō***, v. [2] [→ *1152, 2860*]. to laugh:– laugh (2)

G1152 **γέλως** ***gelōs***, n. [1] [√*1151*]. laughter:– laughter (1)

G1153 **γεμίζω** ***gemizō***, v. [9] [√*1154*]. to fill:– filled (4), fill (2), filled with (1), full (1), swamped (1)

G1154 **γέμω** ***gemō***, v. [11] [→ *1153, 1203*]. to be full:– covered with (3), full (3), full of (3), filled with (2)

G1155 **γενεά** ***genea***, n. [43] [√*1181*]. generation, one's own kind or race, descendant; fig., age, period of time (as in "to all generations"):– generation (29), generations (5), descendants (1), it[S] (1 [+*3836, 4047*]), kind (1), past (1 [+*4233*]), times (1), NDT (4)

G1156 **γενεαλογέω** ***genealogeō***, v. [1] [√*1181 + 3306*]. to trace genealogical descent:– trace descent (1)

G1157 **γενεαλογία** ***genealogia***, n. [2] [√*1181 + 3306*]. genealogy, lineage:– genealogies (2)

G1158 **γενέθλια** ***genethlia***, n. Not used in NIVEBC. [√*1181*]. birthday (celebration)

G1159 **γενέθλιος** ***genethlios***, a. Not used in NIVEBC. [√*1181*]. pertaining to birth, birthday

G1160 **γενέσια** ***genesia***, n. [2] [√*1181*]. birthday (a day that was celebrated):– birthday (2)

G1161 **γένεσις** ***genesis***, n. [5] [√*1181*]. birth; genealogy, descent; (course of one's) life:– birth (2), face (1 [+*4725, 3836*]), genealogy (1 [+*1047*]), life (1)

G1162 **γενετή** ***genetē***, n. [1] [√*1181*]. birth:– birth (1)

G1163 **γένημα** ***genēma***, n. [4] [√*1181*]. fruit, product, yield, harvest:– fruit (3), harvest (1)

G1164 **γεννάω** ***gennaō***, v. [97] [√*1181*]. to become the father of; to bear, give birth to; (pass.) to be conceived, born:– father (45), born (35), gives birth to (2), bear (1), bears children (1), became son[S] (1), birth (1), bore (1), born (1 [+*1666, 3120, 3613*]), came descendants (1), child (1), children (1), conceived (1), gave birth to (1), had (1), mother (1), native (1 [+*1877, 4005*]), produce (1)

G1165 **γέννημα** ***gennēma***, n. [4] [√*1181*]. offspring, brood:– brood (4)

G1166 **Γεννησαρέτ** ***Gennēsaret***, n. pr. [3] Gennesaret:– Gennesaret (3)

G1167 **γέννησις** ***gennēsis***, n. Not used in NIVEBC. [√*1181*]. birth

G1168 **γεννητός** ***gennētos***, a. [2] [√*1181*]. pertaining to birth; "those born among women" means "all humankind":– born (2)

G1169 **γένος** ***genos***, n. [20] [√*1181*]. family, offspring; nation, people, native (of a region); classification or kind:– people (4), offspring (3), different kinds (2), family (2), native (2), born (1), children (1 [+*5626*]), fellow Jews (1), kind (1), kinds (1), sorts (1), NDT (1)

G1170 **Γερασηνός** ***Gerasēnos***, a. pr. g. [3] [√*cf. 1171*]. Gerasene, "*from Gerasa*":– Gerasenes (3)

G1171 **Γεργεσηνός** ***Gergesēnos***, a. pr. g. Not used in NIVEBC. [√*cf. 1170*]. Gergesene, "*from Gergesa*"

G1172 **γερουσία** ***gerousia***, n. [1] [√*1173*]. assembly of the elders:– assembly of elders (1)

G1173 **γέρων** ***gerōn***, n. [1] [→ *1172; cf. 1179*]. old person:– old (1)

G1174 **γεύομαι** ***geuomai***, v. [15] to taste, eat, partake of (implying enjoyment of the experience):– taste (6), tasted (4), eat (2), ate (1), get a taste (1), tasting (1)

G1175 **γεωργέω** ***geōrgeō***, v. [1] [√*1178 + 2240*]. to farm, cultivate:– farmed (1)

G1176 **γεώργιον** ***geōrgion***, n. [1] [√*1178 + 2240*]. (farmer's) field:– field (1)

G1177 **γεωργός** ***geōrgos***, n. [19] [√*1178 + 2240*]. farmer, tenant farmer, share-cropper:– tenants (12), farmers (3), farmer (2), gardener (1), them[S] (1 [+*3836*])

G1178 **γῆ** ***gē***, n. [250] [→ *333, 1127, 1175, 1176, 1177, 2103*]. earth, world, country, region; land, ground, soil:– earth (151), land (31), ground (19), soil (13), Egypt (5 [+*131*]), shore (5), Sodom (2 [+*5047*]), country (2), earthly (2 [+*2093, 3836*]), region (2), world (2), Canaan (1 [+*5913*]), Midian (1 [+*3409*]), ashore (1 [+*1650, 3836*]), ashore (1 [+*2093, 3836*]), countryside (1), earthly (1), earth's (1), its[S] (1 [+*3836*]), landed (1 [+*609, 1650, 3836*]), landed (1 [+*2093, 3836, 2262*]), landed (1 [+*2262, 2093, 3836*]), reptiles (1 [+*2260, 3836*]), them[S] (1 [+*3836, 2997, 2093, 3836*]), world's (1), NDT (2)

G1179 **γῆρας** ***gēras***, n. [1] [→ *1180; cf. 1173*]. old age:– old age (1)

G1180 **γηράσκω** ***gēraskō***, v. [2] [√*1179*]. to grow old, age:– old (1), outdated (1)

G1181 **γίνομαι** ***ginomai***, v. [667] [→ *37, 38, 254, 335, 614, 786, 1155, 1156, 1157, 1158, 1159, 1160, 1161, 1162, 1163, 1164, 1165, 1167, 1168, 1169, 1188, 1189, 1204, 1335, 1681, 2104, 2302, 2441, 3666, 4098, 4100, 4134, 4588, 4591, 5149, 5150, 5151, 5219, 5449, 5450*]. to be, become, happen; to come into existence, be born. It is used in certain contexts to introduce a new section or paragraph in a narrative in Hebrew narrative style: and then, and it came to pass:– was (51), become (46), be (41), came (35), happened (28), became (25), were (19), done (14), is (14), happen (13), made (12), been (11), performed (8), take place (8), are (6), come (6), took place (6), become (5 [+*1650*]), broke out (5), do (5), appeared (4), by no means (4 [+*3590*]), get (4), making (4), not at all (4 [+*3590*]), becoming (3), born (3), comes (3), happening (3), happens (3), reached (3 [+*2093*]), turned into (3), absolutely not (2 [+*3590*]), approached (2), arose (2), arrived (2), became (2 [+*1650*]), becomes (2), being (2), brought (2), came up (2), certainly not (2 [+*3590*]), done (2 [+*4123*]), equaled (2), experienced (2), fell (2), follow example (2 [+*3629*]), heard[S] (2), later (2), lived (2), occurred (2), once (2 [+*1254*]), one day (2 [+*1254*]), promised (2 [+*2039*]), seized (2 [+*2093*]), share in (2 [+*5171*]), stood (2), surpassed (2 [+*1869*]), taken place (2), turned (2), went (2), God forbid[S] (1 [+*3590*]), accomplished (1), afoot (1), after (1), agreed (1 [+*1506, 3924*]), am (1), approached (1 [+*2453*]), approaching (1 [+*1584*]), arriving (1), as a result of (1), bear (1 [+*1666*]), became (1 [+*1639*]), become (1 [+*1650*]), been (1 [+*1639*]), belong (1), brought about (1), came about (1), changed (1 [+*2283*]), come true (1), complained (1 [+*1198*]), dawn (1 [+*2465, 3516*]), daybreak (1 [+*2465*]), daybreak (1 [+*2465, 2002*]), decided (1 [+*1191*]), developed (1), did (1), died (1 [+*2505*]), died (1 [+*3738*]), disappeared from sight (1 [+*908*]), do (1 [+*4475*]), do (1 [+*1869*]), does (1 [+*4048*]), doing (1), fear (1 [+*1873*]), fell headlong (1 [+*4568*]), filled with (1), filled with (1 [+*2093*]), finds (1 [+*2351*]), finished (1), fish (1 [+*243*]), fright (1 [+*1873*]), fulfilled (1), gain (1), go (1), going on (1), grant (1), granted (1), grew (1), grown up (1 [+*3489*]), had (1), happened (1 [+*1639*]), has sexual relations with (1), have (1), heard (1 [+*212*]), heard about (1 [+*1196*]), held (1), here (1), imitate (1 [+*3629*]), in progress (1), in the case of (1), in the morning (1 [+*2465*]), in unison (1 [+*5889, 1651*]), introduced (1), join together in following example (1 [+*5213*]), lead to (1), learned about (1 [+*5745*]), life (1), look (1), looked so much like (1 [+*6059*]), loses saltiness (1 [+*383*]), loved so much (1 [+*28*]), make (1), marries (1), marry[S] (1 [+*4048*]), moths eaten (1 [+*4963*]), murdered (1 [+*5838*]), neared (1 [+*1581*]), need (1 [+*5970, 2400*]), never (1 [+*3590*]), never (1 [+*3590*]), next (1), no longer try (1 [+*3821*]), now (1 [+*2779*]), obey (1 [+*5675*]), on (1), once (1 [+*2779*]), one day (1 [+*2779*]), owns (1), perform (1), perform (1 [+*5679*]), perform (1 [+*1328, 3836, 5931*]), performed (1 [+*1328*]), performed (1 [+*1328, 3836, 5931*]), performing (1), planned (1 [+*1087*]), plotted (1 [+*2101*]), praying (1 [+*4666*]), proved (1), proved to be (1), rang out (1), reach (1 [+*1650*]), reached (1 [+*1650*]), reaching (1 [+*2093*]), receive (1), result in (1 [+*1666*]), revealed (1 [+*1871*]), rewards (1 [+*3633*]), said[S] (1), served as (1), set (1), settled (1), shared in (1 [+*3581*]), show (1 [+*5745*]), spent (1), split (1), spoken[S] (1), stand firm (1 [+*1612*]), starting (1), stop (1 [+*3590*]), succeeded (1), supply (1 [+*1650*]), take charge of (1 [+*2062*]), taken (1), that evening (1 [+*4068*]), the time came (1), thinking (1 [+*3836, 5856*]), thundered (1 [+*1103*]), told (1 [+*4639*]), trembled with fear (1 [+*1958*]), trembling (1 [+*1958*]), turn (1), turned (1 [+*1650*]), turned out (1), undergoes (1 [+*3581*]), unequaled (1 [+*3888, 4024*]), unequaled (1 [+*3888, 4024, 5525*]), united with (1 [+*5242*]), used (1 [+*1877*]), visit (1 [+*4639*]), wake up (1 [+*1213*]), went on (1), wept (1 [+*2653, 3088*]), woke up (1 [+*2031*]), work together (1 [+*5301*]), NDT (66)

G1182 **γινώσκω** ***ginōskō***, v. [221] [→ *51, 52, 53, 57, 58, 183, 336, 341, 342, 1191, 1192, 1193, 1194, 1195, 1196, 1336, 1337, 1338, 2105, 2106, 2841, 2861, 4589, 4590, 5152*]. to know, come to know, recognize, understand; to have sexual relations:– know (99), understand (17), known (12), knows (12), knew (11), find out (6), learned (6), knowing (4), recognize (4), recognized (4), aware (3), aware of (3), found out (3), knowledge (2), made known (2), sure of (2), understood (2), acknowledge (1), am a virgin (1 [+*467, 4024*]), be (1), clear (1), concluded (1), consummate marriage (1), discover (1), evidence (1), evident (1), felt (1), get at truth (1 [+*855*]), had (1), had[S] (1), keep in mind (1), know how (1), knows about (1), learn (1), learned about (1), mark (1), realize (1), realized (1), receive news (1), regarded (1), remember (1), saw (1), see (1), speak (1), sure (1), unaware (1 [+*4024*])

G1183 **γλεῦκος** ***gleukos***, n. [1] [√*1184*]. (sweet) wine:– wine (1)

G1184 **γλυκύς** ***glykys***, a. [4] [→ *1183*]. sweet, fresh (water):– fresh (2), sweet (2)

G1185 **γλῶσσα** ***glōssa***, n. [50] [→ *1186, 2280, 2303*]. tongue; language; sometimes refers to the supernatural gift of tongues (see *2255*):– tongues (21), tongue (19), language (5), languages (2), speaking in tongues (1), speech (1), NDT (1)

G1186 **γλωσσόκομον** ***glōssokomon***, n. [2] [√*1185 + 3180*]. container for money:– money (1), money bag (1)

G1187 **γναφεύς** ***gnapheus***, n. [1] [→ *47; cf. 3117*]. bleacher, fuller, one who cleans and sizes woolen cloth:– anyone[S] (1)

G1188 **γνήσιος** ***gnēsios***, a. [4] [√*1181*]. true, loyal, sincere, genuine:– true (3), sincerity (1)

G1189 **γνησίως** ***gnēsiōs***, adv. [1] [√*1181*]. genuinely, sincerely:– genuine (1)

G1190 **γνόφος** ***gnophos***, n. [1] darkness:– darkness (1)

G1191 **γνώμη** ***gnōmē***, n. [9] [√*1182*]. purpose, resolve; judgment; consent:– judgment (3), purpose (2), agreeing (1 [+*4472, 1651*]), consent (1), decided (1 [+*1181*]), thought (1)

G1192 **γνωρίζω** ***gnōrizō***, v. [25] [√*1182*]. to make known, tell, reveal:– made known (8), make known (5), know (4), tell (3), present (1), remind (1), spread (1), told (1), told about (1)

G1193 **γνώριμος** ***gnōrimos***, a. Not used in NIVEBC. [√*1182*]. acquainted with, known to

G1194 **γνῶσις** ***gnōsis***, n. [29] [√*1182*]. knowledge, understanding:– knowledge (26), considerate (1 [+*2848*]), knowing (1), understanding (1)

G1195 **γνώστης** ***gnōstēs***, n. [1] [√*1182*]. one well acquainted with, expert in:– well acquainted (1)

G1196 **γνωστός** ***gnōstos***, a. [15] [√*1182*]. known:– known (6), know (4 [+*1639*]), explain (1 [+*1639*]), friends (1), heard about (1 [+*1181*]), knew (1), notable (1)

G1197 **γογγύζω** ***gongyzō***, v. [8] [→ *1198, 1199, 1339*]. to grumble, complain, mutter:– grumble (3), grumbling (2), complained (1), did (1), whispering (1)

G1198 **γογγυσμός** ***gongysmos***, n. [4] [√*1197*]. complaint, grumbling; whispering, private talk:– grumbling (2), complained (1 [+*1181*]), whispering (1)

G1199 **γογγυστής** ***gongystēs***, n. [1] [√*1197*]. grumbler, complainer:– grumblers (1)

G1200 **γόης** ***goēs***, n. [1] imposter:– impostors (1)

G1201 **Γολγοθᾶ** ***Golgotha***, n. pr. [3] Golgotha, "*skull*":– Golgotha (3)

G1202 **Γόμορρα** ***Gomorra***, n. pr. [4] Gomorrah, "*to overwhelm with water*":– Gomorrah (4)

G1203 **γόμος** ***gomos***, n. [3] [√*1154*]. cargo, freight:– cargoes (2), cargo (1)

G1204 **γονεύς** ***goneus***, n. [20] [√*1181*]. (pl.) parents:– parents (20)

G1205 **γόνυ** ***gony***, n. [12] [→ *1206*]. knee; "to bend the knee" means "to kneel (in submission or worship)":– knees (5), knee (3), knelt down (2 [+*5502, 3836*]), kneel (1 [+*2828, 3836*]), knelt (1 [+*5502, 3836*])

G1206 γονυπετέω *gonypeteō*, v. [4] [√ *1205 + 4406*]. to kneel (before in submission or worship):– knelt (2), fell on knees before (1), on knees (1)

G1207 γράμμα *gramma*, n. [14] [√ *1211*]. letter (of the alphabet); document, Scriptures, written code; education:– letters (3), written code (3), bill (2), letter (2), get learning (1 [*+3857*]), learning (1), scriptures (1), wrote (1)

G1208 γραμματεύς *grammateus*, n. [63] [√ *1211*]. teacher or expert in the law, scholar, scribe, city clerk:– teachers of the law (57), teacher of the law (3), city clerk (1), man[S] (1), teachers (1)

G1209 γραπτός *graptos*, a. [1] [√ *1211*]. written:– written (1)

G1210 γραφή *graphē*, n. [50] [√ *1211*]. (s.) a passage of Scripture; (pl.) the collective whole of the Scriptures; holy, authoritative collection of writings:– scripture (27), scriptures (18), passage of scripture (3), writings (2)

G1211 γράφω *graphō*, v. [190] [→ *63, 615, 616, 1207, 1208, 1209, 1210, 1582, 2107, 2108, 2863, 4592, 5681, 5934*]. to write:– written (104), write (37), wrote (16), writing (15), described (2), make[S] (2), recorded (2), write down (2), written down (2), wrote down (2), prepared[S] (1), read (1 [*+1639*]), sent letter (1), write an account (1), writes (1), wrote about (1)

G1212 γραώδης *graōdēs*, a. [1] [√ *1626*]. old wives' tale:– old wives (1)

G1213 γρηγορέω *grēgoreō*, v. [22] [√ *1586*]. to keep watch, be on guard:– keep watch (8), watch (3), awake (2), on guard (2), kept watch (1), of sober mind (1), stays awake (1), wake up (1), wake up (1 [*+1181*]), watchful (1), watching (1)

G1214 γυμνάζω *gymnazō*, v. [4] [√ *1218*]. to train, exercise:– experts (1 [*+2840*]), train (1), trained (1), trained (1 [*+2400*])

G1215 γυμνασία *gymnasia*, n. [1] [√ *1218*]. training, exercise:– training (1)

G1216 γυμνητεύω *gymnēteuō*, v. Not used in NIVEBC. [√ *1218*]. to be poorly dressed

G1217 γυμνιτεύω *gymniteuō*, v. [1] [√ *1218*]. to be in ragged clothing, poorly dressed:– in rags (1)

G1218 γυμνός *gymnos*, a. [15] [→ *1214, 1215, 1216, 1217, 1219*]. naked, without clothing; needing (more or better) clothing:– naked (6), needed clothes (2), needing clothes (2), just (1), taken it off (1), uncovered (1), wearing nothing (1 [*+4314, 2093*]), without clothes (1)

G1219 γυμνότης *gymnotēs*, n. [3] [√ *1218*]. nakedness, insufficiently clothed:– nakedness (2), naked (1)

G1220 γυναικάριον *gynaikarion*, n. [1] [√ *1222*]. weak-willed woman, "little woman":– gullible women (1)

G1221 γυναικεῖος *gynaikeios*, a. [1] [√ *1222*]. feminine, weaker:– wives (1)

G1222 γυνή *gynē*, n. [216] [→ *1220, 1221*]. woman; wife:– woman (95), wife (59), women (31), wives (11), faithful to his wife (3 [*+1651, 467*]), widow (3), bride (1), faithful to her husband (1 [*+1651, 467*]), got married (1 [*+1138*]), married (1 [*+2400*]), married (1 [*+3284*]), mother (1), she[S] (1 [*+3836*]), such a commitment[S] (1), were married (1 [*+2400*]), widow (1 [*+5939*]), wife's (1), woman's (1), women's (1), NDT (1)

G1223 Γώγ *Gōg*, n. pr. [1] Gog:– Gog (1)

G1224 γωνία *gōnia*, n. [9] [→ *214, 5481*]. corner; cornerstone, capstone, keystone:– cornerstone (5 [*+3051*]), corners (3), corner (1)

G1225 δ *d*, letter. Not used in NIVEBC. letter of the Greek alphabet

G1226 Δαβίδ *Dabid*, n. pr. Not used in NIVEBC. [√ *1253*]. David

G1227 δαιμονίζομαι *daimonizomai*, v. [13] [√ *1228*]. to be demon-possessed:– demon-possessed (11), possessed by a demon (1), possessed by demons (1)

G1228 δαιμόνιον *daimonion*, n. [63] [→ *1227, 1229, 1230, 1272, 1273*]. demon, (pagan) god:– demons (41), demon (15), demon-possessed (5 [*+2400*]), demonic (1), gods (1)

G1229 δαιμονιώδης *daimoniōdēs*, a. [1] [√ *1228 + 1626*]. of the devil, demonic:– demonic (1)

G1230 δαίμων *daimōn*, n. [1] [√ *1228*]. demon, evil spirit:– demons (1)

G1231 δάκνω *daknō*, v. [1] to bite:– bite (1)

G1232 δάκρυον *dakryon*, n. [10] [→ *1233*]. teardrop:– tears (8), tear (2)

G1233 δακρύω *dakryō*, v. [1] [√ *1232*]. to weep, shed tears:– wept (1)

G1234 δακτύλιος *daktylios*, n. [1] [√ *1235*]. (finger) ring:– ring (1)

G1235 δάκτυλος *daktylos*, n. [8] [→ *1234, 5993; cf. 1259*]. finger:– finger (7), fingers (1)

G1236 Δαλμανουθά *Dalmanoutha*, n. pr. [1] Dalmanutha:– Dalmanutha (1)

G1237 Δαλματία *Dalmatia*, n. pr. [1] Dalmatia, "*deceitful*":– Dalmatia (1)

G1238 δαμάζω *damazō*, v. [4] [→ *1239*]. to tame, subdue, control:– tamed (2), subdue (1), tame (1)

G1239 δάμαλις *damalis*, n. [1] [√ *1238*]. heifer, young cow:– heifer (1)

G1240 Δάμαρις *Damaris*, n. pr. [1] Damaris:– Damaris (1)

G1241 Δαμασκηνός *Damaskēnos*, a. pr. g. [1] [√ *1242*]. Damascene, "*from Damascus*":– of Damascenes (1)

G1242 Δαμασκός *Damaskos*, n. pr. [15] [→ *1241*]. Damascus:– Damascus (15)

G1243 Δάν *Dan*, n. pr. Not used in NIVEBC. Dan

G1244 δανείζω *daneizō*, v. Not used in NIVEBC. [√ *1249*]. to lend, (mid.) to borrow

G1245 δάνειον *daneion*, n. [1] [√ *1249*]. debt, loan:– debt (1)

G1246 δανειστής *daneistēs*, n. Not used in NIVEBC. [√ *1249*]. moneylender, creditor

G1247 δανίζω *danizō*, v. [4] [√ *1249*]. to lend; (mid.) to borrow:– lend (3), borrow (1)

G1248 Δανιήλ *Daniēl*, n. pr. [1] Daniel, "*God [El] is my judge*":– Daniel (1)

G1249 δάνιον *danion*, n. Not used in NIVEBC. [→ *1244, 1245, 1246, 1247, 1250*]. debt, loan

G1250 δανιστής *danistēs*, n. [1] [√ *1249*]. moneylender, creditor:– moneylender (1)

G1251 δαπανάω *dapanaō*, v. [5] [√ *1252*]. to spend; to pay expenses:– spent (2), pay expenses (1), spend (1), spend everything have (1)

G1252 δαπάνη *dapanē*, n. [1] [→ *78, 1251, 1682, 4655*]. cost, expense:– cost (1)

G1253 Δαυίδ *Dauid*, n. pr. [59] [→ *1226*]. David, "*beloved one*":– David (57), David's (2)

G1254 δέ *de*, pt. & c. [2781] [→ *2022, 2023, 2024, 2025, 3592, 3593, 3594, 3595, 3596, 3598, 3599, 4027, 4028, 4029, 4030, 4031, 4032*]. but, and, then, rather:– but (665), and (280), then (89), now (88), so (40), however (24), yet (18), also (6), instead (6), meanwhile (6), or (5), another (4 [*+4005*]), even (4), nevertheless (4), while (4), and yet (3), as it is (3 [*+3814*]), at this (3), otherwise (3 [*+1623, 3590*]), another (2), even though (2), once (2), once (2 [*+1181*]), one day (2 [*+1181*]), otherwise (2 [*+1623, 3590, 1145*]), still (2), though (2), too (2), what is more (2 [*+4024, 3667, 247, 2779*]), a (1 [*+4005, 323*]), after this (1), again (1), all (1), and now (1), and moreover (1), and still (1), another (1 [*+3836*]), as it is (1 [*+3814, 2779*]), at this point (1 [*+4047*]), at other times (1 [*+4047*]), because (1), but as surely as (1), but even (1), but when (1), but (1 [*+3437*]), but also (1), but yet (1), by now (1), finally (1), for (1), in addition (1), instead (1 [*+3814*]), just (1), moreover (1), then (1 [*+2779*]), moreover (1 [*+2779*]), now that (1), only (1), other (1 [*+257*]), other (1 [*+4005*]), others (1 [*+3836*]), others (1 [*+3836*]), others (1 [*+4005*]), rather (2), rather (1 [*+3437*]), rather (1 [*+3437*]), since (1), some (1 [*+257*]), still others (1 [*+3836*]), still another (1), such that (1), the former (1 [*+3836*]), the other (1 [*+4005*]), whatever (1 [*+4005, 323*]), whatever (1 [*+1877, 4005, 323*]), when (1), yes (1), NDT (1457)

G1255 δέησις *deēsis*, n. [18] [√ *1289*]. prayer, request, petition:– prayers (6), prayer (4), pray (2 [*+4472*]), praying (2), ask for help (1), petition (1), petitions (1), requests (1)

G1256 δεῖ *dei*, v. imper. [101] [√ *1313*]. it is a must, it is necessary (one should, ought):– must (56), had to (9), ought to (7), ought (6), should (5), should have (5), have to (4), belong (1), due (1), for (1 [*+1877, 4005*]), is to (1), necessary (1), should be (1), shouldn't (1 [*+4024*]), NDT (2)

G1257 δεῖγμα *deigma*, n. [1] [→ *1258, 1891, 4136, 5682; cf. 1259*]. example:– example (1)

G1258 δειγματίζω *deigmatizō*, v. [2] [√ *1257*]. to expose to public disgrace; to make a spectacle of:– expose to public disgrace (1), made a spectacle (1)

G1259 δείκνυμι *deiknymi*, v. [33] [→ *344, 345, 617, 618, 1260, 1892, 1893, 2109, 5683, 5684; cf. 1235, 1257*]. to show, explain, make known:– show (19), showed (6), shown (3), bring about (1), explain (1), show to prove authority (1), showing (1), shows (1)

G1260 δεικνύω *deiknyō*, v. Not used in NIVEBC. [√ *1259*]. to show, point out, make known

G1261 δειλία *deilia*, n. [1] [√ *1290*]. timidity, cowardice:– timid (1)

G1262 δειλιάω *deiliaō*, v. [1] [√ *1290*]. to be afraid, cowardly, timid:– afraid (1)

G1263 δειλινός *deilinos*, a. Not used in NIVEBC. in the afternoon, toward evening

G1264 δειλός *deilos*, a. [3] [√ *1290*]. afraid, cowardly, timid:– afraid (1), cowardly (1), so afraid (1)

G1265 δεῖνα *deina*, n. [1] a certain one, a person or thing one cannot or does not wish to name:– certain (1)

G1266 δεινός *deinos*, a. Not used in NIVEBC. [√ *1290*]. fearful, terrible

G1267 δεινῶς *deinōs*, adv. [2] [√ *1290*]. terribly, fiercely:– fiercely (1), terribly (1)

G1268 δειπνέω *deipneō*, v. [4] [√ *1270*]. to eat supper, dine:– supper (2), eat (1), supper (1 [*+5515*])

G1269 δειπνοκλήτωρ *deipnoklētōr*, n. Not used in NIVEBC. [√ *1270 + 2813*]. host

G1270 δεῖπνον *deipnon*, n. [16] [→ *1268, 1269, 1271*]. banquet, supper, evening meal:– banquet (4), supper (4), banquets (3), dinner (2), evening meal (1), meal (1), suppers (1)

G1271 δεῖπνος *deipnos*, n. Not used in NIVEBC. [√ *1270*]. banquet, supper, evening meal

G1272 δεισιδαιμονία *deisidaimonia*, n. [1] [√ *1290 + 1228*]. religion:– religion (1)

G1273 δεισιδαίμων *deisidaimōn*, a. [1] [√ *1290 + 1228*]. (very) religious:– very religious (1)

G1274 δέκα *deka*, n. num. [25] [→ *619, 620, 1275, 1276, 1277, 1278, 1279, 1280, 1281, 1282, 1557, 1558, 1559, 1894, 1895, 4298, 5476*]. ten:– ten (24), eighteen (1 [*+2779, 3893*])

G1275 δεκαδύο *dekadyo*, n. num. Not used in NIVEBC. [√ *1274 + 1545*]. twelve

G1276 δεκαέξ *dekaex*, n. num. Not used in NIVEBC. [√ *1274 + 1971*]. sixteen

G1277 δεκαοκτώ *dekaoktō*, n. num. [2] [√ *1274 + 3893*]. eighteen:– eighteen (2)

G1278 δεκαπέντε *dekapente*, n. num. [3] [√ *1274 + 4297*]. fifteen:– fifteen (1), less than two miles (1 [*+6055, 5084*]), ninety feet deep (1 [*+3976*])

G1279 Δεκάπολις *Dekapolis*, n. pr. [3] [√ *1274 + 4484*]. Decapolis, "*[league of] ten cities*":– Decapolis (3)

G1280 δεκατέσσαρες *dekatessares*, n. num. [5] [√ *1274 + 5475*]. fourteen:– fourteen (5)

G1281 δέκατος *dekatos*, a. num. [7] [√ *1274*]. tenth in a series of things or events; as a noun, the tenth part, ten percent of something, tithe:– tenth (6), four in the afternoon (1 [*+6052*])

G1282 δεκατόω *dekatoō*, v. [2] [√ *1274*]. to collect a tenth; (pass.) to pay a tenth:– collected a tenth (1), paid the tenth (1)

G1283 δεκτός *dektos*, a. [5] [√ *1312*]. acceptable, favorable:– favor (2), acceptable (1), accepted (1), accepts (1 [*+1639*])

G1284 δελεάζω *deleazō*, v. [3] [√ *1515*]. to entice, seduce, lure:– entice (1), enticed (1), seduce (1)

G1285 δένδρον *dendron*, n. [25] tree:– tree (17), trees (8)

G1286 δεξιοβόλος *dexiobolos*, n. Not used in NIVEBC. [√ *1288 + 965*]. spearman [?]

G1287 δεξιολάβος *dexiolabos*, n. [1] [√ *1288 + 3284*]. spearman; other sources: bowman, slinger, bodyguard:– spearmen (1)

G1288 δεξιός *dexios*, a. [54] [→ *1286, 1287*]. the right hand or side in contrast to the left; the right is considered culturally to be stronger and of greater prestige than the left; to be seated on the right side of a ruler is a greater position than on the left side; to "give the right hand of fellowship" in Galatians is a sign of friendship, trust, and covenant:– right hand (31), right (21), right side (2)

G1289 δέομαι *deomai*, v. [22] [→ *1255, 1890, 4656*]. to pray; ask, beg, plead:– pray (5), beg (4), begged (3), prayed (3), ask (2), implore (1), plead with (1), pleaded with (1), please (1), tell please (1)

G1290 δέος *deos*, n. [1] [→ *1261, 1262, 1264, 1266, 1267, 1272, 1273*]. awe, fear, reverence:– awe (1)

G1291 Δερβαῖος *Derbaios*, a. pr. g. [1] [√ *1292*]. from Derbe, "*from Derbe*":– from Derbe (1)

G1292 Δέρβη *Derbē*, n. pr. [3] [→ *1291, 1523*]. Derbe:– Derbe (3)

G1293 δέρμα *derma*, n. [1] [√ *1296*]. skin, leather:– goatskins (1 [*+128*])

G1294 δερμάτινος *dermatinos*, a. [2] [√ *1296*]. made of leather:– leather (2)

G1295 δέρρις *derris*, n. Not used in NIVEBC. [√ *1296*]. skin

G1296 δέρω *derō*, v. [15] [→ *1293, 1294, 1295*]. to beat up, strike, flog, slap:– beat (7), beaten with blows (2), beating (2), flogged (2), slaps (1), strike (1)

G1297 δεσμεύω *desmeuō*, v. [3] [√ *1313*]. to tie up, bind; to arrest:– arresting (1), chained hand (1 [+*268*]), tie up (1)

G1298 δεσμέω *desmeō*, v. Not used in NIVEBC. [√ *1313*]. to tie, bind

G1299 δέσμη *desmē*, n. [1] [√ *1313*]. bundle:– bundles (1)

G1300 δέσμιος *desmios*, n. [16] [√ *1313*]. prisoner, one under arrest:– prisoner (11), in prison (2), prisoners (2), arrested (1)

G1301 δεσμός *desmos*, n. [18] [√ *1313*]. chain, fetter, imprisonment:– chains (12), imprisonment (2), bound (1), chained (1), prison (1), NDT (1)

G1302 δεσμοφύλαξ *desmophylax*, n. [3] [√ *1313 + 5875*]. jailer, warden:– jailer (3)

G1303 δεσμωτήριον *desmōtērion*, n. [4] [√ *1313*]. prison, jail:– jail (2), prison (2)

G1304 δεσμώτης *desmōtēs*, n. [2] [√ *1313*]. prisoner:– prisoners (2)

G1305 δεσπότης *despotēs*, n. [10] [→ *3866, 3867; cf. 1313*]. master; Sovereign Lord:– masters (4), sovereign Lord (4), master (1), sovereign (1)

G1306 δεῦρο *deuro*, adv. pl. [9] [→ *1307*]. come, come here:– come (7), go (1), now (1 [+*3836*])

G1307 δεῦτε *deute*, adv. [12] [√ *1306*]. come, come here (pl. of *1306*):– come (12)

G1308 δευτεραῖος *deuteraios*, a. [1] [√ *1545*]. on the following day, on the second day:– on the following day (1)

G1309 δεύτερον *deuteron*, a. [used as adv.] [6] [√ *1545*]. for the second time, secondly:– second time (2), again (1 [+*4099*]), again (1), later (1 [+*3836*]), second (1)

G1310 δευτερόπρωτος *deuteroprōtos*, a. Not used in NIVEBC. [√ *1545 + 4755*]. lit: "second-first"

G1311 δεύτερος *deuteros*, a. [37] [√ *1545*]. second:– second (26), second time (7), another (1), inner (1), middle of the night (1 [+*5871*]), twice (1)

G1312 δέχομαι *dechomai*, v. [56] [→ *99, 346, 450, 587, 621, 622, 627, 628, 1283, 1342, 1345, 1507, 1508, 1509, 1510, 1511, 1531, 1654, 1683, 1693, 1896, 2110, 2347, 2839, 3827, 4104, 4105, 4106, 4107, 4138, 4657, 5685*]. to welcome, receive, accept:– welcomes (15), welcome (7), welcomed (7), receive (6), received (5), accept (3), accepted (3), take (3), obtained (1), receiving (1), refused (1 [+*4024*]), taking (1), tolerate (1), took (1), welcomed (1 [+*3552, 1645*])

G1313 δέω *deō*, v. [43] [→ *1256, 1297, 1298, 1299, 1300, 1301, 1302, 1303, 1304, 1343, 2866, 4317, 5278, 5279, 5686, 5687; cf. 1305*]. to tie, bind, imprison:– bound (15), tied (5), bind (4), as prisoners (2), tie (2), wrapped (2), arrest (1), chained (1), chained hand (1 [+*268*]), compelled (1), had bound (1), in chains (1), in prison (1), pledged (1), prison (1), prisoners (1 [+*1639*]), put in chains (1 [+*1639*]), ties up (1), tying up (1)

G1314 δή *dē*, pt. emph. [5] [→ *1325, 1326, 1327, 2076, 2077, 3889*]. indeed, therefore; can show urgency or certainty:– therefore (1), NDT (4)

G1315 δηλαυγῶς *dēlaugōs*, adv. Not used in NIVEBC. [√ *879*]. very clearly

G1316 δῆλος *dēlos*, a. [3] [→ *83, 84, 85, 1317, 1684, 2867, 4593*]. clear, plain, evident:– clear (1), clearly (1), gives away (1 [+*4472*])

G1317 δηλόω *dēloō*, v. [7] [√ *1316*]. to make clear, bring to light, show, point:– bring to light (1), indicate (1), informed (1), made clear (1), pointing (1), showing (1), told (1)

G1318 Δημᾶς *Dēmas*, n. pr. [3] [√ *1322 or* 1320]. Demas, "*common folks*":– Demas (3)

G1319 δημηγορέω *dēmēgoreō*, v. [1] [√ *1322 + 60*]. to deliver a public address:– delivered a public address (1)

G1320 Δημήτριος *Dēmētrios*, n. pr. [3] [→ *1318?*]. Demetrius, "*of Demeter*":– Demetrius (3)

G1321 δημιουργός *dēmiourgos*, n. [1] [√ *1322 + 2240*]. builder, craftsman, maker:– builder (1)

G1322 δῆμος *dēmos*, n. [4] [→ *623, 624, 1318?, 1319, 1321, 1323, 1685, 1897, 2111, 3773, 4215, 5292*]. people, crowd:– crowd (2), people (1), they[S] (1 [+*3836*])

G1323 δημόσιος *dēmosios*, a. [4] [√ *1322*]. public, publicly:– public (2), publicly (2)

G1324 δηνάριον *dēnarion*, n. [16] denarius [about a day's wage]:– denarius (7), a day's wages (2), denarii (2), more than half a year's wages (2 [+*1357*]), a year's wages (1 [+*5559*]), money worth a year's wages (1 [+*5559*]), silver coins (1)

G1325 δήποτε *dēpote*, adv. Not used in NIVEBC. [√ *1314 + 4544*]. whatever

G1326 δηποτοῦν *dēpotoun*, adv. Not used in NIVEBC. [√ *1314 + 4544 + 4036*]. no matter

G1327 δήπου *dēpou*, adv. [1] [√ *1314 + 4544*]. surely, of course:– surely (1)

G1328 διά *dia*, pp. [672] [→ *88, 89, 90, 91, 442, 507, 626, 1329, 1330, 1331, 1332, 1333, 1334, 1335, 1336, 1337, 1338, 1339, 1340, 1341, 1342, 1343, 1344, 1345, 1346, 1347, 1348, 1349, 1350, 1351, 1352, 1353, 1358, 1359, 1360, 1361, 1362, 1363, 1364, 1365, 1366, 1367, 1368, 1369, 1370, 1371, 1372, 1373, 1374, 1375, 1376, 1377, 1378, 1379, 1380, 1381, 1382, 1383, 1384, 1385, 1386, 1387, 1388, 1389, 1390, 1391, 1392, 1393, 1394, 1395, 1396, 1397, 1398, 1399, 1400, 1401, 1402, 1403, 1404, 1405, 1406, 1407, 1408, 1409, 1410, 1411, 1412, 1413, 1414, 1415, 1416, 1417, 1418, 1419, 1420, 1421, 1422, 1423, 1424, 1425, 1426, 1427, 1428, 1429, 1430, 1431, 1444, 1445, 1446, 1447, 1448, 1449, 1450, 1451, 1452, 1455, 1456, 1457, 1459, 1460, 1461, 1462, 1475, 1476, 1478, 1480, 1481, 1482, 1484, 1494, 1687, 2112, 2114, 4139*]. (gen.) through, by means of; (acc.) because of, for the sake of, therefore:– through (173), by (82), because of (67), for (25), therefore (20 [+*4047*]), because (19 [+*3836*]), in (13), with (13), why (12 [+*5515*]), for sake (10), for the sake of (9), for this reason (9 [+*4047*]), from (7), that is why (7 [+*4047*]), because (6), why (6 [+*5515*]), for (4), out of (4), the reason (4 [+*4047*]), through (4 [+*5125*]), always (3 [+*4246*]), because (3 [+*3836*]), during (3), for benefit (3), on account of (3), the reason (3 [+*4047*]), therefore (3 [+*4047*]), this is why (3 [+*4047*]), why (3 [+*5515*]), afforded by (2), after (2), at (2), because (2 [+*4047*]), because of (2 [+*3836*]), continually (2 [+*4246*]), for (2 [+*3836*]), how is it that (2 [+*5515*]), in answer to (2), of (2), regularly (2 [+*4246*]), since (2 [+*3836*]), so (2 [+*4047*]), so (2 [+*4047*]), so then (2 [+*4047*]), that is why (2 [+*4047*]), why (2 [+*5515, 5516*]), why (2 [+*4005, 162*]), with the help of (2), a few days later (1 [+*2465*]), aroused by (1), as a matter of (1), as the result of (1), at all times (1 [+*4246*]), born of (1), briefly (1 [+*3900*]), bring about (1), by (1 [+*5931*]), by comparing with (1), by means of (1), by the authority of (1), by the will of (1), causes (1), due to (1), for (1 [+*3836*]), for that very reason (1 [+*4047*]), for the benefit of (1), for this reason (1 [+*4047*]), for this very reason (1 [+*4047*]), forever (1 [+*4246*]), give (1), have (1), he (1 [+*3836, 5931, 899*]), how is it that (1 [+*5515*]), in the presence of (1), in view of (1), made (1), on (1), on the basis of (1), on the evidence of (1), over a period (1), patiently (1 [+*5705*]), perform (1 [+*1181, 3836, 5931*]), performed (1 [+*1181*]), performed (1 [+*3836, 5931, 1181*]), quite briefly (1 [+*1099*]), reaching more and more (1 [+*4429, 3836, 4498*]), result (1), said (1 [+*3364*]), since (1), so (1 [+*4005*]), so (1 [+*4005, 162*]), so great (1), that is why (1 [+*4005, 162*]), that was why (1 [+*4047*]), that was why (1 [+*4047*]), the border between (1 [+*3545*]), therefore (1 [+*4005, 162*]), this is why (1 [+*899*]), this is why (1 [+*4047, 1142*]), through (1 [+*3836, 5931*]), to (1), under (1), use (1), used (1), uses (1), using (1 [+*5931*]), visit on the way (1), walked right through (1 [+*1451, 3545*]), what doing (1), when (1), when hears[S] (1), why (1 [+*3836, 162, 4005*]), with (1 [+*5931*]), NDT (48)

G1329 διαβαίνω *diabainō*, v. [3] [√ *1328 + 326*]. to pass through, come over, cross:– come over (1), go (1), passed through (1)

G1330 διαβάλλω *diaballō*, v. [1] [√ *1328 + 965*]. (pass.) to have accusations brought upon someone:– accused (1)

G1331 διαβεβαιόομαι *diabebaioomai*, v. [2] [√ *1328 + 326*]. to confidently affirm, stress, insist on:– confidently affirm (1), stress (1)

G1332 διαβλέπω *diablepō*, v. [3] [√ *1328 + 1063*]. to see clearly; to open eyes wide:– see clearly (2), eyes opened (1)

G1333 διάβολος *diabolos*, a. [used as n.] [38] [√ *1328 + 965*]. devilish, malicious, slanderous; as a noun, the devil, Satan, or a wicked person who is like the devil:– devil (31), devil's (3), he[S] (1 [+*3836*]), malicious talkers (1), slanderers (1), slanderous (1)

G1334 διαγγέλλω *diangellō*, v. [3] [√ *1328 + 34*]. to proclaim (throughout); to give notice:– give notice (1), proclaim (1), proclaimed (1)

G1335 διαγίνομαι *diaginomai*, v. [3] [√ *1328 + 1181*]. to pass, elapse (of time):– later (1), lost (1), over (1)

G1336 διαγινώσκω *diaginōskō*, v. [2] [√ *1328 + 1182*]. to determine, decide:– decide (1), information (1)

G1337 διαγνωρίζω *diagnōrizō*, v. Not used in NIVEBC. [√ *1328 + 1182*]. to give an exact report

G1338 διάγνωσις *diagnōsis*, n. [1] [√ *1328 + 1182*]. decision:– decision (1)

G1339 διαγογγύζω *diagongyzō*, v. [2] [√ *1328 + 1197*]. to mutter, grumble, complain:– mutter (1), muttered (1)

G1340 διαγρηγορέω *diagrēgoreō*, v. [1] [√ *1328 + 1586*]. to become fully awake:– fully awake (1)

G1341 διάγω *diagō*, v. [2] [√ *1328 + 72*]. to live, conduct one's life:– live (1), lived (1)

G1342 διαδέχομαι *diadechomai*, v. [1] [√ *1328 + 1312*]. to receive (in turn):– receiving (1)

G1343 διάδημα *diadēma*, n. [3] [√ *1328 + 1313*]. crown, diadem:– crowns (3)

G1344 διαδίδωμι *diadidōmi*, v. [4] [√ *1328 + 1443*]. to distribute, divide up:– distributed (2), divides up (1), give (1)

G1345 διάδοχος *diadochos*, n. [1] [√ *1328 + 1312*]. successor:– succeeded (1 [+*3284*])

G1346 διαζώννυμι *diazōnnymi*, v. [3] [√ *1328 + 2439*]. to wrap around, tie around, put on:– wrapped around (2), wrapped around waist (1)

G1347 διαθήκη *diathēkē*, n. [33] [√ *1328 + 5502*]. covenant, a solemn agreement between two parties; will, testament, a legal document by which property is transferred to heirs, usually upon death (Heb 9:16):– covenant (28), covenants (3), will (2)

G1348 διαίρεσις *diairesis*, n. [3] [√ *1328 + 145*]. difference, variety:– different kinds (3)

G1349 διαιρέω *diaireō*, v. [2] [√ *1328 + 145*]. to divide, distribute, apportion:– distributes (1), divided (1)

G1350 διακαθαίρω *diakathairō*, v. [1] [√ *1328 + 2754*]. to clear out, clean out (with a possible implication that the cleaning is thorough):– clear (1)

G1351 διακαθαρίζω *diakatharizō*, v. [1] [√ *1328 + 2754*]. to clear out, clean out:– clear (1)

G1352 διακατελέγχομαι *diakatelenchomai*, v. [1] [√ *1328 + 2848 + 1794*]. to refute (thoroughly):– refuted in debate (1)

G1353 διακελεύω *diakeleuō*, v. Not used in NIVEBC. [√ *1328 + 3027*]. to order

G1354 διακονέω *diakoneō*, v. [37] [√ *1356*]. to serve, wait on, help, attend to; this often refers to spiritual and practical ministry in the Church. "To wait upon tables" (Ac 6:2) may mean to literally help in serving food, though some believe it refers (also) to the handling of finances:– serves (6), wait on (6), served (4), administer (2), attended (2), help (2), helped (2), serve (2), care for needs (1), cared for needs (1), do work (1), helpers (1), helping (1), helping to support (1), ministry (1), serve as deacons (1), service (1), serving (1), use to serve (1)

G1355 διακονία *diakonia*, n. [34] [√ *1356*]. ministry, service, this can refer to helps and service of various kinds which can range in meaning from "spiritual" biblical teaching (Ac 6:4) to the "practical" giving of provisions, supplies, support, and finances to those in need (2Co 9:12):– ministry (15), service (9), serve (3), contribution (1), distribution (1), help (1), mission (1), preparations to be made (1), serving (1), task (1)

G1356 διάκονος *diakonos*, n. [29] [→ *1354, 1355*]. servant, minister, a person who renders service and help to others, in some contexts with an implication of lower status; also transliterated as "deacon," a trusted officer of helps and service in the local church:– servant (11), servants (8), minister (3), deacon (2), deacons (2), attendants (1), ministers (1), promotes[S] (1)

G1357 διακόσιοι *diakosioi*, a. num. [8] [√ *1545*]. two hundred:– 1,260 (2 [+*5943, 2008*]), more than half a year's wages (2 [+*1324*]), two hundred (2), 276 (1 [+*1573, 1971*]), a hundred yards (1 [+*4388*])

G1358 διακούω *diakouō*, v. [1] [√ *1328 + 201*]. to give a (legal) hearing:– hear case (1)

G1359 διακρίνω *diakrinō*, v. [19] [√ *1328 + 3212*]. to make a distinction, judge a dispute; (mid./pass.) to doubt, hesitate, waver:– doubt (4), discerning (2), criticized (1), discriminate (1), discriminated (1), disputing (1 [+*1363*]), doubts (1), has doubts (1), have hesitation (1), hesitate (1), interpret (1), judge a dispute (1), makes different (1), waver (1), weigh carefully (1)

G1360 διάκρισις *diakrisis*, n. [3] [√ *1328 + 3212*]. distinguishing, differentiation; passing judgment:– disputable matters (1), distinguish (1), distinguishing between (1)

G1361 διακωλύω *diakōlyō*, v. [1] [√ *1328 + 3266*]. to deter, prevent:– deter (1)

G1362 διαλαλέω *dialaleō*, v. [2] [√ *1328 + 3281*]. to talk about, discuss:– discuss (1), talking about (1)

G1363 διαλέγομαι *dialegomai*, v. [13] [√ *1328 + 3306*]. to reason, discuss, discourse; to argue, dispute:– reasoned with (3), arguing (2), talked (2), addresses (1), argued about (1), disputing (1 [+*1359*]), had discussions (1), reasoned (1), spoke (1)

G1364 διαλείπω *dialeipō*, v. [1] [√ *1328 + 3309*]. to stop, cease:– stopped (1)

G1365 διάλεκτος *dialektos*, n. [6] [√ *1328 + 3306*]. language, dialect, a communication code whether written or oral; in the NT this always refers to known languages commonly spoken in the ancient world:– aramaic (3 [+*1579*]), language (3)

GREEK INDEX

G1366 **διαλιμπάνω** ***dialimpanō***, v. Not used in NIVEBC. [√*1328 + 3309*]. to stop, cease

G1367 **διαλλάσσομαι** ***diallassomai***, v. [1] [√*1328 + 248*]. to become reconciled:– reconciled (1)

G1368 **διαλογίζομαι** ***dialogizomai***, v. [16] [√*1328 + 3306*]. to think, wonder about; to talk, discuss, argue:– thinking (5), discussed (4), arguing about (1), talked the matter over (1 [*+4639, 253*]), talking (1), talking about (1), thought (1), wondered (1), wondering (1)

G1369 **διαλογισμός** ***dialogismos***, n. [14] [√*1328 + 3306*]. thought, doubt; argument, dispute:– thoughts (5), thinking (3), arguing (1), argument (1), disputing (1), doubts (1), quarreling (1), thoughts (1 [*+2840*])

G1370 **διαλύω** ***dialyō***, v. [1] [√*1328 + 3395*]. to disperse, break up:– dispersed (1)

G1371 **διαμαρτύρομαι** ***diamartyromai***, v. [15] [√*1328 + 3459*]. to (solemnly) warn or charge; to (solemnly) testify about:– testified (3), testifying (2), warn (2), warned (2), charge (1), declared (1), give charge (1), testify (1), warns (1), witnessed (1)

G1372 **διαμάχομαι** ***diamachomai***, v. [1] [√*1328 + 3480*]. to argue vigorously, contend sharply:– argued vigorously (1)

G1373 **διαμένω** ***diamenō***, v. [5] [√*1328 + 3531*]. to remain (constantly):– goes on (1), preserved (1), remain (1), remained (1), stood (1)

G1374 **διαμερίζω** ***diamerizō***, v. [11] [√*1328 + 3538*]. to divide, distribute:– divided (5), divided up (2), divide (1), dividing up (1), give (1), separated (1)

G1375 **διαμερισμός** ***diamerismos***, n. [1] [√*1328 + 3538*]. division:– division (1)

G1376 **διανέμω** ***dianemō***, v. [1] [√*1328 + 3795*]. (pass.) to be spread:– spreading (1)

G1377 **διανεύω** ***dianeuō***, v. [1] [√*1328 + 3748*]. to make signs, nod, beckon:– making signs (1)

G1378 **διανόημα** ***dianoēma***, n. [1] [√*1328 + 3808*]. thought:– thoughts (1)

G1379 **διάνοια** ***dianoia***, n. [12] [√*1328 + 3808*]. mind, thinking, understanding; this is a part of the inner person that thinks and processes information into understanding, including the making of choices, the seat of which is the heart:– minds (4), mind (3), thoughts (2), understanding (2), thinking (1)

G1380 **διανοίγω** ***dianoigō***, v. [8] [√*487; cf. 1328*]. to open; (pass.) to be opened; to explain:– opened (5), explaining (1), firstborn (1 [*+3616*]), open (1)

G1381 **διανυκτερεύω** ***dianyktereuō***, v. [1] [√*1328 + 3816*]. to spend the (entire) night:– spent the night (1 [*+1639*])

G1382 **διανύω** ***dianyō***, v. [1] [√*1328 + 539*]. to continue:– continued (1)

G1383 **διαπαντός** ***diapantos***, adv. Not used in NIVEBC. [√*1328 + 4246*]. always, continually, constantly

G1384 **διαπαρατριβή** ***diaparatribē***, n. [1] [√*1328 + 4123 + 5561*]. constant friction:– constant friction (1)

G1385 **διαπεράω** ***diaperaō***, v. [6] [√*1328 + 4305*]. to cross over:– crossed over (4), cross over (1), crossing over (1)

G1386 **διαπλέω** ***diapleō***, v. [1] [√*1328 + 4434*]. to sail across, sail through:– sailed across (1)

G1387 **διαπονέομαι** ***diaponeomai***, v. [2] [√*1328 + 4506*]. to be greatly disturbed, troubled, annoyed:– annoyed (1), greatly disturbed (1)

G1388 **διαπορεύομαι** ***diaporeuomai***, v. [5] [√*1328 + 4513*]. to go through, travel through:– going by (1), going through (1), passing through (1), traveled from town to town (1 [*+3836, 4484*]), went through (1)

G1389 **διαπορέω** ***diaporeō***, v. [4] [√*1328 + 1.1 + 4513*]. to be perplexed, puzzled, in wonder:– perplexed (2), at a loss (1), wondering (1 [*+1877, 1571*])

G1390 **διαπραγματεύομαι** ***diapragmateuomai***, v. [1] [√*1328 + 4556*]. to gain, earn:– gained (1)

G1391 **διαπρίω** ***diapriō***, v. [2] [√*1328 + 4573*]. (pass.) to be furious:– furious (1), furious (1 [*+3836, 2840*])

G1392 **διαρήγνυμι** ***diarēgnymi***, v. Not used in NIVEBC. [√*1328 + 4838*]. to tear, break

G1393 **διαρήσσω** ***diarēssō***, v. Not used in NIVEBC. [√*1328 + 4838*]. to tear, break

G1394 **διαρθρόω** ***diarthroō***, v. Not used in NIVEBC. [√*1328*]. (pass.) to be able to speak

G1395 **διαρπάζω** ***diarpazō***, v. [3] [√*1328 + 773*]. to rob, carry off (many possessions):– plunder (2), NDT (1)

G1396 **διαρρήγνυμι** ***diarrēgnymi***, v. [5] [√*1328 + 4838*]. to tear (clothes), break (chains):– tore (3), break (1), broken (1)

G1397 **διασαφέω** ***diasapheō***, v. [2] [√*1328*]. to tell, explain (in detail):– explain (1), told (1)

G1398 **διασείω** ***diaseiō***, v. [1] [√*1328 + 4940*]. to extort money, as a fig. extension of a violent shaking motion:– extort money (1)

G1399 **διασκορπίζω** ***diaskorpizō***, v. [9] [√*1328 + 5025*]. to scatter:– scattered (5), scattered seed (2), squandered (1), wasting (1)

G1400 **διασπάω** ***diaspaō***, v. [2] [√*1328 + 5060*]. (pass.) to be torn to pieces:– tore apart (1), torn to pieces (1)

G1401 **διασπείρω** ***diaspeirō***, v. [3] [√*1328 + 5062*]. (pass.) to be scattered:– scattered (3)

G1402 **διασπορά** ***diaspora***, n. [3] [√*1328 + 5062*]. scattering, dispersion, Diaspora:– our people live scattered (1 [*+3836*]), scattered among the nations (1), scattered throughout (1)

G1403 **διαστέλλω** ***diastellō***, v. [9] [√*1328 + 5097*]. (mid.) to give orders, command, authorize; (pass.) what was commanded:– commanded (2), did so[S] (2), gave orders (2), authorization (1), ordered (1), warned (1)

G1404 **διάστημα** ***diastēma***, n. [1] [√*1328 + 2705*]. later time, interval:– later (1)

G1405 **διαστολή** ***diastolē***, n. [3] [√*1328 + 5097*]. difference, distinction:– difference (2), distinction (1)

G1406 **διαστρέφω** ***diastrephō***, v. [7] [√*1328 + 5138*]. (act.) to subvert, pervert, make turn away; (pass.) to be perverted, depraved, turned from the truth:– perverse (2), crooked (1), distort the truth (1 [*+3281*]), perverting (1), subverting (1), turn (1)

G1407 **διασῴζω** ***diasōzō***, v. [8] [√*1328 + 5392*]. save, spare, bring safely through a dangerous or distressing situation, with a focus that the rescue is complete or full; to heal, with a focus that the injured or sick person goes from the danger of ill health to the safety of a completely restored or healthy life:– safely (3), escaped (1), heal (1), healed (1), saved through (1), spare life (1)

G1408 **διαταγή** ***diatagē***, n. [2] [√*1328 + 5435*]. putting into effect, institution:– given (1), instituted (1)

G1409 **διάταγμα** ***diatagma***, n. [1] [√*1328 + 5435*]. edict, command:– edict (1)

G1410 **διαταράσσω** ***diatarassō***, v. [1] [√*1328 + 5429*]. (pass.) to be greatly troubled, perplexed, confused:– greatly troubled (1)

G1411 **διατάσσω** ***diatassō***, v. [16] [√*1328 + 5435*]. (act./mid.) to command, order, direct; (pass.) to be required, ordered, put into effect:– told to do (3), directed (2), ordered (2), commanded (1), give directions (1), given (1), instructing (1), made arrangement (1), orders (1), required (1), the rule lay down (1), told (1)

G1412 **διατελέω** ***diateleō***, v. [1] [√*1328 + 5465*]. to continue, remain:– gone (1)

G1413 **διατηρέω** ***diatēreō***, v. [2] [√*1328 + 5498*]. to keep, treasure:– avoid (1), treasured (1)

G1414 **διατί** ***diati***, pt. inter. Not used in NIVEBC. [√*1328 + 5515*]. why?

G1415 **διατίθεμαι** ***diatithemai***, v. Not used in NIVEBC. [√*1328 + 5502*]. to decree, ordain

G1416 **διατίθημι** ***diatithēmi***, v. [7] [√*1328 + 5502*]. to make a covenant or a will; to confer, assign:– made (3), confer (1), conferred (1), establish (1), make (1)

G1417 **διατρίβω** ***diatribō***, v. [9] [√*1328 + 5561*]. to stay, remain, spend some time:– stayed (4), spending (2), remained (1), spent (1), spent some time (1)

G1418 **διατροφή** ***diatrophē***, n. [1] [√*1328 + 5555*]. food, sustenance:– food (1)

G1419 **διαυγάζω** ***diaugazō***, v. [1] [√*1328 + 879*]. to dawn, shine through:– dawns (1)

G1420 **διαυγής** ***diaugēs***, a. [1] [√*1328 + 879*]. transparent:– transparent (1)

G1421 **διαφανής** ***diaphanēs***, a. Not used in NIVEBC. [√*1328 + 5743*]. transparent

G1422 **διαφέρω** ***diapherō***, v. [13] [√*1328 + 5770*]. (tr.) to carry, spread out; (intr.) to differ; to be more valuable than:– more valuable (2), best (1), carry through (1), different (1), differs (1), driven across (1), makes difference (1), spread (1), superior (1), valuable (1), worth more (1), worth more than (1)

G1423 **διαφεύγω** ***diapheugō***, v. [1] [√*1328 + 5771*]. to escape, flee:– escaping (1)

G1424 **διαφημίζω** ***diaphēmizō***, v. [3] [√*1328 + 5774*]. to spread news about, circulate:– spread the news (1), spreading (1), widely circulated (1)

G1425 **διαφθείρω** ***diaphtheirō***, v. [6] [√*1328 + 5780*]. to destroy, corrupt:– corrupt (1), destroy (1), destroyed (1), destroying (1), destroys (1), wasting away (1)

G1426 **διαφθορά** ***diaphthora***, n. [6] [√*1328 + 5780*]. decay:– decay (5), decayed (1 [*+3972*])

G1427 **διάφορος** ***diaphoros***, a. [4] [√*1328 + 5770*]. different; superior, outstanding, excellent:– superior (2), different (1), various (1)

G1428 **διαφυλάσσω** ***diaphylassō***, v. [1] [√*1328 + 5875*]. to guard carefully:– guard carefully (1)

G1429 **διαχειρίζω** ***diacheirizō***, v. [2] [√*1328 + 5931*]. (mid.) to kill, murder, formally, "to lay violent hands on":– kill (1), killed (1)

G1430 **διαχλευάζω** ***diachleuazō***, v. [1] [√*1328 + 5949*]. to make fun of, scoff at, sneer at:– made fun of (1)

G1431 **διαχωρίζω** ***diachōrizō***, v. [1] [√*1328 + 6006*]. (pass.) to be separated:– leaving (1)

G1432 **διγαμία** ***digamia***, n. Not used in NIVEBC. [√*1545 + 1141*]. second marriage

G1433 **δίγαμος** ***digamos***, a. Not used in NIVEBC. [√*1545 + 1141*]. pertaining to a second marriage

G1434 **διδακτικός** ***didaktikos***, a. [2] [√*1438*]. able to teach, skillful at instructing:– able to teach (2)

G1435 **διδακτός** ***didaktos***, a. [3] [√*1438*]. taught, instructed:– taught (3)

G1436 **διδασκαλία** ***didaskalia***, n. [21] [√*1438*]. teaching, doctrine:– teaching (10), doctrine (5), teach (2), teachings (2 [*+1438*]), teachings (1), things taught (1)

G1437 **διδάσκαλος** ***didaskalos***, n. [59] [√*1438*]. teacher, instructor, one who provides instruction, implying authority over the students or followers:– teacher (50), teachers (9)

G1438 **διδάσκω** ***didaskō***, v. [97] [→*1434, 1435, 1436, 1437, 1439, 2281, 2531, 2815, 3791, 6015*]. to teach, instruct, to provide information in a manner intended to produce understanding, either in a formal or informal setting:– teach (34), teaching (32), taught (19), teaches (4), taught (3 [*+1639*]), teachings (2 [*+1436*]), instructed (1), lecture (1), passed on (1)

G1439 **διδαχή** ***didachē***, n. [30] [√*1438*]. (the activity or content of) teaching, instruction:– teaching (23), taught (2), word of instruction (2), careful instruction (1), instruction (1), teachings (1)

G1440 **δίδραχμον** ***didrachmon***, n. [2] [√*1545 + 1533*]. two-drachma (temple tax):– temple tax (1), two-drachma temple tax (1)

G1441 **Δίδυμος** ***Didymos***, n. pr. [3] [√*1545*]. Didymus, "*twin*":– Didymus (3)

G1442 **διδῶ** ***didō***, v. [1] [√*1443*]. I give:– make (1)

G1443 **δίδωμι** ***didōmi***, v. [414] [→*347, 500, 501, 502, 625, 782, 1344, 1442, 1517, 1521, 1522, 1561, 1562, 1563, 1564, 1566, 1686, 1692, 2113, 2331, 2882, 3556, 3632, 3633, 4140, 4142, 4261, 4594, 4595, 4658; cf. 1565*]. to give; that this can have many different specific meanings and referents depending on the context, as noted in the list of NIV translations:– give (113), given (103), gave (76), gives (11), put (9), pay (5), giving (4), grant (4), granted (4), offer (4), let (3), allowed (2), arranged (2), bring (2), commanded (2 [*+1953*]), enable (2), gave up (2), offered (2), perform (2), placed (2), produced (2), show (2), shows (2), slapped in the face (2 [*+4825*]), appoint (1), appointed (1), assigned task (1), be generous to the poor (1 [*+1797*]), bear (1), benefit (1 [*+5921*]), buy (1), cast (1), caused (1), completely healed (1 [*+3836, 3907, 4047*]), does (1), enabled (1), enabled (1 [*+710*]), enabling (1), entrusted (1), gave back (1), gifts (1), give to the poor (1 [*+1797*]), glorified (1 [*+1518*]), glorify (1 [*+1518*]), hand over (1), here is[S] (1), hinder (1 [*+1600*]), is (1), lavished (1), leave (1), make (1), pass on (1), payment (1), plot (1 [*+5206*]), possess (1 [*+1650, 2959*]), poured (1), praised (1 [*+142*]), presented (1), punish (1 [*+1689*]), puts (1), receive (1), repay (1), rescue (1 [*+5401*]), rewarding (1 [*+3836, 3635*]), set (1), sound (1), speak (1), strengthen (1 [*+3194*]), take back (1), took (1), try hard (1 [*+2238*]), venture (1), NDT (4)

G1444 **διεγείρω** ***diegeirō***, v. [6] [√*1328 + 1586*]. to get up, arouse, stimulate:– got up (2), refresh (1), rough (1), stimulate (1), woke (1)

G1445 **διενθυμέομαι** ***dienthymeomai***, v. [1] [√*1328 + 1877 + 2596*]. to think, ponder, reflect:– thinking (1)

G1446 **διεξέρχομαι** ***diexerchomai***, v. Not used in NIVEBC. [√*1328 + 1666 + 2262*]. to come out

G1447 **διέξοδος** ***diexodos***, n. [1] [√*1328 + 1666 + 3847*]. (street) corner:– corners (1)

G1448 **διερμηνεία** ***diermēneia***, n. Not used in NIVEBC. [√*1328 + 2257*]. explanation, interpretation, translation

G1449 **διερμηνευτής** ***diermēneutēs***, n. [1] [√*1328 + 2257*]. interpreter, translator:– interpreter (1)

GREEK INDEX

G1450 διερμηνεύω *diermēneuō*, v. [6] [√*1328* + *2257*]. to interpret, translate, explain:– interpret (3), explained what was said (1), in Greek (1 [+*3306*]), interprets (1)

G1451 διέρχομαι *dierchomai*, v. [42] [√*1328* + *2262*]. to go through, travel throughout:– go through (4), traveled through (3), coming (2), go (2), go over (2), goes through (2), going through (2), passing through (2), traveled about (2), traveled throughout (2), went (2), ascended into (1), came (1), come (1), gone about (1), passed (1), passed through (1), pierce (1), spread (1), took the road through (1), traveled (1), traveled along (1), visit (1), walked around (1), walked right through (1 [+*1328*, *3545*]), went around (1), went on (1), went through (1)

G1452 διερωτάω *dierōtaō*, v. [1] [√*1328* + *2263*]. to find out, ask:– found out (1)

G1453 διετής *dietēs*, a. [1] [√*1545* + *2291*]. two years old:– two years old (1)

G1454 διετία *dietia*, n. [2] [√*1545* + *2291*]. two years:– two years (2)

G1455 διηγέομαι *diēgeomai*, v. [8] [√*1328* + *72*]. to tell, report, describe:– tell (3), told (2), described (1), reported (1), speak of (1)

G1456 διήγησις *diēgēsis*, n. [1] [√*1328* + *72*]. account, narrative:– account (1)

G1457 διηνεκής *diēnekēs*, a. [4] [√*1328* + *5770*]. forever, endless, for all time:– forever (2 [+*1650*, *3836*]), endlessly (1 [+*1650*, *3836*]), for all time (1 [+*1650*, *3836*])

G1458 διθάλασσος *dithalassos*, a. [1] [√*1545* + *2498*]. sandbar, sandbank (surrounded on both sides by sea):– sandbar (1 [+*5536*])

G1459 διϊκνέομαι *diikneomai*, v. [1] [√*1328* + *2653*]. to penetrate, pierce:– penetrates (1)

G1460 διΐστημι *diistēmi*, v. [3] [√*1328* + *2705*]. to leave, pass:– later (2), left (1)

G1461 διϊστορέω *diistoreō*, v. Not used in NIVEBC. [√*1328* + *2707*]. to examine carefully

G1462 διϊσχυρίζομαι *diischyrizomai*, v. [2] [√*1328* + *2709*]. to assert, insist, maintain firmly:– asserted (1), insisting (1)

G1463 δικάζω *dikazō*, v. Not used in NIVEBC. [√*1472*]. to judge, condemn

G1464 δικαιοκρισία *dikaiokrisia*, n. [1] [√*1472* + *3212*]. righteous judgment:– righteous judgment (1)

G1465 δίκαιος *dikaios*, a. [79] [√*1472*]. right, righteous, upright; in the NT this refers to God's proper standards and actions, expressed in the covenants; as a noun it refers to a person in accord with God's standards, in proper relationship with God:– righteous (53), right (9), just (8), innocent (2), upright (2), correctly (1 [+*3213*]), does right (1), faithful to the law (1), righteousness (1), sincere (1)

G1466 δικαιοσύνη *dikaiosynē*, n. [91] [√*1472*]. righteousness, what is right, justice, the act of doing what is in agreement with God's standards, the state of being in proper relationship with God:– righteousness (78), justice (3), right (3), what is right (3), it[s] (1), justified (1), righteous (1), that is right (1)

G1467 δικαιόω *dikaioō*, v. [39] [√*1472*]. to justify, vindicate, declare righteous, to put someone in a proper relationship with another, usually referring to God's relationship to humankind, implying a proper legal or moral relationship:– justified (15), justify (4), considered righteous (3), justifies (3), proved right (3), declared righteous (2), set free (2), acknowledged way right (1), acquitted (1), alienated (1), justification obtain (1), justified before God (1), make innocent (1), vindicated (1)

G1468 δικαίωμα *dikaiōma*, n. [10] [√*1472*]. regulation, requirement, commandment; act of righteousness:– regulations (2), righteous acts (2), decrees (1), justification (1), requirements (1), righteous act (1), righteous decree (1), righteous requirement (1)

G1469 δικαίως *dikaiōs*, adv. [5] [√*1472*]. justly, uprightly, righteously:– justly (2), as ought (1), righteous (1), upright (1)

G1470 δικαίωσις *dikaiōsis*, n. [2] [√*1472*]. justification:– justification (2)

G1471 δικαστής *dikastēs*, n. [2] [√*1472*]. judge:– judge (2)

G1472 δίκη *dikē*, n. [3] [→*92*, *93*, *94*, *95*, *96*, *97*, *508*, *1463*, *1464*, *1465*, *1466*, *1467*, *1468*, *1469*, *1470*, *1471*, *1688*, *1689*, *1690*, *1899*, *2868*, *2869*, *3293*, *3294*, *5688*]. punishment, with a focus that the penalty is justly deserved and right; this can also refer to a pagan Greek goddess, "Justice" (Ac 28:4), who would seek out the guilty and punish the wrongdoer:– goddess Justice (1), punished (1 [+*5514*]), punishment (1)

G1473 δίκτυον *diktyon*, n. [12] (fish) net:– nets (8), net (4)

G1474 δίλογος *dilogos*, a. [1] [√*1545* + *3306*]. insincere, double-tongued:– sincere (1 [+*3590*])

G1475 διό *dio*, c. infer. [53] [√*1328* + *4005*]. therefore, that is why, for this reason:– therefore (28), so (12), that is why (5), this is why (4), for this reason (1), now (1), so then (1), then (1)

G1476 διοδεύω *diodeuō*, v. [2] [√*1328* + *3847*]. to go through, travel through:– passed through (1), traveled about (1)

G1477 Διονύσιος *Dionysios*, n. pr. [1] Dionysius, "*belonging to Dionysus*":– Dionysius (1)

G1478 διόπερ *dioper*, c. infer. [2] [√*1328* + *4005* + *4302*]. therefore, for this reason:– therefore (2)

G1479 διοπετής *diopetēs*, a. [1] [√*2416* + *4406*]. (the image) fallen from heaven (given by the pagan god Zeus):– image which fell from heaven (1)

G1480 διόρθωμα *diorthōma*, n. [1] [√*1328* + *3981*]. reform:– reforms (1)

G1481 διόρθωσις *diorthōsis*, n. [1] [√*1328* + *3981*]. a new order:– new order (1)

G1482 διορύσσω *dioryssō*, v. [4] [√*1328* + *4002*]. to break in:– break in (2), broken into (2)

G1483 Διόσκουροι *Dioskouroi*, n. pr. [1] [√*2416* + *3025*]. the twin gods Castor and Pollux, the Dioscuri, "*sons of Zeus*":– twin gods Castor and Pollux (1)

G1484 διότι *dioti*, c. [23] [√*1328* + *4005* + *5515*]. therefore, because:– because (10), for (6), therefore (2), since (1), so (1), NDT (3)

G1485 Διοτρέφης *Diotrephēs*, n. pr. [1] [√*2416* + *5555*]. Diotrephes, "*nurtured by Zeus*":– Diotrephes (1)

G1486 διπλόος *diploos*, a. Not used in NIVEBC. [√*1545*]. double, twice as much; same as *1487*

G1487 διπλοῦς *diplous*, a. [4] [√*1545*]. double, twice as much; same as *1486*:– double (3), twice as much (1)

G1488 διπλόω *diploō*, v. [1] [√*1545*]. to double, pay back double:– pay back (1)

G1489 δίς *dis*, adv. [6] [√*1545*]. twice, again:– twice (4), again (1), more than once (1 [+*562*, *2779*])

G1490 δισμυριάς *dismyrias*, n. [1] [√*1545* + *3692*]. twenty thousand:– twice ten thousand (1)

G1491 διστάζω *distazō*, v. [2] [√*1545*]. to doubt:– doubt (1), doubted (1)

G1492 δίστομος *distomos*, a. [3] [√*1545* + *5125*]. double-edged:– double-edged (3)

G1493 δισχίλιοι *dischilioi*, a. num. [1] [√*1545* + *5943*]. two thousand:– two thousand in number (1)

G1494 διϋλίζω *diylizō*, v. [1] [√*1328* + *5627*]. to strain out, filter out:– strain out (1)

G1495 διχάζω *dichazō*, v. [1] [√*1545*]. to turn (one against another), cause a separation:– turn (1)

G1496 διχοστασία *dichostasia*, n. [2] [√*1545* + *2705*]. division, dissension:– dissensions (1), divisions (1)

G1497 διχοτομέω *dichotomeō*, v. [2] [√*1545* + *5533*]. to cut to pieces, likely a figure for severe punishment rather than execution:– cut to pieces (2)

G1498 διψάω *dipsaō*, v. [16] [→*1499*]. to be thirsty:– thirsty (13), thirst (3)

G1499 δίψος *dipsos*, n. [1] [√*1498*]. thirst:– thirst (1)

G1500 δίψυχος *dipsychos*, a. [2] [√*1545* + *6038*]. double-minded:– double-minded (2)

G1501 διωγμός *diōgmos*, n. [10] [√*1503*]. persecution:– persecution (5), persecutions (5)

G1502 διώκτης *diōktēs*, n. [1] [√*1503*]. persecutor:– persecutor (1)

G1503 διώκω *diōkō*, v. [45] [→*1501*, *1502*, *1691*, *2870*]. to pursue, persecute, to systematically oppress and harass a person or group, as an extended meaning of pursuing a person on foot in a chase; also from the image of the chase comes the meaning of striving and pressing on to a goal with intensity: to press on:– persecuted (14), persecute (11), persecuting (5), pursue (5), make every effort (2), press on (2), pursued (2), follow (1), practice (1), running off after (1), strive to do (1)

G1504 δόγμα *dogma*, n. [5] [√*1506*]. decree, regulation:– decisions (1), decree (1), decrees (1), legal (1), regulations (1)

G1505 δογματίζω *dogmatizō*, v. [1] [√*1506*]. (pass.) to submit to a rule, regulation:– submit to rules (1)

G1506 δοκέω *dokeō*, v. [63] [→*638*, *1504*, *1505*, *2305*, *2306*, *4659*, *4660*, *5306*; *cf.* *1518*]. to think, consider, regard, an action of the mind and heart for processing information into understanding and choices, sometimes with a focus on appearances. Often in the impersonal form translated, "it seems" (Ac 17:18):– think (25), thought (6), seems (3), thinking (3), thinks (3), decided (2), expect (2), seem (2), agreed (1 [+*1181*, *3924*]), consider (1), considered (1), convinced (1), esteemed (1), esteemed as leaders (1), found (1), glorious (1 [+*1877*, *1518*]), held in high esteem (1), opinion (1), regarded (1), saw (1), seemed good (1), supposing (1), take for (1 [+*1639*]), they[s] (1 [+*3836*]), wants (1)

G1507 δοκιμάζω *dokimazō*, v. [22] [√*1312*]. to test, try, examine; interpret:– test (6), interpret (2), approve (1), approve of (1), approved (1), approves (1), discern (1), examine (1), find out (1), proved (1), refined (1), test and approve (1), tested (1), tests (1), think it worthwhile (1), try out (1)

G1508 δοκιμασία *dokimasia*, n. [1] [√*1312*]. testing, trying, examination:– tried (1)

G1509 δοκιμή *dokimē*, n. [7] [√*1312*]. character, test, proof:– character (2), proved (2), proof (1), severe trial (1 [+*2568*]), stand the test (1)

G1510 δοκίμιον *dokimion*, n. [2] [√*1312*]. testing, proved genuineness:– proven genuineness (1), testing (1)

G1511 δόκιμος *dokimos*, a. [7] [√*1312*]. approved by testing, genuine:– approval (2), approved (2), stood the test (2), test (1)

G1512 δοκός *dokos*, n. [6] plank, beam of wood:– plank (6)

G1513 δόλιος *dolios*, a. [1] [√*1515*]. deceitful, dishonest, tricky:– deceitful (1)

G1514 δολιόω *dolioō*, v. [1] [√*1515*]. to practice deceit, deceive:– practice deceit (1)

G1515 δόλος *dolos*, n. [11] [→*100*, *1284*, *1513*, *1514*, *1516*]. deceit, slyness, trickery, as a fig. extension of the base meaning (not used in the NT) of trapping an animal by baiting or by cunning:– deceit (6), deceitful (1), secretly (1), secretly (1 [+*1877*]), trick (1), trickery (1)

G1516 δολόω *doloō*, v. [1] [√*1515*]. to distort, falsify:– distort (1)

G1517 δόμα *doma*, n. [4] [√*1443*]. gift:– gifts (4)

G1518 δόξα *doxa*, n. [166] [→*1519*, *1901*, *1902*, *3029*, *3030*, *4141*, *5280*; *cf.* *1506*]. This word has a wide range of meanings in the NT, corresponding closely the Hebrew 3883: glory, splendor, brilliance, from the base meaning of the awesome light that radiates from God's presence and is associated with his acts of power; honor, praise, speaking of words of excellence and assigning highest status to God:– glory (120), glorious (13), splendor (9), praise (6), honor (3), celestial beings (2), brilliance (1), divine glory (1), glories (1), glorified (1 [+*1443*]), glorify (1 [+*1443*]), glorious (1 [+*1877*, *1506*]), glorious splendor (1), glory by telling the truth (1), honored (1), with ever-increasing glory (1 [+*608*, *1650*, *1518*]), with ever-increasing glory (1 [+*608*, *1518*, *1650*]), NDT (2)

G1519 δοξάζω *doxazō*, v. [61] [√*1518*]. to glorify, give praise, honor:– glorify (14), glorified (12), praised (11), honored (4), praising (4), glorious (2), praise (2), bring glory (1), brought glory (1), gave praise (1), glorifies (1), glorifying (1), glory (1), glory come (1), glory gave (1), has glory (1), honor (1), take glory (1), take pride in (1)

G1520 Δορκάς *Dorkas*, n. pr. [2] Dorcas, "*gazelle*":– Dorcas (2)

G1521 δόσις *dosis*, n. [2] [√*1443*]. gift, act of giving:– gift (1), giving (1)

G1522 δότης *dotēs*, n. [1] [√*1443*]. giver:– giver (1)

G1523 Δουβέριος *Douberios*, a. pr. g. Not used in NIVEBC. [√*1292*]. Doberian, "*from Doberus*"

G1524 δουλαγωγέω *doulagōgeō*, v. [1] [√*1528* + *72*]. to enslave, bring to subjection:– make slave (1)

G1525 δουλεία *douleia*, n. [5] [√*1528*]. slavery, bondage:– slavery (2), bondage (1), make slaves (1), slaves (1)

G1526 δουλεύω *douleuō*, v. [25] [√*1528*]. to serve (as a slave):– serve (9), serving (3), slaves (3), served (2), enslaved (1), enslaved by (1), in slavery (1), serve as slaves (1), serve humbly (1), serves (1), slave (1), slaving (1)

G1527 δούλη *doulē*, n. [3] [√*1528*]. female servant, female slave:– servant (2), women servants (1)

G1528 δοῦλος[1] *doulos[1]*, n. [124] [→*1524*, *1525*, *1526*, *1527*, *1529*, *1530*, *2871*, *4056*, *5281*]. servant, slave; in the NT a person owned as a possession for various lengths of times (Hebrew slaves no more than seven years, Gentile slaves without time limit), of lower social status than free persons or masters; slaves could earn or purchase their freedom:– servant (53), servants (37), slave (18), slaves (12), servant's (2), servants men (1), slavery (1)

G1529 δοῦλος[2] *doulos[2]*, a. [2] [√*1528*]. slavish, servile, completely controlled, as a fig. extension of a slavery system in the ancient world, see *1528*:– slaves (2)

G1530 δουλόω *douloō*, v. [8] [√*1528*]. to enslave, to cause one to become a slave; (pass.) to become enslaved; see also *1528*:– slaves (3), addicted to (1), bound (1), enslaved (1), in slavery (1), made a slave (1)

GREEK INDEX

G1531 δοχή dochē, n. [2] [√1312]. banquet:– banquet (2)

G1532 δράκων drakōn, n. [13] dragon:– dragon (13)

G1533 δράσσομαι drassomai, v. [1] [→1440, 1534]. to catch, seize:– catches (1)

G1534 δραχμή drachmē, n. [3] [√1533]. silver coin, drachma:– coin (1), silver coins (1), NDT (1)

G1535 δρέπανον drepanon, n. [8] sickle:– sickle (8)

G1536 δρόμος dromos, n. [3] [√5556]. race, course; course (in life), career:– race (2), work (1)

G1537 Δρούσιλλα Drousilla, n. pr. [1] Drusilla:– Drusilla (1)

G1538 δύναμαι dynamai, v. [210] [→104, 105, 1539, 1540, 1541, 1542, 1543, 1904, 2872]. to be able, have ability, to have the power to accomplish an action; humans have variously limited abilities, God is unlimited:– can (84), cannot (39 [+4024]), could (31), able (25), can't (5 [+4024]), could have (3), cannot (2 [+3590]), cannot do (2 [+4028]), couldn't (2 [+4024]), ready (2), and cannot (1 [+4028]), can bear (1), can do (1), cannot (1 [+4046]), competent (1), enables (1), enough (1), has the right (1), hoping (1 [+1623, 4803]), may (1), possible (1), surely cannot (1 [+3590]), unable (1 [+3590]), unable (1 [+4024]), you cannot (1 [+4024])

G1539 δύναμις dynamis, n. [119] [√1538]. power, ability; miracle; ruler, an extended meaning of a person or supernatural being who has administrative power:– power (73), miracles (15), miraculous powers (4), ability (3), bodies (3), powerful (3), powers (3), mighty (2), able (1), brilliance (1), displays of power (1), enabled (1), excessive (1), fury (1), meaning (1), mighty one (1), miracle (1), remarkable miracles (1), so powerfully (1 [+1877]), strength (1), work miracles (1)

G1540 δυναμόω dynamoō, v. [2] [√1538]. (pass.) to be strengthened:– strengthened (1), turned to strength (1)

G1541 δυνάστης dynastēs, n. [3] [√1538]. ruler, sovereign, (court) official:– important official (1), ruler (1), rulers (1)

G1542 δυνατέω dynateō, v. [3] [√1538]. to be able, powerful, strong:– able (2), powerful (1)

G1543 δυνατός dynatos, a. [32] [√1538]. possible (based on power); powerful, able, the Mighty One:– possible (11), able (4), could (3), power (3), strong (3), powerful (2), can (1 [+1639]), impossible (1 [+4024]), influential (1), leaders (1), mighty (1), thorough knowledge (1)

G1544 δύνω dynō, v. [2] [→588, 589, 1550, 1553, 1694, 1898, 1903, 1905, 1906, 1907, 2086, 2087, 2115, 4208]. to set (of the sun):– sunset (1 [+2463]), sunset (1 [+3836, 2463])

G1545 δύο dyo, n. num. [135] [→1275, 1308, 1309, 1310, 1311, 1357, 1432, 1433, 1440, 1441, 1453, 1454, 1458, 1474, 1486, 1487, 1488, 1489, 1490, 1491, 1492, 1493, 1495, 1496, 1497, 1500, 1557, 1558, 1559]. two:– two (126), extra (3), seventy-two (2 [+1573]), 42 (1 [+5477, 2779]), both (1 [+3836, 3938]), forty-two (1 [+5477, 2779]), twenty gallons (1 [+3583])

G1546 δυσβάστακτος dysbastaktos, a. [2] [√1002]. hard to carry:– can hardly carry (1), cumbersome (1)

G1547 δυσεντερία dysenteria, n. Not used in NIVEBC. [→1548; cf. 1877]. dysentery

G1548 δυσεντέριον dysenterion, n. [1] [√1547]. dysentery:– dysentery (1)

G1549 δυσερμήνευτος dysermēneutos, a. [1] [√2257]. hard to explain:– hard to make clear (1 [+3306])

G1550 δύσις dysis, n. Not used in NIVEBC. [√1544]. west

G1551 δύσκολος dyskolos, a. [1] [→1552; cf. 3266]. hard, difficult:– hard (1)

G1552 δυσκόλως dyskolōs, adv. [3] [√1551]. hard, with difficulty:– hard (3)

G1553 δυσμή dysmē, n. [5] [√1544]. west (setting of the sun):– west (5)

G1554 δυσνόητος dysnoētos, a. [1] [√3808]. hard to understand:– hard to understand (1)

G1555 δυσφημέω dysphēmeō, v. [1] [→1556; cf. 5774]. (pass.) to be slandered:– slandered (1)

G1556 δυσφημία dysphēmia, n. [1] [√1555]. bad report, slander:– bad report (1)

G1557 δώδεκα dōdeka, n. num. [75] [√1545 + 1274]. twelve:– twelve (61), 12,000 (13 [+5942]), NDT (1)

G1558 δωδέκατος dōdekatos, a. [1] [√1545 + 1274]. twelfth:– twelfth (1)

G1559 δωδεκάφυλον dōdekaphylon, n. [1] [√1545 + 1274 + 5876]. twelve tribes:– twelve tribes (1)

G1560 δῶμα dōma, n. [7] [→488, 1900, 1908, 2224, 3868, 3869, 3870, 3871, 5325]. roof, housetop:– housetop (3), roof (2), roofs (2)

G1561 δωρεά dōrea, n. [11] [√1443]. gift:– gift (10), it[s] (1 [+3836])

G1562 δωρεάν dōrean, adv. [9] [√1443]. freely, free of charge, without payment:– freely (3), for nothing (1), free gift (1), free of charge (1), without cost (1), without paying (1), without reason (1)

G1563 δωρέομαι dōreomai, v. [3] [√1443]. to give, confer, bestow:– given (2), gave (1)

G1564 δώρημα dōrēma, n. [2] [√1443]. gift:– gift (1), NDT (1)

G1565 δῶρον dōron, n. [19] [→2554; cf. 1443]. gift, offering:– gift (8), gifts (8), devoted to God (2), offerings (1)

G1566 δωροφορία dōrophoria, n. Not used in NIVEBC. [√1443 + 5770]. the bringing of a gift

G1567 ε e, letter. Not used in NIVEBC. letter of the Greek alphabet

G1568 ἔα ea, pt. excl. [1] ha!, aha!:– go away (1)

G1569 ἐάν ean, c. [333] [√1623 + 323]. if (usually used in general conditions or conditions that imply some doubt):– if (183), unless (22 [+3590]), whatever (8 [+4005]), when (8), unless (7 [+3590]), suppose (5), wherever (4 [+3963]), whoever (4 [+4005]), anyone (3 [+4005]), anyone (3 [+5516]), even if (3), whoever (3 [+5516]), anyone (2 [+5516]), what (2 [+4005]), whatever (2 [+4012]), whenever (2 [+4006]), whenever (2 [+3963]), whoever (2 [+5516]), whoever (2 [+4005]), whom (2 [+4005]), without (2 [+3590]), according to what (1 [+2771]), anyone (1 [+4005]), anyone (1 [+4005]), anyone (1 [+4005]), anyone (1 [+4012]), anyone (1 [+4005]), anything (1 [+4005]), anything (1 [+4005]), as often as (1 [+4006]), but (1 [+3590]), every (1 [+4012]), everyone (1), everything (1 [+4246, 4012]), except (1 [+3590]), fail (1 [+3590]), if indeed (1), in keeping with (1 [+4005, 5516]), just as (1 [+6055]), may (1), might have been (1), must (1 [+3590]), on (1), one (1 [+5516]), only (1 [+3590]), only (1 [+4028, 1651, 3590]), or (1 [+5445]), provided that (1), refused (1 [+3590]), since (1), though (1), until (1 [+3590, 4754]), what (1 [+4005]), what (1 [+4012]), what if (1), whatever (1 [+4005]), whatever (1 [+4005, 3836, 5516]), whatever (1), whatever (1 [+4005]), whatever (1 [+5516]), whatever (1 [+4246, 4005, 5516]), whenever (1 [+2471]), wherever (1 [+3963]), wherever (1 [+4023]), whether (1 [+5445]), who (1 [+4015]), whoever (1 [+5516]), whoever (1 [+4015]), NDT (15)

G1570 ἐάνπερ eanper, c. [2] [√1623 + 323 + 4302]. if, if indeed:– if indeed (1), NDT (1)

G1571 ἑαυτοῦ heautou, p. reflex. [319] [√899]. himself, herself, itself, themselves; (pl., in some contexts) reciprocal relationship, to one aother:– himself (56), themselves (48), yourselves (30), ourselves (18), their own (16), their (14), itself (12), his (11), his own (9), one another (8), each other (7), you (7), them (6), they (4), herself (3), your (3), your own (3), he (2), her (2), we (2), accepts (1 [+2400, 1877]), aware (1 [+3857, 1877]), claim (1 [+3306]), claim to be (1 [+3306]), claimed to be (1 [+4472]), claiming (1 [+3306]), claims (1 [+3306]), claims to be (1 [+4472]), conceited (1 [+1877, 5861]), conceited (1 [+5861, 4123]), felt (1 [+1877]), hearts (1), her own (1), him (1), his senses (1), inwardly (1 [+1877]), it (1), jumped (1 [+965]), myself (1), oneself (1), others (1), our (1), proper (1), self-seeking (1 [+2426, 3836]), sum of money[s] (1 [+4123]), their very self (1), wondering (1 [+1877, 1389]), your hearts (1), yours (1), yourself (1), NDT (28)

G1572 ἐάω eaō, v. [11] [→4661]. to let, allow, permit:– let (6), allow (2), allowed (1), left (1), no more (1 [+2401])

G1573 ἑβδομήκοντα hebdomēkonta, n. num. [5] [√2231]. seventy:– seventy-two (2 [+1545]), 276 (1 [+1357, 1971]), seventy (1), seventy-five (1 [+4297])

G1574 ἑβδομηκοντάκις hebdomēkontakis, adv. [1] [√2231]. seventy times:– seventy-seven times (1 [+2231])

G1575 ἕβδομος hebdomos, a. [9] [√2231]. seventh:– seventh (8), one in the afternoon (1 [+6052])

G1576 Ἔβερ Eber, n. pr. [1] Eber, "*[regions] beyond [the river]* or *source of the word "Hebrew"*":– Eber (1)

G1577 Ἑβραϊκός Hebraikos, a. pr. Not used in NIVEBC. [√1578]. Hebrew

G1578 Ἑβραῖος Hebraios, n. pr. g. [4] [→1577, 1579, 1580]. a Hebrew; a Hebraic Jew:– Hebrews (2), Hebraic Jews (1), hebrew (1)

G1579 Ἑβραΐς Hebrais, n. pr. [3] [√1578]. Aramaic, Hebrew dialect:– aramaic (3 [+1365])

G1580 Ἑβραϊστί Hebraisti, adv. pr. [7] [√1578]. in Aramaic, in the Hebrew dialect:– aramaic (5), hebrew (1), in hebrew (1)

G1581 ἐγγίζω engizō, v. [42] [√1584]. come near, draw near:– approached (9), come near (8), near (6), approaching (3), came near (2), came up (2), comes (2), almost (1 [+3588]), almost here (1), come (1), comes near (1), draw near (1), drawing near (1), drew near (1), gathering around (1), gets here (1), neared (1 [+1181])

G1582 ἐγγράφω engraphō, v. [3] [√1877 + 1211]. to write in, write on, record:– written (3)

G1583 ἔγγυος engyos, a. Not used in NIVEBC. (n.) guarantee, guarantor€ [1]:– guarantor (1)

G1584 ἐγγύς engys, adv. [31] [→1581, 1585, 4662]. near, close:– near (22), a Sabbath day's walk from (1 [+4879, 2400, 3847]), almost time (1), almost time for (1), approaching (1 [+1181]), in danger of (1), nearby (1), nearer (1), soon (1), NDT (1)

G1585 ἐγγύτερον engyteron, adv. comp. Not used in NIVEBC. [√1584]. nearer, closer

G1586 ἐγείρω egeirō, v. [143] [→1213, 1340, 1444, 1587, 1995, 2074, 5283]. to arise, to stand from a prone or sleeping position. From this base meaning are several fig. extended meanings: to wake from sleep; to restore from a dead or damaged state: to heal, raise to life; to cause something to exist: raise up (give birth to) a child:– raised (44), get up (16), got up (11), risen (10), rise (8), raised from the dead (7), raised to life (7), raise (5), appear (3), raise up (3), raises (3), come (2), gets up (2), helped up (2), wake up (2), woke (2), woke up (2), appeared (1), go (1), lift out (1), lifted to feet (1), made (1), on feet (1), raise again (1), raised again (1), raised up (1), rise again (1), rising (1), stand up (1), stir up (1), woke up (1 [+608, 3836, 5678])

G1587 ἔγερσις egersis, n. [1] [√1586]. resurrection:– resurrection (1)

G1588 ἐγκάθετος enkathetos, a. [1] [√918; cf. 1877 + 2848]. (n.) spy:– spies (1)

G1589 ἐγκαίνια enkainia, n. [1] [√1877 + 2785]. Feast of Dedication (Hanukkah):– festival of Dedication (1)

G1590 ἐγκαινίζω enkainizō, v. [2] [√1877 + 2785]. (pass.) to be put into effect, inaugurate; (act.) to open:– opened (1), put into effect (1)

G1591 ἐγκακέω enkakeō, v. [6] [√1877 + 2805]. to give up, become discouraged, lose heart:– lose heart (2), discouraged (1), give up (1), tire (1), weary (1)

G1592 ἐγκαλέω enkaleō, v. [7] [√1877 + 2813]. to bring charges, accuse; (pass.) to be charged with, have an accusation brought to:– accusing (2), accusation (1), accusations (1), bring any charge (1), charged with (1), press charges (1)

G1593 ἐγκαταλείπω enkataleipō, v. [10] [√1877 + 2848 + 3309]. to forsake, leave, abandon:– abandoned (2), deserted (2), forsaken (2), abandon (1), forsake (1), giving up (1), left (1)

G1594 ἐγκατοικέω enkatoikeō, v. [1] [√1877 + 2848 + 3875]. to live among:– living among (1)

G1595 ἐγκαυχάομαι enkauchaomai, v. [1] [√1877 + 3016]. to boast:– boast (1)

G1596 ἐγκεντρίζω enkentrizō, v. [6] [√1877 + 3034]. to graft into:– grafted in (2), grafted into (2), graft in (1), they will be grafted in (1)

G1597 ἐγκλείω enkleiō, v. Not used in NIVEBC. [√1877 + 3091]. to lock up

G1598 ἔγκλημα enklēma, n. [2] [√1877 + 2813]. charge, accusation:– charge (1), charges (1)

G1599 ἐγκομβόομαι enkomboomai, v. [1] [√1877]. to clothe (oneself) with, put on:– clothe with (1)

G1600 ἐγκοπή enkopē, n. [1] [√1877 + 3164]. hinderance, restraint:– hinder (1 [+1443])

G1601 ἐγκόπτω enkoptō, v. [5] [√1877 + 3164]. to hinder, stop, impede progress:– blocked way (1), cut in on (1), hinder (1), hindered (1), weary (1)

G1602 ἐγκράτεια enkrateia, n. [4] [√1877 + 3197]. self-control:– self-control (4)

G1603 ἐγκρατεύομαι enkrateuomai, v. [2] [√1877 + 3197]. to have control (of oneself):– control (1), goes into training (1)

G1604 ἐγκρατής enkratēs, a. [1] [√1877 + 3197]. disciplined, self-controlled:– disciplined (1)

G1605 ἐγκρίνω enkrinō, v. [1] [√1877 + 3212]. to classify:– classify (1)

G1606 ἐγκρύπτω enkryptō, v. [2] [√1877 + 3221]. to mix, put into:– mixed (1), mixed into (1)

G1607 ἔγκυος enkyos, a. [1] [√1877 + 3246]. pregnant:– expecting a child (1)

G1608 ἐγχρίω enchriō, v. [1] [√1877 + 5987]. to put on, rub on, anoint:– put on (1)

G1609 ἐγώ egō, p. pers. [2580] [→1831, 1847, 2466, 2743, 3592, 3598, 5652]. I, me, my; we, us, our; often added for emphasis: myself, ourselves:– me (729), my (478), I (428), us (359), our (287), we (183), mine (11), myself (6), me

(5 [+*1847*]), my own (5), ours (5), me (4 [+*3836, 3950*]), I (3 [+*1847*]), I (2 [+*3836, 6034*]), me (2 [+*3836, 3517*]), mine (2 [+*1847*]), our own (2), you (2), your (2), here (1 [+*1877*]), I'm (1 [+*1639*]), me (1 [+*6034*]), me (1 [+*3836, 6034*]), me (1 [+*3836, 4725*]), me (1 [+*3836, 5889*]), my (1 [+*1847*]), my (1 [+*3836, 3950*]), ourselves (1), the (1), them[s] (1 [+*3836, 4252*]), to myself (1 [+*3836, 6034*]), us (1 [+*3836, 3517*]), we (1 [+*3836, 4922*]), we'll (1), what do you want with us (1 [+*5515, 5516, 2779, 5148*]), yes (1 [+*2627*]), NDT (48)

G1610* ἐδαφίζω *edaphizō, v. [1] [√ *1611*]. to dash to the ground, raze:– dash to the ground (1)

G1611* ἔδαφος *edaphos, n. [1] [→ *1610*]. ground:– ground (1)

G1612* ἑδραῖος *hedraios, a. [3] [→ *909, 1613, 1909, 1910, 1911, 2339, 2348, 2757, 4204, 4663, 5284, 5285, 5286; cf. 2757*]. firm, steadfast:– firm (1), settled the matter (1 [+*2705*]), stand firm (1 [+*1181*])

G1613* ἑδραίωμα *hedraiōma, n. [1] [√ *1612*]. foundation:– foundation (1)

G1614* Ἑζεκίας *Hezekias, n. pr. [2] Hezekiah, "*God [El] strengthens*":– Hezekiah (2)

G1615* ἐθελοθρησκία *ethelothrēskia, n. [1] [√ *2527 + 2580*]. self-imposed religion:– self-imposed worship (1)

G1616* ἐθίζω *ethizō, v. [1] [√ *1621*]. (pass.) to be accustomed, required:– custom (1)

G1617* ἐθνάρχης *ethnarchēs, n. [1] [√ *1620 + 806*]. governor:– governor (1)

G1618* ἐθνικός *ethnikos, a. [4] [√ *1620*]. pagan, Gentile:– pagans (3), pagan (1)

G1619* ἐθνικῶς *ethnikōs, adv. [1] [√ *1620*]. like a Gentile, like a pagan:– like a gentile (1)

G1620* ἔθνος *ethnos, n. [162] [→ *1617, 1618, 1619*]. Gentile, pagan; (foreign) nation, a people:– gentiles (83), nations (37), nation (25), pagans (6), people (6), gentile (2), country (1), nations (1 [+*476*]), pagan (1)

G1621* ἔθος *ethos, n. [12] [→ *1616, 1622, 1665, 2456, 2799, 5311*]. custom, practice, habit:– customs (6), custom (4), as usual (1 [+*2848, 3836*]), in the habit of (1)

G1622* ἔθω *ethō, v. Not used in NIVEBC. [√ *1621*]. to be accustomed

G1623* εἰ *ei, pt. cond. [502] [→ *1569, 1570, 1638, 1642, 1643, 1664, 2829, 6059, 6062*]. if, since:– if (297), except (34 [+*3590*]), since (10), though (9), but (7 [+*3590*]), only (7 [+*3590*]), that (6), whether (5), or (4), but (3 [+*3590*]), but only (3 [+*3590*]), never (3), only (3 [+*4024, 3590*]), otherwise (3 [+*1254, 3590*]), except (2 [+*3590, 3667*]), only (2), otherwise (2 [+*1254, 3590, 1145*]), unless (2 [+*1760, 3590*]), when (2), as (1), at least (1 [+*3590*]), because (1 [+*1145, 2779*]), but (1), but (1 [+*3590*]), but if (1 [+*3590*]), even (1), even if (1), even though (1), evidently (1 [+*3590*]), except (1 [+*3614*]), except (1 [+*3590, 3668*]), except for (1 [+*3590*]), had it been (1), hoping (1 [+*4803, 1538*]), if (1 [+*726*]), if only (1), in the hope that (1 [+*726*]), in the hope that (1), may be (1), nevertheless (1 [+*3590*]), no (1), now (1), only (1 [+*3590*]), only (1 [+*3590, 3667*]), only (1 [+*3590, 3668*]), only (1 [+*4029, 3590*]), otherwise (1 [+*1760, 3590*]), perhaps (1 [+*5593*]), perhaps (1 [+*726, 1145*]), since (1 [+*4036*]), so (1), such as (1), surely (1 [+*1145*]), surely (1 [+*3605*]), that (1 [+*4803*]), there may be (1), though (1 [+*247*]), undoubtedly (1 [+*5593*]), unless (1 [+*3590*]), unless (1), unless (1 [+*3590*]), unless (1 [+*3614*]), unless (1 [+*4024*]), until (1 [+*3590, 4020*]), what (1 [+*5516*]), what if (1), when (1 [+*1145*]), whether or not (1), NDT (49)

G1624* εἰδέα *eidea, n. [1] [√ *1626*]. appearance (usually implies a condition of reality):– appearance (1)

G1625* εἶδον *eidon, v. Not used in NIVEBC. [√ *1626*]. to see, watch; realize (used as past tense of *3972*)

G1626* εἶδος *eidos, n. [5] [→ *1212, 1229, 1624, 1625, 2078, 2623, 2624, 2627, 4378, 5653; cf. 1631*]. form, appearance, sight:– form (2), appearance (1), kind (1), sight (1)

G1627* εἰδωλεῖον *eidōleion, n. [1] [√ *1631*]. temple of an idol:– idol's temple (1)

G1628* εἰδωλόθυτος *eidōlothytos, a. [9] [√ *1631 + 2604*]. (food) sacrificed to idols:– food sacrificed to idols (6), food sacrificed to an idol (1), sacrificed to a god (1), sacrificed to idols (1)

G1629* εἰδωλολάτρης *eidōlolatrēs, n. [7] [√ *1631 + 3301*]. idolater, one who worships idols and so practices idolatry:– idolaters (5), idolater (2)

G1630* εἰδωλολατρία *eidōlolatria, n. [4] [√ *1631 + 3301*]. idolatry, the reverence and worship of idols:– idolatry (4)

G1631* εἴδωλον *eidōlon, n. [11] [→ *1627, 1628, 1629, 1630, 2977; cf. 1626*]. idol, an object that is worshiped, formed by casting or carving (with the possible implication that a god or demon is intrinsic to the idol):– idols (8), idol (2), it[s] (1)

G1632* εἰκῇ *eikē, adv. [6] in vain, for nothing, to no purpose:– in vain (3), for no reason (1), idle notions (1), wasted (1)

G1633* εἴκοσι *eikosi, n. num. [11] twenty:– twenty-four (6 [+*5475*]), twenty (2), a hundred and twenty feet deep (1 [+*3976*]), three miles (1 [+*5084, 4297*]), twenty-three (1 [+*5552*])

G1634* εἴκω *eikō, v. [1] [→ *5640*]. to give in, yield:– give in (1 [+*3836, 5717*])

G1635* εἰκών *eikōn, n. [23] [√ *2036*]. image, likeness, portrait:– image (21), images (1), realities (1 [+*3836, 4547*])

G1636* εἰλικρίνεια *eilikrineia, n. [3] [√ *1637*]. sincerity, the positive moral quality of purity (especially in motives), a fig. extension of an unadulterated or unmixed substance:– sincerity (3)

G1637* εἰλικρινής *eilikrinēs, a. [2] [→ *1636; cf. 2463 + 3212*]. pure, wholesome:– pure (1), wholesome (1)

G1638* εἰ μήν *ei mēn, adv. Not used in NIVEBC. [√ *1623 + 3605*]. surely, certainly

G1639* εἰμί *eimi, v. [2463] [→ *582, 707, 1913, 1928, 1930, 1997, 2003, 2026, 2157, 3953, 4045, 4205, 4242, 4342, 5223, 5289, 5542; cf. 2026*]. to be, exist, be present:– is (685), are (382), was (297), be (265), were (131), am (127), been (41), come (16), have (16), had (11), means (10), belong to (8), comes (8), lived (7), happen (6), as (5), become (5 [+*1650*]), isn't (5 [+*4024*]), means (5 [+*3493*]), stands for (5), being (4), belong (4), belong to (4 [+*1666*]), belongs to (4), did (4), it's (4), know (4 [+*1196*]), mean (4), stay (4), stayed (4), will (4), with (4), belonged to (3 [+*1666*]), calls for (3), do (3), go (3), have (3 [+*1877*]), live (3), omega (3 [+*6043, 6042*]), present (3), refers to (3), remain (3), taught (3 [+*1438*]), you (3 [+*6043, 6042*]), aren't (2 [+*3590*]), aren't (2 [+*4024*]), aren't (2 [+*4049*]), at work (2), become (2), cannot (2 [+*4024*]), come with (2 [+*5302*]), deserve (2 [+*2653*]), done (2), follow (2), form (2), get (2), had (2 [+*1877*]), had (2 [+*2400*]), has (2 [+*1877*]), have being (2), last (2), leads to (2), like[s] (2), mean (2 [+*2527*]), meaning (2), meant (2), pleases (2 [+*2298*]), stood (2), though (2), would (2), you (2)6043, *6042*]), above Jesus[s] (1 [+*3963*]), accepts (1 [+*1283*]), alive (1 [+*3836, 6034, 1877, 899*]), approved (1 [+*5306*]), as deserve (1 [+*545*]), asserted authority (1 [+*1877, 983*]), attained (1), be diligent (1), be that as it may (1), bears (1 [+*4472*]), been (1 [+*1181*]), became (1 [+*1181*]), becomes (1), began (1), begging (1 [+*4645*]), belonging to (1), belongs (1), belongs to (1 [+*1666*]), binds together (1 [+*5278*]), boast (1 [+*3017*]), break (1 [+*4127*]), bring (1 [+*1650*]), came about (1), came into being (1), can (1 [+*1543*]), care very little (1 [+*1650, 1788*]), carried out (1), cause (1), come (1 [+*2262*]), companions (1 [+*3552*]), companions (1 [+*3836, 5250*]), consented (1 [+*5163*]), considers (1), consist (1), continued (1), deserve (1 [+*545*]), deserves (1 [+*545*]), devoted to (1 [+*4674*]), disagreed (1 [+*851*]), do (1 [+*4475*]), doesn't (1 [+*4024*]), done (1 [+*2240*]), done (1 [+*4472*]), done (1 [+*4556*]), enjoy (1), enter (1 [+*1656*]), equality (1 [+*3836, 2698*]), exist (1), exists (1), explain (1 [+*1196*]), fail the test (1 [+*99*]), failed the test (1 [+*99*]), fall (1 [+*4406*]), find (1), find (1 [+*2351*]), fish (1 [+*2436*]), forgive (1 [+*2664*]), found (1), fulfill (1 [+*5459*]), gather (1 [+*5251*]), gathered (1), gathered (1 [+*2190*]), gathered (1 [+*5255*]), given (1), going on (1), had to (1 [+*338*]), happened (1), happened (1 [+*1181*]), has (1), hate (1 [+*3631*]), have a place (1), have all want (1 [+*3170*]), have hope (1 [+*1827*]), heard (1 [+*201*]), he's (1), hold (1), how foolish (1 [+*6043, 6042, 485*]), I'm (1 [+*1609*]), implies (1), in all (1 [+*4047*]), in other words (1 [+*4047*]), including (1 [+*4005*]), involves (1), is (1 [+*3493*]), isn't (1 [+*4049*]), joined constantly (1 [+*4674*]), keep (1), kept (1), kept on (1), leading the way (1 [+*4575*]), like (1), live lives (1), local (1), longs for (1 [+*2160*]), looks (1), love husbands (1 [+*5791*]), made (1), made up of (1), making a complaint[s] (1), marveled (1 [+*2513*]), mean (1 [+*3836, 3364, 4047*]), meaning (1 [+*5515, 323*]), means (1 [+*3306*]), meet (1), met with (1), numbering[s] (1), numbering (1 [+*3836, 750*]), one (1), owe (1 [+*4050*]), owed money (1 [+*5971*]), own (1 [+*2625*]), owns (1 [+*3261*]), peddle for profit (1 [+*2836*]), perish (1 [+*1650, 724*]), please (1 [+*2298*]), prisoners (1 [+*1313*]), put aside (1 [+*629*]), put in chains (1 [+*1313*]), put trust (1 [+*4275*]), read (1 [+*1211*]), read (1 [+*2108*]), receive (1), rely (1 [+*4275*]), rely on (1 [+*1666*]), remained (1), represent (1), resembled (1 [+*3927*]), rest (1), riot (1 [+*2573*]), sat (1 [+*5153*]), say (1), say (1 [+*3992*]), say (1 [+*4123*]), see (1 [+*5745*]), seem (1), seem (1 [+*6055*]), seems (1), seen (1), settle matters (1 [+*2333*]), share (1), share in (1 [+*3128*]), share in with (1 [+*5171*]), show favoritism (1 [+*4720*]), show favoritism (1 [+*4721*]), sided (1), sinned (1 [+*281, 4472*]), spent the night (1 [+*1381*]), spread (1), spring up (1), standing (1), staying (1), stood (1 [+*3023*]), stood there (1 [+*2392*]), subject to (1 [+*1877*]), sums up (1), take (1 [+*2400*]), take for (1 [+*1506*]), taken part (1 [+*3128*]), taken part in an uprising (1 [+*3334*]), takes captive (1 [+*3836, 5194*]), tasted[s] (1), testify (1 [+*3459*]), testify (1 [+*1650, 3457*]), that's (1), to come (1), treat (1), try (1), used to (1), using (1), valued highly (1 [+*1952*]), went (1), were (1 [+*4537*]), what shall we do (1 [+*5515, 4036*]), what looks like (1 [+*3961*]), withdrew (1 [+*5723*]), wore clothing (1 [+*1907*]), work with (1 [+*5301*]), worth (1), NDT (110), NDT (2 [+

G1640* εἶμι *eimi, v. Not used in NIVEBC. [→ *583, 717, 1655, 1996, 2079, 2768, 5290*]. to go

G1641* ἕνεκεν *heineken, pp.* [2] [√ *1914*]. because of, on account of:– because (1 [+*4005*]), in comparison with (1 [+*1877, 4047, 3836, 3538*])

G1642* εἴπερ *eiper, pt. cond. [6] [√ *1623 + 4302*]. if indeed, if in fact, since:– if (2), if indeed (2), since (1), NDT (1)

G1643* εἴπως *eipōs, pt. Not used in NIVEBC. [√ *1623 + 4544*]. if perhaps, if somehow

G1644* εἰρηνεύω *eirēneuō, v. [4] [√ *1645*]. to live in peace, be at peace:– live in peace (2), at peace (1), live at peace (1)

G1645* εἰρήνη *eirēnē, n. [92] [→ *1644, 1646, 1647, 1648*]. peace, harmony, tranquility; safety, welfare, health; often with an emphasis on lack of strife or reconciliation in a relation, as when one has "peace with God." Often used as a verbal and written greeting. This word generally follows the meanings and usage of the Hebrew word 8934:– peace (87), blessing of peace (1), peacemakers (1 [+*4472*]), reconcile (1 [+*5261, 1650*]), safe (1 [+*1877*]), welcomed (1 [+*1312, 3552*])

G1646* εἰρηνικός *eirēnikos, a. [2] [√ *1645*]. peace-loving, peaceable, peaceful, with a focus of having freedom from emotional worry and frustration:– peace (1), peace-loving (1)

G1647* εἰρηνοποιέω *eirēnopoieō, v. [1] [√ *1645 + 4472*]. to make peace, to cause reconciliation between two parties, as in Christ causing the believer's peace with God:– making peace (1)

G1648* εἰρηνοποιός *eirēnopoios, a. [1] [√ *1645 + 4472*]. peacemaker, one who restores peace and reconciliation between persons and even nations:– peacemakers (1)

G1649* εἴρω *eirō, v. Not used in NIVEBC. [→ *4694, 4937*]. to say, speak

G1650* εἰς *eis, pp. [1767] [→ *1652, 1653, 1654, 1655, 1656, 1657, 1658, 1659, 1660, 1661, 1662, 2081, 2082, 2269, 2276, 2277, 2278, 4206, 4207, 4208, 4209, 4210, 5291*]. to, toward, into; for. Spatially: movement toward or into an area (extending to a goal); logically: a marker of purpose or result; of time: extending to or up to a certain time:– to (460), into (224), in (174), for (144), on (48), at (34), as (27), forever (23 [+*3836, 172*]), so that (21 [+*3836*]), to (18 [+*3836*]), against (16), among (12), so that (9), of (7), until (7), with (7), about (6), become (6 [+*1181*]), before (6), all over (5 [+*3910*]), become (5 [+*1639*]), entered (5 [+*2262*]), never (5 [+*4024, 3590, 3836, 172*]), in order that (4 [+*3836*]), leads to (4), reached (4 [+*2262*]), that (4 [+*3836*]), to (4 [+*3836*]), toward (4), back (3 [+*3836, 3958*]), for purpose (3), in dealing with (3), leading to (3), where (3 [+*4005*]), among (2 [+*3836, 3545*]), as (2 [+*3950*]), beyond (2), brought[s] (2), entered (2), forever (2 [+*3836, 1457*]), in front of everyone (2 [+*3836, 3545*]), make (2), over (2), receive (2), resulted in (2), that (2), through (2), throughout (2 [+*3910*]), to be (2), to bring (2), why (2 [+*5515*]), why (2 [+*5515*]), able to (1), across (1 [+*3836, 4305*]), across the lake (1 [+*3836, 4305*]), again (1 [+*3836, 172*]), among (1 [+*3847*]), and (1 [+*3836*]), and so (1 [+*3836*]), and thus (1 [+*3836*]), around (1 [+*3836, 3958*]), as a result (1 [+*3836*]), as a result (1 [+*3836*]), as far as (1), as though (1), ashore (1 [+*3836, 1178*]), at all (1 [+*3836, 4117*]), attained (1 [+*5777*]), attaining to (1), away[s] (1 [+*3836, 2557*]), back to (1), bear children (1 [+*2856, 5065, 3284*]), bear testimony (1 [+*609, 3457*]), bearing (1), became (1 [+*1181*]), became (1 [+*1181*]), before (1 [+*3545*]), before (1 [+*3836, 3545*]), bring (1 [+*1639*]), bring into (1), brings (1), brings death (1 [+*1666, 2505, 2505*]), brings life (1 [+*1666, 2437, 2437*]), brought (1), burial (1 [+*5502, 3645*]), by (1), by faith from first to last (1 [+*1666, 4411, 4411*]), care very little (1 [+*1788, 1639*]), completely (1 [+*3836, 4117*]), confirms (1 [+*1012*]), destined to (1), destroyed (1 [+*724*]), discredited (1 [+*4029, 3357*]), do (1), doing (1), drew back (1 [+*599, 3836, 3958*]), endlessly (1 [+*3836, 1457*]), enter (1 [+*4513*]), eventually (1 [+*5465*]), ever (1 [+*3836, 172*]), ever-increasing wickedness (1 [+*490, 490*]), far off (1 [+*3426*]), far outweighs them all (1 [+*2848, 5651, 5651, 983*]), fatal (1 [+*2505*]), for (1 [+*3836*]), for all time (1 [+*3836, 1457*]), for the express purpose (1 [+*899, 4047*]), for the sake of (1), for this purpose (1 [+*4047*]), for this very reason (1 [+*4047, 1142*]), forever (1 [+*172*]), forever (1 [+*2465, 172*]), forevermore (1 [+*4246, 3836, 172*]), from (1), full of (1 [+*5958*]), go back (1 [+*2188, 3836, 3958*]), granted (1), greatly (1 [+*4353*]), grew (1 [+*2262*]), hand over to (1 [+*4140, 5931*]), heard about (1 [+*919*]), held (1 [+*2400*]), how to gratify (1), in agreement (1 [+*3836, 1651*]), in fact (1 [+*4047*]), in order that (1), in order to bring (1), in regard to (1), in this way (1 [+*3836*]), increases (1), indoors (1 [+*3875*]), indoors (1 [+*3836, 3864*]), is[s] (1 [+*3950*]), judged (1 [+*3213, 2262*]), landed (1 [+*609, 3836, 1178*]), led to (1), listen carefully (1 [+*5502, 3836, 4044*]), lose good name (1 [+*591, 2262*]), mutual (1 [+*253*]), never (1 [+*4024, 3836, 172*]), never again (1 [+*4024, 3590, 3836,

172]), next (1 [+3836, 3516]), no never (1 [+4024, 3590, 3836, 172]), on board (1 [+899]), on part (1), on way to (1), onto (1), out of the body (1 [+909, 1675]), out of the body[S] (1 [+3836, 909, 1744]), over to (1), pay attention to who they are (1 [+1063, 4725, 476]), perish (1 [+1639, 724]), permanent (1 [+3836, 172]), possess (1 [+1443, 2959]), prompted (1 [+965, 3836, 2840]), ran ahead (1 [+4731, 3836, 1869]), reach (1 [+1181]), reached (1 [+201]), reached (1 [+1181]), reached (1 [+2262]), reaching (1 [+2262]), reason (1 [+4047]), reconcile (1 [+5261, 1645]), regarding (1), result in (1), return (1 [+2262, 3836, 4099]), right into (1 [+2401, 2276]), saved (1 [+4348, 6034]), share in (1), so (1 [+3836]), so (1 [+3836]), so (1 [+3836]), so as (1 [+3836]), so as to (1), so as to form (1), so then (1 [+3836]), spur on (1 [+4237]), subject to (1 [+5715]), such that (1 [+3836]), supply (1), supply (1 [+1181]), take (1 [+404]), take (1 [+2884]), testify (1 [+3457, 1639]), that (1 [+3836]), the place of (1), then able to (1 [+3836]), there[S] (1 [+3836, 2038]), this is the reason (1 [+4047]), throughout (1), throughout (1 [+4246]), to (1 [+3836]), to (1 [+4047]), to cause (1), to the measure (1), treat (1 [+4472]), turned (1 [+1181]), under (1), up to (1), visited (1 [+2262]), where (1), where (1 [+3836, 5536]), where[S] (1 [+3836, 5596]), with ever-increasing glory (1 [+608, 1518, 1518]), with this in mind (1 [+899]), NDT (270)

G1651 εἷς *heis*, n. num. [347] [→ 1894, 1895, 1942, 2022, 2023, 2024, 2025, 2758, 3594, 3599, 4029, 4032]. one, single:– one (247), a (14), first (9), some (6), the other[S] (6), single (5), each (4 [+1667]), alone (3), an (3), faithful to his wife (3 [+1222, 467]), man (3), the (3), other (2), agreeing (1 [+4472, 1191]), alike (1 [+608]), another (1), any (1), children conceived at the same time (1 [+1666, 3130, 2400]), each (1 [+1651, 2848]), each (1 [+2848, 1651]), each (1), each (1 [+324, 1667]), each (1 [+3836, 2848]), everyone (1 [+1667]), faithful to her husband (1 [+467, 1222]), once (1), one (1 [+5516]), one (1 [+6034]), one at a time (1 [+2848, 1651]), one at a time (1 [+1651, 2848]), only (1), only (1 [+4028, 1569, 3590]), same (1), some (1 [+3538]), someone (1), the next (1 [+3552]), the other (1), the same as (1 [+2779, 3836, 899]), to (1), unity (1), you[S] (1), its[S] (1), final[S] (1), in agreement (1 [+1650, 3836]), in detail (1 [+2848, 1667]), in turn (1 [+2848]), in unison (1 [+5889, 1181]), nothing (1 [+4028]), NDT (4)

G1652 εἰσάγω *eisagō*, v. [11] [√ 1650 + 72]. to bring in, take in:– brought in (2), brought into (2), bring in (1), brings in (1), brought (1), led (1), take into (1), taken into (1), took into (1)

G1653 εἰσακούω *eisakouō*, v. [5] [√ 1650 + 201]. (pass.) to be heard, listened to:– heard (4), listen (1)

G1654 εἰσδέχομαι *eisdechomai*, v. [1] [√ 1650 + 1312]. to receive, welcome:– receive (1)

G1655 εἴσειμι *eiseimi*, v. [4] [√ 1650 + 1640]. to go in, enter:– enter (1), entered (1), went (1), went to (1)

G1656 εἰσέρχομαι *eiserchomai*, v. [193] [√ 1650 + 2262]. to go in, enter:– enter (54), entered (36), went into (15), go into (7), come in (6), enters (6), go in (6), went in (6), come (5), came in (4), went inside (4), went to (4), comes in (3), fall into (3), went (3), arrived (2), came into (2), come and share (2), entering (2), gone (2), appear (1), arrived in (1), came (1), came to (1), comes into (1), enter (1 [+1639]), get in (1), go (1), goes into (1), going into (1), gone into (1), got to (1), in (1), living (1 [+2779, 2002]), reached (1), reaped the benefits of (1), started (1), trying to[S] (1), went back (1), went straight into (1), NDT (1)

G1657 εἰσκαλέομαι *eiskaleomai*, v. [1] [√ 1650 + 2813]. to invite into:– invited into (1)

G1658 εἴσοδος *eisodos*, n. [5] [√ 1650 + 3847]. entering, entrance; reception, welcome:– coming (1), enter (1), reception (1), visit (1), welcome (1)

G1659 εἰσπηδάω *eispēdaō*, v. [1] [√ 403; cf. 1650]. to rush in:– rushed in (1)

G1660 εἰσπορεύομαι *eisporeuomai*, v. [18] [√ 1650 + 4513]. to go in, enter:– come in (3), enter (3), enters (3), going into (2), came (1), go into (1), going (1), moved about freely (1 [+2779, 1744]), went (1), went in (1), went to (1)

G1661 εἰστρέχω *eistrechō*, v. [1] [√ 1650 + 5556]. to run in:– ran back (1)

G1662 εἰσφέρω *eispherō*, v. [8] [√ 1650 + 5770]. to bring in, lead in:– bringing (1), brought (1), brought into (1), carries into (1), do this[S] (1), lead (1), lead into (1), take into (1)

G1663 εἶτα *eita*, adv. [15] [→ 2083, 3575]. then, after that, next:– then (7), and then (3), after that (1), and (1), moreover (1 [+3525]), when (1), NDT (1)

G1664 εἴτε *eite*, pt. [65] [√ 1623 + 5445]. if, whether...or:– or (29), whether (18), if (11), where (3), as for (1 [+5642]), as for (1), such as (1), NDT (1)

G1665 εἴωθα *eiōtha*, v. [4] [√ 1621]. to have a custom:– custom (4)

G1666 ἐκ *ek*, pp. [902] [→ 442, 443, 444, 451, 453, 587, 588, 589, 1446, 1447, 1674, 1675, 1676, 1677, 1678, 1679, 1680, 1681, 1682, 1683, 1684, 1685, 1686, 1687, 1688, 1689, 1690, 1691, 1692, 1693, 1694, 1699, 1700, 1701, 1702, 1703, 1704, 1705, 1706, 1707, 1708, 1709, 1710, 1711, 1712, 1713, 1714, 1715, 1716, 1717, 1718, 1719, 1720, 1721, 1722, 1723, 1724, 1725, 1726, 1727, 1728, 1729, 1732, 1733, 1734, 1735, 1736, 1737, 1738, 1739, 1740, 1741, 1742, 1743, 1744, 1745, 1746, 1747, 1748, 1749, 1750, 1751, 1752, 1754, 1758, 1760, 1762, 1763, 1764, 1765, 1766, 1767, 1768, 1769, 1770, 1771, 1774, 1775, 1972, 1973, 1974, 1975, 1976, 1977, 1978, 1979, 1981, 1982, 1983, 1984, 1985, 1986, 1987, 1988, 1989, 1990, 1992, 1993, 1994, 1995, 1996, 1997, 1998, 1999, 2000, 2001, 2002, 2003, 2004, 2005, 2006, 2007, 2010, 2012, 2013, 2014, 2015, 2016, 2017, 2018, 2019, 2020, 2021, 2022, 2023, 2024, 2025, 2026, 2029, 2030, 2031, 2032, 2033, 2034, 2035, 2274, 2275, 4211, 5292, 5293, 5294, 5655, 5656, 5658; cf. 1753, 1772]. of, out of; from, away from. Spatially: extension from a space to a goal outer in reference, separation; logically: the means or source of an activity, disassociation or separation:– from (313), of (180), by (51), out of (48), at (19), with (19), in (18), on (14), one of (9), some of (9), of origin (7), for (6), belonged to (5), among (4), because of (4), belong to (4 [+1639]), from among (4), mother (4), belonged to (3 [+1639]), depends on (3), have (3), some (3), through (3), based on (2), come from (2), comes from (2), followed (2), from (2 [+3545]), over (2), part of (2), since (2), under (2), Jews (1 [+4364]), according to (1), after (1), as (1), away (1 [+3836, 3545]), away from (1 [+3545]), back (1), bear (1 [+1181]), believers[S] (1 [+899]), belong to household (1), belongs to (1 [+1639]), between (1), born (1 [+3120, 3613]), born (1 [+3120, 3613, 1164]), brings death (1 [+2505, 1650, 2505]), brings life (1 [+2437, 1650, 2437]), brought from (1), by faith from first to last (1 [+4411, 1650, 4411]), came from (1), child[S] (1), children conceived at the same time (1 [+1651, 3130, 2400]), completely (1 [+3336, 4356]), depend on (1), descendant (1 [+3875]), descendant (1 [+3836, 2588]), descended from (1), descended from (1 [+5065]), descended from (1 [+2002, 3836, 4019]), ever (1 [+3836, 172]), ever since (1), free and belong to no one (1 [+1801, 4246]), from then on (1 [+4047]), given through (1), heavenly (1 [+4041]), his native language (1 [+3836, 2625]), illegitimate (1 [+4518]), imposed on (1), in front of (1 [+1885]), in household of (1), kindled[S] (1), lose (1 [+3496]), must (1 [+340]), on (1 [+5931]), on account of (1), on the side of (1), one of (1 [+3836, 750]), out (1), physically (1 [+5882]), reluctantly (1 [+3383]), rely on (1 [+1639]), rely on (1), result in (1 [+1181]), samaritan (1 [+3836, 4899]), say (1 [+201]), say (1 [+3836, 5125]), self-seeking (1 [+2249]), spring from (1), the kind[S] (1), to pay (1), use (1), without (1 [+4024]), NDT (90)

G1667 ἕκαστος *hekastos*, a. [82] [→ 1668]. each, every:– each (55), each (3 [+1651]), each one (2), every (2), all (1), any (1), anyone (1), daily (1 [+2848, 2465]), each (1 [+324, 1651]), each (1 [+1651]), each person (1), every (1 [+2848]), everyone (1 [+1651]), in detail (1 [+2848, 1651]), one (1), other (1), some (1), their (1), them (1), they (1), NDT (4)

G1668 ἑκάστοτε *hekastote*, adv. [1] [√ 1667 + 4005 + 5445]. always, at any time:– always (1)

G1669 ἑκατόν *hekaton*, n. num. [17] [→ 1670, 1671, 1672, 1673]. hundred:– hundred (8), 144,000 (3 [+5477, 5475, 5942]), 144 (1 [+5477, 5475]), 153 (1 [+4299, 5552]), hundreds (1), nine hundred gallons (1 [+1004]), seventy-five pounds (1 [+3354]), thousand bushels (1 [+3174])

G1670 ἑκατονταετής *hekatontaetēs*, a. [1] [√ 1669 + 2291]. a hundred years old:– a hundred years old (1)

G1671 ἑκατονταπλασίων *hekatontaplasiōn*, a. [3] [√ 1669]. a hundred times:– hundred times (3)

G1672 ἑκατοντάρχης *hekatontarchēs*, n. [20] [√ 1669 + 806]. centurion, officer:– centurion (16), centurions (2), centurion's (1), officers (1)

G1673 ἑκατόνταρχος *hekatontarchos*, n. Not used in NIVEBC. [√ 1669 + 806]. centurion, officer

G1674 ἐκβαίνω *ekbainō*, v. [1] [√ 1666 + 326]. to leave, go out:– left (1)

G1675 ἐκβάλλω *ekballō*, v. [81] [√ 1666 + 965]. to take out, remove; to drive out, expel; bring out, send out:– drive out (20), driving out (8), drove out (5), threw out (5), take out (4), brings out (3), drives out (3), driven out (2), get rid of (2), remove (2), send out (2), sent out (2), throw (2), thrown out (2), brought out (1), brought through (1), dragged out (1), drive (1), drove (1), exclude (1 [+2033]), expelled (1), out driven (1), out of the body (1 [+1650, 909]), pluck out (1), put out (1), put outside (1), puts out (1), reject (1), sent away (1), sent off (1), throwing (1), thrown (1), took out (1)

G1676 ἔκβασις *ekbasis*, n. [2] [√ 1666 + 326]. way out; outcome, end, result:– outcome (1), way out (1)

G1677 ἐκβλαστάνω *ekblastanō*, v. Not used in NIVEBC. [√ 1666 + 1056]. to sprout up

G1678 ἐκβολή *ekbolē*, n. [1] [√ 1666 + 965]. throwing out (a ship's cargo), jettisoning:– throw the cargo overboard (1)

G1679 ἐκγαμίζω *ekgamizō*, v. Not used in NIVEBC. [√ 1666 + 1141]. to marry, give in marriage

G1680 ἐκγαμίσκω *ekgamiskō*, v. Not used in NIVEBC. [√ 1666 + 1141]. to give in marriage

G1681 ἔκγονος *ekgonos*, a. [1] [√ 1666 + 1181]. (n.) grandchild:– grandchildren (1)

G1682 ἐκδαπανάω *ekdapanaō*, v. [1] [√ 1666 + 1252]. (pass.) to be completely expended, exhausted:– expend as well (1)

G1683 ἐκδέχομαι *ekdechomai*, v. [6] [√ 1666 + 1312]. to wait for, expect, look forward to:– expecting (1), looking forward to (1), together (1), waiting (1), waits (1), waits for (1)

G1684 ἔκδηλος *ekdēlos*, a. [1] [√ 1666 + 1316]. clear, very evident, plain:– clear (1)

G1685 ἐκδημέω *ekdēmeō*, v. [3] [√ 1666 + 1322]. to be away, absent:– away (2), away from (1)

G1686 ἐκδίδωμι *ekdidōmi*, v. [4] [√ 1666 + 1443]. (mid.) to rent, lease:– rented (3), rent (1)

G1687 ἐκδιηγέομαι *ekdiēgeomai*, v. [2] [√ 1666 + 1328 + 72]. to tell:– told (2)

G1688 ἐκδικέω *ekdikeō*, v. [6] [√ 1666 + 1472]. to avenge, take revenge; to grant justice, get justice:– avenge (1), avenged (1), gets justice (1), grant justice (1), punish (1), take revenge (1)

G1689 ἐκδίκησις *ekdikēsis*, n. [9] [√ 1666 + 1472]. justice; vengeance; punishment:– avenge (2), justice (2), avenged (1 [+4472]), punish (1), punish (1 [+1443]), punishment (1), readiness to see justice done (1)

G1690 ἔκδικος *ekdikos*, a. [2] [√ 1666 + 1472]. punishing, avenging:– agents to bring punishment (1), punish (1)

G1691 ἐκδιώκω *ekdiōkō*, v. [1] [√ 1666 + 1503]. to drive out, persecute (severely):– drove out (1)

G1692 ἔκδοτος *ekdotos*, a. [1] [√ 1666 + 1443]. handed over, given up, delivered up:– handed over (1)

G1693 ἐκδοχή *ekdochē*, n. [1] [√ 1666 + 1312]. expectation:– expectation (1)

G1694 ἐκδύω *ekdyō*, v. [5] [√ 1666 + 1544]. to strip off clothing, unclothe:– took off (2), stripped (1), stripped of clothes (1), unclothed (1)

G1695 ἐκεῖ *ekei*, adv. [95] [→ 1696, 1697, 1698, 2084, 2795, 2796, 2797, 5654]. there, in a place where:– there (67), where (11), nearby (2), among you (1), at Berea[S] (1), here (1), in (1), in that place (1), in the other case (1), the garden[S] (1), there he is (1 [+2627]), NDT (7)

G1696 ἐκεῖθεν *ekeithen*, adv. [27] [√ 1695]. from there, from that place:– from there (8), that place (3), from that place (2), there (2), on (1), on each side of (1 [+1949, 2779]), place (1), that town (1), that town[S] (1), where (1), NDT (6)

G1697 ἐκεῖνος *ekeinos*, p. demo. [237] [√ 1695]. that, those; he, she, it:– that (94), those (27), he (24), they (10), this (7), his (4), them (4), him (3), one (3), she (3), Jesus[S] (2), he[S] (2 [+3836, 476]), himself (2), that same (2), that very (2), their (2), who (2), God[S] (1), Jesus Christ[S] (1), John[S] (1), Judas[S] (1), Mary[S] (1), exact (1), him[S] (1 [+3836, 4737]), it (1), it[S] (1 [+3836, 69]), nearby (1 [+4309, 3836, 5536]), next (1), other (1), others (1), same (1), someone (1), that was the time (1 [+1877, 3836, 2465]), the (1), the Pharisees[S] (1), the father[S] (1), these (1), to come[S] (1), very (1), what (1), which (1), NDT (20)

G1698 ἐκεῖσε *ekeise*, adv. [2] [√ 1695]. there, a place where:– there (1), where (1)

G1699 ἐκζητέω *ekzēteō*, v. [7] [√ 1666 + 2426]. to seek out, seek earnestly; (pass.) to be held responsible:– held responsible for (2), earnestly seek (1), searched intently (1), seek (1), seeks (1), sought (1)

G1700 ἐκζήτησις *ekzētēsis*, n. [1] [√ 1666 + 2426]. controversy, useless speculation:– controversial speculations (1)

G1701 ἐκθαμβέω *ekthambeō*, v. [4] [√ 1666 + 2502]. (pass.) to be overwhelmed with wonder, distressed, alarmed:– alarmed (2), deeply distressed (1), overwhelmed with wonder (1)

G1702 ἔκθαμβος *ekthambos*, a. [1] [√ 1666 + 2502]. (utterly) astonished:– astonished (1)

G1703 ἐκθαυμάζω *ekthaumazō*, v. [1] [√ 1666 + 2513]. to wonder, be (utterly) amazed:– amazed (1)

G1704 ἔκθετος *ekthetos*, a. [1] [√ 1666 + 5502]. thrown out, exposed (to elements), abandoned:– throw out (1)

G1705 ἐκκαθαίρω *ekkathairō*, v. [2] [√ 1666 + 2754]. to cleanse, clean out, get rid of:– cleanse (1), get rid of (1)

G1706 ἐκκαίω *ekkaiō*, v. [1] [√ 1666 + 2794]. (pass.) to be inflamed, have a strong desire:– inflamed (1)

G1707 ἐκκακέω *ekkakeō*, v. Not used in NIVEBC. [√*1666 + 2805*]. to lose heart

G1708 ἐκκεντέω *ekkenteō*, v. [2] [√*1666 + 3034*]. to pierce:– pierced (2)

G1709 ἐκκλάω *ekklaō*, v. [3] [√*1666 + 3089*]. (pass.) to be broken off:– broken off (3)

G1710 ἐκκλείω *ekkleiō*, v. [2] [√*1666 + 3091*]. to alienate, shut out, exclude:– alienate (1), excluded (1)

G1711 ἐκκλησία *ekklēsia*, n. [114] [√*1666 + 2813*]. church, congregation, assembly; a group of people gathered together. It can refer to the OT assembly of believers (Ac 7:38), or a riotous mob (Ac 19:32), but usually to a Christian assembly, a church: as a totality (Eph 3:10), or in a specific locale (Col. 4:15). In the NT a church is never a building or meeting place:– church (74), churches (34), assembly (5), congregations (1)

G1712 ἐκκλίνω *ekklinō*, v. [3] [√*1666 + 3111*]. to turn away, turn aside:– keep away (1), turn from (1), turned away (1)

G1713 ἐκκολυμβάω *ekkolymbaō*, v. [1] [√*1666 + 3147*]. to swim away:– swimming away (1)

G1714 ἐκκομίζω *ekkomizō*, v. [1] [√*1666 + 3180*]. to carry out:– carried out (1)

G1715 ἐκκοπή *ekkopē*, n. Not used in NIVEBC. [√*1666 + 3164*]. hindrance

G1716 ἐκκόπτω *ekkoptō*, v. [10] [√*1666 + 3164*]. to cut off, cut down:– cut down (5), cut off (3), cut from under (1), cut out (1)

G1717 ἐκκρεμάννυμι *ekkremannymi*, v. [1] [√*1666 + 3203*]. (mid.) to hang upon (words), to consider something seriously:– hung on (1)

G1718 ἐκλαλέω *eklaleō*, v. [1] [√*1666 + 3281*]. to tell:– tell (1)

G1719 ἐκλάμπω *eklampō*, v. [1] [√*1666 + 3290*]. to shine:– shine (1)

G1720 ἐκλανθάνομαι *eklanthanomai*, v. [1] [√*1666 + 3291*]. to forget:– completely forgotten (1)

G1721 ἐκλέγομαι *eklegomai*, v. [22] [√*1666 + 3306*]. to chose, pick, select:– chosen (9), chose (8), choose (3), made a choice (1), picked (1)

G1722 ἐκλείπω *ekleipō*, v. [4] [√*1666 + 3309*]. to fail, end, stop:– end (1), fail (1), gone (1), stopped shining (1)

G1723 ἐκλεκτός *eklektos*, a. [23] [√*1666 + 3306*]. elect, chosen, the Chosen One:– chosen (13), elect (10)

G1724 ἐκλογή *eklogē*, n. [7] [√*1666 + 3306*]. election, choice, selection:– chosen (3), election (3), elect (1)

G1725 ἐκλύω *eklyō*, v. [5] [√*1666 + 3395*]. (pass.) to lose heart; give up; collapse in weariness:– collapse (2), give up (1), lose (1), lose heart (1)

G1726 ἐκμάσσω *ekmassō*, v. [5] [√*1666 + 3463*]. to wipe off, dry off:– wiped (4), drying (1)

G1727 ἐκμυκτηρίζω *ekmyktērizō*, v. [2] [√*1666 + 3682*]. to sneer at, ridicule:– sneered at (1), sneering at (1)

G1728 ἐκνεύω *ekneuō*, v. [1] [√*1666 + 3748*]. to slip away, withdraw:– slipped away (1)

G1729 ἐκνήφω *eknēphō*, v. [1] [√*1666 + 3768*]. to come to one's sense, become sober:– come back to senses (1)

G1730 ἑκούσιος *hekousios*, a. [1] [√*1776*]. spontaneous, willing:– voluntary (1 [*+2848*])

G1731 ἑκουσίως *hekousiōs*, adv. [2] [√*1776*]. willingly; deliberately, intentionally:– deliberately (1), willing (1)

G1732 ἔκπαλαι *ekpalai*, adv. [2] [√*1666 + 4093*]. for a long time, long ago:– long (1), long ago (1)

G1733 ἐκπειράζω *ekpeirazō*, v. [4] [√*1666 + 4278*]. to test, put to a test, try, tempt:– put to the test (2), test (2)

G1734 ἐκπέμπω *ekpempō*, v. [2] [√*1666 + 4287*]. to send away, send out:– sent away (1), sent on way (1)

G1735 ἐκπερισσῶς *ekperissōs*, adv. [1] [√*1666 + 4356*]. emphatically:– emphatically (1)

G1736 ἐκπετάννυμι *ekpetannymi*, v. [1] [√*1666 + 4375*]. to hold out, spread out:– held out (1)

G1737 ἐκπηδάω *ekpēdaō*, v. [1] [√*403; cf. 1666*]. to rush out:– rushed out (1)

G1738 ἐκπίπτω *ekpiptō*, v. [10] [√*1666 + 4406*]. to fall off; to fail; to run aground, be dashed to pieces:– run aground (2), dashed (1), drift away (1), failed (1), fall (1), fall from (1), fallen away from (1), falls (1), fell off (1)

G1739 ἐκπλέω *ekpleō*, v. [3] [√*1666 + 4434*]. to sail (from):– sailed (2), sailed from (1)

G1740 ἐκπληρόω *ekplēroō*, v. [1] [√*1666 + 4444*]. to (utterly) fulfill:– fulfilled (1)

G1741 ἐκπλήρωσις *ekplērōsis*, n. [1] [√*1666 + 4444*]. end, completion:– end (1)

G1742 ἐκπλήσσω *ekplēssō*, v. [13] [√*1666 + 4448*]. (pass.) to be amazed, astonished:– amazed (9), astonished (3), amazement (1)

G1743 ἐκπνέω *ekpneō*, v. [3] [√*1666 + 4463*]. to breathe one's last breath, die:– breathed last (2), died (1)

G1744 ἐκπορεύομαι *ekporeuomai*, v. [33] [√*1666 + 4513*]. to go out, come out, leave:– come out (3), comes out (3), coming out (3), leaving (3), went out (3), come (2), came from (1), came out (1), comes (1), comes from (1), flowing from (1), from came (1), go out (1), goes out (1), going (1), leave (1), left (1), moved about freely (1 [*+1660, 2779*]), out came (1), out of the body[S] (1 [*+1650, 3836, 909*]), spread (1), started (1)

G1745 ἐκπορνεύω *ekporneuō*, v. [1] [√*1666 + 4520*]. to engage in sexual immorality:– gave up to sexual immorality (1)

G1746 ἐκπτύω *ekptyō*, v. [1] [√*1666 + 4772*]. to scorn, spit out:– scorn (1)

G1747 ἐκπυρόω *ekpyroō*, v. Not used in NIVEBC. [√*1666 + 4786*]. to set on fire, destroy by fire

G1748 ἐκριζόω *ekrizoō*, v. [4] [√*1666 + 4844*]. to uproot:– uprooted (2), pulled up by the roots (1), uproot (1)

G1749 ἔκστασις *ekstasis*, n. [7] [√*1666 + 2705*]. amazement, astonishment, bewilderment; a trance:– trance (3), amazed (1 [*+3284*]), amazement (1), astonished (1 [*+2014*]), bewildered (1)

G1750 ἐκστρέφω *ekstrephō*, v. [1] [√*1666 + 5138*]. (pass.) to be warped, perverted:– warped (1)

G1751 ἐκσῴζω *eksōzō*, v. Not used in NIVEBC. [√*1666 + 5392*]. to bring safely

G1752 ἐκταράσσω *ektarassō*, v. [1] [√*1666 + 5429*]. to throw into an uproar, into confusion:– throwing into an uproar (1)

G1753 ἐκτείνω *ekteinō*, v. [16] [→*701, 867, 1755, 1756, 1757, 1759, 2085, 2364, 4189, 4727, 4742, 5657, 5936; cf. 1666*]. to stretch out, reach out; point, motion:– stretch out (5), reached out (4), stretched out (2), lay (1), lower (1), motioned (1), pointing (1 [*+5931*]), reached (1 [*+3836, 5931*])

G1754 ἐκτελέω *ekteleō*, v. [2] [√*1666 + 5465*]. to finish, bring to a conclusion:– finish (2)

G1755 ἐκτένεια *ekteneia*, n. [1] [√*1753*]. earnestness:– earnestly (1 [*+1877*])

G1756 ἐκτενής *ektenēs*, a. [1] [√*1753*]. deep, earnest:– deeply (1)

G1757 ἐκτενῶς *ektenōs*, adv. [3] [√*1753*]. deeply, earnestly:– deeply (1), earnestly (1), more earnestly (1)

G1758 ἐκτίθημι *ektithēmi*, v. [4] [√*1666 + 5502*]. (mid.) to explain; (pass.) to be placed out in the elements, exposed, abandoned:– explained (1), explaining about (1), placed outside (1), told (1)

G1759 ἐκτινάσσω *ektinassō*, v. [4] [√*1753*]. to shake off, shake out:– shake off (2), shook off as a warning (1), shook out in protest (1)

G1760 ἐκτός *ektos*, adv. [8] [√*1666*]. outside, beyond, except:– outside (2), unless (2 [*+1623, 3590*]), beyond (1), not include (1), otherwise (1 [*+1623, 3590*]), out of (1)

G1761 ἕκτος *hektos*, a. [14] [√*1971*]. sixth, noon (the sixth hour):– sixth (7), noon (6 [*+6052*]), at noon (1 [*+6052*])

G1762 ἐκτρέπω *ektrepō*, v. [5] [√*1666 + 5572*]. to turn away, wander away from; be disabled:– disabled (1), turn aside (1), turn away from (1), turned (1), turned away (1)

G1763 ἐκτρέφω *ektrephō*, v. [2] [√*1666 + 5555*]. to feed, nourish; to bring up, rear (children):– bring up (1), feed (1)

G1764 ἔκτρομος *ektromos*, a. Not used in NIVEBC. [√*1666 + 5554*]. trembling

G1765 ἔκτρωμα *ektrōma*, n. [1] [√*1666 + 5546*]. abnormal or untimely birth:– abnormally born (1)

G1766 ἐκφέρω *ekpherō*, v. [8] [√*1666 + 5770*]. to bring out, carry out; to produce:– carried out (2), bring (1), brought (1), carry out (1), led (1), produces (1), take out (1)

G1767 ἐκφεύγω *ekpheugō*, v. [8] [√*1666 + 5771*]. to escape:– escape (5), escaped (1), ran (1), slipped through (1)

G1768 ἐκφοβέω *ekphobeō*, v. [1] [√*1666 + 5832*]. to frighten, terrify:– frighten (1)

G1769 ἔκφοβος *ekphobos*, a. [2] [√*1666 + 5832*]. frightened, terrified:– so frightened (1), trembling (1)

G1770 ἐκφύω *ekphyō*, v. [2] [√*1666 + 5886*]. to come out, put forth:– come out (2)

G1771 ἐκφωνέω *ekphōneō*, v. Not used in NIVEBC. [√*1666 + 5889*]. cry out

G1772 ἐκχέω *ekcheō*, v. [22] [→*136, 431, 1773, 2219, 2972, 4717, 5177, 5179, 5180, 5658, 5954, 5959, 5967; cf. 1666*]. to pour out, shed, scatter; (pass.) to be poured out, shed; to rush (for profit):– poured out (11), pour out (3), shed (3), run out (2), rushed (1), scattered (1), spilled out (1)

G1773 ἐκχύννομαι *ekchynnomai*, v. [5] [√*1772*]. to be poured out, shed, spilled:– poured out (3), shed (2)

G1774 ἐκχωρέω *ekchōreō*, v. [1] [√*1666 + 6003*]. to go out, go away:– get out (1)

G1775 ἐκψύχω *ekpsychō*, v. [3] [√*1666 + 6038*]. to die, expire:– died (3)

G1776 ἑκών *hekōn*, a. [2] [→*220, 1730, 1731*]. voluntarily, by one's own choice:– by its own choice (1), voluntarily (1)

G1777 ἐλαία *elaia*, n. [13] [→*66, 1778, 1779, 2814*]. olive, olive tree; when used with *4001* it is the proper name "the Mount of Olives," a ridge on the east side of the Kidron Valley, overlooking Jerusalem and the Temple mount:– olives (9 [*+1779*]), olive (1), olive tree (1), olive trees (1), olives (1)

G1778 ἔλαιον *elaion*, n. [11] [√*1777*]. olive oil:– oil (9), olive oil (2)

G1779 ἐλαιών *elaiōn*, n. [12] [√*1777*]. Mount of Olives, olive grove:– olives (9 [*+1777*]), mount of olives (3)

G1780 Ἐλαμίτης *Elamitēs*, n. pr. g. [1] Elamite, "*highland*":– Elamites (1)

G1781 ἐλάσσων *elassōn*, a. [also used as adv.] [4] [→*1782, 1783, 1784, 1788*]. lesser, cheaper, younger:– cheaper (1), lesser (1), unless over (1), younger (1)

G1782 ἐλαττονέω *elattoneō*, v. [1] [√*1781*]. to have too little:– have too little (1)

G1783 ἐλαττόω *elattoō*, v. [3] [√*1781*]. to make lower than; (pass.) to be made lower than, become lesser, diminish:– made lower (2), less (1)

G1784 ἐλάττων *elattōn*, a. Not used in NIVEBC. [√*1781*]. lesser, cheaper, younger

G1785 ἐλαύνω *elaunō*, v. [5] [→*590, 5295*]. to row (with oars); (pass.) to be driven:– driven (3), rowed (1), the oars[S] (1)

G1786 ἐλαφρία *elaphria*, n. [1] [√*1787*]. lightness, levity:– fickle (1 [*+3836, 5968*])

G1787 ἐλαφρός *elaphros*, a. [2] [→*1786*]. light, not burdensome:– light (2)

G1788 ἐλάχιστος *elachistos*, a. [14] [√*1781*]. least, very small, trivial:– least (6), very little (3), very small (2), care very little (1 [*+1650, 1639*]), less than the least (1), trivial (1)

G1789 Ἐλεάζαρ *Eleazar*, n. pr. [2] Eleazar, "*God [El] is a help*":– Eleazar (2)

G1790 ἐλεάω *eleaō*, v. [3] [√*1799*]. to show mercy, be merciful:– merciful (1), mercy (1), show mercy (1)

G1791 ἐλεγμός *elegmos*, n. [1] [√*1794*]. rebuke, reproof:– rebuking (1)

G1792 ἔλεγξις *elenxis*, n. [1] [√*1794*]. rebuke, reproof:– rebuked (1 [*+2400*])

G1793 ἔλεγχος *elenchos*, n. [1] [√*1794*]. certainty, proof:– assurance (1)

G1794 ἐλέγχω *elenchō*, v. [17] [→*591, 1352, 1791, 1792, 1793, 1998*]. to expose; to rebuke, refute, show fault; to convince, convict:– rebuke (3), exposed (2), convict (1), convicted (1), convicted of sin (1), correct (1), expose (1), point out fault (1), prove guilty (1), prove to be in the wrong (1), rebuked (1), rebukes (1), refute (1), reprove (1)

G1795 ἐλεεινός *eleeinos*, a. [2] [√*1799*]. pitiful:– most to be pitied (1), pitiful (1)

G1796 ἐλεέω *eleeō*, v. [29] [√*1799*]. to have mercy on, pity; to show mercy to, show pity to another who is in serious need, usually with a focus on an act of kindness that will help meet the need:– have mercy (12), had mercy (3), received mercy (3), shown mercy (3), have pity (2), mercy (2), had[S] (1), has mercy (1), receive mercy (1), show mercy (1)

G1797 ἐλεημοσύνη *eleēmosynē*, n. [13] [√*1799*]. gift to the poor, alms, charitable gift; any act of generosity to someone in serious need, often referring to giving gifts of substance or money:– gifts to the poor (2), give to the needy (2 [*+4472*]), be generous to the poor (1 [*+1443*]), beg (1 [*+160*]), begging (1 [*+4639, 3836*]), gave to in need (1 [*+4472*]), gifts for the poor (1), give to the poor (1 [*+1443*]), giving (1), helping the poor (1 [*+4472*]), money (1)

G1798 ἐλεήμων *eleēmōn*, a. [2] [√*1799*]. merciful, including feelings of pity, with a focus of showing compassion to those in serious need:– merciful (2)

G1799 ἔλεος *eleos*, n. [27] [→*446, 447, 1790, 1795, 1796, 1797, 1798*]. mercy, pity; the moral quality of feeling compassion and especially of showing kindness toward someone in need. This can refer to a human kindness and to

God's kindness to humankind:– mercy (24), merciful (2), tender mercy (1 [+*5073*])

G1800 **ἐλευθερία** ***eleutheria***, n. [11] [√*1801*]. freedom, liberty, not enslaved:– freedom (10), free (1)

G1801 **ἐλεύθερος** ***eleutheros***, a. [23] [→*592, 1800, 1802*]. free, released, liberated from various kinds of ownership, confinement, and distress: prison confinement, political domination and oppression, physical sickness, release from the marriage contract in death, and God's release of the sinner from sin. A free person is often contrasted to a slave:– free (18), exempt (1), free and belong to no one (1 [+*1666, 4246*]), freedom (1), released (1), set free (1)

G1802 **ἐλευθερόω** ***eleutheroō***, v. [7] [√*1801*]. to set free, liberate, cause someone to receive liberty or freedom:– set free (5), liberated (1), sets free (1)

G1803 **ἔλευσις** ***eleusis***, n. [1] [√*2262*]. coming, advent:– coming (1)

G1804 **ἐλεφάντινος** ***elephantinos***, a. Not used in NIVEBC. made of ivory (derivative of the Greek word for "elephant," not found in the NT)€ [1]:– made of ivory (1)

G1805 **Ἐλιακείμ** ***Eliakeim***, n. pr. Not used in NIVEBC. [√*cf. 1806*]. Eliakim, "*God [El] establishes*"

G1806 **Ἐλιακίμ** ***Eliakim***, n. pr. [3] [√*cf. 1805*]. Eliakim, "*God [El] establishes*":– Eliakim (3)

G1807 **ἕλιγμα** ***heligma***, n. Not used in NIVEBC. [√*1813*]. package, roll

G1808 **Ἐλιέζερ** ***Eliezer***, n. pr. [1] Eliezer, "*God [El] is [my] help*":– Eliezer (1)

G1809 **Ἐλιούδ** ***Elioud***, n. pr. [2] Eliud, "*God [El] is [my] grandeur*":– Elihud (2)

G1810 **Ἐλισάβετ** ***Elisabet***, n. pr. [9] Elizabeth, "*God [El] is [my] oath*":– Elizabeth (9)

G1811 **Ἐλισαῖος** ***Elisaios***, n. pr. [1] [→*1812*]. Elisha, "*God [El] is [my] salvation*":– Elisha (1)

G1812 **Ἐλισσαῖος** ***Elissaios***, n. pr. Not used in NIVEBC. [√*1811*]. Elisha, "*God [El] is [my] salvation*"

G1813 **ἑλίσσω** ***helissō***, v. [2] [→*1807*]. to roll up:– roll up (1), rolled up (1)

G1814 **ἕλκος** ***helkos***, n. [3] [→*1815*]. sore, abscess:– sores (3)

G1815 **ἑλκόω** ***helkoō***, v. [1] [√*1814*]. (pass.) to be covered with sores:– covered with sores (1)

G1816 **ἑλκύω** ***helkyō***, v. [8] [→*1999*]. to drag, draw, pull in:– dragged (3), dragging (1), draw (1), draws (1), drew (1), haul in (1)

G1817 **Ἑλλάς** ***Hellas***, n. pr. [1] [√*1818*]. Greece:– Greece (1)

G1818 **Ἕλλην** ***Hellēn***, n. pr. [25] [→*1817, 1819, 1820, 1821, 1822*]. Greek; Gentile, a class of person distinguished from the Jewish race and nation (not necessarily Greek):– Greeks (14), gentile (6), Greek (3), gentiles (2)

G1819 **Ἑλληνικός** ***Hellēnikos***, a. pr. [1] [√*1818*]. Greek (language):– Greek (1)

G1820 **Ἑλληνίς** ***Hellēnis***, n. pr. [2] [√*1818*]. Greek, Gentile, a class of person distinguished from the Jewish race and nation (not necessarily Greek):– Greek (2)

G1821 **Ἑλληνιστής** ***Hellēnistēs***, n. pr. g. [3] [√*1818*]. Grecian Jew, Hellenist:– Hellenistic Jews (2), Greeks (1)

G1822 **Ἑλληνιστί** ***Hellēnisti***, adv. pr. [2] [√*1818*]. in Greek (language):– Greek (2)

G1823 **ἐλλογάω** ***ellogaō***, v. [1] [√*1877 + 3306*]. to charge (to one's account):– charge (1)

G1824 **ἐλλογέω** ***ellogeō***, v. [1] [√*1877 + 3306*]. (pass.) to be charged to one's account:– charged against account (1)

G1825 **Ἐλμαδάμ** ***Elmadam***, n. pr. [1] [→*1826*]. Elmadam:– Elmadam (1)

G1826 **Ἐλμωδάμ** ***Elmōdam***, n. pr. Not used in NIVEBC. [√*1825*]. Elmodam

G1827 **ἐλπίζω** ***elpizō***, v. [31] [√*1828*]. to hope, hope for, put hope in, expect, an attitude of confidently looking forward to what is good and beneficial:– hope (11), put hope (4), hope for (2), hoped (2), hoping (2), set hope (2), expect (1), expectations (1), have hope (1 [+*1639*]), hopes (1), hopes for (1), hopes set (1), puts hope (1), trust (1)

G1828 **ἐλπίς** ***elpis***, n. [53] [→*594, 1827, 4598*]. hope, expectation:– hope (52), NDT (1)

G1829 **Ἐλύμας** ***Elymas***, n. pr. [1] [√*cf. 2287*]. Elymas, "[poss.] *wise one hence magician*":– Elymas (1)

G1830 **ἐλωΐ** ***elōi***, l.[n.+p.] [2] [√*cf. 2458*]. Eloi [Aramaic: my God]:– eloi (2)

G1831 **ἐμαυτοῦ** ***emautou***, p. reflex. [37] [√*1609 + 899*]. myself, my own, of my own accord:– myself (17), my own (8), me (4), my (4), I (2), on my own authority (1 [+*608*]), NDT (1)

G1832 **ἐμβαίνω** ***embainō***, v. [16] [√*1877 + 326*]. to get into, step into, embark:– got into (12), get into (2), getting into (1), stepped into (1)

G1833 **ἐμβάλλω** ***emballō***, v. [1] [√*1877 + 965*]. to throw into:– throw into (1)

G1834 **ἐμβαπτίζω** ***embaptizō***, v. Not used in NIVEBC. [√*1877 + 970*]. to dip into

G1835 **ἐμβάπτω** ***embaptō***, v. [2] [√*1877 + 970*]. to dip into:– dipped (1), dips (1)

G1836 **ἐμβατεύω** ***embateuō***, v. [1] [√*1877 + 326*]. to go into great detail about:– goes into great detail (1)

G1837 **ἐμβιβάζω** ***embibazō***, v. [1] [√*1877 + 326*]. to put on board (a vessel):– put (1)

G1838 **ἐμβλέπω** ***emblepō***, v. [12] [√*1877 + 1063*]. to look (closely, directly) at, gaze at:– looked at (4), saw (2), blinded (1 [+*4024*]), look at (1), looked closely at (1), looked directly at (1), looked straight at (1), looking (1)

G1839 **ἐμβριμάομαι** ***embrimaomai***, v. [5] [√*1877 + 1102*]. to warn sternly, rebuke harshly; to be deeply moved:– deeply moved (2), rebuked harshly (1), strong warning (1), warned sternly (1)

G1840 **ἐμέω** ***emeō***, v. [1] to spit out:– spit out (1)

G1841 **ἐμμαίνομαι** ***emmainomai***, v. [1] [√*1877 + 3419*]. to be enraged:– obsessed (1)

G1842 **Ἐμμανουήλ** ***Emmanouēl***, n. pr. [1] Immanuel, "*God with us*":– Immanuel (1)

G1843 **Ἐμμαοῦς** ***Emmaous***, n. pr. [1] [√*cf. 4035*]. Emmaus, "*hot springs*":– Emmaus (1)

G1844 **ἐμμένω** ***emmenō***, v. [4] [√*1877 + 3531*]. to remain in, stay in; remain faithful, continue in:– continue (1), remain faithful (1), remain true (1), stayed in (1)

G1845 **ἐμμέσῳ** ***emmesō***, v. Not used in NIVEBC. [√*1877 + 3545*]. among

G1846 **Ἐμμώρ** ***Hemmōr***, n. pr. [1] Hamor, "*male donkey*":– Hamor (1)

G1847 **ἐμός** ***emos***, a. poss. [86] [√*1609*]. my, mine:– my (48), my own (8), me (7), I (3), me (3 [+*1609*]), I (3 [+*1609*]), mine (3), I have (2 [+*3836*]), it^s (1 [+*3836*]), mine (1 [+*1609*]), me (2 [+*1609*]), mine (1 [+*1609*]), my (1 [+*1609*]), myself (1), of my own (1), NDT (1)

G1848 **ἐμπαιγμονή** ***empaigmonē***, n. [1] [√*1877 + 4089*]. scoffing, mocking:– scoffing (1)

G1849 **ἐμπαιγμός** ***empaigmos***, n. [1] [√*1877 + 4089*]. jeering, scoffing, mocking:– jeers (1)

G1850 **ἐμπαίζω** ***empaizō***, v. [13] [√*1877 + 4089*]. to mock, ridicule:– mocked (8), mock (2), mocking (1), outwitted (1), ridicule (1)

G1851 **ἐμπαίκτης** ***empaiktēs***, n. [2] [√*1877 + 4089*]. scoffer, mocker:– scoffers (2)

G1852 **ἐμπέμπω** ***empempō***, v. Not used in NIVEBC. [√*1877 + 4287*]. to send in

G1853 **ἐμπεριπατέω** ***emperipateō***, v. [1] [√*1877 + 4309 + 4251*]. to walk among:– walk among (1)

G1854 **ἐμπιμπλάω** ***empimplaō***, v. Not used in NIVEBC. [√*1877 + 4398*]. to provide, fill, satisfy

G1855 **ἐμπίμπλημι** ***empimplēmi***, v. [5] [√*1877 + 4398*]. (act.) to provide, fill, satisfy; (pass.) to be filled to satisfaction; to enjoy one's company:– enjoyed company (1), filled (1), had enough to eat (1), provides with plenty (1), well fed (1)

G1856 **ἐμπίμπρημι** ***empimprēmi***, v. [1] [√*1877 + 4399*]. to burn, set on fire:– burned (1)

G1857 **ἐμπιπλάω** ***empiplaō***, v. Not used in NIVEBC. [√*1877 + 4398*]. to provide, fill, satisfy

G1858 **ἐμπίπλημι** ***empiplēmi***, v. Not used in NIVEBC. [√*1877 + 4398*]. to provide, fill, satisfy

G1859 **ἐμπίπρημι** ***empiprēmi***, v. Not used in NIVEBC. [√*1877 + 4399*]. to burn, set on fire

G1860 **ἐμπίπτω** ***empiptō***, v. [7] [√*1877 + 4406*]. to fall into:– fall into (4), fall under (1), falls (1), fell into the hands of (1)

G1861 **ἐμπλέκω** ***emplekō***, v. [2] [√*1877 + 4428*]. (mid./pass.) to be involved in, become entangled:– entangled in (1), gets entangled in (1)

G1862 **ἐμπλοκή** ***emplokē***, n. [1] [√*1877 + 4428*]. braiding (possibly associated with high fashion):– elaborate hairstyles (1 [+*2582*])

G1863 **ἐμπνέω** ***empneō***, v. [1] [√*1877 + 4463*]. to breath:– breathing out (1)

G1864 **ἐμπορεύομαι** ***emporeuomai***, v. [2] [√*1877 + 4513*]. to carry on business; exploit:– carry on business (1), exploit (1)

G1865 **ἐμπορία** ***emporia***, n. [1] [√*1877 + 4513*]. business, trade:– business (1)

G1866 **ἐμπόριον** ***emporion***, n. [1] [√*1877 + 4513*]. market, marketplace:– market (1 [+*3875*])

G1867 **ἔμπορος** ***emporos***, n. [5] [√*1877 + 4513*]. merchant:– merchants (3), merchant (1 [+*476*]), merchants who sold (1)

G1868 **ἐμπρήθω** ***emprēthō***, v. Not used in NIVEBC. [√*1877 + 4399*]. to burn, set on fire

G1869 **ἔμπροσθεν** ***emprosthen***, adv. & pp.* [48] [√*1877 + 4639*]. before, in front of, in the presence of:– before (18), in front of (7), ahead (3), in the presence of (3), at (2), in presence (2), surpassed (2 [+*1181*]), ahead of (1), do (1 [+*1181*]), in faces (1), in front (1), in full view of (1), ran ahead (1 [+*4731, 1650, 3836*]), right in front of (1), to (1), NDT (3)

G1870 **ἐμπτύω** ***emptyō***, v. [6] [√*1877 + 4772*]. to spit on, spit at:– spit on (4), spit (1), spit at (1)

G1871 **ἐμφανής** ***emphanēs***, a. [2] [√*1877 + 5743*]. seen, revealed, visible:– revealed (1 [+*1181*]), seen (1)

G1872 **ἐμφανίζω** ***emphanizō***, v. [10] [√*1877 + 5743*]. to show; report; to present (legal) charges; petition; (pass.) to appear:– show (3), brought charges (2), appear (1), appeared (1), appeared and presented charges (1), petition (1), reported (1)

G1873 **ἔμφοβος** ***emphobos***, a. [5] [√*1877 + 5832*]. afraid, terrified:– afraid (1), fear (1 [+*1181*]), fright (1 [+*1181*]), frightened (1), terrified (1)

G1874 **ἐμφυσάω** ***emphysaō***, v. [1] [√*1877 + 5886*]. to breathe on:– breathed on (1)

G1875 **ἔμφυτος** ***emphytos***, a. [1] [√*1877 + 5886*]. implanted:– planted in (1)

G1876 **ἐμφωνέω** ***emphōneō***, v. Not used in NIVEBC. [√*1877 + 5889*]. to call

G1877 **ἐν** ***en***, pp. [2740] [→*440, 441, 450, 1445, 1582, 1588, 1589, 1590, 1591, 1592, 1593, 1594, 1595, 1596, 1597, 1598, 1599, 1600, 1601, 1602, 1603, 1604, 1605, 1606, 1607, 1608, 1823, 1824, 1832, 1833, 1834, 1835, 1836, 1837, 1838, 1839, 1841, 1844, 1845, 1848, 1849, 1850, 1851, 1852, 1853, 1854, 1855, 1856, 1857, 1858, 1859, 1860, 1861, 1862, 1863, 1864, 1865, 1866, 1867, 1868, 1869, 1870, 1871, 1872, 1873, 1874, 1875, 1876, 1878, 1879, 1880, 1881, 1882, 1887, 1889, 1890, 1891, 1892, 1893, 1896, 1897, 1898, 1899, 1900, 1901, 1902, 1903, 1904, 1905, 1906, 1907, 1908, 1909, 1910, 1911, 1912, 1913, 1918, 1919, 1920, 1921, 1922, 1923, 1924, 1925, 1926, 1927, 1928, 1930, 1931, 1932, 1935, 1936, 1937, 1938, 1939, 1940, 1941, 1943, 1944, 1946, 1947, 1949, 1950, 1951, 1952, 1954, 1955, 1956, 1957, 1958, 1959, 1960, 1961, 1962, 1963, 1964, 1965, 1966, 1967, 1969, 2086, 2087, 2979, 3028, 4212, 4213, 4214, 4599, 5659; cf. 1547, 1953*]. Spatially: in, inside, at, among, with; logically: by means of, with, because of; of time: during, while:– in (1409), with (143), at (126), by (123), on (97), among (92), to (43), through (32), of (20), when (18), for (16), among (14 [+*3545*]), into (11), during (10), this is how (10 [+*4047*]), as (9 [+*3836*]), within (9), as (8), about (7), because of (6), pregnant (6 [+*1143, 2400*]), throughout (6 [+*3910*]), under (6), from (5), on account of (5), where (5 [+*4005*]), while (5 [+*3836*]), against (4), how (4 [+*5515*]), in the realm of (4), there (4 [+*899*]), when (4 [+*3836*]), when (4 [+*3836*]), when (4 [+*4005*]), as (3 [+*3836*]), everywhere (3 [+*4246, 5536*]), had (3), have (3), have (3 [+*1639*]), in (3 [+*3545*]), out of (3), soon (3 [+*5443*]), throughout (3), along (2), as (2 [+*3836*]), at the center of (2 [+*3545*]), before^s (2 [+*213*]), dressed in (2 [+*4314, 2668*]), each other's (2 [+*253*]), full of (2), had (2 [+*1639*]), has (2 [+*1639*]), heavenly (2 [+*3836, 4041*]), in the midst of (2), over (2), soon (2 [+*5443*]), there^s (2 [+*3836, 2639*]), toward (2), truly (2 [+*237*]), uncircumcised (2 [+*213*]), when (2 [+*3836*]), when (2 [+*3836*]), when (2 [+*4005*]), while (2 [+*4005*]), your (2 [+*5148*]), a matter of (1), accepts (1 [+*2400, 1571*]), according to (1), after^s (1 [+*4364*]), after this (1 [+*3836, 2759*]), alive (1 [+*3836, 6034, 899, 1639*]), always (1 [+*4246, 2789*]), and (1), as of first importance (1 [+*4755*]), asserted authority (1 [+*983, 1639*]), at (1 [+*3836*]), at the time of (1), aware (1 [+*3857, 1571*]), based on (1), bear (1), because (1 [+*4005*]), because (1 [+*4005*]), before (1), before (1 [+*3545*]), before (1 [+*3836, 3545*]), before circumcised (1 [+*213*]), before the group (1 [+*3545*]), belong to (1), besides (1), briefly (1 [+*3900*]), by (1 [+*3836*]), by (1 [+*3836*]), by appealing to (1), by following (1), by means of (1), by the power of (1), by the standards (1), caused by (1), cheerfully (1 [+*2660*]), circumcised (1 [+*4364*]), clearly (1 [+*4244*]), complete (1 [+*4246*]), conceited (1 [+*1571, 5861*]), conceive (1 [+*1143, 2400*]), conceive (1 [+*5197, 1143*]), conceived (1 [+*5197, 3836, 3120*]), consists in (1), contain (1), contained (1 [+*2400*]), contained (1 [+*5639*]), continue (1), decided (1 [+*5502, 3836, 4460*]), diligently (1 [+*5082*]), displayed in (1), does work

GREEK INDEX

(1 [+1918, 3586]), down (1), earnestly (1 [+1755]), earthly (1 [+4922]), encircled by (1 [+3545]), enemies (1 [+2397]), entrusted to (1 [+5931]), exposed to (1), expressed in (1), fearlessly (1 [+4244]), felt (1 [+1571]), fidelity to (1), figuratively (1 [+4231]), for (1 [+4005, 1256]), gave (1), generously (1 [+605]), gently (1 [+4559]), gently (1 [+4460, 4559]), glorious (1 [+1518, 1506]), gratifying[S] (1), guilty of (1), he[S] (1 [+3836, 4460, 899, 899]), here (1 [+4047]), here (1 [+899]), here (1 [+1609]), humbly (1 [+4559]), illness (1 [+3836, 4922]), immediately (1 [+5443]), immediately (1 [+899, 3836, 6052]), imperishable (1 [+914]), imprisoned (1 [+5871]), in a manner of speaking (1 [+4130]), in accordance with (1), in addition to (1), in comparison with (1 [+4047, 3836, 3538, 1641]), in handling (1), in midst (1), in presence (1), in the cause of (1), in the face of (1), in the sight of (1), in the way of (1), in your relationships with one another (1 [+5148]), included in (1), inside (1 [+3836, 3864]), invalid (1 [+2400, 3836, 819]), inwardly (1 [+1571]), inwardly (1 [+3836, 3220]), its (1 [+899]), killed (1 [+5840, 633]), made alive[S] (1 [+4005]), made think (1 [+5502, 3836, 2840]), make (1), make up mind (1 [+5502, 3836, 2840]), mark (1), meanwhile (1 [+4005]), meanwhile (1 [+4047]), meanwhile (1 [+3836, 3568]), members of (1), mixed with (1), native (1 [+4005, 1164]), near (1), next to (1 [+3836, 3146]), obey (1 [+5717]), observing (1 [+4513]), old (1 [+4581, 2465]), on (1 [+3836]), on board (1 [+3836, 4450]), on duty (1 [+3836, 5423]), open to (1), out in (1), outward (1 [+3836, 5745]), outwardly (1 [+3836, 5745]), painful (1 [+3383]), perfectly (1 [+4246]), perishable (1 [+5785]), persevered (1 [+4246, 5705]), personally (1 [+4922]), physical (1 [+4922]), possessed by (1), possesses (1), public (1 [+4244]), purpose (1), put on (1), quick (1 [+5443]), quickly (1 [+5443]), relying on (1), safe (1 [+1645]), secretly (1 [+1515]), securely (1 [+4246, 854]), set free (1 [+690, 912]), share (1), show (1), so (1 [+4047]), so powerfully (1 [+1539]), so that (1), soon afterward (1 [+3836, 2009]), strike dead (1 [+650, 2505]), subject to (1 [+1639]), subject to bleeding (1 [+4868, 135]), such[S] (1 [+4922]), suffering[S] (1 [+5393]), that (1 [+3836]), that (1 [+4047]), that was the time (1 [+3836, 2465, 1697]), there (1 [+3836, 5536]), there[S] (1 [+3545]), there[S] (1 [+4047, 3836, 4484]), this is how (1 [+4047]), this kind[S] (1 [+4231]), this makes (1 [+4047]), though (1 [+4005]), thus (1 [+4047]), to show (1), today (1 [+3836, 4958, 2465]), tolerate (1), trying to (1), under care (1), under the control of (1 [+3023]), united (1 [+3836, 899]), united with (1), unseen (1 [+3836, 3220]), unseen (1 [+3836, 3224]), until (1 [+4005]), use (1), use (1 [+4344]), used (1 [+1181]), very old (1 [+4581, 3836, 2465]), wear (1), whatever (1 [+4005, 1254, 323]), when (1 [+4005]), when (1 [+3836]), when (1 [+2465]), when (1 [+3836]), when (1 [+3836]), when (1 [+3836]), when (1 [+4005]), whenever (1), where (1 [+4005, 5536]), while (1 [+3836]), while (1 [+3836]), while (1), while (1 [+4005]), with (1 [+3545]), with regard to (1 [+3538]), with the help of (1), within (1 [+3836, 3517]), wondered about (1 [+5502, 3836, 2840]), wondering (1 [+1571, 1389]), NDT (202)

G1878 ἐναγκαλίζομαι enankalizomai, v. [2] [√1877 + 44]. to take in one's arms:– taking in arms (1), took in arms (1)

G1879 ἐνάλιος enalios, a. [1] [√1877 + 229]. creatures pertaining to the sea:– sea creatures (1)

G1880 ἐνάλλομαι enallomai, v. Not used in NIVEBC. [√1877 + 256]. leap upon

G1881 ἐνανθρωπέω enanthrōpeō, v. Not used in NIVEBC. [√1877 + 476]. to take on human form

G1882 ἔναντι enanti, adv. [used as pp.*] [2] [→595, 1883, 1884, 1885, 2978, 5539, 5641; cf. 1877 + 505]. before (spatial); fig., in the eyes of:– before (2)

G1883 ἐναντίον enantion, adv. [used as pp.*] [5] [√1882]. before (spatial); fig., in the sight of:– before (2), in public (1 [+3836, 3295]), in the sight of (1), of (1)

G1884 ἐναντιόομαι enantioomai, v. Not used in NIVEBC. [√1882]. to oppose

G1885 ἐναντίος enantios, a. [8] [√1882]. against, opposite, in hostility:– against (4), oppose (2), hostile (1), in front of (1 [+1666])

G1886 ἐναργής energēs, a. Not used in NIVEBC. clear, evident, visible

G1887 ἐνάρχομαι enarchomai, v. [2] [√1877 + 806]. to begin:– began (1), beginning (1)

G1888 ἔνατος enatos, a. [10] [√1933]. ninth (ninth hour = three p.m.):– three in the afternoon (6), three in the afternoon (2 [+6052]), ninth (1), three in the afternoon (1 [+6052, 3836, 2465])

G1889 ἐναφίημι enaphiēmi, v. Not used in NIVEBC. [√918; cf. 1877]. to let, permit

G1890 ἐνδεής endeēs, a. [1] [√1877 + 1289]. needy, poor, impoverished:– needy (1)

G1891 ἔνδειγμα endeigma, n. [1] [√1877 + 1257]. evidence, plain indication:– evidence (1)

G1892 ἐνδείκνυμι endeiknymi, v. [11] [√1877 + 1259]. to show, display:– show (6), display (2), be (1), did (1), shown (1)

G1893 ἔνδειξις endeixis, n. [4] [√1877 + 1259]. demonstration, proof, sign:– demonstrate (2), proof (1), sign (1)

G1894 ἕνδεκα hendeka, n. num. [6] [√1651 + 1274]. eleven:– eleven (6)

G1895 ἑνδέκατος hendekatos, a. [3] [√1651 + 1274]. eleventh:– eleventh (1), five in the afternoon (1), five in the afternoon (1 [+6052])

G1896 ἐνδέχομαι endechomai, v. imper. [1] [√1877 + 1312]. it is possible:– can (1)

G1897 ἐνδημέω endēmeō, v. [3] [√1877 + 1322]. to be at home:– at home (3)

G1898 ἐνδιδύσκω endidyskō, v. [2] [√1877 + 1544]. to put on, dress (another); (mid.) dress oneself:– dressed in (1), put on (1)

G1899 ἔνδικος endikos, a. [2] [√1877 + 1472]. just, deserved:– just (2)

G1900 ἐνδόμησις endomēsis, n. Not used in NIVEBC. [√1877 + 1560]. construction, material

G1901 ἐνδοξάζομαι endoxazomai, v. [2] [√1877 + 1518]. to be glorified, honored:– glorified (2)

G1902 ἔνδοξος endoxos, a. [4] [√1877 + 1518]. honored, having high status and so thought to be wonderful, a fig. extension of the feature of an object being radiant or expensive:– expensive (1), honored (1), radiant (1), wonderful (1)

G1903 ἔνδυμα endyma, n. [8] [√1877 + 1544]. clothing, garment:– clothes (7), clothing (1)

G1904 ἐνδυναμόω endynamoō, v. [7] [√1877 + 1538]. to give strength, strengthen; (mid./pass.) to be strong, strengthened:– strong (2), gave strength (1), given strength (1), gives strength (1), powerful (1), strengthened (1)

G1905 ἐνδύνω endynō, v. [1] [√1877 + 1544]. to worm one's way, creep in:– worm their way into (1)

G1906 ἔνδυσις endysis, n. [1] [√1877 + 1544]. putting on:– fine clothes (1 [+2668])

G1907 ἐνδύω endyō, v. [28] [√1877 + 1544]. to clothe, dress; (mid.) clothe oneself:– put on (7), clothe with (3), clothed with (3), dressed in (3), wear (2), wearing (2), clothed (1), in place (1), putting on (1), wore clothing (1 [+1639]), worn (1), NDT (3)

G1908 ἐνδώμησις endōmēsis, n. [1] [√1877 + 1560]. what something is made of, material:– made of (1)

G1909 ἐνέδρα enedra, n. [2] [√1877 + 1612]. plot, ambush:– ambush (1), plot (1)

G1910 ἐνεδρεύω enedreuō, v. [2] [√1877 + 1612]. to wait in ambush, lie in wait for:– waiting (1), waiting in ambush (1)

G1911 ἔνεδρον enedron, n. Not used in NIVEBC. [√1877 + 1612]. plot, ambush

G1912 ἐνειλέω eneileō, v. [1] [√1877]. to wrap in:– wrapped in (1)

G1913 ἔνειμι eneimi, v. [1] [√1877 + 1639]. to be inside; contents:– inside (1)

G1914 ἕνεκα heneka, pp.* Not used in NIVEBC. [→1641, 1915]. for the sake of; for this reason, because

G1915 ἕνεκεν heneken, pp.* [23] [√1914]. for, for the sake of, for this reason, because:– because of (4), for (4), for sake (3), on account of (3), for reason (2), for the sake of (2), all on account of (1), on account (1), that (1), why (1 [+5515]), NDT (1)

G1916 ἐνενήκοντα enenēkonta, n. num. [4] [√1933]. ninety:– ninety-nine (4 [+1933])

G1917 ἐνεός eneos, a. [1] [→1934]. speechless:– speechless (1)

G1918 ἐνέργεια energeia, n. [8] [√1877 + 2240]. working, power, energy:– power (2), working (2), does work (1 [+1877, 3586]), energy (1), powerful (1), works (1)

G1919 ἐνεργέω energeō, v. [21] [√1877 + 2240]. to be at work in; to produce:– at work (11), work (2), works in (2), act (1), effective (1), exerted (1), expressing (1), produces (1), works out (1)

G1920 ἐνέργημα energēma, n. [1] [√1877 + 2240]. working, activity:– working (1)

G1921 ἐνεργής energēs, a. [3] [√1877 + 2240]. active, effective:– active (1), effective (1), effective work (1)

G1922 ἐνευλογέω eneulogeō, v. [2] [√1877 + 2292 + 3306]. (pass.) to be blessed:– blessed (2)

G1923 ἐνέχω enechō, v. [3] [√1877 + 2400]. to oppose, be hostile toward, bear a grudge against; (pass.) to be burdened:– burdened (1), nursed a grudge against (1), oppose (1)

G1924 ἐνθάδε enthade, adv. [8] [√1877]. here, in this place, to this place:– here (6), back (1), there (1)

G1925 ἔνθεν enthen, adv. [2] [√1877]. from here:– from here (2)

G1926 ἐνθυμέομαι enthymeomai, v. [2] [√1877 + 2596]. to consider, reflect on:– considered (1), entertain thoughts (1)

G1927 ἐνθύμησις enthymēsis, n. [4] [√1877 + 2596]. thought, reflection; design, idea:– thoughts (3), design (1)

G1928 ἔνι eni, v. [6] [√1877 + 1639]. there is:– there is (2), does (1), is (1), is there (1), NDT (1)

G1929 ἐνιαυτός eniautos, n. [14] [√899]. year:– year (10), years (2), annual (1 [+2848]), year after year (1 [+2848])

G1930 ἐνίοτε eniote, adv. Not used in NIVEBC. [√1639 + 1877 + 4005]. sometimes

G1931 ἐνίστημι enistēmi, v. [7] [√1877 + 2705]. to be present, (ptcp.) the present:– present (4), be (1), come (1), the present (1)

G1932 ἐνισχύω enischyō, v. [2] [√1877 + 2709]. to strengthen (another); to regain (one's own) strength:– regained strength (1), strengthened (1)

G1933 ἐννέα ennea, n. num. [5] [→1888, 1916]. nine:– ninety-nine (4 [+1916]), nine (1)

G1934 ἐννεός enneos, a. Not used in NIVEBC. [√1917]. speechless

G1935 ἐννεύω enneuō, v. [1] [√1877 + 3748]. to make a sign, nod:– made signs (1)

G1936 ἔννοια ennoia, n. [2] [√1877 + 3808]. attitude, thought:– attitude (1), attitudes (1)

G1937 ἔννομος ennomos, a. [2] [√1877 + 3795]. under law, subject to the law; legal (assembly):– legal (1), under law (1)

G1938 ἐννόμως ennomōs, adv. Not used in NIVEBC. [√1877 + 3795]. subject to the law, in possession of the law

G1939 ἔννυχος ennychos, a. [used as adv.] [1] [√1877 + 3816]. while it is still dark, at night:– while it was still dark (1)

G1940 ἐνοικέω enoikeō, v. [5] [√1877 + 3875]. to live in, live with:– lives in (2), dwell (1), live with (1), lived in (1)

G1941 ἐνορκίζω enorkizō, v. [1] [√1877 + 3992]. to charge by oath, adjure:– charge (1)

G1942 ἑνότης henotēs, n. [2] [√1651]. unity:– unity (2)

G1943 ἐνοχλέω enochleō, v. [2] [√1877 + 4063]. (act.) to cause trouble; (pass.) to be troubled:– cause trouble (1), troubled (1)

G1944 ἔνοχος enochos, a. [10] [√1877 + 2400]. subject to; guilty, liable for:– guilty (2), subject (2), worthy (2), answerable (1), guilty of sinning (1), held in (1), in danger (1)

G1945 ἔνταλμα entalma, n. [3] [√1953]. rule, commandment, precept:– rules (2), commands (1)

G1946 ἐνταφιάζω entaphiazō, v. [2] [√1877 + 5439]. to prepare (a corpse) for burial, bury:– burial (2)

G1947 ἐνταφιασμός entaphiasmos, n. [2] [√1877 + 5439]. preparation for burial, burial:– burial (2)

G1948 ἐντέλλω entellō, v. [15] [√1953]. (mid.) to command, give orders, give instructions:– command (6), commanded (4), commanded to keep (1), gave instructions (1), giving instructions (1), instructed (1), tells (1)

G1949 ἐντεῦθεν enteuthen, adv. [10] [√1877]. from here, from this place:– Galilee[S] (1), from (1), from another place (1 [+4024]), from here (1), leave (1 [+72]), on each side of (1 [+2779, 1696]), on each side (1 [+2779, 1949]), one on each side (1 [+1949, 2779]), out of here (1), this place (1)

G1950 ἔντευξις enteuxis, n. [2] [√1877 + 5593]. prayer, intercession:– intercession (1), prayer (1)

G1951 ἐντίθημι entithēmi, v. Not used in NIVEBC. [√1877 + 5502]. to put in, implant

G1952 ἔντιμος entimos, a. [5] [√1877 + 5507]. highly valued, honored, precious:– precious (2), honor (1 [+2400]), person more distinguished (1), valued highly (1 [+1639])

G1953 ἐντολή entolē, n. [67] [→1945, 1948; cf. 1877]. command, commandment, regulation, an order that has authority:– commands (20), command (18), commandment (11), commandments (5), commanded (2 [+1443]), instructions (2), orders (2), commanded (1 [+3284]), law (1), one[S] (1), regulation (1), regulation (1 [+3795]), requires (1 [+2400, 2848]), what commands (1)

G1954 ἐντόπιος entopios, a. [1] [√1877 + 5536]. resident, local:– people there (1)

G1955 ἐντός entos, adv. [2] [√1877]. inside, within:– in midst (1), inside (1)

G1956 ἐντρέπω entrepō, v. [9] [√1877 + 5572]. to cause shame; (pass.) to be ashamed; (mid.) to care about, respect:–

respect (3), ashamed (1), care what think (1), cared what thought (1), feel ashamed (1), respected (1), shame (1)

G1957 ἐντρέφω entrephō, v. [1] [√1877 + 5555]. (pass.) to be brought up, reared, trained:– nourished (1)

G1958 ἔντρομος entromos, a. [3] [√1877 + 5554]. trembling:– fear (1), trembled with fear (1 [+1181]), trembling (1 [+1181])

G1959 ἐντροπή entropē, n. [2] [√1877 + 5572]. shame, humiliation:– shame (2)

G1960 ἐντρυφάω entryphaō, v. [1] [√1877 + 5588]. to revel, carouse:– reveling (1)

G1961 ἐντυγχάνω entynchanō, v. [5] [√1877 + 5593]. to intercede, appeal, petition:– appealed (1), intercede (1), intercedes (1), interceding (1), petitioned (1)

G1962 ἐντυλίσσω entylissō, v. [3] [√1877]. to wrap up (a body); (pass.) to be folded:– wrapped (1), wrapped around (1), wrapped in (1)

G1963 ἐντυπόω entypoō, v. [1] [√1877 + 5597]. (pass.) to be engraved, carved:– engraved (1)

G1964 ἐνυβρίζω enybrizō, v. [1] [√1877 + 5615]. to insult:– insulted (1)

G1965 ἐνυπνιάζομαι enypniazomai, v. [2] [√1877 + 5678]. to (have supernatural) dreams or visions:– dream (1), on the strength of dreams (1)

G1966 ἐνύπνιον enypnion, n. [1] [√1877 + 5678]. dream:– dreams (1)

G1967 ἐνώπιον enōpion, pp.* [94] [√1877 + 3972]. before, in the presence of; in behalf of, by authority of:– before (34), in the presence of (9), in front of (6), in the sight of (5), to (5), in the eyes of (4), in sight (3), against (2), in presence (2), on behalf (2), at (1), between (1), by (1), entice to sin (1 [+965, 4998]), in eyes (1), in full view of (1), of (1), on (1), on behalf of (1), publicly (1 [+4246]), publicly (1 [+3836, 4436]), sight (1), with (1), NDT (9)

G1968 Ἐνώς Enōs, n. pr. [1] Enosh, "*[mortal] man*":– Enosh (1)

G1969 ἐνωτίζομαι enōtizomai, v. [1] [√1877 + 4044]. to listen carefully, pay attention to:– listen carefully (1)

G1970 Ἑνώχ Henōch, n. pr. [3] Enoch, "*initiated; follower*":– Enoch (3)

G1971 ἕξ hex, n. num. [13] [→1276, 1761, 1980, 2008]. six:– six (7), half (2 [+3604]), 276 (1 [+1357, 1573]), 666 (1 [+1980, 2008]), forty-six (1 [+5477, 2779]), three and a half years (1 [+2291, 5552, 2779, 3604])

G1972 ἐξαγγέλλω exangellō, v. [1] [√1666 + 34]. to declare, proclaim:– declare (1)

G1973 ἐξαγοράζω exagorazō, v. [4] [√1666 + 60]. (act.) to redeem, as a fig. extension of the act of purchasing something in the marketplace; (mid.) to make the most (of the time):– make the most of (1), making the most of (1), redeem (1), redeemed (1)

G1974 ἐξάγω exagō, v. [12] [√1666 + 72]. to lead out, bring out, escort:– led out (6), brought out (2), escort out (1), escorted from (1), lead out (1), leads out (1)

G1975 ἐξαιρέω exaireō, v. [8] [√1666 + 145]. (act.) to gouge, take out, tear out; (mid.) to rescue, set free:– rescued (3), gouge out (2), rescue (2), set free (1)

G1976 ἐξαίρω exairō, v. [1] [√1666 + 149]. to expel, remove, drive away:– expel (1)

G1977 ἐξαιτέω exaiteō, v. [1] [√1666 + 160]. (mid.) to ask for:– asked (1)

G1978 ἐξαίφνης exaiphnēs, adv. [5] [√1666 + 167]. suddenly, unexpectedly:– suddenly (5)

G1979 ἐξακολουθέω exakoloutheō, v. [3] [√1666 + 199 [1.3]]. to follow, obey:– follow (3)

G1980 ἑξακόσιοι hexakosioi, a. num. [2] [√1971]. six hundred:– 1,600 (1 [+5943]), 666 (1 [+2008, 1971])

G1981 ἐξαλείφω exaleiphō, v. [5] [√1666 + 230]. to wipe away, blot out, cancel:– blot out (1), canceled (1), wipe (1), wipe away (1), wiped out (1)

G1982 ἐξάλλομαι exallomai, v. [1] [√1666 + 256]. to jump up:– jumped (1)

G1983 ἐξανάστασις exanastasis, n. [1] [√1666 + 324 + 2705]. resurrection:– resurrection (1)

G1984 ἐξανατέλλω exanatellō, v. [2] [√424; cf. 1666]. to spring up:– sprang up (2)

G1985 ἐξανίστημι exanistēmi, v. [3] [√1666 + 324 + 2705]. to raise up (seed) = have children; (intr.) to stand up:– raise up (2), stood up (1)

G1986 ἐξανοίγω exanoigō, v. Not used in NIVEBC. [√487; cf. 1666]. to open fully

G1987 ἐξαπατάω exapataō, v. [6] [√1666 + 573]. to deceive, cheat:– deceive (3), deceived (3)

G1988 ἐξάπινα exapina, adv. [1] [√1666 + 167]. suddenly:– suddenly (1)

G1989 ἐξαπορέω exaporeō, v. [2] [√1666 + 1.1 + 4513]. (mid.) to despair; (pass.) to be in despair:– despaired (1), in despair (1)

G1990 ἐξαποστέλλω exapostellō, v. [12] [√1666 + 690]. to send out, send away:– sent (6), sent away (3), send away (1), sent off (1), sent on visit (1)

G1991 ἐξαρτάω exartaō, v. Not used in NIVEBC. to be attached to, an adherent

G1992 ἐξαρτίζω exartizō, v. [2] [√1666 + 785]. to finish, complete; (pass.) to be equipped, furnished:– leave (1), thoroughly (1)

G1993 ἐξαστράπτω exastraptō, v. [1] [√1666 + 847]. to flash like lightning:– flash of lightning (1)

G1994 ἐξαυτῆς exautēs, adv. [6] [√1666 + 899]. immediately, at once, right now:– at once (2), as soon as (1 [+6055, 323]), immediately (1), right now (1), right then (1 [+2779, 2627])

G1995 ἐξεγείρω exegeirō, v. [2] [√1666 + 1586]. to raise, awaken (from the dead):– raise (1), raised up (1)

G1996 ἔξειμι exeimi[1], v. [4] [√1666 + 1640]. to leave, go out, go away:– get to (1), leave (1), leaving (1), left (1)

G1997 ἔξειμι exeimi[2], v. Not used in NIVEBC. [√1666 + 1639]. it is permitted, lawful (see 2003)

G1998 ἐξελέγχω exelenchō, v. Not used in NIVEBC. [√1666 + 1794]. to convict

G1999 ἐξέλκω exelkō, v. [1] [√1666 + 1816]. (pass.) to be dragged away:– dragged away (1)

G2000 ἐξέραμα exerama, n. [1] [√1666]. vomit, what is disgorged:– vomit (1)

G2001 ἐξεραυνάω exeraunaō, v. [1] [√1666 + 2236]. to search intently, inquire carefully:– with the greatest care (1)

G2002 ἐξέρχομαι exerchomai, v. [218] [√1666 + 2262]. to go out, leave:– went out (43), left (23), came out (20), come out (15), leave (12), go out (11), gone out (7), came from (6), went (6), spread (5), come (4), go (4), come from (3), gone (3), leaving (3), set out (3), came (2), comes out (2), coming from (2), get out (2), go away (2), going out (2), got out (2), landed (2), out came (2), out come (2), went on (2), bringing a flow (1), came back (1), came down (1), comes (1), coming (1), coming out (1), daybreak (1 [+1181, 2465]), descended from (1 [+1666, 3836, 4019]), driven out (1), escaped (1), flowed out (1), issued (1), known (1), leave (1 [+2032]), led out (1), living (1 [+1656, 2779]), originate (1), out (1), out of (1), rode out (1), set out from (1), slipping away (1), started (1), stepped (1), take on the journey (1), walked out (1), went outside (1), went through (1)

G2003 ἔξεστι exesti, v. imper. [31] [√1666 + 1639]. it is legal, it is proper, it is permitted:– lawful (12), have the right (5), unlawful (4 [+4024]), right (3), can (1), have right (1), law (1), legal (1), may (1), permitted (1), the law forbids (1 [+4024])

G2004 ἐξετάζω exetazō, v. [3] [√458; cf. 1666]. to make a search; to ask, inquire, question:– ask (1), search (1), search for (1)

G2005 ἐξέφνης exephnēs, adv. Not used in NIVEBC. [√1666 + 167]. suddenly, unexpectedly

G2006 ἐξέχω exechō, v. Not used in NIVEBC. [√1666 + 2400]. to stand out, be prominent

G2007 ἐξηγέομαι exēgeomai, v. [6] [√1666 + 72]. to tell, make known, describe, report:– told (2), described (1), made known (1), reported (1), telling about (1)

G2008 ἑξήκοντα hexēkonta, n. num. [9] [√1971]. sixty:– sixty (5), 1,260 (2 [+5943, 1357]), 666 (1 [+1980, 1971]), about seven miles (1 [+600, 5084])

G2009 ἑξῆς hexēs, adv. [5] [√2400]. next, afterward:– next (4), soon afterward (1 [+1877, 3836])

G2010 ἐξηχέω exēcheō, v. [1] [√1666 + 2491]. (pass.) to ring out, be caused to sound out:– rang out (1)

G2011 ἕξις hexis, n. [1] [√2400]. constant use, practice:– constant use (1)

G2012 ἐξιστάνω existanō, v. Not used in NIVEBC. [√1666 + 2705]. to confuse, amaze; (intr.) to be out of one's senses, amazed

G2013 ἐξιστάω existaō, v. Not used in NIVEBC. [√1666 + 2705]. to confuse, amaze; (intr.) to be out of one's senses, amazed

G2014 ἐξίστημι existēmi, v. [17] [√1666 + 2705]. to amaze, astound; (intr.) to be amazed, out of one's senses:– amazed (7), astonished (6), out of mind (2), astonished (1 [+1749]), utterly amazed (1 [+2779, 2513])

G2015 ἐξισχύω exischyō, v. [1] [√1666 + 2709]. to have power, be strong enough:– power (1)

G2016 ἔξοδος exodos, n. [3] [√1666 + 3847]. exodus, departure:– departure (2), exodus (1)

G2017 ἐξολεθρεύω exolethreuō, v. [1] [√1666 + 3897]. (pass.) to be completely cut off from:– completely cut off (1)

G2018 ἐξομολογέω exomologeō, v. [10] [√1666 + 3933]. (act.) to consent; (mid.) to openly confess, admit, praise:– praise (3), acknowledge (2), confessing (2), confess (1), consented (1), openly confessed (1 [+2779, 334])

G2019 ἐξορκίζω exorkizō, v. [1] [√1666 + 3992]. to charge under oath, adjure:– charge under oath (1)

G2020 ἐξορκιστής exorkistēs, n. [1] [√1666 + 3992]. one driving out evil spirits, exorcist:– driving out evil spirits (1)

G2021 ἐξορύσσω exoryssō, v. [2] [√1666 + 4002]. to dig through, tear out:– digging through (1), torn out (1)

G2022 ἐξουδενέω exoudeneō, v. [1] [√1666 + 4024 + 1254 + 1651]. (pass.) to be rejected, treated with contempt:– rejected (1)

G2023 ἐξουδενόω exoudenoō, v. Not used in NIVEBC. [√1666 + 4024 + 1254 + 1651]. (pass.) to be rejected, treated with contempt

G2024 ἐξουθενέω exoutheneō, v. [11] [√1666 + 4024 + 1254 + 1651]. to treat with contempt, look down on, ridicule; (pass.) to be rejected, despised:– treat with contempt (5), amounts to nothing (1), despised (1), looked down on (1), rejected (1), ridiculed (1), scorned (1)

G2025 ἐξουθενόω exouthenoō, v. Not used in NIVEBC. [√1666 + 4024 + 1254 + 1651]. despise, disdain

G2026 ἐξουσία exousia, n. [102] [→2027, 2028, 2980; cf. 1666 + 1639]. authority, power, the right to control or govern; dominion, the area or sphere of jurisdiction; a ruler, human or supernatural:– authority (58), right (10), power (9), authorities (8), charge (2), control (2), ability (1), disposal (1), dominion (1), exercise of rights (1), have (1), in charge (1), jurisdiction (1), kingdom (1), on authority (1 [+3284]), reigns (1), rights (1), that[S] (1), NDT (1)

G2027 ἐξουσιάζω exousiazō, v. [4] [√2026]. to have power over; (pass.) to be mastered:– have authority (2), exercise authority over (1), mastered (1)

G2028 ἐξουσιαστικός exousiastikos, a. Not used in NIVEBC. [√2026]. authoritative

G2029 ἐξοχή exochē, n. [1] [√1666 + 2400]. leading, prominent:– prominent (1 [+2848])

G2030 ἐξυπνίζω exypnizō, v. [1] [√1666 + 5678]. to wake up, arouse:– wake up (1)

G2031 ἔξυπνος exypnos, a. [1] [√1666 + 5678]. awake, aroused:– woke up (1 [+1181])

G2032 ἔξω exō, adv. [60] [√1666]. out, outside:– outside (25), of (8), out (8), away (3), from (2), out of (2), outsiders (2 [+3836]), foreign (1), leave (1 [+2002]), outwardly (1 [+3836, 476]), NDT (7)

G2033 ἔξωθεν exōthen, adv. [13] [√1666]. from the outside:– outside (5), on the outside (3), exclude (1 [+1675]), from outside (1), outer (1), outsiders (1 [+3836]), outward (1)

G2034 ἐξωθέω exōtheō, v. [2] [√723; cf. 1666]. to drive out, expel; to run aground:– out (1), run aground (1)

G2035 ἐξώτερος exōteros, a. [3] [√1666]. outside, farthest out (as a superlative):– outside (3)

G2036 ἔοικα eoika, v. [2] [→1635, 2116, 2117]. to be like, resemble:– like (2)

G2037 ἑορτάζω heortazō, v. [1] [√2038]. to celebrate a festival:– keep the festival (1)

G2038 ἑορτή heortē, n. [25] [→2037]. feast, festival, in the NT this refers the joyous gathering of people for the celebrations of the Jewish calendar year, having a focus on ceremonial eating, such as Passover, Pentecost, and New Moon:– festival (21), festivals (1), passover festival (1), religious festival (1), there[S] (1 [+1650, 3836])

G2039 ἐπαγγελία epangelia, n. [52] [√2093 + 34]. promise:– promise (22), promised (16), promises (9), promised (2 [+1181]), consent (1), fulfill promise (1 [+4005, 3933]), promised (1 [+2040])

G2040 ἐπαγγέλλομαι epangellomai, v. [15] [√2093 + 34]. to promise; to profess, lay claim to:– promised (8), made promise (2), promise (2), profess (1), professed (1), promised (1 [+2039])

G2041 ἐπάγγελμα epangelma, n. [2] [√2093 + 34]. promise:– promise (1), promises (1)

G2042 ἐπάγω epagō, v. [3] [√2093 + 72]. to bring upon; to make guilty:– bringing on (1), brought on (1), make guilty of (1)

G2043 ἐπαγωνίζομαι epagōnizomai, v. [1] [√2093 + 74]. to contend, fight:– contend for (1)

G2044 ἐπαθροίζω epathroizō, v. [1] [√2093 + 125]. (pass.) to increase; to be collected:– increased (1)

G2045 Ἐπαίνετος Epainetos, n. pr. [1] [√*2093 + 142*]. Epenetus, "*praised*":– Epenetus (1)

G2046 ἐπαινέω epaineō, v. [6] [√*2093 + 142*]. to praise, commend:– praise (2), commended (1), extol (1), have praise (1), NDT (1)

G2047 ἔπαινος epainos, n. [11] [√*2093 + 142*]. praise, commendation:– praise (7), commend (1), commended (1 [+*2400*]), praised (1), praiseworthy (1)

G2048 ἐπαίρω epairō, v. [21] [√*2093 + 149*]. to lift up; "to lift up the eyes" means "to look up"; "to lift up the voice" means "to shout" or "talk loudly"; "to lift up the heel" means "to oppose someone" (implying hostility):– called out (3 [+*5889, 3306*]), looked up (3 [+*3836, 4057*]), raised (2), hoisted (1), lift up (1), lifted up (1), lifting up (1), look up (1 [+*3836, 4057*]), looked (1 [+*3836, 4057*]), looking (1 [+*3836, 4057*]), open (1), puts on airs (1), sets up (1), shouted (1 [+*3836, 5889*]), taken up (1), turned against (1 [+*3836, 4761, 899*])

G2049 ἐπαισχύνομαι epaischynomai, v. [11] [√*2093 + 156*]. to be ashamed of:– ashamed (9), ashamed of (1), cause for shame (1)

G2050 ἐπαιτέω epaiteō, v. [2] [√*2093 + 160*]. to beg:– beg (1), begging (1)

G2051 ἐπακολουθέω epakoloutheō, v. [4] [√*2093 + 199 [1.3]*]. to follow after, accompany; be devoted to:– accompanied (1), devoting (1), follow (1), trail behind (1)

G2052 ἐπακούω epakouō, v. [1] [√*2093 + 201*]. to hear, listen to:– heard (1)

G2053 ἐπακροάομαι epakroaomai, v. [1] [√*2093 + 212*]. to listen to:– listening (1)

G2054 ἐπάν epan, c. temp. [3] [√*2093 + 323*]. when, as soon as:– when (2), as soon as (1)

G2055 ἐπάναγκες epanankes, adv. [1] [√*2093 + 340*]. necessarily:– requirements (1)

G2056 ἐπανάγω epanagō, v. [3] [√*2093 + 324 + 72*]. to put out (to sea); to return:– put out (2), on way back (1)

G2057 ἐπαναμιμνήσκω epanamimnēskō, v. [1] [√*2093 + 324 + 3648*]. to remind again:– remind again (1)

G2058 ἐπαναπαύομαι epanapauomai, v. [2] [√*2093 + 324 + 4264*]. to rest on, rely on:– rely on (1), rest (1)

G2059 ἐπανέρχομαι epanerchomai, v. [2] [√*2093 + 324 + 2262*]. to return (home):– return (1), returned home (1)

G2060 ἐπανίστημι epanistēmi, v. [2] [√*2093 + 324 + 2705*]. to rebel against, rise up (in rebellion):– rebel (2)

G2061 ἐπανόρθωσις epanorthōsis, n. [1] [√*2093 + 324 + 3981*]. correcting:– correcting (1)

G2062 ἐπάνω epanō, adv. [19] [√*2093 + 539*]. above, on, upon; more than:– on (7), over (4), above (3), more than (2), of (1), rider (1 [+*2764*]), take charge of (1 [+*1181*])

G2063 ἐπάρατος eparatos, a. [1] [√*2093 + 725*]. accursed:– curse on (1)

G2064 ἐπαρκέω eparkeō, v. [3] [√*2093 + 758*]. to help, aid:– help (2), helping (1)

G2065 ἐπαρχεία eparcheia, n. [2] [√*2093 + 806*]. province:– province (2)

G2066 ἐπάρχειος eparcheios, a. Not used in NIVEBC. [√*2093 + 806*]. belonging to an eparch

G2067 ἐπαρχικός eparchikos, a. Not used in NIVEBC. [√*2093 + 806*]. pertaining to the eparch

G2068 ἔπαυλις epaulis, n. [1] [√*2093 + 885*]. place to live, residence:– place (1)

G2069 ἐπαύριον epaurion, adv. [17] [√*892; cf. 2093*]. the next day, tomorrow:– next day (15), following day (2)

G2070 ἐπαυτοφώρῳ epautophōrō, a. Not used in NIVEBC. [√*2093 + 899*]. pertaining to being caught in the act

G2071 Ἐπαφρᾶς Epaphras, n. pr. [3] Epaphras, "*handsome*":– Epaphras (3)

G2072 ἐπαφρίζω epaphrizō, v. [1] [√*2093 + 931*]. to foam up:– foaming up (1)

G2073 Ἐπαφρόδιτος Epaphroditos, n. pr. [2] Epaphroditus, "*handsome*":– Epaphroditus (2)

G2074 ἐπεγείρω epegeirō, v. [2] [√*2093 + 1586*]. to stir up, arouse, excite:– stirred up (2)

G2075 ἐπεί epei, c. [27] [√*2093*]. since, because, for otherwise:– since (9), because (4), otherwise (4), in that case (2 [+*726*]), as (1), if it were (1), if that were so (1), now (1), now if (1), otherwise (1 [+*726*]), since (1 [+*4036*]), NDT (1)

G2076 ἐπειδή epeidē, c. [10] [√*2093 + 1314*]. when; since, because:– since (4), because (1), for (1), when (1), NDT (3)

G2077 ἐπειδήπερ epeidēper, c. [1] [√*2093 + 1314 + 4302*]. inasmuch as, since, whereas:– NDT (1)

G2078 ἐπεῖδον epeidon, v. [2] [√*2093 + 1626*]. to show favor, concern; to consider, look at:– consider (1), shown favor (1)

G2079 ἔπειμι epeimi, v. [5] [√*2093 + 1640*]. the next day (from a verb that means "to follow, approach"):– next day (3), following (1), next (1)

G2080 ἐπείπερ epeiper, c. Not used in NIVEBC. [√*2093 + 4302*]. since, indeed

G2081 ἐπεισαγωγή epeisagōgē, n. [1] [√*2093 + 1650 + 72*]. introduction, bringing in:– introduced (1)

G2082 ἐπεισέρχομαι epeiserchomai, v. [1] [√*2093 + 1650 + 2262*]. to come in, happen, with a possible implication that it will happen suddenly and forcibly:– come on (1)

G2083 ἔπειτα epeita, adv. [16] [√*2093 + 1663*]. then, later, afterward:– then (11), after that (2), and after that (1), and then (1), and then (1 [+*3552, 4047*])

G2084 ἐπέκεινα epekeina, adv. [1] [√*2093 + 1695*]. beyond, farther on:– beyond (1)

G2085 ἐπεκτείνομαι epekteinomai, v. [1] [√*1753; cf. 2093*]. to strain toward, stretch out:– straining toward (1)

G2086 ἐπενδύομαι ependyomai, v. [2] [√*2093 + 1877 + 1544*]. to be clothed with:– clothed with (2)

G2087 ἐπενδύτης ependytēs, n. [1] [√*2093 + 1877 + 1544*]. outer garment, coat:– outer garment (1)

G2088 ἐπέρχομαι eperchomai, v. [9] [√*2093 + 2262*]. to come, come upon, happen to:– coming on (2), happen (2), attacks (1), came (1), come on (1), comes on (1), coming (1)

G2089 ἐπερωτάω eperōtaō, v. [56] [√*2093 + 2263*]. to ask, question:– asked (35), ask (4), question (4), ask questions (3), asking (2), questioned (2), ask about (1), ask for (1), asked about (1), asking questions (1), demanded (1), plied (1)

G2090 ἐπερώτημα eperōtēma, n. [1] [√*2093 + 2263*]. pledge; some translate "request, appeal":– pledge (1)

G2091 ἐπέχω epechō, v. [5] [√*2093 + 2400*]. (tr.) hold out, hold fast; (intr.) to give attention, watch, notice; to stay, stop:– gave attention (1), hold firmly (1), noticed (1), stayed (1), watch closely (1)

G2092 ἐπηρεάζω epēreazō, v. [2] to mistreat, speak maliciously against:– mistreat (1), speak maliciously against (1)

G2093 ἐπί epi, pp. [884] [→ *258, 454, 455, 2039, 2040, 2041, 2042, 2043, 2044, 2045, 2046, 2047, 2048, 2049, 2050, 2051, 2052, 2053, 2054, 2055, 2056, 2057, 2058, 2059, 2060, 2061, 2062, 2063, 2064, 2065, 2066, 2067, 2068, 2069, 2070, 2072, 2074, 2075, 2076, 2077, 2078, 2079, 2080, 2081, 2082, 2083, 2084, 2085, 2086, 2087, 2088, 2089, 2090, 2091, 2094, 2095, 2096, 2097, 2098, 2099, 2100, 2101, 2102, 2103, 2104, 2105, 2106, 2107, 2108, 2109, 2110, 2111, 2112, 2113, 2114, 2115, 2116, 2117, 2118, 2119, 2120, 2121, 2122, 2123, 2124, 2125, 2126, 2127, 2128, 2129, 2130, 2131, 2132, 2133, 2134, 2135, 2136, 2137, 2138, 2139, 2140, 2141, 2142, 2143, 2144, 2145, 2146, 2147, 2148, 2149, 2150, 2151, 2152, 2153, 2154, 2155, 2156, 2157, 2158, 2159, 2164, 2165, 2166, 2167, 2168, 2169, 2170, 2171, 2172, 2173, 2174, 2175, 2176, 2177, 2178, 2179, 2180, 2181, 2183, 2184, 2185, 2186, 2187, 2188, 2189, 2190, 2191, 2192, 2194, 2195, 2196, 2197, 2198, 2199, 2200, 2201, 2202, 2203, 2204, 2205, 2206, 2207, 2208, 2209, 2210, 2211, 2212, 2213, 2214, 2215, 2216, 2217, 2218, 2219, 2220, 2221, 2222, 2223, 2224, 2225, 2226, 2227, 2228, 2230, 2383, 2384, 2388, 2389, 2390, 2391, 2392, 2393, 2987, 3575, 4215, 4600, 5296, 5297, 5298, 5308; cf. 2160*]. (gen.) on, over, when; (dat.) on, at, in, while; (acc.) across, over, on, to, for, while:– on (269), to (85), in (79), at (40), over (37), against (33), for (33), of (20), before (17), by (11), about (8), with (8), because of (7), upon (5), rider (4 [+*2764*]), together (4 [+*3836, 899*]), from (3), reached (3 [+*1181*]), above (2), after (2), against (2 [+*3836, 5111*]), among (2), around (2), as long as (2 [+*4012, 5989*]), because (2 [+*4005*]), convened the court (2 [+*2767, 3836, 1037*]), earthly (2 [+*3836, 1178*]), generously (2 [+*2330*]), in accordance with (2), in the account of (2), into (2), meaning (2 [+*6055*]), reached (2 [+*2262*]), riders (2 [+*2764*]), right at (2), seized (2 [+*1181*]), seized (2 [+*2095, 3836, 5931*]), toward (2), whatever (2 [+*4012*]), when (2), with face to the ground (2 [+*4725*]), a matter of (1), across (1), along (1), any further (1 [+*4498*]), arrest (1 [+*2095, 3836, 5931*]), arrested (1 [+*2095, 3836, 5931*]), as (1 [+*3836, 3930*]), as long as (1 [+*4012*]), ashore (1 [+*3836, 1178*]), assure (1 [+*237, 3306*]), at the time of (1), because (1), become more and more (1 [+*4498, 4621*]), bedridden (1 [+*2879, 3187*]), beside (1), between (1), by healing[s] (1), certainly (1 [+*237*]), come together (1 [+*5302, 3836, 899*]), comes together (1 [+*5302, 3836, 899*]), conceived (1 [+*326*]), covers (1 [+*3023*]), decided (1 [+*326, 3836, 2840*]), died (1 [+*3738*]), drive out (1), during (1), during the reign of (1), embraced (1 [+*2158, 3836, 5549*]), established (1), facedown to the ground (1 [+*4725*]), fall down (1 [+*4406, 4725*]), filled with (1 [+*1181*]), forward to (1), further (1 [+*4498*]), given (1), got together (1 [+*5251, 3836, 899*]), how true (1 [+*237*]), in addition to (1), in charge of (1), in front of (1), in the days of (1), in the time of (1), inasmuch as (1 [+*4012, 3525, 4036*]), indeed (1 [+*1142, 237*]), just then (1 [+*4047*]), landed (1 [+*2262, 3836, 1178*]), landed (1 [+*3836, 1178, 2262*]), made (1 [+*2400*]), near (1), on and on (1 [+*4498*]), on the basis of (1), only as long as (1 [+*4012, 5989*]), opposes (1 [+*482*]), overcome (1), reaching (1 [+*1181*]), right (1 [+*237*]), seize (1 [+*2095, 3836, 5931*]), shelter with presence (1 [+*5012*]), stake on (1), stone (1 [+*965*]), struck (1 [+*2262*]), the coast (1 [+*3836, 2498*]), them[s] (1 [+*3836, 2997, 3836, 1178*]), threw arms around (1 [+*2158, 3836, 5549*]), threw himself (1 [+*4406, 4725*]), throughout (1 [+*4246*]), to face (1), to see (1), to their number (1 [+*3836, 899*]), to where (1), travel by ship (1 [+*5536, 4434*]), trusted personal servant (1 [+*3836, 3131*]), under (1), up to (1), very (1 [+*4498*]), wearing nothing (1 [+*4314, 1218*]), what (1 [+*4005*]), where (1 [+*4005*]), while (1), while (1 [+*4012*]), NDT (92)

G2094 ἐπιβαίνω epibainō, v. [6] [√*2093 + 326*]. to go up, go upon, ride upon, board (a vessel):– arriving (1), boarded (1), came into (1), go on (1), riding (1), went on board (1)

G2095 ἐπιβάλλω epiballō, v. [18] [√*2093 + 965*]. (tr.) to throw over; to place; lay hold of, seize, arrest; to sew on; (intr.) to break over:– laid (2), seized (2 [+*3836, 5931*]), arrest (1 [+*2093, 3836, 5931*]), arrested (1 [+*3836, 5931*]), arrested (1 [+*3836, 5931, 2093*]), broke down (1), broke over (1), patch (1), puts to (1), restrict (1 [+*1105*]), seize (1 [+*2093, 3836, 5931*]), seized (1 [+*2093, 3836, 5931*]), seized (1 [+*3836, 5931, 2093*]), sews (1), share (1 [+*3538*]), threw over (1)

G2096 ἐπιβαρέω epibareō, v. [3] [√*2093 + 983*]. to burden, weigh down excessively:– burden (2), put it severely (1)

G2097 ἐπιβιβάζω epibibazō, v. [3] [√*2093 + 326*]. to put (someone) on (a mount):– put on (2), taken (1)

G2098 ἐπιβλέπω epiblepō, v. [3] [√*2093 + 1063*]. to look at, show special attention, consider, care about:– look at (1), mindful of (1), show special attention (1)

G2099 ἐπίβλημα epiblēma, n. [4] [√*2093 + 965*]. patch:– patch (3), piece (1)

G2100 ἐπιβοάω epiboaō, v. Not used in NIVEBC. [√*2093 + 1068*]. to cry out loudly

G2101 ἐπιβουλή epiboulē, n. [4] [√*2093 + 1089*]. plan, plot:– plan (1), plot (1), plots (1), plotted (1 [+*1181*])

G2102 ἐπιγαμβρεύω epigambreuō, v. [1] [√*2093 + 1141*]. to marry (as next of kin):– marry (1)

G2103 ἐπίγειος epigeios, a. [7] [√*2093 + 1178*]. being on the earth, earthly, that which is inferior when in contrast to heavenly or divine things:– earthly (5), earthly things (1), on earth (1)

G2104 ἐπιγίνομαι epiginomai, v. [1] [√*2093 + 1181*]. to come up, occur, happen:– came up (1)

G2105 ἐπιγινώσκω epiginōskō, v. [44] [√*2093 + 1182*]. to know (fully), recognize, realize, come to understand:– recognized (6), know (5), realized (4), recognize (4), known (3), learned (3), knew (2), knows (2), understand (2), understood (2), acknowledge (1), find out (1), found out (1), fully known (1), know fully (1), learn the truth (1), realize (1), recognition (1), recognizing (1), took note (1), verify (1)

G2106 ἐπίγνωσις epignōsis, n. [20] [√*2093 + 1182*]. knowledge, understanding, insight:– knowledge (15), conscious of (1), deepening understanding (1), know (1), know better (1), knowing (1)

G2107 ἐπιγραφή epigraphē, n. [5] [√*2093 + 1211*]. inscription, superscription, written notice:– inscription (3), written notice (2)

G2108 ἐπιγράφω epigraphō, v. [5] [√*2093 + 1211*]. (act.) to write; (pass.) to be written (upon), inscribed:– write on (2), inscription (1), on written (1), read (1 [+*1639*])

G2109 ἐπιδείκνυμι epideiknymi, v. [7] [√*2093 + 1259*]. to show, call attention to; to prove, point out:– show (3), call attention to (1), make clear (1), proving (1), showing (1)

G2110 ἐπιδέχομαι epidechomai, v. [2] [√*2093 + 1312*]. to welcome, receive as a guest; to have to do with, accept, recognize:– welcome (2)

G2111 ἐπιδημέω epidēmeō, v. [2] [√*2093 + 1322*]. to live as a visitor, foreigner:– lived there (1), visitors (1)

G2112 ἐπιδιατάσσομαι epidiatassomai, v. [1] [√*2093 + 1328 + 5435*]. to add to (a covenant):– add to (1)

G2113 ἐπιδίδωμι epididōmi, v. [9] [√*2093 + 1443*]. to give, deliver, hand over to:– give (5), delivered (1), gave (1), gave way (1), handed (1)

G2114 ἐπιδιορθόω epidiorthoō, v. [1] [√*2093 + 1328 + 3981*]. to straighten out, correct (in addition):– put in order (1)

G2115 ἐπιδύω epidyō, v. [1] [√*2093 + 1544*]. to go down, set (of the sun):– go down (1)

G2116 ἐπιείκεια epieikeia, n. [2] [√*2093 + 2036*].

gentleness, with an implication of tolerance and graciousness:– gentleness (1), kind (1)

G2117 **ἐπιεικής** ***epieikēs***, a. [5] [*√2093 + 2036*]. gentle, considerate:– considerate (3), gentle (1), gentleness (1)

G2118 **ἐπιζητέω** ***epizēteō***, v. [13] [*√2093 + 2426*]. to look for, run after, seek earnestly:– looking for (3), desire (2), a thorough search made (1), asks for (1), bring up (1), looks for (1), run after (1), runs after (1), sought so earnestly (1), wanted to (1)

G2119 **ἐπιθανάτιος** ***epithanatios***, a. [1] [*√2093 + 2569*]. condemned to die:– condemned to die (1)

G2120 **ἐπίθεσις** ***epithesis***, n. [4] [*√2093 + 5502*]. laying on:– laying on (3), laid on (1)

G2121 **ἐπιθυμέω** ***epithymeō***, v. [16] [*√2093 + 2596*]. to long for, desire; covet, lust:– covet (2), desires (2), long (2), longed (2), coveted (1), desire (1), did[s] (1), eagerly desired (1 [*+2123*]), long to (1), longing (1), lustfully (1 [*+4639, 3836*]), want (1)

G2122 **ἐπιθυμητής** ***epithymētēs***, n. [1] [*√2093 + 2596*]. one who desires, sets heart on (evil):– setting hearts on (1)

G2123 **ἐπιθυμία** ***epithymia***, n. [38] [*√2093 + 2596*]. desire, longing (in contexts where the desire is positive and proper); coveting, craving, lusting (in contexts where the desire is immoral and sinful):– desires (13), evil desires (8), lust (4), coveting (2), desire (2), passions (2), cravings (1), desire (1 [*+2400*]), eagerly desired (1 [*+2121*]), evil desire (1), longed for (1 [*+3836, 6034*]), longing (1), sinful desires (1)

G2124 **ἐπιθύω** ***epithyō***, v. Not used in NIVEBC. [*√2093 + 2604*]. to offer a sacrifice

G2125 **ἐπικαθίζω** ***epikathizō***, v. [1] [*√2093 + 2767*]. to sit down (upon):– sit (1)

G2126 **ἐπικαλέω** ***epikaleō***, v. [30] [*√2093 + 2813*]. (act./pass.) to call (upon), name, be named; (mid.) appeal to, call upon for aid:– called (8), call on (7), appealed (2), calls on (2), made appeal (2), appeal (1), as (1), bear (1), call (1), calling on (1), known as (1), make an appeal (1), prayed (1), to belong (1)

G2127 **ἐπικάλυμμα** ***epikalymma***, n. [1] [*√2093 + 2821*]. cover-up, covering, veil:– cover-up (1)

G2128 **ἐπικαλύπτω** ***epikalyptō***, v. [1] [*√2093 + 2821*]. (pass.) to be covered:– covered (1)

G2129 **ἐπικατάρατος** ***epikataratos***, a. [2] [*√2093 + 2848 + 725*]. cursed:– cursed (2)

G2130 **ἐπίκειμαι** ***epikeimai***, v. [7] [*√2093 + 3023*]. to lay upon; to press, crowd upon, demand insistently:– applying (1), compelled (1 [*+340*]), continued raging (1 [*+4024, 3900*]), crowding around (1), insistently (1), laid across (1), on (1)

G2131 **ἐπικέλλω** ***epikellō***, v. [1] [*√2093 + 3027*]. to run aground:– ran aground (1)

G2132 **ἐπικερδαίνω** ***epikerdainō***, v. Not used in NIVEBC. [*√2093 + 3046*]. to gain in addition

G2133 **ἐπικεφάλαιον** ***epikephalaion***, n. Not used in NIVEBC. [*√2093 + 3051*]. (poll) tax

G2134 **Ἐπικούρειος** ***Epikoureios***, a. pr. *or* n. pr. [1] [*√2093 + 3025*]. Epicurean, "*of Epicurus*":– Epicurean (1)

G2135 **ἐπικουρία** ***epikouria***, n. [1] [*√2093 + 3025*]. help:– helped (1 [*+5593*])

G2136 **ἐπικράζω** ***epikrazō***, v. Not used in NIVEBC. [*√2093 + 3189*]. to shout threats

G2137 **ἐπικρίνω** ***epikrinō***, v. [1] [*√2093 + 3212*]. to decide, determine:– decided (1)

G2138 **ἐπιλαμβάνομαι** ***epilambanomai***, v. [19] [*√2093 + 3284*]. to take hold, catch, trap, seize:– took (5), seized (2), take hold of (2), arrested (1), catch (1), caught (1), helps (1), seizing (1), taking hold of (1), took by (1), trap (1), turned on (1), NDT (1)

G2139 **ἐπιλάμπω** ***epilampō***, v. Not used in NIVEBC. [*√2093 + 3290*]. to shine out, shine forth

G2140 **ἐπιλανθάνομαι** ***epilanthanomai***, v. [8] [*√2093 + 3291*]. to forget:– forget (3), forgotten (2), forgets (1), forgetting (1), forgot (1)

G2141 **ἐπιλέγω** ***epilegō***, v. [2] [*√2093 + 3306*]. (pass.) to be called; (mid.) to choose:– called (1), chose (1)

G2142 **ἐπιλείπω** ***epileipō***, v. [1] [*√2093 + 3309*]. to not have (time); to fail to have:– not have (1)

G2143 **ἐπιλείχω** ***epileichō***, v. [1] [*√2093 + 3314*]. to lick:– licked (1)

G2144 **ἐπιλησμονή** ***epilēsmonē***, n. [1] [*√2093 + 3291*]. forgetfulness:– forgetting (1)

G2145 **ἐπίλοιπος** ***epiloipos***, a. [1] [*√2093 + 3309*]. remaining, the rest:– rest (1)

G2146 **ἐπίλυσις** ***epilysis***, n. [1] [*√2093 + 3395*]. interpretation, explanation:– interpretation (1)

G2147 **ἐπιλύω** ***epilyō***, v. [2] [*√2093 + 3395*]. to explain; (pass.) to be settled, decided:– explained (1), settled (1)

G2148 **ἐπιμαρτυρέω** ***epimartyreō***, v. [1] [*√2093 + 3459*]. to testify that, bear witness about:– testifying (1)

G2149 **ἐπιμέλεια** ***epimeleia***, n. [1] [*√2093 + 3508*]. needs, care, attention:– needs (1)

G2150 **ἐπιμελέομαι** ***epimeleomai***, v. [3] [*√2093 + 3508*]. to take care of, look after:– look after (1), take care of (1), took care of (1)

G2151 **ἐπιμελῶς** ***epimelōs***, adv. [1] [*√2093 + 3508*]. carefully, diligently:– carefully (1)

G2152 **ἐπιμένω** ***epimenō***, v. [16] [*√2093 + 3531*]. to stay, remain; to continue in, keep on, persevere:– stayed (3), continue (2), kept on (2), spend (2), been there (1), go on (1), persevere (1), persist (1), remain (1), stay (1), stay on (1)

G2153 **ἐπινεύω** ***epineuō***, v. [1] [*√2093 + 3748*]. to accept, give consent:– declined (1 [*+4024*])

G2154 **ἐπίνοια** ***epinoia***, n. [1] [*√2093 + 3808*]. thought, intention:– thought (1)

G2155 **ἐπιορκέω** ***epiorkeō***, v. [1] [*√2093 + 3992*]. to break an oath, swear falsely:– break oath (1)

G2156 **ἐπίορκος** ***epiorkos***, a. [1] [*√2093 + 3992*]. perjured; as a noun, perjurer:– perjurers (1)

G2157 **ἐπιούσιος** ***epiousios***, a. [2] [*√2093 + 1639*]. what recurs on a day to day basis, daily:– daily (2)

G2158 **ἐπιπίπτω** ***epipiptō***, v. [11] [*√2093 + 4406*]. to fall upon, come eagerly, embrace; to come on:– came (2), come on (1), embraced (1 [*+2093, 3836, 5549*]), fallen (1), gripped with (1), pushing forward (1), seized with (1), struck (1), threw arms around (1 [*+2093, 3836, 5549*]), threw on (1)

G2159 **ἐπιπλήσσω** ***epiplēssō***, v. [1] [*√2093 + 4448*]. to rebuke, strike at:– rebuke harshly (1)

G2160 **ἐπιποθέω** ***epipotheō***, v. [9] [*→2161, 2162, 2163; cf. 2093*]. to long for, crave, desire:– long (3), crave (1), hearts go out to (1), long for (1), longing (1), longs for (1 [*+1639*]), longs for (1)

G2161 **ἐπιπόθησις** ***epipothēsis***, n. [2] [*√2160*]. longing (for):– longing (2)

G2162 **ἐπιπόθητος** ***epipothētos***, a. [1] [*√2160*]. longed for:– long for (1)

G2163 **ἐπιποθία** ***epipothia***, n. [1] [*√2160*]. longing, desire:– longing (1)

G2164 **ἐπιπορεύομαι** ***epiporeuomai***, v. [1] [*√2093 + 4513*]. to come to, go to:– coming (1)

G2165 **ἐπιράπτω** ***epiraptō***, v. [1] [*√2093 + 4827*]. to sew on:– sews (1)

G2166 **ἐπιρίπτω** ***epiriptō***, v. [2] [*√2093 + 4849*]. to throw on:– cast on (1), threw on (1)

G2167 **ἐπισείω** ***episeiō***, v. Not used in NIVEBC. [*√2093 + 4940*]. to urge on, incite

G2168 **ἐπίσημος** ***episēmos***, a. [2] [*√2093 + 4956*]. notorious, prominent, outstanding:– outstanding (1), well-known (1)

G2169 **ἐπισιτισμός** ***episitismos***, n. [1] [*√2093 + 4992*]. food, something to eat:– food (1)

G2170 **ἐπισκέπτομαι** ***episkeptomai***, v. [11] [*√2093 + 5023*]. to visit, show concern, care for, come to help:– come (2), look after (2), visit (2), care for (1), choose (1), come to help (1), intervened (1), looked after (1)

G2171 **ἐπισκευάζομαι** ***episkeuazomai***, v. [1] [*√2093 + 5007*]. to get ready, make preparations:– started (1)

G2172 **ἐπισκηνόω** ***episkēnoō***, v. [1] [*√2093 + 5008*]. to rest upon, take up residence:– rest on (1)

G2173 **ἐπισκιάζω** ***episkiazō***, v. [5] [*√2093 + 5014*]. to cast a shadow, overshadow; to envelope with a cloud:– covered (3), fall on (1), overshadow (1)

G2174 **ἐπισκοπέω** ***episkopeō***, v. [2] [*√2093 + 5023*]. to see to, care for; to serve as an overseer:– see to it (1), watching over (1)

G2175 **ἐπισκοπή** ***episkopē***, n. [4] [*√2093 + 5023*]. coming, visitation, the coming of divine power for recompense; an office of responsibility and place of leadership referring to an office of apostle in Acts, and the office of overseer or bishop in the local church:– God's coming (1), overseer (1), place of leadership (1), visits (1)

G2176 **ἐπίσκοπος** ***episkopos***, n. [5] [*√2093 + 5023*]. overseer or bishop, a leader in a local church, an extension of one who guards, supervises, and helps:– overseer (3), overseers (2)

G2177 **ἐπισπάομαι** ***epispaomai***, v. [1] [*√2093 + 5060*]. to (attempt to) conceal circumcision, formally "to pull over (the foreskin to conceal circumcision)":– uncircumcised (1)

G2178 **ἐπισπείρω** ***epispeirō***, v. [1] [*√2093 + 5062*]. to sow afterward:– sowed (1)

G2179 **ἐπίσταμαι** ***epistamai***, v. [14] [*√2093 + 2705*]. to understand, know, be aware:– know (7), understand (3), familiar (1), knew (1), know about (1), well aware (1)

G2180 **ἐπίστασις** ***epistasis***, n. [2] [*√2093 + 2705*]. stirring up, rebellion; pressure:– pressure (1), stirring up (1 [*+4472*])

G2181 **ἐπιστάτης** ***epistatēs***, n. [7] [*√2093 + 2705*]. master:– master (7)

G2182 **ἐπιστέλλω** ***epistellō***, v. [3] [*√2186*]. to write a letter:– written (2), write (1)

G2183 **ἐπιστήμη** ***epistēmē***, n. Not used in NIVEBC. [*√2093 + 2705*]. understanding, knowledge

G2184 **ἐπιστήμων** ***epistēmōn***, a. [1] [*√2093 + 2705*]. understanding, expert, learned:– understanding (1)

G2185 **ἐπιστηρίζω** ***epistērizō***, v. [4] [*√2093 + 5114*]. to strengthen:– strengthening (2), strengthen (1), strengthening (1 [*+3836, 6034*])

G2186 **ἐπιστολή** ***epistolē***, n. [24] [*→2182; cf. 2093 + 5097*]. letter, epistle:– letter (15), letters (8), letters of introduction (1)

G2187 **ἐπιστομίζω** ***epistomizō***, v. [1] [*√2093 + 5125*]. to silence, formally, "to stop the mouth":– silenced (1)

G2188 **ἐπιστρέφω** ***epistrephō***, v. [36] [*√2093 + 5138*]. to turn (around, back, from), return:– turn (7), turned (5), returned (3), turned around (3), turning (3), go (2), return (2), turns (2), back (1), bring back (1), come back (1), go back (1), go back (1 [*+1650, 3836, 3958*]), returns (1), turn to (1), turned back (1), turned to (1)

G2189 **ἐπιστροφή** ***epistrophē***, n. [1] [*√2093 + 5138*]. conversion, a fig. extension of *turning* an object, not found in the NT:– converted (1)

G2190 **ἐπισυνάγω** ***episynagō***, v. [8] [*√2093 + 5250 + 72*]. to gather together:– gather (3), gather together (2), gathered (1), gathered (1 [*+1639*]), gathers (1)

G2191 **ἐπισυναγωγή** ***episynagōgē***, n. [2] [*√2093 + 5252*]. gathering, meeting, assembling:– gathered to (1), meeting together (1)

G2192 **ἐπισυντρέχω** ***episyntrechō***, v. [1] [*√2093 + 5250 + 5556*]. to run together to:– running (1)

G2193 **ἐπισυρράπτω** ***episyrraptō***, v. Not used in NIVEBC. to sew on

G2194 **ἐπισύστασις** ***episystasis***, n. Not used in NIVEBC. [*√2093 + 5250 + 2705*]. uprising, disturbance, insurrection

G2195 **ἐπισφαλής** ***episphalēs***, a. [1] [*√2093 + 5378*]. dangerous, unsafe:– dangerous (1)

G2196 **ἐπισχύω** ***epischyō***, v. [1] [*√2093 + 2709*]. to insist:– insisted (1 [*+3306*])

G2197 **ἐπισωρεύω** ***episōreuō***, v. [1] [*√2093 + 5397*]. to gather a great number, accumulate:– gather around a great number (1)

G2198 **ἐπιταγή** ***epitagē***, n. [7] [*√2093 + 5435*]. command, order; authority:– command (5), authority (1), commanding (1 [*+2848, 3306*])

G2199 **ἐπιτάσσω** ***epitassō***, v. [10] [*√2093 + 5435*]. to command, order:– gives orders (2), order (2), ordered (2), command (1), commands (1), directed (1), orders (1)

G2200 **ἐπιτελέω** ***epiteleō***, v. [10] [*√2093 + 5465*]. to finish, complete, end; to perfect, attain a goal; (mid.) to undergo:– finish (2), bring to completion (1), build (1), carry on (1), carry on to completion (1), completed (1), completion (1), perfecting (1), undergoing (1)

G2201 **ἐπιτήδειος** ***epitēdeios***, a. [1] [*√2093 + 3836*]. needful, necessary, suitable:– needs (1)

G2202 **ἐπιτίθημι** ***epitithēmi***, v. [39] [*√2093 + 5502*]. to place, lay upon, put on:– put on (10), placed on (5), place on (4), gave (2), laying on (2), placed (2), add (1), adds (1), attack (1), beat (1 [*+4435*]), burden (1 [*+983*]), flogged (1 [*+4435*]), furnished (1), laid on (1), lay on (1), on lay (1), placing on (1), puts on (1), putting on (1), set on (1)

G2203 **ἐπιτιμάω** ***epitimaō***, v. [29] [*√2093 + 5507*]. to rebuke, warn:– rebuked (16), rebuke (6), sternly (2), warned (2), gave orders (1), rebuked and told (1), strictly warned (1 [*+4133*])

G2204 **ἐπιτιμία** ***epitimia***, n. [1] [*√2093 + 5507*]. punishment:– punishment (1)

G2205 **ἐπιτρέπω** ***epitrepō***, v. [18] [*√2093 + 5572*]. to let, allow, permit, give permission:– let (5), allowed (3), gave permission (2), permitted (2), have permission (1), permission (1), permit (1), permits (1), permitting (1), receiving permission (1)

G2206 ἐπιτροπεύω epitropeuō, v. Not used in NIVEBC. [√2093 + 5572]. to be governor, procurator

G2207 ἐπιτροπή epitropē, n. [1] [√2093 + 5572]. commission, permission:– commission (1)

G2208 ἐπίτροπος epitropos, n. [3] [√2093 + 5572]. foreman, manager, guardian; derived from a Greek verb, "to instruct," not found in the NT:– foreman (1), guardians (1), manager of household (1)

G2209 ἐπιτυγχάνω epitynchanō, v. [5] [√2093 + 5593]. to obtain, receive, gain:– dids (1), gained (1), get (1), obtain (1), received (1)

G2210 ἐπιφαίνω epiphainō, v. [4] [√2093 + 5743]. (act.) to appear, make an appearance, show oneself; (pass.) shine:– appeared (3), shine on (1)

G2211 ἐπιφάνεια epiphaneia, n. [6] [√2093 + 5743]. appearing, appearance; usually referring to the return of Christ, cf. the English word "epiphany":– appearing (5), splendor (1)

G2212 ἐπιφανής epiphanēs, a. [1] [√2093 + 5743]. glorious, splendid:– glorious (1)

G2213 ἐπιφαύσκω epiphauskō, v. [1] [√2093 + 5743]. to shine on:– shine on (1)

G2214 ἐπιφέρω epipherō, v. [2] [√2093 + 5770]. to bring upon, inflict:– bringing on (1), condemn (1 [+3213])

G2215 ἐπιφωνέω epiphōneō, v. [4] [√2093 + 5889]. to shout, cry out loudly:– shouted (2), shouting (2)

G2216 ἐπιφώσκω epiphōskō, v. [2] [√2093 + 5743]. to dawn, begin, shine forth:– about to begin (1), dawn (1)

G2217 ἐπιχειρέω epicheireō, v. [3] [√2093 + 5931]. to attempt, try to:– tried (1), tried to (1), undertaken (1)

G2218 ἐπιχείρησις epicheirēsis, n. Not used in NIVEBC. [√2093 + 5931]. attempt, attack

G2219 ἐπιχέω epicheō, v. [1] [√1772; cf. 2093]. to pour on, pour over:– pouring on (1)

G2220 ἐπιχορηγέω epichorēgeō, v. [5] [√2093 + 5962 + 72]. to support, supply; (pass.) to be supported, receive:– add (1), give (1), receive (1), supplies (1), supported (1)

G2221 ἐπιχορηγία epichorēgia, n. [2] [√2093 + 5962 + 72]. support, help:– provision (1), supporting (1)

G2222 ἐπιχρίω epichriō, v. [2] [√2093 + 5987]. to put on, anoint on, spread on:– put on (2)

G2223 ἐπιψαύω epipsauō, v. Not used in NIVEBC. [√2093 + 6041]. to touch, grasp, attain

G2224 ἐποικοδομέω epoikodomeō, v. [7] [√2093 + 3875 + 1560]. to build up, build on:– build (1), building on (1), building up (1), builds on (1), built (1), built on (1), built up (1)

G2225 ἐποκέλλω epokellō, v. Not used in NIVEBC. [√2093 + 3027]. to run aground

G2226 ἐπονομάζω eponomazō, v. [1] [√2093 + 3950]. (pass.) to be called, named:– call (1)

G2227 ἐποπτεύω epopteuō, v. [2] [√2093 + 3972]. to see, observe:– see (2)

G2228 ἐπόπτης epoptēs, n. [1] [√2093 + 3972]. eyewitness:– eyewitnesses (1)

G2229 ἔπος epos, n. [1] word:– one might even say (1 [+6055, 3306])

G2230 ἐπουράνιος epouranios, a. [19] [√2093 + 4041]. heavenly, celestial; heavenly realms:– heavenly (10), heavenly realms (5), in heaven (2), heavenly things (1), of heaven (1)

G2231 ἑπτά hepta, n. num. [88] [→1573, 1574, 1575, 2232, 2233, 2234]. seven:– seven (85), seventh (1), seventy-seven times (1 [+1574]), week (1 [+2465])

G2232 ἑπτάκις heptakis, adv. [4] [√2231]. seven times:– seven times (4)

G2233 ἑπτακισχίλιοι heptakischilioi, a. num. [1] [√2231 + 5943]. seven thousand:– seven thousand (1)

G2234 ἑπταπλασίων heptaplasiōn, a. Not used in NIVEBC. [√2231]. sevenfold

G2235 Ἔραστος Erastos, n. pr. [3] Erastus, "*beloved*":– Erastus (3)

G2236 ἐραυνάω eraunaō, v. [6] [→451, 2001; cf. 2263]. to search, look into, try to find out:– searches (3), look into (1), study diligently (1), trying to find out (1)

G2237 ἐργάζομαι ergazomai, v. [41] [√2240]. to work, be active, accomplish (something):– work (8), do (5), does (3), done (3), worked (3), doing (2), administered (1), at work (1), brings (1), busy (1), carrying on (1), earn (1), earn living (1), evildoers (1 [+3836, 490]), produce (1), put to work (1), serve (1), sin (1 [+281]), work for a living (1), work hard (1 [+3159]), worked for (1), working (1), works (1)

G2238 ἐργασία ergasia, n. [6] [√2240]. trade, business, making money; indulgence:– business (2), indulge in (1), making money (1), money (1), try hard (1 [+1443])

G2239 ἐργάτης ergatēs, n. [16] [√2240]. worker, laborer, one who does (something):– workers (9), worker (4), evildoers (1 [+94]), evildoers (1 [+2805]), thems (1 [+3836])

G2240 ἔργον ergon, n. [169] [→14, 15, 307, 733, 734, 1175, 1176, 1177, 1321, 1918, 1919, 1920, 1921, 2237, 2238, 2239, 2307, 2308, 2309, 2646, 2806, 2934, 2981, 3310, 3311, 3312, 3313, 4111, 4112, 4318, 4319, 4664, 5300, 5301, 5348; cf. 4816]. work, deed, activity, task, job:– works (36), deeds (32), work (28), done (10), doing (8), actions (7), did (5), do (5), acts (4), deed (4), action (2), thing (2), what did (2), activity (1), assigned task (1), attack (1), behavior (1), done (1 [+1639]), good (1), its (1), its (1 [+5516, 3836]), labor (1), made (1), miracle (1), practices (1), requirements (1), result of work (1), something (1), task (1), things (1), thiss (1 [+3836, 4047]), ways (1), what (1 [+5516, 3836]), what do (1), will (1), NDT (2)

G2241 ἐρεθίζω erethizō, v. [2] to stir up, provoke, arouse; embitter, provoke, irritate:– embitter (1), stirred to action (1)

G2242 ἐρείδω ereidō, v. [1] to stick fast, make immovable, jam:– stuck fast (1)

G2243 ἐρεύγομαι ereugomai, v. [1] to utter, proclaim:– utter (1)

G2244 ἐρημία erēmia, n. [4] [√2245]. remote place, desert, countryside, usually uninhabited areas:– remote place (2), country (1), deserts (1)

G2245 ἔρημος erēmos, a. [49] [→2244, 2246, 2247]. deserted, remote, solitary; as a noun, desert, uninhabited wilderness, or grasslands, implying in some contexts to be a forsaken, desolate place:– wilderness (31), solitary (4), desolate (3), remote (3), desert (2), deserted (1), lonely (1), lonely places (1), open country (1), quiet (1), solitary places (1)

G2246 ἐρημόω erēmoō, v. [5] [√2245]. (pass.) to be brought to ruin, laid waste:– brought to ruin (2), ruined (2), bring to ruin (1 [+4472])

G2247 ἐρήμωσις erēmōsis, n. [3] [√2245]. desolation, devastation, destruction. "The Abomination of Desolation" is a phrase derived from Hebrew, formally, "the detestable thing of desolation." This abomination is a person, thing, or event that defiles a holy place and thus causes it to be abandoned, implying God detests this thing or action. Many refer this to desecration of the temple by Antiochus Epiphanes as analogous to a future event predicted by Jesus:– desolation (2), causes desolation (1)

G2248 ἐρίζω erizō, v. [1] [√2251]. to quarrel:– quarrel (1)

G2249 ἐριθεία eritheia, n. [7] [√2251]. selfish ambition, faction, strife:– selfish ambition (6), self-seeking (1 [+1666])

G2250 ἔριον erion, n. [2] wool:– wool (2)

G2251 ἔρις eris, n. [9] [→2248, 2249]. quarrel, strife, dissension, discord:– discord (2), strife (2), arguments (1), dissension (1), quarreling (1), quarrels (1), rivalry (1)

G2252 ἐρίφιον eriphion, n. [1] [√2253]. goat:– goats (1)

G2253 ἔριφος eriphos, n. [2] [→2252]. (young) goat:– goats (1), young goat (1)

G2254 Ἑρμᾶς Hermas, n. pr. [1] Hermas:– Hermas (1)

G2255 ἑρμηνεία hermēneia, n. [2] [√2257]. interpretation, translation, to translate meaning from one language to another, in the NT a gift of the Spirit necessary for understanding the gift of tongues in assembly:– interpretation (2)

G2256 ἑρμηνευτής hermēneutēs, n. Not used in NIVEBC. [√2257]. translator

G2257 ἑρμηνεύω hermēneuō, v. [3] [→1448, 1449, 1450, 1549, 2255, 2256, 3493]. to translate, give the meaning, interpret, explain:– means (2), translated (1)

G2258 Ἑρμῆς Hermēs, n. pr. [2] Hermes, "[poss.] *rock, cairn*":– Hermes (2)

G2259 Ἑρμογένης Hermogenēs, n. pr. [1] Hermogenes, "*born of Hermes*":– Hermogenes (1)

G2260 ἑρπετόν herpeton, n. [4] reptile:– reptiles (3), reptiles (1 [+3836, 1178])

G2261 ἐρυθρός erythros, a. Not used in NIVEBC. red€ [2]:– red (2)

G2262 ἔρχομαι erchomai, v. [633] [→456, 524, 599, 1446, 1451, 1656, 1803, 2002, 2059, 2082, 2088, 2982, 4209, 4216, 4320, 4601, 4665, 4670, 5291, 5302]. to come, go:– come (190), came (128), coming (62), comes (61), went (51), arrived (13), go (8), returned (6), return (5), entered (4 [+1650]), on way (4), reached (4 [+1650]), arrives (3), came back (3), come back (3), going (3), gone (3), visit (3 [+4639]), went out (3), be disciple (2 [+3958]), joined (2 [+4639]), landed (2 [+2093, 3836, 1178]), reached (2 [+2093]), returns (2), rose (2), to come (2), traveled (2), accompanied (1), alighting (1), approaching (1), arrival (1), been (1), bring (1), brought (1), brought out (1), came along (1), came by (1), came up (1), come (1 [+1639]), entered (1), entered (1 [+1650]), fall (1), falling (1), follow (1 [+3958]), followed (1), gathered (1), get here (1), get in (1), go on (1), goes (1), going to (1), grew (1 [+1650]), happen (1), here (1), hurried off (1 [+5067]), in turn (1), join (1 [+4639]), judged (1 [+1650, 3213]), landed (1), lose good name (1 [+1650, 591]), made way (1), make visit (1), next (1), occurs (1), passed by (1), reached (1), reached (1 [+1650]), reaching (1 [+1650]), rest (1), result (1), return (1 [+1650, 3836, 4099]), returning (1), served (1), set off (1), struck (1 [+2093]), traveled on (1 [+3847]), until (1), visit (1), visited (1 [+1650]), visited (1 [+4639]), went on (1), NDT (6)

G2263 ἐρωτάω erōtaō, v. [63] [→1452, 2089, 2090; cf. 2236]. to ask; beg, urge; pray:– asked (20), ask (18), urged (3), asks (2), begged (2), invited (2), please (2 [+5148]), pray (2), prayer (2), questioned (2), ask questions (1), asking (1), beg (1), praying (1), question (1), questioning (1), request (1), requesting (1)

G2264 ἐσθής esthēs, n. [8] [√2667]. clothing, robe:– clothes (5), dressed (1), robe (1), robes (1)

G2265 ἔσθησις esthēsis, n. Not used in NIVEBC. [√2667]. government

G2266 ἐσθίω esthiō, v. [156] [→2267, 2983, 2984, 5303; cf. 3763, 5741]. to eat, consume, devour:– eat (93), ate (20), eating (20), eats (5), eaten (4), dos (2), does (2), eat (2 [+788]), food (2), abstains (1 [+3590]), consume (1), drink (1), get food (1), have a feast (1), have dinner (1)

G2267 ἔσθω esthō, v. Not used in NIVEBC. [√2266]. to eat, consume, devour

G2268 Ἑσλί Hesli, n. pr. [1] Esli, "*Yahweh sets apart*":– Esli (1)

G2269 ἔσοπτρον esoptron, n. [2] [√1650 + 3972]. mirror:– mirror (2)

G2270 ἑσπέρα hespera, n. [3] [→2271]. evening:– evening (3)

G2271 ἑσπερινός hesperinos, a. Not used in NIVEBC. [√2270]. pertaining to the evening

G2272 Ἑσρώμ Hesrōm, n. pr. [3] Hezron, "*enclosure*":– Hezron (3)

G2273 ἑσσόομαι hessoomai, v. [1] [√2482]. to be inferior, lesser, worse off, with a focus on the manner in which someone is treated:– inferior (1)

G2274 ἔσχατος eschatos, a. [52] [√1666]. last (of a series), least, final:– last (42), end (2), ends (2), final (2), last of all (1), least important (1), lowest (1), now (1)

G2275 ἐσχάτως eschatōs, adv. [1] [√1666]. finally; at the point of death:– dying (1 [+2400])

G2276 ἔσω esō, adv. [9] [√1650]. in, inner, inside, inwardly:– inner (2), inside (2), in (1), into (1), inwardly (1 [+3836]), right into (1 [+2401, 1650]), NDT (1)

G2277 ἔσωθεν esōthen, adv. [12] [√1650]. from within, from inside, inwardly:– inside (4), on the inside (2), from inside (1), from within (1), inwardly (1), on both sides (1 [+2779, 3957]), under (1), within (1)

G2278 ἐσώτερος esōteros, a. [2] [√1650]. inner:– inner (2)

G2279 ἑταῖρος hetairos, n. [3] friend, comrade, companion:– friend (3)

G2280 ἑτερόγλωσσος heteroglōssos, a. [1] [√2283 + 1185]. speaking in a foreign language:– other tongues (1)

G2281 ἑτεροδιδασκαλέω heterodidaskaleō, v. [2] [√2283 + 1438]. to teach false doctrine, teach heresy:– teach false doctrines (1), teaches otherwise (1)

G2282 ἑτεροζυγέω heterozygeō, v. [1] [√2283 + 2413]. to yoke together in a mismatch:– yoked together (1)

G2283 ἕτερος heteros, a. [98] [→2280, 2281, 2282, 2284, 4538]. other, different:– another (29), other (28), others (15), different (4), else (4), some (3), someone else (3), different from (2), changed (1 [+1181]), day after thats (1), elsewhere (1), foreigners (1), new (1), next (1), one kind (1), perversion (1 [+599, 3958, 4922]), the seconds (1), NDT (1)

G2284 ἑτέρως heterōs, adv. [1] [√2283]. differently, other, otherwise:– differently (1)

G2285 ἔτι eti, adv. [93] [→3600, 4033]. still, yet, again:– still (31), again (9), longer (7), more (7), continue (5), any more (3), even (3), any longer (2), anymore (2), yet (2), as (1), as long as still (1), before long (1 [+3625]), besides (1), even before (1), for (1), in a while (1 [+4012, 4012]), just as (1 [+2317]), left (1), longer (1 [+5989]), much (1), only (1), still (1 [+3814]), when (1), while (1), yes (1 [+5445]), NDT (6)

G2286 ἑτοιμάζω hetoimazō, v. [40] [√2289]. to prepare, be ready:– prepared (19), prepare (10), make preparations (5), get ready (3), made ready (1), make ready (1), ready (1)

G2287 **Ἑτοιμᾶς** ***Hetoimas***, n. pr. Not used in NIVEBC. [√*cf. 1829*]. Hetoimas

G2288 **ἑτοιμασία** ***hetoimasia***, n. [1] [√*2289*]. readiness, preparation:– readiness (1)

G2289 **ἕτοιμος** ***hetoimos***, a. [17] [→*2286, 2288, 2290, 4602*]. ready, prepared:– ready (14), do (1), prepared (1), work already done (1)

G2290 **ἑτοίμως** ***hetoimōs***, adv. [3] [√*2289*]. readily:– ready (3)

G2291 **ἔτος** ***etos***, n. [49] [→*1453, 1454, 1670, 5474, 5478, 5562*]. year:– years (42), year (3), three and a half years (1 [+*5552, 2779, 3604, 1971*]), NDT (3)

G2292 **εὖ** ***eu***, adv. [5] [→*460, 1922, 2294, 2295, 2296, 2297, 2298, 2299, 2300, 2301, 2302, 2303, 2304, 2305, 2306, 2307, 2308, 2309, 2310, 2313, 2314, 2315, 2320, 2321, 2322, 2323, 2324, 2325, 2326, 2327, 2328, 2329, 2330, 2331, 2332, 2333, 2334, 2337, 2338, 2339, 2340, 2341, 2342, 2343, 2344, 2345, 2346, 2347, 2348, 2349, 2354, 2355, 2356, 2357, 2358, 2359, 2360, 2361, 2362, 2363, 2364, 2365, 2366, 2367, 2368, 2369, 2370, 2373, 2374, 2375, 2378, 2379, 2380, 2381, 2382, 2986, 4492, 4603, 5306, 5307*]. well; well done!:– well (2), well done (2), help (1 [+*4472*])

G2293 **Εὕα** ***Ehua***, n. pr. [2] Eve, "*life*":– Eve (2)

G2294 **εὐαγγελίζω** ***euangelizō***, v. [54] [√*2292 + 34*]. to preach (bring) the good news (gospel), often with a focus on the content of the message which is brought. In the NT it always refers to the death, burial, resurrection, and witness about Jesus Christ, including its implications for humankind's relationship to God:– preach the gospel (8), preached (8), preached the gospel (3), preaching the gospel (3), proclaiming the good news (3), the good news proclaimed (3), preach (2), preaching (2), proclaimed the good news (2), announced (1), announcing the good news (1), bring good news (1), bring news (1), bringing good news (1), brought good news (1), preach a gospel (1), preaching a gospel (1), preaching the good news (1), proclaim (1), proclaim good news (1), proclaim the good news (1), tell good news (1), tell the good news (1), telling the good news (1), the good news (1), the good news is proclaimed (1), the good news preached (1), the gospel preached (1), told the good news (1)

G2295 **εὐαγγέλιον** ***euangelion***, n. [76] [√*2292 + 34*]. gospel, good news; see also *2294*:– gospel (61), good news (7), preaching the gospel (2), it[s] (1 [+*3836*]), preach the gospel (1), preacher of the gospel (1), proclaimed the gospel (1), proclaiming the gospel (1), work of gospel (1)

G2296 **εὐαγγελιστής** ***euangelistēs***, n. [3] [√*2292 + 34*]. evangelist, preacher of the gospel:– evangelist (2), evangelists (1)

G2297 **εὐαρεστέω** ***euaresteō***, v. [3] [√*2292 + 743*]. to please:– pleased (2), please (1)

G2298 **εὐάρεστος** ***euarestos***, a. [9] [√*2292 + 743*]. pleasing, acceptable:– pleasing (5), pleases (2 [+*1639*]), please (1), please (1 [+*1639*])

G2299 **εὐαρέστως** ***euarestōs***, adv. [1] [√*2292 + 743*]. in an acceptable or pleasing manner:– acceptably (1)

G2300 **Εὔβουλος** ***Euboulos***, n. pr. [1] [√*2292 + 1089*]. Eubulus, "*good counsel*":– Eubulus (1)

G2301 **εὖγε** ***euge***, adv. [1] [√*2292 + 1145*]. well done!, excellent!:– well done (1)

G2302 **εὐγενής** ***eugenēs***, a. [3] [√*2292 + 1181*]. of noble birth, of noble character:– of noble birth (2), of noble character (1)

G2303 **εὐγλωττία** ***euglōttia***, n. Not used in NIVEBC. [√*2292 + 1185*]. glibness, fluency of speech

G2304 **εὐδία** ***eudia***, n. [1] [√*2292 + 2416*]. fair weather:– fair weather (1)

G2305 **εὐδοκέω** ***eudokeō***, v. [21] [√*2292 + 1506*]. to be well pleased, delight:– pleased (9), well pleased (5), delight (2), delighted (1), delighted in (1), prefer (1 [+*3437*]), take pleasure (1), thought it best (1)

G2306 **εὐδοκία** ***eudokia***, n. [9] [√*2292 + 1506*]. goodwill, good purpose, favor, pleasure, desire:– desire (2), pleased (2), favor (1), good pleasure (1), good purpose (1), goodwill (1), pleasure (1)

G2307 **εὐεργεσία** ***euergesia***, n. [2] [√*2292 + 2240*]. act of kindness, good deed:– act of kindness (1), welfare (1)

G2308 **εὐεργετέω** ***euergeteō***, v. [1] [√*2292 + 2240*]. to do good to:– doing good (1)

G2309 **εὐεργέτης** ***euergetēs***, n. [1] [√*2292 + 2240*]. benefactor; in context this is a title:– benefactors (1)

G2310 **εὔθετος** ***euthetos***, a. [3] [√*2292 + 5502*]. fit, fit for service, useable, suitable:– fit (1), fit for service (1), useful (1)

G2311 **εὐθέως** ***eutheōs***, adv. [36] [√*2317*]. immediately, at once:– immediately (19), at once (8), as soon as (1), at that moment (1), at this (1), immediate (1), now (1), quickly (1), right away (1), soon (1), suddenly (1)

G2312 **εὐθυδρομέω** ***euthydromeō***, v. [2] [√*2317 + 5556*]. to sail straight, run a straight course:– sailed straight (2)

G2313 **εὐθυμέω** ***euthymeō***, v. [3] [√*2292 + 2596*]. to keep up one's courage; to be happy, cheerful:– keep up courage (2), happy (1)

G2314 **εὔθυμος** ***euthymos***, a. [1] [√*2292 + 2596*]. encouraged, cheerful, in good spirits:– encouraged (1)

G2315 **εὐθύμως** ***euthymōs***, adv. [1] [√*2292 + 2596*]. gladly, cheerfully:– gladly (1)

G2316 **εὐθύνω** ***euthynō***, v. [2] [√*2317*]. to make straight, straighten; to go straight:– go (1), make straight (1)

G2317 **εὐθύς**[1] ***euthys***[1], adv. [51] [→*2311, 2312, 2316, 2318, 2319, 2985*]. immediately, at once, as soon as:– immediately (14), at once (9), as soon as (8), quickly (4), just as (2), at this (1), just as (1 [+*2285*]), just then (1), right away (1), shortly (1), sudden (1), the moment (1), then (1), very early in the morning (1 [+*4745*]), when (1), without delay (1), NDT (3)

G2318 **εὐθύς**[2] ***euthys***[2], a. [8] [√*2317*]. straight, not crooked; by extension: right, upright, the moral quality of not being wrong or perverse to truth or purity:– straight (6), right (2)

G2319 **εὐθύτης** ***euthytēs***, n. [1] [√*2317*]. righteousness, uprightness, a fig. extension of a straight (not crooked) object, not found in the NT:– justice (1)

G2320 **εὐκαιρέω** ***eukaireō***, v. [3] [√*2292 + 2789*]. to have a chance to, have the opportunity to; to spend one's time:– has the opportunity (1), have a chance (1), spent time (1)

G2321 **εὐκαιρία** ***eukairia***, n. [2] [√*2292 + 2789*]. opportunity, the right moment:– opportunity (2)

G2322 **εὔκαιρος** ***eukairos***, a. [2] [√*2292 + 2789*]. opportune, well timed, suitable; time of need:– opportune (1), time of need (1)

G2323 **εὐκαίρως** ***eukairōs***, adv. [2] [√*2292 + 2789*]. opportunely, in season:– in season (1), opportunity (1)

G2324 **εὔκοπος** ***eukopos***, a. [7] [√*2292 + 3164*]. easy, easier:– easier (7)

G2325 **εὐλάβεια** ***eulabeia***, n. [2] [√*2292 + 3284*]. reverence, reverent submission:– reverence (1), reverent submission (1)

G2326 **εὐλαβέομαι** ***eulabeomai***, v. [1] [√*2292 + 3284*]. to have holy fear, reverence:– holy fear (1)

G2327 **εὐλαβής** ***eulabēs***, a. [4] [√*2292 + 3284*]. devout, godly, God-fearing:– devout (2), God-fearing (1), godly (1)

G2328 **εὐλογέω** ***eulogeō***, v. [41] [√*2292 + 3306*]. to praise, give thanks to, speak well of, extol; (pass.) to be blessed, receive blessing; in some contexts, to give a blessing is to act kindly and impart benefits to the one being blessed:– blessed (19), bless (5), gave thanks (5), praising (3), bless (2 [+*2328*]), blessing (2), given thanks (2), give thanks (1), praise (1), praised (1)

G2329 **εὐλογητός** ***eulogētos***, a. [8] [√*2292 + 3306*]. worthy of being praised, blessed, or commended:– praise (4), praised (3), blessed (1)

G2330 **εὐλογία** ***eulogia***, n. [16] [√*2292 + 3306*]. blessing, praise, thanksgiving, the extolling of another; in some contexts, excessive praise is improper: flattery; by extention, generosity and (giving of) gifts:– blessing (6), praise (4), generous gift (2), generously (2 [+*2093*]), flattery (1), thanksgiving (1)

G2331 **εὐμετάδοτος** ***eumetadotos***, a. [1] [√*2292 + 3552 + 1443*]. generous:– generous (1)

G2332 **Εὐνίκη** ***Eunikē***, n. pr. [1] [√*2292 + 3772*]. Eunice, "*good victory*":– Eunice (1)

G2333 **εὐνοέω** ***eunoeō***, v. [1] [√*2292 + 3808*]. to settle matters by coming to terms:– settle matters (1 [+*1639*])

G2334 **εὔνοια** ***eunoia***, n. [1] [√*2292 + 3808*]. wholeheartedness, enthusiasm, eagerness:– wholeheartedly (1 [+*3552*])

G2335 **εὐνουχίζω** ***eunouchizō***, v. [2] [→*2336; cf. 2400*]. to emasculate, make (oneself) a eunuch; to be celibate, renounce marriage:– choose to live like eunuchs (1), made eunuchs (1)

G2336 **εὐνοῦχος** ***eunouchos***, n. [8] [√*2335*]. eunuch, court official:– eunuch (5), eunuchs (2), those[s] (1)

G2337 **Εὐοδία** ***Euodia***, n. pr. [1] [√*2292 + 3847*]. Euodia, "*good way* poss. *good fragrance*":– Euodia (1)

G2338 **εὐοδόω** ***euodoō***, v. [4] [√*2292 + 3847*]. (pass.) to get along with; to have a way opened; to prosper, get along well:– getting along well (1), income (1), may go well (1), way opened (1)

G2339 **εὐπάρεδρος** ***euparedros***, a. [1] [√*2292 + 4123 + 1612*]. devoted, devotion, service devoted to God:– devotion (1)

G2340 **εὐπειθής** ***eupeithēs***, a. [1] [√*2292 + 4275*]. submissive, obedient, compliant:– submissive (1)

G2341 **εὐπερίσπαστος** ***euperispastos***, a. Not used in NIVEBC. [√*2292 + 4309 + 5060*]. easily distracting

G2342 **εὐπερίστατος** ***euperistatos***, a. [1] [√*2292 + 4309 + 2705*]. easily entangling, constricting, obstructing:– so easily entangles (1)

G2343 **εὐποιΐα** ***eupoiia***, n. [1] [√*2292 + 4472*]. doing good:– do good (1)

G2344 **εὐπορέω** ***euporeō***, v. [1] [√*2292 + 4513*]. to have (financial) ability, have plenty, be well off:– able (1)

G2345 **εὐπορία** ***euporia***, n. [1] [√*2292 + 4513*]. prosperity, prosperous income:– good income (1)

G2346 **εὐπρέπεια** ***euprepeia***, n. [1] [√*2292 + 4560*]. beauty:– beauty (1 [+*3836, 4725*])

G2347 **εὐπρόσδεκτος** ***euprosdektos***, a. [5] [√*2292 + 4639 + 1312*]. acceptable, favorable:– acceptable (3), favor (1), favorably received (1)

G2348 **εὐπρόσεδρος** ***euprosedros***, a. Not used in NIVEBC. [√*2292 + 4639 + 1612*]. constant

G2349 **εὐπροσωπέω** ***euprosōpeō***, v. [1] [√*2292 + 4725*]. to make a good impression, make a good showing:– impress (1)

G2350 **εὐρακύλων** ***eurakylōn***, n. [1] northeast wind, Euraquilo:– northeaster (1)

G2351 **εὑρίσκω** ***heuriskō***, v. [176] [→*461, 2388*]. (act.) to find, discover, meet; (mid.) to obtain; (pass.) to be found:– found (84), find (54), finds (13), met (3), finding (2), and lost (1 [+*4028*]), appeared (1), came to (1), change (1 [+*3567, 5536*]), considered (1), decide (1), discovered (1), enjoyed (1), find (1 [+*1639*]), find out (1), finds (1 [+*1181*]), laid bare (1), looking for (1), obtaining (1), prove (1), provide (1), recovered (1), result (1), was[s] (1), NDT (1)

G2352 **εὐροκλύδων** ***euroklydōn***, n. Not used in NIVEBC. [√*3114*]. southeast wind, Euroclydon

G2353 **εὐρύχωρος** ***eurychōros***, a. [1] [√*6003*]. broad, spacious:– broad (1)

G2354 **εὐσέβεια** ***eusebeia***, n. [15] [√*2292 + 4936*]. godliness, piety:– godliness (10), godly (4), true godliness (1)

G2355 **εὐσεβέω** ***eusebeō***, v. [2] [√*2292 + 4936*]. to worship; to put religion into practice, show piety toward:– put religion into practice by caring for (1), worship (1)

G2356 **εὐσεβής** ***eusebēs***, a. [3] [√*2292 + 4936*]. devout, godly, pious, reverent:– devout (2), godly (1)

G2357 **εὐσεβῶς** ***eusebōs***, adv. [2] [√*2292 + 4936*]. in a godly manner:– godly (2)

G2358 **εὔσημος** ***eusēmos***, a. [1] [√*2292 + 4956*]. intelligible, clear, distinct, easily recognizable:– intelligible (1)

G2359 **εὔσπλαγχνος** ***eusplanchnos***, a. [2] [√*2292 + 5073*]. compassionate, tenderhearted:– compassionate (2)

G2360 **εὐσχημονέω** ***euschēmoneō***, v. Not used in NIVEBC. [√*2292 + 5386*]. to behave in an affected manner

G2361 **εὐσχημόνως** ***euschēmonōs***, adv. [3] [√*2292 + 5386*]. decently, fittingly, becomingly, properly:– decently (1), fitting (1), win the respect (1)

G2362 **εὐσχημοσύνη** ***euschēmosynē***, n. [1] [√*2292 + 5386*]. modesty, presentability:– modesty (1)

G2363 **εὐσχήμων** ***euschēmōn***, a. [5] [√*2292 + 5386*]. presentable, proper, right; prominent, of high standing:– prominent (2), high standing (1), presentable (1), right (1)

G2364 **εὐτόνως** ***eutonōs***, adv. [2] [√*1753; cf. 2292*]. vehemently, vigorously:– vehemently (1), vigorously (1)

G2365 **εὐτραπελία** ***eutrapelia***, n. [1] [√*2292 + 5572*]. coarse joking, vulgar jesting:– coarse joking (1)

G2366 **Εὔτυχος** ***Eutychos***, n. pr. [1] [√*2292 + 5593*]. Eutychus, "*fortunate*":– Eutychus (1)

G2367 **εὐφημία** ***euphēmia***, n. [1] [√*2292 + 5774*]. good report:– good report (1)

G2368 **εὔφημος** ***euphēmos***, a. [1] [√*2292 + 5774*]. admirable, appealing, praiseworthy:– admirable (1)

G2369 **εὐφορέω** ***euphoreō***, v. [1] [√*2292 + 5770*]. to produce a good crop, be fruitful:– yielded an abundant harvest (1)

G2370 **εὐφραίνω** ***euphrainō***, v. [14] [→*2371, 2372; cf. 2292 + 5856*]. (act.) to cause celebration, make glad; (mid./pass.) to celebrate, rejoice, be glad:– celebrate (5), rejoice (3), glad (2), lived in luxury (1 [+*3289*]), make glad (1), merry (1), reveled (1)

G2371 **Εὐφράτης** ***Euphratēs***, n. pr. [2] [√*2370*]. Euphrates:– Euphrates (2)

G2372 **εὐφροσύνη** ***euphrosynē***, n. [2] [*√2370*]. joy, gladness, cheerfulness:– joy (2)

G2373 **εὐχαριστέω** ***eucharisteō***, v. [38] [*√2292 + 5897*]. to thank, give thanks, render gratitude; this can mean words that express gratitude or the emotion of gratitude:– thank (14), given thanks (6), gave thanks (5), giving thanks (5), give thanks (4), thanked (2), gives thanks (1), grateful (1)

G2374 **εὐχαριστία** ***eucharistia***, n. [15] [*√2292 + 5897*]. expression of thanks, thanksgiving, gratitude:– thanksgiving (8), thanks (2), expressions of thanks (1), gratitude (1), thank (1), thankful (1), thankfulness (1)

G2375 **εὐχάριστος** ***eucharistos***, a. [1] [*√2292 + 5897*]. thankful (in word and attitude):– thankful (1)

G2376 **εὐχή** ***euchē***, n. [3] [*√2377*]. vow, oath; prayer:– vow (2), prayer (1)

G2377 **εὔχομαι** ***euchomai***, v. [7] [*→2376, 4666, 4667*]. to pray for; wish for:– pray (4), prayed (1), prayer (1), wish (1)

G2378 **εὔχρηστος** ***euchrēstos***, a. [3] [*√2292 + 5968*]. useful, helpful, serviceable:– useful (2), helpful (1)

G2379 **εὐψυχέω** ***eupsycheō***, v. [1] [*√2292 + 6038*]. to be cheerful, glad:– cheered (1)

G2380 **εὐωδία** ***euōdia***, n. [3] [*√2292 + 3853*]. aroma, fragrance:– fragrant (1 [*+4011*]), fragrant offering (1 [*+4011*]), pleasing aroma (1)

G2381 **εὐώνυμος** ***euōnymos***, a. [9] [*√2292 + 3950*]. left (direction), south:– left (8), south (1)

G2382 **εὐωχία** ***euōchia***, n. Not used in NIVEBC. [*√2292 + 2400*]. banquet, feasting

G2383 **ἐφάλλομαι** ***ephallomai***, v. [1] [*√2093 + 256*]. to jump on, leap upon:– jumped on (1)

G2384 **ἐφάπαξ** ***ephapax***, adv. [5] [*√2093 + 562*]. once for all; at the same time:– once for all (4), at the same time (1)

G2385 **Ἐφεσῖνος** ***Ephesinos***, a. pr. g. Not used in NIVEBC. [*√2387*]. Ephesian

G2386 **Ἐφέσιος** ***Ephesios***, a. pr. g. [5] [*√2387*]. Ephesian, person of Ephesus:– Ephesians (3), Ephesian (1), of Ephesus (1)

G2387 **Ἔφεσος** ***Ephesos***, n. pr. [16] [*→2385, 2386*]. Ephesus:– Ephesus (16)

G2388 **ἐφευρετής** ***epheuretēs***, n. [1] [*√2093 + 2351*]. inventor, contriver:– invent (1)

G2389 **ἐφημερία** ***ephēmeria***, n. [2] [*√2093 + 2465*]. (priestly) division, group, class:– division (1), priestly division (1)

G2390 **ἐφήμερος** ***ephēmeros***, a. [1] [*√2093 + 2465*]. daily, for the day:– daily (1)

G2391 **ἐφικνέομαι** ***ephikneomai***, v. [2] [*√2093 + 2653*]. to come (to), reach (to):– going too far (1), includes (1 [*+948*])

G2392 **ἐφίστημι** ***ephistēmi***, v. [21] [*√2093 + 2705*]. to approach, come near, stand beside, stop; to be imminent, at hand:– appeared (2), came up to (2), stood beside (2), stopped (2), bent (1), came (1), came to (1), close (1), come (1), coming up (1), near (1), prepared (1), rushed (1), stood near (1), stood there (1 [*+1639*]), was (1), NDT (1)

G2393 **ἐφοράω** ***ephoraō***, v. Not used in NIVEBC. [*√2093 + 3972*]. to gaze upon

G2394 **Ἐφραίμ** ***Ephraim***, n. pr. [1] Ephraim, "*doubly fruitful*":– Ephraim (1)

G2395 **ἐφφαθά** ***ephphatha***, l.[v.] [1] ephphatha!, be opened!:– Ephphatha (1)

G2396 **ἐχθές** ***echthes***, adv. [3] [*√5940*]. yesterday:– yesterday (3)

G2397 **ἔχθρα** ***echthra***, n. [6] [*√2398*]. hostility, hatred, antagonism:– hostility (2), enemies (1 [*+1877*]), enmity (1), hatred (1), hostile (1)

G2398 **ἐχθρός** ***echthros***, a. [32] [*→2397*]. (n.) enemy:– enemies (21), enemy (10), enemy (1 [*+476*])

G2399 **ἔχιδνα** ***echidna***, n. [5] viper, snake:– vipers (4), viper (1)

G2400 **ἔχω** ***echō***, v. [708] [*→191, 445, 452, 462, 496, 504, 600, 1923, 1944, 2006, 2009, 2011, 2029, 2091, 2382, 2759, 2807, 2959, 2988, 3576, 3580, 3581, 3807, 4060, 4065, 4218, 4321, 4343, 4430, 4431, 4432, 4604, 4617, 4652, 4668, 4812, 5156, 5212, 5226, 5307, 5309, 5330, 5385, 5660, 5667, 5674; cf. 2335, 5386*]. (tr.) to have, hold, keep; (intr.) to be:– have (214), has (84), had (72), with (23), need (17 [*+5970*]), having (11), is (9), are (8), be (8), sick (8 [*+2809*]), need (7 [*+5970*]), was (7), pregnant (6 [*+1877, 1143*]), demon-possessed (5 [*+1228*]), held (5), possessed by (5), without (5 [*+3590*]), get (4), needs (4 [*+5970*]), take (4), am (3), belongs to (3), guilty of sin (3 [*+281*]), hold (3), holding (3), holds (3), in need (3 [*+5970*]), keep (3), thank (3 [*+5921*]), able (2), been (2), come (2), excuse (2 [*+4148*]), felt (2), had (2 [*+1639*]), hold to (2), love (2 [*+27*]), needed (2 [*+5970*]), of age (2 [*+2461*]), reap (2), received (2), rich (2 [*+3836, 5975*]), were (2), a Sabbath day's walk from (1 [*+1584, 4879, 3847*]), accepts (1 [*+1877, 1571*]), accompanied by (1), answer (1 [*+4639*]), approach (1 [*+4643*]), as follows (1 [*+3836, 5596, 4047*]), been[S] (1), believe (1 [*+4411*]), believers (1 [*+3836, 4411*]), benefit (1 [*+5921*]), boast (1 [*+3018*]), bold (1 [*+4498, 4244*]), bring on (1), bringing (1 [*+3552*]), can (1), cannot (1 [*+4024*]), children conceived at the same time (1 [*+1666, 1651, 3130*]), commended (1 [*+2047*]), conceive (1 [*+1877, 1143*]), consider (1), considered (1 [*+6055*]), contained (1 [*+1877*]), could (1), covered (1 [*+2848*]), crippled (1 [*+819*]), demon-possessed (1 [*+3836, 4460, 3836, 4505*]), dependent on (1 [*+5970*]), desire (1 [*+2123*]), do[S] (1), doing (1), dwell (1 [*+3531*]), dying (1 [*+2275*]), encouraged (1 [*+4155*]), enjoy (1), enjoyed (1), enjoying (1), enough (1), face (1), faced (1 [*+2848, 4725*]), filled with (1), finish (1 [*+5455*]), following (1), for[S] (1), forgiven (1 [*+912*]), functioning (1 [*+5087*]), gained (1), gave[S] (1), give (1), given (1), given (1 [*+608*]), glory (1 [*+3018*]), going through (1), got (1), had charge of (1), harbor (1), hardened (1 [*+4800*]), has to do with (1), have sexual relations with (1), have to do with (1), haven't (1 [*+3590*]), held (1 [*+1650*]), hold (1 [*+6055*]), hold fast (1), holding on (1), honor (1 [*+1952*]), I (1), I must (1 [*+340*]), ill (1 [*+2809*]), in (1), in all (1), in this condition (1), intend (1), invalid (1 [*+1877, 3836, 819*]), is for (1), keep hold of (1), keeper (1), keeping (1), kept (1), lack (1 [*+4024*]), leaves (1), live (1), lived (1 [*+3836, 2998*]), living (1 [*+6034*]), made (1), made (1 [*+2093*]), maintained (1), married (1 [*+1222*]), married to (1), means (1), nearby (1), need (1 [*+340*]), need (1 [*+5790*]), need (1 [*+1181, 5970*]), next (1), next day (1), on (1), persevered (1 [*+5705*]), possess (1), power (1), preached (1 [*+3062*]), reaching (1), rebuked (1 [*+1792*]), remember (1 [*+3644*]), requires (1 [*+1953, 2848*]), resembling (1 [*+926*]), retain (1), rules (1 [*+993*]), sealed (1 [*+3836, 5382*]), see that (1), shallow (1 [*+3590, 958*]), share (1 [*+3538*]), shone with[S] (1), sick (1 [*+819*]), sleeping with (1), spare (1 [*+3590*]), spread (1 [*+3786*]), stop (1 [*+398*]), suffer (1), surrounded by (1), take (1 [*+1639*]), taken (1), trained (1 [*+1214*]), treated with (1), trembling (1 [*+5571*]), uncircumcised (1 [*+213*]), under (1), use (1), want to (1), were married (1 [*+1222*]), whose (1 [*+4005*]), whose[S] (1), wounded (1 [*+3836, 4435*]), NDT (15)

G2401 **ἕως** ***heōs***, c. & pp.* [146] up to, until:– to (31), until (28), until (15 [*+323*]), until (13 [*+4005*]), before (4 [*+323*]), how long (4 [*+4536*]), how long (3 [*+4536*]), still (3 [*+785*]), till (3), until (3 [*+4015*]), while (3), for (2), right up to (2), to the point of (2), up to (2), while (2 [*+4005*]), all the way (1), and (1 [*+4015*]), as far as (1), as long as (1), before (1 [*+4024*]), before (1 [*+4024, 3590, 4005*]), both and (1 [*+608*]), even (1), even in (1), fully (1 [*+5465*]), going on to (1), no more (1 [*+1572*]), right into (1 [*+2276, 1650*]), right on down to (1), till (1 [*+323*]), to the vicinity of (1 [*+4639*]), to where (1), until (1 [*+2465*]), until the time of (1), when (1 [*+4005*]), while still (1 [*+4015*]), NDT (5)

G2402 **ϛ** , letter. Not used in NIVEBC. an obsolete letter (stigma or vau), used as the numeral "six"

G2403 **ζ** ***z***, letter. Not used in NIVEBC. letter of the Greek alphabet

G2404 **Ζαβουλών** ***Zaboulōn***, n. pr. [3] Zebulun, "*honor*":– Zebulun (3)

G2405 **Ζακχαῖος** ***Zakchaios***, n. pr. [3] Zacchaeus, "*righteous one, pure one*":– Zacchaeus (3)

G2406 **Ζάρα** ***Zara***, n. pr. [1] Zerah, "*dawning, shining or flashing [red or scarlet] light*":– Zerah (1)

G2407 **ζαφθάνι** ***zaphthani***, l.[v.+p.] Not used in NIVEBC. [*√cf. 4876*]. sabachthani

G2408 **Ζαχαρίας** ***Zacharias***, n. pr. [11] Zechariah, "*Yahweh remembers*":– Zechariah (10), Zechariah's (1)

G2409 **ζάω** ***zaō***, v. [140] [*→348, 351, 2436, 2437, 2441, 2442, 2443, 5182, 5188*]. to be alive, to live a life; in the NT this can also refer to the resurrection life, Jesus Christ is then "the Living One":– live (50), living (42), alive (19), lives (15), lived (3), life (2), alive again (1), belonged (1), came to life (1), came to life again (1), come to life (1), live a life (1), live lives (1), receive living (1), returned to life (1)

G2410 **ζβέννυμι** ***zbennymi***, v. Not used in NIVEBC. [*√4931*]. to extinguish, put out

G2411 **Ζεβεδαῖος** ***Zebedaios***, n. pr. [12] Zebedee, "*Yahweh bestows*":– Zebedee (10), Zebedee's (2)

G2412 **ζεστός** ***zestos***, a. [2] [*√2417*]. hot:– hot (2)

G2413 **ζεύγνυμι** ***zeugnymi***, v. Not used in NIVEBC. [*→2282, 2414, 2415, 2433, 5183, 5187, 5689*]. to connect, join

G2414 **ζεῦγος** ***zeugos***, n. [2] [*√2413*]. yoke; by extension: a pair:– pair (1), yoke (1)

G2415 **ζευκτηρία** ***zeuktēria***, n. [1] [*√2413*]. rope, band:– ropes (1)

G2416 **Ζεύς** ***Zeus***, n. pr. [2] [*→1479, 1483, 1485, 2304, 2424, 2425*]. Zeus, "*shine, bright*":– Zeus (2)

G2417 **ζέω** ***zeō***, v. [2] [*→2412; cf. 2419, 2434*]. to have great fervor, as a fig. extension something boiling or seething, not found in the NT:– fervor (1), with great fervor (1 [*+3836, 4460*])

G2418 **ζηλεύω** ***zēleuō***, v. [1] [*√2419*]. to be earnest, eager:– earnest (1)

G2419 **ζῆλος** ***zēlos***, n. [16] [*→2418, 2420, 2421, 4143; cf. 2417*]. zeal, ardent concern, enthusiasm, an attitude or emotion of deep, earnest concern; jealousy, envy, rage, morally corrupt zealous ill will:– jealousy (7), envy (2), zeal (2), ardent concern (1), concern (1), enthusiasm (1), raging (1), zealous (1)

G2420 **ζηλόω** ***zēloō***, v. [11] [*√2419*]. to desire, eagerly desire, show zeal, feel an attitude or emotion of deep concern; to be jealous, envious, to experience morally corrupt zealous ill will; covet, as a negative attitude of lust and desire for another's possessions:– jealous (3), eagerly desire (2), zealous (2), covet (1), eager (1), envy (1), have zeal (1)

G2421 **ζηλωτής** ***zēlōtēs***, n. [8] [*√2419*]. zealot, enthusiast, adherent, one who has the feelings or attitudes of deep commitment to a person or cause; in the NT this can technically refer to a person who belonged to a nationalist Jewish group that sought independence from Rome:– zealous (3), eager (2), zealot (2), eager to do (1)

G2422 **ζημία** ***zēmia***, n. [4] [*→2423*]. loss, damage:– loss (4)

G2423 **ζημιόω** ***zēmioō***, v. [6] [*√2422*]. (pass.) to forfeit, suffer loss or damage:– forfeit (3), harmed (1), lost (1), suffer loss (1)

G2424 **Ζηνᾶς** ***Zēnas***, n. pr. [1] [*√2416*]. Zenas, "*gift of Zeus*":– Zenas (1)

G2425 **Ζήνων** ***Zēnōn***, n. pr. Not used in NIVEBC. [*√2416*]. Zeno

G2426 **ζητέω** ***zēteō***, v. [117] [*→349, 1699, 1700, 2118, 2427, 2428, 5184, 5185, 5186*]. to look for, seek out; to try to obtain, desire to possess, strive for:– looking for (17), seek (14), look for (10), seeking (6), seeks (5), tried to (5), want (5), tried (4), trying to (4), looked for a way (3), looking for a way (3), watched for (3), ask for (2), search (2), searching for (2), sought (2), try (2), trying (2), wanting (2), asked for (1), asking (1), asking for (1), asks for (1), attempt (1), demanded (1), demanding (1), gain (1), got ready (1), in search of (1), looks out for (1), required (1), scheming (1), search for (1), searched for (1), self-seeking (1 [*+3836, 1571*]), set heart on (1), set hearts on (1), tries (1), trying to kill (1 [*+3836, 6034*]), trying to take (1), wanted (1), wants to (1), watching for (1)

G2427 **ζήτημα** ***zētēma***, n. [5] [*√2426*]. question for discussion, point of dispute, controversy:– questions (2), controversies (1), points of dispute (1), question (1)

G2428 **ζήτησις** ***zētēsis***, n. [7] [*√2426*]. argument, debate, controversy, discussion:– controversies (2), argument (1), arguments (1), debate (1), discussion (1), investigate (1)

G2429 **ζιζάνιον** ***zizanion***, n. [8] weed, darnel, or some other troublesome weed:– weeds (8)

G2430 **Ζμύρνα** ***Zmyrna***, n. pr. Not used in NIVEBC. [*√5043*]. Smyrna

G2431 **Ζοροβαβέλ** ***Zorobabel***, n. pr. [3] Zerubbabel, "*offspring of Babylon*":– Zerubbabel (3)

G2432 **ζόφος** ***zophos***, n. [5] blackness, darkness, gloom:– blackest (2), darkness (2), gloom (1)

G2433 **ζυγός** ***zygos***, n. [6] [*√2413*]. yoke, a frame and cross bar placed on draft animals to pull various objects; pair of scales, ancient balance-pan scales. "To be under a yoke" means to be in an oppressed condition such as slavery:– yoke (5), pair of scales (1)

G2434 **ζύμη** ***zymē***, n. [13] [*→109, 2435; cf. 2417*]. yeast, leaven:– yeast (10), bread (1), leavened (1), that[S] (1 [*+3836*])

G2435 **ζυμόω** ***zymoō***, v. [4] [*√2434*]. to leaven, ferment, work as yeast:– worked through the dough (2), leavens (1), works through (1)

G2436 **ζωγρέω** ***zōgreō***, v. [2] [*√2409 + 62*]. to capture (alive):– fish (1 [*+1639*]), taken captive (1)

G2437 **ζωή** ***zōē***, n. [135] [*√2409*]. life, physical or spiritual; with *173*, "eternal life":– life (129), brings life (1 [*+1666, 1650, 2437*]), brings life (1 [*+1666, 2437, 1650*]), lifetime (1), live (1), living (1), living thing (1 [*+6034*])

G2438 **ζώνη** ***zōnē***, n. [8] [*√2439*]. belt, sash:– belt (4), belts (2), sash (1), sashes (1)

G2439 **ζώννυμι** ***zōnnymi***, v. [3] [*→350, 1346, 2438, 2440, 4322, 4323, 5690*]. to dress, clothe oneself, put on a belt or sash:– dress (1), dressed (1), put clothes (1)

G2440 **ζωννύω** ***zōnnyō***, v. Not used in NIVEBC. [*√2439*]. to dress, clothe oneself, put on a belt or sash

G2441 **ζῳογονέω** ***zōogoneō***, v. [3] [√*2409* + *1181*]. to give life, make alive; to preserve life, keep alive:– die (1 [+*3590*]), gives life (1), preserve (1)

G2442 **ζῷον** ***zōon***, n. [23] [√*2409*]. living creature, animal:– living creatures (13), living creature (4), animals (3), NDT (3)

G2443 **ζῳοποιέω** ***zōopoieō***, v. [11] [√*2409* + *4472*]. to make alive, give life to:– gives life (5), made alive (2), come to life (1), give life (1), impart life (1), life-giving (1)

G2444 **η** ***ē***, letter. Not used in NIVEBC. letter of the Greek alphabet

G2445 **ἤ** ***ē***, pt. disj. *or* comp. [343] [→ *2472, 2486*]. or; (in a series) either...or; (in comparison) than:– or (249), than (30), and (8), before (4 [+*4570*]), either (2), instead of (2 [+*3437*]), and (1 [+*4099*]), before (1 [+*4570, 323*]), but (1), but (1 [+*247*]), cannot (1 [+*247*]), either or (1), from to (1), more than (1), nor (1), only (1 [+*4024, 4498*]), or (1 [+*3437*]), or again (1), or else (1), or otherwise (1), our (1), some (1), sometimes (1), than (1 [+*3437*]), tune played (1 [+*884, 3068*]), unless (1), whether (1), NDT (27)

G2446 **ἦ** ***ē***, adv. Not used in NIVEBC. [→ *2447*]. truly

G2447 **ἦ μήν** ***ē mēn***, adv. Not used in NIVEBC. [√*2446* + *3605*]. surely

G2448 **ἡγεμονεύω** ***hēgemoneuō***, v. [2] [√*72*]. to govern, lead, rule:– governor (2)

G2449 **ἡγεμονία** ***hēgemonia***, n. [1] [√*72*]. reign, leadership, rulership:– reign (1)

G2450 **ἡγεμών** ***hēgemōn***, n. [20] [√*72*]. ruler, prince, governor, prefect, procurator:– governor (13), governors (4), governor's (2), rulers (1)

G2451 **ἡγέομαι** ***hēgeomai***, v. [28] [√*72*]. to lead, rule, guide; to consider, think, regard:– consider (7), leaders (4), considered (2), ruler (2), think (2), bear in mind (1), chief (1), hold in regard (1), idea (1), regard (1), regarded (1), rules (1), thought (1), treated as (1), understand (1), value (1)

G2452 **ἡδέως** ***hēdeōs***, adv. [5] [√*2454*]. gladly, with delight; in the superlative, most gladly, with utter delight:– gladly (2), liked to (1), very gladly (1), with delight (1)

G2453 **ἤδη** ***ēdē***, adv. [60] already, by this time, even now:– already (34), now (5), as soon as (2 [+*4020*]), by now (2), by this time (2), almost (1), approached (1 [+*1181*]), at last (1 [+*4537*]), even now (1), had been (1), nearly (1), not until (1), now at last (1 [+*4537*]), still (1), NDT (6)

G2454 **ἡδονή** ***hēdonē***, n. [5] [→ *112, 830, 881, 2452, 2455, 5310, 5798*]. pleasure, desire, enjoyment, usually with a negative sense:– pleasures (3), desires (1), pleasure (1)

G2455 **ἡδύοσμον** ***hēdyosmon***, n. [2] [√*2454* + *3853*]. mint:– mint (2)

G2456 **ἦθος** ***ēthos***, n. [1] [√*1621*]. character, habit and custom:– character (1)

G2457 **ἥκω** ***hēkō***, v. [25] [→ *465, 2763*]. to come, to have come, be present:– come (22), arrived (1), here (1), overtake (1)

G2458 **ἠλί[1]** ***ēli[1]***, l.[n.+p.] [2] [√*cf. 1830*]. Eli [Hebrew: my God]:– Eli (2)

G2459 **Ἠλί[2]** ***Ēli[2]***, n. pr. [1] Heli, "*ascent [to God]*":– Heli (1)

G2460 **Ἠλίας** ***Ēlias***, n. pr. [29] Elijah, "*Yahweh is [my] God*":– Elijah (28), Elijah's (1)

G2461 **ἡλικία** ***hēlikia***, n. [8] [√*2462*]. life, time in life, age; stature, height:– life (2), of age (2 [+*2400*]), childbearing age (1 [+*2789*]), short (1 [+*3836, 3625*]), stature (1), whole (1)

G2462 **ἡλίκος** ***hēlikos***, a. [3] [→ *2461, 4383, 5312, 5496*]. how much, how great, how large:– how hard (1), small (1), what a great (1)

G2463 **ἥλιος** ***hēlios***, n. [32] [√*cf. 1637*]. sun:– sun (26), east (1 [+*424*]), east (1 [+*424*]), just after sunrise (1 [+*422, 3836*]), light of the sun (1), sunset (1 [+*1544*]), sunset (1 [+*1544, 3836*])

G2464 **ἧλος** ***hēlos***, n. [2] [→ *4669*]. nail (used in crucifixion):– nail (1), nails (1)

G2465 **ἡμέρα** ***hēmera***, n. [388] [→ *2389, 2390, 2765, 2766, 3540, 3819, 3892, 4958*]. day, time of the day, time, indefinite period of time. "The children of the day" means "God's people," who walk in light. "The day of the Lord" and "the day of Christ" are periods of judgment and vindication, longer than twenty-four hours:– day (181), days (115), time (31), daily (5 [+*2848*]), daylight (4), every day (3 [+*2848*]), Sabbath (2 [+*4879*]), day after day (2 [+*4246*]), daytime (2), morning (2), a few days later (1 [+*1328*]), a week later (1 [+*3552, 3893*]), about noon (1 [+*3545*]), always (1 [+*4246, 3836*]), another[S] (1), broad daylight (1), court (1), daily (1 [+*2848, 1667*]), dawn (1 [+*3516, 1181*]), day after day (1 [+*2848*]), day by day (1 [+*2848, 4246*]), daybreak (1 [+*1181*]), daybreak (1 [+*1181, 2002*]), during[S] (1), festival[S] (1), forever (1 [+*1650, 172*]), in the morning (1 [+*1181*]), late in the afternoon (1 [+*3836, 806, 3111*]), long (1 [+*4498*]), nine in the morning (1 [+*6052, 5569, 3836*]), old (1 [+*4581, 1877*]), some time ago (1 [+*4574, 4047, 3836*]), some time ago (1 [+*608, 792*]), some time ago (1 [+*4574, 4047, 3836*]), that was the time (1 [+*1877, 3836, 1697*]), the last days (1 [+*4958*]), them[S] (1 [+*3836*]), this[S] (1 [+*3836, 4047*]), this[S] (1 [+*4047, 3836*]), this day (1 [+*3836, 4958*]), this very day (1 [+*4958*]), three in the afternoon (1 [+*6052, 1888, 3836*]), today (1 [+*1877, 3836, 4958*]), until (1 [+*2401*]), very day (1 [+*4958*]), very old (1 [+*4581, 1877, 3836*]), week (1 [+*2231*]), when (1 [+*1877*]), while (1), years (1), NDT (1)

G2466 **ἡμέτερος** ***hēmeteros***, a. [7] [√*1609*]. our, our own:– our (4), our own (1), ours (1), us (1)

G2467 **ἡμιθανής** ***hēmithanēs***, a. [1] [√*2468* + *2569*]. half dead:– half dead (1)

G2468 **ἥμισυς** ***hēmisys***, a. [5] [→ *2467, 2469, 2470*]. half (temporal and spacial):– half (5)

G2469 **ἡμιώριον** ***hēmiōrion***, n. [1] [√*2468* + *6052*]. half an hour:– half an hour (1)

G2470 **ἡμίωρον** ***hēmiōron***, n. Not used in NIVEBC. [√*2468* + *6052*]. half an hour

G2471 **ἡνίκα** ***hēnika***, pt. [2] when, whenever, at the time when:– when (1 [+*323*]), whenever (1 [+*1569*])

G2472 **ἤπερ** ***ēper***, pt. comp. [1] [√*2445* + *4302*]. than:– than (1)

G2473 **ἤπιος** ***ēpios***, a. Not used in NIVEBC. gentle, kind€ [1]:– kind (1)

G2474 **Ἤρ** ***Ēr***, n. pr. [1] Er, "*watcher, watchful*":– Er (1)

G2475 **ἤρεμος** ***ēremos***, a. Not used in NIVEBC. peaceful, quiet, tranquil€ [1]:– peaceful (1)

G2476 **Ἡρῴδης** ***Hērōdēs***, n. pr. [43] [→ *2477, 2478, 2479*]. Herod:– Herod (37), Herod's (5), he[S] (1 [+*3836*])

G2477 **Ἡρῳδιανοί** ***Hērōdianoi***, n. pr. g. [3] [√*2476*]. Herodians:– Herodians (3)

G2478 **Ἡρῳδιάς** ***Hērōdias***, n. pr. [6] [√*2476*]. Herodias:– Herodias (6)

G2479 **Ἡρῳδίων** ***Hērōdiōn***, n. pr. [1] [√*2476*]. Herodion:– Herodion (1)

G2480 **Ἠσαΐας** ***Ēsaias***, n. pr. [22] Isaiah, "*Yahweh saves*":– Isaiah (21), book of Isaiah (1)

G2481 **Ἠσαῦ** ***Ēsau***, n. pr. [3] Esau, "*hairy*":– Esau (3)

G2482 **ἥσσων** ***hēssōn***, a. [2] [→ *2273, 2487, 2488, 2489*]. for the worse; (adv.) less:– harm (1), less (1)

G2483 **ἡσυχάζω** ***hēsychazō***, v. [5] [→ *2484, 2485*]. to be silent, have no objection; to rest; to lead a quiet life; to give up:– gave up (1), had no further objections (1), lead a quiet life (1), rested (1), silent (1)

G2484 **ἡσυχία** ***hēsychia***, n. [4] [√*2483*]. quietness, silence; settling down, lack of disturbance:– quiet (2), quietness (1), settle down (1 [+*3552*])

G2485 **ἡσύχιος** ***hēsychios***, a. [2] [√*2483*]. quiet:– quiet (2)

G2486 **ἤτοι** ***ētoi***, pt. disj. [1] [√*2445* + *5520*]. (in a series) whether...or:– whether (1)

G2487 **ἡττάομαι** ***hēttaomai***, v. [2] [√*2482*]. to be mastered, overcome:– mastered (1), overcome (1)

G2488 **ἥττημα** ***hēttēma***, n. [2] [√*2482*]. loss, defeat:– defeated (1), loss (1)

G2489 **ἥττων** ***hēttōn***, a. Not used in NIVEBC. [√*2482*]. for the worse; (adv.) less

G2490 **ἠχέω** ***ēcheō***, v. [1] [√*2491*]. to resound, ring out:– resounding (1)

G2491 **ἦχος[1]** ***ēchos[1]***, n. [3] [→ *2010, 2490, 2492, 2493, 2994, 4654*]. sound, tone, blast (of a trumpet); news, report:– blast (1), news (1), sound (1)

G2492 **ἦχος[2]** ***ēchos[2]***, n. [1] [√*2491*]. roar, sound, noise:– roaring (1)

G2493 **ἠχώ** ***ēchō***, n. Not used in NIVEBC. [√*2491*]. sound

G2494 **θ** ***th***, letter. Not used in NIVEBC. letter of the Greek alphabet

G2495 **θά** ***tha***, l.[v.] Not used in NIVEBC. [√*cf. 3448*]. come!

G2496 **θαβιτα** ***thabita***, l.[n.] Not used in NIVEBC. [√*cf. 5412*]. girl

G2497 **Θαδδαῖος** ***Thaddaios***, n. pr. [2] [√*cf. 3304*]. Thaddaeus, "[poss.] *nipple*":– Thaddaeus (2)

G2498 **θάλασσα** ***thalassa***, n. [91] [→ *1458, 4144; cf. 229*]. sea, lake, a general term for any natural body of water:– sea (56), lake (23), waves (4), water (2), seashore (1), seashore (1 [+*5927, 3836*]), the coast (1 [+*2093, 3836*]), waters (1), water's (1), NDT (1)

G2499 **θάλπω** ***thalpō***, v. [2] to care for, cherish, comfort:– care for (1), cares for (1)

G2500 **Θαμάρ** ***Thamar***, n. pr. [1] Tamar, "*date palm*":– Tamar (1)

G2501 **θαμβέω** ***thambeō***, v. [3] [√*2502*]. (pass.) to be amazed, astounded:– amazed (2), astonished (1)

G2502 **θάμβος** ***thambos***, n. [3] [→ *1701, 1702, 2501*]. amazement, astonishment, wonder:– amazed (1), astonished (1 [+*4321*]), wonder (1)

G2503 **θανάσιμος** ***thanasimos***, a. [1] [√*2569*]. deadly:– deadly poison (1)

G2504 **θανατηφόρος** ***thanatēphoros***, a. [1] [√*2569* + *5770*]. deadly:– deadly (1)

G2505 **θάνατος** ***thanatos***, n. [120] [√*2569*]. death:– death (104), died (2), fatal (2), put to death (2 [+*5462*]), brings death (1 [+*1666, 1650, 2505*]), brings death (1 [+*1666, 2505, 1650*]), deadly peril (1), death sentence (1), die (1 [+*3972*]), died (1 [+*1181*]), fatal (1 [+*1650*]), grounds for the death penalty (1 [+*165*]), plague (1), strike dead (1 [+*650, 1877*])

G2506 **θανατόω** ***thanatoō***, v. [11] [√*2569*]. to put to death, kill:– put to death (6), died (1), face death (1), have executed (1), have put to death (1), killed (1)

G2507 **θάπτω** ***thaptō***, v. [11] [→ *5313; cf. 5439*]. to bury, entomb:– buried (7), bury (4)

G2508 **Θάρα** ***Thara***, n. pr. [1] Terah:– Terah (1)

G2509 **θαρρέω** ***tharreō***, v. [6] [√*2511*]. to have confidence, be bold:– confidence (2), confident (2), as bold (1 [+*3836, 4301*]), bold (1)

G2510 **θαρσέω** ***tharseō***, v. [7] [√*2511*]. take heart!, take courage!, cheer up!:– take courage (3), take heart (3), cheer up (1)

G2511 **θάρσος** ***tharsos***, n. [1] [→ *2509, 2510*]. encouragement, courage:– encouraged (1 [+*3284*])

G2512 **θαῦμα** ***thauma***, n. [2] [√*2513*]. wonder, marvel, astonishment:– greatly astonished (1 [+*2513, 3489*]), wonder (1)

G2513 **θαυμάζω** ***thaumazō***, v. [43] [→ *1703, 2512, 2514, 2515; cf. 2517*]. to be amazed (at), in wonder, astonished, surprised:– amazed (18), astonished (5), surprised (5), amazement (3), astonishment (1), filled with wonder (1), flatter (1 [+*4725*]), greatly astonished (1 [+*2512, 3489*]), marveled (1 [+*1639*]), marveled at (1), marveling (1), surprise (1), utterly amazed (1 [+*2014, 2779*]), wonder (1), wondering (1), wondering why (1)

G2514 **θαυμάσιος** ***thaumasios***, a. [1] [√*2513*]. wonderful, remarkable:– wonderful (1)

G2515 **θαυμαστός** ***thaumastos***, a. [6] [√*2513*]. wonderful, marvelous, remarkable:– marvelous (4), remarkable (1), wonderful (1)

G2516 **θεά** ***thea***, n. [1] [√*2536*]. goddess:– goddess (1)

G2517 **θεάομαι** ***theaomai***, v. [22] [√*cf. 2513, 2519, 2555*]. to see, look at; visit:– seen (8), saw (7), see (5), look at (1), looked at (1)

G2518 **θεατρίζω** ***theatrizō***, v. [1] [√*2519*]. to publicly expose:– publicly exposed (1)

G2519 **θέατρον** ***theatron***, n. [3] [→ *2518; cf. 2517*]. theatre, spectacle, theatrical play:– theater (2), spectacle (1)

G2520 **θεῖον** ***theion***, n. [7] [→ *2523; cf. 2536 or* 2604]. sulfur:– sulfur (7)

G2521 **θεῖος** ***theios***, a. [3] [√*2536*]. divine:– divine (2), divine being (1)

G2522 **θειότης** ***theiotēs***, n. [1] [√*2536*]. divine nature, divinity:– divine nature (1)

G2523 **θειώδης** ***theiōdēs***, a. [1] [√*2520*]. (yellow) as sulfur:– yellow as sulfur (1)

G2524 **Θέκλα** ***Thekla***, n. pr. Not used in NIVEBC. Thecla

G2525 **θέλημα** ***thelēma***, n. [62] [√*2527*]. will, decision, desire:– will (52), decision (1), desires (1), please (1), unwilling (1 [+*4024*]), want (1), wanted (1), wants (1), will (1 [+*2527*]), willing (1), NDT (1)

G2526 **θέλησις** ***thelēsis***, n. [1] [√*2527*]. will, decision:– will (1)

G2527 **θέλω** ***thelō***, v. [207] [→ *1615, 2525, 2526*]. to will, decide, want to; wish, desire:– want (72), wants (21), wanted (17), willing (15), desire (7), like (7), wish (7), refused (6 [+*4024*]), will (6), would (4), want to (3), wanting (3), chosen (2), longed (2), mean (2 [+*1639*]), trying (2), unwilling (2 [+*4024*]), wants to (2), wished (2), wishes (2), about to (1), choose (1), chooses (1), choosing (1), chose (1), decided (1), deliberately (1), delights (1), determined (1), have the desire (1), in order to (1), pleased (1), pleases (1), prefer (1), refuse (1 [+*4024*]), refusing (1 [+*4024*]), request (1), thinking of (1), tries (1), will (1 [+*2525*]), willingness (1), wishing (1), would rather (1)

G2528 **θεμέλιον** ***themelion***, n. [1] [√*2529*]. foundation:– foundations (1)

G2529 **θεμέλιος** ***themelios***, n. [15] [→ *2528, 2530; cf. 5502*]. foundation:– foundation (12), foundations (3)

G2530 **θεμελιόω** ***themelioō***, v. [5] [√ *2529*]. to lay a foundation; to make steadfast:– established (2), foundation (1), laid the foundations (1), steadfast (1)

G2531 **θεοδίδακτος** ***theodidaktos***, a. [1] [√ *2536 + 1438*]. taught by God:– taught by God (1)

G2532 **θεολόγος** ***theologos***, n. Not used in NIVEBC. [√ *2536 + 3306*]. one who speaks of God or divine things

G2533 **θεομαχέω** ***theomacheō***, v. Not used in NIVEBC. [√ *2536 + 3480*]. to fight against God

G2534 **θεομάχος** ***theomachos***, a. [1] [√ *2536 + 3480*]. fighting against God:– fighting against God (1)

G2535 **θεόπνευστος** ***theopneustos***, a. [1] [√ *2536 + 4463*]. God-breathed, inspired by God, referring to a communication from deity:– God-breathed (1)

G2536 **θεός** ***theos***, n. [1315] [→ *117, 2516, 2521, 2522, 2531, 2532, 2533, 2534, 2535, 2537, 2538, 2539, 2540, 2541, 2554, 5510, 5806; cf. 2520*]. God, usually refers to the one true God; in a very few contexts it refers to a (pagan) god or goddess. The "Son of God" as a title of Jesus emphasizes his unique relationship to the Father. "The god of this age" refers to the devil:– God (1149), God's (132), gods (8), his[s] (5), him[s] (4), God-fearing (2 [*+5828, 3836*]), godly (2), he[s] (2 [*+3836*]), God-fearing gentiles (1 [*+5828, 3836*]), divine (1), goddess (1), godly (1 [*+2848*]), godly (1 [*+2848*]), he[s] (1 [*+3836*]), in God's name (1 [*+3991, 3836*]), no ordinary (1 [*+842, 3836*]), this[s] (1), NDT (2)

G2537 **θεοσέβεια** ***theosebeia***, n. [1] [√ *2536 + 4936*]. worship of God, reverence for God:– worship God (1)

G2538 **θεοσεβής** ***theosebēs***, a. [1] [√ *2536 + 4936*]. godly, God-fearing, devout:– godly (1)

G2539 **θεοστυγής** ***theostygēs***, a. [1] [√ *2536 + 5144*]. God-hating:– God-haters (1)

G2540 **θεότης** ***theotēs***, n. [1] [√ *2536*]. Deity, Divinity:– deity (1)

G2541 **Θεόφιλος** ***Theophilos***, n. pr. [2] [√ *2536 + 5813*]. Theophilus, "*friend of God*":– Theophilus (2)

G2542 **θεραπεία** ***therapeia***, n. [3] [√ *2544*]. service, care; (hence) healing:– healing (2), servants (1)

G2543 **θεραπεύω** ***therapeuō***, v. [43] [√ *2544*]. to serve, to give help, take care of another; by extension: to heal, cure; (pass.) to be healed:– healed (21), heal (12), cured (4), healing (3), cure (1), healed ill (1), served (1)

G2544 **θεράπων** ***therapōn***, n. [1] [→ *2542, 2543*]. servant, a person who renders service:– servant (1)

G2545 **θερίζω** ***therizō***, v. [21] [√ *2549*]. to reap, harvest:– reap (10), reaps (3), reap a harvest (2), harvest (1), harvested (1), harvesters (1), harvesting (1), reaper (1), reaping (1)

G2546 **θερισμός** ***therismos***, n. [13] [√ *2549*]. harvest:– harvest (10), harvest field (2), that[s] (1)

G2547 **θεριστής** ***theristēs***, n. [2] [√ *2549*]. harvester, reaper:– harvesters (2)

G2548 **θερμαίνω** ***thermainō***, v. [6] [√ *2549*]. (mid.) to keep warm, warm (oneself):– warming (3), warm (2), warmed (1)

G2549 **θέρμη** ***thermē***, n. [1] [→ *2545, 2546, 2547, 2548, 2550*]. heat:– heat (1)

G2550 **θέρος** ***theros***, n. [3] [√ *2549*]. summer:– summer (3)

G2551 **Θεσσαλία** ***Thessalia***, n. pr. Not used in NIVEBC. [→ *2552, 2553*]. Thessaly

G2552 **Θεσσαλονικεύς** ***Thessalonikeus***, n. pr. g. [4] [√ *2551 + 3772*]. Thessalonian, "*from Thessalonica*":– Thessalonians (2), from Thessalonica (2)

G2553 **Θεσσαλονίκη** ***Thessalonikē***, n. pr. [5] [√ *2551 + 3772*]. Thessalonica:– Thessalonica (5)

G2554 **Θευδᾶς** ***Theudas***, n. pr. [1] [√ *2536 + 1565*]. Theudas, "*gift of God*":– Theudas (1)

G2555 **θεωρέω** ***theōreō***, v. [58] [→ *355, 2556, 4145; cf. 2517*]. to see, look at, watch closely; perceive, experience:– see (24), saw (18), sees (4), watching (3), seeing (2), look at (1), looked on (1), looks at (1), looks to (1), seen (1), think (1), watched (1)

G2556 **θεωρία** ***theōria***, n. [1] [√ *2555*]. sight, spectacle:– sight (1)

G2557 **θήκη** ***thēkē***, n. [1] [√ *5502*]. sheath, scabbard:– away[s] (1 [*+1650, 3836*])

G2558 **θηλάζω** ***thēlazō***, v. [5] [→ *352, 2559*]. to nurse a baby; (n.) nursing infant:– nursing mothers (3), infants (1), nursed (1 [*+3466*])

G2559 **θῆλυς** ***thēlys***, a. [5] [√ *2558*]. female, pertaining to women:– female (3), women (2)

G2560 **θήρα** ***thēra***, n. [1] [√ *2563*]. trap, net:– trap (1)

G2561 **θηρεύω** ***thēreuō***, v. [1] [√ *2563*]. to catch in a mistake, a fig. extension of catching hunted prey, not found in the NT:– catch (1)

G2562 **θηριομαχέω** ***thēriomacheō***, v. [1] [√ *2563 + 3480*]. to fight wild animals:– fought wild beasts (1)

G2563 **θηρίον** ***thērion***, n. [46] [→ *2560, 2561, 2562*]. (wild) animal, (fiendish) beast, snake:– beast (35), animal (2), snake (2), wild beasts (2), animals (1), brutes (1), wild animals (1), NDT (2)

G2564 **θησαυρίζω** ***thēsaurizō***, v. [8] [√ *2565*]. to store up, gather, reserve:– store up (2), hoarded wealth (1), reserved (1), save up (1), saving up (1), stores up (1), storing up (1)

G2565 **θησαυρός** ***thēsauros***, n. [18] [→ *630, 631, 2564; cf. 5502*]. treasure, what is stored up; storeroom:– treasure (8), treasures (5), stored up (4), storeroom (1)

G2566 **θιγγάνω** ***thinganō***, v. [3] to touch:– touch (2), touches (1)

G2567 **θλίβω** ***thlibō***, v. [10] [→ *632, 2568, 5315*]. (act.) to press upon, crowd up to; cause trouble; (pass.) to be narrow; to be pressed, troubled, persecuted:– persecuted (2), crowding (1), distressed (1), harassed (1), hard pressed (1), in trouble (1), narrow (1), trouble (1), troubled (1)

G2568 **θλῖψις** ***thlipsis***, n. [45] [√ *2567*]. trouble, distress, oppression, tribulation:– trouble (8), troubles (8), distress (6), persecution (4), suffering (4), afflictions (2), hardships (2), sufferings (2), trials (2), affliction (1), anguish (1), hard pressed (1), persecuted (1), severe trial (1 [*+1509*]), suffer (1), tribulation (1)

G2569 **θνήσκω** ***thnēskō***, v. [9] [→ *114, 115, 633, 2119, 2467, 2503, 2504, 2505, 2506, 2570, 5271*]. (perf.) to have died, be dead:– dead (9)

G2570 **θνητός** ***thnētos***, a. [6] [√ *2569*]. mortal:– mortal (6)

G2571 **θορυβάζω** ***thorybazō***, v. [1] [√ *2573*]. (pass.) to be upset, distracted:– upset (1)

G2572 **θορυβέω** ***thorybeō***, v. [4] [√ *2573*]. to start a riot, throw into disorder; (pass.) to be alarmed, in commotion, distressed:– alarmed (1), commotion (1), noisy (1), started a riot (1)

G2573 **θόρυβος** ***thorybos***, n. [7] [→ *2571, 2572*]. uproar, riot, commotion, disturbance:– uproar (3), commotion (1), disturbance (1), riot (1), riot (1 [*+1639*])

G2574 **θραυματίζω** ***thraumatizō***, v. Not used in NIVEBC. [√ *2575*]. to break

G2575 **θραύω** ***thrauō***, v. [1] [→ *2574*]. (pass.) to be oppressed, downtrodden, a fig. extension of an object broken in pieces:– oppressed (1)

G2576 **θρέμμα** ***thremma***, n. [1] [√ *5555*]. livestock, domestic animal (usually a sheep or goat):– livestock (1)

G2577 **θρηνέω** ***thrēneō***, v. [4] [→ *2578, 2583; cf. 125*]. to sing a funeral dirge, lament, mourn:– sang a dirge (2), mourn (1), wailed (1)

G2578 **θρῆνος** ***thrēnos***, n. Not used in NIVEBC. [√ *2577*]. dirge, funeral song

G2579 **θρησκεία** ***thrēskeia***, n. [4] [√ *2580*]. religion, worship:– religion (3), worship (1)

G2580 **θρῆσκος** ***thrēskos***, a. [1] [→ *1615, 2579*]. religious:– religious (1)

G2581 **θριαμβεύω** ***thriambeuō***, v. [2] to lead in a triumphal procession:– leads as captives triumphal procession (1), triumphing (1)

G2582 **θρίξ** ***thrix***, n. [15] [→ *5570*]. hair, a hair:– hair (11), hairs (2), elaborate hairstyles (1 [*+1862*]), hair (1 [*+3836, 3051*])

G2583 **θροέω** ***throeō***, v. [3] [√ *2577*]. (pass.) to be alarmed, disturbed:– alarmed (3)

G2584 **θρόμβος** ***thrombos***, n. [1] drop:– drops (1)

G2585 **θρόνος** ***thronos***, n. [62] throne:– throne (51), thrones (7), faces (1), it[s] (1 [*+3836*]), them[s] (1 [*+3836*]), NDT (1)

G2586 **θρύπτω** ***thryptō***, v. Not used in NIVEBC. [→ *5316; cf. 5588*]. to break in pieces

G2587 **Θυάτειρα** ***Thyateira***, n. pr. [4] Thyatira:– Thyatira (4)

G2588 **θυγάτηρ** ***thygatēr***, n. [28] [→ *2589*]. daughter, by extension a term of endearment toward (younger) woman:– daughter (23), daughters (4), descendant (1 [*+1666, 3836*])

G2589 **θυγάτριον** ***thygatrion***, n. [2] [√ *2588*]. little daughter:– little daughter (2)

G2590 **θύελλα** ***thyella***, n. [1] [√ *2596*]. storm:– storm (1)

G2591 **θύϊνος** ***thyinos***, a. [1] [√ *2604*]. citron, from the citron tree (a scented wood):– citron (1)

G2592 **θυμίαμα** ***thymiama***, n. [6] [√ *2604*]. incense; burning incense, offering of incense:– incense (5), burning of incense (1)

G2593 **θυμιατήριον** ***thymiatērion***, n. [1] [√ *2604*]. incense altar:– altar of incense (1)

G2594 **θυμιάω** ***thymiaō***, v. [1] [√ *2604*]. to burn incense, offer incense:– burn incense (1)

G2595 **θυμομαχέω** ***thymomacheō***, v. [1] [√ *2596 + 3480*]. to quarrel, be fighting mad:– quarreling (1)

G2596 **θυμός** ***thymos***, n. [18] [→ *126, 1445, 1926, 1927, 2121, 2122, 2123, 2313, 2314, 2315, 2590, 2595, 2597, 3428, 3429, 3430, 3924, 4608, 4609, 4610*]. wrath, fury, anger, rage, a state of intense displeasure based in some real or perceived wrong. "The anger of God" is due to moral offense and has a focus on righteous punishment:– wrath (4), fury (3), anger (2), fits of rage (2), maddening (2), rage (2), furious (1 [*+4398*]), furious (1 [*+4441*]), fury (1 [*+3489*])

G2597 **θυμόω** ***thymoō***, v. [1] [√ *2596*]. (pass.) to become angry:– furious (1 [*+3336*])

G2598 **θύρα** ***thyra***, n. [39] [→ *2599, 2600, 2601*]. door, gate, entrance:– door (21), doors (6), entrance (5), gate (5), doorway (1), gates (1)

G2599 **θυρεός** ***thyreos***, n. [1] [√ *2598*]. (long, oblong) shield:– shield (1)

G2600 **θυρίς** ***thyris***, n. [2] [√ *2598*]. window:– window (2)

G2601 **θυρωρός** ***thyrōros***, n. [4] [√ *2598*]. doorkeeper, watcher (at door or gate):– gatekeeper (1), one at the door (1), servant girl on duty (1), she[s] (1 [*+3836, 4087, 3836*])

G2602 **θυσία** ***thysia***, n. [28] [√ *2604*]. sacrifice, offering:– sacrifices (14), sacrifice (12), offering (1), offerings (1)

G2603 **θυσιαστήριον** ***thysiastērion***, n. [23] [√ *2604*]. altar:– altar (22), altars (1)

G2604 **θύω** ***thyō***, v. [14] [→ *1628, 2124, 2591, 2592, 2593, 2594, 2602, 2603, 2638; cf. 2520*]. to kill, butcher; to offer sacrifice:– kill (5), sacrificed (2), butchered (1), killed (1), offer sacrifices (1), offered (1), sacrifice (1), sacrificing (1), NDT (1)

G2605 **Θωμᾶς** ***Thōmas***, n. pr. [11] Thomas, "*twin*":– Thomas (11)

G2606 **θώραξ** ***thōrax***, n. [5] breastplate:– breastplates (3), breastplate (2)

G2607 **ι** ***i***, letter. Not used in NIVEBC. [→ *2740*]. letter of the Greek alphabet

G2608 **Ἰάϊρος** ***Iairos***, n. pr. [2] Jairus, "*he gives light*":– Jairus (2)

G2609 **Ἰακώβ** ***Iakōb***, n. pr. [27] [→ *2610*]. Jacob, "*follower, replacer, one who follows the heel*":– Jacob (25), Jacob's (2)

G2610 **Ἰάκωβος** ***Iakōbos***, n. pr. [42] [√ *2609*]. James, "*follower, replacer, one who follows the heel*":– James (41), his[s] (1)

G2611 **ἴαμα** ***iama***, n. [3] [√ *2615*]. healing:– healing (3)

G2612 **Ἰαμβρῆς** ***Iambrēs***, n. pr. [1] Jambres:– Jambres (1)

G2613 **Ἰανναί** ***Iannai***, n. pr. [1] Jannai:– Jannai (1)

G2614 **Ἰάννης** ***Iannēs***, n. pr. [1] Jannes:– Jannes (1)

G2615 **ἰάομαι** ***iaomai***, v. [26] [→ *2611, 2617, 2620*]. (mid.) to heal; (pass.) to be healed, freed:– healed (16), heal (5), healing (2), freed (1), heal the sick (1), heals (1)

G2616 **Ἰάρετ** ***Iaret***, n. pr. [1] Jared, "*servant*":– Jared (1)

G2617 **ἴασις** ***iasis***, n. [3] [√ *2615*]. healing, cure:– heal (1), healed (1), healing (1 [*+699*])

G2618 **ἴασπις** ***iaspis***, n. [4] jasper:– jasper (2), jasper (2 [*+3345*])

G2619 **Ἰάσων** ***Iasōn***, n. pr. [5] Jason, "*to heal*":– Jason (4), Jason's (1)

G2620 **ἰατρός** ***iatros***, n. [6] [√ *2615*]. doctor, physician:– doctor (4), doctors (1), physician (1)

G2621 **Ἰαχίν** ***Iachin***, n. pr. Not used in NIVEBC. Jachin

G2622 **ιβ** ***ib***, n. num. Not used in NIVEBC. two letters representing the number twelve

G2623 **ἴδε** ***ide***, pt. [34] [√ *1626*]. see!, look!; here, there:– look (10), see (10), here (3), here is (3), consider (1), find (1), listen (1), look how (1), mark my words (1), surely (1), NDT (2)

G2624 **ἰδέα** ***idea***, n. Not used in NIVEBC. [√ *1626*]. appearance

G2625 **ἴδιος** ***idios***, a. [114] [→ *2626*]. one's own, private:– his own (27), their own (17), his (10), privately (6 [*+2848*]), your own (5), own (4), their (4), aside (3 [*+2848*]), its own (3), themselves (3), all alone (2 [*+2848, 3668*]), her own (2), our own (2), proper (2), all had (1 [*+3836*]), alone (1 [*+2848*]), belongs (1), friends (1), himself (1), his home (1 [*+3836*]), his native language (1 [*+1666, 3836*]), home (1 [*+3836*]), in private (1 [*+2848*]), its (1), own (1 [*+1639*]), own people (1 [*+5241*]), personal (1), their relatives (1), turn (1 [*+5413*]), whose (1), your (1), your own home (1 [*+3836*]), your own private (1 [*+3836*]), yourselves (1), NDT (4)

G2626 **ἰδιώτης** ***idiōtēs***, n. [5] [√*2625*]. ordinary, untrained person, one who does not understand, an inquirer:– inquirer (2), inquirers (1), ordinary (1), untrained (1)

G2627 **ἰδού** ***idou***, pt. [198] [√*1626*]. look!, suddenly, now; here, there; this particle is used to enliven a Hebrew narrative style, by marking the change of a scene, or emphasize some detail or idea, and is not always translated:– look (18), here (11), see (11), there (11), now (8), and (4 [*+2779*]), just then (3 [*+2779*]), now (3 [*+2779*]), suddenly (3), and (2 [*+2779*]), at that moment (2 [*+2779*]), listen (2), no (2), now (2 [*+3814*]), suddenly (2 [*+2779*]), there is (2), I assure you (1), I tell you (1), and (1 [*+2779*]), and (1 [*+2779*]), as you can see (1 [*+2779*]), as you know (1), at this (1 [*+2779*]), came (1 [*+2779*]), came along (1 [*+2779*]), came up (1), consider (1), even (1 [*+2779*]), he met (1), here I am (1), here he is (1 [*+6045*]), here is (1), here it is (1 [*+6045*]), here's (1), indeed (1 [*+2779*]), on one occasion (1 [*+2779*]), right then (1 [*+2779, 1994*]), so (1), suddenly (1 [*+2779*]), surely (1), take as an example (1), that (1), then (1 [*+2779*]), then (1 [*+2779*]), there (1 [*+2779*]), there (1 [*+2779*]), there he is (1 [*+1695*]), with that (1 [*+2779*]), yes (1 [*+1609*]), yet (1 [*+2779*]), yet (1), NDT (77)

G2628 **Ἰδουμαία** ***Idoumaia***, n. pr. [1] Idumea, "*[land of] Edom*":– Idumea (1)

G2629 **ἱδρώς** ***hidrōs***, n. [1] sweat, perspiration:– sweat (1)

G2630 **Ἰεζάβελ** ***Iezabel***, n. pr. [1] Jezebel, "[poss.] *unexalted, without a husband*":– Jezebel (1)

G2631 **Ἱεράπολις** ***Hierapolis***, n. pr. [1] [√*2641 + 4484*]. Hierapolis, "*[pagan] sacred city*":– Hierapolis (1)

G2632 **ἱερατεία** ***hierateia***, n. [2] [√*2641*]. priestly office, priesthood:– priesthood (1), priests (1)

G2633 **ἱεράτευμα** ***hierateuma***, n. [2] [√*2641*]. priesthood:– priesthood (2)

G2634 **ἱερατεύω** ***hierateuō***, v. [1] [√*2641*]. to serve as a priest:– serving as priest (1)

G2635 **Ἰερεμίας** ***Ieremias***, n. pr. [3] Jeremiah, "*Yahweh loosens [the womb]; Yahweh lifts up, establishes*":– Jeremiah (3)

G2636 **ἱερεύς** ***hiereus***, n. [31] [√*2641*]. priest:– priest (16), priests (15)

G2637 **Ἰεριχώ** ***Ierichō***, n. pr. [13] Jericho, "*moon city*":– the city[S] (7), Jericho (6)

G2638 **ἱερόθυτος** ***hierothytos***, a. [1] [√*2641 + 2604*]. sacrificed to pagan gods:– offered in sacrifice (1)

G2639 **ἱερόν** ***hieron***, n. [71] [√*2641*]. temple, sanctuary; of the temple in Jerusalem, it can denote the entire temple complex:– temple (34), temple courts (32), there[S] (2 [*+1877, 3836*]), its[S] (1 [*+3836*]), temple grounds (1), NDT (1)

G2640 **ἱεροπρεπής** ***hieroprepēs***, a. [1] [√*2641 + 4560*]. reverent, pertaining to proper reverence, worthy of reverence:– reverent (1)

G2641 **ἱερός** ***hieros***, a. [2] [→ *796, 797, 2631, 2632, 2633, 2634, 2636, 2638, 2639, 2640, 2644, 2645, 2646, 2648*]. sacred, holy, set apart for God; (pl.) the holy things:– holy (1), temple (1)

G2642 **Ἱεροσόλυμα** ***Hierosolyma***, n. pr. Not used in NIVEBC. [√*2647*]. Jerusalem

G2643 **Ἱεροσολυμίτης** ***Hierosolymitēs***, n. pr. g. [2] [√*2647*]. inhabitant of Jerusalem:– people of Jerusalem (2)

G2644 **ἱεροσυλέω** ***hierosyleō***, v. [1] [√*2641 + 5195*]. to rob temples:– rob temples (1)

G2645 **ἱερόσυλος** ***hierosylos***, a. [1] [√*2641 + 5195*]. temple robber:– robbed temples (1)

G2646 **ἱερουργέω** ***hierourgeō***, v. [1] [√*2641 + 2240*]. to perform priestly duty, serve as a priest:– priestly duty (1)

G2647 **Ἰερουσαλήμ** ***Ierousalēm***, n. pr. [138] [→ *2642, 2643*]. Jerusalem, "*foundation of Shalem [peace]*":– Jerusalem (136), city of Jerusalem (2)

G2648 **ἱερωσύνη** ***hierōsynē***, n. [3] [√*2641*]. priesthood:– priesthood (3)

G2649 **Ἰεσσαί** ***Iessai***, n. pr. [5] Jesse:– Jesse (5)

G2650 **Ἰεφθάε** ***Iephthae***, n. pr. [1] Jephthah, "*Yahweh opens, frees*":– Jephthah (1)

G2651 **Ἰεχονίας** ***Iechonias***, n. pr. [2] Jeconiah, "*Yahweh supports*":– Jeconiah (2)

G2652 **Ἰησοῦς** ***Iēsous***, n. pr. [914] Jesus, Joshua, "*Yahweh saves*":– Jesus (897), he[S] (6), him[S] (4), Joshua (3), he[S] (2 [*+3836*]), his[S] (1), NDT (1)

G2653 **ἱκανός** ***hikanos***, a. [39] [→ *919, 922, 1459, 2391, 2654, 2655, 2656*]. sufficient, considerable, much; appropriate, competent, worthy, deserving:– many (5), large (4), long (4), worthy (3), deserve (2 [*+1639*]), great (2), number (2), some (2), bright (1), competent (1), considerable (1), deserve (1), enough (1), equal (1), large number (1), large sum (1), made post bond (1 [*+3284, 3836, 4123*]), much (1), qualified (1), satisfy (1 [*+4472*]), sufficient (1), wept (1 [*+3088, 1181*]), NDT (1)

G2654 **ἱκανότης** ***hikanotēs***, n. [1] [√*2653*]. competence, fitness, capability:– competence (1)

G2655 **ἱκανόω** ***hikanoō***, v. [2] [√*2653*]. to make competent, qualify one for, authorize:– made competent (1), qualified (1)

G2656 **ἱκετηρία** ***hiketēria***, n. [1] [√*2653*]. petition, supplication:– petitions (1)

G2657 **ἰκμάς** ***ikmas***, n. [1] moisture:– moisture (1)

G2658 **Ἰκόνιον** ***Ikonion***, n. pr. [6] Iconium:– Iconium (6)

G2659 **ἱλαρός** ***hilaros***, a. [1] [√*2661*]. cheerful, without grudging, with an implication of a gracious attitude; note that the transliteration "hilarious" does not communicate the meaning of this attitude:– cheerful (1)

G2660 **ἱλαρότης** ***hilarotēs***, n. [1] [√*2661*]. cheerfully, not grudgingly, with an implication of a gracious attitude:– cheerfully (1 [*+1877*])

G2661 **ἱλάσκομαι** ***hilaskomai***, v. [2] [→ *480, 2659, 2660, 2662, 2663, 2664*]. (mid.) to make atonement for, with a focus on the means for accomplishing forgiveness, resulting in reconciliation; (pass.) to have mercy on, be merciful to:– have mercy (1), make atonement (1)

G2662 **ἱλασμός** ***hilasmos***, n. [2] [√*2661*]. atoning sacrifice, the means of forgiveness; traditionally propitiation:– atoning sacrifice (2)

G2663 **ἱλαστήριον** ***hilastērion***, n. [2] [√*2661*]. atoning sacrifice; atonement cover, the place where sins are forgiven; traditionally propitiation or mercy seat:– atonement cover (1), sacrifice of atonement (1)

G2664 **ἵλεως** ***hileōs***, a. [2] [√*2661*]. forgiving, gracious; (may God be) gracious!, God forbid!:– forgive (1 [*+1639*]), never (1)

G2665 **Ἰλλυρικόν** ***Illyrikon***, n. pr. [1] Illyricum:– Illyricum (1)

G2666 **ἱμάς** ***himas***, n. [4] (leather) thong, strap:– straps (3), flog (1)

G2667 **ἱματίζω** ***himatizō***, v. [2] [→ *2264, 2265, 2668, 2669; cf. 313*]. (pass.) to be dressed, clothed:– dressed (2)

G2668 **ἱμάτιον** ***himation***, n. [60] [√*2667*]. clothing, cloak, robe:– clothes (21), cloak (11), cloaks (7), garment (6), robe (4), coat (2), dressed in (2 [*+4314, 1877*]), clothed (1), clothing (1), coats (1), fine clothes (1 [*+1906*]), one[S] (1), outer clothing (1), stripped (1 [*+4351, 3836*])

G2669 **ἱματισμός** ***himatismos***, n. [5] [√*2667*]. clothing:– clothes (3), clothing (1), garment (1)

G2670 **ἱμείρομαι** ***himeiromai***, v. Not used in NIVEBC. to desire, long for

G2671 **ἵνα** ***hina***, c. [664] [→ *2672*]. a marker that shows purpose or result: in order that, in order to, so that, then; it can focus on the introduction of a discourse or on the content itself:– so that (209), to (189), that (106), in order that (15), for (13), in order to (12), so (12), then (7), and (5), want (5), or (4 [*+3590*]), so as to (4), reason (3), want to (3), have (2), let (2), meant to (2), must (2), or (2 [*+3590*]), rather than (2 [*+3590*]), see that (2), therefore (2), when (2), aim is (1), allow (1), as (1), as to (1), at the thought of (1), because (1), before (1 [*+3590*]), bent on (1), but rather (1), by (1), expecting to (1), for fear (1 [*+3590*]), for fear that (1 [*+3590*]), from (1 [*+3590*]), goal that (1), hoped (1), if (1), in the hope that (1), instead (1), intent that (1), lest (1 [*+3590*]), otherwise (1 [*+3590*]), please (1), purpose (1), such that (1), to let (1), to make (1), to show that (1), would (1), NDT (30)

G2672 **ἱνατί** ***hinati***, pt. inter. [6] [√*2671 + 5515*]. why?:– why (6)

G2673 **Ἰόππη** ***Ioppē***, n. pr. [10] Joppa, "*beautiful*":– Joppa (10)

G2674 **Ἰορδάνης** ***Iordanēs***, n. pr. [15] Jordan, "*descending*":– Jordan (15)

G2675 **ἰός** ***ios***, n. [3] [→ *2995*]. poison, venom; corrosion, rust:– poison (2), corrosion (1)

G2676 **Ἰουδά** ***Iouda***, n. pr. Not used in NIVEBC. [√*2683*]. Judah, "*praised*"

G2677 **Ἰουδαία** ***Ioudaia***, n. pr. [43] [√*2683*]. Judea, Judean, "*land of the Judahites*":– Judea (41), Judea (1 [*+6001*]), province of Judea (1)

G2678 **ἰουδαΐζω** ***ioudaizō***, v. [1] [√*2683*]. to follow Jewish customs, live as a Jew:– follow Jewish customs (1)

G2679 **Ἰουδαϊκός** ***Ioudaikos***, a. pr. [1] [√*2683*]. Jewish, "*Jewish*":– Jewish (1)

G2680 **Ἰουδαϊκῶς** ***Ioudaikōs***, adv. pr. [1] [√*2683*]. like a Jew, in a Jewish manner, "*Jewish*":– like a Jew (1)

G2681 **Ἰουδαῖος** ***Ioudaios***, a. pr. g. [195] [√*2683*]. Jewish (people), "*Jewish*":– Jews (114), Jewish (24), Jew (18), Jewish leaders (16), they[S] (5 [*+3836*]), Jewish opponents (3), Judean (3), Jew (2 [*+467*]), Jews (2 [*+467*]), they[S] (2 [*+3836*]), Jew (1 [*+476*]), Jewish people (1), leaders[S] (1), people of Judea (1), them[S] (1 [*+3836*]), who[S] (1 [*+3836*])

G2682 **Ἰουδαϊσμός** ***Ioudaismos***, n. pr. [2] [√*2683*]. Judaism, "*Judaism*":– Judaism (2)

G2683 **Ἰούδας** ***Ioudas***, n. pr. [44] [→ *2676, 2677, 2678, 2679, 2680, 2681, 2682*]. Judah, Judas, Jude, "*praised*":– Judas (32), Judah (10), Jude (1), Judea (1)

G2684 **Ἰουλία** ***Ioulia***, n. pr. [1] [√*2685*]. Julia, "*of Julian [the family of Julius Caesar]*":– Julia (1)

G2685 **Ἰούλιος** ***Ioulios***, n. pr. [2] [→ *549, 2684*]. Julius, "*of Julian [the family of Julius Caesar]*":– Julius (2)

G2686 **Ἰουνία** ***Iounia***, n. pr. [1] [→ *2687*]. Junia:– Junia (1)

G2687 **Ἰουνιᾶς** ***Iounias***, n. pr. Not used in NIVEBC. [√*2686*]. Junias

G2688 **Ἰοῦστος** ***Ioustos***, n. pr. [3] Justus, "*just*":– Justus (3)

G2689 **ἱππεύς** ***hippeus***, n. [2] [√*2691*]. horseman, cavalryman:– cavalry (1), horsemen (1)

G2690 **ἱππικός** ***hippikos***, a. [1] [√*2691*]. mounted (troops), pertaining to a horseman:– mounted (1)

G2691 **ἵππος** ***hippos***, n. [17] [→ *68, 800, 2689, 2690, 5803, 5804, 5805*]. horse:– horses (10), horse (7)

G2692 **ἶρις** ***iris***, n. [2] rainbow; some translate as a brilliant halo or circle of light:– rainbow (2)

G2693 **Ἰσαάκ** ***Isaak***, n. pr. [20] Isaac, "*he [God] laughs*":– Isaac (20)

G2694 **ἰσάγγελος** ***isangelos***, a. [1] [√*2698 + 34*]. like an angel:– like angels (1)

G2695 **Ἰσαχάρ** ***Isachar***, n. pr. Not used in NIVEBC. [√*cf. 2704*]. Issachar, "*there is a reward [Ge. 30:18]; may [God] show mercy; hired hand*"

G2696 **Ἰσκαριώθ** ***Iskariōth***, n. pr.[g.?] [→ *2697, 5000, 5001*]. Iscariot, "*man of Kerioth* or *of the assassins*"

G2697 **Ἰσκαριώτης** ***Iskariōtēs***, n. pr.[g.?] [11] [√*2696*]. Iscariot, "*man of Kerioth* or *of the assassins*":– Iscariot (11)

G2698 **ἴσος** ***isos***, a. [8] [→ *2694, 2699, 2700, 2701, 2711*]. equal, same; agreeable:– agree (2), equal (2), as (1), equality (1 [*+3836, 1639*]), in full (1 [*+3836*]), same (1)

G2699 **ἰσότης** ***isotēs***, n. [3] [√*2698*]. equality, fairness:– equality (2), fair (1)

G2700 **ἰσότιμος** ***isotimos***, a. [1] [√*2698 + 5507*]. as precious as, of equal value:– as precious as (1)

G2701 **ἰσόψυχος** ***isopsychos***, a. [1] [√*2698 + 6038*]. like, of like soul, heart or mind:– like (1)

G2702 **Ἰσραήλ** ***Israēl***, n. pr. [68] [→ *2703*]. Israel, "*he struggles with God [El]*":– Israel (52), Israelites (7 [*+5626*]), Israel (3 [*+3875*]), Israel (3 [*+5626*]), people of Israel (2), Israel's (1)

G2703 **Ἰσραηλίτης** ***Israēlitēs***, n. pr. g. [9] [√*2702*]. Israelite, (one) of Israel:– Israelites (5), Israelite (2), of Israel (1), people of Israel (1)

G2704 **Ἰσσαχάρ** ***Issachar***, n. pr. [1] [√*cf. 2695*]. Issachar, "*there is a reward [Ge. 30:18]; may [God] show mercy; hired hand*":– Issachar (1)

G2705 **ἵστημι** ***histēmi***, v. [153] [→ *189, 190, 414, 415, 468, 482, 510, 634, 635, 640, 686, 687, 688, 841, 923, 1404, 1460, 1496, 1749, 1931, 1983, 1985, 2012, 2013, 2014, 2060, 2179, 2180, 2181, 2183, 2184, 2194, 2342, 2392, 2706, 2769, 2770, 2949, 2987, 3495, 3496, 4188, 4224, 4225, 4325, 4613, 4706, 4756, 5084, 5085, 5086, 5087, 5088, 5112, 5308, 5318, 5319, 5363, 5364, 5712; cf. 5089, 5119*]. (intr.) to stand, to stand (firm), be present; to stop; (tr.) to make stand, place, put, establish:– standing (38), stood (29), stand (27), stopped (5), stood up (4), stand firm (3), appear (2), establish (2), established (2), had stand (2), placed (2), standing there (2), stands (2), stood still (2), was (2), counted out (1), got up (1), had brought (1), hold (1), holding (1), is (1), made stand (1), make stand (1), nominated (1), present (1), presented (1), produced (1), put (1), set (1), settled the matter (1 [*+1612*]), stand fast (1), standing around (1), standing firm (1), stands firm (1), stayed (1), stop (1), take stand (1), taken stand (1), there (1), to feet (1), uphold (1), wait (1), waits (1), withstand (1)

G2706 **ἱστίον** ***histion***, n. Not used in NIVEBC. [√*2705*]. sail

G2707 **ἱστορέω** ***historeō***, v. [1] [→ *1461*]. to get acquainted with, visit:– get acquainted with (1)

G2708 **ἰσχυρός** ***ischyros***, a. [28] [√*2709*]. powerful, strong, forceful:– mighty (8), strong (7), more powerful (3), stronger

GREEK INDEX

(3), fervent (1), forceful (1), greatly (1), him^s (1 [+3836]), loud (1), powerful (1), severe (1)

G2709 ἰσχύς ischys, n. [10] [→ *1462, 1932, 2015, 2196, 2708, 2710, 2996*]. strength, power:– strength (7), might (1), power (1), stronger (1)

G2710 ἰσχύω ischyō, v. [28] [√*2709*]. to be strong, powerful, able:– could (6), able (5), strong (3), healthy (2), can do (1), couldn't (1 [+*4024*]), couldn't you (1 [+*4024*]), gave a beating (1), good (1), grew (1), had (1), has value (1), powerful (1 [+*4498*]), takes effect (1), unable (1 [+*4024*]), unable (1 [+*4033*])

G2711 ἴσως isōs, adv. [1] [√*2698*]. perhaps:– perhaps (1)

G2712 Ἰταλία Italia, n. pr. [4] [→ *2713*]. Italy:– Italy (4)

G2713 Ἰταλικός Italikos, a. pr. g. [1] [√*2712*]. Italian:– Italian (1)

G2714 Ἰτουραῖος Itouraios, a. pr. [1] Iturea, "*pertaining to Jetur*":– Iturea (1)

G2715 ἰχθύδιον ichthydion, n. [2] [√*2716*]. little fish:– small fish (2)

G2716 ἰχθύς ichthys, n. [19] [→ *2715*]. fish:– fish (19)

G2717 ἴχνος ichnos, n. [3] [→ *453*]. step, footstep; course of action:– footsteps (2), steps (1)

G2718 Ἰωαθάμ Iōatham, n. pr. [2] Jotham, "*Yahweh will complete*":– Jotham (2)

G2719 Ἰωακίμ Iōakim, n. pr. Not used in NIVEBC. Jehoiakim, "*Yahweh lifts up, establishes*"

G2720 Ἰωανάν Iōanan, n. pr. [1] [√*cf. 2722*]. Joanan, "[prob.] *Yahweh is gracious*":– Joanan (1)

G2721 Ἰωάννα Iōanna, n. pr. [2] [√*cf. 2722*]. Joanna, "[prob.] *Yahweh is gracious*":– Joanna (2)

G2722 Ἰωάννης Iōannēs, n. pr. [135] [√*cf. 2720, 2721, 2728*]. John, "*Yahweh is gracious*":– John (119), John's (15), NDT (1)

G2723 Ἰωάς Iōas, n. pr. Not used in NIVEBC. Joash, "*Yahweh bestows, man of Yahweh*"

G2724 Ἰώβ Iōb, n. pr. [1] Job, "*where is my father* poss. *where is my father, O God?*":– Job's (1)

G2725 Ἰωβήδ Iōbēd, n. pr. [3] [→ *6044*]. Obed, "*servant* or *worshiper*":– Obed (3)

G2726 Ἰωδά Iōda, n. pr. [1] Joda:– Joda (1)

G2727 Ἰωήλ Iōēl, n. pr. [1] Joel, "*Yahweh is God*":– Joel (1)

G2728 Ἰωνάθας Iōnathas, n. pr. Not used in NIVEBC. [√*cf. 2722*]. Jonathas, "*Yahweh has given*"

G2729 Ἰωνάμ Iōnam, n. pr. [1] Jonam, "*Yahweh is gracious*":– Jonam (1)

G2730 Ἰωνάν Iōnan, n. pr. Not used in NIVEBC. Jonan

G2731 Ἰωνᾶς Iōnas, n. pr. [9] Jonah, "*dove*":– Jonah (9)

G2732 Ἰωράμ Iōram, n. pr. [2] Jehoram, "*Yahweh exalts*":– Jehoram (2)

G2733 Ἰωρίμ Iōrim, n. pr. [1] Jorim:– Jorim (1)

G2734 Ἰωσαφάτ Iōsaphat, n. pr. [2] Jehoshaphat, "*Yahweh has judged*":– Jehoshaphat (2)

G2735 Ἰωσή Iōsē, n. pr. Not used in NIVEBC. [√*cf. 2736*]. Jose, "*he will add*"

G2736 Ἰωσῆς Iōsēs, n. pr. [4] [√*cf. 2735*]. Joses, Joseph, "*he will add*":– Joseph (4)

G2737 Ἰωσήφ Iōsēph, n. pr. [34] Joseph, "*he will add*":– Joseph (31), Joseph's (3)

G2738 Ἰωσήχ Iōsēch, n. pr. [1] Josech:– Josek (1)

G2739 Ἰωσίας Iōsias, n. pr. [2] Josiah, "*let* or *may Yahweh give*":– Josiah (2)

G2740 ἰῶτα iōta, n. [1] [√*cf. 2607*]. smallest letter (of the Greek alphabet), which corresponds to the smallest letter of the Hebrew alphabet, *yodh*:– smallest letter (1)

G2741 κ k, letter. Not used in NIVEBC. letter of the Greek alphabet

G2742 κάβος kabos, n. Not used in NIVEBC. cab, a dry measure just less than two quarts

G2743 κἀγώ kagō, contr. [c.+p.] [84] [√*2779 + 1609*]. and I, I also, but I:– I (25), and I (24), I also (9), I too (4), so I (5), me also (3), and I too (2), me (2), and myself (1), and so me (1), and I myself (1), and me (1), but me (1), even I (1), if I (1), myself (1), so that I (1), yes me (1)

G2744 κάδος kados, n. Not used in NIVEBC. jar, container

G2745 καθά katha, c. *or* adv. [1] [√*2848 + 4005*]. (just) as:– as (1)

G2746 καθαίρεσις kathairesis, n. [3] [√*2848 + 145*]. tearing down, demolishment, destruction:– tearing down (2), demolish (1)

G2747 καθαιρέω kathaireō, v. [9] [√*2848 + 145*]. to take down, demolish, overthrow; (pass.) to be robbed of, suffer the loss of:– took down (3), brought down (1), demolish (1), overthrew (1), robbed (1), take down (1), tear down (1)

G2748 καθαίρω kathairō, v. [1] [√*2754*]. to prune, clear unproductive wood, cleanse:– prunes (1)

G2749 καθάπερ kathaper, c. *or* adv. [13] [√*2848 + 4005 + 4302*]. as, just as, like:– just as (6), like (2), as (1), for (1), the same thing (1), which (1), NDT (1)

G2750 καθάπτω kathaptō, v. [1] [√*2848 + 721*]. to fasten, attach, take hold of, seize:– fastened on (1)

G2751 καθαρίζω katharizō, v. [31] [√*2754*]. to make clean, cleanse, purify:– cleansed (9), clean (7), make clean (3), purify (3), cleanse (2), purified (2), cleansing (1), declared clean (1), made clean (1), purifies (1), wash (1)

G2752 καθαρισμός katharismos, n. [7] [√*2754*]. cleansing, purification, washing:– ceremonial washing (2), cleansing (2), cleansed (1), purification (1), purification rites (1)

G2753 κάθαρμα katharma, n. Not used in NIVEBC. [√*2754*]. scapegoat

G2754 καθαρός katharos, a. [26] [→ *174, 175, 176, 1350, 1351, 1705, 2748, 2751, 2752, 2753, 2755, 2760, 4326*]. clean, pure, clear of responsibility, innocent:– clean (11), pure (11), clear (2), innocent (2)

G2755 καθαρότης katharotēs, n. [1] [√*2754*]. cleanness, purity:– clean (1)

G2756 καθέδρα kathedra, n. [3] [√*2757*]. seat, bench:– benches (2), seat (1)

G2757 καθέζομαι kathezomai, v. [7] [→ *2756, 2764, 4149, 4751, 5153; cf. 2848 + 1612*]. to sit down, be seated:– seated (2), sitting (2), sat (1), sat down (1), stayed (1)

G2758 καθεῖς katheis, contr. [pp.+n.] Not used in NIVEBC. [√*2848 + 1651*]. individually

G2759 καθεξῆς kathexēs, adv. [5] [√*2848 + 2400*]. in order, in a sequence:– after this (1 [+*1877, 3836*]), beginning with (1 [+*608, 2779, 3836*]), from place to place (1), orderly (1), the whole story (1)

G2760 καθερίζω katherizō, v. Not used in NIVEBC. [√*2754*]. to make clean, cleanse, purify

G2761 καθεύδω katheudō, v. [22] [√*2848*]. to sleep, fall asleep:– sleeping (11), asleep (6), sleep (2), fell asleep (1), sleeper (1), sleeps (1)

G2762 καθηγητής kathēgētēs, n. [2] [√*2848 + 72*]. teacher; derivative of a verb "to guide, to explain," not found in the NT:– instructor (1), instructors (1)

G2763 καθήκω kathēkō, v. [2] [√*2848 + 2457*]. to be fitting; (pcpl.) things that ought to be, that are proper:– fit (1), ought to be done (1)

G2764 κάθημαι kathēmai, v. [91] [√*2757*]. to sit, seat, ride; to live, stay, reside:– sitting (28), seated (12), sit (11), sits (10), sat (8), rider (4 [+*2093*]), sat down (4), living (3), live (2), rider (2), riders (2 [+*2093*]), sitting down (2), rider (1 [+*2062*]), seat (1), sit enthroned (1)

G2765 καθημέραν kathēmeran, contr. [pp.+n.] Not used in NIVEBC. [√*2848 + 2465*]. every day, daily, day after day

G2766 καθημερινός kathēmerinos, a. [1] [√*2848 + 2465*]. daily:– daily (1)

G2767 καθίζω kathizō, v. [46] [→ *361, 2125, 4150, 4327, 5154*]. (tr.) to place, seat (someone), appoint; (intr.) to sit down, come to rest upon; stay, live. "To sit on the right side" means to be in a position of high status, "to sit on the left" is a lesser position. "To sit on the seat of Moses" means to have the capacity to interpret the Law of Moses with authority:– sat down (15), sit (10), sat (4), sit down (3), convened the court (2 [+*2093, 3836, 1037*]), ridden (2), seated (2), ask for a ruling (1), came to rest (1), place (1), sets up (1), sits (1), sitting down (1), stay (1), stayed (1)

G2768 καθίημι kathiēmi, v. [4] [√*2848 + 1640*]. to let down, lower:– let down (2), lowered (1), lowered (1 [+*5899*])

G2769 καθιστάνω kathistanō, v. Not used in NIVEBC. [√*2848 + 2705*]. see *2770*

G2770 καθίστημι kathistēmi, v. [21] [√*2848 + 2705*]. to put in charge, appoint; to escort, bring, take; (pass.) to be made, become, be appointed:– made (5), put in charge (5), appointed (3), appoint (1), appoints (1), becomes (1), escorted (1), keep (1), puts in charge (1), turn over to (1), NDT (1)

G2771 καθό katho, adv. [4] [√*2848 + 4005*]. insofar as, to the degree that:– according to what (1 [+*1569*]), according to what (1), inasmuch as (1), NDT (1)

G2772 καθολικός katholikos, a. Not used in NIVEBC. [√*2848 + 3910*]. general, universal

G2773 καθόλου katholou, adv. [1] [√*2848 + 3910*]. at all, entirely, completely:– at all (1)

G2774 καθοπλίζω kathoplizō, v. [1] [√*2848 + 3960*]. (mid.) to fully arm or equip (oneself):– fully armed (1)

G2775 καθοράω kathoraō, v. [1] [√*2848 + 3972*]. (pass.) to be clearly seen, perceived:– clearly seen (1)

G2776 καθότι kathoti, c. [6] [√*2848 + 4005 + 5515*]. as, to the degree that; because:– because (3), for (1), NDT (2)

G2777 καθώς kathōs, adv. [182] [√*2848 + 6055*]. as, just as, even as; in accordance with:– as (81), just as (53), even as (3), like (3), for (2), how (2), in accordance with (2), just what (2), and so (1), any more than (1 [+*4024*]), as much as (1), as really (1), as well as (1), because (1), but (1 [+*4024*]), equal with (1), exactly (1), exceeded (1 [+*4024*]), in the same way (1), in the words of (1 [+*3306*]), just as much as (1), only as (1), since (1), so also (1), that (1), that way (1), the same (1 [+*3931*]), this agrees with (1), this is why (1), thus (1), usually (1), what (1), whatever (1), which agrees with (1), NDT (8)

G2778 καθώσπερ kathōsper, adv. [1] [√*2848 + 6055 + 4302*]. just as:– just as (1)

G2779 καί kai, c. [8962] [→ *2743, 2781, 2788, 2792, 2793, 2795, 2796, 2797, 2817, 2829, 4298, 5476*]. (as a connective) and; (connecting and continuing) and then, then; (as a disjuntive) but, yet, however; (as an adv.) also, even, likewise:– and (4802), also (232), then (229), but (166), even (93), so (90), or (57), yet (33), with (30), too (29), and then (25), and also (18), both and (17), both (14), now (12), and yet (11), and so (10), as well (10), in fact (9), still (8), and (7 [+*2627*]), as well as (7), when (7), so that (6), indeed (5), nor (5), that (5), though (5), while (5), and even (4), as (4), because (4), including (4), along with (3), just then (3 [+*2627*]), now (3 [+*2627*]), until (3), whether (3), afterward (2), again (2), and then also (2), and too (2), as for (2), at that moment (2 [+*2627*]), but even (2), in turn (2), later (2), meanwhile (2), nor (2 [+*4024*]), or (2 [+*3590*]), rather than (2 [+*4024*]), since (2), suddenly (2 [+*2627*]), than (2 [+*3590*]), the (2), the same as (2 [+*6055*]), therefore (2), what is more (2 [+*4024, 3667, 1254, 247*]), whether or (2), 42 (1 [+*5477, 1545*]), 430 (1 [+*5484, 5558*]), 450 (1 [+*5484, 4299*]), and (1 [+*2627*]), and (1 [+*247, 1145*]), and (1 [+*5538*]), and as well (1), and indeed (1), and now (1), another (1), as a result (1), as also (1), as it is (1 [+*3814, 1254*]), as you can see (1 [+*2627*]), at all (1), at this (1 [+*2627*]), at this (1), because (1 [+*1623, 1145*]), before (1 [+*4048*]), beginning with (1 [+*608, 3836, 2759*]), both (1 [+*4047*]), both of you (1 [+*5148, 899*]), but also (1), by (1), came (1 [+*2627*]), came along (1 [+*2627*]), eighteen (1 [+*1274, 3893*]), either or (1), especially (1), even (1 [+*1145*]), even (1 [+*2627*]), even so (1 [+*1142*]), even though (1), finally (1), for (1), forty-six (1 [+*5477, 1971*]), forty-two (1 [+*5477, 1545*]), furthermore (1), human being (1 [+*4922, 135*]), if (1), if so (1), in addition (1 [+*247*]), indeed (1 [+*247*]), indeed (1 [+*2627*]), instead of (1 [+*4049*]), it is true (1), likewise (1), living (1 [+*1656, 2002*]), more than once (1 [+*562, 1489*]), more than that (1), moreover (1 [+*1254*]), moved about freely (1 [+*1660, 1744*]), neither (1 [+*4024*]), nor (1 [+*3590*]), nor (1 [+*4024*]), now (1 [+*1181*]), number greatly increased (1 [+*889, 4437*]), on both sides (1 [+*2277, 3957*]), on each side of (1 [+*1949, 1696*]), on one occasion (1 [+*2627*]), on one occasion (1), once (1 [+*1181*]), once (1), one day (1 [+*1181*]), one on each side (1 [+*1949, 1949*]), only (1), openly confessed (1 [+*2018, 334*]), pain (1 [+*6048, 989*]), right then (1 [+*2627, 1994*]), similarly (1), so too (1), sold as slaves (1 [+*5393, 6034*]), soon (1), suddenly (1 [+*2627*]), surplus (1 [+*4246, 19*]), than that (1 [+*3590*]), the same (1 [+*4048*]), the same as (1 [+*1651, 3836, 899*]), the same way (1 [+*6055*]), the two of you (1 [+*5148, 899*]), then (1 [+*2627*]), then (1 [+*1254*]), then (1 [+*2627*]), there (1 [+*2627*]), there (1 [+*2627*]), though (1 [+*1145*]), three and a half years (1 [+*2291, 5552, 3604, 1971*]), thus (1), to be sure (1), together with (1), too (1 [+*3836, 899*]), truly (1), utterly amazed (1 [+*2014, 2513*]), what do want with (1 [+*5515, 5516*]), what do you want with us (1 [+*5515, 5516, 1609, 5148*]), what if (1), why do involve (1 [+*5515, 5516*]), with that (1 [+*2627*]), with that (1), yes (1), yes (1 [+*247*]), yet (1 [+*2627*]), yet even (1), your (1), NDT (2838)

G2780 Καϊάφας Kaiaphas, n. pr. [9] Caiaphas:– Caiaphas (9)

G2781 καίγε kaige, pt. Not used in NIVEBC. [√*2779 + 1145*]. even, even though

G2782 Κάϊν Kain, n. pr. [3] Cain, "*metal worker; brought forth, acquired [Ge. 4:1]*":– Cain (3)

G2783 Καϊνάμ Kainam, n. pr. [2] [→ *2784*]. Cainan, Kenan, "*worker in iron, metal worker*":– Cainan (1), Kenan (1)

G2784 Καϊνάν Kainan, n. pr. Not used in NIVEBC. [√*2783*]. Cainan, "*worker in iron, metal worker*"

G2785 καινός kainos, a. [42] [→ *362, 363, 364, 1589, 1590, 2786, 2787*]. new, latest, anew; in some contexts new is superior to old (Mt 9:17; Heb 8):– new (41), latest (1)

G2786 καινότης kainotēs, n. [2] [√*2785*]. newness:– new (1), new way (1)

G2787 **καινοφωνία** ***kainophōnia***, n. Not used in NIVEBC. [√*2785 + 5889*]. chatter, empty talk

G2788 **καίπερ** ***kaiper***, c. [5] [√*2779 + 4302*]. though, even though, although:– even though (3), though (2)

G2789 **καιρός** ***kairos***, n. [85] [→*177, 178, 2320, 2321, 2322, 2323, 4672*]. time (particular and general); right time, opportune time, proper time, appointed time:– time (49), times (7), appointed time (4), opportunity (4), age (2), dates (2), harvest time (2), proper time (2), seasons (2), a while (1), always (1 [*+1877, 4246*]), appointed season (1), childbearing age (1 [*+2461*]), convenient (1), occasions (1), opportune time (1), present (1 [*+3836, 3814*]), present time (1), season (1), times in history (1)

G2790 **Καῖσαρ** ***Kaisar***, n. pr. [29] [→*2791*]. Caesar:– Caesar (20), Caesar's (9)

G2791 **Καισάρεια** ***Kaisareia***, n. pr. [17] [√*2790*]. Caesarea:– Caesarea (17)

G2792 **καίτοι** ***kaitoi***, pt. [2] [√*2779 + 5520*]. and yet:– and yet (1), yet (1)

G2793 **καίτοιγε** ***kaitoige***, pt. [1] [√*2779 + 5520 + 1145*]. although, and yet:– although in fact (1)

G2794 **καίω** ***kaiō***, v. [11] [→*1706, 2825, 2876, 3008, 3009, 3010, 3011, 3012, 3013, 3014, 3015, 3906*]. to light (a wick), keep burning:– burning (4), blazing (2), burned (2), all ablaze (1 [*+4786*]), fiery (1), light (1)

G2795 **κἀκεῖ** ***kakei***, contr. [c.+adv.] [10] [√*2779 + 1695*]. and there, and where:– there (3), where (3), and there (2), and at house (1), there too (1)

G2796 **κἀκεῖθεν** ***kakeithen***, contr. [c.+adv.] [10] [√*2779 + 1695*]. and from there:– from there (3), and from there (1), from Attalia[s] (1), that place (1), then (1), there (1), NDT (2)

G2797 **κἀκεῖνος** ***kakeinos***, contr. [c.+p. demo.] [22] [√*2779 + 1695*]. and that one:– they (5), the former[s] (2), Priscilla and Aquila (1), and he (1), and that (1), and the one (1), and these (1), he (1), he also (1), he too (1), that (1), them also (1), these (1), this (1), those (1), NDT (2)

G2798 **κακία** ***kakia***, n. [11] [√*2805*]. evil, wickedness, depravity, malice; in some contexts an "evil" situation means a difficult and hard circumstance rather than a morally corrupt circumstance (Mt 6:34):– malice (5), evil (3), depravity (1), trouble (1), wickedness (1)

G2799 **κακοήθεια** ***kakoētheia***, n. [1] [√*2805 + 1621*]. malice:– malice (1)

G2800 **κακολογέω** ***kakologeō***, v. [4] [√*2805 + 3306*]. to curse, malign, speak evil of:– curses (2), maligned (1), say bad about (1)

G2801 **κακοπάθεια** ***kakopatheia***, n. [1] [√*2805 + 4248*]. suffering:– suffering (1)

G2802 **κακοπαθέω** ***kakopatheō***, v. [3] [√*2805 + 4248*]. to suffer trouble, endure hardship:– endure hardship (1), in trouble (1), suffering (1)

G2803 **κακοποιέω** ***kakopoieō***, v. [4] [√*2805 + 4472*]. to do evil, do what is wrong:– do evil (2), does evil (1), doing evil (1)

G2804 **κακοποιός** ***kakopoios***, a. [3] [√*2805 + 4472*]. wrongdoing:– criminal (1), doing wrong (1), those who do wrong (1)

G2805 **κακός** ***kakos***, a. [50] [→*179, 452, 1591, 1707, 2798, 2799, 2800, 2801, 2802, 2803, 2804, 2806, 2807, 2808, 2809, 2810, 5155, 5156*]. evil, wicked, wrong, bad, a perversion of what pertains to goodness; as a noun, an evil thing can refer to any crime, harm, or moral wrong:– evil (24), wrong (8), crime (3), harm (3), bad (2), wicked (2), criminal (1 [*+4472*]), evildoers (1 [*+2239*]), harm (1 [*+4556*]), ill effects (1), ugly (1), wretches (1), wrongdoer (1 [*+4556*]), wrongs (1)

G2806 **κακοῦργος** ***kakourgos***, a. [4] [√*2805 + 2240*]. criminal, evildoer:– criminals (3), criminal (1)

G2807 **κακουχέω** ***kakoucheō***, v. [2] [√*2805 + 2400*]. (pass.) to be mistreated, maltreated, tormented:– mistreated (2)

G2808 **κακόω** ***kakoō***, v. [6] [√*2805*]. to harm, mistreat, oppress, persecute; poison, embitter:– harm (2), mistreated (1), oppressed (1), persecute (1), poisoned (1)

G2809 **κακῶς** ***kakōs***, adv. [16] [√*2805*]. badly, wrongly, terribly; (with *2400*) to be ill:– sick (8 [*+2400*]), diseases (1 [*+3798*]), evil (1), greatly (1), ill (1 [*+2400*]), suffering terribly (1), with wrong motives (1), wretched (1), wrong (1)

G2810 **κάκωσις** ***kakōsis***, n. [1] [√*2805*]. oppression, mistreatment:– oppression (1)

G2811 **καλάμη** ***kalamē***, n. [1] [√*2812*]. straw; note some translate "stubble":– straw (1)

G2812 **κάλαμος** ***kalamos***, n. [12] [→*2811*]. reed, staff, stick, measuring rod, pen:– staff (5), reed (4), rod (2), pen (1)

G2813 **καλέω** ***kaleō***, v. [148] [→*440, 441, 511, 1269, 1592, 1598, 1657, 1711, 2126, 3104, 3105, 3559, 4151, 4155, 4156, 4614, 4673, 4678, 5157, 5220*]. to call, invite, summon. The authority of the speaker dictates the nature of the calling (friends invite; kings summon). This is also translated "to name," the giving of attribution to someone or something:– called (85), call (11), invited (11), calls (8), call (3 [*+3836, 3950*]), host (2), invite (2), invites (2), reckoned (2), called in (1), called to faith (1), consecrated (1 [*+41*]), gave (1), give (1), guests (1), has[s] (1), host invited (1), is[s] (1), known as (1), name (1), name (1 [*+3950*]), name (1 [*+3836, 3950*]), name given (1), named (1 [*+3836, 3950*]), named (1), received[s] (1), said to be (1), tell to come (1), NDT (3)

G2814 **καλλιέλαιος** ***kallielaios***, n. [1] [√*2819 + 1777*]. cultivated olive tree:– cultivated olive tree (1)

G2815 **καλοδιδάσκαλος** ***kalodidaskalos***, a. [1] [√*2819 + 1438*]. teaching what is good:– teach what is good (1)

G2816 **Καλοὶ λιμένες** ***Kaloi limenes***, n. pr. [0] [√*2819 + 3348*]. Fair Havens, "*fair havens*":– Fair Havens Lasea (0)

G2817 **καλοκαγαθία** ***kalokagathia***, n. Not used in NIVEBC. [√*2819 + 2779 + 19*]. nobility of character, excellence

G2818 **καλοποιέω** ***kalopoieō***, v. [1] [√*2819 + 4472*]. to do what is right or good:– doing what is good (1)

G2819 **καλός** ***kalos***, a. [100] [→*2814, 2815, 2816, 2817, 2818, 2822*]. good, right; beautiful, fine, excellent:– good (66), better (8), right (5), beautiful (3), noble (3), excellent (2), fine (2), best (1), better (1 [*+3437*]), choice (1), clear (1), faithful (1), firm (1), goodness (1), well (1), work (1), NDT (2)

G2820 **κάλυμμα** ***kalymma***, n. [4] [√*2821*]. veil, covering:– veil (4)

G2821 **καλύπτω** ***kalyptō***, v. [8] [→*184, 365, 636, 637, 2127, 2128, 2820, 2877, 4152, 4328, 5158*]. cover, veil, hide:– veiled (2), concealed (1), cover (1), cover over (1), covers over (1), hides (1), swept over (1)

G2822 **καλῶς** ***kalōs***, adv. [37] [√*2819*]. rightly, well, sometimes with an implication of correctness:– well (11), good (8), right (6), easily (1), fine way (1), good (1 [*+4472*]), granted (1), honorably (1), please (1), rightly so (1), the right thing (1), the truth (1), truth (1), very well (1), well enough (1)

G2823 **κάμηλος** ***kamēlos***, n. [6] camel:– camel (4), camel's (2)

G2824 **κάμιλος** ***kamilos***, n. Not used in NIVEBC. rope, ship's cable

G2825 **κάμινος** ***kaminos***, n. [4] [√*2794*]. furnace, oven:– furnace (4)

G2826 **καμμύω** ***kammyō***, v. [2] close, shut (the eyes):– closed (2)

G2827 **κάμνω** ***kamnō***, v. [2] to grow weary; be sick:– sick (1), weary (1)

G2828 **κάμπτω** ***kamptō***, v. [4] [→*366, 5159*]. to bend, bow (on a knee):– bow (2), bowed (1), kneel (1 [*+3836, 1205*])

G2829 **κἄν** ***kan***, contr. [c.+pt.] [17] [√*2779 + 1623 + 323*]. and if, even if:– if (4), even if (3), also (1), and when (1), at least (1), even (1), even though (1), I (1), if even (1), just (1), or (1), then would (1)

G2830 **Κανά** ***Kana***, n. pr. [4] [→*2832*]. Cana, "*reed*":– Cana (4)

G2831 **Καναναῖος** ***Kananaios***, n. pr. [2] Zealot, Cananaean (not related to geographical terms Cana or Canaan); same as *2421*, "*zealot*":– zealot (2)

G2832 **Κανανίτης** ***Kananitēs***, n. pr. g. Not used in NIVEBC. [√*2830*]. Canaanite, from Cana

G2833 **Κανδάκη** ***Kandakē***, n. pr. [1] Candace, "[title?] *queen*":– Kandake (1)

G2834 **κανών** ***kanōn***, n. [4] rule, standard; sphere of activity, limit:– rule (1), sphere of activity (1), sphere of service (1 [*+3586, 3836*]), territory (1)

G2835 **Καπερναούμ** ***Kapernaoum***, n. pr. Not used in NIVEBC. [√*cf. 3019*]. Capernaum, "*village of Nahum*"

G2836 **καπηλεύω** ***kapēleuō***, v. [1] to act as a peddler, trade in for profit:– peddle for profit (1 [*+1639*])

G2837 **καπνός** ***kapnos***, n. [13] smoke:– smoke (13)

G2838 **Καππαδοκία** ***Kappadokia***, n. pr. [2] Cappadocia:– Cappadocia (2)

G2839 **καραδοκία** ***karadokia***, n. Not used in NIVEBC. [√*3191 + 1312*]. eager expectation

G2840 **καρδία** ***kardia***, n. [156] [→*2841, 5016*]. heart, mind (seat of thought and emotion). The heart was thought to be the seat of the inner self (composed of life, soul, mind, and spirit). "Heart" is similar in meaning to "soul," but often the "heart" has a focus on thinking and understanding (Mk 2:8; Lk 1:51; 24:38):– hearts (68), heart (61), mind (3), himself (2 [*+3836, 899*]), minds (2), you (2 [*+5148, 3836*]), decided (1 [*+326, 2093, 3836*]), experts (1 [*+1214*]), furious (1 [*+1391, 3836*]), heart's (1), how slow (1 [*+1096, 3836*]), inmost (1), made think (1 [*+5502, 1877, 3836*]), make up mind (1 [*+5502, 1877, 3836*]), prompted (1 [*+965, 1650, 3836*]), self (1 [*+476*]), stand firm (1 [*+5114, 3836*]), themselves (1 [*+899*]), themselves (1 [*+3836, 899*]), thought (1), thoughts (1 [*+1369*]), wondered about (1 [*+5502, 1877, 3836*]), you (1 [*+5148*]), yourselves (1 [*+5148*])

G2841 **καρδιογνώστης** ***kardiognōstēs***, n. [2] [√*2840 + 1182*]. knower of the heart:– know heart (1), knows the heart (1)

G2842 **Κάρπος** ***Karpos***, n. pr. [1] [√*2843*]. Carpus, "*fruit(ful)*":– Carpus (1)

G2843 **καρπός** ***karpos***, n. [66] [→*182, 2842, 2844, 2845*]. fruit, crop, harvest, produce of vegetation; by extension: deed, activity, produce of a person:– fruit (39), crop (6), harvest (4), crops (3), benefit (2), grain (2), child bear (1 [*+3836, 3120*]), contribution (1), crops of fruit (1), descendants (1 [*+3836, 4019*]), fruitful (1), fruitful (1 [*+5770*]), grapes (1), heads (1), more[s] (1 [*+3836*]), seeds (1)

G2844 **καρποφορέω** ***karpophoreō***, v. [8] [√*2843 + 5770*]. to produce a crop, bear fruit:– bearing fruit (2), produce a crop (2), bear fruit (1), bore fruit (1), produces a crop (1), produces grain (1)

G2845 **καρποφόρος** ***karpophoros***, a. [1] [√*2843 + 5770*]. crop, fruitbearing:– crops (1)

G2846 **καρτερέω** ***kartereō***, v. [1] [→*4674, 4675; cf. 3197*]. to persevere, endure:– persevered (1)

G2847 **κάρφος** ***karphos***, n. [6] speck, chip, particle:– speck (4), speck of sawdust (2)

G2848 **κατά** ***kata***, pp. [468] [→*183, 184, 185, 186, 187, 188, 189, 190, 191, 510, 634, 635, 639, 640, 896, 1352, 1588, 1593, 1594, 2129, 2745, 2746, 2747, 2749, 2750, 2757, 2758, 2759, 2761, 2762, 2763, 2765, 2766, 2768, 2769, 2770, 2771, 2772, 2773, 2774, 2775, 2776, 2777, 2778, 2849, 2850, 2851, 2852, 2853, 2854, 2855, 2856, 2857, 2858, 2859, 2860, 2861, 2863, 2864, 2865, 2866, 2867, 2868, 2869, 2870, 2871, 2872, 2874, 2875, 2876, 2877, 2878, 2879, 2880, 2881, 2882, 2883, 2884, 2885, 2886, 2887, 2888, 2889, 2890, 2891, 2892, 2893, 2894, 2895, 2896, 2897, 2898, 2899, 2900, 2901, 2902, 2903, 2904, 2905, 2906, 2907, 2908, 2909, 2910, 2911, 2912, 2913, 2914, 2915, 2916, 2917, 2918, 2919, 2920, 2921, 2922, 2923, 2924, 2925, 2926, 2927, 2928, 2929, 2930, 2931, 2932, 2933, 2934, 2935, 2936, 2937, 2938, 2939, 2940, 2941, 2942, 2943, 2944, 2945, 2946, 2947, 2948, 2949, 2950, 2951, 2952, 2953, 2954, 2955, 2956, 2957, 2958, 2959, 2960, 2961, 2962, 2963, 2964, 2965, 2966, 2967, 2968, 2969, 2971, 2972, 2973, 2974, 2975, 2976, 2977, 2978, 2979, 2980, 2981, 2982, 2983, 2984, 2985, 2986, 2987, 2988, 2989, 2993, 2994, 2995, 2996, 2997, 2998, 2999, 3000, 3001, 3002, 3003, 3004, 3005, 3006, 4153, 4615, 4616, 4617, 5160, 5161, 5162, 5163, 5164, 5691; cf. 2862*]. (gen.) against, contrary to, opposed; down, throughout; (acc.) in, by, with, in accordance with, for:– against (45), according to (43), in (40), by (34), as (15), every (10), in accordance with (8), to (7), about (6), in keeping with (6), privately (6 [*+2625*]), because of (5), daily (5 [*+2465*]), on (5), like (4), with (4), aside (3 [*+2625*]), at (3), based on (3), down (3), every day (3 [*+2465*]), for (3), from house to house (3 [*+3875*]), in every (3), in various (3), of (3), out of (3), through (3), all alone (2 [*+2625, 3668*]), along (2), as for (2), case[s] (2 [*+3836*]), contrary to (2), earthly (2 [*+4922*]), follow (2 [*+4513*]), from one to another (2), in obedience to (2), just as (2), just as (2 [*+4005, 5573*]), meets at (2), natural (2 [*+5882*]), on the basis of (2), over (2), required by (2), that is how (2 [*+3836, 899*]), throughout (2), throughout (2 [*+3910*]), after (1), alone (1 [*+2625*]), alone (1 [*+3668*]), along the coast of (1), among (1), annual (1 [*+1929*]), anywhere else in (1), as far as is concerned (1 [*+3525*]), as far as is concerned (1), as intended (1), as much as (1), as to (1), as usual (1 [*+3836, 899*]), as usual (1 [*+3836, 1621*]), as wants (1), as would (1), at just the right (1), before (1), before (1 [*+4725*]), by means of (1), by the power of (1), by the standards of (1 [*+6055*]), carrying out (1), commanding (1 [*+2198, 3306*]), conformed to (1), conforms to (1), considerate (1 [*+1194*]), covered (1 [*+2400*]), daily (1 [*+1667, 2465*]), day after day (1 [*+2465*]), day by day (1 [*+4246, 2465*]), depends on (1), during (1), each (1 [*+1651, 1651*]), each (1), each (1 [*+3836, 1651*]), every (1 [*+4246*]), every (1 [*+1667*]), extreme (1 [*+958*]), faced (1 [*+4725, 2400*]), far outweighs them all (1 [*+5651, 1650, 5651, 983*]), followed (1), follower of (1), following (1 [*+4513*]), forced (1 [*+340*]), from (1), from everyday life (1 [*+476*]), from one to another (1 [*+4246*]), from point of view (1), from town after town (1 [*+4484*]), from village to village (1 [*+3836, 3267*]), godly (1 [*+2536*]), godly (1 [*+2536*]), great (1 [*+5651*]), had (1), happened (1 [*+5175*]), having (1), how (1 [*+5515*]), how (1 [*+3836*]), human ancestry (1 [*+4922*]), human argument (1 [*+476*]), in accordance with (1 [*+3836, 381*]), in accordance with the will of (1), in conformity with (1), in detail (1 [*+1651, 1667*]), in each (1), in manner (1), in private (1 [*+2625*]), in regard to (1), in response to (1), in the way (1), in this way[s] (1 [*+4922*]), in turn (1 [*+1651*]), in whole

GREEK INDEX

(1), indicating that (1 [+*4005*]), intensely (1 [+*5651*]), just as (1 [+*4012*]), just as (1 [+*4012*]), just as (1 [+*3928*]), just like (1), leads to (1), like (1 [+*3836*, *3928*]), meets in (1), most excellent (1 [+*5651*]), near (1), observer of (1), of origin (1), of own race (1 [+*5150*, *4922*]), off (1), off the coast of (1), on authority (1), one at a time (1 [+*1651*, *1651*]), opposed to (1), opposite (1), orderly way (1 [+*5423*]), over against (1), people (1 [+*4922*]), prescribed by (1), prominent (1 [+*2029*]), reasonable (1 [+*3364*]), required (1), requires (1), requires (1 [+*1953*, *2400*]), the same as (1), thoroughly (1 [+*205*]), to further (1), to suit (1), toward (1), used for (1), utterly (1 [+*5651*]), voluntary (1 [+*1730*]), what deserve (1), what has happened to (1 [+*3836*]), when (1), when face to face (1 [+*4725*]), where (1), with hopes (1), with regard to (1), year after year (1 [+*1929*]), your (1 [+*5148*]), NDT (31)

G2849* καταβαίνω *katabainō, v. [81] [√*2848* + *326*]. to go down, descend:– come down (14), went down (13), came down (12), coming down (9), go down (6), descended (3), descending (3), comes down (2), down (2), goes down (2), going down (2), arrived (1), came (1), come (1), comes (1), descend (1), falling (1), fell (1), go downstairs (1), gone down (1), got down (1), on the way (1), went (1), NDT (1)

G2850* καταβάλλω *kataballō, v. [2] [√*2848* + *965*]. (pass.) to be struck down; (mid.) to lay (a foundation):– laying (1), struck down (1)

G2851* καταβαρέω *katabareō, v. [1] [√*2848* + *983*]. to burden, be a burden:– burden (1)

G2852* καταβαρύνω *katabarynō, v. [1] [√*2848* + *983*]. (pass.) to become heavy, burdened:– heavy (1)

G2853* κατάβασις *katabasis, n. [1] [√*2848* + *326*]. place that goes down, slope, down-grade:– place where the road goes down (1)

G2854* καταβιβάζω *katabibazō, v. Not used in NIVEBC. [√*2848* + *326*]. to bring down

G2855* καταβοάω *kataboaō, v. Not used in NIVEBC. [√*2848* + *1068*]. to cry out, bring charges, complain

G2856* καταβολή *katabolē, n. [11] [√*2848* + *965*]. creation (of the world), beginning, foundation:– creation (9), bear children (1 [+*1650*, *5065*, *3284*]), beginning (1)

G2857* καταβραβεύω *katabrabeuō, v. [1] [√*2848* + *1093*]. to disqualify for a prize, decide against:– disqualify (1)

G2858* καταγγελεύς *katangeleus, n. [1] [√*2848* + *34*]. advocate, proclaimer:– advocating (1)

G2859* καταγγέλλω *katangellō, v. [18] [√*2848* + *34*]. to preach, proclaim, advocate, report:– proclaim (3), proclaimed (3), preach (2), preached (2), proclaiming (2), advocating (1), bring message (1), foretold (1), preaching (1), reported (1), telling (1)

G2860* καταγελάω *katagelaō, v. [3] [√*2848* + *1151*]. to laugh at, mock:– laughed at (3)

G2861* καταγινώσκω *kataginōskō, v. [3] [√*2848* + *1182*]. to condemn, convict; (pass.) to be in the wrong, condemned:– condemn (2), condemned (1)

G2862* κατάγνυμι *katagnymi, v. [4] [→*544*, *3728*; *cf.* *2848*]. to break:– break (2), broke (1), broken (1)

G2863* καταγράφω *katagraphō, v. [1] [√*2848* + *1211*]. to write, with a possible implication that what is written is an accusation:– write (1)

G2864* κατάγω *katagō, v. [9] [√*2848* + *72*]. to bring, bring down, land (on shore):– bring (2), brought (2), bring down (1), landed (1), pulled up (1), put in (1), took down (1)

G2865* καταγωνίζομαι *katagōnizomai, v. [1] [√*2848* + *74*]. (mid.) to conquer, defeat, overcome:– conquered (1)

G2866* καταδέω *katadeō, v. [1] [√*2848* + *1313*]. to bandage, bind up:– bandaged (1)

G2867* κατάδηλος *katadēlos, a. [1] [√*2848* + *1316*]. clear, quite plain:– clear (1)

G2868* καταδικάζω *katadikazō, v. [5] [√*2848* + *1472*]. to condemn:– condemned (4), condemn (1)

G2869* καταδίκη *katadikē, n. [1] [√*2848* + *1472*]. condemnation:– condemned (1)

G2870* καταδιώκω *katadiōkō, v. [1] [√*2848* + *1503*]. to look for, search for:– look for (1)

G2871* καταδουλόω *katadouloō, v. [2] [√*2848* + *1528*]. to make a slave, enslave:– enslaves (1), make slaves (1)

G2872* καταδυναστεύω *katadynasteuō, v. [2] [√*2848* + *1538*]. (act.) to exploit, oppress, dominate; (pass.) to be under the power of, oppressed by:– exploiting (1), under the power (1)

G2873* κατάθεμα *katathema, n. [1] [√*2874*]. cursed thing, that which is under the ban (devoted exclusively to God):– curse (1)

G2874* καταθεματίζω *katathematizō, v. [1] [→*2873*; *cf.* *2848* + *5502*]. to (call down a) curse:– call down curses (1)

G2875* καταισχύνω *kataischynō, v. [13] [√*2848* + *156*]. to dishonor, humiliate, shame, disappoint:– put to shame (4), ashamed (2), dishonors (2), shame (2), embarrassed (1), humiliated (1), humiliating (1)

G2876* κατακαίω *katakaiō, v. [12] [√*2848* + *2794*]. to burn up, consume:– burned (4), burned up (4), burn (1), burn up (1), burning up (1), consumed (1)

G2877* κατακαλύπτω *katakalyptō, v. [3] [√*2848* + *2821*]. (mid.) to cover (the head):– cover (3)

G2878* κατακαυχάομαι *katakauchaomai, v. [4] [√*2848* + *3016*]. to boast about; to triumph over:– boast (1), consider to be superior (1), do[S] (1), triumphs over (1)

G2879* κατάκειμαι *katakeimai, v. [12] [√*2848* + *3023*]. to lie down (in bed); to recline (at dinner):– eating (3), lying (3), in bed (2), bedridden (1 [+*2093*, *3187*]), having dinner (1), lie (1), reclining at the table (1)

G2880* κατακλάω *kataklaō, v. [2] [√*2848* + *3089*]. to break in pieces:– broke (2)

G2881* κατακλείω *katakleiō, v. [2] [√*2848* + *3091*]. to lock up:– locked up (1), put (1)

G2882* κατακληροδοτέω *kataklērodoteō, v. Not used in NIVEBC. [√*2848* + *3102* + *1443*]. to parcel out by lot

G2883* κατακληρονομέω *kataklēronomeō, v. [1] [√*2848* + *3102* + *3795*]. to give as an inheritance:– giving as inheritance (1)

G2884* κατακλίνω *kataklinō, v. [5] [√*2848* + *3111*]. (act.) to cause to sit; (pass.) to recline (at a table):– at the table (1), reclined at the table (1), sat down (1), sit down (1), take (1 [+*1650*])

G2885* κατακλύζω *kataklyzō, v. [1] [√*2848* + *3114*]. (pass.) to be deluged, flooded:– deluged (1)

G2886* κατακλυσμός *kataklysmos, n. [4] [√*2848* + *3114*]. flood, deluge:– flood (4)

G2887* κατακολουθέω *katakoloutheō, v. [2] [√*2848* + *199* *[1.3]*]. to follow:– followed (2)

G2888* κατακόπτω *katakoptō, v. [1] [√*2848* + *3164*]. to cut:– cut (1)

G2889* κατακρημνίζω *katakrēmnizō, v. [1] [√*2848* + *3203*]. to throw down a cliff:– throw off the cliff (1)

G2890* κατάκριμα *katakrima, n. [3] [√*2848* + *3212*]. condemnation:– condemnation (3)

G2891* κατακρίνω *katakrinō, v. [18] [√*2848* + *3212*]. to condemn:– condemn (7), condemned (7), condemned (1 [+*2953*]), condemning (1), condemns (1), finally condemned (1)

G2892* κατάκρισις *katakrisis, n. [2] [√*2848* + *3212*]. condemnation:– condemn (1), condemnation (1)

G2893* κατακύπτω *katakyptō, v. [1] [√*2848* + *3252*]. to stoop down, bend down:– stooped down (1)

G2894* κατακυριεύω *katakyrieuō, v. [4] [√*2848* + *3261*]. to lord it over, gain dominion over, subdue; in some contexts there is an implication that this exercise of authority is harsh:– lord it over (2), lording it over (1), overpowered (1)

G2895* καταλαλέω *katalaleō, v. [5] [√*2848* + *3281*]. to speak against, slander, accuse:– slander (2), speaks against (2), accuse (1)

G2896* καταλαλιά *katalalia, n. [2] [√*2848* + *3281*]. slander, defamation, evil speech:– slander (2)

G2897* κατάλαλος *katalalos, a. [1] [√*2848* + *3281*]. slanderous, defamatory:– slanderers (1)

G2898* καταλαμβάνω *katalambanō, v. [15] [√*2848* + *3284*]. to obtain, attain, take hold of; seize, overtake; (mid.) to grasp, understand, realize, find out:– caught (2), found (1), get (1), grasp (1), obtained (1), overcome (1), overtakes (1), realize (1), realized (1), seizes (1), surprise (1), take hold of (1), taken hold of (1), took hold of (1)

G2899* καταλέγω *katalegō, v. [1] [√*2848* + *3306*]. to put on a list, enroll, select:– put on the list (1)

G2900* κατάλειμμα *kataleimma, n. Not used in NIVEBC. [√*2848* + *3309*]. remnant

G2901* καταλείπω *kataleipō, v. [24] [√*2848* + *3309*]. to leave (behind), neglect; (pass.) remain (behind):– left (11), leave (4), leaving (3), leaves (1), leaving behind (1), neglect (1), passing (1), reserved (1), stands (1)

G2902* καταλιθάζω *katalithazō, v. [1] [√*2848* + *3345*]. to stone to death:– stone (1)

G2903* καταλλαγή *katallagē, n. [4] [√*2848* + *248*]. reconciliation:– reconciliation (4)

G2904* καταλλάσσω *katallassō, v. [6] [√*2848* + *248*]. to reconcile (among human beings or between human beings and God):– reconciled (5), reconciling (1)

G2905* κατάλοιπος *kataloipos, a. [1] [√*2848* + *3309*]. remaining, left over; (n.) remnant, the rest:– rest (1)

G2906* κατάλυμα *katalyma, n. [3] [√*2848* + *3395*]. guest room; inn:– guest room (3)

G2907* καταλύω *katalyō, v. [17] [√*2848* + *3395*]. (tr.) throw down, abolish, destroy; (intr.) to be a guest, rest, find lodging:– destroy (6), thrown down (3), abolish (2), destroyed (2), be the guest (1), fail (1), lodging (1), stop (1)

G2908* καταμανθάνω *katamanthanō, v. [1] [√*2848* + *3443*]. notice carefully, consider closely:– see (1)

G2909* καταμαρτυρέω *katamartyreō, v. [3] [√*2848* + *3459*]. to bring testimony against, bear testimony against:– testimony bringing against (3)

G2910* καταμένω *katamenō, v. [1] [√*2848* + *3531*]. to stay, live:– staying (1)

G2911* καταμόνας *katamonas, a. Not used in NIVEBC. [√*2848* + *3668*]. in private, alone

G2912* κατανάθεμα *katanathema, n. Not used in NIVEBC. [√*2848* + *353*]. curse

G2913* καταναθεματίζω *katanathematizō, v. Not used in NIVEBC. [√*2848* + *353*]. to curse

G2914* καταναλίσκω *katanaliskō, v. [1] [√*2848* + *324* + *274*]. to consume:– consuming (1)

G2915* καταναρκάω *katanarkaō, v. [3] [√*2848*]. to burden, be a burden:– burden (2), burden to (1)

G2916* κατανεύω *kataneuō, v. [1] [√*2848* + *3748*]. to signal, nod:– signaled (1)

G2917* κατανοέω *katanoeō, v. [14] [√*2848* + *3808*]. to pay attention, notice, observe; consider, contemplate; this word has a strong implication that the attention paid is intense, and the contemplation is broad and thorough, resulting in complete understanding:– consider (3), pay attention to (2), faced the fact (1), fix your thoughts on (1), get a closer look (1), look (1), looked (1 [+*867*]), looking at (1), looks at (1), saw (1), saw through (1)

G2918* καταντάω *katantaō, v. [13] [√*2848* + *505*]. to come to, arrive at; attain, reach:– arrived (4), came (2), reach (2), attaining (1), come (1), landed (1), reached (1), see fulfilled (1)

G2919* κατάνυξις *katanyxis, n. [1] [√*2848* + *3817*]. stupor, bewilderment, unable to think:– stupor (1)

G2920* κατανύσσομαι *katanyssomai, v. [1] [√*2848* + *3817*]. to be pierced, stabbed:– cut (1)

G2921* καταξιόω *kataxioō, v. [3] [√*2848* + *545*]. (pass.) to be counted worthy, considered worthy:– counted worthy (2), considered worthy (1)

G2922* καταπατέω *katapateō, v. [5] [√*2848* + *4251*]. to trample (an action that can show disdain):– trample (1), trampled (1), trampled on (1), trampled underfoot (1), trampling on (1)

G2923* κατάπαυσις *katapausis, n. [9] [√*2848* + *4264*]. rest:– rest (8), resting (1)

G2924* καταπαύω *katapauō, v. [4] [√*2848* + *4264*]. to keep from, restrain; to give rest; to rest, cease:– given rest (1), keeping (1), rested (1), rests (1)

G2925* καταπέτασμα *katapetasma, n. [6] [√*2848* + *4375*]. curtain:– curtain (6)

G2926* καταπίμπρημι *katapimprēmi, v. Not used in NIVEBC. [√*2848* + *4399*]. to burn to ashes

G2927* καταπίνω *katapinō, v. [7] [√*2848* + *4403*]. to swallow, devour; (pass.) to be swallowed up, overwhelmed, drowned:– swallowed up (2), devour (1), drowned (1), overwhelmed (1), swallow (1), swallowing (1)

G2928* καταπίπτω *katapiptō, v. [3] [√*2848* + *4406*]. to fall down:– fell (2), fall (1)

G2929* καταπλέω *katapleō, v. [1] [√*2848* + *4434*]. to sail to:– sailed (1)

G2930* καταπονέω *kataponeō, v. [2] [√*2848* + *4506*]. (pass.) to be oppressed, distressed:– distressed (1), him[S] (1 [+*3836*])

G2931* καταποντίζω *katapontizō, v. [2] [√*2848* + *4509*]. (pass.) to be drowned; to sink:– drowned (1), sink (1)

G2932* κατάρα *katara, n. [6] [√*2848* + *725*]. curse, imprecation:– curse (3), accursed (1), cursed (1), cursing (1)

G2933* καταράομαι *kataraomai, v. [5] [√*2848* + *725*]. (mid.) to curse:– curse (3), cursed (2)

G2934* καταργέω *katargeō, v. [27] [√*2848* + *1.1* + *2240*]. to nullify, abolish, make ineffective; (pass.) cease, pass away:– destroyed (3), nullify (3), destroy (2), released (2), transitory (2), abolished (1), break the power (1), cease (1), coming to nothing (1), disappears (1), do away with (1), done away with (1), justified (1), pass away (1), passing away (1), put behind (1), setting aside (1), taken away (1), use up (1), worthless (1)

G2935* καταριθμέω *katarithmeō, v. [1] [√*2848* + *750*]. (pass.) to be numbered among, belong to:– number (1)

G2936 **καταρτίζω** ***katartizō***, v. [13] [√*2848 + 785*]. to restore, put in order, mend; to make complete, equip, train; to prepare, ordain:– prepared (2), preparing (2), restore (2), called forth (1), equip (1), formed (1), fully trained (1), perfectly (1), strive for full restoration (1), supply (1)

G2937 **κατάρτισις** ***katartisis***, n. [1] [√*2848 + 785*]. perfection, completion:– fully restored (1)

G2938 **καταρτισμός** ***katartismos***, n. [1] [√*2848 + 785*]. preparation, training, equipping:– equip (1)

G2939 **κατασείω** ***kataseiō***, v. [4] [√*2848 + 4940*]. to motion, signal by waving or shaking:– motioned (2), motioned (1 [+*3836, 5931*]), motioned for silence (1 [+*3836, 5931*])

G2940 **κατασκάπτω** ***kataskaptō***, v. [2] [√*2848 + 4999*]. (act.) to tear down; (pass.) to be ruined:– ruins (1), torn down (1)

G2941 **κατασκευάζω** ***kataskeuazō***, v. [11] [√*2848 + 5007*]. to prepare, make ready; to build, construct; to set up, arrange, furnish; there is a strong implication that the preparation is thorough, and a possible implication that the act of building may be for a special purpose:– built (3), prepare (3), builder (2), arranged (1), prepared (1), set up (1)

G2942 **κατασκηνόω** ***kataskēnoō***, v. [4] [√*2848 + 5008*]. to perch, nest; to live, dwell:– perch (2), perched (1), rest (1)

G2943 **κατασκήνωσις** ***kataskēnōsis***, n. [2] [√*2848 + 5008*]. nest:– nests (2)

G2944 **κατασκιάζω** ***kataskiazō***, v. [1] [√*2848 + 5014*]. to overshadow:– overshadowing (1)

G2945 **κατασκοπέω** ***kataskopeō***, v. [1] [√*2848 + 5023*]. to spy on, lie in wait for:– spy on (1)

G2946 **κατάσκοπος** ***kataskopos***, n. [1] [√*2848 + 5023*]. spy:– spies (1)

G2947 **κατασοφίζομαι** ***katasophizomai***, v. [1] [√*2848 + 5055*]. to deal treacherously with:– dealt treacherously (1)

G2948 **καταστέλλω** ***katastellō***, v. [2] [√*2848 + 5097*]. (act.) to quiet, restrain:– calm down (1 [+*5639*]), quieted (1)

G2949 **κατάστημα** ***katastēma***, n. [1] [√*2848 + 2705*]. the way one lives, behavior:– way they live (1)

G2950 **καταστολή** ***katastolē***, n. [1] [√*2848 + 5097*]. appearance, behavior:– dress (1)

G2951 **καταστρέφω** ***katastrephō***, v. [2] [√*2848 + 5138*]. to overturn, upset:– overturned (2)

G2952 **καταστρηνιάω** ***katastrēniaō***, v. [1] [√*2848 + 5140*]. to be filled with desires that conflict with dedication to someone:– sensual desires overcome dedication (1)

G2953 **καταστροφή** ***katastrophē***, n. [2] [√*2848 + 5138*]. ruin, destruction:– condemned (1 [+*2891*]), ruins (1)

G2954 **καταστρώννυμι** ***katastrōnnymi***, v. [1] [√*2848 + 5143*]. (pass.) to be scattered:– scattered (1)

G2955 **κατασύρω** ***katasyrō***, v. [1] [√*2848 + 5359*]. to drag away (by considerable force):– drag off (1)

G2956 **κατασφάζω** ***katasphazō***, v. [1] [√*2848 + 5377*]. to kill, slaughter, strike down:– kill (1)

G2957 **κατασφάττω** ***katasphattō***, v. Not used in NIVEBC. [√*2848 + 5377*]. to kill, slaughter, strike down

G2958 **κατασφραγίζω** ***katasphragizō***, v. [1] [√*2848 + 5382*]. (pass.) to be sealed up:– sealed (1)

G2959 **κατάσχεσις** ***kataschesis***, n. [2] [√*2848 + 2400*]. possession, taking into possession:– possess (1 [+*1443, 1650*]), took (1)

G2960 **κατατίθημι** ***katatithēmi***, v. [2] [√*2848 + 5502*]. (mid.) to grant a favor, do a favor:– do (1), grant (1)

G2961 **κατατομή** ***katatomē***, n. [1] [√*2848 + 5533*]. mutilation, cutting away:– mutilators of the flesh (1)

G2962 **κατατοξεύω** ***katatoxeuō***, v. Not used in NIVEBC. [√*2848 + 5534*]. to shoot down

G2963 **κατατρέχω** ***katatrechō***, v. [1] [√*2848 + 5556*]. to run down:– ran down (1)

G2964 **καταυγάζω** ***kataugazō***, v. Not used in NIVEBC. [√*2848 + 879*]. to shine upon, illuminate

G2965 **καταφέρω** ***katapherō***, v. [4] [√*2848 + 5770*]. to cast (a vote) against; to bring (charges); (pass.) to be overwhelmed (by sleep):– brought (1), cast against (1), sinking (1), sound asleep (1 [+*608, 3836, 5678*])

G2966 **καταφεύγω** ***katapheugō***, v. [2] [√*2848 + 5771*]. to flee, take refuge:– fled (2)

G2967 **καταφθείρω** ***kataphtheirō***, v. [1] [√*2848 + 5780*]. (pass.) to be depraved, corrupt:– depraved (1)

G2968 **καταφιλέω** ***kataphileō***, v. [6] [√*2848 + 5813*]. to kiss:– kissed (5), kissing (1)

G2969 **καταφρονέω** ***kataphroneō***, v. [9] [→*2970; cf. 2848 + 5856*]. to despise, look down on, scorn, show contempt:– despise (5), look down on (1), scorning (1), show contempt (1), show disrespect (1)

G2970 **καταφρονητής** ***kataphronētēs***, n. [1] [√*2969*]. scoffer, despiser:– scoffers (1)

G2971 **καταφωνέω** ***kataphōneō***, v. Not used in NIVEBC. [√*2848 + 5889*]. to shout at

G2972 **καταχέω** ***katacheō***, v. [2] [√*1772; cf. 2848*]. to pour out, pour down:– poured (2)

G2973 **καταχθόνιος** ***katachthonios***, a. [1] [√*2848*]. under the earth, subterranean; this may refer to the dead as a class of people, which generally are regarded as inhabiting the underworld. It is likely a more general term than the specific names for the abode of the dead: Hades, Gehenna, Tartaros, etc.:– under the earth (1)

G2974 **καταχράομαι** ***katachraomai***, v. [2] [√*2848 + 5968*]. to make full use of; to be engrossed in:– engrossed in (1), make full use (1)

G2975 **καταψηφίζομαι** ***katapsēphizomai***, v. Not used in NIVEBC. [√*2848 + 6029*]. to be enrolled

G2976 **καταψύχω** ***katapsychō***, v. [1] [√*2848 + 6038*]. to cool off, refresh with:– cool (1)

G2977 **κατείδωλος** ***kateidōlos***, a. [1] [√*2848 + 1631*]. full of idols / images:– full of idols (1)

G2978 **κατέναντι** ***katenanti***, adv. [8] [√*2848 + 1882*]. ahead, before, in the sight of; opposite of:– ahead of (2), in the sight of (2), opposite (2), ahead (1), before (1)

G2979 **κατενώπιον** ***katenōpion***, adv. & pp.* [3] [√*2848 + 1877 + 3972*]. in the sight of, in the presence of; before:– in sight (2), before (1)

G2980 **κατεξουσιάζω** ***katexousiazō***, v. [2] [√*2026; cf. 2848*]. to exercise authority over:– exercise authority over (2)

G2981 **κατεργάζομαι** ***katergazomai***, v. [22] [√*2848 + 2240*]. to produce, accomplish, bring about, do:– do (3), brings (2), doing (2), produced (2), produces (2), accomplished (1), achieving (1), bring about (1), carry out (1), committed (1), demonstrating (1), does (1), done (1), fashioned (1), result in (1), work out (1)

G2982 **κατέρχομαι** ***katerchomai***, v. [15] [√*2848 + 2262*]. to go down, come down:– came down (4), went down (4), landed (3), went (2), came (1), come down (1)

G2983 **κατεσθίω** ***katesthiō***, v. [14] [√*2848 + 2266*]. to eat up, consume:– devour (4), ate up (3), ate (1), consume (1), devoured (1), devours (1), eat (1), exploits (1), squandered (1)

G2984 **κατέσθω** ***katesthō***, v. Not used in NIVEBC. [√*2848 + 2266*]. to eat up, consume

G2985 **κατευθύνω** ***kateuthynō***, v. [3] [√*2848 + 2317*]. to guide, direct, lead:– clear (1), direct (1), guide (1)

G2986 **κατευλογέω** ***kateulogeō***, v. [1] [√*2848 + 2292 + 3306*]. to bless (intensely):– blessed (1)

G2987 **κατεφίσταμαι** ***katephistamai***, v. [1] [√*2848 + 2093 + 2705*]. to make an attack upon, rise up against:– made a attack (1)

G2988 **κατέχω** ***katechō***, v. [17] [√*2848 + 2400*]. to hold back, suppress, restrain; hold fast, possess; (pass.) to be bound:– keep (3), hold (2), hold firmly (2), bound (1), hold on to (1), holding back (1), holding to (1), holds back (1), made for (1), possessing (1), retain (1), suppress (1), take (1)

G2989 **κατηγορέω** ***katēgoreō***, v. [23] [→*2990, 2991, 2992; cf. 2848 + 72*]. to accuse, bring charges against:– accuse (4), accused (3), accusing (3), accuser (1), accuses (1), basis for accusing (1), bring charge against (1), bring charges (1), bring charges against (1), charges (1), charges bringing (1), charges brought (1), charges making (1), presented case (1 [+*806*]), press charges (1), they[S] (1 [+*3836*])

G2990 **κατηγορία** ***katēgoria***, n. [3] [√*2989*]. (legal) charge, accusation:– accusation (1), charge (1), charges (1)

G2991 **κατήγορος** ***katēgoros***, n. [4] [√*2989*]. accuser:– accusers (4)

G2992 **κατήγωρ** ***katēgōr***, n. [1] [√*2989*]. accuser:– accuser (1)

G2993 **κατήφεια** ***katēpheia***, n. [1] [√*2848 + 5743*]. gloominess, a feeling of dejection:– gloom (1)

G2994 **κατηχέω** ***katēcheō***, v. [8] [√*2848 + 2491*]. (act.) to instruct; (pass.) to be instructed, informed:– instructed (2), informed (1), instruct (1), instructor (1), receives instruction (1), reports (1), taught (1)

G2995 **κατιόω** ***katioō***, v. [1] [√*2848 + 2675*]. (pass.) to become corroded, tarnished:– corroded (1)

G2996 **κατισχύω** ***katischyō***, v. [3] [√*2848 + 2709*]. to overcome, prevail; to be able:– able (1), overcome (1), prevailed (1)

G2997 **κατοικέω** ***katoikeō***, v. [44] [√*2848 + 3875*]. to live in, reside in, settle:– inhabitants (9), living (6), live (5), lived in (4), dwell (3), lived (3), dwells (2), live in (2), lives (2), in (1), inhabit (1), living in (1), peoples[S] (1), residents (1), settled (1), staying (1), them[S] (1 [+*3836, 2093, 3836, 1178*])

G2998 **κατοίκησις** ***katoikēsis***, n. [1] [√*2848 + 3875*]. where one lives, residence:– lived (1 [+*3836, 2400*])

G2999 **κατοικητήριον** ***katoikētērion***, n. [2] [√*2848 + 3875*]. dwelling place, home:– dwelling (2)

G3000 **κατοικία** ***katoikia***, n. [1] [√*2848 + 3875*]. where one lives, dwelling place:– lands (1)

G3001 **κατοικίζω** ***katoikizō***, v. [1] [√*2848 + 3875*]. to cause to live in:– caused to dwell (1)

G3002 **κατοπτρίζω** ***katoptrizō***, v. [1] [√*2848 + 3972*]. (mid.) to reflect or to look at, contemplate:– contemplate (1)

G3003 **κατόρθωμα** ***katorthōma***, n. Not used in NIVEBC. [√*2848 + 3981*]. success, prosperity, good order

G3004 **κάτω** ***katō***, adv. [9] [√*2848*]. below; down, downward; bottom:– below (3), down (3), bottom (2), to the ground (1)

G3005 **κατώτερος** ***katōteros***, a. [1] [√*2848*]. lower:– lower (1)

G3006 **κατωτέρω** ***katōterō***, adv. [1] [√*2848*]. under, lower:– under (1)

G3007 **Καῦδα** ***Kauda***, n. pr. [1] [√*cf. 1144, 3084, 3085*]. Cauda:– Cauda (1)

G3008 **καῦμα** ***kauma***, n. [2] [√*2794*]. (scorching) heat:– heat (1), scorching heat (1)

G3009 **καυματίζω** ***kaumatizō***, v. [4] [√*2794*]. (act.) to scorch, burn; (pass.) to be scorched, seared:– scorched (2), scorch (1), seared (1)

G3010 **καυματόω** ***kaumatoō***, v. Not used in NIVEBC. [√*2794*]. to be scorched by the heat

G3011 **καῦσις** ***kausis***, n. [1] [√*2794*]. burning:– burned (1)

G3012 **καυσόω** ***kausoō***, v. [2] [√*2794*]. (pass.) to be consumed by fire, burned up:– fire (1), heat (1)

G3013 **καυστηριάζω** ***kaustēriazō***, v. [1] [√*2794*]. (pass.) to be seared as with a hot iron:– seared as with a hot iron (1)

G3014 **καύσων** ***kausōn***, n. [3] [√*2794*]. (scorching) heat, hot day:– heat (1), hot (1), scorching heat (1)

G3015 **καυτηριάζω** ***kautēriazō***, v. Not used in NIVEBC. [√*2794*]. (pass.) to be seared with a hot iron

G3016 **καυχάομαι** ***kauchaomai***, v. [37] [→*1595, 2878, 3017, 3018*]. to boast, brag about; to rejoice in, glory in; this can refer to proper or improper boasting, depending on the object of the boast:– boast (25), boasting (5), boasts (2), boasted (1), do boasting (1), glory (1), pride (1), take pride (1)

G3017 **καύχημα** ***kauchēma***, n. [11] [√*3016*]. something to boast about, boasting; pride, joy:– boast (3), boasting (3), pride (2), boast (1 [+*1639*]), glory (1), something to boast about (1)

G3018 **καύχησις** ***kauchēsis***, n. [11] [√*3016*]. boasting, pride; glorying in; this can refer to proper or improper boasting, depending on the object of the boast:– boasting (5), pride (2), boast (1), boast (1 [+*2400*]), glory (1), glory (1 [+*2400*])

G3019 **Καφαρναούμ** ***Kapharnaoum***, n. pr. [16] [√*cf. 2835*]. Capernaum, "*village of Nahum*":– Capernaum (16)

G3020 **Κεγχρεαί** ***Kenchreai***, n. pr. [2] Cenchrea:– Cenchreae (2)

G3021 **κέδρος** ***kedros***, n. Not used in NIVEBC. cedar tree

G3022 **Κεδρών** ***Kedrōn***, n. pr. [1] Kidron:– Kidron (1)

G3023 **κεῖμαι** ***keimai***, v. [24] [→*367, 512, 641, 780, 2130, 2879, 3121, 3122, 3130, 3131, 4154, 4329, 4618, 5165, 5263, 5692*]. to lay, lie, be laid, laid out; be destined, appointed:– lying (5), destined (2), is (2), laid (2), there (2), been (1), built (1), covers (1 [+*2093*]), laid out (1), laid up (1), lay (1), made (1), put here (1), stood (1 [+*1639*]), under the control of (1 [+*1877*]), was (1)

G3024 **κειρία** ***keiria***, n. [1] [√*3025*]. strip of linen, bandage, graveclothes:– strips of linen (1)

G3025 **κείρω** ***keirō***, v. [4] [→*1483, 2134, 2135, 3024, 3047, 3048, 3166*]. (act.) to shear (another); (mid.) to have one's hair cut:– have hair cut off (2), cut off (1), shearer (1)

G3026 **κέλευσμα** ***keleusma***, n. [1] [√*3027*]. (loud) command, signal:– loud command (1)

G3027 **κελεύω** ***keleuō***, v. [25] [→*1353, 2131, 2225, 3026*]. to order, direct, command:– ordered (18), gave orders (2), command (1), commanding (1), directed (1), give the order (1), tell (1)

G3028 **κενεμβατεύω** ***kenembateuō***, v. Not used in NIVEBC. [√*3031 + 1877 + 326*]. to step on emptiness, make a misstep

G3029 **κενοδοξία** ***kenodoxia***, n. [1] [√*3031 + 1518*]. vain conceit, empty conceit, a state of pride that has no proper basis:– vain conceit (1)

G3030 **κενόδοξος** ***kenodoxos***, a. [1] [√*3031 + 1518*]. conceited, a state of pride that has no proper basis:– conceited (1)

G3031 **κενός** ***kenos***, a. [18] [→*3028, 3029, 3030, 3032, 3033, 3036*]. empty, empty-handed; by extension: vain, ineffective, useless, foolish:– vain (4), empty-handed (3), empty (2), in vain (2), foolish (1), hollow (1), so^{S} (1), useless (1), without effect (1), without results (1), NDT (1)

G3032 **κενοφωνία** ***kenophōnia***, n. [2] [√*3031 + 5889*]. chatter, empty talk:– chatter (2)

G3033 **κενόω** ***kenoō***, v. [5] [√*3031*]. to empty, deprive; (pass.) to be hollow, emptied, of no value:– deprive (1), emptied of power (1), made nothing (1), means nothing (1), prove hollow (1)

G3034 **κέντρον** ***kentron***, n. [4] [→*1596, 1708*]. sting, goad:– sting (2), goads (1), stingers (1)

G3035 **κεντυρίων** ***kentyriōn***, n. [3] centurion, technically the commander of one hundred:– centurion (3)

G3036 **κενῶς** ***kenōs***, adv. [1] [√*3031*]. without reason, in vain, to no purpose:– without reason (1)

G3037 **κεραία** ***keraia***, n. [2] [√*3043*]. least stroke of a pen, projection [a portion of a letter of the alphabet], referring to the smallest detail of the Law:– least stroke of a pen (2)

G3038 **κεραμεύς** ***kerameus***, n. [3] [√*3041*]. potter:– potter's (2), potter (1)

G3039 **κεραμικός** ***keramikos***, a. [1] [√*3041*]. pertaining to a potter:– pottery (1 [*+5007, 3836*])

G3040 **κεράμιον** ***keramion***, n. [2] [√*3041*]. clay jar:– jar (2)

G3041 **κέραμος** ***keramos***, n. [1] [→*3038, 3039, 3040*]. clay roof tile:– tiles (1)

G3042 **κεράννυμι** ***kerannymi***, v. [3] [→*193, 204, 5166*]. to mix; (pass.) to be poured:– pour (1), poured (1), NDT (1)

G3043 **κέρας** ***keras***, n. [11] [→*3037, 3044*]. horn, often a figure of power and position:– horns (10), horn (1)

G3044 **κεράτιον** ***keration***, n. [1] [√*3043*]. carob pod:– pods (1)

G3045 **κερδαίνω** ***kerdainō***, v. [17] [√*3046*]. to gain; make money; win over; spare:– win (5), gain (4), gained (4), won over (2), make money (1), spared (1)

G3046 **κέρδος** ***kerdos***, n. [3] [→*153, 154, 2132, 3045*]. gain, profit:– gain (2), gains (1)

G3047 **κέρμα** ***kerma***, n. [1] [√*3025*]. coin:– coins (1)

G3048 **κερματιστής** ***kermatistēs***, n. [1] [√*3025*]. money exchanger:– exchanging money (1)

G3049 **κεφάλαιον** ***kephalaion***, n. [2] [√*3051*]. the (main) point; price, sum of money:– main point (1), money (1)

G3050 **κεφαλαιόω** ***kephalaioō***, v. Not used in NIVEBC. [√*3051*]. to strike on the head

G3051 **κεφαλή** ***kephalē***, n. [75] [→*368, 642, 2133, 3049, 3050, 3052, 3053, 4330, 4676*]. head (of a body); top (stone in a building); by extension: someone or something in the primary place, the point of origin:– head (50), heads (18), cornerstone (5 [*+1224*]), hair (1), hair (1 [*+2582, 3836*])

G3052 **κεφαλιόω** ***kephalioō***, v. [1] [√*3051*]. to strike on the head:– struck on the head (1)

G3053 **κεφαλίς** ***kephalis***, n. [1] [√*3051*]. section of a scroll:– scroll (1 [*+1046*])

G3054 **κηδεύω** ***kēdeuō***, v. Not used in NIVEBC. to take care of, bury

G3055 **κημόω** ***kēmoō***, v. [1] to muzzle:– muzzle (1)

G3056 **κῆνσος** ***kēnsos***, n. [4] (poll) tax:– imperial tax (2), tax (1), taxes (1)

G3057 **κῆπος** ***kēpos***, n. [5] [→*3058*]. garden, grove:– garden (5)

G3058 **κηπουρός** ***kēpouros***, n. [1] [√*3057*]. gardener:– gardener (1)

G3059 **κηρίον** ***kērion***, n. Not used in NIVEBC. wax, honeycomb

G3060 **κήρυγμα** ***kērygma***, n. [8] [√*3061*]. preaching, proclamation, message, with a focus on the content of what is preached:– preaching (5), message (1), message proclaim (1), preached (1)

G3061 **κῆρυξ** ***kēryx***, n. [3] [→*3060, 3062, 4619*]. herald, preacher, proclaimer:– herald (2), preacher (1)

G3062 **κηρύσσω** ***kēryssō***, v. [61] [√*3061*]. to preach, proclaim, tell, often urging acceptance of the message, with warnings of consequences for not doing so:– preach (15), preached (14), preaching (8), proclaim (5), proclaiming (5), proclaimed (4), preaches (2), made proclamation (1), message (1), preached (1 [*+2400*]), proclaim message (1), talk (1), talking about (1), tell (1), told (1)

G3063 **κῆτος** ***kētos***, n. [1] huge fish:– huge fish (1)

G3064 **Κηφᾶς** ***Kēphas***, n. pr. [9] Cephas (Aramaic for Peter), "*rock*":– Cephas (9)

G3065 **κιβώριον** ***kibōrion***, n. Not used in NIVEBC. ciborium

G3066 **κιβωτός** ***kibōtos***, n. [6] ark, box, chest:– ark (6)

G3067 **κιθάρα** ***kithara***, n. [4] [→*3068, 3069*]. harp, lyre:– harp (2), harps (2)

G3068 **κιθαρίζω** ***kitharizō***, v. [2] [√*3067*]. to play the harp or lyre:– playing (1), tune played (1 [*+884, 2445*])

G3069 **κιθαρῳδός** ***kitharōdos***, n. [2] [√*3067 + 6046*]. harpist, lyre player:– harpists (2)

G3070 **Κιλικία** ***Kilikia***, n. pr. [8] [√*3071*]. Cilicia:– Cilicia (7), provinces of Cilicia (1)

G3071 **Κίλιξ** ***Kilix***, n. pr. g. Not used in NIVEBC. [→*3070*]. Cilician

G3072 **κινάμωμον** ***kinamōmon***, n. Not used in NIVEBC. [√*3077*]. cinnamon

G3073 **κινδυνεύω** ***kindyneuō***, v. [4] [√*3074*]. to be in danger:– danger (1), endanger (1), in danger (1), in great danger (1)

G3074 **κίνδυνος** ***kindynos***, n. [9] [→*3073*]. danger, risk:– danger (9)

G3075 **κινέω** ***kineō***, v. [8] [→*293, 3076, 3560, 5167*]. to move, remove; to shake, stir up; (pass.) to be moved, removed; be aroused:– move (2), shaking (2), aroused (1), remove (1), removed (1), stirring up (1)

G3076 **κίνησις** ***kinēsis***, n. Not used in NIVEBC. [√*3075*]. motion

G3077 **κιννάμωμον** ***kinnamōmon***, n. [1] [→*3072*]. cinnamon:– cinnamon (1)

G3078 **Κίς** ***Kis***, n. pr. [1] Kish, "*bow, power*":– Kish (1)

G3079 **κίχρημι** ***kichrēmi***, v. [1] [√*cf. 5968, 5969*]. to lend:– lend (1)

G3080 **κλάδος** ***klados***, n. [11] [√*3089*]. branch, twig:– branches (9), twigs (2)

G3081 **κλαίω** ***klaiō***, v. [40] [→*3088*]. to weep, cry, wail, mourn:– weep (10), weeping (6), crying (5), wept (5), mourn (4), wailing (3), cry (2), did^{S} (1), wail (1), weeping (1 [*+4472*]), wept and wept (1 [*+4498*]), with tears (1)

G3082 **κλάσις** ***klasis***, n. [2] [√*3089*]. breaking:– breaking (1), broke (1)

G3083 **κλάσμα** ***klasma***, n. [9] [√*3089*]. broken piece, fragment:– broken pieces (5), pieces (4)

G3084 **Κλαῦδα** ***Klauda***, n. pr. Not used in NIVEBC. [√*cf. 3007*]. Clauda

G3085 **Κλαύδη** ***Klaudē***, n. pr. Not used in NIVEBC. [√*cf. 3007*]. Clauda

G3086 **Κλαυδία** ***Klaudia***, n. pr. [1] [→*3087*]. Claudia, "[poss.] *lame*":– Claudia (1)

G3087 **Κλαύδιος** ***Klaudios***, n. pr. [3] [√*3086*]. Claudius:– Claudius (3)

G3088 **κλαυθμός** ***klauthmos***, n. [9] [√*3081*]. weeping, crying:– weeping (8), wept (1 [*+2653, 1181*])

G3089 **κλάω** ***klaō***, v. [14] [→*1709, 2880, 3080, 3082, 3083, 3097*]. to break:– broke (12), break (2)

G3090 **κλείς** ***kleis***, n. [6] [√*3091*]. key:– key (4), keys (2)

G3091 **κλείω** ***kleiō***, v. [16] [→*643, 1597, 1710, 2881, 3090, 5168*]. to close, shut, lock:– shut (7), locked (5), close (1), has no pity (1 [*+3836, 5073*]), shut up (1), shuts (1)

G3092 **κλέμμα** ***klemma***, n. [1] [√*3096*]. theft, stealing:– thefts (1)

G3093 **Κλεοπᾶς** ***Kleopas***, n. pr. [1] [√*3094 + 4252*]. Cleopas, "*renowned father*":– Cleopas (1)

G3094 **κλέος** ***kleos***, n. [1] [→*3093*]. credit, honor:– credit (1)

G3095 **κλέπτης** ***kleptēs***, n. [16] [√*3096*]. thief:– thief (12), thieves (4)

G3096 **κλέπτω** ***kleptō***, v. [13] [→*3092, 3095, 3113*]. steal:– steal (10), stealing (2), stole away (1)

G3097 **κλῆμα** ***klēma***, n. [4] [√*3089*]. branch (in context, vine branches):– branch (3), branches (1)

G3098 **Κλήμης** ***Klēmēs***, n. pr. [1] Clement, "*mild*":– Clement (1)

G3099 **κληρονομέω** ***klēronomeō***, v. [18] [√*3102 + 3795*]. to inherit, acquire; see also *3100*:– inherit (15), inherited (1), share in the inheritance (1), take inheritance (1)

G3100 **κληρονομία** ***klēronomia***, n. [14] [√*3102 + 3795*]. inheritance, transfer of property and possessions from one generation to another, usually within a family or clan and usually upon the death of the owner. This word often has an implication of a legitimate, historic right to the objects inherited. In some contexts this refers to salvation, an inheritance shared with Jesus Christ, the true heir:– inheritance (14)

G3101 **κληρονόμος** ***klēronomos***, n. [15] [√*3102 + 3795*]. heir, one who inherits:– heir (8), heirs (6), inherit (1)

G3102 **κλῆρος** ***klēros***, n. [11] [→*2882, 2883, 3099, 3100, 3101, 3103, 3729, 3907, 3908, 4677, 5169*]. (casting) lots; share, place, inheritance:– lots (5), entrusted (1), inheritance (1), lot (1), place (1), share (1), shared (1 [*+3275, 3836*])

G3103 **κληρόω** ***klēroō***, v. [1] [√*3102*]. (pass.) to be chosen, appointed:– chosen (1)

G3104 **κλῆσις** ***klēsis***, n. [11] [√*2813*]. call, calling; situation, station in life:– called (4), calling (4), call (1), life (1), situation (1)

G3105 **κλητός** ***klētos***, a. [10] [√*2813*]. called, invited:– called (9), invited (1)

G3106 **κλίβανος** ***klibanos***, n. [2] (fire of a) furnace, oven:– fire (2)

G3107 **κλίμα** ***klima***, n. [3] [√*3111*]. region:– regions (2), Syria (1 [*+3836, 3836, 5353*])

G3108 **κλινάριον** ***klinarion***, n. [1] [√*3111*]. bed, stretcher:– beds (1)

G3109 **κλίνη** ***klinē***, n. [8] [√*3111*]. bed, mat, stretcher:– bed (5), mat (3)

G3110 **κλινίδιον** ***klinidion***, n. [2] [√*3111*]. bed, mat, stretcher (smaller and more temporary than a bed found in a home):– mat (2)

G3111 **κλίνω** ***klinō***, v. [7] [→*195, 369, 804, 1712, 2884, 3107, 3108, 3109, 3110, 3112, 4679, 4680, 4752*]. to bow down, lay down; to be over (late in the day):– lay (2), bowed (1), bowed down (1), late in the afternoon (1 [*+3836, 2465, 806*]), over (1), routed (1)

G3112 **κλισία** ***klisia***, n. [1] [√*3111*]. group reclining for a meal:– groups (1)

G3113 **κλοπή** ***klopē***, n. [2] [√*3096*]. theft, stealing:– theft (2)

G3114 **κλύδων** ***klydōn***, n. [2] [→*2352, 2885, 2886, 3115*]. raging waters, waves:– raging (1), wave (1)

G3115 **κλυδωνίζομαι** ***klydōnizomai***, v. [1] [√*3114*]. to be tossed back and forth by waves:– tossed back and forth by the waves (1)

G3116 **Κλωπᾶς** ***Klōpas***, n. pr. [1] Clopas:– Clopas (1)

G3117 **κνήθω** ***knēthō***, v. [1] [√*cf. 1187*]. (pass.) to feel an itch:– say what itching ears want to hear (1 [*+198*])

G3118 **Κνίδος** ***Knidos***, n. pr. [1] Cnidus, "*age*":– Cnidus (1)

G3119 **κοδράντης** ***kodrantēs***, n. [2] penny, small Roman coin, about one-sixty-fourth of a denarius (a day's wage):– only a few cents (1), penny (1)

G3120 **κοιλία** ***koilia***, n. [23] any and all internal organs, translated in context as: belly, stomach, womb, etc.; by extension: the source of feelings and emotions. "The fruit of the womb" means "a child.":– stomach (8), womb (4), birth (2 [*+3613*]), appetites (1), belly (1), born (1 [*+1666, 3613*]), born (1 [*+1666, 3613, 1164*]), child bear (1 [*+2843, 3836*]), conceived (1 [*+5197, 1877, 3836*]), mother^{S} (1), within (1), wombs (1)

G3121 **κοιμάω** ***koimaō***, v. [18] [√*3023*]. (pass.) to fall asleep, sleep; die:– fallen asleep (6), asleep (3), died (2), fell asleep (2), dies (1), sleep (1), sleep in death (1), sleeping (1), sleeps (1)

G3122 **κοίμησις** ***koimēsis***, n. [1] [√*3023*]. (noun) sleep:– natural sleep (1 [*+5678*])

G3123 **κοινός** ***koinos***, a. [14] [→*3124, 3125, 3126, 3127, 3128, 3129, 5170, 5171*]. common; (ceremonially) unclean, impure, unholy:– impure (4), unclean (3), defiled (2), common (1), in common (1), share (1), shared (1), unholy (1)

G3124 **κοινόω** ***koinoō***, v. [14] [√*3123*]. to make (ceremonially) unclean, impure; to defile:– defile (7), defiles (3), call impure (2), ceremonially unclean (1), defiled (1)

G3125 **κοινωνέω** ***koinōneō***, v. [8] [√*3123*]. to share in, participate in:– share (2), have (1), participate in (1), share in (1), shared (1), shared with (1), shares in (1)

G3126 **κοινωνία** ***koinōnia***, n. [19] [√*3123*]. fellowship, the close association between persons, emphasizing what is common between them; by extension: participation, sharing, contribution, gift, the outcome of such close relationships:– fellowship (9), participation (3), common sharing in (1), contribution (1), partnership (1), partnership with (1), share with others (1), sharing (1), sharing in (1)

G3127 κοινωνικός *koinōnikos*, a. [1] [√3123]. willing to share, generous:– willing to share (1)

G3128 κοινωνός *koinōnos*, n. [10] [√3123]. partner, participant, one who joins in with another in some enterprise or activity, in business or ministry:– participate in (2), partner (2), participants with (1), partners (1), share (1), share in (1 [+1639]), side by side (1), taken part (1 [+1639])

G3129 κοινῶς *koinōs*, adv. Not used in NIVEBC. [√3123]. in the common language or dialect

G3130 κοίτη *koitē*, n. [4] [√3023]. (marriage) bed; conception; sexual immorality:– bed (2), children conceived at the same time (1 [+1666, 1651, 2400]), sexual immorality (1)

G3131 κοιτών *koitōn*, n. [1] [√3023]. bedroom; trusted personal servant, chamberlain:– trusted personal servant (1 [+2093, 3836])

G3132 κόκκινος *kokkinos*, a. [6] [√3133]. scarlet, (bright) red; in some contexts, cloth that is scarlet or (bright) red (Rev 18:12, 16):– scarlet (6)

G3133 κόκκος *kokkos*, n. [7] [→3132]. seed, kernel of grain:– seed (6), kernel (1)

G3134 κολάζω *kolazō*, v. [2] [√3266]. to punish:– punish (1), punishment (1)

G3135 κολακεία *kolakeia*, n. [1] flattery:– flattery (1 [+3364])

G3136 κόλασις *kolasis*, n. [2] [√3266]. punishment:– punishment (2)

G3137 Κολασσαεύς *Kolassaeus*, n. pr. g. Not used in NIVEBC. [√3145]. Colossian

G3138 Κολασσαί *Kolassai*, n. pr. Not used in NIVEBC. [√3145]. Colosse

G3139 κολαφίζω *kolaphizō*, v. [5] to strike with the fists, beat, torment; (pass.) receive a beating, be brutally treated:– struck with fists (2), brutally treated (1), receive a beating (1), torment (1)

G3140 κολλάω *kollaō*, v. [12] [→4681]. (mid.) to join, associate with, cling to; (pass.) to be united, stuck to, piled up; to stay near, follow; to be hired out:– join (2), associate with (1), cling to (1), followers of (1), hired out (1), piled up (1), stay near (1), united (1), united with (1), unites with (1), NDT (1)

G3141 κολλούριον *kollourion*, n. [1] eye salve:– salve (1)

G3142 κολλυβιστής *kollybistēs*, n. [3] money exchanger:– money changers (3)

G3143 κολοβόω *koloboō*, v. [4] [√3266]. to cut short, shorten:– cut short (2), shortened (2)

G3144 Κολοσσαεύς *Kolossaeus*, n. pr. g. Not used in NIVEBC. [√3145]. Colossian

G3145 Κολοσσαί *Kolossai*, n. pr. [1] [→3137, 3138, 3144]. Colosse, "*punishment*":– Colossae (1)

G3146 κόλπος *kolpos*, n. [6] lap area: side, bosom, chest; bay:– side (2), bay (1), closest relationship with (1), lap (1), next to (1 [+1877, 3836])

G3147 κολυμβάω *kolymbaō*, v. [1] [→1713, 3148]. to swim:– swim (1)

G3148 κολυμβήθρα *kolymbēthra*, n. [3] [√3147]. pool:– pool (3)

G3149 κολωνία *kolōnia*, n. [1] Roman colony:– roman colony (1)

G3150 κομάω *komaō*, v. [2] [√3151]. to have long hair:– has long hair (2)

G3151 κόμη *komē*, n. [1] [→3150]. (long) hair:– long hair (1)

G3152 κομίζω *komizō*, v. [10] [√3180]. (act.) to bring; (mid.) to receive (what is due), reward, be repaid:– receive (2), came with (1), receive back (1), receive what is due (1), received (1), received back (1), receiving (1), repaid (1), reward (1)

G3153 κομψότερον *kompsoteron*, adv. comp. [1] [√3180]. better:– better (1)

G3154 κονιάω *koniaō*, v. [2] [→3155]. (pass.) to be whitewashed:– whitewashed (2)

G3155 κονιορτός *koniortos*, n. [5] [√3154 + 3995]. dust:– dust (5)

G3156 κοπάζω *kopazō*, v. [3] [√3164]. to die down, abate:– died down (3)

G3157 κοπετός *kopetos*, n. [1] [√3164]. mourning, sorrowing, lamentation:– mourned (1 [+4472])

G3158 κοπή *kopē*, n. [1] [√3164]. defeat, cutting down:– defeat (1)

G3159 κοπιάω *kopiaō*, v. [23] [√3164]. to work, labor, give effort; to become tired, grow weary:– labor (4), worked hard (3), weary (2), work (2), work hard (2), done the hard work (1), efforts (1), hard work (1), hardworking (1), labors (1), strenuously (1), tired (1), work hard (1 [+2237]), worked (1), worked for (1)

G3160 κόπος *kopos*, n. [18] [√3164]. labor, work; bother, trouble, difficulty:– labor (5), bothering (3 [+4218]), hard work (2), bother (1 [+4218]), labored (1), laboring (1), labors (1), toil (1), trouble (1), work (1), worked (1)

G3161 κοπρία *kopria*, n. [1] [→3162, 3163]. manure pile, rubbish pile:– manure pile (1)

G3162 κόπριον *koprion*, n. [1] [√3161]. fertilizer, manure:– fertilize (1 [+965])

G3163 κόπρος *kopros*, n. Not used in NIVEBC. [√3161]. dung, manure

G3164 κόπτω *koptō*, v. [8] [→370, 644, 718, 737, 1600, 1601, 1715, 1716, 2324, 2888, 3156, 3157, 3158, 3159, 3160, 3273, 4620, 4621, 4682, 4683, 4684]. to cut; (mid.) to mourn, beat one's breast:– mourn (4), cut (2), mourned (1), mourning (1)

G3165 κόραξ *korax*, n. [1] raven, crow:– ravens (1)

G3166 κοράσιον *korasion*, n. [8] [√3025]. (little) girl:– girl (6), little girl (1), she[S] (1 [+3836])

G3167 κορβᾶν *korban*, l.[n.] [1] [→3168]. Corban, a gift dedicated to God:– corban (1)

G3168 κορβανᾶς *korbanas*, n. [1] [√3167]. temple treasury:– treasury (1)

G3169 Κόρε *Kore*, n. pr. [1] Korah, "*shaven, bald*":– Korah's (1)

G3170 κορέννυμι *korennymi*, v. [2] (pass.) to be filled to the full, have enough:– eaten as much as wanted (1 [+5575]), have all want (1 [+1639])

G3171 Κορίνθιος *Korinthios*, n. pr. g. [2] [√3172]. Corinthian:– Corinthians (2)

G3172 Κόρινθος *Korinthos*, n. pr. [6] [→3171]. Corinth, "*decoration*":– Corinth (6)

G3173 Κορνήλιος *Kornēlios*, n. pr. [8] Cornelius, "*of a horn*":– Cornelius (8)

G3174 κόρος *koros*, n. [1] cor (dry measure between ten and twelve bushels):– thousand bushels (1 [+1669])

G3175 κοσμέω *kosmeō*, v. [10] [√3180]. to make beautiful, decorate, dress; trim (a lamp); (pass.) to put in order; be adorned, decorated, beautifully dressed:– put in order (2), adorn (1), adorned (1), adorning (1), beautifully dressed (1), decorate (1), decorated (1), make attractive (1), trimmed (1)

G3176 κοσμικός *kosmikos*, a. [2] [√3180]. earthly, worldly:– earthly (1), worldly (1)

G3177 κόσμιος *kosmios*, a. [2] [√3180]. respectable, honorable:– modestly (1), respectable (1)

G3178 κοσμίως *kosmiōs*, adv. Not used in NIVEBC. [√3180]. modestly

G3179 κοσμοκράτωρ *kosmokratōr*, n. [1] [√3180 + 3197]. (pl.) powers of the world:– powers of world (1)

G3180 κόσμος *kosmos*, n. [186] [→1186, 1714, 3152, 3153, 3175, 3176, 3177, 3178, 3179, 5172]. world: earth, world system, whole universe; adornment. In some contexts, the world is simply the place where people live, in other contexts (especially in John), the world is a system opposed to God:– world (174), its[S] (2 [+3836]), adornment (1), earth (1), its[S] (1), material (1), sky (1), things of the world (1), whole universe (1), worldly (1), world's (1), NDT (1)

G3181 Κούαρτος *Kouartos*, n. pr. [1] Quartus, "*fourth [born]*":– Quartus (1)

G3182 κοῦμ *koum*, l.[v.] [1] [→3183]. koum (Aramaic: stand up!):– koum (1)

G3183 κοῦμι *koumi*, l.[v.] Not used in NIVEBC. [√3182]. koumi (Aramaic: stand up!)

G3184 κουστωδία *koustōdia*, n. [3] guard:– guard (2), guards (1)

G3185 κουφίζω *kouphizō*, v. [1] to lighten, make lighter:– lightened (1)

G3186 κόφινος *kophinos*, n. [6] basket of various sizes and considered typical of the Jews:– basketfuls (2), basketfuls (2 [+4441]), basketfuls (1 [+4445]), baskets (1)

G3187 κράβαττος *krabattos*, n. [11] [→3188]. bed, (sleeping) mat:– mat (8), mats (2), bedridden (1 [+2879, 2093])

G3188 κράββατος *krabbatos*, n. Not used in NIVEBC. [√3187]. bed, (sleeping) mat

G3189 κράζω *krazō*, v. [56] [→371, 372, 2136, 3198, 3199]. call out, cry out, shout, exclaim:– shouted (15), cried out (9), shouting (8), called out (3), cry out (3), crying out (3), called (1), calling out (1), calls out (1), cried (1), cried out (1 [+5889, 3489]), cries out (1), cry (1), exclaim (1), exclaimed (1), gave a shout (1 [+5889]), in a loud voice (1), screams (1), shout (1), shrieked (1), yelling (1)

G3190 κραιπάλη *kraipalē*, n. [1] dissipation:– carousing (1)

G3191 κρανίον *kranion*, n. [4] [→638, 2839]. skull:– skull (4)

G3192 κράσπεδον *kraspedon*, n. [5] edge, border, hem; tassel:– edge (4), tassels on garments (1)

G3193 κραταιός *krataios*, a. [1] [√3197]. mighty, powerful:– mighty (1)

G3194 κραταιόω *krataioō*, v. [4] [√3197]. (pass.) to be strong, become strong:– strong (3), strengthen (1 [+1443])

G3195 κρατέω *krateō*, v. [47] [√3197]. to arrest, seize into custody; to take, grab, hold onto, obtain; (pass.) to be kept from, held:– arrest (8), took (5), arrested (4), seized (4), hold on to (2), hold to (2), clasped (1), connection (1), grabbed (1), have arrested (1), held on (1), hold fast (1), hold firmly (1), hold on (1), holding back (1), holding on to (1), holding to (1), holds (1), kept (1), kept from (1 [+3590]), not forgive (1), not forgiven (1), observe (1), opportunity (1 [+4606]), remain true (1), take charge of (1), take hold (1), take hold of (1)

G3196 κράτιστος *kratistos*, a. [4] [√3197]. most excellent, "your Excellency":– most excellent (3), excellency (1)

G3197 κράτος *kratos*, n. [12] [→202, 203, 1602, 1603, 1604, 3179, 3193, 3194, 3195, 3196, 3201, 3202, 4120, 4331; cf. 2846]. power, strength:– power (7), might (2), mighty (2), mighty deeds (1)

G3198 κραυγάζω *kraugazō*, v. [8] [√3189]. to shout, cry out:– shouted (3), shouting (3), called (1), cry out (1)

G3199 κραυγή *kraugē*, n. [6] [√3189]. crying out, shouting, verbal brawling:– brawling (1), cries (1), cry (1), crying (1), uproar (1), voice (1)

G3200 κρέας *kreas*, n. [2] meat:– meat (2)

G3201 κρείσσων *kreissōn*, a. Not used in NIVEBC. [√3197]. better, superior, greater

G3202 κρείττων *kreittōn*, a. [19] [√3197]. better, superior, greater:– better (14), superior (2), better (1 [+3437]), good (1), greater (1)

G3203 κρεμάννυμι *kremannymi*, v. [7] [→1717, 2889, 3204]. to hang on, hang upon:– hanging (3), hung (2), hang (1), have hung (1)

G3204 κρημνός *krēmnos*, n. [3] [√3203]. steep bank, cliff:– steep bank (3)

G3205 Κρής *Krēs*, n. pr. g. [2] [→3207]. Cretan:– Cretans (2)

G3206 Κρήσκης *Krēskēs*, n. pr. [1] Crescens, "*increasing*":– Crescens (1)

G3207 Κρήτη *Krētē*, n. pr. [5] [√3205]. Crete:– Crete (5)

G3208 κριθή *krithē*, n. [1] [→3209]. barley; barley flour was used in the preparation of cheaper kinds of bread:– barley (1)

G3209 κρίθινος *krithinos*, a. [2] [√3208]. made of barley (flour):– barley (2)

G3210 κρίμα *krima*, n. [27] [√3212]. judgment, condemnation; sentence, punishment:– judgment (13), condemnation (3), punished (2 [+3284]), judge (1), judged (1 [+3284]), judgments (1), lawsuits (1), penalty (1), punishment (1), sentence (1), sentenced (1), the same way[S] (1)

G3211 κρίνον *krinon*, n. [2] lily:– flowers (1), wild flowers (1)

G3212 κρίνω *krinō*, v. [114] [→88, 95, 185, 373, 374, 503, 537, 645, 646, 647, 850, 896, 1359, 1360, 1464, 1605, 1637, 2137, 2890, 2891, 2892, 3210, 3213, 3215, 3216, 3217, 4622, 5173, 5347, 5693, 5694, 5695; cf. 1637]. to decide, consider, as preferring one thing over another or determining the correctness of a matter; by extension: to judge, pass judgment on, condemn in a legal sense:– judge (39), judged (13), judges (9), condemn (5), condemned (5), decided (5), judging (4), pass judgment (4), consider (3), considers (2), judgment (2), on trial (2), stand trial (2), come under judgment (1), condemning (1), convinced (1), decision (1), judgments (1), made up (1), made up mind (1), make up mind (1), passed judgment (1), passing judgment (1), punish (1), reached (1), resolved (1), stand on trial (1), stands condemned (1), sue (1), take for judgment (1), takes to court (1 [+3552]), tried (1)

G3213 κρίσις *krisis*, n. [47] [√3212]. judgment (human or divine), justice, the concept of determining the correctness of a matter; negatively, punishment, condemnation:– judgment (29), justice (5), condemned (2), judge (2 [+4472]), judgments (2), condemn (1 [+2214]), condemned (1 [+5679, 4406]), correctly (1 [+1465]), decisions (1), doom (1), judged (1 [+1650, 2262]), verdict (1)

G3214 Κρίσπος *Krispos*, n. pr. [2] Crispus, "*curled*":– Crispus (2)

G3215 κριτήριον *kritērion*, n. [3] [√*3212*]. court of law; legal dispute, lawsuit:– court (1), disputes (1), judge (1)

G3216 κριτής *kritēs*, n. [19] [√*3212*]. judge:– judge (14), judges (4), sitting in judgment (1)

G3217 κριτικός *kritikos*, a. [1] [√*3212*]. able to discern or judge:– judges (1)

G3218 κρούω *krouō*, v. [9] to knock (on a gate or door):– knock (3), knocks (3), knocking (2), knocked (1)

G3219 κρύπτη *kryptē*, n. [1] [√*3221*]. hidden place:– place hidden (1)

G3220 κρυπτός *kryptos*, a. [17] [√*3221*]. hidden, unseen, secret:– secret (7), hidden (5), secrets (2), inner (1), inwardly (1 [+*1877, 3836*]), unseen (1 [+*1877, 3836*])

G3221 κρύπτω *kryptō*, v. [18] [→*648, 649, 1606, 3219, 3220, 3224, 3225, 3226, 4332*]. to hide:– hidden (9), hid (7), hide (1), secretly (1)

G3222 κρυσταλλίζω *krystallizō*, v. [1] [√*3223*]. to be clear as crystal:– clear as crystal (1)

G3223 κρύσταλλος *krystallos*, n. [2] [→*3222*]. rock crystal; some translate "ice":– crystal (2)

G3224 κρυφαῖος *kryphaios*, a. [2] [√*3221*]. hidden, unseen, secret:– secret (1), unseen (1 [+*1877, 3836*])

G3225 κρυφῇ *kryphē*, adv. [1] [√*3221*]. in secret:– secret (1)

G3226 κρύφιος *kryphios*, a. Not used in NIVEBC. [√*3221*]. hidden, secret

G3227 κτάομαι *ktaomai*, v. [7] [→*3228, 3229, 3230*]. to get, gain, buy; take along; to control:– get (2), bought (1), buy (1), control (1), pay for (1), win (1)

G3228 κτῆμα *ktēma*, n. [4] [√*3227*]. wealth, possessions; piece of property, field:– wealth (2), piece of property (1), property (1)

G3229 κτῆνος *ktēnos*, n. [4] [√*3227*]. (domestic) animal: donkey, horse, cattle:– animals (1), cattle (1), donkey (1), horses (1)

G3230 κτήτωρ *ktētōr*, n. [1] [√*3227*]. (land) owner:– owned (1 [+*5639*])

G3231 κτίζω *ktizō*, v. [15] [→*3232, 3233, 3234*]. to create; (ptcp.) Creator:– created (11), creator (3), create (1)

G3232 κτίσις *ktisis*, n. [19] [√*3231*]. creation, created thing, creature; governmental institution:– creation (15), authority (1), created things (1), creature (1), world (1)

G3233 κτίσμα *ktisma*, n. [4] [√*3231*]. creature, created thing:– created (2), creature (1), creatures (1)

G3234 κτίστης *ktistēs*, n. [1] [√*3231*]. Creator:– creator (1)

G3235 κυβεία *kybeia*, n. [1] cunning, craftiness, trickery:– cunning (1)

G3236 κυβέρνησις *kybernēsis*, n. [1] [→*3237*]. administration; derived from a Greek verb meaning "to steer a ship, to guide," not found in the NT:– guidance (1)

G3237 κυβερνήτης *kybernētēs*, n. [2] [√*3236*]. sea captain, pilot:– pilot (1), sea captain (1)

G3238 κυκλεύω *kykleuō*, v. [1] [√*3241*]. to surround:– surrounded (1)

G3239 κυκλόθεν *kyklothen*, adv. [3] [√*3241*]. (all) around; from all sides:– all around (1), encircled (1), surrounding (1)

G3240 κυκλόω *kykloō*, v. [4] [√*3241*]. to surround: gather around, march around:– gathered around (2), marched around (1), surrounded (1)

G3241 κύκλῳ *kyklō*, adv. [8] [→*3238, 3239, 3240, 4333*]. all around, in a circle, surrounding:– around (3), surrounding (2), encircled (1), from village to village (1 [+*3836, 3267*]), in a circle (1)

G3242 κύλισμα *kylisma*, n. Not used in NIVEBC. [√*3244*]. wallowing, rolling

G3243 κυλισμός *kylismos*, n. [1] [√*3244*]. wallowing, rolling around:– wallowing (1)

G3244 κυλίω *kyliō*, v. [1] [→*375, 653, 3242, 3243, 4685*]. (mid.) to roll around:– rolled around (1)

G3245 κυλλός *kyllos*, a. Not used in NIVEBC. crippled, maimed€ [4]:– crippled (2), maimed (2)

G3246 κῦμα *kyma*, n. [5] [→*652, 1607*]. waves, surf:– waves (4), surf (1)

G3247 κύμβαλον *kymbalon*, n. [1] cymbal:– cymbal (1)

G3248 κύμινον *kyminon*, n. [1] cummin:– cumin (1)

G3249 κυνάριον *kynarion*, n. [4] [√*3264*]. (little or domesticated) dog:– dogs (4)

G3250 Κύπριος *Kyprios*, n. pr. g. [3] [√*3251*]. from Cyprus:– from Cyprus (3)

G3251 Κύπρος *Kypros*, n. pr. [5] [→*3250*]. Cyprus, "*copper*":– Cyprus (5)

G3252 κύπτω *kyptō*, v. [2] [→*376, 2893, 4160, 5174*]. to stoop down, bend down:– bent (1), stoop down (1)

G3253 Κυρεῖνος *Kyreinos*, n. pr. Not used in NIVEBC. [√*3256*]. Quirinius

G3254 Κυρηναῖος *Kyrēnaios*, n. pr. g. [6] [√*3255*]. from Cyrene:– from Cyrene (3), of Cyrene (2), Cyrene (1)

G3255 Κυρήνη *Kyrēnē*, n. pr. [1] [→*3254*]. Cyrene, "*wall*":– Cyrene (1)

G3256 Κυρήνιος *Kyrēnios*, n. pr. [1] [→*3253, 3260*]. Quirinius:– Quirinius (1)

G3257 κυρία *kyria*, n. [2] [√*3261*]. lady (female "lord"):– dear lady (1), lady (1)

G3258 κυριακός *kyriakos*, a. [2] [√*3261*]. pertaining to the Lord, the Lord's:– Lord's (2)

G3259 κυριεύω *kyrieuō*, v. [7] [√*3261*]. to lord over, be master of, have authority over, one who rules or exercises authority; note in some contexts there is an implication that the authority exercised is harsh:– lord it over (2), Lord (1), has authority over (1), has mastery over (1), lords (1), master (1)

G3260 Κυρίνιος *Kyrinios*, n. pr. Not used in NIVEBC. [√*3256*]. Quirinius

G3261 κύριος *kyrios*, n. [717] [→*2894, 3257, 3258, 3259, 3262; cf. 3263*]. lord, master. This can be a title of address to a person of higher status, "lord, sir"; a master of property or slaves; or a NT translation of the Hebrew 151 "Lord" or 3378 "LORD," that is "Yahweh," the proper name of God in the OT:– Lord (602), master (33), Lord's (31), sir (21), masters (7), master's (7), owner (6), lords (3), owners (3), he[S] (1 [+*3836*]), his majesty (1), owns (1 [+*1639*]), sirs (1)

G3262 κυριότης *kyriotēs*, n. [4] [√*3261*]. authority, dominion, power, lordship:– authority (2), dominion (1), powers (1)

G3263 κυρόω *kyroō*, v. [2] [→*218, 4623; cf. 3261*]. to reaffirm; to establish a covenant, ratify, validate:– duly established (1), reaffirm (1)

G3264 κύων *kyōn*, n. [5] [→*3249*]. dog:– dogs (4), dog (1)

G3265 κῶλον *kōlon*, n. [1] dead body, corpse:– bodies (1)

G3266 κωλύω *kōlyō*, v. [23] [→*219, 1361, 3134, 3136, 3143; cf. 1551*]. to hinder, stop, restrain, forbid; oppress; (pass.) to be prevented, kept from:– hinder (3), stop (3), forbid (2), stand in the way (2), hindered (1), keep from (1), kept from (1), kept from carrying out (1), opposes (1), permit (1 [+*3594*]), prevented (1), prevented from (1), restrained (1), stand in way (1), stops (1), told to stop (1), withhold (1)

G3267 κώμη *kōmē*, n. [27] [→*3268, 3269*]. village, town:– village (16), villages (8), from village to village (1 [+*3836, 3241*]), from village to village (1 [+*2848, 3836*]), town (1)

G3268 κωμόπολις *kōmopolis*, n. [1] [√*3267 + 4484*]. village, market town:– villages (1)

G3269 κῶμος *kōmos*, n. [3] [√*3267*]. orgy, revelry, carousing:– orgies (2), carousing (1)

G3270 κώνωψ *kōnōps*, n. [1] gnat, mosquito:– gnat (1)

G3271 Κῶς *Kōs*, n. pr. [1] Cos, "*summit*":– Kos (1)

G3272 Κωσάμ *Kōsam*, n. pr. [1] Cosam, "*diviner*":– Cosam (1)

G3273 κωφός *kōphos*, a. [14] [√*3164*]. unable to talk or speak, mute; deaf:– mute (6), deaf (4), could not talk (1), he[S] (1), man who was deaf (1), unable to speak (1)

G3274 λ *l*, letter. Not used in NIVEBC. letter of the Greek alphabet

G3275 λαγχάνω *lanchanō*, v. [4] to choose by lot, decide by lot; receive (by lot or divine will):– chosen by lot (1), decide by lot (1), received (1), shared (1 [+*3836, 3102*])

G3276 Λάζαρος *Lazaros*, n. pr. [15] Lazarus, "*one whom God helps*":– Lazarus (15)

G3277 λάθρα *lathra*, adv. [4] [√*3291*]. secretly, quietly:– quietly (2), aside (1), secretly (1)

G3278 λαῖλαψ *lailaps*, n. [3] storm, hurricane, whirlwind:– squall (2 [+*449*]), storm (1)

G3279 λακάω *lakaō*, v. [1] [√*cf. 3299*]. to burst open:– burst open (1 [+*3545*])

G3280 λακτίζω *laktizō*, v. [1] to kick:– kick (1)

G3281 λαλέω *laleō*, v. [296] [→*227, 228, 443, 654, 1362, 1718, 2895, 2896, 2897, 3282, 3651, 3652, 4493, 4688, 5196*]. to speak, talk:– speak (59), speaking (39), spoke (32), said (22), spoken (20), say (18), speaks (17), told (16), saying (7), talk (6), talking (5), tell (5), talked (4), proclaim (3), telling (3), declare (2), preached (2), proclaimed (2), promised (2), speaker (2), teach (2), God[S] (1 [+*3836*]), address (1), announced (1 [+*3284*]), boast (1 [+*5665*]), bring (1), bring[S] (1), declaring (1), distort the truth (1 [+*1406*]), insisted (1), lies (1 [+*3836, 6022*]), message (1), preaching (1), presenting (1), promises (1), says (1), speaking (1 [+*4839*]), speaks a word (1), speech (1), spoke about (1), spreading (1), tells (1), use language (1), utter (1), utter words (1), whispered (1), words spoken (1), NDT (2)

G3282 λαλιά *lalia*, n. [3] [√*3281*]. speech, a way of speaking, language:– accent (1), language (1), said (1)

G3283 λαμά *lama*, l.[pp.+p. inter.] Not used in NIVEBC. [→*3316*]. lama (Hebrew: why?)

G3284 λαμβάνω *lambanō*, v. [257] [→*377, 378, 455, 514, 516, 655, 719, 1287, 2138, 2325, 2326, 2327, 2898, 3331, 3335, 3561, 3562, 4161, 4624, 4647, 4689, 4691, 4692, 4719, 4720, 4721, 4722, 4723, 4724, 5197, 5221, 5227, 5269, 5696*]. to take, receive; (pass.) to be received, selected:– receive (40), received (38), took (38), take (22), accept (9), receives (7), taking (7), accepts (5), taken (4), bring (3), collect (3), married (3), take up (3), accepted (2), caught (2), gathered (2), get (2), marry (2), punished (2 [+*3210*]), receiving (2), seized (2), seizing (2), amazed (1 [+*1749*]), announced (1 [+*3281*]), appointed king (1 [+*993*]), be rewarded (1 [+*3635*]), bear children (1 [+*1650, 2856, 5065*]), become (1), choose (1), circumcised (1 [+*4364*]), collected (1), collectors (1), collects (1), commanded (1 [+*1953*]), decided (1 [+*5206*]), devised (1), did[S] (1), draw (1), draws (1), edified (1 [+*3869*]), encouraged (1 [+*2511*]), faced (1 [+*4278*]), filled with (1), forgetting (1 [+*3330*]), gets (1), given (1 [+*4123*]), got (1), guiding (1), had (1), have (1), judged (1 [+*3210*]), laid (1), made (1), made king (1 [+*3836, 993*]), made post bond (1 [+*3836, 2653, 4123*]), married (1 [+*1222*]), obtained (1), on authority (1 [+*2026*]), overtaken (1), picked up (1), plotted (1 [+*5206*]), put on (1), reminded (1 [+*5704*]), repayment (1), seizes (1), selected (1), show favoritism (1 [+*4725, 476*]), show partiality (1 [+*4725*]), succeeded (1 [+*1345*]), take over (1 [+*3836, 5536*]), takes (1), takes advantage (1), took up (1), tried (1 [+*4278*]), with (1), NDT (4)

G3285 Λάμεχ *Lamech*, n. pr. [1] Lamech:– Lamech (1)

G3286 λαμπάς *lampas*, n. [9] [√*3290*]. lamp, lantern, torch:– lamps (6), lamps (1 [+*4786*]), lanterns (1), torch (1)

G3287 λαμπρός *lampros*, a. [9] [√*3290*]. bright, shining, splendorous, elegant:– bright (2), fine (2), shining (2), clear (1), elegant (1), splendor (1)

G3288 λαμπρότης *lamprotēs*, n. [1] [√*3290*]. brightness:– brighter (1)

G3289 λαμπρῶς *lamprōs*, adv. [1] [√*3290*]. in luxury, splendidly:– lived in luxury (1 [+*2370*])

G3290 λάμπω *lampō*, v. [7] [→*1719, 2139, 3286, 3287, 3288, 3289, 4334, 5697*]. to give light, shine:– shine (2), shone (2), gives light (1), lights up (1), made shine (1)

G3291 λανθάνω *lanthanō*, v. [6] [→*237, 238, 239, 240, 242, 1720, 2140, 2144, 3277, 3330*]. to keep secret, escape notice, be hidden:– forget (2), escaped notice (1), go unnoticed (1), keep secret (1), without knowing it (1)

G3292 λαξευτός *laxeutos*, a. Not used in NIVEBC. cut in rock€ [1]:– cut in the rock (1)

G3293 Λαοδίκεια *Laodikeia*, n. pr. [6] [√*3295 + 1472*]. Laodicea:– Laodicea (6)

G3294 Λαοδικεύς *Laodikeus*, n. pr. g. [1] [√*3295 + 1472*]. Laodicean:– Laodiceans (1)

G3295 λαός *laos*, n. [141] [→*793, 3293, 3294, 3310, 3311, 3312, 3313, 3774, 3775*]. people, crowd; often denotes the people of God (either Israel or, by extension, the Christian church):– people (124), peoples (4), people's (3), crowd (2), assembled worshipers (1 [+*4436, 3836*]), band of people (1), crowd (1 [+*4436, 3836*]), in public (1 [+*1883, 3836*]), nations (1), public (1), them[S] (1 [+*3836*]), those[S] (1 [+*3836*])

G3296 λάρυγξ *larynx*, n. [1] throat:– throats (1)

G3297 Λασαία *Lasaia*, n. pr. [0] [→*3298*]. Lasea:– Fair Havens Lasea (0)

G3298 Λασέα *Lasea*, n. pr. Not used in NIVEBC. [√*3297*]. Lasea

G3299 λάσκω *laskō*, v. Not used in NIVEBC. [√*cf. 3279*]. to burst open

G3300 λατομέω *latomeō*, v. [2] to cut, hew (rock):– cut out (2)

G3301 λατρεία *latreia*, n. [5] [→*1629, 1630, 3302*]. worship, ministry, service (to God):– worship (2), ministry (1), service (1), temple worship (1)

G3302 λατρεύω *latreuō*, v. [21] [√*3301*]. to serve, minister (in religious duties):– serve (12), worship (4), minister (1), served (1), worshiped (1), worshiper (1), worshipers (1)

G3303 λάχανον *lachanon*, n. [4] plant, herb, vegetable:– garden plants (2), garden herbs (1), vegetables (1)

G3304 Λεββαῖος *Lebbaios*, n. pr. Not used in NIVEBC. [√*cf. 2497*]. Lebbaeus, "*[one near to] my heart*"

G3305 λεγιών *legiōn*, n. [4] legion, technically an army unit of 6,000 with 6,000 support troops. Twice in the NT it is the proper name of a collective of demons (Mk 5:9; Lk 8:30):– legion (3), legions (1)

G3306 λέγω *legō*, v. [2346] [→ *37, 155, 263, 381, 382, 406, 515, 517, 584, 664, 665, 1006, 1156, 1157, 1363, 1365, 1368, 1369, 1474, 1721, 1723, 1724, 1823, 1824, 1922, 2141, 2328, 2329, 2330, 2532, 2800, 2899, 2986, 3315, 3356, 3357, 3358, 3359, 3360, 3361, 3362, 3363, 3364, 3467, 3468, 3703, 3933, 4162, 4165, 4391, 4494, 4597, 4625, 4690, 5066, 5133, 5198, 5199, 5274, 5293, 5807, 5981, 6016; cf. 3933*]. say, said, the most general term for speaking in the NT, translated contextually with more specific words such as say, tell; ask, answer:– said (773), tell (213), say (190), asked (151), replied (94), told (92), saying (80), says (78), answered (50), called (27), spoken (19), ask (15), speak (15), telling (11), call (9), words (9), talking (8), claim (7), spoke (7), declared (6), declares (6), speaking (6), known as (5), talking about (5), asks (4), claimed (4), claims (4), continued (4), exclaimed (4), speaks (4), asking (3), called out (3 [*+2048, 5889*]), calls (3), claiming (3), meant (3), mention (3), name (3), ordered (3), shouting (3), spoke up (3), tells (3), added (2), addressed (2), calling (2), challenged (2), demanded (2), mean (2), means (2), objected (2), protested (2), said so (2), sent for (2 [*+5888*]), shouted (2), accuse (1), admit (1), advise (1), agree in what say (1 [*+3836, 899*]), announced (1), answer (1), assure (1 [*+2093, 237*]), at this (1 [*+4047*]), began to speak (1 [*+487, 3836, 5125*]), begged (1), boasted (1), boasts (1), call out (1), called out (1 [*+3489, 5889*]), charged (1), claim (1 [*+1571*]), claim to be (1 [*+1571*]), claiming (1 [*+1571*]), claims (1 [*+1571*]), commanded (1), commanding (1 [*+2848, 2198*]), continued[s] (1), cried (1), cried out (1), cry (1), cry out (1), directed (1), discuss (1), explain (1), grant (1), hard to make clear (1 [*+1549*]), have a saying (1), him[s] (1), in Greek (1 [*+1450*]), in the words of (1 [*+2777*]), inquired (1), insisted (1), insisted (1 [*+2196*]), is[s] (1), made statement (1 [*+4839*]), means (1 [*+1639*]), means (1 [*+3493*]), meant (1 [*+4309*]), message (1), named (1), one might even say (1 [*+6055, 2229*]), order (1), plea (1), pleading (1), prayed (1), praying (1), preach (1), present (1), promised (1), question (1), quote (1), referring (1), referring to (1), remarking (1), repeat (1 [*+4099*]), replied[s] (1), reply (1), respond (1), retorted (1), so-called (1), so-called (1 [*+6055*]), state (1), stated (1), take an example (1), talk (1), testified (1), thought (1), turned (1), urged (1), used[s] (1), using (1), using an example (1), warned (1), was[s] (1), welcome (1 [*+5897*]), welcomes (1 [*+5897*]), went on[s] (1), with that (1 [*+4047*]), with the news (1), with this (1 [*+4047*]), word (1), your own idea (1 [*+608, 4932*]), NDT (302)

G3307 λεῖμμα *leimma*, n. [1] [√*3309*]. remnant:– remnant (1)

G3308 λεῖος *leios*, a. Not used in NIVEBC. smooth, level€ [1]:– smooth (1)

G3309 λείπω *leipō*, v. [6] [→ *89, 90, 444, 657, 659, 1364, 1366, 1593, 1722, 2142, 2145, 2900, 2901, 2905, 3307, 3370, 4335, 5698, 5699, 5701*]. to lack, fall short:– have everything need (1 [*+3594*]), lack (1), lacking (1), lacks (1), left (1), NDT (1)

G3310 λειτουργέω *leitourgeō*, v. [3] [√*3295 + 2240*]. to perform religious duties; serve:– performs religious duties (1), share (1), worshiping (1)

G3311 λειτουργία *leitourgia*, n. [6] [√*3295 + 2240*]. religious service, ceremony; service, ministry, help:– service (2), ceremonies (1), help (1), ministry (1), perform (1)

G3312 λειτουργικός *leitourgikos*, a. [1] [√*3295 + 2240*]. ministering, engaged in holy service:– ministering (1)

G3313 λειτουργός *leitourgos*, n. [5] [√*3295 + 2240*]. servant, minister, one who cares for (another), often with a focus on a specific task or duty, which can be practical or spiritual:– servants (2), minister (1), serves (1), take care of (1)

G3314 λείχω *leichō*, v. Not used in NIVEBC. [→ *658, 2143, 4336*]. to lick

G3315 Λέκτρα *Lektra*, n. pr. Not used in NIVEBC. [√*3306*]. Lectra

G3316 λεμά *lema*, l.[pp.+p. inter.] [2] [√*3283*]. lama (Aramaic: why?):– lema (2)

G3317 λέντιον *lention*, n. [2] towel, likely made of linen:– towel (2)

G3318 λεπίς *lepis*, n. [1] [→ *3319, 3320, 3321*]. scale, flake:– scales (1)

G3319 λέπρα *lepra*, n. [4] [√*3318*]. leprosy:– leprosy (4)

G3320 λεπρός *lepros*, a. [9] [√*3318*]. leprous; (n.) leper:– leper (2), man with leprosy (2), those who have leprosy (2), had leprosy (1), have leprosy (1), with leprosy (1)

G3321 λεπτός *leptos*, a. [3] [√*3318*]. very small copper coin, worth about 1/128th of a denarius (a day's wage):– very small copper coins (2), penny (1)

G3322 Λευί *Leui*, n. pr. [8] [→ *3323, 3324, 3325*]. Levi, "[perhaps] *wild cow* or *person pledged for a debt or vow*":– Levi (8)

G3323 Λευίς *Leuis*, n. pr. Not used in NIVEBC. [√*3322*]. Levi, "[perhaps] *wild cow* or *person pledged for a debt or vow*"

G3324 Λευίτης *Leuitēs*, n. pr. g. [3] [√*3322*]. Levite:– Levite (2), Levites (1)

G3325 Λευιτικός *Leuitikos*, a. pr. g. [1] [√*3322*]. Levitical:– Levitical (1)

G3326 λευκαίνω *leukainō*, v. [2] [√*3328*]. to bleach, whiten:– bleach (1), made white (1)

G3327 λευκοβύσσινος *leukobyssinos*, a. Not used in NIVEBC. [√*3328 + 1116*]. white linen

G3328 λευκός *leukos*, a. [25] [→ *3326, 3327*]. white; bright, gleaming:– white (23), bright (1), ripe (1)

G3329 λέων *leōn*, n. [9] lion:– lion (5), lions (3), lion's (1)

G3330 λήθη *lēthē*, n. [1] [√*3291*]. forgetfulness:– forgetting (1 [*+3284*])

G3331 λῆμψις *lēmpsis*, n. [1] [√*3284*]. receiving:– receiving (1)

G3332 ληνός *lēnos*, n. [5] [→ *5700*]. winepress:– winepress (3), press (1), winepress (1 [*+3885*])

G3333 λῆρος *lēros*, n. [1] nonsense, idle talk:– nonsense (1)

G3334 λῃστής *lēstēs*, n. [15] [→ *798*]. robber, bandit; rebel, revolutionary; this word is derived from the Greek verb, "to practice robbery or piracy," not found in the NT:– robbers (6), leading a rebellion (3), rebels (3), bandits (1), robber (1), taken part in an uprising (1 [*+1639*])

G3335 λῆψις *lēpsis*, n. Not used in NIVEBC. [√*3284*]. receiving

G3336 λίαν *lian*, adv. [12] [→ *5663*]. very much, greatly, completely:– great (3), very (3), completely (1 [*+1666, 4356*]), dazzling (1 [*+5118*]), furious (1 [*+2597*]), greatly (1), so (1), strongly (1)

G3337 λίβανος *libanos*, n. [2] [→ *3338*]. frankincense, incense, an aromatic resinous gum:– frankincense (2)

G3338 λιβανωτός *libanōtos*, n. [2] [√*3337*]. censer (bowl for burning incense):– censer (2)

G3339 Λιβερτῖνος *Libertinos*, n. pr. [1] Freedman, "*Freedman*":– freedmen (1)

G3340 Λιβύη *Libyē*, n. pr. [1] [√*cf. 3341*]. Libya:– Libya (1)

G3341 Λιβυστῖνος *Libystinos*, n. pr. g. Not used in NIVEBC. [√*cf. 3340*]. Libyan

G3342 λιθάζω *lithazō*, v. [9] [√*3345*]. to stone:– stone (5), pelted with stones (1), put to death by stoning (1), stoned (1), stoning (1)

G3343 λίθινος *lithinos*, a. [3] [√*3345*]. made of stone:– stone (3)

G3344 λιθοβολέω *lithoboleō*, v. [7] [√*3345 + 965*]. to throw stones:– stone (4), stoned (1), stoned to death (1), stoning (1)

G3345 λίθος *lithos*, n. [59] [→ *2902, 3342, 3343, 3344, 3346, 5994*]. stone, boulder; this can refer to stone as a material or substance, and to a stone as a piece of rock. A "precious stone" is a "gem.":– stone (35), stones (14), another[s] (4), jasper (2 [*+2618*]), boulder (1), jewel (1), millstone (1 [*+3683*]), stone's (1)

G3346 λιθόστρωτος *lithostrōtos*, a. [1] [√*3345 + 5143*]. (n.) stone pavement; translated in the NIV as a place name:– stone pavement (1)

G3347 λικμάω *likmaō*, v. [2] to crush:– crushed (2)

G3348 λιμήν *limēn*, n. [2] [→ *2816, 3349*]. harbor:– harbor (2)

G3349 λίμνη *limnē*, n. [11] [√*3348*]. lake:– lake (10), water's (1)

G3350 λιμός *limos*, n. [12] hunger, famine, starvation:– famine (7), famines (3), hunger (1), starving (1)

G3351 λίνον *linon*, n. [2] linen (garment); wick of a lamp:– linen (1), wick (1)

G3352 Λίνος *Linos*, n. pr. [1] Linus:– Linus (1)

G3353 λιπαρός *liparos*, a. Not used in NIVEBC. costly, rich; (n.) riches€ [1]:– luxury (1)

G3354 λίτρα *litra*, n. [2] (Roman) pound (about 12 oz. or 327 gr.):– about a pint (1), seventy-five pounds (1 [*+1669*])

G3355 λίψ *lips*, n. [1] southwest:– southwest (1)

G3356 λογεία *logeia*, n. [2] [√*3306*]. collection:– collection (1), collections (1)

G3357 λογίζομαι *logizomai*, v. [40] [√*3306*]. to credit, count, reckon; regard, think, consider:– credited (10), think (4), consider (3), realize (2), reasoned (2), regard (2), regarded (2), claim (1), considered (1), count (1), count against (1), counting (1), credit (1), credits (1), discredited (1 [*+1650, 4029*]), expect (1), held (1), keeps record (1), maintain (1), numbered (1), regards (1), think about (1)

G3358 λογικός *logikos*, a. [2] [√*3306*]. spiritual, logical:– spiritual (1), true and proper (1)

G3359 λόγιον *logion*, n. [4] [√*3306*]. (pl.) words, sayings, oracles:– words (3), word (1)

G3360 λόγιος *logios*, a. [1] [√*3306*]. learned, eloquent:– learned (1)

G3361 λογισμός *logismos*, n. [2] [√*3306*]. thought; argument, reasoning:– arguments (1), thoughts (1)

G3362 λογομαχέω *logomacheō*, v. [1] [√*3306 + 3480*]. to quarrel about words:– quarreling about words (1)

G3363 λογομαχία *logomachia*, n. [1] [√*3306 + 3480*]. quarrel about words:– quarrels about words (1)

G3364 λόγος *logos*, n. [330] [√*3306*]. word, spoken or written, often with a focus on the content of a communication (note the many contextual translations in NIV); matter, thing. "The Word" is a title of Christ (Jn 1:1), emphasizing his own deity and communication of who God is and what he is like:– word (121), words (53), message (30), saying (10), teaching (8), account (7), speech (6), news (4), question (4), what[s] (4 [*+3836*]), command (3), said (3), say (3), this[s] (3 [*+3836*]), word of mouth (3), accounts (2), instruction (2), matter (2), preaching (2), speaker (2), talk (2), talking (2), thing (2), this[s] (2 [*+3836, 4047*]), what said (2), account (1 [*+625*]), appearance (1), book (1), conversation (1), eloquence (1), eloquence (1 [*+5667*]), except for (1 [*+4211*]), flattery (1 [*+3135*]), gospel (1), grievance (1), heard (1), mean (1 [*+1639, 3836, 4047*]), ministry (1), nothing (1 [*+4029*]), proposal (1), questions (1), reason (1), reasonable (1 [*+2848*]), reply (1), report (1), rumor (1), said (1 [*+1328*]), sentence (1), something said (1), speak (1), speaking (1), spreading (1 [*+4472*]), stated (1), statement (1), stories (1), story (1), teachings (1), tell (1), testimony (1 [*+3455*]), things (1), this[s] (1), this[s] (1 [*+4047, 3836*]), told (1 [*+550, 3836, 4047*]), took at word (1 [*+4409, 3836*]), truths (1), what say (1), which[s] (1 [*+3836, 899*]), why (1 [*+5515*]), NDT (5)

G3365 λόγχη *lonchē*, n. [1] spear, lance:– spear (1)

G3366 λοιδορέω *loidoreō*, v. [4] [√*3368*]. to insult, curse:– cursed (1), hurled insults (1), hurled insults at (1), insult (1)

G3367 λοιδορία *loidoria*, n. [3] [√*3368*]. insult, slander, verbal abuse:– insult (2), slander (1)

G3368 λοίδορος *loidoros*, n. [2] [→ *518, 3366, 3367*]. slanderer, verbal abuser:– slanderer (1), slanderers (1)

G3369 λοιμός *loimos*, n. & a. Not used in NIVEBC. pestilence; troublemaker, public menace€ [2]:– pestilences (1), troublemaker (1)

G3370 λοιπός *loipos*, a. [55] [√*3309*]. remaining, left over, the rest; in some contexts a marker for a conclusion, "finally," or an adverb of time, "from now on," or "henceforth":– rest (15), other (11), others (9), else (3), finally (2 [*+3836*]), finally (2), from now on (2 [*+3836*]), still (2 [*+3836*]), beyond that (1), everyone else (1), further (1 [*+3836*]), further (1), now (1), now (1 [*+6045*]), remains (1), since that time (1 [*+3836*]), survivors (1)

G3371 Λουκᾶς *Loukas*, n. pr. [3] [√*3372*]. Luke:– Luke (3)

G3372 Λούκιος *Loukios*, n. pr. [2] [→ *3371*]. Lucius:– Lucius (2)

G3373 λουτρόν *loutron*, n. [2] [√*3374*]. washing, bath:– washing (2)

G3374 λούω *louō*, v. [5] [→ *666, 3373*]. to wash, have a bath:– washed (4), had a bath (1)

G3375 Λύδδα *Lydda*, n. pr. [3] Lydda:– Lydda (3)

G3376 Λυδία *Lydia*, n. pr. [2] Lydia:– Lydia (1), Lydia's (1)

G3377 Λυκαονία *Lykaonia*, n. pr. [1] [→ *3378*]. Lycaonia:– Lycaonian (1)

G3378 Λυκαονιστί *Lykaonisti*, adv. pr. [1] [√*3377*]. in (the) Lycaonian (language):– in the Lycaonian language (1)

G3379 Λυκία *Lykia*, n. pr. [1] Lycia:– Lycia (1)

G3380 λύκος *lykos*, n. [6] wolf:– wolves (4), wolf (2)

G3381 λυμαίνω *lymainō*, v. [1] to destroy, damage, ruin:– destroy (1)

G3382 λυπέω *lypeō*, v. [26] [√*3383*]. (act.) to cause sorrow, grief; (pass.) to be sorrowful, sad, distressed:– grieve (5), sad (3), sorrowful (3), distressed (2), grieved (2), hurt (2), sorrow (2), caused grief (1), caused sorrow (1), grief (1), made sorry (1), outraged (1 [*+5379*]), saddened (1), suffer grief (1)

G3383 λύπη *lypē*, n. [16] [→ *267, 3382, 4337, 5200*]. sorrow, grief, pain:– sorrow (7), grief (2), pain (2), distressed (1), painful (1), painful (1 [*+1877*]), reluctantly (1 [*+1666*]), time of grief (1)

G3384 **Λυσανίας** ***Lysanias***, n. pr. [1] Lysanias:– Lysanias (1)

G3385 **Λυσίας** ***Lysias***, n. pr. [2] Lysias:– Lysias (2)

G3386 **λύσις** ***lysis***, n. [1] [√*3395*]. divorce:– released (1)

G3387 **λυσιτελέω** ***lysiteleō***, v. [1] [√*3395* + *5465*]. to be advantageous, (imper. form) it is better:– better (1)

G3388 **Λύστρα** ***Lystra***, n. pr. [6] Lystra:– Lystra (6)

G3389 **λύτρον** ***lytron***, n. [2] [√*3395*]. ransom, the price of release, thus making redemption possible:– ransom (2)

G3390 **λυτρόω** ***lytroō***, v. [3] [√*3395*]. to redeem, free a slave by paying a ransom; from the base meaning of slave redemption in the marketplace comes the figure of sinners redeemed by God from slavery to sin and death:– redeem (2), redeemed (1)

G3391 **λύτρωσις** ***lytrōsis***, n. [3] [√*3395*]. redemption, ransoming, releasing:– redemption (2), redeemed (1 [+*4472*])

G3392 **λυτρωτής** ***lytrōtēs***, n. [1] [√*3395*]. deliverer, redeemer:– deliverer (1)

G3393 **λυχνία** ***lychnia***, n. [12] [√*3394*]. lampstand (not a candlestick):– lampstands (6), stand (4), lampstand (2)

G3394 **λύχνος** ***lychnos***, n. [14] [→*3393*]. lamp, usually of clay or metal, with olive oil to fuel its wick (not a candle):– lamp (12), lamps (1), light (1)

G3395 **λύω** ***lyō***, v. [42] [→*186, 269, 385, 386, 519, 667, 668, 1370, 1725, 2146, 2147, 2906, 2907, 3386, 3387, 3389, 3390, 3391, 3392, 4166, 4167, 4168*]. to loose, release, untie; to break, destroy:– untie (8), untying (4), destroyed (3), released (3), destroy (2), loose (2), loosed (2), set free (2), take off (2), break (1), breaking (1), broken (1), broken to pieces (1), destruction (1), dismissed (1), free (1), freed (1), freeing (1), loosened (1), release (1), set aside (1), sets aside (1), untied (1)

G3396 **Λωΐς** ***Lōis***, n. pr. [1] Lois, "[perhaps] *more desirable, better*":– Lois (1)

G3397 **Λώτ** ***Lōt***, n. pr. [4] Lot:– Lot (3), Lot's (1)

G3398 **μ** ***m***, letter. Not used in NIVEBC. letter of the Greek alphabet

G3399 **Μάαθ** ***Maath***, n. pr. [1] Maath, "*to be small*":– Maath (1)

G3400 **Μαγαδάν** ***Magadan***, n. pr. [1] Magadan:– Magadan (1)

G3401 **Μαγδαλά** ***Magdala***, n. pr. Not used in NIVEBC. [√*cf. 3402*]. Magdala

G3402 **Μαγδαληνή** ***Magdalēnē***, n. pr. g. [12] [√*cf. 3401*]. Magdalene, "*from Magdala*":– Magdalene (12)

G3403 **Μαγεδών** ***Magedōn***, n. pr. Not used in NIVEBC. [√*cf. 762*]. Megiddo

G3404 **μαγεία** ***mageia***, n. [1] [√*3405*]. magic:– sorcery (1)

G3405 **μαγεύω** ***mageuō***, v. [1] [→*3404, 3406, 3407*]. to practice sorcery, magic:– practiced sorcery (1)

G3406 **μαγία** ***magia***, n. Not used in NIVEBC. [√*3405*]. magic

G3407 **μάγος** ***magos***, n. [6] [√*3405*]. sorcerer; (pl.) Magi:– magi (4), sorcerer (2)

G3408 **Μαγώγ** ***Magōg***, n. pr. [1] Magog, "[perhaps] *land of Gog*":– Magog (1)

G3409 **Μαδιάμ** ***Madiam***, n. pr. [1] Midian:– Midian (1 [+*1178*])

G3410 **μαζός** ***mazos***, n. Not used in NIVEBC. [√*3466*]. breast

G3411 **μαθητεύω** ***mathēteuō***, v. [4] [√*3443*]. (act./tr.) to teach; to make a disciple; (pass./intr.) to become a disciple:– become a disciple (2), make disciples (1), won disciples (1)

G3412 **μαθητής** ***mathētēs***, n. [260] [√*3443*]. disciple, student, follower; a committed learner and follower, in the NT usually of Jesus Christ:– disciples (225), disciple (23), them[S] (3 [+*3836, 899*]), student (2), they[S] (2 [+*3836*]), followers (1), gentiles[S] (1), students (1), they[S] (1), NDT (1)

G3413 **μαθήτρια** ***mathētria***, n. [1] [√*3443*]. (female) disciple, student, follower:– disciple (1)

G3414 **Μαθθαῖος** ***Maththaios***, n. pr. [5] [→*3473*]. Matthew, "*gift of Yahweh*":– Matthew (5)

G3415 **Μαθθάτ** ***Maththat***, n. pr. [2] [→*3475*]. Matthat, "*gift of God*":– Matthat (2)

G3416 **Μαθθίας** ***Maththias***, n. pr. [2] [→*3476*]. Matthias, "*gift of Yahweh*":– Matthias (2)

G3417 **Μαθουσαλά** ***Mathousala***, n. pr. [1] Methuselah, "*man of the javelin*":– Methuselah (1)

G3418 **Μαϊνάν** ***Mainan***, n. pr. Not used in NIVEBC. [√*cf. 3527*]. Mainan

G3419 **μαίνομαι** ***mainomai***, v. [5] [→*1841, 3444, 3446*]. to rave, be insane, out of one's mind, to think or reason in an irrational manner manifested by erratic actions or lack of reasonable speech:– out of mind (3), insane (1), raving mad (1)

G3420 **μακαρίζω** ***makarizō***, v. [2] [→*3421, 3422*]. to call blessed; to consider blessed:– call blessed (1), count as blessed (1)

G3421 **μακάριος** ***makarios***, a. [50] [√*3420*]. blessed (receiving God's favor), fortunate, good (in a position of favor), happy (feelings associated with receiving God's favor):– blessed (44), good (4), fortunate (1), happier (1)

G3422 **μακαρισμός** ***makarismos***, n. [3] [√*3420*]. blessedness, joy:– blessedness (2), blessing (1)

G3423 **Μακεδονία** ***Makedonia***, n. pr. [22] [√*3424*]. Macedonia:– Macedonia (21), Macedonian (1)

G3424 **Μακεδών** ***Makedōn***, n. pr. g. [5] [→*3423*]. Macedonian, "*from Macedonia*":– Macedonians (2), Macedonian (1), from Macedonia (1), of Macedonia (1)

G3425 **μάκελλον** ***makellon***, n. [1] meat market, food market:– meat market (1)

G3426 **μακράν** ***makran***, adv. & pp.* [10] [√*3601*]. far away, distant, long way off:– far (5), far away (2), far off (1 [+*1650*]), long (1), some distance (1)

G3427 **μακρόθεν** ***makrothen***, adv. [14] [√*3601*]. from a distance, from far away:– distance (7), far off (3 [+*608*]), at a distance (2), far away (1 [+*608*]), long distance (1)

G3428 **μακροθυμέω** ***makrothymeō***, v. [10] [√*3601* + *2596*]. to have patience; to be patient; to exhibit internal and external control in a difficult circumstance, which control could exhibit itself by delaying an action:– patient (7), patiently waiting (1), putting off (1), waiting patiently (1)

G3429 **μακροθυμία** ***makrothymia***, n. [14] [√*3601* + *2596*]. patience, forbearance, internal and external control in a difficult circumstance, which control could exhibit itself by delaying an action:– patience (11), forbearance (1), patient (1), patiently (1)

G3430 **μακροθύμως** ***makrothymōs***, adv. [1] [√*3601* + *2596*]. patiently:– patiently (1)

G3431 **μακρός** ***makros***, a. [4] [√*3601*]. lengthy, long; distant, far away:– distant (2), lengthy (2)

G3432 **μακροχρόνιος** ***makrochronios***, a. [1] [√*3601* + *5989*]. pertaining to having a long life:– long life (1)

G3433 **μαλακία** ***malakia***, n. [3] [√*3434*]. sickness, ailment:– sickness (3)

G3434 **μαλακός** ***malakos***, a. [4] [→*3433*]. fine, soft; (n.) male prostitute, a male homosexual who is the passive sex partner:– fine clothes (2), fine (1), men who have sex with men (1 [+*780*])

G3435 **Μαλελεήλ** ***Maleleēl***, n. pr. [1] Mahalalel, "*praise of God [El]*":– Mahalalel (1)

G3436 **μάλιστα** ***malista***, adv. super. [12] [√*3437*]. especially:– especially (9), especially so (1), most (1), very (1)

G3437 **μᾶλλον** ***mallon***, adv. comp. [81] [→*3436*]. more, more than; rather, instead:– more (23), rather (13), all the more (7 [+*4498*]), instead (3), greater (2), instead of (2 [+*2445*]), more and more (2), actually (1), better (1 [+*2819*]), better (1 [+*3202*]), but (1 [+*1254*]), do so (1 [+*5968*]), especially (1), especially (1 [+*4359*]), even (1 [+*4531*]), even better (1), even more (1), every (1), greater than ever (1), happier (1 [+*5897*]), instead (1 [+*247, 4047*]), instead (1 [+*5539*]), less (1), more (1 [+*4355*]), more (1 [+*4358*]), more than that (1), much (1), on the contrary (1 [+*247, 4498*]), or (1 [+*2445*]), prefer (1), prefer (1 [+*2305*]), rather (1 [+*1254*]), rather (1 [+*1254*]), than (1 [+*2445*]), very (1), yet (1 [+*247*])

G3438 **Μάλχος** ***Malchos***, n. pr. [1] Malchus, "*king*":– Malchus (1)

G3439 **μάμμη** ***mammē***, n. [1] grandmother:– grandmother (1)

G3440 **μαμωνᾶς** ***mamōnas***, n. [4] wealth, assets:– money (2), wealth (2)

G3441 **Μαναήν** ***Manaēn***, n. pr. [1] Manaen, "*comforter*":– Manaen (1)

G3442 **Μανασσῆς** ***Manassēs***, n. pr. [3] Manasseh, "*one that makes to forget*":– Manasseh (3)

G3443 **μανθάνω** ***manthanō***, v. [25] [→*276, 2908, 3411, 3412, 3413, 5209*]. to learn, study, be instructed:– learn (10), learned (10), get into the habit (1), inquire about (1), instructed (1), learning (1), taught (1)

G3444 **μανία** ***mania***, n. [1] [√*3419*]. insanity, madness:– insane (1)

G3445 **μάννα** ***manna***, n. [4] manna, a food given by God to the generation of the Exodus: "the bread of heaven":– manna (4)

G3446 **μαντεύομαι** ***manteuomai***, v. [1] [√*3419*]. to fortune-tell, divine:– fortune-telling (1)

G3447 **μαραίνω** ***marainō***, v. [1] [→*277, 278*]. (pass.) to fade away, disappear:– fade away (1)

G3448 **μαράνα θά** ***marana tha***, l.[n.+v.] [1] [√*cf. 2495*]. maranatha (Aramaic: "Come, Lord!"):– come Lord (1)

G3449 **μαργαρίτης** ***margaritēs***, n. [9] pearl:– pearls (7), pearl (1), NDT (1)

G3450 **Μάρθα** ***Martha***, n. pr. [13] Martha, "*lady [female lord]*":– Martha (13)

G3451 **Μαρία** ***Maria***, n. pr. [54] [→*3452*]. Mary, "[perhaps] *beloved or plump*":– Mary (52), Mary's (2)

G3452 **Μαριάμ** ***Mariam***, n. pr. Not used in NIVEBC. [√*3451*]. Mary, "[perhaps] *beloved* or *plump*"

G3453 **Μᾶρκος** ***Markos***, n. pr. [8] Mark, "*[Latin] large hammer*":– mark (8)

G3454 **μάρμαρος** ***marmaros***, n. [1] marble:– marble (1)

G3455 **μαρτυρέω** ***martyreō***, v. [75] [√*3459*]. to testify, give testimony; commend, speak well of, vouch for:– testify (26), testifies (8), testified (7), commended (4), witness (3), declared (2), given[S] (2), spoke well (2), confirmed (1), gave this testimony (1), give testimony (1), given testimony (1), highly respected (1), known (1), pointed out (1), respected (1), showed that accepted (1), speak well of (1), spoke well of (1), spread the word (1), testified about (1), testifying (1), testimony (1), testimony (1 [+*3364*]), told about (1), vouch (1), warn (1), well known (1), well spoken of (1)

G3456 **μαρτυρία** ***martyria***, n. [37] [√*3459*]. testimony, evidence; (good) reputation:– testimony (30), bears testimony to (1), evidence (1), it[S] (1 [+*899, 3836*]), reputation (1), saying (1), statements (1), witness (1)

G3457 **μαρτύριον** ***martyrion***, n. [20] [√*3459*]. testimony, proof:– testimony (10), covenant law (2), witnesses (2), bear testimony (1 [+*609, 1650*]), testifies (1), testify (1 [+*625, 3836*]), testify (1 [+*1650, 1639*]), witness (1), witnessed (1)

G3458 **μαρτύρομαι** ***martyromai***, v. [5] [√*3459*]. to testify, declare; to insist on, urge:– declare (2), insist on (1), testify (1), urging (1)

G3459 **μάρτυς** ***martys***, n. [35] [→*282, 1371, 2148, 2909, 3455, 3456, 3457, 3458, 4626, 4753, 5210, 5296, 6018, 6019, 6020*]. witness, testimony; martyr (one who witnessed unto death):– witnesses (20), witness (10), bore testimony (1), martyr (1), testify (1), testify (1 [+*1639*]), testimony of witnesses (1)

G3460 **μασάομαι** ***masaomai***, v. [1] [√*3463*]. to gnaw, bite:– gnawed (1)

G3461 **μασθός** ***masthos***, n. Not used in NIVEBC. [√*3466*]. breast

G3462 **μασσάομαι** ***massaomai***, v. Not used in NIVEBC. [√*3463*]. to gnaw

G3463 **μαστιγόω** ***mastigoō***, v. [7] [→*669, 1726, 3460, 3462, 3464, 3465*]. to flog, whip, scourge; to punish, chastise:– flog (3), flogged (3), chastens (1)

G3464 **μαστίζω** ***mastizō***, v. [1] [√*3463*]. to flog, scourge:– flog (1)

G3465 **μάστιξ** ***mastix***, n. [6] [√*3463*]. flogging device, whip; suffering; disease, sickness:– suffering (2), diseases (1), flogged (1), flogging (1), sicknesses (1)

G3466 **μαστός** ***mastos***, n. [3] [→*3410, 3461*]. breast, chest:– breasts (1), chest (1), nursed (1 [+*2558*])

G3467 **ματαιολογία** ***mataiologia***, n. [1] [√*3469* + *3306*]. meaningless talk, empty talk:– meaningless talk (1)

G3468 **ματαιολόγος** ***mataiologos***, a. [1] [√*3469* + *3306*]. (n.) idle talker:– full of meaningless talk (1)

G3469 **μάταιος** ***mataios***, a. [6] [→*3467, 3468, 3470, 3471, 3472*]. worthless, futile, useless, empty:– futile (2), worthless (2), empty (1), useless (1)

G3470 **ματαιότης** ***mataiotēs***, n. [3] [√*3469*]. emptiness, futility, frustration:– empty (1), frustration (1), futility (1)

G3471 **ματαιόω** ***mataioō***, v. [1] [√*3469*]. (pass.) to become futile, given over to worthlessness:– futile (1)

G3472 **μάτην** ***matēn***, adv. [2] [√*3469*]. in vain, to no end:– in vain (2)

G3473 **Ματθαῖος** ***Matthaios***, n. pr. Not used in NIVEBC. [√*3414*]. Matthew, "*gift of Yahweh*"

G3474 **Ματθάν** ***Matthan***, n. pr. [2] Matthan, "*gift*":– Matthan (2)

G3475 **Ματθάτ** ***Matthat***, n. pr. Not used in NIVEBC. [√*3415*]. Mathat, "*gift*"

G3476 **Ματθίας** ***Matthias***, n. pr. Not used in NIVEBC. [√*3416*]. Matthias, "*gift of Yahweh*"

G3477 **Ματταθά** ***Mattatha***, n. pr. [1] Mattatha, "*gift*":– Mattatha (1)

G3478 **Ματταθίας** ***Mattathias***, n. pr. [2] Mattathias, "*gift of Yahweh*":– Mattathias (2)

G3479 **μάχαιρα** ***machaira***, n. [29] [√*3480*]. (short) sword:– sword (21), swords (7), sword (1 [+*5125*])

G3480 **μάχη** ***machē***, n. [4] [→*285, 1372, 2533, 2534, 2562, 2595, 3362, 3363, 3479, 3481*]. quarrel, conflict, fighting:– quarrels (3), conflicts (1)

G3481 **μάχομαι** ***machomai***, v. [4] [√*3480*]. to fight, quarrel, argue:– argue sharply (1), fighting (1), quarrel (1), quarrelsome (1)

G3482 **μεγαλαυχέω** ***megalaucheō***, v. Not used in NIVEBC. [√*3489 + 902*]. to become proud, boast

G3483 **μεγαλεῖος** ***megaleios***, a. [1] [√*3489*]. (pl. n.) wonders, mighty deeds:– wonders (1)

G3484 **μεγαλειότης** ***megaleiotēs***, n. [3] [√*3489*]. majesty, greatness, grandeur:– divine majesty (1), greatness (1), majesty (1)

G3485 **μεγαλοπρεπής** ***megaloprepēs***, a. [1] [√*3489 + 4560*]. majestic, magnificent:– majestic (1)

G3486 **μεγαλύνω** ***megalynō***, v. [8] [√*3489*]. to glorify, regard highly, praise, exalt; to lengthen, expand:– exalted (1), expand (1), glorifies (1), held in high honor (1), highly regarded (1), long (1), praising (1), shown great (1)

G3487 **μεγάλως** ***megalōs***, adv. [1] [√*3489*]. greatly:– greatly (1)

G3488 **μεγαλωσύνη** ***megalōsynē***, n. [3] [√*3489*]. majesty:– majesty (3)

G3489 **μέγας** ***megas***, a. [194] [→*3482, 3483, 3484, 3485, 3486, 3487, 3488, 3490, 3491, 3492, 3504, 3505*]. great; spatially: large; of quantity or degree: loud, intense, violent; of time: long (time); of position: great, important:– great (89), loud (31), large (10), greatest (5), severe (5), at the top of (4), completely (3), big (2), furious (2), high (2), high officials (2), huge (2), strong (2), terrified (2 [+*5828, 5832*]), violent (2), called out (1 [+*3306, 5889*]), complete (1), cried out (1 [+*3189, 5889*]), deeply (1), enormous (1), filled with (1), fury (1 [+*2596*]), gigantic (1), greatly astonished (1 [+*2513, 2512*]), grown up (1 [+*1181*]), intense (1), intensely (1), long (1), much (1), overcome (1 [+*5309*]), overjoyed (1 [+*5897, 5915, 5379*]), powerfully (1), profound (1), proud (1), richly (1), roar (1 [+*5889*]), shouted (1 [+*5888, 5889*]), shouted (1 [+*3836, 5889, 5774*]), shriek (1 [+*5888, 5889*]), shrieks (1 [+*1066, 5889*]), special (1), surprising (1), terrible (1), terror (1 [+*5832*]), tremendous (1 [+*5496*]), very (1)

G3490 **μέγεθος** ***megethos***, n. [1] [√*3489*]. greatness:– great (1)

G3491 **μεγιστάν** ***megistan***, n. [3] [√*3489*]. great man, prince, high official:– high officials (1), important people (1), princes (1)

G3492 **μέγιστος** ***megistos***, a. super. [1] [√*3489*]. very great:– very great (1)

G3493 **μεθερμηνεύω** ***methermēneuō***, v. [8] [√*3552 + 2257*]. to translate, give the meaning:– means (5 [+*1639*]), is (1 [+*1639*]), means (1), means (1 [+*3306*])

G3494 **μέθη** ***methē***, n. [3] [√*3501*]. drunkenness:– drunkenness (3)

G3495 **μεθιστάνω** ***methistanō***, v. Not used in NIVEBC. [√*3552 + 2705*]. to move, remove; bring, lead astray; (pass.) to lose, be discharged

G3496 **μεθίστημι** ***methistēmi***, v. [5] [√*3552 + 2705*]. to move, remove; bring, lead astray; (pass.) to lose, be discharged:– brought (1), led astray (1), lose (1 [+*1666*]), move (1), removing (1)

G3497 **μεθοδεία** ***methodeia***, n. [2] [√*3552 + 3847*]. scheming, craftiness, strategy:– schemes (1), scheming (1)

G3498 **μεθόριον** ***methorion***, n. Not used in NIVEBC. [√*3552 + 4000*]. boundary; (pl.) region

G3499 **μεθύσκω** ***methyskō***, v. [5] [√*3501*]. (pass.) to be or become drunk, intoxicated:– drunk (3), had too much to drink (1), intoxicated (1)

G3500 **μέθυσος** ***methysos***, n. [2] [√*3501*]. drunkard:– drunkard (1), drunkards (1)

G3501 **μεθύω** ***methyō***, v. [5] [→*287, 3494, 3499, 3500*]. to get drunk:– drunk (4), drunkards (1)

G3502 **μείγνυμι** ***meignymi***, v. [4] [→*3503, 3623, 3624, 5042, 5264*]. to mix, mingle:– mixed (3), glowing (1)

G3503 **μειγνύω** ***meignyō***, v. Not used in NIVEBC. [√*3502*]. to mix, mingle

G3504 **μειζότερος** ***meizoteros***, a. comp. Not used in NIVEBC. [√*3489*]. greater

G3505 **μείζων** ***meizōn***, a. comp. [48] [√*3489*]. greater, larger; older; louder; more:– greater (31), greatest (8), more (3), largest (2), all the louder (1), bigger (1), older (1), weightier (1)

G3506 **μέλας** ***melas***, a. Not used in NIVEBC. the color black; ink, made of soot or other carbon source mixed with oil or resin[s] [6]:– black (3), ink (3)

G3507 **Μελεά** ***Melea***, n. pr. [1] Melea:– Melea (1)

G3508 **μέλει** ***melei***, v. [10] [→*288, 294, 2149, 2150, 2151, 3509, 3520, 3564, 4627*]. (imper.) it is a care, it is a concern; (pers.) to trouble; to concern:– care (2), cares (2), swayed (2), about concerned (1), cared (1), showed concern (1), trouble (1)

G3509 **μελετάω** ***meletaō***, v. [2] [√*3508*]. to plot, think about, meditate on; to give oneself wholly to, practice, cultivate:– give yourself wholly (1), plot (1)

G3510 **μέλι** ***meli***, n. [4] [→*3511, 3512, 3513*]. honey:– honey (4)

G3511 **μελισσεῖον** ***melisseion***, n. Not used in NIVEBC. [√*3510*]. beehive

G3512 **μελισσῖον** ***melission***, n. Not used in NIVEBC. [√*3510*]. beehive

G3513 **μελίσσιος** ***melissios***, a. Not used in NIVEBC. [√*3510*]. pertaining to the bee, honeycomb

G3514 **Μελίτη** ***Melitē***, n. pr. [1] [→*3515*]. Malta:– Malta (1)

G3515 **Μελιτήνη** ***Melitēnē***, n. pr. Not used in NIVEBC. [√*3514*]. Malta

G3516 **μέλλω** ***mellō***, v. [109] to be about to, on the point of; to be destined, must; to intend to; (what is) to come, the future:– about to (21), going to (17), will (16), to come (8), would (7), coming (5), intend (3), later (3), future (2), intended to (2), wanting (2), was (2), about to be (1), am (1), as (1), close to (1), come (1), dawn (1 [+*2465, 1181*]), going to[s] (1), going to happen (1), later to (1), nearly (1), never (1 [+*3600*]), next (1 [+*1650, 3836*]), the future (1), to (1), to be (1), waiting for (1), was to (1), would be (1), yet will (1), NDT (2)

G3517 **μέλος** ***melos***, n. [34] part, member, limb:– part (8), members (6), parts (6), me (2 [+*3836, 1609*]), part of body (2), yourselves (2 [+*3836, 5148*]), each one[s] (1), member (1), nature (1), part of the body (1), parts of the body (1), unite (1 [+*4472*]), us (1 [+*3836, 1609*]), within (1 [+*1877, 3836*])

G3518 **Μελχί** ***Melchi***, n. pr. [2] Melki, "*my king*":– Melki (2)

G3519 **Μελχισέδεκ** ***Melchisedek***, n. pr. [8] Melchizedek, "*[my] king is Zedek [just]*":– Melchizedek (8)

G3520 **μέλω** ***melō***, v. Not used in NIVEBC. [√*3508*]. to care, be concerned; see also *3508*

G3521 **μεμβράνα** ***membrana***, n. [1] parchment, a fine animal leather specially prepared for use in making scrolls:– parchments (1)

G3522 **μέμφομαι** ***memphomai***, v. [2] [→*289, 290, 318, 320, 3523, 3524, 3664, 3699, 3700*]. to find fault with, blame:– blame (1), found fault with (1)

G3523 **μεμψίμοιρος** ***mempsimoiros***, a. [1] [√*3522*]. fault-finding, complaining:– faultfinders (1)

G3524 **μέμψις** ***mempsis***, n. Not used in NIVEBC. [√*3522*]. a reason for complaint

G3525 **μέν** ***men***, pt. aff. [180] [→*3528, 3529, 3530; cf. 3605*]. often untranslated; used with other particles to show contrast: on the one hand, one...or the other:– one (3 [+*4005*]), some (3 [+*3836*]), some (3 [+*4005*]), some (2 [+*4005*]), though (2), to be sure (2), as a result (1 [+*4036*]), as far as is concerned (1 [+*2848*]), certainly (1), even though (1 [+*1142*]), even though (1), fine (1), for (1), in the one case (1 [+*6045*]), inasmuch as (1 [+*2093, 4012, 4036*]), indeed (1), indeed (1 [+*3836*]), moreover (1 [+*1663*]), not only (1), one (1 [+*4005*]), one (1 [+*3836*]), one (1 [+*4005*]), one person (1 [+*4005*]), others (1 [+*3836*]), some (1 [+*3836*]), some (1), some (1 [+*4005*]), sometimes (1 [+*4047*]), the latter (1 [+*3836*]), NDT (142)

G3526 **Μενάμ** ***Menam***, n. pr. Not used in NIVEBC. Menam

G3527 **Μεννά** ***Menna***, n. pr. [1] [√*cf. 3418*]. Menna:– Menna (1)

G3528 **μενοῦν** ***menoun***, pt. [1] [√*3525 + 4036*]. rather, on the contrary:– rather (1)

G3529 **μενοῦνγε** ***menounge***, pt. [2] [√*3525 + 4036 + 1145*]. rather, on the contrary, indeed:– but (1), of course (1)

G3530 **μέντοι** ***mentoi***, pt. [8] [√*3525 + 5520*]. but, yet, nevertheless, really:– but (4), nevertheless (1), really (1), very (1), yet (1)

G3531 **μένω** ***menō***, v. [118] [→*388, 670, 1373, 1844, 2152, 2910, 3665, 4169, 4338, 4693, 5222, 5702, 5705*]. to stay, remain, live, dwell, abide; to be in a state that begins and continues, yet may or may not end or stop. "To abide in Christ" is to follow his example of a life obedient to the will of God:– remain (24), stay (14), lives (13), stayed (12), remains (11), continue (4), endures (3), live (3), enduring (2), living (2), remained (2), staying (2), be (1), before solds[s] (1), belong (1), belongs (1), continues (1), does[s] (1), dwell (1 [+*2400*]), facing (1), has place (1), hold (1), keep on (1), last (1), lasting (1), lasts (1), left (1), lived (1), not move (1 [+*810*]), residing (1), spend (1), spent (1), stand (1), stays (1), still (1), survives (1), waited (1), NDT (1)

G3532 **μερίζω** ***merizō***, v. [14] [√*3538*]. to give, assign; (mid.) to divide, share; (pass.) to be divided:– divided (9), assigned (2), distributed (1), divide (1), gave (1)

G3533 **μέριμνα** ***merimna***, n. [6] [→*291, 3534, 4628; cf. 3538*]. worry, concern, anxiety:– worries (3), anxieties (1), anxiety (1), concern (1)

G3534 **μεριμνάω** ***merimnaō***, v. [19] [√*3533*]. to worry, have anxiety, be concerned:– worry about (5), concerned about (4), worry (4), worrying (2), anxious (1), have concern (1), show concern (1), worried (1)

G3535 **μερίς** ***meris***, n. [5] [√*3538*]. district; part, share, what is common between:– district (1), in common (1), part (1), share (1), what[s] (1)

G3536 **μερισμός** ***merismos***, n. [2] [√*3538*]. dividing, separation; distribution, apportionment:– distributed (1), dividing (1)

G3537 **μεριστής** ***meristēs***, n. [1] [√*3538*]. arbiter:– arbiter (1)

G3538 **μέρος** ***meros***, n. [42] [→*1374, 1375, 3532, 3535, 3536, 3537, 4495, 5211; cf. 3533*]. part, share, portion; (pl.) district, region:– part (10), region (3), extent (2), parts (2), place (2), area (1), consigned (1), detail (1), district (1), in comparison with (1 [+*1877, 4047, 3836, 1641*]), interior (1 [+*541*]), matter (1), one[s] (1), one at a time (1 [+*324*]), piece (1), points (1), regions (1), share (1), share (1 [+*2095*]), share (1 [+*2400*]), shares (1), side (1), some (1 [+*1651*]), the rest (1 [+*5516*]), trade (1), while (1), with regard to (1 [+*1877*]), NDT (1)

G3539 **μεσάζω** ***mesazō***, v. Not used in NIVEBC. [√*3545*]. to be in the middle

G3540 **μεσημβρία** ***mesēmbria***, n. [2] [√*3545 + 2465*]. (of time) noon, midday; (of place) south:– noon (1), south (1)

G3541 **μεσιτεύω** ***mesiteuō***, v. [1] [√*3545*]. to confirm, guarantee:– confirmed (1)

G3542 **μεσίτης** ***mesitēs***, n. [6] [√*3545*]. mediator:– mediator (6)

G3543 **μεσονύκτιον** ***mesonyktion***, n. [4] [√*3545 + 3816*]. midnight:– midnight (3), at midnight (1)

G3544 **Μεσοποταμία** ***Mesopotamia***, n. pr. [2] [√*3545 + 4532*]. Mesopotamia, "*[land] between rivers*":– Mesopotamia (2)

G3545 **μέσος** ***mesos***, a. [58] [→*1845, 3539, 3540, 3541, 3542, 3543, 3544, 3546, 3547, 3548*]. middle, center, among; between; in front of, before:– among (10 [+*1877*]), middle (5), among (4 [+*1877*]), in (3 [+*1877*]), among (2 [+*1650, 3836*]), at the center of (2 [+*1877*]), from (2 [+*1666*]), in front of everyone (2 [+*1650, 3836*]), about noon (1 [+*2465*]), among (1), among (1 [+*324*]), at midnight (1 [+*3816*]), away (1 [+*1666, 3836*]), away from (1 [+*1666*]), before (1 [+*1650*]), before (1 [+*1877*]), before (1 [+*1650, 3836*]), before (1 [+*1877, 3836*]), before the group (1 [+*1877*]), between (1 [+*324*]), burst open (1 [+*3279*]), center (1), encircled by (1 [+*1877*]), fellowship (1), guests[s] (1), in (1), in two (1), into (1 [+*324*]), midnight (1 [+*3836, 3816*]), the border between (1 [+*1328*]), the way (1), there[s] (1 [+*1877*]), walked right through (1 [+*1451, 1328*]), with (1), with (1 [+*1877*]), NDT (1)

G3546 **μεσότοιχον** ***mesotoichon***, n. [1] [√*3545 + 5446*]. dividing wall:– dividing wall (1)

G3547 **μεσουράνημα** ***mesouranēma***, n. [3] [√*3545 + 4041*]. midair:– midair (3)

G3548 **μεσόω** ***mesoō***, v. [1] [√*3545*]. to be halfway through, at midpoint:– halfway through (1)

G3549 **Μεσσίας** ***Messias***, n. pr. [2] Messiah, Anointed One; see also *5986*, "*anointed*":– Messiah (2)

G3550 **μεστός** ***mestos***, a. [9] [→*3551*]. full:– full (5), full of (2), of (1), soaked (1)

G3551 **μεστόω** ***mestoō***, v. [1] [√*3550*]. (pass.) to be filled:– had too much (1)

G3552 **μετά** ***meta***, pp. [468] [→*292, 293, 294, 295, 2331, 3493, 3495, 3496, 3497, 3498, 3553, 3554, 3555, 3556, 3557, 3558, 3559, 3560, 3561, 3562, 3563, 3564, 3565, 3566, 3567, 3568, 3569, 3570, 3571, 3572, 3573, 3574, 3575, 3576, 3578, 3579, 3580, 3581, 3587, 5212*]. (gen.) with, among, a marker of association of various kinds and meanings; (acc.) after, later, a marker of time:– with (259), after (61), to (12), along with (9), against (7), among (7), companions (7 [+*3836*]), later (7), in (4), after (3 [+*3836*]), between (3), later (3 [+*4047*]), later (3 [+*4047*]), after (2 [+*3836*]), after (2 [+*3836*]), afterward (2 [+*4047*]), and (2), away (2), by (2), on (2), through (2), when (2 [+*3836*]), a week later (1 [+2465, 3893]), afterward (1 [+4047]), and as well (1), and then (1 [+2083, 4047]), as (1), as soon as (1), before very long (1 [+4024, 4498]), behind (1), boldly (1 [+4244]), bring (1), bringing (1 [+2400]), carrying (1), close behind (1), companions (1 [+1639]), completely (1 [+4246]), confidently (1 [+4244]), finally (1 [+4047]), first (1 [+3836]), foams at the mouth (1 [+931]), follow (1), followed (1 [+4344]), following (1), humiliated (1 [+158]), hurried (1 [+5082]), hurried (1 [+4513, 5082]), in a manner worthy of (1), involved in (1), is one of (1 [+199]), joyful (1 [+5915]), joyfully (1 [+5915]), other (1 [+4047]), posting (1), settle down (1 [+2484]), some time after this (1 [+4047]), some time later (1 [+4047]), takes to court (1 [+3212]), the next (1 [+1651]), together (1), together with (1), under (1), urgently (1 [+4498, 4155]), use (1), welcomed (1 [+1312, 1645]), when (1), when later (1), wholeheartedly (1 [+2334]), NDT (19)

G3553 μεταβαίνω *metabainō*, v. [12] [√3552 + 326]. to go on, leave, move from:– leave (3), left (2), move (2), crossed over (1), going on (1), move around (1), passed (1), went on (1)

G3554 μεταβάλλω *metaballō*, v. [1] [√3552 + 965]. (mid.) to change one's mind:– changed minds (1)

G3555 μετάγω *metagō*, v. [2] [√3552 + 72]. to turn, steer:– steered (1), turn (1)

G3556 μεταδίδωμι *metadidōmi*, v. [5] [√3552 + 1443]. to impart, share, contribute to needs:– share with (2), giving (1), impart (1), share (1)

G3557 μετάθεσις *metathesis*, n. [3] [√3552 + 5502]. removal, taking up; change, transformation:– changed (1), removing (1), taken (1)

G3558 μεταίρω *metairō*, v. [2] [√3552 + 149]. to move on, leave:– left (1), moved on (1)

G3559 μετακαλέω *metakaleō*, v. [4] [√3552 + 2813]. (mid.) to send for, summon, call to oneself:– for (2), send for (1), sent for (1 [+690])

G3560 μετακινέω *metakineō*, v. [1] [√3552 + 3075]. (pass.) to be moved, removed, shifted from:– move (1)

G3561 μεταλαμβάνω *metalambanō*, v. [7] [√3552 + 3284]. to share in, receive a share:– ate together (1 [+5575]), eat (1 [+5575]), find (1), receive a share (1), receives (1), share in (1), take (1)

G3562 μετάλημψις *metalēmpsis*, n. [1] [√3552 + 3284]. receiving, sharing with:– received (1)

G3563 μεταλλάσσω *metallassō*, v. [2] [√3552 + 248]. to exchange:– exchanged (2)

G3564 μεταμέλομαι *metamelomai*, v. [6] [√3552 + 3508]. (mid.) to regret, repent; (pass.) to be repentant, changed of mind, remorseful:– regret (2), change mind (1), changed mind (1), repent (1), seized with remorse (1)

G3565 μεταμορφόω *metamorphoō*, v. [4] [√3552 + 3671]. (pass.) to be transformed, transfigured, changed in form:– transfigured (2), transformed (2)

G3566 μετανοέω *metanoeō*, v. [34] [√3552 + 3808]. to repent, to change any or all of the elements composing one's life: attitude, thoughts, and behaviors concerning the demands of God for right living:– repent (26), repented (5), repents (2), NDT (1)

G3567 μετάνοια *metanoia*, n. [22] [√3552 + 3808]. change of mind, repentance, the state of changing any or all of the elements composing one's life: attitude, thoughts, and behaviors concerning the demands of God for right living; note that this state can refer to the foundational salvation event in Christ, or to on-going repentance in the Christian life:– repentance (19), change (1 [+5536, 2351]), repent (1), turn in repentance (1)

G3568 μεταξύ *metaxy*, adv. [9] [√3552 + 5250]. (spacial) between; (temporal) meanwhile, next:– between (6), meanwhile (1 [+1877, 3836]), next (1), NDT (1)

G3569 μεταπέμπω *metapempō*, v. [9] [√3552 + 4287]. to summon, send for:– sent for (5), bring back (1), come (1), for (1), transferred (1)

G3570 μεταστρέφω *metastrephō*, v. [2] [√3552 + 5138]. to pervert; to turn into, change:– pervert (1), turned (1)

G3571 μετασχηματίζω *metaschēmatizō*, v. [5] [√3552 + 5386]. (act.) to transform, change (the form); (mid.) to masquerade, disguise (oneself):– applied (1), masquerade (1), masquerades (1), masquerading (1), transform (1)

G3572 μετατίθημι *metatithēmi*, v. [6] [√3552 + 5502]. to change (from one place or position to another); to bring back; to take away:– brought back (1), changed (1), deserting (1), pervert (1), taken away (1), taken from (1)

G3573 μετατρέπω *metatrepō*, v. [1] [√3552 + 5572]. (pass.) to be changed, turned:– change (1)

G3574 μεταφυτεύω *metaphyteuō*, v. Not used in NIVEBC. [√3552 + 5886]. to transplant

G3575 μετέπειτα *metepeita*, adv. [1] [√3552 + 2093 + 1663]. afterward:– afterward (1)

G3576 μετέχω *metechō*, v. [8] [√3552 + 2400]. to share in, partake in, take part in:– belonged to (1), have a part in (1), have support (1), lives on (1), share (1), shared in (1), sharing (1), take part in (1)

G3577 μετεωρίζομαι *meteōrizomai*, v. [1] to worry about, be anxious:– worry about (1)

G3578 μετοικεσία *metoikesia*, n. [4] [√3552 + 3875]. exile, deportation:– exile (4)

G3579 μετοικίζω *metoikizō*, v. [2] [√3552 + 3875]. to send to another place, exile, deport:– send into exile (1), sent (1)

G3580 μετοχή *metochē*, n. [1] [√3552 + 2400]. something in common, sharing, participation:– in common (1)

G3581 μέτοχος *metochos*, a. [6] [√3552 + 2400]. sharing in, partners with:– share in (2), companions (1), partners (1), shared in (1 [+1181]), undergoes (1 [+1181])

G3582 μετρέω *metreō*, v. [11] [√3586]. to measure:– measure (4), measured (4), use[S] (3)

G3583 μετρητής *metrētēs*, n. [1] [√3586]. measure (about nine or ten gallons):– twenty gallons (1 [+1545]); [*also* thirty gallons (1 [+5552])]

G3584 μετριοπαθέω *metriopatheō*, v. [1] [√3586 + 4248]. to deal gently:– deal gently with (1)

G3585 μετρίως *metriōs*, adv. [1] [√3586]. not greatly, moderately:– greatly (1 [+4024])

G3586 μέτρον *metron*, n. [14] [→296, 520, 3582, 3583, 3584, 3585, 4991]. measure, limit, what is apportioned:– measure (5), apportioned (1), does work (1 [+1918, 1877]), in accordance with (1 [+6055]), limit (1), measurement (1), measuring (1), sphere (1), sphere of service (1 [+3836, 2834]), what started[S] (1 [+3836])

G3587 μέτωπον *metōpon*, n. [8] [√3552 + 3972]. forehead:– foreheads (6), forehead (2)

G3588 μέχρι *mechri*, pp.* & c. [17] [→3589]. until, to the point of:– until (5), to (4), until (2 [+4005]), all the way to (1), almost (1 [+1581]), at (1), even to the point of (1), to the point of (1), to the time of (1)

G3589 μέχρις *mechris*, c. & pp.* Not used in NIVEBC. [√3588]. until, to the point of

G3590 μή *mē*, pt. neg. [1041] [→3591, 3592, 3593, 3594, 3595, 3596, 3598, 3599, 3600, 3607, 3608, 3609, 3610, 3612, 3614, 3615]. no, not, (with 4024) absolutely not; a marker that negates a statement. At the beginning of a Greek question, it anticipates a negative response:– not (527), no (58), except (34 [+1623]), don't (25), not (20 [+4024]), unless (14 [+1569]), without (11), never (10 [+4024]), never (9 [+4024]), unless (8 [+1569]), but (7 [+1623]), certainly not (7 [+4024]), never (7 [+4024]), only (7 [+1623]), stop (7), nothing (6), unless (6 [+1569]), never (5 [+4024, 1650, 3836, 172]), never (5), not (5 [+4024]), or (5), without (5 [+2400]), but (4 [+1623]), by no means (4 [+1181]), from (4), keep from (4), neither (4), never (4 [+4024]), not at all (4 [+1181]), or (4 [+2671]), avoid (3), but only (3 [+1623]), cannot (3), don't (3 [+4024]), only (3 [+4024, 1623]), otherwise (3 [+1623, 1254]), prevent from (3), absolutely not (2 [+1181]), against (2), aren't (2 [+1639]), blind (2 [+1063]), cannot (2 [+1538]), certainly not (2 [+1181]), do[S] (2 [+1145]), except (2 [+1623, 3667]), how (2), never (2 [+4024]), never again (2 [+4024]), no (2 [+4024]), none (2), not (2 [+4024]), not (2 [+4024]), not again (2 [+4024]), not at all (2 [+4024]), nothing (2 [+5516]), or (2 [+2671]), or (2 [+2779]), otherwise (2 [+1623, 1254, 1145]), rather than (2 [+2671]), so that not (2 [+4803]), than (2 [+2779]), that (2), that (2 [+4803]), unless (2 [+1760, 1623]), unseen (2 [+1063]), without (2 [+1569]), won't (2), God forbid[S] (1 [+1181]), abstains (1 [+2266]), afraid that (1), anything (1 [+5516]), at least (1 [+1623]), at once (1 [+3890]), before (1 [+2671]), before (1 [+4024, 2401, 4005]), bound to (1 [+450]), but (1 [+1569]), but if (1 [+1623]), could (1), cover (1 [+5746]), didn't (1), die (1 [+2441]), displease (1 [+743]), do[S] (1), doesn't (1), evidently (1 [+1623]), except (1), except (1 [+1569]), except (1 [+1623, 3668]), except for (1 [+1623]), fail (1 [+1569]), fail (1 [+4049]), for (1 [+4803]), for fear (1 [+2671]), for fear that (1 [+2671]), free from (1), from (1 [+2671]), haven't (1 [+2400]), help[S] (1), how (1 [+1142]), isn't at all (1 [+4024]), kept from (1 [+3195]), lest (1 [+2671]), must (1 [+1569]), never (1 [+1181]), never (1 [+4024, 4537]), never (1 [+4024, 4799]), never (1 [+4033, 4024]), never (1 [+1181]), never (1 [+4024]), never again (1 [+4024, 1650, 3836, 172]), nevertheless (1 [+1623]), no ever (1 [+4246, 4024]), no ever (1 [+4024]), no longer (1 [+4024]), no never (1 [+4024, 1650, 3836, 172]), nobody (1 [+5516]), none (1 [+5516]), nor (1 [+2779]), not (1 [+4028]), not by any means (1 [+4024]), not one (1 [+4024]), not only (1), nothing (1 [+4024, 4246]), nothing (1 [+5515]), only (1 [+1623]), only (1 [+1569]), only (1 [+1623, 3667]), only (1 [+1623, 3668]), only (1 [+4029, 1623]), only (1 [+4028, 1651, 1569]), otherwise (1 [+2671]), otherwise (1 [+1760, 1623]), prevent (1), refused (1 [+1569]), shallow (1 [+958]), shallow (1 [+2400, 958]), shouldn't (1), sincere (1 [+1474]), spare (1 [+2400]), stop (1 [+1181]), surely cannot (1 [+1538]), than that (1 [+2779]), that (1 [+4543]), that[S] (1), that don't (1), together with (1 [+6006]), unable (1 [+1538]), unashamed (1 [+159]), unless (1 [+1569]), unless (1 [+1623]), unless (1 [+1623]), until (1 [+1569, 4754]), until (1 [+1623, 4020]), wanted to be sure not (1 [+4803]), what[S] (1), you mean (1), NDT (50)

G3591 μήγε *mēge*, pt. neg. Not used in NIVEBC. [√3590 + 1145]. not

G3592 μηδαμῶς *mēdamōs*, adv. [2] [√3590 + 1254 + 1609]. surely not, by no means, certainly not:– surely not (2)

G3593 μηδέ *mēde*, pt. neg. disj. [56] [√3590 + 1254]. nor, or not, and not, but not:– or (25), not (11), and not (5), nor (4), not even (4), and (1), and don't (1), don't even (1), NDT (4)

G3594 μηδείς *mēdeis*, a. [90] [√3590 + 1254 + 1651]. no one, not anyone, nobody, nothing:– not anyone (13), not (11), no one (10), nothing (10), no (9), don't anyone (5), not anything (4), don't (3), without (3), any (2), any way (1), anyone (1), anyone (1 [+476]), anyone's (1), anything (1), don't any (1), don't anything (1), have everything need (1 [+3309]), haven't anything (1), instead of (1), no more (1), not any (1), not any way (1), not anybody (1), not in the least (1), permit (1 [+3266]), without anything (1), NDT (3)

G3595 μηδέποτε *mēdepote*, adv. [1] [√3590 + 1254 + 4544]. never:– never (1)

G3596 μηδέπω *mēdepō*, adv. [1] [√3590 + 1254]. not yet:– not yet (1)

G3597 Μῆδος *Mēdos*, n. pr. g. [1] Mede:– Medes (1)

G3598 μηθαμῶς *mēthamōs*, adv. Not used in NIVEBC. [√3590 + 1254 + 1609]. by no means, certainly not

G3599 μηθείς *mētheis*, a. Not used in NIVEBC. [√3590 + 1254 + 1651]. no one, nothing

G3600 μηκέτι *mēketi*, adv. [22] [√3590 + 2285]. no longer, never again:– no longer (9), stop (3), again (1), any longer (1), don't anymore (1), leave life of sin (1 [+279]), never (1), never (1 [+3516]), never again (1), no (1), no more (1), not (1)

G3601 μῆκος *mēkos*, n. [3] [→3426, 3427, 3428, 3429, 3430, 3431, 3432, 3602]. length:– long (2), length (1)

G3602 μηκύνω *mēkynō*, v. [1] [√3601]. (pass.) to grow (long), become long:– grows (1)

G3603 μηλωτή *mēlōtē*, n. [1] sheepskin:– sheepskins (1)

G3604 μήν[1] *mēn[1]*, n. [18] [→3741, 3806, 5485, 5564]. month:– months (11), month (4), half year (1 [+1971]), half years (1 [+1971]), three and a half years (1 [+2291, 5552, 2779, 1971])

G3605 μήν[2] *mēn[2]*, pt. [1] [→1638, 2447; cf. 3525]. (with 1623) surely:– surely (1 [+1623])

G3606 μηνύω *mēnyō*, v. [4] to inform, report, tell:– informed of (1), report (1), showed (1), told (1)

G3607 μήποτε *mēpote*, pt. & c. [25] [√3590 + 4544]. never, otherwise, that...not:– or (5), otherwise (4), so that not (3), if (2), if you do (2), for (1), in the hope that (1), never (1), no (1), no (1 [+4024]), none (1 [+5516]), not (1 [+4024]), really (1 [+242]), that none (1 [+5516])

G3608 μήπου *mēpou*, c. Not used in NIVEBC. [√3590 + 4544]. lest, that...somewhere

G3609 μήπω *mēpō*, adv. [2] [√3590]. not yet:– before (1), not yet (1)

G3610 μήπως *mēpōs*, adv. Not used in NIVEBC. [√3590 + 4544]. so that...somehow, lest

G3611 μηρός *mēros*, n. [1] thigh:– thigh (1)

G3612 μήτε *mēte*, c. neg. [34] [√3590 + 5445]. and not, neither, nor:– or (14), no (5), nor (4), not (3), neither (2), and neither (1), and not (1), but (1), either (1), whether (1), without (1)

G3613 μήτηρ *mētēr*, n. [84] [→298, 3616, 3617, 3618, 3619]. mother:– mother (73), mother's (4), birth (2 [+3120]), mothers (2), born (1 [+1666, 3120]), born (1 [+1666, 3120, 1164]), her[S] (1 [+3836])

G3614 μήτι *mēti*, pt. inter. [17] [√3590 + 5516]. often not translated; expects a no answer to a question: surely not, unless:– surely don't (3), could (2), except (1 [+1623]), not (1), of course (1), surely no (1), unless (1 [+1623]), NDT (7)

G3615 μήτιγε *mētige*, pt. inter. [2] [√3590 + 5516 + 1145]. how much more, not to speak of:– how much more (2 [+3615])

G3616 μήτρα *mētra*, n. [2] [√3613]. womb:– firstborn (1 [+1380]), womb (1)

G3617 μητραλῴας *mētralōas*, n. Not used in NIVEBC. [√3613 + 262]. one who kills a mother

G3618 **μητρολῴας** ***mētrolōas***, n. [1] [√*3613 + 262*]. one who kills a mother:– kill mothers (1)

G3619 **μητρόπολις** ***mētropolis***, n. Not used in NIVEBC. [√*3613 + 4484*]. capital city

G3620 **μιαίνω** ***miainō***, v. [5] [→*299, 3621, 3622*]. to pollute, stain, defile; (pass.) to be defiled, corrupted, become ceremonially unclean; this refers to both ceremonial and moral uncleanness:– corrupted (2), ceremonial uncleanness (1), defile (1), pollute (1)

G3621 **μίασμα** ***miasma***, n. [1] [√*3620*]. corruption, defilement:– corruption (1)

G3622 **μιασμός** ***miasmos***, n. [1] [√*3620*]. corruption, pollution, defilement:– corrupt (1)

G3623 **μίγμα** ***migma***, n. [1] [√*3502*]. mixture, compound:– mixture (1)

G3624 **μίγνυμι** ***mignymi***, v. Not used in NIVEBC. [√*3502*]. to mix, mingle

G3625 **μικρός** ***mikros***, a. Not used in NIVEBC. little, small, short, lesser€ [46]:– little (19), little while (7), small (7), least (4), short (2), smallest (2), before long (1 [+*2285*]), little ones (1), low (1), short (1 [+*3836, 2461*]), younger (1)

G3626 **Μίλητος** ***Milētos***, n. pr. [3] Miletus:– Miletus (3)

G3627 **μίλιον** ***milion***, n. [1] (Roman) mile (about 4,854 feet):– mile (1)

G3628 **μιμέομαι** ***mimeomai***, v. [4] [→*3629, 5213*]. to imitate, follow an example, use as a model:– imitate (3), follow example (1)

G3629 **μιμητής** ***mimētēs***, n. [6] [√*3628*]. imitator, an example:– follow example (2 [+*1181*]), imitators (2), imitate (1), imitate (1 [+*1181*])

G3630 **μιμνῄσκομαι** ***mimnēskomai***, v. [23] [√*3648*]. to remember, recall, bring to remembrance, often with an implication that a response or action of some kind will occur:– remember (10), remembered (6), remembering (2), mindful of (1), realize (1), recall (1), recalled (1), recalling (1)

G3631 **μισέω** ***miseō***, v. [40] to hate; (pass.) to be hated, detestable:– hate (14), hates (12), hated (10), hating (2), detestable (1), hate (1 [+*1639*])

G3632 **μισθαποδοσία** ***misthapodosia***, n. [3] [√*3635 + 608 + 1443*]. reward; punishment:– punishment (1), reward (1), rewarded (1)

G3633 **μισθαποδότης** ***misthapodotēs***, n. [1] [√*3635 + 608 + 1443*]. rewarder:– rewards (1 [+*1181*])

G3634 **μίσθιος** ***misthios***, n. [2] [√*3635*]. hired worker:– hired servants (2)

G3635 **μισθός** ***misthos***, n. [29] [→*521, 3632, 3633, 3634, 3636, 3637, 3638*]. wage; reward; what is paid back:– reward (16), wages (6), be rewarded (1 [+*3284*]), paid back (1), payment (1), profit (1), rewarded (1 [+*655*]), rewarding (1 [+*1443, 3836*]), wage (1)

G3636 **μισθόω** ***misthoō***, v. [2] [√*3635*]. to hire:– hire (1), hired (1)

G3637 **μίσθωμα** ***misthōma***, n. [1] [√*3635*]. rented house, rented lodging:– rented house (1)

G3638 **μισθωτός** ***misthōtos***, n. [3] [√*3635*]. hired worker:– hired hand (2), hired men (1)

G3639 **Μιτυλήνη** ***Mitylēnē***, n. pr. [1] Mitylene:– Mitylene (1)

G3640 **Μιχαήλ** ***Michaēl***, n. pr. [2] Michael, "*Who is like God [El]?*":– Michael (2)

G3641 **μνᾶ** ***mna***, n. [7] mina (100 drachmas or denarii, about 100 days' wages):– mina (4), minas (2), more^S (1)

G3642 **μνάομαι** ***mnaomai***, v. Not used in NIVEBC. [→*3650*]. be engaged, betrothed

G3643 **Μνάσων** ***Mnasōn***, n. pr. [1] Mnason:– Mnason (1)

G3644 **μνεία** ***mneia***, n. [7] [√*3648*]. remembrance, mention:– remember (2 [+*4472*]), memories (1), mention (1 [+*4472*]), remember (1), remember (1 [+*2400*]), remembering (1 [+*4472*])

G3645 **μνῆμα** ***mnēma***, n. [8] [√*3648*]. (burial) tomb:– tomb (4), tombs (3), burial (1 [+*5502, 1650*])

G3646 **μνημεῖον** ***mnēmeion***, n. [40] [√*3648*]. tomb, grave:– tomb (31), tombs (5), graves (3), entrance^S (1)

G3647 **μνήμη** ***mnēmē***, n. [1] [√*3648*]. remembrance, recalling, memory:– remember (1 [+*4472*])

G3648 **μνημονεύω** ***mnēmoneuō***, v. [21] [→*389, 390, 2057, 3630, 3644, 3645, 3646, 3647, 3649, 5703, 5704*]. to remember; to think of:– remember (15), consider (1), forgets (1 [+*4033*]), remembered (1), remembering (1), spoke (1), thinking (1)

G3649 **μνημόσυνον** ***mnēmosynon***, n. [3] [√*3648*]. memory, remembrance; memorial offering:– memory (2), memorial offering (1)

G3650 **μνηστεύω** ***mnēsteuō***, v. [3] [√*3642*]. (pass.) to be pledged to marriage, betrothed, become engaged:– pledged to be married (3)

G3651 **μογγιλάλος** ***mongilalos***, a. Not used in NIVEBC. [√*3281*]. pertaining to speaking in a hoarse or weak voice

G3652 **μογιλάλος** ***mogilalos***, a. [1] [√*3653 + 3281*]. hardly able to talk, speaking with difficulty:– could hardly talk (1)

G3653 **μόγις** ***mogis***, adv. [1] [→*3652, 3660, 3677*]. scarcely ever:– scarcely ever (1)

G3654 **μόδιος** ***modios***, n. [3] large bowl (holds about eight dry quarts):– bowl (3)

G3655 **μοιχαλίς** ***moichalis***, n. [7] [√*3659*]. adulteress; (a.) adulterous:– adulterous (4), adulteress (2), adultery (1)

G3656 **μοιχάω** ***moichaō***, v. [4] [√*3659*]. to commit adultery:– commits adultery (4)

G3657 **μοιχεία** ***moicheia***, n. [3] [√*3659*]. (the state or condition of) adultery:– adultery (3)

G3658 **μοιχεύω** ***moicheuō***, v. [15] [√*3659*]. (act.) to commit adultery; (pass.) to become an adulterer:– commit adultery (9), adultery (2), commits adultery (2), committed adultery (1), victim of adultery (1)

G3659 **μοιχός** ***moichos***, n. [3] [→*3655, 3656, 3657, 3658*]. adulterer:– adulterers (2), adulterer (1)

G3660 **μόλις** ***molis***, adv. [6] [√*3653*]. with difficulty, hardly; very rarely:– difficulty (2), hard (1), hardly (1), very rarely (1), with difficulty (1)

G3661 **Μολόχ** ***Moloch***, n. pr. [1] Molech, "*'shameful' king*":– Molek (1)

G3662 **μολύνω** ***molynō***, v. [3] [→*3663*]. to defile, soil, stain, make impure:– defile (1), defiled (1), soiled (1)

G3663 **μολυσμός** ***molysmos***, n. [1] [√*3662*]. contamination, defilement:– contaminates (1)

G3664 **μομφή** ***momphē***, n. [1] [√*3522*]. grievance, cause for complaint:– grievance (1)

G3665 **μονή** ***monē***, n. [2] [√*3531*]. room; dwelling place, abode:– home (1), rooms (1)

G3666 **μονογενής** ***monogenēs***, a. [9] [√*3668 + 1181*]. one and only, unique:– one and only (3), one and only son (3), only (2), only child (1)

G3667 **μόνον** ***monon***, adv. [67] [√*3668*]. only, alone; just, even, simply:– only (40), just (6), alone (3), but (3), except (2 [+*1623, 3590*]), simply (2), what is more (2 [+*4024, 1254, 247, 2779*]), all (1), even (1), merely (1), one (1), only (1 [+*3668*]), only (1 [+*1623, 3590*]), whatever happens (1), NDT (2)

G3668 **μόνος** ***monos***, a. [49] [→*2911, 3666, 3667, 3669, 3670*]. only, alone, by oneself:– only (22), alone (13), all alone (2 [+*2848, 2625*]), alone (1 [+*2848*]), by himself (1 [+*899*]), by myself (1), by ourselves (1), by themselves (1), except (1 [+*247*]), except (1 [+*1623, 3590*]), just (1), only (1 [+*3667*]), only (1 [+*1623, 3590*]), only a single (1), private (1)

G3669 **μονόφθαλμος** ***monophthalmos***, a. [2] [√*3668 + 4057*]. one-eyed:– one eye (1), with one eye (1)

G3670 **μονόω** ***monoō***, v. [1] [√*3668*]. (pass.) to be left alone:– left all alone (1)

G3671 **μορφή** ***morphē***, n. [3] [→*305, 3565, 3672, 3673, 5214, 5215, 5216*]. form, outward appearance; nature, character:– very nature (2), form (1)

G3672 **μορφόω** ***morphoō***, v. [1] [√*3671*]. (pass.) to be formed, take on a form:– formed (1)

G3673 **μόρφωσις** ***morphōsis***, n. [2] [√*3671*]. embodiment, formulation; (outward) form, appearance:– embodiment (1), form (1)

G3674 **μοσχοποιέω** ***moschopoieō***, v. [1] [√*3675 + 4472*]. to make an idol in the shape of a calf:– made an idol in the form of a calf (1)

G3675 **μόσχος** ***moschos***, n. [6] [→*3674*]. calf, ox, young bull:– calf (3), calves (2), ox (1)

G3676 **μουσικός** ***mousikos***, a. Not used in NIVEBC. (n.) musician€ [1]:– musicians (1)

G3677 **μόχθος** ***mochthos***, n. [3] [√*3653*]. toil, hardship, exertion:– hardship (1), toiled (1), toiling (1)

G3678 **μυελός** ***myelos***, n. [1] marrow:– marrow (1)

G3679 **μυέω** ***myeō***, v. [1] [→*3696*]. (pass.) to learn a secret:– learned the secret (1)

G3680 **μῦθος** ***mythos***, n. [5] [→*4170, 4171, 4172*]. myth, story, tale:– myths (4), stories (1)

G3681 **μυκάομαι** ***mykaomai***, v. [1] to roar:– roar (1)

G3682 **μυκτηρίζω** ***myktērizō***, v. [1] [→*1727*]. (pass.) to be mocked, treated with contempt:– mocked (1)

G3683 **μυλικός** ***mylikos***, a. [1] [√*3685*]. pertaining to a grinding mill:– millstone (1 [+*3345*])

G3684 **μύλινος** ***mylinos***, a. [1] [√*3685*]. pertaining to a grinding mill:– millstone (1)

G3685 **μύλος** ***mylos***, n. [4] [→*3683, 3684, 3686, 3687*]. hand mill or millstone for grinding:– large millstone (2 [+*3948*]), hand mill (1), millstone (1)

G3686 **μυλών** ***mylōn***, n. Not used in NIVEBC. [√*3685*]. millhouse

G3687 **μυλωνικός** ***mylōnikos***, a. Not used in NIVEBC. [√*3685*]. pertaining to the millhouse

G3688 **Μύρα** ***Myra***, n. pr. [1] [→*3694*]. Myra:– Myra (1)

G3689 **μυριάς** ***myrias***, n. [8] [√*3692*]. myriad, ten thousand; thousands upon thousands, a practically uncountable number:– thousands (3), thousands upon thousands (2), fifty thousand (1 [+*4297*]), many thousands (1), ten thousand (1)

G3690 **μυρίζω** ***myrizō***, v. [1] [√*3693*]. to pour perfume, anoint:– poured perfume on (1)

G3691 **μύριοι** ***myrioi***, a. num. [1] [√*3692*]. ten thousand; a practically uncountable number:– ten thousand (1)

G3692 **μυρίος** ***myrios***, a. [2] [→*1490, 3689, 3691*]. pertaining to the number ten thousand; a practically uncountable number:– ten thousand (2)

G3693 **μύρον** ***myron***, n. [14] [→*3690*]. perfume, myrrh, ointment:– perfume (11), it^S (1 [+*3836*]), myrrh (1), perfumes (1)

G3694 **Μύρρα** ***Myrra***, n. pr. Not used in NIVEBC. [√*3688*]. Myra

G3695 **Μυσία** ***Mysia***, n. pr. [2] Mysia:– Mysia (2)

G3696 **μυστήριον** ***mystērion***, n. [27] [√*3679*]. mystery, secret; often refers to a misunderstood part of the OT that, with Christ's coming, is now unveiled:– mystery (19), mysteries (3), secret (2), secrets (2), deep truths (1)

G3697 **μυωπάζω** ***myōpazō***, v. [1] to be nearsighted:– nearsighted (1)

G3698 **μώλωψ** ***mōlōps***, n. [1] wound, welt, bruise:– wounds (1)

G3699 **μωμάομαι** ***mōmaomai***, v. [2] [√*3522*]. (mid.) to criticize, find fault, blame; (pass.) to be discredited, have fault found with:– criticism (1), discredited (1)

G3700 **μῶμος** ***mōmos***, n. [1] [√*3522*]. blemish:– blemishes (1)

G3701 **μωραίνω** ***mōrainō***, v. [4] [√*3704*]. (act.) to make foolish, show one foolish; (pass.) to become a fool, be made a fool; (pass.) to become saltless, tasteless, inert:– loses saltiness (2), fools (1), made foolish (1)

G3702 **μωρία** ***mōria***, n. [5] [√*3704*]. foolishness:– foolishness (5)

G3703 **μωρολογία** ***mōrologia***, n. [1] [√*3704 + 3306*]. foolish talk:– foolish talk (1)

G3704 **μωρός** ***mōros***, a. [12] [→*3701, 3702, 3703*]. foolish:– foolish (7), fools (3), fool (1), foolishness (1)

G3705 **Μωσεύς** ***Mōseus***, n. pr. Not used in NIVEBC. [√*3707*]. Moses, "*drawn out* [Ex. 2:10]; [Egyptian] *son*"

G3706 **Μωσῆς** ***Mōsēs***, n. pr. Not used in NIVEBC. [√*3707*]. Moses, "*drawn out* [Ex. 2:10]; [Egyptian] *son*"

G3707 **Μωϋσῆς** ***Mōusēs***, n. pr. [80] [→*3705, 3706*]. Moses, "*drawn out* [Ex. 2:10]; [Egyptian] *son*":– Moses (79), he^S (1)

G3708 **ν** ***n***, letter. Not used in NIVEBC. letter of the Greek alphabet

G3709 **Ναασσών** ***Naassōn***, n. pr. [3] Nahshon, "*small viper*":– Nahshon (3)

G3710 **Ναγγαί** ***Nangai***, n. pr. [1] Naggai:– Naggai (1)

G3711 **Ναζαρά** ***Nazara***, n. pr. Not used in NIVEBC. [→*3712, 3713, 3714, 3715, 3716, 3717*]. Nazareth, "[poss.] *sprout, branch* or *watchtower*"

G3712 **Ναζαρέθ** ***Nazarath***, n. pr. Not used in NIVEBC. [√*3711*]. Nazareth, "[poss.] *sprout, branch* or *watchtower*"

G3713 **Ναζαράτ** ***Nazarat***, n. pr. Not used in NIVEBC. [√*3711*]. Nazareth, "[poss.] *sprout, branch* or *watchtower*"

G3714 **Ναζαρέθ** ***Nazareth***, n. pr. [12] [√*3711*]. Nazareth, "[poss.] *sprout, branch* or *watchtower*":– Nazareth (12)

G3715 **Ναζαρέτ** ***Nazaret***, n. pr. Not used in NIVEBC. [√*3711*]. Nazareth

G3716 **Ναζαρηνός** ***Nazarēnos***, a. pr. g. [6] [√*3711*]. of Nazareth; (n.) Nazarene (in no way connected to the OT Nazirite):– of Nazareth (4), Nazarene (2)

G3717 **Ναζωραῖος** ***Nazōraios***, n. pr. g. [13] [√*3711*]. Nazarene, of Nazareth:– of Nazareth (11), Nazarene (2)

G3718 Ναθάμ *Natham*, n. pr. [1] [→*3719*]. Nathan, "*gift*":– Nathan (1)

G3719 Ναθάν *Nathan*, n. pr. Not used in NIVEBC. [√*3718*]. Nathan, "*gift*"

G3720 Ναθαναήλ *Nathanaēl*, n. pr. [6] Nathanael, "*gift of God [El]*":– Nathanael (6)

G3721 ναί *nai*, pt. aff. *or* emph. [33] yes, indeed, a marker of strong agreement, affirmation, or emphasis:– yes (28), simply yes (2 [+*3721*]), so shall it be (1), wish (1), NDT (1)

G3722 Ναιμάν *Naiman*, n. pr. [1] [→*3737*]. Naaman, "*pleasantness*":– Naaman (1)

G3723 Ναΐν *Nain*, n. pr. [1] Nain, "*pleasant, delightful*":– Nain (1)

G3724 ναός *naos*, n. [45] [→*3753*]. temple; of the temple in Jerusalem, it generally denotes the temple building. Also used figuratively for the church as the dwelling place of the Holy Spirit:– temple (41), temples (2), shrines (1), NDT (1)

G3725 Ναούμ *Naoum*, n. pr. [1] Nahum, "*comfort*":– Nahum (1)

G3726 νάρδος *nardos*, n. [2] nard, the oil of (spike)nard, extracted from the root:– nard (2)

G3727 Νάρκισσος *Narkissos*, n. pr. [1] Narcissus:– Narcissus (1)

G3728 ναυαγέω *nauageō*, v. [2] [√*3730* + *2862*]. to be shipwrecked, have a shipwreck:– shipwrecked (1), suffered shipwreck (1)

G3729 ναύκληρος *nauklēros*, n. [1] [√*3730* + *3102*]. ship owner or captain:– owner of the ship (1)

G3730 ναῦς *naus*, n. [1] [→*3728, 3729, 3731*]. ship:– ship (1)

G3731 ναύτης *nautēs*, n. [3] [√*3730*]. sailor:– sailors (3)

G3732 Ναχώρ *Nachōr*, n. pr. [1] Nahor:– Nahor (1)

G3733 νεανίας *neanias*, n. [3] [√*3742*]. young man:– young man (3)

G3734 νεανίσκος *neaniskos*, n. [11] [√*3742*]. young man:– young man (7), young men (4)

G3735 Νεά πολις *Nea polis*, n. pr. [1] [√*3742* + *4484*]. Neapolis, "*new city*":– Neapolis (1)

G3736 Νεάπολις *Neapolis*, n. pr. Not used in NIVEBC. [√*3742* + *4484*]. Neapolis, "*new city*"

G3737 Νεεμάν *Neeman*, n. pr. Not used in NIVEBC. [√*3722*]. Naaman, "*pleasantness*"

G3738 νεκρός *nekros*, a. [128] [→*3739, 3740*]. dead (can be used physically or fig., of both persons and things); (n.) dead person, corpse:– dead (121), death (3), corpse (1), died (1 [+*1181*]), died (1 [+*2093*]), subject to death (1)

G3739 νεκρόω *nekroō*, v. [3] [√*3738*]. (act.) to put to death; (pass.) to be as good as dead:– as good as dead (1), dead (1), put to death (1)

G3740 νέκρωσις *nekrōsis*, n. [2] [√*3738*]. death, deadness:– dead (1), death (1)

G3741 νεομηνία *neomēnia*, n. [1] [√*3742* + *3604*]. New Moon Celebration:– new Moon celebration (1)

G3742 νέος *neos*, a. [23] [→*391, 3733, 3734, 3735, 3736, 3741, 3743, 3744, 3745, 3754, 3799, 3800, 3801, 3806*]. new, fresh, young, younger:– new (11), younger (9), young (2), youngest (1)

G3743 νεοσσός *neossos*, n. Not used in NIVEBC. [√*3742*]. the young (of a bird)

G3744 νεότης *neotēs*, n. [4] [√*3742*]. youth, childhood:– boy (2), child (1), young (1)

G3745 νεόφυτος *neophytos*, a. [1] [√*3742* + *5886*]. newly converted, a fig. extension of a new plant, not found in the NT:– recent convert (1)

G3746 Νέρων *Nerōn*, n. pr. Not used in NIVEBC. Nero, "*[family name]*"

G3747 Νεύης *Neuēs*, n. pr. Not used in NIVEBC. Neues

G3748 νεύω *neuō*, v. [2] [→*1377, 1728, 1935, 2153, 2916, 5162*]. to motion, nod (as a signal):– motioned (2)

G3749 νεφέλη *nephelē*, n. [25] [→*3751*]. cloud:– cloud (18), clouds (7)

G3750 Νεφθαλίμ *Nephthalim*, n. pr. [3] Naphtali:– Naphtali (3)

G3751 νέφος *nephos*, n. [1] [√*3749*]. cloud:– cloud (1)

G3752 νεφρός *nephros*, n. [1] mind, the part of the inner person that feels, desires, and gives intent; a fig. extension of the kidney (not found in the NT):– minds (1)

G3753 νεωκόρος *neōkoros*, n. [1] [√*3724*]. guardian of the temple:– guardian of the temple (1)

G3754 νεωτερικός *neōterikos*, a. [1] [√*3742*]. pertaining to youth, youthful:– of youth (1)

G3755 νή *nē*, pt. aff. [1] as surely as:– yes just as surely as (1)

G3756 νήθω *nēthō*, v. [2] to spin (yarn):– spin (2)

G3757 νηπιάζω *nēpiazō*, v. [1] [√*3758*]. to be (like) a child:– infants (1)

G3758 νήπιος *nēpios*, a. [15] [→*3757*]. (n.) child, infant; (a.) childlike, childish, infantile, with a negative implication of immaturity or positive implication of innocence, depending on the context:– child (4), little children (3), infants (2), underage (2), childhood (1), children (1), infant (1), young children (1)

G3759 Νηρεύς *Nēreus*, n. pr. [1] Nereus:– Nereus (1)

G3760 Νηρί *Nēri*, n. pr. [1] Neri, "*lamp of Yahweh*":– Neri (1)

G3761 νησίον *nēsion*, n. [1] [√*3762*]. small island:– small island (1)

G3762 νῆσος *nēsos*, n. [9] [→*3761*]. island:– island (9)

G3763 νηστεία *nēsteia*, n. [5] [→*3764, 3765; cf. 2266*]. fasting, going without food:– fasting (2), day of Atonement (1), gone without food (1), hunger (1)

G3764 νηστεύω *nēsteuō*, v. [20] [√*3763*]. to fast, go without food:– fast (11), fasting (6), are[S] (1), fasted (1), NDT (1)

G3765 νῆστις *nēstis*, n. [2] [√*3763*]. hungry, without food:– hungry (2)

G3766 νηφαλέος *nēphaleos*, a. Not used in NIVEBC. [√*3768*]. temperate (in the use of alcohol)

G3767 νηφάλιος *nēphalios*, a. [3] [√*3768*]. temperate (in the use of alcohol):– temperate (3)

G3768 νήφω *nēphō*, v. [6] [→*392, 1729, 3766, 3767*]. to be self-controlled, clear-headed:– sober (3), alert (1), keep head (1), of sober mind (1)

G3769 Νίγερ *Niger*, n. pr. [1] Niger, "*black*":– Niger (1)

G3770 Νικάνωρ *Nikanōr*, n. pr. [1] [√*3772* + *467*]. Nicanor, "*victor*":– Nicanor (1)

G3771 νικάω *nikaō*, v. [28] [√*3772*]. to overcome, overpower; to conquer, triumph:– victorious (10), overcome (7), overcomes (2), conquer (1), conqueror (1), conquest (1), overpower (1), overpowers (1), prevail (1), triumph over (1), triumphed (1), triumphed over (1)

G3772 νίκη *nikē*, n. [1] [→*438, 1022, 2332, 2552, 2553, 3770, 3771, 3773, 3774, 3775, 3776, 3777, 5664*]. victory:– victory (1)

G3773 Νικόδημος *Nikodēmos*, n. pr. [5] [√*3772* + *1322*]. Nicodemus, "*victor over people*":– Nicodemus (5)

G3774 Νικολαΐτης *Nikolaitēs*, n. pr. g. [2] [√*3772* + *3295*]. Nicolaitan, "*follower of Nicolas*":– Nicolaitans (2)

G3775 Νικόλαος *Nikolaos*, n. pr. [1] [√*3772* + *3295*]. Nicolas, "*victor over people*":– Nicolas (1)

G3776 Νικόπολις *Nikopolis*, n. pr. [1] [√*3772* + *4484*]. Nicopolis, "*victory city*":– Nicopolis (1)

G3777 νῖκος *nikos*, n. [4] [√*3772*]. victory:– victory (4)

G3778 Νινευή *Nineuē*, n. pr. Not used in NIVEBC. [→*3779, 3780*]. Nineveh

G3779 Νινευΐ *Nineui*, n. pr. Not used in NIVEBC. [√*3778*]. Nineveh

G3780 Νινευίτης *Nineuitēs*, n. pr. g. [3] [√*3778*]. Ninevite:– Nineveh (2), Ninevites (1)

G3781 νιπτήρ *niptēr*, n. [1] [√*3782*]. basin for washing:– basin (1)

G3782 νίπτω *niptō*, v. [17] [→*481, 672, 3781, 4469*]. to wash; bathe:– wash (10), washed (4), washing (2), give a washing (1)

G3783 νοέω *noeō*, v. [14] [√*3808*]. to understand, see with insight, reflect:– understand (7), see (3), imagine (1), know (1), reflect on (1), understood (1)

G3784 νόημα *noēma*, n. [6] [√*3808*]. thought, mind; scheme, design, plot:– minds (4), schemes (1), thought (1)

G3785 νόθος *nothos*, a. Not used in NIVEBC. illegitimate, born out of wedlock€ [1]:– not legitimate (1)

G3786 νομή *nomē*, n. [2] [√*3795*]. pasture:– pasture (1), spread (1 [+*2400*])

G3787 νομίζω *nomizō*, v. [15] [√*3795*]. to think, suppose, expect, consider:– think (4), thought (4), expected (2), thinking (2), assumed (1), suppose (1), worried (1)

G3788 νομικός *nomikos*, a. [9] [√*3795*]. pertaining to the law; (n.) expert in the law, lawyer:– experts in the law (5), expert in the law (2), about law (1), lawyer (1)

G3789 νομίμως *nomimōs*, adv. [2] [√*3795*]. properly, in accordance to the rules:– according to the rules (1), properly (1)

G3790 νόμισμα *nomisma*, n. [1] [√*3795*]. coin:– coin (1)

G3791 νομοδιδάσκαλος *nomodidaskalos*, n. [3] [√*3795* + *1438*]. teacher of the law:– teachers of the law (2), teacher of the law (1)

G3792 νομοθεσία *nomothesia*, n. [1] [√*3795* + *5502*]. law, legislation:– receiving of the law (1)

G3793 νομοθετέω *nomotheteō*, v. [2] [√*3795* + *5502*]. (pass.) to be given law; to be founded, enacted:– established (1), law given (1)

G3794 νομοθέτης *nomothetēs*, n. [1] [√*3795* + *5502*]. lawgiver:– lawgiver (1)

G3795 νόμος *nomos*, n. [194] [→*490, 491, 492, 671, 1376, 1937, 1938, 2883, 3099, 3100, 3101, 3786, 3787, 3788, 3789, 3790, 3791, 3792, 3793, 3794, 3872, 3873, 3874, 4174, 4175, 5169*]. law, regulation, principle; this has a broad range of meanings and referents, ranging from law as a principle revealed in nature or reason, to the OT Scriptures as a body, the first five books of the Scriptures, or any single command of the Scriptures:– law (184), it[S] (2), lawbreaker (2 [+*4127*]), laws (2), goal[S] (1), law's (1), of law (1), regulation (1 [+*1953*])

G3796 νοσέω *noseō*, v. [1] [√*3798*]. to be unhealthy, ill:– have an unhealthy interest (1)

G3797 νόσημα *nosēma*, n. Not used in NIVEBC. [√*3798*]. disease

G3798 νόσος *nosos*, n. [11] [→*3796, 3797*]. disease, illness:– diseases (5), disease (3), diseases (1 [+*2809*]), illnesses (1), sickness (1 [+*820*])

G3799 νοσσιά *nossia*, n. [1] [√*3742*]. chick, young (of a bird):– chicks (1)

G3800 νοσσίον *nossion*, n. [1] [√*3742*]. young (of a bird):– chicks (1)

G3801 νοσσός *nossos*, n. [1] [√*3742*]. young (of a bird):– young (1)

G3802 νοσφίζω *nosphizō*, v. [3] (mid.) to hold back for oneself, steal by misappropriating:– kept (1), kept back (1), steal (1)

G3803 νότος *notos*, n. [7] south, south wind:– south (4), south wind (3)

G3804 νουθεσία *nouthesia*, n. [3] [√*3808* + *5502*]. warning, admonition; instruction:– instruction (1), warn (1), warnings (1)

G3805 νουθετέω *noutheteō*, v. [8] [√*3808* + *5502*]. to warn, admonish; instruct:– warn (3), admonish (2), admonishing (1), instruct (1), warning (1)

G3806 νουμηνία *noumēnia*, n. Not used in NIVEBC. [√*3742* + *3604*]. New Moon Celebration

G3807 νουνεχῶς *nounechōs*, adv. [1] [√*3808* + *2400*]. wisely, thoughtfully:– wisely (1)

G3808 νοῦς *nous*, n. [24] [→*295, 485, 486, 1378, 1379, 1554, 1936, 2154, 2333, 2334, 2917, 3566, 3567, 3783, 3784, 3804, 3805, 3807, 4173, 4629, 4630, 5706, 5707*]. mind, thinking; understanding, insight; "to open the mind" means "to understand something":– mind (13), minds (4), understanding (3), insight (1), intelligible (1), teaching (1), thinking (1)

G3809 Νύμφαν *Nymphan*, n. pr. [1] [√*3811*]. Nympha:– Nympha (1)

G3810 Νυμφᾶς *Nymphas*, n. pr. Not used in NIVEBC. [√*3811*]. Nymphas

G3811 νύμφη *nymphē*, n. [8] [→*3809, 3810, 3812, 3813*]. bride; daughter-in-law:– bride (5), daughter-in-law (3)

G3812 νυμφίος *nymphios*, n. [16] [√*3811*]. bridegroom:– bridegroom (11), he[S] (2 [+*3836*]), bridegroom's (1), he[S] (1), him[S] (1 [+*3836*])

G3813 νυμφών *nymphōn*, n. [3] [√*3811*]. bridegroom:– bridegroom (3)

G3814 νῦν *nyn*, adv. [149] [→*3815, 5422, 5523*]. now, as it is; (with the article [*3836*]) the present (time):– now (106), present (9), now on (6 [+*3836*]), now (4 [+*3836*]), as it is (3 [+*1254*]), as it is (2), now (2 [+*2627*]), a short while ago (1), again (1 [+*608, 3836*]), as it is (1 [+*1254, 2779*]), at present (1), in fact (1), in the present case (1 [+*3836*]), instead (1 [+*1254*]), just (1), now (1 [+*3836*]), now (1 [+*3836*]), now (1 [+*608, 3836*]), now then (1), present (1 [+*3836, 2789*]), present time (1), still (1 [+*2285*]), this (1 [+*3836*]), NDT (1)

G3815 νυνί *nyni*, adv. [19] [√*3814*]. now, as it is; indeed, in fact:– now (15), as it is (1), in fact (1), indeed (1), NDT (1)

G3816 νύξ *nyx*, n. [61] [→*1381, 1939, 3543, 3819*]. night, evening:– night (51), nights (3), shortly before dawn (2 [+*5480, 5871, 3836*]), at midnight (1 [+*3545*]), evening (1), midnight (1 [+*3545, 3836*]), tonight (1), yes tonight (1 [+*4047, 3836*])

GREEK INDEX

G3817 νύσσω *nyssō*, v. [1] [→2919, 2920]. to pierce, stab:– pierced (1)

G3818 νυστάζω *nystazō*, v. [2] to become drowsy; to sleep, be idle:– drowsy (1), sleeping (1)

G3819 νυχθήμερον *nychthēmeron*, n. [1] [√3816 + 2465]. a night and a day, about 24 hours:– a night and a day (1)

G3820 Νῶε *Nōe*, n. pr. [8] Noah, "*rest, comfort*":– Noah (8)

G3821 νωθρός *nōthros*, a. Not used in NIVEBC. slow to learn; lazy, sluggish€ [2]:– lazy (1), no longer try (1 [+1181])

G3822 νῶτος *nōtos*, n. [1] back (of a human body); to have a "bent back" means to be "in trouble or oppression":– backs (1)

G3823 ξ *x*, letter. Not used in NIVEBC. letter of the Greek alphabet

G3824 ξαίνω *xainō*, v. Not used in NIVEBC. to comb (wool)

G3825 ξενία *xenia*, n. [2] [√3828]. place to stay, guest room:– guest room (1), place where staying (1)

G3826 ξενίζω *xenizō*, v. [10] [√3828]. to receive a guest, entertain; (pass.) to stay as a guest; to think of something as strange, be surprised, astonished:– staying (2), surprised (2), guest (1), guests (1), showed hospitality (1), shown hospitality (1), stay (1), strange (1)

G3827 ξενοδοχέω *xenodocheō*, v. [1] [√3828 + 1312]. to show hospitality:– showing hospitality (1)

G3828 ξένος *xenos*, a. [14] [→3825, 3826, 3827, 5810, 5811]. strange, foreign, alien; (n.) foreigner, stranger, alien; host, one who shows hospitality:– foreigners (5), stranger (4), strange (2), foreign (1), hospitality enjoy (1), strangers (1)

G3829 ξέστης *xestēs*, n. [1] pitcher, jug:– pitchers (1)

G3830 ξηραίνω *xērainō*, v. [15] [√3831]. to wither, shrivel; become rigid:– withered (6), withers (3), dried up (1), rigid (1), ripe (1), shriveled (1), stopped (1), wither (1)

G3831 ξηρός *xēros*, a. [8] [→3830]. dried up, (n.) dry land; shriveled, by extension: withered, paralyzed, of an atrophied limb of the body:– shriveled (4), dry (2), land (1), paralyzed (1)

G3832 ξύλινος *xylinos*, a. [2] [→3833, 3834]. made of wood, wooden:– of wood (1), wood (1)

G3833 ξύλον *xylon*, n. [20] [√3832]. wood; tree; wooden club, stocks:– tree (6), clubs (5), cross (4), wood (3), pole (1), stocks (1)

G3834 ξυράω *xyraō*, v. [3] [√3832]. to have one's hair shaved:– shaved (3)

G3835 ο *o*, letter. Not used in NIVEBC. letter of the Greek alphabet

G3836 ὁ *ho*, art. [19645] [→2201, 3840, 3888, 5422, 5437, 5524, 5525, 5539, 5540, 5541, 6045]. (often not translated) the, this, that, who:– the (7502), who (380), those (352), what (198), a (196), his (183), that (162), their (114), your (95), he (132), the son[s] (75), this (82), our (60), him (55), my (51), whoever (87), you (40), her (28), they (65), which (27), its (25), forever (23 [+1650, 172]), one (24), to (23 [+1650]), anyone (42), because (22 [+1328]), so that (21 [+1650]), an (19), Jesus[s] (16), they (15), all things (14 [+4246]), everything (14 [+4246]), Jesus[s] (14), as (11 [+1877]), things (11), whom (11), these (11), some (10), son[s] (9), birds (8 [+4374, 4041]), she (10), any (7), companions (7 [+3552]), someone (7), we (7), whose (7), now on (6 [+3814]), before (5 [+4574]), never (5 [+4024, 3590, 1650, 172]), now (5 [+3814]), that (5 [+1650]), they[s] (5 [+2681]), when (5 [+1877]), after (4 [+3552]), anything (4), companions (4 [+5250]), every (4), in order that (4 [+1650]), it (5), me (4 [+3950, 1609]), the disciples[s] (4), them (4), them[s] (4 [+476]), together (4 [+2093, 899]), what[s] (4 [+3364]), what[s] (4 [+4839]), while (4 [+1877]), when (8 [+1877]), back (3 [+1650, 3958]), call (3 [+2813, 3950]), footstool (3 [+5711, 4546]), other (3), people[s] (5), God's[s] (3), looked up (3 [+2048, 4057]), others (4), some (3 [+3525]), that (3 [+899]), the very (3), them[s] (3 [+81]), them[s] (3 [+3412, 899]), this[s] (3 [+3364]), affairs (2), after (2 [+3552]), against (2 [+2093, 5111]), all (2), among (2 [+1650, 3545]), as (2 [+1877]), associates (2 [+5250]), because of (2 [+1328]), case[s] (2 [+2848]), convened the court (2 [+2767, 2093, 1037]), each (4), earthly (2 [+2093, 1178]), finally (2 [+3370]), forever (2 [+1650, 1457]), from now on (2 [+3370]), God[s] (2), God-fearing (2 [+5828, 2536]), he[s] (2 [+2536]), he[s] (2 [+2652]), he[s] (2 [+3812]), he[s] (2 [+476, 1697]), heavenly (2 [+1877, 4041]), himself (2), himself (2 [+2840, 899]), his own (2), I (2 [+6034, 1609]), I have (2 [+1847]), in (2), in front of everyone (2 [+1650, 3545]), it[s] (2 [+229]), it[s] (2 [+1046]), it[s] (2 [+3180]), it[s] (2 [+4450]), service[s] (2), knelt down (2 [+5502, 1205]), me (2 [+3517, 1609]), outsiders (2 [+2032]), people (2 [+3836, 5626, 476]), people (2 [+5626, 3836, 476]), property[s] (2), rich (2 [+5975, 2400]), sandals (2 [+5687, 4546]), seized (2 [+2095, 5931]), shortly before dawn (2 [+5480, 5871, 3816]), since (2 [+1328]), sins (2 [+4472, 281]), so (2 [+1650]), still (2 [+3370]), such (2), that is how (2 [+2848, 899]), the man[s] (2), the affairs (2), the mother[s] (2), them[s] (2 [+3836, 5525, 4556]), there[s] (2 [+1877, 2639]), they[s] (2 [+2681]), they[s] (2 [+3412]), this[s] (2 [+3364, 4047]), those who are (2 [+5626]), to (2), what desires[s] (2), what had happened (2), whatever (2), when (2 [+3552]), while (2 [+1877]), when (2 [+1877]), which[s] (2 [+180]), who were hired[s] (2), you (2 [+5148, 2840]), you (2 [+6034, 5148]), yourselves (2 [+3517, 5148]), a person's[s] (1), Abraham's[s] (1), across (1 [+1650, 4305]), across the lake (1 [+1650, 4305]), after (1 [+3552]), after this (1 [+1877, 2759]), again (1 [+608, 3814]), again (1 [+1650, 172]), agree in what say (1 [+899, 3306]), alert (1 [+350, 4019]), alive (1 [+6034, 1877, 899, 1639]), altogether (1 [+4246]), all (1 [+4246]), all about (1 [+4246, 4839]), all had (1 [+2625]), always (1 [+4246, 2465]), and (1), and (1 [+1650]), and so (1 [+1650]), and thus (1 [+1650]), another (1), another (1 [+1254]), any way (1 [+5515]), around (1 [+1650, 3958]), arrest (1 [+2095, 2093, 5931]), arrested (1 [+2095, 5931]), arrested (1 [+2095, 5931, 2093]), as (1 [+1877]), as a result (1 [+1650]), as (1), as (1 [+2093, 3930]), as a result (1 [+1650]), as bold (1 [+2509, 4301]), as follows (1 [+2400, 5596, 4047]), as to (1), as usual (1 [+2848, 899]), as usual (1 [+2848, 1621]), ashore (1 [+1650, 1178]), ashore (1 [+2093, 1178]), assembled worshipers (1 [+4436, 3295]), at first (1 [+4754]), at (1 [+1877]), at all (1 [+1650, 4117]), at once (1 [+899, 6052]), away (1 [+1666, 3545]), away[s] (1 [+1650, 2557]), baptized (1 [+966, 967]), beauty (1 [+2346, 4725]), before (1 [+4574]), before (1 [+4728]), before (1 [+1650, 3545]), before (1 [+1877, 3545]), began[s] (1 [+487, 5125]), began to speak (1 [+487, 5125, 3306]), begging (1 [+4639, 1797]), beginning with (1 [+608, 2779, 2759]), believers (1 [+2400, 4411]), besides everything else (1 [+6006, 4211]), blinded (1 [+5604, 4057]), blindfolded (1 [+4328, 4725]), both (1 [+1545, 3938]), by (1), by (1 [+1877]), by (1 [+1877]), called (1 [+4005, 3950]), Pilate[s] (1), Peter[s] (1), case[s] (1), case[s] (1 [+4309]), child bear (1 [+2843, 3120]), circumstances (1), come together (1 [+5302, 2093, 899]), comes together (1 [+5302, 2093, 899]), companions (1 [+4309]), companions (1 [+5250, 1639]), companions (1 [+5250, 4513]), completely (1 [+1650, 4117]), completely healed (1 [+1443, 3907, 4047]), conceived (1 [+5197, 1877, 3120]), concerns (1), concerns[s] (1), Cornelius[s] (1), crowd (1 [+4436, 3295]), decided (1 [+326, 2093, 2840]), decided (1 [+5502, 1877, 4460]), demon-possessed (1 [+2400, 4460, 3836, 4505]), demon-possessed (1 [+2400, 3836, 4460, 4505]), descendant (1 [+1666, 2588]), descendants (1 [+2843, 4019]), descended from (1 [+2002, 1666, 4019]), done this[s] (1 [+5718, 899, 4246]), dressed ready for service (1 [+4019, 4322]), drew back (1 [+599, 1650, 3958]), each (1 [+2848, 1651]), earlier (1 [+4754]), elementary truths (1 [+5122, 794]), embraced (1 [+2158, 2093, 5549]), endlessly (1 [+1650, 1457]), envious (1 [+4057, 4505]), equal (1 [+899]), equality (1 [+1639, 2698]), ever (1 [+1650, 172]), ever (1 [+1666, 172]), every respect (1 [+4246]), everyone (1 [+4246, 476]), everything (1), everything (1 [+4246, 5007]), evildoers (1 [+2237, 490]), extraordinary (1 [+4024, 5593]), face (1 [+4725, 1161]), family (1 [+4123]), family (1 [+3875, 4252]), family (1 [+3836, 3875, 4252]), family (1 [+3875, 3836, 4252]), fellow (1 [+5250]), fickle (1 [+1786, 5968]), finally (1 [+5465]), first (1 [+3552]), first (1 [+4728]), followers (1 [+4309]), for (1 [+1328]), for (1 [+1328]), for (1 [+1328]), for (1 [+1650]), for all time (1 [+1650, 1457]), forevermore (1 [+1650, 4246, 172]), formerly (1 [+4728]), from house to house (1 [+3864]), from village to village (1 [+3267, 3241]), from village to village (1 [+2848, 3267]), furious (1 [+1391, 2840]), further (1 [+3370]), getting late (1 [+6052, 4216]), give in (1 [+1634, 5717]), go back (1 [+2188, 1650, 3958]), interests[s] (1), God[s] (2), God[s] (1 [+3281]), God-fearing gentiles (1 [+5828, 2536]), God's family (1 [+81]), got together (1 [+5251, 2093, 899]), hair (1 [+2582, 3051]), handed over (1 [+4140, 5931]), has no pity (1 [+3091, 5073]), he[s] (1 [+2536]), he[s] (1 [+3261]), he[s] (1 [+995]), he[s] (1 [+1333]), he[s] (1 [+2476]), he (1 [+4725, 899]), he (1 [+1328, 5931, 899]), he[s] (1 [+4460, 899, 1877, 899]), her[s] (1 [+3613]), her[s] (1 [+4086]), her own (1), him[s] (1 [+467]), him[s] (1 [+801]), him[s] (1 [+2708]), him[s] (1 [+2930]), him[s] (1 [+3812]), him (1 [+3950, 899]), him[s] (1 [+476, 4047]), him[s] (1 [+4737, 1697]), his son[s] (2), his home (1 [+2625]), his native language (1 [+1666, 2625]), home (1 [+2625]), house[s] (1), household (1), household[s] (1), how (1), how (1 [+2848]), how (1 [+4309]), how slow (1 [+1096, 2840]), I (1), illness (1 [+819, 4922]), illness (1 [+1877, 4922]), immediately (1 [+1877, 899, 6052]), in accordance with (1 [+2848, 381]), in agreement (1 [+1650, 1651]), in an uproar (1 [+4398, 5180]), in comparison with (1 [+1877, 4047, 3538, 1641]), in full (1 [+2698]), in order to (1 [+4639]), in person (1 [+4242, 3836, 5393]), in person (1 [+3836, 4242, 5393]), in public (1 [+1883, 3295]), in the early days (1 [+4754]), in the present case (1 [+3814]), in God's name (1 [+3991, 2536]), in the same way (1 [+899]), in this way (1 [+1650]), indeed (1 [+3525]), indoors (1 [+1650, 3864]), inside (1 [+1877, 3864]), interests (1), invalid (1 [+2400, 1877, 819]), inwardly (1 [+2276]), inwardly (1 [+1877, 3220]), it[s] (1 [+3693]), it[s] (1 [+993]), it[s] (1 [+1561]), it[s] (1 [+1847]), it[s] (1 [+2295]), it[s] (1 [+2585]), it[s] (1 [+3954]), it[s] (1 [+4384]), it[s] (1 [+4784]), it[s] (1 [+4839]), it[s] (1 [+5013]), it[s] (1 [+5853]), it[s] (1 [+69, 1697]), it[s] (1 [+899, 3456]), it[s] (1 [+1155, 4047]), it[s] (1 [+5516, 2240]), its[s] (1 [+1178]), its[s] (1 [+2639]), its[s] (1 [+4922]), its[s] (1 [+5393]), its[s] (1 [+4725, 899]), itself (1), just after sunrise (1 [+422, 2463]), keep in suspense (1 [+6034, 149]), kneel (1 [+2828, 1205]), knelt (1 [+5502, 1205]), lame (1 [+105, 4546]), landed (1 [+609, 1650, 1178]), landed (1 [+2093, 1178, 2262]), landed (1 [+2262, 2093, 1178]), late in the afternoon (1 [+2465, 806, 3111]), late (1 [+4070, 6052]), later (1 [+1309]), lies (1 [+3281, 6022]), lift to help (1 [+4718, 5845]), like (1 [+2848, 3928]), like-minded (1 [+899, 5858]), listen carefully (1 [+5502, 1650, 4044]), live in harmony (1 [+899, 5858]), lived (1 [+2998, 2400]), longed for (1 [+2123, 6034]), look up (1 [+4057, 2048]), looked (1 [+149, 4057]), looked (1 [+2048, 4057]), looking (1 [+2048, 4057]), lustfully (1 [+4639, 2121]), made king (1 [+3284, 993]), made post bond (1 [+3284, 2653, 4123]), made think (1 [+5502, 1877, 2840]), make up mind (1 [+5502, 1877, 2840]), mankind (1 [+5882, 474]), Mary[s] (1), matters (1), me (1 [+1609, 5889]), me (1 [+4725, 1609]), me (1 [+6034, 1609]), mean (1 [+1639, 3364, 4047]), meanwhile (1 [+1877, 3568]), met (1 [+3972, 4725]), midnight (1 [+3545, 3816]), mine (1), more[s] (1 [+2843]), motioned (1 [+2939, 5931]), motioned for silence (1 [+2939, 5931]), my (1 [+3950, 1609]), name (1 [+2813, 3950]), named (1 [+2813, 3950]), nearby (1 [+899]), nearby (1 [+4309, 5536, 1697]), never (1 [+4024, 1650, 172]), never again (1 [+4024, 3590, 1650, 172]), next (1 [+1650, 3516]), next to (1 [+1877, 3146]), nine in the morning (1 [+6052, 5569, 2465]), no never (1 [+4024, 3590, 1650, 172]), no ordinary (1 [+842, 2536]), now (1 [+1306]), now (1 [+608, 3814]), now (1 [+3814]), numbering (1 [+1639, 750]), O (1), often (1 [+4498]), on (1), on (1 [+1877]), on board (1 [+1877, 4450]), on duty (1 [+1877, 5423]), once (1 [+4728]), one (1 [+899]), one (1 [+3525]), one of (1 [+1666, 750]), one place (1 [+899]), one's (1), others (1 [+1254]), others (1 [+3525]), others (1 [+1254]), our people live scattered (1 [+1402]), out of the body[s] (1 [+1650, 909, 1744]), outsiders (1 [+2033]), outward (1 [+1877, 5745]), outwardly (1 [+1877, 5745]), outwardly (1 [+2032, 476]), people (1), man[s] (1), Paul[s] (1), performed (1 [+1328, 5931, 1181]), permanent (1 [+1650, 172]), pieces[s] (1), perform (1 [+1181, 1328, 5931]), possessions (1), pottery (1 [+5007, 3039]), present (1 [+3814, 2789]), prompted (1 [+965, 1650, 2840]), proud (1 [+5734, 5858]), publicly (1 [+1967, 4436]), rain (1), ran ahead (1 [+4731, 1650, 1869]), reached (1 [+1753, 5931]), reaching more and more (1 [+4429, 1328, 4498]), realities (1 [+1635, 4547]), reptiles (1 [+2260, 1178]), resolutely (1 [+4725, 5114]), return (1 [+2262, 1650, 4099]), rewarding (1 [+1443, 3635]), samaritan (1 [+1666, 4899]), say (1 [+1666, 5125]), sealed (1 [+2400, 5382]), seashore (1 [+5927, 2498]), seed[s] (1), seize (1 [+2095, 2093, 5931]), seized (1 [+2095, 5931, 2093]), seized (1 [+2095, 2093, 5931]), self-seeking (1 [+2426, 1571]), shared (1 [+3275, 3102]), she[s] (1 [+1222]), she[s] (1 [+3166]), she[s] (1 [+3836, 4087, 2601]), she[s] (1 [+4087, 3836, 2601]), short (1 [+2461, 3625]), shouted (1 [+2048, 5889]), shouted (1 [+3489, 5889, 5774]), sighed deeply (1 [+417, 4460]), sight (1 [+487, 4057]), since that time (1 [+3370]), so (1), so as (1 [+1650]), so overjoyed (1 [+608, 5915]), so (1 [+1650]), so then (1 [+1650]), some time ago (1 [+4574, 4047, 2465]), some (1 [+3525]), some time ago (1 [+4574, 4047, 2465]), someone's (1), something (1), soon afterward (1 [+1877, 2009]), sound asleep (1 [+2965, 608, 5678]), speak (1 [+487, 5125]), speak (1 [+489, 5125]), sphere of service (1 [+3586, 2834]), spoken freely (1 [+5125, 487]), stand firm (1 [+5114, 2840]), still others (1 [+1254]), strengthening (1 [+2185, 6034]), stripped (1 [+4351, 2668]), such that (1 [+1650]), sun moon and stars (1 [+5131, 4041]), sunset (1 [+1544, 2463]), Syria (1 [+3107, 3836, 5353]), Syria (1 [+3836, 3107, 5353]), take over (1 [+3284, 5536]), takes captive (1 [+1639, 5194]), tentmaker (1 [+5010, 5492]), terms (1), terrorists (1 [+467, 4974]), testify (1 [+625, 3457]), that was the time (1 [+1877, 2465, 1697]), that (1 [+1877]), that (1 [+4309]), that[s] (1 [+2434]), that same (1), the expert in the law[s] (1), the former (1 [+1254]), the latter (1 [+3525]), the manager[s] (1), the seed[s] (2), the virgins[s] (1), the workers who were hired[s] (1), the (1 [+4005]), the coast (1 [+2093, 2498]), the father[s] (1), the interests (1), the mother (1), the parts[s] (1 [+5393]), the same as (1 [+1651, 2779, 899]), the soldiers[s] (1), the sons (1), the whole universe (1 [+4246]), the wife (1), their own[s] (1 [+476]), them[s] (1 [+1177]), them[s] (1 [+2239]), them[s] (1 [+2465]), them[s] (1 [+2585]), them[s] (1 [+2681]), them[s] (1 [+3295]), them[s] (1 [+4252, 1609]), them[s] (1 [+4546, 899]), them[s] (1 [+5284, 899]), them[s] (1 [+2997, 2093, 3836, 1178]), them[s] (1 [+3836, 2997, 2093, 1178]), themselves (1 [+2840, 899]), themselves (1 [+6034, 899]), then able to (1 [+1650]), there (1 [+1877, 5536]), there[s] (1 [+3864]), there[s] (1 [+1650, 2038]), there[s] (1 [+1877, 4047, 4484]), they[s] (1 [+476]), they[s] (1 [+1322]), they[s] (1 [+476]), they[s] (1 [+1506]), they[s] (1 [+2989]), they[s] (1 [+5861]), they[s] (1 [+213, 899]), they[s] (1 [+899, 6001]), they[s] (1 [+4057, 899]), they[s] (1 [+5125, 899]), thinking (1 [+1181, 5856]), this (1 [+3814]), this[s]

(1 [+2240, 4047]), this[S] (1 [+2465, 4047]), this[S] (1 [+4047, 2465]), this[S] (1 [+4839, 4047]), this day (1 [+4958, 2465]), this[S] (1 [+4047, 3364]), those[S] (1 [+3295]), thoughts[S] (1), three in the afternoon (1 [+6052, 1888, 2465]), threw arms around (1 [+2158, 2093, 5549]), through (1 [+1328, 5931]), to (1 [+4639]), to myself (1 [+6034, 1609]), to show that (1 [+4639]), to their number (1 [+2093, 899]), today (1 [+1877, 4958, 2465]), told (1 [+550, 3364, 4047]), too (1 [+899, 2779]), took at word (1 [+4409, 3364]), touched (1 [+608, 5999]), traveled from town to town (1 [+1388, 4484]), trusted personal servant (1 [+2093, 3131]), trying to kill (1 [+2426, 6034]), turned against (1 [+2048, 4761, 899]), under (1 [+4123, 4546]), underfoot[S] (1 [+5679, 476]), united (1 [+1877, 899]), unseen (1 [+1877, 3220]), unseen (1 [+1877, 3224]), unusual (1 [+4024, 5593]), us (1), us (1 [+3517, 1609]), very (1), very old (1 [+4581, 1877, 2465]), we (1 [+4922, 1609]), welfare (1 [+4309]), what[S] (1 [+161]), what (1 [+5516, 2240]), what happened[S] (1), what has happened to (1 [+2848]), what started[S] (1 [+3586]), whatever (1 [+4005, 5516, 1569]), whatever (1 [+4246]), whatever (1 [+4005, 5516, 323]), when (1 [+1877]), where (1 [+1650, 5536]), where[S] (1 [+1650, 5596]), which[S] (1 [+3364, 899]), while (1 [+1877]), who[S] (1 [+2681]), who[S] (1 [+476, 4047]), who was hired[S] (1), whose temple[S] (1), why (1 [+5515, 162]), why (1 [+162, 1328, 4005]), wife (1), with great fervor (1 [+2417, 4460]), within (1 [+1877, 3517]), woke up (1 [+1586, 608, 5678]), wondered about (1 [+5502, 1877, 2840]), wounded (1 [+2400, 4435]), yes tonight (1 [+4047, 3816]), you (1 [+3950, 5148]), you (1 [+4725, 5148]), you (1 [+5148, 4725]), you (1 [+5148, 3950]), you[S] (1 [+4364, 5148]), you have (1 [+5050]), your own (1), your own home (1 [+2625]), your own private (1 [+2625]), yourselves (1 [+6034, 5148]), NDT (8581)

G3837 ὀγδοήκοντα ogdoēkonta, n. num. [2] [√3893]. eighty:– eight hundred (1), eighty-four (1 [+5475])

G3838 ὄγδοος ogdoos, a. [5] [√3893]. eighth:– eighth (3), and seven others[S] (1), eight (1)

G3839 ὄγκος onkos, n. [1] [→5665]. hinderance, impediment:– hinders (1)

G3840 ὅδε hode, p. demo. [10] [√3836]. this (one); thus:– these (7), she (1), this or that (1), NDT (1)

G3841 ὁδεύω hodeuō, v. [1] [√3847]. to travel:– traveled (1)

G3842 ὁδηγέω hodēgeō, v. [5] [√3847 + 72]. to lead, guide; explain, instruct:– lead (3), explains (1), guide (1)

G3843 ὁδηγός hodēgos, n. [5] [√3847 + 72]. guide, leader:– guides (3), guide (2)

G3844 ὁδοιπορέω hodoiporeō, v. [1] [√3847 + 4513]. to be on a journey, travel:– on journey (1)

G3845 ὁδοιπορία hodoiporia, n. [2] [√3847 + 4513]. journey:– journey (1), on the move (1)

G3846 ὁδοποιέω hodopoieō, v. Not used in NIVEBC. [√3847 + 4472]. to make a path

G3847 ὁδός hodos, n. [101] [→316, 1447, 1476, 1658, 2016, 2337, 2338, 3497, 3841, 3842, 3843, 3844, 3845, 3846, 4227, 5321, 5322]. road, path, a general term for a thoroughfare to get from one place to another; by extension: way, manner of life; "the Way" is a term for the Christian lifestyle (Ac 9:2; 19:9):– way (51), road (17), path (7), journey (5), ways (5), roadside (3), a Sabbath day's walk from (1 [+1584, 4879, 2400]), among (1 [+1650]), direction (1), do (1), paths (1), roads (1), route (1), street (1), streets (1), the (1), traveled on (1 [+2262]), walked along (1 [+4472]), way of life (1)

G3848 ὀδούς odous, n. [12] tooth:– teeth (10), tooth (2)

G3849 ὀδυνάω odynaō, v. [4] [√3850]. to grieve, be anxious, in agony:– in agony (2), anxiously (1), grieved (1)

G3850 ὀδύνη odynē, n. [2] [→3849]. anguish, grief, pain:– anguish (1), griefs (1)

G3851 ὀδυρμός odyrmos, n. [2] deep sorrow, mourning, lamentation:– deep sorrow (1), mourning (1)

G3852 Ὀζίας Ozias, n. pr. [2] Uzziah, "*Yahweh is [my] strength*":– Uzziah (2)

G3853 ὄζω ozō, v. [1] [→2380, 2455, 4011, 4018]. to give off a bad odor, stink, smell:– bad odor (1)

G3854 ὅθεν hothen, adv. [15] [√4005]. from where, from there; therefore, this is why:– where (3), therefore (2), for this reason (1), from death[S] (1), from there (1), so (1), so then (1), that (1), this is how (1), this is why (1), NDT (2)

G3855 ὀθόνη othonē, n. [2] [→3856]. linen sheet:– sheet (2)

G3856 ὀθόνιον othonion, n. [5] [√3855]. (pl.) strips of linen, bandages:– strips of linen (4), linen (1)

G3857 οἶδα oida, v. [319] [→4631, 5287?, 5288?, 5323]. to know, to possess information; recognize, realize, to come to know; to understand, to be able to use knowledge:– know (219), knew (20), knows (15), knowing (12), realize (8), know how (7), known (6), understand (5), had idea (2), acknowledge (1), acquainted with (1), aware (1 [+1877, 1571]), be (1), convinced (1), did[S] (1), fathom (1), get learning (1 [+1207]), grasp (1), had in mind (1), have idea (1), know about (1), knows how (1), learn (1), meant (1), recognize (1), regard (1), remember (1), see (1), sure (1), take note (1), tell (1), understanding (1), NDT (2)

G3858 οἰκεῖος oikeios, a. [3] [√3875]. belonging to the household, of the immediate family:– belong to the family (1), household (1), members of household (1)

G3859 οἰκετεία oiketeia, n. [1] [√3875]. servant in a household:– servants in household (1)

G3860 οἰκέτης oiketēs, n. [4] [√3875]. house servant, domestic slave:– one[S] (1), servant (1), servants (1), slaves (1)

G3861 οἰκέω oikeō, v. [9] [√3875]. to live, dwell:– living (3), live (2), dwell (1), dwells (1), lives (1), lives in (1)

G3862 οἴκημα oikēma, n. [1] [√3875]. cell, room in a prison:– cell (1)

G3863 οἰκητήριον oikētērion, n. [2] [√3875]. dwelling, home:– dwelling (2)

G3864 οἰκία oikia, n. [93] [√3875]. house, home; family:– house (62), home (13), household (4), houses (4), homes (3), family (1), from house to house (1 [+3836]), indoors (1 [+1650, 3836]), inside (1 [+1877, 3836]), live in (1), there[S] (1 [+3836]), NDT (1)

G3865 οἰκιακός oikiakos, n. [2] [√3875]. member of a household:– members of household (2)

G3866 οἰκοδεσποτέω oikodespoteō, v. [1] [√3875 + 1305]. to manage one's home:– manage homes (1)

G3867 οἰκοδεσπότης oikodespotēs, n. [12] [√3875 + 1305]. head or owner of the house, landowner:– owner of the house (5), landowner (2 [+476]), head of the house (1), landowner (1), owner (1), owner of a house (1 [+476]), owner's (1)

G3868 οἰκοδομέω oikodomeō, v. [40] [√3875 + 1560]. to build, build up, rebuild, a physical edifice; by extension: to edify, strengthen, develop another person's life through acts and words of love and encouragement:– build (12), built (10), builders (4), building (3), build up (2), edifies (2), builds up (1), constructive (1), edified (1), emboldened (1), rebuild (1), rebuild (1 [+4099]), strengthened (1)

G3869 οἰκοδομή oikodomē, n. [18] [√3875 + 1560]. building, construction, a physical edifice; by extension: building up, edification, strengthening, developing another person's life through acts and words of love and encouragement:– building (3), building up (3), buildings (3), build up (2), built up (2), strengthening (2), builds up (1), edification (1), edified (1 [+3284])

G3870 οἰκοδομία oikodomia, n. Not used in NIVEBC. [√3875 + 1560]. edification

G3871 οἰκοδόμος oikodomos, n. [1] [√3875 + 1560]. builder, one who constructs an edifice:– builders (1)

G3872 οἰκονομέω oikonomeō, v. [1] [√3875 + 3795]. to manage:– manager (1)

G3873 οἰκονομία oikonomia, n. [9] [√3875 + 3795]. management, administration, job of administration; what is put into effect, plan:– administration (2), job (2), commission (1), management (1), put into effect (1), trust (1), work (1)

G3874 οἰκονόμος oikonomos, n. [10] [√3875 + 3795]. manager, administrator, director, trustee:– manager (4), director of public works (1), entrusted with (1), given a trust (1), manages household (1), stewards (1), trustees (1)

G3875 οἶκος oikos, n. [113] [→488, 1594, 1940, 2224, 2997, 2998, 2999, 3000, 3001, 3578, 3579, 3858, 3859, 3860, 3861, 3862, 3863, 3864, 3865, 3866, 3867, 3868, 3869, 3870, 3871, 3872, 3873, 3874, 3876, 3877, 3878, 4109, 4228, 4229, 4230, 4340, 4341, 5324, 5325]. house, home, a physical edifice; of royalty: palace; of deity: temple; by extension: family, lineage, people who live in or originated in a particular house:– house (51), home (9 [+899]), household (9), home (8), family (7), home (5 [+5148]), people (4), Israel (3 [+2702]), from house to house (3 [+2848]), descendant (1 [+1666]), descendants (1), family (1 [+3836, 4252]), family (1 [+3836, 3836, 4252]), homes (1), households (1), houses (1), indoors (1 [+1650]), itself[S] (1), market (1 [+1866]), members of household (1), palace (1), palaces (1), sanctuary (1)

G3876 οἰκουμένη oikoumenē, n. [15] [√3875]. the (inhabited) world, (Roman) world; humankind:– world (11), roman world (2), all over world (1), of world (1)

G3877 οἰκουργός oikourgos, a. [1] [√3875]. busy at home, domestic, homemaking:– busy at home (1)

G3878 οἰκουρός oikouros, a. Not used in NIVEBC. [√3875]. staying at home, domestic

G3879 οἰκτείρω oikteirō, v. Not used in NIVEBC. [√3882]. to have compassion on

G3880 οἰκτιρμός oiktirmos, n. [5] [√3882]. compassion, mercy, pity:– compassion (2), mercy (2), compassion (1 [+5073])

G3881 οἰκτίρμων oiktirmōn, a. [3] [√3882]. merciful, compassionate:– merciful (2), mercy (1)

G3882 οἰκτίρω oiktirō, v. [2] [→3879, 3880, 3881]. to have compassion on:– have compassion (2)

G3883 οἶμαι oimai, v. Not used in NIVEBC. [√3887]. to think, suppose, expect

G3884 οἰνοπότης oinopotēs, n. [2] [√3885 + 4403]. drunkard, wine-drinker:– drunkard (2)

G3885 οἶνος oinos, n. [34] [→3884, 3886, 4232]. wine:– wine (32), winepress (1 [+3332]), NDT (1)

G3886 οἰνοφλυγία oinophlygia, n. [1] [√3885 + 5827]. drunkenness:– drunkenness (1)

G3887 οἴομαι oiomai, v. [3] [→3883]. to suppose, think, expect:– expect (1), suppose (1), supposing (1)

G3888 οἷος hoios, p. rel. [14] [→3889, 4481; cf. 3836 + 4005]. what sort of, what kind of:– as (5), how (1), like (1), than (1), the (1), unequaled (1 [+4024, 1181]), unequaled (1 [+4024, 1181, 5525]), what (1), what kinds (1), NDT (1)

G3889 οἱοσδηποτοῦν hoiosdēpotoun, adv. Not used in NIVEBC. [√3888 + 1314 + 4544 + 4036]. no matter what

G3890 ὀκνέω okneō, v. [1] [→3891]. to delay, hesitate:– at once (1 [+3590])

G3891 ὀκνηρός oknēros, a. [3] [√3890]. lazy, idle, not active; troublesome:– lacking (1), lazy (1), trouble (1)

G3892 ὀκταήμερος oktaēmeros, a. [1] [√3893 + 2465]. eighth day:– on the eighth day (1)

G3893 ὀκτώ oktō, n. num. [8] [→1277, 3837, 3838, 3892]. eight:– eight (4), a week later (1 [+3552, 2465]), eighteen (1 [+1274, 2779]), eighth (1), thirty-eight (1 [+5558])

G3894 ὀλεθρευτής olethreutēs, n. Not used in NIVEBC. [√3897]. destroyer

G3895 ὀλεθρεύω olethreuō, v. Not used in NIVEBC. [√3897]. to destroy

G3896 ὀλέθριος olethrios, a. Not used in NIVEBC. [√3897]. deadly, destructive

G3897 ὄλεθρος olethros, n. [4] [→660, 661, 724, 2017, 3894, 3895, 3896, 3904, 3905, 5272]. destruction, ruin:– destruction (3), ruin (1)

G3898 ὀλιγοπιστία oligopistia, n. [1] [√3900 + 4412]. littleness of faith:– little faith (1)

G3899 ὀλιγόπιστος oligopistos, a. [5] [√3900 + 4412]. of little faith:– of little faith (4), little faith (1)

G3900 ὀλίγος oligos, a. [41] [→3898, 3899, 3901, 3902, 3903]. little, small, short; (pl.) few:– few (16), little (8), little while (3), short (3), some (2), a lot of (1 [+4024]), briefly (1 [+1328]), briefly (1 [+1877]), continued raging (1 [+4024, 2130]), great (1 [+4024]), long (1 [+4024]), many (1 [+4024]), sharp (1 [+4024]), small (1)

G3901 ὀλιγόψυχος oligopsychos, a. [1] [√3900 + 6038]. timid, fainthearted, discouraged:– disheartened (1)

G3902 ὀλιγωρέω oligōreō, v. [1] [√3900]. to make light of, despise:– make light of (1)

G3903 ὀλίγως oligōs, adv. [1] [√3900]. scarcely, barely, hardly:– just (1)

G3904 ὀλοθρευτής olothreutēs, n. [1] [√3897]. destroyer:– destroying (1)

G3905 ὀλοθρεύω olothreuō, v. [1] [√3897]. to destroy:– destroyer (1)

G3906 ὁλοκαύτωμα holokautōma, n. [3] [√3910 + 2794]. burnt offering, wholly consumed on the altar as dedicated to God:– burnt offerings (3)

G3907 ὁλοκληρία holoklēria, n. [1] [√3910 + 3102]. completeness, wholeness (in healing):– completely healed (1 [+1443, 3836, 4047])

G3908 ὁλόκληρος holoklēros, a. [2] [√3910 + 3102]. whole, complete:– complete (1), whole (1)

G3909 ὀλολύζω ololyzō, v. [1] to wail, cry out:– wail (1)

G3910 ὅλος holos, a. [108] [→2772, 2773, 3906, 3907, 3908, 3911, 3914]. all, whole, entire; throughout:– whole (53), all (33), throughout (6 [+1877]), all over (5 [+1650]), entire (2), throughout (2 [+1650]), throughout (2 [+2848]), bottom (1), full (1), steeped (1), throughout (1), whole (1 [+4116])

G3911 ὁλοτελής holotelēs, a. [1] [√3910 + 5465]. through and through, wholly, completely:– through and through (1)

G3912 Ὀλυμπᾶς Olympas, n. pr. [1] Olympas:– Olympas (1)

G3913 ὄλυνθος olynthos, n. [1] late fig:– fig tree (1)

G3914 ὅλως ***holōs***, adv. [4] [√*3910*]. completely, (not) at all; actually:– at all (2), actually (1), completely (1)

G3915 ὄμβρος ***ombros***, n. [1] rainstorm (that may include thunder and lightning):– rain (1)

G3916 ὁμείρομαι ***homeiromai***, v. [1] to love, long for:– cared for (1)

G3917 ὁμιλέω ***homileō***, v. [4] [→*3918, 3919, 5326; cf. 3927*]. to talk, converse:– talked (2), talking (2)

G3918 ὁμιλία ***homilia***, n. [1] [√*3917*]. company, associations:– company (1)

G3919 ὅμιλος ***homilos***, n. Not used in NIVEBC. [√*3917*]. crowd, throng

G3920 ὁμίχλη ***homichlē***, n. [1] mist, fog:– mists (1)

G3921 ὄμμα ***omma***, n. [2] [√*3972*]. eye:– eyes (2)

G3922 ὄμνυμι ***omnymi***, v. Not used in NIVEBC. [√*3923*]. to swear, take an oath

G3923 ὀμνύω ***omnyō***, v. [26] [→*3922, 3993, 5350*]. to declare an oath, swear an oath, promise with an oath:– swears (10), swear (5), swore (5), declared on oath (2), promised (1), promised with an oath (1), swear an oath (1), sworn (1)

G3924 ὁμοθυμαδόν ***homothymadon***, adv. [11] [√*3927 + 2596*]. united, in togetherness, as one:– together (4), all (2), agreed (1 [+*1506, 1181*]), all together (1), joined together (1), united (1), with one mind (1)

G3925 ὁμοιάζω ***homoiazō***, v. Not used in NIVEBC. [√*3927*]. to be like, resemble

G3926 ὁμοιοπαθής ***homoiopathēs***, a. [2] [√*3927 + 4248*]. like, of the same quality or kind of desires:– even as (1), like (1)

G3927 ὅμοιος ***homoios***, a. [45] [→*926, 3924, 3925, 3926, 3928, 3929, 3930, 3931, 3932, 3933, 3936, 3937, 3938, 3939, 3940, 4234, 4235, 5327; cf. 3917, 3933*]. like, similar, of a same or similar nature or quality:– like (38), as (2), of (1), resembled (1 [+*1639*]), similar (1), NDT (2)

G3928 ὁμοιότης ***homoiotēs***, n. [2] [√*3927*]. similarity, likeness:– just as (1 [+*2848*]), like (1 [+*2848, 3836*])

G3929 ὁμοιόω ***homoioō***, v. [15] [√*3927*]. to make like, compare; (pass.) to be like, become like:– like (8), compare (4), in form (1), made like (1), say is like (1)

G3930 ὁμοίωμα ***homoiōma***, n. [6] [√*3927*]. likeness; looking like, image; form, appearance:– likeness (2), as (1 [+*2093, 3836*]), like (1), looked like (1), made to look like (1)

G3931 ὁμοίως ***homoiōs***, adv. [31] [√*3927*]. likewise, in the same way, similarly:– in the same way (10), the same (4), also (3), likewise (3), so (3), like (1), received[S] (1), similarly (1), the same (1 [+*2777*]), the same thing (1), too (1), NDT (2)

G3932 ὁμοίωσις ***homoiōsis***, n. [1] [√*3927*]. likeness:– likeness (1)

G3933 ὁμολογέω ***homologeō***, v. [26] [→*469, 2018, 3934, 3935; cf. 3927 + 3306*]. to confess, acknowledge, agree, admit, declare; this can be a profession of allegiance, an admission of bad behavior, or an emphatic declaration of a truth:– acknowledge (5), acknowledges (4), confess (2), acknowledged (1), admit (1), admitting (1), believe (1), claim (1), confessed (1), declare (1), fulfill promise (1 [+*2039, 4005*]), made confession (1 [+*3934*]), openly acknowledge faith (1), openly profess (1), profess faith (1), promised (1), publicly acknowledges (1), tell plainly (1)

G3934 ὁμολογία ***homologia***, n. [6] [√*3933*]. confession, profession, acknowledgment, to openly express commitment and allegiance:– confession (2), acknowledge (1), faith profess (1), made confession (1 [+*3933*]), profess (1)

G3935 ὁμολογουμένως ***homologoumenōs***, adv. [1] [√*3933*]. beyond all question, most certainly:– beyond all question (1)

G3936 ὁμόσε ***homose***, adv. Not used in NIVEBC. [√*3927*]. together

G3937 ὁμότεχνος ***homotechnos***, a. [1] [√*3927 + 5492*]. of the same trade:– as (1)

G3938 ὁμοῦ ***homou***, adv. [4] [√*3927*]. together:– together (3), both (1 [+*3836, 1545*])

G3939 ὁμόφρων ***homophrōn***, a. [1] [√*3927 + 5856*]. living in harmony with, like-minded:– like-minded (1)

G3940 ὅμως ***homōs***, adv. [3] [√*3927*]. just as; at the same time:– at the same time (1), even in the case of (1), just as (1)

G3941 ὄναρ ***onar***, n. [6] dream:– dream (6)

G3942 ὀνάριον ***onarion***, n. [1] [√*3952*]. young donkey:– young donkey (1)

G3943 ὀνειδίζω ***oneidizō***, v. [9] [√*3945*]. to heap insults on, denounce, find fault, rebuke:– insult (3), denounce (1), finding fault (1), heaped insults (1), heaped insults on (1), insulted (1), rebuked (1)

G3944 ὀνειδισμός ***oneidismos***, n. [5] [√*3945*]. disgrace, insult:– disgrace (3), insult (1), insults (1)

G3945 ὄνειδος ***oneidos***, n. [1] [→*3943, 3944*]. disgrace:– disgrace (1)

G3946 Ὀνήσιμος ***Onēsimos***, n. pr. [2] [√*3949*]. Onesimus, "*useful*":– Onesimus (2)

G3947 Ὀνησίφορος ***Onēsiphoros***, n. pr. [2] [√*3949 + 5770*]. Onesiphorus, "*one bringing usefulness*":– Onesiphorus (2)

G3948 ὀνικός ***onikos***, a. [2] [√*3952*]. pertaining to a donkey, millstone worked by a donkey:– large millstone (2 [+*3685*])

G3949 ὀνίνημι ***oninēmi***, v. [1] [→*493, 3946, 3947*]. to have benefit or joy:– have benefit (1)

G3950 ὄνομα ***onoma***, n. [229] [→*2226, 2381, 3951, 5540, 6024*]. name; title; reputation:– name (158), named (32), names (9), call (3 [+*2813, 3836*]), me (3 [+*3836, 1609*]), as (2 [+*1650*]), called (1), called (1 [+*4005*]), called (1 [+*4005, 3836*]), group (1 [+*4063*]), him (1 [+*3836, 899*]), is[S] (1 [+*1650*]), me (1 [+*3836, 1609*]), my (1 [+*3836, 1609*]), name (1 [+*2813*]), name (1 [+*2813, 3836*]), named (1 [+*2813, 3836*]), name's (1), people (1), people (1 [+*476*]), reputation (1), you (1 [+*3836, 5148*]), you (1 [+*5148, 3836*]), NDT (5)

G3951 ὀνομάζω ***onomazō***, v. [9] [√*3950*]. to give a name, designate a name; to confess; (mid.) to call oneself; (pass.) to be named; be known:– a hint of (1), claims (1), confesses (1), derives name (1), designated (1), invoke (1), invoked (1), known (1), named (1)

G3952 ὄνος ***onos***, n. [5] [→*3942, 3948*]. donkey (female or male):– donkey (4), donkey's (1)

G3953 ὄντως ***ontōs***, adv. [10] [√*1639*]. really, certainly, surely:– really (5), certainly (1), indeed (1), it is true (1), surely (1), truly (1)

G3954 ὄξος ***oxos***, n. [6] [√*3955*]. wine vinegar:– wine vinegar (4), drink[S] (1), it[S] (1 [+*3836*])

G3955 ὀξύς ***oxys***, a. [8] [→*3954, 4236, 4237*]. sharp; swift, quick:– sharp (7), swift (1)

G3956 ὀπή ***opē***, n. [2] hole, opening:– holes (1), NDT (1)

G3957 ὄπισθεν ***opisthen***, adv. [7] [√*3958*]. from behind; after:– behind (4), after (1), in back (1), on both sides (1 [+*2277, 2779*])

G3958 ὀπίσω ***opisō***, adv. [35] [→*3957, 5541*]. behind, after, following:– after (8), behind (5), back (3 [+*1650, 3836*]), follow (3), be disciple (2 [+*2262*]), follow (2 [+*4513*]), around (1 [+*1650, 3836*]), back (1), be disciple (1 [+*199*]), drew back (1 [+*599, 1650, 3836*]), follow (1 [+*2262*]), followed (1), followed (1 [+*599*]), go back (1 [+*2188, 1650, 3836*]), led in revolt (1 [+*923*]), overtake (1), perversion (1 [+*599, 4922, 2283*]), NDT (1)

G3959 ὁπλίζω ***hoplizō***, v. [1] [√*3960*]. (mid.) to arm oneself with:– arm (1)

G3960 ὅπλον ***hoplon***, n. [6] [→*2774, 3959, 4110*]. instrument, weapon, armor:– weapons (3), instrument (2), armor (1)

G3961 ὁποῖος ***hopoios***, a. [5] [√*4544*]. what kind of, what sort of:– quality (1), what (1 [+*5525*]), what kind (1), what looks like (1 [+*1639*]), whatever (1 [+*5516*])

G3962 ὁπότε ***hopote***, pt. temp. Not used in NIVEBC. [√*4544*]. when

G3963 ὅπου ***hopou***, pt. pl. [82] [√*4544*]. where, wherever; whenever:– where (57), wherever (4 [+*1569*]), wherever (3), whenever (2 [+*1569*]), wherever (2 [+*323*]), above Jesus[S] (1 [+*1639*]), here (1), in the case of (1), on (1), on the other side[S] (1), since (1), the place where (1), there (1), together (1), wherever (1 [+*1569*]), which (1), yet even (1), NDT (2)

G3964 ὀπτάνομαι ***optanomai***, v. [1] [√*3972*]. (mid.) to appear:– appeared (1)

G3965 ὀπτασία ***optasia***, n. [4] [√*3972*]. (supernatural) vision:– vision (3), visions (1)

G3966 ὀπτός ***optos***, a. Not used in NIVEBC. broiled, roasted€ [1]:– broiled (1)

G3967 ὀπώρα ***opōra***, n. [1] [→*5781*]. fruit:– fruit (1)

G3968 ὅπως ***hopōs***, c. & adv. [53] [√*4544*]. that, so that, (in order) to:– to (16), so that (14), that (9), so (4), how (2), in order to (1), let (1), so that (1 [+*323*]), so that (1 [+*323*]), that (1 [+*323*]), the goal (1), this (1), NDT (1)

G3969 ὅραμα ***horama***, n. [12] [√*3972*]. (supernatural) vision; sight (from God):– vision (10), seen (1), sight (1)

G3970 ὅρασις ***horasis***, n. [4] [√*3972*]. appearance; vision:– appearance of (1), shone (1), vision (1), visions (1)

G3971 ὁρατός ***horatos***, a. [1] [√*3972*]. pertaining to things visible, things seen:– visible (1)

G3972 ὁράω ***horaō***, v. [448] [→*548, 898, 927, 1967, 2227, 2228, 2269, 2393, 2775, 2979, 3002, 3587, 3921, 3964, 3965, 3969, 3970, 3971, 4071, 4238, 4632, 4725, 5034, 5287?, 5288?, 5328, 5666, 5708, 5724, 5864; cf. 4057, 4725*]. to see, notice; perceive; (pass.) to appear, be seen:– saw (183), see (116), seen (63), appeared (17), looked (10), seeing (6), realized (4), look (3), look at (3), noticed (3), perceiving (3), watched (3), careful (2), do that[S] (2), indeed seen (2 [+*3972*]), responsibility (2), see that (2), see to it (2), appear (1), came upon (1), decayed (1 [+*1426*]), die (1 [+*2505*]), experience (1), found (1), had[S] (1), looked at (1), make sure (1), met (1 [+*3836, 4725*]), met with (1), mourn (1 [+*4292*]), noticing (1), recognized (1), sees (1), settle the matter (1), sight (1), to consider (1 [+*4309*]), visit (1), watch out (1), watching (1), NDT (1)

G3973 ὀργή ***orgē***, n. [36] [→*3974, 3975, 4239, 4240; cf. 3977*]. wrath, anger, the feeling and expression of strong displeasure and hostility; this can range from petty human anger to the righteous anger of God toward sinful disobedience:– wrath (27), anger (7), angry (1), punishment (1)

G3974 ὀργίζω ***orgizō***, v. [9] [√*3973*]. (mid./pass.) to be angry, enraged, to feel and express strong displeasure and hostility; this can range from petty human anger to the righteous anger of God toward sinful disobedience:– angry (4), anger (2), enraged (2), indignant (1)

G3975 ὀργίλος ***orgilos***, a. [1] [√*3973*]. quick-tempered, inclined to anger:– quick-tempered (1)

G3976 ὀργυιά ***orguia***, n. [2] [√*3977*]. fathom (about six feet):– a hundred and twenty feet deep (1 [+*1633*]), ninety feet deep (1 [+*1278*])

G3977 ὀρέγω ***oregō***, v. [3] [→*3976, 3979; cf. 3973*]. (mid.) to set one's heart on, strive for, aspire to, desire:– aspires (1), eager for (1), longing for (1)

G3978 ὀρεινός ***oreinos***, a. [2] [√*4001*]. hilly, (n.) hill country:– hill country (2)

G3979 ὄρεξις ***orexis***, n. [1] [√*3977*]. lust, desire:– lust (1)

G3980 ὀρθοποδέω ***orthopodeō***, v. [1] [√*3981 + 4546*]. to act in line with (the truth), act rightly:– acting in line (1)

G3981 ὀρθός ***orthos***, a. [2] [→*494, 1480, 1481, 2061, 2114, 3003, 3980, 3982, 3987*]. straight, level:– at that (1), level (1)

G3982 ὀρθοτομέω ***orthotomeō***, v. [1] [√*3981 + 5533*]. to handle correctly, guide on a straight path:– correctly handles (1)

G3983 ὀρθρίζω ***orthrizō***, v. [1] [√*3986*]. to get up early in the morning:– came early in the morning (1)

G3984 ὀρθρινός ***orthrinos***, a. [1] [√*3986*]. early in the morning:– early morning (1)

G3985 ὄρθριος ***orthrios***, a. Not used in NIVEBC. [√*3986*]. early in the morning

G3986 ὄρθρος ***orthros***, n. [3] [→*3983, 3984, 3985*]. dawn, daybreak, early in the morning:– dawn (1), daybreak (1), early in the morning (1)

G3987 ὀρθῶς ***orthōs***, adv. [4] [√*3981*]. correctly, rightly, plainly:– correctly (2), plainly (1), what is right (1)

G3988 ὁρίζω ***horizō***, v. [8] [√*4000*]. to determine, set, appoint, decree:– appointed (3), decided (1), decreed (1), deliberate (1), marked out (1), set (1)

G3989 ὄρνιξ ***ornix***, n. Not used in NIVEBC. [√*3998*]. bird, hen

G3990 ὅριον ***horion***, n. [12] [√*4000*]. region, area, vicinity:– region (6), vicinity (4), area (1), vicinity (1 [+*4246*])

G3991 ὁρκίζω ***horkizō***, v. [2] [√*3992*]. to command; implore, adjure:– command to come out (1), in God's name (1 [+*3836, 2536*])

G3992 ὅρκος ***horkos***, n. [10] [→*1941, 2019, 2020, 2155, 2156, 3991, 3993*]. oath:– oath (6), oaths (2), say (1 [+*1639*]), vows (1)

G3993 ὁρκωμοσία ***horkōmosia***, n. [4] [√*3992 + 3923*]. oath, taking of an oath:– oath (4)

G3994 ὁρμάω ***hormaō***, v. [5] [√*3995*]. to rush (as in a stampede):– rushed (5)

G3995 ὁρμή ***hormē***, n. [2] [→*929, 3155, 3994, 3996*]. plot, decision; impulse, desire:– pilot (1), plot (1)

G3996 ὅρμημα ***hormēma***, n. [1] [√*3995*]. sudden violence:– violence (1)

G3997 ὄρνεον ***orneon***, n. [3] [√*3998*]. bird:– birds (2), bird (1)

G3998 ὄρνις ***ornis***, n. [2] [→*3989, 3997*]. hen, bird:– hen (2)

G3999 ὁροθεσία ***horothesia***, n. [1] [√*4000 + 5502*]. exact place, fixed boundary:– boundaries (1)

G4000 ὅρος ***horos***, n. Not used in NIVEBC. [→*626, 928, 3498, 3988, 3990, 3999, 4633, 5327, 5329*]. limit

G4001 **ὄρος** ***oros***, n. [65] [→ *3978*]. hill, hillside, mountain, mountainside; this can refer to any elevated place from mounds to high mountains:– mountain (22), mount (15), mountains (9), mountainside (8), hill (5), hills (3), hillside (2), place (1)

G4002 **ὀρύσσω** ***oryssō***, v. [3] [→ *1482, 2021*]. to dig up, dig out:– dug (2), dug a hole (1)

G4003 **ὀρφανός** ***orphanos***, a. [2] [→ *682*]. (n.) an orphan:– orphans (2)

G4004 **ὀρχέομαι** ***orcheomai***, v. [4] to dance:– dance (2), danced (2)

G4005 **ὅς** ***hos***, p. rel. [1417] [→ *1475, 1478, 1484, 1668, 1930, 2745, 2749, 2771, 2776, 3854, 3888, 4007, 4013, 4015, 4020, 4021, 4022, 4023, 4121, 4529, 5538*]. who, which, what, that; anyone, someone, a certain one:– what (125), whom (113), which (108), who (105), that (75), him (54), he (40), the (32), them (27), whose (23), it (19), one (19), this (17), those (16), the people^S (15), they (14), these (13), until (13 [*+2401*]), anyone (12), anyone (10 [*+323*]), whoever (9), whoever (8 [*+323*]), their (7), when (7), when (7 [*+1877*]), his (6), some (6 [*+3525*]), whatever (6), one (5 [*+3525*]), until (5 [*+948*]), whatever (5 [*+1569*]), another (4 [*+1254*]), anyone (4 [*+1569*]), as (4), whatever (4 [*+1569*]), whoever (4 [*+323*]), whoever (4 [*+323*]), anything (3), as (3 [*+5573*]), because (3 [*+505*]), its (3), the one (3), this gospel^S (3), what (3 [*+1569*]), where (3 [*+1877*]), whoever (3 [*+1569*]), whom (3 [*+323*]), a (2), a (2 [*+323*]), another (2), anything (2 [*+1569*]), anyone (2 [*+1569*]), because (2 [*+2093*]), her (2), just as (2 [*+2848, 5573*]), matters (2), others (2), since (2 [*+608*]), some (2), the one (2 [*+323*]), the son^S (2), the gospel^S (2), the life^S (3), theirs (2), things (2), until (2 [*+3588*]), whatever (2 [*+5516, 323*]), where (2 [*+1650*]), where (2 [*+1877*]), while (2 [*+2401*]), whom (2 [*+1569*]), whoever (2 [*+1569*]), whoever (2 [*+323*]), why (2 [*+1328, 162*]), a (1 [*+1254, 323*]), Christ^S (2), idols^S (1), God^S (1), discipline^S (1), faith^S (1), food^S (1), children^S (1), Abraham^S (1), ago (1 [*+608*]), anyone (1 [*+323*]), any (1 [*+323*]), any (1 [*+5516, 323*]), anyone (1 [*+323*]), anyone (1 [*+1569*]), anyone (1 [*+5516*]), as long as (1 [*+948*]), be (1), because (1 [*+1877*]), because (1 [*+505*]), because (1 [*+1641*]), because (1 [*+1877*]), before (1 [*+4024, 3590, 2401*]), called (1 [*+3950*]), called (1 [*+3836, 3950*]), ever since (1 [*+608*]), for (1 [*+1877, 1256*]), from the time (1 [*+608*]), fulfill promise (1 [*+2039, 3933*]), her name^S (1), himself (1), his letters^S (1), his faith^S (1), holiness^S (1), I (1), if any (1 [*+323*]), in keeping with (1 [*+5516, 1569*]), in the same way (1 [*+4048, 5573*]), in that case (1 [*+4309*]), including (1 [*+1639*]), indicating that (1 [*+2848*]), it^S (1 [*+608, 794, 201*]), just as (1 [*+5573*]), just before (1 [*+948*]), just what (1 [*+5516*]), made alive^S (1 [*+1877*]), men^S (1), Mary^S (1), meanwhile (1 [*+1877*]), native (1 [*+1877, 1164*]), now (1 [*+608*]), once (1 [*+608, 323*]), one person (1 [*+3525*]), one person's (1), one of these journeys^S (1), others (1 [*+1254*]), other (1 [*+1254*]), owner of (1 [*+467*]), peace^S (1), Paul^S (1), she (1), so (1), so (1 [*+1328*]), so (1 [*+1328, 162*]), someone (1), something (1), such (2), that day^S (1), that is why (1 [*+1328, 162*]), that tribe^S (1), the death^S (1), the (1 [*+3836*]), the authority^S (1), the glory^S (1), the Jesus^S (1), the lawless one^S (1), the name^S (1), the one meant (1 [*+5642*]), the other (1 [*+1254*]), the promise^S (1), the sacrifices^S (1), the Spirit^S (1), the tabernacle^S (1), then (1 [*+948*]), therefore (1 [*+5920*]), therefore (1 [*+1328, 162*]), these signs^S (1), these ways^S (1), thing (1), third^S (1), this end^S (1), this hope^S (1), this word^S (1), this ark^S (1), this man^S (1), those gentiles^S (1), until (1 [*+1877*]), though (1 [*+1877*]), until (1 [*+948, 323*]), what (1 [*+2093*]), what (1 [*+5515*]), whatever (1 [*+323*]), whatever (1 [*+1569*]), whatever (1 [*+1254, 323*]), whatever (1 [*+1877, 1254, 323*]), whatever (1 [*+3836, 5516, 1569*]), whatever (1 [*+323*]), whatever (1 [*+3836, 5516, 323*]), whatever (1 [*+4246, 5516, 1569*]), when (1 [*+1877*]), when (1 [*+2401*]), where (1), where (1 [*+1650*]), where (1 [*+2093*]), where (1 [*+4123*]), where (1 [*+1877, 5536*]), while (1 [*+1877*]), while (2 [*+1877*]), whoever (1 [*+323*]), who (2 [*+323*]), whoever (1 [*+1569*]), whoever (1 [*+4246, 323*]), whose (1 [*+2400*]), why (1 [*+3836, 162, 1328*]), you (1), your (2), NDT (256)

G4006 **ὁσάκις** ***hosakis***, adv. [3] [√ *4012*]. as often as, whenever:– whenever (2 [*+1569*]), as often as (1 [*+1569*])

G4007 **ὅσγε** ***hosge***, p. rel. & pt. Not used in NIVEBC. [√ *4005 + 1145*]. who

G4008 **ὅσιος** ***hosios***, a. [8] [→ *495, 4009, 4010*]. holy, pious, devout; (n.) Holy One; divine decree (Ac 13:34):– holy (7), holy blessings promised (1)

G4009 **ὁσιότης** ***hosiotēs***, n. [2] [√ *4008*]. holiness:– holiness (2)

G4010 **ὁσίως** ***hosiōs***, adv. [1] [√ *4008*]. holy, in a devout manner:– holy (1)

G4011 **ὀσμή** ***osmē***, n. [6] [√ *3853*]. fragrance, odor:– aroma (3), fragrance (1), fragrant (1 [*+2380*]), fragrant offering (1 [*+2380*])

G4012 **ὅσος** ***hosos***, a. [110] [→ *4006, 4531*]. how great, how much, how far; as, just as:– all (16), whatever (8), everything (6), that (6), who (6), as (5), how much (5), what (5), those (4), all (2 [*+4246*]), as long as (2 [*+2093, 5989*]), as much as (2), in a while (2 [*+2285, 4012*]), whatever (2 [*+1569*]), whatever (2 [*+2093*]), all (1 [*+323*]), all that (1), all whom (1 [*+323*]), anyone (1 [*+1569*]), as long as (1 [*+2093*]), every (1 [*+1569*]), everything (1 [*+4246*]), everything (1 [*+4246, 323*]), everything (1 [*+4246, 1569*]), how many (1), inasmuch as (1 [*+2093, 3525, 4036*]), just as (1 [*+2848*]), just as (1 [*+2848*]), more (1), no matter how many (1), only as long as (1 [*+2093, 5989*]), others (1), people (1), so long as (1 [*+5989*]), the (1), things (1), what (1 [*+1569*]), whatever (1 [*+323*]), whatever (1 [*+4246*]), whatever (1 [*+4246, 323*]), while (1 [*+2093*]), whom (1), NDT (10)

G4013 **ὅσπερ** ***hosper***, p. rel. & pt. Not used in NIVEBC. [√ *4005 + 4302*]. whosoever

G4014 **ὀστέον** ***osteon***, n. [4] [→ *4016*]. bone:– bones (4)

G4015 **ὅστις** ***hostis***, p. rel. & indef. [144] [√ *4005 + 5516*]. who, whoever, whatever; someone, anyone, everyone; with *2401* a marker of time relationships: until, while:– who (41), they (25), which (15), that (5), this (5), whoever (5), it (3), until (3 [*+2401*]), anyone (2), she (2), them (2), these (2), those (2), whoever (2 [*+323*]), you (2), Barabbas^S (1), and (1 [*+2401*]), he (1), her (1), one (1), some (1), such (1), such^S (1), that temple^S (1), the cavalry^S (1), the new covenant^S (1), the one (1), whatever (1), while still (1 [*+2401*]), who (1 [*+1569*]), whoever (1 [*+1569*]), whoever (1 [*+4246*]), your generosity^S (1), NDT (10)

G4016 **ὀστοῦν** ***ostoun***, n. Not used in NIVEBC. [√ *4014*]. bone

G4017 **ὀστράκινος** ***ostrakinos***, a. Not used in NIVEBC. made of clay€ [2]:- clay (1), of clay (1)

G4018 **ὄσφρησις** ***osphrēsis***, n. [1] [√ *3853*]. sense of smell:– sense of smell (1)

G4019 **ὀσφῦς** ***osphys***, n. [8] waist, loins, body; belt:– waist (3), alert (1 [*+350, 3836*]), body (1), descendants (1 [*+2843, 3836*]), descended from (1 [*+2002, 1666, 3836*]), dressed ready for service (1 [*+3836, 4322*])

G4020 **ὅταν** ***hotan***, pt. temp. [120] [√ *4005 + 5445 + 323*]. when, whenever; at once; as soon as:– when (94), whenever (5), after (4), as soon as (2 [*+2453*]), that (2), while (2), any time (1), as soon as (1), before (1), by (1), moment (1), once (1), until (1 [*+1623, 3590*]), NDT (4)

G4021 **ὅτε** ***hote***, pt. temp. [102] [√ *4005 + 5445*]. when, while, after; as, as soon as:– when (83), after (7), as (4), once (2), while (2), as soon as (1), before (1), on (1), NDT (1)

G4022 **ὅτι** ***hoti***, c. [1283] [√ *4005 + 5515*]. that; because, since; for:– that (499), because (210), for (145), to (8), how (6), since (6), as (4), why (3), about (1), although (1), at (1), by (1), for (1 [*+4048*]), here (1), how could (1 [*+5515, 5516*]), if (1), in (1), in this (1), is that why (1), that is (1), the very fact that (1), though (1), though actually (1), to find (1), what (1 [*+5515*]), when (1), which (1), NDT (383)

G4023 **οὗ** ***hou***, adv. pl. [25] [√ *4005*]. where; to which:– where (19), there (2), which (2), the place where (1), wherever (1 [*+1569*])

G4024 **οὐ** ***ou***, adv. neg. [1620] [→ *2022, 2023, 2024, 2025, 4027, 4028, 4029, 4030, 4031, 4032, 4033, 4034, 4037, 4046, 4049*]. no, not, not at all, in no way, (with *3590*) absolutely not. At the beginning of a Greek question, it anticipates a positive response:– not (1023), no (137), don't (55), cannot (39 [*+1538*]), not (29 [*+3590*]), never (27 [*+3590*]), never (18), nothing (12), didn't (8), certainly not (7 [*+3590*]), neither (7), none (7), cannot (6), refused (6 [*+2527*]), without (6), aren't (5), can't (5 [*+1538*]), doesn't (5), isn't (5 [*+1639*]), never (5 [*+3590, 1650, 3836, 172*]), haven't (4), never (4 [*+3590*]), nor (4), unlawful (4 [*+2003*]), don't (3 [*+3590*]), fail (3), more than (3 [*+247*]), no (3 [*+4246*]), only (3 [*+1623, 3590*]), aren't (2 [*+1639*]), cannot (2 [*+1639*]), couldn't (2 [*+1538*]), few (2 [*+4498*]), never (2 [*+3590*]), never again (2 [*+3590*]), no (2 [*+4024*]), no (2 [*+4246*]), no (2 [*+3590*]), no (2 [*+4246*]), no at all (2), no more (2), nor (2 [*+2779*]), not again (2 [*+3590*]), not at all (2 [*+3590*]), nothing (2 [*+5515*]), nothing (2 [*+5516*]), nothing at all (2 [*+4029*]), rather than (2 [*+2779*]), refused (2), stop (2), unwilling (2 [*+2527*]), wasn't (2), what is more (2 [*+3667, 1254, 247, 2779*]), a lot of (1 [*+3900*]), against (1), am a virgin (1 [*+467, 1182*]), any more than (1 [*+2777*]), before (1 [*+2401*]), before (1 [*+3590, 2401, 4005*]), before very long (1 [*+3552, 4498*]), blinded (1 [*+1838*]), but (1 [*+2777*]), cannot (1 [*+2400*]), certainly not (1), childless (1 [*+5451*]), continued raging (1 [*+3900, 2130*]), couldn't (1 [*+2710*]), couldn't you (1 [*+2710*]), declined (1 [*+2153*]), do^S (1), doesn't (1 [*+1639*]), exceeded (1 [*+2777*]), except (1), extraordinary (1 [*+3836, 5593*]), from (1), from another place (1 [*+1949*]), getting nowhere (1 [*+6067, 4029*]), great (1 [*+3900*]), greatly (1 [*+3585*]), hanging over (1 [*+733*]), impossible (1 [*+1543*]), is it possible (1), isn't (1), isn't at all (1 [*+3590*]), lack (1), lack (1 [*+2400*]), long (1 [*+3900*]), lost (1), many (1 [*+3900*]), neither (1 [*+2779*]), never (1 [*+4537*]), never (1 [*+3590, 4537*]), never (1 [*+3590, 4799*]), never (1 [*+4033, 3590*]), never (1 [*+1650, 3836, 172*]), never again (1 [*+3590, 1650, 3836, 172*]), no (1 [*+3607*]), no (1 [*+4029*]), no ever (1 [*+4246, 3590*]), no ever (1 [*+3590*]), no hold (1 [*+4029*]), no longer (1 [*+3590*]), no never (1 [*+3590, 1650, 3836, 172*]), nobody (1 [*+5516*]), nobody (1), none (1 [*+570*]), none (1 [*+4246*]), nor (1 [*+2779*]), not (1 [*+3607*]), not by any means (1 [*+3590*]), not even (1), not one (1 [*+3590*]), nothing (1 [*+3590, 4246*]), nothing (1 [*+4029*]), nothing (1 [*+4246*]), only (1 [*+4498, 2445*]), out of place (1 [*+465*]), quite^S (1), refusal (1), refuse (1), refuse (1 [*+918*]), refuse (1 [*+2527*]), refused (1 [*+1312*]), refusing (1 [*+2527*]), refusing (1 [*+4657*]), sharp (1 [*+3900*]), shouldn't (1), shouldn't (1 [*+1256*]), the law forbids (1 [*+2003*]), unable (1 [*+1538*]), unable (1 [*+2710*]), unaware (1 [*+1182*]), unequaled (1 [*+3888, 1181*]), unequaled (1 [*+3888, 1181, 5525*]), unfinished (1 [*+4444*]), unless (1 [*+1623*]), unlike (1 [*+6055*]), until (1), unusual (1 [*+3836, 5593*]), unwilling (1 [*+2525*]), without (1 [*+1666*]), yet (1 [*+4037*]), you cannot (1 [*+1538*]), NDT (39)

G4025 **οὐά** ***oua***, pt. interj. [1] so!, aha!:– so (1)

G4026 **οὐαί** ***ouai***, pt. interj. [46] woe!, how dreadful!, alas!:– woe (42), how dreadful (3), woes (1)

G4027 **οὐδαμῶς** ***oudamōs***, adv. [1] [√ *4024 + 1254*]. by no means:– by no means (1)

G4028 **οὐδέ** ***oude***, c. neg. [144] [√ *4024 + 1254*]. and not, nor, neither, not either, not even:– or (33), nor (26), not even (17), not (14), neither (8), no (6), and no (5), even not (5), and (4), and not (2), cannot do (2 [*+1538*]), don't (2), never (2), not either (2), and cannot (1 [*+1538*]), and cannot (1), and lost (1 [*+2351*]), and nothing (1), and nothing (1 [*+5516*]), but not either (1), either or (1), even (1), haven't (1), nor (1 [*+4099*]), not (1 [*+3590*]), nothing (1 [*+1651*]), only (1 [*+1651, 1569, 3590*]), NDT (3)

G4029 **οὐδείς** ***oudeis***, a. [234] [√ *4024 + 1254 + 1651*]. no one, not anyone, nothing:– no one (90), nothing (42), no (26), anyone (7), none (7), not (6), not one (6), not any (5), any (3), anything (3), not anyone (3), not anything (3), no at all (2), nothing at all (2 [*+4024*]), others (2), conscience is clear (1 [*+5323*]), discredited (1 [*+1650, 3357*]), getting nowhere (1 [*+4024, 6067*]), haven't anything (1), never (1), no (1 [*+4024*]), no anything (1), no hold (1 [*+4024*]), no way (1), no whatever (1), nobody (1), nor anyone (1), not a thing (1), not anyone's (1), not in the least (1), nothing (1 [*+3364*]), nothing (1 [*+4024*]), nowhere (1), one (1), only (1 [*+1623, 3590*]), without (1), NDT (6)

G4030 **οὐδέποτε** ***oudepote***, adv. [16] [√ *4024 + 1254 + 4544 + 5445*]. never:– never (12), nothing ever (2), never anything (1), no ever (1)

G4031 **οὐδέπω** ***oudepō***, adv. [4] [√ *4024 + 1254*]. not yet, not ever:– not yet (2), ever (1), still not (1)

G4032 **οὐθείς** ***outheis***, a. Not used in NIVEBC. [√ *4024 + 1254 + 1651*]. no one, nobody, not anyone, nothing

G4033 **οὐκέτι** ***ouketi***, adv. [47] [√ *4024 + 2285*]. no longer, not again, not any more, no further:– no longer (26), again (2), any more (2), anymore (2), no more (2), cannot (1), cannot again (1), forgets (1 [*+3648*]), from then on (1), never (1 [*+4024, 3590*]), never again (1), no (1), none ever again (1 [*+4246*]), not (1), not anymore (1), not more (1), still (1), unable (1 [*+2710*])

G4034 **οὐκοῦν** ***oukoun***, adv. [1] [√ *4024 + 4036*]. so, then (to introduce a question):– then (1)

G4035 **Οὐλαμμαούς** ***Oulammaous***, n. pr. Not used in NIVEBC. [√ *cf. 1843*]. Oulammaous

G4036 **οὖν** ***oun***, pt. infer. & trans. [495] [→ *1326, 3528, 3529, 3889, 4034, 5521*]. therefore, then, so then:– then (112), therefore (78), so (72), now (10), and (6), at this (6), but (6), so then (5), when (3), consequently (2 [*+726*]), finally (2), finally (2 [*+5538*]), meanwhile (2), now then (2), therefore (2 [*+726*]), therefore (2 [*+726*]), thus (2), after all (1), again (1), as a result (1 [*+3525*]), as for (1), as soon as (1), at that point (1), because of (1), conclude then (1), however (1), inasmuch as (1 [*+2093, 4012, 3525*]), means (1), now (1 [*+6055*]), since (1), since (1 [*+1623*]), since (1 [*+2075*]), that (1), therefore (1 [*+726*]), this made (1), too (1), under what circumstances (1 [*+4802*]), well then (1), what shall we do (1 [*+5515, 1639*]), NDT (159)

G4037 **οὔπω** ***oupō***, adv. [27] [√ *4024*]. not yet, still not; not ever:– not yet (16), still not (3), before (1), ever (1), not (1), still (1), still no (1), still to come (1), up to that time not (1), yet (1 [*+4024*])

G4038 **οὐρά** ***oura***, n. [5] tail:– tails (4), tail (1)

G4039 **οὐράνιος** ***ouranios***, a. [9] [√ *4041*]. heavenly, in heaven, from heaven:– heavenly (7), from heaven (1), in heaven (1)

G4040 **οὐρανόθεν** ***ouranothen***, adv. [2] [√ *4041*]. from heaven:– from heaven (2)

G4041 **οὐρανός** ***ouranos***, n. [272] [→ *2230, 3547, 4039, 4040*]. sky, air, firmament, any area above the earth; heaven(s), the place of sun, moon, and stars; heaven, in which God dwells. "The third heaven" may be a Jewish technical term for God's dwelling place; "heaven" in some contexts is a euphemism for "God" (Lk 15:18):– heaven (218), heavens (22), sky (16), birds (8 [+*4374, 3836*]), heavenly (2), heavenly (2 [+*1877, 3836*]), air (1), heavenly (1 [+*1666*]), other[S] (1 [+*5679*]), sun moon and stars (1 [+*5131, 3836*])

G4042 **Οὐρβανός** ***Ourbanos***, n. pr. [1] Urbanus, "*refined, elegant*":– Urbanus (1)

G4043 **Οὐρίας** ***Ourias***, n. pr. [1] Uriah, "*Yahweh is [my] flame, light*":– Uriah's (1)

G4044 **οὖς** ***ous***, n. [36] [→ *1969, 6064, 6065*]. ear; listening, responding:– ears (28), ear (5), hearing (1), listen carefully (1 [+*5502, 1650, 3836*]), NDT (1)

G4045 **οὐσία** ***ousia***, n. [2] [√ *1639*]. wealth; estate, property:– estate (1), wealth (1)

G4046 **οὔτε** ***oute***, adv. [used as neg.] [87] [√ *4024* + *5445*]. and not, neither, nor:– nor (29), neither (19), or (14), not (7), and no (1), and none (1 [+*5516*]), and not (1), cannot (1 [+*1538*]), don't (1), either (1), even refuses (1), never (1 [+*4537*]), never (1 [+*4799*]), no (1), nothing (1), nothing (1 [+*5516*]), or even (1), NDT (5)

G4047 **οὗτος** ***houtos***, p. demo. [1382] [→ *4048, 5496, 5525, 5537, 5542*]. this, this one, these; (as object) him, her, it, them; with *1328* or *1650* it means "for this reason":– this (616), these (206), that (40), he (33), they (28), him (20), therefore (20 [+*1328*]), them (17), such (16), it (13), she (12), this is how (10 [+*1877*]), for this reason (9 [+*1328*]), those (8), that is why (7 [+*1328*]), what (7), who (6), their (5), the (4), the reason (4 [+*1328*]), Jesus[S] (3), later (3 [+*3552*]), so (3), the latter[S] (3), the reason (3 [+*1328*]), therefore (3 [+*1328*]), this is why (3 [+*1328*]), this very (3), Jesus[S] (2), above all (2 [+*4754*]), afterward (2 [+*3552*]), because (2 [+*1328*]), for that reason (2 [+*4123*]), for this reason (2 [+*5920*]), his (2), later (2 [+*3552*]), one (2), so (2 [+*1328*]), so (2 [+*1328*]), so then (2 [+*1328*]), that is why (2 [+*1328*]), this[S] (2 [+*3836, 3364*]), very (2), which (2), Andrew[S] (1), John's disciples[S] (1), Judas[S] (1), afterward (1 [+*3552*]), and then (1 [+*2083, 3552*]), appointed[S] (1), as[S] (1), as did (1 [+*899*]), as follows (1 [+*2400, 3836, 5596*]), at other times (1 [+*1254*]), at this (1 [+*3306*]), at this point (1 [+*1254*]), both (1 [+*2779*]), completely healed (1 [+*1443, 3836, 3907*]), everything (1), finally (1 [+*3552*]), following (1), for that very reason (1 [+*1328*]), for the express purpose (1 [+*1650, 899*]), for this purpose (1 [+*1650*]), for this reason (1 [+*1328*]), for this very reason (1 [+*1650, 1142*]), for this very reason (1 [+*899*]), for this very reason (1 [+*1328*]), from then on (1 [+*1666*]), governing[S] (1 [+*899*]), happening[S] (1), her (1), here (1 [+*1877*]), he's (1), him[S] (1 [+*3836, 476*]), in all (1 [+*1639*]), in comparison with (1 [+*1877, 3836, 3538, 1641*]), in fact (1 [+*1650*]), in other words (1 [+*1639*]), instead (1 [+*247, 3437*]), it's (1 [+*3836, 1155*]), just (1), just then (1 [+*2093*]), last (1), later (1 [+*3552*]), man[S] (1), mean (1 [+*1639, 3836, 3364*]), meanwhile (1 [+*1877*]), my (1), one more[S] (1), other (1 [+*3552*]), others (1), our (1), pray[S] (1 [+*4472*]), preach[S] (1 [+*4556*]), present (1), reason (1 [+*1650*]), sacrificed[S] (1 [+*4472*]), same (1), so (1 [+*1877*]), so doing[S] (1), so favored[S] (1), some (1), some time after this (1 [+*3552*]), some time ago (1 [+*4574, 3836, 2465*]), some time ago (1 [+*4574, 3836, 2465*]), some time later (1 [+*3552*]), sometimes (1 [+*3525*]), that (1 [+*1877*]), that was why (1 [+*1328*]), that was why (1 [+*1328*]), the Berean Jews[S] (1), the following (1), the proconsul[S] (1), the reason (1 [+*5920*]), the same (1), the situation[S] (1), the women[S] (1), there[S] (1 [+*1877, 3836, 4484*]), these things (1), thing (1), things (1), this[S] (1 [+*3836, 2240*]), this[S] (1 [+*3836, 2465*]), this[S] (1 [+*3836, 4839*]), this[S] (1 [+*3836, 2465*]), this[S] (1 [+*3836, 3364*]), this is how (1 [+*1877*]), this is the reason (1 [+*1650*]), this is why (1 [+*1328, 1142*]), this makes (1 [+*1877*]), this same (1), this way (1 [+*4246*]), thus (1 [+*1877*]), to (1 [+*1650*]), told (1 [+*550, 3836, 3364*]), what (1 [+*5515, 323*]), what I meant[S] (1 [+*4309*]), what Paul said[S] (1), what happened (1), what is more (1 [+*5250, 4246*]), who[S] (1 [+*3836, 476*]), with that (1 [+*3306*]), with this (1 [+*3306*]), yes tonight (1 [+*3836, 3816*]), you (1), NDT (143)

G4048 **οὕτως** ***houtōs***, adv. [205] [√ *4047*]. in this manner, thus, in the same way, likewise:– so (64), in the same way (14), in this way (12), like this (9), this is how (9), this (8), this is what (6), that is how (4), as (3), likewise (3), then (3), true (3), as is (2), like that (2), such (2), this way (2), accordingly (1), and (1), and (1 [+*1142*]), as a believer[S] (1), as it has (1), at that (1), bear fruit[S] (1), before (1 [+*2779*]), by this kind of (1), does (1 [+*1181*]), for (1 [+*4022*]), how (1), in such a way (1), in the same way (1 [+*4005, 5573*]), in these words (1), in this same way (1), it (1), like (1), marry[S] (1 [+*1181*]), matched by (1), only (1), ready[S] (1), that (1), that is what (1), that is why (1), that way (1), the same (1 [+*2779*]), the way (1), the way of life[S] (1), this is the way (1), this the way (1), this was what (1), what (1), NDT (26)

G4049 **οὐχί** ***ouchi***, adv. neg. [54] [√ *4024*]. not, no!:– not (33), no (7), won't (4), didn't (3), aren't (2 [+*1639*]), doesn't (1), fail (1 [+*3590*]), instead of (1 [+*2779*]), isn't (1 [+*1639*]), shouldn't (1)

G4050 **ὀφειλέτης** ***opheiletēs***, n. [7] [√ *4053*]. debtor, one who owes, is obligated, guilty:– obligated (2), debtors (1), guilty (1), obligation (1), owe (1 [+*1639*]), owed (1)

G4051 **ὀφειλή** ***opheilē***, n. [3] [√ *4053*]. debt; marital duty; (pl.) taxes:– debt (1), duty (1), owe (1)

G4052 **ὀφείλημα** ***opheilēma***, n. [2] [√ *4053*]. debt, obligation, what is owed:– debts (1), obligation (1)

G4053 **ὀφείλω** ***opheilō***, v. [35] [→ *4050, 4051, 4052, 4054, 4695, 5971, 5972*]. to owe, be in debt; be bound by oath; be obligated, ought, must:– ought (9), owe (4), ought to (3), owed (3), should (3), bound by oath (2), must (2), debt (1), debt remain outstanding (1), duty (1), had to (1), has to (1), have to (1), owes (1), should have (1), sins against (1)

G4054 **ὄφελον** ***ophelon***, pt. [4] [√ *4053*]. How I wish! How I hope!:– I wish (1), hope (1), how I wish that (1), wish (1)

G4055 **ὄφελος** ***ophelos***, n. [3] [√ *6067*]. good, gain, benefit:– good (2), gained (1)

G4056 **ὀφθαλμοδουλία** ***ophthalmodoulia***, n. [2] [√ *4057* + *1528*]. eye-service, service performed to attract attention:– eye is on (2)

G4057 **ὀφθαλμός** ***ophthalmos***, n. [100] [→ *535, 3669, 4056; cf. 3972*]. eye, the organ of sight; by extension: the faculty of mental perception and understanding:– eyes (61), eye (25), looked up (3 [+*2048, 3836*]), sight (2), blinded (1 [+*5604, 3836*]), envious (1 [+*3836, 4505*]), envy (1 [+*4505*]), look up (1 [+*3836, 2048*]), looked (1 [+*149, 3836*]), looked (1 [+*2048, 3836*]), looking (1 [+*2048, 3836*]), sight (1 [+*487, 3836*]), they[S] (1 [+*3836, 899*])

G4058 **ὄφις** ***ophis***, n. [14] snake, serpent:– snakes (6), serpent (3), snake (3), serpent's (2)

G4059 **ὀφρῦς** ***ophrys***, n. [1] eyebrow, brow (of a hill):– brow (1)

G4060 **ὀχετός** ***ochetos***, n. Not used in NIVEBC. [√ *2400*]. drain, sewer

G4061 **ὀχλέω** ***ochleō***, v. [1] [√ *4063*]. (pass.) to be tormented, disturbed:– tormented (1)

G4062 **ὀχλοποιέω** ***ochlopoieō***, v. [1] [√ *4063* + *4472*]. to form a mob:– formed a mob (1)

G4063 **ὄχλος** ***ochlos***, n. [175] [→ *1943, 4061, 4062, 4214*]. crowd, people, multitude, mob, a gathering of any size, sometimes with the implication that these are common folk and not leaders or nobility:– crowd (107), people (29), crowds (24), multitude (3), mob (2), numbers of people (2), crowd of people (1), crowds of people (1), group (1 [+*3950*]), many people (1), multitudes (1), number (1), number of people (1), them[S] (1)

G4064 **Ὀχοζίας** ***Ochozias***, n. pr. Not used in NIVEBC. Ahaziah, "*Yahweh has upheld*"

G4065 **ὀχύρωμα** ***ochyrōma***, n. [1] [√ *2400*]. stronghold, fortress; some translate as "prison":– strongholds (1)

G4066 **ὀψάριον** ***opsarion***, n. [5] [→ *4072, 4243*]. (small) fish:– fish (4), small fish (1)

G4067 **ὀψέ** ***opse***, adv. [3] [→ *4068, 4069, 4070*]. in the evening, late in the day; (pp.) after:– after (1), evening (1), in the evening (1)

G4068 **ὀψία** ***opsia***, n. [14] [√ *4067*]. evening:– evening (9), evening (2 [+*4070*]), night (2), that evening (1 [+*1181*])

G4069 **ὄψιμος** ***opsimos***, a. [1] [√ *4067*]. late (in the season, April-May in the modern calendar), spring:– spring rains (1)

G4070 **ὄψιος** ***opsios***, a. [3] [√ *4067*]. late; (n.) evening:– evening (2 [+*4068*]), late (1 [+*3836, 6052*])

G4071 **ὄψις** ***opsis***, n. [3] [√ *3972*]. face; appearance:– face (2), appearances (1)

G4072 **ὀψώνιον** ***opsōnion***, n. [4] [√ *4066* + *6050*]. pay, wage; support, compensation:– expense (1), pay (1), support (1), wages (1)

G4073 **π** ***p***, letter. Not used in NIVEBC. letter of the Greek alphabet

G4074 **παγιδεύω** ***pagideuō***, v. [1] [√ *4381*]. to trap, entrap:– trap (1)

G4075 **παγίς** ***pagis***, n. [5] [√ *4381*]. trap, snare:– trap (4), snare (1)

G4076 **πάγος** ***pagos***, n. Not used in NIVEBC. [→ *740, 741*]. hill, a craggy rock formation

G4077 **πάθημα** ***pathēma***, n. [16] [√ *4248*]. suffering, misfortune; passion:– sufferings (10), passions (2), suffered (2), suffering (2)

G4078 **παθητός** ***pathētos***, a. [1] [√ *4248*]. subject to suffering:– suffer (1)

G4079 **πάθος** ***pathos***, n. [3] [√ *4248*]. lust, sexual passion:– lust (1), lusts (1), passionate (1)

G4080 **παιδαγωγός** ***paidagōgos***, n. [3] [√ *4090* + *72*]. guardian, custodian, supervisor:– guardian (2), guardians (1)

G4081 **παιδάριον** ***paidarion***, n. [1] [√ *4090*]. little boy, child:– boy (1)

G4082 **παιδεία** ***paideia***, n. [6] [√ *4090*]. discipline, training:– discipline (3), training (2), disciplined (1)

G4083 **παιδευτής** ***paideutēs***, n. [2] [√ *4090*]. instructor, teacher; discipliner, corrector:– disciplined (1), instructor (1)

G4084 **παιδεύω** ***paideuō***, v. [13] [√ *4090*]. instruct, train, educate, as an on-going matter, in accord with rules and proper conduct; discipline, punish, for the purpose of better behavior:– disciplined (3), beaten (1), discipline (1), disciplines (1), educated (1), instructed (1), punish (1), punished (1), taught (1), teaches (1), trained (1)

G4085 **παιδιόθεν** ***paidiothen***, adv. [1] [√ *4090*]. from childhood:– childhood (1)

G4086 **παιδίον** ***paidion***, n. [52] [√ *4090*]. child:– child (22), children (8), little children (7), little child (6), child's (2), dear children (2), baby (1), boy's (1), children's (1), friends (1), her[S] (1 [+*3836*])

G4087 **παιδίσκη** ***paidiskē***, n. [13] [√ *4090*]. female servant, female slave, maidservant:– slave woman (4), servant girl (3), female slave (1), servant (1), servant girls (1), she[S] (1 [+*3836, 3836, 2601*]), slave woman's (1), women (1)

G4088 **παιδόθεν** ***paidothen***, adv. Not used in NIVEBC. [√ *4090*]. from childhood

G4089 **παίζω** ***paizō***, v. [1] [→ *1848, 1849, 1850, 1851; cf. 4090*]. to indulge in revelry, play, amuse oneself, dance, sometimes a euphemism for sexual immorality:– indulge in revelry (1)

G4090 **παῖς** ***pais***, n. [24] [→ *553, 4080, 4081, 4082, 4083, 4084, 4085, 4086, 4087, 4088; cf. 4089*]. boy, child, youth, usually below the age of puberty and not necessarily male; a personal servant, slave, attendant, with a possible implication of kind regard or close relationship; the word used in the Greek version of Isaiah, quoted in NT, for "servant" of the Lord:– servant (12), boy (4), attendants (1), boys (1), child (1), children (1), child's (1), servants (1), servants men (1), young (1)

G4091 **παίω** ***paiō***, v. [5] [→ *4697*]. to strike, hit (and so wound):– hit (2), struck (2), strikes (1)

G4092 **Πακατιανός** ***Pakatianos***, a. pr. g. Not used in NIVEBC. Pacatian, "*in Pacatia*"

G4093 **πάλαι** ***palai***, adv. [7] [→ *1732, 4094, 4095, 4096*]. long ago, in the past, already:– long ago (3), all along (1), already (1), in the past (1), past (1)

G4094 **παλαιός** ***palaios***, a. [19] [√ *4093*]. old:– old (19)

G4095 **παλαιότης** ***palaiotēs***, n. [1] [√ *4093*]. the old way, obsoleteness, age:– old way (1)

G4096 **παλαιόω** ***palaioō***, v. [4] [√ *4093*]. (act.) to make obsolete; (pass.) to wear out, become obsolete, become old:– wear out (2), made obsolete (1), obsolete (1)

G4097 **πάλη** ***palē***, n. [1] struggle:– struggle (1)

G4098 **παλιγγενεσία** ***palingenesia***, n. [2] [√ *4099* + *1181*]. renewal; rebirth, regeneration:– rebirth (1), renewal of all things (1)

G4099 **πάλιν** ***palin***, adv. [141] [→ *4098, 4100*]. again, once more; furthermore; on the other hand:– again (83), back (10), once more (9), then (5), another (2), again (1 [+*1309*]), all over again (1 [+*540*]), all over again (1), also (1), and (1 [+*2445*]), another time (1), brought back (1 [+*362*]), elsewhere (1), later (1), nor (1 [+*4028*]), now (1), once again (1), rebuild (1 [+*3868*]), repeat (1 [+*3306*]), return (1 [+*2262, 1650, 3836*]), returned to place (1 [+*404*]), yet (1), NDT (15)

G4100 **παλινγενεσία** ***palingenesia***, n. Not used in NIVEBC. [√ *4099* + *1181*]. rebirth, regeneration

G4101 **παμπληθεί** ***pamplēthei***, adv. [1] [√ *4246* + *4398*]. with one voice, all together:– whole crowd (1)

G4102 **πάμπολυς** ***pampolys***, a. Not used in NIVEBC. [√ *4246* + *4498*]. very great

G4103 **Παμφυλία** ***Pamphylia***, n. pr. [5] [√ *4246* + *5886*]. Pamphylia:– Pamphylia (5)

G4104 **πανδοκεῖον** ***pandokeion***, n. Not used in NIVEBC. [√ *4246* + *1312*]. inn

G4105 **πανδοκεύς** ***pandokeus***, n. Not used in NIVEBC. [√ *4246* + *1312*]. innkeeper

G4106 **πανδοχεῖον** ***pandocheion***, n. [1] [√ *4246* + *1312*]. inn:– inn (1)

G4107 **πανδοχεύς** ***pandocheus***, n. [1] [√ *4246* + *1312*]. innkeeper:– innkeeper (1)

G4108 **πανήγυρις** ***panēgyris***, n. [1] [√ *4246* + *72*]. joyful assembly, festal gathering:– joyful assembly (1)

G4109 **πανοικεί** ***panoikei***, adv. [1] [√*4246* + *3875*]. with one's whole family:– whole household (1)

G4110 **πανοπλία** ***panoplia***, n. [3] [√*4246* + *3960*]. full armor, worn by a heavily armed soldier:– full armor (2), armor (1)

G4111 **πανουργία** ***panourgia***, n. [5] [√*4246* + *2240*]. cunning, craftiness, deception, duplicity:– craftiness (2), cunning (1), deception (1), duplicity (1)

G4112 **πανοῦργος** ***panourgos***, a. [1] [√*4246* + *2240*]. crafty, clever, sly:– crafty (1)

G4113 **πανπληθεί** ***panplēthei***, adv. Not used in NIVEBC. [√*4246* + *4398*]. all together

G4114 **πανταχῇ** ***pantachē***, adv. [1] [√*4246*]. everywhere:– everywhere (1)

G4115 **πανταχόθεν** ***pantachothen***, adv. Not used in NIVEBC. [√*4246*]. from every direction

G4116 **πανταχοῦ** ***pantachou***, adv. [7] [√*4246*]. everywhere; in all directions:– everywhere (6), whole (1 [+*3910*])

G4117 **παντελής** ***pantelēs***, a. [2] [√*4246* + *5465*]. complete, perfect, absolute; at all:– at all (1 [+*1650*, *3836*]), completely (1 [+*1650*, *3836*])

G4118 **πάντῃ** ***pantē***, adv. [1] [√*4246*]. in every way:– every (1)

G4119 **πάντοθεν** ***pantothen***, adv. [3] [√*4246*]. from all directions; completely, entirely:– from everywhere (1), gold-covered (1 [+*4328*, *5992*]), on every side (1)

G4120 **παντοκράτωρ** ***pantokratōr***, n. [10] [√*4246* + *3197*]. Almighty; this title for God translates the Hebrew 7372, [LORD] "of Hosts" (the heavenly armies), and Hebrew 8724, "Shaddai," (probably) God the Mountain, powerful and immovable:– Almighty (10)

G4121 **πάντοτε** ***pantote***, adv. [41] [√*4246* + *4005* + *5445*]. always, at all times, forever:– always (36), at all times (2), any (1), constantly (1), forever (1)

G4122 **πάντως** ***pantōs***, adv. [8] [√*4246*]. surely, certainly, by all possible means, quite:– at all (2), surely (2), by all possible means (1), certainly (1), must (1), quite (1)

G4123 **παρά** ***para***, pp. [193] [→*524*, *563*, *564*, *1384*, *2339*, *4124*, *4125*, *4126*, *4127*, *4128*, *4129*, *4130*, *4131*, *4132*, *4133*, *4134*, *4135*, *4136*, *4138*, *4139*, *4140*, *4141*, *4142*, *4143*, *4144*, *4145*, *4146*, *4147*, *4148*, *4149*, *4150*, *4151*, *4152*, *4153*, *4154*, *4155*, *4156*, *4157*, *4158*, *4159*, *4160*, *4161*, *4162*, *4163*, *4164*, *4165*, *4166*, *4167*, *4168*, *4169*, *4170*, *4171*, *4172*, *4173*, *4174*, *4175*, *4176*, *4177*, *4178*, *4179*, *4180*, *4181*, *4182*, *4183*, *4184*, *4185*, *4186*, *4187*, *4188*, *4189*, *4190*, *4191*, *4192*, *4193*, *4194*, *4195*, *4196*, *4199*, *4200*, *4201*, *4202*, *4204*, *4205*, *4206*, *4207*, *4208*, *4209*, *4210*, *4211*, *4212*, *4213*, *4214*, *4215*, *4216*, *4217*, *4218*, *4219*, *4223*, *4224*, *4225*, *4227*, *4228*, *4229*, *4230*, *4232*, *4233*, *4234*, *4235*, *4236*, *4237*, *4238*, *4239*, *4240*, *4241*, *4242*, *4243*, *4261*, *5219*, *5220*, *5221*, *5222*, *5223*]. (gen.) from; (dat.) with, before, among, in the sight of; (acc.) beside, along side, by, at:– from (46), with (25), by (11), than (11), at (8), along (7), beside (3), contrary to (3), of (3), to (3), among (2), before (2), done (2 [+*1181*]), for that reason (2 [+*4047*]), in presence (2), in sight (2), other than (2), rather than (2), above (1), accepts (1), against (1), any of (1), anyone's (1 [+*5516*]), as responsible to (1), at edge (1), beyond (1), conceited (1 [+*5861*, *1571*]), family (1 [+*3836*]), for (1), give (1), given (1 [+*3284*]), had (1), have (1), in (1), made post bond (1 [+*3284*, *3836*, *2653*]), minus (1), more than (1), near (1), on (1), past (1), say (1 [+*1639*]), say^S (1), sent (1), sum of money^S (1 [+*1571*]), under (1 [+*3836*, *4546*]), unnatural (1 [+*5882*]), what said^S (1), where (1 [+*4005*]), NDT (27)

G4124 **παραβαίνω** ***parabainō***, v. [3] [√*4123* + *326*]. to break, transgress; to leave, turn aside:– break (2), left (1)

G4125 **παραβάλλω** ***paraballō***, v. [1] [√*4123* + *965*]. to come near (by ship); compare:– crossed over (1)

G4126 **παράβασις** ***parabasis***, n. [7] [√*4123* + *326*]. transgression, breaking, violation:– breaking (1), breaking a command (1), sinner (1), sins (1), transgression (1), transgressions (1), violation (1)

G4127 **παραβάτης** ***parabatēs***, n. [5] [√*4123* + *326*]. lawbreaker, transgressor:– lawbreaker (2 [+*3795*]), break (1 [+*1639*]), lawbreaker (1), lawbreakers (1)

G4128 **παραβιάζομαι** ***parabiazomai***, v. [2] [√*4123* + *1040*]. to urge strongly, persuade:– persuaded (1), urged strongly (1)

G4129 **παραβολεύομαι** ***paraboleuomai***, v. [1] [√*4123* + *965*]. to risk, expose to danger:– risked (1)

G4130 **παραβολή** ***parabolē***, n. [50] [√*4123* + *965*]. parable, an illustration that teaches in a story or extended figure of speech; proverb, a short pithy saying:– parable (30), parables (15), lesson (2), illustration (1), in a manner of speaking (1 [+*1877*]), proverb (1)

G4131 **παραβουλεύομαι** ***parabouleuomai***, v. Not used in NIVEBC. [√*4123* + *1089*]. to be careless, have no concern

G4132 **παραγγελία** ***parangelia***, n. [5] [√*4123* + *34*]. order, command; instruction:– command (2), gave strict orders (1 [+*4133*]), instructions (1), orders (1)

G4133 **παραγγέλλω** ***parangellō***, v. [31] [√*4123* + *34*]. to order, command, direct; to give instruction:– command (7), commanded (4), ordered (4), told (3), instructions (2), charge (1), commands (1), directives (1), gave command (1), gave rule (1), gave strict orders (1 [+*4132*]), give command (1), give instructions (1), required (1), strictly warned (1 [+*2203*]), warning (1)

G4134 **παραγίνομαι** ***paraginomai***, v. [37] [√*4123* + *1181*]. to come, arrive, be present; to appear:– came (13), arrived (5), come (4), arriving (3), appeared (2), arrive (1), came back (1), came in (1), came to (1), came to support (1), coming (1), get here (1), present (1), NDT (2)

G4135 **παράγω** ***paragō***, v. [10] [√*4123* + *72*]. to pass by, go on, walk beside; to pass away:– went on (2), going by (1), pass away (1), passing (1), passing away (1), passing by (1), walked along (1), walked beside (1), went along (1)

G4136 **παραδειγματίζω** ***paradeigmatizō***, v. [1] [√*4123* + *1257*]. to subject to public disgrace, hold up to contempt:– subjecting to public disgrace (1)

G4137 **παράδεισος** ***paradeisos***, n. [3] paradise, a place of blessedness, from the base meaning of "garden":– paradise (3)

G4138 **παραδέχομαι** ***paradechomai***, v. [6] [√*4123* + *1312*]. to accept, welcome, receive:– accept (3), accepts (1), entertain (1), welcomed (1)

G4139 **παραδιατριβή** ***paradiatribē***, n. Not used in NIVEBC. [√*4123* + *1328* + *5561*]. useless occupation

G4140 **παραδίδωμι** ***paradidōmi***, v. [119] [√*4123* + *1443*]. to hand over, betray, deliver to prison; to entrust, commit:– handed over (19), betray (17), hand over (9), betrayed (7), delivered (6), entrusted (5), betrayer (4), delivered over (4), gave over (4), gave up (4), passed on (4), betrays (3), committed (3), handed down (3), arrest (2), given over (2), put in prison (2), arrested (1), betraying (1), claimed allegiance (1), commended (1), deliver over (1), delivered over to death (1), gave (1), give over (1), given (1), hand over to (1 [+*1650*, *5931*]), handed over (1 [+*3836*, *5931*]), handing over (1), hands over (1), put (1), putting (1), ripe (1), risked (1), surrendered (1), throwing (1), traitor (1), turn over (1)

G4141 **παράδοξος** ***paradoxos***, a. [1] [√*4123* + *1518*]. remarkable, wonderful:– remarkable (1)

G4142 **παράδοσις** ***paradosis***, n. [13] [√*4123* + *1443*]. tradition; teachings:– tradition (7), traditions (4), teaching (1), teachings (1)

G4143 **παραζηλόω** ***parazēloō***, v. [4] [√*4123* + *2419*]. to make envious, arouse jealousy:– make envious (2), arouse jealousy (1), arouse to envy (1)

G4144 **παραθαλάσσιος** ***parathalassios***, a. [1] [√*4123* + *2498*]. by the lake, by the sea:– by the lake (1)

G4145 **παραθεωρέω** ***paratheōreō***, v. [1] [√*4123* + *2555*]. (pass.) to be overlooked, neglected:– overlooked (1)

G4146 **παραθήκη** ***parathēkē***, n. [3] [√*4123* + *5502*]. deposit, thing entrusted to:– deposit entrusted (1), entrusted (1), entrusted to care (1)

G4147 **παραινέω** ***paraineō***, v. [2] [√*4123* + *142*]. to warn, urge:– urge (1), warned (1)

G4148 **παραιτέομαι** ***paraiteomai***, v. [12] [√*4123* + *160*]. to request, beg; to make excuses; to refuse, reject:– excuse (2 [+*2400*]), have nothing to do with (2), refuse (2), begged (1), do not (1), don't have anything to do with (1), make excuses (1), refused (1), requested (1)

G4149 **παρακαθέζομαι** ***parakathezomai***, v. [1] [√*4123* + *2757*]. to sit beside:– sat (1)

G4150 **παρακαθίζω** ***parakathizō***, v. Not used in NIVEBC. [√*4123* + *2767*]. to sit down beside

G4151 **παρακαλέω** ***parakaleō***, v. [109] [√*4123* + *2813*]. to ask, beg, plead; to comfort, encourage, exhort, urge; to call, invite:– urge (19), encourage (14), begged (13), pleaded with (7), comforted (6), encouraged (6), urged (6), appeal (5), encouraging (5), invited (4), plead with (3), begging (2), comfort (2), comforts (2), answer kindly (1), appease (1), asked (1), asking for help (1), call on (1), exhort (1), exhorted (1), given^S (1), insist on (1), making appeal (1), pleading with (1), receive^S (1), request (1), requested (1), speaking encouragement (1)

G4152 **παρακαλύπτω** ***parakalyptō***, v. [1] [√*4123* + *2821*]. (pass.) to be hidden:– hidden (1)

G4153 **παρακαταθήκη** ***parakatathēkē***, n. Not used in NIVEBC. [√*4123* + *2848* + *5502*]. deposit

G4154 **παράκειμαι** ***parakeimai***, v. [2] [√*4123* + *3023*]. to be present, ready:– have (1), there (1)

G4155 **παράκλησις** ***paraklēsis***, n. [29] [√*4123* + *2813*]. encouragement, comfort, consolation, appeal:– encouragement (9), comfort (8), appeal (2), encouraged (2), exhortation (2), consolation (1), encouraged (1 [+*2400*]), encouraging (1), encouraging message (1), preaching (1), urgently (1 [+*3552*, *4498*])

G4156 **παράκλητος** ***paraklētos***, n. [5] [√*4123* + *2813*]. counselor, intercessor, helper, one who encourages and comforts; in the NT it refers exclusively to the Holy Spirit and to Jesus Christ:– advocate (4), advocate to help (1)

G4157 **παρακοή** ***parakoē***, n. [3] [√*4123* + *201*]. disobedience, unwillingness to hear:– disobedience (2), act of disobedience (1)

G4158 **παρακολουθέω** ***parakoloutheō***, v. [4] [√*4123* + *199* [*1.3*]]. to follow, accompany; to know all about; to investigate:– accompany (1), followed (1), investigated (1), know all about (1)

G4159 **παρακούω** ***parakouō***, v. [3] [√*4123* + *201*]. to refuse to listen, ignore:– refuse (2), overhearing (1)

G4160 **παρακύπτω** ***parakyptō***, v. [5] [√*4123* + *3252*]. to bend over; to look (intently):– bending over (1), bent over (1), bent over to look (1), look (1), looks intently (1)

G4161 **παραλαμβάνω** ***paralambanō***, v. [49] [√*4123* + *3284*]. to take with; take charge of; to receive, accept:– took (12), received (8), take (4), taken (4), took with (4), receive (2), takes (2), took aside (2), accepted (1), instructed (1), receiving (1), take along (1), take home (1), took along (1), took along with (1), took charge of (1), took home (1), traditions (1), NDT (1)

G4162 **παραλέγομαι** ***paralegomai***, v. [2] [√*4123* + *3306*]. to sail past, move along:– moved along (1), sailed (1)

G4163 **παράλιος** ***paralios***, a. [1] [√*4123* + *229*]. (located) by the sea; (n.) seacoast:– coastal region (1)

G4164 **παραλλαγή** ***parallagē***, n. [1] [√*4123* + *248*]. change, variation:– change (1)

G4165 **παραλογίζομαι** ***paralogizomai***, v. [2] [√*4123* + *3306*]. to deceive, delude:– deceive (2)

G4166 **παραλυτικός** ***paralytikos***, a. [10] [√*4123* + *3395*]. (n.) paralytic, lame person:– paralyzed (7), man^S (3)

G4167 **παράλυτος** ***paralytos***, a. Not used in NIVEBC. [√*4123* + *3395*]. (n.) paralytic

G4168 **παραλύω** ***paralyō***, v. [5] [√*4123* + *3395*]. (pass.) to be paralyzed, disabled; (n.) paralytic:– paralyzed (4), weak (1)

G4169 **παραμένω** ***paramenō***, v. [4] [√*4123* + *3531*]. to continue; to remain with:– continue (1), continues in (1), continuing in office (1), stay for a while (1)

G4170 **παραμυθέομαι** ***paramytheomai***, v. [4] [√*4123* + *3680*]. to comfort, encourage, console:– comforting (2), comfort (1), encourage (1)

G4171 **παραμυθία** ***paramythia***, n. [1] [√*4123* + *3680*]. comfort, consolation:– comfort (1)

G4172 **παραμύθιον** ***paramythion***, n. [1] [√*4123* + *3680*]. comfort, consolation, encouragement:– comfort (1)

G4173 **παράνοια** ***paranoia***, n. Not used in NIVEBC. [√*4123* + *3808*]. madness, foolishness

G4174 **παρανομέω** ***paranomeō***, v. [1] [√*4123* + *3795*]. to violate the law, act contrary to the law:– violate the law (1)

G4175 **παρανομία** ***paranomia***, n. [1] [√*4123* + *3795*]. wrongdoing, lawlessness:– wrongdoing (1)

G4176 **παραπικραίνω** ***parapikrainō***, v. [1] [√*4123* + *4395*]. to rebel, disobey:– rebelled (1)

G4177 **παραπικρασμός** ***parapikrasmos***, n. [2] [√*4123* + *4395*]. rebellion, revolt:– rebellion (2)

G4178 **παραπίπτω** ***parapiptō***, v. [1] [√*4123* + *4406*]. to fall away, commit apostasy:– fallen away (1)

G4179 **παραπλέω** ***parapleō***, v. [1] [√*4123* + *4434*]. to sail past:– sail past (1)

G4180 **παραπλήσιος** ***paraplēsios***, a. [1] [√*4123* + *4446*]. (adv.) almost, nearly:– almost (1)

G4181 **παραπλησίως** ***paraplēsiōs***, adv. [1] [√*4123* + *4446*]. in just the same way:– too (1)

G4182 **παραπορεύομαι** ***paraporeuomai***, v. [5] [√*4123* + *4513*]. to pass by, go through:– passed by (2), going (1), passed (1), went along (1)

G4183 **παράπτωμα** ***paraptōma***, n. [20] [√*4123* + *4406*]. trespass, transgression, sin against, to sin as a moral failure to keep a command, fig., stepping out of the bounds of God's law:– sins (8), trespass (5), sin (2), transgression (2), transgressions (2), trespasses (1)

G4184 **παραρρέω** ***pararreō***, v. [1] [√*4123* + *4835*]. to drift away, flow past, slip away:– drift away (1)

G4185 **παράσημος** ***parasēmos***, a. [1] [√*4123* + *4956*]. distinguished, marked; (n.) figurehead, emblem (on a ship):– figurehead (1)

G4186 **παρασκευάζω** ***paraskeuazō***, v. [4] [√*4123* +

5007]. (act.) to prepare; (mid.) to get ready; (mid./pass.) to be ready:– ready (3), prepared (1)

G4187 **παρασκευή** ***paraskeuē***, n. [6] [√*4123* + *5007*]. Preparation Day:– day of preparation (3), preparation day (2), preparation (1)

G4188 **παραστάτις** ***parastatis***, n. Not used in NIVEBC. [√*4123* + *2705*]. supporter

G4189 **παρατείνω** ***parateinō***, v. [1] [√*1753*; *cf.* *4123*]. to keep on, prolong, extend:– kept on (1)

G4190 **παρατηρέω** ***paratēreō***, v. [6] [√*4123* + *5498*]. to watch closely, observe:– watched closely (2), carefully watched (1), keeping a close watch on (1), kept close watch (1), observing (1)

G4191 **παρατήρησις** ***paratērēsis***, n. [1] [√*4123* + *5498*]. careful observation:– something that can be observed (1)

G4192 **παρατίθημι** ***paratithēmi***, v. [19] [√*4123* + *5502*]. (act.) to set before; (mid.) to entrust, commit:– commit (3), distribute to (3), told (2), committed (1), distribute (1), entrust (1), entrusted (1), giving (1), offer (1), offered to (1), proving (1), put before (1), set a meal before (1 [+*5544*]), they did so^{S} (1)

G4193 **παρατυγχάνω** ***paratynchanō***, v. [1] [√*4123* + *5593*]. to happen to be there:– happened to be there (1)

G4194 **παραυτίκα** ***parautika***, adv. [1] [√*4123* + *899*]. (a.) momentary:– momentary (1)

G4195 **παραφέρω** ***parapherō***, v. [4] [√*4123* + *5770*]. to take away, remove; (pass.) to be carried away:– take (2), blown along (1), carried away (1)

G4196 **παραφρονέω** ***paraphroneō***, v. [1] [→*4197*, *4198*; *cf.* *4123* + *5856*]. to be out of one's mind, insane:– out of mind (1)

G4197 **παραφρονία** ***paraphronia***, n. [1] [√*4196*]. madness, insanity:– madness (1)

G4198 **παραφροσύνη** ***paraphrosynē***, n. Not used in NIVEBC. [√*4196*]. madness, insanity

G4199 **παραχειμάζω** ***paracheimazō***, v. [4] [√*4123* + *5946*]. to spend the winter:– winter (2), spend the winter (1), wintered (1)

G4200 **παραχειμασία** ***paracheimasia***, n. [1] [√*4123* + *5946*]. spending the winter:– winter in (1)

G4201 **παραχράομαι** ***parachraomai***, v. Not used in NIVEBC. [√*4123* + *5968*]. to misuse

G4202 **παραχρῆμα** ***parachrēma***, adv. [18] [√*4123* + *5968*]. immediately, instantly, at once:– immediately (9), at once (4), instantly (2), at that moment (1), just (1), so quickly (1)

G4203 **πάρδαλις** ***pardalis***, n. [1] leopard:– leopard (1)

G4204 **παρεδρεύω** ***paredreuō***, v. [1] [√*4123* + *1612*]. to serve regularly, sit beside:– serve (1)

G4205 **πάρειμι** ***pareimi***, v. [24] [√*4123* + *1639*]. to be present, here; to have come:– come (6), present (4), have (2), here (2), am (1), are (1), be (1), be here (1), came (1), now have (1), sought an audience (1), time (1), was (1), was with (1)

G4206 **παρεισάγω** ***pareisagō***, v. [1] [√*4123* + *1650* + *72*]. to bring in secretly:– secretly introduce (1)

G4207 **παρείσακτος** ***pareisaktos***, a. [1] [√*4123* + *1650* + *72*]. brought in secretly, infiltrated:– infiltrated ranks (1 [+*4209*])

G4208 **παρεισδύω** ***pareisdyō***, v. [1] [√*4123* + *1650* + *1544*]. to slip in secretly:– secretly slipped in (1)

G4209 **παρεισέρχομαι** ***pareiserchomai***, v. [2] [√*4123* + *1650* + *2262*]. to come in, sneak in; to add to:– brought in (1), infiltrated ranks (1 [+*4207*])

G4210 **παρεισφέρω** ***pareispherō***, v. [1] [√*4123* + *1650* + *5770*]. to do one's best:– make (1)

G4211 **παρεκτός** ***parektos***, adv. & pp.* [3] [√*4123* + *1666*]. (adv.) besides; (pp.) except for, apart from:– besides everything else (1 [+*6006*, *3836*]), except for (1 [+*3364*]), except for (1)

G4212 **παρεμβάλλω** ***paremballō***, v. [1] [√*4123* + *1877* + *965*]. to build, erect; in context to build a surrounding siege wall:– build (1)

G4213 **παρεμβολή** ***parembolē***, n. [10] [√*4123* + *1877* + *965*]. camp, barracks; army:– barracks (6), camp (3), armies (1)

G4214 **παρενοχλέω** ***parenochleō***, v. [1] [√*4123* + *1877* + *4063*]. to make difficult, trouble:– make it difficult (1)

G4215 **παρεπίδημος** ***parepidēmos***, a. [3] [√*4123* + *2093* + *1322*]. (n.) stranger:– exiles (2), strangers (1)

G4216 **παρέρχομαι** ***parerchomai***, v. [29] [√*4123* + *2262*]. to go by, pass by; (pass.) to pass away, come to an end, disappear; be taken away:– pass away (10), disappear (4), pass (2), after (1), come (1), come along (1), disobeyed (1), getting late (1 [+*3836*, *6052*]), gone (1), neglect (1), pass by (1), passed by (1), passing by (1), spent in the past (1), taken (1), taken away (1)

G4217 **πάρεσις** ***paresis***, n. [1] [√*918*; *cf.* *4123*]. leaving unpunished, passing over:– left unpunished (1)

G4218 **παρέχω** ***parechō***, v. [16] [√*4123* + *2400*]. to present, give; to show, give proof; to cause, bring about, promote; (mid.) to set (an example); to provide; to get for oneself:– bothering (3 [+*3160*]), became (1), bother (1 [+*3160*]), brought in (1), cause (1), do (1), earned (1), given (1), promote (1), provide (1), provides (1), set (1), showed (1), turn to (1)

G4219 **παρηγορία** ***parēgoria***, n. [1] [√*4123* + *72*]. comfort:– comfort (1)

G4220 **παρθενία** ***parthenia***, n. [1] [√*4221*]. virginity:– marriage (1)

G4221 **παρθένος** ***parthenos***, n. [15] [→*4220*]. virgin (male and female), one who has never engaged in sexual relations:– virgin (8), virgins (4), unmarried (1), virgin's (1), NDT (1)

G4222 **Πάρθοι** ***Parthoi***, n. pr. g. [1] Parthian:– Parthians (1)

G4223 **παρίημι** ***pariēmi***, v. [2] [√*918*; *cf.* *4123*]. to leave undone, neglect; (pass.) to be feeble, weakened, listless:– feeble (1), leaving undone (1)

G4224 **παριστάνω** ***paristanō***, v. Not used in NIVEBC. [√*4123* + *2705*]. see *4225*

G4225 **παρίστημι** ***paristēmi***, v. [41] [√*4123* + *2705*]. to place beside, put at disposal; to present, make an offering; (intr.) to stand before, provide, come to aid:– present (7), offer (6), standing near (5), presented (2), stood beside (2), bring near (1), come (1), give (1), handed over (1), nearby (1), prove (1), provide (1), put at disposal (1), rise up (1), stand (1), stand before (1), stand trial before (1), standing around (1), standing by (1), standing nearby (1), stands (1), stood around (1), stood at side (1), stood there (1)

G4226 **Παρμενᾶς** ***Parmenas***, n. pr. [1] Parmenas, "*steady, reliable*":– Parmenas (1)

G4227 **πάροδος** ***parodos***, n. [1] [√*4123* + *3847*]. passing by:– passing visit (1)

G4228 **παροικέω** ***paroikeō***, v. [2] [√*4123* + *3875*]. to live as a stranger, visit; to migrate:– made home (1), visiting (1)

G4229 **παροικία** ***paroikia***, n. [2] [√*4123* + *3875*]. residence as a stranger:– foreigners (1), stay (1)

G4230 **πάροικος** ***paroikos***, a. [4] [√*4123* + *3875*]. strange; (n.) alien, foreigner, stranger:– strangers (2), foreigner (1), foreigners (1)

G4231 **παροιμία** ***paroimia***, n. [5] figure of speech, proverb, maxim:– figuratively (1 [+*1877*]), figure of speech (1), figures of speech (1), proverbs (1), this kind^{S} (1 [+*1877*])

G4232 **πάροινος** ***paroinos***, a. [2] [√*4123* + *3885*]. drunken, given to drunkenness:– given to drunkenness (2)

G4233 **παροίχομαι** ***paroichomai***, v. [1] [√*4123*]. to pass by:– past (1 [+*1155*])

G4234 **παρομοιάζω** ***paromoiazō***, v. [1] [√*4123* + *3927*]. to be like:– like (1)

G4235 **παρόμοιος** ***paromoios***, a. [1] [√*4123* + *3927*]. like, similar:– like (1)

G4236 **παροξύνω** ***paroxynō***, v. [2] [√*4123* + *3955*]. (intr.) to be greatly distressed; to be angered, irritated:– easily angered (1), greatly distressed (1)

G4237 **παροξυσμός** ***paroxysmos***, n. [2] [√*4123* + *3955*]. sharp disagreement; spurring on, encouraging:– sharp disagreement (1), spur on (1 [+*1650*])

G4238 **παροράω** ***paroraō***, v. Not used in NIVEBC. [√*4123* + *3972*]. to overlook, take no notice of

G4239 **παροργίζω** ***parorgizō***, v. [2] [√*4123* + *3973*]. to anger, exasperate:– exasperate (1), make angry (1)

G4240 **παροργισμός** ***parorgismos***, n. [1] [√*4123* + *3973*]. anger:– angry (1)

G4241 **παροτρύνω** ***parotrynō***, v. [1] [√*4123*]. to incite, arouse:– incited (1)

G4242 **παρουσία** ***parousia***, n. [24] [√*4123* + *1639*]. presence; coming, advent; in the NT usually of the second coming of the Son of Man, arriving as a conquering king:– coming (17), comes (3), arrived (1), being (1), in person (1 [+*3836*, *3836*, *5393*]), presence (1)

G4243 **παροψίς** ***paropsis***, n. [2] [√*4123* + *4066*]. dish:– dish (2)

G4244 **παρρησία** ***parrēsia***, n. [31] [√*4246* + *4839*]. boldness, confidence, frankness; public, openness (of speech):– confidence (7), plainly (4), publicly (3), boldness (2), courage (2), assurance (1), bold (1 [+*5968*]), bold (1 [+*4498*, *2400*]), boldly (1 [+*3552*]), clearly (1 [+*1877*]), confident (1), confidently (1 [+*3552*]), fearlessly (1 [+*1877*]), frankness (1), freedom (1), openly (1), public (1), public (1 [+*1877*])

G4245 **παρρησιάζομαι** ***parrēsiazomai***, v. [9] [√*4246* + *4839*]. to speak boldly, preach fearlessly:– speaking boldly (2), answered boldly (1), dared (1), fearlessly (1), freely (1), preached fearlessly (1), speak boldly (1), spoke boldly (1)

G4246 **πᾶς** ***pas***, a. [1241] [→*570*, *1383*, *4101*, *4102*, *4103*, *4104*, *4105*, *4106*, *4107*, *4108*, *4109*, *4110*, *4111*, *4112*, *4113*, *4114*, *4115*, *4116*, *4117*, *4118*, *4119*, *4120*, *4121*, *4122*, *4244*, *4245*]. all, every (thing, one), whole; always:– all (650), every (126), everyone (108), everything (99), whole (24), any (17), all things (14 [+*3836*]), anyone (14), everything (14 [+*3836*]), anything (9), full (8), always (6), great (6), everyone (5 [+*476*]), one (5), one (4 [+*4922*]), always (3 [+*1328*]), everyone's (3), everywhere (3 [+*1877*, *5536*]), no (3 [+*4024*]), whoever (3), all (2 [+*4012*]), continually (2 [+*1328*]), day after day (2 [+*2465*]), entire (2), everyone (2 [+*476*]), no (2 [+*4024*]), regularly (2 [+*1328*]), the country^{S} (2), those^{S} (2), very (2), whatever (2), absolute (1), all (1 [+*476*]), all (1 [+*3836*]), all about (1 [+*3836*, *4839*]), all over (1), altogether (1 [+*3836*]), always (1 [+*1877*, *2789*]), always (1 [+*3836*, *2465*]), any and every (1), anyone (1 [+*6034*]), anything (1 [+*4547*]), at all times (1 [+*1328*]), bless abundantly (1 [+*5921*, *4355*]), complete (1), complete (1 [+*1877*]), completely (1 [+*3552*]), day by day (1 [+*2848*, *2465*]), depth (1), done this^{S} (1 [+*5718*, *899*, *3836*]), every (1 [+*2848*]), every respect (1 [+*3836*]), every way (1), everyone (1 [+*476*]), everyone (1 [+*6034*]), everyone (1 [+*6034*]), everyone (1 [+*3836*, *476*]), everyone (1 [+*476*]), everyone (1 [+*476*]), everyone's (1 [+*476*]), everything (1 [+*4012*]), everything (1 [+*3836*, *5007*]), everything (1 [+*4012*, *323*]), everything (1 [+*4012*, *1569*]), everywhere (1 [+*5536*]), finally (1 [+*5731*]), forever (1 [+*1328*]), forevermore (1 [+*1650*, *3836*, *172*]), free and belong to no one (1 [+*1801*, *1666*]), from one to another (1 [+*2848*]), fully (1 [+*19*]), large (1), no (1 [+*4024*]), no (1 [+*4024*]), no ever (1 [+*4024*, *3590*]), none (1 [+*4024*]), none ever again (1 [+*4033*]), nothing (1 [+*4024*]), nothing (1 [+*4024*, *3590*]), other (1), perfectly (1 [+*1877*]), persevered (1 [+*1877*, *5705*]), profound (1), publicly (1 [+*1967*]), pure (1), securely (1 [+*1877*, *854*]), strict (1), sufficient (1), surplus (1 [+*2779*, *19*]), the whole universe (1 [+*3836*]), they^{S} (1), this way (1 [+*4047*]), throughout (1 [+*1650*]), throughout (1 [+*2093*]), vicinity (1 [+*3990*]), what is more (1 [+*5250*, *4047*]), whatever (1 [+*3836*]), whatever (1 [+*4012*]), whatever (1 [+*4012*, *323*]), whatever (1 [+*4005*, *5516*, *1569*]), whoever (1 [+*4015*]), whoever (1 [+*4005*, *323*]), whole (1 [+*4725*]), without (1 [+*6006*]), world (1), you^{S} (1), NDT (20)

G4247 **πάσχα** ***pascha***, n. [29] Passover, Passover week; Passover meal; Passover lamb:– passover (26), passover lamb (3)

G4248 **πάσχω** ***paschō***, v. [42] [→*2801*, *2802*, *3584*, *3926*, *4077*, *4078*, *4079*, *4557*, *4634*, *5155*, *5217*, *5218*, *5224*]. to experience, suffer, endure (almost always in NT with reference to unpleasant experiences):– suffer (21), suffered (13), suffering (5), suffers (2), experienced (1)

G4249 **Πάταρα** ***Patara***, n. pr. [1] Patara:– Patara (1)

G4250 **πατάσσω** ***patassō***, v. [10] to hit, strike; kill:– strike (4), struck (3), killing (1), strike down (1), struck down (1)

G4251 **πατέω** ***pateō***, v. [5] [→*1853*, *2922*, *4344*]. to trample on, tread on:– trample (1), trample on (1), trampled (1), trampled on (1), treads (1)

G4252 **πατήρ** ***patēr***, n. [413] [→*525*, *526*, *574*, *3093*, *4254*, *4255*, *4256*, *4257*, *4258*, *4259*, *4260*, *4261*, *4262*, *4635*, *5396*, *5399*]. father, a male parent or ancestor; by extension: an honorific title, leader, archetype; (pl.) parents, ancestors (of both genders):– father (337), ancestors (34), father's (19), fathers (12), patriarchs (4), parents (2), ancestor (1), family (1 [+*3875*, *3836*]), family (1 [+*3836*, *3875*, *3836*]), forefathers (1), them^{S} (1 [+*3836*, *1609*])

G4253 **Πάτμος** ***Patmos***, n. pr. [1] Patmos:– Patmos (1)

G4254 **πατραλῴας** ***patralōas***, n. Not used in NIVEBC. [√*4252* + *262*]. one who kills one's father

G4255 **πατριά** ***patria***, n. [3] [√*4252*]. family, family line, clan; people, nation:– family (1), line (1), peoples (1)

G4256 **πατριάρχης** ***patriarchēs***, n. [4] [√*4252* + *806*]. patriarch, father of a nation:– patriarch (2), patriarchs (2)

G4257 **πατρικός** ***patrikos***, a. [1] [√*4252*]. paternal, from one's ancestors:– of fathers (1)

G4258 **πατρίς** ***patris***, n. [8] [√*4252*]. hometown, homeland, land of one's ancestors:– hometown (4), country (1), country of their own (1), own town (1), town (1)

G4259 **Πατροβᾶς** ***Patrobas***, n. pr. [1] [√*4252* + *1050*]. Patrobas, "*father of existence*":– Patrobas (1)

G4260 **πατρολῴας** ***patrolōas***, n. [1] [√*4252* + *262*]. one who kills one's father:– kill fathers (1)

G4261 **πατροπαράδοτος** ***patroparadotos***, a. [1] [√*4252* +

4123 + 1443]. handed down from forefathers:– handed down from ancestors (1)

G4262* πατρῷος *patrōos, a. [3] [√*4252*]. ancestral, from forefathers:– ancestors (2), of ancestors (1)

G4263* Παῦλος *Paulos, n. pr. [158] Paul, Paulus, *"little"*:– Paul (150), Paul's (6), Paulus (1), him[s] (1)

G4264* παύω *pauō, v. [15] [→*187, 188, 398, 399, 2058, 2923, 2924, 5265*]. (act.) to cause to stop; (mid.) to stop, cease, finish:– stopped (6), finished (2), done (1), ended (1), keep from (1), stilled (1), stop (1), stops (1), subsided (1)

G4265* Πάφος *Paphos, n. pr. [2] Paphos:– Paphos (2)

G4266* παχύνω *pachynō, v. [2] to become calloused of heart, make fat, and so unable to understand:– calloused (2)

G4267* πέδη *pedē, n. [3] [√*4269*]. foot shackle, fetter:– foot (2), irons on feet (1)

G4268* πεδινός *pedinos, a. [1] [√*4269*]. level, flat:– level (1)

G4269* πεζεύω *pezeuō, v. [1] [→*4267, 4268, 4270, 4271, 5134, 5135, 5136, 5544, 5545*]. to go on foot, travel by walking:– going on foot (1)

G4270* πεζῇ *pezē, adv. [2] [√*4269*]. on foot:– on foot (2)

G4271* πεζός *pezos, a. Not used in NIVEBC. [√*4269*]. on foot

G4272* πειθαρχέω *peitharcheō, v. [4] [√*4275 + 806*]. to obey; to take advice:– obey (2), obedient (1), taken advice (1)

G4273* πειθός *peithos, a. [1] [√*4275*]. persuasive:– persuasive (1)

G4274* πειθώ *peithō, n. Not used in NIVEBC. [√*4275*]. persuasiveness

G4275* πείθω *peithō, v. [52] [→*400, 577, 578, 579, 2340, 4272, 4273, 4274, 4282, 4301, 4391, 4392; cf. 4412*]. to convince, persuade; to trust in, have confidence in, be persuaded:– convinced (10), confident (7), persuaded (5), persuade (4), followers (2), have confidence (2), put confidence (2), dissuaded (1), follow (1), followed the advice (1), fully persuaded (1), give in to (1), had confidence (1), make obey (1), obeying (1), persuasively (1), put trust (1 [+*1639*]), rely (1 [+*1639*]), satisfy (1), securing support (1), set at rest (1), sure (1), trusted (1), trusts (1), urged (1), win approval (1), won over (1)

G4276* Πειλᾶτος *Peilatos, n. pr. Not used in NIVEBC. [√*4397*]. Pilate

G4277* πεινάω *peinaō, v. [23] [→*4698*]. to be hungry:– hungry (17), go hungry (3), hunger (3)

G4278* πεῖρα *peira, n. [2] [→*585, 586, 1733, 4279, 4280, 4281*]. to try to do, attempt; to face, experience:– faced (1 [+*3284*]), tried (1 [+*3284*])

G4279* πειράζω *peirazō, v. [38] [√*4278*]. to test, tempt; to try to trap; to examine (oneself). The difference between a test and a temptation is found in the tester's motivations and expectations; the devil tempts that the believer might fail God's standards of faith and so sin; God tests that he might determine and sharpen true character, with no focus on making the believer fail:– tempted (11), test (7), tested (7), trap (3), tried (3), tempt (2), tempter (2), did[s] (1), examine (1), tempting (1)

G4280* πειρασμός *peirasmos, n. [21] [√*4278*]. test; trial; temptation:– temptation (8), trials (4), trial (3), testing (2), severe testing (1), tempted (1), tempting (1), test (1)

G4281* πειράω *peiraō, v. [1] [√*4278*]. to try, attempt:– tried to (1)

G4282* πεισμονή *peismonē, n. [1] [√*4275*]. persuasion:– persuasion (1)

G4283* πέλαγος *pelagos, n. [2] open sea; depths:– depths (1), open sea (1)

G4284* πελεκίζω *pelekizō, v. [1] to behead, a derivative of the Greek noun "ax," not found in the NT:– beheaded (1)

G4285* πεμπταῖος *pemptaios, a. Not used in NIVEBC. [√*4297*]. on the fifth day

G4286* πέμπτος *pemptos, a. [4] [√*4297*]. fifth:– fifth (4)

G4287* πέμπω *pempō, v. [79] [→*402, 673, 1734, 1852, 3569, 4636, 5225*]. to send:– sent (45), send (21), sending (6), sent (2 [+*4707*]), take (2), had (1), provide (1), sends (1)

G4288* πένης *penēs, a. [1] [→*4293; cf. 4506*]. poor:– poor (1)

G4289* πενθερά *penthera, n. [6] [√*4290*]. mother-in-law:– mother-in-law (6)

G4290* πενθερός *pentheros, n. [1] [→*4289*]. father-in-law:– father-in-law (1)

G4291* πενθέω *pentheō, v. [10] [√*4292*]. to mourn, grieve (over):– mourn (6), mourning (2), gone into mourning (1), grieved (1)

G4292* πένθος *penthos, n. [5] [→*4291*]. mourning, grief, sadness:– mourning (3), grief (1), mourn (1 [+*3972*])

G4293* πενιχρός *penichros, a. [1] [√*4288*]. poor, needy:– poor (1)

G4294* πεντάκις *pentakis, adv. [1] [√*4297*]. five times:– five times (1)

G4295* πεντακισχίλιοι *pentakischilioi, a. num. [6] [√*4297 + 5943*]. five thousand:– five thousand (6)

G4296* πεντακόσιοι *pentakosioi, a. num. [2] [√*4297*]. five hundred:– five hundred (2)

G4297* πέντε *pente, n. num. [38] [→*1278, 4285, 4286, 4294, 4295, 4296, 4298, 4299, 4300*]. five:– five (35), fifty thousand (1 [+*3689*]), seventy-five (1 [+*1573*]), three miles (1 [+*5084, 1633*])

G4298* πεντεκαιδέκατος *pentekaidekatos, a. [1] [√*4297 + 2779 + 1274*]. fifteenth:– fifteenth (1)

G4299* πεντήκοντα *pentēkonta, n. num. [7] [√*4297*]. fifty:– fifty (3), 153 (1 [+*1669, 5552*]), 450 (1 [+*5484, 2779*]), fifties (1), four hundred and fifty (1)

G4300* πεντηκοστή *pentēkostē, n. [3] [√*4297*]. Pentecost, fiftieth (day after Passover):– pentecost (3)

G4301* πεποίθησις *pepoithēsis, n. [6] [√*4275*]. confidence, trust:– confidence (4), as bold (1 [+*2509, 3836*]), confident (1)

G4302* -περ *-per, pt. emph. Not used in NIVEBC. [→*1478, 1570, 1642, 2077, 2080, 2472, 2749, 2778, 2788, 4013, 6061, 6062*]. an affix for various kinds of emphasis

G4303* Πέραια *Peraia, n. pr. Not used in NIVEBC. [√*4305*]. Peraea

G4304* περαιτέρω *peraiterō, adv. [1] [√*4305*]. further, beyond:– further (1)

G4305* πέραν *peran, adv. [23] [→*527, 596, 1385, 4303, 4304, 4306, 4373, 4405; cf. 4513*]. on the other side; (n.) opposite side, region across:– other side (6), across (3), on the other side of (2), other side of the lake (2), across (1 [+*1650, 3836*]), across the lake (1 [+*1650, 3836*]), beyond (1), crossed (1), on the opposite shore (1), on the other side (1), region across (1), regions across (1), to the far shore (1), NDT (1)

G4306* πέρας *peras, n. [4] [√*4305*]. end, limit:– ends (3), end (1)

G4307* Πέργαμος *Pergamos, n. pr. [2] Pergamum:– Pergamum (2)

G4308* Πέργη *Pergē, n. pr. [3] Perga:– Perga (3)

G4309* περί *peri, pp. [330] [→*597, 598, 1853, 2341, 2342, 4310, 4311, 4312, 4313, 4314, 4315, 4316, 4317, 4318, 4319, 4320, 4321, 4322, 4323, 4324, 4325, 4326, 4327, 4328, 4329, 4330, 4331, 4332, 4333, 4334, 4335, 4336, 4337, 4338, 4339, 4340, 4341, 4342, 4343, 4344, 4345, 4346, 4347, 4348, 4349, 4350, 4351, 4352, 4362, 4363, 4364, 4365, 4366, 4367, 4368, 4369, 4370, 5226, 5227; cf. 4356*]. (gen.) about, concerning, in regard to; (acc.) around, about, nearby:– about (137), for (51), of (17), concerning (13), around (12), because of (4), in (4), on (4), with (4), by (3), to (3), against (2), at (2), from (2), on behalf (2), sin offerings (2 [+*281*]), as (1), as far as is concerned (1), as for (1), as to (1), besiege with questions (1 [+*694, 4498*]), case[s] (1 [+*3836*]), companions (1 [+*3836*]), followers (1 [+*3836*]), had to do with (1), how (1 [+*3836*]), in case (1), in favor (1), in regard to (1), in that case (1 [+*4005*]), meant (1 [+*3306*]), nearby (1 [+*3836, 5536, 1697*]), over (1), over the matter of (1), regarding (1), surrounding (1), that (1 [+*3836*]), to be (1), to consider (1 [+*3972*]), to help (1), welfare (1 [+*3836*]), what I meant[s] (1 [+*4047*]), with regard to (1), NDT (41)

G4310* περιάγω *periagō, v. [6] [√*4309 + 72*]. (tr.) to take (a wife); (intr.) to go about, travel about:– around (1), groped about (1), take along with (1), through (1), travel over (1), went (1)

G4311* περιαιρέω *periaireō, v. [5] [√*4309 + 145*]. to take away; (pass.) to be taken away; to cut loose, set sail; to be given up, abandoned:– cutting loose (1), gave up (1), set sail (1), take away (1), taken away (1)

G4312* περιάπτω *periaptō, v. [1] [√*4309 + 721*]. to kindle (a fire):– kindled (1)

G4313* περιαστράπτω *periastraptō, v. [2] [√*4309 + 847*]. to flash around, shine around:– flashed around (2)

G4314* περιβάλλω *periballō, v. [23] [√*4309 + 965*]. to dress, clothe, wrap around:– dressed in (4), wear (3), clothe (2), clothed in (2), dressed (2), dressed in (2 [+*1877, 2668*]), clothed (1), clothed with (1), dressing in (1), in (1), robed in (1), wearing (1), wearing nothing (1 [+*2093, 1218*]), wrap around (1)

G4315* περιβλέπω *periblepō, v. [7] [√*4309 + 1063*]. to look around at:– looked around (5), looked at (1), looking around (1)

G4316* περιβόλαιον *peribolaion, n. [2] [√*4309 + 965*]. covering, robe:– covering (1), robe (1)

G4317* περιδέω *perideō, v. [1] [√*4309 + 1313*]. to wrap around:– around (1)

G4318* περιεργάζομαι *periergazomai, v. [1] [√*4309 + 2240*]. to be a busybody:– busybodies (1)

G4319* περίεργος *periergos, a. [2] [√*4309 + 2240*]. meddlesome, curious; (n.) busybody; (pl.) sorcery, magical arts:– sorcery (1), talk nonsense (1)

G4320* περιέρχομαι *perierchomai, v. [3] [√*4309 + 2262*]. to go around:– going about (1), went about (1), went around (1)

G4321* περιέχω *periechō, v. [2] [√*4309 + 2400*]. to seize, encircle; to contain, to say:– astonished (1 [+*2502*]), says (1)

G4322* περιζώννυμι *perizōnnymi, v. [6] [√*4309 + 2439*]. to buckle a belt around, gird, dress for service:– around (1), belt buckled around (1), dress to serve (1), dressed ready for service (1 [+*3836, 4019*]), get ready (1), wore (1)

G4323* περιζωννύω *perizōnnyō, v. Not used in NIVEBC. [√*4309 + 2439*]. to buckle a belt around, dress for service, gird

G4324* περίθεσις *perithesis, n. [1] [√*4309 + 5502*]. wearing, putting on:– wearing (1)

G4325* περιΐστημι *periistēmi, v. [4] [√*4309 + 2705*]. to stand around; avoid, shun:– avoid (2), standing here (1), stood around (1)

G4326* περικάθαρμα *perikatharma, n. [1] [√*4309 + 2754*]. scum, refuse:– scum (1)

G4327* περικαθίζω *perikathizō, v. Not used in NIVEBC. [√*4309 + 2767*]. to sit around

G4328* περικαλύπτω *perikalyptō, v. [3] [√*4309 + 2821*]. to blindfold, cover the face or eyes; to cover (with gold):– blindfolded (1), blindfolded (1 [+*3836, 4725*]), gold-covered (1 [+*4119, 5992*])

G4329* περίκειμαι *perikeimai, v. [5] [√*4309 + 3023*]. to surround, place or tie around; to be subject to:– bound with (1), hung (1), subject to (1), surrounded (1), tied around (1)

G4330* περικεφαλαία *perikephalaia, n. [2] [√*4309 + 3051*]. helmet:– helmet (2)

G4331* περικρατής *perikratēs, a. [1] [√*4309 + 3197*]. secure, having power, being in command of, getting under control:– secure (1)

G4332* περικρύβω *perikrybō, v. [1] [√*4309 + 3221*]. to seclude oneself, hide, conceal oneself:– in seclusion (1)

G4333* περικυκλόω *perikykloō, v. [1] [√*4309 + 3241*]. to encircle, surround:– encircle (1)

G4334* περιλάμπω *perilampō, v. [2] [√*4309 + 3290*]. to shine around, blaze around:– blazing around (1), shone around (1)

G4335* περιλείπομαι *perileipomai, v. [2] [√*4309 + 3309*]. to be left, remain:– left (2)

G4336* περιλείχω *perileichō, v. Not used in NIVEBC. [√*4309 + 3314*]. to lick all around, lick off

G4337* περίλυπος *perilypos, a. [4] [√*4309 + 3383*]. overwhelmingly sorrowful; greatly distressing:– overwhelmed with sorrow (2), greatly distressed (1), very sad (1)

G4338* περιμένω *perimenō, v. [1] [√*4309 + 3531*]. to wait for:– wait for (1)

G4339* πέριξ *perix, adv. [1] [√*4309*]. around:– around (1)

G4340* περιοικέω *perioikeō, v. [1] [√*4309 + 3875*]. to live in a neighborhood; (n.) neighbor:– neighbors (1)

G4341* περίοικος *perioikos, a. [1] [√*4309 + 3875*]. neighboring; (n.) neighbor:– neighbors (1)

G4342* περιούσιος *periousios, a. [1] [√*4309 + 1639*]. one's very own, special:– his very own (1)

G4343* περιοχή *periochē, n. [1] [√*4309 + 2400*]. passage (of Scripture), portion:– passage (1)

G4344* περιπατέω *peripateō, v. [95] [√*4309 + 4251*]. to walk (around); to live, conduct one's life:– walk (27), live (17), walking (14), walks (4), walk around (3), walked (3), acting (2), live a life (2), live lives (2), are (1), around (1), behave (1), daily life (1), did[s] (1), do (1), do[s] (1), do so (1), followed (1 [+*3552*]), go (1), go about (1), living (1), moved about (1), passing by (1), prowls around (1), the way act (1), use (1 [+*1877*]), walk along (1), walking around (1), walks around (1), went (1)

G4345* περιπείρω *peripeirō, v. [1] [√*4309*]. to pierce:– pierced (1)

G4346* περιπίπτω *peripiptō, v. [3] [√*4309 + 4406*]. to fall into the hands of; to strike; to face, be involved in:– attacked (1), face (1), struck (1)

G4347* περιποιέω *peripoieō, v. [3] [√*4309 + 4472*]. (mid.) to keep, save; to gain for oneself; to buy, acquire:– bought (1), gain (1), keep (1)

G4348* περιποίησις *peripoiēsis, n. [5] [√*4309 + 4472*].

possession, property; sharing in, gaining; saving:– possession (1), receive (1), saved (1 [+*1650, 6034*]), share in (1), special possession (1)

G4349 **περιραίνω** ***perirainō***, v. Not used in NIVEBC. [√*4309* + *4817*]. to sprinkle all around

G4350 **περιραντίζω** ***perirantizō***, v. Not used in NIVEBC. [√*4309* + *4817*]. to sprinkle all around

G4351 **περιρήγνυμι** ***perirēgnymi***, v. [1] [√*4309* + *4838*]. to strip off, tear off:– stripped (1 [+*3836, 2668*])

G4352 **περισπάω** ***perispaō***, v. [1] [√*4309* + *5060*]. (pass.) to be distracted:– distracted (1)

G4353 **περισσεία** ***perisseia***, n. [4] [√*4356*]. abundance, prevalence:– abundant provision (1), greatly (1 [+*1650*]), overflowing (1), prevalent (1)

G4354 **περίσσευμα** ***perisseuma***, n. [5] [√*4356*]. overflow, plenty; what is left over, scraps:– plenty (2), full of (1), left over (1), what full of (1)

G4355 **περισσεύω** ***perisseuō***, v. [39] [√*4356*]. to have abundance, more than enough, overflow, to have an excessive amount of something, ranging from moderate excess to a very great degree of excess:– left over (5), overflow (4), abound (3), excel (3), do more (2), have an abundance (2), overflowing (2), wealth (2), abounds (1), abundance (1), abundantly (1), better (1), bless abundantly (1 [+*4246, 5921*]), enhances (1), give fully (1), grew (1), have more than enough (1), have plenty (1), have to spare (1), lavished (1), living in plenty (1), more (1 [+*3437*]), surpasses (1 [+*4498*]), welled up (1)

G4356 **περισσός** ***perissos***, a. [6] [→ *1735, 4353, 4354, 4355, 4357, 4358, 4359, 4360, 5655, 5656, 5668, 5669; cf. 4309*]. exceeding, going beyond; full, abundant; (compar.) more than; (n.) advantage:– advantage (1), beyond (1), completely (1 [+*3336, 1666*]), more (1), no need (1), to the full (1)

G4357 **περισσότερον** ***perissoteron***, adv. Not used in NIVEBC. [√*4356*]. even more, so much more

G4358 **περισσότερος** ***perissoteros***, a. [16] [√*4356*]. more than, even more; greater than; with special honor:– more (2), more than (2), most severely (2), special (2), excessive (1), freely (1), greater (1), harder (1), more (1 [+*3437*]), more important (1), much more (1), very (1)

G4359 **περισσοτέρως** ***perissoterōs***, adv. [12] [√*4356*]. to a much greater degree; especially, frequently, extremely:– all the greater (1), all the more (1), depth (1), especially (1), especially (1 [+*3437*]), every (1), extremely (1), harder (1), more (1), more frequently (1), most careful (1), particularly (1)

G4360 **περισσῶς** ***perissōs***, adv. [4] [√*4356*]. even more, all the more:– all the louder (2), even more (1), so (1)

G4361 **περιστερά** ***peristera***, n. [10] dove, pigeon:– doves (5), dove (4), pigeons (1)

G4362 **περιτέμνω** ***peritemnō***, v. [17] [√*4309* + *5533*]. to circumcise:– circumcised (13), circumcise (4)

G4363 **περιτίθημι** ***peritithēmi***, v. [8] [√*4309* + *5502*]. to put on, set on; to treat with:– put on (4), put around (2), set on (1), treat with (1)

G4364 **περιτομή** ***peritomē***, n. [36] [√*4309* + *5533*]. circumcision; fig., the Jews (as a group of people who adhered to the ritual of circumcision):– circumcision (15), circumcised (13), circumcision group (2), Jews (1), Jews (1 [+*1666*]), after[s] (1 [+*1877*]), circumcised (1 [+*1877*]), circumcised (1 [+*3284*]), you[s] (1 [+*3836, 5148*])

G4365 **περιτρέπω** ***peritrepō***, v. [1] [√*4309* + *5572*]. to drive (to insanity):– driving (1)

G4366 **περιτρέχω** ***peritrechō***, v. [1] [√*4309* + *5556*]. to run throughout, run about:– ran throughout (1)

G4367 **περιφέρω** ***peripherō***, v. [3] [√*4309* + *5770*]. to carry, carry around; (pass.) to be blown about, carried here and there:– blown here and there (1), carried to (1), carry around (1)

G4368 **περιφρονέω** ***periphroneō***, v. [1] [√*4309* + *5856*]. to despise, look down on:– despise (1)

G4369 **περίχωρος** ***perichōros***, a. [9] [√*4309* + *6003*]. neighboring; (n.) surrounding country:– region (3), surrounding country (3), country around (1), countryside (1), surrounding (1)

G4370 **περίψημα** ***peripsēma***, n. [1] [√*4309* + *6041*]. refuse, garbage, that which is removed in the process of cleaning:– garbage (1)

G4371 **περπερεύομαι** ***perpereuomai***, v. [1] to boast, brag:– boast (1)

G4372 **Περσίς** ***Persis***, n. pr. [1] Persis, "*female Persian*":– Persis (1)

G4373 **πέρυσι** ***perysi***, adv. [2] [√*4305*]. from last year, since last year:– last year (2)

G4374 **πετεινόν** ***peteinon***, n. [14] [√*4375*]. bird:– birds (8 [+*3836, 4041*]), birds (6)

G4375 **πέτομαι** ***petomai***, v. [5] [→ *1736, 2925, 4374, 4762, 4763, 4764*]. to fly:– flying (4), fly (1)

G4376 **πέτρα** ***petra***, n. [15] [→ *4377, 4378*]. rock, bedrock, rocky crag, or other large rock formation, in contrast to individual stones (cf. *4377*), with a focus that this is a suitable, solid foundation:– rock (10), rocks (3), rocky ground (2)

G4377 **Πέτρος** ***Petros***, n. pr. [155] [√*4376*]. Peter; this has the designative meaning "rock" or "individual stone", "*rock, stone*":– Peter (150), Peter's (5)

G4378 **πετρώδης** ***petrōdēs***, a. [4] [√*4376* + *1626*]. rocky, stony; (n.) rocky place, thin soil with larger rocks or bedrock underneath:– rocky places (3), rocky ground (1)

G4379 **πήγανον** ***pēganon***, n. [1] rue (a garden herb):– rue (1)

G4380 **πηγή** ***pēgē***, n. [11] spring, well (of water); flow (of blood):– springs (5), spring (3), well (2), bleeding (1 [+*135*])

G4381 **πήγνυμι** ***pēgnymi***, v. [1] [→ *4074, 4075, 4699, 5009*]. to set up:– set up (1)

G4382 **πηδάλιον** ***pēdalion***, n. [2] rudder, steering paddle:– rudder (1), rudders (1)

G4383 **πηλίκος** ***pēlikos***, a. [2] [√*2462*]. how great, how large:– how great (1), what large (1)

G4384 **πηλός** ***pēlos***, n. [6] mud, lump of clay:– mud (4), clay (1), it[s] (1 [+*3836*])

G4385 **πήρα** ***pēra***, n. [6] traveler's bag:– bag (6)

G4386 **πηρόω** ***pēroō***, v. Not used in NIVEBC. [→ *401, 4387*]. to disable, maim

G4387 **πήρωσις** ***pērōsis***, n. Not used in NIVEBC. [√*4386*]. nearsightedness, blindness

G4388 **πῆχυς** ***pēchys***, n. [4] measure of length: cubit, or time: hour:– hour (2), a hundred yards (1 [+*1357*]), cubits (1)

G4389 **πιάζω** ***piazō***, v. [12] [√*4390*]. to seize, to grasp an object, usually with the hand; by extension: to arrest, capture, place in confinement:– arrest (3), seize (3), caught (2), arresting (1), captured (1), seized (1), taking (1)

G4390 **πιέζω** ***piezō***, v. [1] [→ *4389*]. (pass.) to be pressed down:– pressed down (1)

G4391 **πιθανολογία** ***pithanologia***, n. [1] [√*4275* + *3306*]. fine-sounding arguments, persuasive speech, a plausible yet false argument:– fine-sounding arguments (1)

G4392 **πιθός** ***pithos***, a. Not used in NIVEBC. [√*4275*]. persuasive

G4393 **πικραίνω** ***pikrainō***, v. [4] [√*4395*]. to turn sour, make bitter; to become sour, embittered:– bitter (1), harsh (1), turn sour (1), turned sour (1)

G4394 **πικρία** ***pikria***, n. [4] [√*4395*]. bitterness:– bitterness (3), bitter (1)

G4395 **πικρός** ***pikros***, a. [2] [→ *4176, 4177, 4393, 4394, 4396*]. bitter, salty:– bitter (1), salt (1)

G4396 **πικρῶς** ***pikrōs***, adv. [2] [√*4395*]. bitterly:– bitterly (2)

G4397 **Πιλᾶτος** ***Pilatos***, n. pr. [55] [→ *4276*]. Pilate, "*[family name]*":– Pilate (54), Pilate's (1)

G4398 **πίμπλημι** ***pimplēmi***, v. [24] [→ *1854, 1855, 1857, 1858, 4101, 4113, 4436, 4437, 4439, 4447, 4496*]. to fill; (pass.) to be filled, completed:– filled with (13), came (2), completed (1), filled (1), filled full (1), fulfillment (1), furious (1 [+*486*]), furious (1 [+*2596*]), in an uproar (1 [+*3836, 5180*]), time (1), was (1)

G4399 **πίμπρημι** ***pimprēmi***, v. [1] [→ *1856, 1859, 1868, 2926*]. to swell:– swell up (1)

G4400 **πινακίδιον** ***pinakidion***, n. [1] [√*4402*]. (small) writing tablet:– writing tablet (1)

G4401 **πινακίς** ***pinakis***, n. Not used in NIVEBC. [√*4402*]. (small) writing tablet

G4402 **πίναξ** ***pinax***, n. [5] [→ *4400, 4401*]. platter, dish:– platter (4), dish (1)

G4403 **πίνω** ***pinō***, v. [73] [→ *2927, 3884, 4503, 4530, 4539, 4540, 4542, 5228, 5234, 5235, 5621; cf. 4532*]. to drink:– drink (50), drinking (10), drank (5), drinks (5), drinks in (1), drunk (1), take (1)

G4404 **πιότης** ***piotēs***, n. [1] richness, nourishing sap:– nourishing sap (1)

G4405 **πιπράσκω** ***pipraskō***, v. [9] [√*4305*]. to sell:– sold (6), sales (1), sold as a slave (1), sold at a price (1)

G4406 **πίπτω** ***piptō***, v. [90] [→ *404, 528, 674, 1206, 1479, 1738, 1860, 2158, 2928, 4178, 4183, 4346, 4637, 4700, 4773, 4774, 5229*]. to fall, collapse; to bow down; to die:– fell (38), fall (12), fallen (8), falls (7), fell down (7), collapsed (2), beat down (1), bow down (1), bowed down (1), came (1), condemned (1 [+*5679, 3213*]), died (1), drop out (1), fails (1), fall (1 [+*1639*]), fall beyond recovery (1), fall down (1), fall down (1 [+*2093, 4725*]), perish (1), perished (1), threw himself (1 [+*2093, 4725*]), NDT (1)

G4407 **Πισιδία** ***Pisidia***, n. pr. [1] [→ *4408*]. Pisidia:– Pisidia (1)

G4408 **Πισίδιος** ***Pisidios***, a. pr. [1] [√*4407*]. Pisidian:– Pisidian (1)

G4409 **πιστεύω** ***pisteuō***, v. [241] [√*4412*]. to believe, put one's faith in, trust, with an implication that actions based on that trust may follow; (pass.) entrust:– believe (121), believed (61), believes (25), believers (8), believing (4), entrusted (3), trusts (3), believed on (1), committed to (1), did[s] (1), do (1), entrust (1), entrusted with (1), entrusted with task (1), faith (1), have faith (1), put faith (1), put trust (1), rely on (1), took at word (1 [+*3836, 3364*]), trust (1), trust with (1), trusted (1)

G4410 **πιστικός** ***pistikos***, a. [2] [√*4412*]. pure:– pure (2)

G4411 **πίστις** ***pistis***, n. [243] [√*4412*]. faith, faithfulness, belief, trust, with an implication that actions based on that trust may follow; "the faith" often refers to the Christian system of belief and lifestyle:– faith (225), faithfulness (4), believing (2), belief (1), believe (1), believe (1 [+*2400*]), believers (1), believers (1 [+*2400, 3836*]), by faith from first to last (1 [+*1666, 1650, 4411*]), by faith from first to last (1 [+*1666, 4411, 1650*]), faithful (1), pledge (1), proof (1), true (1), trusted (1)

G4412 **πιστός** ***pistos***, a. [67] [→ *601, 602, 603, 3898, 3899, 4409, 4410, 4411, 4413; cf. 4275*]. faithful, trustworthy, reliable, believing:– faithful (35), trustworthy (14), believe (5), believer (4), believers (2), trusted (2), believing (1), faith (1), fellow believers (1), reliable (1), sure (1)

G4413 **πιστόω** ***pistoō***, v. [1] [√*4412*]. (pass.) to be convinced of:– convinced (1)

G4414 **πλανάω** ***planaō***, v. [39] [√*4415*]. to lead astray, cause to wander, deceive; (mid./pass.) to be deceived, deluded:– deceived (9), deceive (6), deceives (3), going astray (3), deceiving (2), in error (2), lead astray (2), wandered off (2), deluded (1), leads astray (1), led astray (1), misleads (1), misled (1), mistaken (1), wander (1), wander off (1), wandered (1), wanders away (1)

G4415 **πλάνη** ***planē***, n. [10] [→ *675, 4414, 4416, 4417, 4418*]. error, delusion, deception:– error (6), deceitful (1), deception (1), delusion (1), falsehood (1)

G4416 **πλάνης** ***planēs***, n. Not used in NIVEBC. [√*4415*]. wanderer

G4417 **πλανήτης** ***planētēs***, n. [1] [√*4415*]. wanderer; (a.) wandering:– wandering (1)

G4418 **πλάνος** ***planos***, a. [5] [√*4415*]. deceiving, leading astray; (n.) deceiver, imposter; fig. extensions of the base meaning "to wander off a path," not found in the NT:– deceiver (2), deceivers (1), deceiving (1), impostors (1)

G4419 **πλάξ** ***plax***, n. [3] stone tablet:– tablets (2), stone tablets (1)

G4420 **πλάσμα** ***plasma***, n. [1] [√*4421*]. what is formed, molded:– formed (1)

G4421 **πλάσσω** ***plassō***, v. [2] [→ *4420, 4422*]. to form, mold:– formed (2)

G4422 **πλαστός** ***plastos***, a. [1] [√*4421*]. made up, fabricated, false:– fabricated (1)

G4423 **πλατεῖα** ***plateia***, n. [9] [√*4426*]. (main) street, wide road:– streets (5), great street (2), public square (1), street (1)

G4424 **πλάτος** ***platos***, n. [4] [√*4426*]. width, breadth:– wide (3), breadth (1)

G4425 **πλατύνω** ***platynō***, v. [3] [√*4426*]. to open wide, make wide:– make wide (1), open wide (1), opened wide (1)

G4426 **πλατύς** ***platys***, a. [1] [→ *4423, 4424, 4425*]. wide, broad:– wide (1)

G4427 **πλέγμα** ***plegma***, n. [1] [√*4428*]. something braided or woven:– elaborate hairstyles (1)

G4428 **πλέκω** ***plekō***, v. [3] [→ *1861, 1862, 4427, 4451*]. to twist together, weave, braid:– twisted together (3)

G4429 **πλεονάζω** ***pleonazō***, v. [9] [√*4444*]. to make increase; (intr.) to grow, increase, have abundance:– increase (2), credited (1), have too much (1), increased (1), increasing (1), increasing measure (1), make increase (1), reaching more and more (1 [+*1328, 3836, 4498*])

G4430 **πλεονεκτέω** ***pleonekteō***, v. [5] [√*4444* + *2400*]. to exploit, take advantage of, outwit:– exploit (2), exploited (1), outwit (1), take advantage of (1)

G4431 **πλεονέκτης** ***pleonektēs***, n. [4] [√*4444* + *2400*]. greedy person:– greedy (4)

G4432 **πλεονεξία** ***pleonexia***, n. [10] [√*4444* + *2400*]. greediness, avarice:– greed (9), one grudgingly given (1)

G4433 **πλευρά** ***pleura***, n. [5] side (of the body):– side (5)

G4434 **πλέω** ***pleō***, v. [6] [→ *676, 1095, 1386, 1739, 2929, 4179, 4449, 4450, 4452, 4453, 5709*]. to travel by ship, sail:– sail (2), sailed (2), sailing (1), travel by ship (1 [+*2093, 5536*])

G4435 **πληγή** ***plēgē***, n. [22] [√*4448*]. plague; punishment: beating, flogging, wounding:– plagues (10), plague (3), wound (2), beat (1 [+*2202*]), beatings (1), flogged (1 [+*2202*]), flogged (1), punishment (1), wounded (1 [+*2400, 3836*]), wounds (1)

G4436 **πλῆθος** ***plēthos***, n. [31] [√*4398*]. large number, crowd, multitude, assembly:– number (6), assembly (3), crowd (3), people (3), all (2), multitude (2), assembled worshipers (1 [+*3836, 3295*]), church^S (1), community (1), crowd (1 [+*3836, 3295*]), crowds (1), great company (1), great number (1), group (1), large number (1), numerous (1), pile (1), publicly (1 [+*1967, 3836*])

G4437 **πληθύνω** ***plēthynō***, v. [12] [√*4398*]. to increase, grow in numbers, abound:– in abundance (3), give many descendants (2 [+*4437*]), increase (2), flourish (1), increased (1), increased in numbers (1), number greatly increased (1 [+*889, 2779*]), number increasing (1)

G4438 **πλήκτης** ***plēktēs***, n. [2] [√*4448*]. violent man, bully:– violent (2)

G4439 **πλήμμυρα** ***plēmmyra***, n. [1] [√*4398*]. flood, high water; in context likely a flash flood in a narrow valley (wadi):– flood (1)

G4440 **πλήν** ***plēn***, c. & pp.* [31] [√*4444*]. but, however, only, yet:– but (13), yet (4), however (3), only (3), except (2), beyond (1 [+*4498*]), but now (1), important thing (1), in any case (1), nevertheless (1), NDT (1)

G4441 **πλήρης** ***plērēs***, a. [16] [√*4444*]. full:– full (7), basketfuls (2 [+*3186*]), full of (2), always (1), basketfuls (1 [+*5083*]), covered with (1), fully (1), furious (1 [+*2596*])

G4442 **πληροφορέω** ***plērophoreō***, v. [6] [√*4444 + 5770*]. to fulfill (completely); (pass.) to be fully assured, convinced, persuaded:– discharge all the duties (1), fulfilled (1), fully (1), fully assured (1), fully convinced (1), fully persuaded (1)

G4443 **πληροφορία** ***plērophoria***, n. [4] [√*4444 + 5770*]. full assurance, certainty, conviction:– complete (1), conviction (1), full assurance (1), fully realized (1)

G4444 **πληρόω** ***plēroō***, v. [86] [→ *405, 499, 1740, 1741, 4429, 4430, 4431, 4432, 4440, 4441, 4442, 4443, 4445, 4650, 5230, 5670*]. to fulfill, make full; (pass.) to be filled, full, complete (often used with reference to the fulfillment of the OT Scriptures):– fulfilled (21), fulfill (11), complete (7), filled with (7), filled (6), fill (2), fill with (2), finished (2), full (2), make complete (2), passed (2), amply supplied (1), bring to fruition (1), bring to fulfillment (1), brought to fullness (1), come (1), come true (1), completed (1), completing (1), filled in (1), fills (1), finds fulfillment (1), full number (1), fully (1), fully come (1), fully met (1), gone by (1), greatly (1), happened (1), meet (1), present in fullness (1), unfinished (1 [+*4024*]), was^S (1)

GREEK INDEX

G4445 **πλήρωμα** ***plērōma***, n. [17] [√*4444*]. fullness, fulfillment:– fullness (6), fulfillment (2), basketfuls (1 [+*3186*]), basketfuls (1 [+*5083*]), everything (1), full inclusion (1), full measure (1), full number (1), fully (1), patch (1), piece (1)

G4446 **πλησίον** ***plēsion***, adv. & pp.* & n. [17] [→ *4180, 4181*]. near, close by; (n.) neighbor; (pp.) near:– neighbor (14), near (1), neighbors (1), other (1)

G4447 **πλησμονή** ***plēsmonē***, n. [1] [√*4398*]. indulgence, gratification:– indulgence (1)

G4448 **πλήσσω** ***plēssō***, v. [1] [→ *1742, 2159, 4435, 4438*]. (pass.) to be struck:– struck (1)

G4449 **πλοιάριον** ***ploiarion***, n. [4] [√*4434*]. (small) boat:– boat (2), boats (1), small boat (1)

G4450 **πλοῖον** ***ploion***, n. [68] [√*4434*]. boat, ship:– boat (38), ship (17), boats (6), ships (3), it^S (2 [+*3836*]), on board (1 [+*1877, 3836*]), ship's (1)

G4451 **πλοκή** ***plokē***, n. Not used in NIVEBC. [√*4428*]. braiding, braid

G4452 **πλόος** ***ploos***, n. [3] [√*4434*]. voyage, navigation; same as *4453*:– voyage (2), sailing (1)

G4453 **πλοῦς** ***plous***, n. Not used in NIVEBC. [√*4434*]. voyage, navigation; same as *4452*

G4454 **πλούσιος** ***plousios***, a. [28] [√*4458*]. rich, wealthy; (n.) rich person:– rich (26), wealthy (2)

G4455 **πλουσίως** ***plousiōs***, adv. [4] [√*4458*]. richly, generously, abundantly:– richly (2), generously (1), rich (1)

G4456 **πλουτέω** ***plouteō***, v. [12] [√*4458*]. to be rich; (pf.) to have acquired wealth:– rich (9), acquired wealth (1), gained wealth (1), richly blesses (1)

G4457 **πλουτίζω** ***ploutizō***, v. [3] [√*4458*]. to make rich; (pass.) to be enriched:– enriched (2), making rich (1)

G4458 **πλοῦτος** ***ploutos***, n. [22] [→ *4454, 4455, 4456, 4457*]. riches, wealth:– riches (14), wealth (6), rich (1), value (1)

G4459 **πλύνω** ***plynō***, v. [3] [→ *677*]. to wash (things):– wash (1), washed (1), washing (1)

G4460 **πνεῦμα** ***pneuma***, n. [379] [√*4463*]. wind, breath, things which are commonly perceived as having no material substance; by extension: spirit, heart, mind, the immaterial part of the inner person that can respond to God; spirit being: (evil) spirit, ghost, God the Holy Spirit:– Spirit (328), spirits (32), breath (3), ghost (2), Spirit's (1), attitude (1), decided (1 [+*5502, 1877, 3836*]), demon-possessed (1 [+*2400, 3836, 3836, 4505*]), gently (1 [+*1877, 4559*]), he^S (1 [+*3836, 899, 1877, 899*]), holy (1), inspires (1), mind (1), prophecy (1), sighed deeply (1 [+*417, 3836*]), spiritual (1), wind (1), with great fervor (1 [+*2417, 3836*])

G4461 **πνευματικός** ***pneumatikos***, a. [26] [√*4463*]. spiritual, pertaining to the Spirit; (n.) spiritual person:– spiritual (16), from the Spirit (2), gifts of the Spirit (2), Spirit-taught (1), gifted by the Spirit (1), live by the Spirit (1), people who live by the Spirit (1), that the Spirit gives (1), with the Spirit (1)

G4462 **πνευματικῶς** ***pneumatikōs***, adv. [2] [√*4463*]. spiritually; figuratively:– Spirit (1), figuratively (1)

G4463 **πνέω** ***pneō***, v. [7] [→ *1743, 1863, 2535, 4460, 4461, 4462, 4466, 5710*]. to blow (of wind):– blew (2), blowing (2), blows (2), wind (1)

G4464 **πνίγω** ***pnigō***, v. [3] [→ *678, 4465, 5231*]. to choke or strangle; drown:– choke (1), choked (1), drowned (1)

G4465 **πνικτός** ***pniktos***, a. [3] [√*4464*]. strangled, choked; (n.) meat of strangled animals:– strangled (3)

G4466 **πνοή** ***pnoē***, n. [2] [√*4463*]. wind, breath:– breath (1), wind (1)

G4467 **ποδαπός** ***podapos***, a. Not used in NIVEBC. [√*608 + 4544*]. what kind of; how great!, how magnificent!

G4468 **ποδήρης** ***podērēs***, a. [1] [√*4546*]. reaching to the feet; (n.) robe reaching to the feet:– robe reaching down to feet (1)

G4469 **ποδονιπτήρ** ***podoniptēr***, n. Not used in NIVEBC. [√*4546 + 3782*]. basin for washing feet

G4470 **πόθεν** ***pothen***, adv. [29] from where, from which:– where from (16), where (7), how (2), how far (1), what causes (1), why (1), NDT (1)

G4471 **ποία** ***poia***, n. Not used in NIVEBC. [√*4478 or* 4481]. grass, herb

G4472 **ποιέω** ***poieō***, v. [566] [→ *16, 17, 18, 942, 1647, 1648, 2343, 2443, 2803, 2804, 2818, 3674, 3846, 4062, 4347, 4348, 4473, 4474, 4475, 4701, 5010, 5188, 5935*]. to do, make, practice, produce, a generic term of action or performance: note the many contextual translations in the NIV:– do (157), doing (42), done (36), made (36), did (33), does (23), make (20), performed (13), perform (6), produce (6), bear (5), committed (5), give (4), making (4), treated (4), appointed (3), bears (3), makes (3), practice (3), put (3), put into practice (3), put up (3), wage (3), was (3), work (3), acted (2), carry out (2), formed (2), give to the needy (2 [+*1797*]), judge (2 [+*3213*]), kept (2), performing (2), practiced (2), practices (2), pray (2 [+*1255*]), preparing (2), provide (2), puts into practice (2), send out (2), sins (2 [+*3836, 281*]), spending (2), tell about (2 [+*5745*]), treat (2), accomplish (1), accomplished (1), accomplishing (1), act (1), acts (1), agreeing (1 [+*1651, 1191*]), are (1), attack (1 [+*4483*]), avenged (1 [+*1689*]), be (1), bearing (1), bears (1 [+*1639*]), been (1), began (1), breaks law (1 [+*490*]), bring (1), bring about (1), bring to ruin (1 [+*2246*]), business (1 [+*5515*]), carrying out (1), cause (1), causing (1), celebrate (1), claim to be (1 [+*4932*]), claimed to be (1 [+*1571*]), claims to be (1 [+*1571*]), commits (1), confirm (1 [+*1010*]), consider (1), created (1), criminal (1 [+*2805*]), delay (1 [+*332*]), dividing (1), done (1 [+*1639*]), earned (1), exercise (1), exercised (1), following (1), forced (1), forcing (1), gain (1), gaining (1), gave (1), gave to in need (1 [+*1797*]), get (1), given (1), gives away (1 [+*1316*]), good (1 [+*2822*]), grows (1 [+*890*]), had (1), have (1), healing (1 [+*5618*]), held (1), help (1 [+*2292*]), helping the poor (1 [+*1797*]), involved in (1), keep (1), keeps (1), kept up (1), live out (1), lives by (1), made out to be (1), make out to be (1), mention (1 [+*3644*]), mourned (1 [+*3157*]), obey (1), peacemakers (1 [+*1645*]), pray^S (1 [+*4047*]), prepare (1), prepared (1), provided (1), redeemed (1 [+*3391*]), remember (1 [+*3644*]), remember (1 [+*3644*]), remember (1 [+*3647*]), remembering (1 [+*3644*]), sacrificed^S (1 [+*4047*]), satisfy (1 [+*2653*]), see (1), set up (1), show (1), sin (1 [+*281*]), sinned (1 [+*281, 1639*]), spend (1), spent (1), spreading (1 [+*3364*]), stayed (1), stirring up (1 [+*2180*]), sweep away with the torrent (1 [+*4533*]), think about (1 [+*4630*]), think are (1), treat (1 [+*1650*]), turned into (1), turning into (1), unite (1 [+*3517*]), walked along (1 [+*3847*]), was^S (1), weeping (1 [+*3081*]), win (1), with (1), worked (1), wrote (1), yielded (1), yielding (1), NDT (2)

G4473 **ποίημα** ***poiēma***, n. [2] [√*4472*]. what is made, workmanship, creation:– handiwork (1), made (1)

G4474 **ποίησις** ***poiēsis***, n. [1] [√*4472*]. doing, working:– do (1)

G4475 **ποιητής** ***poiētēs***, n. [6] [√*4472*]. doer, keeper, obeyer; poet:– do (1 [+*1181*]), do (1 [+*1639*]), doing (1), keeping (1), obey (1), poets (1)

G4476 **ποικίλος** ***poikilos***, a. [10] [→ *4497*]. of various kinds, of all kinds:– all kinds (3), various (3), all kinds of (1), many kinds (1), various forms (1), various kinds (1)

G4477 **ποιμαίνω** ***poimainō***, v. [11] [√*4478*]. to shepherd, take care of sheep; to rule, lead:– rule (3), shepherd (2), shepherds (2), looking after the sheep (1), shepherds who feed (1), take care of (1), tends (1)

G4478 **ποιμήν** ***poimēn***, n. [18] [→ *799, 4471?, 4477, 4479, 4480*]. shepherd; pastor:– shepherd (13), shepherds (4), pastors (1)

G4479 **ποίμνη** ***poimnē***, n. [5] [√*4478*]. flock:– flock (3), flocks (1), NDT (1)

G4480 **ποίμνιον** ***poimnion***, n. [5] [√*4478*]. flock:– flock (5)

G4481 **ποῖος** ***poios***, a. [33] [√*3888, 4471?*]. what?, which?, of what kind?:– what (21), which (4), the kind of (3), how (1), the (1), way (1), what kind (1), what kind of (1)

G4482 **πολεμέω** ***polemeō***, v. [7] [√*4483*]. to fight, make war:– fight (2), wage war (2), fought (1), fought back (1), wages war (1)

G4483 **πόλεμος** ***polemos***, n. [18] [→ *4482*]. war, battle, fight:– battle (6), war (5), wars (5), attack (1 [+*4472*]), fights (1)

G4484 **πόλις** ***polis***, n. [162] [→ *315, 1279, 2631, 3268, 3619, 3735, 3736, 3776, 4485, 4486, 4487, 4488, 4489, 5232*]. city, town, village:– city (85), town (50), towns (14), cities (6), city's (1), for town (1), from town after town (1 [+*2848*]), place (1), there^S (1 [+*1877, 4047, 3836*]), traveled from town to town (1 [+*1388, 3836*]), village (1)

G4485 **πολιτάρχης** ***politarchēs***, n. [2] [√*4484 + 806*]. city official, formally, "politarch":– city officials (2)

G4486 **πολιτεία** ***politeia***, n. [2] [√*4484*]. citizenship:– citizenship (2)

G4487 **πολίτευμα** ***politeuma***, n. [1] [√*4484*]. citizenship:– citizenship (1)

G4488 **πολιτεύομαι** ***politeuomai***, v. [2] [√*4484*]. to fulfill one's duty; to conduct oneself, lead one's life:– conduct (1), fulfilled duty (1)

G4489 **πολίτης** ***politēs***, n. [4] [√*4484*]. citizen, subjects of a kingdom; neighbor:– citizen (2), neighbor (1), subjects (1)

G4490 **πολλάκις** ***pollakis***, adv. [18] [√*4498*]. many times, again and again, often, constantly:– often (10), again and again (3), many times (2), constantly (1), many a time (1), NDT (1)

G4491 **πολλαπλασίων** ***pollaplasiōn***, a. [1] [√*4498*]. many times as much:– many times as much (1)

G4492 **πολυεύσπλαγχνος** ***polyeusplanchnos***, a. Not used in NIVEBC. [√*4498 + 2292 + 5073*]. rich in compassion

G4493 **πολύλαλος** ***polylalos***, a. Not used in NIVEBC. [√*4498 + 3281*]. talkative, garrulous

G4494 **πολυλογία** ***polylogia***, n. [1] [√*4498 + 3306*]. speaking many words, wordiness:– many words (1)

G4495 **πολυμερῶς** ***polymerōs***, adv. [1] [√*4498 + 3538*]. at many times, in many ways:– at many times (1)

G4496 **πολυπλήθεια** ***polyplētheia***, n. Not used in NIVEBC. [√*4498 + 4398*]. large crowd

G4497 **πολυποίκιλος** ***polypoikilos***, a. [1] [√*4498 + 4476*]. manifold, (very) many sided:– manifold (1)

G4498 **πολύς** ***polys***, a. [420] [→ *4102, 4490, 4491, 4492, 4493, 4494, 4495, 4496, 4497, 4499, 4500, 4501, 4502*]. many, great, large; (compar.) more than, greater than; (super.) the most; very large:– many (191), great (37), large (31), much (24), more (22), how much (8), most (8), all the more (7 [+*3437*]), greater (6), very (5), long (4), all (3), great deal (3), plenty (3), few (2 [+*4024*]), majority (2), number (2), plentiful (2), rushing (2), strict (2), a great deal (1), a lot of (1), again and again (1), any further (1 [+*2093*]), badly (1), become more and more (1 [+*2093, 4621*]), before very long (1 [+*3552, 4024*]), besiege with questions (1 [+*694, 4309*]), better (1), beyond (1 [+*4440*]), bigger (1), bold (1 [+*4244, 2400*]), by far (1), considerable (1), crowds (1), deep (1), earnestly (1), freely (1), further (1 [+*2093*]), generously (1), greatly (1), hard (1), high (1), intense (1), larger (1), late in the day (1 [+*6052*]), long (1 [+*2465*]), long period (1), loudly (1), many (1 [+*4725*]), often (1), often (1 [+*3836*]), on and on (1 [+*2093*]), on the contrary (1 [+*247, 3437*]), only (1 [+*4024, 2445*]), over (1), powerful (1 [+*2710*]), reaching more and more (1 [+*4429, 1328, 3836*]), several (1), severe (1), severely (1), so many (1), strong (1), strongly (1), surpasses

(1 [+*4355*]), urgently (1 [+*3552, 4155*]), very (1 [+*2093*]), very large (1), very late (1 [+*6052*]), violent (1), violently (1), warmly (1), waters (1), wept and wept (1 [+*3081*]), widespread (1), NDT (1)

G4499 **πολύσπλαγχνος** ***polysplanchnos***, a. [1] [√*4498 + 5073*]. full of compassion, full of mercy:– full of compassion (1)

G4500 **πολυτελής** ***polytelēs***, a. [3] [√*4498 + 5465*]. expensive, of great worth, costly:– expensive (1), great worth (1), very expensive (1)

G4501 **πολύτιμος** ***polytimos***, a. [3] [√*4498 + 5507*]. expensive, of great worth, valuable:– expensive (1), greater worth (1), of great value (1)

G4502 **πολυτρόπως** ***polytropōs***, adv. [1] [√*4498 + 5572*]. in various ways:– in various ways (1)

G4503 **πόμα** ***poma***, n. [2] [√*4403*]. drink:– drink (2)

G4504 **πονηρία** ***ponēria***, n. [7] [√*4505*]. evil, wickedness, malice, in the NT always a negative moral quality opposed to God and his goodness:– evil (3), wickedness (2), malice (1), wicked ways (1)

G4505 **πονηρός** ***ponēros***, a. [78] [→*4504; cf. 4506*]. bad, the negative quality of an object; evil, wicked, crime, the negative moral quality of a person or action opposed to God and his goodness; (n.) wicked deed, wicked thing; the Evil One, a title of Satan:– evil (47), wicked (11), bad (5), more wicked (2), unhealthy (2), crimes (1), demon-possessed (1 [+*2400, 3836, 4460, 3836*]), envious (1 [+*3836, 4057*]), envy (1 [+*4057*]), evildoers (1 [+*476*]), evils (1), festering (1), guilty (1), malicious (1), serious (1), sinful (1)

G4506 **πόνος** ***ponos***, n. [4] [→*1387, 2930; cf. 4288, 4505*]. pain, agony; hard work, toil:– agony (1), pain (1), pains (1), working (1)

G4507 **Ποντικός** ***Pontikos***, a. pr. g. [1] [√*4509*]. from Pontus:– of Pontus (1)

G4508 **Πόντιος** ***Pontios***, n. pr. [3] Pontius, "*[tribal name]*":– Pontius (3)

G4509 **πόντος** ***pontos***, n. Not used in NIVEBC. [→*2931, 4507, 4510*]. open sea

G4510 **Πόντος** ***Pontos***, n. pr. [2] [√*4509*]. Pontus, "*sea*":– Pontus (2)

G4511 **Πόπλιος** ***Poplios***, n. pr. [2] Publius, "*first*":– Publius (1), his[s] (1)

G4512 **πορεία** ***poreia***, n. [2] [√*4513*]. journey, trip; going about one's business, way of life, conduct:– go about business (1), way (1)

G4513 **πορεύομαι** ***poreuomai***, v. [153] [→*679, 680, 1388, 1389, 1660, 1744, 1864, 1865, 1866, 1867, 1989, 2164, 2344, 2345, 3844, 3845, 4182, 4512, 4515, 4516, 4638, 4702, 5233, 5294; cf. 4305*]. to come, go, travel:– go (61), went (19), going (12), goes (5), on way (4), went on (3), follow (2 [+*2848*]), follow (2 [+*3958*]), go back (2), gone (2), living (2), went on way (2), went out (2), about to (1), accompany (1 [+*5250*]), came (1), companions (1 [+*3836, 5250*]), continued on way (1), depart (1), departed (1), enter (1 [+*1650*]), following (1 [+*2848*]), go on way (1), goes on (1), heading (1), hurried (1 [+*3552, 5082*]), journey (1), leave (1), leaving (1), leaving (1 [+*608*]), left (1 [+*608, 4725*]), observing (1 [+*1877*]), press on (1), set out (1), started out (1), taken (1), traveled (1), walking (1), walking away (1), way (1), went along (1), NDT (7)

G4514 **πορθέω** ***portheō***, v. [3] to destroy, annihilate; to raise havoc, pillage:– destroy (2), raised havoc (1)

G4515 **πορία** ***poria***, n. Not used in NIVEBC. [√*4513*]. journey, trip; conduct, way of life

G4516 **πορισμός** ***porismos***, n. [2] [√*4513*]. means of gain:– gain (1), means to financial gain (1)

G4517 **Πόρκιος** ***Porkios***, n. pr. [1] Porcius, "*[tribal name]*":– Porcius (1)

G4518 **πορνεία** ***porneia***, n. [25] [√*4520*]. sexual immorality, fornication, marital unfaithfulness, prostitution, adultery, a generic term for sexual sin of any kind:– sexual immorality (16), adulteries (5), illegitimate (1 [+*1666*]), immorality (1), sexual sin (1), NDT (1)

G4519 **πορνεύω** ***porneuō***, v. [8] [√*4520*]. to commit sexual immorality of any kind, adultery:– committed adultery (3), commit sexual immorality (1), committed sexual immorality (1), did[s] (1), sexual immorality (1), sins sexually (1)

G4520 **πόρνη** ***pornē***, n. [12] [→*1745, 4518, 4519, 4521*]. prostitute, a woman who practices sexual immorality for payment; this can refer to religious unfaithfulness:– prostitute (8), prostitutes (4)

G4521 **πόρνος** ***pornos***, n. [10] [√*4520*]. one who is sexually immoral (male or female), in some contexts distinguished from an adulterer (1Co 6:9):– sexually immoral (7), immoral (1), people immoral (1), sexually immoral people (1)

G4522 **πόρρω** ***porrō***, adv. [4] [√*4574*]. far, a long way off; (compar.) farther:– far (1), far (1 [+*600*]), farther (1), long way off (1)

G4523 **πόρρωθεν** ***porrōthen***, adv. [2] [√*4574*]. from a distance, at a distance:– at a distance (1), from a distance (1)

G4524 **πορρωτέρω** ***porrōterō***, adv. Not used in NIVEBC. [√*4574*]. farther

G4525 **πορφύρα** ***porphyra***, n. [4] [→*4526, 4527, 4528*]. purple (cloth or robe):– purple (2), purple robe (2)

G4526 **πορφύρεος** ***porphyreos***, a. Not used in NIVEBC. [√*4525*]. purple, purple cloth, in some contexts implying royalty; same as *4528*

G4527 **πορφυρόπωλις** ***porphyropōlis***, n. [1] [√*4525 + 4797*]. dealer in purple cloth:– dealer in purple cloth (1)

G4528 **πορφυροῦς** ***porphyrous***, a. [4] [√*4525*]. purple, purple cloth, in some contexts implying royalty; same as *4526*:– purple (4)

G4529 **ποσάκις** ***posakis***, adv. [3] [√*4005*]. how many times?; how often!:– how often (2), how many times (1)

G4530 **πόσις** ***posis***, n. [3] [√*4403*]. drinking; a drink:– drink (2), drinking (1)

G4531 **πόσος** ***posos***, a. [27] [√*4012*]. how great?, how much?, how many?; how great!, how many!, how much!:– how much (12), how many (10), even (1 [+*3437*]), how (1), how great (1), what (1), NDT (1)

G4532 **ποταμός** ***potamos***, n. [17] [→*3544, 4533; cf. 4403*]. river, stream, torrent:– river (9), rivers (4), streams (2), torrent (2)

G4533 **ποταμοφόρητος** ***potamophorētos***, a. [1] [√*4532 + 5770*]. swept away by a torrential flow of a river:– sweep away with the torrent (1 [+*4472*])

G4534 **ποταπός** ***potapos***, a. [7] [√*4544 + 608*]. of what kind?; how great!:– what kind of (4), what great (1), what magnificent (1), what massive (1)

G4535 **ποταπῶς** ***potapōs***, adv. Not used in NIVEBC. [√*4544 + 608*]. in what way, how

G4536 **πότε** ***pote***, adv. inter. [19] [√*4544*]. when? how long?:– when (11), how long (4 [+*2401*]), how long (3 [+*2401*]), NDT (1)

G4537 **ποτέ** ***pote***, pt. [29] [√*4544*]. once, at one time, formerly; now, now at last:– once (5), at one time (3), ever (3), formerly (3), used to (2), when (2), at last (1 [+*2453*]), had been (1), long ago (1), never (1 [+*4024*]), never (1 [+*4046*]), never (1 [+*4024, 3590*]), now at last (1 [+*2453*]), past (1), previous (1), were (1 [+*1639*]), NDT (1)

G4538 **πότερον** ***poteron***, a. *or* pt. [1] [√*4544 + 2283*]. whether:– whether (1)

G4539 **ποτήριον** ***potērion***, n. [31] [√*4403*]. cup:– cup (29), cups (1), gives a cup (1 [+*4540*])

G4540 **ποτίζω** ***potizō***, v. [15] [√*4403*]. to give or offer a drink; to water:– give something to drink (2), waters (2), gave (1), gave something to drink (1), gave to drink (1), give water (1), given to drink (1), gives a cup (1 [+*4539*]), gives water to (1), made drink (1), offered drink (1), offered to drink (1), watered (1)

G4541 **Ποτίολοι** ***Potioloi***, n. pr. [1] Puteoli, "*rotten [sulphur] smell* or *well, spring*":– Puteoli (1)

G4542 **πότος** ***potos***, n. [1] [√*4403*]. carousing, drinking party, orgy:– carousing (1)

G4543 **πού** ***pou***, adv. [4] [√*4544*]. somewhere, a place where; about, approximately:– about (1), place where (1), somewhere (1), that (1 [+*3590*])

G4544 **ποῦ** ***pou***, adv. inter. pl. [48] [→*1325, 1326, 1327, 1643, 3595, 3607, 3608, 3610, 3889, 3961, 3962, 3963, 3968, 4030, 4467, 4534, 4535, 4536, 4537, 4538, 4543*]. where?, at what place?:– where (44), place (3), what (1)

G4545 **Πούδης** ***Poudēs***, n. pr. [1] Pudens, "*modest*":– Pudens (1)

G4546 **πούς** ***pous***, n. [93] [→*435, 3980, 4468, 4469, 5488, 5711*]. foot; leg:– feet (75), foot (8), footstool (3 [+*5711, 3836*]), sandals (2 [+*5687, 3836*]), hand (1), lame (1 [+*105, 3836*]), legs (1), them[s] (1 [+*3836, 899*]), under (1 [+*4123, 3836*])

G4547 **πρᾶγμα** ***pragma***, n. [11] [√*4556*]. thing, matter, practice:– matter (2), things (2), anything (1 [+*4246*]), dispute (1), help (1), practice (1), realities (1 [+*1635, 3836*]), thing (1), what[s] (1)

G4548 **πραγματεία** ***pragmateia***, n. [1] [√*4556*]. (pl.) affairs, concerns:– civilian affairs (1 [+*1050*])

G4549 **πραγματεύομαι** ***pragmateuomai***, v. [1] [√*4556*]. to put capital to work, do business:– put to work (1)

G4550 **πραιτώριον** ***praitōrion***, n. [8] Praetorium; palace (of the governor); palace guard:– palace (4), praetorium (2), palace guard (1), palace of the roman governor (1)

G4551 **πράκτωρ** ***praktōr***, n. [2] [√*4556*]. officer, a bailiff or constable in charge of a debtor's prison:– officer (2)

G4552 **πρᾶξις** ***praxis***, n. [6] [√*4556*]. deed, action, practice; function:– done (2), action (1), function (1), misdeeds (1), practices (1)

G4553 **πρᾶος** ***praos***, a. Not used in NIVEBC. [√*4558*]. gentle, humble, considerate

G4554 **πραότης** ***praotēs***, n. Not used in NIVEBC. [√*4558*]. gentleness, humility, courtesy, considerateness

G4555 **πρασιά** ***prasia***, n. [2] [→*5995*]. group; in context this word is doubled: group by group:– in groups (2 [+*4555*])

G4556 **πράσσω** ***prassō***, v. [39] [→*407, 1390, 4547, 4548, 4549, 4551, 4552*]. to do, act, practice:– do (9), done (6), doing (5), acted (1), collect (1), collected (1), deeds (1), defying (1 [+*595*]), demonstrate (1 [+*545*]), does (1), done (1 [+*1639*]), harm (1 [+*2805*]), indulged (1), live (1), mind business (1), observe (1), practice (1), practiced (1), preach[s] (1 [+*4047*]), put into practice (1), them[s] (1 [+*3836, 3836, 5525*]), wrongdoer (1 [+*2805*])

G4557 **πραϋπαθία** ***praupathia***, n. [1] [√*4558 + 4248*]. gentleness:– gentleness (1)

G4558 **πραΰς** ***praus***, a. [4] [→*4553, 4554, 4557, 4559*]. gentle, meek, the positive moral quality of dealing with people in a kind manner, with humility and consideration:– gentle (3), meek (1)

G4559 **πραΰτης** ***prautēs***, n. [11] [√*4558*]. gentleness, meekness, humility:– gentle (3), gentleness (3), humility (2), gently (1 [+*1877*]), gently (1 [+*1877, 4460*]), humbly (1 [+*1877*])

G4560 **πρέπω** ***prepō***, v. [7] [→*2346, 2640, 3485*]. to be proper, appropriate, fitting:– proper (2), appropriate (1), appropriate for (1), fitting (1), improper[s] (1), meets need (1)

G4561 **πρεσβεία** ***presbeia***, n. [2] [√*4565*]. delegation, ambassador:– delegation (2)

G4562 **πρεσβευτής** ***presbeutēs***, n. Not used in NIVEBC. [√*4565*]. old man

G4563 **πρεσβεύω** ***presbeuō***, v. [2] [√*4565*]. to be an ambassador:– ambassador (1), ambassadors (1)

G4564 **πρεσβυτέριον** ***presbyterion***, n. [3] [√*4565*]. body or council of the elders, Sanhedrin:– body of elders (1), council (1), council of the elders (1)

G4565 **πρεσβύτερος** ***presbyteros***, a. [66] [→*4561, 4562, 4563, 4564, 4566, 4567, 5236*]. older; ancestral; (n.) in the Gospels and Acts, "elder," usually as an official leader of the Jewish community, in the epistles, "older man" and "older woman," who may or may not be official leaders of the church, depending on the context:– elders (57), older (4), elder (3), ancients (1), old (1)

G4566 **πρεσβύτης** ***presbytēs***, n. [3] [√*4565*]. older man, possibly an official of the church in some contexts:– old man (2), older (1)

G4567 **πρεσβῦτις** ***presbytis***, n. [1] [√*4565*]. older woman, possibly an official of the church in context:– older (1)

G4568 **πρηνής** ***prēnēs***, a. Not used in NIVEBC. headlong, headfirst in prone position; some translate as "swollen, distended"€ [1]:– fell headlong (1 [+*1181*])

G4569 **πρίζω** ***prizō***, v. [1] [√*4573*]. (pass.) to be sawn in two:– sawed in two (1)

G4570 **πρίν** ***prin***, adv. [13] [√*4574*]. before:– before (8), before (4 [+*2445*]), before (1 [+*2445, 323*])

G4571 **Πρίσκα** ***Priska***, n. pr. [6] [→*4572*]. Prisca, Priscilla:– Priscilla (6)

G4572 **Πρίσκιλλα** ***Priskilla***, n. pr. Not used in NIVEBC. [√*4571*]. Priscilla, Prisca

G4573 **πρίω** ***priō***, v. Not used in NIVEBC. [→*1391, 4569*]. (pass.) to be sawn in two

G4574 **πρό** ***pro***, pp. [47] [→*4522, 4523, 4524, 4570, 4575, 4576, 4577, 4578, 4579, 4580, 4581, 4582, 4583, 4584, 4585, 4586, 4587, 4588, 4589, 4590, 4591, 4592, 4593, 4594, 4595, 4596, 4597, 4598, 4599, 4600, 4601, 4602, 4603, 4604, 4605, 4606, 4607, 4608, 4609, 4610, 4611, 4612, 4613, 4614, 4615, 4616, 4617, 4618, 4619, 4620, 4621, 4622, 4623, 4624, 4625, 4626, 4627, 4628, 4629, 4630, 4631, 4632, 4633, 4634, 4635, 4636, 4637, 4638, 4640, 4706, 4710, 4711, 4726, 4727, 4728, 4729, 4730, 4731, 4732, 4733, 4734, 4735, 4740, 4741, 4742, 4743, 4749, 5864; cf. 4745, 4755*]. (of place) before, at; (of time) before, some time ago:– before (23), before (5 [+*3836*]), ahead of (4 [+*4725*]), at (3), above (2), ago (1), ahead of (1), before (1 [+*3836*]), before (1 [+*4725*]), just before (1), just outside (1), on ahead (1 [+*4725*]), some time ago (1 [+*4047, 3836, 2465*]), some time ago (1 [+*4047, 3836, 2465*]), NDT (1)

G4575 **προάγω** ***proagō***, v. [20] [√*4574 + 72*]. to go on ahead, lead the way; to bring out, bring to trial:– went ahead (3), brought (2), go ahead (2), go on ahead (2), going ahead (2), bring out (1), bring to trial (1), entering ahead (1), former

GREEK INDEX

(1), leading the way (1 [+1639]), led the way (1), once made (1), reaching ahead of (1), runs ahead (1)

G4576 προαιρέω proaireō, v. [1] [√4574 + 145]. (mid.) to decide, determine:– decided (1)

G4577 προαιτιάομαι proaitiaomai, v. [1] [√4574 + 162]. to make a charge beforehand:– already made the charge (1)

G4578 προακούω proakouō, v. [1] [√4574 + 201]. to hear about beforehand:– already heard (1)

G4579 προαμαρτάνω proamartanō, v. [2] [√4574 + 279]. to sin earlier, to have sinned beforehand:– sinned earlier (2)

G4580 προαύλιον proaulion, n. [1] [√4574 + 885]. entryway, gateway:– entryway (1)

G4581 προβαίνω probainō, v. [5] [√4574 + 326]. (spacial) to go on, go on farther; (temporal) to be well along (in years), advanced (in age):– going on (1), gone farther (1), old (1 [+1877, 2465]), very old (1 [+1877, 3836, 2465]), well along (1)

G4582 προβάλλω proballō, v. [2] [√4574 + 965]. to push to the front, cause to come to the front; to sprout, put forth:– pushed to the front (1), sprout leaves (1)

G4583 προβατικός probatikos, a. [1] [√4574 + 326]. pertaining to sheep; (pr.n.) the Sheep (Gate):– sheep Gate (1)

G4584 προβάτιον probation, n. Not used in NIVEBC. [√4574 + 326]. lamb

G4585 πρόβατον probaton, n. [39] [√4574 + 326]. sheep:– sheep (38), sheep's (1)

G4586 προβιβάζω probibazō, v. [1] [√4574 + 326]. (pass.) to be prompted, caused to come forward:– prompted (1)

G4587 προβλέπω problepō, v. [1] [√4574 + 1063]. (mid.) to plan, select, provide:– planned (1)

G4588 προγίνομαι proginomai, v. [1] [√4574 + 1181]. to commit beforehand, happen previously:– committed beforehand (1)

G4589 προγινώσκω proginōskō, v. [5] [√4574 + 1182]. to know beforehand, foreknow; (mid.) to choose beforehand:– foreknew (2), chosen before (1), forewarned (1), known (1)

G4590 πρόγνωσις prognōsis, n. [2] [√4574 + 1182]. foreknowledge:– foreknowledge (2)

G4591 πρόγονος progonos, a. [2] [√4574 + 1181]. (pl.) parents, forefathers, ancestors:– ancestors (1), parents and grandparents (1)

G4592 προγράφω prographō, v. [4] [√4574 + 1211]. to write beforehand; to show clearly, advertise, proclaim:– already written (1), clearly portrayed (1), written about (1), written in the past (1)

G4593 πρόδηλος prodēlos, a. [3] [√4574 + 1316]. obvious, clear, evident:– obvious (2), clear (1)

G4594 προδίδωμι prodidōmi, v. [1] [√4574 + 1443]. to give beforehand:– given (1)

G4595 προδότης prodotēs, n. [3] [√4574 + 1443]. traitor, betrayer, treacherous one:– betrayed (1), traitor (1), treacherous (1)

G4596 πρόδρομος prodromos, a. [1] [√4574 + 5556]. going before, forerunner:– forerunner (1)

G4597 προεῖπον proeipon, v. Not used in NIVEBC. [√4574 + 3306]. to foretell, tell beforehand

G4598 προελπίζω proelpizō, v. [1] [√4574 + 1828]. to be the first to hope, hope beforehand:– the first to put hope (1)

G4599 προενάρχομαι proenarchomai, v. [2] [√4574 + 1877 + 806]. to begin beforehand, begin previously:– earlier made a beginning (1), first (1)

G4600 προεπαγγέλλω proepangellō, v. [2] [√4574 + 2093 + 34]. (mid.) to promise beforehand; (pass.) to be promised previously:– promised (1), promised beforehand (1)

G4601 προέρχομαι proerchomai, v. [9] [√4574 + 2262]. to go on ahead; to lead; to visit in advance:– going farther (2), went on ahead (2), go on (1), got ahead of (1), leading (1), visit (1), walked the length (1)

G4602 προετοιμάζω proetoimazō, v. [2] [√4574 + 2289]. to prepare in advance:– prepared in advance (2)

G4603 προευαγγελίζομαι proeuangelizomai, v. [1] [√4574 + 2292 + 34]. to announce the gospel in advance:– announced the gospel in advance (1)

G4604 προέχω proechō, v. [1] [√4574 + 2400]. (mid.) to be better off, have an advantage:– advantage (1)

G4605 προηγέομαι proēgeomai, v. [1] [√4574 + 72]. to put above, go before:– above (1)

G4606 πρόθεσις prothesis, n. [12] [√4574 + 5502]. setting forth: plan, purpose, will; (a.) consecrated (bread):– purpose (5), consecrated (4), opportunity (1 [+3195]), plan (1), true (1)

G4607 προθεσμία prothesmia, n. [1] [√4574 + 5502]. set time, fixed or limited time:– time set (1)

G4608 προθυμία prothymia, n. [5] [√4574 + 2596]. eagerness, willingness, readiness:– eagerness (3), eager (1), willingness (1)

G4609 πρόθυμος prothymos, a. [3] [√4574 + 2596]. willing, eager:– willing (2), eager (1)

G4610 προθύμως prothymōs, adv. [1] [√4574 + 2596]. eagerly, willingly:– eager (1)

G4611 πρόϊμος proimos, a. [1] [√4574]. early; (n.) autumn rains (in October of the modern calendar):– autumn rains (1)

G4612 πρωϊνός proinos, a. Not used in NIVEBC. [√4574]. early, belonging to the morning

G4613 προΐστημι proistēmi, v. [8] [√4574 + 2705]. (act/mid) to manage, direct, lead; (mid.) to devote oneself, busy oneself to:– manage (3), care for (1), devote (1), devote to (1), direct affairs (1), lead (1)

G4614 προκαλέω prokaleō, v. [1] [√4574 + 2813]. (mid.) to provoke, challenge:– provoking (1)

G4615 προκαταγγέλλω prokatangellō, v. [2] [√4574 + 2848 + 34]. to foretell, predict, announce beforehand:– foretold (1), predicted (1)

G4616 προκαταρτίζω prokatartizō, v. [1] [√4574 + 2848 + 785]. to arrange for in advance, get ready beforehand:– in advance finish the arrangements (1)

G4617 προκατέχω prokatechō, v. Not used in NIVEBC. [√4574 + 2848 + 2400]. to gain possession of or occupy previously

G4618 πρόκειμαι prokeimai, v. [5] [√4574 + 3023]. (pass.) to be set before, present:– set before (2), marked out (1), serve as (1), there (1)

G4619 προκηρύσσω prokēryssō, v. [1] [√4574 + 3061]. to preach beforehand:– preached (1)

G4620 προκοπή prokopē, n. [3] [√4574 + 3164]. progress, advancement:– progress (2), advance (1)

G4621 προκόπτω prokoptō, v. [6] [√4574 + 3164]. to go ahead, go forward, advance:– advancing (1), become more and more (1 [+2093, 4498]), get far (1), go (1), grew (1), nearly over (1)

G4622 πρόκριμα prokrima, n. [1] [√4574 + 3212]. partiality, discrimination, prejudice:– partiality (1)

G4623 προκυρόω prokyroō, v. [2] [√4574 + 3263]. to establish previously, ratify beforehand:– previously established (1), to (1)

G4624 προλαμβάνω prolambanō, v. [3] [√4574 + 3284]. to take beforehand; to go on ahead; (pass.) to be caught, detected:– beforehand (1), caught (1), go ahead with (1)

G4625 προλέγω prolegō, v. [15] [√4574 + 3306]. to tell beforehand; to speak in the past:– told ahead of time (2), already gave a warning (1), already quoted (1), already said (1), did before[S] (1), foretold (1), repeat (1), said before (1), said previously (1), spoke long ago (1), spoken in the past (1), telling (1), told before (1), warn (1)

G4626 προμαρτύρομαι promartyromai, v. [1] [√4574 + 3459]. to predict, bear witness to beforehand:– predicted (1)

G4627 προμελετάω promeletaō, v. [1] [√4574 + 3508]. to worry beforehand; some translate "to plan ahead":– worry beforehand (1)

G4628 προμεριμνάω promerimnaō, v. [1] [√4574 + 3533]. to worry or be anxious beforehand:– worry beforehand about (1)

G4629 προνοέω pronoeō, v. [3] [√4574 + 3808]. to provide for, care for; to consider, have regard for:– careful (1), provide for (1), taking pains (1)

G4630 πρόνοια pronoia, n. [2] [√4574 + 3808]. foresight, provision, care:– foresight (1), think about (1 [+4472])

G4631 πρόοιδα prooida, v. Not used in NIVEBC. [√4574 + 3857]. to know beforehand, know previously

G4632 προοράω prooraō, v. [4] [√4574 + 3972]. to see previously; to see ahead, foresee; (mid.) to see in front of:– foresaw (1), previously seen (1), saw (1), seeing what was to come (1)

G4633 προορίζω proorizō, v. [6] [√4574 + 4000]. to predestine, decide beforehand:– predestined (4), decided beforehand (1), destined (1)

G4634 προπάσχω propaschō, v. [1] [√4574 + 4248]. to suffer previously:– previously suffered (1)

G4635 προπάτωρ propatōr, n. [1] [√4574 + 4252]. forefather, ancestor:– forefather (1)

G4636 προπέμπω propempō, v. [9] [√4574 + 4287]. to accompany, escort; to send on one's way, help on one's journey:– send on way (3), accompanied (2), assist on journey (1), help on journey (1), help on way (1), sent on way (1)

G4637 προπετής propetēs, a. [2] [√4574 + 4406]. rash, reckless, thoughtless:– rash (2)

G4638 προπορεύομαι proporeuomai, v. [2] [√4574 + 4513]. to go before:– go before (1), go on (1)

G4639 πρός pros, pp. [695] [→717, 718, 1869, 2347, 2348, 4641, 4642, 4643, 4644, 4645, 4646, 4647, 4648, 4649, 4650, 4651, 4652, 4653, 4654, 4655, 4656, 4657, 4658, 4659, 4660, 4661, 4662, 4663, 4664, 4665, 4666, 4667, 4668, 4669, 4670, 4671, 4672, 4673, 4674, 4675, 4676, 4677, 4678, 4679, 4680, 4681, 4682, 4683, 4684, 4685, 4688, 4689, 4690, 4691, 4692, 4693, 4694, 4695, 4696, 4697, 4698, 4699, 4700, 4701, 4702, 4703, 4704, 4705, 4707, 4708, 4709, 4712, 4713, 4714, 4715, 4716, 4717, 4718, 4725; cf. 4686]. (gen.) to, for; (dat.) on, at, near, by; (acc.) to, toward; with; in order to; against:– to (373), with (45), for (26), at (20), against (15), in (8), toward (8), before (7), among (6), of (5), around (4), back to (4), lead to (3), so that (3), visit (3 [+2262]), as (2), because (2), into (2), joined (2 [+2262]), together (2 [+253]), about (1), answer (1 [+2400]), approaching (1), at edge (1), begging (1 [+3836, 1797]), beside (1), between (1), bring (1), by (1), comparing with (1), concerning (1), end in (1), in order to (1 [+3836]), in order to (1), in relations with (1), in response to (1), jealously (1 [+5784]), join (1 [+2262]), leads to (1), lustfully (1 [+3836, 2121]), nearly (1), on (1), one another (1 [+257, 257]), outside (1), over to (1), related to (1), replied (1), return to (1), so as to (1), talked the matter over (1 [+1368, 253]), to (1 [+3836]), to see (1), to show that (1 [+3836]), to the vicinity of (1 [+2401]), told (1 [+1181]), up to (1), visit (1 [+1181]), visited (1 [+2262]), why (1 [+5515]), NDT (116)

G4640 προσάββατον prosabbaton, n. [1] [√4574 + 4879]. day before the Sabbath (Friday):– the day before the Sabbath (1)

G4641 προσαγορεύω prosagoreuō, v. [1] [√4639 + 72]. to designate:– designated (1)

G4642 προσάγω prosagō, v. [4] [√4639 + 72]. to bring to; to approach, come near:– approaching (1), bring (1), bring to (1), brought before (1)

G4643 προσαγωγή prosagōgē, n. [3] [√4639 + 72]. access; approach:– access (2), approach (1 [+2400])

G4644 προσαιτέω prosaiteō, v. [2] [√4639 + 160]. to beg:– beg (1), begging (1)

G4645 προσαίτης prosaitēs, n. [2] [√4639 + 160]. beggar:– begging (1 [+1639]), NDT (1)

G4646 προσαναβαίνω prosanabainō, v. [1] [√4639 + 324 + 326]. to move up, go up:– move up (1)

G4647 προσαναλαμβάνω prosanalambanō, v. Not used in NIVEBC. [√4639 + 324 + 3284]. to take in besides, welcome

G4648 προσαναλίσκω prosanaliskō, v. Not used in NIVEBC. [√4639 + 324 + 274]. to spend lavishly or in addition

G4649 προσαναλόω prosanaloō, v. Not used in NIVEBC. [√4639 + 324 + 274]. to spend lavishly or in addition

G4650 προσαναπληρόω prosanaplēroō, v. [2] [√4639 + 324 + 4444]. to supply, fill up:– supplied (1), supplying (1)

G4651 προσανατίθημι prosanatithēmi, v. [2] [√4639 + 324 + 5502]. to add; to consult, ask advice:– added (1), consult (1)

G4652 προσανέχω prosanechō, v. Not used in NIVEBC. [√4639 + 324 + 2400]. to rise up toward

G4653 προσαπειλέω prosapeileō, v. [1] [√4639 + 581]. to threaten further:– further threats (1)

G4654 προσαχέω prosacheō, v. Not used in NIVEBC. [√4639 + 2491]. to resound

G4655 προσδαπανάω prosdapanaō, v. [1] [√4639 + 1252]. to spend extra:– extra expense have (1)

G4656 προσδέομαι prosdeomai, v. [1] [√4639 + 1289]. to need:– needed (1)

G4657 προσδέχομαι prosdechomai, v. [14] [√4639 + 1312]. to receive, welcome, accept; to wait for, anticipate:– waiting for (4), wait for (2), accepted (1), looking forward to (1), receive (1), refusing (1 [+4024]), waiting (1), welcome (1), welcomes (1), NDT (1)

G4658 προσδίδωμι prosdidōmi, v. Not used in NIVEBC. [√4639 + 1443]. to give (over)

G4659 προσδοκάω prosdokaō, v. [16] [√4639 + 1506]. to look forward to, expect, wait for:– expect (5), expecting (3), looking forward to (2), expected (1), in suspense (1), look forward to (1), waiting (1), waiting expectantly (1), waiting for (1)

G4660 προσδοκία prosdokia, n. [2] [√4639 + 1506]. anticipation, expectation; apprehension:– apprehensive (1), hoping would happen (1)

G4661 προσεάω proseaō, v. [1] [√4639 + 1572]. to allow to go farther:– allow to hold course (1)

G4662 προσεγγίζω prosengizō, v. Not used in NIVEBC. [√4639 + 1584]. to approach, come near

G4663* προσεδρεύω *prosedreuō, v. Not used in NIVEBC. [√*4639* + *1612*]. to serve, wait upon

G4664* προσεργάζομαι *prosergazomai, v. [1] [√*4639* + *2240*]. to earn more:– earned more (1)

G4665* προσέρχομαι *proserchomai, v. [86] [√*4639* + *2262*]. to come to, approach, draw near; to agree to:– came to (26), came (19), went to (8), come to (4), came up (3), going to (3), came forward (2), came up to (2), went (2), went up (2), agree to (1), approach (1), approached (1), comes to (1), coming (1), draw near (1), draw near to worship (1), go to (1), going (1), stepped forward (1), to (1), visit (1), went over (1), went to see (1), NDT (1)

G4666* προσευχή *proseuchē, n. [36] [√*4639* + *2377*]. prayer; place of prayer:– prayer (16), prayers (12), place of prayer (2), pray (2), praying (2), prayed earnestly (1 [+*4667*]), praying (1 [+*1181*])

G4667* προσεύχομαι *proseuchomai, v. [85] [√*4639* + *2377*]. to pray:– pray (44), prayed (17), praying (14), prayer (4), prays (3), make prayers (2), prayed earnestly (1 [+*4666*])

G4668* προσέχω *prosechō, v. [24] [√*4639* + *2400*]. to watch out, be on guard, beware; to pay attention, devote, apply oneself:– on guard (4), careful (2), pay attention (2), beware (1), consider carefully (1), devote (1), devote to (1), follow (1), followed (1), gave attention (1), guard (1), indulging in (1), keep watch over (1), paid close attention (1), pay attention to (1), respond (1), served at (1), watch (1), watch out (1)

G4669* προσηλόω *prosēloō, v. [1] [√*4639* + *2464*]. to nail to:– nailing to (1)

G4670* προσήλυτος *prosēlytos, n. [4] [√*4639* + *2262*]. Gentile convert (to Judaism), transliterated as "proselyte":– converts to Judaism (2), convert (1), convert to Judaism (1)

G4671* πρόσθεσις *prosthesis, n. Not used in NIVEBC. [√*4639* + *5502*]. presentation, setting forth

G4672* πρόσκαιρος *proskairos, a. [4] [√*4639* + *2789*]. lasting only for a short time, temporary:– short time (2), fleeting (1), temporary (1)

G4673* προσκαλέω *proskaleō, v. [29] [√*4639* + *2813*]. (mid.) to call, summon, send for; gather together:– called to (9), called (5), called in (3), call (2), called together (2), calling to (2), sent for (2), called over to (1), calling (1), gathered together (1), summoning (1)

G4674* προσκαρτερέω *proskartereō, v. [10] [√*4639* + *2846*]. to join, adhere to; to be ready; to give attention, be faithful; to spend much time together:– attendants (1), continued (1), devote (1), devoted to (1 [+*1639*]), faithful (1), followed everywhere (1), give attention (1), give full time (1), joined constantly (1 [+*1639*]), ready (1)

G4675* προσκαρτέρησις *proskarterēsis, n. [1] [√*4639* + *2846*]. perseverance, patience:– keep on (1)

G4676* προσκεφάλαιον *proskephalaion, n. [1] [√*4639* + *3051*]. cushion, pillow:– cushion (1)

G4677* προσκληρόω *prosklēroō, v. [1] [√*4639* + *3102*]. (pass.) to be joined with, associated with:– joined (1)

G4678* πρόσκλησις *prosklēsis, n. Not used in NIVEBC. [√*4639* + *2813*]. summons, invitation

G4679* προσκλίνω *prosklinō, v. [1] [√*4639* + *3111*]. (pass.) to be rallied to, associated with:– rallied (1)

G4680* πρόσκλισις *prosklisis, n. [1] [√*4639* + *3111*]. favoritism, partiality:– favoritism (1)

G4681* προσκολλάω *proskollaō, v. [2] [√*4639* + *3140*]. (pass.) to be united to:– united (1), united to (1)

G4682* πρόσκομμα *proskomma, n. [6] [√*4639* + *3164*]. stumbling block, something that causes one to stumble:– causes to stumble (2), stumbling block (2), stumble (1), stumbling (1)

G4683* προσκοπή *proskopē, n. [1] [√*4639* + *3164*]. stumbling block, occasion for stumbling; fig. of sinning:– stumbling block (1)

G4684* προσκόπτω *proskoptō, v. [8] [√*4639* + *3164*]. to strike, beat; (intr.) to stumble, fall:– stumble (3), beat against (1), cause to fall (1), strike (1), strike against (1), stumbled over (1)

G4685* προσκυλίω *proskyliō, v. [2] [√*4639* + *3244*]. to roll in front of, roll up to:– rolled (1), rolled in front of (1)

G4686* προσκυνέω *proskyneō, v. [60] [→*4687*; *cf.* *4639*]. to worship, pay homage, show reverence; to kneel down (before):– worship (29), worshiped (17), knelt before (3), worshipers (3), fall down (1), fell on knees in front of (1), in reverence (1), kneeling down (1), on knees before (1), paid homage (1), worshiping (1), worships (1)

G4687* προσκυνητής *proskynētēs, n. [1] [√*4686*]. worshiper:– worshipers (1)

G4688* προσλαλέω *proslaleō, v. [2] [√*4639* + *3281*]. to talk with:– talk with (1), talked with (1)

G4689* προσλαμβάνω *proslambanō, v. [12] [√*4639* + *3284*]. to take aside, take along; to partake; to welcome, accept:– accept (2), accepted (2), took aside (2), ate (1), eaten (1), invited to home (1), rounded up (1), welcome (1), welcomed (1)

G4690* προσλέγω *proslegō, v. Not used in NIVEBC. [√*4639* + *3306*]. to answer

G4691* πρόσλημψις *proslēmpsis, n. [1] [√*4639* + *3284*]. acceptance:– acceptance (1)

G4692* πρόσληψις *proslēpsis, n. Not used in NIVEBC. [√*4639* + *3284*]. acceptance

G4693* προσμένω *prosmenō, v. [7] [√*4639* + *3531*]. to be with, continue in, remain, stay:– been with (2), continue (1), continues (1), remain (1), stay (1), stayed on (1)

G4694* προσορμίζω *prosormizō, v. [1] [√*4639* + *1649*]. (pass.) to be anchored, come into harbor:– anchored (1)

G4695* προσοφείλω *prosopheilō, v. [1] [√*4639* + *4053*]. to owe (in addition):– owe (1)

G4696* προσοχθίζω *prosochthizō, v. [2] [√*4639*]. to be angry, provoked:– angry (2)

G4697* προσπαίω *prospaiō, v. Not used in NIVEBC. [√*4639* + *4091*]. to strike against, beat against

G4698* πρόσπεινος *prospeinos, a. [1] [√*4639* + *4277*]. hungry:– hungry (1)

G4699* προσπήγνυμι *prospēgnymi, v. [1] [√*4639* + *4381*]. to nail to (the cross):– nailing to cross (1)

G4700* προσπίπτω *prospiptō, v. [8] [√*4639* + *4406*]. to fall down before; to beat against, strike against:– fell at feet (3), beat against (1), fell (1), fell at (1), fell before (1), fell down before (1)

G4701* προσποιέω *prospoieō, v. [1] [√*4639* + *4472*]. to act as if, pretend:– continued on as if (1)

G4702* προσπορεύομαι *prosporeuomai, v. [1] [√*4639* + *4513*]. to come to, approach:– came to (1)

G4703* προσρήγνυμι *prosrēgnymi, v. [2] [√*4639* + *4838*]. to strike upon:– struck (2)

G4704* προσρήσσω *prosrēssō, v. Not used in NIVEBC. [√*4639* + *4838*]. to strike upon

G4705* προστάσσω *prostassō, v. [7] [√*4639* + *5435*]. (act./mid.) to command, order; (pass.) to be set, prescribed:– commanded (5), appointed (1), ordered (1)

G4706* προστάτις *prostatis, n. [1] [√*4574* + *2705*]. helper:– benefactor (1)

G4707* προστίθημι *prostithēmi, v. [18] [√*4639* + *5502*]. to add to, increase ; (pass.) to be brought to, given:– added (3), add (2), given as well (2), sent (2 [+*4287*]), added to (1), added to number (1), brought to (1), buried (1), even more (1), increase (1), proceeded (1), spoken to (1), went on (1)

G4708* προστρέχω *prostrechō, v. [3] [√*4639* + *5556*]. to run up to:– ran up to (2), ran (1)

G4709* προσφάγιον *prosphagion, n. [1] [√*4639* + *5741*]. (little) fish:– fish (1)

G4710* πρόσφατος *prosphatos, a. [1] [√*4574* + *5777* or 5840]. new:– new (1)

G4711* προσφάτως *prosphatōs, adv. [1] [√*4574* + *5777* or 5840]. recently:– recently (1)

G4712* προσφέρω *prospherō, v. [47] [√*4639* + *5770*]. to bring to, present, offer; to treat as, deal with:– brought (12), offered (8), offer (7), offer sacrifices (3), bringing to (2), offering (2), bring (1), brought to (1), get to (1), lifted (1), made (1), offered as a sacrifice (1), offered up (1), offers (1), presented with (1), repeated[S] (1), sacrifice (1), sacrificed (1), treating (1)

G4713* προσφιλής *prosphilēs, a. [1] [√*4639* + *5813*]. lovely, pleasing:– lovely (1)

G4714* προσφορά *prosphora, n. [9] [√*4639* + *5770*]. offering, presentation:– offering (4), sacrifice (3), offerings (2)

G4715* προσφωνέω *prosphōneō, v. [7] [√*4639* + *5889*]. to call out; speak to, address:– calling out (2), appealed to (1), called forward (1), called to (1), said to (1), speak to (1)

G4716* προσχαίρω *proschairō, v. Not used in NIVEBC. [√*4639* + *5897*]. to be glad

G4717* πρόσχυσις *proschysis, n. [1] [√*1772*; *cf.* *4639*]. sprinkling:– application (1)

G4718* προσψαύω *prospsauō, v. [1] [√*4639* + *6041*]. to touch:– lift to help (1 [+*3836*, *5845*])

G4719* προσωπολημπτέω *prosōpolēmpteō, v. [1] [√*4725* + *3284*]. to show favoritism, partiality:– show favoritism (1)

G4720* προσωπολήμπτης *prosōpolēmptēs, n. [1] [√*4725* + *3284*]. one who shows favoritism, partiality:– show favoritism (1 [+*1639*])

G4721* προσωπολημψία *prosōpolēmpsia, n. [4] [√*4725* + *3284*]. favoritism, partiality:– favoritism (3), show favoritism (1 [+*1639*])

G4722* προσωποληπτέω *prosōpolēpteō, v. Not used in NIVEBC. [√*4725* + *3284*]. to show favoritism, partiality

G4723* προσωπολήπτης *prosōpolēptēs, n. Not used in NIVEBC. [√*4725* + *3284*]. one who shows favoritism, partiality

G4724* προσωποληψία *prosōpolēpsia, n. Not used in NIVEBC. [√*4725* + *3284*]. favoritism, partiality

G4725* πρόσωπον *prosōpon, n. [76] [→*719*, *2349*, *4719*, *4720*, *4721*, *4722*, *4723*, *4724*; *cf.* *4639* + *3972*]. face, a part of the body; by extension: in someone's presence, sight; (with various pp.) before, in front of, on the surface of:– face (21), faces (6), ahead of (4 [+*4574*]), presence (4), appearance (2), sight (2), with face to the ground (2 [+*2093*]), appearances (1), beauty (1 [+*2346*, *3836*]), before (1 [+*4574*]), before (1 [+*608*]), before (1 [+*2848*]), blindfolded (1 [+*4328*, *3836*]), face (1 [+*3836*, *1161*]), faced (1 [+*2848*, *2400*]), facedown to the ground (1 [+*2093*]), fall down (1 [+*4406*, *2093*]), flatter (1 [+*2513*]), from (1 [+*608*]), he (1 [+*3836*, *899*]), its[S] (1 [+*3836*, *899*]), left (1 [+*4513*, *608*]), many (1 [+*4498*]), me (1 [+*3836*, *1609*]), met (1 [+*3972*, *3836*]), on ahead (1 [+*4574*]), pay attention to who they are (1 [+*1063*, *1650*, *476*]), person (1), personally (1), reach (1), resolutely (1 [+*3836*, *5114*]), see (1), show favoritism (1 [+*476*, *3284*]), show partiality (1 [+*3284*]), threw himself (1 [+*4406*, *2093*]), throne (1), what is seen (1), when face to face (1 [+*2848*]), who they are (1 [+*476*]), whole (1 [+*4246*]), you (1 [+*3836*, *5148*]), you (1 [+*5148*, *3836*])

G4726* προτάσσω *protassō, v. Not used in NIVEBC. [√*4574* + *5435*]. to determine beforehand, allot beforehand

G4727* προτείνω *proteinō, v. [1] [√*1753*; *cf.* *4574*]. to stretch out:– stretched out (1)

G4728* πρότερος *proteros, a. [11] [√*4574*]. before; (adv.) before, formerly, an earlier time:– earlier (2), first (2), before (1 [+*3836*]), first (1 [+*3836*]), former (1), formerly (1 [+*3836*]), formerly (1), once (1 [+*3836*]), when (1)

G4729* προτίθημι *protithēmi, v. [3] [√*4574* + *5502*]. (mid.) to plan, purpose; to present, bring forth:– planned (1), presented (1), purposed (1)

G4730* προτρέπω *protrepō, v. [1] [√*4574* + *5572*]. to encourage, urge on:– encouraged (1)

G4731* προτρέχω *protrechō, v. [2] [√*4574* + *5556*]. to run ahead:– outran (1 [+*5441*]), ran ahead (1 [+*1650*, *3836*, *1869*])

G4732* προϋπάρχω *prouparchō, v. [2] [√*4574* + *5679* + *806*]. to exist formerly:– before (1), for some time (1)

G4733* πρόφασις *prophasis, n. [6] [√*4574* + *5743*]. excuse; pretense, show, cover:– show (2), excuse (1), false motives (1), mask to cover up (1), pretending (1)

G4734* προφέρω *propherō, v. [2] [√*4574* + *5770*]. to bring out:– brings out (2)

G4735* προφητεία *prophēteia, n. [19] [→*4736*, *4737*, *4738*, *4739*, *6021*; *cf.* *4574* + *5774*]. prophecy, an inspired message, sometimes encouraging obedience to God, sometimes proclaiming the future as a warning to preparedness and continued obedience:– prophecy (13), prophecies (3), prophesying (2), gift of prophecy (1)

G4736* προφητεύω *prophēteuō, v. [28] [√*4735*]. to prophesy, to speak an inspired message, sometimes encouraging obedience to God, sometimes proclaiming the future as a warning to preparedness and continued obedience:– prophesy (12), prophesied (8), prophesies (5), prophecy (1), prophesying (1), spoke (1)

G4737* προφήτης *prophētēs, n. [144] [√*4735*]. prophet, one who speaks inspired utterances; the writings of the OT prophets; see also *4735*:– prophets (80), prophet (60), prophet's (2), him[S] (1 [+*3836*, *1697*]), prophet (1 [+*467*])

G4738* προφητικός *prophētikos, a. [2] [√*4735*]. prophetic, prophesy; see also *4735*:– prophetic (2)

G4739* προφῆτις *prophētis, n. [2] [√*4735*]. prophetess, a woman who speaks inspired utterances; see also *4735*:– prophet (2)

G4740* προφθάνω *prophthanō, v. [1] [√*4574* + *5777*]. to anticipate, come before:– first (1)

G4741* προχειρίζω *procheirizō, v. [3] [√*4574* + *5931*]. (mid.) to choose, appoint:– appoint (1), appointed (1), chosen (1)

G4742* προχειροτονέω *procheirotoneō, v. [1] [√*1753*; *cf.* *4574* + *5931*]. to choose beforehand, appoint beforehand:– already chosen (1)

G4743* Πρόχορος *Prochoros, n. pr. [1] [√*4574* + *5962*]. Procorus:– Procorus (1)

G4744* πρύμνα *prymna, n. [3] stern (of a vessel):– stern (3)

G4745* πρωΐ *prōi, adv. [12] [→*4746*, *4747*, *4748*; *cf.*

4574]. early in the morning:– early (3), early in the morning (2 [+*275*]), in the morning (2), at dawn (1), early in the morning (1), early morning (1), morning (1), very early in the morning (1 [+*2317*])

G4746* πρωΐα *prōia, n. [2] [√*4745*]. early morning:– early in the morning (2)

G4747* πρώϊμος *prōimos, a. Not used in NIVEBC. [√*4745*]. early; (n.) autumn rains

G4748* πρωϊνός *prōinos, a. [2] [√*4745*]. early, pertaining to the morning:– morning (2)

G4749* πρῷρα *prōra, n. [2] [√*4574*]. bow (of a vessel):– bow (2)

G4750* πρωτεύω *prōteuō, v. [1] [√*4755*]. to be supreme, first, have first place:– supremacy (1)

G4751* πρωτοκαθεδρία *prōtokathedria, n. [4] [√*4755* + *2757*]. most important seat, seat of honor:– most important seats (4)

G4752* πρωτοκλισία *prōtoklisia, n. [5] [√*4755* + *3111*]. place of honor:– place of honor (2), places of honor (2), places of honor at the table (1)

G4753* πρωτόμαρτυς *prōtomartys, n. Not used in NIVEBC. [√*4755* + *3459*]. first martyr

G4754* πρῶτον *prōton, adv. [60] [√*4755*]. first; earlier; above all:– first (45), first of all (4), above all (2 [+*4047*]), first (2 [+*4755*]), after (1), at first (1 [+*3836*]), begins (1), earlier (1 [+*3836*]), in the early days (1 [+*3836*]), in the first place (1), until (1 [+*1569, 3590*])

G4755* πρῶτος *prōtos, a. [97] [→*1310, 4750, 4751, 4752, 4753, 4754, 4756, 4757, 4758, 4759, 5812; cf. 4574*]. first (chronologically or in order of importance):– first (75), leaders (3), leading (3), before (2), first (2 [+*4754*]), most important (2), worst (2), as of first importance (1 [+*1877*]), beginning (1), best (1), chief (1), former (1), old order of things (1), outer (1), prominent (1)

G4756* πρωτοστάτης *prōtostatēs, n. [1] [√*4755* + *2705*]. ringleader, leader:– ringleader (1)

G4757* πρωτοτόκια *prōtotokia, n. [1] [√*4755* + *5503*]. inheritance rights (of the firstborn):– inheritance rights as the oldest son (1)

G4758* πρωτότοκος *prōtotokos, a. [8] [√*4755* + *5503*]. firstborn (human or animal). In biblical culture, the firstborn had higher status and received a greater share of the inheritance. Jesus Christ, as the firstborn of God, is of supreme status and inherits all things:– firstborn (8)

G4759* πρώτως *prōtōs, adv. [1] [√*4755*]. for the first time:– first (1)

G4760* πταίω *ptaiō, v. [5] [→*720*]. to stumble, fall, trip:– stumble (3), at fault (1), stumbles (1)

G4761* πτέρνα *pterna, n. [1] heel:– turned against (1 [+*2048, 3836, 899*])

G4762* πτερύγιον *pterygion, n. [2] [√*4375*]. highest point:– highest point (2)

G4763* πτέρυξ *pteryx, n. [5] [√*4375*]. wing:– wings (5)

G4764* πτηνός *ptēnos, a. [1] [√*4375*]. what is winged or feathered; (n.) bird:– birds (1)

G4765* πτοέω *ptoeō, v. [2] [→*4766*]. (pass.) to be startled, frightened:– frightened (1), startled (1)

G4766* πτόησις *ptoēsis, n. [1] [√*4765*]. something alarming:– fear (1)

G4767* Πτολεμαΐς *Ptolemais, n. pr. [1] Ptolemais:– Ptolemais (1)

G4768* πτύον *ptyon, n. [2] [√*4772*]. winnowing fork or shovel:– winnowing fork (2)

G4769* πτύρω *ptyrō, v. [1] (pass.) to be frightened:– frightened (1)

G4770* πτύσμα *ptysma, n. [1] [√*4772*]. saliva, spit:– saliva (1)

G4771* πτύσσω *ptyssō, v. [1] [→*408*]. to roll up:– rolled up (1)

G4772* πτύω *ptyō, v. [3] [→*1746, 1870, 4768, 4770*]. to spit (saliva):– spit (3)

G4773* πτῶμα *ptōma, n. [7] [√*4406*]. dead body, carcass, corpse:– body (3), bodies (2), carcass (1), NDT (1)

G4774* πτῶσις *ptōsis, n. [2] [√*4406*]. falling, crash:– crash (1), falling (1)

G4775* πτωχεία *ptōcheia, n. [3] [√*4777*]. poverty:– poverty (3)

G4776* πτωχεύω *ptōcheuō, v. [1] [√*4777*]. to be or become poor:– poor (1)

G4777* πτωχός *ptōchos, a. [34] [→*4775, 4776*]. poor; (n.) poor, beggar, a person of few resources, culturally considered oppressed, despised, and miserable. "The poor in spirit" are not lacking in spirit, but have the positive moral quality of humility, realizing they have nothing to offer God but are in need of his free gifts:– poor (31), beggar (2), miserable (1)

G4778* πυγμή *pygmē, n. [1] [→*4781, 4782*]. fist; with a fist = NIV "ceremonial":– ceremonial[s] (1)

G4779* Πύθιος *Pythios, n. pr. Not used in NIVEBC. Pythian

G4780* πύθων *pythōn, n. [1] spirit of divination:– which predicted the future (1)

G4781* πυκνός *pyknos, a. [3] [√*4778*]. (a.) often, frequent, numerous; (adv.) often, as a comparative: quite often, as often as possible:– frequent (1), frequently (1), often (1)

G4782* πυκτεύω *pykteuō, v. [1] [√*4778*]. to fight with the fist, box:– fight (1)

G4783* πύλη *pylē, n. [10] [→*4784*]. (city) gate:– gate (6), city gate (2), city gates (1), gates (1)

G4784* πυλών *pylōn, n. [18] [√*4783*]. gate, door, entryway:– gates (7), gate (3), city gates (1), door (1), gateway (1), it[s] (1 [+*3836*]), outer (1), NDT (3)

G4785* πυνθάνομαι *pynthanomai, v. [12] to ask, inquire, question:– asked (5), ask (2), asking (1), information (1), inquired (1), learning (1), question (1)

G4786* πῦρ *pyr, n. [71] [→*351, 1747, 4787, 4789, 4790, 4791, 4792, 4793, 4794, 4795, 4796*]. fire, flames:– fire (57), burning (5), blazing (2), fiery (2), flames (2), all ablaze (1 [+*2794*]), lamps (1 [+*3286*]), spark (1)

G4787* πυρά *pyra, n. [2] [√*4786*]. fire:– fire (2)

G4788* πύργος *pyrgos, n. [4] tower, watchtower:– tower (2), watchtower (2)

G4789* πυρέσσω *pyressō, v. [2] [√*4786*]. to burn with a fever:– fever (1), with a fever (1)

G4790* πυρετός *pyretos, n. [6] [√*4786*]. fever:– fever (6)

G4791* πύρινος *pyrinos, a. [1] [√*4786*]. fiery red, the color of fire:– fiery red (1)

G4792* πυρόω *pyroō, v. [6] [√*4786*]. to burn; to burn inwardly:– burn (1), burn with passion (1), fire (1), flaming (1), glowing (1), refined (1)

G4793* πυρράζω *pyrrazō, v. [2] [√*4786*]. to be red, the color of fire:– red (2)

G4794* πυρρός *pyrros, a. [2] [√*4786*]. fiery red, the color of fire:– fiery red (1), red (1)

G4795* Πύρρος *Pyrros, n. pr. [1] [√*4786*]. Pyrrhus, "*fiery red*":– Pyrrhus (1)

G4796* πύρωσις *pyrōsis, n. [3] [√*4786*]. burning, painful:– burning (2), fiery (1)

G4797* πωλέω *pōleō, v. [22] [→*4527*]. to sell:– sold (8), sell (7), selling (5), buying (2)

G4798* πῶλος *pōlos, n. [12] colt:– colt (12)

G4799* πώποτε *pōpote, adv. [6] ever, at any time:– ever (3), never (1), never (1 [+*4046*]), never (1 [+*4024, 3590*])

G4800* πωρόω *pōroō, v. [5] [→*4801*]. to harden, deaden, make dull:– hardened (3), hardened (1 [+*2400*]), made dull (1)

G4801* πώρωσις *pōrōsis, n. [3] [√*4800*]. hardening, stubbornness:– hardening (2), stubborn (1)

G4802* πῶς *pōs, pt. inter. [103] how? in what way?; how!:– how (79), how is it (5), what (4), why (3), even (1), how (1 [+*323*]), how then (1), some way (1), under what circumstances (1 [+*4036*]), way (1), with care (1 [+*1063*]), NDT (5)

G4803* πώς *pōs, pt. [14] somehow, in some way:– somehow (4), so that not (2 [+*3590*]), that (2 [+*3590*]), for (1 [+*3590*]), hoping (1 [+*1623, 1538*]), in some way (1), that (1), that (1 [+*1623*]), wanted to be sure not (1 [+*3590*])

G4804* ρ *r, letter. letter of the Greek alphabet

G4805* Ῥαάβ *Rhaab, n. pr. [2] Rahab, "*spacious, broad*":– Rahab (2)

G4806* ῥαββί *rhabbi, l.[n.] [15] [→*4807, 4808, 4809*]. Rabbi, a title of a teacher:– rabbi (15)

G4807* ῥαββονί *rhabboni, l.[n.] Not used in NIVEBC. [√*4806*]. Rabboni

G4808* ῥαββουνί *rhabbouni, l.[n.] [2] [√*4806*]. Rabboni:– rabbi (1), rabboni (1)

G4809* ῥαββωνί *rhabbōni, l.[n.] Not used in NIVEBC. [√*4806*]. Rabboni

G4810* ῥαβδίζω *rhabdizō, v. [2] [√*4811*]. to beat with a rod:– beaten with rods (2)

G4811* ῥάβδος *rhabdos, n. [12] [→*4810, 4812, 4824, 4825*]. rod, staff, stick; measuring rod; scepter:– scepter (5), staff (5), measuring rod (1), rod of discipline (1)

G4812* ῥαβδοῦχος *rhabdouchos, n. [2] [√*4811* + *2400*]. officer, the Roman *lictor,* a policeman:– officers (2)

G4813* ῥαβιθά *rhabitha, l.[n.] Not used in NIVEBC. [√*cf. 5420*]. (Aramaic) little girl

G4814* Ῥαγαύ *Rhagau, n. pr. [1] Reu, "*friend [of God]*":– Reu (1)

G4815* ῥᾳδιούργημα *rhadiourgēma, n. [1] [√*4816*]. crime, legal infraction:– crime (1)

G4816* ῥᾳδιουργία *rhadiourgia, n. [1] [→*4815; cf. 2240*]. trickery:– trickery (1)

G4817* ῥαίνω *rhainō, v. Not used in NIVEBC. [→*4349, 4350, 4822, 4823*]. (pass.) to be sprinkled

G4818* Ῥαιφάν *Rhaiphan, n. pr. [1] [→*4833, 4834, 4854*]. Rephan:– Rephan (1)

G4819* ῥακά *rhaka, l.[a.] [1] [→*4828*]. Raca (a term of abuse, derived from Aramaic *rîqa',* meaning "empty[-headed] one"), "*empty-headed [?]*":– raca (1)

G4820* ῥάκος *rhakos, n. [2] piece of cloth:– cloth (2)

G4821* Ῥαμά *Rhama, n. pr. [1] Ramah, "*elevated spot*":– Ramah (1)

G4822* ῥαντίζω *rhantizō, v. [4] [√*4817*]. to sprinkle:– sprinkled (3), sprinkled to cleanse (1)

G4823* ῥαντισμός *rhantismos, n. [2] [√*4817*]. sprinkling:– sprinkled (2)

G4824* ῥαπίζω *rhapizō, v. [2] [√*4811*]. to strike, slap:– slapped (1), slaps (1)

G4825* ῥάπισμα *rhapisma, n. [3] [√*4811*]. slap, strike:– slapped in the face (2 [+*1443*]), beat (1)

G4826* ῥάσσω *rhassō, v. Not used in NIVEBC. [√*4838*]. to strike, dash, throw down

G4827* ῥαφίς *rhaphis, n. [2] [→*731, 2165*]. needle:– needle (2)

G4828* ῥαχά *rhacha, l.[a.] Not used in NIVEBC. [√*4819*]. Raca, "*empty-headed [?]*"

G4829* Ῥαχάβ *Rhachab, n. pr. [1] Rahab, "*spacious, broad*":– Rahab (1)

G4830* Ῥαχήλ *Rachēl, n. pr. [1] Rachel, "*ewe*":– Rachel (1)

G4831* Ῥεβέκκα *Rhebekka, n. pr. [1] Rebekah, "[poss.] *choice calf*":– Rebekah's (1)

G4832* ῥέδη *rhedē, n. [1] carriage:– carriages (1)

G4833* Ῥεμφάν *Rhemphan, n. pr. Not used in NIVEBC. [√*4818*]. Remphan

G4834* Ῥεφάν *Rhephan, n. pr. Not used in NIVEBC. [√*4818*]. Rephan

G4835* ῥέω *rheō, v. [1] [→*137, 4184, 4868, 5929*]. to flow:– flow (1)

G4836* Ῥήγιον *Rhēgion, n. pr. [1] Rhegium:– Rhegium (1)

G4837* ῥῆγμα *rhēgma, n. [1] [√*4838*]. destruction, ruin:– destruction (1)

G4838* ῥήγνυμι *rhēgnymi, v. [7] [→*1392, 1393, 1396, 4351, 4703, 4704, 4826, 4837, 4841, 5357*]. to burst, break forth; to tear to pieces; to throw violently:– burst (3), shout for joy (1), tear to pieces (1), threw to the ground (1), throws to the ground (1)

G4839* ῥῆμα *rhēma, n. [68] [→*394, 395, 777, 4244, 4245, 4842, 4843*]. word, saying; matter; thing:– word (17), words (16), things (6), say (4), what[s] (4 [+*3836*]), matter (2), meant (2), message (2), all about (1 [+*4246, 3836*]), charge (1), command (1), it[s] (1 [+*3836*]), made statement (1 [+*3306*]), meaning (1), promised (1), saying (1), sayings (1), says (1), speaking (1 [+*3281*]), thing (1), this[s] (1 [+*3836, 4047*]), what[s] (1), what said (1)

G4840* Ῥησά *Rhēsa, n. pr. [1] Rhesa:– Rhesa (1)

G4841* ῥήσσω *rhēssō, v. Not used in NIVEBC. [√*4838*]. to throw violently

G4842* ῥήτωρ *rhētōr, n. [1] [√*4839*]. lawyer:– lawyer (1)

G4843* ῥητῶς *rhētōs, adv. [1] [√*4839*]. clearly, exactly:– clearly (1)

G4844* ῥίζα *rhiza, n. [17] [→*1748, 4845*]. root, rootstock:– root (16), roots (1)

G4845* ῥιζόω *rhizoō, v. [2] [√*4844*]. (pass.) to be rooted, with the associative meaning that a rooted object is strong and healthy:– rooted (2)

G4846* ῥιπή *rhipē, n. [1] [√*4849*]. twinkling, rapid movement (of the eye); some translate as "the blink (of an eye)":– twinkling (1)

G4847* ῥιπίζω *rhipizō, v. [1] [√*4849*]. (pass.) to be tossed about:– tossed (1)

G4848* ῥιπτέω *rhipteō, v. [1] [√*4849*]. to throw off:– throwing off (1)

G4849 ῥίπτω rhiptō, v. [7] [→*681, 2166, 4846, 4847, 4848*]. to throw, drop; to lay; (pass.) to be helpless, laid out:– dropped (1), helpless (1), laid (1), threw (1), threw down (1), threw overboard (1), thrown (1)

G4850 Ῥοβοάμ Rhoboam, n. pr. [2] Rehoboam, "*[my] people will enlarge, expand*":– Rehoboam (2)

G4851 Ῥόδη Rhodē, n. pr. [1] Rhoda, "*rose*":– Rhoda (1)

G4852 Ῥόδος Rhodos, n. pr. [1] Rhodes, "*rose*":– Rhodes (1)

G4853 ῥοιζηδόν rhoizēdon, adv. [1] with a roar; a derivative of a Greek noun meaning, "the noise made by a passing arrow," not found in the NT:– roar (1)

G4854 Ῥομφά Rhompha, n. pr. Not used in NIVEBC. [√*4818*]. Rompha

G4855 ῥομφαία rhomphaia, n. [7] (long) sword:– sword (7)

G4856 ῥοπή rhopē, n. Not used in NIVEBC. downward movement, twinkling

G4857 Ῥουβήν Rhoubēn, n. pr. [1] Reuben, "*See, a son! [Ge. 29:32]; substitute a son*":– Reuben (1)

G4858 Ῥούθ Rhouth, n. pr. [1] Ruth, "*friendship*, poss. *comrade, companion; refreshed*":– Ruth (1)

G4859 Ῥοῦφος Rhouphos, n. pr. [2] Rufus, "*red-haired*":– Rufus (2)

G4860 ῥύμη rhymē, n. [4] street, alley, lane:– street (2), alleys (1), streets (1)

G4861 ῥύομαι rhyomai, v. [17] to rescue, deliver:– rescue (5), deliver (3), delivered (3), rescued (3), deliverer (1), kept safe (1), rescues (1)

G4862 ῥυπαίνω rhypainō, v. [1] [√*4866*]. to be vile:– vile (1)

G4863 ῥυπαρεύω rhypareuō, v. Not used in NIVEBC. [√*4866*]. (pass.) to be fouled, defiled

G4864 ῥυπαρία rhyparia, n. [1] [√*4866*]. (moral) filth:– moral filth (1)

G4865 ῥυπαρός rhyparos, a. [2] [√*4866*]. shabby, dirty; moral vileness, filthiness:– filthy (1), vile (1)

G4866 ῥύπος rhypos, n. [1] [→*4862, 4863, 4864, 4865, 4867*]. dirt:– dirt (1)

G4867 ῥυπόω rhypoō, v. Not used in NIVEBC. [√*4866*]. to defile, pollute

G4868 ῥύσις rhysis, n. [3] [√*4835*]. flow (of blood), bleeding:– bleeding (2 [+*135*]), subject to bleeding (1 [+*1877, 135*])

G4869 ῥυτίς rhytis, n. [1] wrinkle:– wrinkle (1)

G4870 Ῥωμαϊκός Rhōmaikos, a. pr. Not used in NIVEBC. [√*4873*]. Roman, Latin

G4871 Ῥωμαῖος Rhōmaios, a. pr. g. [12] [√*4873*]. Roman, from Rome; (n.) Roman citizen:– roman citizen (5 [+*476*]), Romans (3), roman citizens (2 [+*476*]), from Rome (1), roman (1)

G4872 Ῥωμαϊστί Rhōmaisti, adv. pr. [1] [√*4873*]. in Latin (language):– latin (1)

G4873 Ῥώμη Rhōmē, n. pr. [8] [→*4870, 4871, 4872*]. Rome:– Rome (8)

G4874 ῥώννυμι rhōnnymi, v. [1] [→*778, 779*]. to be strong; (pass.) farewell, goodbye, as the closing of a letter:– farewell (1)

G4875 σ s, letter. Not used in NIVEBC. letter of the Greek alphabet

G4876 σαβαχθάνι sabachthani, l.[v.+p.] [2] [√*cf. 2407*]. sabachthani (Aramaic: "you have forsaken me"):– sabachthani (2)

G4877 Σαβαώθ Sabaōth, l.[pr. n.] [2] Almighty ["of Hosts"], a Greek transliteration of the Hebrew word 7372, "armies, hosts." This title has the associative meanings of power and potent authority, and pictures the Lord as a great, powerful, supreme general:– Almighty (2)

G4878 σαββατισμός sabbatismos, n. [1] [√*4879*]. Sabbath-rest, Sabbath observance; used with *3847* "a sabbath's day journey" reckoned at 800 to 900 yards (2,000 cubits):– Sabbath-rest (1)

G4879 σάββατον sabbaton, n. [68] [→*4640, 4878*]. Sabbath:– Sabbath (53), week (9), Sabbath (2 [+*2465*]), Sabbath day (1), Sabbath days (1), Sabbath duty (1), a Sabbath day's walk from (1 [+*1584, 2400, 3847*])

G4880 σαγήνη sagēnē, n. [1] (large) dragnet, a net with weights on the bottom and dragged through the water:– net (1)

G4881 Σαδδουκαῖος Saddoukaios, n. pr. [14] [√*cf. 4882*]. Sadducee, "[poss.] *followers of Zadok; righteous*":– Sadducees (14)

G4882 Σαδώκ Sadōk, n. pr. [2] [√*cf. 4881*]. Zadok, "*righteous one*":– Zadok (2)

G4883 σαίνω sainō, v. [1] (pass.) to be unsettled, disturbed:– unsettled (1)

G4884 σάκκος sakkos, n. [4] sackcloth, a heavy coarse cloth used for making sacks, but worn by the penitent or mournful as a sign of contrition and sorrow:– sackcloth (4)

G4885 Σαλά Sala, n. pr. [1] Sala, "*missile [a weapon], sprout*":– Shelah (1)

G4886 Σαλαθιήλ Salathiēl, n. pr. [3] Shealtiel, "*I have asked [him] of God [El]*; poss. *God [El] is a shield*":– Shealtiel (3)

G4887 Σαλαμίς Salamis, n. pr. [1] Salamis, "*peace*":– Salamis (1)

G4888 σαλεύω saleuō, v. [15] [→*810, 4893; cf. 256*]. to shake up; agitate; (pass.) to be shaken, swayed, unsettled:– shaken (8), swayed (2), agitating (1), shake (1), shaken together (1), shook (1), unsettled (1)

G4889 Σαλήμ Salēm, n. pr. [2] Salem, "*peace*":– Salem (2)

G4890 Σαλίμ Salim, n. pr. [1] Salim:– Salim (1)

G4891 Σαλμών Salmōn, n. pr. [3] Salmon, "*little spark*":– Salmon (3)

G4892 Σαλμώνη Salmōnē, n. pr. [1] Salmone:– Salmone (1)

G4893 σάλος salos, n. [1] [√*4888*]. tossing motion, rolling motion (of the surging waves):– tossing (1)

G4894 σάλπιγξ salpinx, n. [11] [√*4895*]. trumpet:– trumpet (7), trumpet call (2), trumpets (2)

G4895 σαλπίζω salpizō, v. [12] [→*4894, 4896*]. to sound a trumpet, announce with a trumpet:– sounded trumpet (7), announce with trumpets (1), sound (1), sound trumpet (1), sounded (1), trumpet sound (1)

G4896 σαλπιστής salpistēs, n. [1] [√*4895*]. trumpeter:– trumpeters (1)

G4897 Σαλώμη Salōmē, n. pr. [2] Salome, "*peaceful, prosperous one*":– Salome (2)

G4898 Σαλωμών Salōmōn, n. pr. Not used in NIVEBC. [√*5048*]. Solomon

G4899 Σαμάρεια Samareia, n. pr. [11] [→*4900, 4901, 4902*]. Samaria, "*belonging to the clan of Shemer [1Ki 16:24]*":– Samaria (10), samaritan (1 [+*1666, 3836*])

G4900 Σαμαρία Samaria, n. pr. Not used in NIVEBC. [√*4899*]. Samaria, "*belonging to the clan of Shemer [1Ki 16:24]*"

G4901 Σαμαρίτης Samaritēs, n. pr. g. [9] [√*4899*]. Samaritan:– samaritan (5), Samaritans (4)

G4902 Σαμαρῖτις Samaritis, n. pr. g. & a. [2] [√*4899*]. Samaritan:– samaritan (2)

G4903 Σαμοθράκη Samothrakē, n. pr. [1] Samothrace, "*Thracian Samos*":– Samothrace (1)

G4904 Σάμος Samos, n. pr. [1] Samos, "*heights, lofty place*":– Samos (1)

G4905 Σαμουήλ Samouēl, n. pr. [3] Samuel, "*his name is God [El]; heard of God [El]; the unnamed god is El*":– Samuel (3)

G4906 Σαμφουρειν Samphourein, n. pr. Not used in NIVEBC. Sepphoris

G4907 Σαμψών Sampsōn, n. pr. [1] Samson, "*little one of Shemesh [pagan sun god]* or *sunny*":– Samson (1)

G4908 σανδάλιον sandalion, n. [2] sandal:– sandals (2)

G4909 σανίς sanis, n. [1] plank, board:– planks (1)

G4910 Σαούλ Saoul, n. pr. [9] Saul, "*asked of God* or poss. *dedicated to God*":– Saul (9)

G4911 σαπρός sapros, a. [8] [√*4960*]. bad, rotten, decayed; unwholesome:– bad (7), unwholesome (1)

G4912 Σάπφιρα Sapphira, n. pr. [1] [√*4913*]. Sapphira, "*beautiful*":– Sapphira (1)

G4913 σάπφιρος sapphiros, n. [1] [→*4912*]. sapphire stone:– sapphire (1)

G4914 σαργάνη sarganē, n. [1] (large flexible) basket, possibly made of ropes:– basket (1)

G4915 Σάρδεις Sardeis, n. pr. [3] Sardis:– Sardis (3)

G4916 σάρδινος sardinos, n. Not used in NIVEBC. [√*4917*]. carnelian, sard

G4917 σάρδιον sardion, n. [2] [→*4916, 4918*]. carnelian (a reddish precious stone):– ruby (2)

G4918 σαρδόνυξ sardonyx, n. [1] [√*4917*]. sardonyx (a variety of agate):– onyx (1)

G4919 Σάρεπτα Sarepta, n. pr. [1] Zarephath, "[poss.] *smelting place; place of pigmenting, staining*":– Zarephath (1)

G4920 σαρκικός sarkikos, a. [7] [√*4922*]. material; worldly, sinful; pertaining to the flesh; see also *4922*:– worldly (3), material (2), of the world (1), sinful (1)

G4921 σάρκινος sarkinos, a. [4] [√*4922*]. fleshly, made of flesh; human; worldly, unspiritual; see also *4922*:– as to ancestry (1), human (1), people who are worldly (1), unspiritual (1)

G4922 σάρξ sarx, n. [147] [→*4920, 4921*]. flesh, body, the soft tissue of a creature, often in contrast to bone, ligament, or sinew; by extension human, humankind, with a focus on the fallen human nature, which is frail and corrupt in contrast to immaterial (spiritual) things:– flesh (74), body (16), people (5), one (4 [+*4246*]), human (3), the world (3), earthly (2 [+*2848*]), human standards (2), sinful nature (2), worldly (2), birth (1), bodies (1), by physical descent (1), earthly (1 [+*1877*]), earthly life (1), external (1), fellow man (1), human ancestry (1 [+*2848*]), human being (1 [+*2779, 135*]), illness (1 [+*819, 3836*]), illness (1 [+*1877, 3836*]), in this way[S] (1 [+*2848*]), it[S] (1), its[S] (1 [+*3836*]), life (1), life on earth (1), of own race (1 [+*5150, 2848*]), one (1), outwardly (1), people (1 [+*2848*]), personally (1 [+*1877*]), perversion (1 [+*599, 3958, 2283*]), physical (1), physical (1 [+*1877*]), sensual (1), such[S] (1 [+*1877*]), this world (1), unspiritual (1), we (1 [+*3836, 1609*]), NDT (5)

G4923 Σαρούχ Sarouch, n. pr. Not used in NIVEBC. [√*4952*]. Serug, "*descendant, i.e., younger branch*"

G4924 σαρόω saroō, v. [3] to sweep, sweep clean:– swept clean (2), sweep (1)

G4925 Σάρρα Sarra, n. pr. [4] Sarah, "*princess*":– Sarah (3), Sarah's (1)

G4926 Σαρών Sarōn, n. pr. [1] [√*cf. 838*]. Sharon, "*plain, level country*":– Sharon (1)

G4927 Σατάν Satan, n. pr. Not used in NIVEBC. [→*4928*]. Satan, "*hostile opponent*"

G4928 Σατανᾶς Satanas, n. pr. [36] [√*4927*]. Satan, "*hostile opponent*":– Satan (35), Satan's (1)

G4929 σάτον saton, n. [2] seah (dry measure of about 12 quarts):– about sixty pounds (2 [+*5552*])

G4930 Σαῦλος Saulos, n. pr. [15] Saul, "*asked for* poss. *dedicated to God*":– Saul (15)

G4931 σβέννυμι sbennymi, v. [6] [→*812, 2410*]. to extinguish, quench, snuff out:– quenched (2), extinguish (1), going out (1), quench (1), snuff out (1)

G4932 σεαυτοῦ seautou, p. reflex. [43] [√*5148 + 899*]. yourself:– yourself (31), you (3), your (2), claim to be (1 [+*4472*]), your life (1), your own (1), your own idea (1 [+*608, 3306*]), your very self (1), yourselves (1), NDT (1)

G4933 σεβάζομαι sebazomai, v. [1] [√*4936*]. to worship:– worshiped (1)

G4934 σέβασμα sebasma, n. [2] [√*4936*]. object of worship; some translate as a place of worship: sanctuary:– objects of worship (1), worshiped (1)

G4935 σεβαστός sebastos, a. [3] [√*4936*]. (a.) revered, worthy of reverence, imperial (not found in the NT); (n.) Emperor, a title of reverence or veneration:– emperor (1), emperor's (1), imperial (1)

G4936 σέβω sebō, v. [10] [→*813, 814, 815, 2354, 2355, 2356, 2357, 2537, 2538, 4933, 4934, 4935, 4948, 4949*]. (mid.) to worship, be devout, God-fearing:– worship (3), God-fearing (2), worshiper (2), God-fearing Greeks (1), devout (1), worshiped (1)

G4937 σειρά seira, n. [1] [√*1649*]. chain:– chains (1)

G4938 σειρός seiros, n. Not used in NIVEBC. [√*4987*]. pit, cave

G4939 σεισμός seismos, n. [14] [√*4940*]. earthquake; storm:– earthquake (9), earthquakes (3), quake (1), storm (1)

G4940 σείω seiō, v. [5] [→*411, 1398, 2167, 2939, 4939*]. to cause to shake; (pass.) to be shaken, stirred up:– shook (2), shake (1), shaken (1), stirred (1)

G4941 Σεκοῦνδος Sekoundos, n. pr. [1] Secundus, "*second*":– Secundus (1)

G4942 Σελεύκεια Seleukeia, n. pr. [1] Seleucia:– Seleucia (1)

G4943 σελήνη selēnē, n. [9] [→*4944*]. moon:– moon (9)

G4944 σεληνιάζομαι selēniazomai, v. [2] [√*4943*]. (pass.) to have a seizure:– has seizures (1), having seizures (1)

G4945 Σεμεΐ Semei, n. pr. Not used in NIVEBC. [√*4946*]. Semei, "*Yahweh has heard*"

G4946 Σεμεΐν Semein, n. pr. [1] [→*4945*]. Semein, "*Yahweh has heard*":– Semein (1)

G4947 σεμίδαλις semidalis, n. [1] finely ground flour:– fine flour (1)

G4948 σεμνός semnos, a. [4] [√*4936*]. worthy of respect, noble:– worthy of respect (3), noble (1)

G4949 σεμνότης semnotēs, n. [3] [√*4936*]. holiness, seriousness, respect:– holiness (1), respect (1), seriousness (1)

G4950 Σέργιος Sergios, n. pr. [1] Sergius:– Sergius (1)

G4951 Σερούκ Serouk, n. pr. Not used in NIVEBC. [√*4952*]. Serug, "*descendant, i.e., younger branch*"

G4952 Σερούχ Serouch, n. pr. [1] [→*4923, 4951*]. Serug, "*descendant, i.e., younger branch*":– Serug (1)

G4953 Σήθ Sēth, n. pr. [1] Seth, "*determined, granted [Ge 4:25]; restitution*":– Seth (1)

G4954 Σήμ Sēm, n. pr. [1] Shem, "*name, fame*":– Shem (1)

G4955 σημαίνω sēmainō, v. [6] [√*4956*]. to make known; to indicate (beforehand), predict, foretell:– about[S] (1), indicate (1), made known (1), predicted (1), show (1), specifying (1)

G4956 σημεῖον sēmeion, n. [77] [→*817, 2168, 2358, 4185, 4955, 4957, 5361*]. (miraculous) sign, signal, mark:– signs (38), sign (32), distinguishing mark (1), marks (1), miraculously (1), signal (1), NDT (3)

G4957 σημειόω sēmeioō, v. [1] [√*4956*]. (mid.) to take special note of:– take special note (1)

G4958 σήμερον sēmeron, adv. [41] [√*2465*]. today, this day:– today (33), this day (2), day (1), the last days (1 [+*2465*]), this day (1 [+*3836, 2465*]), this very day (1 [+*2465*]), today (1 [+*1877, 3836, 2465*]), very day (1 [+*2465*])

G4959 σημικίνθιον sēmikinthion, n. Not used in NIVEBC. [√*4980*]. apron

G4960 σήπω sēpō, v. [1] [→*4911*]. to rot, decay:– rotted (1)

G4961 σηρικός sērikos, a. Not used in NIVEBC. silken; (n.) silk (cloth)

G4962 σής sēs, n. [3] [→*4963*]. moth:– moths (2), moth (1)

G4963 σητόβρωτος sētobrōtos, a. [1] [√*4962 + 1048*]. moth-eaten:– moths eaten (1 [+*1181*])

G4964 σθενόω sthenoō, v. [1] [→*819, 820, 821, 822*]. to strengthen, make strong:– firm (1)

G4965 σιαγών siagōn, n. [2] cheek:– cheek (2)

G4966 σιαίνομαι siainomai, v. Not used in NIVEBC. to be disturbed, annoyed

G4967 σιγάω sigaō, v. [10] [→*4968*]. to be or become silent; (pass.) to be hidden, concealed:– quiet (3), silent (3), finished (1), hidden (1), kept to themselves (1), speaker stop (1)

G4968 σιγή sigē, n. [2] [√*4967*]. silence:– silence (1), silent (1)

G4969 σιδήρεος sidēreos, a. Not used in NIVEBC. [√*4970*]. made of iron; same as *4971*

G4970 σίδηρος sidēros, n. [1] [→*4969, 4971*]. iron:– iron (1)

G4971 σιδηροῦς sidērous, a. [5] [√*4970*]. made of iron; same as *4969*:– iron (5)

G4972 Σιδών Sidōn, n. pr. [9] [→*4973*]. Sidon, "*fishery*":– Sidon (9)

G4973 Σιδώνιος Sidōnios, a. pr. g. [2] [√*4972*]. Sidonian, a person of Sidon:– people of Sidon (1), region of Sidon (1)

G4974 σικάριος sikarios, n. [1] [√*cf. 5000, 5001 [?]*]. terrorist, assassin:– terrorists (1 [+*467, 3836*])

G4975 σίκερα sikera, l.[n.] [1] fermented drink, beer:– fermented drink (1)

G4976 Σίλας Silas, n. pr. [12] [→*4977*]. Silas, "*asked for* poss. *dedicated to God*":– Silas (12)

G4977 Σιλουανός Silouanos, n. pr. [4] [√*4976*]. Silas, Silvanus, "*asked for* poss. *dedicated to God*":– Silas (4)

G4978 Σιλωάμ Silōam, n. pr. [3] Siloam, "*sent*":– Siloam (3)

G4979 Σιμαίας Simaias, n. pr. Not used in NIVEBC. Simaias

G4980 σιμικίνθιον simikinthion, n. [1] [→*4959*]. apron:– aprons (1)

G4981 Σίμων Simōn, n. pr. [75] [→*5208*]. Simon, "*he has heard* or *obedient one*":– Simon (70), Simon's (4), his[S] (1)

G4982 Σινά Sina, n. pr. [4] Sinai, "*Sin [pagan moon god]; glare [from white chalk]*":– Sinai (4)

G4983 σίναπι sinapi, n. [5] mustard plant:– mustard (5)

G4984 σινδών sindōn, n. [6] linen (cloth or garment):– linen cloth (3), garment (1), linen (1), linen garment (1)

G4985 σινιάζω siniazō, v. [1] to sift, shake in a sieve:– sift (1)

G4986 σιρικός sirikos, a. Not used in NIVEBC. made of silk, silken; (n.) silk (cloth)€ [1]:– silk cloth (1)

G4987 σιρός siros, n. Not used in NIVEBC. [→*4938*]. dungeon, pit, cave

G4988 σιτευτός siteutos, a. [3] [√*4992*]. fattened:– fattened (3)

G4989 σιτίον sition, n. [1] [√*4992*]. (food made from) grain:– grain (1)

G4990 σιτιστός sitistos, a. [1] [√*4992*]. fattened; (n.) fattened cattle:– fattened cattle (1)

G4991 σιτομέτριον sitometrion, n. [1] [√*4992 + 3586*]. measured allowance of food, ration of grain:– food allowance (1)

G4992 σῖτος sitos, n. [14] [→*826, 827, 2169, 4988, 4989, 4990, 4991*]. wheat, grain:– wheat (11), grain (2), kernel (1)

G4993 Σιχάρ Sichar, n. pr. Not used in NIVEBC. [√*5373*]. Sychar

G4994 Σιών Siōn, n. pr. [7] Zion, "*citadel*":– Zion (7)

G4995 σιωπάω siōpaō, v. [10] [→*4996*]. to be quiet, remain silent; to be calm, not agitated:– quiet (5), silent (4), remained silent (1)

G4996 σιωπῇ siōpē, adv. Not used in NIVEBC. [√*4995*]. quietly, privately

G4997 σκανδαλίζω skandalizō, v. [29] [→*4998*]. to cause to sin, cause to fall (into sin), offend; to fall away (from the faith), go astray; to take offense:– causes to stumble (9), fall away (7), stumble (2), took offense (2), cause offense (1), cause to fall (1), cause to stumble (1), causes to fall into sin (1), led into sin (1), offend (1), offended (1), turn away from the faith (1), will[S] (1)

G4998 σκάνδαλον skandalon, n. [15] [√*4997*]. stumbling block, obstacle, offense; something that causes sin:– stumbling block (3), makes fall (2), causes sin (1), entice to sin (1 [+*965, 1967*]), make stumble (1), obstacle (1), obstacles in way (1), offense (1), such things[S] (1), they[S] (1), things that cause people to stumble (1), things that cause to stumble (1)

G4999 σκάπτω skaptō, v. [3] [→*2940, 5002*]. to dig:– dig (2), dug (1)

G5000 Σκαριώθ Skariōth, n. pr.[g.?] [√*2696; cf. 4974 [?]*]. Scarioth

G5001 Σκαριώτης Skariōtēs, n. pr.[g.?] [√*2696; cf. 4974 [?]*]. Scariot

G5002 σκάφη skaphē, n. [3] [√*4999*]. lifeboat, (small) boat:– lifeboat (3)

G5003 σκέλος skelos, n. [3] leg:– legs (3)

G5004 σκέπασμα skepasma, n. [1] clothing, covering; this can refer to shelter or personal covering:– clothing (1)

G5005 Σκευᾶς Skeuas, n. pr. [1] Sceva:– Sceva (1)

G5006 σκευή skeuē, n. [1] [√*5007*]. (ship's) tackle, gear:– tackle (1)

G5007 σκεῦος skeuos, n. [23] [→*412, 564, 683, 2171, 2941, 4186, 4187, 5006*]. possession, merchandise, object, thing; jar, vessel, dish; a general term that can refer to a human being:– articles (2), objects (2), possessions (2), something (2 [+*5516*]), body (1), clay jar (1), everything (1 [+*4246, 3836*]), instrument (1), instruments (1), jar (1), jars (1), merchandise (1), partner (1), pottery (1), pottery (1 [+*3836, 3039*]), sea anchor (1), sheet (1), NDT (2)

G5008 σκηνή skēnē, n. [20] [→*2172, 2942, 2943, 5009, 5010, 5011, 5012, 5013*]. tabernacle; tent, shelter, dwelling:– tabernacle (10), shelters (3), dwelling place (2), room (2), dwellings (1), tent (1), tents (1)

G5009 σκηνοπηγία skēnopēgia, n. [1] [√*5008 + 4381*]. (Feast of) Tabernacles:– tabernacles (1)

G5010 σκηνοποιός skēnopoios, n. [1] [√*5008 + 4472*]. tentmaker; some translate more generally: leather worker:– tentmaker (1 [+*3836, 5492*])

G5011 σκῆνος skēnos, n. [2] [√*5008*]. tent:– tent (2)

G5012 σκηνόω skēnoō, v. [5] [√*5008*]. to live, dwell; to spread a tent:– dwell (2), live (1), made dwelling (1), shelter with presence (1 [+*2093*])

G5013 σκήνωμα skēnōma, n. [3] [√*5008*]. tent, dwelling place, lodging place:– dwelling place (1), it[S] (1 [+*3836*]), tent (1)

G5014 σκιά skia, n. [7] [→*684, 2173, 2944*]. shadow, shade:– shadow (6), shade (1)

G5015 σκιρτάω skirtaō, v. [3] to leap, with an implication that the one leaping is joyful:– leaped (2), leap for joy (1)

G5016 σκληροκαρδία sklērokardia, n. [3] [√*5020 + 2840*]. hardness of heart, stubbornness, obstinacy:– hearts hard (2), stubborn (1)

G5017 σκληρός sklēros, a. [5] [√*5020*]. hard, harsh:– hard (3), defiant (1), strong (1)

G5018 σκληρότης sklērotēs, n. [1] [√*5020*]. hardness, stubbornness:– stubbornness (1)

G5019 σκληροτράχηλος sklērotrachēlos, a. [1] [√*5020 + 5549*]. stiff-necked, stubborn:– stiff-necked (1)

G5020 σκληρύνω sklērynō, v. [6] [→*5016, 5017, 5018, 5019*]. to harden (the heart), make obstinate, make stubborn; (pass.) to be hardened, become obstinate:– harden (3), hardened (1), hardens (1), obstinate (1)

G5021 σκολιός skolios, a. Not used in NIVEBC. crooked; corrupt€ [4]:– corrupt (1), crooked (1), harsh (1), warped (1)

G5022 σκόλοψ skolops, n. [1] thorn; some translate this as a "splinter":– thorn (1)

G5023 σκοπέω skopeō, v. [6] [→*258, 2170, 2174, 2175, 2176, 2945, 2946, 5024, 5297*]. to watch out for, take notice of, look to:– fix eyes on (1), keep eyes on (1), looking to (1), see to it (1), watch (1), watch out (1)

G5024 σκοπός skopos, n. [1] [√*5023*]. goal:– goal (1)

G5025 σκορπίζω skorpizō, v. [5] [→*1399, 5026*]. to scatter, disperse:– scatters (3), freely scattered (1), scattered (1)

G5026 σκορπίος skorpios, n. [5] [√*5025*]. scorpion:– scorpions (3), scorpion (2)

G5027 σκοτεινός skoteinos, a. [3] [√*5030*]. dark:– full of darkness (2), dark (1)

G5028 σκοτία skotia, n. [16] [√*5030*]. darkness, the dark:– darkness (11), dark (5)

G5029 σκοτίζομαι skotizomai, v. [5] [√*5030*]. (pass.) to be or become dark, be darkened:– darkened (4), turned dark (1)

G5030 σκότος skotos, n. [31] [→*5027, 5028, 5029, 5031*]. darkness, the dark:– darkness (29), dark (2)

G5031 σκοτόω skotoō, v. [3] [√*5030*]. (pass.) to be or become darkened:– darkened (2), plunged into darkness (1)

G5032 σκύβαλον skybalon, n. [1] rubbish, refuse, dung; this can refer to any of a number of rotten, decaying things, all that is worth getting rid of:– garbage (1)

G5033 Σκύθης Skythēs, n. pr. g. [1] Scythian:– Scythian (1)

G5034 σκυθρωπός skythrōpos, a. [2] [√*3972*]. to look somber, appear downcast, implying a sad or sullen attitude:– faces downcast (1), somber (1)

G5035 σκύλλω skyllō, v. [4] [→*5036*]. to bother, annoy; (pass.) to be harassed; (mid.) to trouble oneself:– bother (2), harassed (1), trouble (1)

G5036 σκῦλον skylon, n. [1] [√*5035*]. (pl.) spoils, booty:– plunder (1)

G5037 σκωληκόβρωτος skōlēkobrōtos, a. [1] [√*5038 + 1048*]. eaten by worms:– eaten by worms (1)

G5038 σκώληξ skōlēx, n. [1] [→*5037*]. worm:– worms (1)

G5039 σμαράγδινος smaragdinos, a. [1] [√*5040*]. (of) emerald:– emerald (1)

G5040 σμάραγδος smaragdos, n. [1] [→*5039*]. emerald:– emerald (1)

G5041 σμῆγμα smēgma, n. Not used in NIVEBC. ointment, salve

G5042 σμίγμα smigma, n. Not used in NIVEBC. [√*3502*]. mixture, compound

G5043 σμύρνα[1] smyrna[1], n. [2] [→*2430, 5044, 5045, 5046*]. myrrh, an aromatic resinous gum:– myrrh (2)

G5044 Σμύρνα[2] Smyrna[2], n. pr. [2] [√*5043*]. Smyrna:– Smyrna (2)

G5045 Σμυρναῖος Smyrnaios, a. pr. g. Not used in NIVEBC. [√*5043*]. Smyrnaean

G5046 σμυρνίζω smyrnizō, v. [1] [√*5043*]. to mix with myrrh, referring to wine mixed with myrrh as a drug to deaden the senses and mind:– mixed with myrrh (1)

G5047 Σόδομα Sodoma, n. pr. [9] Sodom:– Sodom (7), Sodom (2 [+*1178*])

G5048 Σολομών Solomōn, n. pr. [12] [→*4898*]. Solomon, "*peace, well being*":– Solomon (7), Solomon's (5)

G5049 σορός soros, n. [1] coffin, bier:– bier (1)

G5050 σός sos, a. poss. [30] [√*5148*]. (s.) your, yours:– your (12), yours (7), you (3 [+*5148*]), your own (3), you (2), belongs to you (1), you have (1 [+*3836*]), NDT (1)

G5051 σουδάριον soudarion, n. [4] piece of cloth, burial cloth, handkerchief:– cloth (2), handkerchiefs (1), piece of cloth (1)

G5052 Σουσάννα Sousanna, n. pr. [1] Susanna, "*lily*":– Susanna (1)

G5053 σοφία sophia, n. [51] [√*5055*]. wisdom (either secular or divine). Christ is called "the wisdom of God"

GREEK INDEX

in 1Co 1:24, 30. On the basis of the OT, wisdom can be personified:– wisdom (49), wise (2)

G5054 σοφίζω sophizō, v. [2] [√5055]. to make wise; (pass.) to be cleverly invented:– cleverly devised (1), make wise (1)

G5055 σοφός sophos, a. [20] [→831, 2947, 5053, 5054, 5814, 5815]. wise; expert, skilled; (n.) a person who is skilled or expert, often as a class or kind, a wise man or woman:– wise (18), sages (1), wiser (1)

G5056 Σπανία Spania, n. pr. [2] Spain:– Spain (2)

G5057 σπαράσσω sparassō, v. [3] [√5060]. to convulse, shake violently:– convulsed (1), shook violently (1), throws into convulsions (1)

G5058 σπαργανόω sparganoō, v. [2] to wrap (in cloth), to bind a newborn infant in strips of long cloth, a normal act of child care for warmth, security, etc.:– wrapped in cloths (2)

G5059 σπαταλάω spatalaō, v. [2] to live in pleasure, in self-indulgence:– lives for pleasure (1), self-indulgence (1)

G5060 σπάω spaō, v. [2] [→413, 597, 685, 1400, 2177, 2341, 4352, 5057, 5360]. (mid.) to draw (a sword):– drew (2)

G5061 σπεῖρα speira, n. [7] company of soldiers, cohort; technically one tenth of a Roman legion: 600 fighting men:– company of soldiers (2), detachment of soldiers (2), regiment (2), roman troops (1)

G5062 σπείρω speirō, v. [52] [→1401, 1402, 2178, 5065, 5066, 5076, 5077, 5078]. to sow seed, scatter seed:– sow (9), sown (9), sows (8), farmer (4), seed sown (4), scattering seed (3), seed falling (3), sower (3), planted (2), sow seed (2), sowed (2), plant (1), sown seed (1), NDT (1)

G5063 σπεκουλάτωρ spekoulatōr, n. [1] executioner:– executioner (1)

G5064 σπένδω spendō, v. [2] [→836]. (pass.) to be poured out like a drink offering:– poured out like a drink offering (2)

G5065 σπέρμα sperma, n. [43] [√5062]. seed, the part of a plant or animal that can propagate the species (cf. "sperm"); by extension: children, offspring, descendants:– descendants (11), offspring (11), seed (10), children (3), seeds (3), descendant (2), bear children (1 [+1650, 2856, 3284]), child (1), descended from (1 [+1666])

G5066 σπερμολόγος spermologos, a. [1] [√5062 + 3306]. babbler, chatterer, implying the person has low status, living by picking up scraps:– babbler (1)

G5067 σπεύδω speudō, v. [6] [→5079, 5080, 5081, 5082]. to hurry, hasten:– at once (1), hurried off (1 [+2262]), immediately (1), in a hurry (1), quick (1), speed (1)

G5068 σπήλαιον spēlaion, n. [6] den, cave, hideout:– den (3), caves (2), cave (1)

G5069 σπιλάς spilas, n. [1] [√5070]. blemish, spot:– blemishes (1)

G5070 σπίλος spilos, n. [2] [→834, 5069, 5071]. stain, blot:– blots (1), stain (1)

G5071 σπιλόω spiloō, v. [2] [√5070]. to corrupt; (pass.) to be stained, defiled:– corrupts (1), stained (1)

G5072 σπλαγχνίζομαι splanchnizomai, v. [11] [√5073]. to have compassion on, have pity on:– had compassion (4), have compassion (2), took pity (2), filled with compassion (1), heart went out (1), take pity (1)

G5073 σπλάγχνον splanchnon, n. [11] [→2359, 4492, 4499, 5072]. inward parts of body: intestines; of emotion: *heart, affection, tenderness, compassion*:– affection (3), compassion (1 [+3880]), has no pity (1 [+3091, 3836]), heart (1), hearts (1), intestines (1), tender mercy (1 [+1799]), tenderness (1), very heart (1)

G5074 σπόγγος spongos, n. [3] sponge:– sponge (3)

G5075 σποδός spodos, n. [3] ashes:– ashes (3)

G5076 σπορά spora, n. [1] [√5062]. seed:– seed (1)

G5077 σπόριμος sporimos, a. [3] [√5062]. what is sown; (pl.n.) grainfield:– grainfields (3)

G5078 σπόρος sporos, n. [6] [√5062]. seed:– seed (5), store of seed (1)

G5079 σπουδάζω spoudazō, v. [11] [√5067]. to be eager, make every effort, do one's best:– do best (4), make every effort (4), eager (1), made effort (1), make effort (1)

G5080 σπουδαῖος spoudaios, a. [3] [√5067]. zealous, eager, earnest; (compar.) more enthusiastic, very earnest:– enthusiasm (1), so[S] (1), zealous (1)

G5081 σπουδαίως spoudaiōs, adv. [4] [√5067]. earnestly, zealously, with vigor; (compar.) all the more eager, with special urgency:– all the more eager (1), earnestly (1), everything can (1), hard (1)

G5082 σπουδή spoudē, n. [12] [√5067]. hurry, haste; earnestness, diligence, zeal, eagerness:– earnestness (3), concern (1), devoted (1), diligence (1), diligently (1 [+1877]), eager (1), effort (1), hurried (1 [+3552]), hurried (1 [+4513, 3552]), zeal (1)

G5083 σπυρίς spyris, n. [5] basket:– basketfuls (2), basket (1), basketfuls (1 [+4441]), basketfuls (1 [+4445])

G5084 στάδιον stadion, n. [7] [√2705]. arena, stadium, race course; a unit of length: stade (about 200 yards):– stadia (2), about seven miles (1 [+600, 2008]), distance (1), less than two miles (1 [+6055, 1278]), race (1), three miles (1 [+1633, 4297]); [*also* four miles (1 [+5558])]

G5085 στάμνος stamnos, n. [1] [√2705]. jar:– jar (1)

G5086 στασιαστής stasiastēs, n. [1] [√2705]. insurrectionist, revolutionary:– insurrectionists (1)

G5087 στάσις stasis, n. [9] [√2705]. continuance, state of existence; uprising, insurrection, riot; dispute, discord:– dispute (3), insurrection (2), functioning (1 [+2400]), rioting (1), riots (1), uprising (1)

G5088 στατήρ statēr, n. [1] [√2705]. four-drachma coin, stater (four days' wages):– four-drachma coin (1)

G5089 σταυρός stauros, n. [27] [→416, 5090, 5365; *cf.* 2705]. cross:– cross (26), crosses (1)

G5090 σταυρόω stauroō, v. [46] [√5089]. to crucify:– crucified (31), crucify (15)

G5091 σταφυλή staphylē, n. [3] (bunch of) grapes:– grapes (3)

G5092 στάχυς[1] stachys[1], n. [5] [→5093]. head of grain:– heads of grain (3), head (2)

G5093 Στάχυς[2] Stachys[2], n. pr. [1] [√5092]. Stachys, "*head of grain*":– Stachys (1)

G5094 στέγη stegē, n. [3] [√5095]. roof:– roof (3)

G5095 στέγω stegō, v. [4] [→689, 5094, 5566]. to put up with, stand, endure; to protect, cover:– stand (2), protects (1), put up with (1)

G5096 στεῖρα steira, n. [5] [√5104]. (state of) barrenness, infertility:– barren (1), childless women (1), not able to conceive (1), unable to conceive (1), NDT (1)

G5097 στέλλω stellō, v. [2] [→690, 1403, 1405, 2186, 2948, 2950, 5124, 5366, 5713, 5714]. (mid.) to avoid, keep away from:– avoid (1), keep away (1)

G5098 στέμμα stemma, n. [1] [√5110]. wreath, garland:– wreaths (1)

G5099 στεναγμός stenagmos, n. [2] [√5101]. groan, sigh:– groaning (1), groans (1)

G5100 στενάζω stenazō, v. [6] [√5101]. to groan, sigh; to grumble:– groan (3), burden (1), deep sigh (1), grumble (1)

G5101 στενός stenos, a. [3] [→417, 5099, 5100, 5102, 5103, 5367]. narrow:– narrow (2), small (1)

G5102 στενοχωρέω stenochōreō, v. [3] [√5101 + 6003]. (pass.) to be crushed; to withhold, be restricted:– withholding (2), crushed (1)

G5103 στενοχωρία stenochōria, n. [4] [√5101 + 6003]. distress, hardship, difficulty:– difficulties (1), distress (1), distresses (1), hardship (1)

G5104 στερεός stereos, a. [4] [→5096, 5105, 5106]. solid, strong; standing firm, steadfast:– solid (3), standing firm (1)

G5105 στερεόω stereoō, v. [3] [√5104]. to make strong; (pass.) to become strong, be strengthened:– made strong (1), strengthened (1), strong (1)

G5106 στερέωμα stereōma, n. [1] [√5104]. firmness, steadfastness:– firm (1)

G5107 Στεφανᾶς Stephanas, n. pr. [3] [√5110]. Stephanas, "*victor's wreath*":– Stephanas (3)

G5108 Στέφανος[1] Stephanos[1], n. pr. [7] [√5110]. Stephen, "*victor's wreath*":– Stephen (7)

G5109 στέφανος[2] stephanos[2], n. [18] [√5110]. woven crown, wreath, victory garland; of various shapes and various materials, leaves, twigs, flowers, even metal, as a sign of victory, honor, and in some contexts, authority:– crown (14), crowns (3), victor's crown (1)

G5110 στεφανόω stephanoō, v. [3] [→5098, 5107, 5108, 5109]. to crown, present a wreath:– crowned (2), receive the victor's crown (1)

G5111 στῆθος stēthos, n. [5] chest, breast:– against (2 [+2093, 3836]), breast (1), breasts (1), chests (1)

G5112 στήκω stēkō, v. [9] [√2705]. to stand, stand firm, be steadfast:– stand firm (5), stand (2), standing (1), standing firm (1)

G5113 στηριγμός stērigmos, n. [1] [√5114]. security, firmness:– secure position (1)

G5114 στηρίζω stērizō, v. [13] [→844, 2185, 5113]. to strengthen, establish, stand firm; to be resolute:– strengthen (6), make strong (2), establish (1), firmly established (1), resolutely (1 [+3836, 4725]), set in place (1), stand firm (1 [+3836, 2840])

G5115 στιβάς stibas, n. [1] leafy branch:– branches (1)

G5116 στίγμα stigma, n. [1] [→5117]. mark, scar; in context Paul is likely referring to the scars he received in service to Jesus as marks of ownership by his master:– marks (1)

G5117 στιγμή stigmē, n. [1] [√5116]. instant, moment:– instant (1 [+5989])

G5118 στίλβω stilbō, v. [1] to dazzle, be radiant:– dazzling (1 [+3336])

G5119 στοά stoa, n. [4] [→5121, 5147; *cf.* 2705]. covered colonnade, portico:– colonnade (3), covered colonnades (1)

G5120 στοιβάς stoibas, n. Not used in NIVEBC. leafy branch

G5121 Στοϊκός Stoikos, a. pr. [1] [√5119]. Stoic:– Stoic (1)

G5122 στοιχεῖον stoicheion, n. [7] [√5123]. principle, basic principle; element (of nature); elementary truths:– elemental spiritual forces (3), elements (2), elementary truths (1 [+3836, 794]), forces (1)

G5123 στοιχέω stoicheō, v. [5] [→5122, 5368]. to follow, walk in, adhere to:– follow (2), keep in step with (1), live up to (1), living (1)

G5124 στολή stolē, n. [9] [√5097]. (flowing) robe:– robes (4), robe (3), flowing robes (2)

G5125 στόμα stoma, n. [78] [→694, 1492, 2187, 5126]. mouth; by extension: edge (of a sword):– mouth (39), mouths (9), lips (6), face (4), through (4 [+1328]), testimony (2), words (2), began[S] (1 [+487, 3836]), began to speak (1 [+487, 3836, 3306]), edge (1), say (1 [+1666, 3836]), speak (1 [+487, 3836]), speak (1 [+489, 3836]), spoken freely (1 [+3836, 487]), sword (1 [+3479]), that[S] (1), they[S] (1 [+3836, 899]), voice (1), NDT (1)

G5126 στόμαχος stomachos, n. [1] [√5125]. stomach:– stomach (1)

G5127 στρατεία strateia, n. [2] [√5131]. warfare; fight:– battle (1), fight with (1)

G5128 στράτευμα strateuma, n. [8] [√5131]. army, troops, soldiers:– troops (3), armies (2), army (2), soldiers (1)

G5129 στρατεύομαι strateuomai, v. [7] [√5131]. (mid.) to serve as a soldier; to wage war, fight, battle:– wage war (2), battle (1), fight (1), serves as a soldier (1), serving as a soldier (1), soldiers (1)

G5130 στρατηγός stratēgos, n. [10] [√5131 + 72]. magistrate, praetor; captain, officer:– magistrates (5), captain of guard (2), captain (1), officers of guard (1), officers of the temple guard (1)

G5131 στρατιά stratia, n. [2] [→529, 5127, 5128, 5129, 5130, 5132, 5133, 5134, 5135, 5136, 5369]. host, army (of heaven), (celestial) bodies:– host (1), sun moon and stars (1 [+3836, 4041])

G5132 στρατιώτης stratiōtēs, n. [26] [√5131]. soldier:– soldiers (22), soldier (3), them[S] (1)

G5133 στρατολογέω stratologeō, v. [1] [√5131 + 3306]. to gather an army; (ptcp.) commanding officer, with a focus on enlisting soldiers:– commanding officer (1)

G5134 στρατοπεδάρχης stratopedarchēs, n. Not used in NIVEBC. [√5131 + 4269 + 806]. military commander, commander of a camp

G5135 στρατοπέδαρχος stratopedarchos, n. Not used in NIVEBC. [√5131 + 4269 + 806]. military commander, commander of a camp

G5136 στρατόπεδον stratopedon, n. [1] [√5131 + 4269]. army:– armies (1)

G5137 στρεβλόω strebloō, v. [1] [√5138]. to distort, twist:– distort (1)

G5138 στρέφω strephō, v. [21] [→418, 419, 695, 1406, 1750, 2188, 2189, 2951, 2953, 3570, 5137, 5266, 5370, 5371, 5715]. to turn, turn away, return; to change, repent, turn one's life:– turned (9), turn (5), turning (2), change (1), returned (1), turned away from (1), turned back (1), turning around (1)

G5139 στρηνιάω strēniaō, v. [2] [√5140]. to live in luxury, with an implication that this luxury contributes to improper sensuality and immorality:– luxury (1), shared luxury (1)

G5140 στρῆνος strēnos, n. [1] [→2952, 5139]. luxury:– luxuries (1)

G5141 στρουθίον strouthion, n. [4] sparrow:– sparrows (4)

G5142 στρώννυμι strōnnymi, v. Not used in NIVEBC. [√5143]. to spread out; (pass.) to be furnished

G5143 στρωννύω strōnnyō, v. [6] [→2954, 3346, 5142, 5716]. to spread out; (pass.) to be furnished:– spread (3), all furnished (1), furnished (1), roll up mat (1)

G5144 στυγητός *stygētos*, a. [1] [→*696, 2539, 5145*]. hated:– hated (1)

G5145 στυγνάζω *stygnazō*, v. [2] [√*5144*]. to be gloomy, sad, others translate "shocked, appalled"; (of weather) to be overcast, gloomy:– face fell (1), overcast (1)

G5146 στῦλος *stylos*, n. [4] pillar, column; (fig.) leader:– pillar (2), pillars (2)

G5147 Στωϊκός *Stōikos*, a. pr. Not used in NIVEBC. [√*5119*]. Stoic

G5148 σύ *sy*, p. pers. [2891] [→*4932, 5050, 5629*]. you, your:– you (2007), your (685), yours (14), your own (13), yourselves (13), home (5 [+*3875*]), yourself (4), you (3 [+*5050*]), please (2 [+*2263*]), you (2 [+*3836, 6034*]), you (2 [+*3836, 4725*]), you (2 [+*3836, 3950*]), you (2 [+*3836, 2840*]), your (2 [+*1877*]), yourselves (2 [+*3836, 3517*]), both of you (1 [+*2779, 899*]), he (1), in your relationships with one another (1 [+*1877*]), the two of you (1 [+*2779, 899*]), them[s] (1 [+*81*]), what do you want with us (1 [+*5515, 5516, 1609, 2779*]), you (1 [+*2840*]), you (1 [+*6034*]), you[s] (1 [+*3836, 4364*]), you yourselves (1), your (1 [+*2848*]), yourselves (1 [+*2840*]), yourselves (1 [+*3836, 6034*]), you're (1), NDT (119)

G5149 συγγένεια *syngeneia*, n. [3] [√*5250* + *1181*]. family, relative, one's own people:– family (1), people (1), relatives (1)

G5150 συγγενής *syngenēs*, a. [11] [√*5250* + *1181*]. family, relative, one's own race or people:– relatives (6), fellow Jews (2), fellow Jew (1), of own race (1 [+*2848, 4922*]), relative (1)

G5151 συγγενίς *syngenis*, n. [1] [√*5250* + *1181*]. (female) relative:– relative (1)

G5152 συγγνώμη *syngnōmē*, n. [1] [√*5250* + *1182*]. concession:– concession (1)

G5153 συγκάθημαι *synkathēmai*, v. [2] [√*5250* + *2757*]. to sit with:– sat (1 [+*1639*]), sitting with (1)

G5154 συγκαθίζω *synkathizō*, v. [2] [√*5250* + *2767*]. to sit down together; to be seated together:– sat down together (1), seated with (1)

G5155 συγκακοπαθέω *synkakopatheō*, v. [2] [√*5250* + *2805* + *4248*]. to suffer together with, endure hardship with:– join with in suffering (2)

G5156 συγκακουχέομαι *synkakoucheomai*, v. [1] [√*5250* + *2805* + *2400*]. (pass.) to be mistreated with:– mistreated along with (1)

G5157 συγκαλέω *synkaleō*, v. [8] [√*5250* + *2813*]. (act.) to call together; (mid.) to call to one's side, summon:– called together (6), calls together (2)

G5158 συγκαλύπτω *synkalyptō*, v. [1] [√*5250* + *2821*]. to conceal:– concealed (1)

G5159 συγκάμπτω *synkamptō*, v. [1] [√*5250* + *2828*]. (pass.) to be bent over:– bent (1)

G5160 συγκαταβαίνω *synkatabainō*, v. [1] [√*5250* + *2848* + *326*]. to come, go down with:– come with (1)

G5161 συγκατάθεσις *synkatathesis*, n. [1] [√*5250* + *2848* + *5502*]. agreement:– agreement (1)

G5162 συγκατανεύω *synkataneuō*, v. Not used in NIVEBC. [√*5250* + *2848* + *3748*]. to agree, consent

G5163 συγκατατίθημι *synkatatithēmi*, v. [1] [√*5250* + *2848* + *5502*]. (mid.) to consent, agree with:– consented (1 [+*1639*])

G5164 συγκαταψηφίζομαι *synkatapsēphizomai*, v. [1] [√*5250* + *2848* + *6029*]. (pass.) to be added, chosen together with:– added (1)

G5165 σύγκειμαι *synkeimai*, v. Not used in NIVEBC. [√*5250* + *3023*]. to recline together

G5166 συγκεράννυμι *synkerannymi*, v. [2] [√*5250* + *3042*]. to combine, unite:– put together (1), share (1)

G5167 συγκινέω *synkineō*, v. [1] [√*5250* + *3075*]. to stir up, arouse:– stirred up (1)

G5168 συγκλείω *synkleiō*, v. [4] [√*5250* + *3091*]. to catch (fish hemmed up in a net); to confine, imprison, lock up:– locked up (2), bound (1), caught (1)

G5169 συγκληρονόμος *synklēronomos*, a. [4] [√*5250* + *3102* + *3795*]. inheriting together; (n.) co-heir:– heirs with (2), co-heirs (1), heirs together (1)

G5170 συγκοινωνέω *synkoinōneō*, v. [3] [√*5250* + *3123*]. to share with, be connected with:– share in (2), have to do with (1)

G5171 συγκοινωνός *synkoinōnos*, n. [4] [√*5250* + *3123*]. sharer, companion, participant, partner:– share in (2 [+*1181*]), companion (1), share in with (1 [+*1639*])

G5172 συγκομίζω *synkomizō*, v. [1] [√*5250* + *3180*]. to bury, entomb:– buried (1)

G5173 συγκρίνω *synkrinō*, v. [3] [√*5250* + *3212*]. to express, explain; to compare:– compare (2), explaining (1)

G5174 συγκύπτω *synkyptō*, v. [1] [√*5250* + *3252*]. to bend over, be crippled:– bent over (1)

G5175 συγκυρία *synkyria*, n. [1] [√*5250*]. event that just happens, coincidence:– happened (1 [+*2848*])

G5176 συγχαίρω *synchairō*, v. [7] [√*5250* + *5897*]. to rejoice with:– rejoice with (4), rejoices with (2), shared joy (1)

G5177 συγχέω *syncheō*, v. [5] [√*1772; cf. 5250*]. to baffle, confuse; to stir up, cause trouble; (pass.) to be bewildered, confused; to be in an uproar, stirred up:– baffled (1), bewilderment (1), in an uproar (1), in confusion (1), stirred up (1)

G5178 συγχράομαι *synchraomai*, v. [1] [√*5250* + *5968*]. to associate with, have (friendly) dealings with:– associate with (1)

G5179 συγχύνω *synchynō*, v. Not used in NIVEBC. [√*1772; cf. 5250*]. to baffle, confuse; to stir up, cause trouble; (pass.) to be confused; to be in an uproar, stirred up

G5180 σύγχυσις *synchysis*, n. [1] [√*1772; cf. 5250*]. uproar, confusion:– in an uproar (1 [+*4398, 3836*])

G5181 συγχωρέω *synchōreō*, v. Not used in NIVEBC. [√*5250* + *6003*]. to permit

G5182 συζάω *syzaō*, v. [3] [√*5250* + *2409*]. to live with:– live with (3)

G5183 συζεύγνυμι *syzeugnymi*, v. [2] [√*5250* + *2413*]. to join together:– joined together (1), together (1)

G5184 συζητέω *syzēteō*, v. [10] [√*5250* + *2426*]. to discuss; to debate, argue:– question (2), argue with (1), arguing (1), arguing about (1), asked (1), debated (1), debating (1), discussed (1), discussing (1)

G5185 συζήτησις *syzētēsis*, n. Not used in NIVEBC. [√*5250* + *2426*]. dispute, discussion

G5186 συζητητής *syzētētēs*, n. [1] [√*5250* + *2426*]. philosopher, debater:– philosopher (1)

G5187 σύζυγος *syzygos*, a. [1] [√*5250* + *2413*]. yokefellow, comrade:– companion (1)

G5188 συζωοποιέω *syzōopoieō*, v. [2] [√*5250* + *2409* + *4472*]. to make alive with (someone):– made alive with (2)

G5189 συκάμινος *sykaminos*, n. [1] mulberry tree:– mulberry tree (1)

G5190 συκῆ *sykē*, n. [16] [√*5192*]. fig tree:– fig tree (14), figs (1), tree (1)

G5191 συκομορέα *sykomorea*, n. [1] [√*5192*]. sycamore-fig tree:– sycamore-fig tree (1)

G5192 σῦκον *sykon*, n. [4] [→*5190, 5191, 5193*]. fig:– figs (4)

G5193 συκοφαντέω *sykophanteō*, v. [2] [√*5192* + *5743*]. to accuse falsely, oppress; to cheat, extort:– accuse falsely (1), cheated out of (1)

G5194 συλαγωγέω *sylagōgeō*, v. [1] [√*5195* + *72*]. to take captive:– takes captive (1 [+*1639, 3836*])

G5195 συλάω *sylaō*, v. [1] [→*2644, 2645, 5194*]. to rob:– robbed (1)

G5196 συλλαλέω *syllaleō*, v. [6] [√*5250* + *3281*]. to talk with, discuss with, confer with:– talking with (2), conferred (1), discussed (1), said (1), talking (1)

G5197 συλλαμβάνω *syllambanō*, v. [16] [√*5250* + *3284*]. to seize, arrest, capture; to become pregnant, conceive; to help, come to the aid of:– arrested (2), capture (2), help (2), seized (2), conceive (1 [+*1877, 1143*]), conceived (1), conceived (1 [+*1877, 3836, 3120*]), have (1), pregnant (1), seize (1), seizing (1), taken (1)

G5198 συλλέγω *syllegō*, v. [8] [√*5250* + *3306*]. to pick, pull up, collect:– pick (2), collect (1), collected (1), pull up (1), pulled up (1), pulling (1), weed out (1)

G5199 συλλογίζομαι *syllogizomai*, v. [1] [√*5250* + *3306*]. to discuss together:– discussed (1)

G5200 συλλυπέω *syllypeō*, v. [1] [√*5250* + *3383*]. (pass.) to be deeply distressed, grieved with:– deeply distressed (1)

G5201 συμβαίνω *symbainō*, v. [8] [√*5250* + *326*]. to happen; to come about:– happened (3), are (1), had to (1), happen (1), happening (1), in the midst of (1)

G5202 συμβάλλω *symballō*, v. [6] [√*5250* + *965*]. to dispute with; to confer with, meet with; to ponder; to engage in (war); (mid.) to help, assist:– conferred (1), debate with (1), go (1), help (1), met (1), pondered (1)

G5203 συμβασιλεύω *symbasileuō*, v. [2] [√*5250* + *995*]. to reign with, be king with:– reign with (2)

G5204 συμβιβάζω *symbibazō*, v. [7] [√*5250* + *326*]. (pass.) to be held together; to be united; (act.) to conclude; to prove; to instruct, teach, advise:– held together (2), concluding (1), instruct (1), proving (1), shouted instructions (1), united (1)

G5205 συμβουλεύω *symbouleuō*, v. [4] [√*5250* + *1089*]. to advise, counsel; (mid.) to plot, conspire, consult:– advised (1), conspiracy (1), counsel (1), schemed (1)

G5206 συμβούλιον *symboulion*, n. [8] [√*5250* + *1089*]. plan, plot; decision; council:– plans (3), council (1), decided (1 [+*3284*]), plan (1), plot (1 [+*1443*]), plotted (1 [+*3284*])

G5207 σύμβουλος *symboulos*, n. [1] [√*5250* + *1089*]. counselor, advisor:– counselor (1)

G5208 Συμεών *Symeōn*, n. pr. [7] [√*4981*]. Simeon, Simon, "*he has heard* or *obedient one*":– Simeon (5), Simon (2)

G5209 συμμαθητής *symmathētēs*, n. [1] [√*5250* + *3443*]. fellow disciple:– rest of disciples (1)

G5210 συμμαρτυρέω *symmartyreō*, v. [3] [√*5250* + *3459*]. to testify with; to confirm:– also bearing witness (1), confirms (1), testifies with (1)

G5211 συμμερίζομαι *symmerizomai*, v. [1] [√*5250* + *3538*]. to share with:– share in (1)

G5212 συμμέτοχος *symmetochos*, a. [2] [√*5250* + *3552* + *2400*]. sharing with, being partner with, derived from the Greek verb "to share in the possession of something," not found in the NT:– partners with (1), sharers together (1)

G5213 συμμιμητής *symmimētēs*, n. [1] [√*5250* + *3628*]. fellow imitator:– join together in following example (1 [+*1181*])

G5214 συμμορφίζω *symmorphizō*, v. [1] [√*5250* + *3671*]. (pass.) to become like, be conformed to:– becoming like (1)

G5215 σύμμορφος *symmorphos*, a. [2] [√*5250* + *3671*]. conformed, being like:– be like (1), conformed to (1)

G5216 συμμορφόω *symmorphoō*, v. Not used in NIVEBC. [√*5250* + *3671*]. to give the same form

G5217 συμπαθέω *sympatheō*, v. [2] [√*5250* + *4248*]. to sympathize with:– empathize with (1), suffered along with (1)

G5218 συμπαθής *sympathēs*, a. [1] [√*5250* + *4248*]. sympathetic:– sympathetic (1)

G5219 συμπαραγίνομαι *symparaginomai*, v. [1] [√*5250* + *4123* + *1181*]. (mid.) to come together:– gathered (1)

G5220 συμπαρακαλέω *symparakaleō*, v. [1] [√*5250* + *4123* + *2813*]. (pass.) to be mutually encouraged:– mutually encouraged (1)

G5221 συμπαραλαμβάνω *symparalambanō*, v. [4] [√*5250* + *4123* + *3284*]. to take along with:– take (1), take with (1), taking with (1), took along (1)

G5222 συμπαραμένω *symparamenō*, v. Not used in NIVEBC. [√*5250* + *4123* + *3531*]. to stay with (someone) to help

G5223 συμπάρειμι *sympareimi*, v. [1] [√*5250* + *4123* + *1639*]. to be present with:– present with (1)

G5224 συμπάσχω *sympaschō*, v. [2] [√*5250* + *4248*]. to suffer with, share in suffering:– share in sufferings (1), suffers with (1)

G5225 συμπέμπω *sympempō*, v. [2] [√*5250* + *4287*]. to send with:– sending along (1), sending with (1)

G5226 συμπεριέχω *symperiechō*, v. Not used in NIVEBC. [√*5250* + *4309* + *2400*]. to surround, stand around together

G5227 συμπεριλαμβάνω *symperilambanō*, v. [1] [√*5250* + *4309* + *3284*]. to put one's arms around, embrace:– put arms around (1)

G5228 συμπίνω *sympinō*, v. [1] [√*5250* + *4403*]. to drink with:– drank (1)

G5229 συμπίπτω *sympiptō*, v. [1] [√*5250* + *4406*]. to collapse:– collapsed (1)

G5230 συμπληρόω *symplēroō*, v. [3] [√*5250* + *4444*]. (pass.) to be swamped, become full; to be fulfilled, come to an end:– approached (1), came (1), swamped (1)

G5231 συμπνίγω *sympnigō*, v. [5] [√*5250* + *4464*]. to choke; to crush:– choke (2), choked (2), crushed (1)

G5232 συμπολίτης *sympolitēs*, n. [1] [√*5250* + *4484*]. fellow citizen:– fellow citizens (1)

G5233 συμπορεύομαι *symporeuomai*, v. [4] [√*5250* + *4513*]. to go with, come together:– came (1), traveling with (1), walked along with (1), went along with (1)

G5234 συμποσία *symposia*, n. Not used in NIVEBC. [√*5250* + *4403*]. common meal

G5235 συμπόσιον *symposion*, n. [2] [√*5250* + *4403*]. group:– in groups (2 [+*5235*])

G5236 συμπρεσβύτερος *sympresbyteros*, n. [1] [√*5250* + *4565*]. fellow elder:– fellow elder (1)

G5237 συμφέρω *sympherō*, v. [15] [√*5250* + *5770*]. to bring together; to be helpful, be gained; (n.) common good; (imper. verb) it is good, better, beneficial:– better (5), good

(3), beneficial (2), best (1), brought together (1), common good (1), gained (1), helpful (1)

G5238 **σύμφημι** ***symphēmi***, v. [1] [√*5250 + 5774*]. to agree with:– agree (1)

G5239 **σύμφορος** ***symphoros***, a. [2] [√*5250 + 5770*]. beneficial, advantageous; (n.) good, a benefit, an advantage:– good (2)

G5240 **συμφορτίζω** ***symphortizō***, v. Not used in NIVEBC. [√*5250 + 5770*]. to burden together with others

G5241 **συμφυλέτης** ***symphyletēs***, n. [1] [√*5250 + 5876*]. (pl.) one's own countrymen, people:– own people (1 [*+2625*])

G5242 **σύμφυτος** ***symphytos***, a. [1] [√*5250 + 5886*]. united, being one with:– united with (1 [*+1181*])

G5243 **συμφύω** ***symphyō***, v. [1] [√*5250 + 5886*]. to grow up with:– grew up with (1)

G5244 **συμφωνέω** ***symphōneō***, v. [6] [√*5250 + 5889*]. to agree with; to match, fit in with:– agree (2), agreed (1), conspire (1), in agreement (1), match (1)

G5245 **συμφώνησις** ***symphōnēsis***, n. [1] [√*5250 + 5889*]. harmony, agreement:– harmony (1)

G5246 **συμφωνία** ***symphōnia***, n. [1] [√*5250 + 5889*]. music:– music (1)

G5247 **σύμφωνος** ***symphōnos***, a. [1] [√*5250 + 5889*]. mutually consenting, agreeing; (n.) mutual agreement:– mutual consent (1)

G5248 **συμψηφίζω** ***sympsēphizō***, v. [1] [√*5250 + 6029*]. to calculate, compute:– calculated (1)

G5249 **σύμψυχος** ***sympsychos***, a. [1] [√*5250 + 6038*]. united in spirit, harmonious:– one in spirit (1)

G5250 **σύν** ***syn***, pp. [128] [→*850, 851, 852, 853, 2190, 2192, 2194, 3568, 5149, 5150, 5151, 5152, 5153, 5154, 5155, 5156, 5157, 5158, 5159, 5160, 5161, 5162, 5163, 5164, 5165, 5166, 5167, 5168, 5169, 5170, 5171, 5172, 5173, 5174, 5175, 5176, 5177, 5178, 5179, 5180, 5181, 5182, 5183, 5184, 5185, 5186, 5187, 5188, 5196, 5197, 5198, 5199, 5200, 5201, 5202, 5203, 5204, 5205, 5206, 5207, 5209, 5210, 5211, 5212, 5213, 5214, 5215, 5216, 5217, 5218, 5219, 5220, 5221, 5222, 5223, 5224, 5225, 5226, 5227, 5228, 5229, 5230, 5231, 5232, 5233, 5234, 5235, 5236, 5237, 5238, 5239, 5240, 5241, 5242, 5243, 5244, 5245, 5246, 5247, 5248, 5249, 5251, 5252, 5253, 5254, 5255, 5256, 5257, 5258, 5260, 5261, 5262, 5263, 5264, 5265, 5266, 5267, 5268, 5269, 5270, 5271, 5272, 5273, 5274, 5275, 5276, 5277, 5278, 5279, 5280, 5281, 5282, 5283, 5284, 5285, 5286, 5287, 5288, 5289, 5290, 5291, 5292, 5293, 5294, 5295, 5296, 5297, 5298, 5299, 5300, 5301, 5302, 5303, 5304, 5305, 5306, 5307, 5308, 5309, 5310, 5311, 5312, 5313, 5314, 5315, 5316, 5317, 5318, 5319, 5320, 5321, 5322, 5323, 5324, 5325, 5326, 5327, 5328, 5329, 5330, 5331, 5332, 5333, 5334, 5335, 5336, 5337, 5338, 5339, 5340, 5341, 5342, 5343, 5344, 5345, 5346, 5347, 5348, 5349, 5350, 5357, 5360, 5361, 5362, 5363, 5364, 5365, 5366, 5367, 5368, 5369, 5370, 5371, 5372*]. with; as, besides, a marker which shows association with another thing or person:– with (75), and (11), together with (7), along with (6), companions (4 [*+3836*]), associates (2 [*+3836*]), accompanied by (1), accompany (1 [*+4513*]), along (1), as (1), attendant (1), both and (1), companions (1 [*+3836, 1639*]), companions (1 [*+3836, 4513*]), fellow (1 [*+3836*]), including (1), join in (1), on (1), present (1), so (1), through (1 [*+5931*]), what is more (1 [*+4246, 4047*]), when (1), NDT (6)

G5251 **συνάγω** ***synagō***, v. [59] [√*5250 + 72*]. to gather together, assemble; invite, call together:– gathered (11), gather (9), gathered together (5), met (5), assembled (3), gathering (2), invite in (2), meeting (2), met together (2), store (2), band (1), bring together (1), called a meeting (1), called together (1), came together (1), caught (1), gather (1 [*+1639*]), gather together (1), gathered around (1), got together (1 [*+2093, 3836, 899*]), got together (1), harvests (1), invited in (1), picked up (1), store away (1), went (1)

G5252 **συναγωγή** ***synagōgē***, n. [56] [→*697, 801, 2191; cf. 5250 + 72*]. synagogue, congregation, meeting, a gathering of worshipers, usually a Jewish congregation, though in some contexts it may refer to a Christian assembly; a synagogue building:– synagogue (31), synagogues (23), congregation (1), meeting (1)

G5253 **συναγωνίζομαι** ***synagōnizomai***, v. [1] [√*5250 + 74*]. to join in a struggle, help, assist:– join in struggle (1)

G5254 **συναθλέω** ***synathleō***, v. [2] [√*5250 + 123*]. to contend at one's side, together:– contended at side (1), striving together (1)

G5255 **συναθροίζω** ***synathroizō***, v. [2] [√*5250 + 125*]. to bring together; (pass.) to be gathered:– called together (1), gathered (1 [*+1639*])

G5256 **συναίρω** ***synairō***, v. [3] [√*5250 + 149*]. to settle (monetary accounts):– settle (1), settled (1), settlement (1)

G5257 **συναιχμάλωτος** ***synaichmalōtos***, n. [3] [√*5250 + 171*]. fellow prisoner:– fellow prisoner (2), in prison with (1)

G5258 **συνακολουθέω** ***synakoloutheō***, v. [3] [√*5250 + 199 [1.3]*]. to follow, accompany:– follow (1), followed (1), following (1)

G5259 **συναλίζω** ***synalizō***, v. [1] to eat with:– eating with (1)

G5260 **συναλίσκομαι** ***synaliskomai***, v. Not used in NIVEBC. [√*5250 + 274*]. to be made captive together with

G5261 **συναλλάσσω** ***synallassō***, v. [1] [√*5250 + 248*]. to reconcile:– reconcile (1 [*+1650, 1645*])

G5262 **συναναβαίνω** ***synanabainō***, v. [2] [√*5250 + 324 + 326*]. to come with, travel with:– come up (1), traveled with (1)

G5263 **συνανάκειμαι** ***synanakeimai***, v. [7] [√*5250 + 324 + 3023*]. to eat with, have dinner with:– dinner guests (2), other guests (2), at the table with (1), ate with (1), eating with (1)

G5264 **συναναμείγνυμι** ***synanameignymi***, v. [3] [√*5250 + 324 + 3502*]. to associate with:– associate with (2), associate (1)

G5265 **συναναπαύομαι** ***synanapauomai***, v. [1] [√*5250 + 324 + 4264*]. to find rest together, be refreshed together:– in company be refreshed (1)

G5266 **συναναστρέφομαι** ***synanastrephomai***, v. Not used in NIVEBC. [√*5250 + 324 + 5138*]. to associate with, go about with

G5267 **συναντάω** ***synantaō***, v. [6] [√*5250 + 505*]. to meet; to happen to:– met (4), happen (1), meet (1)

G5268 **συνάντησις** ***synantēsis***, n. Not used in NIVEBC. [√*5250 + 505*]. meeting

G5269 **συναντιλαμβάνομαι** ***synantilambanomai***, v. [2] [√*5250 + 505 + 3284*]. to help, come to the aid of:– help (1), helps (1)

G5270 **συναπάγω** ***synapagō***, v. [3] [√*5250 + 608 + 72*]. (pass.) to be led away, carried off; to associate with (the lowly):– associate with (1), carried away (1), led astray (1)

G5271 **συναποθνῄσκω** ***synapothnēskō***, v. [3] [√*5250 + 608 + 2569*]. to die with:– die with (2), died with (1)

G5272 **συναπόλλυμι** ***synapollymi***, v. [1] [√*5250 + 608 + 3897*]. (mid.) to die with, perish with:– killed with (1)

G5273 **συναποστέλλω** ***synapostellō***, v. [1] [√*5250 + 690*]. to send with:– sent with (1)

G5274 **συναρμολογέω** ***synarmologeō***, v. [2] [√*5250 + 764 + 3306*]. (pass.) to be joined together, fit together:– joined (1), joined together (1)

G5275 **συναρπάζω** ***synarpazō***, v. [4] [√*5250 + 773*]. to seize; (pass.) to be caught, seized:– seized (3), caught (1)

G5276 **συναυλίζομαι** ***synaulizomai***, v. Not used in NIVEBC. [√*5250 + 887*]. (mid.) to spend the night with

G5277 **συναυξάνω** ***synauxanō***, v. [1] [√*5250 + 889*]. to grow together:– grow together (1)

G5278 **σύνδεσμος** ***syndesmos***, n. [4] [√*5250 + 1313*]. bond; sinew; captive:– binds together (1 [*+1639*]), bond (1), captive (1), sinews (1)

G5279 **συνδέω** ***syndeō***, v. [1] [√*5250 + 1313*]. (pass.) to be imprisoned with, bound with:– together with in prison (1)

G5280 **συνδοξάζω** ***syndoxazō***, v. [1] [√*5250 + 1518*]. (pass.) to be glorified with, share glory with:– share in glory (1)

G5281 **σύνδουλος** ***syndoulos***, n. [10] [√*5250 + 1528*]. fellow servant, fellow slave:– fellow servant (6), fellow servants (3), other servants (1)

G5282 **συνδρομή** ***syndromē***, n. [1] [√*5250 + 5556*]. running together:– running from all directions (1)

G5283 **συνεγείρω** ***synegeirō***, v. [3] [√*5250 + 1586*]. to raise up with:– raised with (2), raised up with (1)

G5284 **συνέδριον** ***synedrion***, n. [22] [√*5250 + 1612*]. Sanhedrin; (local) council:– sanhedrin (17), local councils (2), court (1), members of the sanhedrin (1), them[S] (1 [*+3836, 899*])

G5285 **συνέδριος** ***synedrios***, n. Not used in NIVEBC. [√*5250 + 1612*]. member of the council

G5286 **σύνεδρος** ***synedros***, n. Not used in NIVEBC. [√*5250 + 1612*]. member of the council

G5287 **συνείδησις** ***syneidēsis***, n. [30] [√*5250 + 3857 or* 3972]. conscience:– conscience (24), consciences (4), conscious (1), guilty (1)

G5288 **συνείδω** ***syneidō***, v. Not used in NIVEBC. [√*5250 + 3857 or* 3972]. to consider, know

G5289 **σύνειμι[1]** ***syneimi[1]***, v. [2] [√*5250 + 1639*]. to be with; (n.) companion:– companions (1), were with (1)

G5290 **σύνειμι[2]** ***syneimi[2]***, v. [1] [√*5250 + 1640*]. to gather together, come together:– gathering (1)

G5291 **συνεισέρχομαι** ***syneiserchomai***, v. [2] [√*5250 + 1650 + 2262*]. to enter together with:– entered with (1), he went with into (1)

G5292 **συνέκδημος** ***synekdēmos***, n. [2] [√*5250 + 1666 + 1322*]. traveling companion:– accompany (1), traveling companions (1)

G5293 **συνεκλεκτός** ***syneklektos***, a. [1] [√*5250 + 1666 + 3306*]. chosen together with:– chosen together (1)

G5294 **συνεκπορεύομαι** ***synekporeuomai***, v. Not used in NIVEBC. [√*5250 + 1666 + 4513*]. to go out with

G5295 **συνελαύνω** ***synelaunō***, v. Not used in NIVEBC. [√*5250 + 1785*]. to drive, force, bring

G5296 **συνεπιμαρτυρέω** ***synepimartyreō***, v. [1] [√*5250 + 2093 + 3459*]. to testify at the same time:– testified (1)

G5297 **συνεπίσκοπος** ***synepiskopos***, n. Not used in NIVEBC. [√*5250 + 2093 + 5023*]. fellow overseer

G5298 **συνεπιτίθημι** ***synepitithēmi***, v. [1] [√*5250 + 2093 + 5502*]. (mid.) to join in an accusation, join in an attack:– joined in (1)

G5299 **συνέπομαι** ***synepomai***, v. [1] [√*5250*]. to accompany:– accompanied (1)

G5300 **συνεργέω** ***synergeō***, v. [5] [√*5250 + 2240*]. to work together, work with; (n.) fellow worker:– co-workers (1), joins in the work (1), worked with (1), working together (1), works (1)

G5301 **συνεργός** ***synergos***, a. [13] [√*5250 + 2240*]. fellow worker:– co-worker (4), co-workers (3), co-worker in service (1), co-workers in service (1), fellow worker (1), fellow workers (1), work together (1 [*+1181*]), work with (1 [*+1639*])

G5302 **συνέρχομαι** ***synerchomai***, v. [30] [√*5250 + 2262*]. to come together, gather, assemble; to go along with, accompany:– came together (3), come together (3), gathered (3), come with (2 [*+1639*]), accompanied (1), assemble (1), assembled (1), been with (1), came (1), came with (1), come along with (1), come together (1 [*+2093, 3836, 899*]), comes together (1 [*+2093, 3836, 899*]), continued with (1), gather (1), gathered around (1), gathering (1), going with (1), meet together (1), meetings (1), there (1), went along (1), went with (1)

G5303 **συνεσθίω** ***synesthiō***, v. [5] [√*5250 + 2266*]. to eat with:– ate with (2), eat with (2), eats with (1)

G5304 **σύνεσις** ***synesis***, n. [7] [√*918; cf. 5250*]. understanding, insight; intelligence, the faculty of comprehension, often referring to wisdom and insight in spiritual matters:– understanding (4), insight (2), intelligence (1)

G5305 **συνετός** ***synetos***, a. [4] [√*918; cf. 5250*]. intelligent, learned, with good sense:– intelligent (2), learned (2)

G5306 **συνευδοκέω** ***syneudokeō***, v. [6] [√*5250 + 2292 + 1506*]. to approve of, give approval; to be willing:– approve of (2), willing (2), approved (1 [*+1639*]), giving approval (1)

G5307 **συνευωχέομαι** ***syneuōcheomai***, v. [2] [√*5250 + 2292 + 2400*]. to partake in a feast together:– eating with (1), feast with (1)

G5308 **συνεφίστημι** ***synephistēmi***, v. [1] [√*5250 + 2093 + 2705*]. to join in an attack:– joined in the attack (1)

G5309 **συνέχω** ***synechō***, v. [12] [√*5250 + 2400*]. to cover (ears); to crowd (against); to guard, hold in custody; to compel, urge on; (pass.) to suffer, be distressed; to be devoted to:– suffering (2), compels (1), constraint under (1), covered (1), crowding (1), devoted exclusively (1), guarding (1), hem in (1), overcome (1 [*+3489*]), suffering from (1), torn (1)

G5310 **συνήδομαι** ***synēdomai***, v. [1] [√*5250 + 2454*]. to delight in agreement:– delight in (1)

G5311 **συνήθεια** ***synētheia***, n. [3] [√*5250 + 1621*]. custom, practice:– accustomed to (1), custom (1), practice (1)

G5312 **συνηλικιώτης** ***synēlikiōtēs***, n. [1] [√*5250 + 2462*]. person of one's own age, contemporary:– of own age (1)

G5313 **συνθάπτω** ***synthaptō***, v. [2] [√*5250 + 2507*]. (pass.) to be buried with:– buried with (2)

G5314 **συνθλάω** ***synthlaō***, v. [2] [√*5250*]. (pass.) to be broken to pieces:– broken to pieces (2)

G5315 **συνθλίβω** ***synthlibō***, v. [2] [√*5250 + 2567*]. to press around, crowd against:– crowding against (1), pressed around (1)

G5316 **συνθρύπτω** ***synthryptō***, v. [1] [√*5250 + 2586*]. to break:– breaking (1)

G5317 **συνίημι** ***syniēmi***, v. [26] [√*918; cf. 5250*]. to understand, realize:– understand (14), understood (4), understanding (3), understands (2), did[S] (1), realize (1), wise (1)

G5318 **συνιστάω** ***synistaō***, v. Not used in NIVEBC. [√*5250 + 2705*]. see *5319*

G5319 συνίστημι *synistēmi*, v. [16] [√*5250* + *2705*]. to commend, recommend; to demonstrate, bring out, prove to be; (intr.) to stand with; to hold together; to be formed:– commend (6), commends (2), brings out more clearly (1), commended (1), demonstrates (1), formed (1), hold together (1), proved (1), really would be (1), standing with (1)

G5320 συνίω *syniō*, v. Not used in NIVEBC. [√*918*; *cf. 5250*]. to understand, realize

G5321 συνοδεύω *synodeuō*, v. [1] [√*5250* + *3847*]. to travel with:– traveling with (1)

G5322 συνοδία *synodia*, n. [1] [√*5250* + *3847*]. company of travelers, caravan:– company (1)

G5323 σύνοιδα *synoida*, v. [2] [√*5250* + *3857*]. to share knowledge with; to be conscious (of oneself):– conscience is clear (1 [+*4029*]), full knowledge (1)

G5324 συνοικέω *synoikeō*, v. [1] [√*5250* + *3875*]. to live with:– live with (1)

G5325 συνοικοδομέω *synoikodomeō*, v. [1] [√*5250* + *3875* + *1560*]. (pass.) to be built up together:– built together (1)

G5326 συνομιλέω *synomileō*, v. [1] [√*5250* + *3917*]. to talk with, converse with:– talking with (1)

G5327 συνομορέω *synomoreō*, v. [1] [√*5250* + *3927* + *4000*]. to be next door to:– next door (1)

G5328 συνοράω *synoraō*, v. [2] [√*5250* + *3972*]. to realize, become aware:– dawned on (1), found out (1)

G5329 συνορία *synoria*, n. Not used in NIVEBC. [√*5250* + *4000*]. neighboring country

G5330 συνοχή *synochē*, n. [2] [√*5250* + *2400*]. anguish, distress:– anguish (2)

G5331 συνταράσσω *syntarassō*, v. Not used in NIVEBC. [√*5250* + *5429*]. to throw into confusion, disturb

G5332 συντάσσω *syntassō*, v. [3] [√*5250* + *5435*]. to command, direct, instruct:– commanded (1), directed (1), instructed (1)

G5333 συντέλεια *synteleia*, n. [6] [√*5250* + *5465*]. end, close, completion:– end (4), culmination (1), very end (1)

G5334 συντελέω *synteleō*, v. [6] [√*5250* + *5465*]. to finish, accomplish; (pass.) to be fulfilled, be over, accomplished:– end (1), finality (1), finished (1), fulfilled (1), make (1), over (1)

G5335 συντέμνω *syntemnō*, v. [1] [√*5250* + *5533*]. to cut short, speed up:– speed (1)

G5336 συντεχνίτης *syntechnitēs*, n. Not used in NIVEBC. [√*5250* + *5492*]. one who follows the same trade

G5337 συντηρέω *syntēreō*, v. [3] [√*5250* + *5498*]. to protect, defend; to treasure, preserve in memory; (pass.) to be preserved:– preserved (1), protected (1), treasured up (1)

G5338 συντίθημι *syntithēmi*, v. [3] [√*5250* + *5502*]. (mid.) to agree, decide:– agreed (2), decided (1)

G5339 συντόμως *syntomōs*, adv. [1] [√*5250* + *5533*]. briefly:– briefly (1)

G5340 συντρέχω *syntrechō*, v. [3] [√*5250* + *5556*]. to run together, go together; by extension, to be closely associated in a particular behavior or undertaking:– came running (1), join (1), ran (1)

G5341 συντρίβω *syntribō*, v. [7] [√*5250* + *5561*]. to break, destroy; (pass.) to be broken, bruised, dashed to pieces:– broke (2), broken (1), bruised (1), crush (1), dash to pieces (1), destroying (1)

G5342 σύντριμμα *syntrimma*, n. [1] [√*5250* + *5561*]. ruin, destruction:– ruin (1)

G5343 σύντροφος *syntrophos*, a. [1] [√*5250* + *5555*]. brought up with (in a family); this can refer to a foster sibling or an intimate friend:– brought up with (1)

G5344 συντυγχάνω *syntynchanō*, v. [1] [√*5250* + *5593*]. to come together with, meet:– get near (1)

G5345 Συντύχη *Syntychē*, n. pr. [1] [√*5250* + *5593*]. Syntyche, "*coincidence, success*":– Syntyche (1)

G5346 συντυχία *syntychia*, n. Not used in NIVEBC. [√*5250* + *5593*]. occurrence, incident

G5347 συνυποκρίνομαι *synypokrinomai*, v. [1] [√*5250* + *5679* + *3212*]. to join in one's hypocrisy:– joined in hypocrisy (1)

G5348 συνυπουργέω *synypourgeō*, v. [1] [√*5250* + *5679* + *2240*]. to join to help:– help (1)

G5349 συνωδίνω *synōdinō*, v. [1] [√*5250* + *6047*]. to join in the pains of childbirth, suffer agony together:– in the pains of childbirth (1)

G5350 συνωμοσία *synōmosia*, n. [1] [√*5250* + *3923*]. plot, conspiracy:– plot (1)

G5351 Σύρα *Syra*, n. pr. Not used in NIVEBC. [√*5354*]. Syrian woman

G5352 Συράκουσαι *Syrakousai*, n. pr. [1] Syracuse:– Syracuse (1)

G5353 Συρία *Syria*, n. pr. [8] [√*5354*]. Syria:– Syria (7), Syria (1 [+*3836*, *3107*, *3836*])

G5354 Σύρος *Syros*, n. pr. g. [1] [→*5351*, *5353*, *5355*, *5356*]. Syrian:– Syrian (1)

G5355 Συροφοινίκισσα *Syrophoinikissa*, n. pr. g. [1] [√*5354* + *5836*]. woman of Syrian Phoenicia:– Syrian Phoenicia (1)

G5356 Συροφοίνισσα *Syrophoinissa*, n. pr. g. Not used in NIVEBC. [√*5354* + *5836*]. Syrophoenician

G5357 συρρήγνυμι *syrrēgnymi*, v. Not used in NIVEBC. [√*5250* + *4838*]. to dash together

G5358 Σύρτις *Syrtis*, n. pr. [1] [√*5359*]. Syrtis:– sandbars of Syrtis (1)

G5359 σύρω *syrō*, v. [5] [→*2955*, *5358*]. to drag, tow; to sweep:– dragged (2), dragged off (1), swept out of (1), towing (1)

G5360 συσπαράσσω *sysparassō*, v. [2] [√*5250* + *5060*]. to cause to convulse:– convulsion (1), threw into a convulsion (1)

G5361 σύσσημον *syssēmon*, n. [1] [√*5250* + *4956*]. signal:– signal (1)

G5362 σύσσωμος *syssōmos*, a. [1] [√*5250* + *5393*]. co-member of a body:– members together of one body (1)

G5363 συστασιαστής *systasiastēs*, n. Not used in NIVEBC. [√*5250* + *2705*]. fellow insurrectionist

G5364 συστατικός *systatikos*, a. [1] [√*5250* + *2705*]. commendatory, recommended:– recommendation (1)

G5365 συσταυρόω *systauroō*, v. [5] [√*5250* + *5089*]. (pass.) to be crucified with:– crucified with (5)

G5366 συστέλλω *systellō*, v. [2] [√*5250* + *5097*]. to wrap up, cover up; (pass.) to be shortened, limited:– short (1), wrapped up (1)

G5367 συστενάζω *systenazō*, v. [1] [√*5250* + *5101*]. to join in groaning, groan together:– groaning (1)

G5368 συστοιχέω *systoicheō*, v. [1] [√*5250* + *5123*]. to correspond:– corresponds to (1)

G5369 συστρατιώτης *systratiōtēs*, n. [2] [√*5250* + *5131*]. fellow soldier:– fellow soldier (2)

G5370 συστρέφω *systrephō*, v. [2] [√*5250* + *5138*]. to gather up, bring together:– came together (1), gathered (1)

G5371 συστροφή *systrophē*, n. [2] [√*5250* + *5138*]. commotion, disorderly gathering, mob; conspiracy, plot:– commotion (1), conspiracy (1)

G5372 συσχηματίζω *syschēmatizō*, v. [2] [√*5250* + *5386*]. (mid.) to conform to a pattern or mold; (pass.) to be conformed to a pattern or mold:– conform to (1), conform to the pattern (1)

G5373 Συχάρ *Sychar*, n. pr. [1] [→*4993*]. Sychar:– Sychar (1)

G5374 Συχέμ *Sychem*, n. pr. [2] Shechem, "[poss.] *shoulder [saddle of a hill]; shoulders [and upper back]*":– Shechem (2)

G5375 σφαγή *sphagē*, n. [3] [√*5377*]. slaughter:– slaughter (2), slaughtered (1)

G5376 σφάγιον *sphagion*, n. [1] [√*5377*]. offering for slaughter:– sacrifices (1)

G5377 σφάζω *sphazō*, v. [10] [→*2956*, *2957*, *5375*, *5376*]. to kill, slay, murder:– slain (5), had a wound (1), kill (1), murder (1), murdered (1), slaughtered (1)

G5378 σφάλλω *sphallō*, v. Not used in NIVEBC. [→*854*, *855*, *856*, *857*, *2195*]. (pass.) to slip, stumble, fall

G5379 σφόδρα *sphodra*, adv. [11] [→*5380*]. very, greatly, exceedingly:– very (3), terrified (2 [+*5828*]), filled with (1), greatly (1), outraged (1 [+*3382*]), overjoyed (1 [+*5897*, *5915*, *3489*]), rapidly (1), so (1)

G5380 σφοδρῶς *sphodrōs*, adv. [1] [√*5379*]. violently:– violent (1)

G5381 σφραγίζω *sphragizō*, v. [15] [√*5382*]. to seal, to put a mark on an object to show possession, authority, identity, or security:– sealed (4), seal up (2), certified (1), made sure that received (1), marked with a seal (1), placed seal of approval (1), put a seal (1), putting a seal on (1), set seal of ownership on (1), NDT (2)

G5382 σφραγίς *sphragis*, n. [16] [→*2958*, *5381*]. seal:– seal (10), seals (5), sealed (1 [+*2400*, *3836*])

G5383 σφυδρόν *sphydron*, n. [1] [√*5384*]. ankle:– ankles (1)

G5384 σφυρόν *sphyron*, n. Not used in NIVEBC. [→*5383*]. ankle or heel

G5385 σχεδόν *schedon*, adv. [3] [√*2400*]. nearly, almost:– almost (1), nearly (1), practically (1)

G5386 σχῆμα *schēma*, n. [2] [→*858*, *859*, *860*, *2360*, *2361*, *2362*, *2363*, *3571*, *5372*; *cf. 2400*]. form, outward appearance:– appearance (1), form (1)

G5387 σχίζω *schizō*, v. [11] [→*5388*]. to tear, divide; (pass.) to be torn, divided, split (in opinion):– torn (5), divided (2), split (1), tear (1), tears (1), torn open (1)

G5388 σχίσμα *schisma*, n. [8] [√*5387*]. tear, split, divide an object into parts, with an implication that the object is now damaged; by extension: division, dissension, implying discord and damage to the unity of the original group:– divided (3), divisions (2), tear (2), division (1)

G5389 σχοινίον *schoinion*, n. [2] (pl.) cords, ropes:– cords (1), ropes (1)

G5390 σχολάζω *scholazō*, v. [2] [√*5391*]. to devote oneself to; to be unoccupied, stand empty:– devote to (1), unoccupied (1)

G5391 σχολή *scholē*, n. [1] [→*5390*]. lecture hall, a building in which students meet for discussion and study, school:– lecture hall (1)

G5392 σῴζω *sōzō*, v. [106] [→*420*, *861*, *862*, *1407*, *1751*, *5396*, *5399*, *5400*, *5401*, *5402*, *5403*]. to save, rescue, deliver; to heal; by extension: to be in right relationship with God, with the implication that the condition before salvation was one of grave danger or distress:– saved (47), save (37), healed (13), survive (2), bring safely (1), cured (1), delivered (1), get better (1), made well (1), make well (1), saves (1)

G5393 σῶμα *sōma*, n. [142] [→*5362*, *5394*, *5395*]. body, the mass of anything, usually a corporeal tissue, human, animal, or plant, though it can also refer to a heavenly body; the church is said to be like a (human) body, emphasizing its essential unity with very important diversities of function within the unity:– body (114), bodies (15), animal (1), dead (1), dead body (1), in person (1 [+*3836*, *4242*, *3836*]), its[s] (1 [+*3836*]), physical (1), physically (1), reality (1), sold as slaves (1 [+*2779*, *6034*]), suffering[s] (1 [+*1877*]), the parts[s] (1 [+*3836*]), whole self (1), NDT (1)

G5394 σωματικός *sōmatikos*, a. [2] [√*5393*]. bodily, physical:– bodily (1), physical (1)

G5395 σωματικῶς *sōmatikōs*, adv. [1] [√*5393*]. in bodily form, corporeally:– in bodily form (1)

G5396 Σώπατρος *Sōpatros*, n. pr. [1] [√*5392* + *4252*]. Sopater, "*saving one's father*":– Sopater (1)

G5397 σωρεύω *sōreuō*, v. [2] [→*2197*]. to heap up, pile up; (pass.) to be loaded down:– heap on (1), loaded down with (1)

G5398 Σωσθένης *Sōsthenēs*, n. pr. [2] Sosthenes:– Sosthenes (2)

G5399 Σωσίπατρος *Sōsipatros*, n. pr. [1] [√*5392* + *4252*]. Sosipater, "*saving one's father*":– Sosipater (1)

G5400 σωτήρ *sōtēr*, n. [24] [√*5392*]. Savior, one who delivers from grave danger; note that in the NT this always refers to God the Father and Jesus Christ as Savior of believers from righteous wrath to a proper relationship with God:– savior (24)

G5401 σωτηρία *sōtēria*, n. [45] [√*5392*]. salvation, rescue, deliverance, the state of not being in grave danger and so being safe; this can refer to ordinary dangers and conditions on earth, but it usually refers to the state of believers being safe from righteous wrath in a proper relationship with God:– salvation (36), saved (5), deliverance (1), rescue (1 [+*1443*]), save (1), survive (1)

G5402 σωτήριον *sōtērion*, n. [4] [√*5392*]. salvation; this word can focus on the message or means of salvation:– salvation (4)

G5403 σωτήριος *sōtērios*, a. [1] [√*5392*]. bringing salvation, saving, delivering:– offers salvation (1)

G5404 σωφρονέω *sōphroneō*, v. [6] [→*5405*, *5406*, *5407*, *5408*, *5409*; *cf. 5856*]. to be in a right state of mind, have sober judgment; to be self-controlled:– in right mind (3), alert (1), self-controlled (1), sober judgment (1)

G5405 σωφρονίζω *sōphronizō*, v. [1] [√*5404*]. to train, encourage, advise, urge:– urge (1)

G5406 σωφρονισμός *sōphronismos*, n. [1] [√*5404*]. self-discipline, with an implication that this discipline demonstrates prudence and wisdom:– self-discipline (1)

G5407 σωφρόνως *sōphronōs*, adv. [1] [√*5404*]. in self-control:– self-controlled (1)

G5408 σωφροσύνη *sōphrosynē*, n. [3] [√*5404*]. propriety, appropriateness; reasonableness, mental soundness:– propriety (2), reasonable (1)

G5409 σώφρων sōphrōn, a. [4] [√*5404*]. self-controlled, implied to be wise and prudent in nature:– self-controlled (4)

G5410 τ t, letter. Not used in NIVEBC. letter of the Greek alphabet

G5411 ταβέρναι tabernai, n. Not used in NIVEBC. [→ *5553*]. tavern, shop, store

G5412 Ταβιθά Tabitha, n. pr. [2] [√*cf. 2496*]. Tabitha, "*gazelle*":– Tabitha (2)

G5413 τάγμα tagma, n. [1] [√*5435*]. turn, order, arrangement:– turn (1 [+*2625*])

G5414 τακτός taktos, a. [1] [√*5435*]. appointed, fixed:– appointed (1)

G5415 ταλαιπωρέω talaipōreō, v. [1] [√*5417*]. to grieve, lament:– grieve (1)

G5416 ταλαιπωρία talaipōria, n. [2] [√*5417*]. misery, distress:– misery (2)

G5417 ταλαίπωρος talaipōros, a. [2] [→*5415, 5416*]. wretched, miserable:– wretched (2)

G5418 ταλαντιαῖος talantiaios, a. [1] [√*5419*]. weighing a talent (about 57 to 80 lbs.):– weighing a hundred pounds (1)

G5419 τάλαντον talanton, n. [13] [→*5418*]. talent (weight and monetary unit; about 57 to 80 lbs.); a talent of silver was about 6,000 days' wages (denarii) of a common laborer and a talent of gold was about 180,000 day's wages, often implying a vast, unattainable amount:– bags of gold (7), bag of gold (2), bags (1), gold (1), NDT (2)

G5420 ταλιθά talitha, l.[n.] [1] [√*cf. 4813*]. talitha (Aramaic: "little girl"):– talitha (1)

G5421 ταμεῖον tameion, n. [4] [√*5533*]. room, inner room, storeroom:– inner rooms (2), room (1), storeroom (1)

G5422 τανῦν tanyn, contr. [art.+adv.] Not used in NIVEBC. [√*3836 + 3814*]. concerning the present, now

G5423 τάξις taxis, n. [9] [√*5435*]. order, succession; kind, nature:– order (6), disciplined (1), on duty (1 [+*1877, 3836*]), orderly way (1 [+*2848*])

G5424 ταπεινός tapeinos, a. [8] [→*5425, 5426, 5427, 5428*]. humble, lowly, downcast, timid:– humble (4), downcast (1), in humble circumstances (1), of low position (1), timid (1)

G5425 ταπεινοφροσύνη tapeinophrosynē, n. [7] [√*5424 + 5856*]. humility, humbleness, modesty:– humility (6), humble (1)

G5426 ταπεινόφρων tapeinophrōn, a. [1] [√*5424 + 5856*]. humble:– humble (1)

G5427 ταπεινόω tapeinoō, v. [14] [√*5424*]. (act.) to humble (oneself), lower (oneself); (pass.) to be humbled, brought low, in need:– humble (6), humbled (4), in need (1), lower (1), made low (1), takes the lowly position (1)

G5428 ταπείνωσις tapeinōsis, n. [4] [√*5424*]. humbleness, lowliness, humiliation:– humiliation (2), humble state (1), lowly (1)

G5429 ταράσσω tarassō, v. [17] [→*1410, 1752, 5331, 5430, 5431*]. to trouble, disturb, throw into confusion; (pass.) to be disturbed, terrified, confused; to be stirred up:– troubled (6), disturbed (2), terrified (2), throwing into confusion (2), frightened (1), startled (1), stirred (1), stirring up (1), thrown into turmoil (1)

G5430 ταραχή tarachē, n. Not used in NIVEBC. [√*5429*]. disturbance

G5431 τάραχος tarachos, n. [2] [√*5429*]. commotion; disturbance:– commotion (1), disturbance (1)

G5432 Ταρσεύς Tarseus, n. pr. g. [2] [√*5433*]. Tarsus:– from Tarsus (2)

G5433 Ταρσός Tarsos, n. pr. [3] [→*5432*]. Tarsus:– Tarsus (3)

G5434 ταρταρόω tartaroō, v. [1] to send to hell, hold captive in Tartarus; a derivative of the Greek noun "Tartarus," a place of torture and torment lower than Hades in Greek and Jewish apocalyptic literature, not found in the NT:– sent to hell (1)

G5435 τάσσω tassō, v. [8] [→*421, 530, 538, 698, 863, 864, 865, 1408, 1409, 1411, 2112, 2198, 2199, 4705, 4726, 5332, 5413, 5414, 5423, 5717, 5718*]. (act./mid.) to appoint, determine, arrange; devote; (pass.) to be established, appointed, assigned:– appointed (2), arranged (1), assigned (1), devoted (1), established (1), told (1), NDT (1)

G5436 ταῦρος tauros, n. [4] bull, ox:– bulls (3), oxen (1)

G5437 ταὐτά tauta, contr. [art.+p.] Not used in NIVEBC. [√*3836 + 899*]. the same things

G5438 ταφή taphē, n. [1] [√*5439*]. burial place:– burial place (1)

G5439 τάφος taphos, n. [7] [→*1946, 1947, 5438; cf. 2507*]. tomb, grave:– tomb (4), tombs (2), graves (1)

G5440 τάχα tacha, adv. [2] [√*5444*]. perhaps, possibly:– perhaps (1), possibly (1)

G5441 ταχέως tacheōs, adv. [15] [√*5444*]. quickly, in haste; very soon:– quickly (6), soon (4), as soon as possible (1 [+*6055*]), easily (1), hasty (1), outran (1 [+*4731*]), very soon (1)

G5442 ταχινός tachinos, a. [2] [√*5444*]. swift; soon, imminent:– soon (1), swift (1)

G5443 τάχος tachos, n. [8] [√*5444*]. quickness, immediateness; (in pp. phrase) quickly, immediately, soon:– soon (4 [+*1877*]), immediately (1 [+*1877*]), quick (1 [+*1877*]), quickly (1 [+*1877*]), soon (1 [+*1877*])

G5444 ταχύς tachys, a. [13] [→*5440, 5441, 5442, 5443*]. quick, swift; (adv.) quickly, momentarily, soon:– soon (6), quickly (3), quick (2), hurried (1), in the next moment (1)

G5445 τέ te, pt. [214] [→*1664, 1668, 3612, 4020, 4021, 4030, 4046, 4121, 5538, 6063*]. and, but (often not translated) ; with *2779*, "both...and":– and (48), both (14), then (5), but (4), so (3), alike (2), and also (2), even (2), also (1), as (1), because (1), including (1), or (1 [+*1569*]), really (1), that is (1), whether (1), whether (1 [+*1569*]), yes (1 [+*2285*]), NDT (124)

G5446 τεῖχος teichos, n. [9] [→*3546, 5526*]. wall:– wall (6), walls (3)

G5447 τεκμήριον tekmērion, n. [1] convincing proof:– convincing proofs (1)

G5448 τεκνίον teknion, n. [8] [√*5503*]. dear children, little children:– dear children (7), children (1)

G5449 τεκνογονέω teknogoneō, v. [1] [√*5503 + 1181*]. to have children, bear a child:– have children (1)

G5450 τεκνογονία teknogonia, n. [1] [√*5503 + 1181*]. childbearing:– childbearing (1)

G5451 τέκνον teknon, n. [99] [√*5503*]. child, son, daughter, offspring, descendant:– children (73), son (14), child (5), children's (2), brood (1), childless (1 [+*4024*]), daughters (1), deserving of (1), sons (1)

G5452 τεκνοτροφέω teknotropheō, v. [1] [√*5503 + 5555*]. to bring up children:– bringing up children (1)

G5453 τεκνόω teknoō, v. Not used in NIVEBC. [√*5503*]. to bear (a child)

G5454 τέκτων tektōn, n. [2] [√*5492*]. carpenter, woodworker; more generally: construction worker, including stonemason and metalworker:– carpenter (1), carpenter's (1)

G5455 τέλειος teleios, a. [19] [√*5465*]. perfect, mature, finished:– perfect (9), mature (5), adults (1), completeness (1), finish (1 [+*2400*]), fully mature (1), mature (1 [+*467*])

G5456 τελειότης teleiotēs, n. [2] [√*5465*]. perfection, maturity, completeness:– maturity (1), perfect unity (1)

G5457 τελειόω teleioō, v. [23] [√*5465*]. to perfect, complete, finish; (pass.) to reach a goal, be fulfilled, completed, made perfect:– made perfect (7), made complete (4), finish (3), make perfect (2), arrived at goal (1), clear (1), complete (1), finishing (1), fulfilled (1), over (1), reach goal (1)

G5458 τελείως teleiōs, adv. [1] [√*5465*]. fully, completely, perfectly:– fully (1)

G5459 τελείωσις teleiōsis, n. [2] [√*5465*]. perfection, accomplishment, fulfillment:– fulfill (1 [+*1639*]), perfection (1)

G5460 τελειωτής teleiōtēs, n. [1] [√*5465*]. perfecter:– perfecter (1)

G5461 τελεσφορέω telesphoreō, v. [1] [√*5465 + 5770*]. to mature (to fruitfulness):– mature (1)

G5462 τελευτάω teleutaō, v. [11] [→*5463; cf. 5465*]. to die:– died (5), die (2), put to death (2 [+*2505*]), dead (1), end was near (1)

G5463 τελευτή teleutē, n. [1] [√*5462*]. death:– death (1)

G5464 τελέω teleō, v. [28] [√*5465*]. to finish, complete, fulfill; (pass.) to be finished, be completed, fulfilled, perfected:– finished (9), completed (3), fulfilled (3), ended (2), pay (2), accomplished (1), carried out (1), done (1), finish (1), gratify (1), keep (1), made perfect (1), obeys (1), over (1)

G5465 τέλος telos, n. [40] [→*269, 699, 1412, 1754, 2200, 3387, 3911, 4117, 4500, 5333, 5334, 5455, 5456, 5457, 5458, 5459, 5460, 5461, 5464; cf. 5462, 5467*]. end, result, outcome, finish, goal; revenue, tax, duty:– end (21), culmination (2), outcome (2), revenue (2), destiny (1), duty (1), end result (1), eventually (1 [+*1650*]), finally (1 [+*3836*]), finally brought about (1), fulfillment (1), fully (1 [+*2401*]), goal (1), last (1), result (1), result in (1), very end (1)

G5466 τελωνεῖον telōneion, n. Not used in NIVEBC. [√*5467*]. revenue or tax office

G5467 τελώνης telōnēs, n. [21] [→*803, 5466, 5467, 5468; cf. 5465 + 6050*]. tax collector:– tax collectors (15), tax collector (6)

G5468 τελώνιον telōnion, n. [3] [√*5467*]. tax collector's booth:– tax collector's booth (2), tax booth (1)

G5469 τέρας teras, n. [16] wonder, miracle, which is by implication a sign or portent:– wonders (16)

G5470 Τέρτιος Tertios, n. pr. [1] Tertius, "*third*":– Tertius (1)

G5471 Τέρτουλλος Tertoullos, n. pr. Not used in NIVEBC. Tertullus, "*third*"

G5472 Τέρτυλλος Tertyllos, n. pr. [2] Tertullus, "*third*":– Tertullus (2)

G5473 τεσσαράκοντα tessarakonta, n. num. Not used in NIVEBC. [√*5475*]. forty

G5474 τεσσαρακονταετής tessarakontaetēs, a. num. Not used in NIVEBC. [√*5475 + 2291*]. (of) forty years

G5475 τέσσαρες tessares, n. num. [41] [→*1280, 5473, 5474, 5476, 5477, 5478, 5479, 5480, 5481, 5482, 5483, 5484, 5485, 5486, 5487, 5488, 5489, 5490, 5544, 5545*]. four:– four (29), twenty-four (6 [+*1633*]), 144,000 (3 [+*1669, 5477, 5942*]), 144 (1 [+*1669, 5477*]), by four (1), eighty-four (1 [+*3837*])

G5476 τεσσαρεσκαιδέκατος tessareskaidekatos, a. num. [2] [√*5475 + 2779 + 1274*]. fourteenth:– fourteen (1), fourteenth (1)

G5477 τεσσεράκοντα tesserakonta, n. num. [22] [√*5475*]. forty:– forty (15), 144,000 (3 [+*1669, 5475, 5942*]), 144 (1 [+*1669, 5475*]), 42 (1 [+*2779, 1545*]), forty-six (1 [+*2779, 1971*]), forty-two (1 [+*2779, 1545*])

G5478 τεσσερακονταετής tesserakontaetēs, a. num. [2] [√*5475 + 2291*]. (of) forty years:– forty years (1), forty years (1 [+*5989*])

G5479 τεταρταῖος tetartaios, a. [1] [√*5475*]. fourth (day):– four days (1)

G5480 τέταρτος tetartos, a. [10] [√*5475*]. fourth in a series or collection; (n.) the fourth (fractional) part of something:– fourth (7), shortly before dawn (2 [+*5871, 3836, 3816*]), three ago (1 [+*608*])

G5481 τετράγωνος tetragōnos, a. [1] [√*5475 + 1224*]. square, cubical:– square (1)

G5482 τετράδιον tetradion, n. [1] [√*5475*]. squad of four soldiers:– squads of four each (1)

G5483 τετρακισχίλιοι tetrakischilioi, a. num. [5] [√*5475 + 5943*]. four thousand:– four thousand (5)

G5484 τετρακόσιοι tetrakosioi, a. num. [4] [√*5475*]. four hundred:– four hundred (2), 430 (1 [+*2779, 5558*]), 450 (1 [+*2779, 4299*])

G5485 τετράμηνος tetramēnos, a. [1] [√*5475 + 3604*]. (for) four months:– four months (1)

G5486 τετραπλόος tetraploos, a. [used as adv.] Not used in NIVEBC. [√*5475*]. four times (as much); same as *5487*

G5487 τετραπλοῦς tetraplous, a. [used as adv.] [1] [√*5475*]. four times (as much); same as *5486*:– four times (1)

G5488 τετράπους tetrapous, a. [3] [√*5475 + 4546*]. four-footed; (n.) four-footed animal of any kind:– four-footed animals (2), animals (1)

G5489 τετραρχέω tetrarcheō, v. [3] [√*5475 + 806*]. to be a tetrarch:– tetrarch (3)

G5490 τετράρχης tetrarchēs, n. [4] [√*5475 + 806*]. tetrarch, a ruler of less rank and authority than a king:– tetrarch (4)

G5491 τεφρόω tephroō, v. [1] [√*5606*]. to reduce to ashes by fire:– burning to ashes (1)

G5492 τέχνη technē, n. [3] [→*802, 3937, 5336, 5454, 5493; cf. 5503*]. skill, trade, craft:– skill (1), tentmaker (1 [+*5010, 3836*]), trade (1)

G5493 τεχνίτης technitēs, n. [4] [√*5492*]. craftsman, skilled worker, architect, designer, one who engages in a craft or trade, in some contexts with a focus or the design and planning of what is crafted:– craftsmen (2), architect (1), worker (1)

G5494 τήκομαι tēkomai, v. [1] (pass.) to be melted:– melt (1)

G5495 τηλαυγῶς tēlaugōs, adv. [1] [√*879*]. clearly, plainly:– clearly (1)

G5496 τηλικοῦτος tēlikoutos, p. demo. [4] [√*2462 + 4047*]. so great, so large:– so great (1), so large (1), such (1), tremendous (1 [+*3489*])

G5497 τηνικαῦτα tēnikauta, adv. Not used in NIVEBC. at that time, then

G5498 τηρέω tēreō, v. [70] [→*1413, 4190, 4191, 5337, 5499*]. to keep, guard, obey, observe:– keep (18), kept (11), obey (5), keeps (4), held (3), obeys (3), obeyed (2), protect

GREEK INDEX

(2), reserved (2), careful (1), do (1), does (1), guard (1), guarding (1), guards (1), held over (1), hold (1), hold fast (1), keep under guard (1), keeps safe (1), kept watch over (1), not marry (1), observe (1), protected (1), remains (1), save (1), saved (1), stood (1), take to heart (1)

G5499 **τήρησις** ***tērēsis***, n. [3] [√*5498*]. jail, prison, custody; keeping, observance:– jail (2), keeping (1)

G5500 **Τιβεριάς** ***Tiberias***, n. pr. [3] [√*5501*]. Tiberias:– Tiberias (2), Galilee (1)

G5501 **Τιβέριος** ***Tiberios***, n. pr. [1] [→*5500*]. Tiberius:– Tiberius (1)

G5502 **τίθημι** ***tithēmi***, v. [100] [→*118, 119, 120, 127, 292, 423, 460, 507, 509, 629, 700, 853, 1347, 1415, 1416, 1704, 1758, 1951, 2120, 2202, 2310, 2557, 2874, 2960, 3557, 3572, 3792, 3793, 3794, 3804, 3805, 3999, 4146, 4153, 4192, 4324, 4363, 4606, 4607, 4651, 4671, 4707, 4729, 5161, 5163, 5298, 5338, 5625, 5719; cf. 353, 2529, 2565, 2874*]. (act.) to place, put; (pass.) to be placed or put; (mid.) to set, appoint, decide, arrange:– put (21), laid (11), placed (10), lay down (8), lay (5), made (5), appointed (4), make (3), assign (2), knelt down (2 [+*3836, 1205*]), put in (2), puts (2), appoint (1), appointing (1), brings out (1), burial (1 [+*1650, 3645*]), committed (1), decided (1 [+*1087*]), decided (1 [+*1877, 3836, 4460*]), destined (1), falling on (1), fastened (1), fell on (1), got down on (1), knelt (1 [+*3836, 1205*]), laid down (1), lays down (1), listen carefully (1 [+*1650, 3836, 4044*]), made think (1 [+*1877, 3836, 2840*]), make up mind (1 [+*1877, 3836, 2840*]), offer (1), planted (1), set (1), set aside (1), took off (1), use to describe (1), wondered about (1 [+*1877, 3836, 2840*])

G5503 **τίκτω** ***tiktō***, v. [18] [→*866, 4757, 4758, 5448, 5449, 5450, 5451, 5452, 5453, 5527, 5817; cf. 5492*]. to give birth to; bear, produce:– born (3), give birth to (3), gave birth to (2), give birth (2), baby to be born (1), bore a child (1), gave birth (1), given birth (1), gives birth to (1), giving birth to a child (1), have baby (1), produces (1)

G5504 **τίλλω** ***tillō***, v. [3] to pick (heads of grain):– pick (3)

G5505 **Τιμαῖος** ***Timaios***, n. pr. [1] [√*5507*]. Timaeus, "*precious, valuable*":– Timaeus (1)

G5506 **τιμάω** ***timaō***, v. [21] [√*5507*]. to honor, show respect, give recognition:– honor (16), give proper recognition (1), honored (1 [+*5507*]), price set (1 [+*5507*]), show proper respect (1), NDT (1)

G5507 **τιμή** ***timē***, n. [41] [→*869, 870, 871, 872, 873, 988, 1952, 2203, 2204, 2700, 4501, 5505, 5506, 5508, 5509, 5510, 5511, 5512, 5513, 5818*]. honor, value, respect; nobility, specialness; money, cost:– honor (23), money (4), special purposes (3), price (2), respect (2), value (2), honorable (1), honored (1 [+*5506*]), precious (1), price set (1 [+*5506*]), sum (1)

G5508 **τίμιος** ***timios***, a. [13] [√*5507*]. precious, valuable, honored; costly:– precious (6), costly (2), honored (2), valuable (1), very precious (1), worth (1)

G5509 **τιμιότης** ***timiotēs***, n. [1] [√*5507*]. wealth:– wealth (1)

G5510 **Τιμόθεος** ***Timotheos***, n. pr. [24] [√*5507 + 2536*]. Timothy, "*precious one of God*":– Timothy (24)

G5511 **Τίμων** ***Timōn***, n. pr. [1] [√*5507*]. Timon, "*precious, valuable*":– Timon (1)

G5512 **τιμωρέω** ***timōreō***, v. [2] [√*5507 + 149*]. to punish:– punished (2)

G5513 **τιμωρία** ***timōria***, n. [1] [√*5507 + 149*]. punishment:– punished (1)

G5514 **τίνω** ***tinō***, v. [1] [→*702*]. to pay (a price or penalty), in context the penalty is suffering:– punished (1 [+*1472*])

G5515 **τίς** ***tis***, p. inter. [558] [→*1414, 1484, 2672, 2776, 4022*]. who?, what?, which?, why?:– what (166), who (93), why (40), what (30 [+*5516*]), which (19), who (13 [+*5516*]), whom (9), why (8 [+*1328*]), who (7 [+*5516*]), whose (7), why (7 [+*1328*]), how (6), what (6 [+*5516*]), why (6 [+*5516*]), what (5 [+*5516*]), what (5 [+*5516*]), who (5 [+*5516*]), why (5 [+*5516*]), why (5 [+*5516*]), how (4 [+*1877*]), why (4 [+*5516*]), why (4 [+*1328*]), what (3 [+*5516*]), what (3 [+*5516*]), what (3 [+*5516*]), why (3 [+*5516*]), why (3 [+*5516*]), a (2), anything (2), how is it that (2 [+*1328*]), nothing (2 [+*4024*]), one (2), something (2), what do want with (2 [+*5516*]), why (4 [+*5516*]), why (2 [+*1328, 5516*]), why (2 [+*1328*]), why (2 [+*1650*])5516]), all (1), any (1), any (1 [+*5516, 476*]), any one (1), any way (1 [+*3836*]), business (1 [+*4472*]), but (1 [+*5516*]), each (1), how (1 [+*2848*]), how could (1 [+*5516, 4022*]), how far (1), how is it that (1 [+*1328*]), meaning (1 [+*323, 1639*]), nothing (1 [+*3590*]), which (1 [+*476*]), which (1 [+*323*]), which one (1 [+*323*]), who (1 [+*476*]), why (2 [+*1650*]), why (1 [+*5516*]), who (1 [+*5516*]), why (1 [+*5516*]), one (1 [+*5516*]), one (1 [+*5516, 476*]), some (1), supper (1 [+*1268*]), that (1), the (1), those (1), was there ever (1), was there ever (1 [+*5516*]), what (1 [+*4022*]), what (1 [+*5516*]), what (1 [+*5516, 323*]), what do want with (1 [+*5516, 2779*]), what do want with (1), what do you want with us (1 [+*5516, 1609, 2779, 5148*]), what shall we do (1 [+*4036, 1639*]), what (1 [+*4005*]), what (1 [+*5516*]), what (1 [+*323, 4047*]), what does it matter (1 [+*5516*]), what's (1), where (1), who (1 [+*5516*]), why (1 [+*3836, 162*]), why (1 [+*1915*]), why (1 [+*3364*]), why (1 [+*4639*]), why (1 [+*5920*]), why do involve (1 [+*5516, 2779*]), NDT (11), NDT (2 [+

G5516 **τις** ***tis***, p. indef. [659] [→*3614, 3615, 4015*]. one, anyone, anything; some, someone, something:– some (101), a (71), anyone (68), anything (30), one (37), any (26), someone (30), what (46 [+*5515*]), something (16), why (15 [+*5515*]), who (14 [+*5515*]), why (12 [+*5515*]), who (12 [+*5515*]), certain (8), what (7 [+*5515*]), whoever (6), an (5), anybody (4), what (4 [+*5515*]), a certain (5), anyone (3 [+*1569*]), others (3), those (3), whoever (3 [+*1569*]), whoever (3 [+*1569*]), why (3 [+*5515*]), few (2), nothing (2 [+*3590*]), nothing (2 [+*4024*]), several (3), something (2 [+*5007*]), what do want with (2 [+*5515*]), what (2), whatever (3), whatever (2 [+*4005, 323*]), who (2 [+*323*]), why (2 [+*1328, 5515*]), why (2 [+*5515*]), you (2)5515]), a (1 [+*467*]), a kind of (1), and none (1 [+*4046*]), and nothing (1 [+*4028*]), another (1 [+*257*]), any (1 [+*4005, 323*]), any (1 [+*5515, 476*]), anyone (1 [+*1569*]), anyone (1 [+*4005*]), anyone (1 [+*323*]), anyone (1 [+*476*]), anyone's (1), anyone's (1 [+*4123*]), anything (1 [+*3590*]), but (1 [+*5515*]), favor[S] (1), group (1), how could (1 [+*5515, 4022*]), in keeping with (1 [+*4005, 1569*]), it[S] (1 [+*3836, 2240*]), just what (1 [+*4005*]), man's[S] (1), members (1), nobody (1 [+*4024*]), nobody (1 [+*3590*]), none (1 [+*3590*]), none (1 [+*3607*]), nothing (1 [+*4046*]), some (1 [+*476*]), one (1 [+*476*]), one (1 [+*1569*]), anyone (1 [+*1569*]), one (1 [+*1651*]), one (1 [+*5515*]), one (1 [+*5515, 476*]), other (1), people (1), person (1), persons (1), some sort (1), somebody (1), somewhat (1), that none (1 [+*3607*]), the (1), the rest (1 [+*3538*]), them (1), they (1), thing (1), things (1), was there ever (1 [+*5515*]), what (1 [+*5515, 323*]), what do want with (1 [+*5515, 2779*]), what do you want with us (1 [+*5515, 1609, 2779, 5148*]), what (1 [+*1623*]), what (1 [+*3836, 2240*]), what does it matter (1 [+*5515*]), whatever (1 [+*4005, 3836, 1569*]), whatever (1 [+*323*]), whatever (1 [+*1569*]), whatever (1 [+*3961*]), whatever (1 [+*4005, 3836, 323*]), whatever (1 [+*4246, 4005, 1569*]), who (1), who (1 [+*5515*]), why do involve (1 [+*5515, 2779*]), NDT (29), NDT (2 [+

G5517 **Τίτιος** ***Titios***, n. pr. [1] [√*5519*]. Titius:– Titius (1)

G5518 **τίτλος** ***titlos***, n. [2] sign, prepared notice, inscription:– notice (1), sign (1)

G5519 **Τίτος** ***Titos***, n. pr. [13] [→*5517*]. Titus:– Titus (13)

G5520 **τοί** ***toi***, pt. Not used in NIVEBC. [→*2486, 2792, 2793, 3530, 5521, 5522, 5523*]. surely (emphasizing reliability)

G5521 **τοιγαροῦν** ***toigaroun***, pt. [2] [√*5520 + 1142 + 4036*]. therefore, then:– therefore (2)

G5522 **τοίγε** ***toige***, pt. Not used in NIVEBC. [√*5520 + 1145*]. indeed

G5523 **τοίνυν** ***toinyn***, pt. infer. [3] [√*5520 + 3814*]. then, therefore:– then (2), therefore (1)

G5524 **τοιόσδε** ***toiosde***, a. [1] [√*3836*]. such as this, of this kind:– the (1)

G5525 **τοιοῦτος** ***toioutos***, a. [57] [√*3836 + 4047*]. such, such as this, of such a kind:– such (27), these (3), him (2), so (2), such as these (2), that (2), this (2), blemish[S] (1), he (1), like him (1), like that (1), like this (1), marry[S] (1), none other than (1), of a kind (1), other (1), related (1), similar (1), the kind of (1), them[S] (1 [+*3836, 3836, 4556*]), unequaled (1 [+*3888, 4024, 1181*]), what (1 [+*3961*]), NDT (2)

G5526 **τοῖχος** ***toichos***, n. [1] [√*5446*]. wall:– wall (1)

G5527 **τόκος** ***tokos***, n. [2] [√*5503*]. interest (on a monetary loan):– interest (2)

G5528 **τολμάω** ***tolmaō***, v. [16] [→*703, 5529, 5530, 5531, 5532*]. to dare, be bold, courageous:– dare (7), dared (5), be[S] (1), boldly (1), dares (1), venture (1)

G5529 **τολμηρός** ***tolmēros***, a. [1] [√*5528*]. bold, daring, audacious; (comp. adv.) quite boldly:– boldly (1)

G5530 **τολμηρότερον** ***tolmēroteron***, adv. comp. Not used in NIVEBC. [√*5528*]. rather boldly

G5531 **τολμηροτέρως** ***tolmēroterōs***, adv. Not used in NIVEBC. [√*5528*]. rather boldly

G5532 **τολμητής** ***tolmētēs***, n. [1] [√*5528*]. bold man, daring man:– bold (1)

G5533 **τομός** ***tomos***, a. [1] [→*598, 704, 705, 875, 1497, 2961, 3982, 4362, 4364, 5335, 5339, 5421*]. cutting, sharp; (compar.) sharper:– sharper (1)

G5534 **τόξον** ***toxon***, n. [1] [→*2962*]. bow (weapon):– bow (1)

G5535 **τοπάζιον** ***topazion***, n. [1] topaz (a bright yellow precious stone):– topaz (1)

G5536 **τόπος** ***topos***, n. [93] [→*876, 1954*]. place, location; passage (in a book); position; possibility, opportunity:– place (63), places (6), everywhere (3 [+*1877, 4246*]), area (2), room (2), change (1 [+*3567, 2351*]), everywhere (1 [+*4246*]), foothold (1), nearby (1 [+*4309, 3836, 1697*]), opportunity (1), ports (1), position (1), rocks (1 [+*5550*]), sandbar (1 [+*1458*]), seat (1), spot (1), take over (1 [+*3284, 3836*]), temple[S] (1), there (1 [+*1877, 3836*]), travel by ship (1 [+*2093, 4434*]), where (1 [+*1650, 3836*]), where (1 [+*1877, 4005*])

G5537 **τοσοῦτος** ***tosoutos***, a. [19] [√*4047*]. so great, so many, so large, so long:– so many (3), such great (3), as much (2), this (2), all (1), all these (1), enough (1), long (1), so much (1), such (1), such a great (1), such a long (1), that (1)

G5538 **τότε** ***tote***, adv. [160] [√*4005 + 5445*]. then, when, at that time:– then (106), at that time (11), so (5), finally (2 [+*4036*]), that time on (2), when (2), after (1), and (1), and (1 [+*2779*]), at that (1), formerly (1), of that time (1), once (1), that time (1), then on (1), NDT (23)

G5539 **τοὐναντίον** ***tounantion***, contr. [art.+pp.*] [3] [√*3836 + 1882*]. but, on the contrary:– on the contrary (2 [+*247*]), instead (1 [+*3437*])

G5540 **τοὔνομα** ***tounoma***, contr. [art.+n.] [1] [√*3836 + 3950*]. named, by name:– named (1)

G5541 **τοὐπίσω** ***toupisō***, contr. [art.+adv.] Not used in NIVEBC. [√*3836 + 3958*]. back, behind

G5542 **τουτέστιν** ***toutestin***, contr. [art.+v.] Not used in NIVEBC. [√*4047 + 1639*]. that is to say, by this we mean

G5543 **τράγος** ***tragos***, n. [3] [√*5592*]. male goat:– goats (3)

G5544 **τράπεζα** ***trapeza***, n. [15] [√*5475 + 4269*]. table:– table (9), tables (4), deposit (1), set a meal before (1 [+*4192*])

G5545 **τραπεζίτης** ***trapezitēs***, n. [1] [√*5475 + 4269*]. banker:– bankers (1)

G5546 **τραῦμα** ***trauma***, n. [1] [→*1765, 5547*]. (pl.) wounds:– wounds (1)

G5547 **τραυματίζω** ***traumatizō***, v. [2] [√*5546*]. to wound:– bleeding (1), wounded (1)

G5548 **τραχηλίζω** ***trachēlizō***, v. [1] [√*5549*]. (pass.) to be laid bare:– laid bare (1)

G5549 **τράχηλος** ***trachēlos***, n. [7] [→*5019, 5548*]. neck, throat:– neck (3), embraced (1 [+*2158, 2093, 3836*]), lives (1), necks (1), threw arms around (1 [+*2158, 2093, 3836*])

G5550 **τραχύς** ***trachys***, a. [2] [→*5551*]. rough, uneven:– rocks (1 [+*5536*]), rough (1)

G5551 **Τραχωνῖτις** ***Trachōnitis***, n. pr. [1] [√*5550*]. Traconitis, "*rough, stony district*":– Traconitis (1 [+*6001*])

G5552 **τρεῖς** ***treis***, n. num. [68] [→*804, 5553, 5558, 5559, 5560, 5562, 5564, 5565, 5566, 5567, 5568, 5569*]. three:– three (61), about sixty pounds (2 [+*4929*]), 153 (1 [+*1669, 4299*]), six pounds (1 [+*5955*]), thirty gallons (1 [+*3583*]), three and a half years (1 [+*2291, 2779, 3604, 1971*]), twenty-three (1 [+*1633*])

G5553 **Τρεῖς ταβέρναι** ***Treis tabernai***, n. pr. [1] [√*5552 + 5411*]. Three Taverns, "*three taverns*":– three Taverns (1)

G5554 **τρέμω** ***tremō***, v. [3] [→*1764, 1958, 5571*]. to tremble, fear:– trembling (2), afraid (1)

G5555 **τρέφω** ***trephō***, v. [9] [→*427, 1418, 1485, 1763, 1957, 2576, 5343, 5452, 5575, 5576, 5577, 5578*]. to care for, feed, nurse; (pass.) to be nurtured, cared for:– feeds (2), taken care of (2), brought up (1), fattened (1), feed (1), food supply (1), nursed (1)

G5556 **τρέχω** ***trechō***, v. [20] [→*1536, 1661, 2192, 2312, 2963, 4366, 4596, 4708, 4731, 5282, 5340, 5579, 5580, 5720*]. to run; to strive, give effort:– ran (6), run (5), running (3), effort (1), runners (1), running a race (1), running race (1), rushing (1), spread rapidly (1)

G5557 **τρῆμα** ***trēma***, n. [1] eye (the hole in a needle through which thread is passed):– eye (1)

G5558 **τριάκοντα** ***triakonta***, n. num. [11] [√*5552*]. thirty:– thirty (8), 430 (1 [+*5484, 2779*]), four miles (1 [+*5084*]), thirty-eight (1 [+*3893*])

G5559 **τριακόσιοι** ***triakosioi***, a. num. [2] [√*5552*]. three hundred:– a year's wages (1 [+*1324*]), money worth a year's wages (1 [+*1324*])

G5560 **τρίβολος** ***tribolos***, n. [2] [√*5552 + 965*]. thistle:– thistles (2)

G5561 **τρίβος** ***tribos***, n. [3] [→*1384, 1417, 4139, 5341, 5342, 5990*]. path:– paths (3)

G5562 **τριετία** ***trietia***, n. [1] [√*5552 + 2291*]. (for) three years:– three years (1)

G5563 **τρίζω** ***trizō***, v. [1] to gnash, grind:– gnashes (1)

G5564 **τρίμηνος** ***trimēnos***, a. [1] [√*5552 + 3604*]. a period of three months:– for three months (1)

G5565 **τρίς** ***tris***, adv. [12] [√*5552*]. three times:– three times (12)

G5566 **τρίστεγον *tristegon***, n. [1] [*√5552 + 5095*]. third story (of a building):– third story (1)

G5567 **τρισχίλιοι *trischilioi***, a. num. [1] [*√5552 + 5943*]. three thousand:– three thousand (1)

G5568 **τρίτον *triton***, adv. [8] [*√5552*]. third, for the third time; (n.) the third (fractional) part of something:– third time (5), third (3)

G5569 **τρίτος *tritos***, a. [48] [*√5552*]. third:– third (42), nine in the morning (2 [*+6052*]), daybreak (1), nine (1 [*+6052*]), nine in the morning (1 [*+6052, 3836, 2465*]), third time (1)

G5570 **τρίχινος *trichinos***, a. [1] [*√2582*]. made of hair, hairy:– made of goat hair (1)

G5571 **τρόμος *tromos***, n. [5] [*√5554*]. trembling, fear:– trembling (3), fear (1), trembling (1 [*+2400*])

G5572 **τροπή *tropē***, n. [1] [*→426, 706, 1762, 1956, 1959, 2205, 2206, 2207, 2208, 2365, 3573, 4365, 4502, 4730, 5573, 5574*]. shifting, turning, variation, change:– shifting (1)

G5573 **τρόπος *tropos***, n. [13] [*√5572*]. manner, way, kind; way of life:– way (5), as (3 [*+4005*]), just as (2 [*+2848, 4005*]), in the same way (1 [*+4048, 4005*]), just as (1 [*+4005*]), lives (1)

G5574 **τροποφορέω *tropophoreō***, v. [1] [*√5572 + 5770*]. to endure, put up with:– endured conduct (1)

G5575 **τροφή *trophē***, n. [16] [*√5555*]. food, nourishment:– food (12), ate together (1 [*+3561*]), eat (1 [*+3561*]), eaten as much as wanted (1 [*+3170*]), keep (1)

G5576 **Τρόφιμος *Trophimos***, n. pr. [3] [*√5555*]. Trophimus, "*nourished [child]*":– Trophimus (3)

G5577 **τροφός *trophos***, n. [1] [*√5555*]. mother, nurse:– nursing mother (1)

G5578 **τροφοφορέω *trophophoreō***, v. Not used in NIVEBC. [*√5555 + 5770*]. to care for (as a nurse)

G5579 **τροχιά *trochia***, n. [1] [*√5556*]. path, course:– paths (1)

G5580 **τροχός *trochos***, n. [1] [*√5556*]. wheel; (fig.) whole course (of life):– course (1)

G5581 **τρύβλιον *tryblion***, n. [2] bowl:– bowl (2)

G5582 **τρυγάω *trygaō***, v. [2] to gather or pick (grapes):– gather (1), gathered (1)

G5583 **τρυγών *trygōn***, n. [1] (pl.) doves, turtledoves:– doves (1)

G5584 **τρυμαλιά *trymalia***, n. [1] [*→5585*]. eye (the tear-drop shaped hole of a needle through which thread is passed):– eye (1)

G5585 **τρύπημα *trypēma***, n. [1] [*√5584*]. eye (of a needle):– eye (1)

G5586 **Τρύφαινα *Tryphaina***, n. pr. [1] [*√5588*]. Tryphena, "*dainty*":– Tryphena (1)

G5587 **τρυφάω *tryphaō***, v. [1] [*√5588*]. to live in luxury, lead a life of self-indulgence:– lived in luxury (1)

G5588 **τρυφή *tryphē***, n. [2] [*→1960, 5586, 5587, 5589; cf. 2586*]. luxury, splendor; carousal, indulgence, reveling:– carouse (1), luxury (1)

G5589 **Τρυφῶσα *Tryphōsa***, n. pr. [1] [*√5588*]. Tryphosa, "*delicate*":– Tryphosa (1)

G5590 **Τρῳάς *Trōas***, n. pr. [6] Troas:– Troas (6)

G5591 **Τρωγύλλιον *Trōgyllion***, n. pr. Not used in NIVEBC. Trogyllium

G5592 **τρώγω *trōgō***, v. [6] [*→5543*]. to eat, feed on:– eats (2), feeds on (2), eating (1), shared (1)

G5593 **τυγχάνω *tynchanō***, v. [12] [*→1950, 1961, 2209, 2366, 4193, 5344, 5345, 5346, 5608, 5659*]. to take part in; to obtain, provide; (intr.) to happen a certain way, to be extraordinary; perhaps:– enjoyed (1), extraordinary (1 [*+4024, 3836*]), gain (1), helped (1 [*+2135*]), obtain (1), perhaps (1), perhaps (1 [*+1623*]), provide for (1), received (1), taking part (1), undoubtedly (1 [*+1623*]), unusual (1 [*+4024, 3836*])

G5594 **τυμπανίζω *tympanizō***, v. [1] [*√5597*]. (pass.) to be tortured, tormented:– tortured (1)

G5595 **τυπικῶς *typikōs***, adv. [1] [*√5597*]. as an example:– examples (1)

G5596 **τύπος *typos***, n. [15] [*√5597*]. pattern, model, example, type, a visual form to be copied, such as in crafting an idol; by extension: a pattern of behavior to be emulated:– pattern (4), model (3), example (2), examples (2), as follows (1 [*+2400, 3836, 4047*]), idols (1), marks (1), where[S] (1 [*+1650, 3836*])

G5597 **τύπτω *typtō***, v. [13] [*→531, 1963, 5594, 5595, 5596, 5721*]. to strike, beat, wound:– beat (5), struck (3), strike (2), beating (1), slaps (1), wound (1)

G5598 **Τύραννος[1] *Tyrannos[1]***, n. pr. [1] [*√5599*]. Tyrannus, "*ruler*":– Tyrannus (1)

G5599 **τύραννος[2] *tyrannos[2]***, n. Not used in NIVEBC. [*→5598*]. despotic ruler, tyrant

G5600 **τυρβάζω *tyrbazō***, v. Not used in NIVEBC. (mid.) trouble oneself; (pass.) to be troubled

G5601 **Τύριος *Tyrios***, n. pr. g. [1] [*√5602*]. Tyrian:– people of Tyre (1)

G5602 **Τύρος *Tyros***, n. pr. [11] [*→5601*]. Tyre, "*rocky place*":– Tyre (11)

G5603 **τυφλός *typhlos***, a. [49] [*→5604*]. blind; (n.) blind person:– blind (49)

G5604 **τυφλόω *typhloō***, v. [3] [*√5603*]. to cause blindness, deprive of sight:– blinded (2), blinded (1 [*+3836, 4057*])

G5605 **τυφόομαι *typhoomai***, v. [3] [*√5606*]. (pass.) to be or become conceited, implying foolishness:– conceited (3)

G5606 **τύφω *typhō***, v. [1] [*→5491, 5605*]. (pass.) to smolder, smoke:– smoldering (1)

G5607 **τυφωνικός *typhōnikos***, a. Not used in NIVEBC. of hurricane force€ [1]:– of hurricane force (1)

G5608 **Τυχικός *Tychikos***, n. pr. [5] [*√5593*]. Tychicus, "*good fortune*":– Tychicus (5)

G5609 **υ *y***, letter. Not used in NIVEBC. letter of the Greek alphabet

G5610 **ὑακίνθινος *hyakinthinos***, a. [1] [*√5611*]. dark blue, *poss.* dark red:– dark blue (1)

G5611 **ὑάκινθος *hyakinthos***, n. [1] [*→5610*]. jacinth:– jacinth (1)

G5612 **ὑάλινος *hyalinos***, a. [3] [*√5613*]. of glass:– glass (2), NDT (1)

G5613 **ὕαλος *hyalos***, n. [2] [*→5612*]. glass, some translate "crystal":– glass (2)

G5614 **ὑβρίζω *hybrizō***, v. [5] [*√5615*]. to insult, mistreat:– insult (2), mistreat (1), mistreated (1), treated outrageously (1)

G5615 **ὕβρις *hybris***, n. [3] [*→1964, 5614, 5616*]. insult, mistreatment; disaster, damage:– damage (1), disastrous (1), insults (1)

G5616 **ὑβριστής *hybristēs***, n. [2] [*√5615*]. insolent man, violent man:– insolent (1), violent (1)

G5617 **ὑγιαίνω *hygiainō***, v. [12] [*√5618*]. to be healthy, sound:– sound (8), enjoy good health (1), healthy (1), safe and sound (1), well (1)

G5618 **ὑγιής *hygiēs***, a. [11] [*→5617*]. healthy, sound, well:– well (4), cured (1), freed (1), healed (1), healing (1 [*+4472*]), made well (1), sound (1), soundness (1)

G5619 **ὑγρός *hygros***, a. [1] [*√5624*]. moist, green:– green (1)

G5620 **ὑδρία *hydria***, n. [3] [*√5623*]. water jar:– jars (1), water jar (1), water jars (1)

G5621 **ὑδροποτέω *hydropoteō***, v. [1] [*√5623 + 4403*]. to drink water (exclusively):– drinking only water (1)

G5622 **ὑδρωπικός *hydrōpikos***, a. [1] [*√5623*]. suffering from dropsy (edema, abnormal swelling from accumulated fluids):– suffering from abnormal swelling of body (1)

G5623 **ὕδωρ *hydōr***, n. [76] [*→536, 5620, 5621, 5622; cf. 5624*]. water:– water (65), waters (10), rushing (1)

G5624 **ὑετός *hyetos***, n. [5] [*→5619; cf. 5623*]. rain:– rain (3), rain (1 [*+1101*]), raining (1)

G5625 **υἱοθεσία *huiothesia***, n. [5] [*√5626 + 5502*]. adoption as sons, sonship; in NT culture a son received greater inheritance and honor, but in Christ men and women inherit equally:– adoption to sonship (5)

G5626 **υἱός *huios***, n. [375] [*→5625*]. son, child (of either gender), descendant (in any generation); by extension: a term of endearment; one of a class or kind, for example, a "son of the resurrection" is one who participates in the resurrection. "The Son of Man" is an OT phrase usually meaning "human being," that in the NT is used almost exclusively as a messianic title (see Da 7:13), emphasizing Jesus' humanity:– son (292), children (18), sons (18), people (10), Israelites (7 [*+2702*]), child (6), Israel (3 [*+2702*]), descendants (2), guests (2), people (2 [*+3836, 3836, 476*]), sons and daughters (2), those who are (2 [*+3836*]), children (1 [*+1169*]), descended from (1), foal (1), followers (1), friends (1), heirs (1), man (1), one doomed to (1), someone who promotes (1), subjects (1), whose[S] (1)

G5627 **ὕλη *hylē***, n. [1] [*→1494*]. forest, wood:– forest (1)

G5628 **Ὑμέναιος *Hymenaios***, n. pr. [2] Hymenaeus, "*of [pagan god] Hymen*":– Hymenaeus (2)

G5629 **ὑμέτερος *hymeteros***, a. [11] [*√5148*]. (pl.) your, your own:– you (5), your (2), your own (2), yours (2)

G5630 **ὑμνέω *hymneō***, v. [4] [*√5631*]. to sing hymns, sing praises:– sung a hymn (2), sing praises (1), singing hymns (1)

G5631 **ὕμνος *hymnos***, n. [2] [*→5630*]. hymn, song of praise:– hymns (2)

G5632 **ὑπάγω *hypagō***, v. [79] [*√5679 + 72*]. to go (away):– go (44), going (20), get (2), going away (2), went (2), away from (1), goes (1), going out (1), going over (1), heading (1), leave (1), leaving (1), on way (1), returning (1)

G5633 **ὑπακοή *hypakoē***, n. [15] [*√5679 + 201*]. obedience:– obedience (8), obedient (5), obey (1), obeying (1)

G5634 **ὑπακούω *hypakouō***, v. [21] [*√5679 + 201*]. to obey, be obedient; to answer (the door):– obey (15), obeyed (3), accepted (1), answer (1), obedient (1)

G5635 **ὕπανδρος *hypandros***, a. [1] [*√5679 + 467*]. married, legally bound to a man in marriage:– married (1)

G5636 **ὑπαντάω *hypantaō***, v. [10] [*√5679 + 505*]. to go out to meet; to oppose:– met (6), went out to meet (2), meet (1), oppose (1)

G5637 **ὑπάντησις *hypantēsis***, n. [3] [*√5679 + 505*]. meeting:– meet (3)

G5638 **ὕπαρξις *hyparxis***, n. [2] [*√5679 + 806*]. property, goods, possessions:– possessions (2)

G5639 **ὑπάρχω *hyparchō***, v. [60] [*√5679 + 806*]. to have, possess; (n.) possessions; to be, exist:– was (11), is (9), possessions (9), are (8), be (2), have (2), possess (2), am (1), been (1), being (1), calm down (1 [*+2948*]), contained (1 [*+1877*]), gone (1), indulge in (1), loved money (1 [*+5795*]), means (1), need (1), owned (1), owned (1 [*+3230*]), property (1), wasn't (1), wealth (1), NDT (2)

G5640 **ὑπείκω *hypeikō***, v. [1] [*√5679 + 1634*]. to submit, yield:– submit to authority (1)

G5641 **ὑπεναντίος *hypenantios***, a. [2] [*√5679 + 1882*]. opposing, being against; (n.) enemy:– against and condemned (1), enemies (1)

G5642 **ὑπέρ *hyper***, pp. [149] [*→5643, 5644, 5645, 5646, 5647, 5648, 5649, 5650, 5651, 5652, 5653, 5654, 5655, 5656, 5657, 5658, 5659, 5660, 5661, 5662, 5663, 5664, 5665, 5666, 5667, 5668, 5669, 5670, 5671, 5672, 5673*]. (acc.) above, beyond, more than; (gen.) for, in behalf of, for the sake of; in place of:– for (92), about (8), above (4), for the sake of (4), in (4), more than (4), on behalf (4), beyond (3), than (3), concerning (2), for sake (2), on behalf of (2), over (2), to (2), as for (1 [*+1664*]), because of (1), better than (1), follower (1), go beyond (1), in order to fulfill (1), more (1), more than is warranted (1), represent (1), take place (1), the one meant (1 [*+4005*]), NDT (2)

G5643 **ὑπεραίρομαι *hyperairomai***, v. [3] [*√5642 + 149*]. to become conceited, exalt oneself:– conceited (1), exalt (1), NDT (1)

G5644 **ὑπέρακμος *hyperakmos***, a. [1] [*√5642 + 216*]. past one's prime, getting along in years:– passions too strong (1)

G5645 **ὑπεράνω *hyperanō***, adv. [3] [*√5642 + 539*]. far above, high above:– above (1), far above (1), higher (1)

G5646 **ὑπερασπίζω *hyperaspizō***, v. Not used in NIVEBC. [*√5642 + 835*]. to shield, protect

G5647 **ὑπεραυξάνω *hyperauxanō***, v. [1] [*√5642 + 889*]. to grow more and more, increase abundantly:– growing more and more (1)

G5648 **ὑπερβαίνω *hyperbainō***, v. [1] [*√5642 + 326*]. to wrong, transgress against, sin against:– wrong (1)

G5649 **ὑπερβαλλόντως *hyperballontōs***, adv. [1] [*√5642 + 965*]. more severely, to a much greater degree:– more severely (1)

G5650 **ὑπερβάλλω *hyperballō***, v. [5] [*√5642 + 965*]. to go beyond, surpass, be incomparable:– surpassing (2), incomparable (1), incomparably (1), surpasses (1)

G5651 **ὑπερβολή *hyperbolē***, n. [8] [*√5642 + 965*]. all-surpassing, surpassingly great, most excellent, beyond measure:– all-surpassing (1), far outweighs them all (1 [*+2848, 1650, 5651, 983*]), far outweighs them all (1 [*+2848, 5651, 1650, 983*]), great (1 [*+2848*]), intensely (1 [*+2848*]), most excellent (1 [*+2848*]), surpassingly great (1), utterly (1 [*+2848*])

G5652 **ὑπερεγώ *hyperegō***, adv. [pp.+p.] Not used in NIVEBC. [*√5642 + 1609*]. (adv.) even more

G5653 **ὑπερείδω *hypereidō***, v. Not used in NIVEBC. [*√5642 + 1626*]. to overlook, not punish

G5654 **ὑπερέκεινα *hyperekeina***, adv. [1] [*√5642 + 1695*]. beyond; (n.) regions beyond:– regions beyond (1)

G5655 **ὑπερεκπερισσοῦ *hyperekperissou***, adv. [3] [*√5642 + 1666 + 4356*]. immeasurably; most earnestly; in the highest regard:– highest (1), immeasurably more (1), most earnestly (1)

G5656 **ὑπερεκπερισσῶς *hyperekperissōs***, adv. Not used in NIVEBC. [*√5642 + 1666 + 4356*]. beyond all measure, most highly

G5657 **ὑπερεκτείνω *hyperekteinō***, v. [1] [*√1753; cf.*

5642]. to go too far, overextend, stretch out beyond:– come (1)

G5658 ὑπερεκχύννω *hyperekchynnō*, v. [1] [√*1772; cf. 5642 + 1666*]. (pass.) to be running over, overflowing:– running over (1)

G5659 ὑπερεντυγχάνω *hyperentynchanō*, v. [1] [√*5642 + 1877 + 5593*]. to intercede:– intercedes (1)

G5660 ὑπερέχω *hyperechō*, v. [5] [√*5642 + 2400*]. to govern, have authority; to be better than, transcend; (n.) surpassing greatness:– above (1), governing (1), supreme authority (1), surpassing worth (1), transcends (1)

G5661 ὑπερηφανία *hyperēphania*, n. [1] [√*5642 + 5743*]. arrogance, pride:– arrogance (1)

G5662 ὑπερήφανος *hyperēphanos*, a. [5] [√*5642 + 5743*]. proud, arrogant:– proud (4), arrogant (1)

G5663 ὑπερλίαν *hyperlian*, adv. [2] [√*5642 + 3336*]. exceedingly, beyond measure; (with *693*) super-apostles:– super-apostles (2 [+*693*])

G5664 ὑπερνικάω *hypernikaō*, v. [1] [√*5642 + 3772*]. to thoroughly conquer, go beyond conquest:– more than conquerors (1)

G5665 ὑπέρογκος *hyperonkos*, a. [2] [√*5642 + 3839*]. boastful, bombastic:– boast (1 [+*3281*]), boastful (1)

G5666 ὑπεροράω *hyperoraō*, v. [1] [√*5642 + 3972*]. to overlook, disregard:– overlooked (1)

G5667 ὑπεροχή *hyperochē*, n. [2] [√*5642 + 2400*]. authority, superiority:– authority (1), eloquence (1 [+*3364*])

G5668 ὑπερπερισσεύω *hyperperisseuō*, v. [2] [√*5642 + 4356*]. to increase all the more, exceed bounds, overflow:– increased all the more (1), knows no bounds (1)

G5669 ὑπερπερισσῶς *hyperperissōs*, adv. [1] [√*5642 + 4356*]. beyond all measure, exceedingly:– overwhelmed (1)

G5670 ὑπερπλεονάζω *hyperpleonazō*, v. [1] [√*5642 + 4444*]. to be (greatly) abundant:– poured out abundantly (1)

G5671 ὑπερυψόω *hyperypsoō*, v. [1] [√*5642 + 5737*]. to exalt to the highest place:– exalted to the highest place (1)

G5672 ὑπερφρονέω *hyperphroneō*, v. [1] [√*5642 + 5856*]. to think too highly of oneself:– think of yourself more highly (1)

G5673 ὑπερῷον *hyperōon*, n. [4] [√*5642*]. upstairs room, upper story:– upstairs room (4)

G5674 ὑπέχω *hypechō*, v. [1] [√*5679 + 2400*]. to experience:– suffer (1)

G5675 ὑπήκοος *hypēkoos*, a. [3] [√*5679 + 201*]. obedient:– obedient (2), obey (1 [+*1181*])

G5676 ὑπηρετέω *hypēreteō*, v. [3] [√*5677*]. to serve, care for needs:– served (1), supplied (1), take care of needs (1)

G5677 ὑπηρέτης *hypēretēs*, n. [20] [→*5676; cf. 5679*]. servant, attendant, helper, one who serves or attends, not distinguished in status from other words for servant:– officials (5), guards (4), servants (3), officers (2), temple guards (2), attendant (1), helper (1), officer (1), servant (1)

G5678 ὕπνος *hypnos*, n. [6] [→*70, 71, 934, 1965, 1966, 2030, 2031*]. sleep, slumber:– natural sleep (1 [+*3122*]), sleep (1), slumber (1), sound asleep (1 [+*2965, 608, 3836*]), very sleepy (1 [+*976*]), woke up (1 [+*1586, 608, 3836*])

G5679 ὑπό *hypo*, pp. [218] [→*537, 538, 4732, 5347, 5348, 5632, 5633, 5634, 5635, 5636, 5637, 5638, 5639, 5640, 5641, 5674, 5675, 5680, 5681, 5682, 5683, 5684, 5685, 5686, 5687, 5688, 5689, 5690, 5691, 5692, 5693, 5694, 5695, 5696, 5697, 5698, 5699, 5700, 5701, 5702, 5703, 5704, 5705, 5706, 5707, 5708, 5709, 5710, 5711, 5712, 5713, 5714, 5715, 5716, 5717, 5718, 5719, 5720, 5721, 5722, 5723, 5724; cf. 5677*]. (gen.) by, by means of; (acc.) under (in space as well as in status or authority); at (a time of day):– by (96), under (37), from (7), in (2), of (2), to (2), at (1), at hands (1), condemned (1 [+*3213, 4406*]), end (1), established (1), for (1), on (1), other[s] (1 [+*4041*]), perform (1 [+*1181*]), subject to (1), the result of (1), the way (1), under the control of (1), under the power of (1), underfoot[s] (1 [+*3836, 476*]), NDT (57)

G5680 ὑποβάλλω *hypoballō*, v. [1] [√*5679 + 965*]. to secretly persuade, instigate secretly:– secretly persuaded (1)

G5681 ὑπογραμμός *hypogrammos*, n. [1] [√*5679 + 1211*]. example, model:– example (1)

G5682 ὑπόδειγμα *hypodeigma*, n. [6] [√*5679 + 1257*]. example, model, pattern, copy:– example (4), copies (1), copy (1)

G5683 ὑποδείκνυμι *hypodeiknymi*, v. [6] [√*5679 + 1259*]. to show; to warn:– show (3), warned (2), showed (1)

G5684 ὑποδεικνύω *hypodeiknyō*, v. Not used in NIVEBC. [√*5679 + 1259*]. to show; to warn

G5685 ὑποδέχομαι *hypodechomai*, v. [4] [√*5679 + 1312*]. to welcome, receive as a guest:– gave lodging (1), opened home to (1), welcomed (1), welcomed into house (1)

G5686 ὑποδέω *hypodeō*, v. [3] [√*5679 + 1313*]. (mid.) to put on (sandals):– fitted (1), on (1), wear (1)

G5687 ὑπόδημα *hypodēma*, n. [10] [√*5679 + 1313*]. sandal:– sandals (8), sandals (2 [+*3836, 4546*])

G5688 ὑπόδικος *hypodikos*, a. [1] [√*5679 + 1472*]. accountable, answerable:– accountable (1)

G5689 ὑποζύγιον *hypozygion*, n. [2] [√*5679 + 2413*]. donkey:– donkey (2)

G5690 ὑποζώννυμι *hypozōnnymi*, v. [1] [√*5679 + 2439*]. to undergird, brace:– under to hold together (1)

G5691 ὑποκάτω *hypokatō*, adv. [11] [√*5679 + 2848*]. (pp.*) under:– under (9), NDT (2)

G5692 ὑπόκειμαι *hypokeimai*, v. Not used in NIVEBC. [√*5679 + 3023*]. to lie below, be found

G5693 ὑποκρίνομαι *hypokrinomai*, v. [1] [√*5679 + 3212*]. to pretend, make believe; see also *5695*:– pretended (1)

G5694 ὑπόκρισις *hypokrisis*, n. [6] [√*5679 + 3212*]. hypocrisy (an extension of an actor in a play, not found in the NT), implying arrogance and hardness of heart, utterly devoid of sincerity and genuineness:– hypocrisy (5), hypocritical (1)

G5695 ὑποκριτής *hypokritēs*, n. [17] [√*5679 + 3212*]. hypocrite (an extension of an actor in a play, not found in the NT), implying arrogance and hardness of heart, utterly devoid of sincerity and genuineness:– hypocrites (15), hypocrite (2)

G5696 ὑπολαμβάνω *hypolambanō*, v. [5] [√*5679 + 3284*]. to take up; to show hospitality; to reply; to suppose, think, believe:– suppose (2), hid (1), reply (1), show hospitality (1)

G5697 ὑπολαμπάς *hypolampas*, n. Not used in NIVEBC. [√*5679 + 3290*]. window, opening

G5698 ὑπόλειμμα *hypoleimma*, n. [1] [√*5679 + 3309*]. remnant:– remnant (1)

G5699 ὑπολείπω *hypoleipō*, v. [1] [√*5679 + 3309*]. (pass.) to be left, remaining:– left (1)

G5700 ὑπολήνιον *hypolēnion*, n. [1] [√*5679 + 3332*]. pit for a winepress:– pit for the winepress (1)

G5701 ὑπολιμπάνω *hypolimpanō*, v. [1] [√*5679 + 3309*]. to leave behind:– leaving (1)

G5702 ὑπομένω *hypomenō*, v. [17] [√*5679 + 3531*]. to stay behind; to stand firm, endure, persevere:– endure (4), endured (3), stands firm (3), perseveres (2), endure hardship (1), patient (1), persevered (1), stayed (1), stayed behind (1)

G5703 ὑπομιμνῄσκω *hypomimnēskō*, v. [7] [√*5679 + 3648*]. to remind, call to mind; (pass.) to remember:– remind (4), call attention to (1), remembered (1), reminding (1)

G5704 ὑπόμνησις *hypomnēsis*, n. [3] [√*5679 + 3648*]. reminder, memory, remembrance:– memory (1), reminded (1 [+*3284*]), reminders (1)

G5705 ὑπομονή *hypomonē*, n. [32] [√*5679 + 3531*]. perseverance, endurance, patience:– perseverance (12), endurance (8), patient endurance (4), endure patiently (1), patiently (1 [+*1328*]), persevere (1), persevered (1 [+*2400*]), persevered (1 [+*1877, 4246*]), persevering (1), persistence (1), stand firm (1)

G5706 ὑπονοέω *hyponoeō*, v. [3] [√*5679 + 3808*]. to think, suppose; expect; to sense, suspect:– expected (1), sensed (1), suppose (1)

G5707 ὑπόνοια *hyponoia*, n. [1] [√*5679 + 3808*]. suspicion:– suspicions (1)

G5708 ὑποπιάζω *hypopiazō*, v. Not used in NIVEBC. [√*5679 + 3972*]. to wear out, weaken; to beat up, treat roughly

G5709 ὑποπλέω *hypopleō*, v. [2] [√*5679 + 4434*]. to sail to the lee of, to move to the side that offers protection or shelter:– passed to the lee of (1), sailed to the lee of (1)

G5710 ὑποπνέω *hypopneō*, v. [1] [√*5679 + 4463*]. to blow gently (of wind):– gentle blow (1)

G5711 ὑποπόδιον *hypopodion*, n. [7] [√*5679 + 4546*]. footstool:– footstool (3), footstool (3 [+*3836, 4546*]), on the floor by feet (1)

G5712 ὑπόστασις *hypostasis*, n. [5] [√*5679 + 2705*]. confidence, trust, being sure; being, essence:– being (1), confidence (1), confident (1), conviction (1), self-confident (1)

G5713 ὑποστέλλω *hypostellō*, v. [4] [√*5679 + 5097*]. (act.) to draw back, withdraw; (mid.) to hesitate, shrink back:– hesitated (2), draw back (1), shrinks back (1)

G5714 ὑποστολή *hypostolē*, n. [1] [√*5679 + 5097*]. shrinking back:– shrink back (1)

G5715 ὑποστρέφω *hypostrephō*, v. [35] [√*5679 + 5138*]. to turn back toward, return; to turn one's back on, turn away:– returned (18), return (4), came back (2), left (2), go back (1), on way home (1), returning (1), returning home (1), subject to (1 [+*1650*]), turn backs (1), went away (1), went back (1), went home (1)

G5716 ὑποστρωννύω *hypostrōnnyō*, v. [1] [√*5679 + 5143*]. to spread out:– spread (1)

G5717 ὑποταγή *hypotagē*, n. [4] [√*5679 + 5435*]. obedience, submission:– give in (1 [+*1634, 3836*]), obedience (1), obey (1 [+*1877*]), submission (1)

G5718 ὑποτάσσω *hypotassō*, v. [38] [√*5679 + 5435*]. to put in subjection, subject, subordinate; (pass.) to submit, be subject to:– submit (14), put under (5), subject (5), subjected (3), in submission (2), bring under control (1), done this[s] (1 [+*899, 3836, 4246*]), made subject (1), obedient (1), placed under (1), putting under (1), subject to control (1), submits (1), submitted (1)

G5719 ὑποτίθημι *hypotithēmi*, v. [2] [√*5679 + 5502*]. (act.) to risk, lay down (a life); (mid.) to point out, teach:– point out (1), risked (1)

G5720 ὑποτρέχω *hypotrechō*, v. [1] [√*5679 + 5556*]. to sail to the lee of, to move to the side that offers protection or shelter:– passed to the lee of (1)

G5721 ὑποτύπωσις *hypotypōsis*, n. [2] [√*5679 + 5597*]. example, pattern:– example (1), pattern (1)

G5722 ὑποφέρω *hypopherō*, v. [3] [√*5679 + 5770*]. to endure, bear up under, stand up under:– bears up (1), endure (1), endured (1)

G5723 ὑποχωρέω *hypochōreō*, v. [2] [√*5679 + 6003*]. to withdraw, retreat:– withdrew (1), withdrew (1 [+*1639*])

G5724 ὑπωπιάζω *hypōpiazō*, v. [2] [√*5679 + 3972*]. to wear out, weaken; to beat up, treat roughly:– attack (1), strike a blow (1)

G5725 ὗς *hys*, n. [1] female pig, sow:– sow (1)

G5726 ὑσσός *hyssos*, n. Not used in NIVEBC. javelin

G5727 ὕσσωπος *hyssōpos*, n. [2] hyssop, highly aromatic leaves used in purification rites and at Passover:– branches of hyssop (1), stalk of the hyssop plant (1)

G5728 ὑστερέω *hystereō*, v. [16] [√*5731*]. to lack, be in need, destitute; to be inferior; to fall short:– lack (4), inferior (2), destitute (1), fall short (1), fallen short (1), falls short (1), gone (1), in need (1), in want (1), lacked (1), needed (1), worse (1)

G5729 ὑστέρημα *hysterēma*, n. [9] [√*5731*]. what is lacking; poverty; what is needed:– lacking (3), need (2), could not give (1), needed (1), needs (1), poverty (1)

G5730 ὑστέρησις *hysterēsis*, n. [2] [√*5731*]. need, poverty, lack:– need (1), poverty (1)

G5731 ὕστερος *hysteros*, a. [12] [→*935, 5728, 5729, 5730*]. (comp.) later, second; (neu.) finally, last of all:– later (5), after (2), finally (2), finally (1 [+*4246*]), last of all (1), later on (1)

G5732 ὑφαίνω *hyphainō*, v. Not used in NIVEBC. [→*5733*]. to weave

G5733 ὑφαντός *hyphantos*, a. [1] [√*5732*]. woven:– woven (1)

G5734 ὑψηλός *hypsēlos*, a. [12] [√*5737*]. high, mighty; proud, arrogant; highly valued; (compar.) more exalted:– high (6), arrogant (1 [+*5858*]), exalted above (1), heaven (1), mighty (1), proud (1 [+*3836, 5858*]), value highly (1)

G5735 ὑψηλοφρονέω *hypsēlophroneō*, v. [1] [√*5737 + 5856*]. to be arrogant, proud:– arrogant (1)

G5736 ὕψιστος *hypsistos*, a. [13] [√*5737*]. highest, most exalted; (as a title of God) the Most High:– most High (9), highest heaven (3), highest (1)

G5737 ὕψος *hypsos*, n. [6] [→*5671, 5734, 5735, 5736, 5738, 5739*]. height, high position, heaven:– high (3), heaven (1), high position (1), on high (1)

G5738 ὑψόω *hypsoō*, v. [20] [√*5737*]. to lift up, elevate, exalt:– lifted up (6), exalted (5), exalt (3), lift up (2), lifted (2), elevate (1), made prosper (1)

G5739 ὕψωμα *hypsōma*, n. [2] [√*5737*]. height; pretension:– height (1), pretension (1)

G5740 φ *ph*, letter. Not used in NIVEBC. letter of the Greek alphabet

G5741 φάγος *phagos*, n. [2] [→*4709; cf. 2266*]. glutton:– glutton (2 [+*476*])

G5742 φαιλόνης *phailonēs*, n. [1] [→*5769*]. cloak:– cloak (1)

G5743 φαίνω *phainō*, v. [31] [→*428, 905, 906, 907, 908, 1421, 1871, 1872, 2210, 2211, 2212, 2213, 2216, 2993, 4733, 5193, 5661, 5662, 5745, 5746, 5747, 5748, 5749, 5751, 5752, 5753, 5762?, 5763?, 5833, 5890, 5891, 5892, 5893, 5894, 5895*]. (act.) to shine, give light; (mid./pass.) to appear, be visible;:– appeared (7), shine (3), shining (3), appear (2), seen (2), visible (2), appears (1), become of (1), gave light (1), light (1), look (1), obvious (1), recognized (1), see (1), seemed (1), shines (1), show (1), think (1)

G5744* Φάλεκ *Phalek, n. pr. [1] Peleg, "*water canal*":– Peleg (1)

G5745* φανερός *phaneros, a. [18] [√*5743*]. visible, clear, plain, known:– open (2), tell about (2 [+*4472*]), clear (1), disclosed (1), know (1), knows (1), laid bare (1), learned about (1 [+*1181*]), obvious (1), outward (1 [+*1877, 3836*]), outwardly (1 [+*1877, 3836*]), plain (1), see (1 [+*1639*]), show (1 [+*1181*]), shown for what it is (1), well known (1)

G5746* φανερόω *phaneroō, v. [49] [√*5743*]. (act.) to reveal, make known, show; (pass.) to appear, be disclosed, displayed, revealed:– appeared (10), revealed (9), appears (4), disclosed (3), appear (2), made known (2), plain (2), show (2), showed (2), brought to light (1), clearly (1), cover (1 [+*3590*]), displayed (1), expose (1), happened (1), illuminated (1), made clear (1), made plain (1), see (1), seen plainly (1), spread (1), visible (1)

G5747* φανερῶς *phanerōs, adv. [3] [√*5743*]. openly, publicly:– distinctly (1), openly (1), publicly (1)

G5748* φανέρωσις *phanerōsis, n. [2] [√*5743*]. manifestation, disclosure, revelation:– manifestation (1), setting forth plainly (1)

G5749* φανός *phanos, n. [1] [√*5743*]. torch, lantern:– torches (1)

G5750* Φανουήλ *Phanouēl, n. pr. [1] Phanuel, "*face of God [El]*":– Penuel (1)

G5751* φαντάζω *phantazō, v. [1] [√*5743*]. (pass.) to become visible; (n.) a sight:– sight (1)

G5752* φαντασία *phantasia, n. [1] [√*5743*]. pomp, pageantry:– pomp (1)

G5753* φάντασμα *phantasma, n. [2] [√*5743*]. ghost, apparition, transliterated as "phantasm":– ghost (2)

G5754* φάραγξ *pharanx, n. [1] valley, ravine:– valley (1)

G5755* Φαραώ *Pharaō, n. pr. [5] Pharaoh, "*the great house*":– Pharaoh (3), Pharaoh's (2)

G5756* Φαρές *Phares, n. pr. [3] Perez, "*breaking out*":– Perez (3)

G5757* Φαρισαῖος *Pharisaios, n. pr. [98] Pharisee, "*separate ones*":– Pharisees (84), Pharisee (12), Pharisee's (2)

G5758* φαρμακεία *pharmakeia, n. [2] [√*5760*]. witchcraft, magic, the use of spells and potions of magic, often involving drugs:– magic spell (1), witchcraft (1)

G5759* φαρμακεύς *pharmakeus, n. Not used in NIVEBC. [√*5760*]. magician, sorcerer

G5760* φάρμακον *pharmakon, n. [1] [→*5758, 5759, 5761*]. magic potion, charm; (pl.) magic arts, with a focus on the use of drugs and potions:– magic arts (1)

G5761* φάρμακος *pharmakos, n. [2] [√*5760*]. one who practices magical arts, magician:– those who practice magic arts (1), who practice magic arts (1)

G5762* φάσις *phasis, n. [1] [√*5774 or* 5743]. news, report:– news (1)

G5763* φάσκω *phaskō, v. [3] [√*5774 or* 5743]. to claim, assert:– claimed (2), asserting (1)

G5764* φάτνη *phatnē, n. [4] manger, stall:– manger (3), stall (1)

G5765* φαῦλος *phaulos, a. Not used in NIVEBC. evil, bad€ [6]:– bad (3), evil (3)

G5766* φέγγος *phengos, n. [2] light, radiance:– light (2)

G5767* φείδομαι *pheidomai, v. [10] [→*910, 5768*]. to spare, refrain from:– spare (9), refrain (1)

G5768* φειδομένως *pheidomenōs, adv. [2] [√*5767*]. sparingly:– sparingly (2)

G5769* φελόνης *phelonēs, n. Not used in NIVEBC. [√*5742*]. cloak

G5770* φέρω *pherō, v. [65] [→*429, 708, 711, 1022, 1422, 1427, 1457, 1566, 1662, 1766, 2214, 2369, 2504, 2844, 2845, 2965, 3947, 4195, 4210, 4367, 4442, 4443, 4533, 4712, 4714, 4734, 5237, 5239, 5240, 5461, 5574, 5578, 5722, 5841, 5843, 5844, 5845, 5846, 5892*]. to bring, bear, carry; lead:– brought (16), bring (11), bear (6), bringing (4), came (2), driven along (2), bearing (1), bears (1), blowing (1), bore (1), brought back (1), brought in (1), carried (1), carried along (1), carry (1), carrying (1), charge (1 [+*162*]), fruitful (1 [+*2843*]), had origin (1), lead (1), leading (1), multiplying (1), produces (1), prove (1), put (1), reach out (1), sustaining (1), take (1), taken (1), took (1)

G5771* φεύγω *pheugō, v. [29] [→*709, 1423, 1767, 2966, 5868, 5870*]. flee, escape, elude:– flee (11), fled (7), escape (3), ran off (3), elude (1), escaped (1), fled away (1), run away (1), runs away (1)

G5772* Φῆλιξ *Phēlix, n. pr. [9] Felix, "*fortunate, lucky*":– Felix (9)

G5773* φήμη *phēmē, n. [2] [√*5774*]. news, report:– news (2)

G5774* φημί *phēmi, v. [65] [→*1424, 2367, 2368, 4735, 5238, 5762?, 5763?, 5773, 5775; cf. 1059, 1555, 4735*]. to say, declare, affirm:– said (25), replied (17), answered (7), asked (3), declared (2), mean (2), say (2), claim (1), declare (1), shouted (1 [+*3489, 3836, 5889*]), NDT (4)

G5775* φημίζω *phēmizō, v. Not used in NIVEBC. [√*5774*]. to spread (news) by saying

G5776* Φῆστος *Phēstos, n. pr. [13] Festus, "*festal, joyful*":– Festus (13)

G5777* φθάνω *phthanō, v. [7] [→*4710?, 4711?, 4740*]. to precede; to arrive, attain, come:– come upon (2), attained (1), attained (1 [+*1650*]), come (1), get (1), precede (1)

G5778* φθαρτός *phthartos, a. [6] [√*5780*]. perishable, not lasting, mortal:– perishable (4), mortal (1), that will not last (1)

G5779* φθέγγομαι *phthengomai, v. [3] [→*710, 5782*]. to speak, proclaim:– mouth words (1), speak (1), spoke (1)

G5780* φθείρω *phtheirō, v. [9] [→*91, 914, 915, 917, 1425, 1426, 2967, 5778, 5781, 5785*]. to destroy, corrupt; (pass.) to be corrupted, destroyed, perish; to be led astray:– corrupted (3), destroy (2), corrupts (1), destroys (1), led astray (1), perish (1 [+*5785*])

G5781* φθινοπωρινός *phthinopōrinos, a. [1] [√*5780 + 3967*]. pertaining to the (late) autumn:– autumn (1)

G5782* φθόγγος *phthongos, n. [2] [√*5779*]. voice, sound; note, musical tone:– notes (1), voice (1)

G5783* φθονέω *phthoneō, v. [1] [√*5784*]. to envy, be jealous of:– envying (1)

G5784* φθόνος *phthonos, n. [9] [→*916, 5783*]. envy:– envy (6), self-interest (2), jealously (1 [+*4639*])

G5785* φθορά *phthora, n. [9] [√*5780*]. perishableness, destruction, corruption; depravity:– corruption (1), decay (1), depravity (1), destroyed (1), destruction (1), perish (1), perish (1 [+*5780*]), perishable (1), perishable (1 [+*1877*])

G5786* φιάλη *phialē, n. [12] bowl:– bowl (7), bowls (5)

G5787* φιλάγαθος *philagathos, a. [1] [√*5813 + 19*]. loving what is good:– loves what is good (1)

G5788* Φιλαδέλφεια *Philadelpheia, n. pr. [2] [√*5813 + 81 [1.3]*]. Philadelphia, "*love of brother/sister*":– Philadelphia (2)

G5789* φιλαδελφία *philadelphia, n. [6] [√*5813 + 81 [1.3]*]. brotherly love; brotherly kindness:– mutual affection (2), love (1), love for each other (1), love for one another (1), loving one another as brothers and sisters (1)

G5790* φιλάδελφος *philadelphos, a. [2] [√*5813 + 81 [1.3]*]. loving as brothers:– love one another (1), need (1 [+*2400*])

G5791* φίλανδρος *philandros, a. [1] [√*5813 + 467*]. loving one's husband:– love husbands (1 [+*1639*])

G5792* φιλανθρωπία *philanthrōpia, n. [2] [√*5813 + 476*]. love, kindness:– kindness (1), love (1)

G5793* φιλανθρώπως *philanthrōpōs, adv. [1] [√*5813 + 476*]. in kindness, kindly:– kindness (1 [+*5968*])

G5794* φιλαργυρία *philargyria, n. [1] [√*5813 + 738*]. love of money, avarice, greed:– love of money (1)

G5795* φιλάργυρος *philargyros, a. [2] [√*5813 + 738*]. money-loving, avaricious, greedy:– loved money (1 [+*5639*]), lovers of money (1)

G5796* φίλαυτος *philautos, a. [1] [√*5813 + 899*]. loving oneself, selfish:– lovers of themselves (1)

G5797* φιλέω *phileō, v. [25] [√*5813*]. to love, to have affection and regard of a very high order, not unlike *27*, and overlapping in meaning in some contexts:– love (13), loves (6), kiss (3), loved (3)

G5798* φιλήδονος *philēdonos, a. [1] [√*5813 + 2454*]. loving pleasure:– lovers of pleasure (1)

G5799* φίλημα *philēma, n. [7] [√*5813*]. kiss:– kiss (7)

G5800* Φιλήμων *Philēmōn, n. pr. [1] [√*5813*]. Philemon, "*beloved*":– Philemon (1)

G5801* Φίλητος *Philētos, n. pr. [1] [√*5813*]. Philetus, "*beloved*":– Philetus (1)

G5802* φιλία *philia, n. [1] [√*5813*]. friendship, love:– friendship (1)

G5803* Φιλιππήσιος *Philippēsios, n. pr. g. [1] [√*5813 + 2691*]. Philippian:– Philippians (1)

G5804* Φίλιπποι *Philippoi, n. pr. [4] [√*5813 + 2691*]. Philippi:– Philippi (4)

G5805* Φίλιππος *Philippos, n. pr. [36] [√*5813 + 2691*]. Philip, "*horse lover*":– Philip (32), Philippi (2), Philip's (2)

G5806* φιλόθεος *philotheos, a. [1] [√*5813 + 2536*]. loving God:– lovers of God (1)

G5807* Φιλόλογος *Philologos, n. pr. [1] [√*5813 + 3306*]. Philologus, "*lover of words [education]*":– Philologus (1)

G5808* φιλονεικία *philoneikia, n. [1] [→*5809; cf. 5813*]. dispute, strife:– dispute (1)

G5809* φιλόνεικος *philoneikos, a. [1] [√*5808*]. contentious, quarrelsome:– contentious (1)

G5810* φιλοξενία *philoxenia, n. [2] [√*5813 + 3828*]. hospitality, entertainment of strangers:– hospitality (1), show hospitality to strangers (1)

G5811* φιλόξενος *philoxenos, a. [3] [√*5813 + 3828*]. hospitable:– hospitable (2), offer hospitality (1)

G5812* φιλοπρωτεύω *philoprōteuō, v. [1] [√*5813 + 4755*]. to love to be first:– loves to be first (1)

G5813* φίλος *philos, a. [29] [→*920, 921, 2541, 2968, 4713, 5787, 5788, 5789, 5790, 5791, 5792, 5793, 5794, 5795, 5796, 5797, 5798, 5799, 5800, 5801, 5802, 5803, 5804, 5805, 5806, 5807, 5810, 5811, 5812, 5814, 5815, 5816, 5817, 5818, 5819, 5820; cf. 5808*]. (a.) friendly; (n.) friend (male or female):– friends (16), friend (11), close (1), friendship (1)

G5814* φιλοσοφία *philosophia, n. [1] [√*5813 + 5055*]. philosophy, human wisdom:– philosophy (1)

G5815* φιλόσοφος *philosophos, n. [1] [√*5813 + 5055*]. philosopher:– philosophers (1)

G5816* φιλόστοργος *philostorgos, a. [1] [√*5813*]. devoted, loving dearly:– devoted (1)

G5817* φιλότεκνος *philoteknos, a. [1] [√*5813 + 5503*]. loving one's children:– love children (1)

G5818* φιλοτιμέομαι *philotimeomai, v. [3] [√*5813 + 5507*]. to have an ambition, aspire to a goal:– ambition (1), make it ambition (1), make it goal (1)

G5819* φιλοφρόνως *philophronōs, adv. [1] [√*5813 + 5856*]. hospitably, in a friendly manner:– generous (1)

G5820* φιλόφρων *philophrōn, a. Not used in NIVEBC. [√*5813 + 5856*]. well disposed, friendly, kind

G5821* φιμόω *phimoō, v. [7] to muzzle; to silence; (pass.) to be quiet:– quiet (2), muzzle (1), silence talk (1), silenced (1), speechless (1), still (1)

G5822* φλαγελλόω *phlagelloō, v. Not used in NIVEBC. [√*5848*]. to flog

G5823* Φλέγων *Phlegōn, n. pr. [1] [√*5825*]. Phlegon, "*burning*":– Phlegon (1)

G5824* φλογίζω *phlogizō, v. [2] [√*5825*]. to set on fire:– set on fire (1), sets on fire (1)

G5825* φλόξ *phlox, n. [7] [→*5823, 5824*]. flame, blaze:– blazing (4), flames (2), fire (1)

G5826* φλυαρέω *phlyareō, v. [1] [√*5827*]. to gossip, talk nonsense:– nonsense (1)

G5827* φλύαρος *phlyaros, a. [1] [→*3886, 5826*]. gossipy:– busybodies (1)

G5828* φοβέομαι *phobeomai, v. [95] [√*5832*]. to fear, be afraid, alarmed, in some contexts improper and an impediment to faith and love; to reverence, respect, worship, in other contexts a proper fear for God, a deep reverence and awe:– afraid (53), fear (15), feared (5), God-fearing (2 [+*3836, 2536*]), alarmed (2), fearing (2), fears (2), terrified (2 [+*5379*]), terrified (2 [+*5832, 3489*]), God-fearing gentiles (1 [+*3836, 2536*]), careful (1), filled with awe (1), frightened (1), give way to (1), respect (1), revere (1), reverence (1), tremble (1), worship (1)

G5829* φοβερός *phoberos, a. [3] [√*5832*]. fearful, dreadful, terrible:– dreadful (1), fearful (1), terrifying (1)

G5830* φοβέω *phobeō, v. Not used in NIVEBC. [√*5832*]. to fear, be afraid, alarmed; to reverence, respect, worship

G5831* φόβητρον *phobētron, n. [1] [√*5832*]. fearful event:– fearful events (1)

G5832* φόβος *phobos, n. [47] [→*925, 1768, 1769, 1873, 5828, 5829, 5830, 5831*]. fear, terror; respect, reverence; see also *5399*:– fear (20), awe (4), respect (4), reverence (3), afraid (2), reverent fear (2), terrified (2 [+*5828, 3489*]), terrified (2), terror (2), alarm (1), feared (1), fears (1), terror (1 [+*3489*]), threats (1), warning (1)

G5833* Φοίβη *Phoibē, n. pr. [1] [√*5743*]. Phoebe, "*radiant*":– Phoebe (1)

G5834* Φοινίκη *Phoinikē, n. pr. [3] [√*5836*]. Phoenicia, "*land of purple [dye]; poss. land of date palms*":– Phoenicia (3)

G5835* Φοινίκισσα *Phoinikissa, n. pr. Not used in NIVEBC. [√*5836*]. Phoenician

G5836* φοῖνιξ¹ *phoinix¹, n. [2] [→*5355, 5356, 5834, 5835, 5837*]. palm tree, palm branch:– palm (1), palm branches (1)

G5837* Φοῖνιξ² *Phoinix², n. pr. [1] [√*5836*]. Phoenix:– Phoenix (1)

G5838* φονεύς *phoneus, n. [7] [√*5840*]. murderer:–

murderers (3), murderer (2), murdered (1 [+1181]), murderer (1 [+467])

G5839 φονεύω *phoneuō*, v. [12] [√5840]. to commit murder, kill:– murder (6), murdered (3), commit murder (1), kill (1), murders (1)

G5840 φόνος *phonos*, n. [9] [→439, 4710?, 4711?, 5838, 5839]. murder, killing:– murder (6), killed (1 [+1877, 633]), murderous (1), murders (1)

G5841 φορέω *phoreō*, v. [6] [√5770]. to wear, bear:– bear (2), wearing (2), borne (1), wear (1)

G5842 φόρον *phoron*, n. [1] forum, used only as a compound proper name "Forum of Appius," a market town south of Rome:– forum (1)

G5843 φόρος *phoros*, n. [5] [√5770]. tax:– taxes (5)

G5844 φορτίζω *phortizō*, v. [2] [√5770]. to load down (with a burden); (pass.) to be burdened:– burdened (1), load down (1)

G5845 φορτίον *phortion*, n. [6] [√5770]. burden, load, cargo:– burden (1), burdens (1), cargo (1), lift to help (1 [+4718, 3836]), load (1), loads (1)

G5846 φόρτος *phortos*, n. Not used in NIVEBC. [√5770]. cargo

G5847 Φορτουνᾶτος *Phortounatos*, n. pr. [1] Fortunatus, "*fortunate*":– Fortunatus (1)

G5848 φραγέλλιον *phragellion*, n. [1] [→5822, 5849]. whip:– whip (1)

G5849 φραγελλόω *phragelloō*, v. [2] [√5848]. to flog:– flogged (1), had flogged (1)

G5850 φραγμός *phragmos*, n. [4] [√5852]. barrier, wall, country lane:– wall (2), barrier (1), country lanes (1)

G5851 φράζω *phrazō*, v. [1] to explain, interpret:– explain (1)

G5852 φράσσω *phrassō*, v. [3] [→5850]. to shut; (pass.) to be stopped, silenced:– shut (1), silenced (1), stop (1)

G5853 φρέαρ *phrear*, n. [7] well, shaft, Abyss:– well (3), abyss (1), it[S] (1 [+3836]), shaft (1), NDT (1)

G5854 φρεναπατάω *phrenapataō*, v. [1] [√5856 + 573]. to deceive:– deceive (1)

G5855 φρεναπάτης *phrenapatēs*, n. [1] [√5856 + 573]. deceiver:– deception (1)

G5856 φρήν *phrēn*, n. [2] [→932, 933, 3939, 4368, 5425, 5426, 5672, 5735, 5819, 5820, 5854, 5855, 5858, 5859, 5860, 5861, 5862, 5863; cf. 2370, 2969, 4196, 5404]. (pl.) thinking, understanding:– thinking (1), thinking (1 [+1181, 3836])

G5857 φρίσσω *phrissō*, v. [1] to shudder:– shudder (1)

G5858 φρονέω *phroneō*, v. [28] [√5856]. to think, regard, hold an opinion; to set one's mind on; to have a (certain) attitude:– does so[S] (3), mind (3), have in mind (2), think (2), arrogant (1 [+5734]), attitude of mind (1), concern (1), concerned (1), feel (1), have minds set on (1), have mindset (1), like-minded (1 [+3836, 899]), live in harmony (1 [+3836, 899]), mind set (1), proud (1 [+3836, 5734]), regards as special (1), set minds on (1), take a view of things (1), take view (1), thought (1), views (1), NDT (1)

G5859 φρόνημα *phronēma*, n. [4] [√5856]. mind:– mind (4)

G5860 φρόνησις *phronēsis*, n. [2] [√5856]. wisdom, understanding:– understanding (1), wisdom (1)

G5861 φρόνιμος *phronimos*, a. [14] [√5856]. wise, sensible, shrewd; (with 4123 + 4932) conceited:– wise (8), shrewd (2), conceited (1 [+1877, 1571]), conceited (1 [+4123, 1571]), sensible (1), they[S] (1 [+3836])

G5862 φρονίμως *phronimōs*, adv. [1] [√5856]. shrewdly, wisely:– shrewdly (1)

G5863 φροντίζω *phrontizō*, v. [1] [√5856]. to be careful, concerned:– careful (1)

G5864 φρουρέω *phroureō*, v. [4] [√4574 + 3972]. to guard; (pass.) to be held prisoner; to be shielded:– guard (1), guarded (1), held in custody (1), shielded (1)

G5865 φρυάσσω *phryassō*, v. [1] to rage, rave:– rage (1)

G5866 φρύγανον *phryganon*, n. [1] brushwood, firewood:– brushwood (1)

G5867 Φρυγία *Phrygia*, n. pr. [3] Phrygia:– Phrygia (3)

G5868 φυγαδεύω *phygadeuō*, v. Not used in NIVEBC. [√5771]. (tr.) to cause to become a fugitive; (intr.) to be a fugitive, live in exile

G5869 Φύγελος *Phygelos*, n. pr. [1] Phygelus, "*fugitive*":– Phygelus (1)

G5870 φυγή *phygē*, n. [1] [√5771]. flight, fleeing:– flight (1)

G5871 φυλακή *phylakē*, n. [47] [√5875]. prison, jail, haunt; guard; watch (of the night):– prison (30), haunt (3), jail (3), shortly before dawn (2 [+5480, 3836, 3816]), cell (1), guard (1), guards (1), imprisoned (1 [+1877]), imprisonment (1), imprisonments (1), keeping watch (1 [+5875]), middle of the night (1 [+1311]), time of night (1)

G5872 φυλακίζω *phylakizō*, v. [1] [√5875]. to imprison:– imprison (1)

G5873 φυλακτήριον *phylaktērion*, n. [1] [√5875]. phylactery, a small box containing Scripture verses, traditionally bound on the forehead and arm by the Jews during prayer:– phylacteries (1)

G5874 φύλαξ *phylax*, n. [3] [√5875]. guard, sentry:– guards (2), sentries (1)

G5875 φυλάσσω *phylassō*, v. [31] [→1126, 1302, 1428, 5871, 5872, 5873, 5874]. to obey, keep; to guard, watch; to keep away from, abstain:– keep (7), guard (4), kept (3), on guard (3), kept under guard (2), obey (2), abstain (1), guarded (1), guarding (1), guards (1), in obedience to (1), keeping watch (1 [+5871]), kept safe (1), obeyed (1), protect (1), protected (1)

G5876 φυλή *phylē*, n. [31] [→260, 1559, 5241; cf. 5886]. tribe; people, nation:– tribe (24), tribes (5), peoples (2)

G5877 φύλλον *phyllon*, n. [6] leaf:– leaves (5), leaf (1)

G5878 φύραμα *phyrama*, n. [5] lump (of clay), batch (of dough); derived from a Greek verb, "to mix (wet or dry) substances," not found in the NT:– batch (2), batch of dough (2), lump (1)

G5879 φυσικός *physikos*, a. [3] [√5886]. pertaining to things of nature: natural, instinctive; (n.) creatures of instinct:– natural (2), creatures of instinct (1)

G5880 φυσικῶς *physikōs*, adv. [1] [√5886]. by instinct, naturally:– by instinct (1)

G5881 φυσιόω *physioō*, v. [7] [√5886]. to puff up, inflate; (pass.) to be proud, arrogant:– arrogant (2), proud (2), puffed up (2), puffs up (1)

G5882 φύσις *physis*, n. [14] [√5886]. nature; natural state of being or characteristics:– nature (6), natural (2 [+2848]), birth (1), kinds (1), mankind (1 [+3836, 474]), nature of things (1), physically (1 [+1666]), unnatural (1 [+4123])

G5883 φυσίωσις *physiōsis*, n. [1] [√5886]. arrogance, pride:– arrogance (1)

G5884 φυτεία *phyteia*, n. [1] [√5886]. plant:– plant (1)

G5885 φυτεύω *phyteuō*, v. [11] [√5886]. to plant:– planted (5), plants (3), growing (1), planted seed (1), planting (1)

G5886 φύω *phyō*, v. [3] [→1770, 1874, 1875, 3574, 3745, 4103, 5242, 5243, 5879, 5880, 5881, 5882, 5883, 5884, 5885; cf. 5876]. to grow up, come up, referring to plant growth:– came up (2), grows (1)

G5887 φωλεός *phōleos*, n. [2] hole (in the ground), den:– dens (2)

G5888 φωνέω *phōneō*, v. [42] [√5889]. to call (out), summon:– called (10), crows (7), call (3), called out (3), calling (3), crowed (3), sent for (2 [+3306]), summoned (2), asking for (1), called aside (1), called in (1), calls (1), crow (1), invite (1), said (1), shouted (1 [+3489, 5889]), shriek (1 [+5889, 3489])

G5889 φωνή *phōnē*, n. [141] [→231, 430, 851, 936, 1771, 1876, 2215, 2787, 2971, 3032, 4715, 5244, 5245, 5246, 5247, 5888]. voice, sound, tone, noise of any kind; by extension: speaking, language:– voice (86), sound (9), voices (6), rumblings (4), called out (3 [+2048, 3306]), roar (2), shouts (2), words (2), blasts (1), call (1), called out (1 [+3306, 3489]), cried out (1 [+3189, 3489]), cry (1), gave a shout (1 [+3189]), in a loud voice (1 [+149]), in unison (1 [+1181, 1651]), languages (1), me (1 [+1609, 3836]), music (1), peal (1), peals (1), roar (1 [+3489]), say (1), saying (1), shouted (1 [+2048, 3836]), shouted (1 [+5888, 3489]), shouted (1 [+3489, 3836, 5774]), shriek (1 [+5888, 3489]), shrieks (1 [+1066, 3489]), sounded (1), sounds (1), thing[S] (1), thundering (1), tone (1), NDT (1)

G5890 φῶς *phōs*, n. [73] [√5743]. light; daylight; firelight:– light (67), daylight (2), lights (2), fire (1), firelight (1)

G5891 φωστήρ *phōstēr*, n. [2] [√5743]. star; brilliance, splendor:– brilliance (1), stars (1)

G5892 φωσφόρος *phōsphoros*, a. [1] [√5743 + 5770]. light-bearing; (n.) morning star, likely referring to the planet Venus:– morning star (1)

G5893 φωτεινός *phōteinos*, a. [5] [√5743]. full of light; bright:– full of light (3), bright (1), light (1)

G5894 φωτίζω *phōtizō*, v. [11] [√5743]. to give light, shine; (pass.) to be enlightened, illuminated:– enlightened (2), bring to light (1), brought to light (1), give light (1), gives light (1), gives light to (1), illuminated (1), make plain (1), received light (1), shines (1)

G5895 φωτισμός *phōtismos*, n. [2] [√5743]. light, illumination:– give light (1), light (1)

G5896 χ *ch*, letter. Not used in NIVEBC. letter of the Greek alphabet

G5897 χαίρω *chairō*, v. [74] [→940, 2373, 2374, 2375, 4716, 5176, 5915, 5919, 5920, 5921, 5922, 5923]. to rejoice, be glad, delighted; (as a greeting) Hail!, Greetings!:– rejoice (20), glad (14), greetings (6), delighted (4), hail (3), rejoicing (3), delight (2), happy (2), joyfully (2), full of joy (1 [+5915]), gave joy (1), given joy (1), gladly (1), gloat (1), happier (1 [+3437]), have[S] (1), joy (1), joyful (1), overjoyed (1), overjoyed (1 [+22]), overjoyed (1 [+5915, 3489, 5379]), pleased (1), rejoiced (1), rejoices (1), welcome (1 [+3306]), welcomes (1 [+3306]), were[S] (1)

G5898 χάλαζα *chalaza*, n. [4] hail, hailstorm, hailstone:– hail (2), hailstones (1), hailstorm (1)

G5899 χαλάω *chalaō*, v. [7] [→5902, 5903, 5904]. to lower, let down:– lowered (3), let down (2), I will let down (1), lowered (1 [+2768])

G5900 Χαλδαῖος *Chaldaios*, n. pr. g. [1] Chaldean:– Chaldeans (1)

G5901 χαλεπός *chalepos*, a. Not used in NIVEBC. difficult, harsh; violent€ [2]:– terrible (1), violent (1)

G5902 χαλιναγωγέω *chalinagōgeō*, v. [2] [√5899 + 72]. to keep in check, keep a rein on one's mouth:– keep a tight rein on (1), keep in check (1)

G5903 χαλινός *chalinos*, n. [2] [√5899]. bit, bridle:– bits (1), bridles (1)

G5904 χαλινόω *chalinoō*, v. Not used in NIVEBC. [√5899]. to bridle, hold in check

G5905 χάλκεος *chalkeos*, a. Not used in NIVEBC. [√5910]. made of bronze; same as 5911

G5906 χαλκεύς *chalkeus*, n. [1] [√5910]. metalworker:– metalworker (1)

G5907 χαλκηδών *chalkēdōn*, n. [1] [√5910]. chalcedony:– agate (1)

G5908 χαλκίον *chalkion*, n. [1] [√5910]. (copper or bronze) kettle:– kettles (1)

G5909 χαλκολίβανον *chalkolibanon*, n. [2] [√5910]. burnished bronze, fine bronze:– bronze (1), burnished bronze (1)

G5910 χαλκός *chalkos*, n. [5] [→5905, 5906, 5907, 5908, 5909, 5911]. copper, bronze; objects of copper:– money (2), bronze (1), copper (1), gong (1)

G5911 χαλκοῦς *chalkous*, a. [1] [√5910]. made of bronze; same as 5905:– bronze (1)

G5912 χαμαί *chamai*, adv. [2] to the ground, on the ground:– ground (1), on the ground (1)

G5913 Χανάαν *Chanaan*, n. pr. [2] [→5914]. Canaan, "*land of purple* hence *merchant trader*":– Canaan (1), Canaan (1 [+1178])

G5914 Χαναναῖος *Chananaios*, a. pr. g. [1] [√5913]. Canaanite:– Canaanite (1)

G5915 χαρά *chara*, n. [59] [√5897]. joy, rejoicing, happiness, gladness:– joy (46), happiness (2), rejoicing (2), filled with joy (1 [+22]), full of joy (1 [+5897]), glad (1), happy (1), joyful (1 [+3552]), joyfully (1 [+3552]), overjoyed (1 [+5897, 3489, 5379]), pleasant (1), so overjoyed (1 [+608, 3836])

G5916 χάραγμα *charagma*, n. [8] [→5917, 5918, 5925]. mark, stamp; image, idol:– mark (7), image (1)

G5917 χαρακτήρ *charaktēr*, n. [1] [√5916]. exact representation, reproduction:– exact representation (1)

G5918 χάραξ *charax*, n. [1] [√5916]. barricade, palisade (a defensive line or fence):– embankment (1)

G5919 χαρίζομαι *charizomai*, v. [23] [√5897]. to give grace; to forgive, cancel (a debt); to grant; to hand over into custody:– forgive (5), forgave (4), forgiven (2), gave (2), hand over (2), forgiving (1), freely given (1), graciously give (1), graciously given (1), granted (1), in grace gave (1), released (1), restored (1)

G5920 χάριν *charin*, c. *or* pp.* [10] [√5897]. therefore, because of this, for this reason:– for (2), for this reason (2 [+4047]), because of (1), for the sake of (1), grace (1 [+5921]), the reason (1 [+4047]), therefore (1 [+4005]), why (1 [+5515])

G5921 χάρις *charis*, n. [155] [√5897]. grace, the state of kindness and favor toward someone, often with a focus on a benefit given to the object; by extension: gift, benefit; credit; words of kindness and benefit: thanks, blessing:– grace (116), favor (8), thanks (6), credit (3), thank (3 [+2400]), commendable (2), gift (2), act of grace (1), benefit (1 [+1443]), benefit (1 [+2400]), bless abundantly (1 [+4246, 4355]), favor (1 [+160]), goodwill (1), grace (1 [+5920]), grace of giving (1), gracious (1), gracious gift (1), gratitude (1), offering (1), privilege (1), thankful (1), thankfulness (1)

G5922 χάρισμα *charisma*, n. [17] [√5897]. gracious gift;

GREEK INDEX

see also *5921*:– gift (8), gifts (7), gracious favor (1), spiritual gift (1)

G5923 **χαριτόω** ***charitoō***, v. [2] [√*5897*]. to give graciously, to show acts of kindness by freely giving; (n.) one highly favored; see also *5921*:– freely given (1), highly favored (1)

G5924 **Χαρράν** ***Charran***, n. pr. [2] Haran, "[earlier] *mountaineer;* perhaps *sanctuary*":– Harran (2)

G5925 **χάρτης** ***chartēs***, n. [1] [√*5916*]. (papyrus) paper:– paper (1)

G5926 **χάσμα** ***chasma***, n. [1] chasm:– chasm (1)

G5927 **χεῖλος** ***cheilos***, n. [7] lip; edge (of a shoreline):– lips (6), seashore (1 [+*3836, 2498*])

G5928 **χειμάζω** ***cheimazō***, v. [1] [√*5930*]. (pass.) to be battered in a storm:– took such a battering from the storm (1)

G5929 **χείμαρρος** ***cheimarros***, n. [1] [√*5930 + 4835*]. valley, ravine, wadi:– valley (1)

G5930 **χειμών** ***cheimōn***, n. [6] [→*5928, 5929*]. winter; stormy weather:– winter (4), storm (1), stormy (1)

G5931 **χείρ** ***cheir***, n. [177] [→*901, 942, 1429, 2217, 2218, 4741, 5932, 5933, 5934, 5935; cf. 4742, 5936*]. hand, area or portion of the hand; power, control:– hand (73), hands (71), power (2), seized (2 [+*2095, 3836*]), arms (1), arrest (1 [+*2095, 2093, 3836*]), arrested (1 [+*2095, 3836*]), arrested (1 [+*2095, 3836, 2093*]), by (1 [+*1328*]), clutches (1), entrusted to (1 [+*1877*]), finger (1), foot (1), grasp (1), hand over to (1 [+*4140, 1650*]), handed over (1 [+*4140, 3836*]), he (1 [+*1328, 3836, 899*]), help (1), motioned (1 [+*2939, 3836*]), motioned for silence (1 [+*2939, 3836*]), on (1 [+*1666*]), perform (1 [+*1181, 1328, 3836*]), performed (1 [+*1328, 3836, 1181*]), pointing (1 [+*1753*]), reached (1 [+*1753, 3836*]), seize (1 [+*2095, 2093, 3836*]), seized (1 [+*2095, 3836, 2093*]), seized (1 [+*2093, 2095, 3836*]), through (1 [+*5250*]), through (1 [+*1328, 3836*]), using (1 [+*1328*]), with (1 [+*1328*]), wrists (1)

G5932 **χειραγωγέω** ***cheiragōgeō***, v. [2] [√*5931 + 72*]. to lead by the hand:– by the hand (1), led by the hand (1)

G5933 **χειραγωγός** ***cheiragōgos***, n. [1] [√*5931 + 72*]. someone who leads by the hand, leader:– someone to lead by the hand (1)

G5934 **χειρόγραφον** ***cheirographon***, n. [1] [√*5931 + 1211*]. written code, record of debt:– charge of indebtedness (1)

G5935 **χειροποίητος** ***cheiropoiētos***, a. [6] [√*5931 + 4472*]. hand-made, man-made:– made with human hands (3), built by human hands (1), done by human hands (1), made by human hands (1)

G5936 **χειροτονέω** ***cheirotoneō***, v. [2] [√*1753; cf. 5931*]. to appoint, choose:– appointed (1), chosen (1)

G5937 **χείρων** ***cheirōn***, a. Not used in NIVEBC. worse (than); more severe than€ [11]:– worse (9), more severely (1), worse off (1)

G5938 **Χερούβ** ***Cheroub***, n. pr. [1] (pl.) cherubim:– cherubim (1)

G5939 **χήρα** ***chēra***, n. [26] widow:– widow (12), widows (12), widow (1 [+*1222*]), NDT (1)

G5940 **χθές** ***chthes***, adv. Not used in NIVEBC. [→*2396*]. yesterday

G5941 **χιλίαρχος** ***chiliarchos***, n. [21] [√*5943 + 806*]. military officer, commander; technically an officer of 1,000 soldiers; in the ancient Roman military an officer of a cohort, one tenth of a legion, about 600 soldiers:– commander (17), generals (2), high-ranking military officers (1), military commanders (1)

G5942 **χιλιάς** ***chilias***, n. [23] [√*5943*]. thousand:– 12,000 (13 [+*1557*]), thousand (5), 144,000 (3 [+*1669, 5477, 5475*]), ten thousand (2)

G5943 **χίλιοι** ***chilioi***, a. num. [11] [→*1493, 2233, 4295, 5483, 5567, 5941, 5942*]. thousand:– thousand (8), 1,260 (2 [+*1357, 2008*]), 1,600 (1 [+*1980*])

G5944 **Χίος** ***Chios***, n. pr. [1] Kios:– Chios (1)

G5945 **χιτών** ***chitōn***, n. [11] tunic, robe, clothing, undergarment:– shirt (5), clothes (1), clothing (1), garment (1), robes (1), shirts (1), undergarment (1)

G5946 **χιών** ***chiōn***, n. [2] [→*4199, 4200*]. snow:– snow (2)

G5947 **χις** ***chi***, n. num. Not used in NIVEBC. [√*cf. 5953*]. 616

G5948 **χλαμύς** ***chlamys***, n. [2] robe, cloak, a heavy outer garment used by soldiers and travelers:– robe (2)

G5949 **χλευάζω** ***chleuazō***, v. [1] [→*1430*]. to sneer, mock, scoff:– sneered (1)

G5950 **χλιαρός** ***chliaros***, a. Not used in NIVEBC. lukewarm€ [1]:– lukewarm (1)

G5951 **Χλόη** ***Chloē***, n. pr. [1] [→*5952*]. Chloe, "*tender shoot*":– Chloe's (1)

G5952 **χλωρός** ***chlōros***, a. [4] [√*5951*]. light green; pale; (n.) green plant:– green (2), pale (1), plant (1)

G5953 **χξς** ***chx***, n. num. Not used in NIVEBC. [√*cf. 5947*]. 666

G5954 **χοϊκός** ***choikos***, a. [4] [√*1772*]. made of dust, of the earth:– earthly (2), dust (1), of earth (1)

G5955 **χοῖνιξ** ***choinix***, n. [2] (almost one liter or) quart:– six pounds (1 [+*5552*]), two pounds (1)

G5956 **χοῖρος** ***choiros***, n. [12] pig:– pigs (12)

G5957 **χολάω** ***cholaō***, v. [1] [√*5958*]. to be angry:– angry (1)

G5958 **χολή** ***cholē***, n. [2] [→*5957*]. gall, bile:– full of (1 [+*1650*]), gall (1)

G5959 **χόος** ***choos***, n. Not used in NIVEBC. [√*1772*]. dust; same as *5967*

G5960 **Χοραζίν** ***Chorazin***, n. pr. [2] [→*6002*]. Korazin:– Chorazin (2)

G5961 **χορηγέω** ***chorēgeō***, v. [2] [√*5962 + 72*]. to supply, provide:– provides (1), supply (1)

G5962 **χορός** ***choros***, n. [1] [→*2220, 2221, 4743, 5961*]. dance; (pl.) dancing:– dancing (1)

G5963 **χορτάζω** ***chortazō***, v. [15] [√*5965*]. to feed; (pass.) to be filled to satisfaction, eat one's fill:– satisfied (6), feed (2), well fed (2), eat (1), eat all want (1), filled (1), gorged (1), had fill (1)

G5964 **χόρτασμα** ***chortasma***, n. [1] [√*5965*]. food:– food (1)

G5965 **χόρτος** ***chortos***, n. [15] [→*5963, 5964*]. grass, plant; this can refer to plants in various forms and stages: hay, stalk, field, etc.:– grass (9), field (1), hay (1), plant (1), stalk (1), wheat (1), wild flower (1 [+*470*])

G5966 **Χουζᾶς** ***Chouzas***, n. pr. [1] Cuza, "*little judge*":– Chuza (1)

G5967 **χοῦς** ***chous***, n. [2] [√*1772*]. dust; same as *5959*:– dust (2)

G5968 **χράομαι** ***chraomai***, v. [11] [→*712, 945, 946, 947, 2378, 2974, 3079, 4201, 4202, 5178, 5970, 5971, 5972, 5973, 5974, 5975, 5978, 5979, 5980, 5981, 5982, 5983; cf. 5969*]. to make use of, use; to do, act, proceed:– use (4), bold (1 [+*4244*]), do so (1 [+*3437*]), fickle (1 [+*3836, 1786*]), kindness (1 [+*5793*]), passed (1), used (1), uses (1)

G5969 **χράω** ***chraō***, v. Not used in NIVEBC. [→*5976, 5977; cf. 3079, 5968*]. to lend

G5970 **χρεία** ***chreia***, n. [48] [√*5968*]. need, necessity:– need (20 [+*2400*]), need (5), needs (5), need (4 [+*2400*]), needs (4 [+*2400*]), in need (3 [+*2400*]), needed (2), needed (2 [+*2400*]), dependent on (1 [+*2400*]), need (1 [+*1181, 2400*]), responsibility (1)

G5971 **χρεοφειλέτης** ***chreopheiletēs***, n. [2] [√*5968 + 4053*]. debtor:– debtors (1), owed money (1 [+*1639*])

G5972 **χρεωφειλέτης** ***chreōpheiletēs***, n. Not used in NIVEBC. [√*5968 + 4053*]. debtor

G5973 **χρή** ***chrē***, pt. *or* v. imper. [1] [√*5968*]. it should, it is necessary:– should (1)

G5974 **χρῄζω** ***chrēzō***, v. [5] [√*5968*]. to need, have need of:– need (5)

G5975 **χρῆμα** ***chrēma***, n. [6] [√*5968*]. money, wealth, possessions:– money (3), rich (2 [+*3836, 2400*]), bribe (1)

G5976 **χρηματίζω** ***chrēmatizō***, v. [9] [√*5969*]. to warn; (pass.) to bear a name; to be warned, told about, revealed to:– warned (5), called (2), revealed (1), told to ask (1)

G5977 **χρηματισμός** ***chrēmatismos***, n. [1] [√*5969*]. proclamation or answer from God:– God's answer (1)

G5978 **χρήσιμος** ***chrēsimos***, n. [1] [√*5968*]. pertaining to value, usefulness, advantage:– value (1)

G5979 **χρῆσις** ***chrēsis***, n. [2] [√*5968*]. relations, functions:– relations (1), sexual relations (1)

G5980 **χρηστεύομαι** ***chrēsteuomai***, v. [1] [√*5968*]. to be kind:– kind (1)

G5981 **χρηστολογία** ***chrēstologia***, n. [1] [√*5968 + 3306*]. smooth talk, attractive speech:– smooth talk (1)

G5982 **χρηστός** ***chrēstos***, a. [7] [√*5968*]. easy, good; kind, loving, benevolent:– good (2), kind (2), better (1), easy (1), kindness (1)

G5983 **χρηστότης** ***chrēstotēs***, n. [10] [√*5968*]. kindness, goodness:– kindness (9), good (1)

G5984 **χρῖσμα** ***chrisma***, n. [3] [√*5987*]. anointing:– anointing (3)

G5985 **Χριστιανός** ***Christianos***, n. pr. g. [3] [√*5986*]. Christian:– Christian (2), Christians (1)

G5986 **Χριστός** ***Christos***, n. pr. [529] [→*532, 5985, 6023; cf. 5987*]. Christ, Anointed One, Messiah, the Greek translation of the Hebrew 5431 (cf. Greek *3549*). The Messiah is the Son of David, an anointed leader expected to bring in an age of peace and liberty from all oppression. In the NT, the Messiah is Jesus, who came first to bring liberty from sin and peace with God and who will come again to bring all things under his control:– Christ (449), Messiah (66), Christ's (11), anointed (1), him[s] (1), this[s] (1)

G5987 **χρίω** ***chriō***, v. [5] [→*1608, 2222, 5984; cf. 5986*]. to anoint (physically, with oil; spiritually, with the Holy Spirit), to assign a person to a special task, implying a giving of power by God to accomplish the task:– anointed (4), anointing (1)

G5988 **χρονίζω** ***chronizō***, v. [5] [√*5989*]. to take a long time, delay; to stay a long time:– a long time in coming (1), delay (1), stayed so long (1), staying away a long time (1), taking a long time (1)

G5989 **χρόνος** ***chronos***, n. [54] [→*3432, 5988, 5990*]. time, period of time:– time (32), times (5), as long as (2 [+*2093, 4012*]), beginning of time (2 [+*173*]), long (2), delay (1), forty years (1 [+*5478*]), instant (1 [+*5117*]), lives (1), longer (1), longer (1 [+*2285*]), old (1), only as long as (1 [+*2093, 4012*]), past (1), so long as (1 [+*4012*]), while (1)

G5990 **χρονοτριβέω** ***chronotribeō***, v. [1] [√*5989 + 5561*]. to spend time:– spending time (1)

G5991 **χρύσεος** ***chryseos***, a. Not used in NIVEBC. [√*5996*]. made of gold; same as *5997*

G5992 **χρυσίον** ***chrysion***, n. [12] [√*5996*]. gold; gold jewelry or coins:– gold (11), gold-covered (1 [+*4328, 4119*])

G5993 **χρυσοδακτύλιος** ***chrysodaktylios***, a. [1] [√*5996 + 1235*]. having or wearing a gold ring:– wearing a gold ring (1)

G5994 **χρυσόλιθος** ***chrysolithos***, n. [1] [√*5996 + 3345*]. chrysolite:– chrysolite (1)

G5995 **χρυσόπρασος** ***chrysoprasos***, n. [1] [√*5996 + 4555*]. chrysoprase (an apple-green quartz):– turquoise (1)

G5996 **χρυσός** ***chrysos***, n. [10] [→*5991, 5992, 5993, 5994, 5995, 5997, 5998*]. gold:– gold (10)

G5997 **χρυσοῦς** ***chrysous***, a. [18] [√*5996*]. made of gold; same as *5991*:– golden (12), gold (5), of gold (1)

G5998 **χρυσόω** ***chrysoō***, v. [2] [√*5996*]. (pass.) to be adorned with gold:– glittering (2)

G5999 **χρώς** ***chrōs***, n. [1] skin, surface of the body:– touched (1 [+*608, 3836*])

G6000 **χωλός** ***chōlos***, a. Not used in NIVEBC. lame, crippled€ [14]:– lame (11), crippled (2), that way[s] (1)

G6001 **χώρα** ***chōra***, n. [28] [√*6003*]. country, land, region; countryside, field:– country (8), region (8), fields (3), land (2), Judea (1 [+*2677*]), Traconitis (1 [+*5551*]), area (1), countryside (1), ground (1), they[s] (1 [+*899, 3836*]), NDT (1)

G6002 **Χωραζίν** ***Chōrazin***, n. pr. Not used in NIVEBC. [√*5960*]. Korazin

G6003 **χωρέω** ***chōreō***, v. [10] [→*432, 713, 1774, 2353, 4369, 5102, 5103, 5181, 5723, 6001, 6005*]. to go, come; to accept; to make room, have room:– accept (3), have room (2), come (1), goes (1), holding (1), make room for (1), room (1)

G6004 **χωρίζω** ***chōrizō***, v. [13] [√*6006*]. to divide, separate, leave; (pass.) to be separated from, set apart:– separate (5), leave (2), does[s] (1), leaves (1), left (1), separated (1), set apart (1), so[s] (1)

G6005 **χωρίον** ***chōrion***, n. [10] [√*6003*]. place, parcel of land, field:– field (3), land (3), place (2), estate (1), plot of ground (1)

G6006 **χωρίς** ***chōris***, adv. [41] [→*714, 1431, 6004, 6007*]. (adv.) by itself, separately; (pp.*) without, besides, apart from, independent from:– without (22), apart from (7), not (3), besides (2), independent of (2), besides everything else (1 [+*3836, 4211*]), separate (1), separate from (1), together with (1 [+*3590*]), without (1 [+*4246*])

G6007 **χωρισμός** ***chōrismos***, n. Not used in NIVEBC. [√*6006*]. division

G6008 **χῶρος** ***chōros***, n. [1] northwest:– northwest (1)

G6009 **ψ** ***ps***, letter. Not used in NIVEBC. letter of the Greek alphabet

G6010 **ψάλλω** ***psallō***, v. [5] [→*6011*]. to sing hymns, sing songs of praise:– sing (2), make music (1), sing praises (1), sing songs of praise (1)

G6011 **ψαλμός** ***psalmos***, n. [7] [√*6010*]. Psalms (book of or section of OT); psalm, hymn of praise:– psalms (5), hymn (1), psalm (1)

G6012 **ψευδάδελφος** ***pseudadelphos***, n. [2] [√*6017 + 81 1.3*]. false brother:– false believers (2)

G6013 **ψευδαπόστολος** ***pseudapostolos***, n. [1] [√*6017 + 690*]. false apostle:– false apostles (1)

G6014 **ψευδής** ***pseudēs***, a. [3] [√*6017*]. false, lying; (n.) liar:– false (2), liars (1)

G6015 ψευδοδιδάσκαλος *pseudodidaskalos*, n. [1] [√*6017* + *1438*]. false teacher:– false teachers (1)

G6016 ψευδολόγος *pseudologos*, a. [1] [√*6017* + *3306*]. false of speech; (n.) liar:– liars (1)

G6017 ψεύδομαι *pseudomai*, v. [12] [→*950, 6012, 6013, 6014, 6015, 6016, 6018, 6019, 6020, 6021, 6022, 6023, 6024, 6025, 6026*]. to lie, speak untruths:– lie (4), lying (3), lied (2), deny (1), falsely (1), liars (1)

G6018 ψευδομαρτυρέω *pseudomartyreō*, v. [5] [√*6017* + *3459*]. to give false testimony:– give false testimony (3), gave false testimony (1), testified falsely (1)

G6019 ψευδομαρτυρία *pseudomartyria*, n. [2] [√*6017* + *3459*]. false testimony:– false evidence (1), false testimony (1)

G6020 ψευδόμαρτυς *pseudomartys*, n. [2] [√*6017* + *3459*]. false witness, one who gives false testimony:– false witnesses (2)

G6021 ψευδοπροφήτης *pseudoprophētēs*, n. [11] [√*6017* + *4735*]. false prophet:– false prophets (7), false prophet (4)

G6022 ψεῦδος *pseudos*, n. [10] [√*6017*]. lie, falsehood, deception:– lie (5), falsehood (2), counterfeit (1), deceitful (1), lies (1 [+*3281, 3836*])

G6023 ψευδόχριστος *pseudochristos*, n. [2] [√*6017* + *5986*]. (pl.) false Christs:– false messiahs (2)

G6024 ψευδώνυμος *pseudōnymos*, a. [1] [√*6017* + *3950*]. falsely called or identified:– falsely called (1)

G6025 ψεῦσμα *pseusma*, n. [1] [√*6017*]. falsehood, untruth:– falsehood (1)

G6026 ψεύστης *pseustēs*, n. [10] [√*6017*]. liar:– liar (8), liars (2)

G6027 ψηλαφάω *psēlaphaō*, v. [4] [√*6041*]. to touch, handle:– touched (2), reach out (1), touch (1)

G6028 ψηφίζω *psēphizō*, v. [2] [√*6029*]. to calculate; to estimate:– calculate (1), estimate (1)

G6029 ψῆφος *psēphos*, n. [3] [→*2975, 5164, 5248, 6028; cf. 6041*]. stone, vote (cast by stones); in NT times a white stone usually meant a vote for innocence, a black stone a vote for guilt; the white stone of Rev 2:17 may picture the innocence of its owner:– it^s (1), stone (1), vote (1)

G6030 ψιθυρισμός *psithyrismos*, n. [1] [→*6031*]. whispering gossip:– gossip (1)

G6031 ψιθυριστής *psithyristēs*, n. [1] [√*6030*]. gossip, whisperer:– gossips (1)

G6032 ψίξ *psix*, n. Not used in NIVEBC. [→*6033*]. bit, crumb

G6033 ψιχίον *psichion*, n. [2] [√*6032*]. crumb, very small piece:– crumbs (2)

G6034 ψυχή *psychē*, n. [101] [√*6038*]. life, soul; heart, mind; a person; the immaterial (and eternal) part of inner person, often meaning the animate self, which can be translated by pronouns: "my soul" = "I, myself":– life (33), soul (20), lives (5), souls (5), heart (3), I (2 [+*3836, 1609*]), minds (2), you (2 [+*3836, 5148*]), alive (1 [+*3836, 1877, 899, 1639*]), all^s (1), everyone (1 [+*4246*]), everyone (1 [+*4246*]), anyone (1 [+*4246*]), being (1), keep in suspense (1 [+*3836, 149*]), living (1 [+*2400*]), living thing (1 [+*2437*]), longed for (1 [+*2123, 3836*]), me (1 [+*1609*]), me (1 [+*3836, 1609*]), mind (1), one (1 [+*1651*]), people (1), saved (1 [+*1650, 4348*]), sold as slaves (1 [+*5393, 2779*]), strengthening (1 [+*2185, 3836*]), them (1 [+*899*]), them^s (1), themselves (1 [+*3836, 899*]), to myself (1 [+*3836, 1609*]), trying to kill (1 [+*2426, 3836*]), unstable (1 [+*844*]), us^s (1), you^s (1), you (1 [+*5148*]), yourselves (1 [+*3836, 5148*]), NDT (1)

G6035 ψυχικός *psychikos*, a. [6] [√*6038*]. pertaining to the natural state: physical, unspiritual, without the Spirit:– natural (3), follow mere natural instincts (1), unspiritual (1), without the Spirit (1)

G6036 ψῦχος *psychos*, n. [3] [√*6038*]. cold:– cold (3)

G6037 ψυχρός *psychros*, a. [4] [√*6038*]. cold:– cold (3), one^s (1)

G6038 ψύχω *psychō*, v. [1] [→*433, 434, 715, 953, 1500, 1775, 2379, 2701, 2976, 3901, 5249, 6034, 6035, 6036, 6037*]. (pass.) to grow cold:– grow cold (1)

G6039 ψωμίζω *psōmizō*, v. [2] [√*6040*]. to feed; to give to the poor:– feed (1), give to the poor (1)

G6040 ψωμίον *psōmion*, n. [4] [→*6039; cf. 6041*]. piece of bread:– bread (2), piece of bread (2)

G6041 ψώχω *psōchō*, v. [1] [→*2223, 4370, 4718, 6027; cf. 6029, 6040*]. to rub:– rub (1)

G6042 Ὦ¹ *Ō¹*, letter; n. pr. [9] letter of the Greek alphabet; Omega:– omega (3 [+*6043, 1639*]), you (3 [+*6043, 1639*])6043, 1639]), how foolish (1 [+*6043, 1639, 485*]), NDT (2 [+

G6043 ὦ² *ō²*, pt. interj. [20] O!, Oh!:– omega (3 [+*1639, 6042*]), you (3 [+*1639, 6042*]), you (3)1639, 6042]), how foolish (1 [+*1639, 6042, 485*]), oh (1), NDT (7), NDT (2 [+

G6044 Ὠβήδ *Ōbēd*, n. pr. Not used in NIVEBC. [√*2725*]. Obed, "*servant* or *worshiper*"

G6045 ὧδε *hōde*, adv. [61] [√*3836*]. here:– here (48), this (5), here he is (1 [+*2627*]), here it is (1 [+*2627*]), here's (1), in the one case (1 [+*3525*]), now (1 [+*3370*]), there (1), NDT (2)

G6046 ᾠδή *ōdē*, n. [7] [→*106, 3069*]. song:– song (4), songs (2), NDT (1)

G6047 ὠδίν *ōdin*, n. [4] [→*5349, 6048*]. labor, birth pain; agony (of death):– birth pains (2), agony (1), labor pains (1)

G6048 ὠδίνω *ōdinō*, v. [3] [√*6047*]. to suffer the pains of childbirth:– in labor (1), in the pains of childbirth (1), pain (1 [+*2779, 989*])

G6049 ὦμος *ōmos*, n. [2] (pl.) shoulders:– shoulders (2)

G6050 ὠνέομαι *ōneomai*, v. [1] [→*4072; cf. 5467*]. to buy:– bought (1)

G6051 ᾠόν *ōon*, n. [1] egg:– egg (1)

G6052 ὥρα *hōra*, n. [103] [→*2469, 2470, 6053*]. hour, portion of time, while, moment:– hour (41), time (25), moment (8), noon (6 [+*1761*]), hours (3), little while (2), nine in the morning (2 [+*5569*]), three in the afternoon (2 [+*1888*]), at noon (1 [+*1761*]), at once (1 [+*899, 3836*]), five in the afternoon (1 [+*1895*]), four in the afternoon (1 [+*1281*]), getting late (1 [+*3836, 4216*]), immediately (1 [+*1877, 899, 3836*]), late (1 [+*4070, 3836*]), late in the day (1 [+*4498*]), nine (1 [+*5569*]), nine in the morning (1 [+*5569, 3836, 2465*]), one in the afternoon (1 [+*1575*]), short (1), three in the afternoon (1 [+*1888, 3836, 2465*]), very late (1 [+*4498*])

G6053 ὡραῖος *hōraios*, a. [4] [√*6052*]. beautiful:– beautiful (4)

G6054 ὠρύομαι *ōryomai*, v. [1] to roar:– roaring (1)

G6055 ὡς *hōs*, pt. & c. [502] [→*2777, 2778, 6056, 6058, 6059, 6061, 6062, 6063*]. as, that, how, about, when; like, as:– as (155), like (123), when (32), just as (21), about (19), as if (15), how (11), after (5), as though (5), while (5), and (4), of (4), so (3), to (3), looked like (2), meaning (2 [+*2093*]), on (2), on the pretext of (2), regarded as (2), resembled (2), that (2), the same as (2 [+*2779*]), though (2), when (2 [+*323*]), according to (1), allegedly (1), as soon as (1), as soon as (1 [+*323, 1994*]), as soon as possible (1 [+*5441*]), asserting (1), at (1), because (1), blood red (1 [+*135*]), by the standards of (1 [+*2848*]), compared with (1), considered (1 [+*2400*]), for (1), for that (1), hold (1 [+*2400*]), in accordance with (1 [+*3586*]), just as (1 [+*1569*]), just like (1), less than two miles (1 [+*5084, 1278*]), now (1 [+*4036*]), one might even say (1 [+*2229, 3306*]), seem (1 [+*1639*]), seemed (1), since (1), so-called (1 [+*3306*]), somehow or other (1 [+*323*]), that is (1), the same way (1 [+*2779*]), the size of (1), trying to (1 [+*323*]), trying to (1), unlike (1 [+*4024*]), what (1), whatever (1), NDT (43)

G6056 ὡσάν *hōsan*, rel. adv. + pt. Not used in NIVEBC. [√*6055* + *323*]. as if, as it were, so to speak

G6057 ὡσαννά *hōsanna*, l.[v.+pt.] [6] Hosanna! (exclamation of praise, originally "Save [us]!"):– hosanna (6)

G6058 ὡσαύτως *hōsautōs*, adv. [17] [√*6055* + *899*]. in the same way, so also, likewise, similarly:– in the same way (7), the same thing (2), also (1), likewise (1), same (1), similarly (1), so also (1), the same (1), the same way (1), too (1)

G6059 ὡσεί *hōsei*, pt. comp. [21] [√*6055* + *1623*]. like, as; about (an approximation):– about (12), like (6), as (1), looked so much like (1 [+*1181*]), what seemed to be (1)

G6060 Ὡσηέ *Hōsēe*, n. pr. [1] Hosea, "*salvation*":– Hosea (1)

G6061 ὥσπερ *hōsper*, pt. comp. [36] [√*6055* + *4302*]. as, just as; like:– as (15), just as (9), like (6), as indeed (1), since (1), the way (1), unlike (1), what (1), NDT (1)

G6062 ὡσπερεί *hōsperei*, pt. comp. [1] [√*6055* + *4302* + *1623*]. like, as though, as it were:– as (1)

G6063 ὥστε *hōste*, pt. [83] [√*6055* + *5445*]. a marker for introducing clauses: for this reason, therefore, so; so that, resulting in; to, for the purpose of:– so that (19), so (18), therefore (12), that (6), so then (5), such that (5), to (4), as a result (3), and (2), now (2), consequently (1), how to (1), in order to (1), then (1), NDT (3)

G6064 ὠτάριον *ōtarion*, n. [2] [√*4044*]. ear:– ear (2)

G6065 ὠτίον *ōtion*, n. [3] [√*4044*]. ear:– ear (3)

G6066 ὠφέλεια *ōpheleia*, n. [2] [√*6067*]. value, advantage:– advantage (1), value (1)

G6067 ὠφελέω *ōpheleō*, v. [15] [→*543, 4055, 6066, 6068*]. to be of good use; to have value; to help; to devote (as a gift) to God:– good (3), help (2), of value (2), benefit (1), counts for (1), gain (1), getting (1), getting better (1), getting nowhere (1 [+*4024, 4029*]), good for (1), has value (1)

G6068 ὠφέλιμος *ōphelimos*, a. [4] [√*6067*]. valuable, useful, profitable:– value (2), profitable (1), useful (1)

GREEK INDEX

NUMBERING SYSTEM INDEXES

FEATURES OF THE INDEX OF STRONG → GOODRICK/KOHLENBERGER NUMBERS

STRONG NUMBER
Non-italic "roman" numbers are Hebrew or Aramaic; *italic* numbers are Greek (see pages xii, xviii).

G/K NUMBER
Hebrew numbers start with "H"; Aramaic numbers start with "A"; Greek numbers are *italic* and start with "*G.*"

STRONG............ G/K

1............................ H3
2.................... A10003

ONE-TO-ONE CORRESPONDENCE
Most Strong numbers have a one-to-one correspondence to a G/K number (see page xviii).

11........................ H10
"......................... H11

DITTO MARKS (")
Indicates a Strong number corresponds to more than one G/K number (see page xviii).

1508..... G1623+3590
1509............... G1623
+3590+5516

PLUS MARKS (+)
Indicates a Strong number corresponds to a combination of G/K numbers (see page xviii).

2467

NO LEADER DOTS; NO G/K/ NUMBER
Indicates a Strong number has no equivalent in the G/K numbering system (limited to conjectured roots and word fragments not found in the biblical texts).

INDEX OF STRONG → GOODRICK/KOHLENBERGER NUMBERS

STRONG	G/K
531	H576
532	H577
533	H579
534	H580
535	H581
"	H582
536	H583
537	H584
538	H585
539	H586
"	H587
540	A10041
541	H587
542	H588
543	H589
544	H590
545	H594
546	H593
547	H595
548	H591
549	H592
550	H578
"	H596
551	H597
552	H598
553	H599
554	H600
555	H601
556	H602
557	H603
558	H604
"	H605
559	H606
"	H607
560	A10042
561	H609
"	H610
"	H611
562	H608
563	A10043
564	H612
"	H613
565	H614
"	H615
566	H617
567	H616
568	H618
"	H619
569	H620
570	H621
571	H622
572	H623
573	H624
574	A10028
575	H625
576	A10044
577	H626
"	H629
578	H627
579	H628
580	H630
581	A10045
582	H632
"	A10046
583	H633
584	H634
585	H635
586	A10047
587	H636
588	H637
589	H638
590	H639
591	H641
592	H640
593	H642
594	H643
595	H644
596	H645
597	H646
598	A10048
599	H647
600	A10049
601	H649
602	H650
603	H651
604	H652
605	H631
"	H653
606	A10050
607	A10051
"	A10052
608	A10053
609	H654
610	H655
611	H656
612	H657
613	A10054
614	H658
615	H659
616	H660
617	H661
618	H662
619	H663
620	A10055
621	H664
622	H665
"	H4417
623	H666
624	H667
625	H668
626	H669
627	H670
628	H671
629	A10056
630	H672
631	H673
632	H674
633	A10057
634	H675
635	H676
636	A10058
637	H677
638	A10059
639	H678
"	H690
640	H679
641	H681
642	H682
643	H683
644	H684
"	H685
645	H686
646	H680
647	H688
648	H689
649	H691
650	H692
"	H693
651	H695
652	H694
653	H696
654	H697
655	H698
656	H699
657	H700
"	H701
658	H702
"	H1956
659	H703
660	H704
661	H705
662	H706
663	H707
664	H708
665	H709
666	H710
667	H711
668	H712
669	H713
670	A10060
671	A10061
"	A10062
672	H714
"	H715
"	H716
"	H717
673	H718
674	A10063
675	H719
676	H720
677	A10064
678	H721
"	H722
679	H723
680	H724
681	H725
682	H727
"	H728
683	H729
684	H730
685	H731
686	H732
687	H733
688	H734
689	H735
690	H736
691	H737
692	H739
"	H740
693	H741
694	H742
695	H743
696	H744
697	H746
698	H747
699	H748
700	H749
701	H750
702	H752
703	A10065
704	H753
705	H754
706	H752
707	H755
708	H756
709	H758
"	H759
710	H760
711	A10066
712	H761
713	H763
714	H764
715	H765
716	H766
717	H768
718	A10067
719	H770
720	H769
721	H773
722	H771
"	H772
723	H774
"	H795
724	H776
725	H777
726	H145
727	H778
728	H779
"	H819
729	H775
730	H780
731	H781
732	H782
733	H783
734	H784
735	A10068
736	H785
737	H786
738	H787
"	A10069
739	H738
740	H790
"	H791
741	H789
742	H767
743	H792
744	H793
745	H794
746	H796
"	A10070
747	H798
748	H799
"	H837
749	A10071
750	H800
"	H803
751	H804
752	H801
753	H802
754	A10073
755	A10072
756	A10074
757	H805
758	H806
759	H810
760	H809
761	H812
"	H8246
762	H811
763	H808
"	H5645
764	H813
765	H814
766	H815
767	H816
768	H817
769	H818
770	H820
771	H821
772	A10075
773	A10076
774	H822
775	H823
776	H824
777	H825
778	A10077
779	H826
780	H827
781	H829
782	H830
783	H831
"	A10078
784	H836
785	A10080
786	H838
787	A10079
788	H839
789	H840
790	H841
791	H842
792	H843
793	H845
794	H844
795	H846
796	H847
797	H848
798	H849
799	H850
800	H836
801	H852
802	H851
803	H853
"	H859
804	H855
805	H856
"	H857
806	H858
807	H860
808	H861
809	H862
810	H863
811	H864
812	H865
"	H866
813	H867
814	H868
815	H869
816	H870
817	H871
818	H872
819	H873
820	H875
821	H874
822	H876
823	H877
824	H878
825	H879
826	A10081
827	H880
828	H881
829	H882
830	H883
831	H884
832	H885
833	H886
"	H887
834	H889
"	H948
"	H3876
"	H4424
835	H890
"	H897
836	H888
837	H891
838	H892
"	H893
"	H894
839	H9309
840	H832
841	H833
842	H895
843	H896
"	H898
844	H835
845	H834
846	A10082
847	H900
848	H901
849	A10083
850	H902
851	H903
"	H904
852	A10084
853	H254
"	H906
854	H907
"	H4425
855	H908
856	H909
857	H910
858	A10085
859	H905
"	H911
"	H914
"	H917
"	H920
860	H912
861	A10086
862	H913
"	H916
863	H416
"	H915
864	H918
865	H919
866	H921
867	H922
868	H925
869	H924
870	A10087
"	A10092
871	H926
872	H929
873	A10090
874	H930
875	H931
876	H932
877	H934
878	H938
879	H935
880	H939
881	H940
882	H941
883	H936
"	H4307
"	H8022
884	H933
"	H937
"	H8682
885	H942
886	H943
887	H944
888	A10091
889	H945
890	H947
891	H946
892	H949
893	H950
894	H951
895	A10093
896	A10094
897	H952
898	H953
899	H954
"	H955
900	H956
901	H957
902	H958
903	H960
904	H961
"	H962
905	H963
"	H964
"	H4224
906	H965
907	H966
"	H967
908	H968
909	H969
910	H970
911	H971
912	H973
913	H974
"	H975
914	H976
915	H977
916	H978
917	H979
918	H980
919	H981
920	H982
921	A10095
922	H983
923	H985
924	A10096
925	H986
926	H987
927	A10218
"	A10097
928	H988
929	H989
930	H990
931	H984
"	H991
932	H992
933	H993
934	H994
935	H995
"	H4215
936	H996
937	H997
938	H998
939	H999
940	H1000
941	H1001
942	H1002
943	H1003
944	H1005
"	H1006
945	H1004
946	H1007
947	H1008
948	H1009
949	H1010
950	H1011
951	H1012
952	H1013
953	H1014
"	H1071
954	H1017
"	H1018
955	H1019
956	A10102
957	H1020
958	H1021
959	H1022
"	H5802
960	H1022
961	H1023
962	H1024
963	H1025
964	H1026
965	H1027
966	H1028
967	H1029
968	H1030
969	H1031
970	H1033
"	H1037
971	H1032
"	H1039
972	H1040
973	H1041
"	H1042
974	H1043
975	H1044
976	H1046
977	H1034
"	H1047
"	H1048
978	H1049
979	H1035
980	H1036
"	H1038
981	H1051
982	H1052
"	H1053
"	H1054
983	H1055
984	H1056
985	H1057
986	H1059
987	H1058
988	H1060
989	A10098
990	H1061
991	H1062
992	H1063
993	H1064
994	H1065
995	H1067
996	H1068
"	H1075
997	A10099
998	H1069
999	A10100
1000	H1070
1001	A10101
1002	H1072
1003	H1073
1004	H1074
"	H1428
1005	A10103
1006	H1076
1007	H1077
1008	H1078
1009	H745
"	H1079
1010	H1081
"	H1110
1011	H1082
"	H1348
1012	H1083
1013	H1084
1014	H1085
1015	H1086
"	H1814
1016	H1087
1017	H1088
"	H2029
1018	H726
"	H1089
"	H2032
1019	H1090
1020	H1093
"	H2127
"	H3811
1021	H1094
"	H2130
1022	H1095
"	H2140
1023	H1092
1024	H1096
"	H1112
"	H2175
1025	H1097
"	H2195
1026	H1098
"	H2196
1027	H1099
"	H2234
1028	H1100
1029	H1101
"	H2242
1030	H1128
"	H9090
1031	H1102
1032	H1103
"	H2582
1033	H1105
"	H4122
1034	H1106
1035	H1107
1036	H1108
"	H4364
"	H6765
1037	H1109
1038	H1111
1039	H1113
1040	H1114
1041	H1115
1042	H1116
"	H6712
1043	H1117
1044	H1118
"	H6820
1045	H1119
1046	H1120
1047	H1121
1048	H1122
"	H7208
1049	H1123
"	H7449
1050	H1124
1051	H1125
1052	H1126
"	H8632
"	H9093
1053	H1127
1054	H1130
1055	H1131
1056	H1133
1057	H1132
1058	H1134
1059	H1135
1060	H1147
1061	H1137
1062	H1148
1063	H1136
1064	H1138
1065	H1140
1066	H1141
1067	H1142
1068	H1143
1069	H1144
1070	H1145
1071	H1146
1072	H1149
1073	H1136
1074	H1150
1075	H1152
1076	H1151
1077	H1153
"	H1154
1078	H1155
1079	A10104
1080	A10106
1081	H1156
1082	H1158
1083	H1159
1084	H1160
1085	H1161
1086	H1162
1087	H1165
1088	H1163
1089	H1164
1090	H1167
"	H1168
1091	H1166
1092	H1169
1093	A10107
1094	H1170
1095	H1171
1096	A10108
1097	H1172
"	H4442
1098	H1173
1099	H1174
1100	H1175
1101	H1176
"	H1177
1102	H1178
1103	H1179
1104	H1180
"	H1181
"	H1182
1105	H1183
"	H1184
1106	H1185
"	H1186
1107	H1187
1108	H1188
1109	H1189
"	H1190
1110	H1191
"	H4444
1111	H1192
1112	H1157
1113	A10105
"	A10109
1114	H1193
1115	H1194
1116	H1195
1117	H1196
1118	H1197
1119	H1198
1120	H1199
"	H1200
1121	H1201
"	H1217
"	H4240
1122	H1202
1123	A10110
1124	A10111
1125	H1203
1126	H1204
1127	H1205
1128	H1206
1129	H1215
1130	H1207
1131	H1218
1132	H1209
1133	H1210
1134	H1211
1135	H1212
1136	H1213
1137	H1220
1138	H1221
1139	H1222
"	H1400
1140	H1224
1141	H1225
"	H1226
1142	H1223
1143	H1227
1144	H1228
1145	H1229
1146	H1230
1147	A10112
1148	H1231
1149	A10113
1150	H1232
1151	H1214
1152	H1233
1153	H1234
1154	H1235
1155	H1235
1156	A10114
1157	H1237
"	H1238
1158	H1239
"	H1240
1159	A10115
1160	H1242
1161	H1243
1162	H1244
"	H1245
1163	H1246
1164	H1247
1165	H1248
1166	H1241
"	H1249
1167	H1250
"	H1251
1168	H1252
1169	A10116
1170	H1253
1171	H1254
1172	H1266
1173	H1267
1174	H1255
1175	H1268
"	H6599
1176	H1256
1177	H1257
1178	H1258
1179	H1259
1180	H1266
1181	H1252+1195
1182	H1269
1183	H1270
1184	H1270
1185	H1271
1186	H1260
1187	H1261
1188	H1262
1189	H1263
1190	H1264
1191	H1272
1192	H1273
1193	H1265

STRONG	G/K
1194	H1274
1195	H1275
1196	H1276
1197	H1277
"	H1278
"	H1279
1198	H1280
1199	H1281
1200	H1282
1201	H1284
1202	H1283
1203	H1285
1204	H1286
1205	H1287
1206	H1288
1207	H1289
1208	H1290
1209	H1291
1210	H1292
"	H1293
1211	H1294
1212	H1295
1213	H1296
"	H1297
1214	H1298
1215	H1299
1216	H1301
1217	H1302
1218	H1304
1219	H1305
"	H1306
"	H1307
1220	H1309
1221	H1310
"	H1311
1222	H1309
1223	H1312
1224	H1313
"	H7652
1225	H1315
"	H7394
1226	H1314
"	H1316
1227	H1317
1228	H1318
1229	H1319
1230	H1320
1231	H1321
1232	H1322
1233	H1323
1234	H1324
1235	H1325
1236	A10117
1237	H1326
1238	H1327
"	H1328
1239	H1329
1240	A10118
1241	H1330
1242	H1331
"	H1332
1243	H1333
1244	H1334
1245	H1335
1246	H1336
1247	A10120
1248	H1337
1249	H1338
1250	H1339
"	H1340
1251	A10119
1252	H1341
1253	H1342
1254	H1343
"	H1344
"	H1345
1255	H1347
1256	H1349
1257	H1350
1258	H1351
1259	H1352
1260	H1354
"	H1355
1261	H1353
1262	H1346
"	H1356
"	H1357
1263	H1358
1264	H1394
1265	H1360
1266	H1361
1267	H1362
1268	H1363
"	H1408
1269	H1364
"	H1365
1270	H1366
1271	H1367
1272	H1368
"	H1369

STRONG	G/K
"	H1370
1273	H1372
1274	H1356
"	H1357
1275	H1373
1276	H1379
1277	H1374
1278	H1375
1279	H1376
1280	H1378
1281	H1371
1282	H1377
1283	H1380
1284	H1381
1285	H1382
1286	H451
1287	H1383
1288	H1384
"	H1385
1289	A10121
"	A10122
1290	H1386
1291	A10123
1292	H1387
1293	H1388
1294	H1389
"	H1390
1295	H1391
1296	H1392
"	H1393
1297	A10124
1298	H1396
1299	H1397
1300	H1398
1301	H1399
1302	H1401
1303	H1402
1304	H1403
"	H1404
1305	H1359
"	H1405
"	H1406
1306	H1407
1307	H1409
1308	H1410
1309	H1415
1310	H1418
1311	H1419
1312	H1420
1313	H1411
1314	H1411
1315	H1412
1316	H1421
"	H1422
1317	H1423
1318	H1424
1319	H1413
1320	H1414
1321	A10125
1322	H1425
1323	H1426
1324	H1427
1325	A10126
1326	H1429
1327	H1431
1328	H1432
"	H1433
1329	H1434
1330	H1435
1331	H1436
1332	H1437
1333	H1438
1334	H1439
1335	H1440
1336	H1441
1337	H1442
1338	H1443
1339	H1444
1340	H1445
1341	H1447
1342	H1448
1343	H1450
1344	H1449
1345	H1451
1346	H1452
1347	H1454
1348	H1455
1349	H1456
1350	H1453
"	H1457
1351	H1458
1352	H1459
1353	H1460
1354	H1461
"	H1462
1355	A10128
1356	H1463
"	H1464
1357	H1466
1358	A10129

STRONG	G/K
1359	H1570
1360	H1465
1361	H1467
1362	H1468
1363	H1470
1364	H1469
1365	H1471
1366	H1473
1367	H1474
1368	H1475
1369	H1476
1370	A10130
1371	H1477
1372	H1478
1373	H1480
1374	H1481
1375	H1483
1376	H1484
1377	H1485
1378	H1486
1379	H1487
1380	H1488
1381	H1489
1382	H1490
1383	H1491
1384	H1492
1385	H1482
1386	H1493
1387	H1494
1388	H1495
1389	H1496
1390	H1497
1391	H1500
1392	H1499
1393	H1498
1394	H1501
"	H1502
1395	H1503
1396	H1504
1397	H1505
1398	H1506
1399	H1504
1400	A10131
1401	A10132
1402	H1507
1403	H1508
1404	H1509
1405	H1510
1406	H1511
1407	H1512
1408	H1513
1409	H1513
1410	H1514
1411	A10133
1412	H1516
1413	H1517
"	H1518
1414	A10134
1415	H1519
1416	H1522
1417	H1521
1418	H1523
1419	H1472
"	H1524
"	H2045
1420	H1525
1421	H1526
"	H1528
1422	H1527
1423	H1531
1424	H1533
1425	H1532
1426	H1534
1427	H1535
1428	H1536
1429	H1537
1430	H1538
"	H1539
1431	H1540
1432	H1541
1433	H1542
1434	H1544
1435	H1543
1436	H1545
"	H1546
1437	H1547
1438	H1548
1439	H1549
1440	H1550
1441	H1551
1442	H1552
1443	H1553
1444	H1555
1445	H1554
1446	H1529
"	H1530
1447	H1555
1448	H1556
"	H1560
1449	H1557

STRONG	G/K
1450	H1558
1451	H1559
1452	H1561
1453	H1562
1454	H1563
1455	H1564
1456	H1565
1457	H1566
1458	H1567
1459	A10135
1460	H1568
"	H1569
1461	H1572
1462	H1479
"	H1571
1463	H1573
1464	H1574
1465	H1576
1466	H1576
1467	H1575
"	A10136
1468	H1577
1469	H1578
1470	H1579
1471	H1580
"	H1582
1472	H1581
1473	H1583
1474	H1584
1475	H1585
1476	H1586
1477	H1587
1478	H1588
1479	H1589
1480	H1590
1481	H1591
"	H1592
"	H1593
1482	H1594
1483	H1595
1484	H1596
1485	H1597
1486	H1598
1487	H1599
"	H1641
1488	H1600
1489	H1601
1490	A10139
1491	H1602
1492	H1603
1493	H1604
1494	H1605
1495	H1606
1496	H1607
1497	H1608
1498	H1610
1499	H1609
1500	H1611
1501	H1612
1502	H1613
1503	H1614
1504	H1615
"	H1616
1505	A10140
1506	H1617
1507	H1618
1508	H1619
1509	H1620
1510	A10141
1511	H1621
"	H1747
1512	H1623
1513	H1624
"	H1625
1514	H1626
1515	H1627
1516	H1628
1517	H1630
1518	H1622
"	H1631
1519	A10137
1520	H1632
1521	H1633
1522	H1634
1523	H1635
1524	H1636
"	H1637
1525	H1638
1526	H1639
1527	H1640
1528	A10142
1529	H1642
1530	H1643
"	H1644
1531	H1646
1532	H1647
1533	H1648
1534	H1649
"	H1650
1535	A10143

STRONG	G/K
1536	H1651
1537	H1652
"	H2055
1538	H1653
1539	H1654
1540	H1655
1541	A10144
1542	H1656
1543	H1657
"	H1684
1544	H1658
1545	H1659
1546	H1661
1547	A10145
1548	H1662
1549	H1663
1550	H1664
1551	H1665
1552	H1666
1553	H1667
1554	H1668
1555	H1669
1556	H1670
"	H1671
1557	H1672
1558	H1673
1559	H959
"	H1674
1560	A10146
1561	H1645
1562	H1675
1563	H1676
1564	H1677
1565	H1678
1566	H1679
1567	H1681
1568	H1680
1569	H1682
1570	H1683
1571	H1685
1572	H1686
1573	H1687
1574	H1688
1575	H1689
1576	H1691
1577	H1690
1578	H1692
1579	H1693
1580	H1694
1581	H1695
1582	H1696
1583	H1697
1584	H1698
1585	A10147
1586	H1699
"	H1700
1587	H1701
"	H1702
1588	H1703
"	H2056
1589	H1704
1590	H1705
1591	H1706
1592	H1707
1593	H1708
1594	H1708
1595	H1709
"	H1710
1596	A10148
1597	H1711
1598	H1713
1599	H1714
"	H1715
1600	H1716
1601	H1717
1602	H1718
1603	H1720
1604	H1719
1605	H1721
1606	H1722
1607	H1723
1608	H1724
1609	H1725
1610	H1726
"	H1727
1611	A10149
1612	H1728
1613	H1729
1614	H1730
1615	H1732
1616	H1731
1617	H1733
1618	H1734
1619	H1735
"	H1736
1620	H1737
1621	H1738
1622	H1739
1623	H1740
1624	H1741

STRONG	G/K
1625	H1742
1626	H1743
1627	H1744
1629	H1746
1630	H1748
1631	H1749
1632	H1754
1633	H1750
"	H1751
1634	H1752
1635	A10150
1636	H1753
1637	H1755
1638	H1756
1639	H1757
"	H1758
1640	H1759
1641	H1760
1642	H1761
1643	H1762
1644	H1763
"	H1764
1645	H1765
1646	H1766
1647	H1768
1648	H1767
1649	H1769
1650	H1770
1651	H1771
1652	H1772
1653	H1773
1654	H1774
"	H1776
1655	A10151
1656	H1775
1657	H1777
1658	H1778
1659	H1779
1660	H1780
1661	H1781
1662	H1783
1663	H1785
1664	H1786
1665	H1787
1666	H1788
1667	H1784
1668	A10154
1669	H1790
1670	H1791
1671	H1792
1672	H1793
1673	H1795
"	H1869
1674	H1796
1675	H1797
1676	H1798
1677	H1800
1678	A10155
1679	H1801
1680	H1803
1681	H1804
1682	H1805
1683	H1806
1684	A10156
1685	A10157
1686	H1807
1687	H1808
1688	H1809
"	H1810
"	H4255
1689	H1812
1690	H1811
1691	H1813
1692	H1815
1693	A10158
1694	H1817
1695	H1816
1696	H1818
"	H1819
"	H1820
1697	H1821
1698	H1822
"	H1823
1699	H1824
1699'	H1825
1700	H1826
1701	A10159
1702	H1827
1703	H1830
1704	H1828
1705	H1829
1706	H1831
1707	H1832
1708	H1833
1709	H1794
"	H1834
1710	H1836
1711	H1835
1712	H1837
1713	H1838

STRONG	G/K
"	H1839
"	H5609
1714	H1840
1715	H1841
1716	H1842
1717	H1843
1718	H1844
1719	H1847
"	H1848
1720	H1848
1721	H1849
"	H8102
"	H8114
1722	A10160
1723	A10161
"	A10162
1724	H1850
1725	H1851
1726	H1852
1727	H1853
1728	H1854
1729	H1855
1730	H1856
1731	H1857
1732	H1858
1733	H1860
1734	H1846
"	H1861
1735	H1845
1736	H1859
"	H1863
1737	H1862
1738	H1864
1739	H1865
1740	H1866
1741	H1867
1742	H1868
1743	H1870
1744	H1871
1745	H1872
1746	H1873
"	H1874
1747	H1875
1748	H1876
1749	H1880
1750	H1881
1751	H1882
1752	H1883
"	H1884
1753	A10163
1754	H1885
"	H3903
1755	H1886
"	H1887
1756	H1799
"	H1888
1757	A10164
1758	H1889
1759	A10165
1760	H1890
"	H1891
1761	A10166
1762	H1892
1763	A10167
1764	H1893
1765	H1894
1766	H1895
1767	H972
"	H1896
"	H3904
"	H4514
1768	A10168
1769	H1897
1770	H1899
1771	H1900
1772	H1901
1773	H1902
1774	H1903
1775	H1904
1776	H1905
1777	H1878
"	H1879
"	H1906
1778	A10169
1779	H1907
"	H8723
"	H8726
1780	A10170
1781	H1908
1782	A10171
1783	H1909
1784	A10172
1785	H1911
1786	H1912
1787	H1914
1788	H1913
1789	H1915
1790	H1916
1791	A10173
1792	H1917

STRONG	G/K
1793	H1918
"	H1919
1794	H1920
1795	H1921
1796	H1922
1797	A10174
1798	A10175
1799	A10176
"	A10177
1800	H1924
1801	H1925
1802	H1926
"	H1927
1803	H1929
"	H1930
1804	H1931
1805	H1932
1806	H1933
"	H1934
1807	H1935
1808	H1936
1809	H1937
"	H1938
1810	H1939
1811	H1940
"	H1941
1812	H1942
1813	H1943
1814	H1944
1815	A10178
1816	H1945
1817	H1923
"	H1928
"	H1946
1818	H1947
1819	H1948
1820	H1949
"	H1950
1821	A10179
1822	H1951
1823	H1952
1824	H1953
"	H1954
1825	H1955
1826	H1957
"	H1958
"	H1959
1827	H1960
1828	H1961
1829	H1962
1830	H1963
1831	H1964
1832	H1965
1833	H1967
1834	H1877
"	H1966
"	H2008
1835	H1968
"	H1969
1836	A10180
1837	H1972
1838	H1973
1839	H1974
1840	H1971
"	H1975
1841	A10181
1842	H1970
1843	H1976
1844	H1978
1845	H1979
1846	H1980
1847	H1981
"	H1982
"	H1983
1848	H1984
1849	H1985
1850	H1986
1851	H1987
1852	H1988
1853	H1989
1854	H1990
1855	A10182
1856	H1991
1857	H1992
1858	H1993
1859	A10183
1860	H1994
1861	H1995
"	H1996
1862	H1997
1863	H1998
1864	H1999
1865	H2001
"	H2002
1866	H2000
1867	H2003
1868	A10184
1869	H2005
1870	H2006
1871	H2007

STRONG	G/K
1872	A10185
1873	H2009
1874	H2010
1875	H2004
"	H2011
1876	H2012
1877	H2013
1878	H2014
1879	H2015
1880	H2016
1881	H2017
1882	A10186
1883	A10187
1884	A10188
1885	H2018
1886	H2019
1887	H2026
1888	A10194
"	A10195
1889	H2027
1890	H2037
1891	H2038
1892	H2039
1893	H2040
1894	H2041
1895	H2042
1896	H2043
"	H2051
1897	H2047
1898	H2048
1899	H2049
1900	H2050
1901	H2052
1902	H2053
1903	H2054
1904	H2057
1905	H2058
1906	H2059
1907	A10196
1908	H2060
1909	H2061
1910	H2062
1911	H2063
1912	H2064
1913	H2066
"	H2067
1914	H2068
1915	H2070
1916	H2071
1917	A10197
1918	H2072
1919	H2073
1920	H2074
1921	H2065
"	H2075
1922	A10198
1923	A10199
1924	H2076
1925	H2078
1926	H2077
1927	H2079
1928	H2080
1929	H2081
1930	H2082
1931	H2085
"	H2115
1932	A10200
"	A10205
1933	H2092
"	H2093
1934	A10201
1935	H2086
1936	H2087
1937	H2088
1938	H2089
1939	H2069
"	H2090
1940	H2091
1941	H2091
1942	H2094
"	H2095
1943	H2096
1944	H2097
1945	H2098
1946	A10202
1947	H2099
1948	H2100
1949	H2101
1950	H2102
1951	H2103
1952	H2104
1953	H2106
1954	H2107
1955	H2108
1956	H2110
1957	H2111
1958	H2113
1959	H2116
1960	H2117
1961	H181
"	H2118
1962	H2119
1963	H2120
1964	H2121
1965	A10206
1966	H2122
1967	H2123
1968	H2124
1969	H2125
1970	H2128
"	H2686
1971	H2129
1972	H2133
1973	H2131
"	H2134
1974	H2136
1975	H2137
"	H4208
1976	H2138
1977	H2139
1978	H2141
1979	H2142
1980	H2143
1981	A10207
1982	H2144
1983	A10208
1984	H2145
"	H2146
"	H2147
1985	H2148
1986	H2150
1987	H2152
1988	H2151
1989	H2153
1990	H2154
1991	H2155
1992	H2156
"	H2160
"	H2161
1993	H2159
1994	A10210
1995	H2162
"	H2171
1996	H2163
1997	H2164
1998	H2166
1999	H2167
2000	H2169
"	H2170
2001	H2172
2002	A10211
"	A10212
2003	H2173
2004	H2177
2005	H2176
2006	A10213
2007	H2179
2008	H2178
2009	H2180
2010	H2182
2011	H1208
"	H2183
2012	H2184
2013	H2187
"	H2188
2014	H2198
2015	H2200
2016	H2201
2017	H2201
2018	H2202
2019	H2203
2020	H2208
2021	H2210
2022	H2215
2023	H2216
2024	H2217
2025	H2219
2026	H2222
2027	H2223
2028	H2224
2029	H2105
"	H2225
2030	H2226
"	H2230
2031	A10217
2032	H2228
"	H2231
2033	H2229
2034	H2232
2035	H2233
2036	H2235
2037	H2227
2038	H2236
2039	H2237
2040	H2238
2041	H2239
2042	H2215
2043	H828
"	H2034
"	H2240
2044	H2244
2045	H2245
2046	H2247
2047	H2251
2048	H2252
"	H9438
2049	H2253
2050	H2109
"	H2254
2051	H2258
2052	H2259
2053	H2260
2054	H2261
2055	H2262
2056	H2263
2057	H2264
2058	H2265
2059	H2266
2060	H2267
2061	H2269
2062	H2270
2063	H2271
2064	H2272
2065	H2273
2066	H2274
2067	H2275
2068	H2276
2069	H2277
"	H2278
2070	H2279
2071	H2280
2072	H2281
2073	H2291
"	H2292
2074	H2282
2075	H2283
2076	H2284
2077	H2285
2078	H2286
2079	H2287
2080	H2288
2081	H2289
2082	H2290
2083	H2291
2084	A10223
2085	H2293
2086	H2294
2087	H2295
2088	H2296
2089	H8445
2090	H2297
2091	H2298
2092	H2299
2093	H2300
2094	H2301
"	H2302
2095	A10224
2096	H2303
2097	H2305
2098	H2306
2099	H2304
2100	H2307
2101	H2308
2102	H2326
2103	A10225
2104	H2309
2105	H2311
2106	H2312
2107	H2313
2108	H2314
2109	H2315
"	H3469
2110	A10226
2111	H2316
"	H2398
2112	A10227
2113	H2317
2114	H2319
"	H2320
2115	H2318
2116	H2318
2117	H2321
2118	H2310
"	H2322
2119	H2323
"	H2324
2120	H2325
2121	H2327
2122	A10228
2123	H2328
"	H2329
2124	H2330
2125	H2331
2126	H2332
2127	H2333
2128	H2334
"	H2335
2129	H2336
2130	H2337
2131	H2338
"	H2414
"	H2415
2132	H2339
2133	H2340
2134	H2341
2135	H2342
2136	A10229
2137	H2343
2138	H2344
"	H2345
2139	H2346
2140	H2347
2141	H2348
2142	H2349
"	H2350
"	H4654
2143	H2352
"	H2354
2144	H2353
2145	H2351
2146	H2355
2147	H2356
2148	H2357
"	H2358
"	A10230
2149	H2359
2150	H2360
2151	H2361
"	H2362
2152	H2363
2153	H2364
2154	H2365
2155	H2366
2156	H2367
2157	H2368
2158	H2369
2159	H2370
2160	H2371
2161	H2372
2162	H2373
2163	H2374
2164	A10231
2165	H2375
2166	A10232
2167	H2376
2168	H2377
2169	H2378
2170	A10233
2171	A10234
2172	H2379
2173	H2380
2174	H2381
"	H2382
2175	H2383
2176	H2384
2177	H2385
2178	A10235
2179	H2386
2180	H2387
2181	H2388
"	H2389
"	H2390
2182	H2391
"	H2392
2183	H2393
2184	H2394
2185	H2390
2186	H2395
"	H2396
2187	H2397
2188	H2399
2189	H2400
2190	H2401
2191	H2402
2192	A10236
2193	H2403
2194	H2404
2195	H2405
2196	H2406
"	H2407
2197	H2408
2198	H2409
2199	H2410
2200	A10237
2201	H2411
2202	H2412
2203	H2413
2204	H2416
2205	H2418
2206	H2417
2207	H2419
2208	H2421
2209	H2420
2210	H2422
2211	A10238
2212	H2423
2213	H2425
2214	H2424
"	H2426
2215	H2427
2216	H2428
2217	A10239
2218	H2429
2219	H2430
"	H2431
"	H4664
"	H4668
2220	H2432
2221	H2433
2222	H2434
"	H2449
2223	H2435
2224	H2436
2225	H2437
2226	H2438
2227	H2439
2228	H2440
2229	H2441
"	H2442
2230	H2443
2231	H2444
2232	H2445
2233	H2446
2234	A10240
2235	H2447
"	H2448
2236	H2450
"	H2451
2237	H2452
"	H2453
2238	H2454
2239	H2455
2240	H2456
2241	H2457
2242	H2458
2243	H2460
2244	H2461
2245	H2462
2246	H2463
2247	H2464
2248	A10242
2249	H2466
2250	H2467
2251	H2468
2252	H2469
2253	H2470
2254	H2471
"	H2472
"	H2473
2255	A10243
2256	H2474
"	H2475
"	H2476
"	H2477
"	H2482
2257	A10244
2258	H2478
"	H2481
2259	H2480
2260	H2479
2261	H2483
2262	H2484
2263	H2485
2264	H2486
2265	H2487
2266	H2248
"	H2488
"	H2489
2267	H2490
2268	H2491
2269	A10245
2270	H2492
2271	H2493
2272	H2494
2273	A10246
2274	H2495
2275	H2496
"	H2497
"	H6306
2276	H2498
2277	H2499
2278	H2500
2279	H2501
2280	H2502
2281	H2503
2282	H2504
2283	H2505
2284	H2506
2285	H2507
2286	H2508
"	H2509
2287	H2510
2288	H2511
2289	H2513
2290	H2512
"	H2514
2291	H2515
2292	H2516
"	A10247
2293	H2517
2294	H2518
2295	H2519
2296	H2520
2297	H2522
2298	A10248
2299	H2521
2300	H2523
"	H2527
2301	H2524
2302	H2525
"	H2526
2303	H2529
2304	H2530
2305	A10250
2306	A10249
2307	H2531
2308	H2532
"	H2533
2309	H2535
2310	H2534
2311	H2536
2312	H2537
2313	H2538
2314	H2539
2315	H2540
2316	H2540
2317	H2541
2318	H2542
2319	H2543
2320	H2544
2321	H2545
2322	H2546
2323	A10251
2324	A10252
2325	H2549
2326	H2550
2327	H2551
2328	H2552
2329	H2553
2330	H2554
2331	H2555
"	H2556
2332	H2558
2333	H2557
2334	H2596
2335	H2559
2336	H2560
2337	H2561
2338	A10253
2339	H2562
2340	H2563
2341	H2564
2342	H2565
"	H2655
"	H2656
2343	H2566
2344	H2567
"	H2568
2345	H2569
2346	H2570
2347	H2571
2348	H2572
2349	H2573
2350	H2574
2351	H2575
2352	H2987
2353	H2580
2354	H2581
2355	H2583
2356	H2986
2357	H2578
2358	A10254
2359	H2585
2360	H2584
2361	H2586
"	H2587
2362	H2588
2363	H2590
"	H2591
2364	H2592
2365	H2593
2366	H2594
"	H3123
"	H3131
2367	H2595
2368	H2597
2369	H2598
2370	A10255
2371	H2599
"	H2604
2372	H2600
2373	H2601
2374	H2602
"	H2603
2375	H2605
2376	A10256
2377	H2606
2378	H2608
2379	A10257
2380	H2607
2381	H2609
2382	H2610
2383	H2611
2384	H2612
2385	H2613
2386	H2614
2387	H2615
2388	H2616
2389	H2617
2390	H2618
2391	H2619
2392	H2620
2393	H2621
2394	H2622
2395	H2623
2396	H2624
"	H2625
2397	H2626
2398	H2627
"	H2630
"	H3148
2399	H2628
2400	H2629
2401	H2631
2402	A10258
2403	H2632
"	H2633
2404	H2634
2405	H2635
2406	H2636
2407	H2637
2408	A10259
2409	A10260
2410	H2638
2411	H2639
2412	H2640
2413	H2641
2414	H2642
2415	H2643
2416	H2644
"	H2645
"	H2646
"	H2651
"	H2652
"	H2653
2417	A10261
2418	A10262
2419	H2647
2420	H2648
2421	H2649
2422	H2650
2423	A10263
2424	H2654
2425	H2649
2426	H2658
2427	H2659
"	H2660
2428	H2657
"	H2662
2429	A10264
2430	H2658
2431	H2663
"	H2691
2432	H2661
"	H2664
2433	H2665
2434	H2666
2435	H2667
2436	H2576
"	H2668
2437	H2669
2438	H2670
"	H2671
2439	H2590
2440	H2673
2441	H2674
2442	H2675
2443	H2676
2444	H2677
2445	A10265
2446	H2678
2447	H2679
2448	H2680
2449	H2681
2450	H2682
2451	H2683
2452	A10266
2453	H2685
2454	H2684
2455	H2687
2456	H2688
2457	H2689
2458	H2690
2459	H2693
2460	H2694
2461	H2692
2462	H2695
2463	H2696
2464	H2697
2465	H2698
2466	H2699
2467	H2700
2468	H2701
2469	H2702
2470	H2703
"	H2704
2471	H2705
2472	H2706
2473	H2708
2474	H2707
"	H2709
2475	H2710
2476	H2711
2477	H2712
2478	H2713
2479	H2714
2480	H2715
2481	H2717
2482	H2718
2483	H2716
2484	H2719
2485	H2720
2486	H2721
2487	H2722
2488	H2723
2489	H2724
"	H3875
2490	H2725
"	H2726
"	H2727
2491	H2728
"	H2729
2492	H2730
"	H2731
2493	A10267
2494	H2732
2495	H2733
2496	H2734
2497	H2735
2498	H2736
"	H2737
2499	A10268
2500	H2739
2501	H2738
2502	H2740
"	H2741
2503	H2742
2504	H2743
2505	H2744
"	H2745
"	H2746
2506	H2749
"	H2750
2507	H2751
2508	A10269
2509	H2747
2510	H2748
2511	H2747
2512	H2752
2513	H2753
"	H2754
2514	H2756
2515	H2755
2516	H2757
2517	H2758
2518	H2759
"	H2760
2519	H2761
2520	H2762
2521	H2211
"	H2763
2522	H2764
"	H2765
2523	H2766
2524	H2767
2525	H2768
2526	H2769
2527	H2770
2528	A10270
2529	H2772
2530	H2773
"	H2776
2531	H2774
2532	H2775
2533	H2777
2534	H2771
"	H2778
"	H2779
2535	H2780
2536	H2781
2537	H2782
"	H2795
2538	H2783
2539	H2784
2540	H2785
2541	H2787
2542	H2788
2543	H2789
"	H2790
2544	H2791

STRONG	G/K	STRONG	G/K	STRONG	G/K	STRONG	G/K	STRONG	G/K	STRONG	G/K	STRONG	G/K	STRONG	G/K
2545	H2792	2622	H2882	2703	H2965	2779	H3074	"	H3165	2942	A10302	3029	A10312	3115	H3425
2546	H2793	2623	H2883	"	H6541	2780	H3073	2860	H3163	2943	H3250	3030	H3339	3116	H3426
2547	H2794	2624	H2884	2704	H2966	2781	H3075	2861	H3164	2944	H3249	3031	H3340	3117	H3427
2548	H2796	2625	H2885	2705	H2967	2782	H3024	2862	H3166	2945	H3251	3032	H3341	"	H3428
2549	H2797	2626	H2886	2706	H2976	"	H3076	2863	H3167	"	H3252	3033	H3342	3118	A10317
2550	H2798	2627	A10276	2707	H2977	"	H3077	2864	H3168	2946	H3253	3034	H3343	3119	H3429
"	H2800	2628	H2887	2708	H2978	2783	A10284	2865	H3169	"	H3254	"	H3344	3120	H3430
2551	H2799	2629	H2888	2709	H2979	2784	H3078	2866	H3170	2947	H3255	3035	H3345	3121	H3431
2552	H2801	2630	H2889	2710	H2980	2785	H3079	2867	H3171	"	H3257	"	H3346	3122	H3432
2553	H2802	2631	A10277	2711	H2981	2786	H3080	2868	A10293	"	H3258	"	H3350	3123	H3433
2554	H2803	2632	A10278	2712	H2577	2787	H2579	2869	A10294	2948	H3256	3036	H3347	3124	H3434
"	H2804	2633	H2890	"	H2982	"	H3014	2870	H3174	2949	H3259	3037	H3348	3125	H3436
2555	H2805	2634	H2891	2713	H2983	"	H3081	"	H3175	2950	H3260	3038	H3349	3126	H3437
2556	H2786	2635	A10279	2714	H2984	"	H3082	2871	H3178	2951	H3261	"	H3353	3127	H3438
"	H2806	2636	H2892	2715	H2985	2788	H3083	2872	H3179	2952	H3262	"	H3357	3128	H3439
"	H2807	2637	H2893	2716	H2989	2789	H3084	2873	H3180	2953	A10303	3039	H3351	3129	H3440
"	H2808	2638	H2894	2717	H2990	2790	H3086	2874	H3181	2954	H3263	3040	H3352	3130	H3441
2557	H2809	2639	H2895	"	H2991	"	H3087	"	H3183	2955	H3264	3041	H3354	3131	H3442
"	H4721	2640	H2896	2718	A10281	2791	H3089	2875	H3182	2956	H3265	3042	H3355	3132	H3443
2558	H2810	2641	H2897	2719	H2995	2792	H3090	2876	H3184	2957	A10304	3043	H3356	3133	H3444
2559	H2811	2642	H2898	2720	H2992	2793	H3091	2877	A10295	2958	H3266	3044	H3358	3134	H3445
2560	H2812	2643	H2899	2721	H2996	"	H3092	2878	H3186	2959	H3267	3045	H1977	3135	H3447
"	H2813	2644	H2901	"	H2997	2794	H3086	2879	H3185	2960	H3268	"	H3359	3136	H3449
"	H2814	2645	H2902	2722	H2998	2795	H3094	2880	H3187	2961	H3269	3046	A10313	"	A10318
2561	H2815	2646	H2903	2723	H2999	2796	H3088	2881	H3188	2962	H3270	3047	H3360	3137	H3451
2562	A10271	2647	H2904	2724	H3000	"	H3093	2882	H3189	2963	H3271	3048	H3361	3138	H3453
2563	H2816	2648	H2905	2725	H3001	2797	H3095	2883	H3190	2964	H3272	3049	H3362	3139	H3454
"	H2817	2649	H2906	2726	H3002	2798	H1629	2884	H3191	2965	H3273	3050	H3363	3140	H3455
"	H2818	2650	H2907	"	H3003	"	H3096	2885	H3192	2966	H3274	3051	H2035	3141	H3456
2564	H2819	2651	H2908	2727	H3004	2799	H3098	2886	H3193	2967	A10305	"	H3364	3142	H3457
2565	H2798	2652	H2909	2728	H3005	2800+1471	H2046	2887	H3194	2968	H3277	3052	A10314	3143	H3458
2566	H2820	2653	H2910	2729	H3006	2800+1471	H3099	2888	H3195	2969	H3278	3053	H3365	3144	H3459
2567	H2821	2654	H2911	2730	H3007	2801	H3100	2889	H3196	2970	H3279	3054	H3366	3145	H3460
2568	H2822	"	H2912	2731	H3010	2802	H3101	2890	H3196	"	H3280	3055	H3372	3146	H3461
2569	H2823	2655	H2913	2732	H3011	2803	H3108	2891	H3197	2971	H3281	3056	H3367	3147	H3462
2570	H2824	2656	H2914	2733	H3009	"	H3110	2892	H3198	2972	H3285	3057	H3368	3148	H3463
2571	H2821	2657	H2915	"	H3012	2804	A10285	"	H3199	2973	H3282	3058	H3369	3149	H3464
2572	H2825	2658	H2916	2734	H3013	2805	H3109	"	H4756	2974	H3283	3059	H3370	"	H3465
"	H2826	2659	H2917	2735	H1515	2806	H3111	2893	H3200	2975	H3284	3060	H3371	3150	H3466
2573	H2827	2660	H2918	"	H2044	2807	H3112	2894	H3173	2976	H3286	3061	A10315	3151	H3467
2574	H2828	"	H2919	"	H2988	2808	H3113	2895	H3512	2977	H3287	3062	A10316	3152	H3468
"	H4217	2661	H7249	2736	H3015	2809	H3114	2896	H3176	"	H3288	3063	H3373	3153	H3470
2575	H2829	2662	H2920	"	H3029	2810	H3115	"	H3177	2978	H415	3064	H3374	"	H3471
"	H2830	2663	H2921	2737	H3016	2811	H3116	"	H3201	"	H3289	3065	H3375	3154	H3472
2576	H2831	2664	H2924	2738	H3017	"	H3117	"	H3202	2979	H3290	3066	H3376	3155	H3473
2577	H2833	2665	H2925	2739	H3018	2812	H3118	"	H3205	2980	H3291	3067	H3376	3156	H3474
2578	H2832	2666	H2926	2740	H3019	2813	H3119	"	H3208	2981	H3292	"	H3377	3157	H3475
2579	H2828+8041	2667	H2927	2741	H3020	2814	H3120	2897	H3203	2982	H3293	3068	H3378	"	H3476
2580	H2834	2668	H2928	"	H3042	2815	H3121	"	H3204	2983	H3294	3069	H3378	3158	H3477
2581	H2835	2669	H2929	2742	H3021	2816	A10286	2898	H3206	2984	H3295	3070	H3378+8011	3159	H3477
2582	H2836	"	H2931	"	H3022	2817	H3102	2899	H3207	2985	H3296	3071	H3378+5812	3160	H2465
2583	H2837	2670	H2930	"	H3023	2818	A10287	2900	H3209	2986	H3297	3072	H3378+7404	"	H3478
2584	H2839	2671	H2932	"	H3025	"	A10288	"	H3210	2987	A10308	3073	H3378+8934	3161	H3479
2585	H2840	2672	H2933	"	H3026	2819	A10289	2901	H3211	2988	H3298	3074	H3378+9004	3162	H3480
"	H2841	"	H2934	2743	H3027	2820	H3104	"	H3684	2989	H3299	3075	H3379	"	H3481
2586	H2842	"	H2935	2744	H3028	2821	H3124	2902	H3212	2990	H3301	3076	H3380	3163	H3482
2587	H2843	2673	H2936	2745	H3030	"	H3127	"	H3220	2991	H3300	3077	H3381	3164	H3484
2588	H2844	2674	H2937	2746	H3031	2822	H3125	2903	H3213	2992	H3302	3078	H3382	3165	H3485
2589	H2838	"	H2938	2747	H3032	2823	H3126	2904	H3214	2993	H3303	3079	H3383	3166	H3487
2590	H2845	2675	H2548	2748	H3033	2824	H3128	2905	H3215	2994	H3304	"	H3451	3167	H3488
"	H2846	"	H2939	2749	A10282	2825	H3128	2906	A10296	2995	H3305	3080	H3384	3168	H3489
"	H2847	2676	H2940	2750	H3034	2826	H3129	2907	H3216	2996	H3306	3081	H3385	3169	H3490
2591	A10272	2677	H2942	2751	H3035	2827	A10290	2908	A10297	2997	H3307	3082	H3386	"	H3491
2592	H2848	"	H2944	2752	H3036	2828	H3130	2909	H3217	2998	H3308	3083	H3387	3170	H3492
2593	H2849	2678	H2943	2753	H3037	2829	H3132	2910	H3219	2999	H3309	3084	H3388	3171	H3486
2594	H2850	2679	H4971	2754	H3038	2830	H3133	2911	H3218	3000	H3310	3085	H3389	"	H3493
2595	H2851	2680	H4971	2755	H3039	2831	H3134	2912	H3221	3001	H3312	3086	H3390	3172	H3494
2596	H2852	2681	H2948	2756	H3040	2832	H3135	"	H3223	3002	H3313	"	H3391	3173	H3495
2597	A10273	2682	H2945	2757	H3043	2833	H3136	2913	H3222	3003	H3314	3087	H3392	3174	H3496
2598	H2853	"	H2946	"	H3044	2834	H3103	2914	H3224	"	H3315	3088	H3393	3175	H3497
2599	H2854	"	H2947	2758	H3045	"	H3106	2915	H3225	"	H3316	"	H3454	3176	H3498
2600	H2855	2683	H2949	2759	H3046	"	H3107	2916	H3226	3004	H3317	3089	H3394	3177	H3499
2601	H2856	2684	H2950	2760	H3047	2835	H3105	2917	A10298	3005	H3311	3090	H3395	3178	H3500
2602	H2857	2685	A10280	2761	A10283	2836	H3137	2918	H3227	3006	H3318	3091	H3397	3179	H3501
2603	H2858	2686	H2951	2762	H3048	"	H3138	2919	H3228	3007	A10309	3092	H3398	3180	H3502
"	H2859	"	H2952	2763	H3049	2837	H3139	2920	A10299	3008	H3319	"	H3399	3181	H3503
2604	A10274	2687	H2953	"	H3050	2838	H3122	2921	H3229	3009	H3320	3093	H3400	3182	H3504
2605	H2860	2688	H2954	2764	H3051	2839	H3140	2922	H3231	3010	H3321	3094	H3401	3183	H3505
2606	H2861	2689	H2956	"	H3052	2840	H3141	2923	H3230	3011	H3322	3095	H3402	3184	H3506
2607	H2862	2690	H2955	2765	H3054	2841	H3142	2924	H3231	3012	H3323	3096	H3403	3185	H3507
2608	H2863	"	H2957	2766	H3053	2842	H3143	2925	H3232	3013	H3324	"	H3404	3186	H3508
"	H2864	2691	H2958	2767	H3055	2843	H3144	2926	H3233	"	H5652	3097	H3405	3187	H3509
"	A10275	"	H2973	2768	H3056	2844	H3145	2927	A10300	3014	H3325	3098	H3406	3188	H2249
2609	H2865	2692	H2960	2769	H3057	"	H3146	2928	H3234	3015	H3326	3099	H3407	"	H3510
2610	H2866	2693	H1520	2770	H3058	2845	H3147	"	H3235	3016	H3328	3100	H3408	3189	H3511
2611	H2867	"	H2961	2771	H3059	2846	H3149	2929	H3236	3017	H3327	3101	H3409	3190	H3512
"	H2868	2694	H2250	"	H3060	2847	H3150	2930	H3237	3018	H3330	3102	H3410	3191	A10320
2612	H2869	"	H2959	2772	H3061	2848	H3151	"	H3239	3019	H3329	3103	H3411	3192	H3513
2613	H2870	"	H2962	2773	H2589	2849	H3152	2931	H3238	3020	H3332	"	H3412	3193	H3514
2614	H2871	2695	H2968	2774	H3062	2850	H3153	2932	H3240	3021	H3333	3104	H3413	3194	H3420
2615	H2872	"	H2974	2775	H3063	2851	H3154	2933	H3241	3022	H3334	3105	H3414	3195	H3515
2616	H2873	2696	H2969	"	H3064	2852	H3155	"	H3242	3023	H3335	3106	H3415	3196	H3516
"	H2874	"	H2970	"	H3066	2853	H3156	2934	H3243	3024	H3331	3107	H3416	3197	H3517
2617	H2875	2697	H2971	2776	H3065	2854	H3157	2935	H3244	3025	H3336	3108	H3417	3198	H3519
"	H2876	2698	H2972	2777	H3067	2855	H3158	2936	H3245	3026	H3337	3109	H3418	3199	H3520
2618	H2877	2699	H2958	"	H3068	2856	H3159	2937	H3246	"	H8447	3110	H3419	"	H3521
2619	H2878	2700	H2975	2778	H3069	2857	A10291	2938	H3247	"	A10310	3111	H3421	3200	H3522
2620	H2879	2701	H2963	"	H3070	2858	H3160	2939	A10301	"	A10679	3112	H3422	3201	H3523
2621	H2880	2702	H2964	"	H3071	2859	H3161	2940	H3248	3027	H3338	3113	H3423	3202	A10321
"	H2881	"	H6065	"	H3072	"	H3162	2941	A10301	3028	A10311	3114	H3424	3203	H3524

STRONG	G/K
"	H3525
3204	H3518
"	H3526
"	H3527
3205	H3528
"	H4256
3206	H3529
3207	H3530
3208	H3531
3209	H3533
3210	H3534
3211	H3535
3212	H2143
3213	H3536
3214	H3537
3215	H3538
3216	H4363
3217	H3539
3218	H3540
3219	H3541
3220	H3542
3221	A10322
3222	H3553
3223	H3543
3224	H3544
3225	H3545
3226	H3546
3227	H3549
3228	H3547
3229	H3550
"	H3551
3230	H3552
3231	H3554
3232	H3555
3233	H3548
"	H3556
3234	H3557
3235	H3558
3236	H3559
3237	H3560
3238	H3435
"	H3561
3239	H3562
"	H3563
3240	H4965
3241	H3564
"	H3565
3242	H3566
3243	H3567
"	H4787
"	H5682
3244	H3568
3245	H3569
"	H3570
3246	H3571
3247	H3572
3248	H3573
3249	H6073
3250	H3574
3251	H3575
3252	H3576
3253	H3577
3254	H3578
"	H6231
3255	A10323
3256	H3579
"	H3580
"	H3581
3257	H3582
3258	H3583
"	H3584
3259	H3585
3260	H3587
"	H3588
3261	H3589
3262	H3590
3263	H3591
3264	H3623
3265	H3592
"	H3600
3266	H3593
3267	H3594
3268	H3595
3269	H3596
3270	H3597
3271	H3598
3272	A10324
"	A10325
3273	H3599
3274	H3601
3275	H3602
3276	H3603
3277	H3604
3278	H3605
3279	H3606
"	H3608
3280	H3607
3281	H3609
3282	H3610
3283	H3612
"	H6720
3284	H3613
3285	H3614
3286	H3615
3287	H3617
3288	H3616
"	H3618
3289	H3446
"	H3619
"	H6805
3290	H3620
3291	H3621
3292	H3622
3293	H3623
"	H3624
"	H3625
3294	H3586
"	H3628
3295	H3626
"	H3627
3296	H762
"	H3629
3297	H3630
3298	H3631
3299	H3632
"	H3633
3300	H3634
3301	H3635
3302	H3636
3303	H3637
3304	H3638
"	H3645
3305	H3639
3306	H3640
3307	H3641
3308	H3642
3309	H3643
"	H3644
3310	H3646
3311	H3647
3312	H3648
3313	H3649
3314	H3650
3315	H3651
3316	H3652
"	H3653
3317	H3654
3318	H3448
"	H3655
"	H7361
3319	A10707
3320	H3656
"	H7388
3321	A10326
3322	H3657
3323	H3658
3324	H3659
3325	H3660
3326	H3661
"	H3662
"	H3666
3327	H3663
3328	H3664
3329	H3665
3330	A10327
3331	H3667
3332	H3668
3333	H3669
3334	H7674
3335	H3450
"	H3670
3336	H3671
3337	H3672
3338	H3674
3339	H3673
3340	H3672
3341	H3675
3342	H3676
3343	H3677
3344	H3678
"	H3683
3345	A10328
3346	A10329
3347	H3680
3348	H3681
3349	H3682
3350	H3679
3351	H3685
3352	H3686
3353	H3687
3354	H3688
3355	H3690
3356	H3691
3357	H3692
3358	A10330
3359	H3693
3360	H3694
3361	H3695
3362	H3696
3363	H3697
3364	H3699
3365	H3700
3366	H3702
3367	A10331
3368	H3698
"	H3701
"	H3703
"	H7941
3369	H3704
3370	H3705
3371	H3706
3372	H3707
"	H3708
3373	H3710
3374	H3711
3375	H3712
3376	H3713
3377	H3714
3378	H3715
3379	H3716
3380	H3717
3381	H3718
3382	H3719
3383	H3720
3384	H3452
"	H3709
"	H3721
"	H3722
"	H3723
3385	H3725
3386	H3726
3387	H3728
3388	H3729
"	H3730
3389	H3731
3390	A10332
3391	H3732
3392	H3733
3393	A10333
3394	H3734
3395	H3736
3396	H3737
3397	H3738
3398	H3739
3399	H3740
"	H8184
3400	H3741
3401	H3742
3402	H3743
3403	H3744
3404	H3745
"	H3746
3405	H3735
"	H3747
3406	H3748
"	H3755
"	H3756
3407	H3749
3408	H3750
3409	H3751
3410	A10334
3411	H3752
3412	H3754
3413	H3757
3414	H3758
"	H3759
3415	H3760
3416	H3761
3417	H3762
3418	H3764
3419	H3763
3420	H3766
3421	H3767
3422	H3768
3423	H3769
3424	H3771
3425	H3772
3426	H3780
3427	H3782
"	H3794
3428	H3784
3429	H3783
3430	H3785
"	H3787
3431	H3786
3432	H3795
3433	H3788
3434	H3790
3435	H3791
3436	H3792
3437	H3793
"	H3806
3438	H3796
3439	H3797
3440	H3798
3441	H3799
3442	H3800
"	H3801
3443	A10336
3444	H3802
3445	H3803
3446	H3773
3447	H3804
3448	H414
"	H3805
3449	H3807
"	H3808
3450	H3774
3451	H3809
"	H3812
3452	H3810
3453	H3813
3454	H3814
3455	H3775
3456	H3815
3457	H3816
3458	H3817
3459	H3818
3460	H3819
"	H3820
3461	H3821
3462	H3822
"	H3823
3463	H3825
3464	H3826
3465	H3824
3466	H3827
3467	H3828
"	H3830
"	H4635
3468	H3829
3469	H3831
3470	H3832
"	H3833
3471	H3835
3472	H3834
3473	H3836
3474	H3837
"	H9223
3475	H3840
3476	H3841
3477	H3838
"	H3839
3478	H3776
3479	A10335
3480	H3777
3481	H3778
3482	H3778
3483	H3842
3484	H3843
3485	H3779
3486	H3844
3487	A10337
3488	A10338
3489	H3845
3490	H3846
3491	H3847
3492	H3848
3493	A10339
3494	H3849
3495	H3850
3496	H3853
3497	H3854
3498	H3855
3499	H3856
"	H3857
3500	H3858
3501	H3859
3502	H3860
3503	H3861
3504	H3862
3505	H3863
3506	H3864
3507	H3865
3508	H3866
3509	H3867
3510	H3872
3511	H3873
3512	H3874
3513	H3877
3514	H3880
3515	H3878
3516	H3879
3517	H3881
3518	H3882
3519	H3883
3520	H3884
"	H3885
3521	H3886
3522	H3887
3523	H3889
3524	H3888
3525	H3890
3526	H3891
3527	H3892
3528	H3893
3529	H3894
3530	H3896
3531	H3895
3532	H3897
3533	H3899
3534	H3900
3535	H3898
3536	H3901
3537	H3902
3538	A10343
3539	H3905
3540	H3906
3541	H3907
3542	A10345
3543	H3908
"	H3909
3544	H3910
3545	H3911
3546	A10346
3547	H3912
3548	H3913
3549	A10347
3550	H3914
3551	A10348
3552	H3915
3553	H3916
3554	H3917
3555	H3918
3556	H3919
3557	H3920
3558	H3921
3559	H3922
"	H5787
"	H5788
3560	H3923
3561	H3924
3562	H3925
3563	H3926
"	H3927
3564	H3929
3565	H3930
3566	H3931
3567	A10350
3568	H3932
"	H3933
3569	H3934
3570	H3935
3571	H3934
3572	H3936
3573	H3937
"	H8403
3574	H3938
3575	H3939
"	H3940
3576	H3941
3577	H3942
3578	H3943
3579	H3944
3580	H3945
3581	H3946
"	H3947
3582	H3948
3583	H3949
3584	H3950
3585	H3951
3586	H3952
3587	H3953
3588	H3954
3589	H3957
3590	H3958
3591	H3959
3592	H3961
3593	H3960
3594	H3962
3595	H3963
3596	H3964
3597	H3965
3598	H3966
3599	H3967
3600	H3968
3601	H3969
3602	H3970
3603	H3971
3604	A10352
3605	H3972
3606	A10353
3607	H3973
"	H3974
"	H3984
3608	H3975
3609	H3976
3610	H3977
3611	H3978
3612	H3979
"	H3981
3613	H3980
3614	H3982
3615	H3983
3616	H3985
3617	H3986
3618	H3987
3619	H3990
3620	H3991
3621	H3992
3622	H3988
"	H3993
3623	H3994
3624	H3995
3625	H3996
3626	H3997
3627	H3998
3628	H3989
"	H3999
3629	H4000
3630	H4002
3631	H4001
3632	H4003
3633	H4004
3634	H4005
3635	A10354
3636	H4006
3637	H4007
3638	H4008
3639	H4009
3640	H4010
3641	H4011
"	H4012
3642	H4014
3643	H4016
"	H4018
3644	H4017
3645	H4019
"	H4020
3646	H4021
3647	H4022
3648	H4023
3649	H4024
3650	H4025
3651	H4026
"	H4027
"	H4028
"	H4338
3652	A10357
3653	H4029
"	H4030
3654	H4031
"	H4038
3655	H4033
3656	H4034
3657	H4035
3658	H4036
3659	H4037
3660	A10358
3661	
3662	H4039
3663	H4040
"	H4041
"	H4042
3664	H4043
3665	H4044
3666	H4045
3667	H4046
"	H4047
3668	H4049
3669	H4048
"	H4050
"	H4051
3670	H4052
3671	H4053
3672	H4054
"	H4055
3673	A10359
3674	H4056
3675	A10360
3676	H4058
3677	H4057
"	H4060
3678	H4058
"	H4061
3679	A10361
3680	H4059
3681	H4062
3682	H4064
3683	H4065
3684	H4067
3685	H4068
3686	H4069
3687	H4070
3688	H4071
3689	H4072
"	H4073
3690	H4074
3691	H4075
3692	H4077
3693	H4076
3694	H4063
3695	H4078
3696	H4079
3697	H4080
3698	H4081
3699	H4082
3700	H4083
3701	H4084
3702	A10362
3703	H4085
3704	H4086
3705	A10363
3706	A10364
"	A10365
"	A10563
3707	H4087
3708	H4088
"	H4089
3709	H4090
3710	H4091
3711	H4092
3712	H4093
3713	H4094
"	H4095
3714	H4096
3715	H4097
"	H4099
3716	H4098
3717	H4100
3718	H4101
3719	H4102
3720	H4103
3721	H4104
3722	H4105
"	H4106
3723	H4107
3724	H4108
"	H4109
"	H4110
"	H4111
3725	H4113
3726	H2194
"	H4112
"	H6671
3727	H4114
3728	H4115
3729	A10366
3730	H4117
3731	H4116
3732	H4118
3733	H4119
"	H4120
"	H4121
3734	H4123
"	A10367
3735	A10369
3736	H4124
3737	A10368
3738	H3928
"	H4125
"	H4127
"	H4128
3739	H4126
3740	H4130
3741	H4129
3742	H4131
3743	H4132
3744	A10370
3745	A10371
3746	H4133
3747	H4134
3748	H4135
3749	H4136
3750	H4137
3751	H4138
3752	H4139
3753	H4140
3754	H4142
"	H4148
3755	H4141
"	H4144
3756	H4145
3757	H4146
3758	H4147
3759	H4149
"	H4152
3760	H4150
"	H4151
3761	H4153
3762	H4153
3763	H4154
3764	A10372
3765	H4155
3766	H4156
3767	H4157
3768	H4158
3769	H4159
3770	H4160
3771	H4161
3772	H4162
3773	H4164
3774	H4165
3775	H4166
3776	H4167
3777	H4168
3778	H4169
3779	A10373
3780	H4170
3781	H4172
3782	H4173
3783	H4174
3784	H4175
3785	H4176
3786	H4177
3787	H4178
3788	H4179
3789	H4180
3790	A10374
3791	H4181
3792	A10375
3793	H4182
3794	H4183
3795	H4184
3796	H4185
3797	A10376
3798	H4186
3799	H4187
3800	H4188
3801	H4189
3802	H4190
3803	H4192
"	H4193
"	H4194
3804	H4195
3805	H4196
3806	H4197
3807	H4198
3808	H2132
"	H4202
"	H4257
3809	A10379
"	A10384
3810	H4203
"	H4274
3811	H4206
3812	H4207
3813	H4209
3814	H4319
3815	H4210
3816	H4211
3817	H4212
3818	H4204
"	H6652
3819	H4205
"	H8170
3820	H4213
3821	A10380
3822	H4219
3823	H4220
"	H4221
3824	H4222
3825	A10381
3826	H4226
3827	H4225
3828	H4227
"	H4247
3829	H4228
3830	H4229
"	H4230
3831	A10382
3832	H4231
3833	H4216
"	H4218
"	H4232
"	H4233
"	H4234
3834	H4223
3835	H4235
"	H4236
3836	H4237
3837	H4238
"	H4239
3838	H4241
"	H4245
3839	H4242
3840	H4246
3841	H4243
3842	H4244
3843	H4246
3844	H4248
3845	H4249
3846	H4250
3847	H4252
3848	A10383
3849	H4253
3850	H4254
3851	H4258
3852	H4259
3853	H4260
3854	H4261
3855	H4262
3856	H3532
"	H4263
"	H4264
"	H4271
3857	H4265
"	H4266
3858	H4267
"	H4268

STRONG	G/K
3859	H4269
3860	H2176
3861	A10385
"	A10386
3862	H4272
3863	H4273
3864	H4275
3865	H4276
3866	H4276
3867	H4277
"	H4278
3868	H4279
3869	H4280
3870	H4281
3871	H4283
3872	H4284
"	H4304
3873	H2135
"	H4285
3874	H4286
3875	H4287
3876	H4288
3877	H4289
3878	H4290
"	H4291
3879	A10387
3880	H4292
3881	H4291
3882	H4293
3883	H4294
3884	H4295
3885	H4296
"	H4328
"	H4349
3886	H4362
3887	H4329
"	H4370
"	H4885
3888	H4297
3889	H4298
3890	A10388
3891	H4299
3892	H4300
3893	H4301
3894	H4302
"	H4303
3895	H4305
3896	H4306
3897	H4308
3898	H4309
"	H4310
3899	H4312
3900	A10389
3901	H4311
3902	H4313
3903	H4314
3904	A10390
3905	H4315
3906	H4316
3907	H4317
3908	H4318
3909	H4319
3910	H4320
3911	H4321
3912	H4322
3913	H4323
3914	H4324
3915	H4325
"	H4326
3916	A10391
3917	H4327
3918	H4330
3919	H4298
"	H4331
"	H4332
"	H4333
3920	H4334
3921	H4335
3922	H4336
3923	H4337
3924	H4339
3925	H4340
3926	H4344
3927	H4345
3928	H4341
3929	H4347
3930	H4350
3931	H4351
3932	H4352
3933	H4353
3934	H4354
3935	H4355
3936	H4356
3937	H4357
3938	H4358
3939	H4360
3940	H4365
3941	H4366
3942	H7156
3943	H4369
3944	H4371
3945	H4372
3946	H4373
3947	H3689
"	H4374
"	H7774
3948	H4375
3949	H4376
3950	H4377
3951	H4378
3952	H4379
3953	H4380
3954	H4381
3955	H4382
3956	H4383
3957	H4384
3958	H4385
3959	H4386
3960	H4387
3961	A10392
3962	H4388
3963	H4390
3964	A10394
3965	H4393
3966	H4394
3967	H4395
"	H4405
3968	H4396
3969	A10395
3970	H4397
3971	H4398
"	H4583
3972	H4399
3973	H4400
3974	H4401
3975	H4402
3976	H4404
3977	A10396
3978	H4407
3979	H4408
3980	H4409
3981	H4410
3982	H4411
3983	A10397
3984	A10398
3985	H4412
3986	H4413
3987	H4414
3988	H4415
"	H4416
"	H5806
3989	H4418
3990	H4419
3991	H4420
3992	H4421
3993	H4422
3994	H4423
3995	H4426
3996	H4427
3997	H4427
3998	H4428
3999	H4429
4000	H4430
4001	H4431
4002	H4432
4003	H4433
4004	H4435
4005	H4436
4006	H4437
4007	H4438
4008	H4439
4009	H4440
4010	H4443
4011	H4445
4012	H4446
4013	H4448
"	H4450
4014	H4449
4015	H4451
4016	H4434
4017	H4452
4018	H4453
4019	H4455
4020	H4456
4021	H4457
4022	H4458
4023	H4459
"	H4461
4024	H4460
"	H4465
4025	H4462
4026	H4463
4027	H4466
"	H4464+446
4028	H4467
4029	H4468
4030	H4469
"	H4458
4031	H4470
4032	H4471
4033	H4472
"	H4473
4034	H4475
4035	H4476
4036	H4474
"	H4992
4037	H4477
4038	H4478
4039	H4479
4040	A10399
4041	H4480
4042	H4481
4043	H4482
"	H4483
"	H4484
4044	H4485
4045	H4486
4046	H4487
4047	H4488
4048	H4489
4049	A10400
4050	H4490
4051	H4491
4052	H4492
4053	H4493
4054	H4494
"	H4495
4055	H4496
4056	A10401
4057	H4497
"	H4498
4058	H4499
4059	H4499
4060	H4500
"	H4501
"	H4515
4061	A10402
"	A10429
4062	H4502
"	H5290
4063	H4503
4064	H4504
4065	H4505
4066	H4506
4067	H4517
"	H4528
4068	H4507
4069	H4508
4070	A10403
4071	H4509
4072	H4510
4073	H4511
4074	H4512
4075	H4513
4076	A10404
4077	A10404
4078	H4537+1896
4079	H4506
4080	H4518
4081	H4516
4082	H4519
4083	A10406
4084	H4520
4085	H4521
4086	H4522
4087	H4523
4088	H4524
4089	H4525
"	H4526
4090	H4506
4091	H4527
4092	H4520
4093	H4529
4094	H4532
4095	H4533
4096	H4534
4097	H4535
4098	H4536
4099	H2158
4100	H4342
"	H4537
"	H4768
"	H8975
4101	A10408
4102	H4538
4103	H4539
4104	H4540
4105	H4541
4106	H4542
4107	H4543
4108	H4544
4109	H4544
4110	H4545
4111	H4546
4112	H4547
4113	H4549
4114	H4550
4115	H4551
4116	H4554
4117	H4555
"	H4556
4118	H4557
4119	H4558
4120	H4559
4121	H4560
4122	H4561
4123	H4562
4124	H4565
"	H4566
4125	H4567
4126	H4569
4127	H4570
4128	H4571
4129	H4530
4130	H4531
4131	H4572
4132	H4573
4133	H4574
4134	H4575
4135	H4576
"	H4577
4136	H4346
"	H4568
"	H4578
4137	H4579
4138	H4580
4139	H4581
4140	H4582
4141	H6015
4142	H6015
4143	H4586
4144	H4587
4145	H4588
4146	H4589
4147	H4591
"	H4593
4148	H4592
4149	H4594
"	H5035
4150	H4595
4151	H4596
4152	H4597
4153	H4598
4154	H5048
4155	H4599
4156	H4600
4157	H4601
4158	H4602
"	H4789
4159	H4603
4160	H5160
4161	H4604
4162	H4605
4163	H4606
4164	H4607
4165	H4608
4166	H4609
4167	H4610
4168	H4611
4169	H4612
4170	H4613
4171	H4614
"	H4615
4172	H4616
"	H4624
4173	H4617
4174	H4618
4175	H4619
"	H4620
"	H4621
4176	H4622
4177	H4623
4178	H5307
4179	H5317
4180	H4625
"	H4626
4181	H4627
4182	H4628
4183	H4629
4184	H4630
4185	H4631
4186	H4632
4187	H4633
4188	H4634
4189	H5436
4190	H4636
4191	H4637
4192	H4637
4193	A10409
4194	H4638
4195	H4639
4196	H4640
4197	H4641
4198	H4642
4199	H4645
4200	H4646
4201	H4647
4202	H4648
4203	A10410
4204	H4650
4205	H4649
4206	H4651
"	H4652
"	H4653
4207	H4656
"	H4657
"	H4658
4208	H4655
4209	H4659
4210	H4660
4211	H4661
4212	H4662
4213	H4663
4214	H4665
4215	H4668
4216	H4666
4217	H4667
4218	H4669
4219	H4670
4220	H4671
4221	H4672
4222	H4673
4223	A10411
4224	H4675
"	H4676
4225	H4678
4226	H4677
4227	H4679
4228	H4680
4229	H4674
"	H4681
"	H4682
"	H4683
4230	H4684
4231	H4685
4232	H4686
"	H4696
4233	H4687
4234	H4688
4235	H4689
4236	H4690
4237	H4691
4238	H4692
4239	H4693
4240	H4694
4241	H4695
4242	H4697
4243	H4698
4244	H4702
4245	H4700
"	H4701
4246	H4703
4247	H4704
4248	H4705
4249	H4706
4250	H4707
4251	H4708
4252	H4709
4253	H4710
4254	H4711
4255	A10412
4256	H4713
4257	H4714
4258	H4715
4259	H4716
4260	H4717
4261	H4718
4262	H4719
4263	H4720
4264	H4722
4265	H4723
4266	H4724
4267	H4725
4268	H4726
4269	H4727
4270	H4728
4271	H4729
4272	H4730
4273	H4731
4274	H4732
4275	H4733
4276	H4734
4277	H4735
4278	H4736
4279	H4737
4280	H4738
4281	H4739
4282	H4739
4283	H4740
4284	H4742
4285	H4743
4286	H4741
4287	H4744
4288	H4745
4289	H4746
4290	H4747
4291	A10413
4292	H4748
4293	H4749
4294	H4751
4295	H4752
4296	H4753
4297	H4754
4298	H4755
4299	H4757
4300	H4758
4301	H4759
4302	H4760
4303	H4761
4304	H4762
4305	H4763
4306	H4764
4307	H4766
4308	H4765
4309	H4767
4310	H4769
4311	H4772
4312	H4773
4313	H2126
"	H3765
"	H4770
4314	H4771
4315	H4774
4316	H4775
4317	H4776
4318	H4777
4319	H4778
4320	H4779
4321	H4781
4322	H4780
4323	H4782
4324	H4783
4325	H4784
4326	H4785
4327	H4786
4328	H4588
4329	H4590
"	H4788
4330	H4790
4331	H4791
4332	H4792
4333	A10414
4334	H4793
4335	H4794
4336	A10415
4337	H4796
4338	H4795
4339	H4797
4340	H4798
4341	H4799
4342	H3892
4343	H4800
4344	H4801
4345	H4803
4346	H4802
4347	H4804
4348	H4805
4349	H4806
4350	H4807
4351	H4808
4352	H4809
4353	H4810
4354	H4811
4355	H4812
4356	H4813
4357	H4816
4358	H4814
4359	H4817
4360	H4815
4361	H4818
4362	H4819
4363	H4820
"	H4825
4364	H4821
4365	H4822
"	H4823
"	H4824
4366	H4826
4367	H4827
4368	H4828
4369	H4807
4370	H4829
4371	H4830
4372	H4832
4373	H4831
4374	H4833
4375	H4834
4376	H4835
4377	H4836
4378	H4837
4379	H4838
4380	H4839
4381	H4840
4382	H4841
4383	H4842
4384	H4843
4385	H4844
4386	H4845
4387	H4846
4388	H4847
4389	H4847
4390	H4848
"	H4862
4391	A10416
4392	H4849
4393	H4850
4394	H4854
4395	H4852
4396	H4853
4397	H4855
4398	A10417
4399	H4856
4400	H4857
4401	H4858
4402	H4859
4403	H4860
4404	H4861
"	H4905
4405	H4863
4406	A10418
4407	H4851
"	H4864
4408	H4865
4409	H4866
"	H4868
"	H4883
4410	H4867
4411	H4869
4412	H4870
4413	H4871
4414	H4872
"	H4873
4415	A10419
4416	A10420
4417	H4875
4418	H4874
4419	H4876
4420	H4877
4421	H4878
4422	H4880
"	H4881
4423	H4879
4424	H4882
4425	H4884
4426	H4886
4427	H4887
"	H4888
4428	H4889
"	H4890
4429	H4889
4430	A10421
4431	A10422
4432	H4891
4433	A10423
4434	H4892
4435	H4894
4436	H4893
4437	A10424
4438	H4895
4439	H4896
4440	H4897
4441	H4898
"	H4899
4442	H4900
4443	H4901
4444	H4902
4445	H4903
"	H4904
4446	H4906
4447	H2168
"	H4907
4448	H4910
"	H4911
4449	A10425
4450	H4912
4451	H4913
4452	H4914
4453	H4915
4454	H4916
4455	H4917
"	H4918
4456	H4919
4457	H4920
4458	H4921
4459	H4922
4460	H4923
4461	H4924
4462	H4584
"	H4925
4463	H4926
4464	H4927
4465	H4928
4466	H4929
4467	H4930
4468	H4931
4469	H4932
4470	H4933
4471	H4934
"	H4935
4472	H4936
4473	H4937
4474	H4938
4475	H4939
4476	H4940
4477	H4941
4478	H4942
"	H4943
4479	A10426
4480	H4946
"	H4974
4481	A10427
4482	H4944
"	H4945
4483	A10431
4484	A10428
4485	H4947
4486	A10430
4487	H4948
4488	H4949
4489	H4951
4490	H4950
4491	H4952
4492	H4953
4493	H4954
4494	H4955
4495	H4956
4496	H4957
"	H4967
4497	H4959
4498	H4960
4499	H4961
4500	H4962
4501	H4963
4502	H4964
4503	H4966
4504	A10432
4505	H4968
4506	H4969
"	H4970
4507	H4972
4508	H4973
4509	H4975
4510	A10433
4511	H4976
"	H4977
4512	H4978
4513	H4979
4514	H4980
4515	H4981
4516	H4982
4517	H4983
4518	H4984
4519	H4985
4520	H4986
4521	H4987
4522	H4989
4523	H4988
4524	H4990
"	H4991
4525	H4993
"	H4994
4526	H4995
4527	H4996
4528	H4997
4529	H4998
4530	H5002
4531	H4999
"	H5000
4532	H5001
4533	H5003
4534	H5004
4535	H5005
4536	H5006
4537	H5007
4538	H5008
4539	H5009
4540	H5010
4541	H5011
"	H5012
"	H5013
4542	H5014
4543	H5016
4544	H5017
4545	H5018
4546	H5019
4547	H5020
4548	H5021
4549	H5022
4550	H5023
4551	H5024
"	H5025
4552	H5026
4553	H5027
4554	H5028
4555	H5029
4556	H5030
4557	H5031
4558	H5032
4559	H5033
4560	H5034

STRONG	G/K
4561	H5036
4562	H5037
4563	H5039
4564	H5040
4565	H5041
4566	H5042
4567	A10434
4568	H5043
4569	H5044
"	H5045
4570	H5046
"	H5047
4571	H5048
4572	H5049
4573	H5050
4574	H5052
4575	H5051
4576	H5053
4577	A10435
4578	H5055
4579	H5054
4580	H5056
4581	H5057
"	H5058
4582	H5059
4583	H5060
"	H5061
"	H5079
4584	H5062
"	H5063
4585	H5104
4586	H5064
4587	H5065
4588	H5066
4589	H5067
4590	H5068
"	H5069
4591	H5070
4592	H5071
4593	H6487
4594	H5073
4595	H5074
4596	H5075
4597	H5076
4598	H5077
4599	H5078
4600	H5080
4601	H5081
"	H5082
"	H5083
4602	H5084
4603	H5085
4604	H5086
4605	H5087
"	H5093
4606	A10436
4607	H5089
4608	H5090
4609	H5091
"	H5092
4610	H5090+6832
4611	H5094
"	H5095
4612	H5096
4613	H5097
4614	H5098
4615	H5099
4616	H4348
"	H5100
4617	H5101
"	H5102
4618	H5103
"	H5105
4619	H5106
4620	H5107
4621	H5108
4622	H5109
4623	H5110
4624	H5111
4625	H5112
4626	H5113
4627	H5114
4628	H5115
4629	H5116
4630	H5120
4631	H5117
4632	H5118
"	H6869
4633	H5119
4634	H5120
4635	H5121
4636	H5122
4637	H5124
4638	H5125
4639	H5126
4640	H5127
4641	H5128
"	H5129
4642	H5131
4643	H5130
4644	H5132
4645	H5133
4646	H5134
4647	H5135
4648	H5136
4649	H5137
4650	H5138
4651	H5139
4652	H5140
4653	H5141
4654	H5142
"	H5143
4655	H5144
4656	H5145
4657	H5146
4658	H5147
4659	H5148
"	H5149
4660	H5150
4661	H5151
4662	H5152
4663	H5152
4664	H5153
4665	H5154
4666	H5155
4667	H5156
4668	H5158
4669	H5157
4670	H5159
4671	H5161
4672	H5162
4673	H5163
4674	H5164
4675	H5165
"	H5166
4676	H5167
4677	H5168
4678	H5169
"	H5170
4679	H5171
4680	H5172
4681	H5173
4682	H5174
4683	H5175
4684	H5177
4685	H5178
"	H5179
"	H5182
"	H5183
4686	H5180
"	H5181
"	H5192
4687	H5184
4688	H5185
"	H5198
4689	H5186
4690	H5187
4691	H5188
4692	H5189
"	H5190
4693	H5191
4694	H5193
"	H5211
4695	H5194
4696	H5195
4697	H5196
4698	H5197
4699	H5185
4700	H5199
4701	H5200
4702	H5201
4703	H5202
4704	H7582
4705	H5203
4706	H5204
4707	H5205
4708	H5206
4709	H5207
4710	H5208
4711	H5209
4712	H5210
4713	H5212
4714	H5213
4715	H5214
4716	H5215
4717	H5216
4718	H5216
"	H5217
4719	H5218
4720	H5219
4721	H5220
4722	H5221
4723	H5223
"	H5224
"	H7745
"	H7750
4724	H5225
4725	H5226
4726	H5227
4727	H5228
4728	H5229
4729	H5230
4730	H5233
4731	H5234
4732	H5235
4733	H5236
4734	H5237
4735	H5238
4736	H5239
4737	H5240
4738	H5241
4739	H5242
4740	H5243
4741	H5244
4742	H7910
4743	H5245
4744	H5246
4745	H5247
4746	H5248
4747	H5249
4748	H5250
4749	H5251
4750	H5252
4751	H5253
"	H5287
4752	H5254
4753	H5255
4754	H5256
"	H5257
4755	H5259
4756	A10437
4757	H5282
4758	H5260
4759	H5261
"	H5262
4760	H5263
4761	H5265
4762	H5358
"	H5359
4763	H5265
"	H8039
4764	H5266
4765	H5267
4766	H5269
4767	H5268
4768	H5270
4769	H5271
4770	H5272
4771	H5273
4772	H5274
4773	H5275
4774	H5276
4775	H5277
4776	A10438
4777	H5278
4778	H5279
4779	A10439
4780	H5280
4781	H5281
4782	H5283
4783	H5284
4784	H5286
4785	H5288
4786	H5289
4787	H5285
4788	H5291
4789	H5292
4790	H5293
4791	H5294
4792	H5295
4793	H5296
4794	H5297
4795	H5299
4796	H5300
4797	H5301
4798	H5301
4799	H5302
4800	H5303
4801	H5305
4802	H5306
4803	H5307
4804	A10440
4805	H5308
4806	H5258
"	H5309
4807	H5311
"	H5314
4808	H5312
4809	H5313
4810	H5311
4811	H5316
4812	H5318
4813	H5319
4814	H5320
4815	H5321
4816	H5322
4817	H5323
4818	H5324
4819	H5326
4820	H5327
4821	H5328
4822	H5329
4823	H5330
4824	H5331
4825	H5332
4826	H5333
4827	H5334
4828	H5335
4829	H5337
4830	H5338
4831	H5339
4832	H5340
"	H5341
"	H5342
4833	H5343
4834	H5344
4835	H5298
4836	H5345
4837	H5346
4838	H5347
4839	H5348
4840	H5349
4841	H5350
4842	H5351
4843	H5352
4844	H5353
4845	H5354
4846	H5355
4847	H5356
4848	H5357
4849	H5360
4850	H5361
4851	H5390
4852	H5392
4853	H5362
"	H5363
4854	H5364
4855	H5391
4856	H5365
4857	H5393
4858	H5366
4859	H5394
4860	H5396
4861	H5398
4862	H5399
4863	H5400
4864	H5367
"	H5368
4865	H5401
4866	H5402
4867	H5403
4868	H5404
4869	H5369
"	H5370
4870'	H5405
4871	H5406
4872	H5407
4873	A10441
4874	H5408
4875	H5409
4876	H5397
"	H5410
4877	H5411
4878	H5412
4879	H5413
4880	H5414
"	H5415
4881	H5372
"	H5379
4882	H5416
4883	H5373
4884	H5374
4885	H5375
"	H5376
4886	H5417
4887	A10442
4888	H5418
"	H5419
"	H5420
"	H5421
4889	H5422
4890	H5377
4891	H5423
4892	H5424
4893	H5425
"	H5426
4894	H5427
4895	H5378
4896	H5428
4897	H5429
4898	H5430
4899	H5431
4900	H5432
4901	H5433
4902	H5434
4903	A10444
4904	H5435
4905	H5380
4906	H5381
4907	A10445
4908	H5438
4909	H5382
4910	H5440
4911	H5439
"	H5441
4912	H5442
4913	H5443
4914	H5446
4915	H5444
"	H5445
4916	H5447
"	H5448
4917	H5449
4918	H5450
4919	H5451
4920	H5452
"	H5453
4921	H5454
4922	H5455
4923	H5457
4924	H5458
"	H5460
"	H9044
4925	H5459
4926	H5461
4927	H5462
4928	H5463
4929	H5464
"	H5465
4930	H5383
4931	H5466
4932	H5467
4933	H5468
4934	H5469
4935	H5470
4936	H5471
4937	H5472
"	H5473
4938	H5474
"	H5475
4939	H5384
4940	H5476
4941	H5477
4942	H5478
4943	H5479
4944	H5480
4945	H5482
"	H5483
4946	H5484
4947	H5485
4948	H5486
4949	H5487
4950	H5488
4951	H5385
4952	H5489
4953	A10446
4954	H5490
4955	H5386
4956	H5387
4957	H5388
4958	H5389
4959	H5491
4960	H5492
4961	A10447
4962	H5493
"	H5494
4963	H5495
4964	H5496
4965	H566
"	H2031
"	H5497
4966	H5498
4967	H5499
4968	H5500
4969	H5501
4970	H5503
4971	H5504
4972	H5505
4973	H5506
4974	H5507
4975	H5516
4976	H5508
4977	H5509
4978	A10448
4979	H5510
4980	H5511
4981	H5512
4982	H5513
4983	H5514
"	H5515
4984	H5951
4985	H5517
4986	H5518
4987	H5519
4988	H5517
4989	H5520
4990	H5521
4991	H5522
4992	H5523
4993	H5524
"	H5525
4994	H5528
4995	H5529
4996	H5530
4997	H5532
4998	H5533
4999	H5661
5000	H5534
5001	H5535
5002	H5536
5003	H5537
5004	H5539
5005	H5538
5006	H5540
5007	H5541
"	H5542
5008	H5543
5009	H5544
5010	H5545
5011	H5546
5012	H5547
5013	A10451
5014	H5548
"	H5554
5015	H5549
"	H5550
"	H5551
5016	H5553
5017	A10452
5018	H5555
5019	H5556
"	H5557
5020	A10453
5021	H5558
5022	H5559
5023	A10454
5024	H5560
5025	H5561
"	H5562
5026	H5563
5027	H5564
5028	H5565
5029	A10455
5030	H5566
5031	H5567
5032	H5568
5033	H5569
5034	H5570
"	H5571
5035	H5574
"	H5575
5036	H5572
5037	H5573
5038	H5577
5039	H5576
5040	H5578
5041	H5579
5042	H5580
5043	A10456
5044	H5581
5045	H5582
5046	H5583
5047	A10457
5048	H5584
5049	A10458
5050	H5585
5051	H5586
5052	H5587
5053	A10459
5054	H5588
5055	H5590
5056	H5591
5057	H5592
5058	H5593
5059	H5594
5060	H5595
5061	H5596
5062	H5597
5063	H5598
5064	H5599
"	H5600
5065	H5601
5066	H5602
5067	H5603
5068	H5605
5069	A10461
"	A10219
5070	H5606
5071	H5607
5072	H5608
5073	A10462
5074	H5610
5075	A10463
5076	H5611
5077	H5604
"	H5612
5078	H5613
5079	H5614
5080	H5615
"	H5616
5081	H5618
5082	H5619
5083	H5621
5084	H5620
5085	A10464
5086	H5622
5087	H5623
5088	H5624
5089	H5625
5090	H5627
"	H5628
5091	H5629
"	H5630
5092	H5631
5093	H5632
5094	A10466
"	A10467
"	A10465
5095	H5633
5096	H5634
"	H5636
5097	H5635
5098	H5637
5099	H5638
5100	H5639
5101	H5640
5102	H5641
"	H5642
5103	A10468
5104	H5643
5105	H5644
5106	H5648
5107	H5649
5108	H5650
"	H5762
5109	H5651
"	H5763
5110	H5653
5111	A10469
5112	H5617
"	H5654
5113	H5655
5114	H5656
5115	H5657
"	H5658
5116	H5659
"	H5660
5117	H5663
"	H5664
"	H5698
5118	H5665
5119	H5666
5120	H5667
5121	H5662
"	H5668
"	H5766
5122	A10470
5123	H5670
5124	H5671
5125	H5672
"	H5768
5126	H5673
5127	H5674
5128	H5675
5129	H5676
5130	H2185
"	H5677
"	H5678
5131	H5679
5132	H5680
5133	H5681
"	H5901
"	H5902
5134	H3567
5135	A10471
5136	H5683
5137	H5684
"	H5685
5138	H5686
5139	H5687
5140	H5688
"	H5689
5141	H5690
5142	A10472
5143	H5691
5144	H5692
"	H5693
5145	H5694
5146	H5695
5147	H5696
5148	H5697
5149	H5700
5150	H5719
5151	H5699
5152	H5701
5153	H5702
5154	H5703
5155	H5704
5156	H5705
5157	H5706
5158	H5707
"	H5708
"	H5711
5159	H5709
5160	H5712
5161	H5713
5162	H5714
5163	H5715
5164	H5716
5165	H5717
5166	H5718
5167	H5720
5168	H5721
5169	H5722
5170	H5724
"	H5725
5171	H5726
5172	H5727
5173	H5728
5174	A10473
5175	H5729
5176	H5731
5177	H5732
5178	H5733
"	H5734
5179	H5735
5180	H5736
5181	H5737
5182	A10474
5183	H5738
"	H5739
5184	H5740
5185	H5741
5186	H5742
5187	H5744
5188	H5755
5189	H5746
5190	H5747
5191	A10475
5192	H5748
5193	H5749
5194	H5750
5195	H5745
5196	H5751
5197	H5752
5198	H5753
"	H5754
5199	H5756
5200	H5743
5201	H5757
"	H5758
5202	A10476
5203	H5759
5204	H5760
5205	H5764
5206	H5765
5207	H5767
5208	A10478
5209	H5769
5210	H5770
5211	H5771
5212	H5772
5213	H5773
5214	H5774
5215	H5776
5216	H5775
"	H5944
5217	H5777
5218	H5778
"	H5779
5219	H5780
5220	H5781
5221	H5782
5222	H5784
5223	H5783
5224	H5786
"	H5785
5225	H5789
5226	H5790
5227	H5790
5228	H5791
5229	H5791
5230	H5792
5231	H5793
5232	A10479
5233	H5794
5234	H5795
"	H5796
5235	H5798
5236	H5797
5237	H5799
5238	H5800
5239	H5801
5240	H1022
5241	H5803
5242	H5804
5243	H4908
"	H4909
5244	H5805
5245	A10480

STRONG	G/K
5246	H5807
5247	H5809
5248	H5808
5249	H5810
5250	H5811
5251	H5812
5252	H5813
5253	H8450
5254	H5814
5255	H5815
5256	A10481
5257	H5816
"	H5817
5258	H5818
"	H5820
5259	H5819
5260	A10482
5261	A10483
5262	H5821
"	H5822
5263	H5823
5264	H5824
5265	H5825
5266	H5826
5267	A10513
5268	H5827
5269	H5828
5270	H5829
5271	H5830
"	H5831
5272	H5832
5273	H5833
"	H5834
5274	H5835
"	H5836
5275	H5837
5276	H5838
5277	H5839
5278	H5840
5279	H5841
"	H5842
5280	H5844
5281	H5843
5282	H5846
5283	H5845
5284	H5847
5285	H5848
5286	H5849
5287	H5850
"	H5851
5288	H5853
5289	H5852
5290	H5854
5291	H5855
5292	H5856
"	H5857
5293	H5858
5294	H5859
5295	H5860
5296	H5861
5297	H5862
5298	H5863
5299	H5864
"	H5865
5300	H5866
"	H5867
"	H5875
5301	H5870
5302	H5871
5303	H5872
5304	H5873
5305	H5874
5306	H5876
5307	H5877
5308	A10484
5309	H5878
5310	H5879
"	H5880
5311	H5881
5312	A10485
5313	A10486
5314	H5882
5315	H5883
5316	H5868
"	H5884
5317	H5885
5318	H5886
5319	H5887
5320	H5888
5321	H5889
5322	H5890
"	H5891
5323	H5892
5324	H2205
"	H5893
"	H5894
"	H5895
5325	H5896
5326	A10487
5327	H5897
"	H5898
5328	H5900
5329	H5904
5330	A10488
5331	H5905
5332	H5906
5333	H5907
5334	H5908
5335	H5909
5336	H5910
5337	H5911
5338	A10489
5339	H5912
5340	H5913
5341	H5903
"	H5915
"	H5917
5342	H5916
5343	A10490
5344	H5918
"	H5919
5345	H5920
5346	H2186
"	H5921
5347	H5922
5348	H5923
5349	H5924
5350	H5926
5351	H5925
5352	H5927
5353	H5928
5354	H7752
5355	H5929
"	H5930
5356	H5931
"	H7734
5357	H5932
5358	H5933
5359	H5934
5360	H5935
5361	H5936
5362	H5937
"	H5938
5363	H5939
5364	H5940
5365	H5941
5366	H5942
5367	H5943
5368	A10491
5369	H5945
5370	H5946
5371	H5947
5372	H8087
5373	H5948
5374	H5949
"	H5950
5375	H5951
5376	A10492
5377	H5958
5378	H5957
"	H5961
5379	H5951
5380	H5959
5381	H5371
"	H5952
5382	H5960
5383	H5957
5384	H5962
5385	H5953
5386	H5963
5387	H5954
"	H5955
5388	H5964
5389	A10493
5390	H5965
5391	H5966
"	H5967
5392	H5968
5393	H5969
5394	H5970
5395	H5971
5396	A10494
5397	H5972
5398	H5973
5399	H5974
5400	H5956
5401	H5975
"	H5976
5402	H5977
"	H5978
5403	A10495
5404	H5979
5405	H5980
5406	H5981
5407	A10496
5408	H5983
5409	H5984
5410	H5985
"	H5986
5411	H5982
"	H5987
5412	A10497
5413	H5988
5414	H3851
"	H3852
"	H5989
5415	A10498
5416	H5990
5417	H5991
5418	H5992
"	H5993
5419	H5994
5420	H5995
5421	H5996
5422	H5997
5423	H5998
5424	H5999
5425	H6000
"	H6001
"	H6002
5426	A10499
5427	H6003
5428	H6004
5429	H6006
5430	H6007
5431	H6008
5432	H6009
5433	H6010
"	H6012
5434	H6013
5435	H6011
5436	H6014
5437	H6015
5438	H6016
5439	H4585
"	H6017
5440	H6018
5441	H6020
5442	H6019
5443	A10501
"	A10676
5444	H6021
5445	H6022
5446	A10502
5447	H6023
5448	H6024
5449	H6025
5450	H6026
5451	H6027
5452	A10503
5453	H6028
5454	H6029
"	H6030
5455	H6031
5456	H6032
5457	A10504
5458	H6033
5459	H6035
5460	A10505
5461	H6036
5462	H6034
"	H6037
"	H6038
5463	A10506
5464	H6039
5465	H6040
5466	H6041
5467	H6042
5468	H6043
5469	H6044
5470	H6045
5471	H6046
5472	H6047
5473	H6048
5474	H6050
5475	H6051
5476	H6052
5477	H6053
5478	H6054
5479	H6055
5480	H6057
5481	A10507
5482	H6059
5483	H6061
"	H6062
"	H6101
5484	H6063
5485	H6064
5486	H6066
5487	A10508
5488	H6068
5489	H6069
5490	H6067
5491	A10509
5492	H6070
"	H6071
5493	H6073
"	H6233
"	H8462
5494	H6074
"	H6076
5495	H6075
5496	H6077
5497	H6078
5498	H6079
5499	H6080
5500	H6081
5501	H6082
5502	H2900
"	H6085
5503	H6086
5504	H6087
5505	H6086
5506	H6088
5507	H6089
5508	H6090
5509	H6049
"	H6092
"	H6213
5510	H6094
5511	H6095
5512	H6096
"	H6097
5513	H6098
5514	H6099
5515	H6060
"	H6100
5516	H6102
5517	H6103
"	H6104
5518	H6105
"	H6106
5519	H6107
5520	H6108
5521	H6109
5522	H6110
5523	H6111
5524	H6112
5525	H6113
5526	H6056
"	H6058
"	H6114
"	H6115
"	H6116
"	H8503
5527	H6117
5528	H6118
5529	H6120
5530	H6119
5531	H6121
"	H8508
5532	H6122
"	H6125
5533	H5015
"	H6123
"	H6124
5534	H6126
"	H6127
5535	H6129
5536	H6130
5537	H6131
5538	H6133
5539	H6134
5540	H6135
5541	H6136
"	H6137
5542	H6138
5543	H6132
"	H6139
"	H6140
"	H6144
5544	H6141
5545	H6142
5546	H6143
5547	H6145
5548	H6146
5549	H6147
"	H6148
5550	H6149
5551	H6150
5552	H6151
5553	H6152
5554	H6153
5555	H2165
"	H4712
"	H6154
5556	H6155
5557	H6156
5558	H6157
5559	A10513
5560	H6159
5561	H6160
5562	H5552
"	H6161
"	H6162
5563	H6163
5564	H6164
5565	H6165
5566	H6166
5567	H6168
5568	H6169
5569	H6170
5570	H2189
"	H2190
"	H6171
5571	H6172
5572	H6174
5573	H6175
5574	H6176
5575	H6177
5576	H6178
5577	H6180
5578	H6179
5579	H6181
5580	H6182
5581	H6183
5582	H6184
5583	A10514
5584	H6185
5585	H6186
"	H6187
5586	H6188
5587	H6191
"	H8546
5588	H6189
5589	H6190
5590	H6192
5591	H6193
"	H6194
5592	H6195
"	H6196
"	H6197
5593	H6198
5594	H6199
5595	H6200
5596	H6202
"	H6203
"	H8558
5597	H6204
5598	H6205
5599	H6206
"	H6207
5600	H6208
5601	H6209
5602	H6210
5603	H6201
"	H6211
5604	H6212
5605	H6214
5606	H6215
"	H6216
5607	H6217
"	H8565
5608	H6218
"	H6221
5609	A10515
5610	H6222
5611	H6223
5612	H6219
"	H6220
"	H6225
5613	A10516
5614	H6224
5615	H6228
5616	H6227
5617	H6226
5618	H2191
"	H6072
"	H6230
5619	H6232
5620	H6234
5621	H6235
5622	A10517
5623	H6236
5624	H6237
5625	H6238
5626	H6241
5627	H6239
"	H6240
5628	H6242
"	H6243
"	H6244
5629	H6245
5630	H6246
5631	H6247
5632	A10518
5633	H6248
"	H6249
5634	H6250
5635	H6251
5636	H6252
5637	H6253
5638	H6255
"	H6257
5639	H6256
5640	H6258
"	H8608
5641	H6259
5642	A10519
"	A10520
5643	H6260
"	H6261
5644	H6262
5645	H6265
"	H6266
"	H6267
5646	H6264
5647	H6268
5648	A10522
5649	A10523
5650	H6269
5651	H6270
5652	H6271
5653	H6272
5654	H6273
5655	H6274
5656	H6275
5657	H6276
5658	H6277
"	H6278
5659	H6285
5660	H6279
5661	H6280
5662	H6281
"	H6282
5663	H6283
5664	H5589
"	H6284
5665	A10524
5666	H6286
5667	H6287
5668	H6288
5669	H6289
5670	H6292
"	H6293
5671	H6294
5672	H6295
5673	A10525
5674	H6296
"	H6297
5675	A10526
5676	H6298
5677	H6299
5678	H6301
5679	H6302
5680	H6303
5681	H6304
5682	H6305
5683	H2496
5684	H6307
5685	H6308
5686	H6309
5687	H6290
5688	H6291
"	H6310
5689	H6311
5690	H6313
5691	H6312
5692	H6314
5693	H6315
5694	H6316
5695	H6319
5696	H6318
5697	H6320
5698	H6321
5699	H6317
"	H6322
5700	H6323
"	H6324
5701	H6327
5702	H6328
5703	H6329
5704	H6330
5705	A10527
5706	H6331
5707	H6332
5708	H6340
5709	A10528
5710	H6334
"	H6335
5711	H6336
5712	H6337
5713	H6338
5714	H6333
"	H6341
"	H6342
"	H6345
"	A10529
5715	H6343
5716	H6344
5717	H6346
5718	H6347
"	H6348
5719	H6349
5720	H6350
5721	H6351
5722	H6352
5723	H6353
5724	H6354
5725	H6355
5726	H6356
5727	H6357
5728	H6362
"	H6364
5729	H6361
5730	H6358
"	H6366
5731	H6359
"	H6360
5732	A10530
5733	H6363
5734	H6365
"	H6367
5735	H6368
"	H6900
5736	H6369
5737	H6370
"	H6371
"	H6372
5738	H6376
5739	H6373
5740	H6374
"	H6375
5741	H6377
5742	H6378
5743	H6380
5744	H6381
5745	H6382
5746	H6383
5747	H6384
5748	H6385
5749	H6386
"	H6387
5750	H6388
5751	A10531
5752	H6389
5753	H6390
"	H6391
5754	H6392
5755	H6379
"	H6393
"	H6394
5756	H6395
5757	H6398
5758	A10532
5759	H6396
5760	H6397
5761	H6398
"	H6399
5762	H6400
"	H6511
5763	H6402
5764	H6403
5765	H6401
5766	H6404
"	H6406
"	H6593
"	H6637
5767	H6405
5768	H6407
"	H6408
5769	H6409
5770	H6523
5771	H6411
5772	H6703
5773	H6413
5774	H6414
"	H6415
"	H6545
"	H6758
"	H9507
5775	H6416
5776	A10533
5777	H6769
5778	H6417
"	H6550
5779	H6418
5780	H6419
"	H6420
5781	H6421
5782	H6424
"	H6749
5783	H6423
5784	A10534
5785	H6425
5786	H6422
5787	H6426
5788	H6427
"	H6428
5789	H6429
5790	H6431
5791	H6430
5792	H6432
5793	H6433
5794	H6434
"	H6435
5795	H6436
5796	A10535
5797	H6437
5798	H6438
"	H6446
5799	H6439
5800	H6440
"	H6441
5801	H6442
5802	H6443
5803	H6444
5804	H6445
5805	H6447
5806	H6448
5807	H6449
5808	H6450
5809	H6473
5810	H6451
5811	H6452
5812	H6453
5813	H6454
5814	H6455
5815	H6456
5816	H6457
5817	H6458
5818	H6459
"	H6460
5819	H6461
5820	H6462
"	H6463
5821	H6464
5822	H6465
5823	H6466
5824	A10536
5825	H6467
5826	H6468
5827	H6470
5828	H6469
5829	H6470
"	H6472
5830	H6474
5831	A10537
5832	H6475
5833	H6476
5834	H6477
5835	H6478
5836	H6479
5837	H6480
5838	H6481
"	H6482
5839	A10538
5840	H6483
5841	H6484
5842	H6485
5843	A10539
5844	H6486
"	H6487
5845	H6489
5846	H6490
5847	H6491
5848	H6488
"	H6493
"	H6494
5849	H6496
"	H6497
5850	H6498
5851	H6499
5852	H6500
5853	H6501
5854	H6502
5855	H6503
"	H8794
5856	H6505
5857	H6504
"	H6509
"	H6569
5858	H6506
"	H6507
"	H6508
5859	H6510
5860	H6512
"	H6513
5861	H6514
5862	H6515
5863	H2192
"	H6300
"	H6516
5864	H6517
5865	H6518
5866	H6519
5867	H6520
"	H6521
5868	H6522
5869	H6412
"	H6524
5870	A10540
5871	H6526
5872	H6527
5872 to 5887	H6525
5873	H1712
"	H6528
5874	H6529
5875	H2213
"	H6530

STRONG	G/K
5876	H6532
5877	H6533
5878	H3008
"	H6534
5879	H6542
"	H6543
5880	H6535
5881	H6544
5882	H6325
"	H6536
5883	H6537
"	H8080
5884	H6538
5885	H6539
5886	H5624+9478
5887	H6540
5888	H6545
5889	H6546
5890	H6547
5891	H6548
"	H6549
5892	H6551
"	H6552
5893	H6553
5894	A10541
5895	H6554
"	H6555
5896	H6562
5897	H6563
5898	H6558
5899	H6559
5900	H6564
5901	H6565
5902	H6566
5903	H6567
5904	H5730
"	H6560
5905	H6561
5906	H6568
5907	H6570
5908	H6571
5909	H6572
5910	H6573
5911	H6574
5912	H6575
5913	H6576
5914	H6577
5915	H6578
5916	H6579
5917	H6580
5918	H6581
5919	H6582
5920	H6583
5921	H6584
5922	A10542
5923	H6585
5924	A10543
5925	H6587
5926	H6589
5927	H6158
"	H6590
5928	A10545
5929	H6591
5930	H6592
5931	A10544
5932	H6594
5933	H6595
"	H6607
5934	H6596
5935	H6597
"	H6615
5936	H6598
5937	H6600
5938	H6601
5939	H6602
5940	H6605
5941	H6603
5942	H6604
"	H6606
5943	A10546
5944	H6608
5945	H6609
"	H6610
5946	A10548
5947	H6611
5948	H6612
5949	H6613
5950	H6614
5951	H6617
5952	A10547
5953	H6618
"	H6619
"	H6620
"	H6621
5954	A10549
5955	H6622
5956	H6623
5957	A10550
5958	H6624
5959	H6625
5960	H6626
5961	H6628
5962	A10551
5963	H6627
5964	H6630
"	H6631
5965	H6632
5966	H6633
5967	A10552
5968	H6634
5969	H6635
5970	H6636
5971	H6638
"	H6639
5972	A10553
5973	H6640
5974	A10554
5975	H6641
5976	H5048
5977	H6642
5978	H6643
5979	H6644
5980	H6645
5981	H6646
5982	H6647
5983	H6648
5984	H6649
5985	H6649
5986	H6650
5987	H6651
5988	H6653
5989	H6654
5990	H6655
5991	H6656
5992	H6657
5993	H5816+6639
5994	A10555
5995	H6658
5996	H6659
5997	H6660
5998	H6661
5999	H6662
6000	H6663
6001	H6664
"	H6665
6002	H6667
6003	H6668
6004	H6669
"	H6670
6005	H6672
6006	H6673
6007	H6674
6008	H6675
6009	H6676
6010	H6677
6011	H6679
6012	H6680
6013	H6678
6014	H6682
"	H6683
6015	A10556
6016	H6684
"	H6685
6017	H6686
6018	H6687
6019	H6688
6020	H6689
6021	H6690
6022	H6691
6023	H6692
6024	H6693
6025	H6694
6026	H6695
6027	H6696
6028	H6697
6029	H6698
6030	H4361
"	H6410
"	H6699
"	H6702
6031	H6700
"	H6701
6032	A10558
6033	A10559
6034	H6704
6035	H6705
"	H6718
6036	H6707
6037	H6709
6038	H6708
6039	H6713
6040	H6715
6041	H6714
6042	H6706
"	H6716
6043	H6717
6044	H6719
6045	H6721
6046	H6722
6047	H6723
6048	H6724
6049	H6725
"	H6726
6050	A10560
6051	H6727
6052	H6728
6053	H6729
6054	H6730
6055	H6731
"	H6732
6056	A10561
6057	H6733
6058	H6734
6059	H6735
6060	H6736
6061	H6710
6062	H6737
6063	H6738
"	H6739
6064	H6711
"	H6740
6065	A10562
6066	H6741
6067	H6742
6068	H6743
"	H6744
6069	H6745
6070	H6746
6071	H6747
6072	H6748
6073	H6751
6074	A10564
6075	H6752
"	H6753
6076	H6754
6077	H6755
6078	H6756
6079	H6757
6080	H6759
6081	H6761
6082	H6762
6083	H6760
6084	H6763
"	H6764
6085	H6766
"	H6767
"	H6768
6086	H6770
6087	H6771
"	H6772
6088	A10565
6089	H6775
"	H6776
6090	H6777
"	H6778
6091	H6773
6092	H6774
6093	H6779
6094	H6780
6095	H6781
6096	H6782
6097	H6785
6098	H6783
"	H6784
6099	H6786
6100	H6787
6101	H6788
6102	H6789
6103	H6790
"	H6792
6104	H6791
6105	H6793
"	H6794
6106	H6795
"	H6799
6107	H6796
6108	H6797
"	H6798
6109	H6800
6110	H6802
6111	H6801
6112	H6804
6113	H6806
6114	H6807
6115	H6808
6116	H6809
6117	H6810
6118	H6813
6119	H6811
6120	H6812
6121	H6814
"	H6815
6122	H6817
6123	H6818
6124	H6819
6125	H6821
6126	H6822
6127	H6823
6128	H6824
6129	H6825
6130	H6826
6131	H6827
"	H6828
6132	A10566
6133	H6830
6134	H6831
6135	H6829
6136	A10567
6137	H6832
6138	H6833
6139	H6834
6140	H6835
6141	H6836
6142	H6837
6143	H6838
6144	H6840
6145	H6839
6146	A10568
6147	H6841
6148	H6842
"	H6843
6149	H6844
6150	H6845
6151	A10569
6152	H6846
"	H6851
"	H6852
6153	H6847
6154	H6848
"	H6849
"	H6850
6155	H6857
6156	H6853
6157	H6856
6158	H6854
6159	H6855
6160	H6858
6161	H6859
6162	H6860
6163	H6861
"	H6862
6164	H6863
6165	H6864
6166	H6865
"	H6866
6167	A10570
6168	H6867
6169	H6868
6170	H6870
6171	H6871
6172	H6872
6173	A10571
6174	H6873
6175	H6874
6176	H6875
"	H6898
6177	H6876
6178	H6877
6179	H6878
6180	H6879
6181	H6880
6182	H6881
6183	H6882
6184	H6883
6185	H6884
6186	H6885
6187	H6886
6188	H6887
6189	H6888
6190	H2197
"	H6889
6191	H6891
6192	H6890
6193	H6892
6194	H6894
6195	H6893
6196	H6895
6197	H6896
6198	H6897
6199	H6899
6200	H6901
6201	H6903
6202	H6904
6203	H6902
6204	H6905
6205	H6906
6206	H5123
"	H6907
6207	H6908
6208	H6909
6209	H6910
6210	H6911
6211	H6931
"	H6932
"	H6933
6211'	A10572
6212	H6912
6213	H6913
6214	H6915
6215	H6916
6216	H6934
6217	H6935
6218	H6917
6219	H6936
6220	H6937
6221	H6918
6222	H6919
6223	H6938
6224	H6920
6225	H6939
6226	H6942
6227	H6940
6228	H6941
6229	H6921
6230	H6922
6231	H6943
6232	H6944
6233	H6945
6234	H6946
6235	H6924
"	H6927
6236	A10573
6237	H6923
6238	H6947
6239	H6948
6240	H6925
"	H6926
"	H6930
6241	H6928
6242	H6929
6243	A10574
6244	H6949
6245	H6950
"	H6951
6246	A10575
6247	H6952
6248	H6953
6249	H6954
6250	H6955
6251	H6957
6252	H6958
6253	H6956
6254	H6960
6255	H6959
6256	H6961
6257	H6963
6258	H6964
6259	H6965
6260	H6966
6261	H6967
6262	H6968
6263	A10577
6264	H6969
6265	H6970
6266	H6971
6267	H6972
6268	A10578
6269	H6973
6270	H6974
6271	H6975
"	H6976
6272	H6977
6273	H6978
6274	H6979
6275	H6980
6276	H6982
6277	H6981
6278	H6962
6279	H6983
6280	H6984
6281	H6987
6282	H6985
"	H6986
6283	H6988
6284	H6990
6285	H6991
"	H6992
"	H6993
6286	H6994
"	H6995
6287	H6996
6288	H6997
"	H6998
6289	H6999
6290	H7000
6291	H7001
6292	H7002
6293	H7003
6294	H7004
6295	H7005
6296	H7006
6297	H7007
6298	H7008
6299	H7009
6300	H7010
6301	H7011
6302	H7012
6303	H7013
6304	H7014
"	H7151
6305	H7015
"	H7016
6306	H7017
"	H7018
6307	H7019
"	H7020
6308	H7021
6309	H7022
6310	H7023
6311	H7024
6312	H7025
"	H7026
"	H7030
6313	H7028
6314	H7029
6315	H7031
"	H7032
6316	H7033
6317	H7034
6318	H7035
6319	H7036
"	H7280
6320	H7037
6321	H7038
6322	H7039
"	H7040
6323	H687
"	H7041
6324	H7027
"	H7043
6325	H7044
6326	H7045
6327	H7046
"	H7047
"	H7207
6328	H7048
6329	H7048
"	H7049
6330	H7050
6331	H7051
6332	H7052
6333	H7053
6334	H7054
6335	H7055
"	H7056
6336	H7057
6337	H7058
6338	H7059
6339	H7060
6340	H7061
6341	H7062
"	H7063
6342	H7064
6343	H7065
6344	H7066
6345	H7067
6346	H7068
6347	A10580
6348	H7069
6349	H7070
6350	H7071
6351	H7072
6352	H7073
6353	A10581
6354	H7074
6355	H7075
6356	H7076
6357	H7077
6358	H7080
6359	H7078
6360	H7079
6361	A10582
6362	H7080
6363	H7081
"	H7082
6364	H7083
6365	H7085
6366	H7023
6367	H2112
"	H2672
"	H7084
6368	H7086
6369	H7087
6370	H7108
6371	H7089
6372	H7090
6373	H7091
6374	H7092
6375	H7211
6376	H7093
6377	H7094
6378	H7095
6379	H7096
6380	H2207
"	H7097
6381	H7098
6382	H7099
6383	H7100
6384	H7101
6385	H7103
6386	A10583
6387	A10584
6388	H7104
6389	H7105
6390	H7106
6391	H7107
6392	A10585
6393	H7110
6394	H7109
6395	H7111
6396	H7112
6397	H7113
6398	H7114
6399	A10586
6400	H7115
6401	H7116
6402	A10587
6403	H7117
6404	H7118
6405	H7119
6406	H7120
6407	H7121
6408	H7122
6409	H7123
6410	H7124
"	H7125
6411	H7102
"	H7126
6412	H7127
"	H7128
6413	H7129
6414	H7130
6415	H7131
6416	H7132
6417	H7133
6418	H7134
"	H7135
6419	H7136
"	H7137
6420	H7138
6421	H7139
6422	H7140
6423	H7141
6424	H7142
"	H7143
6425	H7144
6426	H7145
6427	H7146
6428	H7147
6429	H7148
6430	H7149
6431	H7150
6432	H7152
6433	A10588
6434	H7157
6435	H7153
6436	H7154
6437	H7042
"	H7155
6438	H7157
6439	H7158
"	H7159
"	H7160
"	H7161
6440	H4367
"	H4368
"	H7156
6441	H7163
6442	H7164
6443	H7162
"	H7165
6444	H7166
6445	H7167
6446	H7168
6447	A10589
6448	H7170
6449	H7171
6450	H7169
6451	H7172
6452	H7173
"	H7174
6453	H7175
6454	H7176
6455	H7177
6456	H7178
6457	H7179
6458	H7180
6459	H7181
6460	A10590
6461	H7182
6462	H7183
6463	H7184
6464	H7185
"	H7187
6465	H7186
6466	H7188
6467	H7189
6468	H7190
6469	H7191
6470	H7192
6471	H7193
6472	H7194
6473	H7196
6474	H7197
6475	H7198
6476	H7199
"	H7200
6477	H7201
6478	H7202
6479	H7203
6480	H7204
6481	H7205
6482	H7206
6483	H2204
"	H7209
6484	H7210
6485	H7212
"	H7217
"	H7227
6486	H7213
6487	H7214
6488	H7215
6489	H7216
6490	H7218
6491	H7219
6492	H7220
6493	H7221
6494	H7222
6495	H7223
"	H7751
6496	H7224
6497	H7225
6498	H7226
6499	H7228
6500	H7229
6501	H7230
"	H7241
6502	H7231
6503	H7232
"	H7247
6504	H7233
6505	H7234
6506	H7235
6507	H7237
6508	H7236
6509	H7238
"	H7311
6510	H7239
6511	H7240
6512	H7051
6513	H7242
6514	H7243
"	H7263
6515	H7245
6516	H7246
6517	H7248
6518	H7250
6519	H7244
"	H7252
6520	H7251
6521	H7253
6522	H7254
6523	A10591
6524	H7255
"	H7256
"	H7257
6525	H7258
6526	H7259
6527	H7260
6528	H7261
6529	H7262
6530	H7264
"	H7265
6531	H7266
6532	H7267
6533	H7268
6534	H7269
6535	H7270
6536	H7271
6537	A10592
"	A10593
6538	H7272
6539	H7273
6540	A10594
6541	H7274
6542	H7275
6543	A10595
6544	H7276
"	H7277
6545	H7279
6546	H7278
6547	H7281
6548	H2922
6549	H7281+5785
6550	H7282
6551	H7283
6552	H7284
6553	H7285
6554	H7286

STRONG	G/K
6555	H7287
6556	H7288
6557	H7289
6558	H7291
6559	H7292
6560	H7290
6561	H7293
6562	A10596
6563	H7294
6564	H7295
6565	H7296
"	H7297
6566	H7298
6567	H7300
"	H7301
6568	A10597
6569	H7302
6570	H7303
6571	H7304
"	H7305
6572	H7306
"	H7358
6573	A10598
6574	H7307
6575	H7308
6576	H7299
6577	H7309
6578	H7310
6579	H7312
6580	H7317
6581	H7313
6582	H7318
6583	H7319
6584	H7320
6585	H7314
6586	H7321
6587	H7315
6588	H7322
6589	H7316
6590	A10599
6591	A10600
6592	H7323
6593	H7324
6594	H7325
6595	H7326
"	H7336
6596	H7327
6597	H7328
6598	H7329
6599	H7330
6600	A10601
6601	H7331
"	H7332
6602	H7333
6603	H7334
6604	H7335
6605	H7337
"	H7338
6606	A10602
6607	H7339
6608	H7340
6609	H7347
6610	H7341
6611	H7342
6612	H7343
"	H7344
6613	A10603
6614	H7345
6615	H7346
6616	H7348
6617	H7349
"	H9520
6618	H7350
6619	H7351
6620	H7352
6621	H7353
6622	H7354
6623	H7355
6624	H7356
6625	H7357
6626	H7359
6627	H7362
6628	H7365
6629	H7366
6630	H7367
6631	H7368
6632	H7369
"	H7370
6633	H7371
6634	A10605
6635	H7372
"	H7378
6636	H7375
"	H7387
6637	H2206
"	H7376
6638	H7377
6639	H7379
6640	A10606
6641	H7380
6642	H7381
6643	H7373
"	H7374
"	H7382
"	H7383
6644	H7384
6645	H7385
6646	H7386
6647	A10607
6648	H7389
6649	H7390
6650	H7391
6651	H7392
6652	H7393
6653	H7395
6654	H7396
"	H7397
6655	A10608
6656	A10609
6657	H7398
6658	H7399
"	H7400
6659	H7401
6660	H7402
6661	H7403
6662	H7404
6663	H7405
6664	H7406
6665	A10610
6666	H7407
6667	H7408
"	H7409
6668	H5176
"	H7410
6669	H7411
6670	H7412
"	H7413
6671	H7414
6672	H7415
"	H7416
6673	H7417
6674	H7364
6675	H7363
6676	A10611
6677	H7418
"	H7454
6678	H7419
"	H7420
6679	H7421
"	H7472
6680	H7422
6681	H7423
6682	H7424
6683	H7425
6684	H7426
6685	H7427
6686	H7428
6687	H7429
6688	H7430
6689	H7431
"	H7433
"	H7434
"	H7487
6690	H7432
6691	H7436
6692	H7437
"	H7438
6693	H7439
6694	H7440
6695	H7441
"	H7442
6696	H7443
"	H7444
6697	H7445
"	H7446
"	H7447
6698	H7448
6699	H7451
6700	H7452
6701	H7453
6702	H7455
6703	H7456
6704	H7457
6705	H7458
6706	H7460
6707	H7461
6708	H7459
6709	H7462
6710	H7463
6711	H7464
6712	H7465
6713	H7466
6714	H7468
6715	H7467
6716	H7469
6717	H7471
6718	H7473
"	H7474
6719	H7475
6720	H7476
6721	H7477
6722	H7479
6723	H7480
6724	H7481
6725	H7483
6726	H7482
6727	H7484
6728	H7470
6729	H7485
6730	H7486
6731	H7488
"	H7578
"	H7490
6732	H7489
6733	H7491
6734	H7492
6735	H7493
"	H7494
"	H7495
"	H7496
6736	H7497
6737	H7493
"	H7494
"	H7495
"	H7496
6738	H7498
6739	A10612
6740	H7499
6741	H7500
6742	H7501
"	H7508
6743	H7502
"	H7503
6744	A10613
6745	H7505
6746	H7504
6747	H7505
"	H7506
6748	H7507
6749	H7510
6750	H7509
6751	H7511
6752	H7498
6753	H2209
6754	H7512
"	H7513
6755	A10614
6756	H7514
"	H7515
6757	H7516
6758	H7517
6759	H7518
6760	H7519
6761	H7520
6762	H7522
6763	H7521
6764	H7523
6765	H7524
6766	H7525
6767	H7526
"	H7527
"	H7528
"	H7529
6768	H7530
6769	H7531
6770	H7532
6771	H7534
6772	H7533
6773	H7535
6774	H7536
6775	H7537
6776	H7538
6777	H7539
6778	H7540
6779	H7541
6780	H7542
6781	H7543
"	H7544
6782	H7545
6783	H7552
6784	H7546
6785	H7547
6786	H7548
6787	H7549
6788	H7550
6789	H7551
6790	H7554
6791	H7553
6792	H7555
"	H7556
6793	H7557
"	H7558
"	H7559
6794	H7562
6795	H7563
6796	H7564
6797	H7561
"	H7565
"	H7566
6798	H7567
"	H7568
6799	H7569
6800	H7560
"	H7570
6801	H7571
6802	H7572
6803	H7573
6804	H7574
6805	H7575
6806	H7576
6807	H7577
"	H7578
6808	H7579
6809	H7581
6810	H7582
6811	H7583
6812	H7584
6813	H7585
6814	H7586
6815	H1300
"	H7587
"	H7588
6816	H7589
6817	H7590
6818	H7591
6819	H7592
6820	H7580
"	H7593
6821	H7594
6822	H7595
6823	H7596
6824	H7597
6825	H7598
"	H7609
6826	H7599
6827	H7602
6828	H7600
6829	H7601
6830	H7603
6831	H7604
"	H7612
6832	H7605
"	H7616
6833	H7606
6834	H7607
6835	H7608
6836	H7610
6837	H7611
6838	H7613
6839	H7614
6840	H7615
6841	A10615
6842	H7618
6843	H7619
6844	H7620
6845	H7621
"	H7636
6846	H7622
"	H7623
6847	H7195
"	H7624
6848	H7625
"	H7626
6849	H7617
6850	H7627
6851	H7628
6852	H7629
6853	A10616
6854	H7630
6855	H7631
6856	H7632
6857	H7634
6858	H7633
6859	H7635
6860	H7637
6861	H7638
6862	H7639
"	H7640
"	H7641
6863	H7643
6864	H7644
6865	H7450
"	H7645
6866	H7646
6867	H7647
"	H7648
6868	H7649
6869	H7650
"	H7651
"	H7659
"	H7676
6870	H7653
6871	H7654
6872	H7655
"	H7656
"	H7657
6873	H7658
6874	H7662
6875	H7661
6876	H7660
6877	H7663
6878	H7664
6879	H7665
6880	H7667
6881	H7666
6882	H7668
"	H7670
6883	H7669
6884	H7671
6885	H7672
6886	H7673
6887	H7674
"	H7675
"	H7677
6888	H7678
6889	H7679
6890	H2241
"	H7680
6891	H7681
6892	H7683
"	H7795
6893	H7684
6894	H7685
6895	H7686
6896	H7687
6897	H7687
6898	H7688
6899	H7689
6900	H7690
6901	H7691
6902	A10618
6903	A10619
6904	H7692
6905	H7692
6906	H7693
6907	H7694
6908	H7695
6909	H7696
6910	H7697
6911	H7698
6912	H7699
6913	H7700
6914	H2246
"	H7701
6915	H7702
6916	H7703
6917	H7704
6918	H7705
6919	H7706
6920	H7707
6921	H7708
6922	A10620
6923	H7709
6924	H7710
"	H7711
"	H7714
6925	A10621
6926	H7713
6927	H7712
6928	A10622
6929	H7715
6930	H7716
6931	H7719
6932	H7717
6933	A10623
6934	H7718
6935	H7720
6936	H7721
6937	H7722
6938	H7723
6939	H7724
6940	H7725
6941	H7726
6942	H7727
6943	H7730
6944	H7731
6945	H7728
6946	H7729
6947	H1395
"	H7732
6948	H7728
6949	H7733
6950	H7735
6951	H7736
6952	H7737
6953	H7738
6954	H7739
6955	H7740
6956	H7741
6957	H7742
"	H7743
"	H7744
6958	H7794
"	H7796
6959	H7746
6960	H7747
"	H7748
6961	H7749
6962	H7752
"	H7753
6963	H7754
"	H7825
"	H7826
6964	H7755
6965	H7756
"	H7856
"	H9539
6966	A10624
6967	H7757
6968	H7758
6969	H7759
"	H7801
6970	H7760
6971	H7761
6972	H7763
6973	H7762
6974	H7763
"	H7810
6975	H7764
"	H7765
6976	H2212
"	H7766
6977	H7767
6978	H7743+7743
6979	H7769
"	H7979
"	H7981
"	H7982
6980	H7770
6981	H7927
6982	H7771
6983	H7772
6984	H7773
6985	H7775
6986	H7776
6987	H7776
6988	H7777
6989	H7778
6990	H3684
6991	H7779
6992	A10625
6993	H7780
6994	H7781
6995	H7782
6996	H7783
"	H7785
6997	H2214
"	H7784
6998	H7786
6999	H5231
"	H5232
"	H7787
7000	H7788
7001	A10626
7002	H7789
7003	H7790
7004	H7792
7005	H7793
7006	H7794
7007	A10627
7008	H7798
7009	H7799
7010	A10628
7011	A10629
7012	H7800
7013	H7802
7014	H7803
"	H7804
"	H7805
7015	H7806
7016	H7807
7017	H7808
7018	H7809
7019	H7811
7020	H7812
7021	H7813
7022	H7814
7023	H7815
7024	H7816
"	H7817
7025	H3085
"	H3097
"	H7818
"	H7819
7026	H7820
7027	H7821
7028	H7822
7029	H7823
7030	A10644
"	A10630
7031	H7824
7032	A10631
7033	H7828
7034	H7829
7035	H7827
7036	H7830
7037	H7831
7038	H7832
7039	H7833
7040	H7834
7041	H7835
7042	H7836
7043	H7837
7044	H7838
7045	H7839
7046	H7840
7047	H7841
7048	H7842
7049	H7843
"	H7844
7050	H7845
"	H7846
7051	H7847
7052	H7848
7053	H7849
7054	H7850
7055	H7851
7056	H7852
7057	H7853
7058	H7854
7059	H7855
7060	H7857
7061	H7858
7062	H7859
7063	H7853
7064	H7860
7065	H7861
7066	A10632
7067	H7862
7068	H7863
7069	H7864
"	H7865
7070	H7866
7071	H7867
7072	H7868
7073	H7869
7074	H7870
7075	H7871
7076	H7872
7077	H7873
7078	H7874
7079	H7875
7080	H7876
7081	H7877
7082	H7878
7083	H7879
7084	H7881
7085	H7882
7086	H7883
7087	H7884
"	H7885
7088	H7886
7089	H7888
7090	H7887
7091	H7889
7092	H7890
7093	H7891
7094	H7892
7095	H7893
7096	H7894
7097	H7895
"	H7897
7098	H7896
"	H7901
7099	H7898
7100	H7902
7101	H7903
7102	H7904
7103	H7905
7104	H6681
"	H7906
7105	H7907
"	H7908
7106	H7909
"	H7910
7107	H7911
7108	A10633
7109	A10634
7110	H7912
"	H7913
7111	H7914
7112	H7899
"	H7915
7113	A10635
7114	H7900
"	H7917
"	H7918
7115	H7919
7116	H7920
7117	H7921
7118	A10636
7119	H7922
7120	H7923
7121	H7924
7122	H7925
7123	A10637
7124	H7926
7125	H7925
7126	H7928
7127	A10638
7128	H7930
7129	A10639
7130	H7931
7131	H7929
7132	H7932
7133	H7933
"	H7934
7134	H7935
7135	H7938
7136	H7936
"	H7939
7137	H7937
7138	H7940
7139	H7942
7140	H7943
7141	H7946
7142	H7944
7143	H7945
7144	H7942
7145	H7948
7146	H7947
"	H7949
7147	H7950
7148	H7951
7149	A10640
7150	H7952
7151	H7953
"	H7956
7152	H7954
7153	H7957
"	H7959
7154	H7958
7155	H2941
"	H7960
7156	H7964
7157	H7961
7158	H6173
"	H7962
"	H7963
7159	H7965
7160	H7966
7161	H7967
"	H7969
7162	A10641
7163	H2199
"	H7968
7164	H7970
7165	H7971
7166	H7972
7167	H7973
7168	H7974
7169	H7975
7170	A10642
7171	H7976
7172	H7977
7173	H7978
7174	H7980
7175	H7983
7176	H7984
7177	H7985
7178	H7986
7179	H7990
7180	H7991
7181	H7992
7182	H7993
7183	H7994
"	H7995
7184	H7987
7185	H7996
7186	H7997
7187	A10643
7188	H7998
7189	H7999
"	H8000
7190	H8001
7191	H8002
7192	H7988
7193	H7989
7194	H8003
7195	H8004
7196	H8005
7197	H8006
"	H8007
7198	H8008
7199	H8009
7200	H8011
"	H8013
"	H8021
7201	H8012
7202	H8011
7203	H8014
"	H8015
7204	H2218
7205	H8017
7206	H8018
7207	H8019
7208	H8020
7209	H8023
7210	H8024
7211	H8016
"	H8025

STRONG	G/K
7212	H8026
7213	H8027
7214	H8028
7215	H8029
7216	H8030
7217	A10646
7218	H8031
"	H8034
7219	H8032
7220	H8033
"	H8396
7221	H8035
7222	H8036
7223	H8037
7224	H8038
7225	H8040
7226	H8031
7227	H8041
"	H8042
7228	H8043
7229	A10647
7230	H8044
7231	H8045
7232	H8046
7233	H8047
7234	H8048
7235	H2220
"	H2221
"	H8049
"	H8050
7236	A10648
7237	H8051
7238	A10650
7239	H8052
7240	A10649
7241	H8053
7242	H8054
7243	H8055
"	H8068
7244	A10651
7245	H8056
7246	H8057
7247	H8058
7248	H4454
"	H8059
7249	H8060
"	H8042+6247
7250	H8061
7251	H8062
7252	H8061
7253	H8063
7254	H8061
"	H8064
7255	H8065
"	H8066
7256	H8067
7257	H8069
7258	H8070
7259	H8071
7260	A10647
7261	A10652
7262	H8072
7263	H8073
7264	H8074
7265	A10653
7266	A10654
7267	H8075
7268	H8076
7269	H8077
7270	H8078
7271	A10655
7272	H8079
7273	H8081
7274	H8082
7275	H8083
7276	H8084
7277	H8086
7278	H8085
7279	H8087
7280	H8088
"	H8089
"	H8090
7281	H8092
7282	H8091
7283	H8093
7284	A10656
7285	H8094
"	H8095
7286	H8096
7287	H8097
"	H8098
7288	H8099
7289	H8100
7290	H8101
7291	H8103
7292	H8104
7293	H8105
7294	H8105
7295	H8107
7296	H8106
7297	H3724
"	H8109
7298	H8110
"	H8111
7299	A10657
7300	H8113
7301	H8115
7302	H8116
7303	H8108
"	H8117
7304	H8118
7305	H8119
7306	H8193
7307	H8120
7308	A10658
7309	H8121
7310	H8122
7311	H3727
"	H3753
"	H8123
"	H8225
"	H8249
7312	H8124
7313	A10659
7314	A10660
7315	H8125
7316	H8126
7317	H8127
7318	H8128
7319	H8129
7320	H6471
"	H8251
7321	H8131
7322	H8344
7323	H8132
"	H8350
7324	H8197
7325	H8201
7326	H8133
7327	H8134
7328	A10661
7329	H8135
7330	H8136
7331	H8139
7332	H8137
7333	H8138
7334	H8140
7335	H8141
7336	H8142
7337	H8143
7338	H8144
7339	H8148
7340	H8149
"	H8150
7341	H8145
7342	H8146
7343	H8147
7344	H8151
7345	H8152
"	H8153
7346	H8154
7347	H8160
7348	H8156
"	A10662
7349	H8157
7350	H8158
7351	H8112
"	H8159
7352	A10663
7353	H8161
7354	H8162
7355	H8163
7356	H8166
"	H8171
7357	H8165
7358	H8167
7359	A10664
7360	H8164
"	H8168
7361	H8169
7362	H8172
7363	H8173
"	H8174
7364	H8175
7365	A10665
7366	H8176
7367	H8177
7368	H8178
7369	H8179
7370	H8180
7371	H8181
7372	H8182
7373	H8183
7374	H8185
7375	H8186
7376	H8187
7377	H8188
7378	H8189
7379	H8190
"	H8191
7380	H8192
7381	H8194
7382	A10666
7383	H8195
7384	H1910
"	H8196
7385	H8198
7386	H8199
7387	H8200
7388	H8202
7389	H8203
7390	H8205
7391	H8204
7392	H8206
7393	H8207
7394	H8209
"	H8211
7395	H8208
7396	H8210
7397	H8212
7398	H8213
7399	H8214
7400	H8215
7401	H8216
7402	H8217
7403	H8218
7404	H8219
7405	H8220
7406	H8221
7407	H8222
7408	H8223
7409	H8224
7410	H8226
7411	H8227
"	H8228
7412	A10667
7413	H8229
7414	H8230
"	H8259
7415	H8231
7416	H8232
7417	H8233
"	H8234
"	H8235
"	H8237
7418	H8238
"	H8241
7419	H8239
7420	H8242
7421	H811
7422	H8243
7423	H8244
"	H8245
7424	H8247
7425	H8248
7426	H8250
7427	H8129
7428	H8236
7429	H8252
7430	H8253
7431	H8254
7432	H8255
7433	H8240
7434	H2174
"	H8256
7435	H8258
7436	H7435
7437	H8257
7438	H8260
7439	H8261
7440	H8262
7441	H8263
7442	H8130
"	H8264
7443	H8266
7444	H8264
7445	H8265
7446	H8267
7447	H8268
"	H8269
7448	H8270
7449	H8271
7450	H8272
7451	H8273
"	H8274
7452	H8275
7453	H8276
7454	H8277
7455	H8278
7456	H8279
"	H8281
7457	H8280
7458	H8280
7459	H8282
7460	H8283
7461	H8284
"	H8285
7462	H8287
"	H8289
7463	H8291
7464	H8292
"	H8300
7465	H8288
7466	H8293
7467	H8294
7468	H8295
7469	H8296
7470	A10668
7471	H8297
7472	H8298
7473	H8286
7474	H8299
7475	H8301
7476	A10669
7477	H8302
7478	H8303
7479	H8304
7480	H8305
7481	H8306
"	H8307
7482	H8308
7483	H8309
"	H8310
7484	H8311
"	H8312
7485	H8313
7486	H8314
7487	A10670
7488	H8315
"	H8316
7489	H5336
"	H8317
"	H8318
7490	A10671
7491	H8319
7492	H8320
7493	H8321
"	H8322
7494	H8323
7495	H8324
7496	H8327
7497	H8328
"	H8329
7498	H8325
"	H8334
7499	H8337
7500	H8326
7501	H8330
7502	H8331
7503	H8332
7504	H8333
7505	H8336
7506	H8338
7507	H8339
7508	H8340
7509	H8341
7510	H8335
"	H8342
7511	H8346
7512	A10672
7513	H8343
7514	H8345
7515	H8346
7516	H8347
7517	H8348
7518	H8349
7519	H8351
7520	H8353
7521	H8352
"	H8354
"	H8355
7522	H8356
7523	H8357
7524	H8358
7525	H8359
7526	H8360
7527	H8361
7528	H8362
7529	H8363
7530	H8364
7531	H8365
"	H8367
7532	H8366
7533	H8368
7534	H8369
7535	H8370
7536	H8371
7537	H8372
7538	H8373
"	H8374
7539	H8375
7540	H8376
7541	H8377
7542	H8378
7543	H8379
7544	H8380
7545	H8381
7546	H8382
7547	H8383
7548	H8384
7549	H8385
7550	H8386
7551	H8387
7552	H8388
"	H8389
"	H8390
7553	H8391
7554	H8392
7555	H8393
7556	H8394
7557	H8395
7558	H8397
7559	H8398
7560	A10673
7561	H8399
7562	H8400
7563	H8401
7564	H8402
7565	H8404
7566	H8405
7567	H8406
7568	H8407
7569	H8408
7570	H8409
7571	H8410
7572	H8411
7573	H8412
7574	H8413
7575	H8414
7576	H8415
7577	H8416
7578	H8417
7579	H8612
7580	H8613
7581	H8614
7582	H8615
"	H8616
7583	H8617
7584	H8618
7585	H8619
7586	H8620
7587	H8621
7588	H8622
"	H8623
7589	H8624
7590	H8764
7591	H8625
7592	H8626
"	H8628
7593	A10689
7594	H8627
7595	A10690
7596	H8629
7597	H8630
"	H9003
7598	A10691
7599	H8631
7600	H8633
7601	
7602	H8634
"	H8635
7603	H8419
7604	H8636
7605	H8637
7606	A10692
7607	H8638
7608	H8640
7609	H8641
7610	H8639
7611	H8642
7612	H8643
7613	H8420
"	H8421
7614	H8644
7615	H8645
7616	H8646
7617	H8647
7618	H8648
7619	H8649
"	H8742
7620	H8651
"	H8652
7621	H8678
7622	H8654
"	H8669
7623	H8655
"	H8656
7624	A10693
7625	A10694
7626	H8657
7627	H8658
7628	H8660
"	H8665
7629	H8661
7630	H8662
7631	A10695
7632	H8663
7633	H8664
7634	H8499
7635	H8666
7636	H8667
7637	H8668
7638	H8422
7639	H8422
7640	H8670
7641	H8672
"	H8673
7642	H8671
7643	H8423
"	H8424
7644	H8674
"	H8675
7645	H8676
"	H8677
7646	H8425
7647	H8426
7648	H8427
7649	H8428
7650	H8678
7651	H8679
7652	H8680
"	H8681
7653	H8430
7654	H8429
7655	A10696
7656	H8683
7657	H8684
7658	H8685
7659	H8686
7660	H8687
7661	H8688
7662	A10697
7663	H8431
"	H8432
7664	H8433
7665	H8653
"	H8689
7666	H8690
7667	H8691
"	H8694
7668	H8692
7669	H8693
7670	H8695
7671	H8696
7672	A10698
7673	H8697
"	H8698
7674	H8700
7675	H8699
7676	H8701
7677	H8702
7678	H8703
7679	H8434
7680	A10677
7681	H8707
7682	H8435
7683	H1417
"	H8704
7684	H8705
7685	H8436
7686	H8706
7687	H8437
"	H8439
7688	H8708
7689	H8438
7690	A10678
7691	H8709
7692	H8710
7693	H8711
7694	H8712
7695	A10699
7696	H8713
7697	H8714
7698	H8715
7699	H8716
"	H8718
7700	H8717
7701	H8719
7702	H8440
7703	H8720
7704	H8441
"	H8442
7705	H8721
7706	H8724
7707	H8725
7708	H8443
7709	H8727
7710	H8728
7711	H8729
"	H8730
7712	A10700
7713	H8444
7714	H8731
7715	A10701
7716	H8445
7717	H8446
7718	H8732
7719	H8733
7720	H8448
7721	H5951
7722	H8738
"	H8739
7723	H8736
7724	H8737
7725	H8740
7726	H8743
7727	H8744
7728	H8745
7729	H8746
7730	H8449
7731	H8747
7732	H8748
7733	H8749
7734	H6047
7735	H8451
7736	H8720
7737	H8750
"	H8751
7738	H9589
7739	A10702
7740	H8753
7741	H8754
7742	H8452
7743	H8755
7744	H8756
7745	H8757
7746	H8758
7747	H8760
7748	H8761
7749	H8762
7750	H6091
"	H8454
7751	H8763
7752	H8765
"	H8766
"	H8867
7753	H8455
7754	H8456
"	H8457
7755	H8458
"	H8459
7756	H8460
7757	H8767
7758	H8768
"	H8871
7759	H8769
7760	H8461
"	H8492
7761	A10682
7762	H8770
7763	H9071
7764	H8771
7765	H8772
7766	H8773
7767	H8774
7768	H8775
7769	H8780
"	H8782
7770	H8781
7771	H8779
7772	H8778
"	H8779
7773	H8776
7774	H8783
7775	H8784
7776	H8785
7777	H8786
"	H8787
7778	H8788
7779	H8789
"	H8790
7780	H8791
7781	H8793
7782	H8795
7783	H8796
7784	H8798
7785	H8797
7786	H8606
7787	H8492
7788	H8801
7789	H8800
7790	H8803
7791	H8805
7792	A10703
7793	H8804
7794	H8802
7795	H8463
7796	H8604
7797	H8464
7798	H8807
7799	H8808
7800	H8809
7801	A10704
7802	H8808+6343
7803	H8811
7804	A10706
7805	H8812
7806	H8813
7807	H8814
7808	H8465
7809	H8815
7810	H8816
7811	H8466
7812	H8817
7813	H8467
7814	H8468
7815	H8818
7816	H8819
7817	H8820
"	H8863
7818	H8469
7819	H8821
"	H8822
"	H8823
7820	H8822
7821	H8824
7822	H8825
7823	H6084
"	H8826
7824	H8470
7825	H8827
7826	H8828
7827	H8829
7828	H8830
7829	H8831
7830	H8832
7831	H8833
"	H8834
7832	H8471
7833	H8835
7834	H8836
7835	H8837
7836	H8838
7837	H8840
7838	H8839
7839	H8841
7840	H8842
7841	H8843
7842	H8844
7843	H8845
7844	A10705
7845	H8846
7846	H8473
7847	H8474
7848	H8847
7849	H8848
7850	H8849
7851	H8850
7852	H8475
7853	H8476
7854	H8477
7855	H8478
7856	H8479
7857	H8851
7858	H8852
7859	A10680
7860	H8853
7861	H8855
"	H9231
7862	H8856
7863	H8480
7864	H8857
7865	H8481
7866	H8858
7867	H8482
7868	A10681
"	A10675
7869	H8483
7870	H8860
7871	H8859
7872	H8484
7873	H8485
7874	H8486
7875	H6093
"	H8487
7876	H8861
7877	H8862
7878	H8488
7879	H8490
7880	H8489
7881	H8491
7882	H8864
7883	H8865
7884	H4251
"	H8866
7885	H8868
7886	H8869
7887	H8870
"	H8926
"	H8931
7888	H8872
7889	H8873
7890	H8875
7891	H8876
7892	H8877
"	H8878
7893	H8880
7894	H8881
7895	H8810
"	H8882

STRONG	G/K
7896	H8883
7897	H8884
7898	H8885
7899	H8493
7900	H8494
7901	H8886
7902	H8887
7903	H8888
7904	H8889
7905	H8496
7906	H8497
7907	H8498
7908	H8890
7909	H8891
"	H8892
7910	H8893
7911	H4171
"	H8894
7912	A10708
7913	H8895
7914	H8500
7915	H8501
7916	H8502
7917	H8502
7918	H8896
7919	H8505
"	H8506
7920	A10683
7921	H5437
"	H8897
7922	H8507
7923	H8898
7924	A10684
7925	H8899
7926	H8900
7927	H8901
"	H8902
7928	H8903
7929	H8900
7930	H8904
7931	H8905
7932	A10709
7933	H8905
7934	H8907
7935	H8908
"	H8909
7936	H6128
"	H8509
7937	H8910
"	H8912
7938	H8512
7939	H8510
7940	H8511
7941	H8911
7942	H8914
7943	H8913
7944	H8915
7945	H8611
7946	H8916
7947	H8917
7948	H8918
7949	H8919
7950	H8920
"	H8921
7951	H8922
7952	H8923
7953	H8923
7954	A10710
7955	A10685
"	A10711
7956	H8924
"	H8925
7957	H8927
"	H8928
7958	H8513
7959	H8930
7960	A10712
7961	H8929
7962	H8932
7963	A10713
7964	H8933
7965	H8934
7966	H8936
7967	H8935
7968	H8937
7969	H5456
"	H8993
7970	H9001
7971	H8938
7972	A10714
7973	H8939
"	H8945
7974	H8941
7975	H8940
"	H8942
7976	H8943
7977	H8944
7978	H8946
7979	H8947
7980	H8948
7981	A10715
7982	H8949
7983	H8950
7984	A10716
7985	A10717
7986	H8951
7987	H8952
7988	H8953
7989	H8954
7990	A10718
7991	H8955
"	H8956
"	H8957
"	H8998
7992	H8958
"	H8999
7993	H8959
7994	H8960
7995	H8961
7996	H8962
7997	H8963
"	H8964
7998	H8965
7999	H8966
8000	A10719
8001	A10720
8002	H8968
8003	H8969
8004	H8970
8005	H8972
8006	H8973
8007	H8514
8008	H8515
8009	H8516
8010	H8976
8011	H8974
8012	H8517
8013	H8977
8014	H8518
8015	H8979
8016	H8980
8017	H8981
8018	H8982
"	H8983
8019	H8984
"	H8985
8020	H8986
8021	H8988
8022	H8987
8023	H8989
8024	H8989
8025	H8990
8026	H8991
8027	H8992
8028	H8994
8029	H9000
8030	H8996
8031	H8995
8032	H8997
8033	H9004
8034	H9005
8035	H9006
8036	A10721
8037	H9007
8038	H9008
8039	H9009
8040	H8520
8041	H8520
"	H8521
8042	H8522
8043	H9010
8044	H9011
8045	H9012
8046	A10722
8047	H9014
8048	H9015
8049	H9016
8050	H9017
8051	H9018
8052	H9019
8053	H9020
8054	H9021
8055	H8523
8056	H8524
8057	H8525
8058	H9023
8059	H9024
8060	H9025
8061	H9026
8062	H9027
8063	H8526
8064	H9028
8065	A10723
8066	H9029
8067	H9030
8068	H9031
"	H9032
8069	H9033
"	H9034
8070	H9035
"	H9082
8071	H8529
8072	H8528
8073	H8530
"	H8978
"	H9036
8074	H9037
8075	A10724
8076	H9038
8077	H9039
"	H9040
8078	H9041
8079	H8532
8080	H9042
8081	H9043
8082	H9045
8083	H9046
8084	H9047
8085	H9048
"	H9049
8086	A10725
8087	H9050
8088	H9051
8089	H9053
8090	H9054
8091	H9052
8092	H9055
8093	H9056
8094	H9057
8095	H9058
8096	H9059
8097	H9060
8098	H9061
"	H9062
8099	H9063
8100	H9064
8101	H9065
8102	H9066
8103	H9067
8104	H9068
8105	H9069
8106	H9070
"	H9013
8107	H9081
8108	H9072
8109	H9073
8110	H9074
"	H9075
8111	H9076
8112	H5264
"	H9077
8113	H9078
8114	H9079
"	H9080
8115	A10726
8116	H9083
8117	H9084
8118	H9085
8119	H9086
8120	A10727
8121	H9087
8122	A10728
8123	H9088
8124	A10729
8125	H9091
8126	H9092
8127	H9094
8128	A10730
8129	H9095
8130	H8533
8131	A10686
8132	H9096
"	H9101
8133	A10731
8134	H9098
8135	H8534
8136	H9099
8137	H9100
8138	H9101
8139	A10733
8140	A10732
8141	H9102
8142	H9097
"	H9104
8143	H2036
"	H9105
8144	H9106
8145	H9108
8146	H8535
8147	H9109
8148	H9110
8149	H8536
8150	H9111
"	H9112
8151	H9113
8152	H9114
8153	H3822
8154	H9115
8155	H9116
8156	H9117
8157	H9118
8158	H9119
8159	H9120
8160	A10734
8161	H9121
8162	H9122
8163	H8537
"	H8538
"	H8539
8164	H8540
8165	H8541
"	H8542
"	H8543
8166	H8544
8167	H8545
8168	H9123
8169	H9124
"	H9125
8170	H9126
8171	H9127
8172	H9128
8173	H9129
"	H9130
8174	H9131
8175	H8547
"	H8548
"	H8549
8176	H9132
8177	A10687
8178	H8550
"	H8551
8179	H9133
8180	H9134
8181	H8552
8182	H9135
8183	H8554
8184	H8555
8185	H8553
8186	H9136
8187	H9137
"	H9138
8188	H8556
8189	H9139
8190	H9140
8191	H9141
8192	H9142
8193	H8557
8194	H9147
8195	H9143
"	H9156
8196	H9144
8197	H8792
"	H9145
"	H9146
8198	H9148
8199	H9149
8200	A10735
8201	H9150
8202	H9151
8203	H9152
"	H9153
8204	H9154
8205	H9155
8206	H9157
"	H9158
8207	H9159
8208	H9160
8209	A10736
8210	H8564
"	H9161
8211	H9162
8212	H9163
8213	H9164
8214	A10737
8215	A10738
8216	H9165
8217	H9166
8218	H9168
8219	H9169
8220	H9170
8221	H9172
8222	H8559
8223	H9171
8224	H8560
8225	H9175
8226	H8561
8227	H9176
"	H9177
8228	H9179
8229	H9180
8230	H9181
8231	H9182
8232	A10739
8233	H9183
8234	H9184
8235	H9185
8236	H9186
8237	H9187
"	H9188
8238	A10740
8239	H9189
8240	H9190
"	H9191
8241	H9192
8242	H8566
8243	A10741
8244	H8567
8245	H9193
"	H9194
"	H9195
8246	H5481
8247	H9196
8248	H9197
8249	H9198
8250	H9198
8251	H9199
8252	H9200
8253	H9201
8254	H9202
8255	H9203
8256	H9204
8257	H9205
8258	H9206
8259	H9207
8260	H9208
8261	H9209
8262	H9210
8263	H9211
8264	H8799
"	H9212
8265	H8568
8266	H9213
8267	H9214
8268	H9216
8269	H6254
"	H8569
8270	H9218
"	H9219
8271	A10742
8272	H8570
8273	H9220
8274	H9221
8275	H9222
8276	H8571
8277	H8572
8278	H8573
8279	H8574
8280	H8575
8281	H9223
"	H9224
8282	H8576
8283	H8577
8284	H9224
8285	H9217
"	H9225
8286	H8578
8287	H9226
8288	H8579
8289	H4389
"	H9227
8290	H9228
8291	H8602
"	H8604
8292	H9229
"	H9241
8293	H9230
8294	H8580
8295	H8581
8296	H8582
"	H8583
8297	H8584
8298	H9232
8299	H8585
8300	H8586
8301	H8587
8302	H9233
"	H9234
8303	H8590
8304	H8588
"	H8589
8305	H8591
8306	H9235
8307	H9244
8308	H8592
8309	H9173
"	H9236
8310	H8593
8311	H8594
8312	H8595
8313	H8596
8314	H8597
8315	H8598
8316	H8599
8317	H9237
8318	H9238
8319	H9239
8320	H8601
8321	H8603
8322	H8605
"	H9240
8323	H8606
8324	H8806
8325	H9242
"	H9243
8326	H9247
8327	H9245
8328	H9247
8329	H9246
8330	A10743
8331	H9249
8332	A10744
"	A10745
8333	H9248
"	H9249
8334	H9250
8335	H9251
8336	H9253
"	H9254
8337	H9252
8338	H9255
8339	H9256
8340	A10746
8341	H9257
8342	H8607
8343	H9258
8344	H9259
8345	H9261
8346	H9262
8347	H9263
8348	H9264
8349	H9265
8350	H9266
8351	H9268
8352	H9269
8353	A10747
8354	H9272
8355	A10748
8356	H9271
8357	H9268
8358	H9275
8359	H9274
8360	H9276
8361	A10749
8362	H9278
8363	H9277
8364	H9279
8365	H9280
"	H9281
8366	H8874
"	H9282
8367	H9284
8368	H8609
8369	H9285
8370	A10750
8371	H9286
8372	H9288
8373	H9289
8374	H9290
8375	H9291
8376	H9292
8377	H9293
8378	H9294
8379	H9295
8380	H9296
"	H9339
8381	H9297
8382	H9298
8383	H9303
8384	H9300
8385	H9299
"	H9301
8386	H9302
8387	H9304
8388	H9305
"	H9306
8389	H9307
8390	H9308
8391	H9309
8392	H9310
8393	H9311
8394	H9312
"	H9341
8395	H9313
8396	H9314
8397	H9316
8398	H9315
8399	H9318
8400	H9319
8401	H9320
8402	H9321
8403	H9322
8404	H9323
8405	H9324
8406	A10752
8407	H9325
"	H9433
8408	H9326
8409	H9327
8410	H9329
8411	A10753
8412	H9330
8413	H9331
8414	H9332
8415	H9333
8416	H9335
8417	H9334
8418	H9336
8419	H9337
8420	H9338
8421	A10754
8422	H9317
8423	H9340
8424	H9342
8425	H9328
8426	H9343
8427	H9344
8428	H9345
8429	A10755
8430	H9346
8431	H9347
8432	H9348
8433	H9349
"	H9350
8434	H9351
8435	H9352
8436	H9353
"	H9400
8437	H9354
8438	H9355
"	H9357
8439	H9356
8440	H9358
8441	H9359
8442	H9360
8443	H9361
8444	H9362
8445	H9363
8446	H9365
8447	H9366
8448	H9366
8449	H9367
8450	A10756
8451	H9368
8452	H9368
8453	H9369
8454	H9370
8455	H9371
8456	H9372
8457	H9373
8458	H9374
8459	H9375
8460	A10757
8461	H9376
8462	H9378
8463	H9377
8464	H9379
8465	H9380
8466	H9381
"	H9385
"	H9386
8467	H9382
8468	H9383
8469	H9384
8470	H9385
8471	H9387
8472	H9388
8473	H9389
8474	H3013
8475	H9390
8476	H9391
8477	H9392
8478	H5502
"	H9393
8479	A10757
8480	H9394
"	H9395
8481	H9396
8482	H9397
8483	H2547
"	H9398
8484	H9399
8485	H9401
8486	H9402
8487	H9403
8488	H9405
8489	H9404
8490	H9406
8491	H9407
8492	H3770
"	H9408
8493	H9409
8494	H9410
8495	H9411
8496	H9412
8497	H9413
8498	H9414
8499	H9414
8500	H9415
8501	H9412
8502	H9416
8503	H9417
8504	H9418
8505	H9419
8506	H9420
8507	H9421
8508	H9422
8509	H9423
8510	H9424
8511	H9428
8512	H9425
8513	H9430
8514	H9429
8515	H9431
"	H9445
8516	H9432
8517	A10758
8518	H9434
8519	H9442
8520	H9436
8521	H9426
8522	H9437
8523	A10759
8524	H9435
8525	H9439
8526	H9440
8527	H9441
8528	H9427
8529	H9443
8530	H9444
8531	A10760
8532	A10761
8533	A10762
8534	H9446
8535	H9447
8536	A10764
8537	H9448
8538	H9450
8539	H9449
8540	A10763
8541	H9451
8542	H9452
8543	H9453
8544	H9454
8545	H9455
8546	H9456
8547	H9457
8548	H9458
8549	H9459
8550	H9460
8551	H9461
8552	H9462
8553	H9463
8554	H9464
8555	H9465
8556	H9466
"	H9467
8557	H9468
8558	H9469
8559	H9470
"	H9471
8560	H9472
"	H9473
8561	H9474
8562	H9475
8563	H9476
8564	H9477
8565	H9478
8566	H9479
8567	H9480
8568	H9478
8569	H9481
8570	H9482
8571	H9483
8572	H9484
8573	H9485
8574	H9486
8575	H9487
"	H9488
8576	H9489
8577	H9490
8578	A10765
8579	A10766
8580	H9491
"	H9492
8581	H9493
8582	H9494
8583	H9495
"	H9497
8584	H9496
8585	H9498
"	H9499
8586	H9500
8587	H9502
8588	H9503
8589	H9504
8590	H9505
8591	H9506
8592	H9508
8593	H9509
8594	H9510

STRONG	G/K
8595	H9511
8596	H4191
"	H9512
"	H9513
8597	H9514
8598	H9515
8599	H9516
"	H9517
8600	H9518
8601	H9519
8602	H9521
"	H9522
8603	H9523
8604	H9524
8605	H9525
8606	H9526
8607	H9527
8608	H9528
8609	H9529
8610	H9530
8611	H9531
8612	H9532
8613	H9533
8614	A10767
8615	H9535
"	H9536
8616	H9534
"	H9537
8617	H9538
8618	H9539
8619	H9540
8620	H9541
8621	H9542
8622	H9543
8623	H9544
8624	A10768
8625	A10769
"	A10770
8626	H9545
8627	A10771
8628	H9364
"	H9546
8629	H9547
8630	H9548
8631	A10772
8632	A10773
"	A10774
8633	H9549
8634	H9550
8635	H9551
8636	H9552
8637	H8078
8638	H9553
8639	H9554
8640	H9555
8641	H9556
8642	H9557
8643	H9558
8644	H9559
8645	H9560
8646	H9561
"	H9562
8647	H9563
8648	A10775
"	A10778
8649	H9564
"	H9566
"	H9567
"	H9569
8650	H9568
8651	A10776
8652	A10777
8653	H9570
8654	H9571
8655	H9572
8656	H9573
"	H9574
8657	H9575
8658	H9577
8659	H9576
"	H9578
8660	H9579
8661	H9580
8662	H9581
8663	H9583
"	H9589
8664	H9585
"	H9586
8665	H9587
8666	H9588
8667	H9582
8668	H9591
8669	H9592
8670	H9593
8671	H9595
8672	H9596
8673	H9597
8674	A10779

GREEK NEW TESTAMENT

STRONG	G/K
1	*G1*
"	*G270*
2	*G2*
3	*G3*
4	*G4*
5	*G5*
6	*G6*
7	*G7*
8	*G8*
9	*G9*
10	*G10*
11	*G11*
12	*G12*
13	*G13*
14	*G14*
15	*G16*
16	*G17*
17	*G18*
18	*G19*
19	*G20*
20	*G21*
21	*G22*
22	*G23*
23	*G24*
24	*G25*
25	*G26*
26	*G27*
27	*G28*
28	*G29*
29	*G30*
30	*G31*
"	*G35*
31	*G32*
32	*G34*
33	*G72*
34	*G36*
35	*G37*
36	*G38*
37	*G39*
"	*G420*
38	*G40*
39	*G41*
40	*G41*
41	*G42*
42	*G43*
43	*G44*
44	*G45*
45	*G46*
46	*G47*
47	*G48*
48	*G49*
49	*G50*
50	*G51*
51	*G52*
52	*G53*
53	*G54*
54	*G55*
55	*G56*
56	*G57*
57	*G58*
58	*G59*
59	*G60*
60	*G61*
61	*G62*
62	*G63*
63	*G64*
64	*G65*
65	*G66*
66	*G67*
67	*G68*
68	*G69*
69	*G70*
70	*G71*
71	*G72*
72	*G73*
73	*G74*
74	*G75*
75	*G76*
76	*G77*
77	*G78*
78	*G79*
79	*G80*
80	*G81*
81	*G82*
82	*G83*
83	*G84*
84	*G85*
85	*G194*
"	*G86*
86	*G87*
87	*G88*
88	*G89*
89	*G90*
90	*G91*
"	*G916*
"	*G917*
91	*G92*
92	*G93*
93	*G94*
94	*G96*
95	*G97*
96	*G99*
97	*G100*
98	*G101*
99	*G102*
100	*G103*
101	*G104*
102	*G105*
103	*G106*
104	*G107*
105	*G108*
106	*G109*
107	*G110*
108	*G111*
109	*G113*
110	*G114*
111	*G116*
112	*G117*
113	*G118*
114	*G119*
115	*G120*
116	*G121*
117	*G122*
118	*G123*
119	*G124*
120	*G126*
121	*G127*
122	*G128*
123	*G129*
124	*G130*
125	*G131*
126	*G132*
127	*G133*
"	*G1290*
128	*G134*
129	*G135*
130	*G136*
131	*G137*
132	*G138*
133	*G139*
134	*G140*
135	*G141*
136	*G142*
137	*G143*
138	*G145*
139	*G146*
140	*G147*
141	*G148*
142	*G149*
143	*G150*
144	*G151*
145	*G152*
146	*G153*
147	*G154*
148	*G155*
149	*G156*
150	*G156*
151	*G157*
152	*G158*
153	*G159*
154	*G160*
155	*G161*
156	*G162*
157	*G163*
"	*G166*
158	*G165*
159	*G165*
160	*G167*
161	*G168*
162	*G169*
163	*G170*
164	*G171*
165	*G172*
166	*G173*
167	*G174*
168	*G175*
169	*G176*
170	*G177*
171	*G178*
172	*G179*
173	*G180*
174	*G181*
175	*G182*
176	*G183*
177	*G184*
178	*G185*
179	*G186*
180	*G187*
"	*G188*
181	*G189*
182	*G190*
183	*G191*
184	*G192*
185	*G193*
186	*G195*
187	*G196*
188	*G197*
189	*G198*
190	*G199*
191	*G200*
"	*G201*
192	*G202*
193	*G203*
194	*G204*
195	*G205*
196	*G206*
197	*G209*
198	*G208*
199	*G209*
200	*G210*
201	*G211*
202	*G212*
203	*G213*
204	*G214*
205	*G215*
206	*G216*
207	*G217*
208	*G218*
209	*G219*
210	*G220*
211	*G222*
"	*G223*
212	*G224*
213	*G225*
214	*G226*
215	*G227*
216	*G228*
217	*G221*
"	*G229*
218	*G230*
219	*G231*
220	*G232*
221	*G233*
222	*G234*
223	*G235*
224	*G236*
225	*G237*
226	*G238*
227	*G239*
228	*G240*
229	*G241*
230	*G242*
231	*G243*
232	*G244*
233	*G245*
234	*G246*
235	*G247*
236	*G248*
237	*G249*
238	*G251*
239	*G252*
240	*G253*
241	*G254*
242	*G256*
"	*G380*
243	*G257*
244	*G258*
245	*G259*
246	*G260*
247	*G261*
248	*G262*
249	*G263*
250	*G264*
251	*G265*
252	*G266*
253	*G267*
254	*G268*
255	*G269*
256	*G271*
257	*G272*
258	*G273*
259	*G274*
260	*G275*
261	*G276*
262	*G277*
263	*G278*
264	*G279*
265	*G280*
266	*G281*
267	*G282*
268	*G283*
269	*G285*
270	*G286*
271	*G287*
272	*G288*
273	*G289*
274	*G290*
275	*G291*
276	*G292*
277	*G293*
278	*G294*
279	*G295*
280	*G296*
281	*G297*
282	*G298*
283	*G299*
284	*G300*
285	*G302*
286	*G303*
287	*G304*
288	*G306*
289	*G307*
290	*G308*
291	*G309*
292	*G310*
293	*G312*
294	*G313*
"	*G314*
295	*G315*
296	*G316*
297	*G317*
298	*G318*
299	*G320*
300	*G321*
301	*G322*
302	*G323*
303	*G324*
304	*G325*
305	*G326*
306	*G327*
307	*G328*
308	*G329*
309	*G330*
310	*G331*
311	*G332*
312	*G334*
313	*G335*
314	*G336*
315	*G337*
316	*G338*
317	*G339*
318	*G340*
319	*G341*
320	*G342*
321	*G343*
322	*G344*
323	*G345*
324	*G346*
325	*G347*
326	*G348*
327	*G349*
328	*G350*
329	*G351*
330	*G352*
331	*G353*
332	*G354*
333	*G355*
"	*G1461*
334	*G356*
335	*G357*
336	*G358*
337	*G359*
338	*G360*
339	*G361*
340	*G362*
341	*G363*
342	*G364*
343	*G365*
344	*G366*
345	*G367*
346	*G368*
347	*G369*
348	*G370*
349	*G371*
350	*G373*
351	*G374*
352	*G376*
353	*G377*
354	*G378*
355	*G379*
"	*G384*
356	*G381*
357	*G382*
358	*G383*
359	*G385*
360	*G386*
361	*G387*
362	*G388*
363	*G389*
364	*G390*
365	*G391*
366	*G392*
367	*G393*
368	*G394*
369	*G395*
370	*G396*
371	*G397*
372	*G398*
373	*G399*
374	*G400*
375	*G402*
376	*G401*
377	*G404*
378	*G405*
379	*G406*
380	*G408*
381	*G409*
382	*G410*
383	*G411*
384	*G412*
385	*G413*
386	*G414*
387	*G415*
388	*G416*
389	*G417*
390	*G418*
391	*G419*
392	*G421*
393	*G422*
394	*G423*
395	*G424*
396	*G426*
397	*G427*
398	*G428*
399	*G429*
400	*G430*
401	*G431*
402	*G432*
403	*G433*
404	*G434*
405	*G435*
406	*G436*
407	*G437*
408	*G438*
409	*G439*
410	*G441*
411	*G442*
412	*G443*
413	*G444*
414	*G445*
415	*G446*
416	*G448*
417	*G449*
418	*G450*
419	*G451*
420	*G452*
421	*G453*
422	*G454*
423	*G455*
424	*G456*
425	*G457*
426	*G458*
427	*G459*
428	*G460*
429	*G461*
430	*G462*
431	*G463*
432	*G464*
433	*G465*
434	*G466*
435	*G467*
436	*G468*
437	*G469*
438	*G470*
439	*G471*
440	*G472*
441	*G473*
442	*G474*
443	*G475*
444	*G476*
445	*G477*
446	*G478*
447	*G479*
448	*G447*
"	*G480*
449	*G481*
450	*G403*
"	*G482*
451	*G483*
452	*G484*
453	*G485*
"	*G493*
454	*G486*
455	*G487*
"	*G1986*
456	*G488*
457	*G489*
458	*G490*
459	*G491*
460	*G492*
461	*G494*
462	*G495*
463	*G496*
464	*G497*
465	*G498*
466	*G499*
467	*G500*
468	*G501*
469	*G502*
470	*G503*
471	*G515*
472	*G504*
473	*G505*
474	*G506*
475	*G507*
476	*G508*
477	*G509*
478	*G510*
479	*G511*
480	*G512*
481	*G513*
482	*G514*
483	*G515*
484	*G516*
485	*G517*
486	*G518*
487	*G519*
488	*G520*
489	*G521*
490	*G522*
491	*G523*
492	*G524*
493	*G525*
494	*G526*
495	*G527*
496	*G528*
497	*G529*
498	*G530*
499	*G531*
500	*G532*
501	*G533*
502	*G534*
503	*G535*
504	*G536*
505	*G537*
506	*G538*
507	*G539*
508	*G333*
509	*G540*
510	*G425*
"	*G541*
511	*G542*
512	*G543*
513	*G544*
514	*G545*
515	*G546*
516	*G547*
517	*G548*
518	*G33*
"	*G550*
519	*G551*
520	*G552*
521	*G553*
522	*G554*
523	*G555*
524	*G556*
525	*G557*
526	*G558*
527	*G559*
528	*G560*
529	*G561*
530	*G562*
531	*G563*
532	*G564*
533	*G565*
534	*G567*
535	*G568*
536	*G569*
537	*G570*
538	*G572*
539	*G573*
540	*G574*
541	*G575*
542	*G927*
543	*G577*
544	*G578*
545	*G579*
546	*G580*
547	*G581*
548	*G582*
549	*G583*
550	*G584*
551	*G585*
552	*G586*
553	*G587*
554	*G588*
555	*G589*
556	*G590*
557	*G591*
558	*G592*
559	*G593*
560	*G594*
561	*G584*
"	*G595*
562	*G596*
563	*G597*
564	*G598*
565	*G599*
566	*G600*
567	*G600*
568	*G600*
569	*G601*
570	*G602*
"	*G3898*
571	*G603*
572	*G605*
573	*G604*
"	*G606*
574	*G607*
575	*G608*
576	*G609*
577	*G610*
578	*G611*
579	*G612*
580	*G613*
581	*G614*
582	*G615*
583	*G616*
584	*G617*
585	*G618*
586	*G619*
"	*G620*
587	*G621*
588	*G622*
589	*G623*
590	*G624*
591	*G625*
592	*G626*
593	*G627*
594	*G628*
595	*G629*
596	*G630*
597	*G631*
598	*G632*
599	*G633*
600	*G634*
"	*G635*
601	*G636*
602	*G637*
603	*G638*
"	*G2839*
604	*G639*
605	*G640*
606	*G641*
607	*G642*
608	*G643*
609	*G644*
610	*G645*
611	*G646*
612	*G647*
613	*G648*
614	*G649*
615	*G650*
"	*G651*
616	*G652*
617	*G375*
"	*G653*
618	*G655*
619	*G656*
620	*G657*
621	*G658*
"	*G2143*
"	*G3314*
"	*G4336*
622	*G660*
623	*G661*
624	*G662*
625	*G663*
626	*G664*
627	*G665*
628	*G666*
629	*G667*
630	*G668*
631	*G669*
632	*G671*
633	*G672*
634	*G674*
635	*G675*
636	*G676*
637	*G677*
638	*G678*
639	*G679*
640	*G680*
641	*G681*
642	*G682*
643	*G683*
"	*G2171*
644	*G684*
645	*G685*
646	*G686*
647	*G687*
648	*G689*
649	*G690*
"	*G1852*
650	*G691*
"	*G935*
651	*G692*
652	*G693*
653	*G694*
654	*G695*
655	*G696*
656	*G697*
657	*G698*
658	*G699*
659	*G700*
660	*G701*
661	*G702*

STRONG	G/K
662	G703
663	G704
664	G705
665	G706
666	G707
667	G708
668	G709
669	G710
670	G711
671	G712
672	G713
673	G714
674	G715
675	G716
676	G717
677	G718
678	G719
679	G720
680	G721
681	G721
"	G4312
682	G722
683	G723
684	G724
685	G725
686	G726
687	G727
688	G728
689	G98
"	G730
"	G763
690	G732
691	G733
692	G734
693	G735
"	G739
694	G736
695	G737
696	G738
697	G740
"	G4076
698	G741
699	G742
700	G743
701	G744
702	G745
703	G746
704	G748
705	G749
706	G750
707	G751
708	G752
709	G753
710	G754
711	G755
712	G756
713	G757
714	G758
715	G759
"	G760
716	G761
717	G762
"	G3403
718	G764
719	G765
720	G766
721	G768
722	G769
723	G770
724	G771
725	G772
726	G773
727	G774
728	G775
729	G731
730	G776
"	G781
731	G777
732	G778
"	G779
733	G780
734	G782
735	G783
736	G784
737	G785
738	G786
739	G787
740	G788
741	G789
742	G790
743	G791
744	G792
745	G793
746	G794
747	G795
748	G796
749	G797
750	G799
751	G800
752	G801
753	G802
754	G803
755	G804
756	G806
757	G806
758	G807
759	G808
760	G809
"	G811
761	G810
762	G812
763	G813
764	G814
765	G815
766	G816
767	G817
761	G818
769	G819
770	G820
771	G821
772	G822
773	G823
774	G824
775	G825
776	G826
777	G827
778	G828
779	G829
780	G830
781	G831
782	G571
"	G832
783	G833
784	G834
"	G5646
785	G835
786	G836
787	G837
788	G839
789	G840
790	G841
791	G842
792	G843
793	G844
794	G845
795	G846
796	G847
797	G848
798	G849
799	G850
800	G851
801	G852
802	G853
803	G854
804	G855
805	G856
806	G857
807	G858
"	G2360
808	G859
809	G860
810	G861
811	G862
812	G863
813	G864
814	G865
815	G866
816	G867
817	G868
818	G869
"	G870
819	G871
820	G872
821	G873
822	G874
823	G875
824	G876
825	G877
826	G878
"	G2964
827	G879
828	G880
829	G881
830	G882
831	G883
832	G884
833	G885
834	G886
835	G887
836	G888
837	G889
"	G891
"	G3824
838	G890
839	G892
840	G893
841	G894
842	G895
843	G896
844	G897
845	G898
846	G899
847	G898
848	G898
849	G901
850	G903
851	G904
852	G905
853	G906
854	G907
855	G908
856	G909
"	G4060
857	G910
858	G911
859	G912
860	G913
861	G914
862	G915
863	G918
"	G1889
864	G919
865	G920
866	G921
867	G922
868	G923
869	G924
870	G925
871	G926
872	G927
873	G928
874	G929
875	G930
876	G931
877	G932
878	G933
879	G934
880	G936
"	G305
881	G937
"	G941
882	G938
883	G939
884	G940
885	G943
886	G942
887	G944
888	G945
889	G946
890	G947
891	G948
892	G949
893	G950
894	G951
"	G952
895	G953
896	G955
897	G956
898	G957
899	G958
900	G959
901	G960
902	G961
903	G962
904	G963
905	G964
906	G965
907	G966
908	G967
909	G968
910	G969
911	G970
"	G4817
912	G972
913	G973
914	G974
915	G975
916	G976
917	G977
918	G978
919	G979
920	G971
"	G980
"	G981
921	G982
922	G983
923	G984
924	G985
925	G986
"	G2852
926	G987
927	G988
928	G989
929	G990
930	G991
931	G992
932	G993
933	G994
934	G994
935	G995
936	G996
937	G997
"	G998
938	G999
939	G1000
940	G1001
941	G1002
942	G1003
943	G1004
"	G2742
"	G2744
944	G1005
945	G1006
946	G1007
947	G1008
948	G1009
949	G1010
950	G1011
951	G1012
952	G1013
953	G1014
954	G1015
955	G1016
956	G1018
957	G1019
958	G1020
"	G1021
959	G1022
960	G1023
961	G1024
962	G1028
"	G1030
963	G1029
964	G1031
"	G1032
965	G1033
966	G1034
"	G1035
967	G1036
968	G1037
969	G1039
970	G1040
971	G1041
972	G1042
973	G1043
974	G1044
"	G1045
975	G1046
976	G1047
977	G1048
978	G1049
979	G1050
980	G1051
981	G1052
982	G1053
983	G1054
984	G1055
985	G1056
"	G1057
986	G1058
987	G1059
"	G1555
988	G1060
989	G1061
990	G1062
991	G1063
992	G1064
993	G1065
994	G1066
995	G1068
996	G1069
997	G1070
998	G1071
999	G1072
"	G1073
1000	G1074
1001	G1075
1002	G1076
1003	G1067
"	G1077
"	G1078
1004	G1079
1005	G1080
1006	G1081
1007	G1026
"	G1027
"	G1082
1008	G1083
1009	G1084
1010	G1085
1011	G1086
1012	G1087
1013	G1088
1014	G1089
1015	G1090
1016	G1091
1017	G1092
1018	G1093
1019	G1094
1020	G1095
1021	G1096
1022	G1097
1023	G1098
1024	G1099
1025	G1100
1026	G1101
1027	G1103
1028	G1104
1029	G1105
1030	G1106
1031	G1107
1032	G1108
1033	G1109
1034	G1110
1035	G1111
1036	G1112
1037	G1113
1038	G1114
1039	G1115
"	G3327
1040	G1116
1041	G1117
1042	G1119
1043	G1120
1044	G1121
1045	G1122
1046	G1123
1047	G1125
1048	G1124
1049	G1126
1050	G1127
1051	G1128
1052	G1129
1053	G1130
"	G1135
1054	G1131
1055	G1132
1056	G1133
1057	G1134
1058	G1136
1059	G1137
1060	G1138
1061	G1139
"	G1140
1062	G1141
1063	G1142
1064	G1143
1065	G1145
1066	G1146
1067	G1147
1068	G1148
"	G1149
1069	G1150
1070	G1151
1071	G1152
1072	G1153
1073	G1154
1074	G1155
1075	G1156
1076	G1157
1077	G1158
"	G1159
"	G1160
1078	G1161
1079	G1162
1080	G1164
1081	G1163
"	G1165
1082	G1166
1083	G1167
1084	G1168
1085	G1169
1086	G1170
"	G1171
1087	G1172
1088	G1173
1089	G1174
1090	G1175
1091	G1176
1092	G1177
1093	G1178
1094	G1179
1095	G1180
1096	G1181
1097	G1182
1098	G1183
1099	G1184
1100	G1185
1101	G1186
1102	G1187
1103	G1188
1104	G1189
1105	G1190
1106	G1191
1107	G1192
1108	G1194
1109	G1195
1110	G1193
"	G1196
1111	G1197
1112	G1198
1113	G1199
1114	G1200
1115	G1201
1116	G1202
1117	G1203
1118	G1204
1119	G1205
1120	G1206
1121	G1207
1122	G1208
1123	G1209
1124	G1210
1125	G1211
"	G2863
1126	G1212
1127	G1213
1128	G1214
1129	G1215
1130	G1216
"	G1217
1131	G1218
1132	G1219
1133	G1220
1134	G1221
1135	G1222
1136	G1223
1137	G1224
1138	G1226
"	G1253
1139	G1227
1140	G1228
1141	G1229
1142	G1230
1143	G1231
1144	G1232
1145	G1233
1146	G1234
1147	G1235
1148	G1236
1149	G1237
1150	G1238
1151	G1239
1152	G1240
1153	G1241
1154	G1242
1155	G1244
"	G1247
1156	G1245
"	G1249
1157	G1246
"	G1250
1158	G1248
1159	G1251
1160	G1252
1161	G1254
1162	G1255
1163	G1256
1164	G1257
1165	G1258
1166	G1259
"	G1260
1167	G1261
1168	G1262
1169	G1264
1170	G1265
1171	G1267
1172	G1268
1173	G1270
"	G1271
1174	G1273
1175	G1272
1176	G1274
1177	G1275
1178	G1278
1179	G1279
1180	G1280
1181	G1281
1182	G1281
1183	G1282
1184	G1283
1185	G1284
1186	G1285
1187	G1286
"	G1287
1188	G1288
1189	G1289
1190	G1291
"	G1523
1191	G1292
1192	G1293
1193	G1294
1194	G1296
1195	G1297
1196	G1298
1197	G1299
1198	G1300
1199	G1301
1200	G1302
1201	G1303
1202	G1304
1203	G1305
1204	G1306
1205	G1307
1206	G1308
1207	G1310
1208	G1309
"	G1311
1209	G1312
1210	G1313
1211	G1314
1212	G1316
1213	G1317
1214	G1318
1215	G1319
1216	G1320
1217	G1321
1218	G1322
1219	G1323
1220	G1324
1221	G1325
1222	G1327
1223	G1328
1224	G1329
1225	G1330
1226	G1331
1227	G1332
1228	G1333
1229	G1334
1230	G1335
1231	G1336
1232	G1337
1233	G1338
1234	G1339
1235	G1340
1236	G1341
1237	G1342
1238	G1343
1239	G1344
1240	G1345
1241	G1346
1242	G1347
1243	G1348
1244	G1349
1245	G1350
"	G1351
1246	G1352
1247	G1354
1248	G1355
"	G1566
1249	G1356
1250	G1357
1251	G1358
1252	G1359
1253	G1360
1254	G1361
1255	G1362
1256	G1363
1257	G1364
1258	G1365
1259	G1367
1260	G1368
1261	G1369
1262	G1370
1263	G1371
1264	G1372
1265	G1373
1266	G1374
1267	G1375
1268	G1376
1269	G1377
1270	G1378
1271	G1379
1272	G1380
1273	G1381
1274	G1382
1275	G1383
1276	G1385
1277	G1386
1278	G1387
1279	G1388
1280	G1389
1281	G1390
1282	G1391
1283	G1395
1284	G1392
"	G1393
"	G1396
1285	G1397
1286	G1398
1287	G1399
1288	G1400
1289	G1401
1290	G1402
1291	G1403
1292	G1404
1293	G1405
1294	G1406
1295	G1407
1296	G1408
1297	G1409
1298	G1410
1299	G1411
1300	G1412
1301	G1413
1302	G1414
1303	G1415
"	G1416
1304	G1417
1305	G1418
1306	G1419
1307	G1420
"	G1421
1308	G1422
1309	G1423
1310	G1424
"	G5775
1311	G1425
1312	G1426
1313	G1427
1314	G1428
1315	G1429
1316	G1431
1317	G1434
1318	G1435
1319	G1436
1320	G1437
1321	G1438
1322	G1439
1323	G1440
1324	G1441
1325	G1442
"	G1443
1326	G1444
1327	G1447
1328	G1449
"	G2256
1329	G1450
1330	G1451
1331	G1452
1332	G1453
1333	G1454
1334	G1455
1335	G1456
1336	G1457
1337	G1458
1338	G1459
1339	G1460
1340	G1462
1341	G1464
1342	G1465
1343	G1466
1344	G1467
1345	G1468
1346	G1469
1347	G1470
1348	G1471
1349	G1472
"	G2869
1350	G1473
1351	G1474
1352	G1475
1353	G1476
1354	G1477
1355	G1478
1356	G1479
1357	G1481
1358	G1482
1359	G1483
1360	G1484
1361	G1485
1362	G1486
"	G1487
1363	G1488
1364	G1489
1365	G1491
1366	G1492
1367	G1493
1368	G1494
1369	G1495
1370	G1496
1371	G1497
1372	G1498
1373	G1499
1374	G1500
1375	G1501
1376	G1502
1377	G1503
1378	G1504
1379	G1505
1380	G1506
1381	G1507
"	G1508
1382	G1509
1383	G1510
1384	G1511
1385	G1512
1386	G1513
1387	G1514
1388	G1515

STRONG	G/K
1389	G1516
1390	G1517
1391	G1518
1392	G1519
1393	G1520
1394	G1521
1395	G1522
1396	G1524
1397	G1525
1398	G1526
1399	G1527
1400	G1528
1401	G1528
"	G1529
1402	G1530
1403	G1531
1404	G1532
1405	G1533
1406	G1534
1407	G1535
1408	G1536
1409	G1537
1410	G1538
1411	G1539
1412	G1540
1413	G1541
1414	G1542
1415	G1543
1416	G1544
1417	G1545
1418	
1419	G1546
1420	G1547
"	G1548
1421	G1549
1422	G1551
1423	G1552
1424	G1553
1425	G1554
1426	G1556
1427	G1557
1428	G1558
1429	G1559
1430	G1560
1431	G1561
1432	G1562
1433	G1563
1434	G1564
1435	G1565
1436	G1568
1437	G1569
1438	G1571
1439	G1572
1440	G1573
1441	G1574
1442	G1575
1443	G1576
1444	G1577
1445	G1578
1446	G1579
1447	G1580
1448	G1581
1449	G1582
1450	G1583
1451	G1584
1452	G1585
1453	G1586
1454	G1587
1455	G1588
1456	G1589
1457	G1590
1458	G1592
1459	G1593
1460	G1594
1461	G1596
1462	G1598
1463	G1599
1464	G1600
"	G1715
1465	G1601
1466	G1602
1467	G1603
1468	G1604
1469	G1605
1470	G1606
1471	G1607
1472	G1608
1473	G1609
1474	G1610
1475	G1611
1476	G1612
1477	G1613
1478	G1614
1479	G1615
1480	G1616
1481	G1617
1482	G1618
1483	G1619
1484	G1620
1485	G1621
1486	G1622
"	G1665
1487	G1623
1488	G1639
1489	G1623+1145
1490	G1623+1254
	+3590+1145
1491	G1626
1492	G3857
1493	G1627
1494	G1628
"	G2638
1495	G1630
1496	G1629
1497	G1631
1498	G1639
1499	G1623+2779
1500	G1632
1501	G1633
1502	G1634
1503	G2036
1504	G1635
1505	G1636
1506	G1637
1507	G1813
1508	G1623+3590
1509	G1623
	+3590+5516
1510	G1639
1511	G1639
1512	G1642
1513	G1643
1514	G1644
1515	G1645
1516	G1646
1517	G1647
1518	G1648
1519	G1650
1520	G1651
1521	G1652
1522	G1653
1523	G1654
1524	G1655
1525	G1656
1526	G1639
1527	G1651+2848
1528	G1657
1529	G1658
1530	G1659
"	G1737
1531	G1660
1532	G1661
1533	G1662
1534	G1663
1535	G1664
1536	G1623+5516
1537	G1666
1538	G1667
1539	G1668
1540	G1669
1541	G1670
1542	G1671
1543	G1672
"	G1673
1544	G1675
1545	G1676
1546	G1678
1547	G1679
1548	G1680
1549	G1681
1550	G1682
1551	G1683
1552	G1684
1553	G1685
1554	G1686
1555	G1687
1556	G1688
1557	G1689
1558	G1690
1559	G1691
1560	G1692
1561	G1693
1562	G1694
1563	G1695
1564	G1696
1565	G1697
1566	G1698
1567	G1699
1568	G1701
1569	G1702
1570	G1704
1571	G1705
1572	G1706
1573	G1591
"	G1707
1574	G1708
1575	G1709
1576	G1710
1577	G1711
1578	G1712
1579	G1713
1580	G1714
1581	G1716
1582	G1717
1583	G1718
1584	G1719
1585	G1720
1586	G1721
1587	G1722
1588	G1723
1589	G1724
1590	G1725
"	G2287
1591	G1726
1592	G1727
1593	G1728
1594	G1729
1595	G1730
1596	G1731
1597	G1732
1598	G1733
1599	G1734
1600	G1736
1601	G1738
1602	G1739
1603	G1740
1604	G1741
1605	G1742
1606	G1743
1607	G1744
1608	G1745
1609	G1746
1610	G1748
1611	G1749
1612	G1750
1613	G1752
1614	G1753
1615	G1754
1616	G1755
1617	G1757
1618	G1756
1619	G1757
1620	G1758
1621	G1759
1622	G1760
1623	G1761
1624	G1762
1625	G1763
1626	G1765
1627	G1766
1628	G1767
1629	G1768
1630	G1769
1631	G1770
1632	G1772
"	G1773
1633	G1774
1634	G1775
1635	G1776
1636	G1777
1637	G1778
1638	G1779
1639	G1780
1640	G1781
"	G1784
1641	G1782
1642	G1783
1643	G1785
1644	G1786
1645	G1787
1646	G1788
1647	G1788
1648	G1789
1649	G1792
1650	G1791
"	G1793
1651	G1794
1652	G1795
1653	G1790
"	G1796
1654	G1797
1655	G1798
1656	G1799
1657	G1800
1658	G1801
1659	G1802
1660	G1803
1661	G1804
1662	G1805
"	G1806
1663	G1808
1664	G1809
1665	G1810
1666	G1811
"	G1812
1667	G1813
1668	G1814
1669	G1815
1670	G1816
1671	G1817
1672	G1818
1673	G1819
1674	G1820
1675	G1821
1676	G1822
1677	G1823
"	G1824
1678	G1825
"	G1826
1679	G1827
1680	G1828
1681	G1829
"	G2287
1682	G1830
1683	G1831
1684	G1832
1685	G1833
1686	G1834
"	G1835
1687	G1836
1688	G1837
1689	G1838
1690	G1102
"	G1839
1691	G1609
1692	G1840
1693	G1841
1694	G1842
1695	G1843
"	G4035
1696	G1844
1697	G1846
1698	G1609
1699	G1847
1700	G1609
1701	G1849
1702	G1850
1703	G1851
1704	G1853
1705	G1854
"	G1855
"	G1857
"	G1858
1706	G1860
1707	G1861
1708	G1862
"	G4451
1709	G1863
1710	G1864
1711	G1865
1712	G1866
1713	G1867
1714	G1856
"	G1859
"	G1868
1715	G1869
1716	G1870
1717	G1871
1718	G1872
1719	G1873
1720	G1874
1721	G1875
1722	G1877
1723	G1878
1724	G1879
1725	G1882
1726	G1883
1727	G1885
1728	G1887
1729	G1890
1730	G1891
1731	G1892
1732	G1893
1733	G1894
1734	G1895
1735	G1896
1736	G1897
1737	G1898
1738	G1899
1739	G1900
"	G1908
1740	G1901
1741	G1902
1742	G1903
1743	G1904
1744	G1905
1745	G1906
1746	G1907
1747	G1909
1748	G1910
1749	G1911
1750	G1912
1751	G1913
1752	G1641
"	G1914
"	G1915
1753	G1918
1754	G1919
1755	G1920
1756	G1886
"	G1921
1757	G1922
1758	G1923
1759	G1924
1760	G1445
"	G1926
1761	G1927
1762	G1928
1763	G1929
1764	G1931
1765	G1932
1766	G1888
1767	G1933
1768	G1916
1769	G1917
"	G1934
1770	G1935
1771	G1936
1772	G1937
1773	G1939
1774	G1940
1775	G1942
1776	G1943
1777	G1944
1778	G1945
1779	G1946
1780	G1947
1781	G1353
"	G1948
1782	G1925
"	G1949
1783	G1950
1784	G1952
1785	G1953
1786	G1954
1787	G1955
1788	G1956
1789	G1957
1790	G1764
"	G1958
1791	G1959
1792	G1960
1793	G1961
1794	G1962
1795	G1963
1796	G1964
1797	G1965
1798	G1966
1799	G1967
1800	G1968
1801	G1969
1802	G1970
1803	G1971
1804	G1972
1805	G1973
1806	G1974
1807	G1975
1808	G1976
1809	G1977
1810	G1978
"	G2005
1811	G1979
1812	G1980
1813	G1981
1814	G1982
1815	G1983
1816	G1677
"	G1984
1817	G1985
1818	G1987
1819	G1988
1820	G1989
1821	G1990
1822	G1992
1823	G1993
1824	G1994
1825	G1995
1826	G1996
1827	G1998
1828	G1999
1829	G2000
1830	G2001
1831	G2002
"	G1446
"	G1674
1832	G1997
"	G2003
1833	G2004
1834	G2007
1835	G2008
1836	G2009
1837	G2010
1838	G2011
1839	G2012
"	G2013
"	G2014
1840	G2015
1841	G2016
1842	G2017
1843	G2018
1844	G2019
1845	G2020
1846	G2021
1847	G2022
"	G2023
1848	G2024
"	G2025
1849	G2026
1850	G2027
1851	G2029
1852	G2030
1853	G2031
1854	G2032
1855	G2033
1856	G2034
1857	G2035
1858	G2037
1859	G2038
1860	G2039
1861	G2040
1862	G2041
1863	G2042
1864	G2043
1865	G2044
1866	G2045
1867	G2046
1868	G2047
1869	G2048
1870	G2049
1871	G2050
1872	G2051
1873	G2052
1874	G2053
1875	G2054
1876	G2055
1877	G2056
1878	G2057
1879	G2058
1880	G2059
1881	G2060
1882	G2061
1883	G2062
1884	G2064
1885	G2065
"	G2066
1886	G2068
1887	G2069
1888	G900
"	G2070
1889	G2071
1890	G576
"	G2072
1891	G2073
1892	G2074
1893	G2075
1894	G2076
1895	G2077
1896	G2078
"	G2393
1897	G2080
1898	G2081
1899	G2083
1900	G2084
1901	G2085
1902	G2086
1903	G2087
1904	G2082
"	G2088
1905	G2089
1906	G2090
1907	G2091
1908	G2092
1909	G2093
1910	G2094
1911	G2095
1912	G2096
1913	G2097
1914	G2098
1915	G2099
1916	G2100
1917	G2101
1918	G2102
1919	G2103
1920	G2104
1921	G2105
1922	G2106
1923	G2107
1924	G2108
1925	G2109
1926	G2110
1927	G2111
1928	G2112
1929	G2113
"	G4658
1930	G2114
1931	G2115
1932	G2116
1933	G2117
1934	G2118
1935	G2119
1936	G2120
1937	G2121
1938	G2122
1939	G2123
1940	G2125
1941	G2126
1942	G2127
1943	G2128
1944	G2063
"	G2129
1945	G2130
1946	G2134
1947	G2135
1948	G2137
1949	G2138
1950	G2140
1951	G2141
1952	G2142
1953	G2144
1954	G2145
1955	G2146
1956	G2147
1957	G2148
1958	G2149
1959	G2150
1960	G2151
1961	G2152
1962	G2153
1963	G2154
1964	G2155
1965	G2156
1966	G2079
1967	G2157
1968	G2158
1969	G2159
1970	
1971	G2160
1972	G2161
1973	G2162
1974	G2163
1975	G2164
1976	G2165
"	G2193
1977	G2166
1978	G2168
1979	G2169
1980	G2170
1981	G2172
1982	G2173
1983	G2174
1984	G2175
1985	G2176
1986	G2177
1987	G2179
1988	G2181
1989	G2182
1990	G2184
1991	G2185
1992	G2186
1993	G2187
1994	G2188
1995	G2189
1996	G2190
1997	G2191
1998	G2192
1999	G2180
"	G2194
2000	G2195
2001	G2196
2002	G2197
2003	G2198
2004	G2199
2005	G2200
2006	G2201
2007	G2202
2008	G2203
2009	G2204
2010	G2205
"	G5181
2011	G2207
2012	G2208
2013	G2209
2014	G2210
2015	G2211
2016	G2212
2017	G2213
"	G2223
2018	G2214
2019	G2215
"	G2971
2020	G2216
2021	G2217
2022	G2219
2023	G2220
2024	G2221
2025	G2222
2026	G2224
2027	G2131
"	G2225
2028	G2226
2029	G2227
2030	G2228
2031	G2229
2032	G2230
2033	G2231
2034	G2232
2035	G2233
2036	G3306
2037	G2235
2038	G2237
2039	G2238
2040	G2239
2041	G2240
2042	G2241
2043	G2242
2044	G2243
2045	G2236
2046	G3306
2047	G2244
2048	G2245
2049	G2246
2050	G2247
2051	G2248
2052	G2249
2053	G2250
2054	G2251
2055	G2252
2056	G144
"	G2253
2057	G2254
2058	G1448
"	G2255
2059	G2257
2060	G2258
2061	G2259
2062	G2260
2063	G2261
2064	G2262
2065	G2263
2066	G2264
2067	G2265
2068	G2266
"	G2267
2069	G2268
2070	G1639
2071	G1639
2072	G2269
2073	G2270
2074	G2272
2075	G1639
2076	G1639
2077	G1639
2078	G2274
2079	G2275
2080	G2276
2081	G2277
2082	G2278
2083	G2279
2084	G2280
2085	G2281
2086	G2282
2087	G255
"	G2283
2088	G2284
2089	G2285
2090	G2286
2091	G2288
2092	G2289
2093	G2290
2094	G2291
2095	G2292
"	G2301
2096	G2293
2097	G2294
2098	G2295
2099	G2296
2100	G2297
2101	G2298
2102	G2299
2103	G2300
2104	G2302
2105	G2304
2106	G2305
2107	G2306
2108	G2307
2109	G2308
2110	G2309
2111	G2310
2112	G2311
2113	G2312
2114	G2313
2115	G2314
"	G2315
2116	G2316
2117	G2317
"	G2318
2118	G2319
2119	G2320
2120	G2321
2121	G2322
2122	G2323

STRONG	G/K
2123	*G2324*
2124	*G2325*
2125	*G2326*
2126	*G2327*
2127	*G2328*
"	*G2986*
2128	*G2329*
2129	*G2303*
"	*G2330*
2130	*G2331*
2131	*G2332*
2132	*G2333*
2133	*G2334*
2134	*G2335*
2135	*G2336*
2136	*G2337*
2137	*G2338*
2138	*G2340*
2139	*G2341*
"	*G2342*
2140	*G2343*
2141	*G2344*
2142	*G2345*
2143	*G2346*
2144	*G2347*
2145	*G2339*
"	*G2348*
2146	*G2349*
2147	*G2351*
2148	*G2350*
"	*G2352*
2149	*G2353*
2150	*G2354*
2151	*G2355*
2152	*G2356*
2153	*G2357*
2154	*G2358*
2155	*G2359*
2156	*G2361*
2157	*G2362*
2158	*G2363*
2159	*G2364*
2160	*G2365*
2161	*G2366*
2162	*G2367*
2163	*G2368*
2164	*G2369*
2165	*G2370*
2166	*G2371*
2167	*G2372*
2168	*G2373*
2169	*G2374*
2170	*G2375*
2171	*G2376*
2172	*G2377*
2173	*G2378*
2174	*G2379*
2175	*G2380*
2176	*G2381*
2177	*G1880*
"	*G2383*
2178	*G2384*
2179	*G2385*
2180	*G2386*
2181	*G2387*
2182	*G2388*
2183	*G2389*
2184	*G2390*
2185	*G2391*
2186	*G2392*
2187	*G2394*
2188	*G2395*
2189	*G2397*
2190	*G2398*
2191	*G2399*
2192	*G2400*
2193	*G2401*
2194	*G2404*
2195	*G2405*
2196	*G2406*
2197	*G2408*
2198	*G2409*
2199	*G2411*
2200	*G2412*
2201	*G2414*
2202	*G2415*
2203	*G2416*
2204	*G2417*
2205	*G2419*
2206	*G2418*
"	*G2420*
2207	*G2421*
2208	*G2421*
2209	*G2422*
2210	*G2423*
2211	*G2424*
2212	*G2426*
2213	*G2427*
2214	*G1700*
"	*G2428*

STRONG	G/K
2215	*G2429*
2216	*G2431*
2217	*G2432*
2218	*G2433*
2219	*G2434*
2220	*G2435*
2221	*G2436*
2222	*G2437*
2223	*G2438*
2224	*G2439*
"	*G2440*
2225	*G2441*
2226	*G2442*
2227	*G2443*
2228	*G2445*
2229	*G2446*
2230	*G2448*
2231	*G2449*
2232	*G2450*
2233	*G2206*
"	*G2451*
2234	*G2452*
2235	*G2453*
2236	*G2452*
2237	*G2454*
2238	*G2455*
2239	*G2456*
2240	*G2457*
2241	*G2458*
2242	*G2459*
2243	*G2460*
2244	*G2461*
2245	*G2462*
2246	*G2463*
2247	*G2464*
2248	*G1609*
2249	*G1609*
2250	*G2465*
2251	*G2466*
2252	*G1639*
2253	*G2467*
2254	*G1609*
2255	*G2468*
2256	*G2469*
"	*G2470*
2257	*G1609*
2258	*G1639*
2259	*G2471*
2260	*G2472*
2261	*G2473*
2262	*G2474*
2263	*G2475*
2264	*G2476*
2265	*G2477*
2266	*G2478*
2267	*G2479*
2268	*G2480*
2269	*G2481*
2270	*G2483*
2271	*G2484*
2272	*G2485*
2273	*G2486*
2274	*G2273*
"	*G2487*
2275	*G2488*
2276	*G2482*
"	*G2489*
2277	*G1639*
2278	*G2490*
2279	*G2491*
"	*G2492*
"	*G2493*
2280	*G2497*
2281	*G2498*
2282	*G2499*
2283	*G2500*
2284	*G2501*
2285	*G2502*
2286	*G2503*
2287	*G2504*
2288	*G2505*
2289	*G2506*
2290	*G2507*
2291	*G2508*
2292	*G2509*
2293	*G2510*
2294	*G2511*
2295	*G2512*
2296	*G1703*
"	*G2513*
2297	*G2514*
2298	*G2515*
2299	*G2516*
2300	*G2517*
2301	*G2518*
2302	*G2519*
2303	*G2520*
2304	*G2521*
2305	*G2522*
2306	*G2523*

STRONG	G/K
2307	*G2525*
2308	*G2526*
2309	*G2527*
2310	*G2528*
"	*G2529*
2311	*G2530*
2312	*G2531*
2312'	*G2532*
2313	*G2533*
2314	*G2534*
2315	*G2535*
2316	*G2536*
2317	*G2537*
2318	*G2538*
2319	*G2539*
2320	*G2540*
2321	*G2541*
2322	*G2542*
"	*G3859*
2323	*G2543*
2324	*G2544*
2325	*G2545*
2326	*G2546*
2327	*G2547*
2328	*G2548*
2329	*G2549*
2330	*G2550*
2331	*G2552*
2332	*G2553*
2333	*G2554*
2334	*G2555*
2335	*G2556*
2336	*G2557*
2337	*G2558*
2338	*G2559*
2339	*G2560*
2340	*G2561*
2341	*G2562*
2342	*G2563*
2343	*G2564*
2344	*G2565*
2345	*G2566*
2346	*G2567*
2347	*G2568*
2348	*G2569*
2349	*G2570*
2350	*G2572*
2351	*G2573*
2352	*G2574*
"	*G2575*
2353	*G2576*
2354	*G2577*
2355	*G2578*
2356	*G2579*
2357	*G2580*
2358	*G2581*
2359	*G1295*
"	*G2582*
2360	*G2583*
2361	*G2584*
2362	*G2585*
2363	*G2587*
2364	*G2588*
2365	*G2589*
2366	*G2590*
2367	*G2591*
2368	*G2592*
2369	*G2593*
2370	*G2594*
2371	*G2595*
2372	*G2596*
2373	*G2597*
2374	*G2598*
2375	*G2599*
2376	*G2600*
2377	*G2601*
2378	*G2602*
2379	*G2603*
2380	*G2124*
"	*G2604*
2381	*G2605*
2382	*G2606*
2383	*G2608*
2384	*G2609*
2385	*G2610*
2386	*G2611*
2387	*G2612*
2388	*G2613*
2389	*G2614*
2390	*G2615*
2391	*G2616*
2392	*G2617*
2393	*G2618*
2394	*G2619*
2395	*G2620*
2396	*G2623*
2397	*G1624*
"	*G2624*
2398	*G2625*
2399	*G2626*

STRONG	G/K
2400	*G2627*
2401	*G2628*
2402	*G2629*
2403	*G2630*
2404	*G2631*
2405	*G2632*
2406	*G2633*
2407	*G2634*
2408	*G2635*
2409	*G2636*
2410	*G2637*
2411	*G2639*
2412	*G2640*
2413	*G2641*
2414	*G2642*
2415	*G2643*
2416	*G2644*
2417	*G2645*
2418	*G2646*
2419	*G2647*
2420	*G2648*
2421	*G2649*
2422	*G2650*
2423	*G2651*
2424	*G2652*
2425	*G2653*
2426	*G2654*
2427	*G2655*
2428	*G2656*
2429	*G2657*
2430	*G2658*
2431	*G2659*
2432	*G2660*
2433	*G2661*
2434	*G2662*
2435	*G2663*
2436	*G2664*
2437	*G2665*
2438	*G2666*
2439	*G2667*
2440	*G2668*
2441	*G2669*
2442	*G2670*
"	*G3916*
2443	*G2671*
2444	*G2672*
2445	*G2673*
2446	*G2674*
2447	*G2675*
2448	*G2676*
2449	*G2677*
2450	*G2678*
2451	*G2679*
2452	*G2680*
2453	*G2681*
2454	*G2682*
2455	*G2683*
"	*G2726*
2456	*G549*
"	*G2684*
"	*G2686*
2457	*G2685*
2458	*G2687*
2459	*G2688*
"	*G5517*
2460	*G2689*
2461	*G2690*
2462	*G2691*
2463	*G2692*
2464	*G2693*
2465	*G2694*
2466	*G2695*
"	*G2704*
2467	
2468	*G1639*
2469	*G2696*
"	*G2697*
"	*G5000*
"	*G5001*
2470	*G2698*
2471	*G2699*
2472	*G2700*
2473	*G2701*
2474	*G2702*
2475	*G2703*
2476	*G2705*
2477	*G2707*
2478	*G2708*
2479	*G2709*
2480	*G2710*
2481	*G2711*
2482	*G2712*
2483	*G2713*
2484	*G2714*
2485	*G2715*
2486	*G2716*
2487	*G2717*
2488	*G2718*
2489	*G2720*
"	*G2721*

STRONG	G/K
2490	*G2722*
2491	*G2722*
"	*G2728*
2492	*G2724*
2493	*G2727*
2494	*G2729*
"	*G2730*
2495	*G2731*
2496	*G2732*
2497	*G2733*
2498	*G2734*
2499	*G2735*
2500	*G2736*
2501	*G2737*
"	*G2738*
2502	*G2739*
2503	*G2740*
2504	*G2743*
2505	*G2745*
2506	*G2746*
2507	*G2747*
2508	*G2748*
2509	*G2749*
"	*G2778*
2510	*G2750*
2511	*G2751*
"	*G2760*
2512	*G2752*
2513	*G2754*
2514	*G2755*
2515	*G2756*
2516	*G2757*
2517	*G2759*
2518	*G2761*
2519	*G2762*
2520	*G2763*
2521	*G2764*
2522	*G2766*
2523	*G2767*
2524	*G2768*
2525	*G2769*
"	*G2770*
2526	*G2771*
2526'	*G2772*
2527	*G2773*
2528	*G2774*
2529	*G2775*
2530	*G2776*
2531	*G2777*
2532	*G2779*
2533	*G2780*
2534	*G2781*
2535	*G2782*
2536	*G2783*
"	*G2784*
2537	*G2785*
2538	*G2786*
2539	*G2788*
2540	*G2789*
2541	*G2790*
2542	*G2791*
2543	*G2792*
2544	*G2793*
2545	*G2794*
2546	*G2795*
2547	*G2796*
2548	*G2797*
2549	*G2798*
2550	*G2799*
2551	*G2800*
2552	*G2801*
"	*G2817*
2553	*G2802*
2554	*G2803*
2555	*G2804*
2556	*G2805*
2557	*G2806*
2558	*G2807*
2559	*G2808*
2560	*G2809*
2561	*G2810*
2562	*G2811*
2563	*G2812*
2564	*G2813*
2565	*G2814*
2566	*G2819*
2567	*G2815*
2568	*G2816*
2569	*G2818*
2570	*G2819*
2571	*G2820*
2572	*G2821*
2573	*G2822*
2574	*G2823*
"	*G2824*
2575	*G2825*
2576	*G2826*
2577	*G2827*
2578	*G2828*
2579	*G2829*

STRONG	G/K
2580	*G2830*
2581	*G2831*
"	*G2832*
2582	*G2833*
2583	*G2834*
2584	*G2835*
"	*G3019*
2585	*G2836*
2586	*G2837*
2587	*G2838*
2588	*G2840*
2589	*G2841*
2590	*G2843*
2591	*G2842*
2592	*G2844*
2593	*G2845*
2594	*G2846*
2595	*G2847*
2596	*G2848*
2597	*G2849*
2598	*G2850*
2599	*G2851*
2600	*G2853*
2601	*G2854*
2602	*G2856*
2603	*G2857*
2604	*G2858*
2605	*G2859*
2606	*G2860*
2607	*G2861*
2608	*G2862*
2609	*G2864*
2610	*G2865*
2611	*G2866*
2612	*G2867*
2613	*G1463*
"	*G2868*
2614	*G2870*
2615	*G2871*
2616	*G2872*
2617	*G2875*
2618	*G2876*
2619	*G2877*
2620	*G1595*
"	*G2878*
2621	*G2879*
2622	*G2880*
2623	*G1597*
"	*G2881*
2624	*G2882*
"	*G2883*
2625	*G2884*
2626	*G2885*
2627	*G2886*
2628	*G2887*
2629	*G2888*
2630	*G2889*
2631	*G2890*
2632	*G2891*
2633	*G2892*
2634	*G2894*
2635	*G2895*
2636	*G2896*
2637	*G2897*
2638	*G2898*
2639	*G2899*
2640	*G2900*
"	*G5698*
2641	*G2901*
2642	*G2902*
2643	*G2903*
2644	*G2904*
2645	*G2905*
2646	*G2906*
2647	*G2907*
2648	*G2908*
2649	*G2909*
2650	*G2910*
2651	*G2911*
2652	*G2873*
"	*G2912*
2653	*G2874*
"	*G2913*
2654	*G2914*
2655	*G2915*
2656	*G2916*
2657	*G2917*
2658	*G2918*
2659	*G2919*
2660	*G2920*
2661	*G2921*
2662	*G2922*
2663	*G2923*
2664	*G2924*
2665	*G2925*
2666	*G2927*
2667	*G2928*
2668	*G2929*
2669	*G2930*
2670	*G2931*

STRONG	G/K
2671	*G2932*
2672	*G2933*
2673	*G2934*
2674	*G2935*
2675	*G2936*
2676	*G2937*
2677	*G2938*
2678	*G2939*
2679	*G2940*
2680	*G2941*
2681	*G2942*
2682	*G2943*
2683	*G2944*
2684	*G2945*
2685	*G2946*
2686	*G2947*
2687	*G2948*
2688	*G2949*
2689	*G2950*
2690	*G2951*
2691	*G2952*
2692	*G2953*
2693	*G2954*
2694	*G2955*
2695	*G2956*
"	*G2957*
2696	*G2958*
2697	*G2959*
2698	*G2960*
2699	*G2961*
2700	*G2962*
2701	*G2963*
2702	*G2965*
2703	*G2966*
2704	*G2967*
2705	*G2968*
2706	*G2969*
2707	*G2970*
2708	*G2972*
2709	*G2973*
2710	*G2974*
"	*G4201*
2711	*G2976*
2712	*G2977*
2713	*G2978*
2714	*G2979*
2715	*G2980*
2716	*G2981*
[2717	*Omitted by Strong]*
2718	*G2982*
2719	*G2983*
"	*G2984*
2720	*G2985*
2721	*G2987*
2722	*G2988*
2723	*G2989*
2724	*G2990*
2725	*G2991*
"	*G2992*
2726	*G2993*
2727	*G2994*
2728	*G2995*
2729	*G2996*
2730	*G2997*
"	*G3001*
2731	*G2998*
2732	*G2999*
2733	*G3000*
2734	*G3002*
2735	*G1480*
"	*G3003*
2736	*G3004*
"	*G3006*
2737	*G3005*
2738	*G3008*
2739	*G3009*
"	*G3010*
2740	*G3011*
2741	*G3012*
2742	*G3014*
2743	*G3013*
"	*G3015*
2744	*G3016*
2745	*G3017*
2746	*G3018*
2747	*G3020*
2748	*G3021*
"	*G3022*
2749	*G3023*
2750	*G3024*
2751	*G3025*
2752	*G3026*
2753	*G3027*
2754	*G3029*
2755	*G3030*
2756	*G3031*
2757	*G2787*
"	*G3032*
2758	*G3033*

STRONG	G/K
2759	*G3034*
2760	*G3035*
2761	*G3036*
2762	*G3037*
2763	*G3038*
2764	*G3039*
2765	*G3040*
2766	*G3041*
2767	*G3042*
2768	*G3043*
2769	*G3044*
2770	*G2132*
"	*G3045*
2771	*G3046*
2772	*G3047*
2773	*G3048*
2774	*G3049*
2775	*G3050*
"	*G3052*
2776	*G3051*
2777	*G3053*
2778	*G2133*
"	*G3056*
2779	*G3057*
2780	*G3058*
2781	*G3059*
2782	*G3060*
2783	*G3061*
2784	*G3062*
2785	*G3063*
2786	*G3064*
2787	*G3066*
2788	*G3067*
2789	*G3068*
2790	*G3069*
2791	*G3070*
"	*G3071*
2792	*G3072*
"	*G3077*
2793	*G3073*
2794	*G3074*
2795	*G3075*
2796	*G3076*
2797	*G3078*
2798	*G3080*
2799	*G3081*
2800	*G3082*
2801	*G3083*
2802	*G1144*
"	*G3007*
"	*G3084*
"	*G3085*
2803	*G3086*
2804	*G3087*
2805	*G3088*
2806	*G3089*
2807	*G3090*
2808	*G3091*
2809	*G3092*
2810	*G3093*
2811	*G3094*
2812	*G3095*
2813	*G3096*
2814	*G3097*
2815	*G3098*
2816	*G3099*
2817	*G3100*
2818	*G3101*
2819	*G3102*
2820	*G3103*
2821	*G3104*
2822	*G3105*
2823	*G3106*
2824	*G3107*
2825	*G3108*
"	*G3109*
2826	*G3110*
2827	*G3111*
2828	*G3112*
2829	*G3113*
2830	*G3114*
2831	*G3115*
2832	*G3116*
2833	*G3117*
2834	*G3118*
2835	*G3119*
2836	*G3120*
2837	*G3121*
2838	*G3122*
2839	*G3123*
2840	*G3124*
2841	*G3125*
2842	*G3126*
2843	*G3127*
2844	*G3128*
2845	*G3130*
2846	*G3131*
2847	*G3132*
2848	*G3133*
2849	*G3134*

STRONG	G/K
2850	G3135
2851	G3136
2852	G3139
2853	G3140
2854	G3141
2855	G3142
2856	G3143
2857	G3138
"	G3145
2858	G3137
"	G3144
2859	G3146
2860	G3147
2861	G3148
2862	G3149
2863	G3150
2864	G3151
2865	G3152
2866	G3153
2867	G3154
2868	G3155
2869	G3156
2870	G3157
2871	G3158
2872	G3159
2873	G3160
2874	G3161
"	G3162
"	G3163
2875	G3164
2876	G3165
2877	G3166
2878	G3167
"	G3168
2879	G3169
2880	G3170
2881	G3171
2882	G3172
2883	G3173
2884	G3174
2885	G3175
2886	G3176
2887	G3177
"	G3178
2888	G3179
2889	G3180
2890	G3181
2891	G3182
"	G3183
2892	G3184
2893	G3185
2894	G3186
2895	G3187
"	G3188
2896	G3189
2897	G3190
2898	G3191
2899	G3192
2900	G3193
2901	G3194
2902	G3195
2903	G3196
2904	G3197
2905	G3198
2906	G3199
2907	G3200
2908	G3201
2909	G3202
2910	G3203
2911	G3204
2912	G3205
2913	G3206
2914	G3207
2915	G3208
2916	G3209
2917	G3210
2918	G3211
2919	G3212
2920	G3213
2921	G3214
2922	G3215
2923	G3216
2924	G3217
2925	G3218
2926	G3219
2927	G3220
"	G3224
"	G3226
2928	G3221
2929	G3222
2930	G3223
2931	G3225
2932	G3227
2933	G3228
2934	G3229
2935	G3230
2936	G3231
2937	G3232
2938	G3233
2939	G3234
2940	G3235
2941	G3236
2942	G3237
2943	G3239
2944	G3238
"	G3240
2945	G3241
2946	G3242
"	G3243
2947	G3244
2948	G3245
2949	G3246
2950	G3247
2951	G3248
2952	G3249
2953	G3250
2954	G3251
2955	G3252
2956	G3253
"	G3254
2957	G3255
2958	G3256
"	G3260
2959	G3257
2960	G3258
2961	G3259
2962	G3261
2963	G3262
2964	G3263
2965	G3264
2966	G3265
2967	G3266
2968	G3267
2969	G3268
2970	G3269
2971	G3270
2972	G3271
2973	G3272
2974	G3273
2975	G3275
2976	G3276
2977	G3277
"	G4996
2978	G3278
2979	G3280
2980	G654
"	G3281
2981	G3282
2982	G3283
"	G3316
2983	G3284
2984	G3285
2985	G3286
"	G5697
2986	G3287
2987	G3288
2988	G3289
2989	G2139
"	G3290
2990	G3291
2991	G3292
2992	G3295
2993	G3293
2994	G3294
2995	G3296
2996	G3297
"	G3298
2997	G3279
"	G3299
2998	G3300
2999	G3301
3000	G3302
3001	G3303
3002	G3304
3003	G3305
3004	G1649
"	G3306
3005	G3307
3006	G3308
3007	G3309
3008	G3310
3009	G3311
3010	G3312
3011	G3313
3012	G3317
3013	G3318
3014	G3319
3015	G3320
3016	G3321
3017	G3322
3018	G3323
3019	G3324
3020	G3325
3021	G3326
3022	G3328
3023	G3329
3024	G3330
3025	G3332
3026	G3333
3027	G798
"	G3334
3028	G3331
"	G3335
3029	G3336
3030	G3337
3031	G3338
3032	G3339
"	G3341
3033	G3340
3034	G3342
3035	G3343
3036	G3344
3037	G3345
3038	G3346
3039	G3347
3040	G3348
3041	G3349
3042	G3350
3043	G3351
3044	G3352
3045	G3353
3046	G3354
3047	G3355
3048	G3356
3049	G3357
3050	G3358
3051	G3359
3052	G3360
3053	G3361
3054	G3362
3055	G3363
3056	G3364
3057	G3365
3058	G3366
3059	G3367
3060	G3368
3061	G3369
3062	G3370
3063	G3370
3064	G3370
3065	G3371
3066	G3372
3067	G3373
3068	G3374
3069	G3375
3070	G3376
3071	G3377
3072	G3378
3073	G3379
3074	G3380
3075	G3381
3076	G3382
3077	G3383
3078	G3384
3079	G3385
3080	G3386
3081	G3387
3082	G3388
3083	G3389
3084	G3390
3085	G3391
3086	G3392
3087	G3393
3088	G3394
3089	G3395
3090	G3396
3091	G3397
3092	G3399
3093	G3400
"	G3401
3094	G3402
3095	G3404
"	G3406
3096	G3405
3097	G3407
3098	G3408
3099	G3409
3100	G3411
3101	G3412
3102	G3413
3103	G3417
3104	G3418
"	G3526
3105	G3419
3106	G3420
3107	G3421
3108	G3422
3109	G3423
3110	G3424
3111	G3425
3112	G3426
3113	G3427
3114	G3428
3115	G3429
3116	G3430
3117	G3431
3118	G3432
3119	G3433
3120	G3434
3121	G3435
3122	G3436
3123	G3437
3124	G3438
3125	G3439
3126	G3440
3127	G3441
3128	G3ber
3129	G3443
3130	G3444
3131	G3445
3132	G3446
3133	G3447
3134	G2495
"	G3448
3135	G3449
3136	G3450
3137	G3451
"	G3452
3138	G3453
3139	G3454
3140	G3455
3141	G3456
3142	G3457
3143	G3458
3144	G3459
"	G4753
3145	G3460
"	G3462
3146	G3463
3147	G3464
3148	G3465
3149	G3461
"	G3461
"	G3466
3150	G3467
3151	G3468
3152	G3469
3153	G3470
3154	G3471
3155	G3472
3156	G3414
"	G3473
3157	G3474
3158	G3415
"	G3475
3159	G3416
"	G3476
3160	G3477
3161	G3478
3162	G3479
3163	G3480
3164	G3481
3165	G1609
3166	G902
"	G3482
3167	G3483
3168	G3484
3169	G3485
3170	G3486
3171	G3487
3172	G3488
3173	G3489
3174	G3490
3175	G3491
3176	G3492
3177	G3493
3178	G3494
3179	G3495
"	G3496
3180	G3497
3181	G3498
3182	G3499
3183	G3500
3184	G3501
3185	G3505
3186	G3504
3187	G3505
3188	G3506
3189	G3506
3190	G3507
3191	G3509
3192	G3510
3193	G3511
"	G3512
"	G3513
3194	G3514
"	G3515
3195	G3516
3196	G3517
3197	G3518
3198	G3519
3199	G3508
"	G3520
3200	G3521
3201	G3522
3202	G3523
[3202 to 3304 Omitted by Strong]	
3303	G3525
3304	G3528
"	G3529
3305	G3530
3306	G3531
3307	G3532
3308	G3533
3309	G3534
3310	G3535
3311	G3536
3312	G3537
3313	G3538
3314	G3540
3315	G3541
3316	G3542
3317	G3543
3318	G3544
3319	G3545
3320	G3546
3321	G3547
3322	G3539
"	G3548
3323	G3549
3324	G3550
3325	G3551
3326	G3552
3327	G3553
3328	G3554
3329	G3555
3330	G3556
3331	G3557
3332	G3558
3333	G3559
3334	G3560
3335	G3561
3336	G3562
3337	G3563
3338	G3564
3339	G3565
3340	G3566
3341	G3567
3342	G3568
3343	G3569
3344	G3570
"	G3573
3345	G3571
3346	G3572
3347	G3575
3348	G3576
3349	G3577
3350	G3578
3351	G3579
3352	G3580
3353	G3581
3354	G3582
3355	G3583
3356	G3584
3357	G3585
3358	G3586
3359	G3587
3360	G3588
"	G3589
3361	G3590
3362	G1569+3590
3363	G2671+3590
3364	G4024+3590
3365	G3592
"	G3598
3366	G3593
3367	G3594
"	G3599
3368	G3595
3369	G3596
3370	G3597
3371	G3600
3372	G3601
3373	G3602
3374	G3603
3375	G3604
3376	G3605
3377	G3606
3378	G3590+4024
3379	G3607
3380	G3609
3381	G3610
3382	G3611
3383	G3612
3384	G3613
3385	G3614
3386	G3615
3387	G3614
3388	G3616
3389	G3617
"	G3618
3390	G3619
3391	G1651
3392	G3620
3393	G3621
3394	G3622
3395	G1807
"	G3623
"	G5041
"	G5042
3396	G3502
"	G3503
"	G3624
3397	G3625
3398	G3625
3399	G3626
3400	G3627
3401	G3628
3402	G3629
3403	G3630
3404	G3631
3405	G3632
3406	G3633
3407	G3634
3408	G3635
3409	G3636
3410	G3637
3411	G3638
3412	G3639
3413	G3640
3414	G3641
3415	G3642
3416	G3643
3417	G3644
3418	G3645
3419	G3646
3420	G3647
3421	G3648
3422	G3649
3423	G3650
3424	G3651
"	G3652
3425	G3653
3426	G3654
3427	G1609
3428	G3655
3429	G3656
3430	G3657
3431	G3658
3432	G3659
3433	G3660
3434	G3661
3435	G3662
3436	G3663
3437	G3524
"	G3664
3438	G3665
3439	G3666
3440	G3667
3441	G3668
3442	G3669
3443	G3670
3444	G3671
3445	G3672
3446	G3673
3447	G3674
3448	G3675
3449	G3677
3450	G1609
3451	G3676
3452	G3678
3453	G3679
3454	G3680
3455	G3681
3456	G3682
3457	G3683
3458	G3684
"	G3685
3459	G3686
3460	G3688
"	G3694
3461	G3689
3462	G3690
3463	G3691
"	G3692
3464	G3693
3465	G3695
3466	G3696
3467	G3697
3468	G3698
3469	G3699
3470	G3700
3471	G3701
3472	G3702
3473	G3703
3474	G3704
3475	G3705
"	G3706
"	G3707
3476	G3709
3477	G3710
3478	G3711
"	G3712
"	G3713
"	G3714
"	G3715
3479	G3716
3480	G3717
3481	G3718
"	G3719
3482	G3720
3483	G3721
3484	G3723
3485	G3724
3486	G3725
3487	G3726
3488	G3727
3489	G3728
3490	G3729
3491	G3730
3492	G3731
3493	G3732
3494	G3733
3495	G3734
3496	G3735
"	G3736
3497	G3722
"	G3737
3498	G3738
3499	G3739
3500	G3740
3501	G3742
3502	G3743
"	G3801
3503	G3744
3504	G3745
3505	G3746
3506	G3748
3507	G3749
3508	G3750
3509	G3751
3510	G3752
3511	G3753
3512	G3754
3513	G3755
3514	G3756
3515	G3757
3516	G3758
3517	G3759
3518	G3760
3519	G3761
3520	G3762
3521	G3763
3522	G3764
3523	G3765
3524	G3766
"	G3767
3525	G3768
3526	G3769
3527	G3770
3528	G3771
3529	G3772
3530	G3773
3531	G3774
3532	G3775
3533	G3776
3534	G3777
3535	G3778
"	G3779
3536	G3780
3537	G3781
"	G4469
3538	G3782
3539	G3783
3540	G3784
3541	G3785
3542	G3786
3543	G3787
3544	G3788
3545	G3789
3546	G3790
3547	G3791
3548	G3792
3549	G3793
3550	G3794
3551	G3795
3552	G3796
3553	G3797
3554	G3798
3555	G3799
3556	G3800
3557	G3802
3558	G3803
3559	G3804
3560	G3805
3561	G3741
"	G3806
3562	G3807
3563	G3808
3564	G3809
"	G3810
3565	G3811
3566	G3812
3567	G3813
3568	G3814
3569	G5422
3570	G3815
3571	G3816
3572	G3817
3573	G3818
3574	G3819
3575	G3820
3576	G3821
3577	G3822
3578	G3825
3579	G3826
3580	G3827
3581	G3828
3582	G3829
3583	G3830
3584	G3831
3585	G3832
3586	G3833
3587	G3834
3588	G3836
3589	G3837
3590	G3838
3591	G3839
3592	G3840
3593	G3841
3594	G3842
3595	G3843
3596	G3844
3597	G3845
3598	G3847
3599	G3848
3600	G3849
3601	G3850
3602	G3851
3603	G4005+1639
3604	G3852
3605	G3853
3606	G3854
3607	G3855
3608	G3856
3609	G3858
3610	G3860
3611	G3861
3612	G3862
3613	G3863
3614	G3864
3615	G3865
3616	G3866
3617	G3867
3618	G3868
"	G3871
3619	G3869
3620	G3870
3621	G3872
3622	G3873
3623	G3874
3624	G3875
3625	G3876
3626	G3877
"	G3878
3627	G3879
"	G3882
3628	G3880
3629	G3881
3630	G3884
3631	G3885
3632	G3886
3633	G3883
"	G3887
3634	G3888
3635	G3890
3636	G3891
3637	G3892
3638	G3893
3639	G3896
"	G3897
3640	G3899
3641	G3900
3642	G3901
3643	G3902
3644	G3894
"	G3904
3645	G3895
"	G3905
3646	G3906
3647	G3907
3648	G3908
3649	G3909
3650	G3910
3651	G3911
3652	G3912
3653	G3913
3654	G3914
3655	G3915
3656	G3917
3657	G3918
3658	G3919
3659	G3921
3660	G3922
"	G3923
3661	G3924
3662	G3925
3663	G3926
3664	G3927

STRONG	G/K
3665	G3928
3666	G3929
3667	G3930
3668	G3931
3669	G3932
3670	G3933
3671	G3934
3672	G3935
3673	G3937
3674	G3938
3675	G3939
3676	G3940
3677	G3941
3678	G3942
3679	G3943
3680	G3944
3681	G3945
3682	G3946
3683	G3947
3684	G3948
3685	G3949
3686	G3950
3687	G3951
3688	G3952
3689	G3903
"	G3953
3690	G3954
3691	G3955
3692	G3956
3693	G3957
3694	G3958
"	G5541
3695	G3959
3696	G3960
3697	G3961
3698	G3962
3699	G3963
3700	G3964
3701	G3965
3702	G3966
3703	G3967
3704	G3968
3705	G3969
3706	G3970
3707	G3971
3708	G1625
"	G3972
3709	G3973
3710	G3974
3711	G3975
3712	G3976
3713	G3977
3714	G3978
3715	G3979
3716	G3980
3717	G3981
3718	G3982
3719	G3983
3720	G3984
3721	G3985
3722	G3986
3723	G3987
3724	G3988
3725	G3990
3726	G1941
"	G3991
3727	G3992
3728	G3993
3729	G3994
3730	G3995
3731	G3996
3732	G3997
3733	G3989
"	G3998
3734	G3999
3735	G4001
3736	G4002
3737	G4003
3738	G4004
3739	G4005
3740	G4006
3741	G4008
3742	G4009
3743	G4010
3744	G4011
3745	G4012
3746	G4013
3747	G4014
"	G4016
3748	G4015
3749	G4017
3750	G4018
3751	G4019
3752	G4020
3753	G4021
3754	G4022
3755	G4015
3756	G4024
3757	G4023
3758	G4025
3759	G4026
3760	G4027
3761	G4028
3762	G4029
"	G4032
3763	G4030
3764	G4031
3765	G4033
3766	G4034
3767	G4036
3768	G4037
3769	G4038
3770	G4039
3771	G4040
3772	G4041
3773	G4042
3774	G4043
3775	G4044
3776	G4045
3777	G4046
3778	G4047
3779	G4048
3780	G4049
3781	G4050
3782	G4051
3783	G4052
3784	G4053
3785	G4054
3786	G4055
3787	G4056
3788	G4057
3789	G4058
3790	G4059
3791	G4061
3792	G4062
3793	G4063
3794	G4065
3795	G4066
3796	G4067
3797	G4069
3798	G4068
"	G4070
3799	G4071
3800	G4072
3801	G3836+1639 +2779+2262
3802	G4074
3803	G4075
3804	G4077
3805	G4078
3806	G4079
3807	G4080
3808	G4081
3809	G4082
3810	G4083
3811	G4084
3812	G4085
"	G4088
3813	G4086
3814	G4087
3815	G4089
3816	G4090
3817	G4091
3818	G4092
3819	G4093
3820	G4094
3821	G4095
3822	G4096
3823	G4097
3824	G4098
"	G4100
3825	G4099
3826	G4101
"	G4113
3827	G4102
3828	G4103
3829	G4104
"	G4106
3830	G4105
"	G4107
3831	G4108
3832	G4109
3833	G4110
3834	G4111
3835	G4112
3836	G4115
3837	G4114
"	G4116
3838	G4117
3839	G4118
3840	G4119
3841	G4120
3842	G4121
3843	G4122
3844	G4123
3845	G4124
3846	G4125
3847	G4126
3848	G688
"	G4127
3849	G4128
3850	G4130
3851	G4129
"	G4131
3852	G4132
3853	G4133
3854	G4134
3855	G4135
3856	G4136
3857	G4137
3858	G4138
3859	G1384
"	G4139
3860	G4140
3861	G4141
3862	G4142
3863	G4143
3864	G4144
3865	G4145
3866	G4146
3867	G4147
3868	G4148
3869	G4149
"	G4150
3870	G4151
3871	G4152
3872	G4153
3873	G4154
3874	G4155
3875	G4156
3876	G4157
3877	G4158
3878	G4159
3879	G4160
3880	G4161
3881	G4162
3882	G4163
3883	G4164
3884	G4165
3885	G4166
"	G4167
3886	G4168
3887	G4169
3888	G4170
3889	G4171
3890	G4172
3891	G4174
3892	G4175
3893	G4176
3894	G4177
3895	G4178
3896	G4179
3897	G4180
3898	G4181
3899	G4182
3900	G4183
3901	G4184
3902	G4185
3903	G4186
3904	G4187
3905	G4189
3906	G4190
3907	G4191
3908	G4192
3909	G4193
3910	G4194
3911	G4195
3912	G4196
3913	G4173
"	G4197
"	G4198
3914	G4199
3915	G4200
3916	G4202
3917	G4203
3918	G4205
3919	G4206
3920	G4207
3921	G4208
3922	G4209
3923	G4210
3924	G4211
3925	G4213
3926	G4214
3927	G4215
3928	G4216
3929	G4217
3930	G4218
3931	G4219
3932	G4220
3933	G4221
3934	G4222
3935	G4223
3936	G4224
"	G4225
3937	G4226
3938	G4227
3939	G4228
3940	G4229
3941	G4230
3942	G4231
3943	G4232
3944	G4233
3945	G4234
3946	G4235
3947	G4236
3948	G4237
3949	G4239
3950	G4240
3951	G4241
3952	G4242
3953	G4243
3954	G4244
3955	G4245
3956	G4246
3957	G4247
3958	G4248
3959	G4249
3960	G4250
3961	G4251
3962	G4635
"	G4252
3963	G4253
3964	G4254
"	G4260
3965	G4255
3966	G4256
3967	G4257
3968	G4258
3969	G4259
3970	G4261
3971	G4262
3972	G4263
3973	G4264
3974	G4265
3975	G4266
3976	G4267
3977	G4268
3978	G4269
3979	G4270
"	G4271
3980	G4272
3981	G4273
"	G4274
"	G4392
3982	G2167
"	G4275
3983	G4277
3984	G4278
3985	G4279
3986	G4280
3987	G4281
3988	G4282
3989	G4283
3990	G4284
3991	G4286
3992	G4287
3993	G4288
3994	G4289
3995	G4290
3996	G4291
3997	G4292
3998	G4293
3999	G4294
4000	G4295
4001	G4296
4002	G4297
4003	G4298
4004	G4299
4005	G4300
4006	G4301
4007	G4302
4008	G4305
4009	G4306
4010	G4307
4011	G4308
4012	G4309
4013	G4310
4014	G4311
4015	G4313
4016	G4212
"	G4314
4017	G4315
4018	G4316
4019	G4317
4020	G4318
4021	G4319
4022	G4320
4023	G4321
4024	G4322
"	G4323
4025	G4324
4026	G4325
4027	G2753
"	G4326
4028	G4328
4029	G4329
4030	G4330
4031	G4331
4032	G4332
4033	G4333
4034	G4334
4035	G4335
4036	G4337
4037	G4338
4038	G4339
4039	G4340
4040	G4341
4041	G4342
4042	G4343
4043	G4344
4044	G4345
4045	G4346
4046	G4347
4047	G4348
4048	G4351
4049	G4352
4050	G4353
4051	G4354
4052	G4355
4053	G4356
4054	G4357
4055	G4358
4056	G4359
4057	G4360
4058	G4361
4059	G4362
4060	G4363
4061	G4364
4062	G4365
4063	G4366
4064	G4367
4065	G4368
4066	G4369
4067	G4370
4068	G4371
4069	G4372
4070	G4373
4071	G4374
4072	G4375
4073	G4376
4074	G4377
4075	G4378
4076	G4379
4077	G4380
4078	G4381
4079	G4382
4080	G4383
4081	G4384
4082	G4385
4083	G4388
4084	G4389
4085	G4390
4086	G4391
4087	G4393
4088	G4394
4089	G4395
4090	G4396
4091	G4276
"	G4397
4092	G4399
4093	G4400
"	G4401
4094	G4402
4095	G4403
4096	G4404
4097	G4405
4098	G4406
"	G5229
4099	G4407
"	G4408
4100	G4409
4101	G4410
4102	G4411
4103	G4412
4104	G4413
4105	G4414
4106	G4415
4107	G4416
"	G4417
4108	G4418
4109	G4419
4110	G4420
4111	G4421
4112	G4422
4113	G4423
4114	G4424
4115	G4425
4116	G4426
4117	G4427
4118	G4498
4119	G4498
4120	G4428
4121	G4429
4122	G4430
4123	G4431
4124	G4432
4125	G4433
4126	G4434
4127	G4435
4128	G4436
4129	G4437
4130	G4398
4131	G4438
4132	G4439
4133	G4440
4134	G4441
4135	G4442
4136	G4443
4137	G4444
4138	G4445
4139	G4446
4140	G4447
4141	G4448
4142	G4449
4143	G4450
4144	G4452
"	G4453
4145	G4454
4146	G4455
4147	G4456
4148	G4457
4149	G4458
4150	G4459
4151	G4460
4152	G4461
4153	G4462
4154	G4463
4155	G4464
4156	G4465
4157	G4466
4158	G4468
4159	G4470
4160	G4472
4161	G4473
4162	G4474
4163	G4475
4164	G4476
4165	G4477
4166	G4478
4167	G4479
4168	G4480
4169	G4471
"	G4481
4170	G4482
4171	G4483
4172	G4484
4173	G4485
4174	G4486
4175	G4487
4176	G4488
4177	G4489
4178	G4490
"	G1930
4179	G2234
"	G4491
4180	G4494
4181	G4495
4182	G4497
4183	G4498
4184	G4492
"	G4499
4185	G4500
4186	G4501
4187	G4502
4188	G4503
4189	G4504
4190	G4505
4191	G4505
4192	G4506
4193	G4507
4194	G4508
4195	G4510
4196	G4511
4197	G4512
"	G4515
4198	G4513
4199	G4514
4200	G4516
4201	G4517
4202	G4518
4203	G4519
4204	G4520
4205	G4521
4206	G4522
4207	G4523
4208	G4524
4209	G4525
4210	G4526
"	G4528
4211	G4527
4212	G4529
4213	G4530
4214	G4531
4215	G4532
4216	G4533
4217	G4467
"	G4534
4218	G4537
4219	G4536
4220	G4538
4221	G4539
4222	G4540
4223	G4541
4224	G4542
4225	G4543
4226	G4544
4227	G4545
4228	G4546
4229	G4547
4230	G4548
4231	G4549
4232	G4550
4233	G4551
4234	G4552
4235	G4553
4236	G4554
"	G4557
4237	G4555
4238	G407
"	G4556
4239	G4558
4240	G4559
4241	G4560
4242	G4561
4243	G4563
4244	G4564
4245	G4565
4246	G4562
"	G4566
4247	G4567
4248	G4568
4249	G4569
"	G4573
4250	G4570
4251	G4571
4252	G4572
4253	G4574
4254	G4575
4255	G4576
4256	G164
"	G4577
4257	G4578
4258	G4579
4259	G4580
4260	G4581
4261	G4582
4262	G4583
4263	G4584
"	G4585
4264	G4586
4265	G4587
4266	G4588
4267	G4589
4268	G4590
4269	G4591
4270	G4592
4271	G4593
4272	G4594
4273	G4595
4274	G4596
4275	G4632
4276	G4598
4277	G4625
"	G4597
4278	G4599
4279	G4600
4280	G4625
"	G4597
4281	G4601
4282	G4602
4283	G4603
4284	G4604
"	G4617
4285	G4605
4286	G4606
"	G4671
4287	G4607
4288	G4608
4289	G4609
4290	G4610
4291	G4613
4292	G4614
4293	G4615
4294	G4616
4295	G4618
4296	G4619
4297	G4620
4298	G4621
4299	G4622
4300	G4623
4301	G4624
4302	G4625
"	G4597
4303	G4626
4304	G4627
4305	G4628
4306	G4629
4307	G4630
4308	G4631
"	G4632
4309	G4633
4310	G4634
4311	G4636
4312	G4637
4313	G4638
4314	G4639
4315	G4640
4316	G4641
4317	G4642
"	G4652
"	G4654
4318	G4643
4319	G4644
"	G4645
4320	G4646
4321	G4648
"	G4649
4322	G4650
4323	G4651
4324	G4653
4325	G4655
4326	G4656
4327	G4657
4328	G4659
4329	G4660
4330	G4661
4331	G4662
4332	G4204
"	G4663
4333	G4664
4334	G4665
4335	G4666
4336	G4667
4337	G4668
4338	G4669
4339	G4670
4340	G4672
4341	G4673
4342	G4674
4343	G4675
4344	G4676
4345	G4677
4346	G4678
"	G4680
4347	G4681
"	G4679
4348	G4682
4349	G4683
4350	G4684
4351	G4685
4352	G4686
4353	G4687
4354	G4688
4355	G4647
"	G4689
4356	G4691
"	G4692
4357	G4693
4358	G4694
4359	G4695
4360	G4696
4361	G4698
4362	G4699
4363	G4700
4364	G4701
4365	G4702
4366	G4703
"	G4704
4367	G4705
4368	G4188
"	G4706
4369	G4707
4370	G4708
"	G4716
4371	G4709
4372	G4710
4373	G4711
4374	G4712
4375	G4713
4376	G4714
4377	G4715
4378	G4717
4379	G4718
4380	G4719
"	G4722
4381	G4720
"	G4723
4382	G4721
"	G4724
4383	G4725
4384	G4726
4385	G4727
4386	G4728
4387	G4728
4388	G4729
4389	G4730
4390	G4731
4391	G4732
4392	G4733

STRONG	G/K
4393	G4734
4394	G4735
4395	G4736
4396	G4737
4397	G4738
4398	G4739
4399	G4740
4400	G4741
4401	G4742
4402	G4743
4403	G4744
4404	G4745
4405	G4746
4406	G4611
"	G4747
4407	G4612
"	G4748
4408	G4749
4409	G4750
4410	G4751
4411	G4752
4412	G4754
"	G4759
4413	G4755
4414	G4756
4415	G4757
4416	G4758
4417	G4760
4418	G4761
4419	G4762
4420	G4763
4421	G4764
4422	G4765
4423	G4766
4424	G4767
4425	G4768
4426	G4769
4427	G4770
4428	G4771
4429	G4772
4430	G4773
4431	G4774
4432	G4775
4433	G4776
4434	G4777
4435	G4778
4436	G4780
4437	G4781
4438	G4782
4439	G4783
4440	G4784
4441	G4785
4442	G4786
4443	G4787
4444	G4788
4445	G4789
4446	G4790
4447	G4791
4448	G4792
4449	G4793
4450	G4794
4451	G4796
4452	G4803
4453	G4797
4454	G4798
4455	G4799
4456	G4386
"	G4800
4457	G4387
"	G4801
4458	G4535
"	G4803
4459	G4802
4460	G4805
4461	G4806
4462	G4807
"	G4808
"	G4809
4463	G4810
4464	G4811
4465	G4812
4466	G4814
4467	G4815
4468	G4816
4469	G4819
"	G4828
4470	G4820
4471	G4821
4472	G4822
4473	G4823
4474	G4824
4475	G4825
4476	G1017
"	G4827
4477	G4829
4478	G4830
4479	G4831
4480	G4832
4481	G4818
"	G4833
"	G4834
"	G4854
4482	G4835
4483	G3306
4484	G4836
4485	G4837
4486	G4826
"	G4838
"	G4841
4487	G4839
4488	G4840
4489	G4842
4490	G4843
4491	G4844
4492	G4845
4493	G4846
"	G4856
4494	G4847
4495	G4848
4496	G4849
4497	G4850
4498	G4851
4499	G4852
4500	G4853
4501	G4855
4502	G4857
4503	G4858
4504	G4859
4505	G4860
4506	G4861
4507	G4864
4508	G4865
4509	G4866
4510	G4862
"	G4863
"	G4867
4511	G4868
4512	G4869
4513	G4870
4514	G4871
4515	G4872
4516	G4873
4517	G4874
4518	G2407
"	G4876
4519	G4877
4520	G4878
4521	G4879
4522	G4880
4523	G4881
4524	G4882
4525	G4883
"	G4966
4526	G4884
4527	G4885
4528	G4886
4529	G4887
4530	G4890
4531	G4888
4532	G4889
4533	G4891
4534	G4892
4535	G4893
4536	G4894
4537	G4895
4538	G4896
4539	G4897
4540	G4899
"	G4900
4541	G4901
4542	G4902
4543	G4903
4544	G4904
4545	G4905
4546	G4907
4547	G4908
4548	G4909
4549	G4910
4550	G4911
4551	G4912
4552	G4913
4553	G4914
4554	G4915
4555	G4916
4556	G4917
4557	G4918
4558	G4919
4559	G4920
4560	G4921
4561	G4922
4562	G4923
"	G4951
"	G4952
4563	G4924
4564	G4925
4565	G838
"	G4926
4566	G4927
4567	G4928
4568	G4929
4569	G4930
4570	G2410
"	G4931
4571	G5148
4572	G4932
4573	G4933
4574	G4934
4575	G4935
4576	G4936
4577	G4937
"	G4938
"	G4987
4578	G4939
4579	G4940
4580	G4941
4581	G4942
4582	G4943
4583	G4944
4584	G4945
"	G4946
4585	G4947
4586	G4948
4587	G4949
4588	G4950
4589	G4953
4590	G4954
4591	G4955
4592	G4956
4593	G4957
4594	G4958
4595	G4960
4596	G4961
"	G4986
4597	G4962
4598	G4963
4599	G4964
4600	G4965
4601	G4967
4602	G4968
4603	G4969
"	G4971
4604	G4970
4605	G4972
4606	G4973
4607	G4974
4608	G4975
4609	G4976
4610	G4977
4611	G4978
4612	G4959
"	G4980
4613	G4981
4614	G4982
4615	G4983
4616	G4984
4617	G4985
4618	G4988
4619	G4990
4620	G4991
4621	G4989
"	G4992
4622	G4994
4623	G4995
4624	G4997
4625	G4998
4626	G4999
4627	G5002
4628	G5003
4629	G5004
4630	G5005
4631	G5006
4632	G5007
4633	G5008
4634	G5009
4635	G5010
4636	G5011
4637	G5012
4638	G5013
4639	G5014
4640	G5015
4641	G5016
4642	G5017
4643	G5018
4644	G5019
4645	G5020
4646	G5021
4647	G5022
4648	G5023
4649	G5024
4650	G5025
4651	G5026
4652	G5027
4653	G5028
4654	G5029
4655	G5030
4656	G5031
4657	G5032
4658	G5033
4659	G5034
4660	G5035
4661	G5036
4662	G5037
4663	G5038
4664	G5039
4665	G5040
4666	G5043
4667	G2430
"	G5044
4668	G5045
4669	G5046
4670	G5047
4671	G5148
4672	G4898
"	G5048
4673	G5049
4674	G5050
4675	G5148
4676	G5051
4677	G5052
4678	G5053
4679	G5054
4680	G5055
4681	G5056
4682	G5057
4683	G5058
4684	G5059
4685	G5060
4686	G5061
4687	G2178
"	G5062
4688	G5063
4689	G5064
4690	G5065
4691	G5066
4692	G5067
4693	G5068
4694	G5069
4695	G5071
4696	G5070
4697	G5072
4698	G5073
4699	G5074
4700	G5075
4701	G5076
4702	G5077
4703	G5078
4704	G5079
4705	G5080
4706	G5080
4707	G5080
4708	G5081
4709	G5081
4710	G5082
4711	G5083
4712	G5084
4713	G5085
4714	G5087
4715	G5088
4716	G5089
4717	G5090
4718	G5091
4719	G5092
4720	G5093
4721	G5094
4722	G5095
4723	G5096
4724	G5097
4725	G5098
4726	G5099
4727	G5100
4728	G5101
4729	G5102
4730	G5103
4731	G5104
4732	G5105
4733	G5106
4734	G5107
4735	G5109
4736	G5108
4737	G5110
4738	G5111
4739	G5112
4740	G5113
4741	G5114
4742	G5116
4743	G5117
4744	G5118
4745	G5119
4746	G5115
"	G5120
4747	G5122
4748	G5123
4749	G5124
4750	G5125
4751	G5126
4752	G5127
4753	G5128
4754	G5129
4755	G5130
4756	G5131
4757	G5132
4758	G5133
4759	G5134
"	G5135
4760	G5136
4761	G5137
4762	G5138
4763	G5139
4764	G5140
4765	G5141
4766	G5142
"	G5143
4767	G5144
4768	G5145
4769	G5146
4770	G5121
"	G5147
4771	G5148
4772	G5149
4773	G5150
"	G5151
4774	G5152
4775	G5153
4776	G4327
"	G5154
4777	G5155
4778	G5156
4779	G5157
4780	G5158
4781	G5159
4782	G5160
4783	G5161
4784	G5163
4785	G2975
"	G5164
4786	G5166
4787	G5167
4788	G5168
4789	G5169
4790	G5170
4791	G5171
4792	G5172
4793	G5173
4794	G5174
4795	G5175
"	G5346
4796	G5176
4797	G5177
"	G5179
4798	G5178
4799	G5180
4800	G5182
4801	G2413
"	G5183
4802	G5184
4803	G5185
4804	G5186
4805	G5187
4806	G5188
4807	G5189
4808	G5190
4809	G5191
4810	G5192
4811	G5193
4812	G5194
4813	G5195
4814	G5196
4815	G5197
4816	G5198
4817	G5199
4818	G5200
4819	G5201
4820	G5202
4821	G5203
4822	G5204
4823	G5205
4824	G5206
4825	G5207
4826	G5208
4827	G5209
4828	G5210
4829	G5211
4830	G5212
4831	G5213
4832	G5215
4833	G5214
"	G5216
"	G5240
4834	G5217
4835	G5218
4836	G5219
4837	G5220
4838	G5221
4839	G5222
4840	G5223
4841	G5224
4842	G5225
4843	G5227
4844	G5228
4845	G5230
4846	G5231
4847	G5232
4848	G5233
4849	G5234
"	G5235
4850	G5236
4851	G5237
"	G5239
4852	G5238
4853	G5241
4854	G5242
4855	G5243
4856	G5244
4857	G5245
4858	G5246
4859	G5247
4860	G5248
4861	G5249
4862	G5250
4863	G5251
4864	G5252
4865	G5253
4866	G5254
4867	G125
"	G5255
4868	G5256
4869	G5257
4870	G5258
4871	G5259
"	G5260
"	G5276
4872	G5262
4873	G5263
"	G5165
4874	G5264
4875	G5265
4876	G5267
4877	G5268
4878	G5269
4879	G5270
4880	G5271
4881	G5272
4882	G5273
4883	G5274
4884	G5275
4885	G5277
4886	G5278
4887	G5279
4888	G5280
4889	G5281
4890	G5282
4891	G5283
4892	G5284
4893	G5287
4894	G5288
"	G5323
"	G5328
4895	G5289
4896	G5290
4897	G5291
4898	G5292
4899	G5293
4900	G5261
"	G5295
4901	G5296
4902	G5299
4903	G5300
4904	G5301
4905	G5302
4906	G5303
4907	G5304
4908	G5305
4909	G5306
4910	G5307
4911	G5308
4912	G5309
4913	G5310
4914	G5311
4915	G5312
4916	G5313
4917	G5314
4918	G5315
4919	G5316
4920	G5317
"	G5320
4921	G5318
"	G5319
4922	G5321
4923	G5322
4924	G5324
4925	G5325
4926	G5326
4927	G5327
4928	G5330
4929	G5332
4930	G5333
4931	G5334
4932	G5335
4933	G5337
4934	G5298
"	G5338
4935	G5339
4936	G5340
4937	G5341
4938	G5342
4939	G5343
4940	G5344
4941	G5345
4942	G5347
4943	G5348
4944	G5349
4945	G5350
4946	G5352
4947	G5353
4948	G5354
4949	G5351
"	G5355
"	G5356
"	G5835
4950	G5358
4951	G5359
4952	G5331
"	G5360
4953	G5361
4954	G5362
4955	G5086
"	G5363
4956	G5364
4957	G5365
4958	G5366
4959	G5367
4960	G5368
4961	G5369
4962	G5370
4963	G5371
4964	G5372
4965	G4993
"	G5373
4966	G5374
4967	G5375
4968	G5376
4969	G5377
4970	G5379
4971	G5380
4972	G5381
4973	G5382
4974	G5383
"	G5384
4975	G5385
4976	G5386
4977	G5387
4978	G5388
4979	G5389
4980	G5390
4981	G5391
4982	G1751
"	G5392
4983	G5393
4984	G5394
4985	G5395
4986	G5396
4987	G5397
4988	G5398
4989	G5399
4990	G5400
4991	G5401
4992	G5402
"	G5403
4993	G5404
4994	G5405
4995	G5406
4996	G5407
4997	G5408
4998	G5409
4999	G5411
5000	G5412
5001	G5413
5002	G5414
5003	G5415
5004	G5416
5005	G5417
5006	G5418
5007	G5419
5008	G2496
"	G5420
5009	G5421
5010	G5423
5011	G5424
5012	G5425
5013	G5427
5014	G5428
5015	G5429
5016	G5430
5017	G5431
5018	G5432
5019	G5433
5020	G5434
5021	G5435
5022	G5436
5023	G4047
5024	G5437
5025	G4047
5026	G4047
5027	G5438
5028	G5439
5029	G5440
5030	G5441
5031	G5442
5032	G5441
5033	G5441
5034	G5443
5035	G5444
5036	G5444
5037	G5445
5038	G5446
5039	G5447
5040	G5448
5041	G5449
5042	G5450
5043	G5451
5044	G5452
5045	G5454
5046	G5455
5047	G5456
5048	G5457
5049	G5458
5050	G5459
5051	G5460
5052	G5461
5053	G5462
5054	G5463
5055	G5464
5056	G5465
5057	G5467
5058	G5466
"	G5468
5059	G5469
5060	G5470
5061	G5472
5062	G5473
"	G5477
5063	G5474
"	G5478
5064	G5475
5065	G5476
5066	G5479
5067	G5480
5068	G5481
5069	G5482
5070	G5483
5071	G5484
5072	G5485
5073	G5486
"	G5487
5074	G5488
5075	G5489
5076	G5490
5077	G5491
5078	G5492
5079	G5493
5080	G5494
5081	G1315
"	G5495
5082	G5496
5083	G5498
5084	G5499
5085	G5500
5086	G5501
5087	G5502
5088	G5503
5089	G5504
5090	G5505
5091	G5506
5092	G5507
5093	G5508
5094	G5509
5095	G5510
5096	G5511
5097	G5512
5098	G5513
5099	G5514
5100	G5516
5101	G5515
5102	G5518
5103	G5519
5104	G5520
5105	G5521
"	G5522
5106	G5523
5107	G5524
5108	G5525
5109	G5526
5110	G5527
5111	G5528
5112	G5529
"	G5530
"	G5531
5113	G5532
5114	G5533
5115	G5534

STRONG	G/K
5116	G5535
5117	G5536
"	G4509
5118	G5537
5119	G5538
5120	G3836
5121	G5539
5122	G5540
5123	G5542
5124	G4047
5125	G4047
5126	G4047
5127	G4047
5128	G4047
5129	G4047
5130	G4047
5131	G5543
5132	G5544
5133	G5545
5134	G5546
5135	G5547
5136	G5548
5137	G5549
5138	G5550
5139	G5551
5140	G5552
5141	G5554
5142	G5555
5143	G5556
5144	G5558
5145	G5559
5146	G5560
5147	G5561
5148	G5562
5149	G5563
5150	G5564
5151	G5565
5152	G5566
5153	G5567
5154	G5568
"	G5569
5155	G5570
5156	G5571
5157	G5572
5158	G5573
5159	G5574
"	G5578
5160	G5575
5161	G5576
5162	G5577
5163	G5579
5164	G5580
5165	G5581
5166	G5582
5167	G5583
5168	G5584
5169	G5557
"	G5585
5170	G5586
5171	G5587
5172	G5588
5173	G5589
5174	G5590
5175	G5591
5176	G5592
5177	G5593
5178	G5594
5179	G5595
"	G5596
5180	G5597
5181	G5598
5182	G2571
"	G5600
5183	G5601
5184	G5602
5185	G5603
5186	G5604
5187	G5605
5188	G5606
5189	G5607
5190	G5608
5191	G5610
5192	G5611
5193	G5612
5194	G5613
5195	G5614
5196	G5615
5197	G5616
5198	G5617
5199	G5618
5200	G5619
5201	G5620
5202	G5621
5203	G5622
5204	G5623
5205	G5624
5206	G5625
5207	G5626
5208	G5627
5209	G5148
5210	G5148
5211	G5628
5212	G5629
5213	G5148
5214	G5630
5215	G5631
5216	G5148
5217	G5632
5218	G5633
5219	G5634
5220	G5635
5221	G5636
5222	G5637
5223	G5638
5224	G5639
5225	G5639
5226	G5640
5227	G5641
5228	G5642
5229	G5643
5230	G5644
5231	G5645
5232	G5647
5233	G5648
5234	G5649
5235	G5650
5236	G5651
5237	G4238
"	G5653
"	G5666
5238	G5654
5239	G5657
5240	G5655
"	G5656
"	G5658
5241	G5659
5242	G5660
5243	G5661
5244	G5662
"	G5663
5245	G5664
5246	G5665
5247	G5667
5248	G5668
5249	G5669
5250	G5670
5251	G5671
5252	G5672
5253	G5673
5254	G5674
5255	G5675
5256	G5676
5257	G5677
5258	G5678
5259	G5679
5260	G5680
5261	G5681
5262	G5682
5263	G5683
"	G5684
5264	G5685
5265	G5686
5266	G5687
5267	G5688
5268	G5689
5269	G5690
5270	G5691
5271	G5693
5272	G5694
5273	G5695
5274	G5696
5275	G5699
5276	G5700
5277	G659
"	G5701
5278	G670
"	G5702
5279	G5703
5280	G5704
5281	G5705
5282	G5706
5283	G5707
5284	G5709
5285	G5710
5286	G5711
5287	G5712
5288	G5713
5289	G5714
5290	G5715
5291	G5716
5292	G5717
5293	G5718
5294	G5719
5295	G5720
5296	G5721
5297	G5722
5298	G5723
5299	G5708
"	G5724
5300	G5725
5301	G5727
5302	G5728
5303	G5729
5304	G5730
5305	G5731
5306	G5731
5307	G5733
5308	G5734
5309	G5735
5310	G5736
5311	G5737
5312	G5738
5313	G5739
5314	G5741
5315	G2266
5316	G5743
5317	G5744
5318	G5745
5319	G5746
5320	G5747
5321	G5748
5322	G5749
5323	G5750
5324	G5751
5325	G5752
5326	G5753
5327	G5754
5328	G5755
5329	G5756
5330	G5757
5331	G5758
"	G5760
5332	G5759
5333	G5761
5334	G5762
5335	G5763
5336	G5764
5337	G5765
5338	G5766
5339	G5767
5340	G5768
5341	G5742
"	G5769
5342	G5770
5343	G5771
5344	G5772
5345	G5773
5346	G5774
5347	G5776
5348	G5777
5349	G5778
5350	G5779
5351	G5780
5352	G5781
5353	G5782
5354	G5783
5355	G5784
5356	G5785
5357	G5786
5358	G5787
5359	G5788
5360	G5789
5361	G5790
5362	G5791
5363	G5792
5364	G5793
5365	G5794
5366	G5795
5367	G5796
5368	G5797
5369	G5798
5370	G5799
5371	G5800
5372	G5801
5373	G5802
5374	G5803
5375	G5804
5376	G5805
5377	G5806
5378	G5807
5379	G5808
5380	G5809
5381	G5810
5382	G5811
5383	G5812
5384	G5813
5385	G5814
5386	G5815
5387	G5816
5388	G5817
5389	G5818
5390	G5819
5391	G5426
"	G5820
5392	G3055
"	G5821
5393	G5823
5394	G5824
5395	G5825
5396	G5826
5397	G5827
5398	G5829
5399	G5828
"	G5830
5400	G5831
5401	G5832
5402	G5833
5403	G5834
5404	G5836
5405	G5837
5406	G5838
5407	G5839
5408	G5840
5409	G5841
5410	G5842
5411	G5843
5412	G5844
5413	G5845
5414	G5846
5415	G5847
5416	G5848
5417	G5849
"	G5822
5418	G5850
5419	G5851
5420	G5852
5421	G5853
5422	G5854
5423	G5855
5424	G5856
5425	G5857
5426	G5858
5427	G5859
5428	G5860
5429	G5861
5430	G5862
5431	G5863
5432	G5864
5433	G5865
5434	G5866
5435	G5867
5436	G5869
5437	G5870
5438	G5871
5439	G5872
5440	G5873
5441	G5874
5442	G5875
5443	G5876
5444	G5877
5445	G5878
5446	G5879
5447	G5880
5448	G5881
5449	G5882
5450	G5883
5451	G5884
5452	G5885
5453	G5886
5454	G5887
5455	G1876
"	G5888
5456	G5889
5457	G5890
5458	G5891
5459	G5892
5460	G5893
5461	G5894
5462	G5895
5463	G5897
5464	G5898
5465	G5899
5466	G5900
5467	G5901
5468	G5902
"	G5904
5469	G5903
5470	G5905
"	G5911
5471	G5906
5472	G5907
5473	G5908
5474	G5909
5475	G5910
5476	G5912
5477	G5913
5478	G5914
5479	G5915
5480	G5916
5481	G5917
5482	G5918
5483	G5919
5484	G5920
5485	G5921
5486	G5922
5487	G5923
5488	G5924
5489	G5925
5490	G5926
5491	G5927
5492	G5928
5493	G5929
5494	G5930
5495	G5931
5496	G5932
5497	G5933
5498	G5934
5499	G5935
5500	G5936
5501	G5937
5502	G5938
5503	G5939
5504	G2396
"	G5940
5505	G5942
5506	G5941
5507	G5943
5508	G5944
5509	G5945
5510	G5946
5511	G5948
5512	G1430
"	G5949
5513	G5950
5514	G5951
5515	G5952
5516	G5947
"	G5953
5517	G5954
5518	G5955
5519	G5956
5520	G5957
5521	G5958
5522	G5967
"	G5959
5523	G5960
"	G6002
5524	G5961
5525	G5962
5526	G5963
5527	G5964
5528	G5965
5529	G5966
5530	G5968
5531	G3079
"	G5969
5532	G5970
5533	G5971
"	G5972
5534	G5973
5535	G5974
5536	G5975
5537	G5976
5538	G5977
5539	G5978
5540	G5979
5541	G5980
5542	G5981
5543	G5982
5544	G5983
5545	G5984
5546	G5985
5547	G5986
5548	G5987
5549	G5988
5550	G5989
5551	G5990
5552	G5991
"	G5997
5553	G5992
5554	G5993
5555	G5994
5556	G5995
5557	G5996
5558	G5998
5559	G5999
5560	G6000
5561	G6001
5562	G6003
5563	G6004
5564	G6005
5565	G6006
5566	G6008
5567	G6010
5568	G6011
5569	G6012
5570	G6013
5571	G6014
5572	G6015
5573	G6016
5574	G6017
5575	G6020
5576	G6018
5577	G6019
5578	G6021
5579	G6022
5580	G6023
5581	G6024
5582	G6025
5583	G6026
5584	G6027
5585	G6028
5586	G6029
5587	G6030
5588	G6031
5589	G6032
"	G6033
5590	G6034
5591	G6035
5592	G6036
5593	G6037
5594	G6038
5595	G6039
5596	G6040
5597	G6041
5598	G6042
5599	G6043
5600	G1639
5601	G2725
"	G6044
5602	G6045
5603	G6046
5604	G6047
5605	G6048
5606	G6049
5607	G1639
5608	G6050
5609	G6051
5610	G6052
5611	G6053
5612	G6054
5613	G6055
5614	G6057
5615	G6058
5616	G6059
5617	G6060
5618	G6061
5619	G6062
5620	G6063
5621	G6064
"	G6065
5622	G6066
5623	G6067
5624	G6068

FEATURES OF THE INDEX OF GOODRICK/ KOHLENBERGER → STRONG NUMBERS

G/K NUMBER
Hebrew numbers start with "H"; Aramaic numbers start with "A"; Greek numbers are *italic* and start with "*G*."

STRONG NUMBER
Non-italic "roman" numbers are Hebrew or Aramaic; *italic* numbers are Greek (see pages xii, xviii).

G/K............STRONG

H3............................1
A10003...................2

ONE-TO-ONE CORRESPONDENCE
Most G/K numbers have a one-to-one correspondence to a Strong number (see page xviii).

H63........................57
"..............................59

DITTO MARKS (")
Indicates a G/K number corresponds to more than one Strong number (see page xviii).

G1276......1176+1803
G1277............... 1176
+2532+3638

PLUS MARKS (+)
Indicates a G/K number corresponds to a combination of Strong numbers (see page xviii).

H1
A10001
G207

NO LEADER DOTS; NO G/K/ NUMBER
Indicates a G/K number has no equivalent in the Strong numbering system (see page xviii).

HEBREW OLD TESTAMENT

G/K	STRONG
H1	
H2	
H3	1
H4	3
H5	5
H6	6
H7	8
H8	9
H9	10
H10	11
H11	11
H12	12
H13	13
H14	14
H15	16
H16	17
H17	18
H18	19
H19	20
H20	15
H21	
H22	
H23	21
H24	22
H25	23
H26	24
H27	
H28	26
H29	27
H30	28
H31	29
H32	29
H33	30
H34	31
H35	32
H36	34
H37	35
H38	32
H39	36
H40	37
H41	38
H42	39
H43	40
H44	41
H45	42
H46	74
H47	43
H48	44
H49	33
H50	45
H51	46
H52	47
H53	48
H54	49
H55	50
H56	51
H57	52
H58	53
H59	54
H60	55
H61	56
H62	56
H63	57
"	59
H64	58
"	59
H65	60
H66	61
H67	180
H68	62
H69	63
H70	64
H71	65
H72	66
H73	67
H74	68
H75	72
H76	71
H77	73
H78	70
H79	74
H80	75
H81	76
H82	77
H83	78
H84	79
H85	80
H86	81
H87	82
H88	83
H89	84
H90	85
H91	86
H92	87
H93	52
H94	53
H95	88

G/K	STRONG
H96	89
H97	90
H98	91
H99	92
H100	93
H101	94
H102	95
H103	96
H104	97
H105	
H106	98
H107	98
H108	99
H109	100
H110	101
H111	102
H112	103
H113	105
H114	106
H115	107
H116	108
H117	109
H118	110
H119	111
H120	112
H121	123
H122	130
H123	113
H124	114
H125	138
H126	115
H127	151
H128	182
H129	117
H130	118
H131	119
H132	120
H133	120
H134	121
H135	120
H136	121
H137	122
H138	124
H139	123
H140	125
H141	127
H142	128
H143	127
H144	126
H145	132
"	726
H146	129+5346
H147	131
H148	133
H149	134
H150	135
H151	136
H152	137
H153	138
H154	138
H155	139
H156	140
H157	141
H158	142
H159	145
H160	143
H161	146
H162	146
H163	150
H164	151
H165	152
H166	152
H167	154
H168	155
H169	156
H170	157
H171	159
H172	158
H173	160
H174	160
H175	
H176	161
H177	162
H178	163
H179	164
H180	165
H181	1961
H182	167
H183	166
H184	174
H185	168
H186	169
H187	428
H188	170
H189	174
H190	171
H191	172
H192	173
H193	174
H194	

G/K	STRONG
H195	175
H196	176
H197	176
H198	177
H199	178
H200	178
H201	179
H202	181
H203	183
H204	184
H205	185
H206	186
H207	187
H208	188
H209	189
H210	190
H211	191
H212	193
H213	192
H214	193
H215	193
H216	196
H217	195
H218	194
H219	199
H220	198
H221	197
H222	200
H223	201
H224	205
H225	206
H226	202
H227	203
H228	204
H229	207
H230	205
H231	208
H232	209
H233	210
H234	211
H235	211
H236	212
H237	213
H238	214
H239	215
H240	216
H241	217
H242	224
H243	218
H244	218
H245	219
H246	219
H247	221
H248	222
H249	223
H250	223
H251	224
H252	225
H253	226
H254	853
H255	227
H256	229
H257	231
H258	232
H259	233
H260	234
H261	235
H262	237
H263	238
H264	239
H265	241
H266	240
H267	242
H268	243
H269	244
H270	244
H271	245
H272	246
H273	247
H274	248
H275	249
H276	250
H277	253
H278	251
H279	254
H280	255
H281	256
H282	256
H283	257
H284	258
H285	259
H286	260
H287	261
H288	264
H289	262
H290	270
H291	265
H292	266
H293	267
H294	268

G/K	STRONG
H295	269
H296	270
H297	270
H298	271
H299	272
H300	273
H301	274
H302	274
H303	275
H304	276
H305	278
H306	277
H307	279
H308	281
H309	281
H310	282
H311	283
H312	284
H313	285
H314	286
H315	287
H316	288
H317	289
H318	290
H319	291
H320	292
H321	293
H322	294
H323	295
H324	296
H325	297
H326	298
H327	299
H328	300
H329	301
H330	302
H331	303
H332	305
H333	304
H334	306
H335	308
H336	309
H337	312
H338	313
H339	310
H340	314
H341	315
H342	316
H343	310
H344	319
H345	322
H346	323
H347	325
H348	325
H349	326
H350	327
H351	328
H352	
H353	329
H354	329
H355	330
H356	328
H357	331
H358	332
H359	333
H360	334
H361	335
H362	339
H363	338
H364	336
H365	337
H366	340
H367	341
H368	342
H369	343
H370	344
H371	345
H372	346
H373	347
H374	348
H375	349
H376	350
H377	349
H378	351
H379	349
H380	352
H381	352
H382	352
H383	352
H384	353
H385	354
H386	364
H387	355
"	365
H388	337
H389	357
H390	356
H391	356
H392	358
H393	359

G/K	STRONG
H394	360
H395	361
H396	362
H397	359
H398	366
H399	367
H400	368
H401	369
H402	370
H403	371
H404	372
H405	373
H406	374
H407	375
H408	376
H409	376
H410	378
H411	382
H412	379
H413	380
H414	3448
H415	2978
H416	863
H417	384
H418	385
H419	386
H420	387
H421	389
H422	390
H423	391
H424	392
H425	393
H426	394
H427	395
H428	396
H429	397
H430	398
H431	400
H432	401
H433	402
H434	403
H435	403
H436	404
H437	405
H438	406
H439	407
H440	408
H441	
H442	352
H443	352
H444	352
H445	410
H446	410
H447	411
H448	413
H449	415
H450	416
H451	1286
H452	414
H453	417
H454	418
H455	419
H456	420
H457	422
H458	421
H459	428
H460	423
H461	424
H462	425
H463	425
H464	427
H465	428
H466	430
H467	432
H468	433
H469	435
H470	434
H471	436
H472	356
H473	437
H474	438
H374.5	
H475	439
H476	441
H477	441
H478	442
H479	443
H480	444
H481	445
H482	446
H483	447
H484	448
H485	419
"	449
H486	450
H487	451
H488	452
H489	452
H490	453
H491	453

G/K	STRONG
H492	454
H493	454
H494	455
H495	456
H496	457
H497	458
H498	460
H499	461
H500	463
H501	462
H502	464
H503	465
H504	466
H505	467
H506	468
H507	469
H508	470
H509	471
H510	472
H511	473
H512	474
H513	475
H514	476
H515	477
H516	478
H517	448
H518	480
H519	481
H520	481
H521	482
H522	483
H523	484
H524	485
H525	486
H526	487
H527	488
H528	488
H529	489
H530	490
H531	491
H532	492
H533	440
H534	493
H535	494
H536	495
H537	496
H538	497
H539	498
H540	499
H541	500
H542	500
H543	501
H544	502
H545	503
H546	504
H547	505
H548	505
H549	507
H550	467
H551	508
H552	509
H553	469
H554	510
H555	511
H556	512
H557	513
H558	514
H559	514
H560	515
H561	518
H562	517
H563	519
H564	520
H565	522
H566	4965
H567	520
H568	367
H569	523
H570	525
"	527
"	539
H571	526
H572	527
"	528
H573	529
H574	529
H575	530
H576	531
H577	532
H578	550
H579	533
H580	534
H581	535
H582	535
H583	536
H584	537
H585	538
H586	539
H587	539
"	541

G/K	STRONG
H588	542
H589	543
H590	544
H591	548
H592	549
H593	546
H594	545
H595	547
H596	550
H597	551
H598	552
H599	553
H600	554
H601	555
H602	556
H603	557
H604	558
H605	558
H606	559
H607	559
H608	562
H609	561
H610	561
H611	561
H612	564
H613	564
H614	565
H615	565
H616	567
H617	566
H618	568
H619	568
H620	569
H621	570
H622	571
H623	572
H624	573
H625	575
H626	577
H627	578
H628	579
H629	577
H630	580
H631	605
H632	582
H633	583
H634	584
H635	585
H636	587
H637	588
H638	589
H639	590
H640	592
H641	591
H642	593
H643	594
H644	595
H645	596
H646	597
H647	599
H648	
H649	601
H650	602
H651	603
H652	604
H653	605
H654	609
H655	610
H656	611
H657	612
H658	614
H659	615
H660	616
H661	617
H662	618
H663	619
H664	621
H665	622
H666	623
H667	624
H668	625
H669	626
H670	627
H671	628
H672	630
H673	631
H674	632
H675	634
H676	635
H677	637
H678	639
H679	640
H680	646
H681	641
H682	642
H683	643
H684	644
H685	644
H686	645
H687	6323

G/K	STRONG
H688	647
H689	648
H690	639
H691	649
H692	650
H693	650
H694	652
H695	651
H696	653
H697	654
H698	655
H699	656
H700	657
H701	657
H702	658
H703	659
H704	660
H705	661
H706	662
H707	663
H708	664
H709	665
H710	666
H711	667
H712	668
H713	669
H714	672
H715	672
H716	672
H717	672
H718	673
H719	675
H720	676
H721	678
H722	678
H723	679
H724	680
H725	681
H726	1018
H727	682
H728	682
H729	683
H730	684
H731	685
H732	686
H733	687
H734	688
H735	689
H736	690
H737	691
H738	739
H739	692
H740	692
H741	693
H742	694
H743	695
H744	696
H745	1009
H746	697
H747	698
H748	699
H749	700
H750	701
H751	1835
"	3120
H752	702
"	706
H753	704
H754	705
H755	707
H756	708
H757	
H758	709
H759	709
H760	710
H761	712
H762	3296
H763	713
H764	714
H765	715
H766	716
H767	742
H768	717
H769	720
H770	719
H771	722
H772	722
H773	721
H774	220
"	723
H775	723
H776	724
H777	725
H778	727
H779	728
H780	730
H781	731
H782	732
H783	733
H784	734

G/K	STRONG
H785	736
H786	737
H787	738
H788	221
H789	741
H790	740
H791	740
H792	743
H793	744
H794	745
H795	723
H796	746
H797	224
H798	747
H799	748
H800	750
H801	752
H802	753
H803	750
H804	751
H805	757
H806	758
H807	758+4601
H808	763
H809	760
H810	759
H811	762
"	7421
H812	761
H813	764
H814	765
H815	766
H816	767
H817	768
H818	769
H819	728
H820	770
H821	771
H822	774
H823	775
H824	776
H825	777
H826	779
H827	780
H828	2043
H829	781
H830	782
H831	783
H832	840
H833	841
H834	845
H835	844
H836	784
"	800
H837	748
H838	786
H839	788
H840	789
H841	790
H842	791
H843	792
H844	794
H845	793
H846	795
H847	796
H848	797
H849	798
H850	799
H851	802
H852	801
H853	803
H854	380
H855	804
H856	805
H857	805
H858	806
H859	803
H860	807
H861	808
H862	809
H863	810
H864	811
H865	812
H866	812
H867	813
H868	814
H869	815
H870	816
H871	817
H872	818
H873	819
H874	821
H875	820
H876	822
H877	823
H878	824
H879	825
H880	827
H881	828
H882	829
H883	830
H884	831
H885	832
H886	833
H887	833
H888	836
H889	834
H890	835
H891	837
H892	838
H893	838
H894	838
H895	842
H896	843
H897	835
H898	843
H899	377
H900	847
H901	848
H902	850
H903	851
H904	851
H905	859
H906	853
H907	854
H908	855
H909	856
H910	857
H911	859
H912	860
H913	862
H914	859
H915	863
H916	862
H917	859
H918	864
H919	865
H920	859
H921	866
H922	867
H923	388
H924	869
H925	868
H926	871
H927	
H928	
H929	872
H930	874
H931	875
H932	876
H933	884
H934	877
H935	879
H936	883
H937	884
H938	878
H939	880
H940	881
H941	882
H942	885
H943	886
H944	887
H945	889
H946	891
H947	890
H948	834
H949	892
H950	893
H951	894
H952	897
H953	898
H954	899
H955	899
H956	900
H957	901
H958	902
H959	1559
H960	903
H961	904
H962	904
H963	905
H964	905
H965	906
H966	907
H967	907
H968	908
H969	909
H970	910
H971	911
H972	1767
H973	912
H974	913
H975	913
H976	914
H977	915
H978	916
H979	917
H980	918
H981	919
H982	920
H983	922
H984	931
H985	923
H986	925
H987	926
H988	928
H989	929
H990	930
H991	931
H992	932
H993	933
H994	934
H995	935
H996	936
H997	937
H998	938
H999	939
H1000	940
H1001	941
H1002	942
H1003	943
H1004	945
H1005	944
H1006	944
H1007	946
H1008	947
H1009	948
H1010	949
H1011	950
H1012	951
H1013	952
H1014	953
H1015	953+5626
H1016	953+6228
H1017	954
H1018	954
H1019	955
H1020	957
H1021	958
H1022	959
"	960
"	5240
H1023	961
H1024	962
H1025	963
H1026	964
H1027	965
H1028	966
H1029	967
H1030	968
H1031	969
H1032	971
H1033	970
H1034	977
H1035	979
H1036	980
H1037	970
H1038	980
H1039	971
H1040	972
H1041	973
H1042	973
H1043	974
H1044	975
H1045	
H1046	976
H1047	977
H1048	977
H1049	978
H1050	
H1051	981
H1052	982
H1053	982
H1054	982
H1055	983
H1056	984
H1057	985
H1058	987
H1059	986
H1060	988
H1061	990
H1062	991
H1063	992
H1064	993
H1065	994
H1066	15
H1067	995
H1068	996
H1069	998
H1070	1000
H1071	953
H1072	1002
H1073	1003
H1074	1004
H1075	996
H1076	1006
H1077	1007
H1078	1008
H1079	1009
H1080	1004+791
H1081	1010
H1082	1011
H1083	1012
H1084	1013
H1085	1014
H1086	1015
H1087	1016
H1088	1017
H1089	1018
H1090	1019
H1091	1004+1588
H1092	1023
H1093	1020
H1094	1021
H1095	1022
H1096	1024
H1097	1025
H1098	1026
H1099	1027
H1100	1028
H1101	1029
H1102	1031
H1103	1032
H1104	358
H1105	1033
H1106	1034
H1107	1035
H1108	1036
H1109	1037
H1110	1010
H1111	1038
H1112	1024
H1113	1039
H1114	1040
H1115	1041
H1116	1042
H1117	1043
H1118	1044
H1119	1045
H1120	1046
H1121	1047
H1122	1048
H1123	1049
H1124	1050
H1125	1051
H1126	1052
H1127	1053
H1128	1030
H1129	1004+8425
H1130	1054
H1131	1055
H1132	1057
H1133	1056
H1134	1058
H1135	1059
H1136	1063
"	1073
H1137	1061
H1138	1064
H1139	439
H1140	1065
H1141	1066
H1142	1067
H1143	1068
H1144	1069
H1145	1070
H1146	1071
H1147	1060
H1148	1062
H1149	1072
H1150	1074
H1151	1076
H1152	1075
H1153	1077
H1154	1077
H1155	1078
H1156	1081
H1157	1112
H1158	1082
H1159	1083
H1160	1084
H1161	1085
H1162	1086
H1163	1088
H1164	1089
H1165	1087
H1166	1091
H1167	1090
H1168	1090
H1169	1092
H1170	1094
H1171	1095
H1172	1097
H1173	1098
H1174	1099
H1175	1100
H1176	1101
H1177	1101
H1178	1102
H1179	1103
H1180	1104
H1181	1104
H1182	1104
H1183	1105
H1184	1105
H1185	1106
H1186	1106
H1187	1107
H1188	1108
H1189	1109
H1190	1109
H1191	1110
H1192	1111
H1193	1114
H1194	1115
H1195	1116
H1196	1117
H1197	1118
H1198	1119
H1199	1120
H1200	1120
H1201	1121
H1202	1122
H1203	1125
H1204	1126
H1205	1127
H1206	1128
H1207	1130
H1208	2011
H1209	1132
H1210	1133
H1211	1134
H1212	1135
H1213	1136
H1214	1151
H1215	1129
H1216	
H1217	1121
H1218	1131
H1219	
H1220	1137
H1221	1138
H1222	1139
H1223	1142
H1224	1140
H1225	1141
H1226	1141
H1227	1143
H1228	1144
H1229	1145
H1230	1146
H1231	1148
H1232	1150
H1233	1152
H1234	1153
H1235	1154
"	1155
H1236	
H1237	1157
H1238	1157
H1239	1158
H1240	1158
H1241	1166
H1242	1160
H1243	1161
H1244	1162
H1245	1162
H1246	1163
H1247	1164
H1248	1165
H1249	1166
H1250	1167
H1251	1167
H1252	1168
H1253	1170
H1254	1171
H1255	1174
H1256	1176
H1257	1177
H1258	1178
H1259	1179
H1260	1186
H1261	1187
H1262	1188
H1263	1189
H1264	1190
H1265	1193
H1266	1172
"	1180
H1267	1173
H1268	1175
H1269	1182
H1270	1183
"	1184
H1271	1185
H1272	1191
H1273	1192
H1274	1194
H1275	1195
H1276	1196
H1277	1197
H1278	1197
H1279	1197
H1280	1198
H1281	1199
H1282	1200
H1283	1202
H1284	1201
H1285	1203
H1286	1204
H1287	1205
H1288	1206
H1289	1207
H1290	1208
H1291	1209
H1292	1210
H1293	1210
H1294	1211
H1295	1212
H1296	1213
H1297	1213
H1298	1214
H1299	1215
H1300	6815
H1301	1216
H1302	1217
H1303	
H1304	1218
H1305	1219
H1306	1219
H1307	1219
H1308	
H1309	1220
"	1222
H1310	1221
H1311	1221
H1312	1223
H1313	1224
H1314	1226
H1315	1225
H1316	1226
H1317	1227
H1318	1228
H1319	1229
H1320	1230
H1321	1231
H1322	1232
H1323	1233
H1324	1234
H1325	1235
H1326	1237
H1327	1238
H1328	1238
H1329	1239
H1330	1241
H1331	1242
H1332	1242
H1333	1243
H1334	1244
H1335	1245
H1336	1246
H1337	1248
H1338	1249
H1339	1250
H1340	1250
H1341	1252
H1342	1253
H1343	1254
H1344	1254
H1345	1254
H1346	1262
H1347	1255
H1348	1011
H1349	1256
H1350	1257
H1351	1258
H1352	1259
H1353	1261
H1354	1260
H1355	1260
H1356	1262
"	1274
H1357	1262
"	1274
H1358	1263
H1359	1305
H1360	1265
H1361	1266
H1362	1267
H1363	1268
H1364	1269
H1365	1269
H1366	1270
H1367	1271
H1368	1272
H1369	1272
H1370	1272
H1371	1281
H1372	1273
H1373	1275
H1374	1277
H1375	1278
H1376	1279
H1377	1282
H1378	1280
H1379	1276
H1380	1283
H1381	1284
H1382	1285
H1383	1287
H1384	1288
H1385	1288
H1386	1290
H1387	1292
H1388	1293
H1389	1294
H1390	1294
H1391	1295
H1392	1296
H1393	1296
H1394	1264
H1395	6947
H1396	1298
H1397	1299
H1398	1300
H1399	1301
H1400	1139
H1401	1302
H1402	1303
H1403	1304
H1404	1304
H1405	1305
H1406	1305
H1407	1306
H1408	1268
H1409	1307
H1410	1308
H1411	1313
"	1314
H1412	1315
H1413	1319
H1414	1320
H1415	1309
H1416	
H1417	7683
H1418	1310
H1419	1311
H1420	1312
H1421	1316
H1422	1316
H1423	1317
H1424	1318
H1425	1322
H1426	1323
H1427	1324
H1428	1004
H1429	1326
H1430	
H1431	1327
H1432	1328
H1433	1328
H1434	1329
H1435	1330
H1436	1331
H1437	1332
H1438	1333
H1439	1334
H1440	1335
H1441	1336
H1442	1337
H1443	1338
H1444	1339
H1445	1340
H1446	
H1447	1341
H1448	1342
H1449	1344
H1450	1343
H1451	1345
H1452	1346
H1453	1350
H1454	1347
H1455	1348
H1456	1349
H1457	1350
H1458	1351
H1459	1352
H1460	1353
H1461	1354
H1462	1354
H1463	1356
H1464	1356
H1465	1360
H1466	1357
H1467	1361
H1468	1362
"	1364
H1469	1364
H1470	1363
H1471	1365
H1472	1419
H1473	1366
H1474	1367
H1475	1368
H1476	1369
H1477	1371
H1478	1372
H1479	1462
H1480	1373
H1481	1374
H1482	1385
H1483	1375
H1484	1376
H1485	1377
H1486	1378
H1487	1379
H1488	1380
H1489	1381
H1490	1382
H1491	1383
H1492	1384
H1493	1386
H1494	1387
H1495	1388
H1496	1389
H1497	1390
H1498	1393
H1499	1392
H1500	1391
H1501	1394
H1502	1394
H1503	1395
H1504	1396
"	1399
H1505	1397
H1506	1398
H1507	1402
H1508	1403
H1509	1404
H1510	1405
H1511	1406
H1512	1407
H1513	1408
"	1409
H1514	1410
H1515	2735
H1516	1412
H1517	1413
H1518	1413
H1519	1415
H1520	2693
H1521	1417
H1522	1416
H1523	1418
H1524	1419
H1525	1420
H1526	1421
H1527	1422
H1528	1421
H1529	1446
H1530	1446
H1531	1423
H1532	1425
H1533	1424
H1534	1426
H1535	1427
H1536	1428
H1537	1429
H1538	1430
H1539	1430
H1540	1431
H1541	1432
H1542	1433
H1543	1435
H1544	1434
H1545	1436
H1546	1436
H1547	1437
H1548	1438
H1549	1439
H1550	1440
H1551	1441
H1552	1442
H1553	1443
H1554	1445
H1555	1444
"	1447
H1556	1448
H1557	1449
H1558	1450
H1559	1451
H1560	1448
H1561	1452
H1562	1453
H1563	1454
H1564	1455
H1565	1456
H1566	1457
H1567	1458
H1568	1460

G/K	STRONG
H1569	1460
H1570	1359
H1571	1462
H1572	1461
H1573	1463
H1574	1464
H1575	1467
H1576	1465
"	1466
H1577	1468
H1578	1469
H1579	1470
H1580	1471
H1581	1472
H1582	1471
H1583	1473
H1584	1474
H1585	1475
H1586	1476
H1587	1477
H1588	1478
H1589	1479
H1590	1480
H1591	1481
H1592	1481
H1593	1481
H1594	1482
H1595	1483
H1596	1484
H1597	1485
H1598	1486
H1599	1487
H1600	1488
H1601	1489
H1602	1491
H1603	1492
H1604	1493
H1605	1494
H1606	1495
H1607	1496
H1608	1497
H1609	1499
H1610	1498
H1611	1500
H1612	1501
H1613	1502
H1614	1503
H1615	1504
H1616	1504
H1617	1506
H1618	1507
H1619	1508
H1620	1509
H1621	1511
H1622	1518
H1623	1512
H1624	1513
H1625	1513
H1626	1514
H1627	1515
H1628	1516
H1629	2798
H1630	1517
H1631	1518
H1632	1520
H1633	1521
H1634	1522
H1635	1523
H1636	1524
H1637	1524
H1638	1525
H1639	1526
H1640	1527
H1641	1487
H1642	1529
H1643	1530
H1644	1530
H1645	1561
H1646	1531
H1647	1532
H1648	1533
H1649	1534
H1650	1534
H1651	1536
H1652	1537
H1653	1538
H1654	1539
H1655	1540
H1656	1542
H1657	1543
H1658	1544
H1659	1545
H1660	
H1661	1546
H1662	1548
H1663	1549
H1664	1550
H1665	1551
H1666	1552
H1667	1553
H1668	1554
H1669	1555
H1670	1556
H1671	1556
H1672	1557
H1673	1558
H1674	1559
H1675	1562
H1676	1563
H1677	1564
H1678	1565
H1679	1566
H1680	1568
H1681	1567
H1682	1569
H1683	1570
H1684	1543
H1685	1571
H1686	1572
H1687	1573
H1688	1574
H1689	1575
H1690	1577
H1691	1576
H1692	1578
H1693	1579
H1694	1580
H1695	1581
H1696	1582
H1697	1583
H1698	1584
H1699	1586
H1700	1586
H1701	1587
H1702	1587
H1703	1588
H1704	1589
H1705	1590
H1706	1591
H1707	1592
H1708	1593
"	1594
H1709	1595
H1710	1595
H1711	1597
H1712	5873
H1713	1598
H1714	1599
H1715	1599
H1716	1600
H1717	1601
H1718	1602
H1719	1604
H1720	1603
H1721	1605
H1722	1606
H1723	1607
H1724	1608
H1725	1609
H1726	1610
H1727	1610
H1728	1612
H1729	1613
H1730	1614
H1731	1616
H1732	1615
H1733	1617
H1734	1618
H1735	1619
H1736	1619
H1737	1620
H1738	1621
H1739	1622
H1740	1623
H1741	1624
H1742	1625
H1743	1626
H1744	1627
H1745	1628+3643
H1746	1629
H1747	1511
H1748	1630
H1749	1631
H1750	1633
H1751	1633
H1752	1634
H1753	1636
H1754	1632
H1755	1637
H1756	1638
H1757	1639
H1758	1639
H1759	1640
H1760	1641
H1761	1642
H1762	1643
H1763	1644
H1764	1644
H1765	1645
H1766	1646
H1767	1648
H1768	1647
H1769	1649
H1770	1650
H1771	1651
H1772	1652
H1773	1653
H1774	1654
H1775	1656
H1776	1654
H1777	1657
H1778	1658
H1779	1659
H1780	1660
H1781	1661
H1782	1662
"	1667
H1783	1662
H1784	1667
H1785	1663
H1786	1664
H1787	1665
H1788	1666
H1789	
H1790	1669
H1791	1670
H1792	1671
H1793	1672
H1794	1709
H1795	1673
H1796	1674
H1797	1675
H1798	1676
H1799	1756
H1800	1677
H1801	1679
H1802	
H1803	1680
H1804	1681
H1805	1682
H1806	1683
H1807	1686
H1808	1687
H1809	1688
H1810	1688
H1811	1690
H1812	1689
H1813	1691
H1814	1015
H1815	1692
H1816	1695
H1817	1694
H1818	1696
H1819	1696
H1820	1696
H1821	1697
H1822	1698
H1823	1698
H1824	1699
H1825	1699'
H1826	1700
H1827	1702
H1828	1704
H1829	1705
H1830	1703
H1831	1706
H1832	1707
H1833	1708
H1834	1709
H1835	1711
H1836	1710
H1837	1712
H1838	1713
H1839	1713
H1840	1714
H1841	1715
H1842	1716
H1843	1717
H1844	1718
H1845	1735
H1846	1734
H1847	1719
H1848	1719
"	1720
H1849	1721
H1850	1724
H1851	1725
H1852	1726
H1853	1727
H1854	1728
H1855	1729
H1856	1730
H1857	1731
H1858	1732
H1859	1736
H1860	1733
H1861	1734
H1862	1737
H1863	1736
H1864	1738
H1865	1739
H1866	1740
H1867	1741
H1868	1742
H1869	1673
H1870	1743
H1871	1744
H1872	1745
H1873	1746
H1874	1746
H1875	1747
H1876	1748
H1877	1834
H1878	1777
H1879	1777
H1880	1749
H1881	1750
H1882	1751
H1883	1752
H1884	1752
H1885	1754
H1886	1755
H1887	1755
H1888	1756
H1889	1758
H1890	1760
H1891	1760
H1892	1762
H1893	1764
H1894	1765
H1895	1766
H1896	1767
H1897	1769
H1898	1769+1410
H1899	1770
H1900	1771
H1901	1772
H1902	1773
H1903	1774
H1904	1775
H1905	1776
H1906	1777
H1907	1779
H1908	1781
H1909	1783
H1910	7384
H1911	1785
H1912	1786
H1913	1788
H1914	1787
H1915	1789
H1916	1790
H1917	1792
H1918	1793
H1919	1793
H1920	1794
H1921	1795
H1922	1796
H1923	1817
H1924	1800
H1925	1801
H1926	1802
H1927	1802
H1928	1817
H1929	1803
H1930	1803
H1931	1804
H1932	1805
H1933	1806
H1934	1806
H1935	1807
H1936	1808
H1937	1809
H1938	1809
H1939	1810
H1940	1811
H1941	1811
H1942	1812
H1943	1813
H1944	1814
H1945	1816
H1946	1817
H1947	1818
H1948	1819
H1949	1820
H1950	1820
H1951	1822
H1952	1823
H1953	1824
H1954	1824
H1955	1825
H1956	658
"	6450
H1957	1826
H1958	1826
H1959	1826
H1960	1827
H1961	1828
H1962	1829
H1963	1830
H1964	1831
H1965	1832
H1966	1834
H1967	1833
H1968	1835
H1969	1835
H1969.5	
H1970	1842
H1971	1840
H1972	1837
H1973	1838
H1974	1839
H1975	1840
H1976	1843
H1977	3045
H1978	1844
H1979	1845
H1980	1846
H1981	1847
H1982	1847
H1983	1847
H1984	1848
H1985	1849
H1986	1850
H1987	1851
H1988	1852
H1989	1853
H1990	1854
H1991	1856
H1992	1857
H1993	1858
H1994	1860
H1995	1861
H1996	1861
H1997	1862
H1998	1863
H1999	1864
H2000	1866
H2001	1865
H2002	1865
H2003	1867
H2004	1875
H2005	1869
H2006	1870
H2007	1871
H2008	1834
H2009	1873
H2010	1874
H2011	1875
H2012	1876
H2013	1877
H2014	1878
H2015	1879
H2016	1880
H2017	1881
H2018	1885
H2019	1886
H2020	
H2021	
H2022	
H2023	
H2024	
H2025	
H2026	1887
H2027	1889
H2028	326
H2029	1017
H2030	507
H2031	4965
H2032	1018
H2033	7151+704
H2034	2043
H2035	3051
H2036	8143
H2037	1890
H2038	1891
H2039	1892
H2040	1893
H2041	1894
H2042	1895
H2043	1896
H2044	2735
H2045	1419
H2046	2800+1471
H2047	1897
H2048	1898
H2049	1899
H2050	1900
H2051	1896
H2052	1901
H2053	1902
H2054	1903
H2055	1537
H2056	1588
H2057	1904
H2058	1905
H2059	1906
H2060	1908
H2061	1909
H2062	1910
H2063	1911
H2064	1912
H2065	1921
H2066	1913
H2067	1913
H2068	1914
H2069	1939
H2070	1915
H2071	1916
H2072	1918
H2073	1919
H2074	1920
H2075	1921
H2076	1924
H2077	1926
H2078	1925
H2079	1927
H2080	1928
H2081	1929
H2082	1930
H2083	
H2084	
H2085	1931
H2086	1935
H2087	1936
H2088	1937
H2089	1938
H2090	1939
H2091	1940
"	1941
H2092	1933
H2093	1933
H2094	1942
H2095	1942
H2096	1943
H2097	1944
H2098	1945
H2099	1947
H2100	1948
H2101	1949
H2102	1950
H2103	1951
H2104	1952
H2105	2029
H2106	1953
H2107	1954
H2108	1955
H2109	2050
H2110	1956
H2111	1957
H2112	6367
H2113	1958
H2114	
H2115	1931
H2116	1959
H2117	1960
H2118	1961
H2119	1962
H2120	1963
H2121	1964
H2122	1966
H2123	1967
H2124	1968
H2125	1969
H2126	4313
H2127	1020
H2128	1970
H2129	1971
H2130	1021
H2131	1973
H2132	3808
H2133	1972
H2134	1973
H2135	3873
H2136	1974
H2137	1975
H2138	1976
H2139	1977
H2140	1022
H2141	1978
H2142	1979
H2143	1980
"	3212
H2144	1982
H2145	1984
H2146	1984
H2147	1984
H2148	1985
H2149	1984+3050
H2150	1986
H2151	1988
H2152	1987
H2153	1989
H2154	1990
H2155	1991
H2156	1992
H2157	
H2158	4099
H2159	1993
H2160	1992
H2161	1992
H2162	1995
H2163	1996
H2164	1997
H2165	5555
H2166	1998
H2167	1999
H2168	4447
H2169	2000
H2170	2000
H2171	1995
H2172	2001
H2173	2003
H2174	7434
H2175	1024
H2176	2005
"	3860
H2177	2004
H2178	2008
H2179	2007
H2180	2009
H2181	
H2182	2010
H2183	2011
H2184	2012
H2185	5130
H2186	5346
H2187	2013
H2188	2013
H2189	5570
H2190	5570
H2191	5618
H2192	5863
H2193	72
H2194	3726
H2195	1025
H2196	1026
H2197	6190
H2198	2014
H2199	7163
H2200	2015
H2201	2016
"	2017
H2202	2018
H2203	2019
H2204	6483
H2205	5324
H2206	6637
H2207	6380
H2208	2020
H2209	6753
H2210	2021
H2211	2521
H2212	6976
H2213	5875
H2214	6997
H2215	2022
"	2042
H2216	2023
H2217	2024
H2218	7204
H2219	2025
H2220	7235
H2221	7235
H2222	2026
H2223	2027
H2224	2028
H2225	2029
H2226	2030
H2227	2037
H2228	2032
H2229	2033
H2230	2030
H2231	2032
H2232	2034
H2233	2035
H2234	1027
H2235	2036
H2236	2038
H2237	2039
H2238	2040
H2239	2041
H2240	2043
H2241	6890
H2242	1029
H2243	63
H2244	2044
H2245	2045
H2246	6914
H2247	2046
H2248	2266
H2249	3188
H2250	2694
H2251	2047
H2252	2048
H2253	2049
H2254	2050
H2255	
H2256	
H2257	
H2258	2051
H2259	2052
H2260	2053
H2261	2054
H2262	2055
H2263	2056
H2264	2057
H2265	2058
H2266	2059
H2267	2060
H2268	
H2269	2061
H2270	2062
H2271	2063
H2272	2064
H2273	2065
H2274	2066
H2275	2067
H2276	2068
H2277	2069
H2278	2069
H2279	2070
H2280	2071
H2281	2072
H2282	2074
H2283	2075
H2284	2076
H2285	2077
H2286	2078
H2287	2079
H2288	2080
H2289	2081
H2290	2082
H2291	2073
"	2083
H2292	2073
H2293	2085
H2294	2086
H2295	2087
H2296	2088
H2297	2090
H2298	2091
H2298.5	
H2299	2092
H2300	2093
H2301	2094
H2302	2094
H2303	2096
H2304	2099
H2305	2097
H2306	2098
H2307	2100
H2308	2101
H2309	2104
H2310	2118
H2311	2105
H2312	2106
H2313	2107
H2314	2108
H2315	2109
H2316	2111
H2317	2113
H2318	2115
"	2116
H2319	2114
H2320	2114
H2321	2117
H2322	2118
H2323	2119
H2324	2119
H2325	2120
H2326	2102
H2327	2121
H2328	2123
H2329	2123
H2330	2124
H2331	2125
H2332	2126
H2333	2127
H2334	2128
H2335	2128
H2336	2129
H2337	2130
H2338	2131
H2339	2132
H2340	2133
H2341	2134
H2342	2135
H2343	2137
H2344	2138
H2345	2138
H2346	2139
H2347	2140
H2348	2141
H2349	2142
H2350	2142
H2351	2145
H2352	2143
H2353	2144
H2354	2143

G/K	STRONG
H2355	2146
H2356	2147
H2357	2148
H2358	2148
H2359	2149
H2360	2150
H2361	2151
H2362	2151
H2363	2152
H2364	2153
H2365	2154
H2366	2155
H2367	2156
H2368	2157
H2369	2158
H2370	2159
H2371	2160
H2372	2161
H2373	2162
H2374	2163
H2375	2165
H2376	2167
H2377	2168
H2378	2169
H2379	2172
H2380	2173
H2381	2174
H2382	2174
H2383	2175
H2384	2176
H2385	2177
H2386	2179
H2387	2180
H2388	2181
H2389	2181
H2390	2181
"	2185
H2391	2182
H2392	2182
H2393	2183
H2394	2184
H2395	2186
H2396	2186
H2397	2187
H2398	2111
H2399	2188
H2400	2189
H2401	2190
H2402	2191
H2403	2193
H2404	2194
H2405	2195
H2406	2196
H2407	2196
H2408	2197
H2409	2198
H2410	2199
H2411	2201
H2412	2202
H2413	2203
H2414	2131
H2415	2131
H2416	2204
H2417	2206
H2418	2205
H2419	2207
H2420	2209
H2421	2208
H2422	2210
H2423	2212
H2424	2214
H2425	2213
H2426	2214
H2427	2215
H2428	2216
H2429	2218
H2430	2219
H2431	2219
H2432	2220
H2433	2221
H2434	2222
H2435	2223
H2436	2224
H2437	2225
H2438	2226
H2439	2227
H2440	2228
H2441	2229
H2442	2229
H2443	2230
H2444	2231
H2445	2232
H2446	2233
H2447	2235
H2448	2235
H2449	2222
H2450	2236
H2451	2236
H2452	2237
H2453	2237
H2454	2238
H2455	2239
H2456	2240
H2457	2241
H2458	2242
H2459	
H2460	2243
H2461	2244
H2462	2245
H2463	2246
H2464	2247
H2465	3160
H2466	2249
H2467	2250
H2468	2251
H2469	2252
H2470	2253
H2471	2254
H2472	2254
H2473	2254
H2474	2256
H2475	2256
H2476	2256
H2477	2256
H2478	2258
H2479	2260
H2480	2259
H2481	2258
H2482	2256
H2483	2261
H2484	2262
H2485	2263
H2486	2264
H2487	2265
H2488	2266
H2489	2266
H2490	2267
H2491	2268
H2492	2270
H2493	2271
H2494	2272
H2495	2274
H2496	2275
"	5683
H2497	2275
H2498	2276
H2499	2277
H2500	2278
H2501	2279
H2502	2280
H2503	2281
H2504	2282
H2505	2283
H2506	2284
H2507	2285
H2508	2286
H2509	2286
H2510	2287
H2511	2288
H2512	2290
H2513	2289
H2514	2290
H2515	2291
H2516	2292
H2517	2293
H2518	2294
H2519	2295
H2520	2296
H2521	2299
H2522	2297
H2523	2300
H2524	2301
H2525	2302
H2526	2302
H2527	2300
H2528	
H2529	2303
H2530	2304
H2531	2307
H2532	2308
H2533	2308
H2534	2310
H2535	2309
H2536	2311
H2537	2312
H2538	2313
H2539	2314
H2540	2315
"	2316
H2541	2317
H2542	2318
H2543	2319
H2544	2320
H2545	2321
H2546	2322
H2547	8483
H2548	2675
H2549	2325
H2550	2326
H2551	2327
H2552	2328
H2553	2329
H2554	2330
H2555	2331
H2556	2331
H2557	2333
H2558	2332
H2559	2335
H2560	2336
H2561	2337
H2562	2339
H2563	2340
H2564	2341
H2565	2342
H2566	2343
H2567	2344
H2568	2344
H2569	2345
H2570	2346
H2571	2347
H2572	2348
H2573	2349
H2574	2350
H2575	2351
H2576	2436
H2577	2712
H2578	2357
H2579	2787
H2580	2353
H2581	2354
H2582	1032
H2583	2355
H2584	2360
H2585	2359
H2586	2361
H2587	2361
H2588	2362
H2589	2773
H2590	2363
"	2439
H2591	2363
H2592	2364
H2593	2365
H2594	2366
H2595	2367
H2596	2334
H2597	2368
H2598	2369
H2599	2371
H2600	2372
H2601	2373
H2602	2374
H2603	2374
H2604	2371
H2605	2375
H2606	2377
H2607	2380
H2608	2378
H2609	2381
H2610	2382
H2611	2383
H2612	2384
H2613	2385
H2614	2386
H2615	2387
H2616	2388
H2617	2389
H2618	2390
H2619	2391
H2620	2392
H2621	2393
H2622	2394
H2623	2395
H2624	2396
H2625	2396
H2626	2397
H2627	2398
H2628	2399
H2629	2400
H2630	2398
H2631	2401
H2632	2402
H2633	2403
H2634	2404
H2635	2405
H2636	2406
H2637	2407
H2638	2410
H2639	2411
H2640	2412
H2641	2413
H2642	2414
H2643	2415
H2644	2416
H2645	2416
H2646	2416
H2647	2419
H2648	2420
H2649	2421
"	2425
H2650	2422
H2651	2416
H2652	2416
H2653	2416
H2654	2424
H2655	2342
H2656	2342
H2657	2428
H2658	2426
"	2430
H2659	2427
H2660	2427
H2661	2432
H2662	2428
H2663	2431
H2664	2432
H2665	2433
H2666	2434
H2667	2435
H2668	2436
H2669	2437
H2670	2438
H2671	2438
H2672	6367
H2673	2440
H2674	2441
H2675	2442
H2676	2443
H2677	2444
H2678	2446
H2679	2447
H2680	2448
H2681	2449
H2682	2450
H2683	2451
H2684	2454
H2685	2453
H2686	1970
H2687	2455
H2688	2456
H2689	2457
H2690	2458
H2691	2431
H2692	2461
H2693	2459
H2694	2460
H2695	2462
H2696	2463
H2697	2464
H2698	2465
H2699	2466
H2700	2467
H2701	2468
H2702	2469
H2703	2470
H2704	2470
H2705	2471
H2706	2472
H2707	2474
H2708	2473
H2709	2474
H2710	2475
H2711	2476
H2712	2477
H2713	2478
H2714	2479
H2715	2480
H2716	2483
H2717	2481
H2718	2482
H2719	2484
H2720	2485
H2721	2486
H2722	2487
H2723	2488
H2724	2489
H2725	2490
H2726	2490
H2727	2490
H2728	2491
H2729	2491
H2730	2492
H2731	2492
H2732	2494
H2733	2495
H2734	2496
H2735	2497
H2736	2498
H2737	2498
H2738	2501
H2739	2500
H2740	2502
H2741	2502
H2742	2503
H2743	2504
H2744	2505
H2745	2505
H2746	2505
H2747	2509
"	2511
H2748	2510
H2749	2506
H2750	2506
H2751	2507
H2752	2512
H2753	2513
H2754	2513
H2755	2515
H2756	2514
H2757	2516
H2758	2517
H2759	2518
H2760	2518
H2761	2519
H2762	2520
H2763	2521
H2764	2522
H2765	2522
H2766	2523
H2767	2524
H2768	2525
H2769	2526
H2770	2527
H2771	2534
H2772	2529
H2773	2530
H2774	2531
H2775	2532
H2776	2530
H2777	2533
H2778	2534
H2779	2534
H2780	2535
H2781	2536
H2782	2537
H2783	2538
H2784	2539
H2785	2540
H2786	2556
H2787	2541
H2788	2542
H2789	2543
H2790	2543
H2791	2544
H2792	2545
H2793	2546
H2794	2547
H2795	2537
H2796	2548
H2797	2549
H2798	2550
"	2565
H2799	2551
H2800	2550
H2801	2552
H2802	2553
H2803	2554
H2804	2554
H2805	2555
H2806	2556
H2807	2556
H2808	2556
H2809	2557
H2810	2558
H2811	2559
H2812	2560
H2813	2560
H2814	2560
H2815	2561
H2816	2563
H2817	2563
H2818	2563
H2819	2564
H2820	2566
H2821	2567
"	2571
H2822	2568
H2823	2569
H2824	2570
H2825	2572
H2826	2572
H2827	2573
H2828	2574
H2829	2575
H2830	2575
H2831	2576
H2832	2578
H2833	2577
H2834	2580
H2835	2581
H2836	2582
H2837	2583
H2838	2589
H2839	2584
H2840	2585
H2841	2585
H2842	2586
H2843	2587
H2844	2588
H2845	2590
H2846	2590
H2847	2590
H2848	2592
H2849	2593
H2850	2594
H2851	2595
H2852	2596
H2853	2598
H2854	2599
H2855	2600
H2856	2601
H2857	2602
H2858	2603
H2859	2603
H2860	2605
H2861	2606
H2862	2607
H2863	2608
H2864	2608
H2865	2609
H2866	2610
H2867	2611
H2868	2611
H2869	2612
H2870	2613
H2871	2614
H2872	2615
H2873	2616
H2874	2616
H2875	2617
H2876	2617
H2877	2618
H2878	2619
H2879	2620
H2880	2621
H2881	2621
H2882	2622
H2883	2623
H2884	2624
H2885	2625
H2886	2626
H2887	2628
H2888	2629
H2889	2630
H2890	2633
H2891	2634
H2892	2636
H2893	2637
H2894	2638
H2895	2639
H2896	2640
H2897	2641
H2898	2642
H2899	2643
H2900	5502
H2901	2644
H2902	2645
H2903	2646
H2904	2647
H2905	2648
H2906	2649
H2907	2650
H2908	2651
H2909	2652
H2910	2653
H2911	2654
H2912	2654
H2913	2655
H2914	2656
H2915	2657
H2916	2658
H2917	2659
H2918	2660
H2919	2660
H2920	2662
H2921	2663
H2922	6548
H2923	2661+6512
H2924	2664
H2925	2665
H2926	2666
H2927	2667
H2928	2668
H2929	2669
H2930	2670
H2931	2669
H2932	2671
H2933	2672
H2934	2672
H2935	2672
H2936	2673
H2937	2674
H2938	2674
H2939	2675
H2940	2676
H2941	7155
H2942	2677
H2943	2678
H2944	2677
H2945	2682
H2946	2682
H2947	2682
H2948	2681
H2949	2683
H2950	2684
H2951	2686
H2952	2686
H2953	2687
H2954	2688
H2955	2690
H2956	2689
H2957	2690
H2958	2691
"	2699
H2959	2694
H2960	2692
H2961	2693
H2962	2694
H2963	2701
H2964	2702
H2965	2703
H2966	2704
H2967	2705
H2968	2695
H2969	2696
H2970	2696
H2971	2697
H2972	2698
H2973	2691
H2974	2695
H2975	2700
H2976	2706
H2977	2707
H2978	2708
H2979	2709
H2980	2710
H2981	2711
H2982	2712
H2983	2713
H2984	2714
H2985	2715
H2986	2356
H2987	2352
H2988	2735
H2989	2716
H2990	2717
H2991	2717
H2992	2720
H2993	2717
H2994	
H2995	2719
H2996	2721
H2997	2721
H2998	2722
H2999	2723
H3000	2724
H3001	2725
H3002	2726
H3003	2726
H3004	2727
H3005	2728
H3006	2729
H3007	2730
H3008	5878
H3009	2733
H3010	2731
H3011	2732
H3012	2733
H3013	2734
"	8474
H3014	2787
H3015	2736
H3016	2737
H3017	2738
H3018	2739
H3019	2740
H3020	2741
H3021	2742
H3022	2742
H3023	2742
H3024	2782
H3025	2742
H3026	2742
H3027	2743
H3028	2744
H3029	2736
H3030	2745
H3031	2746
H3032	2747
H3033	2748
H3034	2750
H3035	2751
H3036	2752
H3037	2753
H3038	2754
H3039	2755
H3040	2756
H3041	
H3042	2741
H3043	2757
H3044	2757
H3045	2758
H3046	2759
H3047	2760
H3048	2762
H3049	2763
H3050	2763
H3051	2764
H3052	2764
H3053	2766
H3054	2765
H3055	2767
H3056	2768
H3057	2769
H3058	2770
H3059	2771
H3060	2771
H3061	2772
H3062	2774
H3063	2775
H3064	2775
H3065	2776
H3066	2775
H3067	2777
H3068	2777
H3069	2778
H3070	2778
H3071	2778
H3072	2778
H3073	2780
H3074	2779
H3075	2781
H3076	2782
H3077	2782
H3078	2784
H3079	2785
H3080	2786
H3081	2787
H3082	2787
H3083	2788
H3084	2789
H3085	7025
H3086	2790
"	2794
H3087	2790
H3088	2796
H3089	2791
H3090	2792
H3091	2793
H3092	2793
H3093	2796
H3094	2795
H3095	2797
H3096	2798
H3097	7025
H3098	2799
H3099	2800+1471
H3100	2801
H3101	2802
H3102	2817
H3103	2834
H3104	2820
H3105	2835
H3106	2834
H3107	2834
H3108	2803
H3109	2805
H3110	2803
H3111	2806
H3112	2807
H3113	2808
H3114	2809
H3115	2810
H3116	2811
H3117	2811
H3118	2812
H3119	2813
H3120	2814
H3121	2815
H3122	2838
H3123	2366
H3124	2821
H3125	2822
H3126	2823
H3127	2821
H3128	2824
"	2825
H3129	2826
H3130	2828
H3131	2366
H3132	2829
H3133	2830
H3134	2831
H3135	2832
H3136	2833
H3137	2836
H3138	2836
H3139	2837
H3140	2839
H3141	2840

G/K	STRONG
H3142	2841
H3143	2842
H3144	2843
H3145	2844
H3146	2844
H3147	2845
H3148	2398
H3149	2846
H3150	2847
H3151	2848
H3152	2849
H3153	2850
H3154	2851
H3155	2852
H3156	2853
H3157	2854
H3158	2855
H3159	2856
H3160	2858
H3161	2859
H3162	2859
H3163	2860
H3164	2861
H3165	2859
H3166	2862
H3167	2863
H3168	2864
H3169	2865
H3170	2866
H3171	2867
H3172	
H3173	2894
H3174	2870
H3175	2870
H3176	2896
H3177	2896
H3178	2871
H3179	2872
H3180	2873
H3181	2874
H3182	2875
H3183	2874
H3184	2876
H3185	2879
H3186	2878
H3187	2880
H3188	2881
H3189	2882
H3190	2883
H3191	2884
H3192	2885
H3193	2886
H3194	2887
H3195	2888
H3196	2889
"	2890
H3197	2891
H3198	2892
H3199	2892
H3200	2893
H3201	2896
H3202	2896
H3203	2897
H3204	2897
H3205	2896
H3206	2898
H3207	2899
H3208	2896
H3209	2900
H3210	2900
H3211	2901
H3212	2902
H3213	2903
H3214	2904
H3215	2905
H3216	2907
H3217	2909
H3218	2911
H3219	2910
H3220	2902
H3221	2912
H3222	2913
H3223	2912
H3224	2914
H3225	2915
H3226	2916
H3227	2918
H3228	2919
H3229	2921
H3230	2923
H3231	2922
"	2924
H3232	2925
H3233	2926
H3234	2928
H3235	2928
H3236	2929
H3237	2930
H3238	2931
H3239	2930
H3240	2932
H3241	2933
H3242	2933
H3243	2934
H3244	2935
H3245	2936
H3246	2937
H3247	2938
H3248	2940
H3249	2944
H3250	2943
H3251	2945
H3252	2945
H3253	2946
H3254	2946
H3255	2947
H3256	2948
H3257	2947
H3258	2947
H3259	2949
H3260	2950
H3261	2951
H3262	2952
H3263	2954
H3264	2955
H3265	2956
H3266	2958
H3267	2959
H3268	2960
H3269	2961
H3270	2962
H3271	2963
H3272	2964
H3273	2965
H3274	2966
H3275	
H3276	
H3277	2968
H3278	2969
H3279	2970
H3280	2970
H3281	2971
H3282	2973
H3283	2974
H3284	2975
H3285	2972
H3286	2976
H3287	2977
H3288	2977
H3289	2978
H3290	2979
H3291	2980
H3292	2981
H3293	2982
H3294	2983
H3295	2984
H3296	2985
H3297	2986
H3298	2988
H3299	2989
H3300	2991
H3301	2990
H3302	2992
H3303	2993
H3304	2994
H3305	2995
H3306	2996
H3307	2997
H3308	2998
H3309	2999
H3310	3000
H3311	3005
H3312	3001
H3313	3002
H3314	3003
H3315	3003
H3316	3003
H3317	3004
H3318	3006
H3319	3008
H3320	3009
H3321	3010
H3322	3011
H3323	3012
H3324	3013
H3325	3014
H3326	3015
H3327	3017
H3328	3016
H3329	3019
H3330	3018
H3331	3024
H3332	3020
H3333	3021
H3334	3022
H3335	3023
H3336	3025
H3337	3026
H3338	3027
H3339	3030
H3340	3031
H3341	3032
H3342	3033
H3343	3034
H3344	3034
H3345	3035
H3346	3035
H3347	3036
H3348	3037
H3349	3038
H3350	3035
H3351	3039
H3352	3040
H3353	3038
H3354	3041
H3355	3042
H3356	3043
H3357	3038
H3358	3044
H3359	3045
H3360	3047
H3361	3048
H3362	3049
H3363	3050
H3364	3051
H3365	3053
H3366	3054
H3367	3056
H3368	3057
H3369	3058
H3370	3059
H3371	3060
H3372	3055
H3373	3063
H3374	3064
H3375	3065
H3376	3066
H3377	3067
H3378	3068
"	3069
H3379	3075
H3380	3076
H3381	3077
H3382	3078
H3383	3079
H3384	3080
H3385	3081
H3386	3082
H3387	3083
H3388	3084
H3389	3085
H3390	3086
H3391	3086
H3392	3087
H3393	3088
H3394	3089
H3395	3090
H3396	
H3397	3091
H3398	3092
H3399	3092
H3400	3093
H3401	3094
H3402	3095
H3403	3096
H3404	3096
H3405	3097
H3406	3098
H3407	3099
H3408	3100
H3409	3101
H3410	3102
H3411	3103
H3412	3103
H3413	3104
H3414	3105
H3415	3106
H3416	3107
H3417	3108
H3418	3109
H3419	3110
H3420	3194
H3421	3111
H3422	3112
H3423	3113
H3424	3114
H3425	3115
H3426	3116
H3427	3117
H3428	3117
H3429	3119
H3430	3120
H3431	3121
H3432	3122
H3433	3123
H3434	3124
H3435	3238
H3436	3125
H3437	3126
H3438	3127
H3439	3128
H3440	3129
H3441	3130
H3442	3131
H3443	3132
H3444	3133
H3445	3134
H3446	3289
H3447	3135
H3448	3318
H3449	3136
H3450	3335
H3451	3079
"	3137
H3452	3384
H3453	3138
H3454	3088
"	3139
H3455	3140
H3456	3141
H3457	3142
H3458	3143
H3459	3144
H3460	3145
H3461	3146
H3462	3147
H3463	3148
H3464	3149
H3465	3149
H3466	3150
H3467	3151
H3468	3152
H3469	2109
H3470	3153
H3471	3153
H3472	3154
H3473	3155
H3474	3156
H3475	3157
H3476	3157
H3477	3158
"	3159
H3478	3160
H3479	3161
H3480	3162
H3481	3162
H3482	3163
H3483	
H3484	3164
H3485	3165
H3486	3171
H3487	3166
H3488	3167
H3489	3168
H3490	3169
H3491	3169
H3492	3170
H3493	3171
H3494	3172
H3495	3173
H3496	3174
H3497	3175
H3498	3176
H3499	3177
H3500	3178
H3501	3179
H3502	3180
H3503	3181
H3504	3182
H3505	3183
H3506	3184
H3507	3185
H3508	3186
H3509	3187
H3510	3188
H3511	3189
H3512	2895
"	3190
H3513	3192
H3514	3193
H3515	3195
H3516	3196
H3517	3197
H3518	3204
H3519	3198
H3520	3199
H3521	3199
H3522	3200
H3523	3201
H3524	3203
H3525	3203
H3526	3204
H3527	3204
H3528	3205
H3529	3206
H3530	3207
H3531	3208
H3532	3856
H3533	3209
H3534	3210
H3535	3211
H3536	3213
H3537	3214
H3538	3215
H3539	3217
H3540	3218
H3541	3219
H3542	3220
H3543	3223
H3544	3224
H3545	3225
H3546	3226
H3547	3228
H3548	3233
H3549	3227
H3550	3229
H3551	3229
H3552	3230
H3553	3222
H3554	3231
H3555	3232
H3556	3233
H3557	3234
H3558	3235
H3559	3236
H3560	3237
H3561	3238
H3562	3239
H3563	3239
H3564	3241
H3565	3241
H3566	3242
H3567	3243
"	5134
H3568	3244
H3569	3245
H3570	3245
H3571	3246
H3572	3247
H3573	3248
H3574	3250
H3575	3251
H3576	3252
H3577	3253
H3578	3254
H3579	3256
H3580	3256
H3581	3256
H3582	3257
H3583	3258
H3584	3258
H3585	3259
H3586	3294
H3587	3260
H3588	3260
H3589	3261
H3590	3262
H3591	3263
H3592	3265
H3593	3266
H3594	3267
H3595	3268
H3596	3269
H3597	3270
H3598	3271
H3599	3273
H3600	3265
H3601	3274
H3602	3275
H3603	3276
H3604	3277
H3605	3278
H3606	3279
H3607	3280
H3608	3279
H3609	3281
H3610	3282
H3611	
H3612	3283
H3613	3284
H3614	3285
H3615	3286
H3616	3288
H3617	3287
H3618	3288
H3619	3289
H3620	3290
H3621	3291
H3622	3292
H3623	3264
"	3293
H3624	3293
H3625	3293
H3626	3295
H3627	3295
H3628	3294
H3629	3296
H3630	3297
H3631	3298
H3632	3299
H3633	3299
H3634	3300
H3635	3301
H3636	3302
H3637	3303
H3638	3304
H3639	3305
H3640	3306
H3641	3307
H3642	3308
H3643	3309
H3644	3309
H3645	3304
H3646	3310
H3647	3311
H3648	3312
H3649	3313
H3650	3314
H3651	3315
H3652	3316
H3653	3316
H3654	3317
H3655	3318
H3656	3320
H3657	3322
H3658	3323
H3659	3324
H3660	3325
H3661	3326
H3662	3326
H3663	3327
H3664	3328
H3665	3329
H3666	3326
H3667	3331
H3668	3332
H3669	3333
H3670	3335
H3671	3336
H3672	3337
"	3340
H3673	3339
H3674	3338
H3675	3341
H3676	3342
H3677	3343
H3678	3344
H3679	3350
H3680	3347
H3681	3348
H3682	3349
H3683	3344
H3684	2901
"	6990
H3685	3351
H3686	3352
H3687	3353
H3688	3354
H3689	3947
H3690	3355
H3691	3356
H3692	3357
H3693	3359
H3694	3360
H3695	3361
H3696	3362
H3697	3363
H3698	3368
H3699	3364
H3700	3365
H3701	3368
H3702	3366
H3703	3368
H3704	3369
H3705	3370
H3706	3371
H3707	3372
H3708	3372
H3709	3384
H3710	3373
H3711	3374
H3712	3375
H3713	3376
H3714	3377
H3715	3378
H3716	3379
H3717	3380
H3718	3381
H3719	3382
H3720	3383
H3721	3384
H3722	3384
H3723	3384
H3724	7297
H3725	3385
H3726	3386
H3727	7311
H3728	3387
H3729	3388
H3730	3388
H3731	3389
H3732	3391
H3733	3392
H3734	3394
H3735	3405
H3736	3395
H3737	3396
H3738	3397
H3739	3398
H3740	3399
H3741	3400
H3742	3401
H3743	3402
H3744	3403
H3745	3404
H3746	3404
H3747	3405
H3748	3406
H3749	3407
H3750	3408
H3751	3409
H3752	3411
H3753	7311
H3754	3412
H3755	3406
H3756	3406
H3757	3413
H3758	3414
H3759	3414
H3760	3415
H3761	3416
H3762	3417
H3763	3419
H3764	3418
H3765	4313
H3766	3420
H3767	3421
H3768	3422
H3769	3423
H3770	8492
H3771	3424
H3772	3425
H3773	3446
H3774	3450
H3775	3455
H3776	3478
H3777	3480
H3778	3481
"	3482
H3779	3485
H3780	3426
H3781	
H3782	3427
H3783	3429
H3784	3428
H3785	3430
H3786	3431
H3787	3430
H3788	3433
H3789	
H3790	3434
H3791	3435
H3792	3436
H3793	3437
H3794	3427
H3795	3432
H3796	3438
H3797	3439
H3798	3440
H3799	3441
H3800	3442
H3801	3442
H3802	3444
H3803	3445
H3804	3447
H3805	3448
H3806	3437
H3807	3449
H3808	3449
H3809	3451
H3810	3452
H3811	1020
H3812	3451
H3813	3453
H3814	3454
H3815	3456
H3816	3457
H3817	3458
H3818	3459
H3819	3460
H3820	3460
H3821	3461
H3822	3462
"	8153
H3823	3462
H3824	3465
H3825	3463
H3826	3464
H3827	3466
H3828	3467
H3829	3468
H3830	3467
H3831	3469
H3832	3470
H3833	3470
H3834	3472
H3835	3471
H3836	3473
H3837	3474
H3838	3477
H3839	3477
H3840	3475
H3841	3476
H3842	3483
H3843	3484
H3844	3486
H3845	3489
H3846	3490
H3847	3491
H3848	3492
H3849	3494
H3850	3495
H3851	5414
H3852	5414
H3853	3496
H3854	3497
H3855	3498
H3856	3499
H3857	3499
H3858	3500
H3859	3501
H3860	3502
H3861	3503
H3862	3504
H3863	3505
H3864	3506
H3865	3507
H3866	3508
H3867	3509
H3868	
H3869	
H3870	
H3871	
H3872	3510
H3873	3511
H3874	3512
H3875	2489
H3876	834
H3877	3513
H3878	3515
H3879	3516
H3880	3514
H3881	3517
H3882	3518
H3883	3519
H3884	3520
H3885	3520
H3886	3521
H3887	3522
H3888	3524
H3889	3523
H3890	3525
H3891	3526
H3892	3527
"	4342
H3893	3528
H3894	3529
H3895	3531
H3896	3530
H3897	3532
H3898	3535
H3899	3533
H3900	3534
H3901	3536
H3902	3537
H3903	1754
H3904	1767
H3905	3539
H3906	3540
H3907	3541
H3908	3543
H3909	3543
H3910	3544
H3911	3545
H3912	3547
H3913	3548
H3914	3550
H3915	3552
H3916	3553
H3917	3554
H3918	3555
H3919	3556
H3920	3557
H3921	3558
H3922	3559
H3923	3560
H3924	3561
H3925	3562
H3926	3563
H3927	3563

G/K	STRONG
H3928	3738
H3929	3564
H3930	3565
H3931	3566
H3932	3568
H3933	3568
H3934	3569
"	3571
H3935	3570
H3936	3572
H3937	3573
H3938	3574
H3939	3575
H3940	3575
H3941	3576
H3942	3577
H3943	3578
H3944	3579
H3945	3580
H3946	3581
H3947	3581
H3948	3582
H3949	3583
H3950	3584
H3951	3585
H3952	3586
H3953	3587
H3954	3588
H3955	3588+518
H3956	3588+408+3651
H3957	3589
H3958	3590
H3959	3591
H3960	3593
H3961	3592
H3962	3594
H3963	3595
H3964	3596
H3965	3597
H3966	3598
H3967	3599
H3968	3600
H3969	3601
H3970	3602
H3971	3603
H3972	3605
H3973	3607
H3974	3607
H3975	3608
H3976	3609
H3977	3610
H3978	3611
H3979	3612
H3980	3613
H3981	3612
H3982	3614
H3983	3615
H3984	3607
H3985	3616
H3986	3617
H3987	3618
H3988	3622
H3989	3628
H3990	3619
H3991	3620
H3992	3621
H3993	3622
H3994	3623
H3995	3624
H3996	3625
H3997	3626
H3998	3627
H3999	3628
H4000	3629
H4001	3631
H4002	3630
H4003	3632
H4004	3633
H4005	3634
H4006	3636
H4007	3637
H4008	3638
H4009	3639
H4010	3640
H4011	3641
H4012	3641
H4013	
H4014	3642
H4015	3588+4100
H4016	3643
H4017	3644
H4018	3643
H4019	3645
H4020	3645
H4021	3646
H4022	3647
H4023	3648
H4024	3649
H4025	3650
H4026	3651
H4027	3651
H4028	3651
H4029	3653
H4030	3653
H4031	3654
H4032	
H4033	3655
H4034	3656
H4035	3657
H4036	3658
H4037	3659
H4038	3654
H4039	3662
H4040	3663
H4041	3663
H4042	3663
H4043	3664
H4044	3665
H4045	3666
H4046	3667
H4047	3667
H4048	3669
H4049	3668
H4050	3669
H4051	3669
H4052	3670
H4053	3671
H4054	3672
H4055	3672
H4056	3674
H4057	3677
H4058	3676
"	3678
H4059	3680
H4060	3677
H4061	3678
H4062	3681
H4063	3694
H4064	3682
H4065	3683
H4066	3678+3050
H4067	3684
H4068	3685
H4069	3686
H4070	3687
H4071	3688
H4072	3689
H4073	3689
H4074	3690
H4075	3691
H4076	3693
H4077	3692
H4078	3695
H4079	3696
H4080	3697
H4081	3698
H4082	3699
H4083	3700
H4084	3701
H4085	3703
H4086	3704
H4087	3707
H4088	3708
H4089	3708
H4090	3709
H4091	3710
H4092	3711
H4093	3712
H4094	3713
H4095	3713
H4096	3714
H4097	3715
H4098	3716
H4099	3715
H4100	3717
H4101	3718
H4102	3719
H4103	3720
H4104	3721
H4105	3722
H4106	3722
H4107	3723
H4108	3724
H4109	3724
H4110	3724
H4111	3724
H4112	3726
H4113	3725
H4114	3727
H4115	3728
H4116	3731
H4117	3730
H4118	3732
H4119	3733
H4120	3733
H4121	3733
H4122	1033
H4123	3734
H4124	3736
H4125	3738
H4126	3739
H4127	3738
H4128	3738
H4129	3741
H4130	3740
H4131	3742
H4132	3743
H4133	3746
H4134	3747
H4135	3748
H4136	3749
H4137	3750
H4138	3751
H4139	3752
H4140	3753
H4141	3755
H4142	3754
H4143	
H4144	3755
H4145	3756
H4146	3757
H4147	3758
H4148	3754
H4149	3759
H4150	3760
H4151	3760
H4152	3759
H4153	3761
"	3762
H4154	3763
H4155	3765
H4156	3766
H4157	3767
H4158	3768
H4159	3769
H4160	3770
H4161	3771
H4162	3772
H4163	
H4164	3773
H4165	3774
H4166	3775
H4167	3776
H4168	3777
H4169	3778
H4170	3780
H4171	7911
H4172	3781
H4173	3782
H4174	3783
H4175	3784
H4176	3785
H4177	3786
H4178	3787
H4179	3788
H4180	3789
H4181	3791
H4182	3793
H4183	3794
H4184	3795
H4185	3796
H4186	3798
H4187	3799
H4188	3800
H4189	3801
H4190	3802
H4191	8596
H4192	3803
H4193	3803
H4194	3803
H4195	3804
H4196	3805
H4197	3806
H4198	3807
H4199	
H4200	
H4201	
H4202	3808
H4203	3810
H4204	3818
H4205	3819
H4206	3811
H4207	3812
H4208	1975
H4209	3813
H4210	3815
H4211	3816
H4212	3817
H4213	3820
H4214	3820+6965
H4215	935
H4216	3833
H4217	2574
H4218	3833
H4219	3822
H4220	3823
H4221	3823
H4222	3824
H4223	3834
H4224	905
H4225	3827
H4226	3826
H4227	3828
H4228	3829
H4229	3830
H4230	3830
H4231	3832
H4232	3833
H4233	3833
H4234	3833
H4235	3835
H4236	3835
H4237	3836
H4238	3837
H4239	3837
H4240	1121
H4241	3838
H4242	3839
H4243	3841
H4244	3842
H4245	3838
H4246	3840
"	3843
H4247	3828
H4248	3844
H4249	3845
H4250	3846
H4251	7884
H4252	3847
H4253	3849
H4254	3850
H4255	1688
H4256	3205
H4257	3808
H4258	3851
H4259	3852
H4260	3853
H4261	3854
H4262	3855
H4263	3856
H4264	3856
H4265	3857
H4266	3857
H4267	3858
H4268	3858
H4269	3859
H4270	
H4271	3856
H4272	3862
H4273	3863
H4274	3810
H4275	3864
H4276	3865
"	3866
H4277	3867
H4278	3867
H4279	3868
H4280	3869
H4281	3870
H4282	
H4283	3871
H4284	3872
H4285	3873
H4286	3874
H4287	3875
H4288	3876
H4289	3877
H4290	3878
H4291	3878
"	3881
H4292	3880
H4293	3882
H4294	3883
H4295	3884
H4296	3885
H4297	3888
H4298	3889
"	3919
H4299	3891
H4300	3892
H4301	3893
H4302	3894
H4303	3894
H4304	3872
H4305	3895
H4306	3896
H4307	883
H4308	3897
H4309	3898
H4310	3898
H4311	3901
H4312	3899
H4313	3902
H4314	3903
H4315	3905
H4316	3906
H4317	3907
H4318	3908
H4319	3814
H4223	3909
H4320	3910
H4321	3911
H4322	3912
H4323	3913
H4324	3914
H4325	3915
H4326	3915
H4327	3917
H4328	3885
H4329	3887
H4330	3918
H4331	3919
H4332	3919
H4333	3919
H4334	3920
H4335	3921
H4336	3922
H4337	3923
H4338	3651
H4339	3924
H4340	3925
H4341	3928
H4342	4100
H4343	
H4344	3926
H4345	3927
H4346	4136
H4347	3929
H4348	4616
H4349	3885
H4350	3930
H4351	3931
H4352	3932
H4353	3933
H4354	3934
H4355	3935
H4356	3936
H4357	3937
H4358	3938
H4359	
H4360	3939
H4361	6030
H4362	3886
H4363	3216
H4364	1036
H4365	3940
H4366	3941
H4367	6440
H4368	6440
H4369	3943
H4370	3887
H4371	3944
H4372	3945
H4373	3946
H4374	3947
H4375	3948
H4376	3949
H4377	3950
H4378	3951
H4379	3952
H4380	3953
H4381	3954
H4382	3955
H4383	3956
H4384	3957
H4385	3958
H4386	3959
H4387	3960
H4388	3962
H4389	8289
H4390	3963
H4391	
H4392	
H4393	3965
H4394	3966
H4395	3967
H4396	3968
H4397	3970
H4398	3971
H4399	3972
H4400	3973
H4401	3974
H4402	3975
H4403	
H4404	3976
H4405	3967
H4406	369
H4407	3978
H4408	3979
H4409	3980
H4410	3981
H4411	3982
H4412	3985
H4413	3986
H4414	3987
H4415	3988
H4416	3988
H4417	622
H4418	3989
H4419	3990
H4420	3991
H4421	3992
H4422	3993
H4423	3994
H4424	834
H4425	854
H4426	3995
H4427	3996
"	3997
H4428	3998
H4429	3999
H4430	4000
H4431	4001
H4432	4002
H4433	4003
H4434	4016
H4435	4004
H4436	4005
H4437	4006
H4438	4007
H4439	4008
H4440	4009
H4441	
H4442	1097
H4443	4010
H4444	1110
H4445	4011
H4446	4012
H4447	
H4448	4013
H4449	4014
H4450	4013
H4451	4015
H4452	4017
H4453	4018
H4454	7248
H4455	4019
H4456	4020
H4457	4021
H4458	4022
"	4030
H4459	4023
H4460	4024
H4461	4023
H4462	4025
H4463	4026
H4464	4027
"	4028
H4465	4024
H4466	4027
H4467	4028
H4468	4029
H4469	4030
H4470	4031
H4471	4032
H4472	4033
H4473	4033
H4474	4036
H4475	4034
H4476	4035
H4477	4037
H4478	4038
H4479	4039
H4480	4041
H4481	4042
H4482	4043
H4483	4043
H4484	4043
H4485	4044
H4486	4045
H4487	4046
H4488	4047
H4489	4048
H4490	4050
H4491	4051
H4492	4052
H4493	4053
H4494	4054
H4495	4054
H4496	4055
H4497	4057
H4498	4057
H4499	4058
"	4059
H4500	4060
H4501	4060
H4502	4062
H4503	4063
H4504	4064
H4505	4065
H4506	4066
"	4079
"	4090
H4507	4068
H4508	4069
H4509	4071
H4510	4072
H4511	4073
H4512	4074
H4513	4075
H4514	1767
H4515	4060
H4516	4081
H4517	4067
H4518	4080
H4519	4082
H4520	4084
"	4092
H4521	4085
H4522	4086
H4523	4087
H4524	4088
H4525	4089
H4526	4089
H4527	4091
H4528	4067
H4529	4093
H4530	4129
H4531	4130
H4532	4094
H4533	4095
H4534	4096
H4535	4097
H4536	4098
H4537	4100
H4538	4102
H4539	4103
H4540	4104
H4541	4105
H4542	4106
H4543	4107
H4544	4108
"	4109
H4545	4110
H4546	4111
H4547	4112
H4548	
H4549	4113
H4550	4114
H4551	4115
H4552	65
H4553	
H4554	4116
H4555	4117
H4556	4117
H4557	4118
H4558	4119
H4559	4120
H4560	4121
H4561	4122
H4562	4123
H4563	
H4564	
H4565	4124
H4566	4124
H4567	4125
H4568	4136
H4569	4126
H4570	4127
H4571	4128
H4572	4131
H4573	4132
H4574	4133
H4575	4134
H4576	4135
H4577	4135
H4578	4136
H4579	4137
H4580	4138
H4581	4139
H4582	4140
H4583	3971
H4584	4462
H4585	5439
H4586	4143
H4587	4144
H4588	4145
"	4328
H4589	4146
H4590	4329
H4591	4147
H4592	4148
H4593	4147
H4594	4149
H4595	4150
H4596	4151
H4597	4152
H4598	4153
H4599	4155
H4600	4156
H4601	4157
H4602	4158
H4603	4159
H4604	4161
H4605	4162
H4606	4163
H4607	4164
H4608	4165
H4609	4166
H4610	4167
H4611	4168
H4612	4169
H4613	4170
H4614	4171
H4615	4171
H4616	4172
H4617	4173
H4618	4174
H4619	4175
H4620	4175
H4621	4175
H4622	4176
H4623	4177
H4624	4172
H4625	4180
H4626	4180
H4627	4181
H4628	4182
H4629	4183
H4630	4184
H4631	4185
H4632	4186
H4633	4187
H4634	4188
H4635	3467
H4636	4190
H4637	4191
"	4192
H4638	4194
H4639	4195
H4640	4196
H4641	4197
H4642	4198
H4643	4100+2088
H4644	4100+2088
H4645	4199
H4646	4200
H4647	4201
H4648	4202
H4649	4205
H4650	4204
H4651	4206
H4652	4206
H4653	4206
H4654	2142
H4655	4208
H4656	4207
H4657	4207
H4658	4207
H4659	4209
H4660	4210
H4661	4211
H4662	4212
H4663	4213
H4664	2219
H4665	4214
H4666	4216
H4667	4217
H4668	2219
"	4215
H4669	4218
H4670	4219
H4671	4220
H4672	4221
H4673	4222
H4674	4229
H4675	4224
H4676	4224
H4677	4226
H4678	4225
H4679	4227
H4680	4228
H4681	4229
H4682	4229
H4683	4229
H4684	4230
H4685	4231
H4686	4232
H4687	4233
H4688	4234
H4689	4235
H4690	4236
H4691	4237
H4692	4238
H4693	4239
H4694	4240
H4695	4241
H4696	4232
H4697	4242
H4698	4243
H4699	2256+392
H4700	4245
H4701	4245
H4702	4244
H4703	4246
H4704	4247
H4705	4248
H4706	4249
H4707	4250

G/K	STRONG
H4708	4251
H4709	4252
H4710	4253
H4711	4254
H4712	5555
H4713	4256
H4714	4257
H4715	4258
H4716	4259
H4717	4260
H4718	4261
H4719	4262
H4720	4263
H4721	2557
H4722	4264
H4723	4265
H4724	4266
H4725	4267
H4726	4268
H4727	4269
H4728	4270
H4729	4271
H4730	4272
H4731	4273
H4732	4274
H4733	4275
H4734	4276
H4735	4277
H4736	4278
H4737	4279
H4738	4280
H4739	4281
"	4282
H4740	4283
H4741	4286
H4742	4284
H4743	4285
H4744	4287
H4745	4288
H4746	4289
H4747	4290
H4748	4292
H4749	4293
H4750	
H4751	4294
H4752	4295
H4753	4296
H4754	4297
H4755	4298
H4756	2892
H4757	4299
H4758	4300
H4759	4301
H4760	4302
H4761	4303
H4762	4304
H4763	4305
H4764	4306
H4765	4308
H4766	4307
H4767	4309
H4768	4100
H4769	4310
H4770	4313
H4771	4314
H4772	4311
H4773	4312
H4774	4315
H4775	4316
H4776	4317
H4777	4318
H4778	4319
H4779	4320
H4780	4322
H4781	4321
H4782	4323
H4783	4324
H4784	4325
H4785	4326
H4786	4327
H4787	3243
H4788	4329
H4789	4158
H4790	4330
H4791	4331
H4792	4332
H4793	4334
H4794	4335
H4795	4338
H4796	4337
H4797	4339
H4798	4340
H4799	4341
H4800	4343
H4801	4344
H4802	4346
H4803	4345
H4804	4347
H4805	4348
H4806	4349

G/K	STRONG
H4807	4350
"	4369
H4808	4351
H4809	4352
H4810	4353
H4811	4354
H4812	4355
H4813	4356
H4814	4358
H4815	4360
H4816	4357
H4817	4359
H4818	4361
H4819	4362
H4820	4363
H4821	4364
H4822	4365
H4823	4365
H4824	4365
H4825	4363
H4826	4366
H4827	4367
H4828	4368
H4829	4370
H4830	4371
H4831	4373
H4832	4372
H4833	4374
H4834	4375
H4835	4376
H4836	4377
H4837	4378
H4838	4379
H4839	4380
H4840	4381
H4841	4382
H4842	4383
H4843	4384
H4844	4385
H4845	4386
H4846	4387
H4847	4388
"	4389
H4848	4390
H4849	4392
H4850	4393
H4851	4407
H4852	4395
H4853	4396
H4854	4394
H4855	4397
H4856	4399
H4857	4400
H4858	4401
H4859	4402
H4860	4403
H4861	4404
H4862	4390
H4863	4405
H4864	4407
H4865	4408
H4866	4409
H4867	4410
H4868	4409
H4869	4411
H4870	4412
H4871	4413
H4872	4414
H4873	4414
H4874	4418
H4875	4417
H4876	4419
H4877	4420
H4878	4421
H4879	4423
H4880	4422
H4881	4422
H4882	4424
H4883	4409
H4884	4425
H4885	3887
"	3945
H4886	4426
H4887	4427
H4888	4427
H4889	4428
"	4429
H4890	4428
H4891	4432
H4892	4434
H4893	4436
H4894	4435
H4895	4438
H4896	4439
H4897	4440
H4898	4441
H4899	4441
H4900	4442
H4901	4443
H4902	4444

G/K	STRONG
H4903	4445
H4904	4445
H4905	4404
H4906	4446
H4907	4447
H4908	5243
H4909	5243
H4910	4448
H4911	4448
H4912	4450
H4913	4451
H4914	4452
H4915	4453
H4916	4454
H4917	4455
H4918	4455
H4919	4456
H4920	4457
H4921	4458
H4922	4459
H4923	4460
H4924	4461
H4925	4462
H4926	4463
H4927	4464
H4928	4465
H4929	4466
H4930	4467
H4931	4468
H4932	4469
H4933	4470
H4934	4471
H4935	4471
H4936	4472
H4937	4473
H4938	4474
H4939	4475
H4940	4476
H4941	4477
H4942	4478
H4943	4478
H4944	4482
H4945	4482
H4946	4480
H4947	4485
H4948	4487
H4949	4488
H4950	4490
H4951	4489
H4952	4491
H4953	4492
H4954	4493
H4955	4494
H4956	4495
H4957	4496
H4958	5186+4512
H4959	4497
H4960	4498
H4961	4499
H4962	4500
H4963	4501
H4964	4502
H4965	3240
"	5117
H4966	4503
H4967	4496
H4968	4505
H4969	4506
H4970	4506
H4971	2679
"	2680
H4972	4507
H4973	4508
H4974	4480
H4975	4509
H4976	4511
H4977	4511
H4978	4512
H4979	4513
H4980	4514
H4981	4515
H4982	4516
H4983	4517
H4984	4518
H4985	4519
H4986	4520
H4987	4521
H4988	4523
H4989	4522
H4990	4524
H4991	4524
H4992	4036
H4993	4525
H4994	4525
H4995	4526
H4996	4527
H4997	4528
H4998	4529
H4999	4531
H5000	4531

G/K	STRONG
H5001	4532
H5002	4530
H5003	4533
H5004	4534
H5005	4535
H5006	4536
H5007	4537
H5008	4538
H5009	4539
H5010	4540
H5011	4541
H5012	4541
H5013	4541
H5014	4542
H5015	5533
H5016	4543
H5017	4544
H5018	4545
H5019	4546
H5020	4547
H5021	4548
H5022	4549
H5023	4550
H5024	4551
H5025	4551
H5026	4552
H5027	4553
H5028	4554
H5029	4555
H5030	4556
H5031	4557
H5032	4558
H5033	4559
H5034	4560
H5035	4149
H5036	4561
H5037	4562
H5038	
H5039	4563
H5040	4564
H5041	4565
H5042	4566
H5043	4568
H5044	4569
H5045	4569
H5046	4570
H5047	4570
H5048	4154
"	4571
"	5976
H5049	4572
H5050	4573
H5051	4575
H5052	4574
H5053	4576
H5054	4579
H5055	4578
H5056	4580
H5057	4581
H5058	4581
H5059	4582
H5060	4583
H5061	4583
H5062	4584
H5063	4584
H5064	4586
H5065	4587
H5066	4588
H5067	4589
H5068	4590
H5069	4590
H5070	4591
H5071	4592
H5072	
H5073	4594
H5074	4595
H5075	4596
H5076	4597
H5077	4598
H5078	4599
H5079	4583
H5080	4600
H5081	4601
H5082	4601
H5083	4601
H5084	4602
H5085	4603
H5086	4604
H5087	4605
H5088	4480+5921
H5089	4607
H5090	4608
H5091	4609
H5092	4609
H5093	4605
H5094	4611
H5095	4611
H5096	4612
H5097	4613
H5098	4614

G/K	STRONG
H5099	4615
H5100	4616
H5101	4617
H5102	4617
H5103	4618
H5104	4585
H5105	4618
H5106	4619
H5107	4620
H5108	4621
H5109	4622
H5110	4623
H5111	4624
H5112	4625
H5113	4626
H5114	4627
H5115	4628
H5116	4629
H5117	4631
H5118	4632
H5119	4633
H5120	4630
"	4634
H5121	4635
H5122	4636
H5123	6206
H5124	4637
H5125	4638
H5126	4639
H5127	4640
H5128	4641
H5129	4641
H5130	4643
H5131	4642
H5132	4644
H5133	4645
H5134	4646
H5135	4647
H5136	4648
H5137	4649
H5138	4650
H5139	4651
H5140	4652
H5141	4653
H5142	4654
H5143	4654
H5144	4655
H5145	4656
H5146	4657
H5147	4658
H5148	4659
H5149	4659
H5150	4660
H5151	4661
H5152	4662
"	4663
H5153	4664
H5154	4665
H5155	4666
H5156	4667
H5157	4669
H5158	4668
H5159	4670
H5160	4160
H5161	4671
H5162	4672
H5163	4673
H5164	4674
H5165	4675
H5166	4675
H5167	4676
H5168	4677
H5169	4678
H5170	4678
H5171	4679
H5172	4680
H5173	4681
H5174	4682
H5175	4683
H5176	6668
H5177	4684
H5178	4685
H5179	4685
H5180	4686
H5181	4686
H5182	4685
H5183	4685
H5184	4687
H5185	4688
"	4699
H5186	4689
H5187	4690
H5188	4691
H5189	4692
H5190	4692
H5191	4693
H5192	4686
H5193	4694
H5194	4695
H5195	4696

G/K	STRONG
H5196	4697
H5197	4698
H5198	4688
H5199	4700
H5200	4701
H5201	4702
H5202	4703
H5203	4705
H5204	4706
H5205	4707
H5206	4708
H5207	4709
H5208	4710
H5209	4711
H5210	4712
H5211	4694
H5212	4713
H5213	4714
H5214	4715
H5215	4716
H5216	4717
"	4718
H5217	4718
H5218	4719
H5219	4720
H5220	4721
H5221	4722
H5222	
H5223	4723
H5224	4723
H5225	4724
H5226	4725
H5227	4726
H5228	4727
H5229	4728
H5230	4729
H5231	6999
H5232	6999
H5233	4730
H5234	4731
H5235	4732
H5236	4733
H5237	4734
H5238	4735
H5239	4736
H5240	4737
H5241	4738
H5242	4739
H5243	4740
H5244	4741
H5245	4743
H5246	4744
H5247	4745
H5248	4746
H5249	4747
H5250	4748
H5251	4749
H5252	4750
H5253	4751
H5254	4752
H5255	4753
H5256	4754
H5257	4754
H5258	4806
H5259	4755
H5260	4758
H5261	4759
H5262	4759
H5263	4760
H5264	8112
H5265	4761
"	4763
H5266	4764
H5267	4765
H5268	4767
H5269	4766
H5270	4768
H5271	4769
H5272	4770
H5273	4771
H5274	4772
H5275	4773
H5276	4774
H5277	4775
H5278	4777
H5279	4778
H5280	4780
H5281	4781
H5282	4757
H5283	4782
H5284	4783
H5285	4787
H5286	4784
H5287	4751
H5288	4785
H5289	4786
H5290	4062
H5291	4788
H5292	4789
H5293	4790

G/K	STRONG
H5294	4791
H5295	4792
H5296	4793
H5297	4794
H5298	4835
H5299	4795
H5300	4796
H5301	4797
"	4798
H5302	4799
H5303	4800
H5304	4800+3050
H5305	4801
H5306	4802
H5307	4178
"	4803
H5308	4805
H5309	4806
H5310	4807
"	4810
H5311	4807
"	4810
H5312	4808
H5313	4809
H5314	4807
H5315	4809+6946
H5316	4811
H5317	4179
H5318	4812
H5319	4813
H5320	4814
H5321	4815
H5322	4816
H5323	4817
H5324	4818
H5325	
H5326	4819
H5327	4820
H5328	4821
H5329	4822
H5330	4823
H5331	4824
H5332	4825
H5333	4826
H5334	4827
H5335	4828
H5336	7489
H5337	4829
H5338	4830
H5339	4831
H5340	4832
H5341	4832
H5342	4832
H5343	4833
H5344	4834
H5345	4836
H5346	4837
H5347	4838
H5348	4839
H5349	4840
H5350	4841
H5351	4842
H5352	4843
H5353	4844
H5354	4845
H5355	4846
H5356	4847
H5357	4848
H5358	4762
H5359	4762
H5360	4849
H5361	4850
H5362	4853
H5363	4853
H5364	4854
H5365	4856
H5366	4858
H5367	4864
H5368	4864
H5369	4869
H5370	4869
H5371	5381
H5372	4881
H5373	4883
H5374	4884
H5375	4885
H5376	4885
H5377	4890
H5378	4895
H5379	4881
H5380	4905
H5381	4906
H5382	4909
H5383	4930
H5384	4939
H5385	4951
H5386	4955
H5387	4956
H5388	4957
H5389	4958

G/K	STRONG
H5390	4851
H5391	4855
H5392	4852
H5393	4857
H5394	4859
H5395	
H5396	4860
H5397	4876
H5398	4861
H5399	4862
H5400	4863
H5401	4865
H5402	4866
H5403	4867
H5404	4868
H5405	4870'
H5406	4871
H5407	4872
H5408	4874
H5409	4875
H5410	4876
H5411	4877
H5412	4878
H5413	4879
H5414	4880
H5415	4880
H5416	4882
H5417	4886
H5418	4888
H5419	4888
H5420	4888
H5421	4888
H5422	4889
H5423	4891
H5424	4892
H5425	4893
H5426	4893
H5427	4894
H5428	4896
H5429	4897
H5430	4898
H5431	4899
H5432	4900
H5433	4901
H5434	4902
H5435	4904
H5436	4189
H5437	7921
H5438	4908
H5439	4911
H5440	4910
H5441	4911
H5442	4912
H5443	4913
H5444	4915
H5445	4915
H5446	4914
H5447	4916
H5448	4916
H5449	4917
H5450	4918
H5451	4919
H5452	4920
H5453	4920
H5454	4921
H5455	4922
H5456	7969
H5457	4923
H5458	4924
H5459	4925
H5460	4924
H5461	4926
H5462	4927
H5463	4928
H5464	4929
H5465	4929
H5466	4931
H5467	4932
H5468	4933
H5469	4934
H5470	4935
H5471	4936
H5472	4937
H5473	4937
H5474	4938
H5475	4938
H5476	4940
H5477	4941
H5478	4942
H5479	4943
H5480	4944
H5481	8246
H5482	4945
H5483	4945
H5484	4946
H5485	4947
H5486	4948
H5487	4949
H5488	4950
H5489	4952

G/K	STRONG
H5490	4954
H5491	4959
H5492	4960
H5493	4962
H5494	4962
H5495	4963
H5496	4964
H5497	4965
H5498	4966
H5499	4967
H5500	4968
H5501	4969
H5502	8478
H5503	4970
H5504	4971
H5505	4972
H5506	4973
H5507	4974
H5508	4976
H5509	4977
H5510	4979
H5511	4980
H5512	4981
H5513	4982
H5514	4983
H5515	4983
H5516	4975
H5517	4985
"	4988
H5518	4986
H5519	4987
H5520	4989
H5521	4990
H5522	4991
H5523	4992
H5524	4993
H5525	4993
H5526	
H5527	
H5528	4994
H5529	4995
H5530	4996
H5531	527+4996
H5532	4997
H5533	4998
H5534	5000
H5535	5001
H5536	5002
H5537	5003
H5538	5005
H5539	5004
H5540	5006
H5541	5007
H5542	5007
H5543	5008
H5544	5009
H5545	5010
H5546	5011
H5547	5012
H5548	5014
H5549	5015
H5550	5015
H5551	5015
H5552	5562
H5553	5016
H5554	5014
H5555	5018
H5556	5019
H5557	5019
H5558	5021
H5559	5022
H5560	5024
H5561	5025
H5562	5025
H5563	5026
H5564	5027
H5565	5028
H5566	5030
H5567	5031
H5568	5032
H5569	5033
H5570	5034
H5571	5034
H5572	5036
H5573	5037
H5574	5035
H5575	5035
H5576	5039
H5577	5038
H5578	5040
H5579	5041
H5580	5042
H5581	5044
H5582	5045
H5583	5046
H5584	5048
H5585	5050
H5586	5051
H5587	5052
H5588	5054
H5589	5664
H5590	5055
H5591	5056
H5592	5057
H5593	5058
H5594	5059
H5595	5060
H5596	5061
H5597	5062
H5598	5063
H5599	5064
H5600	5064
H5601	5065
H5602	5066
H5603	5067
H5604	5077
H5605	5068
H5606	5070
H5607	5071
H5608	5072
H5609	1713
H5610	5074
H5611	5076
H5612	5077
H5613	5078
H5614	5079
H5615	5080
H5616	5080
H5617	5112
H5618	5081
H5619	5082
H5620	5084
H5621	5083
H5622	5086
H5623	5087
H5624	5088
H5625	5089
H5626	
H5627	5090
H5628	5090
H5629	5091
H5630	5091
H5631	5092
H5632	5093
H5633	5095
H5634	5096
H5635	5097
H5636	5096
H5637	5098
H5638	5099
H5639	5100
H5640	5101
H5641	5102
H5642	5102
H5643	5104
H5644	5105
H5645	763
H5646	
H5647	
H5648	5106
H5649	5107
H5650	5108
H5651	5109
H5652	3013
H5653	5110
H5654	5112
H5655	5113
H5656	5114
H5657	5115
H5658	5115
H5659	5116
H5660	5116
H5661	4999
H5662	5121
H5663	5117
H5664	5117
H5665	5118
H5666	5119
H5667	5120
H5668	5121
H5669	
H5670	5123
H5671	5124
H5672	5125
H5673	5126
H5674	5127
H5675	5128
H5676	5129
H5677	5130
H5678	5130
H5679	5131
H5680	5132
H5681	5133
H5682	3243
H5683	5136
H5684	5137
H5685	5137
H5686	5138
H5687	5139
H5688	5140
H5689	5140
H5690	5141
H5691	5143
H5692	5144
H5693	5144
H5694	5145
H5695	5146
H5696	5147
H5697	5148
H5698	5117
H5699	5151
H5700	5149
H5701	5152
H5702	5153
H5703	5154
H5704	5155
H5705	5156
H5706	5157
H5707	5158
H5708	5158
H5709	5159
H5710	
H5711	5158
H5712	5160
H5713	5161
H5714	5162
H5715	5163
H5716	5164
H5717	5165
H5718	5166
H5719	5150
H5720	5167
H5721	5168
H5722	5169
H5723	2734
"	2787
H5724	5170
H5725	5170
H5726	5171
H5727	5172
H5728	5173
H5729	5175
H5730	5904
H5731	5176
H5732	5177
H5733	5178
H5734	5178
H5735	5179
H5736	5180
H5737	5181
H5738	5183
H5739	5183
H5740	5184
H5741	5185
H5742	5186
H5743	5200
H5744	5187
H5745	5195
H5746	5189
H5747	5190
H5748	5192
H5749	5193
H5750	5194
H5751	5196
H5752	5197
H5753	5198
H5754	5198
H5755	5188
H5756	5199
H5757	5201
H5758	5201
H5759	5203
H5760	5204
H5761	
H5762	5108
H5763	5109
H5764	5205
H5765	5206
H5766	5121
H5767	5207
H5768	5125
H5769	5209
H5770	5210
H5771	5211
H5772	5212
H5773	5213
H5774	5214
H5775	5216
H5776	5215
H5777	5217
H5778	5218
H5779	5218
H5780	5219
H5781	5220
H5782	5221
H5783	5223
H5784	5222
H5785	5224
"	6549
H5786	5224
H5787	3559
H5788	3559
H5789	5225
H5790	5226
"	5227
H5791	5228
"	5229
H5792	5230
H5793	5231
H5794	5233
H5795	5234
H5796	5234
H5797	5236
H5798	5235
H5799	5237
H5800	5238
H5801	5239
H5802	959
H5803	5241
H5804	5242
H5805	5244
H5806	3988
H5807	5246
H5808	5248
H5809	5247
H5810	5249
H5811	5250
H5812	5251
H5813	5252
H5814	5254
H5815	5255
H5816	5257
H5817	5257
H5818	5258
H5819	5259
H5820	5258
H5821	5262
H5822	5262
H5823	5263
H5824	5264
H5825	5265
H5826	5266
H5827	5268
H5828	5269
H5829	5270
H5830	5271
H5831	5271
H5832	5272
H5833	5273
H5834	5273
H5835	5274
H5836	5274
H5837	5275
H5838	5276
H5839	5277
H5840	5278
H5841	5279
H5842	5279
H5843	5281
H5844	5280
H5845	5283
H5846	5282
H5847	5284
H5848	5285
H5849	5286
H5850	5287
H5851	5287
H5852	5289
H5853	5288
H5854	5290
H5855	5291
H5856	5292
H5857	5292
H5858	5293
H5859	5294
H5860	5295
H5861	5296
H5862	5297
H5863	5298
H5864	5299
H5865	5299
H5866	5300
H5867	5300
H5868	5316
H5869	5299+1756
H5870	5301
H5871	5302
H5872	5303
H5873	5304
H5874	5305
H5875	5300
H5876	5306
H5877	5307
H5878	5309
H5879	5310
H5880	5310
H5881	5311
H5882	5314
H5883	5315
H5884	5316
H5885	5317
H5886	5318
H5887	5319
H5888	5320
H5889	5321
H5890	5322
H5891	5322
H5892	5323
H5893	5324
H5894	5324
H5895	5324
H5896	5325
H5897	5327
H5898	5327
H5899	
H5900	5328
H5901	5133
H5902	5133
H5903	5341
H5904	5329
H5905	5331
H5906	5332
H5907	5333
H5908	5334
H5909	5335
H5910	5336
H5911	5337
H5912	5339
H5913	5340
H5914	5006
"	5132
H5915	5341
H5916	5342
H5917	5341
H5918	5344
H5919	5344
H5920	5345
H5921	5346
H5922	5347
H5923	5348
H5924	5349
H5925	5351
H5926	5350
H5927	5352
H5928	5353
H5929	5355
H5930	5355
H5931	5356
H5932	5357
H5933	5358
H5934	5359
H5935	5360
H5936	5361
H5937	5362
H5938	5362
H5939	5363
H5940	5364
H5941	5365
H5942	5366
H5943	5367
H5944	5216
H5945	5369
H5946	5370
H5947	5371
H5948	5373
H5949	5374
H5950	5374
H5951	4984
"	5375
"	5379
"	7721
H5952	5381
H5953	5385
H5954	5387
H5955	5387
H5956	5400
H5957	5378
"	5383
H5958	5377
H5959	5380
H5960	5382
H5961	5378
H5962	5384
H5963	5386
H5964	5388
H5965	5390
H5966	5391
H5967	5391
H5968	5392
H5969	5393
H5970	5394
H5971	5395
H5972	5397
H5973	5398
H5974	5399
H5975	5401
H5976	5401
H5977	5402
H5978	5402
H5979	5404
H5980	5405
H5981	5406
H5982	5411
H5983	5408
H5984	5409
H5985	5410
H5986	5410
H5987	5411
H5988	5413
H5989	5414
H5990	5416
H5991	5417
H5992	5418
H5993	5418
H5994	5419
H5995	5420
H5996	5421
H5997	5422
H5998	5423
H5999	5424
H6000	5425
H6001	5425
H6002	5425
H6003	5427
H6004	5428
H6005	
H6006	5429
H6007	5430
H6008	5431
H6009	5432
H6010	5433
H6011	5435
H6012	5433
H6013	5434
H6014	5436
H6015	4141
"	4142
"	5437
H6016	5438
H6017	5439
H6018	5440
H6019	5442
H6020	5441
H6021	5444
H6022	5445
H6023	5447
H6024	5448
H6025	5449
H6026	5450
H6027	5451
H6028	5453
H6029	5454
H6030	5454
H6031	5455
H6032	5456
H6033	5458
H6034	5462
H6035	5459
H6036	5461
H6037	5462
H6038	5462
H6039	5464
H6040	5465
H6041	5466
H6042	5467
H6043	5468
H6044	5469
H6045	5470
H6046	5471
H6047	5472
"	7734
H6048	5473
H6049	5509
H6050	5474
H6051	5475
H6052	5476
H6053	5477
H6054	5478
H6055	5479
H6056	5526
H6057	5480
H6058	5526
H6059	5482
H6060	5515
H6061	5483
H6062	5483
H6063	5484
H6064	5485
H6065	2702
H6066	5486
H6067	5490
H6068	5488
H6069	5489
H6070	5492
H6071	5492
H6072	5618
H6073	3249
"	5493
H6074	5494
H6075	5495
H6076	5494
H6077	5496
H6078	5497
H6079	5498
H6080	5499
H6081	5500
H6082	5501
H6083	
H6084	7823
H6085	5502
H6086	5503
"	5505
H6087	5504
H6088	5506
H6089	5507
H6090	5508
H6091	7750
H6092	5509
H6093	7875
H6094	5510
H6095	5511
H6096	5512
H6097	5512
H6098	5513
H6099	5514
H6100	5515
H6101	5483
H6102	5516
H6103	5517
H6104	5517
H6105	5518
H6106	5518
H6107	5519
H6108	5520
H6109	5521
H6110	5522
H6111	5523
H6112	5524
H6113	5525
H6114	5526
H6115	5526
H6116	5526
H6117	5527
H6118	5528
H6119	5530
H6120	5529
H6121	5531
H6122	5532
H6123	5533
H6124	5533
H6125	5532
H6126	5534
H6127	5534
H6128	7936
H6129	5535
H6130	5536
H6131	5537
H6132	5543
H6133	5538
H6134	5539
H6135	5540
H6136	5541
H6137	5541
H6138	5542
H6139	5543
H6140	5543
H6141	5544
H6142	5545
H6143	5546
H6144	5543
H6145	5547
H6146	5548
H6147	5549
H6148	5549
H6149	5550
H6150	5551
H6151	5552
H6152	5553
H6153	5554
H6154	5555
H6155	5556
H6156	5557
H6157	5558
H6158	5927
H6159	5560
H6160	5561
H6161	5562
H6162	5562
H6163	5563
H6164	5564
H6165	5565
H6166	5566
H6167	
H6168	5567
H6169	5568
H6170	5569
H6171	5570
H6172	5571
H6173	7158
H6174	5572
H6175	5573
H6176	5574
H6177	5575
H6178	5576
H6179	5578
H6180	5577
H6181	5579
H6182	5580
H6183	5581
H6184	5582
H6185	5584
H6186	5585
H6187	5585
H6188	5586
H6189	5588
H6190	5589
H6191	5587
H6192	5590
H6193	5591
H6194	5591
H6195	5592
H6196	5592
H6197	5592
H6198	5593
H6199	5594
H6200	5595
H6201	5603
H6202	5596
H6203	5596
H6204	5597
H6205	5598
H6206	5599
H6207	5599
H6208	5600
H6209	5601
H6210	5602
H6211	5603
H6212	5604
H6213	5509
H6214	5605
H6215	5606
H6216	5606
H6217	5607
H6218	5608
H6219	5612
H6220	5612
H6221	5608
H6222	5610
H6223	5611
H6224	5614
H6225	5612
H6226	5617
H6227	5616
H6228	5615
H6229	
H6230	5618
H6231	3254
H6232	5619
H6233	5493
H6234	5620
H6235	5621
H6236	5623
H6237	5624
H6238	5625
H6239	5627
H6240	5627
H6241	5626
H6242	5628
H6243	5628
H6244	5628
H6245	5629
H6246	5630
H6247	5631
H6248	5633
H6249	5633
H6250	5634
H6251	5635
H6252	5636
H6253	5637
H6254	8269
H6255	5638
H6256	5639
H6257	5638
H6258	5640
H6259	5641
H6260	5643
H6261	5643
H6262	5644
H6263	
H6264	5646
H6265	5645
H6266	5645
H6267	5645
H6268	5647
H6269	5650
H6270	5651
H6271	5652
H6272	5653
H6273	5654
H6274	5655

G/K	STRONG
H6275	5656
H6276	5657
H6277	5658
H6278	5658
H6279	5660
H6280	5661
H6281	5662
H6282	5662
H6283	5663
H6284	5664
H6285	5659
H6286	5666
H6287	5667
H6288	5668
H6289	5669
H6290	5687
H6291	5688
H6292	5670
H6293	5670
H6294	5671
H6295	5672
H6296	5674
H6297	5674
H6298	5676
H6299	5677
H6300	5863
H6301	5678
H6302	5679
H6303	5680
H6304	5681
H6305	5682
H6306	2275
H6307	5684
H6308	5685
H6309	5686
H6310	5688
H6311	5689
H6312	5691
H6313	5690
H6314	5692
H6315	5693
H6316	5694
H6317	5699
H6318	5696
H6319	5695
H6320	5697
H6321	5698
H6322	5699
H6323	5700
H6324	5700
H6325	5882
H6326	5697+7992
H6327	5701
H6328	5702
H6329	5703
H6330	5704
H6331	5706
H6332	5707
H6333	5714
H6334	5710
H6335	5710
H6336	5711
H6337	5712
H6338	5713
H6339	
H6340	5708
H6341	5714
H6342	5714
H6343	5715
H6344	5716
H6345	5714
H6346	5717
H6347	5718
H6348	5718
H6349	5719
H6350	5720
H6351	5721
H6352	5722
H6353	5723
H6354	5724
H6355	5725
H6356	5726
H6357	5727
H6358	5730
H6359	5731
H6360	5731
H6361	5729
H6362	5728
H6363	5733
H6364	5728
H6365	5734
H6366	5730
H6367	5734
H6368	5735
H6369	5736
H6370	5737
H6371	5737
H6372	5737
H6373	5739
H6374	5740

G/K	STRONG
H6375	5740
H6376	5738
H6377	5741
H6378	5742
H6379	5755
H6380	5743
H6381	5744
H6382	5745
H6383	5746
H6384	5747
H6385	5748
H6386	5749
H6387	5749
H6388	5750
H6389	5752
H6390	5753
H6391	5753
H6392	5754
H6393	5755
H6394	5755
H6395	5756
H6396	5759
H6397	5760
H6398	5757
"	5761
H6399	5761
H6400	5762
H6401	5765
H6402	5763
H6403	5764
H6404	5766
H6405	5767
H6406	5766
H6407	5768
H6408	5768
H6409	5769
H6410	6030
H6411	5771
H6412	5869
H6413	5773
H6414	5774
H6415	5774
H6416	5775
H6417	5778
H6418	5779
H6419	5780
H6420	5780
H6421	5781
H6422	5786
H6423	5783
H6424	5782
H6425	5785
H6426	5787
H6427	5788
H6428	5788
H6429	5789
H6430	5791
H6431	5790
H6432	5792
H6433	5793
H6434	5794
H6435	5794
H6436	5795
H6437	5797
H6438	5798
H6439	5799
H6440	5800
H6441	5800
H6442	5801
H6443	5802
H6444	5803
H6445	5804
H6446	5798
H6447	5805
H6448	5806
H6449	5807
H6450	5808
H6451	5810
H6452	5811
H6453	5812
H6454	5813
H6455	5814
H6456	5815
H6457	5816
H6458	5817
H6459	5818
H6460	5818
H6461	5819
H6462	5820
H6463	5820
H6464	5821
H6465	5822
H6466	5823
H6467	5825
H6468	5826
H6469	5828
H6470	5827
"	5829
H6471	7320
H6472	5829

G/K	STRONG
H6473	5809
H6474	5830
H6475	5832
H6476	5833
H6477	5834
H6478	5835
H6479	5836
H6480	5837
H6481	5838
H6482	5838
H6483	5840
H6484	5841
H6485	5842
H6486	5844
H6487	4593
"	5844
H6488	5848
H6489	5845
H6490	5846
H6491	5847
H6492	
H6493	5848
H6494	5848
H6495	
H6496	5849
H6497	5849
H6498	5850
H6499	5851
H6500	5852
H6501	5853
H6502	5854
H6503	5855
H6504	5857
H6505	5856
H6506	5858
H6507	5858
H6508	5858
H6509	5857
H6510	5859
H6511	5762
H6512	5860
H6513	5860
H6514	5861
H6515	5862
H6516	5863
H6517	5864
H6518	5865
H6519	5866
H6520	5867
H6521	5867
H6522	5868
H6523	5770
H6524	5869
H6525	5872 to 5887
H6526	5871
H6527	5872
H6528	5873
H6529	5874
H6530	5875
H6531	
H6532	5876
H6533	5877
H6534	5878
H6535	5880
H6536	5882
H6537	5883
H6538	5884
H6539	5885
H6540	5887
H6541	2703
H6542	5879
H6543	5879
H6544	5881
H6545	5774
"	5888
H6546	5889
H6547	5890
H6548	5891
H6549	5891
H6550	5778
H6551	5892
H6552	5892
H6553	5893
H6554	5895
H6555	5895
H6556	5892+2041
H6557	
H6558	5898
H6559	5899
H6560	5904
H6561	5905
H6562	5896
H6563	5897
H6564	5900
H6565	5901
H6566	5902
H6567	5903
H6568	5906
H6569	5857
H6570	5907

G/K	STRONG
H6571	5908
H6572	5909
H6573	5910
H6574	5911
H6575	5912
H6576	5913
H6577	5914
H6578	5915
H6579	5916
H6580	5917
H6581	5918
H6582	5919
H6583	5920
H6584	5921
H6585	5923
H6586	5921+3651
H6587	5925
H6588	45
H6589	5926
H6590	5927
H6591	5929
H6592	5930
H6593	5766
H6594	5932
H6595	5933
H6596	5934
H6597	5935
H6598	5936
H6599	1175
H6600	5937
H6601	5938
H6602	5939
H6603	5941
H6604	5942
H6605	5940
H6606	5942
H6607	5933
H6608	5944
H6609	5945
H6610	5945
H6611	5947
H6612	5948
H6613	5949
H6614	5950
H6615	5935
H6616	
H6617	5951
H6618	5953
H6619	5953
H6620	5953
H6621	5953
H6622	5955
H6623	5956
H6624	5958
H6625	5959
H6626	5960
H6627	5963
H6628	5961
H6629	5921+4192
H6630	5964
H6631	5964
H6632	5965
H6633	5966
H6634	5968
H6635	5969
H6636	5970
H6637	5766
H6638	5971
H6639	5971
H6640	5973
H6641	5975
H6642	5977
H6643	5978
H6644	5979
H6645	5980
H6646	5981
H6647	5982
H6648	5983
H6649	5984
"	5985
H6650	5986
H6651	5987
H6652	3818
H6653	5988
H6654	5989
H6655	5990
H6656	5991
H6657	5992
H6658	5995
H6659	5996
H6660	5997
H6661	5998
H6662	5999
H6663	6000
H6664	6001
H6665	6001
H6666	
H6667	6002
H6668	6003
H6669	6004

G/K	STRONG
H6670	6004
H6671	3726
H6672	6005
H6673	6006
H6674	6007
H6675	6008
H6676	6009
H6677	6010
H6678	6013
H6679	6011
H6680	6012
H6681	7104
H6682	6014
H6683	6014
H6684	6016
H6685	6016
H6686	6017
H6687	6018
H6688	6019
H6689	6020
H6690	6021
H6691	6022
H6692	6023
H6693	6024
H6694	6025
H6695	6026
H6696	6027
H6697	6028
H6698	6029
H6699	6030
H6700	6031
H6701	6031
H6702	6030
H6703	5772
H6704	6034
H6705	6035
H6706	6042
H6707	6036
H6708	6038
H6709	6037
H6710	6061
H6711	6064
H6712	1042
H6713	6039
H6714	6041
H6715	6040
H6716	6042
H6717	6043
H6718	6035
H6719	6044
H6720	3283
H6721	6045
H6722	6046
H6723	6047
H6724	6048
H6725	6049
H6726	6049
H6727	6051
H6728	6052
H6729	6053
H6730	6054
H6731	6055
H6732	6055
H6733	6057
H6734	6058
H6735	6059
H6736	6060
H6737	6062
H6738	6063
H6739	6063
H6740	6064
H6741	6066
H6742	6067
H6743	6068
H6744	6068
H6745	6069
H6746	6070
H6747	6071
H6748	6072
H6749	5782
H6750	
H6751	6073
H6752	6075
H6753	6075
H6754	6076
H6755	6077
H6756	6078
H6757	6079
H6758	5774
H6759	6080
H6760	6083
H6761	6081
H6762	6082
H6763	6084
H6764	6084
H6765	1036
H6766	6085
H6767	6085
H6768	6085
H6769	5777

G/K	STRONG
H6770	6086
H6771	6087
H6772	6087
H6773	6091
H6774	6092
H6775	6089
H6776	6089
H6777	6090
H6778	6090
H6779	6093
H6780	6094
H6781	6095
H6782	6096
H6783	6098
H6784	6098
H6785	6097
H6786	6099
H6787	6100
H6788	6101
H6789	6102
H6790	6103
H6791	6104
H6792	6103
H6793	6105
H6794	6105
H6795	6106
H6796	6107
H6797	6108
H6798	6108
H6799	6106
H6800	6109
H6801	6111
H6802	6110
H6803	
H6804	6112
H6805	3289
H6806	6113
H6807	6114
H6808	6115
H6809	6116
H6810	6117
H6811	6119
H6812	6120
H6813	6118
H6814	6121
H6815	6121
H6816	
H6817	6122
H6818	6123
H6819	6124
H6820	1044
H6821	6125
H6822	6126
H6823	6127
H6824	6128
H6825	6129
H6826	6130
H6827	6131
H6828	6131
H6829	6135
H6830	6133
H6831	6134
H6832	6137
H6833	6138
H6834	6139
H6835	6140
H6836	6141
H6837	6142
H6838	6143
H6839	6145
H6840	6144
H6841	6147
H6842	6148
H6843	6148
H6844	6149
H6845	6150
H6846	6152
H6847	6153
H6848	6154
H6849	6154
H6850	6154
H6851	6152
H6852	6152
H6853	6156
H6854	6158
H6855	6159
H6856	6157
H6857	6155
H6858	6160
H6859	6161
H6860	6162
H6861	6163
H6862	6163
H6863	6164
H6864	6165
H6865	6166
H6866	6166
H6867	6168
H6868	6169
H6869	4632

G/K	STRONG
H6870	6170
H6871	6171
H6872	6172
H6873	6174
H6874	6175
H6875	6176
H6876	6177
H6877	6178
H6878	6179
H6879	6180
H6880	6181
H6881	6182
H6882	6183
H6883	6184
H6884	6185
H6885	6186
H6886	6187
H6887	6188
H6888	6189
H6889	6190
H6890	6192
H6891	6191
H6892	6193
H6893	6195
H6894	6194
H6895	6196
H6896	6197
H6897	6198
H6898	6176
H6899	6199
H6900	5735
H6901	6200
H6902	6203
H6903	6201
H6904	6202
H6905	6204
H6906	6205
H6907	6206
H6908	6207
H6909	6208
H6910	6209
H6911	6210
H6912	6212
H6913	6213
H6914	6213
H6915	6214
H6916	6215
H6917	6218
H6918	6221
H6919	6222
H6920	6224
H6921	6229
H6922	6230
H6923	6237
H6924	6235
H6925	6240
H6926	6240
H6927	6235
H6928	6241
H6929	6242
H6930	6240
H6931	6211
H6932	6211
H6933	6211
H6934	6216
H6935	6217
H6936	6219
H6937	6220
H6938	6223
H6939	6225
H6940	6227
H6941	6228
H6942	6226
H6943	6231
H6944	6232
H6945	6233
H6946	6234
H6947	6238
H6948	6239
H6949	6244
H6950	6245
H6951	6245
H6952	6247
H6953	6248
H6954	6249
H6955	6250
H6956	6253
H6957	6251
H6958	6252
H6959	6255
H6960	6254
H6961	6256
H6962	6278
H6963	6257
H6964	6258
H6965	6259
H6966	6260
H6967	6261
H6968	6262
H6969	6264

G/K	STRONG
H6970	6265
H6971	6266
H6972	6267
H6973	6269
H6974	6270
H6975	6271
H6976	6271
H6977	6272
H6978	6273
H6979	6274
H6980	6275
H6981	6277
H6982	6276
H6983	6279
H6984	6280
H6985	6282
H6986	6282
H6987	6281
H6988	6283
H6989	
H6990	6284
H6991	6285
H6992	6285
H6993	6285
H6994	6286
H6995	6286
H6996	6287
H6997	6288
H6998	6288
H6999	6289
H7000	6290
H7001	6291
H7002	6292
H7003	6293
H7004	6294
H7005	6295
H7006	6296
H7007	6297
H7008	6298
H7009	6299
H7010	6300
H7011	6301
H7012	6302
H7013	6303
H7014	6304
H7015	6305
H7016	6305
H7017	6306
H7018	6306
H7019	6307
H7020	6307
H7021	6308
H7022	6309
H7023	6310
"	6366
H7024	6311
H7025	6312
H7026	6312
H7027	6324
H7028	6313
H7029	6314
H7030	6312
H7031	6315
H7032	6315
H7033	6316
H7034	6317
H7035	6318
H7036	6319
H7037	6320
H7038	6321
H7039	6322
H7040	6322
H7041	6323
H7042	6437
H7043	6324
H7044	6325
H7045	6326
H7046	6327
H7047	6327
H7048	6328
"	6329
H7049	6329
H7050	6330
H7051	6331
"	6512
H7052	6332
H7053	6333
H7054	6334
H7055	6335
H7056	6335
H7057	6336
H7058	6337
H7059	6338
H7060	6339
H7061	6340
H7062	6341
H7063	6341
H7064	6342
H7065	6343
H7066	6344

G/K	STRONG
H7067	6345
H7068	6346
H7069	6348
H7070	6349
H7071	6350
H7072	6351
H7073	6352
H7074	6354
H7075	6355
H7076	6356
H7077	6357
H7078	6359
H7079	6360
H7080	6358
"	6362
H7081	6363
H7082	6363
H7083	6364
H7084	6367
H7085	6365
H7086	6368
H7087	6369
H7088	
H7089	6371
H7090	6372
H7091	6373
H7092	6374
H7093	6376
H7094	6377
H7095	6378
H7096	6379
H7097	6380
H7098	6381
H7099	6382
H7100	6383
H7101	6384
H7102	6411
H7103	6385
H7104	6388
H7105	6389
H7106	6390
H7107	6391
H7108	6370
H7109	6394
H7110	6393
H7111	6395
H7112	6396
H7113	6397
H7114	6398
H7115	6400
H7116	6401
H7117	6403
H7118	6404
H7119	6405
H7120	6406
H7121	6407
H7122	6408
H7123	6409
H7124	6410
H7125	6410
H7126	6411
H7127	6412
H7128	6412
H7129	6413
H7130	6414
H7131	6415
H7132	6416
H7133	6417
H7134	6418
H7135	6418
H7136	6419
H7137	6419
H7138	6420
H7139	6421
H7140	6422
H7141	6423
H7142	6424
H7143	6424
H7144	6425
H7145	6426
H7146	6427
H7147	6428
H7148	6429
H7149	6430
H7150	6431
H7151	6304
H7152	6432
H7153	6435
H7154	6436
H7155	6437
H7156	3942
"	6440
H7157	6434
"	6438
H7158	6439
H7159	6439
H7160	6439
H7161	6439
H7162	6443
H7163	6441
H7164	6442
H7165	6443
H7166	6444
H7167	6445
H7168	6446
H7169	6450
H7170	6448
H7171	6449
H7172	6451
H7173	6452
H7174	6452
H7175	6453
H7176	6454
H7177	6455
H7178	6456
H7179	6457
H7180	6458
H7181	6459
H7182	6461
H7183	6462
H7184	6463
H7185	6464
H7186	6465
H7187	6464
H7188	6466
H7189	6467
H7190	6468
H7191	6469
H7192	6470
H7193	6471
H7194	6472
H7195	6847
H7196	6473
H7197	6474
H7198	6475
H7199	6476
H7200	6476
H7201	6477
H7202	6478
H7203	6479
H7204	6480
H7205	6481
H7206	6482
H7207	6327
H7208	1048
H7209	6483
H7210	6484
H7211	6375
H7212	6485
H7213	6486
H7214	6487
H7215	6488
H7216	6489
H7217	6485
H7218	6490
H7219	6491
H7220	6492
H7221	6493
H7222	6494
H7223	6495
H7224	6496
H7225	6497
H7226	6498
H7227	6485
H7228	6499
H7229	6500
H7230	6501
H7231	6502
H7232	6503
H7233	6504
H7234	6505
H7235	6506
H7236	6508
H7237	6507
H7238	6509
H7239	6510
H7240	6511
H7241	6501
H7242	6513
H7243	6514
H7244	6519
H7245	6515
H7246	6516
H7247	6503
H7248	6517
H7249	2661
H7250	6518
H7251	6520
H7252	6519
H7253	6521
H7254	6522
H7255	6524
H7256	6524
H7257	6524
H7258	6525
H7259	6526
H7260	6527
H7261	6528
H7262	6529
H7263	6514
H7264	6530
H7265	6530
H7266	6531
H7267	6532
H7268	6533
H7269	6534
H7270	6535
H7271	6536
H7272	6538
H7273	6539
H7274	6541
H7275	6542
H7276	6544
H7277	6544
H7278	6546
H7279	6545
H7280	6319
H7281	6547
H7282	6550
H7283	6551
H7284	6552
H7285	6553
H7286	6554
H7287	6555
H7288	6556
H7289	6557
H7290	6560
H7291	6558
H7292	6559
H7293	6561
H7294	6563
H7295	6564
H7296	6565
H7297	6565
H7298	6566
H7299	6576
H7300	6567
H7301	6567
H7302	6569
H7303	6570
H7304	6571
H7305	6571
H7306	6572
H7307	6574
H7308	6575
H7309	6577
H7310	6578
H7311	6509
H7312	6579
H7313	6581
H7314	6585
H7315	6587
H7316	6589
H7317	6580
H7318	6582
H7319	6583
H7320	6584
H7321	6586
H7322	6588
H7323	6592
H7324	6593
H7325	6594
H7326	6595
H7327	6596
H7328	6597
H7329	6598
H7330	6599
H7331	6601
H7332	6601
H7333	6602
H7334	6603
H7335	6604
H7336	6595
H7337	6605
H7338	6605
H7339	6607
H7340	6608
H7341	6610
H7342	6611
H7343	6612
H7344	6612
H7345	6614
H7346	6615
H7347	6609
H7348	6616
H7349	6617
H7350	6618
H7351	6619
H7352	6620
H7353	6621
H7354	6622
H7355	6623
H7356	6624
H7357	6625
H7358	6572
H7359	6626
H7360	
H7361	3318
H7362	6627
H7363	6675
H7364	6674
H7365	6628
H7366	6629
H7367	6630
H7368	6631
H7369	6632
H7370	6632
H7371	6633
H7372	6635
H7373	6643
H7374	6643
H7375	6636
H7376	6637
H7377	6638
H7378	6635
H7379	6639
H7380	6641
H7381	6642
H7382	6643
H7383	6643
H7384	6644
H7385	6645
H7386	6646
H7387	6636
H7388	3320
H7389	6648
H7390	6649
H7391	6650
H7392	6651
H7393	6652
H7394	1225
H7395	6653
H7396	6654
H7397	6654
H7398	6657
H7399	6658
H7400	6658
H7401	6659
H7402	6660
H7403	6661
H7404	6662
H7405	6663
H7406	6664
H7407	6666
H7408	6667
H7409	6667
H7410	6668
H7411	6669
H7412	6670
H7413	6670
H7414	6671
H7415	6672
H7416	6672
H7417	6673
H7418	6677
H7419	6678
H7420	6678
H7421	6679
H7422	6680
H7423	6681
H7424	6682
H7425	6683
H7426	6684
H7427	6685
H7428	6686
H7429	6687
H7430	6688
H7431	6689
H7432	6690
H7433	6689
H7434	6689
H7435	7436
H7436	6691
H7437	6692
H7438	6692
H7439	6693
H7440	6694
H7441	6695
H7442	6695
H7443	6696
H7444	6696
H7445	6697
H7446	6697
H7447	6697
H7448	6698
H7449	1049
H7450	6865
H7451	6699
H7452	6700
H7453	6701
H7454	6677
H7455	6702
H7456	6703
H7457	6704
H7458	6705
H7459	6708
H7460	6706
H7461	6707
H7462	6709
H7463	6710
H7464	6711
H7465	6712
H7466	6713
H7467	6715
H7468	6714
H7469	6716
H7470	6728
H7471	6717
H7472	6679
H7473	6718
H7474	6718
H7475	6719
H7476	6720
H7477	6721
H7478	7227+6721
H7479	6722
H7480	6723
H7481	6724
H7482	6726
H7483	6725
H7484	6727
H7485	6729
H7486	6730
H7487	6689
H7488	6731
H7489	6732
H7490	6731
H7491	6733
H7492	6734
H7493	6735
"	6737
H7494	6735
"	6737
H7495	6735
"	6737
H7496	6735
"	6737
H7497	6736
H7498	6738
"	6752
H7499	6740
H7500	6741
H7501	6742
H7502	6743
H7503	6743
H7504	6746
H7505	6745
"	6747
H7506	6747
H7507	6748
H7508	6742
H7509	6750
H7510	6749
H7511	6751
H7512	6754
H7513	6754
H7514	6756
H7515	6756
H7516	6757
H7517	6758
H7518	6759
H7519	6760
H7520	6761
H7521	6763
H7522	6762
H7523	6764
H7524	6765
H7525	6766
H7526	6767
H7527	6767
H7528	6767
H7529	6767
H7530	6768
H7531	6769
H7532	6770
H7533	6772
H7534	6771
H7535	6773
H7536	6774
H7537	6775
H7538	6776
H7539	6777
H7540	6778
H7541	6779
H7542	6780
H7543	6781
H7544	6781
H7545	6782
H7546	6784
H7547	6785
H7548	6786
H7549	6787
H7550	6788
H7551	6789
H7552	6783
H7553	6791
H7554	6790
H7555	6792
H7556	6792
H7557	6793
H7558	6793
H7559	6793
H7560	6800
H7561	6797
H7562	6794
H7563	6795
H7564	6796
H7565	6797
H7566	6797
H7567	6798
H7568	6798
H7569	6799
H7570	6800
H7571	6801
H7572	6802
H7573	6803
H7574	6804
H7575	6805
H7576	6806
H7577	6807
H7578	6807
H7579	6808
H7580	6820
H7581	6809
H7582	4704
"	6810
H7583	6811
H7584	6812
H7585	6813
H7586	6814
H7587	6815
H7588	6815
H7589	6816
H7590	6817
H7591	6818
H7592	6819
H7593	6820
H7594	6821
H7595	6822
H7596	6823
H7597	6824
H7598	6825
H7599	6826
H7600	6828
H7601	6829
H7602	6827
H7603	6830
H7604	6831
H7605	6832
H7606	6833
H7607	6834
H7608	6835
H7609	6825
H7610	6836
H7611	6837
H7612	6831
H7613	6838
H7614	6839
H7615	6840
H7616	6832
H7617	6849
H7618	6842
H7619	6843
H7620	6844
H7621	6845
H7622	6846
H7623	6846
H7624	6847
H7625	6848
H7626	6848
H7627	6850
H7628	6851
H7629	6852
H7630	6854
H7631	6855
H7632	6856
H7633	6858
H7634	6857
H7635	6859
H7636	6845
H7637	6860
H7638	6861
H7639	6862
H7640	6862
H7641	6862
H7642	
H7643	6863
H7644	6864
H7645	6865
H7646	6866
H7647	6867
H7648	6867
H7649	6868
H7650	6869
H7651	6869
H7652	1224
H7653	6870
H7654	6871
H7655	6872
H7656	6872
H7657	6872
H7658	6873
H7659	6869
H7660	6876
H7661	6875
H7662	6874
H7663	6877
H7664	6878
H7665	6879
H7666	6881
H7667	6880
H7668	6882
H7669	6883
H7670	6882
H7671	6884
H7672	6885
H7673	6886
H7674	3334
"	6887
H7675	6887
H7676	6869
H7677	6887
H7678	6888
H7679	6889
H7680	6890
H7681	6891
H7682	
H7683	6892
H7684	6893
H7685	6894
H7686	6895
H7687	6896
"	6897
H7688	6898
H7689	6899
H7690	6900
H7691	6901
H7692	6904
"	6905
H7693	6906
H7694	6907
H7695	6908
H7696	6909
H7697	6910
H7698	6911
H7699	6912
H7700	6913
H7701	6914
H7702	6915
H7703	6916
H7704	6917
H7705	6918
H7706	6919
H7707	6920
H7708	6921
H7709	6923
H7710	6924
H7711	6924
H7712	6927
H7713	6926
H7714	6924
H7715	6929
H7716	6930
H7717	6932
H7718	6934
H7719	6931
H7720	6935
H7721	6936
H7722	6937
H7723	6938
H7724	6939
H7725	6940
H7726	6941
H7727	6942
H7728	6945
"	6948
H7729	6946
H7730	6943
H7731	6944
H7732	6947
H7733	6949
H7734	5356
H7735	6950
H7736	6951
H7737	6952
H7738	6953
H7739	6954
H7740	6955
H7741	6956
H7742	6957
H7743	6957
H7744	6957
H7745	4723
H7746	6959
H7747	6960
H7748	6960
H7749	6961
H7750	4723
H7751	6495
H7752	5354
H7656	6962
H7753	6962
H7754	6963
H7755	6964
H7756	6965
H7757	6967
H7758	6968
H7759	6969
H7760	6970
H7761	6971
H7762	6973
H7763	6972
"	6974
H7764	6975
H7765	6975
H7766	6976
H7767	6977
H7768	
H7769	6979
H7770	6980
H7771	6982
H7772	6983
H7773	6984
H7774	3947
H7775	6985
H7776	6986
"	6987
H7777	6988
H7778	6989
H7779	6991
H7780	6993
H7781	6994
H7782	6995
H7783	6996
H7784	6997
H7785	6996
H7786	6998
H7787	6999
H7788	7000
H7789	7002
H7790	7003
H7791	
H7792	7004
H7793	7005
H7794	6958
"	7006
H7795	6892
H7796	6958
H7797	
H7798	7008
H7799	7009
H7800	7012
H7801	6969
H7802	7013
H7803	7014
H7804	7014
H7805	7014
H7806	7015
H7807	7016
H7808	7017
H7809	7018
H7810	6974
H7811	7019
H7812	7020
H7813	7021
H7814	7022
H7815	7023
H7816	7024
H7817	7024
H7818	7025
H7819	7025
H7820	7026
H7821	7027
H7822	7028
H7823	7029
H7824	7031
H7825	6963
H7826	6963
H7827	7035
H7828	7033
H7829	7034
H7830	7036
H7831	7037
H7832	7038
H7833	7039
H7834	7040
H7835	7041
H7836	7042
H7837	7043
H7838	7044
H7839	7045
H7840	7046
H7841	7047
H7842	7048
H7843	7049
H7844	7049
H7845	7050
H7846	7050
H7847	7051
H7848	7052

G/K	STRONG
H7849	7053
H7850	7054
H7851	7055
H7852	7056
H7853	7057
"	7063
H7854	7058
H7855	7059
H7856	6965
H7857	7060
H7858	7061
H7859	7062
H7860	7064
H7861	7065
H7862	7067
H7863	7068
H7864	7069
H7865	7069
H7866	7070
H7867	7071
H7868	7072
H7869	7073
H7870	7074
H7871	7075
H7872	7076
H7873	7077
H7874	7078
H7875	7079
H7876	7080
H7877	7081
H7878	7082
H7879	7083
H7880	
H7881	7084
H7882	7085
H7883	7086
H7884	7087
H7885	7087
H7886	7088
H7887	7090
H7888	7089
H7889	7091
H7890	7092
H7891	7093
H7892	7094
H7893	7095
H7894	7096
H7895	7097
H7896	7098
H7897	7097
H7898	7099
H7899	7112
H7900	7114
H7901	7098
H7902	7100
H7903	7101
H7904	7102
H7905	7103
H7906	7104
H7907	7105
H7908	7105
H7909	7106
H7910	4742
"	7106
H7911	7107
H7912	7110
H7913	7110
H7914	7111
H7915	7112
H7916	
H7917	7114
H7918	7114
H7919	7115
H7920	7116
H7921	7117
H7922	7119
H7923	7120
H7924	7121
H7925	7122
"	7125
H7926	7124
H7927	6981
H7928	7126
H7929	7131
H7930	7128
H7931	7130
H7932	7132
H7933	7133
H7934	7133
H7935	7134
H7936	7136
H7937	7137
H7938	7135
H7939	7136
H7940	7138
H7941	3368
H7942	7139
"	7144
H7943	7140
H7944	7142
H7945	7143
H7946	7141
H7947	7146
H7948	7145
H7949	7146
H7950	7147
H7951	7148
H7952	7150
H7953	7151
H7954	7152
H7955	2696+7152
H7956	7151
H7957	7153
H7958	7154
H7959	7153
H7960	7155
H7961	7157
H7962	7158
H7963	7158
H7964	7156
H7965	7159
H7966	7160
H7967	7161
H7968	7163
H7969	7161
H7970	7164
H7971	7165
H7972	7166
H7973	7167
H7974	7168
H7975	7169
H7976	7171
H7977	7172
H7978	7173
H7979	6979
H7980	7174
H7981	6979
H7982	6979
H7983	7175
H7984	7176
H7985	7177
H7986	7178
H7987	7184
H7988	7192
H7989	7193
H7990	7179
H7991	7180
H7992	7181
H7993	7182
H7994	7183
H7995	7183
H7996	7185
H7997	7186
H7998	7188
H7999	7189
H8000	7189
H8001	7190
H8002	7191
H8003	7194
H8004	7195
H8005	7196
H8006	7197
H8007	7197
H8008	7198
H8009	7199
H8010	
H8011	7200
"	7202
H8012	7201
H8013	7200
H8014	7203
H8015	7203
H8016	7211
H8017	7205
H8018	7206
H8019	7207
H8020	7208
H8021	7200
H8022	883
H8023	7209
H8024	7210
H8025	7211
H8026	7212
H8027	7213
H8028	7214
H8029	7215
H8030	7216
H8031	7218
"	7226
H8032	7219
H8033	7220
H8034	7218
H8035	7221
H8036	7222
H8037	7223
H8038	7224
H8039	4763
H8040	7225
H8041	7227
H8042	7227
H8043	7228
H8044	7230
H8045	7231
H8046	7232
H8047	7233
H8048	7234
H8049	7235
H8050	7235
H8051	7237
H8052	7239
H8053	7241
H8054	7242
H8055	7243
H8056	7245
H8057	7246
H8058	7247
H8059	7248
H8060	7249
H8061	7250
"	7252
"	7254
H8062	7251
H8063	7253
H8064	7254
H8065	7255
H8066	7255
H8067	7256
H8068	7243
H8069	7257
H8070	7258
H8071	7259
H8072	7262
H8073	7263
H8074	7264
H8075	7267
H8076	7268
H8077	7269
H8078	7270
"	8637
H8079	7272
H8080	5883
H8081	7273
H8082	7274
H8083	7275
H8084	7276
H8085	7278
H8086	7277
H8087	5372
"	7279
H8088	7280
H8089	7280
H8090	7280
H8091	7282
H8092	7281
H8093	7283
H8094	7285
H8095	7285
H8096	7286
H8097	7287
H8098	7287
H8099	7288
H8100	7289
H8101	7290
H8102	1721
H8103	7291
H8104	7292
H8105	7293
"	7294
H8106	7296
H8107	7295
H8108	7303
H8109	7297
H8110	7298
H8111	7298
H8112	7351
H8113	7300
H8114	1721
H8115	7301
H8116	7302
H8117	7303
H8118	7304
H8119	7305
H8120	7307
H8121	7309
H8122	7310
H8123	7311
H8124	7312
H8125	7315
H8126	7316
H8127	7317
H8128	7318
H8129	7319
"	7427
H8130	7442
H8131	7321
H8132	7323
H8133	7326
H8134	7327
H8135	7329
H8136	7330
H8137	7332
H8138	7333
H8139	7331
H8140	7334
H8141	7335
H8142	7336
H8143	7337
H8144	7338
H8145	7341
H8146	7342
H8147	7343
H8148	7339
H8149	7340
H8150	7340
H8151	7344
H8152	7345
H8153	7345
H8154	7346
H8155	7344+5892
H8156	7348
H8157	7349
H8158	7350
H8159	7351
H8160	7347
H8161	7353
H8162	7354
H8163	7355
H8164	7360
H8165	7357
H8166	7356
H8167	7358
H8168	7360
H8169	7361
H8170	3819
H8171	7356
H8172	7362
H8173	7363
H8174	7363
H8175	7364
H8176	7366
H8177	7367
H8178	7368
H8179	7369
H8180	7370
H8181	7371
H8182	7372
H8183	7373
H8184	3399
H8185	7374
H8186	7375
H8187	7376
H8188	7377
H8189	7378
H8190	7379
H8191	7379
H8192	7380
H8193	7306
H8194	7381
H8195	7383
H8196	7384
H8197	7324
H8198	7385
H8199	7386
H8200	7387
H8201	7325
H8202	7388
H8203	7389
H8204	7391
H8205	7390
H8206	7392
H8207	7393
H8208	7395
H8209	7394
H8210	7396
H8211	7394
H8212	7397
H8213	7398
H8214	7399
H8215	7400
H8216	7401
H8217	7402
H8218	7403
H8219	7404
H8220	7405
H8221	7406
H8222	7407
H8223	7408
H8224	7409
H8225	7311
H8226	7410
H8227	7411
H8228	7411
H8229	7413
H8230	7414
H8231	7415
H8232	7416
H8233	7417
H8234	7417
H8235	7417
H8236	7428
H8237	7417
H8238	7418
H8239	7419
H8240	7433
H8241	7418
H8242	7420
H8243	7422
H8244	7423
H8245	7423
H8246	761
H8247	7424
H8248	7425
H8249	7311
H8250	7426
H8251	7320
H8252	7429
H8253	7430
H8254	7431
H8255	7432
H8256	7434
H8257	7437
H8258	7435
H8259	7414
H8260	7438
H8261	7439
H8262	7440
H8263	7441
H8264	7442
"	7444
H8265	7445
H8266	7443
H8267	7446
H8268	7447
H8269	7447
H8270	7448
H8271	7449
H8272	7450
H8273	7451
H8274	7451
H8275	7452
H8276	7453
H8277	7454
H8278	7455
H8279	7456
H8280	7457
"	7458
H8281	7456
H8282	7459
H8283	7460
H8284	7461
H8285	7461
H8286	7473
H8287	7462
H8288	7465
H8289	7462
H8290	
H8291	7463
H8292	7464
H8293	7466
H8294	7467
H8295	7468
H8296	7469
H8297	7471
H8298	7472
H8299	7474
H8300	7464
H8301	7475
H8302	7477
H8303	7478
H8304	7479
H8305	7480
H8306	7481
H8307	7481
H8308	7482
H8309	7483
H8310	7483
H8311	7484
H8312	7484
H8313	7485
H8314	7486
H8315	7488
H8316	7488
H8317	7489
H8318	7489
H8319	7491
H8320	7492
H8321	7493
H8322	7493
H8323	7494
H8324	7495
H8325	7498
H8326	7500
H8327	7496
H8328	7497
H8329	7497
H8330	7501
H8331	7502
H8332	7503
H8333	7504
H8334	7498
H8335	7510
H8336	7505
H8337	7499
H8338	7506
H8339	7507
H8340	7508
H8341	7509
H8342	7510
H8343	7513
H8344	7322
H8345	7514
H8346	7511
"	7515
H8347	7516
H8348	7517
H8349	7518
H8350	7323
H8351	7519
H8352	7521
H8353	7520
H8354	7521
H8355	7521
H8356	7522
H8357	7523
H8358	7524
H8359	7525
H8360	7526
H8361	7527
H8362	7528
H8363	7529
H8364	7530
H8365	7531
H8366	7532
H8367	7531
H8368	7533
H8369	7534
H8370	7535
H8371	7536
H8372	7537
H8373	7538
H8374	7538
H8375	7539
H8376	7540
H8377	7541
H8378	7542
H8379	7543
H8380	7544
H8381	7545
H8382	7546
H8383	7547
H8384	7548
H8385	7549
H8386	7550
H8387	7551
H8388	7552
H8389	7552
H8390	7552
H8391	7553
H8392	7554
H8393	7555
H8394	7556
H8395	7557
H8396	7220
H8397	7558
H8398	7559
H8399	7561
H8400	7562
H8401	7563
H8402	7564
H8403	3573
H8404	7565
H8405	7566
H8406	7567
H8407	7568
H8408	7569
H8409	7570
H8410	7571
H8411	7572
H8412	7573
H8413	7574
H8414	7575
H8415	7576
H8416	7577
H8417	7578
H8418	
H8419	7603
H8420	7613
H8421	7613
H8422	7638
"	7639
H8423	7643
H8424	7643
H8425	7646
H8426	7647
H8427	7648
H8428	7649
H8429	7654
H8430	7653
H8431	7663
H8432	7663
H8433	7664
H8434	7679
H8435	7682
H8436	7685
H8437	7687
H8438	7689
H8439	7687
H8440	7702
H8441	7704
H8442	7704
H8443	7708
H8444	7713
H8445	2089
"	7716
H8446	7717
H8447	3026
H8448	7720
H8449	7730
H8450	5253
H8451	7735
H8452	7742
H8453	
H8454	7750
H8455	7753
H8456	7754
H8457	7754
H8458	7755
H8459	7755
H8460	7756
H8461	7760
H8462	5493
H8463	7795
H8464	7797
H8465	7808
H8466	7811
H8467	7813
H8468	7814
H8469	7818
H8470	7824
H8471	7832
H8472	
H8473	7846
H8474	7847
H8475	7852
H8476	7853
H8477	7854
H8478	7855
H8479	7856
H8480	7863
H8481	7865
H8482	7867
H8483	7869
H8484	7872
H8485	7873
H8486	7874
H8487	7875
H8488	7878
H8489	7880
H8490	7879
H8491	7881
H8492	7760
"	7787
H8493	7899
H8494	7900
H8495	
H8496	7905
H8497	7906
H8498	7907
H8499	7634
H8500	7914
H8501	7915
H8502	7916
"	7917
H8503	5526
H8504	
H8505	7919
H8506	7919
H8507	7922
H8508	5531
H8509	7936
H8510	7939
H8511	7940
H8512	7938
H8513	7958
H8514	8007
H8515	8008
H8516	8009
H8517	8012
H8518	8014
H8519	
H8520	8040
"	8041
H8521	8041
H8522	8042
H8523	8055
H8524	8056
H8525	8057
H8526	8063
H8527	
H8528	8072
H8529	8071
H8530	8073
H8531	
H8532	8079
H8533	8130
H8534	8135
H8535	8146
H8536	8149
H8537	8163
H8538	8163
H8539	8163
H8540	8164
H8541	8165
H8542	8165
H8543	8165
H8544	8166
H8545	8167
H8546	5587
H8547	8175
H8548	8175
H8549	8175
H8550	8178
H8551	8178
H8552	8181
H8553	8185
H8554	8183
H8555	8184
H8556	8188
H8557	8193
H8558	5596
H8559	8222
H8560	8224
H8561	8226
H8562	5606
H8563	5606
H8564	8210
H8565	5607
H8566	8242
H8567	8244
H8568	8265
H8569	8269
H8570	8272
H8571	8276
H8572	8277
H8573	8278
H8574	8279
H8575	8280
H8576	8282
H8577	8283
H8578	8286
H8579	8288
H8580	8294
H8581	8295
H8582	8296
H8583	8296
H8584	8297
H8585	8299
H8586	8300
H8587	8301
H8588	8304
H8589	8304
H8590	8303
H8591	8305
H8592	8308
H8593	8310
H8594	8311
H8595	8312
H8596	8313
H8597	8314
H8598	8315
H8599	8316
H8600	
H8601	8320
H8602	8291
H8603	8321
H8604	7796
"	8291
H8605	8322
H8606	7786
"	8323
H8607	8342
H8608	5640
H8609	8368
H8610	
H8611	7945
H8612	7579
H8613	7580
H8614	7581
H8615	7582
H8616	7582
H8617	7583
H8618	7584
H8619	7585
H8620	7586
H8621	7587
H8622	7588
H8623	7588
H8624	7589
H8625	7591
H8626	7592

G/K	STRONG
H8627	7594
H8628	7592
H8629	7596
H8630	7597
H8631	7599
H8632	1052
H8633	7600
H8634	7602
H8635	7602
H8636	7604
H8637	7605
H8638	7607
H8639	7610
H8640	7608
H8641	7609
H8642	7611
H8643	7612
H8644	7614
H8645	7615
H8646	7616
H8647	7617
H8648	7618
H8649	7619
H8650	
H8651	7620
H8652	7621
H8653	7665
H8654	7622
H8655	7623
H8656	7623
H8657	7626
H8658	7627
H8659	
H8660	7628
H8661	7629
H8662	7630
H8663	7632
H8664	7633
H8665	7628
H8666	7635
H8667	7636
H8668	7637
H8669	7622
H8670	7640
H8671	7642
H8672	7641
H8673	7641
H8674	7644
H8675	7644
H8676	7645
H8677	7645
H8678	7650
H8679	7651
H8680	7652
H8681	7652
H8682	884
H8683	7656
H8684	7657
H8685	7658
H8686	7659
H8687	7660
H8688	7661
H8689	7665
H8690	7666
H8691	7667
H8692	7668
H8693	7669
H8694	7667
H8695	7670
H8696	7671
H8697	7673
H8698	7673
H8699	7675
H8700	7674
H8701	7676
H8702	7677
H8703	7678
H8704	7683
H8705	7684
H8706	7686
H8707	7681
H8708	7688
H8709	7691
H8710	7692
H8711	7693
H8712	7694
H8713	7696
H8714	7697
H8715	7698
H8716	7699
H8717	7700
H8718	7699
H8719	7701
H8720	7703
"	7736
H8721	7705
H8722	
H8723	1779
H8724	7706
H8725	7707
H8726	1779
H8727	7709
H8728	7710
H8729	7711
H8730	7711
H8731	7714
H8732	7718
H8733	7719
H8734	
H8735	
H8736	7723
H8737	7724
H8738	7722
H8739	7722
H8740	7725
H8741	
H8742	7619
H8743	7726
H8744	7727
H8745	7728
H8746	7729
H8747	7731
H8748	7732
H8749	7733
H8750	7737
H8751	7737
H8752	
H8753	7740
H8754	7741
H8755	7743
H8756	7744
H8757	7745
H8758	7746
H8759	
H8760	7747
H8761	7748
H8762	7749
H8763	7751
H8764	7590
H8765	7752
H8766	7752
H8767	7757
H8768	7758
H8769	7759
H8770	7762
H8771	7764
H8772	7765
H8773	7766
H8774	7767
H8775	7768
H8776	7773
H8777	7771
H8778	7772
H8779	7771
H8780	7769
H8781	7770
H8782	7769
H8783	7774
H8784	7775
H8785	7776
H8786	7777
H8787	7777
H8788	7778
H8789	7779
H8790	7779
H8791	7780
H8792	8197
H8793	7781
H8794	5855
H8795	7782
H8796	7783
H8797	7785
H8798	7784
H8799	8264
H8800	7789
H8801	7788
H8802	7794
H8803	7790
H8804	7793
H8805	7791
H8806	8324
H8807	7798
H8808	7799
H8809	7800
H8810	7895
H8811	7803
H8812	7805
H8813	7806
H8814	7807
H8815	7809
H8816	7810
H8817	7812
H8818	7815
H8819	7816
H8820	7817
H8821	7819
H8822	7819
"	7820
H8823	7819
H8824	7821
H8825	7822
H8826	7823
H8827	7825
H8828	7826
H8829	7827
H8830	7828
H8831	7829
H8832	7830
H8833	7831
H8834	7831
H8835	7833
H8836	7834
H8837	7835
H8838	7836
H8839	7838
H8840	7837
H8841	7839
H8842	7840
H8843	7841
H8844	7842
H8845	516
"	7843
H8846	7845
H8847	7848
H8848	7849
H8849	7850
H8850	7851
H8851	7857
H8852	7858
H8853	7860
H8854	
H8855	7861
H8856	7862
H8857	7864
H8858	7866
H8859	7871
H8860	7870
H8861	7876
H8862	7877
H8863	7817
H8864	7882
H8865	7883
H8866	7884
H8867	7752
H8868	7885
H8869	7886
H8870	7887
H8871	7758
H8872	7888
H8873	7889
H8874	8366
H8875	7890
H8876	7891
H8877	7892
H8878	7892
H8879	
H8880	7893
H8881	7894
H8882	7895
H8883	7896
H8884	7897
H8885	7898
H8886	7901
H8887	7902
H8888	7903
H8889	7904
H8890	7908
H8891	7909
H8892	7909
H8893	7910
H8894	7911
H8895	7913
H8896	7918
H8897	7921
H8898	7923
H8899	7925
H8900	7926
"	7929
H8901	7927
H8902	7927
H8903	7928
H8904	7930
H8905	7931
"	7933
H8906	
H8907	7934
H8908	7935
H8909	7935
H8910	7937
H8911	7941
H8912	7937
H8913	7943
H8914	7942
H8915	7944
H8916	7946
H8917	7947
H8918	7948
H8919	7949
H8920	7950
H8921	7950
H8922	7951
H8923	7952
"	7953
H8924	7956
H8925	7956
H8926	7887
H8927	7957
H8928	7957
H8929	7961
H8930	7959
H8931	7887
H8932	7962
H8933	7964
H8934	7965
H8935	7967
H8936	7966
H8937	7968
H8938	7971
H8939	7973
H8940	7975
H8941	7974
H8942	7975
H8943	7976
H8944	7977
H8945	7973
H8946	7978
H8947	7979
H8948	7980
H8949	7982
H8950	7983
H8951	7986
H8952	7987
H8953	7988
H8954	7989
H8955	7991
H8956	7991
H8957	7991
H8958	7992
H8959	7993
H8960	7994
H8961	7995
H8962	7996
H8963	7997
H8964	7997
H8965	7998
H8966	7999
H8967	
H8968	8002
H8969	8003
H8970	8004
H8971	
H8972	8005
H8973	8006
H8974	8011
H8975	4100
H8976	8010
H8977	8013
H8978	8073
H8979	8015
H8980	8016
H8981	8017
H8982	8018
H8983	8018
H8984	8019
H8985	8019
H8986	8020
H8987	8022
H8988	8021
H8989	8023
"	8024
H8990	8025
H8991	8026
H8992	8027
H8993	7969
H8994	8028
H8995	8031
H8996	8030
H8997	8032
H8998	7991
H8999	7992
H9000	8029
H9001	7970
H9002	
H9003	7597
H9004	8033
H9005	8034
H9006	8035
H9007	8037
H9008	8038
H9009	8039
H9010	8043
H9011	8044
H9012	8045
H9013	8106
H9014	8047
H9015	8048
H9016	8049
H9017	8050
H9018	8051
H9019	8052
H9020	8053
H9021	8054
H9022	
H9023	8058
H9024	8059
H9025	8060
H9026	8061
H9027	8062
H9028	8064
H9029	8066
H9030	8067
H9031	8068
H9032	8068
H9033	8069
H9034	8069
H9035	8070
H9036	8073
H9037	8074
H9038	8076
H9039	8077
H9040	8077
H9041	8078
H9042	8080
H9043	8081
H9044	4924
H9045	8082
H9046	8083
H9047	8084
H9048	8085
H9049	8085
H9050	8087
H9051	8088
H9052	8091
H9053	8089
H9054	8090
H9055	8092
H9056	8093
H9057	8094
H9058	8095
H9059	8096
H9060	8097
H9061	8098
H9062	8098
H9063	8099
H9064	8100
H9065	8101
H9066	8102
H9067	8103
H9068	8104
H9069	8105
H9070	8106
H9071	7763
H9072	8108
H9073	8109
H9074	8110
H9075	8110
H9076	8111
H9077	8112
H9078	8113
H9079	8114
H9080	8114
H9081	8107
H9082	8070
H9083	8116
H9084	8117
H9085	8118
H9086	8119
H9087	8121
H9088	8123
H9089	8124
H9090	1030
H9091	8125
H9092	8126
H9093	1052
H9094	8127
H9095	8129
H9096	8132
H9097	8142
H9098	8134
H9099	8136
H9100	8137
H9101	8132
"	8138
H9102	8141
H9102.5	
H9103	
H9104	8142
H9105	8143
H9106	8144
H9107	
H9108	8145
H9109	8147
H9110	8148
H9111	8150
H9112	8150
H9113	8151
H9114	8152
H9115	8154
H9116	8155
H9117	8156
H9118	8157
H9119	8158
H9120	8159
H9121	8161
H9122	8162
H9123	8168
H9124	8169
H9125	8169
H9126	8170
H9127	8171
H9128	8172
H9129	8173
H9130	8173
H9131	8174
H9132	8176
H9133	8179
H9134	8180
H9135	8182
H9136	8186
H9137	8187
H9138	8187
H9139	8189
H9140	8190
H9141	8191
H9142	8192
H9143	8195
H9144	8196
H9145	8197
H9146	8197
H9147	8194
H9148	8198
H9149	8199
H9150	8201
H9151	8202
H9152	8203
H9153	8203
H9154	8204
H9155	8205
H9156	8195
H9157	8206
H9158	8206
H9159	8207
H9160	8208
H9161	8210
H9162	8211
H9163	8212
H9164	8213
H9165	8216
H9166	8217
H9167	
H9168	8218
H9169	8219
H9170	8220
H9171	8223
H9172	8221
H9173	8309
H9174	
H9175	8225
H9176	8227
H9177	8227
H9178	
H9179	8228
H9180	8229
H9181	8230
H9182	8231
H9183	8233
H9184	8234
H9185	8235
H9186	8236
H9187	8237
H9188	8237
H9189	8239
H9190	8240
H9191	8240
H9192	8241
H9193	8245
H9194	8245
H9195	8245
H9196	8247
H9197	8248
H9198	8249
"	8250
H9199	8251
H9200	8252
H9201	8253
H9202	8254
H9203	8255
H9204	8256
H9205	8257
H9206	8258
H9207	8259
H9208	8260
H9209	8261
H9210	8262
H9211	8263
H9212	8264
H9213	8266
H9214	8267
H9215	
H9216	8268
H9217	8285
H9218	8270
H9219	8270
H9220	8273
H9221	8274
H9222	8275
H9223	3474
"	8281
H9224	8281
"	8284
H9225	8285
H9226	8287
H9227	8289
H9228	8290
H9229	8292
H9230	8293
H9231	7861
H9232	8298
H9233	8302
H9234	8302
H9235	8306
H9236	8309
H9237	8317
H9238	8318
H9239	8319
H9240	8322
H9241	8292
H9242	8325
H9243	8325
H9244	8307
H9245	8327
H9246	8329
H9247	8326
"	8328
H9248	8333
H9249	8333
H9250	8334
H9251	8335
H9252	8337
H9253	8336
H9254	8336
H9255	8338
H9256	8339
H9257	8341
H9258	8343
H9259	8344
H9260	
H9261	8345
H9262	8346
H9263	8347
H9264	8348
H9265	8349
H9266	8350
H9267	
H9268	8351
"	8352
"	8357
H9269	8352
H9270	
H9271	8356
H9272	8354
H9273	
H9274	8359
H9275	8358
H9276	8360
H9277	8363
H9278	8362
H9279	8364
H9280	8365
H9281	8365
H9282	8366
H9283	
H9284	8367
H9285	8369
H9286	8371
H9287	
H9288	8372
H9289	8373
H9290	8374
H9291	8375
H9292	8376
H9293	8377
H9294	8378
H9295	8379
H9296	8380
H9297	8381
H9298	8382
H9299	8385
H9300	8384
H9301	8385
H9302	8386
H9303	8383
H9304	8387
H9305	8388
H9306	8388
H9307	8389
H9308	8390
H9309	839
"	8391
H9310	8392
H9311	8393
H9312	8394
H9313	8395
H9314	8396
H9315	8398
H9316	8397
H9317	8422
H9318	8399
H9319	8400
H9320	8401
H9321	8402
H9322	8403
H9323	8404
H9324	8405
H9325	8407
H9326	8408
H9327	8409
H9328	8425
H9329	8410
H9330	8412
H9331	8413
H9332	8414
H9333	8415
H9334	8417
H9335	8416
H9336	8418
H9337	8419
H9338	8420
H9339	8380
H9340	8423
H9341	8394
H9342	8424
H9343	8426
H9344	8427
H9345	8428
H9346	8430
H9347	8431
H9348	8432
H9349	8433
H9350	8433
H9351	8434
H9352	8435
H9353	8436
H9354	8437
H9355	8438
H9356	8439
H9357	8438
H9358	8440
H9359	8441
H9360	8442
H9361	8443
H9362	8444
H9363	8445
H9364	8628
H9365	8446
H9366	8447
"	8448
H9367	8449
H9368	8451
"	8452
H9369	8453
H9370	8454
H9371	8455
H9372	8456
H9373	8457
H9374	8458
H9375	8459
H9376	8461
H9377	8463
H9378	8462
H9379	8464
H9380	8465
H9381	8466
H9382	8467
H9383	8468
H9384	8469
H9385	8466
"	8470
H9386	8466
H9387	8471
H9388	8472
H9389	8473
H9390	8475
H9391	8476
H9392	8477
H9393	8478
H9394	8480
H9395	8480
H9396	8481
H9397	8482
H9398	8483
H9399	8484
H9400	8436
H9401	8485
H9402	8486
H9403	8487
H9404	8489
H9405	8488
H9406	8490
H9407	8491

G/K	STRONG
H9408	8492
H9409	8493
H9410	8494
H9411	8495
H9412	8496
"	8501
H9413	8497
H9414	8498
"	8499
H9415	8500
H9416	8502
H9417	8503
H9418	8504
H9419	8505
H9420	8506
H9421	8507
H9422	8508
H9423	8509
H9424	8510
H9425	8512
H9426	8521
H9427	8528
H9428	8511
H9429	8514
H9430	8513
H9431	8515
H9432	8516
H9433	8407
H9434	8518
H9435	8524
H9436	8520
H9437	8522
H9438	2048
H9439	8525
H9440	8526
H9441	8527
H9442	8519
H9443	8529
H9444	8530
H9445	8515
H9446	8534
H9447	8535
H9448	8537
H9449	8539
H9450	8538
H9451	8541
H9452	8542
H9453	8543
H9454	8544
H9455	8545
H9456	8546
H9457	8547
H9458	8548
H9459	8549
H9460	8550
H9461	8551
H9462	8552
H9463	8553
H9464	8554
H9465	8555
H9466	8556
H9467	8556
H9468	8557
H9469	8558
H9470	8559
H9471	8559
H9472	8560
H9473	8560
H9474	8561
H9475	8562
H9476	8563
H9477	8564
H9478	8565
"	8568
H9479	8566
H9480	8567
H9481	8569
H9482	8570
H9483	8571
H9484	8572
H9485	8573
H9486	8574
H9487	8575
H9488	8575
H9489	8576
H9490	8577
H9491	8580
H9492	8580
H9493	8581
H9494	8582
H9495	8583
H9496	8584
H9497	8583
H9498	8585
H9499	8585
H9500	8586
H9501	
H9502	8587
H9503	8588
H9504	8589
H9505	8590
H9506	8591
H9507	5774
H9508	8592
H9509	8593
H9510	8594
H9511	8595
H9512	8596
H9513	8596
H9514	8597
H9515	8598
H9516	8599
H9517	8599
H9518	8600
H9519	8601
H9520	6617
H9521	8602
H9522	8602
H9523	8603
H9524	8604
H9525	8605
H9526	8606
H9527	8607
H9528	8608
H9529	8609
H9530	8610
H9531	8611
H9532	8612
H9533	8613
H9534	8616
H9535	8615
H9536	8615
H9537	8616
H9538	8617
H9539	6965
"	8618
H9540	8619
H9541	8620
H9542	8621
H9543	8622
H9544	8623
H9545	8626
H9546	8628
H9547	8629
H9548	8630
H9549	8633
H9550	8634
H9551	8635
H9552	8636
H9553	8638
H9554	8639
H9555	8640
H9556	8641
H9557	8642
H9558	8643
H9559	8644
H9560	8645
H9561	8646
H9562	8646
H9563	8647
H9564	8649
H9565	
H9566	8649
H9567	8649
H9568	8650
H9569	8649
H9570	8653
H9571	8654
H9572	8655
H9573	8656
H9574	8656
H9575	8657
H9576	8659
H9577	8658
H9578	8659
H9579	8660
H9580	8661
H9581	8662
H9582	8667
H9583	8663
H9584	
H9585	8664
H9586	8664
H9587	8665
H9588	8666
H9589	7738
"	8663
H9590	
H9591	8668
H9592	8669
H9593	8670
H9594	
H9595	8671
H9596	8672
H9597	8673

ARAMAIC OLD TESTAMENT

G/K	STRONG
A10001	
A10002	
A10003	2
A10004	4
A10005	7
A10006	69
A10007	104
A10008	116
A10009	144
A10010	147
A10011	148
A10012	149
A10013	153
A10014	230
A10015	228
A10016	236
A10017	252
A10018	263
A10019	280
A10020	307
A10021	311
A10022	320
A10023	317
A10024	318
A10025	321
A10026	324
A10027	363
A10028	574
A10029	383
A10030	399
A10031	409
A10032	412
A10033	426
A10034	429
A10035	431
A10036	459
A10037	479
A10038	506
A10039	521
A10040	524
A10041	540
A10042	560
A10043	563
A10044	576
A10045	581
A10046	582
A10047	586
A10048	598
A10049	600
A10050	606
A10051	607
A10052	607
A10053	608
A10054	613
A10055	620
A10056	629
A10057	633
A10058	636
A10059	638
A10060	670
A10061	671
A10062	671
A10063	674
A10064	677
A10065	703
A10066	711
A10067	718
A10068	735
A10069	738
A10070	746
A10071	749
A10072	755
A10073	754
A10074	756
A10075	772
A10076	773
A10077	778
A10078	783
A10079	787
A10080	785
A10081	826
A10082	846
A10083	849
A10084	852
A10085	858
A10086	861
A10087	870
A10088	
A10089	
A10090	873
A10091	888
A10092	870
A10093	895
A10094	896
A10095	921
A10096	924
A10097	927
A10098	989
A10099	997
A10100	999
A10101	1001
A10102	956
A10103	1005
A10104	1079
A10105	1113
A10106	1080
A10107	1093
A10108	1096
A10109	1113
A10110	1123
A10111	1124
A10112	1147
A10113	1149
A10114	1156
A10115	1159
A10116	1169
A10117	1236
A10118	1240
A10119	1251
A10120	1247
A10121	1289
A10122	1289
A10123	1291
A10124	1297
A10125	1321
A10126	1325
A10127	
A10128	1355
A10129	1358
A10130	1370
A10131	1400
A10132	1401
A10133	1411
A10134	1414
A10135	1459
A10136	1467
A10137	1519
A10138	
A10139	1490
A10140	1505
A10141	1510
A10142	1528
A10143	1535
A10144	1541
A10145	1547
A10146	1560
A10147	1585
A10148	1596
A10149	1611
A10150	1635
A10151	1655
A10152	
A10153	
A10154	1668
A10155	1678
A10156	1684
A10157	1685
A10158	1693
A10159	1701
A10160	1722
A10161	1723
A10162	1723
A10163	1753
A10164	1757
A10165	1759
A10166	1761
A10167	1763
A10168	1768
A10169	1778
A10170	1780
A10171	1782
A10172	1784
A10173	1791
A10174	1797
A10175	1798
A10176	1799
A10177	1799
A10178	1815
A10179	1821
A10180	1836
A10181	1841
A10182	1855
A10183	1859
A10184	1868
A10185	1872
A10186	1882
A10187	1883
A10188	1884
A10189	
A10190	
A10191	
A10192	
A10193	
A10194	1888
A10195	1888
A10196	1907
A10197	1917
A10198	1922
A10199	1923
A10200	1932
A10201	1934
A10202	1946
A10203	
A10204	
A10205	1932
A10206	1965
A10207	1981
A10208	1983
A10209	
A10210	1994
A10211	2002
A10212	2002
A10213	2006
A10214	
A10215	
A10216	
A10217	2031
A10218	927
A10219	5069
A10220	
A10221	
A10222	
A10223	2084
A10224	2095
A10225	2103
A10226	2110
A10227	2112
A10228	2122
A10229	2136
A10230	2148
A10231	2164
A10232	2166
A10233	2170
A10234	2171
A10235	2178
A10236	2192
A10237	2200
A10238	2211
A10239	2217
A10240	2234
A10241	
A10242	2248
A10243	2255
A10244	2257
A10245	2269
A10246	2273
A10247	2292
A10248	2298
A10249	2306
A10250	2305
A10251	2323
A10252	2324
A10253	2338
A10254	2358
A10255	2370
A10256	2376
A10257	2379
A10258	2402
A10259	2408
A10260	2409
A10261	2417
A10262	2418
A10263	2423
A10264	2429
A10265	2445
A10266	2452
A10267	2493
A10268	2499
A10269	2508
A10270	2528
A10271	2562
A10272	2591
A10273	2597
A10274	2604
A10275	2608
A10276	2627
A10277	2631
A10278	2632
A10279	2635
A10280	2685
A10281	2718
A10282	2749
A10283	2761
A10284	2783
A10285	2804
A10286	2816
A10287	2818
A10288	2818
A10289	2819
A10290	2827
A10291	2857
A10292	
A10293	2868
A10294	2869
A10295	2877
A10296	2906
A10297	2908
A10298	2917
A10299	2920
A10300	2927
A10301	2939
A10302	2942
A10303	2953
A10304	2957
A10305	2967
A10306	
A10307	
A10308	2987
A10309	3007
A10310	3026
A10311	3028
A10312	3029
A10313	3046
A10314	3052
A10315	3061
A10316	3062
A10317	3118
A10318	3136
A10319	
A10320	3191
A10321	3202
A10322	3221
A10323	3255
A10324	3272
A10325	3272
A10326	3321
A10327	3330
A10328	3345
A10329	3346
A10330	3358
A10331	3367
A10332	3390
A10333	3393
A10334	3410
A10335	3479
A10336	3443
A10337	3487
A10338	3488
A10339	3493
A10340	
A10341	
A10342	
A10343	3538
A10344	
A10345	3542
A10346	3546
A10347	3549
A10348	3551
A10349	
A10350	3567
A10351	
A10352	3604
A10353	3606
A10354	3635
A10355	
A10356	4101
A10357	3652
A10358	3660
A10359	3673
A10360	3675
A10361	3679
A10362	3702
A10363	3705
A10364	3706
A10365	3706
A10366	3729
A10367	3734
A10368	3737
A10369	3735
A10370	3744
A10371	3745
A10372	3764
A10373	3779
A10374	3790
A10375	3792
A10376	3797
A10377	
A10378	
A10379	3809
A10380	3821
A10381	3825
A10382	3831
A10383	3848
A10384	3809
A10385	3861
A10386	3861
A10387	3879
A10388	3890
A10389	3900
A10390	3904
A10391	3916
A10392	3961
A10393	
A10394	3964
A10395	3969
A10396	3977
A10397	3983
A10398	3984
A10399	4040
A10400	4049
A10401	4056
A10402	4061
A10403	4070
A10404	4076
"	4077
A10405	4076
"	4077
A10406	4083
A10407	4070
A10408	4101
A10409	4193
A10410	4203
A10411	4223
A10412	4255
A10413	4291
A10414	4333
A10415	4336
A10416	4391
A10417	4398
A10418	4406
A10419	4415
A10420	4416
A10421	4430
A10422	4431
A10423	4433
A10424	4437
A10425	4449
A10426	4479
A10427	4481
A10428	4484
A10429	4061
A10430	4486
A10431	4483
A10432	4504
A10433	4510
A10434	4567
A10435	4577
A10436	4606
A10437	4756
A10438	4776
A10439	4779
A10440	4804
A10441	4873
A10442	4887
A10443	4887
A10444	4903
A10445	4907
A10446	4953
A10447	4961
A10448	4978
A10449	
A10450	
A10451	5013
A10452	5017
A10453	5020
A10454	5023
A10455	5029
A10456	5043
A10457	5047
A10458	5049
A10459	5053
A10460	5665
A10461	5069
A10462	5073
A10463	5075
A10464	5085
A10465	5094
A10466	5094
A10467	5094
A10468	5103
A10469	5111
A10470	5122
A10471	5135
A10472	5142
A10473	5174
A10474	5182
A10475	5191
A10476	5202
A10477	
A10478	5208
A10479	5232
A10480	5245
A10481	5256
A10482	5260
A10483	5261
A10484	5308
A10485	5312
A10486	5313
A10487	5326
A10488	5330
A10489	5338
A10490	5343
A10491	5368
A10492	5376
A10493	5389
A10494	5396
A10495	5403
A10496	5407
A10497	5412
A10498	5415
A10499	5426
A10500	
A10501	5443
A10502	5446
A10503	5452
A10504	5457
A10505	5460
A10506	5463
A10507	5481
A10508	5487
A10509	5491
A10510	5481
A10511	7859
A10512	5481
A10513	5559
"	5267
A10514	5583
A10515	5609
A10516	5613
A10517	5622
A10518	5632
A10519	5642
A10520	5642
A10521	
A10522	5648
A10523	5649
A10524	5665
A10525	5673
A10526	5675
A10527	5705
A10528	5709
A10529	5714
A10530	5732
A10531	5751
A10532	5758
A10533	5776
A10534	5784
A10535	5796
A10536	5824
A10537	5831
A10538	5839
A10539	5843
A10540	5870
A10541	5894
A10542	5922
A10543	5924
A10544	5931
A10545	5928
A10546	5943
A10547	5952
A10548	5946
A10549	5954
A10550	5957
A10551	5962
A10552	5967
A10553	5972
A10554	5974
A10555	5994
A10556	6015
A10557	3705
A10558	6032
A10559	6033
A10560	6050
A10561	6056
A10562	6065
A10563	3706
A10564	6074
A10565	6088
A10566	6132
A10567	6136
A10568	6146
A10569	6151
A10570	6167
A10571	6173
A10572	6211
A10573	6236
A10574	6243
A10575	6246
A10576	3706
A10577	6263
A10578	6268
A10579	
A10580	6347
A10581	6353
A10582	6361
A10583	6386
A10584	6387
A10585	6392
A10586	6399
A10587	6402
A10588	6433
A10589	6447
A10590	6460
A10591	6523
A10592	6537
A10593	6537
A10594	6540

G/K	STRONG
A10595	6543
A10596	6562
A10597	6568
A10598	6573
A10599	6590
A10600	6591
A10601	6600
A10602	6606
A10603	6613
A10604	
A10605	6634
A10606	6640
A10607	6647
A10608	6655
A10609	6656
A10610	6665
A10611	6676
A10612	6739
A10613	6744
A10614	6755
A10615	6841
A10616	6853
A10617	
A10618	6902
A10619	6903
A10620	6922
A10621	6925
A10622	6928
A10623	6933
A10624	6966
A10625	6992
A10626	7001
A10627	7007
A10628	7010
A10629	7011
A10630	7030
A10631	7032
A10632	7066
A10633	7108
A10634	7109
A10635	7113
A10636	7118
A10637	7123
A10638	7127
A10639	7129
A10640	7149
A10641	7162
A10642	7170
A10643	7187
A10644	7030
A10645	
A10646	7217
A10647	7229
"	7260
A10648	7236
A10649	7240
A10650	7238
A10651	7244
A10652	7261
A10653	7265
A10654	7266
A10655	7271
A10656	7284
A10657	7299
A10658	7308
A10659	7313
A10660	7314
A10661	7328
A10662	7348
A10663	7352
A10664	7359
A10665	7365
A10666	7382
A10667	7412
A10668	7470
A10669	7476
A10670	7487
A10671	7490
A10672	7512
A10673	7560
A10674	
A10675	7868
A10676	5443
A10677	7680
A10678	7690
A10679	3026
A10680	7859
A10681	7868
A10682	7761
A10683	7920
A10684	7924
A10685	7955
A10686	8131
A10687	8177
A10688	
A10689	7593
A10690	7595
A10691	7598
A10692	7606
A10693	7624
A10694	7625
A10695	7631
A10696	7655
A10697	7662
A10698	7672
A10699	7695
A10700	7712
A10701	7715
A10702	7739
A10703	7792
A10704	7801
A10705	7844
A10706	7804
A10707	3319
A10708	7912
A10709	7932
A10710	7954
A10711	7955
A10712	7960
A10713	7963
A10714	7972
A10715	7981
A10716	7984
A10717	7985
A10718	7990
A10719	8000
A10720	8001
A10721	8036
A10722	8046
A10723	8065
A10724	8075
A10725	8086
A10726	8115
A10727	8120
A10728	8122
A10729	8124
A10730	8128
A10731	8133
A10732	8140
A10733	8139
A10734	8160
A10735	8200
A10736	8209
A10737	8214
A10738	8215
A10739	8232
A10740	8238
A10741	8243
A10742	8271
A10743	8330
A10744	8332
A10745	8332
A10746	8340
A10747	8353
A10748	8355
A10749	8361
A10750	8370
A10751	
A10752	8406
A10753	8411
A10754	8421
A10755	8429
A10756	8450
A10757	8460
"	8479
A10758	8517
A10759	8523
A10760	8531
A10761	8532
A10762	8533
A10763	8540
A10764	8536
A10765	8578
A10766	8579
A10767	8614
A10768	8624
A10769	8625
A10770	8625
A10771	8627
A10772	8631
A10773	8632
A10774	8632
A10775	8648
A10776	8651
A10777	8652
A10778	8648
A10779	8674

GREEK NEW TESTAMENT

G/K	STRONG
G1	1
G2	2
G3	3
G4	4
G5	5
G6	6
G7	7
G8	8
G9	9
G10	10
G11	11
G12	12
G13	13
G14	14
G15	18+2041
G16	15
G17	16
G18	17
G19	18
G20	19
G21	20
G22	21
G23	22
G24	23
G25	24
G26	25
G27	26
G28	27
G29	28
G30	29
G31	30
G32	31
G33	518
G34	32
G35	30
G36	34
G37	35
G38	36
G39	37
G40	38
G41	39
"	40
G42	41
G43	42
G44	43
G45	44
G46	45
G47	46
G48	47
G49	48
G50	49
G51	50
G52	51
G53	52
G54	53
G55	54
G56	55
G57	56
G58	57
G59	58
G60	59
G61	60
G62	61
G63	62
G64	63
G65	64
G66	65
G67	66
G68	67
G69	68
G70	69
G71	70
G72	33
"	71
G73	72
G74	73
G75	74
G76	75
G77	76
G78	77
G79	78
G80	79
G81	80
G82	81
G83	82
G84	83
G85	84
G86	85
G87	86
G88	87
G89	88
G90	89
G91	90
G92	91
G93	92
G94	93
G95	94+2923
G96	94
G97	95
G98	689
G99	96
G100	97
G101	98
G102	99
G103	100
G104	101
G105	102
G106	103
G107	104
G108	105
G109	106
G110	107
G111	108
G112	
G113	109
G114	110
G115	2288+1
G116	111
G117	112
G118	113
G119	114
G120	115
G121	116
G122	117
G123	118
G124	119
G125	4867
G126	120
G127	121
G128	122
G129	123
G130	124
G131	125
G132	126
G133	127
G134	128
G135	129
G136	130
G137	131
G138	132
G139	133
G140	134
G141	135
G142	136
G143	137
G144	2056
G145	138
G146	139
G147	140
G148	141
G149	142
G150	143
G151	144
G152	145
G153	146
G154	147
G155	148
G156	149
"	150
G157	151
G158	152
G159	153
G160	154
G161	155
G162	156
G163	157
G164	4256
G165	158
"	159
G166	157
G167	160
G168	161
G169	162
G170	163
G171	164
G172	165
G173	166
G174	167
G175	168
G176	169
G177	170
G178	171
G179	172
G180	173
G181	174
G182	175
G183	176
G184	177
G185	178
G186	179
G187	180
G188	180
G189	181
G190	182
G191	183
G192	184
G193	185
G194	85
G195	186
G196	187
G197	188
G198	189
G199	190
G200	191
G201	191
G202	192
G203	193
G204	194
G205	195
G206	196
G207	
G208	198
G209	199
"	197
G210	200
G211	201
G212	202
G213	203
G214	204
G215	205
G216	206
G217	207
G218	208
G219	209
G220	210
G221	217
G222	211
G223	211
G224	212
G225	213
G226	214
G227	215
G228	216
G229	217
G230	218
G231	219
G232	220
G233	221
G234	222
G235	223
G236	224
G237	225
G238	226
G239	227
G240	228
G241	229
G242	230
G243	231
G244	232
G245	233
G246	234
G247	235
G248	236
G249	237
G250	
G251	238
G252	239
G253	240
G254	241
G255	2087
G256	242
G257	243
G258	244
G259	245
G260	246
G261	247
G262	248
G263	249
G264	250
G265	251
G266	252
G267	253
G268	254
G269	255
G270	1
G271	256
G272	257
G273	258
G274	259
G275	260
G276	261
G277	262
G278	263
G279	264
G280	265
G281	266
G282	267
G283	268
G284	
G285	269
G286	270
G287	271
G288	272
G289	273
G290	274
G291	275
G292	276
G293	277
G294	278
G295	279
G296	280
G297	281
G298	282
G299	283
G300	284
G301	
G302	285
G303	286
G304	287
G305	880
G306	288
G307	289
G308	290
G309	291
G310	292
G311	906+293
G312	293
G313	294
G314	294
G315	295
G316	296
G317	297
G318	298
G319	
G320	299
G321	300
G322	301
G323	302
G324	303
G325	304
G326	305
G327	306
G328	307
G329	308
G330	309
G331	310
G332	311
G333	508
G334	312
G335	313
G336	314
G337	315
G338	316
G339	317
G340	318
G341	319
G342	320
G343	321
G344	322
G345	323
G346	324
G347	325
G348	326
G349	327
G350	328
G351	329
G352	330
G353	331
G354	332
G355	333
G356	334
G357	335
G358	336
G359	337
G360	338
G361	339
G362	340
G363	341
G364	342
G365	343
G366	344
G367	345
G368	346
G369	347
G370	348
G371	349
G372	
G373	350
G374	351
G375	617
G376	352
G377	353
G378	354
G379	355
G380	242
G381	356
G382	357
G383	358
G384	355
G385	359
G386	360
G387	361
G388	362
G389	363
G390	364
G391	365
G392	366
G393	367
G394	368
G395	369
G396	370
G397	371
G398	372
G399	373
G400	374
G401	376
G402	375
G403	450
G404	377
G405	378
G406	379
G407	4238
G408	380
G409	381
G410	382
G411	383
G412	384
G413	385
G414	386
G415	387
G416	388
G417	389
G418	390
G419	391
G420	37
G421	392
G422	393
G423	394
G424	395
G425	510
G426	396
G427	397
G428	398
G429	399
G430	400
G431	401
G432	402
G433	403
G434	404
G435	405
G436	406
G437	407
G438	408
G439	409
G440	507+2821
G441	410
G442	411
G443	412
G444	413
G445	414
G446	415
G447	448
G448	416
G449	417
G450	418
G451	419
G452	420
G453	421
G454	422
G455	423
G456	424
G457	425
G458	426
G459	427
G460	428
G461	429
G462	430
G463	431
G464	432
G465	433
G466	434
G467	435
G468	436
G469	437
G470	438
G471	439
G472	440
G473	441
G474	442
G475	443
G476	444
G477	445
G478	446
G479	447
G480	448
G481	449
G482	450
G483	451
G484	452
G485	453
G486	454
G487	455
G488	456
G489	457
G490	458
G491	459
G492	460
G493	453
G494	461
G495	462
G496	463
G497	464
G498	465
G499	466
G500	467
G501	468
G502	469
G503	470
G504	472
G505	473
G506	474
G507	475
G508	476
G509	477
G510	478
G511	479
G512	480
G513	481
G514	482
G515	471
"	483
G516	484
G517	485
G518	486
G519	487
G520	488
G521	489
G522	490
G523	491
G524	492
G525	493
G526	494
G527	495
G528	496
G529	497
G530	498
G531	499
G532	500
G533	501
G534	502
G535	503
G536	504
G537	505
G538	506
G539	507
G540	509
G541	510
G542	511
G543	512
G544	513
G545	514
G546	515
G547	516
G548	517
G549	2456
G550	518
G551	519
G552	520
G553	521
G554	522
G555	523
G556	524
G557	525
G558	526
G559	527
G560	528
G561	529
G562	530
G563	531
G564	532
G565	533
G566	575+737
G567	534
G568	535
G569	536
G570	537
G571	782
G572	538
G573	539
G574	540
G575	541
G576	1890
G577	543
G578	544
G579	545
G580	546
G581	547
G582	548
G583	549
G584	550
"	561
G585	551
G586	552
G587	553
G588	554
G589	555
G590	556
G591	557
G592	558
G593	559
G594	560
G595	561
G596	562
G597	563
G598	564
G599	565
G600	566
"	567

G/K	STRONG
G600	568
G601	569
G602	570
G603	571
G604	573
G605	572
G606	573
G607	574
G608	575
G609	576
G610	577
G611	578
G612	579
G613	580
G614	581
G615	582
G616	583
G617	584
G618	585
G619	586
G620	586
G621	587
G622	588
G623	589
G624	590
G625	591
G626	592
G627	593
G628	594
G629	595
G630	596
G631	597
G632	598
G633	599
G634	600
G635	600
G636	601
G637	602
G638	603
G639	604
G640	605
G641	606
G642	607
G643	608
G644	609
G645	610
G646	611
G647	612
G648	613
G649	614
G650	615
G651	615
G652	616
G653	617
G654	2980
G655	618
G656	619
G657	620
G658	621
G659	5277
G660	622
G661	623
G662	624
G663	625
G664	626
G665	627
G666	628
G667	629
G668	630
G669	631
G670	5278
G671	632
G672	633
G673	575+3992
G674	634
G675	635
G676	636
G677	637
G678	638
G679	639
G680	640
G681	641
G682	642
G683	643
G684	644
G685	645
G686	646
G687	647
G688	3848
G689	648
G690	649
G691	650
G692	651
G693	652
G694	653
G695	654
G696	655
G697	656
G698	657
G699	658
G700	659
G701	660
G702	661
G703	662
G704	663
G705	664
G706	665
G707	666
G708	667
G709	668
G710	669
G711	670
G712	671
G713	672
G714	673
G715	674
G716	675
G717	676
G718	677
G719	678
G720	679
G721	680
"	681
G722	682
G723	683
G724	684
G725	685
G726	686
G727	687
G728	688
G729	
G730	689
G731	729
G732	690
G733	691
G734	692
G735	693
G736	694
G737	695
G738	696
G739	693
G740	697
G741	698
G742	699
G743	700
G744	701
G745	702
G746	703
G747	
G748	704
G749	705
G750	706
G751	707
G752	708
G753	709
G754	710
G755	711
G756	712
G757	713
G758	714
G759	715
G760	715
G761	716
G762	717
G763	689
G764	718
G765	719
G766	720
G767	
G768	721
G769	722
G770	723
G771	724
G772	725
G773	726
G774	727
G775	728
G776	730
G777	731
G778	732
G779	732
G780	733
G781	730
G782	734
G783	735
G784	736
G785	737
G786	738
G787	739
G788	740
G789	741
G790	742
G791	743
G792	744
G793	745
G794	746
G795	747
G796	748
G797	749
G798	3027
G799	750
G800	751
G801	752
G802	753
G803	754
G804	755
G805	
G806	756
"	757
G807	758
G808	759
G809	760
G810	761
G811	760
G812	762
G813	763
G814	764
G815	765
G816	766
G817	767
G818	768
G819	769
G820	770
G821	771
G822	772
G823	773
G824	774
G825	775
G826	776
G827	777
G828	778
G829	779
G830	780
G831	781
G832	782
G833	783
G834	784
G835	785
G836	786
G837	787
G838	4565
G839	788
G840	789
G841	790
G842	791
G843	792
G844	793
G845	794
G846	795
G847	796
G848	797
G849	798
G850	799
G851	800
G852	801
G853	802
G854	803
G855	804
G856	805
G857	806
G858	807
G859	808
G860	809
G861	810
G862	811
G863	812
G864	813
G865	814
G866	815
G867	816
G868	817
G869	818
G870	818
G871	819
G872	820
G873	821
G874	822
G875	823
G876	824
G877	825
G878	826
G879	827
G880	828
G881	829
G882	830
G883	831
G884	832
G885	833
G886	834
G887	835
G888	836
G889	837
G890	838
G891	837
G892	839
G893	840
G894	841
G895	842
G896	843
G897	844
G898	845
G899	846
"	847
"	848
G900	1888
G901	849
G902	3166
G903	850
G904	851
G905	852
G906	853
G907	854
G908	855
G909	856
G910	857
G911	858
G912	859
G913	860
G914	861
G915	862
G916	90
G917	90
G918	863
G919	864
G920	865
G921	866
G922	867
G923	868
G924	869
G925	870
G926	871
G927	542
"	872
G928	873
G929	874
G930	875
G931	876
G932	877
G933	878
G934	879
G935	650
G936	880
G937	881
G938	882
G939	883
G940	884
G941	881
G942	886
G943	885
G944	887
G945	888
G946	889
G947	890
G948	891
G949	892
G950	893
G951	894
G952	894
G953	895
G954	
G955	896
G956	897
G957	898
G958	899
G959	900
G960	901
G961	902
G962	903
G963	904
G964	905
G965	906
G966	907
G967	908
G968	909
G969	910
G970	911
G971	920
G972	912
G973	913
G974	914
G975	915
G976	916
G977	917
G978	918
G979	919
G980	920
G981	920
G982	921
G983	922
G984	923
G985	924
G986	925
G987	926
G988	927
G989	928
G990	929
G991	930
G992	931
G993	932
G994	933
G994	934
G995	935
G996	936
G997	937
G998	937
G999	938
G1000	939
G1001	940
G1002	941
G1003	942
G1004	943
G1005	944
G1006	945
G1007	946
G1008	947
G1009	948
G1010	949
G1011	950
G1012	951
G1013	952
G1014	953
G1015	954
G1016	955
G1017	4476
G1018	956
G1019	957
G1020	958
G1021	958
G1022	959
G1023	960
G1024	961
G1025	
G1026	1007
G1027	1007
G1028	962
G1029	963
G1030	962
G1031	964
G1032	964
G1033	965
G1034	966
G1035	966
G1036	967
G1037	968
G1038	
G1039	969
G1040	970
G1041	971
G1042	972
G1043	973
G1044	974
G1045	974
G1046	975
G1047	976
G1048	977
G1049	978
G1050	979
G1051	980
G1052	981
G1053	982
G1054	983
G1055	984
G1056	985
G1057	985
G1058	986
G1059	987
G1060	988
G1061	989
G1062	990
G1063	991
G1064	992
G1065	993
G1066	994
G1067	1003
G1068	995
G1069	996
G1070	997
G1071	998
G1072	999
G1073	999
G1074	1000
G1075	1001
G1076	1002
G1077	1003
G1078	1003
G1079	1004
G1080	1005
G1081	1006
G1082	1007
G1083	1008
G1084	1009
G1085	1010
G1086	1011
G1087	1012
G1088	1013
G1089	1014
G1090	1015
G1091	1016
G1092	1017
G1093	1018
G1094	1019
G1095	1020
G1096	1021
G1097	1022
G1098	1023
G1099	1024
G1100	1025
G1101	1026
G1102	1690
G1103	1027
G1104	1028
G1105	1029
G1106	1030
G1107	1031
G1108	1032
G1109	1033
G1110	1034
G1111	1035
G1112	1036
G1113	1037
G1114	1038
G1115	1039
G1116	1040
G1117	1041
G1118	
G1119	1042
G1120	1043
G1121	1044
G1122	1045
G1123	1046
G1124	1048
G1125	1047
G1126	1049
G1127	1050
G1128	1051
G1129	1052
G1130	1053
G1131	1054
G1132	1055
G1133	1056
G1134	1057
G1135	1053
G1136	1058
G1137	1059
G1138	1060
G1139	1061
G1140	1061
G1141	1062
G1142	1063
G1143	1064
G1144	2802
G1145	1065
G1146	1066
G1147	1067
G1148	1068
G1149	1068
G1150	1069
G1151	1070
G1152	1071
G1153	1072
G1154	1073
G1155	1074
G1156	1075
G1157	1076
G1158	1077
G1159	1077
G1160	1077
G1161	1078
G1162	1079
G1163	1081
G1164	1080
G1165	1081
G1166	1082
G1167	1083
G1168	1084
G1169	1085
G1170	1086
G1171	1086
G1172	1087
G1173	1088
G1174	1089
G1175	1090
G1176	1091
G1177	1092
G1178	1093
G1179	1094
G1180	1095
G1181	1096
G1182	1097
G1183	1098
G1184	1099
G1185	1100
G1186	1101
G1187	1102
G1188	1103
G1189	1104
G1190	1105
G1191	1106
G1192	1107
G1193	1110
G1194	1108
G1195	1109
G1196	1110
G1197	1111
G1198	1112
G1199	1113
G1200	1114
G1201	1115
G1202	1116
G1203	1117
G1204	1118
G1205	1119
G1206	1120
G1207	1121
G1208	1122
G1209	1123
G1210	1124
G1211	1125
G1212	1126
G1213	1127
G1214	1128
G1215	1129
G1216	1130
G1217	1130
G1218	1131
G1219	1132
G1220	1133
G1221	1134
G1222	1135
G1223	1136
G1224	1137
G1225	
G1226	1138
G1227	1139
G1228	1140
G1229	1141
G1230	1142
G1231	1143
G1232	1144
G1233	1145
G1234	1146
G1235	1147
G1236	1148
G1237	1149
G1238	1150
G1239	1151
G1240	1152
G1241	1153
G1242	1154
G1243	
G1244	1155
G1245	1156
G1246	1157
G1247	1155
G1248	1158
G1249	1156
G1250	1157
G1251	1159
G1252	1160
G1253	1138
G1254	1161
G1255	1162
G1256	1163
G1257	1164
G1258	1165
G1259	1166
G1260	1166
G1261	1167
G1262	1168
G1263	
G1264	1169
G1265	1170
G1266	
G1267	1171
G1268	1172
G1269	
G1270	1173
G1271	1173
G1272	1175
G1273	1174
G1274	1176
G1275	1177
G1276	1176+1803
G1277	1176 +2532+3638
G1278	1178
G1279	1179
G1280	1180
G1281	1181
"	1182
G1282	1183
G1283	1184
G1284	1185
G1285	1186
G1286	1187
G1287	1187
G1288	1188
G1289	1189
G1290	127
G1291	1190
G1292	1191
G1293	1192
G1294	1193
G1295	2359
G1296	1194
G1297	1195
G1298	1196
G1299	1197
G1300	1198
G1301	1199
G1302	1200
G1303	1201
G1304	1202
G1305	1203
G1306	1204
G1307	1205
G1308	1206
G1309	1208
G1310	1207
G1311	1208
G1312	1209
G1313	1210
G1314	1211
G1315	5081
G1316	1212
G1317	1213
G1318	1214
G1319	1215
G1320	1216
G1321	1217
G1322	1218
G1323	1219
G1324	1220
G1325	1221
G1326	
G1327	1222
G1328	1223
G1329	1224
G1330	1225
G1331	1226
G1332	1227
G1333	1228
G1334	1229
G1335	1230
G1336	1231
G1337	1232
G1338	1233
G1339	1234
G1340	1235
G1341	1236
G1342	1237
G1343	1238
G1344	1239
G1345	1240
G1346	1241
G1347	1242
G1348	1243
G1349	1244
G1350	1245
G1351	1245
G1352	1246
G1353	1781
G1354	1247
G1355	1248
G1356	1249
G1357	1250
G1358	1251
G1359	1252
G1360	1253
G1361	1254
G1362	1255
G1363	1256
G1364	1257
G1365	1258
G1366	
G1367	1259
G1368	1260
G1369	1261
G1370	1262
G1371	1263
G1372	1264
G1373	1265
G1374	1266
G1375	1267
G1376	1268
G1377	1269
G1378	1270
G1379	1271
G1380	1272
G1381	1273
G1382	1274
G1383	1275
G1384	3859
G1385	1276
G1386	1277
G1387	1278
G1388	1279
G1389	1280
G1390	1281
G1391	1282

G/K	STRONG
G1392	1284
G1393	1284
G1394	
G1395	1283
G1396	1284
G1397	1285
G1398	1286
G1399	1287
G1400	1288
G1401	1289
G1402	1290
G1403	1291
G1404	1292
G1405	1293
G1406	1294
G1407	1295
G1408	1296
G1409	1297
G1410	1298
G1411	1299
G1412	1300
G1413	1301
G1414	1302
G1415	1303
G1416	1303
G1417	1304
G1418	1305
G1419	1306
G1420	1307
G1421	1307
G1422	1308
G1423	1309
G1424	1310
G1425	1311
G1426	1312
G1427	1313
G1428	1314
G1429	1315
G1430	5512
G1431	1316
G1432	
G1433	
G1434	1317
G1435	1318
G1436	1319
G1437	1320
G1438	1321
G1439	1322
G1440	1323
G1441	1324
G1442	1325
G1443	1325
G1444	1326
G1445	1760
G1446	1831
G1447	1327
G1448	2058
G1449	1328
G1450	1329
G1451	1330
G1452	1331
G1453	1332
G1454	1333
G1455	1334
G1456	1335
G1457	1336
G1458	1337
G1459	1338
G1460	1339
G1461	333
G1462	1340
G1463	2613
G1464	1341
G1465	1342
G1466	1343
G1467	1344
G1468	1345
G1469	1346
G1470	1347
G1471	1348
G1472	1349
G1473	1350
G1474	1351
G1475	1352
G1476	1353
G1477	1354
G1478	1355
G1479	1356
G1480	2735
G1481	1357
G1482	1358
G1483	1359
G1484	1360
G1485	1361
G1486	1362
G1487	1362
G1488	1363
G1489	1364
G1490	1417+3461
G1491	1365
G1492	1366
G1493	1367
G1494	1368
G1495	1369
G1496	1370
G1497	1371
G1498	1372
G1499	1373
G1500	1374
G1501	1375
G1502	1376
G1503	1377
G1504	1378
G1505	1379
G1506	1380
G1507	1381
G1508	1381
G1509	1382
G1510	1383
G1511	1384
G1512	1385
G1513	1386
G1514	1387
G1515	1388
G1516	1389
G1517	1390
G1518	1391
G1519	1392
G1520	1393
G1521	1394
G1522	1395
G1523	1190
G1524	1396
G1525	1397
G1526	1398
G1527	1399
G1528	1400
"	1401
G1529	1401
G1530	1402
G1531	1403
G1532	1404
G1533	1405
G1534	1406
G1535	1407
G1536	1408
G1537	1409
G1538	1410
G1539	1411
G1540	1412
G1541	1413
G1542	1414
G1543	1415
G1544	1416
G1545	1417
G1546	1419
G1547	1420
G1548	1420
G1549	1421
G1550	
G1551	1422
G1552	1423
G1553	1424
G1554	1425
G1555	987
G1556	1426
G1557	1427
G1558	1428
G1559	1429
G1560	1430
G1561	1431
G1562	1432
G1563	1433
G1564	1434
G1565	1435
G1566	1248
G1567	
G1568	1436
G1569	1437
G1570	1437+4007
G1571	1438
G1572	1439
G1573	1440
G1574	1441
G1575	1442
G1576	1443
G1577	1444
G1578	1445
G1579	1446
G1580	1447
G1581	1448
G1582	1449
G1583	1450
G1584	1451
G1585	1452
G1586	1453
G1587	1454
G1588	1455
G1589	1456
G1590	1457
G1591	1573
G1592	1458
G1593	1459
G1594	1460
G1595	2620
G1596	1461
G1597	2623
G1598	1462
G1599	1463
G1600	1464
G1601	1465
G1602	1466
G1603	1467
G1604	1468
G1605	1469
G1606	1470
G1607	1471
G1608	1472
G1609	1473
"	1691
"	1698
"	1700
"	2248
"	2249
"	2254
"	2257
"	3165
"	3427
"	3450
G1610	1474
G1611	1475
G1612	1476
G1613	1477
G1614	1478
G1615	1479
G1616	1480
G1617	1481
G1618	1482
G1619	1483
G1620	1484
G1621	1485
G1622	1486
G1623	1487
G1624	2397
G1625	3708
G1626	1491
G1627	1493
G1628	1494
G1629	1496
G1630	1495
G1631	1497
G1632	1500
G1633	1501
G1634	1502
G1635	1504
G1636	1505
G1637	1506
G1638	2229+3375
G1639	1488
"	1498
"	1510
"	1511
"	1526
"	2070
"	2071
"	2252
"	2258
"	2277
"	2468
"	5600
"	5607
G1640	
G1641	1752
G1642	1512
G1643	1513
G1644	1514
G1645	1515
G1646	1516
G1647	1517
G1648	1518
G1649	3004
G1650	1519
G1651	1520
"	3391
G1652	1521
G1653	1522
G1654	1523
G1655	1524
G1656	1525
G1657	1528
G1658	1529
G1659	1530
G1660	1531
G1661	1532
G1662	1533
G1663	1534
G1664	1535
G1665	1486
G1666	1537
G1667	1538
G1668	1539
G1669	1540
G1670	1541
G1671	1542
G1672	1543
G1673	1543
G1674	1831
G1675	1544
G1676	1545
G1677	1816
G1678	1546
G1679	1547
G1680	1548
G1681	1549
G1682	1550
G1683	1551
G1684	1552
G1685	1553
G1686	1554
G1687	1555
G1688	1556
G1689	1557
G1690	1558
G1691	1559
G1692	1560
G1693	1561
G1694	1562
G1695	1563
G1696	1564
G1697	1565
G1698	1566
G1699	1567
G1700	2214
G1701	1568
G1702	1569
G1703	2296
G1704	1570
G1705	1571
G1706	1572
G1707	1573
G1708	1574
G1709	1575
G1710	1576
G1711	1577
G1712	1578
G1713	1579
G1714	1580
G1715	1464
G1716	1581
G1717	1582
G1718	1583
G1719	1584
G1720	1585
G1721	1586
G1722	1587
G1723	1588
G1724	1589
G1725	1590
G1726	1591
G1727	1592
G1728	1593
G1729	1594
G1730	1595
G1731	1596
G1732	1597
G1733	1598
G1734	1599
G1735	1537+4053
G1736	1600
G1737	1530
G1738	1601
G1739	1602
G1740	1603
G1741	1604
G1742	1605
G1743	1606
G1744	1607
G1745	1608
G1746	1609
G1747	
G1748	1610
G1749	1611
G1750	1612
G1751	4982
G1752	1613
G1753	1614
G1754	1615
G1755	1616
G1756	1618
G1757	1617
"	1619
G1758	1620
G1759	1621
G1760	1622
G1761	1623
G1762	1624
G1763	1625
G1764	1790
G1765	1626
G1766	1627
G1767	1628
G1768	1629
G1769	1630
G1770	1631
G1771	1537+5455
G1772	1632
G1773	1632
G1774	1633
G1775	1634
G1776	1635
G1777	1636
G1778	1637
G1779	1638
G1780	1639
G1781	1640
G1782	1641
G1783	1642
G1784	1640
G1785	1643
G1786	1644
G1787	1645
G1788	1646
"	1647
G1789	1648
G1790	1653
G1791	1650
G1792	1649
G1793	1650
G1794	1651
G1795	1652
G1796	1653
G1797	1654
G1798	1655
G1799	1656
G1800	1657
G1801	1658
G1802	1659
G1803	1660
G1804	1661
G1805	1662
G1806	1662
G1807	3395
G1808	1663
G1809	1664
G1810	1665
G1811	1666
G1812	1666
G1813	1507
"	1667
G1814	1668
G1815	1669
G1816	1670
G1817	1671
G1818	1672
G1819	1673
G1820	1674
G1821	1675
G1822	1676
G1823	1677
G1824	1677
G1825	1678
G1826	1678
G1827	1679
G1828	1680
G1829	1681
G1830	1682
G1831	1683
G1832	1684
G1833	1685
G1834	1686
G1835	1686
G1836	1687
G1837	1688
G1838	1689
G1839	1690
G1840	1692
G1841	1693
G1842	1694
G1843	1695
G1844	1696
G1845	1722+3319
G1846	1697
G1847	1699
G1848	
G1849	1701
G1850	1702
G1851	1703
G1852	649
G1853	1704
G1854	1705
G1855	1705
G1856	1714
G1857	1705
G1858	1705
G1859	1714
G1860	1706
G1861	1707
G1862	1708
G1863	1709
G1864	1710
G1865	1711
G1866	1712
G1867	1713
G1868	1714
G1869	1715
G1870	1716
G1871	1717
G1872	1718
G1873	1719
G1874	1720
G1875	1721
G1876	5455
G1877	1722
G1878	1723
G1879	1724
G1880	2177
G1881	
G1882	1725
G1883	1726
G1884	
G1885	1727
G1886	1756
G1887	1728
G1888	1766
G1889	863
G1890	1729
G1891	1730
G1892	1731
G1893	1732
G1894	1733
G1895	1734
G1896	1735
G1897	1736
G1898	1737
G1899	1738
G1900	1739
G1901	1740
G1902	1741
G1903	1742
G1904	1743
G1905	1744
G1906	1745
G1907	1746
G1908	1739
G1909	1747
G1910	1748
G1911	1749
G1912	1750
G1913	1751
G1914	1752
G1915	1752
G1916	1768
G1917	1769
G1918	1753
G1919	1754
G1920	1755
G1921	1756
G1922	1757
G1923	1758
G1924	1759
G1925	1782
G1926	1760
G1927	1761
G1928	1762
G1929	1763
G1930	4178
G1931	1764
G1932	1765
G1933	1767
G1934	1769
G1935	1770
G1936	1771
G1937	1772
G1938	1722+3551
G1939	1773
G1940	1774
G1941	3726
G1942	1775
G1943	1776
G1944	1777
G1945	1778
G1946	1779
G1947	1780
G1948	1781
G1949	1782
G1950	1783
G1951	
G1952	1784
G1953	1785
G1954	1786
G1955	1787
G1956	1788
G1957	1789
G1958	1790
G1959	1791
G1960	1792
G1961	1793
G1962	1794
G1963	1795
G1964	1796
G1965	1797
G1966	1798
G1967	1799
G1968	1800
G1969	1801
G1970	1802
G1971	1803
G1972	1804
G1973	1805
G1974	1806
G1975	1807
G1976	1808
G1977	1809
G1978	1810
G1979	1811
G1980	1812
G1981	1813
G1982	1814
G1983	1815
G1984	1816
G1985	1817
G1986	455
G1987	1818
G1988	1819
G1989	1820
G1990	1821
G1991	
G1992	1822
G1993	1823
G1994	1824
G1995	1825
G1996	1826
G1997	1832
G1998	1827
G1999	1828
G2000	1829
G2001	1830
G2002	1831
G2003	1832
G2004	1833
G2005	1810
G2006	
G2007	1834
G2008	1835
G2009	1836
G2010	1837
G2011	1838
G2012	1839
G2013	1839
G2014	1839
G2015	1840
G2016	1841
G2017	1842
G2018	1843
G2019	1844
G2020	1845
G2021	1846
G2022	1847
G2023	1847
G2024	1848
G2025	1848
G2026	1849
G2027	1850
G2028	
G2029	1851
G2030	1852
G2031	1853
G2032	1854
G2033	1855
G2034	1856
G2035	1857
G2036	1503
G2037	1858
G2038	1859
G2039	1860
G2040	1861
G2041	1862
G2042	1863
G2043	1864
G2044	1865
G2045	1866
G2046	1867
G2047	1868
G2048	1869
G2049	1870
G2050	1871
G2051	1872
G2052	1873
G2053	1874
G2054	1875
G2055	1876
G2056	1877
G2057	1878
G2058	1879
G2059	1880
G2060	1881
G2061	1882
G2062	1883
G2063	1944
G2064	1884
G2065	1885
G2066	1885
G2067	
G2068	1886
G2069	1887
G2070	1888
G2071	1889
G2072	1890
G2073	1891
G2074	1892
G2075	1893
G2076	1894
G2077	1895
G2078	1896
G2079	1966
G2080	1897
G2081	1898
G2082	1904
G2083	1899
G2084	1900
G2085	1901
G2086	1902
G2087	1903
G2088	1904
G2089	1905
G2090	1906
G2091	1907
G2092	1908
G2093	1909
G2094	1910
G2095	1911
G2096	1912
G2097	1913
G2098	1914
G2099	1915
G2100	1916
G2101	1917
G2102	1918
G2103	1919
G2104	1920
G2105	1921
G2106	1922
G2107	1923
G2108	1924
G2109	1925
G2110	1926
G2111	1927
G2112	1928
G2113	1929
G2114	1930
G2115	1931
G2116	1932
G2117	1933
G2118	1934
G2119	1935
G2120	1936
G2121	1937
G2122	1938
G2123	1939
G2124	2380
G2125	1940
G2126	1941
G2127	1942
G2128	1943
G2129	1944
G2130	1945
G2131	2027
G2132	2770
G2133	2778
G2134	1946
G2135	1947
G2136	
G2137	1948
G2138	1949
G2139	2989
G2140	1950
G2141	1951
G2142	1952
G2143	621
G2144	1953
G2145	1954
G2146	1955
G2147	1956
G2148	1957
G2149	1958
G2150	1959
G2151	1960
G2152	1961
G2153	1962
G2154	1963
G2155	1964
G2156	1965
G2157	1967
G2158	1968
G2159	1969
G2160	1971
G2161	1972
G2162	1973
G2163	1974
G2164	1975

G/K	STRONG
G2165	1976
G2166	1977
G2167	3982
G2168	1978
G2169	1979
G2170	1980
G2171	643
G2172	1981
G2173	1982
G2174	1983
G2175	1984
G2176	1985
G2177	1986
G2178	4687
G2179	1987
G2180	1999
G2181	1988
G2182	1989
G2183	
G2184	1990
G2185	1991
G2186	1992
G2187	1993
G2188	1994
G2189	1995
G2190	1996
G2191	1997
G2192	1998
G2193	1976
G2194	1999
G2195	2000
G2196	2001
G2197	2002
G2198	2003
G2199	2004
G2200	2005
G2201	2006
G2202	2007
G2203	2008
G2204	2009
G2205	2010
G2206	2233
G2207	2011
G2208	2012
G2209	2013
G2210	2014
G2211	2015
G2212	2016
G2213	2017
G2214	2018
G2215	2019
G2216	2020
G2217	2021
G2218	
G2219	2022
G2220	2023
G2221	2024
G2222	2025
G2223	2017
G2224	2026
G2225	2027
G2226	2028
G2227	2029
G2228	2030
G2229	2031
G2230	2032
G2231	2033
G2232	2034
G2233	2035
G2234	4179
G2235	2037
G2236	2045
G2237	2038
G2238	2039
G2239	2040
G2240	2041
G2241	2042
G2242	2043
G2243	2044
G2244	2047
G2245	2048
G2246	2049
G2247	2050
G2248	2051
G2249	2052
G2250	2053
G2251	2054
G2252	2055
G2253	2056
G2254	2057
G2255	2058
G2256	1328
G2257	2059
G2258	2060
G2259	2061
G2260	2062
G2261	2063
G2262	2064
G2263	2065
G2264	2066
G2265	2067
G2266	2068
"	5315
G2267	2068
G2268	2069
G2269	2072
G2270	2073
G2271	
G2272	2074
G2273	2274
G2274	2078
G2275	2079
G2276	2080
G2277	2081
G2278	2082
G2279	2083
G2280	2084
G2281	2085
G2282	2086
G2283	2087
G2284	2088
G2285	2089
G2286	2090
G2287	1681
G2288	2091
G2289	2092
G2290	2093
G2291	2094
G2292	2095
G2293	2096
G2294	2097
G2295	2098
G2296	2099
G2297	2100
G2298	2101
G2299	2102
G2300	2103
G2301	2095
G2302	2104
G2303	2129
G2304	2105
G2305	2106
G2306	2107
G2307	2108
G2308	2109
G2309	2110
G2310	2111
G2311	2112
G2312	2113
G2313	2114
G2314	2115
G2315	2115
G2316	2116
G2317	2117
G2318	2117
G2319	2118
G2320	2119
G2321	2120
G2322	2121
G2323	2122
G2324	2123
G2325	2124
G2326	2125
G2327	2126
G2328	2127
G2329	2128
G2330	2129
G2331	2130
G2332	2131
G2333	2132
G2334	2133
G2335	2134
G2336	2135
G2337	2136
G2338	2137
G2339	2145
G2340	2138
G2341	2139
G2342	2139
G2343	2140
G2344	2141
G2345	2142
G2346	2143
G2347	2144
G2348	2145
G2349	2146
G2350	2148
G2351	2147
G2352	2148
G2353	2149
G2354	2150
G2355	2151
G2356	2152
G2357	2153
G2358	2154
G2359	2155
G2360	807
G2361	2156
G2362	2157
G2363	2158
G2364	2159
G2365	2160
G2366	2161
G2367	2162
G2368	2163
G2369	2164
G2370	2165
G2371	2166
G2372	2167
G2373	2168
G2374	2169
G2375	2170
G2376	2171
G2377	2172
G2378	2173
G2379	2174
G2380	2175
G2381	2176
G2382	
G2383	2177
G2384	2178
G2385	2179
G2386	2180
G2387	2181
G2388	2182
G2389	2183
G2390	2184
G2391	2185
G2392	2186
G2393	1896
G2394	2187
G2395	2188
G2396	5504
G2397	2189
G2398	2190
G2399	2191
G2400	2192
G2401	2193
G2402	
G2403	
G2404	2194
G2405	2195
G2406	2196
G2407	4518
G2408	2197
G2409	2198
G2410	4570
G2411	2199
G2412	2200
G2413	4801
G2414	2201
G2415	2202
G2416	2203
G2417	2204
G2418	2206
G2419	2205
G2420	2206
G2421	2207
"	2208
G2422	2209
G2423	2210
G2424	2211
G2425	
G2426	2212
G2427	2213
G2428	2214
G2429	2215
G2430	4667
G2431	2216
G2432	2217
G2433	2218
G2434	2219
G2435	2220
G2436	2221
G2437	2222
G2438	2223
G2439	2224
G2440	2224
G2441	2225
G2442	2226
G2443	2227
G2444	
G2445	2228
G2446	2229
G2447	2229+3375
G2448	2230
G2449	2231
G2450	2232
G2451	2233
G2452	2234
"	2236
G2453	2235
G2454	2237
G2455	2238
G2456	2239
G2457	2240
G2458	2241
G2459	2242
G2460	2243
G2461	2244
G2462	2245
G2463	2246
G2464	2247
G2465	2250
G2466	2251
G2467	2253
G2468	2255
G2469	2256
G2470	2256
G2471	2259
G2472	2260
G2473	2261
G2474	2262
G2475	2263
G2476	2264
G2477	2265
G2478	2266
G2479	2267
G2480	2268
G2481	2269
G2482	2276
G2483	2270
G2484	2271
G2485	2272
G2486	2273
G2487	2274
G2488	2275
G2489	2276
G2490	2278
G2491	2279
G2492	2279
G2493	2279
G2494	
G2495	3134
G2496	5008
G2497	2280
G2498	2281
G2499	2282
G2500	2283
G2501	2284
G2502	2285
G2503	2286
G2504	2287
G2505	2288
G2506	2289
G2507	2290
G2508	2291
G2509	2292
G2510	2293
G2511	2294
G2512	2295
G2513	2296
G2514	2297
G2515	2298
G2516	2299
G2517	2300
G2518	2301
G2519	2302
G2520	2303
G2521	2304
G2522	2305
G2523	2306
G2524	
G2525	2307
G2526	2308
G2527	2309
G2528	2310
G2529	2310
G2530	2311
G2531	2312
G2532	2312′
G2533	2313
G2534	2314
G2535	2315
G2536	2316
G2537	2317
G2538	2318
G2539	2319
G2540	2320
G2541	2321
G2542	2322
G2543	2323
G2544	2324
G2545	2325
G2546	2326
G2547	2327
G2548	2328
G2549	2329
G2550	2330
G2551	
G2552	2331
G2553	2332
G2554	2333
G2555	2334
G2556	2335
G2557	2336
G2558	2337
G2559	2338
G2560	2339
G2561	2340
G2562	2341
G2563	2342
G2564	2343
G2565	2344
G2566	2345
G2567	2346
G2568	2347
G2569	2348
G2570	2349
G2571	5182
G2572	2350
G2573	2351
G2574	2352
G2575	2352
G2576	2353
G2577	2354
G2578	2355
G2579	2356
G2580	2357
G2581	2358
G2582	2359
G2583	2360
G2584	2361
G2585	2362
G2586	
G2587	2363
G2588	2364
G2589	2365
G2590	2366
G2591	2367
G2592	2368
G2593	2369
G2594	2370
G2595	2371
G2596	2372
G2597	2373
G2598	2374
G2599	2375
G2600	2376
G2601	2377
G2602	2378
G2603	2379
G2604	2380
G2605	2381
G2606	2382
G2607	
G2608	2383
G2609	2384
G2610	2385
G2611	2386
G2612	2387
G2613	2388
G2614	2389
G2615	2390
G2616	2391
G2617	2392
G2618	2393
G2619	2394
G2620	2395
G2621	
G2622	
G2623	2396
G2624	2397
G2625	2398
G2626	2399
G2627	2400
G2628	2401
G2629	2402
G2630	2403
G2631	2404
G2632	2405
G2633	2406
G2634	2407
G2635	2408
G2636	2409
G2637	2410
G2638	1494
G2639	2411
G2640	2412
G2641	2413
G2642	2414
G2643	2415
G2644	2416
G2645	2417
G2646	2418
G2647	2419
G2648	2420
G2649	2421
G2650	2422
G2651	2423
G2652	2424
G2653	2425
G2654	2426
G2655	2427
G2656	2428
G2657	2429
G2658	2430
G2659	2431
G2660	2432
G2661	2433
G2662	2434
G2663	2435
G2664	2436
G2665	2437
G2666	2438
G2667	2439
G2668	2440
G2669	2441
G2670	2442
G2671	2443
G2672	2444
G2673	2445
G2674	2446
G2675	2447
G2676	2448
G2677	2449
G2678	2450
G2679	2451
G2680	2452
G2681	2453
G2682	2454
G2683	2455
G2684	2456
G2685	2457
G2686	2456
G2687	2458
G2688	2459
G2689	2460
G2690	2461
G2691	2462
G2692	2463
G2693	2464
G2694	2465
G2695	2466
G2696	2469
G2697	2469
G2698	2470
G2699	2471
G2700	2472
G2701	2473
G2702	2474
G2703	2475
G2704	2466
G2705	2476
G2706	
G2707	2477
G2708	2478
G2709	2479
G2710	2480
G2711	2481
G2712	2482
G2713	2483
G2714	2484
G2715	2485
G2716	2486
G2717	2487
G2718	2488
G2719	
G2720	2489
G2721	2489
"	2490
G2722	2491
G2723	
G2724	2492
G2725	5601
G2726	2455
G2727	2493
G2728	2491
G2729	2494
G2730	2494
G2731	2495
G2732	2496
G2733	2497
G2734	2498
G2735	2499
G2736	2500
G2737	2501
G2738	2501
G2739	2502
G2740	2503
G2741	
G2742	943
G2743	2504
G2744	943
G2745	2505
G2746	2506
G2747	2507
G2748	2508
G2749	2509
G2750	2510
G2751	2511
G2752	2512
G2753	4027
G2754	2513
G2755	2514
G2756	2515
G2757	2516
G2758	2596+1520
G2759	2517
G2760	2511
G2761	2518
G2762	2519
G2763	2520
G2764	2521
G2765	2596+2250
G2766	2522
G2767	2523
G2768	2524
G2769	2525
G2770	2525
G2771	2526
G2772	2526′
G2773	2527
G2774	2528
G2775	2529
G2776	2530
G2777	2531
G2778	2509
G2779	2532
G2780	2533
G2781	2534
G2782	2535
G2783	2536
G2784	2536
G2785	2537
G2786	2538
G2787	2757
G2788	2539
G2789	2540
G2790	2541
G2791	2542
G2792	2543
G2793	2544
G2794	2545
G2795	2546
G2796	2547
G2797	2548
G2798	2549
G2799	2550
G2800	2551
G2801	2552
G2802	2553
G2803	2554
G2804	2555
G2805	2556
G2806	2557
G2807	2558
G2808	2559
G2809	2560
G2810	2561
G2811	2562
G2812	2563
G2813	2564
G2814	2565
G2815	2567
G2816	2568
G2817	2552
G2818	2569
G2819	2566
"	2570
G2820	2571
G2821	2572
G2822	2573
G2823	2574
G2824	2574
G2825	2575
G2826	2576
G2827	2577
G2828	2578
G2829	2579
G2830	2580
G2831	2581
G2832	2581
G2833	2582
G2834	2583
G2835	2584
G2836	2585
G2837	2586
G2838	2587
G2839	603
G2840	2588
G2841	2589
G2842	2591
G2843	2590
G2844	2592
G2845	2593
G2846	2594
G2847	2595
G2848	2596
G2849	2597
G2850	2598
G2851	2599
G2852	925
G2853	2600
G2854	2601
G2855	
G2856	2602
G2857	2603
G2858	2604
G2859	2605
G2860	2606
G2861	2607
G2862	2608
G2863	1125
G2864	2609
G2865	2610
G2866	2611
G2867	2612
G2868	2613
G2869	1349
G2870	2614
G2871	2615
G2872	2616
G2873	2652
G2874	2653
G2875	2617
G2876	2618
G2877	2619
G2878	2620
G2879	2621
G2880	2622
G2881	2623
G2882	2624
G2883	2624
G2884	2625
G2885	2626
G2886	2627
G2887	2628
G2888	2629
G2889	2630
G2890	2631
G2891	2632
G2892	2633
G2893	2596+2955
G2894	2634
G2895	2635
G2896	2636
G2897	2637
G2898	2638
G2899	2639
G2900	2640
G2901	2641
G2902	2642
G2903	2643
G2904	2644
G2905	2645
G2906	2646
G2907	2647
G2908	2648
G2909	2649
G2910	2650
G2911	2651
G2912	2652
G2913	2653
G2914	2654
G2915	2655
G2916	2656
G2917	2657
G2918	2658
G2919	2659
G2920	2660
G2921	2661
G2922	2662
G2923	2663
G2924	2664
G2925	2665
G2926	
G2927	2666
G2928	2667
G2929	2668
G2930	2669
G2931	2670
G2932	2671
G2933	2672
G2934	2673
G2935	2674
G2936	2675
G2937	2676
G2938	2677
G2939	2678
G2940	2679
G2941	2680
G2942	2681
G2943	2682
G2944	2683
G2945	2684
G2946	2685
G2947	2686
G2948	2687
G2949	2688
G2950	2689
G2951	2690
G2952	2691
G2953	2692
G2954	2693
G2955	2694
G2956	2695
G2957	2695
G2958	2696
G2959	2697

G/K	STRONG
G2960	2698
G2961	2699
G2962	2700
G2963	2701
G2964	826
G2965	2702
G2966	2703
G2967	2704
G2968	2705
G2969	2706
G2970	2707
G2971	2019
G2972	2708
G2973	2709
G2974	2710
G2975	4785
G2976	2711
G2977	2712
G2978	2713
G2979	2714
G2980	2715
G2981	2716
G2982	2718
G2983	2719
G2984	2719
G2985	2720
G2986	2127
G2987	2721
G2988	2722
G2989	2723
G2990	2724
G2991	2725
G2992	2725
G2993	2726
G2994	2727
G2995	2728
G2996	2729
G2997	2730
G2998	2731
G2999	2732
G3000	2733
G3001	2730
G3002	2734
G3003	2735
G3004	2736
G3005	2737
G3006	2736
G3007	2802
G3008	2738
G3009	2739
G3010	2739
G3011	2740
G3012	2741
G3013	2743
G3014	2742
G3015	2743
G3016	2744
G3017	2745
G3018	2746
G3019	2584
G3020	2747
G3021	2748
G3022	2748
G3023	2749
G3024	2750
G3025	2751
G3026	2752
G3027	2753
G3028	
G3029	2754
G3030	2755
G3031	2756
G3032	2757
G3033	2758
G3034	2759
G3035	2760
G3036	2761
G3037	2762
G3038	2763
G3039	2764
G3040	2765
G3041	2766
G3042	2767
G3043	2768
G3044	2769
G3045	2770
G3046	2771
G3047	2772
G3048	2773
G3049	2774
G3050	2775
G3051	2776
G3052	2775
G3053	2777
G3054	
G3055	5392
G3056	2778
G3057	2779
G3058	2780
G3059	2781

G/K	STRONG
G3060	2782
G3061	2783
G3062	2784
G3063	2785
G3064	2786
G3065	
G3066	2787
G3067	2788
G3068	2789
G3069	2790
G3070	2791
G3071	2791
G3072	2792
G3073	2793
G3074	2794
G3075	2795
G3076	2796
G3077	2792
G3078	2797
G3079	5531
G3080	2798
G3081	2799
G3082	2800
G3083	2801
G3084	2802
G3085	2802
G3086	2803
G3087	2804
G3088	2805
G3089	2806
G3090	2807
G3091	2808
G3092	2809
G3093	2810
G3094	2811
G3095	2812
G3096	2813
G3097	2814
G3098	2815
G3099	2816
G3100	2817
G3101	2818
G3102	2819
G3103	2820
G3104	2821
G3105	2822
G3106	2823
G3107	2824
G3108	2825
G3109	2825
G3110	2826
G3111	2827
G3112	2828
G3113	2829
G3114	2830
G3115	2831
G3116	2832
G3117	2833
G3118	2834
G3119	2835
G3120	2836
G3121	2837
G3122	2838
G3123	2839
G3124	2840
G3125	2841
G3126	2842
G3127	2843
G3128	2844
G3129	
G3130	2845
G3131	2846
G3132	2847
G3133	2848
G3134	2849
G3135	2850
G3136	2851
G3137	2858
G3138	2857
G3139	2852
G3140	2853
G3141	2854
G3142	2855
G3143	2856
G3144	2858
G3145	2857
G3146	2859
G3147	2860
G3148	2861
G3149	2862
G3150	2863
G3151	2864
G3152	2865
G3153	2866
G3154	2867
G3155	2868
G3156	2869
G3157	2870
G3158	2871
G3159	2872

G/K	STRONG
G3160	2873
G3161	2874
G3162	2874
G3163	2874
G3164	2875
G3165	2876
G3166	2877
G3167	2878
G3168	2878
G3169	2879
G3170	2880
G3171	2881
G3172	2882
G3173	2883
G3174	2884
G3175	2885
G3176	2886
G3177	2887
G3178	2887
G3179	2888
G3180	2889
G3181	2890
G3182	2891
G3183	2891
G3184	2892
G3185	2893
G3186	2894
G3187	2895
G3188	2895
G3189	2896
G3190	2897
G3191	2898
G3192	2899
G3193	2900
G3194	2901
G3195	2902
G3196	2903
G3197	2904
G3198	2905
G3199	2906
G3200	2907
G3201	2908
G3202	2908
"	2909
G3203	2910
G3204	2911
G3205	2912
G3206	2913
G3207	2914
G3208	2915
G3209	2916
G3210	2917
G3211	2918
G3212	2919
G3213	2920
G3214	2921
G3215	2922
G3216	2923
G3217	2924
G3218	2925
G3219	2926
G3220	2927
G3221	2928
G3222	2929
G3223	2930
G3224	2927
G3225	2931
G3226	2927
G3227	2932
G3228	2933
G3229	2934
G3230	2935
G3231	2936
G3232	2937
G3233	2938
G3234	2939
G3235	2940
G3236	2941
G3237	2942
G3238	2944
G3239	2943
G3240	2944
G3241	2945
G3242	2946
G3243	2946
G3244	2947
G3245	2948
G3246	2949
G3247	2950
G3248	2951
G3249	2952
G3250	2953
G3251	2954
G3252	2955
G3253	2956
G3254	2956
G3255	2957
G3256	2958
G3257	2959
G3258	2960

G/K	STRONG
G3259	2961
G3260	2958
G3261	2962
G3262	2963
G3263	2964
G3264	2965
G3265	2966
G3266	2967
G3267	2968
G3268	2969
G3269	2970
G3270	2971
G3271	2972
G3272	2973
G3273	2974
G3274	
G3275	2975
G3276	2976
G3277	2977
G3278	2978
G3279	2997
G3280	2979
G3281	2980
G3282	2981
G3283	2982
G3284	2983
G3285	2984
G3286	2985
G3287	2986
G3288	2987
G3289	2988
G3290	2989
G3291	2990
G3292	2991
G3293	2993
G3294	2994
G3295	2992
G3296	2995
G3297	2996
G3298	2996
G3299	2997
G3300	2998
G3301	2999
G3302	3000
G3303	3001
G3304	3002
G3305	3003
G3306	2036
"	2046
"	3004
"	4483
G3307	3005
G3308	3006
G3309	3007
G3310	3008
G3311	3009
G3312	3010
G3313	3011
G3314	621
G3315	
G3316	2982
G3317	3012
G3318	3013
G3319	3014
G3320	3015
G3321	3016
G3322	3017
G3323	3018
G3324	3019
G3325	3020
G3326	3021
G3327	1039
G3328	3022
G3329	3023
G3330	3024
G3331	3028
G3332	3025
G3333	3026
G3334	3027
G3335	3028
G3336	3029
G3337	3030
G3338	3031
G3339	3032
G3340	3033
G3341	3032
G3342	3034
G3343	3035
G3344	3036
G3345	3037
G3346	3038
G3347	3039
G3348	3040
G3349	3041
G3350	3042
G3351	3043
G3352	3044
G3353	3045
G3354	3046
G3355	3047

G/K	STRONG
G3356	3048
G3357	3049
G3358	3050
G3359	3051
G3360	3052
G3361	3053
G3362	3054
G3363	3055
G3364	3056
G3365	3057
G3366	3058
G3367	3059
G3368	3060
G3369	3061
G3370	3062
"	3063
"	3064
G3371	3065
G3372	3066
G3373	3067
G3374	3068
G3375	3069
G3376	3070
G3377	3071
G3378	3072
G3379	3073
G3380	3074
G3381	3075
G3382	3076
G3383	3077
G3384	3078
G3385	3079
G3386	3080
G3387	3081
G3388	3082
G3389	3083
G3390	3084
G3391	3085
G3392	3086
G3393	3087
G3394	3088
G3395	3089
G3396	3090
G3397	3091
G3398	
G3399	3092
G3400	3093
G3401	3093
G3402	3094
G3403	717
G3404	3095
G3405	3096
G3406	3095
G3407	3097
G3408	3098
G3409	3099
G3410	3149
G3411	3100
G3412	3101
G3413	3102
G3414	3156
G3415	3158
G3416	3159
G3417	3103
G3418	3104
G3419	3105
G3420	3106
G3421	3107
G3422	3108
G3423	3109
G3424	3110
G3425	3111
G3426	3112
G3427	3113
G3428	3114
G3429	3115
G3430	3116
G3431	3117
G3432	3118
G3433	3119
G3434	3120
G3435	3121
G3436	3122
G3437	3123
G3438	3124
G3439	3125
G3440	3126
G3441	3127
G3442	3128
G3443	3129
G3444	3130
G3445	3131
G3446	3132
G3447	3133
G3448	3134
G3449	3135
G3450	3136
G3451	3137
G3452	3137
G3453	3138

G/K	STRONG
G3454	3139
G3455	3140
G3456	3141
G3457	3142
G3458	3143
G3459	3144
G3460	3145
G3461	3149
G3462	3145
G3463	3146
G3464	3147
G3465	3148
G3466	3149
G3467	3150
G3468	3151
G3469	3152
G3470	3153
G3471	3154
G3472	3155
G3473	3156
G3474	3157
G3475	3158
G3476	3159
G3477	3160
G3478	3161
G3479	3162
G3480	3163
G3481	3164
G3482	3166
G3483	3167
G3484	3168
G3485	3169
G3486	3170
G3487	3171
G3488	3172
G3489	3173
G3490	3174
G3491	3175
G3492	3176
G3493	3177
G3494	3178
G3495	3179
G3496	3179
G3497	3180
G3498	3181
G3499	3182
G3500	3183
G3501	3184
G3502	3396
G3503	3396
G3504	3186
G3505	3185
"	3187
G3506	3188
"	3189
G3507	3190
G3508	3199
G3509	3191
G3510	3192
G3511	3193
G3512	3193
G3513	3193
G3514	3194
G3515	3194
G3516	3195
G3517	3196
G3518	3197
G3519	3198
G3520	3199
G3521	3200
G3522	3201
G3523	3202
G3524	3437
G3525	3303
G3526	3104
G3527	
G3528	3304
G3529	3304
G3530	3305
G3531	3306
G3532	3307
G3533	3308
G3534	3309
G3535	3310
G3536	3311
G3537	3312
G3538	3313
G3539	3322
G3540	3314
G3541	3315
G3542	3316
G3543	3317
G3544	3318
G3545	3319
G3546	3320
G3547	3321
G3548	3322
G3549	3323
G3550	3324
G3551	3325

G/K	STRONG
G3552	3326
G3553	3327
G3554	3328
G3555	3329
G3556	3330
G3557	3331
G3558	3332
G3559	3333
G3560	3334
G3561	3335
G3562	3336
G3563	3337
G3564	3338
G3565	3339
G3566	3340
G3567	3341
G3568	3342
G3569	3343
G3570	3344
G3571	3345
G3572	3346
G3573	3344
G3574	
G3575	3347
G3576	3348
G3577	3349
G3578	3350
G3579	3351
G3580	3352
G3581	3353
G3582	3354
G3583	3355
G3584	3356
G3585	3357
G3586	3358
G3587	3359
G3588	3360
G3589	3360
G3590	3361
G3591	3361+1065
G3592	3365
G3593	3366
G3594	3367
G3595	3368
G3596	3369
G3597	3370
G3598	3365
G3599	3367
G3600	3371
G3601	3372
G3602	3373
G3603	3374
G3604	3375
G3605	3376
G3606	3377
G3607	3379
G3608	3361+4225
G3609	3380
G3610	3381
G3611	3382
G3612	3383
G3613	3384
G3614	3385
"	3387
G3615	3386
G3616	3388
G3617	3389
G3618	3389
G3619	3390
G3620	3392
G3621	3393
G3622	3394
G3623	3395
G3624	3396
G3625	3397
"	3398
G3626	3399
G3627	3400
G3628	3401
G3629	3402
G3630	3403
G3631	3404
G3632	3405
G3633	3406
G3634	3407
G3635	3408
G3636	3409
G3637	3410
G3638	3411
G3639	3412
G3640	3413
G3641	3414
G3642	3415
G3643	3416
G3644	3417
G3645	3418
G3646	3419
G3647	3420
G3648	3421
G3649	3422

G/K	STRONG
G3650	3423
G3651	3424
G3652	3424
G3653	3425
G3654	3426
G3655	3428
G3656	3429
G3657	3430
G3658	3431
G3659	3432
G3660	3433
G3661	3434
G3662	3435
G3663	3436
G3664	3437
G3665	3438
G3666	3439
G3667	3440
G3668	3441
G3669	3442
G3670	3443
G3671	3444
G3672	3445
G3673	3446
G3674	3447
G3675	3448
G3676	3451
G3677	3449
G3678	3452
G3679	3453
G3680	3454
G3681	3455
G3682	3456
G3683	3457
G3684	3458
G3685	3458
G3686	3459
G3687	
G3688	3460
G3689	3461
G3690	3462
G3691	3463
G3692	3463
G3693	3464
G3694	3460
G3695	3465
G3696	3466
G3697	3467
G3698	3468
G3699	3469
G3700	3470
G3701	3471
G3702	3472
G3703	3473
G3704	3474
G3705	3475
G3706	3475
G3707	3475
G3708	
G3709	3476
G3710	3477
G3711	3478
G3712	3478
G3713	3478
G3714	3478
G3715	3478
G3716	3479
G3717	3480
G3718	3481
G3719	3481
G3720	3482
G3721	3483
G3722	3497
G3723	3484
G3724	3485
G3725	3486
G3726	3487
G3727	3488
G3728	3489
G3729	3490
G3730	3491
G3731	3492
G3732	3493
G3733	3494
G3734	3495
G3735	3496
G3736	3496
G3737	3497
G3738	3498
G3739	3499
G3740	3500
G3741	3561
G3742	3501
G3743	3502
G3744	3503
G3745	3504
G3746	3505
G3747	
G3748	3506
G3749	3507

G/K	STRONG
G3750	3508
G3751	3509
G3752	3510
G3753	3511
G3754	3512
G3755	3513
G3756	3514
G3757	3515
G3758	3516
G3759	3517
G3760	3518
G3761	3519
G3762	3520
G3763	3521
G3764	3522
G3765	3523
G3766	3524
G3767	3524
G3768	3525
G3769	3526
G3770	3527
G3771	3528
G3772	3529
G3773	3530
G3774	3531
G3775	3532
G3776	3533
G3777	3534
G3778	3535
G3779	3535
G3780	3536
G3781	3537
G3782	3538
G3783	3539
G3784	3540
G3785	3541
G3786	3542
G3787	3543
G3788	3544
G3789	3545
G3790	3546
G3791	3547
G3792	3548
G3793	3549
G3794	3550
G3795	3551
G3796	3552
G3797	3553
G3798	3554
G3799	3555
G3800	3556
G3801	3502
G3802	3557
G3803	3558
G3804	3559
G3805	3560
G3806	3561
G3807	3562
G3808	3563
G3809	3564
G3810	3564
G3811	3565
G3812	3566
G3813	3567
G3814	3568
G3815	3570
G3816	3571
G3817	3572
G3818	3573
G3819	3574
G3820	3575
G3821	3576
G3822	3577
G3823	
G3824	837
G3825	3578
G3826	3579
G3827	3580
G3828	3581
G3829	3582
G3830	3583
G3831	3584
G3832	3585
G3833	3586
G3834	3587
G3835	
G3836	3588
"	5120
G3837	3589
G3838	3590
G3839	3591
G3840	3592
G3841	3593
G3842	3594
G3843	3595
G3844	3596
G3845	3597
G3846	3598+4160
G3847	3598
G3848	3599
G3849	3600
G3850	3601
G3851	3602
G3852	3604
G3853	3605
G3854	3606
G3855	3607
G3856	3608
G3857	1492
G3858	3609
G3859	2322
G3860	3610
G3861	3611
G3862	3612
G3863	3613
G3864	3614
G3865	3615
G3866	3616
G3867	3617
G3868	3618
G3869	3619
G3870	3620
G3871	3618
G3872	3621
G3873	3622
G3874	3623
G3875	3624
G3876	3625
G3877	3626
G3878	3626
G3879	3627
G3880	3628
G3881	3629
G3882	3627
G3883	3633
G3884	3630
G3885	3631
G3886	3632
G3887	3633
G3888	3634
G3889	
G3890	3635
G3891	3636
G3892	3637
G3893	3638
G3894	3644
G3895	3645
G3896	3639
G3897	3639
G3898	570
G3899	3640
G3900	3641
G3901	3642
G3902	3643
G3903	3689
G3904	3644
G3905	3645
G3906	3646
G3907	3647
G3908	3648
G3909	3649
G3910	3650
G3911	3651
G3912	3652
G3913	3653
G3914	3654
G3915	3655
G3916	2442
G3917	3656
G3918	3657
G3919	3658
G3920	
G3921	3659
G3922	3660
G3923	3660
G3924	3661
G3925	3662
G3926	3663
G3927	3664
G3928	3665
G3929	3666
G3930	3667
G3931	3668
G3932	3669
G3933	3670
G3934	3671
G3935	3672
G3936	
G3937	3673
G3938	3674
G3939	3675
G3940	3676
G3941	3677
G3942	3678
G3943	3679
G3944	3680
G3945	3681
G3946	3682
G3947	3683
G3948	3684
G3949	3685
G3950	3686
G3951	3687
G3952	3688
G3953	3689
G3954	3690
G3955	3691
G3956	3692
G3957	3693
G3958	3694
G3959	3695
G3960	3696
G3961	3697
G3962	3698
G3963	3699
G3964	3700
G3965	3701
G3966	3702
G3967	3703
G3968	3704
G3969	3705
G3970	3706
G3971	3707
G3972	3708
G3973	3709
G3974	3710
G3975	3711
G3976	3712
G3977	3713
G3978	3714
G3979	3715
G3980	3716
G3981	3717
G3982	3718
G3983	3719
G3984	3720
G3985	3721
G3986	3722
G3987	3723
G3988	3724
G3989	3733
G3990	3725
G3991	3726
G3992	3727
G3993	3728
G3994	3729
G3995	3730
G3996	3731
G3997	3732
G3998	3733
G3999	3734
G4000	
G4001	3735
G4002	3736
G4003	3737
G4004	3738
G4005	3739
G4006	3740
G4007	3739+1065
G4008	3741
G4009	3742
G4010	3743
G4011	3744
G4012	3745
G4013	3746
G4014	3747
G4015	3748
"	3755
G4016	3747
G4017	3749
G4018	3750
G4019	3751
G4020	3752
G4021	3753
G4022	3754
G4023	3757
G4024	3756
G4025	3758
G4026	3759
G4027	3760
G4028	3761
G4029	3762
G4030	3763
G4031	3764
G4032	3762
G4033	3765
G4034	3766
G4035	1695
G4036	3767
G4037	3768
G4038	3769
G4039	3770
G4040	3771
G4041	3772
G4042	3773
G4043	3774
G4044	3775
G4045	3776
G4046	3777
G4047	3778
G4047	5023
"	5025
"	5026
"	5123
"	5124
"	5125
"	5126
"	5127
"	5128
"	5129
"	5130
G4048	3779
G4049	3780
G4050	3781
G4051	3782
G4052	3783
G4053	3784
G4054	3785
G4055	3786
G4056	3787
G4057	3788
G4058	3789
G4059	3790
G4060	856
G4061	3791
G4062	3792
G4063	3793
G4064	
G4065	3794
G4066	3795
G4067	3796
G4068	3798
G4069	3797
G4070	3798
G4071	3799
G4072	3800
G4073	
G4074	3802
G4075	3803
G4076	697
G4077	3804
G4078	3805
G4079	3806
G4080	3807
G4081	3808
G4082	3809
G4083	3810
G4084	3811
G4085	3812
G4086	3813
G4087	3814
G4088	3812
G4089	3815
G4090	3816
G4091	3817
G4092	3818
G4093	3819
G4094	3820
G4095	3821
G4096	3822
G4097	3823
G4098	3824
G4099	3825
G4100	3824
G4101	3826
G4102	3827
G4103	3828
G4104	3829
G4105	3830
G4106	3829
G4107	3830
G4108	3831
G4109	3832
G4110	3833
G4111	3834
G4112	3835
G4113	3826
G4114	3837
G4115	3836
G4116	3837
G4117	3838
G4118	3839
G4119	3840
G4120	3841
G4121	3842
G4122	3843
G4123	3844
G4124	3845
G4125	3846
G4126	3847
G4127	3848
G4128	3849
G4129	3851
G4130	3850
G4131	3851
G4132	3852
G4133	3853
G4134	3854
G4135	3855
G4136	3856
G4137	3857
G4138	3858
G4139	3859
G4140	3860
G4141	3861
G4142	3862
G4143	3863
G4144	3864
G4145	3865
G4146	3866
G4147	3867
G4148	3868
G4149	3869
G4150	3869
G4151	3870
G4152	3871
G4153	3872
G4154	3873
G4155	3874
G4156	3875
G4157	3876
G4158	3877
G4159	3878
G4160	3879
G4161	3880
G4162	3881
G4163	3882
G4164	3883
G4165	3884
G4166	3885
G4167	3885
G4168	3886
G4169	3887
G4170	3888
G4171	3889
G4172	3890
G4173	3913
G4174	3891
G4175	3892
G4176	3893
G4177	3894
G4178	3895
G4179	3896
G4180	3897
G4181	3898
G4182	3899
G4183	3900
G4184	3901
G4185	3902
G4186	3903
G4187	3904
G4188	4368
G4189	3905
G4190	3906
G4191	3907
G4192	3908
G4193	3909
G4194	3910
G4195	3911
G4196	3912
G4197	3913
G4198	3913
G4199	3914
G4200	3915
G4201	2710
G4202	3916
G4203	3917
G4204	4332
G4205	3918
G4206	3919
G4207	3920
G4208	3921
G4209	3922
G4210	3923
G4211	3924
G4212	4016
G4213	3925
G4214	3926
G4215	3927
G4216	3928
G4217	3929
G4218	3930
G4219	3931
G4220	3932
G4221	3933
G4222	3934
G4223	3935
G4224	3936
G4225	3936
G4226	3937
G4227	3938
G4228	3939
G4229	3940
G4230	3941
G4231	3942
G4232	3943
G4233	3944
G4234	3945
G4235	3946
G4236	3947
G4237	3948
G4238	5237
G4239	3949
G4240	3950
G4241	3951
G4242	3952
G4243	3953
G4244	3954
G4245	3955
G4246	3956
G4247	3957
G4248	3958
G4249	3959
G4250	3960
G4251	3961
G4252	3962
G4253	3963
G4254	3964
G4255	3965
G4256	3966
G4257	3967
G4258	3968
G4259	3969
G4260	3964
G4261	3970
G4262	3971
G4263	3972
G4264	3973
G4265	3974
G4266	3975
G4267	3976
G4268	3977
G4269	3978
G4270	3979
G4271	3979
G4272	3980
G4273	3981
G4274	3981
G4275	3982
G4276	4091
G4277	3983
G4278	3984
G4279	3985
G4280	3986
G4281	3987
G4282	3988
G4283	3989
G4284	3990
G4285	
G4286	3991
G4287	3992
G4288	3993
G4289	3994
G4290	3995
G4291	3996
G4292	3997
G4293	3998
G4294	3999
G4295	4000
G4296	4001
G4297	4002
G4298	4003
G4299	4004
G4300	4005
G4301	4006
G4302	4007
G4303	
G4304	4012+2087
G4305	4008
G4306	4009
G4307	4010
G4308	4011
G4309	4012
G4310	4013
G4311	4014
G4312	681
G4313	4015
G4314	4016
G4315	4017
G4316	4018
G4317	4019
G4318	4020
G4319	4021
G4320	4022
G4321	4023
G4322	4024
G4323	4024
G4324	4025
G4325	4026
G4326	4027
G4327	4776
G4328	4028
G4329	4029
G4330	4030
G4331	4031
G4332	4032
G4333	4033
G4334	4034
G4335	4035
G4336	621
G4337	4036
G4338	4037
G4339	4038
G4340	4039
G4341	4040
G4342	4041
G4343	4042
G4344	4043
G4345	4044
G4346	4045
G4347	4046
G4348	4047
G4349	
G4350	
G4351	4048
G4352	4049
G4353	4050
G4354	4051
G4355	4052
G4356	4053
G4357	4054
G4358	4055
G4359	4056
G4360	4057
G4361	4058
G4362	4059
G4363	4060
G4364	4061
G4365	4062
G4366	4063
G4367	4064
G4368	4065
G4369	4066
G4370	4067
G4371	4068
G4372	4069
G4373	4070
G4374	4071
G4375	4072
G4376	4073
G4377	4074
G4378	4075
G4379	4076
G4380	4077
G4381	4078
G4382	4079
G4383	4080
G4384	4081
G4385	4082
G4386	4456
G4387	4457
G4388	4083
G4389	4084
G4390	4085
G4391	4086
G4392	3981
G4393	4087
G4394	4088
G4395	4089
G4396	4090
G4397	4091
G4398	4130
G4399	4092
G4400	4093
G4401	4093
G4402	4094
G4403	4095
G4404	4096
G4405	4097
G4406	4098
G4407	4099
G4408	4099
G4409	4100
G4410	4101
G4411	4102
G4412	4103
G4413	4104
G4414	4105
G4415	4106
G4416	4107
G4417	4107
G4418	4108
G4419	4109
G4420	4110
G4421	4111
G4422	4112
G4423	4113
G4424	4114
G4425	4115
G4426	4116
G4427	4117
G4428	4120
G4429	4121
G4430	4122
G4431	4123
G4432	4124
G4433	4125
G4434	4126
G4435	4127
G4436	4128
G4437	4129
G4438	4131
G4439	4132
G4440	4133
G4441	4134
G4442	4135
G4443	4136
G4444	4137
G4445	4138
G4446	4139
G4447	4140
G4448	4141
G4449	4142
G4450	4143
G4451	1708
G4452	4144
G4453	4144
G4454	4145
G4455	4146
G4456	4147
G4457	4148
G4458	4149
G4459	4150
G4460	4151
G4461	4152
G4462	4153
G4463	4154
G4464	4155
G4465	4156
G4466	4157
G4467	4217
G4468	4158
G4469	3537
G4470	4159
G4471	4169
G4472	4160
G4473	4161
G4474	4162
G4475	4163
G4476	4164
G4477	4165
G4478	4166
G4479	4167
G4480	4168
G4481	4169
G4482	4170
G4483	4171
G4484	4172
G4485	4173
G4486	4174
G4487	4175
G4488	4176
G4489	4177
G4490	4178
G4491	4179
G4492	4184
G4493	
G4494	4180
G4495	4181
G4496	
G4497	4182
G4498	4118
"	4119
"	4183
G4499	4184
G4500	4185
G4501	4186
G4502	4187
G4503	4188
G4504	4189
G4505	4190
"	4191
G4506	4192
G4507	4193
G4508	4194
G4509	5117
G4510	4195
G4511	4196
G4512	4197
G4513	4198
G4514	4199
G4515	4197
G4516	4200
G4517	4201
G4518	4202
G4519	4203
G4520	4204
G4521	4205
G4522	4206
G4523	4207
G4524	4208
G4525	4209
G4526	4210
G4527	4211
G4528	4210
G4529	4212
G4530	4213
G4531	4214
G4532	4215
G4533	4216

G/K	STRONG
G4534	4217
G4535	4458
G4536	4219
G4537	4218
G4538	4220
G4539	4221
G4540	4222
G4541	4223
G4542	4224
G4543	4225
G4544	4226
G4545	4227
G4546	4228
G4547	4229
G4548	4230
G4549	4231
G4550	4232
G4551	4233
G4552	4234
G4553	4235
G4554	4236
G4555	4237
G4556	4238
G4557	4236
G4558	4239
G4559	4240
G4560	4241
G4561	4242
G4562	4246
G4563	4243
G4564	4244
G4565	4245
G4566	4246
G4567	4247
G4568	4248
G4569	4249
G4570	4250
G4571	4251
G4572	4252
G4573	4249
G4574	4253
G4575	4254
G4576	4255
G4577	4256
G4578	4257
G4579	4258
G4580	4259
G4581	4260
G4582	4261
G4583	4262
G4584	4263
G4585	4263
G4586	4264
G4587	4265
G4588	4266
G4589	4267
G4590	4268
G4591	4269
G4592	4270
G4593	4271
G4594	4272
G4595	4273
G4596	4274
G4597	4302
G4598	4276
G4599	4278
G4600	4279
G4601	4281
G4602	4282
G4603	4283
G4604	4284
G4605	4285
G4606	4286
G4607	4287
G4608	4288
G4609	4289
G4610	4290
G4611	4406
G4612	4407
G4613	4291
G4614	4292
G4615	4293
G4616	4294
G4617	4284
G4618	4295
G4619	4296
G4620	4297
G4621	4298
G4622	4299
G4623	4300
G4624	4301
G4625	4302
"	4277
"	4280
G4626	4303
G4627	4304
G4628	4305
G4629	4306
G4630	4307
G4631	4308
G4632	4275
"	4308
G4633	4309
G4634	4310
G4635	3962
G4636	4311
G4637	4312
G4638	4313
G4639	4314
G4640	4315
G4641	4316
G4642	4317
G4643	4318
G4644	4319
G4645	4319
G4646	4320
G4647	4355
G4648	4321
G4649	4321
G4650	4322
G4651	4323
G4652	4317
G4653	4324
G4654	4317
G4655	4325
G4656	4326
G4657	4327
G4658	1929
G4659	4328
G4660	4329
G4661	4330
G4662	4331
G4663	4332
G4664	4333
G4665	4334
G4666	4335
G4667	4336
G4668	4337
G4669	4338
G4670	4339
G4671	4286
G4672	4340
G4673	4341
G4674	4342
G4675	4343
G4676	4344
G4677	4345
G4678	4346
G4679	4347
G4680	4346
G4681	4347
G4682	4348
G4683	4349
G4684	4350
G4685	4351
G4686	4352
G4687	4353
G4688	4354
G4689	4355
G4690	
G4691	4356
G4692	4356
G4693	4357
G4694	4358
G4695	4359
G4696	4360
G4697	
G4698	4361
G4699	4362
G4700	4363
G4701	4364
G4702	4365
G4703	4366
G4704	4366
G4705	4367
G4706	4368
G4707	4369
G4708	4370
G4709	4371
G4710	4372
G4711	4373
G4712	4374
G4713	4375
G4714	4376
G4715	4377
G4716	4370
G4717	4378
G4718	4379
G4719	4380
G4720	4381
G4721	4382
G4722	4380
G4723	4381
G4724	4382
G4725	4383
G4726	4384
G4727	4385
G4728	4386
"	4387
G4729	4388
G4730	4389
G4731	4390
G4732	4391
G4733	4392
G4734	4393
G4735	4394
G4736	4395
G4737	4396
G4738	4397
G4739	4398
G4740	4399
G4741	4400
G4742	4401
G4743	4402
G4744	4403
G4745	4404
G4746	4405
G4747	4406
G4748	4407
G4749	4408
G4750	4409
G4751	4410
G4752	4411
G4753	3144
G4754	4412
G4755	4413
G4756	4414
G4757	4415
G4758	4416
G4759	4412
G4760	4417
G4761	4418
G4762	4419
G4763	4420
G4764	4421
G4765	4422
G4766	4423
G4767	4424
G4768	4425
G4769	4426
G4770	4427
G4771	4428
G4772	4429
G4773	4430
G4774	4431
G4775	4432
G4776	4433
G4777	4434
G4778	4435
G4779	
G4780	4436
G4781	4437
G4782	4438
G4783	4439
G4784	4440
G4785	4441
G4786	4442
G4787	4443
G4788	4444
G4789	4445
G4790	4446
G4791	4447
G4792	4448
G4793	4449
G4794	4450
G4795	
G4796	4451
G4797	4453
G4798	4454
G4799	4455
G4800	4456
G4801	4457
G4802	4459
G4803	4452
"	4458
G4804	
G4805	4460
G4806	4461
G4807	4462
G4808	4462
G4809	4462
G4810	4463
G4811	4464
G4812	4465
G4813	
G4814	4466
G4815	4467
G4816	4468
G4817	911
G4818	4481
G4819	4469
G4820	4470
G4821	4471
G4822	4472
G4823	4473
G4824	4474
G4825	4475
G4826	4486
G4827	4476
G4828	4469
G4829	4477
G4830	4478
G4831	4479
G4832	4480
G4833	4481
G4834	4481
G4835	4482
G4836	4484
G4837	4485
G4838	4486
G4839	4487
G4840	4488
G4841	4486
G4842	4489
G4843	4490
G4844	4491
G4845	4492
G4846	4493
G4847	4494
G4848	4495
G4849	4496
G4850	4497
G4851	4498
G4852	4499
G4853	4500
G4854	4481
G4855	4501
G4856	4493
G4857	4502
G4858	4503
G4859	4504
G4860	4505
G4861	4506
G4862	4510
G4863	4510
G4864	4507
G4865	4508
G4866	4509
G4867	4510
G4868	4511
G4869	4512
G4870	4513
G4871	4514
G4872	4515
G4873	4516
G4874	4517
G4875	
G4876	4518
G4877	4519
G4878	4520
G4879	4521
G4880	4522
G4881	4523
G4882	4524
G4883	4525
G4884	4526
G4885	4527
G4886	4528
G4887	4529
G4888	4531
G4889	4532
G4890	4530
G4891	4533
G4892	4534
G4893	4535
G4894	4536
G4895	4537
G4896	4538
G4897	4539
G4898	4672
G4899	4540
G4900	4540
G4901	4541
G4902	4542
G4903	4543
G4904	4544
G4905	4545
G4906	
G4907	4546
G4908	4547
G4909	4548
G4910	4549
G4911	4550
G4912	4551
G4913	4552
G4914	4553
G4915	4554
G4916	4555
G4917	4556
G4918	4557
G4919	4558
G4920	4559
G4921	4560
G4922	4561
G4923	4562
G4924	4563
G4925	4564
G4926	4565
G4927	4566
G4928	4567
G4929	4568
G4930	4569
G4931	4570
G4932	4572
G4933	4573
G4934	4574
G4935	4575
G4936	4576
G4937	4577
G4938	4577
G4939	4578
G4940	4579
G4941	4580
G4942	4581
G4943	4582
G4944	4583
G4945	4584
G4946	4584
G4947	4585
G4948	4586
G4949	4587
G4950	4588
G4951	4562
G4952	4562
G4953	4589
G4954	4590
G4955	4591
G4956	4592
G4957	4593
G4958	4594
G4959	4612
G4960	4595
G4961	4596
G4962	4597
G4963	4598
G4964	4599
G4965	4600
G4966	4525
G4967	4601
G4968	4602
G4969	4603
G4970	4604
G4971	4603
G4972	4605
G4973	4606
G4974	4607
G4975	4608
G4976	4609
G4977	4610
G4978	4611
G4979	
G4980	4612
G4981	4613
G4982	4614
G4983	4615
G4984	4616
G4985	4617
G4986	4596
G4987	4577
G4988	4618
G4989	4621
G4990	4619
G4991	4620
G4992	4621
G4993	4965
G4994	4622
G4995	4623
G4996	2977
G4997	4624
G4998	4625
G4999	4626
G5000	2469
G5001	2469
G5002	4627
G5003	4628
G5004	4629
G5005	4630
G5006	4631
G5007	4632
G5008	4633
G5009	4634
G5010	4635
G5011	4636
G5012	4637
G5013	4638
G5014	4639
G5015	4640
G5016	4641
G5017	4642
G5018	4643
G5019	4644
G5020	4645
G5021	4646
G5022	4647
G5023	4648
G5024	4649
G5025	4650
G5026	4651
G5027	4652
G5028	4653
G5029	4654
G5030	4655
G5031	4656
G5032	4657
G5033	4658
G5034	4659
G5035	4660
G5036	4661
G5037	4662
G5038	4663
G5039	4664
G5040	4665
G5041	3395
G5042	3395
G5043	4666
G5044	4667
G5045	4668
G5046	4669
G5047	4670
G5048	4672
G5049	4673
G5050	4674
G5051	4676
G5052	4677
G5053	4678
G5054	4679
G5055	4680
G5056	4681
G5057	4682
G5058	4683
G5059	4684
G5060	4685
G5061	4686
G5062	4687
G5063	4688
G5064	4689
G5065	4690
G5066	4691
G5067	4692
G5068	4693
G5069	4694
G5070	4696
G5071	4695
G5072	4697
G5073	4698
G5074	4699
G5075	4700
G5076	4701
G5077	4702
G5078	4703
G5079	4704
G5080	4705
"	4706
"	4707
G5081	4708
"	4709
G5082	4710
G5083	4711
G5084	4712
G5085	4713
G5086	4955
G5087	4714
G5088	4715
G5089	4716
G5090	4717
G5091	4718
G5092	4719
G5093	4720
G5094	4721
G5095	4722
G5096	4723
G5097	4724
G5098	4725
G5099	4726
G5100	4727
G5101	4728
G5102	4729
G5103	4730
G5104	4731
G5105	4732
G5106	4733
G5107	4734
G5108	4736
G5109	4735
G5110	4737
G5111	4738
G5112	4739
G5113	4740
G5114	4741
G5115	4746
G5116	4742
G5117	4743
G5118	4744
G5119	4745
G5120	4746
G5121	4770
G5122	4747
G5123	4748
G5124	4749
G5125	4750
G5126	4751
G5127	4752
G5128	4753
G5129	4754
G5130	4755
G5131	4756
G5132	4757
G5133	4758
G5134	4759
G5135	4759
G5136	4760
G5137	4761
G5138	4762
G5139	4763
G5140	4764
G5141	4765
G5142	4766
G5143	4766
G5144	4767
G5145	4768
G5146	4769
G5147	4770
G5148	4571
"	4671
"	4675
"	4771
"	5209
"	5210
"	5213
"	5216
G5149	4772
G5150	4773
G5151	4773
G5152	4774
G5153	4775
G5154	4776
G5155	4777
G5156	4778
G5157	4779
G5158	4780
G5159	4781
G5160	4782
G5161	4783
G5162	
G5163	4784
G5164	4785
G5165	4873
G5166	4786
G5167	4787
G5168	4788
G5169	4789
G5170	4790
G5171	4791
G5172	4792
G5173	4793
G5174	4794
G5175	4795
G5176	4796
G5177	4797
G5178	4798
G5179	4797
G5180	4799
G5181	2010
G5182	4800
G5183	4801
G5184	4802
G5185	4803
G5186	4804
G5187	4805
G5188	4806
G5189	4807
G5190	4808
G5191	4809
G5192	4810
G5193	4811
G5194	4812
G5195	4813
G5196	4814
G5197	4815
G5198	4816
G5199	4817
G5200	4818
G5201	4819
G5202	4820
G5203	4821
G5204	4822
G5205	4823
G5206	4824
G5207	4825
G5208	4826
G5209	4827
G5210	4828
G5211	4829
G5212	4830
G5213	4831
G5214	4833
G5215	4832
G5216	4833
G5217	4834
G5218	4835
G5219	4836
G5220	4837
G5221	4838
G5222	4839
G5223	4840
G5224	4841
G5225	4842
G5226	
G5227	4843
G5228	4844
G5229	4098
G5230	4845
G5231	4846
G5232	4847
G5233	4848
G5234	4849
G5235	4849
G5236	4850
G5237	4851
G5238	4852
G5239	4851
G5240	4833
G5241	4853
G5242	4854
G5243	4855
G5244	4856
G5245	4857
G5246	4858
G5247	4859
G5248	4860
G5249	4861
G5250	4862
G5251	4863
G5252	4864
G5253	4865
G5254	4866
G5255	4867
G5256	4868
G5257	4869
G5258	4870
G5259	4871
G5260	4871
G5261	4900
G5262	4872
G5263	4873
G5264	4874
G5265	4875
G5266	
G5267	4876
G5268	4877
G5269	4878
G5270	4879
G5271	4880
G5272	4881
G5273	4882
G5274	4883
G5275	4884
G5276	4871
G5277	4885
G5278	4886
G5279	4887
G5280	4888
G5281	4889
G5282	4890
G5283	4891
G5284	4892
G5285	
G5286	
G5287	4893
G5288	4894
G5289	4895
G5290	4896
G5291	4897
G5292	4898
G5293	4899
G5294	
G5295	4900
G5296	4901
G5297	4862+1985
G5298	4934
G5299	4902
G5300	4903
G5301	4904
G5302	4905
G5303	4906
G5304	4907
G5305	4908
G5306	4909
G5307	4910
G5308	4911
G5309	4912
G5310	4913
G5311	4914
G5312	4915
G5313	4916
G5314	4917
G5315	4918
G5316	4919
G5317	4920
G5318	4921

G/K	STRONG
G5319	4921
G5320	4920
G5321	4922
G5322	4923
G5323	4894
G5324	4924
G5325	4925
G5326	4926
G5327	4927
G5328	4894
G5329	
G5330	4928
G5331	4952
G5332	4929
G5333	4930
G5334	4931
G5335	4932
G5336	
G5337	4933
G5338	4934
G5339	4935
G5340	4936
G5341	4937
G5342	4938
G5343	4939
G5344	4940
G5345	4941
G5346	4795
G5347	4942
G5348	4943
G5349	4944
G5350	4945
G5351	4949
G5352	4946
G5353	4947
G5354	4948
G5355	4949
G5356	4949
G5357	
G5358	4950
G5359	4951
G5360	4952
G5361	4953
G5362	4954
G5363	4955
G5364	4956
G5365	4957
G5366	4958
G5367	4959
G5368	4960
G5369	4961
G5370	4962
G5371	4963
G5372	4964
G5373	4965
G5374	4966
G5375	4967
G5376	4968
G5377	4969
G5378	
G5379	4970
G5380	4971
G5381	4972
G5382	4973
G5383	4974
G5384	4974
G5385	4975
G5386	4976
G5387	4977
G5388	4978
G5389	4979
G5390	4980
G5391	4981
G5392	4982
G5393	4983
G5394	4984
G5395	4985
G5396	4986
G5397	4987
G5398	4988
G5399	4989
G5400	4990
G5401	4991
G5402	4992
G5403	4992
G5404	4993
G5405	4994
G5406	4995
G5407	4996
G5408	4997
G5409	4998
G5410	
G5411	4999
G5412	5000
G5413	5001
G5414	5002
G5415	5003
G5416	5004
G5417	5005
G5418	5006
G5419	5007
G5420	5008
G5421	5009
G5422	3569
G5423	5010
G5424	5011
G5425	5012
G5426	5391
G5427	5013
G5428	5014
G5429	5015
G5430	5016
G5431	5017
G5432	5018
G5433	5019
G5434	5020
G5435	5021
G5436	5022
G5437	5024
G5438	5027
G5439	5028
G5440	5029
G5441	5030
"	5032
"	5033
G5442	5031
G5443	5034
G5444	5035
"	5036
G5445	5037
G5446	5038
G5447	5039
G5448	5040
G5449	5041
G5450	5042
G5451	5043
G5452	5044
G5453	
G5454	5045
G5455	5046
G5456	5047
G5457	5048
G5458	5049
G5459	5050
G5460	5051
G5461	5052
G5462	5053
G5463	5054
G5464	5055
G5465	5056
G5466	5058
G5467	5057
G5468	5058
G5469	5059
G5470	5060
G5471	
G5472	5061
G5473	5062
G5474	5063
G5475	5064
G5476	5065
G5477	5062
G5478	5063
G5479	5066
G5480	5067
G5481	5068
G5482	5069
G5483	5070
G5484	5071
G5485	5072
G5486	5073
G5487	5073
G5488	5074
G5489	5075
G5490	5076
G5491	5077
G5492	5078
G5493	5079
G5494	5080
G5495	5081
G5496	5082
G5497	
G5498	5083
G5499	5084
G5500	5085
G5501	5086
G5502	5087
G5503	5088
G5504	5089
G5505	5090
G5506	5091
G5507	5092
G5508	5093
G5509	5094
G5510	5095
G5511	5096
G5512	5097
G5513	5098
G5514	5099
G5515	5101
G5516	5100
G5517	2459
G5518	5102
G5519	5103
G5520	5104
G5521	5105
G5522	5105
G5523	5106
G5524	5107
G5525	5108
G5526	5109
G5527	5110
G5528	5111
G5529	5112
G5530	5112
G5531	5112
G5532	5113
G5533	5114
G5534	5115
G5535	5116
G5536	5117
G5537	5118
G5538	5119
G5539	5121
G5540	5122
G5541	3694
G5542	5123
G5543	5131
G5544	5132
G5545	5133
G5546	5134
G5547	5135
G5548	5136
G5549	5137
G5550	5138
G5551	5139
G5552	5140
G5553	5140+4999
G5554	5141
G5555	5142
G5556	5143
G5557	5169
G5558	5144
G5559	5145
G5560	5146
G5561	5147
G5562	5148
G5563	5149
G5564	5150
G5565	5151
G5566	5152
G5567	5153
G5568	5154
G5569	5154
G5570	5155
G5571	5156
G5572	5157
G5573	5158
G5574	5159
G5575	5160
G5576	5161
G5577	5162
G5578	5159
G5579	5163
G5580	5164
G5581	5165
G5582	5166
G5583	5167
G5584	5168
G5585	5169
G5586	5170
G5587	5171
G5588	5172
G5589	5173
G5590	5174
G5591	5175
G5592	5176
G5593	5177
G5594	5178
G5595	5179
G5596	5179
G5597	5180
G5598	5181
G5599	
G5600	5182
G5601	5183
G5602	5184
G5603	5185
G5604	5186
G5605	5187
G5606	5188
G5607	5189
G5608	5190
G5609	
G5610	5191
G5611	5192
G5612	5193
G5613	5194
G5614	5195
G5615	5196
G5616	5197
G5617	5198
G5618	5199
G5619	5200
G5620	5201
G5621	5202
G5622	5203
G5623	5204
G5624	5205
G5625	5206
G5626	5207
G5627	5208
G5628	5211
G5629	5212
G5630	5214
G5631	5215
G5632	5217
G5633	5218
G5634	5219
G5635	5220
G5636	5221
G5637	5222
G5638	5223
G5639	5224
"	5225
G5640	5226
G5641	5227
G5642	5228
G5643	5229
G5644	5230
G5645	5231
G5646	784
G5647	5232
G5648	5233
G5649	5234
G5650	5235
G5651	5236
G5652	5228+1473
G5653	5237
G5654	5238
G5655	5240
G5656	5240
G5657	5239
G5658	5240
G5659	5241
G5660	5242
G5661	5243
G5662	5244
G5663	5244
G5664	5245
G5665	5246
G5666	5237
G5667	5247
G5668	5248
G5669	5249
G5670	5250
G5671	5251
G5672	5252
G5673	5253
G5674	5254
G5675	5255
G5676	5256
G5677	5257
G5678	5258
G5679	5259
G5680	5260
G5681	5261
G5682	5262
G5683	5263
G5684	5263
G5685	5264
G5686	5265
G5687	5266
G5688	5267
G5689	5268
G5690	5269
G5691	5270
G5692	
G5693	5271
G5694	5272
G5695	5273
G5696	5274
G5697	2985
G5698	2640
G5699	5275
G5700	5276
G5701	5277
G5702	5278
G5703	5279
G5704	5280
G5705	5281
G5706	5282
G5707	5283
G5708	5299
G5709	5284
G5710	5285
G5711	5286
G5712	5287
G5713	5288
G5714	5289
G5715	5290
G5716	5291
G5717	5292
G5718	5293
G5719	5294
G5720	5295
G5721	5296
G5722	5297
G5723	5298
G5724	5299
G5725	5300
G5726	
G5727	5301
G5728	5302
G5729	5303
G5730	5304
G5731	5305
"	5306
G5732	
G5733	5307
G5734	5308
G5735	5309
G5736	5310
G5737	5311
G5738	5312
G5739	5313
G5740	
G5741	5314
G5742	5341
G5743	5316
G5744	5317
G5745	5318
G5746	5319
G5747	5320
G5748	5321
G5749	5322
G5750	5323
G5751	5324
G5752	5325
G5753	5326
G5754	5327
G5755	5328
G5756	5329
G5757	5330
G5758	5331
G5759	5332
G5760	5331
G5761	5333
G5762	5334
G5763	5335
G5764	5336
G5765	5337
G5766	5338
G5767	5339
G5768	5340
G5769	5341
G5770	5342
G5771	5343
G5772	5344
G5773	5345
G5774	5346
G5775	1310
G5776	5347
G5777	5348
G5778	5349
G5779	5350
G5780	5351
G5781	5352
G5782	5353
G5783	5354
G5784	5355
G5785	5356
G5786	5357
G5787	5358
G5788	5359
G5789	5360
G5790	5361
G5791	5362
G5792	5363
G5793	5364
G5794	5365
G5795	5366
G5796	5367
G5797	5368
G5798	5369
G5799	5370
G5800	5371
G5801	5372
G5802	5373
G5803	5374
G5804	5375
G5805	5376
G5806	5377
G5807	5378
G5808	5379
G5809	5380
G5810	5381
G5811	5382
G5812	5383
G5813	5384
G5814	5385
G5815	5386
G5816	5387
G5817	5388
G5818	5389
G5819	5390
G5820	5391
G5821	5392
G5822	5417
G5823	5393
G5824	5394
G5825	5395
G5826	5396
G5827	5397
G5828	5399
G5829	5398
G5830	5399
G5831	5400
G5832	5401
G5833	5402
G5834	5403
G5835	4949
G5836	5404
G5837	5405
G5838	5406
G5839	5407
G5840	5408
G5841	5409
G5842	5410
G5843	5411
G5844	5412
G5845	5413
G5846	5414
G5847	5415
G5848	5416
G5849	5417
G5850	5418
G5851	5419
G5852	5420
G5853	5421
G5854	5422
G5855	5423
G5856	5424
G5857	5425
G5858	5426
G5859	5427
G5860	5428
G5861	5429
G5862	5430
G5863	5431
G5864	5432
G5865	5433
G5866	5434
G5867	5435
G5868	
G5869	5436
G5870	5437
G5871	5438
G5872	5439
G5873	5440
G5874	5441
G5875	5442
G5876	5443
G5877	5444
G5878	5445
G5879	5446
G5880	5447
G5881	5448
G5882	5449
G5883	5450
G5884	5451
G5885	5452
G5886	5453
G5887	5454
G5888	5455
G5889	5456
G5890	5457
G5891	5458
G5892	5459
G5893	5460
G5894	5461
G5895	5462
G5896	
G5897	5463
G5898	5464
G5899	5465
G5900	5466
G5901	5467
G5902	5468
G5903	5469
G5904	5468
G5905	5470
G5906	5471
G5907	5472
G5908	5473
G5909	5474
G5910	5475
G5911	5470
G5912	5476
G5913	5477
G5914	5478
G5915	5479
G5916	5480
G5917	5481
G5918	5482
G5919	5483
G5920	5484
G5921	5485
G5922	5486
G5923	5487
G5924	5488
G5925	5489
G5926	5490
G5927	5491
G5928	5492
G5929	5493
G5930	5494
G5931	5495
G5932	5496
G5933	5497
G5934	5498
G5935	5499
G5936	5500
G5937	5501
G5938	5502
G5939	5503
G5940	5504
G5941	5506
G5942	5505
G5943	5507
G5944	5508
G5945	5509
G5946	5510
G5947	5516
G5948	5511
G5949	5512
G5950	5513
G5951	5514
G5952	5515
G5953	5516
G5954	5517
G5955	5518
G5956	5519
G5957	5520
G5958	5521
G5959	5522
G5960	5523
G5961	5524
G5962	5525
G5963	5526
G5964	5527
G5965	5528
G5966	5529
G5967	5522
G5968	5530
G5969	5531
G5970	5532
G5971	5533
G5972	5533
G5973	5534
G5974	5535
G5975	5536
G5976	5537
G5977	5538
G5978	5539
G5979	5540
G5980	5541
G5981	5542
G5982	5543
G5983	5544
G5984	5545
G5985	5546
G5986	5547
G5987	5548
G5988	5549
G5989	5550
G5990	5551
G5991	5552
G5992	5553
G5993	5554
G5994	5555
G5995	5556
G5996	5557
G5997	5552
G5998	5558
G5999	5559
G6000	5560
G6001	5561
G6002	5523
G6003	5562
G6004	5563
G6005	5564
G6006	5565
G6007	
G6008	5566
G6009	
G6010	5567
G6011	5568
G6012	5569
G6013	5570
G6014	5571
G6015	5572
G6016	5573
G6017	5574
G6018	5576
G6019	5577
G6020	5575
G6021	5578
G6022	5579
G6023	5580
G6024	5581
G6025	5582
G6026	5583
G6027	5584
G6028	5585
G6029	5586
G6030	5587
G6031	5588
G6032	5589
G6033	5589
G6034	5590
G6035	5591
G6036	5592
G6037	5593
G6038	5594
G6039	5595
G6040	5596
G6041	5597
G6042	5598
G6043	5599
G6044	5601
G6045	5602
G6046	5603
G6047	5604
G6048	5605
G6049	5606
G6050	5608
G6051	5609
G6052	5610
G6053	5611
G6054	5612
G6055	5613
G6056	5613+302
G6057	5614
G6058	5615
G6059	5616
G6060	5617
G6061	5618
G6062	5619
G6063	5620
G6064	5621
G6065	5621
G6066	5622
G6067	5623
G6068	5624